The New York Times

CROSSWORD PUZZLE
DICTIONARY

The New York Times

CROSSWORD PUZZLE DICTIONARY

• Third Edition •

By Tom Pulliam and Clare Grundman

A HUDSON GROUP BOOK

TIMES
T
BOOKS

Library of Congress Cataloging in Publication Data

Pulliam, Tom.
    The New York Times crossword puzzle dictionary.

    "A Hudson Group book."
    1. Crossword puzzles—Glossaries, vocabularies, etc.
I. Grundman, Clare, 1913–   . II. New York Times.
III. Title
GV1507.C7P83   1984   793.73′2′03   84-40108
ISBN: 0-8129-2823-7

Random House Website address:
http://www.randomhouse.com/

Manufactured in the United States of America on acid-free paper

98765432

First Paperback Edition

PREFACE to the First Edition

THE NEW YORK TIMES CROSSWORD PUZZLE DICTIONARY exceeds in completeness and scope all other puzzle dictionaries. No useful word has been omitted. Not only have puzzles themselves been combed for synonyms that are used over and over, but also a word-for-word reading of major unabridged dictionaries, both current and old, has produced a thoroughly complete and extensive checklist.

Each of us has been solving and compiling puzzles for many years, and our chief purpose has been to design a practical and easy-to-use dictionary, in the belief that your needs and requirements for such a volume closely reflect our own. For example, the synonyms are arranged by the number of letters, and then alphabetized so you can quickly find the very word that fills the spaces in the puzzle. Another feature, one that seems obvious for a crossword puzzle dictionary but is not found in most of them, is that all words are printed in easy-to-read capital letters. The type has been chosen with great care for its legibility, and the three-column format not only provides a short line of type to scan but also enables us to get a very large number of words on each page.

Synonyms of great length have been omitted to give room for the shorter, more useful words. The puzzler can always "fill in" the very long words provided he has a good supply of short common synonyms. We have placed, therefore, an arbitrary ceiling of eight-letter word-lengths, knowing this will satisfy almost all needs. Here and there, however, you will find occasional exceptions to this rule. These are synonyms of such frequent, interesting, and normal usage that their omission might handicap the puzzler.

The "shaded boxes" scattered through the book are a notable and unique feature of THE NEW YORK TIMES CROSSWORD PUZZLE DICTIONARY. They collect under one heading a variety of categories and synonyms that you would have a hard time finding in other dictionaries. For example, when you are confronted by the clue "Brazilian river" merely turn to the shaded area marked BRAZIL, where you will find several excellent possibilities. Similarly, look for a "Philippine native" under PHILIPPINES, or a "Scottish measure" under SCOTLAND.

Another useful feature is the lavish listing of phrases. For instance, instead of being confronted by the simple clue "Sword," you may run up against "Double-edged sword." Under the entry word SWORD in this dictionary you will find ample phrases that qualify the entry word or more sharply specify its meaning. Also, given the definition "Turn aside," simply look under TURN and find that phrase, along with many others.

THE NEW YORK TIMES CROSSWORD PUZZLE DICTIONARY is a versatile reference book that you will want to keep on your desk or next to your chair for help, not only with crossword puzzles, but also for a large variety of other puzzles and contests. In addition, it will be invaluable for writers, speakers, and the like, for (with more than one-half million words) it is one of the largest books of synonyms ever published. Its simple arrangement makes it far easier to use than the standard thesauri.

Our hope is that you will come to use this new word book as we might. Get to know it and be adventuresome! If the first entry you consult does not corner the exact word you are seeking, let any listing at that spot lead you to a cross-reference. Follow this track until you have the right word "treed."

A project of this scope may well have been beyond the ability of only two to accomplish. We have required and welcomed top-flight support during our work. Although many might be named, special note must be given to the efforts of Richard Martz and David House of Dartmouth College, who were responsible for much of the computerization; also, to Gorton Carruth and Robert O'Brien of Morningside Associates. Each made his individual contributions, which we gratefully acknowledge.

Happy word hunting!

Tom Pulliam
Clare Grundman

1974

PREFACE to the Second Edition

This Second Edition of THE NEW YORK TIMES CROSSWORD PUZZLE DICTIONARY greatly augments the First Edition. We have added approximately 100,000 new entry words and synonyms into a new four-column format, which maintains the same easy-to-read features and the large numbers of words per page, including many new longer words. An outstanding innovation of this Second Edition is the inclusion of the titles of major works of literature and music, as well as their authors and composers, and the names of characters in books, plays, operas, etc. Another very important addition is the listing of famous people from various walks of life—painters, physicians, playwrights, botanists, etc.—as well as those men and women who have won Nobel Prizes and who have been inducted into the Hall of Fame. We have also assembled what we believe to be the most comprehensive listing of prefixes, suffixes, and combining forms, which are *listed by meaning,* and the largest list of biblical, mythological, and literary relationships ever to appear in a crossword puzzle dictionary. And, of course, we have retained from the First Edition the unique ''shaded boxes'' that feature pertinent facts about geographical locations.

We would like to acknowledge once more the excellent assistance of Gorton Carruth and Robert O'Brien of Morningside Editorial Associates and to thank the many puzzlers who have sent us their compliments and suggestions.

Again, we wish you happy word hunting!

T.P.
C.G.

1984

PREFACE to the Third Edition

In the decade since the Second Edition of THE NEW YORK TIMES CROSSWORD PUZZLE DICTIONARY was published, the nature of crossword puzzles has changed in several ways, some obvious and some subtle. These changes, which we determined several years ago would require a Third Edition in order to have an up-to-date dictionary, are reflected in the many alterations and additions you will find in the text. In the last few years writers of crossword puzzles have made the clues less obvious, thus making the puzzles more difficult to solve. We believe that the average solver appreciates this additional challenge. You will discover in this Third Edition, therefore, many alternate and uncommon synonyms of finding words. You will also discover many synonyms consisting of phrases of two or more words unaccompanied by qualifying explanations, such as "two words." For example, under the finding word "succeed" you will find MAKEIT. Consider, AT HOME under "in," SHOOIN under "winner (easy)," the slangy GOAPE under "flip," and the three-word phrase INARUT under "stuck." Please remember that all phrases are listed, just as they are written in puzzles, as one word. This use of phrases makes solving crossword puzzles more interesting, as does the use of "gimmicks" or unifying themes, slang, and words and phrases associated with the space age and the drug culture. You will find a more extensive coverage of these kinds of subjects in this new edition. We have also included a list of "partners," a category that has come into increasing use. For example, the clue asks for the "partner of hither," intending you to fill in YON. These pairings are all listed under the finding word "partners" and written in the dictionary as one word: HITH-ERYON, KITHKIN, YINYANG, etc. You will find a similar listing under "alterna-tives," which suggests the use of *or* instead of *and,* as in "alternative of hit" is MISS and is entered as HITMISS. Particularly useful new categories of finding words are those dealing with sports teams and players. For example, under "hockey" or "football" you will find lists of players and teams. Other similar finding words include baseball, golf, and tennis. Finally, we have updated many lists, such as Nobel Prize winners and persons who are well-known for their achievements in their professions, such as "author," "playwright," and "statesman." In short, all these additions confirm that this Third Edition of THE NEW YORK TIMES CROSS-WORD PUZZLE DICTIONARY remains the most comprehensive and current puz-zle dictionary available.

Once again we would like to acknowledge the excellent and necessary assist-ance of Gorton Carruth of Morningside Editorial Associates. For this Third Edition we are grateful for the contributions of Edmund Yee, who guided us through the intricacies of the computer, and Bruce Wetterau, who updated the geographical boxes and expanded the categories of occupations. Our thanks also go to Henry Griffin for much of the keyboarding. We are especially grateful to the many puz-zlers who have written us over the years with their suggestions and well wishes.

Happy word hunting!

T.P.
C.G.

1995

The New York Times

CROSSWORD PUZZLE
DICTIONARY

A

A AY HA AIR ARY PER ALFA EACH
ALPHA
(EVER —) ARROW
AA LAVA
AAL AL MULBERRY
AARDVARK ANTEATER EARTHHOG
EDENTATE
AARDWOLF HYAENID
AARON (BROTHER OF —) MOSES
(BURIAL PLACE OF —) HOR
(FATHER OF —) AMRAM
(MOTHER OF —) JOCHEBED
(SISTER OF —) MIRIAM
(SON OF —) ABIHU NADAB ELEAZAR
ITHAMAR
(WIFE OF —) ELISHEBA
AARONIC LEVITIC LEVITICAL
AARON'S ROD MULLEIN
AB HATI
ABA ABAYAH
ABACA HEMP FIBER LUPIS LINAGA
MANILA
ABACK SHORT
ABACUS SOROBAN SHWANPAN
ABADDON PIT HELL ABYSS SATAN
APOLLYON
ABAFT AFT BACK BAFT ADAFF
ASTERN BEHIND REARWARD
(— THE BEAM) LARGE
ABALONE EAR PAUA AWABI NACRE
ORMER UHLLO ASSEIR MOLLUSK
ABANDON EGO CAST DROP FLEE
JUNK QUIT SINK ABAND ALLAY
CHUCK DITCH EXPEL LEAVE PLANT
REMIT SCRAP WAIVE YIELD
ABJURE BANISH BETRAY DESERT
DEVEST DISUSE DIVEST EXPOSE
FOREGO FORHOO FORLET
MAROON RECANT REFUSE REJECT
RELENT RESIGN SLOUGH STRAND
VACATE DEPLORE DISCARD
FORFEIT FORSAKE SCUTTLE
ABDICATE FORHOOIE FORSWEAR
JETTISON RASHNESS RENOUNCE
SURCEASE RELINQUISH
(— EVIL WAYS) REFORM
(WITH —) DESPERATELY
ABANDONED BAD LEFT LORN LOST
VACANT WICKED CORRUPT
FORLORN PROJECT DEPRAVED
DERELICT DESERTED DESOLATE
FLAGRANT FORSAKEN
ABANDONING
(PREF.) LIPO
ABANDONMENT BURIAL DUNKIRK
APOSTASY ABATEMENT
(— OF RESTRAINT) LETUP
ABANGA ADY
ABAS (FATHER OF —) CELEUS
LYNCEUS
(MOTHER OF —) METANIRA
HYPERMNESTRA
(SON OF —) PROETUS ACRISIUS

ABASE SINK VAIL AVALE AVILE
BLAME DEMIT DIMIT LOWER
SHAME ABJECT BEMEAN DEBASE
DEFAME DEJECT DEMEAN DEPOSE
GROVEL HUMBLE LESSEN MEEKEN
REDUCE DEGRADE DEPRESS
MORTIFY DIMINISH DISGRACE
DISHONOR
ABASED ABAISSE DEJECTED
ABASH AWE COW BASH BAZE DASH
AVALE ESBAY SHAME HUMBLE
AFFRONT CONFUSE MORTIFY
BEWILDER BROWBEAT CONFOUND
ABASHED BLANK CHEAP SHAMED
ASHAMED FOOLISH SHEEPISH
ABASHMENT VERGOYNE
ABATE EBB END LOW CALM CURB
FAIK FALL MEND OMIT SLOW SOFT
VAIL VOID WANE ALLAY ALLOW
ANNUL APPAL BREAK CHECK
LOWER QUASH RELAX REMIT
SLAKE SWAGE ASLAKE DEDUCT
LESSEN PACIFY REBATE REDUCE
RELENT ABOLISH ASSUAGE
CASSARE CHANCER NULLIFY
QUALIFY SLACKEN SUBSIDE
DECREASE DIMINISH MITIGATE
MODERATE OVERBLOW PALLIATE
ABATEMENT DELF FALL ALLAY
DELFT DELPH LETUP GUSSET
MIOSIS RABATE DECREASE
DISCOUNT PROSTRATION
(— OF DISEASE) LYSIS
ABATIS OBSTACLE SLASHING
ABAXIAL DORSAL
ABBA FATHER
ABBAY ABBACY
ABBE MONK CLERIC CURATE PRIEST
ABBESS AMMA VICARESS
ABBEY ABADIA ABBAYE PRIORY
CONVENT NUNNERY CLOISTER
ABBOT ABBAS COARB
ARCHIMANDRITE
(— OF MISRULE) BISHOP
ABBREVIATE CUT CLIP DOCK
PRUNE DIGEST ABRIDGE BOBTAIL
CURTAIL SHORTEN CONDENSE
CONTRACT TRUNCATE
ABBREVIATED SHORT BOBTAIL
CRYPTIC MUTILATE
ABBREVIATION LAPSE SIGLUM
SYMBOL
(PL.) SIGLA
ABC ALPHABET
ABDA (FATHER OF —) SHAMMUA
(SON OF) ADONIRAM
ABDEEL (SON OF —) SHELEMIAH
ABDERITE FOOL SCOFFER
SIMPLETON
ABDI (SON OF —) KISHI
ABDICATE CEDE QUIT DEMIT EXPEL
LEAVE REMIT DEPOSE DISOWN

FOREGO RESIGN RETIRE VACATE
ABANDON DISCLAIM RENOUNCE
ABDICATION DRIFT
ABDIEL (FATHER OF —) GUNI
(SON OF —) AHI
ABDOMEN BOUK WOMB ALVUS
APRON BELLY MELON MIRAC
PLEON THARM PAUNCH VENTER
STOMACH
(PREF.) CELI COELI VENTR(I)(O)
ABDOMINAL BELLY HEMAL CELIAC
COELIAC VENTRAL VISCERAL
ABDON (FATHER OF —) MICAH
HILLEL JEHIEL SHASHAK
ABDUCT LURE TAKE STEAL ABDUCE
KIDNAP RAVISH SPIRIT CAPTURE
ABDUCTED RAPT
ABDUCTION APAGOGE RAPTURE
ABDUCTION FROM THE
SERAGLIO (CHARACTER IN —)
OSMIN PASHA BLONDE BELMONTE
PEDRILLO CONSTANZE
(COMPOSER OF —) MOZART
ABDUCTOR SPIRIT
ABEAM ABREAST
ABECEDARIAN TYRO NOVICE
LEARNER BEGINNER
ABECEDARIUS ABC
ABED SICK RESTING RETIRED
SLEEPING
ABEL (BROTHER OF —) CAIN SETH
(FATHER OF —) ADAM
(MOTHER OF —) EVE
(PARENT OF —) ADAM
ABE LINCOLN IN ILLINOIS
(AUTHOR OF —) SHERWOOD
(CHARACTER IN —) ABE ANN GALE
MARY SETH TODD GREEN SPEED
GRAHAM JIMMIE MENTOR NINIAN
BOWLING DOUGLAS EDWARDS
HERNDON RUTLEDGE
ABELMOSK MUSK MALLOW
ABENCERAGES (CHARACTER IN —)
ALMANSOR
(COMPOSER OF —) CHERUBINI
ABENCERRAJE (AUTHOR OF —)
VILLEGAS
(CHARACTER IN —) JARIFA
NARVAEZ RODRIGO ABINDARRAEZ
ABERDEEN ANGUS BLACK DODDY
DODDIE
ABERRANT WILD CLAMMY DEVIANT
ABNORMAL STRAYING VARIABLE
ABERRATION SLIP WARP ERROR
FAULT LAPSE MANIA DELIRIUM
DELUSION INSANITY
ABESSIVE CARITIVE
ABET AID EGG BACK HELP BOOST
COACH ASSIST FOMENT INCITE
SECOND SUCCOR UPHOLD
COMFORT CONNIVE ESPOUSE
FORWARD FURTHER SUPPORT
SUSTAIN ADVOCATE BEFRIEND

ABETO ACXOYATL
ABETTING CONFEDERATE
ABETTOR FAUTOR ADVOCATE
PROMOTER
ABEYANCE ABEYANCY DORMANCY
(IN —) ONICE
ABEYANT LATENT
ABHIMANYU (FATHER OF —)
ARJUNA
(VICTIM OF —) LAKSHMANA
ABHOR UG IRK HATE SHUN AGRISE
DETEST LOATHE DESPISE DISLIKE
EXECRATE ABOMINATE
ABHORRENCE HATE ODIUM
HATRED HORROR DISGUST DISLIKE
SCUNNER AVERSION LOATHING
ABHORRENT ODIOUS UGSOME
HATEFUL ABSONANT INFAMOUS
REPUGNANT
ABI (SON OF —) HEZEKIAH
ABIA (FATHER OF —) BECHER
SAMUEL JEROBOAM REHOBOAM
(HUSBAND OF —) HEZRON
ABIATHAR (FATHER OF —)
AHIMELECH
ABIDA (FATHER OF —) MIDIAN
ABIDE BE WIN WON BEAR BIDE
KEEP LAST LEND LENG LIVE REST
STAY WAIT ABEAR AWAIT DELAY
EXIST HABIT PAUSE STAND SWELL
TARRY ENDURE HARBOR LINGER
REMAIN RESIDE SUBMIT INHABIT
SOJOURN SUBSIST SUSTAIN
CONTINUE TOLERATE
(— BY) HOLD
ABIDING ABY FAST STABLE LASTING
ABIDINGNESS PERMANENCE
ABIEL (SON OF —) KISH
ABIES FIRS CONIFERS
ABIETATE SYLVATE
ABIEZER (FATHER OF —) GILEAD
ABIGAIL MAID
(HUSBAND OF —) DAVID NABAL
JETHER
(SON OF —) AMASA DANIEL
CHILEAB
ABIGEUS ABACTOR
ABIHAIL (DAUGHTER OF —) ESTHER
(FATHER OF —) HURI ELIAB
(HUSBAND OF —) ABISHUR
REHOBOAM
(SON OF —) ZURIEL
ABIHU (BROTHER OF —) NADAB
(FATHER OF —) AARON
(MOTHER OF —) ELISHEBA
ABIHUD (FATHER OF —) BELA
ABIJAH (FATHER OF —) DAVID
SAMUEL JEROBOAM REHOBOAM
(SON OF —) ASA HEZEKIAH
ABILITY G CAN MAY CLAY EASE
FORM HAND CLASS FLAIR FORCE
MIGHT POWER SKILL STUFF VERVE
ENERGY ENGINE INGINE MAUGHT

STROKE TALENT CALIBER CUNNING FACULTY POTENCY APTITUDE CAPACITY STRENGTH
(— TO ENTER) ACCESS
(— TO THROW) ARM
(BATTING —) STICKWORK
(CREATIVE —) IMAGINATION
(FIELDING —) GLOVE
(INVENTIVE —) CONTRIVANCE
(MENTAL —) INGENY BRAINPOWER
ABIMELECH (BROTHER OF —) JOTHAM
(FATHER OF —) GIDEON ABIATHA
ABINADAB (FATHER OF —) SAUL JESSE
ABINOAM (SON OF —) BARAK
ABIPON CORONADO
ABIRAM (FATHER OF —) HIEL ELIAB
ABISHAI (BROTHER OF —) JOAB ASAHEL
(MOTHER OF —) ZERUIAH
ABISHALOM (DAUGHTER OF —) MAACHAH
ABISHUA (FATHER OF —) BELA PHINEHAS
(SON OF —) BUKKI
ABISHUR (FATHER OF —) SHAMMAI
ABITAL (HUSBAND OF —) DAVID
ABITUB (FATHER OF —) SHAHARAIM
(MOTHER OF —) HUSHIM
ABJECT LOW BASE MEAN POOR SUNK VILE HELOT PRONE SORRY CRAVEN MENIAL PALTRY SORDID SUPINE FAWNING FORLORN IGNOBLE SERVILE SLAVISH BEGGARLY CRINGING DEGRADED DOWNCAST LISTLESS WRETCHED
ABJOINT ABSTRICT
ABJURE DENY NITTE SPURN ESCHEW RECALL RECANT REJECT RESIGN REVOKE ABANDON DISAVOW EJURATE RETRACT ABNEGATE DISCLAIM FORSWEAR RENOUNCE
ABLAUT APOPHONY
ABLAZE ALOW AFIRE ALOWE ABLEEZE BURNING GLOWING RADIANT GLEAMING INFLAMED
ABLE APT BIG CAN FIT FERE ADEPT HABIL SMART THERE CLEVER EXPERT FACILE FITTED HABILE POTENT STRONG BASTANT CAPABLE DOUGHTY DEXTROUS POSSIBLE POWERFUL SKILLFUL SUITABLE TALENTED VIGOROUS
(— TO WALK) FEERIE FEIRIE
(SUFF.) (— TO) FUL
ABLE-BODIED YAL YALD YAULD
ABLENESS
(SUFF.) ABILITY IBILITY
ABLUTION BATH WIDU WUDU WUZU LOTION BAPTISM BATHING WASHING
ABNAKI WABANAKI
ABNEGATE DENY ABJURE FOREGO REFUSE REJECT DISAVOW DISCLAIM FORSWEAR IMMOLATE RENOUNCE
ABNER (BROTHER OF —) KISH
(FATHER OF —) NER
(SLAYER OF —) JOAB
(SON OF —) JAASIEL
(WIFE OF —) RIZPAH

ABNORMAL ENORM QUEER UTTER ERRATIC UNUSUAL VICIOUS ABERRANT ATYPICAL FREAKISH TERATOID ANOMALOUS MONSTROUS
(PREF.) ANOM(O) DYS MAL PARA POLY PSEUD(O)
ABNORMALITY ATAXY ATAXIA LETHAL ANOMALY BROWNING DEMENTIA ENORMITY
(CATTLE —) SAWDUST
ABOARD ON ONTO ACROSS ATHWART
ABODE COT DAR HUT INN WON BODE CELL FLAT HALL HOME NEST OMEN REST SEAT TENT WOON BEING BOWER DELAY HAUNT HOUSE MANOR PITCH RESET SIEGE SUITE ABIDAL BIDING ESTATE ADDRESS COTTAGE HABITAT LODGING MANSION SITTING CUNABULA DOMICILE DWELLING RESIANCE TENEMENT
(— OF DEAD) DAR AARU HELL ARALU HADES ORCUS SHEOL HEAVEN SHADES XIBALBA NIFLHEIM
(— OF DELIGHT) ELYSIUM
(— OF EVIL POWERS) ABYSS
(— OF GIANTS) UTGARD
(— OF GODS) MERU ASGARD OLYMPUS
(— OF LOST SOULS) ABADDON
(— OF MEN) MIDGARD
(— OF SOULS) LIMBO
(— OF SPIRITS) HELL
(ANIMAL —) ZOO MENAGERIE
(CELESTIAL —) HEAVEN
(FILTHY —) STY STYE
(MISERABLE —) DOGHOLE
(SHELTERED —) SHADE
ABOLISH END BLOT KILL ABATE ANNUL ERASE FORDO QUASH CANCEL EFFACE FOREDO RECALL REPEAL REVOKE VACATE DESTROY NULLIFY RESCIND REVERSE ABROGATE
ABOLITION EXTINCTION
ABOMA BOA BOM BOMA
ABOMASUM READ REED
ABOMINABLE VILE NASTY RUSTY CURSED ODIOUS ROTTEN BEASTLY HATEFUL HEINOUS MALEDICT NEFANDOUS
ABOMINABLY BEASTLY
ABOMINATE HATE ABHOR DETEST LOATHE EXECRATE
ABOMINATION EVIL CRIME CURSE HORROR PLAGUE DISGUST AVERSION
ABONGO BABONGO
ABORAL DORSAL ABACTINAL
ABORIGINAL ABO YAO FIRST NATAL BINGHI NATIVE SAVAGE NATURAL PRIMARY ORIGINAL
(— WOMAN) GIN
ABORIGINE KA KHA AINU TODA ALFUR BAIGA BLACK BOONG DASYU MAORI MYALL ALFURO ARANDA ARANTA ARUNTA BINGHI INDIAN KIPPER KODAGA NATIVE SAVAGE ADIBASI CHINHWAN WARRAGAL WARRIGAL
(AUSTRALIAN —) ABO

ABORT SLIP
ABORTION ABORT FAILURE CASTLING FETICIDE MISBIRTH
ABORTIVE IDLE VAIN BLIND FUTILE BOOTLESS
ABOUND SNY FLOW SNEE TEEM COVER FLEET SWARM REDOUND OVERFLOW
(SUFF.) ULENT
ABOUNDING RIFE FLUSH ROUTH COPIOUS REPLETE TEEMING UBEROUS ABUNDANT AFFLUENT PROLIFIC
(— IN POSSESSIONS) RICH
(SUFF.) IOUS OSE OUS
ABOUT BY IN OF ON RE SAY ASTO AWAY NEAR SOME UMBE UPON ANENT ASTIR CIRCA ABROAD ACTIVE ALMOST ANENST AROUND CIRCUM TOWARD ENVIRON CIRCITER
(PREF.) AMB(I) AMPH(I)(O) CIRCUM HYPER PERI
ABOUT-FACE FLOP
ABOVE ON UP OER SUP ATOP OVER PAST UPON ABEEN ABOON ABUNE ALOFT SUPRA BEFORE BEYOND HIGHER THEREUP OVERHEAD SUPERIOR
(— GENERAL LEVEL) APART
(PREF.) EP EPH EPI HYPER OVER SUPER SUPRA SUR
ABOVEBOARD HONEST
ABRADE RAW RUB BARK FILE FRET GALL RASP SAND WEAR CHAFE ERASE GRATE GRAZE GRIND SCORE SCUFF TOUCH SCOTCH SCRAPE IRRITATE
ABRADER FILE RASP EMERY SANDER ABRASER GRINDER SCRAPER
ABRAHAM (BIRTHPLACE OF —) UR
(BROTHER OF —) HARAN NAHOR
(CONCUBINE OF —) HAGAR
(FATHER OF —) TERAH
(GRANDFATHER OF —) NAHOR
(GRANDSON OF —) ESAU
(NEPHEW OF —) LOT
(SON OF —) ISAAC MEDAN SHUAH MIDIAN ZIMRAN ISHMAEL JOKSHAN
(WIFE OF —) SARAH KETURAH
ABRASION BURN GALL OUCH SCAR SORE GRAZE BRUISE BLASTING
ABRASIVE SAND EMERY PUMICE QUARTZ SILICA ALUNDUM BORAZON ERODENT ABRADANT CORUNDUM PUMICITE SCRUBBER
ABRAXAS GEM STONE AMULET ABRASAX
ABREAST EVEN AFRONT BESIDE HANGING
ABRET BREAD WAFER
ABRI SHED COVER DUGOUT SHELTER
ABRIDGE CUT DOCK LASK BRIEF ELIDE LIMIT RASEE RAZEE BRIDGE REDUCE SHRINK CURTAIL DEPRIVE REWRITE SHORTEN ABSTRACT BREVIATE COMPRESS CONDENSE CONTRACT DIMINISH RETRENCH SIMPLIFY ABBREVIATE
ABRIDGED TAIL

ABRIDGEMENT BRIEF ABREGE DIGEST PRECIS RESUME SKETCH COMPEND EPITOME PANDECT SUMMARY SUMMULA ABSTRACT BOILDOWN BREVIARY SYNOPSIS ABBREVIATION ABBREVIATURE
ABROAD OFF ASEA AWAY ABOUT ASTIR FORTH ABREED AFIELD ASTRAY WIDELY DISTANT OUTWARD OVERSEA OFFSHORE
ABROGATE ANNUL QUASH REMIT CANCEL REPEAL REVOKE VACATE ABOLISH NULLIFY RESCIND RETRACT DISSOLVE OVERRULE
ABROGATION REPEAL
ABRUPT BOLD CURT DEAD FAST RUDE BLUFF BLUNT BRIEF BRUSK HASTY ICTIC PLUMP QUICK ROUGH SHARP SHEER SHORT STEEP STUNT SURLY TERSE TOTAL CHOPPY CRAGGY CRUSTY PROMPT RUGGED SUDDEN ANGULAR BRUSQUE PRERUPT VIOLENT HEADLONG VERTICAL PRECIPITATE
(NOT —) SOFT
ABRUPTLY BANG SHARP SHORT STEEPLY SUDDENLY
ABSALOM (FATHER OF —) DAVID
(MOTHER OF —) MAACHAH
(SISTER OF —) TAMAR
(SLAYER OF —) JOAB
ABSALOM, ABSALOM (AUTHOR OF —) FAULKNER
(CHARACTER IN —) BON ROSA ELLEN HENRY JUDITH SHREVE SUTPEN THOMAS CHARLES-COMPSON GOODHUE QUENTIN MCCANNON COLDFIELD
ABSAROKA CROW
ABSCESS BOIL MORO SORE ULCER FESTER INCOME LESION QUINSY VOMICA EXITURE GUMBOIL PARULIS APOSTEME SQUINACY
ABSCISIC ACID DORMIN
ABSCISSA X COSINE
ABSCISSION APOCOPE
ABSCOND GO FLY RUN BOLT FLEE HIDE QUIT ELOPE SCRAM SMOKE DECAMP DEPART DESERT ELOINE ESCAPE LEVANT WITHDRAW
ABSEILING RAPPEL
ABSENCE CUT LACK VOID WANT BLANK LEAVE DEFECT REMOVE VACUUM DEFAULT FAILURE VACANCY FURLOUGH
(— FROM DUTY) LIBERTY
(— FROM ONE'S COUNTRY) EXILE
(— OF AN ORGAN) AGENESIA AGENESIS
(— OF BIAS) DETACHMENT
(— OF CEREMONY) FAMILIARITY
(— OF FAMILIARITY) DISTANCE
(— OF FEELING) APATHY
(— OF FEVER) APYREXY APYREXIA
(— OF FORM) ENTROPY
(— OF GOVERNMENT) ANARCHY
(— OF INHIBITIONS) ANIMALITY
(— OF LIGHT) BLACK DARKNESS
(— OF MARRIAGE) AGAMY
(— OF MIND) ABSTRACTION
(— OF NAILS) ANONYCHIA
(— OF PAIN) ANODYNIA

(— OF PIGMENTATION) ACHROMA ACHROMIA
(— OF SKULL) ACRANIA
(— OF TAIL) ANURY
(— OF TASTE) AGEUSIA
(— OF TRUMPS) CHICANE
(— OF TRUTH) FALSEHOOD
(PERMITTED —) LEAVE
(PREF.) DYS ECTRO NON
ABSENT CUT OFF OUT AWAY AWOL GONE LOST WANE DESERT MUSING LACKING MISSING NOTHERE WANTING ABSORBED DREAMING
(— IN MIND) ABSTRACT
(PREF.) ECTRO
ABSENTMINDED FLAKY MUSED MUSING DISTRAIT DREAMING ABSTRACTED
ABSENTMINDEDNESS STARGAZING
ABSINTHE AJENJO GENIPI
ABSOLUTE GOD ONE TAO TAT DEAD DOWN FAIR FINE FREE MEAR MEER MERE PLAT PLUM PURE RANK REAL SELF TRUE VERY BLANK CLEAR FIXED PLUMB SHEER STARK STONE TOTAL UTTER WHOLE ENTIRE PROPER SEVERE SIMPLE SQUARE BRAHMAN CERTAIN PERFECT PLENARY ABSTRACT COMPLETE DESPOTIC EVENDOWN EXPLICIT IMPLICIT POSITIVE
(— TEMPERATURE) T
(NOT —) NISI FINITE CONDITIONAL
ABSOLUTELY YEA YES AMEN BONE COLD DEAD FAIR JUST PLAT SLAP PLAIN PLUMB STARK BARELY FAIRLY FLATLY SIMPLY WHOLLY SHEERLY ENTIRELY EVENDOWN
ABSOLUTION EXCUSE PARDON SHRIFT LOOSING SHRIVING
ABSOLUTISM CAESARISM DESPOTISM
ABSOLVE FREE QUIT CLEAR LOOSE REMIT ACQUIT ASSOIL EXCUSE EXEMPT FINISH PARDON SHRIVE UNBIND CLEANSE FORGIVE JUSTIFY RELEASE DISPENSE LIBERATE OVERLOOK
ABSORB EAT FIX SOP SUP BLOT SOAK SUCK TAKE AMUSE DRINK MERGE RIVET UNITE DEVOUR ENGAGE ENGULF ENWRAP IMBIBE INGEST INSORB INWRAP OCCUPY SPONGE STIFLE COMBINE CONSUME ENGROSS IMMERSE INVOLVE OCCLUDE SWALLOW
(— GRADUALLY) OSMOSE
ABSORBED DEEP GONE LOST RAPT SUNK FIXED ABSENT BURIED ENRAPT HIPPED INTENT PLUNGED RIVETED WRAPPED IMMERSED ABSTRACTED
(— BY) ALL
ABSORBENT BASE DOPE FOMES BARYTA SPONGY ANTACID SORBENT ANTIACID BIBULOUS DRINKING
ABSORBER SNUBBER
(— OF MONEY) LICKPENNY
(SHOCK —) BUFFER DAMPER

ABSORPTION AUTISM PREOCCUPATION
(— UNIT) SABIN
ABSORPTIVE SPONGY
ABSQUATULATE DECAMP ABSCOND
ABSTAIN DENY FAST KEEP STAY AVOID CEASE SPARE SPURN WAIVE DESIST DISUSE ESCHEW FOREGO REFUSE REJECT FORBEAR REFRAIN RESTRAIN TEETOTAL WITHHOLD
(— FROM) FAST FORGO LEAVE ABJURE ESCHEW FOREGO REFRAIN
ABSTAINER TOTE RECHABITE
ABSTEMIOUS SOBER ACETIC SLENDER MODERATE
ABSTENTION CELIBACY CHASTITY
ABSTERGE WIPE BATHE CLEAN PURGE RINSE
ABSTINENCE ENCRATY
ABSTINENT SOBER ABSTEMIOUS
ABSTRACT CULL DEED DRAW NOTE PART PURE TAKE BRIEF IDEAL STEAL ABSORB DEDUCT DETACH DIGEST DIVERT DOCKET NOETIC PRECIS REMOVE ABRIDGE COMPEND EPITOME EXCERPT ISOLATE PURLOIN SECRETE SUMMARY VIDIMUS ABSTRUSE ACADEMIC ARGUMENT BREVIATE DISCRETE PRESCIND SEPARATE SYLLABUS SYNOPSIS TABLEITY WITHDRAW METAPHYSICAL
(— SECRETLY) SUBDUCT
(NOT —) CONCRETE
(PL.) PARATITLA PARATITLES
ABSTRACTED REMOTE
ABSTRACTION STUDY ENTITY ABSENCE REVERIE ABSTRACT QUODDITY
(MENTAL —) REVERY REVERIE
ABSTRUSE DARK DEEP HIGH HIDDEN MYSTIC REMOTE SECRET SUBTLE CURIOUS OBSCURE RETIRED ABSTRACT ACROATIC ESOTERIC PROFOUND METAPHYSICAL
ABSTRUSENESS DEPTH
ABSURD HOT RICH WILD DOTTY DROLL FALSE INANE INEPT SILLY SCREWY STUPID ASININE FATUOUS FOOLISH LAPUTAN ABSONANT DOGGEREL FABULOUS COCKAMAMY MONSTROUS RIDICULOUS PREPOSTEROUS
ABSURDITY BETISE FATUITY FOOLERY FOPPERY WALTROT MAGGOTRY NONSENSE UNREASON
ABUNA METRAN
ABUNDANCE WON COPY FLOW MORT SONS WONE CHEAP DEPTH FLUSH FOUTH POWER RIVER ROUTH ROWTH SCADS SONSE STORE WRECK BOUNTY FOISON GALORE LAVISH OODLES PLENTY POWDER RICHES TALENT UBERTY WEALTH FLUENCY LASHINS PLEROMA SATIETY BELLYFUL FULLNESS LASHINGS OPULENCE

PLEURISY RIMPTION PLENITUDE REDUNDANCY
(IN —) APLENTY
ABUNDANT FAT OLD FREE LUSH MUCH RANK RICH RIFE AMPLE FLUSH HEFTY LARGE OPIME ROUTH ROWTH STORE DEMOID GALORE HEARTY ROUTHY APLENTY COPIOUS FERTILE FULSOME LIBERAL OPULENT PROFUSE REPLETE TEEMING UBERANT UBEROUS WEALTHY AFFLUENT FRUITFUL GENEROUS NUMEROUS PLENTIFUL
(NOT —) LIGHT SPARE
(PREF.) HADR(O) LARGI
ABUNDANTLY RIFE WELL FREELY PLENTY LARGELY HEARTILY
ABUSE MAR MOB TAX BUSE CALL DRUB FLAY GAFF HARM HURT LACK MAUL RAIL RUIN SLAM TEEN VAIN BASTE BLAST CRIME CURSE FAULT GRIEF SCOLD SLANG SNASH SPOIL BERATE DEFILE INJURE INSULT MALIGN MISSAY MISUSE MUMBLE PUNISH RAVISH REVILE TANCEL TANSEL VILIFY YATTER AFFRONT BACKJAW BEDEVIL DECEIVE DESPITE FALSIFY MISBEDE MISCALL MISNAME OBLOQUY OUTRAGE PERVERT PROFANE SLANDER TRADUCE UPBRAID VIOLATE BALLARAG BUSINESS DISHONOR FRUMPERY LANGUAGE MALTREAT MISAPPLY MISTREAT REPROACH SLAPDASH
(— OF FREEDOM) LICENCE LICENSE
ABUSED DOWNTROD DOWNTRODDEN
ABUSIVE FOUL DIRTY SHREWD CORRUPT SATIRIC CHEATING INSOLENT LIBELOUS
ABUT BUTT JOIN REST TOUCH ADJOIN BORDER BUTTAL PROJECT
ABUTILON MALLOW
ABUTMENT CRIB PIER ALETTE BUTTRESS
ABUTTING FLUSH ADJACENT
ABY ABIDING
ABYSM ABIME BISME DOWNFALL
ABYSMAL DEEP DREARY PROFOUND UNENDING WRETCHED
ABYSS PIT POT DEEP GULF HELL HOLE VOID ABYSM CHAOS CHASM DEPTH GORGE ABRUPT BOTTOM VORAGO ABADDON AVERNUS GEHENNA SWALLOW DOWNFALL INTERVAL
ABYSSAL ABYSMAL BASSALIAN
ABYSSINIA (SEE ETHIOPIA)
ABYSSINIAN SIDI ABASSIN
(— BANANA) ENSETE
ACACALLIS (FATHER OF) MINOS
(MOTHER OF —) PASIPHAE
(SON OF —) GARAMAS AMPHITHEMIS
ACACIA GUM JAM KOA WELD WOLD BABUL GIDYA MULGA MYALL SIRIS THORN TIMBE VEREK WOALD WOULD ARABIC BABLAH BINDER GIDGEA GIDGEE GIDYEA HASHAB LEGUME LOCUST

MIMOSA SALLEE WATTLE YARRAN BLUEBUSH BRIGALOW CHAPARRO IRONWOOD ROSEWOOD
ACADEMIC IVY MOOT RIGID FORMAL ACADEME CLASSIC DONNISH ERUDITE LEARNED POMPIER PEDANTIC PLATONIC
(— HEAD) DEAN
ACADEMY LYCEE CRUSCA LYCEUM MANEGE SCHOOL ACADEME COLLEGE SOCIETY YESHIVA SEMINARY
(FRENCH —) FORTY
(RIDING —) MANAGE MANEGE
ACADIAN CAJUN
ACAJOU CAJU CAJOO CAJOU
ACALEPH MEDUSA MEDUSAN
ACAMAS (BROTHER OF —) ARCHELOCHUS
(FATHER OF —) ANTENOR THESEUS EUSSORUS
(MOTHER OF —) THEANO PHAEDRA
(SLAYER OF —) AJAX MERIONES
(SON OF —) MUNITUS
ACANA ALMIQUE
ACANTHA FIN SPINE THORN PRICKLE ACANTHON
ACAPU WALNUT WACAPOU CHAPERNO
ACARID MITE NYMPH NYMPHA OCTOPOD DIBRANCH PROTONYMPH
ACARNAN (BROTHER OF —) AMPHOTERUS
(FATHER OF —) ALCMAEON
(MOTHER OF —) CALLIRRHOE
ACASTUS (FATHER OF —) PELIAS
(SLAYER OF —) PELEUS
(WIFE OF —) HIPPOLYTE
ACAUDAL BOBBED ANUROUS ECAUDATE TAILLESS
ACAULESCENT STEMLESS
ACCEDE LET AGREE ALLOW ENTER GRANT YIELD ACCORD ASSENT ATTAIN COMPLY CONCUR CONCEDE CONFORM CONSENT
ACCELERATE GUN REV RUN HYPO JAZZ RACE SPUR URGE DRIVE FAVOR FORCE HURRY LINAC SPEED HASTEN ADVANCE FORWARD FURTHER QUICKEN ANTEDATE DISPATCH EXPEDITE INCREASE THROTTLE
ACCELERATED
(PREF.) TACHY
ACCELERATING
(PREF.) AUXO
ACCELERATION PICKUP SPEEDUP
(— OF REACTION) CATALYSIS
(— UNIT) STAPP
ACCELERATOR GAS GUN SPEEDER BETATRON BEVATRON THROTTLE
(LINEAR —) LINAC
ACCENT BEAT BIRR BLAS BURR MARK TONE ACUTE GRAVE ICTUS PITCH PULSE SOUND THROB VERGE BROGUE LENGTH RHYTHM STRESS THESIS EMPHASIS
(DORIC —) PLATEASM
(IRISH —) BROGUE
(MUSICAL —) BEAT
(WITHOUT AN —) ATONIC

ACCENTED FZ SFZ TONIC STRONG MARCATO MARCANDO SFORZATO

ACCENTUATE ACCENT

ACCENTUATION DECLAMATION ENHANCEMENT

ACCEPT BUY EAT BEAR FANG HAVE HOLD JUMP TAKE ADMIT ADOPT AGREE ALLOW HONOR INFER MARRY ASSENT ASSUME AVOUCH POCKET RATIFY AGREEON AGREETO APPROVE BELIEVE CONCEDE EMBRACE ESPOUSE RECEIVE SETTLEFOR
(— AS ONE'S OWN) NOSTRIFICATE
(— AS TRUE) ACCREDIT
(— AT RANDOM) DRAW
(— BETS) BOOK
(— EAGERLY) LEAP
(— INHERITANCE) ADIATE
(— READILY) SWALLOW
(— WITHOUT QUESTION) ABIDE

ACCEPTABLE LIEF VALID SIGHTLY WELCOME GRACIOUS PASSABLE PLEASANT

ACCEPTANCE PASS SNAFF ADITIO TAQLID PASSAGE CREDENCE CURRENCY
(— OF INHERITANCE) CERNITURE
(— OF ORDER) ALLOTMENT

ACCEPTATION MEANING ACCEPTANCE

ACCEPTED GOING VULGAR POPULAR APPROVED CREDITED ORTHODOX STANDARD
(NOT —) OUT
(WIDELY —) INVETERATE

ACCEPTOR BASE

ACCESS FIT WAY ADIT DOOR GATE PATH ROAD ENTRY GOING ROUTE ACCOST AVENUE COMING ENTREE PORTAL STREET ADVANCE APPROACH ENTRANCE PAROXYSM RECOURSE
(— OF DISEASE) ATTACK

ACCESSIBILITY EXPOSURE

ACCESSIBLE NEAR OPEN HANDY PATENT AFFABLE PRESENT FAMILIAR PERVIOUS SOCIABLE GETATABLE

ACCESSION ENTER ACCESS AFFLUX ALLUVIO ILLAPSE ADDITION ALLUVION ENTRANCE INCREASE

ACCESSORY HAT AIDE ALLY DOME TOOL EXTRA SCARF HELPER ABETTOR ADAPTER ADAPTOR ADJUNCT ANCILLA ENCLAVE FITTING FIXTURE ADDITIVE HATSTAND ORNAMENT
(PL.) ADDENDA FIXINGS STAFFAGE

ACCIACCATURA MORDENT

ACCIDENT HAP CASE LUCK EVENT GRIEF PRANG SHUNT CHANCE HAZARD INJURY MISHAP FORTUNE QUALITY CALAMITY CASUALTY DISASTER FORTUITY INCIDENT ROLLOVER
(— IN CAR RACING) SHUNT
(AUTOMOBILE —) FATAL
(EUCHARISTIC —S) SPECIES
(HAVE — WITH) PRANG

ACCIDENTAL ODD CASUAL CHANCE RANDOM EXTERNAL

ACCIPITER ERNE HAWK

ACCLAIM CRY CLAP FAME HAIL LAUD ROOT CHEER CLAIM ECLAT EXTOL SHOUT PRAISE APPLAUD HOSANNA OVATION PLAUDIT RECLAME WELCOME APPLAUSE
(NOISY —) RIOT

ACCLAMATION CRY VOTE CHEER SHOUT ACCLAIM HOSANNA PLAUDIT APPLAUSE

ACCLIMATE ENURE INURE HARDEN SEASON ACCUSTOM

ACCLIMATIZE SALT ADAPT HARDEN ORIENT SEASON

ACCLIVITY BANK BROW HILL RISE GRADE PITCH SLANT SLOPE TALUS ASCENT HEIGHT INCLINE

ACCOLADE EMMY KISS RITE SIGN AWARD HONOR KUDOS MEDAL OSCAR TOKEN EULOGY SYMBOL EMBRACE GARLAND CEREMONY

ACCOMMODATE AID BED BOW FIT CAMP GIVE HELP HOLD LEND SORT SUIT ADAPT BOARD DEFER FAVOR HOUSE LODGE SERVE YIELD ADJUST COMPLY FAVOUR OBLIGE SETTLE CONFORM CONTAIN FASHION ATTEMPER GARRISON

ACCOMMODATING OBLIGING

ACCOMMODATION LOAN BERTH CLASS BERTHAGE GIFFGAFF
(— BILL) KITE
(PL.) PASSAGE

ACCOMPANIED FRAUGHT

ACCOMPANIMENT SON ALBA BACKUP BURDEN ESCORT OOMPAH ADJUNCT DESCANT SUPPORT OBLIGATO
(IMPROVISED —) VAMP
(PLAY JAZZ —) COMP
(PL.) FIXINGS

ACCOMPANIST JONGLEUR

ACCOMPANY SEE BACK FARE FERE JOIN LEAD TEND WAIT BRING PILOT ASSIST ATTEND CONCUR CONVEY CONVOY ESCORT FOLLOW SECOND SQUIRE COEXIST CONDUCT CONSORT SUPPORT CHAPERON

ACCOMPANYING FELLOW ADJUNCT
(PREF.) SYMPHORI

ACCOMPLICE PAL AIDE ALLY CHUM BUDDY CRONY LOUKE SHILL TILER BONNET COHORT FELLOW HELPER ABETTOR FEODARY FEUDARY HUSTLER PARTNER STEERER

ACCOMPLISH DO GO END WIN CHAR FILL WORK ENACT EQUIP FETCH FORTH SWING AFFORD ATTAIN EFFECT FINISH FULFIL MANAGE VIRTUE ABSOLVE ACHIEVE CHEVISE COMPASS EXECUTE EXPLETE FULFILL FURNISH OPERATE PERFECT PERFORM REALIZE SUCCEED COMPLETE CONTRIVE DISPATCH ENGINEER OUTCARRY NEGOTIATE

ACCOMPLISHED APT ABLE ARCH DONE ADEPT ENDED GREAT TERSE BESEEN EXPERT HANDSOME TALENTED

ACCOMPLISHMENT ART END DEED FEAT PASS CRAFT SKILL EFFECT TALENT VIRTUE EARNING QUALITY FRUITION LEARNING
(PRIOR —) ANTICIPATION

ACCORD GIVE JIBE JUMP SUIT UNIT AGREE ALLOW ATONE AWARD BEFIT CHIME CHORD CORDE GRANT LEVEL STAND TALLY UNITY ACCEDE ADJUST ASSENT BESTOW BETEEM COMPLY CONCUR SETTLE UNISON COMPORT COMPOSE CONCEDE CONCERT CONCORD CONGREE CONSENT CONSORT HARMONY RAPPORT RESPOND UNANIME DIAPASON SYMPATHY
(— WITH) SUIT
(IN —) ALONG

ACCORDANCE CONCERT CONSENT
(IN —) ALONG

ACCORDANT EVEN ATTUNED AGREEING COHERENT SUITABLE

ACCORDING (— TO) AD BY AUX SEC EMFORTH ENFORTH PURSUANT SECUNDUM
(— TO ART) SA
(— TO LAW) SL

ACCORDINGLY SO ERGO THEN THUS HENCE IGITUR

ACCORDION LANTUM FLUTINA FLAUTINO

ACCOST BAIL HAIL MASH MEET ABORD ASSAY BOARD GREET SPEAK ACCESS BROACH HALLOO SALUTE ACCOAST ADDRESS SOLICIT APPROACH GREETING

ACCOUCHEUR OBSTETRICIAN

ACCOUCHEUSE MIDWIFE

ACCOUNT TAB BILL BOOK DEEM DRAW ITEM NICK NOTE RATE REDE SAKE TAIL TALE TELL TEXT WORD AUDIT BLAME CHALK COUNT JUDGE SCORE STATE STORY VALUE WORTH BATTEL CREDIT DETAIL ESTEEM HORARY LEGEND NOTICE PROFIT REASON RECKON RECORD REGARD RELATE RENDER REPORT REPUTE TREATY ACCOMPT COMPOST COMPUTE EXPLAIN JOURNAL LEXICON NARRATE PROCESS RECITAL TAILZIE BREVIARY CONSIDER ESTIMATE RELATION TREATISE BORDEREAU MONOGRAPH RECKONING PRESENTATION
(— FOR) SAVE EXPLAIN
(—S FOR PROVISIONS) BATTELS
(ACCURATE —) GRIFF GRIFFIN
(CREDIT —) TICK
(KIND OF —) IRA NOW
(LONG —) ILIAD MEGILLAH
(LONG, INVOLVED —) MEGILLA MEGILLAH
(OFFICIAL —) PROTOCOL
(SAVINGS —) IRA
(SHORT —) KETCH
(TRAVEL —) ITINERARY
(PL.) BATTELS

ACCOUNTABILITY DETAIL LIABILITY

ACCOUNTABLE LIABLE AMENABLE

ACCOUNTANT CLERK SIRCAR SIRKAR AUDITOR PESHKAR PUTWARI KULKARNI MUTSUDDY RECKONER

ACCOUNTANT-GENERAL DAFTARDAR DEFTERDAR

ACCOUNTING TASK REASON COSTING

ACCOUTER ARM RIG GIRD ARRAY DRESS EQUIP ATTIRE CLOTHE OUTFIT BEDIGHT FURNISH HARNESS PROVIDE

ACCOUTERMENTS GEAR TIRE DRESS ATTIRE GRAITH

ACCREDIT ALLOT VOUCH CREDIT DEPUTE APPOINT APPROVE ASCRIBE BELIEVE CERTIFY CONFIRM ENDORSE LICENSE SANCTION

ACCRETION SUM GAIN GROWTH DEPOSIT EXUDATE ADDITION ADHESION INCREASE
(INJURIOUS —) RUST

ACCRUAL ACCRUE DEMERIT

ACCRUE ADD WIN EARN GAIN GROW PILE ARISE ENSUE ENURE INCUR INURE ISSUE MATURE RESULT SPRING ACQUIRE COLLECT REDOUND ACCRESCE CUMULATE INCREASE

ACCUMULATE DRAW FUND GROW HEAP HIVE MASS PILE SAVE AMASS DRIFT HOARD STACK STORE TOTAL ACCRUE GARNER GATHER MUSTER RACKUP SCRAPE COLLECT CONGEST HARVEST INCREASE

ACCUMULATION DRIP DUMP FUND GAIN HEAP MASS PILE LODGE STACK STORE ANLAGE BACKUP BUDGET COLUMN DEBRIS GARNER BACKLOG CUMULUS DEPOSIT DOSSIER MORAINE DIVIDEND INTEREST
(— OF FLUID) EDEMA OEDEMA ASCITES
(— OF FORCE) CHARGE
(— OF SNOW) ALIMENTATION
(— OF TRIFLES) FLOTSAM
(— ON CONCRETE) LAITANCE

ACCURACY NICETY FIDELITY JUSTNESS PRECISION
(— OF ADJUSTMENT) TRAM
(HISTORICAL —) SYNCHRONISM

ACCURATE JUST LEAL NICE TRUE CLOSE EXACT FLUSH RIGHT DEADON NARROW PROPER SEVERE STRICT CAREFUL CORRECT CURIOUS PRECISE FAITHFUL PERQUEER PUNCTUAL RIGOROUS TRUTHFUL
(NOT —) IMPURE
(UNPLEASANTLY —) BRUTAL

ACCURATELY JUST FAIRLY JUSTLY CLOSELY EXACTLY INSOOTH

ACCURSED FEY CURSED DAMNED DOOMED FORBID SACRED WARIED BLASTED MALEDICT

ACCUSATION BEEF WITE BLAME CAUSE CRIME POINT WHITE APPEAL ATTACK CHARGE THREAP THREEP ACCUSAL SCANDAL DELATION
(FALSE —) SUGGESTION

ACCUSATORY WRAYFUL

ACCUSE TAX WRY CALL FILE NOTE SHOW SLUR TASK WITE WRAY

ACOUP ARGUE BLAME PEACH
TAINT TOUCH WHITE APPEAL
ATTACH ATTACK BECALL BEWRAY
CHARGE DEFAME DELATE DETECT
INDICT INTENT MURMUR APPEACH
ARRAIGN ATTAINT CENSURE
IMPEACH IMPLEAD TRADUCE
CHASTISE COMPLAIN DENOUNCE
QUESTION REDARGUE REPROACH
(— UNJUSTLY) SLANDER
ACCUSER CHARGER DELATOR
LIBELANT
ACCUSING CULPATORY
DENUNCIATORY
ACCUSTOM URE USE WIN WON
HAFT WONT ADAPT BREAK DRILL
ENURE FLESH HABIT HAUNT INURE
TRAIN ADDICT ADJUST CUSTOM
INDUCE ORIENT SEASON CONSORT
EDUCATE TOUGHEN ACQUAINT
(— HORSE TO BIT) MOUTH
(— TO PASTURE) HAFT
ACCUSTOMED TAME USED WONE
WONT USANT USUAL INURED
CHRONIC CURRENT HABITED
CONSUETE
ACCUSTOMEDNESS HABIT
ACE AS ALS JOT ONE PIP TIB ATOM
CARD HERO MARK TOPS UNIT
WHIZ ADEPT BASTO FLYER POINT
BULLET EXPERT AVIATOR BRISQUE
PARTICLE
(— OF CLUBS) BASTA BASTO
(— OF SPADES) SPADILLE SPADILLO
(— OF TRUMPS) TIB HONOR PUNTO
(THREE —S) GLEEK
ACEDIA SLOTH ACCIDIA ACCIDIE
ACEPHALOUS HEADLESS
ACER NEGUNDO
ACERB ACID HARD SOUR TART
ACRID HARSH SHARP BITTER
SEVERE
ACERBAS (WIFE OF —) ELISSA
ACERBATE EMBITTER IRRITATE
ACERBITY ACRIMONY ASPERITY
CYNICISM SEVERITY TARTNESS
ACESTES (FATHER OF —) CRIMISUS
(MOTHER OF —) EGESTA
(WIFE OF —) ENTELLA
ACETABULUM PAN PYXIS CUPULE
ACETABLE HOLDFAST
ACETAL KETAL FORMAL KETATE
BUTYRAL
ACETALDEHYDE ETHYL ETHANAL
ALDEHYDE
ACETIC SOUR SHARP ZOONIC
ACETOPHENETIDIN PHENACETIN
ACETYLENE TOLAN ALKINE ALKYNE
ETHINE ETHYNE TOLANE
ACHAEMENES (BROTHER OF —)
XERXES
(FATHER OF —) DARIUS
(SLAYER OF —) INARUS
ACHAEUS (FATHER OF —) XUTHUS
(MOTHER OF —) CREUSA
ACHBOR (FATHER OF —) MICHAIAH
(SON OF —) BAALHANAN
ACHE AKE NAG NIP ECHE GELL HURT
LONG PAIN PANG PINE RACK WARK
WERK HACHE SMART STANG
STOUN THROB THROE WARCH
YEARN DESIRE MISERY STITCH

STOUND TWINGE TWITCH
ANGUISH EARACHE SORENESS
ACHENE CYPSELA UTRICLE
ACHIEVE DO END GET WIN EARN
GAIN HACK HAVE MAKE FETCH
FORCE NOTCH REACH SCORE
AFFORD ARRIVE ATTAIN EFFECT
FINISH OBTAIN CHEVISE COMPASS
EXPLOIT FULFILL PERFORM
PROCURE PRODUCE REALIZE
SUCCEED TRIUMPH COMPLETE
CONCLUDE CONTRIVE
ACCOMPLISH
(— HARMONY) AGREE
(— ORIENTATION) ADJUST
ACHIEVED (SOMETHING EASILY —)
GIMME
ACHIEVEMENT ACT JOB DEED
FEAT WORK ACTION CAREER
RESULT STROKE EXPLOIT HARVEST
PROWESS SUCCESS FELICITY
(COMPLETE —) TRIUMPH
ACHILLEA PTARMICA
ACHILLES PELIDES
(COMPANION OF —) PATROCLUS
(FATHER OF —) PELEUS
(FRIEND OF —) PATROCLUS
(GRANDFATHER OF —) AEACUS
(HORSE OF —) XANTHUS
(MOTHER OF —) THETIS
(SLAYER OF —) PARIS
ACHIM (FATHER OF —) SADOC
(SON OF —) ELIUD
ACHING SORE
ACHIOTE OLEANA ACHUETE
ANNATTO ARNATTA ARNATTO
ACHRAS SAPOTA
ACHROMACYTE SHADOW
ACHROMATIC GRAY GREY
NEUTRAL
ACHSAH (FATHER OF —) CALEB
(HUSBAND OF —) OTHNIEL
ACICULAR SPLINTERY
ACID DRY LSD YAR DIAL DOPA KEEN
PABA SOUR TART ACERB ACRID
ALGIN AMINO CERIN EAGER
HARSH LYSIN MALIC OLEUM RHEIN
SHARP ULMIC ABRINE ALLIIN
BITING BITTER DORMIN FOLATE
GLYCIN LYSINE NIACIN PROLIN
SERINE TWEAKY VALINE ACERBIC
ACETOSE CERASIN FILICIN
GLYCINE PROLINE STEARIN
VINEGAR ORNITHINE PENICILLIN
(CRYSTALLINE —) EDTA
(KIND OF —) MALIC ADIPIC KAINIC
MURAMIC
(NITRIC —) AQUAFORTIS
(NUCLEIC —) DNA RNA
(SEQUENCE OF NUCLEIC —)
INTRON
(PREF.) ACETO OXY
(SUFF.) — RADICAL) OYL
ACID HYDROGEN
(SUFF.) HYDRIC
ACIDITY ACOR VERDURE ACERBITY
SOURNESS VERJUICE
ACIDULOUS TART
ACIS (FATHER OF —) FAUNUS
(LOVER OF —) GALATEA
(MOTHER OF —) SYMAETHIS
(SLAYER OF —) POLYPHEMUS

**ACIS & GALATEA (CHARACTER IN
—)** ACIS GALATEA POLYPHEMUS
(COMPOSER OF —) HANDEL
ACKNOWLEDGE NOD OWN AVER
AVOW SIGN ADMIT ADOPT ALLOW
GRANT KITHE KYTHE THANK YIELD
ACCEDE ACCEPT AGNIZE ANSWER
ASSENT AVOUCH BEKNOW
COUTHE FATHER REWARD
CONCEDE CONFESS DECLARE
OBSERVE PROFESS DISCLOSE
RECOGNIZE
ACKNOWLEDGEMENT GRANT
THANK AVOWAL CREDIT SHRIFT
APOLOGY AGNITION COGNOVIT
COGNISANCE COGNIZANCE
RECOGNITION
(— OF MISTAKE) JEOFAIL
(— OF SERVICE) GRAVITY
(— OF SIN) PECCAVI
(WRITTEN —) RECEIPT
ACLE AKLE IRUL JAMBA IRONWOOD
PYENGADU
ACLYS HURLBAT
ACME IT ACE CAP TOP APEX CULM
HIGH PEAK CREST PITCH POINT
STATE APOGEE CLIMAX COMBLE
CRISIS CULMEN HEIGHT HEYDAY
SUMMIT ZENITH CUMULUS
SUBLIME CAPSHEAF CAPSTONE
PINNACLE
ACNE WHELK ROSACEA
ACOLYTE BOY HELPER NOVICE
SERVER LEARNER PATENER
THURIFER
ACOMIA BALDNESS
ACONITE BIKH ACONITUM
NAPELLUS
ACORN NUT MAST GLAND OVEST
BAI ANUS BELLOTA BELLOTE
(— CUPS) VALONIA
(PL.) MAST CAMATA PANNAGE
CAMATINA
(PREF.) BALAN(I)(O) GLANDI
GLANDULI
ACORN-SHAPED BALANOID
ACOUSTICS SONICS PHONICS
ACQUAINT KNOW TELL TEACH
VERSE ADVISE INFORM NOTIFY
SCHOOL APPRISE APPRIZE
POSSESS RESOLVE
ACQUAINTANCE KITH HABIT
COUSIN FRIEND GOSSIP PICKUP
AFFINITY FAMILIAR INTIMATE
(CLOSE —) HABIT INWARDNESS
(PRACTICAL —) PRACTICE PRACTISE
(PL.) KITH SOCIETY
ACQUAINTED VERSED ACQUENT
VERSANT
(CLOSELY —) INTIMATE
ACQUIESCE BOW ABIDE AGREE
CHIME YIELD ACCEDE ACCEPT
ASSENT COMPLY CONCUR SUBMIT
CONCEDE CONFIRM CONFORM
CONSENT
ACQUIESCENCE ASSENT
ACQUIRABLE
(PREF.) CTETO
ACQUIRE ADD BAG BUY GET WIN
EARN FORM GAIN GRAB HAVE
MAKE REAP ADOPT AMASS ANNEX
BEGET CHEVY CHIVY GLEAN INCUR
LEARN REACH SEIZE STEAL ATTAIN

CHIVEY CHIVVY DERIVE EFFECT
GARNER OBTAIN SECURE SNATCH
COLLECT CONQUER DEVELOP
PROCURE RECEIVE CONTRACT
(— DESIRABLE QUALITY) AGE
(— KNOWLEDGE) LERE
ACQUIRED (NOT —) NATURAL
ACQUIREMENT (— OF CONTROL)
TAKEOVER
ACQUISITION WIN GAIN LUCRE
ACQUEST ACQUIST GETTING
CONQUEST ACCESSION
(DISHONEST —) GRAFT
(VALUED —) PRIZE
ACQUISITIVE GRABBY
ACQUIT PAY FREE QUIT CLEAR
QUIET ASSOIL BEHAVE BESTOW
EXCUSE PARDON ABSOLVE
COMPORT CONDUCT RELEASE
REQUITE LIBERATE OVERLOOK
UNCHARGE ASSOILZIE
ACQUITTAL EXCUSE DISCHARGE
ABSOLUTION
ACQUITTANCE QUIETUS RELEASE
ACRE AKER LAND ACKER FIELD
STANG ARPENT COLLOP
FARMHOLD
(QUARTER —) ROOD
(120 —S) HIDE
(2-3RDS —) COVER
(PL.) ACREAGE
ACREMAN CARUCARIUS
ACRID HOT ACID BASK KEEN SOUR
HARSH ROUGH SHARP SURLY
BITING BITTER CAUSTIC PUNGENT
REEKING UNSAVORY VIRULENT
ACRIMONIOUS MAD ACID KEEN
ACRID ANGRY GRUFF HARSH IRATE
SHARP SNELL SURLY BITTER
CAUSTIC STINGING VIRULENT
ACRIMONY VIRUS ACERBITY
ASPERITY PUNGENCY SOURNESS
ANIMOSITY
ACRISIUS (BROTHER OF —)
PROETUS
(DAUGHTER OF —) DANAE
(FATHER OF —) ABAS
(MOTHER OF —) AGLAIA
(SLAYER OF —) PERSEUS
(WIFE OF —) AGANIPPE EURYDICE
ACROBAT ZANY KINKER GYMNAST
TOPPLER TUMBLER BALANCER
AERIALIST ROPEWALKER
ACRONYM INITIALISM
ACROPOLIS FORT HILL POLIS
CADMEA CITADEL LARISSA
ACROSOME IDIOSOME IDIOZOME
ACROSS OVER SPAN YOND CROSS
ABOARD THWART ATHWART
OPPOSITE TRAVERSE
(CLEAN —) SHORT
(PREF.) DIA OVER TRANS
ACROSTIC ABC AGLA DORA GAME
POEM TANAK PHRASE PUZZLE
TANACH
ACRYLIC PROPENOIC
ACT BE DO GO APE LAW LET ACTU
AUTO BILL COME DEAL DEED
DORA FACT FEAT HOCK JEST MAKE
MOVE PART PASS PLAY SKIT SLIM
TAKE TURN WORK ACTUS DRAMA
EDICT EMOTE ENTRY EXERT FEIGN
GRACE KARMA MODEL SCENE

SHIFT SHTIK STUNT ACTION
BEHAVE BESTIR DECREE DEMEAN
FACTUM MANAGE RAGMAN
SHTICK COMPORT EXECUTE
EXPLOIT PERFORM PORTRAY
PRETEND STATUTE FUNCTION
PRETENSE SIMULATE
(— AFFECTEDLY) MIMP POSTURE
(— AGGRESSIVELY) HUSTLE
(— AS WANTON) RIG
(— AWKWARDLY) HOCKER
(— BADLY) HAMFATTER
(— BEFORE) ANTICIPATE
(— BLUNDERINGLY) BULL
(— DECEITFULLY) DOUBLE
(— DISHONESTLY) FUDGE
(— FIRST) LEAD
(— FOOLISHLY) FON FONNE FOLEYE
FOOTER FOOTLE
(— FRIVOLOUSLY) FRIVOL FRIBBLE
(— IN A NERVOUS WAY) JITTER
(— INDECISIVELY) DITHER
(— INDEPENDENTLY) SEVER
(— IN THEATER) GAFF
(— OF APPROVAL) EUGE
(— OF BEGGING) CADGE
(— OF CIVILITY) CURTSY DEVOIR
CURTSEY
(— OF KINDNESS) CARESS BENEFIT
(— OF LABOR) DILIGENCE
(— OF PRAYER) DEVOTION
(— OF STUPIDITY) BETISE
(— OF TRICKERY) COG
(— OF UNKINDNESS) CUT
(— OUT) ENACT DRAMATIZE
(— PLAYFULLY) DALLY BANTER
(— QUICKLY) GIRD
(— RASHLY) RACKLE
(— SLOWLY) DAWDLE
(— SPORTIVELY) DAFF
(— SUDDENLY) FLASH
(— TIMIDLY) NESH
(— TOGETHER) AGREE COACT
CONCUR CONCORD
(— TRIFLINGLY) JANK
(— UPON) TOUCH AFFECT HANDLE
(— UP TO) EVEN
(— VIGOROUSLY) TWIG TURNTO
(— WITHOUT RESTRAINT)
FREEWHEEL
(COMICAL —) JIG
(CONVENTIONAL —) AMENITY
(CORRUPT —) DEPRAVITY
(CRIMINAL —) INFAMY
(DARING —) ESCAPADE
(DECEITFUL —) ABUSE
(DECEPTIVE —) FEINT
(ECCENTRIC —) CANTRIP
(EVIL —) MALEFICENCE
(FAULTY —) PARAPRAXIS
(FOOLISH —) DIDO IDIOTISM
(FORBIDDEN —) CRIME
(FORMAL —) CEREMONY
(FRAUDULENT —) SCAM
(HABITUAL—) EXERCISE
(HASTY —) FLING
(HOSTILE —) BLOW
(INJURIOUS —) SPOIL
(KIND OF —) RIOT
(LAUDATORY —) COUP
(LITURGICAL —) LAVABO
(LIVELY —) JIG
(MERITORIOUS —) MITZVAH

(MISCHIEVOUS —) DIDO CANTRAP
CANTRIP
(OFFENSIVE —) AFFRONT
(OFFICIAL —S) ACTA
(PLAYFUL —) RALLERY RAILLERY
(PRAISEWORTHY —) DEMERIT
(RUDE —) INCIVILITY
(SUDDEN VIOLENT —) BENSEL
BENSIL
(THOUGHTLESS —) FOLLY
(UNMANNERLY —) SOLECISM
(UNUSUAL —) STUNT
(VALOROUS —) WORSHIP
(VARIETY —) SKETCH
(WRONG —) DERELICT DERELICTUM
(PL.) DOINGS
(SUFF.) ADE ATE CY ICE ION ISM
TH
ACTAEON (FATHER OF —)
ARISTAEUS
(MOTHER OF —) AUTONOE
ACTINAL ORAL
ACTING AGENT SERVING
HISTRIONIC
(— AGAINST) ADVERSE
(— BY TURN) ALTERN
(— IN RETURN) RECIPROCAL
(— ODDLY) HAYWIRE
(— RAPIDLY) DRASTIC
(UNSKILLFUL —) BUNGLING
ACTINIAN OPELET VESTLET
ACTINOST RADIAL RADIALE
ACTINOZOAN SEAFLOWER
ACTION ACT AIR DAP JOB PAS ACTO
CASE DEED FACT FRAY GEST PLAY
PLOY PUSH SHOW STEP SUIT
WORK ACTIO DOING EDICT FIGHT
FLING GESTE ISSUE THING TREAD
VENUE AFFAIR AGENCY BATTLE
BEFOOT COMBAT PRAXIS
CONDUCT FACTION GESTURE
MEASURE PROCESS TANQUAM
ACTIVITY BEHAVIOR BUSINESS
CONFLICT FUNCTION PRACTICE
PRACTISE
(— BETWEEN HORSE AND RIDER)
APPUI
(— OF DRAMA) EPITASIS
(— OF WIND) EOLATION
(— PAINTING) TACHISM
(— POTENTIAL) SPIKE
(ABSURD —S) BOSH
(ANTAGONISTIC —) ATOMISM
(BLAMEWORTHY —) WITE
(CAPRICIOUS —) FREAK
(CHEMICAL —) ACTINISM
(COARSE —) HARLOTRY
(CONCLUDING —) MOPUP
(CONVULSIVE —) SPASM
(COOPERATIVE —) SYNERGISM
(COURT —) LAW SUIT ASSIZE
LAWSUIT QUERELA QUERELE
(CRUEL —) RUTH
(CUSTOMARY —) COURSE
(DIVINE —) THEURGY
(DUE —) ORDER
(EXAGGERATED —) PRODUCTION
(EXTEMPORE —) SCHEDIASM
(FANTASTIC —) ABTIC
(FINAL —) CATASTROPHE
(FOOLISH —) FOPPERY INEPTITUDE
(FRISKY —) FRISKIN
(FRIVOLOUS —) DALLIANCE

(HOSTILE —) OPPOSITION
(IMPULSIVE —) STAMPEDE
(INDIRECT —) WINDLASS
(INITIAL —) LEADOFF INDUCTION
(INTRODUCTORY —) PROLOGUE
(JOINT —) COACTION
(LEGAL —) DEBT SUIT ACCOUNT
DETINET DETINUE PROCEEDING
(MEAN —S) DOGGERY
(MILITARY —) SWEEP OPERATION
(ODD —S) JIMJAMS
(PLAYFUL —) FUN FROLIC
(RASH —) HASTE
(REPEATED —) DRUM DOUBLE
(SUDDEN —) FLISK
(SYMBOLIC —) CHARADE
(TACTLESS —) GAUCHERIE
(UNAVOIDABLE —) FORCEPUT
(UNINTERMITTED —) HEAT
(VIOLENT —) AFFRAY
(WHIMSICAL —S) HUMORS
HUMOURS
(WILY —) WRINKLE
(PREF.) CIN(O) CINET(O) KIN(O)
KINESI KINET(O)
(SUFF.) ADE AL ANCE ANT ARD
ATION CY ENCE ESIS ING ISATION
IVE IZATION MENT OSIS PRACTIC
PRAXIA PRAXIS SIS SOME LE LING
ACTIS (FATHER OF —) RHODE
(MOTHER OF —) HELIUS
ACTIVATE SPARK ACTIFY ELICIT
(— BY MIXING WITH WATER)
PROOF
ACTIVATION
(SUFF.) KINESIS
ACTIVATOR GOAD
ACTIVE UP YAL YAP YEP BUSY GAIN
LISH LIST PERT RASH SPRY TRIG
WHAT YALD YARE YEPE YERN
ABOUT AGILE ALERT ALIVE ASTIR
BRISK DEEDY FRESH LIGHT LINGY
LUSTY NIPPY PEART QUICK READY
SMART SNELL SPICY SPRIG STOUT
SWANK VIVID WIGHT YAULD YERNE
ACTUAL BOUNCY CLEVER DIRECT
FEERIE FEIRIE FIERCE HEARTY
LIVELY LIVING MOVING NIMBLE
PROMPT QUIVER SEMMIT SPEEDY
SPRACK SPROIL SPRUCE SPRUNT
SWANKY WIMBLE DASHING
DEEDFUL DELIVER DYNAMIC
HOPPING HUMMING KINETIC
STHENIC THRODDY YANKING
ANIMATED ATHLETIC BRAWLING
DILIGENT SPIRITED VIGOROUS
(EXCESSIVELY —) MANIC
(NORMALLY —) ABOUT
ACTIVELY DOWN BUSILY DEEDILY
HEARTILY
ACTIVITIES
(PL.) DOINGS
ACTIVITY ACT ADO GOG VIR FIZZ
LIFE PLAY PUSH STIR BLAST CAPER
EVENT HEART RAJAS RALLY TRADE
VIGOR ACTION AGENCY BUSTLE
ENERGY HUSTLE SATTVA SPROIL
AGILITY CALLING BUSINESS
EXERCISE FUNCTION MOVEMENT
PARERGON STIRRING OCCUPATION
(— OF INTELLECT) NOESIS
(BUSTLING —) RUSH

(CHOICE OF —) THING
(FRENZIED —) HUSTLE
(FUNCTIONAL —) SHOP
(GAY —) MERRYMAKING
(MENTAL —) CONCEIT BRAINWORK
MENTATION
(SHARED —) COMMUNITY
(SPHERE OF —) SCENE
(STORMY —) RAGE
(TEACHING —) REALIA
(TROUBLESOME —) COIL
(PL.) GOINGSON
(SUFF.) OR
(OUTBURST OF —) FEST
ACTON HOGTON HAQUETON
ACTOR HAM DOER HERO LEAD
MIME STAR AGENT BUFFO COMIC
DROLL EXTRA HEAVY MIMIC PLANT
SERIO SUPER ARTIST BUSKER
COWBOY DISEUR FEEDER FIDDLE
MUMMER PLAYER PUPPET STAGER
TOMMER ARTISTE CABOTIN
DISEUSE HISTRIO PRIMOMO
ROSCIUS STORMER TROUPER
AISTEOIR COMEDIAN HISTRION
JUVENILE STROLLER THESPIAN
(BROTHER OF —) AUGEAS
(DAUGHTER OF —) POLYMELA
(FATHER OF —) DIOMEDES
MYRMIDON
(INDIFFERENT —) JAY
(INEPT —) HAM
(INFERIOR —) SHINE
(MOTHER OF —) DEION PASIDICE
(SON OF —) CTEATUS EURYTUS
MENOETIUS
(PREF.) HISTRIO
ACTRESS DIVA STAR INGENUE
STARLET FARCEUSE PREMIERE
THESPIAN
ACTUAL GOOD HARD REAL TRUE
VERY POSIT RIGHT BODILY
FACTUAL GENUINE CONCRETE
DEFINITE EXISTING MATERIAL
POSITIVE TANGIBLE
ACTUALITY ACT FACT BEING VERITY
REALITY ENERGEIA REALNESS
ACTUALLY BUT DONE TRULY
FAIRLY ITSELF REALLY
(NOT —) NOMINALLY
ACTUATE ACT EGG RUN DRAW
MOVE URGE ENACT IMPEL ROUSE
START AROUSE COMPEL EXCITE
INCITE INDUCE AGITATE ANIMATE
ENLIVEN INSPIRE POINTED
SHARPEN MOTIVATE PERSUADE
ACUITY FINENESS
ACUMEN WIT INSIGHT CAPACITY
KEENNESS SAGACITY
ACUMINATE TAPE
ACUTE ACID FINE HIGH KEEN TART
HEAVY QUICK SHARP SMART
SNACK SNELL ARGUTE ASTUTE
CRYING SHREWD SHRILL SUBTLE
TREBLE URGENT CRUCIAL FEELING
INTENSE POINTED VIOLENT
CRITICAL INCISIVE POIGNANT
ACUMINATE PENETRATING
PENETRATIVE
(MOST —) DIRE
(NOT —) SLOW GRAVE CHRONIC
(PREF.) OXY

ACUTENESS DEPTH SENSE ACUITY ACUMEN NOSTRIL INCISION SAGACITY SUBTLETY
(— OF SMELL) HYPEROSMIA
ACYCLIC SPIRAL ALIPHATIC
ACYLOIN
(SUFF.) OIN
ADA (BROTHER OF —) PIXODARUS
(HUSBAND & BROTHER OF —) IDRIEUS
ADAD RAMMAN
ADAGE SAW DICT REDE TEXT WORD AXIOM MAXIM MOTTO HOMILY SAYING TRUISM WHEEZE BROMIDE PRECEPT PROVERB APHORISM APOTHEGM PAROEMIA
ADAGIO ADAGE ADAGIETTO
ADAH (HUSBAND OF —) ESAU LAMECH
(SON OF —) JABAL JUBAL ELIPHAZ
ADAIAH (FATHER OF —) SHIMHI JEROHAM
ADALIA (FATHER OF —) HAMAN
ADAM ADE EDIE ADKIN
(GRANDSON OF —) ENOS ENOCH
(SON OF —) ABEL CAIN SETH
(TEACHER OF —) RAISEL
(WIFE OF —) EVE LILITH
ADAM-AND-EVE CRAWFOOT
ADAMANT FIRM GRIM HARD SOLID STONY ADAMAS DIAMOND UNMOVED OBDURATE SOLIDITY STUBBORN
ADAMANTINE FIRM HARD BORON STONE VAJRA ADAMANT
ADAM BEDE (AUTHOR OF —) ELIOT
(CHARACTER IN —) ADAM SETH DINAH HETTY ARTHUR BARTLE IRVINE MARTIN MASSEY MORRIS POYSER SORREL DONNITHORNE
ADAMITE NUDIST PICARD
ADAMS ANSEL
ADAM'S APPLE GUZZLE THROATBOLL
ADAM'S FLANNEL MULLEIN
ADAM'S NEEDLE YUCCA
ADAPT APT FIT PLY PUT EDIT MOLD SORT SUIT AGREE HUMOR INURE SHAPE TALLY ADJUST CHANGE COMPLY DERIVE DOCTOR HUMOUR TEMPER ARRANGE CONFORM CONVERT FASHION PREPARE QUALIFY ATTEMPER CONTRIVE EQUALIZE MODULATE REGULATE ACCOMMODATE
ADAPTABILITY FLUIDITY ELASTICITY
ADAPTABLE LABILE ELASTIC PLASTIC PLIABLE FLEXUOUS
ADAPTATION CONSERTION
(— TO MUSIC) SETTING
ADAPTED FIT FOR FITTED SUITED CONGENIAL
ADAPTER KIT ARRANGER
ADAXIAL SUPERIOR POSTERIOR
ADBEEL (FATHER OF —) ISHMAEL
ADD AD EIK EKE SAY SUM TOT CAST FOOT GAIN JOIN LEND PLUS TOTE AFFIX ANNEX GIVEN PUTON TOTAL UNITE ACCRUE ADJECT APPEND ATTACH CONFER FIGURE RECKON SUPPLY ACCRETE AUGMENT COMBINE COMPILE COMPUTE

ENLARGE SUBJOIN SUMMATE INCREASE
(— ALCOHOL) SPIKE
(— AN ENTRY) RUNON
(— FUEL) BEET
(— IN WRITING) ASCRIBE
(— ON) AFFIX ANNEX
(— STRENGTH) HEARTEN
(— TO) ADORN ENRICH AUGMENT ENHANCE
(— UP) SUM TOT COUNT TALLY TOTAL AMOUNT
(— WORT TO BEER) KRAUSEN
ADDA SCINK SKINK LIZARD
ADDAR (FATHER OF —) BELA
ADDAX PYGARG PYGARGUS
ADDED AND EKE PLUS ADJUNCT
(— SOMETHING) TILLY
(RECENTLY —) FRESH
ADDEND SUMMAND
ADDENDUM RIDER
ADDER ATHER KRAIT VIPER ELAPID NADDER NEDDER CRIBBER ELAPOID HAGWORM HOGNOSE HYPNALE
(KIND OF —) MILK
ADDERING (KIND OF —) CRIB
ADDER'S-TONGUE LILY LILIUM COXCOMB ROOSTERS
ADDERWORT BISTORT
ADDI (FATHER OF —) COSAM
(SON OF —) MELCHI
ADDICT FAN BUFF DOPE DOPY HYPE USER WINO COKEY COKIE FIEND HOPPY HOUND JUNKY SLAVE BOTARY DEVOTE JUNKER JUNKIE DELIVER DEVOTEE HABITUE HOPHEAD SNIFTER ACCUSTOM DOPEHEAD SNOWBIRD
ADDICTED GIVEN PRONE HOOKED BIBULOUS
ADDICTION HABIT JONES MONKEY BIBACITY
ADDITION AND EIK EKE ELL TAB TOO ALSO ELSE GAIN PLUS AFFIX ICING RIDER ACCESS ACCRUE AUGEND ENCORE GANSEL INCOME PREFIX ADJUNCT ADVANCE AUCTARY CODICIL JOINING PENDANT UNITING ADDENDUM INCREASE MANTISSA ACCESSION
(— TO ARTICLE) SHIRTTAIL
(— TO BEEHIVE) IMP
(— TO CALENDAR) EPACT
(— TO MASS) FARCE FARSE
(— TO PRICE) ADVANCE
(— TO WORD) PARAGOGE
(EXTRANEOUS —) ACCRETION
(TRIVIAL —) FILIP FILLIP
(PREF.) IN —) SUPER
ADDITIONAL NEW ELSE MORE ADDED EXTRA FRESH OTHER TIDDER TOTHER ANOTHER BESIDES FURTHER ACCESSORY PIGGYBACK
ADDITIVE CUMOL CUMENE PRESERVATIVE
(HAND-CREAM —) ALOE
ADDLE EARN HOME IDLE MIRE AMAZE FILTH RIPEN SPOIL CURDLE MUDDLE THRIVE AGITATE CONFUSE BEFUDDLE BEWILDER

ADDLED ASEA EMPTY PUTRID MUDDLED UNSOUND
ADDRA DAMA NANGER
ADDRESS AIM SUE WOO BACK CALL EASE HAIL HOME MINT PRAY TACT TALK TULK TURN ABODE APPLY BOARD COURT DRESS ELOGE GREET POISE SKILL SPEAK TREAT ACCOST ADJUST APPEAL BOUNCE CHARGE DEVOTE DIRECT EULOGY MANNER PARLEY SALUTE SERMON SPEECH BEHIGHT CONDUCT CONSIGN ENTRUST LECTURE ORATION TUTOYER APPROACH DEDICATE DELIVERY DISPATCH FACILITY HARANGUE INSCRIBE PETITION
(— FAMILIARLY) TOM TUTOYER
(— FOR GI) APO
(— SAUCILY) CHYAK CHYACK
(METHOD OF —) TONE
(PART OF —) ZIP
(PULPIT —) KHUTBA KHUTBAH
ADDUCE BEAR CITE GIVE NAME ALLAY ARGUE BRING INFER OFFER QUOTE ALLEGE ASSIGN OBJECT ADVANCE COUNTER MENTION PRESENT
ADE SQUASH
ADELIE PENGUIN
ADEPS FAT LARD
ADEPT ACE APT DON ABLE HANDY ADROIT ARTIST CRAFTY DEACON EXPERT MASTER VERSED ANCIENT ARTISTE CAPABLE DABSTER MAHATMA DEXTROUS SKILLFUL PROFICIENT
ADEQUATE DUE FIT ABLE ENOW FAIR FULL GOOD MEET WELL AMPLE DIGNE EQUAL COMMON DECENT ENOUGH PROPER CONDIGN PASSABLE SUITABLE COMMENSURATE SATISFACTORY
(BARELY —) BRIEF
ADER (FATHER OF —) BERIAH
ADHERE HEW HUG CLAG CLAM CLOG GLUE HOLD JOIN KEEP LINK ABIDE AFFIX APPLY CLEAM CLING STICK UNITE ATTACH CEMENT CLEAVE COHERE FREEZE ACCRETE ANNERRE PERSIST
ADHERENCE CLING ABIDANCE ADHESION ARIANISM FIDELITY
ADHERENT IST ITE AIDE ALLY JAIN SIKH ADEPT BAHAI BLACK BONPA DEIST JAINA SIDER SPIKE STOOP FACTOR KIRKER VOTARY APRISTA BAHAIST CHANIST FASCIST FLACIAN GNOSTIC NICAEAN OWENIAN SECTARY SEQUELA THOMIST AGATHIST BELIEVER BUDDHIST CABALIST DISCIPLE FAITHFUL FATALIST FOLLOWER HUMANIST HYLICIST IMPERIAL PARTISAN RETAINER SERVITOR SOCINIAN UPHOLDER MONTANIST
(PL.) FOLD FOLLOWING
(SUFF.) ITE
ADHERING PERTINACIOUS
ADHESION BLOCKING STICKAGE SYNECHIA
ADHESIVE GUM WAX BOND CLAM GLUE SIZE TAPE DABBY DAUBY

PASTE TACKY BINDER CEMENT CLINGY GLUTEN MASTIC PLUCKY SMEARY STICKY HOTMELT MOUNTANT MUCILAGE TENACIOUS
(PREF.) GLUT
ADHESIVENESS STICK
ADHIBIT USE ADMIT AFFIX APPLY ATTACH
ADIANTUM MAIDENHAIR
ADIEL (SON OF —) AZMAVETH
ADIEU ADEW CIAO ADDIO ADIOS LEAVE FAREWELL
AD INFINITUM EVER
ADIPOCERE GRAVEWAX
ADIPOSE FAT HARD SUET FATTY OBESE PURSY SQUAT TALLOW
ADIT DOOK DOOR ENTRY SOUGH STULM ACCESS TUNNEL PASSAGE APPROACH ENTRANCE
ADJACENT NEAR NIGH CLOSE FLUSH HANDY BESIDE NEARBY MEETING VICINAL ABUTTING TOUCHING CONTIGUOUS
(PREF.) (— TO) AC AD AF AG AL AP AS AT
ADJECTIVE ADNOUN DIPTOTE EPITHET NOMINAL MODIFIER
ADJOIN ADD ABUT BUTT JOIN LINE TACK COAST MARCH TOUCH UNITE ACCOST APPEND ATTACH BORDER CONTACT NEIGHBOR
ADJOINING VICINAL
ADJOURN END MOVE RISE STAY ARISE CLOSE DEFER DELAY RECESS SUSPEND DISSOLVE POSTPONE PROROGUE
ADJUDGE TRY ARET DEEM FIND GIVE HOLD RATE ALLOT AREAD AREED ARETT AWARD GRANT JUDGE ORDER ADDEEM ADDICT ADDOOM ASSIGN DECERN DECIDE DECREE ORDAIN REGARD BEHIGHT CONDEMN SENTENCE
(— GUILTY) DAMN
(— NOT GUILTY) ABSOLVE
ADJUDICATE ACT TRY HEAR PASS RULE JUDGE DECIDE ESTEEM RECKON REGARD SETTLE ADJUDGE CONSIDER SENTENCE
ADJUNCT AID HELP PART WORD ANNEX DEVICE PHRASE ADJOINT ANCILLA APENAGE EPITHET FITTING GARNISH PERTAIN TEACHER ADDITION ADDITIVE APPANAGE APPENDIX ORNAMENT
ADJURATION OATH APPEAL SWEARING
ADJURE ASK BEG BID BIND ETHE PRAY CRAVE PLEAD SWEAR APPEAL CHARGE OBTEST BESEECH COMMAND CONJURE CONTEST ENTREAT REQUEST UNSWEAR
ADJUST FIT FIX KEY SET CAST EASE FORM FREE GEAR JUST LINE PARE RATE SIZE SORT SUIT TRAM TRIM TRUE TUNE ADAPT ADMIT ALIGN ALINE ALTER ANGLE COAPT EQUAL FRAME PATCH RANGE RIGHT SHAPE ACCORD ATTUNE HAMMER JUSTEN ORIENT SETTLE SQUARE TEMPER WANGLE ADDRESS ARRANGE BALANCE CHANCER

COMPOSE CONCERT CONFORM CORRECT DISPOSE JUSTIFY PREPARE RECTIFY COMPOUND REGULATE CALIBRATE ACCOMMODATE
(— A LOOM) GATE
(— DULY) CONCENT
(— SAIL) FLATTEN
(PREF.) CO
ADJUSTABLE ELASTIC
ADJUSTED KEYED
(ACCURATELY —) TRUE
ADJUSTER FIXER FITTER ASSESSOR
ADJUSTMENT FIT GEAR MISE TRIM FITNESS FITTING CHANCERY
(— OF DISPUTE) MISE
(COST —) COLA
(HARMONIOUS —) TUNE
ADJUTANT AIDE ALLY STORK ARGALA HELPER HURGILA MARABOU OFFICER
ADJUVANT AIDE HELPER ADJUNCT HELPFUL
ADLAI (SON OF —) SHAPHAT
AD-LIB FAKE
ADMAN HUCKSTER
ADMEASURE METE
ADMETUS (FATHER OF —) PHERES
(WIFE OF —) ALCESTIS
ADMINISTER DO RUN DEAL DEEM DOSE GIVE MOVE RULE APPLY SERVE TREAT DIRECT GOVERN MANAGE SETTLE SUPPLY TENDER ADHIBIT CONDUCE CONDUCT CONTROL EXECUTE EXHIBIT FURNISH HUSBAND DISPENSE MINISTER
(— FORCIBLY) HAND
(— SACRAMENT) BISHOP HOUSEL
ADMINISTRATION HELM RULE SWAY POLICY TAHSIL CONDUCT DIOCESE ECONOMY RECTORY REGIMEN CARRIAGE DISPOSAL MINISTRY
(— OF OATH) JURATION
(CORRUPT —) MALVERSATION
(REVENUE —) HACIENDA
ADMINISTRATOR CAID HELM QAID GABBAI ALCAIDE MANAGER TRUSTEE DIRECTOR EXECUTOR MINISTER PROVICAR PROCONSUL
(— OF COMPUTER BOARD) SYSOP
(INCA —) CURACA
(MORMON —) APOSTLE
ADMIRABLE FINE GOOD HIGH NEAT GRAND GREAT LUMMY PROUD DIVINE AMIABLE CAPITAL ELEGANT MIRANDA RIPPING
ADMIRAL (ALSO SEE NAVAL OFFICER) FLAG AMREL AMRELLE CAPITAN FLAGMAN GENERAL NAVARCH
(KIND OF —) RED REAR VICE
ADMIRATION CULT FUROR GLORY ESTEEM LIKING WONDER CONCEIT WORSHIP ADULATION
(— FOR BIGNESS) JUMBOISM
(EXTRAVAGANT —) FUREUR
ADMIRE DIG LIKE LOVE ADORE EXTOL HONOR PRIZE VALUE ESTEEM MARVEL REGARD REVERE WONDER ADULATE APPROVE

DELIGHT IDOLIZE RESPECT VENERATE
ADMIRER FAN BEAU LOVER SWAIN AMATEUR DEVOTEE FOLLOWER IDOLATER
(PL.) FOLLOWING
ADMISSION FEE ADIT CALL ENTRY ACCESS CHARGE ENTREE TICKET APOLOGY CONSENT INGRESS ENTRANCE RECEPTION CONCESSION
(— TO BAR) CALL
(— TO MINISTRY) ORDINATION
(CONCLUSIVE —) ESTOPPEL
ADMIT COP KEN LET OWN AVER AVOW BEAR TAKE AGREE ALLOW ENTER GRANT IMMIT INLET ACCEDE ACCEPT ADJUST ASSENT AVOUCH ENROLL INDUCT PERMIT SUFFER ADHIBIT CONCEDE CONFESS INCLUDE PROFESS RECEIVE SUFFICE INITIATE
(— AS MEMBER) INDUCT
(— AS VALID) ALLOW
(— OPENLY) OWNUPTO
(— TO HOLY ORDERS) ORDAIN
ADMITTANCE ACCESS ADMITTY ENTRANCE
ADMITTED GIVEN GRANTED
ADMITTING THOUGH
(REGRETFULLY —) AFRAID
ADMIX DALLOP DOLLOP
ADMIXTURE DASH ALLOY BLEND SHADE SPICE TINGE DALLOP DOLLOP FLAVOR LEAVEN STREAK MIXTURE SOUPCON COMPOUND INFUSION
ADMONISH WARN CHIDE SCOLD ADVISE ENJOIN EXHORT NOTIFY REBUKE REMIND SCHOOL CAUTION COUNSEL MONITOR REPROVE
ADMONITION ITEM ADVICE CAVEAT HOMILY CAUTION LECTURE REPROOF WARNING DOCUMENT REMINDER
ADNATE ADHERENT EPIGYNOUS
(— TO CALYX) INFERIOR
ADO DO COIL DEED FLAP FUSS ROUT STIR TODO WORK HOOHA HURRY TOUSE TOWSE BOTHER BUSTLE EFFORT FLURRY HUBBUB POTHER RUCKUS BLATHER BLETHER SPUTTER TROUBLE TURMOIL BUSINESS FOOFARAW
ADOBE MUD CLAY DOBE DOBY SILT BRICK DOBIE TAPIA MUDCAP
ADOLESCENCE TEENS YOUTH NONAGE PUBERTY MINORITY
ADOLESCENT LAD TEEN YOUNG YOUTH TEENER IMMATURE TEENAGER
(DISRUPTIVE —) NED
(PROSPECTIVE —) PRETEEN
ADONIJAH (BROTHER OF —) AMNON ABSALOM CHILEAB
(FATHER OF —) DAVID
(MOTHER OF —) HAGGITH
(SLAYER OF —) BENAIAH
ADONIS ADON
(FATHER OF —) CINYRAS
(MOTHER OF —) MYRRH MYRRHA

ADOPT TAKE STEAL ACCEPT ASSUME ATTACH BORROW CHOOSE FATHER FOLLOW FOSTER MOTHER TAKEON ACQUIRE EMBRACE ESPOUSE RECEIVE WELCOME ADVOCATE ARROGATE MAINTAIN
ADOPTION ESPOUSAL
(— OF DEBTS) ASSUMPTION
ADORABLE LOVELY LOVABLE CHARMING
ADORATION HOMAGE WORSHIP DEVOTION
(— OF GOD) LOVE
ADORE DOTE LAUD LOVE EXALT EXTOL HONOR WURTH ADMIRE ESTEEM PRAISE REVERE GLORIFY IDOLIZE WORSHIP VENERATE
ADORN DUB FIG GEM ORN SET BEAD BUSK DECK DILL DINK FOIL GAUD GILD LACE OUCH PICK PINK POSH STUD SWAG TRIM ADORE ANORN ARRAY BEDUB BEGEM BELAY BESEE BRAVE CROWN DIGHT DRAPE DRESS FRONT GRACE HIGHT INLAY JEWEL MENSK PRANK PRICK PRIDE PRIMP PRINK ROUGE SPLAY SPRIG TRICK AGUISE ATTIRE ATTRAP BECOME BEDECK BETRIM BLAZON BROOCH CLOTHE COLLAR DAMASK DIADEM EMBOSS ENAMEL ENRICH ENROBE FIGURE FINIFY FRIEZE FRINGE GRAITH INSTAL INVEST ORNIFY POUNCE PURFLE QUAINT STATUE SUBORN TASSEL ADONISE APPAREL BEDIGHT BEDIZEN COMMEND CORONET DEPAINT DIGNIFY EMPEARL FEATHER FOLIAGE FURNISH GARNISH GLORIFY GRATIFY IMPLUME SPANGLE VARNISH BEAUTIFY DECORATE EMBLAZON FLOURISH ORNAMENT SPLENDOR
(— WITH MOSAIC) TESSELLATE
ADORNED CLAD BESEEN DAEDAL ORNATE PICKED BRAIDED CLOTHED COLORED DAISIED FIGURED OVERHUNG
(GAUDILY —) TAWDRY
(SHOWILY —) BEPRANKED
ADORNMENT TIRE ADORN DRESS PRIDE BEAUTY DECORE TAHALI TINSEL DECKING OUNDING PRANKING TIREMENT
ADOXY TENET
ADRAMMELECH (BROTHER OF —) SHAREZER
(FATHER OF —) SENNACHERIB
ADRASTUS (BROTHER OF —) MECISTEUS
(DAUGHTER OF —) AEGIA DEIPYLE
(FATHER OF —) TALAUS GORDIUS
(MOTHER OF —) LYSIMACHE
(SISTER OF —) ERIPHYLE
ADRESTUS (BROTHER OF —) AMPHIUS
(FATHER OF —) MENOPS
(SLAYER OF —) DIOMEDES
ADRIANA LECOUVREUR
(CHARACTER IN —) ADRIANA MAURICE BOUILLON MICHONNET
(COMPOSER OF —) CILEA

ADRIEL (FATHER OF —) BARZILLAI
(WIFE OF —) MERAB
ADRIFT ASEA LOST AWAFT LIGAN LOOSE AFLOAT DERELICT FLOATING UNMOORED
ADROIT DEFT EASY FEAT GOOD NEAT SLIM ADEPT HANDY READY SMART SNACK TIGHT TRICK ARTFUL CLEVER EXPERT HABILE NIMBLE CUNNING DEXTROUS HANDSOME SKILLFUL
ADROITNESS ART EASE TACT KNACK SKILL ADDRESS FACILITY
ADSORBENT BASE EARTH SILICA
ADULATE FAWN LAUD GLOSS GLOZE PRAISE REVERE FLATTER
ADULATION GLOSE GLOZE PRAISE INCENSE FLATTERY
ADULT MAN FULL MANLY MATURE EPHEBIC GROWNUP THRIVEN
(SCIENCE OF TEACHING —S) ANDRAGOGY
(YOUNG COLLEGE-EDUCATED —) YUP YUPPIE
ADULTERANT DOPE MULTUM ALMEIDINA
ADULTERATE CUT MIX CARD DASH LOAD ABUSE ALLOY HOCUS TAINT DEACON DEBASE DEFILE DILUTE EXTEND MANAGE WEAKEN BASTARD CORRUPT FALSIFY VITIATE DENATURE IMPURIFY SPURIOUS
(— WINE) LIME
ADULTERATED CUT SHAM IMPURE CORRUPT SPURIOUS
ADULTEROUS ERRING
ADULTERY AVOUTRY CUCKOLDOM CUCKOLDRY MISCONDUCT
ADUMBRATE IMAGE SHADE VAGUE OBSCURE SUGGEST INTIMATE
ADUMBRATION SHADE SHADOW PHANTASM
ADUNCOUS BENT HOOKED
ADUST BURNT FIERY GLOOMY SALLOW PARCHED SCORCHED SUNBURNT
ADVANCE GO AID PAY SOP WAY BULL CITE COME DASH GAIN HELP INCH LAUD LEND LIFT LOAN MARK MOVE NEAR NOSE PASS PUSH RISE SHOW STEP WORM AVANT BOOST BRING CREEP ENTER EXALT EXTOL FAVOR FORGE MARCH OFFER PLACE PREST RAISE SERVE SPEED STAIR STAKE THROW ADDUCE ADMOVE ALLEGE AMOUNT ASSIGN ASSIST AVAUNT BETTER DEGREE EXTEND FAVOUR GROWTH HASTEN INCEDE INROAD PREFER PREPAY SCHOOL STRIDE STRIKE THRIVE TRAVEL VAUNCE BENEFIT DEVELOP ELEVATE ENHANCE FORTHGO FORWARD FURTHER HEADWAY IMPREST IMPROVE PROCEED PROCESS PROMOTE PROMOVE PROPOSE PROSPER PROVECT SUCCEED ADDITION DEVELOPE HEIGHTEN INCREASE PROGRESS PROGRESSION
(— BY CUTTING) DRIVE
(— BY LEAPS) SALTATION

(— IN LIFE) WAY
(— LABORIOUSLY) STRIVE
(— OBLIQUELY) SIDLE
(— OF MONEY) IMPREST
(— ONE'S POINT) TAKE
(— RUDELY) ELBOW
(— SLOWLY) INCH WORM CRAWL
CREEP
(— WAVERINGLY) HOBBLE
(— WITH EFFORT) DRAG
(DIFFICULT —) SLOG
(GRADUAL —) ILLAPSE
(STEADY —) SWING
(SUDDEN —) SHOOT
(VIGOROUS —) SWING
(PL.) APPROACHES
ADVANCED FAR DEEP GONE HIGH
LATE AHEAD OUTER FORWARD
IMPREST LIBERAL VANWARD
FOREMOST
(— IN AGE) DEEP ANTIQUATED
(— IN YEARS) SENIOR AGEABLE
ELDERLY
(MOST —) EXTREME FARTHEST
FOREMOST HEADMOST
(WELL —) AGED
ADVANCEMENT UP GOOD ASCENT
INCREASE
ADVANCING RISING
(— BY DEGREES) GRADUAL
(— RAPIDLY) RAKING
ADVANTAGE AD BOT USE VAN
BEST BOOT BOTE DRAW DROP
EDGE GAIN GOOD HANK JUMP
MEND NOTE ODDS PULL SAKE VAIL
ASSET AVAIL BULGE BUNCE FAVOR
FRAME FRUIT KINCH LAUGH POINT
SPEED START STEAD USAGE
BEHALF BEHOOF BETTER CARROT
EFFECT PROFIT ACCOUNT BENEFIT
CAPITAL EXPLOIT FORDEAL
FURTHER PROMOTE PURPOSE
UTILITY VANTAGE HANDICAP
INTEREST LEVERAGE OVERHAND
OVERPLUS PERCENTAGE
(ACCIDENTAL —) FLUKE
(UNDUE —) ABUSE
(UNEXPECTED —) WINDFALL
ADVANTAGEOUS GOOD JOLI
WELL JOLIE GOLDEN PLUMMY
SPEEDY USEFUL ELIGIBLE
BEHOVEFUL PROPITIOUS
(PREF.) EU
ADVENT DAWN COMING INCOME
ARRIVAL APPROACH PAROUSIA
ADVENTITIOUS CASUAL FOREIGN
STRANGE ACQUIRED EPISODIC
ACCESSORY
ADVENTURE GEST LARK RISK SEEK
WAGE EVENT GESTE PERIL QUEST
AUNTER AUNTRE CHANCE DANGER
HAZARD EMPRISE EMPRIZE
FORTUNE VENTURE ESCAPADE
JEOPARDY
(TALE OF —) CONTE
ADVENTURER ROUTIER ARGONAUT
PICAROON
ADVENTURESS DEMIREP
DEMIMONDAINE
ADVENTUROUS BOLD RASH
DARING ERRANT AUNTROUS
RECKLESS

ADVERSARY FOE ENEMY RIVAL
SATAN FOEMAN OPPONENT
(— OF GOD) DEVIL
(PREF.) ENSTATO
ADVERSE FOE ILL EVIL CROSS
LOATH THRAW AVERSE INFEST
WITHER AWKWARD COUNTER
DIVERSE FROWARD HOSTILE
OPPOSED CONTRARY INIMICAL
OPPOSING OPPOSITE OVERWART
THRAWART
(PREF.) COUNTER
ADVERSITY ILL WOE CROSS DECAY
NIGHT MISERY SORROW WITHER
ILLNESS TROUBLE CALAMITY
DISTRESS MISFORTUNE
ADVERT HEED AVERT RECUR REFER
ALLUDE ATTEND RETURN REVERT
OBSERVE CONSIDER
ADVERTISE CRY BARK BILL CALL
PLUG PUFF STAR WARN BLURB
INFORM NOTIFY PARADE DECLARE
DISPLAY OBSERVE PLACARD
PUBLISH ANNOUNCE PROCLAIM
ADVERTISED AFFICHE
ADVERTISEMENT AD BILL SIGN
BLURB CHANT PITCH PROMO
ADVERT CACHET DODGER NOTICE
POSTER TEASER AFFICHE
PLACARD STUFFER CIRCULAR
HANDBILL
ADVERTISING BUSH BILLING
PUFFERY
(EXTRAVAGANT —) HYPE
(MASS-MEDIA —) ADMASS
(RADIO OR TV —) PLUGOLA
ADVICE AVIS AVYS LORE NEWS
REDE AVYSE INPUT STEER ADVISO
DEVICE NOTICE CAUTION CONSEIL
COUNSEL OPINION TIDINGS
GUIDANCE MONITION
(PL.) INFORMATION
ADVICE-BOAT AVISO
ADVISABLE BOOK PROPER
PRUDENT
ADVISE SAY READ REDE TELL VISE
WARN WISE AREAD AREED COACH
GUIDE WEISE WEIZE ADJURE
ADVISO BEREDE CONFER DEVISE
EXHORT INFORM PONDER REVEAL
APPRISE APPRIZE COUNSEL
ACQUAINT ADMONISH CONSIDER
RECOMMEND
(— AGAINST) DISSUADE
(— STRONGLY) URGE
(— WRONGLY) MISCOUNSEL
ADVISED DELIBERATE
ADVISER AIDE TOUT COACH COMES
TUTOR DOCTOR EGERIA LAWYER
NESTOR ADVISOR MONITOR
STARETS TEACHER ATTORNEY
CROUPIER DIRECTOR FIELDMAN
PREACHER
ADVISORY URGING PRUDENT
ADVOCACY BOOM FAVOR AVOWRY
FAVOUR ARIANISM
ADVOCATE PRO ABET BACK PUSH
URGE VOGT ACTOR ADOPT FAVOR
PLEAD ASSERT AVOWRY BACKER
DEFEND IDEIST LAWYER PATRON
SYNDIC ABETTOR APOSTLE
DECLAIM ENDORSE ESPOUSE
EXPOUND FASCIST GOLDBUG

PATRIOT PLEADER PROCTOR
PROMOTE SCHOLAR SUPPORT
ATTORNEY CHAMPION CLUBBIST
DEFENSOR EXPONENT HUMANIST
PARTISAN PREACHER PARACLETE
PROPONENT
(— FAVORED BY JUDGE) PEAT
(— OF REVOLT) ANARCH
(SUFF.) ARIAN CRAT
ADVOWSON ADVOCACY
TENEMENT PATRONAGE
ADZ AX AXE ADZE EDGE ADDIS
ADDICE EATCHE THIXLE HATCHET
AEACUS (FATHER OF —) ZEUS
JUPITER
(MOTHER OF —) AEGINA
(SON OF —) PELEUS PHOCUS
TELAMON
(WIFE OF —) ENDEIS
AECHMAGORAS (FATHER OF —)
HERCULES
(MOTHER OF —) PHIALO
AECIUM CAEOMA
AEDON (BROTHER OF —) AMPHION
(FATHER OF —) PANDAREUS
(HUSBAND OF —) ZETHUS
POLYTECHNUS
(MOTHER OF —) HARMOTHOE
(SON OF —) ITYLUS
AEETES (DAUGHTER OF —) MEDEA
(FATHER OF —) HELIOS
(MOTHER OF —) PERSA PERSEIS
(SON OF —) APSYRTUS
AEGAEON (BROTHER OF —) GYGES
COTTUS
(FATHER OF —) URANUS
(MOTHER OF —) GE GAEA
(WIFE OF —) AEMILIA
AEGEAN SEA (ANCIENT PEOPLE OF
—) PSARA PSYRA SAMIAN LELEGES
SAMIOTE
(GULF OF —) SAROS
(ISLAND OF —) COS IOS KEOS NIOS
RODI SCIO CHIOS LEROS MELOS
NAXOS PAROS PATMO SAMOS
SIROS TENOS THERA ANDROS
IKARIA IMBROS LEMNOS LESBOS
RHODES SKYROS
(RIVER INTO —) STRUMA VARDAR
MARISTA
(TOWN ON —) CHIOS VATHY
MYTILENE
AEGEON (WIFE OF —) AEMILIA
AEGEUS (BROTHER OF —) LYCUS
NISUS PALLAS
(FATHER OF —) PANDION
(SON OF —) THESEUS
(WIFE OF —) PYLIA
AEGIA (FATHER OF —) ADRASTUS
(HUSBAND OF —) POLYNICES
(SON OF —) THERSANDER
AEGINA (FATHER OF —) ASOPUS
(MOTHER OF —) METOPE
(SON OF —) AEACUS
AEGIR HLER GYMIR
(WIFE OF —) RAN
AEGIRITE ACMITE
AEGIS EGIS SHIELD AUSPICE
DEFENCE DEFENSE
AEGISTHUS (FATHER OF —)
THYESTES
(MOTHER OF —) PELOPIA
(SLAYER OF —) ORESTES

AEGLE (BROTHER OF —) PHAETHON
(FATHER OF —) HELIUS
(MOTHER OF —) CLYMENE
AEGYPTUS (BROTHER OF —)
DANAUS
(FATHER OF —) BELUS
(MOTHER OF —) ANCHINOE
(SON OF —) LYNCEUS
AENEAS (COMPANION OF —)
ACHATES
(FATHER OF —) ANCHISES
(GREAT-GRANDSON OF —) BRUT
(MOTHER OF —) VENUS APHRODITE
(SON OF —) IULUS ASCANIUS
(WIFE OF —) CREUSA LAVINIA
AENEID (AUTHOR OF —) VIRGIL
(CHARACTER IN —) ANNA DIDO
JUNO VENUS AENEAS PALLAS
TURNUS EVANDER LATINUS LAVINIA
ANCHISES ASCANIUS
AENGUS (MOTHER OF —) BOANN
AEOLUS (BROTHER OF —) DORUS
XUTHUS
(DAUGHTER OF —) ARNE CANACE
ALCYONE HALCYONE
(FATHER OF —) HELLEN HIPPOTES
(MOTHER OF —) ARNE ORSEIS
(SON OF —) ATHAMAS CRETHEUS
SISYPHUS SALMONEUS
AEON AGE EON ERA AION AEVUM
CYCLE KALPA PERIOD
(PAIR OF —S) SYZYGY
AEPYTUS (FATHER OF —)
CRESPHONTES
(MOTHER OF —) MEROPE
AERATE AERIFY CHARGE INFLATE
AERIAL AERY AIRY TWIN AERIE
LOFTY DIPOLE UNREAL AEOLIAN
ANTENNA ETHEREAL
(ROTATING —) SCANNER
(WIRELESS —) RADIATOR
AERIALIST FLIER FLYER
AERIE AERY AIRE AYRE EYRY NEST
AIERY BROOD EYRIE
AERIFORM UNREAL GASEOUS
AEROBE BACTERIUM
AERODROME AIRPORT AIRFIELD
AEROEMBOLISM BENDS
AEROFOIL FOIL SLAT ROTOR
CONTROL SURFACE
AEROLITE AEROLITH
AERONAUT PILOT SKYMAN
AERONAUTICS AVIATION
AEROPE (DAUGHTER OF —)
ANAXIBIA
(FATHER OF —) CATREUS CERHEUS
(HUSBAND OF —) ATREUS
PLISTHENES
(LOVER OF —) THYESTES
(SISTER OF —) CLYMENE
(SON OF —) MENELAUS
AGAMEMNON
AEROPLANE (SEE AIRPLANE)
FANJET JALOPY RAIDER PARASOL
PROPJET SOCIABLE SPITFIRE
AEROSE BRASSY
AEROSTAT AIRSHIP BALLOON
AIRCRAFT
AERUGO RUST PATINA
AESACUS (FATHER OF —) PRIAM
(LOVER OF —) HESPERIA
(MOTHER OF —) ARISBE
ALEXIRRHOE

AESEPUS (BROTHER OF —) PEDASUS
(FATHER OF —) BUCOLION
(MOTHER OF —) ABARBAREA
(SLAYER OF —) EURYALUS
AESON (BROTHER OF —) PELIAS
(FATHER OF —) CRETHEUS
(MOTHER OF —) TYRO
(SON OF —) JASON
(WIFE OF —) ALCIMEDA
AESTHETIC ARTISTIC ESTHETIC TASTEFUL
AETA ITA
AETHALIDES (FATHER OF —) HERMES MERCURY
(MOTHER OF —) EUPOLEMIA
AETHRA (FATHER OF —) OCEANUS PITTHEUS
(MOTHER OF —) TETHYS
(SON OF —) HYAS THESEUS
AETOLUS (FATHER OF —) ENDYMION
(SON OF —) CALYDON PLEURON
(WIFE OF —) PRONOE
AFAR OFF AWAY SAHO FERNE FERREN REMOTE YFERRE DANAKIL DANKALI DISTANT
AFARA LIMBA
AFFABLE FAIR OPEN BLAND CIVIL FRANK SUAVE BENIGN FACILE FORTHY GENIAL SOCIAL URBANE AMIABLE CORDIAL GENERAL LIKABLE CHARMING FAMILIAR FRIENDLY GRACIOUS PLEASANT SOCIABLE TOWARDLY CONVERSABLE
AFFAIR DO JOB PIE BLOW CASE DEAL DUEL GEAR PLOY BRAWL CAUSE EVENT FIGHT LEVEE PARTY THING ACTION BATTLE BEHALF DOMENT EFFEIR MATTER SETOUT SHAURI BLOWOUT CONCERN FUNERAL HOEDOWN JOURNEY LIAISON PALAVER SHEBANG BUSINESS COMETHER ENDEAVOR HYPOTHEC INTRIGUE OCCASION PROCEEDING
(CONFUSED —) SCHEMOZZLE
(CRITICAL —) KANKEDORT
(LOVE —) LOVE AMOUR INTRIGUE
(SOCIAL —) FORMAL JUNKET SUPPER
(STATE —S) ESTATE
(PL.) SQUARES OCCASIONS
AFFECT AIL AIR HIT BEAR MELT MOVE POSE RINE SHAM STIR SWAY ALLOT ALTER ANNOY ASSAY COLOR DRIVE FANCY FEIGN HAUNT IMPEL MINCE SHOCK TOUCH ASPIRE ASSIGN ASSUME CHANGE DESIRE MOLEST SOFTEN STRIKE THRILL ATTAINT ATTINGE BEWITCH CONCERN EMOTION FEELING IMPRESS OPERATE PASSION PRETEND PROFESS ALLOCATE DISPOSED FREQUENT INTEREST SIMULATE
(— BY HANDLING) TOUCH
(— DEEPLY) CUT
(— FAVORABLY) LIKE
(— INJURIOUSLY) INTERESS
(— STRONGLY) HIT HOLD SURPRISE

(— WITH EXCITEMENT) BLOW
(— WITH FEELING) SMITE
AFFECTATION AIR AIRS POSE SHAM FRILL GRACE MINCE CHICHI CONCEIT DISPLAY FOPPERY FROUNCE GRIMACE PIETISM FONDNESS PRETENSE PUPPYISM
(PL.) LUGS
AFFECTED MOY AIRY CAMP FEAT AILED APISH MOVED POSEY CHICHI FALLAL FEISTY FORMAL PRETTY QUAINT SEIZED FEIGNED MINIKIN MISSISH REACHED SMITTEN STILTED TAFFETA TAFFETY TOUCHED INVOLVED PRECIEUX PRECIOUS RECHERCHE
(— BY DECAY) DOTY
(— WITH RABIES) MAD
(EASILY —) SENSIBLE
(SOMETHING —) CAMP
(SUFF.) IC ICAL PATH(IA)(IC)(Y)
AFFECTING AIRIFIED FRAPPANT POIGNANT TOUCHING
AFFECTION LOVE WAFF ALOHA AMOUR BOTCH FLAME HEART CHERTE DOTAGE ESTEEM HYDROA MALADY REGARD THRUSH AILMENT CHARITY EMOTION FEELING PASSION SYMPTOM CHLOASMA DEARNESS DEVOTION FONDNESS KINDNESS MELICERA TENDENCY
(LASTING —) WARMSPOT
(MORBID —) SEQUELA
(PARENTAL —) STORGE
(PROFOUND —) WORSHIP
(PL.) HEART HEARTSTRING
(SUFF.) OMA PATHY
AFFECTIONATE DEAR FOND WARM ARDENT DOTING LOVING TENDER AMOROUS CORDIAL DEVOTED EARNEST ZEALOUS ATTACHED PARENTAL SISTERLY
AFFECTIVE SENSIBLE
AFFERENT BEAR ESODIC SENSORY ADVEHENT INFERENT
AFFIANCE AFFY FAITH TRUST ASSURE ENGAGE ENSURE FIANCE PLEDGE PLIGHT SPOUSE BETROTH PROMISE CONTRACT RELIANCE
AFFIANCED INTENDED
AFFIANT DEPONENT AFFIDAVIT
AFFIDAVIT DAVY OATH AFFIANT AFFIDAVY AFFYDAVY
AFFILIATE ALLY UNIT ADOPT MERGE UNITE ATTACH BRANCH RELATE ASCRIBE CHAPTER CONNECT FILIATE
AFFINITY KIN TELE FAMILY LIKING AVIDITY CHEMISM KINDRED KINSHIP RAPPORT ALLIANCE GOSSIPRY HOMOLOGY RELATION SYMPATHY COGNATION
(PREF.) **(— FOR)** TROP(IDO)(O)
(SUFF.) **(— FOR)** PHIL(A)(AE)(E)(IA)(ISM)(IST)(OUS)(US) TROPE TROPISM
AFFIRM PUT AFFY AVER AVOW TAKE POSIT STATE SWEAR TRUTH VOUCH ADHERE ALLEGE ASSERT ATTEST AVOUCH DEPOSE RATIFY SUBMIT THREAP THREEP VERIFY ASSEVER CONFIRM DECLARE

PROFESS PROTEST TESTIFY MAINTAIN PREDICATE
AFFIRMATION SAY VOW YES AMEN OATH WORD DIXIT PONENT THESIS AVERRAL AVERMENT
AFFIRMATIVE AY AYE NOD YAH YEA YEP YES AMEN ATEN YEAH PONENT DOGMATIC POSITIVE
AFFIX ADD FIX PEN PIN SET CASE CLIP FAST JOIN NAIL SEAL SIGN ADDON ANNEX INFIX STAMP UNITE ANCHOR APPEND ATTACH FASTEN SETTLE STAPLE ADHIBIT CONNECT ENTITLE FORMANT IMPRESS PLASTER SUBJOIN
AFFLATUS FURY FUROR FRENZY VISION IMPULSE
AFFLICT AIL RUE TRY VEX COMB FIRE HOLD HURT PAIN PINE RACK TUKE ARRAY ASSAY BESET CURSE GRILL GRIPE HARRY PINCH PRESS SEIZE SMITE TRYST VISIT WOUND WRING BURDEN GRIEVE HARASS HUMBLE INFECT MOLEST PESTER REMORD SCORCH STRAIN STRESS STRIKE CHASTEN INFLICT OPPRESS SCOURGE TORMENT TROUBLE DISTRESS LACERATE STRAITEN
AFFLICTED JOB SAD SORRY AILING WOEFUL GRIEVED HAUNTED SMITTEN IMPAIRED STRICKEN TROUBLED
AFFLICTION WOE EVIL LOSS PAIN SORE TEEN TINE TRAY ASSAY CROSS GRIEF PRESS SMART STOUR BUFFET DURESS MISERY PATHOS PLAGUE SORROW STRESS THRONG AILMENT DISEASE ILLNESS PASSION PURSUIT SCOURGE TORTURE TROUBLE CALAMITY DISTRESS HARDSHIP SEVERITY SICKNESS VEXATION MARTYRDOM
(SECRET —) HAIRSHIRT
(PL.) CUP
(SUFF.) **(— WITH)** ITIS
AFFLICTIVE SAD DIRE SORE SOUR HEAVY SEVERE
AFFLUENCE EASE AFFLUX INFLUX PLENTY RICHES WEALTH FORTUNE OPULENCE
AFFLUENT FAT RICH FLUSH RIVER BRANCH SPRUIT STREAM COPIOUS FLOWING HALCYON OPULENT WEALTHY ABUNDANT INFLUENT
AFFORD GO BEAR GIVE LEND GRANT INCUR OFFER STAND THOLE YIELD CONFER ENDURE MANAGE SUPPLY ACHIEVE FORWARD FURNISH FURTHER PRODUCE PROVIDE MINISTER
AFFRAY FEUD FRAY RIOT ALARM BRAWL BROIL CLASH FIGHT MELEE SCARE SPURN ATTACK BATTLE COMBAT EFFRAY ENFRAI FRIGHT STRIFE TERROR TUMULT ASSAULT CONTEST QUARREL SCUFFLE STARTLE FRIGHTEN STRUGGLE
AFFRIGHT COW FEAR AGAST ALARM DAUNT DOUBT DREAD SCARE AGRISE APPALL DISMAY

CONFUSE STARTLE TERRIFY FRIGHTEN
AFFRONT CUT DEFY SLAP ABUSE BEARD PEEVE HARASS INJURE INSULT NETTLE OFFEND SLIGHT STRUNT ASSAULT OFFENCE OFFENSE OUTRAGE PROVOKE CONFRONT DISGRACE ILLTREAT IRRITATE CONTUMELY
AFFUSION POURING INFUSION
AFGHAN RUG GHAN COVER DURANI HASARA HAZARA PATHAN BLANKET PAKHTUN PUKHTUN ACHAKZAI COVERLET
AFGHAN FOX CORSAC CORSAK

AFGHANISTAN	
CAPITAL:	KABUL
COIN:	PUL ABBASI AMANIA AFGHANI
LAKE:	HELMAND
LANGUAGE:	DARI PASHTO PUSHTU BALOCHI BALUCHI
MEASURE:	JERIB KAROH
MOUNTAIN:	KOH SAFEO CHAGAI PAMIRS SULAIMAN HIMALAYAS
NATIVE:	SISTANI
PARLIAMENT:	SHURA
PROVINCE:	GHOR FARAH HERAT KABUL KUNAR KUNUZ LOGAR MAZAR ZABUL GHAZNI KAPISA PARWAN WARDAK
RIVER:	LORA OXUS CABUL FARAH HARUT INDUS KABUL KHASH KUNAR KOKCHA KUNDUZ HELMAND MURGHAB AMUDARYA
SEA:	DARYA
TOWN:	RUI JURM NANI WAMA ASMAR BALKH DOSHI HERAT KABUL KUNAR MARUF MATUN MUKUR PAHRA TULAK URGAN CHAMAN GHAZNI KUNDUZ NAUZAD PANJAO RUSTAK SANGAN SAROBI TUKZAR WASHIR BAGHLAN BAMIYAN DILARAM KANDAHAR MAZARESHARIF
TRIBE:	SAFI TURK ULUS KAFIR TAJIK UZBEK BALOCH BALUCH HAZARA KIRGIZ PATHAN
WEIGHT:	PAU PAW SER SIR KARWAR KHURDS

AFICIONADO FAN AMATEUR DEVOTEE GROUPIE FOLLOWER
AFIELD ABROAD ASTRAY
AFIRE ALOW ALOWE EAGER ABLAZE AFLAME ARDENT BURNING FLAMING
A-FLAT AS AIS
AFLOAT ASEA ASWIM AWAFT AWASH ADRIFT BUOYED NATANT ABROACH FLOODED UNFIXED FLOATING
AFOOT ABOUT AGATE ASTIR ABROAD TOWARD WALKING
AFORE ERE
AFOREMENTIONED SAID SUCH
AFORESAID SAME DITTO NAMED PRIOR PREVIOUS
AFORETIME ERE FORMER FORMERLY
AFRAID RAD REDE ADRAD FRAID PAVID REDDE TIMID AGHAST

CRAVEN FEARED SCARED WROTHE
AFEARED ALARMED ANXIOUS
ASCARED CHICKEN FEARFUL
GASTFUL COWARDLY GHASTFUL
TIMOROUS
AFREET JINN AFRIT DEMON GIANT
IFRIT JINNI AFRITE EFREET
AFRESH ANEW ANON OVER AGAIN
NEWLY DENOVO ENCORE
REPEATED

AFRICA
(ALSO SEE SPECIFIC COUNTRIES)
DESERT: NAMIB NEFUD NUBIAN
SAHARA ARABIAN KALAHARI
LAKE: CHAD CONGO NYASA VOLTA
ALBERT KARIBA MALAWI RUDOLF
TURKANA VICTORIA TANGANYIKA
MOUNTAIN: MERU ATLAS ELGON
KENYA TEIDE TOUBKAL KARISIMBI
RASDASHAN RUWENZORI
DRAKENSBERG KILIMANJARO
NATION: CHAD MALI TOGO BENIN
CONGO EGYPT GABON GHANA
KENYA LIBYA NIGER SUDAN ZAIRE
ANGOLA GAMBIA GUINEA
MALAWI RWANDA UGANDA
ZAMBIA ALGERIA BURUNDI
LESOTHO LIBERIA MOROCCO
NAMIBIA NIGERIA SENEGAL
SOMALIA TUNISIA BOTSWANA
CAMEROON DJIBOUTI ETHIOPIA
TANZANIA ZIMBABWE
SWAZILAND IVORYCOAST
MADAGASCAR MAURITANIA
MOZAMBIQUE UPPERVOLTA
BURKINAFASO SIERRALEONE
SOUTHAFRICA GUINEABISSAU
RIVER: NILE ORANGE LIMPOPO
SENEGAL ZAMBEZI
WATERFALL: FINCHA TUGELA
KALAMBO RUACANA TESSISAT
VICTORIA

AFRICAINE, L' (CHARACTER IN —)
INEZ DAGAMA SELIKA NELUSKO
(COMPOSER OF —) MEYERBEER
AFRICAN BOER AFRIC
AFRICAN MARIGOLD KHAKIBOS
AFRIKAANS TAAL DUTCH
AFRO NATURAL
AFT BACK REAR ABAFT AFTER
ASTERN BEHIND
(FARTHEST —) AFTERMOST
AFTER A AB BY TO AFT EFT FOR SIN
ANON NEXT PAST POST SYNE
ABAFT APRES ARTER EFTER
INFRA LATER SINCE ASTERN
BEHIND BEYOND FOLLOW
HINDER
(— MEALS) PC
(PREF.) EPH EPI INFRA META
POST
AFTERBIRTH HEAM SECUNDINE
SOOTERKIN
AFTERBODY TONNEAU
AFTERBURNER AUGMENTER
AFTEREFFECT SEQUEL SEQUELA
(PL.) HANGOVER
AFTERGRASS FOG AFTERFEED
AFTERIMAGE SPECTRUM
PHOTOGENE SENSATION
(KIND OF —) PURKINJE

AFTERMATH FOG ETCH LOSS ISSUE
ROWEN ROWET TRAIL TRAIN
ARRISH EDDISH EDGREW EDGROW
EFFECT PROFIT RESULT SEQUEL
UPSHOT EAGRASS STUBBLE
BACKWASH
AFTERMOST LAST HINDMOST
AFTERNOON AFTER TARDE
UNDERN EVENING TEATIME
AFTERPIECE JIG EPODE EXODE
EXODIUM POSTLUDE
AFTERSONG EPODE
AFTERSWARM CAST SPEW SPUE
CASTLING
AFTERTASTE TWANG FAREWELL
AFTERTHOUGHT FOOTNOTE
AFTERWARD EFT POST SITH THEN
APRES LATER INABIT EFTSOON
EFTSOONS
AFTERWARDS SYNE
AGA AGHA LORD CHIEF
(WIFE OF —) BEGUM
AGAIN OR TO BIS EFT YET AGIN
ANEW ANON AYEN AYIN BACK
MORE OVER NEWLY AFRESH
DENOVO ENCORE ITERUM
EFTSOON FRESHLY FURTHER
EFTSOONS MOREOVER
(— AND AGAIN) AND
(PREF.) ANA OVER PALI RE
AGAINST BY IN UP CON GIN NON
AGIN ANTI GAIN INTO WITH AGAIN
ANENT AYENS UNTIL ANENST
AVERSE AYENST CONTRA GAINST
UPTILL VERSUS FERNENT FORNENT
OPPOSED ADVERSUS CONTRAIR
FORENENT FORNENST FORINST
(— HOPE) AGLEE AGLEY
(PREF.) ANTH ANTI CAT(A) CATH
CONTRA ENANTIO GAIN OB
AGAL HEADROPE
AGALLOCH AGGUR ALOES GAROO
GARROO GARROW TAMBAC
LINALOE AGALWOOD CALAMBAC
AGAMA AGA AGHA GUANA AGAMID
IGUANA LIZARD AGAMIAN
AGAMEDE (FATHER OF —) AUGEAS
(HUSBAND OF —) MULIUS
AGAMEMNON (BROTHER OF —)
MENELAUS
(DAUGHTER OF —) ELECTRA
IPHIGENIA
(FATHER OF —) PLISTHENES
(GRANDFATHER OF —) ATREUS
(MOTHER OF —) AEROPE
(SON OF —) ORESTES
(WIFE OF —) CLYTEMNESTRA
AGAMETE SPORE
AGAMID AGA AGHA BALETE BALITI
AGAPANTHUS TULBAGHIA
LOVEFLOWER
AGAPE LOVE OPEN FEAST GAPING
YAWNING
AGAR MOSS GELOSE KANTEN
GELOSIN GELOSINE
AGARIC BLEWITS BLUSHER
FLYBANE LEPIOTA
AGASP EAGER GASPING
AGATE TAW ONYX RUBY SARD
ACHATE GAGATE MARBLE PEBBLE
QUARTZ
(KIND OF —) MOSS
AGATI SESBANIA

AGAVE ALOE LILY PITA AGAUE
AMOLE DATIL SISAL LILIUM
MAGUEY MESCAL PULQUE ZAPUPE
CANTALA KARATTO KERATTO
TEQUILA HENEQUEN HENIQUEN
JINIQUEN SOAPWEED
(BROTHER OF —) POLYDORUS
(FATHER OF —) CADMUS
(HUSBAND OF —) ECHION
(MOTHER OF —) HARMONIA
(SISTER OF —) INO SEMELE
AUTONOE
(SON OF —) PENTHEUS
AGE ALD BIN DAY ELD EON ERA
AEON EDGE GRAY OLAM TIME
YUGA AETAT CYCLE EPOCH GETON
OLDEN RIPEN SECLE WORLD
YEARS MATURE MELLOW PERIOD
SIECLE WITHER CENTURY
DEVELOP GLACIAL OLDNESS
SECULUM SENESCE VORHAND
ANCIENTY DURATION ETERNITY
LIFETIME MAJORITY MATURITY
(— OF MOON) EPACT
(— OF 100 YEARS) CENTENARY
(ADVANCED —) DOTAGE
(BEING UNDER 13 YEARS OF —)
PRETEEN
(EARLY MIDDLE —) SUMMER
(FULL —) MAJORITY
(GREAT —) ANTIQUITY GRANDEVITY
(OLD —) CRUTCH SENIUM VETUSTY
SENILITY
(PREF.) (OLD —) GERONT(O)
PRESBY(O)
(SUFF.) AEVAL EVAL
(HAVING APPROXIMATE — OF) ISH
ISTIC
AGED AE AET AGY OLD RIPE ANILE
HOARY OLDEN PASSE FEEBLE
INFIRM MATURE SENILE WINTRY
YEARED ANCIENT ELDERLY
OGYGIAN WINTERED
(NOT —) GREEN
(WELL —) STALE
AGEE AJEE AWRY AGLEY ASKEW
(SON OF —) SHAMMAH
AGELESS ETERNAL TIMELESS
AGELONG SECULAR SAECULAR
AGENCY DINT HAND CHECK FORCE
LEVER MEANS MOYEN ORGAN
PROXY ACTION BUREAU MEDIUM
OFFICE ARBITER BENEFIT
BROKERY FACULTY LIBRARY
MACHINE ACTIVITY COMPTOIR
COURTESY MINISTRY
(PUBLIC —) AUTHORITY
(REGULATORY —) QUANGO
(RESTORATIVE —) BALM
(SUPPOSITITIOUS —) ENTELECHY
(THERAPEUTIC —) MODALITY
(WORLD WAR II —) WPA
AGENDA LIST PLAN ROTA OUTLINE
AGENDUM ITEM SLATE DOCKET
RECORD RITUAL PROGRAM
AGENOR (BROTHER OF —) BELUS
(DAUGHTER OF —) EUROPA
(FATHER OF —) ANTENOR NEPTUNE
(MOTHER OF —) LIBYA
(SON OF —) CILIX CADMUS
PHOENIX
(WIFE OF —) TELEPHASSA

AGENT SPY AMIN DOER ETCH GENE
ACTOR AMEEN BUYER CAUSE
ENVOY MEANS ORGAN PROXY
REEVE RIDER VAKIL WALLA
ADUROL ASSIGN ATOPEN BROKER
BURSAR COMMIS DEALER DEPUTY
ENGINE FACTOR FITTER KEHAYA
LEDGER MEDIUM MINION MUKTAR
PESKAR SELLER SYNDIC VAKEEL
WALLAH BAILIFF BLISTER
CHANNEL COUCHER DRASTIC
FACIENT FEDERAL HUSBAND
LEAGUER MOOKTAR MOUNTAR
MUKTEAR MUTAGEN OFFICER
PESHKAR PROCTOR SCALPER
APPROVER ATTORNEY AUMILDAR
CATALYST EMISSARY EXECUTOR
GOMASHTA GOMASTAH
IMPROVER INCITANT INSTITOR
MINISTER MITICIDE MOOKHTAR
OPERATOR PROMOTER QUAESTOR
RESIDENT SALESMAN VIRUCIDE
MIDDLEMAN OPERATIVE
SATELLITE SENESCHAL
MAINSPRING PROCURATOR
PLENIPOTENTIARY
(— AGAINST LEPROSY) DAPSONE
(— INVESTIGATING DRUG
VIOLATIONS) NARC NARK
(— OF CROMWELL) AGITATOR
(ANTIKNOCK —) ADDITIVE
ALKYLATE
(BINDING —) CHELATOR
(CLEANSING —) SOAP
(CONFIDENTIAL —) AMIN AMEEN
(DESTRUCTIVE —) DEVOURER
(EMPLOYMENT —) PADRONE
(ENFORCEMENT —) LAW
(ENVIRONMENTAL —) ZEITGEBER
(ESPIONAGE —) COURIER
(FISCAL —) STEWARD
(FIXING —) HYPO
(GOVERNMENT —) NARC NARCO
(HEALING —) BALSAM
(LIGHTLY-VALUED —) PAWN
(MEDICINAL —) DRASTIC
(MILK-CURDLING —) RENNET
(NARCOTIC —) NARC NARK GAZER
(OXIDIZING —) NINHYDRIN
(PRESS —) FLACK
(PUBLICITY —) BEATER
(PURCHASING —) CIRCAR SIRCAR
SIRKAR
(SECRET —) SBIRRO OPERATIVE
(SPECIAL —) TMAN
(SPIRITUAL —) POWER
(STIMULATING —) FILIP FILLIP
(SUBVERSIVE —) STOOGE
(SWEETENING —) DULCIN
(UNDERCOVER —) SPOOK
(VOLATILE —) SPIRIT
(WETTING —) SPREADER
(SUFF.) ANT FIER STAT(IC)(ICS)
AGE-OLD TIMEWORN
AGESILAUS (BROTHER OF —) AGIS
(FATHER OF —) ARCHIDAMUS
(MOTHER OF —) EUPOLIA
AGGLOMERATE HEAP LUMP MASS
PILE SELF SLAG WIND CHAOS
GATHER CLUSTER COLLECT
AGGLOMERATION HORDE
CONGERY FAVELLA CONGERIE

AGGRANDIZE LIFT BOOST EXALT RAISE ADVANCE AUGMENT DIGNIFY ELEVATE ENLARGE MAGNIFY PROMOTE INCREASE

AGGRAVATE IRK NAG VEX FEED LOAD TWIT ANGER ANNOY TAUNT TEASE BURDEN PESTER WORSEN AGGREGE BEDEVIL ENHANCE ENLARGE MAGNIFY PROVOKE AGGRIEVE HEIGHTEN INCREASE IRRITATE

AGGRAVATED ACUTE

AGGREEABLE ACCEPTABLE

AGGREGATE ADD ALL SET SUM AUGE BAND BULK CLON CLUB COMB DEME FLOC GOUT LATH MASS BLOCK BUNCH CLASS CLONE COVER CROWD FIELD GROSS SHOOT SMEAR TOTAL UNITE WHOLE AMOUNT BALLAS DOMAIN PLUREL VOLUME ASBOLAN COLLECT SCHMEAR SCHMEER ARCULITE ASBOLANE ASBOLITE AXIOLITE COMPOUND COVERAGE CUMULITE ENSEMBLE MANIFOLD MULTEITY TOTALITY
(— OF CELLS) TISSUE
(— OF CRYSTALS) TREE
(— OF MICA) BOOK
(— OF MINERALS) EYE
(— OF ORE) KIDNEY
(— OF POINTS) CELL
(— OF RELATED THINGS) SHMEAR SCHMEAR
(— OF STATEMENTS) AUTHORITY
(— OF TISSUES) BODY
(MATHEMATICAL —) FIELD SEQUENCE
(MOLECULAR —) MICELLE
(SOIL —) PED
(SUFF.) ERY

AGGREGATION HEAD HERD NEST CLUMP CUTIN FLOCK GORGE GROUP LURRY SWARM COLONY FAMILY NATION SYSTEM CLUSTER CONGERY GALLERY SORITES CONGERIE EUMERISM

AGGRESSION WAR RAID ATTACK INJURY ASSAULT OFFENSE INVASION

AGGRESSIVE BUTCH PUSHY PUSHING AGONISTIC TRUCULENT

AGGRESSIVENESS CRUST DEFIANCE BELLICOSITY

AGGRIEVE TRY HARM HURT PAIN HARRY WRONG INJURE AFFLICT OPPRESS TROUBLE DISTRESS

AGGRIEVED SORE OFFENDED

AGHAST AGAST AFRAID

AGHRERATH (FATHER OF —) PESHENG
(SLAYER OF —) AFRASIAB

AGILAWOOD AGALLOCH AGALLOCHUM

AGILE DEFT FAST LISH SPRY WIRY ADEPT ALERT BRISK CATTY ELFIN FLEET LITHE NIFTY NIPPY QUICK WANLE WITHY ACTIVE ADROIT FEERIE FEIRIE LIMBER LISSOM LITHER LIVELY LUTHER NIMBLE QUIVER SUPPLE WANDLE LISSOME SALIENT SPRINGE SPRINGY ATHLETIC

AGILITY LEVITY SPROIL SLEIGHT ACTIVITY LEGERITY SALIENCE

AGING BINNING
(PREMATURE —) GERODERMA GERODERMIA

AGIO BATTA DISAGIO PREMIUM DISCOUNT EXCHANGE

AGIST TAX FEED RATE GRAZE PASTURE

AGITATE FAN IRK JAR VEX WEY FRET FUSS MOVE PLOT RILE ROCK ROIL SEEK STIR TEEM ALARM ALTER BREAK BROIL CHURN DRIVE HARRY IMPEL QUAKE ROUSE SHAKE AROUSE BETOSS BUSKLE DEBATE DEVISE EXCITE FOMENT HARASS INCITE JABBLE JOSTLE JUMBLE JUSTLE LATHER MANAGE RATTLE RUFFLE SEETHE ACTUATE CANVASS COMMOVE CONCUSS DISCUSS DISTURB PERTURB REVOLVE TEMPEST TORMENT TROUBLE ACTIVATE CONTRIVE CONVULSE DISQUIET DISTRACT TRANSACT
(— A LIQUID) SPARGE

AGITATED WILD HECTIC STEWED STORMY YEASTY AGITATO ESTUOUS UNQUIET AESTUOUS FEVERISH FLURRIED SEETHING OVERWROUGHT

AGITATION GOG JAR JOG BOIL FEAR FLAP FRET FURY GUST HEAT ITCH JERK JOLT SNIT STEW ALARM DANCE HURRY QUAKE SHAKE STORM STOUR TWEAK YEAST BREEZE BUSTLE DITHER ENERGY FIZZLE FLIGHT FLURRY FRENZY JABBLE MOTION PUCKER QUIVER RIPPLE SHAKES TAKING TREMOR TUMULT UNREST WELTER EMOTION FERMENT FLUSTER FLUTTER MADNESS RAMPAGE STICKLE SWITHER TEMPEST TURMOIL DISQUIET PAROXYSM UPHEAVAL COMMOTION
(— AND PROPAGANDA) AGITPROP
(— IN LIQUID) JABBLE
(BODILY —) JACTATION
(MENTAL —) STEW

AGITATOR HOG TREATER

AGLAIA (FATHER OF —) JUPITER
(MOTHER OF —) EURYNOME
(SISTER OF —) THALIA EUPHROSYNE

AGLET TAB TAG LACE STUD PLATE AIGLET PENDANT SPANGLE HAWTHORN STAYLACE

AGLEY AWRY AGLEE ASIDE ASKEW WRONG

AGLYCON GENIN NONSUGAR SAPOGENIN

AGNATE AKIN ALLIED COGNATE KINDRED

AGNEL MOUTON

AGNOETE THEMISTIAN

AGNOMEN NAME ALIAS EPITHET SURNAME COGNOMEN NICKNAME

AGNOSTIC ATHEIST DOUBTER SKEPTIC NESCIENT

AGO BY SIN BACK ERST GONE PAST SENS SYNE YGOE YORE ABACK AGONE SINCE YGONE SINSYNE BACKWARD
(LONG —) ANCIENTLY

AGOG AVID KEEN ASTIR EAGER LIVELY EXCITED VIGILANT

AGOING AGATE

AGONIZE BEAR RACK STRAIN WRITHE

AGONIZING GRINDING HARROWING

AGONY ACHE PAIN PANG DOLOR GRIEF GRIPE PANIC STOUR THRAW THROE TRIAL ACHING ANGUISH ANXIETY EMOTION TORMENT TORTURE TRAVAIL DISTRESS PAROXYSM

AGOUTI CAPA CAVY PACA ACUCHI AGOUTY ACOUCHI ACOUCHY

AGRAFFE CLASP

AGRARIAN RURAL PASTORAL PRAEDIAL

AGRAULOS (DAUGHTER OF —) HERSE PANDROSOS
(FATHER OF —) ACTAEUS
(HUSBAND OF —) CECROPS

AGREE FAY FIT GEE HIT PAN YES GIBE GREE JIBE JUMP MEET SIDE SORT SUIT ADMIT ALLOW ATONE BLEND CHECK CLICK CLOSE FADGE GRANT HITCH JUTTY LEVEL MATCH PIECE STAND TALLY UNITE YIELD ACCEDE ACCEPT ACCORD ADHERE ASSENT ASSORT COMPLY CONCUR CONDOG COTTON ENGAGE REWARD SETTLE SQUARE SUBMIT ARRANGE BARGAIN COMPORT CONCEDE CONFORM CONGREE CONGRUE CONSENT CONSIGN DARESAY PACTION PROMISE COINCIDE COMPOUND CONTRACT COVENANT QUADRATE
(— MUTUALLY) STIPULATE
(— TO) ACCEPT
(— TO JOIN) ADHERE
(— UPON) TAILYE TAILZEE TAILZIE
(— WITH) SIT LIKE SIDE TAIL ANSWER

AGREEABLE AMEN EASY FAIR FINE GOOD KIND LIEF NICE SOFT WEME AMENE CANNY DULCE GRATE JOLIE JOLLY LITHE LUSTY QUEME READY SAPID SMIRK SUANT SUAVE SUENT SWEET COMELY COWDIE DAINTY DULCET KINDLY LIKELY MELLOW SAVORY SMOOTH SUITED ADAPTED AMABILE AMIABLE COUTHIE DOUCEUR TUNABLE WELCOME WILLING WINSOME AMENABLE CHARMING DELICATE GRATEFUL LIKESOME LOVESOME OBLIGING PLACABLE PLAUSIVE PLEASANT PLEASING PURSUANT SOCIABLE SUITABLE THANKFUL CONGENIAL PALATABLE
(NOT —) ABHORRENT
(UNPLEASANTLY —) SACCHARINE

AGREED ON DONE CONTENT

AGREEING CONNATE CONTENT ACCORDANT ACCORDING

AGREEMENT GO FIT NOD AXIS BOND DEAL FINE LINE MISE PACT TACK TAIL TRUE WHIZ ATONE COVIN LEASE MATCH TERMS TOUCH TRUTH TRYST UNITY WHIZZ

ACCORD ACTION ASSENT CARTEL CAUTIO COMART COMITY COVINE DICKER LEAGUE PACTUM PLEDGE TREATY UNISON ANALOGY BARGAIN CLOSING CLOSURE COMPACT CONCERT CONSENT CONSORT CONSULT ENTENTE HARMONY ONENESS PACTION RAPPORT CONTRACT DIAPASON SANCTION SORTANCE SYMPATHY ACCEPTANCE ACCORDANCE
(— OF SOUND) CHIME
(— TO JOIN) ADHESION
(GRAMMATICAL —) ATTRACTION
(IN —) ASONE
(REPURCHASE —) REPO
(SECRET —) CAHOOT CAHOOTS COLLUSION

AGRICANE (SLAYER OF —) ORLANDO

AGRICULTURAL ARABLE GEOPONIC GEOPONICAL

AGRICULTURE FARMING GAINAGE TILLAGE AGRONOMY
(— SYSTEM) KOLKHOZ
(PREF.) AGRO

AGRICULTURIST THO FARMER GROWER SANTAL PLANTER RANCHER
AMERICAN REID MORTON RUFFIN TAYLOR THOMAS WATSON BORLAUG
CANADIAN MACKAY SAUNDERS
ENGLISH TULL YOUNG
GERMAN NAUMANN
SWISS SAUSSURE

AGRIMONY CLIVE BONESET BORWORT HEMPWEED

AGRIPPINA (SON OF —) NERO

AGRITO AGARITA MAHONIA ALGERITO ASHBERRY

AGRIUS (BROTHER OF —) LATINUS TELEGONUS
(FATHER OF —) ULYSSES ODYSSEUS PORTHAON
(MOTHER OF —) GAEA CIRCE EURYTE
(SON OF —) THERSITES

AGRONOMIST (ALSO SEE AGRICULTURIST)

AGROUND SEWED ASHORE BEACHED STRANDED

AGRYPHA LOGION

AGRYPNIA INSOMNIA SLEEPLESSNESS

AGUACATE AHUACA AVOCADO

AGUAMAS PINGUIN

AGUE CHILL EXIES FEVER MALARIA QUARTAN SHAKING SHIVERS

AGUE TREE SASSAFRAS

AGUEWEED BONESET

AGUR (FATHER OF —) JAKEH

AH AY ACH

AHAB (FATHER OF —) OMRI
(NEIGHBOR OF —) NABOTH
(WIFE OF —) JEZEBEL

AHAR AGEE AJEE

AHARAH (FATHER OF —) BENJAMIN

AHARTALAV YARROW MILFOIL

AHASBAI (SON OF —) ELIPHELET

AHAZ (FATHER OF —) MICAH JOTHAM

AHAZIAH (FATHER OF —) AHAB
JEHORAM
(MOTHER OF —) JEZEBEL ATHALIAH
AHBAN (FATHER OF —) ABISUR
(MOTHER OF —) ABIHAIL
AHEAD ON UP ALEE FORE AFORE
ALONG DORMY BEFORE DORMIE
ONWARD ALREADY ENDWAYS
ENDWISE FORWARD LEADING
ADELANTE ADVANCED ANTERIOR
(— OF TIME) FAST
(STRAIGHT —) FORERIGHT
AHEM HUM
AHIAH (FATHER OF —) AHITUB
JERAHMEEL
(SON OF —) BAASHA
AHIAM (FATHER OF —) SHARAR
AHIEZER (FATHER OF —)
AMMISHADDAI
AHIHUD (FATHER OF —) SHELOMI
(SON OF —) GEDALIAH
AHILUD (SON OF —) BAANA
JEHOSHAPHAT
AHIMAAZ (DAUGHTER OF —)
AHINOAM
(FATHER OF —) ZADOK
AHIMELECH (FATHER OF —) AHITUB
AHINADAB (FATHER OF —) IDDO
AHINOAM (FATHER OF —) AHIMAAZ
(HUSBAND OF —) SAUL DAVID
(SON OF —) AMNON
AHIO (FATHER OF —) BERIAH JEHIEL
ABINADAB
AHIRAM (FATHER OF —) BENJAMIN
AHISAMACH (SON OF —) AHOLIAB
AHISHAHAR (FATHER OF —) BILHAN
AHITUB (FATHER OF —) AMARIAH
PHINEHAS
(SON OF —) ZADOK AHIJAH
AHIMELECH
AHLAI (FATHER OF —) SHESHAN
(HUSBAND OF —) JARHA
(SON OF —) ZABAD
AHOAH (FATHER OF —) BENJAMIN
AHOLIBAMAH (FATHER OF —) ANAH
(HUSBAND OF —) ESAU
AHOY AVAST
AHUEHUETE CEDAR SABINO
CYPRESS
AHURA MAZDA ORMAZD
AHUZAM (FATHER OF —) ASHUR
(MOTHER OF —) NAARAH
AH WILDERNESS (AUTHOR OF —)
ONEILL
(CHARACTER IN —) BELLE DAVID
MILLER MURIEL RICHARD
MCCOMBER
AIAH (BROTHER OF —) ANAH
(DAUGHTER OF —) RIZPAH
(FATHER OF —) ZIBEON
AID KEY ABET BACK BEET HAND
HELP PONY REDE ALLAY BOOST
COACH FAVOR GRANT SERVE
SPEED TREAT ASSIST CRUTCH
FAVOUR FRIEND PROFIT RELIEF
REMEDY RESCUE SECOND
SUCCOR SUPPLY UPHOLD
ADVANCE AIDANCE ANCILLA
BACKING BENEFIT COMFORT
ENDORSE FORWARD FURTHER
INDORSE RELIEVE SECOURS

SERVICE SUBSIDY SUPPORT
ADJUVATE AUXILIUM BEFRIEND
SUFFRAGE
(— A VESSEL) HOVEL
(— A WAITER) BUS
(— IN MONEY) SUBSIDY
(— SECRETLY) SUBAID
(COMPLEXION —) FUCUS
(FAMILY —) AFDC
(MORMON —) COUNSELOR
COUNSELLOR
AIDA (CHARACTER IN —) AIDA
AMNERIS RADAMES AMONASRO
(COMPOSER OF —) VERDI
AIDAN (FATHER OF —) GABRAN
AIDE AID BEAGLE DEPUTY SECOND
OFFICER ORDERLY ADJUTANT
GALLOPER PARAPROFESSIONAL
(BULLFIGHTER'S —) CAPEADOR
AIDS (— VIRUS) HIV
AIGRETTE EGRET HERON PLUME
SPRAY AIGRET FEATHERS
AIL ILE AILD EILE EYLE FAIL PAIN
PINE AFFECT BOTHER FALTER
SUFFER AFFLICT DECLINE
TROUBLE COMPLAIN DISTRESS
AILANTHUS SUMAC SUMACH
AILING SICK CRAZY CRONK DONCY
DONSY SOBER DONSIE SICKLY
UNWELL CRAICHY CREACHY
AILMENT AIL ILL PIP COUGH
MALADY DISEASE ILLNESS
DISORDER SICKNESS WEAKNESS
(SUDDEN —) WAFF
(WINTER —) STREP
AIM END LAY TRY BEAD BEAM BEND
BENT BUTT FINE GLEE GOAL HEAD
HOLD LEAD MARK MINT PLAN
SAKE SEEK TEMP VIEW VIZY WINK
ACIES BLANK DRIVE ESSAY ETTLE
GUESS LEVEL POINT PRICK SCOPE
SIGHT TRAIN VISIE VIZZY ASPIRE
DESIGN DIRECT ESTEEM INTEND
INTENT OBJECT SCHEME STRIVE
ADDRESS ATTEMPT CHIMERA
MEANING PRETEND PURPOSE
RESPECT STAGGER CHIMAERA
CONSIDER ENDEAVOR ESTIMATE
PRETENSE STEERING TENTAMEN
(— A BROADCAST) NARROWCAST
(— A KICK) FLING
(— AT) EYE AFFECT
(— FURTIVELY) STEAL
(— HIGH) LOB
(— INDIRECTLY) GLANCE
AIMED FAST
(— AT) AFFECTED
AIMING LEVEL GUNLAYING
AIMLESS IDLE BLIND CHANCE
RANDOM DRIFTING
AIMLESSNESS FLANERIE
AIR AER PEW SKY AERE ARIA AURA
AYRE BROW DIRT FEEL LILT LOFT
MIEN PORT POSE SONG TELL TUNE
VENT WIND AVION ETHER FRILL
OZONE UTTER VOICE AERATE
AETHER ALLURE ASPECT BROACH
CACHET MANNER MELODY
OSTENT PIAFFE REGARD REGION
STRAIN VANITY WELKIN WITHER
BEARING DISPLAY EXHIBIT
EXPRESS FANFARE MALARIA

NEPHELE PIAFFER ATTITUDE
BEHAVIOR CARRIAGE PRESENCE
(— COOLED) WATERLESS
(— EXHALED) BLAST
(— IN MOTION) BREATH
(— OUT) VENT
(— PLANT) LIFELEAF
(AFFECTED —S) FRILLS
(BOASTFUL —) PARADO
(CHEERFUL —) LILT
(CONFIDENT —) BRAVURA
(COOL —) FRESCO
(COQUETTISH —) MINAUDERIE
(FETID —) REEK
(FOUL —) DIRT
(HAUGHTY —S) ALTITUDES
(MUSICAL —) ARIA SOLO TUNF
BRAWL MELODY ARIETTA ARIETTE
BRAVURA CANZONE MUSETTE
CAVATINE
(OPEN —) OUTDOORS
OUTOFDOORS
(POISONOUS —) MALARIA
(POMPOUS —) SWELL
(PRETENTIOUS —) SIDE
(PURE —) SERENE
(PUT ON —S) PROSS
(PUT ON THE —) TELEVISE
BROADCAST
(STALE —) STEAM
(STIFLING —) SMORE
(THE —) GATE
(WARM —) OAM
(PL.) LUGS FRONT
(PREF.) AER(O) ATM(O) PNEO
PNEUM(A)(ATA)(O)(ON)(UNO)
PNEUSTA
AIRBORNE ALOFT
AIRCRAFT KITE ABORT BLIMP
CRAFT FLYER PLANE GLIDER
TRIJET AEROBUS AERONEF
AIRSHIP BALLOON AEROBOAT
AERODYNE AEROSTAT AIRLINER
AIRPLANE AUTOGIRO AUTOGYRO
GYRODYNE TILTROTOR
GYROCOPTER ROTORCRAFT
ORNITHOPTER
(— DESIGN) STEALTH
(— WAITING TO LAND) STACK
(ARMED —) GUNSHIP
(LARGE JET —) WIDEBODY
(SMALL —) STOL
(UNIDENTIFIED —) UFO BOGY
BOGEY BOGIE
(UNMANNED —) RPV
AIRCRAFTSMAN ERK
AIRCREWMAN KICKER AIREDALE
AIRFARE (CLASS OF —) APEX
AIRFIELD AERODROME SATELLITE
AIRFOIL FIN FLAP SLAT BLADE
CANARD SURFACE AEROFOIL
ELEVATOR
**AIR FORCE (WOMEN COMPONENTS
OF —)** WAF
AIRHEAD SAP
AIRILY JAUNTILY
AIRING OUTING
AIRLESS STUFFY STIFLING
AIRLINE KLM SAS TWA BWIA ELAL
ALOHA DELTA USAIR FEEDER
IBERIA QANTAS SABENA SKYWAY
UNITED NONSKED LUFTHANSA

AIRMAN ACE FLIER FLYER BIRDMAN
WARBIRD AERONAUT WASTEMAN
AIRPLANE BUS CUB JET MIG SST
BAKA GYRO KILL KITE SHIP ZERO
AVION CAMEL CRATE FLIER FLYER
FRITZ GOTHA HEINE JENNY LINER
PLANE SCOUT SNOOP AIRBUS
BOMBER CANARD CESSNA
CHASER COPTER FANJET FERRET
FESSEL FOKKER GLIDER JENNIE
PUSHER SMOKER TANDEM VESSEL
VIMANA AERONEF AVIATIK AVIETTE
BIPLANE CLIPPER FIGHTER FLIVVER
FLYAWAY HOTSHOT PENGUIN
SNOOPER SPOTTER STINSON
TRACTOR WARBIRD AEROSTAT
ALBATROS KAMIKAZE SEAPLANE
SKYCOACH SKYCRAFT SOCIABLE
STRUTTER TRIPLANE TURBOJET
WARPLANE AEROPLANE
MONOPLANE
(— ENGINE) RAMJET
(COMMANDEER —) SKYJACK
(JET —) AIRBUS
(JUMPING FROM —) SKYDIVING
(PART OF —) FIN POD TAB FLAP
WING BLADE CABIN PYLON RADAR
ENGINE RUDDER AILERON COCKPIT
COWLING SPOILER ELEVATOR
REVERSER STABILIZER SUPPRESSOR
(REMOTE-CONTROLLED —) DRONE
(TYPE OF —) TRIJET
AIR PLANT LIFELEAF LIVELEAF
AIRPORT DROME AIRPARK JETPORT
SCUTTLE AIRDROME AIRFIELD
AIRSCREW PUSHER
**AIRSHIP (SEE ALSO AIRPLANE AND
AIRCRAFT)** SHIP BLIMP GASBAG
AERONAT AEROSTAT PARSEVAL
ZEPPELIN
AIRSTREAM PEW DOWNWASH
AIRSTRIP LILY
AIRTIGHT SEALED AIRPROOF
HERMETIC
AIRWAY MONKEY RETURN SKYWAY
AIRWAVE WINDWAY WINDROAD
AIRY GAY COOL RARE THIN EMPTY
HUFFY LIGHT MERRY WINDY
AERIAL BLITHE BREEZY FLUFFY
JAUNTY JOCUND LIVELY STARRY
AIRLIKE AIRSOME HAUGHTY
JOCULAR SFOGATO AFFECTED
ANIMATED DEBONAIR DELICATE
ETHEREAL FLIPPANT GRACEFUL
SPARKISH TRIFLING VOLATILE
AISLE WAY YLE AILE LANE NAVE
WALK ALLEE ALLEY FEEDWAY
GANGWAY PASSAGE CORRIDOR
AIT OAT EYOT HOLM ILOT ISLE
EIGHT ISLET ISLOT
AITCH ACHE
AITCHBONE ICEBONE EDGEBONE
AJA (FATHER OF —) RAGHU DILIPA
AJAR OPEN DISCORDANT
AJAX AIAS
(FATHER OF —) OILEUS TELAMON
(MOTHER OF —) ERIBOEA
PERIBOEA
AJIGARTA (SON OF —) SUNAHSEPA
AJONJOLI SESAME
AJOWAN AJAVA AIWAIN
AKALI SHAHIDI
AKAN (FATHER OF —) EZER

AKEAKE AKE HOPBUSH IRONWOOD
AKHA KAW
AKIMBO ANGLED AKEMBOLL AKENBOLD
AKIN SIB LIKE NEAR NIGH ALIKE CLOSE AGNATE ALLIED COUSIN SIBBED TENDER COGNATE CONNATE GERMANE RELATED SIMILAR
  (— ON MALE SIDE) AGNATIC
  (NOT —) UNSIB
AKKUB (FATHER OF —) ELIOENAI
AKRA ACCRA INKRA
AKU VICTORFISH
AL AAL AWL MULBERRY
ALA AXIL DRUM WING AXILLA RECESS NOSEWING

ALABAMA
CAPITAL: MONTGOMERY
COUNTY: LEE BIBB CLAY DALE PIKE COOSA HENRY LAMAR MACON PERRY BLOUNT BUTLER COFFEE DALLAS ELMORE ETOWAH GENEVA GREENE MARION MONROE MORGAN SHELBY SUMTER WILCOX CHILTON
LAKE: MARTIN
MOUNTAIN: CHEAHA LOOKOUT RACCOON
NATIVE: LIZARD
RIVER: PEA COOSA CAHABA MOBILE SIPSEY TENSAW CONECUH PERDIDO SEPULGA WARRIOR TOMBIGBEE TALLAPOOSA
STATE BIRD: YELLOWHAMMER
STATE FISH: TARPON
STATE FLOWER: CAMELLIA
STATE TREE: PINE LONGLEAF
TOWN: OPP PIPER SELMA ATHENS CORONA HEFLIN JASPER LANETT LINDEN MARION MOBILE SAMSON BREWTON FLORALA GADSDEN ANNISTON SYLACAUGA TUSCALOOSA

ALABASTER GYPSUM TECALI ONYCHITE
ALACK ALAS ALAKE
ALACRITY HASTE SPEED CELERITY RAPIDITY
ALAMEDA MALL WALK
ALAMETH (FATHER OF —) BECHER
ALAN ALAND ALANT ALAUNT
ALANG-ALANG COGON KOGON
ALANS GHUZ OGHUZ
ALANTIN INULIN
ALAR PTERIC WINGED AXILLARY WINGLIKE
ALARBUS (MOTHER OF —) TAMORA
ALARDO (BROTHER OF —) BRADAMANT
ALARM COW DIN BELL FEAR FRAY GAST LARM ALERT BROIL CLOCK DAUNT FEEZE LARUM NOISE PANIC ROUSE SCARE SIREN START STILL UPSET AFFRAY ALARUM APPALL AROUSE ATTACK BUZZER DISMAY EXCITE FRIGHT OUTCRY SIGNAL TERROR TOCSIN DISTURB GLOPPEN GLOPPEN MOUNTEE STARTLE TERRIFY TORPEDO

WARNING AFFRIGHT DISQUIET FRIGHTEN SURPRISE CONSTERNATION
  (FIRE —) STILL FIREBOX
ALARMED SCARY SCAREY FEARFUL GASTFUL AFFRAYED GHASTFUL SCAREFUL STREAKED
ALARMER HUER
ALARMING SCARY SCAREY FEARFUL SCAREFUL
ALARMIST JITTERBUG
ALAS AY ACH HEU LAS OCH TSK VAE WOE EHEU HECH OIME WALY ALACK HALAS HELAS OIMEE SOSAD HARROW OCHONE OTOTOI WAESUCK ULLAGONE WAESUCKS WELLADAY WELLAWAY

ALASKA
CAPITAL: JUNEAU
GLACIER: MUIR
ISLAND: ADAK ATKA ATTU UMNAK KODIAK UNIMAK AFOGNAK DIOMEDE NUNIVAK
ISLAND GROUP: RAT ALEUTIAN PRIBILOF ANDREANOF
LAKE: NAKNEK ILIAMNA
MOUNTAIN: BONA VETA SPURR KATMAI PAVLOF FORAKER MCKINLEY
MOUNTAIN RANGE: CRAZY BROOKS KAIYUH CHUGACH KILBUCK WRANGELL
NATIVE: ALEUT AHTENA ESKIMO INGALIK KOYUKON TLINGIT
PENINSULA: KENAI SEWARD
PURCHASER: SEWARD
RIVER: CHENA KOBUK YUKON COPPER NOATAK TANANA KOYUKUK SUSITNA CHULITNA COLVILLE KUSKOKWIM PORCUPINE
STATE BIRD: PTARMIGAN
STATE FLOWER: FORGETMENOT
STATE TREE: SPRUCE
TOWN: EEK NOME RUBY KENAI SITKA UMIAT BARROW JUNEAU KODIAK NENANA SKAGWAY KOTZEBUE ANCHORAGE FAIRBANKS KETCHIKAN
VOLCANO: KUKAK SPURR GRIGGS KATMAI MAGEIK MARTIN PAVLOF DOUGLAS ILIAMNA REDOUBT TORBERT TRIDENT WRANGELL

ALASTRIM AMAAS
ALATE WINGY
ALB ALBE AUBE CAMISIA CHRISOM VESTMENT
ALBACORE TUNA TUNNY GERMAN GERMON LONGFIN ALALONGA ALALUNGA MACKEREL SCOMBRID

ALBANIA
ANCIENT PEOPLE: ILLYRIAN
CAPITAL: TIRANA TIRANE
COIN: LEK FRANC QINTAR QINTARKA
KING: ZOG
LAKE: ULZE OHRID PRESPA SCUTARI OHRIDSKO
MOUNTAIN: KORAB SHALA PINDUS KORITNIK

REGION: EPIRUS
RIVER: MAT DRIN OSUM SEMAN BOJANA ERZENI SEMENI VIJOSE SHKUMBI
TOWN: LIN FIER KLOS LESH BERAT CROIA DUKAT KORCE KRUJE PECIN PEQIN QUKES RUBIC SPASH VLONE VLORE AVLONA BERATI BITSAN DARDHE DURRES KORRCE PERMET PRESHE TIRANA VALONA ALESSIO DURAZZO KORITZA SCUTARI SHKODER
TRIBE: GEG CHAM GHEG TOSK

ALBANIAN GEG GHEG GUEG ARNAUT SKIPETAR
ALBATROSS GONY GOON GONEY GOONY NELLY FABRIC GOONEY GOONIE QUAKER SEABIRD ALCATRAS BLUEBIRD STINKPOT
ALBEIT ALL ALBE ALBEE ALLBE THOUGH HOWBEIT
ALBERIC (WIFE OF —) MAROZIA
ALBERTA (CAPITAL OF —) EDMONTON
  (LAKE OF —) BANFF JASPER WATERTON
  (RIVER OF —) BOW OLDMAN WAPITI ATHABASCA
  (TOWN OF —) CALGARY REDDEER LETHBRIDGE MEDICINEHAT
ALBIGENSIANS CATHARI
ALBINISM ALPHOSIS
ALBINO LEUCAETHIOP
ALBITE PERICLINE
ALBIZZIA SIRIS
ALBOIN (FATHER OF —) ALDUIN
  (SLAYER OF —) HELMICHIS
  (WIFE OF —) ROSAMUNDA
ALBUM ALBE BOOK RECORD VOLUME REGISTER
ALBUMEN WHITE
ALBUMIN ALBUMEN PHASELIN SYNTONIN
ALBUMINOID ELASTIN FIBROIN KERATIN PROTEIN SERICIN COLLAGEN GORGONIN
ALBURNUM SAP BLEA SPLINT SAPWOOD
ALBUS BLANCO
ALCAEUS (DAUGHTER OF —) ANAXO
  (FATHER OF —) PERSEUS ANDROGEUS
  (MOTHER OF —) ANDROMEDA
  (SON OF —) AMPHITRYON
ALCAIDE CADE CAID QAID JUDGE ALCADE
ALCATHOUS (FATHER OF —) PELOPS
  (MOTHER OF —) HIPPODAMIA
  (SLAYER OF —) OENOMAUS IDOMENEUS
  (WIFE OF —) EUACHME
ALCESTIS (AUTHOR OF —) EURIPIDES
  (CHARACTER IN —) APOLLO ADMETUS ALCESTIS HERCULES THANATOS
  (FATHER OF —) PELIAS
  (HUSBAND OF —) ADMETUS
ALCHEMIST ADEPT ARTIST CHEMIC CHEMICK CHEMIST HERMETIC

  (AUTHOR OF —) JONSON
  (CHARACTER IN —) DOL ABEL FACE SURLY COMMON DAPPER MAMMON PLIANT SUBTLE ANANIAS DRUGGER EPICURE KASTRIL LOVEWIT WHOLESOME TRIBULATION
ALCHEMY ART MAGIC ALCUMY CHYMIA SPAGYRIC
  (GOD OF —) HERMES
ALCHFRITH (FATHER OF —) OSWIU
  (MOTHER OF —) EANFLAED
  (WIFE OF —) CYNEBURH
ALCHORNEA DOVEWOOD
ALCIBIADES (FATHER OF —) CLINIAS
  (MOTHER OF —) DINOMACHE
ALCIMEDE (FATHER OF —) PHYLACUS
  (HUSBAND OF —) AESON
  (MOTHER OF —) CLYMENE
  (SON OF —) JASON
ALCIMEDES (BROTHER OF —) ARGUS MEDEUS PHERES MERMERUS TISANDER THESSALUS
  (FATHER OF —) JASON
  (MOTHER OF —) MEDEA
ALCINA (SISTER OF —) MORGANA LOGISTILLA
  (VICTIM OF —) RUGGIERO
ALCINOUS (DAUGHTER OF —) NAUSICAA
  (FATHER OF —) NAUSITHOUS
  (MOTHER OF —) PERIBOEA
  (WIFE OF —) ARETE
ALCIPPE (DAUGHTER OF —) MARPESSA
  (HUSBAND OF —) EVENUS METION
  (SON OF —) DAEDALUS
ALCIS (FATHER OF —) ANTIPOENUS
  (SISTER OF —) ANDROCLEA
ALCITHOE (FATHER OF —) MINYAS
  (SISTER OF —) ARSIPPE LEUCIPPE
ALCMAEON (FATHER OF —) AMPHIARAUS
  (MOTHER OF —) ERIPHYLE
  (WIFE OF —) CALLIRRHOE ALPHESIBOEA
ALCMENE (FATHER OF —) ELECTRYON
  (HUSBAND OF —) AMPHITRYON
  (SON OF —) HERCULES IPHICLES
ALCOHOL ALKY ETHAL ETHYL IDITE LEDOL NEROL VINYL AMYROL ANDROL CEDROL ELEMOL GLYCOL GUAIOL HYDROL IDITOL LUPEOL LUTEIN METHYL PHYTOL SPIRIT STERIN STERNO STEROL TALITE ACRITOL ADONITE ALDITOL ALKANOL ANISOIN BORNEOL BUTANOL CAROTOL DECANOL ETHANOL FENCHOL HEPTITE HEXITOL INOSITE MANNITE MENTHOL PHORBOL PULEGOL QUINITE SCOPINE SORBITE STETHAL STYRONE TAGETOL TALITOL TROPINE XYLITOL CATECHOL LINALOOL MANNITOL METHANOL GLYCERINE PYRIDOXINE
  (ETHYL —) METHS
  (NOT USING —) STRAIGHT
ALCOHOLATE SPIRIT ESSENCE

ALCOHOLIC ALKY
(HERBAL — DRINK) SNAPS
(NOT —) SOFT
ALCOHOLOMETER GENOMETER
VINOMETER
ALCOVE BAY NOOK BOWER NICHE
ORIEL STALL CARREL RECESS
CARRELL CUBICLE DINETTE
RETREAT SERVERY ALHACENA
SNUGGERY TABLINUM
ALCYONARIAN SEAPEN
ALCYONE (BROTHER OF —)
EURYSTHEUS
(FATHER OF —) ATLAS AEOLUS
(HUSBAND OF —) CEYX
(MOTHER OF —) ENARETE PLEIONE
(SON OF —) ANTHAS HYRIEUS
ALDABELLA (BROTHER OF —)
OLIVIERO BRANDIMARTE
(FATHER OF —) MONODANTES
(HUSBAND OF —) ORLANDO
ALDEHYDE ALDOL CITRAL ALKANAL
CHLORAL COGENER DECANAL
GLYOXAL HEXANAL RETINAL
RETINEL ACROLEIN CONGENER
FURFURAL PIPERONAL
PYRIDOXINE
ALDER AHN OLER ALNUS ELDER
OWLER SAGEROSE
(PREF.) ALNI
ALDERMAN BAILIE SENIOR
HEADMAN
ALDFRITH (BROTHER OF —)
ECGFRITH
(FATHER OF —) OSWIU
ALE MUM NOG BASS BEER BOCK
BREW FLIP MILD NOGG PURL
SCUD YELL AUDIT CLINK DARBY
JOUGH KVASS LAGER NAPPY
STOUT ALEGAR PORTER STINGO
SWANKY BITTERS MOROCCO
OCTOBER PHARAOH HUGMATEE
**(— BREWED WITH BRACKISH
WATER)** TIPPER
(— MIXED WITH SWEETENER)
BRAGGET
(INFERIOR —) SWANKY SWANKEY
(NEW —) SWATS
(SOUR —) ALEGAR
(SPICED —) SWIG
(STRONG —) MUM HUFF BURTON
STINGO HUFFCAP
(WEAK —) TWOPENNY
ALEATORY HAZARDOUS
ALEBION (BROTHER OF —) BERGION
DERCYNUS
(FATHER OF —) NEPTUNE
POSEIDON
(SLAYER OF —) HERCULES
ALECOST COSTMARY
ALECTRYON TITOKI
ALEE AHEAD LEEWARD
ALEHOUSE PUB TAVERN BARROOM
MUGHOUSE POTHOUSE
ALEKO (CHARACTER IN —) ALEKO
ARENSKY ZEMFIRA
(COMPOSER OF —) RACHMANINOFF
ALEMBIC LIMBEC LIMBECK
CUCURBIT
(PART OF —) HEAD LAMP CUCURBIT
RECEIVER
ALERT APT GAY HEP HIP YAL YEP
FOXY GLEG KEEN LIVE PERT SNAP

TRIG WAKE WARN WARY YALD
YEPE ACUTE AGILE ALARM ALIVE
AWAKE AWARE BREME BRISK
EAGER ERECT LEERY MERRY NIPPY
PEART PEERT QUICK READY SHACK
SHARP SIREN SLICK SWIFT TIGHT
WAKER YAULD ACTIVE ALARUM
ARRECT BRIGHT DAPPER LIVELY
NIMBLE PROMPT SLIPPY SPRACK
SUDDEN TIPTOE TOCSIN WACKER
CAREFUL KNOWING WAKEFUL
WORKING PREPARED THOUGHTY
VIGILANT WAKERIFE WATCHFUL
ALERTNESS NOUS SNAP ANTENNA
APTNESS APTITUDE
(MENTAL —) WIT
ALETES (FATHER OF —) HIPPOTES
AEGISTHUS
(MOTHER OF —) CLYTEMNESTRA
(SLAYER OF —) ORESTES
ALETTE WING ABUTMENT
ALEUT ATKA ORARIAN UNALASKA
**ALEUTIANS (ISLANDS AND ISLAND
GROUPS OF —)** FOX RAT ADAK
ATKA ATTU NEAR KISKA UMNAK
KODIAK
(TOWN OF —) UNALASKA
(VOLCANO ON —) SHISHALDIN
ALEWIFE BANG ALLICE ALOOFE
BUCKIE ALEWHAP HERRING
OLDWIFE POMPANO WALLEYE
GRAYBACK GREYBACK SAWBELLY
SKIPJACK
ALEXANDER ALEX PARIS SAWNY
ELLICK SAWNEY SAWNIE
ISKANDER
(BIRTHPLACE OF —) PELLA
(FATHER OF —) SIMON
(HORSE OF —) BUCEPHALUS
ALEXIARES (FATHER OF —)
HERCULES
(MOTHER OF —) HEBE
ALFA HALFA ESPARTO
ALFALFA HAY MEDIC FODDER
LEGUME LUCERN LUCERNE
ALFILARIA ERODIUM FILAREE
FILARIA PINWEED PINGRASS
ALFORJA BAG POUCH WALLET
ALFARGA ALFORGE
ALGA NORI ALGAL BROWN FUCUS
JELLY SLAKE SLOAK SLOKE
DESMID DIATOM FUNORI NOSTOC
AMANORI GULAMAN HAITSAI
OARWEED SEAWEED ANABAENA
FERNLEAF GELIDIUM HAIRWEED
ROCKWEED SEABEARD SILKWEED
SPOROGEN WHIPCORD ZOOGLOEA
ALGAE
(PREF.) PHYC(O)
(SUFF.) PHYCEAE
ALGARROBA CAROB CALDEN
ALGEBRA LOGISTIC
(KIND OF —) LIE LINEAR BOOLEAN
ALGEBRAIC COSSIC
ALGENIB MIRFAK

ALGERIA
BERBER: KABYLE SHAWIA TUAREG
BERBER DIALECT: ZENATA SENHAJA
CAPITAL: ALGIERS
CAVALRYMAN: SPAHI SPAHEE
DEPARTMENT: ORAN ALGER
ALGIERS CONSTANTINE

GRASS: ESPARTO
HILL: TELL
HOLY MAN: MARABOUT
MEASURE: PIK REBIS TARRI TERMIN
MONASTERY: RIBAT
MOUNTAIN: AISSA ATLAS AURES
DAHRA TAHAT CHELIA AHAGGAR
MOUYDIR DJURJURA
NAME: ALGERIE NUMIDIA
NATIVE: BERBER KABYLE
PIRATE: CORSAIR
RIVER: SHELIF CHELIFF MEDJERDA
RULER: BEY DEY BEVLERBEY
SECT: SUNNITE
SETTLER: COLON PIEDNOIR
SHIP: XEBEC
TERRITORY: AINSEFRA GHARDALA
TOUGGOURT
TOWN: BONE ORAN AFLOU ARZEW
BATNA BLIDA MEDEA SAIDA
SETIF TENES ABADLA ANNABA
AUMALE BARIKA BECHAR BEJAIA
BENOUD BISKRA BOUGIE DELLYS
DJANET DJELFA DZIOUA FRENDA
GUELMA SKIKDA BOGHARI
MASCARA MILIANA NEGRINE
NEMOURS OUARGLA TEBESSA
TLEMCEN
WEIGHT: ROTL

ALGERINE COOLOOLY KOOLOOLY
ALGID COLD COOL CHILLY CLAMMY
ALGOLOGY VERATRIN PHYCOLOGY
ALGONKIAN CREE EOZOIC
(— ROCKS) UNKAR
ALIAS AKA ELSE OTHER ANONYM
AYLESS ASSUMED EPITHET
PSEUDONYM
(UNDER AN —) INCOGNITO
ALIBI PLEA EXCUSE APOLOGY
PRETEXT
ALIDADE INDEX DIOPTER
ALIEN ET GER DEED FREMD METIC
ALAUNT ALLTUD AUBAIN CONVEY
EXOTIC INMATE REMOTE ADVERSE
DENIZEN FOREIGN FRAMMIT
INVADER OUTLAND STRANGE
DETAINEE STRANGER TRANSFER
ALIENATE PART WEAN ALIEN AVERT
ANNALY CONVEY DEMISE DEVEST
FREEZE FORFEIT SUBVERT
AMORTIZE DISUNITE ESTRANGE
MORTMAIN SEPARATE STRANGER
TRANSFER WITHDRAW
ALIENATION GIFT DISTASTE
DISUNION DISUNITY DIVISION
DONATION INSANITY
ALIENIST PSYCHOPATH
PSYCHIATRIST
ALIGHT DROP LAND LEND REST
STOP AVALE LATCH LIGHT LODGE
PERCH ROOST STOOP SWOOP
ARRIVE SETTLE BURNING
DESCEND
ALIGN LINE TRAM TRUE ALINE
ARRAY DRESS RANGE ADJUST
ARRANGE MARSHAL
(— PAPER) JOG
ALIGNED FAIR COLORED
COLLINEAR
ALIGNMENT KELTER KILTER
GROUPING ORIENTATION
ALII ARIKI

ALIKE AKIN BOTH LIKE SAME EQUAL
INLIKE SQUARE YLICHE EQUALLY
SIMILAR UNIFORM
(PREF.) HOM(O) ISO
ALIMENT PAP FOOD FUEL BROMA
MANNA VIANDS ALIMONY
PABULUM RATIONS
ALIMONY ALIMENT
ALINDA (FATHER OF —) ALPHONSO
ALIPHATIC FATTY ACYCLIC
ALIVE VIF BUSY KEEN SPRY VIVE
AGILE ALERT ALIFE ASTIR AWARE
BEING BRISK FRESH GREEN QUICK
VITAL AROUND EXTANT LIVING
SLIPPY ANIMATE VIBRANT
ANIMATED EXISTENT SENSIBLE
SWARMING
(PREF.) VIVI
ALKALI LYE REH BASE BRAK KALI
SALT SODA USAR BRACK CAUSTIC
(PREF.) KALI
ALKALINITY (REDUCED —) ACIDOSIS
ALKALOID BASE ERGOT ESERE
ARICIN BRUCIN CEVINE CODEIN
CONINE CURINE ESERIN QUINIA
QUININ ACONINE ARABINE ARICINE
ATROPIA BOGAINE BOLDINE
BRUCINE CAFFEIN COCAINE
CODEINE CONIINE EMETINE
HARMINE HYGRINE JERVINE
KAIRINE NARCEIN NEOPINE
OUABAIN PTOMAIN QUININE
SCOPINE SINAPIN SOLANIN
SOPHORA VIOLINE CURARINE
CYTISINE PIPERINE MESCALINE
QUINIDINE YOHIMBINE
PAPAVERINE PILOCARPINE
VINBLASTINE VINCRISTINE
CAMPTOTHECIN
ALKANE BUTANE PARAFFIN
ALKANET BUGLOSS PUCCOON
REDROOT
ALKANNIN ORCANET ANCHUSIN
ORCHANET
ALKENE OLEFIN
ALKYD GLYPTAL
ALL A AL ANY SUM EACH FULL TOTE
AUGHT EVERY GROSS OMNES
OUGHT QUITE TOTAL TOTUM
TUTTA TUTTO WHOLE ENTIRE
SOLELY WHOLLY PLENARY
ENTIRELY EVERYONE TOTALITY
(— BUT ABSOLUTELY) ALMOST
(— IN) ALTOGETHER
(— TOGETHER) COLLECTEDLY
(AND —) ANA
(AT —) AVA ANYWISE ANYTHING
ANYWHERE
(OF —) AVA
(PREF.) CUNCTI OMN(I) PAM PAN
PANT(A)(O) PASI
ALLANITE CERINE CERITE ORTHITE
ALLAY AID LAY CALM CITE COOL
EASE HELP HUSH STAY ABATE
AGATE ALLOY CHARM CHECK
DELAY QUELL QUIET SALVE SLAKE
STILL ADDUCE LESSEN PACIFY
QUENCH REDUCE SOFTEN SOLACE
SOOTHE STANCH SUBDUE TEMPER
APPEASE ASSUAGE COMFORT
COMPOSE LIGHTEN MOLLIFY
RELIEVE REPRESS STAUNCH
MITIGATE PALLIATE

ALLAYED DEFERRED
ALL-CREATING OMNIFIC
ALLEGATION PLEA COUNT VOUCH
CHARGE ESSOIN AVERRAL FICTION
PROFERT SCANDAL SURMISE
AVERMENT SCIENTER PRETENSION
ALLEGE LAY SAY AVER AVOW CITE
SHOW URGE ALLAY CLAIM FEIGN
INFER LEDGE OFFER PLEAD QUOTE
STATE SWEAR TRUMP VOUCH
ADDUCE AFFIRM ASSERT ASSIGN
CHARGE DEPOSE ESSOIN OBTEND
RECITE ADVANCE ASCRIBE
DECLARE LIGHTEN PRESENT
PROFESS PROPOSE MAINTAIN
ALLEGED SUPPOSED SURMISED
ALLEGIANCE FOY TIE DUTY FAITH
HONOR FEALTY HOMAGE LYANCE
LOYALTY SERVAGE SERVICE
TRIBUTE CIVILITY DEVOTION
FIDELITY LIGEANCE
ALLEGORICAL PARABOLIC
SYMBOLICAL
ALLEGORICALLY SECRETLY
ALLEGORIZE TALMUDIZE
ALLEGORY MYTH TALE FABLE
STORY EMBLEM PARABLE
APOLOGUE METAPHOR
ALLELE GENE
ALLELOMORPH GENE
ALLELUIA AEVIA LAUDS
ALL-EMBRACING INFINITE
SWEEPING
ALLERGEN INHALANT GOLDENROD
ALLERGY ATOPY IDIOBLAPSIS
ALLEVIATE AID BALM CALM CURE
EASE HELP ABATE ALLAY QUIET
ALIGHT ALLEGE LENIFY LESSEN
PACIFY SOFTEN SOLACE SOOTHE
SUCCOR SUPPLE TEMPER
ASSUAGE COMPOSE CONSOLE
CORRECT LENIATE LIGHTEN
MOLLIFY RELEASE RELIEVE
DIMINISH MITIGATE MODERATE
PALLIATE
ALLEVIATION ALAY SOLACE
ALLEY MIG ROW WAY CHAR LANE
LEAD MALL MEWS PASS PATH
VENT WALK WENT WIND WYND
AISLE ALLEE BLIND BYWAY CHARE
ENTRY TEWER WEENT ALLEGE
PEEWEE SMOOTH TRANCE VENNEL
PASSAGE
(BLIND —) LOKE STOP CLOSE
POCKET RUELLE IMPASSE
ALL FOR LOVE (AUTHOR OF —)
DRYDEN
(CHARACTER IN —) ANTONY
OCTAVIA OCTAVIUS CLEOPATRA
DOLABELLA VENTIDIUS
ALLHALLOWTIDE HOLLANTIDE
ALLHEAL PANACEA VALERIAN
WOUNDWORT
ALL-HOLY PANAGIA PANHAGIA
ALLIANCE AXIS PACT UNION
ACCORD FUSION LEAGUE LYANCE
TREATY COMPACT ENTENTE
SOCIETY AFFINITY AGNATION
CACTALES COVENANT DREIBUND
FEDERACY FUNGALES LILIALES
TRIPLICE CONSOCIATION
(— IN WAR) SYMMACHY
ALLICE SHAD ALEWIFE POMPANO

ALLIED SIB AKIN AGNATE COUSIN
JOINED LINKED UNITED COGNATE
CONNATE FEDERAL GERMANE
KINDRED RELATED SIMILAR
RELATIVE
ALLIGATOR GATOR NIGER CAIMAN
CAYMAN CROTCH JACARE LIZARD
TRAVOY YACARE CRAWLER
CREEPER LAGARTO TRAVOIS
ALAGARTO LORICATE
(— PEAR) ZABOCA AVOCADO
AGUACATE
(— TURTLE) LOGGERHEAD
(MALE —) BULL
ALLIGATORING WEBBING
ALLIGATOR PEAR AVOCADO
ALL-INCLUSIVE WIDE GLOBAL
ALLITERATION RHYME LETTER
ALLITERATIVE LITERAL
ALLIUM LILY ONION GARLIC
ALLNESS OMNEITY OMNITUDE
ALLOCATE DEAL DOLE METE RATE
ALLOT AWARD SHARE AFFECT
ASSIGN DEVOTE OUTPLACE
ALLOCATION DRAW DESIGNATION
ALLODIAL UDAL
ALLODIUM ESTATE
ALLONGE RIDER
ALLOT FIX SET ARET BILL CAST
DEAL DOLE GIVE MARK METE PART
RATE SORT ALLOW ARETT AWARD
CAVEL GRANT SHARE ACCORD
AFFECT ASSIGN BESTOW DEPUTE
DESIGN DIRECT INTEND ORDAIN
RATION ACCOUNT APPOINT
DESTINE PRORATE QUARTER
SPECIFY TRIBUTE ALLOCATE
PROPORTION
(— QUARTERS) CANTON
ALLOTHEIST PAGAN
ALLOTMENT CUT LOT DOLE CAVEL
SHARE RATION SIZING LOTMENT
LOTTERY PORTION DIVISION
PITTANCE
ALL-OUT DEAD
ALLOW LET LOW BEAR GIVE HAVE
LEND LOAN ADMIT DEFER GRANT
LEAVE STAND THOLE YIELD
ACCEPT ACCORD ASSIGN BESTOW
BETEEM ENABLE ENDURE PERMIT
SUFFER APPROVE CONCEDE
CONFESS LICENCE LICENSE
SUFFICE SUPPOSE SUSTAIN
CONSIDER DISPENSE SANCTION
TOLERATE
(— UNWILLINGLY) GRUDGE
ALLOWABLE FREE LICIT LAWFUL
PERMISSIBLE
ALLOWANCE BOT FEE ICE AGIO
BOTE DOLE EASE EDGE GIFT HIRE
ODDS RATE SALT SIZE ARRAS
BATTA CLOFF GRANT LEAVE RATIO
SHARE STENT STINT BOUCHE
BOUNTY CORODY FODDER
MARGIN RATING REGAIN SALARY
SEQUEL TANTUM ALIMENT
ALIMONY CORRODY DIETARY
DIOBELY LEAKAGE LOWANCE
PENSION PORTION PREBEND
SCALAGE STIPEND TEARAGE
APPENAGE APPROVAL BREAKAGE
DISCOUNT DRAFTAGE ORDINARY

QUANTITY SANCTION SOLATIUM
VIATICUM
(— FOR EXPENSES) DIET
(— FOR MAINTENANCE) ALIMENT
(— FOR THICKNESS) BOXING
(— FOR WASTE) TARE TRET
(— FOR WEIGHT) BUG TARE DRAFT
DRAUGHT
(— OF ARROWS) SHEAF
(— OF FOOD) DIET BOUCHE
DIETARY
(— OF TIME OR DISTANCE) LAW
(— TO WORKER'S) MAGS MAGGS
(CLOTHING —) INLAY
(CORRECTIVE —) SALT
(EXTRA —) BUCKSHEE
(NEGATIVE —) INTERFERENCE
(SERVANT'S —) LIVERY
ALLOWED VENIAL LICENTIATE
(NOT —) ILLICIT FORBIDDEN
ALLOWING THOUGH
ALLOY LAY LOY MIX AICH ASEM
ALPAX BIDRI BIDRY BRASS CALIN
DURAL FLINT INVAR MOKUM
MONEL TERNE ALBATA ALNICO
ALUMEL BIDREE BILLON BRONZE
CERMET GARBLE ILLIUM LATTEN
LEAVEN NEOGEN NIELLO OCCAMY
OREIDE OROIDE PEWTER SOLDER
TAMBAC TOMBAC TOMBAK
ACIERAL ALCHEMY AMALGAM
BABBITT BIDDERY ELINVAR
INCONEL MIXTURE NITINOL
PAKTONG PERLITE RHEOTAN
RHODITE SEMILOR SIMILOR
TAENITE TUTANIA TUTENAG
ALFENIDE ARGENTON ARSEDINE
AWARUITE CALAMINE CARACOLI
CARACOLY DORALIUM ELECTRUM
EUTECTIC GUNMETAL HARDENER
KAMACITE METALINE NICHROME
ORICHALC ROMANIUM STELLITE
ZIRCALOY PINCHBECK PORPORINO
ALL-PERVADING UNIVERSAL
ALL-PURPOSE VERSATILE
ALL QUIET ON WESTERN FRONT
(AUTHOR OF —) REMARQUE
(CHARACTER IN —) PAUL KROPP
ALBERT BAUMER MULLER TJADENS
KEMMERICH STANILAUS
KATCYINSKY
ALL RIGHT OK YES OKAY AGREED
OKEYDOKE
ALL-ROUND OVERALL OVERHEAD
ALLSEED FLAXSEED BURSTWORT
ALL SOULS' DAY SOULMASS
ALLSPICE BUBBY PIMENTO
ALL'S WELL THAT ENDS WELL
(AUTHOR OF —) SHAKESPEARE
(CHARACTER IN —) DIANA LAFEU
HELENA BERTRAM LAVACHE
MARIANA PAROLLES VIOLENTA
ALLTHORN JUNCO
ALLUDE HINT IMPLY POINT REFER
ADVERT GLANCE RELATE
CONNOTE MENTION SUGGEST
INDICATE INTIMATE
ALLURE IT AIR COY WIN WOO BAIT
DRAW LEAD LURE MOVE SWAY
WILE ANGLE BRIBE CHARM COURT
DECOY SNARE TEMPT ALLECT
ENTICE ENTRAP ILLURE INDUCE
INVITE SEDUCE ATTRACT BEGUILE

ENSNARE BLANDISH INESCATE
INVEIGLE PERSUADE SIRENING
ALLUREMENT BAIT CORD LURE
SNARE ALLURE GLAMOR
GUDGEON AGACERIE
SOLICITATION
ALLURING GREEN TAKING
AGACANT SIRENIC SUGARED
TAKEFUL CATCHING CHARMING
ENTICING FETCHING TEMPTING
ALLUSION HINT TWIT TOUCH
GLANCE REFLEX INKLING MENTION
INNUENDO INSTANCE REFERENCE
ALLUSIVE CANTING
ALLUVIUM WASH
ALLY PAL AIDE JOIN RANGE UNION
UNITE BACKER COHORT COXCOX
FRIEND HELPER LEAGUE ALLIANT
CONNECT PARTNER ADHERENT
CONFEDER FEDERATE
(PL.) FOEDERATI
ALMANAC ORDO PADDY
CALENDAR
ALMANDINE GARNET CARBUNCLE
ALMEMAR BEMA BIMA BIMAH
ALMIGHTY GOD GREAT MAKER
CREATOR EXTREME JEHOVAH
INFINITE POWERFUL PUISSANT
OMNIPOTENT
ALMOND DOE PILI BADAM CHUFA
JORDAN KAMANI KANARI
AMYGDAL BISCUIT TALISAY
ALMANDER ALMENDRO
AMYGDALA ROSACEAN VALENCIA
(— BROWN) WOOD
(— SHAPED OBJECT) MANDORLA
(PREF.) AMYGDAL(O) MANDEL(O)
ALMONRY AMBRY
ALMOST JUST LIKE MOST MUCH
NEAR NIGH ABOUT ANEAR CLOSE
AMAIST FECKLY MOSTLY NEARLY
NIGHLY MUCHWHAT WELLMOST
WELLNEAR WELLNIGH
PRACTICALLY
(PREF.) PARA PEN(E)
ALMS DOLE GIFT ALMOIN AUMOUS
AWMOUS BOUNTY CORBAN
MAUNDY RELIEF ALMOIGN
CHARITY HANDOUT PASSAGE
DEVOTION DONATION GRATUITY
OFFERING PITTANCE BENEFACTION
(GIVER OF —) ALMONER
ALMSHOUSE POORHOUSE
WORKHOUSE
ALMSMAN BLUECOAT
ALMUCE HOOD AMICE VAGAS
TIPPET VAKASS VARKAS
ALODIUM ODAL ODEL ODHAL
ESTATE PROPERTY
ALOE PITA AGAVE
(— EXTRACT) ORCIN ORCINAL
ALOEUS (FATHER OF —) NEPTUNE
POSEIDON
(MOTHER OF —) CANACE
(SON OF —) OTUS EPHIALTES
(WIFE OF —) IPHIMEDIA
ALOFT UP HIGH ABOVE AHIGH
UPWARD AHEIGHT SKYWARD
OVERHEAD
(PREF.) HYPS(I)(O)
ALONE ALL ONE BARE LANE LORN
ONLY SOLE SOLO ALOOF APART

SOLUS SIMPLY SINGLE SOLEIN SOLELY SULLEN UNIQUE ALONELY FORLORN UNAIDED DESOLATE DETACHED ISOLATED SEPARATE SOLITARY
(ALL —) LEELANE LEELONE
(PREF.) MANI MON(O) SOLI
(SUFF.) MONAS

ALONG ON UP VIA AWAY LANG WITH YOND AHEAD LONGS BESIDE FORBYE FOREBY ONWARD ALONGST ENDLONG FORWARD PARALLEL TOGETHER
(— THE MARGIN) DOWN
(— WITH) AND
(WELL —) ENDWAYS ENDWISE
(PREF.) (— WITH) SYM

ALONGSIDE AT BY ASIDE CLOSE ABOARD BESIDE ABREAST FORNENT SIDLINS FORNENST PARALLEL
(PREF.) PAR(A)

ALONSOA MASKFLOWER

ALOOF DRY ICY SHY COLD COOL ABACK ALONE APART PROUD ABEIGH FROSTY OTIOSE REMOTE SILENT SKEIGH DISTANT REMOVED STUCKUP RESERVED

ALOPECIA PELADE ATRICHIA BALDNESS

ALOPECIC BALD

ALOPECURUS FOXTAIL

ALOT SLEW

ALOUD OUT

ALPACA PACO

ALPENGLOW AFTERGLOW

ALPENSTOCK STOCK BERGSTOCK

ALPHABET ABC ABCEE ABSEY CUFIC KUFIC LATIN ONMUN ORDER BISAYA BRAHMI CIPHER GLAGOL HANGUL HANKUL KAITHI NAGARI PRIMER ROMAJI SARADA SCRIPT TAGALA VISAYA ALJAMIA FUTHARK KALEKAH LETTERS PESHITO ALJAMIAH CROSSROW GUJARATI GURMUKHI
(— SQUARE) TABLEAU
(ARABIC —) BA FA HA RA TA YA ZA AYN DAD DAL JIM KAF KHA LAM MIM NUN QAF SAD SIN THA WAW ZAY ALIF DHAL SHIN GHAYN
(CELTIC —) OGAM OGHAM
(GREEK —) MU NU PI XI CHI ETA PHI PSI RHO TAU BETA IOTA ZETA ALPHA DELTA GAMMA KAPPA OMEGA SIGMA THETA LAMBDA EPSILON OMICRON UPSILON
(HEBREW —) HE PE MEM NUN SIN TAW VAV WAW AYIN BETH HETH KAPH QOPH RESH SHIN TETH YODH ALEPH GIMEL SADHE ZAYIN DALETH LAMEDH SAMEKH
(OLD IRISH —) OGAM OGHAM

ALPHAEUS (SON OF —) JAMES MATTHEW

ALPHESIBOEA (FATHER OF —) BIAS PHEGEUS
(HUSBAND OF —) ALCMAEON
(SON OF —) ADONIS

ALPS (LAKE IN —) ZUG COMO ISEO THUN GARDA BRIENZ GENEVA ZURICH LUCERNE MAGGIORE CONSTANCE

(PASS IN —) SPLUGA ARLBERG BRENNER SIMPLON SPLUGEN SEMPIONE
(PEAK IN —) ROSA VISO BLANC LEONE TRIGLAV VOLJNAC EISENHUT PARADISO HOCHSTUHL MARMOLADA MONTBLANC KELLERWAND SACCARELLO
(VALLEY IN —) ZERMATT CHAMONIX ENGADINE INTERLAKEN GRINDELWALD LAUTERBRUNNEN

ALREADY EEN NOW DONE EVEN SINCE BEFORE

ALSACE-LORRAINE REICHSLAND

ALSINE ALLBONE

ALSO SO ALS AND EKE TOO YET ERST ITEM MORE PLUS ALONG DITTO BESIDES FURTHER THERETO LIKEWISE MOREOVER
(— KNOWN AS) AKA

ALSO-RAN SLOWPOKE BACKMARKER

ALTAMONT (WIFE OF —) CALISTA

ALTAR ARA BEMA BOMOS TABLE WEVED ACERRA AUTERE HAIKAL SHRINE TRIPOD VEDIKA CHANCEL CHANTRY ESCHARA SCROBIS THYMELE OMPHALOS REPOSOIR REPOSITORY
(— BACK) TABLE
(— TOP) MENSA

ALTARPIECE ANCONA DIPTYCH TRIPTYCH

ALTAZIMUTH ABA

ALTER COOK DRAW EDIT GELD MOVE RASE TURN VARY VEER WEND ADAPT AMEND BREAK ELIDE EMEND FORGE RESET SHAPE SHIFT ADJUST BUSHEL CENSOR CHANGE DEFORM IMMUTE JIGGER MODIFY MUTATE NEUTER REVISE TEMPER UNSAME CHAFFER COMMUTE CONVERT CORRECT CORRUPT DISTORT FASHION QUALIFY RECYCLE STRANGE ACTIVATE EXCHANGE REJIGGER
(— APPEARANCE) WRY
(— BOUNDARIES) DEACON
(— BRANDS) DUFF
(— DIRECTION) BREAK
(— FRAUDULENTLY) FIDDLE
(— STANCE) CLOSE

ALTERATION DOWN CROSS ACTION CHANGE JANGLE DISEASE HEMIOLA MUTATION UPHEAVAL
(— OF BOUNDARY) ERUB ERUV

ALTERATIVE LAPPA FUMARIA

ALTERCATE JANGLE STICKLE WRANGLE

ALTERCATION SPAT TIFF TILT BRAWL BROIL CRASH CROSS FIGHT BARNEY BICKER FRACAS JANGLE STRIFE BRABBLE CONTEST DISPUTE PASSAGE QUARREL WRANGLE SQUABBLE

ALTERED BURNT BROKEN VARIED ANOTHER FEIGNED ADJUSTED
(— BY AGE) STALE
(PREF.) EPH EPI META

ALTERNATE ELSE SWAY VARY OTHER RECUR SHIFT ALTERN

CHANGE RINGER ROTATE SECOND SEESAW SPIRAL EXCHANGE INTERMIT TRAVERSE
(— LEAPS AND DIVES) GREYHOUND
(— PLAYERS) PLATOON
(PREF.) CO COUNTER

ALTERNATELY ABOUT RECIPROCALLY

ALTERNATION ADDITION
(— OF GENERATIONS) METAGENESIS

ALTERNATIVE OR FORK HORN BACKUP CHOICE EITHER OPTION DISJUNCT ELECTION
(PREF.) ALLELO

ALTERNATIVES (SEE PARTNERS) DODIE INOUT ONOFF HITMISS WINLOSE FISHFOWL HIDEHAIR ONEOTHER SINKSWIM WHITERYE FACTFANCY HERETHERE WHEREWHEN ALLNOTHING TRICKTREAT

ALTERNATOR MAGNETO

ALTHAEA MALLOW
(FATHER OF —) THESTIUS
(HUSBAND OF —) OENEUS
(SON OF —) MELEAGER

ALTHAEMENES (FATHER OF —) CATREUS
(SISTER OF —) AEROPE CLYMENE APEMOSYNE

ALTHORN SAX ALTO ALTUS SAXHORN

ALTHOUGH ALL EEN SET ALBE ALIF EVEN THAT WHEN WHILE ALBEIT THOUGH WHENAS DESPITE HOWBEIT WHEREAS

ALTITUDE APEX PEAK HIGHT LEVEL PITCH HEIGHT STATURE
(SUN'S GREATEST —) APOGEE

ALTO MEAN ALTUS ALTHORN SAXHORN

ALTOGETHER ALL NUDE QUITE SHEER STICK AGREAT ALGATE BODILY FREELY WHOLLY EXACTLY TOTALLY UTTERLY ALLTHING ENTIRELY

ALTRUISM OTHERISM

ALTRUISTIC HEROIC HEROICAL

ALUDEL POT LUDEL UDELL

ALULA LOBE WING ALULET SQUAMA TEGULA LOBULUS WINGLET CALYPTER

ALULIM ALOROS

ALUM AUM ALME GRAD ALUMEN MIGITE TSCHER STYPTIC HARDENER KALINITE
(FEATHER —) ALUNOGEN

ALUMINA ARGIL ALOXITE

ALUMNUS GRAD PUPIL GRADUATE

ALUMROOT HEUCHERA

ALUR LUR LURI

ALVAN (FATHER OF —) SHOBAL

ALVEARY HIVE BEEHIVE

ALVELOZ SAP

ALVEOLA FAVEOLUS

ALVEOLAR SPUMOID GINGIVAL

ALVEOLATE FAVOSE FAVOUS PITTED

ALWAYS O AY AYE EEN EER EVER SIMLE STILL ALWISE SEMPRE ALGATES FOREVER EVERMORE

ALYSSUM ALISON MADWORT

ALZIRA (CHARACTER IN —) ALZIRA GUSMAN ZAMORO
(COMPOSER OF —) VERDI

AM M AME HAM
(— NOT) NAM AINT AMNT
(I —) CHAM CHYM

AMA CUP AMULA CRUET DIVER VESSEL CHALICE

AMABILE GENTLE TENDER

AMACRATIC AMASTHENIC

AMADAVAT WAXBILL TIGERBIRD

AMADIS (COMPOSER OF —) LULLY

AMADOU PUNK TINDER

AMAH NURSE SERVANT

AMAHL AND THE NIGHT VISITORS (COMPOSER OF —) MENOTTI

AMAIN GREATLY FORCIBLY

AMAL (FATHER OF —) HELEM

AMALA AMLAH

AMALASONTHA (FATHER OF —) THEODORIC

AMALEK (FATHER OF —) ELIPHAZ
(MOTHER OF —) TIMNAH

AMALGAM ALLOY MAGNESIA ARQUERITE

AMALGAMATE MIX FUSE JOIN ALLOY BLEND MARRY MERGE UNITE BLUNGE MINGLE COMBINE COALESCE COMPOUND

AMALGAMATION MERGER ADDITION

AMALGAMATOR PLATEMAN

AMANORI NORI LAVER

AMANUENSIS PENMAN SCRIBE TYPIST RECORDER

AMARANTA (HUSBAND OF —) BARTOLUS

AMARANTH JATACO PIGWEED FLORAMOR
(PL.) LIGHTHOUSES

AMARETTO LIQUEUR MACAROON

AMARIAH (FATHER OF —) BANI MERAIOTH
(SON OF —) AHITUB

AMARILLO FUSTIC

AMARYLLIS LILY AGAVE CRINUM SNOWFLAKE

AMASA (FATHER OF —) ITHRA HADLAI JETHER
(MOTHER OF —) ABIGAIL

AMASAI (SON OF —) MAHATH

AMASHAI (FATHER OF —) AZAREEL

AMASIAH (FATHER OF —) ZICHRI

AMASS HEAP HILL MASS PILE SAVE GROSS HOARD STACK STORE GATHER COLLECT COMPILE CONGEST ENGROSS ASSEMBLE OVERHEAP ACCUMULATE

AMASSMENT HEAP

AMATA (DAUGHTER OF —) LAVINIA
(HUSBAND OF —) LATINUS

AMATEUR HAM LAY TIRO TYRO NOVICE SUNDAY VOTARY ADMIRER DABBLER DEVOTEE FANCIER JACKLEG PATRIOT VARMENT VARMINT BEGINNER
(GOLF —) DUFFER

AMATEURISH BUSH TYRONIC

AMATORY EROTIC LOVING TENDER AMOROUS GALLANT ANACREONTIC

AMAZE AWE WOW MAZE STAM STUN ALARM FERLY FLOOR ASTONY AWHAPE WONDER ASTOUND CONFUSE IMPRESS PERPLEX STAGGER STUPEFY ASTONISH BEWILDER CONFOUND DUMFOUND FRIGHTEN SURPRISE

AMAZED AGAPE INAWE AGAZED BUSHED ASTONIED

AMAZEMENT STAM AMAZE FERLY GHAST FERLIE FRENZY WONDER MADNESS SURPRISE CONSTERNATION **(INTERJECTION TO EXPRESS —)** YIKES

AMAZIAH (FATHER OF —) JOASH

AMAZON VIRAGO

AMBARI KANAF KENAF KANAFF

AMBASSADOR AGENT ELCHI ENVOY VAKIL DEPUTY ELCHEE LEDGER LEGATE NUNCIO VAKEEL EMBASSY LEAGUER CAPUCIUS DIPLOMAT MINISTER

AMBASSADORIAL FECIAL FETIAL

AMBASSADORS (AUTHOR OF —) JAMES **(CHARACTER IN —)** JIM MAMIE MARIA SARAH JEANNE POCOCK GOSTREY LAMBERT NEWSOME CHADWICK STRETHER WAYMARSH

AMBER GRIS LIME AWMER RESIN FUSTIC LAMMER SUCCIN YELLOW BURMITE AMBEROID ELECTRUM SUNSTONE **(PREF.)** ELECTRO SUCCIN(I)(O)

AMBERFISH JUREL CARANX KAHALA RUNNER CARANGID CARANGIN KINGFISH MACKEREL MEDREGAL

AMBERGRIS AMBER AMBRACAN

AMBERINA (KIND OF —) PLATED

AMBERJACK ALMICORE CORONADO

AMBIENCE MILIEU AMBIANCE

AMBIGUITY AMBAGE PARADOX

AMBIGUOUS DARK VAGUE DOUBLE FORKED LOUCHE CRYPTIC DUBIOUS DOUBTFUL SLIPPERY SPURIOUS **(NOT —)** EXPRESS

AMBIT LIMIT SCOPE SPACE BOUNDS EXTENT SPHERE CIRCUIT COMPASS BOUNDARY PRECINCT

AMBITION ATE GOAL HOPE WISH GLORY DESIRE PURPOSE PRETENSION

AMBITIONLESS DRIFTING

AMBITIOUS AVID BOLD HIGH KEEN EAGER ETTLE SHOWY EMULOUS ASPIRANT ASPIRING

AMBITUS TENOR

AMBIVALENCE BIPOLARITY

AMBIVALENT EQUIVOCAL

AMBLE FOOL GAIT MOOCH PADNAG MEANDER SAUNTER TRIPPLE

AMBLING TOLUTATION

AMBLYOPIA SNOWBLINDNESS

AMBO DESK PULPIT

AMBOCEPTOR COPULA MEDIATOR

AMBOYNA LINGOA KIABOOCA

AMBROSIA AMRITA AMBROSE HONEYDEW KINGWEED

AMBROSIAL DIVINE FRAGRANT

AMBRY SAFE CHEST NICHE AUMRIE CLOSET PANTRY RECESS ALMONRY ARMOIRE ARMARIUM CUPBOARD

AMBULANCE PANNIER AUXILIUM BRANCARD **(— ATTENDANT)** EMT

AMBULATE GAD HIKE MOVE WALK

AMBULATORY ALURE GALLERY PORTICO CLOISTER PERAMBLE

AMBUSCADE WATCH WAYLAY BUSHMENT

AMBUSH NAB LURE LURK TRAP WAIT AWAIT BLIND BUSSE CATCH COVER LURCH SHOMA SNARE STALE TRAIN WATCH INBUSH THREAT WAYLAY FORELAY SCUPPER DISGUISE ENBUSSHE AMBUSCADE **(SUFF.) (ONE IN —)** DOLOPS

AMCHOOR AMHAR

AMELIA (AUTHOR OF —) FIELDING **(CHARACTER IN —)** BOOTH JAMES TRENT AMELIA HARRIS ATKINSON HARRISON MATTHEWS ELIZABETH

AMELIORATE EASE HELP MEND AMEND EMEND BETTER REFORM IMPROVE PROMOTE

AMEN YEA TRULY ASSENT SOBEIT VERILY APPROVAL SANCTION

AMENABLE GAME OPEN LIABLE PLIANT SUBJECT OBEDIENT MALLEABLE

AMEND END BEET HEAL MEND ALTER ATONE BEETE EMEND REDUB BETTER CHANGE DOCTOR REFORM REMEDY REPAIR REPEAL REVISE CONVERT CORRECT ENLARGE IMPROVE RECOVER RECTIFY REDRESS RESTORE CHASTISE

AMENDING COMPENSATION

AMENDMENT RIDER AMENDS REFORM SLEEPER

AMENDS BOOT MEND ASSETH ASSYTH REWARD APOLOGY REDRESS

AMENITY JOY COMITY FEATURE SUAVITY CIVILITY COURTESY MILDNESS **(PL.)** AGREMENS FROUFROU NICETIES

AMENT JUL CHAT IDIOT IULUS MORON CATKIN CACHRYS CATTAIL GOSLING IMBECILE NUCAMENT

AMERCE FINE MERCE MULCT TREAT AFFEER PUNISH SCONCE CONDEMN FORFEIT

AMERCEMENT MULCT UNLAW BLOODWIT

AMERICA INDIA

AMERICAN YANK GRINGO YANKEE YANQUI AMERICA WESTERN JONATHAN COLUMBIAN **(— OF EUROPEAN STOCK)** WASP **(— OF MEXICAN DESCENT)** CHICANA CHICANO **(AUTHOR OF —)** JAMES **(CHARACTER IN —)** BREAD CINTRE CLAIRE NEWMAN NIOCHE TRISTRAM VALENTIN BELLEGARDE CHRISTOPHER

AMERICAN GRAY JAKO

AMERICANISM HECKERISM

AMERICAN TRAGEDY (AUTHOR OF —) DREISER **(CHARACTER IN —)** ALDEN CLYDE SAMUEL SONDRA ROBERTA FINCHLEY GRIFFITHS

AMESTRIS (FATHER OF —) OTANES ONOPHAS **(WIFE OF —)** XERXES

AMETHYST ONEGITE CORUNDUM

AMIABILITY DOUCEUR

AMIABLE GOOD KIND WARM SWEET CLEVER GENIAL GENTLE LOVING MELLOW SMOOTH TENDER AFFABLE LOVABLE WINSOME CHARMING ENGAGING FRIENDLY OBLIGING PLEASING

AMICABLE KIND FRIENDLY NEIGHBORLY

AMICE AMIT AMYS CAPE COWL HOOD EPHOD ALMUCE DOMINO TIPPET VAKASS AMICTUS VESTMENT

AMID IN OMEL AMELL AMONG AMIDST DURING IMELLE AMONGST BETWEEN

AMIDAS (BROTHER OF —) BRACIDAS

AMIDE LACTAM SULTAM ANILIDE ARYLIDE PEPTIDE

AMIDST AMONG AMONGST

AMILDAR AUMIL

AMIN IDI

AMINE ANILIN ANILINE PSILOCIN

AMINO ALANINE

AMINO-ACID LYSINE

AMISS ILL MIS AWRY BIAS AGATE AGLEY ASKEW WONKY WRONG ACROSS AGRIEF ASTRAY FAULTY MISTAKE IMPROPER **(PREF.)** MIS PAR(A)

AMITRIPTYLINE ELAVIL

AMITTAI (SON OF —) JONAH

AMITY PEACE ACCORD CONCORD HARMONY

AMMA ABBESS MOTHER

AMMIEL (DAUGHTER OF —) BATHSHEBA **(FATHER OF —)** OBEDEDOM **(SON OF —)** MACHIR

AMMIHUD (SON OF —) TALMAI PEDAHEL SHEMUEL ELISHAMA

AMMINADAB (FATHER OF —) RAM ARAM KOHATH UZZIEL **(SON OF —)** NAASSON

AMMISHADDAI (SON OF —) AHIEZER

AMMIZABAD (FATHER OF —) BENAIAH

AMMO BBS **(— FOR TOY GUN)** CAP CAPS

AMMONIA HARTSHORN

AMMONIAC OSHAC

AMMONITE POLYPOD AMMONOID BACULITE CACULOID CERATITE SALIGRAM

AMMONIUM CARBONATE HARTSHORN

AMMOPHILA STAR STARR

AMMUNITION AMMO AMMU ARMS SHOT BOMBS FODDER POWDER SHELLS BULLETS BUCKSHOT GRENADES MATERIAL MATERIEL ORDNANCE SHRAPNEL

AMNESIA LAPSE FORGETFULNESS

AMNESTY COWLE PARDON OBLIVION

AMNION SAC CAUL SEROSA INDUSIUM MEMBRANE

AMNON (FATHER OF —) DAVID **(HALF-SISTER OF —)** TAMAR

AMOBARBITAL AMYTAL

AMOEBA AMEBA AMEBULA PROTEUS AMOEBULA RHIZOPOD

AMOK MAD AMUCK CRAZY CRAZED VIOLENT FRENZIED **(RUNNING —)** ARIOT

AMOLE EMOL AMOULI AMOLILLA MANFREDA

AMON (FATHER OF —) MANASSEH **(SON OF —)** JOSIAH

AMONG IN MID AMID INTO MANG MONG OMEL WITH AMANG AMELL MIDST AMIDST BIMONG IMELLE WITHIN BETWEEN **(— OTHER THINGS)** IA **(PREF.)** EPH EPI INTER

AMOR EROS LOVE CUPID AMOROSO

AMORAL NEUTRAL NONMORAL

AMORET (HUSBAND OF —) SCUDAMORE **(SISTER OF —)** BELPHOEBE

AMORINO CUPID

AMORITE CANAANITE

AMOROUS FOND GAMY SOFT WARM CADGY JOLLY MUSHY NUTTY ARDENT COQUET EROTIC LOVELY LOVING SPOONY TENDER WANTON AMATIVE AMATORY AMIABLE FERVENT GALLANT JEALOUS SMICKER LOVESOME VENEREAN

AMOROUSLY SMICKLY

AMORPHOUS VAGUE ATELENE HYALINE DEFORMED FORMLESS INCHOATE RESINOUS

AMORT ALAMORT DEJECTED LIFELESS

AMORTIZE DESTROY MORTISE ALIENATE

AMOUNT GO GOB LOT SUM SUP TOT ANTE BODY COME DOSE DRAW FECK KIND LEVY MESS REAM RISE SOUD SOWD TALE UNIT WARE ADDUP CHUNK COUNT GROSS MOUNT PRICE REACH STACK STORE STUFF TOTAL WHOLE BUDGET DEGREE DOLLOP DOSAGE EFFECT EXTENT FIGURE MATTER NUMBER SUPPLY ADVANCE FOOTING QUANTUM SCRUPLE SIGNIFY SLATHER TODDICK INCREASE QUANTITY SPOONFUL SURMOUNT VALLIDOM **(— BORNE BY BEAST)** SEAM **(— CARRIED AT ONE TIME)** GANG **(— DUE)** BILL SCORE **(— HELD)** CAPACITY **(— LEFT IN VESSEL)** ULLAGE **(— OF BASS)** BOOMINESS **(— OF CONCRETE)** LIFT **(— OF DYE)** STRIKE **(— OF FLOW)** STRENGTH **(— OF FREIGHT)** CARLOAD **(— OF GAS)** BREATH **(— OF HERRINGS)** CRANNAGE

(— OF LEAKAGE) SLIP
(— OF LIQUOR) SLUG
(— OF MEDICINE) DOSAGE
(— OF MONEY) BEAN BOND CASH SCOT
(— OF OIL) ALLOWABLE
(— OF PAYMENT) FOOTAGE
(— OF POWDER) INCREMENT
(— OF SOIL) INTHROW
(— OF WATER) CATCHMENT
(— OF WORK) ASSIGNMENT
(— OWED) LIABILITY OBLIGATION
(— PAID) COST
(— PROVIDED) SUPPLY
(— TURNED BY SPADE) GRAFT
(APPRECIABLE —) BEANS
(COMPLETE —) FULL
(CONSIDERABLE —) MIGHT HANTLE HATFUL
(EXACT —) NICK
(EXTRA —) BONUS
(GREAT —) MICKLE INFINITY MOUNTAIN
(GREATEST —) MAXIMUM
(GROSS —) SLUMP
(INADEQUATE —) DEFICIENCY
(INDEFINITE —) BAIT SNAG SOME
(INFINITESIMAL —) IOTA
(INSIGNIFICANT —) SCRAT PEANUTS PEPPERCORN
(LARGE —) GOB LOB JUNT LUMP MINT RAFT SNAG SWAG SIEGE SLASH SPATE BOODLE SOMDEL BONANZA SOMDIEL CARTLOAD MUCHNESS SOMEDEAL
(LAVISH —) SLATHER
(LEAST —) DIDDLY
(LEAST POSSIBLE —) GRAIN AMBSACE
(LIMITED —) SPRINKLING
(MEDICINAL —) DOSAGE
(MINUTE —) HAIR FLEABITE
(RENT —) GALE
(SIZABLE —) CHUNK SMART
(SLIGHT —) ADDED SNACK TILLY TINGE
(SLIGHTEST —) BEANS
(SMALL —) ACE BIT DAB TAD DITE DOIT DRAB DRAM DRIB FLOW HAET HINT HOOT INCH LICK MITE SNAP SONG SPOT SKOSH SPECK SPURT TRACE DRAPPY PICKLE SMIDGE TICKET CAPSULE DRAPPIE GLIMMER KENNING SMIDGEN SMIDGIN THOUGHT
(SMALLEST —) JOT STIVER MINIMUM STEEVER STUIVER
(SMALLEST —S) MINIMA
(TENFOLD —) DECUPLE
(USUAL —) GRIST
(WHOLE —) ALL SUBSTANCE
(YEARLY —) ANNUITY
(SUFF.) ANCE ANT ENCE
AMOUR DRURY DRUERY AMOURET INTRIGUE PARAMOUR
AMOZ (SON OF —) ISAIAH
AMPERSAND AND ALSO PLUS AMPASSY IPSEAND
AMPHETAMINE SPEED UPPER BENZEDRINE
AMPHIALUS (MOTHER OF —) CECROPIA

AMPHIARAUS (DAUGHTER OF —) EURYDICE DEMONASSA
(FATHER OF —) OICLES
(MOTHER OF —) HYPERMNESTRA
(SON OF —) ALCMAEON AMPHILOCHUS
(WIFE OF —) ERIPHYLE
AMPHIBIA BATRACHIA
AMPHIBIAN EFT OLM FROG HYLA NEWT RANA TOAD ANURA SIREN SNAKE AMPHIB AXOLOTL CAUDATE ERYOPID PROTEUS TADPOLE AISTOPOD SALAMANDER
AMPHIBOLE EDENITE ORALITE URALITE ASBESTOS CROSSITE TREMOLITE SMARAGDITE
AMPHICARPA FALCATA
AMPHICTYON (FATHER OF —) DEUCALION
(MOTHER OF —) PYRRHA
AMPHIGASTRIUM UNDERLEAF
AMPHIGORIC INANE
AMPHILOCHUS (FATHER OF —) AMPHIARAUS
(MOTHER OF —) ERIPHYLE
AMPHION (BROTHER OF —) ZETHUS
(FATHER OF —) ZEUS IASUS JUPITER
(MOTHER OF —) ANTIOPE
(WIFE OF —) NIOBE
AMPHIOXUS LANCELET
AMPHIPOD SHRIMP
AMPHISSA (FATHER OF —) ECHETUS MACAREUS
(MOTHER OF —) CANACHE
AMPHISSUS (FATHER OF —) APOLLO
(MOTHER OF —) DRYOPE
AMPHITHEA (DAUGHTER OF —) ANTICLEA
(HUSBAND OF —) AUTOLYCUS
AMPHITHEATER BOWL OVAL ARENA CAVEA CIRCUS CIRQUE STADIUM THEATER
AMPHITRITE (FATHER OF —) NEREUS OCEANUS
(HUSBAND OF —) NEPTUNE POSEIDON
(MOTHER OF —) TETHYS
(SON OF —) TRITON
AMPHITRYON (AUTHOR OF —) PLAUTUS
(CHARACTER IN —) SOSIA ALCMENA JUPITER MERCURY AMPHITRYON
(DOG OF —) LAELAPS
(FATHER OF —) ALCAEUS
(MOTHER OF —) HIPPONOME
(WIFE OF —) ALCMENE
AMPHORA JUG URN VASE CADUS DIOTA PELIKE
AMPHOTERUS (BROTHER OF —) ACARNAN
(FATHER OF —) ALCMAEON
(MOTHER OF —) CALLIRRHOE
AMPLE BIG FAIR FULL GOOD MUCH RICH SIDE WIDE BROAD GREAT LARGE LUCKY PLUMP ROOMY ROUND SONSY WALLY ENOUGH HEARTY PLENTY PROLIX COPIOUS LIBERAL OPULENT WEALTHY ABUNDANT ADEQUATE BARONIAL GENEROUS HANDSOME SPACIOUS PLENTIFUL

AMPLIFICATION GAIN
AMPLIFIED EXTENDED
AMPLIFIER BOOSTER REPEATER
AMPLIFY PAD FARCE FARSE SWELL WIDEN DILATE EXPAND EXTEND STRESS AUGMENT ENLARGE STRETCH AMPLIATE HEIGHTEN INCREASE LENGTHEN MULTIPLY
AMPLITUDE BULK BREADTH LATITUDE OPULENCE
AMPLY LARGE
AMPUTATE CUT LOP PRUNE SEVER CURTAIL
AMPUTATION APOCOPE ABLATION
AMPYCUS (FATHER OF —) PELIAS
(MOTHER OF —) CHLORIS
(SON OF —) MOPSUS
AMRAM (FATHER OF —) BANI DISHON
(SON OF —) MOSES
AMRITA RASA
AMULA AMA VESSEL
AMULET GEM MET ANKH HAND JUJU MOJO PLUM CHARM IMAGE MENAT SAFFI SAFIE TOKEN FETISH GRIGRI MASCOT SAPHIE SCROLL TABLET ABRAXAS AMALETT ICHTHUS ICHTHYS PERIAPT CHURINGA GREEGREE HAGSTONE LIGATURE ORNAMENT TALISMAN PHYLACTERY
AMULIUS (BROTHER OF —) NUMITOR
(FATHER OF —) PROCAS
(NEPHEW OF —) LAUSUS
AMURRU MARTU
AMUSE GAME LAKE ENJOY MIRTH SHORT SPORT ABSORB DELUDE DIVERT ENGAGE FROLIC PLEASE POPJOY SOLACE TICKLE BEGUILE DISPORT GRATIFY PASTIME BEWILDER DISTRACT RECREATE
(— IMMENSELY) SLAY
(— ONESELF) POPJOY
(— VERY MUCH) SLAY
AMUSEMENT FAD FUN JEU GAME JEST LAKE PLAY MIRTH SPORT LAKING MUSERY PASTIME COTTABUS LAUGHTER PLEASURE (PL.) MIDWAY
AMUSING RICH COMIC DROLL FUNNY MERRY WITTY COMICAL FOOLISH KILLING RISIBLE FARCICAL HUMOROUS PLEASANT SPORTFUL
(SOMEONE —) GIGGLE
(SOMETHING OR SOMEONE —) HOOT
AMYCLAS (FATHER OF —) LACEDAEMON
(MOTHER OF —) SPARTE
(SON OF —) HYACINTHUS
AMYCUS (FATHER OF —) NEPTUNE POSEIDON
(MOTHER OF —) MELIA
(SLAYER OF —) POLLUX
AMYGDALA TONSIL
AMYL AMYDON PENTYL ISOAMYL
AMYLASE PTYALIN DIASTASE
AMYMONE (FATHER OF —) DANAUS
(HUSBAND OF —) ENCELADUS
(SON OF —) NAUPLIUS

AMYNTOR (FATHER OF —) ORMENUS
(SON OF —) PHOENIX
(WIFE OF —) CLEOBULE
AMYTHAON (BROTHER OF —) AESON PHERES
(FATHER OF —) CRETHEUS
(MOTHER OF —) TYRO
(SON OF —) BIAS MELAMPUS
(WIFE OF —) IDOMENE
AN ONE ARTICLE
ANA EVENTS OMNIANA SAYINGS
ANABAPTIST DIPPER ABECEDARIAN
ANABAS MARTINICO
ANABATIC DESCENDING
ANABLEPS FOUREYES
ANABO NABO ANABONG
ANABRANCH BRANCH TALLYWALKA
ANACAONA (BROTHER OF —) BEHECHIO
(HUSBAND OF —) CAONABO
ANACHARSIS (BROTHER OF —) SAULIUS
ANACHRONISM SOLECISM
ANACONDA BOA ABOLLA SUCURI SUCURY CAMOUDIE SUCURUJU
ANACREONTIC TEIAN
ANACRUSIS UPBEAT
ANADEM CROWN DIADEM FILLET WREATH CHAPLET CORONET GARLAND
ANAGNOST LECTOR READER
ANAGOGICAL MYSTICAL
ANAGRAM REBUS PUZZLE METAGRAM LOGOGRIPH (PL) VERBARIUM
ANAGUA KNACKAWAY KNOCKAWAY
ANAH (DAUGHTER OF —) AHOLIBAMAH
(FATHER OF —) ZIBEON
ANAL PODICAL
ANALABOS CLOAK
ANALGESIC ANODYNE CODEINE QUININE ANTIPYRIN PHENALGIN
ANALOGICAL NORMAL
ANALOGOUS LIKE SIMILAR
ANALOGUE DFDT ANALOG
ANALOGY QIYAS PARALLEL PREDISONE
(CLOSE —) PARITY
ANALYSIS TEST INDEX STUDY ANATOMY AUTOPSY SCANSION SOLUTION
(BLOWPIPE —) PYROLOGY
(CHARACTER —) PSYCHOGRAPH
(ECONOMIC —) DYNAMICS
(LOGICAL —) SYLLOGISM
ANALYST SHRINK
ANALYTIC SUBTLE REGULAR
(NOT —) SYNTHETIC SYNTHETICAL
ANALYTICAL CLINICAL DIVISIVE
ANALYZE RUN PART SIFT ASSAY BREAK PARSE SENSE STUDY WEIGH ASSESS DIVIDE REDUCE DISSECT EXAMINE ITEMIZE RESOLVE TITRATE UNPIECE APPRAISE CONSTRUE DIAGNOSE SEPARATE
(— ACCOUNT) AGE
(— VERSE) SCAN

ANAMITE TWINE
ANANAS ANANA PINGUIN
ANANI (FATHER OF —) ELIOENAI
ANANIAS LIAR SIDRACH
   (FATHER OF —) NEDEBAEUS
   (WIFE OF —) SAPPHIRA
ANANSI NANCY
ANAPEST ANTIDACTYL
ANARCHIST RED PROVO REBEL
   ANARCH NIHILIST REDSHIRT
   SOLECIST
ANARCHY RIOT CHAOS REVOLT
   LICENSE MISRULE DISORDER
ANASARCA EDEMA DROPSY
ANASAZI PUEBLO PLATEAU
ANASCHISTIC EUMITOTIC
ANASTOMOSIS GLOMUS
ANASTROPHE INVERSION
ANATASE OCTAHEDRITE
ANATH (SON OF —) SHAMGAR
ANATHEMA WO BAN MUD WOE
   OATH CURSE CENSURE
ANATHEMATIZE BAN CURSE
   ACCURSE EXECRATE
ANATHOTH (FATHER OF —) BECHER
ANATOMIST **AMERICAN** TODD
   ALLEN EVANS SABIN WYMAN
   DWIGHT KNOWER COGHILL
   HERRICK STOCKARD
   AUSTRIAN HYRTL
   BELGIAN VESALIUS
   DANISH STENO
   DUTCH TULP GRAAF CAMPER
   COITER DUBOIS
   ENGLISH GRAY OWEN JONES
   QUAIN COWPER HARVEY HAVERS
   HILTON HUNTER WILLIS
   FRENCH ROBIN DUVERNEY
   DUPUYTREN POISEUILLE
   CRUVEILHIER
   GERMAN HIS FICK ROUX HENLE
   MEYER BRAUNE EBERTH KRAUSE
   MECKEL MULLER RATHKE WAGNER
   FRORIEP SIEBOLD ANDERSCH
   BISCHOFF HARTMANN MEISSNER
   SCHULTZE SCHWALBE WRISBERG
   GEGENBAUR HELMHOLTZ
   LIEBERKUHN SOEMMERRING
   WEIDENREICH
   GREEK RUFUS HEROPHILUS
   ERASISTRATUS
   ITALIAN CORTI ASELLI PACINI
   SCARPA VAROLI CALDANI
   COLOMBO COTUGNO ROLANDO
   MALPIGHI EUSTACHIO FALLOPIUS
   PACCHIONI
   SCOTTISH BELL MONRO FERRIER
   GOODSIR PETTIGREW MACALISTER
   SWEDISH KEY
   SWISS BAUHIN HALLER HARDER
   BRUNNER
ANATOMIZE ANALYZE DISSECT
ANATOMY TOPOLOGY
   (— OF HORSE) HIPPOTOMY
   (MICROSCOPIC —) HISTOLOGY
   (VEGETABLE —) PHYTOTOMY
ANAX (FATHER OF —) URANUS
   (MOTHER OF —) GE GAEA
   (SON OF —) ASTERIUS
ANAXARETE (LOVER OF —) IPHIS
ANAXIBIA (DAUGHTER OF —)
   PELOPEA ALCESTIS PISIDICE
   (FATHER OF —) BIAS

   (HUSBAND OF —) PELIAS
   (SON OF —) ACASTUS
ANAXO (BROTHER OF —)
   AMPHITRYON
   (DAUGHTER OF —) ALCMENE
   (FATHER OF —) ALCAEUS
   (HUSBAND OF —) ELECTRYON
ANCAEUS (FATHER OF —) ALEUS
   NEPTUNE LYCURGUS POSEIDON
   (MOTHER OF —) ASTYPALAEA
   (SON OF —) AGAPENOR
ANCESTOR ION MIL ADAM EBER
   HETH ROOT SIRE DORUS ELDER
   STOCK APETUS ATAVUS AUTHOR
   BELDAM EPONYM FATHER
   MANNUS MILEDH PARENT STIPES
   ANCIENT BELDAME BELSIRE
   EPAPHUS FLEANCE FORBEAR
   IAPETUS ISHMAEL KACHINA
   SAKULYA DARDANUS FOREBEAR
   FOREGOER MILESIUS MYRMIDON
   RELATIVE PREDECESSOR
   PRIMOGENITOR
   (— CULT) MANISM
   (—S OF GOTLANDERS) GEAT
   (MAORI —) TIKI TUPUNA
   (PL.) OLDERS ANCESTY
ANCESTRAL AVAL AVITAL AVITIC
   LINEAL FAMILIAL
ANCESTRY KIN RACE SEED ATHEL
   FAMILY ORIGIN PEOPLE SOURCE
   STRAIN DESCENT KINDRED
   LINEAGE BREEDING PEDIGREE
ANCHINOE (FATHER OF —) NILUS
   (HUSBAND OF —) BELUS
   (SON OF —) DANAUS AEGYPTUS
ANCHISES (FATHER OF —) CAPYS
   (MOTHER OF —) THEMIS
   (SON OF —) AENEAS
ANCHOR FIX BIND DRAG DRUG
   HOOK MOOR REST SLUG SPUD
   STOP AFFIX BERTH BOWER KEDGE
   RIVET SHEET STOCK ATTACH
   DROGUE FASTEN HERMIT KEDGER
   KELLEG SECURE STREAM CHAPLET
   CONNECT DEADMAN GRAPNEL
   GROUSER KILLICK MUDHOOK
   SUPPORT COCKBILL
   (— IN PLACE) ACOCKBILL
   (— RING) TORUS
   (AT —) ASTAY
   (BEAM —) WALL
   (PART OF —) ARM EYE KEY PEE PIN
   BALL BILL HEAD HOOP PALM RING
   CROWN FLUKE STOCK TREND
   THROAT
ANCHORAGE DOCK STAY HARBOR
   REFUGE RIDING MOORAGE
   ABUTMENT BERTHAGE ROOTHOLD
ANCHORITE MONK LONER HERMIT
   ASCETIC EREMITE RECLUSE
   STYLITE ANCHORET
ANCHOVY NEHU BOCON SPRAT
   HERRING SARDINE
   (— SAUCE) ALEC
   (PL.) ALICI
ANCHUSA OXTONGUE
ANCHUSIN ALKANET
ANCIENT ELD OLD AGED AULD
   FERN HIGH HOAR IAGO YORE
   EARLY ELDER HOARY OLDEN
   BYGONE ENSIGN FORMER NOETIC
   PISTOL PRIMAL VETUST ANTIENT

   ANTIQUE ARCHAIC ARCHEAN
   CLASSIC OGYGEAN OGYGIAN
   HISTORIC NOACHIAN OBSOLETE
   PRIMEVAL PRISTINE TIMEWORN
   (MOST —) ELDEST
   (PREF.) ARCHAE PALAE(O) PALE(O)
   PALE PALE(O)
ANCIENTLY OLD HIGH
ANCILLA HELPER ADJUNCT
   SERVANT
ANCON ELBOW CORBEL CONSOLE
AND N U AN ET SO ANT TOO ALSO
   PLUS BESIDES FURTHER
   MOREOVER AMPERSAND
   (— SO FORTH) ETC USW
   (SYMBOL OF —) AMPERSAND
ANDAMAN MINCOPI MINKOPI
   MINCOPIE
ANDESITE BONINITE TIMAZITE
   PROPYLITE
ANDHAKA (FATHER OF —) KASYAPA
   (MOTHER OF —) DITI
   (SLAYER OF —) SHIVA
ANDIRON DOG CHENET COBIRON
   FIREDOG HESSIAN HANDIRON
   LANDIRON
ANDORRA (LANGUAGE OF —)
   CATALAN
   (NATIVE OF —) ANDOSIAN
   (RIVER OF —) VALIRA
ANDRADITE APLOME GARNET
ANDRAEMON (FATHER OF —)
   OXYLUS
   (MOTHER OF —) GORGE DRYOPE
   (SON OF —) THOAS
ANDREA CHENIER (CHARACTER IN
   —) ANDREA COIGNY GERARD
   CHENIER MADELEINE
   (COMPOSER OF —) GIORDANO
ANDROCLES AND THE LION
   (AUTHOR OF —) SHAW
   (CHARACTER IN —) LAVINIA
   MEGAERA ANDROCLES FERROVIUS
ANDROCONIUM STIGMA PLUMULE
ANDROGEUS (FATHER OF —)
   MINOS
   (MOTHER OF —) PASIPHAE
ANDROID ROBOT AUTOMATON
ANDROMACHE (AUTHOR OF —)
   EURIPIDES
   (CHARACTER IN —) PELEUS THETIS
   ORESTES PYRRHUS HERMIONE
   MENELAUS MOLOSSUS
   ANDROMACHE NEOPTOLEMUS
   (FATHER OF —) EETION
   (HUSBAND OF —) HECTOR
   HELENUS NEOPTOLEMUS
   (SON OF —) PIELUS ASTYANAX
   MOLOSSUS PERGAMUS
ANDROMEDA (FATHER OF —)
   CEPHEUS
   (MOTHER OF —) CASSIOPEA
   (RESCUER OF —) PERSEUS
ANDROMEDE BIELID
ANDRON (FATHER OF —) ANIUS
   (SISTER OF —) OENO ELAIS
   SPERMO
ANECDOTAL LITERARY
ANECDOTE GAG TOY JOKE TALE
   YARN EVENT STORY SKETCH
   HAGGADA EXEMPLUM HAGGADAH
   (COLLECTION OF —S) ANA
ANECHOIC DEAD

ANEMIA SURRA SURRAH ANAEMIA
   HYPAEMA HYPHEMA HYPHEMIA
   ISCHEMIA SPANEMIA CHLOROSIS
ANEMIC LOW PALE WEAK MEALY
   WATERY LIFELESS
   (PREF.) CHLOR(O)
ANEMONE LILY CRASS EMONY
   POLYP OPELET ACTINIA
   BOWBELLS SNOWDROP
   (KIND OF —) RUE
ANENT ON RE ASTO ABOUT ANENST
   BESIDE TOWARD AGAINST
   OPPOSITE
ANESTHESIA BLOCK CORYL SPINAL
ANESTHETIC GAS CRNA ETHER
   ACOINE EVIPAN OBTUSE OPIATE
   COCAINE DULLING MENTHOL
   METOPRYL PARAFORM PROCAINE
   SEDATIVE PHENOCAIN
   METHOXYFLURANE
   (SUFF.) CAINE
ANESTHETIST CRNA
ANESTHETIZE FREEZE ETHERIZE
ANEW OVER AGAIN NEWLY AFRESH
   ITERUM NEWLINS NEWLINGS
   RECENTLY
   (PREF.) RE
ANFRACTUOUS SPIRAL BENDING
   SINUOUS WINDING TORTUOUS
ANGEL MAH DEVA EBUS ANGLE
   ARDOR ARIEL DAEVA DULIA NAKIR
   YAKSA ABDIEL ARIOCH BACKER
   BELIAL CHERUB MONKIR MUNKAR
   NEKKAR SERAPH SPIRIT THRONE
   UZZIEL YAKSHA ANGELET
   EGREGOR ISRAFEL RAPHAEL
   SPONSOR WATCHER ZADKIEL
   ZOPHIEL APOLLYON GUARDIAN
   ITHURIEL SUPERNAL
   (— OF DEATH) AZRAEL SAMMAEL
   (DESTROYING —) ABADDON
   (FALLEN —) SATAN
   (FALLEN —S) HELL
   (GUARDIAN —) YAKSA YAKSHA
   YAKSHI
   (RECORDING —) SIJIL SIJILL
   (PL.) HOST FRAVASHI SERAPHIM
ANGELFISH MONK MUNK ANGEL
   QUOTT RHINA SQUAT MONACH
   CICHLID FLATFISH KINGSTON
   MONKFISH SQUATINA
ANGELIC SAINTLY BEATIFIC
   CHERUBIC HEAVENLY SERAPHIC
ANGELICA JELLICA ARCHANGEL
   (FATHER OF —) GALAPHRON
   (LOVER OF —) ORLANDO
ANGELIN PACAY ANGELEEN
ANGELIQUE (CHARACTER IN —)
   CHARLOT BONIFACE ANGELIQUE
   (COMPOSER OF —) IBERT
ANGER ARR IRE IRK MAD VEX BATE
   BILE BURN CRAB FELL FUME FURY
   GALL GRIM HUFF MOOD RAGE
   RILE ROIL RUFF TEEN TIFF ANNOY
   BIRSE GRAME GRIPE HATEL IRISH
   PIQUE SPONK SPUNK STURT
   THRAW WRATH BOTHER CHOLER
   DANDER ENRAGE EXCITE GRIEVE
   MADDEN MONKEY NETTLE
   OFFEND RANCOR SPLEEN TALENT
   TEMPER WARMTH BURNING
   DESPITE DUDGEON EMOTION

INCENSE INFLAME PASSION PROVOKE STOMACH ACRIMONY DISTRESS EBENEZER IRRITATE VEXATION
ANGERED SORE AGRAMED PELTISH INCENSED
ANGICO CURUPAY
ANGINA PRUNELLA
ANGIOSPERM HARDWOOD METASPERM
ANGLE IN BOB DIP ELL OUT TEE WRO CANT COIN COOK DRAW FISH FORK HADE KEEN KNEE LEAD NOOK PEAK SITE WICK ANCON ARRIS AXIAL BEVEL BIGHT CHOIL COIGN DRAFT DRIFT ELBOW FLEAM GROIN GUISE INGLE PHASE POINT QUOIN SLANT SLOPE ALLURE ANGULE ASPECT CANTON CORNEL CORNER DIRECT ENGHLE EPAULE HADING LAGGEN LAGGIN OCTANT SCHEME SQUARE TORNUS ANGLIAN ANGULUS ANOMALY AZIMUTH BASTION DRAUGHT GIMMICK KNUCKLE PERIGON RAVELIN SALIENT ARGUMENT DECALAGE DIHEDRAL FISHHOOK INTRIGUE SHOULDER OBLIQUITY
(— OF BEVEL) FLEAM FLEEM
(— OF BOWSPRIT) STEEVE STEEVING
(— OF CLUB HEAD) LIE
(— OF EYELIDS) CANTHUS
(— OFF) JAG
(— OF HAT BRIM) BREAK
(— OF HIPBONE) HOOK
(— OF LEAF) AXIL
(— OF RAFTER) HEEL
(— OF TIMBER KNEE) BRECCII
(DRIFT —) LEEWAY
(OBTUSE —) HEEL BULLNOSE
(ROCK —) DIEDRE
(ROOF —) HIP FASTIGIUM
(ROUND —) PERIGON
(SALIENT —) ARIS ARRIS PIEND
(PREF.) ANGULO GON(I)(IO)(Y)(YO)
(SUFF.) GON
ANGLED CANTED NOOKED ANGULATE
(PREF.) ACUTI
ANGLER MONK FRIAR THIEF SLIMER LOPHIID RODSTER SPINNER WIDEGAB WIDEGAP ALLMOUTH FROGFISH MONKFISH PISCATOR TOADFISH WALTONIAN
ANGLESMITH SLABMAN
ANGLEWORM ESS WORM FISHWORM
ANGLICAN EPISCOPAL
ANGLO CAUCASIAN

ANGORA CAT GOAT ANGOLA RABBIT
ANGRILY ANGERLY IRATELY FUMINGLY
ANGRY MAD ASHY EVIL GRIM GRUM HIGH RILY ROID ROSY SORE WARM WAXY WILD WRAW CROOK CROSS GRAME HUFFY IRATE IROUS MOODY RATTY RILEY SNAKY STUNT VEXED WEMOD WROTH BIRSIT CHAFED CROUSE FRENZY FUMING FUMOUS HEATED IREFUL LOADED SHIRTY SNAKEY STUFFY TICKED ENRAGED FRETFUL FURIOUS HOPPING IRACUND PAINFUL RILEDUP ROPABLE SNAKISH SPLEENY TEEDOFF UPTIGHT CHOLERIC INFLAMED RIGOROUS SEETHING SPITFIRE TEMPERED VEHEMENT WREAKFUL INDIGNANT PASSIONATE
(BE —) STEAM
(MAKE —) FROST
ANGRY-LOOKING THUNDERY
ANGUISH WOE ACHE HARM HURT PAIN PANG RACK TRAY AGONY ANGST ANGUS GRIEF THROE MISERY REGRET SORROW ANGOISE ANGWICH REMORSE TORMENT TORTURE TRAVAIL DISTRESS
(CHRIST'S —) AGONY
ANGUISHED GRIEFFUL
ANGULAR BONE BONY EDGY LEAN SLIM THIN GAUNT SHARP ABRUPT POINTED SCRAWNY CORNERED
(NOT —) SOFT
(PREF.) ANG
ANGULARITY EDGINESS
ANGUS FORFAR FORFARSHIRE
ANHYDRIDE LACTAM SULTAM FULGIDE LACTIDE SULTONE GLUCOSAN MANNITAN SORBITAN
ANHYDRITE VULPINITE
ANHYDROUS DRY DESICCATED
ANI WITCH CUCKOO JEWBIRD KEELBILL KEELBIRD TICKBIRD
ANIAM (FATHER OF —) SHEMIDAH
ANIARA (COMPOSER OF —) BLOMDAHL
ANIMADVERSION BLAME REMARK CENSURE COMMENT REPROOF WARNING MONITION REPROACH REFLECTION
ANIMAL (ALSO SEE UNDER SPECIFIC HEADINGS) FAT DEER BEAST BIPED BLACK BRUTE GRADE GROSS LUSTY STORE STRAY BRUTAL CARNAL DAPPLE DESPOT FLESHY KICKER MAMMAL RODENT SILVAN SORREL SPONGE SYLVAN BEASTIE BREEDER CARRION CRITTER EPIZOON FATLING LINSANG SENSUAL BURROWER CREATURE EMIGRANT ORGANISM PREDATOR
(— COLLECTION) LARDER
(— FOR MARKET) STOCKER
(— INHABITED BY SPIRIT) GUACA HUACA
(— LIVING IN CAVES) TROGLOBITE
(— OF LITTLE VALUE) SCALAWAG SKALAWAG
(— RESEMBLING MAN) HOMINOID
(— S AS RENT) CAIN
(— SHOT) KILL
(— VICTIM OF MOTOR VEHICLE) ROADKILL
(— WITH BLACK COAT AND MARKINGS) PARSON
(— WITH DOCKED TAIL) CURTAL
(BEEF —) BONER GRASSER
(BOVINE —) BOSS BRUTE
(BROKEN-DOWN —) CROCK
(CARNIVOROUS —) GENET GENETTE SARCOPHILE
(CASTRATED —) SEG SEGG SPAY SPADO GELDING
(COLD-BLOODED —) ECTOTHERM
(CREATED —) BARAMIN
(DECOY —) COACH
(DOMESTIC —) DOER SCRUB BESTIAL FOLLOWER SCRUBBER
(DRAFT —) AVER AIVER
(EMACIATED —) FRAME SKELETON
(FABULOUS —) KYLIN BUNYIP DRAGON ACEPHAL GRIFFIN GRIFFON GRYPHON UNICORN SEMITAUR TRAGELAPH
(FARM —S) STOCK
(FEMALE —) HEN SHE LADY JENNY SHEDER
(FERAL —) CIMAROON CIMARRON CIMMARON
(FLEA-RIDDEN —) FLEABAG
(FOOTLESS —) APOD APODE
(FOSSIL —) ZOOLITE
(FREAKISH —) FERLY FERLIE
(GRASSHOPPER-EATING —) WHANGAM
(GRAY —) GRIZZLE
(GRAZING —) HERBAGER
(GREEDY —) GORB
(HORNED —) HORN REEM
(HORNLESS —) POLLARD
(HUNTED —) QUARRY
(HYPOTHETICAL —) PROAVIS
(IMAGINARY —) WHANGAM CATAWAMPUS
(LOWER —) BEAST CREATURE
(LUSTY OR PLUMP —) BILCH BILSH
(MALE —) HE TOM BUCK BULL JACK STAG JOHNNY BACHELOR
(MARINE —) LANCELET
(MATURE —) SENIOR
(MEAT —) CHOPPER
(MISCHIEVOUS —) ELF
(MYTHICAL —) HODAG KYLIN MOONACK
(ODD —) SPLACKNUCK
(PACK —) HUNIA SUMPTER
(PARTY —) STAG
(PET —) CADE
(PREMATURE —) SLINK
(PURSUED —S) GAME
(ROASTED —) BARBECUE BARBEQUE

(SADDLE —) LOPER
(SCRAWNY —) SCRAG
(SHORN —) SHEAR
(SKINNY —) SCRAE
(SLUGGISH —) DRUMBLE
(SOLID-HOOFED —) SOLIPED
(SPOTTED —) CALICO
(STOCKY —) BLOCK
(STUNTED —) SHARGAR SHARGER
(THICKSET —) NUGGET
(TOTEM —) EPONYM
(UNBRANDED —) SLICK
(UNCASTRATED —) ENTIRE
(UNDERSIZED —) DURGAN DURGEN SCALAWAG SCALLYWAG
(UNHOUSED —) OUTLER OUTLIER
(UNMANAGEABLE —) OUTLAW
(UNWEANED —) SUCKER
(WANDERING —) STRAY ESTRAY
(WARM-BLOODED —) ENDOTHERM HAEMATHERM
(WATER —) AQUATIC AQUATILE
(WEAK —) DRAG DOWNER
(WILD —) SAVAGE WILDLING
(WING-FOOTED —) ALIPED
(WORNOUT —) KANCKER
(WORTHLESS —) CARRION
(YOUNG —) HOG BIRD HOGG JOEY SHOT TOTO STORE JUNIOR PULLUS FATLING LITTLIN KINDLING LITTLING SUCKLING YOUNGLET
(2-HORNED —) BICORN BICORNE
(4-FOOTED —) TETRAPOD
(PL.) ZOA FAUNA NECTON NEKTON
(PREF.) ZO(E)(IDIO)(IDO)(O) ZOOLOGICO
(RUMINATING —) MERYC(O)
(SUFF.) ACEA AD THERE THERIA THERIUM ZOA ZOIC ZOON
ANIMALCULISM SPERMISM
ANIMALITY HOGGERY
ANIMALS
(SUFF.) ATA IDA IDEA INI
ANIMA MUNDI WELTGEIST
ANIMATE ACT PEP FIRE MOVE PERK STIR URGE ALIVE BRISK CHEER DRIVE FLUSH IMBUE IMPEL LIGHT LIVEN QUICK ROUSE VITAL AROUSE BRIGHT ENSOUL EXCITE INCITE INDUCE INFORM KINDLE LIVING PROMPT SPIRIT VIVIFY ACTUATE COMFORT ENLIVEN INSPIRE QUICKEN ACTIVATE ENERGIZE INSPIRIT VITALIZE
(NOT —) BRUTE
ANIMATED UP GAY VIF GLAD VIVE ALIVE ANIME BRISK QUICK VITAL VIVID ACTIVE ARDENT BLITHE BOUNCY BRISKY LIVELY LIVING SPARKY SPUNKY BUOYANT JOCULAR STHENIC BOUNCING INSTINCT LIFESOME SPIRITED VIGOROUS
ANIMATION BRIO ELAN FIRE HEAT LIFE VERVE SPIRIT SPARKLE
ANIMATOR INFORMER
ANIME COPAL ELEMI RESIN ROSIN ANIMATO
ANIMIKEAN LAWSON
ANIMISM NATURISM
ANIMOSITY HATE PIQUE SPITE ANIMUS ENMITY HATRED MALICE RANCOR DISLIKE ACRIMONY

ANIMUS MIND ONDE WILL EFFORT ENMITY SPIRIT TEMPER ATTITUDE

ANIRUDDHA (FATHER OF —) PRADYUMNA

ANISE ANET DILL CUMEN UMBEL FENNEL SIKIMI SHIKIMI

ANIUS (DAUGHTER OF —) OENO ELAIS SPERMO
(FATHER OF —) APOLLO
(MOTHER OF —) RHOEO CREUSA
(SON OF —) ANDRON
(WIFE OF —) DORIPPE

ANKH TAU

ANKLE COOT CUIT HOCK QUIT ANCLE QUEET TALUS WRIST TARSUS SHACKLE
(COCKED —S) KNUCKLING
(PREF.) TAL(I)(O) TARS(I)(O)

ANKLEBONE TALUS ASTRAGAL

ANKLET SHOE SOCK BANGLE FETTER SHACKLE

ANLAGE INCEPT PROTON INITIAL BLASTEMA

ANNA (FATHER OF —) BELUS
(SISTER OF —) DIDO

ANNA BOLENA (CHARACTER IN —) ANNE JANE HENRY PERCY BOLEYN SEYMOUR
(COMPOSER OF —) DONIZETTI

ANNA KARENINA (AUTHOR OF —) TOLSTOY
(CHARACTER IN —) ANNA KITTY LEVIN ALEXEI STEPAN KARENIN VRONSKY OBLONSKY KONSTANTINE SHTCHERBATSKY

ANNALIST WRITER RECORDER

ANNALS FASTI NIHONGI REGISTER

ANNAM (ALSO SEE VIETNAM) VIETNAM
(BOAT OF —) GAYYOU GAYDIANG
(MEASURE OF —) LY GON NGU QUO SAO TAT PHAN THAT SHITA THUOC TRUONG
(TOWN OF —) HUE VINH TOURANE QUANGTRI
(WEIGHT OF —) CAN BINH DONG

ANNAS (FATHER OF —) SETHI

ANNATTO OTTER URUCU ORLEAN ROUCOU SALMON ACHIOTE ACHUETE ANNOTTO ARNATTO ORLEANS

ANNEAL BAKE FUSE HEAT SMELT TEMPER INFLAME TOUGHEN GRAPHITE

ANNEALER TUBER HEATER

ANNEALING LIGHTING

ANNELID NAID WORM LUGWORM SERPULA ANNULATE SANDWORM SERPULAN OLIGOCHAETE

ANNEX ADD ELL LAY JOIN WING AFFIX SEIZE UNITE ADJECT ANNECT APPEND ATTACH FASTEN ACQUIRE CONNECT FIXTURE POSTFIX SUBJOIN ADDITION ANNEXURE DOCUMENT PENTHOUSE

ANNIE OAKLEY PASS TICKET FREEBEE FREEBIE

ANNIHILATE END OUT KILL RAZE RUIN SLAY ABATE ANNUL ERASE WRECK DELETE DEVOUR NOUGHT QUENCH REDUCE ABOLISH DESTROY EXPUNGE DECIMATE UNCREATE DISCREATE PULVERIZE

ANNIHILATION FANA NEGATION

ANNIVERSARY FETE MASS EMBER FEAST ANNUAL JUBILEE YEARDAY BIRTHDAY FESTIVAL YAHRZEIT
(100TH —) CENTENNIAL
(1000TH —) MILLENIUM
(150TH —) SESQUICENTENNIAL
(200TH —) BIMILLENARY BIMILLENIUM
(25TH —) SEMIJUBILEE
(50TH —) SEMICENTENNIAL

ANNONA ATIS ATTA ATEES

ANNOTATE EDIT NOTE STET GLOSS BENOTE NOTIFY POSTIL REMARK APOSTIL COMMENT EXPLAIN FOOTNOTE

ANNOTATION APOSTIL COMMENT SCHOLION SCHOLIUM

ANNOTATOR NOTIST SCHOLIAST

ANNOUNCE BID CRY BODE CALL DEEM MAKE SCRY SHOW SING TELL BRUIT CLAIM KNELL STATE VOICE ASSERT BLAZON BROACH DENOTE HERALD INFORM PREACH REPORT REVEAL SIGNAL SPRING STEVEN DECLARE DIVULGE FORERUN GAZETTE PUBLISH SIGNIFY DENOUNCE FORETELL INTIMATE PROCLAIM RENOUNCE SENTENCE

ANNOUNCEMENT BID CRY HAT BILL CALL LEAD ALARM BANCO BANNS BLURB EDICT ALARUM DECREE DICTUM NOTICE GAZETTE SENSING BULLETIN CIRCULAR DECISION RESCRIPT PROCLAMATION
(— OF DAWN) AUBADE
(STAGE —) SENNET

ANNOUNCER NEBO PAGE CRIER EMCEE CALLER DEEJAY HERALD NUNCIO VEEJAY GONGMAN GRINDER SPIELER NUNCIATE SPRUIKER

ANNOY ARR BUG DUN EAT EGG GET GIG HOX IRE IRK NAG NOY NYE TRY VEX BAIT BORE BURN FASH FRET FUSS GALL GRIG HALE HARM HAZE HUFF HUMP MIFF NARK PAIN RILE ROIL CHAFE CHASE CHEVY CHIVY DEVIL GRAMY GRATE HARRY PEEVE PIQUE SPITE STURT TEASE THORN UPSET WEARY WORRY BADGER BOTHER CADDLE CHIVEY CHIVVY EARWIG ENRAGE GRAVEL HAGGLE HARASS HATTER HECKLE HECTOR INFEST INJURE MADDEN MOLEST NEEDLE NETTLE OFFEND PESTER POTTER PUTOUT RATTLE REHETE RUFFLE TICKLE BEDEVIL DISTURB HOTFOOT JACKSON TERRIFY TROUBLE ACERBATE CONTRARY DISTRESS IRRITATE PERSECUTE

ANNOYANCE VEX DRAG FASH PEST WEED CROSS GRIEF LOATH SPITE STALL THORN INSECT PESTER DISGUST FASHERY NOYANCE TROUBLE UMBRAGE FASHERIE FLEABITE NOISANCE NUISANCE PINPRICK

ANNOYED SORE TEEDOFF INSULTED

ANNOYING TARE PESKY NOYOUS DISEASY HATEFUL IRKSOME NOISOME PAINFUL TARSOME FASHIOUS FRETSOME NIGGLING SPITEFUL TIRESOME PROVOKING PESTIFEROUS

ANNOYINGLY CONFOUNDED CONFOUNDEDLY

ANNUAL BOOK BUGLE PLANT FLOWER YEARLY ANNUARY BUGSEED BUGWEED ETESIAN GIFTBOOK PERIODIC YEARBOOK
(OLD WORLD —) WELD

ANNUITY CENSO CONSOL INCOME PENSION TONTINE PERPETUITY

ANNUL TOL CASS NULL TOLL UNDO VOID ADNUL AVOID BLANK ELIDE ERASE QUASH REMIT RETEX UNLAW CANCEL FRIVOL NEGATE RECALL REPEAL REVERT REVOKE UNLIVE VACATE ABOLISH CASHIER CASSARE CASSATE DESTROY NULLIFY RESCIND RETRACT REVERSE VACUATE ABROGATE ARROGATE DEROGATE DISANNUL DISSOLVE IMBECILE OVERRIDE OVERRULE

ANNULAR BANDED CYCLIC RINGED ANNULATE CINGULAR CIRCULAR

ANNULARLY RINGWISE

ANNULET RING RIDGE FILLET ANNULUS MOLDING

ANNULLING VACATUR

ANNULMENT UNDOING ABATEMENT

ANNULUS RING ANNULE COLLAR GYROMA INDUSIUM

ANNUNCIATION MARYMASS

ANNUNCIATOR TELLER INDICATOR

ANOA BUFFALO SAPIUTAN

ANODE PLATE ZINCOID

ANODIC ASCENDING

ANODYNE BALM ACOPON BROMAL OPIATE REMEDY EUGENOL SOOTHER NARCOTIC SEDATIVE CHLORODYNE

ANOINT FAT OIL RUB BALM BEAT CERE NARD ANELE ANOIL CREAM CROWN ENOIL LATCH NUNCT PRUNE SALVE SMARM SMEAR SMERL CHRISM GREASE INUNCT SPREAD THRASH MOISTEN UNGUENT

ANOINTMENT CHRISMATORY

ANOMALOUS ODD DIFFORM STRANGE UNUSUAL ABERRANT ABNORMAL ATYPICAL PECULIAR

ANOMALY CREEPER CYCLOPY EPILOIA PARADOX CYCLOPIA

ANON NAN ANEW ONCE SOON AGAIN LATER AFRESH BEDEEN BEDENE THENCE SHORTLY

ANONYMITY NOBODYNESS

ANONYMOUS UNKNOWN NAMELESS UNAVOWED UNSIGNED

ANOPLURA PARASITA PEDICULINA

ANORAK CAGOUL KAGOOL KAGOUL KAGOULE

ANOTHER NEW THAT ALIAS FRESH SECOND TIDDER TOTHER ANITHER FURTHER

(PREF.) ALTERO
(ONE —) ALLELO

ANOXIA ASPHYXIA

ANSHUMAN (FATHER OF —) ASAMANJAS
(GRANDFATHER OF —) SAGARA

ANSWER DO IT SAY SIT ECHO MEET PLEA REIN SUIT ATONE AVAIL COMES COVER JAWAB REACT REPLY SERVE LETTER REJOIN RESULT RETORT RETURN RIPOST ACCOUNT COUNTER DEFENCE DEFENSE FULFILL RESPOND SATISFY ANTIPHON COMEBACK PLEADING REBUTTAL REPARTEE RESPONSE SOLUTION
(— BACK) CHOP
(— FOR) FORM VANG
(— IN FUGUE) COMES
(— OF POPE) RESCRIPT
(— SHARPLY) SNAP
(— THE PURPOSE) DO FIT SUIT AVAIL SERVE
(— TO CHARGE) PLEA
(DECISIVE —) SOCKDOLAGER SOCKDOLOGER
(EXAM —) TRUE FALSE
(GIVE IMPROMPTU —) FIELD
(LEGAL —) DUPLY

ANSWERABLE EQUAL LIABLE FITTING ADEQUATE AMENABLE

ANSWERER USHABTI

ANSWERING
(PREF.) COUNTER

ANT ANAI ANAY ANER ATTA GYNE MIRE AMPTE EMMET KELEP MAXIM MINIM NURSE SAUBA SIAFU SLAVE AMAZON DRIVER ERGATE NASUTE NEUTER WORKER BULLDOG FORAGER FORMICE OUVRIER PISMIRE PISSANT PONERID REPLETE SOLDIER TERMITE ACULEATA DORYLINE FORMICID GYNECOID HONEYPOT MACRANER MICRANER MYRMICID TAPINOMA
(— LION) DOODLEBUG
(— SHRIKE) BATARA
(— STUDY) MYRMECOLOGY
(— THRUSH) PITTA
(— TREE) WORMIGO
(PART OF —) EYE WAIST GASTER ANTENNA MANDIBLE
(WINGED —) ALATE
(WORKER —) ERGATE
(PREF.) FORMI(CI) MYRMECO MYRMO TERMITO
(SUFF.) MYRMEX

ANTA PIER PARASTAS PEDESTAL PILASTER

ANTACID SATURANT

ANTAEUS (FATHER OF —) NEPTUNE POSEIDON
(MOTHER OF —) GE GAEA

ANTAGONISM WAR ANIMUS ENMITY QUARREL AVERSION CONFLICT
(IN —) COUNTER

ANTAGONIST FOE ENEMY PARTY RIVAL FOEMAN BATTLER WARRIOR COPEMATE OPPONENT OPPOSITE WRANGLER

(— OF DRUGS) NALAXONE
NALOXONE
ANTAGONISTIC ADVERSE
COUNTER HOSTILE ANTERGIC
CONTRARY INIMICAL OPPONENT
OPPOSITE
(— TO GROWTH) ANTIBLASTIC
(NOT —) SYMPATHETIC
(PREF.) ENANTIO
ANTAGONIZE OPPOSE CONTEST
ANTARCTICA (— CAPE) ADARE
(MOUNTAIN ON —) TYREE
GARDNER KIRKPATRICK
(VOLCANO ON —) EREBUS
MELBOURNE
ANT BEAR BEAR ERDVARK
AARDVARK ANTEATER EDENTATE
TAMANOIR
ANTE PAY STAKE
(— UP) KICKIN
ANTEATER TAPIR NUMBAT
ECHIDNA TAMANDU AARDVARK
AARDWOLF DASYURID EDENTATE
PANGOLIN TAMANDUA TAMANOIR
ANTEBRACHIUM CUBIT CUBITAL
CUBITUS FOREARM
ANTECEDENT FORE CAUSE PRIOR
FORMER REASON WHENCE
PREMISE ANTERIOR PREVIOUS
PRECEDING PRECEDENCE
PREVENIENT
(— OF CANON) GUIDA
ANTECHAMBER LIWAN
ANTEDATE PRECEDE PREDATE
FOREDATE PREEXIST
ANTEDATED FORETIMED
ANTELOPE GNU GOA KID KOB RAM
SUS ASTE BISA BUCK DODA DUST
GUIB IBEX KODA KUDU ORYX PALA
PUKU ROAN SUNI TOPI TORA
ADDAX BAIRA BEIRA BEISA BEKRA
BOHOR BONGO BOVID BUBAL
CHIRU ELAND GORAL GUIBA IPETE
LICHI NAGOR NYALA ORIBI PEELE
PERON SABLE SAIGA SASIN
SEROW TAKIN YAKIN BAGWYN
BHOKRA BUBALE CABREE CABRET
CABRIE CABRIT CHOUKA DIKDIK
DUIKER DUYKER DZEREN DZERIN
DZERON GOORAL GRIMME
HEROLA IMPALA INYALA KOODOO
LECHWE LELWEL NAKONG NILGAI
NILGAU PALLAH POOKOO PYGARG
RHEBOK ALGAZEL BLAUBOK
BLESBOK BUBALIS CHAMOIS
CHIKARA DEFASSA GAZELLE
GEMSBOK GERENUK GREENUK
GRYSBOK MADOQUA REDBUCK
RHEEBOK SASSABY STEMBOK
AGACELLA BLEEKBOK BLESBUCK
BONTEBOK BOSCHBOK BUSHBUCK
KORRIGUM LEUCORYX REEDBUCK
STEENBOK PRONGHORN
HARTEBEEST
(YOUNG —) KID LAMB
ANTEMERIDIEM ACKEMMA
ANTENNA DISH HORN LOOP PALP
TIER YAGI AERIAL DIPOLE FEELER
TACTOR DOUBLET WHISKER
MONOPOLE PARABOLA RADIATOR
(SHORTWAVE —) YAGI
ANTENNATA INSECTA

ANTENOR (FATHER OF —) AESYETES
(MOTHER OF —) CLEOMESTRA
(WIFE OF —) THEANO
ANTERIOR FORNE FRONT PRIOR
ATLOID BEFORE FORMER ANTICUS
PRORSAL VENTRAL ATLANTAL
INFERIOR PREVIOUS PRECEDING
(PREF.) ANTER(O) EPH EPI PRE PRO
ANTEROOM HALL FOYER LOBBY
ENTRANCE
ANTEROS (BROTHER OF —) EROS
(FATHER OF —) ARES MARS
(MOTHER OF —) APHRODITE
ANTEWAR PREBELLUM
ANTHAS (FATHER OF —) NEPTUNE
POSEIDON
(MOTHER OF —) ALCYONE
ANTHELION HALO NIMBUS
ANTISUN AUREOLE
ANTHELMINTIC CUNIC BRAYERA
EMRELIN PINKROOT SCAMMONY
SANTONICA PIPERAZINE
PHENOTHIAZINE
ANTHEM HYMN SONG AGNUS
MOTET PAEAN PSALM INTROIT
RESPOND ASPERGES ISODICON
(JAPANESE —) KIMIGAYO
ANTHEMIUS (FATHER OF —)
PROCOPIUS
ANTHER TIP AGLET CHIVE THECA
ANTHESIS BLOOM BLOSSOM
ANTHILL BANK TUMP
ANTHOCYANIN ENIN OENIN
BETANIN PUNICIN VIOLANIN
ANTHOLOGIST RHAPSODE
RHAPSODIST
ANTHOLOGY ANA POSY ALBUM
SYLVA CORPUS READER GARLAND
SYNTAGMA CHRESTOMATHY
ANTHOZOAN CORAL POLYP
ANEMONE GULINULA
ANTHRACITE CULM
ANTHRACITIC HARD
ANTHRACONITE STINKSTONE
SWINESTONE
ANTHRAX SANG CHARBON
BLACKLEG
ANTHROPOLOGIST TOTEMIST
CULTURALIST
AMERICAN BIRD BOAS COON MEAD
BEALS DIXON HOUGH JENKS LEWIS
SAPIR STARR BUTLER DORSEY
GEERTE HOLMES HOOTON LAUFER
LINTON MERCER POWELL PUTNAM
RIPLEY WEAVER BATESON BRINTON
FOLKMAR KROEBER LAFARGE
MONTAGU SPINDEN WISSLER
BENEDICT GWALTNEY HRDLICKA
MACCURDY KLUCKHOHN
MACDONALD HERSKOVITS
GOLDENWEISER
AUSTRALIAN DART
AUSTRIAN LUSCHAN
BELGIAN BIEBUYCK
ENGLISH HODGE KEITH PERRY
SMITH TYLOR BEDDOE HADDON
HOWITT LEAKEY MARETT RIVERS
GOODALL TURNBULL MALINOWSKI
FINNISH WESTERMARCK
FRENCH HAMY BROCA DENIKER
LAPOUGE TOPINARD DUCHAILLU
MORTILLET HOVELACQUE
MANOUVRIER

GERMAN WAITZ GUNTHER
HARTMANN SCHWALBE
BLUMENBACH WEIDENREICH
SCHOETENSACK
ITALIAN SERGI MANTEGAZZA
NORWEGIAN HEYERDAHL
SCOTTISH FRAZER MONBODDO
ANTHROPOPHAGITE CANNIBAL
ANTIA (BELOVED OF —)
BELLEROPHON
(FATHER OF —) IOBATES
(HUSBAND OF —) PROETUS
ANTIAIRCRAFT ARCHIE
ANTIANEIRA (FATHER OF —)
MENETES
(SON OF —) ECHION ERYTUS
ANTIBALLOONER SEPARATOR
ANTIBIOTIC BIOTIC ABIOTIC FILIPIN
HUMULON TYLOSIN CIRCULIN
CITRININ CLAVACIN CLAVATIN
COLISTIN FRADICIN HUMULONE
NEOMYCIN NYSTATIN RIFAMPIN
SUBTILIN VIOMYCIN POLYMYCIN
PUROMYCIN RIFAMICIN
GENTAMICIN OLIGOMYCIN
PENICILLIN RIFAMPICIN
ANTIBODY LYSIN REAGIN BLOCKER
GLUTININ PRECIPITIN
ANTIC TOY DIDO FOOL LARK WILD
CAPER CLOWN COMIC DROLL
MERRY PRANK STUNT GAMBOL
BUFFOON CAPRICE GAMBADE
GAMBADO
ANTICHRIST BEAST
ANTICIPATE BALK BEAT HOPE
JUMP WISH ALLOT AUGUR AWAIT
DREAD PSYCH SENSE STALL
DIVINE EXPECT PSYCHE THWART
DEVANCE FORERUN FORESEE
OBVIATE PORTEND PREPARE
PREVENE PREVENT PROPOSE
RESPECT SUPPOSE ANTEDATE
FORECAST FOREFEEL FORETAKE
PROSPECT
ANTICIPATION TYPE ODIUM
AUGURY OPINION THOUGHT
PROSPECT PROLEPSIS
PRESCIENCE PREMONITION
ANTICIPATORY PREVENIENT
ANTICLEA (FATHER OF —)
AUTOLYCUS
(HUSBAND OF —) LAERTES
(SON OF —) ULYSSES ODYSSEUS
ANTICLIMAX BATHOS
ANTICLINE ARCH DOME NAPPE
ISOCLINE OVERFOLD
ANTICOAGULANT WARFARIN
ANTICYCLONE HIGH
ANTIDEPRESSANT DOXEPIN
NIALAMIDE PARGYLINE
NORTRIPTYLINE
ANTIDOTE GUACO BEZOAR EMETIC
GALENA REMEDY THERIAC
DELETERY THERIACA BEZOARDIC
MITHRIDATE BLEXIPHARMIC
(— TO POISON) ORVIETAN
ANTIGEN N LYSOGEN BIOLOGIC
PRECIPITINOGEN
ANTIGERMANISM VANSITTARTISM
ANTIGONE (AUTHOR OF —)
SOPHOCLES
(BROTHER OF —) POLYNICES

(CHARACTER IN —) CREON
HAEMON ISMENE ANTIGONE
TIRESIAS
(FATHER OF —) OEDIPUS
(MOTHER OF —) JOCASTA
(SISTER OF —) ISMENE
ANTIGORITE SERPENTINE
ANTIGUA & BARBUDA (CAPITAL:)
SAINTJOHNS
(COIN:) DOLLAR
(ISLAND:) ANTIGUA BARBUDA
REDONDA
(LANGUAGE:) ENGLISH
(TOWN:) CODRINGTON
ANTILOCHUS (FATHER OF —)
NESTOR
(MOTHER OF —) ANAXIBIA
(SLAYER OF —) MEMNON
ANTIMALARIAL PENTAQUIN
PENTAQUINE
ANTIMASK ANTIC ANTICK
ANTIMONIAL STIBIAL
ANTIMONY SB KOHL REGULUS
STIBIUM
(PREF.) STIB(IO)
ANTIMONY SULFIDE SURMA
SOORMA
ANTINOMIAN FIDUCIARY
ANTINOMY PARADOX
ANTIOPE (FATHER OF —) NYCTEUS
(HUSBAND OF —) LYCUS THESEUS
(SISTER OF —) HIPPOLYTE
(SON OF —) ZETHUS AMPHION
HIPPOLYTUS
ANTIOXIDANT BHA SESAMOL
ANTIPATHY HATE ODIUM ENMITY
NAUSEA RANCOR ALLERGY
DISGUST DISLIKE AVERSION
DISTASTE DYSPATHY LOATHING
ANTIPHON SALVE GRADUAL
PLACEBO GRADUALE
ANTIPHONALLY CHOIRWISE
ANTHEMWISE
ANTIPHONARY LEDGER
ANTIPHUS (BROTHER OF —)
MESTHLES
(FATHER OF —) PRIAM
TALAEMENES
(HALF-BROTHER OF —) ISUS
(MOTHER OF —) HECUBA
ANTIPODAL ANTARCTIC
ANTIPYRETIC SALOL MALARIN
THALLIN THALLINE
ANTIQUARY ARCHAIST
ANTIQUARIAN
ANTIQUATED OLD AGED FUSTY
MOSSY PASSE FOGRAM FOSSIL
VOIDED ANCIENT ARCHAIC
FOGYISH NOACHIAN OBSOLETE
OUTDATED OUTMODED
TIMEWORN
ANTIQUE ANTIC RELIC SIRUP SYRUP
VIRTU ANTICK NOETIC ANCIENT
ARCHAIC NOACHIC NOACHIAN
OUTMODED ARCHAICAL
(PERSON WHO LOCATES —S)
PICKER
ANTIQUITY ELD OLD PAST YORE
RELIC OLDNESS ANCIENCE
ANCIENCY
(PL.) ARCHEOLOGY
ARCHAEOLOGY
ANTIRED WHITE

ANTI-SEMITISM JUDOPHOBIA
ANTISEPTIC CAVA EGOL KAVA SALT
AMIDO AMINE EUPAD EUSOL
IODOL SALOL AMADOL IATROL
IODINE KRELOS PHENOL PICROL
ALCOHOL ALUMNOL ARBUTIN
ASEPTIC COLYTIC LORETIN
STERILE TACHIOL TEUCRIN
THALLIN CREOSOTE ICHTHYOL
KAVAKAVA METAPHEN TEREBENE
THALLINE MERBROMIN
ACRIFLAVINE
(SUFF.) IOM
ANTISOCIAL HOSTILE ANARCHIST
ANTISPASMODIC KELLIN SAMBUL
SUMBAL SUMBUL KHELLIN
PAPAVERINE STRAMONIUM
PENTOBARBITAL
ANTISTROPHE REVERT
COUNTERTURN
ANTITHESIS AND CONTRAST
ANTITHETICAL OPPOSITE
ANTITOXIN SERUM BIOLOGIC
ANTIVIVISECTIONIST BESTIARIAN
ANTIWAR (— GROUP) DOVES
ANTLER DAG HORN KNOB RIAL
TRAY DAGUE RIGHT ROYAL SHOOT
SPIKE BOSSET SHOVEL TROCHE
SPELLER DEERHORN SURROYAL
TROCHING
(— POINT) TROCHING
(BRANCH OF —) TINE PRONG
(PL.) HEAD ATTIRE
ANT LION LACEWING DOODLEBUG
NEUROPTERAN
ANTONINA (HUSBAND OF —)
BELISARIUS
ANTONY AND CLEOPATRA
(AUTHOR OF —) SHAKESPEARE
(CHARACTER IN —) EROS IRAS
MENAS PHILO ALEXAS ANTONY
GALLUS SCARUS SEXTUS SILIUS
TAURUS AGRIPPA LEPIDUS
MARDIAN OCTAVIA THYREUS
VARRIUS CANIDIUS CHARMIAN
DERCETAS DIOMEDES DOMITIUS
MECAENAS OCTAVIUS SELEUCUS
CLEOPATRA DEMETRIUS
DOLABELLA VENTIDIUS
EUPHRONIUS MENECRATES
PROCULEIUS
ANTONYM OPP OPPOSITE
ANTOTHIJAH (FATHER OF —)
JEROHAM
ANTSHRIKE BATARA
ANTSY EDGY FUSSY TENSE FIDGETY
ANT THRUSH PITTA
ANT TREE HORMIGO
ANUB (FATHER OF —) COZ
ANUS ASS ARSE BUNG VENT SIEGE
TEWEL
(PREF.) ANO PROCT(O)
(SUFF.) PROCTA
ANVIL BLOCK INCUS SNARL STAKE
STITH TEEST STETHY STITHY
ANDVILE ANFEELD BICKERN
BEAKIRON
(— SUPPORT) STOCK
(MINIATURE —) STAKE STUMP
(PREF.) INCUD(O)
ANXIETY HOW CARE CARK FEAR
FRAY PAIN ALARM ANGOR ANGST

DOUBT DREAD PANIC WORRY
KIAUGH NERVES PUCKER ANGUISH
CAUTION CHAGRIN CONCERN
SCRUPLE TENSION THOUGHT
TROUBLE DISQUIET SUSPENSE
SOLICITUDE
(— ABOUT HEALTH)
HYPOCHONDRIA
(EXTREME —) RACK
ANXIOUS AGOG BUSY FOND TOEY
EAGER FIRST UPSET AFRAID
UNEASY ANGUISH CAREFUL
CARKING EARNFUL FORWARD
TIDIOSE UNQUIET DESIROUS
RESTLESS THOUGHTY WATCHFUL
CONCERNED
ANY A AN AY AIR ALL ARY ONI ONY
AIRY EVER PART SOME WHAT
(— WHATEVER) ALL
(NOT —) NARY
ANYBODY ANY ONE ANYONE
SOMEONE
ANYHOW HOW NOHOW NOWAY
ALWAYS ANYWAY
ANYONE HE MAN ANYBODY
ANYTHING THAT AUGHT OUGHT
ANYWAY NOHOW ALWAYS
ANYWHERE EIHWER OWHERE
UBIQUE ANYPLACE
ANYWISE ANYHOW ANYWAY
ANYWAYS
AOUDAD ARUI UDAD AUDAD SHEEP
CHAMOIS
APACE FAST QUICK QUICKLY
RAPIDLY SPEEDILY
APACHE YUMA PADUCA CIBECUE
VAQUERO QUERECHO
MESCALERO
APAGOGE ABDUCTION
APAP EPIPHI
APAR APARA BOLITA MATACO
APART BY OFF AWAY BOUT ELSE
ALONE ALOOF AROOM ASIDE
RIVEN SOLUS SPLIT YTWYN ABREID
ATWAIN LONELY SUNDRY
ASUNDER ENISLED REMOVED
SEVERAL SEVERED SEPARATE
PIECEMEAL
(— FROM) BARRING
(TAKE —) UNRIG
(WIDE —) ASPAR
(WIDELY —) ABROAD
(PREF.) CHORI DI DICH
APARTMENT BUT PAD WON DIGS
FLAT HALL LOFT ROOM STEW
WENE WONE WOON ABODE
BOWER OECUS ORIEL ROOMS
SALON SOLAR SUITE ANDRON
CLOSET DECKER DINGLE DUPLEX
GROTTO LYCEUM SALOON SINGLE
SOLLAR SPENCE STANZA BUTTERY
CHAMBER COCKPIT GALLERY
MANSION PRIVACY BUILDING
EPHEBEUM SHOWROOM
SOLARIUM TENEMENT THALAMUS
MAISONETTE
(— FOR IDOL) TING
(— IN CASTLE) BOWER
(— IN CHURCH) SACRISTY
(— OF WARSHIP) COCKPIT
(BACHELOR —) GARCONNIERE
(OUTER —) BUT

(PRIVATE —) MAHAL PARADISE
(RENTED —) LET
(PL.) GYNAECEUM
APATHETIC CALM COLD COOL
DEAD DOWF DULL BLASE DOWFF
INERT STOIC GLASSY SUPINE
TORPID ADENOID PASSIVE
UNMOVED LISTLESS SLUGGISH
LETHARGIC PERFUNCTORY
APATHY SLOTH ACEDIA CAFARD
PHLEGM TORPOR LANGUOR
DOLDRUMS DULLNESS LETHARGY
OMISSION STOICISM STOLIDITY
(EXTREME —) STUPOR
APATITE IJOLITE MOROXITE
PHOSPHORITE
APAYAO ISNEG
APE KRA LAR PAN BOOR COPY DUPE
FOOL MAHA MIME MOCK SHAM
WILD BEROK CLOWN CRAZY
MAGOT MIMIC ORANG PONGO
PYGMY APELET BABOON GELADA
GIBBON LANGUR MARTEN MARTIN
MIRROR MONKEY OURANG
PARROT PONGID SIMIAN SIMIID
BUFFOON COPYCAT EMULATE
GORILLA IMITATE PORTRAY
PRIMATE SATYRUS SIAMANG
DURUKULI IMITATOR MANTEGAR
SIMULATE ORANGUTAN
(— STUDY) PITHECOLOGY
(GO —) FLIP FLIPOUT
(PREF.) PITHEC(O)
(SUFF.) PITHECUS
APEAK VERTICAL
APEIRON MATTER
APELIKE SIMIAN
APER BOAR MIME SNOB CLOWN
MOCKER BUFFOON COPYCAT
APERCU DIGEST GLANCE PRECIS
SKETCH INSIGHT OUTLINE
APERIENT LAX OPENER CASCARA
APERIODIC DEADBEAT
APERITIF KIR WHET CINZANO
DUBONNET
APERTURE F EYE GAP OPE VUE
BOLE BORE HOLE LEAK PASS
PORE RENT RIMA SLIT SLOT VENT
BREAK CHASM CLEFT CRACK
LIGHT MOUTH PUPIL STOMA
CUTOUT HIATUS KEYWAY LOUVER
WINDOW FISSURE KEYHOLE
OPENING ORIFICE OSTIOLE
PINHOLE PUNCTUM SWALLOW
TROMPIL APERTION FENESTRA
LOOPHOLE OVERTURE SPIRACLE
(— OF COROLLA) RICTUS
APEX EPI PIN TIP TOP ACME AUGE
CONE CUSP NOON PEAK RUFF
CREST HIGHT PITCH POINT SPIRE
APOGEE CLIMAX CRISIS CUPULA
GENION HEIGHT SUMMIT TITTLE
VERTEX ZENITH CACUMEN
EVEREST PAPILLA PUNCTUM
PINNACLE
(— OF HELMET) CREST
(— OF OBELISK) PYRAMIDION
(PREF.) APIC(O)
(SUFF.) ACE
APHAREUS (BROTHER OF —)
LEUCIPPUS
(FATHER OF —) PERIERES
(MOTHER OF —) GORGOPHONE

(SON OF —) IDAS LYNCEUS
(WIFE OF —) ARENE
APHASIA ALALIA ALEXIA JARGON
APHEMIA ASYMBOLIA
APHID APHIS LOUSE APTERA BLIGHT
COLLIER DIMERAN MIGRANS
PUCERON BLACKFLY GREENFLY
GYNOPARA HOMOPTER
APHIDAS (DAUGHTER OF —) ANTIA
(FATHER OF —) ARCAS
(MOTHER OF —) ERATO MEGANIRA
CHRYSOPELIA
(SON OF —) ALEUS
APHIS ANTCOW GREENFLY
APHORISM SAW ADAGE AXIOM
GNOME MAXIM MOTTO SUTRA
SUTTA CLICHE DICTUM SAYING
WISDOM EPIGRAM PRECEPT
PROVERB APOTHEGM PISHOGUE
APHORISTIC GNOMIC
APHRODISIAC DEWTRY DAMIANA
VENEREAL VENEREOUS
APHRODITE VENUS CYPRIS URANIA
ANTHEIA MYLITTA CYTHEREA
PANDEMOS
(FATHER OF —) ZEUS JUPITER
(HUSBAND OF —) VULCAN
(LOVER OF —) ARES
(MOTHER OF —) DIONE
(SON OF —) EROS CUPID AENEAS
APIARIST SKEPPIST
APIARY HIVE SKEP BEEYARD
BEEHOUSE
APICULTURE BEEKEEPING
APIECE UP ALL PER APOP EACH
SERIATIM
APIKORES BECORESH
APIO ARRACACH ARRACACHA
APIOS SOIA SOJA GLYCINE
APIS HAPI
(FATHER OF —) APOLLO
PHORONEUS
(MOTHER OF —) LAODICE
APISH SILLY FOPPISH AFFECTED
APITONG BAGAC HAPITON KERUING
APIUM UMBEL
APLENTY GALORE
APLITE HAPLITE
APLOMB TACT NERVE POISE
SURETY COOLNESS
APOCALYPSE DOOM SHOWING
REVELATION
APOCRISIARY RESPONSAL
APOCRYPHA (— BOOK) BEL EZRA
ABGAR ENOCH TOBIT BARUCH
DANIEL ESDRAS JUDITH AERAPHA
JUBILEES MANASSES MACCABEES
ECCLESIASTICUS
APOCRYPHAL SHAM FALSE
UNREAL DOUBTFUL FABULOUS
FICTIOUS
APODAL FOOTLESS
APODE EEL
APOGEE ACME APEX AUGE PEAK
CLIMAX ZENITH
APOGON AMIA CARDINAL
APOLLO SUN PAEAN DELIUS
AGYIEUS APOLLON LYKEIOS
PATROUS PHOEBUS PYTHIUS
CYNTHIUS PYTHAEUS
(FATHER OF —) ZEUS JUPITER
(MOTHER OF —) LETO LATONA
(SISTER OF —) DIANA ARTEMIS

APOLLYON DEVIL SATAN ABADDON
APOLOGETIC SORRY
APOLOGUE MYTH FABLE STORY
APOLOGY PARABLE ALLEGORY
APOLOGY PLEA ALIBI AMENDS
EXCUSE PARDON REGRET PRETEXT
SCRUPLE APOLOGIA
(INTERJECTION EXPRESSING —)
OOPS WOOPS
APOPHONY ABLAUT
APOPHYGE SCAPE ESCAPE
APOPLEXY ESCA SHOCK STROKE
POPLESIE
APOSTASY FALL LAPSE
APOSTATE RAT LAPSED CONVERT
HERETIC PERVERT SECEDER
DEFECTOR DESERTER DISLOYAL
RECREANT RENEGADE TURNCOAT
APOSTATIZE DESERT
APOSTLE ESCAPE TEACHER
DISCIPLE FOLLOWER PREACHER
(BIBLICAL —) JOHN JUDE LEVI PAUL
DENIS JAMES JUDAS PETER SIMON
ANDREW PHILIP THOMAS DIDYMUS
MATTHEW BARNABAS MATTHIAS
APOSTLE BIRD CATBIRD
APOSTROPHE TUISM TURNWAY
TURNTALE
APOTHECARY CHEMIC SPICER
CHEMICK DRUGGIST
APOTHECIUM CUP PELTA TRICA
SHIELD ARDELLA LIRELLA PATELLA
APOTHEGM SAW DICT ADAGE
AXIOM GNOME MAXIM SUTRA
DICTUM SAYING SUTTAH PROVERB
APHORISM SENTENCE
APOTHEOSIS DEIFICATION
CONSECRATION
APOTHEOSIZE DEIFY EXALT
ELEVATE GLORIFY CANONIZE
APPAIM (FATHER OF —) NADAB
APPALL STUN APPAL DAUNT SHOCK
DISMAY REDUCE REVOLT WEAKEN
ASTOUND DEPRESS DISGUST
DISMISS HORRIFY PETRIFY
TERRIFY AFFRIGHT ASTONISH
ENFEEBLE FRIGHTEN OVERCOME
APPALLING AWFUL AWESOME
FEARFUL TERRIBLE TERRIFIC
APPANAGE GRANT ADJUNCT
APANAGE
APPARATUS AID BOX GUN LOG SET
ADON DRAG ETNA FAKE GEAR GRIP
HECK HELM LAMP LIFT STOW TIRE
TOOL BURET GANCH HOIST HORSE
LEECH RELAY SCUBA SHEAR SIREN
SONAR SPRAY STILL STOVE SWING
BUDDLE BUFFER COILER COOKER
DEVICE DINGUS ENGINE FEEDER
FILTER FOGGER GADGET GEYSER
GRAITH LADDER LIFTER MILKER
ORRERY OUTFIT REFLUX RUDDER
SEESAW SHEARS SMOKER
SMUDGE TACKLE TIPPLE TREMIE
TROMPE AERATOR AIRBATH
ALEMBIC APPAREL AUTOMAT
BAGGAGE BALANCE BASCULE
BURETTE DERRICK ECHELON
FURNACE GASOGEN GRILLER
HOISTER INHALER ISOTRON
MACHINE MEGAFOG PINCERS
PRESSER SOUNDER SOXHLET
SPRAYER STEAMER STIRRER

TELEPIX TREMOLO TRIMMER
UTENSIL AGITATOR AQUALUNG
BLOWDOWN CALUTRON
CONVEYER CONVEYOR CRYOSTAT
DIALYZER DIAPHOTE DIGESTER
DRENCHER DUMBBELL EOLIPILE
EQUIPAGE ERGOSTAT GASIFIER
GAZOGENE INJECTOR ISOSCOPE
JACQUARD OSMOGENE OZONIZER
PULMOTOR PURIFIER RECORDER
REDUCTOR REHEATER SCRUBBER
SOFTENER STRIPPER HANGLIDER
ABSORPTIOMETER
(— IN STOMACH OF LOBSTER)
LADY
(SEGMENTAL —) BRAINSTEM
(SWIMMING —) SCUBA
(SUFF.) STAT(IC)(ICS)
APPAREL DECK FARE GARB GEAR
ROBE SECT TIRE WEAR WEDE
ADORN ARRAY BESEE CLOTH
DRESS EQUIP HABIT MITER TUNIC
ATTIRE CLOTHE GRAITH INFULA
OUTFIT PARURE ROBING CLOBBER
COSTUME FURNISH GARMENT
HARNESS PREPARE RAIMENT
VESTURE CLOTHING FOOTWEAR
HEADWEAR WARDROBE
(ECCLESIASTIC —) FANON ORALE
MANIPLE CHASUBLE CORPORAL
(HEAD —) MILLINERY
(MILITARY —) WARENTMENT
(MOURNING —) WEEDS
(RICH —) ARRAY
APPARENT OPEN BREEM BREME
CLEAR OVERT PLAIN FORMAL
PARENT PATENT PHANIC CERTAIN
EVIDENT GLARING OBVIOUS
SEEMING SHALLOW VISIBLE
DISTINCT ILLUSORY MANIFEST
PALPABLE PROBABLE SEMBLANT
SEMBLABLE OSTENSIBLE
APPARENTLY
(PREF.) QUASI
APPARITION HUE HANT SHOW
DREAM FANCY FETCH GHOST
HAUNT IMAGE LARVA PHASM
SHADE SHAPE SPOOK ASPECT
DOUBLE IDOLUM SOWLTH SPIRIT
SPRITE STOUND SWARTH TAISCH
THURSE VISION WRAITH DISPLAY
EIDOLON FANTASY FEATURE
PHANTOM SPECTER SPECTRE
EPIPHANY ILLUSION PHANTASM
PRESENCE REVENANT SPECTRUM
SEMBLANCE
APPARITOR BEADLE PARURE
PARITOR SUMMONER
APPEAL ASK BEG BID CRY CALL
CASE PLEA SEEK SUIT APPLY
CHARM CLEPE REFER SPEAK
ACCUSE ADJURE AVOUCH INVOKE
PRAYER SUMMON ADDRESS
CONJURE ENTREAT IMPLORE
REQUEST SOLICIT APPROACH
ENTREATY PETITION ADJURATION
(— FOR CONTRIBUTIONS) WHIP
(— FOR HELP) SOS
(— FOR QUARTER) KAMERAD
(— TO) APPLY AVOUCH INVOKE
ARRAIGN
(SEX —) IT OOMPH
(SOLEMN —) OATH

APPEALING CUTE NICE CATCHY
CLEVER NELLOW CUNNING
SUGARED PLEASANT
(STRIKINGLY —) ZINGY
APPEAR BID CAR EYE GET COME
DAWN FARE LOOK LOOM MAKE
MEET PEER REAR RISE SEEM WALK
ARISE ENTER ISSUE KITHE KYTHE
OCCUR SOUND THINK ARRIVE
BESEEM EMERGE INFORM
REGARD SPRING BLOSSOM
COMPEAR DEVELOP OUTCROP
RESEMBLE
(— ABOVE GROUND) BREER
BRAIRD
(— AND DISAPPEAR) COOK
(— BETTER) GAIN
(— BRIEFLY) GLINT
(— DIRECTLY BEFORE) AFFRONT
(— FAINTLY) GLIMMER
(— SUDDENLY) BURST
(— UNEXPECTEDLY) BLOOM
IRRUPT
(PREF.) PHANER(O) PHANTA
PHANTO
APPEARANCE AIR CUT HUE CAST
FARE FORM GARB IDEA LATE LEEN
LOOK MIEN SHOW VIEW BLUSH
COLOR EIDOS FAVOR FRONT
GUISE HABIT LOOKS PHASE
PHASM SHAPE SIGHT SOUND
SPICE ASPECT EFFECT FACIES
FAVOUR MANNER OBJECT OSTENT
REGARD VISAGE ARRIVAL DISPLAY
FARRAND FASHION FEATURE
GLIMPSE OUTSIDE RESPECT
SHOWING SPECIES ARTEFACT
ARTIFACT EPIPHANY ILLUSION
LIKENESS PRESENCE PRETENSE
SEMBLANCE
(— OF LIGHT ON HAIR) HAG
(BRILLANT —) SHINE
(CLOUDED —) HAZE CHILL
(CONSPICUOUS —) FIGURE
(DISTINCTIVE —) AURA
(FIRST —) DAWN DEBUT SPRING
(GENERAL —) RIG
(GUEST —) CAMEO
(IMPOVERISHED —) BEGGARY
(MERE —) INTENTIONAL
(MOCK —) SIMULACRUM
(MOTTLED —) ROE DAPPLE
(MOTTLED SKY —) BLINK
(OF NEAT —) PREPPY PREPPIE
(OUTWARD —) FACE SEEM SHOW
FACADE APPAREL BALLOON
SEEMING SURFACE
(PERSONAL —) PRESENCE
(SERIES OF —S) ROAD
(STRIPED —) ROE
(SUPERNATURAL —) APPARITION
(SURFACE —) TOUR BLOOM
(UNGAINLY —) ANGULARITY
(VAGUE —) BLUR
(PREF.) SPECTRO
(SUFF.) OPSIA OPSIO OPSIS OPSY
PHANE PHANOUS PHANT PHANY
APPEASE LAY PAY CALM EASE
HUSH SATE ALLAY ALONE ATONE
MEASE PEACE PEASE QUIET SLAKE
STILL DEFRAY GENTLE MEEKEN
MODIFY PACIFY PLEASE SOFTEN
SOOTHE ASSUAGE CONTENT

DULCIFY GRATIFY MOLLIFY
PLACATE SATISFY STICKLE SUFFICE
SWEETEN MITIGATE PROPITIATE
(— APPETITE) STAY
APPEASEMENT MUNICHISM
APPELLATION NAME TERM GODDY
STYLE TITLE APPEAL CALLING
EPITHET GOODMAN SURNAME
COGNOMEN METRONYM
NICKNAME
APPEND ADD PIN TAG CLIP HANG
JOIN TACK AFFIX ANNEX ADJOIN
ATTACH FASTEN AUGMENT
POSTFIX SUBJOIN
APPENDAGE ARM AWN FIN LEG
TAB TAG ARIL BARB CAUD FLAP
HOOK HORN LIMB LOBE SPUR TAIL
AFFIX BEARD CAUDA CERAS EXITE
RIDER SCALE TROLL WHISK
CERCUS CIRRUS CORONA ELATER
ENDITE LAGENA LIGULE PALPUS
PAPPUS STIPEL STYLET SUFFIX
UROPOD ADJUNCT ANTENNA
AURICLE CODICIL EARLOBE
EMBLAST FIXTURE FURCULA
GONOPOD HOUSING MALELLA
PENDANT STIPULE SWIMMER
THIMBLE TRAILER WINGLET
ADDITION ADHERENT ASCIDIUM
BRACHIUM EMPODIUM FILAMENT
GNATHITE PEDIPALP PENDICLE
PHYLLOID PREDELLA RHABDITE
SYNTROPE MAXILLIPED
(— ON MOCCASIN) TRAILER
(EAR-SHAPED —) AURICLE
(PL.) ADNEXA ANNEXA FORCEPS
APPENDIX EKE ANNEX LABEL
APPEND VERMIX AURICLE CODICIL
PENDANT ADDENDUM AURICULA
EPILOGUE
APPERCEPTION RECOGNITION
APPERTAIN LIE FALL REFER
BELONG EFFEIR RELATE CONCERN
PERTAIN
APPETITE MAW YEN LUST PICA
TUCK URGE WILL ZEST BELLY
BLOOD GORGE GREED GUSTO
TASTE TWIST BULIMY DESIRE
FAMINE GENIUS GODOWN
HUNGER LIKING OREXIS RELISH
STROKE TALENT BULIMIA CRAVING
EDACITY LONGING PASSION
STOMACH SWALLOW WANTING
CUPIDITY FONDNESS GULOSITY
TENDENCY
(— LOSS) ANOREXIA
(ANIMAL —) BLOOD
(CANINE —) PHAGEDENA
(EXCESSIVE —) LIMOSIS GULOSITY
POLYPHAGIA
(PERVERTED —) MALACIA
(RAVENOUS —) LIMOSIS
(SUFF.) OREXIA PHIL(A)(AE)(E)(IA)
(ISM)(IST)(OUS)(US)
APPETIZER WET WHET SAUCE
CANAPE RAMAKI RELISH RUMAKI
SAVORY CEVICHE SASHIMI
APERITIF COCKTAIL DUBONNET
(CHICKEN LIVER —) RUMAKI
APPETIZING NICE GUSTY SAVORY
GUSTFUL GUSTABLE PALATABLE
APPLAUD HUM CLAP LAUD RISE
ROOT RUFF CHEER EXTOL HUZZA

PRAISE ACCLAIM APPROVE
COMMENT ENDORSE HOSANNA
PLAUDIT
(GROUP HIRED TO —) CLAQUE
APPLAUDER
(PL.) CLAQUE
APPLAUSE CLAP HAND BRAVO
CHEER ECLAT HUZZA SALVO
HURRAH PRAISE ACCLAIM
OVATION CLAPPING
(— WITH THE FEET) RUFF
APPLE MAC PIP CRAB OHIA POME
COPEI JAMBO BEEFIN BIFFIN
CODLIN DOUCIN ESOPUS GOLDIN
KARELA KAVIKA MACUPA MAKOPA
PIPPIN PUFFIN RENNET RUSSET
BALDWIN BEAUFIN CODLING
COSTARD FAMEUSE GOLDING
PEELING POMEROY RAMBURE
RIBSTON RUDDOCK WAGENER
WEALTHY WINESAP AMPALAYA
COCCAGEE CORTLAND GREENING
JONATHAN MCINTOSH NONESUCH
PARADISE PEARMAIN POMANDER
POROPORO QUEENING REINETTE
ROSACEAN SWEETING WHITSOUR
QUARENDEN QUARANTINE
(— OF PERU) JIMSON JIMPSON
SHOOFLY
(— OF THE EYE) PUPIL
(BITTER —) COLOCYNTH
(CRAB —) CRAB SCRAB WHARRE
POWITCH
(CRUSHED —) POMACE
(EMU —) COLANE
(GOLDEN —) BEL BAEL
(LIKE AN —) POMACEOUS
(PEARLIKE —) SORB
(PEELED —) DUMPLING
(SHRIVELED —) CRUMPLING
(SLICED DRIED —S) SNITS SNITZ
SCHNITZ
(SMALL —) CODLIN CODLING
(SMALL —S) GRIGGLES
(STUNTED —) SCRUNT
(THORN —) MAD METEL
(PREF.) POMI POMO
APPLEBERRY DUMPLING
APPLEJOHN DEUSAN DEUZAN
APPLE-POLISH BROWNNOSE
APPLIANCE GEAR GRAB IRON TOOL
BRACE CLAMP DEVIL FLIER FLYER
GLODE SHADE BONNET BREWER
DEVICE ENGINE FABRIC GADGET
GAITER JUICER SPLINT WINDLE
CHARGER MACHINE SCRAPER
STOPPER UTENSIL BALANCER
DEVIATOR
(PL.) FURNITURE
APPLICABLE APT FIT MEET PROPER
USEFUL FITTING PLIABLE APPOSITE
RELATIVE RELEVANT SUITABLE
(STRICTLY —) PROPER
(UNIVERSALLY —) CATHOLIC
(WIDELY —) BROAD
APPLICANT PROSPECT
APPLICATION USE DAUB FORM
BLANK TOPIC APPEAL EFFORT
ADDRESS EPITHEM REQUEST
EPITHEME LENITIVE PETITION
PRACTICE SEDULITY
(— OF KNOWLEDGE) PRACTICE
PRACTISE

(— OF TESTS) DOCIMASY
(— OF THE MIND) STUDY
(— TO WRONG PURPOSE) ABUSE
(MEDICINAL —) PLASTER DRESSING
FRONTING LENITIVE
(MENTAL —) INTENTION
APPLICATOR COLPOSTAT
APPLIED (CLOSELY —) ACCUMBENT
(PREF.) TECHNO
APPLIQUE DAG DAGGE ATTACH
DESIGN ORNAMENT
APPLY ASK LAY PLY PUT RUB SET
USE BEAR BEND CLAP DAUB GIVE
HOLD MOVE SEEK TOIL TURN
WORK ADAPT GRIND IMPLY LABOR
LIKEN REFER SMEAR ADDICT
APPEAL APPOSE BESTOW BETAKE
BUCKLE COMPLY DEVOTE DIRECT
EMPLOY EXTEND RESORT ADHIBIT
COMPARE CONFORM IMPRESS
OVERLAY PERTAIN REQUEST
SOLICIT UTILIZE DEDICATE
DISPENSE MINISTER PETITION
(— BRAKE) BUR
(— COSMETICS) DO POP
(— GRAPHITE) BLACKLEAD
(— GREASE) ARM
(— HOT CLOTHS) FOMENT
(— IMPROPERLY) ABUSE
(— ONESELF) ATTEND INTEND
MUCKLE ADDRESS
(— PIGMENT) DRAG
(— TO) CONSULT CONTACT
APPOGGIATURA BACKFALL
ACCIACCATURA
(DOUBLE —) FALL
APPOINT ARM FIX SET CALL DECK
GIVE MAKE NAME ALLOT ARRAY
AWARD COOPT CREST DIGHT
ELECT ENACT EQUIP INSET PITCH
PLACE POINT SHAPE SLATE
ASSIGN ASSIZE ATTACH CREATE
DECREE DEPUTE DETAIL DEVISE
DIRECT ENTAIL ORDAIN OUTFIT
SETTLE STEVEN TAILYE ARRAIGN
CONFIRM DESTINE DISPOSE
FURNISH GAZETTE RESOLVE
TAILZIE DELEGATE DEPUTIZE
INDICATE NOMINATE ORDINATE
(— A CLERIC) COLLATE
(— BEFOREHAND) STALL
(— TO BENEFICE) PRESENT
APPOINTED DUE DATIVE
APPOINTEE PLACEMAN
APPOINTMENT SET DATE BERTH
ORDER TRYST BILLET OFFICE
STEVEN COMMAND STATION
CREATION DELEGACY POSITION
(— OF HEIR) INSTITUTION
APPORTION LOT DEAL DOLE MARK
METE PART RATE ALLOT AWARD
CAVEL GRANT PARAL SHARE SHIFT
WEIGH APPLOT ASSESS ASSIGN
DIVIDE PARCEL RATION TAVERN
ARRANGE BALANCE QUARTER
ALLOCATE DESCRIBE ADMEASURE
PROPORTION
APPORTIONMENT DIVISION
APPOSITE APT PAT COGENT TIMELY
GERMANE INCIDENT RELATIVE
RELEVANT SUITABLE
APPRAISAL APPRIZAL

APPRAISE GAGE LOVE METE RATE
ASSAY GAUGE JUDGE PRICE PRIZE
VALUE ASSESS ESTEEM EVALUE
PONDER PRAISE SIZEUP SURVEY
ADJUDGE ANALYZE COMMEND
ESTIMATE EVALUATE
APPRECIABLE ANY SENSIBLE
PERCEPTIBLE
APPRECIATE DIG FEEL LOVE JUDGE
PRIZE RAISE SAVOR TASTE VALUE
ADMIRE ESTEEM SAVOUR
ADVANCE APPRIZE APPROVE
CHERISH REALIZE INCREASE
TREASURE
APPRECIATION EYE GUSTO SENSE
CONCEIT PERCEPTION
APPRECIATIVE AWAKE GRATEFUL
(— OF BEAUTY) ESTHETIC
AESTHETIC
APPREHEND COP GET LAG NAB SEE
FEAR HEAR KNOW NOTE SCAN
TAKE VIEW CATCH DREAD GRASP
GRIPE INTUE SEIZE ARREST
BEHOLD DETAIN INTEND INTUIT
BELIEVE CAPTURE CONCEIT
ENDOUTE FORESEE IMAGINE
REALIZE RECEIVE SENSATE
SUPPOSE CONCEIVE DISCOVER
OVERTAKE PERCEIVE
APPREHENDED GRIPPIT
APPREHENSIBLE NOETIC SENSATE
SENSIBLE
APPREHENSION CARE FEAR FRAY
PAIN PANG SCAN WERE ALARM
DOUBT DREAD FANCY WORRY
ARREST DISMAY NOESIS ANXIETY
CAPTURE CONCERN PRESAGE
SUSPECT DISTRUST MISTRUST
SUSPENSE COGNITION
PREHENSION
APPREHENSIVE APT ANTSY JUMPY
FEARED MORBID ANXIOUS
FEARFUL JEALOUS NERVOUS
STREAKY UPTIGHT DOUBTFUL
SOLICITOUS
APPRENTICE CUB BIND BOOT SNOB
TYRO CADET DEVIL BURSCH
HELPER JOCKEY NOVICE
BANKMAN GROMMET LEARNER
TRAINEE WAISTER APRENDIZ
BEGINNER JACKAROO PRENTICE
SERVITOR TURNOVER
(— ON SHIP) BRASSBOUNDER
(LONDON —) FLATCAP
(SHOEMAKER'S —) SNOB
APPRENTICESHIP SERVITUDE
APPRISE WARN LEARN TEACH
ADVISE INFORM NOTIFY REVEAL
APPRIZE ACQUAINT DISCLOSE
INSTRUCT
APPROACH TRY ADIT BUMP BURN
CHAT COME COST DRAW NEAR
NERE NIGH ROAD ABORD BOARD
CLOSE COAST ESSAY STALK VERGE
ACCEDE ACCESS ACCOST ADVENT
ANIMUS APPEAL BORDER BREAST
BROACH COMING GATHER
GONEAR IMPEND PROACH TRENCH
ADVANCE AGGRESS APPULSE
CONTACT PREFACE SEAGATE
SUCCEED CONVERGE NEIGHBOR
ONCOMING

(— FROM WINDWARD) BEAR
(— GAME) DRAW
(— HOSTILELY) SWAY
(— NEAR) TOUCH
(— OF DEATH) FIT
(— OF NIGHT) FALL
(— TENDENCY) ADIENCE
(GOLF —) SHIPSHOT
(INDIRECT —) FEELER
(INVITING —) PASS
APPROACHABLE COMMON
AFFABLE ACCESSIBLE
APPROACHING LIKE COMING
TOWARD ONCOMING
APPROBATION TEST FAVOR PROOF
TRIAL ASSENT FAVOUR LOANGE
PRAISE REGARD REPUTE PLAUDIT
APPLAUSE APPROVAL SANCTION
APPROPPRIATELY APROPOS
APPROPRIATE ADD APT DUE FIT
LAY PAT AKIN CRIB FEAT GOOD
GRAB GRIP HELP JUST MEET SINK
SUIT TAKE ALLOT ANNEX FITTY
HAPPY RIGHT STEAL USURP
ASSELF ASSIGN ASSUME BORROW
DECENT DEVOTE DEVOUR DIGEST
GATHER GENTIL KINDLY PILFER
PIRATE POCKET PROPER TIMELY
WORTHY APPROVE APROPOS
CABBAGE CONDIGN CONVERT
FITTING GERMANE GRABBLE
GRADELY IMPOUND PREEMPT
PURLOIN RELATED SECRETE
SWALLOW ACCROACH APPOSITE
ARROGATE BECOMING DESERVED
EMBEZZLE GRACEFUL HANDSOME
IDONEOUS PECULIAR PROPERTY
RELEVANT RIGHTFUL SUITABLE
(— UNLAWFULLY) HEIST STEAL
(MOST —) CHOICE
APPROPRIATED ASSUMED
PECULIAR
APPROPRIATENESS APTNESS
DECENCY FITNESS APTITUDE
(NICE —) ELEGANCE
APPROPRIATION FUND VOTE
DEVOTION
(FRAUDULENT —) CON
EMBEZZLEMENT
APPROVAL AMEN ECLAT ASSENT
ESTEEM APPROOF CONSENT
PLAUDIT SUPPORT APPLAUSE
BLESSING SANCTION SUFFRAGE
AGREEMENT
(EXPRESSION OF —) VOILA
(FLIGHT —) AOK
APPROVE DO OK BUY DIG TRY
AMEN HAVE LIKE OKAY OKEH PASS
TEST VOTE ALLOW BLESS CLEAR
FAVOR PROVE VALUE ACCEPT
ADMIRE BISHOP CONCUR RATIFY
AGREEON APPLAUD CERTIFY
COMMEND CONFIRM CONSENT
ENDORSE EXHIBIT INDORSE
SUPPORT ACCREDIT MANIFEST
SANCTION
APPROVED TRYE EXPERT PROBAL
ACCEPTED ORTHODOX
(NOT —) OUT
APPROVING HEARTY
APPROXIMATE NEAR ABOUT CIRCA
CLOSE COAST ROUGH COARSE

GENERAL NOMINAL APPROACH ESTIMATE
APPROXIMATELY SAY AWAY GAIN MUCH NIGH SOME ABOUT CIRCA ALMOST AROUND NEARLY TOWARD CRUDELY ROUGHLY
APPROXIMATING COMPARATIVE
APPROXIMATION CIRCA COUNTERFEIT
APPURTENANCE GEAR ANNEX ASSIGN EFFEIR ADJUNCT COMFORT APPANAGE PENDICLE
(PL.) ADDENDA
APRICOT COT UME ANSU MUME ABRICOCK BLENHEIM
(DRIED —S) MEBOS MEEBOS
A PRIORI PURE
APRON BIB CAP BASE BOOT BRAT DICK RAMP SLOP TAYO TIER COVER EPHOD BARVEL BISHOP CANVAS DAIDLE DICKEY NAPRON RUNWAY SHIELD TARMAC TOUSER BRATTLE CANVASS DAIDLIE GREMIAL TABLIER LAMBSKIN PINAFORE PRASKEEN BARMCLOTH
(— OF FURNITURE) PETTICOAT
(— OF SEAT) FALL
(CHILD'S —) TIER BISWOP SLIPPER
(LEATHER —) DICK DICKY BARVEL DICKEY BARMFEL BARVELL BARMSKIN
(MASON'S —) LAMBSKIN
(SILKEN —) GREMIAL
(PL.) ARMITAS
APROPOS APT FIT PAT MEET TIMELY RELEVANT SUITABLE
APSE BEMA APSIS NICHE CHEVET CONCHA EXEDRA RECESS EXHEDRA PROTHESIS
APSIS APSE AUGE
APSYRTUS (FATHER OF —) AEETES
(MOTHER OF —) IDYIA ASTERODIA
(SISTER OF —) MEDEA
APT FIT PAT YAP ABLE DEFT FAIN FEAT GLEG KEEN VAIN WONT ADEPT ALERT HAPPY PRONE QUICK READY ASPERT CLEVER DOCILE KITTLE LIABLE LIKELY PRETTY SUITED TOWARD APROPOS CAPABLE FITTING IDONEAL WILLING APPOSITE DEXTROUS DISPOSED HANDSOME IDONEOUS INCLINED POIGNANT PRACTIVE PREPARED SKILLFUL SUITABLE
(— TO CHANGE) LABILE
(— TO TURN) WALT
APTERYX KIWI RATITE KIVIKIVI KIWIKIWI
APTITUDE ART BENT GIFT HEAD TURN CRAFT FLAIR HABIT KNACK SKILL VERVE GENIUS TALENT ABILITY CONDUCT FACULTY FITNESS LEANING CAPACITY INSTINCT TENDENCY
APTLY PAT
APTNESS GIFT KNACK SKILL APTITUDE FELICITY
APUS CYPSELUS MICROPUS
AQUARIUS SKINKER
AQUATIC (RARE —) MONKSEAL
AQUEDUCT AQUA DUCT CANAL AQUAGE SPECUS

CHANNEL CONDUIT PASSAGE
(— OF SILVIUS) ITER
AQUEOUS HYDATOID WATERISH
AQUILA (WIFE OF —) PRISCILLA
AQUILANT (BROTHER OF —) GRYPHON
ARA MACAW
(FATHER OF —) JETHER
ARAB AHL AUS IBAD OMAN SLEB WAIF ARABY GAMIN NOMAD SAUDI TATAR SEMITE SLUBBI URCHIN ARABIAN BEDOUIN SARACEN SOLUBBI AZZAZAME KABABISH LARRIKIN SLOUBBIE YEMENITE
ARABELLA (CHARACTER IN —) MATTEO ZDENKA WALDNER ARABELLA MANDRYKA
(COMPOSER OF —) STRAUSS
ARABESQUE ORNATE MORISCO

ARABIA

COIN: LARI CARAT DINAR KABIK RIYAL
DESERT: NYD ANKAF DEHNA NAFUD NEFUD
DISTRICT: ASIR
GARMENT: ABA HAIK CABAAN BURNOUS
GODDESS: ALLAT
HOLY CITY: MECCA MEDINA
HOLY LAND: HEJAZ
ISLAND: SOCOTRA
JUDGE: CADI
KINGDOM: NEJD
MEASURE: DEN SAA FERK KIST ACHIR RARID CABDA CAFIZ COVID CUDDY MAKUK QASAB TEMAN WOIBE ZUDDA ARTABA ASSBAA COVIDO FEDDAN GARIBA GHALVA CAPHITE FARSAKH FARSANG KILADJA MARHALE NUSFIAH
MOUNTAIN: NEBO HOREB SINAI
PORT: ADEN
RULER: AMIR EMIR AMEER EMFER
STATE: ASIR OMAN YEMEN KUWAIT
TOWN: ABHA ADEN BEDA BERA HAIL RIAD SANA TAIF DUBAI HAUTA HOFUF JIDDA MECCA MOCHA QATIF TAIZZ YENBO ANAIZA MANAMA MATRAH MEDINA RIYADH SALALA SHAQRA BURAIDA HODEIDA MUKALLA ONEIZAH SHARJAH
TRIBE: AUS ASIR IRAD TEMA KEDAR DIENDEL SHUKRIA
WEIGHT: ROTL BAHAR CHEKI KELLA MAUND NASCH NEVAT OCQUE OUKIA RATEL TOMAN VAKIA BOKARD DIRHEM MISKAL FARSALAH

ARABIC CARSHUNI GARSHUNI KARSHUNI THAMUDIC
(— ALPHABET) BA FA HA RA TA YA ZA AYN DAD DAL JIM KAF KHA LAM MIM NUN QAF SAD SIN THA WAW ZAY ALIF DHAL SHIN GHAYN
ARABLE FERTILE PLOWABLE TILLABLE
ARACHNID CRAB MITE TICK TAINT ACARID ACARUS CARTER SPIDER CARTARE OCTOPOD PEDIPALP

SCORPION SOLPUGID PSEUDOSCORPION
ARACHNOID KINGCRAB
ARAD (FATHER OF —) BERIAH
ARAGONITE ALABASTER
ARAIN ARRAND
ARAKANESE MAGHI
ARAM (FATHER OF —) ESROM HEZRON KEMUEL SHAMER
ARAMAIC SYRIAC MANDAEAN
(— TRANSLATION) TARGUM
ARAN (BROTHER OF —) UZ
(FATHER OF —) DISHAN
ARANEA EPEIRA
ARAPAIMA PIRARUCU
ARAPONGA BELLBIRD
ARAROBA ZEBRAWOOD
ARAROS (FATHER OF —) ARISTOPHANES
ARAUCANIAN AUCA PAMPA MAPOCHE MOLUCHE PAMPERO PICUNCHE
ARAWA AOTEA MATATUA
ARAWAK ARUA BARE URAN ARAUA BAURE CAMPA CHANE GUANA INERI SIUSI BAINOA BANIVA GUINAU IGNERI GOAJIRO IPURINA CAQUETIO CUSTENAU
ARBALEST BALISTER CROSSBOW
ARBITER REF UMP JUDGE CRITIC ODDMAN UMPIRE ADVISER DAYSMAN ODDSMAN OVERMAN REFEREE DICTATOR STICKLER
ARBITRAGE SHUNTING
ARBITRARY SEVERE THETIC WILLFUL ABSOLUTE DESPOTIC MASTERLY
(NOT —) FREE
ARBITRATE DECIDE MEDIATE
ARBITRATION DAYMENT
ARBITRATOR ARB REF JUDGE UMPIRE ARBITER MUNSIFF REFEREE MEDIATOR
ARBOR BAR AXLE BEAM ABODE BOWER SHAFT STAFF STALK TRAIL ARBOUR BOWERY GARDEN HERBER PANDAL RAMADA VOIDER BERCEAU HARBOUR MANDREL MANDRIL ORCHARD PERGOLA RETREAT SPINDLE TRELLIS FRESCADE TONNELLE
ARBORVITAE AKEKI ALERCE
ARBUTUS IVY MAYFLOWER
ARC BOW ARCH BEND FOIL HALO CURVE HANCE ORBIT SPARK SWING FOGBOW FOLIUM OCTANT RADIAN COMPASS RAINBOW FROSTBOW
(— OF HORIZON) AZIMUTH AMPLITUDE
(ELECTRIC —) SPARK
ARCA BOX CHEST PATEN ARCULA
ARCADE ORB AVENUE LOGGIA STREET GALLERY PORTICO ARCATURE CLOISTER
ARCADIAN CAJUN
ARCANE RUNIC HIDDEN SECRET MYSTERIOUS
ARCAS (FATHER OF —) ZEUS JUPITER
(MOTHER OF —) CALLISTO
ARCESIUS (FATHER OF —) ZEUS JUPITER CEPHALUS

(MOTHER OF —) PROCRIS EURYODIA
(SON OF —) LAERTES
ARCH ARC BOW COY SET SLY BACK BEND COPE COVE DOME HARP HOOP IRIS LEER OGEE PASS PEND PERT SPAN ARCUS CHIEF CURVE FAULD GREAT HANCE HUNCH INBOW JOWEL OGIVE PAUKY PAWKY POKEY PRIME ROACH SAUCY SWEEP VAULT ARCADE BRIDGE CALCAR CAMBER CLEVER DIADEM FOGBOW FORNIX GIRDLE IMPISH INVERT LANCET MANTEL SPRING SUNBOW WICKET ZYGOMA ARCHWAY CONCAVE CUNNING EMINENT GATEWAY ROGUISH SEGMENT SQUINCH SUPPORT TESTUDO TRIUMPH WAGGISH ALVEOLAR ESPIEGLE FOGEATER OVERCAST SCUNCHEON
(— OF FIREPLACE) MANTEL MANTELTREE
(— OF SKY) FIRMAMENT
(— OF WATER) CURL TUBE TUNNEL
(DENTAL —) ARCADE
(LOGGING —) SULKY
(PART OF —) PIER CHORD IMPOST PILLAR ABUTMENT EXTRADOS INTRADOS KEYSTONE SKEWBACK SPANDREL SPRINGER VOUSSOIR
(POINTED —) OGIVE
(PL.) SUBARARCUATION
ARCHAEOCYTE SORITE
ARCHAEOLOGIST POTHUNTER PREHISTORIAN
AMERICAN CLAY LOVE DAVIS EVANS HAWES SHEAR SOREN BARBER BUTLER GLUECK GORDON GORMAN HAYNES HEWETT HOLMES KIDDER MORELY PARKER PORTER SNYDER SQUIER MERRIAM NUTTALL REISNER SAVILLE SPEISER ALBRIGHT BREASTED CUMMINGS HANFMANN ROBINSON STERRETT THOMPSON BANDELIER CARPENTER MOOREHEAD RICHARDSON FROTHINGHAM
AUSTRALIAN CHILDE
AUSTRIAN ARNETH STUDNICZKA
CANADIAN CURRELLY
CZECH HROZNY
DANISH ZOEGA MULLER POULSEN WORSAAE BRONDSTED MATHIASSEN STEENSTRUP
DUTCH GRUYTERE
ENGLISH BELL COOK GANN GELL HALL BIBBY BUDGE EVANS RYMER STEIN CARTER CHILDE LAYARD MURRAY NEWTON PETRIE WARREN BEAZLEY BRAYLEY BURROWS DAWKINS DODWELL FELLOWS GARDNER HERBERT HOGARTH PENROSE WHEELER WOOLLEY GARSTANG HAMILTON LAWRENCE MALLOWAN RIDGEWAY STEPHENS THOMPSON BABINGTON
FRENCH LEBAS MAURY PUGIN VOGUE BORDES BREUIL CAGNAT CHOISY CLARAC COCHET FORBIN GAIDOZ LARTET MORGAN PERROT SAULCY BABELON CHANTRE

CHARNAY DELATRE HOMOLLE LEBLANT PEIRESC POTTIER BERTRAND DIEULAFOY LENORMANT DECHELETTE QUATREMERE WADDINGTON LECHEVALIER **GERMAN** MAU ROSS TREU ADLER BRAUN BRUNN CONZE SARRE ANDRAE BECKER HELBIG HILLER MULLER NISSEN SCHOLL CURTIUS GERHARD LASAULX WELCKER WIEGAND BENNDORF BOTTIGER KOLDEWEY KOSSINNA PETERSEN ESSENWEIN LOESCHCKE MICHAELIS SCHLIEMANN FURTWANGLER WINCKELMANN **GREEK** TSOUNTAS **ICELANDIC** MAGNUSSON **IRISH** STOKES ODONOVAN MACALISTER **ISRAELI** YADIN SUKENIK **ITALIAN** BONI LANZI ROSSI CANINA CESNOLA FIORELLI LANCIANI MARUCCHI VISCONTI **POLISH** MICHALOWSKI **RUSSIAN** KOPPEN POGODIN CHWOLSON **SCOTTISH** RAMSAY BURGESS **SWEDISH** BRENNER MONTELIUS **SWISS** KELLER
ARCHAIC OLD ANCIENT ANTIQUE HISTORIC OBSOLETE (PREF.) PALE
ARCHAISM (USE OF —S) GADZOOKERY
ARCHANGEL SATAN URIEL GABRIEL MICHAEL RAPHAEL HIERARCH
ARCHBISHOP HATTO PRELATE PRIMATE ORDINARY
ARCHDEMON BELFAGOR BELFAZOR
ARCHDIOCESE EPARCHY
ARCHDUKE ERZHERZOG
ARCHEAN EOZOIC
ARCHED ARCHY CONVEX ARCUATE EMBOWED VAULTED HOOPLIKE CAMERATED (— IN) CONCAVE (PREF.) TOXIC(O) TOX(I)(O)
ARCHEGONIUM CALYPTRA OOANGIUM
ARCHELAUS (BROTHER OF —) PHILIP ANTIPAS (FATHER OF —) HEROD (MOTHER OF —) MALTHAKE
ARCHEMORUS (FATHER OF —) LYCURGUS (MOTHER OF —) EURYDICE (NURSE OF —) HYPSIPYLE
ARCHER BOW CLIM CLYM BOWER BUTTY CUPID ROVER BOWBOY BOWMAN BOWYER SHOOTER PANDARUS (EQUIPMENT OF —) TACKLE
ARCHER-FISH DARTER
ARCHERY TOXOLOGY ARTILLERY (— SPACE) PETTICOAT (PREF.) TOX(I)(O) TOXIC(O)
ARCHETYPE IDEA MODEL FIGURE SAMPLE ESSENCE EXAMPLE PARAGON PATTERN EXEMPLAR FRAVASHI ORIGINAL PARADIGM PROTOTYPE

ARCHIL CORKE CORCIR CORKER PERSIS CUDBEAR LECANORA ORCHILLA ORSEILLE
ARCHING CAMBER
ARCHITECT MAKER ARTIST ARTISAN BUILDER CREATOR PLANNER BEZALEEL DESIGNER SURVEYOR **AMERICAN** DAY ORR PEI COBB COPE CRAM CRET HOOD HOWE HUNT JAHN KAHN MIES PELZ POPE POST SERT TOWN VAUX WANK WARE YEON ADLER ALLEN BACON BAYER BUTTS CASEY CRAMP DAVIS FLAGG GEHRY GOULD HEINS HOBAN MAHER MCKIM MILLS OBATA PELLI PRICE RODIA TANGE WAUGH WHITE BARBER BREUER GEDDES GILMAN GRAHAM HAIGHT HEJDUK HOWARD ITTNER JENNEY KASKEY MIZNER NEUTRA OWINGS ROGERS UPJOHN WALKER WALTER WARREN WRIGHT BRAGDON BRUNNER BURNHAM CARRERE CORBETT EIDLITZ GILBERT GOODHUE GRIFFIN HOWELLS KENDALL KIESLER KIMBALL LAFARGE LATROBE LESCAZE PARSONS PEABODY PEREIRA PLOWMAN RAYMOND STURGIS TUTHILL BENJAMIN BOGARDUS BOSWORTH BULFINCH COOLIDGE DINKELOO HARRISON HASTINGS HOLABIRD MCINTIRE SULLIVAN THOMPSON THORNTON VANBRUNT YAMASAKI MAGONIGLE RICHARDSON STEWARDSON STRICKLAND HARDENBERGH WHEELWRIGHT **AUSTRIAN** NULL URBAN GRAVES WAGNER FERSTEL HASENAUER HOLZMEISTER **BELGIAN** VELDE POELAERT **BRAZILIAN** COSTA NIEMEYER **CZECH** ZITEK **DANISH** NYROP UTZON HANSEN JACOBSEN **DUTCH** OUD KEYSER BERLAGE CUYPERS LOMBARD MOREELSE **EGYPTIAN** CALLINICUS **ENGLISH** KENT NASH SHAW TITE WEBB WREN ADAMS BAKER BARRY BLORE DANCE GLOAG GOTCH GWILT JONES MOULD SCOTT SOANE STONE WYATT BODLEY CLARKE COOPER HANSOM HUSSEY PAXTON STREET STUART BECKETT BENTLEY GIBBERD JACKSON KNOWLES LUTYENS PEARSON PENROSE RICKMAN ATKINSON CHAMBERS COCKERAM FLETCHER NESFIELD VANBRUGH CHAMPNEYS HAWKSMOOR NICHOLSON WILKINSON CATHERWOOD LANCHESTER WATERHOUSE ABERCROMBIE BUTTERFIELD PENNETHORNE **FINNISH** EERO AALTO SAARINEN GESELLIUS **FRENCH** DUC ETEX COTTE DUBAN LEVAU MAROT PUGET BENARD BERAIN BROSSE LEDOUX LEFUEL LESCOT NEPVEU ANTOINE BALTARD

BLONDEL BULLANT DAVIOUD DELORME FORMIGE GABRIEL GARDNER GARNIER LENOTRE MANSART PERCIER PEVSNER VIOLLET ANDROUET CHALGRIN CUVILLES FELIBIEN FONTAINE HITTORFF LEPAUTRE PERRAULT SOUFFLOT LEMERCIER LECORBUSIER **GERMAN** HOLL LENZ ADLER ERWIN GEDON LENNE SPEER KLENZE MESSEL MOLLER SEMPER STULER BEHRENS FRIESEN GROPIUS HOLBEIN NEUMANN OLBRICH POELZIG HEGEMANN LANGHANS SCHINKEL SCHLUTER ALTDORFER ESSENWEIN MENDELSOHN POPPELMANN KNOBELSDORFF **GREEK** ICTINUS DOXIADIS MNESICLES SOSTRATUS DINOCRATES HIPPODAMUS POLYCLITUS CALLICRATES **HUNGARIAN** STEINDL **IRISH** MAGINNIS **ISRAELI** SAFDIE **ITALIAN** BONI DANTI DOLCI GENGA NERVI PONTI PORTA POZZO VINCI AGNOLO ALESSI BONOMI CIGOLI COSIMO GIOTTO IUVARA PISANO ROMANO SERING SOLARI SUARDI VASARI ALBERTI ALGARDI BELLINI BERNINI BIBIENA CAGNOLA CONTINO CORTONA FONTANA GIORGIO GUARINI LAURANA MADERNA PERUZZI TIBALDI TRIBOLO VIGNOLA AGOSTINO AMMANATI BRAMANTE CIVITALI GIOCONDO LOMBARDO PALLADIO PALLASIO PIRANESI SCAMOZZI BORROMINI PIERMARINI SANMICHELI SERVANDONI VANVITELLI PRIMATICCIO BRUNELLESCHI MICHELANGELO **JAPANESE** ISOZAKI **MEXICAN** BARRAGAN **POLISH** NOWICKI SPYCHALSKI **ROMAN** COSMATI COSSUTIUS **RUSSIAN** BRYULOV **SCOTTISH** ADAM ROSS GIBBS STIRLING MACKINTOSH **SPANISH** CANO GAUDI CANDELA HERRERA VILLANUEVA **SWEDISH** TESSIN ASPLUND OSTBERG TENGBOM **SWISS** FRISCH LECORBUSIER **TURKISH** SINAN
ARCHITECTURAL TECTONIC OECODOMIC
ARCHITECTURE DRAVIDA
ARCHITRAVE EPISTYLE PLATBAND
ARCHIVES TABULARY TABULARIUM
ARCHIVOLT RING ARCHBAND HEADBAND
ARCHLUTE THEORBO
ARCHON RULER DIRECTOR OFFICIAL THESMOTHETE
ARCHWAY ARCH PEND ARCUS PAILOO PAILOU
ARC LAMP MONOPHOTE
ARCOGRAPH BOW
ARCO SALTANDO SPICCATO
ARCTIC ICY COLD COOL GELID POLAR BOREAL CHILLY FRIGID

GALOSH NORTHERN OVERSHOE (— VEHICLE) SNOCAT
ARCTIUM LAPPA
ARCTOID URSINE
ARD (FATHER OF —) BELA
ARDENT HOT AVID FOND KEEN LIVE WARM EAGER FIERY GLEDY RETHE SHARP ABLAZE FERVID FIERCE IGNITE STRONG TORRID AMOROUS BURNING CORDIAL DEVOTED EARNEST FEELING FERVENT FLAMING FORWARD GLOWING INTENSE SHINING ZEALOUS DESIROUS EMPRESSE FEVERISH FLAGRANT ROMANTIC SANGUINE SCALDING SPORTIVE VEHEMENT PERFERVID
ARDON (FATHER OF —) CALEB (MOTHER OF —) AZUBAH
ARDOR DASH EDGE ELAN FIRE GLOW HEAT LOVE ZEAL ZEST ESTRO FLAME GUSTO HEART TAPAS VERVE WRATH DESIRE FERVOR FOUGUE METTLE SPIRIT SPLEEN WARMTH ARDENCY EARNEST ENTRAIN PASSION DEVOTION FEROCITY VIOLENCE VIVACITY
ARDUOUS HARD LOFTY STEEP STIFF SEVERE TRYING ONEROUS EXACTING TIRESOME TOILSOME
ARDYS (FATHER OF —) GYGES
ARE MU RE AIR ARN ARUN HARE
AREA BELT PALE SIZE TREF ZONE BASIN COAST COURT FIELD PLACE RANGE REALM SCENE SCOPE SPACE TRACT ACCENT AREOLA EXTENT GROUND LOCALE MOARIA REGION SECTOR SPHERE SPREAD VOLUME ACREAGE AMENITY AREAWAY CIRCUIT COMPASS CONTENT COUNTRY ENVIRON EXPANSE KINGDOM PURLIEU SURFACE CAPACITY DISTRICT ENCEINTE PLOTTAGE PROVINCE (— ALONG HIGHWAY) STRIP (— AROUND MOUTH) DELTA PERISTOME (— AT INTERSECTION) CIRCUS (— BETWEEN FILLETS) CANALIS (— IN BACTERIAL CULTURE) PLAQUE (— IN CARTOON) BALLOON (— IN CULTURE) PLAQUE (— IN FRONT OF HOCKEY GOAL) CREASE (— IN HOSTILE TERRITORY) AIRHEAD (— OF ACTIVITY) METIER (— OF EXPERIENCE) BOOK (— OF FLAG) CANTON (— OF INTEREST) SCENE (— OF OLDER LAND) KIPUKA (— OF OPEN WATER AMID ICE) POLYNYA (— OF RIDGES) BILO (— OF TIMBERLAND) CHENA (— ON MOON) MARE WANE TERRA (— OVER GATE) PORTAL (— RELATE) SPACIAL SPATIAL (— UNIT) TAN YOKE LABOR VIRGATE PLETHRON PLOWGANG PLOWGATE (BLANK —) BITE HOLE

(BORDER —) OUTSKIRT OUTSKIRTS
(BORDERED —) PANEL
(COMBAT —) GLACIS
(CONTINENTAL —) MOARIA
(CULTURAL —) HORIZON
(CURLING —) PARISH
(DARK — OF MOON) MARE MARIA
(DENUDED —) BURN
(DIKED —) SLUSHPIT
(DISEASED —) PLAQUE
(ELONGATED —) BELT
(ENCLOSED —) FOLD SEPT
(EXTRAMURAL —) BANLIEUE
(FENCED —) CAGE COMPOUND
(FERTILE —) HAMMOCK
(FLOORING —) SQUARE
(FORTIFIED —) BASTION ENCEINTE
(GATHERING —) MANDAPA
(HOCKEY —) GOALMOUTH
(HOSPITAL —) ICU
(HUNTING —) SURROUND
(IMMOBILE — OF EARTH'S CRUST)
CRATON
(INFESTED —) FLYBELT
(ISOLATED —) POCKET
(LARGE —) LANDMASS
(LIMITED —) SPOT
(LOW-LYING —) GLADE SWALE
COULEE COULIE GUTTER
(LUMINOUS —) AUREOLA AUREOLE
(MINE —) SQUEEZE
(NUCLEAR —) HEARTH ECUMENE
(OPEN —) COURT LAUND PLAZA
CAMPUS SQUARE HAGGARD
(OVERGROWN —) COGONAL
(PASTURE —) SOUM
(PAVED —) CAUSEY
(PLOWED —) BREAK
(RAISED —) TRIBUNE
(RESIDENTIAL —) BANLIEU
BANLIEUE
(RURAL —) STICKS BOONIES
BOONDOCKS
(SHOPPING —) MALL MART ARCADE
EMPORIUM
(SLUM —) STEW
(SMALL —) AREOLA
(SMOKING —) BULLPEN
(STERN —) AFTERPART
(STORAGE —) STACK
(SUBURBAN —) ADDITION
FAUBOURG
(SUNKEN —) SAG
(SWAMPY —) SLASH
(TEST —) MILACRE
(TIDAL —) CLAMFLAT
(TRANSITION —) ECOTONE
(TREELESS —) SLICK
(TUMID —) CERE
(UNCLEARED —) BUSH
(UPLAND —) COTEAU
(VOLCANIC —) SOLFATARA
(WASTE —) FOREST
(WOODED —) HAG BOSK BOSQUE
(SUFF.) **(GEOGRAPHIC —)** GAEA
GEA
ARECA ARAK ARCHA BETEL
ARELI (FATHER OF —) GAD
ARENA AREA LIST OVAL RING RINK
COURT FIELD SCENE SCOPE SPACE
STAGE CIRCUS CIRQUE REGION
SPHERE COCKPIT STADIUM
TERRAIN THEATER BULLRING

(ATLANTA —) OMNI
(JAI ALAI —) FRONTON
ARENACEOUS SANDY GRITTY
SABULOUS
AREOLA PIT AREA RING SPOT
SPACE CAVITY
ARES MARS ENYALIUS GRADIVUS
QUIRINUS
(FATHER OF —) ZEUS JUPITER
(MOTHER OF —) ENYO HERA JUNO
(SON OF —) REMUS CYCNUS
ROMULUS
ARETE CREST
(FATHER OF —) DIONYSIUS
(HUSBAND OF —) DION ALCINOUS
(MOTHER OF —) ARISTOMACHE
AREUS (BROTHER OF —) TALAUS
LEODOCUS
(FATHER OF —) BIAS
(MOTHER OF —) PERO
ARGALA STORK MARABOU
ARGALI AMMON ARKAR AOUDAD
ARGAN IRONWOOD
ARGANTE (DAUGHTER OF —)
OCTAVIA ZERBINETTE
ARGENT LUNA MOON PEARL WHITE
BLANCH SILVER CRYSTAL SHINING
SILVERY

ARGENTINA
CAPITAL: BUENOSAIRES
COIN: PESO CENTAVO ARGENTINO
DANCE: TANGO CUANDO GAUCHO
FALLS: GRANDE IGUAZU
INDIAN: LULE GUARANI
LAKE: VIEDMA CARDIEL FAGNANO
MUSTERS
MEASURE: SINO VARA LEGUA
CUADRA FANEGA LASTRE
MANZANA
MONEY: AUSTRAL
MOUNTAIN: TORO ANDES CHATO
LAUDO MAIPU POTRO CONICO
PISSIS RINCON FAMATINA
MURALLON OLIVARES TRONADOR
ZAPALERI ACONCAGUA
INCAHUASI TUPUNGATO
MERCEDARIO LLULLAILLACO
PLAIN: PAMPA PAMPAS
PORT: ROSARIO
PROVINCE: CHACO JUJUY SALTA
CHUBUT CORDOBA FORMOSA
LARIOJA MENDOZA NEUQUEN
TUCUMAN MISIONES PATAGONIA
REGION: CHACO PATAGONIA
RIVER: SALI ATUEL CHICO COYLE
DULCE LIMAY NEGRO PLATA
TEUCO BLANCO CHUBUT CUARTO
FLORES GRANDE PARANA
QUINTO SALADO BERMEJO
DESEADO MENDOZA TERCERO
TUNUYAN SENGUERR
TOWN: AZUL GOYA ORAN PUAN
BAHIA JUNIN LANUS LUJAN
METAN SALTA PARANA RAWSON
RUFINO VIEDMA ZARATE BOLIVAR
CORDOBA DOLORES FORMOSA
LABANDA MENDOZA NEUQUEN
POSADAS RAFAELA ROSARIO
TUCUMAN USHUAIA GALLEGOS
CATAMARCA
VOLCANO: LANIN MAIPU DOMUYO
PETEROA TUPUNGATO

WATERFALL: IGUAZU
WEIGHT: LAST GRANO LIBRA
QUINTAL TONELADA

ARGES (BROTHER OF —) BRONTES
STEROPES
(FATHER OF —) URANUS
(MOTHER OF —) GE GAEA
ARGIA (FATHER OF —) OCEANUS
ADRASTUS
(HUSBAND OF —) INACHUS
POLYBUS POLYNICES
ARISTODEMUS
(MOTHER OF —) TETHYS
AMPHITHEA
(SON OF —) ARGUS PROCLES
EURYSTHENES
ARGIL CLAY ALUMINA
ARGIOPE (DAUGHTER OF —)
EUROPA
(HUSBAND OF —) AGENOR
(SON OF —) CILIX CADMUS THASUS
CERCYON PHINEUS PHOENIX
ARGOL TARTAR
ARGOSY SHIP FLEET GALLEON
RAGUSYE
ARGOT CALO CANT FLASH LINGO
SLANG JARGON PATOIS PATTER
DIALECT
ARGUE JAW ARGY CHOP FUSS
MEAN MOOT MOVE SPAR TIFF
WORD ARGIE CAVIL ORATE PLEAD
PROVE TREAT ACCUSE ADDUCE
CAFFLE DEBATE EVINCE HASSLE
REASON ARRAIGN CONTEND
CONTEST COUNTER DISCUSS
DISPUTE WRANGLE ERGOTIZE
INDICATE MAINTAIN PERSUADE
QUESTION TRAVERSE
(— DEDUCTIVELY) SYLLOGIZE
(— SNAPPISHLY) YAFF
(— SUBTLY) DISTINGUISH
ARGUEBUS HAGBUT HACKBUT
ARGUER JAW
ARGUMENT ROW AGON BEEF BLUE
CASE FUSS MOOT PLEA SPAR SPAT
TEXT TIFF CLASH DEBAT INDEX
KNIFE LEMMA PROOF THEME
TOPIC BARNEY COMBAT CORKER
DEBATE DUSTUP ELENCH HASSLE
MATTER TUSSLE APAGOGE
CLAMPER DEFENCE DEFENSE
DILEMMA DISPUTE ESSENCE
FLUBDUB POLEMIC RHUBARB
SOPHISM SORITES SUMMARY
ABSTRACT CLINCHER COURSING
EVIDENCE SPARRING TRILEMMA
REASONING PARALOGISM
PERSUASION
(— FOR) PRO
(— IN FAVOR) PRO
(ART OF —) POLEMICS
(CONSLUSIVE —) SOCKDOLAGER
SOCKDOLOGER
(DECISIVE —) SETTLER
(ILLOGICAL —) FALLACY
(INVALID —) SOPHISM
(SCHOLASTIC —) QUODLIBET
(THEORETICAL —) ACADEMICS
ARGUMENTATION DEBATE
DISPUTE ERGOTISM CHOPLOGIC
ARGUMENTATIVE ERISTIC
FRATCHY FORENSIC

ARGUS (FATHER OF —) ZEUS
JUPITER PHRIXUS
(MOTHER OF —) ARGIA NIOBE
CHALCIOPE
(SLAYER OF —) HERMES MERCURY
ARGUSFISH SCAT
ARHAT MONK LOHAN RAKAN SAINT
ARAHANT
ARIA AIR SOLO SONG TUNE
MELODY SORTIE ARIETTA ARIETTE
SORTITA
ARIADNE (FATHER OF —) MINOS
(HUSBAND OF —) THESEUS
(MOTHER OF —) PASIPHAE
ARIADNE AUF NAXOS
(CHARACTER IN —) ARIADNE
BACCHUS ZERBINETTA
(COMPOSER OF —) STRAUSS
ARIAN AGNOETE AGNOITE
HOMOEAN ANOMOIAN EUSEBIAN
ARID DRY BALD BARE DULL LEAN
BARREN DESERT JEJUNE MEAGER
DROUTHY PARCHED STERILE
THIRSTY DROUGHTY WITHERED
ARIDAI (FATHER OF —) HAMAN
ARIDATHA (FATHER OF —) HAMAN
ARIDITY DROUTH DROUGHT SICCITY
ARIFS RAM
ARIKARA REE
ARIL POD ANILLUS COATING
ARILLODE
ARIODANTE (COMPOSER OF —)
HANDEL
ARIODANTES (LOVER OF —)
GENEURA
ARISAI (FATHER OF —) HAMAN
ARISBE (FATHER OF —) MEROPS
(HUSBAND OF —) PRIAM
DARDANUS HYRTACUS
(SON OF —) ASIUS NISUS AESACUS
ARISE WAX COME FLOW FORM
GROW LIFT REAR RISE SOAR STEM
AWAKE BEGIN BUILD EXIST ISSUE
MOUNT RAISE SPRAY STAND
START SURGE TOWER WAKEN
ACCRUE AMOUNT APPEAR
ASCEND ATTAIN DERIVE EMERGE
HAPPEN KITTLE SPRING DEVELOP
EMANATE EXSURGE PROCEED
REDOUND SOURDRE
(— FROM) STEM
ARISING LEVEE EMERGENT
(PREF.) (— WITHIN) IDIO
ARISTAEUS (DAUGHTER OF —)
MACRIS
(FATHER OF —) APOLLO
(MOTHER OF —) CYRENE
(SON OF —) ACTAEON
(WIFE OF —) AUTONOE
ARISTE (BROTHER OF —) CHRYSALE
ARISTO (BROTHER OF —)
SGANARELLE
ARISTOCRACY CLASS ELITE
GENTRY ARISTOI SAMURAI
NOBILITY OPTIMACY
ARISTOCRAT LORD NOBLE ARISTO
JUNKER GRANDEE PARVENU
EUPATRID OPTIMATE PATRICIAN
(RUSSIAN —) BOIAR BOYAR
BOYARD
(PL.) ARISTOI
ARISTOCRATIC HIGH TONY NOBLE
QUALITY CAVALIER BELGRAVIAN

ARISTODEMUS (BROTHER OF —)
TEMENUS CRESPHONTES
(FATHER OF —) ARISTOMACHUS
(SON OF —) PROCLES
EURYSTHENES
(WIFE OF —) ARGEIA
ARISTOTELIAN PERIPATETIC
ARITHMETIC SUM AUGRIM
ALGORISM
(— FIGURE) ADDEND
ARITHMOMETER MULTIPLIER

ARIZONA

CAPITAL: PHOENIX
COUNTY: GILA PIMA YUMA PINAL
APACHE MOHAVE NAVAJO
COCHISE YAVAPAI COCONINO
GREENLEE MARICOPA
SANTACRUZ
INDIAN: HOPI PIMA YUMA NAVAHO
NAVAJO PAPAGO HUALAPAI
MOUNTAIN: BANGS GROOM
LEMMON TURRET HUALPAI
PASTORA MERIDIAN
MOUNTAIN RANGE: GILA KOFA
MOHAWK GALIURO HUALPAI
AQUARIUS BUCKSKIN
PEAK: HUMPHREYS
RIVER: GILA SALT ZUNI VERDE
PUERCO COLORADO
STATE BIRD: CACTUSWREN
STATE FLOWER: SAGUARO
STATE NICKNAME: OCOTILLO
STATE TREE: PALOVERDE
TOWN: AJO ELOY MESA NACO
YUMA GLOBE LEUPP TEMPE
BISBEE JEROME MCNARY
SALOME TOLTEC TUCSON
CLIFTON CORTARO KINGMAN
MORENCI NOGALES PHOENIX
SAFFORD FREDONIA PRESCOTT
FLAGSTAFF TOMBSTONE

ARJUN KUMBUK
ARJUNA (FATHER OF —) PANDU
(SON OF —) ABHIMANYU
ARK BIN BOX BOAT SHIP BARGE
CHEST HUTCH BASKET COFFER
REFUGE WANGAN RETREAT
SHELTER WANIGAN FLATBOAT
ARKANSAN ARKANSAWYER

ARKANSAS

CAPITAL: LITTLEROCK
COUNTY: LEE CLAY DREW PIKE
POLK POPE YELL BOONE CROSS
DESHA IZARD LOGAN SHARP
STONE BAXTER CHICOT LONOKE
SEARCY CALHOUN PRAIRIE
PULASKI OUACHITA
INDIAN: CADDO OSAGE QUAPAW
CHOCTAW CHEROKEE
LAKE: CONWAY NIMROD GREESON
NORFORK OUACHITA
MOUNTAIN: RICH GAYLOR
MAGAZINE
MOUNTAIN RANGE: OZARK
OUACHITA
NATIVE: TOOTHPICK
NICKNAME: WONDER
PRESIDENT: CLINTON
RIVER: RED WHITE SALINE BUFFALO
CURRENT COSSATOT OUACHITA

STATE BIRD: MOCKINGBIRD
STATE FLOWER: APPLE BLOSSOM
STATE TREE: SHORTLEAFPINE
TOWN: COY CUY KEO OLA ROE ULM
ALMA BONO CASA DELL DIAZ
MORO ENOLA PERLA RISON
RONDO WYNNE ALICIA JASPER
PIGGOTT

ARKOSE ARENITE SANDSTONE
ARLECCHINO (CHARACTER IN —)
LEANDRO BOMBASTO COLUMBINE
HARLEQUIN
(COMPOSER OF —) BUSONI
ARLESIANA, L' (CHARACTER IN —)
ROSA MAMMAI METIFIO VIVETTE
FEDERICO
(COMPOSER OF —) CILEA
ARM FIN OAR TOE BOOM HEEL LIMB
WING BLADE BOUGH CRANE EQUIP
FENCE FIORD FIRTH FJORD FORCE
GARDY INLET MIGHT OXTER
POWER RIFLE SNORD STOCK
BRANCH CRUTCH ENERGY FRETUM
GIBBET MEMBER OUTFIT PINION
RADIAL SLEEVE TAPPET WEAPON
CATCHER DERRICK DRAWARM
FLIPPER FOREARM FORTIFY
FURNISH GARNISH HARNESS
OCKSTER PREPARE PROTECT
PROVIDE QUILLON SUPPORT
ARMORIAL CROSSARM FOLLOWER
FORELIMB PULLDOWN SOUPBONE
STRENGTH TRANSEPT
(— FORCES) MIRV
(— HOLDING FLINT) HAMMER
(— OF BARNACLE) CIRRUS CIRRHUS
(— OF CHAIR) ELBOW
(— OF CRANE) JIB GIBBET
RAMHEAD
(— OF GIN) START
(— OF PROPELLER) BLADE
(— OF RECORD PLAYER) PICKUP
(— OF SEA) COVE FLOW MEER
MERE BRACE CANAL FIRTH FRITH
GRAIN FRETUM ESTUARY EURIPUS
(— OF SPINNING MULE) SICKLE
(— OF WINDMILL) VANE WHIP
(— WITH GAFF) HEEL
(INDEX —) DIOPTER
(IRON —) CRANE
(KIND OF —) BOSTON
(LEVER —) SWEEP
(PITCHING —) SOUPBONE
(WINDMILL —) VANE
(PL.) ARMORY ARMAMENT
(PREF.) BRACHI
ARMADA NAVY FLEET FLOTILLA
ARMADILLO APAR PEBA TATU
APARA POYOU TATOU BOLITA
MATACO MATICO MULITA PELUDO
DASYPOD TATOUAY TATUASU
EDENTATE KABASSOU LORICATE
PANGOLIN
(SMALL —) PICHI PICHICIAGO
ARMAMENT ARMADA BATTERY
ARMATURE ARMING KEEPER
LIFTER
ARMBAND BRASSARD
ARMCHAIR CHAIR ELBOW BERGERE
FAUTEUIL LOVESEAT
ARMED FLUTE HEELED DAGGERED
WEAPONED

ARMENIA

ANCIENT CAPITAL: ANI ARTASHAT
ARTAXATA
ANCIENT NAME: MINNI
CAPITAL: EREVAN ERIVAN YEREVAN
COIN: RUBLE
FORTRESS: EREBUNI
HERO: ARA ARAM HAIK ARAME
VARTAN
KING: ASHOT GAGIK TRDAT ZAREH
DIKRAN ARTAKIAS ARTASHES
TIGRANES ZARIADES
KINGDOM: URARTU VANNIC CILICIA
SOPHENE ARDSRUNI
LAKE: VAN SEVAN URMIA
LANGUAGE: ARMENIAN
MOUNTAIN: ARA ALAGEZ ARARAT
TAURUS ALADAGH ARAGATS
KARABAKH
NATIVE: ARMEN GOMER
PLAIN: ARARAT
RIVER: KUR ARAS KURA ARAKS
CYRUS DEBET HALYS ZANGA
AGSTEV ARAXES RAZDAN TIGRIS
HRAZDAN VOROTAN AKHURYAN
EUPHRATES
SAINT: SAHAK MESROP
TOWN: VAN SIVAS BITLIS EREVAN
KUMAYN SPITAK ERZURUM
KUMAIRI TRABZON LENINAKAN

ARMENIAN ERMYN HADJI HAIKH
ARMFUL LOCK YAFFLE
ARMHOLE MAIL SCYE OXTER
ARMSCYE ARMSEYE ARMSIZE
ARMIDE (CHARACTER IN —) ARMIDA
RINALDO
(COMPOSER OF —) GLUCK
ARMINIO (COMPOSER OF —)
HANDEL
ARMISTICE LULL PEACE TRUCE
INDUCIAE
ARMLET BANGLE TABLET TORQUE
ARMHOOP
ARMONI (FATHER OF —) SAUL
(MOTHER OF —) RIZPAH
ARMOR (AND SPECIFIC PIECES
THEREOF) ARMS BACK BOOT EGIS
JAMB MAIL TACE WEED ACTON
AMURE BARDS BRACE CUISH
CULET DORON GUARD GUIGE
JAMBE PIECE PLATE PROOF SCALE
STEEL TAPUL TASSE TRUSS
ARMLET ARMOUR BEAVER BRINIE
BRUNIE BYRNIE CAMAIL CORIUM
COUTER CRANET CUISSE GORGET
GRAITH GREAVE JAMBER POLEYN
RONDEL SECRET SHIELD TASSET
THORAX TONLET TUILLE VOIDER
AILETTE ARMHOOP BESAGNE
BROIGNE CORSLET CUIRASS
DEFENSE EPAULET HARNESS
HAUBERK JAZERAN KNEELET
LAMBOYS PALETTF PANOPLY
PLACATE POITREL REREDOS
ROUNDEL SABATON VENTAIL
BRASSARD PAULDRON
RAMENTUM VAMBRACE
BAINBERGS RONDACHEPALLETTE
(— ON TREE) TROPHY
(— PLATE) TUILLE
(ELBOW —) CUBITIERE

(FOOT —) SABATON SABBATON
SOLLERET
(HEAD —) ARMET CASQUE HELMET
PALLET SCONCE VENTAIL AVENTAIL
(HORSE —) BARB BARD BARDE
CRINET CHAMFRON CRINIERE
CHAMFRAIN
(LEATHER —) CORIUM
(LEG —) BOOT JAMB CUISH JAMBE
CUISSE GREAVE JAMBER TUILLE
JAMBEAU CHAUSSES
(NECK —) COLLAR GORGET
(PADDED —) GAMBESON
(SUIT OF —) CAST STAND
(PREF.) HOPL(O)
ARMOR-BEARER SQUIRE ARMIGER
CUSTREL
ARMORED PANZER
ARMORER GUNSMITH ARTIFICER
ARMORICAN BRETON
ARMORY ARSENAL HERALDRY
ARMPIT ALA OXTER AXILLA
ARMHOLE
ARMS TACKLE
(PREF.) HOPL(O)
**ARMS AND THE MAN (AUTHOR OF
—)** SHAW
(CHARACTER IN —) LOUKA RAINA
NICOLA PETKOFF SERGIUS
CATHERINE BLUNTSCHLI
ARMY FERD HERE HOST IMPI LEVY
MAIN ARRAY CROWD FORCE
HERSE HORDE POWER RANKS
ZOMBI COHORT HONVED LEGION
NUMBER THRONG TROOPS MILITIA
BATTALIA CHIVALRY MILITARY
(HOSTILE —) FOE
(MEMBER OF IRISH REPUBLICAN —)
PROVO
(VOLUNTEER —) VOLAR
(PL.) SABAOTH
(PREF.) STRATO
**ARMY OFFICER (ALSO SEE
SOLDIER)**
ARMYWORM GRASSWORM
ARNE (FATHER OF —) AEOLUS
(HUSBAND OF —) METAPONTUS
(MOTHER OF —) THEA
(SON OF —) AEOLUS BOEOTUS
ARNOTTO ROUCOU
AROAR REBOANT
AROD (FATHER OF —) GAD
AROID APII ARAD TARO APIUM
KRUBI TANIA KONJAK TANIER
YAUTIA PINUELA CALADIUM
CUNJEVOI MOCOMOCO
CUCKOOPINT
AROMA AURA NOSE ODOR NIDOR
SAVOR SCENT SMELL SNUFF SPICE
FLAVOR BOUQUET PERFUME
REDOLENCE
(— OF WINE) BLOOM
AROMATIC BALMY SPICY SWEET
MASTIC ODOROUS PIQUANT
PUNGENT FRAGRANT REDOLENT
SPICEFUL
AROUND NEAR UMBE ABOUT CIRCA
CIRCUM ENVIRON
(PREF.) AMBI AMPHI CIRCUM PERI
AROUSAL INDUCTION
AROUSE SOW CALL CITE FIRE GAIN
HEAT MOVE REAR SPUR STIR
WAKE WHET ADAWE ALARM

ALERT AWAKE EVOKE FLESH
PIQUE RAISE RALLY ROUSE ROUST
SHAKE STEER WAKEN ABRAID
AWAKEN ELICIT EXCITE FOMENT
INCITE INDUCE KINDLE REVIVE
STIRUP SUMMON THRILL TURNON
ACTUATE AGITATE CONNOTE
INCENSE INFLAME INSPIRE
PROVOKE STEAMUP SUGGEST
WHOMPUP INSPIRIT
(— DISPLEASURE) AGGRAVATE
(— ENMITY) ESTRANGE
(— WRATH) SPLEEN
ARPEGGIATE BREAK
ARPEGGIO SWEEP ROULADE
FLOURISH
(— EFFECT) RASGADO
ARPHAXAD (FATHER OF —) SHEM
ARRACACHA APIO ARRA
ARRACK ARAK RACK ARAKI
RACKAPEE
ARRAIGN TRY CITE ARGUE PEACH
ACCUSE CHARGE IMPUTE INDICT
INDITE SUMMON APPOINT
IMPEACH DENOUNCE
ARRANGE DO FIX LAY RAY SET
CAST COMB EDIT FILE FORM PLAN
PLAT RAIL RULE SIDE SIZE SORT
TIGH TIFT WORK ADAPT AGREE
ALIGN ALINE ARRAY BESEE CURRY
DRAPE DRESS ETTLE FANCY
FRAME GRADE ORDER PITCH
RANGE SCORE SHAPE SHIFT SPACE
STALL TRICK ADJUST BRANCH
CODIFY DAIKER DESIGN DEVISE
FETTLE FORMAT INFORM ORDAIN
SETTLE SOLUTE TAILYE ADDRESS
APPOINT BESPEAK CATALOG
COLLATE COMPONE COMPOSE
CONCERT DISPOSE ENRANGE
GRADATE MARSHAL PERMUTE
PREPARE REDRESS SERIATE
TAILZEE TAILZIE ALPHABET
CLASSIFY CONCLUDE ORGANIZE
REGULATE TABULATE COLLOCATE
CONJOBBLE NEGOTIATE
STIPULATE ORCHESTRATE
(— BEFOREHAND) FORLAY
FORELAY
(— FANTASTICALLY) HARLEQUINIZE
(— FASTIDIOUSLY) PREEN
(— HAIR) SET TED COIF TRUSS
COIFFE
(— HARMONIOUSLY) GRADATE
(— IN FLOCKS) HIRSEL HIRSLE
(— IN FOLDS) DRAPE
(— IN LAYERS) DESS TIER
(— IN ROW) RACE
(— STRAW) HAULM
(— SYSTEMATICALLY) DIGEST
(— WITH BEST AT TOP) DEACON
ARRANGEMENT FIX FLY LAY RAY
DEAL FLOW PLAT RANK TIFF
ARRAY BUILD DRAPE INDEX ORDER
SETUP BORDER DESIGN HOOKUP
LAYOUT SCHEME SETOUT SYNTAX
SYSTEM TREATY BLEEDER INTERIM
POSTURE TONTINE ATTITUDE
CONTRACT DISPOSAL GROUPING
POSITURE SEQUENCE
ORDONNANCE ORIENTATION
BANDSTRATION ORCHESTRATION

(— IN LINE) RANK SERIES
(— IN LOCK) DETECTOR
(— OF BRISTLES) CHAETOTAXY
(— OF CHESS PAWNS) CHAIN
(— OF COMPUTER ELEMENTS)
ARRAY
(— OF DRAPERIES) CAST
(— OF FLOWERS) CASCADE
CORSAGE IKEBANA PARTERRE
(— OF GRADES) CURVE
(— OF GUNS) ARMADA
(— OF HAIRDO) FORETOP
(— OF HAIRS) SCOPA
(— OF HOOKS) GIG
(— OF LOOM BARS) GRIFF GRIFFE
(— OF PARTS) STRUCTURE
(OF ROCKS) BEDDING
(— OF TACKLE) BURTON
(— OF TIMBER) ANCHOR
(— OF TROOPS) ECHELON
(BETTING —) PERM
(CIRCULAR —) CYCLE
(DISHONEST —) CROSS
(GEOMETRICAL —) LATTICE
(MUSICAL —) CHART
(ORDERED —) PERMUTATION
(SECRET —) PACK
(TRADITIONAL —) AKOLUTHIA
AKOLOUTHIA
(TRAVEL —) CHARTER
(PREF.) TAX(EO)(I)(O)
(LACK OF —) ATAXO
(SUFF.) OSIS TACTIC TAXIS TAXY
ARRANGEMNET (SECRET —) PACKK
ARRANGING ORDONNANT
(JAPANESE ART OF FLOWER —)
IKEBANA
ARRANNGEMENT (MUSICAL—)
SCORE INSTRUMENTATION
ARRANT BAD THIEF OUTLAW
ROBBER VAGRANT OUTRIGHT
PRECIOUS RASCALLY
ARRAS ORRIS ARISTE DRAPERY
TAPESTRY
ARRASTRA TAHONA
ARRAU JURARA
ARRAY DON DUB FIG ARMY BUSK
DECK DOLL FYRD GALA GARB
HOST POMP RAIL RANK ROBE VEST
ADORN ALIGN ALINE ATOUR
DRESS EQUIP HABIT HARKA HEDGE
ORDER ADIGHT AGUISE ATTIRE
ATTRAP BEDECK CLOTHE DEVISE
FETTLE FINERY GRAITH INVEST
LAYOUT MUSTER PLIGHT SERIES
SETOUT SHROUD ADDRESS
AFFAITE AFFLICT APPAREL
ARRANGE BATTERY BEDIGHT
COMPANY DISPLAY DISPOSE
ENVELOP FURNISH FYRDUNG
MARSHAL PANOPLY REPAREL
ACCOUTER
(— OF CHEMICALS) ARA
(— OF GUNS) BROADSIDE
(— OF TROOPS) PAREL
(— OF WEAPONS) ARMORY
(— TASTELESSLY) DAUB
(BATTLE —) ACIES HERSE BATTALIA
(MATHEMATICAL —) MATRIX
ARRAYED HABITED ABULYEIT
ARREAR DEBT BEHIND UNPAID
ARRIERE
(IN —S) BACK BEHIND

ARREST CAP COP FIX FOB LAG NAB
NIP VAG BALK BUST CURB FALL
GLOM GRAB HALT HOLD JAIL KEEP
NAIL NICK PULL REST SHOP SIST
STAY STEM STOP ARRET CATCH
CHECK DELAY PINCH REEST SEIZE
STILL STUNT ATTACH BRIDLE
COLLAR DECREE DETAIN ENGAGE
FINGER HAULIN HINDER PLEDGE
PULLIN RETARD SLOUGH SNEEZE
THWART CAPTION CAPTURE
CUSTODY SUSPEND IMPRISON
OBSTRUCT RESTRAIN
(— DEVELOPMENT) FIXATE
(— OF BLEEDING) HEMOSTASIS
(— OF DEVELOPMENT) ABORTION
(— OF GROWTH) STASIS
(PUT UNDER —) BUST
ARRESTER (SPARK —) BONNET
ARRESTING BOLD SEIZING
MAGNETIC PLEASING STRIKING
ARRET EDICT ARREST DECREE
DECISION JUDGMENT
ARRHA HANDGELD
ARRIGANTLY HIGH
ARRIS PIEN ANGLE PIEND ARRIDGE
ARRIVAL COMER IKBAL VENUE
ADVENT COMING INCOMING
REACHING
(— TIME) TOUCHDOWN
(— TIME RECORD) OS
(NEW —) ROOINEK
(UNTIMELY —) LATECOMER
ARRIVE GO SEY COME FALL FLOW
GAIN LAND LEND RIVE GETIN LIGHT
OCCUR REACH WORTH ACCEDE
APPEAR ATTAIN HAPPEN OBTAIN
UPCOME CHECKIN COMPASS
(— AT) GET HIT FIND GAIN HENT
MAKE BRING EDUCE FETCH GUESS
SEIZE ATTAIN DERIVE ESTIMATE
(— AT LAST) ROLLIN
ARRIVED-IN DONE
ARROBA ROVE
ARROGANCE PRIDE SWANK
TUMOR BOWWOW HUBRIS
BOBANCE CONCEIT DISDAIN
EGOTISM HAUTEUR STOMACH
BOLDNESS SUCCUDRY SURQUIDY
ARROGANT BOLD COXY HIGH
MOOD COBBY COCKY GREAT
HUFFY JOLLY LOFTY PROUD
STOUT SURLY WLONK ASSUME
CHESTY FIERCE LORDLY UPPISH
UPPITY WANTON FORWARD
FROSTED HAUGHTY HAUTAIN
HUFFISH POMPOUS STATELY
TOPPING AFFECTED ASSUMING
CAVALIER FASTUOUS IMPUDENT
SNUFFING SUPERIOR TUMOROUS
OVERBEARING OVERWEENING
ARROGATE GRAB TAKE CLAIM
SEIZE USURP ASSUME ADROGATE
ARROW FLO PIN ROD SEL BOLT
DART REED SELF SELL SHOT VIRE
BLUNT DEATH FLANE ROVER
SHAFT ARCHER FLIGHT GANYIE
GARROT QUARRY SPRITE TACKLE
WEAPON BOBTAIL DOGBOLT
MISSILE POINTER PROJECT
QUARREL SAGITTA SPINNER
FISHTAIL FORKHEAD

(— ARUM) TUCKAHOE
(— IN GRASS) GREEN SNAKE
(— IN LEG OF STAND) FOOT
(FIRE —) MALLEOLUS
(PART OF —) TIP BUTT HEAD NOCK
PILE POINT SHAFT FEATHER
FLETCHING
(POISONED —) DERRID SUMPIT
(WOBBLING —) FISHTAIL
(PREF.) BELO(NO) HASTATO
SAGITTI SAGITTO TOX(I)(ICO)(O)
ARROWHEAD BUNT FORK HEAD
PILE FLUKE POINT NEOLITH
ARTIFACT CROWBILL FORKHEAD
SPICULUM
ARROWROOT PIA ARUM MUSA
SAGU ARARU CANNA TACCA TIKOR
ARARAO CURCUMA
ARROWSMITH (AUTHOR OF —)
LEWIS
(CHARACTER IN —) MAX ALMUS
JOYCE LEORA SILVA TERRY LANYON
MARTIN GUSTAVE WICKETT
GOTTLIEB SONDELIUS
ARROWSMITH PICKERBAUGH
ARROWWORM SAGITTA
CHAETOGNATH
ARROYO DRAW WADI BROOK
CREEK GULCH GULLY HONDO
ZANJA COULEE RAVINE STREAM
CHANNEL BARRANCA BARRANCO
ARRRANGED (— IN BUNDLES)
DESMOID
ARSENAL ARMORY SUPPLY
MAGAZINE
ARSENOPYRITE MISPICKEL
ARSHIN ARCHIN ALTSCHIN
(ONE-24TH OF —) PARMAK
PARMACK
ARSINOE (DAUGHTER OF —)
ERIOPIS
(FATHER OF —) PHEGEUS
LEUCIPPUS
(HUSBAND OF —) ALCMAEON
(MOTHER OF —) PHILODICE
(SISTER OF —) PHOEBE HILAIRA
ARSIS BEAT ICTUS ACCENT RHYTHM
UPBEAT DOWNBEAT
ARSON FIRE CRIME FELONY
BURNING
ARSONIST ARSONITE
ARSPHENAMINE SIX SALVARSAN
ART WILE CRAFT KNACK KUNST
MAGIC SKILL TRADE MISTER
TECHNE ARTWORK CALLING
CUNNING DESCANT DISCANT
FACULTY FINESSE MYSTERY
SCIENCE APTITUDE ARTIFICE
BUSINESS LEARNING PRACTICE
PRACTISE
(— OF APPLYING TESTS) DOCIMASY
(— OF BLAZONING) ARMORY
(— OF CALCULATING) ALGORISM
ALGORITHM
(— OF DEFENSE) SKIRMISH
(— OF FLOWER ARRANGEMENT)
IKEBANA
(— OF FLOWER ARRANGING)
IKEBANA
(— OF HEALING) LEECHCRAFT
(— OF HORSEMANSHIP) MANEGE
(— OF PREPARING COLORS)
GUMPTION

(— OF SELF-DEFENSE) AIKIDO
(— OF SPEECH) RHETORIC
(— OF TYING KNOTS IN PATTERN) MACRAME
(— SUPPLIES) OILS
(DIABOLIC —) DEVILRY DEVILTRY
(DRAMATIC —) STAGE
(IRRATIONAL —) DADA
(JAPANESE — MOVEMENT) YAMATO YAMATOE
(JUNK —) NEODADA
(KIND OF —) OP POP CLIP JUNK MARTIAL OPTICAL
(LEG —) CHEESECAKE
(MAGIC —) WITHERCRAFT
(MYSTERIOUS —) CABALA KABALA CABBALA KABBALA QABBALA CABBALAH KABBALAH QABBALAH
(NOT —) SHLOCK
(OCCULT —) THEURGY
(RUN AN — SHOW) CURATE
(SHODDY —) BONDIEUSERIE
(TYPE OF —) STREETSCAPE
(PREF.) TECHNI TECHNO TYP(I)(O)
(SUFF.) ERY SHIP TECHNICS TECHNY TYPAL TYPE TYPIC TYPY
(RELATING TO —) METRIC
ARTAXERXES (COMPOSER OF —) ARNE
ART DECO DECO MODERNE
(— MASTER) ERTE
(— PAINTER) ERTE
ARTEMIS UPIS DELIA DIANA PHOEBE CYNTHIA AMARYSIA
ARTERY WAY PATH ROAD AORTA PULSE ROUTE COURSE DENTAL FACIAL RADIAL STREET VESSEL ANONYMA CAROTID COELIAC CONDUIT HIGHWAY SCIATIC VAGINAL CEREBRAL CERVICAL CORONARY DORSALIS EMULGENT PROFUNDA
(NECK —) CAROTID
ARTFUL APT FLY SLY FOXY WILY AGILE DOWNY PAWKY SUAVE ADROIT CLEVER CRAFTY FACILE PRETTY QUAINT SCHEMY SHREWD SMOOTH TRICKY CROOKED CUNNING KNOWING PLAITED POLITIC PRACTIC SUBTILE VULPINE DEXTROUS SCHEMING STEALTHY
ARTFULNESS CUNNING ARTIFICE SUBTLETY
ART GRAY QUAKER SEAMIST
ARTHRITIS GOUT CARPITIS
ARTHROPOD GOLACH GOLOCH SPIDER CHILOPOD DIPLOPOD PERIPATUS
ARTHUR (FATHER OF —) UTHER
ARTICHOKE BUR CANADA CYNARA CARDOON CHOROGI CROSNES KNOTROOT
ARTICLE A AN YE LOT ONE THE BOOK ITEM TERM BRIEF CHEAT ESSAY GEANE PAPER PIECE PLANK POINT STORY THEME THING CLAUSE DETAIL LEADER NOTICE OBJECT REPORT PARTICLE BROCHURE CAUSERIE DOCTRINE PARTICLE POSTFACE TREATISE
(— OF CLOTHING) DUD DIDO APRON CLOUT DICKY FANCY THING

CASUAL DICKEY GARMENT COINTISE CREATION
(— OF FOOD) CATE KNACK
(— OF FURNITURE) STICK
(— OF LITTLE WORTH) DIDO
(— OF SILK) SQUEEZE
(— OF TRADE) PADNAG
(— OF UNUSUAL SIZE) IMPERIAL
(—S OF FAITH) CREDENDA
(—S OF MERCHANDISE) CHAFFER
(CAST-IRON —S) KENTLEDGE
(CHEAP —) CAMELOT
(CHOICE —) VALUABLE
(CONTERFEIT —) DUMMY
(DECORATIVE —) LACKER LACQUER
(FANCY —) CONCEIT
(FIVE —S) HAND
(GENUINE —) GOODS
(HANDICRAFT —) BOONDOGGLE
(INFERIOR —S) SHODDY
(METAL —S) BATTERY
(MISCELLANEOUS —S) SUNDRIES
(NESWPAPER —) STORY LEADER FEATURE
(NONDESCRIPT —) DODAD DOODAB DOODAD WHATNOT
(PALTRY —) GIMCRACK JIMCRACK
(PERSONAL —) CHOSE
(SECONDHAND —) JUNK
(SHOWY —) FRIPPERY
(TRIFLING —) KNICKKNACK
(VALUABLE —S) SWAG
(WORTHLESS —) TRANGAM
(PL.) WARES
ARTICULAATE (INDISTINCTLY —) THICK
ARTICULATE BACK JOIN CLEAR FRAME JOINT SPEAK UNITE UTTER VOCAL ACCENT FLUENT VERBAL EXPRESS JOINTED PHONATE DISTINCT SYLLABLE
(— ASCHILD) LISP
(— CONFUSEDLY) SPUTTER
ARTICULATED BACK BLADE DENTAL DORSAL LABIAL JOINTED ALVEOLAR CEREBRAL VERTEBRATE
ARTICULATION NODE JOINT VOICE SUTURE ARTHRON JUNCTURE SYNTAXIS
(DEFECTIVE —) LALLATION LAMBDACISM
ARTIFACT CELT DISC DISK BATON GUACA HUACA AMGARN BRONZE EOLITH FABRIC GORGET REJECT RONDEL SAGAIE SKEWER ABRADER ARTEFAC DISCOID RACLOIR SCRAPER ARTEFACT DATEMARK RONDELLE TRANCHET
(JAPANESE —S) HANIWA
(PL.) CACHE CERAUNIA
ARTIFICE ART GIN JET GAUD HOAX JOUK PLAN PLOT RUSE TURN WILE BLIND CHEAT COVIN CRAFT CROCK CROOK DODGE DRAFT FEINT FETCH FRAUD GUILE SHIFT SKILL STALL TRAIN TRICK CAUTEL DECEIT DEVICE DOUBLE ENGINE CHICANE COMPASS CUNNING DODGERY DRAUGHT EVASION FINESSE SHUFFLE SLEIGHT COZENAGE DISGUISE DOUBLING INTRIGUE

MANAGERY MANEUVER PRACTICE PRACTISE PRETENSE STRATEGY TRICKERY WINDLASS
(PL.) CABAL CRANS
ARTIFICER WRIGHT ARTIFEX WORKMAN DAEDALUS LAPIDARY MECHANIC OPIFICER TVASHTAR TVASHTRI
ARTIFICIAL CUTE SHAM BOGUS DUMMY FAKED FALSE ARTFUL ERSATZ FORCED FORGED STAGEY UNREAL ASSUMED BASTARD FEIGNED PLASTIC AFFECTED FABULOUS FALSETTO POSTICHE POSTIQUE SPURIOUS
(NOT —) REAL NATURAL
(OVERLY —) ALEXANDRIAN
(SOMETHING —) CAMP
ARTIFICIALITY MANNERISM
ARTILLERY (OR PIECE THEREOF) ARMS GUNS DRAKE SAKER CANNON MINION HEAVIES LANTACA LANTAKA CANNONRY ORDNANCE
(— FIRE) STONK RAFALE
ARTILLERYMAN GUN GUNNER LASCAR REDLEG LASHKAR ENGINEER TOPECHEE
ARTISAN FEVER SMITH ARTIST COOPER ARTIFEX TARKHAN WORKMAN KAMMALAN LETTERER MECHANIC OPIFICER OPERATIVE SILVERSMITH
ARTISANSHIP FOLKCRAFT
ARTIST (ALSO SEE PAINTER) DAB NABI POET ACTOR ADEPT BRUSH HILDA RAPIN DANCER ETCHER EXPERT FICTOR MASTER SINGER WIZARD ARTISAN ARTISTE ARTSMAN FAUVIST OPERANT PAINTER PONTIST SCHEMER ANIMATOR COLORIST FUSINIST IDEALIST LADISLAW LETTERER MAGICIAN MUSICIAN SCULPTOR SKETCHER STIPPLER PASTELIST PRIMITIVE MINIMALIST PASTELLIST
(— SCHOOL) LUMINISM
(SIDEWALK —) SCREEVER
(PL.) SCHOOL
ARTISTIC ARTLY DAEDAL EXPERT ESTHETIC PAINTERLY
(— MATERIAL) KITSCH
(— QUALITY) VERTU VIRTU
ARTISTRY FOLKCRAFT
ARTLESS NAIF OPEN FRANK NAIVE PLAIN SEELY CANDID RUSTIC SIMPLE GIRLISH NATURAL INNOCENT
ARTS TRIVIUM
(MARTIAL —) BUDO
ART-SONG LIED
ARTY CHICHI
ARUGULA RUGOLA
ARUM ARAD TARO AROID CALALU DRAGON TAWKEE WAMPEE MANDRAKE TUCKAHOE
ARVIRAGUS CADWAL
(FATHER OF —) CYMBELINE
(WIFE OF —) DORIGEN
ARYAN MEDE SLAV OSSET NORDIC OSSETE
(NOT —) ANARYA
ARZA (SLAYER OF —) ZIMRI

AS S SO ALS FOR HOW QUA ALSO INTO LIKE SOME THAT THUS TILL WHEN EQUAL QUOAD SINCE WHILE BRONZE THEWAY WHENAS BECAUSE EQUALLY SIMILAR QUATENUS
(— FAR AS) TO INTO QUATENUS
(— IT WERE) FAIRLY
(— LONG AS) SOBEIT
(— MUCH) ALSMEKILL
(— SOON) ALSOON ASTITE ALSWITH DIRECTLY
(— TO) QUOAD
(— WELL) EVEN
(— WELL AS) FORBY FORBYE
(— YET) HITHERTO
ASA (FATHER OF —) ABIJAH
ASAFETIDA HING LASER FERULA
ASAHEL (BROTHER OF —) JOAB
(MOTHER OF —) ZERUIAH
(SLAYER OF —) ABNER
(SON OF —) JONATHAN
(UNCLE OF —) DAVID
ASANDER (BROTHER OF —) PARMENION
(FATHER OF —) PHILOTAS
ASAPH (FATHER OF —) BECHERIAH
(SON OF —) JOAH ASARELAH
ASARABACCA HAZEL FOALFOOT
ASAREEL (FATHER OF —) JEHALELEEL
ASARELAH (FATHER OF —) ASAPH
ASBESTOS ABBEST XYLITE AMIANTH ABSISTOS ALBESTON AMIANTUS WOODROCK EARTHFLAX
(BLUE —) CROCIDOLITE
ASCALAPHUS (BROTHER OF —) IALMENUS
(FATHER OF —) ARES MARS ACHERON
(MOTHER OF —) ORPHNE GORGYRA ASTYOCHE
(SLAYER OF —) DEIPHOBUS
ASCEND UP STY RISE SOAR STYE UPGO ARISE CLIMB MOUNT SCALE STAIR TOWER AMOUNT ASPIRE BREAST CLIMAX UPRISE CLAMBER UPCLIMB ESCALATE PROGRESS
ASCENDANCY SWAY POWER CONTROL MASTERY SUCCESS DOMINION OWERANCE PRESTIGE
ASCENDANT ARISING MOUNTANT ASSURGENT
ASCENDING ANODAL ANODIC ORIENT UPHILL UPWARD ANABATIC ASPIRANT SUBERECT
(— WITHOUT A TURN) FLYING
ASCENSION APOTHEOSIS
ASCENT STY HILL RAMP RISE RIST UPGO CLIMB GLORY GRADE MOUNT RAISE SCEND SLOPE STEEP STEPS STILL UPWAY SOURCE STAIRS UPCOME UPGANG UPHILL UPRISE UPWITH INCLINE SCALING UPGRADE UPSWING EMINENCE GRADIENT
ASCERTAIN GET SEE SET TRY FEEL FIND TELL COUNT GLEAN LEARN PITCH PROVE ASSURE ATTAIN FIGURE ANALYSE ANALYZE APPRISE APPRIZE COMPUTE MEASURE UNEARTH DISCOVER

ASCETIC NUN MONK SOFI SUFI YATI YOGI DANDY FAKIR FRIAR SADHU SOFEE STOIC YOGIN CHASTE ESSENE HERMIT SADDHU SEVERE SOOFEE STRICT ADAMITE AUSTERE BHIKSHU DEVOTEE EREMITE RECLUSE SRAMANA STYLITE TAPASVI AVADHUTA MARABOUT NAZARITE SANNYASI (PL.) THERAPEUTAE

ASCIDIAN POLYP CUNGEBOI CUNGEVOI TETHYDAN TUNICATE

ASCIDIUM PITCHER VASCULUM

ASCOCARP ASCOMA

ASCOGONIUM ARCHICARP

ASCOMA CUPULE

ASCRIBABLE DUE

ASCRIBE LAY ARET EVEN GIVE APPLY BLAME COUNT GUESS IMPLY INFER PLACE REFER TITLE ACCUSE ALLEGE ARETTE ASSIGN ATTACH CHARGE CREDIT IMPUTE PREFER RECKON RELATE ASCRIVE ENTITLE ACCREDIT ARROGATE DEDICATE INSCRIBE INTITULE

ASCRIPTION LAUD CREDIT ADDITION

ASCUS BAG SAC THECA ASCELLUS

ASEA LOST ADDLED ADRIFT PUZZLED SAILING CONFUSED

ASEMIA ASYMBOLIA

ASENATH (FATHER OF —) POTIPHERAH
(HUSBAND OF —) JOSEPH
(SON OF —) EPHRAIM MANASSEH

ASEXUAL AGAMIC NEUTER AGAMOUS
(PREF.) AGAM(O)

ASGARD (GODS OF —) AESIR

ASH AS ALS ASE ASS FIG RON COKE SORB ARTAR ASHEN EMBER TRAIN ROWAN CINDER CORPSE DOTTEL DOTTLE TEPHRA WICKEN CLINKER RESIDUE DOGBERRY FRAXINUS HOOPWOOD WINETREE
(BARILLA —) PULVERINE
(FRUIT OF —) SAMARA
(SILKY —) CEDAR
(PL.) ASE AXAN KELP SOIL ASHEN VAREC WASTE BREEZE CINDERS CREMAINS PULVERIN

ASHAMED MEAN NACE NAIS ABASHED HANGDOG HONTOUS SHAMEFACED

ASHBEL (FATHER OF —) BENJAMIN

ASH-BLOND CENDRE

ASH-COLORED CINEREAL CINEREOUS

ASHEN WAN GRAY GREY PALE WAXEN WHITE PALLID GHASTLY BLANCHED CINEREAL

ASHER (FATHER OF —) JACOB
(MOTHER OF —) ZILPAH

ASHES (— OF CREMATED BODY) CREMAINS
(HUMAN —) CREMAINS
(PREF.) CINE SPODO TEPHRA TEPHRO

ASHKENAZ (FATHER OF —) GOMER

ASHKOKO CONY DAMAN HYRAX

ASHLAR ASELAR RANGEWORK

ASHORE ACOST ALAND AGROUND BEACHED STRANDED

ASHTAVAKRA (FATHER OF —) KAHODA

ASHTRAY SPITKID SPITKIT

ASHUR FEROHER
(FATHER OF —) HEZRON
(MOTHER OF —) ABIAH
(WIFE OF —) HELAH

ASHVATH (FATHER OF —) JAPHLET

ASHY WAN CINEREAL

ASIA (FATHER OF —) OCEANUS
(HUSBAND OF —) IAPETUS
(MOTHER OF —) TETHYS
(SON OF —) ATLAS EPIMETHEUS PROMETHEUS

ASIA
(ALSO SEE SPECIFIC COUNTRIES)
DESERT: GOBI TAKLAMAKAN
LAKE: ARAL URMIA BAYKAL CASPIAN BALKHASH
MOUNTAIN: FUJI DJAJA JANNU KAMET PAMIR ARARAT KUNGUR KUNLUN LHOTSE MAKALU MUZTAG NOSHAQ NUPTSE SEMERU TRIVOR EVEREST RATHONG ANNAPURNA
NATION: IRAN IRAQ LAOS OMAN BURMA CHINA INDIA JAPAN NEPAL QATAR SYRIA TIBET YEMEN BHUTAN ISRAEL JORDAN RUSSIA TAIWAN TURKEY ARMENIA BAHRAIN CROATIA LEBANON VIETNAM CAMBODIA HONGKONG MALAYSIA MONGOLIA PAKISTAN THAILAND INDONESIA KAMPUCHEA SINGAPORE AZERBAIJAN BANGLADESH NORTHKOREA SOUTHKOREA AFGHANISTAN SAUDIARABIA
RANGE: ALTAI KOLYMA HIMALAYA
RIVER: OB SI AMUR LENA URAL INDUS GANGES MEKONG TIGRIS HWANGHO SALWEEN TANGTZE YENISEI EUPHRATES IRRAWADDY
VOLCANO: APO USU FUGI GEDE TAAL AGUNG ALAID DEMPO MAYON RAUNG MARAPI MERAPI SEMERU SINILA SLAMET ULAWUN TAMBORA TJAREME GAMALAMA KERINTJE RINDJANI TOLBACHIK BULOSANSUNDORO
WATERFALL: JOG GOKAK KEGON MEKONG CAUVERY

ASIA MINOR (ANCIENT REGION OF —) IONIA

ASIAN LAO THAI

ASIDE BY BYE OFF AGEE AWAY GONE NEAR PAST AGLEY ALOOF APART ASKEW FORBY ASLANT ASTRAY BESIDE BEYOND BYHAND FORBYE FORTHBY LATERAL PRIVATE WHISPER OVERHAND RESERVED SECRETLY SEPARATE SIDEWISE OVERBOARD TOTHEWIND

ASININE DULL CRASS DENSE INEPT SILLY ABSURD ASSISH OBTUSE SIMPLE STUPID DOLTISH FATUOUS FOOLISH IDIOTIC MORONIC

ASIUS (FATHER OF —) DYMAS HYRTACUS

(SISTER OF —) HECUBA
(SLAYER OF —) AJAX IDOMENUS

ASK BEG SPY SUE FAND PRAY QUIZ CLAIM CRAVE EXACT FRAYN PLEAD QUERY SPEAK SPEER SPEIR SPELL SPERE ADJURE DEMAND DESIRE EXAMIN EXPECT FRAIST FRAYNE INVITE BESEECH BESPEAK CONSULT ENTREAT IMPLORE INQUIRE REQUEST REQUIRE SOLICIT PETITION QUESTION
(— ALMS) CANT THIG
(— FOR) BEG BID CRY DUN LAIT SEEK BESPEAK INQUIRE REQUEST
(— PAYMENT) CHARGE

ASKANCE AWRY ASKEW ASKILE CROOKED SIDEWAYS

ASKEW CAM AGEE ALOP AWRY AZEW AGLEE AGLEY AMISS ATILT CRAZY GLEED TIPSY ASKANT ASLANT ATWIST FLOOEY SKEWED SKIVIE ASQUINT CROOKED OBLIQUE BIASWISE COCKEYED SIDELING

ASKING ROGATION ROGATORY

ASKWARD HAMHANDED

ASLANT ASIDE SLOPE
(PREF.) PLAGI(O)

ASLEEP DEAD FAST IDLE LATENT NUMBED DORMANT NAPPING

ASOCIAL EGREGIOUS

ASOKA (FATHER OF —) BINDUSARA

ASOPUS (DAUGHTER OF —) ORNIA THEBE AEGINA ASOPIS CLEONE PIRENE SINOPE CHALCIS CORCYRA SALAMIS TANAGRA THESPEIA
(SON OF —) ISMENUS PELASGUS
(WIFE OF —) METOPE

ASP ESP ASPIC COBRA SNAKE VIPER ASPIDE URAEUS CERASTES

ASPAR (FATHER OF —) ARDABURIUS

ASPARAGUS LILY GRASS SPRUE ASPERGE SPARAGE SPERAGE
(— GARNISH) PRINCESS
(— UNIT) SPEAR
(INFERIOR —) SPRUE

ASPATHA (FATHER OF —) HAMAN

ASPECT AIR HUE WAY AURA BROW FACE HAND KIND LEER LOOK MIEN SIDE VIEW VULT ANGLE COLOR DECIL FACET GUISE IMAGE NORMA PHASE SIGHT STAGE TRINE VISOR VIZOR DECILE FACIES FIGURE GLANCE MANNER PHASIS REGARD VISAGE APPAREL BEARING ESSENCE FEATURE MALEFIC OUTLOOK RESPECT RETRAIT SEXTILE SHOWING SPECIES CARRIAGE CONSPECT FOREHEAD OUTSIGHT PROSPECT QUINTILE CHARACTER SEMBLANCE
(— OF CURVE) INSIDE
(— OF EMOTION) AFFECT
(— OF MOON) CRESCENT
(— OF MUSICAL NUANCES) AGOGICS
(BALEFUL —) DISASTER
(CULTURAL —) EMANATION
(DETERMINING —) HEART
(DORSAL —) NOTUM
(EXTERNAL —) PHYSIOGNOMY
(FACIAL —) EXPRESSION
(LANGUAGE —) DURATIVE

(OF PLANETS) QUARTILE
(OF STARS) QUINCUNX
(PRIMARY —) HIGHWAY
(QUARTILE —) SQUARE
(SECONDARY —) BYWAY

ASPEN APS ASP ALAMO NITHER POPLAR POPPLE QUAKER QUAKING TREMBLE

ASPER AKCHA AKCHEH OTHMANY

ASPERGILLUM HYSSOP SPRINKLE STRINKLE

ASPERITY IRE RIGOR ACERBITY ACRIMONY TARTNESS ANIMOSITY

ASPERSE SKIT SLUR SPOT ABUSE DECRY LIBEL SPRAY DEFAME DEFILE MALIGN REVILE SHOWER VILIFY APPEACH BLACKEN DETRACT LAMPOON SLANDER TARNISH TRADUCE BESMIRCH FORSPEAK SPRINKLE

ASPERSION SLUR BAPTISM CALUMNY INNUENDO

ASPHALT BREA PITCH SLIME FILLER MANJAK BITUMEN CUTBACK MANJACK BYERLITE UINTAITE GILSONITE

ASPHALTUM CONGO

ASPHODEL KNAVERY AFFODILL

ASPHYXIA APNEA APNOEA ACROTISM SUFFOCATION

ASPIC JELLY GELATIN GELATINE LAVENDER

ASPIRANT (— TO KNIGHTHOOD) DONZEL SQUIRE

ASPIRATE ROUGH SPIRITUS

ASPIRATION GOAL IDEAL DESIRE RECOIL SIGHTS AMBITION PRETENSION

ASPIRE AIM STY HOPE LONG MINT RISE SEEK SOAR WISH ETTLE MOUNT TOWER YEARN ASCEND ATTAIN DESIRE PRETEND

ASPIRIN FEBRIFUGE

ASPIRING ASPIRANT

ASRIEL (FATHER OF —) GILEAD

ASS DOLT FOOL JADE KHUR MOKE BURRO CHUMP CUDDY DICKY DUNCE EQUID GUDDA HINNY NINNY CUDDIE DAPPLE DICKEY DONKEY ONAGER ASINEGO ASSHEAD JACKASS LONGEAR MALTESE SOLIPED IMBECILE
(FEMALE —) JENNY JENNET
(MALE —S) JACKSTOCK
(WILD —) KIANG KULAN KYANG KIYANG KOULAN ONAGER HEMIPPE CHIGETAI GHORKHAR HEMIONUS
(PL.) JACKSTOCK
(PREF.) ONISCI ONO

ASSAI MANICOLE

ASSAIL WOO BASH BEAT FRAY HOOT JUMP PELT SAIL ASSAY BESET FLYAT PRESS SETAT SHOCK STONE WHACK WHANG ACCUSE ATTACK BATTER BICKER BULLET HURTLE IMPUGN INFEST INSULT INVADE MALIGN MOLEST OFFEND OPPUGN RAGEAT RATTLE SAILYE SCATHE STRIKE ASSAULT ATTEMPT BELABOR BESEIGE BOMBARD CATCALL ENFORCE ASSEMBLE BLUDGEON TOMAHAWK
(— WITH DIN) PEAL

(— WITH LANGUAGE) REVILE BULLYRAG BALLLYRAG
(— WITH RAILLERY) BANTER
(— WITH WORDS) TONGUE
ASSAILANT ONSETTER
ASSAM (MOUNTAIN OF —) JAPVO
(STATE OF —) KHASI MANIPUR
(TOWN OF —) IMPHAL SADIYA GAUHATI SHILLONG
(TRIBE OF —) AO AKA AOR AHOM GARO NAGA
ASSARACUS (BROTHER OF —) ILUS GANYMEDE
(FATHER OF —) TROS
(MOTHER OF —) CALLIRRHOE
(SISTER OF —) CLEOPATRA
(SON OF —) CAPYS
ASSART SART THWAITE
ASSASSIN THAG THUG BRAVE BRAVO FEDAI FIDAI NINJA CUTTLE FIDAWI HITMAN KILLER SLAYER RUFFIAN STABBER TORPEDO HACKSTER MURDERER SICARIUS
ASSASSINATE KILL SLAY MURDER REMOVE
ASSASSINATION THUGGEE
ASSAULT MUG BEAT BLOW COSH FRAY RAID SLUG ABUSE ALARM ASSAY BRUNT HARRY ONSET POISE POUND SHOCK SMITE STORM STOUR VENUE AFFRAY ALARUM ASSAIL ATTACK BREACH BUFFET CHARGE ENGINE EXTENT HOLDUP INSULT INVADE NAPALM ONFALL STOUND STOUSH THRUST YOKING ATTEMPT BOMBARD DESCENT LAMBAST PURSUIT RUNNING VIOLATE INVASION OUTBURST BUSHWHACK
ASSAY RUN SAY TRY TEST ESSAY PROOF PROVE TOUCH TRIAL ASSAIL ATTACK EFFORT ANALYZE ATTEMPT EXAMINE TASTING ANALYSIS APPRAISE ENDEAVOR ESTIMATE HARDSHIP
ASSAYER POTDAR TESTER
(CONTAINER OF —) CUPEL
ASSAYING DOCIMASY
ASSEMBLAGE ARMY BODY CAMP CLOT COMA CREW HERD HOST MASS PACK RUCK BUNCH CHOIR COURT CROWD DRIFT DROVE FLOCK GROUP LEVEE POSSE QUIRE SALON SHOCK SWARM TRIBE CONVOY GALAXY HOOKUP RESORT SPREAD SYSTEM THRONG CIRCUIT CLUSTER COLLEGE COMPANY COMPLEX CONVENT CULTURE SOCIETY STATION STATUTE TABAGIE ASSEMBLY AUDITORY CONGRESS MULTIPLE PARLIAMENT
(— OF FOSSILS) COLONY
(— OF INTEGERS) IDEAL
(CONFUSED —) FARRAGO
ASSEMBLE FIT LAY POD SAM BULK CALL HERD HOST KNOT MASS MEET ROUT SAMM AMASS ASAME FLOCK GROUP PIECE RALLY TROOP UNITE COUPLE GATHER HUDDLE MUSTER SUMMON COLLATE COLLECT COMPILE

CONDUCE CONVENE CONVOKE RECRUIT CONGRESS CONGREGATE
(— CARDS) BUNCH
ASSEMBLED ACCOYLD
ASSEMBLER BONDER
ASSEMBLING MUSTER PARADE ROUNDUP
ASSEMBLY HUI SUM BAUD BEVY BOGY DIET DRUM DUMA FEIS HOEY MALL MOOT RAAD ROUT SEJM SEYM TING AGORA BOGEY BOULE COURT COVEN CURIA DOUMA FORUM GROUP JUNTA LEVEE PARTY PRESS SABHA SETUP SOBOR SYNOD THING TROOP AENACH AONACH ASSIZE BOBBIN BUSING CHAPEL COETUS COVINE GEMOTE MAJLIS PARADE PLENUM POWWOW SEIMAS SENATE STEVEN CHAMBER CHAPTER COLLEGE COMITIA COMMAND COMPANY CONCION CONSORT CONVENT COUNCIL DIETINE EOTATES FOLKMOT HUSTING LANDTAG MEETING PENSION SERVICE SESSION SOCIETY SYNAGOG SYNAXIS TEMPEST TYNWALD ZEMSTVO AUDIENCE CONCLAVE CONGRESS ECCLESIA FOLKMOOT PLACITUM PORTMOTE PRESENCE SEDERUNT SOBRANJE TINEWALD TRIBUNAL VOLKSTAG WARDMOTE CONCOURSE
(— HOUSE) KASHIM
(— OF BLESSED) HEAVEN
(— OF CONDUCTORS) BUS
(— OF DEPUTIES) AMPHICTYONA
(— OF ELDERS) KGOTLA
(— OF WITCHES) COVEN SABBAT SABBATH
(AFTERNOON —) LEVEE
(BOY SCOUT —) JAMBOREE
(CLOSED —) CONCLAVE
(CROWDED —) SQUEEZE
(EVENING —) ROUT
(FASTENER —) SEMS
(FULL —) PLENUM
(GRENADE —) BOUCHON
(IRELAND —) DAIL SEANAD
(IRISH —) DAIL
(RIOTOUS —) MOB DONNYBROOK
(PL.) PLENA COMITIA
ASSENT AYE BOW NOD YEA YES AMEN SEAL SENT ADMIT AGREE GRANT YIELD ACCEDE ACCEPT ACCORD BELIEF CHORUS COMPLY CONCUR SUBMIT UNISON APPROVE CONCEDE CONFESS CONFORM CONSENT ADHESION CONSTATE OKEYDOKE SANCTION SUFFRAGE ACCESSION OKEYDOKEY
(— TO) GOWITH
ASSERT LAY BRAG SHOW POSIT VOICE AFFIRM ALLEGE ASSURE AVOUCH DEFEND DEPONE DEPOSE INTEND INTENT THREAP UPHOLD ADVANCE BETOKEN CONFIRM CONTEND DECLARE PROTEST SUPPORT ADVOCATE CHAMPION CONSTATE MAINTAIN OUTSTAND POSITIVE PREDICATE
ASSERTING (POSITIVELY —) THETIC

ASSERTION VOW FACT HOTI CLAIM VOUCH AVERMENT
(— OF MASCULINITY) MACHISMO
(BOASTFUL —) JACTATION
(DUBIOUS —) PLINYISM
ASSERTIVE BRASH DOGMATIC POSITIVE
ASSESS LAY TAX CESS DOOM LEVY MISE RATE SCOT TOLL AGIST CENSE PRICE STENT SUMUP TEIND VALUE AFFEER ASSIZE CHARGE EXTEND IMPOSE SAMPLE MEASURE APPRAISE ESTIMATE
ASSESSMENT FEE LUG TAX CESS DUTY LEVY SCOT TOLL CULET JUMMA PRICE RATAL STENT TITHE WORTH EXTENT IMPOST PURVEY SURTAX TARIFF SCUTAGE BRIGBOTE TAXATION
ASSESSOR JUDGE MUFTI RATER TAXER CESSOR LISTER TASKER AUDITOR STENTOR TAXATOR
(PL.) FINTADORES
ASSET PLUS HONOR GETPENNY PROPERTY RESOURCE STRENGTH
ASSETS GOODS MEANS MONEY STOCK CREDIT WEALTH CAPITAL EFFECTS ACCOUNTS PROPERTY RESOURCE
ASSEVERATE SAY VOW AVER AVOW STATE SWEAR AFFIRM ALLEGE ASSERT ASSURE DECLARE PROTEST
ASSEVERATION VOW OATH STATING
ASSHUR (FATHER OF —) SHEM
ASSIDUOUS BUSY GREAT ACTIVE DEVOTED PENIBLE STUDIED DILIGENT FREQUENT SEDULOUS STUDIOUS
ASSIGN FIX LET PUT SET ARET CAST CEDE DEAL DOLE DRAW GIVE METE RATE SEAL SHOW SIGN ALLOT ALLOW APPLY ARETT AWARD DIGHT ENDOW REFER SHIFT TITLE ADDUCE AFFECT ALLEGE ATTACH CHARGE CONVEY DESIGN DIRECT ENTAIL ORDAIN ACCOUNT ADJUDGE APPOINT ASCRIBE CONSIGN DISPOSE ENTITLE SPECIFY STATION TRIBUTE ALLOCATE ANTEDATE ARROGATE DELEGATE INSCRIBE TRANSFER
(— QUARTERS) BILLET
(— TASK) STINT
ASSIGNATION DATE MEET TRYST MEETING
ASSIGNMENT DECK DUTY TASK CHORE GRIND STENT STINT TUNCA CESSIO LESSON CESSION BUSINESS HOMEWORK PLACEMENT
(FOREIGN —) POST
ASSIGNOR CEDOR CEDENS CEDENT
ASSIMILATE MIX ONE FUSE ADAPT ALTER BLEND LEARN MERGE ABSORB DIGEST IMBIBE COMPARE CONCOCT RESEMBLE
ASSIMILATION ECHOISM HOMEOSIS RECOGNITION
(— OF FOOD) CONCOCTION
ASSINIBOIN HOHE

ASSIR (FATHER OF —) KORAH EBIASAPH JECONIAH
ASSIST AID ABET BACK HELP JOIN AVAIL BOOST COACH FAVOR NURSE SERVE SPEED STEAD ATTEND ESCORT PROMPT SECOND SQUIRE SUCCOR BENEFIT COMFORT FURTHER RELIEVE SUPPORT SUSTAIN ADJUVATE BEFRIEND
(— A READER) FESCUE
(— AT) STAY
ASSISTANCE AID ALMS CAST GIFT HAND HELP LIFT BOOST FAVOR HEEZE RELIEF REMEDY SUCCOR SUPPLY ADJUTOR COMFORT SECOURS SUBSIDY SUPPORT AUXILIUM EASEMENT GIFFGAFF LARGESSE
ASSISTANT CAD AIDE ALLY HAND HELP MAID MATE PUNK SOUS ZANY CLERK GROOM USHER VALET AIDANT BUMPER COMMIS CURATE DEPUTY FLUNKY HELPER LEGATE NIPPER SECOND TULTUL YEOMAN ABETTOR ACOLYTE ADJOINT ADJUNCT DOORMAN DRESSER HOGGLER PADRINO PARTNER PROVOST RUBBLER SHIFTER STRIKER SWAMPER ADJUTANT ADJUVANT FELDSHER GOMASHTA LECTURER MINISTER OFFSIDER PARASITE SERVITOR SIDESMAN SUBPRIOR
(— TO ANIMAL SHOW JUDGE) STEWARD
(AUCTIONEER'S —) SPOTTER
(BOY —) NIPPER
(DOCTOR'S —) FELDSHER
(DYEING —) CARRIER
(GUNNER'S —) MATROSS
(MASON'S —) GOUJAT
(MATADOR'S —) CHULO
(POLICE —) CORPORAL
(SURVEYOR'S —) CHAINMAN
(WAITER'S —) BUSBOY OMNIBUS
ASSOCIATE MIX PAL AIDE ALLY BAND CHUM HERD JOIN LINK MATE MOOP MOUP PEER WALK WIFE YOKE BLEND BUDDY CRONY HABER MATCH TRAIN TROOP ASSORT ATTACH ATTEND CHABER COHORT COUSIN FASTEN FELLOW FRIEND HELPER HOBNOB MARROW MEDDLE MEMBER MINGLE PUISNE PUISNY RELATE SOCIUS SPOUSE TRAVEL ADJUNCT ASSOCIE BRACKET COALITE COMMUNE COMPANY COMPEER COMRADE CONNECT CONSORT HUSBAND PARTNER PEWMATE SOCIATE COMPLICE CONFRERE CONJOINT CONVERSE COPEMATE FAMILIAR FEDERATE FOLLOWER FREQUENT GADSHILL IDENTIFY INTIMATE PARTAKER ACCOMPANY ACCOMPLICE
(— WITH) FRAT MOOP MOUP
(DEMON —) FLY
(PL.) ENTOURAGE
ASSOCIATED
(PREF.) SYM
(SUFF.) (— WITH) IC(AL)

ASSOCIATION HUI BODY BOND BUND CLUB GILD HONG HUNT TONG ARTEL BOARD GUILD HANSA HANSE SANGH TRUCK UNION CARTEL CERCLE CHAPEL COMITY CONGER GRANGE LEAGUE LEGION LYCEUM PLEDGE SANGHA SCHOLA VEREIN CIRCUIT COMBINE COMPANY CONSORT CONTACT CONVENT COUNCIL SOCIETY SOROSIS SYNOECY AFFINITY ALLIANCE ASSEMBLY ATHENEUM CONVERSE HABITUDE INTIMACY SODALITY SYNOMOSY TAALBOND ORGANIZATION
(— OF FOSSILS) FAUNULA FAUNULE
(ANTAGONISTIC —) ANTIBIOSIS
(BANK —) SANDL
(BOOK-SELLERS' —) CONGER
(CLOSE —) HARNESS INTIMACY
(EMPLOYERS' —) GREMIO
(FARMERS' —) GRANGE
(IN —) ALONG
(LABOR —) ARTEL UNION
(RELIGIOUS —) SAMAJ
(SECRET —) CABAL
(STUDENTS' —) CORPS
(SYMBIOTIC —) ACAROPHILY
ASSOIL RID SOIL ATONE CLEAR SOLVE ACQUIT PARDON REFUTE ABSOLVE DELIVER EXPIATE UNGIVE RELEASE RESOLVE
ASSONANCE PUN RHYME PARAGRAM
ASSORT BOLT CULL SUIT WINNOW
(— COINS) SHROFF
ASSORTED CHOW CHOWCHOW
ASSORTER FEEDER LOOKER
ASSORTMENT BAG LOT SET OLIO BATCH BUNCH GROUP SUITE RAGBAG MIXTURE
(— OF COLORS) PALETTE
(— OF TYPE) BILL FONT
(COMPLETE —) STANDARD
ASSUAGE BEET CALM EASE LIOS LISS ABATE ALLAY CHARM DELAY LISSE MEASE SALVE SLAKE STILL SWAGE LENIFY LESSEN MODIFY PACIFY QUENCH REDUCE SOFTEN SOLACE SOOTHE TEMPER APPEASE COMFORT MOLLIFY QUALIFY RELIEVE SATISFY DIMINISH MITIGATE MODERATE
ASSUASIVE MILD LENIENT LENITIVE SOOTHING
ASSUME DON PUT SAY SET BEAR DARE FANG GIVE MASK PULL SHAM SHIP TAKE ADOPT ANNEX CLOAK ELECT ENDUE FEIGN GUESS INDUE INFER RAISE USURP ACCEPT AFFECT DETAKE CLOTHE FIGURE ASSUMPT BELIEVE PREMISE PRESUME PRETEND RECEIVE SUBSUME SUPPOSE SURMISE ACCROACH ARROGATE SIMULATE PERSONATE POSTULATE UNDERTAKE
(— CHARACTER) ACT AFFECT
(— FORM) ENGENDER
(— OFFICE) ACCEDE
(— PAINTING STANCE) BACK
ASSUMED ALIAS FALSE GIVEN FEIGNED AFFECTED BORROWED

ASSUMING LOFTY UPPISH UPPITY AFFECTED ARROGANT SUPERIOR
ASSUMPTION ALSOB DONNEE THESIS BALLOON FICTION SURMISE HOMEOSIS MARYMASS PRETENCE PRETENSE PRESUMPTION
(BASIC —) BEGINNING
(EMPTY —) IMAGINATION
ASSURANCE FACE GALL SEAL BRASS CHEEK FAITH NERVE POISE TRUST APLOMB AVOUCH BELIEF CAUTIO CREDIT PLEVIN PLIGHT SAFETY COURAGE PROMISE WARRANT AUDACITY BOLDNESS COOLNESS FIRMANCE FOREHEAD SECURITY SUREMENT
ASSURE AFFY AVER SURE TELL CINCH HIGHT SEWUP VOUCH AFFEER ASSERT AVOUCH ENSURE INSURE PLEDGE SECURE SEKERE SICCAR SICKER WITTER BETROTH CERTIFY CONFIRM DECLARE HEARTEN PROMISE PROTEST RESOLVE WARRANT AFFIANCE CONVINCE EMBOLDEN PERSUADE
ASSURED BOLD CALM COLD FIRM PERT SURE BOUND SIKER SLUSH FACILE PROBAL SECURE SICCAR SICKER CERTAIN POSITIVE
(— OF SUCCESS) MADE
(BLUNTLY —) KNOCKDOWN
ASSUREDLY AMEN SOON INDEED PERDIE REDELY SICCAR SICKER SURELY VERILY HARDILY WITTERLY
ASSYRIA ASHUR ASSUR ASSHUR
(CAPITAL OF —) CALAH NINEVEH
ASSYRIAN NESTORIAN
(— PLUM) SEBESTEN
ASTER ARNICA COCASH AMELLUS BEEWEED BONESET EUASTER ASTROFEL COMPOSIT CYTASTER MONASTER STARWORT STOKESIA
ASTERIA (DAUGHTER OF —) HECATE
(FATHER OF —) COEUS
(HUSBAND OF —) PERSES
(MOTHER OF —) PHOEBE
(SISTER OF —) LETO LATONA
ASTERISK MARK STAR ASTER ASTERISM WINDMILL
(THREE —S) ASTERISM
ASTERIUS (BROTHER OF —) AMPHION
(FATHER OF —) ANAX HYPERASIUS
(SLAYER OF —) MILETUS
ASTERN AFT BAFT HIND REAR ABAFT APOOP BEHIND OCCIPUT BACKWARD
ASTEROID EROS HEBE IRIS JUNO CERES DIONE FLORA IRENE METIS VESTA ASTREA EGERIA EUROPA HYGEIA PALLAS PLANET PSYCHE THALIA THEMIS THETIS ELECTRA EUNOMIA FORTUNA LUTETIA CALLIOPE MASSALIA PLANTOID STARFISH STARLIKE VICTORIA
ASTHMA PHTHISIC
ASTHMATIC POUCY PURSY POUCEY WHEEZY PANTING PUFFING
ASTIR UP AGOG ABOUT AFOOT AGATE ALERT GOING ACTIVE

AROUND ASTEER MOVING ROUSED ABROACH EXCITED STIRRING VIGILANT
ASTONISH AWE DAZE STAM AMAZE KNOCK SHOCK DAMMER MARVEL STOUND ASTOUND GLOPPEN IMPRESS STARTLE AMERVEIL BEWILDER CONFOUND SURPRISE
ASTONISHING AMAZING FABULOUS MARVELOUS MARVELLOUS MINDBOGGLING
ASTONISHMENT MUSE FERLY DISMAY FARLEY MARVEL STOUND WONDER SURPRISE
ASTOUND BEAT STUN ABASH AMAZE APPAL SHOCK STOUN APPALL STOUND STAGGER STUPEFY STUPEND TERRIFY ASTONISH CONFOUND SURPRISE
ASTOUNDED STUPENT
ASTOUNDING STUNNING
ASTRAEA (FATHER OF —) ZEUS JUPITER
(MOTHER OF —) THEMIS
(SISTER OF —) PUDICITIA
ASTRAEUS (BROTHER OF —) PALLAS PERSES
(FATHER OF —) CRIUS
(MOTHER OF —) EURYBIA
ASTRAGAL TALUS CHAPLET CORNICE BAGUETTE
ASTRAGALAR
(PREF.) TALO
ASTRAGALUS TALUS VETCH HUCKLEBONE
ASTRAKHAN BOKHARA
ASTRAL REMOTE STARRY STELLAR ASTRAEAN SIDEREAL STARLIKE
ASTRAY AWRY LOST WILL ABORD AGATE AGLEE AGLEY AMISS ASIDE GLEED WRONG ABROAD AFIELD ERRANT ERRING FAULTY DEPAYSE DEVIOUS FORLORN SINNING WILSOME MISTAKEN STRAYING
ASTRIDE ATOP ABOARD ACHEVAL SPANNING
ASTRINGENCY ACERBITY ACRIMONY
ASTRINGENT ACID ALUM COTO SOUR TART ACERB HARSH ROUGH SAPAN STERN TONER CORNUS MASTIC PONTIC SEVERE TANNIN ALUMNOL AUSTERE BINDING CATECHU PUCKERY RHATANY STYPTIC GERANIUM TRILLIUM
(NOT —) SOFT
ASTROLOGER JOTI JOSHI ARTIST JOTISI MERLIN ZADKIEL SCHEMIST
ASTROLOGY STARCRAFT MATHEMATICALS
ASTRONAUT (— ACTIVITY) SPACEWALK
ASTRONOMER JOTI JOSHI JOTISI
AMERICAN BOK SEE BOND BOSS HALE HALL HILL POOR REES TODD VERY ABELL ADAMS BAADE BAUER BOWEN CHASE ELKIN FROST HOUGH HYNEK MAURY PEASE SAGAN SWIFT YOUNG AITKEN BAILEY CANNON DRAPER HOLDEN HUBBLE HUSSEY JACOBY KEELER KUIPER LOOMIS LOWELL PEIRCE PETERS PORTER RENIZE ROGERS

SEARES STRUVE WALKER WATSON WILSON BARNARD BURNHAM EASTMAN FLEMING GILLIES JASTROW LANGLEY LITTELL MERRILL MITCHEL MOULTON NEWCOMB PERRINE RITCHEY RUSSELL SAFFORD SHAPLEY SLIPHER WHITNEY ASHBROOK BOWDITCH CAMPBELL CHANDLER COMSTOCK DOUGLASS HARKNESS STEBBINS TOMBAUGH WINTHROP WOODWARD ALEXANDER DOOLITTLE LEUSCHNER MOREHOUSE PICKERING PRITCHETT HARRINGTON RUTHERFURD SCHAEBERLE RITTENHOUSE SCHLESINGER EICHELBERGER
AUSTRIAN FALB HAGEN LITTROW PURBACH
BELGIAN QUETELET
CANADIAN KLOTZ PLASKETT
CZECH KOHOUTEK
DANISH BRAHE DREYER HANSEN ROEMER SCHUMACHER LONGOMONTANUS
DUTCH BLAEU SITTER HUYGENS KAPTEYN
EGYPTIAN PTOLEMY
ENGLISH AIRY HIND POND DYLE TODD WARD ADAMS DAILY DIXON DYSON INNES JEANS JONES MASON MILNE MURIS WALES CLERKE DARWIN HALLEY LOVELL BRADLEY CHALLIS CLAXTON DELARUE GREGORY HUGGINS LOCKYER LUBBOCK MICHELL PARSONS PENROSE PROCTOR BRISBANE COPELAND EDDINTON GLAISHER GOMPERTZ HERSCHEL HORROCKS EDDINGTON FLAMSTEED MASKELYNE PRITCHARD CARRINGTON GELLIBRAND GROOMBRIDGE SHEEPSHANKS
FINNISH STONE
FRENCH BIOT FAYE LYOT PONS WOLF HENRY LOEWY RAYET BAILLY FERNEL MOREUX PICARD VALLOT BORELLY BOUVARD CASSINI DELISLE JANSSEN LALANDE LAPLACE MARALDI MESSIER MOUCHEZ PUISEUX DELAMBRE DELAUNAY LACAILLE LAGRANGE BIGOURDAN CHACORNAC LEMONNIER LEVERRIER TISSERAND BURCKHARDT FLAMMARION MAUPERTUIS
GERMAN BEER BODE WOLF ZACH BAYER BIELA ENCKE GALLE GAUSS GRAFF KEMPF KNOPF MAYER ARNOLD ARREST AUWERS BESSEL BRUHNS HANSEN HARZER IDELER KEPLER LAMONT MADLER MARIUS MOBIUS MULLER OLBERS PETERS RUMKER SPORER STRUYE TEMPEL AMBRONN APIANUS BRENDEL BRUNNOW EINMART SCHONER SCHWABE FOERSTER GUTHNICK HARTMANN HERSCHEL HEVELIUS LINDENAU MERCATOR RHATICUS SCHEINER WINNECKE FABRICIUS PALITZSCH SCHONFELD
GREEK CONON METON PTOLEMY AUTOLYCUS CALLIPPUS

CLEOMEDES OENOPIDES SOSIGENES HIPPARCHUS THEODOSIUS ANAXIMANDER ARISTARCHUS CLEOSTRATUS ERATOSTHENES **INDIAN** ARYABHATA BRAHMAGUPTA **IRISH** BALL PARSONS HAMILTON MOLYNEUX **ITALIAN** AMICI FRISI DONATI ORIANI PIAZZI SECCHI BORELLI GALILEI GALILEO RICCIOLI TACCHINI BIANCHINI BOSCOVICH FRACASTORO SCHIAPARELLI **NORWEGIAN** HANSTEEN **POLISH** COPERNICUS **RUSSIAN** BREDICHIN SHKLOVSKY **SCOTTISH** GILL NICHOL WILSON GREGORY ANDERSON FERGUSON HENDERSON **SWEDISH** DUNER BOHLIN GYLDEN CELSIUS ANGSTROM BACKLUND BRANTING STROMGREN **SWISS** ZWICKY

ASTRONOMICAL FAR HUGE GREAT URANIC DISTANT IMMENSE URANIAN COLOSSAL INFINITE **(— INSTRUMENT)** ARMILL

ASTRONOMY WAGON WAGONER WAGGONER

ASTROPHEL PENTHIA STARLIGHT

ASTUTE SLY FOXY KEEN WILY ACUTE CANNY QUICK SHARP SMART CLEVER CRAFTY NASUTE SHREWD CUNNING KNOWING SKILLED

ASTYAGES (FATHER OF —) CYAXARES

ASTYANAX (FATHER OF —) HECTOR **(MOTHER OF —)** ANDROMACHE

ASTYDAMIA (FATHER OF —) PELOPS **(MOTHER OF —)** HIPPODAMIA **(SON OF —)** AMPHITRYON

ASTYOCHE (DAUGHTER OF —) PHYLEUS **(LOVER OF —)** HERCULES **(SON OF —)** TLEPOLEMUS

ASUNDER ATWO APART SPLIT ATWAIN SUNDER SUNDRY DIVIDED DIVORCED YSOWNDIR **(PREF.)** AP(H) DI DICH(O)

ASURA VARUNA

ASVATTHAMAN (FATHER OF —) DRONA **(MOTHER OF —)** KRIPA

ASYLUM ARK HOME JAIL ALTAR COVER GRITH HAVEN BEDLAM HARBOR REFUGE ALSATIA COLLEGE HOSPICE RETREAT SHELTER BUGHOUSE MADHOUSE NUTHOUSE

ASYMMETRIC PEDIAL

AS YOU LIKE IT (AUTHOR OF —) SHAKESPEARE **CHARACTER IN —** ADAM CELIA CORIN PHEBE AMIENS AUDREY DENNIS JAQUES LEBEAU OLIVER CHARLES MARTEXT ORLANDO SILVIUS WILLIAM ROSALIND FREDERICK TOUCHSTONE

AT A AL AU BY IN TO ALS TIL TILL UNTO ATTEN THERE HEREAT

(— ALL) ANY AVA EER EVER HALF OUGHT SOEVER HOWEVER

ATABAL DRUM TABOR ATTABAL

ATALANTA (CHARACTER IN —) MERCURY ATALANTA MELEAGER **(COMPOSER OF —)** HANDEL **(FATHER OF —)** IASUS **(HUSBAND OF —)** MELANION HIPPOMENES **(MOTHER OF —)** CLYMENE

ATAMAN CHIEF JUDGE HETMAN HEADMAN

ATARAH (HUSBAND OF —) JERAHMEEL **(SON OF —)** ONAM

ATAVISM REVERSION

ATELIER SHOP STUDIO BOTTEGA WORKSHOP

ATEO WAKEA

ATES SWEETSOP

ATHALARIC (FATHER OF —) EUTHELRIC **(MOTHER OF —)** AMALASUINTHA

ATHALIAH (FATHER OF —) AHAB **(HUSBAND OF —)** JEHORAM **(MOTHER OF —)** JEZEBEL

ATHAMAS (DAUGHTER OF —) HELLE **(FATHER OF —)** AEOLUS **(MOTHER OF —)** ENARETE **(SON OF —)** PHRIXUS LEARCHUS PALAEMON **(WIFE OF —)** INO NEPHELE

ATHANAGILD (DAUGHTER OF —) BRUNEHILDE GALESWINTHA

ATHANOR OVEN ATHENOR FURNACE

ATHAPASKAN HAW HARE HUPA KATO KASKA AHTENA BEAVER CHETCO GILENO LASSIK SARCEE SEKANI CARRIER CHILULA KOYUKON KUTCHIN

ATHEIST ZENDIK DOUBTER INFIDEL NASTIKA AGNOSTIC APIKOROS NETHEIST

ATHENA ALEA AUGE NIKE ALERA AREIA ERGANE HIPPIA HYGEIA ITONIA PALLAS POLIAS AIANTIS MINERVA APATURIA

ATHENIAN ATTIC CHORAGUS CHOREGUS

ATHLAI (FATHER OF —) BEBAI

ATHLETE PRO BLUE JOCK KEMP STAR BOXER COLOR CRACK CUTEY CUTIE TURNER ACROBAT AMATEUR GYMNAST STICKER TUMBLER VARMINT GAMESTER REPEATER WRESTLER PENTATHLETE **(COLLEGE —)** REDSHIRT

ATHLETIC AGILE BURLY LUSTY VITAL BRAWNY GYMNIC ROBUST SINEWY STRONG BOARDLY BOORDLY MUSCULAR POWERFUL VIGOROUS

ATHLETICS GAMES SPORT EXERCISE

AT-HOME ASSEMBLY

ATHWART CROSS ABOARD ACROSS ASLANT OBLIQUE SIDEWISE TRAVERSE

ATLANTIC CROAKER HARDHEAD

ATLANTIC OCEAN POND MILLPOND

ATLAS BOOK LIST MAPS TOME TITAN TELAMON MAINSTAY **(DAUGHTERS OF —)** ATLANTIDES **(FATHER OF —)** IAPETUS **(MOTHER OF —)** CLYMENE **(WIFE OF —)** PLEIONE

ATLE ETHEL

ATMAN ATMA ATTA SELF

ATMOSPHERE AIR SKY AURA FEEL LIFT MOOD TONE AROMA CLIME DECOR ETHER PLACE SMELL FROWST MIASMA NIMBUS SPHERE WELKIN FEELING HYALINE QUALIFY AMBIANCE AMBIENCE **(— OF DISCOURAGEMENT)** CHILL **(CHARACTERISTIC —)** VIBE **(EMOTIONAL —)** VIBE VIBES **(NOXIOUS —)** MIASMA **(OUTERMOST PART OF —)** GEOCORONA **(SECTION OF —)** SOLENOID **(SENSED —)** KARMA **(STALE —)** FROUST FROWST **(STUFFY —)** FUG **(SUFFOCATING —)** STIFLE

ATMOSPHERIC AERIAL METEORIC

ATMOSPHERICS STATIC STRAYS SFERICS SPHERICS

ATOLL LAGOON

ATOM ACE BIT ION JOT DIAD DYAD HAET HATE IOTA MITE MOTE WHIT ATOMY HENAD LABEL MONAD SHADE SPECK TINGE ADATOM BRIDGE CARBYL HEPTAD ISOBAR TETRAD ATOMIZE BODIKIN IONOGEN ISOTOPE NUCLIDE RADICAL SPECIES FUNCTION ISOSTERE MOLECULE PARTICLE PERISSAD QUANTITY CORPUSCLE SCINTILLA **(— TOTALITY)** MATTER **(COMBINING —)** ACCEPTOR **(TAGGED —)** TRACER **(PL.)** SMITHERS SMITHEREENS

ATOMIC TINY MINUTE NUCLEAR **(— PARTICLE)** MUON

ATOMIZE PULVERIZE

ATOMIZER SPRAY SPARGE SCENTER SPRAYER AIRBRUSH ODORATOR PERFUMER **(CONTENTS OF —)** SCENTS

ATOMS **(PREF.) (CONTAINING 20 —)** EICOS **(CONTAINING 4 CARBON —)** BUT **(HAVING ARRANGEMENT OF —)** GALA GALACTO **(PRESENCE OF 2 NITROGEN —)** DIAZ

ATONE AGREE AMEND ACCORD ANSWER ASSOIL RANSOM REDEEM REPENT APPEASE EXPIATE RESTORE SATISFY **(— FOR)** ABY BYE ABYE MEND ABIDE ABEGGE

ATONEMENT MEND RANSOM MICHTAM PENANCE SATISFACTION ACCEPTILATION

ATOP ACOR OVER UPON

ATORAI DAURI

ATOSSA (FATHER OF —) CYRUS **(HUSBAND OF —)** DARIUS SMERDIS CAMBYSES

ATRABILIOUS SAD GLUM ADUST GLOOMY MOROSE SULLEN

ATRAMENTOUS INKY

ATRAX (DAUGHTER OF —) CAENIS HIPPODAMIA **(FATHER OF —)** PENEUS **(MOTHER OF —)** BURA

ATREUS (BROTHER OF —) THYESTES **(FATHER OF —)** PELOPS **(HALF-BROTHER OF —)** THYESTES **(MOTHER OF —)** HIPPODAMIA **(SON OF —)** MENELAUS **(WIFE OF —)** AEROPE

ATRIP AWEIGH

ATRIUM HALL ATRIO COURT CAVITY AURICLE CHAMBER PASSAGE

ATROCIOUS BAD DARK RANK VILE AWFUL BLACK CRUEL GROSS ATROCE BRUTAL ODIOUS SAVAGE WICKED HEINOUS UNGODLY VIOLENT FLAGRANT GRIEVOUS HORRIBLE TERRIBLE MONSTROUS

ATROPHIC AUANTIC

ATROPHY RUST STUNT TABES MACIES MOLDER SHRINK STARVE SWEENY WITHER SWINNEY WASTING STULTIFY **(PREF.)** NECR(O)

ATROPINE DATURINE

ATTACH ADD FIX PUT SET SEW TAG TIE BIND BOLT GLUE HANG JOIN LINK NAIL SPAN TAKE VEST WELD ADOPT AFFIX ANNEX BEWED CLING FOUND HINGE HITCH LATCH PASTE SCREW SEIZE SPEND STICK TACHE TATCH UNITE ACCUSE ADDICT ADHERE ADJOIN APPEND ARREST CEMENT DEVOTE ENGAGE ENTAIL ENTIRE FASTEN FATHER INDICT SPLINE ADHIBIT APPOINT ASCRIBE CONNECT ESPOUSE SUBJOIN **(— TEMPORARILY)** SECOND

ATTACHED FAST FOND ADNATE DOTING ADJUNCT BIGOTED SESSILE ADSCRIPT INSERTED

ATTACHING INCIDENT ALLIGATION

ATTACHMENT ARM GAG BAIL BALE DRUM FLAY HEAD HECK LOVE MOTE SHIM SHOE AMOUR CHUCK CRUSH DOBBY DODAD FENCE GUARD STRIG AFFAIR BEATER BINDER BUMPER DAMSEL DOBBIE DOCTOR DOODAD DREDGE FELLER FETICH FETISH HEMMER HILLER LAPPET LAYBOY MARKER PACKER PICKUP SECTOR SHIELD SIDING ADAPTOR AFFAIRE BIGOTRY BRAIDER CREASER DROPPER FAGOTER FITTING GIGBACK HEADSET HOLDING JOINTER KNOCKUP LEVELER SPANNER SPRAYER DEVOTION DINGDONG FASTNESS FIXATION FONDNESS GOVERNOR HEADREST

ATTACK FIT HIT HOP MUG SIC BAIT BOMB BOUT CLAW COSH DINT FAKE FANG FORK FRAY GANG GIVE HOOK JUMP MACE PAIL PANG RAID RISE RUSH SAIL SICK SLOW

TACK TURN WADE YOKE ABUSE
ALARM ASSAY BEGIN BESET BLAST
BLITZ BOARD BRASH BRUNT
CATCH CHECK DRIVE FIGHT FLUSH
FORAY FORCE GLIDE HARRY
HOUND ICTUS ONSET POISE PULSE
SALLY SCUFF SETON SMITE SOUSE
SPASM SPELL STORM ACCESS
ACCUSE ACTION AFFRAY AFFRET
ASSAIL ATTAME BATTLE BICKER
BODRAG CHARGE CRISIS DOUBLE
ENVAYE EXPUGN EXTENT GRUDGE
INDICT INFEST INSULT INVADE
OFFEND ONFALL ONRUSH POUNCE
RUFFLE SAVAGE SHOWER SORTIE
STOUND STRIKE STROKE TACKLE
TAKING THRUST AGGRESS
ASPERSE ASSAULT ATTEMPT
BARRAGE BELABOR BELIBEL
BESEIGE BOMBARD CENSURE
CRUSADE DESCENT OFFENSE
PICKOUT POTSHOT RUNNING
SCALING SEIZURE STACKER
CAMISADE CAMISADO ENDEAVOR
ESCALADE PAROXYSM SKIRMISH
SURPRISE TOMAHAWK OFFENSIVE
ONSLAUGHT PENETRATION
(— FEEDBAG) TIEIN
(— IN COCKFIGHT) SHUFFLE
(— OF ILLNESS) GO
(— OFILLNESS) FIT
(— OF ILLNESS) DWAM DWALM
ACCESS
(— OFILLNESS) ONFALL SEIZURE
(— FETCH SICKNESS) WHIP SEIZURE
(— TO ROB) THUG
(— WITH SHOUTS) HUE
(— WITH WORDS) STOUSH
(— ZEALOUSLY) CRUSADE
(BOMBING —) PRANG
(CHESS —) FORK
(CRITICAL —) SLATING
(FENCING —) GLIDE
(LIGHT —) TOUCH
(NIGHT —) CAMISADO
(PROLONGED —) SIEGE
(SLIGHT —) WAFF
(SUDDEN —) ICTUS RAPTUS
SURPRISE
(SUICIDAL —) KAMIKAZE
(SURPRISE —) ALARM ALARUM
(VERBAL —) FIRE SALVO BLUDGEON
(SUFF.) LEPSIA LEPSIS LEPSY
LEPT(IC)
ATTACKER AGGRESSOR
OFFENDANT
(SUFF.) MASTIX
ATTACK ON THE MILL
(CHARACTER IN —) MERLIER
DOMINIQUE FRANCOISE
MARCELLINE
(COMPOSER OF —) BRUNEAU
ATTAI (FATHER OF —) REHOBOAM
(MOTHER OF —) AHLAI MAACHAH
ATTAIN GO GET HIT WIN BUMP
COME EARN GAIN RISE SORT
ARISE CATCH COVER CROSS
FETCH PROVE REACH TOUCH
ACCEDE AMOUNT ARRIVE ASPIRE
EFFECT OBTAIN SECURE STRIKE
ACHIEVE ACQUIRE COMPASS
PROCURE SUCCEED OVERTAKE
(— TO ACCOMPLISH) FIND FORCE

ATTAINMENT ARRIVAL ADEPTION
ENERGEIA PURCHASE
(— OF NIRVANA) MOKSHA
(SCHOLARLY —) LETTERS
ATTAR ITR OIL ATAR OTTO ATHAK
OTTAR ESSENCE PERFUME
ATTEMPT GO PUT SAY SHY TRY
BASH BOUT BURL DARE DASH
FAND FIST FOND HACK JUMP MIND
MINT MIRD OSSE SEEK SHOT SLAP
STAB WAGE WORK ASSAY BEGIN
ESSAY ETTLE FLING FRAME OFFER
ONSET PRESS PROOF PROVE
START TEMPT TRIAL WHACK
ASSAIL ATTACK EFFORT FRAIST
STRIVE ENFORCE IMITATE
PRETEND PROFFER STAGGER
VENTURE CONATION ENDEAVOR
EXERTION PURCHASE TENTAMEN
(— TO AROUSE) AGITATE
(— TO BRIBE) APPROACH
(— TO INFLUENCE) AGITATION
(— TO THROW RIDER) ESTRAPADE
(ABORTIVE —) FUTILITY
(FIRST —) DEBUT
(PREF.) PEIRA
ATTEND GO HO HOA HOO SEE BEAT
FAND HARK HEAR HEED LIST MIND
OYEO OYEZ STAY TEND WAIT WALK
APPLY AUDIT AWAIT GUARD
NURSE SERVE TREAT VISIT WATCH
ASSIST CONVEY ESCORT FOLLOW
HARKEN INTEND LACKEY LISTEN
SECOND SHADOW SQUIRE
CONDUCT CONSORT ESQUIRE
HEARKEN LACQUEY PERPEND
RETINUE ACCOMPANY
(— A LADY) WAIT
(— FUNERAL) FOLLOW
(— REGULARLY) KEEP
(— TO) MIND TREAT FETTLE INTEND
(— UPON) TENT CHASE CHAPERON
ATTENDANCE GATE SUIT CHAPEL
NUMBER OFFICE REGARD SERVICE
PRESENCE
ATTENDANT BOY FLY LAD JACK
MAID MUTE PAGE PEON SYCE
ZANY CADDY COMES GILLY
GROOM GUIDE JAGER USHER
VALET ALEXAS CADDIE DACTYL
DAMSEL EMILIA ESCORT FRIEND
GESITH GILLIE HAIDUK HOGMAN
JAEGER KAVASS MINION PORTER
SQUIRE STOCAH TUBMAN VARLET
VERGER WAITER YEOMAN ALIPTES
ARMORER BULLDOG CHOBDAR
COURIER CROSSER DAMOSEL
FAMULUS FENELLA FOOTBOY
GHILLIE HALLMAN HOSTESS
JACKMAN LINKMAN ORDERLY
PAGEBOY PIQUEUR PRESSER
SEQUENT SERVANT SHIPBOY
SPOUTER TRABANT TRESSEL
ATTENDEE BEACHBOY CHASSEUR
CORYBANT CRUTCHER FEWTERER
FOLLOWER GATHERER HANDMAID
HENCHBOY HENCHMAN
HOUSEMAN MINISTER MYRMIDON
OBSERVER OUTRIDER ROSALINE
SERGEANT SERJEANT STAFFIER
TIPSTAFF WATERMAN OBSERVANT
PURSUIVANT CHAMBERLAIN

(— OF CYBELE) CORYBANT
(ARMED —) CAVASS KAVASS
(CROSSING —) GATEMAN
(FLIGHT —) STEW STEWARD
STEWARDESS
(FUNERAL —) MUTE
(KNIGHT'S —) SWAIN CUSTREL
ESQUIRE
(PALACE —S) BOSTANGI
(PROCTOR'S —) BULLDOG
(SHIP'S —) STEWARD
(YOUNG —) BOY LAD JACK PAGE
KNIGHT
(PL.) MEINY STAFF CORTEGE
RETINUE
ATTENDED FRAUGHT
ATTENDER (HABITUAL —) PATRON
ATTENTION EAR CARE GAUM HEED
HIST MARK MIND NOTE RUSH
SHUN TENT COURT FLOOR GUARD
STUDY TASTE DETAIL FAVORS
NOTICE REGARD ACCOUNT
ACHTUNG ADDRESS EARNEST
HEARING RESPECT THOUGHT
AUDIENCE
(— FROM SUPERIOR) TASHRIF
TASHREEF
(— TO PETTY ITEMS) MICROLOGY
(AMOROUS —) GALLANTRY
(FIXED —) DHARANA
(FLATTERING —) HOMAGE
(INTERJECTION TO ATTRACT —)
YOOHOO
(PLEASING —) INCENSE
(SPECIAL —) ACCENT
(PL.) FUSS
ATTENTIVE WARY ALERT AWAKE
CIVIL CLOSE SHARP TENTY ARRECT
INTENT POLITE ALLEARS CAREFUL
GALLANT HEEDFUL LISTFUL
MINDFUL PRESENT DILIGENT
OBEDIENT STUDIOUS THOUGHTY
VIGILANT WATCHFUL
(— TO) IMMINENT
ATTENUATE SAP DRAW FINE THIN
WATER DILUTE LESSEN RAREFY
REDUCE WEAKEN SLENDER
AVIANIZE DECREASE DIMINISH
EMACIATE ENFEEBLE TAPERING
ATTENUATED RARE THIN GAUNT
AERIAL DILUTED SPINDLY
FINESPUN SMORZATO
ATTENUATION LOSS
ATTENUATOR PAD
ATTEST CHOP SEAL SIGN PROVE
STATE SWEAR VOUCH ADJURE
AFFIRM INVOKE RECORD WITTEN
CERTIFY CONFESS CONFIRM
CONSIGN TESTIFY WARRANT
WITNESS EVIDENCE INDICATE
MANIFEST
ATTESTATION VOUCH DOCKET
RECORD
ATTESTED SWORN CERTIFIED
ATTIC LOFT CELER SOLAR SOLER
GARRET TALLET GRENIER
COCKLOFT
(— SIDE) SKEELING
ATTILA (BROTHER OF —) BLEDA
(CHARACTER IN —) LEO EZIO
ATTILA FORESTO ODABELLA
(COMPOSER OF —) VERDI

(FATHER OF —) MUNDZUK
(WIFE OF —) HILDA ILDICO
ATTIRE (ALSO SEE DRESS) BEGO
BUSK GARB SUIT TIRE ADORN
ARRAY BIGAN DRESS GETUP HABIT
AGUISE ENROBE PLIGHT REVEST
TOILET ADDRESS APPAREL
DUBBING PANOPLY ACCOUTER
CLEADING EQUIPAGE FEATHERS
(EPISCOPAL —) PONTIFICAL
(FORMAL —) BALLDRESS
(SHINING —) SHEEN
ATTIRED TRICKSY
(— IN FINERY) BRAW
ATTITUDE AIR CUE SET BIAS MIEN
MOOD POSE SIDE ANGLE FRAME
HEART PHASE SHAPE SHELL SIGHT
SLANT STAND ACTION ANIMUS
ASPECT MANNER SPIRIT STANCE
BEARING FEELING GESTURE
POSTURE STATION STOMACH
BEHAVIOR CARAPACE CROTCHET
HABITUDE POSITION
PREPOSSESSION
(— OF HUNTING DOG) POINT
(HABITUAL —) SONG
(MENTAL —) SENSE
(PREVAILING —) STREAM
ATTITUDINIZE POSE POSTURE
ATTORNEY DOER AGENT AVOUE
PROXY VAKIL DEPUTY FACTOR
FISCAL LAWYER LEGIST MUKTAR
SYNDIC VAKEEL PROCTOR
ADVOCATE PROSECUTOR
ATTRACT BAIT CALL DRAW LURE
PULL TILL WIND BRING CATCH
CHARM COURT FETCH TEMPT
ALLURE ATTACH ENGAGE ENLIST
ENTICE GATHER INVITE SEDUCE
STRIKE BEWITCH PROCURE
INTEREST MAGNETIZE
(— FISH) CHUM
ATTRACTANT (MOTH SEX)
GYPLURE
ATTRACTION TUG BAIT CALL CARD
CLOU DRAW PULL CHARM DRAFT
FAVOR SPELL TRACT APPEAL
DESIRE FAVOUR MAGNET
BLOWOFF COITION DRAUGHT
GRAVITY INDRAFT ADHESION
AFFINITY COHESION CONTRACT
PENCHANT SIDESHOW WITCHERY
(KIND OF —) ADDED
(SEX —) GYPLURE
ATTRACTIVE FLY BRAW CHIC CUTE
FAIR FOXY GOOD NICE BONNY
DISHY FATAL JOLLY NIFTY QUEME
SONSY SWEET COMELY FLASHY
FRUITY HEPPEN LOVELY LURING
PRETTY SAVORY SEEMLY SNAZZY
TAKING TRICKY AMIABLE CIRCEAN
CUNNING EYEABLE EYESOME
GRADELY LIKABLE WINNING
WINSOME ALLURING CHARMING
ENGAGING ENTICING FEATURED
FETCHING GRACEFUL GRACIOUS
HANDSOME INVITING SPECIOUS
TEMPTING VENEREAN
PERSONABLE PREPOSSESSING
(— TO OPPOSITE SEX) EPIGAMIC
(FALSELY —) MERETRICIOUS
(NOT —) FOUL INCURIOUS
(STRIKINGLY —) ZINGY

ATTRACTIVENESS CHARM GRACE LOOKS BEAUTY GLAMOR AMENITY GLITTER AFFINITY HARLOTRY
ATTRIBUTABLE DUE
ATTRIBUTE FOX OWE PUT GIVE MARK SIGN TYPE ALLOT BADGE BLAME CHARM PLACE POWER REFER TRAIT ALLEGE ALLUDE ARRECT ASSERT ASSIGN BESTOW CHARGE CREDIT IMPUTE PREFER REPUTE SYMBOL ADJUNCT APANAGE ASCRIBE COUNTER ESSENCE PERTAIN QUALITY ACCREDIT APPANAGE ARROGATE GRANDITY INTITULE PROPERTY PROPRIUM STRENGTH
  (—S OF ROCKS) GEOLOGY
  (— WRONGFULLY) FOIST
  (PL.) SARIRA SHARIRA
ATTRIBUTION ACCENT THEORY ANIMISM ETIOLOGY
ATTRITION WEAR GRIEF REGRET SORROW ANGUISH ABRASION BLASTING FRICTION
ATTUNE KEY TUNE ADAPT AGREE ACCORD ADJUST TEMPER PREPARE
ATUA AKUA DEMON SPIRIT
ATYPICAL RARE BIZARRE ABERRANT GROTESQUE
AUBADE ALBA
AUBERGE INN ALBERGO
AUBERGINE EGGPLANT
AUBURN ABRAM BLOND CACHA CUTCH BLONDE CACHOU CATECHU GOREVAN TULIPWOOD
AU COURANT CONTEMPORARY
AUCTION CANT ROUP SALE SELL VEND COKER TRADE BARTER BRIDGE HAMMER OUTCRY TROVER VENDUE OUTROOP UNCTION DISPOSAL KNOCKOUT PORTSALE
AUCTIONEER CRIER CRYER OUTCRIER
AUDACIOUS BOLD BRASH BRAVE FRACK HARDY SAUCY AUDACE BRAZEN CHEEKY DARING FORWARD ARROGANT FEARLESS IMPUDENT INSOLENT INTREPID SPIRITED BAREFACED DEVILMAYCARE
  (NOT —) CIVIL
  (PIQUANTLY —) SASSY SAUCY
AUDACITY CHEEK NERVE COURAGE BOLDNESS TEMERITY HARDIHOOD PRESUMPTION
AUDIBLE RIFE ALOUD CLEAR HEARD AUTOMATIC
AUDIBLY ALOUD
AUDIENCE EAR PIT FANS AUDIT COURT FLOOR HOUSE PUBLIC GALLERY HEARING ASSEMBLY AUDITORY TRIBUNAL
AUDIT SCAN CHECK PROBE APPOSE RECKON VERIFY ACCOUNT EXAMINE INQUIRE INSPECT ESTIMATE
AUDITION READ HEARING
AUDITOR CENSOR HEARER APPOSER AUDIENT PITTITE COUNTOUR DISCIPLE LISTENER

AUDITORIUM HALL ROOM CAVEA FRONT ODEUM THEATER AUDITORY
AUDITORY ORAL OTIC AURAL AUDILE ACOUSTIC AUDITIVE
AUGE (FATHER OF —) ALEUS
  (HUSBAND OF —) TEUTHRAS
  (MOTHER OF —) NAERA
  (SON OF —) TELEPHUS
AUGER BIT POD BORE BORAL BORER GRILL BORING GIMLET NAUGER WIMBLE PIERCER TEREBRA
  (PREF.) TRYPAN(O)
AUGHT ACHT EAWT AUCHT OWNED CIPHER NAUGHT WORTHY NOTHING VALIANT ANYTHING
AUGMENT ADD EKE FEED GROW HELP URGE BOOST EXALT SWELL APPEND DILATE EXPAND EXTEND AMPLIFY BALLOON ENHANCE ENLARGE IMPROVE INFLAME MAGNIFY COMPOUND HEIGHTEN INCREASE MAJORATE MULTIPLY
  (— IN STRENGTH) INGROSS
AUGMENTATION RISE EKING SWELL GROWTH AUCTARY ADDITION
AUGMENTED SHARP EXTREME
AUGUR BODE OMEN SEER SPEAK AUSPEX DIVINE BETOKEN CONJECT FORESEE OMINATE PORTEND PREDICT PRESAGE PROMISE PROPHET SIGNIFY DENOUNCE FOREBODE FORESHOW FORETELL FOREWARN INDICATE PROPHESY
AUGURY ORE OMEN RITE SIGN SOOTH TOKEN HANSEL RITUAL AUSPICE HANDSEL PRESAGE CEREMONY
AUGUST AWFUL GRAND NOBLE KINGLY SERENE SOLEMN EXALTED STATELY IMPOSING MAJESTIC
  (FIRST DAY OF —) LAMMAS LUGNAS LUGHNAS LUGNASAD
  (PREF.) SEBASTO
AUGUSTINIAN AUSTIN ASSUMPTIONIST
AUHUHU HOLA
AUK FALK LOOM ARRIE DIVER LEMOT MURRE NODDY SCOOT SCOUT SKOUT MARROT PUFFIN ROTCHE STARIK TINKER DOVEKEY DOVEKIE PENGUIN PYGOPOD SEAFOWL WILLOCK GAIRFOWL GAREFOWL ROCKBIRD RAZORBILL
AULA HALL COURT EMBLIC
AUNT TIA BAWD AUNTY NAUNT TANTA TANTE AUNTIE GOSSIP
  (— SALLY) STICKS
AURA AIR HALO ODOR PUFF AROMA NUMEN SAVOR SMELL BREEZE NIMBUS BUZZARD ESSENCE FEELING
  (CHARACTERISTIC —) VIBE
  (SENSED —) KARMA
  (VITALIZING —) VIBE VIBES
AURAL OTIC AUDIAL
AUREATE GOLDEN ORNATE ROCOCO YELLOW

AUREOLE HALO CROWN GLORY LIGHT AREOLA CORONA GLORIA NIMBUS VESICA GLORIOLE MANDORLA
AUREUS (HALF —) SEMIS
AURICLE EAR PINNA ATRIUM EARLET TRUMPET PAVILION
AURICULAR OTIC
AURICULATE EARED
AURIGA WAGONER WAGGONER
AURIST OTOLOGIST
AUROCHS TUR UROX URUS BISON WISENT BONASUS
AURORA EOS DAWN DRAPERY MORNING
AURORA BOREALIS DANCERS STREAMERS
AUSPICE CARE OMEN SIGN AUGURY PORTENT GUIDANCE
  (PL.) EGIS AEGIS
AUSPICIOUS FAIR GOOD TWINE WHITE BRIGHT CHANCY DEXTER CHANCEY FAVORING PROPITIOUS PROSPEROUS
AUSTERE BARE COLD HARD SOUR BLEAK BUDGE GRAVE GRUFF HARSH RIGID ROUGH SHARP STERN STIFF STOUR BITTER CHASTE FORMAL RUGGED SEVERE SIMPLE SOMBER STRICT SULLEN TETRIC ASCETIC CRABBED DANTEAN EARNEST SERIOUS GRANITIC RIGOROUS TETRICAL ASTRINGENT PURITANICAL
AUSTERITY RIGOR CATOISM RIGORISM SIMPLICITY
AUSTRAL SOUTHERN

AUSTRALIA

ABORIGINE: MYALL
CAPE: HOWE
CAPITAL: CANBERRA
COIN: DUMP POUND SHILLING
DESERT: STURT GIBSON TANAMI SIMPSON
HARBOR: DARWIN BRISBANE FREMANTLE MELBOURNE NEWCASTLE
ISLAND: CATO COCOS FRASER KOOLAN CORINGA KANGAROO LACEPEDE MELVILLE ROTTNEST TASMANIA
LAKE: EYRE COWAN FROME BARLEE BULLOO LEFROY AMADEUS BLANCHE EVERARD GREGORY TORRENS GAIRDNER NABBEROO DISAPPOINTMENT
LANGUAGE: YABBER
MEASURE: SAUM
MOUNTAIN: OLGA BRUCE LEGGE CRADLE GARNET GAWLER MAGNET STUART BONGONG GREGORY WILHELM CUTHBERT JUSGRAVE MULLIGAN KOSCIUSKO
MOUNTAIN RANGE: DARLING FLINDERS
NATIVE: ABO MARA BINGE ARANDA ARUNTA AUSSIE DIGGER BILLIJIM KANGAROO WARRAGAL WARRIGAL JINDYWOROBAK
PENINSULA: EYRE
RIVER: DALY SWAN BULLO COMET FINKE ISAAC PAROO ROPER

SNOWY YARRA BARCOO BARWON CULGOA DAWSON DEGREY DARLING FITZROY LACHLAN STAATEN WARREGO BURDEKIN FLINDERS GEORGINA VICTORIA
SEA: CORAL TIMOR TASMAN ARAFURA
SOLDIER: DIGGER SWADDY BILLIJIM
STATE: TASMANIA VICTORIA QUEENSLAND
STRAIT: TORRES
TOWN: AYR YASS DUBBO PERTH WAGGA ALBURY AUBURN CAIRNS CASINO COBURG DARWIN HOBART MACKAY SYDNEY BENDIGO GEELONG KOGARAH MILDURA MITCHAM ADELAIDE BRISBANE ESSENDON RANDWICK RINGWOOD MELBOURNE TOOWOOMBA
VALLEY: GROSE JAMIESON MEGALONG
WATERFALL: TULLY COOMERA WALLAMAN WENTWORTH WOLLOMOMBI
WATER HOLE BILLABONG
WOMAN: LUBRA

AUSTRALIAN ANZAC AUSSIE DIGGER AUSTRAL CURRENCY KANGAROO WARRAGAL WARRIGAL
  (— GIRL) LUBRA

AUSTRIA

ANCIENT PEOPLE: HUNS AVARS RAETIANS SLOVENES BAVARIANS
CAPITAL: WIEN VIENNA
CELTIC KINGDOM: NORICUM
COIN: DUCAT KRONE FLORIN HELLER ZEHNER GROSCHEN SCHILLING
DUCHY: STYRIA CARNIOLA CARINTHIA
EMPEROR: CHARLES FRANCIS FERDINAND
LAKE: ALMSEE FERTOTO MONDSEE BODENSEE TRAUNSEE CONSTANCE NEUSIEDLER
MEASURE: FASS FUSS JOCH MASS MUTH YOKE HALBE LINIE MEILE METZE PFIFF PUNKT ACHTEL BECHER SEIDEL DLAFTER VIERTEL DREILING
MOUNTAIN: STUBAI EISENERZ RHATIKON KITZBUHEL
NATIVE: STYRIAN TYROLEAN
NOBILITY: RITTER
PASS: LOIBL ARLBERG BRENNER PLOCKEN
PROVINCE: TIROL TYROL STYRIA VIENNA SALZBURG CARINTHIA VORARLBERG
RIVER: INN MUR DRAU ENNS KAMP LECH MURZ RAAB DONAU MARCH SALZA THAYA TRAUN DANUBE SALZACH
RIVER PORT: LINZ KREMS VIENNA
ROMAN PROVINCE: RAETIA NORICUM PANNONIA
TOWN: ENNS GRAZ LECH LINZ RIED WELS WIEN GMUND LIENZ STEYR

TRAUN LEOBEN VIENNA BREGENZ
MODLING SPITTAL VILLACH
DORNBIRN SALZBURG
INNSBRUCK
WATERFALL: KRIMML GASTEIN
GOLLING
WEIGHT: MARC SAUM UNZE DENAT
KARCH PFUND STEIN CENTNER
PFENNIG VIERLING

AUTACOID HORMONE INCRETION
AUTARCHIC FREE
AUTHENTIC ECHT PURE REAL SURE
TRUE EXACT PUCCA PUCKA PUKKA
RIGHT VALID ACTUAL DINKUM
PROPER CORRECT CURRENT
GENUINE SINCERE CREDIBLE
OFFICIAL ORIGINAL RELIABLE
AUTHENTICATE SEAL PROVE
VOUCH ATTEST SIGNET VERIFY
APPROVE CONFIRM LEGALIZE
AUTHOR DOER JUDE SIRE JUDAS
MAKER RULER AUCTOR FACTOR
FORGER LOKMAN PARENT
PENMAN SCRIBE SOURCE WRITER
ANCIENT CLASSIC CREATOR
ELOHIST FOUNDER LOLLIUS
ANCESTOR BEGETTER COMPILER
COMPOSER IDEALIST IMMORTAL
INVENTOR JEHOVIST ORIGINAL
PAYYETAN PRODUCER
(BAD —) BLOTTER
(PL.) SS
AMERICAN ADE BOK GAY ILG LEA
LEE NIN NYE POE ZIM AGAR AGEE
AUEL BABB BATE BAUM BEER BELL
BODE BOVA BOYD BUCK BURT CAIN
CARO CARR COIT COOK DANA DAHL
DYER EDDY EDEL ERTE EWEN FARB
GALE GANN GASS GRAU GREY HALL
HAHN HUIE HUMF HUNT JONG
KEMP KREY KYNE LANE LASH LONG
LOOS LUCE MACY MAYO NASH
PAUL POST POHL PUZO RAND ROTH
SHAW SUHL URIS WARD WATT
WEBB WEST WOOD WOUK AARON
ADAMS ADLER AIKEN ALBEE ALGER
ALSOP AMORY ANSON ANTIN
ARNOW BACON BARTH BASSO
BATES BAUGH BEACH BEEBZ BENET
BINNS BOLES BOYLE BRITT BROWN
BRUSH CABLE CAHAN CANBY CHILD
CLAPP COOKE CORLE CRANE
CREWS CUPPY DAVIS DEISS DIETZ
DOBIE DODGE DRURY DUNNE
EARLE EATON ELLIS EVANS FAUST
FOESS FOOTE GATES GOYEN GRAFF
GREEN HARTE HECHT HOBAN
HORAN HULME HURST HYAMS
IRWIN JAFFE JAKES KELLY KESEY
KEYES KIELY KOVEL LAPPE LEECH
LEWIS LILLY LODGE LORTZ LYNES
LYTLE MABEE MAJOR MARCH
MASON MASUR MCFEE MERTZ
NIZER OATES ODELL OGDEN OHARA
PAINE PANEK POOLE POTOK PUSEY
QUEEN RAINE RECHY REESE REEVE
RIVES ROARK SELBY SEUSS SIMAK
SIMMS SMITH STEIN STONE STONG
STOUT STOWE TEALE TEVIS THANE
THARP TRINE TRYON TUDOR TULLY
TWAIN UHNAK VANCE VIDAL VORSE
WALSH WATTS WELTY WEEMS

WELLS WHITE WHYTE WILEY
WOLFE WYLIE YERBY ADAMIC
ALCOTT ALGREN ANGELL ARTHUR
ASIMOV AUSTIN BAILEY BARNES
BECKER BELLOW BESSIE BISHOP
BOWLES BRALEY BRINIG BROWNE
BURMAN BURNET CABELL CAPOTE
CARMER CARSON CATHER CATLIN
CATTON CHIANG CLARKE COLTON
COOPER CORBIN CORLEY CROUSE
DANNAY DARGAN DAVIES DELAND
DEVOTO DIDION DILLON DOWNEY
ELLROY EVARTS FARSON FERBER
FIELDS FINLEY FISHER FLAVIN
FLEBBE FORBES FULLER GADDIS
GILMAN GINOTT GORMAN GUNTER
HALPER HARRIS HAWKES HERBST
HOBART HOLMES HOLZER HOOKER
HORGAN HOSMER HOWARD
HUGHES IRVING JAHODA JEWETT
KELLER KESTER KUMMER LAIKEN
LARCOM LEGUIN LIBBEY LONDON
LOVETT LUDLUM LUMMIS MAILER
MANNES MARCUM MARTIN
MCEVOY MILLAY MILLER MORLEY
MORROW MUNSON NATHAN
NORRIS PARKER PITKIN POLITI
PORTER POWELL PROUTY RHODES
RIFKIN RIPLEY ROURKE RUNYON
SALTUS SENDAK SEVERN SHEEHY
SONTAG STEELE STREET STRONG
STYRON SUCKOW SWADOS TALESE
TAYLOR TERKEL THAYER THOMAS
TOLAND TOOMER TRUMAN TUTTLE
UPDIKE VEBLEN WALLOP WARNER
WATKIN WERNER WILDER WILLIS
WILSON WINTER WINWAR WISTER
WRIGHT YERKES ALDRICH
ANDREWS BABBITT BANNING
BELLAMY BENNETT BIGELOW
BIGGERS BOYESEN BOYNTON
BURGESS BURNETT CALKINS
CARROLL CHEEVER CHILTON
CLEMENS COMFORT COURNOS
COZZENS CUMMINS CURWOOD
DERLETH DREISER EDMONDS
ELLIOTT ELLISON ERSKINE FARRELL
FAWCETT FERNALD FINEMAN
FOLLETT FRANKEN FREEMAN
GALLICO GARLAND GIFFORD
GLASGOW GRATTAN GUNTHER
HAMMETT HEYWARD HOLDING
HOPKINS JANIFER JOHNSON
KAILLOR KELLAND KEROUAC
KILVERT KOMROFF LAFARGE
LARDNER LINCOLN LINDSAY
LOSSING MASTERS MULFORD
MUMFORD MURFREE NABOKOV
OSTENSO OURSLER PARRISH
PARROTT PEATTIF PRESTON
PRUETTE ROBERTS ROLVAAG
SAMPSON SAROYAN SEIFERT
SKINNER TARBELL TERHUNE
THEROUX THOREAU THURBER
TRAUBEL VANDINE VANDYKE
VANLOON VOELKER VOLLMER
WAKEMAN WEBSTER WESCOTT
WHARTON WHITNEY WINSLOW
WOOLSEY WOOLSON YOUMANS
ATHERTON ATKINSON AYSCOUGH
BAKELESS BARRETTO BENCHLEY
BILLINGS BRADFORD BURDETTE
CALDWELL CANTWELL CHAMBERS

CLEGHORN COLLISON CONNOLLY
CONVERSE CRAWFORD DONNELLY
FAULKNER FERGUSON FREDERIC
GELLHORN GLASPELL GOODRICH
HAGEDORN HARRISON HEINLEIN
JOHNSTON KEMELMAN KIRKLAND
KOSINSKI KRUMGOLD LATHBURY
MACAULAY MACGRATH MARQUAND
MELVILLE MICHENER MITCHELL
NORDHOFF PERELMAN PETERKIN
PHILLIPS PROKOSCH RAWLINGS
REPPLIER RICHARDS RINFHART
SALINGER SANDBURG SEDGWICK
SINCLAIR SPILLANE SPINGARN
SPOFFORD STANFORD STARRETT
STEPHENS STOCKTON STODDARD
TIETJENS TOLEDANO TORRENCE
TURNBULL VANDOREN VONNEGUT
WESTCOTT WIDDEMER WILLIAMS
ALTSHELER BACHELLER BERCOVICI
BODENHEIM BROMFIELD
BURROUGHS CARPENTER
CHURCHILL DOSPASSOS
EGGLESTON GRANBERRY
HAWTHORNE HEMINGWAY
ISHERWOOD KORZYBSKI
LANCASTER LOCKRIDGE
MCCULLERS NICHOLSON
OSULLIVAN SANTAYANA
SCHULBERG SIGOURNEY STALLINGS
STEINBECK STEVENSON STRIBLING
WOOLLCOTT CLENDENING
FITZGERALD MCCUTCHEON
SOUTHWORTH TARKINGTON
TROWBRIDGE UNTERMEYER
VANVECHTEN CANTACUZENE
CHAMBERLAIN GERSTENBERG
MINNIGERODE SCHLESINGER
STRATEMEYER HERGESHEIMER
ARGENTINIAN PUIG BORGES
GALVEZ MARMOL SABATO
CANDIOTI TIMERMAN CAPDEVILA
AUSTRALIAN STOW WEST RECKE
COWAN GREER WHITE BROWNE
CLARKE LAWSON PORTER POWELL
CALVERT COLLINS DAVISON
EGERTON TRAVERS PRICHARD
SOUTHALL VILLIERS BRINSMEAD
CAMBRIDGE MOOREHEAD
RICHARDSON
AUSTRIAN LIND ADLER BAYER
KAFKA PRAED ZWEIG WERFEL
BARTSCH COLERUS NEUMANN
PICHLER ROSEGGER SCHREKER
ALTENBERG BURCKHARD
SCHREIBER SCHNITZLER
VONDODERER
BELGIAN COSTER HYMANS PICARD
EEKHOUD SIMENON DECOSTER
LEMONNIER
BRAZILIAN AMADO CUNHA
MORAES TAUNAY GUIMARAES
LISPECTOR VERISSIMO
BULGARIAN VAZOV CANETTI
CANADIAN COX ROY CARR GROVE
MOWAT SETON SULTE ATWOOD
BIRNEY BRIAND ERDMAN HAILEY
LEVINE MILLAR MOODIE PARKER
CAMERON GLASSCO LEACOCK
MCLUHAN NEUHAUS RICHLER
SERVICE TRUDEAU CHAMBERS
LAURENCE MCDOWELL STRINGER
SULLIVAN CALLAGHAN DELAROCHE

MACDONALD MACLENNAN
PICKTHALL VANPAASEN
CHILEAN CORTES ALLENDE
COLOMBIAN CARO REYES CUERVO
CARRASQUILLA
CZECH HASEK MUCHA LANGER
HOLECEK JIRASEK KUNDERA
COMENIUS VANCURRA
DANISH BANG NEXO HERTZ KIDDE
SKRAM BLIXEN LARSEN RORDAM
BAUDITZ CLAUSEN DINESEN
PALUDAN TANDRUP ANDERSEN
FREUCHEN INGEMANN JACOBSEN
BUCHHOLTZ COUPERIUS
DRACHMANN GJELLERUP
JORGENSEN MICHAELIS
BREGENDAHL KIERKEGAAD
DUTCH LOOY EEDEN BEKKER
CREMER DEJONG EMANTS JENSEN
LENNEP DEVRIES ERAMUS
DEHARTOG MAARTENS
ENGLISH DAY LEE PYM AMIS AYER
BECK BEHN BELL BRAY COLE DANE
ERTZ FENN FORD GLYN HONE HULL
HUME KOPS LAMB LEEK LEON LEVY
LONG LYLY MORE MUIR PAUL PAYN
REED REID PHYS RICE SAKI SHAW
SNOW WAIN WARD WEBB WEST
WOOD WREN ADAMS AMORY
AYRES BARRY BATES BAYLY BERRY
BLOOM BRETT BRYCE BURKE CAINE
COMBE CORVO CRABB CRAIK CRISP
CROWE DAVIE DEFOE DIGBY DIXON
DOYLE ELIOT ELLIS EWING FRAYN
GIBBS HARDY HEARD HEVER HINDE
HOLME INNES JAMES JEANS
KEOWN LEVER LEWIS LOCKE LOFTS
LOWRY LUCAS MASON MAYNE
MCFEE MILNE MOORE MUNRO
MURRY ORCZY OUIDA POWYS
RAMEE READE ROPES SCOTT
SHARP SHIEL SHUTE SMITH STEEL
STERN SWIFT WAUGH WELLS
WOOLF WYLIE YONGE YOUNG
ALDISS ALLSOP AMBLER ANGELL
ASCHAM ASHTON ASTELL AUBREY
AUSTEN AUSTIN BARING BARRIE
BAWDEN BELLOC BENSON BESANT
BLOUNT BLYTON BORROW BRAINE
BRIDGE BRONTE BROPHY BULLEN
BUNYAN BURGIN BURTON CALDER
CANNAN CASTLE CHURCH CONRAD
CRONIN ESSLIN FARNOL FELKIN
FOSTER GODWIN GOUDGE GRAHAM
GRAVES GREENE HILTON HOBBES
HOLTBY HORLER HOWELL HOWITT
HUDSON HUGHES HUXLEY JEROME
LANDON LANDOR LYTTON MACHEN
MORGAN MORTON MOSLEY
MURRAY NESBIT NORTON ONIONS
ORMSBY ORWELL PALMER PORTER
POWELL PUDNEY REEVES RUSKIN
SANDYS SANSOM SAYERS SEWELL
SHANKS SOUTAR SPRING STERNE
SYMONS TAYLOR WALTON WARNER
WARREN WARTON WATSON
WEYMAN WRIGHT AGUILAR
ASHFORD BAGNOLD BALCHIN
BALDWIN BARCLAY BENNETT
BENTLEY BERNERS BIRRELL
BOLITHO BOTTOME BULLETT
BUNBURY CHAMIER CHATWIN
CLELAND COCKTON COLLINS

CORELLI CRISPIN DAICHES DEEPING DICKENS DODGSON DOUGLAS DUDENEY EDWARDS FARJEON FIRBANK FORSTER FORSYTH FREEMAN GARNETT GASKELL GIBBONS GISSING GOLDING GUTHRIE HAGGARD HASSALL HAWKINS HAZLITT HEWLETT HICHENS HORNUNG HOUSMAN JACKSON JOHNSON KENNEDY KIPLING LAMBURN LECARRE LEHMANN LESSING LOVESEY LOWNDES MARRYAT MAUGHAM MAXWELL MCKENNA MITFORD MONTAGU MORISON NICHOLS OXENHAM PEACOCK PERTWEE RANSOME RITCHIE ROBERTS SASSOON SHELLEY SITWELL SMEDLEY SOWERBY SPENDER SURTEES TOLKIEN TOYNBEE VACHELL WADDELL WALLACE WALPOLE ZIMMERN BARBAULD BARTLETT BEERBOHM BRITTAIN CHRISTIE DASHWOOD DEIGHTON FIELDING FLETCHER FORESTER HAMILTON HARRADEN KERNAHAN KINGSLEY KNOBLOCK KOESTLER LAWRENCE LEIGHTON MACAULAY MARRIOTT MEREDITH MORDAUNT OLIPHANT OLLIVANT PATTISON SINCLAIR SMOLLETT STANNARD STOPPARD STRETTON THIRKELL TROLLOPE WALMSLEY ZANGWILL AINSWORTH ALDINGTON BERESFORD BLACKMORE BLACKWOOD BROUGHTON CARPENTER CHURCHILL DEQUINCEY DUMAURIER GERHARDIE GOLDSMITH GREENWELL GREENWOOD HENRIQUES KINGSMILL LINKLATER LITVINOFF LLEWELLYN MANSFIELD MITCHISON MONKHOUSE OPPENHEIM PEMBERTON PHILLPOTS PICKTHALL PRIESTLEY PRITCHETT RADCLIFFE ROBERTSON SCHREINER SOUTHWOLD STACPOOLE STAPLEDON THACKERAY TREVELYAN WHITEHEAD WILKINSON WILLCOCKS WODEHOUSE FOTHERGILL GALSWORTHY HUTCHINSON MEYERSTEIN MUGGERIDGE RICHARDSON SHORTHOUSE SWINNERTON WILLIAMSON DANGERFIELD YOUNGHUSBAND
ESTONIAN TAMMSAARE
FINNISH AHO KIVI CANTH KALLAS CYGNAUS SALMINEN SILLANPAA TAVASTSTJERNA
FRENCH FOA GAY NAU SUE AIDE ARON AYME BLOY GIDE HUGO KARR MAEL SADE SAND UZES ZOLA ABOUT BAZIN BEDEL BLOCH BOVET BUTOR CAMUS CARCO CEARD COLET DUMAS DURAS FABRE GENET GIONO HEMON LOUYS OHNET PEYRE ROSNY SAGAN VERNE ACHARD AGOULT ARAGON ARGENS ARLAND AULNOY AVENEL BALZAC BEDIER BENOIT BERAUD BISSON BIYIDI BLOUET BODARD

BOULLE BRUEYS BUFFON CASSOU CLADEL CRAVEN DAUDET DONIOL EPINAY ELUARD FAYARD FRANCE HALEVY HUZARD IMBERT JAMMES LACLOS LEROUX LESAGE MOULIE PROUST REBOUX SARTRE SCHURE TROYAT VERCEL VOLNEY ANCELOT ARNAULT BAUMANN BEHAINE BERNARD BERQUIN BONNARD BOSSUET BOURGET BOUVIER CAZOTTE COCTEAU COLETTE DEBERLY DELTEIL DURTAIN FEYDEAU FONTANE GAUTIER HERMANT HERVIEU HOFFMAN IONESCU LAVEDAN LEBLANC LERMINA MALRAUX MAURIAC MAROIS MERIMEE MONNIER PREVOST REGNIER ROLLAND ROMAINS SANDEAU SARASIN SIMENON TENDRON ASSOLANT BANVILLE BARBUSSE BEAUVOIR BENJAMIN BERENGER BERNANOS BERTRAND BONVALOT BORDEAUX BOYLESVE BRUNHOFF CENDRARS CHARTIER CLARETIE DORGELES DUFRESNY ESTAUNIE FEUILLET FLAUBERT FOUCAULT GENEVOIX GONCOURT GREVILLE HOUSSAYE HUYSMANS KOCKLOTI LATAILLE MALHERBE MARIETON MARIVAUX MONTEPIN MONTFORT PERRAULT RABELAIS ROUSSEAU SAVIGNON SCHOPFER SOUPAULT STENDHAL VALLETTE VOLTAIRE BEAUCHAMP BOUHELIER CHERVILLE COULEVAIN DESCHANEL FONTAINAS MARMONTEL MIOMANDRE POURTALES SENANCOUR BAZANCOURT CHARLEVOIX DESJARDINS FAUCONNIER MAUPASSANT APOLLINAIRE MARGUERITTE
GERMAN APEL BALL BAUM BOLL BURG HEYM HOLZ HUCH KURZ MANN ARNDT BULOW BUSSE EBERS ERNST GRASS GROTH HAGEN HALBE HAUFF HESSE HEYSE HUBER KUHNE LANGE LAUBE MAREK MUGGE MUNDT RAABE UNRUH ZESEN ZWEIG BECKER BEREND BINZER BLUNCK BUICKE CONRAD DAUMER DEWOHL DREYER HAUSER HEYDEN JENSEN JOHNST KLEIST KNIGGE LEWALD LUDWIG MILLER MORIKE MUSAUS REUTER SCHMID VIEBIG WERNER BERTUCH BRONNEN CONRADI DAUBLER FALLADA FREYTAG GLAESER GUTZKOW HEIBERG KASTNER KRETZER LAROCHE NEUMANN OSTWALD REDWITZ RICHTER SEGHERS VULPIUS AUERBACH BORKENAU BRENTANO ECKSTEIN FRAENKEL HAUSMANN HOCHHUTH HOFFMANN KOTZEBUE LIENHARD MEISSNER REMARQUE ROQUETTE WOLZOGEN ZSCHOKKE BEYERLEIN GANGHOFER IMMERMANN SCHUCKING SIODMAKK SUDERMANN UECHTRITZ WILBRANDT WITZLEBEN ZERKAULEN ZOBELTITZ FLAISCHLEN GERSTACKER KELLERMANN

SPIELHAGEN WASSERMANN WILDERMUTH HASENCLEVER FEUCHTWANGER SCHOPENHAUER
GREEK AESOP HOMER BARDIS IOPHON LONGUS LUCIAN BABRIUS PLUTARCH ARISTOTLE ONOSANDER KAZANTZAKIS
GUATEMALAN ASTRUIAS
HUNGARIAN FAY BIRO JOKAI DOBOZY FARAGO FOLDES JOSIKA KARMAN SALTEN HEGEDUS VAMBERY HARSANYI KOESTLER KORMENDI
ICELANDIC KAMBAN ARNASON LAXNESS SAEMUND GUNNARSSON THORODDSEN GUDMUNDSSON
INDIAN ALI ABBAS ANAND GHOSE MEHTA RUSHDIE SORABJI CHATTERJI SHRIDHARANI KRISHNAMURTI
IRISH DALY WEST BEHAN BOWEN COYLE CROLY DOYLE GWYNN JOYCE KEANE LECKY LETTS LOVER MOORE MOYES STERN TYNAN WILDE BARLOW BROOKE CROFTS ERVINE GRAVES LEFANU LESLIE MARTIN OBRIEN OGRADY OKELLY PEARSE STOKER TREVOR BECKETT CCOGARTY ORKERY DUNSANY LARDNER LAWLESS MACGILL MATURIN MAXWELL MURDOCH OCONNER STARKIE CARELTON CHILDERS KAVANAGH ODONNELL OFAOLAIN ORIORDAN STEPHENS OFLAHERTY TODHUNTER WARBURTON WIBBERLEY BARRINGTON MCALLISTER SOMERVILLE
ISRAELI OZ BROD AGNON BUBER
ITALIAN VARE BRUNO PULCI SERAO TASSO AMICIS FARINA MAFFEI PAPINI PAVESE SILONE ALBERTI BARRILI BARZINI BONATTI CARCANO DELEDDA GALIANI GIACOMO MANZONI MOHAVIA PELLICO ALBRIZZI BERSEZIO SABATINI BOCCACCIO CHIARELLI CORRADINI DANNUNZIO FOGAZZARO GUERRAZZI BELGIOIOSO BERTINELLI PREZZOLINI CASTELNUOVO PIRANDELLO
JAPANESE ENDO BAKIN NAGAI OZAKI TAMAI MISHIMA FUKUZAWA KAWABATA MURASAKI
LATVIAN RAINIS
MEXICAN AZUELA GAMBOA TRAVEN FUENTES
NEW ZEALAND EDEN ADAMS MARSH DUGGAN BOLITHO LYTTLETON MANSFIELD RUSSELL
NIGERIAN ALUKO ACHEBE DELANO SOYINKA TUTUOLA
NORWEGIAN LIE BULL BOJER FONHUS HAMSUN UNDSET COLLETT GARRORG INGSTAD ELVESTAD KIELLAND ASBJORNSEN
PERUVIAN PALMA URETA ALEGRIA CACERES
POLISH REJ ASCH PRUS STRUG ANCZYC BERENT CONRAD GOETEL BALUCKI REYMONT WITTLIN ZAPOLSKA ZELENSKI ZEROMSKI ZULAWSKI MILKOWSKI NALKOWSKA

DANILOWSKI KONOPNICKA KRASZEWSKI CHMIELOWSKI OSSENDOWSKI SIENKIEWICZ KORZENIOWSKI ANDREZEJEWSKI
PORTUGUESE LOBO BRAGA SOUSA DANTAS MORAES
ROMAN LUCAN APULEIUS PHAEDRUS VELLEIUS PETRONIUS
RUMANIAN BEIN GOGA NEGRUZZI CARAGIALE RADULESCU
RUSSIAN BLOK BABEL BUNIN FEDIN GOGOL GORKI FADEEV GLINKA HERZEN KRYLOV KUPRIN LEONOV LESKOV AKSAKOV ALDANOV AMALRIK ANDREEV CHEKHOV GARSHIN GLADKOV KATAYEV PILNYAK PUSHKIN ROMANOV TOLSTOI BULGAKOV KARAMZIN POTEKHIN SHALAMOV SHUKSHIN TURGENEV USPENSKI VERESAEY BESTUZHEV EHRENBURG GONCHAROV KOROLENKO LERMONTOV PASTERNAK SHOLOKHOV SUMAROKOV USPENSKII DOSTOEVSKI YUSHKEVICH ZOSHCHENKO AMFITEATROV ARTSYBASHEV GRIGOROVICH LAZHECHNIKOV SOLZHENITSYN
SCOTTISH TEY DENT GALT GUNN HOGG LANG BEITH BROWN COMBE JACOB MUNRO SCOTT SHARP SPARK YOUNG AYTOUN BARRIE BROGAN BUCHAN GIBBON SHAIRP WATSON BALFOUR CHESNEY FERRIER HERRIOT MACLEAN MACLEOD BUCHANAN CRAUFURD CROCKETT LOCKHART MAITLAND MARSHALL OLIPHANT URQUHART FINDLATER MACDONALD MACKENZIE MITCHISON MOLESWORTH
SOUTH AFRICA HEAD SEED PATON CLOETE MILLIN PLOMER
SOUTH AFRICAN BLOOM COETZEE GORDIMER BALLINGER
SPANISH ALAS BAREA PEREZ RIVAS ROJAS TRIGO ALEMAN BAROJA ESPRIU PEREDA SENDER AGUILAR ALARCON ESPINEL MACHADO CABALLERO CERVANTES
SWEDISH AURELL CARLEN EDGREN MOBERG MWRDAL WAHLOO AHLGREN LIDGREN SJOWALL ALMQVIST LAGERLOF SCHWARTZ BACKSTROM LUNDEGARD LAGERKVIST STRINDBERG STREINDBERG WETTERBERGH
SWISS ROD FREY HEER KING HESSE WYSS SPYRI FRISCH FUSELI KAISER BITZIUS FEDERER KERLLER OLIVIER DURRENMATT
WELSH MAP EVANS PRYCE WYNNE DAVIES THOMAS ARUNDEL POLLETT LLEWELLYN
YUGOSLAVIAN ANDRIC DJILAS DEDIER
AUTHORITATIVE GRAVE CLASSIC OFFICIAL ORACULAR POSITIVE TEXTUARY MAGISTERIAL (PREF.) CURIO
AUTHORITY LAW ROD SEE BALL RULE SWAY ADEPT BOARD FAITH

POWER RICHE RIGHT SAYSO
STAMP SWING TITLE ARTIST
AUTHOR CREDIT DANGER EMPERY
EXPERT FASCES PUNDIT REGENT
REGIME SWINGE WEIGHT AMITATE
COMMAND CONTROL DYNASTY
FACULTY LEADING LICENCE
LICENSE POTENCY SCEPTER
WARRANT DISPOSAL DOMINION
DOMINIUM HEGEMONY LORDSHIP
PRESTIGE SANCTION STRENGTH
PROCURATION
(— OF SWITZERLAND) BUNDESRAT
(ARBITRARY —) ABOVE
(CHALLENGE —) REBEL
(COLLEGE —) DON
(MORAL —) MANA
(ONE HIGHEST IN —) SUPREMO
(PAPAL —) VATICAN
(ROYAL —) SCEPTRE SOVRANTY
(SPIRITUAL —) KEYS KHILAFAT
(SUPREME —) SAY SIRCAR SIRKAR
(TEACHING —) MAGISTERIUM
(UNLIMITED —) AUTOCRACY
(PL.) ISNAD SIRCAR
(SUFF.) CRACY CRAT(IC)
AUTHORIZATION FIAT BARAT
BERAT PASSPORT SANCTION
WARRANTY PERMISSION
AUTHORIZE LET LEAL VEST ALLOW
CLEAR CLOTHE PERMIT RATIFY
APPROVE EMPOWER ENDORSE
ENTITLE INDORSE JUSTIFY
LICENSE WARRANT ACCREDIT
DELEGATE LEGALIZE SANCTION
AUTHORIZED LEGAL OFFICIAL
AUTHORSHIP PENCRAFT
PATERNITY
AUTO (ALSO SEE AUTOMOBILE)
CRATE CHUMMY LIZZIE
(— RACING MANEUVER)
SLINGSHOT
(— RACING PROBLEM) SPINOUT
(CONVERTIBLE —) RAGTOP
(UNSATISFACTORY —) LEMON
AUTOBIOGRAPHY VITA MEMOIR
AUTOCHTHONOUS NATIVE
EDAPHIC ENDEMIC
AUTOCLAVE DIGESTER DIGESTOR
AUTOCRACY MONARCHY
AUTOCRAT CHAM CZAR TSAR TZAR
MOGUL CAESAR DESPOT
AUTARCH MONARCH DICTATOR
MONOCRAT
AUTOCRATIC ABSOLUTE
AUTO-DA-FE AUTO SERMO
AUTOGRAPH NAME SIGN MANUAL
INSCRIBE
AUTOLYCUS (DAUGHTER OF —)
ANTICLEA
(FATHER OF —) HERMES MERCURY
(HALF-BROTHER OF —)
PHILAMMON
(MOTHER OF —) CHIONE
AUTOMATIC REFLEX MACHINE
MECHANICAL
(PREF.) SELF
AUTOMATON GOLEM ROBOT
AUTOMA ANDROID MACHINE
AUTOMOBILE BUG BUS CAR SIX
AUTO FOUR HEAP JEEP PONY TRAP
BUGGY COACH COUPE CRATE
EDSEL EIGHT MOTOR PONEY

RACER SEDAN BUCKET CHUMMY
CUSTOM JALOPY JUNKER SALOON
WHEELS AUTOCAR COMPACT
FLIVVER HACKNEY HARDTOP
MACHINE MINICAR MINIVAN
PHAETON STEAMER TORPEDO
VOITURE CARRYALL DRAGSTER
ELECTRIC FASTBACK ROADSTER
SQUADROL SUBURBAN VICTORIA
HATCHBACK NOTCHBACK
(CONVERTIBLE —) RAGTOP
DROPHEAD
(DEMONSTRATOR —) DEMO
(KIND OF —) RENTACAR
(MIDGET —) DOODLEBUG
(NOISY —) BANGER
(SMALL —) MINI
AUTONOE (FATHER OF —) CADMUS
(HUSBAND OF —) ARISTAEUS
(MOTHER OF —) HARMONIA
(SISTER OF —) AGAVE
(SON OF —) ACTAEON
AUTONOMOUS FREE SEPARATE
AUTONOMY SOVEREIGNTY
SEPARATENESS
(— OF GOD) ASEITY ASEITAS
AUTOPSY NECROPSY
AUTUMN FALL KHARIF AUTOMPNE
FALLTIME MATURITY
AUXILIARY AID SUB AIDE ALLY
ANSAR AIDING BRANCH DONKEY
HELPER ABETTER ABETTOR
ADJUNCT HELPING PARTNER
ADJUTANT ANCILLARY
PERIPHERAL
(PL.) FOEDERATI
AVAIL DO AID DOW USE BOOT HELP
FADGE SERVE SKILL STEAD VALUE
MOMENT PROFIT BENEFIT
BESTEAD PREVAIL SERVICE
SUCCEED SUFFICE UTILIZE
SUBSERVE
(— ONESELF) EMBRACE IMPROVE
SUBSERVE
AVAILABLE FIT FREE OPEN FLUSH
HANDY LOOSE ONTAP READY
PATENT USABLE PRESENT VISIBLE
ATSTORES
AVALANCHE SLIDE LAWINE
VOLLEGE
AVANT-COURIER HERALD
SCURRIER
AVANT-GARDE LITERATI
AVARICE GREED MAMMON MISERY
AVIDITY CUPIDITY RAPACITY
AVARICIOUS CLOSE SLOAN
GREEDY HAVING HUNGRY SORDID
STINGY GRIPING GRIPPLE ITCHING
MISERLY COVETOUS GRASPING
AVATAR BALARAMA EPIPHANY
AVELLANEOUS HAZEL
AVENGE REPAY RIGHT VISIT WRACK
WREAK AWREAK PUNISH
BEWREAK REQUITE REVENGE
SATISFY CHASTISE
AVENGER KANAIMA NEMESIS
WREAKER
AVENS GEUM BENNET BAREFOOT
AVENTURINE SUNSTONE
GOLDSTONE
AVENUE RUE WAY GATE MALL PIKE
ROAD ALLEE ALLEY DRIVE ENTRY

ACCESS ARCADE ARTERY DROMOS
RIDING STREET AVENIDA OPENING
PASSAGE
AVER SAY AIVER CLAIM PROVE
STATE SWEAR AFFIRM ALLEGE
ASSERT ASSURE AVOUCH DEPOSE
VERIFY DECLARE JUSTIFY PROFESS
PROTEST
AVERAGE PAR SUM DUTY FAIR
MEAN NORM RULE SOSO RATIO
USUAL VALUE CHARGE MEDIAL
MEDIAN MEDIUM MIDDLE
NORMAL TARIFF ARRIAGE
ESTIMATE MEDIOCRE MIDDLING
MODERATE ORDINARY OVERHEAD
QUANTITY STANDARD
(DOW-JONES —) DOW
(NOT —) BORDERLINE
AVERNAL HELLISH INFERNAL
AVERSE LOTH BALKY LOATH
AFRAID ADVERSE AGAINST
OPPOSED BACKWARD INIMICAL
OPPOSITE PERVERSE RELUCTANT
(— TO) ABOVE
AVERSION TOY HATE DERRY
ODIUM ENMITY HATRED HORROR
PHOBIA REGRET DESPITE DISDAIN
DISGUST DISLIKE MISLIKE
DISTASTE ABOMINATION
(— TO FOOD) APOSITIA
(— TO WORK) ERGOPHOBIA
AVERT WRY BEND FEND MOVE
SHUN TURN WARD AVOID DETER
DODGE EVADE PARRY SHEER
TWIST DEFRAY DIVERT RETARD
SHIELD DECLINE DEFLECT EXPIATE
PREVENT ALIENATE ESTRANGE
FOREFEND WITHTURN
AVESTA ZEND
AVIARY CAGE HOUSE VOLARY
ORNITHON
AVIATOR ACE FLIER FLYER PILOT
AIRMAN FLYING ICARUS BIRDMAN
LOOPIST LUFBERY MANBIRD
SOLOIST
AVID LSD AGOG KEEN WARM EAGER
ARDENT GREEDY HUNGRY JEJUNE
ANXIOUS ATHIRST CRAVING
LONGING THIRSTY DESIROUS
GRASPING
AVIDITY AVARICE CUPIDITY
AVIFAUNA BIRDS ORNIS BIRDLIFE
AVIKOM JACKS
AVOCADO COYO PEAR PALTA
AHUACA CHININ MARROW PERSEA
ZABOCA ABACATE ABBOGADA
AGUACATE ALLIGATO
AVOCET BARKER TILTER YELPER
SCOOPER
AVOID FLY SHY BALK FLEE HELP
MISS PASS QUIT SAVE SHUN VOID
WARE ABHOR ANNUL AVERT
BURKE DITCH DODGE ELUDE
EVADE EVITE FEIGN HEDGE PARRY
SHIFT SHIRK SKIRT SKULK SLACK
SPAIR SPARE START WANGE
WONDE ABJURE BLENCH BYPASS
DETOUR ESCAPE ESCHEW REFUTE
REMOVE VACATE ABSTAIN
DECLINE EVITATE FORBEAR
FORSAKE REFRAIN
(— A PUNCH) SLIP
(— COMMITMENT) FUDGE

(— EXPENSE) HELP MISS SKIVE
(— OVERWORKING) FAVOR
(— RESPONSIBILITY) BLUDGE
(— SUPERHIGHWAY) SHUNPIKE
(PREF.) PHYGO
AVOIDANCE DODGE OUTLET
EVASION ESCHEWAL
(— OF RISK) CAUTION
(PREF.) PHOB(O)
AVOIDING (— BATTLE) FABIAN
AVOIRDUPOIS HEFT
AVOUCH AVER ASSERT
AVOW OWN BIND WARE ADMIT
STATE AFFIRM ASSERT AVOUCH
DEPONE DEPOSE DEVOTE
CONFESS DECLARE JUSTIFY
PROFESS MAINTAIN
AVOWAL OATH WORD AVOURE
PROTEST
AVOWED FRANK SWORN STATED
DECLARED
AWAIT BIDE HEED KEEP PEND STAY
TEND WAIT ABIDE TARRY WATCH
ATTEND EXPECT IMPEND REMAIN
WAYLAY
(— PAYMENT) CARRY
AWAITING BEFORE BIDING
AWAKE DAW STIR WAKE ADAWE
ALERT ALIVE AWARE ROUSE
ABRADE ABRAID ACTIVE AROUSE
AWAKEN EXCITE CAREFUL
HEEDFUL STARTLE VIGILANT
AWAKEN DAW STIR ALERT AROUSE
BESTIR EXCITE KINDLE
AWAKENER (ARMY —) BUGLE
AWAKENING REVIVAL WAKEFUL
AWARD LAW ARET CLIO GIVE HUGO
KUDO MARK MEED METE OBIE
TONY WARD AI LOT ARETT EDGAR
GRANT MEDAL PRICE PRIZE
ACCORD ACTION ADDEEM
ADDOOM ADWARD ASSIGN
BESTOW BOUNTY CONFER
DECIDE GRAMMY MODIFY
ADJUDGE APPOINT CONSIGN
CUSTODY KEEPING ACCOLADE
SENTENCE
(ATHLETIC —) LETTER
(DETECTIVE FICTION —) EDGAR
(MOVIE —) OSCAR
(MYSTERY-NOVEL WRITING —)
EDGAR
(RADIO OR TELEVISION —) CLIO
(RECORDING —) GRAMMIE
(STATUETTE —) GRAMMY REUBEN
(TELEVISION —) EMMY
(THEATER —) OBIE
(THEATRICAL —) TONY
(WRITING —) HUGO
(PL.) DESERTS
AWARE HEP HIP RECK SURE WARE
WARY WISE ALERT ALIVE AWAKE
JERRY BEWARE KNOWING
MINDFUL APPRISED INFORMED
SENSIBLE SENTIENT VIGILANT
WATCHFUL
(— OF) ONTO
(KEENLY —) HIP
AWARENESS EAR FEEL
SENSE FEELING INSIGHT
COGNITION SENSATION
PERCEPTION

(— OF SUPERNATURAL) VISION
(— OF WORTH) APPRECIATION
AWASH ASEA ADRIFT AFLOAT
FLOODED SWAMPED FLOATING
AWAY BY TO AWA FRO OFF OUT VIA
WAY AFAR GONE PAST SCAT YOND
ALONG APART ASIDE FORTH
HENCE ABROAD ABSENT BEGONE
ONWARD THENCE DISTANT
FROWARD FAREWELL TOTHEWIND
(— FROM) DOWN WITH ALONE
ALOOF APART BESIDE
(— FROM HOME) AFIELD OUTLAND
(— FROM MOUTH) ABORAL
(— FROM PORT) AFLOAT
(FARTHER —) BEYOND
(PREF.) DE E
(— FROM) APH APO
AWE COW WOW FEAR AMAZE
DAUNT DREAD SCARE FRIGHT
HORROR REGARD TERROR
WONDER BUFFALO RESPECT
ASTONISH BEWILDER OVERCOME
RELIGION
AWED SOLEMN
AWEIGH ATRIP
AWE-INSPIRING GODFUL SOLEMN
AWESOME RELIGIO FEARSOME
OLYMPIAN
AWESOME EERY FELL HOLY AWFUL
EERIE WEIRD SOLEMN DREADED
GHOSTLY
AWESTRUCK SILENT
AWETO WERI
AWFUL DIRE FINE UGLY DREAD
GHAST AUGUST HORRID
AWESOME FEARFUL HIDEOUS
SATANIC DREADFUL SHOCKING
TERRIBLE
AWFULLY AWFUL FIERCE
AWHILE FORABIT
AWKWARD AWK CAR GAUM UNCO
BLATE CRANK DODGY FALSE
FUDGY GAUMY GAWKY GOATY
INAPT INEPT SPLAY STIFF UNCOW
UNKED UNKID CLUMSY GAUCHE
RUSTIC STICKY THUMBY UNEASY
WOODEN ADVERSE BOORISH

CUBBISH FROWARD HALTING
LOUTISH LUMPISH STILTED
UNCANNY UNCOUTH UNHANDY
UNREADY BUNGLING CLOWNISH
FECKLESS LUBBERLY PERVERSE
UNGAINLY UNTOWARD UNWIELDY
CLOUTERLY GRACELESS
MALADROIT
(— LOOKING) HORSY
(— PERSON) CLOUT KLUTZ TAWPY
TUMFIE
(NOT —) FACILE
AWKWARD PERSON GALOOT
AWL BROD BROG NAIL NALL PROD
PROG ALENE BRODE ELSEN NALLE
BROACH DRIVER ELSHIN FIBULA
GIMLET BRADAWL SCRIBER
STABBER
AWN AIL EAR JAG BARB BEAK JAGG
PILE ARISTA BRISTLE
(— OF BARLEY) HORN
(— OF OATS) JAG JAGG
(PL.) BEARD
AWNED BARBATE
AWNING TILT BLIND SHADE VELUM
CANOPY SEMIAN SHADER TIENDA
TENTORY SEMIANNA SUNBLIND
SUNSHADE VELARIUM
AWNLESS NOT NOTT HUMBLE
HUMMEL POLLARD MUTICOUS
AWRY CAM WRY AGEE BIAS SKEW
AGLEY AMISS ASKEW GLEED
GLEYD SNAFU WONKY WRONG
ACROSS ASIDEN BLOOEY BLOOIE
CAMMED FLOOEY SKIVIE THRAWN
ASKANCE ASQUINT ATHWART
CROOKED OBLIQUE PERVERSE
AX ADZ AXE CAN ADZE EAWT FIRE
HACHE MATAX BIFACE CANCEL
CUTOUT PICKEL PIOLET POLEAX
THIXLE TWIBIL BESAGUE BOUCHER
BROADAX CHOPPER CLEAVER
HATCHET JEDDING PULASKI
TWIBILL FRANCISC PALSTAVE
SUNDERER TOMAHAWK
(DOUBLE —) LABRYS
(HEADSMAN'S —) MANNAIA
(MASON'S —) CAVEL

(PART OF —) EAR EYE BUTT FACE
HAFT HEAD POLL BLADE HELVE
HANDLE
(WOODEN —) MACANA
(PREF.) SECURI
AXENIC GERMFREE
AXHAMMER CAVEL CAVIL KEVEL
KNAPPER
AXIAL VENTRAL
AXIL ALA
AXILLA AXIS ARMPIT SHOULDER
AXILLARY ALAR
AXIOM SAW ADAGE MAXIM MOTTO
BYWORD DICTUM SAYING TRUISM
DIGNITY PRECEPT PROVERB
APHORISM APOTHEGM DIGNITAS
PETITION SENTENCE POSTULATE
AXIOMATIC PRIMITIVE
AXIS AXE NUT AXLE STEM ARBOR
HINGE STALK ARBOUR CAUDEX
CENTER CHITRA RACHIS CAULOME
CORNCOB DENTATA POLAXIS
SPINDLE SUCCULA SYMPODE
TENDRIL AXLETREE MONOPODE
(— OF A FLOWER) CYME SPIKE
UMBEL CORYMB RACEME PANICLE
(— OF COCHLEA) MODIOLUS
(PREF.) AX(I)(IO)(O)(ONO)
AXLE EX BAR COD PIN AXIS BOGY
ARBOR BOGEY BOGIE EXTRE
SHAFT AXTREE SLEEVE MANDREL
SPINDLE SUCCULA
AXOLOTL SIREDON
AXON PROCESS
AYAH IYA CHAY EYAH MAID NURSE
AYE I AY EY EYE PRO YEA YES EVER
ALWAYS ASSENT FOREVER
AYESHA (HUSBAND OF —)
MOHAMMED
AYU AI SWEETFISH
AZALEA ERICA MINERVA CARDINAL
AZALIAH (SON OF —) SHAPHAN
AZANIAH (SON OF —) JESHUA
AZAREEL (FATHER OF —) BANI
JEROHAM
(SON OF —) AMASHAI MAASIAI
AZARIAH (FATHER OF —) JEHU
ODED ETHAN NATHAN AHIMAAZ

JEROHAM JOHANAN MAASEIAH
JEHALELEL ZEPHANIAH
JEHOSHAPHAT
(SON OF —) JOEL
AZAZ (SON OF —) BELA
AZAZEL EBLIS
AZAZIAH (SON OF —) HOSHEA
AZERBAIJAN (ALSO SEE RUSSIA)
(CAPITAL OF —) BAKU
(CAPITOL OF —) BAKU
AUTONOMOUS REGION:
NAGORNOKARABAKH
AUTONOMOUS REPUBLIC:
NAKHICHEVAN
CANAL: SHIRVAN KARABAKH
CAPITAL: BAKU BAKY
COIN: MANAT
LAKE: GEYGYOL
LANGUAGE: AZERI
MOUNTAIN: TUFAN SHAKHDAG
BAZARDYUZYU KYUMYURKYOY
MOUNTAIN RANGE: TALISH TALYSH
CAUCASUS MUROVDAG
SHAKHDAG ZANGEZUR
PLAIN: MUGAN SHIRVAN LENKORAN
MILSKAYA
RIVER: ARAS KURA ARAKS
TOWN: GANJA SUMGAIT
KIROVABAD
AZIMUTH ZN ARC BEARING
AZMAVETH (SON OF —) PELET
JEZIEL
AZOLE PYRROLE
AZOR (FATHER OF —) ELIAKIM
AZRIEL (SON OF —) SERAIAH
AZRIKAM (FATHER OF —) AZEL
NEARIAH
(SLAYER OF —) ZICHRI
AZTEC AZTECA MEXICA MEXICAN
TENOCHCA
AZUBAH (HUSBAND OF —) CALEB
(SON OF —) JEHOSHAPHAT
AZUR (SON OF —) HANANIAH
JAAZANIAH
AZURE BICE BLUE HURT JOVE
COBALT JOVIAL JUPITER
CERULEAN SAPPHIRE
AZZAN (SON OF —) PALTIEL

B

B SI BEE BAKER BRAVO
  (**— FLAT**) ZA BEMOL
BA TRIPOS
BAA MAA MAE BLEAT
BAAL BEEZEBUB
BAANA (FATHER OF —) AHILUD
  (**SON OF —**) ZADOK
BAANAH (BROTHER OF —) RECHAB
  (**FATHER OF —**) HUSHAI RIMMON
  (**SLAYER OF —**) DAVID
  (**SON OF —**) HELEB HELED
BAARA (HUSBAND OF —)
  SHAHARAIM
BAASHA (FATHER OF —) AHIJAH
BABBAR UTU UTUO
BABBITT PHILISTINE
  (**AUTHOR OF —**) LEWIS
  (**CHARACTER IN —**) TED MYRA PAUL
  TANIS ZILLA GEORGE VERONA
  BABBITT JUDIQUE REISLING
BABBLE CHAT GASH KNAP PURL
  TOVE BABIL BLATE CLACK CLYDE
  GLOCK HAVER PRATE TAVER
  WLAFF CACKLE DITHER GABBLE
  GAGGLE GLAVER GOSSIP JANGLE
  MURMUR PALTER PIFFLE RABBLE
  TAIVER TUMULT BLABBER
  BLATHER BLETHER BLUSTER
  BRABBLE CHATTER CHIPPER
  CLATTER PRATTLE SMATTER
  TWADDLE TWATTLE GLAISTER
BABBLER CACKI FR BLATEROON
  STIPITURE
BABBLING LALLATION
  (**PREF.**) LALO
BABE NAIF INFANT
BABEL DIN MEDLEY TUMULT
  CHARIVARI CONFUSION
BABESIA APIOSOMA NUTTALIA
  PIROPLASMA
BABOON APE PAP PAPA DRILL
  ADONIS BAVIAN CHACMA GIRRIT
  PAPION SPHINX BABUINA
  MANDRILL HAMADRYAD
BABUL SANT SUNT ACACIA BABOOT
  GARRAT GONAKE NEBNEB
  ATTALEH GONAKIE
BABUSHKA SCARF KERCHIEF
BABY MOP BABA BABE CHAP DOLL
  JOEY NENE TOTO WEAN BAIRN
  CHILD HUMOR SPOIL WAYNE
  CHRISM CODDLE FONDLE INFANT
  MOPPET PAMPER POUPEE PUPPET
  SQUALL WEANIE BAMBINO
  CHRISOM INDULGE PAPOOSE
  PREEMIE WADDLER PAPPOOSE
  (**— FOOD**) PAP
BABY CARRIAGE PRAM BUGGY
  WAGON GOCART STROLLER
  PERAMBULATOR
BABYISH TIDDY PULING SIMPLE
  PUERILE CHILDISH
BABYLONIA CHALDEA

BABYLONIAN (— CYCLE) SAROS
BABY'S BREATH GYP GYPSOPHILA
BACALAO MURRE SCAMP ABADEJO
  CODFISH GROUPER GUILLEMOT
BACCATE BERRIED
BACCHANAL DEVOTEE REVELER
  CAROUSER
BACCHANTE FROW MAENAD
BACCHUS LIBER LYAEUS BROMIUS
  DIONYSUS
  (**AUNT OF —**) INO
  (**FATHER OF —**) ZEUS JUPITER
  (**MOTHER OF —**) SEMELE
BACHELOR BACH SEAL BATCH
  GARCON WANTER BACULERE
  BENEDICT CELIBATE
BACILLUS GERM VIRUS MICROBE
BACK AID FRO TUB VAT ABET BAKE
  BECK FULL HIND HINT NAPE NATA
  REAR TAIL ABACK AGAIN ANGEL
  BOOST BROAD CHINE DORSE
  FAVOR NOTUM SPINE SPLAT
  STERN VOUCH ASSIST DORSUM
  HINDER RETRAL SECOND SOOTHE
  TERGUM TROUGH UPHOLD VERIFY
  CISTERN ENDORSE FINANCE
  POSTERN RIGGING SPONSOR
  SUPPORT SUSTAIN BACKWARD
  FULLBACK HALFBACK MAINTAIN
  (**— A ROWBOAT**) STERN
  (**— OF ANIMAL**) RIG TERGUM
  (**— OF ARCHERY TARGET**) BOSS
  (**— OF AWNING**) RIDGEROPE
  (**— OF BOOK**) DORSE SPINE
  (**— OF BULL**) ROOF
  (**— OF HAND**) OPISTHENAR
  (**— OF HEAD**) INION NODDLE
  NIDDICK OCCIPUT
  (**— OF INSECT**) NOTUM
  (**— OF NECK**) NAPE NUQUE SCRUFF
  (**— OF PAGE**) FV
  (**— OUT**) BEG JIB DUCK FLUNK
  CRAWFISH
  (**— TO BACK**) ADDORSED
  (**— UP**) ABET PROVE VERIFY
  (**— WATER**) STERN SHEAVE
  (**ANIMALS' —S**) DORSA
  (**BROUGHT —**) REDUX
  (**SHOWING —**) TERGANT
  (**PREF.**) ANA DORSI DORSO NOT(O)
  OPISTH(O) POST RE RETRO TERGI
  TERGO
  (**AT THE — OF**) OPISTH(O) POSTERO
  (**BENT —**) POSTERO RECURVI
  RECURVO
  (**SUFF.**) NOTUS
BACKACHE NOTALGIA
BACKBAND RIGWIDDIE RIGWOODIE
BACKBITING CATTY DETRACTION
BACKBOARD BANK MONITOR
BACKBONE BACK GRIT GUTS CHINE
  NERVE PLUCK RIDGE SPINA SPINE
  LADDER METTLE SPIRIT GRISTLE

  RIGBANE SPINULE STAMINA
  VERTEBRA
  (**— OF FISH**) GRATE
BACKCHAT MOUTH CROSSTALK
BACK-COMB TEASE
BACKCOUNTRY BUSH STICKS
  BOONIES BACKLAND BACKVELD
  BOONDOCKS
BACKDROP OLEO SCENERY
  SETTING
BACKER ANGEL
BACKFIELD SECONDARY
BACKFIRE BOOMERANG
BACKFLASH GUTTER
BACKGAMMON IRISH LURCH
  TABLE FAYLES GAMMON TABLES
  BACKGAME TICKTACK VERQUERE
  (**— MAN**) BLOT TABLEMAN
BACKGROUND FOND REAR
  GROUND OFFING LINEAGE SETTING
  BACKDROP DISTANCE EXTERIOR
  OFFSCAPE TRAINING EDUCATION
  (**— OF FLOWERS**) BOCAGE
  (**MUSICAL —**) SUPPORT
BACKHANDED AWKWARD
BACKHOE PULLSHOVEL
BACKHOUSE PRIVY OUTHOUSE
BACKING AID EGIS AEGIS BACKUP
  BEHIND LINING MUSI IN REFUSE
  SUPPORT HEARTING FINANCING
  (**LEGAL —**) STRENGTH
BACKLASH LASH SHAKE SLACK
BACKLOG RESERVE SURPLUS
  BACKBRAND
BACKPACK GEAR LOAD
BACKPIECE DOSSIERE
BACKPLATE REREDOS
BACKREST LAZYBACK
BACKROPE GOBLINE
BACKSEY SEY SIRLOIN
BACKSLIDE FALL LAPSE DESERT
  REVERT RELAPSE
BACKSPIN DRAG UNDERCUT
  UNDERSPIN
BACKSTITCH PURL PEARL
BACKSTOP BUTT
BACK TALK LIP SASS
BACKWARD FRO JAY LAX YON
  BACK CRAB DANK DULL LOTH
  ABACK AREAR BLATE INAPT LOATH
  THRAW UNAPT ARREAR ASTERN
  AVERSE BYGONE POSTIC RETRAD
  RETRAL STUPID ARRIERE BASHFUL
  LAGGARD LAGGING REVERSE
  UPSTAGE DILATORY IGNORANT
  LATEWARD PERVERSE REARWARD
  RINKYDINK TAILFIRST
  (**PREF.**) OPISTH(O) RE RETRO
BACKWARDNESS DARKNESS
  BARBARISM
BACKWARDS YON ABACK AROUND
  (**PREF.**) OPISO PALI(M)(N)
BACKWASH SLIPSTREAM

BACKWATER EBB COVE SLEW SLUE
  SNYE BAYOU BOGAN SHEAVE
  SLOUGH RETRACT RETREAT
  BACKWASH BILLABONG
BACKWOODS BRUSH
BACKWOODSMAN HICK WOODSY
  BUCKSKIN HILLBILLY
BACKWORT COMFREY
BACON PIG BARD MEAT PORK
  BARDE JAMON PRIZE SPECK
  FLITCH GAMMON RUSTIC SAWNEY
  GAMBONE SOWBELLY
  (**UNSMOKED —**) PANCETTA
BACOPA BRAMIA
BACTERIOLOGIST AMERICAN GAY
  KAHN NOVY PARK BURKE CRAIG
  ERNST MOORE PLOTZ BERGEY
  ENDERS JORDAN FRANCIS KENDALL
  NOGUCHI THEILER ZINSSER
  BELGIAN BORDET
  BRAZILIAN CHAGAS
  CANADIAN WESBROOK
  CUBAN AGRAMONTE
  ENGLISH TWORT FLEMING
  FRENCH ROUX RAMON MARTIN
  LAVERAN NICOLLE CHAMBERLAND
  GERMAN KOCH FLUGGE GAFFKY
  GRUBER HUEPPE BEHRING EHRLICH
  GARTNER LOFFLER FRAENKEL
  PFEIFFER UHLENHUTH
  WASSERMANN
  JAPANESE HATA SHIGA KITAZATO
  RUMANIAN BABES
  RUSSIAN METCHNIKOFF
  SPANISH FERRAN
  SWISS YERSIN
BACTERIUM ROD COLI GERM
  AEROBE COCCUS CYTODE
  ANTHRAX CHOLERA LYSOGEN
  MICROBE PROTEUS SARCINA
  VIBRION BACILLUS LISTERIA
  PATHOGEN SHIGELLA BOTULINUS
  CYTOPHAGA HEMOPHILE
  INFECTANT INFECTION SPIRILLUM
  MICROCOCCUS PNEUMOCOCCUS
  SCHIZOMYCETE PNEUMOBACILLUS
BAD BIG DUD ILL SAD EVIL FULL
  HARD LEWD POOR PUNK QUED
  SICK SOUR VILE WICK ADDLE
  GAMMY LOUSY NASTY SORRY
  WEARY WORST WRONG ARRANT
  FAULTY LITHER LUTHER NOUGHT
  ROTTEN SEVERE SHREWD SINFUL
  UNGOOD UNKIND WICKED
  BALEFUL BANEFUL CHRONIC
  CORRUPT FEARFUL HARMFUL
  HEINOUS HURTFUL IMMORAL
  INUTILE NAUGHTY SPOILED
  TAINTED UNLUCKY UNMORAL
  UNSOUND VICIOUS ANNOYING
  CRIMINAL DEPRAVED DOGGEREL
  FIENDISH FLAGRANT INFERIOR
  PRECIOUS SINISTER UNSUITED

(— MANNERS) TROLLOPE
(ASTROCIOUSLY —) PIACULAR
(OUTRAGEOUSLY —) GRIEVOUS
(OUTSTANDINGLY —) ARRANT
PIACULAR
(RATHER —) INDIFFERENT
(VERY —) FEARFUL ALMIGHTY
GODAWFUL EXECRABLE
(PREF.) CAC(O) CACH DYS KAK(O)
MAL(E) MIS
(SUFF.) CACE
BADDERLOCKS MURLIN PURSES
HENWARE SEAWEED HONEYWARE
BADEBEC (HUSBAND OF —)
GARGANTUA
(SON OF —) PANTAGRUEL
BADGE PIN BLUE MARK SIGN STAR
COLOR CREST CROSS FAVOR
HONOR ORDER PATCH TOKEN
WINGS BUTTON BUZZER COLLAR
EMBLEM ENSIGN FASCES GARTER
GIGLIO PLAQUE SHIELD SYMBOL
TIPONI WEEPER CHEVRON
EPAULET FEATHER BRASSARD
EPISEMON INSIGNIA SCAPULAR
VERNICLE EPAULETTE
COGNISANCE
(— OF VIRGINITY) SNOOD
(JAPANESE —) MON KIRIMON
(PILGRIM —) SCALLOP
(RUSSIAN —) ZNAK
(PL.) INSIGNIA
BADGER NAG PAT BAIT GRAY GREY
GRIS MELE PATE ANNOY BRACE
BROCK BRUSH CHEVY CHIVY
HURON MELES PAHMI RATED
RATEL TAXEL TAXUS TEASE
WORRY BAUSON BAWSON
BOTHER BRAROW CHIVVY HAGGLE
HARASS HAWKER HECKLE KIDDER
MELINE PESTER TELEDU WOMBAT
BAUSOND GRISARD TORMENT
BRAIREAU BULLYRAG CARCAJOU
HUCKSTER IRRITATE STINKARD
MISTONUSK
(— STATE) WISCONSIN
(AUSTRALIAN —) WOMBAT
(BURROW OF —) SET SETT
(COMPANY OF —S) CETE
(LIKE A —) MELINE
BADGER-DOG DACHSHUND
BADINAGE FOOL CHAFF JOKER
BANTER RAILLERY TRIFLING
BADLANDS MALPAIS
BADLY BAD ILL EVIL HARD ILLY SICK
SADLY EVILLY HARDLY POORLY
UNWELL FAULTILY WICKEDLY
VICIOUSLY
(PREF.) MAL
BADMINTON POONA
BADNESS MALICE PRAVITY
UNVALUE EVILNESS
(SUFF.) CACE
**BADROULBOUDOUR (HUSBAND
OF —)** ALADDIN
BAD-TEMPERED CRANKY STROPPY
CROTCHETY FOUL ANGRY STINGY
CRABBED GROUCHY
BAFF LOFT
BAFFLE FOX GET BALK BEAT FOIL
LICK MATE POSE STOP UNDO
CHEAT CHECK ELUDE EVADE FLING
STICK STUMP BLENCH BOGGLE

DEFEAT DELUDE FICKLE INFAMY
OUTWIT PUZZLE RESIST THWART
BUFFALO CONFUSE DECEIVE
QUIBBLE STONKER BEWILDER
CONFOUND DISGRACE JUGGLING
BAFFLED FOXED BEATEN
BAFFLING SHREWD ELUSIVE
BAG COD KIT LOT MAT NET PAD POD
POT SAC CELL DRAG GRIP HOBO
KILL LAND LOBE MAIL POCK POKE
SACK TOOT TOTE TRAP WOMB
BELLY BOUGE BULSE CATCH DILLI
DILLY EMERY FLOAT HUSSY PETER
POUCH PURSE SCRIP SEIZE SHOOT
SNARE STEAL BLOUSE BUDGET
CAVITY ENTRAP FOLLIS GASBAG
MATAPI PAGGLE POCKET POUNCE
SACHET SEABAG VALISE WALLET
ALFORJA BALLOON BEANBAG
BLISTER BUCKRAM CANTINA
CAPCASE CAPTURE CUSHION
DESTROY GAMEBAG GOMUKHI
HANDBAG HOLDALL RETICLE
SANDBAG SARPLER SATCHEL
TRAVOIS BALLONET CARRYALL
CORNSACK ENTRAILS ENVELOPE
FOLLICLE KNAPSACK MONEYBAG
OVERSLIP POCHETTE RETICULE
RUCKSACK SUITCASE WINESKIN
MULTIWALL WEEKENDER
PORTMANTEAU
(— BULGING) SWAG
(— FOR DIAMONDS) BULSE
(— FOR LETTERS) MAIL POUCH
KAREETA MAILBAG POSTBAG
(— FOR TOOLS) WALLET
(— OF ANISEED) DRAG
(— OF PERFUME) SACHET
(— OF WOOL) POCKET
(— WITH POCKETS) TIDE TIDY
(ANATOMICAL —) CECUM CAECUM
STOMACH
(AUSTRALIAN —) SWAG DILLI SHIRT
SHAMMY
(GAS —) CELL
(GRAB —) FISHPOND
(HAWSE —) JACKASS
(KIND OF —) DOGGY DOUGLAS
(LEATHER —) JAG JAGG ASKOS
BUDGE BOUGET MUSSUK
(NET —) SNOOD GARLAND
(SEWING —) HUSSY
(SLEEPING —) FUMBA FLEABAG
SLEEPER
(WATER —) CHAGAL CHAGEN
CHAGUL
(PREF.) UTRI
(SUFF.) SACCATE SACCI SACCO
BAGASSE BEGASS LINAGA MEGASS
BAGATELLE CANON TRUNK VERSE
CANNON TRIFLE NOTHING
BAGEL ROLL BIALY
(PARTNER OF —) LOX
BAGGAGE ARMS GEAR MINX SWAG
CUTTY HUZZY NASTY SAMAN
STUFF TENTS TRASH WENCH
HARLOT REFUSE TRASHY TRUNKS
CLOTHES DUNNAGE EFFECTS
FARDAGE PLUNDER RUBBISH
SALMARY SUMPTER VALISES
CARRIAGE HARLOTRY RUBBISHY
UTENSILS
BAGGAGE CAR WAGON FOURGON

BAGGER SACKER BATCHER
BAGGING SOUTAGE
BAGGY LOOSE POCKY PURSY
FLABBY PUFFED PURSIVE SACCATE
BAGNIO BAIN BATH BAGNE PRISON
BROTHEL HOTHOUSE
BAGPIPE MUSE PIPE PIVA DRONE
TITTY BIGNOU BINIOU CHORUS
GEWGAW MUSETTE PIFFERO
SAMBUKE DULCIMER SYMPHONY
ZAMPOGNA CORNAMUTE
CORNEMUSE SYMPHONIA
(PART OF —) BAG CORD PIPE
DRONE MOUNT STOCK TASSEL
CHANTER WINDBAG BLOWPIPE
BAGUETTE CHAPLET
BAH PO FIE FOH PAH POH ROT RATS
FAUGH PSHAW NONSENSE
BAHAMAS (CAPITAL OF —) NASSAU
(ISLAND OF —) ABACO EXUMA
ANDROS BIMINI
(TOWN IN —) FREEPORT
BAHIA (CAPITAL OF —) SALVADOR
BAHRAIN (CAPITAL OF —) MANAMA
(MONEY OF —) FILS DINAR
(TOWN OF —) RIFAA JIDHAFS
BAIL BOW DIP ANDI BALE BOND
HOOP LADE LAVE RING RYND YOKE
LADLE SCOOP THROW VOUCH
BUCKET HANDLE PLEDGE SECURE
SURETY VADIUM CAUTION
CUSTODY DELIVER RELEASE
REPLEVY BAILSMAN BULWARKS
SECURITY GUARANTEE
(— OUT) ABANDON
BAILEE LESSEE POSITOR
CONDUCTOR
BAILER SPOUCHER
BAILIFF FOUD GRAB HIND AGENT
REEVE SAFFO SCULT STAFF BAILIE
BAILLI BEADLE BEAGLE DEPUTY
FACTOR GRIEVE LOOKER OFFICE
PORTER PREVOT SCHOUT VARLET
BUMTRAP GRIPPER PROVOST
PUTTOCK SHERIFF STEWARD
APPROVER HUISSIER OVERSEER
TIPSTAFF CATCHPOLE CATCHPOLL
CONSTABLE HUNDREDER
PORTREEVE SENESCHAL
WAPENTAKE
BAILIWICK AREA FIELD DOMAIN
OFFICE SPHERE PROVINCE
BAILMENT MUTUUM
BAILOR LESSOR
BAIN NEAR LITHE READY SHORT
DIRECT LIMBER SUPPLE FORWARD
WILLING
BAIRN WEAN
BAIT BAD BOB COG DAP LUG BITE
CAST CHUM FEED HALT HANK
LURE PLUG TAIL DECOY HOUND
LEGER SHACK SLATE SQUID STALE
TEMPT TRAIN WORRY ALLURE
APPAST ATTACK BADGER BERLEY
ENTICE HARASS HECKLE HECTOR
KILLER LEDGER REPAST SHRAPE
SLIVER FULCRUM GUDGEON
PROVOKE TAGTAIL TOLLING
TORMENT BRANLING CUNGEBOI
BRANDLING
(— FOR BIRDS) SHRAP SHRAPE
(— FOR COD) CAPELIN
(— WITH DOGS) SLATE

(GREASY —) ROGUE
(GROUND —) BERLEY
(MAGGOT —) GENTLE
(SCENTED —) DRAG
(SPINNING —) PROPELLER
BAITING HANK
BAIZE BAY BAYES BAYETA DOMETT
BOCKING
BAKE DRY BURN COCT COOK FIRE
BATCH BROIL GRILL PARCH ROAST
ANNEAL HARDEN BISCUIT PISTATE
SCALLOP CLAMBAKE ESCALLOP
(— EGGS) SHIRR
(— THOROUGHLY) SOAK
BAKED CASINO COCTILE
(— IN EARTH OVEN) KALUA
(— PRODUCT) KICHEL
BAKER OVEN FIRER BAXTER
BURNER FURNER PISTOR FURNACE
OVENMAN ROASTER
BAKER BIRD HORNERO
BAKERY PIZZERIA
BAKING CUIT BATCH COCTION
FURNAGE ASSATION
BAKONGO FIOT
BALAAM (FATHER OF —) BEOR
BALACHONG NGAPI
BALAK (FATHER OF —) ZIPPOR
BALANCE BEAM EVEN PEIS REST
SWAY TRIM COVER ERASE PEISE
POISE SCALE TRONE WEIGH WEIHE
ADJUST AUNCEL CANCEL EMBLEM
EQUATE KELTER KELVIN KILTER
LAUNCE OFFSET SANITY SQUARE
STRIKE DESEMER LIBRATE
OVERRUN RESIDUE TRABUCH
TRUTINE EQUALITY EQUALIZE
EQUATION SERENITY WESTPHAL
TREBUCHET PROPORTION
(— DUE) ARREAR
(— IN ACCOUNT) CREDIT
(— OF SAILS) ATRY
(MAKE —) EQUATE
(MENTAL —) HEAD
(PREF.) STATO
BALANCED EVEN EQUAL LEVEL
TRUED APOISE KITTLE WEIGHED
COMPLETE QUADRATE TOGETHER
(PREF.) SYM
BALANCER HALTER ACROBAT
GYMNAST HALTERE
BALATA ICICA BULLACE BEEFWOOD
BORRACHA
BALCONY POY ORIEL PORCH
STOOP CIRCLE GAZEBO PIAZZA
PODIUM SOLLAR BALAGAN
GALLERY MIRADOR PERGOLA
TERRACE BRATTICE CANTORIA
VERANDAH MEZZANINE
BALD RAW BARE BASE BOLD CRUDE
DODDY NAKED PLAIN CALLOW
PALTRY PEELED PILLED SIMPLE
CALVOUS EPILOSE LITERAL
POLLARD GLABROUS HAIRLESS
TONSURED
(— HEAD) PILGARLIC
(— SPOT) TONSURE
(PREF.) PHALACRO
BALDACHIN CANOPY CIBORIUM
BALDER BALDR BALDUR BAELDAEG
(CHILD OF —) FORSETE FORSETI
(FATHER OF —) ODIN

(SLAYER OF —) HOTH LOKE LOKI HOTHR

(WIFE OF —) NANNA

BALDERDASH ROT GUFF PUNK GOOEY TRASH TRIPE DRIVEL JARGON FLUBDUB NONSENSE BALDUCTUM RIGMAROLE

BALDMONEY MEU SPIGNEL SPICKNEL

BALDNESS ACOMIA CALVITY ALOPECIA ATRICHIA OPHIASIS CALVITIES

BALDPATE ZUISIN POACHER

BALDRIC BELT LACE GIRDLE ZODIAC BALTEUS SUPPORT NECKLACE

BALE NO GIB NOT WOE EVIL FIRE HARM LAVE PACK PYRE BLOCK CRATE DEATH FARDO SERON BALLOT BUNDLE EMBALE SEROON SORROW PACKAGE SARPLER

BALEARIC ISLANDS (ISLAND OF —) IBIZA CABRERA MAJORCA MINORCA CONEJERA

(MEASURE OF —) PALMO MISURA QUARTA QUARTIN BARCELLA

(TOWN OF —) IBIZA MAHON PALMA

(WEIGHT OF —) CARGO CORTA QUARTANO

BALEEN WHALEBONE

BALEFUL BAD EVIL DEADLY MALIGN SACRED SULLEN MALEFIC NOXIOUS RUINOUS SIDERAL SINISTER WRETCHED MALEFICENT

BALI (CAPITAL OF —) DENPASAR

(DANCE OF —) ARDJA BARIS KRISS BARONG KETJAK MONKEY DJANGER

(MOUNTAIN OF —) AGOENG

(MUSICAL INSTRUMENT OF —) GAMELAN

(RICE FIELD OF —) SAWAH

(STRAIT OF —) LOMBOK

(TOWN OF —) SINGARADJA

BALIN (BROTHER OF —) SUGRIVA

(SLAYER OF —) RAMA

BALINGHASAY ANAM ANAN

BALK GAG HEN HUE JIB JUB SHY BEAM BILK BUCK BULL COND FOIL GORM HADE HEAP LICK LOFT MISS OMIT PROP SHUN SKIP SLIP STAY STOP AVOID BAULK BLOCK CHECK CLAMP DEMUR HUNCH MOUND REBEL REEST RIDGE STAKE STICK WAVER BAFFLE DEFEAT FALTER HINDER IMPEDE OUTWIT RAFTER REFUSE STRAIN THWART BLUNDER CODLING GALLOWS ISTHMUS MISTAKE

(— IN FISHING) HUE COND

(HALF —) FLITCH

(PL.) MIDDLES

BALKAN (— COIN) NOVCIC

(— COUNTRY) GREECE SERBIA ALBANIA RUMANIA BULGARIA

(— INSTRUMENT) GUSLA

(— RIVER) JIU OLT IBAR JIUL SAVA TISA OLTUL DANUBE MORAVA

(— SEA) BLACK AEGEAN IONIAN ADRIATIC

BALKER HUER CONNER

BALKY NAPPY STICK MULISH REESTY RESTIVE CONTRARY STUBBORN OBSTINATE

BALL IN BAL BOB FLY HOP NOB ORB PEA TOY BEAD BOWL CLEW CLUE KNOB KNOP KNUR PICK PILL POME PROM TRAP DANCE EDGER FAULT FLOAT GLOBE GLOME HURLY ORBIT PEARL PUPPY SHAPE SNACK SPORT TRUCK BULLET BUTTON HOOKER HURLEY MOONIE MUDDLE PEELEE PELLET PELOTA POMMEL POMPON RONDEL RUNDLE SPHERE SQUASH BALLOON CONFUSE FLOATER GLOBULE INCURVE INSHOOT KNAPPAN LEATHER MANDREL PELOTON RIDOTTO SLITTER ASSEMBLY BASEBALL BISCAYEN FANDANGO FOOTBALL GROUNDER HANDBALL QUENELLE SOFTBALL SPHEROID TRAPBALL

(— AS SHIP'S SIGNAL) SHAPE

(— FOR MUSKET) GOLI SLUG

(— OF CLAY) KNICKER

(— OF FIRE) DYNAMO

(— OF RICE OR MEAT) PINDA

(— OF THREAD) COP CLEW CLUF GOME BOTTOM COPPIN WHARROW

(— OF THUMB) THENAR CUSHION

(— OF WASTE IRON) COBBLE

(—S OF MEDICI FAMILY) PALLE

(— USED IN SHINTY) PEG

(BILLIARD —) SPOT IVORY SNOOKER

(BOWLED —) TICE CURVE SKYER BAILER BUMPER FIZZER GOOGLY KICKER POODLE SEAMER YORKER CREEPER SNORTER SPINNER BREAKBACK CROSSOVER INSWINGER

(BOWLING —) DODO JACK

(CORK —) PLUMBER

(CRICKET —) SNICK SHOOTER

(CROQUET —) ROVER

(DECORATIVE —) DRAGEE

(FIVES —) SNACK

(FORCEMEAT —) QUENELLE

(FRIED —) RISSOLE

(GOLF —) PUTTY

(HARD —) SNUG

(HOCKEY —) NUN NUR ORR

(INK —) PUMPET

(JAI ALAI —) PELOTA

(KIND OF —) MINIE

(MEAT —S) CECILS

(PLASTIC —) WIFFLE

(SKITTLE —) CHEESE

(SPONGE —) NERF

(TENNIS —) PALM

(WOODEN —) KNUR

(PREF.) GLOBI GLOBO SPHAER(O) SPHER(O)

(SUFF.) SPHAERA SPHERE SPHERIC(AL)

BALLAD JIG LAI LAY LILT MELE POEM SONG CAROL DERRY FANCY BALLET BYLINA CARVAL SONNET BALLANT CANZONE CORRIDO GWERZIOU SINGSONG

BALLAST BED CRIB LOAD TRIM METAL POISE STONE BOTTOM BURDEN GRAVEL WEIGHT BALANCE LASTAGE SANDBAG DRAGROPE KENTLEDGE SABURRATE

BALLERINA DANCER DANSEUSE

BALLET BALLAD MASQUE BOURREE PANTOMIME

(— COACH) REPETITEUR

(— LEAP) CABRIOLE ENTRECHAT

(— MOVEMENT) VOLE FERME TEMPS APLOMB CHASSE OUVERT POINTE RELEVE RETIRE ALLONGE ARRONDI ASSEMBLE ATTITUDE ARABESQUE

(— POSE) ARABESQUE

(— PROP) BARRE

(— SPIN) PIROUETTE

BALLHOOTER BRUTTER

BALLISTA SWEEP MANGONEL

BALLOON BAG BALL BLIMP EXPAND GASBAG AIRSHIP DISTEND DRACHEN INFLATE SAUSAGE SKYHOOK AEROSTAT ENVELOPE DIRIGIBLE

(TRIAL —) KITE

BALLOONING BOSOMY

BALLOONIST AERONAUT AEROSTAT

BALLOON VINE FAROLITO HEARTPEA HEARTSEED

BALLOT BALE POLL PROX VOTE ELECT PROXY VOICE BILLET CHOICE POLICY TICKET SUFFRAGE

BALLROOM SALOON

BALLYHOO BALLY HOOPLA

BALM OIL BEEB BITO DAUB ODOR SALVE ANOINT BALSAM EMBALM LOTION RELIEF SOLACE SOOTHE ANODYNE BESMEAR COMFORT PERFUME UNGUENT OINTMENT

(— OF GILEAD) CANADA OPOBALSAM

(BURN —) ALOE

BALMORAL CAP BOOT SHOE

BALMY DAFT MILD SOFT BLAND DAFFY MOONY SPICY SUNNY SWEET GENTLE INSANE SERENE HEALING LENIENT AROMATIC BALSAMIC DRESSING FRAGRANT SOOTHING

BALONEY BULL BUNK CROCK HOOEY BUNKUM BUSHWA BUSHWAH

BALSA RAFT FLOAT GUANO POLAK POLACK BOBWOOD CORKWOOD

BALSAM BALM RIGA TOLU UMIRI COPALM GURJAN GURJUN STORAX AMPALEA COPAIBA CREEPER AMPALAYA BDELLIUM BENJAMIN OINTMENT

BALSAM APPLE KARELA AMARGOSA AMPALAYA BALSAMINE

BALSAM FIR SAPIN BAUMIER

BALSAM POPLAR TACAMAHAC

BALSAMROOT SUNFLOWER

BALSAMWEED MOONSHINE FEATHERWEED

BAIT YOD ESTH LETT ESTONIAN

BALTIC (— GULF) RIGA DANZIG BOTHNIA FINLAND

(— ISLAND) AERO DAGO FARO OSEL ALAND ALSEN OESEL OLAND GOTLAND HIIUMAA BORNHOLM

(— PORT) KIEL RIGA MEMEL REVAL DANZIG GDANSK TALINN LEIPAJA

(— RIVER) ODER ODRA DVINA VIADUA

(— TOWN) MEMEL DANZIG GDANSK LEIPAJA

BALUCHISTAN (— CULTURE) QUETTA

BALUSTER SPOKE COLUMEL BANISTER COLUMELLA

BALUSTRADE BARRER PARAPET RAILING BALCONET BANISTER

BAMBI (AUNT OF —) ENA

BAMBOO DHA CANE REED BATAK GLUMAL GUADUA TONKIN BATAKAN WANGHEE WHANGEE

(SACRED —) NANDIN

(WOVEN —) SAWALI

BAMBOOZLE DUPE HAVE CHEAT COZEN GRILL CAJOLE HUMBUG BUFFALO BUMBAZE DECEIVE DEFRAUD MYSTIFY PERPLEX

BAN BAR WOE TABU VETO BANAL BANUS BLOCK CURSE EDICT ORDER TABOO BANISH CENSOR ENJOIN FORBID HINDER INVOKE NOTICE OUTLAW CONDEMN EXCLUDE ANATHEMA DENOUNCE EXECRATE PROHIBIT

(— ON NEWS) BLACKOUT

(LEGAL —) ESTOP

BANA (DAUGHTER OF —) USHA

BANAK UCUUBA

BANAL FLAT CORNY INANE SILLY STALE TRITE VAPID JEJUNE INSIPID MUNDANE TRIVIAL

BANANA FEI FIG MUSA SABA BERRY ENSETE FINGER SAGING LACATAN PLATANO SAGUING SUNBEAM PLANTAIN

(KIND OF —) TOP

BANANAS BALMY BATTY DAFFY

BAND BAR GAD HUB TIE TUB ZON BEAD BELT BEND BOND CAME CASH CORD CREW CUFF FALL FERD FESS GANG GATE GIRT HOOP HOOP KNOT LACE LIST RING SASH SHOE TAPE WISP ZONA ZONE AMPYX BANDY BRAID CHOIR CLAMP CORSE COVEY COVIN CRAPE CROWN FEMUR FLOCK FRAME GIRTH GORGE GUARD JATHA LABEL MEINY NOISE PANEL PATTE PRIDE QUIRE SABOT SNOOD STRAP STRIP STROP TAPIS TORSE TRACK TRIBE UNITE WERED WITHE ARMLET BENDEL BINDER BORDER BOYANG BRIDGE BUNDLE CIMBIA CLAVUS COHORT COLLAR COLLET COPULA COVINE CRANCE CRAVAT DECKLE FASCIA FETTER FILLET FRIEZE FRINGE FUNNEL GAMMON GARTER GASKET GIRDLE HYPHEN LEGLET MATRIX NIPPER NORSEL PLEDGE RADULA REGULA ROLLER SCREED STRAKE STRING STRIPE SWATHE TAENIA TETHER TISSUE WEEPER BINDING BLANKET CHAMBUL CIRCLET COMPANY ENOMOTY FERRULE FRONTAL GARLAND HATBAND HEADING NECKTIE ORPHREY PALLIUM PIGTAIL PROMISE SEQUELA SHACKLE SHOEING SWADDLE VINCULUM

(— ACROSS SUNSPOT) BRIDGE

(— AROUND MAST) PARREL

(— AT BOTTOM OF WALL) PLINTH
(— FOR HEAD) VITTA
(— IN BRAIN) LIGULA FRENULUM FUNICULUS
(— IN ROCKS) FAHLBAND
(— OF CLAY) COTTLE
(— OF COLOR) SOCK SLASH STRIA LACING FASCIOLE SPECTRUM
(— OF CRAPE) WEED SCARF
(— OF FUR) TIPPET
(— OF INDIANS) SHIVWITS
(— OF LIGHT) STREAMER
(— OF PILLAGERS) SKINNERS
(— OF PIPERS) POVERTY
(— OF PLASTER) SCREED
(— OF PURPLE) CLAVUS
(— OF STARS) GALAXY
(— OF STRAW) GAD SIMMON
(— OF TISSUE) TENDON TISSUE
(— OF 13 WITCHES) COVEN
(— ON HORSE'S HOOF) FROG
(— ON SHIELD) ENDORSE
(— TO COMPRESS CHEEKS) CAPISTRUM
(— TOGETHER) BANDY
(— UNDER TONGUE) LYTTA
(ARMED —) JATHA POSSE
(ARMOR —) TONLET
(CIRCULAR —) HOOP RING ANNULE WREATH
(DANCE —) CHORO COMBO
(DECORATIVE —) PATTE LEGLET CORNICE ARCHIVOLT
(DIVIDING —) CLOISON
(EUCHARISTIC —) MANIPLE
(FOREHEAD —) INFULA
(HEAD —) BANDEAU
(IRON —) FRET GATE TRUSS FUNNEL STRAKE
(LACE —) SCALLOP
(MUSICIANS —) CONCERT
(NOISY —) CALLITHUMP
(RADIO —) CHANNEL
(RAISED —) RIB
(RESONANCE —) FORMANT
(STREET —) MARIACHI
(TRIBAL —) AIMAK
(PL.) GRIPES INTERLACERY
(PREF.) TAENI(A)(O) ZON(I)(O)
(SUFF.) (CILIATED —) TROCH(A)(AL) (OUS)(US)

BANDAGE BAND BELT BIND TAPE BLIND BRACE CLOUT DRESS GALEA LINEN SLING SPICA SWARF SWATH TRUSS BINDER COLLAR CRAVAT FASCIA FETTLE FILLET LIGATE NIPPER ROLLER SWARTH SWATHE SWEATH REVERSE ROLLING SWADDLE TRUSSER ACCIPTER CAPELINE CINCTURE GAUNTLET LIGAMENT LIGATURE SCAPULAR STOCKING CAPISTRUM
(— FOR NOSE) ACCIPITER
(EYE —) MUFFLER
(FINGER —) HOVEL
(JAW —) FUNDA
(PL.) SWADDLING
BANDALORE QUIZ
BANDANNA WEB TURBAN BANDANA PULICATE PULICATE PULLICAT
BANDAR RHESUS

BANDEAU BRA BAND STRIP FILLET BRASSIERE
BANDICOOT RAT MARL BILBI BILBY BADGER BIELBY PINKIE QUENDA
BANDIT CACA TORY BRAVO THIEF BANISH HAIDUK HEYDUK OUTLAW ROBBER BANDIDO BRIGAND LADRONE TULISAN BUSHWACK MARAUDER MIQUELET PICAROON RAPPAREE BANDOLERO
(PL.) MANZAS
BANDLEADER MASTER MAESTRO CHORAGUS CONDUCTOR
BANDORE PANDORA PANDURA (PREF.) PANDURI
BANDSMAN WINDJAMMER
BANDSTAND KIOSK STAND
BANDY VIE BAND CART CHOP SWAP TRADE LEAGUE RACKET STRIVE CHAFFER CONTEND DISCUSS CARRIAGE EXCHANGE SHUTTLECOCK
(— WORDS) REVIE GIFFGAFF
BANE BAN WOE BONE EVIL HARM KILL PEST RUIN CURSE DEATH VENOM INJURY MURDER POISON SLAYER NEMESIS SCOURGE MISCHIEF MURDERER NUISANCE
BANEBERRY COHOSH REDBERRY TOADROOT GRAPEWORT
BANEFUL BAD ILL EVIL VILE SWART HARMFUL HURTFUL NOXIOUS RUINOUS VENOMOUS SINISTRAL PERNICIOUS
BANG POM RAP BAFF BEAT BLOW BOOT DASH DOCK DRUB POUF RUSH SCAT SLAM SWAP SWOP TANK BLAFF CLASH CRACK DRIVE EXCEL FORCE IMPEL POUND SLAKE SLUMP SOUND SPANG STRAM THUMP WHACK WHANG WHUMP BOUNCE CUDGEL ENERGY FRINGE STRIKE THRASH THUNGE THWACK SARDINE SURPASS THUNDER FORELOCK
(— ON HEAD) BRAIN
BANGLADESH (CAPITAL OF —) DACCA
(MONEY OF —) TAKA
(NATIVE OF —) BENGALI
(PAISA OF —) POISHA
(RIVER OF —) GANGES
(TOWN IN —) KHULNA CHITTAGONG
COIN: TAKA
BANGLE ORNAMENT
BANGTAIL NAG
BANG-UP SLAP CRACK TIPTOP
BANISH BAN FREE ABAND EJECT EXILE EXPEL FLEME WAIVE WREAK BANDIT DEPORT DISPEL DISTER FORSAY OUTLAW ABANDON CONDEMN CONFINE DISMISS DIVORCE EXCLUDE DISPLACE RELEGATE EXPATRIATE
BANISHED FUGITIVE
BANISHMENT EXILE BANNIMUS OUTLAWRY XENELASY OSTRACISM XENELASIA
BANISTER RAILING BALUSTER
BANJO BOX BANJORE BANJORINE
(— SITE) KNEE
BANK BAR BAY COP JUG RIM ROW BINK BRAE BREW BUTT CAJA DIKE

DUNE DYKE EDGE HEAD HILL LINK MASS PILE RAKE RAMP RELY RIPA RIVE SAND SCAR SEAT SIDE TIER WEIR BANCO BENCH BLUFF BRINK COAST DITCH EARTH FENCE HOVER HURST LEVEE MARGE MOUND MOUNT RIDGE SAVER SHARE SHELF SHOAL SHORE SLOPE STACK STAGE TRUST BANQUE BORROW CAISSE CAUSEY CRADGE DEGREE DEPEND DOUBLE MARGIN RANDOM RECKON RIVAGE STRAND ANTHILL BANKING CUSHION DEPOSIT LOMBARD POTTERY SANDBAG SHALLOW WINDROW BARRANCA PLATFORM TRAVERSE
(— A FIRE) REST
(— ASSOCIATION) SANDL
(— FOR DRYING BRICKS) HACK
(— OF CANAL) BERM BERME HEELPATH
(— OF EARTH) COP DAM DITCH
(— OF RIVER) RIPA WHARF STRAND
(— OF SAND OR MUD) BAR SCALP
(— OF SNOW) WREATH SNOWDRIFT
(— OF TURF) SUNK
(KIND OF —) STILL
(OVERHANGING —) BREW HOVER
(RUSSIAN —) CRAPETTE
(SAVINGS —) THRIFT
(STEEP —) HEUCH HEUGH WOUGH BARRANCA BARRANCO
(PREF.) RIPI
BANKER BOOK SETH SETT FACTOR FINDER SAHKAR SHROFF SOUCAR SOWCAR LOMBARD MARWARI MONEYER SPONSOR TAILLEUR BANQUETER FINANCIER
BANKNOTE CRISP FLIMSY SCREEN
(— FORGED) STUMER
(PL.) CABBAGE
BANKRUPT SAP BONG BUNG BUST DUCK RUMP BREAK BROKE DRAIN SMASH STRIP BROKEN BUSTED DYVOUR QUISBY CRACKED DEPLETE
BANKRUPTCY SMASH FAILURE SMASHUP
BANKSMAN LANDER HILLMAN
BANLIEUE LOWY ENVIRONS
BANNER FANE FLAG JACK SIGN COLOR BUMPER ENSIGN FANNON PENNON LABARUM LEADING PENNANT SALIENT BANDEROL BRATTACH FOREMOST GONFALON ORIFLAMB STANDARD STREAMER VEXILLUM BEAUSEANT ORIFLAMME
(— ON TRUMPET) TABARD
(FUNERAL —) BANNEROL GUMPHEON GUMPHION
(PL.) ENSIGNRY
BANNOCK PANAK DIGGER JANNOCK
BANNS CRY BANS CRIES NOTICE SIBRET SIBRIT SIBREDE SPURRINGS
BANQUET FETE MEAL DIFFA FEAST DINNER JUNKET MANGER REGALE REGALO REPAST SEUDAH SPREAD AHAAINA CONVITO CONVIVE

NAMGERY REGALIO CAROUSAL FESTIVAL SYMPOSIUM SYSSITION
BANQUETER CONVIVE SYMPOSIAST
BANQUETING EPULATION TRENCHERING
BANQUETTE FIRESTEP
BANSHEE BOW SIDHE TROLL
BANTAM COCK GRIG BANTY DANDY SAUCY CHICKEN SEBRIGHT COMBATIVE
BANTENG OX TSINE BANTIN TEMADAU
BANTER COD KID RAG ROT CHIP FOOL JEST JOKE JOSH MOCK QUIZ RAIL RAZZ BORAK CHAFF DRAPE JOLLY QUEER RALLY ROAST TAUNT TRICK DELUDE DERIDE HAGGLE SATIRE BADINER STASHIE BADINAGE CHAFFING GIFFGAFF RAILLERY RIDICULE
BANTING DIET DUGOUT
BANTU ILA BULU GOGO GUHA HEHE YAKA ZULU DUALA KAFIR KAMBA KIOKO KONDE KONGO LAMBA SHONA SWAZI BANYAI BASUTO DAMARA HERERO KAFFIR NATIVE THONGA WAGUHA YAKALA CABINDA MASHONA SWAHILI WACHAGA
(— LANGUAGE) ILA RONGA NYANJA THONGA KIRUNDI NYAMWEZI
BANTUSTAN HOMELAND
BANYAN BUR BURR BANIYA BUNNIA JAGUEY
BAOBAB MOWANA IMBONDO TEBELDI CALABASH ADANSONIA
BAPTISM CLEANSING IMMERSION PALINGENY PERFUSION
BAPTISMAL FONTAL
BAPTIST DIPPER DOPPER DIDAPPER SEPARATE TRASKITE
BAPTIZE DIP DEPE FULL NAME HEAVE VOLOW PLUNGE PURIFY ASPERSE CLEANSE IMMERSE CHRISTEN SPRINKLE
BAPTIZED ILLUMINATE
BAR BAN DAM FID FOX GAD INN LAW LEG RIB ROD TAP AXLE BALK BAND BANK BAUR BEAM BOLT BOOM BULL CAKE CHAR CORE CROW DRAG FLAT GATE HIDE JOKE LOCK MAKE OUST POLE RACK RAIL REEF SAVE SETT SHUT SKID SLAB SLAT SLIP SLOT SNIB STOP TREE YARD ARBOR BAULK BENCH BETTY BILBO BLOCK BLOOM BRACE CATCH CLASP CLOSE COURT CRAMP CREEL DEBAR DETER DOLLY EASER EMBAR ESTOP FENCE FORCE GEMEL HEDGE HORSE HUMET LEVER PERCH PILOT PINCH PITCH RANCE RATCH SHADE SHAFT SHAPE SIGHT SLOTE SNEEK SPELL SPOON SPRAG STAFF STANG STAVE STEEK STRAP STRIP STRUT SWIPE TRACE YAIRD ANCONY BARRET BATTEN BILLET BISTRO BODEGA BROOCH BUMPER CRUTCH DOFFER DOLLEY DOLLIE EVENER EXCEPT EYEBAR FASTEN FORBAR FORBID FORCER FORSET GRILLE HEAVER HINDER LADDER

MEAGRE NORMAN PEELER
RABBLE RADIAL RETURN RIFFLE
SALOON SHADES SHANTY STOWER
STRIPE TABLET TANGLE TILLER
TOGGLE BARRACE BARRAGE
BARRIER BOBSTAY BOLSTER
BUVETTE CHANNEL CHARIOT
CONFINE COUNTER DRAWBAR
EXCLUDE GALLOWS MANDREL
MANDRIL OVERARM PREVENT
SCRATCH SIDEBAR SNIBBLE
SPINDLE STEMMER TOMBOLO
TOPRAIL TRUNDLE WIREBAR
ASTRAGAL KNIFEWAY MURDERER
PESSULUS
(— FOR TAPPING FURNACE)
LANCET
(— IN CHIMNEY) SWEE
(— IN FABRIC) BARRE
(— IN RIVER) CHAR SANDBAR
(— IN SEA) SWASH
(— OF CULTIVATOR) ARCH
(— OF DOOR) SLOT STANG
(— OF ELECTRIC SWITCH) BLADE
(— OF GATE) SPAR LEDGE
(— OF HARROW) BULL
(— OF LOOM) EASER SWORD
BATTEN BACKSTAY
(— OF METAL) ZED
(— OF RAYS) SHOOT
(— OF SAND) TOMBOLO
(— OF STEEL) BLOOM BILLET
STIRRUP
(— OF WAGON) SHETH
(— OF WHEEL) SPOKE
(— ON BOWSPRIT) WHISKER
(— ON SIDE OF BOWSPRIT)
WHISKER
(— ON WINDMILL) UPLONG
(— SUPPORTING MILLSTONE)
MOLINE
(WITH SHACKLES) BILBOES
(WITH SPIKES) HERISSON
(CAST IRON —) SOW
(CONNECTING —) ZYGON
(HERALDIC —) FESS FESSE HUMET
LABEL
(JOINTED —) CHILL
(KIND OF —) RAW WET CASH FERN
NERF OPEN SWAY SALAD DATING
OYSTER SINGLES
(MINING —) MOIL
(NOTCHED —) RISP SKEY
(PAIR OF —S) GEMEL GEMMEL
(REFRESHMENT —) BUFFET
CANTEEN
(SOAP FRAME —) SESS
(STIRRING —) CRUTCH
(TAMPING —) STEMMER
(TYPEWRITER —) BAIL BALE
SPACER SHUTTLE
(UNSAVORY —) DIVE
(WEAVING —) TEMPLE
(WHEEL —) AXLE SPOKE
BARABARA HUT
BARACHEL (SON OF —) ELIHU
BARAK (FATHER OF —) ABINOAM
BARANI BRANDY
BARB AWN BUR JAG MOW BURR
CLIP FILE FLUE HAIR HERL HOOK
JAGG BEARD HORSE POINT RIDGE
SHAFT SPEAR PIGEON STRAIN

TIPPET WITTER BARBARY BARBULE
BRISTLE FILAMENT KINGFISH
(— OF ANCHOR) FLUKE
(— OF ARROW) HOOK WING BEARD
WITTER
(— OF FEATHER) HARL HERL
RAMUS PINNULA FILAMENT
(— OF HARPOON) FLUE FLUKE
(THROW —S AT) ZING
(PREF.) ONC(O)
BARBADOS (CAPITAL OF —)
BRIDGETOWN
(MOUNTAIN OF —) HILLABY
(NATIVE OF —) BIM BAJAN
BARBADOS CHERRY ACEROLA
BARBADOS PRIDE SANDALWOOD
BARBAREA CAMPE
BARBARIAN HUN BOOR GOTH
RUDE WILD ALIEN BRUTE SAVAGE
VANDAL RUFFIAN FOREIGNER
HOTTENTOT UNTUTORED
TRAMONTANE
BARBARIC GROSS ATROCIOUS
BARBARISM CANT DATISM
SAVAGISM SOLECISM
BARBARITY FERITY CRUELTY
FELLNESS FEROCITY RUDENESS
SAVAGERY BRUTALITY
BARBAROUS FELL RUDE WILD
CRUEL BRUTAL FIERCE GOTHIC
BESTIAL FOREIGN HUNNISH
INHUMAN SLAVISH UNCIVIL
IGNORANT CUTTHROAT
FEROCIOUS PRIMITIVE
BARBARY MAGOT MAGHRIB
MOGHRIB
(— STATE) TUNIS ALGIERS
MOROCCO TRIPOLI
BARBASCO CUBE JOEWOOD
BARBECUE ASADO BOCAN BUCCAN
(— ITEM) KABOB
BARBEL BEARD CIRRUS WATTLE
BARBLET CYPRINID
BARBER NAI FIGARO POLLER
SHAVER TONSOR SCRAPER
TONSURE
(— FISH) TANG
**BARBER OF BAGDAD (CHARACTER
IN —)** ABUL BEKAR CALIPH
MARGIANA NUREDDIN
(COMPOSER OF —) CORNELIUS
**BARBER OF SEVILLE (CHARACTER
IN —)** BERTHA FIGARO ROSINA
BARTOLO LINDORO ALMAVIVA
(COMPOSER OF —) ROSSINI
BARBERRY MAHONIA
BARBET BARBION BARMKIN
DREAMER BARBICAN PUFFBIRD
WATERRUG IRONSMITH
PEARLBIRD THICKHEAD TIGERBIRD
BARBITAL VERONAL
BARBITURATE DOWNER SECONAL
GOOFBALL SECOBARBITAL
PENTOBARBITAL PHENOBARBITAL
BARBULE RADIUS RADIOLUS
**BARCHESTER TOWERS (AUTHOR
OF —)** TROLLOPE
(CHARACTER IN —) BOLD SLOPE
ARABIN BERTIE NERONI ELEANOR
GRANTLY HARDING OBADIAH
PROUDIE SEPTIMUS STANHOPE
CHARLOTTE ETHELBERT QUIVERFUL

BARD BHAT MUSE POET SCOP
SWAN DRUID OVATE RUNER
SCALD SKALD OSSIAN SHAPER
SINGER BARDING PENBARD
MINSTREL MUSICIAN TALIESEN
DEMODOCUS SEANNACHIE
BARE DRY BALD LEAN MERE NUDE
POOR THIN ALONE BLEAK CRUDE
EMPTY NAKED PLAIN PLUME
SCANT STARK STRIP WASTE
BARISH BARREN CALLOW DENUDE
DIVERT DIVEST EXPOSE HISTIE
MARGIN MEAGER MEAGRE
PALTRY PILLED REVEAL SCARRY
SIMPLE DIVULGE EXPOSED
UNARMED UNCOVER DENUDATE
DESOLATE DISCLOSE STRIPPED
DESTITUTE
(— SKIN) BUFF
(— TEETH) TUCK
(NOT —) COOL
(PREF.) GYMN NUDI PSIL(O)
BAREFACED GLARING IMPUDENT
AUDACIOUS SHAMELESS
BAREFOOT UNSHOD
BARELY JIMP JUST ONLY FANIT
HARDLY MERELY POORLY SIMPLY
UNEATH UNNETH NAKEDLY
UNNETHE EDGEWAYS SCANTILY
SCARCELY SLIGHTLY
BARER NAVVY DELVER FEIGHER
MUCKMAN CALLOWER
BARFISH DORAB
BARFLY SOT TOSSPOT
BARGAIN GO BUY RUG WOD COPE
DEAL HUCK KOOP MART MISE
PACT PICK RUGG SALE SELL SNIP
SONG TROG WHIZ CHEAP FIGHT
PRICE STEAL TROKE TRUCK
WHACK WHIZZ BARTER DICKER
HAGGLE HIGGLE INDENT NIFFER
PALTER CHAFFER CHEAPEN
COMPACT CONTEND CONTEST
DISPOSE PACTION TRAFFIC
CONTRACT COVENANT PENNORTH
PURCHASE STRUGGLE
WANWORTH PENNYWORTH
(— HARD) PRIG
(— IN MINING) STURT
BARGAINER NIP KITE COPER
COWPER CHAFFERER
(SHARP —) SCREW
BARGAINING MART ACHATE
CHAFFER CHEAPING HUCKSTERY
(KIND OF —) PLEA
BARGE ARK BOX BOY HOY TOW TUB
BARK BOAT FUST LUMP PRAM
RAFT SCOW TROW BARCA CASCO
DUMMY FOIST LUNGE LURCH
PRAAM SCOLD SHREW VIXEN
BARQUE BERATE BUGERO DREDGE
GALLEY GYASSA PRAHAM REBUKE
STUMPY TENDER THRUST WHERRY
BALLOON BIRLING BIRLINN
CHALANA DROGHER GABBARD
GABBART GONDOLA LIGHTER
OMNIBUS TOWBOAT TUMBLER
TUMBRIL BILLYBOY BUDGEROW
CARRIAGE BUCENTAUR
MOORPUNKY
(COAL —) KEEL
(FRENCH —) TOUE
(TOWED —) BUTTY

BARGEMAN PUG BARGEE BARGER
HOYMAN HUFFLER
BARGHEST PADFOOT
BARITE CAUK CAWK TIFF CAULK
BARYTES BARYTINE HEPATITE
BARITONE DEEP
BARK AGO BAG BAY OUF RUB TAN
WAP YAP YIP BAFF BOAT BOOF
COAT COTO DITA HOWL HUSK
OPEN PEEL PELT PILL REND RIND
ROSS SKIN SNAP TAPA WAFF YAFF
YAWP YELP YIPE AABEC BALAT
BARCA BARGE COUGH MOCHA
NIEPA SHELL SHOUT SPEAK STRIP
TIMBE YAMPH YOUFF ABRADE
AGAMID AVARAM BARKEY
BOWWOW CASSIA CORNUS
CORTEX GIRDLE MASSOY SINTOC
TRANKY WAFFLE YAFFLE CASCARA
MALAMBO MESENNA PEREIRA
PHLOEUM SOLICIT TANDARK
DOUNDAKE EUONYMUS
FRANGULA GRANATUM
MEZEREUM WOODSKIN
RHYTIDOME QUERCITEON
(AROMATIC —) CANELLA
CULILAWAN
(EXTERIOR OF —) ROSS
(INNER —) BAST
(LAVER OF —) HAT
(PREF.) CORTICI CORTICO PHELLO
PHLO(E)(EO) QUIN(O)
BARKER BUFFER DOORMAN
GRINDER SPIELER SPUDDER
SPRUIKER CHARLATAN
BARKING BAY SPUD QUEST
LATRANT LATRATION
BARLEY BIG BEAR BENT BERE BIGG
GRAIN SPRAT LICORN HORDEUM
WHITECORN
(AWN OF —) HORN
(GROUND —) TSAMBA
(HULLED —) PTISAN
(REFUSE —) SHAG FLINTS
(PREF.) ALPHITO CRITHO
BARLEY CAKE
(PREF.) MAZO
BARN BYRE AMBAR LATHE STALL
GRANGE STABLE SKIPPER
COWHOUSE
(— OWL) LULU MADGE
(COW —) SAUR SHIPPON
(PART OF —) BAY HIP DOOR EAVE
APRON GABLE RIDGE VERGE
AWNING CUPOLA DORMER
PENTHOUSE VENTILATOR
WEATHERVANE
BARNACLE BRAY BREY ACORN
LEPAS CYPRIS ANATIFA BALANID
LEPADID CIRRIPED GNATHOPOD
SACCULINA
BARNBURNER SOFT
BARNSTORM TOUR
BARNYARD PIGHTLE BACKSIDE
FARMYARD STRAWYARD
BAROMETER GLASS ANEROID
OROMETER STATOSCOPE
BARON THANE DAIMIO BARONET
FREEMAN FREIHERR
(COURT —) HALLMOOT
BARONET SIR
BARONY HAN DOMAIN

BAROQUE GOTHIC ORNATE ROCOCO GROTESQUE IRREGULAR

BAROTO VINTA

BARRACK CAMP BOTHY CASERN CANNABA CUARTEL

BARRACKS HOOCH HOOTCH **(DETENTION —)** GLASSHOUSE

BARRACUDA CUDA KAKU SPET BARRY PELON SNAKE SNOEK SNOOK BECUNA PICUDA SCOOTS SENNET VICUDA KATONKEL SCOOTERS

BARRAGE BAR SALVO ATTACK VOLLEY BARRIER DRUMBEAT DRUMFIRE UMBRELLA CANNONADE FUSILLADE

BARRAMUNDA SALMON CYCLOID DIPNOAN FLATHEAD CERATODUS

BARRED CUCKOO RIBBED STRIPED

BARREL FAT HUB KEG TUN VAT BUTT CADE CASK DRUM KANG TREE WOOD BOWIE QUILL SHELL STAND UNION FESSEL GIRNAL GIRNEL HOGGET RUMBLE RUNLET TIERCE TUMBLE VESSEL CALAMUS CISTERN PACKAGE RATTLER RUNDLET TUMBLER CYLINDER HOGSHEAD KILDERKIN **(— OF FEATHER)** CALAMUS **(— OF REVOLVER)** CHAMBER **(— ROW)** LONGER **(— WITH CRANKS)** VANGEE **(CAPSTAN —)** SPOOL **(CORE —)** LANTERN **(HERRING —)** CADE CRAN **(PART OF —)** HEAD HOOP CHIME STAVE BOTTOM **(SMALL —)** KEG KIT CADE KNAG RUNLET BARRICO RUNDLET **(TAR —)** CLAVIE **(PL.)** ALOT

BARRELHOUSE GUTBUCKET

BARREN DRY ARID BARE BOWY DEAD DEAF DOUR DULL EILD GAST GELD LEAN NUDE POOR SALT SECK YELD YELL ADDLE BLEAK BLUNT BOWEY DRAPE DUSTY EMPTY GAUNT GHAST GUESS NAKED STARK STERN WASTE YEILD DESERT EFFETE FALLOW HISTIE HUNGRY JEJUNE MEAGER STUPID SAPLESS STERILE DESOLATE IMPOTENT TEEMLESS TREELESS **(NOT —)** FACILE FECUND **(PL.)** LANDES **(PREF.)** STEIRO

BARREN GROUND (AUTHOR OF —) GLASGOW **(CHARACTER IN —)** JASON RUFUS GENEVA JOSIAH NATHAN OAKLEY PEDLAR DORINDA ELLGOOD GREYLOCK

BARRENNESS DEARTH VACANCY EMPTINESS

BARRICADE BAR STOP BLOCK CLOSE FENCE ABATIS PRISON BARRAGE BARRIER DEFENSE FORTIFY OBSTRUCT RAMFORCE REVETMENT ROADBLOCK **(— OF TREES)** ABATIS

BARRIER ALP BAR DAM BALK BOMA BOOM CRIB CROY DIKE DOOR DYKE FOSS GATE LINE LOCK PALE

STOP WALL WEIR BAULK BOUND CHAIN FENCE FOSSE GRILL HEDGE LIMIT STILE STUMP CORDON GLACIS GRILLE HURDLE SCREEN TREBLE BARRAGE CEILING CHICANE CURTAIN GALLERY PARAPET RAILING RAMPART BOUNDARY FORTRESS FRONTIER STOCKADE STRENGTH TRAVERSE **(— ACROSS RIVER)** STILL KIDDLE **(— IN TRUCK)** HEADER **(— OF STAKES)** STOCKKADE **(— OF TREES)** SHELTERBELT **(ARTIFICIAL —)** FOSS FOSSE **(OIL SPILL —)** BOOM **(PROTECTIVE —)** REDOUBT **(RACECOURSE —)** RAILS **(SPIKED —)** TURNPIKE **(TRAFFIC —)** SEPARATOR **(PL.)** BAIL **(PREF.)** HERCO

BARRING BUT SAVE CLOSED

BARRISTER COLT BARMAN JUNIOR LAWYER TUBMAN COUNSEL POSTMAN TEMPLAR ADVOCATE ATTORNEY SERJEANT **(PL.)** BAR

BARROOM PUB CAFE HOUSE BISTRO SALOON CANTINA DOGGERY GROCERY TAPROOM DRAMSHOP DRINKERY EXCHANGE GROGGERY GROGSHOP

BARROW HOD HOG BANK BIER DUNE GALT HILL MOTE TUMP CARRY GRAVE GURRY HURLY MOUND SEDAN TRUCK BURROW GALGAL KURGAN NAVETA HILLOCK TROLLEY TUMULUS MOUNTAIN PUSHCART

BARRULET VIVRE

BARTENDER MIXER BARMAN BARMAID SKINKER TAPSTER

BARTER CHAP CHOP COPE COUP HAWK MANG MONG SELL SWAP TROG VEND CORSE TRADE TROKE TRUCK DICKER NIFFER SCORSE BARGAIN CAMBIUM CHAFFER PERMUTE TRAFFIC TRUCKLE COMMERCE EXCHANGE TRUCKAGE

BARTERED BRIDE (CHARACTER IN —) JASEK JENIK KECAL MICHA TOBIAS MARENKA ESMERALDA **(COMPOSER OF —)** SMETANA

BARTERER COPER COWPER TRUCKER

BARUCH (FATHER OF —) NERIAH ZABBAI COLHOZEH

BARYTES CAUK CAWK HEPATITE

BARZILLAI (SON OF —) ADRIEL

BASAL BASIC BASILAR RADICAL

BASALT MARBLE NAVITE DIABASE GHIZITE KULAITE POTTERY AUGANITE BANDAITE BASANITE DOLERITE ANAMESITE ARAPAHITE MELAPHYRE SUDBURITE VARIOLITE **(DECOMPOSED —)** WACKE

BASE BED DEN HUB LOW TUT ANIL CLAM EVIL FOOT FOUL HUBB HUNK LEWD MEAN POOR RELY REST ROOT SACK STAY STEM STEP VILE BASIS BLOCK CHEAP DIRTY FIRST FLOOR FOUND LACHE

MUDDY PETTY SNIDE SOCLE STAND STOOL WORSE ABJECT BOTTOM BRASSY COARSE COMMON DEMISS GROUND GRUBBY HARLOT HUMBLE MENIAL NOUGHT PALTRY PATAND PATTEN PERRON PODIUM RASCAL SECOND SHABBY SORDID VULGAR BASTARD CAITIFF COMICAL CURRISH DEBASED FOOTING HANGDOG HILDING HOUSING IGNOBLE OUTPOST PEASANT ROINISH SERVILE SLAVISH STADDLE STANDER SUBBASE SUPPORT CHURLISH COISTREL COISTRIL DEGRADED DRAWHEAD HARLOTRY HOLDFAST INFAMOUS INFERIOR MECHANIC MESCHANT PEDESTAL PEDIMENT RASCALLY SCULLION SHAMEFUL STANDARD STEPPING SUBSTRAT UNWORTHY WRETCHED NIDDERING **(— IN GAME)** HOME **(— IN QUALITY)** LEADEN **(— OF BRANCK)** KNOT **(— OF CANNON)** SOUL **(— OF OPERATIONS)** BOOK HOME **(— OF OVULE)** CHALAZA **(— OF PETAL)** CLAW **(— OF PILLAR)** PATTEN **(— OF PLANT)** CAUDEX **(— OF POLLINIUM)** DISC DISK **(— OF ROCK)** MAGMA MAGMO **(— OF TUBER)** HEEL **(— OF WORD)** STEM **(CHEMICAL —)** ALKALI ACRIDAN ADENINE ANSERIN CHOLINE GUANINE ACRIDANE ACTININE AGMATINE ALDIMINE ALKALOID ANSERINE CONYRINE GALEGINE KETIMINE LEPIDINE SEMIDINE **(HIDDEN —)** LAIR **(HOME —)** DEN **(LEAF —)** FOVEA **(LOGARITHM —)** E RADIX **(OFF —)** AWOL **(PROJECTING —)** PLINTH **(SECOND —)** KEYSTONE **(STALKLIKE —)** CNIDOPOD **(PREF.)** BASI TAPIN(O) **(SUFF.)** HEDRAL

BASEBALL PILL APPLE DUSTER FLOATER INSHOOT LEATHER BEANBALL HARDBALL HORSEHIDE STICKBALL **(— DOUBLEHEADER)** TWINIGHT **(— FLY)** POPUP **(— PLAYER)** OTT COBB DEAN FORD MAYS ROSE RUTH RYAN AARON BANKS BENCH BERRA BROCK CAREW EVERS LYONS PAIGE REESE SPAHN YOUNG FELLER GEHRIG GOSLIN KEELER KOUFAX MANTLE MUSIAL SEAVER CARLTON DYKSTRA HORNSBY JACKSON JOHNSON CLEMENTE DIMAGGIO DRYSDALE ROBINSON STARGELL WILLIAMS YANNIGAN BOTTOMLEY KILLEBREW CAMPANELLA STRAWBERRY YASTRZEMSKI **(— PRACTICE)** FUNGO **(— TEAM)** CUBS METS REDS EXPOS TWINS ANGELS ASTROS BRAVES

GIANTS PADRES REDSOX ROYALS TIGERS BREWERS DODGERS INDIANS MARLINS ORIOLES PIRATES RANGERS ROCKIES YANKEES BLUEJAYS MARINERS PHILLIES WHITESOX ATHLETICS CARDINALS **(— THROW)** PEG TOSS **(HIGH-BOUNCING —)** CHOPPER **(MODIFIED —)** TBALL

BASEBOARD GRIN SKIRT PLINTH EASEMENT MOPBOARD SKIRTING WASHBOARD

BASE-DEALING BROKING

BASELESS IDLE UNFOUNDED

BASEMAN SACKER

BASEMENT BASE CELLAR TAHKHANA

BASENESS FELONY VILITY BEGGARY SQUALOR TURPITUDE

BASH BAT LAM TRY BEAT BLOW DENT GALA MASH SWAT WHAM WHOP ABASH BEANO PARTY SLOSH SMASH ASSAIL BRUISE STRIKE ATTEMPT BLOWOUT JAMBOREE

BASHEMATH (FATHER OF —) ISHMAEL **(HUSBAND OF —)** ESAU

BASHFUL COY SHY HELO SHAN BLATE HELOE TIMID MODEST PUDENT ASHAMED DAUNTED BACKWARD BLUSHING DAPHNEAN DISMAYED LOATHFUL PUDIBUND RETIRING SACKLESS SHAMEFUL SHEEPISH SKITTISH VERECUND SHAMEFACED

BASHFULNESS PUDOR SHYNESS

BASIC NET BASE BASAL VITAL BOTTOM BEDROCK CANONIC CENTRAL CLASSIC PRIMARY ZINCOUS CARDINAL ULTIMATE ELEMENTAL ESSENTIAL SUBSTRATE

BASIL TULASI

BASILICA (PART OF —) APSE BEMA NAVE AISLE ALTAR NARTHEX TRANSEPT

BASIN DOP PAN BOWL COMB COVE DISH DOCK EWER FLOW FONT GULF LAKE PARK SINK SLAD TALA TANK COMBE LAVER SLAKE STOUP BASSON BULLAN CHAFER CIRQUE HOLLOW LAVABO LEKANE LOUTER MARINA VALLEY VESSEL CUVETTE PISCINA RECEIPT URCEOLE BIRDBATH CESSPOOL LAVATORY RECEPTOR VANITORY WASHBOWL GEMELLION **(— FOR RAINWATER)** IMPLUVIUM **(DESERT —)** PLAYA **(GEOLOGICAL —)** BOLSON **(MOUNTAIN —)** HOYA PUNA **(OYSTER —)** PISCINA **(ROCK —)** KEEVE KIEVE **(SEA —)** FLOW **(PREF.)** LECAN(O)

BASIS BASE FOND FOOT FORM FUND ROOT SILL AXIOM RADIX STOCK ANLAGE BOTTOM GROUND ACCOUNT BEDROCK FOOTING PREMISE SUPPORT GRAVAMEN STRENGTH AUTHORITY CRITERION

FUNDAMENT GROUNDSEL SUBSTANCE

BASK SUN BEEK LAZE WARM ACRID BATHE ENJOY REVEL BITTER REJOICE APRICATE

BASKET IE ARK COB FAN HOT KIT LUG PAD PED PEG POT RIP TAP TOP BUCK CAUL COBB COOP CORB CORF CRIB FLAT GOAL HOTT IEIE KIPE KISH KIST KITT LEAP MAND MAUN SKEP TAPE TILL TOUR TRUG WEEL CABAS CASSY CESTA CHEST CRAIL CRASH CRATE CREEL DEVIL DILLI DILLY FRAIL GRATE MAUND MOLLY NATTE RUSKY SCULL SWILL WILLY BEACON ROKARK CASSIE CLEAVE COFFIN COURGE CRADLE DORSEL DORSER DOSSER FANNER FASCET GABION HAMPER HOBBET HOBBIT HOPPET JICARA JUNKET KIBSEY KIPSEY MOCOCK MOLLIE MURLIN PEGALL PETARA POTTLE PUNNET SEQUIN SERPET TAPPET TEANAL TOPNET VOIDER WINDEL WINDLE WISKET ZEQUIN CANASTA CORBEIL CRESSET FLASKET HANAPER MURLAIN PANNIER PATTARA PITARAH PRICKLE SCUTTLE SEEDLIP SHALLOW SKEOUGH SKIPPET WATTAPE WHISKET CALATHUS CANISTER CHEQUEEN ZECCHINO

(— BOTTOM) SLATH
(— FOR CRUMBS) VOIDER
(— FOR EELS) BUCK COURGE
(— FOR FIGS) TAP CABAS FRAIL TAPNET
(— FOR FISH) CREEL
(— FOR FRUIT) CALA MOLLY CALATHOS
(FISH —) CRAN HASK
(JAI ALAI —) CESTA
(PART OF —) RIB RIM FOOT JOIN RAND SLEW WALE FITCH STAKE UPSET BORDER HANDLE
(REFUSE —) SIEVE
(WICKER —) RIP

BASKETBALL HOOP
(— ATTEMPT) SETSHOT
(— FOUL) HACK
(— GOAL) TIPIN
(— PLAYER) BIRD REED WEST EWING ONEAL PIVOT BAYLOR ERVING JABBAR JORDAN MALONE MCHALE PARISH PETTIT THOMAS UNSELD WALTON WORTHY BARKLEY FRAZIER GRUENIG JOHNSON RUSSELL ALCINDOR HAVLICEK OLAJUWON PIVOTMAN SWINGMAN ROBERTSON STEINMETZ DEBUSSCHERE
(— SHOT) JAM DUNKSHOT SLAMDUNK
(— TEAM) BING HEAT JAZZ NETS SUNS BARRY BUCKS BULLS COUSY HAWKS KINGS MAGIC SPURS LAKERS PACERS BRADLEY BULLETS CELTICS HORNETS NUGGETS PISTONS ROCKETS CLIPPERS WARRIORS CAVALIERS MAVERICKS CHAMBERLAIN SUPERSONICS

TIMBERWOLVES TRAILBLAZERS SEVENTYSIXERS KNICKERBOCKERS
(DUNK SHOT) JAM
(FREE-THROW LANE IN —) PAINT
(KIND OF — PASS) SPOT OUTLET
BASKET MAKER ANASAZI
BASKETRY UPSET
BASKETWORK TEE SLEW WALE SLATH STAKE SLATHE STROKE SLEWING
BASMATH (FATHER OF —) SOLOMON
(HUSBAND OF —) AHIMAAZ
BASQUE VASCON EUSCARA EUSCARO IBERIAN BISCAYAN
(— DIALECT) LABOURDIN
(PL.) VASCONA VASCONES
BAS-RELIEF PLAQUETTE
BASS LOW PES CHUB DEEP DRUM FOOT ROCK BASSO DRONE HURON ROCHE SWEGO VOICE BORDUN BRASSE BURDEN CHERNA GROUND JUMPER REDEYE SINGER STRIPE ACHIGAN BARFISH BOURDON BROWNIE GROWLER JEWFISH STRIPER BACHELOR BIGMOUTH BLUEFISH CABRILLA CONTINUO ROCKFISH SPOTTAIL STREAKER TALLYWAG WELSHMAN LINESIDES
(— DRUM) TAMBURONE
(— PART) ALBERTI
(DRONE —) BOURDON
(GROUND —) OSTINATO
(LEADING —) SUCCENTOR
(THOROUGH —) BC
BASSOON REED CURTAL FAGOTI BOMBARD FAGOTTE FAGOTTO WOODWIND
(PART OF —) BELL BOOT BUTT WING CROOK JOINT
BASSWOOD LIN BASS WAHOO LINDEN WICOPY DADDYNUT WHITEWOOD
BAST LIBER RAMIE PHLOEM NOSEBURN
BASTARD GET SOB BASE FALSE CANNON COWSON GALLEY HYBRID IMPURE MAMZER BYSPELL GETLING LOWBRED MONGREL WOSBIRD BANTLING BASEBORN MISBEGET NAMELESS SPURIOUS WHORESON
(PREF.) NOTH(O)
BASTE SEW BEAT CANE COOK DRUB LARD TACK FLAMB SAUCE CUDGEL JIPPER PUNISH STITCH THRASH
BASTION JETTY BULWARK LUNETTE MOINEAU
(PART OF —) FACE RAMP ANGLE FLANK GORGE CURTAIN BANQUETTE
BAT CAT HIT WAD BACK BAKE BATE BEAT CLUB FOWL GAIT JACK LUMP MASS SWAT TRAP WINK BANDY BATON BRICK CHUCK FUNGO HARPY PIECE SPREE STICK ALIPED BACKIE BASTON BEETLE CUDGEL DRIVER KALONG PADDLE POMMEL RACKET STRIKE STROKE WILLOW BAUCKIE FLUTTER JAVELIN MORMOPS NOCTULE VAMPIRE BLUDGEON ROUSETTE SEROTINE

BARBASTEL REARMOUSE REREMOUSE CHEIROPTER
(GO TO — FOR) AID
(PART OF —) KNOB MEAT LABEL BARREL HANDLE SIGNATURE
(PREF.) NYCTERI
(SUFF.) NYCTERIS
BATAK (— DIALECT) TOBA
BATCH LOT BAKE BREW CAST CROP FINE MASS MESS RAFT SORT BUNCH FLOOR GROUP BAKING CHEESE MAKING BOILING BREWING FORMULA MIXTURE RAISING QUANTITY
(— OF EGGS) SETTING
(— OF GRAIN) GRIST
(— OF MAIL) SEPARATION
BATCHER BAGGER
BATE BAIT BEET PARE PUER PURE GRAIN
BATELEUR BERGHAAN
BATEMAN DRENCHER
BATFISH ANGLER DIABLO MALTHE DEVILFISH
BATH DIP TUB BAIN BATE LOSS PERT TOSH BATHE LAVER STEEP THERM BAGNIO DOUCHE LIQUOR MIKVAH PICKLE PLUNGE SHOWER SPONGE BALNEUM LAVATIE ABLUTION BALNEARY
(FOOT —) PEDILUVIUM
(HOT —) STEW SCALD STUFE THERM STUPHE THERME
(HOT-AIR —) STOVE
(MUD —) ILLUTATION
(PHOTOGRAPHIC —) FIXER
(SITZ —) BIDET SITZBAD SEMICUPE INSESSION
(SPINNING —) DOPE
(STEAM —) SAUNA
(TANNING —) BATE SOAK
(TURKISH —) HAMMAM HUMMUM HOTHOUSE
(WHIRLPOOL —) JACUZZI
(PREF.) BALNE(O)
BATHE BAY TUB BAIN BASK DOOK LAVE STEW WASH CLEAN DOUSE DOWSE EMBAY SOUSE STEEP ENWRAP FOMENT SHOWER SPLASH EMBATHE IMMERSE PERVADE SUFFUSE PERMEATE
BATHHOUSE SEW STEW SAUNA STUFF BAGNIO CABANA HAMMAM STUPHE BALNEARY
BATHING LAVACRE LAVEMENT
(— SUIT) SLIP TOGS MAILLOT
(SAND —) SABURRATION
BATHROBE PEIGNOIR
BATHROOM BIFFY BALNEARY
BATHSHEBA (FATHER OF —) ELIAM AMMIEL
(HUSBAND OF —) DAVID URIAH
(SON OF —) NATHAN SHIMEA SHOBAB SOLOMON
BATHTUB TUB TOSH LAVACRE
BATIA (FATHER OF —) TEUCER
(HUSBAND OF —) DARDANUS
(SON OF —) HIPPOCOON ERICHTHONIUS
BATON ROD BEND BURN WAND STAFF STICK BAGUET BASTON CUDGEL BOURDON SCEPTER

SCEPTRE BAGUETTE CROSSBAR TRUNCHEON
BATSMAN BAT BATTER HITTER SLOGGER SLUGGER STRIKER
BATTALION WARD CONREY
BATTEN END LAY RIB SLAT SLEY CLEAT LEDGE BATTON BEATER ENRICH FATTEN REEPER THRIVE FERTILIZE
(PL.) SPARRING
BATTER RAM BEAT DENT MAIM MAUL PELT CLOUR DINGE FRUSH PASTE POUND SMASH BALLER BRUISE BUFFET HAMMER HATTER HITTER PUMMEL THRING TUMBLE BATSMAN BOMBARD CRIPPLE DESTROY FRITTER SHATTER SLUGGER STRIKER DEMOLISH
BATTERCAKE WAFFLE CRUMPET
BATTERING BLAST LACING
BATTERY PILE SINK TIRE TROOP RADEAU EXCITER SINKBOX SINKBOAT ACCUMULATOR
(GUN —) SWINGER
BATTLE WAR CAMP DUEL FEUD FRAY MART MEET TILT TOIL UNDO BRUSH FIELD FIGHT JOUST STOUR ACTION AFFAIR AFFRAY CAMLAN COMBAT SHOWER STRIVE CONTEND CONTEST HOSTING JOURNAL JOURNEY WARFARE CONFLICT SKIRMISH STRUGGLE ENCOUNTER NAUMACHIA THEOMACHY
(PREF.) MACHO
(SUFF.) MACHIA MACHY
BATTLE-AX WIFLE POLEAX SPARTH TWIBIL BROADAX HAI BERD TWIBILL WHIFFLE FAUCHARD FRANCISC
BATTLE CRY CRY BANZAI ENSIGN GERONIMO SLUGHORN BEAUSEANT
BATTLEFIELD ARENA BLAIR CHAMP TAHUA CHAMPAIGN
BATTLEGROUND COCKPIT TERRAIN
BATTLEMENT KERNEL MERION PINION BARMKIN CORNELLE MURDRESS
(PART OF —) CRENEL MERLON MACHIOLATION
BATTLE OF LEGNANO
(CHARACTER IN —) LIDA ARRIGO ROLANDO FREDERICK BARBAROSSA
(COMPOSER OF —) VERDI
BATTLESHIP MAINE CARRIER
BATTOLOGIZE ITERATE
BATTUS (FATHER OF —) POLYMNESTUS
(MOTHER OF —) PHRONIMA
BATTY BATS BUGGY CRAZY SILLY BANANAS BATLIKE FOOLISH
BAUBLE BOW TOY BEAD GAUD BUTTON GEWGAW TRIFLE MAROTTE TRINKET GIMCRACK PLAYTHING
BAWD AUNT HARE DIRTY MADAM DEFILE MADAME PANDER COMMODE MACKEREL PROCURER PURVEYOR
BAWDINESS RAUNCH
BAWDRY SCULDUDDERY

BAWDY LEWD DIRTY SCARLET SKULDUGGERY

BAWL CRY HOWL ROAR ROUT YAUP YAWP BLORE GOLLY SHOUT BELLOW BOOHOO GOLLAR OUTCRY GLAISTER
(**— OUT**) JUMP CRACK SCOLD

BAY ARM COD DAM RIA VOE BANK BARK CHOP COVE GULF HOLE HOPE HOWL LOCH ROAN TREE WICK YAUP YAWP BAHIA BASIN BAYOU BERRY BIGHT COLOR CREEK FIORD FJORD FLEET HAVEN HORSE INLET LOUGH MOUTH ORIEL QUEST SINUS SPEAK TRAVE BABBLE HARBOR LAUREL RECESS SEVERY TONGUE WINDOW BADIOUS BAYGALL ENCLOSE ESTUARY MALABAR SILANGA ULULATE BREWSTER CHESTNUT
(**— OF BARN**) GOAF SKEELING SKILLING SKILLION
(**— OF LIBRARY**) CLASSIS
(**— STATE**) MASSACHUSETTS
(**SWEET —**) BREWSTER BEAVERWOOD

BAYBERRY AUSU PIMIENTA WAXBERRY

BAYOU SLEW SLOO SLUE BROOK CREEK INLET RIVER OUTLET SLOUGH STREAM RIVULET BACKWATER

BAY WINDOW ORIEL MIRADOR

BAZAAR FAIR FETE SALE AGORA BURSE CHAWK CHOWK MARKET ALCAZAR CANTEEN BOOKFAIR EMPORIUM BEZESTEEN

BDELLIUM GUGAL GUGUL GOOGUL

BE ABE ARE BES BEEN BETH BIST LIVE ABIDE EXIST OCCUR WORTH REMAIN BREATHE CONSIST SUBSIST CONTINUE
(**TO —**) SER ETRE SEIN

BEACH AIR BANK CHIP MOOR NARD RIPA SAND SLIP COAST PLAGE PLAYA PRAYA SHORE GROUND SHILLA STRAND HARDWAY SEASIDE SHINGLE LAKESHORE
(**— PROTECTOR**) SEAWALL
(**— RIDGE**) FULL
(**PROJECTING —**) CUSP
(**SANDY —**) MACHAIR
(**PREF.**) THIN(O)

BEACH APPLE CANAJONG
BEACHCOMBER SEASONER STRANDLOOPER
BEACHED AGROUND
BEACH FLEA SCUD SCREW SANDBOY
BEACH GRASS STAR SPIRE MARRAM BENTSTAR
BEACON MARK PIKE SIGN BAKEN FANAL GUIDE PHARE RACON ENSIGN PHAROS RAMARK SIGNAL CRESSET SEAMARK WARNING BALEFIRE NEEDFIRE SIGNPOST STANDARD
(**RADAR —**) RACON NAVAID

BEAD NIB POT DROP FOAM GAUD AGGRI AGGRY BUGLE FILET GRAIN KNURL PEARL QUIRK SIGHT STAFF ARANGO BAGUET BAUBLE BICONE BUBBLE CORNET FILLET HEISHE HEISHI PELLET PIPPER POPPET PRAYER RONDEL WAMPUM CABLING DEWDROP GLOBULE MOLDING SPARKLE TRINKET AVEMARIA CABOCHON
(**PREHISTORIC —**) ADDERSTONE
(**ROSARY —**) GAUD PATERNOSTER
(**SHELL —S**) SEWAN

BEADING VEINING
(**PL.**) TASBIH

BEADLE CRIER MACER POKER USHER BEDRAL BUMBLE HARMAN HERALD BAILIFF NUTHOOK OFFICER SERVITOR SUMMONER APPARITOR MESSENGER

BEADSMAN BEGGAR HERMIT BLUEGOWN GOWNSMAN

BEAK NEB NIB BECK BILL CLAP NOSE PIKE PROW LORUM SNOUT SWORD TUTEL MASTER NOZZLE SPERON WEAPON EMBOLON EMBOLUM FOREBOW MOLDING ROSTRUM BEAKHEAD MANDIBLE CAPITULUM
(**— OF SHELL**) UMBO
(**— OF SHIP**) SPERON
(**— OF SWORDFISH**) SWORD
(**PREF.**) RHAMPH(O) RHYNCH(O) ROSTR(I)(O)
(**SUFF.**) RHYNCHUS RHYNCUS ROSTRAL

BEAKED NASUTE
BEAKER CUP HORN TASS BIKER BOCAL BOUSE GLASS BARECA
BEAM BAR LEG RAY TIE BALK BEAK BOOM EMIT GLOW GRIN PLAT SILE SILL SKID SPAR STUD ARBOR BAULK CABER FLASH GLEAM GLEED JOIST LIGHT RAYON SHAFT SHAPE SHINE SHOOT SMILE SPEAR STANG STOCK TRAVE BINDER BULKER CAMBER CHEESE COLLAR FLITCH GIRDER GLANCE HEADER MANTEL NEEDLE RAFTER SUMMER TIMBER TRABES TREVIS WALKER BALANCE BUMPKIN CATHEAD CHANNEL CHEVRON DORMANT DRAWBAR FRIJOLE MADRIER PINRAIL RADIATE SLEEPER SUPPORT TRANSOM TRIMMER TYNDALL AXLETREE BROWPOST HERISSON PADSTONE PLOWHEAD ROOFTREE STENTREL TEMPLATE BRESSUMMER
(**— OF LIGHT**) CHINK GLEED RAYON SHAFT PENCIL SIGNAL STREAM SUNBEAM STRICTURE
(**HIGH —**) BRIGHTS
(**LARGE —**) BALK LACE BAULK SUMMER
(**LOW —**) DIM
(**POWERFUL —**) LASER
(**SANIO'S —**) CRASSULA
(**WEAVER'S —**) TRAM TAVIL
(**PL.**) CRANEWAY
(**PREF.**) DOCO

BEAMER SMILER SCUDDER
BEAMING GAY ROSY BRIGHT LUCENT MASSIVE RADIANT SHINING
BEAMY BROAD BRIGHT JOYOUS LUCENT MASSIVE RADIANT MIRTHFUL

BEAN BON NIB URD CHAP FABA FAVA GRAM HABA HEAD LIMA POLE SNAP TEKE TICK BRAIN CARAT PULSE SIEVA SKULL TONKA CACOON CASTER COLLAR FELLOW KIDNEY LABLAB LENTIL NIPPLE NOGGIN RUNNER RUTTEE SEEWEE STRIKE TEPARY THRASH TRIFLE CALABAR FRIJOLE MAZAGAN PHASEMY SNAPPER WINDSOR BONAVIST BONNYVIS RAMBUTAN TICKBEAN TORNILLO
(**— CURD**) TOFU
(**— OF CHINA AND JAPAN**) ADZUKI
(**BROKEN COFFEE —S**) TRIAGE
(**KIND OF —**) GOA MOTH MUNG PINTO TONKA TEPARY WINGED
(**LOCUST —**) CAROB
(**MESCAL —**) SOPHORA
(**PL.**) NIBS FASELS FESELS PODDER PODWARE
(**PREF.**) FABI

BEANFEAST BEANO
BEANIE DINK
BEAN-SHAPED FABIFORM
BEANSHOOTER TRUNK PEASHOOTER
BEAN TREE BOGUM
BEAN TREFOIL LABURNUM
BEAR GO CUB LUG BALU BERN BORN CAST DREE DUBB FURE GEST GIVE HAVE HOLD LIFT TEEM TOTE URSA WEAR YEAN ABEAR ABIDE ALLOW BALOO BEGET BHALU BREED BRING BROOK BROWN BRUIN CARRY DREIE DRIVE GESTE ISSUE KOALA POLAR PRESS SPARE STAND STICK THOLE THROW WEIGH WIELD YIELD AFFORD BEHAVE BRUANG CONVEY ENDURE IMPORT INFANT KADIAK KINDLE KODIAK PIERCE RENDER SUFFER THRUST UPHOLD URSULA WOMBAT WOOBUT ABROOKE ARCTOID BROWNIE COMPORT CONDUCT EPHRAIM FORBEAR GRIZZLY MUSQUAW PRODUCE STOMACH SUPPORT SUSTAIN UNDERGO FISSIPED SILVERTIP
(**— A PART**) CONTRIBUTE
(**— DOWN**) BROWBEAT OVERSWAY
(**— EVIDENCE**) ASSERT
(**— EXPENSES**) DEFRAY
(**— FLOWERS**) FLOURISH
(**— FRUIT**) FRUCTIFY
(**— IN MIND**) REMEMBER
(**— INVESTIGATION**) WASH
(**— ON**) CONCERN
(**— OUT**) PROPORT
(**— PATIENTLY**) DIGEST
(**— UP**) CAPE ENDURE SUSTAIN
(**— WITH CREDIT**) BROOK
(**— WITNESS**) TEEM SPEAK ATTEST DEPOSE
(**— YOUNG**) FIND YEAN CALVE CHILD
(**MALE —**) BOAR
(**NYMPH CHANGED TO —**) CALLISTO
(**SLOTH —**) ASWAIL
(**STUFFED —**) TEDDY
(**PREF.**) ARCT(O) URSI
(**SUFF.**) FER(ENCE)(ENT)(OUS)

GEN(E)(ESIA)(ESIS)(FTIC)(IC)(IN) (OUS)(Y) GER(ENCE)(ENT)(OUS)
BEARBERRY LARB WHORTLE BILBERRY DOGBERRY FOXBERRY CREASHAKS
BEARCAT PANDA
BEARD ANE AWN AVEL BARB DEFY FACE FUZZ NECK NOSE PEAK TUFT ZIFFS ARISTA BEAVER GOATEE TASSEL AFFRONT BARBULE CHARLEY CHARLIE VANDYKE IMPERIAL STILETTO WHISKERS BILLYGOAT
(**— OF GRAIN**) AIL AWN
(**— TREATISE**) POGONOLOGY
(**KIND OF —**) GYPSUM
(**SMALL —**) BARBET
(**PREF.**) ATHERO POGON(O)
(**SUFF.**) POGON

BEARDED AWNIE HAIRY BARBED BARBATE HIRSUTE POGONIATE WHISKERED
BEARDLESS NOT NOTT IMBERBE POLLARD
BEARDTONGUE PENSTEMON
BEARER NEWS HAMAL MACER BEADLE HAMMAL HOLDER PACKER PORTER ANCIENT CARRIER JAMPANI PINCERN CHAPRASI ESCUDERO PORTATOR STANDARD MESSENGER SUPPORTER
(**— OF GREAT BURDEN**) ATLAS
(**ARMOR —**) ESQUIRE
(**BURDEN —**) HAMAL HAMMAL
(**CROZIER —**) CROCIARY
(**CUP —**) SAKI COPPER
(**PALANQUIN —**) BOY SIRDAR MUSAHAR
(**SHIELD —**) SQUIRE ESCUDERO
(**STANDARD —**) ANCIENT
(**STRETCHER —**) BRANCARDIER
(**SWORD —**) PORTGLAVE PORTGLAIVE
(**PREF.**) PORTE

BEARING AIM AIR COD BALL DUCT GEST MIEN ORLE PORT RUBY BIRTH FRONT GESTE HABIT JEWEL POISE SETUP TENUE TREND ALLURE APPORT ASPECT BILLET CHARGE COURSE DEPORT GERENT GIGLIO MANNER ORIENT SADDLE STANCE THRUST VOIDER ADDRESS AZIMUTH CONDUCT FASHION GESTURE MEANING POSTURE PURPORT RHODING SUPPORT AMENANCE ATTITUDE BEHAVIOR BIRTHING CARRIAGE DELIVERY DEMEANOR FOOTSTEP PEDESTAL PRESENCE PRESSURE RELATION STANDARD TENDENCY TOURNURE YIELDING REFERENCE
(**— AWAY**) DEFERENT
(**— FRUIT**) FRUCTED
(**— OUTWARD**) EFFERENT
(**— UPON**) RELEVANT
(**ARROGANT —**) HUFF
(**CONSEQUENTIAL —**) POMP
(**HERALDIC —**) GAD DELF ENTE GORE MARK ORLE PALL WEEL CROWN DELFT DELPH FUSIL LAVER PHEON BILLET DEVICE ENSIGN

GOUTTE CHAPLET CLARION
DEMIVOL PLASQUE QUARTER
ORDINARY QUENTISE TRESSURE
(PERSONAL —) GARB
(PREF.) PHOR(O)
(SUFF.) GEROUS IGEROUS PARA
PAROUS PHORA PHORE(SIS)
PHORIA PHOROUS PHORUS
BEARLIKE URSINE
BEAR'S-EAR AURICULA
BEAR'S-FOOT OXHEAL PEGROOTS
BEARSKIN BUSBY
BEAR STATE ARKANSAS
BEAST BETE HOOF BRUTE VACHE
ANIMAL JUMENT CRITTER
MONSTER MUSIMON VENISON
BEHEMOTH BLIGHTER OPINICUS
(— OF BURDEN) JUMENT SUMPTER
(CASTRATED —) SPADO
(DEAD —) MORKIN
(FABULOUS —) YALE THRIS
BAGWYN BICORN TRICORN
UNICORN DINGMAUL EPIMACUS
OPINICUS GYASCUTUS
(HORNED —) RETHER ROTHER
(STURDY —) NUGGET
(WILD —) FERIN FERINE OUTLAW
UNBEAST
(WILD —S) ZIIM
(3-HORNED —) TRICORN
(PREF.) THER(A)(IO)(O)
(SUFF.) THERE THERIA THERIUM
BEASTLIKE THEROID
BEASTLY GROSS PRONE ANIMAL
BRUTAL WICKED BESTIAL BRUTISH
INHUMAN SWINISH OFFENSIVE
BEAT BAT BUM COB DAD FAN FIR
LAM PIP PLY PUG PUN RUN TAN
TAP TAW TEW TIE WAX BAFF BAIT
BANG BASH BATE BELT BEST
BLOW BOLT BRAY BUFF BURN
CANE CAST CHAP CLAP CLUB COIL
COLT COMB CRAB DAUD DING
DINT DRUB DUMP DUNT FELL FIRK
FLAP FLAX FLOG FRAM FRAP FRAT
GROW HAZE JOWL KILL LACE
LAMP LASH LICK LOUK LUMP LUSH
MAUL MELL MEND MILL PAIK PALE
PANT PELT POLT POSS PRAT ROUT
SCAT SLAM SLAT SLOG SOCK SOLE
SOWL STUB SWAP SWOP TACK
TAKD TICK TRIM TUCK TUND TWIG
WALK WARP WELT WHIP WHOP
WIPE BANDY BASTE BATON BEPAT
BERRY BIRCH BLESS CHURN CLINK
CREAM CURRY DOUSE DRASH
DRESS DRIVE FEEZE FIGHT FILCH
FLAIL FLANK FORGE ICTUS INLAY
KNOCK LABOR NEVEL NOINT
PASTE PATCH POUND PULSE
PUNCH ROUGH ROUND SCATT
SCOOP SCOUR SKELP STAMP
STRAP SWACK SWING TARGE
THREP THROB THUMP TREAD
TRUMP UPEND WADDY WHACK
WHANG WORST ACCENT ANOINT
BAMBOO BATTER BENSEL BETTLE
BOUNCE BUFFET COTTON CUDGEL
DEFEAT DOWSEL FEAGUE FETTLE
HAMMER HAMPER JACKET KNEVEL
LARRUP LATHER NEAVIL NODDLE
OUTRUN PUMMEL RADDLE

REBUKE REESLE RHYTHM SCUTCH
SQUASH STOUND STOUSH STRIKE
STRIPE STROKE SUGGIL SWINGE
SWITCH TANSEL TEWTAW TEWTER
THRASH THREAP THREIP THREPE
THRESH TICKLE WAGGLE WALLOP
WATTLE WUTHER ASSAULT
BATTUTA BELABOR BLATTER
BLISTER CADENCE CANVASS
CONQUER CONTUSE EXHAUST
FATIGUE FLYFLAP KNUCKLE
LAMBACK LAMBAST LOBTAIL
LOUNDER PULSATE REESHIE
SHELLAC SURPASS SWABBLE
SWADDLE TROLLOP TROUNCE
VIBRATE MALLEATE PALPITATE
SPIFLICATE
(— ABOUT) BUSK BANGLE
(— AGAINST) BLAD
(— AGAINST THE WIND) LAVEER
(— BACK) REBUFF
(— BARLEY) PAIL WARM
(— CLOTHES) BATTLE
(— COVERT) TUFT
(— DOWN) LAY FELL FULL ABATE
FLASH
(— EGGS) CAST
(— FIBERS) BRUSH
(— FLAX) SCUTCH
(— HIGH) LEAP
(— IT) LAM
(— OF DRUM) RUFF RAPPEL RATTAN
(— OF HEART) DUNT STROKE
(— ON BUTTOCKS) COB
(— OUT) THRESH
(— SEVERELY) DRUB LUMP SOAK
BASTE SOUSE LATHER
(— SMALL) CHAP
(— TO AND FRO) BANDY
(— TO WINDWARD) LAVEER
(— UP) WHISK SWITCH WORKOVER
(— VIOLENTLY) WETHER
(— WINGS) BATE FLAP
(— WITH HAMMER) DOLLY
(— WITH WHIP) SJAMBOK
(— WOODS) TUSK
(MUSICAL —) SALSA BOUNCE
BATTUTA
(WEAK —) ARSIS
(PREF.) TYPTO
BEATEN BEAT BETE BATTU PARTY
TRITE TRADED
BEATER RAB MAUL SEAL CANER
LACER STOCK DASHER DRIVER
MALLET TRIMMER SCUTCHER
THRESHER
BEATIFIC DEIFIC ELYSIAN
BEATIFIED BLEST BLESSED
BEATIFY SAINT HALLOW HEAVEN
ENCHANT GLORIFY SANCTIFY
BEATING COB COBB LICK TUND
BEANS DOUSE JESSE PULSE STICK
HAZING HIDING HOSING ROPAND
TATTOO BASHING BATTERY
BELTING CLANKER DASHING
DUSTING LICKING SKELPIN
WELTING WHALING BIRCHING
DRESSING DRUBBING RIBROAST
SLOSHING WHIPPING JACKETING
STRAPPADO PERCUSSION
BEATITUDE JOY BLISS BENISON
MACARISM HAPPINESS

**BEATRICE DI TENDA (CHARACTER
IN —)** AGNESE FILIPPO BEATRICE
VISCONTI OROMBELLO
(COMPOSER OF —) BELLINI
**BEATRICE ET BENEDICT
(CHARACTER IN —)** HERO CLAUDIO
BEATRICE BENEDICT SOMARONE
(COMPOSER OF —) BERLIOZ
BEAU BEW BOY CHAP BLADE
DANDY FLAME LOVER SPARK
SWELL ADONIS ESCORT FELLOW
GARCON STEADY SUITOR TATTLE
ADMIRER AIMWELL BRAVERY
COURTER COXCOMB CUPIDON
GALLANT SPARKER FOLLOWER
BEAU GREGORY COCKEYE
BEAUISH DOGGY
BEAUT PIP DILLY
BEAUTIFUL FAIR FINE GLAD GOOD
MEAR MEER MERE WALY BELLE
BONNY KALON LUSTY SILLEN
WLITY WLONK BLITHE BONNIE
COMELY DECORE FREELY LOVELY
POETIC PRETTY VENUST ANGELIC
ELEGANT FORMOSE FORMOUS
TEMPEAN TOKALON CHARMING
DELICATE ESTHETIC FAIRSOME
GORGEOUS GRACEFUL
HANDSOME LUCULENT SPECIOUS
MAGNIFICENT
(PREF.) CALI CALLI CALLO CALO
PULCHRI
BEAUTIFY FAIR GILD ADORN GRACE
HIGHT PREEN PRIMP PRUNE
BEAUTY BEDECK DECORE ENAMEL
QUAINT ADONIZE ENHANCE
GARNISH GLORIFY DECORATE
FAIRHEAD EMBELLISH PULCHRIFY
BEAUTY GEM FACE FAIR FORM
GLEE BEAUT BELLE CHARM FAVOR
GLORY GRACE PRIDE WLITE
FINERY LOOKER LOVELY POLISH
DECORUM FEATURE TOKALON
SPLENDOR FORMOSITY
(— OF FORM) SYMMETRY
(— OF STYLE) ELEGANCE
(PREF.) CALI CALLI CALLO CALO
PULCHRI
BEAVER BOOMER CASTOR RODENT
PRALINE MUSHROOM SEWELLEL
STARLING
(— SKIN) PLEW
(— STATE) OREGON
(DARK —) NUTMEG
BEBAI (SON OF —) ZECHARIAH
BEBEERINE CURINE
BEBEERU SWEETWOOD
GREENHEART
BECAUSE AS SO FOR THAT BEING
CAUSE SINCE THEN FORWHY
THROUGH INASMUCH
BECCAFICO FIGEATER FIGPECKER
BECHE-DE-MER PIDGIN TREPANG
BECHER (FATHER OF —) EPHRAIM
BENJAMIN
BECHORATH (FATHER OF —)
APHIAH
BECK RUN VAT BECON BROOK
CREEK
(— AND CALL) DEVOTION
BECKEN CYMBALS
BECKET SQUILGEE SQUILGEE

BECKON BOW NOD WAG BECK
WAFT WAVE CURTSY SUMMON
BIDDING COMMAND CURTSEY
GESTURE
BECKONING WAFTURE
BECLOUD HIDE MASK BEDIM
DARKEN MUDDLE MYSTIFY
OBSCURE OBNUBILATE
BECLOUDED FOGGY
BECOME GO FIT GET RAX SET SIT
WAX COME FALL GROW LIKE PASS
SUIT TALE TILL WEAR ADORN
BEFIT GRACE PROVE WORTH
ACCORD BEFALL BESEEM BETIDE
CHANGE IWORTH BEHOOVE
FLATTER PROCEED
(— A PARTY) ACCEDE
(— AUDIBLE) ARISE
(— BETTER) GAIN
(— BIGGER) SPREAD
(— DAMP) EVE
(— DAZED) DWAM DWALM
(— DIM) DASWEN
(— DROWSY) DOW
(— EVENTUALLY) ENDUP
(— FAT) GRAZE
(— FLUID) FLOW FLUX LEACH
(— KNOWN) GO KITHE KYTHE
SPUNK
(— MEMBER) JOIN
(— MOLDY) FUST MOUL FINEW
(— MOROSE) SOUR
(— ROUND) GLOBE
(— SOUR) FOX BLINK CARVE
(SUFF.) IZE
BECOMING FIT FEAT GOOD BHAVA
FITTY RIGHT COMELY DUEFUL
GAINLY PROPER DECORUM
FARRAND FARRANT DECOROUS
HANDSOME SUITABLE WISELIKE
(SUFF.) ESCENT ESCENCE
ESCENCE
BECOMINGLY TALLY
BED COT HAY KIP LIT PAD PAN TYE
BAND BASE BODY BUNK DOSS
DOWN FLOP FORM LAIR PLOT
SACK VEIN WADI WADY BERTH
BOIST COUCH FLASK FLOCK GRATE
GROVE LAYER ROOST THORE
BORDER BOTTOM COUCHE
CRADLE GIRDLE HOTBED LIBKEN
LIBKIN LITTER MATRIX OSIERY
PALLET STRATA CHANNEL
CHARPOY FLEABAG HAMMOCK
LODGING QUARTER REPOSAL
SEEDBED SETTING STRATUM
SUBSOIL TRUCKLE TRUNDLE
BASSINET CAPSTONE LENTICLE
PLANCHER SHAKEDOWN
(— DOWN) DOSS
(— IN WAGON) KATEL
(— OF ANIMAL) LAIR KENNEL
(— OF CLAY) CLOD
(— OF COAL) BRAT DELF SEAM
(— OF EMBERS) GRIESHOCH
(— OF FIRE CLAY) THILL
(— OF FURNACE) HEARTH
(— OF GUN-CARRIAGE) FLASK
(— OF HAND PRESS) COFFIN
(— OF OYSTERS) PLANT
(— OF REFUSE) NITRIARY
(— OF ROCK) CAP PLUM
(— OF ROSES) ROSARY

(— OF SEDIMENT) WARP
(— OF SHELLFISH) BANK
(— OF STONES) SHINGLE
(— OF STREAM) DRAW WASH
NULLAH BILLABONG STREAMWAY
(— SIZE) KING TWIN QUEEN
DOUBLE SINGLE
(CREEK —) COULEE COULIE
(DRIED LAKE —) CHOTT SEBKA
SHOTT
(FEATHER —) TIE TYE
(FOLDING —) SLAWBANK
(GO TO —) SACKOUT
(LOW —) LOWBOY
(OYSTER —) STEW LAYER SCALP
CLAIRE LAYING OYSTERAGE
(RUBBLE —) CALLOW
(SEED —) SEMINARY
(WATER-BEARING —) AQUAFER
AQUIFER
(WOODEN —) RUSTBANK
(PREF.) CLIN(O) STRATI STROMATI
STROMATO
(SUFF.) STROMA
BEDAD (SON OF —) HADAD
BEDAN (FATHER OF —) GILEAD
BEDAUB CLAG CLAT DAUB MOIL
SOIL SLAKE SMEAR PARGET
SLUBBER SLAISTER BEPLASTER
BEDBUG BUG CHINK CIMEX CHINCH
CHINTZ COREID PUNESE VERMIN
CIMICID PUNAISE REDCOAT
CONENOSE HEMIPTER HOUSEBUG
BEDCHAMBER RUELLE BEDROOM
CUBICLE
BEDCLOTHES COVER BEDDING
CLOTHES
BEDCOVER COMFORTER
PALAMPORE
BEDDING BEDROLL DOMESTICS
BEDECK GEM BEDO LARD TRAP
ADORN ARRAY DIGHT GRACE
PRINK ORNAMENT EMBELLISH
BEDECKED PRINKY
BEDEGUAR SPONGE
BEDEIAH (FATHER OF —) BANI
BEDEVIL ABUSE ANNOY BESET
WORRY HARASS MUDDLE PESTER
BEWITCH CONFUSE TORMENT
BEDEW DEW DAMPEN SHOWER
EMBATHE IRRORATE
BEDIZEN DAUB ADORN ARRAY
DIZEN BEDAUB
BEDLAM ZOO RIOT NOISE RUDAS
ASYLUM TUMULT UPROAR
MADNESS MADHOUSE
BETHLEHEM
BEDLAMITE MADMAN
BEDOUIN ABSI ARAB BEDU MOOR
NOMAD BADAWI BEDAWEE
SHAMMAR HOWEITAT
BEDQUILT POURPOINT
BEDRAGGLE DAG DRABBLE
TRACHLE
BEDRAGGLED FORLORN
SHOPWORN
BEDRAIL RAVE RATHE
BEDRIDDEN ILL AILING BEDFAST
(NOT —) AFOOT
BEDROCK LEDGE NADIR SHELF
BOTTOM HARDPAN STONEHEAD
BEDROLL BINDLE

BEDROOM FLAT BERTH CABIN
BEDDER DORMER BOUDOIR
CHAMBER CUBICULO WARDROBE
GARDEROBE
BEDSORE ANACLISIS DECUBITUS
BEDSPREAD ALEZE STRAIL
BEDCOVER COVERLET COVERLID
BEDSTAFF SLAT
BEDSTEAD BED COT CRIB HATCH
STEAD STAPLE ANGAREP
CHARPOY
BEDSTRAW CRUDWORT
CURDWORT FLEAWEED
BEDFLOWER CROSSWORT
SCRAMBLER
BED TESTER SPARVER
BEDWARMER CURATE
BEDWEAR PJS
BEE DOR FLY APIS BEVY KING RING
KARBI MASON NOMIA NURSE
PARTY DINGAR DRONEL DRONER
FROLIC INSECT NOTION TORQUE
TSETSE WORKER ANDRENA
DEBORAH KOOTCHA MELISSA
RAISING SERPENT STINGER
SWERVER TRIGONA ANDRENID
ANGELITO HONEYBEE QUILTING
SCOPIPED SHUCKING WAXMAKER
GATHERING
(KIND OF —) KILLER
(PERTAINING TO —S) APIAN
(QUEEN —) KING
(PL.) BEEN BONE HIVE SPEW
SOCIALES
(PREF.) API
BEEBREAD CERAGO AMBROSIA
BEECH BUCK BIRCH MYRTLE
FLINDOSA FLINDOSY
(PREF.) FAGI FAGO
BEECHNUT SPLITNUT
(PL.) BUCK MAST PANNAGE
BEEF JERK BEEVE BULLY GRIPE
JERKY VIFDA VIVDA CASSON
CUTTER CHARQUI TOPSIDE
COMPLAIN COMPOUND PASTRAMI
PIPIKAULA
(— FOR SLAUGHTER) MART
(BOILED —) BOUILLI
(BROILED —) CHURRASCO
(CORN —) BULLY
(CUT OF —) SEY LOIN RUMP SIDE
BARON CHINE CHUCK FLANK ROAST
ROUND SHANK STEAK ALOYAU
CUTLET SADDLE BRISKET KNUCKLE
QUARTER SIRLOIN EDGEBONE
SHOULDER AITCHBONE NINEHOLES
RATTLERAN
(GROUND —) HAMBURGER
(INFERIOR —) COMPOUND
(JERKED —) TASAJO BILTONG
CHARQUE CHARQUI
(LEAN —) LIRE
(PIECE OF —) PAILLARD
(SALTED —) JUNK VIFDA
(STRIPS OF —) FAJITA
BEEF BREAD SWEETBREAD
BEEFEATER OXBIRD BUPHAGA
OXBITER OXPECKER TICKBIRD
BEEFWOOD TOA BELAH BELAR
FILAO
BEEFY HEAVY HEFTY SOLID
BRAWNY FLESHY
BEE GLUE PROPOLIS

BEEHIVE GUM BUTT GUME HIVE
SKEP PYCHE STAND STATE STOCK
SWARM APIARY HAIRDO HOPPET
ALVEARY SWARMER BEEHOUSE
PRAESEPE
(— STATE) UTAH
(— TOMB) TREASURY
BEEKEEPER HIVER BEEMAN
BEEHERD APIARIST SKEPPIST
BEELIADA (FATHER OF —) DAVID
BEELZEBUB DEVIL
BEEN BE BON SEE BONE
BEEPER PAGER
BEE PLANT GUACO STINKWEED
BEER ALE MUM BIER BOCK BREW
FARO GAIL GROG GYLE HOPS KVAS
MALT MILD QUAS SCUD SUDS
BELCH CHANG CHICA GROUT
KVASS LAGER POMBE QUASS
SCUDS STOUT WEISS CHICHA
DOUBLE GATTER LIQUOR PORTER
SPRUCE STINGO SWANKY SWIPES
WALLOP ZYTHUM CERVEZA
PANGASI PHARAOH PILSNER
TANKARD TAPLASH TAPWORT
CERVISIA PILSENER
(ADD TO —) KRAUSEN
(BAD —) TACK TAPLASH
(HOT — AND GIN) PURL
(INFERIOR —) BELCH SWANKY
(KIND OF —) NEAR
(SMALL —) TIFF GROUT
(SOUR —) BEEREGAR
(STRONG —) HUFF NAPPY DOUBLE
STINGO
(THIN —) PRITCH SWIPES
(TIBETAN —) CHANG
(WARM — AND OATMEAL) STORRY
(WEAK —) BEVERAGE
BEERA (FATHER OF —) ZOPHAH
BEER-GARDEN BRASSERIE
BEERHOUSE KNEIPE TIDDLYWINK
BEERI (DAUGHTER OF —) JUDITH
(SON OF —) HOSEA
BEESWAX CAPPING
BEET CHARD MANGEL MANGOLD
STECHLING
(SUGAR —) BOLTER
BEETLE BAT BOB BUG DOR JUT
RAM BEAT BUZZ FLEA FOWL GOGA
GOGO IPID MAUL MELL STAG
TROX TURK UANG AMARA ATLAS
BORER BULGE CAROB CHUCK
CLOCK DRIVE FIDIA GOGGA HISPA
LYCID MELOE SAGRA TIGER
BATLET CHAFER CLERID COCUYO
CUCUYO ELATER GOLACH
GOLOCH HISTER JUTOUT KHAPRA
LICTUS MALLET MELOID PESTLE
PRUNER PTINID SAWYER SCARAB
WEAVER WEEVIL ADELOPS
BRUCHID BUZZARD CADELLE
CARABID CARABUS CLOCKER
CUCUJID FIDDLER FIREFLY
GIRDLER GOLDBUG HORNBUG
LADYBUG LUCANID PAUSSID
PRIONID PROJECT SILPHID
SKIPPER SNAPPER SOLDIER
TANBARK TICKLER ATEUCHUS
CALOSOMA CETONIAN COCKTAIL
CURCULIO DYTISCID ENGRAVER
EROTYLID FIGEATER GLOWWORM
HARDBACK LADYBIRD LAMPYRID

LOWFRING OVERHANG RUTELIAN
SCOLYTID SEARCHER SHARNBUD
SHARNBUG SKIPJACK SPHINDID
SQUASHER SQUEAKER SYMPHILE
TOKTOKJE WHIRLWIG DEDEMERID
LONGICORN OSTOMATID
TUMBLEBUG TWIRLIGIG
WHIRLIGIG SCAPHIDIUM
RHYNCHOPHORAN
(KIND OF —) OIL
(RHINOCEROS —) UANG
SCARABAEID
(PL.) XYLOPHAGA
BEEWEED ASTER TONGUE
BEFALL HAP COME LIMP SORT TIDE
TIME CHEFE CHIVE OCCUR SHAPE
ASTART BECOME BETIDE HAPPEN
PERTAIN
BEFIT DOW SIT COME LONG SEEM
SORT SUIT BESET SERVE BECOME
BEHOVE BESEEM BETIDE
BEHOOVE
BEFITTING FIT AFTER DECENT
PROPER WORTHY SEEMING
THRIFTY BECOMING DECOROUS
SORTABLE
(PROFESSIONALLY —) ETHICAL
(SUFF.) LY
BEFOG GAUM CLOUD OBSANE
CONFUSE MYSTIFY
BEFOOL BOB FON SOT BURN COLT
CRAP DOLT DUPE FODE JADE
POOP ASSOT ELUDE FONNE
BEFLUM DIDDLE TRIFLE FOOLIFY
BEFOOLING BITE
BEFORE OR TO AIR BUT ERE FOR
GIN TIL ANTE FORE SAID TILL YORE
AFORE AHEAD ANENT AVANT
CORAM FIRST FORBY FORNE
FRONT PRIOR SOPRA UNTIL
ERENOW FORBYE FORMER
RATHER SOONER TOFORE WITHIN
AGAINST ALREADY EARLIER
FORTHBY FORWARD
(— LONG) SOON ERELONG
(JUST —) TOWARD FORMERLY
(PREF.) FORE OB PRAE PRE PRO
PROTER(O)
BEFOREHAND AFORE
BEFORE-MENTIONED SAID SUCH
BEFOUL FILE SLUT SOIL BERAY
DIRTY GRUFT BEMIRE DAGGLE
DARKEN DEFILE DRABBLE
FEWMAND POLLUTE SLUTTER
BESQUIRT ENTANGLE
BEFOULED SHARNY
BEFRIEND AID ABET HELP FAVOR
ASSIST FOSTER FRIEND SUCCOR
BENEFIT SUPPORT SUSTAIN
BEFUDDLE BOX GAS ADDLE BESOT
MUDDLE BECLOUD CONFUSE
FLUSTER MYSTIFY STUPEFY
BEFUDDLED REE MUSED
BEG ASK BID CRY SUE WOO CANT
COAX KICK MOVE MUMP PRAY
PRIG SEEK SORN SUIT THIG TRAM
CADGE CRAVE MAUND MOOCH
PLEAD SCAFF SHOOL TEASE
YEARN ADJURE FLEECH BESEECH
ENTREAT IMPLORE MAUNDER
REQUEST SKELDER SOLICIT
PETITION OBSECRATE PANHANDLE

BEGET GET WIN BEAR HAVE KIND SIRE BREED YIELD BIGATE CREATE FATHER ACQUIRE ENGRAFF CONCEIVE ENGENDER GENERATE PROCREATE
(PREF.) GONIDIO GONIMO GONIO GON(O)

BEGETTER SIRE AUTHOR FATHER MOTHER PARENT

BEGETTING
(SUFF.) GON(E)(IDIUM)(IMO)(IUM)(Y)

BEGGAR BLOB PROG RUIN ASKER HALFY LAZAR RANDY ROGUE THRUM TRAMP ARMINE BACACH BIDDER CADGER CANTER DYVOUR MUMPER PARIAH PAUPER SORNER WRETCH ABRAHAM ALMSMAN BAIRAGI BEGSTER JAHKMAN LAZARUS MAUNDER PARDHAN PROCTOR RUFFLER SCAFFER SORNARI STEMMER THIGGER ABRAMMAN BADGEMAN BEADSMAN BESOGNIO BEZONIAN BLUEGOWN DUMMERER GLASSMAN PALLIARD STRÖLLER WHIPJACK MENDICANT SCHNORRER
(— DESCRIPTION) PASS
(SWINDLING —) JARKMAN
(VIOLENT —) RANDY RANDIE
(PL.) GUEUX

BEGGARED PEELED

BEGGARLY MEAN POOR CHEAP PETTY SORRY ABJECT PALTRY PILLED PEGRALL BANKRUPT INDIGENT HUNGARIAN

BEGGAR'S-LICE STICKWEED
BEGGARS' OPERA (AUTHOR OF —) GAY
(CHARACTER IN —) LUCY POLLY LOCKIT PEACHUM MACHEATH

BEGGAR-TICK CUCKOLD
(PL.) BOOTJACKS

BEGGARY THIG WANT INDIGENCE PAUPERISM

BEGGING MAUND CRAVING OPENERS MENDICANT THOMASING
(— FOR FOOD) SCRANNING
(FRAUDULENT —) TRUANDISE

BEGHARD PICARD

BEGIN GIN GYN HIT FALL FANG HEAD JUMP LEAD OPEN RISE TAME YOKE ARISE ENTER FRONT START ATTACK ATTAME INCEPT SPRING STREAK TEEOFF INSTATE COMMENCE GETGOING INCHOATE INITIATE
(— AGAIN) RENEW REOPEN RESUME
(— IN EARNEST) SETTO
(— TO APPEAR) PEEP
(— TO MELT) GIVE
(— TO WORK) GEL

BEGINNER BOOT PUNK TIRO TYRO ROOKY SOFTA GINNER NOVICE ROOKIE SOPHTA AMATEUR ENTRANT RECRUIT RUBBLER STUDENT TRAINEE FRESHMAN INCEPTOR NEOPHYTE NEWCOMER NOVELIST ABECEDARIAN

BEGINNING EGG ORD DAWN EDGE GERM HEAD RISE ROOT SEED ALPHA BIRTH DEBUT ENTRY FIRST FRONT ONSET START VAUNT AURORA INCOME INSTIL ONCOME ORIGIN OUTSET SETOUT SOURCE SPRING CALENDS DAWNING GENESIS HANDSEL INCIPIT INFANCY INITIAL INITION KALENDS NASCENT OPENING SUNRISE ENTRANCE EXORDIUM INCHOATE OUTSTART RUDIMENT
(— OF A TRILL) RIBATTUTA
(FROM THE —) ABOVO
(NEW —) EPOCH
(PL.) INCUNABULA
(PREF.) ACR(O)
(SUFF.) ARCH ARCHIC ARCHY ESCENT

BEGONE OFF OUT VIA AWAY SCAT SHOO SCOOT SCRAM AROINT AVAUNT DEPART SKIDOO SKIDDOO VAMOOSE

BEGONIA GAIETY GAYETY

BEGRIME COOM SOIL COLLY DITCH GRIME BECOOM SMIRCH SMUDGE BRUCKLE

BEGRIMED DIRTY GRIMY SMUDGY CINDERY SMIRCHY

BEGRUDGE ENVY GRUDGE MALIGN JALOUSE

BEGTI NAIR COCKUP

BEGUILE FOX COAX FODE FOIL FOND GULL LURE VAMP WILE WISE AMUSE CHARM CHEAT COZEN ELUDE EVADE GUILE TEMPT TRICK TROLL TRYST WEIZE BRIGUE BUTTER DELUDE DIVERT ENTRAP JUGGLE VAMPEY DECEIVE ENSNARE FLATTER FLUMMER MISLEAD MOUNTEBANK

BEHALF HALF PART SAKE SIDE FAVOR SCORE STEAD AFFAIR MATTER PROFIT BENEFIT DEFENCE SUPPORT INTEREST

BEHAVE DO ACT LET BEAR FARE HAVE KEEP MAKE PLAY WALK WORK ABEAR CARRY REACT TREAT ACQUIT DEMEAN DEPORT HANDLE COMPORT CONDUCT CONTAIN DISPORT GESTURE MANAGER FUNCTION REGULATE RESTRAIN
(— AFFECTEDLY) MOP
(— AWKWARDLY) GAUM HOCKER
(— BOLDLY) GAUSTER
(— BRASHLY) HOOK
(— CHURLISHLY) CARL
(— EVASIVELY) DODGE
(— FOOLISHLY) DOLT
(— IRRATIONALLY) FREAK
(— MEANLY) SNEAK
(— MISCHIEVOUSLY) LARK
(— NOISILY) HELL REHAYTE
(— OSTENTATIOUSLY) SWANK
(— RIOTOUSLY) ROLLICK GALRAVAGE GILRAVAGE
(— VULGARLY) RAMP

BEHAVING
(SUFF.) ANT ENT

BEHAVIOR AIR MIEN PORT RULE THEW WALK FRONT GUISE HABIT LATES USAGE ACTION COURSE GOINGS MANNER ACTIONS BEARING BIGOTRY COMPORT CONDUCT DECORUM ERGASIA FACTION FASHION HAVANCE HAVINGS AMENANCE ATTITUDE BLINDISM BREEDING BYRONICS CARRIAGE FUNCTION MAINTAIN PERFORMANCE
(AMOROUS —) SPORT
(ARROGANT —) SIDE SWAGGER
(COURTEOUS —) COMITY COURTESY
(DECENT —) CIVILITY
(EXCITED —) RAMPAGE RAMPAUGE
(FOOLISH —) SIMPLES SOTTISE
(GOAL-DIRECTED —) HORME
(GOOD —) STRAIGHT
(IMPROPER —) MISCONDUCT
(LIVELY —) TITTUP
(LOUTISH —) BUFFOONERY
(RIOTOUS —) RAMPAGE
(SILLY —) SPOONISM
(SLEAZY —) SMARM
(STUDIED —) ART
(SUSPICIOUS —) SUS
(UNDERHANDED —) SKULLDUGGERY
(VIOLENT —) THUGGERY

BEHEAD NECK

BEHEST BID LAW HEST RULE ORDER DEMAND BIDDING COMMAND MANDATE

BEHIND AFT HINT PAST RUMP ABACK ABAFF ABAFT AFTER AHIND AREAR LATER PASSE TARDY ARREAR ASTERN DERERE BACKWARD DILATORY
(— TIME) OVERDUE
(PREF.) META POST POSTERO RETRO

BEHINDHAND TARDY LAGGARD DILATORY HINDERLY

BEHOLD LA LO EYE SEE SPY ECCE ESPY GAZE HOLD KEEP LOOK SCAN STOP TOOT VIEW VISE WAIT HOLDE OCULE SIGHT VOILA WATCH ASPECT DESCRY MIRROR REGARD RETAIN DISCERN OBSERVE SURVISE WITNESS

BEHOLDEN OWING AFFINED BOUNDEN OBLIGED INDERTED

BEHOOVE DOW FIT NEED SUIT THAR BEFIT OUGHT THARF BELONG PROPER REQUIRE

BEIGE HOP TAN ECRU HOPI GREGE DORADO GREIGE STRING SUNBURN

BEING ENS ESSE FEAL SELF ENTIA GNOME HUMAN SHAPE TROLL ANIMAL ENTITY EXTANT LIVING MORTAL PERSON SYSTEM ESSENCE PRESENT REALITY VIVENCY CREATURE EXISTENT ONTOLOGY PRESENCE STANDING
(ANIMATE —) LIFE JAGAT
(BIONIC HUMAN —) CYBORG
(CELESTIAL —) ANGEL CHERUB SERAPH WATCHER DIVINITY
(DIMINUTIVE —) ELF GNOME
(DIVINE —) DEV DEVA DEMIGOD
(ESSENCE OF —) SAT
(ETERNAL —) EON AEON
(EVIL —) DEVIL GHOUL
(FABULOUS —) TENGU TORNIT
(HAVING REAL —) ONTIC
(HUMAN —) BODY BUCK JACK SOUL BLADE HUMAN SLIME ANIMAL ADAMITE CREATURE RATIONAL CHRISTIAN
(IDEAL —) IMMORTAL
(ILL-FAVORED —) BLASTIE
(IMAGINARY —) SYLPH TERMAGANT
(INNER —) INWARD SPRITE INBEING
(INNERMOST —) HEART
(INTRINSIC —) ESSENCE
(LEGENDARY —) GIANT
(LIVING —) BLOOD WIGHT
(MATERIAL —) HYLIC
(PERFECT —) GOD
(PHYSICAL —) FLESH
(SEMIDIVINE —) SHEDU LAMASSU
(SMALL —) INCHLING
(SO —) SAEBEINS
(SUPERNATURAL —) DEV MAN AKUA ATUA DEVA JANN ZEMI ADARO BALAM DAEVA DEMON FAIRY TROLL WIGHT DAEMON GARUDA GODKIN SPIRIT GODLING FOLLETTO HAMINGJA
(SUPREME —) DEITY MONAD NYAMBE NZAMBI CREATOR
(TRUE —) OUSIA
(PREF.) ONT(O) ZO(E)(IDIO)(IDO)(O) ZOOLOGICO
(HUMAN —) ANTHROP(O)
(SUFF.) IC(AL) ZOA ZOIC ZOON

BELA (FATHER OF —) AZAZ BEOR BENJAMIN

BELABOR PLY BEAT DRUB LASH WORK ASSAIL BOUNCE CUDGEL HAMMER HAMPER THRASH THWACK

BELARUS (ALSO SEE RUSSIA)
CANAL: DNIEPERBUG
CAPITAL: MINSK
COIN: RUBLE
LAKE: NARACH NAROCH DRISVYATY DRYSVYATY ASVEYSKAYE OSVEYSKOYE
MARSH: PRIPET PALESSE POLESYE
MOUNTAIN: DZERZHINSKAYA DZYARZHINSKAYA
NAME: BYELARUS BELORUSSIA BYELORUSSIA
PEOPLE: BELARUS RUSSIAN BELORUSSIAN WHITERUSSIAN
PLAIN: BEREZINA
RIVER: BUG DRUT SOZH DISNA DNEPR DVINA DYSNA NEMAN SLUCH DNEPRO PRIPET PTITCH DAUGAVA DNIEPER NEMUNAS PRIPYAT SHCHARA YASELDA BEREZINA PRYPYATS SVISLOCH BYAREZINA MUKHAVETS
TOWN: BREST GOMEL HOMEL PINSK GRODNO HRODNA BORISOV MOGILEV VITEBSK ZHODINO BOBRUISK BOBRUYSK MOGILYOV MOLODECHNO BRESTLITOVSK

BELAY BESET BELAGE INVEST WAYLAY BESEIGE

BELCH YEX BOCK BOKE BOLK BURP GALP RASP RIFT ERUCT FRUCT REBOKE ERUCTATE

BELCHING BRASH

BELDAM HAG FURY TROT CRONE RUDAS ALECTO ERINYS RUDOUS

VIRAGO BELDAME JEZEBEL
TISIPHONE
BELEAGUER BELAY BESET INVEST
ASSAULT BESEIGE LEAGUER
BLOCKADE SURROUND
BELEAGUERING SIEGE
BELEM PARA
BELEMNITE ARTIFACT KERAUNION
BELFRY SHED TOWER BEFFROY
CLOCHER CLOGHEAD BELLHOUSE
BELGIAN FLEMING
BELGIAN CONGO (CAPITAL OF —)
LEOPOLDVILLE
(LAKE IN —) KIVU MWERU ALBERT
(PROVINCE OF —) KIVA KASAI
EQUATOR KATANGA ORIENTAL
(RIVER IN —) RUKI KASAI LINDI
LOMAMI LUKUGA UBANGI ARUWIMI
LULONGA
(TOWN IN —) BOMA LULUABOURG

BELGIUM
CANAL: YSER UNION ALBERT
CAMPINE
CAPITAL: BRUSSELS BRUXELLES
GAUL TRIBE: REMI BELGAE NERVII
MEASURE: VAT AUNE LAST PIED
CARAT PERCHE BOISSEAU
MOUNTAIN: BOTRANGE
NAME: BELGIE BELGIQUE
PLATEAU: ARDENNES HOHEVENN
PORT: OSTEND ANTWERP
PROVINCE: LIEGE NAMUR ANTWERP
BRABANT HAINAUT LIMBURG
FLANDERS HAINAULT
RIVER: LYS DYLE LEIE MAAS MARK
YSER BOUCQ DEMER LESSE
MEUSE NETHE RUPEL SENNE
DENDER ESCAUT MANJEL
OURTHE SAMBRE SEMOIS
VESDRE WARCHE AMBLEVE
SCHELDT
TOWN: AS AAT ANS ATH HAL HUY
MOL SPA AATH AMAY ASSE
BOOM BREE DOEL GAND GEEL
GENK GENT HOEI LIER LOOZ
MONS VISE WAHA ZELE AALST
ALOST ARLON CINEY EEKLO
ESSEN EUPEN EVERE GENCK
GHENT HEIST IEPER JETTE JUMET
LIEGE NAMUR RONSE TIELT
UCCLE VORST WEZET YNOIR
YPRES AARLEN ANVERS BERGEN
BILZEN BRUGES DEURNE ELSENE
IZEGEM LEUVEN LIERRE MERXEM
OPWIJK OSTEND ANTWERP
ARDOOIE BERCHEM DOORWIK
HERSTAL HOBOKEN IXELLES
LOUVAIN MECHLIN ROULERS
SERAING TONGRES TOURNAI
BRUSSELS COURTRAI KORTRIJK
MECHELEN MOUSCRON
TONGEREN TURNHOUT VERVIERS
WATERLOO
WEIGHT: LAST CARAT LIVRE POUND
CHARGE CHARIOT ESTERLIN

BELIE BELONG DEFAME BESEIGE
FALSIFY PERTAIN SLANDER
TRADUCE DISGUISE STRUMPET
SURROUND MISREPRESENT
BELIEF CRY FAY ISM LEVE MIND
SECT TAKE TROW VIEW VOTE
WEEN CAUSE CREDO CREED
DOGMA FAITH OBEAH TENET
TROTH TRUST CREDIT GROUND
CRIANCE FEELING HOLDING
OPINION TROWING ARYANISM
BITHEISM CREDENCE DOCTRINE
FINALISM HUMANISM RELIANCE
THANATISM PREPOSSESSION
(— HANDED DOWN) TRADITION
(— IN DEVILS) DIABOLISM
(— IN GHOSTS) EIDOLISM
(— IN GOD) DEISM THEISM
(— IN MAGIC) OBEAH
(CONVENTIONAL —) PIETY
(FALSE —) DELUSION
(GROUNDLESS —) CANARD
(MORTAL —) HALL
(READY —) ACCEPTATION
(SHALLOW —) BALLOON
(SUPERSTITIOUS —) FREET
(TRADITIONAL —) ICON IKON EIKON
(UNFOUNDED —) FICTON
(UNIMPORTANT —) FAD
BELIEVABLE PLAUSIBLE
BELIEVE BUY WIS DEEM FEEL HOLD
TAKE TREW TROW WEEN CREED
FAITH FANCY GUESS JUDGE SEPAD
THINK TRUST ACCEPT CREDIT
ESTEEM EXPECT DARESAY
SUPPOSE ACCREDIT CONSIDER
CREDENCE
(— ERRONEOUSLY) FEIGN
(— NAIVELY) SWALLOW
(— UNCRITICALLY) EAT
(HARD TO —) TALL
BELIEVER IST LEVER BOTARY KITABI
CREDENS ADHERENT ARMINIAN
(SUFF.) ARIAN
BELIEVING CREDENT FAITHFUL
BELISARIO (CHARACTER IN —)
ANTONIA EUTRIPIO BELISARIUS
(COMPOSER OF —) DONIZETTI
BELISE (BROTHER OF —)
PHILAMINTE
BELITTLE DIS DUMP DECRY DWARF
SNEER BEMEAN DEMEAN MINISH
SLIGHT DETRACT DIMINUE
LIGHTLY MINIMIZE VILIPEND
DENIGRATE DISCREDIT DISPARAGE
BELITTLER ZOILUS
BELIZE (CAPITAL OF —) BELMOPAN
BELL HUB TOM CALL FAIR GONG
HUBB RING ROAR CHIME CLOAK
CLOCK CODON FLARE KNELL
SWELL TENOR BASKET BELLOW
BUBBLE CLOCHE CROTAL CURFEW
PHONIC SOCKET TAPPER TOCSIN
TOLLER TREBLE TRIPLE VESPER
ANGELUS BLOSSOM CAMPANA
CAMPANE COROLLA COWBELL
JANGLER JINGLER LOWBELL
SKELLAT SKILLET TAMBOUR
TANTONY TINKLER CASCABEL
COCKBELL DINGDONG DOORBELL
HANDBELL HAWKBELL MORTBELL
PAVILLON STARTLER TINGTANG
(ALARM —) TOCSIN
(CLOSED —) CROTAL
(EVENING —) CURFEW
(FUNERAL —) TELLER
(HAND —) CLAG
(LARGE —) SIGNUM
(LOWEST —) BORDON BOURDON
(PART OF —) BOW LIP HEAD
CROWN MOUTH WAIST CLAPPER
SHOULDER
(PASSING —) KNELL
(SACRING —) SQUILLA
(SLEIGH —) GRELOT CROTALUM
(PREF.) CAMPANI CAMPANO
BELLABELLA HAELTZUK HEILTSUK
BELLADONNA DWALE MANICON
BANEWORT DAFTBERRY
DWAYBERRY MYDRIATIC
NIGHTSHADE
BELLARIA (HUSBAND OF —)
PANDOSTO
BELLARMINE GRAYBEARD
GREYBEARD LONGBEARD
BELLBIRD MAKO SHRIKE COTINGA
ARAPUNGA KORIMAKO
MAKOMAKO CAMPANERO
BELLBOY BUTTONS
BELLE SPARK TOAST
(SPANISH —) MAJA
BELLEEK POTTERY CHAMPAGNE
**BELLE HELENE, LE (COMPOSER OF
—)** OFFENBACH
BELLEROPHON (FATHER OF —)
GLAUCUS
(MOTHER OF —) EURYMEDE
BELLFLOWER LOBELIA RAMPION
BELLWORT HASKWORT IVYBELLS
MILKWORT
BELLHOP PAGE BELLBOY HALLBOY
CHASSEUR
BELLICOSE MAD IRATE WARFUL
HOSTILE WARLIKE MILITANT
BELLIGERENT BRISTLY HOSTILE
SCRAPPY STROPPY WARLIKE
CHOLERIC FIGHTING JINGOIST
COMBATIVE IRASCIBLE LITIGIOUS
WRANGLING PUGNACIOUS
BELLISANT (HUSBAND OF —)
ALEXANDER
(SON OF —) ORSON VALENTINE
BELLOW CRY LOW MOO YAP BAWL
BEAL BELL GAPE ROAR ROME
ROUT YAUP YAWP BELVE BLART
BLORE CROON ROUST SHOUT
TROAT BULLER CLAMOR RUMMES
BLUSTER RUMMISH THUNDER
ULULATE
BELLOWING ROUT ROUST BELLING
BLATANT BOATION MUGIENT
BELLOWS BELY LUNGS BULIES
FEEDER SANDER WINKER
SYLPHON WINDBAG EXPELLER
(SMALL —) PLUFF
(STORAGE —) RESERVOIR
(PREF.) PHYSA PHYSALLO PHYSO
BELLOWS FISH BUGLER SNIPEFISH
BELL RINGER TOLL YOUTH TOLLER
CLINKUM
BELL-TOWER BELFRY CAMPANILE
BELLWETHER MASTER
BELLY BAG COD GIE GUT MAW POD
BOUK BUNT FILL KYTE MARY
WAME WEAM WOMB BINGY
BOSOM BULGE FRONT GORGE
PLEON TABLE THARM THERM
TRIPE BAGGIE BINGEE HUNGER
PAUNCH VENTER ABDOMEN
BALLOON STOMACH TUMBREL
APPETITE
(PREF.) CELI COELI(O) GASTER(O)
GASTR(I)(O) VENTRI VENTRO
(SUFF.) GASTER GASTRIA
BELLYACHE CARP YAMMER
COMPLAIN COLLYWOBBLES
BELLYBAND WANTY
BELLYING BUNTING PREGNANT
BELLY-UP BANKRUPT
BELONE SEAPIKE
BELONG BE GO FIT LIE BEAR FALL
RELY APPLY BELIE GROUP AFFEIR
INHERE RELATE RETAIN BEHOOVE
PERTAIN APPERTAIN SUBSCRIBE
BELONGING
(SUFF.) EAE
(— TO) AR ARY EAN INE ISE ORIUM
BELONGINGS ALLS DUDS FARE
GEAR GOODS TRAPS ASSETS
DUFFEL DUFFLE ESTATE USINGS
BAGGAGE EFFECTS CHATTELS
PROPERTY PURPRISE FURNITURE
HOUSEHOLD PARAPHERNALIA
BELOVED DEAR IDOL LIEF AIMEE
BOSOM CHERI SWEET ADORED
CHERIE MINION DARLING
PRECIOUS INAMORATA
INAMORATO
(MOST —) ALDERLIEFEST
BELOW ALOW BAJO DOWN ABLOW
AFTER INFRA NEATH SOTTO
UNDER BEHIND BENEATH
(PREF.) INFERO INFRA SUB
BELT LAS AREA BAND BEAT BLOW
CEST FELT GIRD LACE LIST MARK
RING SASH SLUG ZONE GIRTH
MITER MITRE PATTE STRAP STRIP
SWATH TRACT WAIST WHACK
ZONAR ZONIC BODICE CENTER
CESTUS CINGLE FETTLE GIRDLE
INVEST LUNGER REGION STRAIT
STRIPE SWATHE ZONNAR ZONULE
BALDRIC BALTEUS CIRCUIT
PASSAGE BALTHEUS CEINTURE
CINCTURE CINGULUM ELEVATOR
ENCIRCLE MECHANIC SURROUND
CUMBERBUND CUMMERBUND
(— OF FOG) BLANKET
(AMMUNITION —) BANDOLEER
BANDOLIER
(ASTROLOGICAL —) CLIMATE
(CONVEYOR —) HAUL
(ENDLESS —) APRON CREEPER
(GREEK —) ZOSTER
(HINDU SWAMP —) TERAI
(KIND OF —) VANALLEN
(MACHINE —) SWIFTER
(MINERAL —) RANGE
(PACKHORSE'S —) WANTY
(PART OF —) TIP HOLE FRAME
PANEL PRONG BUCKLE FILLER
KEEPER LINING PIPING TONGUE
STITCHING
(TREE —) BERM BERME
(PL.) BALTEI
(PREF.) ZON(O)
BELTED ZONATE GIRDLED
CINCTURED
(— WITH WHITE) SHEETED
BELUGA HUSE HUSO HAUSEN
MARSOON WHITEFISH
BELUS (BROTHER OF —) AGENOR
(FATHER OF —) NEPTUNE
POSEIDON
(MOTHER OF —) LIBYA EURYNOME

(SON OF —) DANAUS CEPHEUS AEGYPTUS

BELVEDERE GAZEBO LOOKOUT

BELVIDERA (FATHER OF —) PRIULI

   (HUSBAND OF —) JAFFIER

BELVIDERE MIRADOR

BEMIRE DAG SOIL JARBLE

BEMOAN RUE MEAN MOAN SIGH WEEP MOURN PLAIN BEWAIL LAMENT DEPLORE

BEMUSE SOT BULL DAZE AMUSE

BEMUSED DOPY DOPEY PIXILATED MOONSTRUCK

BENAIAH (FATHER OF —) JEHOIADA

   (SON OF —) PELATIAH

BENCH PEW BANC BANK BENK BERM BINK DAIS DEAS FORM MESA SEAT SILL STEP TRAM BASIN BASON BERME BREAK CARIN CHAIR FORME JUDGE PLANK STALL STOOL BANCUS BANKER SCONCE SEDILE SETTEE SETTLE SITTER COUNTER DRESSER REPOSAL SHAMBLE SITTING TRESTLE TRIBUNE ALEBENCH

   (— FOR DAIRY TUBS) TRAM

   (— FOR KNEADING DOUGH) BREAK

   (CHURCH —) PEW

   (KNEELING —) PRIEDIEU

   (OUTDOOR —) EXEDRA EXHEDRA

   (PLAYER'S —) WOOD

   (ROWER'S —) BANK THOFT ZYGON THWART

   (SHOEMAKER'S —) FORME

   (TAILOR'S —) SHOPBOARD

   (WORKMAN'S —) SIEGE

BEND BOW ESS NID NIP PLY SAG SET SNY WIN WRY ABOW ARCH BENT BOOL BUCK COPE CURB DOME FAUD FLEX FOLD GENU HOOK KINK LEAN LOUT PLOY RUMP TURN VENT WEEP ANGLE BATON BIGHT BREAK COUCH COUDE COURB CRANK CRIMP CRINK CROOK CULGE CURVE DROOP FLECT FRESE HINGE HUNCH INBOW KNEEL PLASH PLICA QUIRL ROUND SCRAG SKELP SLANT STOOP TREND TWINE TWIST BOUGHT BUCKLE CAMBER CONVEX COTICE CROUCH SPRING COMPASS FLEXURE RECLINE GENUFLECT

   (— IN) INFLECT

   (— IN HANDRAIL) RAMP

   (— IN PIPE) TRAP DIPTRAP

   (— IN REVERENCE) PROSTRATE

   (— IN SHIP'S TIMBER) SNY

   (— KNEE) KNUCKLE

   (RIVER —) OXBOW

   (SUFF.) FLECT(ION) FLEX(ION)

BENDER BUM JAG LEG BUST KNEE TEAR DRUNK SPREE BRIDGE WHOPPER GUZZLING SIXPENCE BRANNIGAN INFLECTOR

BENDING BOW SAG KNEE KNOT PLIE CROOK CURVE LITHE TWIST PLIANT SUPPLE TWISTY ANFRACT FLEXION HOGGING SINUOUS BUCKLING FLECTION

   (— DOWNWARD) RECLINATE

   (— OF ROCK) DRAG

(BALLET —) PLIE

(PREF.) SPHINGO

BENDLETS FRET

BENDY TREE MIRO MAHOE

BENEATH ALOW ANETH BELOW LOWER UNDER ANEATH

   (PREF.) HYPO INFRA SUB

BENEDICITE BENISON CANTICLE

BENEDICT NEOGAMIST

BENEDICTINE CLUNIAC CAMALDOLESE TIRONENSIAN

BENEDICTION ABOT AMEN ABOTH NANDI AMIDAH BROCHO PRAYER BENISON BERAKAH BLESSING

BENEFACTION ALMS BOON GIFT PRESENT DONATION GRATUITY

BENEFACTOR AGENT ANGEL DONOR FRIEND HELPER PATRON SAVIOR MAECENAS PROMOTER

BENEFICE FEE FEU FEUD FIEF FAVOR SCARF CURACY LIVING BENEFIT CANONRY PRELACY RECTORY TOTQUOT DONATIVE KINDNESS SINECURE VICARAGE PLURALITY

BENEFICENCE BOON GIFT GRACE BOUNTY CHARITY GOODNESS KINDNESS

BENEFICENT KINDLY AMIABLE BENEFIC GRACIOUS

BENEFICIAL GOOD USEFUL HEALTHY HELPFUL BONITARY SALUTARY SANATIVE SINGULAR AVAILABLE BENIGNANT DESIRABLE ENJOYABLE HEALTHFUL LUCRATIVE REWARDING WHOLESOME PROFITABLE

BENEFICIARY HEIR USER DONEE CESTUI CESTUY USUARY VASSAL LEGATEE FEUDATORY

   (SUFF.) EE

BENEFIT AID USE BOON BOOT GAIN GIFT GOOD HELP PERK PROW SAKE AVAIL BOOST FRUIT SELTH STEAD VISIT ASSIST BEHALF BEHOOF BETTER FRINGE PROFIT SALUTE USANCE ADVANCE BESPEAK CONCERT DESERVE IMPROVE SERVICE UTILITY BEFRIEND INTEREST

   (— SUCCESSFULLY) FLY

BENEVOLENCE JEN BOUNTY GOODNESS GOODWILL HUMANITY

BENEVOLENT GOOD KIND BENIGN KINDLY LOVING AMIABLE LIBERAL GENEROUS AVUNCULAR BENIGNANT ALTRUISTIC PROPITIOUS HUMANITARIAN PHILANTHROPIC

   (WEAKLY —) GOODYGOODY

BENHANAN (FATHER OF —) SHIMON

BEN HUR (AUTHOR OF —) WALLACE

   (CHARACTER IN —) HUR IRAS JUDAH ESTHER TIRZAH MESSALA BALTHASAR SIMONIDES

BENIGN BOON GOOD KIND MILD BLAND SWEET TRINE GENIAL GENTLE AFFABLE BENEFIC BENEDICT GRACIOUS INNOCENT SALUTARY FAVORABLE WHOLESOME

BENIGNANT KIND BLAND GENIAL LIBERAL GRACIOUS MERCIFUL

BENIN (CAPITAL OF —) PORTONOVO

   (TOWN IN —) COTONOU

BENISON BOON BENEDICTION

BENJAMIN BENZOIN

   (FATHER OF —) HARIM JACOB BILHAN

   (MOTHER OF —) RACHEL

   (SON OF —) ARD EHI BELA GERA ROSH ASHBEL BECHER HUPPIM MUPPIM NAAMAN

BENNET CLOVEWORT

BENNISEED SESAME

BENO TUBA

BENT AIM BOW SET BIAS CAST CURB GIFT TURN BANDY BOUND BOWED BOWLY COUDE COURB CRANK CRUMP FLAIR HUMOR KNACK LURCH PRONE SQUAT SWING TASTE TREND AKIMBO ANLAGE BENNET BIASED BRACED COURBE COURSE CURVED DOGLEG ENERGH GENIUS HOOKED INTENT LIKING NECKED SQUINT SWAYED TALENT ADUNCAL ARCUATE BUCKLED CROOKED CURVANT EMBOWED FLEXION FLEXURE IMPETUS INTENSE LEANING LEVELED PRONATE PURPOSE STOOPED TENSION ADUNCOUS APTITUDE ARCUATED CRUMPLED DECLINED FLECTION IMMINENT INFLEXED PENCHANT REFLEXED TENDENCY

   (— AT THE END) HAMATE HOGGED GRYPANIAN

   (— DOWNWARD) BOWED DECURVED INCUMBENT RECLINATE

   (— IN) INCAVATE

   (— INWARD) ADUNC

   (— OF MIND) GEME AFFECTION

   (EASILY —) LITHY

   (NATURAL —) SWING

   (SPECIAL —) VERVE

   (PREF.) ANKYL(O) CAMPTO CURVI CYPH(O) CYRT(O) SCOLIO

BEN-TEAK NANDI NANAWOOD

BENT-GRASS FIBRIN REDTOP

BENUMB NIP DAZE DUNT NUMB STUN CHILL DAVER DOZEN SCRAM SHRAM CUMBER DEADEN PERISH STOUND BINOMEN FRETISH FRETIZE STIFFEN STUPEFY TORPEDO TORPEFY

BENUMBED CHILL SCRAM ASLEEP CLUMSE CLUMSY FROZEN TORPID CLUMPST SHRAMMED

BENUMBING LEADEN

BENVENUTO CELLINI (CHARACTER IN —) POMPEO TERESA ASCANIO CELLINI BALDUCCI SALVIATA BENVENUTO FIERAMOSCA

   (COMPOSER OF —) BERLIOZ

BENZAYDA (LOVER OF —) OZWY

BENZENE PHENE BENZIN BENZOL PHENENE

   (SUFF.) PHEN(E)

BENZINE

   (PREF.) PHEN(O)

BENZOIN BENJOIN LINDERA BENJAMIN FIXATIVE

   (SUFF.) OIN

BEOR (SON OF —) BELA BALAAM

BEOWULF (AUTHOR OF —) UNKNOWN

   (CHARACTER IN —) WIGLAF BEOWULF GRENDEL HIGELAC UNFERTH AESCHERE HONDSCIO HROTHGAR

BEQUEATH GIVE WILL ENDOW LEAVE OFFER BESTOW COMMIT DEMISE DEVISE LEGATE QUETHE BEQUEST COMMEND TRANSMIT

BEQUEST GIFT WILL LEGACY BEQUEATH HERITAGE PITTANCE ENDOWMENT BENEFACTION

BERACHIAH (SON OF —) ASAPH

BERAIAH (FATHER OF —) SHIMHI

BERATE JAW NAG DRUB LASH RAIL ABUSE BASTE CHIDE SCOLD SCORE SLATE REVILE CENSURE REPROVE UPBRAID CHASTISE

BERBER RIF RIFF KABYL SHLUH KABYLE SHILHA HARATIN MZABITE SHILLUH HARRATIN MOZABITE

   (— CHIEF) CAID

BERCEUSE CRADLESONG WIEGENLIED

BEREAVE ROB STRIP WIDOW DIVEST SADDEN DEPRIVE DESPOIL

BEREAVED ORB BEREFT VIDUOUS WIDOWED DESOLATE

BEREAVEMENT ORBITY ORBITUDE VIDUATION

BERECHIAH (SON OF —) ASAPH MESHULLAM ZECHARIAH

BEREFT ORB LORN LOST POOR QUIT WIDOW ORBATE FORLORN FORFAIRN DESTITUTE

BERG FLOE BARROW ICEBERG FLOEBERG

BERGAMOT BOSE BERGAMA BURGAMOT

BERGERE SEAT

BERGYLT ROSEFISH

BERI (FATHER OF —) ZOPHAH

BERIAH (FATHER OF —) ASHER EPHRAIM

BERIBERI KAKKE

BERITH BRIS BRISS BRITH

BERM BERME LISIERE HEELPATH

BERMUDA PETREL CAHOW

BERNICE (FATHER OF —) HEROD

BERRY BAY DEW HAW ALEY BEAT CRAN POHA RASP BACCA BLACK CUBEB FRUIT GRAIN GRAPE LANSA MOUND SALAL SAVIN BURROW LANSAT LANSEH SABINE THRESH CURRANT ETAERIO HILLOCK ACROSARC ALLSPICE COWBERRY DEWBERRY HAWEBAKE PERSIMMON POKEBERRY SASKATOON PEPPERCORN SHEEPBERRY POMEGRANATE

   (ACID —) CURRANT

   (COFFEE —) CHERRY

   (DRIED —) PASA

   (JUMPER —) ABHAL

   (LAUREL —) BAY

   (POISONOUS —) BANEBERRY

   (PREF.) BACCI COCC(I)(O)

BERRY-LIKE BACCATE ACINIFORM

BERTH BED JOB BUNK DOCK SLIP SOPT CABIN PLACE UPPER BILLET OFFICE SECURE LODGING

MOORING SLIPWAY POSITION ANCHORAGE
BERTHA (FATHER OF —) CARIBERT
(HUSBAND OF —) PEPIN HEREWARD
(SON OF —) CHARLES
BERYL EMERALD AEROIDES HELIODOR GOSHENITE MORGANITE AQUAMARINE
BERYLLIA GLUCINA GLUCINE
BERYLLIUM GLUCINUM
BESEECH ASK BEG BID CRY SUE WOO PRAY CRAVE HALSE PLEAD PRESS ADJURE APPEAL OBTEST CONJURE ENTREAT IMPLORE SOLICIT IMPETRATE OBSECRATE
BESET PLY SET SIT BEGO SAIL STUD ALLOT BELAY BIGAN HARRY PRESS SIEGE SPEND STEAD ASSAIL ATTACK HARASS INFEST OBSESS WAYLAY ARRANGE BESIEGE OVERSET PERPLEX BLOCKADE ENCUMBER ENTHRONG OBSTRUCT SURROUND BELEAGUER
(— WITH DIFFICULTIES) SCABROUS
BESHOW SKIL CUDDY CUDDEN CUDDIE BADDOCK COALFISH SKILFISH
BESIDE BY HEAR INBY NEXT ALONG ANENT ASIDE FORBY ABREAST AGAINST FORNENT ADJACENT FORNENST
(— ONE ANOTHER) ABREAST
(— ONESELF) FEY
(PREF.) EPH EPI PAR(A)
BESIDES BY TO AND BUT TOO YET ALSO ELSE MORE OVER PLUS THEN UNTO WITH ABOVE AGAIN FORBY SUPRA BESIDE BEYOND EXCEPT FORBYE WITHAL THERETO WITHOUT LIKEWISE MOREOVER
(PREF.) EPH EPI PROS
BESIEGE GIRD GIRT BELAY BELIE BESET SIEGE STORM ATTACK OBSESS OBSIDE PESTER PLAGUE COMPASS SOLICIT SURROUND BELEAGUER
BESMEAR RAY BALM DAUB SOIL APPLY COVER GRIME GRUFT MUDDY SLAKE SMEAR SULLY TAINT BEDAUB PLATCH BESLIME SMOTHER BESMIRCH BESLUBBER
BESMIRCH TAR DASH SLUR SOIL SMEAR SULLY TAINT SLURRY SMIRCH ASPERSE BLACKEN DRAGGLE TURPIFY DISCOLOR
BESMIRCHED MACULATE MACULATED
BESMUT CROCK
BESOM COW MAP DRAB BISME BROOM SWEEP SLOVEN HEATHER
BESOT DULL ASOTE ASSOT MUDDLE STUPID STUPEFY BEFUDDLE
BESOTTED BEDAZED DRUNKEN INFATUATED
BESPANGLE DOT STAR STUD ADORN JEWEL INVENT SPRINKLE
BESPATTER BLOT DASH JAUP SOIL SPOT MUDDY PLASH STAIN SULLY BEGARY SPARGE ASPERSE SCATTER SMOTTER REPROACH SPRINKLE

BESPEAK CITE HINT SHOW ARGUE IMPLY ORDER SPEAK TRYST ACCOST ATTEST ENGAGE STEVEN ADDRESS ARRANGE BENEFIT BETOKEN DISCUSS EXCLAIM RESERVE FORETELL INDICATE
BESPECKLE DASH
BESPECTACLED SPECCY
BESPRINKLE DROP SHED POWDER ASPERSE BESTREW BESPRING SPRINKLE BEQUIRTLE
BEST O ACE BEAT GOOD LACE MOST PICK TOPS WALE CREAM ELITE EXCEL PRIZE WORST CHOICE DEFEAT FINEST FLOWER OUTWIT SUNDAY TIPTOP UTMOST ARISTOS CONQUER GARLAND LARGEST OPTIMUM PALMARY DAMNDEST GREATEST KOHINOOR OUTMATCH OUTSTRIP POSSIBLE TOPNOTCH VANQUISH
(SUNDAY —) BRAWS
(PREF.) ARIST(O)
BESTIAL LOW VILE WILD BRUTE FERAL PRONE BRUTAL FILTHY BEASTLY BRUTISH INHUMAN SENSUAL BARBARIC BELLUINE DEPRAVED
BESTIR STIR AWAKE SHIFT STEER AROUSE HUSTLE
(— ONESELF) LEG
BEST MAN PARANYMPH
BESTOW ADD PUT USE CAST DEAL DOTE GIVE SEND STOW TAKE WARE ALLOT ALLOW APPLY AWARD BESET GRANT INFER LODGE PLACE SPEND THOLE WREAK ACCORD BETEEM CONFER DEMISE DEVOTE DIVIDE DONATE DOTATE EMPLOY ENTAIL ESTATE EXTEND IMPART IMPOSE RENDER SHOWER COLLATE COMMEND DISPOSE ENLARGE EROGATE INDULGE INSTATE PARTAKE PRESENT QUARTER TRIBUTE BEQUEATH
(— LAVISHLY) HEAP
(— UPON) GIFT
BESTOWAL DOLE DISPOSAL COLLATION LARGITION
(— OF PRAISE) ACCOLADE
BESTOWED GIVEN
BESTRIDE HORSE STRIDE STRADDLE OVERSTRIDE
BET GO UP BAS BOX LAY PUT SET VIE WAD ANTE BACK BRAG CHIP GAGE HOLD JACK NOIR PAIR PLAY PLOT PUNT RISK WAGE BOUND CARRE HEDGE ROUGE SAVER SPORT STAKE WAGER GAMBLE HAZARD IMPAIR MANQUE MILIEU PLEDGE DERNIER PREMIER ACCUMULATOR
(— AGAINST) MILK COPPER
(— AT LONG ODDS) SKINNER
(— BOLDLY) BLUFF
(— CHIP) CHECK
(FARO —) SLEEPER
(HEDGING —) SAVER
(MULTIPLE —) PARLAY
(POKER —) BLIND

(RACE —) WIN SHOW PLACE DOUBLE EXACTA PARLAY TRIPLE TRIFECTA
(RACING —) WIN SHOW PLACE DOUBLE EXACTA PARLAY TRIPLE PERFECTA QUINELLA TRIFECTA
(UP THE —) RAISE
BETA AND GAMMA GUARDS
BETA-BLOCKER TIMOLOL
BETAKE GO GET HIE MOVE TAKE APPLY CATCH GRANT ASSUME COMMIT REMOVE REPAIR RESORT COMMEND JOURNEY WITHDRAW
(— ONESELF) BUN HIT BOUN MARK PIKE TEEM AVOID FOUND HAUNT REFER TRUSS YIELD
(— ONESELF TO MILL) SUE
BETEL PAN IKMO ITMO SERI SIRI SIRIH PINANG PUPULO
BETEL LEAF PAN BUYO PAUN PAWNE
BETEL NUT BONGA BONYA BUNGA SUPARI
BETHABARA NOIBWOOD GREENHEART
BETHEL BETHESDA
BETHINK TAKE THINK ADVISE DEVISE RECALL REFLECT CONSIDER REMEMBER RECOLLECT
(— ONE'S SELF) MIN MINE UMBETHINK
BETHLEHEM BEDLAM
BETHROOT TRILLIUM
BETHUEL (DAUGHTER OF —) REBEKAH
(FATHER OF —) NAHOR
(MOTHER OF —) MILCAH
(UNCLE OF —) ABRAHAM
BETHUMP POUND PUMMEL LOUNDER
BETIDE HAP TIDE BEFIT OCCUR TRITE WORTH BECOME BEFALL CHANCE HAPPEN BETOKEN PRESAGE
BETIMES ANON RATH SOON EARLY RATHE TIMEOUS SPEEDILY FORTHWITH
BETOKEN MARK NOTE SHOW SIGN AUGUR TOKEN ASSERT BETIDE DENOTE EVINCE IMPORT SHADOW BESPEAK EXPRESS OBLIQUE PORTEND PRESAGE SIGNIFY FOREBODE FORESHOW INDICATE
BETONY BROOMWORT
BETRAY BLAB BLOW BOIL GULL SELL SHOP SILE SING SPOT TELL TRAY UNDO WRAY ABUSE CROSS FALSE PEACH ROUND SPILL SPLIT SWICK SWIKE ACCUSE BEWRAY DELUDE DESCRY DESERT QUATCH REVEAL SEDUCE SNITCH SQUEAL BEGUILE DECEIVE FALSIFY MISLEAD PROMOTE TRAITOR DISCLOSE DISCOVER
(— CONFIDENCES) SPILL
BETRAYAL RAP ABUSE ACCUSE TREASON GIVEAWAY PRODITION
BETRAYER RAT JUDAS SKUNK SEDUCER TRAITOR DERELICT RECREANT SQUEALER
BETRAYING TELLTALE
BETROTH AFFY EARL TOKEN TROTH TRUTH ASSURE ENGAGE ENSURE

PLEDGE PLIGHT ESPOUSE PROMISE AFFIANCE CONTRACT DESPOUSE HANDFAST
BETROTHAL ESPOUSAL HANDFAST
BETROTHED SURE VOWED ASSURED ENGAGED HANDFAST INTENDED COMBINATE
(AUTHOR OF —) MANZONI
(CHARACTER IN —) LUCIA RENZO RODRIGO ABBONDIO BORROMEO CRISTOFORO
BETTA PLAKAT
BETTER AID TOP BEET MEND AMEND EMEND EXCEL SAFER WISER BIGGER EXCEED REFORM ADVANCE CHOICER CORRECT GREATER IMPROVE PROMOTE RECTIFY RELIEVE SUPPORT SURPASS EMINENCE INCREASE SUPERIOR
(— A SCORE) BREAK
(— THAN ORDINARY) EXTRA
BETTING ACTION GAMBLING
(— ARRANGEMENT) PERM
(— SYSTEM) PAROLI ALEMBERT
BETTOR ORALER
BETTY JENNY COTBETTY JOCRISSE MOLLYCOT WIFECARL
BETWEEN AMID EMEL AMELL AMONG ENTRE TWEEN YTWYN ATWEEN ATWIXT TWEESH AVERAGE BETWIXT
(PREF.) DI INTER INTRA
BEUDANITE CORKITE
BEVEL BLOW CANT CONE EDGE PUSH REAM ANGLE BEARD BEZEL MITER MITRE SLANT SLOPE SNAPE SPLAY ASLANT CIPHER RHYMER CHAMFER INCLINE OBLIQUE
(— EDGES) BEARD
(WITHOUT —) FLAT
BEVERAGE ADE ALE AVA CUP NOG POP RUM SAP TEA BEER BREW CHIA GROG MABI MATE MEAD MILK NIPA SODA WHIG WINE CHOCA CIDER CLARY COCOA DRAFT DRINK JULEP LAGER LEBAN MORAT MULSE NEGUS PUNCH SHRUB SMASH TREAT TWIST WATER BISHOP COFFEE EGGNOG LIQUID LIQUOR NECTAR PORTER SPRUCE TISWIN BUNNELL CASSINA CORDIAL LIMEADE OENOMEL POTABLE STEPONY TULAPAI ALEBERRY COCKTAIL LEMONADE LIBATION PIQUETTE POTATION SANGAREE SWITCHEL BADMINTON CALIBOGUS CHOCOLATE GINGERADE ORANGEADE POMPERKIN SOMETHING
(— FROM COW'S MILK) KEFIR KEPHIR
(— FROM PEPPERS) KAVA KAVAKAVA
(— FROM SAP) TUBA
(— OF BUTTERMILK AND WATER) BLAND
(— OF CHAMPAGNE) POPE
(— OF GODS) NECTAR
(— OF HONEY AND WATER) HYDROMEL METHEGLIN
(— OF HOT MILK) POSSET
(— OF PORT WINE) BISHOP

(— OF VINEGAR AND WATER) POSCA
(— OF WINE AND WATER) SPRITZER
(ALCOHOLIC —) DEW ARAK SAKE SAKI ARRAK BASIG SHRUB SNAPS STUFF ARRACK FIREWATER STIMULANT
(COLA —) DOPE
(EFFERVESCENT —) FIZZ
(FERMENTED —) BASI KAVA KUMYS KUMISS
(FRUIT —) BEVERAGE
(INSIPID —) WASH
(JAPANESE —) SAKE SAKI
(MEXICAN —) TEPACHE
(POLYNESIAN —) AVA KAVA
(WEAK —) LAP
(PL.) WAIPIRO
BEVY HERD PACK COVEY DROVE FLOCK GROUP SWARM FLIGHT SCHOOL COMPANY
BEWAIL CRY RUE WEY KEEN MOAN RAME SIGH WAIL WEEP MOURN PLAIN BEMOAN GRIEVE LAMENT PLAINT SORROW THROPE DEPLORE COMPLAIN
BEWARE WAR CAVE GARE HEED SHUN TENT WARD AVOID SPEND ESCHEW WARNING
BEWILDER FOG FOX MAR BEAT DAZE FOIL GAUM MAZE STUN ABASH ADDLE AMAZE AMUSE DEAVE DIZZY BAFFLE REMIST BEMUSE BOTHER DAZZLE DUDDER MOIDER MOMBLE MUDDLE PUZZLE WANDER WILDER BUFFALO BUMBAZE CONFUSE FLASKER MYSTIFY NONPLUS PERPLEX STAGGER STUPEFY ASTONISH CONFOUND DISTRACT ENTANGLE OVERMUSE SQUATTER SURPRISE
(PREF.) PLAZO
BEWILDERED MAR ASEA LOST MANG WILL AGAPE ATSEA DAZED MAZED MUZZY BUSHED MAPPED BEMAZED STUPENT WILSOME CONFUSED HELPLESS WILLYARD PERPLEXED
BEWILDERMENT AWE FOG DAZE MISMAZE STICKLE AMAZEMENT CONFUSION PERPLEXITY
BEWITCH HEX WISH BLINK CHARM MAGIC OBEAH SPELL WITCH ENAMOR ENTICE GLAMOR GRIGRI HOODOO STRIKE THRILL ATTRACT BEDEVIL DELIGHT ENCHANT GLAMOUR ENSORCEL FORSPEAK GREEGREE OVERLOOK
BEWITCHED RAPT ENRAPT HAGGED
BEWITCHING SIREN
BEYOND BY FREE OVER YOND ABOVE ASIDE AYOND FORBY ULTRA BEHIND BEYANT YONDER BENEATH BESIDES FORTHBY FURTHER OUTGATE PASSING WITHOUT OVERMORE SUPERIOR HEREAFTER
(— CONTROL) MASTERLESS
(— DOUBT) ASSURED
(— HOPE) DESPERATE
(— ORDINARY METHODS) AFIELD
(— THE MARK) GONE

(— THE MOUNTAINS) TRAMONTANE
(— THE SEA) ULTRAMARINE
(— THIS) STILL
(GO —) OVERSHOOT
(PREF.) EXTRA HYPER META OVER PARA PERI PRETER SUPER TRANS ULTRA
BEYOND HUMAN POWER
(AUTHOR OF —) BJORNSON
(CHARACTER IN —) SANG CLARA ELIAS HANNA ADOLPH RACHAEL ROBERTS
BEZALEEL (FATHER OF —) URI
BEZANT SOLIDUS
BEZEL RIM TOP EDGE OUCH SEAL BEVIL BEZIL CROWN FACET CLIATON FLANGE MARQUISE TEMPLATE
BEZER (FATHER OF —) ZOPHAH
BEZIQUE PENCHANT
BEZOAR GOATSTONE HIPPOLITH
B-GIRL SITTER
BHAKTA BHAGAVATA
BHANG BANG BENG BENJ HEMP HASHISH
BHARAL TUR HALL NAHOOR BURRHEL
BHARTRIHARI (BROTHER OF —) VIKHAMADITYA
BHIKSHU GELONG
BHIMA (FATHER OF —) VAYU PANDU
(MOTHER OF —) KUNTI PRITHA
BHUTAN (ASSEMBLY OF —) TSONGDU
(CAPITAL OF —) THIMPHU
(COIN OF —) CHETRUM
(CURRENCY OF —) PAISA RUPEE CHETRUM NGULTRUM
(LANGUAGE OF —) DZONGKHA
(MONEY OF —) NGULTRUM
(RIVER OF —) MACHU MANAS AMOCHU
BHUTAN PINE KAIL
BIANCA (HUSBAND OF —) FAZIO LEONTIO
(SISTER OF —) KATHERINE
BIANNUAL BIYEARLY
BIANOR (FATHER OF —) TIBERIS
(MOTHER OF —) MANTO
BIAS PLY WRY AWRY BENT CANT SWAY WARP AMISS COLOR FAVOR POISE SLANT SLOPE SWING TWIST BIGOTRY INCLINE OBLIQUE SUGGEST CLINAMEN COLORING DIAGONAL TENDENCY PREJUDICE PROCEDURE SPECTACLE
(— IN NEWS REPORTING) PLUGOLA
(BROTHER OF —) MELAMPUS
(FATHER OF —) AMYTHAON
(MOTHER OF —) IDOMENE
(WIFE OF —) PERO IPHIANASSA
BIASED SLANT ANGLED COLORED OBLIQUE PARTIAL SLANTED
(— ONE) BIGOT
BIB SIP BRAT POUT APRON BLAIN DRINK BRASSY FEEDER TIPPLE TUCKER BAVETTE
(CHILD'S —) BISHOP
(LEATHER —) DICK
BIBLE BOOK ITALA VULGATE SCRIPTURE

(— TEXT) MIKRA MIQRA
(BOOK OF —) EX CHR COL COR DAN EPH GAL GEN HAB HAG HEB HOS JER JOB KIN LAM LEV MAL MIC NAH NEH NUM PET REV ROM SAM TIM ACTS AMOS CANT DEUT EZEK EZRA JOEL JOHN JUDE JUDG LUKE MARK MATT OBAD PHIL PROV RUTH SONG ZECH ZEPH HOSEA JAMES JONAH KINGS MICAH NAHUM PETER THESS TITUS DANIEL ECCLES ESTHER EXODUS HAGGAI ISAIAH JOSHUA JUDGES PHILEM PSALMS ROMANS SAMUEL EZEKIEL GENESIS HEBREWS MALACHI MATTHEW NUMBERS OBADIAH TIMOTHY JEREMIAH NEHEMIAH PHILEMON PROVERBS CANTICLES EPHESIANS GALATIANS LEVITICUS ZECHARIAH ZEPHANIAH CHRONICLES COLOSSIANS REVELATION CORINTHIANS DEUTERONOMY PHILIPPIANS ECCLESIASTES LAMENTATIONS THESSALONIANS
(SYRIAC VERSION OF —) PESHITO
BIBLE LEAF COSTMARY
BIBULOUS DRINKING BIBACIOUS
BICEPS HAMSTRING
BICKER JAR WAR BOWL SPAR TIFF ARGUE BRAWL CAVIL FIGHT SCRAP ASSAIL ATTACK BATTLE CONTEND DISPUTE PICKEER QUARREL QUIBBLE WRANGLE PETTIFOG SKIRMISH SQUABBLE
BICKERN ANVIL BEAKIRON
BICUSPID PREMOLAR
BICYCLE BIKE QUAD CORGI CORGY CYCLE HOBBY MOUNT STEED WHEEL JIGGER ORNARY SAFETY TANDEM ORDINAR TRIPLET ORDINARY ROADSTER TENSPEED
(— FOR TWO) TANDEM
(— MANEUVER) WHEELIE
(PART OF —) ARM LUG RIM CLIP FORK POST RACK RING SEAT STAY STEM TIRE CHAIN GUARD PEDAL SHIFT SPOKE FENDER HANGER SADDLE DOWNTUBE SPROCKET CHAINWHEEL DERAILLEUR
(PLACE WHERE —S ARE SERVICED) CYCLERY
(STATIONARY —) EXERCYCLE
BID GO BEG NAP BEDE BODE CALL GIVE HEST HIST PRAY TELL WISH CHEAP CLEPE FRAGE OFFER ORDER ADJURE CHARGE DIRECT ENJOIN INVITE REVEAL SIMPLE SUMMON TENDER BALANCE CHEAPEN COMMAND DECLARE DROPVIE ENTREAT PROFFER ANNOUNCE PROCLAIM PROPOSAL
(— ADIEU) TEACH
(— AT AUCTION) CRY
(— IN CARDS) CUE FROG JUMP PASS SKIP SOLO FRAGE GRAND NULLO SHIFT BOSTON DEFEND DEMAND DENIAL DOUBLE SMUDGE BLUCHER COMMAND SHUTOUT SUPPORT CONTRACT REDOUBLE SCHMEISS
(FIRST —) OPENER OPENERS
(MAKE FIRST —) OPEN
(SEALED —) TICKET

BIDDING BEHEST AUCTION BIDDANCE DIRECTIVE
BIDE FACE STAY WAIT ABIDE AWAIT DWELL TARRY WATCH ENDURE REMAIN SUFFER SOJOURN CONTINUE TOLERATE
BIDENS CUCKOLD MANZANILLA
BIDET SITZBAD INSESSION
BIDRI VIDRY BIDDERY TUTENAG
BIENNIAL TRIETERIC
BIER BEAR PYRE FRAME GRAVE HANDY HORSE TABUT COFFIN HEARSE LITTER SUPPORT FERETORY FERETRUM
BIFURCATION WYE FORK SPLIT BRANCH CROTCH CRUTCH FORKING DIVISION DICHOTOMY
BIG FAT BARO BOLD HUGE MUCH VAST BULKY CHIEF GAUCY GRAND GREAT GROSS HUSKY LARGE GAUCIE MIGHTY BIGGISH BUMPING EMINENT HUMMING LEADING MASSIVE POMPOUS UPRIGHT VIOLENT BOASTFUL BOUNCING ENORMOUS GENEROUS GIGANTIC IMPOSING PLUMPING PREGNANT SLAPPING SWANKING SWAPPING THUMPING
(— C) CANCER
(— WITH YOUNG) FULL GRAVID
(FAIRLY —) TIDY
(MARVELOUSLY —) TREMENDOUS
(VERY-) SKELPING SLASHING
(PREF.) MAGNI
BIGFOOT SASQUATCH
BIGHORN ARGAL AOUDAD ARGALI CIMARRON
BIGHT BAY BEND BITE COIL GULF LOOP ROVE ANGLE CURVE INLET NOOSE BOUGHT CORNER HOLLOW POCKET
BIGMOUTH BLAB
BIGNESS BULK
BIGOT CAFARD ZEALOT FANATIC MUMPSIMUS
BIGOTED BIASED NARROW HIDEBOUND ILLIBERAL SECTARIAN
BIGOTRY INTOLERANCE
BIGROOT MANROOT BITTERROOT
BIG SHOT HEAVY MUCKAMUCK
BIG SKY COUNTRY MONTANA
BIGWIG SWELL
BIKE (KIND OF —) MOTOR TRAIL
BIKINI TANGA
(TOPLESS —) MONOKINI
BILE BOIL GALL HUMP VENOM CHOLER GROWTH RANCOR ATRABILE MELANCHOLY
(PREF.) BILI CHOL(E)(O)
(SUFF.) CHOLIA CHOLY
BILGE PUMP SCUM BOUGE BULGE BILLAGE THURROCK
BILHAH (SON OF —) DAN NAPHTALI
BILHAN (FATHER OF —) JEDIAEL
BILIMBI CAMIAS KAMIAS CUCUMBER
BILINGUAL DIGLOT
BILIOUS GALLISH LIVERISH
BILIOUSNESS LIVER CHOLER
BILK DO GYP BALK DUPE HOAX CHEAT COZEN TRICK DELUDE FLEECE SWEDGE DECEIVE DEFRAUD SWINDLE

BILL ACT DUN GET LAW NEB NIB TAB BEAK CHIT CLAP GETT KITE NOTE PECK SHOT CHECK ENTRY LIBEL SCORE VISOR CARESS CHARGE DOCKET INDICT LAWING PECKER PICKAX POSTER STRIKE DERTRUM INVOICE LAMPOON MATTOCK PLACARD PROGRAM REMANET STATUTE BILLHOOK DOCUMENT HEADLAND INNOCENT PETITION TREASURY RECKONING ACCEPTANCE

(— OF ANCHOR) PEE PEAK

(— OF COMPLAINT) QUERELA

(— OF CREDIT) ANGEL

(— OF DIVORCE) GET GETT

(— OF EXCHANGE) SOLA HUNDI DEVISE

(— OF FARE) MENU CARTE

(— OF PARCELS) FACTURE

(ACCOMMODATION —) KITE

(COUNTERFEIT —S) STIFF

(DOLLAR —) BUCK SPOT SINGLE FROGSKIN

(POSTPONED —) REMANET

(REVOLUTIONARY —) ASSIGNAT

(TAVERN —) RECKONING

(10-DOLLAR —) TEN TENNER SAWBUCK

(100-DOLLAR —) CENTURY

(2-DOLLAR —) DEUCE

(5-DOLLAR —) FIN VEE FIVE FIVER

BILLET BAR GAD HUT LAY LOG LOOP NOTE PASS POST SPOT BERTH ENROL HOUSE LODGE ORDER SHIDE SPRAG STICK STRAP BALLOT BULLET COUPON ENROLL HARBOR LETTER LIBBET NOTICE TICKET BEARING EPISTLE MISSIVE POLLACK COALFISH DOCUMENT FIREWOOD ORNAMENT POSITION QUARTERS

(— SOLDIERS) CESS

BILLET-DOUX CAPON

BILLETING LIVERY

BILLFISH GAR LONGJAWS SAILFISH SPEARFISH

BILLFOLD WALLET NOTECASE

BILLHOOK BILL DHAW HOOK PAWPAW SLASHER SNAGGER SCIMITAR

BILLIARD (— STROKE) LAG

(KIND OF — SHOT) BANK CAROM

BILLIARD BALL IVORY

BILLIARD CUE MACE MAST

(TIP OF —) LEATHER

BILLIARDS PILLS TRUCKS

(— SHOT) CAROM

(LAWN —) TROCO

BILLIKEN MASCOT

BILLINGSGATE ABUSE SLAPDASH

BILLION MILLIARD

(PREF.) GIGA

BILLIONTH

(PREF.) BICRO NANO

BILL OF MARRIAGE (CHARACTER IN —) MILL FANNY SLOOK TOBIAS EDOARDO

(COMPOSER OF —) ROSSINI

BILLON BAIOC VELLON BAJOCCO

BILLOW SEA BLOW WAVE BULGE CLOUD FLOAT SURGE SWELL RESACA RIPPLE ROLLER WALLOW BREAKER UNDULATE

BILLY CAW CHAP CLUB GOAT MACE MATE BATON FANNY NEDDY CUDGEL FANNIE FELLOW BROTHER COMRADE BILLIKIN BILLYCAN BLUDGEON JACKSHAY BLACKJACK TRUNCHEON

BILLY BUDD (CHARACTER IN —) BUDD VERE BILLY CLAGGART

(COMPOSER OF —) BRITTEN

BILLYCOCK DERBY

BILSHAN (COMPANION OF —) ZERUBBABEL

BIMAH ALMEMAR ALMEMOR

BIMHAL (FATHER OF —) JAPHLET

BIN ARK BOX CUB GUM BING BONE CART CRIB VINA FRAME HUTCH KENCH PUNGI STALL STORE WAGON BASKET BUNKER GARNER HAMPER MANGER POCKET TROUGH WITHIN BLEACHER

(— FOR CEMENT) SILO

(— FOR FISH) KENCH

(— FOR GRAIN) ARK

BINARY HYDRIDE

BINATE DUAL DOUBLE PAIRED COUPLED TWOFOLD GEMINATE

BINAURAL DIOTIC

BIND JAM LAP TIE WAP EARL FAST FRAP GIRD GYVE HOLD HOOP JOIN KNIT KNOT LASH MAIL NAIL TAPE YERK BRACE CADGE CHAIN CINCH EDDER GIRTH SNAKE STICK STRAP TRUSS ATTACH BUNDLE COMMIT EMBIND ENGAGE FETTER FREEZE GARTER GIRDLE LIGATE OBLIGE PICKLE STRAIN SWATHE TETHER WRITHE ARTICLE ASTRAIN BANDAGE CONFINE EMBOUND ENCHAIN GRAPPLE SHACKLE SWADDLE ASTRINGE CONCLUDE FLIGHTER HANDFAST INNODATE LIGATURE OBLIGATE RESTRAIN

(— A FALCON) MAIL

(— BY LEASE) THIRL

(— BY OATH) SACRAMENT

(— BY PLEDGE) GAGE SWEAR

(— IN BUNDLE) KID BAVIN

(— INTO SHEAVES) GAVEL THRAVE

(— ONESELF) ADHERE

(— ROUND) WHIP

(— TOGETHER) LIME FAGOT SEIZE CEMENT FAGGOT ASTRINGE RELIGATE COLLIGATE

(— TO SECRECY) TILE

(— UP) KILT BAVIN TRUSS UPBAND ASTRICT REVOLVE

(— WINGS) PINION

(— WITH THREAD) OOP

(PREF.) SPHINGO

(SUFF.) SPHINX

BINDER BAND BEAM BOND CORD ROPE BALER COVER FRAME LEVER FILLET FOLDER GIRDER HEADER LIGNIN STAPLE TARMAC HAYBAND BONDSTONE BOOKMAKER

(— OF SAND-DUNES) MARRAM MARRUM

BINDING TAG BAND CORD GARD HARD LEAR ROPE TAPE YAPP COVER VALID CADDIS EDGING RIBBON BOUNDEN CADDICE GALLOON LAPPING MOUSING WEBBING FAITHFUL LIGATIVE LIGATORY STRINGENT OBLIGATORY

(— FAST) IRON

(— OF BOOK) BOCK FACE YAPP

(— OF GOLD) BISSET

(— ON DRESS) FENT

(SUFF.) DESIS

BINDLESTIFF BUM

BINDLE STIFF HOBO

BINDWEED BINE WIRE CREEPER TIEVINE BEARBIND BEARBINE BELLBINE BINEWEED CORNBIND HELLWEED MILKMAID WOODBINE WITHYWIND

BINE WIRE

BINGE BAT BOW HIT BLOW BUST SOAK TEAR TOOT TOPE BEANO PARTY SOUSE SPRAY SPREE CRINGE BLOWOFF CAROUSAL

(ON A —) ONATEAR

BINGO KENO BEANO LOTTO BRANDY SCREENO TOMBOLA

BINNACLE PYX BITTACLE

BINNUI (FATHER OF —) HENADAD

(SON OF —) NOADIAH

BINOCULARS GLASS

BINOMIAL DIONYM BINOMEN

BIOCHEMIST AMERICAN LI BERG CORI LOEB BLOCH BOYER DOISY KAMEN MOORE OCHOA SHEAR TATUM ASIMOV BEADLE CORDES SLOTTA WATSON ALSBERG AXELROD LIPMANN OSBORNE SCHALLY SHAFFER KORNBERG NORTHRUP NIRENBERG

ARGENTINIAN LELOIR

CANADIAN COLLIP

DANISH DAM

ENGLISH CHAIN KREBS PERUTZ PORTER SANGER HOPKINS MITCHELL

FRENCH MONOD DUCLAUX

GERMAN LYNEN LIPMANN

SWISS THEORELL

BIODEGRADABLE SOFT

BIOGEOGRAPHY CHOROLOGY

BIOGRAPHER PLUTARCH

AMERICAN DAY BEER COFFIN HENDRICK VANDOREN

ENGLISH CECIL ROWSE FORSTER DRINKWATER

ROMAN SUETONIUS

SCOTTISH BOSWELL LOCKHART

BIOGRAPHY BIO LIFE VITA MEMOIR ACCOUNT HISTORY RECOUNT PSYCHOGRAPH

(— OF A SORT) OBIT

(— OF SAINTS) HAGIOGRAPHA HAGIOGRAPHY

(KIND OF —) TELLALL

BIOLOGIST NATURALIST

AMERICAN EAST JUST LUTZ MAYR WALD BRONK CHILD CLARK LURIA MINOT PEARL SABIN SAGAN SHULL TYLER WOODS BAILEY BEADLE BUMPUS CARREL COTTAM FISHER JORDAN LITTLE OSBORN PALADE SPERRY WELLER CONKLIN EHRLICH HERRICK HERSHEY WETMORE CHAMBERS DELBRUCK DISABATO HARRISON SEDGWICK STOCKARD VISHNIAC

AUSTRALIAN BURNET

AUSTRIAN STEINACH

BELGIAN CLAUDE

CUBAN FINLAY

ENGLISH CRICK GEDDES HUXLEY MIVART SANGER BATESON COBBOLD KENDREW MEDAWAR ROMANES CUMMINGS MILSTEIN NICHOLSON ABERCROMBIE

FRENCH GIARD CARREL NOCARD BOUCHARD LEDANTEC

GERMAN WOLFF DRIESCH EHRLICH HAECKEL SPEMANN UEXKULL WEISMANN MUCKERMANN

IRISH ALLMAN

NORWEGIAN MJOEN

RUSSIAN BAER GURVICH LYSENKO MEDVEDEV METCHNIKOFF

SCOTTISH GEDDES THOMSON

SWISS ARBER

BIONIC (— HUMAN BEING) CYBORG

BIOPHORE BIOGEN PLASOME

BIOPLAST MICELLA MICELLE

BIOTITE MICA ANOMITE MEROXENE RUBELLAN

BIOTOPE STATION

BIPARTITE

(PREF.) DIPHY

BIPED DIPODE HINDQUARTERS

BIRCH COW BIRK CANE FLOG WHIP ALDER ALNUS CANOE SWISH BETULA BIRKEN TAWHAI HICKORY

BIRCHBARK CANOE

BIRD ANI DAW DOG JAY NUN PIE TIT TUI CHAT COOT CROW DOVE FOWL HERN IBIS JACK KAGU KITE KNOT LARK QUIT RUFF TERN TODY WING WREN BAKER BRANT CHUCK CLEAR COVEY EGRET FINCH FLIER FLYER GOOSE HOBBY JUNCO LARID LIVER PEWEE PEWIT RAVEN ROBIN SNIPE STILT SWIFT TEREK TURCO TWITE VIREO BULBUL DICKEY DIPPER DRIVER DRONGO DUCKER DUNLIN FALCON FINGER GROUSE GUINEA HOOPOE HOOTER JACANA JAEGER LINNET MARTEN MOCKER NESTER ORIOLE OSCINE PHOEBE PLOVER SHRIKE SILVAN SINGER SITTER SYLVAN THRUSH TROGON TURNIX VERDIN YAWPER ANTBIRD BABBLER BLUEJAY BUNTING BUSTARD BUZZARD CATBIRD CHIRPER COTINGA COURLAN FEATHER FLAPPER FLICKER FLIGGER FLOPPER GRACKLE HALCYON HORNERO HURGILA INCOMER IRRISOR JACAMAR JACKDAW KINGLET MINIVET MOULTER ORTOLAN PEACOCK PERCHER QUILLER REDWING SCRAPER SKINNER SKYLARK SPARROW SUNBIRD SWALLOW TANAGER TINAMOU TITLARK TOMFOOL WARBLER WAXWING WAYBUNG ACCENTOR AIRPLANE AMADAVAT ANNOTINE BLACKCAP BLACKNEB BLUEBIRD BOATBILL BOBOLINK BOBWHITE BUBBLING CAGELING CARINATE COCKBIRD COCORICO

DREPANID FERNBIRD FIREBIRD FIRETAIL GROSBEAK GRUIFORM IBISBILL JUVENILE KILLDEER KINGBIRD LOBEFOOT LONGSPUR OXPECKER PALMIPED PHEASANT PLUMIPED POORWILL PREACHER REDSTART SALTATOR SONGBIRD STARLING SURFBIRD SWAMPHEN TAPACOLO THRASHER THROSTLE TITMOUSE TREMBLER UMBRETTE WHINCHAT WOODCHAT WOODCOCK YEARBIRD COCKYOLLY CROSSBILL ROADRUNNER MOCKINGBIRD
(— CHASED BY HAWK) QUARRY
(— OF BRILLIANT PLUMAGE) TODY JALAP BARBET ORIOLE TROGON JACAMAR KIROMBO MINIVET TANAGER
(— OF INDIA) BAYA KALA SHAMA
(— OF OMEN) WAYBIRD
(— OF PREY) OWL HAWK KITE EAGLE ELANT GLEAD GLEDE STOOP EAGLET ELANET BUZZARD GOSHAWK STOOPER VULTURE ACCIPITER
(AFRICAN —) TAHA QUELEA TOURACO UMBRETTE NAPECREST
(AUSTRALIAN —) EMU ROA LORY ARARA LEIPOA BOOBOOK BUSTARD FIGBIRD WAYBUNG BELLBIRD LOWRIKEET LYREBIRD MANUCODE
(BIG-BEAKED —) BECARD HORNBILL
(CRESTED —) KAGU COPPY HOATZIN TOPKNOT
(CROCODILE —) TROCHIL
(DECOY —) CALL STOOL
(DIVING —) AUK LOON GREBE DARTER DOPPER DUCKER GRAYLING PLUNGEON
(EUROPEAN —) ANI DAW MEW QUA CIRL DARR KITE MALL MORO QUIS ROOK STAG WHIM YITE AMSEL BOONK GLEDE MAVIS MERLE OUSEL OUZEL SACER SAKER SERIN TARIN TEREK TERIN WHAUP AVOCET CUCKOO CUSHAT GAYLAG GODWIT MARTEN MERLIN MISSEL REDCAP WHEWER WINDLE WINNEL WRANNY BITTERN BUSTARD HAYBIRD KESTREL MOTACIL ORTOLAN SAKERET STARNEL WHISKEY WINNARD WITWALL BARGOOSE CHEPSTER DOTTEREL GARGANEY REDSTART WHEATEAR WHEYBIRD WHIMBREL WRANNOCK YOLDRING
(EXTINCT —) MOA DODO JIBI KIWI MAMO RUKH OFFBIRD
(FABULOUS —) FUM ROC FUNG HALCYON OOFBIRD WHISTLER
(FEMALE —) HEN JENNY
(FICTITIOUS —) JAYHAWK PHOENIX
(FISH-CATCHING —) OSPREY CRABIER
(FLEDGLING —) SQUAB
(FLIGHTLESS —) EMU GOR MOA DODO EYAS GORB GULL KAGU KIWI CALLOW GORLIN APTERYX GORLING NESTLER OSTRICH PENGUIN BUBBLING NESTLING
(FRIGATE —) IOA IWA
(FRUIT-EATING —) COLY

(GALLOWS —) HEMPY HEMPIE
(GAME —) QUAIL SNIPE COLIMA GROUSE INCOME FLAPPER INCOMER PHEASANT PARTRIDGE
(GREEN —) SIRGANG
(HAWAIIAN —) IO OO AVA IOA IWA OOA IIWI JIBI KOAE MAMO MOHO OMAO OOAA KAMAO PALILA
(HORN-HEADED —) KAMICHI
(INJURED —) CRIPPLE
(LARGEST —) LAMMERGEIER
(LIMICOLINE —) PRATINCOLE
(LONG-TOED —) JACANA
(MADAGASCAR —) KIROMBO
(MECHANICAL —) ORTHOPTER
(MYTHICAL —) FUM ROC GANZA SIMURG SIMURGH
(NEW ZEALAND —) KEA MOA OII ROA HUIA KAKA KIWI KOKO KUKU KULU PEHO RURU TITI WEKA POAKA KAKAPO KOKAKO KUKUPA APTERYX KORIMAKO MOREPORK NOTORNIS
(NIGHT —) OWL OWLET
(NOISY —) PIE MAGPIE
(PASSERINE —) QUIT FINCH SPARROW STARNEL SWALLOW SYLVIID DREPANID FALCONET FERNBIRD GRALLINA JACKBIRD OVENBIRD
(PERTAINING TO —S) OSCINE
(PISCATORY —) ERNE TERN
(RAPACIOUS —) SKUA JAEGER
(RASORIAL —) SCRATCHER
(RUNNING —) COURSER
(SAMOAN —) IAO
(SEA —) AUK ERN ERNE GONY GULL PINK SKUA SMEW TERN EIDER MURRE SOLAN FULMAR GANNET HAGDON OSPREY PETREL PUFFIN PELICAN SEAFOWL MURRELET MALLEMUCK
(SHORE —) REE RAIL SORA SNIPE STILT WADER AVOCET CURLEW PLOVER WILLET WRYBILL SHEATHBILL
(SHORT-TAILED —) BREVE
(SINGING —) LARK WREN PIPIT ROBIN VEERY VIREO CANARY LINNET MOCKER ORIOLE OSCINE SINGER THRUSH WARBLER FAUVETTE REDSTART NIGHTINGALE
(SMALL —) TIT TODY WREN DICKY PEGGY PIPIT TYDIE VIREO DICKEY LINNET SISKIN TOMTIT CREEPER SPARROW TITLARK COCORICO GNATSNAP PERCOLIN STARLING WHEATEAR
(SOUTH AMERICAN —) GUAN MINA MITU MYNA RARA TOCA BAKER CHAJA JOPIM TURCO BARBET BECARD CHUNGA TOUCAN CARIAMA OILBIRD BELLBIRD BOATBILL CARACARA GUACHARO HOACTZIN PUFFBIRD SCREAMER TAPACOLO TAPACULO TERUTERO
(STYLIZED —) DISTELFINK
(TROPICAL —) ANI GUAN KOAE TODY BOS'N BOSUN JALAP BARBET BECARD MOTMOT TROGON JACAMAR MANAKIN WIGTAIL LONGTAIL SALTATOR
(WADING —) HERN IBIS RAIL SORA CRANE HERON SNIPE STILT STORK

ARGALA AVOCET GODWIT JACANA LIMPKIN BOATBILL FLAMINGO SHOEBILL SHOEBIRD SANDERLING
(WILD —S) GALLINAE
(WITCH —) ANI
(YEAR-OLD —) ANNOTINE
(YOUNG —) EYA GULL PIPER CHEEPER FLAPPER NESTLER BIRDIKIN NESTLING
(PL.) AVIFAUNA POLYMYODI PRAECOCES
(PREF.) AVI ORNIS ORNITH(I)(O)
(SUFF.) ORNIS ORNITHES
BIRD BOLT BURBOLT QUARREL
BIRDBRAIN SIMP
BIRD CAGE AVIARY PINJRA VOLARY VOLERY PADDOCK
BIRDCATCHER FOWLER
BIRD CHERRY DOGWOOD EGGBERRY HACKWOOD HAGBERRY
BIRDLIFE ORNIS
BIRD-LIKE ORNITHOID
BIRDLIME GLUE LIME BELIME VISCUM BIRDGLUE
BIRD OF PARADISE APUS MANUCODE RIFLEBIRD
BIRD-REARING AVINCULTURE
BIRDS (AUTHOR OF —) ARISTOPHANES
(CHARACTER IN —) EPOPS TEREUS BASILEIA EUELPIDES PISTHETAERUS
BIRD'S-FOOT FOWLFOOT SERRADELLA
BIRD'S KNEE SUFFRAGO
BIRD'S MANTLE STRAGULUM
BIRDY AVIAN
BIRENO (WIFE OF —) OLIMPIA
BIRETTA SARRET
BIRI BIDI
BIRL ROTATE
BIRTH KIN BEAR FALL YEAN BLOOD BURDEN GENTRY ORIGIN BEARING BORNING DESCENT GENESIS LINEAGE DELIVERY GENITURE NASCENCY NATALITY NATIVITY
(FALSE —) SOOTERKIN
(GENTLE —) GENTILITY
(GENTLE —)0 GENTRICE
(GIVE —) CALVE
(HIGH —) PARAGE
(HONORABLE —) BLOOD
(OF LOW —) CRESTLESS
(OF NOBLE —) CORONETED
(PREF.) NATI
(SUFF.) (GIVING —) PARA PAROUS
BIRTHMARK MOLE IMAGE NAEVE NEVUS BLEMISH SPILOMA SIGNATURE
BIRTHPLACE INCUNABULA
BIRTHRATE NATALITY FERTILITY
BIRTHRIGHT KIND BIRTHDOM HERITAGE
BIRTHROOT BATHROOT BATHWORT DEATHROOT DISHCLOTH SQUAWROOT
BIRTHSTONE (APRIL —) DIAMOND
(AUGUST —) SARDONYX
(DECEMBER —) TURQUOISE
(FEBRUARY —) AMETHYST
(JANUARY —) GARNET
(JULY —) RUBY
(JUNE —) PEARL

(MARCH —) BLOODSTONE
(MAY —) EMERALD
(NOVEMBER —) TOPAZ
(OCTOBER —) OPAL
(SEPTEMBER —) SAPPHIRE
BIRTHWORT GUACO ASARUM BATHROOT
BISAYAN AKLAN CEBUAN AKLANON CEBUANO
BISCUIT BUN NUT BAKE ROLL RUSK SNAP WOOD BREAD COOKY SCONE WAFER BISQUE COOKIE DODGER MALLOW MUFFIN PARKIN PERKIN SIMNEL CRACKER GALETTE PENTILE PRETZEL RATAFIA RATIFIA CRACKNEL HARDTACK ZWIEBACK GINGERSNAP
(ALMOND —) RARAFIA
(BROKEN —S) DUNDERFUNK
(COLOR —) DOE PAWNEE
(SHIP —) HARDTACK DANDYFUNK DUNDERFUNK
BISECT FORK CROSS HALVE SPLIT CLEAVE DIVIDE MIDDLE SEPARATE
BISECTION MEDIATION
BISEXUAL ACDC
BISHOP EP ABBA EPUS LAWN PAPA POPE ANGEL COARB DENIS ARCHER BUSTLE DESPOT EPARCH EXARCH MAGPIE PRESUL PRIEST PRIMUS ROCHET ROCKAT PONTIFF PRELATE PRIMATE TULCHAN ANTISTES DIOCESAN DIRECTOR ORDINARY OVERSEER PONTIFEX PATRIARCH METROPOLITAN
(— AND MARTYR) EM
(ANGLICAN —) MAGPIE
(CHESS —) ALFIN ALPHYN ARCHER
(NEIGHBOR OF —) KING QUEEN KNIGHT
(PL.) PURPLE
BISHOPRIC SEE
BISHOP'S-WEED AMMI AMMEOS KHELLA WILLIAM BOLEWORT BULLWORT GOUTWEED TOOTHPICK
BISHOPWEED GOUTWEED GOUTWORT
BISKOP BRUSHER STEENBRAS
BISMARK KRAPFE KRAPFEN
BISMUTH WISMUTH TINGLASS
BISON BUGLE BOVINE MITHAN WISENT AUROCHS BONASUS BUFFALO
BISTORT PATIENCE ADDERWORT ASTROLOGE SNAKEWEED SNAKEWORT
BISTRO BAR CAFE TAVERN WINESHOP ESTAMINET NIGHTCLUB
BIT ACE FID FIP GAG JOT NIP ORT PIP TAD WEE ATOM BITE BITT CHIP CROP CURB DITE DOIT DRIB FLAW FOOD GRUE HAFT HATE HOOT IOTA ITEM LEVY MITE MOTE PART RIFF SLUT SNAP SNIP SPOT TOOL WHIT AUGER BLADE CHECK CRUMB DRILL GROAT PATCH PEZZO PIECE POINT SCRAP SHRED SHTIK SKOSH SMACK SNACK SPECK STEEK TASTE THRUM WIGHT BITTIE BRIDLE CANNON EATING MORSEL PELHAM PICKLE

SCATCH SHTICK SIPPET SMIDGE
SPLICE STITCH STIVER TITTLE
TRIFLE BRADOON BRIDOON
CHILENO GLIMMER MODICUM
MORCEAU PALLION PORTION
SCHTICK SMIDGEN SMIDGIN
SNAFFLE THOUGHT TRANEEN
FISHTAIL FRACTION FRAGMENT
QUANTITY SMIDGEON SMITCHIN
TWOPENNY
(— OF GOSSIP) HEARING
(— OF INFORMATION) GRIFF
GRIFFIN WRINKLE
(— OF KEY) WEB
(— OF LAND) CROOK
(— OF METAL) FLITTER
(— OF TOAST) SNIPPET
(—S AND PIECES) GUBBINS
GUBBINGS
(—S OF COKE) BREEZE
(—S OF WRITING) EXCERPTA
(— TO EAT) MUNGEY
(A —) SOME
(COMIC —) SIGHTGAG
(CUTTING —) CHASER
(DRILL —) CROWN
(FANCIFUL —) FLAM
(FIPPENY —) SIXPENCE
(FLORID —) FLOURISH
(HORSE'S —) KEVEL SNODE
CANNON PELHAM SCATCH SNAFFLE
BASTONET
(LEAST —) FIG JOT RAP DAMN
HANG LICK GHOST GROAT RIZZOM
STITCH
(LITTLE —) PICK TOUCH BITTOCK
REMNANT SOUPCON
(ONE — PER SECOND) BAUD
(ONE-QUARTER —) GILL
(ONE BILLION —S) GIGABIT
(SEQUENCE OF —S) BYTE
(SMALL —) BLEB GLIM SPUNK
(SMALL —S) SMATTER
(THEATRICAL —) SHTICK SCHTICK
(TINY —) TAD SPECK DRIBBLE
SCRINCH TODDICK
(PL.) SMITHERS SMITHEREENS
BITCH DO GYP BICK LAMP SLUT
BRACH BROOD CHEAT GROUSE
COMPLAIN
BITE BIT CUT EAT JAW NIP BAIT
CHAM CHEW ETCH FOOD GASH
GNAP GNAW HOLD KNAP MEAL
RIVE SNAP TAKE CHACK CHAMM
CHAMP CHEAT GNASH PINCH
SEIZE SMART SNACK STING TOOTH
TRICK CRUNCH MORSEL NIBBLE
PIERCE SAVAGE BUGBITE CHEATER
CORRODE FORBITE IMPRESS
MORSURE MUNCHET PARTAKE
SHARPER SLANDER
(— AT) HIT
(— GREEDILY) HANCH
(— REPEATEDLY) CHAMP
BITER
(SUFF.) DECTES
BITHIAH (HUSBAND OF —) MERED
BITING BIT HOT ACID HOAR KEEN
ACRID NIPPY QUICK SHARP SNELL
BITTER RODENT SEVERE SHREWD
STINGY TEETHY TWEAKY CAUSTIC
CUTTING MORDANT MORSURE
NIPPING PUNGENT SUBACID

DRILLING INCISIVE PIERCING
POIGNANT SCALDING SCATHING
STINGING ACIDULOUS
MORDACIOUS
BITIS ECHIDNA
BITO BALM HAJILIJ
BITON (BROTHER OF —) CLEOBIS
(MOTHER OF —) CYDIPPE
BITT BLOCK KNIGHT BOLLARD
(PL.) RANGEHEADS
BITTER AWA GAL ACID ACRE ASIM
BASK KEEN MARA RUDE SALT
SORE SOUR TART ACERB ACRID
AMARA ASPER BLEAK EAGER
HARSH IRATE SHARP SNELL BITING
PICRIC SEVERE AUSTERE CAUSTIC
CRABBED CUTTING FERVENT
GALLING GALLISH PAINFUL
PUNGENT SATIRIC POIGNANT
SARDONIC STINGING SUBAMARE
VIRULENT ASTRINGENT
ACRIMONIOUS
(NOT —) MILD
(PREF.) PICR(O)
(SUFF.) PICRIN
BITTER APPLE COLOCYNTH
BITTER BIT SMALLPOX
BITTERBUSH SNAKEROOT
BITTER CLOVER YELLOWTOP
BITTERLY SOUR FELLY BITTER
ROUNDLY CURSEDLY
BITTERN BUMP SOCO BOONK
BUTOR EGRET HERON BITORE
BUMBLE BUMMLE BUTTAL KAKKAK
BLITTER BUMMLER ERICIUS
DUNKADOO GRUIFORM LONGNECK
(FLOCK OF —) SEDGE SIEGE
BITTERNESS RUE ACOR BILE FELL
GALL ATTER MARAH ENMITY
MALICE RANCOR AMARITY
ACERBITY ACRIDITY ACRIMONY
ASPERITY FERVENCY SEVERITY
WORMWOOD
(EXTREME —) VIRULENCE
(WITH —) AMAREVOLE
BITTER PIT STIPPEN
BITTERROOT LEWISIA
TOBACCOROOT
BITTERS AMER
BITTER SPAR DOLOMITE
BITTERSWEET FELLEN DOGWOOD
LOBSTER SOLANUM WAXWORK
DULCAMARA FELONWOOD
FELONWORT FEVERTWIG
WITHYWIND WOLFBERRY
BITTER VETCH ERS
BITTERWEED RAGWEED
HORSEWEED
BITTERWORT FELWORT
DANDELION
BITUMEN TAR CONGO PITCH SLIME
MALTHA ASPHALT CARBENE
ALKITRAN ALCHITRAN ELATERITE
BIVALENT DIATOMIC
BIVALVE HEN CLAM SPAT PINNA
COCKLE DIATOM MUSSEL OYSTER
MOLLUSK NUCULID PANDORA
SCALLOP TOHEROA
BIVOUAC CAMP ETAPE WATCH
ENCAMP SHELTER
BIZARRE ODD ANTIC DEDAL GONZO
OUTRE QUEER QUAINT ANTICAL
BAROQUE CURIOUS FANCIFUL

ECCENTRIC FANTASTIC
GROTESQUE OUTLANDISH
BLAB LAB CHAT BLART BLATE
CHEEP CLACK PEACH PRATE
BABBLE BETRAY GOSSIP REVEAL
SQUEAL TATTLE BLABBER
CHATTER CLATTER
BLABBERMOUTH YENTA
BLACK DHU JET WAN CALO CROW
DARK EBON FOUL INKY NOIR PIKY
SOOT BUGLE COLLY DUSKY
DWALE MURKY NEGRO NOIRE
RAVEN SABLE SOOTY TARRY THICK
ATROUS BRUNET DISMAL ETHIOP
GLOOMY MURREY PITCHY SULLEN
ABAISER AFRICAN BLACKEN
DIAMOND MELANIC NEGRITO
NIGRINE NIGROUS PICEOUS
SCHWARZ SWARTHY UNCLEAN
MOURNFUL
(— AND BLUE) LIVID
(— OUT) CONK
(BONE —) SPODIUM
(BROWNISH —) LAVA
(GREENISH —) CORBEAU
(IVORY —) ABAISER
(LIGHT-SKINNED —) BROWN
(RATHER —) DUSKISH
(VIOLET —) CROW
(PREF.) ATRO MAVRO MEL(A)
MELAN(O) NIGRI
(SUFF.) MELANE
BLACKAMOOR BLECK NEGRO
MORIAN NEGRESS ETHIOPIAN
BLACK ARROW (AUTHOR OF —)
STEVENSON
(CHARACTER IN —) DICK ELLIS
OATES DANIEL JOANNA OLIVER
SEDLEY LAWLESS RICHARD
SHELTON BRACKLEY DUCKWORTH
BLACK ASH HOOPWOOD
BLACKBALL PIP PILL BALLOT
EXCLUDE HEEBALL OSTRACIZE
BLACK BASS HURON TROUT
ACHIGAN GROWLER OCHIGAN
BLACKBERRY AGAWAM LAWTON
BRAMBLE DEWBERRY MULBERRY
ROSACEAN
(— BUSH) MORE
BLACKBIRD ANI DAW PIE CROW
MERL AMSEL COLLY MERLE
OUSEL OUZEL RAVEN BLACKY
COLLEY MAIZER BLACKIE
COWBIRD GRACKLE JACKDAW
REDWING WOOFELL TROOPIAL
BLACKBOARD SLATE CHALKBOARD
GREENBOARD
BLACKBREAM TARWHINE
BLACK-BROWED GLOOMY
BLACK BRYONY LILY LILIUM
OXBERRY BINDWEED MANDRAKE
BLACK BUCK SASIN
BLACKCAP GULL JACK PEGGY
HAYBIRD WARBLER MOCKBIRD
TITMOUSE JACKSTRAW
RASPBERRY
BLACKCOCK GROUSE
BLACKDAMP STYTH STYTHE
CHOKEDAMP
BLACKDRINK YAPON YAUPON
BLACKEN INK TAR CHAR CORK
SMUT SOIL SOOT BLECK CLOUD
COLLY JAPAN SMOKE SULLY

BEFOUL BLATCH DARKEN DEFAME
MALIGN SMEETH SMIRCH SMUTCH
VILIFY ASPERSE BENEGRO NIGRIFY
SLANDER SMOLDER TRADUCE
BESMIRCH
BLACKENED REECHY
BLACKENING SWART SWARTH
BLACKEYE COWPEA
BLACKFELLOW BLACKBOY
YAMMADJI
BLACKFIN CISCO SESIS
BLACKFISH GRIND TAUTOG
BORLASE DOGFISH GRAMPUS
POTHEAD HARDHEAD
BLACKFLY GNAT SIMULIID
BLACKFOOT BLOOD KAINAH
PIEGAN SIKSIKA SIHASAPA
BLACK GROUPER MERO AGUAJI
WARSAW GARRUPA
BLACKGUARD CUR SHAG BLECK
CATSO GAMIN GUARD SNUFF
SWEEP ROTTER LADRONE
SKELLUM VAGRANT BLAGGARD
CRIMINAL LARRIKIN VAGABOND
SCOUNDREL
BLACK GUILLEMOT CUTTY TYSTE
SCRABE DOVEKEY DOVEKIE
SCRABER PUFFINET
BLACK GUM TUPELO HORNPIPE
STINKWOOD
BLACK HAW SLOE BOOTS ALISIER
STAGBUSH VIBURNUM
BLACKHEAD COMEDO
BLACK HOLE COLLAPSAR
BLACK HOREHOUND HENBIT
ARCHANGEL
BLACK HORSE SUCKER SUCKEREL
BLACKING LINK BLECK BLATCH
BLEACH ATRAMENT
BLACK IRONWOOD AXMASTER
AXEMASTER
BLACKISH DUSKY MOREL SWART
BLACKY
BLACKJACK OAK SAP CLUB COSH
DUCK FLAG JACK BILLY BEETLE
BLENDE JERKIN BOMBARD
NATURAL BLUDGEON
BLACKLEG LEG FIRE SCAB SNOB
ANTHRAX GAMBLER JACKLEG
APOSTATE BLACKNEB BLACKNOB
SWINDLER KNOBSTICK
BLACK LETTER GOTHIC
BLACKLY SABLY
BLACK MAGIC VODUN VODOUN
DIABLERIE
BLACKMAIL BLEED BRIBE CHOUT
COERCE EXTORT RANSOM
TRIBUTE CHANTAGE
BLACKMAILER GHOUL BRIBER
LEECHER
BLACK MANGROVE COURIDA
BLACK MEDIC HOP TREFOIL
NONESUCH SHAMROCK
BLACKNESS GRIME DARKNESS
NIGRITUDE
BLACK NIGHTSHADE MOREL
DUSCLE SOLANUM BLUEBERRY
MOONSHADE TROMPILLO
BLACK OLIVE OXHORN
BLACKOUT SKIT
BLACK PEPPER PIMENTA
BLACK PINE MATAI
BLACK POISON WALNUT

BLACK RHINOCEROS BORELE KEITLOA UPEYGAN

BLACK SALLY SALLEE MUZZLEWOOD

BLACK SANICLE LUNGWORT MASTERWORT

BLACK SHANK LANAS

BLACK SKIMMER CUTWATER SHEARBILL

BLACKSMITH GOW SMUG LOHAR SHOER SMITH PLOVER SMITHY VULCAN BROOKIE FARRIER STRIKER BURNEWIN IRONSMITH

BLACKSNAKE WHIP QUIRT RACER ELAPID RUNNER COLUBRID

BLACK SPECK DARTROSE

BLACK SPURGE FLUXWEED

BLACKTAIL DASSY DASSIE

BLACK TERN DARR STARN

BLACKTHORN HAW SLOE SNAG SCROG GRIBBLE SLOEBUSH SLOETREE SNAGBUSH

BLACKTOP PAVE

BLACK-VARNISH TREE THEETSEE

BLACK VULTURE URUBU CORBIE ZOPILOTE

BLACK WALNUT NOGAL

BLACKWATER STATE NEBRASKA

BLACK WIDOW POKOMOO

BLACK WOLF KARAKURT

BLACKWOOD BITTERLIGHTWOOD

BLACKWORT COMFREY

BLADDER SAC VES ASCO VESICA AMPULLA BLATHER BLISTER INFLATE UROCYST UTRICLE VESICLE

(**AIR —**) POKE SWIM SOUND SINGALLY

(**PL.**) ASCI

(**PREF.**) ASC(I)(IDI)(IDIO)(O) CYST(I)
(O) PHYSO VESICO

(**SUFF.**) CYST(IS)

BLADDER-AND-STRING BUMBASS

BLADDER CAMPION BEHN BEHEN SILENE COWBELL SNAPPER RATTLEBOX

BLADDER KETMIE MODESTY

BLADDERNUT BAGNUT

BLADDER-WORM CESTODE

BLADDERWORT POPWEED

BLADDER WRACK CUTWEED KELPWARE

BLADE BIT FIN FOP OAR SAW WEB BLOW BONE BOWL EDGE EPEE FLAG HEAD LEAF LIMB TANG WEAK BLOOD BRAND DANDY FLUKE GRAIN GUIDE HEALD KNIFE LANCE SHEAR SPARK SPEAR SPIRE SWORD BLUNGE BUCKET BUSTER CUTTER DOCTOR FOIBLE HEDDLE LAMINA PAGINA RIPPER ROARER SCYTHE SICKLE TOLEDO BAYONET CHIPPER GALLANT POLESAW SCALPEL SCAPULA SCRAPER SPINNER MOLDBOARD PROPELLER

(**— OF FAN**) VANE

(**— OF GRASS**) PILE CHIRE SPEAR SPIRE STRAP TRANEEN

(**— OF KNIFE**) TANG GRAIN

(**— OF LEAF**) LIMB LAMINA

(**— OF MORION**) COMB

(**— OF OAR**) PALM PEEL PELL WASH

(**— OF PROPELLER**) FAN

(**— OF SCISSORS**) BILL

(**— OF YOUNG GRAIN**) SORAGE

(**BROAD —**) SPATULA

(**CULTIVATOR —**) SWEEP DUCKFOOT

(**MIXER —**) BEATER

(**NARROW —**) DISC

(**SKATE —**) RUNNER

(**SURGICAL —**) LEUCOTOME

(**SUFF.**) SPATH

BLAES CAM CAN CALM CAUM

BLAFFERT PLAPPERT

BLAGGERMOUTH YENTA GOSSIP

BLAH DRAB DULL MEDIOCRE

BLAIN RUBY SORE BULLA BLISTER INFLAME PUSTULE

BLAKE MCKAY

BLAMABLE FAULTY CULPABLE

BLAME RAP CALL CHOP HURT LACK ONUS SAKE SPOT TWIT WITE CHIDE FAULT GUILT ODIUM PINCH PINON SHEND SNAPE SWICK SWIKE THANK TOUCH WHITE ACCUSE ATTASK BUMBLE BURDEN CHARGE DIRDUM PLIGHT REBUKE REVILE SCANCE APPOINT ASCRIBE CENSURE CONDEMN CULPATE OBLOQUY REPROOF REPROVE SLANDER UPBRAID WITHNIM REPROACH

BLAMED BLINDING BLISTERING

BLAMELESS PURE ENTIRE PERFECT INNOCENT SACKLESS SPOTLESS WITELESS RIGHTEOUS

BLAMEWORTHY GUILTY CRIMINAL CULPABLE REPROBATE

BLANCH FADE PALE BLENK CHALK SCALD WHITE APPALL ARGENT BIANCA BLEACH BLENCH FALLOW WHITEN ETIOLATE

BLANCHED ASHEN MEALY ETIOLATE BLOODLESS COLORLESS

BLANCMANGE FLUMMERY

BLAND COLD KIND MILD OILY OPEN SOFT SLEEK SUAVE BENIGN BREEZY GENIAL GENTLE SMOOTH URBANE AFFABLE AMIABLE LENIENT VANILLA FAVONIAN GRACIOUS UNCTUOUS

BLANDISH COAX CHARM ALLURE BLANCH CAJOLE FONDLE SMOOTH FLATTER WHEEDLE HONEYFUGLE

BLANDISHMENT SOOTH LISALVE

(**PL.**) TREACLE

BLANDLY CREAMILY

BLANK BARE BURR FLAN FORM SHOT VOID ANNUL BLIND BREAK CHASM CLEAN EMPTY FALSE RANGE SPACE WASTE WHITE COUPON VACANT ANTIQUE BRINDLE NONPLUS UNMIXED VACUOUS UNFILLED

(**MAY BE —**) STARE

BLANKED BLIND

BLANKET RUG BROT MAUD WRAP BLUEY COTTA COVER CUMLY LAYER MANTA PATTU QUILT SHEET SUGAN THROW AFGHAN COOLER CUMBLY GLOBAL KAMBAL MANTLE PALLET PONCHO PUTTOO SERAPE SOOGAN SPREAD STIFLE STROUD TILPAH CHIRIPA DOUBLER

SMOTHER WHITTLE COVERLET MACKINAW

(**— A VESSEL**) WRONG

(**— OF SKINS**) KAROSS

(**— WITH BOMBS**) SATURATE

(**BUSHMAN'S —**) BLUEY

(**HORSE —**) MANTA

(**QUILTED —**) BROT

(**SADDLE —**) CORONA

(**PREF.**) REGO

BLANKETING DUFFEL DUFFLE

BLANKNESS VACUITY NEGATION

BLARE PEAL BLART BLAST BLEAR NOISE BLAZON SCREAM FANFARE TANTARA TRUMPET

BLARNEY CON TAFFY BUTTER CAJOLE SAWDER FLATTER WHEEDLE

BLAS GIL RUY

BLASPHEME ABUSE CURSE DEFAME REVILE PROFANE

BLASPHEMOUS BAD RIBALD IMPIOUS PROFANE

BLASPHEMY CALUMNY CURSING IMPIETY ANATHEMA SWEARING

BLAST BUB NIP WAP BANG BLOW FRAP GALE GUST RUIN RUST SHOT TOOT WAFF WIND BLAME BLIST BLORE SPLIT STUNT TRUMP ATTACK BLIGHT BUGGER FORBID NIDDER NITHER REBUFF VOLLEY WITHER BLUSTER DESPOIL EXPLODE SHATTER SHRIVEL DYNAMITE OUTBURST PROCLAIM WHIRLPUFF

(**— OFF**) START

(**— OF WIND**) GUST RISE PERRY PIRRIE VENTOSITY

(**— ON HORN**) TOOT PRYSE

(**— WITH COLD**) SNEAP

(**FURIOUS —**) SNIFTER

(**MILITARY —**) SALVO

(**RAINY —**) BLATTER

BLASTED BLAME BLAMED BLIGHTED BLINDING BLINKING

BLASTER FROSTER SHOOTER SHOTMAN

BLASTING SCATHING SHOOTING STELLATION

(**— METHOD**) MUDCAP

BLASTOMERE MESOMERE MACROMERE MICROMERE

BLASTULA PLACULA PLANULA PLANULAN

BLATANT GLIB LOUD BRASH GROSS NOISY SILLY VOCAL COARSE GARISH TONANT VULGAR BRAWLING STRIDENT

BLATHER ADO RAVE STIR BLEAT BABBLE WAFFLE BLITHER PRATTLE NONSENSE

BLAUBOK ETAAC BLUEBUCK

BLAZE LOW BURN FIRE GLOW HACK LEAM LOWE LUNT MARK SHOT SPOT FLAME FLARE FLASH GLARE GLEAM GLORY INGLE RATCH SHINE STARE STEAM TORCH BLAZON BLEEZE BONFIRE PIONEER SPLENDOR

(**— OUT**) FLAP

(**HEAVENLY —**) NOVA

BLAZING AFIRE FIERY FLAMY LIGHT TORRID FLAMING FLARING

BLAZING STAR LIATRIS GRUBROOT SNAKEROOT

BLAZON DECK SHOW ADORN BLARE BLAZE BOAST DEPICT SHIELD DECLARE DISPLAY EXHIBIT PUBLISH EMBLAZON INSCRIBE

BLAZONED ARMED BANNERED

BLEACH SUN WASH BLEAK CHALK CROFT POACH BLANCH BLENCH CHLORE PURIFY WHITEN DECOLOR LIGHTEN BLONDINE ETIOLATE PEROXIDE

(**— PULP**) POTCH

BLEACHER WHITSTER

BLEACHERS SCAFFOLD

BLEAK DIM RAW BLAE BLAY COLD DOUR GRAY PALE ABLET OURIE SPRAT STARK SWALE ALBURN BITTER BLEACH DISMAL DREARY FRIGID PALLID CUTTING DESOLATE CHEERLESS

BLEAK HOUSE (**AUTHOR OF —**) DICKENS

(**CHARACTER IN —**) JO ADA JOHN ALLAN CLARE FLITE GUPPY KROOK BUCKET ESTHER RAWDON DEDLOCK JELLYBY RICHARD WILLIAM CARSTONE CHADBAND JARNDYCE SKIMPOLE LEICESTER SUMMERSON WOODCOURT TULKINGHORN

BLEAT BAA MAA BLAT BLEA YARM BLART BLATE BLATHER BLUSTER WHICKER

BLEATING BALANT

BLEB BLOB BULLA BUBBLE BLISTER PUSTULE VESICLE SWELLING

BLEED RUN FLUX MILK WEEP BLOOD LEECH MULCT SWEAT SWINDLE TEICHER PHLEBOTOMIZE

BLEEDER STICKER

BLEEDING BLOODY SANGLANT

BLEEDING HEART EARDROP DICENTRA

BLEMISH MAR BLOT BLUR DENT FLAW GALL LACK MAIM MARK MOIL MOLE RIFT SAKE SCAR SLUR SPOT TASH VICE WANT AMPER BLAME BOTCH BRECK CLOUD CRACK FAULT FLECK MULCT NAEVE SPECK STAIN SULLY TACHE TAINT TOUCH BLOTCH BREACH DEFAME DEFECT IMPAIR INJURE MACULA MACULE MAYHEM SMIRCH STIGMA BUBUKLE CATFACE DEFAULT FAILING FISSURE SUNSPOT MACULATION

(**— IN CLOTH**) AMPER SULLY

(**— IN PAPER**) FISHEYE

(**PRINTING —**) MACKLE

BLEMISHED BAD WEMMY

BLENCH FOIL SHUN WILE AVOID ELUDE EVADE QUAIL SHAKE SHIRK TRICK BAFFLE BLANCH BLEACH FLINCH RECOIL SHRINK DECEIVE

BLEND MIX RUN BLOT FADE FUSE JOIN MELD MELT MENG MOLD ADMIX BLIND CREAM GRADE MERGE MOULD PUREE SHADE SMEAR SPOIL STAIN TINGE UNITE BLUNGE COMMIX CRASIS DAZZLE MINGLE TEMPER COMBINE CONFUSE CORRUPT DECEIVE

GRADATE MIXTURE POLLUTE
COALESCE CONCRETE IMMINGLE
TINCTURE CONTEMPER
(— OF NOISES) CHARM
(— OF SHERRY) SOLERA
(— OF WINES) CUVEE
BLENDE JACK SPHALERITE
BLENDED FONDU FUSED MIXED
MERGED MINGLED CONFLATE
CONFLUENT
BLENDING FUSION HOTCHPOT
BLENNY GUNNEL SHANNY EELPOUT
JUGULAR KELPFISH SENORITA
WOLFFISH WRYMOUTH QUILLFISH
ROCKSKIPPER
BLESBOK NUNNI BLESBUCK
BLESS KEEP SAIN WAVE ADORE
ANELE BENSH CROSS EXTOL
FAVOR GUARD THANK VISIT
WOUND CROUCH FAVOUR
HALLOW PRAISE THRASH
APPROVE BEATIFY EMBLISS
GLORIFY PROTECT MACARIZE
PRESERVE SANCTIFY
BLESSED HOLY BLEST HAPPY SEELY
DIVINE JOYFUL SACRED SEELFUL
BENEDICT BHAGAVAT BLISSFUL
BLOOMING HALLOWED HEAVENLY
CELESTIAL
(— MAN) BEATI
(— WOMAN) BEATA
BLESSEDNESS BLISS FELICITY
BEATITUDE HAPPINESS
BLESSING BOON GIFT SAIN BLISS
DUKAN GRACE SORRA BARAKA
DUCHAN PRAISE BENISON
DARSHAN WORSHIP BERACHAH
FELICITY MACARISM BEATITUDE
(PL.) CUP
BLEU DE ROI SEVRES
BLIGHT NIP FIRE RUIN RUST SMUT
SOKA BLAST BRANT EDEMA FROST
SNEAP MILDEW NITHER TAKING
WITHER DESTROY
(— OF HOPS) FIREBLAST
(PREF.) UREDO
BLIGHTER GUY SOD FELLOW
BLIND BET POT ANTE BOMA DARK
DEAD DULL HIDE HOOD SEEL
BISME BLANK BLEND CHICK CLOAK
DUNCH SHADE STAKE STALL
WAGER AMBUSH BISSON BLENDE
DARKEN DAZZLE SCREEN SECRET
AIMLESS ANTIQUE BANDAGE
BATTERY BENIGHT ECLIPSE
EYELESS OBSCURE PRETEXT
RAYLESS SHUTTER ABORTIVE
ARTIFICE BAYARDLY BLINDING
EXCECATE HOODWINK IGNORANT
INVOLVED JALOUSIE OUTSHINE
PURBLIND UMBRELLA VENETIAN
(— IN ONE EYE) PEED GLEED GLEYD
(— MAN) MOLE
(HALF —) STARBLIND
(PART OF —) SLAT
(PL.) PERSIENNES
(PREF.) CECO TYPHL(O)
BLIND ALLEY LOKE STOP POCKET
IMPASSE
BLINDER FLAP HOOD BLIND BLUFF
LUNET WINKER BLINKER EYEFLAP
LUNETTE HOODWINK BLINDFOLD

BLINDFOLD MOP DARK BLINK
BLUFF SCARF MUFFLE BANDAGE
BLINDER OBSCURE ENCLOSER
HEEDLESS HOODWINK RECKLESS
CONCEALED
BLINDING BISME BISSON
BLINDMAN'S BLUFF POST
HOODWINK
BLINDNESS BISSON CECITY
MYOPSY ABLEPSY ANOPSIA
MEROPIA ABLEPSIA DARKNESS
IGNORANCE
(— TO TRUTH) AVIDYA AVIJJA
(COLOR —) ACHROBIA
MONOCHROMATISM
(DAY —) HEMERALOPIA
(NIGHT —) NYCTALOPIA
(PARTIAL —) MEROPIA HEMIOPSIA
(RED-GREEN —) DALTONISM
(SNOW —) CHIONABLEPSIA
(STUDY OF —) TYPHLOLOGY
(TEMPORARY —) MOONBLINK
BLINDSTITCH FELL
BLINDWORM SLOW ORVET ANGUID
HAGWORM SLOWWORM
BLIND-YOUR-EYES GANGWA
ALIPATA
BLINK BAT PINK SHUN WINK BLUSH
CHEAT FLASH GLEAM SHINE TRICK
GLANCE IGNORE OBTUSE WAPPER
BLINTER CONDONE GLIMMER
GLIMPSE NEGLECT NICTATE
SPARKLE TWINKLE
BLINKER EYE BLINK BLUFF LIGHT
EYELID SIGNAL WAPPER WINKER
BLINDER FLASHER GOGGLES
COQUETTE HOODWINK MACKEREL
BLINKING PINK OWLISH
BLINTZE BLIN BLINTZ PANCAKE
BLIP PIP ECHO
(SONAR —) ECHO
BLISS JOY EDEN KAIF SEEL SEIL
BLESS GLORY ANANDA HEAVEN
DELIGHT ECSTASY GLADDEN
NIRVANA RAPTURE FELICITY
GLADNESS PARADISE PLEASURE
BLISSFUL HOLY SEELY BLITHE
EDENIC BLESSED ELYSIAN
UTOPIAN BEATIFIED GLORIFIED
BLISTER BEAT BLAB BLEB BLOB
BLOW BOIL BURN LASH QUAT
APTHA BLAIN BLIBE BULGE BULLA
TOPIC VESIC APHTHA BUBBLE
CUPOLA SCORCH SOTTER TETTER
BLADDER BLUSTER SCALDER
SKELLER VESICLE VESICATE
(PREF.) PUSTULI VESICUL(O)
BLISTERED BULLATE
BLISTERING VESICANT
BLITHE GAY GLAD BONNY BUXOM
HAPPY JOLLY MERRY BONNIE
JOVIAL JOYOUS LIVELY GAYSOME
JOCULAR WINSOME CHEERFUL
GLADSOME SPRIGHTLY
BLITZ REDDOG
BLIZZARD BLOW GALE WIND
BURAN PURGA RETORT SNIFTER
SQUELCHER
(— STATE) SD SDAK
BLOAT BLOW BLAST BLOWN FLOAT
HOOVE HOVEN PUFFY SWELL
BOWDEN EXPAND TUMEFY
DISTEND FERMENT INFLATE

BLOATED FOZY BLOAT BROSY
CURED FOGGY HOVEN PUFFY
TUMID GOTCHY SODDEN TURGID
POMPOUS REPLETE
BLOATER MOONEYE
BLOB LIP WEN BEAD BLEB BLOT
BOIL CLOT DAUB DROP GLOB
GOUT LUMP MARK MASS BUBBLE
DALLOP DOLLOP PIMPLE SPLASH
BLEMISH BLISTER BLOSSOM
GLOBULE PUSTULE SPLOTCH
BLOC RING BLOCK CABAL PARTY
UNION CLIQUE BENELUX FACTION
BLOCK AME BAR COB COG DAM DIE
DIT DOG FID HOB HUB JAM KEY
NOG ROW TOP VOL BALK BASE
BEAR BILK BLOC BUCK BUNT CAKE
CLOG CUBE DRUM FOIL FOUL
FROG GLUT HEAD JAMB LEAD
MASK MASS MOCK QUAR STAY
STEP STOP TRIG BAULK BRICK
CHAIR CHECK CHEEK CHUMP
CLAMP CLEAT CLOSE COVER
DETER DOLLY DUMMY EMBAR
FLOAT HEART HORST JUMBO
NUDGE PARRY PATCH SHAPE
SLUMP SPIKE SPOKE STOCK STUFF
STUMP ASSIZE DENTIL DOLLEY
DOMINO FIPPLE FORMER HAMPER
HINDER IMPEDE KIBOSH MONKEY
MUFFLE MUTULE OPPOSE OUTWIT
QUERRE RIPPER SADDLE SCOTCH
SNATCH SQUARE STREET STYMIE
TAPLET THWART TROLLY WAYLAY
BOLLOCK BOLSTER BUCKLER
CONDEMN DEADEYE ERRATIC
INHIBIT OUTLINE PREVENT
QUADREL RAMHEAD STONKER
TRIGGER TROLLEY BLOCKADE
DEADHEAD ELECTRET FOLLOWER
KEYSTONE MONOLITH OBSTACLE
OBSTRUCT STOPPAGE WITHSPAR
BRIQUETTE
(— AT SPAR END) STEEVE
(— A WHEEL) SCOTE
(— FOR SKIDDING LOGS) BICYCLE
(— FOR SLAVE SALES) CATASTA
(— IN SPEAKING) STAMMER
(— OF BUILDINGS) INSULA
(— OF COAL) JUD JUDD
(— OF EARTH'S CRUST) HORST
(— OF GRANITE) SET
(— OF ICE) SERAC
(— OF LAND) FORTY
(— OF SEATS) CUNEUS
(— OF SHARES) TRANCHE
(— OF TIMBER) BOLT JUGGLE
(—S OF STONE) DIMENSION
(— SUPPORTING MAST) STEP
(— THE WAY) SCOAT
(— UP) BAR DAM CLOY QUIRT
CONDEMN OPPILATE FORECLOSE
(— WITH HOLE IN IT) WAPP
EUPHROE
(— WITH PROJECTING CORE)
SETTLE
(ARCHITECTURAL —) DRUM STONE
DENTIL IMPOST MUTULE PLINTH
DOSSERET
(BUILDING —) MEGALITH
(CHOPPING —) HACKLOG
(CLAY —) DRAWBAR
(FAULT —) MASSIF

(FELTED —) DAMPER
(FOOTBALL —) CRACKBACK
(FULCRUM —) GLUT
(FUSE —) CUTOUT
(HOSPITAL —) PAVILION
(IRON —) USE VOL BITT ANVIL
CHAIR
(LOGGING —) LEAD JUMBO
(NAUTICAL —) CHOCK HEART
STOCK SADDLE DEADEYE FAIRLEAD
(ORNAMENTAL —) BOSS
MODILLION
(PAVING —) SET CUBE SETT STONE
WHEELER
(PLASTER —) BATTER
(POLISHING —) BUFF FLOAT RABOT
(PRINTING —) CUT QUAD RISER
QUADRAT
(PULLEY —) CRAWL
(SANDSTONE —) SARSEN
(SQUARED —) MITCHEL
(STUMBLING —) HURTING
(TACKLE —) CALO TONGUE
(VAULTING —) BUCK HORSE
BLOCKADE DAM FERM BESET
BLOCK EMBAR SIEGE WHISKY
BESIEGE EMBARGO BLOCKAGE
OBSTRUCT BARRICADE
BELEAGUER
BLOCKAGE LOGJAM
BLOCKER CASER BRACER
(CHANNEL —) NIFEDEPINE
BLOCKHEAD ASS LUG OAF SAP
BUST CLOT COOF COOT DAFF
DOLT FOOL MOME NOWT STUB
BLOCK BOOBY CHUMP CUDDY
GOLEM GOOSY IDIOT NINNY SNIPE
SUMPH CUDDIE DIMWIT DISARD
NITWIT NOODLE TUMPHY TURNIP
ASSHEAD BUZZARD DIZZARD
DULBERT JACKASS LACKWIT
MUDHEAD NOGHEAD TOMFOOL
BEEFHEAD BONEHEAD CLODPATE
CLODPOLL CODSHEAD DULLHEAD
DULLPATE DUMBHEAD
DUMMKOPF GAMPHREL
HARDHEAD JOLTHEAD LUNKHEAD
BLOCKHOUSE SPUR PUNTAL
GARRISON
BLOCKING JAM JAMB DUNNAGE
BLOCKADE CROSSING
BLOCKISH STOLID
BLOKE EGG GUY MAN CHAP COVE
TOFF BLOAK JOKER FELLOW
BLOLLY BEEFWOOD CORKWOOD
PORKWOOD
BLOND BAN FAIR LIGHT BLONDE
FLAXEN GOLDEN YELLOW
LEUCOUS BLONDINE
(AUTUMN —) FAWN
BLOOD KIN SAP GORE LIFE MASS
MOOD RACE SANG SANK BLADE
BLUDE BLUID CRUOR FLESH FLUID
SERUM STOCK CLARET INDRED
KAINAH SLUDGE GALLANT KINSHIP
KINSMAN LINEAGE RELATION
TROPHEMA
(— CONDITION) SICKLEMIA
(— OF GREEK GODS) ICHOR
(— RELATED) HEMAL
(CORRUPT —) YOUSTIR
(HALF —) DEMISANG
(PREF.) HAEM(A)(O) HAEMAT(O)

HEM(A)(O) HEMAT(O) SANGUI SANGUINO SANO (SUFF.) AEMIA EMIA HAEMIA HEMIA

BLOOD CLOT (PREF.) THROMB(O)

BLOODCURDLING GORY HORROR

BLOODFLOWER HIPPO REDHEAD BLOODWEED

BLOODHOUND LYM LYAM LYME HOUND LIMER SLOTH BANDOG LEAMER SLEUTH TIEDOG LYAMHOUND SLEUTHHOUND

BLOODIED BEBLED

BLOODLESS DEAD ANEMIC ANAEMIC INHUMAN TURNIPY LIFELESS UNFEELING

BLOODLETTER BLEEDER

BLOOD-LETTING PHLEBOTOMY

BLOODLIKE HEMATOID HAEMATOID

BLOOD PHEASANT ITHAGINE

BLOOD PUDDING BLUTWURST

BLOOD-RED SANGUINE

BLOODROOT PUCCOON REDROOT BOLOROOT COONROOT CORNROOT TURMERIC SANGUINARIA

BLOODSHED DEATH CARNAGE VIOLENCE SLAUGHTER

BLOODSHOT RED INFLAMED

BLOODSTAINED GORY

BLOODSTONE SANGUINE HEMACHATE

BLOODSUCKER LEECH SPONGER VAMPIRE

BLOODTHIRSTINESS ACHARNEMENT

BLOODTHIRSTY BLOODY CARNAL SANGUINE TIGERISH FEROCIOUS MURDEROUS SANGUINARY

BLOOD VESSEL VEIN COMES HEMAD ARTERY CAPILLARY (PREF.) ANGIO

BLOODWOOD AJHAR JAROOL

BLOODY GORY RUDE BALLY BLODE CRUEL RUDDY BLUGGY CRUENT GRISLY PLUCKY CRIMSON BLEEDING DEATHFUL HEMATOSE INFAMOUS SANGLANT BUTCHERLY CRUENTOUS FEROCIOUS MERCILESS MURDEROUS SANGUINARY

BLOODY BARK LANCEPOD

BLOOM DEW BLOW CAST HAZE KNOT BLURT BLUSH CHILL BLOOTH BLOWTH BLOSSOM BLOWING ANTHESIS BLOOMING FLOREATE FLOURISH (— OF WILLOW) GULL (— ON INSECT) POLLEN (— ON SHELL) CUTICLE (— ON TREE) GOSLING (FULL —) HEYDAY (METAL —S) HEAT (POWDERY —) PRUINA

BLOOMER ERROR BLOWER BLUNDER FAILURE

BLOOMERS KNICKERS PANTALETS

BLOOMERY FORGE HEARTH FURNACE

BLOOMING PERT ROSY FLUSH FRESH GREEN PRIME ABLOOM FLORID BLOWING FLAMING ROSEATE BLINKING

BLOOPER BLOOMER

BLOSSOM BUD BELL BLOB BLOW CHIP SILK BLOOM LEHUA FLOWER BLOWING BURGEON PROSPER BOURGEON FLOURISH (BLIGHTED —) BLAST (HERALDIC —) FRASE FRAISE (PL.) SET BLOSSOMRY

BLOSSOMING BLOWTH FLORAISON FLORULENT (— AFTER NOON) POMERIDIAN

BLOT MAR BLOB BLUR DAUB SOIL SPOT BLACK BLANK BLEND BLOTE ERASE SMEAR SPECK STAIN SULLY BLOTCH CANCEL DAMAGE EFFACE IMPAIR MACULA SHADOW SMIRCH SMOUCH SMUDGE SMITCH STIGMA BLEMISH ECLIPSE EXPUNGE INKBLOT OBSCURE SPLOTCH TARNISH DISGRACE REPROACH (— OUT) OUT BURY ANNUL ERASE CANCEL DELETE EXPUNGE

BLOTCH DAB BLOT DASH GOUT MONK SPOT AMPER PATCH SMEAR SPLAT STAIN MACULA MOTTLE PLOTCH PURPLE SMIRCH SPLASH STIGMA BLEMISH PUSTULE SPLOTCH ERUPTION MACULATE (PL.) BLIBE (PREF.) MACUL(I)(O)

BLOTCHED SCABBY PIEBALD MACULATE SCABROUS SPLASHED MACULATED (SUFF.) MACULATE

BLOTCHY SCOVY

BLOTTER BLAD

BLOTTO LIT

BLOUSE CHOLI MIDDY SHIRT SMOCK TUNIC WAIST CAMISA GUIMPE JUMPER CASAQUE VAREUSE CAMISOLE CASAQUIN JIRKINET (ABBREVIATED —) HALTER (BUSHMAN'S —) BLUEY (KIND OF —) PEASANT

BLOW BOB COB COP CUT DAB DAD DUB FAN FIB HIT JAB JAR NAP ONE PAT PEG POP RAP TAP TIP TIT WAP ANDE BAFF BANG BASH BEAT BELT BIFF BIRR BLAD BLAW BRAG BUFF BULL BUMP BUTT CHAP CHOP CONK COUP CRIG CUFF DASH DAUD DENT DING DINT DIRD DOLE DRAW DRUB DUNT DUSH FLAP FLEG FLIG FUFF FUNK GALE GOWF GUST HACK HUFF HURT JOLT KNAP KNEE LASH LEAD LEFT LICK LOUK LUSH MINT ONER PAIK PALT PANT PASS PICK PIRR PLUG POLT PUCK PUFF PUSH SCAT SCUD SHOT SLAM SLAP SLAT SLUG SOCK SPAT STOP SWAP SWAT SWOP SWOT THUD WELT WHAP WHOP WIND WIPE YANK BINGE BLADE BLAST BLIZZ BLOOM BOAST BRUNT BURST CLAUT CLINK CLOUR CLOUT CLUMP CLUNK CRUMP CRUNT CURSE DEVEL DOUSE DOWSE DUNCH FACER FILIP FLACK

FLICK FLIRT GOWFF ICTUS IMPEL KNOCK OUTER PALMY PANDY PASTE PEISE PLUMP PLUNK PUNCH RIGHT SHAKE SHOCK SKELP SKIRL SKITE SLASH SLIPE SLOSH SMACK SMASH SMITE SNICK SOUND SOUSE SPANK SPEND STORM STRIP SURGE SWACK SWEEP SWIPE THROW THUMP TOUCH TRICE WHACK WHANG WHIFF WHOOF WHUFF BELTER BENSEL BENSIL BETRAY BOUNCE BUFFET CONKER DEPART DIRDUM DUNDER EXPAND FILLIP FISTER FLOWER FROLIC HANDER HUFFLE LARRUP REBUKE SIFFLE STOUSH STRIPE STROKE SWITCH THUNGE THWACK WALLOP WINDER AFFLATE ASSAULT ATTAINT BELLOWS BENSAIL BLOSSOM BLOWOUT BLUSTER BOASTER COUNTER CRUSHER DESTROY INFLATE KNOCKER LAMBACK LOUNDER MOUTHER PUBLISH SHATTER SMACKER SPANKER SQUELCH WHAMPLE WHIFFLE WHIRRET WHITHER CALAMITY DISASTER KNOCKOUT PASHWAFF SASARARA SICKENER SIDEWINDER (— ABRASIVES) BLAST (— CEMENT) KIBOSH (— GUSTILY) FLAW TUCK WINNOW (— IN PUFFS) FAFF (— NOSE) SNITE (— OFF STEAM) SNIFT (— OF WHALE) SPOUT (— ON CHEEK) ALAPA (— ON HEAD) NOB CONK CLOUR CONKER NOBBER TOPPER NOBBLER (— ON NOSE) NOSER CANKER NOZZLER SMELLER (— SMOKE) NOSE (— SOFTLY) BREATHE (— UP) BOMB BLAST DYNAMITE SUFFLATE (— UPON) WINNOW (— VIOLENTLY) STORM (— WITH CUDGEL) DUB DRUB CRUNT (— WITH FIST) BOP BOX PEG BELT HOOK CLOUT BUFFET ROUNDHOUSE (— WITH FOOT) BOOT KICK SPURN (BOXING —) BLAST FACER (DECISIVE —) SOCKDOLAGER SOCKDOLOGER (FENCING —) MONTANT (GENTLE —) CHUCK (GLANCING —) SCUFF (HARD —) SLOG STOT YANK BEVEL SWACK TWITCHER (HEAVY —) DAD DONG DRUB DUNT ONER SLAM SLUG CLOUT KNOCK POISE SOUSE SQUAT STAVE SWASH STOUND PLUMPER REEMISH (LIGHT —) WAFF (MOCK —) FEINT (NOISY —) DUNDER DUNNER (RESOUNDING —) CLAP CRACK (SHARP —) BAT NAP CLIP KNAP SLAP SPAT CLICK FLICK FLEWIT STINGER (SLIGHT —) SCLAFF

(SMART —) CLIP FLIP SKELP SKITE YANKER (SUDDEN —) ZAP

BLOWCASE EGG

BLOWER PAN DRIER DRYER WHALE FANNER PUFFER BELLOWS BLOOMER BOOSTER MUMBLER BRAGGART OUTBURST (GLASS —) GAFFER

BLOWGUN SUMPIT SUMPITAN SARBACANE PEASHOOTER

BLOWHOLE BLOW GLOUP SPOUT SPIRACLE (— IN STEEL) ROAK

BLOWING ABLOW BLAST BLORE GUSTY BLUSTER BLUSTERY (— AT LOW SPEED) SLACK (— AT RIGHT ANGLES) SIDE (— OF WHALE) SPOUT

BLOWN STALE TIRED OPENED WINDED BLOSSOM SWOLLEN TAINTED BETRAYED FLYBLOWN INFLATED

BLOWOUT BASH BLOW FEED MEAL BURST VALLEY FLAMEOUT WINGDING WHINGDING

BLOWPIPE HOD SUMPIT SUMPITAN SARBACANE (PEWTERER'S —) HOD

BLOWSY DOWDY BLOUSY BLOWZY FROWZY

BLOWY DUSTY

BLUBBER CRY FAT SOB BLUB FOAM WAIL WEEP BIBLE MELON PIECE SPECK SPICK SWELL THICK WHINE BURBLE FLITCH LIPPER LUDDER MEDUSA NETTLE SEETHE BLABBER BLUSTER SLOBBER SWOLLEN WHIMPER (— AT WHALE'S NECK) CANT (CUT WHALE —) FLENSE (REFUSE —) FENKS FOOTING FRITTERS

BLUDGEON BAT HIT SAP CLUB COSH MACE BILLY STICK TOWEL COERCE COURSE BLACKJACK TRUNCHEON

BLUE (ALSO SEE COLOR) HAW LOW SAD SKY AQUA BICE BLAE BLEU CYAN GLUM SAXE TEAL WOAD AZURE BERYL LIVID NIKKO PERSE SMALL WAGET COBALT GLOOMY INDIGO LUPINE ORIENT PEWTER RISQUE SEVERE TRYPAN CELESTE CYANINE GENTIAN GOBELIN HYPPISH LEARNED LIBERTY LOBELIA MATELOT MISTBLU MURILLO NATTIER PEACOCK QUIMPER REGATTA WATCHET CERULEAN DEJECTED LABRADOR LARKSPUR LITERARY MAZARINE MIDNIGHT NATIONAL SAPPHIRE WEDGWOOD POMPADOUR (— DYE) METHYL (BLACKISH —) BLO BLOO (DEEP —) SMALT (DULL —) HAW (ROYAL —) HATHOR (SHADE OF —) INDE COPEN (PREF.) CYAN(O) INDICO IND(I)(O) (SUFF.) (— PIGMENT) CYAN(IC)

BLUEBELL CROWBELL HAREBELL

BLUEBERRY OHELO STONER
PALBERRY RABBITEYE VACCINIUM
BLUEBIRD (— GUIDE) LEADER
BLUE-BLACK BLO
BLUEBLOSSOM LILAC
BLUEBONNET CAP SCOT BLUECAP
BLUEBOTTLE BLUET BLAVER
BARBEAU BLAWORT BLOWFLY
BLUECAP BLUECUP BRUSHES
HARDOCK BLUEBLAW HYACINTH
CORNBINKS
BLUE CREEPER LOVE
BLUE CURLS FLEASEED FLEAWEED
BLUE-EYED GRASS PIGROOT
SATINFLOWER
BLUEFIN TUNNY
BLUEFISH ELF BASS ELFT SHAD
TUNA HORSE SAURY DARZEE
TAILER TAILOR FATBACK SKIPJACK
WEAKFISH
(YOUNG OF —) SNAPPER
WHITEFISH
BLUEGILL BREAM SUNFISH
PONDFISH PUMPKINSEED
BLUE GOOSE BALDHEAD
BLUEGRASS STATE KENTUCKY
BLUE GREEN VENICE
BLUE GUM FEVERGUM
EUCALYPTUS
BLUE HEN STATE DELAWARE
BLUE HERON CRANE NAILROD
BLUEJACKET SAILOR DRAGMAN
BLUEJOINT REDTOP BLUETOPS
BLUENESS CYANOSIS
(— OF SKIN) CYANOSIS
BLUENOSE PRUDE
BLUE-PENCIL EDIT EMEND
BLUE PETER ASK
BLUE PINE LIM
BLUE POINTER MAKO
BLUEPRINT MAP PLAN PLOT DRAFT
TRACE SKETCH DIAGRAM PROJECT
CYANOTYPE
BLUE RUNNER JUREL
BLUES MARE DUMPS CAFARD
DISMAL GLOOMS DISMALS
HORRORS HUMDRUM MEGRIMS
SADNESS DOLDRUMS DOLEFULS
MULLIGRUBS
BLUE SHEEP BURHEL
BLUE SLATE SKAILLIE
BLUESTOCKING BLUE PEDANT
BASBLEU
BLUE SUCCORY CATNACHE
CUPIDONE
BLUET PISSABED EYEBRIGHT
INNOCENCE
BLUE TIT NUN STONECHAT
BLUE TITMOUSE YAUP TYDIE
TIDIFE BLUECAP
BLUETONGUE THICKHEAD
BLUE VERVAIN IRONWEED
BLUE VINNY DORSET
BLUEWEED ECHIUM IRONWEED
ADDERWORT
BLUFF ALTO BANK BRAG CURT
FOOL RUDE BLUNT BRAVE BURLY
CLIFF FRANK GRUFF SHORT SURLY
SWANK WINDY ABRUPT BOUNCE
CRUSTY BLINDER BLINKER
BLUFTER BRUSQUE DECEIVE
UNCIVIL BARRANCA BARRANCO
CHURLISH HOODWINK IMPOLITE

BLUISH BLEUATRE
BLUISH-GRAY MERLE
BLUISH-GREEN AQUAMARINE
BLUMEA PLACUS
BLUNDER ERR MIX BALK BONE
BOOB BUBU BULL DOLT FLUB
GAFF ROIL SKEW SLIP STIR TRIP
BEVUE BLOOP BONER BOTCH
BREAK ERROR FAULT FLUFF GAFFE
LAPSE MISDO BOGGLE BOOBOO
BUMBLE BUMMLE BUNGLE
ESCAPE FUMBLE GAZEBO
HOWLER MAFFLE MINGLE
MUDDLE SLIPUP BLOOMER
BLOOPER CLANGER CONFUSE
DERANGE FAILURE FLOATER
MISSTEP MISTAKE OVERSEE
SOTTISE STUMBLE PRATFALL
SOLECISM
((AMUSING —) HOWLER
(— IN LANGUAGE) BULL
(— IN SPEECH) SOLECISM
(HUMILIATING —) PRATFALL
(VERBAL —) SLIPSLAP SLIPSLOP
BLUNDERBUSS TRABU TRABUCO
TRABUCHO TROMBONE
ESPINGOLE
BLUNDERER BUMBLER BUMMLER
KNOTHEAD LUMBERER
BLUNDERING AWKWARD
BUMBLING
BLUNT BALD BATE BULL CURT
DAMP DULL FLAT MULL SNUB
ABATE BLATE BLUFF BRUSK
DUBBY FRANK INERT MORNE
PLAIN PLUMP STUNT TERSE
CANDID CLUMSY DEADEN DIRECT
OBTUND OBTUSE REBATE RETUND
SHEATH STUBBY STUPID BRUSQUE
DISEDGE HACKNEY SHEATHE
SNUBBED SPADISH STUBBED
STUPEFY HEBETATE
BLUNTED MORNED
(PREF.) OBTUSI
BLUNTLY PLAT PLUMP FLATLY
CRUDELY FRANKLY
BLUR DIM FOG HUM BLOB BLOT
FADE FUZZ MIST SLUR SOIL SPOT
BLEAR CLOUD FUDGE SHAKE
SMEAR STAIN SULLY MACKLE
MACULE SMUDGE STIGMA
BLEMISH CONFUSE FEATHER
OBSCURE TAILING
BLURB AD BOLT PUFF RAVE BRIEF
PROMO NOTICE
(PROMOTIONAL —) PROMO
BLURRED FAINT FUZZY MUZZY
VAGUE WOOZY BLEARY BLURRY
CLOUDY SMEARY SMUDGY
SWIMMY WOOLLY CLOUDED
COMATIC EDGELESS FLANNELLY
BLURRING HALATION
BLURT BLAT BOLT PLUMP BLUNDER
EXCLAIM
BLUSH BLUE GLOW BLINK COLOR
FLUSH GLEAM PAINT ROUGE
TINGE CHANGE GLANCE MANTLE
REDDEN CRIMSON FLICKER
SCARLET LIKENESS JOSEPHINE
BLUSHING RED ROSY ABLUSH
ROSEATE FLUSHING ROSACEOUS
BLUSTER GAS BEEF BLOW DING
HUFF RAGE RAIL RANT RAVE

BLAST BLEAT BLORE BOAST
BRACE BULLY NOISE STORM
SWANK BABBLE BELLOW BOUNCE
FRAPLE HECTOR HUFFLE TUMULT
WUTHER BLUBBER BRAVADO
FLUSTER GAUSTER ROISTER
SWAGGER WHITHER BOASTING
BULLYING THREATEN
RODOMONTADE
BLUSTERER SWAG FLASH HECTOR
HUFFER FRAPLER HUFFCAP
TEARCAT CACAFOGO FANFARON
BLUSTERING BOG LOUD BLUFF
BRASH BULLY VAPORS HUFFCAP
VAPOURS ARROGANT BULLYING
BLUSTERY RAW
BOA BOM BOID BOMA ABOMA
JIBOA SCARF THROW ABOLLA
ADJIGA GIBOIA JOBOYA PYTHON
ADJIGER CAMOODI EMPEROR
PEROPOD ANACONDA CORALLUS
BOADICEA (HUSBAND OF —)
PRASUTAGUS
BOAR HOG APER SUID BRAWN
SWINE BARROW HOGGET TUSKER
BRAWNER SOUNDER SUIDIAN
VENISON WILRONE BRISTLER
SANGLIER HOGGASTER
(— CRY) FREAM
(— HEAD) HURE
(— IN 2ND YEAR) HOGGET
(— IN 3RD YEAR) HOGSTEER
HOGGASTER
(— STY) FRANK
(YOUNG —) GRISE SOUNDER
(PREF.) SUI
BOARD EAT LAG PAX TOE DAIL DEAL
DECK DIET EATS FARE FLIP HACK
JOIN KEEP LATH MEAT SHIP SIGN
SLAT TRAY TRIP ASTEL BUIRD
CHESE CLEAR COARD COUCH
COURT ENTER FOUND GETIN
GETON HOUSE LODGE MEALS
PANEL PLANK RATCH SHIDE STAGE
STALL SWALE TABLE THEAL
ABACUS ACCOST ASTYLL
COMMON PALLET PLANCH
RANDOM RIBBON SHIELD SIDING
TUCKER CABINET CHAMBER
COUNCIL CRIMPER DUOVIRI
ENPLANE ENTRAIN KNEELER
PALETTE PENSION PLANCHE
SCRAPER TABLING TRANSOM
WHATMAN APPROACH ASSEMBLY
BOXBOARD CUPBOARD EXCLUDER
FETIALES KEYBOARD LAPBOARD
PEGBOARD TRIBUNAL
PRESSBOARD MORTARBOARD
(— FOR FALCON'S MEAT) HACK
(— OF BRIDGE) CHESS
(— OF LOOM) CARD
(— OF MILL WHEEL) AWE
(— ON CALF'S NOSE) BLAB
(— OVER) BERTH
(— WITH GROOVE) COULISSE
(— WITH HANDLE) CLAPPER
(— WITH NUMBER) SLATE
(— WITH PINS) RIDDLE
(— WITH TEETH) HACKLE RUFFER
(BLOCKHEAD —) DOLL
(CHANNEL —) PAN
(CHESS —) TABLER

(DRAWING —) COQUILLE
(EXHIBITION —) FRAME
(FLOOR —) KEY
(GAME —) HALMA
(HEART-SHAPED —) PLANCHET
(KIND OF —) OUIJA MALIBU
(MORTAR —) HAWK
(NOTCHED —) HORSE
(OTTER —) DOOR
(POLING —) RUNNER
(PRESSED —S) FELT
(PULP-PRESSING —) COUCH
(RABBETED —S) SHIPLAP
(SHEATHING —S) SARKING
(STRIKE —) SCREED
(TANNING —) BEAM
(THIN —) SHIDE SARKING
(THIN —S) SLITWORK
(WARPING —) BARTREE
BOARDED PLANCHED
BOARDER MEALER TABLER
GRAINER PENSIONER SOJOURNER
TRANSIENT
BOARDING LIVERY
BOARDINGHOUSE FONDA HOUSE
PENSION
BOARDWALK MARINA DUCKBOARD
BOARWOOD CHEWSTICK
BOAST BOG GAB JET BEEF BLAW
BLOW BRAG CROW POMP PUFF
RAVE VANT WIND WOST YELP
BLAST BRAVE CRACK CRAKE
EXTOL EXULT GLORY PRATE
QUACK ROOSE SCOLD SKITE
VAPOR VAUNT VOUST YOLPE
AVAUNT BLAZON BLEEZE BOUNCE
CLAMOR FLAUNT INSULT MENACE
OUTCRY SPLORE BLUSTER
BRAVING CLAMOUR DEVAUNT
DISPLAY GLORIFY SWAGGER
FLOURISH THREATEN VANTERIE
VAUNTERY
BOASTER BLOW HUFF GALAH SKITE
BLOWER CROWER GASCON
PEDANT PRATER SHAKER
BLOWOFF BOUNCER BRAGGER
BRAVADO CRACKER RUFFLER
BLOWHARD BRAGGART
CACAFUGO FANFARON GLORIOSO
JINGOIST RODOMONT TARTARIN
WOUSTOUR
BOASTFUL BIG BRAG HIGH COCKY
LARGE BRAGGY PARADO BOBADIL
JACTANT VAUNTIE FANFARON
GLORIOUS GASCONADE
THRASONIC
BOASTFULLY SIDE LARGE
BOASTFULNESS GLORY EGOTISM
WINDINESS
BOASTING BLOW HUFF YELP
BOAST CRACK PRATE ROOSE
QUACKY BOBANCE GASSING
JACTANCE JACTANCY QUACKISH
VAPORING VAUNTAGE VENTOSITY
RODOMONTADE
(EMPTY —) GAS
BOAT ARK BUM BUN CAT COG COT
DOW GIG MON TUB ACON BAIT
BARK BOOT BRIG CARV CHOP
COCK DHOW DINK DORY DUMP
FLAT FOUZ JUNK PAIR PLAT PRAM
PUNT RAFT SCOW SHIP SKAG TACK
TODE TOPO TROW WAKA YAWL

YOLE ACCON AVISO BANCA BARCA BARGE BARIS BATEL BIDAR BOLIA BOYER BULLY BUYER CANOE COBLE CRAFT DHONI DINGY FERRY FOIST FORTY FUNNY JOLLY KETCH LAKER LINER NADIR OOLAK PIECE PILOT PRAAM RACER SHELL SHOUT SIKAR SKIFF SKIFT SMACK TOPPO UMIAK WAAPA WHIFF XEBEC ZEBEC BAIDAK BANGKA BATEAU BAWLEY BELLUM BILALO BORLEY BOTTOM BOUTRE CAIQUE CARVEL CAYUCO CHEBEC COCKLE CRUISE CUTTER DINGHY DREDGE DRIVER DROVER DUGOUT FLATTY GALLEY GARVEY GAYYOU GLIDER HOOKER JAGGER JIGGER KEELER KICKER KUPHAR LATEEN LERRET MAILER NAGGAR NUGGAR PACKET PEAPOD PEDULE PICARD PINKIE PLAYTE PULWAR RANDAN ROCKER SANDAL SCAPHE SCHOUW SCHUYT SETTEE SINGLE SKERRY STRUSE TANKER TENDER TIMBER TOGGER TORPID TRANKY TROUGH VESSEL WAFTER WHERRY ZEBECK AIRBOAT ALMADIA ANGEYOK BALLOEN BALLOON BAULEAH BUMBOAT CAISSON CARRIER CATCHER CORACLE COBOLAN CRUISER CURRACH DOODODY DRIFTER DROGHER FLATTIE FLEETER FLYBOAT FOYBOAT FRIGATE GAIASSA GASBOAT GEORDIE GONDOLA HOVELER HUFFLER KELLECK LIGHTER MACHINE MASOOLA NACELLE PEARLER PEDIWAK PINNACE PIRAGUA POOKAWN PUTELEE SCOOTER SCULLER SHALLOP SHARPIE SHIKARA SIKHARA SKAFFIE SKIPPET SPONGER SPYBOAT STEAMER TRAWLER TUCKNER TUMRREL TUMBRIL VEDETTE WHIRREY BALANGAY BARANGAY BILLYBOY BOOMBOAT BULLBOAT BUMBARGE CANALLER CHALOUPE CHEBACCO CHELINGA CHELINGO COCKBOAT COROCORE DAHABEAH DUCKBOAT FIREBOAT FLAGBOAT KEELBOAT LIFEBOAT MACKINAW MONOXYLE NEWSBOAT OYSTERER PALANDER PANCHWAY PESSONER PESSULUS PULLBOAT SAILBOAT SCHOKKER SCHOONER SURFBOAT TONGKANG TRANSFER OUTRIGGER

(— OF MALTA) DGHAISA
(— WITH SAILS AND OARS) LYMPHIAD
(ABANDONED —) DERELICT
(CANAL — OF VENICE) VAPORETTO
(CHEMICAL —) CAPSULE
(CHINESE —) JUNK SAMPAN
(CLUMSY —) HOOKER DROGHER
(COLLEGE —) TORPID
(DISPATCH —) AVISO PACKET
(ESKIMO —) KAMIK UMIAK OOMIAC UMIACK
(FERRY —) BAC CUTT
(FISHING —) COG BOVO BUSS DONI CANOA COBLE DHONI NOBBY PYKAR SMACK VINTA BALDIE

BAWLEY BORLEY DOGGER DROVER FISHER KUPHAR NICKEY SANDAL SCAFFY SEINER SEXERN TOSHER VOLYER WHALER CARAVEL CRABBER DRAGGER FOLLYER POOKAUN SHARPIE SKAFFIE TRAWLER DRAGBOAT GAROOKUH SHRIMPER

(FLAT-BOTTOM —) ARK BAC BUN DORY FLAT PLAT PRAM PUNT SCOW BARGE COBLE DOREY FLOAT MOSES PRAAM SHOUT BATEAU BUGEYE GAYYOU PUTELI GONDOLA LIGHTER FLATBOAT GUNDELOW JOHNBOAT
(FLY —) BUSS FLUTE FLIGHT
(GANGES —) PUTELI
(HIGHLAND —) BIRLINN
(INCENSE —) NEF SHIP NAVICULA
(MALAY —) COROCORE GALLIVAT
(MORTAR —) PALANDER
(OPEN —) WHIFF LERRET SHALLOP
(PATROL —) SPITKID SPITKIT
(PLEASURE —) FUNNY PEDALO
(RACING —) SIX FOUR EIGHT SCULL SHELL SINGLE TORPID SCULLER
(SHIP'S —) GIG MOSES DINGEY DINGHY LAUNCH TENDER PINNACE
(SKIN —) BIDAR BAIDAR ANGEYOK BIDARKA BULLBOAT
(SMALL —) CARTOPPER
(WICKER —) KUFA GOOFA GOOFAH CORACLE
(3-OAR —) RANDAN
(6-OAR —) SEXERN
(8-OAR —) SHIP
(PL.) LIGHTERAGE
(PREF.) CYMBI CYMBO
(SUFF.) SCAPH
BOATBUILDING SETWORK
BOATHOOK STOWER HITCHER
BOATMAN DANDI DANDY PHAON BARGER BOWMAN CHARON YAWLER HOBBLER HOVELER HUFFLER COBLEMAN VOYAGEUR WATERMAN GONDOLIER
BOAT SEAT TAFT
BOAT-SHAPED NAVICULAR
(PREF.) SCAPH(O)
BOAT SHELL YET SWEETMEAT
BOATSWAIN BOSN BOSUN SERANG TINDAL
BOAZ (FATHER OF —) SALMA SALMON
(SON OF —) OBED
(WIFE OF —) RUTH
BOB BAB BOW CUT DAB DIP HOD JOG POP RAP TAP BALL BLOW BUFF CALF CLIP CLOD COIN CORK DUCK GRUB JEER JERK JEST KNOB MOCK WORM BUNCH CHEAT DANCE FILCH FLOAT FLOUT SHAKE TAUNT TRICK BINGLE BOBBER BOBBLE BUFFET CURTSY DELUDE HOBBLE POMMEL POPPLE STRIKE WEIGHT BOBSLED BOBTAIL CLUSTER HAIRCUT PAGEBOY PENDANT PLUMMET REFRAIN SHINGLE SHILLING
(— UP) LOLLOP
BOBAC PAHMI TARBAGAN
BOBBER CORK DUCK FLOAT BOBFLY

BOBBIN PIN CONE CORD PIRN REEL BRAID QUILL SPOOL BROCHE HANGER SKREEL TAVELL WORKER RATCHET SPINDLE TARELLE TORCHON
(PL.) BONES
BOBBINET ILLUSION
BOBBING DOOK
BOBBLE ERROR
BOBOLINK DEER REED SUCKER BUNTING MAYBIRD ORTOLAN REEDBIRD RICEBIRD
BOBSLED BOB DRAY BOBLET RIPPER TRAVERSE
BOBWHITE COLIN QUAIL PARTRIDGE
BOBWIG DALMAHOY
BOCACCIO JACK TOMCOD
BOCCACCIO TRECENTIST
BOCCARELLA NOSEHOLE
BOCCARO YIHSING
BOCE BOGUE OXEYE
BOCHERU (FATHER OF —) AZEL
BODE OMEN SIGN STOP AUGUR OFFER HERALD MESSAGE PORTEND PRESAGE FOREBODE FORECAST FORESHOW FORETELL INDICATE
BODHISATTVA KWANNON MAITREYA AVALOKITA PADMAPANI
BODICE JUPE CHOLI GILET JUMPS WAIST BASQUE BOLERO CORSET JELICK LYFKIE CORSAGE OVERBODY SLIPBODY
BODIERON BOREGAT
BODILESS MOONSHINE
BODILY SOLID SOMAL ACTUAL CARNAL FLESHLY SOMATIC CORPORAL ENTIRELY EXTERNAL MATERIAL PERSONAL PHYSICAL SARKICAL VISCERAL CORPOREAL
(NOT —) INTERIOR
BODKIN AWL PIN POINT BROACH DAGGER NEEDLE POPPER HAIRPIN PONIARD STILETTO EYELETEER
BODLE TURNER
BODO CACHARI
BODY BOD BAND BELL BOLE BOOK BOUK BUCK BULK CREW DEHA FORM HEAD LICH MASS MOLD NAVE RIND RUPA SOMA STEM ATOMY FLESH FRAME HABIT MOULD SHANK STIFF TORSO TRUNK CORMUS CORPSE CORPUS CUERPO EXTENT FUSEAU LICHAM PERSON SARIRA AIRFOIL ANATOMY CADAVER CARCASS COMPANY ECONOMY QUANTUM SKINFUL SUPTION TEXTURE CORSAINT DEMARCHY EXTENSUM MAJORITY PHYSIQUE QUARROME TENEMENT PERSONNEL
(— OF ARROW) SHAFT STELE
(— OF BASILICA) NAVE
(— OF BEES) SWARM
(— OF BELIEVERS) FAITH
(— OF CANONS) CHAPTER
(— OF CARDINALS) CONCLAVE
(— OF CEREMONIES) RITUAL
(— OF CHILDREN) INFANTRY
(— OF CHRISTIANS) KOINONIA COMMUNION
(— OF CONSTABLES) POSSE

(— OF CORINTHIAN CAPITAL) VASE
(— OF DOCTRINES) DOGMA
(— OF ECHINODERM) DISC DISK
(— OF EVIDENCE) CASE CORPUS
(— OF FIBERS) FORNIX
(— OF FOLLOWERS) SECT
(— OF GUARDS) WARD
(— OF HELMET) BELL
(— OF ISLAMIC CUSTOM) SUNNA SUNNAH
(— OF JUDGES) JUDICIARY
(— OF KNOWLEDGE) STUFF
(— OF LAW) CODE SHAR HALAKA SHARIA PANDECT SHARIAT HALACHAH
(— OF LEGEND) SAGA
(— OF MANKIND) HERD
(— OF MUSCLE) BELLY
(— OF NOTIONS) FOLKLORE
(— OF OFFICERS) BUREAU
(— OF ORE) BUNCH MANTO
(— OF PIGMENT) EYESPOT IMPASTO
(— OF POETRY) EPOS
(— OF PRINCIPLES) ORGANON
(— OF ROCK) DIKE DYKE HORSE STOCK BIOHERM MUDFLOW INTRUSION
(— OF SINGERS) CHORUS
(— OF STATUTE) PURVIEW
(— OF STUDENTS) CLASS
(— OF TEN) DECURY
(— OF TENANTS) GAVEL HOMAGE
(— OF THIEVES) SCHOOL
(— OF TRADITIONS) HADIT HADITH
(— OF TROOPS) FORCE TAXIS AMBUSH BATTLE CONREY SCREEN SQUARE BRIGADE LASHKAR SUPPORT BATTALIA GARRISON
(— OF TYPE) SHANK
(— OF VASSALS) BAN MANRED
(— OF WARRIORS) IMPI
(— OF WATER) BAY RIP SEA BAHR FORD HEAD LAKE LAVE POND POOL WAVE ABYSS BAYOU DRINK FLOOD OCEAN SHARD SHERD SWASH LAGOON NYANZA STREAM FLOWAGE SWALLOW
(— OF WELLBORN MEN) COMITATUS
(— OF WRITINGS) SMRTI SMRITI
(— OF 12 MEN) DOUZAINE
(— POLITIC) ESTATE
(— RIDDLED BY BULLETS) SIEVE
(CAROTID —) GLOMUS
(CART —) SIRPEA
(CELESTIAL —) SUN BALL COMET PLANET SPHERE ELEMENT ASTEROID PLANETOID SATELLITE PLANETESIMAL
(CIRCULAR —) DISC DISK
(COMPACT —) GLOBE
(CONDUCTING —) GROUND
(CORPORATE —) SOCIETY
(DEAD —) LICH MORT GHOST CADAVER CARCASS CARRION SUBJECT
(DEFEATED —) ROUT
(ECCLESIASTICAL —) CLASSIS
(ELASTIC —) CUSHION
(EXTENDED) LENGTH
(FAT —) EPIPLOON
(FRUITING —) CONK CLAVA ASCOCARP MAZAEDIUM

(GALACTIC —) SPINAR
(GLOBULAR —) NOB KNOB
(GOVERNING —) KAHAL SYNOD DURBAR SENATE DECARCHY DIRECTORY
(HAT —) HOOD
(HEAVENLY —) SUN LAMP STAR COMET LIGHT CANDLE
(HOLLOW —) TUBE
(HUMAN —) EARTH
(HYALINE —) DRUSE
(IMMUNE —) DESMON
(JUDICIAL —) FORUM
(KIND OF —) LIFTING
(LEGISLATIVE —) CHAMBER ASSEMBLY CONGRESS LAGTHING PARLIAMENT
(MAIN — OF ARMY) BATTLE
(MATHEMATICAL —) FILAMENT
(MORMON —) BISHOPRIC
(MORTAL —) KHET
(POROUS —) MADREPORITE
(PRESBYTERIAN —) SESSION JUDICATORY
(RELIGIOUS —) SECT CONVENT
(REPRODUCTIVE —) EGG GEMMA SPORE GEMMULA
(ROUND —) GLOBE
(SONOROUS —) PHONIC
(SPIRITUAL —) SAHU
(SWELLING —) BOSS
(UNICELLUAR —) SPORE
(WAGON —) BED BUCK PUNT
(PREF.) CORPORI SOMAT(O) SOMATICO SOMO
(SUFF.) CY DEMA SOMA(TO)(TOUS) SOME SOMIA SOMIC SOMOUS SOMUS
(— OF A KIND) ID
BODYGUARD THANE ESCORT INWARD HUSCARL RETINUE TRABANT THINGMAN WARDCORS
(CRIMINAL'S —) MINDER
BOER TAKHAAR AFRIKANER
BOG BUG CAR DUB FEN GOG HAG BOLD CARR CESS FLOW MIRE MOOR MOSS OOZE QUAG SINK SLEW SLUE SPEW STOG SUDS SYRT WASH LETCH MARSH MIZZY SAUCY SLADE SLOCK SWAMP MORASS MUSKEG POLDER SLOUGH CRIPPLE FORWARD PEATERY TURBARY QUAGMIRE
(MARSH —) QUAG
(PEAT —) CESS MOSS PETARY YARPHA
(PREF.) HELO
BOG ASPHODEL KNAVERY
BOGEY BUG COW HAG BOGIE BOGLE DEVIL GNOME TRUCK BOGGLE BOOGER GOBLIN BOGGARD BOGGART BUGABOO BUGBEAR SPECTER SPECTRE
BOGGED SLOUGHED
BOGGLE JIB SHY BALK FOIL STOP ALARM BOTCH DEMUR SCARE START STICK BAFFLE BUNGLE GOBLIN SHRINK BAUCHLE BLUNDER PERPLEX SCRUPLE STUMBLE FRIGHTEN HESITATE
BOGGY WET DEEP MIRY SOFT FENNY FOGGY GOUTY HAGGY

MOSSY SNAPY SPEWY MARISH MARSHY QUAGGY SLOBBY SWAMPY WAUGHY BOGGISH QUEACHY SQUASHY
BOGIER RIDER GEARMAN
BOGLAND SLADE
BOGLE GOBLIN
BOG MANGANESE WAD LAMPADITE
BOGO ABILO ABILAO
BOGOMILE PATARIN PATARINE
BOGUS FAKE SHAM FALSE PHONY SPURIOUS
BOGY GOBLIN
BOHEME, LA (CHARACTER IN —) MIMI COLLINE MUSETTA RODOLFO MARCELLO SCHAUNARD
(COMPOSER OF —) PUCCINI
BOHEMIAN ARTY PICARA PICARD PICARO ARTISTIC
(— RIVER) ELBE VLTAVA LUZNICE BEROUNKA
(— TOWN) PISEK PLZEN PRAHA TABOR PILSEN PRAGUE
BOHEMIAN GIRL (COMPOSER OF —) BALFE
BOHOR REEDBUCK
BOIL FRY PET STY BILE BLOB BOLL BRAN BREW BUCK BUMP COCT COOK COWL LEEP PLAY PUSH QUAT RAGE SEED SORE STEW STYE TEEM WALL WALM WELL BLAIN BOTCH BREDE STEAM BETRAY BUBBLE BULDER BULLER BURBLE DECOCT GALLOP PIMPLE RISING SEETHE SIMMER TOTTLE WABBLE WOBBLE ANTHRAX BEALING BREEDER CATHAIR ELIXATE ESTUATE INFLAME AESTUATE EBULLATE FURUNCLE PHLEGMON CARBUNCLE
(— IN LYE) BUCK
(— SYRUP) PEARL
(SAND —) BLOWOUT
(PREF.) COCTO DOTHI(EN)(O) ZEO
BOILED SOD SODDEN
(— WITHOUT SAUCE) ANGLAISE
BOILER YET REEF STILL COPPER KETTLE RETORT TEACHE ALEMBIC CALDRON FURNACE
(SALT —) WELLER
BOILERMAKER (PART OF —) BEER
BOILING WALM ABOIL FERVID COCTION FERVENT SCALDING SEETHING ELIXATION
BOILING POINT
(PREF.) COCTO
BOISTERER (MASTER OF —) FORTUNIO
BOISTEROUS GURL HIGH LOUD RUDE WILD BURLY GURLY NOISY RANDY ROARY ROUGH WINDY COARSE RUGGED SHANDY STOCKY STORMY STRONG UNRULY FURIOUS MASSIVE ROARING VIOLENT BIGMOUTH CUMBROUS LARRIKIN STRIDENT VEHEMENT ROBUSTIOUS
BOLD BIG BOG MOD YEP DERF HARD KEEN PERT RASH RUDE TALL WHAT YEPE APERT BARDY BIELD BRASH BRAVE BRENT FRACK

FREAK FRECK GALLY HARDY JOLLY LARGE MANLY NERVY PAWKY PEART POKEY RUDAS SAUCY STEEP STOUT WLONK ABRUPT AUDACE BRASSY BRAZEN CROUSE DARING FIERCE HEROIC PLUCKY PRETTY STRONG ASSURED DASHING DEFIANT FORWARD GRIVOIS HAUGHTY MASSIVE VALIANT ARROGANT FAMILIAR FEARLESS IMMODEST IMPUDENT INTREPID MALAPERT POWERFUL RESOLUTE TEMEROUS
(NOT —) GENTEEL
BOLDFACE BOLD BLACK FULLFACE
BOLDLY CRANK BARELY CROUSE HARDLY HARDILY ROUNDLY STRONGLY
BOLDNESS BROW DARE FACE GALL BIELD CHEEK NERVE PLUCK VIGOR DARING BRAVERY COURAGE FREEDOM AUDACITY TEMERITY HARDIHOOD
(— OF SPEECH) PARRHESIA
BOLDO NUTMEG
BOLE CLAY DOSE STEM BOLUS CRYPT TRUNK RUDDLE TIMBER
BOLETUS CEPE
BOLIDE METEOR FIREBALL
BOLIVIA PILE

BOLIVIA	
CAPITAL:	LAPAZ SUCRE
COIN:	TOMIN CENTAVO
DEPARTMENT:	LAPAZ ORURO PANDO ELBENI POTOSI TARIJA
FORMER CAPITAL:	ORURO
INDIAN:	URO INCA ITEN MOXO URAN ARAWAK AYMARA CHARCA CHICHA IXIAMA TACANA PUQUINA QUECHUA SIRIONE TUMUPASA
LAKE:	POOPO COIPASA ROGAGUA AULLAGAS TITICACA
MEASURE:	LEAGUE CELEMIN
MOUNTAIN:	JARA CUSCO CUZCO PUPUYA SAJAMA SORATA ILLAMPU ANCOHUMA ILLIMANI ZAPALERI
MOUNTAINS:	ANDES SUNSAS SANSIMON SANTIAGO
PANPIPE:	SICU SIKU
PLATEAU:	ALTIPLANO
RIVER:	BENI YATA ABUNA APERE BOOPI LAUCA ORTON BAURES GRANDE ICHILO ITENEZ MADIDI MAMORE MIZQUE TARIJA YACUMA GUAPORE ITONAMA MACHUPO BENECITO INAMBARI PARAGUAY PARAPETI
SALT DEPOSIT:	UYUNI EMPEXA
SWAMP:	IZOZOG
TOWN:	IVO ICLA ITAU MOJO POJO SAYA YACO YATA YURA CLIZA LAPAZ LLICA ORURO QUIME SUCRE UNCIA UYUNI ZONGO GUAQUI POTOSI TARIJA
VOLCANO:	OLLAGUE
WEIGHT:	LIBRA MARCO

BOLL BOW POD BULB KNOB SNAP ONION BUBBLE CAPSULE
(FOURTH —) FIRLOT

BOLLARD BITT KEVEL DOLPHIN DEADHEAD
(—S AND BITTS) APOSTLES
BOLLER STRIPPER
BOLL WEEVIL PICUDO
BOLO MACHETE SUNDANG
BOLSHEVIK RED MAXIMALIST
BOLSHEVISM COMMUNISM SOVIETISM
BOLSHEVIST BOLO
BOLSTER AID PAD JACK PILLOW CUSHION HEADING STIFFEN SUPPORT BACKSTOP BALUSTER COMPRESS MAINTAIN
BOLT BAR JAG KEY LUE PEN PIN ROD RUN BEAT BURR CRAM DART DUMP FLEE GULP LOCK PAWL SHUT SIFT SLOT SNIB SPAR STUD ARROW BILBO CLOSE ELOPE FLASH FLOUR GORGE LATCH RIVET SETUP SHAFT STOCK ASSORT DECAMP DESERT FASTEN FLIGHT GANYIE GARBLE MOOTER PINTLE PURIFY QUARRY REFINE SAFETY SEARCE SECURE SNIBEL STREAK STRONG TOGGLE WINNOW ABSCOND BAYBOLT DOGBOLT EYEBOLT MISSILE QUARREL SETBOLT SHACKLE SLABBER THUNDER DRAWBOLT FASTENER FISHBOLT FLATHEAD KINGBOLT RINGBOLT SEPARATE SLUMMOCK STAMPEDE
(— FOOD) SKOFF
(DOOR —) DRAWBOLT
(FIERY —) RESHEPH
(LIGHTNING —) SHAFT
(THUNDER —) FULMEN
(PREF.) GOMPHO
BOLTER BOLT SIEVE DRESSER MUGWUMP
BOLTHEAD MATRASS
BOLUS BALL PILL
BOMB DUD EGG ROC AZON BOOM FRAG BLARE CRUMP PRANG RAZON SHELL SQUIB ASHCAN SALUTE AEROSOL BALLOON BOMBARD GRENADE MARMITE TORPEDO AEROBOMB FIREBALL WHIZBANG PINEAPPLE INCENDIARY
(— RELEASE) TOGGLE
(FLYING —) DOODLEBUG
(KIND OF —) SKIP
(TRENCH —) MINNIE
(UNEXPLODED —) DUD
(PL.) STICK
BOMBARD BOMB PELT CRUMP SHELL ATTACK BATTER BOTTLE STRAFE
BOMBARDMENT BLITZ SIEGE ATTACK RAFALE STRAFE BATTERY SHELLING
BOMBARDON TUBA NICOLO POMMER BRUMMER
BOMBAST GAS PAD PUFF RAGE RANT RAVE STUFF TUMOR BLUSTER FUSTIAN TYMPANY BALLYHOO BOASTING RHAPSODY TURGIDITY
BOMBASTIC PUFFY TUMID VOCAL WINDY FLUENT HEROIC MOUTHY TURGID BLOATED BOMBAST

FLOWERY FUSTIAN OROTUND
POMPOUS RANTING STILTED
SWOLLEN INFLATED SWELLING
(— STYLE) TYMPANY
BOMBAY DUCK BUMALO
BUMMALO
BOMBER (TYPE OF —) STEALTH
BOMBINATE HUM BUZZ
BONACE TREE NOSEBURN
BONACI AGUAJI
BONA FIDE LEVEL GENUINE
AUTHENTIC
BONANZA BUNCH
BONANZA STATE MONTANA
BONBON CANDY CREAM GOODY
DAINTY CARAMEL COSAQUE
SNAPPER CONFETTO
(PL.) CONFETTI
BOND BON DOG TIE VOW ANDI BAIL
BAND DUTY FIVE FOUR GILT GLUE
GYVE HOLD CHAIN KNOT LINK NOTE YOKE
BOUND CHAIN NEXUS SWATH
BINDER CEDULA CEMENT CONNEX
COPULA COUPLE ENGAGE
ESCROW FETTER LEAGUE PLEDGE
SOLDER SWATHE FOREIGN
HUSBAND LIAISON LIBERTY
LINKAGE MANACLE SHACKLE
STATUTE ADHESIVE CONTRACT
COVENANT LIGAMENT LIGATION
LIGATURE MORTGAGE SECURITY
VADIMONY VINCULUM
(EMOTIONAL —) RAPPORT
(KIND OF —) JUNK
(PL.) IRON KHAKIS SHORTS
(PREF.) DESM(A)(IDI)(IDIO)(O)
ETHMO OSSE(O) OSSI OST(E)(EO)
(SUFF.) (CONTAINING TRIPLE —)
OLIC
BONDAGE YOKE THRALL HELOTRY
SERFDOM SLAVERY BONDSHIP
THIRLING CAPTIVITY SERVITUDE
BONDED CATTED ENGAGED
BONDMAN CARL ESNE PEON SERF
CHURL HELOT SLAVE STOOGE
SURETY THRALL VASSAL CHATTEL
PEASANT SERVANT VILLEIN
BONDSMAN
BONDSTONE BINDER BONDER
KEYSTONE
BONE OS DIB HIP LUZ RIB TOT BANE
ULNA BLADE FEMUR HYOID ILIUM
INCUS JUGAL MALAR SLATE
STONE TALUS TIBIA UNION VOMER
CANNON COCCYX CONCHA
COPULA CUBOID EPURAL FIBULA
FILLET HAMATE NUCHAL PECTEN
RADIAL SPLINT STAPES TRIPOD
UNGUIS ZYGOMA DENTARY
PAI ATAI PROOTIC CORACOID
PALATINE PARIETAL PERIOTIC
PISIFORM QUADRATE TEMPORAL
NAVICULAR OPERCULAR
METACARPAL
(— OF ARM) RADIU
(— OF DIGIT) PHALANX
(— OF NOSE) VOMER TURBINAL
(ANKLE —) TALUS
(EAR —) INCUS HAMMER STAPES
MALLEUS TYMPANIC
(HEEL —) CALCANEUM
(HIP —) HUGGIN
(HORSE'S —) RACK

(PELVIC —) PUBIS
(PUBIC —) PECTEN
(SHIN —) CNEMIS
(SKULL —) SQUAMOSAL
(SMALL —) OSSICLE
(THIGH —) FEMUR
(WRIST —) RADIALE SCAPHOID
TRAPEZOID
(PL.) DICE CLAPPERS ETHMO
KNACKERS SKELETON
(PREF.) ETHMO OSSE(O) OSSI
OST(E)(EO)
(SUFF.) OST(EON)(EUS)(OSIS)
BONE-BLACK SPODE SPODIUM
BONED
(SUFF.) OSTEUS
BONEFISH OIO MACABI GRUBBER
BONYFISH LADYFISH
BONEHEAD SAP BOOB STUPE
BONER BUBU FLUB ROCK ERROR
BRODIE STAYER STUMER
BLOOMER BLOOPER BLUNDER
MISTAKE STEELER STUMOUR
BONES
(PREF.) (— OF HAND OR FOOT)
PHALANGI(A)
BONESET COMFREY AGUEWEED
EUPATORY HEMPWEEK
BONEYARD STOCK
BONFIRE BLAZE TANDLE TAWNIE
BALEFIRE BURNFIRE NEEDFIRE
BONGO DOR BUNGO CANOE
BONI MUNI
BONIFACE HOST
BONING SAP
BONITO AKU ATU NICE COBIA
SARDA BONITA ROBALO
ALBACORE KATONKEL MACKEREL
SCOMBRID SKIPJACK
BONNET CAP HAT COWL HOOD
POKE POXY SCON COVER DECOY
SCONE SHAPE TOQUE CAPOTE
MOBCAP SLOUCH CHAPEAU
COMMODE CORONET LEGHORN
SOWBACK VOLUPER BALMORAL
BONGRACE HEADGEAR
BONNET MONKEY ZATI MUNGA
TOQUE MACACO RILAWA
MACAQUE
BONNY GAY FINE MERRY PLUMP
BLITHE BONNIE PRETTY STRONG
HEALTHY BUDGEREE HANDSOME
BEAUTIFUL
BONTOK IGOROT
BONUS GIN TIP GIFT MEED PLUM
PLUS AWARD BRIBE BUNCE BUNTS
PILON PRIZE SPIFF REGALO
REWARD CUMSHAW DOUCEUR
PREMIUM SUBSIDY BOUNTITH
DIVIDEND TANTIEME LAGNIAPPE
BON VIVANT SPORT EPICURE
GOURMET
BON VIVEUR FLANEUR
BONY HARD LANK THIN LANKY STIFF
TOUGH OSTEAL SKINNY ANGULAR
OSSEOUS SCRAGGY SKELETAL
BONYFISH MENHADEN
BOO FIE HUMBUG
BOOB ASS OAF FOOL GOON GOOP
DUNCE GOONY NEDDY NITWIT
BOOBOOK OWL PEHO RURU
CUCKOO MOPOKE MOPEHAWK
MOREPORK

BOOB TUBE BOX
BOOBY GAWK GONY SULA DUNCE
IDIOT LOSER PATCH PRIZE SILLY
SLEIGH STUPID CAMANAY
PIQUERO GOOSECAP
BOOBYALLA DOGWOOD
WATERBUSH
BOODLE LOOT SWAG CROWD
GRAFT BUDDLE NOODLE PAYOFF
PLUNDER CABOODLE
BOOGEYMAN PADFOOT
TANKERABOGUS
BOOJUM SNARK
BOOK MO LIL LOG CHAP CODE
FORM HEFT OPUS PAGE TEXT
TOME ALBUM ALDUS BIBLE
CANON CANTO CODEX DETUR
DIARY DIVAN ENTER FI ETA FOLIO
FROST GUIDE KITAB LIBEL LIBER
QUAIR QUIRE RAZEE ZOHAR
ALDINE ANONYM BODONI CURSUS
DOCKET ENGAGE HERBAL LEDGER
MAHZOR MANUAL MISSAL
NUMBER REBIND RECORD RITUAL
SCHOOL TICKET TROPER VOLUME
BLOTTER CATALOG COUCHER
DIETARY DISCARD FEODARY
GARLAND GRAMMAR JOURNAL
LAWBOOK LEXICON MANDALA
OCTAPLA OMNIBUS ORDINAL
OUTBOOK PEERAGE RECITER
SAMHITA SERVICE SLEEPER
SPEAKER SPELLER SYNAXAR
TERRIER TICKLER TRAVAIL TRIGLOT
TYPICON TYPICUM WRITING
BANKBOOK BROCHURE CALCULUS
CASEBOOK CASHBOOK CHAPBOOK
COOKBOOK COPYBOOK DECRETAL
DOCUMENT FESTIVAL GIFTBOOK
GOSPELER HANDBOOK HARDBACK
HERDBOOK JESTBOOK JUVENILE
LIBRETTO PASTORAL POMANDER
POSTBOOK REGISTER SONGBOOK
STUDBOOK SYNAXARY TALEBOOK
TRIODION TWENTYMO VESPERAL
PAPERBACK PONTIFICAL
NOMENCLATOR PROCESSIONAL
PHARMACOPOEIA
(— BACK) DORSE
(— FOR HARVARD GRADUATE)
DETUR
(— OF CHARTS) WAGONER
PORTOLAN
(— OF DEVOTIONS) ORARIUM
(— OF HERALDRY) ARMORY
ARMORIAL
(— OF HOMILIES) POSTIL
(— OF MAPS) ATLAS
(— OF PSALMS) PSALTER TEHILLIM
(— OF RULES) HOYLE
(— OF SERVICES) PIE
(— OF SOLUTIONS) KEY
(— OF THE MASS) ORDO
(— SECTION) OCTAVO QUARTO
(—S KEPT IN PRINT) BACKLIST
(— THAT DOESN'T SELL) PLUG
(CHEAP —) BLOOD
(CHINESE —) CHING
(COMIC —) COMIX
(COMMONPLACE —) ADVERSARIA
(ELEMENTARY —) PRIMER
(FIRST READING —) ABC ABCEE
ABSEY

(FOLDED —) ORIHON
(HOLY —) VEDA
(IMPROPER —S) FACETIAE
(INSTRUCTION —) METHOD
(JOKE —) JOE JESTBOOK
(LOST HEBREW —) JASHAR JASHER
(MEMORANDUM —) AGENDA
JOTTER TICKLER
(MINIATURE —) BIBELOT
(PART OF —) CASE FLAP COVER
HINGE JOINT SPINE TITLE JACKET
LINING ENDLEAF BACKBONE
ENDPAPER HEADBAND BACKSTRIP
SHELFBACK
(PRAYER —) PORTAS SIDDUR
PORTASS PORTHORS
(READING —) ABC ABCEE ABSEY
(RECORD —) LIBER TICKLER
(RELIGIOUS —) KITAB KORAN
QURAN GOSPEL HORARY KYRIAL
PROSAR GRADUAL KYRIALE
BREVIARY MEGILLAH ORDINARY
SYNAXARY
(SACRED —) KORAN QURAN
PURANA
(SERVICE —) COMES GRAIL TEXTUS
(SLOW-SELLING —) PLUG
(STRANGE —S) CURIOSA
(UNBOUND —) CAHIER
(PL.) LIBRI SHELF STUDY EROTICA
SCRIPTURE
(PREF.) BIBLIO LIBRI
BOOKBINDING STUB YAPP STRING
BOOKBINDINNG LAWCALF
BOOKCASE DESK STAGE STALL
SCRINE PLUTEUS CREDENZA
BOOK COVER LID SIDE FOREL
RECTO VERSO FORREL REVERSE
REVERSO
BOOKISH BOOKY ERUDITE INKHORN
PEDANTIC STUDIOUS
BOOKLET FOLDER NOVELET
BROCHURE
BOOK LOUSE PSOCID
BOOKMAKER LAYER BOOKER
BOOKIE
BOOKMARK MARKER TASSEL
REGISTER
BOOK PALM TARA TALIERA
BOOKSELLER STATIONER
BIBLIOPOLE
BOOKSHELF DESK PLUTEUS
(PL.) CLASSIS
BOOKWORM GOME GRUB NERD
TOOL WONK CEREB GNURD GRIND
SQUID SPIDER WEENIE
BOOM JIB BEAM BOMB BUMP CRIB
POLE ROAR SPAR BRAIL CHAIN
CRANE CROON PROBE BUMPKIN
CATHEAD CURTAIN RESOUND
SUPPORT BOWSPRIT FLOURISH
(CRANE —) ARM GIB JIB
BOOMBOX (SOUND FROM —)
BLARE
BOOMER TNT
BOOMERANG KALIE KILEY KYLIE
WANGO ATLATL BOUNCE RECOIL
LEEWILL REBOUND WOMERAH
WOOMERA BACKFIRE HORNERAH
LEEANGLE RICOCHET TROMBASH
BOOMING HUMMING ROARING
BOOM IRON WITHE CRANCE

BOON GAY BENE GIFT GOOD KIND
BOUND FAVOR GRANT MERRY
ORDER BENIGN BOUNTY GOODLY
JOVIAL PRAYER BENEFIT
COMMAND PRESENT BLESSING
INTIMATE PETITION BENEFACTION
BOONDOCKS STICKS BOONIES
BOOR CAD OAF BOER BORE CARL
HICK JACK KERN LOUT PILL RUNT
SLOB CARLE CHUFF CHURL
CLOWN KERNE SLAVE BUMKIN
CARLOT CLUNCH HOBLOB
JOBSON JOSKIN LUBBER LUMMOX
RUSTIC BUMPKIN CAUBOGE
GROBIAN PEASANT VILLAIN
BOEOTIAN BOSTHOON
CLODHOPPER
BOORISH ILL RUDE CRASS GAWKY
ROUGH RUNTY SURLY CLUMSY
RUSTIC SAVAGE SULLEN VULGAR
WOOLEN AWKWARD CRABBED
HIRSUTE HOBLIKE KERNISH
LOUTISH PEAKISH ROISTER
UNCOUTH VILLAIN WOOLLEN
BOEOTIAN CARTERLY CHURLISH
CLODDISH CLOWNISH LUBBERLY
SWAINISH TACTLESS UNGAINLY
BOORISHNESS VILLAINY
GROBIANISM
BOOST AID ABET BACK BOOM
HELP LIFT LEG PLUG PUSH COACH
EXALT HOIST HOOSH RAISE ASSIST
ADVANCE COMMEND ELEVATE
ENDORSE PROMOTE INCREASE
BOOT PAC PAD USE CURE GAIN
HALF HELP HOOF KICK PUNT SHOE
SOCK AVAIL BOOTY DERBY EJECT
EVICT JEMMY KAMIK PEWEE SPOIL
BOOTEE BUDGET BUSKIN CASING
CHUKKA CRAKOW ENRICH FUMBLE
GAITER GALOSH INSHOE JEMIMA
JOCKEY MUKLUK PEDULE SHEATH
BENEFIT BOTTINE COTHURN
COWHIDE CRUISER HESSIAN
HIGHLOW SEABOOT SHOEPAC
VANTAGE BALMORAL BOTTEKIN
CHASSURE COVERING FINNESKO
JACKBOOT LARRIGAN NAPOLEON
COTHURNUS WAFFLESTOMPER
(— OF CARRIAGE) FOREBOOT
(— ON SADDLE) GAMBADE
GAMBADO
(CAR —) BUSTLE
(CLIMBING —) SCARPETTO
(HALF —) PAC BUSKIN COCKER
SKILTY BRODEKIN
(HIKING —) WAFFLESTOMPER
(HOB-NAILED —) BAT
(HORSE'S —) SCALPER
(KIND OF —) DENVER
(LUMBERMAN'S —) CRUISER
(MARINE —) SKINHEAD
(RIDING —) JEMMY JIMMY
JODHPUR
(SEALSKIN —) KAMIK
(STOUT —) STOGA STOGY
(TO —) ALSO
(TORTURE —) SQUEEZER
(WATERPROOF —) WADER
(PL.) OVERS WADER FINNESKO
HESSIANS
BOOTBLACK SHINER BLACKER
SHOEBOY

BOOTED OCREATE
BOOTES WAINMAN HERDSMAN
BOOTH BOX BULK COOP DESK LOGE
SHED SHOP SOOK BOTHY CABIN
CRAME HOUSE KIOSK LIWAN
LODGE PITCH SLANG STALL STAND
BOTHAN PAGODA PANDAL
PAYBOX SUCCAH SUKKAH TIENDA
BALAGAN COCKSHY TABERNA
BOOTLACE LACET THONG
BOOTLEG SHY SLY ILLEGAL ILLICIT
BOOTY BOOT FANG GAIN LOOT
PELF PREY SACK SWAG BUTIN
CHEAT FORAY GRAFT PRIZE
CREAGH FLEECE SPOILS DESPOIL
PILLAGE PLUNDER SPREAGH
SPREATH STEALTH PURCHASE
SPUILZIE STEALAGE
BOOZE BOLL BOUT BUDGE DRINK
HOOCH SPREE FUDDLE LIQUOR
BOOZY TIPPLE LIQUORY
BOP POP JIVE DANCE SHUFFLE
**BOPHUTHATSWANA (CAPITAL OF
—)** MMABATHO
(TOWN OF —) TEMBA MABOPANE
GARANKUWA
BORAGE ANCHUSA
BORAX FLUX TINCAL
(— SOURCE) KERNITE
BORDER CUT HEM RIM TAB ABUT
BABK BRIM CURB DADO EAVE
EDGE LIMB LINE LIST LOVE MARK
NARK ORLE RAND ROON RUND
SIDE TRIM WELL WELT BOARD
BOUND BRAID BRINK CHEEK
COAST COSTA DRAFT FILET FLANK
FOREL FRAME FRILL GUARD LIMIT
MARCH MARGE MARLI PLAIT
SHORE SKIRT STRIP SWAGE TOUCH
VERGE ACCOST ADJOIN COTISE
EDGING FILLET FORREL FRINGE
IMPALE LACING LIMBUS LISERE
MARGIN ORFRAY PURFLE QUADRA
SCREED STRIPE TANIKO WEEPER
CONFINE DRAUGHT FIMBRIA
FLOROON MARGENT SELVAGE
VALANCE BOUNDARY DOUBLING
FRONTIER MARCHESE NEIGHBOR
OUTSKIRT PLATBAND SKIRTING
SURROUND TERMINUS TRESSOUR
TRESSURE
(— OF EXTERNAL EAR) HELIX
(— OF LACE) PICOT
(— OF ROCK) SALBAND
(— OF SAIL) DOUBLING
(— OF SHIELD) BORDURE
(— OF STREAM) ROND
(— ON) ABUT ACCOST AFFRONT
NEIGHBOR
(FLOWERED —) FLOROON
(ORNAMENTAL —) PURL WAGE
FRAME FRINGE MATTING DENTELLE
TRESSURE
(RIBBON —) FRILAL
(PL.) CONFIN PURLIEU CONFINS
(PREF.) CRASPEDO LIMBI
BORDERED ORLE LIMBATE
BORDERER MARCHMAN
BORDERING MARGENT FRONTIER
BORDERLAND BOUNDS
(— OF HELL) LIMBO
BORE BIT CUT EAT IRK JET TAP
DRAG FLAT HOLE JUMP PALL PILL

POKE REAM RUSH SINK SIZE TIDE
TIRE TOOL ANNOY AUGER CHINK
DRILL EAGRE ENNUI GAUGE
GOUGE OUGHT PLONK PRICK
PUNCH SUGUR TEWEL THIRL TRICK
VAPOR WEARY BEFOOL CANNON
GIMLET PIERCE THRILL THRUST
TUNNEL WIMBLE YAWNER
BROMIDE CALIBER CALIBRE
CONCAVE CREVICE HUMDRUM
NUDNICK OPENING AIGUILLE
CAPILLUS DIAMETER DRAWBORE
GRATIANO POROROCA
(— OF CANNON) SOUL CHASE
(PREF.) FORAMINI
BOREAL NORTHERN
BOREAS AQUILO AQUILON
(BROTHER OF —) NOTUS HESPERUS
ZEPHYRUS
(DAUGHTER OF —) CLEOPATRA
(FATHER OF —) ASTRAEUS
(MOTHER OF —) EOS AURORA
(SON OF —) ZETES CALAIS
BORED BLASE HOHUM WEARY
ENNUYEE TEDIOUS SATIATED
BOREDOM YAWN BLAHS ENNUI
ACEDIA TEDIUM
(FEELING OF —) BLAHS
BORELE KEITLOA UPEYGAN
BORER MOLE BARDEE WIMBLE
HAGFISH TANBARK TERMITE
TERRIER FLATHEAD SHIPWORM
WOODWORM
(PREF.) TRYPAN(O)
BORING DIM DRY FLAT SLOW
HOHUM BROACH STODGY STUPID
TIRING LUMPISH TEDIOUS
PIERCING TIRESOME TEREBRANT
(— TOOL) AUGER GIMLET WIMBLE
AIGUILLE
(SOMETHING —) DRAG
**BORIS GODUNOV (CHARACTER IN
—)** BORIS PIMEN DMITRY GRIGORY
MISSAIL RANGONI SHUISKY
VARLAAM
(COMPOSER OF —) MUSSORGSKY
BORN N NEE NATE INNATE NASCENT
NATURAL UTERINE ORIGINAL
(— OUT OF WEDLOCK) BASTARD
(NEWLY —) NEONATE
(NOBLY —) GENEROUS
(PREMATURELY —) SLINK ABORTIVE
(WELL —) FREE EUGENIC
(SUFF.) GEN(E)(ESIA)(ESIS)(ETIC)(IC)
(IN)(OUS)(Y)
BORNE RODE NARROW CARRIED
ENDURED
(— AFFRONTEE) CABOCHED
(— LOWER THAN USUAL) ABASED
(— ON WATER) AFLOAT
(WIND —) EOLIAN

BORO MARIANA
BORON BORAX ULEXITE
BORORO COROADO
BOROUGH BURG CITY PORT TOWN
WICK BORGO BRUSH BURGH
CASTLE COUNTY CITADEL
FORTESS VILLAGE TOWNSHIP
(SUFF.) BURG
BORROW BOT BITE COPY HIRE KICK
LOAN SHIN TAKE THIG ADOPT
STEAL TOUCH DESUME DUPLEX
PLEDGE STRIKE SURETY CHEVISE
HOSTAGE MUTUATE TITHING
BORROWED SECONDHAND
BORROWER BOT CRIB MUTUARY
BORROWING ECLECTIC
BORS (BROTHER OF —) BAN
(UNCLE OF —) LANCELOT
BORSCHT (— INGREDIENT) BEETS
BOS OX NEAT TAURUS
BOSH END ROT JOKE SHOW TALK
TOSH FUDGE TRASH BUSHWA
FIGURE FLAUNT HUMBUG TRIVIA
HOGWASH TOSHERY GALBANUM
NONSENSE POPPYCOCK
BOSKY BUSHY TIPSY WOODY
FUDDLED
**BOSNIA & HERZEGOVINA (ALSO
SEE YUGOSLAVIA)**
CAPITAL: SARAJEVO
COIN: DINAR
LANGUAGE: BOSNIAN
SERBOCROATIAN
MOUNTAIN: MAGLIC
MOUNTAIN RANGE: GRMEC
CINCAR RADUSA VITOROG
KLEKOVACA PLJESIVICA
PEOPLE: SERB SLAV CROAT
RIVER: UNA SAVA BOSNA DRINA
VRBAS NERETVA
SEA: ADRIATIC
TOWN: MOSTAR RAGUSA
BANJALUKA DUBROVNIK
**BOSNIA-HERZEGOVINA (RIVER OF
—)** BOSNA DRINA NERETVA
(TOWN OF —) TUZLA MAGLAJ
MOSTAR VISOKO SARAJEVO
BOSOM LAP BARM BUST CLOSE
DICKY HEART SINUS BREAST
CAVITY DESIRE DICKEY RECESS
BELOVED EMBRACE GREMIAL
INCLOSE INTIMATE POITRINE
(— OF DRESS) SQUARE
(FALSE —) PLUMPER
BOSS BUR HUB MOP NOB ORB PAD
POP BAAS BEAD BOCE BUHR BURR
CAPO COCK CZAR KNOB KNOP
KNOT NAIL NAVE NULL STUD TSAR
BULLA BULLY BWANA CHIEF
EMPTY JEWEL KNOSP ORDER
OWNER PEARL ANCHOR BROOCH
BUCKRA BUTTON CHEESE DIRECT
HOLLOW HONCHO MANAGE
MASTER OCULUS PATERA PELLET

SHIELD BULLION CACIQUE
CAPATAZ CAPTAIN CUSHION
FOREMAN HASSOCK HEADMAN
HOBNAIL MANAGER PADRONE
PHALERA SPANGLE SPONSON
DIRECTOR DOMINATE DOMINEER
MISERERE OMPHALOS OVERSEER
UMBILICUS
(— OF LOGGING CAMP) BULLY
(— OF SHIELD) UMBO
(FIRE —) GASMAN
(LEATHER —) BUTTON
(MINE —) SHIFTER SHIFTMAN
(POLITICAL —) CACIQUE CAUDILLO
(STRAW —) BULL LEADER
(PREF.) UMBO
BOSSY PUSHY
BOSTONIAN HUBBITE
BOT OESTRUM OESTRUS
BOTANIST HERBALIST HERBARIAN
AMERICAN AMES BEAL COOK GRAY
HOWE ROSE BROWN CLUTE GAGER
HEALD JAMES JONES LOGAN
MOORE PURSH SEARS SHULL
SMALL VASEY BAILEY BESSEY
CANNON CARVER CUTLER DUDLEY
DUGGAR FARLOW HARRIS HOWELL
JEPSON LEMMON PEIRCE SHANTZ
TAYLOR TORREY WATSON
BARTRAM BIGELOW BRITTON
COULTER CROCKER ELLIOTT
FERNALD GOODALE HOLLICK
JOHNSON MERRILL PEATTIE
POLLARD RYDBERG SWINGLE
THURBER CALDWELL CAMPBELL
COPELAND KNOWLTON MARSHALL
TRELEASE BLAKESLEE FAIRCHILD
LONGWORTH NIEUWLAND
OSTERHOUT SULLIVANT
UNDERWOOD CHAMBERLAIN
AUSTRIAN UNGER KERNER MENDEL
JACQUIN HABERLANDT
BELGIAN LINDEN
CANADIAN SAUNDERS
DANISH HANSEN WARMING
JOHANNSEN RAUNKIAER
DUTCH TREUB DODOENS
ENGLISH WARD BOWER BUDDLE
CLARKE DARWIN GERARD HOOKER
HUDSON MARTYN PAXTON TURNER
BENNETT FORSYTH HAWORTH
HENSLOW JACKSON LINDLEY
DRYANDER SIBTHORP BABINGTON
FRENCH BORNET MAGNOL MIRBEL
THURET TRECUL BONNIER JUSSIEU
LECLUSE MICHAUX TULASNE
DECAISNE MILLARDET
JACQUEMONT TOURNEFORT
VANTIEGHEM DESFONTAINES
GERMAN BOCK COHN KOCH LINK
MOHL ZINN BLUME DRUDE FUCHS
KUNTH SACHS ENGLER GLOXIN
GMELIN GOEBEL HEDWIG KUNTZE
MIGULA REINKE CORRENS EICHLER
FITTING GARTNER JUNGIUS
KARSTEN KUTZING MOLISCH
PFEFFER RIVINUS WARBURG
BRUNFELS LEDEBOUR LONITZER
SPRENGEL DILLENIUS GRISEBACH
KOLREUTER CAMERARIUS
HOFMEISTER PRINGSHEIM
REICHENBACH STRASBURGER
HUNGARIAN ENDLICHER

IRISH HARVEY
ITALIAN TONI CORTI ALPINI
BECCARI CESALPINO
JAPANESE IKENO
NORWEGIAN GUNNERUS
RUSSIAN BUNGE FAMINTSYN
SCOTTISH AITON BROWN DOUGLAS
FORTUNE MORISON FALCONER
SPANISH CAVANILLES
SWEDISH DAHL KALM FRIES
RETZIUS ACHARIUS AFZELIUS
LINNAEUS THUNBERG ANDERSSON
BROMELIUS
SWISS BAUHIN VAUCHER
CANDOLLE
BOTANY HERBARISM PHYTOLOGY
BOTCH MAR MUX BOIL BOSS FLUB
MEND MESS MULL SORE BITCH
BODGE BUTCH FLUFF FUDGE
SPOIL STICK BOGGLE BOLLIX
BUMBLE BUNGLE COBBLE JUMBLE
MUCKER REPAIR TINKER BLUNDER
BUTCHER CLAMPER SCAMBLE
SCLATCH SLUBBER SWELLING
BOTCHER GRILSE SALMON TINKER
BUNGLER BUTCHER CLOUTER
COBBLER
BOTCHERY PATCHERY
BOTE KINBOT MAGBOTE CARTBOTE
FRITHBOT PLOWBOTE WAINBOTE
BOTFLY BOTT BREEZE GADBEE
GADFLY NITTER CANOPID OESTRID
TORSALO DIPTERAN OESTRIAN
BOTH BO ALL TWO BAITH EQUALLY
(PREF.) AMBI AMBO AMPH(I)(O) BIS
(— SIDES) AMPHI
BOTHER ADO AIL BUG IRK NAG VEX
FASH FAZE FUSS JADE WORK
ANNOY DEAVE HARRY KNOCK
PHASE TEASE TRADE WORRY
BADGER BUSTLE CUMBER DITHER
FLURRY GRAVEL HARASS HASSLE
MEDDLE MITHER MOIDER MOLEST
MUCKLE PESTER PLAGUE POTHER
POTTER PUTTER PUZZLE TAMPER
CONFUSE DISTURB FASHERY
GRIZZLE PERPLEX TERRIFY
TRACHLE TROUBLE BEWILDER
DISTRESS IRRITATE NUISANCE
BOTOCUDO BORUN AIMORE
AYMORO
BOTONEE TREFLEE FLEURONE
BO TREE PIPAL

BOTSWANA
CAPITAL: GABORONE GABERONES
COIN: PULA RAND THEBE
DESERT: KALAHARI
LAKE: DOW NGAMI
LANGUAGE: BANTU CLICK KHOISAN
SETSWANA
MONEY: PULA THEBE
MOUNTAIN: TSODILO
NATIVE: BANTU TSWANA BUSHMAN
RIVER: NATA OKWA CHOBE NOSOB
CUANDO MOLOPO SHASHI
CUBANGO LIMPOPO OKAVANGO
TOWN: KANYE ORAPA TSANE
SEROWE LOBOTSI MOCHUDI
PALAPYE THAMAGA GABERONES

BOTTLE JUG BOSS SKIN VIAL VIOL
AMPUL ASKOS BETTY BOCAL

BUIRE BURET CADUS COOJA
CROFT CRUET CRUSE FIFTH FLASK
GIRBA GLASS GOURD HOUSE
PHIAL SPLIT VERRE ALUDEL
BACBUC BUNDLE CARAFE CARBOY
CASTER CASTOR CHAGUL CHATTY
CREWET DORUCK DUBBER FESSEL
FIASCO FLACON FLAGON GOGLET
GUTTUS JORDAN LAGENA
MAGNUM MARINE MATARA
NURSER PACKER SIPHON VESSEL
WOULFF BALLOON BIBERON
BOMBARD BOMBOLA BURETTE
CANTEEN CARAFON COSTREL
DEADMAN FLACKET FLOATER
GRENADE INKHORN BOMBONNE
BORACHIO BUILDING CALABASH
DECANTER DEMIJOHN GARDEVIN
JEROBOAM MARIOTTE PRESERVE
REHOBOAM PEPPERBOX
(— IN WICKER) CARBOY DEMIJOHN
(EGYPTIAN —) DORUCK
(EMPTY —) MARINE
(HOT-WATER —) PIG
(LARGE —) KIT JEROBOAM
(LEATHER —) BOOT JACK DUBBA
BUDGET DUBBER DUPPER MATARA
BOMBARD BORACHIO WHINNOCK
WINESKIN
(MEDICINE —) VIAL PHIAL
(OVERSIZED —) BALTHAZAR
(PAIR OF —S) GEMEL GEMMEL
(PART OF —) LIP CORK KICK NECK
PUNT MOUTH MUZZLE CAPSULE
SHOULDER
(PILGRIM'S —) AMPULLA
(SMALL —) VIAL AMPUL CRUET
PHIAL SPLIT FLACON AMPOULE
TICKLER CRUISKEN CRUISKEEN
(10 — 0 OF WINE) RIDDLE
(40 —$) KEMPLE
(PREF.) UTRI
BOTTLE CAP CAPSULE
BOTTLE CARRIER FASCET
BOTTLE CASE CELLAR
BOTTLEHEAD DOEGLING
BOTTLER COOPER
BOTTOM ASS BED ARSE BASE DALE
DOUP FLAT FOND FOOT FUND
HOLM LEES REAR ROOT ABYSS
BASIS DREGS FLOOR LAIGH NADIR
BATHOS FOUNCE FUNDUS
GROUND GUTTER LAAGTE LEEGTE
BEDROCK LOWLAND SUPPORT
SURFACE BUTTOCKS INTERVAL
SEDIMENT TETRAPOD
(— LINE) NET
(— OF BENCH) TOE
(— OF CUPOLA) HEARTH
(— OF FURROW) SOLE
(— OF GRATE) NIGGARD
(— OF PAGE) TAIL
(— OF PISTOL GRIP) BUTT
(— OF POT) POTSTONE
(— OF PRINTER'S GALLEY) SLICE
(— OF PULLEY BLOCK) BREECH
(— OF SEA) GROUND BENTHOS
(— OF SOLE) NAUMK NAUMKEAG
(— OF STACK) STADDLE
(MARSHY —) SIKE
(ROCK —) HARDPAN
(PL.) HOLM HOLME
BOTTOM-DWELLING DEMERSAL

BOTTOMER FOOTMAN
STATIONMAN
BOTTOMLAND STRATH
BOTTOMLESS ABYSMAL
BOTTOM LINE CRUX UPSHOT
OUTCOME SUMMARY
CONCLUSION
BOTULISM LAMSIEKTE LAMZIEKTE
BOUDOIR ROOM BOWER CABIN
BEDROOM CABINET
BOUGH ARM LEG LIMB TWIG
CHUCK SHOOT SPRAY SPRIG
BRANCH RAMAGE SHROUD
GALLOWS PHYLLIS OFFSHOOT
SHOULDER
(— ON TAVERN) BUSH
(— USED AS TORCH) ROUGHIE
(DRY —) ROUGHY ROUGHIE
(PL.) RAMAGE DUNNAGE
RAMMAGE
BOUGHT KEFT STORE ZEBINA
BOUGIE CANDLE COLLYRIE
FILIFORM
BOUILLABAISSE POTPOURRI
BOULDER NOB KELK KNOR ROCK
STONE GIBBER BOOTHER DORNICK
ERRATIC GRAYBACK HARDHEAD
MEGALITH POTSTONE
BOULE BIRNE
BOULEVARD DRIVE PRADO AVENUE
STREET ALAMEDA HIGHWAY
TERRACE CORNICHE
BOULTER TRAWL SPILLER SPILLET
BOUNCE DAP HOP BANG BLOW
BRAG BUMP DING DIRD FIRE GATE
JUMP LEAP OUST SACK STOT
BOAST BOUND BULLY CAROM
CHUCK EJECT KNOCK SCOLD
THUMP VERVE BLAGUE MORGAY
SPIRIT SPRING STRIKE ADDRESS
BLUSTER CHOUNCE DISMISS
REBOUND SWAGGER PINGPONG
PROCLAIM RICOCHET
(— A BABY) DANDLE
(— BACK) RECOVER
BOUNCER BUMPER CHUCKER
SCROUGER
BOUNCING BIG BUXOM LUSTY
STOUT BOUNCY HEALTHY
WALLOPING
(— OF TONGUE) FLAP
BOUNCING BET SOAPWORT
BOUND DAP END HOP LOP BENT
BIND BOND BONE BROW BUTT
DART GIRT JUMP LEAP LIST MERE
RAMP RISE SCUD SKIP STEM STOT
SURE TERM WALL AMBIT BORNE
BOURN FIXED GOING LIMIT READY
SALLY SCOUP SKELP START STEND
STING TILED VAULT VERGE
BORDER BOUNCE BOURNE
BUTTAL CAVORT CURVET DEFINE
DOMAIN FINISH GAMBOL GIRDED
HURDLE JETTED LIABLE LOLLOP
OBLIGE PRANCE SPRING AFFINED
BARRIER CERTAIN CHAINED
CLOSURE CONFINE CONTAIN
COSTIVE DELIMIT DRESSED
GAMBADO INCLUDE REBOUND
SALTATE SECURED SUBSULT
TERMINE TRUSSED BOUNDARY
CONFINED DESTINED ENCLOSED
FASCIATE FRONTIER HANDFAST

LANDMARK LIMITATE OBLIGATE
PINIONED PRECINCT PREPARED
RESTRICT SHACKLED
(— ALONG) SLING
(— BY OATH) SWORN
(— BY OBLIGATION) AFFINED
(— CLUMSILY) LOLLOP
(NOT —) SOLUTE
(RIGIDLY —) STATIC STATICAL
(PL.) PALE AMBIT MOUND
CLOSURE COMPASS CONFINE
PURLIEUS PERIPHERY

BOUNDARY AHU END RIM DOLE
DOOL EDGE FINE FORM LINE LIST
MARK MEAR MEER MERE META
METE PALE SURF TERM TRIG WALL
AMBIT BOURN CLOSE FENCE
FRAME FRONT HEDGE LIMES LIMIT
MARCH MEITH MOUND SHORE
VERGE BORDER COLLET DEFINE
OCTROI OCTROY TROPIC BARRIER
BOUNDER BUTTING COMPASS
FURLONG OUTLINE CURBLINE
FRONTIER LANDLINE LIMITARY
PRECINCT TERMINUS UMSTROKE
PERIMETER PERIPHERY
MAGNETOPAUSE
(— OF EARTH'S CRUST-MANTLE)
MOHO
(PL.) ABUTTALS ENVIRONS
(PREF.) HORO LIMI ORI TERMINO
(— OF AIR MASS) FRONTO
TERMINO

BOUNDER CAD HARE RAKE ROUE
ROTTER

BOUNDING (— LINE) RUBICON

BOUNDLESS VAST UNTOLD
ENDLESS ETERNAL INFINITE
UNLIMITED

BOUNDLESSNESS INFINITY

BOUNTEOUS BOON CROWNED
LIBERAL PLENTEOUS

BOUNTIFUL GOOD LUSH RICH
AMPLE FREELY LAVISH LIBERAL
PROFUSE ABUNDANT GENEROUS

BOUNTY BOON GIFT MEED AWARD
BONUS GRANT LARGE VALOR
WORTH BONTEE REWARD VIRTUE
LARGESS PREMIUM PRESENT
PROWESS SUBSIDY DONATIVE
GOODNESS GRATUITY KINDNESS

BOUQUET BOB AURA ODOR POSY
AROMA BLOOM CIGAR POSEY
SHEAF SPRAY BOWPOT BUSKET
SHOWER CORSAGE NOSEGAY
BOUGHPOT
(— GARNI) FAGOT FAGGOT
(DEVELOP —) BREATHE

BOURDON BURDEN

BOURGEOIS ORGON COMMON
POOTER STUPID BOORISH
BURGHER
(KIND OF —) PETIT

BOURGEOIS GENTILHOMME
(AUTHOR OF —) MOLIERE
(CHARACTER IN —) CLEANTE
LUCILLE COVIELLE JOURDAIN

BOURSE SALE BOLSA BORSE
CAMBIO

BOURTREE ELDER

BOUT GO JOB BOOT FALL PULL
TURN BOOZE BRASH CRASH ESSAY
FIGHT MATCH PLUCK ROUND

SCRAP SIEGE TRIAL VENNY VENUE
ATTACK COURSE FRACAS YOKING
ASSAULT ATTEMPT CAROUSE
CIRCUIT CONTEST DEBAUCH
OUTSIDE WITHOUT CONFLICT
(— OF INDULGENCE) JAG
(DRINKING —) BAT BEND BUST TIRL
BOOZE SPRAY SPREE RANDAN
SCREED SPLORE CAROUSE
GAEDOWN WASSAIL POTATION

BOUTONNIERE BOUQUET
BUTTONHOLE

BOUW BAHU BAHOE

BOVAARISM EGO

BOVATE OSKEN OXGANG OXGATE
OXLAND
(TWO —S) HUSBANDLAND

BOVINE OX BOS COW BOSS BULL
CALF DULL NEAT SLOW ZEBU
BEAST BISON STEER ANIMAL
COWISH HUMLIE HUMMEL OXLIKE
ROTHER BULLOCK TAURINE
BANGTAIL LEPTOBOS

BOW ARC LEG LUG NOD SAW TIE
YEW ARCH BAIL BEAK BECK BEND
BENT CURB DUCK FOLD FORE
GORA JOUK KNEE KNOT LATH
LOUT MOVE PROW SELF STEM
SWIM TRUE TURN WEND BINGE
CLINE CONGE COQUE COUCH
CROOK CRUSH CURVE DEFER
GOURA HONOR KNEEL NOEUD
SHIKO STICK STOOP VENIE YIELD
ARCHER ASSENT BAUBLE BUCKLE
CONGEE CRINGE CROUCH CURTSY
FIDDLE FOGBOW RIBBON SALAAM
SALUTE SCRAPE SUBMIT SWERVE
TOURTE WEAPON DEPRESS
FOREBOW FORMBOW HANDBOW
INCLINE INFLECT LONGBOW
NECKTIE RAINBOW ARBALEST
COURTESY CRESCENT ENTRANCE
FOGEATER GREETING STONEBOW
TRUELOVE OBEISANCE
(— DOWN) ALOUT HUMBLE
(— IN ONE PIECE) SELF
(— LOW) BINGE
(— OF PLOW) DRAIL
(— OF VESSEL) HEAD PROW STEM
HAWSE ENTRANCE
(— ON SCRAPER) BAIL BALE
(— ON SEA) ATRY
(— OUTWARD) CONVEX
(— SLIGHTLY) ADDRESS
(OVERHANGING —) SWIM
(PART OF —) DIP TIP BACK FACE
GRIP LIMB LOOP NOCK BELLY
BRIDGE HANDLE RECURVE SERVING
BOWSTRING
(PART OF VIOLIN —) NUT TIP FROG
HAIR HEAD POINT SCREW STICK
(WITH THE —) ARCO
(PREF.) ARCI ARCO TOX(I)(ICO)(O)

BOWDLERIZE EDIT

BOWED ARCO BENT BANDY KNEED
ARCATE ARCATO CURVED
BULGING CURVANT SHAMBLE
DOWNBENT
(PREF.) TOX(I)(O)

BOWELS GUT GUTS WOMB BELLY
COLON ROPES VISCERA ENTRAILS
(PREF.) VISCER(I)(O)

BOWER RUN BOOR JACK NOOK
SALE ABODE ARBOR JOKER KNAVE
ANCHOR BOWERY LEFSEL PANDAL
BERCEAU CABINET CHAMBER
COTTAGE EMBOWER ENCLOSE
LEVESEL PERGOLA RETREAT
SHELTER TRELLIS THALAMUS
(— FOR SNAKES) KISI
(GARDEN —) ALCOVE

BOWERBIRD CATBIRD COLLARBIRD

BOWFIN AMIA GANOID LAWYER
MORGAY SAWYER CHOUPIC
DOGFISH GRINDAL GRINDLE
GRINNEL MUDFISH

BOWIE STATE ARKANSAS

BOWING CERNUOUS FEATHERING

BOWL CAP CUP PAN TUN COUP
ROLL TASS TRAY WOOD ARENA
BASIN BOWIE DEPAS GUARD
JORUM KITTY LAVER MAZER PHIAL
PITCH ROGAN SCALE TANOA
TAZZA TREEN TROLL BEAKER
BICKER CHAWAN CLOSET COOTIE
CRATER FESSEL JICARA KETTLE
LEKANE MAZARD MORTAR PIGGIN
TROUGH TUREEN VESSEL
BRIMMER DITCHER DOUBLER
DUGGLER SCYPHUS SKYPHOS
SPILLER STADIUM TOUCHER
TRINDLE TRUNDLE WHISKIN
AQUARIUM BRIDECUP FISHBOWL
JEROBOAM LAVATORY MONTEITH
REHOBOAM PORRINGER
(— ILLEGALLY) JERK
(— OF PIPE) CHILLUM STUMMEL
(— ON PEDESTAL) TAZZA SALVER
(— OUT) YORK
(— THAT TOUCHED JACK)
TOUCHER
(— WITH TWO HANDLES) CAP
DEPAS
(DRINKING —) TUN TASS
(MARBLE CUTTER'S —) SEBILLA
(OBLONG —) PITCHI
(PUNCH —) SNEAKER
(SHALLOW —) CAP COUPE WHISKIN
(SMALL —) JACK
(SOUP —) ECUELLE
(SUGAR —) SUGAR SUCRIER
(TOILET —) HOPPER
(WOODEN —) CAP BOWIE COGIE
KITTY ROGAN BASSIE BICKER
COGGIE COOTIE

BOWLEG OUTKNEE

BOWLEGGED BANDY VALGUS

BOWLER HAT POT DERBY KEGLER
PINMAN SPINNER TRUNDLER
(CRICKET —S) ATTACK

BOWLINE BOWLIN FARGOOD

BOWLING BOWLS ATTACK KEGLING
TENPINS
(— GAME) BOCCI

BOWLS RINK BOCCE DOCCIE

BOWMAN ARCHER

BOW-SHAPED ARCATE

BOWSPRIT SPAR

BOWSTRING SERVING

BOWYER BOWER ARTILLER

BOX BED BIN CAR EAR FUR GIG KIT
LOB LUG PIX PYX TYE ARCA BARK
BODY BOOT CAGE CAJA CASE CIST
CRIB CUFF CYST DRAB FLAT HEAD
LOGE MILL PACK PUNG SCOB SEAT

SLAP SLUG SPAR STOW TILL TRAY
ARBOR BARGE BIJOU BOIST BUIST
BUXUS CADDY CAPSA CHEST
CLOUT CRATE FIGHT FRAME
HUTCH LADLE POUCH PUNCH
SHRUB STALL TRUNK ASCHAM
BRUISE BUFFET BUNKER CARTON
CASKET COFFER COFFIN DRAWER
GRILLE HAMPER HATBOX HAYBOX
HOPPER ICEBOX MAROON
MOCUCK PATRON PETARA PILLAR
SAGGER SHRINE STRIKE TARBOX
VANITY ARCANUM BANDBOX
BATTERY BOXTREE BOXWOOD
CABINET CAISSON CARRIER
CASHBOX CASQUET CASSONE
COFFRET CONFINE COREBOX
DICEBOX DREDGER DUSTBOX
ENCLOSE EXHAUST FOSTELL
FREEZER HANAPER JACKBOX
PACKAGE PILLBOX PITARAH
PRINTER SANDBOX SCATULA
SHELTER TRUMMEL WHERRET
BOXTHORN DOVECOTE DRAGEOIR
JUNCTION LAVARIUM MATCHBOX
POMANDER SHOWCASE SLIPCASE
SOLANDER SWEATBOX
PEPPERBOX PHYLACTERY
(— FOR CARRYING COAL) DAN
(— FOR CARRYING ICE) YAKHDAN
(— FOR CLOTHES) PETARA PITARA
PITARAH
(— FOR COSMETICS) PUFFBOX
(— FOR CUTLERY) CANTEEN
(— FOR FIRE) CHAUFFER
(— FOR FISH) CAR NID
(— FOR MONEY OFFERING) ARCA
LADLE
(— FOR SALT) DRAB
(— FOR SEAL) SKIPPET
(— FOR SEED) LEAP
(— FOR TOBACCO) BUTT DOSS
CADDY SARATOGA
(— FOR TROUSSEAU) GLORYBOX
(— IN TIMEPIECE) BARREL
(— IN WHEEL HUB) FUR
(— OF BIRCHBARK) MOCUCK
(— OF CYLINDER) BUSH
(— OF FIRE CLAY) SAGGAR SAGGER
(— OF ORGAN) BOOT SWELL
(— SHAPED LIKE BOOK) SOLANDER
(— TO SHELTER BELL) SCONCE
(— USED AS DARKROOM) TENT
(BALLOT —) URN
(BERRY —) HALLOCK
(BREAD —) BARGE
(CANDLE —) BARK
(CIRCULAR —) THIMBLE
(COLLECTION —) BROD
(COMPASS —) KETTLE BINNACLE
(DICE —) RATTLE
(FANCY —) ETUI ETWEE
(FLOATING —) CAISSON
(FOUNDRY —) FRAME
(IRON —) HANGER
(JAPANESE —) INRO
(JUGGLER'S —) TRANKA
(KIND OF —) FUZZ READY
(MONEY —) CASH SAFE PIRLIE
(ORE —) SKIP
(PERFUME —) CASSOLETTE
(PIVOTING —) TOUR
(PRESENTATION —) COFFRET

(PRINTING —) TURTLE
(REFRIGERATOR —) COOLER
(SHADOW —) SPAR
(SHALLOW —) FLAT BACKET HARBOR
(SNUFF —) MILL MULL
(TEA —) CADDY
(TELEPHONE —) KIOSK
(TIN —) TRUMMEL VASCULUM
(WITNESS —) PETER STAND
(PREF.) CAPSULI CAPSULO CISTO PYXID(O)
BOX BRIER INDIGO INKBERRY
BOXCAR LOWRY STOCKCAR
BOX ELDER MAPLE NEGUNDO
BOXER PUG CHAMP DARES
BANTAM MILLER NOBBER TANKER
WELTER BRUISER CRUISER
FIGHTER SLUGGER SPARRER
BUFFETER PUGILIST SOUTHPAW
BOXFISH CHAPIN COWFISH
SHELLFISH TRUNKFISH
BOXING PLUG RING FANCY SAVATE
PARINGS SCIENCE SPARRING
(— GLOVE) MUFFLE
(— JAB) LEFT RIGHT
BOXING-GLOVE CESTUS MUFFLE
BOX TORTOISE COOTER
BOXWOOD KNYSNA DUDGEON
BOXY BLOCKY
BOY BO BUB FAG GUY HIM LAD PUR
TAD BOYO CHAP LOON NINO PAGE
PUER BILLY BUBBY BUDDY CHABO
CHILD CRACK GAMIN GILPY
GROOM KNAVE PUTTO ROGUE
SWAIN VALET YOUTH BIRKIE
BUTTON CALLAN CHOKRA GAFFER
GARCON MANNIE MASTER NIPPER
RASCAL SHAVER STIRRA UMFAAN
URCHIN BOUCHAL CALLANT
DRAWBOY GLEANER GOSSOON
GRUMMET JACKBOY RUBRI FR
SERVANT SPADGER TRAPPER
CLERGION HENCHBOY MUCHACHO
SPALPEEN
(— DRESSED AS WOMAN) MALINCHE
(— IN LIVERY) TIGER
(— NOT YET 13) PRETEEN
(— OF FREE BIRTH) CAMILLUS
(ALTAR —) ACOLYTE THURIFER
(AWKWARD —) CUB CALF GRUMMET
(BABY —) NENE
(BLESSED —) BEATUS
(BOISTEROUS —) GILPY GILPEY
(BOLD —) SPALPEEN
(CHIMNEY SWEEPER'S —) CHUMMY
(CHOIR —) CHILD
(CLEANING —) BUSBOY
(COLLIER'S —) HODDER
(EFFEMINATE —) SISSY MOLLYCODDLE
(ERRAND —) GALOPIN
(FIRST-YEAR —) GYTE
(FIRST YEAR —) GYTE
(GOOD OLD —) BUBBA
(HEAD —) SENIOR CAPTAIN
(HOMELESS —) ARAB
(ILL-MANNERED —) CUB
(LOVER —) ROMEO
(MESSENGER —) PAGE
(MISCHIEVOUS —) NICKUM

(MY —) AVICK
(NATIVE —) MOWGLI
(NON-JEWISH —) SHEGETZ
(OFFICE —) DUFTRY DUFTERY
(PERT —) CRACK
(POOR —) HERO
(ROGUISH —) CRACK GAMIN URCHIN
(SAUCY —) NACKET
(SERVING —) KNAVE PEDEE
CHOKRA MOUSSE FOOTBOY
GOSSOON
(SILLY —) CALF
(SMALL —) BO BUDDY UMFAAN SPADGER
(SPRIGHTLY —) CRACK
(STABLE —) MAFU MAFOO MEHTAR
(TEDDY —) DUCKTAIL
(TOWN —) CAD
(WINGED —) PUTTO
(YOUNG —) LAD SONNY YOUTH NIPPER
(PL.) BOYHOOD
(PREF.) PAED(O) PAID(O) PED(O)
BOYCOTT MITE SHUN AVOID DEBAR
BLACKBALL
BOYFRIEND BEAU STEADY
BOYISH GAMIN GAMINE
BRA BANDEAU
BRABANTIO (DAUGHTER OF) DESDEMONA
BRACE DUO LEG MAN TIE TWO
BEND BIND CASE FRAP GIRD JACK
KNEE LACE MARK PAIR PROP SPUR
STAY STEM STUD CLAMP CRANK
DWANG GIRTH HOUND NERVE
POISE RIDER SHORE STEEL STOCK
STRUT ANKLET BINDER BRACHE
CLENCH COLLAR COUPLE CRUTCH
FASTEN FATHOM HURTER SPLINT
STRING WIMBLE BOTTINE
BRACKET EMBRACE REFRESH
SPANNER STIFFEN SUPPORT
ACCOLADE BITBRACE BITSTALK
BITSTOCK BUTTRESS CROSSBAR
ENCIRCLE ORTHOTIC
(— ACROSS CABLE) STUD
(— AND HALF) LEASH
(— A YARD) TRAVERSE
(— BETWEEN FRAMES) TOM
(— FOR POST) SPUR
(— UP) ACCINGE SHARPEN
(PART OF —) BOW HEAD JAWS
PAWL RING CHUCK CRANK QUILL
SHELL HANDLE RATCHET
(PL.) BRIDGING
BRACED BENT
(— ABACK) ABOX
BRACELET BAND RING ARMIL
CHAIN ARMLET BANGLE GRIVNA
ARMILLA CIRCLET MANACLE
POIGNET RACETTE WRISTER
BARRULET HANDCUFF MUFFETEE
WRISTLET
(— USED AS MONEY) MANILLA
(SHELL —) SANKHA
BRACER TONIC SHORER BLOCKER
ARMGUARD STIFFENER
STIMULANT
BRACHIAL HUMERAL
BRACHIOPOD ATREMATE ATRYPOID
SPIRIFER
BRACHIUM ARM

BRACHYCEPHALIC ROUNDHEADED
BRACING CRISP QUICK TONIC DUNNAGE
BRACKEN FERN TARA BRAKE PLAID
BRACKET BIBB COCK CONK FORK
GATE PUNK ANCON BELOW BRACE
CLASS CONCH COUCH CRANE
CRANK CROOK LEVEL SHELF
STRUT TRUSS ANCONE BECKET
BRIDGE CORBEL COUPLE GUSSET
HANGER LADDER MUTULE SADDLE
SCONCE BECKETT CONSOLE
DERRICK FEATHER FIXTURE
GATELEG LOOKOUT POTENCE
SPONSON SPOTTED BRAGWORT
CATEGORY CROTCHET MISERERE
SPECKLED STRADDLE MODILLION
CANTILEVER
(PL.) HOOKS CROOKS
BRACKISH YAR FOIST SALTY
BRACKY SALINE BREACHY SALTISH
NAUSEOUS
BRACT HUSK LEAF GLUME LEMMA
PALEA PALET SCALE SPADIX
SPATHE BRACTLET PHYLLARY
BRACTEOLE PROPHYLL
BRAD PIN NAIL PRIG RIVET SPRIG
BRADAMANT (BROTHER OF —) RINALDO
(HUSBAND OF —) ROGERO
BRAE BANK BRAY BROW HILL CLEVE
SLOPE WOUGH CLEEVE VALLEY
BRAG GAB JET BLAH BLAW BLOW
CROW DEFY FACE HUFF PUFF
WIND WOST YELP BLUFF BOAST
CRACK FLIRD PREEN SKITE STRUT
VAUNT BLEEZE BOUNCE INSULT
SPLORE SPROSE SQUIRT DISPLAY
GAUSTER ROISTER SWAGGER
BRAGGART FLOURISH PRETENSE
THREATEN
BRAGGART BRAG PUFF BOAST
FACER BLOWER CROWER GASBAG
GASCON HECTOR ROTGUN SKITER
THRASO BLOWOFF BOASTER
BOBADIL BOUNCER CRACKER
RUFFLER SHALLOW VAPORER
BANGSTER BLOWHARD
CACAFUGO FANFARON PAROLLES
PUCKFIST RENOWNER RODOMONT
SKIPJACK
BRAGGARTISM COCKALORUM
BRAGGING ROOSE JACTANCE
RODOMONT THRASONIC
BRAHMA KA SELF BRAMAH
BRAHMAN ARYAN HINDU PUNDIT
SMARTA BRAHMIN
BRAID CUE BRAY GIMP JERK LACE
PLAT TAIL TRIM BREDE FANCY
FREAK JIFFY LACET MILAN ONSET
ORRIS PLAIT PLEAT QUEUE START
TAGAL TRACE TRADE TRESS TRICK
TWINE VOMIT WEAVE BOBBIN
BORDER CORDON EDGING
GALLON LACING MOMENT PLIGHT
RIBBON RICRAC SENNET SNATCH
STRING BANDING BULLION
CAPRICE ENTWINE UPBRAID
BRANDISH ORNAMENT REPROACH
RICKRACK SOUTACHE TRIMMING
(— FOR HATS) SENNET SINNET
(— OF WIG) SNAKE
(LINEN —) INKLE

BRAIDER RATCHER
BRAIDING FROG BREDE
BRAIDWORK LACET
BRAIN MAD BEAN HARN MIND PATE
UTAC WITS AXION HAIRN HAURN
SKULL GENIUS NODDLE PSYCHE
FURIOUS SENSORY THINKER
CEREBRUM HEADPIECE
(— WAVE PATTERN) THETA
(IN THE —) UPSTAIRS
(KIND OF —) PEA
(MUDDLED —) SMOKEJACK
(PART OF —) PONS CORTEX FORNIX
THALAMUS VENTRICLE
(PL.) HARN PATE SCONCE HEADPIECE
(PREF.) CEREBELLI CEREBELLO
CEREBR(I)(O) ENCEPHAL(O)
(SUFF.) ENCEPHALIA ENCEPHALUS
ENCEPHALY
BRAINCHILD IDEA
BRAINLESS SILLY STUPID FOOLISH
WITLESS
BRAINPAN PAN HARNPAN
PANNICLE
BRAIN SAND SABULUM
BRAIZE BECKER
BRAKE COW BULL BURR CAGE
CLOG CURB DRAG FERN LOCK
RACK SKID SLOW STAY TARA TRAP
TRIG BLOCK CHECK COPSE DELAY
DETER GRIPE SNARE SPOKE SPRAG
VOMIT BRIDLE CONVOY HARROW
HINDER REMORA RETARD STAYER
WARABI BRACKEN DEADMAN
DILEMMA SLIPPER STOPPER
THICKET TRIGGER DRAGROPE
RETARDER
(— PART) DISC SHOE
BRAKEMAN GUARD SHACK SHAKE
BRAKIE NIPPER DILLIER SNAPPER
SWAMPER DILLYMAN INCLINER
TRAINMAN
BRAKES ANCHORS
BRAMBLE WHIN BRIER RHAMN
THIEF THORN BUMBLE JAGGER
LAWYER STICKER DEWBERRY
MAYBERRY NESSBERRY
(PREF.) BATO
BRAMBLE BUSH TUTU GRANJENO
BRAMBLING KATE SNOWHAMMER
BRAMBLY DUMAL SPINY THORNY
PRICKLY
BRAN GRIT SEED DARAK TREAT
CEREAL CHESIL CHISEL POLLARD
TOPPING BEESWING
(— AND MEAL) SHORTS
(CORNMEAL —) HUSK
(FINE —) POLLEN
(UNSORTED —) RUBBLES
(PREF.) PITYRO
BRANCH ARM BOW COW KOW LAP
LEG LOP RAY RUN BARB BROG
BUSH CHAT FANG FORK LIMB
PALM PART RAME RICE RISE SNAG
SNUG SPUR STEM STUD TANG
TWIG YARD AXITE BAYOU BOUGH
BREAK BRIAR BRIER CREEK DRUPA
GRAIN LAYER LULOV PLASH
PRONG RAMUS REISE SCROG
SHOOT SHRAG SPRAY SPRIG STICK
TWIST VIMEN WITHE BUREAU
CLADUS DIVIDE DRUKPA EXOPOD

GERMEN GREAVE GROWTH
LEADER MEMBER OFFSET OUTLET
PHYLUM PORTIO RADDLE RAMAGE
RAMIFY RUNNER SHROUD SPRANG
STOLON STREAM TAPOUN
CHAPTER CLADODE DIALECT
DIVERGE ENDOPOD FURCATE
LATERAL PHYLLIS RAMULUS
TENDRIL TORRENT ANAPHYTE
BRONCHUS DISTRICT EFFLUENT
OFFSHOOT PEASTICK SCAFFOLD
SPRANGLE TRAILING
PHYLLOCLADE RAMIFICATION
(— OF ANTLER) SPELLER
ADVANCER
(— OF COLONY) STIPE
(— OF CRAFT) INDUSTRY
(— OF FAMILY) SEPT
(— OF FEATHER) BARB
(— OF HORN) RIAL ANTLER
(— OF IVY) BUSH
(— OF LEARNING) ART STUDY
FACULTY KNOWLEDGE
(— OF MATHEMATICS) ALGEBRA
CALCULUS
(— OF THALLUS) STICHID
(— OF TREASURY) FISCUS
(DEAD —) FLAG
(EVERGREEN —S) GREENS
(LANGUAGE —) INDIC
(LOCAL —) COURT
(MINE —) LEADER
(PALM —) LULAB
(RAILWAY —) LYE
(SHORT THICK —) STUMP
(SLENDER —) WHIP
(SMALL —) RICE
(YOUNGER —) CADET
(PL.) LOFT RAMI SKIRT SPRAY
RAMAGE CYPRESS DEADWOOD
(PREF.) CLON(O) FRONDI RAMI
RAMOSO RAMULI
(SUFF.) RAMOSE
BRANCHED FORKY FORKED
RAMATE RAMOSE CLADOSE
TROCHED RAMIFORM
(SUFF.) CLADOUS
BRANCHES
(SUFF.) (HAVING —) CLEMA
BRANCHIA GILL
BRANCHING ARMY RAMOSE
FURCATE DICHOTOMY
BRANCHIOPOD SHRIMP
BRANCHLET RAMULUS SPILLER
BRAND BIRN BLOT BURN CHOP
FLAW KIND MARK NOTE SEAR SMIT
SMOT SORT VENT WIPE BUIST
INURE LABEL SCEAR STAIN STAMP
SWORD TAINT TORCH BARREL
MARQUE STIGMA FLAMBEAU
NAMEPLATE STIGMATIZE
BRANDED INFAMOUS
BRANDIMART (SLAYER OF —)
GRADASSO
(WIFE OF —) FLORDELIS
BRANDING IRON BRAND CAUTER
SEARER CAUTERY
BRANDISH WAG DART STIR WAVE
WIND BLESS BRAID SHAKE SWING
WIELD FLAUNT HURTLE QUAVER
RUFFLE STRAIN WINNOW FLUTTER
GLITTER SWAGGER VIBRATE
WAMPISH FLOURISH VAMBRASH

BRANDY DOP VSO BOOF FINE JACK
MARC VSOP BINGO MOBBY NANTS
NANTZ PEACH RAKIA VVSOP
CINDER COGNAC GRAPPA KIRSCH
PUPELO RAKIJA VISNEY ANISADO
AQUAVIT QUETSCH ARMAGNAC
CALVADOS SLIVOVIC SLIVOVITZ
AGUARDIENTE
(— AND WATER) MAHOGANY
(PLUM —) SLIVOVITZ SLIVOVITCH
(SOUTH AFRICAN —) SMOKE
BRANDYWINE (VICTOR AT —)
HOWE
BRANK MUMPS BRIDLE PILLORY
BRANLE BRAWL
BRAN-LIKE PITYROID
BRANT ROUT ERECT PROUD QUINK
SHEER STEEP ROUGHT
BRASH GAY BOLD FACY RASH
HASTY NERVY SAUCY STORM
ATTACK RUBBLE BRITTLE
FORWARD IMPUDENT TACTLESS
BALDFACED
BRASQUE STEEP
BRASS CASH ALLOY CHEEK MONEY
NERVE BRAZEN BRONZE MASLIN
ORMOLU OFFICER ORICHALC
(— PLAYER) WINDJAMMER
(PREF.) CHALC(O) CHALK(O)
BRASSARD ARMBAND
BRASSEY BIB
BRASSICA CABBAGE
BRASSIERE BANDEAU
BRASSWARE DINANDERIE
BRASSY LOUD RUDE BRAZEN
COARSE SHRILL IMPUDENT
STRIDENT OVERBLOWN
BRAT BIB GET IMP BROT FILM SCUM
APRON BAIRN BILSH BROLL CHILD
CLOAK GAITT SCAMP INFANT
MANTLE TERROR URCHIN
GARMENT BANTLING
BRATTICER AIRMAN CANVASMAN
BRAVADO POMP BRAVE PRIDE
STORM SWASH HECTOR BLUSTER
BOMBAST BRAVERY SWAGGER
VAUNTERY GASCONISM
BRAVE BOLD BRAW DARE DEFY
FACE FINE GAME GOOD PROW
TALL WILD ADORN BOAST BRAVO
BULLY FELON HARDY JOLLY
MANLY MOODY ORPED ROMAN
STIFF STOUT VAUNT WIGHT
BRAWLY BREAST DARING HEROIC
MANFUL PLUCKY SANNUP STURDY
BRAVADO DOUGHTY GALLANT
HAUTAIN SOLDIER SWAGGER
VALIANT VENTURE WARRIOR
CAVALIER DEFIANCE EMBOLDEN
FEARLESS INTREPID LIONLIKE
STALWART SUPERIOR VALOROUS
VIRTUOUS
BRAVELY BIG FINELY
BRAVE NEW WORLD (AUTHOR OF
—) HUXLEY
(CHARACTER IN —) JOHN MARX
MOND CROWNE LENINA WATSON
BERNARD MUSTAPHA HELMHOLTZ
BRAVERY GRIT VALOR SPIRIT
VIRTUE BRAVADO BRAVURA
COURAGE HEROISM JOLLITY
MANHEAD MANHOOD PROWESS
BOLDNESS CHIVALRY

BRAVO OLE RAH EUGE THUG BRAVE
BULLY BANDIT CUTTER BRAVADO
SHABASH VILLAIN APPLAUSE
ASSASSIN
BRAWL DIN ROW BEEF CLEM DUST
FRAY RIOT BLIND BROIL CHIDE
CLASH FIGHT FLYTE MELEE REVEL
RISSA SCOLD SCRAP AFFRAY
BICKER FRACAS FRATCH HABBLE
REVILE RUFFLE RUMPUS SHINDY
STOUSH STRIFE TUMULT UPROAR
YATTER BAGARRE BOBBERY
BRABBLE BRANGLE DISCORD
DISPUTE QUARREL SCUFFLE
TUILYIE WRANGLE COMPLAIN
RIXATION SQUABBLE STRAMASH
BRAWLER FRATCH NICKER
SQUARER FRAMPLER NIGHTCAP
OUTCRIER
BRAWLING NOISY BLATANT FLITING
SCAMBLING SHEMOZZLE
BRAWN BEEF BOAR LIRE PORK
FLESH SINEW FATTEN MUSCLE
MANPOWER STRENGTH
(MOCK —) HEADCHEESE
BRAWNY BEEFY FLESHY ROBUST
SINEWY SQUARE STRONG STURDY
CALLOUS MUSCULAR POWERFUL
STALWART
BRAXY BRADSOT
BRAY CRY MIX RUB BEAT ROUT
TOOL CRUSH GRIND NOISE POUND
STAMP BRUISE HEEHAW OUTCRY
PESTLE THRASH WHINNY
BRAYERA KOSO CUSSO KOSSO
BRAZEN BOLD CALM HARD PERT
BRASS HARDY HARSH SASSY
AENEAN BRASSY BLATANT
CALLOUS FORWARD IMMODEST
IMPUDENT INSOLENT METALLIC
BRAZENFACED CHEEKY
BRAZIER HEARTH MANGAL
BRASERO HIBACHI REREDOS
SCALDINO

BRAZIL ROSET
BAY: MARAJO IGRANDE SEPETIBA
GUANABARA
BIRD: MITU MITUA
CAPE: FRIO BLANCO BUZIOS
GURUPY ORANGE SAOTOME
SAOROQUE
CAPITAL: BRASILIA
COIN: JOE REIS CONTO DOBRA
CENTAVO HALFJOE MILREIS
CRUZEIRO
DAM: FURNAS ITAIPU PEIXOTO
DANCE: SAMBA MAXIXE
ESTUARY: PARA
FALLS: IGUACU IGUASSU
INDIAN: ANTA ACROA ARARA
ARAUA BRAVO CARIB GUANA
ARAWAK CARAJA CARAYAN
JAVAHAI TARIANA BOTOCUDO
CHAMBIOA
ISLAND: MARACA MARAJO
BANANAL CARDOSO CAVIANA
MEXIANA COMPRIDA
LAKE: AIMA FEIA MIRIM
MEASURE: PE MOIO PIPA SACK
VARA BRACA FANGA LEGOA
MILHA PALMO PASSO TONEL
CANADA COVADO CUARTA

LEAGUE QUARTO TAREFA
ALQUIER GARRAFA ALQUEIRE
MONETARY UNIT: CRUZADO
MOUNTAIN: URUCUM BANDEIRA
ITATIAIA
MOUNTAINS: MAR GERAL ORGAN
PIAUI ACARAI GURUPI ORGAOS
PARIMA AMAMBAI CARAJAS
GRADAUS RONCADOR
TOMBADOR
NATIVE: CABOCLO CURIBOCA
MAMELUCO PAULISTA
PORT: RIO PARA BAHIA BELEM
CEARA NATAL SANTOS PELOTAS
SALVADOR
PRESIDENT: BRAS DUTRA FILHO
VARGAS
RIVER: APA ICA DOCE GEIO IVAI JARI
PARA PARU SONO TEFE ABUNA
ANAUA APORE CAPIM CLARO
CORUA ICANA IRIRI ITAPI JURUA
JUTAI MANSO NEGRO PARDO
PIAUI PRETO TIETE TURVO URUBU
VERDE XINGU AJUANA AMAZON
ARINOS BALSAS BRANCO
CANUMA CONTAS CUIABA DEMINI
GRAJAU GRANDE GURUPI IBICUI
IGUACU JAPURA JAVARI MEARIM
MORTES MUCURI PARANA
PURPUS RONURO SANGUE
TACUTU TIBAGI UATUMA UAUPES
VELHAS CORUMBA IGUASSU
MADEIRA PARAIBA SUCURIU
TAPAJOS TAQUARI TEODORO
URUGUAI ARAGUAIA PADAUIRI
PARACATU PARAGUAI PARNAIBA
SOLIMOES TARAUACA
STATE: ACRE PARA AMAPA BAHIA
CEARA GOIAS GOYAZ PIAUI
PARANA PIAUHY ALAGOAS
GUAPORE PARAIBA RORAIMA
SERGIPE AMAZONAS MARANHAO
PARAHIBA PARAHYBA RONDONIA
SAOPAULO
TOWN: ACU EXU ICO IPU ITU JAU
LUZ RIO UBA BAGE FARO IBIA IJUI
ITAI LAPA LINS PARA PIUI TUPA
UNAI BAHIA BAIAO BAURU BELEM
CEARA NATAL NEVES CAMPOS
CUIABA ILHEUS MACEIO MANAOS
MANAUS OLINDA RECIFE SANTOS
ARACAJU CARUARU CITORIA
GOIANIA ITABUNA JUNDIAI
NITEROI PELOTAS TAUBATE
UBERABA ANAPOLIS BRASILIA
CAMPINAS CURITIBA LONDRINA
SALVADOR SOROCABA TERESINA
TREE: APA ICICA UCUUBA ARARIBA
WALLABA
WATERFALL: GLASS IGUAZU
WEIGHT: BAG ONCA LIBRA ARROBA
OITAVA ARRATEL QUILATE
QUINTAL TONELADA

BRAZIL NUT JUVIA CASTANA
BRAZILWOOD SAPPAN VERZINO
HYPERNIC PEACHWOOD
SAPPANWOOD
BREACH GAP CHAP FLAW GOOL
RENT RIFT SLAP BRACK BRECK
BURST CHASM CLEFT CRACK
PAUSE SPLIT WOUND BRUISE
HARBOR HERNIA HIATUS INROAD

SCHISM SCREED SLUICE ASSAULT
BLEMISH DISPUTE FISSURE
OPENING QUARREL RUPTURE
BREAKING CREVASSE FRACTION
FRACTURE INTERVAL OUTBREAK
SOLUTION TRESPASS
(— IN DIKE) GOOL
(— IN SEAWAY) GOOL
(— OF CHASTITY) SCULDUDDRY
SKULDUDDERY
(— OF CONTINUITY) SALTUS
(— OF DUTY) BARRATRY
(— OF ETIQUETTE) SOLECISM
(— OF FAITH) TREASON
(— OF GRAMMAR) SOLECISM
(— OF MORALITY) SCAPE VAGARY
(— OF PEACE) AFFRAY DISORDER
FRACTION
(— OF RULES) FOUL
(— OF SYNTAX) SOLECISM
(— OF UNITY) SOHISM
BREAD BAP BUN NAN PAN BODY
BRAD DIET FARE FOOD LOAF NAAN
PAIN PITA PONE RIMA ROLL ROTI
RUSH RUSK TOKE AZYME BABKA
BATCH BATON BOXTY CAPER
CHEAT KISRA LIMPA MICHE POORI
ROOTY TOMMY CHALLA CHAPON
COCKET DAMPER DODGER
ENZYME HALLAH KANKIE MASLIN
MATZOS PANNAM SIMNEL TAMMIE
WASTEL YANNAM ALIMENT
ANADAMA BANNOCK CHALLAH
EULOGIA MANCHET POPOVER
STOLLEN TOASTER CORNCAKE
FOCACCIA HARDTACK SOFTTACK
TORTILLA ZWIEBACK
PUMPERNICKEL
(AND MILK) PODS PANADA
POBBIES
(— BOX) PANETIERE
(— QUALITY) PANEITY
(BATCH OF —) CAST
(BUTTERED —) CAPER
(DRY —) TOKE
(EUCHARISTIC —) BODY HOST
AZYME
(FANCY —) BRAID
(INDIAN —) NAN
(ITALIAN —) FOCACCIA
(KIND OF —) FRY PITA POCKET
(MAIZE —) PIKI
(OATMEAL —) ANACK JANNOCK
(POTATO —) FADGE
(QUICK —) SCONE
(S. AFRICAN —) DIKA
(SLICE OF —) TARTINE TRENCHER
(SMALL LOAF OF —) COB
(SMALL PIECE OF —) SIPPET
MEALOCK
(SOPPED —) MISER BREWIS
BROWIS
(SWEET —) BUN BROWNIE STOLLEN
(TOASTED —) SIPPET
(TWICE-BAKED —) ZWIEBACK
(UNLEAVENED —) AZYM AZYME
BANNOCK CHAPATTI
(WHEAT —) CHEAT HOVIS COCKET
MANCHET PARATHA
(YEAST-LEAVENED —) SALLYLUNN
(PREF.) ARTO PANI
BREADBOARD PANEL
BREADED ANGLAISE

BREADFRUIT MASI RIMA RIMAS
DUGDUG NANGCA CAMANSI
CASTANA ANTIPOLO BREADNUT
CHESTNUT
BREADNUT RAM
BREADROOT PSORALEA
BREADTH BEAM WIDTH LATITUDE
(— OF PLANK) STRAIK STRAKE
(FINGER'S —) DIGIT
BREADWINNING GAP BOON BUST
DASH HINT KNAP PICK PLOW REND
RENT RIFT RIVE
BREAK GO CUT JAR LOP TEN ABRA
BUST CHIP DRAG FALL FLAW KNAP
PART RUIN RUSH SLIP SNAP STEP
STOP TEAR TURN UNDO WASH
WORK ALTER BLANK BRACK BURST
CHECK CHINK CLEFT COMMA
CRACK CRAZE DAUNT FALSE
FRACT FRUSH LAPSE PAUSE PLUCK
ROUGH SEVER SMASH SOLVE
SPAWN SPELT STAVE SWING
WOUND BRUISE CABBLE CHANGE
CLEAVE CRANNY CUTOUT DEFEAT
HIATUS IMPAIR LACUNA PIERCE
SALTUS SHREND SPRING TEWTAW
TEWTER BLUNDER CAESURA
CRACKLE CRANKLE CREVICE
CRUMBLE DESTROY DISABLE
DISPART DISRUPT EXHAUST
FISSURE GRITTLE INFRACT
INTERIM OPENING RESPITE
RUPTURE SHATTER TAILING
VARIATE BREATHER CREVASSE
DIERESIS DIFFRACT FRACTION
FRACTURE FRAGMENT INFRINGE
INTERVAL SEPARATE SOLUTION
STRAMASH
(— APART) SUNDER DISRUPT
SHATTER
(— AWAY) BOLT PEEL ESCAPE
(— BOULDERS) BULLDOZE
(— DOWN) CONK FAIL GIVE CRAZE
CROCK PLASH TRAIK UNMAN
BRUISE TUMBLE ANALYZE
FOUNDER REFRACT COLLAPSE
INFRINGE
(— FORCE) BAFFLE
(— FORTH) BOIL ERUPT EVENT
FLASH EXPLODE
(— FROM ICE MASS) CALVE
(— GLASS) SHREND DRAGADE
(— IN) ENTER
(— IN PIECES) CHAP DICE KNAP
CRASH CRAZE SMASH SMOKE
SHIVER CRUMBLE FRITTER
SMATTER DEMOLISH DIFFRACT
DISJOINT SPLINTER STRAMASH
(— INTO) BROACH IRRUPT
(— INTO FOAM) COMB
(— INWARD) STAVE
(— IN WAVES) JABBLE
(— IN YARN) SMASH
(— LANCE) TAINT
(— OF CONTINUITY) SALTUS
(— OFF) NUB DROP SNAP CEASE
LEAVE ABRUPT DIREMPT INTERMIT
PRETERMIT
(— OFF END) SNUB
(— OPEN) BUST CHOP FORCE
(— ORE) COB SPALL SPAWL
(— OUT) ERUPT START ASSURD
STRIKE

(— RANKS) DISMISS
(— SHARPLY) KNACK
(— SILENCE) QUATCH QUETCH
(— SKIN) GALL
(— SLATE) SCULP
(— STONE) CAVIL KEVEL
(— THE BACK) CHINE
(— THROUGH) BEAT FORCE
BREACH
(— THROUGH SHELL) PIP
(— UP) BUCK FALL MELT FLOUR
SEVER SPALE SPLIT STASH INCIDE
DEGRADE DIFFUSE DISBAND
DISSECT DISTURB REFRACT SCARIFY
SCATTER CROSSCUT DISJOINT
DISPERSE DISSOLVE DISUNIFY
FRAGMENT
(— UP EARTH) HACK FALLOW
(— UP SIEGE) LEVY
(— WATER) FIN
(— WINDOWS) NICK
(INDUSTRY —) SHAKEOUT
(STEM —) BROWNING
(SUFF.) CLASE CLASIA CLAST(IC)
BREAKABLE BRITTLE BRUCKLE
FRIABLE DELICATE FRANGIBLE
BREAKAGE GRIEF
BREAKAX IRONWOOD
BREAKDOWN JUBA EDGER
BURNOUT DEBACLE HOEDOWN
ANALYSIS COLLAPSE DILUTION
(— OF RIND) ADUSTIOSIS
(ELECTRIC —) AVALANCHE
BREAKER JUMP SURF WAVE
BARECA BEAKER BILLOW COMBER
ROLLER CRACKER SLEDGER
LEDGEMAN SCRAPPER
(— OF WORD) WARLOCK
(CIRCUIT —) CUTOUT
(ROCK —) ALLIGATOR
(PL.) BREACH
(SUFF.) CLASTIC
BREAKFAST BRUNCH DEJEUNE
DISJUNE DEJEUNER DISJEUNE
(— FOOD) GRANOLA
BREAKING BREACH BREAKUP
FRACTION FRACTURE SOLUTION
(— COVER) GETAWAY
(— DOWN) LYSIS
(— FORTH) ERUPTIVE
(— OFF) CHIPPING ABRUPTION
(— OF OATH) PERJURY
(— UP) DEBACLE ANALYSIS
DISUNION
(SUFF.) CLASE CLASIA CLAST(IC)
(— INTO SMALL PIECES) THRIPSIS
BREAKSTONE SAXIFRAGE
BREAK-UP DEBACLE
BREAKWATER COB DAM COBB
CROY DIKE MOLE PIER PILE QUAY
JETTY GROYNE REFUGE BULWARK
STOCKADE
BREAM TAI BRIM CARP CHAD SCUP
SHAD ZOPE BROOM ROMAN
BALEEN BARWIN BRAISE SARGUS
OLDWIFE SUNFISH WAREHOU
CYPRINID FLATFISH TARWHINE
STEENTJIE
BREAST DUG BOOB BUMP CROP
FACE BOOBY BOSOM BRAVE
BUBBY CHEST HEART MAMMA
PETTO STALL BAZOOM PECTUS
POMMEL THORAX BRISKET

COUNTER KNOCKER FOREBOWS
(— OF HORSE) COUNTER
(PHOTOGRAPH OF —S)
MAMMOGRAM
(PL.) BUST
(PREF.) MAMM(I)(ILLI) MAST(O)
MAZ(O) PECTORI STERN(O)
STETH(O)
BREASTBAND HORSE
BREASTBONE BREAST STERNUM
XIPHOID
BREASTHOOK CRUTCH FOREHOOK
BREASTPIECE RABAT RABBI
BREASTPLATE EGIS URIM AEGIS
BREAST BYRNIE GORGET LORICA
ORACLE SHIELD THORAX CUIRASS
PALETTE POITREL PECTORAL
PLASTRON RATIONAL
(HIGH PRIEST'S —) RATIONAL
BREASTS
(SUFF.) MASTIA
BREASTWORK FORT REDAN
SANGAR SCHANZ SCHERM
SCONCE SUNGAR BRATTLE
PARAPET PLUTEUS RAMPART
BARBETTE BRATTICE
BREATH AIR ANDE GASP HUFF LIFF
ONDE PANT PECH PUFF SIGH WAFT
WIND BLAST PAUSE SCENT SMELL
VAPOR WHIFF WHIFT BREEZE
FLATUS PNEUMA HALITUS
INSTANT RESPITE SUSPIRE
SPIRACLE
(— OF WIND) SPIRIT
(BAD —) OZOSTOMIA
(DIVINE —) NEPHESH
(LIFE —) PRANA SPIRIT
(STINKING —) FUMOSITY
(PREF.) PNEO PNEUM(A)(O)
PNEUMATO PNEUMON(O) RESPIRO
SPIRACULI SPIRO
(SUFF.) PNEA PNEUSTA PNOEA
BREATHE ANDE LIVE ONDE PANT
PECH PUFF SIGH VENT EXIST
EXUDE SPEAK SPIRE UTTER ASPIRE
EXHALE INHALE WHEEZE AFFLATE
EMANATE RESPIRE SUSPIRE
(— HEAVILY) FOB PECH FNESE
SOUGH THROTTLE
(— LABORIOUSLY) GASP
(— NOISILY) SOUGH SNOTTER
(— OUT) EXPIRE
(— UPON) FAN
BREATHER PAUSE
BREATHING AIR ALIVE PNEUMA
SPIRIT GASPING AFFLATUS
SPIRITUS SPIRATION
(— HEAVILY) SUSPIRIOUS
(LABORED —) ASTHMA
(ROUGH —) ASPER
(SMOOTH —) LENE LENIS
BREATHING-SPACE BARLEY
RESPIRATION
BREATHLESSNESS TIFT
BREATHY HOLLOW ADENOID
BRECCIA BROCKRAM
BRED (WELL —) FREE
BREECH BORE BUTT DOUP BLOCK
BRICK CULOTTE DRODDUM
BUTTOCKS CYLINDER DERRIERE
(— OF SECURITY) LEAK
BREECHBLOCK BLOCK VENTPIECE
BREECHCLOTH HIPPEN HIPPING

BREECHES HOSE CHAPS JEANS
LEVIS SLOPS STOCK TREWS
BRACAE BRAGAS BREEKS GASKIN
SMALLS TIGHTS TROUSE TRUSSES
BOMBARDS BREEKUMS
JODHPURS KICKSIES KNICKERS
LEATHERS TROUSERS PANTALOON
SMALLCLOTHES
(KNEE —) SMALLS
BREED GET ILK BEAR KIND RACE
REAR SORT BEGET BROOD CASTE
CAUSE CLASS FANCY HATCH ISSUE
RAISE STOCK STORE TRAIN
CREATE GENDER STRAIN EDUCATE
NOURISH PRODUCE PROGENY
SPECIES VARIETY ENGENDER
GENERATE INSTRUCT MULTIPLY
PULLULATE
(— OF BEEF CATTLE) BEEFALO
(— OF CATS) RAGDOLL
(— OF SWINE) LACOMBE
(DWARF —) TOY
(DWARF —) TOY
BREEDER RANCHER AURELIAN
HERDSMAN HORSEMAN
(FISH —) MILTER
BREEDING ORIGIN DESCENT
NURTURE TUPPING BEHAVIOR
CIVILITY PREGNANT TRAINING
(— PLACE) NIDUS
(GOOD —) GENTRY
BREEZE AIR AURA BLOW FLAW
GALE GUST PIRR SNAP STIR WIND
BLAST RUMOR SLANT WALTZ
BREATH DOCTOR REPORT SLATCH
SPIRIT ZEPHYR FRESHEN MUZZLER
QUARREL VIRASON WHISPER
(COOL —) DOCTOR
(GENTLE —) AIR AURA ZEPHYR
(LAND —) TERRAL
(SHOOT THE —) GAB JAW
(STIFF —) STOUR TIFTER
BREEZE FLY WHAME
BREEZY AIRY BRISK FRESH WINDY
AIRISH
BRETHREN IKHWAN
BRETON ARMORICAN
BREVE NOTE WRIT BRIEF MINIM
ORDER SHORT PRECEPT
BREVIARY ORDO CURSUS DIGEST
LEDGER PORTAS COUCHER
EPITOME SUMMARY ABSTRACT
PORTESSE PORTHORS
(— CONTENTS) PRAYERS
BREVITY SYNTOMY LACONISM
UNLENGTH BRIEFNESS
SHORTNESS TERSENESS
BRACHYLOGY
BREW ALE MIX BEER BOIL MAKE
PLOT POUR DRINK HATCH STEEP
STOUT BROWST DEVISE DILUTE
FOMENT GATHER LIQUOR SEETHE
CONCOCT INCLINE PREPARE
CONTRIVE
(HOME —) SAMOGON
BREWER TUNNER
BREWERY BRASSERIE
BREWING GAIL GYLE BROWST
BUMMOCK
BRIBE BUD BUY FEE FIX OIL ROB
SOP TIP BAIT DASH GIFT HAVE
HIRE MEED MOIL PALM VAIL WAGE
BONUS CUDDY GRAFT OFFER

STEAL SUGAR TEMPT TOUCH
BOODLE EXTORT GREASE HAMPER
NOBBLE PAYOLA SQUARE SUBORN
CORRUPT DOUCEUR SWEETEN
TICKLER GRATUITY VENALIZE
(— TO A POLICEMAN) NUT
(— TO POLICEMAN) NUT
BRIBERY MEED
(OPEN TO —) VENAL
BRIC-A-BRAC CURIO VERTU VIRTU
BIBELOT TROCKERY TRUMPERY
BRICK BAT BUR BURR GLUT MARL
PAVE TILE BLOCK GAULT QUARL
SLOPE SPLIT STOCK STONE TOOTH
CUTTER FELLOW HEADER PAMENT
PAVIOR BACKING CLINKER
FLETTON GRIZZLE PERPEND
SOLDIER BURNOVER
(— WALL) NECK
(CRACKED —) CHUFF SHUFF
(FINAL HALF —) JACK
(IMPERFECT —) SHIPPER
BURNOVER
(PILE OF —S) HACK CLAMP
(PULVERIZED —) SOORKY SOORKEE
(SECOND-RATE —) GRIZZLE
(SECOND QUALITY —S) BRINDLES
(SOFT —) CUTTER RUBBER PICKING
(SQUARE —) QUADREL
(STACK OF —) LIFT
(SUN-DRIED —) BAT ADOBE
(UNBURNT —) ADOBE
(WOODEN —) DOOK
(PL.) CLAYWARE
(PREF.) PLINTHI
BRICKBAT GIBE
BRICKLAYER BRICKY MASONER
BRICKMAKER MOLDER
BRICKWORK HOB BRICKING
BRIDAL NUPTIAL BRIDALTY
BRIDE KALLAH SPOUSE SHULAMITE
SWEETENER
BRIDE OF LAMMERMOOR
(AUTHOR OF —) SCOTT
(CHARACTER IN —) LUCY CALEB
EDGAR FRANK ASHTON HAYSTON
WILLIAM RAVENSWOOD
BALDERSTONE
BRIDE-PRICE LOBOLD LOBOLO
BRIDESHEAD REVISITED (AUTHOR
OF —) WAUGH
(CHARACTER IN —) BOY REX CARA
KURT BERYL CELIA JULIA RYDER
BRIDEY ANTHONY BLANCHE
CHARLES MOTTRAM CORDELIA
MUSPRATT SAMGRASS
MARCHMAIN MULCASTER
SEBASTIAN BRIDESHEAD
BRIDESMAID PARANYMPH
BRIDEWELL JAIL MILLDOLL
BRIDGE WAY BRIG LINK NOSE PONS
PONT REST SPAN WIEN CROSS
SIRAT TOWIE GANTRY ISLAND
JIGGER RIALTO RUNWAY SANGAR
AUCTION BASCULE BIFROST
CHANNEL CONNECT CULVERT
EXOSTRA PASSAGE PASSING
PINNOCK PONCEAU PONTOON
PROPONS TRAJECT TRESTLE
VIADUCT CONTRACT TRAVERSE
DUPLICATE
(— BID) SPLINTER
(— BUILDER) PONTIFEX

(— HAND) YARBOROUGH
(— HOLDING) HONORS TENACE
YARBOROUGH
(— MARKER) PYLON
(— OF MUSICAL INSTRUMENT)
MAGAS CHEVALET CHEVILLE
(— PLAY) RUFF UPPERCUT
(— SEAT) EAST WEST DUMMY
NORTH SOUTH
(— TO PARADISE) ALSIRAT
(ARCADED —) RIALTO
(BILLIARDS —) JIGGER
(CONTRACT —) CHICAGO GHOULIE
PLAFOND
(FLUE —) ALTAR
(GATEWAY —) GOUT
(HOSE —) JUMPER
(IMPEDANCE —) DIPLEXER
(NATURAL —) ARCH
(PLANK —) LIGGER
(RAISE — BID) JUMP
(ROPE SUSPENSION —) JOOLA
(RUDE —) CLAPPER
(PREF.) GEPHYR(O) PONTI PONTO
BRIDGEMAKER PONTIFEX
BRIDGEMAN EBBMAN
BRIDGE OF SAN LUIS REY
(AUTHOR OF —) WILDER
(CHARACTER IN —) PIO JAIME
PILAR MANUEL PEPITA ESTEBAN
JUNIPER PERICHOLE MONTEMAYOR
BRIDGING ASTRIDE STRUTTING
BRIDLE BIT CURB REIN RULE BRAKE
BRANK BRIDE CHECK GUARD
GUIDE STRUT DIRECT GOVERN
HALTER MASTER SIMPER SUBDUE
BLINDER CONTROL LORMERY
REPRESS SNAFFLE SWAGGER
CAVESSON RESTRAIN SUPPRESS
BRIDLE PATH SPURWAY
BRIEF FEW CURT LIST RIFE WRIT
BLURB BREVE CHARM PITHY
QUICK SHORT TERSE ABRUPT
COMMON CURTAL FLYING HOURLY
LETTER LITTLE SNIPPY SUDDEN
ABRIDGE CAPSULE COMPACT
COMPOSE CONCISE CRYPTIC
INVOICE LACONIC MANDATE
OUTLINE PRECEPT SUMMARY
BREVIATE CONDENSE FLEETING
FLITTING SNATCHED SNIPPETY
SUCCINCT SYLLABUS
(PL.) BIKINI
(PREF.) BREVI
BRIEF CASE FOLIO TASHIE
BRIEFED (WELL —) UPON
BRIEFLY BRIEF ENFIN SHORTLY
BRIEFS JOCKEY
BRIER BARB PIPE BRIAR ERICA
THORN SMILAX BRUYERE PRICKER
INKBERRY
BRIER TREE PIPER
BRIG RIG JAIL PRISON GEORDIE
BRIGADE TERZO CAMPOO
BRIGAND THIEF USKOK BANDIT
KLEPHT LATRON PIRATE ROBBER
CATERAN KETTRIN LADRONE
ROUTIER SOLDIER PICAROON
BANDOLERO
(PL.) TCHETNITSI
BRIGANDAGE DACOITY
BRIGANDINE PLACCATE

BRIGHT APT GAY NET FINE GILD
GLAD GLEG HIGH LIVE ROSY
ACUTE AGLOW ALERT ANIME
BEAMY BRAVE CLEAR CRISP
EAGLE FLARY FRESH GEMMY
JOLLY LIGHT LUCID NITID PRINT
QUICK RIANT SHARP SHEEN SHEER
SHINY SMART SMOLT STEEP
SUNNY TINNY VIVID WHITE WITTY
BERTHA CHEERY CLEVER FLASHY
FLORID GARISH LIMPID LIVELY
LUCENT ORIENT SERENE SHRILL
SILVER BEAMISH DIAMOND
DILUCID FORWARD FULGENT
LAMBENT RADIANT RINGING
SHINING ANIMATED CHEERFUL
FLASHING GLEAMING LIGHTFUL
LUMINOUS LUSTROUS SPLENDID
SPLENDOR STARLIKE SUNSHINY
(— IN COLOR) NEON
(BLINDINGLY —) GLARING
(NOT —) SOFT
(OFFENSIVELY —) GARISH
(SOFTLY —) LAMBENT
(TOO —) ROARY ROARIE
(VULGARLY —) GAUDY
(PREF.) AETHIO AGLAO LAMPR(O)
BRIGHTEN GILD LAMP BLOOM
CHEER CLEAR FLAME GLOZE LIGHT
LIVEN SHINE SNUFF CANTLE
ENGILD POLISH ANIMATE BURNISH
EMBRAVE ENLIVEN FURBISH
LIGHTEN REFRESH SMARTEN
ILLUMINE
BRIGHTENED LITUP
BRIGHTENER FLUOROL
BRIGHTLY GAY CLEAR LIGHT SHEEN
BRIGHT FRESHLY SHEENLY
BRIGHTNESS SUN BLAZE BLOOM
ECLAT FLAME GLARE GLEAM
GLINT GLORY GLOSS LIGHT NITOR
SHEEN SHINE ACUMEN BRIGHT
CANDOR FULGOR LUSTER CLARITY
GLISTEN GLITTER LAMBERT
NITENCY SPARKLE RADIANCE
SPLENDOR BRILLIANCE
(— OF TOBACCO) FLASH
(— UNIT) STILB
(UNIT OF —) NIT
(PREF.) GANO
BRIGUE BLAT
BRILLIANCE FAME BLARE BLAZE
ECLAT FLAME GLARE GLORY
SHINE VALUE KEENNESS
RADIANCE SPLENDOR VIVACITY
REFULGENCE
BRILLIANCY FIRE BLARE ECLAT
GLORY REFLET CLARITY GLITTER
ORIENCY RADIANCE SPLENDOR
BRILLIANT GAY GOOD KEEN SAGE
WISE BREME QUICK VIVID BRIGHT
CLEVER GIFTED LIVELY PURPLE
SIGNAL BRAVURA BRITTLE
EMINENT FLAMING GLARING
LAMBENT LAMPING LOZENGE
PRISMAL RADIANT SHINING
BLINDING DAZZLING DIZZYING
GLORIOUS INSPIRED LUCULENT
LUMINOUS SLASHING SPLENDID
PRISMATIC
(TRANSIENTLY —) METEORIC
BRIM LIP RIM RUT SEA EDGE TURF
BLUFF BRINK MARGE OCEAN

VERGE WATER BORDER MARGIN
TURNUP COPULATE STRUMPET
(— OF HAT) FLAP LEAF POKE BRINK
TARFE SLOUCH
BRIMFUL TIPFUL TOPFUL CROWNED
BRIMMING BIG FULL ABRIM
BRIMSTONE SULFUR VIRAGO
SULPHUR BRINSTON SPITFIRE
(PREF.) THI(O)
BRIMSTONY LURID
BRINDLED TABBY TAWNY BRANDED
FLECKED STREAKED
BRINE SEA MAIN SALT BRACK
LEACH OCEAN TEARS PICKLE
MARINADE
BRINER COBBERER
BRING DO LAY TEE WIN BEAR BUCK
CALL FIRK LEAD STOP TAKE TEEM
CARRY DRIVE ENDUE FETCH INCUR
APPORT ARRIVE CONVEY DEDUCE
CONDUCE CONDUCT EXHIBIT
PROCURE PRODUCE
(— ABOUT) DO SEE BREW MAKE
STAY TEEM CAUSE DIGHT FRAME
INFER MOYEN SETUP SHAPE SWING
CREATE EFFECT INVOKE SECURE
BRING COMPASS CONDUCE INSPIRE
OPERATE PROCURE PRODUCE
CATALYZE OCCASION TRANSACT
PERPETRATE
(— ABOUT CAPTURE) ACCOUNT
(— BACK) REFER EFFECT RECALL
REDUCE REDUCT RELATE RETURN
REVIVE REVOKE PRODUCE RESTORE
OCCASION RETRIEVE TRANSACT
(— BEFORE) HAUL
(— CHARGE) APPEACH
(— DOWN) LAY DROP FALL FELL
STOP ABATE COUCH EMBASE
SOFTEN DECLINE DESCEND
DISMOUNT OVERTHROW
(— DOWN STEER) HOOLIHAN
(— FORTH) CAST FOAL GIVE MAKE
TEEM YEAN EDUCE HATCH ISSUE
SPAWN THROW PROFER DELIVER
TRADUCE ENGENDER PROCREATE
(— FORTH YOUNG) EAN KID YEAN
(— FORWARD) CITE LEAD INFER
ADDUCE ALLEGE ADJUST
ADVANCE PROPOSE
(— IN) EARN INFER USHER IMPORT
INDUCE INVECT REPORT RETURN
ADHIBIT
(— INTO BATTLE) COMMIT
(— INTO COURT) SIST
(— INTO DISGRACE) FOUL
(— LOW) AVALE DEGRADE
SUPPLANT
(— ON) INFER INDUCE
(— ONESELF) GET
(— OUT) DRAW ACCENT ELICIT
DISINTER HEIGHTEN
(— OVER) CONVERT
(— SHIP INTO POSITION) EASE
(— TO A HALT) STICK
(— TO AN END) DO END FIT DOCK
DRAW REDD CEASE FORDO DECIDE
EXPIRE FINISH FOREDO FULFIL
DISJOIN INCLUDE COMPLETE
CONCLUDE DISSOLVE SURCEASE
(— TO BAY) CORNER
(— TO BEAR) EXERT
(— TOGETHER) JOIN AMASS RAISE

UNITE ADDUCT CONFER CORRAL
ENGAGE ENLINK GATHER SUMMON
COLLATE COLLECT COMPILE
COMPORT ASSEMBLE CONFLATE
ENSEMBLE
(— TO HEEL) FACE
(— TO LIFE) EVOKE ANIMATE
(— TO LIGHT) GRUB REAP DREDGE
ELICIT EXPOSE REVEAL UNEARTH
DISCLOSE DISCOVER
(— TO NAUGHT) DASH FOIL UNDO
NEGATE CONFUTE DESTROY
(— TO PERFECTION) RIPEN
(— TO STOP) CURB HALT ARREST
(— TO THE GROUND) GRASS
(— UP) REAR BREED NURSE RAISE
TRAIN NURSLE NUZZLE UPREAR
EDUCATE NOURISH
(SUFF.) FER(ENCE)(ENT)(OUS)
(— ABOUT) FIC(AL)(ATE)(ATION)
(ATIVE)(ATOR)(ATORY)(E)(ENCE)(ENT)
(IAL)(IARY)(IENT) FIQUE
BRING-DOWN LETDOWN
COMEDOWN
BRINGER (— OF BABIES) STORK
(— OF BAD LUCK) JINX JONAH
(— OF BAD NEWS) SCREECHOWL
(— OF DREAMS) MAB
(— OF GOOD LUCK) MASCOT
BRINGING-UP BREEDING
EDUCATION
BRINJAL EGGPLANT
BRINK END EVE LIP RIM SEA BANK
BRIM EDGE FOSS MARGE SHORE
VERGE BORDER MARGIN
MARGENT PRECIPICE THRESHOLD
BRINY BRACK SALTY SALINE
BRACKISH MURIATED
BRIOCHE ROLL STICH SAVARIN
BRISE-SOLEIL BLIND SUNBREAK
SUNSHADE
BRISK GAY BRAG BUSY CANT FAST
KEEN PERK PERT RACY RASH SPRY
TRIG VIVE YARE YERN AGILE ALERT
ALIVE BUDGE BUXOM CANTY
COBBY CRANK CRISP FRESH FRISK
KEDGE NIPPY PEART PEPPY PERKY
QUICK ROUND ZIPPY ACTIVE
BREEZY COCKET CROUSE DAPPER
FLICKY LIVELY NIMBLE SNAPPY
SPRACK SPRUNT TROTTY VIVACE
ALLEGRO CHIPPER HUMMING
ROUSING ANIMATED BRUSHING
FRISKFUL GALLIARD RATTLING
SMACKING SPANKING SPIRITED
(SOMEWHAT —) ALLEGRETTO
BRISKLY YERN SHARP YERNE
BUSILY CROUSE ALLEGRO
ROUNDLY
BRISKNESS ALACRITY VIRITOOT
BRISTLE AWN JAG RIB BARB HAIR
JAGG SETA TELA BIRSE BRUSH
PARCH PREEN STARE STRUT STYLE
TOAST AVISTA CHAETA PALPUS
RUFFLE SETULA STIVER STRIGA
STYLET GLOCHIS SMELLER
STUBBLE WHISKER ACICULUM
FRENULUM SPICULUM VIBRISSA
VIBRACULUM
(PREF.) CHAET(I)(O) CHETO
HIRSUTO HORRI SETI SETULI
(SUFF.) CHAETA CHAETES
CHAETUS

BRISTLED HERISSE HORRENT
BRISTLE-SHAPED STYLOID
BRISTLING ROUGH HISPID HORRID
SETOSE THORNY HORRENT
SCRUBBY SPINOUS
BRISTLY BIRSY PENNY SETOSE
STUBBY SCRUBBY STICKLE
BRITAIN
(PREF.) BRITO
BRITISH ENGLISH BRITANNIC
WHITEHALL
**BRITISH COLUMBIA (CAPITAL OF
—)** VICTORIA
(MOUNTAINS OF —) COAST
CARIBOO CASCADE PURCELL
SELKIRK MONASHEE
(RIVER OF —) NASS LIARD PEACE
FRASER SKEENA STIKINE
(TOWN OF —) KELOWNA
KAMLOOPS VANCOUVER
BRITISH GUM DEXTRIN DEXTRINE
BRITISH HONDURAS (BAY OF —)
CHETUMAL
(CAPITAL OF —) BELMOPAN
(FORMER CAPITAL OF —) BELIZE
(MOUNTAIN RANGE OF —) MAYA
(TOWN OF —) CAYO STANN
COROZAL
BRITOMARTIS (FATHER OF —) ZEUS
JUPITER
(MOTHER OF —) CARME
BRITON BRIT CELT SCOT BRYTHON
BRITTANY ARMORICA
(NATIVE OF —) BRETON
BRITTLE DRY FROW WEAK BRASH
CANDY CRIMP CRISP CRUMP
EAGER FRAIL FROWY FRUSH
SHORT SPALT CRISPY CRUMPY
FEEBLE FICKLE FROUGH GINGER
INFIRM SLIGHT BRICKLE BRUCKLE
CRACKLY FRAGILE FRIABLE
REDSEAR SHIVERY SMOPPLE
BRITCHEL DELICATE SNAPPISH
(— AT HIGH HEAT) REDSHORT
BRITTLEBUSH ENCELIA
BRITTLE STAR OPHIUROID
BROACH AIR AWL CUT PIN ROD TAP
OPEN OUCH SHED SPIT SPUR STAB
TAME VEER VENT BEGIN DRESS
DRIFT PRICK RIMER SPOOL START
VOICE ATTAME BORING BROOCH
DRIVER FIBULA LAUNCH PIERCE
REAMER RHYMER STRIKE
ENLARGE EXPRESS PUBLISH
SPINDLE SQUARER VIOLATE
WIDENER APPROACH DEFLOWER
DRIFTPIN INCISION PORPOISE
BROAD DEEP FREE VAST WIDE
AMPLE BEAMY BRAID DORIC
GROSS LARGE LARGO PLAIN
ROOMY SPLAY SQUAB STOUT
THICK WOMAN COARSE GLOBAL
BELCHER EVIDENT GENERAL
GRIVOIS LIBERAL OBVIOUS
PLATOID BARNYARD SPACIOUS
TOLERANT
(— AND FLAT) PLATOID
(NOT —) STRAIT
(PREF.) EURY LATI PLAT(Y)
BROADBILL GAYA RAYA GAPER
SCAUP BOATBILL SHOVELER
SWORDFISH

BROADCAST AIR SOW SEED SEND
CARRY RADIO STREW AIRING
SPREAD DECLARE DIFFUSE
PUBLISH SCATTER ANNOUNCE
TELEVISE TRANSMIT
BROADCLOTH CASTOR SUCLAT
TAUNTON
BROADEN BREDE WIDEN DILATE
EXPAND EXTEND SPREAD
ENNOBLE
BROADHORN ARK
BROADLOOM CARPET
BROAD-MINDED LIBERAL
BROADNESS BIGNESS LIBERALITY
BROADSIDE RAM TIRE BROAD
GARLAND
BROADSWORD BILL KRIS GLAIVE
HANGER SPATHA CUTLASS
FERRARA CLAYMORE MONTANTO
SCIMITAR
BROBDINGNAGIAN HUGE
BROCADE ACCA BROCHE KINCOB
KINKHAB NISHIKI BAUDEKIN
DAMASSIN
BROCADED BROCHE
BROCCOLI ASPARAGUS
BROCCOLI BROWN GOAT LOAM
PLOVER RABBIT
BROCCOLI RABE RAPINI RAPPINI
BROCHURE TRACT BOOKLET
PAMPHLET TREATISE
BROCKET PITA STAG BROCK
SPITTER
BRODIAEA GRASSNUT
BROGAN STOGA STOGY BROGUE
STOGIE
BROGUE STOGY STOGIE
BROIL ROW BURN CHAR FEUD FRAY
GRID HEAT TOIL ALARM BRAWL
GRILL MELEE SCRAP SWELT
AFFRAY BIRSLE BRAISE GRILLY
SPLORE SQUEAL TUMULT
BRANDER BRULYIE CARBONE
CONTEST DISCORD DISPUTE
EMBROIL FRIZZLE GARBOIL
QUARREL SIMULTY BARBECUE
BLOODWIT CONFLICT GRILLADE
STRAMASH
BROILED CASINO
BROILER GRILL SEARER CHICKEN
POUSSIN
BROKE HOG LOW BUST SKINT
STONY STONEY CHICANE UPTIGHT
BANKRUPT
BROKEN DOWN DUFF RENT RUDE
TORN BLOWN BROKE BURST
FRACT GAPPY HAIRY KAPUT
ROMPU ROUGH TAMED BRASHY
HACKLY RUINED SHAKEN CRACKED
CRUSHED FRACTED REDUCED
SUBDUED VICIOUS WHIPPED
BANKRUPT CONTRITE OUTLAWED
RUPTURED TATTERED WEAKENED
(— BUT NOT TRAINED) GREEN
(— IN) STOVEN
(— IN HEALTH) CRAZY
(— OFF) ABRUPT
(EASILY —) GINGER
(PREF.) FRACTO
BROKEN-DOWN HAYWIRE
DISJASKED DISJASKIT
BROKER AGENT CRIMP BANIAN
BANYAN CORSER DEALER FACTOR

JOBBER BROGGER CHANGER COURSER MONEYER PEDDLER REALTOR SCALPER HUCKSTER INSTITOR MERCHANT
BROKERAGE AGIOTAGE
BROMATIUM KOHLRABI
BROME CHEAT
BROMEGRASS CHESS
BROMIA (HUSBAND OF —) SOSIA
BROMO ACID EOSIN EOSINE
BROMUS DRAWK
BRONCHITIS HUSK HOOSE HOOZE
BRONCO PONY PONEY CAYUSE BRONCHO MUSTANG
BRONCOBUSTER BUSTER GINETE BUCKAROO
BRONZE AES TAN BUST ALLOY BROWN COWBOY ORMOLU STATUE ASIATIC GUNMETAL
(— AGE CULTURE) UBAID
(ANTIQUE —) CACAO
(GILDED —) VERMEIL
(MEDAL —) CALABASH
(PREF.) CHALC(O) CHALK(O)
BRONZEWING SQUATTER
BROOCH BAR PIN BOSS LACE OUCH PRIN PROP CAMEO CLASP MORSE PREEN SLIDE SPRAY SPRIG FIBULA NOUCHE PLAQUE SHIELD FERMAIL PETALON CROTCHET ORNAMENT SUNBURST
BROOD EYE FRY NYE SET SIT MOPE NEST NIDE RACE STEW TEAM TRIP WEEP AERIE BREED CLOCK COVER COVEY FLOCK GLOOM GROUP HATCH HOVER ISSUE SEDGE STOCK WORRY YOUNG CLETCH CLUTCH FAMILY KINDLE LITTER PONDER PROGENY SPECIES CLECKING COGITATE INCUBATE KINDLING MEDITATE
(— OF BIRDS) AERY AERIE COVEY EYRIE SEDGE SIEGE
(— OF PHEASANTS) EYE NID NYE NIDE
BROODER HOVER MOTHER NURSERY
BROOK RUN BEAR BECK BURN GHYL GILL LAKE RILL RUSH SIKE ABIDE BAYOU BOURN CREEK FLEET GLIDE STAND STELL TCHAI ARROYO BRANCH CANADA DIGEST ENDURE GUTTER RINDLE RIVOSE RUNLET RUNNEL SICKET STREAM SUFFER ABROOKE COMPORT CONCOCT STOMACH QUEBRADA TOLERATE
(RIPPLING —) PURL
(SALT —) LICK
BROOKLET BECK DOKE RILL RILLET RUNNEL RILLOCK RIVULET
BROOM COW MOP FRAY SWAB WISP BESOM BISME BREAM BRUSH SCRUB SPART SWEEP UALIS WHISK GENISTA HAGWEED WHISKER HACKWEED SPLINTER
(DYER'S —) GENET DYEWOOD
(NATIVE —) DOGWOOD
(TOPS OF —) SCOPARIUS
(PREF.) SCOPI SCOPULI
BROOMCORN HURL
BROOMCORN MILLET HIRSE PANIC PANICLE KADIKANE

BROOMRAPE HELLROOT HERBBANE
BROOMROOT SACATON ZACATON
BROSE ATHOLE CROWDIE
BROTH SEW BREE BROO FOND KAIL KALE SOUP DASHI GLAZE STOCK BREWIS CULLIS JUSSAL JUSSEL LIQUOR SKILLY CALDERA POTTAGE SOUCHIE SUPPING BOUILLON CONSOMME PISHPASH POSSODIE POWSOWDY
(FISH —) DASHI
BROTHEL KIP CRIB STEW BAGNE HOUSE BAGNIO BORDEL CORINTH LUPANAR SHEBANG BORDELLO CATHOUSE HOOKSHOP HOTHOUSE JOYHOUSE SERAGLIO
BROTHER FR BUB FRA KIN PAL SIB BHAI BRER EGIL FRAY MATE MONK PEER BILLY BUBBY BUDDY CADET FRERE FRIAR FELLOW FRAILE FRATER GERMAN COMRADE SIBLING FOSTERER
(HUSBAND'S —) LEVIR
(LAY —) SCOLOG
(WIFE'S —) AFFINE
(YOUNGER —) CADET
(PL.) FF ADELPHI BRETHREN CURIATII HARLUNGEN
(PREF.) ADELPHO FRATRI
(SUFF.) ADELPHIA ADELPHOUS
BROTHERHOOD GILD GUILD LODGE ORDER PAPEY FRIARY BRATSVO CHISHTI THIASOS THIASUS BRODHULL SODALITY
(— OF FREEMASONS) CRAFT
(LITERARY —) FELIBRIGE
BROTHER-IN-LAW MAUGH
BROTHERS KARAMAZOV
(AUTHOR OF —) DOSTOEVSKI
(CHARACTER IN —) IVAN ALEXEY DMITRI FYODOR ALYOSHA KATRINA ZOSSIMA GRUSHENKA SMERDYAKOV
BROUGHAM PILLBOX CARRIAGE
BROUGHT BROCHT
(— FROM ELSEWHERE) DERIVED
(— TO BAY) CORNERED
(— TOGETHER) CONFLATE
(— UP BY HAND) CADE
BROUHAHA SCRAP
BROW TOP BRAE EDGE MIEN SNAB BOUND BRINK CREST EAVES FRONT RIDGE SLOPE BOLDNESS FOREHEAD
BROWBEAT BOSS CARP FACE ABASH BULLY BOUNCE HECTOR DEPRESS DUMBCOW OUTFACE SWAGGER
BROWBEATEN HACKED
BROWN (ALSO SEE COLOR) ART DUN LES TAN ARAB COIN COOK DARK GOAT LION SEAR ABRAM ACORN ARGUS BRUNO DUSKY HAZEL KAFFA MOSUL PABLO PENNY QUAIL SEDGE SEPIA TAWNY TENNE TOAST UMBER APACHE BEAVER BRUNET BURNET GLOOMY MALAGA MANILA MASTIC MOHAWK PALOMA PLOVER PONGEE RABBIT RUSSET SENNET TANNED TURTLE WIGWAM ASPHALT FUSCOUS HARVEST

LIBERIA MUSCADE OAKWOOD OXBLOOD POMPEII PRAIRIE REDWOOD TANBARK TOBACCO VESUVIN BRUNETTE MOCCASIN MUSHROOM PHEASANT PERSIMMON PYGMALION
(CONDOR —) TIFFIN
(DARK —) BURNET
(GRAYISH —) DUN
(HAIR —) ARGALI
(LIGHT —) BRAN ALOMA ALESAN STRING
(OLIVE —) BARK AUTUMN
(REDDISH —) BAY ROAN SORE SEPIA AUBURN CROTAL GINGER RUSSET SORREL AMBROSIA
(YELLOWISH —) AZTEC ALMOND BAMBOO BLONDE BEESWAX ALDERNEY
(PREF.) AITHO
BROWNBACK DOWITCH DOWITCHER
BROWNED ADUST
BROWN HEART RAAN
BROWNIE ELF NIS COOKY DOBBY NISSE URISK DOBBIE GOBLIN URUISG
BROWNING SCALD SCORCH SUNTAN
BROWNISH UMBER BURNET
(— BLACK) LAVA
BROWN LUNG DISEASE BYSSINOSIS
BROWNSTONE CHESTNUT
BROWSE BRUT CROP FEED GRAZE FORAGE NIBBLE PASTURE
BRUCITE NEMALITE
BRUISE JAM BASH BRAY BUBU DENT DUNT HURT JAMB MAIM MAUL SORE STUN TUND BLACK BREAK BRIZZ CRUSH CURRY DELVE DINGE FRUSH POUND PUNCH SQUAT BATTER BREACH HATTER INJURY INTUSE MANGLE POUNCE SHINER STOUND SUGGIL BATTERY CONTUND CROWNER DAMMISH DISABLE
(— FLAX) BRAKE
BRUISED HURT LIVID FROISSE
BRUIT DIN FAME RALE ROAR TELL NOISE RUMOR SOUND BLAZON CLAMOR REPORT DECLARE HEARSAY
BRUNEI (— WEIGHT) PARA CHAPAH
(COIN OF —) SEN
(TOWN OF —) SERIA
BRUNET DARK BLACK BROWN GIPSY GYPSY MORENA SWARTHY BRUNETTE MORENITA
BRUNHILD (HUSBAND OF —) GUNTHER
BRUNT JAR BLOW JOLT CLASH FORCE ONSET SHOCK ATTACK EFFORT IMPACT STRAIN STRESS ASSAULT OUTBURST VIOLENCE
BRUSH DIP DUB PIG TIP BOSH CARD COMB DUST FLAP FLAT FRAY KIYI SKIM SWAB BROOM CHAPE CLEAN COPSE FIGHT FITCH GRAZE LINER SABLE SCOPA SCRUB SCUFF SWEEP SWOOP WHISK BADGER BATTLE BRIGHT BROSSE DABBER

DAUBER DUSTER MOGOTE PALLET PENCIL PICKUP PUTOIS RIGGER RUBBER SPONGE STROKE TEASEL CLEANSE FOXTAIL GRAINER GROOMER MOTTLER STIPPLE STRIPER THICKET SCRUBBER SKIRMISH SOFTENER STIPPLER TARBRUSH NAILBRUSH PAINTBRUSH
(— ASIDE) SCUFF
(— IN DANCING) SCUFFLE
(— OF HIR) PENCIL
(— OF TWIGS) COW
(— TO CLEAN SHIP BOTTOM) HOG
(BLUNT —) BLENDER
(DENSE —) BUNDOCKS BOONDOCKS
(ELECTRIC —) DOCTOR
(EMPHASIZED —) SLAP
(FLESH —) SCRAPER STRIGIL
(GROWTH OF —) SYLVAGE
(POLLEN —) SCOPA SAROTHRUM
(SMALL —) TOOL FITCH FITCHEW
(PREF.) MUSCARI SCOPI
BRUSHER LIMBER LIPPER
BRUSH MAKER FLIRTY FLICKER
BRUSH SHUNT PIGTAIL
BRUSHWOOD HAG RICE RONE RUSH BAVIN BRAKE BRUSH COPSE FRITH REISE SCROG SCRUB SPRAY COPPET GARSIL MALLEE RAMMEL SCRAWL SCRUNT SHROGS TINNET TINSEL COPPICE ROUGHIE TEENAGE THICKET WOODRIS BUSHWOOD OVENWOOD
BRUSQUE CURT RUDE BLUFF BLUNT GRUFF HASTY ROUGH SHORT ABRUPT VIOLENT CAVALIER IMPOLITE
BRUT DRY
BRUTAL CRUEL FERAL GROSS CARNAL COARSE FERINE SAVAGE BEASTLY BESTIAL BRUTISH CADDISH DOGGISH INHUMAN BELLUINE INHUMANE INSOLENT RUTHLESS
BRUTALITY SADISM
BRUTE BETE BEAST GROSS YAHOO ANIMAL BRUTAL SAVAGE BEASTLY BESTIAL BRUTISH GORILLA RUFFIAN
BRUTISH FELL CRUEL BRUTAL CARNAL FIERCE SAVAGE STUPID BESTIAL INHUMAN SENSUAL GADARENE
BRYONY HOP NEP ALRAUN COWBIND MANDRAKE
(— FRUIT) OXBERRY
BRYOPHYTE MOSS ANOPHYTE LIVERWORT
BRYOPHYTIC MOSSY MOSSED
BRYOZOAN POLYZOAN
BRYTHONIC CYMRIC KYMRIC BRITTONIC
BUBBLE AIR BUB BEAD BELL BLEB BLOB BOIL BOLL DUPE FOAM GLOB SCUM SEED CAPER CHEAT EMPTY VAPOR BURBLE DELUDE HOTTER POPPLE SEETHE SOTTER TRIFLE BLISTER BLUBBER DECEIVE GLOBULE DELUSIVE
(— IN GLASS) BOIL REAM SEED BLISTER

(FORMATION OF —S) EBULLISM
(PL.) SUDS
(PREF.) BULLI
BUBBLING GAY BULLER BURBLY
BOILING GASSING EFFUSIVE
BUBINGA KEVAZINGO
BUBO EMEROD
BUCCANEER PIRATE RIFLER
ROBBER VIKING CORSAIR
MARINER SPOILER MAROONER
PICAROON
BUCHMANITE GROUPER
BUCHU BUKA DIOSMA
BUCK FOB RAM BOIL BUTT DEER
DUDE MALE PRIG REAR SOAK
STAG TOFF WASH BLOOD DANDY
MONEY PITCH SASIN STEEP
BASKET DOLLAR OPPOSE RESIST
STRIVE SAWBUCK BUCKJUMP
BUCKWASH
(— IN 1ST YEAR) FAWN
(— IN 2ND YEAR) PRICKET
(— IN 3RD YEAR) SORREL
(— IN 4TH YEAR) SORE
(STEADILY) SUNFISH
(— UP) BRACE
BUCKBEAN BOGBEAN THREEFOLD
BUCKER DOLLYMAN
BUCKET SAY TUB BAIL BOOT BOWK
CAGE GRAB MEAL PAIL SKIP
BOWIE CHEAT SCOOP SKEEL
STOOP STOUP BAILER DIPPER
DRENCH HOPPET KIBBLE SITULA
SUCKER VESSEL FERMAIL
GRAPPLE SNAPPER SWINDLE
CANNIKIN HEDGEHOG PAINTPOT
(— ON MILL WHEEL) AW AWE EIE
(— ON WHEELS) SKIP
(GLASS-MAKING —) CUVETTE
(GRAVEL —) GRAB
(HOISTING —) HUDGE
(PART OF —) EAR RIM BAIL BODY
CURL HANDLE
(TWO —S OF WATER) GAIT
BUCKEYE CANOE
BUCKEYE STATE OHIO
BUCKLAW HAYSTON
BUCKLE BOW BEND CURL KINK
OUCH TACH TACK WARP BRACE
CLASP MARRY STRAP TACHE
TWIST FIBULA CONTEND FERMAIL
GRAPPLE FASTENER STRUGGLE
BUCKLER CRAB BLOCK PELTA
SCUTE TARGE SHIELD TAIRGE
TARGET BUCKLUM BUCKRAM
ROTELLA ROUNDEL SHUTTER
RONDACHE
BUCKLING KINK UPSET
BUCK RAKE SWEEP
BUCKRAM STIFFENER
BUCKS BREAD DOUGH MONEY
MOOLA DINERO
BUCKTHORN COMA RHAMN
SCROG WAHOO ALATERN
CASCARA BEARWOOD FRANGULA
LOTEBUSH WAYTHORN
STINKWOOD
BUCKTHORN BROWN SUMAC
SUMACH
BUCKWHEAT BUCK CRAP BRANK
WRIGHT KNOTWEED SARRAZIN
POLYGONUM
(PL.) FAGOPYRUM

BUCOLIC IDYL LOCAL NAIVE RURAL
FARMER RUSTIC SIMPLE
COWHERD ECLOGUE AGRESTIC
HERDSMAN PASTORAL
BUCOLION (FATHER OF —)
LAOMEDON
(SON OF —) AESEPUS PEDASUS
(WIFE OF —) ABARBAREA
BUD BUR EYE GEM IMP PIP BULB
BURR CION FORM GERM GIRL
GROW KNOP KNOT WORK CAPOT
CHILD CLOVE GEMMA GRAFT
SCION SHOOT SPRIT SPURT YOUTH
BUDLET BULBIL BUTTON FLOWER
GERMIN OCULUS OILLET SPROUT
BLOSSOM BROTHER CABBAGE
GEMMULE PLUMULE ROSEBUD
TENDRON BOURGEON BULBILLA
(BLIGHTED —) BLAST
(BROOD —) SOREDIUM
(UNDERGROUND —) TURION
(UNDEVELOPED —) EYE
(UNOPENED —) KNOSP
(PL.) CAPERS
(PREF.) BLAST(O) GEMMI GEMMO
BUDDENBROOKS (AUTHOR OF —)
MANN
(CHARACTER IN —) TOM JEAN TONI
ERICA GERDA HANNO JOHANN
THOMAS ANTONIE GRUNLICH
CHRISTIAN PERMANEDER
BUDDHA FO FOH BUTSU JATAKA
GAUTAMA SRAMANA DAIBUTSU
(STORY) JATAKA
(FATHER OF —) SUDDHODANA
(SON OF —) KAHULA
BUDDHISM DAIJO FOISM KEGON
CHANISM LAMAISM HINAYANA
(— CODE) VINAYA
(BRANCH OF —) MAHAYANA
BUDDHIST (— DOCTRINE) ANATTA
TRIKAWA
(— FESTIVAL) WESAK
(— MOUNTAIN) OMEI
(— PATH) VEHICLE
(— SCHOOL) RITSU
(— SECT) SHIN TENDAI
(— TEACHER) GURU
(— WHO ATTAINED NIRVANA)
ARHAT ARAHAT
BUDDLE TYE FRAME BODDLE
SLIMER STRIPE TROUGH
BUDDY BO BOY BUD DOC PAL JACK
MATE COBBER DIGGER BROTHER
COMRADE COMPADRE TENTMATE
BUDGE FUR JEE BOGY MOVE STIR
BOOZE BRISK MUDGE STIFF THIEF
JOCUND LIQUOR SOLEMN
AUSTERE POMPOUS MOVEMENT
BUDGET BAG BOGY BOOT PACK
PLAN ROLL BATCH BOGEY BOGIE
BUNCH STOCK STORE BOTTLE
BUNDLE PARCEL SOCKET WALLET
PROGRAM
BUFF ASH BOB FAN TAN BLOW
COAT CURT FIRM SHINE SNUFF
SPARK BUFFET POLISH STURDY
DEVOTEE STAMMER STUTTER
NAUMKEAG
(TILLEUL —) ALABASTER
BUFFALO OX ANOA ARNA ARNI
BUFF STAG ARNEE BISON BUGLE
BUFFLE HAMPER KERBAU

MURRAH WUNTEE CARABAO
CARIBOU GAZELLE OVERAWE
TIMARAU ZAMOUSE BEWILDER
SAPIUTAN SELADANG
(WATER —) ARNEE
BUFFALO CHIPS BODEWASH
BUFFALO FISH SUCKER BUFFALO
BIGMOUTH GOURDHEAD
BUFFER DOG PAD FROG RACK
BUMPER FENDER HURTER PISTOL
CUSHION
BUFFET BAR BOB BOX BEAT BLAD
BLOW BUFF CUFF GOWF PLAT
SCAT SLAP TOSS YANK FILIP
KNOCK SCUFF SCUFT SMITE
STOOL ABACUS BATTER FILLIP
FLEWIT SERVER SETOUT STRIKE
STRIVE THRASH COLPHEG
CONTEND COUNTER HASSOCK
SMACKER SQUELCH CREDENCE
CREDENZA CUPBOARD SPANGHEW
BUFFETING DIRD SKITE DUSTING
BUFFLEHEAD DUCK FOOL CLOWN
BUFFLE DIPPER DOPPER
MARIONET WOOLHEAD
MERRYWING
BUFFOON DOR WAG WIT APER
FOOL JAPE MIME MOME VICE
ZANY ACTOR ANTIC BUFFO CLOWN
COMIC DROLE DROLL HARLOT
JESTER MUMMER STOOGE
ANTIQUE BOUFFON FARCEUR
JUGGLER PIERROT PLAYBOY
SCOGGIN TOMFOOL BALATRON
GRACIOSO HUMORIST MACAROON
MERRYMAN OWLGLASS PLEASANT
RIDICULE PANTALOON
SCARAMOUCH PUNCHINELLO
BUFFOONERY JAPERY ZANYISM
CLOWNERY TOMFOOLERY
BUFO TOAD
BUG (ALSO SEE INSECT) DOR FLU
FLAW GERM IDEA MITE BOGEY
BULGE FIEND LYGUS ROACH
ARADID BEDBUG BEETLE BUGGER
CAPSID CHINCH COREID CORUCO
ELATER GLITCH INSECT SALDID
SCHEME TINGID BELLIED
BOATMAN BUGBEAR CIMICID
CORSAIR FORWARD POMPOUS
STRIDER ASSASSIN BARBEIRO
CONENOSE HEMIPTER HOBBYIST
NAUCORID VINCHUCA
(— OFF) LEAVE
(KIND OF —) LYGUS DAMSEL
(RED —) CHIGGA CHIGGER
(SOW —) SLATER
(PREF.) CIMI(CI)
(SUFF.) CORIS
BUGABOO BOGY FEAR GOGA GOGO
OGRE TURK ALARM BOGEY BOGIE
GOGGA RODACH GOBLIN
BUGBEAR SPECTER SPECTRE
WORRICOW
BUGANDA (— KING) KABAKA
BUGBANE COHOSH BUGWORT
RICHWEED HELLEBORE
BUGBEAR BUG COW BOGY OGRE
BOGEY BOGIE CADDY MORMO
POKER BOGGLE BOGGART
BUGABOO FEARBABE SCAREBUG
BUGGER SOD CHAP BOOGER
FELLOW PERSON RASCAL HERETIC

BUGGY CART NUTS PRAM SHAY
TRAP NUTTY CALESA CABOOSE
CALESIN FOOLISH VEHICLE
DEMENTED INFESTED ROADSTER
STANHOPE
BUGLE BEAD HORN AJUGA BLACK
BUFFALO BULLOCK CLARION
HUTCHET TRUMPET KEYBUGLE
(— CALL) WARISON
(PART OF —) CUP RIM BELL BITE
EDGE
(YELLOW —) IVA
BUGLER WINDJAMMER
BUGLEWEED IVA AJUGA
BUGLOSS ALKANET ANCHUSA
BLUEWEED OXTONGUE
BUILD BIG SET FORM LEVY MAKE
REAR TELD DRIVE EDIFY ERECT
FOUND FRAME HOUSE PUTUP
RAISE SHAPE THROW CREATE
FABRIC GRAITH TAILLE TIMBER
COMPILE EXTRUCT FASHION
ASSEMBLE PHYSIQUE
(— FIRE) CHUNK
(— HASTILY) CLAP
(— NEST) AERIE NIDIFY
(— UP) AGGRADE
(BODY —) HABITUS STATURE
BUILDER EPEUS MAKER BIGGAR
EPEIUS HANGER ERECTOR
ENGINEER TECTONIC
(DAM —) DAMMER
(PREF.) TECTO
(SUFF.) TECT
BUILDING GIN CASA CRIB DOME
FLAT HALL IGLU UNIT PILE
SHED SHOP SI AB SPOT TELD
ABBEY AEDES ARENA BLOCK
COURT FOLLY FRAME HOTEL
HOUSE IGLOO JAWAB STORE
STUDY ARMORY RIGGIN BOTTLE
CASING CHAPEL FABRIC GARAGE
HAMMAM INSULA LYCEUM
PALACE SCHOOL SUCCOR
BREWERY BROODER CARBARN
COLLEGE DIORAMA EDIFICE
FACTORY FLATTOP FOUNDRY
KURHAUS MANSION PALAZZO
SALTERN STATION SYNAGOG
ATHENEUM BAGHOUSE BASILICA
BROLETTO CHANCERY DIPTEROS
DRYHOUSE DWELLING DYEHOUSE
ELEVATOR EPHEBEUM FIRETRAP
FOURPLEX GASHOUSE GINHOUSE
HOTHOUSE ICEHOUSE MAGAZINE
NYMPHEUM PANORAMA
SERAPEUM STEMMERY TAXPAYER
TENEMENT VELODROME
OBSERVATORY OUTBUILDING
PLANETARIUM MEETINGHOUSE
(— BLOCK) MEGALITH
(— FOR AIRCRAFT) DOCK
(— GROUPS) HAM
(— OF STONE) KAABA CASHEL
TRUDDO TRULLO
(— ON POSTS) PATAKA
(— WITH TRIANGULAR FRONT)
AFRAME
(BUDDHIST —) TOPE
(CIRCULAR —) THOLE THOLOS
ROTUNDA
(CRUDE —) SHANTY

(DILAPIDATED —) FLEAPIT ROOKERY FIRETRAP
(EXHIBITION —) MUSEUM
(FARM —) BARN STABLE HACIENDA
(FORTIFIED —) CASTLE
(GLOOMY —) MAUSOLEUM
(GRAIN —) GARNER
(GROUP OF —S) CLUSTER
(JAI ALAI —) FRONTON
(MOVABLE —) TURRET
(ORNAMENTAL —) ALCOVE
(PUBLIC —) CASINO THEATER THEATRE COLISEUM
(QUADRANGULAR —) TETRAGON
(QUARANTINE —) LAZARET
(ROUND —) THOLUS
(SACRED —) CHURCH MOSQUE TEMPLE SACRARY PANTHEON SARAPEUM
(SERIES OF —S) SWEEP
(SLIGHT —) SHED
(SMALL —) HUT COOP HOCK EDICULE
(SPORTS —) CAGE
(STATELY —) DOME
(STORAGE —) BARN HORREUM
(SUBSIDIARY —) ANNEX
(TALL —) SKYSCRAPER
(TRADE —) HALL
(UNCOMFORTABLE —) ARK
(PL.) FUNDUS
BUILD-UP GROWTH
BUILT SET BOUKIT STACKED TIMBERED
(COMPACTLY —) CORKY
(HEAVILY —) BLOCKY
(LOOSELY —) GANGLING
(STRONGLY —) BURLY GROSS QUARRY
(WELL —) BUIRDLY
BUKIDNON MONTES BINOKID
BUKKI (FATHER OF —) JOGLI ABISHUA
(SON OF —) UZZI
BULB BUD SET BLUB CORM IXIA KNOB LAMP ROOT SEED SEGO CAMAS CHIVE CLOVE FLOAT GLOBE ONION SWELL TUBER BULBIL BULBUS CAMASS CROCUS GARLIC OFFSET SCILLA BABIANA GALTONIA SPARAXIS TRITONIA PHOTOFLASH
(— OF PERCUSSION) CONCHOID
(CUBICAL —) FLASHCUBE
(LIGHT —) HELION
(ONION —) BUTTON
(PL.) SQUILL
(PREF.) BULBI BULBO
BULBIL CHIVE BULBLET
(PL.) SPAWN
BULBLET CHIVE CORMEL BULBULE NUCLEUS PROPAGO
BULBUL KALA BUHLBUHL GREENBUL LEAFBIRD

BULGARIA
ASSEMBLY: SOBRANJE SOBRANYE
CAPE: EMINE SABLA KURATAN
CAPITAL: SOFIA
COIN: LEV LEW STOTINKA
COMMUNE: SLIVEN SLIVNO SISTOVA
GULF: BURGAS

MEASURE: OKA OKE KRINE LEKHE
MOUNTAIN: BOTEV SAPKA MUSALA VIKHREN
MOUNTAINS: PIRIN BALKAN RHODOPE
PEOPLE: SLAV TATAR BULGAR SLAVIC
RIVER: LOM VIT ARDA OSMA ISKER MESTA DANUBE MARICA OGOSTA STRUMA YANTRA MARITSA STRYAMA TUNDZHA
TOWN: RILA RUSE AYTOS BUTAN BYCLU ELENA ISKRA STARA VARNA BLEVEN BURGAS DULOVO LEVSKY PLEVNA SHUMEN SHUMLA SLIVEN SLIVNO WIDDIN YAMBOL ZAGORA GABROVO KARLOVO PLOVDIV SISTOVA TIRNOVO RUSTCHUK
WEIGHT: OKA OKE TOVAR

BULGARIAN POMAK
BULGE BAG BUG JUT SAG BIAS BULB BUMP CASK HUMP KNOB LUMP PANT BILGE BLOAT BOUGE FLASK POUCH START STRUT SWELL BEETLE BILLOW COCKLE EXTEND PUCKER WALLET BLISTER PROJECT OVERHANG PROTRUDE SWELLING PROJECTION
(— OUT) TUT BELLY BOWDEN STRUNT
(OFFENSIVE —) SALIENT
BULGING FULL BOMBE BOWED BUGGY GOUTY PUDGY TUMID BAGGED BUNCHY CONVEX GOOGLY TOROSE GAMPISH GIBBOUS GOUTISH SWOLLEN BOUFFANT PROPTOSIS
BULK BODY BOUK FECK HEAP HEFT HOLD HULK HULL LUMP MASS MOLE PILE SIZE BURLY CARGO GROSS MIGHT POWER SLUMP STALL SWELL CORPSE EXPAND EXTENT FIGURE VOLUME BIGNESS MAJORITY QUANTITY
(PREF.) ONCO
BULKHEAD CHECK BATTERY PARTITION
BULKY BIG MAIN BURLY GROSS LARGE LUSTY PUDGY STOUT CLUMSY STODGY HULKING LUMPING MASSIVE VOLUMED WEIGHTY CUMBROUS UNWIELDY
(PREF.) PYCN(O)
BULL COP SEG APIS BEEF BILL JEST MALE ROAN SEAL SEGG SLIP STOT TORO ZEBU BACIS BEEVE BOBBY BONER BOVID BRUTE CROCK DRINK EDICT ERROR ANIMAL BOVINE BUSHWA LETTER PEELER TAURUS BULLOCK BUSHWAH CRITTER CRUSADE NOVILLO TAURINE CAJOLERY DOCUMENT FLATTERY IRISHISM
(— AREA) QUERENCIA
(— KILLING) VOLAPIE
(HORNLESS —) DODDY DODDIE
(HUMAN-HEADED —) SHEDU CAMASSU
(YOUNG —) STOT BUGLE MICKY STIRK STOTT BULLOCK

(PL.) BATTERY
(PREF.) TAUR(I)(O)
BULLA BLEB BULL SEAL BLAIN BLISTER VESICLE
BULL CELL TORIL
BULLDOG BULL BULLER BULLDOZE
BULLDOZE COW RAM BULLY FORCE SCOOP COERCE BROWBEAT BULLYRAG RESTRAIN
BULLDOZER (PART OF —) ARM EYE SHOE TANK BLADE FRAME IDLER LEVER LIGHT STRUT TRACK CANOPY FENDER GRILLE ROLLER CLEANER HOUSING MUFFLER CYLINDER
BULLET ACE GUN BALL LEAD PILL SHOT SLUG TOWEL CONOID DUMDUM PELLET PICKET SINKER TRACER DINGBAT MISSILE PELLOCK PROJECT SPITZER BISCAYAN MUSHROOM WADCUTTER
(— SIZE) CALIBER
(KIND OF —) MAGIC
(PL.) BALL LEAD STUFF
BULLETIN ITEM MEMO NOTICE POSTER REPORT SERIAL PROGRAM NEWSBILL
BULLETIN BOARD (OPERATOR OF —) SYSOP
BULLFIGHT CORRIDA NOVILLADA
BULLFIGHTER TORERO MATADOR PICADOR CAPEADOR TOREADOR NOVILLERO
BULLFIGHTING REJONEO TAUROMACHY
(— MOVEMENT) PASE
(PASE IN —) VERONICA
BULLFINCH ALP OLP HOOP MAWP MONK NOPE OLPH POPE HEDGE TANNY TAWNY MONACH REDBIRD REDHOOP SHIRLEY BLOODALP TONYHOOP
BULLHEAD CUR POUT POGGE COTTOID
BULLHEADED SET
BULLHORN HAILER LOUDHAILER
BULLIMONG FARRAGE
BULLION BILLOT
BULLISH STIFF
BULLOCK HOG HOGG NEAT NOWT STOT BUGLE COACH KNOUT STEER STIRK BOVINE
(AUSTRALIAN —) SNAIL
(BAD-TEMPERED —) RAGER
(DECOY —) COACH
BULL-ROARER BUZZ BUMMER BUZZER ROARER TUNDUN HUMBUZZ TURNDUN WHIZZER
BULL'S-EYE EYE BULL DUMP GOLD BLANK OXEYE WHITE TARGET ROUNDEL
BULL SNAKE GOPHER
BULL TROUT TRUFF
BULLY COW NUT BOAT BOSS FACE FINE GOOD HAZE HUFF MATE BRAVE BRAVO GREAT JOLLY SNOOL TIGER VAPOR BOUNCE CUTTER CUTTLE HARASS HECTOR HUFFER JOVIAL RUFFLE TYRANT BLUSTER BOUNCER BULLOCK DARLING DASHING GALLANT GAUSTER HUFFCAP ROISTER RUFFIAN RUFFLER SLASHER

SOLDIER SWAGGER BANGSTER BARRATER BLUDGEON BROWBEAT BULLDOZE DOMINEER FRAMPLER NIGHTCAP RABIATOR
(MASTIC —) ACOMA
BULLY TREE BALATA BULLACE GAUSTER BEEFWOOD
BULRUSH REED RISP RUSH TULE SEDGE BUMBLE GLUMAL AKAAKAI CATTAIL PAPYRUS SCIRPUS TUSSOCK
BULWARK BAIL FORT WALL FENCE JETTY MANTA MOUND TOWER SCONCE WARDER BASTION DEFENCE DEFENSE PARAPET PROTECT RAMPART WEREWALL
BUM BEG DIN BOMB BOOM HOBO DRINK DRONE IDLER MOOCH SHACK STIFF TRAMP FROLIC GUZZLE ROTTER SPONGE SQUEEF GUZZLER LAYABOUT VAGABOND BINDLESTIFF
BUMBERSHOOT GAMP
BUMBLE ERR
BUMBLEBEE DOR CLOCK BUMBEE BUMBLE CARDER BUMBLER
BUMBLER OAF IDIOT KLUTZ
BUMMER FLOP FAILURE SKIDDER STINKER
BUMP CRY HIP HIT NOB BANG BLOW BOOM BUNK DIRD JOLT JOWL KNOB LUMP NERF WHAP WHOP BARGE BULGE CLASH CLOUR CLOUT DUNCH KNOCK ORGAN THUMP BOUNCE CANNON IMPACT JOUNCE NODULE STRIKE BITTERN COLLIDE CONFLICT SWELLING
(— IMPOLITELY) KNEE
(— IN SKI RUN) MOGUL
(— OFF) KILL SCRAG MURDER
(— ON SKI RUN) MOGUL
(— ON WHALE'S HEAD) HOVEL
BUMPER BOWL FINE GOOD FACER GLASS ROUSE BUFFER CASABE FENDER GOBLET HURTER KELTIE BOUNCER BRIMMER DINGMAN CARANGID
(— GUARD) OVERRIDER
BUMPER CAR DODGEM
BUMPKIN JAY YAP BEAM BOOM BOOR CHAW CLOD GAWK HICK LOUT PUTT RUBE SWAB SWAD TIKE TYKE CHURL CLOWN ROBIN YAHOO YOKEL FARMER JOSKIN LUMMOX RUSTIC BUCOLIC CAUBOGE HAWBUCK CHAWBACON
BUMPTIOUS COXY BRASH COCKSY
BUN PUG CHOU BRICK COOKIE CRESCENT
(PL.) BUTTOCKS
BUNAH (FATHER OF —) JERAHMEEL
BUNCH BOB SET WAD BALE BOSS CHOU CLEW CLOT CLUB CLUE COMA KICK KNOB KNOT PACK SWAD TUFT WISP BREAK CLUMP FAGOT FLOCK KNOLL PAHIL THUMP CLUTCH GAGGLE HUDDLE CLUSTER
(— OF BANANAS) HAND STEM
(— OF FEATHERS) LURE PLUME

(— OF FLAX) HEAD STRICK
(— OF FLOWERS) POSY BOWPOT
BOUQUET BOUQUET NOSEGAY
BOUGHPOT
(— OF FOLIAGE) FINIAL
(— OF FRUIT) HOG STRAP
(— OF GRAIN) RIP
(— OF GRAPES) RAISIN
(— OF GRASS) WHISK
(— OF HAIR) COB
(— OF HERBS) BOUQUET
(— OF IVY) BUSH
(— OF RAGS) MOP
(— OF TOBACCO LEAVES) HAND
BREAK
(— OF TWIGS) COW KOW ROD
(— UP) SHRUG
(LONG —) STRING
(SMALL —) WISP
BUNCHER BINDER
BUNCHY TRUSS
BUNCO SCAM CHEAT
BUNCOMBE HOOEY BUNKUM
BUND BAND QUAY PRAYA LEAGUE
SOCIETY
BUNDLE KID LOT PAD TOD WAD
WAP BALE BAND BEAT BOLT BOOK
BUNG DRUG DRUM GARB HANK
HAUL HEAD KNOT LOCK PACK
ROLL SWAG BLUEY BULTO BUNCH
FADGE FAGOT GAVEL GLEAN
GROUP LITCH NICKY PETER SHEAF
SKEIN TARRY TRACE TRUSS TURSE
WADGE BARSOM BATTEN BINDLE
BOTTLE BUDGET DRIVER DUFTER
FAGGOT FARDEL FASCES FUMBLE
GATHER KNITCH LOGGIN NUMBER
PACKET PARCEL SCROLL THRAVE
DORLACH FASCINE GARBAGE
MATILDA PACKAGE FASCICLE
TROUSSEAU
(— BARLEY) SHEAVE
(— OF BOARDS) BOLT
(— OF CELLULOSE) MICROFIBRIL
(— OF FASCINES) ROULEAU
(— OF FIBRILS) AXONEME
(— OF FILAMENTS) BYSSUS
(— OF FLAX) BEET HEAD
(— OF HAIR) LEECH
(— OF HAY, STRAW, ETC.) WAP
WASE WISP GAVEL SHEAF
BATTEN BOLTIN BOTTLE TIPPLE
WINDLING
(— OF HEATH) KID
(— OF HIDES) KIP
(— OF NERVE FIBERS) TRACT
COLUMN
(— OF PAPERS) SPUR DUFTER
(— OF RODS) FASCES
(— OF SACKS) BADGER
(— OF SACRED TWIGS) BARSOM
(— OF THONGS) KNOUT
(— OF TOBACCO) CARROT
(— OF TWIGS) BIRCH BROOM
FAGGOT
(— OF WOOD) PIMP BAVIN FAGOT
(— OF YARN) HAUL SLIP
(— OF 60 SKINS) TURN
(— UP) EMBALE
(BUSHMAN'S —) DRUM BLUEY
BUNG CORK DOOK PLUG SHIVE
SPILE STOPPER

BUNGEY KIT
BUNGI-BUNGI STAVEWOOD
BUNGLE ERR BOOB DUFF FLUB
GOOF MESS MUCK MUFF MULL
BLUNK BOTCH FAULT FLUFF
FUDGE MISDO SPOIL STICK
BOGGLE BOLLIX BUMBLE FOOZLE
FUMBLE MANGLE MOMBLE
MUCKER MUDDLE TAILOR TOGGLE
BAUCHLE BLUNDER BUTCHERY
SHAMMOCK
BUNGLER MUFF LUMMOX PUDDLE
TINKER BLUNKER BUMBLER
BUMMLER FOOZLER DAUBSTER
SCHLEMIEL
BUNGLING FLUFF FUDGY INERT
CLUMSY AWKWARD TINKERLY
MUDDLEHEADED
BUNGO BONGO CANOE
BUNG START FLOGGER
BUNION ONION WYROCK
CARBUNCLE
BUNJI-BUNJI CUDGERIE
BUNK BED CAR BLAA BLAH CASE
JUNK SACK ABIDE BERTH BUNKO
FRAME HOKUM HOOEY LEAVE
LODGE SLEEP TRUCK BUNKUM
TIMBER BALONEY BOLSTER
CHICORY HEMLOCK TWADDLE
BUNCOMBE COBBLERS MALARKEY
NONSENSE
BUNKHOUSE BULLPEN
BUNKUM BLAH BULL BUNK CROCK
FUDGE HOKUM HOOPLA BALONEY
BUNCOMBE MALARKEY
BUNTAL BURI BANGKOK
BUNTING EBB POP GIRL FLAG PAPE
POPE CHINK DUMPY FINCH PLUMP
COTTON STOCKY TOWHEE UNTIDY
COWBIRD ETAMINE GARMENT
OATFOWL ORTOLAN ROUNDED
BELLYING BOBOLINK PRUSIANO
RICEBIRD RINGBIRD SLOVENLY
NONPAREIL
BUNTON DIVIDER
BUNUS (FATHER OF —) HERMES
(MOTHER OF —) ALCIDAMEA
BUOY DAN NUN WAFT BAKEN ELATE
FLOAT LAGAN RAISE BEACON
MARKER DOLPHIN SUSTAIN
DEADHEAD LEVITATE MAKEFAST
SONOBUOY
(KIND OF —) SONOBUOY
BUOYANCY BALON BALLON LEVITY
SPRING ELATION
BUOYANT GAY CORKY HAPPY
LIGHT BLITHE BOUNCY FLOATY
LIVELY ELASTIC HOPEFUL
JOCULAR LILTING SPRINGY
ANIMATED CHEERFUL SANGUINE
SPIRITED VOLATILE
BUPHAGUS (FATHER OF —) IAPETUS
(MOTHER OF —) THORNAX
(SLAYER OF —) ARTEMIS
BUR BUZZ TEAZEL STICKER
BURBARK AKONGE BOXBUSH
BURRBARK
BURBOT COD CONY CUSK LING
LOTA CONEY LOCHE LAWYER
MORGAY DOGFISH EELPOUT
GUDGEON BIRDBOLT
BURBUNG BORA

BURDEN TAX VEX BIRN CARE CARK
CLAG CLOG DRAG DUTY FARE
FOOT GANG LADE LOAD MUCK
ONUS PORT SEAM TACK TASK
BIRTH CARGO CROWD CRUSH
DRONE HEAVY LABOR MIDST
CHARGE CUMBER ENTAIL FARDEL
HAMPER IMPOSE LADING SADDLE
THRACK WEIGHT BALLAST
BURTHEN CONVETH FRAUGHT
FREIGHT HAGRIDE ONERATE
OPPRESS REFRAIN REPRISE
SUMPTER TROUBLE CAPACITY
CARRIAGE ENCUMBER ENGREGGE
HANDICAP OVERCOME PRESSURE
QUANTITY RUMBELOW
MILLSTONE RESPONSIBILITY
(— OF SONG) WHEEL FADING
HOLDING OVERTURN OVERWORD
(FINANCIAL —) EXPENSE
BURDENED HEAVY LADEN GRAVID
FRAUGHT HARASSED
BURDENER INCUBUS
BURDENSOME HEAVY IRKSOME
ONEROUS WEIGHTY CUMBROUS
GRIEVOUS GRINDING LOADSOME
BURDOCK DOCK GOBO CLITE
CLOTE CLOTS DRAIN LAPPA
BARDANE BURWEED BUZZIES
CADILLO CLOTBUR HARDOCK
HAREBUR CLEAVERS HAULBACK
BUREAU DESK CHEST AGENCY
EXCISE OFFICE CENTRAL DRESSER
AGITPROP
BUREAUCRAT MANDARIN
BURFISH ATINGA
BURGEON BUD GROW ERUPT
SHOOT SPROUT
BURGESS CITIZEN FREEMAN
PORTMAN COMMONER GURGIBUS
(PL.) BURGWARE
BURG GRASS SANDBUR
COCKSPUR SANDSPUR
BURGH ROYALTY
BURGLAR YEGG CRACK THIEF
GOPHER ROBBER RAFFLES
YEGGMAN PETERMAN PICKLOCK
(— TOOL) LOID
BURGLARY BREAK CRACK THEFT
LARCENY ROBBERY STEALAGE
BURGLE ROB SCREW
BURGUNDY MACON POMMARD
VOUGEOT TONNERRE
BURIAL FUNERARY INTERMENT
(— MOUND) TOLA HUACA
BURIAL PLACE AHU TOMB GRAVE
BURIAL GIGUNU LAYSTOW
PYRAMID CATACOMB CEMETERY
GOLGOTHA LAYSTALL
BURIED HIDDEN HUMATE SEPULT
ABSORBED IMBEDDED
(NOT —) UNRESTED
(RECENTLY —) GREEN
BURIN GRAVER PLASTIC
BURKINA FASO (CAPITAL OF —)
OUAGADOUGOU
(LANGUAGE OF —) BOBO LOBI
SAMO MANDE MOSSI
(MOUNTAIN IN —) TEMA
(NATIVE OF —) BOBO LOBI SAMO
BISSA HAUSA MANDE MARKA

MOSSI PUEHL TUAREG SENOUFO
VOLTAIC YATENGA MANDINGO
(RIVER IN —) VOLTA SOUROU
(TOWN OF —) PO LEO DORI PAMA
YAKO DJIBO GAOUA LAWRA
HOUNDE TOUGAN BANFORA
BURL BURR KNAR KNOT LUMP
KNAUR PIMPLE PUSTULE
BURLAP GUNNY CROCUS BAGGING
HESSIAN SACKING WRAPPING
BURLER LECKER SPILER
BURLESQUE APE ODD COPY JEST
MIME SKIT BURLY DROLL FARCE
REVUE COMEDY OVERDO PARODY
BUFFOON JOCULAR MIMICRY
MOCKERY OVERACT DOGGEREL
RIDICULE TRAVESTY
BURLY BIG FAT BLUFF BULKY
GROSS HEAVY HUSKY LARGE
LUSTY NOBLE OBESE STOUT THICK
TRAMP BOWERLY BUIRDLY
MASTIFF STATELY IMPOSING
BUR MARIGOLD BACLIN CUCKOLD
BURMESE KADU BIRMAN
ARAKANESE
BURN GYP BREN BREW CHAR FIRE
GLOW PLOT RAZE BILL SEAR SERE
TEND TIND ADUST BLAZE BROIL
BROOK CENSE CHARK CLAMP
FLAME FLARE OUTDO PARCH
PLOUT QUICK ROAST SCALD
SCAUM SINGE SWEAL WASTE
WATER CLOZLE IGNIFY SCORCH
SIZZLE STREAM CHARPIT
COMBURE COMBUST CONSUME
CREMATE CROZZLE FLICKER
FRIZZLE INCENSE OXIDIZE RIVULET
SCOWDER SMOLDER SWINDLE
FLAGRATE SQUANDER
AMBUSTION
(— FEEBLY) GUTTER
(— FITFULLY) FLICKER
(— IN) INURE
(— MIDNIGHT OIL) LUCUBRATE
(— OUT) GUT
(— THOROUGHLY) ASH
(— UP) ADUST EXUST
(— WITH LITTLE FLAME) SMUDGE
(LET —) BISHOP
(PREF.) COMBURI
BURNED ADUST COMBUST
(PREF.) AITHO
BURNER BEAK ETNA KORO BAKER
PILOT ARGAND BUNSEN CENSER
BATSWING CALCINER GASLIGHT
THURIBLE WELSBACH
BURNET SELFHEAL BLOODWORT
BURNING HOT FIRE LIVE ADUST
AFIRE ANGRY BLAZE CALID EAGER
FIERY FLAME GLEDY QUICK SCALD
URENT ABLAZE ARDENT FERVID
FIRING LIVING TORRID USTION
ADURENT CAUSTIC CAUTERY
FERVENT FLAMING GLARING
GLOWING INTENSE MORDANT
SCOWDER SHINING ARDUROUS
EXCITING FLAGRANT INUSTION
MUIRBURN PARCHING SCOUTHER
(— BRIGHTLY) LIGHT
(— OF FORESTS IN INDIA) JHOOM
(MALICIOUS —) ARSON
(NO LONGER —) EXTINCT
(PREF.) IGNI

BURNING BUSH WAHOO
BURNISH RUB GLAZE GLOSS INLAY
POLISH FURBISH
BURNISHED BROWN WHITE
BURNISHER AGATE BUFFER
GLAZER FROTTON POLISHER
BURNT ADUST BRULE COMBUST
BURP BOKE BELCH BUBBLE
BURR NUT PAD RIB BARB BIRR BOSS
BUZZ HALO KNOB PILE RING ROVE
SLUG WHIR BRIAR BURGH CROUP
WHARL WHIRR BANYAN CIRCLE
CORONA TEASEL TUNNEL WASHER
CORONET STICKER PARASITE
(— IN WOOD) GNAR KNAR
(— OF ANTLER) CORONET
(— ON TYPE) RAG
BURRO ASS DONKEY
BURROW BED DEN DIG SET BURY
HEAP HOLE HOWK MINE MOLE
PIPE ROOT TUBE BERRY COUCH
EARTH MOUND FURROW ROOTLE
TUNNEL CLAPPER GALLERY
PASSAGE SHELTER EXCAVATE
WORMHOLE
(— AS EEL) MUD
(— IN) MOIL
(— OF BADGER) SET
(— OF OTTER) COUCH
(FOSSIL —) SCOLITE
BURROWS TOWN
BURSA SAC SACK POUCH CAVITY
BURSULA
BURSAR BOWSER PURSER TERRAR
BOUCHER CASHIER
BURSE CASE SHOP FOREL BAZAAR
BOURSE POCKET
BURST FIT FLY POP BLOW BUST
DASH GUSH GUST LOSS LOUP
REND SCAT TILT BLAST BLOUT
BREAK CRACK ERUPT FLAFF FLASH
GRAZE REAVE SALVO SCATT
SHOUT SPASM SPLIT START STAVE
BROKEN DAMAGE INJURY SPROUT
EXPLODE IMPLODE RUPTURE
SHATTER AIRBURST OUTBREAK
SUNDERED
(— ASUNDER) OUTRIVE
(— FORTH) ERUPT SALLY EXPIRE
BALLOON
(— IN) IRRUPT IMPLODE
(— INTO FRAGMENTS) FLITTER
(— INTO LAUGHTER) BUFF
(— OF ACTIVITY) BRASH SPURT
SPRINT SPLURGE
(— OF ARTILLERY) GRAZE RAFALE
(— OF CHEERS) SALVO
(— OF ENERGY) BANG
(— OF FIRING) COUGH
(— OF HARMONIOUS SOUND)
DIAPASON
(— OF LIGHT) FLASH GLORY
(— OF SPEED) KICK FLUTTER
(— OF TEARS) BLURT
(— OF TEMPER) FUFF BOUTADE
(— OF WIND) FLAW
(— OPEN) DEHISCE UPBRAST
(— OUT) BUFF PRORUMP
(— THE HEART) RIVE
(SUFF.) RRHAGIA RRHAGY
BURSTER GALE LUGGER CRACKER
BURSTING TUMID ABURST
BLOWOUT RUPTION ERUPTING

BURY URN CAMP HIDE MOOL RAKE
TURF VEIL CLOAK COVER EARTH
GRAVE INTER INURN PLANT VAULT
WHELM ENTOMB ENWOMB
HEARSE INHUME SEPULT SHROUD
BEDELVE CONCEAL ENGROSS
IMMERSE PITHOLE REPRESS
SECRETE FUNERATE INHEARSE
SUBMERGE SEPULCHER
BUS CLEAR CAMION JITNEY
JEEPNEY MINIBUS DOUBLEDECKER
(PRIVATE —) PIRATE
BUSBOY OMNIBUS PICCOLO
BUSH TOD BUTT BOSCH BURSE
CLUMP GROVE PLASH SCRAY
SHRUB BOUCHE BRANCH BUSKET
MAQUIS TAVERN BOSCAGE
BOUCHON CLUSTER OUTBACK
THICKET BUSHLAND
(— OF HAIR) GLIB
(— SICKNESS) TAURANGA
(BLACKBERRY —) BRAMBLE
(PRICKLY —) GORSE
(ROSE —) ROSIER ROSIERE
(STUNTED —) SCROG
(WILD ROSE —) BRIAR BRIER
(PL.) RUFFMANS
(PREF.) THAMN(O)
BUSHBUCK BONGO
BUSH CLOVER HAGI
BUSH COW ZAMOUSE
BUSHEL FOO FOU GOB LOT MET
EPHA EPHI EPHAH BUCKET
MODIUS STRICK
(1.6 —) FANEGA
(1-HALF —) TOVET
(1-HALF TO 3-4THS —) CABOT
(1-4TH —) PECK
(3-4THS —) SKIPPLE
(3 TO 5 —S) SACK
(4 —S) COMB COOMB
(41.28 —) WEY
(8 —S) SEAM
BUSHER SWAMPER
BUSHGRASS WOODREED
BUSHING BUSH COAK DRILL LINER
BOUCHE COLLET LINING SLEEVE
BOUCHON FERRULE GROMMET
PADDING
(HALF —) STEP
BUSHMAN GUNG BUSHY KHUAI
ABATOA ABATWA WHALER
BUSHBOY SWAGMAN NEGRILLO
(PL.) SAN SAAN
BUSHMASTER CURUCUCU
SURUCUCU
BUSHWHACKER PAPAW PAWPAW
BUSHY BOSKY SHOCK DUMOSE
DUMOUS BUSHMAN QUEACHY
BUSIED VERSANT

BUSILY THRANG
BUSINESS ADO ART BIZ FAT JOB
PIE CARE FEAT FIRM FUSS GAME
GEAR LINE NOTE TASK WORK
CAUSE CRAFT ERGON TRADE
TRUCK AFFAIR CUSTOM EMPLOY
ERRAND MATTER METIER NEGOCE
OFFICE PIDGIN PIGEON RACKET
TURKEY ACCOUNT BEESWAX
CALLING CONCERN JOURNEY
PALAVER TRADING TRAFFIC
ACTIVITY AGIOTAGE BESOIGNE
COMMERCE FOLLOWER INDUSTRY
INTEREST VOCATION OCCASIONS
OCCUPATION
(— WITHOUT ASSETS) SHELL
(COMIC —) LAZZO
(MONKEY —) JOUKERY PAWKERY
(STAGE —) BYPLAY
BUSINESSMAN TYCOON POACHER
BOURGEOIS CONVERTER
BUSKIN BOOT SHOE CALIGA
BOTTINE COTHURN BRODEKIN
COTHURNUS
BUSS SMOUCH
BUSSU UBUSSU TROOLIE
BUST BUMP FAIL RUIN TAME
BOSOM BREAK BURST BUSTO
CHEST EDGAR FLUNK SPREE
BRONZE DEMOTE REDUCE STATUE
TURKEY DEGRADE DISMISS
FAILURE PROTOME PORTRAIT
(— SHAPE) TAILLE
BUSTARD KORI OTIS WATO PAAUW
TURKEY BEBILYA HOUBARA
KORHAAN FLORICAN GOMPAAUW
(PREF.) OTIDI
BUSTIC AUSUBO CASSADA
BUSTLE ADO TEW BUZZ FIKE FRAY
FUSS JUMP STIR WHEW WHIR
FRISK HASTE HYPER KNOCK PAVIE
STEER WHIRL WHIRR BISHOP
BUMBLE ENERGY FISSLE FISTLE
FLURRY FUSTLE HUDDLE HUSTLE
POTHER PUDDER RACKET ROMAGE
RUFFLE TATTER THRONG TUMULT
UNREST UPROAR CLATTER
CLUTTER CONTEND LOUSTER
SCOWDER SCUFFLE SCUFTER
SPUFFLE ACTIVITY IMPROVER
SPLUTTER STRUGGLE TOURNURE
CRINOLETTE
(—ABOUT) TROT
BUSTLING ADO BUSY FUSSY
SPOFFISH STIRRING
BUST-UP SCUFFLE
BUSY FAST FELL APPLY BRISK
QUICK ACTIVE ATWORK EIDENT
EMPLOY INTENT LIVELY OCCUPY
ORNATE STEERY THRONG UNIDLE
ENGAGED HOPPING HUMMING
OPEROSE TROUBLE WORKING
DILIGENT EMPLOYED EXERCISE
OCCUPIED SEDULOUS TIRELESS
UNTIRING PRAGMATIC
PRAGMATICAL
(— ONESELF) STRAP
(— WITH TRIFLES) FIDDLE FIDDLING
(NOT —) SLACK
BUSYBODY BUSY SNOOP YENTA
EARWIG SPOFFY ARDELIO
MARPLOT MEDDLER SNOOPER

FACTOTUM QUIDNUNC
PRAGMATIC
BUT AC LO MA BIT SED YEA YET
MERE ONLY SAVE ARRAH STILL
ALWAYS EXCEPT UNLESS BESIDES
HOWBEIT HOWEVER
BUTCHER KILL SLAY BUTCH SPOIL
BUNGLE KIDDER LEGGER LEMMER
MURDER VENDOR BOTCHER
BRAINER BRITTEN FLESHER
MEATMAN PORKMAN KILLCALF
PIGSTICK SLAUGHTER
BUTCHERBIRD SHRIKE MATAGASSE
BUTCHER'S-BROOM RUSCUS
BRUSCUS
BUTCHERY MURDER CARNAGE
MASSACRE SHAMBLES
SLAUGHTER
BUTEA DHAK
BUTEO BUZZARD
BUTES (BROTHER OF —)
ERECHTHEUS
(FATHER OF —) NEPTUNE PANDION
POSEIDON
(SISTER OF —) PROCNE PHILOMELA
(WIFE OF —) CHTHONIA
BUTLER SOMLER YEOMAN
BOTELER SERVANT SPENCER
STEWARD CELLARER CONSUMAH
KHANSAMA STEPHANO
MAJORDOMO
BUTT JUR JUT MOT PIT PUT RAM
RUN TOY TUP BUCK BUNT BURT
BUSH CART CASK DISH DOSS FOOL
GOAD GOAL GOAT HORN JOLT
JURR PIPE POLL PUCK PUSH STUB
TANG TOPE TURR BOUND DUNCH
HINGE JOINT MOUND ROACH
SCOPE STOCK STUMP BREECH
TARGET THRUST BEEHIVE
BUTTOCK PARAPET PROJECT
REVERSE STUMMEL ARIETATE
FLATFISH FLOUNDER RIDICULE
SACKBUTT
(— FOR RIDICULE) GAME SPORT
STALE COCKSHY
(— OF CIGAR) DOCK SNIPE
(— OF HORSEHIDE) SHELL
(— OF JOKE) JEST SCOGGIN
JESTWORD
(CIGARETTE —) BUMPER
(HALF —) BEND
BUTTE HILL PICACHO
BUTTER RAM GOAT SHEA CLART
COCUM BAMBUK BEURRE CAJOLE
LEKVAR SPREAD BLARNEY
FLATTER
(— MEASURE) SPAN
(— SUBSTITUTE) VANASPATI
(ARTIFICIAL —) BOSH OLEO BOSCH
MARGARINE
(ASTRONOMICAL —) ARIES
(BROWNED IN —) NOISETTE
(PRUNE —) LEKVAR
(SEMIFLUID —) GHI GHEE
BUTTER-AND-EGGS RANSTEAD
TOADFLAX
BUTTERBUR CLEAT CLOTE ELDIN
GALON GALLON OXWORT GILTCUP
FLEADOCK
BUTTERCUP BOLT CYME CRAZY
ANEMONE CRAISEY CROWTOE
GILTCUP GOLDCUP KINGCOB

KINGCUP CRAWFOOT CROWFOOT FROGWORT PASQUEFLOWER

BUTTERFISH GUNNEL POMPANO WHITING PALOMETA SKIPJACK

BUTTERFLY IO BLUE ARGUS COMMA ELFIN GHOST NYMPH QUEEN SATYR SWIFT WHITE ZEBRA ADONIS ALPINE APOLLO CALIGO COPPER DANAID HOPPER IDALIA JUGATE MORPHO PIERID PROGNE PSYCHE SULFUR THECLA URSULA VIOLET YELLOW ADMIRAL BUCKEYE DIURNAL DOLPHIN EMPEROR FRENATE MONARCH PIERINE SATYRID SKIPPER SULPHUR TROILUS TUSSOCK VANESSA VICEROY ARTHEMIS CECROPIA CRESCENT GRAYLING HESPERID ITHOMIID WANDERER METALMARK
(— BREEDER) AURELIAN

BUTTERFLY FISH MOJARRA FLATFISH

BUTTERFLY WEED FLUXROOT MILKWEED WINDROOT

BUTTERMILK WHIG JOCOQUE SOURDOOK
(— AND WATER) BLAND

BUTTERSCOTCH TOFFY

BUTTERTREE MAHWA

BUTTERWORT BEANWEED ROTGRASS SHEEPWEED

BUTTERY BOTRY LARDER SPENCE BUTLERY SPICERY

BUTTOCK CHEEK

BUTTOCKS ASS BUM BUN CAN FUD HAM ARSE BUNS BUTT CULE DOCK DOUP DUFF LEND MOON POOP PRAT SEAT TAIL TOBY TUSH CROUP FANNY NATES SLATS

STERN TOUTE TUSHY BEHIND BOTTOM BREECH CHEEKS CURPIN HEINIE HINDER TUSHIE CROUPON CRUPPER DRODDUM HURDIES KEISTER BACKSIDE DERRIERE NATIFORM POSTERIOR
(PRACTICE OF EXPOSING —) MOONING
(PREF.) NATI PYG(O)
(SUFF.) PROCTA PYGAL PYGE PYGIA(N) PYGOUS PYGUS

BUTTON BUD ZIP BOSS CHIN DOME HOOK KNOB KNOP SPUR TUFT BADGE CATCH GLIDE OLIVE PEARL PRILL BARREL BAUBLE BOUTON BUCKLE GLIDER SHINER TOGGLE TROCHE DEWDROP HORNTIP KNICKER NETSUKE PRESSEL REGULUS DOORBELL FASTENER OLIVETTE
(— MAN) SOLDIER
(KIND OF —) PANIC

BUTTONBUSH BUCKBRUSH SWAMPWOOD

BUTTONHOLE EYE LOOP SLIT

BUTTON SNAKEROOT LIATRIS SAWWORT

BUTTONWOOD COTONIER

BUTTRESS NOSE PIER PILE PROP SPUR STAY BRACE BRICK ALLETTE OUTCAST OUTSHOT SUPPORT TAMBOUR ABUTMENT
(— MEMBER) TIRE

BUTYL TETRYL

BUXOM MILD AMPLE JOLLY PLUMP PRONE SONSY BLITHE CRUMBY CRUMMY FLORID FODGEL HUMBLE PLIANT SONSIE BOWERLY BOUNCING FLEXIBLE OBEDIENT OBLIGING YIELDING JUNOESQUE

BUY CHAP COFF COUP GAIN HAVE SHOP SNIP TAKE BRIBE CLAIM TRADE ABEGGE MARKET RANSOM REDEEM SECURE ACQUIRE CHAFFER PURCHASE
(— BACK) REPRISE
(— OFF) BRIBE APPEASE
(— UP STOCKS) COVER
(GOOD —) DEAL

BUYER CHAP AGENT CATER BEGGER EMPTOR PATRON VENDEE CHAPMAN SHOPPER ACHATOUR CUSTOMER PROSPECT
(— OF CLOTH) REDUBBER

BUYING ACATE ACHATE EMPTION
(— MANIA) ONIOMANIA

BUZ (FATHER OF —) NAHOR
(MOTHER OF —) MILCAH

BUZI (SON OF —) EZEKIEL

BUZZ HUM BURR CALL DASH HISS HUSS HUZZ RING WHIR FANCY FLING PHONE RUMOR BUMBLE NOTION WHOOSH WHISPER

BUZZARD AURA FOOL HAWK PERN BUTEO GLADE GLEDE HARPY STOOP BEETLE CURLEW PREYER STUPID PUDDOCK PUTTOCK VULTURE BROMVOEL

BUZZER BEE BELL ALARM HOWLER SIGNAL WHIZZER

BY A P X AB AT OF TO AGO BYE GIN PAR PER TIL ABUT ANON INTO NEAR PAST TILL APART ASIDE CLOSE FORBY BESIDE TOWARD BESIDES THROUGH
(— AND —) ANON
(— AND BY) BELIVE BIMEBY
(— FAR) EASILY
(— HEART) PERQUEIR
(— HOOK OR CROOK) HABNAB

(— MEANS OF) PER MOYENANT
(— NO MEANS) NA
(— REASON OF THIS) HEREAT
(— STEALTH) STOWLINS
(— SURPRISE) ABACK
(— THE DAY) PD
(— THE ORDER OF) O
(— THE WAY) APROPOS
(— THIS TIME) ALREADY
(— WAY OF) VIA
(GONE —) AGO PAST
(NEAR —) GIN
(PREF.) PRETER

BY-BIDDER FUNK CAPPER PUFFER

BYBLIS (BROTHER OF —) CAUNUS
(FATHER OF —) MILETUS
(MOTHER OF —) IDOTHEA

BY-CHANNEL BAYOU BRANCH

BYCOKET ABACOT ABOCOCKET

BYGONE PAST YORE OLDEN BYPAST FORMER ANCIENT ANTIQUE ELAPSED BACKWARD DEPARTED FOREPAST PRETERIT

BYPASS JUMP SHUN AVOID BURKE EVADE SHUNT CUTOFF DETOUR CIRCUIT OUTFLANK

BYPATH LANE BYWAY UNDERWALK

BY-PRODUCT SPINOFF SCRAP SHORTS EFFLUVIUM MIDDLINGS OUTGROWTH

BYRE SHIPPEN COWHOUSE

BYRNIE ARMOR

BYROAD BOREEN

BYWAY LANE PATH ALLEY BYPATH BYWALK OUTWAY SIDEWAY

BYWORD ADAGE AXIOM MOTTO BYNAME DIVERB PHRASE SAYING NAYWORD PROVERB NICKNAME REPROACH

BY-WORK PARERGON

C

C DO CEE DOH COCA CHARLIE HUNDRED

CAAMA FOX ASSE SILVER

CAB FLY KAB HACK TAXI ARABA ARANA CABIN NODDY GHARRI CRAWLER HACKNEY SHOWFUL TAXICAB VETTURA COUPELET MOTORCAB
(HINDU —) JUDKA
(KIND OF —) GYPSY
(LOW-HUNG —) HERDIC
(2-PONY —) KOSONG
(4-WHEELED —) BOUNDE BOUNDER DROSHKY GROWLER

CABAL PLOT RING JUNTA JUNTO PARTY BRIGUE CLIQUE SCHEME SECRET CHATTER CONSULT COUNCIL DISPUTE FACTION TALKING INTRIGUE CAMARILLA

CABALASSOU ARMADILLO

CABALISTIC MYSTIC

CABARET CAFE TAVERN

CABASSOU XENURUS

CABBAGE CAB CHOU CRIB KALE WORT CROUT FILCH SAVOY STEAL STOCK PECHAY PILFER TAILOR BOWKAIL OXHEART PAKCHOI PALMITO PURLOIN BORECOLE COLEWORT CRUCIFER CULTIGEN DRUMHEAD KOHLRABI KERGUELEN
(CHINESE —) BOKCHOY PAKCHOI
(KIND OF —) NAPA
(STUFFED —) HOLISHKES
(PL.) WORTS

CABBAGE BARK ANGELIM ANGELIN

CABBAGE SOUP SHCHI STCHI SHTCHEE

CABBAGE STALK CASTOCK

CABBIE HACK

CABDRIVER HACK MUSH CABBY CABMAN COCHER MUSHER COCHERO HACKMAN

CABIN BOX CAB COT DEN HUT CAVE CELL CREW CRIB SHED TILT BOOTH CHOZA COACH CUDDY FELZE HOVEL LODGE SHACK BOHAWN CABANA CASITA LITTER REFUGE SALOON SHANTY SHELTY WIGWAM BEDROOM BOUDOIR COTTAGE HUDDOCK MUDSILL
(— ON SHIP'S DECK) TEXAS ROUNDHOUSE
(DOUBLE —) SADDLEBAG
(PASSENGER —) VAN
(RUSSIAN LOG —) IZBA

CABIN-BOY GRUMMET

CABINET ARK BOX BUHL CASE FILE SINK AMBRY BAHUT BOARD CABIN CHEST BAFFLE BUREAU CLOSET ICEBOX ALMIRAH BOUDOIR COMMODE CONSOLE COUNCIL ETAGERE FREEZER JUKEBOX WHATNOT CELLARET CUPBOARD MINISTRY SHOWCASE VARGUENO MONOCLEID
(FILING —) MORGUE

CABINET-MAKER EBENISTE

CABINETMAKER EBENISTE

CABLE GUY TOW BOOM COAX CORD FAST JUNK LINK ROPE STAY WIRE CABLET GANGER STRAND TETHER COAXIAL GUNLINE SKYLINE CATENARY HIGHLINE TELEGRAM UMBILICAL
(— WITH EYE AT EACH END) STRAP
(— WOUND) KECKLING
(CHAIN —) BOOM
(DERRICK —) BACKSTAY
(SPLICED —) SHOT
(SUSPENDED —) ROPEWAY

CABLE CAR TELFER TELPHER

CABLED RUDENTED

CABMAN IZVOZCHIK

CABOCHON CAB SHELL CARBUNCLE

CABOODLE KIT LOT CALABASH

CABOOSE CAB CAR VAN CRIB HACK BUGGY CRUMMY GALLEY PALACE BOUNCER COOKROOM DOGHOUSE

CABRILLA CONY GAPER GROUPER

CABRIOLE LEG

CABSTAND HASARD HAZARD

CABUYA PITEIRA

CACAO BROMA COCOA ARRIBA COCKER CRIOLLO FORASTERO

CACHARI BODA

CACHE BURY HIDE DEPOT STASH STORE MEMORY SCREEN CONCEAL DEPOSIT TREASURE

CACHELOT WHALE

CACHET SEAL STAMP WAFER ESSENCE KONSEAL

CACIQUE BUNYAH CASSICAN HANGNEST

CACKEREL MENDOLE

CACK-HANDED CLUMSY AWKWARD

CACKLE CANK CONK CLACK LAUGH BABBLE GABBLE GAGGLE GIGGLE GOSSIP KECKLE TITTER CHACKLE CHATTER SNICKER TWADDLE LAUGHTER

CACKLING GAGGLING

CACKLING GOOSE GREASER

CACOMISTLE CIVET ARCTOID RINGTAIL BASSARISK

CACOON SEGRA SEQUA

CACOPHONOUS HARSH RAUCOUS JANGLING STRIDENT

CACTUS BLEO DILDO NOPAL BAVOSO CARDON CEREUS CHAUTE CHENDE CHINOA CHOLLA COCHAL MESCAL PEYOTE PEYOTL TASAJO AIRAMPO BISAGRE BISNAGA SAGUARO ALICOCHE CHICHIPE PITAHAYA XEROPHIL
(— FRUIT) MUYUSA
(KIND OF —) RATTAIL

CAD CUR BOOR CHUM HEEL CHURL LOUSE SWEEP BRAKJE MUCKER RASCAL ROTTER BOUNDER BUDMASH DASTARD BLIGHTER ASSISTANT

CADASTRAL UNIT YOKE

CADAVER BODY STIFF CORPSE CARCASS SUBJECT SKELETON

CADAVEROUS PALE GAUNT LIVID PALLID GHASTLY HAGGARD

CADDIE NACKET

CADDIS FLY DUN CADEW SEDGE CADBIT

CADDISWORM PIPER

CADDO ADAI TEXAS EYEISH HAINAI KICHAI HASINAI

CADE LAMB SOCK

CADENAS NEF

CADENCE BEAT FALL IAMB LILT PACE TONE CLOSE METER METRE PULSE SOUND SWING THROB DACTYL IAMBUS JINGLE RHYTHM BACCHIC ANAPAEST CLAUSULA MOVEMENT MEDIATION
(GREGORIAN —) TROPE

CADENZA MELISMA BARIOLAGE

CADET SON DODO GOAT PLEBE YOUTH EMBRYO JUNIOR SERGEANT

CADGE BEG BOT BUM TIE BIND HAWK CARRY MOOCH PEDDLE SPONGE SCROUNGE

CADGER BOT BUM DEALER HAWKER CARRIER PACKMAN SPONGER HUCKSTER SCAMBLER

CADGY KEDGY MERRY WANTON AMOROUS LUSTFUL CHEERFUL MIRTHFUL

CADMUS (DAUGHTER OF —) INO AGAVE SEMELE AUTONOE
(FATHER OF —) AGENOR
(MOTHER OF —) TELEPHASSA
(SISTER OF —) EUROPA
(SON OF —) POLYDORUS
(WIFE OF —) HARMONIA

CADRE CORE FRAME

CADUCEUS WAND STAFF SCEPTER SCEPTRE KERYKEION

CAECUM TYPHLON
(PREF.) ILEO TYPHL(O)

CAESAR (WORDS FROM —) ETTU

CAESURA REST STOP BREAK PAUSE INTERVAL DIAERESIS

CAFE BAR PUB CAFF AGOGO TAVERN BARROOM CABARET TAVERNA ESTAMINET
(— AU LAIT) ALESAN
(ROADSIDE —) BUVETTE

CAFE CREME SUEDE

CAFETERIA AUTOMAT

CAFFEINE THEIN THEINE

CAGAYAN IBANAG

CAGE BOX CAR GIG MEW PEN COOP CORF CRIB GOAL BRAKE CAVEA GRATE HUTCH AVIARY BASKET BUCKET CHAPEL ENCAGE FLIGHT PRISON CHANTRY CONFINE ENCLOSE LANTERN SHELTER TUMBREL TUMBRIL CARRIAGE ELEVATOR IMPRISON LAVARIUM RETAINER SCAFFOLD STRAINER
(— FOR HAWKS) MEW
(— FOR HENS) CAVEY CAVIE
(— FOR MOUTH) MUZZLE
(— OF MINE SHAFT) GIG
(— OF TRAM) CABIN
(BIRD —) AVIARY PINJRA VOLARY BIRDCAGE
(FIRE —) CRESSET
(KIND OF —) RIB
(LOBSTER —) CORF CREEL
(REVOLVING —) TUMBLER

CAGED PENT CAPTIVE

CAGER ONSETTER

CAGEY CAGY WARY COONY

CAGMAG KEGMEG

CAGOT AGOTE

CAHITA YAQUI

CAHOT PITCHHOLE

CAIMAN CAYMAN JACARE ALLIGATOR

CAIN (BROTHER OF —) ABEL SETH
(FATHER OF —) ADAM
(MOTHER OF —) EVE
(SON OF —) ENOCH

CAINAN (FATHER OF —) ENOS ARPHAXAD
(SON OF —) SALA MAHALALEEL

CAINGANG COROADO AWEIKOMA CORONADO

CAIRN MAN PIKE MOUND RAISE GALGAL CATSTONE STONEMAN

CAIRNGORM MORION SMOKESTONE

CAISSON BOX PONT CAMEL CHEST WAGON COFFER PONTON SAUCER CAMAILE CHAMBER LACUNAR PONTOON
(— DISEASE) BENDS

CAITIFF BASE MEAN VILE COWARD WICKED CAPTIVE COWARDLY PRISONER WRETCHED

CAJOLE COG CON JIG COAX FLAM FLUM PALP WORD CARNY CHEAT CURRY DECOY FRAIK INGLE JOLLY TEASE BEFLUM CARNEY DELUDE DIDDLE ENTICE FRAISE HUMBUG WHILLY BEGUILE BEHONEY CUITTLE FLATTER PALAVER SOOTHER TWEEDLE WHEEDLE BLANDISH

CAJOLERY FRAIK SOOTH TAFFY WILES BUTTER FRAISE WHILLY BLARNEY DAUBERY FLATTERY

CAKE BAR BUN NUT WIG BAKE BALL FLAE FOOL LUMP MASS MOLE PUFF TART ARVAL BATTY BLOCK BOXTY COOKY CRUST CUPID FADGE KYAAK PATTY SCONE SHIVE TORTE WAFER WEDGE BARKLE CIMBAL COOKIE DAMPER ECLAIR GATEAU HALLAH HARDEN KICHEL KUCHEN NACKET PARKIN PASTRY POPLIN SIMNEL TABLET WASTEL ASHCAKE BANBURY BANNOCK BRIOCHE BROWNIE CAKETTE CARAWAY CASSATA CROZZLE CRUMPET CUPCAKE FAIRING GALETTE GENOISE HOECAKE MANCHET NUTCAKE OATCAKE PANCAKE PLASTER POPADAM CHRIMSEL CLAPCAKE KUGELHOF MADELINE MARZIPAN SEEDCAKE SOLIDIFY SOULCAKE TORTILLA TURNPIKE
(— OF CLAY) PLATTEN
(— OF COCONUT PULP) POONAC
(— OF MEAL) DODGER
(— OF RUBBER) BISCUIT
(ALMOND —) RATAFIA
(CORN —) PONE
(CREOLE RICE —) CALA
(EASTER —) TANSY
(FANCY —) SUNKET
(FLAT —) PLATE BUNUELO GALETTE PLACENT CHRIMSEL
(FOURTH PART OF —) FARL FARLE
(FRIED —) WONDER CRULLER DOUGHNUT
(GINGER —) BOLIVAR
(GRIDDLE —) LATKE FLIPPER FRITTER FLAPJACK
(HOLIDAY —) SIMNEL
(HONEY —) LEKACH
(INDIAN —) PARATHA
(KIND OF —) LANE FUNNEL
(LAMB AND WHEAT —) KIBBE KIBBEH
(LEAVENED —) BAP
(NEW YEAR'S —) HAGMENA HOGMANAY
(OATEN —) BANNOCK
(OIL —) GRIT POONAC
(PIECE OF —) CINCH BREEZE
(PLUM —) SIMNEL
(POTATO —) FADGE
(PRESS —) CACHAZA
(RAISIN —) BABA
(RUM —) BABA
(SEED —) WIG SEEDCAKE
(TEA —) LUNN SCONE PIKELET
(THIN —) WAFER JUMBLE BANNOCK TORTILLA
(UNLEAVENED —) CHAPATI CHAPATTI
(YEAST —) KOJI SAVARIN
(PL.) AMSATH COLYBA

CAKED CLIT

CAKE PULLER KNOCKER

CAKES AND ALE (AUTHOR OF —) MAUGHAM
(CHARACTER IN —) AMY KEAR KEMP ALROY ROSIE EDWARD

GEORGE ASHENDEN TRAFFORD DRIFFIELD

CALABA BIRMA GALBA

CALABASH GOURD CURUBA JICARA

CALABASH TREE HIGUERO

CALABOOSE JUG BRIG JAIL STIR POKEY COOLER PRISON CABOOSE BASTILLE HOOSEGOW

CALABUR TREE CAPULI CAPULIN SILKWOOD

CALAIS (BROTHER OF —) ZETES
(FATHER OF —) BOREAS
(MOTHER OF —) ORITHYIA

CALAMANCO MANKIE

CALAMINE CADMIA

CALAMINT BASIL

CALAMITOUS BAD SAD DIRE EVIL BLACK FATAL BITTER DISMAL TRAGIC WOEFUL ADVERSE BALEFUL DIREFUL HAPLESS RUINOUS UNHAPPY UNLUCKY GRIEVOUS TRAGICAL WRETCHED

CALAMITY ILL WOE BLOW DOOM EVIL RUIN RUTH SLAP HYDRA STORM WRACK MISERY ONCOME PLAGUE SORROW EXTREME SCOURGE ACCIDENT DISASTER DISTRESS FATALITY JUDGMENT MISCHIEF

CALAMONDIN ORANGE CALAMANSI

CALAMUS PEN CANE REED QUILL ACORUS RATTAN ROTANG

CALANGAY ABACAY COCKATOO

CALANTHA (FATHER OF —) AMYCLAS

CALASH CALESA GALECHE

CALCANEUM FIBULARE HYPOTARSUS

CALCAR OVEN SPUR FURNACE CALCARIUM PREHALLUX

CALCEOLARIA FAGELIA IONIDIUM

CALCIFY CRETIFY

CALCINING BURNING

CALCINO MUSCADINE

CALCITE APHRITE CALCSPAR ALABASTER ARAGONITE ARGENTINE HISLOPITE

CALCIUM LIME

CALCIUM CARBONATE WHITING DRIPSTONE

CALCIUM HYDROXIDE LIME

CALCIUM SULPHATE PLASTER

CALCULATE AIM SUM CALK CAST PLAN RATE TELL COUNT FRAME THINK CIPHER DESIGN EXPECT FIGURE NUMBER RECKON ACCOUNT AVERAGE CALLATE COMPUTE PREPARE CONSIDER ESTIMATE FORECAST
(— BY ASTROLOGY) ERECT

CALCULATED COLD MEASURED

CALCULATING COLD WISE BRITTLE CAUTIOUS

CALCULATION CARE SHARE CALCUL ACCOUNT CAUTION WORKING CALCULUS FORECAST HINDCAST PRUDENCE
(PL.) FIGURES

CALCULATOR TABLE ABACUS ABACIST SOROBAN CALCULER COMPUTER ISOGRAPH

CALCULUS STONE UROLITH ANALYSIS
(PREF.) LITH(O)
(SUFF.) LITE LITH(IC) LITIC

CALDRON POT RED VAT LEAD ALFET BOILER KELDER KETTLE TRIPOD VESSEL CALDERA CAULDRON

CALEB (DAUGHTER OF —) ACHSAH
(FATHER OF —) HEZRON JEPHUNNEH
(SON OF —) HUR

CALENDAR ORDO DIARY FASTI ALMANAC CALENDS JOURNAL KALENDS REGISTER SCHEDULE
(— ADDITION) EPACT
(— OF MARTYRS) MENOLOGY
(— SIGN) ZODIAC
(ADDITION TO —) EPACT
(PL.) FASTI

CALENDER TABBY SCHREINER

CALENDERER CANROYER SMOOTHER

CALENDS K KAL

CALF CA BOB BOX BOY LEG BOSS BUSS DOLT VEAL VEAU BOBBY BOSSY BUNCH DOGIE MOGGY PODDY RANNY SOOKY YOUTH MUSCLE VEALER WEANER BULCHIN FATLING SLEEPER CALFLING
(LIKE A —) VITULINE
(OF LEG —) SURAL
(PREMATURE —) SLINK
(STRAY —) MAVERICK
(UNBRANDED —) LONGEAR SLEEPER
(YEARLING —) BUD DAIRT
(YOUNG —) DEACON
(PL.) CAURE

CALF'S-FOOT JELLY SULZE FISNOGA

CALFSKIN OOZE COROVA VELLUM GRASSER TULCHAN VEALSKIN

CALIBER BORE RANK DEGREE TALENT ABILITY BREADTH COMPASS QUALITY CAPACITY DIAMETER MAGNITUDE
(HIGH —) STATURE

CALIBRATED BRIX BEAUME BALLING

CALICHE CALCRETE TEPETATE NITRATINE

CALICO BLAY PINTO SALLO CHINTZ SALLOO CROYDON SPOTTED DUNGAREE GOLDFISH

CALICO ASTER WISEWEED

CALICOBACK STINKBUG

CALICO BASS CRAPPIE BACHELOR

CALICO-BUSH KALMIA

CALICUT KOZHIKODE

CALIFORNIA
CAPITAL: SACRAMENTO
COLLEGE: MILLS POMONA WHITTIER
COUNTY: INYO KERN MONO NAPA YOLO YUBA MARIN MODOC COLUSA LASSEN MERCED PLACER PLUMAS SHASTA SOLANO SONOMA SUTTER TEHAMA TULARE ALAMEDA VENTURA SISKIYOU CALAVERAS
DESERT: MOJAVE COLORADO
INDIAN: HUPA POMO YANA YUKI KAROK MAIDU MIWOK WAPPO WIYOT YUROK PATWIN SHASTA TOLOWA YOKUTS CHUMASH LUISENO SALINAN SERRANO DIEGUENO
LAKE: MONO SODA EAGLE OWENS TAHOE SALTON TULARE ALMANOR BERRYESSA
MOUNTAIN: MUIR LASSEN SHASTA WHITNEY
NAME: ELDORADO
PARK: LASSEN SEQUOIA YOSEMITE
PRESIDENT: NIXON
PRISON: ALCATRAZ
RESORT: OJAI
RIVER: EEL MAD PIT KERN OWENS PUTAH STONY FEATHER KLAMATH RUBICON TRINITY SACRAMENTO
STATE BIRD: QUAIL
STATE FLOWER: POPPY
STATE NICKNAME: GOLDEN
STATE TREE: REDWOOD
TOWN: LODI AZUSA CHICO CHINO INDIO BLYTHE CARMEL COVINA EUREKA FRESNO LOMPOC MERCED OXNARD POMONA SONOMA TULARE ALAMEDA BURBANK GARDENA NEEDLES SALINAS VALLEJO VISALIA ALTADENA BERKELEY PASADENA REDLANDS CUCAMONGA
UNIVERSITY: USC UCLA CALTECH STANFORD

CALIPER JENNY ODDLEGS CALIPERS

CALIPH ABU ALI BEKR IMAM OMAR CALIF OTHMAN ABBASID UMAYYAD

CALISTA (HUSBAND OF —) ALTAMONT CLEANDER
(LOVER OF —) LOTHARIO LYSANDER

CALISTO, LA (CHARACTER IN —) PAN JOVE JUNO DIANA LYCAON CALISTO MERCURY ENDYMION
(COMPOSER OF —) CAVALLI

CALIXTINE UTRAQUIST

CALK (ALSO SEE CAULK) JAG NAP PAY COPY CORK FILL STOP CAULK CLOSE HORSE ROUGH CAREEN CALTROP CHINTZE OCCLUDE SILENCE

CALKING OAKUM

CALL HO KA BAN BID CRY CUP DUB HOY SAY SEE CITE COOP DIAL HAIL JERK NAME NOTE PAGE PIST ROUP STOP TERM TOOT YELL BEDUB CHUCK CLAIM CLEPE CLOCK ELECT HALLO HIGHT HOLLA PHONE ROUSE SHOUT SPEAK STYLE UTTER VISIT VOUCH WAKEN YODEL ACCUSE APPEAL AROUSE BECALL CHANGE DEMAND HALLOA HALLOO INVITE INVOKE MUSTER QUETHE SUMMON TEKIAH TERUAH YELPER ACCLAIM ADDRESS APPOINT BEHIGHT BETITLE COLLECT COMMAND CONVENE CONVOKE DECLARE ENTITLE IMPEACH INQUIRE INSTYLE MOUNTEE WHISTLE ANNOUNCE

APPELATE ASSEMBLE NOMINATE PROCLAIM TRANSFER VOCATION
(— A BET) STAY
(— ALOUD) COUNT
(— BACK) RSVP RECALL REVOKE
(— COARSELY) ROOP ROUP
(— DOWN) BRAWL DEVOCATE IMPRECATE
(— FOR) CRY TAKE CLAIM EXACT DEMAND DESIRE COLLECT SOLICIT
(— FOR HELP) SOS
(— FOR HOGS) SOOK SOOEY
(— FOR PARLEY) CHAMADE
(— FORTH) STIR EVOKE BECKON ELICIT INDUCE INVOKE ATTRACT PROVOKE SUGGEST
(— HOUNDS) LIFT
(— IN ANGER) GREET
(— IN CHILDRENS' GAMES) FAN FEN FIN VENTS
(— IN MARBLES) DUBS
(— INTO QUESTION) IMPUGN OPPUGN
(— IN WHIST) ABUNDANCE
(— LOUDLY) CRY HAIL ACCLAIM
(— MAN BY MAN) ARRAY
(— ON TELEPHONE) BUZZ
(— OUT) HAIL LURE ASCRY EVOKE HALLO GOLLAR GOLLER HOLLER HULLOO
(— THE GAME) UMP
(— TO ACCOUNT) AREASON CONTROL
(— TO ARMS) ALARM ALARUM RAPPEL
(— TO BELLBOY) FRONT
(— TO CAT) CHEET
(— TO COURT) ARRAIGN
(— TO COWS) PROO SOOK COBOSS SOOKIE
(— TO DUTY) TURNOUT
(— TO FOOD) SOSS
(— TO HORSE) HIE HUP WAY PROO
(— TO MIND) CITE MING RECORD BETHINK RECOLLECT
(— TO PRAYER) ADAN AZAN
(— TO READINESS) ALERT
(— TO SPARROW) PHIP PHIPPE
(— TO WITNESS) APPEAL
(— UPON) ASK SEE CITE GREDE HALSE BECALL DEPOSE ENGAGE SUMMON ADDRESS BESEECH IMPLORE
(BIRD'S —) WEET
(BOATSWAIN'S —) WINDING
(BRIDGE —) DOUBLE
(BUGLE —) POST HALLALI STABLES
(CLOSE —) TOUCH
(DUCK —) SQUAWKER
(FRIENDLY —) CEILIDH
(HUNTING —) MOT RECHATE RECHEAT
(KIND OF —) ROLL COLLECT
(MORNING —) MATIN
(NAUTICAL —) AHOY
(SHEPHERD'S —) OVEY
(SOCIAL —) VISIT
(SPORTSMAN'S —) HOICKS YOICKS HALLALI
(SQUARE DANCE —) GEE HAW
(STAGE TRUMPET —) SENNET SINNET
(TRUMPET —) BERLOQUE

CALLA ARUM LILY DRAGON MAYFLOWER
CALLBOY FRONT CALLER HALLBOY
CALLED NEMPT
CALLER FLOORMAN
CALLIGRAPHER PENMAN WRITER COPYIST ENGROSSER
CALLIGRAPHY LETTERING CHIROGRAPHY
CALLING ART JOB WAY CALL HAIL RANK TRADE CAREER METIER NAMING OUTCRY MISSION MYSTERY PURSUIT STATION SUMMONS WARNING BUSINESS FUNCTION POSITION SHOUTING VOCATION
(— TO ACCOUNT) AUDIT
(— TOGETHER) MUSTER
CALLIOPE (FATHER OF —) ZEUS JUPITER
(MOTHER OF —) MNEMOSYNE
(SON OF —) ORPHEUS
CALLIRRHOE (FATHER OF —) OCEANUS
(HUSBAND OF —) TROS ALCMAEON
(SON OF —) ILUS GANYMEDE ASSARACUS
CALLISTO (FATHER OF —) LYCAON
(SON OF —) ARCAS
CALLITHRIX HAPALE JACCHUS
CALLOP YELLOWBELLY
CALLOSAL TRABAL
CALLOSITY SEG CALLUS SITFAST TYLOSIS CHESTNUT
CALLOUS HARD HORNY TOUGH BRAWNY OBTUSE SEARED TORPID WAUKIT DEDOLENT OBDURATE HEARTLESS
CALLOUSED BRAWNY
CALLOW BALD BARE CRUDE GREEN SQUAB JEJUNE MARSHY IMMATURE UNFORMED YOUTHFUL
CALLUS SEG POROMA TYLOMA CALLOUS
(— ON HORSE) RINGBONE
(PREF.) PORA PORO
CALM LAY LEE COOL DILL EASY EVEN FAIR FLAT HUSH LOWN LULL MEES MILD REST SOFT STAY ABATE ALLAY CHARM LEVEL LITHE LOUND MEASE PEACE QUELL QUIET SLEEK SMOLT SOBER STILL STOIC STREW APLOMB DEFUSE DOCILE GENTLE GLASSY IRENIC PACIFY PLACID SEDATE SERENE SETTLE SILENT SLATCH SLIGHT SMOOTH SOOTHE STEADY APPEASE ASSUAGE CALMATO COMPOSE GLACIAL HALCYON MOLLIFY PACIFIC PATIENT PLACATE QUALIFY QUIETEN RESTFUL UNMOVED CALMNESS COMPOSED DECOROUS MODERATE PEACEFUL PLACABLE RESTRAIN SERENITY TRANQUIL UNRUFFLE POSSESSED PHILOSOPHIC
(INTERNAL —) HARMONY
(NOT —) BOISTEROUS
CALMING SEDATIVE
CALMLY COOLY COOLLY STILLY
CALMNESS CALM LULL POISE PHLEGM REPOSE SERENE TEMPER

ATARAXY COOLNESS SERENITY SOBRIETY STILLNESS
CALNO KULLANI
CALOMEL TURPETH
CALORIC THERMOGEN
CALORIE THERM THERME
CALQUE LOANSHIFT
CALTROP CROWTOE GALTRAP BULLHEAD CROWFOOT
CALUMET PIPE PEACEPIPE
CALUMNIATE BLOT SLUR TEEN BELIE LIBEL ACCUSE ATTACK BEFOUL DEFAME MALIGN REVILE VILIFY ASPERSE BLACKEN SLANDER TRADUCE
CALUMNIATION SATIRE ASPERSION
CALUMNY SLUR ATTACK DEPRAVE OBLOQUY SLANDER ASPERSION
CALVA CALOTTE SINCIPUT
CALVARIA SKULLCAP
CALVARY GOLGOTHA
CALVE FRESHEN
CALVINIST GENEVAN GOMARIAN
CALYCE (FATHER OF —) AEOLUS
(MOTHER OF —) ENARETE
(SON OF —) ENDYMION
CALYCULUS CELL CALYX
CALYPTER ALULA SQUAMA
CALYPTRA CAP VEIL EPIGONIUM
CALYX CUP POP HULL HUSK LEAF CULOT SEPAL SHUCK
(PREF.) CALYC(I)(O)
CAM COG AWRY LOBE TRIG ASKEW CATCH SNAIL WIPER LIFTER TAPPET CROOKED TRIPPET KNOCKOFF PERVERSE ROLLBACK
CAMACHILE INGA HUAMUCHIL
CAMAGON MABOLO
CAMAS LOBELIA
CAMBER SET ARCH BEND SWEEP ROUNDUP CROSSFALL

CAMBODIA

CAPE: SAMIT
CAPITAL: PNOMPENH PHNOMPENH
COIN: SEN RIEL PUTTAN PIASTER
GULF: SIAM
LAKE: TONLESAP
MOUNTAIN: PAN AURAL
MOUNTAINS: DANGREK CARDAMOM ELEPHANT
NAME: CAMBOJA CAMBODGE KAMPUCHEA
NATIVE: CHAM KHMER
RIVER: SAN SEN BASSAC MEKONG PORONG SREPOK SEKHONG TONLESAP
RUINS: ANGKORWAT
TOWN: REAM TAKEO KAMPOT KRATIE PURSAT KOHNIEH KRACHEH ROVIENG SAMRONG PNOMPENH SISOPHON
WEIGHT: MACE TAEL

CAMBODIAN KHMER
CAMBRIC LAWN BATISTE PERCALE
CAMBUSCAN (SON OF —) CANACE CAMBALLO ALGARSIFE
CAME BAND CALM
CAMEL COLT OONT DELOUL DROMED FENDER HAGEEN MEHARI CAISSON TYLOPOD

BACTRIAN RUMINANT DROMEDARY
CAMEL GRASS SCHOENANTH
CAMELLIA JAPONICA
CAMEL LIP CHILOMA
CAMELOPARD GIRAFFE
CAMEO GEM GAMAHE CAMAIEU CARVING PHALERA RELIEVO ANAGLYPH
(— MATERIAL) ONYX
CAMERA KINO KODAK CHAMBER MINICAM PANORAM ENLARGER MINIATURE VERASCOPE CAMCVORDER
(— AND RECORDER) PORTAFAX PORTAPACK
(— SHOT) PAN
(— TUBE) VIDICON
(KIND OF —) REFLEX
(PART OF —) LUG BODY DOOR KNOB LENS LOCK CRANK DRIVE FOCUS LATCH SCALE STRAP TIMER BUTTON SENSOR SOCKET WINDOW ADVANCE BELLOWS LANYARD RELEASE SHUTTER PHOTOCELL TRANSDUCER VIEWFINDER
(SHIELD FOR —) GOBO
(VIDEO —) CAMCORDER
CAMERAMAN LENSMAN
CAMEROON (CAPITAL OF —) YAOUNDE
(RIVER OF —) DJA NYONG SANAGA
(TOWN OF —) EDEA POLI YOKO BAFIA KRIBI DOUALA
CAMILLA (FATHER OF —) METABUS
(SLAYER OF —) ARUNS
CAMILLE (AUTHOR OF —) DUMAS
(CHARACTER IN —) DUVAL ARMAND NANINE CAMILLE GAUTIER PRUDENCE VARVILLE
CAMIRUS (FATHER OF —) CERCAPHUS
(MOTHER OF —) CYDIPPE
CAMISOLE WAISTCOAT
CAMLET MOHAIR PARAGON BARRACAN
CAMOMILE OXEYE MORGAN MAYWEED
CAMOUFLAGE FAKE HIDE DAZZLE MUFFLE SCREEN CONCEAL DISGUISE
CAMOUFLET STIFLER
CAMP TAN PEST TENT DOUAR ETAPE HORDE SIEGE TABOR CASTLE LAAGER SUGARY BIVOUAC HUTMENT LASHKAR LODGING MAHALLA PALANKA ZAREEBA QUARTERS
(— OF INDIAN SOLDIERS) LASHKAR
(— OUT) MAROON OUTLIE
(HOBO —) JUNGLE
(LABOR —) GULAG
(LUMBER —) CHANTIER
(PRISONER —) OFLAG STALAG
(PREF.) CASTRA
(SUFF.) CASTER CESTER CHESTER
CAMPA ANDA ANDI ANTI
CAMPAIGN BLITZ DRIVE PLAIN WHOOP CANVASS CRUSADE JOURNEY SERVICE SOLICIT WARFARE
(STUNT —) JIHAD

CAMPANA GUTTA
CAMPANERO COTINGA ARAPUNGA BELLBIRD COTINGID
CAMPANILE TOWER BELFRY CLOCHER STEEPLE CARILLON
CAMPANULA BELLWORT
CAMPESTRAL AGRARIAN
CAMP-FOLLOWER BOY BUMMER LASCAR
CAMPHOL BORNEOL
CAMPHOR ASARONE BORNEOL MENTHOL
(ANISE —) ANETHOLE
CAMPHOR TREE KADUR KAPOR
CAMPING BIVOUAC
CAMPION ROBIN COWBELL
CAMPUS GATE QUAD YARD FIELD
CAN CUP JUG MAY MOW POT TIN ABLE FIRE JAIL SACK BILLY CADDY COULD ESHIN OILER PUTUP SHALL SKILL BOTTLE VESSEL ABILITY BOMBARD CANIKIN CAPABLE CREAMER DISMISS GROWLER PIPETTE BILLYCAN CONSERVE PRESERVE
(— FOR LIQUOR) JACK
(— ON WHEELS) DANDY
(BULGED —) SWELL FLIPPER
(DEFECTIVE —) SPRINGER
(LEAKY —) LEAKER
(MILK —) CHURN
(SPRAY —) AEROSOL
(TIN —) DESTROYER
(TRASH —) DUSTBIN
(PREF.) SCYPH(I)(O)
CANAAN (FATHER OF —) HAM
CANAANITE ARKITE HIVITE AMORITE HIVVITE JEBUSITE
CANACE (BROTHER OF —) MACAREUS
(FATHER OF —) AEOLUS
(MOTHER OF —) ENARETE
(SON OF —) TRIOPAS

CANADA
(ALSO SEE SPECIFIC PROVINCES)
BAY: JAMES HUDSON UNGAVA GEORGIAN
CAPITAL: OTTAWA
INDIAN: CREE COMOX HAIDA NISKA SARSI STALO MICMAC NAHANE NOOTKA SARCEE SEKANE CARRIER NANAIMO SHUSWAP SONGISH TAHLTAN ALGONKIN COWICHAN LILLOOET MALECITE SQUAMISH TSATTINE
ISLAND: READ BANKS BYLOT COATS DEVON SABLE BAFFIN MANSEL VICTORIA ANTICOSTI VANCOUVER
ISLANDS: PARRY BELCHER BATHURST MAGDALEN
LAKE: BEAR CREE GARRY RAINY SLAVE LOUISE SIMCOE ABITIBI DUBAWNT NIPIGON KOOTENAY OKANAGAN NIPISSING
MEASURE: MINOT PERCH ARPENT CHAINON
MOUNTAIN: LOGAN ROYAL ROBSON TREMBLANT
MOUNTAIN RANGE: SKEENA CARIBOO PEMBINA STELIAS COLUMBIA LAURENTIAN
NATIVE: CANUCK

PARK: YOHO BANFF ACADIA JASPER
PENINSULA: GASPE BOOTHIA MELVILLE
PROVINCE: BC NB NS MAN ONT PEI QUE ALTA SASK QUEBEC ALBERTA ONTARIO MANITOBA NOVASCOTIA NEWBRUNSWICK NEWFOUNDLAND SASKATCHEWAN
PROVINCIAL CAPITAL: QUEBEC REGINA STJOHN HALIFAX TORONTO EDMONTON VICTORIA WINNIPEG CHARLOTTETOWN
RIVER: HAY RED BACK PEEL PEACE SLAVE YUKON FRASER NELSON OTTAWA SKEENA THELON KOKOSAK PEMBINA PETAWAWA SAGUENAY MACKENZIE RICHELIEU
STRAIT: CABOT DEASE HECATE HUDSON GEORGIA
SYMBOL: MAPLELEAF
TERRITORY: YUKON
TOWN: HULL BANFF LAVAL GUELPH OSHAWA REGINA SARNIA CALGARY HALIFAX LACHINE MONCTON NANAIMO SUDBURY TORONTO WELLAND WINDSOR KINGSTON MONTREAL VICTORIA WINNIPEG SASKATOON VANCOUVER
UNIVERSITY: MCGILL DALHOUSIE
WATERFALL: DELLA PANTHER TAKAKKAW

CANADA BLUEBERRY SOURTOP
CANADA GOOSE HONKER BUSTARD OUTARDE
CANADA JAY MEATBIRD MOOSEBIRD
CANADA LYNX PISHU LUCIVEE
CANADA PLUM CHENEY
CANADA VIOLET JUNEFLOWER
CANADIAN CANUCK
CANAILLE MOB FLOUR RABBLE DOGGERY RIFFRAFF
CANAL CUT CANO DUCT LODE PIPE SHAT TUBE BAYOU DITCH DRAIN FOSSA GRAFF KLONG SCALA ZANJA ESTERO GROOVE KENNEL STRAIT TRENCH VAGINA ACEQUIA APHODUS CHANNEL CONDUIT FOREBAY RACEWAY SHIPWAY TOWPATH AQUEDUCT EMISSARY IRRIGANT MILLRACE PROSODUS VOLKMANN
(— LABORER) NAVIGATOR
(ALIMENTARY —) GUT ENTERON INTESTINE
(ANATOMICAL —) SCALA MEATUS
(CARINAL —) LACUNA
(PREF.) MEATO
CANARD DUCK HOAX RUMOR GRAPEVINE
CANARY DICKY FRILL SERIN LIZARD ROLLER CAYENNE CHOPPER JONQUIL SQUEALER
(— HYBRID) MULE

CANARY ISLAND
CAPITAL: SANTACRUZ
ISLAND: ROCA CLARA FERRO LOBOS PALMA ROCCA GOMERA HIERRO INFERNO GRACIOSA TENERIFE LANZAROTE
MEASURE: FANEGADA
MOUNTAIN: TEYDE LACRUZ ELCUMBRE TENERIFE
PROVINCE: LASPALMAS
TOWN: LAGUNA ARRECIFE VALVERDE
VOLCANO: TENEGUIA

CANARY MOSS CORKIR
CANASTA SAMBA BOLIVIA
(— PLAY) MELD
CANCEL AX BLOT DASH DELE OMIT UNDO VENT WIPE ABORT ADEEM ANNUL BELAY CROSS ERASE QUASH REMIT SCORE SCRUB DELETE EFFACE KILL ER RECALL REMOVE REVOKE STROKE ABOLISH DESTROY EXPUNGE NULLIFY RESCIND RETRACT SCRATCH SUBLATE UNWRITE ABROGATE OVERRIDE WRITEOFF OBLITERATE
CANCELED OFF NOGO
CANCELER BUMPER STAMPER
CANCELLATION GRID CANCEL REVOKE RECISION SURRENDER
CANCER BIGC WOLF KASHYAPA SCIRRHUS
(PREF.) CARCIN(O)
CANCERWORT FLUELLIN
CANDAREEN FAN FEN
CANDELABRUM PHAROS MENORAH GIRANDOLE
CANDID FAIR JUST OPEN PURE BLUNT CLEAR FRANK NAIVE PLAIN HONEST ARTLESS JANNOCK SINCERE EVENDOWN INNOCENT SPLENDID STRAIGHT PLAINSPOKEN
CANDIDA (AUTHOR OF —) SHAW
(CHARACTER IN —) MORELL CANDIDA MARCHBANKS
CANDIDATE AGREGE LEGACY ESQUIRE NOMINEE ASPIRANT GRADUAND ORDINAND PROSPECT
(DOCTORAL) ABD
(DOCTORAL —) ABD
(LIST OF —S) SLATE
(TEACHING —) AGREGE
CANDIDE (AUTHOR OF —) VOLTAIRE
(CHARACTER IN —) CACAMBO CANDIDE PANGLOSS PAQUETTE CUNEGONDE
CANDIDIASIS MONILIASIS
CANDIED GLACE
CANDLE DIP WAX GLIM SIZE SLUT LIGHT SPERM TAPER TOLLY TORCH BOUGIE CIERGE MORTAR PLANET SHAMUS SLUSHY TALLOW TORTIS CANDELA PERCHER PRICKET SHAMMES AMANDINE
(IMITATION —) JUDAS
(SQUARE —) QUARRIER
CANDLEFISH SKIL EULACHON HOOLAKIN OOLACHAN SKILFISH SABLEFISH
CANDLEHOLDER SPIDER
CANDLEMAKER CHANDLER TALLOWER
CANDLEMAS TERM MARYMASS

CANDLENUT AMA LAMA BIABO KUKUI IGUAPE KEMIRI LUMBANG ABURAGIRI
CANDLESNUFFER DOUTER
CANDLESTAND TORCHERE
CANDLESTICK BUGIA DYKER JESSE STICK CRUSIE LAMPAD MORTAR SCONCE PASCHAL PRICKET CHANDLER DICERION FLAMBEAU STANDARD TORCHERE TRIKERION
(TALL ORNAMENTAL —) TORCHERE
CANDLEWICK MATCH SNAST SHROUD
(CHARRED PART OF —) SNOT SNUFF SNUFFING
CANDLEWOOD CIRIO OCOTILLO TABANUCO
CANDOR PURITY FAIRNESS KINDNESS INTEGRITY SIMPLICITY
CANDY DROP DUMP KISS PIPE ROCK CREAM CRISP DULCE FUDGE GLACE GUNDY LOLLY NABIT SPICE SQUIB SWEET TAFFY BONBON COMFIT DRAGEE HUMBUG NOGADA NOUGAT PATTIE PENIDE BRITTLE CANDIEL CARAMEL CONGEAL FLATTER FONDATE GUMDROP SWEETEN SWEETIE TORRONE ALPHENIC LOLLIPOP STICKJAW PEPPERMINT
(DECORATIVE —) DRAGEE
(PL.) CUTS CONFETTI
CANDYTUFT CRUCIFER
(PL.) IBERIS
CANE ROD BEAT CRAB DART FLOG PIPE REED STEM TUBE WAND WHIP BIRCH GIBBY GUNDY LANCE STAFF STICK SWISH TOLLY WADDY BAMBOO JAMBEE KEBBIE PUNISH RATTAN CALAMUS HICKORY KIPPEEN MALACCA SCOURGE STADDLE TICKLER WHANGEE GIBSTAFF
(BLACK —) JAPAN
(END OF —) FRAZE
(SPLIT —) CANEWORK
(TIP OF —) FERRULE
CANELLA CINNAMON WHITEWOOD
CANELO CIXO
CANESCENT HOARY
CANE TREE BEJUCO
CANFIELD KLONDIKE
CANICULA SIRIUS
CANINE CUR DOG FOX PUP FISC TUSH WOLF DOGLY DOGLIKE LANIARY EYETOOTH
CANING RATTAN BIRCHING
CANISTEL TIES EGGFRUIT
CANNA ACHIRA GOLDBIRD
CANNABIS BHANG GANJA GUAZA GUNJA HEMPWORT
(— TOPS) TAKROURI
CANNEL BONE FURCULE
CANNEL COAL AMPELITE
CANNER CANMAN TINNER
CANNIBAL WINDIGO LESTRIGON THYESTEAN
CANNON BIT EAR GUN BASE SHOT TUBE ASPIC CAROM CRACK MOYEN PIECE SACRE SACRI SAKER SHANK SLING THIEF BARKER BICORN CURTAL FALCON FOWLER JINGAL LICORN MORTAR POTGUN

BASTARD BOMBARD BULLDOG CHAMBER HANDGUN LOMBARD MOYENNE ROBINET SERPENT STINGER UNICORN BASILISK CULVERIN HOWITZER MURDERER OERLIKON ORDNANCE SPITFIRE CARAMBOLE CARRONADE ZUMBOORUK
(— OF BELL) EAR
(CARRIAGE OF —) NADRIER
(DISCHARGE OF —) TIRE
(DUMMY —) QUAKER
(PART OF —) BASE BORE FACE KNOB NECK OGEE RING VENT CHASE FILET SWELL BREECH BUTTON FILLET MUZZLE CHAMBER DOLPHIN GUNLOCK RIMBASE ASTRAGAL CASCABEL TRUNNION REINFORCE
CANNONBALL GUN PILL TEAR BULLET GUNSTONE
CANNON BOSS TRUNNION
CANNON PLUG TAMPION
CANNOT CANT CANNA DONNA DOWNA UNABLE
CANNULA TROCAR
CANNY SLY COZY SNUG WARY WILY WISE COONY LUCKY PAWKY QUIET SAVVY CLEVER FRUGAL GENTLE SHREWD STEADY CAREFUL CUNNING KNOWING PRUDENT QUIETLY THRIFTY CAUTIOUS SKILLFUL WATCHFUL
CANOE AMA KIAK LISI PAHI PROA WAKA AOTEA ARAWA BANCA BIRCH BONGO BUNGO CANKA KAYAK KOLEK PRAHU SKIFF TONEE UMIAK VINTA WAAPA BAIDAR BALLAM BAROTO CORIAL CUNNER DUGOUT OOMIAK PAOPAO PITPAN PUNGEY TAINUI TROUGH WHERRY ALMADIA BIDARKA BUCKEYE CANADER CASCARA CORACLE CURIARA CURRANE HOROUTA LAKATOI PIRAGUA PIROGUE BALANGAY BARANGAY FALTBOAT FOLDBOAT MONOXYLE MONTARIA TAKITUMU THAMAKAU TSUKUPIN WOODSKIN
CANON FEN LAW CODE FUGA HYMN LAUD LIST ROTA RULE SONG AXIOM GORGE GULCH MODEL NODUS ROUND TABLE TENET ACTION DECREE GNOMON BROCARD LIBRARY PRECEPT STATUTE DECISION MATHURIN STAGIARY STANDARD SACRISTAN PREBENDARY PREMONSTRATENSIAN
(BODY OF —S) CHAPTER
CANONICAL CANONIC ACCEPTED ORTHODOX
(NOT —) APOCHRYPHAL
CANOODLE PET CARESS FONDLE
CAN OPENER CHURCHKEY
CANOPY SKY CEIL COPE DAIS HOOD TILT CHUPA CROWN HOVEL SHADE STATE VAULT AWNING BUBBLE CELURE ESTATE FINIAL GABLET HUPPAH PELMET SHADOW TESTER CEILING HEAVENS MARQUEE SHELTER SPARVER BASILICA CIBORIUM COVERING OVERWOOD

PAVILION SEMIANNA SHAMIANA TABERNACLE
(— ABOVE THRONE) STATE
(— FOR LIVESTOCK) HOVEL
(— OF ALTAR) DAIS CIBORIUM
(— OF HEAVEN) VAULT
(— OVER BROODER) HOVER
(BED —) TESTER SPARVER
(HEARSE —) MAJESTY
CANT TIP COAX HEEL LEAN LIST NOOK SING TILT TURN ARGOT BEVEL CHANT DRIFT FLASH HIELD LINGO LUSTY MERRY NICHE PITCH SHARE SLANG SLANT SLOPE WHINE CAREEN CASTER CORNER INTONE JARGON LIVELY PATOIS PATTER SNIVEL AUCTION DIALECT INCLINE PORTION SINGING WHEEDLE CHEERFUL PRETENSE VIGOROUS
CANTABRIGIAN CANTAB CAMBRIDGE
CANTALA MAGUEY
CANTALOUPE MELON MUSKMELON
CANTANKEROUS ILL CURSED CUSSED ORNERY KICKISH PIGGISH CANKERED CONTRARY PERVERSE
CANTATA MOTET SERENATA PASTORALE VILLANCICO
(CHILDREN'S —) KINDERSPIEL
CANTEEN BAR FLASK BAZAAR CANTINA
CANTER JOG RUN GAIT LOPE PACE RACK AUBIN ROGUE BEGGAR WHINER TRIPPLE SNUFFLER VAGABOND
CANTERBURY BELL MILKWORT CAMPANULA
CANTERBURY TALES (AUTHOR OF —) CHAUCER
(CHARACTER IN —) NUN COOK DYER HOST MONK WIFE CLERK FRIAR REEVE DOCTOR KNIGHT MILLER PARSON PRIEST SQUIRE WEAVER YEOMAN CHAUCER PLOWMAN SHIPMAN FRANKLIN MANCIPLE MERCHANT PARDONER PRIORESS SERGEANT SUMMONER CARPENTER HABERDASHER
CANTICLE ODE HYMN LAUD SONG CANTO ANTHEM CANTIC HIRMOS BRAVURA MAGNIFICAT
CANTILEVER LOOKOUT SEMIBEAM CARTOUCHE
CANTING CANT PIOUS SNUFFLING
CANTO AIR FIT BOOK DUAN PACE RUNE SONG VERSE MELODY PASSUS CANTICLE
CANTON ANGLE UNION CORNER VOLOST PORTION QUARTER SECTION DISTRICT DIVISION
(HALF —) ESQUIRE
CANTOR HAZAN HAZZAN SINGER CHANTER CHAZZAN SOLOIST PSALMIST
CANVAS FLY PAT DUCK GLUT PATA SAIL TARP TENT TEWK CLOTH COAST SCRIM TOILE VITRY BALINE BURLAP CATGUT LINING MUSLIN PICTURE POLDAVY SACKING SCUTAGE DRABBLER PAINTING VANDELAS SAILCLOTH

(— COVER) TARP
(— FOR CONVEYING GRAIN) APRON
(OLD CONDEMNED —) RUMBOWLINE
(RUBBERIZED —) TOSH
(STUFFED —) BOLSTER
(TARRED —) COAT
CANVASBACK CAN DIVER CHEVAL DUCKER POCHARD BULLNECK
CANVASS BEAT CASE DRUM HAWK POLL SIFT RANDY STUDY DEBATE PEDDLE SEARCH AGITATE DISCUSS EXAMINE SOLICIT TROUNCE CAMPAIGN CONSIDER
CANVASSER AGENT POLLER ROADMAN
CANYON CAJON CHASM COULE GORGE GULCH ARROYO CANADA RAVINE
CANZONE ODE
CAOUTCHOUC RUBBER ELATERITE
CAP CUP FEZ HAT LID PAD POT TAJ TAM TIP TOP ACME CALL COIF CORK COWL DINK DOME DOWD ETON GAGE HOOD HURE JOAN KEEP KEPI MATE SHOE SHOW TOPI BERET BOINA BUSBY CHIEF COVER CROWN EXCEL FANON GALEA HOUVE KULAH MATCH MUTCH OUTDO PHANO PUNCH SEIZE SHAKO TOPEE TRUMP ARREST BARRAD BARRET BEANIE BIGGIN BIRRUS BONNET CALPAC CLIMAX COCKUP CORNET GALERA HELMET HUBCAP JINNAH MOBCAP PILEUS PINNER PRIMER PUZZLE SUMMIT TABARD TURBAN ALOPEKE BIRETTA CALOTTE CAMAURO CAPITAL CEREVIS CHAPEAU CHECHIA CLOSURE COMMODE FERRULE FLATCAP FORAGER HEADCAP OVERLIE OVERTOP PERPLEX PETASOS PILLBOX PILLION SOWBACK SURPASS THIMBLE TURNCAP ACROSOME BALMORAL BEARSKIN BYCOCKET CAPELINE CHAPERON COONSKIN ELECTRIC FOLLOWER HEADGEAR PHRYGIUM SKEWBACK SKULLCAP SURPRISE TARBOOSH
(— FOR PILEDRIVER) PUNCH
(— OF FLAGSTAFF) TRUCK
(— OF FOAM) HOOD
(— OF MUSHROOM) PILEUS
(— OF PIER) CUSHION
(— OF PYXIDIUM) LID
(— OF WATCH) DOME CROWN
(— ON MAST) TRUCK
(ACADEMIC —) MORTARBOARD
(BISHOP'S —) HURA HURE
(CANADIAN —) TUQUE
(CHIMNEY —) GRANNY
(HORSEMAN'S —) MONTERO
(HUNTER'S —) MONTERA MONTERO
(ICE —) BRAE CALOTTE
(JESTER'S —) COXCOMB FOOLSCAP
(MILITARY —) KEPI BUSBY SHAKO CHAPKA CZAPKA
(MOUNTAIN —) SCALP
(OLD WOMAN'S —) TOY
(PERCUSSION —) AMORCE CAPSULE

(PERUVIAN —) CHULLO
(POPE'S —) CAMAURO
(ROMAN —) PILEUS
(ROOT —) CALYPTRA
(TRIANGULAR —) CALPAC KALPAK CALPACK
(WOMAN'S —) TOY CAUL DOWD JOAN KELL MUTCH COMMODE VOLUPER BIGGONET
(WOOLEN —) BOINA TOQUE TUQUE
(PREF.) PILEI PILEO PILO
CAPABILITY POWER STROIL ABILITY CONDUCT FACULTY POTENCY CAPACITY
CAPABLE APT CAN FIT ABLE GOOD ADEPT CAPAX FENDY TIGHT EXPERT SKILLED POWERFUL
(— OF BEING DEFENDED) TENABLE
(— OF BEING DRAWN OUT) DUCTILE
(— OF BEING SEVERED) SEVTILE
(— OF BEING THROWN) MISSILE
(— OF BEING UTTERED) EFFABLE
(— OF FLYING) VOLANT
(— OF SUBMISSION) AMENABLE
(NORMALLY —) ABOUT
(SUFF.) ABLE IBLE
(— OF) ILE
CAPACIOUS FULL SIDE WIDE AMPLE BROAD LARGE ROOMY WOMBY GOODLY ROOMFUL CAPTIOUS ROOMSOME SPACIOUS
CAPACITOR CONDENSER
CAPACITY BACK BENT BIND DISH GIFT GIVE SIZE TURN BLAST FLAIR FORCE KNACK MODEL POWER SKILL SPACE AGENCY BOTTOM BURDEN ENERGY ENGINE EXTENT GENIUS MODULE SPREAD TALENT VOLUME ABILITY CALIBER CALIBRE CONTENT FACULTY FITNESS QUALITY APTITUDE INSTINCT STRENGTH INFLUENCE
(— FOR EATING) STROKE
(— FOR ENDURANCE) STAY
(— FOR HIGHER KNOWLEDGE) INTELLECT
(— OF LATHE) SWING
(— OF SHIP) BURDEN
(— TO UNDERSTAND LANGUAGE) ORACY
(CIVIL —) CAPUT
(INNATE —S) STAMINA
(INTELLECTUAL —) BROW
(LOAD-PULLING —) DRAFT DRAUGHT
(MENTAL —S) BELFRY
(SPECIAL —) KNACK
(UNIT OF —) MUD MUID LAGEN KISHEN MEDIMNUS KILDERKIN
(UNLIMITED —) INFINITY
CAPANEUS (FATHER OF —) HIPPONOUS BELLEROPHON
(SLAYER OF —) JUPITER
(SON OF —) STHENELUS
(WIFE OF —) EVADNE
CAPARISON DECK TRAP HOUSE COVERING TRAPPING
CAPARISONED BARDED
CAPE RAS COPE GAPE HEAD HOOK LOOK NAZE NECK NESS SKAW TANG WRIT AMICE CAPPA CLOAK FICHU ORALE POINT SAGUM

STARE STOLE TALMA BERTHA BYRRUS CABAAN CHAPEL DOLMAN MANTLE SONTAG TABARD TIPPET CHLAMYS LEATHER MANTEEL MOZETTA SALIENT TANJONG VANDYKE CIRCULAR COLLARET HEADLAND LAMBSKIN MANTILLA MOZZETTA PALATINE PELERINE SEALSKIN INVERNESS RAINPROOF
(— OF SKINS) KAROSS
(— OF STRAW) MINO
(BULLFIGHTER'S —) CAPA
(CLERGICAL —) ALMUCE
(DRESSING —) TOILET
(FEATHER —) AHUULA
(HOODED —) HUKE DOMINO
(LACE OR SILK —) VISITE
(LOW —) TANG
(PAPAL —) FANO FANON FANUM ORALE PHANO
(RAIN —) CAPOTE
CAPE ANTEATER AARDVARK
CAPE ARMADILLO PANGOLIN
CAPE DUTCH TAAL
CAPE GOOSEBERRY POHA
CAPE HARTEBEEST CAAMA
CAPE HEN STINKER STINKPOT
CAPEK (— DRAMA) RUR
CAPELIN SMELT ICEFISH
CAPE PIGEON PINTADO
CAPE POLECAT ZORIL MUISHOND
CAPER HOP JET DIDO HOIT JUMP LEAP ROMP SKIP SKIT ANTIC BRANK DANCE FLING FLISK FRISK PRANK SAUCE SCOUP SHRUB CAVORT CURVET FRISCO FROLIC GAMBOL GAMOND PRANCE SPRING TITTUP VAGARY CORSAIR COURANT FRISCAL GAMBADO PRANKLE CAPRIOLE MARIGOLD
(ABOUT) FLING CAVORT
(SILLY —) SHINE
CAPER SPURGE CATEPUCE
CAPE TOWN BOVENLAND
CAPE VERDE ISLANDS (CAPITAL OF —) PRAIA
(TOWN OF —) MINDELO
(VOLCANO ON —) FOGO
CAPHITE KIST
CAPITAL CAP CASH CITY FUND GOOD LIMA MAIN RARE SEAT BASIC CHIEF FATAL GREAT MAJOR MONEY MUANG STOCK VITAL DEADLY HEADLY IMPOST LETTER LISBON MORTAL PRIMAL UNCIAL WEALTH CENTRAL CHATTEL DRESDEN LEADING RADICAL SERIOUS WEIGHTY CABECERA CATALLUM CHAPITER CHAPTREL DOSSERET SWINGING
(— OF HEAVEN) AMARAVATI
(— OF HELL) PANDEMONIUM
(DIVISION OF —) ABACUS
(GAMBLER'S —) STAKE
(INADEQUATE —) SHOESTRING
CAPITALIST MONEYER
CAPITATUM MAGNUM
CAPITELLUM KNOP
CAPITOL STATEHOUSE
CAPITOLINE SATURNIAN
CAPITULATE DEFER
CAPITULATION MUNICH TREATY

CAPITULUM HEAD KNOP ANTHODIUM
CAPO DON BOSS HEAD
CAPOTE HOOD CAPPO CLOAK BONNET MANTLE TOPPER
CAPPED PILEATE PILEATED
CAPPER CORKER SEALER STEERER
CAPPY TALLOWY
CAPRICCIO (CHARACTER IN —) FLAMAND OLIVIER MADELEINE
(COMPOSER OF —) STRAUSS
CAPRICE FAD TOY KINK MOOD WHIM ANTIC BRAID CRANK FANCY FREAK HUMOR QUIRK CHANGE MAGGOT NOTION SPLEEN TEMPER VAGARY WHIMSY BOUTADE CONCEIT CROCHET IMPULSE TANTRUM WHIMSEY
CAPRICIOUS DIZZY DODDY FLUKY MOODY CHANCY FICKLE FITFUL KITTLE PLATTY WANTON COMICAL ERRATIC FLIGHTY MAGGOTY MOONISH PEEVISH VAGRANT WAYWARD EPISODAL FANCIFUL FREAKISH HUMOROUS PERVERSE SKITTISH UNSTEADY VARIABLE VOLATILE CROTCHETY FANTASTIC VAGARIOUS
CAPRICIOUSNESS FREAK
CAPRICORN GOAT
CAPRIPEDE SATYR
CAPRYL RUTYL DECANOYL
CAPSHEAF CAP HOOD
CAPSICUM AJI PEPPER PAPRIKA
(— SAUCE) TABASCO
CAPSID MIRID
CAPSIZE COUP KEEL PURL UPEND UPSET WRONG WHEMMLE OVERTURN
CAPSTAN CRAB DRUM DANDY HOIST LEVER CYLINDER WINDLASS
CAPSTONE ACME LECH TOPSTONE
CAPSULE CAP POD URN BOLL CASE CYST PILL SEED PEARL PERLE SHELL THECA WAFER AMPULE BARROW CACHET COCOON OOCYST SHEATH AMPOULE EYEBALL OTOCYST SEEDBOX SILIQUE VANILLA PERICARP PYXIDIUM
(— OF LSD) MICRODOT
(DRUG —S) RED REDS
(PERSON WHO TAKES —S) PILLHEAD
(SPACE —) TERRELLA
(PREF.) THEC(A)(I)(O)
CAPTAIN BO BOH CID BAAS HEAD JOAB RAIS REIS BARAK CHIEF LEADER MASTER NAAMAN SOTNIK CAPITAN FOREMAN HEADMAN MANAGER PATROON SKIPPER FLUELLEN GOVERNOR SUBAHDAR
(— OF ARAB VESSEL) NACODAR
(— OF CAVALRY) RESSAI DAR RITMASTER
(— OF CRICKET TEAM) SKIPPER
(— OF CURLING TEAM) SKIP
(— OF PRIVATEER) CAPER
(— OF SHIP) WAFTER
(STRICT —) SUNDOWNER
CAPTAINS COURAGEOUS (AUTHOR OF —) KIPLING
(CHARACTER IN —) DAN JACK

DISKO TROOP CHEYNE HARVEY MANUEL SALTERS
CAPTAIN'S DAUGHTER (AUTHOR OF —) PUSHKIN
(CHARACTER IN —) MARIA PETER ALEXEI ZOURIN EMELYAN GRINEFF GRINYEV EGOROVNA IVANOVNA MIRONOFF PUGACHEV SHVABRIN VASILISA SAVELITCH POUGATCHEFF
CAPTION TITLE LEADER LEGEND CUTLINE HEADING SUBHEAD CITATION HEADLINE SUBTITLE
CAPTIOUS CRAFY TESTY CRAFTY SEVERE CARPING CYNICAL FRETFUL PEEVISH TETTISH ALLURING CATCHING CAVILING CONTRARY CRITICAL
CAPTIOUSLY TUTLY
CAPTIVATE WIN TAKE CATCH CHARM RIVET ALLURE ENAMOR PLEASE RAVISH SUBDUE ATTRACT BEWITCH CAPTIVE CAPTURE ENCHANT ENTHRALL INTEREST OVERTAKE SURPRISE
CAPTIVATED EPRIS EPRISE CAPTIVE
CAPTIVATING TAKING KILLING WINNING WINSOME CATCHING
CAPTIVE SLAVE DANIEL ENAMOR THRALL BRISEIS CAITIFF CAITIVE PRISONER
(— OF HERCULES) IOLE
CAPTIVITY BOND IRON BONDS CHAINS DURESS BONDAGE SERFDOM SLAVERY
(— OF THE JEWS) EXILE
CAPTOR TAKER VICTOR CATCHER
CAPTURE BAG COP FIX GET NAB NET WIN FALL FANG GRAB HOOK LAND PREY SNIB TAKE TRAP TREE CARRY CATCH FORCE PINCH PRIZE PURSE RAVEN SEIZE SWOOP ARREST COLLAR CORRAL ENTRAP GOBBLE OBTAIN PIRACY REDUCE TAKING CAPTIVE LOWBELL SEIZURE WINNING EXCHANGE SURPRISE UNDERNIM
(— BACKGAMMON PIECE) HIT
(— BIRDS) TOODLE
(— GAME) SATCHEL
(— OF ALL PRIZES) SWEEP
(— TROUT) TICKLE
CAPTURED COLLARED
CAPUCHIN MONKEY CAY SAI CEPID SAJOU WEEPER SAPAJOU RINGTAIL
CAPULIN CEREZA
CAPYBARA CAVY CARPINCHO
CAPYS (FATHER OF —) ASSARACUS
(SON OF —) ANCHISES
(WIFE OF —) THEMISTE
CAR BOX BUS PIG AUTO BOGY BUNK DOLL DRAG DUMP GRIP JEEP RATH TRAM ZULU BOGEY COACH CRATE DINER DUMMY GURRY HUTCH JIMMY RATHA SEDAN STOCK TRAIN TRUCK WRONG BASKET BOXCAR BUFFET CHIPPY DINGEY DINGHY DUPLEX HOPPER JIGGER JINGLE SALOON SETOFF SMOKER TOURER AWKWARD CARROCH CHARIOT COMBINE FLATCAR FREEZER GIRAFFE GONDOLA HANDCAR MINIVAN SIDECAR

TELPHER TRAILER TROLLEY VEHICLE VETTURA AMPHICAR DRAGSTER HORSECAR OUTSIDER QUADRIGA ROADSTER SINISTER
(— FOR TRAIN CREW) CABOOSE
(— ON RAIL) TROLLEY
(BAGGAGE —) BLIND
(BRAND OF —) FORD SAAB CHEVY DODGE MAZDA VOLVO PLYMOUTH
(CABLE —) GONDOLA
(COAL —) HUTCH JIMMY WAGON WAGGON
(CONVERTIBLE —) RAGTOP
(DEALER'S —) DEMO
(ELECTRIC —) TELFER TELPHER
(ELEVATOR —) CAB CAGE
(EMPTY —) EMPTY IDLER
(ENCLOSED CABLE —) GONDOLA
(FUNNY —) DRAGSTER
(GO BY —) AUTO MOTOR
(JAUNTING —) SIDECAR
(KIND OF —) PACE PROWL SQUAD HEARSE MUSCLE
(KIND OF POLICE —) PANDA
(LOG —) BUNK
(LOW-WHEELED —) HUTCH TRUCKLE
(MINE —) SKIP LARRY BARNEY GIRAFFE GUNBOAT
(MONORAIL —) GYROCAR
(OBSERVATION —) BUGGY
(OLD —) HEAP CRATE JUNKER
(OLD-TIME —) REO NASH EDSEL ESSEX STUTZ DESOTO HUDSON MAXWELL
(POLICE —) CRUISER
(POLICE PATROL —) PANDA
(SMALL —) MINICAB ECONOBOX
(STYLE OF —) COUPE SEDAN
(TOURING —) PHAETON
(TOY RACING —) SLOTCAR
(TROLLEY —) SHORT
(USED —) DOG
CARABAO BUFF BUFFALO
CARACAL GORKUN SYAGUSH
CARACARA HAWK CARANCHA CHIMANGO
CARACOLE FRISK CAREER
CARADOC BALA CRADOCK
CARAFE CROFT BOTTLE
CARAGUATA CHAGUAR
CARAJURA CHICA
CARAMBOLA BLIMBING BALIMBING
CARAMEL BLACKJACK
CARAPA CRAB CRAPPO CRABWOOD
CARAPACE CRUST SHELL LORICA SHIELD CALAPASH
(SUFF.) STEGE STEGITE
CARAT (HUNDREDTH OF —) POINT
CARATE PINTA
CARATHIS (SON OF —) VATHEK
CARAVAN VAN TREK TRIP FLEET TRAIN CAFILA COFFLE CONVOY SAFARI TRAVEL JOURNEY VEHICLE CONDUCTA
CARAVANSARY INN CHAN KHAN HOTEL SERAI ZAYAT HOSTEL IMARET CHOULTRY HOSTELRY SERAGLIO
CARAVEL NINA
CARAWAY CARVY UMBEL
CARBAMATE MEPROBAMATE
CARBAMIDE UREA

CARBINE STEN DRAGON MUSKET DRAGOON ESCOPET
(BRITISH —) STEN
CARBOHYDRATE SUGAR AMYLAN GELOSE INULIN STARCH FUCOSAN GLUCIDE CELLULIN DEXTRINE DEXTROSE GLYCOGEN GRAMININ PENTOSAN TRITICIN CELLULOSE PARAMYLUM POLYSACCHARIDE
CARBON COAL COKE COPY SOOT NORIT CRAYON DIAMOND REPLICA CHARCOAL GRAPHITE SCHUNGITE
(PREF.) ANTHRAC(O)
(SUFF.) ANE
CARBONADO BORT BOART BOORT CARBON
CARBONATE BURN CHAR FIZZ AERATE ALKALI ENLIVEN ENERGIZER
CARBONATOR GASMAN
CARBON DIOXIDE CHOKEDAMP
(SUFF.) CAPNIA
CARBONIZE CHAR
CARBONIZER PICKLER
CARBORUNDUM EMERY ABRASIVE SILUNDUM
CARBOXYL
(SUFF.) (CONTAINING —) OIC ONIC
CARBUNCLE RUBY PYROPE ANTHRAX CHARBOCLE
(PREF.) ANTHRAC(O)
CARBURETOR CARB DIFFUSER VAPORIZER
CARCASS BEEF BODY BOUK CASE CULL BLOCK MUMMY CORPSE CARRION
(— OF WHALE) CRANG KRANG KRENG
CARCERULE SARCOBASIS
CARD ACE MAP PAM WAG CLUB COMB DRAW FACE FIVE FOUR JACK KING MENU PLAN ROVE STOP BALOP BLANK CARTE CHART CHECK DEUCE DUMMY EIGHT ENTRY EQUAL FICHE FLATS GREEN HEART HONOR JOKER LOSER PIECE QUEEN SPADE STAMP STIFF TAROT TEASE BENDER CARTEL CONVEX FILLER KICKER KNIGHT PIGEON READER SECOND TICKET TOWSER BRAGGER BRISQUE DIAMOND PROGRAM RELEASE STARTER STOPPER TAROCCO TRIUMPH BOOKMARK COMOQUER DECKHEAD DRAWCARD SCHEDULE SCRIBBLE SQUEEZER STRIPPER TIMECARD
(— GAME) WAR
(— IN OMBRE) MANILLE
(— LAST IN BOX) HOCK HOCKELTY
(— WOOL) TUM ROVE
(ACE OF CLUBS —) BASTA BASTO MATADOR PUPPYFOOT
(ACE OF SPADES —) MATADOR SPADILLE
(ACE OF TRUMPS —) TIB
(AVIATOR'S —) CARNET
(CLUB —) OAK
(COMPASS —) FLY ROSE
(CREDIT —) PLASTIC
(CRIBBAGE —S) CRIB
(DEAD —) SLEEPER
(DIAMOND —) PICK CARREAU

(DISCARDED —S) CRIB
(DRAWING —) BLOWOFF
(FARO —) SODA
(FOUR —) CATER QUATRE
(FOURTH —) CASE
(HIGHEST UNPLAYED —) COMMAND
(IN THE —S) PROBABLE
(JOKER —) BRAGGER MISTIGRIS
(KIND OF —) PUNCH REPORT HOLLERITH
(KING, QUEEN OR KNAVE —) COST FACE
(KNAVE —) PAM TOM JACK BOWER EQUES MAKER NODDY COQUIN KNIGHT PICARO VARLET WENZEL CUSTREL PEASANT VILLAIN VARLETTO
(LAYOUT OF —S) TABLEAU
(LOW —) GUARD
(MARKED —) STAMP
(POSTAL —) COVER
(PULLING —S) TIRE
(QUEEN AND KNAVE —S) INTRIGO INTRIGUE
(RUN OF —S) SEQUENCE
(SPADE —) PICK DIGGER
(STOCK —) TALON
(THIRD HIGHEST TRUMP —) BASTA
(THREE —) TREY THREE
(WILD —) FREAK
(3 —S IN SEQUENCE) TIERCE FOURCHETTE
(3 —S OF KIND) TRIO TRICON PAIRIAL TRIPLET
(3 ACE —S) CORONA
(3 FACE —S) GLEEK
(4 OF TRUMPS —) TIDDY
(5 FACE —S) BLAZE
(7, 8 AND 9 —S) VOIDS
CARDAMOM KNOBWOOD
CARDBOARD CARD PALL BLANK BOGUS CARTON BRISTOL TAGBOARD PAPERBOARD
(SMALL PIECES OF —) CHAD
(TWO —S) SPHEROGRAPH
CARDER TOZER TEASER TUMMER
CARDIALGIA HEARTBURN
CARDIGAN CORGI WAMUS FABRIC JACKET WAMPUS SWEATER
CARDINAL RED MAIN BASIC CHIEF CLOAK VITAL ALEPHA CLERIC DATARY PRINCE RADICAL ALEFNULL ALEFZERO CAMPEIUS PENITENTIARY
CARDINALATE PURPLE
CARDINAL BIRD CARNAL REDBIRD REDLEGS GROSBEAK REDSHANK
CARDINAL FISH FUCINITA ALFONCINO
CARDSHARP TRAMPOSO
CARDSHARPER GREEK SHARPER SPIELER
CARE DO DOW HOW CARK CURE DUTY FASH FRET HEED KEEP KEPE MIND PASS RECK SOIN TEND TENT WISH YEME COUNT GRIEF GUARD NURSE PAINS SORGE TRUST WORRY BURDEN CARIEN CHARGE CUMBER DESIRE GRIEVE KIAUGH LAMENT REGARD SORROW ANXIETY AUSPICE CAUTION CHERISH CONCERN CULTURE

CUSTODY KEEPING RESPECT RUNNING SCRUPLE THOUGHT TUITION BUSINESS PERIERGY TENDMENT NURTURANCE PRECAUTION SOLICITUDE
(— FOR) KNOW MIND RECK TEND WARD FORCE NURSE SAVOR FATHER MATTER REGARD CHERISH PROCURE
(— FOR ONESELF) BACH
(— OF HOUSEHOLD) HUSBANDRY
(— OF LIVESTOCK) CHORE
(— OF THE OLD) GERIATRY
(GIVE EXCESSIVE — TO) WETNURSE
(JUDICIOUS —) LEISURE
(WATCHFUL —) TENDANCE OVERSIGHT
CAREEN GIP CANT HEEL KEEL LIST TILT VEER LURCH SLOPE SWIFT INCLINE
CAREENING ALIST AREEL
CAREER RUN WAY LIFE ROAD RUSH SPEED TRADE CHARGE COURSE GALLOP CALLING CARIERE PURSUIT
(— SUMMARY) BIO VITA
(MILITARY —) ARMS SERVICE
(SELECT A —) GOINTO
CAREFREE EASY FRANK HAPPY BREEZY DEGAGE HOLIDAY DEBONAIR
CAREFUL BUSY WARY CANNY CHARY CLOSE EXACT HOOLY TENTY CHOICE DAINTY EIDENT EYEFUL FRUGAL NARROW TENDER ANXIOUS CURIOUS ENVIOUS GUARDED HEEDFUL PAINFUL PRUDENT THRIFTY ACCURATE CAUTIOUS CRITICAL DILIGENT DISCREET DREADFUL GINGERLY MOURNFUL PUNCTUAL TROUBLED VIGILANT WATCHFUL OBSERVANT METICULOUS SOLICITOUS PUNCTILIOUS
CAREFULLY HOOLY NARROW CANNILY CHARILY TENTILY CHOICELY GINGERLY
CAREFULNESS CAUTION
CARELESS LAX COOL EASY LASH RASH MESSY SLACK CASUAL OVERLY RAKISH REMISS SECURE SLOPPY SUPINE UNTIDY UNWARY CURSORY LANGUID SLIGHTY UNCANNY HEEDLESS LISTLESS MINDLESS RECKLESS SLATTERN SLIPSHOD SLOVENLY YEMELESS NEGLECTFUL SLATTERNLY
CARELESSLY SLACK OVERLY SLACKLY SLIGHTLY
CARELESSNESS LACHES LAXITY INCAUTION
CARESS COY HUG PAT PET BILL CLAP DAUT DAWT KISS MUCH NECK INGLE NURSE CODDLE COSSET CUDDLE FONDLE PAMPER STROKE CHERISH EMBRACE FLATTER BLANDISH CANOODLE LALLYGAG
CARETAKER KEEPER WARDER JANITOR
CAREWORN HAGGARD

CARGO BULK LAST LOAD BURDEN LADING FREIGHT PACKAGE PORTAGE CARGASON PROPERTY SHIPLOAD SHIPMENT TRAFFICS
CARIAMA CHUNGA SERIEMA
CARIB GALIBI CALINAGO
CARIBBEAN (— GULF) DARIEN HONDURAS
(— ISLAND) CUBA SABA ARUBA HAITI NEVIS BEQUIA NASSAU TOBAGO ANTIGUA BARBUDA BONAIRE CURACAO GRENADA JAMAICA TORTOLA ANGUILLA BARBADOS DOMINICA TRINIDAD GUADELOUPE MONTSERRAT
(— ISLAND GROUP) TURKS CAICOS CAYMAN LEEWARD ANTILLES WINDWARD
CARIBE PIRAI PIRANHA CHARACINE
CARIBOU STAG RANGIFER REINDEER
CARICATURE APE COPY MOCK SKIT FARCE LIBEL MIMIC SQUIB OVERDO PARODY SATIRE CARTOON TRAVESTY BURLESQUE
CARILLON PEAL
CARILLONNEUR CAMPANIST BELLMASTER
CARINA KEEL
CARIOUS ROTTEN
CARMELITE EXTERN TERESIAN
CARMEN (CHARACTER IN —) JOSE CARMEN ZUNIGA MICAELA ESCAMILLO
(COMPOSER OF —) BIZET
CARMI (FATHER OF —) REUBEN
(SON OF —) ACHAN
CARMINATIVE GINGER CALAMUS CAMPHOR ANETHOLE VALERIAN
CARMINE RED LAKE CRIMSON SCARLET
CARNAGE WAL MURDER POGROM STRAGE BUTCHERY MASSACRE BLOODSHED SLAUGHTER
CARNAL CROW LEWD GROSS ANIMAL BODILY SEXUAL BESTIAL BRUTISH EARTHLY FLESHLY SECULAR SENSUAL WORLDLY MATERIAL PANDEMIC PHYSICAL TEMPORAL
CARNATION JACK PINK FLAKE BIZARRE PICOTEE DAYBREAK DIANTHUS GRENADINE MALMAISON
CARNELIAN SARD COPPER
(BEAD OF —) ARANGO
CARNIVAL FETE SHOW CARNY CANVAS APOKREA CANVASS REVELRY FASCHING FESTIVAL
CARNIVORE CAT DOG FOX BEAR COON LION LYNX MINK PUMA SEAL WOLF CIVET GENET HYENA OTTER PANDA PEKAN RATEL SABLE STOAT TIGER BADGER COUGAR ERMINE FELINE FERRET FISHER FOUSSA JACKAL JAGUAR MARTEN OCELOT POSSUM SERVAL WEASEL DASYURE GLUTTON LEOPARD MEERKAT POLECAT RACCOON TIGRESS AARDWOLF MONGOOSE OPPOSSUM PREDACEAN ZOOPHAGAN
(FOSSIL —) CREODONT

CARNIVOROUS SARCOPHAGOUS
CAROB HUSK LOCUST ALGAROBA
CAROL LAY NOEL SING SONG DITTY
YODEL WARBLE WASSAIL
MADRIGAL AGUINALDO
CAROLINA ALLSPICE SHRUB
CAROLINE ISLANDS (— ISLAND
GROUP) PALAU
(ISLAND OF —) YAP HALL PALU
TRUK PELEW PULAP OROLUK
PONAPE WOLEAI PELELIU
(TOWN OF —) LOT NIF RUNU
KOROR MUTOK TOMIL PONAPE
MALAKAL GARUSUUN
CAROLINGIAN KARLING
CAROM SHOT BOUNCE CANNON
GLANCE STRIKE REBOUND
BILLIARD CARAMBOLE
CAROUSAL BAT GELL LARK ORGY
RIOT ROMP TOOT BINGE FEAST
RANDY REVEL ROUSE SPRAY
SPREE FROLIC SHINDY SPLORE
BANQUET CAROUSE REVELRY
WASSAIL DRINKING FESTIVAL
JAMBOREE
CAROUSE JET BOUT HELL RANT
TEAR TOOT BINGE BIRLE BOUSE
DRINK QUAFF RANDY REVEL
ROUSE SPREE TOAST COURANT
JOLLIFY WASSAIL CAROUSAL
CAROUSER BACCHANT
BACCHANAL
CAROUSING REVEL RAFFING
(— OF ICEBOUND SEAMEN) MALLE
MOLLIE
CARP KOI NAG BITE DRUM SING
SNAG TALK YERK CAVIL PINCH
PRATE SCOLD SPEAK CENSOR
GROUSE NIBBLE RECITE TWITCH
CENSURE CHATTER CRUCIAN
QUIBBLE COMPLAIN CYPRINID
GOLDFISH
(CRUCIAN —) GIBEL
(LAKE —) DRUM LAKER
(PREF.) CYPRIN(O)
CARPAL ACTINOST
CARPEL ACHENE CARPID COCCUS
MERICARP CARPOPHYL
(PL.) CORE
CARPENTER ANT LOHAR FITTER
FRAMER HOUSER JOINER PINNER
WRIGHT BUILDER HOWSOUR
WOODMAN INDENTER TECTONIC
TIMBERER PITWRIGHT
SHIPWRIGHT
(SHIP'S —) CHIPS
(PREF.) TECTO
CARPENTRY WOODWORK
WRIGHTRY
CARPER MOME CRITIC KNOCKER
CARPET MAT RUG AGRA KALI KUBA
HERAT KILIM SARUK SCOLD
SUMAK TAPET TAPIS TEKKE USHAK
AFGHAN FLOSSA FRIEZE KASHAN
KIDDER KIRMAN LAVEHR NAMMAD
RUNNER SAROUK SAXONY SELJUK
SMYRNA TABRIZ VELVET WILTON
DHURRIE GIORDES HAMADAN
INGRAIN ISFAHAN ISPAHAN
SHEMAKA TEHERAN AKHISSAR
AMRITSAR BRUSSELS COVERING
FOOTPACE KARABAGH MOQUETTE

TAPESTRY TURCOMAN VENETIAN
AXMINSTER SITRINGEE
(HOLY —) KISWA
(PILELESS —) KILIM GELEEM
CARPETING FILLING
CARPET SHARK WOBBEGONG
CARPET SHELL EEROCK PULLET
CARPETWEED FICOID FICOIDAL
MESEMBRYANTHEMUM
CARPING CRAB CAPTIOUS CAVILING
CRITICAL
CARPSUCKER QUILLBACK
CARPUS WRIST CARPOPODITE
CARRAGEEN KILLEEN
CARREL STALL CUBICLE
CARRIAGE AIR CAB CAR FLY GIG
RIG RUT SET VIS ARBA BIGA CART
CHAR DRAG DUKE EKKA GAIT GARB
HACK LOAD MIEN PORT RUTH
SHAY TEAM TRAP WYNN ARABA
BANDY BRAKE BREAK BRETT
BUGGY CHAIR COACH COUPE
ESSED FRONT JUTKA MIDGE
NODDY PANEL POISE SADOO
SETUP SULKY TENUE TONGA
TRUCK WAGON BURDEN CALASH
CHAISE CHARET CISIUM CONVOY
DENNET DROSKY FIACRE GHARRY
GOCART HANSOM HERDIC
KOSUNG LANDAU MANNER
MOTION PORTER REMISE SADDLE
SPIDER SURREY SURREY TANDEM
TELEGA TROIKA BAGGAGE
BEARING BERLINE BOUNDER
BRITSKA CALECHE CALESIN
CARAVAN CARIOLE CAROCHE
CHARIOT COACHEE CONDUCT
CROYDON DOGCART DOSADOS
DROSHKY FORECAR GESTURE
HACKMAN HACKNEY MINIBUS
PHAETON POSCHAY SHANDRY
SKYHOOK TALLYHO TARTANA
TILBURY TRANSIT TROLLEY
UNICORN VECTURE VEHICLE
VETTURA VOITURE VOLANTE
WAFTAGE BAROUCHE BEHAVIOR
BROUGHAM CARRIOLE CARRYALL
CLARENCE CURRICLE DEARBORN
DEMEANOR DORMEUSE EQUIPAGE
PORTANCE PRESENCE ROCKAWAY
SOCIABLE STANHOPE TARANTAS
TOURNURE VICTORIA
(— IN PHILIPPINES) CALESA
(— OF HANDPRESS) COFFIN
(— OF HORSE) AIR
(AMMUNITION —) CAISSON
(CEREMONIAL —) RATH
(ELEVATED —) LIFT
(GUN —) CHASSIS
(INDIAN —) RUT EKKA BANDY
GHARRI GHARRY
(JAVANESE —) SADO SADOO
(LIVERY —) REMISE
(LOG —) DRAG
(PUBLIC —) FLY OMNIBUS
CARRIAGE HOUSE REMISE
CARRIAGEWAY SWEE
CARRIED (— AWAY) RAPT ENLEVE
CARRIER HOD BASE JEEP SHIP
TRAM BUGGY HAMAL KAHAR
MACER PLANE SABOT TAMEN
TIGER BARKIS BEARER CADGER
COOLIE HAMMAL HODMAN

JAGGER PACKER PORTER RUNNER
TAILER WEASEL DRAYMAN
DROGHER FLATTOP POSTMAN
REMOVER TACULLI TROTTER
VEHICLE CARGADOR CARRYALL
PORTATOR RAILROAD TEAMSTER
SUBSTRATE
(— OF DISEASE) VECTOR
(COAL —) FLATIRON
(COLOR —) LURRIER
(CRANE —) GANTRY
(ENDLESS —) TAILER
(FIRE —) PORTFIRE
(MAIL —) COURIER POSTMAN
(ORE —) BARGE BOXCAR
(WATER —) BHISTI BHEESTY
(PREF.) PORTE
CARRION KET VILE OFFAL CORPSE
HOODIE REFUSE ROTTEN CARCASS
CORRUPT DOGMEAT CROWBAIT
CARRION BIRD SCAVENGER
CARRION CROW DOWP HOODY
URUBU CORBIE HOODIE
GERCROW
CARROT UMBEL CONIUM DAUCUS
CACHRYS SECRETE BUPLEVER
HILLTROT
(DEADLY —) DRIAS
(PERUVIAN —) ARRACACHA
(PREPARED WITH —S) CRECY
CARROTING SECRETAGE
CARROUSEL RIDE WHIRLGIG
QUADRILLE
CARRY CAR HUG JAG LUG BEAR
BUCK CART DRAY FARE GEST HAUL
HAVE HOLD HUMP LEAD PACK
PORT SHOW TAKE TOTE TUMP
BRING BROOK CADGE CROSS
FERRY GESTE GUIDE POISE WALTZ
WEIGH BEHAVE CONVEY CONVOY
DELATE DEPORT DERIVE EXTEND
COMPORT CONDUCT CONTAIN
ENTRAIN PORTAGE PRODUCE
SUPPORT SUSTAIN UNDERGO
BAJULATE CONTINUE TRANSFER
TRANSMIT
(— AWAY) FIRK DRAIN REAVE
SWEEP TRUSS ABLATE ASPORT
(— CLUBS) CADDY CADDIE
(— EFFIGY) GUY
(— FORWARD) EXTEND
(— IN OXCART) KURVEY
(— INTO EFFECT) FULFIL FULFILL
(— IN TRIUMPH) CHAIR
(— LIQUOR) BOOTLEG
(— OFF) RAP HENT LIFE SACK FETCH
HEAVE RIFLE SCOUR SWOOP
ABDUCT ASPORT BRAZEN KIDNAP
SPIRIT
(— ON) DO RUN WAR HAVE LEAD
LEVY WAGE APPLY DRIVE ENSUE
FIGHT TRAIN CREATE DEMEAN
FOLLOW MANAGE OCCUPY
CONDUCT EXERCISE MAINTAIN
TRANSACT
(— ONESELF) HOLD
(— ONWARD) CONTINUE
(— OUT) DO ACT END GIVE LAST
HONOR AFFORD EFFECT ACHIEVE
EXECUTE FULFILL PERFORM
SATISFY PERPETRATE
(— TOO FAR) OVERDO

(— UPWARD) RAP ESCALATE
(SUFF.) GER(ENCE)(ENT)(OUS)
PHER PHORA PHORE(SIS) PHORIA
PHOROUS PHORUS
(— ON) IZE
CARRYALL BUS CASE WAGON
CARRIAGE
CARRY-ALONG TOTE
CARRYING BURDEN GERENT
FRAUGHT
(— AWAY) REVEHENT
(— ON) GESTION
(— WEIGHT) EFFECTIVE
(PREF.) (— ON) PHORO
CART CAR JAG POT RUT BUTT CHAR
COOP COUP DRAY HAUL JANG
LEAD LOAD PLOW PUTT RUTH
TOTE WAIN ARABA BANDY BOGEY
BOGIE CADDY CARRY DANDY DILLY
DOLLY SULKY TONGA TRUCK
WAGON BARROW CADDIE CHAISE
CHARET CISIUM CONVEY DOLLIE
DUMPER GHARRI GHARRY JIGGER
JINKER KURUMA LIMBER PLOUGH
SPIDER CARIOLE CARRETA
CHARIOT DOGCART GUJERAT
HACKERY MORFREY SHALLOW
SHANDRY TROLLEY TRUNDLE
TUMBLER TUMBREL TUMBRIL
VEHICLE BUCKCART DUMPCART
HANDCART PUSHCART
(— WITH TANK) TUMBLER
(BULLOCK —) BANDY HACKERY
(COSTER'S —) TROLL
(COVERED —) JINGLE CARIOLE
(FARMER'S —) PUTT GAMBO
MORPHREY
(FREIGHT —) CARRETON
(LOG —) TUG BUNK
(LUMBER —) GILL BUMMER
(MILKMAN'S —) PRAM
(OX —) RECKLA
(PARCELS —) FLY
(TIMBER —) CUTS
(TIP —) COOP COUP COUPE
(UNDERSLUNG —) FLOAT
(2-PONY —) KOSONG
(2-WHEELED —) BANDY BUGGY
SULKY CARRETA TUMBREL
(3-WHEELED —) PORTER
CARTE MAP CARD LIST MENU
CHART CHARTER DIAGRAM
CARTE BLANCHE BLANK
CARTEL CARD DEFY PACT POOL
SHIP PAPER TRUST CORNER
LETTER TREATY CONTRACT
SYNDICATE
CARTER CARMAN JAGGER LEADER
DRAYMAN LADEMAN TRUCKER
HORSEMAN TEAMSTER
CART-HORSE AVER
CARTILAGE COPULA TISSUE
CRICOID EPIURAL GRISTLE
RADIALE STERNUM TARSALE
THYROID CHONDRUS EPIPUBIS
HYPOHYAL SESAMOID TURBINAL
(— UNDER DOG'S TONGUE) LYTTA
(PREF.) CHONDR(I)(IO)(O) CRICO
(SUFF.) CHONDRIA CHONDRY
CRINUS
CARTILAGINOUS CHONDRIC
CARTLOAD SEAM FOTHER
CARTOGRAPH MAP PLAT CHART

CARTOGRAPHER CHARTIST MAPMAKER
AMERICAN GANNETT HUTCHINS SOUTHACK STEVENSON
ENGLISH SPEED
GERMAN KIEPERT STIELER PETERMANN WALDSEEMULLER
RUSSIAN KAULBARS
SWISS SIEGFRIED
CARTON BOX CASE SHELL
CARTOON EPURE ANIMATION
CARTOONING (— AWARD) REUBEN
CARTOONIST AMERICAN DAY FOX KEY REA ARNO BAER BALD BODE CADY CAPP DODD DUNN HELD HESS LUKS NAST BARKS BLOCK BURCK CRUMB DARCY DIRKS DUFFY EDSON ERNST GOULD HATLO KIRBY LANTE MCCAY NEHER OPPER PLUMB SAXON SEGAR STEIG TERRY YATES YOUNG ADDAMS BERNDT BRIGGS CANIFF DEITCH DISNEY DORGAN FISHER KEMBLE KOTSKY MUSIAL NEWELL NOWLAN POWERS RIPLEY SCHULZ SOGLOW DARLING GRUELLE KEPPLER MAULDIN MCMANUS TRUDEAU WEBSTER GOLDBERG HERBLOCK OUTCAULT SCHULTZE WESTOVER WILLIAMS NANKIVELL STEINBERG HERSHFIELD FITZPATRICK
AUSTRALIAN LINDSAY
BELGIAN CULLIFORD
DUTCH RAEMAEKERS
ENGLISH LOW SPY DYSON LEECH SMYTHE FURNISS GILLRAY HAMPSON TENNIEL ROBINSON LANCASTER BAIRNSFATHER
FRENCH GOSCINNY
GERMAN MEGGENDORFER
MEXICAN ARRIOLA COVARRUBIAS
WELSH BATEMAN ILLINGWORTH
CARTOUCHE MESA OVAL DURANGO CARTRIDGE
CARTRIDGE BAG CASE HULL BLANK SHELL SHORT BULLET MAGNUM PATRON CAPSULE TORPEDO HANDLOAD SHOTSHELL
(PART OF —) RIM CASE HEAD NOSE SLUG CRIMP BULLET JACKET PRIMER
(TAPE —) CASSETTE
(TYPE OF —) POPIN
CARTULARY COUCHER
CARTWHEEL CLOGWHEEL
CARUCATE CARVE PLOWLAND
(ONE EIGHTH —) OXGANG OXGATE OXLAND
CARUNCLE ARIL COMB STROPHIOLE
CARVE CUT ALAY SIDE BEHEW BREAK GRAVE KIRVE MINCE SHEAR SPLAY SPOIL THIGH INCISE QUINSE SCULPT THWITE TRENCH UNLACE ENCHASE ENGRAIL ENGRAVE DISJOINT MALAHACK SCULLION
(— A BIRD) WING
(— AN EEL) TRUNCHEON
(— CHICKEN) FRUSH
(— GOOSE) REAR
(— HEN) SPOIL
(— PEACOCK) DISFIGURE

(— PLOVER) MINCE
(— SWAN) LIFT
(PREF.) GLYPHO GLYPT(O) SCULPTO
(SUFF.) GLYPH
CARVED CARVEN GLYPHIC INCISED
(PREF.) GLYPT(O)
CARVER BODGER KIRVER CROPPER FROSTER IVORIST CISELEUR TRENCHER
CARVING CAMEO GLYPH IVORY ENTAIL SCRIVE GLYPTIC MASKOID NICKING APLUSTRE INTAGLIO TRIPTYCH PETROGLYPH
(— ON MOLDING) GADROON
(— ON TREE) DENDROGLYPH
(CIRCULAR —) TONDO
CARYA HICORIA
CARYATID TELAMON CANEPHORA
(PART OF —) GAINE
CARYOCAR SOUARI
CARYOPHYLLUS JAMBOSA
CARYOPSIS SEED
CASABLANCA (CHARACTER IN —) ILSA
CASANOVA AMORIST
CASCABEL POMMEL POMMELION
CASCADE LIN FALL LINN FORCE SPOUT CATARACT
CASCARA BUCKTHORN WAHOO SHITTIM
CASCARILLA CROTON GOATWEED SWEETWOOD
CASE BAG BOX CUP HAP LEG POD POT PYX BIND BOOT BUNK BURR CASK COPE DEED DESK DOCK DOME FILE PACK PAIR ROLL SUIT TICK BRACE BRIEF BULLA BURSE CADDY CASUS CAUSE CHAPE COVER CRATE EVENT FOLIO FOREL HUSSY HUTCH PRESS PYXIS SHELL STATE THECA THING TRIAL ACTION AFFAIR APPEAL BARREL BINDER BOXING CARTON CASING CELLAR CHANCE CHRISM COFFIN COUPLE LOCKET LORICA MATTER PATRON PENNER PETARD POPPET QUIVER RIDDLE SHEATH SHRINE STATOR SURVEY TASHIE TWEEZE VALISE VANITY CABINET CAMISIA CAPCASE CAPSULE COUNTER CUSHION DIECASE ENCLOSE ENVELOP EXAMPLE GEARBOX HOLDALL HOLSTER HOUSING HUMIDOR INCLOSE LAWSUIT LUNETTE PACKAGE REMANET SATCHEL SHIPPER WARDIAN ACCIDENT ARGUMENT BOOKCASE CARRYALL CUPBOARD ENVELOPE EQUIPAGE EXEMPLAR GARDEVIN INSTANCE KNAPSACK PACKSACK PORTFIRE SHOWCASE SITUATED SOLANDER TANTALUS CARTRIDGE PORTFOLIO
(— CONTAINING ELEVATOR BELT) LEG
(— ENCLOSING CLOCK DIAL) HOOD
(— FOR BOTTLES) CELLARET
(— FOR CARDS) SHOE
(— FOR COMPASS) BINNACLE
(— FOR DECANTERS) TANTALUS
(— FOR EXPLOSIVES) TRUNK
(— FOR JEWELS) TYE

(— FOR MAINSPRING) BARILLET
(— FOR MOLD) COPE CHAPE
(— FOR MONEY) WALLET
(— FOR MUMMY) SLEDGE
(— FOR PISTOL) HOLSTER
(— FOR PULLEY) BLOCK
(— FOR RIFLE) BOOT
(— FOR SEWING ITEMS) HUSSY
(— FOR TOOLS) TROUSSE
(— FOR TWEEZERS) BUBBLEBOW
(— FOR WRITING MATERIALS) STANDISH
(— IN WATCH) DOME BARREL
(— OF) A
(— OF FLOUR BOLTER) HUTCH
(— OF VENETIAN BLIND) HEADBOX
(— WITH COMPARTMENTS) RIDDLE
(BONY —) CARAPACE
(CARTRIDGE —) DOP CARTOUCHE
(COSMETIC —) COMPACT
(COURT —) LAWSUIT
(EGG —) OVISAC OOTHECA
(EMPTY —) SHELL
(FIREWORKS —) LANCE
(GRAMMATICAL —) DATIVE ESSIVE LATIVE ELATIVE FACTIVE ABLATIVE EQUATIVE ERGATIVE GENITIVE ILLATIVE LOCATIVE VOCATIVE ACCUSATIVE
(HOPELESS —) GONER
(LARVA —) INDUSIUM
(LUGGAGE —) IMPERIAL
(ORNAMENTAL —) ETUI
(PAPER —) COFFIN
(PILLOW —) SLIP
(SMALL —) MINAUDIERE
(SPORE —) ASCUS
(WICKER —) HASK BARROW HANAPER
(WING —) SHARD
(WRITING —) KALAMDAN
(PREF.) THEC(A)(I)(O)
(EGG —) OOTHEC(O)
(SUFF.) THECA THECIUM
CASED BOUND
CASEMENT SASH LUKET WINDOW
CASE OF SERGEANT GRISCHA
(AUTHOR OF —) ZWEIG
(CHARACTER IN —) BABKA LYCHOW GRISCHA WILHELMI WINFRIED BJUSCHEFF PAPROTKIN PONSANSKI SCHIEFFENZAHN
CASH (SHORT OF —) STRAPPED
CASHEW ACAJOU ANACARD
CASHEW TREE ACAJOU
CASHIER CASS CAST BREAK DEALER POTDAR PURSER TELLER CHECKER DISMISS
CASHIERED BROKEN DEGOMME
CASHMERE KASHMIR PRUNELL
CASH REGISTER DAMPER REGEST GREFFIER RECORDER REGISTER
CASING BODY BOOT BUNG CASE CURB HULL SHOE SKIN TIRE APRON BELLY DERMA EPHOD GAINE LINER ROUND STOCK TRUNK BOXING COFFIN COLLET JACKET KISHKE LINING SCROLL SHEATH VOLUTE COWLING FEEDBOX HOUSING MANHEAD OUTCASE STAVING THIMBLE CACHEPOT COVERING PLOWSHOE SHIRTING WHEELBOX

(— FOR BRAIN) HARNPAN
(— FOR SHAFT) TUB
(BOILER —) JACKET
CASINO BAKED BROILED
(— CALL) HITME
(— EMPLOYEE) DEALER
CASK KEG PIN TUB TUN VAT BOSS BUTT CADE COWL DRUM KNAG PIPE RAPE RIER SLIP TREE WOOD ANKER BOWIE BULGE FOIST STAND UNION BARECA BARREL CARDEL CASQUE DOLIUM FIRKIN FOODER LONGER OCTAVE TIERCE WINGER BARRICO BREAKER FOSTELL LEAGUER RUNDLET SACKBUT CASSETTE HOGSHEAD PUNCHEON QUARDEEL ROUNDLET KILDERKIN
(BREWING —) UNION
(LOCKED —) TANTALUS
(PERFORATED —) POT
(SMALL —) KEG TUB KNAG STOOP STOUP
(WINE —) FAT TUN BOSS BUTT PIPE TIERCE HOGSHEAD
(PL.) COOPERAGE
CASKET BOX PIX TYE CASE CASK CIST TILL TOMB BUIST CHEST ACERRA CHASSE COFFER COFFIN SHRINE CADENAS FOSTELL CASSETTE
CASK-STAND STILLAGE STILLION
CASPIAN (— FEEDER) YSER
CASQUE CASK HORN GALEA HELMET BRASSET
CASSABANANA CURUBA
CASSANDRA SEER
(BROTHER OF —) HELENUS
(FATHER OF —) PRIAM
(HUSBAND OF —) AGAMEMNON
(MOTHER OF —) HECUBA
(SLAYER OF —) CLYTEMNESTRA
CASSAREEP CAXIRI
CASSAVA AIPI YUCA AIPIM YUCCA CASIRI CAZIBI MANIOC TAPIOCA
(— DISH) TAPIOCA
CASSEROLE TUREEN COCOTTE MARMITE TERRINE TZIMMES
CASSETTE TAPE MAGAZINE CARTRIDGE
CASSIA KEZIA SENNA SICKLEPOD
CASSIA FISTULA AMALTAS
CASSIMERE ZEPHYR
CASSINI OLEG
CASSITERITE TINSTONE
CASSITES KUSHSHU
CASSOCK GOWN SLOP VEST APRON GIPPO SIMAR SYMAR PRIEST PELISSE SIMARRE SOUTANE ZIMARRA
CASSOWARY EMU MURUP MOORUP RATITE
CAST MEW PUT SET AURA BILL DART HURL MOLD MOLT PICK SHED SLAT SLIP SPEW SWAK TINT TOSS TREE TURN WHAP WHOP WURP BLOCK BRAID CHUCK COOST DEUCE DRIVE EJECT ERECT FLING FLIRT FOUND FUSIL HEAVE IMAGE KEIST PITCH SHADE SHAPE SHOOT SLING STAMP THROW TINGE COLLAR INJECT NOSING

STRIKE STRIND THRILL AGARWAL CASHIER DEPOSIT DISCARD MOULAGE VIBRATE CASTLING CONSPECT OUTSLING POLYTYPE TINCTURE

(— ASIDE) DICE FLING

(— A SPELL) TAKE HOODOO BESPELL BEWITCH FORSPEAK

(— ASPERSIONS) SLUR SKLENT APPEACH

(— AWAY) DUMP SHOVE DEJECT REJECT

(— DICE) WHIRL

(— DISCREDIT) GLANCE

(— DOWN) DASH DUMP HURL SINK ABASE AMATE AMORT AWARP STREW ABATTU ABJECT DECAST DEJECT DEMISS THRING ECLIPSE RUINATE DEJECTED

(— FORTH) SPEW SPUE WARP BELCH BRAID LAUNCH

(— GLOOM) DUSK CLOUD DARKEN DEPRESS

(— IN A MOLD) STRIKE

(— LOTS) CAVEL

(— METAL) YET

(— OF DICE) COUP DEUCE

(— OFF) DAFF JILT MOLT SHED DITCH LOSSE SHAKE SLIRT SLUFF WAIVE CASTEN DEVEST REFUSE REJECT SLOUGH ABDICATE RENOUNCE

(— OF HERRINGS) WARP

(— OF LANGUAGE) IDIOM

(— OF NET) SHOT SHOOT

(— ON GROUND) TERRE

(— OUT) EGEST EJECT EXPEL BANISH ABANDON EXTRUDE OSTRACIZE

(— SHADOW) ADUMBRATE

(— UP) SUM LEVY UPBRAID

(FRESHLY —) GREEN

(PLASTER —) CUIRASS

(SUFF.) JECT

CASTANET CLICKER KNACKER KNOCKER SNAPPER TCHAPAN CROTALUM

CASTAWAY WAIF WEFT TRAMP CRUSOE REJECT OUTCAST DERELICT STRANDED

CASTE (OR CASTE MEMBER) DOM MEO AHIR BHAR BHAT GOLA JATI KOLI KORI MALI MINA PASI TELI BAGDI BANIA DHOBY GOALA IRAVA KAHAR KUMNI KUNBI KURMI LADHA LOHAR MAHAR PALLI PUGGI SAMAR SANSI SINGH SONAR SUDRA TANTI VARNA ARORAS BAIDYA BALIJA BANIAN BHANGI CHAMAR CHETTY CHUHRA DHANUK DHOBIE DOSADH DURZEE HOLEYA HOLIYA ILAVAN JAJMAN KALWAR KAMBOH KHATRI KUMHAR KURUBA LOHANA MADIGA NATION PALLAR PRABHU PULAYA PULIAN PURVOE RAJPUT VAISYA AGARWAL BRAHMAN BRAHMIN DHANGAR GADARIA HARIJAN KAYASTH KOMATRI KURUMBA NISHADA VELLALA KAMMALAN KHANDAIT PARAIYAN POVINDAH RAJBANSI VAKKALIGA

(LOWER —S) PANCHAMA

CASTER VIAL CRUET CRUSE PHIAL CASTOR HORRAL HURLER MASTER ROLLER FOUNDER PITCHER TRUCKLE TRUNDLE

(SURF —) SQUIDDER

CASTIGATE LASH EMEND SCARE SCORE BERATE PUNISH REVISE STRAFE SUBDUE CANVASS CENSURE CHASTEN CORRECT LEATHER REPROVE CHASTISE KEELHAUL LAMBASTE FUSTIGATE OBJURGATE

CASTIGATION HELL LASHING DRESSING

CASTILIAN BROWN TANAGRA

CASTING DIE PIG CAST FONT KEEP MOLD TYMP BLOCK CHOCK CHUCK FOUND MOULD BILLET BUMPER MATRIX MISRUN SPIDER COULAGE DARTING SEGMENT SEPARATOR SORTILEGE

(— LOTS) SORTITION

(— OF HOROSCOPE) APOTELESM

(— OF NET) SHOT

(— OVERBOARD) JETTISON

(PL.) SPRAY FOUNDRY

CAST IRON YETLING

CASTLE BURY FONT HALL KEEP ROCK ROOK ABODE BROCH COURT MORRO PIECE CASBAH BASTILE BOROUGH CHATEAU CITADEL SCHLOSS UDOLPHO BASTILLE CASTELET CASTILLO FASTNESS FORTRESS STAROSTY TINTAGEL

(— IN CHESS) JUEZ ROOK TOUR JUDGE TOWER

(PART OF —) KEEP MOAT WARD MOUNT TOWER WHARF BAILEY BRIDGE DONJON TURRET BASTION BULWARK DUNGEON OUTWORK RAMPART BARBICAN CASEMATE GATEHOUSE BATTLEMENT DRAWBRIDGE PORTCULLIS

(SMALL —) PEEL TOWER CASTLET CHATELET

CASTLE OF OTRANTO (AUTHOR OF —) WALPOLE

(CHARACTER IN —) CONRAD JEROME MANFRED MATILDA ISABELLA THEODORE

CAST-OFF DISCARD

CASTOR BEAVER LEATHER TRUCKLE TRUNDLE BARKSTONE

(— AND POLLUX) TWINS GEMINI DIOSCURI

(MOTHER OF —) LEDA

CASTOR AND POLLUX

(CHARACTER IN —) CASTOR PHOEBE POLLUX JUPITER MERCURY TELAIRA

(COMPOSER OF —) RAMEAU

CASTOR-OIL

(PREF.) RICIN(I)

CASTOR-OIL PLANT KIKI MAMONA PALMCRIST

CASTRATE CUT FIX GIB LIB GELD GLIB SPAY SWIG TRIM ALTER CAPON DESEX PRUNE STEER CHANGE DOCTOR EUNUCH NEUTER EVIRATE CAPONIZE MUTILATE SATURNIZE

CASTRATED CUT GIBBED NEUTER UNPAVED

(NOT —) STONE ENTIRE

CASTRATO EUNUCH EVIRATO TENORINO

CASUAL GLIB ORRA STRAY BLITHE BYHAND CHANCE FOLKSY RANDOM CASALTY CURSORY LEISURE NATURAL OFFHAND RUNNING GLANCING INFORMAL PROMISCUOUS

CASUALTY LOSS DEATH CADUAC CHANCE HAZARD INJURY MISHAP ACCIDENT DISASTER

CASUARINA BEEFWOOD

CASUIST JESUIT

CAT GIB RAT REX SOW TAB CHAT EYRA FLOG GATO LION LYNX MANX MISS PARD CHAUS PUSS CHAUS CIVET FELID GATOL KITTY KORAT MANUL MEWER MOGGY OUNCE PUSSY SMOKE TABBY TIGER TILER WHITE ZIBET ANGORA BIRMAN BOMBAY COUGAR FELINE JAGUAR KITTEN KODKOD MALKIN MARGAY MAWKIN MIAUER MOGGIE MOUSER MUSION NEUTER OCELOT PAJERO PURRER SERVAL SOMALI TIBERT TORTIE BURMESE CARACAL CATHEAD CATLING CHEETAH KITLING KUICHUA LEOPARD LINSANG PANTHER PERSIAN SIAMESE TIGRESS WILDCAT WRAWLER BAUDRONS DASYURID FISSIPED PUSSYCAT RINGTAIL TONKINESE

(— CRY) WAW MEOW MIAOW

(— GROUP) CLOWDER

(BREED OF —) CYMRIC CHARTREUX

(BREED OF —S) RAGDOLL

(FAMOUS —) MORRIS GARFIELD MEHITABEL HEATHCLIFF

(FEMALE —) QUEEN WHEENCAT

(MALE —) GIB TOM TOMCAT

(PART OF —) EAR EYE PAW TOE HEEL KNEE LIPS LOIN NAPE NECK RUMP TAIL BELLY BREAK ELBOW FLANK SHANK THIGH WRIST FEELER DEWCLAW LEATHER WHISKER FOREHEAD SHOULDER VIBRISSA METATARSUS

(ROOF-PROWLING —) TILER

(TAILLESS —) RUMPY

(PREF.) AELUR(O) AILUR(O) FELIN(O)

CATACHRESIS ABUSION

CATACHRESTICAL ABUSIVE

CATACLYSM FLOOD DELUGE DEBACLE DISASTER UPHEAVAL

CATACOMB TOMB CRYPT VAULT CEMETERY HYPOGEUM

(PL.) ARENARIAE

CATADROMOUS SEAGOING

CATAFALQUE BIER COFFIN

CATALECTIC HEMIAMB TRUNCATED

CATALEPSY TRANCE SEIZURE CATATONY

CATALOG PIE PYE BILL BOOK LIST ROLL ROTA BRIEF CANON FLIER FLYER INDEX PINAX AUTHOR RAGGER RAGMAN RECORD ROSTER ARRANGE BEADROW DIPTYCH NOTITIA BEADROLL BULLETIN CALENDAR CLASSIFY REGISTER SCHEDULE SYLLABUS CATALOGUE DIDASCALY INVENTORY

CATALUFA SCAD TORO BIGEYE

CATALYST CARRIER SAUSAGE ZIEGLER CATALYTE HOPCALITE

(NEGATIVE —) INHIBITER

CATAMARAN NAG RAFT TROW BALSA FLOAT NAGGER GUNBOAT JANGADA MONITOR AUNTSARY

CATAMITE INGLE GUNSEL NINGLE PATHIC BARDASH GANYMEDE

CATAMOUNT LION LYNX PUMA COUGAR

CATAPLASM PELOID POULTICE

CATAPULT GUN BIBLE SLING SWEEP THROW HURTLE LAUNCH ONAGER TREPAN ALACRAN BRICOLE PEDRERO TORMENT TRABUCH WARWOLF BALLISTA CROSSBOW DONDAINE LAUNCHER MANGONEL MARTINET SCORPION SPRINGAL STONEBOW

CATARACT LIN FALL LINN FALLS FLOOD PEARL DELUGE CASCADE NIAGARA CATADUPE OVERFALL VICTORIA

CATARRH MUR COLD MURR POSE RHEUM CORYZA NASITIS

CATASTROPHE ACCIDENT CALAMITY DISASTER CATACLYSM

CATCALL HOOT

CATCH BAG COB COG COP GET GIN KEP NAB NET NIP DRAW FANG GLOM HASP HAUL HAWK HENT HOLD HOOK LAND MAKE MEET MESS NAIL NICK PAWL SAVE SEAR SNAG SNAP SNIB STOP TAKE TRAP TREE VANG BENET CHAPE CLASP CLEEK CREEL FETCH GLOVE GRASP HITCH KETCH KNACK LASSO LATCH PLANT SEIZE SNARE SNICK SWOOP TRICK TROLL ARREST ATTAIN BUTTON CLUTCH CORNER CORRAL DETECT DETENT ENGAGE ENMESH ENTRAP IMMESH LOCKET NOBBLE NOODLE SNATCH SPRENT TAIGLE TAKING TURNEL ATTRACT CAPTURE ENSNARE GIMMICK GRAPNEL RELEASE SNIGGLE SPRINGE TRIGGER CONTRACT CRANNAGE ENTANGLE FASTNESS HOLDBACK HOLDFAST OVERTAKE SNAPHAAN SURPRISE

(— A FLYBALL) SHAG

(— AT PROPER TIME) NICK

(— ATTENTION) FLAG

(— BIRDS) BATFOWL BIRDLIME

(— EELS) SNIGGLE

(— FIRE) SPUNK IGNITE KINDLE

(— FISH) JAB JIG GILL HANG GILLNET

(— FISH WITH HANDS) GUDDLE GRABBLE HANDFAST

(— HOLD OF) GRIP GRASP

(— IN THE ACT) NAB

(— IN VOICE) FETCH

(— OF DOOR) LATCH SNECK SNICK

(— OF FISH) FARE HAUL SHOT TACK TRIP SHACK

(— ON) GET GETIT

(— ONE'S BREATH) GASP CHINK
(— SIGHT OF) SPY ESPY SPOT
DESCRY
(CRICKET —) DOLLY
(EASY —) POPUP
(RATCHET —) CLICK
(SAFETY —) CLEVIS
CATCHALL RAGBAG
CATCHER TAKER BIRDER FANGER
LARKER RECEIVER
CATCHFLY SILENE FLYBANE
CATCHING CATCHY TAKING
ALLURING ARRESTING
CATCH-PHRASE SLOGAN WHEEZE
CATCHPOLE BAILIFF PUTTOCK
CATCHWEED CLEAVERS
CATCHWORD CUE TAG MOTTO
BYWORD PHRASE SLOGAN
STARTER CATCHCRY SHIBBOLETH
CATCHY CATCHING APPEALING
CATCH-22 DILEMMA
CATECHISE QUIZ
CATECHISM QUIZ GUIDE MANUAL
CARRITCH QUESTIONS
CATECHU COTCH CUTCH KHAIR
GAMBIER
CATECHUMEN PUPIL AUDIENT
AUDITOR CONVERT BEGINNER
NEOPHYTE COMPETENT
CATEGORICAL DIRECT ABSOLUTE
EXPLICIT KNOCKDOWN
CATEGORIZE ZAG CODE HAVE
SORT
CATEGORY WAY KING RANK TALE
CLASS FIELD GENRE GENUS
ORDER STYLE FAMILY LEAGUE
NUMBER RUBRIC SERIES SPECIES
DIVISION PIGEONHOLE
PREDICAMENT
(— OF TENSES) INFECTUM
(BIOLOGICAL —) TAXON
(HIGHEST —) IDEA
(PRIMARY —) SUBSTANCE
(TAXONOMIC —) TAXON FORMA
GENUS TAXON COHORT LEGION
SUBCLASS SUBGENUS SUBFAMILY
CATENARY ARC
CATER CUT FEED HUMOR SERVE
TREAT PANDER PURVEY SUPPLY
PROVIDE
(PREF.) OPSONI OPSONO
CATERCOUSIN PAL FRIEND
CATERER ACATER MANCIPLE
**CATERINA CORNARO (CHARACTER
IN —)** ANDREAS GERARDO
CATERINA MOCENIGO LUSIGNANO
(COMPOSER OF —) DONIZETTI
CATERPILLAR CAT MUGA AWETO
ERUCA CANKER LOOPER PALMER
PORINA RISPER TAILOR WOUBIT
CUTWORM TRACTOR WEBWORM
HANGWORM HORNWORM
SILKWORM SKINWORM
WORTWORM PALMERWORM
(PREF.) CAMPO ERUCI
(SUFF.) CAMPA
CATERWAUL CRY HOWL WAIL
MIAUL WRAWL
CATFACE ARR SCAR
CATFISH MUD CUSK ELOD POUT
RAAD SHAL WOOF BAGRE DORAD
RAASH BARBER DOCMAC GLANIS
GOONCH GOUJON HASSAR

MADTOM MUDCAT BARBUDO
CANDIRU COBBLER FIDDLER
PYGIDID SILURID WALLAGO
BULLHEAD BULLPOUT CORYDORA
FLATHEAD MATHEMEG PLOTOSID
SQUEAKER STONECAT
CATGUT THARM THAIRM CATLING
WHIPCORD
CATHARI BULGARI PATARINE
CATHARTIC ALOIN BRYONY PHYSIC
CALOMEL RHUBARB SCOURER
EUONYMUS EVACUANT
HYDRAGOG KALADANA LAPACTIC
LAXATIVE SCAMMONY SOLUTIVE
SOLUTORY PURGATIVE
PODOPHYLLIN
CATHAYAN KITAN
CATHEDRA SEE
CATHEDRAL DOM SEE DUOMO
SOBOR MARTYRY MEMORIA
MINSTER BASILICA
(PART OF —) ARCH ROOF CROSS
GABLE IMAGE LABEL SPIRE TOWER
BELFRY FINIAL LINTEL LOUVER
PORTAL WINDOW CROCKET
GALLERY LOZENGE MOLDING
MULLION TRACERY TREFOIL
PINNACLE TYMPANUM DRIPSTONE
THROATING TRIFORIUM
CINQUEFOIL CLERESTORY
QUATREFOIL
CATHEXIS CHARGE
CATHODE K KA FILAMENT
ELECTRODE HYDROGODE
CATHOLIC BROAD GENERAL
LIBERAL TOLERANT
(— ORDER) MARIST DOMINICAN
FRANCISCAN
CATHOLICISM PAPISM POPERY
CATHOLICON PANACEA
CATKIN RAG TAG CHAT GULL AGLET
AMENT IULUS PUSSY CACHRYS
CATTAIL GOSLING
(PREF.) AMENTI
CATMINT NEP NIP
CATNAP NAP DOZE
CATNIP NEP CATARIA CATMINT
CATWORT
CATREUS (DAUGHTER OF —)
AEROPE CLYMENE APEMOSYNE
(FATHER OF —) MINOS
(MOTHER OF —) PASIPHAE
(SON OF —) ALTHAEMENES
CAT'S-CLAW LONGPOD
ESCAMBRON
CAT'S CRADLE HEI
CAT'S-EAR GOSMORE CAPEWEED
FLATWEED
CAT'S EYE CHATOYANT
CAT'S-FOOT PUSSYTOE
CAT'S-PAW TOOL PROPERTY
CAT'S-TAIL BULRUSH
CATTAIL DOD DODD FLAG MUSK
RUSH TULE AMENT BAYON BLECK
CLOUD RAUPO REREE WONGA
CATKIN GLADEN TOTORA
BULRUSH GLADDON MATREED
BLACKCAP CARBUNGI FLAXTAIL
CAT THYME HULWORT
CATTLE ZO BOW FEE GIR AVER
DHAN GAUR KINE NEAT NOWT
OXEN ZEBU ZOBO DEVON STOCK
ANKOLI DURHAM GALYAK ONGOLE

ROTHER SINDHI SUSSEX BESTIAL
NELLORE REDPOLL COMPOUND
OUTSIGHT TUBICORN
(— CARRIED OFF) SPREATH
(ASIAN DAIRY —) REDSINDHI
(BREED OF —) ANGUS BORAN
DEVON FJALL KERRY KYLOE SANGA
SANGU ANGONI ANKOLE ANKOLI
DEXTER DURHAM FULANI JERSEY
SUSSEX BAROTSE BRAFORD
BRAHMAN BRANGUS COASTER
CRIOLLA GUZERAT HARIANA
SAHIWAL ALDERNEY AYRSHIRE
CHARBRAY FRIBOURG FRIESIAN
GALLOWAY GUERNSEY HEREFORD
HOLSTEIN KANGAYAM LIMOUSIN
LONGHORN
(DWARF —) NATA NIATA
(WILD YOUNG —) KANGAROO
(PREF.) BOVI
CATTLE-BREEDER AHIR ALUR
CATTLE DEALER DROVER
CATTLEHIDE BUFF CROUPON
CATTLEMAN FAZENDEIRO
CATTLE MARKET SALEYARD
CATTLE PEN KRAAL
CATTLE RAID SPRAITH SPREAGH
CATTLE RUN STATION
CATTLE STEALER ABACTOR
ABIGEUS
CATTLE YARD CANCHA
CATTY KIN KATI SNIDE
CAUCASIAN OSSET WHITE OSSETE
IRANIAN EUROPEAN JAPHETIC
PALEFACE
(— LANGUAGE) UDI UDIC UDIN
(PL.) MELANOI
CAUCHO ULE RUBBER
CAUCUS BLOC PRIMARY
CAUDAL POSTERIOR
(PREF.) UR(O)
CAUDATA URODELA
CAUDEX STEM STIPE
CAUGHT GRIPPIT ENTANGLED
(— AT FAULT) TARDY
CAUL HOW WEB KEEL KELL TRUG
VEIL GALEA HOUVE DORLOT
CREPINE KERCHER NETWORK
OMENTUM MEMBRANE SILLYHOW
TRESSOUR TRESSURE
(PREF.) AMNIO OMENT(O)
CAULDRON KOHUA CALDRON
CAULICLE SCAPEL ROSTELLUM
CAULIFLOWER BROCCOLI
SNOWBALL CHOUFLEUR
CAULK CALK CORK FILL FLAG
CHINSE
CAUNUS (FATHER OF —) MILETUS
(MOTHER OF —) CYANEE
(SISTER OF —) BYBLIS
CAUSAL GENETIC
CAUSE DO AIM GAR ISM KEY LET
WAY CASE CHAT FATE HOTI LEAD
MAKE MOVE ROOT SAKE SPUR
SUIT AGENT ARCHE BASIS BREED
CAUSA FRAME PARTY SETUP SKILL
SLAKE WREAK YIELD ADDICT
CREATE EFFECT ELICIT GOSSIP
GROUND INDUCE INVOKE MALADY
MANNER MATTER MOTIVE OBJECT
ORIGIN PARENT REASON RESORT
SOURCE SPEECH SPRING
CHESOUN CONCERN DISEASE

LAWSUIT PROCURE PRODUCE
PROVOKE QUARREL SUBJECT
BUSINESS ENGENDER GENERATE
INSTANCE MOVEMENT OCCASION
WHEREFORE MAINSPRING
(— A SORE) RANKLE
(— DAMAGE) DAMNIFY
(— FOR COMPLAINT) COMEBACK
(— OF ANXIETY) BUGABOO
(— OF IRRITATION) GALL
(— OF PAIN) DISEASE
(— OF QUARREL) GRUDGE
(— OF RUIN) BANE
(— OF SORROW) GRIEF
(— OF TERROR) AFFRIGHT
(— OF TROUBLE) TRACHLE
(— PAIN) URN
(— TO ARCH) ROACH
(— TO CONTRACT) PUCKER
(— TO CROUCH) COUCH
(— TO DESERT) DEFECT
(— TO END) ACHIEVE
(— TO GO) HAVE
(— TO MOVE RAPIDLY) GIG
(— TO PROJECT) JET
(— TO RESULT) ISSUE
(— TO STICK) MIRE
(— TO SWELL) BINGE EMBOSS
(— TO THICKEN) CURD
(COMMITTED TO A —) ENGAGE
(FINAL —) END
(FORM-GIVING —) IDEA
(IMMEDIATE —) SIGNAL
(PRIMAL —) URGRUND
(PREF.) AETIO AITIO CAUSI ETIO
(SUFF.) FIC(AL)(ATE)(ATION)(ATIVE)
(ATOR)(ATORY)(E)(ENCE)(ENT)(IAL)
(IARY)(IENT) FIQUE
CAUSED
(SUFF.) (— BY) IC(AL)
CAUSER (— OF TROUBLE)
BOLSHEVIK
CAUSERIE CHAT
CAUSEWAY WAY DIKE ROAD
HIGHWAY CHAUSSEE
CAUSING
(SUFF.) ABLE FACIENT FACT(ION)
(IVE)(ORY) FIC IBLE
CAUSTIC LYE ACID TART ACRID
QUICK SALTY SHARP SNELL ACIDIC
BITING BITTER SEVERE BURNING
CAUTERY CUTTING ERODENT
MORDANT NIPPING PUNGENT
PYROTIC SATIRIC ALKALINE
DIERETIC SCATHING SNAPPISH
STINGING ACIDULOUS SARCASTIC
MORDACIOUS
CAUSTICITY ACRIMONY
CAUTERIZATION USTION INUSTION
CAUTERIZE BURN CHAR FIRE SEAR
BRAND INUST SINGE
CAUTERY MOXA
CAUTION CARE FEAR HEED WARN
GUARD ADVICE CAUTEL CAVEAT
EXHORT ANXIETY COUNSEL
PRECEPT PROVISO WARNING
ADMONISH FORECAST FOREWARN
MONITION PRUDENCE WARINESS
CAUTIOUS SHY CAGY SAFE WARE
WARY ALERT CANNY CHARY SIKER
FABIAN HOOLIE SICKER TENDER
TIPTOE CAREFUL CURIOUS
ENVIOUS FEARFUL FERDFUL

GUARDED PRUDENT DISCREET SUSPENSE VIGILANT CAUTELOUS

CAUTIOUSLY CANNY CANNILY CHARILY EASYLIKE GINGERLY TENDERLY

CAVAL
(PREF.) VEN(I)(O)

CAVALCADE RAID RIDE MARCH TRAIN PARADE SAFARI COMPANY JOURNEY PAGEANT

CAVALIER GAY CAVY CURT EASY FINE BOSSY BRAVE FRANK MOUNT RIDER ESCORT KNIGHT BRUSQUE GALLANT HAUGHTY OFFHAND SOLDIER CAVALERO ROYALIST CHAMBERER CHEVALIER COMMANDER

CAVALLA CERO JACK TORO ULUA JUREL CARANX CARANGID CREVALLE SCOMBRID

CAVALLERIA RUSTICANA
(CHARACTER IN —) LOLA ALFIO TURIDDU SANTUZZA
(COMPOSER OF —) MASCAGNI

CAVALRY HORSE HEAVIES CHIVALRY HORSEMEN YEOMANRY

CAVALRYMAN SOWAR SPAHI SUWAR HUSSAR JINETE LANCER REITER ARGOLET COURIER DRAGOON PLUNGER SABREUR TROOPER GENDARME HORSEMAN SILLADAR STRADIOT
(PRUSSIAN —) UHLAN
(PL.) FORAGERS

CAVATINA SOLO

CAVE DEN TIP COVE HOLE LAIR MINE REAR SINK TOSS WEEM ANTAR ANTRE CABIN CACHE CALVE CAVEA CRYPT DELVE FOGOU SLADE SPEOS STORE UPSET BEWARE CAVERN CAVITY CELLAR DUGOUT GROTTO HOLLOW LARDER LUSTER PANTRY PLUNGE SHROUD MANSION RESERVE SPELUNK CASTILLO COLLAPSE OVERTURN MITHRAEUM
(— IN) COLT
(ANIMAL LIVING IN —) TROGLODYTE
(ONE WHO EXPLORES —S) SPELUNKER
(PREF.) SPELEO

CAVEAT BEWARE NOTICE CAUTION WARNING

CAVE-DWELLER HORITE TROGLODYTE

CAVE-DWELLING NATUFIAN
(PREF.) TROGLO

CAVEMAN NEANDERTHAL

CAVER SPELUNKER

CAVERN DEN CAVE COVE GROT HOLE LAIR WEEM CROFT VAULT ANTRUM CAVITY GROTTO HOLLOW SPELUNK
(PREF.) ANTR(O)

CAVERNOUS ERECTILE

CAVESSON CHAIN

CAVETTO GULA GORGE

CAVIAR OVA ROE IKRA GARUM IKARY BELUGA OSETRA OSSETRA SEVRUGA

CAVIL CARK CARP HAFT QUIP HAGGLE CAPTION CHICANE QUARREL QUIBBLE PETTIFOG QUIDDITY FORMALIZE

CAVILER CRITIC GIRDER HAFTER ZOILUS

CAVILING CAPTIOUS CRITICAL PICAYUNE

CAVITIED
(SUFF.) COELOUS COELUS

CAVITY BAG CUP PIT SAC ABRI AXIL CASE CAVE CELL DALK DENT DUCT HOLE MIND MINE VEIN VOID WELL WOMB ABYSS BOSOM BURSA CRYPT DRUSE FOSSA GEODE GOUGE LUMEN MOUTH ORBIT SCOOP SINUS ANTRUM AREOLA AREOLE ATRIUM AXILLA BORING CAECUM CAMERA CAVERN COELIA COELOM COTYLE CRATER DEBLAI GROTTO HOLLOW LACUNA POCKET RECESS SCAPHA SOCKET VACUUM VOMICA ABDOMEN CHAMBER CISTERN CYATHUS DIOCOEL KYATHOS LOCULUS MORTISE VACUITY VACUOLE VESICLE ALVEOLUS BROODSAC EPICOELE FOLLICLE WELLHOLE VESTIBULE
(— IN BONE) LACUNA
(— IN CASTING) PIPE
(— IN FRUIT) VITTA
(— IN GLASS) TEAR
(— IN HEAD OF WHALE) CASE
(— IN HEART) AURICLE
(IN HILLSIDE) ABRI
(— IN LAVA) AMYGDALE AMYGDULE
(— IN MINE) DAG
(— IN ROCK) KETTLE
(— MADE BY SEALS) IGLOO
(— OF SEA-SHELL) FLUE
(ALTAR —) TOMB
(ANATOMICAL —) LUMEN
(BAKING —) OVEN
(BODY —) GUT BELLY CLOACA THORAX ABDOMEN STOMACH PSEUDOCOEL PERICARDIUM
(CHEST —) THORAX
(CRYSTAL-LINED —) VUGG DRUSE GEODE
(DEEP —) WOMB
(EAR —) CONCHA COCHLEA
(GUN —) BORE
(NASAL —) CAVUM
(SUBTERRANEAN —) SLUGGA
(UNFILLED — IN ROCK) VUG
(PREF.) ALVEOL(I)(O) ANTR(O) CAEC(I)(O) CEC(I)(O) CEL(I)(O) COEL(I)(O)
(SUFF.) CELE COELE COELUS

CAVORT PLAY BOUND CAPER CURVET GAMBOL PRANCE

CAVY PACA PONY AGOUTI APEREA CAYUSE CAPYBARA
(FEMALE —) SOW

CAW KA CRY CALL CROAK QUARK QUAWK

CAY ILOT

CAYMAN JACARE

CAYSTER (DAUGHTER OF —) SEMIRAMIS

(FATHER OF —) ACHILLES
(MOTHER OF —) PENTHESILEA

CAYUSE CAVY PONY BRONCO MUSTANG

CEASE HO BOW CUT DIE END LIN BALK BLIN DROP FINE HALT HOLD LIFT LISS QUIT REST SACE SHUT STAY STOP STOW AVAST CLOSE DOWSE LEAVE PAUSE PETER STINT SWICK WAIVE DESIST DEVALL EXPIRE FINISH FORGET ABSTAIN OUTGIVE REFRAIN SUSPEND INTERMIT OVERGIVE SURCEASE
(— FIGHTING) YIELD
(— MILKING COW) SINE
(— TEMPORARILY) LIFT
(— TO ASSERT) ABANDON
(— TO EXIST) VANISH
(— TO FLOW) STANCH STAUNCH

CEASELESS EVER ENDLESS ETERNAL IMMORTAL UNENDING

CEASING CESSER CESSATION

CEBUS SAI

CECILIA SIS SISSU

CECROPS (DAUGHTER OF —) HERSE AGLAUROS PANDROSOS
(WIFE OF —) AGLAURUS

CECUM
(PREF.) TYPHL(O)

CEDAR SUGI TOON SAVIN AROLLA DEODAR SABINA TUMION CYPRESS JUNIPER WAXWING CALANTAS PAHAUTEA

CEDAR SWAMP GREENING

CEDAR WAXWING RECOLLET

CEDE CESS GIVE AWARD GRANT LEAVE WAIVE YIELD ASSIGN RESIGN SUBMIT CONCEDE RENOUNCE TRANSFER

CEDILLA TITTLE

CEIBA KAPOK BENTANG POCHOTE

CEIL LINE SYLE OVERLAY WAINSCOT

CEILING CAP TOP DOME LACE LOFT CHUTT CUPOLA LINING SCREEN SOFFIT SYLING CURTAIN LACUNAR PLAFOND TESTUDO COVERING DECKHAND OVERHEAD PANELING PLANCHER SEMIDOME

CELAENO (FATHER OF —) ATLAS
(MOTHER OF —) PLEIONE
(SON OF —) LYCUS NYCTEUS

CELANDINE FICARY KILLWORT PILEWORT WARTWEED WARTWORT FELONWORT JEWELWEED

CELEBES (GULF OF —) BONE TOLO TOMINI
(ISLAND OF —) MUNA BUTUNG PELENG SULAWESI
(PEOPLE OF —) TORAJA
(TOWN OF —) BUOL LUWUK MANADO MAKASAR

CELEBRANT REVELER

CELEBRATE FETE KEEP SING CHANT DITTY EXTOL HONOR REVEL SACRE SOUND SPEAK BESING CHAUNT EXTOLL PRAISE RECORD RENOWN REPEAT ELEGIZE EXECUTE GLORIFY MAFFICK OBSERVE TRUMPET EMBLAZON EULOGIZE PROCLAIM
(— VICTORY) TRIUMPH
(— 2 MASSES) BINATE DUPLICATE

CELEBRATED KEPT FAMED NOTED FAMOUS EMINENT FEASTED RENOMME STORIED FABULOUS GLORIOUS NOTIFIED OBSERVED RENOWNED

CELEBRATION EED FETE GALA POPE RITE FESTA REVEL COOLIN CUSTOM DOMENT EASTER FIESTA HOOPLA POWWOW RENOWN SIMHAH BLOWOUT HAGMENA HOLIDAY JUBILEE PASCHAL SHINDIG SIMCHAH BINATION BIRTHDAY HOGMANAY MAKAHIKI OCCASION OLYMPIAD POTLATCH SHIVAREE FESTIVITY HOOLAULEA JUNKETING MERRIMENT MILLENIUM
(LIVELY —) RAVEUP
(STUDENT —) GAUDEAMUS
(UNRESTRAINED —) ORGY
(WILD —) ORGY SATURNALIA

CELEBRATOR JUBILIST

CELEBRITY FAME LION NAME STAR CELEB ECLAT RENOWN REPUTE
(PL.) GLITTERATI

CELERITY HASTE HURRY SPEED DISPATCH RAPIDITY VELOCITY SWIFTNESS

CELERY SIT ACHE STICK UMBEL KARPAS SALARY CELERIAC SMALLAGE

CELESTIAL HOLY ASTRAL DIVINE HEAVEN URANIC ANGELIC CHINESE ETHERED EMPYREAL ETHEREAL HEAVENLY OLYMPIAN
(— OBJECT) QUASAR

CELESTITE APOTOME

CELEUS (SON OF —) DEMOPHON TRIPTOLEMUS
(WIFE OF —) METANIRA

CELIBACY CHASTITY VIRGINITY

CELIBATE CLERK CHASTE SINGLE BACHELOR SPINSTER

CELL BOX EGG BAND BOOT CAGE CYTE DISC DISK GERM GONE HOLE JAIL KILL ASCUS CABIN CAROL CLINK CRYPT CYTON FIBER FIBRE GHOST GLAND GROUP OOTID TMEMA TORIL VAULT ZOOID ANAXON CEPTOR COCCUS COOLER CYTODE GAMETE GONIUM INAXON NEURON PRISON SHIELD SIPHON SYPHON WESTON ZYGOTE AGAMETE AMEBULA APOCYTE CELLULE CHAMBER CLOCHAN CLOSTER COCCOID CUBICLE DIPLOID DUNGEON ELEMENT EPICYTE EUPLOID HAPLOID HEMATID INITIAL LOCULUS MYOCYTE NEURONE OOBLAST PAPILLA PLASTID RENETTE SEGMENT SPORONT STEREID TRISOME UTRICLE VESICLE AMACRINE BASOCYTE BASOPHIL BIFORINE BIOPLAST CLOGHAUN DIKARYON FAVEOLUS GLIOCYTE GONIDIUM GONOCYTE HEMOCYTE HOLDOVER IDIOSOME LOCELLUS MYOBLAST ORGANULE PROSORUS RECEPTOR SCLEREID SPERMULE SYNERGID TRACHEID TRIPLOID ZOOBLAST MACROCYTE MICROCYTE MYELOCYTE

OSTEOCYTE PHAGOCYTE
PROGAMETE MELANOCYTE
MOTONEURON NEUTROPHIL
OSTEOCLAST MELANOBLAST
MELANOPHORE ODONTOBLAST
(— CONTAINING LATEX) LATICIFER
(— OF LEADERS) CADRE
(— OF TEMPLE) NAOS
(BEE —) PIPE
(CLUSTER OF —S) MORULA
(DETENTION —) BULLPEN
(DRY —) NICAD
(EGG —) OVUM
(KIND OF —) LIP HELA KILLER
MOTHER
(NERVE —) NEURON NEURONE
(PART OF —) SAP NUCLEUS PLASTID
VACUOLE MEMBRANE CENTRIOLE
ECTOPLASM ENDOPLASM
NUCLEOLUS RETICULUM
CENTROSOME CHONDRIOSOME
(PHOTOELECTRIC —) EYE PEC
PHOTOCELL
(PLANT —) LATICIFER
(PRISON —) BING HOLE CABIN
CLINK COOLER JIGGER
(RECLUSE'S —)) ANCHORAGE
(STAB —) BAND
(THIN-WALLED —S) STOMIUM
(VOLTAIC —) BATTERY
(PL.) SPOR LAURA POTLINE
SWEATBOX
(PREF.) CYT(IO)(O) GAMET(O)
GONIDI ONT(O) THYRE(O) THYRO
(SUFF.) BLAST(IC)(Y) CYTE PHAG(A)
(E)(O)(OUS)(US)(Y) PLASIA PLASIS
PLASM(A)(IA)(IC) PLAST PLATI(IC)(Y)
SPONGIA(E)(N) SPONGIUM THYRIS
CELLA NAOS
CELLAR CAVE VAULT BODEGA
PALACE FAVISSA HYPOGEE
BASEMENT HYPOGEUM
MATAMORO VAULTAGE
(WINE —) BODEGA
CELLARET TANTALUS
CELLARMAN SOMMELIER
CELL-DIVISION MEIOSIS
CELLULAR
(SUFF.) ENCHYMA ENCHYMATA
CELLULOID XYLONITE
CELLULOSE CRUMB AMYLOID
LIGNOSE TAMIDINE
CELT GAEL GAUL KELT MANX IRISH
WELSH BRETON BRITON EOLITH
GADHEL GOIDEL BRYTHON
CORNISH PALSTAFF PALSTAVE
(PL.) CYMRY KYMRY
CELTIC ERSE GAEL SCOTCH
CEMBALO DULCIMER ZIMBALON
CEMENT FIX KIT TIE GLUE HEAL
JOIN KNIT LIME LUTE SLIP BETON
GROUT IMBED PASTE PUTTY
SIMON STICK TABBY UNITE BINDER
CHUNAM COHERE FASTEN FILLER
GULGUL KIBOSH MALTHA MASTIC
MORTAR OOGLEA SOLDER
ASPHALT MIXTION ADHESIVE
ALBOLITE ALBOLITH CEMENTUM
HADIGEON SOLIDIFY SOLUTION
(BEES' —) PROPOLIS
(SUFF.) LITE LITH(IC) LITIC
CEMENTER GLUER GLUEMAN
SMEARER

CEMENT MIXER TEMPERER
CEMETERY HOWF KILL LAIR LITTEN
CHARNEL BONEYARD CATACOMB
GOLGOTHA URNFIELD
NECROPOLIS
CENCHRIAS (FATHER OF —)
POSEIDON
(MOTHER OF —) PIRENE
(SLAYER OF —) ARTEMIS
CENCI (AUTHOR OF —) SHELLEY
(CHARACTER IN —) CENCI MARZIO
ORSINO CAMILLO GIACOMO
OLIMPIO SAVELLA BEATRICE
BERNARDO LUCRETIA
CENERENTOLA, LA (CHARACTER IN
—) TISBE RAMIRO ALIDORO
DANDINI ANGELINA CLORINDA
MAGNIFICO CINDERELLA
(COMPOSER OF —) ROSSINI
CENOBITE NUN MONK FRIAR
ESSENE RECLUSE MONASTIC
SYNODITE
CENOTAPH TOMB
CENSE THURIFY
CENSER INCENSER THURIBLE
CASSOLETTE
CENSOR CRITIC SCREEN SYNDIC
LAUNDER RESTRICT SUPPRESS
CENSORIOUS SEVERE BLAMING
CARPING BLAMEFUL CAPTIOUS
CRITICAL CULPABLE SLASHING
CENSORSHIP WRAPS ASSIZE
CENSURE
CENSURABLE TAXABLE BLAMABLE
CULPABLE
CENSURE BAN HIT NIP RAP TAP TAX
WIG CALL CARP DEEM DRUB FLAY
HELL LASH RATE SLAP TASK WITE
BEANS BLAME CHIDE CURSE
DECRY FAULT HOKER JUDGE
PINCH SCOLD SLANG SLASH SLATE
TAUNT TOUCH WHITE ACCUSE
ATTACK BERATE CHARGE REBUFF
REBUKE REFORM REMORD STRAFE
TARGUE TIRADE APPEACH BLISTER
CHASTEN CONDEMN CONTROL
DECRIAL DYSLOGY IMPEACH
IMPROVE INVEIGH REPROOF
REPROVE SCARIFY TRADUCE
TROUNCE UPBRAID BACKBITE
CHASTISE DISALLOW JUDGMENT
LANGUAGE REPROACH SATIRIZE
SENTENCE STRICTURE
ADMONITION
(GOD OF —) MOMUS
CENSUS LIST POLL CENSE COUNT
LUSTER LUSTRUM CAPITATION
CENT RED DUIT SANT BROWNIE
CENTAVO STUIVER
(FIVE —S) JITNEY NICKEL
(ODD —S) BREAKAGE
(ONE —) PENNY
(TEN —S) DIME
(TWENTY-FIVE —S) QUARTER
(12 1-2 —S) LEVY
CENTAUR CHIRON NESSUS
HORSEMAN BUCENTAUR
SAGITTARY
CENTAURUS (FATHER OF —) IXION
(MOTHER OF —) NEPHELE
CENTAURY BEHN BEHEN SABBATIA
EARTHGALL

CENTENNIAL STATE COLORADO
CENTER COR EYE GIG HUB MID AXIS
CORE NAVE SEAT SNAP YOLK
FOCUS FOYER GLOME HEART
MIDST NEXUS PIVOT SPINE
BOTTOM CENTRE MIDDLE PIPPER
STAPLE TEMPLE CENTRUM
ESSENCE LINEMAN NUCLEUS
UMBILIC INCENTER OMPHALOS
SNAPBACK
(— FOR SPINDLE) GIG
(— FOR TARGET) EYE PIN PINHOLE
(— OF ACTIVITY) HUB HIVE
(— OF ARCH) COOM
(— OF ASSURANCE) FORTRESS
(— OF ATTRACTION) FOCUS STAGE
CYNOSURE POLESTAR
(— OF BASKET) SLATHER
(— OF CITY) DOWNTOWN
(— OF CULTIVATION) HOME
(— OF CULTURE) ATHENS
(— OF DIAMOND) WELL
(— OF ESCUTCHEON) NOMBRIL
(— OF FIGURE) CENTROID
(— OF FISHING NET) BUNT
(— OF FLOWER) EYE
(— OF HURRICANE) EYE
(— OF OPERATIONS) SHOP
(— OF POPULATION) CITY
(— OF POWER) SEE SIEGE
(— OF STAGE) LIMELIGHT
(— OF STRENGTH) GANGLION
(— PIECE) HUB
(BASKETBALL —) PIVOTMAN
(COLLECTION —) ENTREPOT
(COMMERCIAL —) MALL MART
MACHI EMPORIUM
(HARD —) KNOT
(INTIMATE —) BOSOM
(KIND OF —) NERVE
(LATHE —) PIKE
(NERVOUS —) BRAIN NIDUS
(NEURAL —) APPESTAT
(OFF —) ALOP
(PROPAGANDA —) AGITPUNKT
(RECREATION —) ARCADE
(REHABILITATION —) HOSTEL
(SHOPPING —) MALL
(TOWARD —) ENTAD
(TRADING —) BEACH EXCHANGE
(VITAL —) HEARTH HEARTBEAT
(PREF.) CENTR(I)(O)
(SUFF.) CENTRIC
CENTERING COOM COOMB
CENTRY FANTAIL
CENTERPIECE ROSACE DORMANT
EPERGNE DUCHESSE
CENTETES TENREC
CENTIARE LI
CENTIGRADE CELSIUS
CENTIME RAPPEN
CENTIMETER GAL
CENTIPEDE VEI VERI EARWIG
GOLACII GOLOCII POLYPOD
CHILOPOD MULTIPED MYRIAPOD
SANTAPEE SCUTIGER
SCOLOPENDRA
CENTRAL MID AXIAL BASIC CHIEF
FOCAL MIXED POLAR PRIME
MEDIAN MIDDLE CAPITAL CENTRIC
LEADING NUCLEAR PIVOTAL
PRIMARY CARDINAL DOMINANT
(PREF.) CENTR(I)(O)

CENTRAL AFRICAN REPUBLIC
CAPITAL: BANGUI
COIN: FRANC
NATIVE: BAYA SARA BANDA BWAKA
SANGO YAKOMA BANZIRI
MANDJIA
RIVER: BOMU NANA CHARI KOTTO
MBARI MPOKO OUAKA OUHAM
CHINKO LOBAYE SANGHA
UBANGI
TOWN: OBO IPPY BIRAO BOUAR
KEMBE NDELE NGOTO PAOUA
RAFAI ZEMIO BABOUA BAKALA
BANGUI BOZOUM BAMBARI
GRIMARI ZEMONGO BERBERATI
BOSSANGOA

CENTRAL AMERICAN LADINO
(— NATION) BELIZE PANAMA
HONDURAS COSTARICA
(— TREE) TUNO TUNU
CENTRANTH SPURFLOWER
CENTRIFUGAL EFFERENT
RADIATING
CENTRIFUGE CYCLONE SEPARATOR
CENTRIPETAL AFFERENT
CENTROSOME CENTRUM
CENTRIOLE
CENTRUM CORE
CENTURIED SECULAR
CENTURY AGE TON SECLE SIECLE
(14TH —) TRECENTO
(17TH —) SEICENTO
CENTURY PLANT ALOE PITA
AGAVE MAGUEY CANTALA
TEQUILA MONOCARP
CENWALH (FATHER OF —) CYNEGILS
CEPHALALGIA SODA HEADACHE
CEPHALIC CRANIAL ATLANTAL
CEREBRAL
CEPHALOPOD SQUID CUTTLE
INKFISH OCTOPUS SPIRULA
DIBRANCH SCAPHITE
CEPHALOTHORAX PROSOMA
CEPHALUS (FATHER OF —) DEION
(MOTHER OF —) DIOMEDE
(WIFE OF —) PROCRIS
CEPHEUS (BROTHER OF —) DANAUS
AEGYPTUS AMPHIDAMAS
(DAUGHTER OF —) ANDROMEDA
(FATHER OF —) ALEUS BELUS
(MOTHER OF —) ANCHINOE
(WIFE OF —) CASSIOPEA
CERAMIC (— WARE) WEDGWOOD
CERAMICS TILES POTTERY
CERAMUS (FATHER OF —) BACCHUS
DIONYSUS
(MOTHER OF —) ARIADNE
CERASTES ASP VIPER
CERATE WAX LARD SALVE
UNGUENT OINTMENT
CERCYON (DAUGHTER OF —) ALOPE
(FATHER OF —) NEPTUNE
POSEIDON HEPHAESTUS
(SLAYER OF —) THESEUS
CEREAL RYE BEAN BRAN CORN
MUSH OATS RICE SAMP TEFF
ARZUN GRAIN MAIZE SPELT
WHEAT BARLEY BINDER FARINA
HOMINY PABLUM OATMEAL
SOYBEAN PORRIDGE
CEREAL LEAF FLAG

CEREBRAL CEPHALIC INVERTED
(PREF.) PSYCH(O)
CEREBRATION THOUGHT
CEREBROSIDE KERASIN
CEREMENT SHROUD
CEREMONIAL FORM PRIM RITE
STIFF FORMAL RIALTY RITUAL
SOLEMN PRECISE STUDIED
TRIUMPH UPANAYA AVERSION
SPLENDOR
(FOOLISH —) MUMMERY
CEREMONIOUS GRAND LOFTY
STIFF FORMAL PROPER SOLEMN
PRECISE STATELY STUDIED
CEREMONY BRIS FETE FORM GAUD
HAKO ORGY POMP RITE SEAL
SHOW SIGN SING BERIT DANCE
DOSEH STATE ACTION AUGURY
BERITH BRIDAL BURIAL EXEQUY
GOMBAY HOMAGE KERIAH
MALKAH MAUNDY NIPTER OFFICE
PARADE POWWOW REVIEW
RITUAL SALUTE BAPTISM DISPLAY
KIDDUSH MEI AVFH OVATION
PAGEANT PANAGIA PORTENT
PRODIGY TAHARAH ACCOLADE
APOLUSIS ASPERGES COEMPTIO
CRIOBOLY ENCAENIA EXERCISE
FUNCTION HADDALAH HAKAFOTH
HERALDRY MARRIAGE OCCASION
SKEYTING INAUGURAL INDUCTION
ORDINANCE CORONATION
OBSERVANCE
(GRADUATION —) CAPPING
(HAZING —) CREELING
(MARRIAGE —) ESPOUSAL
(TEA —) CHANOYU
(PL.) DEGREE HOLIES AGENDUM
FERALIA JUSTMENTS
CERES DEMETER
(DAUGHTER OF —) PROSERPINE
PHERREPHATTA
(FATHER OF —) SATURN
(MOTHER OF —) VESTA
CERINTHE HONEYWORT
CERO SEARER SIERRA CAVALLA
PINTADO KINGFISH
CERTAIN COLD COOL DEAD FAST
FIRM FREE REAL SEAL SURE TRUE
BOUND CLEAR EXACT FIXED PLAIN
SIKER ACTUAL MEMORY SECURE
SICKER STATED WITTER ASSURED
PERFECT PRECISE SETTLED
SRADDHA ABSOLUTE APPARENT
CONSTANT DEFINITE OFFICIAL
PALPABLE POSITIVE RELIABLE
RESOLVED UNERRING CONFIDENT
CERTAINLY AY AYE WIS AMEN IWIS
SOON SURE WHAT YWIS TRULY
CERTES INDEED PERDIE SICCAR
SICKER SURELY VERILY HARDLY
EVERMORE FORSOOTH SECURELY
NATURALLY
(MOST —) SO
CERTAINTY YEA CERT PIPE SNIP
CINCH POLICY SURETY SURENESS
CONSTANCY
(LACK OF —) SCRUPLE
CERTIFICATE BOND CHIT CHECK
DEMIT JURAT LIBEL SCRIP TALON
TITLE AMPARO ATTEST CEDULA
COUPON INDENT PATENT POTTAH

RETURN TICKET VERIFY CERTIFY
CONSTAT DIPLOMA VOUCHER
WARRANT WAYBILL AEGROTAT
JUDGMENT KABBALAH NAVICERT
REGISTER REGISTRY SECURITY
TESCARIA TESTAMUR TEZKIRAH
NOTARIZATION
(CUSTOMHOUSE —) COCKET
(MARRIAGE —) LINES
(MINER'S —) LICENCE LICENSE
(PILOT'S —) BRANCH
(SERVANT'S —) CHIT
CERTIFICATION PASS STAMP
APPROVAL HECHSHER CLEARANCE
DISCHARGE
CERTIFIED SWORN
CERTIFY AVOW VISE AUDIT SWEAR
AFFIRM ASSURE ATTEST DEPOSE
EVINCE VERIFY WITTER APPROVE
ENDORSE LICENSE TESTIFY
ACCREDIT
CERTITUDE CERTAIN CONFIDENCE
CERULEAN BLUE AZURE COELIN
CYANEAN CYANEOUS
CERUMEN WAX EARWAX
CERVIX NECK
CESS BOG TAX CEDE DUTY LEVY
LUCK RATE ABWAB SLOPE YIELD
IMPOST MEASURE SURRENDER
(BAD —) SORRA
CESSATION HO END HOO BLIN
HALT HUSH LISS LULL REST STAY
STOP BREAK CEASE CLOSE DEVAL
LETUP LISSE PAUSE SLACK STINT
TRUCE CUTOFF DEMISE DISUSE
OFFSET PERIOD RECESS CEASING
CLOSURE RESPITE ABEYANCE
BLACKOUT DESITION INTERVAL
SHUTDOWN STOPPAGE SURCEASE
SUSPENSE
(— OF HOSTILITIES) TRUCE
INDUCIAE ARMISTICE
(— OF LIFE) DEATH
(— OF RESPIRATION) APNEA
APNOEA
(— OF WAR) PEACE
(— OF WORK) HARTAL
(DECREED —) MORATORIUM
(TEMPORARY —) RESPITE
CESSPOOL SINK SUMP SINKER
CISTERN JAWHOLE SINKHOLE
SUSPIRAL
CESTODE POLYZOAN TAPEWORM
CESTRUM POISONBERRY
CESTUS CEST CESTON HURLBAT
GAUNTLET WHIRLBAT
CETACEAN ORC CETE ORCA SUSU
WHALE BELUGA COWFISH
DOLPHIN GRAMPUS NARWHAL
MUTILATE PORPOISE
CETO (BROTHER OF —) PHORCYS
(DAUGHTERS OF —) GRAEAE
GORGONS HESPERIDES
(FATHER OF —) PONTUS
(MOTHER OF —) GAEA
CEYLON (SEE SRI LANKA) SERENDIP
TAPROBANE
CEYLONESE CEYLON BURGHER
CEYLON MOSS GULAMAN
CGS UNIT STILB STOKE
CHA TSIA CHAIS
CHACMA BAVIAN BOBBEJAAN

CHAD
CAPITAL: NDJAMENA
COIN: FRANC FRANCCFA
LAKE: CHAD
NATIVE: ARAB SARA KREDA
MASSA TOUBOU KAMADJA
MOUNDAN
PLATEAU: ENNEDI
RIVER: CHARI SHARI LOGONE
BAHRAOUK
TOWN: ATI BOL LAI MAO FADA
FAYA MONGO ABECHE BOKORO
BONGOR LARGEAU MOUNDOU
FORTLAMY MOUSSORO

CHADOR PHULKARI
CHAETA UNCINUS
CHAETOCHLOA SETARIA
CHAETOPOD SCALEBACK
CHAETURA DRAB BEAR
CHAFE IRK RUB VEX FRET FRIG FROT
FUME GALD GALL HEAT JOSH
RAGE STEW WARM WEAR ANGER
ANNOY CHAFF GRIND SCOLD
SNUFF WORRY WRING ABRADE
BANTER EXCITE FRIDGE HARASS
INJURY NETTLE RANKLE INCENSE
INFLAME SNUFFLE FRICTION
IRRITATE RAILLERY
CHAFER CRESSET
CHAFF GUY HAY PUG RAG ROT
BRAN CAFF CHIP GRIT GUFF JOSH
MOCK PULU QUIZ RAZZ BORAK
CHIAK CHYAK DROSS GLUME
HULLS HUSKS JOLLY RALLY SLACK
STOUR STRAW TEASE TRASH
BANTER BHOOSA REFUSE
CAVINGS TAILING RAILLERY
RIDICULE SHELLING
CHAFFER BANDY SIEVE WARES
BUYING DICKER HAGGLE HIGGLE
MARKET PALTER BARGAIN
CHATTER SELLING TRAFFIC
EXCHANGE
CHAFFINCH PINK CHINK SPINK
TWINK ROBERD SCOBBY SHILFA
SKELLY ROBINET SNABBIE
WETBIRD
CHAFFY SCALY ACEROSE ACEROUS
PALEATE
CHAFING GALLING IMPATIENCE
CHAFING-DISH HEARTH
CHAGRIN ENVY SPITE VEXATION
CHAGRINED SICK ASHAMED
CHAIN FOB GUY NET ROW SET TEW
TIE TOE TOW TUG TYE BIND BOND
CURB FALL FAST FILE GYVE JOIN
LINE LINK SEAL SOAM TEAM BRAII
CABLE GROUP GUARD LEASH
SHANK SHEET SLANG SLING SUITE
TRACE TRAIN WRASE CARCAN
CATENA COLLAR CORDON FASTEN
FETTER GANGER HANGER HOBBLE
JACKER JIGGER LINKER RACKAN
SECURE SERIES STRING TETHER
TOGGLE BOBSTAY CATFALL
CHIGNON CONNECT EMBRACE
ENSLAVE LASHING MANACLE
NETWORK PAINTER PENDANT
SAUTOIR SHACKLE TACKLER
BACKROPE BRACELET CARCANET
GLEIPNIR LINKWORK NECKLACE

RECEPTOR RESTRAIN RIGWIDDY
STROBILA WOOLDING
(— FOR ANCHOR) CATFALL PAINTER
(— FOR BINDING) JACKER TACKLER
(— FOR WRAPPING MAST)
WOOLDING
(— OF AUTHORITIES) ISNAD
(— OF DUNES) SAIF SEIF
(— OF MOUNTAINS) RANGE
(— OF ROCKS) REEF
(— ON CONVICT'S LEG) SLANG
(— TO BIND CATTLE) SEAL
(DECORATIVE —) FESTOON
(ENDLESS —) CREEPER
(KIND OF —) MARKOV
(MAGIC —) GLEIPNIR
(SHORT —) SHANK
(SUSPENDED —) CATENARY
(WATCH —) FOB ALBERT
(PL.) IRONS CONVEYOR
(PREF.) HORMO STREPHO STREPSI
STREPT(O)
CHAIN LINK SHUT COPULA SWIVEL
CHAINMAN CLASHY CLASHEE
LINEMAN TAPEMAN
CHAIN-SHAPED CATENOID
CHAIR KEEP SEAT SHOP HORSE
SEDAN STOOL ESTATE OFFICE
PULPIT ROCKER SADDLE SITTER
TONJON CACOLET COMMODE
FANBACK GONDOLA SITTING
VOYEUSE WINDSOR ARMCHAIR
CARRIAGE CATHEDRA FAUTEUIL
KANGAROO SGABELLO VOLTAIRE
(— FOR PRAYING) PRIEDIEU
(— OF SANCTUARY) FRITHSTOOL
(— OF STATE) THRONE
(— SLUNG FROM POLE) KAGO
TALABON
(— WITH CANOPY) STATE
(BISHOP'S —) CATHEDRA
FALDSTOOL
(EASY —) COGSWELL
(GREEK —) KLISMOS
(KIND OF —) EAMES
(LEAVE THE —) ARISE
(MINING —) DOG
(PART OF —) ARM EAR LEG BACK
POST RUNG SEAT SLAT CREST
SPLAT STILE STUMP ROCKER
ARMREST SPINDLE BACKRAIL
HEADPIECE
(PORTABLE —) SEDAN
(SEDAN —) NORIMONO
(SPRING —) PERCH
(THRONE —) SHINZA
CHAIRMAN HEAD CHAIR EMCEE
PRESES SPEAKER CONVENER
DIRECTOR MODERATOR
PROLOCUTOR
(PREF.) SYMPOSI
CHAISE GIG SHAY CHAIR CALESIN
CARRIAGE CURRICLE
SHANDRYDAN
CHAISE LONGUE DAYBED
DUCHESSE
CHALAZA TREAD TREADLE
GALLATURE
CHALAZION STYE
CHALCEDONY ONYX OPAL SARD
AGATE CHERT PRASE CATEYE
JASPER PLASMA QUARTZ

CARNEOL OPALINE SARDINE SARDIUS ENHYDROS CORNELIAN **(RED —)** CARNELIAN

CHALCIOPE (FATHER OF —) AEETES
(HUSBAND OF —) PHRIXUS
(MOTHER OF —) ASTERODIA
(SISTER OF —) MEDEA
(SON OF —) ARGUS MELAS PHRONTIS CYTISSORUS

CHALCIS (CHILDREN OF —) CURETES CORYBANTES
(FATHER OF —) ASOPUS
(MOTHER OF —) METOPE

CHALCOPYRITE RUN

CHALDEAN SEER KALDANI BABYLONIAN
(— MEASURE) CANE FOOT MAKUK QASAB ARTABA GARIBA GHALVA MANSION
(— RIVER) TIGRIS EUPHRATES
(— TOWN) UR

CHALICE AMA CUP BOWL CALIX GRAIL REGAL GOBLET KRASIS

CHALK CAUK CORK PALE SCAR TALC TICK CRETA FLOUR SCORE BLANCH BLEACH CRAYON CREDIT RUBBLE WHITEN ACCOUNT WHITING
(GREEN —) PRASINE
(HARD —) HURLOCK
(RED —) RUBRIC
(SURVEYOR'S —) KEEL
(PREF.) CALCAREO CALC(I)(IO)(O)

CHALKBOARD GREENBOARD

CHALKSTONE TOPHUS

CHALKY CRETACIC CRETACEOUS

CHALLENGE HEN VIE BRAG CALL DARE DEFY FACE GAGE ASSAY BANCO BLAME BRAVE CLAIM QUERY STUMP ACCUSE APPEAL BANTER CARTEL CHARGE DACKER DAIKER DEMAND DESCRY FORBID IMPUGN INFIRM INVITE RECUSE SERDAB ARRAIGN CENSURE IMPEACH PROVOKE REPROVE SOLICIT SUMMONS CHAMPION DARRAIGN DEFIANCE GAUNTLET QUESTION REPROACH
(— A BULL) CITE

CHALLENGING PIQUANT BLOODSHOT

CHALONE AUTACOID

CHALYBEATE MARTIAL

CHALYBITE SIDERITE

CHAMBER ODA AGER CELL CIST DOME FLAT FOLD HALL IWAN KIVA ROOM SALE TOMB BOWER CAVUM COURT GOMER HOUSE SENAT SHAFT SOLAR SOLER STOVE ATRIUM CAMARA CAMERA COFFER HEADER HOLLOW MIHRAB SENADO SENATE SOLLAR SPRING STANZA WILSON BEDROOM CAISSON CHAI MER CHANNEL CHAUMER CONCAVE CUBICLE FAVISSA FIREBOX GALLERY GEHENNA MANSION RECEIPT CASEMATE CYLINDER DIFFUSER FOUNTAIN GROSSRAT SMOKEBOX SNEMOVNA THALAMUS
(— FOR MOLTEN GLASS) FONT
(— IN FURNACE) SHAFT DOGHOUSE

(— OF EAR) SACCULE UTRICLE
(— POT) JORDAN JEROBOAM
(AIR —) SPONSON
(AUDIENCE —) DURBAR
(BOMBPROOF —) CASEMATE
(CLIMATE CONTROL —) BIOTRON
(FIRE —) ARCH STOVE COCKLE FIREBOX
(FORTIFICATION —) BUNKER
(JUDGE'S —) CAMERA
(OPEN —) LANTERN
(ORGAN —) SWELL
(PERTAINING TO —) CAMERAL
(PISTON —) BARREL
(PRIVATE —) CLOSET CONCLAVE
(PUEBLO —) KIVA ESTUFA
(SLEEPING —) BEDROOM WARDROBE
(SMALL —) LOCULUS
(SUPPLY —) MAGAZINE
(UNDERGROUND —) CAVE CRYPT CAVERN SERDAB HYPOGEE
(WATERTIGHT —) CAISSON
(PREF.) THALAM(I)(O)
(SUFF.) CELE COELE COELUS

CHAMBERLAIN EUNUCH FACTOR SERVANT STEWARD PALATINE POLONIUS

CHAMBERPOT POT JERRY POTTY JORDAN

CHAMELEON ANOLE ANOLI LACERT SAURIAN

CHAMFER BEVEL CHIMB CHIME CHINE FLUTE CIPHER FURROW GROOVE

CHAMOIS GEMS IZARD AOUDAD SHAMMY ANTELOPE

CHAMOMILE MAYWEED MARGUERITE

CHAMONT (SISTER OF —) MONIMIA

CHAMP BITE CHAW FIRM HARD MASH CHANK CHOMP FIELD GNASH TRAMPLE

CHAMPAGNE AY BUBBLY SIMKIN BELLEEK SILLERY CHAMPERS
(IMITATION —) GOOSEBERRY

CHAMPAIGN PLAIN

CHAMPION ACE AID FAN ABET BACK BOSS DEFY HERO KEMP GHAZI ASSERT ATTEND DEFEND KEMPER KNIGHT PATRON SQUIRE VICTOR APOSTLE ESPOUSE FIGHTER PALADIN PROTECT ADVOCATE DEFENDER PALMERIN PROTAGONIST

CHAMPIONING
(PREF.) PRO

CHAMPIONSHIP TITLE LAURELS ADVOCACY

CHAMPLEVE ENAMEL INLAID

CHANCE DIE HAP LOT CASE CAST DINT DRAW FATE LINE LUCK ODDS RISK SHOT SHOW TIDE BREAK ETTLE STAKE WHACK BETIDE CASUAL GAMBLE HAPPEN HAZARD MISHAP RANDOM SQUEAK STRIKE TUMBLE AIMLESS FORTUNE OPENING STUMBLE VANTAGE VENTURE ACCIDENT CASUALTY EVENTUAL FORTUITY QUESTION ALEATORIC OPPORTUNITY PERADVENTURE

(— OF LOSS) RISK
(— OF SUCCESS) PROSPECT
(ADVERSE —) HAZARD
(EVEN —) TOSSUP
(HAPPY-) MERCY
(ILL —) MISHAP
(SLIGHT —) PRAYER
(SLIM —) PRAYER
(UNFORTUNATE —) PITY
(PL.) PROSPECTS
(PREF.) TYCH(O)

CHANCEL BEMA CHOIR ADYTUM

CHANCELLOR LOGOTHETE

CHANCY DODGY ALEATORY

CHANDELIER CORONA LUSTER PHAROS PENDANT CHANDLER GASELIER GIRANDOLE

CHANDLER TALLOWER

CHANE OREJON

CHANGE MEW CHOP FLOP MOLT MOVE ODDS PEAL TURN VARY VEER WARP WEND ADAPT ALTER AMEND BREAK COINS EMEND MOULT SHIFT THROW ADJUST BECOME DIFFER DIGEST IMMUTE MODIFY MUANCE MUTATE REMOVE REVAMP REVISE SWITCH WISSEL WRIXLE COMMUTE CONVERT CUTOVER DEVIATE FLUXION MORTIFY BECOMING DENATURE EXCHANGE INNOVATE LENITION MUTATION REVISION TRANSFER TRANSUME VARIANCE PERMUTATION METAMORPHY MODIFICATION METAMORPHOSIS
(— APPEARANCE) DISGUISE
(— BACK) REVERT
(— COLOR) TURN
(— COURSE) GYBE JIBE
(— DIRECTION) CUT CANT CHOP HAUL KNEE VEER ANGLE BREAK SHIFT
(— FOR BETTER) HELP
(— FORM) DEVELOP
(— FOR WORSE) BEDEVIL
(— GAIT) BREAK
(— GRADUALLY) PASS GRADUATE
(— IN COURSE) SHEER
(— IN DIRECTION) JOG KNEE STEP
(— IN ELEVATION) FORK
(— IN LAKE LEVEL) SEICHE
(— IN SIZE) ASTOGENY
(— INTO VAPOR) FLASH
(— MONEY) WISSEL
(— OF FORM) SET
(— OF FORTUNE) PERIPETY
(— OF GEAR) KICKDOWN
(— OF HABITAT) MIGRATE
(— OF KEY) TRANSITION
(— OF LIFE) MENOPAUSE
(— OF MIND) CAPRICE
(— OF MOOD) VARY
(— OF PITCH) MOTION INFLECT
(— OF POLICY) TACK
(— OF POSITION) KINESIS
(— OF SEA LEVEL) EUSTACY
(— OF SOUND) BREAKING
(— OF WORD) ANAGRAM
(— ONE'S HEART) REPENT
(— PACE) BREAK
(— POSITION) STIR FLEET HOTCH
(— QUICKLY) FLY
(— RESIDENCE) FLIT

(— SHAPE) DRAW CREEP DEFORM
(— SIDES) RAT
(ABNORMAL —) LESION
(ABRUPT —) DOGLEG SALTATION
(GEAR —) KICKDOWN
(GRADUAL —) DRIFT
(MAKE NO —) STANDPAT
(ONE WHO OPPOSES —) AGINNER
(PRESSURE —) ALLOBAR
(SHORT —) FLUFF
(SMALL —) GROCERY
(UNEXPECTED —) SWITCH
(PL.) DOUBLES PLASTIQUE
(PREF.) ALLAGO ALLASSO AMOEBI AMOEBO MUTA MUTO
(SUFF.) MUTE

CHANGEABLE EEMIS GIDDY IMMIS LIGHT WINDY CHOPPY FICKLE FITFUL GERFUL KETCHY LABILE MOBILE MOTLEY MUABLE SHIFTY WANKLE BRUCKLE ERRATIC MUTABLE PROTEAN UNSTAID VARIANT VARIOUS VOLUBLE AMENABLE CATCHING GLIBBERY MOVEABLE SKITTISH TICKLISH UNSTABLE VARIABLE VEERABLE VOLATILE WEATHERY CHAMELEON VERSATILE

CHANGEABLENESS LEVITY CAPRICE VIBRATION

CHANGED VARIED ANOTHER
(PREF.) META

CHANGEFUL FICKLE SHIFTY MUTABLE RESTLESS

CHANGELESS CONSISTENT

CHANGELING AUF AWF OAF DOLT FOOL CHILD DUNCE IDIOT WAVERER IMBECILE KILLCROP RENEGADE TURNCOAT

CHANGEOVER SWITCH

CHANGING FLUXIBLE ALTERNATE
(— MONEY) AGIO
(CONTINUALLY —) FLOATING

CHANK SANK CONCH

CHANNEL CUT GAT POD REE RUT SOW CANO CAVA DEEP DIKE DUCT DYKE FLUE GATE GOOL GOTE GOUT GURT KILL KYLE LAKE LANE PACE PIPE RACE SLEW SLOO VALE VEIN WADI WADY WASH BAYOU CANAL CARRY CHASE COWAL DITCH DRAIN DRILL FLUME FLUTE GLYPH GUIDE INSET LATCH QUIRK RIVER SINUS SLIDE SOUND STOOL STOVE STRIA SWASH AIRWAY ALVEUS ARROYO ARTERY BRANCH COURSE CUTOFF ESTERO FURROW GROOVE GULLET GUTTER HOLLOW KENNEL KEYWAY LAGOON MEDIUM OFFLET OILWAY RABBET RESACA RIVOSE RUNWAY SLOUGH SLUICE SPECUS STRAIT STRAND STREAM THROAT TROUGH CHAMFER CONDUCT CONDUIT CULVERT CUNETTE EURIPUS OFFTAKE PASSAGE RACEWAY RIVULET SHIPWAY SILANGA STRIGIL THALWEG TIDEWAY WASHOUT AQUEDUCT FLOODWAY GUIDEWAY GUNKHOLE RACELINE SCOURWAY SPILLWAY CANNELURE

(**— FOR MOLTEN METAL**) SOW GATE RUNNER
(**— IN CLOTH**) FLUTE
(**— IN ICE FIELD**) LEAD
(**— IN MOLD**) SPRAY
(**— OF AQUEDUCT**) SPECUS
(**— OF BRAIN**) ITER
(**— ON A DECK**) CHIMB CHIME
(**— ON WHALE**) SCARF
(**ARTIFICIAL —**) GAT GOUT
(**DRAINAGE —**) GAW
(**ENGLISH —**) SLEEVE
(**INCLINED —**) SHOOT
(**INFORMATION —**) PIPELINE
(**IRRIGATION —**) AUWAI DROVE
(**LYMPH —**) CISTERNA
(**SECONDARY —**) BINNACLE
(**SLOPING —**) CHUTE SHUTE
(**PREF.**) CANALI RHYN(O) SOLEN(O) VAS(I)(O)

CHANNELBILL RAINFOWL
CHANNELED FLUTED
CHANT CANT MELE SING SONG TONE CAROL PSALM SOUGH ANTHEM CANTUS INTONE LITANY MANTRA WARBLE CHORTLE INTROIT PROSODE REQUIEM WORSHIP ALLELUIA ANTIPHON CANTICLE INTONATE SINGSONG PLAINSONG CANTILLATE
CHANTER STICK CANTOR SINGER BAGPIPE SONGSTER CHALUMEAU
(**— OF BAGPIPE**) OBOE
CHANTERELLE CANTINO
CHANTING RAP CHARM HAZANUT ANTIPHONY CHAZZANUT
CHANTLATE SPROCKET
CHANTRY CAGE
CHAOS NU NUN PIE APSU GULF HYLE MESS VOID ABYSS BABEL CHASM BEDLAM JUMBLE MATTER TOPHET ANARCHY MIXTURE DISORDER SHAMBLES TAILSPIN TOHUBOHU
CHAOTIC MUDDLED CONFUSED FORMLESS TUMULTUARY
CHAP BOY BUY DOG LAD MAN RAP WAG BEAN BEAT BIRD BLOW CHIP CHOP COVE DICK DUCK HIND JOHN KIBE MASH MATE NABS SNAP BILLY BLOKE BUCKO BULLY BUYER CHAFT CHINK CLEFT CRACK FRUIT KNOCK LOVER RUMMY SCOUT SPLIT SPORT SPRAY SWIPE TRADE YOUTH BARTER BOHUNK BREACH BUGGER CALLAN CHOOSE CODGER CUFFIN FELLOW FOUTER FOUTRA GAFFER GEEZER JOSSER KIPPER SHAVER STRIKE STROKE TURNIP BASTARD BROTHER CALLANT FISSURE HUSBAND ROUGHEN BLIGHTER CUSTOMER DIVISION MERCHANT
(**— HANDS**) RACK SPRAY
(**— IN SKIN**) KIN KIBE
(**FINE —**) BULLY
(**OLD —**) BO GEEZER
(**PLUCKY —**) COCK
(**QUEER —**) GALOOT
(**S.AFRICAN —**) KEREL
(**YOUNG —**) GAFFER
(**PL.**) CHOPS

CHAPARRAL MONTE CHAMISAL BUCKTHORN
CHAPARRO YAYA
CHAPBOOK CHAP GARLAND
CHAPE CRAMPET MORDANT
CHAPEL CAGE CAPE COPE COWL HOOD CLOAK CRYPT PORCH SALEM BETHEL BEULAH CHARRE CHURCH HAIKAL MORADA SHRINE CAPELLA CHANTRY CHAPLET CHARNEL CHHATRI GALILEE MARTYRY MEETING MEMORIA ORATORY SACRARY SERVICE BETHESDA DEACONRY DIACONIA FERETORY FERETRUM PARABEMA SACELLUM SODALITY
(**UNDERGROUND —**) SHROUDS
CHAPERON HOOD ATTEND DUENNA ESCORT MATRON GRIFFIN PROTECT GUARDIAN SHEEPDOG TRAPPING
CHAPLAIN PADRE LEVITE ALMONER CONDUCT ALTARIST ORDINARY
CHAPLAINCY SCARF
CHAPLET BEAD ORLE STUD CROWN ANADEM ANCHOR CIRCLE FILLET JAMBER JAMMER ROSARY STAPLE TROPHY WREATH CORONAL CORONET GARLAND MOULDING NECKLACE ORNAMENT
(**PREF.**) STEMMATI
CHAPLIN (**WIFE OF —**) OONA
CHAPMAN CHAP BUYER DEALER HAWKER TRADER COPEMAN PEDDLER CUSTOMER MERCHANT
CHAPPIE JOCKEY
CHAPS FLEWS BREECHES LEGGINGS OVERALLS
CHAPTER BODY CELL PACE POST CAPUT COURT LODGE BRANCH CABILDO CAPITAL CORRECT COUNCIL MEETING SECTION ASSEMBLY
(**— OF BOOK**) CAPITAL
(**— OF KORAN**) SURA SURAH
(**— OF SOCIETY**) CAMP CIRCLE
CHAPTER-HOUSE FRATRY
CHAR BURN CART COAL SEAR BROIL CHARK CHORE SHARD SINGE TROUT SCORCH BLACKEN CHARIOT TORGOCH REDBELLY SAIBLING SALMONID SANDBANK
(**PL.**) SALVELINI
CHARA MUSKGRASS
CHARACIN DORADO DOURADE BLOODFIN
CHARACTER AURA BALL BENT CARD CASE CLAY CLEF DASH ECAD FLAT FOND FORM HAIR KIND MAKE MARK MOLD NOTE PART ROLE RUNE SIGN SORT TONE TRIM TYPE BRAND COLOR ETHIC ETHOS FIBER HABIT HEART HUMOR INDEX SAVOR STAMP TENOR TOKEN TRAIT WRITE CARACT CIPHER COCKUP DAGGER DIRECT EMBLEM FIGURE GENIUS HANGER LETTER MANNER METTLE NATURE REPUTE SIGLUM SPIRIT STRIPE SYMBOL CALIBER CLOTHES EDITION ENGRAVE ESSENCE IMPRESS QUALITY CAPACITY FRACTION IDENTITY IDEOGRAM INFERIOR

INSCRIBE LIGATURE SELFHOOD SYLLABIC DESCENDER PARAGRAPH PERSONAGE
(**— IN DRAMA**) CHORUS
(**— IN PLAY**) DAME BESSY
(**— OF SOIL**) LAIR
(**ASSUMED —**) ROLE FIGURE INCOGNITO
(**BAD —**) DROLE BUDMASH
(**BASIC —**) BOTTOM
(**CELTIC —**) OGAM OGHAM
(**CHIEF —**) AGONIST
(**CHINESE —**) SHOU RADICAL
(**COMIC —**) PIERROT
(**COMMON —**) COMMUNITY
(**ESSENTIAL —**) ALLOY
(**FICTIONAL —**) PERSONA
(**FIRM —**) BACKBONE
(**GIVE — TO**) TONE
(**GREEK —**) SAMPI
(**JAPANESE —S**) HIBUNCI
(**MENDELIAN —**) ALLEL ALLELE
(**PHYSICAL —**) ARMENOID
(**PRIME —**) ESSENCE
(**SHIFTLESS —**) BEAT
(**STOCK —**) BESSY MACCUS
(**TESTED —**) ASSAY
(**TRIED —**) TOUCH
(**VULGAR —S**) ONMUN
(**PL.**) MANA
(**SUFF.**) ERY
(**HAVING — OF**) IC(AL)
CHARACTERISTIC CAST COST MARK MIEN ANGLE AROMA GRACE POINT TACHE TOKEN TRAIT TRICK ACCENT BEAUTY NATURE STIGMA STROKE ADJUNCT AMENITY FEATURE IMPRESS QUALITY SPECIES TYPICAL ACTIVITY HEADMARK PECULIAR PROPERTY SYMBOLIC PARAMETER PROPRIETY PECULIARITY PARTICULARITY QUALIFICATION
(**— OF ANTIBODIES**) AVIDITY
(**— OF PARTICLES**) CHARM
(**ADVENTITIOUS —**) ACCIDENT
(**DISTINGUISHING —**) SPECIES HALLMARK BIRTHMARK
(**PECULIAR —**) IDIOPATHY
(**PL.**) CORNERS FACULTY
(**SUFF.**) IC(AL)
(**— OF**) ISH ISTIC LY
CHARACTERIZATION ELOGY ELOGIUM
CHARACTERIZE MARK STYLE DEFINE DEPICT TITULE ENGRAVE ENTITLE IMPRINT PORTRAY DESCRIBE INDICATE INSCRIBE
CHARACTERIZED
(**SUFF.**) (**— BY**) AL FUL IAL IC(AL) LEW
CHARACTERLESS INANE
CHARADES GAME
CHARCOAL COAL CARBO CHARK CARBON FUSAIN PENCIL BLACKEN SPODIUM SCRIBBET
CHARD BEET
CHARGE FEE LAP LAY RAP TAX BEEF BILL BUCK CALL CARE CARK CAST COST CURE DUES DUTY FILL GIBE KEEP LADE LIEN LOAD NICK NOTE ONUS RACK RATE REST RUSH

SHOT SIZE SOAK SPAR TASK TOLL WARD WIKE AGIST BLAME CAUSE CHALK COUNT CRIME DEBIT EXTRA GYRON ONSET ORDER PRICE REFER SCORE SHOCK STICK STING THING TRUST ACCUSE ADJURE ALLEGE APPEAL ASSESS ATTACK BEHEST BURDEN CAREER CENSUS COURSE CREDIT DAMAGE DEFAME DEMAND DITTAY ENJOIN ENURNY EXCESS IMPOSE IMPUTE METAGE OBJECT OFFICE PIPAGE REATUS SURMIT SURTAX TARIFF TOWAGE WEIGHT ACIDIZE ANNULET ARRAIGN ARTICLE ASCRIBE ASSAULT AVERAGE BOATAGE CARTAGE CENSURE CHEVRON CLAMPER COMMAND CONCERN CONJURE CORKAGE CORNAGE CUSTODY DOCKAGE DRAYAGE EMBASSY EXPENSE FLOTAGE HAULAGE IGNITER IMPEACH KEEPING MANDATE MILEAGE MISSION MIXTURE MOORAGE PANNAGE QUAYAGE REPRISE SIDEAGE SLANDER SLIDAGE SURMISE WARPAGE BILLBACK BRASSAGE CASUALTY CHASTISE CRESCENT DELAYAGE DENOUNCE LEGATION ORDINARY OVERLOAD PLANKAGE POUNDAGE PROVINCE QUESTION SLINGING SPENDING STANDAGE TUTORAGE VIGORISH COMPLAINT ACCUSATION ACCUSEMENT
(**— AGAINST**) TILT
(**— BATTERY**) SOAK BOOST
(**— EXCESSIVELY**) FLEECE
(**— FALSELY**) SURMISE
(**— FOR GRAZING**) AGIST
(**— OF FIREARM**) LOAD AMORCE
(**— OF MENTAL ENERGY**) CATHEXIS
(**— OF METAL**) HEAT
(**— OF ORE**) POST
(**— TO BE PAID**) LAW
(**— UPON PROPERTY**) LIEN
(**— WITH CRIME**) ACCUSE DELATE INDICT ARTICLE ATTAINT IMPEACH
(**— WITH GAS**) AERATE
(**AGGREGATE —S**) BOOK
(**CANNON —**) GRAPE
(**COVER —**) COUVERT
(**DEPTH —**) CAN ASHCAN
(**EXPLOSIVE —**) CAP BLAST SNAKE SQUIB TULIP BOOSTER BURSTER IGNITER
(**FALSE —**) CALUMNY
(**HERALDIC —**) DELF DROP GIRON GYRON LABEL BEZANT BILLET DRAGON GURGES BEARING ESQUIRE
(**MAILING —**) FRANKAGE
(**POWDER —**) GRAIN
(**SHAPED —**) BEEHIVE
(**SPIRITUAL —**) CURE
(**TEMPORARY —**) CARE
(**WINE —**) CORKAGE
CHARGEABLE GUILTY
CHARGED UP HOT LADEN BELAST BILLETY BILLETTE ELECTRIC INSTINCT
(**— WITH EMOTION**) SWOLLEN

CHARGEHAND CLICKER
CHARGEMAN BLASTER
CHARGER DISH HORSE MOUNT
STEED ACCUSER COURSER
PLATTER TROOPER
CHARILY FRUGALLY GINGERLY
CHARIOT CAR BIGA CART CHAR
RATH WAIN BUGGY CHAIR ESSED
RATHA TRIGA WAGON CHARET
QUADRIGA
CHARIOTEER AURIGA CARTER
DRIVER IOLAUS LEADER CARTARE
WAGONER MYRTILUS
AUTOMEDON
CHARITABLE KIND BENIGN
HUMANE LENIENT LIBERAL
GENEROUS
CHARITY ALMS DOLE GIFT LOVE
PITY RUTH MERCY BASKET
BOUNTY CARITAS HANDOUT
LARGESS LENIENCE TZEDAKAH
(SYMBOL OF —) PELICAN
CHARIVARI BABEL SHALLAL
SERENADE SHIVAREE
CHARLATAN FAKE CHEAT FAKER
FRAUD QUACK CABOTIN EMPIRIC
IMPOSTER MAGICIAN SYCOPHANT
MOUNTEBANK QUACKSALVER
CHARLES II DAVID
CHARLIE MCCARTHY STOOGE
CHARLOCK KRAUT RUNCH
HARLOCK KEDLOCK KERLOCK
MUSTARD SINAPIS YELLOWS
CHARDOCK CHEDLOCK SKEDLOCK
SKELLOCH
CHARM IT GBO KEY OBI CALM CHIC
HAND JINX JUJU JYNX LUCK MOJO
PLAY RUNE SNOW SONG TAKE TILL
ZOGO ALLAY AROMA BRIEF CATCH
FAVOR FREET FREIT GRACE LAMIN
MAGIC OBEAH OOMPH SAFFI
SAFIE SPELL VENUS WANGA
WEIRD ALLURE AMULET BEAUTY
CARACT DEASIL DISARM ENAMOR
ENGAGE ENTICE FETISH GLAMOR
GRIGRI INCANT MANTRA MELODY
PLEASE SAPHIE SCARAB SOOTHE
SUBDUE SUMMON VOODOO
ABRAXAS ASSUAGE ATTRACT
BEGUILE BEWITCH CANTION
CANTRIP CONJURE CONTROL
DELIGHT ENCHANT ENTHRAL
FLATTER HEITIKI PERIAPT PHILTER
PHILTRE SINGING SORCERY
BLESSING BRELOQUE COMETHER
COQUETRY ENTHRALL ENTRANCE
GLAUMRIE GREEGREE PISHOGUE
PRACTICE TALISMAN CAPTIVATE
MAGNETIZE PATERNOSTER
(MAGNETIC —) CHARISMA
CHARMED CAPTIVE
CHARMER HOURI SIREN EXORCIST
MAGICIAN SORCERER ENCHANTER
CHARMING LEPID SWEET GOLDEN
WIZARD AMIABLE DARLING
EYESOME TEMPEAN WINNING
WINSOME ADORABLE DELICATE
GRACEFUL LOVESOME
PICTURESQUE
CHARNEL GHASTLY CEMETERY
GOLGOTHA
CHARNEL-HOUSE OSSUARY
GOLGOTHA

CHARON (FATHER OF —) EREBUS
(MOTHER OF —) NOX
CHARPOY BED COT
CHARQUI JERKY XARQUE
CHART MAP BILL CARD MARK PLAN
PLAT PLOT ROSE CARTE GRAPH
SCORE STILL RECORD SCHEME
DIAGRAM EMAGRAM EXPLORE
ISOTYPE OUTLINE PROJECT
DOCUMENT DOPEBOOK
MERCATOR PLATFORM
(— BOOK) WAGONER
(— FROM AIR) AEROVIEW
(— MARK) VIGIA
(— OF A COURSE) RUTTER
(MARINER'S —) ROSE RUTTER
(WEATHER —) ANALOGUE
NEPHANALYSIS
CHARTER FIX LET BOND BOOK
DEED HIRE RENT CARTE CHART
FUERO GRANT LEASE SANAD
CHARTA PERMIT SUNNUD
DIPLOMA CONTRACT GRUNDLOV
HEIRLOOM LANDBOOK
MONOPOLY PANCHART
CHARTERHOUSE OF PARMA
(AUTHOR OF —) STENDHAL
(CHARACTER IN —) GINA CONTI
DONGO MOSCA CLELIA FAUSTA
GILETTI FABRIZIO FERRANTE
MARIETTA PIETRANERA
CHARWOMAN CHARER CHARLADY
PORTRESS JANITRESS
CHARY SHY DEAR WARY CHERE
SCANT SPARE DAINTY FRUGAL
PRIZED SKIMPY CAREFUL CURIOUS
SPARING CAUTIOUS HESITANT
PRECIOUS RESERVED SPAREFUL
VIGILANT
CHASE FOG SIC SUE FALL HUNT
JERL SHAG SHOO SICK ANNOY
CATCH CHEVY CHIVY DRIVE HARRY
HOUND SCORE SHACK CACCIA
CHIVVY CHOUSE EMBOSS FOLLOW
FRIEZE FURROW GALLOP GROOVE
HALLOO HARASS HOLLOW INDENT
PURSUE QUARRY SCORSE TRENCH
CHANNEL ENGRAVE HUNTING
PURSUIT ORNAMENT PURCHASE
(— GAME) COURSE
(— HARD) RATTLE
CHASER RAM DRINK HOUND
FROGGER
(WOMAN —) SHEEPBITER
CHASING CISELURE
(— OF GAME) DRIVE
CHASM GAP KIN PIT GULF RIFT
YAWN ABYSS BLANK CANON
CHAOS CLEFT GORGE BREACH
CANYON HIATUS FISSURE
MEGARON SWALLOW VACANCY
APERTURE CREVASSE INTERVAL
VACATION
CHASSE SLIP GLIDE SASHAY
CHASSEUR HUNTER BELLBOY
DOORMAN FOOTMAN HUNTSMAN
CHASSIS SASH FRAME FIGURE
CHASTE CAST PURE ATTIC CLEAN
ZONED DECENT HONEST MODEST
PROPER SEVERE VESTAL VIRGIN
CLEANLY PUDICAL REFINED
CELIBATE INNOCENT VIRGINLY
VIRTUOUS CONTINENT

CHASTEN RATE ABASE SMITE
SMOTE SNEAP SOBER HUMBLE
PUNISH REBUKE REFINE SUBDUE
TEMPER AFFLICT CENSURE
CORRECT NURTURE CHASTISE
MODERATE RESTRAIN
CHASTISE BEAT FIRK FLOG LASH
SLAP TRIM WHIP AMEND BLAME
FEEZE SCOLD SPANK SPILL STRAP
TAUNT ACCUSE ANOINT BERATE
CHARGE DISPLE PUNISH PURIFY
REBUKE REFINE STRAFE SWINGE
TEMPER THRASH TICKLE CHASTEN
CORRECT REPROVE SCOURGE
SHINGLE SUSPECT CASTIGATE
CHASTISEMENT ROD HELL TOCO
TOKO CENSURE PAYMENT
FLOGGING
(DIVINE —) WRATH
CHASTITY HONOR PURITY VIRTUE
HONESTY MODESTY PUDENCY
CELIBACY GOODNESS PUDICITY
INNOCENCE
CHASUBLE CASULA DEACON
INFULA PLANET PAENULA PIANETA
VESTMENT
CHAT GAS JAW MAG RAP BIRD CHIN
CONE COZE DISH GIST TALK TELL
TOVE TWIG YARN AMENT CAUSE
COOSE CRACK DALLY PITCH POINT
PRATE PROSE PROSS SPEAK SPIKE
VISIT BABBLE BRANCH CATKIN
CONFAB COURSE DEVICE GABBLE
GIBBER GOSSIP GOSTER HOBNOB
JABBER NATTER POTATO POTTER
SAMARA CHAFFER CHATTER
SHMOOZE CAUSERIE CHATTERY
CONVERSE SCHMOOZE SPIKELET
STROBILE
CHATEAU HOUSE TOWER CASTLE
MANSION SCHLOSS CHATELET
FORTRESS
CHATON BASIL BEZEL BEZIL STONE
COATING SETTING
CHATTEL CATTLE PLEDGE
DEODAND FIXTURE CATALLUM
PERSONAL
(DISTRAINT OF —S) NAAM
(PL.) STUFF FARLEU FARLEY
COMODATO HOUSEHOLD
CHATTER GAB JAW MAG RAP YAK
YAP BLAB CARP CHAT CHIN CLAP
CLAT DISH GASH HACK KNAP RICK
TALK TEAR YIRR CABAL CLACK
CLASH GARRE HAVER PRATE
SHAKE BABBLE BRUDGE CACKLE
CLAVER GABBLE GIBBER GOSSIP
JABBER JANGLE JARGON PALTER
RATTLE SHIVER TATTER TATTLE
TINKLE YAMMER YATTER BLABBER
BRABBLE CHACKLE CHAFFER
CHIPPER CHITTER CLACKET
CLATTER CLITTER GABNASH
NASHGOB PALAVER PRABBLE
PRATING PRATTLE SHATTER
SMATTER TRATTLE TWATTLE
TWITTER TWITTLE WHITTER
BABBLING LOLLYGAG SCHMOOSE
SCHMOOZE VERBIAGE
(SUFF.) LALIA
CHATTERBOX JAY MAG PIET
BUCCO CLACK CRYSTE GOSSIP
MAGPIE

CHATTERER JAY MAG PIE BLAB
CHUET CHEWET GABBER MAGPIE
RATTLE HAVERER
CHATTERING PIET BABBLY
CHAVISH POPPING TWITTER
BABBLING
CHATTY CHIRRUPY GARRULOUS
CHAUFFEUR DRIVER SHOVER
TESTER
CHAUVINISM JINGOISM
CHAUVINIST JINGO JINGOIST
CHAW JAW VEX CHEW ENVY MULL
GRIND PONDER
CHAYOTE CHOCHO TALLOTE
HUISQUIL MIRLITON
CHEAP LOW BASE GAIN POOR VILE
BORAX CLOSE FLASH GAUDY
GROSS KITCH LIGHT MUCKY NASTY
PRICE SNIDE TATTY TIGHT TINNY
VALUE ABJECT BRUMMY CHEESY
COMMON CRUMBY CRUMMY
JITNEY LEADEN PLENTY SHODDY
SLEAZY SORDID STINGY TAWDRY
TRASHY UNDEAR BARGAIN
CHINTZY POPULAR TINHORN
INFERIOR PENNORTH SIXPENNY
TWOPENNY BRUMMAGEM
PINCHBECK
(— ITEM) TWOFER
(PREF.) VILI
CHEAPEN DOCK STALE VILIFY
SMALLEN
CHEAPSKATE PIKER STIFF
CHEAT DO BAM BOB COG CON FOB
FOP FUB GIP GUM GYP JIG NIP TOP
BEAT BILK BITE BULL BURN CLIP
COLT CRIB DISH DUFF DUPE FAKE
FIRK FLAM FLUM GECK GULL HAVE
HOAX HOSE JILT JINK JOUK KNAP
LIAR MACE MUMP NAIL NICK NOSE
POOP PULL REAM ROOK SCAM
SELL SHAM SILE SKIN SLUR SNAP
SWAP SWOP TRIM WEED WIPE
BITCH BLINK BOOTY BUNCO
BUNKO COZEN CROOK CULLY
DODGE FAKER FLING FOIST FOURB
FRAUD FUDGE GLEEK GOUGE
GREEK GUILE HOCUS KNAVE
LURCH MULCT PINCH PLOAT
RATON ROGUE SCAMP SCREW
SHARP SHORT SLANG SPOIL STICK
STIFF STING SWICK SWIKE TOUCH
TRICK VERSE WRINK BAFFLE
BLANCH BUBBLE BUCKET CHIAUS
CHISEL CHOUSE CLOYNE COGGER
DADDLE DECEIT DELUDE DERIDE
DIDDLE DOODLE DUFFER EMUNGE
EUCHRE FIDDLE FLEECE GAZUMP
GREASE HUMBUG HUMMER
HUSTLE ILLUDE INTAKE JOCKEY
NIGGLE NOBBLE NUZZLE OUTWIT
RADDLE RENEGE RIPOFF SHAVER
SHICER SNUDGE SUCKER TWICER
ABUSION BEGUILE BUBBLER
CHICANE COZENER CULLION
DECEIVE DEFRAUD ESCHEAT
FAITOUR FINAGLE FINESSE
FOISTER GUDGEON JUGGLER
MISLEAD PLUNDER QUIBBLE
SHARPER SHIFTER SKELDER
SLICKER SWINDLE VERNEUK
ARTIFICE BEJUGGLE CHALDESE
CHISELER DELUSION HOODWINK

IMPOSTOR INTRIGUE OUTREACH OVERTAKE PICAROON SHAMMOCK SWINDLER BAMBOOZLE CIRCUMVENT SHORTCHANGE
CHEATED SOLD
CHEATER BITE GULL SPEC KNAVE BILKER INTAKE TOPPER SHARPER FINAGLER TREACHER
CHEATING HOCUS BARRAT ODLING ABUSIVE FUBBERY MICHERY ROGUERY CHEATERY JUGGLING TRICKERY
CHECH DUD BOUNCER
CHECK BIT DAM HAP LID NAB NIP SAY SET TAB BAIL BALK BEAT BILK BILL CHIP CHIT COOK CRIB CURB DAMP FACE FOIL GAGE HURT ITEM KITE PAWL REIN SKID SNEB SNIB SNIP SNUB STAY STEM STOP STUB TAKE TEST TICK TRIG TURN TWIT WERE ABORT ALLAY ANNUL BAULK BLOCK BRAKE CATCH CHIDE CHILL CHING CHOKE CRACK CROOK DAUNT DELAY DETER DRAFT EMBAR FACER FAULT GAUGE LIMIT MODER PAUSE QUELL REPEL SNAPE SPOKE STALL STILL STUNT TALLY TAUNT THROW TOKEN TRASH WAVER ARAYNE ARREST ATTACK BAFFLE BOTTLE BRIDLE CHEQUE COUPON DAMPEN DEFEAT DETAIN DETENT DURESS GRAVEL HAFFET HAFFIT HINDER IMPEDE OPPOSE OUTWIT PULLUP QUENCH RABBET REBATE REBUFF REBUKE RETURN SCOTCH STANCH STAYER STIFLE STYMIE TICKET VERIFY ANSTOSS AWEBAND BACKSET BECLOUD COMMAND CONTAIN CONTROL COUNTER CURTAIN DRAUGHT INHIBIT MONITOR REFRAIN REPRESS REPROOF REPROVE REPULSE REVERSE SETBACK SNAFFLE STAUNCH STOPPER TRAMMEL TROUBLE BULKHEAD ENCUMBER HOLDBACK OBSTRUCT PULLBACK RESTRAIN WITHHOLD
(— ENTHUSIASM) DISMAY
(— GRADUALLY) CUSHION
(— GROWTH) BLAST STINT STUNT
(— IN) ARRIVE
(— IN GLASS) SPLIT
(— IN TIMBER) STARSHAKE
(— MOTION) SPRAG
(— OF HORSE) SACCADE
(— PASSER) PAPERHANGER
(— PROGRESS) DEFEAT
(FORGED —) STIFF STUMER
(HOLD IN —) COMPESCE
(ILLEGAL — IN HOCKEY) SPEARING
(RESTAURANT —) LAWING
(WORTHLESS —) DUD STUMER
(WRITE A BAD —) BOUNCE
(PREF.) ISCH(O)
CHECKED CHECK BEATEN CLOSED CAPTIVE STOPPED
CHECKER DAM DICE FRET KING CHECK FREAK FRECK PIECE WHITE DAMPER DRAUGHT
CHECKERBERRY JINKS DRUNKARD TEABERRY

CHECKERBOARD TABLE DAMBROD DAMBOARD
CHECKERED PIED VAIR DICED PLAID CHECKY MOTLEY
CHECKERS DRAFTS CHEQUERS DRAUGHTS
CHECKERWORK TESSEL CHECKER TESSERA
CHECKING REST BLOCK SETBACK EBRILLADE
(— OF HEMORRHAGE) TORSION
(SUFF.) SCHESIS SCHETIC
CHECKMATE LICK MATE STOP UNDO BAFFLE CORNER DEFEAT OUTWIT STYMIE THWART SUIMATE
CHECKSTONE CHUCK
CHEDDAR CHEESE
CHEEK CHAP CHOP GALL GENA JAMB JOLE JOWL LEER SASS WANG WANK BUCCA CHOKE CHYAK CRUST NERVE SAUCE SHICK CHYACK HAFFET HAFFIT OXCHEEK AUDACITY TEMERITY
(— OF SPUR) SHANK
(— OF VISE) CHAP
(PREF.) BUCCO MEL PAREI(A)
CHEEKBONE MALAR ZYGOMA
CHEEK-POUCH (— OF BABOON) ALFORJA
CHEEKY BOLD FRESH
CHEEP PIP YAP YIP CHIP HINT PEEP PULE CHIRP CREAK TWEET SQUEAK TATTLE
CHEER OLE RAH FARE FOOD MIND ROOT VIVA YELL BRAVO BRISK CHIRK ELATE ERECT FEAST HEART HUZZA JOLLY MIRTH SHOUT SPORT TIGER WHOOP CANTLE CHERRY GAIETY HOORAY HURRAH HUZZAH REHETE SOLACE VIANDS ACCLAIM ANIMATE APPLAUD CHERISH COMFORT CONSOLE ENCHEER GLADDEN HEARTEN JOLLITY LIGHTEN REFRESH REJOICE SUPPORT UPRAISE APPLAUSE BRIGHTEN HILARITY INSPIRIT RECREATE VIVACITY
(BURST OF —S) SALVO
(GOOD —) WELFARE
(JAPANESE —) BANZAI
(SORRY —) PENANCE
CHEERFUL GAY CANT GLAD GLEG GOOD HIGH ROSY BONNY CADGY CANTY CHIRK DOUCE HAPPY JOLLY LIGHT MERRY PEART READY RIANT SAPPY SUNNY VAUDY BLITHE BRIGHT CHEERY CHIRPY CROUSE GAWSIE GENIAL HEARTY HILARY JOCUND LIVELY RIDENT BUOYANT CHEERLY CHIPPER HOLIDAY JOCULAR SMILING WINSOME CHEERING CHIRRUPY EUPEPTIC FRIENDLY GLADSOME HOMELIKE SANGUINE SUNBEAMY SUNSHINE (PREF.) HILARO
CHEERFULLY GLADLY CANTILY CHEERLY JOLLILY LIGHTLY CHEERILY GENIALLY
CHEERFULNESS JOY GLEE TAIT CHEER CHERTE GAIETY GAYETY LEVITY SPIRIT JOLLITY BUOYANCY FESTIVAL GLADNESS HILARITY
(MORE THAN —) GLEE

CHEERING GLAD CORDIAL CHEERFUL CHIRPING
CHEERIO BYE CIAO TATA LATER HOORAY HOOROO
CHEERLESS SAD BLAE COLD DIRE DRAB GLUM GRAY BLEAK DREAR ELYNG WASTE DISMAL DREARY GLOOMY WINTRY DOLEFUL FORLORN JOYLESS SUNLESS DEJECTED DESOLATE LITHLESS
CHEER PINE CHIL
CHEERY BUXOM BRIGHT BOBBISH GAYSOME
CHEESE OKA BLUE BRIE EDAM FETA HAND JACK TOME TRIP APPLE BRICK COLBY CREAM DAISY DERBY GOUDA GRANA KENNO MAHON QUESO SWISS TOMME WHEEL ZIEGA ZIGER ASIAGO BARRIE BONDON BRYNZA BURGOS CANTAL CASSAN DUNLOP GLARUS JUNKET MYSOST ROMANO RONCAL SAANEN SBRINZ TILSIT ZAMORA ZIEGER ANGELOT CHEDDAR CHEVRET COTTAGE CROWDIE FONTINA FROMAGE GJEDOST GRUYERE HAVARTI KASSERI KEBBUCK LASELVA PRIMOST PROVOLA RICOTTA SAPSAGO SERRANO STILTON TETILLA TRUCKLE AMERICAN CABRALES CHESHIRE EMMENTAL LONGHORN MUENSTER PARMESAN PECORINO RACLETTE SANSIMON SLIPCOAT TRONCHON LEICESTER MOUSETRAP PROVOLONE ROQUEFORT WILTSHIRE MOZZARELLA NEUFCHATEL SERVILLETA
(— COATING) MOLD
(— DISH) RACLETTE
(— FANCIER) TUROPHILE
(— IN OATMEAL) CABOC
(— ROLLED IN OATMEAL) CABOC
(COTTAGE —) CROWDIE
(CREAM —) JUNKET
(DANISH —) HAVARTI
(GOAT —) CHEVRE
(HUNGARIAN —) LIPTAUER
(INCIPIENT —) CURD
(INFERIOR —) DICK
(KIND OF —) RAT RATTRAP
(LARGE —) KEBBOC
(MELTED —) FONDUTA
(MILD FRENCH —) REBLOCHON
(SAY —) SMILE
(SOFT —) STRACCHINO
(STORE —) CHEDDAR
(WELSH —) CAERPHILLY
(PREF.) CASE(O) TURO TYR(O)
CHEESELIKE CASEOUS
CHEESEPARING STINGY
CHEESE VAT CHESSEL CHESSART
CHEESEWOOD BONEWOOD WHITEWOOD
CHEETAH CAT OUNCE YOUSE YOUZE GUEPARD
CHEF COOK COMMIS SAUCIER CUISINIER
(PASTRY —) PATISSIER
CHEFOO YENTAI
CHELA HAND MANUS NIPPER PINCER

CHELATE COMPLEX
CHELICERA FALX FANG FALCER MANDIBLE
CHELLIAN ABBEVILLIAN
CHELONIAN TURTLE TURTOISE
CHELUBAI (FATHER OF —) HEZRON
CHEMICAL (ALSO SEE SPECIFIC HEADINGS) ACID BASE SALT ALKALI BLEACH CHEMIC DODGER SAFENER ADDITIVE ALGICIDE CATALYST DEHORNER
(— FROM HEMP RESIN) THC
(— IN MARIJUANA) THC
(— WARFARE AGENT) SARIN
(PREF.) ACETO ALCO ALDO AMIDO AMYL(II)(O) AZ(O) BENZ(O) BOR(O) BROM(O) BUT(YR)(YRO) CADM(I)(O) CAPRO CARB(O) CHAVI(O) CUMO DIAZO DIOL DUPLO EKA ESTERI FORM(O) GLY(O) IDO IMIDO IMINO KER(O) KET(O) LAUR LIP LYSO LYXO MAL(O) MENTH(O) MERCUR(O) METH MOLYBD MURIO NAPH ITH NITRATO NITRILO NITROSO NOR OLEO ORTHO OSMIO OX OXAL(O) OXIDI OXIDO OXIMIDO OXO OXY OZO PENT(A) PERI PHLOR(O) PHTHAI(O) PIPTO PLUMB(I)(O) POLY PROP PROS PROTE(O) PYRROL(O) SYN TOI (U)
(SUFF.) AMIN(E)(O) ANE ASE ATE ENE ID(E) ILE INE INOL INONE ION ITE ITOL IUM OIC OIN OL OLE OLIC OLID(E) ON(E) ONIC ONIUM OSAN OSE OSIDE OUS OYL PHORE RETIN THIN(E) YL YNE ZYME
CHEMIN-DE-FER SHIMMY
CHEMISE SARK SHIFT SHIRT SIMAR SMOCK CAMISA SHIMMY LINGERIE
CHEMISETTE SHAM GUIMPE TUCKER PARTLET
CHEMIST ANALYST ASSAYER CHEMICK BENCHMAN COLORIST DRUGGIST
AMERICAN DOW ABEL CADY CRAM DANA HALE HALL HARE HART HASS HUNT KING LAMB LIND LOEB LONG MARK REID UREY WATT CLARK COOKE CROSS DEBYE DROWN DUMEZ FLORY GIBBS GOOCH HAMOR HERTY KRAUS LEWIS LIBBY MOORE NOYES POWER SEMON SMITH SNELL STINE WILEY BROWNE BUCHER BURTON CALVIN CARVER CLARKE CRAFTS DARKEN DEDUVE DORSET DUDLEY EGLOFF HOLMES HOOVER JULIAN LANDIS LEVENE MENDEL MORGAN MUNROE PALMER REMSEN ROBLIN ROGERS SHIMER SUMNER TORREY WARREN WESSON ALDRICH ANDREWS ATWATER CASSIDY CASTNER CUSHMAN DUSHMAN EDELMAN GIAUQUE GODLOVE GOMBERG GUTHRIE HARKINS KHORANA MIDGLEY ONSAGER PAULING SEABORG SHERMAN SLOSSON WHITNEY BANCROFT BENEDICT CHANDLER COOLIDGE COTTRELL DJERASSI FRANKLIN KOSSFORD LANGMUIR LIPSCOMB MCCOLLUM MCMILLAN MIDGELEY MULLIKEN RICHARDS SILLIMAN SPRINGER

STODDARD WILLIAMS WOODWARD
ALEXANDER CAROTHERS
HENDERSON NIEUWLAND
PATTERSON CHITTENDEN
HILLEBRAND
ARGENTINE LELOIR
AUSTRIAN KUHN EMICH PREGL
PRECHTL WELSBACH ZSIGMONDY
BELGIAN STAS SOLVAY HELMONT
BAEKELAND PRIGOGINE
CANADIAN HERZBERG
MCLAUGHLIN
CZECH BRAUNER HEYROVSKY
DANISH OERSTED THOMSEN
BRONSTED KJELDAHL SORENSEN
DUTCH COHEN MULDER HOMBERG
ENGLISH ABEL BELL DAVY POPE
SWAN TODD ABNEY BOYLE CROSS
DAKIN DEWAR HENRY MARSH
PROUT SODDY SYNGE YOUNG
BARTON BRANDE DALTON DONNAN
GREGOR HARDEN INGOLD MARTIN
MILLER PERKIN PORTER RAMSAY
THORPE TILDEN WATSON ANDREWS
CROOKES DANIELL FARADAY
HAWORTH HODGKIN NORRISH
TENNANT TRAVERS HATCHETT
MITCHELL PLAYFAIR ROBINSON
WILLIAMS ARMSTRONG CAVENDISH
CORNFORTH FRANKLAND
GLADSTONE PRIESTLEY WILKINSON
HINSHELWOOD
FINNISH VIRTANEN
FRENCH LEHN BAUME BEHAL
CONTE CURIE DUFAY DUMAS
FREMY LEBEL LEBON WURTZ
BALARD CLAUDE DARCET DULONG
GERNEZ GUIMET LEMERY NAQUET
ORFILA PERRIN PROUST RAOULT
WERNER CHAPTAL DAUBENY
FRIEDEL GLENARD LAURENT
LEBLANC LUMIERE MACQUER
MOISSAN PASTEUR PELOUZE
THENARD BERTRAND CAVENTOU
CHEVREUL COURTOIS DEBIERNE
DEMARCAY FOURCROY FOURNEAU
GERHARDT GRIGNARD KUHLMANN
REGNAULT SABATIER BERTHELOT
LAVOISIER LECLANCHE
LENORMAND PELLETIER
VAUQUELIN BERTHOLLET
CHARDONNET DUBRUNFAUT
LECHATELIER BOUSSINGAULT
SCHUTZENBERGER
GERMAN CARO HAHN KOPP KUHN
MOND ADLER ALDER BOSCH DIELS
EIGEN FRANK HABER KNORR KOLBE
LUNGE MEYER STAHL ACHARD
BAEYER BECHER BREDIG BUNSEN
DOMAGK FITTIG GIESEL GRAEBE
KOSSEL LIEBIG MAGNUS NERNST
TRAUBE WOHLER BERGIUS
BISCHOF BORRGER BUCHNER
CASSIUS CURTIUS ERDMANN
FEHLING FISCHER GLAUBER
HOFMANN OSTWALD TIEMANN
WALLACH WIELAND WINDAUS
ZIEGLER KLAPROTH MARGGRAF
SPRENGEL BEILSTEIN BUTENANDT
FRESENIUS LADENBURG
LAMPADIUS SCHEIBLER SCHONBEIN
STRASSMAN WIEDEMANN
ZSIGMONDY BODENSTEIN

DOBEREINER ERLENMEYER
LIEBERMANN STAUDINGER
STROHMEYER WILLSTATTER
GOLDSCHMIDT UNVERDORBEN
WILLSTATTER MITSCHERLICH
HUNGARIAN HEVESY
IRISH KIRWAN STEWART
ITALIAN LEVI NATTA SOVET COVELLI
FABRONI SOBRERO AVOGADRO
CIAMICIAN CANNIZZARO
BRUGNATELLI
JAPANESE FUKUI TAKAMINE
NORWEGIAN WAAGE HASSEL
GULDBERG
POLISH CURIE MOSCICKI
RUSSIAN BACH WALDEN SEMENOV
BUTLEROV MENDELEV ZELINSKI
PRIGOGINE
SCOTTISH URE BELL HALL BLACK
BROWN DEWAR YOUNG BEILBY
GRAHAM THOMSON MACINTOSH
SPANISH RODRIGUEZ
SWEDISH GAHN CLEVE BERGMAN
SCHEELE MOSANDER SEFSTROM
SVEDBERG TISELIUS ARRHENIUS
BERZELIUS CRONSTEDT
BLOMSTRAND ABDERHALDEN
SWISS NEF GLASER KARRER
MULLER PICTET PRELOG WERNER
RUZICKA MARIGNAC SAUSSURE
REICHSTEIN
CHEMOSTERILANT METEPA
CHENAANAH (FATHER OF —)
BILHAN
CHENDE CHINOA
CHENFISH KINGFISH
CHENILLE SNAIL
CHEQUEEN BASKET SEQUIN
ZEQUIN CECCHINE ZECCHINO
CHEQUER DICE
CHERAN (FATHER OF —) DISHON
CHERAW SARA
CHEREMIS MARI
CHERISH AID HUG PET BEAR DOTE
HAVE HOPE LIKE LOVE SAVE
ADORE BOSOM BROOD CHEER
CLING COWER ENJOY NURSE
PRIZE VALUE CARESS ESTEEM
FADDLE FONDLE FOSTER GRUDGE
HARBOR MOTHER NESTLE NUZZLE
PAMPER PETTLE REVERE
COMFORT EMBOSOM EMBRACE
INDULGE NOURISH NURTURE
PROTECT SUPPORT SUSTAIN
ENSHRINE INSPIRIT PRESERVE
TREASURE
CHERISHED PET DEAR BOSOM
DANDILY AFFECTED PRECIOUS
CHEROOT MANILA TRICHI TRICHY
CHERRY BING CHOP DUKE FUJI
GEAN MERRY MOREL CORNEL
MAZARD BURBANK CAPULIN
CHAPMAN LAMBERT MAHALEB
MARASCA MAYDUKE MORELLO
OXHEART PITANGA WINDSOR
AMARELLE DURACINE EGGBERRY
LUKEWARD NAPOLEON ROSACEAN
BIGARREAU MARASCHINO
MONTMORENCY
CHERRY BLOSSOM HEBE
CHERRY-COLORED CERISE
CHERRY ORCHARD (AUTHOR OF —)
CHEKHOV

(CHARACTER IN —) ANYA GAYEV
VARYA YASHA DUNYASHA
LOPAKHIN RANEVSKY TROFIMOV
CHARLOTTE
CHERRY PLUM MYROBALAN
CHERRY STONE PAIP
CHERT BOONE WHINSTONE
CHERUB AMOR EROS ANGEL CUPID
SERAPH SPIRIT AMORINO
AMORETTO CHERUBIM
CHERVIL BUN KECK ARFOIL CERFOIL
COWWEED HONEWORT
MILKWEED RATSBANE
CHESED (FATHER OF —) NAHOR
CHESS CHEAT SHOGI CHECKER
SKITTLES
(— CHAMPION) TAL
(— EXPERT) TAL
(— MOVE) ZUGZWANG
(INEPT — PLAYER) PATZER POTZER
CHESSBOARD CHESS TABLE
CHECKER
CHESSMAN PIN KING PIECE
CHECKER CHEQUER
(— SET) MEINY MEINIE
(ANY — BUT PAWN) OFFICER
(BISHOP —) ALFIN ALPHIN ARCHER
(CASTLE —) JUEZ ROOK TOUR
UDGE JUDGE LEDGE TOWER
(KNIGHT —) HORSE CHEVALIER
(PAWN —) PON POUNE
(QUEEN —) FERS FIERS PHEARSE
CHEST ARK BOX CUB FIX KIT PIX PYX
ARCA BUST CAJA CASH CIST CYST
FUND KIST SAFE SCOB AMBRY
BAHUT BUIST CADDY FRONT
HOARD HUTCH RAZEE SISTA
TRUNK ALMOIN BASKET BREAST
BUNKER BUREAU CAISSE CAJETA
CASKET COFFER COFFIN FORCER
GIRNAL GIRNEL HAMPER JORDAN
LARNAX LOCKER LOWBOY SCRINE
SHRINE SPRUCE STRIPE THORAX
WANGAN BRAZIER BRISKET
CAISSON CAPCASE CASSONE
COMMODE DEPOSIT DRAWERS
DRESSER ENCLOSE HIGHBOY
TOOLBOX WANIGAN WINDBAG
CISTVAEN CUPBOARD FORCELET
MANIFOLD STANDARD TREASURE
TREASURY
(— FOR CUTLERY) CANTEEN
(— FOR FISH) CAUF
(— OF ORES) CAXON
(— PROTECTOR) BIB
(FRONT OF —) BREAST
(MEDICINE —) INRO
(SMALL —) COFFRET
(PREF.) STERN(O) STETH(O)
THORAC(I)(O)
CHESTERFIELD COAT SOFA
CHESTNUT GAG JOKE LING RATA
BROWN HORSE STORY CASTOR
MARRON SATIVA CRENATA
DENIATA
(HORSE —) CONKER
(POLYNESIAN —) RATA
(WATER —) LING
(PREF.) CASTANO
CHESTNUT-COLORED BAY ROAN
BADIOUS
CHEST PROTECTOR PECTORAL
CHEVAL-DE-FRISE TURNPIKE

CHEVAL GLASS PSYCHE
CHEVALIER CADET NOBLE KNIGHT
GALLANT CAVALIER HORSEMAN
CHEVET APSE
CHEVILLE PEG
CHEVIN CHUB CHEVESNE
CHEVRON BEAM MARK WOUND
RAFTER STRIPE ZIGZAG
CHEVROTAIN MUSK NAPU DEERLET
KANCHIL MEMINNA PLANDOK
TRAGULE BOOMORAH PEESOREH
RUMINANT
CHEVY TEASE
CHEW CUD EAT GUM TAW BITE
CHAM CHAW GNAW NOSH QUID
CHAMP CHONK GRIND MUNCH
RUMEN CRUNCH MUMBLE
CHUMBLE MEDITATE RUMINATE
MANDUCATE
(— OUT) SCOLD
(— THE CUD) KUMINATE
(— THE FAT) GAB JAW YAK
(— UP NOISILY) CHANK GROUSE
CHEWING GUM GUM CHICCLE
CHEWINK FINCH JOREE TOWHEE
GRASSET
CHEYENNE DOG
CHIAN SCIAN
CHIANTI FLORENCE
CHIASTOLITE MACLE ANDALUSITE
CHIBCHA MUISCA
CHIC GOGO PERT POSH TRIG TRIM
KIPPY NATTY NIFTY SMART CHICHI
DAPPER GIGOLO JAUNTY MODISH
TRENDY ELEGANT STYLISH
(KIND OF —) RADICAL
(NO LONGER —) OUT
CHICAGO PORKOPOLIS
CHICANE DECEPTION
CHICANERY DIRT RUSE WILE FEINT
TRICK ARTIFICE INTRIGUE
TRICKERY DECEPTION
PETTIFOGGERY
CHICHI ARTY TONY
CHICK BIRD GIRL PEEP TICK CHILD
NATTY POULET SCREEN SEQUIN
SPROUT CHICKEN CHUCKIE
CHICKADEE TOMTIT BLACKCAP
TITMOUSE
CHICKAREE BOOMER
CHICKEN HEN KIP COCK FOWL
BIDDY CAPON CHICK CHILD
CHOOK CHUCK DEEDY FRYER
LAYER MANOC POULT SILKY TIMID
AFRAID CHICKY PULLET SULTAN
SUSSEX TURKEN ANCOBAR
BOARDER BROILER DIBBLER
LEGHORN POUSSIN ROASTER
ROOSTER SCRATCH ARAUCANA
COCKEREL PHASANID SPRINGER
(— OUT) WIMPOUT
(— PIECES ON SKEWER) YAKITORI
(— SHELTER) MOTHER
(FRIED —) ESCABECHE
(STRIPS OF —) FAJITA
CHICKEN COOP CAVY CAVIE
CHICKEN-FEED PEANUTS
CHICKEN POX SOREHEAD
VARICELLA
CHICK-PEA CHIT GRAM CHICH
CICER COWGRAM SOWGRAM
GARBANZO GARVANCE
(PL.) FASELS

CHICKWEED BLINK BLINKS SPURRY ALLBONE STARWORT

CHICO SAPODILLA

CHICORY BUNK CREPIS ENDIVE SUCCORY WITLOOF BLUEWEED COMPOSIT RADICCHIO

CHIDE BAN FUSS RAIL RATE BLAME CHECK FLITE FLYTE SCOLD SNEAP BERATE REBUFF REBUKE SCHOOL THREAP THREAT THREEP TONGUE CENSURE REPROVE UPBRAID WRANGLE ADMONISH BETONGUE LAMBASTE REPROACH

CHIDING ROW

CHIEF (ALSO SEE CHIEFTAIN) BO AGA BIG BOH CAP CID COR DUX MIR MOI TOP AGHA ALII AMIR ARCH ARII BOSS CAID CHEF COCK DATO DEAN DOEG DUCE DUKE EMIR HEAD HIER HIGH INCA JARL JEFE KAID KHAN KING MAIN MICO MOST NAIK ONLY QAID RAIS RAJA REIS TYEE ALDER ALPHA ARIKI DATTO ELDER FIRST GREAT MAJOR MATAI NAYAK PRIMA PRIME PRIMO RAJAH RULER THANE TITAN VITAL ZAQUE ZIPPA ADALID CABEZA DEPUTY FLAITH HEADLY INKOSI KEHAYA KUBERA KUVERA LEADER LUUHAI MASTER MIRDHA NAIQUE PENLOP PRARHU PRIMAL RECTOR SACHEM SAYYID SHAYKH SHEIKH SHERIF STAPLE SUDDER TOPMAN TURNUS CAPITAL CAPTAIN CENTRAL EMINENT FOREMAN GENERAL HEADMAN INGOMAR LEADING LEMPIRA MUGWUMP OVERMAN PADRONE PALMARY POLYGAR PRELATE PREMIER PRIMARY SHEREEF STELLAR SUPREME TOPSMAN TRIBUNE CABOCEER CAPITANO CARDINAL DECURION DIRECTOR DOMINANT ELDORADO ESPECIAL FOREMOST GOVERNOR HEADSMAN HIERARCH INTIMATE MOKADDAM PREMIERE SAGAMORE STAROSTA SUBCHIEF PENDRAGON

(— IN INDIA) PRABHU SIRDAR

(— OF ADVOCATES) BATONNIER

(— OF RELIGIOUS ORDER) GENERAL

(— OF TITHING) BORSHOLDING

(— OF 10 MEN) DEAN

(CHINOOK —) TYEE

(CLAN —) TOISECH

(INDIAN —) SUNCK SACHEM SUNCKE CACIQUE MOCUDDUM SAGAMORE

(MALAY —) RAJA RAJAH

(MOHAMMEDAN —) DATO DATTO SAYID SAYYID

(SCHOOL —) DUX

(SCOTTISH —) MAORMOR

(TIBETAN —) POMBO

(TURKISH —) AGA AGHA

(VIKING —) SEAKING

(PREF.) ARCH(I) PROT(O)

CHIEFLY MAINLY LARGELY

CHIEFTAIN BEG AMIR CHAM EMIR HEAD JARL KHAN ASTUR CHIEF EMEER LEADER SIRDAR CAUDILLO HIAWATHA

CHIEFTAINCY STOOL CHIEFRY

CHIEFTAINESS QUEEN

CHIFFCHAFF PEGGY CHIPCHAP CHIPCHOP

CHIFFON SHEER

CHIFFONIER BUREAU CABINET COMMODE

CHIGGER BICHO PIQUE CHIGGA CHIGOE GIGGER JIGGER LEPTUS REDBUG WHEELWORM

CHIGNON COB KNOT COBBE TWIST

CHIGOE FLEA SIKA BICHO NIGUA PIQUE SCREW CHIGGA ENIGUA JIGGER SANDBOY SANDWORM

CHIH FU PREFECT

CHILBLAIN KIBE MULE BLAIN MOOLS MOULS PERNIO

CHILD BEN BOY BUD ELF GET IMP KID LAD SON SOT TAD TOT WAY BABA BABE BABY BATA BIRD BRAT CHAP CHIT CION FOOD GIRL GYTE PAGE PUSS TIKE TINY TOTO TROT TYKE WEAN BAIRN BIRTH BROLL BROWL CHICK CHIEL COOKY ELFIN GAMIN ISSUE KEIKI OLIVE POULT SCION TIDDY TRICK WAYNE WENCH WHELP CHERUB COLLOP COOKIE ENFANT FILIUS FOSTER INFANT MOPPET NIPPER PLEDGE PROLES SHAVER STUMPY TACKER TODDLE URCHIN BAMBINO CHOOKIE CHOPPER CHRISOM COCKNEY DICKENS GANGREL GYTLING KINCHIN KITLING LAMBKIN PAPOOSE PRETEEN PROGENY STICHEL SUBTEEN TIDDLER TODDLER TROTTIE WRAWLER YOUNKER BANTLING CHISELER DAUGHTER EPIGONUS JUVENILE LITTLING NURSLING PRATTLER RUNABOUT WEANLING WHIMLING PRESCHOOLER

(— AT BAPTISM) CHRISOM CHRISTOM

(— IN THE WOMB) BURDEN

(— OF THE WORLD) WELTKIND

(— UNDER 7 YEARS) INFANS

(ANNOYING —) BRAT

(BAD-MANNERED —) GOOP

(BAPTISMAL —) CHRISOM

(CHUBBY —) CHUNK

(CODDLED —) COCKNEY

(ELF'S —) AUF OAF CHANGELING

(FAVORITE —) BENJAMIN

(FAVORITE —) BENJAMIN

(FORWARD —) JACKANAPES

(FOSTER —) DAULT NORRY NURRY FOSTER REARLING

(ILLEGITIMATE —) MISHAP BASTARD

(INNOCENT —) CHRISOM

(LAST-BORN —) DILLING

(LOVED —) JOY

(MERRY —) SUNBEAM

(MEXICAN —) NINO

(MISCHIEVOUS —) IMP LIMB TIKE DICKENS

(NAKED —) SCUDDY

(NEGLECTED —) WAIF WASTREL

(NEWBORN —) NEONATE STRANGER

(NURSERY —) PREEMIE

(PAUPER —) MINDER

(PLAYFUL —) ELF WANTON

(PLUMP —) FOB FUB

(PRECOCIOUS —) PRODIGY

(PURE —) DOVE

(ROWDY —) HOODLUM

(SMALL —) TAD TOT MITE SPUD GAITT KIDDY TIDDY TOTUM KIDLET PEEWEE TACKER BAIRNIE

(SPOILED —) CADE COSSET WANTON COCKNEY

(STUNTED —) URF

(SWEET —) CHERUB

(TROUBLESOME —) PICKLE STICHEL

(UNMANNERLY —) SMATCHET

(UNWEANED —) SUCKLING

(YOUNG —) BABY JOEY INFANT SQUIRT GANGREL NESTLER TODDLER BANTLING INNOCENT LITTLING SUCKLING

(YOUNGEST —) WRIG DILLING

(PREF.) INFANTI PAED(O) PAID(O) PED(O) TECHNO TECNO TEKNO

CHILDBED JIZZEN

CHILDBIRTH LABOR CRYING INLYING TRAVAIL OXYTOCIA

(— WOMAN) PUERPERA

(OF A METHOD OF —) LAMAZE

(PREF.) LOCHIO LOCHO TOCO TOKO

(SUFF.) TOCIA TOCO(US) TOKIA TOKO(US)

CHILDHOOD INFANCY CHILDAGE

(2ND —) DOTAGE TWICHILD

CHILDISH TID WEAK DANSY NAIVE PETTY SILLY YOUNG CHITTY PULING SIMPLE WEANLY ASININE BABYISH CHILDLY FOOLISH KIDDISH PEEVISH PROGENY PUERILE UNMANLY BAIRNISH BRATTISH IMMATURE TOOTLING

CHILDISHNESS DOTAGE

CHILDLESS ORBATE

CHILDREN ISSUE PROLES STRAIN PROGENY OFFSPRING

(NUMBER OF —) PARITY

(SUFF.) PAEDES

CHILE SOCOMPA

(— INDIAN) FUEGIAN

CHILE

BAY: COOK EYRE NENA TARN LOMAS OTWAY SARCO DARWIN INUTIL MORENO STOKES TONGOY DYNELEY INGLESA SKYRING DESOLATE

CAPE: DYER HORN CHOROS HORNOS QUILAN TABLAS DESEADO BASCUNAN CARRANZA

CAPITAL: SANTIAGO

CHANNEL: ANCHO CHEAP BEAGLE COCKBURN MORALEDA

COIN: PESO LIBRA CONDOR ESCUDO CENTAVO CONDORS CONDORES

DESERT: ATACAMA

GULF: ANCUD GUAFO PENAS ARAUCO

INDIAN: ONA AUCA INCA ONAN ARAUCA CHANGO YAHGAN FUEGIAN MAPUCHE MOLUCHE PAMPEAN PATAGON RANQUEL ALIKULUF PICUNCHE TSONECAN

ISLAND: LUZ PRAT BYRON GUAFO HOSTE MOCHA NUEVA NUNEZ VIDAL CHILOE DAWSON EASTER LENNOX PIAZZI PICTON QUILAN RIESCO STOSCH TALCAN ANGAMOS CAMPANA HANOVER REFUGIO TRANQUI CLARENCE HUAMBLIN NALCAYEC NAVARINO TRAIGUEN

ISLANDS: CHONOS HERMITE PAJAROS CHAUQUES

ISTHMUS: OFQUI

LAKE: TORO RANCO YELCHO PUYEHUE RUPANCO

MEASURE: VARA LEGUA LINEA CUADRA FANEGA

MOUNTAIN: MACA TORO CHATO MAIPO PAINE POTRO PULAR TORRE YOGAN APIWAN BURNEY CONICO JERVIS POQUIS RINCON CHALTEL COPIAPO FITZROY PALPANA VELLUDA COCHRANE TRONADOR YANTELES

MOUNTAINS: ANDES DARWIN ALMEIDA DOMEYKO

NATIVE: PATAGONIAN

PENINSULA: HARDY LACUY TAITAO TUMBES

POINT: TORO GALLO LILES LOBOS LOROS MORRO TALCA TETAS VIEJA CACHOS GALERA MOLLES ANGAMOS LAVAPIE

PORT: LOTA TOME ARICA COQUIMBO

PROVINCE: AISEN ARICA AYSEN MAULE NUBLE TALCA ARAUCO BIOBIO CAUTIN CHILOE CURICO OSORNO ATACAMA LINARES MALLECO COQUIMBO OHIGGINS SANTIAGO TARAPACA VALDIVIA

RIVER: LOA LAJA YALI ALHUE AZAPA BRAVO BUENO ELQUI ITATA LAUCA LLUTA MAIPO MAULE PUELO RAHUE RAPEL VITOR BIOBIO CAMINA CHOAPA CHOROS CISNES COLINA HUASCO LIMARI MORADO PALENA POSCUA TOLTEN COPIAPO VALDIVIA

SHRUB: LITRE

STRAIT: NELSON MAGELLAN

TOWN: BOCO CUYA LEBU LOTA OCOA TOCO TOME ARICA TALCA ARAUCO CURICO GATICO OSORNO SERENA TEMUCO VICUNA YUMBEL YUNGAY CALDERA CHILLAN COPIAPO COQUIMBO RANCAGUA SANTIAGO VALDIVIA

TREE: RAULI

VOLCANO: LANIN MAIPO ANTUCO LASCAR LLAIMA OSORNO OYAHUE TACORA LAUTARO PETEROA SOCOMAP VILLARICA GUALLATIRI

WEIGHT: GRANO LIBRA QUINTAL

WIND: SURES

CHILEAB (FATHER OF —) DAVID

(MOTHER OF —) ABIGAIL

CHILE-BELLS COPIHUE LAPAGERIA

CHI-LIN KYLIN UNICORN

CHILION (DAUGHTER OF —) ORPAH

(MOTHER OF —) NAOMI

CHILL ICE RAW AGUE COLD COOL DAZY ALGID ALGOR DAVER GELID OURIE RIGOR SCHEL SHAKE FRAPPE FREEZE FRIGID FROSTY SHIVER SNELLY DEPRESS FRETISH FRISSON MALARIA COLDNESS **(— OUT)** RELAX
CHILLED ICED ACOLD CHILL FROZEN STARVEN
CHILLING ICY COLD EERY BLEAK EERIE NIPPY CHILLY WINTRY GLACIAL NIPPING SHIVERY
CHILLNESS COLD
CHILLY ICY RAW COLD COOL LASH ALGID BLEAK HUNCH NIPPY PARKY AGUISH AIRISH ARCTIC CRIMMY FROSTY FROZEN LEEPIT CAULDRIFE
CHIMAERA BELUE DRAGON CATFISH PLACOID RATFISH RATTAIL DOODSKOP
CHIME DIN RIM BELL EDGE PEAL RING SUIT TING TINK AGREE CHIMB CHINE PRATE ACCORD CLOCHE CYMBAL JINGLE MELODY CONCORD HARMONY SINGSONG **(PL.)** BELL
CHIMER CYMAR SIMAR CHIMAR TABARD
CHIMERA FANCY MIRAGE MOSAIC POMATO ILLUSION
CHIMERE ROBE
CHIMERICAL VAIN WILD INSANE UTOPIAN DELUSIVE FANCIFUL ROMANTIC IMAGINARY
CHIMNEY BAG LUM TUN FLUE LUMM PIPE TUBE VENT GULLY STACK STALK TEWEL CHIMLA FUNNEL LOUVER SMOKER TUNNEL FISSURE OPENING ORIFICE FUMIDUCT SMOKESTACK
CHIMNEY CAP TURNCAP
CHIMNEY CORNER FIRESIDE INGLENOOK
CHIMNEY COWL COW
CHIMNEY HOOD JACK
CHIMNEY PIECE PAREL
CHIMNEY PIPE TALLBOY
CHIMNEY POST SPEER
CHIMNEY-POT TOPHAT
CHIMNEY SEAT SCONCE
CHIMNEY SWEEP SWEEP CHUMMY FLUEMAN RAMONEUR
CHIMP (SPACE —) ENOS
CHIMPANZEE APE CHIMP JACKO JOCKO PIGMY PYGMY NCHEGA PIGMEW PYGMEAN
CHIN JAW RAP CHAT TSIN MENTUM CHOLLER **(— POINT)** MENTON POGONION **(DOUBLE —)** BUCCULA CHOLLER (PREF.) GENIO MENTI MENTO
CHINA WARE JAPAN LENOX SPODE CATHAY PARIAN SEVRES TEASET CERAMIC CHEENEY DRESDEN LIMOGES MEISSEN POTTERY CINCHONA CROCKERY EGGSHELL **(BONE —)** WEDGWOOD **(KIND OF —)** HOTEL

CHINA
ABORIGINE: YAO MANS MIAO MANTZU YAOMIN MIAOTSE

AREA UNIT: MU MOU MOW
BASIN: TARIM
BAY: LAICHOW HANGCHOW
BUDDHA: FO
CAPE: OLWANPI
CAPITAL: PEKING TAIPEI PEIPING
CHANNEL: BASHI
COIN: PU CASH CENT MACE TAEL TIAO YUAN CHIAO SYCEE DOLLAR
CURRENCY: RENMINBI
DEPRESSION: TURFAN
DESERT: GOBI ORDOS SHAMO ALASHAN TAKLAMAKAN
DIALECT: WU MIN AMOY HAKKA CANTON HSIANG SWATOW FOOCHOW WENCHOW KANHAKKA MANDARIN
DRY LAKE: LOPNOR
DYNASTY: WU HAN SHU SUI WEI YIN CHIN CHOU HSIA HSIN MING SUNG TANG YUAN CHING SHANG
GULF: POHAI CHIHLI TONKIN PECHILI LIAOTUNG
ISLAND: AMOY FLAT MACAO MATSU NAMKI CHUSAN HAINAN PRATAS QUEMOY TAIWAN YUHWAN FORMOSA HUNGTOW TUNGSHA CHOUCHAN KULANGSU STAUNTON
ISLANDS: PENGHU TACHEN CHUSHAN MIAOTAO
LAKE: TAI CHAO KAOYU OLING TELLI BAMTSO BORNOR EBINOR ERRHAI KHANKA LOPNOR NAMTSO POYANG CHALING HUNGTSE KARANOR KOKONOR HULUNNOR MONTCALM TAROKTSO TELLINOR TIENCHIH TSINGHAI TUNGTING
MEASURE: HO HU KO LI MU PU TO TU FAN FEN PAU TOU TUN YIN CHIH FANG KISH PARA QUEI SHIH TSUN CHANG CHING SHENG SHING CHUPAK KUNGHO KUNGLI KUNGMU KUNGFEN KUNGYIN KUNGCHIH
MOUNTAIN: OMI OMEI SUNG KAILAS POBEDA EVEREST MUZTABH SUNGSHAN
MOUNTAINS: ALTAY KUNLUN ALASHAN KUENLUN MEILING MINSHAN NANLING NANSHAN TANGLHA BOGDOULA HIMALAYA TAPASHAN TAYULING TIENSHAN WUYLISHAN
NAME: CATHAY
NATIVE: PAT
PENINSULA: LEICHU LUICHOW LIAOTUNG
PORT: AMOY WUHU AIGUN SHASI ANTUNG CANTON CHEFOO DAIREN ICHANG NINGPO PAKHOI SWATOW SZEMAO WUCHOW YOCHOW FOOCHOW HUNCHUN MENGTSZ NANKING SAMSHUI SANTUAO SOOCHOW WENCHOW CHANGSHA HANGCHOW KIUKIANG KONGMOON LUNGCHOW SHANGHAI TENGYUEH TIENTSIN TSINGTAO WANHSIEN
PROVINCE: HONAN HOPEH HOPEI HUNAN HUPEI HUPEN JEHOL

KANSU KIRIN TIBET ANHWEI FUKIEN SHANSI SHENSI TAIWAN YUNNAN KIANGSI KWANGSI NGANHUI CHEKIANG KWEICHOW LIAONING MONGOLIA SHANTUNG SZECHWAN TSINGHAI MANCHURIA
RELIGION: JU SHINTO TAOISM BUDDHISM
RESERVOIR: SUNGARI
RIVER: SI HAN ILI MIN NEN PEI WEI AMUR HUAI LIAO LOHO TUNG YALU YUAN YUEN ARGUN FENHO MACHU PEIHO TARIM TUMEN WEIHO CHUMAR DRECHU DZACHU KHOTAN KUMARA LIAOHO MANASS MEKONG OCHINA URUNGU YELLOW HOANGHO HWANGHO KERULEN KIALING SALWEEN SIKIANG SUNGARI TSANGPO WUKIANG YANGTZE YARKAND YUKIANG CHERCHEN HANKIANG HUNGSHUI MINKIANG
RULER: WANG
SEA: ECHINA SCHINA YELLOW
STRAIT: HAINAN TAIWAN FORMOSA
TOWN: BAI NOH AHPA AMOY ANSI ANTA AQSU FUYU GUMA HAMI HUMA IPIN KIAN KISI LINI LOHO LUTA MOHO MOYU MULI NIYA NOHO NURA OMIN OWPU RIMA SAKA SIAN TALI TAYU WUHU WUSU WUTU YAAN CHIAI FUSIN HOFEI ICHUN JEHOL KIRIN KOKLU LHASA MACAO PENKI SHASI TAIAN TALAI TUTZE TUYUN TZEPO WUHAN WUSIH YENKI YULIN YUMEN ANSHAN ANTUNG CANTON CHENDU DAIREN FUCHAU FUSHUN HANKOW HANTAN HARBIN HOIHOW KALGAN LOYANG LUSHUN MUKDEN NINGPO PAOTOW PEKING PENGPU SUCHOW SWATOW TAINAN TAIPEI TALIEN TSINAN YUNNAN CHUNGTU FATSHAN FOOCHOW HANYANG HUHEHOT KAIFENG KUNMING KWEISUI LANCHOW NANKING PAOTING PEIPING SOOCHOW TAIYUAN TIANJIN TZEKUNG URUMCHI WUCHANG YENPING CHANGSHA CHAOCHOW CHENGTEH CHINCHOW HANGCHOW KIAOCHOW KWEIYANG NANCHANG QARAQASH SHANGHAI SHENYANG SIANGTAN TANGSHAN TENGCHOW TIENTSIN TSINGTAO TUNGCHOW CHUNGKING
WEIGHT: LI TA FAN FEN HAO KIN SSU TAN YIN CHEE CHIN DONG MACE SHIH TAEL CATTY CHIEN LIANG PICUL TCHIN HAIKWAN KUNGFEN KUNGSSU KUNGCHIN

CHINABERRY LILAC AZEDARACH CHINABALL SOAPBERRY
CHINA BLUE NIKKO
CHINA-GRASS RAMI RAMEE RAMIE
CHINA HAT HAELTZUK HEILTSUK

CHINAMAN CHOW JOHN JOHNNY CELESTIAL (PL.) TANKA
CHINA ROSE MANETTI HIBISCUS
CHINA STONE PETUNSE
CHINA TREE LILAC HAGBUSH
CHINAWARE CRACKLE
CHINCHILLA ABROCOME VIZCACHA
CHINE BACK IKAT CHINK CRACK CREST GORGE RIDGE SPINE CLEAVE RAVINE SPROUT CREVICE
CHINESE PAT BABA CHOW CERAI CHINK SERES SERIC SINIC MANZAS MONGOL ASIATIC CATAIAN CHINOIS PIGTAIL SANGLEY **(COMMUNIST —)** CHICOM (PREF.) CHINO SINICO SINO
CHINESE ARTICHOKE CROSNE CHOROGI CROSNES STACHYS KNOTROOT
CHINESE CABBAGE PECHAY PAKCHOI
CHINESE DATE BER JUJUBE
CHINESE GELATIN AGAR
CHINESE PARSLEY CILANTRO
CHING TSING
CHINGPAW KACHIN SINGPHO YAWYINS
CHINIOFON YATREN
CHINK GAP BORE CASH CHAP COIN JINK KINK RENT RIFT RIME SCAR BOORE CHECK CHINE CHUNK CLEFT CRACK GRIKE KNACK MONEY CRANNY RICTUS SPRAIN CHINKLE CREVICE FISSURE APERTURE
CHINPIECE BARBEL
CHINQUAPIN OAK BONNET NUTLET BONNETS CANDOCK CHESTNUT WANKAPIN YOCKERNUT
CHINTZ PINTADO SALAMPORE
CHIONE (FATHER OF —) BOREAS DAEDALION **(HUSBAND OF —)** NEPTUNE **(MOTHER OF —)** ORITHYIA DAEDALION **(SLAYER OF —)** DIANA **(SON OF —)** EUMOLPUS AUTOLYCUS PHILAMMON
CHIOT SCIOT
CHIP BIT CPU CUT DIB GAG HEW NIG BONE CHAP CLIP HACK KNAP KNOP NICK PARE SAND SKIN SNIP SNUB BEACH CHECK CRACK FLAKE PIECE SCRAP SKELF SLICE SPALE SPALL SPALT SPAWL SPELL SPOON WASTE BORING CHISEL GALLET MARKER NOODLE COUNTER SHAVING CHIPPING COSSETTE FRAGMENT SPLINTER WHITLING **(— IN)** ANTE **(— OF SOLDER)** LINK **(— OF WOOD)** SPOON **(— OUT)** DESEAM **(BUFFALO —S)** BODEWASH **(COMPUTER MEMORY —)** DRAM **(CORN —S)** FRITOS **(MEMORY —)** DRAM **(POTATO —)** CRISP **(SUPPLY OF —S)** STACK **(TORTILLA —)** NACHO
CHIP BASKET PUNNET
CHIPMAN SCRAPMAN

CHIPMUNK CHIPPY GOPHER GRINNY HACKEE GRINNIE SQUIRREL
CHIPOLATA SAUSAGE
CHIPPENDALE AFGHAN
CHIPPER GAY SPRY CHIRP PERKY BABBLE COCKEY FIERCE HACKER KIPPER LIVELY CHATTER CHIRRUP TWITTER CHEERFUL
CHIPPINGS SWARF
CHIRO BONYFISH FRANCESCA
CHIROGRAPHY WRITING
CHIRON (— AS CONSTELLATION) SAGITTARIUS
 (FATHER OF —) SATURN
 (MOTHER OF —) PHILYRA
CHIROPODIST PEDICURE CORNCUTTER
CHIROPTEROUS BATTY
CHIRP PEW PIP PEEK PEEP PIPE PULE TWIT WEAK CHEEP CHELP CHIRK CHIRL CHIRM CHIRT TWEET TWINK CHIPPER CHIRRUP CHITTER REJOICE SHATTER TWEEDLE TWITTER WHEETLE WHITTER
CHIRPPING TWITTER
CHIRR PITTER
CHIRU SUS
CHISEL BUR CUT GAD CHIP ETCH FORM MOIL PARE SEAT SETT TANG TOOL BRUZZ BURIN CARVE CHEAT DROVE GOUGE HARDY POINT SCOOP SLICK STIFF BROACH CHESIL FIRMER FORMER GRAVEL HAGGLE POMMEL QUARRY REAMER TOOLER BARGAIN BOASTER BOLSTER CHIPPER ENGRAVE GRADINE GRUBBER POINTER QUARREL SCOOPER SCORPER SHINGLE CROSSCUT SPLITTER
 (BLACKSMITH'S —) HARDY HARDIE
 (FLINT —) TRANCHET
 (ICE —) GRUD
 (JEWELER'S —) SCAUPER SCORPER
 (PREHISTORIC —) CELT
 (STONEMASON'S —) TOOL DROVE POMMEL TOOLER SPLITTER
 (TOOTHED —) GRADINE
 (TRIANGULAR —) BUR BURR
 (WHEELWRIGHT'S —) BRUZZ
 (PREF.) CELTI
CHISELER CHEAT CROOK COYOTE GOUGER
CHISLON (SON OF —) ELIDAD
CHIT DAB IOU TAB BILL NOTE DRAFT LETTER VOUCHER
CHITARRONE ARCHLUTE
CHITCHAT GAB GASH GUFF TALK BANTER GOSSIP GOSSIPRY BAVARDAGE
CHITINOUS SHELLY
CHITON EXOMIS DIPLOIS EXOMION
CHITTAMWOOD IRONWOOD
CHITTERLINGS SOULFOOD
CHIVALROUS BRAVE CIVIL NOBLE PREUX GENTLE POLITE GALLANT GENTEEL VALIANT WARLIKE KNIGHTLY
CHIVE CIVE SIVE CIVET SITHE ALLIUM
CHIVY RUN VEX BAIT HUNT RACE CHASE CHEVY TEASE BADGER

CHIVVY FLIGHT HARASS PURSUE PURSUIT SCAMPER TORMENT MANEUVER
CHLAMYDIA BEDSONIA
CHLOASMA MOTH
CHLOR LEMON
CHLORDIAZEPOXIDE LIBRIUM
CHLORIDE BUTTER CALOMEL MURIATE VIOLOGEN ALEMBROTH
CHLORINE OXYGEN
CHLORION SPHEX
CHLORIS (BROTHER OF —) AMYCLAS
 (FATHER OF —) AMPHION
 (HUSBAND OF —) NELEUS ZEPHYRUS
 (MOTHER OF —) NIOBE
 (SON OF —) NESTOR
CHLORITE AMESITE
CHOANA COLLAR
CHOBDAR USHER CHOPDAR
CHOCK COG PAD BLOCK BRACE CHUCK CLEAT SPOKE SPRAG WEDGE SCOTCH
 (PL.) STOWWOOD
CHOCKABLOCK SOLID
CHOCOLATE BUD CANDY COCOA NORFOLK JACOLATT
 (— MIXTURE) GANACHE
 (— SNACK) OREO
CHOGAK SHOQ
CHOICE BET ODD TRY BEST FINE FORE GOOD MIND PICK RARE WALE WEAL WILL CREAM ELITE PRIME VOICE CHOSEN DAINTY DESIRE FLOWER OPTION PICKED PLUMMY SELECT DILEMMA ELEGANT EXCERPT PERMISS DELICATE ELECTION EXIMIOUS UNCOMMON VOLITION RECHERCHE PREFERENCE
 (FAVORITE —) STANDBY
 (FREE —) SWING DRUTHERS
 (PARTICULARLY —) RECHERCHE
CHOICEST PICK PRIMROSE
CHOIR KERE QUIRE CHAPEL CHORUS CHORALE CONCERT KAPELLE PSALMODY
CHOIRBOY CLERGEON CHORISTER
CHOIR LEADER CANTOR CHORAGUS CHORISTER PRECENTOR
CHOIRMASTER CHORAGUS
CHOKE DAM GAG GOB CLOG DAMP PLUG QUAR STOP WARP CHECK CHOCK CLOSE GRAIN GRANE SCRAG WORRY ACCLOY HINDER IMPEDE STIFLE SWARVE CONGEST QUACKLE QUEAZEN QUERKEN REPRESS SILENCE SMOLDER SMOTHER OBSTRUCT QUEASOME SCUMFISH STOPPAGE STRANGLE SUPPRESS THROTTLE
 (— OFF) BESET
 (— UP) CLOY GORGE STUFF
CHOKEBERRY DOGBERRY SOAPBERRY
CHOKED FOUL WOOLY WOOLLY CLOTTED
CHOKEDAMP STYTHE BLACKDAMP
CHOKERMAN CHAINER CHAINMAN
CHOKWE KIOKO
CHOLER IRE BILE FURY RAGE

ANGER WRATH SPLEEN TEMPER DISTEMPER
CHOLERIC MAD ANGRY CROSS FIERY HUFFY TESTY FUMISH IREFUL TOUCHY BILIOUS ENRAGED IRACUND PEEVISH PEPPERY WASPISH WRATHFUL IMPATIENT
CHOLIAMB SCAZON
CHONDRIOME CYTOME
CHOOSE OPT TRY CHAP CULL LIKE LIST LOVE LUST PICK TAKE VOTE WALE WEAL ADOPT ELECT PRICK ANOINT DECIDE GOWITH PLEASE PREFER SELECT EMBRACE ESPOUSE EXTRACT SEPARATE
 (— ABRUPTLY) PLUMP
 (— A CAREER) GOINTO
 (— EASIEST COURSE OF ACTION) WIMPOUT
 (— TO WEAR) FAVOR
CHOOSING OPTION ECLECTIC
CHOOSY PICKY CHOICY FINICAL
CHOP AX AXE CUT HAG HEW JAW LOP CHAP CHIP DICE GASH HACK HASH HOWL RIVE SLIT CARVE CLEFT CRACK KNOCK MINCE NOTCH SLASH STAMP TRADE TRUCK WHANG BARTER CHANGE CLEAVE INCISE EXCHANGE
 (— OFF) SNIG
 (— SMALL) DEVIL MINCE
 (— UP) HACKLE
 (— WITH DULL AX) BUTTE
 (DOG'S —) FLEW
 (PORK —) GRISKIN
CHOPINE CIOPPINO PANTOFLE
CHOPPED CUT CHAPPED
CHOPPER SAX MINCER CLEAVER SLASHER TRANCHET
CHOPPINESS CHOP JABBLE
CHOPPING BLOCK HACKLOG
CHOPPING TOOL (— CULTURE) SOAN SOHAN
CHOPPY BUMPY LOPPY LUMPY PECKY ROUGH SHORT POPPLY
CHORAL (— SOCIETY) ORPHEON
CHORD CORD DYAD ROLL TONE CORDE NERVE TRIAD TRINE ACCORD STRING TENDON TETRAD CADENCE CONCORD HARMONY ARPEGGIO DIAMETER FILAMENT SFORZANDO
 (STRIKE A —) RESONATE
 (TOUCH A —) RESONATE
CHORDATA VERTEBRA
CHORE JOB JOT CHAR DUTY TASK CHARE KNACK STINT ERRAND BUSINESS
CHOREA JUMP JERKS
CHOREOGRAPHY TERPSICHORE
CHORION SEROSA
CHORISTER SINGER CHANTER CHOIRBOY
CHORTLE TITTER
CHORUS SONG CHOIR DRONE QUIRE ACCORD ASSENT BURDEN UNISON CHORALE HOLDING REFRAIN RESPONSE THYMELICI
 (— IN PLAY) GREX
CHOSEN ELECT ELITE SORTED ELECTED FANCIED AFFECTED SELECTED

 (CAREFULLY —) RECHERCHE
 (PREF.) LECTO
CHOUGH COW CHANK CHEWET CORBIE CHOCARD
CHOWDER BOUILLABAISSE
CHOWRY COWTAIL
CHRISM CREAM CREME MURON MYRON
CHRIST X KING LORD TRUE JUDGE RANSOM VERITY MESSIAH SAVIOUR DRIGHTEN PARAMOUR
 (INFANT —) BAMBINO
CHRISTEN DUB NAME KIRSEN BAPTIZE
CHRISTENING GOSSIPING
CHRISTIAN XN XT XTIAN UNIATE GENTILE THOMEAN CHRISTEN EBIONITE GALILEAN MELCHITE NAZARENE ORIENTAL STONEITE TRADITOR COLOSSIAN
 (— MONOGRAM) IHS
 (— VISITOR TO JERUSALEM) HAJI HADJI HAJJI
 (EARLY —) COPT
 (EASTERN —) UNIAT
 (JEWISH —) JUDAIZER
 (PL.) FLOCK LAPSED ACEPHALI FAITHFUL
CHRISTIANIA CRISTY
CHRISTIANITY WAY XTY XNTY
CHRISTMAS NOEL YULE HOLIDAY NATIVITY YULETIDE MIDWINTER
CHRISTMAS ROSE BEARFOOT LUNGWORT MELAMPOD PEDELION
CHRISTOPHE COLOMB
 (COMPOSER OF —) MILHAUD
CHRIST'S-THORN NABK JUJUBE ZIZYPHUS
CHROMA COLOR QUALITY
CHROMATIC HUEFUL FLAMING SEMITONAL
CHROMATOPHORE ALLOPHORE LIPOPHORE UNIVALENT RHODOPLAST
CHROMOLITHOGRAPH OLEOGRAPH
CHROMOSOME DIAD DYAD IDANT HOMOLOG ALLOSOME AUTOSOME IDIOSOME MONOSOME KARYOMERE LEPTONEMA PLANOSOME
 (ENLARGED REGION OF —) PUFF
 (PL.) GEMINI
 (SUFF.) (HAVING — NUMBER) PLOID
CHROMOSPHERE SIERRA
CHROMOTROPE DYE
CHRONIC FIXED SEVERE INTENSE CONSTANT STUBBORN
CHRONICLE BRUT ANNAL DIARY ENACT RECORD ACCOUNT HISTORY RECITAL CORNICLE REGISTER
 (PL.) ANNALS ARCHIVE PARALIPOMENON
CHRONICLER WRITER CHRONIST COMPILER RECORDER HISTORIAN SEANNACHIE
CHRONOLOGICAL TEMPORAL
CHRONOMETER DIAL HACK CLOCK TIMER WATCH
CHRYSAL FRET
CHRYSALIS KELL PUPA AURELIA

CHRYSANTHEMUM MUM KIKU
OXEYE SPOON BRUTUS POMPON
KIKUMON KIRIMON AZALEAMUM
PYRETHRUM MARGUERITE
CHRYSEIS (FATHER OF —) CHRYSES
CHRYSIN FLAVONE
CHRYSIPPUS (FATHER OF —)
PELOPS
(MOTHER OF —) ASTYOCHE
(SLAYER OF —) HIPPODAMIA
CHRYSOBERYL CATEYE
CHRYSOPAL CYMOPHANE
CHRYSOLITE OLIVINE PERIDOT
CHRYSOPAL
CHRYSOTILE ASBESTOS
CHTHONIAN INFERNAL
CHUB DACE DOLT FOOL KIYI LOUT
POLL CHOPA CHEVIN SHINER
CYPRINID FALLFISH MACKEREL
CHAVENDER HORNYHEAD
CHUBBY FAT CHUFF FUBSY PLUMP
PUDGY CHOATY CHUFFY PLUMPY
ROTUND ROLYPOLY
CHUB MACKEREL TINK TINKER
HARDHEAD SCOMBRID
CHUCK HEN LOG PIG CHUG GRUB
HURL JERK LUMP TOSS CHOCK
CLUCK HEAVE PITCH THROW
BOUNCE CHUCKY COLLET
CHUCKLE DISCARD
CHUCK-A-LUCK SWEAT HAZARD
BIRDCAGE
CHUCKER CROZER
CHUCK-FARTHING CHUCK KNICKER
CHUCKHOLE CAHOT CHUGHOLE
CHUCKIE-STANES DIBS
CHUCKLE CHUCK CLUCK EXULT
LAUGH GIGGLE GIZZEN KECKLE
SMUDGE TITTER CHORTLE
CHUCKLEHEAD DIMWIT
CHUD VEPS VEPSE
CHUDDAR PHULKARI
CHUFA SEDGE GLUMAL CYPRESS
EARTHNUT GALANGAL TIGERNUT
GROUNDNUT
CHUM CAD PAL BAIT MATE PARD
TOLE TOLL BUDDY BUTTY CRONY
SPROG AIKANE CHUMMY COBBER
COPAIN FRIEND PARDNER
ROOMMATE
(— AROUND) HOBNOB
CHUMMY GREAT MATEY PALLY
FAMILIAR
CHUMP ASS DOLT HEAD BLOCK
PUMPKIN ENDPIECE SCHLEMIEL
CHUNCHO CHAMA
CHUNK DAB DAD FID GOB PAT WAD
JUNK JUNT SLUG CHOCK CHUCK
CLAUT PIECE THROW WHANG
WHANK GOBBET DORNICK
KNUCKLE LUNCHEON
CHUNKY LUMPY PLUMP SQUAT
STOUT THICK TRUSS BLOCKY
CHURRY STOCKY CHUNKED
CHURCH DOM SEE DOME FANE
FOLD HIGH KILL KIRK KURK TERA
ABBEY AUTEM FAITH FLOCK KOVIL
SAMAJ TITLE BETHEL CHAPEL
CHARGE HIERON SPOUSE TEMPLE
EDIFICE FANACLE IGLESIA
LATERAN MEMORIA MINSTER
ORATORY RECTORY STATION
TEMPLET BASILICA EBENEZER

ECCLESIA PECULIAR
PROCATHEDRAL
(— BOOK) TRIODION
(AREA OF —) APSE BEMA
(CHRISTIAN —) BODY ISRAEL
HERITAGE
(EASTERN —) UNIATE
(KIND OF —) STAVE
(MEMBER OF UNIFICATION —)
MOONIE
(PREF.) ECCLESIASTICO
ECCLESI(O)
CHURCHMAN ALDER ELDER
DEACON KIRKMAN PRELATE
(HIGH —) PUSEYITE PRELATIST
(LOW —) SIM LOWBOY SIMEONITE
CHURCH-OFFICER BEADLE BEDRAL
BEDERAL
CHURCH SERVICE HEARING
TENEBRAE
CHURCHWARDEN PIPE STRAW
WARDEN WARNER
CHURCHYARD HAW LITTEN
CEMETERY KIRKYARD LYNCHGATE
CHURL CAD MAN OAF BOOR CARL
GNOF HIND LOUT SERF CARLE
CEORL CHUFF GNOFF KNAVE
MISER BODACH CARLOT HARLOT
LUBBER RUSTIC VASSAL YEOMAN
BONDMAN FREEMAN HASKARD
HUSBAND NIGGARD PEASANT
VILLAIN VILLEIN CURMUDGEON
CHURLISH MEAN BLUFF GRUFF
ROUGH RUNTY SURLY URSAL
CRABBY RUSTIC SORDID SULLEN
VULGAR BOORISH CARLAGE
CARLISH CRABBED CURRISH
DOGGISH INCIVIL PEEVISH VIOLENT
CHURN BEAT BOIL KIRN MOIL STIR
DRILL SHAKE BUBBLE SEETHE
AGITATE BARATTE TRUNDLE
CHUTE RUSH SLIP TUBE FLUME
HURRY RAPID SHOOT SLIDE
HOPPER TROUGH DECLINE
DESCENT DOWNFALL STAMPEDE
TELEGRAPH
(MINING —) PASS TELEGRAPH
CHUTZPAH CRUST
CHUZA (WIFE OF —) JOANNA
CIBOL SYBO ONION SYBOW
SHALLOT
CIBORIUM PIX PYX CANOPY CIVORY
COFFER CIMBORIO
CICADA CAD CIGALE JARFLY
LOCUST TETTIX LYREMAN
HOMOPTER
(SOUND OF —) CHIRR
CICATRICE FESTER
CICATRICLE TREAD GALLATURE
CICATRIX EYE MARK SCAB SCAR
SEAM
CICATRIZE FESTER SCARIFY
CICELY MYRRH
CICERO TULLY
CICERONE GUIDE PILOT MENTOR
ORATOR COURIER SIGHTSMAN
CICERONIAN TULLIAN
CICHLID JEWELFISH
CID HERO CAMPEADOR
(AUTHOR OF —) CORNEILLE
(CHARACTER IN —) GOMES DIEGUE
SANCHE CHIMENE FERNAND
URRAQUE RODRIGUE

CID, EL (COMPOSER OF —)
MASSENET
CIDER PERRY PERKIN SWANKY
SYDDYR POMMAGE SCRUMPY
BEVERAGE COCCAGEE
(HARD —) APPLEJACK
(INFERIOR —) SWANKY
CIGAR PURO TOBY WEED BREVA
CLARO SEGAR SHUCK SMOKE
CONCHA CORONA HAVANA
MADURA MADURO MANILA
STOGIE TWOFER BOUQUET
CHEROOT CULEBRA LONDRES
REGALIA TRABUCO COLORADO
LOCOFOCO PANATELA PERFECTO
PICKWICK PURITANO
(PART OF —) BAND FOOT HEAD
TUCK FILLER WRAPPER
CIGARETTE CIG FAG BIRI BUTT KING
PILL SKAG CIGGY CUBEB JOINT
SHUCK SMOKE WHIFF CIGGIE
GASPER REEFER CIGARITO
(— BUTT) ROACH
(— SUBSTANCE) TAR
(MARIHUANA —) JOINT STICK
(MARIJUANA —) JAY JOINT SPLIFF
(PART OF —) BAND FOOT PAPER
FILTER
CIGARFISH SCAD QUIAQUIA
CILIATION
(SUFF.) TRICHA TRICHI(A)
TRICHOUS TRICHY
CILIUM HAIR LASH EYELASH
UNCINUS BARBICEL CILIOLUM
(PREF.) BLEPHAR(O)
CILIX (BROTHER OF —) CADMUS
THANUS PHINEUS PHOENIX
(FATHER OF —) AGENOR
(MOTHER OF —) TELEPHASSA
(SISTER OF —) EUROPA
CILLOSIS LIFEBLOOD
CIMBALOM CEMBALON DULCIMER
CIMEX BEDBUG ACANTHIA
CIMON (FATHER OF —) MILTIADES
(MOTHER OF —) HEGESIPYLE
CINCH BELT GIRD GRIP PIPE SNAP
GIMME GIRTH GRAVY BREEZE
CINCHA FASTEN WRAPUP PIANOLA
SINECURE
CINCHONA CHINA QUINA
CINCHONA BARK
(PREF.) QUIN(O)
CINCINNATI PORKOPOLIS
CINCTURE BAND BELT GIRD HALO
LIST RING ZONE GIRTH CENTER
CESTUS COLLAR FILLET GIRDLE
BALDRIC COMPASS ENCIRCLE
SURCINGLE
CINDER ASH TAP COAL GRAY SCAR
SLAG CHARK DROSS EMBER
DANDER SCORIA CLINKER FOXTAIL
RESIDUE
(REFUSE —) BREEZE
(VOLCANIC —) LAPILLUS
(PL.) GLEEDS
CINEMA FILMS DRIVEIN THEATER
CINEMATIZE FILMIZE
CINEMATOGRAPH KINO
VERISCOPE VITAGRAPH
CINEPHILE CINEAST
CINERARIA URNS SENECIO
CINGULUM BAND RIDGE GIRDLE
CINNABAR MINIUM

CINNAMON CANEL SPICE CASSIA
SANELA STACTE CANELLA
BARBASCO
(WILD —) BAYBERRY
CINNAMONROOT FLYBANE
FLEAWORT
CINNAMON STONE GARNET
ESSONITE
CINQUEFOIL FRASIER COWBERRY
HARDHACK ROSACEAN QUINTFOIL
SILVERWEED
CINYRAS (DAUGHTER OF —)
MYRRHA
(FATHER OF —) APOLLO
(SON OF —) ADONIS
CION BUD IMP SECT SLIP GRAFT
SCION SHOOT UVULA SARMENT
GRAFTING
CIPHER KEY NIL CODE NULL ZERO
ALBAM AUGHT OUGHT DECODE
DEVICE FIGURE LETTER NAUGHT
NOUGHT NUMBER SYMBOL
ATHBASH NULLITY MONOGRAM
VIGENERE NOTHINGLY
CIRCASSIAN ADIGHE KABARD
CHERKESS KABARDIN
CIRCE SIREN TEMPTER
(BROTHER OF —) AEETES
(FATHER OF —) SOL
(LOVER OF —) ULYSSES ODYSSEUS
(MOTHER OF —) PERSE
(NIECE OF —) MEDEA
(SON OF —) TELEGONUS
CIRCINATE SCORPIOID
CIRCLE DOT LAP ORB RED SET CLUE
CULT DISK GYRE HALO HOOP IRIS
LOOP MARU ORBE RING RINK
ROLL TOUR TURN ZONE BLACK
CAROL CLASS CROWN CYCLE
FETCH FRAME GROUP KREIS
MONDE ORBIT PEARL REALM
RHOMB RIGOL ROUND ROWEL
SKIRT SWIRL TWIRL BEZANT
BROUGH CIRCUS CIRQUE CLIQUE
COLLET COLURE CORDON
CORONA DIADEM EQUANT GIRDLE
RONDEL ROTATE RUNDLE SPIRAL
SYSTEM TROPIC AZIMUTH
CHUKKAR CHUKKER CIRCLET
CIRCUIT COMPANY COMPASS
CORONET COTERIE ENCLOSE
HORIZON MONTHON REVOLVE
RINGLET DEFERENT ECLIPTIC
FROSTBOW ROUNDURE
SURROUND
(— AROUND ORGAN) ANNULET
(— IN BULL'S-EYE) CARTON
(— OF FRIED DOUGH) POPADUM
(— OF HELL) MALEBOLGE
(— OF MONOLITHS) CROMLECH
(— TRACED BY HORSE) VOLT
(ASTRONOMICAL —) EQUANT
EPICYCLE
(DANCE —) GALLEY
(EIGHTH PART OF —) OCTANT
(FAIRY —) RINGLET
(FULL —) AMBIT
(GREAT —) EQUATOR ECLIPTIC
MERIDIAN
(IMAGINARY —) CYCLE DEFERENT
(INNER —) BOSOM
(MYSTIC —) MANDALA
(PARHELIC —) FROSTBOW

(QUARTER —) ARC
(STONE —) CAROL HURLER
GORSEDD CROMLECH
(TRAVERSE —) RACER
(TWO —S) CACHET
(PREF.) CYCL(O) GYRO
CIRCLET BAND HALO HOOP RING
CROWN RIGOL VERGE BANGLE
CIRQUE CORONA WREATH CIRCUIT
CORONET VALLARY BRACELET
HEADBAND
(PREF.) STEPHAN(O)
CIRCUIT LAP AREA BOUT EYRE ITER
LOOP TOUR WEND ZONE AMBIT
CHAIN CYCLE ORBIT ROUND
ROUTE VIRON AMBAGE BUFFER
CIRCLE DETOUR DOUBLE HOOKUP
SPHERE UMGANG ZODIAC
ADAPTER ADDRESS COMARCA
COMPASS COUNTER DIOCESE
ACCEPTER DIPLEXER DISTRICT
PERIPLUS PROGRESS
(BRANCH —) LEG
(COMPUTER —) NOR NAND
(ELECTRIC —) LEG LOOP DOUBLER
SQUELCH SECONDARY
(ELECTRONIC —) GATE
(INTEGRATED —) CHIP MICROCHIP
(JUNCTION —) TRUNK
CIRCUITOUS MAZY CURVED
CROOKED DEVIOUS OBLIQUE
SINUOUS TWISTED VAGRANT
WINDING FLEXUOUS INDIRECT
RAMBLING TORTUOUS
AMBAGIOUS DECEITFUL
DEVIATING WANDERING
ROUNDABOUT
(— METHOD) WINDLASS
CIRCUITOUSLY ROUND
CIRCULAR O BILL FLIER FLYER
LIBEL ORBAL ORBED ROUND
DODGER FOLDER RINGED WHEELY
ANNULAR COMPASS CYCLOID
DISCOID DISLIKE HANDOUT
PERFECT RUNDLED COMPLETE
DOPEBOOK ENCYCLIC GLOBULAR
INFINITE NUMMULAR PAMPHLET
DOPESHEET ORBICULAR
CIRCULAR-KNIT SEAMLESS
CIRCULATE GO AIR MIX MOVE PASS
RISE TURN WALK WIND BANDY
TROLL CANARD PURVEY ROTATE
SCURRY SPHERE SPREAD WANDER
CANVASS CONVECT DIFFUSE
PUBLISH CONVOLVE
CIRCULATING WAIF AFLOAT
AMBIENT CURRENT
CIRCULATION ISSUE COURSE
COVERAGE CURRENCY
CIRCUMCISER MOHEL
CIRCUMCISION BRITH PERITOMY
CIRCUMFERENCE ARC AUGE
AMBIT APSIS GIRTH VERGE
BORDER BOUNDS CIRCLE LIMITS
COMPASS BOUNDARY SURROUND
(— OF SHELL) LIMBUS
CIRCUMFERENTOR PLANCHETTE
CIRCUMFLEX DOGHOUSE
(INVERTED —) HACEK
CIRCUMLOCUTION AMBAGE
CIRCUIT WINDING VERBIAGE
CIRCUMLOCUTORY WORDY
CIRCUMNAVIGATION PERIPLUS

CIRCUMSCRIBE BOUND FENCE
LIMIT DEFINE CAPTURE CONFINE
ENCLOSE ENVIRON ENCIRCLE
RESTRAIN RESTRICT SURROUND
CONSCRIBE
CIRCUMSCRIBED NARROW
INSULAR LIMITED
(PREF.) CIRCUM
CIRCUMSPECT SHY WARY WISE
ALERT CHARY CAREFUL GUARDED
PRUDENT CAUTIOUS DISCREET
VIGILANT WATCHFUL
CIRCUMSPECTION RESPECT
PRUDENCE WARINESS
CIRCUMSTANCE GO FIX CASE FACT
ITEM NOTE EVENT PHASE POINT
START STATE THING AFFAIR DETAIL
FACTOR PICKLE CALLING ELEMENT
EPISODE INCIDENT INSTANCE
POSITION OCCURRENCE
PARTICULAR
(BAFFLING —) WARK
(CRITICAL —S) EXTREMES
(DIFFICULT —) WANTS
(EXECRABLE —) ATROCITY
(LUDICROUS —) JEST
(PL.) CIRCS STATE TERMS ESTATE
FORTUNE
CIRCUMSTANCED OFF
CIRCUMSTANTIAL EXACT FORMAL
MINUTE PRECISE DETAILED
ITEMIZED PARTICULAR
CIRCUMSTANTIATE SUPPORT
EVIDENCE
CIRCUMVENT BALK BEAT DISH
DUPE FOIL CHEAT CHECK COZEN
EVADE OUTGO TRICK BAFFLE
DELUDE ENTRAP NOBBLE OUTWIT
THWART CAPTURE DECEIVE
DEFRAUD ENSNARE PREVENT
OUTFLANK SURROUND
UNDERFONG
CIRCUS RING SHOW ARENA CANVAS
CIRCLE CIRQUE CARNIVAL
(— LOT) TOBER
(— RING) TAN
CIRQUE CWM CIRC BASIN CIRCLE
CIRCUS CORRIE RECESS CIRCLET
EROSION
CIS SYN NERAL NORMAL
CISCO KIYI BLOAT BLOATER
BLUEFIN LONGJAW MOONEYE
BLACKFIN GRAYBACK TULLIBEE
WHITEFIN
CISKEI (CAPITAL OF —) BISHO
(TOWN OF —) ALICE ZWELITSHA
CISSA SIRGANG
CISSEUS (BROTHER OF —) GYAS
(COMPANION OF —) HERCULES
(FATHER OF —) MELAMPUS
(SLAYER OF —) AENEAS
CISSUS TREEBINE
CIST BOX KIST TOMB CHEST CISTA
QUOIT CASKET CHAMBER
KISTVAEN
CISTERCIAN TRAPPIST
CISTERN BAC FAT SAC TUB URN VAT
BACK PANT SUMP TANK URNA
WELL LAVER CAVITY CAISSON
CHULTUN CUVETTE STEEPER
FEEDHEAD
CITADEL ARX FORT HALL ALAMO
BURSA BYRSA TOWER CASTLE

BOROUGH CHESTER KREMLIN
ALHAMBRA FASTNESS FORTRESS
TOOTHILL ACROPOLIS
CITATION CITAL NOTICE MENTION
SUMMONS EPIGRAPH MONITION
AUTHORITY EVOCATION
CITE CALL NAME SIST TELL ALLAY
EVOKE QUOTE REFER ACCITE
ACCUSE ADDUCE ALLEGE AROUSE
AVOUCH EXCITE INVOKE NOTIFY
RECITE REPEAT SUMMON
ADVANCE ARRAIGN BESPEAK
CONVENT EXCERPT EXTRACT
IMPEACH MENTION INDICATE
INSTANCE REHEARSE
CITHARA CITHER CITOLE PHORMINX
CITHERN ZITTERN LANGSPEL
CITIZEN CIT ALLY VOTER NATIVE
BURGESS BURGHER CITOYEN
CLERUCH DENIZEN ELECTOR
FLATCAP FREEMAN OPPIDAN
SUBJECT TOWNMAN AMERICAN
CIVILIAN COMMONER CONSCIVE
DOMESTIC NATIONAL OCCUPANT
RESIDENT
(— OF SECOND CLASS) KNIGHT
HIPPEUS
(—S OF MEDINA) ANSAR
(FOREIGN-BORN —) ALIEN
(LATIN — OF U.S.) YANQUI
(PL.) SUBJECT PERIOECI CITIZENRY
(SUFF.) ITE
CITIZENRY COUNTRY SUBJECT
CITRAL GERANIAL
CITRON LIME CEDRA LEMON
CEDRAT ETHROG YELLOW
BERGAMOT
CITTERN LAUD CITHERN PENORCON
CITY FU WON BURG DORP TOWN
URBS WOON ZION DUNUM CALNO
EKRON JEBUS LILLE MANOA PIECE
PLACE POLIS SETTE STEAD VILLE
CALNEH CENTER CIUDAD CUTHAH
GILEAD JAMNIA JEBUSI LAGADO
NAGARA PITHOM STAPLE
BABYLON CAMBALU CHESTER
ELLASAR FREEDOM JABNEEL
MECHLIN CABECERA ELDORADO
MAGAZINE PALENQUE
(— LIFE) ASHCAN
(— OF GOD) SION ZION
(ANCIENT —) PERGAMUM
(CAPITAL —) SEAT
(CATHEDRAL —) SEE
(CHIEF —) CAPITAL CABECERA
MEGAPOLIS
(RICH —) MAGAZINE
(TREASURE —) RAAMSES
(WICKED —) BABYLON
(PREF.) URBI
(SUFF.) GRAD POLE POLIS
POLITAN POLITE
CITY-STATE POLIS CIVITAS
CIVET CAT CIT GENET RASSE ZIBET
BONDAR FOUSSA MUSANG
PAGUMA ZIBETH CIVETTA
FOSSANE LINSANG NANDINE
POLECAT ZIBETUM ZINSANG
FANALOKA MONGOOSE
TANGALUNG
CIVIC LAY CIVIL SUAVE URBAN
POLITE URBANE CIVICAL SECULAR
CIVIL FAIR HEND HENDE SUAVE

POLITE URBANE AFFABLE AMIABLE
COURTLY ELEGANT GALLANT
POLITIC REFINED SECULAR
DISCREET GRACIOUS OBLIGING
POLISHED WELLBRED
CIVILIAN CIT CIVIE CIVIL CIVVY
PEKIN MOHAIR CITIZEN TEACHER
CIVILIST GOWNSMAN OUTSIDER
NONCOMBATANT
(— ENTERTAINING SOLDIER) PYKE
CIVILITY BONTE COURT COMITY
NOTICE AMENITY COURTESY
URBANITY GENTILITY
(PL.) HONORS HONOURS
CIVILIZATION ISLAM KULTUR
POLICE CULTURE ECUMENE
CIVILITY
(GREEK —) HELLENISM
CIVILIZE TAME TEACH TRAIN POLISH
REFINE EDUCATE HUMANIZE
URBANIZE
CIVILIZED CHRISTIAN
CIVVIES MUFTI
CLABBER LOP MUD MIRE CURDLE
LOPPER CLAUBER
CLACKDISH CLICKET
CLAD DREST ROBED BESEEN
CLEDDE DECKED ADORNED
ARRAYED ATTIRED CLOTHED
COVERED DRESSED SHEATHED
(— IN PURPLE) PORPORATE
(SCANTILY —) SINGLY
CLADOSE RAMOSE CLADINE
BRANCHED
CLAIM ASK DUE AVER AVOW CALL
CASE DIBS LIEN MINE NAME PLEA
COLOR DRAFT EXACT PLEAD RIGHT
SHOUT TITLE ALLEGE ASSERT
DEMAND DESIRE ELICIT EQUITY
INTEND RECKON ACCLAIM
COLLECT DERECHO DRAUGHT
PRETEND PRETEXT PROFESS
RECLAIM REQUIRE SOLICIT
ARROGATE DARRAIGN INTEREST
MAINTAIN PRETENCE PRETENSE
PROCLAIM SUBCLAIM CHALLENGE
POSTULATE PRETENSION
PRESCRIPTION
(— IN BUSINESS) CAPITAL
(— IN LEASE) REDDENDO
REDDENDUM
(— TO BE BELIEVED) AUTHORITY
(FALSE —) JACTATION
(FORESTER'S —) PUTURE
(INDIAN LEGAL —) HAK HAKH
(JUST —) RIGHT
(MINING —) SHICER
CLAIMANT CLAIMER USURPER
PRETENDER
CLAIRE PARK
CLAIRVOYANCE ESP INSIGHT
VOYANCE LUCIDITY SAGACITY
TELOPSIS PRECOGNITION
CLAIRVOYANT FEY SEER OMENER
PROPHET SEERESS
CLAM MYA BASE CLOG DAUB GLAM
HUSH MEAN BLUNT CLAMP CRASH
GAPER GLAUM GRASP GROPE
PAHUA RAZOR SHELL SMEAR
SOLEN SPOUT STICK VENUS
ADHERE CLUTCH GWEDUC
QUAHOG STICKY BIVALVE
CLANGOR COQUINA MOLLUSK

STEAMER ADHESIVE ARROGATE
BULLNOSE SHIPWORM
NANNINOSE
(KIND OF —) RAZOR
(PART OF —) BEAK FOOT SHELL
VALVE MANTLE SIPHON UMBONE
ORIFICE
CLAMBAKE BAKE RALLY
CLAMAROO SQUANTUM
CLAMBER CLIMB SCALE CLAVER
SCRAWM SPRAWL RAMMACK
SCRABBLE SCRAMBLE SPRACHLE
STRUGGLE
CLAMMY DAMP DANK SOFT WACK
MOIST SAMMY STICKY WAUGHY
FLACCID SQUIDGY CLAMMISH
CLAMOR CRY DIN HUE BARK BERE
BUNK GAFF RANE RERD ROAR
ROUP ROUT SONG UTAS WAIL
BLARE BOAST BRUIT CHIDE CHIRM
NOISE OUTAS RERDE RUMOR
SHOUT BELLOW BOWWOW
HUBBUB OUTCRY QUETHE RACKET
TUMULT UPROAR YATTER
CLAMOUR EXCLAIM ORATION
STASHIE NORATION PILILLOO
PULLALUE SHOUTING
(— AGAINST) DECRY
CLAMOROUS NIP LOUD AROAR
NOISY VOCAL BLATANT CLAMANT
DINSOME YELLING BRAWLING
DECRYING OPENMOUTHED
OBSTREPEROUS
CLAMP DOG HOG LUG NIP PIN SET
BAIL BALE BEND BOLT BURY CLAM
GLAM GRIP JACK MUTE NAIL VISE
YOKE BLOCK BRACE CLASP CRAMP
GLAND GLAUM HORSE CLINCH
FASTEN MOPHEAD STIRRUP
FASTENER HOLDFAST
(— FOR BASS DRUM) SPUR
(— FOR CORK) AGRAFE AGRAFFE
(— FOR FLASK) GLAND
(— ON TUBE) PINCHCOCK
(STORAGE —) GRAVE
CLAMSHELL CLAM GRAB SHUCK
CLAN ATI HAN KIN SET SIB CULT
GENS HAPU NAME RACE SECT
SEPT SIOL UNIT AIMAK AYLLU
CLASS GENOS GROUP HORDE
PARTY TRIBE ABUSUA CLIQUE
FAMILY SENAAH ABIEZER KINDRED
PHRATRY SATSUMA SOCIETY
ZADRUGA CALPULLI DIVISION
(— SUBDIVISION) OBE
CLANDESTINE BYE SLY FOXY
HEDGE PRIVY QUIET SNEAK
COVERT HIDDEN SECRET BOOTLEG
FURTIVE ILLICIT BACKDOOR
HIDLINGS STEALTHY
CLANG DIN DING PEAL RING TONK
CLANK CLASH NOISE JANGLE
TIMBRE
CLANGER STUMER
CLANGING JANGLE
CLANGOR DIN CLAM ROAR CLANG
HUBBUB UPROAR
CLANGOROUS BRAZEN PLANGENT
CLANGULA HARELDA
CLANK RING RACKLE
CLAP BANG CHOP FLAP PEAL SLAP
SPAT TACK CHEER CLINK CRACK
SMITE POSTER STRIKE STROKE

APPLAUD CHATTER CLAPPER
PLAUDIT HANDCLAP
(— OF THUNDER) DINT
(— ON) CRACK
CLAPBOARD KNAPPLE CLAPHOLT
CLAPNET DAYNET
CLAPPER CLAP CLACK RATTLE
TONGUE JINGLET KNACKER
KNOCKER CROTALUM
(— OF BELL) TONGUE
(PL.) BONES
CLAPPING APPLAUSE
CLAPTRAP HOKUM TRASH TRIPE
BLAGUE BUNKUM DEVICE
EYEWASH FUSTIAN BUNCOMBE
NONSENSE TRICKERY
CLARE MINORESS
CLARENCE GROWLER
CLARET TERSE PONTAC LAFITTE
BORDEAUX BADMINTON
CLARIAS HARMOOT KARMOUTH
CLARIBEL (HUSBAND OF —) PHAON
CLARICE (BROTHER OF —) HUON
(HUSBAND OF —) RINALDO
CLARIFIED PURED LAUTER
CLARIFY CLAY FINE CLEAN CLEAR
PURGE SNUFF PURIFY REFINE
RENDER SERENE SETTLE CLEANSE
DESPUME EXPLAIN GLORIFY
DEFECATE DEPURATE ELIQUATE
SIMPLIFY
CLARIN ACOCOTL
CLARINET BEN BIN BON BEEN BONE
REED AULOS CLARY PUNGI
CLARONE LAUNEDDAS
(PART OF —) KEY PAD BELL CORK
REED CLAMP COVER BARREL
LIGATURE MOUTHPIECE
FINGERPLATE
CLARION REST CLARE CLARY CLEAR
CLARINO SUFFLUE TRUMPET
**CLARISSA HARLOWE (AUTHOR OF
—)** RICHARDSON
(CHARACTER IN —) HOWE JOHN
JAMES MORDEN ROBERT SOLMES
BELFORD HARLOWE WILLIAM
ARABELLA CLARISSA LOVELACE
SINCLAIR
CLARITY GLORY SPLENDOR
STRENGTH CLEARNESS SIMPLICITY
CLARY ORVAL CLARRE SALVIA
CLASH JAR BANG BOLT BUMP DASH
FRAY NEWS SLAM BRAWL BRUNT
CHECK CRASH CROSS FIGHT
FRUSH KNOCK OCCUR PRATE
SHOCK AFFRAY DIFFER GOSSIP
HURTLE IMPACT JOSTLE STRIFE
STRIKE TATTLE THRUST THWART
COLLIDE DISCORD SCANDAL
ARGUMENT CONFLICT
(— OF WORDS) BARGE
CLASHING HARSH CONFLICT
FRICTION COLLISION
CLASP HUG PIN CLIP DOME FOLD
GRAB GRIP HASP HOLD HOOK
HOOP KEEP OUCH STAY TACH
BRACE CATCH CLING GRASP
MORSE PREEN SEIZE SLIDE SPANG
TACHE ACCOLL AGRAFE AMPLEX
BECLIP BROOCH BUCKLE CLENCH
CLUTCH ENFOLD ENWRAP FASTEN
FIBULA GIMMER GIMMOR INCLIP
INFOLD JIMMER STRAIN TASSEL

AGRAFFE AMPLECT EMBRACE
ENTWINE FERMAIL HOLDING
MOUSING TENDRIL BARRETTE
CORSELET FASTENER SURROUND
(— HANDS) SHAKE WRING
CLASPING AMPLECTANT
CLASS ILK BRAN CHOP FORM KIND
RACE RANK RATE SECT SORT SUIT
TYPE YEAR BREED CASTE GENRE
GENUS GRADE GROUP ORDER
RANGE TRIBE VARNA VERGE
ASSORT CIRCLE CLINIC DECURY
FAMILY GENDER LEAGUE MISTER
NATION PHYLUM RATING RECKON
REMOVE RUBRIC STRAIN STRIPE
CATALOG FACTION LECTURE
REGIMEN SEMINAR SPECIES
VARIETY CATEGORY DESCRIBE
DIVISION GENOTYPE GEOMOROI
(— OF BARDS) THULIR
(— OF GOODS) BRAND
(— OF OUTCASTS) ETA
(— OF PEOPLE) FOLK SALARIAT
(— OF SECURITIES) LEGAL
(— OF SHASTRAS) SRUTI SHRUTI
(— OF SLAVES) HELOTRY
(— OF SOUNDS) ENDING
(— OF TEASELS) KINGS
(ARISTOCRATIC —) ARISTOI
(CHOICEST —) ROBUR
(DEPRESSED —) PANCHAMA
(FIRST —) GAY
(HEREDITARY —) CASTE
(INTERMEDIATE —) SHELL REMOVE
(JAPANESE —) HEIMIN KWAZOKU
(LABORING —) PARAIYAN
PROLETARIAT
(LEARNED —) VATES CLERISY
(LOWER —) BELOW GENTE
(LOWER —S) MASSES
(LOWEST —) LAG SCUM
(MIDDLE —) BOURGERIS
BOURGEOISIE
(PEASANT —) JACQUERIE
(PRIVILEGED —) ARISTOCRACY
(SLAVEHOLDING —) CHIVALRY
(SOCIAL —) ESTATE SHIZOKU
(WAGE EARNINNG —)
PROLETARIAT
(WEALTHY —) PLUTOCRACY
(WITH —) INTASTE
(WORKING —) TOIL
(PREF.) CRATO
(SUFF.) CY OIDA OIDEA OIDEI
CLASSIC VINTAGE AUGUSTAN
TEXTBOOK
CLASSICAL PURE ATTIC GREEK
LATIN ROMAN CHASTE CLASSIC
ACADEMIC HELLENIC MASTERLY
(NOT —) BASE
CLASSICALLY IDEALLY
CLASSIFICATION FILE RANK RATE
SORT CODEN GENRE GENUS
GRADE ORDER TAXIS RATING
SYSTEM ANALYSIS CATEGORY
DIVISION TAXONOMY BREAKDOWN
CLASSIFIED SECRET
CLASSIFIER COUNTER SEPARATOR
CLASSIFY CODE LIST RANK RATE
SIZE SORT SUIT TAPE TYPE BREAK
CLASS DRAFT GRADE GROUP
LABEL RANGE TRIBE ASSORT
CODIFY DIGEST DIVIDE IMPOST

TICKET ACCOUNT ARRANGE
BRACKET BRIGADE CATALOG
DISPOSE DRAUGHT GRAMMAR
MARSHAL SUBSUME REGISTER
PIGEONHOLE
(— TOGETHER) SLUMP
CLASSIS CONFERENCE
CLASSY TONY SMOOTH
CLATHRATE LATTICED
CLATTER DIN JAR CLACK NOISE
RUMOR BABBLE GABBLE GOSSIP
HOTTER HURTLE RACKLE RATTLE
TATTLE BLATTER CHATTER
CLUNTER CLUTTER PRATTLE
REESHLE SHATTER SLAMBANG
CLATTERING CLATTERY
SLITHERING
CLAUSE ITEM PART CLOSE COMMA
JOKER PLANK RIDER SALVO TROPE
MEMBER PHRASE ADJUNCT
ARTICLE COMMATA PASSAGE
PROVISO SLEEPER APODOSIS
CLAUSULA PARTICLE PETITION
REDDENDO SENTENCE TENENDAS
TENENDUM NOVODAMUS
(— IN CREED) FILIOQUE
(— IN WRIT) TESTE
(— OF DEED) TESTATUM
(— OF WILL) DEVISE
(ADDED —) RIDER
(ADDITIONAL —) RIDER
(CONDITIONAL —) PROTASIS
(SAAVING —) SALVO
(SUBORDINATE —) PROTASIS
CLAVACIN PATULIN
CLAVER PRATE CLOVER GOSSIP
CHATTER CLABBER CLAIVER
CLAMBER
CLAVICHORD CLAVIER MANICORD
UNICHORD CLARIGOLD
MONOCHORD
CLAVICLE FURCULE COLLARBONE
CLAVICOR HORN
CLAVIER MANUAL KLAVIER
CLAVUS CORN BUNION HELOMA
CLAW DIG PEG CLEE CRAB FANG
FAWN HAND HOOK NAIL PULL
SERE TEAR UNCE CHELA CLAUT
CLOOF CLUFE COURT GRASP
GRIFF ONGLE SCLAW SEIZE TALON
UNCUS CLUNCH CLUTCH CRATCH
NIPPER POUNCE SCRAPE SINGLE
UNGUAL UNGUIS UNGULA
WEAPON CRUBEEN FALCULA
FLATTER SCRATCH SHUTTLE
WHEEDLE SCRABBLE
(HAWK'S —) POUNCE
(LOBSTER —) CHELA
(PL.) CLUTCH
(PREF.) CHEL(I)(O) ONYCH(O)
UNGUI
(SUFF.) ONYCHA ONYCHES
ONYCHIA ONYCHUS ONYX
CLAY BAT COB PUG WAD WAX BASS
BEND BODY BOLE ROTT GALT
GLEY LOAM LUTE MARL MIRE
PAPA SMIT TILL ARGIL BRICK
CLOAM EARTH GAULT LOESS
OCHRE PASTE RABAT TASCO
BINDER CLEDGE CLUNCH KAOLIN
PUDDLE SAGGER DAUBING
MOULDER RASHING CAMSTANE
CAMSTONE CIMOLITE FIRECLAY

GUMBOTIL LATERITE LIFELESS SINOPITE SMECTITE
(— FOR MELTING POTS) TASCO
(— IN GLASS) TEAR
(— IRON) BULL
(— LAYER) VARVE
(— USED MEDICALLY) FANGO
(COVERED WITH —) LUTOSE
(HARD —) BEND
(HARDENED —) METAL
(INDURATED —) BASS CLUNCH
(PIECE OF FIRED —) TILE
(PIPE —) CAMSTANE CAMSTONE
(POTTER'S —) SLIP ARGIL PETUNTSE
(REMOVE —) UNLUTE
(SURPLUS —) SPARE
(TOUGH —) LECK
(3-ARMED, HARD-FIRED —) STILT
(PREF.) ARGILL(O) ARGILLACEO PEL(O)
CLAYEY BOLAR HEAVY MALMY MARLY CLEDGY LUTOSE ARGILLIC
CLAYMORE FERRARA MORGLAY
CLAY PIGEON BIRD CLAY
CLAYSTONE LECK
CLAYWARE GLOST
CLEADING CLOTHING
CLEAN DO FAY FEY HOE MOP NET DRUM DUST FAIR NEAT PURE REDD RIPE SIDE SMUG SWAB TRIM WASH WIPE CLEAR CURRY EMPTY FEIGH GRAVE SCOUR SCRUB SMART SWEEP TERSE TOSHY BARREL CHASTE CLEVER KOSHER PURIFY SPANDY APINOID BANDBOX CHAMOIS CLEANLY CLEANSE CLEARLY FURBISH PERFECT SWINGLE ABSTERGE BACKWASH BRIGHTLY DEXTROUS ENTIRELY RENOVATE SCAVENGE SPOTLESS UNSOILED
(— A FUR) DRUM
(— A PIPE) REAM
(— A QUILL) DUTCH
(— BOAT) CAREEN
(— BY SCRAPING) GRAVE
(— BY SMOKE) SMEEK
(— CANNON) SCALE
(— FEATHERS) PREEN
(— FIREARM) WORM
(— FLAX) SWINGLE
(— IN ACID) BLANCH
(— OUT) USH SPEAR
(— SHIP'S BOTTOM) HOG BREAM GRAVE
(— UP) DISPATCH
(— WITH VACUUM) HOOVER
(COME —) FESSUP
(RITUALLY —) KOSHER
CLEAN-CUT CRISP
CLEANED BRIGHT
CLEANER SOAP BORAX PURER FOLDER GUMMER RAMROD FLUEMAN SPOTTER CLEANSER
(AIR —) CAN
(GRAIN —) KICKER
(STREET —) ORDERLY
CLEAN-LIMBED CLEVER
CLEAN-LINED SPRUCE
CLEANLY PURE CLEAN ADROIT ARTFUL CHASTE FAIRLY SPANDY CORRECT ELEGANT INNOCENT SKILLFUL

CLEANNESS PURITY
CLEANSE FAY BRAN CARD COMB FARM HEAL PICK SOAP WASH BROOM BRUSH CLEAN CLEAR DIGHT DRESS FEIGH FLAME FLUSH PURGE RINSE SCOUR SCRUB SNUFF BOTTOM CAREEN EMUNGE PICKLE PURIFY REFINE SPONGE WILLOW BAPTIZE CLARIFY DEBRIDE DETERGE EXPIATE LAUNDER MUNDIFY SWEETEN ABSTERGE DEPURATE OFFSCOUR RENOVATE SCAVENGE SPRINKLE
CLEANSER LYE SOAP CLEANER PURIFIER DETERGENT DETERSIVE
CLEANSING BATH FLUSH ABLUENT CLYSMIC WASHING ABLUTION CLEANING LAVATION DETERGENT MENDATORY PURGATORY ABSTERGENT
(CEREMONIAL —) LAVABO PURGATION
CLEANTE (FATHER OF —) HARPAGON
(LOVER OF —) ANGELIQUE
(SISTER OF —) ELMIRE
CLEANTHE (BROTHER OF —) SIPHAX
CLEANTHIS (HUSBAND OF —) SOSIA
CLEANUP KILLING SWEEPUP
CLEAR HOT JAM NET PEN RID WAY CAST EASY FAIR FINE FLAT FREE GAIN GRUB JAIL JUMP NEAT OPEN OVER PURE PUTE QUIT REDD RIFE SHUT SLAM VOID ACUTE ATRIP AZURE BREAK BREME BRENT BROAD CHUCK CLEAN CRISP DRIVE LIGHT LUCID NAKED PLAIN PRINT PRUNE SCOUR SHARP SMOLT SUNNY SUTEL SWEEP UNTIE VIVID ACQUIT AERIAL ASSOIL BRIGHT CANDID CLEVER EXCUSE EXEMPT FLUTED LAUTER LIMPID LIQUID LUCENT PATENT PURIFY REMBLE SERENE SETTLE SHRILL SMOOTH UNSTOP ABSOLVE CAPITAL CLARIFY CLARION CRYSTAL DELIVER DILUCID EVIDENT EXPLAIN EXPRESS GLARING GRAPHIC LIGHTEN OBVIOUS PERVIAL RELEASE SILVERY THROUGH ACCREDIT APPARENT BRIGHTEN BULLDOZE DEFINITE DISTINCT EXPLICIT LUCULENT LUMINOUS MANIFEST PELLUCID REVELANT PERSPICUOUS
(— AWAY) FAY FEY FEIGH BANISH DISPEL DISCUSS
(— FROM) ALOOF
(— FROM CRITICISM) VINDICATE
(— IN TONE) SILVER
(— LAND) CURE BRUSH SLASH DEADEN BUSHHOG
(— OF BLAME) QUIT
(— OFF) QUIT
(— OF FINE HAIR) SLATE
(— OF GROUND) ATRIP AWEIGH
(— OF GUILT) PURGE
(— OF MUD) SLUTCH
(— OF SCUM) SKIM
(— OF SEEDS) GIN RIPPLE
(— OF TUFTS) HOB
(— OUT) BLOW HOOK SWAMP SKIDDOO HIGHTAIL DISCHARGE

(— PATH) FRAY HACK BUSHWACK
(— TABLE) DISSERVE
(— TABLES) BUS
(— THROAT) HOICK HOUGH HARRUMPH
(— UP) SOLVE ASSOIL RESOLVE DISSOLVE UNSHADOW
(ALL —) COPACETIC COPESETTIC
(NOT —) DULL DUSKY FOGGY INEVIDENT
CLEARANCE CHOP ROOM RUNBY BACKLASH ALLOWANCE
(— FOR SHIP) PRATIQUE
CLEAR-CUT LUCID SHARP DIRECT CONCISE DECIDED CHISELED DEFINITE DISTINCT INCISIVE TRENCHANT
CLEARED (— FOR ACTION) PREDY
CLEARHEADED LUCID
CLEARING SART FIELD FRITH GLADE SHADE TRACT ALCOVE ASSART RIDING RIDDING SLASHING
(FOREST —) SLASH SLASHING
CLEARLY FAIR CLEAR LIGHT REDLY FAIRLY FRANKLY PATENTLY WITTERLY
CLEAR-MINDEDNESS LUCIDITY
CLEARNESS CLARITY FINESSE EVIDENCE FINENESS
CLEAR-SIGHTED SEEING
CLEARWEED RICHWEED
CLEAT BITT STUD BLOCK CHOCK KEVEL LEDGE RANGE WEDGE BATTEN RIFFLE BOLLARD COXCOMB GROUSER SIRMARK SUPPORT SURMARK
CLEAVAGE RIFT CLEFT WASSIE FISSION FISSURE WEDGING DIVISION SCISSION
(PREF.) SCHISTO SCHIZ(O)
(SUFF.) CLASE SCHISIS SCHIST
CLEAVE CUT RIP CHOP HANG HOLD JOIN LINK PART RELY REND RIFT RIVE SLIT TEAR BREAK CARVE CHAWN CHINE CLAVE CLEFT CLING CLOVE CRACK KNIFE SEVER SHALE SHARE SHEAR SLIVE SPLAT STICK ADHERE BISECT COHERE DIVIDE FURROW PIERCE SLEAVE SUNDER DISPART FISSURE SEPARATE
(— OFF) AXE SCIND
CLEAVER CLIVE CLEAVE FROWER PARANG CHOPPER HATCHET PARANGI
CLEAVERS GRIP CLOTE CLOTS CLITHE HAIRIF HAIRUP BURHEAD LOVEMAN PIGTAIL BIRDLIME
CLEAVING DYSTOME FISSION DYSTOMIC
(— READILY) EUTOMOUS
CLECHE URDE URDY URDEE
CLEF KEY CLIVE CHIAVETTA
CLEFT CUT GAP JAG CHAP CHOP FENT FLAW GASH NOCK REFT RIFT RILL RIMA RIVE SLIT BIFID BREAK CHASM CHAWN CHINK CLOFF CLOVE CRACK CREEK CRENA GULCH KLOOF RILLE RIVEN SINUS SPLIT BREACH CHAPPY CLEAVE CLOUGH CLOVEN CRANNY CROTCH DIVIDE LISSOM PARTED RECESS RICTUS STIGMA BLASTED CHIMNEY CREVICE DIVIDED

FISSURE OPENING SLIFTER APERTURE CREVASSE FRACTURE INCISION INCISURA MULTIFID SCISSURA SCISSURE PALMATIFID
(— BETWEEN HILLS) SLACK RAVINE
(— IN HOOF) SEAM
(— IN ROCK) RIVA
(— IN THE POSTERIORS) NOCK
(— OF BUTTOCKS) CREASE
(PREF.) FISSI SCHISTO SCHIZ(O)
(SUFF.) FID FIDATE
CLEMATIS PIPESTEM CURLYHEAD
CLEMENCY ORE PITY GRACE MERCY LENITY QUARTER KINDNESS LENIENCY MILDNESS
CLEMENT MILD SOFT WARM GENTLE LENIENT MERCIFUL
CLEMENZA DI TITO (CHARACTER IN —) TITUS ANNIUS SEXTUS BERENICE SERVILIA VITELLIA
(COMPOSER OF —) MOZART
CLENCH FIST GRIP GRIT HOLD NAIL BRACE CLASP CLENK CLINT CLOSE GRASP CLINCH CLUTCH DOUBLE
(— FIST) GRIPE
CLEONTE (LOVER OF —) LUCILLE
CLEOPATRA (BROTHER OF —) ILUS ZETES CALAIS GANYMEDE ASSARACUS
(FATHER OF —) IDAS TROS BOREAS PTOLEMY
(HUSBAND OF —) PHILIP PHINEUS PTOLEMY MELEAGER
(MOTHER OF —) MARPESSA ORITHYIA CALLIRRHOE
CLEPE CLUPIEN
CLEPSYDRA GURRY GHURRY
CLERGY CLOTH CRAPE CHURCH CLERISY MINISTRY
(BODY OF —) PUI PIT
CLERGYMAN ADDA ABBE DEAN PAPA CANON CLERK FROCK PADRE PILOT PRIOR RABBI VICAR BISHOP CLERIC CURATE DEACON DIVINE DOMINE PAROCH PARSON PASTOR PRIEST RECTOR SUPPLY CASSOCK PRELATE CARDINAL CHAPLAIN CLERICAL DIOCESAN EMERITUS LECTURER MINISTER ORDINARY PREACHER REVEREND SQUARSON PRESBYTER PREBENDARY REVIVALIST
CLERIC ABBE CURE CLERK FROCK DEACON GALLAH LEVITE PRIEST ACOLYTE GOLIARD ANAGNOST
(DISREPUTABLE —) GOLIARD
CLERICAL BLACK CLERIC CLERKISH PARSONIC PARSONLY
(NOT —) LAIC
CLERIMOND (BROTHER OF —) FERRAGUS
(HUSBAND OF —) VALENTINE
CLERIMONT (LOVER OF —) CLARINDA
CLERK NUN BABU MONK AGENT AWARD BABOO CLARK FILER RALPH WRITE BILLER CHASER CLERIC COMMIS GRADER HERMIT KITMAN LAYMAN MAPPER MASTER MUNSHI PANDIT PENMAN PRIEST PUNDIT RALPHO SCRIBE SIRCAR TELLER WRITER YEOMAN ACOLYTE ACTUARY BOOKMAN CARCOON

COMPOSE DOPSTER GOMASTA PIARIST SCHOLAR SHIPPER SHOPMAN STUFFER CLERGEON CLERGION CLERKESS CURSITOR EMPLOYEE GREFFIER MUTSUDDY PENCLERK RECORDER SALESMAN
(— OF ST PAUL) BARNABITE
(CHIEF —) PROTHONOTARY
(HOTEL —) DESKMAN

CLERKLY LEARNED SCRIBAL CLERGIAL SCHOLARLY

CLEVE BRAE CLIFF CLEEVE HILLSIDE

CLEVER APT SLY ABLE CUTE DEFT FEAT FELL FINE FOXY GLEG GNIB GOOD HEND KEEN NEAT SLIM SPRY AGILE ALERT CANNY CLEAN CLEAR CUNNY FALSE FEATY FENDY HANDY HEADY HENDE LITHE QUICK SHARP SLICK SMART SNACK WITTY ACTIVE ADROIT ARTFUL ASTUTE BRIGHT CRAFTY EXPERT HABILE HEPPEN KITTLE KNACKY NEATLY NIMBLE PRETTY SHREWD SPIFFY STALKY SUBTLE AMIABLE CUNNING GNOSTIC PARLISH PARLOUS VARMENT VARMINT DEXTROUS HANDSOME OBLIGING SKILLFUL TALENTED

CLEVERLY SLICK FEATLY TIDELY SMARTLY ASTUTELY

CLEVERNESS CAN CHIC NOUS TACT KNACK SKILL ESPRIT INDUSTRY DEXTERITY

CLEVIS COP DEE HAKE CLEVY COPSE BRIDGE BRIDLE MUZZLE SHACKLE PLOWHEAD

CLEW BALL CLUE HINT GLOBE GLOME SKEIN BOTTOM HURDLE THREAD

CLICHE COMMONPLACE

CLICK DOG DOT DASH MESH PAWL SLAP TICK AGREE CATCH FORGE SNECK SNICK DETENT PALLET RATCHET
(— HORSE'S SHOES) FORGE
(HEEL —S) BELLS
(TELEGRAPH —) DASH

CLICK BEETLE DOR ELATER

CLICKER CASTANET

CLIENT CEILE JAJMAN PATRON PATIENT CUSTOMER HENCHMAN RETAINER

CLIENTELE TRADE PUBLIC CLIENTRY

CLIFF HOE NIP CRAG HILL KLIP ROCK SCAR BLUFF CLEVE CLINT HEUCH HEUGH KRANS SCARP SHORE SLOPE STEEP CLEEVE HEIGHT KRANTZ PISKUN CLOGWYN HILLSIDE PALISADE TRAVERSE
(BROKEN —) CRAG
(ICE —) ICEBLINK
(LINE OF —S) PALISADE
(PREF.) CREMNO

CLIFFY SCARRY

CLIMATE SKY SUN MOOD CLIME HEAVEN REGION TEMPER ATTITUDE
(SCIENCE OF —) PHENOLOGY
(PREF.) METEOR(O)

CLIMAX CAP TOP ACME APEX HEAD NEAR PEAK SHUT CREST CROWN MOUNT SCALE TIGHT APOGEE

ASCEND FINISH HEIGHT PAYOFF SHINNY SUMMIT ZENITH BLOWOFF EVEREST CAPSHEAF CAPSTONE EPIPLOCE CULMINATION

CLIMB GAD STY COON RAMP RISE SHIN SKIN SOAR STYE CREEP GRIMP MOUNT SCALE SKLIM SPEED SPEEL SWARM TWINE ASCEND ASCENT BREAST SCLIMB SCRAWM SHINNY SWARVE SWERVE CLAMBER SCRAMBLE TRAVERSE
(— ABOARD) HOP
(— DOWN) LIGHT UNSCALE
(— IN MOUNTAINEERING) CHIMNEY
(— OVER) SURMOUNT

CLIMBER CUBE AKALA AKELA KAIWI TIMBO RIGGER SCALER COWHAGE CRAMPON CREEPER
(MOUNTAIN —) ALPINIST

CLIMBING RAMPANT SCANDENT
(MOUNTAIN —) ALPINISM

CLIMBING FERN NITO AGSAM

CLIMBING IRON SPUR PRICK CRAMPET CRAMPIT CRAMPON CREEPER PRICKER CRAMPBIT

CLIMBING PALM RATTAN

CLIMBING PEPPER BETEL

CLIMBING ROSE SCRAMBLE

CLINCH FIX GET HUG ICE TOE BIND GRIP LOCK NAIL SEAL CLAMP CLING CLINK CLINT GRASP RIVET SEIZE CLENCH CLUTCH FASTEN SECURE SNATCH CONFIRM EMBRACE GRAPPLE SCUFFLE COMPLETE CONCLUDE HOLDFAST

CLING HUG BANK HANG HOLD RELY CLASP HITCH STICK TRUST ADHERE CLEAVE CLINCH COHERE DEPEND FASTEN SHRINK WITHER CHERISH EMBRACE SHRIVEL CONTRACT

CLINGER LIMPET

CLINGFISH SUCKER TESTAR TETARD SUCKFISH

CLINGING CLUNG HUGGING ADHAMANT ADHERENT OSCULANT

CLINK ALE JUG PUT RAP BEAT BLOW BRIG CASH CLAP COIN JAIL MOVE RING SLAP CHINK KLINK LATCH MONEY RHYME SEIZE CLINCH JINGLE LOCKUP MOMENT PRISON STRIKE TINKLE INSTANT JINGLING

CLINKER BUR DUD BUHR BURR SCAR SLAG WASTE HOLLANDER
(PL.) BREEZE

CLINKER-BUILT SHINGLED LAPSTRAKE

CLINKSTONE PHONOLITE

CLINOMETER TRIMMER

CLINTONIA BLUEBEAD DOGBERRY COWTONGUE

CLIP BAT BOB CUT DOD HUG LIP LOP MOW NIG NIP BARB BEAK CHIP COLL CROP DOCK DODD FLAG HOLD PACE PARE POLL SNIP TRIM BRUSH CLASP DRESS FORCE LUNET MINCE PRUNE SHAVE SHEAR SHRIP SNICK STEEK CLUPPE CLUTCH CRUTCH FASTEN GADGET HINDER HOLDER LACING CALIPER CURTAIL CURTAIN EMBRACE

HICKORY LUNETTE SCISSOR SHORTEN DIMINISH ENCIRCLE RETAINER
(— A COIN) SHORTEN
(— OF LEAD) TINGLE
(— WOOL) CRUTCH
(CARTRIDGE —) CHARGER
(HAIR —) BARRETTE
(SPRING —) JACK

CLIP-FASTENER DOME

CLIPPED SHORN TONSURED

CLIPPER BOAT SHIP DOCKER SLICER CHAINER CLAMMER CLEANER GRABMAN GRIPPER SHEARER SNAPPER

CLIPPING BOB SCROW CUTTING SNIPPING
(—S OF METAL) SCISSEL
(PL.) BRASH SHORTS EXCERPTA

CLIQUE COT MOB SET BLOC CLAN CLUB GANG KNOT PUSH RING CABAL CROWD GROUP JUNTO MAFIA WRITE CIRCLE CLETCH SCHISM COTERIE FACTION CONCLAVE SODALITY CAMARILLA

CLISTHENES (FATHER OF —) MEGACLES
(MOTHER OF —) AGARISTA

CLITANDRE (LOVER OF —) LUCINDE CELIMENE ANGELIQUE

CLITELLUM GIRDLE SADDLE CINGULUM

CLOAK ABA HAP BRAT CAPA CAPE COPE HIDE HUKE IZAR MANT MASK PALL RAIL ROBE VEIL WRAP AMICE BURKA CAPOT CHOGA COVER GREGO GUISE JELAB MANTA MANTO PILCH SAGUM SHUBA TALAR TALMA TILMA ABOLLA AHUULA ASSUME BAUTTA CAMAIL CAPOTE CASTER CHAMMA CHAPEL CHIMER DOLMAN JOSEPH MANTLE MANTUA PHAROS PONCHO RHASON SCREEN SERAPE SHIELD SHROUD TABARD VISITE ALICULA BAVAROY CASSOCK CHLAMYS CHUDDAR CONCEAL COURTBY GARMENT MANTEAU PAENULA PALLIUM PELISSE PELLARD PRETEXT ROKELAY SHELTER SURCOAT ZIMARRA ALBORNOZ BURNOOSE CAPUCHIN CARDINAL DISGUISE INTRIGUE MANTILLA PALLIATE ROQUELAURE
(— OF FEATHERS) MAMO AHUULA
(— WITH CROSSES) ANALABOS
(ARAB —) GALABIA GALLABIA GALABIYAH
(BULLFIGHTER'S —) CAPA
(CORONATION —) SACCOS
(FUR —) PILCH
(HOODED —) HUKE CAPOT BAUTTA BIRRUS BAVAROY CARDINAL DJELLABA
(INQUISITION —) SANBENITO
(RED —) CAPE
(RUSSIAN —) SARAFAN
(SHORT —) MANTELET
(SOLDIER'S —) SAGUM MANTEEL
(WATERPROOF —) GOSSAMER
(PREF.) PALLIO

CLOAKED PALLIATE

CLOAKROOM VESTRY VESTIARY

CLOAM DAUB CLOMB CROCKERY

CLOCHE BELL

CLOCK NEF BELL CALL DIAL GOER GONG TIME WRAP BUNDY CLUCK GURRY HATCH HURRY KNOCK METER QUIRK STYLE VERGE WATCH BEETLE CROUCH GHURRY ORLAGE TICKER SKELPER STRIKER TATTLER HOROLOGE INCUBATE ORNAMENT RECORDER SOLARIUM TELLTALE
(— IN FORM OF SHIP) NEF
(— ON STOCKING) QUIRK GUSHET GUSSET
(— WITH PENDULUM) PENDULE
(KIND OF —) CESIUM
(PART OF —) BOB ROD BASE DIAL DOOR FACE FOOT HAND HOOD RING ROPE CHAIN CREST PLATE TRUCK FINIAL PLINTH WEIGHT CHAPTER NUMERAL PENDULUM SPANDREL
(TIME —) BUNDY
(WATER —) GURRY GHURRY SOLARIUM CLEPSYDRA

CLOCKER SIZER TIMER RAILBIRD

CLOCKWISE DEASIL DESSIL SUNWISE POSITIVE

CLOD SOD CLAT CLOT DOLT DULL LOUT LUMP SLOB TURF CLOUT CLOWN DIVOT EARTH GLEBE GROSS KNOLL YOKEL CLATCH GROUND STUPID BUMPKIN

CLODDISH GROSS STUPID BOORISH

CLODDY GLEBY GLEBOUS

CLODHOPPER BOOR CLOD SHOE RUSTIC HOBNAIL PLOWMAN

CLODIA LESBIA

CLODPATE CLOT DOLT FOOL RAMHEAD CLODPOLE CLODPOLL IMBECILE

CLODPOLE BOOR BUMPKIN

CLOG FUR GUM JAM LOG BALL CLAG CLAM CLOY CURB DRAG GAUM GLUB LEAD LOAD LUMP SHOE SKID STOP BLIND BLOCK CHECK CHOKE DANCE SABOT SPOKE TRASH ACCLOY ADHERE BURDEN CHOPIN COBCAB DAGGLE ENCLOG FETTER FREEZE GALOSH HAMPER HOBBLE IMPEDE PATINE PATTEN REMORA SANDAL SECQUE WEIGHT CONGEST CREEPER ENGLEIM FETLOCK PERPLEX SHACKLE SPANCEL TRAMMEL TRIGGER BEDAGGLE COALESCE ENCUMBER OBSTRUCT OVERSHOE RESTRAIN
(— A FILE) PIN
(WOODEN —S) GETA GETAS

CLOG ALMANAC STAFF

CLOGGED FOUL FURRY PINNY FROZEN CLOTTED BEGUMMED

CLOGGING CLOGGY FOULING CUMBROUS

CLOGGY DULL HEAVY LUMPY STICKY

CLOISONNE SHIPPO

CLOISTER HALL STOA ABBEY AISLE ARCADE FRIARY IMMURE PIAZZA PRIORY CLOSTER CONVENT NUNNERY MONASTERY

CLOISTER AND THE HEARTH
(AUTHOR OF —) READE
(CHARACTER IN —) KATE DENYS
ELIAS GILES MARIE PETER BRANDT
GERARD MARTIN PIETRO ELIASON
MARGARET GHYSBRECHT

CLOISTERED RECLUSE
CLONE DESMA REPLICA SPICULE
CLORINDA (SLAYER OF —) TANCRED
CLOSE BY IN CAP END GUM HAW
HOT TYE ZOP AKIN BUNG CHOP
CLAP CLIT DAUB FAST FILL FINE
FIRM GRIP HARD HIDE LOUK MEET
NEAR NIGH QUIT SEAL SHUT SLAM
SNUG SPAR STOP TINE WINK
WYND ZERO ANEAR BLOCK
BOSOM BREAK CEASE CHEAP
CHIEF COAPT DENSE FENCE FINIS
FLIRT GARTH GROSS ISSUE MUGGY
SNECK SOLID STEEK STICK STIVY
THICK TIGHT BUCKLE BUTTON
CLAUSE CLENCH CLUTCH DOUBLE
EFFECT EXPIRY FINALE FINISH
INSTOP INWARD NARROW NEARBY
PERIOD SECRET SETTLE SILENT
STANCH STINGY STITCH STRAIT
STRICT STUFFY THRONG ADJOURN
BOROUGH CLOSING CLOSISH
COMPACT CONDEMN CONTEXT
COSTIVE EXTREME GRAPPLE
MISERLY OCCLUDE POCKETY
PUTHERY RAMPIRE RECLUDE
SHUTTER SIMILAR STAUNCH
STOPPER ACCURATE ADJACENT
BLOCKADE CLAUSULA COMPLETE
COMPRESS CONCLUDE ENCEINTE
ESPECIAL FAMILIAR FINALIZE
HAIRLINE IMMINENT INTIMATE
OBTURATE PARCLOSE PRECLUDE
STIFLING PROXIMATE
(— BY) FORBY AROUND BESIDE
FORERY HEREBY FORTHBY
SISTERING
(— EYES OF HAWK) SEEL
(— IN) RESET ENCLOSE INCLOSE
(— IN ON) TAKE
(— THE MOUTH) STOPPLE
(— TIGHTLY) SEALOFF
(— TO) BY INBY NEAR NIGH ANEAR
INBYE ALMOST AGAINST
(— TO BATSMAN) SILLY
(— TO COMMUNICATION) CORDON
(— TOGETHER) COLLAPSE
(— TO QUARRY) HOT
(— TO THE HEART) DEAR
(— TO THE WIND) SHARP
(— UP) DIT CORK DITT FILL FOLD
STOP SERRY UPCLOSE
(— WITH) BIND
(— WITH A CLICK) SNECK
(AS — AS POSSIBLE) CHOCK
(NOT —) UNNEAR
(PARTIALLY —) HOOD
(VERY —) CHIEF STINGY
(PREF.) PLESI(O) PYCN(O) STEN(O)
(SUFF.) STENOSIS
CLOSE-COUPLED COMPACT
CLOSE-CUT SHAVEN
CLOSED DARK DOWN SHUT CLOSE
LUCKEN UNOPEN BLOCKED
COVERED
(— AT ONE END) BLIND
(PREF.) CLEIST CLIST OCCLUSO

CLOSEFISTED MEAN NEAR FISTY
TIGHT SNIPPY STINGY MISERLY
HANDFAST
CLOSE-FITTING FIT HARD MEET
SNUG THEAT THEET TIGHT THIGHT
PRINCESS SUCCINCT PRINCESSE
CLOSE-IN SILLY
CLOSE-KNIT TRUSSED
CLOSE-LIPPED SILENT
CLOSELY FAST JUST NEAR WELL
SADLY ALMOST BARELY HARDLY
NARROW NEARLY JUNCTLY
STRICTLY
CLOSEMOUTHED SECRET SILENT
TACITURN
(NOT —) LEAKY
CLOSENESS DENSITY SECRECY
FIDELITY INTIMACY NEARNESS
PARSIMONY
CLOSER VAMPER CLOSURE
CLOSE-SET THICK SERRIED
CLOSE-SMELLING FROWSTY
CLOSEST NEXT NEAREST
CLOSESTOOL STOLE
CLOSET ARK LOO EWRY ROOM
SAFE ZETA AMBRY CUBBY CUDDY
PRESS LOCKER PANTRY SECRET
CABINET CONCEAL PRIVATE
STORAGE CONCLAVE CUPBOARD
GARDEVIN WARDROBE
CLOSING FLY SLAM SNAP CLINCH
CLOSURE CLOTURE CLAUDENT
PHASEOUT BUTTONING
(— DOWN OF OPERATIONS)
PHASEOUT
(MUSICAL —) CODA
(TEMPORARY —) SHUTDOWN
CLOSURE END GAG BOLT SEAL
BOUND LIMIT POPTOP ATRESIA
CLOTURE FERRULE TENSION
CLAUSURE FINALITY KANGAROO
(FABRIC —) VELCRO
(SUFF.) CLEISIS CLISIS
CLOT DOT GEL CLAG CLAT GOUT
JELL LUMP MASS MOLE SHED
CLART CLUMP GRUME BALTER
COTTER LAPPER LOPPER CLODDER
CONGEAL EMBOLUS THICKEN
CLODPATE COAGULUM CONCRETE
SOLIDIFY THROMBUS
(— OF BLOOD) THRUMBUS
(— OF DIRT) SPLATCH
(PREF.) THROMB(O)
CLOTH DAB RAG BLUE COAT DRAB
DRAP ECRU FELT FILE PALL SEAM
WARE WOOF BEIGE BLUET CABAN
CLOUT DITTO FOULE GOODS
GREEN KENTE LODEN LUNGI
MOORY PRINT STUPE TAMMY
TAWNY TIBET TOILE TWEED TWILL
WIGAN ALPACA AWNING BENGAL
BYSSUS CANAMO CANVAS
CHADOR CLAITH CLERGY COVERT
DOMETT DORSEL DOSSAL DOSSER
DRAPET DUSTER FABRIC LIVERY
LONGYI LOWELL MELLAY MULETA
NAPKIN RENGUE REXINE SARONG
SURNAP TILLOT WITNEY ACETATE
BAGGING BOULTEL CHADDAR
CHRISOM COATING CRIMSON
DRAPERY DUSTRAG FALDING
GARMENT JACONET ORLEANS
PANUELO RAIMENT SACKING

SURNAPE TEXTILE WATCHET
WORSTED BATSWING CHRISMAL
COMPRESS CORPORAL CRAMOISY
DWELLING FROCKING HOMESPUN
LAMBSKIN MATERIAL PHULKARI
RADEVORE SHAATNEZ SHEETING
THICKSET TOILINET
(— FOR BELT) SHROUD
(— FOR SWEAT) SUDARY
SUDARIUM
(— FOR WIPING TABLE) FILE
(— FOR WRAPPING CHILD) PILCH
(— FOR WRAPPING FABRICS) TILLET
(— FOR WRAPPING THE DEAD)
CEREMENT
(— HANGING FROM WAISTBAND)
LANGOOTY
(— OF GOLD) LAME
(— OF GOLD) SONERI
(— OF GOLD) SONERIE CICLATON
CHECKLATON
(— OF SINGLE WIDTH) STRAITS
(— REMAINING AFTER CUTTING)
CABBAGE
(— TEXTURE) WALE
(— WORN LIKE KILT) LAVALAVA
(ALTAR —) TOWEL PENDLE
PALLIUM VESPERAL CATASARKA
(ARABIAN —) HAIK CABAN CABAAN
(BAPTISMAL —) CHRISOM
(BARK —) TAPA TAPPA
(BED —) COVER SPREAD
(BLACK —) KISWA KISWAH
(BLUE —) PERSE
(COARSE —) KELT DOZEN DUROY
RUDGE BURREL CANGAN DOWLAS
DOZENS FORFAR FRIEZE HODDEN
KERSEY KHARVA KHARWA STAMIN
STROUD TAPALO WADMAL
CAMBAYE COTONIA DRUGGET
FORFARS RAPLOCH RUGGING
SARPLER SOUTAGE FLUSHING
RADEVORE SARCILIS
(COMMUNION —) FANON SINDON
ANIMETTA CORPORAL PURIFICATOR
(CORDED —) REP REPP
(COTTON —) BAFT JEAN TOBE
ADATI BLUET CAFFA CRASH DURRY
JEANS KHADI KHAKI SURAT BEAVER
CALICO CANGAN DOWLAS DURRIE
GANZIE HUMHUM KALMUK NANKIN
PENANG CAMBAYE FUSTIAN
GALATEA GINGHAM JACONET
KHADDAR LASTING NANKEEN
REGATTA BOGOTANA CRETONNE
DOMESTIC MUSLINET
(CRIMSON —) CRAMASIE
CRAMOISY
(DECORATIVE —) SCARF
(DRAB —) KHAKI
(DRIVING —) TOWEL
(EMBROIDERED —) SAMPLER
BAUDEKIN
(FINE —) SINDON SCARLET
(FIORE —) PINA
(GLASS —) DORON
(GOAT-WOOL —) ABA ABBA ABAYA
SLING
(GREEN —) KENDAL
(GUNNY —) TAT
(HAIR —) ABA ABBA CILICE
(HEMP —) PINAYUSA

(HOMESPUN —) KELT KHADI PATTU
PUTTOO HEADING KHADDAR
(INFERIOR —) MOCKADO
(KIND OF —) LOIN PINA
(LAP —) GREMIAL
(LINEN —) BRIN LINE GULIX
DOWLAS FORFAR BRABANT
LOCKRAM SILESIA BLANCARD
CORPORAL DRILLING GAMBROON
GHENTING LINCLOTH
(LONG —) LUNGI WHITE LUNGEE
(ORNAMENTAL —) TRAP DOSSAL
DOSSEL
(PACK —) MANTA
(PACKING —) SOUTAGE
(PIECE OF —) APRON CLOUT GODET
LANGOOTY
(PURLOINED —) CABBAGE
(RICH —) SCARLET
(ROUGH —) PETERSHAM
(ROYAL —) PURPLE
(SADDLE —) PANEL NUMNAH
SHABRACK
(SILK —) CAFFA BENGAL PATOLA
LUSTRINE LUSTRING
(SOAKED —) BUCK
(SOFT —) RUGINE
(STAGE —) BACKDROP
(STARCHED —) GUIMPE
(STRIPED —) RAY
(STRONG —) CANVAS DURANCE
BARRACAN
(TARTAN —) PLAID
(TURBAN —) SASH
(TWILLED —) JANE JEAN BARATHEA
GAMBROON
(UNDYED —) HODDEN
(VARI-COLORED —) MEDLEY
MOTLEY
(WASHING —) SHAMMY CHAMOIS
(WATERPROOF —) MAC MACK
(WAX —) MUMJUMA
(WET —) DAB
(WOOL —) SAY DRAB PUKE BEIGE
BUREL DOZEN DUROY LAINE STARA
TAMIS TAMMY BURNET DOZENS
DUFFEL HODDEN KENDAL KERSEY
MEDLEY MELTON MUSTER SATARA
SAXONY STAMIN TAMINY TARTAN
BASTARD BLANKET DUNSTER
FLANNEL RAPLOCH ROPLOCH
RUGGING BEARSKIN BOMBAZET
BUCKSKIN FLORENCE SARCILIS
VENETIAN PETERSHAM
BOMBAZETTE
(WORSTED —) RASH SHAG BOTANY
BOMBAZET
(PREF.) HISTI(O)
CLOTHE DON DUB HAP LAP RIG TOG
BUSK COAT DECK GARB GIRD
GOWN ROBE VEST ADORN ARRAY
CLEAD CLEED DRESS ENDOW
ENDUE FLESH FROCK HABIT INDUE
ATTIRE BEWRAP SHRIDE SHROUD
SWATHE ADDRESS APPAREL
FEATHER RAIMENT VESTURE
ACCOUTER ACCOUTRE
(PLAIN —) MUFTI
CLOTHED CLAD BECLAD HABITED
CLOTHES CASE DUDS GARB GEAR
GORE KAPA SUIT TACK TOGS
WEAR BRAWS CLAES DUCKS
HABIT ATTIRE FARDEL SHROUD

THREAD TROGGS APPAREL
BAGGAGE COSTUME IRONING
RAIMENT REGALIA THREADS
TOGGERY VESTURE WEARING
CLOTHING FEATHERS FRIPPERY
GARMENTS INDUMENT
(CASTOFF —) FRIPPERY
(CIVILIAN —) MUFTI CIVVIES
(COLORFUL —) TRAPPINGS
(DAINTY —) PRETTIES
(DRESS —) WAMPUM
(FINE —) BRAWS
(HANDSOME —) BRAVERY
(MOURNING —) DOLE
(READY-TO-WEAR —)
PRETAPORTER
(SHOWY —) LUGS
(SOAKED —) BUCK
(TRACK —) SILKS
CLOTHES DRYER AIRER TUMBLER
CLOTHES-HORSE MAIDEN SCREEN
CLOTHESPIN PEG
CLOTHESPRESS ARMOIRE
TALLBOY WARDROBE
CLOTH FOLDER CUTTLER
CLOTHING (ALSO SEE CLOTHES)
BACK BLUE BRAT COAT GARB
GEAR SEAM WEAR ARRAY BUREL
CLOTH DRESS GREEN HABIT
JABOT STUFF ATTIRE FARDEL
ROBING VESTRY APPAREL
CLOBBER CLOTHES CRIMSON
DRAPERY FISHNET OUTWALL
RAIMENT THREADS VESTURE
WEEDERY INDUMENT KNITWEAR
MENSWEAR ORNAMENT
SLOPWORK VESTIARY VESTMENT
BEACHWEAR
(ARTICLE OF —) VINE
(BLACK —) SABLE
(COARSE —) BUREL
(INFORMAL —) PLAYWEAR
(LOWER —) LAP
(MUSLIM —) IHRAM
(NAUTICAL —) SLOPS
(OF CLASSIC —) PREPPY PREPPIE
(SHEER —) FLIMSIES
(SHOWY —) SHEEN FINERY
(WOMEN'S —) FRILLIES
(WORK —) FATIGUES
(SUFF.) ESTHES
CLOTHING DEALER HOSIER
CLOTHWORKER FULLER
CLOTILDA (FATHER OF —)
CHILPERIC
(HUSBAND OF —) CLOVIS
AMALARIC
(UNCLE OF —) GUNDEBALD
CLOTTED GORY CLOTTY CLOUTED
GARGETY GRUMOUS LIVERED
CLOTURE GAG CLOSURE
CLOUD DOG FOG NUE SKY BLUR
DAMP DARK DUST FOOL HAZE
HELM HIDE MIST PUFF REEK SMUR
ARCUS BEDIM BEFOG BLOOM
DRIFT GLOOM MUDDY NUBIA
OXEYE SHADE STAIN SULLY
SWARM TAINT VAPOR CIRRUS
DAMAGE DARKEN DEEPEN
DEFAME FUNNEL MUDDLE
NEBULA NIMBUS PILEUS POTHER
SCREEN SHADOW STIGMA
BLACKEN CONFUSE CUMULUS

ECLIPSE FUMULUS GRANULE
OBSCURE POOTHER STRATUS
SUNSPOT TARNISH CLOUDCAP
CLOUDLET COCKTAIL NIGHTCAP
NUBILATE OVERCAST WOOLPACK
(— BEFORE STORM) MESSENGER
(— OF DROPS) SPRAY
(— OF DUST OR VAPOR) STEW
SMOTHER
(— OF MIST) SOP
(— OVER MOUNTAIN) HELM
(CIRRUS —S) GOATSHAIR
(DRIVINNG —) SCUD
(FLYING —) RACK
(FUNNEL —) TORNADO
(HIGH —) CIRRUS
(HORIZONTAL —) STRATUS
(KIND OF —) OORT
(LAYER OF —S) DECK
(MASS OF HIGH —S) RACK
(MASSY —) CUMULUS
(NUCLEAR —) FIREBALL
(RAIN —) NIMBUS
(PL.) SCUD SOUP CARRY GASHES
(PREF.) CIRR(I)(O) CIRRH(I)(O)
NEBULI NEPHEL(I)(O) NEPHO NIMBI
NUBI
CLOUDBERRY AKPEK MOLKA
AVERIN
(FRUIT OF —) NOOP
CLOUDED HAZY DIRTY DUSTY FILMY
JASPE MUCKY SHADY ACLOUD
GLOOMY TURBID INFUMATE
NEBULOUS
CLOUDINESS FAIR HAZE GLOOM
MUDDLE NUBECULA
CLOUDING DAPPLE
(— OF EYE) CATARACT
CLOUDLESS AZURE CLEAR BRIGHT
CLOUDLIKE NEBULOUS NUBIFORM
CLOUDY DIM DARK DULL HAZY
BLEAR FILMY FOGGY MISTY
MUDDY MURKY SHADY GLOOMY
LOWERY OPAQUE SMURRY VEILED
BLURRED CLOUDED NEBULAR
OBSCURE CONFUSED NEBULOSE
NUBILOUS OVERCAST VAPOROUS
CLOUGH CLUF CLEFT CLOES
CLEUCH CLEUGH RAVINE VALLEY
CLOUT BAT BOX DAB HIT LAP BEAT
BLOW BUMP CLOD CLUB CUFF
JOIN MEND NAIL PULL SLAP SLUG
SWAT JUICE PATCH SMITE WHACK
KLOWET STRIKE TACKET TARGET
THRASH WASHER BANDAGE
BOSTHOON INFLUENCE
CLOVE GAP NAIL CHIVE CLEFT GILLY
BUTTON CLEAVE RAVINE SHERRY
GILLIVER
CLOVE BROWN EAGLE
CLOVEN CLEFT SPLIT DIVIDED
BISULCATE
CLOVEN-FOOTED SLIT FISSIPED
CLOVE PINK GELOFER GRENADIN
CLOVER RED HAGI SEED HUBAM
LOTUS MEDIC NARDU PUSSY
ALSIKE BERSIM LADINO LEGUME
LUXURY NARDOO ALFALFA
BERSEEM BERSINE CLAIVER
COMFORT LUCERNE MELILOT
SAPLING TREFOIL TRIFOLY
COWGRASS HAREFOOT

NAPOLEON PUSSYCAT SHAMROCK
SUCKLING YELLOWTOP
(KIND OF —) LADINO
CLOVER DODDER AILWEED
EPITHYME HAILWEED HAIRWEED
HALEWEED
CLOWN HOB OAF PUT APER BOOR
FOOL GAUM GOFF JOEY LOUT
MIME MOME SWAD ZANY ANTIC
BUFFO CHUFF CHURL COMIC
FESTE IDIOT MIMER PATCH PUNCH
WAMBA ZANNI AUGUST BODACH
CHOUGH HOBBIL JESTER JOSKIN
LUBBER RUSTIC STOOGE AUGUSTE
BODDAGH BUFFOON BUMPKIN
CHARLEY COSTARD KOSHARE
LAVACHE LOBSTER MUDHEAD
PEASANT PIERROT PLAYBOY
SCOFFER TOMFOOL COVIELLO
KOYEMSHI MERRYMAN
WHITEFACE PUNCHINELLO
CLOWNISH RAW RUDE ZANY
GAWKY ROUGH BORREL CLUMSY
COARSE RUSTIC AWKWARD
BOORISH BORRELL HOBLIKE
KERNISH LOBBISH LOUTISH
UNCIVIL VILLAIN BOEOTIAN
CLUBBISH SWADDISH UNGAINLY
CLOY CLOG GLUT NAIL PALL SATE
GORGE PRICK ACCLOY PIERCE
SATIATE SATISFY SURFEIT
SATURATE
(— WITH ADORATION) BESOT
CLOYED BLASE
CLOYER SNAP
CLOYING GOOEY SWEET VANILLA
CLOYSOME LUSCIOUS
SACCHARINE
CLUB BAT DOG HIT HUI SET BEAT
CANE JOIN MACE MALL MAUL
MERE POLT TEAM BAFFY BANDY
BATON BILLY BUNCH CLOUT
HURLY KEBBY LODGE MASHY
ORDER STAFF STICK TOWEL UNITE
YOKEL ZONTA BULGER CERCLE
CIRCLE CLIQUE CUDGEL HURLEY
KEBBIE LIBBET MACANA MASHIE
MENAGE MUCKLE NULLAH PRIEST
STRIKE TAIAHA VEREIN WEAPON
WHITES BOURDON CAMBUCA
COLLEGE COUNCIL HETAERY
HETAIRY SOROSIS ATHENEUM
BLUDGEON CATSTICK SODALITY
SORORITY SPONTOON TERTULIA
KNOBKERRY
(— IN PLAYING CARDS) OAK
(— OF ANTENNA) CLAVUS
(BASEBALL —) FARM
(GOLF —) IRON WOOD BAFFY CLEEK
MASHY SPOON STICK WEDGE
BRASSY BULGER DRIVER JIGGER
LOFTER MASHIE PUTTER BLASTER
MIDIRON NIBLICK PITCHER
(INTERNATIONAL SERVICE —)
GYRO
(MAORI —) MERE MERAI MARREE
(MEMBER OF SERVICE —)
SERTOMAN
(POLICEMAN'S —) SAP BILLY
PANTOON SPONTON SPONTOON
NIGHTSTICK LATHI
(POLITICAL —) ROTA FASCIO
HETAERY HETAIRY

(SINGERS' —) GLEE
(SPIKED —) ALLIDE
(SPORTS —) BAT
(WAR —) WADDY
(WOMEN'S —) SOROSIS SORORITY
CIRCLE
(PREF.) CLAVI CORDYL(O)
RHOPAL(O)
(SUFF.) CORYNUS
CLUB CARRIER CLAVIGER
CLUBFOOT TALUS VARUS VALGUS
TALIPES CYLLOSIS POLTFOOT
CLUB, GOLF (PART OF —) TOE FACE
GRIP HEAD HEEL NECK NOSE SOLE
HOSEL SHAFT
CLUB MOSS MOSS FOFEET
LYCOPOD PILIGAN CROWFOOT
FERNWORT
CLUBROOT CLUB ANBURY
ANBERRY HANBURY CLUBBING
CLUBFOOT
CLUB RUSH RUSH SEDGE GLUMAL
DEERHAIR
CLUB-SHAPED CLAVATE
CLUCK HEN FUSS CHUCK CLACK
CLICK CLOCK CLOOK
CLUE KEY TIP BALL CLEW HINT IDEA
LEAD GUIDE TWINE BOTTOM
CLAVIS THREAD INNUENDO
CLUMP SOP TOD BLOW BUSH CLOT
HEAP KNOT LUMP MASS MOSS
MOTT TOPE TUFT TUMP TURB
BLUFF BUNCH CLAMP GROUP
GROVE HOUSE PATCH PLUMP
STUMP TREAD WUDGE CLUNCH
DOLLOP LUMPER BOSCAGE
CLUMPER CLUSTER THICKET
(— OF BRIERS OR ROSES) ROAN
RONE
(— OF CELLS) SLUDGE
(— OF SHRUBS) BUSH
(— OF SPORANGIA) SORUS
(— OF TREES) BLUFF HOUSE HURST
HYRST BOSQUE
CLUMSILY SOUSE GREENLY
GAUCHELY
CLUMSINESS GAUCHERIE
CLUMSY AWK FLOB LEWD NUMB
RUDE BLUNT BULKY GAUMY
GAWKY HOGGY HULKY INAPT
INEPT SCRAM SPLAY STIFF STOGY
CLUMPY CLUNKY GAUCHE LUBBER
NOGGEN THUMBY WOODEN
AWKWARD BOORISH CHUCKLE
LOUTISH LUMPISH UNHANDY
UNREADY BENUMBED BUNGLING
CLOWNISH FOOTLESS GAUMLESS
HANDLESS LUMBERLY TACTLESS
UNGAINLY UNWIELDY CLOUTERLY
PONDEROUS HIPPOPOTAMIC
(— PERSON) KLUTZ
(NOT —) FINE
CLUPEID HERRING
CLUSTER ROB BOG BUSH CLOT
COMA CONE CYME KNOT LUMP
TUFT BUNCH CLUMP DRUSE
GROUP PLUMP SHEAF SORUS
CENTER COLONY GATHER
MORULA PLEIAD REGIME
BOUROCK CLUTHER DOLPHIN
ENVIRON FOLIAGE FASCICLE
NUCLEATE SURROUND

(— AS BEES) BALL KNIT
(— OF BANANAS) HAND
(— OF BRANCHES) SPRAY
(— OF CELLS) ROSETTE
(— OF CRYSTALS) DRUSE
(— OF FEATHERS) MUFF
(— OF FIBERS) NEP
(— OF FLOWERS) CYME TRUSS
CORYMB ANTHEMY PANICLE
(— OF HAIRS) MYSTAX
(— OF METAL BALLS) GRAPE
(— OF NODULES) GRAPES
(— OF PILES) DOLPHIN
(— OF PLANTS) BED
(— OF RAYS) AIGRETTE
(— OF SPORES) SORUS
(— OF STARS) PRAESEPE
(— OF TINES) TROCHE
(— OF WOOL) NEP
(CONFUSED —) SPLATTER
(GERM CELL —) MORULA
(SUSPENDED —) SWAG
(PREF.) CORYMDI CYM(I)(O) K'I'M(I)
(O) RACEMI RACEMO
CLUSTER BEAN GUAR
CLUSTERED TUFTED RACEMOSE
AGGREGATE CONGLOMERATE
CLUTCH HUG NAB SET CLAM CLAW
CLEM CLIP FIST GLAM GRAB GRIP
NEST BROOD CATCH CLASP CLAUT
CLEEK CLICK GLAUM GRASP GRIPE
GRISP HATCH LEVER POWER SEIZE
TALON CLEACH CLENCH CLETCH
CLINCH CUTOUT FASTEN RETAIN
SNATCH CLAUGHT CONTROL
CRAMPON COUPLING
(— OF EGGS) SET LAWTER LAYING
SETTING SITTING LAUGHTER
CLUTCHING GRIP GRIPING
CLUTTER MESS STUFF BUSTLE
CUMBER LITTER CLATTER
DISORDER CONFUSION
CLUTTERED CLATTY CLOTTED
CLYMENE (DAUGHTER OF —)
ALCIMEDE
(FATHER OF —) MINYAS CATREUS
OCEANUS
(HUSBAND OF —) IAPETUS
NAUPLIUS PHYLACUS
(MOTHER OF —) TETHYS
(SON OF —) OEAX ATLAS IPHICLUS
PHAETHON MENOETIUS
PALAMEDES
CLYPEUS NASUS EPISTOME
PRELABRUM
CLYSTER LAVEMENT INJECTION
CLYTEMNESTRA (BROTHER OF —)
CASTOR POLLUX POLYDEUCES
(DAUGHTER OF —) ELECTRA
LAODICE IPHIGENIA IPHINASSA
CHRYSOTHEMIS
(FATHER OF —) TYNDAREUS
(HUSBAND OF —) TANTALUS
AGAMEMNON
(LOVER OF —) AEGISTHUS
(MOTHER OF —) LEDA
(SISTER OF —) HELENA
(SON OF —) ORESTES
CLYTIUS (BROTHER OF —) PRIAM
(FATHER OF —) EURYTUS
LAOMEDON
(MOTHER OF —) GAEA

(SLAYER OF —) HERCULES
(SON OF —) CALETOR
COACH BUS CAR FLY DRAG HACK
HELP ARABA BOGEY BOGIE BRIEF
CABIN FLIER FLYER PILOT PRIME
STAGE TEACH TRAIN TUTOR
ADVISE DIRECT FIACRE JARVEY
MENTOR SALOON ADVISER
CHARIOT COACHER CONCORD
GONDOLA PREPARE RATTLER
TALLYHO TRAINER CARRIAGE
DORMEUSE PUPILIZE
(BALLET —) REPETITEUR
(FAST —) FLIER FLYER
(HACKNEY —) FIACRE JARVEY
(HEAVY —) DRAG
(SLOW —) SLOWPOKE
(3-WHEELED —) TRICYCLE
COACHDOG DALMATIAN
COACH-HOUSE REMISE
COACHMAN FLY FISH JEHU WHIP
PILOT COACHY DRIVER COACHEE
COACHER YAMSHIK YEMSCHIK
COACTION EXPLOITATION
COADJUTOR PRIOR
COAGULANT CURD RENNET
STYPTIC COAGULUM GELATINE
COAGULATE GEL SET CAKE CLOD
CLOT CURD JELL QUAIL YEARN
COTTER CURDLE LAPPER LOBBER
LOPPER POSSET CLABBER
CLOTTER CONGEAL PECTIZE
THICKEN COAGULUM CONCRETE
SOLIDIFY
COAGULATED CRUDY CURDY
LIVERED
COAGULATION GOUT CLOTTER
COAGULUM CLOT THROMBUS
COAK-LIKE PHELLOID
COAL BID BASS DUFF FUEL SWAD
BLOCK CHARK EMBER GHOST
GLEED STOKE BARING BRAZIL
BURGEE CANNEL CARBON CINDER
FIRING SPLINT BACKING BOGHEAD
BRIGHTS BYERITE CORRLES
LIGNITE RATTLER VITRAIN
AMPELITE LANDSALE
(— IN PLACE) SOLID
(— MINE) COLLIERY
(— MINER) COLLIER
(— PILLAR) STOOK
(— SLAB) SKIP
(BAD —) SMUT
(BED OF —) SEAM
(BROWN-) LIGNITE
(DIRTY —) RASH
(FINE —) DUFF SCREENINGS
(IMPURE —) SWAD
(INFERIOR —) CROW
(LARGE BLOCK OF —) JUD JUDD
(LIVE OR GLOWING —) GLEED
GLEYD
(REFUSE —) BREEZE
(SIZE OF —) EGG NUT PEA LUMP
RICE SLACK STOVE BARLEY BROKEN
CHESTNUT WALLSEND BUCKWHEAT
(SLATY —) BASS BONE BONY
(SMALL LUMP OF —) NUBBLING
(SMALL PORTION OF UNCUT —)
PANEL
(PREF.) ANTHRAC(O) CARBONI
COAL BED SEAM
COALBIN BUNKER

COAL BROKER CRIMP
COAL CAR JIMMY
COAL CHUTE DOCK
COAL DUST COOM CULM SMUT
COOMB
COALESCE MIX CLOG FUSE JOIN
BLEND MERGE UNITE COHERE
EMBODY MINGLE SINTER
COMBINE
COALESCENCE UNION FUSION
LEAGUE CAPTURE SYNANTHY
COAL-FACE BANK
COALFISH SEY PARR COLEY CUDDY
SEITH BESHOW BILLET CUDDEN
PODLER SAITHE SILLOC BADDOCK
GLASHAN GLASSIN PILTOCK
POLLACK
(YOUNG —) PODLER PODI FY
COMAMIE POODLER SILLOCK
GRAYFISH
COALITION FRONT TRUST UNION
FUSION LEAGUE MERGER ENTENTE
ALLIANCE
COAL OIL KEROSENE
COALRAKE HOE FREGGIN FRUGGAN
SCRAPPLE
COAL WORKER GEORDIE HURRIER
COAL YARD REE
COAMING CURB LEDGE COMBING
COARSE FAT LOW RAW BASE BULL
DANK FOUL HARD HASK LEWD
LOUD RANK RUDE SOUR VILE
BAWDY BRASH BROAD CRASS
CRUDE DIRTY GREAT GROFF
GROSS HARSH HASKY HEAVY
LARGE LOOSE PLAIN RANDY
ROUGH ROUTH ROWTY RUDAS
STOGY STOUR THICK UNORN
BLOWSY BRAZEN BRUTAL
CALLOW CHUFFY COMMON
DUDGEN EARTHY IMPURE INCULT
RANDIE RIBALD ROUDAS RUDOUS
RUGGED RUSSET RUSTIC SORDID
SULTRY UNFELE VULGAR BLATANT
CARLAGE CARLISH CRIBBLE
FULSOME GOATISH LOUTISH
LOWBRED OBSCENE PROFANE
RAPLOCH RAUCOUS ROINISH
SENSUAL BARBARIC CLOWNISH
HOMESPUN IMMODEST INDECENT
PLEBEIAN STUBBORN UNCHASTE
COARSE-FIBERED STRONG
COARSE-GRAINED DRY GRUFF
COARSELY BROADLY HARSHLY
COARSEN HACKNEY
COARSENESS RAUNCH HOGGERY
COAST BANK LAND RIPA BEACH
BOARD CLIFF SHORE SLIDE
WARTH ADJOIN BORDER RIVAGE
STRAND BOBSLED SEASIDE
APPROACH SEABOARD SEASHORE
ROLLALONG
COASTAL ORARIAN
COASTER MAT SLED TILE DOLLY
TROUT BARCON CRADLE CREEPER
MISTICO TOBOGGAN
COAST GUARD (U.S. — WOMAN)
SPAR
COASTLAND MAREMMA
COAT FUR LAY PEE SAC TOG BARK
BLUE BUFF CONY DAUB FOIL FOLD
HIDE HUSK JACK JAMA JUPE MIDI
PINK RIND SACK SCAB SEAL TOGE

ZINC BENNY CLOTH CONEY COVER
CRUST FLASH FROCK GLACE
GLAZE HABIT JAMAH JEMMY
LAYER OILER PAINT PLATE QUYTE
SAQUE SHELL TERVE ALPACA
BYRNIE COATEE DUSTER ENAMEL
ENROBE EXTIMA GROUND HACKLE
INTIMA INVEST JACKET JOSEPH
KIRTLE LACKER MANTLE MELOTE
PARGET PELAGE RABBIT REEFER
SEALER SILVER SLOUGH STUCCO
TABARD VENEER BEESWAX
BOBTAIL CASSOCK COATING
COURTBY CRISPIN CUTAWAY
GARMENT GROGRAM INCRUST
KARAKUL LACQUER OILCOAT
OVERLAY PALETOT PELISSE
PLASTER SHELLAC SHOOTER
SPENCER STRATUM SUBCOAT
SURCOAT SURTOUT SWAGGER
TOGEMAN TOPCOAT VESTURE
BENJAMIN COURTEPY GRAPHITE
INTONACO MACKINAW
MEMBRANE OVERCOAT ROCKELAY
SEALSKIN SHERWANI SILICATE
TEGUMENT TRENCHER
OUTERCOAT PETERSHAM
REDINGOTE CHESTERFIELD
(— FOOD) DREDGE
(— LENS) BLOOM
(— OF ARMS) CREST BLAZON
BEARINGS
(— OF BIRD SKINS) TEMIAK
(— OF BLOOD VESSEL) MEDIA
(— OF CARIBOU SKINS) KOOLETAH
(— OF DEFENSE) JACK
(— OF EYE) CHOROID
(— OF EYEBALL) SCLERA
(— OF GRAVEL) BLOTTER
(— OF INDIA) ACHKAN
(— OF MAIL) FROCK BRINIE BYRNIE
SECRET HAUBERK HABERGEON
CATAPHRACT
(— OF ORGAN) INTIMA
(— OF OVULE) PRIMINE
(— OF PLASTER) SET ARRICCIO
BROWNING INTONACO
(— OF SEED) ARIL BRAN EPISPERM
(— OF WOOL) FLEECE
(— WITH ALLOY) TERNE
(— WITH PITCH) PAY
(— WORN UNDER ARMOR)
GAMBESON
(CLOSE-FITTING —) TRUSS
(DEER'S WINTER —) BLUE
(FIRST — OF TIN) LIST
(FUR —) ANARAK ANORAK
(HAIR —) MELOTE
(HERALD'S —) TABARD
(HOODED —) GREGO CAPOTE
(KIND OF —) TRENCH
(LONG —) MAXI JIBBA JIBBAH
KAPOTE DJIBBAH MAXICOAT
NEWMARKET
(LOOSE —) CASSOCK PALETOT
INVERNESS
(MILITARY —) TUNIC BLOUSE
BUFFCOAT
(OLD —) MUMMOCK
(RIDING —) JOSEPH
(SACKCLOTH —) SANBENITO
(SEALSKIN —) NETCHA
(SEED —) ARIL

(SHEEPSKIN —) ZAMARRA ZAMARRO
(SHORT —) PEA JUMP MIDI SACK TERNE JERKIN REEFER PEACOAT
(THREE-QUARTER LENGTH —) ACHKAN
(WATERPROOF —) BURSATI SLICKER
(WOMAN'S —) CARACO DOLMAN
(WOOLLY —) LANUGO
COATED GLACE BACKED FURRED LOADED PLATED CANDIED
(— WITH FLOUR AND CRUMBS) MILANESE
COAT HANGER SHOULDER
COATI NASUA TEJON NARICA PISOTE ARCTOID
COATING (ALSO SEE COAT) FUR GUM ARIL DOPE DRAB FILM FLOR HAIR HOAR SKIN BLOOM FLASH GLACE GLAZE ICING SCALE BEAVER CHATON COVERT CRUSTA FINISH JACKET PATINA VENEER BACKING DIPCOAT FURRING GILDING LACQUER OVERLAY PLATING TINNING ACIERAGE CAMBOUIS CLADDING EMULSION FLOODING MUCILAGE OVERCOAT PERIDIUM PLASTERING
(— FOR METAL) SLUSH
(— OF BACTERIA) SLIME
(— OF GLASS) MOILES FOLIATION
(— OF GLUE) ENAMEL
(— OF ICE) GLAZE
(— OF SEED) TESTA
(— OF TONGUE) ATTER
(CHEESE —) MOLD
(CORROSION —) RUST
(METAL —) CLAD CLADDING
(MIRROR —) FOIL
(OUTSIDE —) CRUST
(POWDERY —) DOWN
(PROTECTIVE —) RESIST
(PRUINOUS —) FARINA
(SEED —) TESTA
(WALL —) GROUT
COATLICUE (HUSBAND OF —) MIXCOATL
(SON OF —) HUITZILOPOCHTLI
COATTAIL LABIE LAPPET
COAX BEG COY PET CANT DUPE FAGE FAWN LURE URGE WILE JOLLY TEASE BANTER CAJOLE CUITLE CUTTER ENTICE FLEECH SEDUCE BEGUILE CROODLE CROWDLE CRUDDLE FLATTER IMPLORE SOOTHER WHEEDLE BLANDISH COLLOGUE INVEIGLE PERSUADE
COAXIAL CONCENTRIC
COB EAR LOB MEW COBB
COBALT (— EXPORTER) ZAIRE
COBBERER ROARER ROUSER
COBBLE DARN MEND PAVE SOLE BOTCH PATCH STONE BUNGLE COGGLE REPAIR RESOLE
COBBLER PIE SNOB SHEEP SOLER SUTOR ARTIST COZIER SOUTER BOTCHER CATFISH CRISPIN POMPANO SADDLER CHUCKLER SCORPION SNOBSCAT
COBBLERFISH COBBLER SUNFISH SHOEMAKER

COBBLESTONE COGGLE
COBBY STOUT HEARTY LIVELY STOCKY COMPACT
COBIA SNOEK SNOOK
COBLE MULE KOBIL
COBNUT COB OUABE HOGNUT PIGNUT
COBRA ASP NAG HAJE NAGA NAJA KRAIT VIPER ELAPID URAEUS
COBWEB NET TRAP SNARE WEVET GOSSAMER
COCA CUCA KHOKA TRUXILLO
COCAINE BLOW COKE SNOW TOOT CRACK FLAKE FREEBASE
(— MIXED WITH HEROIN) SPEEDBALL
(— USER) COKEHEAD
(— WITH HEROIN) SPEEDBALL
(TAKE —) SPEEDBALL
COCASH ASTER SWANWEED
COCCOID BERRYLIKE
COCCULUS CEBATHA FISHBERRY
COCCUS COFFEEBUG
COCCYX RUMPBONE
(PREF.) COCCYGEO COCCYG(O)
COCHE MOCOA
COCHINEAL GRAIN BLANCO COCCUS GRANILLA
COCHINEAL FIG NOPAL
COCHINEAL INSECT VERMIL VERMEIL VERMILION
COCK COX TAP BANK BOOT COIL FOWL HEAP KORA PILE RICK SPAN COCKY COQUE FIGHT FUGIE GALLO SHOCK STACK STRUT VALVE YOWLE CRAVEN FAUCET HAMMER HEELER LEADER CONTEND GORCOCK PETCOCK ROOSTER SWAGGER ASTROLOG COCKBIRD COCKEREL COXBONES GAMECOCK JERMONAL STOPCOCK
(— GUNLOCK) NAB
(— OF HAY) HIPPLE
(— OF THE WALK) KINGFISH
(— WITHOUT COURAGE) CRAVEN
(— WITHOUT SPURS) MUCKNA
(FIGHTING —) FUGIE HEELER TURNPOKE
(TURKEY —) STAG
(WATER —) KORA
(WEATHER —) FANE VANE
(PREF.) ALECTORO ALECTRYO GALLI
COCKADE KNOT BADGE COCKARD ROSETTE TRICOLOR
COCKATIEL QUARRION
COCKATOO ARA ARARA COCKY GALAH MACAW ABACAY COCKIE PARROT CORELLA JACATOO CALANGAY GANGGANG
COCKATOO BUSH BLUEBERRY
COCKBOAT COG COCK SCULL COGBOAT
COCKCHAFER MAYBUG OAKWEB BUZZARD HUMBUZZ MAYBEETLE
COCKCROW DAWN
COCKED HAT SCRAPER RAMILLIE
COCKER CODDLE COGGER CUITER QUIVER SPANIEL
COCKEREL COCK SLIP BANTAM
COCKFIGHT MAIN SPAR
COCKINESS BRAVADO SWAGGER

COCKLE COCK GALL GITH KILN OAST BULGE KAKEL SHELL STOVE DARNEL NUCULA PALOUR PUCKER RIPPLE WABBLE ZIZANY CUCKOLD WRINKLE HARDHEAD
(PREF.) CONCH(O)
COCKLEBUR COTS CLOTE COCKLE BURDOCK BURWEED CADILLO CLOTBUR CUCKOLD CLOTWEED DITCHBUR
COCKNEY ARRY ORTHERIS LONDONESE
COCKPIT PIT RING RINK WELL ARENA CABIN FIELD GALLERA
COCKROACH BUG DRUM ROACH BEETLE BLATTID DRUMMER KNOCKER
COCKSCOMB CREST COXCOMB
COCKSFOOT HARDGRASS
COCKSPUR FINGRIGO GARABATO
COCKTAIL SOUR ZOOM BRONX CRUSTA GIBSON GIMLET MAITAI COBBLER MARTINI NEGRONI SAZERAC SIDECAR STINGER SWIZZLE APERITIF DAIQUIRI MARGARITA GRASSHOPPER TEQUILASUNRISE
(— INGREDIENT) SAZERAC
(KIND OF —) MOLOTOV
COCK-UP MESS
COCKY PERK PERT CRANK PERKY CROUSE FARMER JAUNTY COCKING ARROGANT
COCO KOKO BROMA COCOA COKER YUNTIA
COCOA MAHAL TURTLE PATASHTE
COCOA BROWN PUEBLO
COCONUT COCO COCKER NARGIL COCOANUT
COCONUT FIBER COIR KAIR KYAR CAYAR
COCONUT MEAT COPRA
COCONUT PALM KOKO NIOG
COCOON POD CLEW CLUE KELL SCAB SHED SHELL BOTTOM DOUPION FOLLICLE
COCO PLUM ICACO HICACO
COCOWOOD KOKRA
COCOYAM TARO YAUTIA
COCUSWOOD KOKRA
COD BAG BIB COR KID POD AXLE BANK CUSK FOOL GADE HOAX HUSK POOR ROCK BELLY DORSE DROUD GADID POUCH SCROD SHALE SHAUP TORSK BURBOT CODGER CULTUS ESCROD FELLOW MULVEL PILLOW POCKET TOMCOD WACHNA BACALAO CODFISH CODLING CUSHION KEELING KILLING MILWELL MORRHUA SCROTUM CABELIAU DOLEFISH KABBELOW KLIPFISH ROCKLING
(BUFFALO —) LING
(CURED —) DUNFISH
(DRIED —) STOCK
(PILE OF DRIED —) YAFFLE
(SALTED —) COR KLIPFISH HABERDINE
(YOUNG —) SPRAG
CODA END CAUDA RONDO EPILOG FINALE CODETTA EPILOGUE POSTLUDE

CODDLE PET BABY CADE COOK MUCH HUMOR NURSE SMALM SPOIL CARESS COCKER COSSET COTTON FONDLE PAMPER PTISAN QUADLE PARBOIL
CODE BCD LAW FLAG ASCII CANON CODEX DOGMA FUERO CIPHER DIGEST SECRET SIGNAL MULTEKA PRECEPT DOOMBOOK MICROCODE
(— OF CEREMONIES) RITUAL
(— OF CHIVALRY) BUSHIDO
(— OF LAWS) ADA ADAT PANDECT SHERIAT DOOMBOOK
(— OF REGULATIONS) RULE
(— OF RULES) VINAYA
(— OF WHAT IS FITTING) DECORUM PROTOCOL
(— WORD) ALFA XRAY ZULU ROGER ROMEO TANGO SIERRA VICTOR YANKEE WHISKEY
(COMPUTER —) BCD ASCII
(INFORMATION —) EBCDIC
(KIND OF —) ZIP AREA MORSE PENAL
(PUNCHCARD —) HOLLERITH
(PUNCH CARD —) HOLLERITH
(READ BAR —S) SCAN
CODETTA CONDUIT
CODE WORD EUPHEMISM
CODEX ALEF CODE ALEPH ANNAL
CODFISH POOR SPRAG TORSK KEELING
CODGER COD CUFF CHURL CRANK MISER FELLOW NIGGARD
CODICIL ANNEX LABEL SCRIPT
CODIFY INDEX DIGEST CLASSIFY
CODLING HAKE
CODOL RETINOL
CODON TRIPLET
CODSWALLOP TRIPE
COEFFICIENT CUMULANT AUSTAUSCH
COELENTERATE POLYP MEDUSA ACALEPH RADIATE ACALEPHE
COENOBIUM COLONY
COENOCYTE SYMPLASM SYMPLAST SYNCYTIUM
COENZYME NAD NADH NADP NADPH COFACTOR
COERCE COW CURB MAKE BULLY CHECK DRIVE FORCE ORDER COHERT COMPEL HIJACK CONCUSS ENFORCE REPRESS SANDBAG BLUDGEON BULLDOZE DISTRAIN RESTRAIN RESTRICT BLACKJACK
COERCION HEAT FORCE DURESS COMMAND
COEUR D'ALENE SKITSWISH
COEUS (BROTHER OF —) ENCELADUS
(DAUGHTER OF —) LETO LATONA ASTERIA
(FATHER OF —) URANUS
(MOTHER OF —) GAEA
(SISTER OF —) FAMA RUMOR
(WIFE OF —) PHOEBE
COFFEE JO JOE RIO CAFE COHO COHU JAVA MILD DECAF MOCHA BOGOTA BRAZIL CAUFLE CHAOUA JAMOKE SANTOS TRIAGE ARABICA BOURBON MELANGE SUMATRA

ESPRESSO MAZAGRAN MEDELLIN TRILLADO CAPUCCINO CAPPUCCINO
(— DISPENSER) URN
(DECAFFEINATED —) DECAF
(KIND OF —) DECAF
(MORNING —) ELEVENS
COFFEE BEAN QUAKER
COFFEEBERRY JOJOBA CASCARA SOYBEAN PEABERRY
COFFEE CAKE KUCHEN
COFFEECAKE (ROUND —) TEARING
COFFEE-CUP FINGAN FINJAN
COFFEEHOUSE INN CAFE CAFENEH CAFENER CAFENET
COFFEEMAKER SILEX
COFFEEPOT PERCOLATOR
COFFEE TREE BONDUC CHICOT VIRGILIA
COFFER ARK BOX DAM PYX CHEST HUTCH TRUNK CASKET FORCER FORCET SPRUCE TRENCH CAISSON CASHBOX CASSOON COFFRET LACUNAR LAQUEAR CIBORIUM STANDARD
COFFIN BIER CASE CIST KIST MOLD PALL SHELL BASKET CASING CASKET COFFER HEARSE TROUGH THROUGH
(LEADEN —) COPE
COG CAM LIE NOG CAUK COCK GEAR JEST CATCH CHEAT CHOCK CHUCK COGUE COZEN TENON TOOTH TRICK WEDGE WHEEL CAJOLE COGGING DECEIVE PRODUCE QUIBBLE WHEEDLE
COGENT GOOD PITHY VALID POTENT STRONG TELLING FORCIBLE POWERFUL PREGNANT
COGITATE MULL MUSE PLAN THINK PONDER CONNATE MEDIATE REFLECT CONSIDER
COGNATE KIN AKIN ALIKE ALLIED COGENER KINDRED RELATED SIMILAR BANDHAVA RELATIVE APOPHONIC
COGNITION GNOSIS NOESIS KENNING KNOWLEDGE PERCEPTION
(SUFF.) GNOSIA GNOSIS GNOSTIC GNOSY
COGNITIVE KNOWING EPISTEMIC
COGNIZANCE KEN WIT HEED MARK BADGE CREST EMBLEM NOTICE BEARING COCKADE KNOWING PRIVITY WITTING
COGNIZANT WARE WISE AWAKE AWARE GUILTY KNOWING WITTING ACKNOWNE SENSIBLE
(BE —) DEEM
COGNIZE KNOW
COGNOMEN NAME BYNAME AGNOMEN SURNAME NICKNAME PATRONYM
COGON ILLUK KUNAI LALANG
COGWOOD CERILLO
COHABIT BED LIVE DWELL ADHERE OCCUPY COMPANY ACCUSTOM
CO-HEIR PARCENER
COHERE FIT BOND GLUE SUIT AGREE CLING SEIZE STICK UNITE ADHERE CEMENT CLEAVE CONNECT COINCIDE

COHERENCE UNION CONSENT CONTEXT COHESION STRENGTH
COHERENT SERRIED
COHESION BOND ADHESION HARDNESS STRENGTH
COHESIVE FATTY GLUEY TENACIOUS
COHESIVENESS TENACITY
COHOBA PARICA
COHORT PAL ALLY BUDDY FRIEND PARTNER
COHOSH SQUAWROOT PAPOOSEROOT
COHUNE COROJO COROZO
COIF CAP HOW HOOD HOUVE BEGGIN BIGGIN BURLET HAIRDO QUAIFE ARRANGE CALOTTE BIGGONET COIFFURE SKULLCAP
COIFFURE COIF HEAD HAIRDO TUTULUS TRESSURE
(KIND OF —) BOB BUN AFRO PAGEBOY
COIL ADO WIN WIP ANSA CLEW CURL FAKE FANK FURL FUSS HANK LINK LOOP ROLL TUFT WIND ENROL FLAKE HELIX QUERL QUILE ROUND SPIRE TENSE TESLA TWINE TWIRL TWIST WHORL WRING BOBBIN BOTTOM DOUGHT DIMMER ENROLL GLOMUS HEATER RENDER RUNDLE SPIRAL TEASER TOROID TUMULT UPWIND VOLUME WINDUP WREATH ENTRAIL HAYCOCK INVOLVE PRIMARY RINGLET ROULEAU SNAKING TICKLER TROUBLE WREATHE COFUSION CONVOLVE ENCIRCLE INDUCTOR OVERCOIL
(— IN STILL) SCROLL
(— INTO BALL) WIRF
(— OF CAPILLARIES) TUFT
(— OF HAIR) BUN PUG
(— OF SNAKE) FOLD
(— OF WIRE) BOBBIN SOLENOID
(— OF YARN) SKEIN
(INDUCTION —) JIGGER
(PREF.) SPIRILLO SPIR(I)(O)
COILED GYRATE TORTILE WRITHEN TURBINAL
COILER FLARER
COILING SPIRY
COIN AS BU PU AVO BAN BIT BOO COB DAM DIE DUB ECU FIL JOE KIP LAT LEK LEU LEV LEY ORI PUL SEN SOL TRA WEN WON ZUZ ABAS ANNA ATTE BAHT BATZ BESA CASH CENT CHIP CHON DEMY DIME DOIT DONG DOTT DUMP DURO FELS FILS GILL GROS GROT HARP HOON HWAN JACK JANE KRAN KYAT LEVY LION MAIL MAKE MERK MILL MINT MITE MULE OBAN ONZA OORD PARA PAUL PESA PESO PICE POND POUL QUAN RAND RIAL ROCK RYAL SCAD SENT SINK SIZE SLUG TAEL TARA TARE TARI TARO TIAO TREY TYPE UNIT ACKEY AGNEL AGORA AKCHA ALBUS ALTIN ALTUN AMANI ANGEL ANGLE ASPER BAIOC BAIZA BATTE BEKAR BELGA BETSO BEZZO BISTI BLANC BLANK BODLE BROAD BROWN CHINK CLINK COIGN CONTO

COROA CROSS CROWN CUNYE DARIC DINAR DISME DOBLA DUCAT EAGLE EYRIR FANAM FANON FODDA FRANC GAZET GRANO GROAT GROSZ HALER HECTE JACOB JULIO JUSTO KOBAN KRONA KRONE KROON LIARD LIBRA LITRA LIVRE LOUIS MEDAL MEDIN MEDIO MILAN MOHUR MOPUS NOBLE NOMOS OBANG ORKEY ORKYN PAISA PAOLO PARDO PENNY PERAU PESSA PIECE PLACK PLATE POALI POALO PROOF PRUTA QUART QUINE RAPPE REBIA RIDER RIYAL ROYAL RUBLE RUPIA SAIGA SAPEK SCEAT SCUDO SCUTE SEMIS SHAHI SICCA SMASH SOLDO STAMP STYCA SUCRE TALER TANGA TANKA TEMPO THRIP TICAL TRIME UNCIA UNITE WHITE ABASSI ABBASI AFGHAN AHMADI ARGENT ASSARY AUREUS AZTECA BALBOA BAUBEE BAWBEE BEAVER BEZANT BIANCO BI ANCO BOGACH BRONZE CARLIN CENTAS CHAISE COBANG CONDOR COPPER CORONA CUARTO CUNZIE DECIME DENARY DENIER DERHAM DINDER DIOBOL DIRHAM DIXAIN DIZAIN DORI ON DODKIN DOLLAR DOPPIA DOUBLE ESCUDO FILLER FLORIN FOLLIS FORINT GEORGE GIULIO GOURDE GRIVNA GROSSO GUINEA GULDEN HARPER HELLER ICHIBU ITZEBU JUSLIK KLIPPE KOPECK KORONA KORUNA LAUREL LEPTON MACUTA MAHBUB MAIDEN MANCUS MEDINO MISKAL NICKEL NORKYN OCHAVO OCTAVE UNGARO PADUAN PAGUDA PARDAO PATACA PATART PHILIP PRUTAH QUEZAL ROSARY SALUNG SALUTE SATANG SEQUIN SESKIN SHEKEL SHIELD SIGLOS SINKER SIXAIN SOMALO SOVRAN STATER STELLA STIVER TALENT TARGET TESTAO TESTER TESTON THALER THOMAN TOSTON TRIENS TUMAIN TUNGAH TURNER TURNEY TURTLE UNGARO VINTEM XERIFF YUZLIK ZECHIN ZEHNER ZEQUIN ALFONSO ALTILIK ANGELET ANGELOT ANGOLAR ANGSTER BAIOCCO BAJOCCO BARBONE BOLIVAR CARDECU CARLINE CARLINO CAROLIN CAROLUS CENTAVO CHALCUS CHALKOS CORDOBA COUNTER CRUSADO DAMPANG DRACHMA DUCATON DUPLONE ESCALAN FANTASY JACOBUS JOANNES KASBEKE KREUZER LEMPIRA LEONINE LEOPARD LUIGINO MANGOUR MARENGO MOIDORE MONARCH MUZOONA NOUMMOS ONCETTA PAHLAVI PARISIS PATACAO PATAGON PATAQUE PENNING PFENNIG PISTOLE QUADRIN QUARTER QUATTIE QUETZAL QUINYIE REDDOCK RUDDOCK RUSPONE SANTIMS SCRUPLE SEXTANS SILIQUA SIZEINE SOLIDUS SPECIES

STAMPEE STOOTER STUIVER SULTANE TALLERO TEECALL THRYMSA TORNESE TRIOBOL UNICORN XERAFIN ALBERTIN AMBROSIN AQUILINO AUGUSTAL AUKSINAS BAETZNER BAGATINE BECHTLER BLAFFERT BLANKEEL BLANKILO BROCKAGE CAVALIER CHINKERS CHUCKRAM COLONIAL COURONNE CROCKARD CRUZEIRO DECUSSIS DENARIUS DIDRACHM DIOBOLON DOUBLOON EQUIPAGA FARTHING FILIPPIC FREDERIK GAZZETTA GENOVINO GIGLIATO GIUSTINA GROSCHEN HARDHEAD HYPERPER IMPERIAL ISABELLA JOHANNES KREUTZER LUSHBURG MACARONI MAJIDIEH MARAVEDI MARCELLO METALLIK MILESIMA PATACOON PAVILION PICAYUNE PIEDFORT PISTOLET PLAPPERT PORTAGUE QUADRANS QUADRINE QUARTINE QUINCUNX RESTRIKE RIGMAREE RISDALER RIXDALER SCUDDICK SEMUNCIA SESTERCE SHILLING SIXPENCE SKILLING SLEEPING SOLIDARE STERLING SIQUINKA SULTANIN TENPENNY TETROBOL THIRTEEN TWOPENCE ZECCHINO DRACHEATE
(— AROUND NECK) TALI
(— FLIP CALL) HEADS TAILS
(— HAVING MINTING ERROR) FIDO
(— IMPERFECTLY MINTED) BROCKAGE
(— OF TRIFLING VALUE) RAP
(BASE —) SHAND SHEEN SINKER
(CLAD —) SANDWICH
(COUNTERFEIT —) RAP GRAY GREY SLIP SHEEN SHOFUL STUMER STUMOR
(ISRAEL —) AGORA
(ISRAEL —S) AGOROT
(PLUGGED —) PLUG
(SMALL THICK —) DUMP
(PL.) AGOROT CHANGE CHINKS SERIES COINAGE
(PREF.) NUMISMATO NUMMI
COINAGE FICTION GALUMPH MINTAGE
COINCIDE FIT GEE JIBE JUMP AGREE TALLY CONCUR
COINCIDENCE SYNCHRONY
COINCIDENT EVEN TOGETHER
COINCIDING CONGRUENT CONSILIENT
COINER MONIER MONEYER SMASHER
COINS CHANGE
COITION SOIL VENERY MEETING CONGRESS
COKE ASK COAL COLK CORE DOPE CHARK COCAINE
(BROKEN —) BREEZE
COL GAP NEK HALS JOCH PASS HALSE SWIRE SADDLE
COLANDER SIEVE STRAINER
COLAXAIS (BROTHER OF —) ARPOXAIS LIPOXAIS
(FATHER OF —) TARGITAUS
COLCOTHAR SAFFRON TUSCANY
COLD FLU ICY MUR NIP COOL DEAD DULL FRIO HARD HASK HOAR

MURR ROUP SOUR ACALE ACOLD
AGUED ALGID BLEAK CHILL CRISP
FISHY FROID FRORE GELID GLACE
GLARE OORIE OURIE PARKY
POOSE RHEUM SHARP SNELL
STONY VIRUS ARCTIC BITTER
BOREAL CHILLY CLAMMY CRIMMY
FREDDO FRIGID FRIGOR FROSTY
GLASSY MARBLY STECKY WAIRCH
WINTRY BRITTLE CATARRH
CHILLED COLDISH COSTIVE
DISTANT FROSTED GLACIAL
INHUMAN MORFOND SHIVERY
STRANGE FREEZING MORFOUND
PIERCING RESERVED RHIGOSIS
STANDOFF UNHEATED REPULSIVE
(— IN HEAD) POSE POOSE CORYZA
CATARRH GRAVEDO SNIVELS
SNIFFLES SNIFTERS
(BITTER —) ARCTIC
(VERY —) ICY GELID FRIGID PEEVISH
(PREF.) CRY(O) FRIGO FRIGORI
KRY(O) PSYCHRO
COLD-BLOODED BRUTAL LEEPIT
COLD CUTS ASSIETTE
COLD-HEARTED COLD FROZEN
BLOODLESS
COLDLY DRILY DRYLY
COLDNESS COLD FROST STEEL
PHLEGM ALGIDITY ASPERITY
DISTANCE FROIDEUR
COLDONG FRIARBIRD
COLE CALE KAIL KALE COLZA
FRIGOR COLEWORT
COLE-SEED COLZA NAVEW
COLESEED NAVEW
COLEUS KOORKA
COLEWORT COLE KALE RIBE STOCK
CABBAGE
(SPROUT OF —) STOVEN
COLIC BATS FRET BATTS GUTTIE
BELLYACHE
COLICROOT UNICORN ALOEROOT
HUSKROOT HUSKWORT
STARWORT
COLIMA TAPA IRONWOOD
COLISEUM HALL STADIUM
THEATER COLOSSEUM
COLL HUG CLIP CULL POLL PRUNE
EMBRACE
COLLABORATE AID ASSIST
COOPERATE
COLLAGEN OSSEIN
COLLAPSE CAVE FALL FLOP FOLD
GIVE SINK WILT CRASH SLUMP
WRECK BUCKLE SHRINK TUMBLE
CAPSIZE CROPPER CRUMBLE
CRUMPLE DEBACLE DEFLATE
FAILURE FLUMMOX FOUNDER
SMASHUP CONTRACT DOWNFALL
MELTDOWN TAILSPIN
PROSTRATION
(— OF NUCLEUS) SYSTOLE
COLLAPSED QUAT CLUNG
COLLAPSIBLE FOLDING
COLLAPSING FAILURE COLLABENT
COLLAR CAP FUR NAB BAND BOSS
ETON FALL FANO GILL GRAB POKE
RING RUFF CHAIN DICKY FANON
FANUM FICHU PHANO RUCHE
SEIZE STOCK TRASH WHISK
BERTHA CARCAN CHOKER COLLET
COLLUM DICKEY GORGET PARRAL

PARREL RABATO REBATO SADDLE
SLEEVE TACKLE TORQUE TUCKER
TURNUP BOBACHE BOBECHE
CAPTURE CHIGNON CIRCLET
PANUELO PARTLET POTHOOK
REBATER SHACKLE STICKUP
VANDYKE CARCANET CINCTURE
NECKBAND NECKLACE RABATINE
STARCHER TURNDOWN
(— FOR HORSE) BARGHAM
BRECHAM
(HIGH —) GILLS JAMPOT
(HORSE —) BRECHAM
(IRON —) JOUG JOUGS CARCAN
POTHOOKS
(LACE —) SCALLOP
(MAGISTRATE'S —) GOLILLA
(ROMAN —) RABAT
(WHEEL-SHAPED —) RUFF
(WOODEN —) CANG CANGUE
COLLAR BEAM SPANNER
SPANPIECE
COLLARBONE CLAVICLE
COLL'ARCO ARCATO
COLLARED ACCOLLE ACCOLLEE
TORQUATE
COLLAR PAD AFTERWALE
COLLATE BESTOW CONFER VERIFY
COMPARE
COLLATERAL SIDE ASSETS MARGIN
OBLIQUE INDIRECT PARALLEL
SECURITY
COLLATION TEA MEAL BEVER
LUNCH REPAST SERMON ADDRESS
READING DEJEUNER HOTCHPOT
TREATISE
COLLEAGUE AIDE ALLY UNITE
DEPUTY SOCIUS ADJUNCT
COLLEGE COMPEER CONSORT
PARTNER CONFRERE CONSPIRE
COLLECT JUG SAM TAX CALL CARD
CULL DRAW HEAP LEVY LIFT PICK
PILE POOL REAR SAMM SAVE
AMASS CROWD GLEAN GROUP
HOARD RAISE STORE SWEEP
ACCOIL ACCRUE CENTER CONFER
GARNER GATHER MUSTER PRAYER
SEMBLE SHEAVE UPTAKE ARCHIVE
CLUSTER COMPILE CONGEST
ENGROSS IMPOUND RAMMASS
RECUEIL SCAMBLE SYNAPTE
ASSEMBLE CONFLATE CONTRACT
CUPBOARD INGATHER RESEMBLE
SCRAMBLE SCROUNGE
(— AND DRIVE INTO ENCLOSURE)
WEAR
(— FOOD) FORAGE
(— GRAIN) GAVEL
(— INTO COVEY) JUG
(— MONEY) NOB
(— WAGES) UPLIFT
COLLECTED CALM COOL SOBER
SERENE PRESENT COMPOSED
(PREF.) ATHRO
COLLECTION ANA BAG KIT SET
BAND BEVY BOOK CLAN CROP FILE
HEAD HEAP KNOT LEVY OLIO RAFT
SORT ALBUM ANNEX ARRAY
BATCH BUDGE BUNCH DEPOT
FLOCK GLEAN GROUP HOARD
KITTY SHEAF STORE SUITE SWATH
TROVE AFFLUX BUDGET BUNDLE

CONGER CORPUS FARDEL MISHNA
PARCEL RAGBAG RECULE SORITE
SPRING SWATHE TUMBLE
ACCOUNT BOILING BULLARY
CLUSTER COLLECT CONGERY
EXHIBIT FERNERY FISTFUL
FLUTTER GALLERY QUOTITY
RECUEIL SAMHITA SMATTER
SMYTRIE SYLLOGE TERRIER
ASSEMBLY CABOODLE CONGERIE
CUSTOMAL FASCICLE GATHERUM
GLOSSARY JINGBANG ROMESCOT
ROMESHOT SYNTAGMA
(— AT FOX HUNT) CAP
(— OF ALMS) QUEST
(— OF ANIMALS) ZOO HEAD
(— OF BOOKCASES) STACK
(— OF BOOKS) SET BIBLE CANON
LIBRARY
(— OF CONIFERS) PINETUM
(— OF DATA) GROUND
(— OF FORMULAS) CODEX
(— OF FOUR) TETRAD
(— OF HUTS) BUSTEE
(— OF JOKES) SOTTISIER
(— OF LAWS) CODE
(— OF MAPS) ATLAS
(— OF OBJECTS) AFFAIR
(— OF OPINIONS) SYMPOSIUM
(— OF PERSONS) BOODLE
(— OF PLANTS) SERTULE
(— OF POEMS) DIVAN DIWAN SYLVA
ANTHOLOGY
(— OF PUS) ABSCESS HYPOPYON
(— OF REVENUES) TAHSIL TEHSIL
(— OF ROCKS) SUITE
(— OF RULES) SUTRA SUTTA
(— OF SAMPLES) SWATCH
(— OF SAYINGS) ANA SUTRA SUTTA
(— OF SMALL THINGS) SMYTRIE
(— OF SPECIMENS) CABINET
(— OF STAFFS) SYSTEM
(— OF STORIES) LEGEND
(— OF TIPS) TRONC
(— OF TOOLS) LAYOUT
(— OF TREES) SERINGAL
(— OF UNWANTED ANIMALS)
LARDER
(— OF VIEWS) SYMPOSIUM
(— OF WIVES) SERAGLIO
(— OF WRITINGS) CORPUS
(— OF 24 SHEETS) QUIRE
(CHURCH —) PLATE
(CONFUSED —) CLUTTER
(MISCELLANEOUS —) OLIO FARDEL
SMYTRIE
(VALUABLE —) TROVE
(VAST —) CLOUD
(SUFF.) ERY
COLLECTION-BOX LADLE
COLLECTIVE ARTEL GROUP
AGGREGATE
COLLECTIVELY ASONE
COLLECTIVIST COMMUNIST
SOCIALIST
COLLECTOR COMB CAMEIST
CURIOSO DUSTMAN FURIOSO
UPTAKER ANTIQUER COUNTOUR
GATHERER OOLOGIST STAMPMAN
VIRTUOSO ZAMINDAR
(— ITEMS) RARIORA
(— OF BUTTERFLIES) AURELIAN

(— OF HERBS) SIMPLER
(— OF REVENUE) AUMIL AUMILDAR
TALUKDAR ZAMINDAR
(— OF UNNEEDED ITEMS) PACKRAT
(BILL —) DUNNER
(CUSTOMS —) HOPPO CUSTOMER
(INDISCRIMINATE —) MAGPIE
(ITEMS OF —) VIRTU
(TAX —) CAID QAID GABBAI
PUBLICAN TAHSILDAR
COLLECTORATE TALUK
COLLEEN GIRL LASS MISS BELLE
CAILIN DAMSEL
COLLEGE TOL HALL AGGIE HOUSE
LYCEE CAMPUS COLAGE SCHOOL
SIWASH ACADEMY MADRASA
SEMINARY SORBONNE
(KIND OF —) CLUSTER
(MUSLIM —) MADRASA
MADRASAH
COLLEGER TUG
COLLET BAND NECK RING CHUCK
CULET CASING CIRCLE COLLAR
COLLUM FLANGE BUSHING
COLLIDE HIT RAM BUMP DASH FRAY
HURT BARGE CLASH CRASH
KNOCK SHOCK SMITE WRECK
CANNON HURTLE STRIKE THRUST
(— HEAD-ON) RAM
(— WITH) PRANG
(— WITH) IMPINGE
COLLIE KELPIE BEARDIE
COLLIER MINER PLOVER GEORDIE
COILYEAR FLATIRON SCUTCHER
COLLIERY MINE
COLLIMATE ALIGN
COLLINATE ALIGN
COLLIQUATION SYNTEXIS
COLLISION HIT FOUL CLASH CRASH
PRANG SHOCK SHUNT HURTLE
IMPACT JOSTLE PILEUP SMASHUP
CLASHING CONFLICT
COLLOCATE SET PLACE ARRANGE
COLLOID GEL
COLLOP PIECE
COLLOQUIAL FAMILIAR INFORMAL
COLLOQUIUM INDUCEMENT
COLLOQUY CHAT TALK PARLEY
DIALOGUE
COLLOTYPE ARTOTYPE HELIOTYPE
COLLUDE PLOT SCHEME CONNIVE
COLLOGUE CONSPIRE
COLLUM NECK
COLLUSION DECEIT CAHOOTS
SECRECY PRACTICE PRACTISE
COLLUSIVE COVINOUS COLLUSORY

COLOMBIA

CAPE: VELA AGUJA MARZO
AUGUSTA
CAPITAL: BOGOTA
CAY: VELA VIGIA RONCADOR
COIN: PESO REAL CONDOR PESETA
CENTAVO
FORMER NAME: DARIEN
NEWGRANADA
GULF: URABA CUPICA DARIEN
TIBUGA TORTUGAS
INDIAN: BORO CUNA HOKA MACU
MUZO PAEZ CARIB CATIO CHOCO
COFAN COGUI CUBEO GUANE
PIJAO SEONA ARAWAK BETOYA
CALIMA INGANO SALIVA TAHAMI

TUCANO TUNEBO YAHUNA
ACHAGUA ANDAQUI CHIBCHA
CHIMILA GUAHIBO GUAJIRO
PANCHES PUINAVE PUITOTO
QUECHUA TAIRONA GUARAUNO
MOTILONE
INLET: TUMACO
ISLAND: BARU NAIPO FUERTE
GORGONA CUSACHON
MEASURE: VARA AZUMBRE
CELEMIN
MOUNTAIN: CHITA HUILA PURACE
TOLIMA
MOUNTAINS: ABIBE ANDES BAUDO
COCUY AYAPEL PERIJA TUNAHI
CHAMUSA ORIENGAL
PLAINS: LLANOS
POINT: CRUCES LACRUZ SOLANO
CARIBANA GALLINAS
PORT: LORICA CARTAGENA
PROVINCE: META CAUCA CHOCO
HUILA VALLE ARAUCA BOYACA
CALDAS NARINO TOLIMA VAUPES
BOLIVAR CAQUETA GUAJIRE
VICHADA AMAZONAS PUTUMAYO
RIVER: UVA BITA META MUCO SINU
TOMO UPIA YARI BAUDO CAUCA
CESAR ISANA MESAI NECHI PATIA
PAUTO SUCIO AMAZON ARAUCA
ARIARI ATRATO CAGUAN VAUPES
YAPURA CAQUETA GUAINIA
INIRIDA TRUANDO VICHADA
APAPORIS CASANARE GUAVIARE
PUTUMAYO MAGDALENA
TOWN: TEN ANZA BUGA CALI MITU
MUZO PAEZ SIPI TADO TOLU YARI
BELLO CHINU GUAPI NEIVA PASTO
TUNJA BOGOTA CUCUTA IBAGUE
QUIBDO SANGIL CARTAGO
LETICIA PALMIRA PEREIRA
POPAYAN GIRARDOT MEDELLIN
MONTERIA CARTAGENA
TREE: ARBOLOCO
VOLCANO: PURACE
WEIGHT: BAG SACO CARGA LIBRA
QUILATE QUINTAL

COLON CROWN POINT HEMISTICH
MESYMNION
COLONEL (— OF LIFEGUARDS)
GOLDSTICK
COLONIAL OVERSEA OVERSEAS
COLONIST BOOR COLON FATHER
CUTHEAN PIONEER PLANTER
SETTLER EMIGRANT
(— IN AFRICA) BOER
(— IN SICILY) SIKELIOT
(AUSTRALIAN —) STERLING
(PL.) DEHAITES DEHAVITES
COLONIZE ECIZE FOUND PLANT
GATHER SETTLE MIGRATE
COLONIZER OECIST OEKIST
COLONNADE ROW STOA PORCH
PARVIS PIAZZA XYSTUS EUSTYLE
GALLERY PARVISE PERGOLA
PORTICO TERRACE CHOULTRY
DIASTYLE PERISTYLE
COLONNETTE COLUMELLA
COLONUS SERF TENANT
COLONY STATE STOCK SWARM
CENOBE CORMUS APOIKIA
COLONIA CENOBIUM GANNETRY
PLANTATION POLYZOARIUM

(— OF BEES) HIVE SKEP SWARM
(BRYOZOAN —) ESCHARA
COLOPHONY ROSIN
COLOR (ALSO SEE SPECIFIC COLOR)
DIP DYE HUE BLEE CAST FAKE
FLAG PUKE SUIT TINT TONE BADGE
BLUSH GLAZE GLOSS GRAIN PAINT
SHADE STAIN TAINT TASTE TENNE
TINCT TINGE TOUCH BANNER
BLEACH BOTTOM BRIDGE
CHROMA ENSIGN INFECT LOCKET
MANTLE RADDLE REDDEN STREAK
TEMPER COULEUR DEPAINT
DISTORT ENGRAIN PENNANT
PIGMENT SPECKLE COLORING
STANDARD TERTIARY TINCTURE
(— IMPARTED TO HERRINGS)
GILDING
(— LOSS) POLIOSIS
(— OF BIRD) SMUT
(— OF BODY) HEAT
(— OF EYES OF FOWLS) DAW
(— OF HONEY) AMBER
(— OF HUMAN FLESH) CARNATION
(— OF REFLECTED LIGHT)
OVERTONE
(— OF ROCK) STONE
(AUTUMN —) OCHER
(BLUE —) FOG JAY SKY WAD AQUA
BICE CIEL CYAN DELF DUSK IRIS
NAVY PAON SAXE WADE WOAD
ZINC AZURE BERYL BLUET CADET
CAPRI CHING COPEN DELFT DELPH
DIANA DRAKE EMAIL GRAPE METAL
NIKKO ORION PEARL ROYAL SLATE
SMALT SMOKE VANDA CANTON
CENDRE COELIN ENSIGN GROTTO
HATHOR INDIGO LUPINE MARINE
MASCOT MIGNON ORIENT PENSEE
ROMANY SEVRES VENICE ZENITH
CELESTE CERAMIC CHICORY
DUSTBLU GOBELIN HORIZON
LIBERTY LOBELIA LOGWOOD
MATELOT PEACOCK PETUNIA
RAMESES SISTINE SIXTINE
ABSINTHE BLUEBIRD BLUEWOOD
BRITTANY CAESIOUS CATTLEYA
CERULEAN CERULEUM DUCKLING
ELECTRIC GENDARME HYACINTH
INFANTRY LABRADOR LARKSPUR
MASCOTTE MAZARINE MIDNIGHT
MOONBEAM NATIONAL SAPPHIRE
TWILIGHT WEDGWOOD
(BROWN —) BAY ELK FOX OAK TAN
ARAB BARK BOLE BRAN BURE CAIN
CLAY CORK CUBA DATE DEER DRAB
DUST ECRU FAON FAWN GOAT
GOLD HOPI IRON LAMA LION MAST
MESA MUSK PUCE SEAL SIAM TEAK
ACORN ADUST ALOMA AZTEC BEIGE
BISON BLOND BLUSH BOLUS BRIAR
BRICK BRIER BROWN BUNNY
CACAO CAMEL CANNA CLOVE
COCOA CONGO EAGLE FRIAR
FUDGE GIPSY GRAIN GYPSY HAZEL
HENNA KAFFA KHAKI LIVER MAHAL
MALAY MECCA MINIM MUMMY
NEGRO OTTER PABLO QUAIL SABEL
SEDGE SEPIA SIENA SIRUP SNUFF
SUDAN SUEDE SUMAC SYRUP
TABAC TAFFY TENNE TOAST TOPAZ
AFGHAN ALESAN ALMOND APACHE
ARGALI AUBURN BAMBOO BEAVER

BISQUE BISTER BISTRE BLONDE
BRONCO BRONZE BURNET COCHIN
COFFEE CONDOR COOKIE COWBOY
CROTAL DORADO ESKIMO FALLOW
GINGER GRAVEL GROUSE HAVANA
ISABEL LOUTRE MAROON MERIDA
MOHAWK MUFFIN NUTMEG ORIOLE
PAWNEE PLOVER PUEBLO RABBIT
RACKET RUDDLE RUSSET SAHARA
SANTOS SHERRY SORREL SPHINX
SPONGE STRING STUCCO SUMACH
SUNTAN THRUSH TIFFIN TURTLE
ASPHALT BADIOUS BEESWAX
BITUMEN BRACKEN BRONCHO
CALDRON CATTAIL CIGARET
COCONUT COTRINE CRACKER
DOGWOOD DURANGO FEUILLE
FILBERT GAZELLE GOREVAN
HARVEST LEATHER LIBERIA
MALABAR MIRADOR MORDORE
MOROCCO MUSCADE MUSTANG
NORFOLK OAKWOOD PERIQUE
PRALINE RACQUET ROSARIO
SABELLA SUNBURN SUNDOWN
TALLYHO TANBARK TOBACCO
TUSCANY ALDERNEY ALGERIAN
AMBROSIA BISMARCK BOBOLINK
CALABASH CARTOUCH CAULDRON
CINNAMON CLAYBANK CORDOVAN
DOUBLOON ETRUSCAN EUCHROME
HAZELNUT ISABELLA KOLINSKY
LEAFMOLD MANDALAY MOCCASIN
MOLESKIN MOROCCAN
MUSHROOM NOISETTE PHEASANT
SAUTERNE SHAGBARK STARLING
TAMARACK TEAKWOOD TERRAPIN
TORTOISE WOODBARK
(DEAD-LEAF —) FILEMOT
(DEEP —) DARK
(FAST —) GRAIN
(FAWN —) WHEATEN
(GREEN —) BOA FIR IVY ALOE BICE
FERN JADE LEEK MOSS NILE SAGE
ALOES CEDRE CHLOR DRAKE FAIRY
HOLLY KELLY LOVAT OLIVE SPRAY
CANNON EMPIRE HUNTER JASPER
LAUREL LIERRE LIZARD MEADOW
MOUSSE MYRTLE SPRUCE VERDET
CELADON CITRINE CORBEAU
CRESSON CYPRESS EMERALD
INGENUE JADEITE JUNIPER
MESANGE NEPTUNE OLIVINE
PERIDOT SEAFOAM SERPENT
TILLEUL VERDURE BAYBERRY
CHASSEUR COPPERAS EMERAUDE
GLAUCOUS GLOWWORM PARAKEET
PERRUCHE PISTACHE POPINJAY
SHAMROCK TARRAGON VIRIDIAN
WOODLAND
(GRIZZLED —) AGOUTI AGOUTY
(LACK OF —) PALLOR
(LOSE —) FADE
(OF A DARKISH —) SUBFUSE
(OTHER —S) OR ASH BAT DOE DUN
JET TEA CHIP CORN CROW DAWN
DOVE GRAY GREY GULL HEMP LAVA
LEAD MODE MOLE NICE NUDE
PLUM PORT PUKE ROAN RUST SAND
SOOT WOOD AMBER BEACH BLACK
CAMEO CERES CHILE CHILI COPRA
CRANE CRASH CREAM DWALE
EBONY FLESH GRAPE GREBE GREGE
MAUVE MOUSE PANSY PHLOX

PLOMB PRAWN PRUNE PUTTY RIFLE
SABLE SPICE STEEL THYME TWINE
ANATTO AURORA AUTUMN CASTOR
CINDER COLLIE CORCIR DAHLIA
DAMSON DENVER EVEQUE FIESTA
FUSTIC GAMBIA GRIEGE KASPER
MALLOW MODENA NAVAHO
NAVAJO NIMBUS NUTRIA ONDINE
ORCHID OXFORD OYSTER PEANUT
PEBBLE PIGEON QUAKER RAISIN
RESEDA ROUCOU SEASAN SILVER
TUSCAN VANITY VESTAL VIOLET
WALNUT ADMIRAL ANNATTO
ARBUTUS ARDOISE ARNATTA
BEGONIA BERMUDA BLOSSOM
BRINDLE CARAIBE CARAMEL
CORBEAU COTRINE COWSLIP
CRACKER CRUISER MORELLO
MURILLO NATURAL OPHELIA
PELICAN PONTIFF POPCORN
PRELATE PUMPKIN QUIMPER
REGATTA ROSEBUD SAKKARA
SANDUST SPARROW SUNBEAM
THISTLE TUSSORE VERVAIN VIOLINE
WEIGELA WHEATEN ALUMINUM
AMARANTH AMETHYST BLONDINE
CARMETTA CHARCOAL CLEMATIS
COCOBOLO COQUETTE CREVETTE
CYCLAMEN EGGPLANT EMINENCE
FELDGRAU FLAMINGO GILLIVER
GRAPHITE GUNMETAL HONEYDEW
IMPERIAL JACINTHE LAVENDER
MARATHON MORILLON MULBERRY
PALMETTO ROSEWOOD SAUTERNE
SQUIRREL SUNBURST WIRELESS
WISTARIA WISTERIA CARNELIAN
(RED —) DAWN FLEA GOLF GOYA
HEBE LAKE MIST PUCE RUBY TULY
WINE AGATE BRASS BRICK CANNA
CANON CEDAR CORAL CUTCH
EMBER FLAME FLASH GULES LILAC
MELON NYMPH PEACH PEONY
POPPY ROSET SIENA SPARK TOTEM
ACAJOU ARCHIL AURORE AUTUMN
AZALEA BRAZIL CANYON CARROT
CATSUP CERISE CHERRY CHERUB
CLARET COGNAC DAMASK FRAISE
GAIETY GARNET GAYETY GRANET
JOCKEY KERMES MADDER MALAGA
MIKADO MURREY NECTAR ORCHIL
PATISE SALMON SANDIX SHRIMP
SIERRA SULTAN TITIAN TOMATO
AFRICAN ANAMITE ANEMONE
BEGONIA BISCUIT BOKHARA
CARMINE CASTORY CATAWBA
CATCHUP CATECHU CRIMSON
CURRANT FIREFLY FUCHSIA
FUCHSIN GRANATE GRANITE
HEATHER INDIANA KETCHUP
LACQUER LOBSTER MAGENTA
MASCARA NACARAT OXBLOOD
PAPRIKA POMPEII PONCEAU
REDWOOD ROSETAN ROSETTE
RUBELLE SAFFLOR SARAVAN
SCARLET SINOPLE STAMMEL
SULTANA VERMEIL ALKERMES
AMARANTH ARCHILLA BISMARCK
BORDEAUX BURGUNDY CAMELLIA
CARDINAL CHAUDRON CHEROKEE
CHERUBIM CHESTNUT COCOANUT
CONFETTI DAMONICO DIANTHUS
DUBONNET EVENGLOW GERANIUM
GRENADIN GRIDELIN MAHOGANY

MANDARIN MAROCAIN NACARINE TOREADOR
(SOLID —) SOLID
(TONE —) TIMBRE
(YELLOW —) HAY RAT WAX BEAR BUFF CLAY CORN CUIR ECRU FLAX GOLD LARK LIME MOTH WELD WOLD ACIER ALOMA AZTEC BEIGE BLAKE BRASS CHALK CREAM GRAIN HONEY IVORY LEMON MAIZE MAPLE SHELL STRAW TAUPE WOULD ACACIA ALMOND BANANA CANARY CATHAY CHROME CITRON CITRUS CROCUS DORADO FALLOW MANILA MASTIC MIMOSA NANKIN NUGGET OXGALL SULFUR SUNRAY SUNSET ANTIQUE APRICOT BISCUIT CAVALRY CHAMOIS GAMBOGE JASMINE JONQUIL LEGHORN MEXICAN NANKEEN PRAIRIE RHUBARB SAFFRON SULPHUR SUNGLOW ANTELOPE CALABASH CAPUCINE COCKATOO DAFFODIL EGGSHELL GENERALL GOLDMIST MARIGOLD ORPIMENT PRIMROSE SNOWSHOE
(PL.) FLAG
(PREF.) CHROM(AT)(ATO)(I)(IDIO)(O)
(HAVING DARK —) FUSCO
(SUFF.) CHROIA CHROIC CHROID CHROMASIA CHROME CHROMIA CHROMY CHROOUS
COLORABLE SPECIOUS PLAUSIBLE

COLORADO

CAPITAL: DENVER
COLLEGE: REGIS
COUNTY: BACA MESA YUMA OTERO OURAY ROUTT GILPIN CHAFFEE
MOUNTAIN: OSO LONGS PIKES ELBERT
MOUNTAIN RANGE: ROCKY
NATIVE: ROVER
PARK: ESTES
RIVER: YAMPA DOLORES APISHAPA ARIKAREE GUNNISON PURGATOIRE
STATE FLOWER: COLUMBINE
STATE NICKNAME: CENTENNIAL
STATE TREE: SPRUCE
TOWN: ASPEN DELTA LAMAR GOLDEN PUEBLO SALIDA ALAMOSA BOULDER DURANGO GREELEY GUNNISON LOVELAND TRINIDAD

COLORANT STAIN
COLORATION BLEE PILE FLASH CLOUDING COLORISM SCHILLER PIGMENTATION
COLORATURA GORGIA SOPRANO
COLOR-BLIND MONOCHROMATIC
(— TO RED) PROTANOPIC
COLOR-BLINDNESS DALTONISM
COLORED FAW HUED MALE TINCT BIASED DEPAINT STAINED
(— IN RED) RUBRIC
(— LIKE PIPE BOWL) TROUSERED
(BRILLIANTLY —) SUPERB FLAMING PSYCHEDELIC
(GORGEOUSLY —) FLAMBOYANT
(HIGHLY —) CHROMATIC PRISMATIC
(PARTI —) PIED PIEBALD

(UNIFORMLY —) HARD
(PREF.) CHROM(AT)(ATO)(I)(IDIO)(O)
(SUFF.) CHROME CHROOUS
COLORFUL GAY BRAVE JUICY VIVID COLORY GOLDEN FREAKED GORGEOUS
COLORING DYE BLEE TINT PAINT TINGE TINGENT BRONZING PAINTING TINCTURE
(— FOR EYELASHES) MASCARA
(— MATTER) TINCTION
(GARISH —) JAZZ
(SUFF.) CHROMY
COLORING MATTER
(SUFF.) PHYLL(A)(OUS)(UM)(Y)
COLORLESS WAN DRAB DULL PALE ASHEN BLAKE BLANK PLAIN ANEMIC MOUSEY PALLID HUELESS NEUTRAL ACHROMIC ACHROOUS BLANCHED ETIOLATE LIFELESS
(PREF.) LEUC(O)
COLOSSAL BIG HUGE VAST GREAT JUMBO LARGE IMMENSE TITANIC ENORMOUS GIGANTIC MONSTROUS
COLOSSUS GIANT TITAN STATUE COLOSSO MONOLITH
COLOSTRUM FOREMILK AFTERINGS
COLT FOAL STAG FILLY POTRO STAIG HOGGET POLEYN STAGGIE EQUULEUS
COLTER LAVER COOTER COULTER FOREIRON
COLTSFOOT DOCK CLOTE HOOFS CLEATS FARFARA LAGWORT SOWFOOT BULLFOOT CLAYWEED FOALFOOT
COLUGO COBEGO
COLUMBATE NIOBATE
COLUMBIA SINKIUSE
COLUMBINE AQUILEGE BLUEBELL CHUCKIES ROCKBELL
COLUMBITE DIANITE NIOBITE
COLUMBUS (BIRTHPLACE OF —) GENOA
COLUMELLA STALACE
COLUMN COG LAT ROW ANTA FILE FUST GOAL LINE POLE POST PROP STUB BAGUE LALLY SHAFT STELA STELE TORSO TRUNK WURTZ ASOKAN CORNER GNOMON PILLAR SCAPUS STAPLE STRING TSWETT COLUMEL SUPPORT VIGREUX CYLINDER PILASTER
(— IN EAR) MODIOLUS
(— OF FIGURES) SUM
(— OF FILAMENTS) SYNEMA
(— OF MOLTEN ROCK) PLUME
(BUDDHIST —) LAT
(FIGURE USED AS —) ATLAS TELAMON
(PART OF —) BASE DADO NECK OVOLO SHAFT TORUS ABACUS PLINTH REGLET SCOTIA CAPITAL ECHINUS FLUTING ASTRAGAL CINCTURE COLARENO PEDESTAL
(PART OF A —) SOCLE
(ROCK —) HOODOO
(ROULETTE —) DERNIER
(SPINAL —) HORN SPINE BACKBONE
(STRUCTURAL —) LALLY
(TWISTED —) TORSO

COLUMNAR TERETE STELENE COLUMNAL VERTICAL
COLUMNIST WRITER ANALYST
COLY MOUSEBIRD
COLZA SARSON
COMA TUFT BUNCH CARUS SLEEP SOPOR STUPOR SUBETH TORPOR TRANCE SEMICOMA CHEVELURE
COMATOSE OUT DROWSY LETHARGIC
COMB CARD GILL KAME LASH PICK RACK RAKE REDD REED SEEK TOZE BREAK BRUSH CAMBE CLEAN CREST CTENE CURRY FLISK RAVEL TEASE HACKLE SMOOTH CUSHION HATCHEL WRAITHE BEATILLE CARUNCLE TORTOISE
(KIND OF —) HOT
(WEAVING —) RADDLE
(PREF.) CTEN(O) LOPH(I)(IO)(O) PECTINATO
COMBAT WAR BLOW BOUT COPE DUEL FRAY MEEK MEET RUSH TILT CLASH FIGHT JOUST REPEL STOUR ACTION AFFRAY BATTLE MEDLEY OPPOSE RESIST SHOWER STRIFE CONTEND CONTEST COUNTER DERAIGN DISPUTE EXPLOIT SCUFFLE SERVICE ARGUMENT CONFLICT STRUGGLE
(— BETWEEN KNIGHTS) JOUST
(FUTILE —) SCIAMACHY
(SHAM —) SCIOMACHY
(SINGLE —) DUOMACHY
COMBATANT DUELER BATTLER FIGHTER CHAMPION GLADIATOR
COMBATIVE BANTAM MILITANT AGONISTIC BELLICOSE DEPENDENT PUGNACIOUS AGONISTICAL
COMBE HOPE
COMBED CRESTED
COMBER WAVE HANDER BREAKER KEMPSTER
COMBINATION KEY BLOC CLUB GANG PACT POOL RING CABAL COMBO GROUP JUNTO PARTY TRUST UNION CARTEL CLIQUE CORNER CRASIS FUSION LEAGUE MEDLEY MERGER AMALGAM BATTERY COMBINE CONSORT COTERIE FACTION HARMONY JOINING MIXTURE ADDITION ALLIANCE ENSEMBLE MONOPOLY GOODLIBET
(— OF CARDS) SET BUILD FLUSH SPREAD STRAIGHT
(— OF CIRCUMSTANCES) ACTION
(— OF COLORS) HARLEQUIN
(— OF FACES) FORM
(— OF FIRMS) TRUST
(— OF INTAGLIO FORMS) GRYLLI
(— OF NUMBERS) GIG SADDLE
(— OF TACKLES) JEERS
(— OF TONES) CHORD
(— OF 10) DECUPLET
(DANCE —) SEQUENCE
(HARMONIOUS —) CONCORD
(NOSE-JAW —) LAYBACK
(SCORING —) IMPERIAL
(PREF.) HAPT(O)
COMBINE ADD FIX MIX WED BIND BLOC CLUB JOIN NICK POOL

BLEND GROUP JOINT MARRY MERGE TOTAL UNITE ABSORB CONCUR LEAGUE MEDDLE MERGER MINGLE SPLICE ACCRETE AMALGAM COMPACT CONJOIN CONJURE MACHINE COALESCE COMPOUND CONCRETE CONDENSE CONFLATE CONSTRUE CONTRACT CUMULATE FEDERATE ORCHESTRATE
(— AGAINST) BOYCOTT
(— WITH GAS) AERATE
(— WITH WATER) AQUATE
COMBINED GUM BOUND FIXED JOINT UNITED CONJOINT
COMB-LIKE PECTINAL
COMBO (SMALL —) TRIO
COMBUST START
COMBUSTIBLE FUEL FIERY ARDENT CINDER PICEOUS BURNABLE
COMBUSTION FIRE HEAT FLAME THERM TUMULT BURNING BACKFIRE
COME BE GET LAY COOP DRAW FALL GROW HAUL PASS WHEN ARISE CHIVE FETCH ISSUE LIGHT OCCUR REACH ACCRUE ADVENE APPEAR ARRIVE BECOME BEFALL EMERGE HAPPEN OBTAIN SPRING ADVANCE DEVELOP EMANATE PROCEED APPROACH PRACTICE
(— ABOUT) ARISE OCCUR CHANCE
(— AFTER) SUE FOLLOW
(— APART) FRAY SHED BREAK STAVE
(— BACK) REVERSE
(— BACK TO LIFE) REVIVE
(— BEFORE) FORERUN PREVENE ANTECEDE ANTEDATE
(— BETWEEN) INTERPOSE INTERVENE
(— DOWN) AVALE SWOOP ALIGHT DESCEND SUCCEED DISMOUNT
(— FORTH) EMIT BREAK ISSUE ACCEDE FORTHGO FURNACE
(— FORWARD) ACCEDE
(— IN CONTACT) ATTINGE
(— IN SECOND) PLACE
(— IN THIRD) SHOW
(— INTO BLOOM) BURST BLOSSOM
(— INTO COLLISION) MEET CLASH COLLIDE
(— INTO EXISTENCE) FORM BEGIN ACCRUE HAPPEN SPRING
(— INTO POSSESSION) ACQUIRE INHERIT
(— OF AGE) MAJORIZE
(— OFF) HARL PEEL
(— OUT) ISSUE APPEAR EMERGE EMANATE
(— SUDDENLY) CLAP PLUMP
(— THROUGH) DELIVER
(— TO) TOUCH ADVENE STRIKE RECOVER REVERSE
(— TO AN END) PASS
(— TO BELIEVE IN) ADOPT
(— TO CONCLUSION) DECIDE
(— TO DIE) DO DIE SET DROP EXPIRE FINISH SURCEASE
(— TOGETHER) ADD HERD JOIN MEET AMASS CONCUR COUPLE GATHER COLLECT COMBINE CONVENE ASSEMBLE

(— TO GRIEF) FOUNDER
(— TO HAND) OFFER
(— TO LIGHT) SPUNK DEVELOP
(— TO MIND) OCCUR STRIKE
(— TO NOTHING) ABORT
(— TO PASS) SORT BREAK LIGHT BEFALL BETIDE HAPPEN
(— TO PERFECTION) RIPEN
(— TO REST) LODGE SETTLE
(— TO STAND STILL) STOP
(— TO TERMS) AGREE TRYST ACCORD BARGAIN COMPOSE COMPOUND ACCOMMODATF
(— TO THE SURFACE) RISE
(— UNDER) SUBVENE
(— UPON) FIND CROSS INVENT STRIKE OVERTAKE
(FULLY —) EXPIATE
COMEBACK RALLY ANSWER RETORT RETURN REBOUND RIPOSTE HAULBACK RECOVERY REPARTEE
COMECRUDO CARRIZO
COMEDIAN WAG WIT CARD ACTOR ANTIC CLOWN COMIC GAGMAN JESTER BUFFOON FUNSTER COMOEDUS FUNMAKER FUNNYMAN PATTERER
COMEDO BLACKHEAD
COMEDOWN RATHOS DESCENT LETDOWN
COMEDY SOCK DRAMA FARCE LAZZO REVUE SITCOM COMEDIA TEMACHA COMOEDIA TRAVESTY BACCHIDES SLAPSTICK
(HEROIC —) NATAKA
(KIND OF —) STANDUP
(SITUATION —) SITCOM
(PREF.) COMICO
COMEDY OF ERRORS (AUTHOR OF —) SHAKESPEARE
(CHARACTER IN —) LUCE PINCH AEGEON ANGELO DROMIO ADRIANA AEMILIA EPHESUS LUCIANA SOLINUS BALTHAZAR ANTIPHOLUS
COMELINESS GRACE DECORUM FEATURE VENUSTY PULCHRITUDE
COMELY FAIR GOOD HEND PERT TALL TIDY WEME BONNY BUXOM HENDE QUEME SONCY SONSY TIGHT DECENT FORMAL GOODLY LIKELY LIKING LOVELY PRETTY PROPER SEEMLY SONSIE VENUST FARRANT FORMFUL SIGHTLY BECOMING DECOROUS FEATURED GRACEFUL HANDSOME PLEASING SUITABLE
COME-ON TEASER
COMET STAR METEOR XIPHIAS SUNGRAZER
(— HEAD) COMA
COMEUPPANCE REBUKE DESERTS BUSINESS
COMFIT CANDY SUCKLE CONFECT PRALINE CONSERVE PRESERVE
(PL) CONFETTI
COMFORT AID EASE REST STAY BIELD CHEER LIGHT SOOTH VISIT ENDURE RELIEF REPOSE SOLACE SOOTHE SUCCOR ANIMATE ASSUAGE CHERISH CONFIRM CONSOLE ENLIVEN GLADDEN REFRESH RELIEVE SUPPORT

SUSTAIN INSPIRIT NEPENTHE PLEASURE REASSURE GEMUTLICH
COMFORTABLE RUG BEIN BIEN COSH COSY COZY EASY FEEL FEIL LIKE SNUG TOSH TRIG CANNY COMFY COUTH CUSHY LITHE QUEME QUILT SCARF SONCY COUTHY HEPPEN PENTIT SONSIE RELAXED RESTFUL CHEERFUL DELICATE EUPHORIC HOMELIKE WRISTLET GEMUTLICH
COMFORTABLE-LOOKING SONSY SONSIE
COMFORTABLY SWEETLY
COMFORTED CONSOLATE
COMFORTER PUFF COVER DUVET EIDER NAHUM QUILT SCARF TIPPET CHEERER PACIFIER
COMFORTING TOSY TOSIE FRIENDLY
COMFORTLESS DREARY FORLORN UNCOUTH DESOLATE EITHLESS
COMFREY DAISY BONESET BACKWORT KNITBACK BRUISEWORT
COMIC WAG CLOWN DROLL FUNNY STRIP BUFFONE COMIQUE THALIAN COMEDIAN FARCICAL
COMICAL LOW BASE BUFFO DROLL FUNNY MERRY QUEER STRIP WITTY BOUFFE AMUSING CARTOON JOCULAR RISIBLE STRANGE TRIVIAL HUMOROUS TICKLISH BURLESQUE SPLITTING
COMING DUE ANON COME NEXT VENUE ADVENT FUTURE TOWARD ARRIVAL FOOTING FORWARD BECOMING DESERVED NAISSANT PAROUSIA
(— AFTER) LATTER
(— AND GOING) FITFUL
(— FORTH) NAISSANT
(— INTO BEING) BIRTH GENESIS
(— NEAR) ACCESSION
(— NEXT) FOLLOWING
(— OUT) DEBUT ISSUE EGRESS
(— TO) ADIT
(— TOGETHER) SEANCE CONGRESS COUPLING GATHERING
(— TO OFFICE) ACCESS ACCESSION
(SECOND —) PAROUSIA
(SECOND — OF CHRIST) PAROUSIA
COMMA POINT VIRGULE
(SCRATCH —) DIAGONAL
COMMAND DO BID SAW SOH BECK BODE BOON CALL COME EASY FIAT HEST HETE MAND RATE RULE SWAY WARN WILL WISH WORD BEKEN CHECK COVER EDICT EXACT FORCE HIGHT ORDER POWER SWEEP UKASE ADJURE BEHEST CHARGE COMPEL DECREE DEMAND DEVICE DIRECT ENJOIN GOVERN HOOKUM IMPOSE MASTER ORACLE ORDAIN STEVEN SUMMON APPOINT BEHIGHT BIDDING CONCERN CONTROL DICTATE JUSSION JUSSIVE LEADING MANDATE OFFICER PRECEPT REQUIRE SKIPPER WARRANT BIDDANCE DOMINEER IMPERATE INSTRUCT MANDAMUS RESTRAIN

(— EMOTIONS) GRIP
(— OF ARMY) CONDUCT
(— TO COMPUTER TO STORE DATA) SAVE
(— TO DOGS) MUSH
(— TO HORSE) GEE HAW HUP HUPP WHOA GIDDAP HUDDUP
(— TO TURN LEFT) HAW
(— TO TURN RIGHT) GEE HUP HUPP
(EXCLUSIVE —) MONOPOLY
(MAGICIAN'S —) PRESTO
(NAUTICAL —) AVAST
(ORGANIC —) PERACID
COMMANDANT GOVERNOR KILLADAR
COMMANDED IMPERATE
COMMANDEER PRESS HIJACK
(— AIRCRAFT) SKYJACK
(— AN AIRPLANE) SKYJACK
COMMANDER CID CIO DUX DUKE EMIR HEAD JEFE BLOKE CHIFF EMEER ADALID LEADER MASTER RAMMER TARTAN ALCALDE CAPTAIN CROWNER DECARCH DEKARCH DRUNGAR EMPEROR GENERAL KHALIFA MARSHAL NAVARCH OFFICER VAIVODE HERETOGA HIPPARCH LOCHAGER LOCHAGUS MYRIARCH PHYLARCH RISALDAR SERASKER TAXIARCH TETRARCH VINTENER PROCONSUL
(— IN CHIEF) SIRDAR TARTAN TURTAN ADMIRAL GENERAL
(ANGLO-ASIAN) SIRDAR
(CAVALRY —) RISALDAR
COMMANDERY PRECEPTORY
COMMANDING DOMINANT IMPERANT IMPERIAL IMPOSING
COMMANDMENT LAW RULE ORDER COMMAND MITZVAH PRECEPT BODEWORD
(DIVINE —) LAW
(TEN —S) DECALOG DECALOGUE
COMMANDO RAIDER RANGER CHINDIT FEDAYEE STORMER
(MEMBER OF — GROUP) FEDAYEE
COMMELINA DEWFLOWER
COMMEMORATE FETE KEEP FEAST REMENE EPITAPH MEMORATE MONUMENT REMEMBER MEMORIALIZE
COMMEMORATION AWARD MEDAL COMMEM PLAQUE JUBILEE MEMORIA MENTION SERVICE EBENEZER ENCAENIA MEMORIAL REMEMBRANCE
COMMEMORATIVE HONORARY MEMORIAL
COMMENCE FALL FANG FILE MOVE OPEN ARISE BEGIN FOUND START ARRAME EMBARK INCEPT LAUNCH SPRING STREAK STREEK INITIATE
COMMENCEMENT ONSET ORIGIN OUTSET KICKOFF OPENING ENTRANCE
COMMENCING INITIAL NASCENT INCIPIENT
COMMEND KEN PAT GIVE LAUD ADORN ALOSE BEKEN BOOST EXTOL GRACE OFFER BESTOW BETAKE COMMIT PRAISE RESIGN APPLAUD APPROVE BESPEAK

BETEACH DELIVER ENTRUST INTRUST BEQUEATH
COMMENDABLE GOOD WORTHY LOVABLE LOWABLE LAUDABLE
COMMENDATION LAUD PRAISE CITATION
(EFFUSIVE —) SLAVER
(MARKED —) APPLAUSE
COMMENSAL EPIZOON MESSMATE
COMMENSALISM SYNOECY SYMPHILY COMMUNISM
COMMENSURATE EVEN EQUAL ENOUGH ADEQUATE RELEVANT
COMMENT BARB BRAG GIBE JIBE NOTE TALK WORD ASIDE BREAK DUNCE GLOSS GLOZE INPUT CUTTER DILATE GAMBIT NOTATE POSTIL REMARK SCANCE CAPTION DESCANT DISCUSS EXPLAIN EXPOUND ADDENDUM SCHOLION SCHOLIUM DISPRAISE
(— DISAPPROVINGLY) HARRUMPH
(BITING —) BARB
(CAUSTIC —) SATIRE
(ILL-TIMED —) CLANGER
(MARGINAL —) APOSTIL
(WITTY —) RIFF
COMMENTARY GLOSS GEMARA MEMOIR SATIRE ACCOUNT COMMENT MEKILTA POSTILS FOOTNOTE GLOSSARY TREATISE
(RABBINICAL —) HAKAM AGADAH HAGGADA HAGGADAH
(PL.) MIDRASHIM
COMMENTATOR HAKAM CRITIC GLOZER ANALYST GLOSSIST SCHOLIAST
COMMERCE TRADE BARTER CHANGE TRAFFIC BUSINESS EXCHANGE MERCATURE NAVIGATION
COMMERCIAL STORE TRADY TRADAL MERCHANT TRADEFUL
(— ESTABLISHMENT) HONG
COMMERCIALISM HUCKSTERISM MERCANTILISM
COMMINGLE MIX FUSE JOIN BLEND IMMIX MERGE UNITE MINGLE COMBINE COMINGE EMBROIL COMEDDLE
COMMINUTE MILL CRUSH GRIND POUND POUNCE POWDER
COMMINUTED FINE
COMMISERATE PITY
COMMISERATION EMPATHY SYMPATHY
COMMISSION PLAT SEND TASK BOARD PRESS TRUST BRANCH BREVET CHARGE DEMAND DEPUTE ERRAND LEGACY OFFICE ORDAIN PERMIT COMMAND CONSIGN DUOVIRI EMPOWER FITTAGE GOSPLAN MANDATE MISSION SQUEEZE WARRANT CORNETCY DELEGATE ENCHARGE INTERPOL OVERRIDE POUNDAGE
(— AS CAPTAIN) POST
(CHARGING NO —) NOLOAD
COMMISSIONAIRE CADDY CADDIE DUBASH
COMMISSIONER ENVOY TRIER LEDGER ARRAYER OFFICER PRISTAW DELEGATE

COMMISSURE VINCULUM
COMMIT DO GIVE PULL STOW TAKE
ALLOT ARRET HIGHT LEAVE REFER
TEACH ARETTE ASSIGN BETAKE
ENGAGE PERMIT REMAND
BEHIGHT BETEACH COMMAND
COMMEND COMMISE CONFIDE
CONSIGN DELIVER DEPOSIT
ENTRUST INTRUSE INTRUST
BEQUEATH DEDICATE DELEGATE
IMPRISON RELEGATE
RECOMMEND PERPETRATE
(— ERROR) SNAPPER
(— MONEY) INVEST
(— TO BATTLE) LAUNCH
(— TO JAIL) JUG
(— TO MEMORY) CON LEARN
MEMORIZE
(— VIOLENCE) TOUCH
(— WASTE) ESTREPE
COMMITMENT OBLIGATION
COMMITTAL COMPROMISE
COMMITTED ENGAGED
(— TO) ENGAGE
COMMITTEE BODY JURY RUMP
BOARD GROUP JUNTA TABLE
BUREAU SOVIET COUNCIL
DELEGACY POLITBURO PRESIDIUM
SYNDICATE
COMMIXTURE MIXTURE
HOTCHPOT CONFUSION
IMMISSION
COMMODE CAP CHEST STOOL
TOPKNOT CUPBOARD FONTANGE
COMMODIOUS FIT AMPLE ROOMY
PROPER USEFUL SPACIOUS
SUITABLE CAVERNOUS
COMMODITY ITEM WARE GOODS
STUFF EXPORT FUTURE STAPLE
ARTICLE SHIPMENT
(— SOLD SHORT) BEAR
(UNSALABLE —) DRUG
(PL.) KIND SPOTS CHANDLERY
COMMON LAY LOW NOA TYE BASE
MEAN RIFE TOWN VILE BANAL
BRIEF CHEAP EJIDO EXIDO GREEN
GRIMY GROSS JOINT LEASE OFTEN
SLACK STALE TACKY TRITE USUAL
COARSE DEMOID FAMOUS
MODERN MUTUAL ORNERY
PROPIO PUBLIC SIMPLE VULGAR
AVERAGE CURRENT DEMOTIC
GENERAL GENERIC IGNOBLE
NATURAL POPULAR PROFANE
RAFFISH REGULAR TRIVIAL
UNNOBLE VILLAIN BANAUSIC
EPIDEMIC FAMILIAR FREQUENT
HABITUAL MECHANIC MEDIOCRE
ORDINARY PANDEMIC PLEBEIAN
TRIFLING TRITICAL RECIPROCAL
(— OF ESTOVERS) BOT BOTE
(IN —) ALIKE
(NOT —) UNTRADED
(PL.) COMMUNE
(PREF.) CAEN(O) CEN(O) COEN(O)
HOM(O)
COMMONER SNOB CEORL PLEBE
SIMPLE BURGESS CITIZEN
STUDENT ROTURIER
COMMONLY OFTEN VULGO
FAMILIARLY
COMMONNESS IDIOTISM
COMMUNITY VULGARITY

COMMON PEOPLE VULGUS
COMMONPLACE DULL FADE WORN
BANAL DAILY PLAIN PROSE PROSY
STALE TOPIC TRIPY TRITE USUAL
COMMON DEJAVU GARDEN
HOMELY MODERN TRUISM
VULGAR FADAISE HUMDRUM
INSIPID PROSAIC TEDIOUS TRIVIAL
BANALITY BROMIDIC COPYBOOK
EVERYDAY ORDINARY RUMTYTOO
PLATITUDE PEDESTRIAN
COMMONPLACENESS BATHOS
HUMDRUM
COMMON SENSE WIT NOUS SALT
GUMPTION
COMMONWEAL WEAL REPUBLIC
COMMONWEALTH POLIS STATE
ESTATE PUBLIC WEALTH
COMONTE COUNTRY COMMONTY
(IDEAL —) UTOPIA
**COMMONWEALTH OF
INDEPENDENT STATES** (SEE
RUSSIA)
COMMOTION DO ADO DIN BREE
DUST FLAP FRAY FUSS HEAT HELL
RIOT STIR TODO TOSS WHIR
ALARM FLARE FUROR HURLY
HURRY STORM STOUR WHIRL
BUSTLE CATHRO FISSLE FISTLE
FLURRY FRACAS FRAISE FURORE
GARRAY HOOPLA HOTTER MOTION
MUTINY PHRASE POTHER RUFFLE
SHINDY SPLORE SQUALL STEERY
TUMULT UNREST UPSTIR WELTER
BLATHER BLUSTER CATOUSE
CLATTER KIPPAGE SHINDIG
TAMASHA TEMPEST TURMOIL
DISORDER ERUPTION REMOTION
STIRRAGE STRAMASH TIRRIVEE
UPHEAVAL UPRISING
COMMUNAL EJIDAL
COMMUNE MIR AREA DEME TALK
ARGUE REALM SHARE TREAT
ADVISE CONFER DEBATE IMPORT
PARLEY REVEAL CONSULT
DISCUSS DIVULGE COMMERCE
CONVERSE DISTRICT STANITZA
TOWNSHIP
(DUTCH —) EDE
COMMUNICABLE OPEN FRANK
CATCHING SOCIABLE
COMMUNICATE SAY GIVE SHOW
SIGN TELL BREAK DRILL SPEAK
TELEX YIELD BESTOW COMMON
CONVEY IMPART INFECT INFORM
REVEAL SIGNAL ADDRESS
BREATHE DECLARE DICTATE
DIVULGE CONVERSE DESCRIBE
INTIMATE
(— BY ALLUSION) IMPLY
COMMUNICATION CALL NOTE
WORD CABLE FAVOR LETTER
SPEECH ADDRESS DIVULGE
GALLERY MESSAGE COMETHER
LANGUAGE TELEGRAM
MEMORANDUM
(— SERVICE) TELEX
(— SYSTEM) VOICEMAIL
(ESTABLISH —) LOGIN LOGON
COMMUNICATIVE FREE SOCIABLE
EXPANSIVE
COMMUNION CULT HOST MASS
SECT TALK CREED FAITH SHARE

UNITY CHURCH HOMILY
COMMUNE CONCORD NAGMAAL
SYNAGOG ANTIPHON COMMERCE
CONVERSE KOINONIA VIATICUM
(— SERVICE) ACTION
COMMUNISM LENINISM
SOVIETISM
COMMUNIST RED COMMIE SOVIET
COMRADE
COMMUNITY MIR BODY BURG CITY
CLAN DESA MARK MURA DESSA
FIRCA STATE THORP CENOBY
CLIMAX COLONY FAMILY HAMLET
MILLET NATION POLITY PUBLIC
SOCIES ANTHILL BOHEMIA
COMMUNE COMONTE CONVENT
HERONRY KINGDOM PHALANX
SOCIETY VILLAGE ZADRUGA
AUTONOMY COMMONTY DISTRICT
LIKENESS PRIORATE PROVINCE
SODALITY SWEEPDOM TOWNSHIP
(— OF ANCHORITES) LAURA
(— OF INTERESTS) KINSHIP
(— OF KNIGHTS TEMPLARS)
PRECEPTORY
(— OF NATURE) RACE
(— OF ORGANISMS) GAMODEME
(— OF TURKS) KIZILBASH
(ANCIENT GREEK —) DEME
(CHURCH —) BODY FOLD FLOCK
SYNOD PARISH
(COOPERATIVE —) PHALANSTERY
(ECOLOGICAL —) SERE PROCLIMAX
(JEWISH —) JEWRY KOLEL ALJAMA
SHTETL JUDAISM SHTETEL
SYNAGOG KEHILLAH
(MAORI —) KAIK KAIKA
(PERUVIAN —) AYLLU COMUNIDAD
(PLANT —) HEATH FOREST ALTERNE
ENCLAVE
(RELIGIOUS —) CENOBY SAMGHA
SANGHA CONVENT CENOBIUM
(RUSSIAN —) MIR
(UTOPIAN —) PANTISOCRACY
(VILLAGE —) IKHWAN
COMMUTATE COMMUTE
UNDIRECT
COMMUTATIVE ABELIAN
COMMUTATOR BREAK BREAKER
RHEOTROPE
COMMUTE ALTER CHANGE TRAVEL
CONVERT EXCHANGE
COMMUTER (GROUP OF —S)
VANPOOL
COMOROS (CAPITAL OF —) MORONI
(ISLAND OF —) MWALI MOHELI
NZWANI ANJOUAN NJAZIDJA
(VOLCANO OF —) KARTHALA
COMPACT SAD BALL BOND CASE
FAST FIRM HARD KNIT PACK PACT
PLOT SNUG TRIM TRUE BRIEF
CLOSE COVIN CROWD DENSE
GROSS HARDY HORNY MATCH
PITHY SOLID SPISS TERSE THICK
TIGHT BEETLE COMART HARDEN
LEAGUE SHRINK SPISSY STOCKY
TREATY VANITY BARGAIN CONCISE
CONCORD CROWDED NUGGETY
PACTION SERRIED TABLOID
ALLIANCE CONDENSE CONTRACT
COVENANT FLAPJACK HEAVYSET
SOLIDIFY SUCCINCT PELLETIZE

(PREF.) GLOMERO GLOMERULO
PYCN(O) PYKN(O)
COMPACTED SAD CROWDED
(PREF.) PECTO
COMPACTNESS BODY DENSITY
FASTNESS SOLIDITY INTENSITY
COMPANION PAL SOC CHUM FERE
MAKE MATE PEER TWIN WIFE
BILLY BUDDY BULLY BUTTY CHINA
COMES CRONY CULLY DARES
GREEK MATCH MATEY MAUGH
RIVAL SPORT ATTEND BELAMY
BILLIE BROLGA COBBER COHORT
COMATE CUMMER CUPMAN
DUENNA EGERIA ESCORT FELLOW
FRIEND GESITH GOSSIP KIMMER
MARROW PANION SHADOW
SPOUSE STEADY TROJAN ACHATES
COMPANY COMPEER COMRADE
CONSORT ELPENOR FRANION
HUSBAND PARTNER SOCIATE
SOCIETY SPECIAL BARNACLE
BEAUPERE COMPADRE CORRIVAL
EPHESIAN EPHESINE FAITHFUL
FAMILIAR HELPMATE PARALLEL
PLAYFERE SYNODITE
(ARCHER'S —) BUTTY
(DRINKING —) CUPMATE
(POT —) ALEKNIGHT
(READING —) LECTRICE
(TABLE —) CONVICTOR
(PL.) SOCIETY
(PREF.) HETAERO
COMPANIONABLE FERE MATEY
SOCIAL CORDIAL FELLOWLY
GRACIOUS SOCIABLE
COMPANION-AT-LARGE BILLY
BILLIE
COMPANIONS (SEE PARTNERS)
COMPANIONSHIP FERE SHIP
HAUNT COMPANY SOCIETY
AFFINITY
COMPANY CIE CRY MOB SET BAND
BEVY BODY CORE CREW CRUE
FARE FERE FIRM GANG GEST GING
HERD HOST MANY PUSH ROUT
SORT TEAM TURM AERIE COVEN
COVEY CROWD FLOCK FLOTE
GESTE GROUP GUEST HORDE
JATHA MEINY PARTY SQUAD SUITE
TROOP TURMA CIRCLE CLIQUE
COHORT COVINE CURNEY DECURY
LOCHUS OUTFIT RESORT THRAVE
THRONG TROUPE TWENTY VOLLEY
BATTERY COLLEGE CONDUCT
CONSORT HOLDING JIMBANG
MANIPLE SOCIETE SOCIETY
THIASOS THIASUS VISITOR
ASSEMBLY FAISCEAU FOLKMOOT
JINGBANG PRESENCE
(— OF BADGERS) CETE
(— OF BIRDS) BANK
(— OF BOOKSELLERS) CONGER
CONGENER
(— OF DANCERS) COMPARSA
(— OF HERDSMEN) BOOLY BOOLEY
(— OF HERONS) SEDGE SIEGE
(— OF HORSEMEN) TROOP
(— OF LIONS) PRIDE
(— OF MARTENS) RICHESSE
(— OF MUSICIANS) ORCHESTRA
(— OF PEACOCKS) MUSTER
(— OF PERFORMERS) TROUPE

(— OF PLOVERS) STAND
(— OF SINGERS) CHOIR QUIRE CHORUS
(— OF SWANS) BANK
(— OF TEN) DECURY DECURIA
(— OF THE FAITHFUL) FOLD
(— OF TRAVELERS) CAFILA CAVALCADE
(— OF WOMEN) GAGGLE
(— OF WORSHIPERS) THIASUS
(— OF WORSHIPPERS) THIASUS
(EXCLUSIVE —) CROWD
(FINANCIAL —) FACTOR
(FIRE —) SQUAD
(MILITARY —) WATCH DECURY VENLIN PELOTON VEXILLUM
(RECORDING —) LABEL
(SUITABLE —) BESORT
COMPARABLE LIKE SAME SIMILAR
COMPARATIVE
(SUFF.) ER IOR
COMPARE VIE EVEN LIKE SIZE APPLY EQUAL LIKEN MATCH SCALE TALLY ALLUDE CONFER PARIFY RELATE SEMBLE BALANCE BRACKET COLLATE EXAMINE SENIBLE SIGNIFY STACKUP ASSEMBLE CONFRONT CONTRAST ESTIMATE PARALLEL RESEMBLE SIMILIZE
(— WITH) TO
COMPARISON SIMILE ANALOGY BALANCE COMPARE PARABLE PARAGON DISIMILE LIKENESS LIKENING METAPHOR PARALLEL
(— OF HOROSCOPES) SYNASTRY
COMPARTMENT BAY BIN BOX CAB POD CELL DECK FLUE PANE PART SLOT WELL ABODE CABIN HATCH HUTCH PANEL STALL VOLET ABACUS ALCOVE BUNKER GARAGE HOPPER MUFFLE REGION SEVERY SMOKER ALVEOLE CABINET CAPSULE CELLULE CHAMBER FIREBOX HOUSING KITCHEN LOCULUS MANSION ROTONDE SECTION ALVEOLUS COALHOLE DIVISION FOREPEAK GRINTERN LOCELLUS STEERAGE TRAVERSE PIGEONHOLE
(— FOR COAL) BUNKER
(— FOR TREATING ORE) KITCHEN
(— IN BAR) SNUG SNUGGERY
(— IN BARN) BAY
(— IN CAR) BOOT
(— IN STOVE) BROILER
(— OF COACH) IMPERIAL
(— OF ROOF) SEVERY
(— OF VAULTING) SEVERY
(— OF WINDOW) LIGHT
(— ON GAMEBOARD) STORE
(— ON ROULETTE WHEEL) EAGLE
(— ON TRAIN) COUCHETTE
(CARGO —) HOLD
(DECOMPRESSION —) POD
(DETACHABLE —) POD
(GAS-TIGHT —) BALLONET
(GUNNER'S —) BLISTER
(REFRIGERATOR —) CHILLER
(SCREENED —) TRAVERSE
(SLEEPING —) CUBICLE
(STAGECOACH —) COUPE
(STORAGE—) BOOT

COMPASS BOW AREA DIAL GAIN ROOM ROSE SIZE TOUR AMBIT FIELD GAMUT RANGE REACH SCOPE SWEEP TENOR WHEEL ARRIVE ATTAIN BOUNDS CIRCLE DEGREE DIACLE DIACLE EFFECT EXTENT MERIST MODULE SPHERE SPREAD VOLUME ACHIEVE AZIMUTH CALIBER CIRCUIT CONFINE DIVIDER EMBRACE ENCLOSE ENVIRON HORIZON IMAGINE PELORUS PURVIEW TRAMMEL BOUNDARY CINCTURE CIRCUITY DIAPASON PRACTICE PRACTISE SURROUND
(— IN SHIP'S CABIN) TELLTALE
(— NEEDLE END) LILY
(— OF MELODY) AMBITUS
(— OF TONES) DIAPASON
(— OF VOICE) GAMUT SCALE
(— POINT) RHUMB
(BELL-MAKING —) CROOK
(PART OF —) PIN CARD DOME HOOD PIVOT HOUSING BINNACLE
COMPASS BOX KETTLE
COMPASS CARD ROSE PEDRERO PERRIER
COMPASSION RUE PITY RUTH GRACE HEART MERCY PIETY SORRY KARUNA LENITY REMORSE STOMACH CLEMENCY HUMANITY KINDNESS SYMPATHY
COMPASSIONATE MEEK RUTH SOFT HUMAN GENTLE TENDER CLEMENT PIETOSO PITEOUS PITIFUL GRACIOUS MERCIFUL
COMPASS PLANT PILOTWEED ROSINWEED
COMPASS QUARTER PLAGE
COMPASS SIGHT VANE
COMPATIBILITY MATCH
COMPATIBLE AKIN CIVIL ARTISTIC SUITABLE
COMPATRIOT NATIVE PATRIOT SYNETHNIC
COMPEL GAR MAKE MOVE URGE BRING CAUSE COACT DRIVE EXACT FORCE IMPEL PRESS SHOVE COERCE ENJOIN EXTORT INCITE OBLIGE THREAT ACTUATE AFFORCE ATTRACT COMMAND DRAGOON ENFORCE NECESSE REQUIRE VIOLENCE NECESSITATE
(— TO GO) HALE
(— TO PAY) STICK
COMPELLED HAS FAIN MUST BOUND FORCED ENFORCED
COMPELLING COGENT STRONG TELLING BRUISING FORCEFUL
COMPELLINGLY BADLY
COMPENDIOUS BRIEF SHORT TERSE DIRECT COMPACT CONCISE SUMMARY SUCCINCT
COMPENDIUM LIST BRIEF APERCU DIGEST PRECIS SKETCH SURVEY CATALOG COMPEND EPITOME LEXICON MEDULLA OUTLINE PANDECT SUMMARY SYLLOGE ABSTRACT BREVIARY BREVIATE LANDSKIP SYLLABUS SYNOPSIS ABRIDGEMENT
(— OF DOCTRINE) SYMBOL

COMPENSATE PAY JIBE AGREE ATONE COVER REPAY TALLY OFFSET RECOUP REDEEM REWARD SQUARE COMMUTE CORRECT PLASTER REDRESS REPRISE REQUITE RESTORE SATISFY COMPENSE DISPENSE EQUALIZE
COMPENSATION BOT FEE PAY UTU BOOT BOTE HIRE MEND TOLL BONUS LOWER WAGES AMENDS ANGILD GERSUM OFFSET REWARD SALARY SETOFF DAMAGES FREIGHT PAYMENT REDRESS SALVAGE STIPEND BREAKAGE DONATIVE EARNINGS INTEREST OCTOGILD PILOTAGE PITTANCE REQUITAL SOLATIUM
(— FOR INJURY) SATISFACTION
(— FOR KILLING MAN) MANBOT MANBOTE
(MEAGER —) PITTANCE
(WORKER'S —) COMPO
COMPENSATORILY EVEN
COMPETE PIT VIE COPE KEMP TEND CLASH MATCH RIVAL STRIVE CONTEND CONTEST EMULATE CORRIVAL
(WITH) DUCK
COMPETENCE SKILL ABILITY FACULTY CAPACITY
COMPETENCY MAY CAPACITY
COMPETENT UP APT CAN FIT ABLE GOOD HOME MEET SANE ADEPT CAPAX SMART SWEET TIGHT INTACT LAWFUL WORTHY CAPABLE ENDOWED SKILLED ADEQUATE SUITABLE QUALIFIED
COMPETITION VIE DRAW GAME HEAT JUMP RACE MATCH PRIZE TRIAL WAGER CONTEST PARAGON RIVALRY BIATHLON CONCOURS CONFLICT
(— AMONG REAPERS) KEMP
(ATHLETIC —) MEET
(DRIVING —) RALLY RALLYE
(VERSE —) TENSON
COMPETITOR FOE ENEMY MATCH RIVAL WAGER COUSIN PLAYER AGONIST ENTRANT CORRIVAL FAVORITE GAMESTER OPPONENT
(FORMIDABLE —) TIGER
COMPILATION ANA BOOK CODE CENTO DIGEST CASEBOOK DIRECTORY GATHERING
COMPILE ADD EDIT AMASS GATHER SELECT ARRANGE COLLECT COMPOSE PREPARE
COMPILER AUTHOR EDITOR COLLATOR GATHERER GLOSSIST SCISSORER
COMPLACENT CALM SMUG PLACID FATUOUS PRIGGISH
COMPLACENTLY FATLY
COMPLAIN AIL NAG YAP YIP BEEF CARP CRIB FRET FUSS GREX KEEN KICK KREX MEAN MOAN MOOT MUTE RAIL RULE WAIL YELP YIRN BITCH BLEAT BRAWL CRAKE CROAK CROON GRIPE GROWL GRUMP GRUNT PINGE PLAIN WHINE BEWAIL CHARGE COTTER CREATE GRIEVE GROUSE GRUTCH

HOLLER KVETCH MURMUR PEENGE REPINE SQUAWK THREAP THROPE WHINGE YAMMER CHUNNER DEPLORE GRIZZLE GRUMBLE INVEIGH NITPICK PROTEST BELLYACHE
COMPLAINANT ACTOR ASKER ORATOR ACCUSER PLAINER QUERENT RELATOR
COMPLAINER CRAB WHINER CRYBABY KVETCHER
COMPLAINING BRAY PULY WHINY LATRANT QUERENT DOLEANCE QUERULOUS
COMPLAINT RAP BEEF CARP FUSS HOWL MEAN MOAN WAIL BITCH GRIPE GROWL WHINE CHESON GROUCH GROUSE GRUDGE GRUTCH HOLLER KVETCH LAMENT MALADY NIGGLE PLAINT REPINE SQUAWK AILMENT DISEASE GRUMBLE ILLNESS PROTEST QUARREL QUERELE RECLAMA TRAGEDY COMPLAIN DISORDER DOLEANCE GRAVAMEN JEREMIAD
(SUBDUED —) MURMUR
COMPLAISANCE AMENITY SUAVITY FACILITY URBANITY
COMPLAISANT BON ABLE EASY KIND BUXOM CIVIL SUAVE BONAIR POLITE SMOOTH SUPPLE URBANE AFFABLE AMIABLE BOWABLE LENIENT GRACIOUS OBLIGING PLEASING
COMPLEMENT CREW GANG FORCE TALLY ALEXIN AMOUNT COUSIN ADJUNCT OBVERSE PENDANT
(MILITARY —) STRENGTH
COMPLEMENTARY OPPOSITE
(PREF.) COUNTER
COMPLETE DO ALL CAP END BLUE DASH DEAD DEEP DONE FAIR FILL FINE FULL JUST PASS PURE RANK VERY CLEAN CLOSE CROWN EVERY GROSS LARGE PLAIN PLUMB POINT PUCCA PUKKA QUITE RIPEN ROUND SOLID SOUND STARK STONE TOTAL UTTER WHOLE CHOATE DAMPEN DEADLY EFFECT ENTIRE FINISH GLOBAL HOLLOW INTACT MATURE PROPER SINGLE STRICT VESTED ACHIEVE CONFIRM EXECUTE EXPLETE FULFILL GERMANE OUTWORK PERFECT PLENARY REALIZE REPLETE SPHERAL ABSOLUTE BLINKING CIRCULAR CONCLUDE FINALIZE IMPLICIT INTEGRAL OUTRIGHT OVERCOME PRECIOUS PROFOUND THOROUGH BODACIOUS NEGOTIATE ACCOMPLISH
(— CARELESSLY) HUDDLE
(— IN SYLLABLES) ACATHLECTIC
(REMARKABLY —) SPLENDID
(PREF.) HOL(O) TEL(E)(EO)
COMPLETED PAU OVER CLOSED SUMMED COMPLETE FINISHED
(NOT —) DURATIVE
COMPLETELY ALL JAM BARE BUCK FAIR FLAT GOOD SLAM SLAP SPAN BLACK CLEAN CLOSE FULLY PLUMB QUITE SHEER SMACK

COMPLETELY SPANG STARK STICK STOCK UTTER BODILY ENTIRE GAINLY HOLLOW PURELY SPANDY WHOLLY ALGATES BLANKLY THROUGH CLEVERLY DIRECTLY ENTIRELY HEARTILY OUTRIGHT WHOLEHOG (PREF.) DE DIS OB PAN

COMPLETENESS DEPTH ALLNESS FULLNESS RIPENESS INTEGRITY PLENITUDE

COMPLETION END CROWN FINISH (PREF.) TELEUT(O)

COMPLEX HARD MAZY BEING ETHOS FIELD HYOID MIXED ADDUCT DESERT KNOTTY SYSTEM CULTURE NETWORK SAMKARA SINUOUS TANGLED TWISTED ABSTRUSE COMPOUND EQUATION EXCHANGE INVOLVED MANIFOLD SAMSKARA SYNDROME CISPLATIN MACROCOSM
(— OF CHARACTERISTICS) PERSONALITY
(— OF DIALECTS) HINDI
(— OF HORMONES) CALINE
(— OF IDEAS) EGO SYSTEM
(— OF SHOPS) MALL
(BASEMENT —) FLOOR
(NOT —) SIMPLE

COMPLEXION HUE RUD BLEE CAST LEER LOOK RUDD TINT COLOR HUMOR STATE TENOR TINGE ASPECT TEMPER COLORING
(BAD —) DYSCHROA

COMPLEXITY NODUS SCHEME TANGLE INTRIGUE

COMPLIANCE TRUE ASSENT MUNICH CESSION CONSENT HARMONY OBSEQUY ABIDANCE CIVILITY FACILITY FORMALITY

COMPLIANT EASY MEEK OILY SOFT BUXOM FACILE PLIANT SUPPLE COMMODE DUCTILE DUTIFUL WILLING AMENABLE OBEDIENT TOWARDLY YIELDING TRACTABLE

COMPLICATE INTORT PUZZLE TANGLE EMBROIL INVOLVE PERPLEX BEWILDER INTRIGUE INTRICATE

COMPLICATED HARD KNOTTY PROLIX COMPLEX GORDIAN SNARLED TANGLED INVOLVED PLEXIFORM

COMPLICATION KNOT NODE PLOT NODUS SNARL TANGLE INTRIGUE
(— IN STORY) NODE

COMPLIMENT GIFT KUDO LAUD EXTOL EULOGY PRAISE SALAAM SALUTE ADULATE APPLAUD BOUQUET COMMEND DOUCEUR FLATTER TRIBUTE ENCOMIUM FLUMMERY GRATUITY GREETING
(EMPTY —) FLUMMERY

COMPLY PLY CEDE OBEY ABIDE ADAPT AGREE APPLY YIELD ACCEDE ACCORD ASSENT ENFOLD SUBMIT CONFORM EMBRACE OBSERVE
(— WITH) OBEY SERVE OBSERVE SATISFY

COMPONE GOBONE GOBONY

COMPONENT KEY DRAG FORM ITEM PART UNIT GIVEN FACTOR MEMBER SIMPLE ELEMENT FORMANT PARTIAL CONJUNCT INTEGRAL
(— OF ARMY) CAVALRY
(— OF CELL WALLS) CALLOSE
(ELECTRIC —S) CIRCUITRY
(PHYSICAL —S) HARDWARE
(PRINCIPAL —) BASIS

COMPORT ACT BEAR HAVE HOLD JIBE KEEP SUIT ABEAR AGREE BROOK CARRY TALLY ACCORD ACQUIT BEHAVE DEMEAN ENDURE SQUARE CONDUCT

COMPORTMENT DEALING BEHAVIOR DEMEANOR

COMPOSE BAT PEN SET CALM COMP DITE FORM LULL MAKE ALLAY BREVE BRIEF CLERK CLINK COUCH DIGHT DRAFT FRAME ORDER PATCH PIECE SPELL STICK WRITE ACCORD ADJUST CREATE DESIGN GRAITH INDITE NOTATE RECITE REDACT SETTLE SOOTHE STEADY ARRANGE COMPACT COMPILE COMPONE CONCOCT CONFORM DICTATE DISPOSE DRAUGHT FASHION PATIENT PRODUCE TYPESET COMPOUND COMPRISE REGULATE
(— POETRY) MAKE SING

COMPOSED SET CALM COOL QUIET SOBER WROTE DEMURE DIGEST PLACID SEDATE SERENE COMPACT WRITTEN COMPOUND DECOROUS TOGETHER TRANQUIL
(— IN METER) FOOTED
(ILL —) LAME

COMPOSEDNESS SOSSIEGO

COMPOSER BARD POET LYRIC ODIST AUTHOR LYRIST PENMAN WRITER CONTEUR ELEGIST FANTAST MAESTRO COLORIST ELEGIAST IDYLLIST ILIADIST MELODIST MONODIST MUSICIAN PHANTAST TUNESMITH
AMERICAN FRY BIRD BOND CAGE COLE IVES KERN ROOT BEACH BLOCH DANKS FOOTE HANDY HAYDN HOMER LEHAR NEVIN OHARA PRATT ROREM SCOTT SOUSA WEILL BARBER CADMAN HARRIS KRENEK LOOMIS PALMER PARKER PISTON PORTER SEEGER SPEAKS SUESSE TAYLOR WINNER ANTHEIL BRISTOW CHASINS COPLAND DEKOVEN GILBERT GOLDMAN HAESCHE HERBERT MENOTTI PARROTT RODGERS SCHUMAN THOMSON YOUMANS BARTLETT BROCKWAY BURLEIGH CHADWICK CONVERSE GERSHWIN GOODRICH GRAINGER KREISLER SESSIONS THOMPSON ARMSTRONG BERNSTEIN CARPENTER ELLINGTON MACDOWELL
ARGENTINIAN CASTRO
AUSTRIAN FUX GAL BERG WOLF BRULL DRDLA MOTTL ZAYTZ BLEYLE CZERNY EYBLER LANNER MOZART BITTNER NEUKOMM STRAUSS BRUCKNER DIABELLI GYROWETZ KORNGOLD REZNICEK SCHUBERT HEUBERGER MILLOCKER SCHONBERG GANSBACHER ALBRECHTSBERGER
BELGIAN FETIS LEKEU BENOIT BERIOT BLOCKX BRASIN DUMONT FRANCK GRISAR JONGEN GEVAERT HUBERTI LEMMENS MATHIEU CAMPENHOUT
BRAZILIAN GOMES VILLALOBOS
CANADIAN BRANSCOMB
CZECH BENDL NOVAK DVORAK FIBICH FORSTER JANACEK KUBELIK SMETANA DESPAUER NESWADBA KALLIWODA KOVAROVIC MYSLIVECEK
DANISH ENNA GADE HAMERIK NIELSEN HARTMANN
DUTCH FODOR OBRECHT ARCADELT WAGENAAR SWEELINCK
ENGLISH BAX TYE ARNE BLOW BYRD CARR CLAY HOOK MONK BACHE BLISS BOYCE CAREY COOKE COWEN CROFT ELGAR ELVEY FIELD HOLST LAWES LOCKE PARRY SCOTT TOVEY ARNOLD ASHTON AUSTIN AVISON BARNBY BISHOP BRIDGE COATES COWARD CRAMER CROTCH CROUCH CUSINS DAVIES DELIUS DIBDIN GERMAN GLOVER GREENE HANDEL LAMOND LINLEY MCEWEN ONEILL PARKER TALLIS THOMAS WALTON WILSON ATTWOOD BANTOCK BARNETT BENNETT CELLIER COLEMAN DUNHILL FARRANT GIBBONS HORSLEY IRELAND JACKSON LATROBE NOVELLO PURCELL STAINER STORACE BENJAMIN BOUGHTON SULLIVAN TYRWHITT ARMSTRONG CALDICOTT HESELTINE MACFARRNE MACKENZIE SOMERVELL GOLDSCHMIDT RAVENSCROFT
FINNISH PACIUS KAJANUS MADETOJA MELARTIN PALMGREN SIBELIUS WEGELIUS JARNEFELT MERIKANTO
FRENCH ERB HUE ADAM INDY LALO ALARD ALKAN AUBER AURIC BAZIN BIZET COHEN DAVID DUKAS FAURE GOUVY HERVE IBERT LULLY MASSE MEHUL RAVEL REBER REYER SATIE WIDOR AUBERT AUDRAN CAMPRA CHOPIN DANCLA DAQUIN DUBOIS DUPARC GODARD GOSSEC GOUNOD HALEVY HEROLD LECOCQ LEROUX PIERNE STRAUS THOMAS BERLIOZ BERTINI BOESSET BRUNEAU CAMBERT CHELARD COQUARD DEBUSSY DELIBES DUCASSE GUIRAUD LACOMBE LAPARRA LECLAIR LESUEUR MARTINI MILHAUD POULENC SCHMITT CHABRIER CHAUSSON COUPERIN DALAYRAC ERLANGER GOUDIMEL GUILMANT HONEGGER LEFEBVRE MAILLART MASSENET MESSAGER MONSIGNY BOELLMANN BOIELDIEU CHAMINADE OFFENBACH WECKERLIN BURGMULLER DESAUGIERS DESTOUCHES PLANQUETTE WALDTEUFEL CHARPENTIER
GERMAN ABT ETT AHLF BACH BOHM BOTT DORN GOTZ HAAS KAUN LOBE ORFF RAFF ABERT BIBER BLECH BOEHE BRUCH DANZI EBERS FASCH FESCA FINCK FRANK GENEE GLUCK GRAUN GRELL KLEIN LOEWE NEEFE WEBER ALBERT AMBROS BECKER BERGER BOHNER BRAHMS COMMER CRUGER ECKERT EITNER FLOTOW HILLER JENSEN KOHLER KUCKEN KUHLAU KUHNAU LINCKE MAHLER WAGNER WINTER BARGIEL CONRADI EBERLIN HASSLER JARNACH MOLIQUE NAUMANN RICHTER SILCHER STRAUSS WULLNER ZOLLNER AGRICOLA BENEDICT BRAMBACH DIETRICH DRAESEKE EBERWEIN HOFFMANN HOLSTEIN KAMINSKI KEUSSLER KIRCHNER KREUTZER PFITZNER REINECKE SCHUMANN VOLKMANN AIBLINGER AMBROSIUS BEETHOVEN BRAUNFELS BUXTEHUDE CANNABICH DELLINGER HINDEMITH KLUGHARDT MARSCHNER MATTHESON MEYERBEER NEITHARDT REICHARDT BELLERMANN BLUMENTHAL DESTOUCHES PRAETORIUS SCHARWENKA HUMPERDINCK MENDELSSOHN FRANCKENSTEIN LEICHTENTRITT
HUNGARIAN ERKEL HUBAY LEHAR LISZT BARTOK KODALY KUSSER JOACHIM ROMBERG DOHNANYI GOLDMARK
IRISH BALFE OSBORNE WALLACE
ITALIAN LOTI PAER PERI ARAIA BAINI BOITO BRAGA CESTI CLARI COSTA VERDI ALFANO ANERIO ARDITI ARTUSI BUSONI CIAMPI COCCIA MERULO NANINI PACINI PEROSI VECCHI ALBERTI ALLEGRI ANFOSSI ARIOSTI BASSANI BAZZINI BELLINI BERTONI BIANCHI CACCINI CALDARA CAMBINI CASELLA CAVALLI COLONNA CONCONE CORELLI DURANTE FERRARI FLORIMO PICCINI PORPORA PUCCINI ROSSINI SALIERI TARTINI TOSELLI VIADANA VIVALDI ZACCONI ZARLINO AGOSTINI ALBINONI BERNABEI CLEMENTI FIORILLO GABRIELI GAGLIANO GIORDANI GIORDANO JOMMELLI LEGRENZI MARCELLO MASCAGNI PRATELLA RAIMONDI RESPIGHI SPONTINI ANIMUCCIA BANCHIERI BONONCINI BOTTESINI BRAMBILLA CARISSIMI CAVALIERI CHERUBINI DONIZETTI GUGLIELMI LOCATELLI MALIPIERO MARCHETTI MORLACCHI PAISIELLO PERGOLESI SCARLATTI TOMMASINI VICENTINO BOCCHERINI CAMPAGNOLI MERCADANTE MONTEVERDI PALESTRINA PONCHIELLI ZINGARELLI LEONCAVALLO
MEXICAN CHAVEZ CARRILLO
NORWEGIAN GRIEG KJERULF NORDRAAK SVENDSEN SCHJELDERUP

POLISH KOLBERG FITELBERG KAMIENSKI KARLOWICZ MONIUSZKO NOSKOWSKI SZYMANOWSKI
PORTUGUESE ARNEIRO MACHADO BOMTEMPO PORTOGALLO
RUMANIAN ENESCO OTESCUA
RUSSIAN LVOV SEROV GLINKA LIADOV ONEGIN TANEEV ARENSKI BORODIN REBIKOV GODOWSKY LIPAUNOV SCRIABIN BALAKIREY CHEREPNIN GLAZOUNOV KASHPEROV KASTALSKI MUSORGSKI PROKOFIEV KALINNIKOV MOUSORGSKY STRAVINSKY AZANCHEVSKI BORTNYANSKI TCHAIKOVSKY KHACHATURIAN RACHMANINOFF SHOSTAKOVICH
SCOTTISH GOW SPOTTISWOODE
SPANISH ARBOS FALLA CASALS ALBENIZ MARTINI PEDRELL BARBIERI GUERRERO VICTORIA
SWEDISH ALFVEN HALLEN ATTERBERG HALLSTROM WENNERBERG
SWISS EGLI HEGAR HUBER
VENEZUELAN CARRENO
WELSH EVANS PARRY
COMPOSITE HYBRID ITALIC MOTLEY COMPLEX COMPOSED CONCRETE INTEGRAL
COMPOSITION ANA DITE MASS OPUS WORK CENTO DITTY DRAMA FUGUE GETUP MURKY PIECE POESY STUCK THEME ACCORD EULOGY FILLER HAIKAI LESSON MAGGOT MONODY THESIS THREAD VULGUS ARTICLE COMPOST CONSIST DISPLAY EBURINE EPISTLE MIXTURE PICTURE STOPPER WRITING ACROSTIC CAUSERIE COMPOUND DIALOGUE DIAPENTE EXERCISE FANTASIA FROTTAGE HEELBALL
(— FOR BILLIARD BALLS) COMPO
(— TO BE ACTED) PLAY DRAMA
(— TO FILL LEATHER) STUFF
(AMOROUS —) EROTIC
(ARTISTIC —) COLLAGE
(BAGPIPE —) PORT
(BANKRUPT'S —) COMPO
(BUILDING —) STAFF
(CHORAL —) MOTET CANTATA ORATORIO
(GUMMY —) GROUND
(HAND —) CASEWORK
(HUMOROUS —) BURLA
(IMPERFECT —) SOOTERKIN
(INSTRUMENTAL —) AIR GATO FANCY RONDO GROUND SKETCH SONATA TIENTO BOURREE CANZONE BERCEUSE CONCERTO FANTASIA RHAPSODY SYMPHONY PASSACAGLIA
(LITERARY —) BOOK CENTO DEBAT ESSAY PIECE COMEDY SATIRE SKETCH THESIS TREATISE
(MAGIC —) HELLBROTH
(MUSICAL —) DUET GLEE IDYL OPUS SOLO SONG TRIO BURLA CANON DANCE ELEGY ETUDE FUGUE GAZEL IDYLL MESTO MOTET NONET SCORE STUDY ADAGIO

ARIOSO AZIONE ENTREE GHAZEL HOCKET HOQUET SEPTET SEXTET BALLADE BOURREE BOUTADE BRAVURA ORGANUM QUARTET SCHERZO TOCCATA CAVATINA CHACONNE CLAUSULA CONCERTO INNOMINE SERENADE SINFONIA STANDARD SYMPHONY ANTIPHONY OFFERTORY PROCESSIONAL
(NARRATIVE —) BALLAD
(PLASTIC —) CEMENT
(POETIC —) GLOSS KAVYA
(RAMBLING —) SATIRE RHAPSODY
(RELIGIOUS —) MOTET ANTHEM HYMNIC CANTATA ORATORIO
(RUBBER —) GUM
(VEDIC —) GAYATRI
(VITREOUS —) ENAMEL
(VOCAL —) ARIA SOLO SONG CANON ANTHEM ELEVATIO CONDUCTUS
(WORDLESS —) VOCALISE
(PL.) JUVENILIA LITERATURE
COMPOSITOR COMP TYPO ADMAN SETTER BANKMAN CASEMAN CLICKER PRINTER STONEMAN
COMPOST PELF SOIL MINGLE COMPOTE MIXTURE COMPOUND DRESSING
COMPOSURE BOND MIEN POISE QUIET UNION REPOSE TEMPER BALANCE POSTURE CALMNESS SERENITY
(LOSE —) CHOKE
COMPOTATION SYMPOSIUM
COMPOTE BOWL COMPORT COMPOST
COMPOUND LSD MIX NTA BASE DIOL ENOL FILL JOIN MIXT SOUR TEPA ALKYL ALLOY AMIDE AMINE BLEND DIENE ESTER FURIL IMIDE OXIDE UNION ACETAL ADJUST ALKIDE DORANE COMMIX COPULA IODIDE JUMBLE KETONE MEDLEY PHENOL POLYOL PTERIN PYRONE SETTLE TEMPER URACIL URAMIL AGATHIN ALCOHOL ALLICIN ALLOXAN AMALGAM AMIDATE AMIDINE AMINATE AMMONIA ARGYROL CARBENE COMBINE COMPLEX COMPONE COMPOSE COMPOST DVANDVA KAMPONG KHELLIN PHORBIN PREPARE SPIRANE STEROID AGLUCONE AGLYCONE ALIZARIN ALKOXIDE AMMONATE ANTIPODE APIGENIN BRAZILIN CEROMIDE COMPOSED FUCHSONE GARDENIN GENTISIN GOSSYPOL IODOFORM ISOLOGUE STYRACIN CARBORANE YELLOWCAKE
(ADHESIVE —) SALVE
(CHEMICAL —) PCB
(COLORLESS —) FURAN FURANE
(COMBINING —) ACCEPTOR
(CRYSTALLINE —) TEPA
(EXPLOSIVE —) TNT
(HALOCARBON —) DBCP
(OF A CHEMICAL —) ORGANO
(ORGANIC —) ENOL
(POISONOUS —) KETENE CACODYL GLYCINE HELENIN STIBINE

(SYNTHETIC —) ANDROGEN SORBITAN
(PREF.) **(PARENT —)** NOR
(SUFF.) GENIN
(CARBON —) ENE
COMPOUNDED CONCRETE COMPOSITE
COMPOUNDER TANKER
COMPOUNDING INTIMACY
COMPREHEND GET SEE KNOW TAKE TWIG COVER GRASP IMPLY LATCH REACH SAVVY SEIZE SENSE SKILL SMOKE SPELL ATTAIN BOTTOM DIGEST EMBODY FATHOM FOLLOW PIERCE UPTAKE COMPASS CONTAIN DISCERN EMBRACE ENCLOSE IMAGINE INCLUDE INVOLVE REALIZE RECEIVE SWALLOW COMPRISE CONCEIVE CONCLUDE PERCEIVE
COMPREHENSIBLE EXOTERIC INCLUDED SENSABLE SCRUTABLE
COMPREHENSION HOLD SABE GRASP SAVVY SENSE ESPRIT FATHOM NOESIS UPTAKE EPITOME INSIGHT KNOWING SUMMARY BEARINGS PREHENSION
(OF READING —) CLOZE
COMPREHENSIVE BIG FULL WIDE BROAD GRAND LARGE GLOBAL SCOPIC CAPABLE CONCISE GENERAL GENERIC CATHOLIC ENCYCLIC SPACIOUS
COMPREHENSIVENESS POWER SCOPE EXTENT BREADTH WIDENESS LARGENESS
COMPRESS NIP TIE BALE BIND FIRM LACE WRAP CLING CRAMP CROWD CRUSH PINCH PRESS SMASH BUNDLE DEFORM DIGEST GATHER SHRINK STRAIN THRONG ABRIDGE ASTRICT BOLSTER CABBAGE COMPACT CURTAIL DEFLATE EMBRACE FLATTEN PLEDGET REPRESS SQUEEZE SQUINCH ASTRINGE CONDENSE CONTRACT LAMINATE PEMMICAN RESTRAIN SUPPRESS
(— WOOL) DUMP
(HOT —) STUPE
(MEDICAL —) BOLSTER PLEDGET
COMPRESSED STRICT CROWDED SUCCINCT ANGUSTATE COARCTATE
COMPRESSION CRUSH SQUEEZE PRESSURE THLIPSIS
(PREF.) SYMPIESO SYMPIEZO
COMPRESSOR PUMP ROTARY CONDENSER
COMPRISE HOLD COVER IMPLY SEIZE ATTACH CONFER EMBODY EMPLOY MUSTER COMPOSE CONTAIN EMBRACE ENCLOSE INCLUDE INVOLVE CONCEIVE PERCEIVE
COMPROMISE FINE TRIM COMMIT INTERIM COMPOUND ENDANGER PALLIATE TEMPORIZE
COMPROMISED BRULE
COMPROMISING FALSE
COMPULSION NEED URGE FORCE PRESS DURESS STRESS IMPULSE

COACTION COERCION DISTRESS EXACTION PERFORCE NECESSITY
COMPULSORY COERCIVE FORCIBLE NECESSARY
(NOT —) OPTIONAL
COMPUNCTION QUALM REGRET SORROW REMORSE SCRUPLE PENITENCE
COMPURGATOR COJUROR COSWEARER
COMPUTATION COMPOT ACCOUNT COMPUTE CALCULUS COMPUTUS ESTIMATE RECKONING
COMPUTE ADD SUM CAST ITEM RATE COUNT TALLY VALUE ASSESS CIPHER FIGURE NUMBER RECKON ACCOUNT BALANCE SUPPUTE ESTIMATE CALCULATE
COMPUTER HOST MINI ADDER ENIAC LAPTOP MANIAC DESKTOP MAINFRAME PROCESSOR MINICOMPUTER
(— ADD-ON) ESE
(— ALL-PURPOSE CODE) BASIC
(— BINARY DIGIT) BIT
(— CAPACITY) RAM ROM
(— CHIP) CPU
(— CIRCUIT) NOR NAND
(— CIRCUIT BOARD) SIMM
(— CODE) BCD ASCII
(— COLLECTION OF DATA) DATABASE
(— COMPANY) AST IBM NEC ACER DELL APPLE COMPAQ GATEWAY MACINTOSH PACKARDBELL HEWLETTPACKARD
(— COMPONENT) CHIP
(— CORRECTION) PATCH
(— CURSOR MOVER) MOUSE TRACKBALL
(— DATA) FILE PUSHDOWN
(— DEVICE) WAND MOUSE
(— DISK) FLOPPY MINIFLOPPY
(— DISK OPERATING SYSTEM) MSDOS PCDOS
(— FAILURE) CRASH
(— GATE) AND
(— GATEWAY) PORT
(— HARDWARE) PC CPU DRIVE MONITOR PRINTER KEYBOARD
(— INDEX) KWIC
(— INFORMATION) DATA DATABASE
(— INFORMATION UNIT) BYTE MEGABYTE
(— INSERT) DISK
(— INSTRUCTION) MACRO
(— INTERFACE) PORT
(— KEY) ALT END ESC TAB CTRL HOME ENTER
(— LANGUAGE) ADA APL BCD RPG LISP LOGO ALGOL BASIC COBOL PASCAL PROLOG FORTRAN
(— LIST) MENU
(— MEMORY) RAM ROM PAGE CACHE EPROM STACK SCRATCHPAD
(— MEMORY CHIP) DRAM
(— MEMORY MODULE) CHIP SIMM
(— MONITOR) VGA SVGA
(— MOVIE) HAL
(— NERD) WEENIE
(— NETWORK) LAN
(— PRINTED TEXT) HARDCOPY PRINTOUT

(— PROGRAM) WORM VIRUS EDITOR LOADER FORTRAN SPREADSHEET BULLETINBOARD
(— PROGRAMMABLE MEMORY) EPROM
(— PROGRAMS) SOFTWARE
(— SEQUENCE OF BITS) BYTE
(— SOCKET) BANK PORT
(— SOFTWARE) DRIVER MONITOR
(— SOFTWARE NAME) LOTUS
(— SOUND) BEEP
(— STORAGE) FIELD
(— SYMBOL) ICON
(— SYSTEM) KLUGE KLUDGE TRSDOS
(— SYSTEMS COMMUNICATION) GATEWAY
(— UNIT) BIT BYTE ONEK
(— VIDEO DEVICE) MONITOR
(— VIDEO DISPLAY OF TASKS) MENU
(— WHIZ) HACKER
(ADMINISTRATOR OF — BOARD) SYSOP
(COMMAND TO — TO STORE DATA) SAVE
(COPY OF — FILE) BACKUP
(ENTER — DATA INTO MEMORY) WRITE
(ENTER A — PROGRAM) LOAD
(FLASHING — CUE) CURSOR
(FUNCTIONING PERIOD OF —) UPTIME
(HEART OF —) CPU
(HINT ON — TO CONTINUE) PROMPT
(INDICATOR ON — SCREEN) CURSOR
(INTEGRATED — CIRCUIT) CHIP
(KIND OF) ANALOG HYBRID DIGITAL
(KIND OF —) DESKTOP
(LINK FOR TWO —S BY PHONE) MODEM
(MAGNETIC — RECORD) DISK
(MOVE — DISPLAY UP OR DOWN) SCROLL
(NETWORK —) HOST
(OPERATOR OF — PROGRAM) SYSOP
(PARTS OF — SYSTEM) HARDWARE
(PHYSICAL PARTS OF — SYSTEM) HARDWARE
(PRODUCER OF — SYSTEMS) OEM
(READY A —) BOOT
(RELATING TO — DISK) WINCHESTER
(STORED — MEMORY) FIRMWARE
(STORE OF — DATA) PUSHDOWN
(PL.) CYBER
COMRADE PAL ALLY CHUM MATE PEER BILLY BUDDY BUTTY CRONY HABER HAVER TOWNY BURSCH CHABER CHAVER COPAIN COUSIN DIGGER ENGIDU FELLOW FRATER FRIEND GOSSIP HEARTY BROTHER COMPEER CONVIVE BEAUPERE CAMARADA CAMARADE COMORADO CONFRERE COPEMATE TOVARICH SKAINSMATE
(— AT TABLE) CONVIVE
(PL.) SOCE
COMRADESHIP CAMARADERIE

CON DO RAP ANTI KNOW LEAD LOOK PORE QUIN READ SCAN CHEAT CUNNE GUIDE KNOCK LEARN STEER STUDY DIRECT PERUSE REGARD VERSUS AGAINST DECEIVE EXAMINE INSPECT OPPOSED SWINDLE
CONCAVE CAVE VOID CAMUS MINUS ARCHED DISHED HOLLOW SIMOUS VAULTY VAULTED CRESCENT INCURVED
(SUFF.) COELOUS COELUS
CONCAVITY COVE DISH CONCHA HOLLOW VENTER KNEEPAN
CONCEAL MEW WRY BURY DERN FEAL HIDE KEEP LENE MASK SCUG SILE VEIL VEST WRAP BLIND BOSOM CACHE CLOAK COUCH COVER FEIGN LAYNE PLANT SHADE BURROW CLOSET DOCTOR ELOIGN EMBOSS HUDDLE HUGGER IMBOSK OCCULT POCKET SCREEN SHADOW SHIELD SHROUD STIFLE VIZARD ABSCOND ENVELOP OPPRESS PLASTER SECRETE SMOTHER BESCREEN DISGUISE ENSCONCE PALLIATE PRETENCE PRETENSE WITHHOLD
(— A FUGITIVE) HARBOR
(— A TRAIL) TRASH
(— INFORMATION) LAYNE
(— PROFITS) SKIM
(— TO AVOID TAX) SKIM
CONCEALED DERN SCUG SNUG BLIND PERDU PRIVY BURROW COVERT HIDDEN LATENT OCCULT PERDUE SECRET VEILED COVERED LARVATE WRAPPED ABSTRUSE CRYPTOUS HIDEAWAY RECONDITE
(— BY) BENEATH
(PREF.) ADEL(O)
CONCEALING DESIGNING OBVELATION
CONCEALMENT MEW LAIN COVER FRAUD NIGHT STALE SECRECY CELATION VELATION SECRETION
(— OF TREASURE) MISPRISION
(IN —) DOGGO
CONCEDE OWN CEDE GIVE ADMIT AGREE ALLOW GRANT WAIVE YETTE YIELD ACCORD ASSENT BETEEM CONFESS OTTROYE BEGRUDGE ACKNOWLEDGE
(— AS ADVANTAGE) SPOT
CONCEIT EGO TOY IDEA SIDE WIND CRANK FANCY KNACK POESY PRIDE QUIRK BABERY DEVICE NOTION VAGARY VANITY BIGHEAD CAPRICE EGOTISM OUTRAGE TYMPANY CONCETTO FLIMFLAM
(VIVID —) VISION
CONCEITED BUG BRAG COXY FESS VAIN CHUFF COCKY FLORY HUFFY PENSY PROUD SAUCY CLEVER BIGGETY BIGGITY ARROGANT DOGMATIC NOSEWISE PENSEFUL PRIGGISH SNOBBISH
CONCEIVABLE EARTHLY POSSIBLE
CONCEIVE FORM HOLD MAKE PLAN TEEM WEEN BEGIN BRAIN CATCH DREAM FANCY FRAME GUESS IMAGE THINK DESIGN DEVISE

IDEATE INTEND PONDER SETTLE GESTATE IMAGINE REALIZE SUPPOSE SUSPECT COMPRISE CONTRIVE ENVISAGE
CONCENTRATE AIM FIX MASS PILE BUNCH COACT EXALT FOCUS PURSE UNIFY ARREST ATTEND CENTER CITRIN DECOCT DISTIL FIXATE GATHER SINGLE COMPACT CONGEST DISTILL ENGROSS ESSENCE EXTRACT THICKEN ABSOLUTE APPROACH ASSEMBLE CONDENSE CONTRACT FOCALIZE GRADUATE
(— ORE) STRAKE
CONCENTRATED HARD DENSE FIXED INTENT STRONG EXALTED INTENSE
(NOT —) DIFFUSE
CONCENTRATION BRIX TITER CENTER BALLING SAMADHI ACTIVITY FIXATION PELMANISM
(— OF ARTILLERY FIRE) STONK
(— OF ENERGY) EXCITON
(— OF GRAPE JUICE) BESHMET
(— OF PLANTS) BED
(— OF SOLUTION) MOLARITY
(EXCESS —) MONOMANIA
CONCEPT GUT GUTS IDEA PLAN FANCY IMAGE BEGRIFF CONCEIT OPINION THOUGHT ABSOLUTE CATEGORY PLURALISM PERCEPTION
CONCEPTION ENS IDEA VIEW EIDOS FANCY FETUS IMAGE BELIEF DESIGN EMBRYO ENTITY NOTION CONCEIT CONCEPT PROJECT PURPOSE CATEGORY ESTHETIC NOTATION RATIONAL
(— OF IDEA) HENT
(— OF ONESELF) BOVARISM BOVARYSM
(ABSTRACT —) ARCHETYPE
(FALSE —) IDOL DELUSION
(QUICKNESS OF —) PREGNANCY
CONCEPTUAL IDEAL NOTIONAL
CONCEPTUALISM SERMONISM
CONCERN BUG BEAR CARE FEAR FIRM GEAR HAND PART RECK SAKE APPLY CAUSE CERNE DRIVE EVENT GRIEF HEART SORGE STAND TOUCH WORRY AFFAIR AFFECT BEHOLD CHARGE DIRECT EMPLOY FINGER IMPORT MATTER REGARD THRUST ANXIETY ARTICLE BOTTLER COMPANY DISTURB FUNERAL INVOLVE PERTAIN RESPECT SHEBANG SOLICIT TROUBLE BUSINESS HYPOTHEC INTEREST JEALOUSY
(— ONESELF) DEAL PASS TOUCH INTERMIT
(INDUSTRIAL —) COLOSSUS
(PRUDISH —) COMSTOCKERY
(SOMETHING CAUSING —) ALBATROSS
(SPECIAL —) ACCENT
(WORLDLY —S) EARTH
(SUFF.) **(— FOR)** ITIS
CONCERNED INTENT ANXIOUS VERSANT WORRIED ATWITTER BOTHERED

CONCERNING BY OF ON RE TO FOR TIL TILL ABOUT ANENT ANENST APROPOS TOUCHING
CONCERT POP PLAN RECK UNITE ACCORD DEVISE SMOKER ARRANGE BENEFIT CONCENT CONCORD CONSORT CONSULT HARMONY POPULAR RECITAL NEGOTIATE
CONCERT-HALL ODEON ODEUM
CONCERTINA ORGAN LANTUM SQUIFFER BANDONION MELOPHONE
CONCESSION BOON FAVOR GRANT LEASE STOOP ASSENT GAMBIT OCTROY CESSION EPITROPE MYNPACHT ADMISSION ALLOWANCE PRIVILEGE
CONCESSIONAIRE GRIFTER
CONCH CONK PUNK SHELL COCKLE MUSSEL STROMB STROMBUS SCUNGILLI
CONCIERGE SUPER PORTER SUISSE WARDEN DVORNIK JANITOR
CONCILIATE GET CALM EASE GAIN ATONE HONEY THING ADJUST PACIFY SOFTEN ACQUIRE APPEASE CONCILE MOLLIFY PLACATE SATISFY PROPITIATE
CONCILIATOR ARBITRATOR
CONCILIATORY MILD SOFT GENTLE GIVING IRENIC LENIENT PACIFIC WINNING IRENICAL LENITIVE TREATABLE
CONCISE CURT NEAT TRIG BRIEF CRISP PITHY SHORT TERSE COGENT CUTTED COMPACT LACONIC POINTED PRECISE SERRIED SUMMARY TABLOID MUTILATE PREGNANT SUCCINCT
CONCISELY PRESSLY ELLIPTICALLY
CONCISENESS BREVITY ECONOMY SYNTOMY FASTNESS SYNTOMIA BRACHYOLOGY
CONCLAMATION SHOUT
CONCLAVE SOBOR CLOSET CHAMBER MEETING AREOPAGY ASSEMBLY
CONCLUDE BAR END AMEN FINE REST TAKE CLOSE DRIVE ESTOP INFER JUDGE LIMIT CLINCH DECIDE DEDUCE EXPIRE FIGURE FINISH GATHER INDUCE PERIOD REASON RECKON SETTLE ACHIEVE ARRANGE COLLECT CONFINE EMBRACE ENCLOSE RESOLVE SUPPOSE COMPLETE DISPATCH ESTIMATE GRADUATE PARCLOSE RESTRAIN
CONCLUDED OVER COMPLETE
CONCLUDING LAST DESITIVE
CONCLUSION END AMEN CODA ERGO FINE LAST TERM CLOSE ENVOY EVENT FINIS ISSUE LOOSE OMEGA POINT ENDING FINALE FINISH PERIOD RESULT SEQUEL THIRTY UPSHOT CLOSURE CURTAIN FINDING OUTCOME SEQUELA VERDICT APODOSIS DECISION EPILOGUE FINALITY FRUITION GODSPEED ILLATION ILLATIVE JUDGMENT PARCLOSE SENTENCE

(— OF ARIA) CABALETTA
(FINAL —) ISSUE
(RANDOM —) SURMISE
(PL.) COLLATION
CONCLUSIVE LAST FINAL VALID
COGENT CERTAIN EVIDENT
EXTREME TELLING DECISIVE
DEFINITE ULTIMATE
CONCOCT MIX BREW COOK FAKE
PLAN PLOT VAMP FRAME HATCH
THINK DECOCT DEVISE DIGEST
INVENT MINGLE REFINE SCHEME
COMPOSE CONFECT DREAMUP
PERFECT PREPARE COMPOUND
INTRIGUE
CONCOCTION PLAN PLOT MUMMY
DEVICE MUMMIA BREWING
MIXTURE SNEEZER BUSINESS
COMPOUND
CONCOMITANT SEQUELA
INCIDENT ACCESSORY ASSOCIATE
ATTENDANT ATTENDING
COMPANION CONJOINED
COOPERANT SATELLITE
CONCORD PART AGREE AMITY
PEACE TERMS UNION UNITY
TREATY UNISON COMPACT
CONCENT CONCERT HARMONY
ONENESS QUARTER COVENANT
SYMPATHY COMMUNITY
(— OF SOUNDS) SYMPHONIA
CONCORDANT UNISON TUNABLE
TUNEFUL HARMONIC UNISONAL
UNISONOUS
CONCORDE SST
CONCOURSE CROWD HAUNT
PLACE POINT REPAIR RESORT
THRONG COMPANY ASSEMBLY
FREQUENCE
(INFERNAL —) HELL
CONCRESCENCE ADHESION
CONCRETE CLOT FIRM HARD REAL
BETON GROUT SOLID UNITE
ACTUAL CEMENT GUNITE
COMBINE CONGEAL SPECIAL
COALESCE COMPOUND POSITIVE
TANGIBLE AEROCRETE
CONCRETION CLOT KNOT MESS
FLINT FUSIL PEARL STONE BEZOAR
DOGGER NODULE TOPHUS LITHITE
OTOLITH CALCULUS HAIRBALL
POTSTONE SEBOLITH GALLSTONE
(— IN BAMBOO) TABASHIR
TABASHEER
CONCUBINAGE KARAO KAREWA
HETAERISM
CONCUBINE DASI MOLL HAGAR
RIZPAH BEDMATE HETAIRA
ODALISK MISTRESS ODALISQUE
CONCUPISCENCE DESIRE
CONCUPISCENT ANTSY
CONCUR HAND JIBE JOIN AGREE
CHECK CHIME UNITE ACCEDE
ACCORD ASSENT CONDOG
APPROVE COMBINE CONSENT
CONVENT COINCIDE CONSPIRE
CONVERGE
(— IN) SUBSCRIBE
CONCURRENCE UNION ASSENT
BESTOW CONSENT CONSORT
MEETING ADHESION SYNDROME
ADMISSION

CONCURRENT COEVAL UNITED
MEETING COPUNCTAL
CONCUSSION BUMP SHOCK
IMPACT ICEQUAKE COMMOTION
CONDEMN BAN CAST DAMN DEEM
DOOM FILE FINE HISS BLAME
BLESS DECRY JUDGE AMERCE
ATTAIN AWREAK BANISH DETEST
ADJUDGE CENSURE CONVICT
DENOUNCE FORJUDGE REPROACH
SENTENCE PROSCRIBE
(— AS SPURIOUS) OBELIZE
CONDEMNATION BAN DOOM
BLAME CENSURE DECRIAL
BRICKBAT
CONDEMNATORY SEVERE
ADVERSE
CONDEMNED FATAL DAMNED
CONDENSATION BAN STORY
DIGEST CAPSULE BOILDOWN
CONDENSE CUT JIG BRIEF UNITE
DECOCT DIGEST HARDEN LESSEN
NARROW REDUCE SHRINK
ABRIDGE CAPSULE COMBINE
COMPACT DEFLATE DENSATE
DISTILL SHORTEN SQUEEZE
THICKEN COMPRESS CONTRACT
DIMINISH PEMMICAN SOLIDIFY
CONDENSED CURT BRIEF CAPSULE
COMPACT CONCISE SUMMARY
TABLOID ABSORBED
CONDENSER ALUDEL REFLUX
BALANCER CAPACITOR
CONDER HUER
CONDESCEND DEIGN FAVOR
GRANT SNOOT STOOP ASSENT
OBLIGE SUBMIT CONCEDE
DESCEND
CONDESCENDING AVUNCULAR
CONDESCENSION STOOP DISDAIN
COURTESY DIGNATION
CONDIGN DUE FIT FAIR JUST
SEVERE WORTHY ADEQUATE
SUITABLE
CONDIMENT SOY HERB KARI MACE
SAGE SALT CAPER CURRY DULCE
DULSE SAUCE SPICE THYME
AIWAIN AJOWAN CATSUP CLOVES
GARLIC PEPPER RELISH SAMBAL
TAMARA BADIANE CANELLA
CHUTNEY KETCHUP MUSTARD
OREGANO PAPRIKA VINEGAR
ALLSPICE BALACHAN BLATJANG
DRESSING SEASONER TURMERIC
CONDITION IF AND FIG PLY WAY
CASE FORM HOOD MODE NICK
PASS RANK ROTE TERM TIFF TRIM
ANGLE BIRTH CAUSE CENSE CLASS
COLOR COVIN ESTRE FACET JOKER
PLACE POINT SHAPE STAGE STATE
THEAT WHACK AGENCY DEGREE
DONNEE ESTATE FETTLE GENTRY
MORALE MUSCLE PLIGHT STATUS
STRING ARTICLE CALLING FEATHER
FOOTING PLISKIE PREMISE
PREPARE PROVISO STATION
SUSPEND COVENANT OCCASION
POSITION PROTASIS STANDING
PREDICAMENT REQUIREMENT
(— IN LIFE) NICHE SPHERE
(— OF ANXIETY) CARK
(— OF BODY) HEAT AFFECTION
(— OF FATIGUE) FRAZZLE

(— OF FLUCTUATION) EURIPUS
(— STATED BEFOREHAND)
PREMISE
(BEING IN DIRTY —) GRUNGY
(CHANCE —) ACCIDENT
(CRUSHED —) MASH
(DEBASED —) CACHEXY CACHEXIA
(DEPRESSED —) DOWNBEAT
(DETERMINING —) GROUND
(DIRTY —) CLAT
(DISEASED —) DIEBACK
(DISGRACEFUL —) IGNOMINY
(DRUNKEN —) BUN
(DUE —) ORDER
(FAULTY —) MALADY
(FLOURISHING —) HEALTH
(GENERAL —) VOGUE
(HABITUAL —) TENOR
(LOW —) NOTHING
(MEAN —) DUST
(MISERABLE —) SQUALOR
(MORBID —) HOLDOVER
(MOST APPROPRIATE —) CHECKER
(NECESSARY —) MEAN
(NEUROTIC —) LATAH
(ORDERLY —) DECENCY
(PAINFUL —) CRICK
(PERMANENT —) HEXIS
(PROPER —) KILTER
(PROTECTIVE —) CALLUS CALLOUS
(SCURFY —) BUCKSKIN
(STATIONARY —) JIB
(SUBLIME —) HEAVEN
(SURROUNDING —) AIR
(TRUE —) SIZE
(UNEQUAL —) ODDS
(UNPROSPEROUS —) ILLTH
(UNWHOLESOME —) MALADY
(WEATHER —S) ELEMENTS
(PL.) HAND TERMS STRINGS
(SUFF.) ACITY ATION DOM ERY ICE
ICITY ILITY ION ISM MENT NESS OR
OSIS SHIP TH TY
(MORBID —) IASIS
CONDITIONAL EVENTUAL
CONNEXIVE PROVISORY QUALIFIED
CONDITIONED FINITE LIMITED
CONDITIONER DEGGER
CONDITIONING EDUCATION
HYPOTHESIS
CONDOLE MOAN
CONDOLENCE PITY RUTH EMPATHY
SYMPATHY
CONDOM JOHNNY RUBBER
JOHNNIE PROPHYLACTIC
CONDONE BLINK REMIT ACQUIT
EXCUSE FORGET IGNORE PARDON
ABSOLVE FORGIVE OVERLOOK
CONDOR TIFFIN BUZZARD VULTURE
CONDUCE GO AID HELP HIRE LEAD
TEND BRING GUIDE CONFER
EFFECT ENGAGE ADVANCE
CONDUCT FURTHER REDOUND
CONDUCT ACT CON RUN USE WIN
BEAR CALL COND CONN DEED
FACT FARE FIRK FORM GARB GEST
HAND KEEP LEAD MIEN PLAY QUIT
RULE SHOW TAKE WAGE WALK
BATON CARRY CHAIR DRESS DRIVE
FETCH GESTE GUARD GUIDE HABIT
MAYNE SITHE TRADE TRAIN USAGE
USHER ACTION ATTEND BEHAVE
COLORS CONVEY CONVOY

COURSE DEDUCE DEMEAN
DEPORT DIRECT ESCORT GOVERN
INDUCT MANAGE MANNER SQUIRE
ACTIONS BEARING CHANNEL
COMPERE COMPORT CONDITE
CONDUCE CONDUIT CONTAIN
CONTROL EXECUTE GALLANT
GESTION OFFICER OPERATE
WIREWAY ARRIVISM BEHAVIOR
CARRIAGE CHAPLAIN COURTESY
DEMEANOR GUIDANCE REGULATE
SHEPHERD TRANSACT
(— AROUND) TROT
(— ONESELF) DO ACT ACQUIT
BEHAVE BESTOW DEMEAN DEPORT
COMPORT CONTAIN DISPORT
ENTREAT MAINTAIN
(APPROPRIATE —) DHARMA
(BRASH —) FACE
(CONVENTIONAL —) PRAXIS
(DISORDERLY —) RANDAN
(DORMANT —) LATENCY
(DUTIFUL —) PIETY
(ETHICAL —) HONOR
(MORAL —) LIFE
(NORMAL —) WAY
(PROPER —) CRICKET
(RECKLESS —) DEVILRY DEVILTRY
(RIGHT —) TE TAO
(RIOTOUS —) RANDAN
(SAFE —) KOWL COWLE
(SEDITIOUS —) MISPRISION
(SHOWY —) BRAVADO
(SLOPPY —) SWASH
(SOCIAL —) MANNERS
(VAINGLORIOUS —) HEROICS
(WANTON —) RUFF
(WEAK —) FOLLY
CONDUCTANCE G
(UNIT OF —) MHO SIEMENS
CONDUCTION COURSING
CONDUCTOR CON BOND CADE
LEAD MAIN BRUSH GUARD SHUNT
SPOUT TRUNK BRIDGE BUSMAN
CARMAN CONVOY COPPER
ESCORT FEEDER LEADER OFFSET
RETURN CAPTAIN CATHODE
MAESTRO MANAGER AQUEDUCT
BATONIST CICERONE CONVEYOR
DIRECTOR EMPLOYEE FILAMENT
STICKMAN ANELECTRIC
(— OF FESTIVAL) SKUDLER
(ELECTRIC —) FILAMENT
(LIGHTNING —) ROD
(OMNIBUS —) CAD
(WOMAN —) CLIPPIE
(PL.) SERVICE
(SUFF.) EER
CONDUIT BOSS DUCT GOUT MAIN
PIPE SINK TUBE WIRE CABLE
CANAL CUNDY SEWER STACK
HEADER SLUICE TROUGH CARRIER
CHANNEL CHIMNEY CONDITE
CONDUCT CULVERT CUNDITE
EXHAUST FOGGARA LATERAL
LAUNDER PASSAGE WIREWAY
AQUEDUCT OLEODUCT PENSTOCK
UTILIDOR WASTEWAY
(PL.) LIMBERS
CONDYLOMA SYCOMA
CONE CAP YOW CHAT KING MOXA
PINA TOOT CONUS CRACK SCREW
SHAPE SPIRE YOWIE BOBBIN

CONOID MONTRE PASTIL CLUSTER
CONELET CONIOLE FISSURE
FRUSTUM PROLONG PYRAMID
STROBIL THIMBLE CANNELON
DUMPLING GALBULUS PASTILLE
PINECONE STROBILE STROBILUS
(— OF CLOTH) VANE
(— OF FIR) YOW YOWIE STROBIL
STROBILE STROBILUS
(— OF GUNPOWDER) PEEOY
(— OF HOP PLANT) BUR BURR
(— OF SILVER AMALGAM) PINA
(— ON LOG END) CAP
(— ON SHOE) CLEAT
(— STRUCTURE) NURAGHE
(HALF —) FORME NAPPE
(ICE CREAM —) ICE CORNET
(INVERTED —) HOPPER
(KIND OF —) NOSE
(PAPER —) SPILL COFFIN
(ROPE-MAKING —) TOP
(TOP CUT FROM —) UNGULA
(TRAFFIC —) PYLON
(VOLCANIC —) PUY MONTICULE
(PL.) HOPS
(PREF.) CON(I)(ICO)(O) STROBILI
CONENOSE BEDBUG BARBEIRO
CONE-SHELL ADMIRAL
CONESTOGA WAGON CARAVAN
CONEY CONY HYRAX HYRACID
GUATIBERO
CONFAB CHAT TALK POWWOW
CONFLAB PRATTLE
CONFABULATE TALK
CONFECTION CHOW MOSS CANDY
DULCE FUDGE MEBOS SWEET
BONBON COCKLE COMFIT DAINTY
DRAGEE HALVAH JUNKET MAJOON
NOUGAT SWEETY TABLET
CARAMEL CONFECT FONDANT
MIXTURE POMFRET PRALINE
SEATRON SUCCADE ANGELICA
CHOWCHOW CODINIAC
COMPOUND CONSERVE DELICACY
MARZIPAN PRESERVE QUIDDANY
SUBTLETY MARSHMALLOW
(TURKISH —) HALVAH
CONFECTIONERY CIMBAL
TUCKSHOP CONFISERIE
CONFEDERACY BUND COVIN
CREEK JUNTA KEDAR UNION
COVINE LEAGUE COMPLOT
ALLIANCE COVENANT FEDERACY
ILLINOIS BLACKFOOT
CONFEDERATE AID PAL REB ALLY
BAND PUFF COVER REBEL STALL
UNITE LEAGUE SANTAR ABETTER
ABETTOR CONJURE FEDARIE
FEDERAL FEODARY PARTNER
STEERER CONSPIRE FEDERARY
FEDERATE
(— SOLDIER) CONFED JOHNNY
GRAYBACK GRAYCOAT GREYBACK
(PICKPOCKET'S —) STALL
CONFEDERATION BODY BUND
ZUPA GUEUX UNION LEAGUE
COMPACT HASINAI SOCIETY
ALLIANCE COVENANT
(— OF VILLAGES) ZUPA
CONFER DUB GIVE MEET TALK
AWARD ENDOW FEOFF GRANT
INFER PARLE SPEND TREAT ADVISE
BESTOW COMMON CONFAB

DONATE ENTAIL HUDDLE IMPARL
IMPART INVEST PARLEY POWWOW
COLLATE COMMUNE COMPARE
CONDUCE CONSULT CONTACT
COUNSEL DISCUSS INSTATE
PRESENT COLLOGUE COMPRISE
CONVERGE NEGOTIATE
(— DEGREE UPON) CAP
(— KNIGHTHOOD UPON) DUB
CONFERENCE DIET TALK SYNOD
TREAT TRUST CAUCUS CONFAB
HUDDLE INDABA KORERO PARLEY
PARVIS POWWOW SUMMIT
CIRCUIT COUNCIL MEETING
PALAVER PARLING SEMINAR
COLLOQUE COLLOQUY CONCLAVE
CONGRESS PRACTICE PRACTISE
TUTORIAL PARLIAMENT
(SCIENCE —) PUGWASH
CONFERRING GRANT DATION
CONFESS OWN AVOW FESS KNOW
SING ADMIT GRANT KITHE
ACKNOW AGNISE ATTEST AVOUCH
BEKNOW COUTHE RENDER REVEAL
SHRIFT SHRIVE SQUEAK CONCEDE
DIVULGE PROFESS WHITTLE
DISBOSOM DISCLOSE DISCOVER
MANIFEST ACKNOWLEDGE
CONFESSION ALHET CREDO CREED
GRANT AVOWAL SHRIFT SHRIVE
VIDDUI ASHAMNU FORMULA
PECCAVI COGNOVIT
(MUTUAL —) SHARING
CONFESSIONAL SHRIFT MALCHUS
CONFESSOR FATHER SHRIFT
SHRIVER
CONFIDANT PRIVY FRIEND INWARD
INSIDER PRIVADO INTIMATE
CONFIDE AFFY RELY TELL TRUST
COMMIT DEPEND LIPPEN BELIEVE
CONSIGN ENTRUST INTRUST
(— IN) VENTURE
CONFIDENCE FACE HARK HOPE
BIELD CHEEK FAITH STOCK TRUST
APLOMB BELIEF CREDIT FIANCE
FIDUCE METTLE MORALE SECRET
SPIRIT SURETY COUNSEL
COURAGE PRIVITY AFFIANCE
BOLDNESS CREDENCE RELIANCE
SECURITY SURENESS
(—GAME) SCAM STING
CONFIDENT BOLD SMUG SURE
COCKY CRANK HARDY SIKER
CROUSE SECURE SICKER TRAIST
ASSURED CERTAIN HOPEFUL
RELIANT CONSTANT FEARLESS
FIDUCIAL IMPUDENT POSITIVE
SANGUINE TRUSTFUL
CONFIDENTIAL PACK BOSOM
PRIVY CLOSET COVERT HUSHED
INWARD SECRET PRIVATE
ESOTERIC FAMILIAR INTIMATE
CONFIDING TRUSTY CREDENT
RELIANT TRUSTFUL CONFIDENT
CONFIGURATION FORM SHAPE
FIGURE BANDING CONTOUR
DIAMOND GESTALT OUTLINE
GEOMETRY POSTURE OPPOSITION
PERSPECTIVE
(CELESTIAL —) SYZYGY
CONFINE BAR BOX CUB DAM HEM
MEW NUN PEN PIN STY TIE BAIL
BIND BOOM CAGE COOP CRIB

FOLD HASP JAIL KEEP LACE LOCK
PEND SEAL SHUT SPAN STEW
STOP STOW BOUND CABIN CHAIN
COART CRAMP CROWD DELAY
FENCE HOUSE LIMIT MARCH
PINCH POUND STICK STINT THIRL
BORDER BOTTLE COARCT CORRAL
EMBANK FETTER FORBAR HAMPER
HURDLE IMMURE IMPALE IMPARK
INTERN KENNEL PINION POCKET
PRISON SHUTIN STRAIN TETHER
ASTRICT CHAMBER COMPASS
CONTAIN IMPOUND INCLUDE
MANACLE PINFOLD POISTER
RECLOSE SECLUDE SHACKLE
TRAMMEL BASTILLE BOUNDARY
CLOISTER CONCLUDE DISTRAIN
FOCALIZE IMPRISON RESTRAIN
STRAITEN WAREHOUSE
(— IN HANDKERCHIEF) MAIL
(PL.) AMBIT PURLIEU PERIPHERY
CONFINED ILL FAST PENT BOUND
CAGED CLOSE CRAMP BEDRID
IMPALE IMPENT PENTIT SEALED
CAPTIVE CRAMPED CRIBBED
LIMITED SQUEEZY IMPENDED
IMPLICIT INTERNED PAROCHIAL
(— TO CERTAIN AREA) ENDEMIC
(—TO ONE) PROPER
(— TO SELECT GROUP) ESOTERIC
CONFINEMENT MEW BOND HOLD
JAIL WARD CRYING GATING
DURANCE INLYING JANKERS
WARDING CLAUSURE FIRMANCE
GROANING LOCKDOWN SOLITARY
CONFINES AMBIT
CONFINING NARROW
CONFIRM FIX SET FIRM SEAL PROVE
VOUCH AFFEER AFFIRM ASSENT
ASSURE ATTEST AVOUCH BISHOP
CLINCH FASTEN HARDEN RATIFY
REABLE SECOND SETTLE STABLE
VERIFY APPROVE COMFORT
COMPACT CONSIGN ENDORSE
FORTIFY JUSTIFY PROPORT
SUPPORT SUSTAIN THICKEN
ACCREDIT CONVINCE CORROBER
ENTRENCH INSTRUCT SANCTION
STRENGTH VALIDATE
CORROBORATE REDETERMINE
CONFIRMATION PROOF CHRISM
SANCTION
CONFIRMED SET FIXED SWORN
ARRANT STABLE CERTAIN
CHRONIC AFFEERED HABITUAL
HARDENED RATIFIED
CONFISCATE GRAB SEIZE USURP
CONDEMN CONFISK ESCHEAT
PUBLISH DISTRAIN
CONFISCATION ESCHEAT
INCENSION
CONFLAGRATION WAR FIRE BLAZE
FEVER BURNING INFERNO
CONFLICT JAR WAR AGON BATE
BOUT BUMP CAMP DUEL FRAY
MEET MUSS RIFT AGONY BROIL
BRUSH CLASH FIGHT GRIPS MIXUP
STOUR ACTION BATTLE COMBAT
MUTINY OPPOSE SCRAPE SHOWER
STRIFE CONTEND CONTEST
DISCORD SCUFFLE WARFARE
ANTIMONY CLASHING DISAGREE
MILITATE SKIRMISH STRIVING

STRUGGLE COLLISION
COLLUCTATION
(DRAMATIC —) AGON
(FINAL —) ARMAGEDDON
CONFLICTING ADVERSE
ABHORRENT
CONFLUENCE FORK CROWD
INFALL CONFLUX MEETING
JUNCTION
CONFLUENT FORK
CONFORM DO GO FIT HEW BEND
LEAN OBEY SORT SUIT ABIDE
ADAPT AGREE APPLY SHAPE YIELD
ACCEDE ADJUST ASSENT COMPLY
CONFER SETTLE SQUARE SUBMIT
COMPOSE CONFIRM
(— TO) KEEP MEET ANSWER
BEHAVE SATISFY
CONFORMABLE DONE SUING
SUITED CONFORM PURSUANT
QUADRANT
CONFORMATION FORM BUILD
(MENTAL —) SAMSKARA
CONFORMING FAIR SAME COMELY
DECENT CORRECT CONGRUOUS
CONFORMIST BOY COMPLIER
CONFORMITY FIT ACCORD
DHARMA EQUITY REASON
HARMONY JUSTICE KEEPING
ACCURACY AFFINITY JUSTNESS
LIKENESS SYMMETRY CONGRUITY
FORMALITY ACCORDANCE
CONSERTION
(— TO LAW) DECENCY LEGALITY
(— WITH GOOD MANNERS)
PROPRIETY
CONFOUND MIX BLOW DASH MATE
MAZE ROUT STAM STUN WHIP
ABASH ADDLE AMAZE APPAL
BLAST FOUND SHEND SPOIL
STUMP WASTE AWHAPE BAFFLE
BUNKER COMMIT DISMAY DUDDER
MINGLE MUDDLE RABBIT RATTLE
ASTOUND BUMBAZE CONFUSE
CONFUTE CORRUPT DESTROY
FLUMMOX FORLESE MISTAKE
NONPLUS PERPLEX PETRIFY
STUMBLE STUPEFY ASTONISH
BABELIZE BEWILDER DISTRACT
DUMFOUND SURPRISE SPIFLICATE
CONFOUNDED MATE BALLY BLAME
RUDDY BLAMED DEUCED POCKED
BLASTED BLESSED MURRAIN
PEEVISH DUMMERED JIGGERED
SWITCHED CONSARNED
(BE —) ABAVE ABAWE
CONFRATERNITY BODY UNION
SOCIETY CONFRAIRY
CONFRONT DARE DEFY FACE MEET
NOSE BEARD BRACE BRAVE
CROSS FRONT STAND ACCOST
ASSAIL BREAST OPPOSE RESIST
VISAGE AFFRONT COMPARE
OUTFACE PROPOSE ENVISAGE
THREATEN
CONFRONTATION FACEOFF
CONFRONTING BEFORE ADVERSE
ABUTTING CONFRONT
CONFUSE BOX FOX MIX BALL DASH
DAZE DOIT DOZE DUST GAUM
HARL MAZE MUSS ROIL ROUT
ABASH ADDLE AMAZE BEFOG
BITCH BLEND CLOUD DEAVE DIZZY

MUDDY SHEND SHENT SNARL STEER TWIST UPSET BAFFLE BEDAZE BEMUSE BOTHER BURBLE CADDLE COMMIT CORPSE DUDDER DUDDLE FLURRY FUDDLE GRAVEL JUMBLE MADDLE MAFFLE MAMMER MASKER MIZZLE MOIDER MOMBLE MUDDLE PUZZLE RAFFLE RATTLE TWITCH WIMPLE BECLOUD BEDEVIL BLUNDER BUMBAZE DERANGE DIFFUSE EMBROIL FLUSTER GARBOIL GIDDIFY MISTAKE MYSTIFY NONPLUS PERPLEX PERTURB SCATTER SHUFFLE STUPEFY UNRAVEL BEFUDDLE BEWILDER CONFLATE CONFOUND DISORDER DISTRACT DUMFOUND ENTANGLE MISORDER SQUATTER OBFUSCATE

(— AN ACTOR) CORPSE
(— BY NOISE) DUDDER
CONFUSED ASEA LOST ADDLE DIZZY FOGGY FUZZY HEAVY MISTY MUDDY MUZZY VAGUE WESTY WOOLY BLOTTO CLOUDY DOILED DOITED DRUMLY JUMBLY MEDLEY MOPISH MUSHED SHAGGY TAVERT WOOLLY BEMUSED BLURRED CHAOTIC CLOUDED CONFUSE DIFFUSE MIFFLED OBSCURE RATTLED STUPENT COCKEYED DERANGED FLURRIED INVOLVED STREAKED FLUSTERED INDISTINCT SCRAMBLING MUDDLEHEADED
(— IN LANGUAGE) BABYLONIAN
(EASILY —) BASHFUL
CONFUSEDLY PELLMELL
CONFUSING DIZZY MAZEFUL BAFFLING BLINDING DIZZYING
CONFUSION PI DIN PIE COIL DUST FLAP FUSS HARL MESS MOIL RIOT AMAZE ATAXY BABEL CHAOS CHEVY CHIVY DERAY FRASE HAVOC HURLY LARRY LURRY SNAFU SNARL STROW ATAXIA BABBLE BAFFLE BALLUP BEDLAM BUMBLE CHIVVY DUDDER FRAISE HABBLE HOBBLE HUBBUB HUDDLE JABBLE JUMBLE MASTIC MUCKER MUDDLE POTHER PUCKER RABBLE RUFFLE RUMPUS THRONG TOPHET TUMULT UPROAR WELTER ANARCHY BLUNDER BLUSTER CLUTTER COBWEBS FARRAGE FLUTTER GARBOIL HURLING KIPPAGE LOUSTER MISMAZE MISRULE ROOKERY RUMMAGE SCADDLE SCOWDER TOPHETH TURMOIL WHEMMEL WIDDRIM BABELISM DISARRAY DISORDER EQUIVOKE HOOROOSH SCOUTHER SHAMBLES SPLUTTER STRAMASH TOHUBOHU
CONFUTATION DISPROOF
CONFUTE DENY EVICT REBUT EVINCE EXPOSE REFUTE FALSIFY IMPROVE SILENCE SUBVERT CONCLUDE CONFOUND CONVINCE DISPROVE INFRINGE OVERCOME REDARGUE
CONGEAL GEL ICE SET GEAL JELL CANDY COTTER CURDLE FREEZE

HARDEN STIFFEN STORKEN THICKEN CONCRETE SOLIDIFY
(— INTO HOARFROST) RIME
CONGEALED FROZEN
CONGELATION FROST
CONGENER BEAVER DOTTREL DOTTEREL
CONGENIAL SIB BOON HAPPY NATAL NATIVE AMIABLE CONNATE KINDRED
CONGENITAL INNATE CONNATE CONNATAL GENETOUS
CONGER SEAEEL
CONGERIES CALCULARY COLLECTION
CONGEST STUFF IMPACT
CONGESTED INJECTED
CONGESTION JAM HEAP LAMPAS LAMPERS CROWDING STOPPAGE
CONGLOMERATE HEAP MASS PILE ROCK STACK BANKET PSEPHITE NAGELFLUH
(—S OF JAPAN) ZAIBATSU
(JAPANESE —) ZAIBATSU
CONGLOMERATION HUDDLE GLOMMOX IMBROGLIO
CONGO MUMMY ASPHALTUM

CONGO

CAPITAL: BRAZZAVILLE
COIN: FRANC FRANCCFA
LAKE: MWERU TUMBA UPEMBA LEOPOLD
NATIVE: SUSA VILI MANTU PYGMY BATEKE MBOCHI WABUMA DAKONGO BANGALA
PLATEAU: BATEKE
RIVER: UELE CONGO KWILU LUUA NGOKO NIARI SANGA WAMBA KWENGE LOANGE SANGHA UBANGI KOUILOU LUDILAGII
TOWN: EWO EPENA HOLLE JACOB OKOYO SEMBE MAKOUA OUESSO ZANAGA DOLISIE ENYELLE LOUBOMO SOUANKE DJAMBALA BRAZZAVILLE
TRIBUTARY: LOMAMI UBANGI ARUWIMA LUALABA LUAPULA ITIMBIRI

CONGOU KEEMUN
CONGRATULATE HUG JOY LAUD GREET SALUTE FLATTER MACARIZE
(— ONESELF) PREEN
CONGRATULATION PARABIEN
(PL.) GRATTERS
CONGREGATE HERD MASS MEET PACK TEEM GROUP SWARM TROOP GATHER MUSTER COLLECT CONVENE ASSEMBLE
CONGREGATION PEW BODY FOLD HERD HOST MASS FLOCK SAMAJ SWARM CHURCH PARISH COMPANY MEETING ORATORY SYNAXIS ASSEMBLY BRETHREN CHAPELRY
(— OF WITCHES) COVEN
(JEWISH —) KOLEL ALJAMA SYNAGOG
(PL.) CHARGE
CONGRESS MOD DAIL DIET SYNOD UYEZD OBLAST OUYEZD

POWWOW COUNCIL GORSEDD MEETING ASSEMBLY CONCLAVE
(— OF BARDS) EISTEDDFOD
CONGRESSMAN SENATOR DOUGHFACE
CONGRUITY ACCORD CONCORD FITNESS HARMONY KEEPING SYMMETRY COHERENCE
CONGRUOUS CONGRUE HARMONIC SUITABLE ACCORDING
CONICAL CONIC TAPER COPPED MITRAL COPPLED TAPERING
(PREF.) TURBINATO TURBIN(I)(O)
CONICALLY
(PREF.) TURBINATO
CONIDIUM CIDIUM ARTHROSPORE
CONIFER FIR YEW PINE CEDAR LARCH SPRUCE SOFTWOOD EVERGREEN
CONIFERAE PINALES
CONIUM HEMLOCK
CONJECTURE AIM CAST PLOT ROVE SHOT VIEW AUGUR ETTLE FANCY GUESS OPINE THINK BELIEF DIVINE THEORY CONJECT IMAGINE OPINION PRESUME SUPPOSE SURMISE SUSPECT HINDCAST SUPPOSAL
CONJOIN JOIN KNIT ATTEND EMPALE IMPALE ALLIGATE
CONJOINED JOINED JUGATE LINKED JUGATED CONJUNCT TOUCHING
CONJOINTLY JUNCTLY TOGETHER
CONJUGAL SPOUSAL CONNUBIAL
CONJUGATE YOKED JOINED UNITED COUPLED INFLECT PARONYMOUS
CONJUGATION SYNGAMY ZYGOSIS CYTOGAMY ENDOGAMY SYNOPSIS
CONJUNCTION AS ET IF OR AND BUT NOR TIE THAN JOINT SINCE SYNOD UNION UNITY THOUGH COITION CONSORT JOINDER CONJUNCT RATIONAL
(PREF.) (IN —) CO
CONJUNCTIVITIS PINKEYE
CONJUNCTURE SEASON
CONJURATION ART CHARM MAGIC SPELL VOODOO EXORCISM
CONJURE PRAY WISH CHARM HALSE ADJURE ENJOIN INVENT INVOKE SUMMON BESEECH COMBINE ENTREAT IMAGINE CONSPIRE CONTRIVE EXORCIZE
(— UP) RAISE
CONJURE MAN CUNJAH CUNJER GOOFER GUFFER
CONJURER MAGE PELLAR POWWOW SHAMAN WIZARD JUGGLER WARLOCK WIELARE ANGEKKOK JONGLEUR MAGICIAN PYTHONIC SORCERER
CONJURING JADU JADOO CONJURY VOODOOISM
CONK FAIL HEAD KONK NOSE FAINT KNOCK STALL BRACKET
CONNECT COG PUT TIE ALLY BIND BOND GEAR GLUE JOIN KNIT KNOT LINK AFFIX CHAIN MARRY NITCH UNITE ATTACH BRIDGE CEMENT COHERE COMMIT CONNEX COUPLE ENLINK FASTEN PLUGIN

RELATE SPLICE COMBINE ENCHAIN INVOLVE APPARENT CATENATE CONTINUE DOVETAIL INTERTIE
(— TREADLE) CORD
CONNECTED ALLIED CONNEX AFFINED COUPLED HANGING
(— WITH) ABOUT
(ELECTRICALLY —) ALIVE
(NOT —) FOREIGN ASYNARTETE
(SYNTACTICALLY —) ABSOLUTE
(SUFF.) (— WITH) ARIA ARIUM AST ORIAL

CONNECTICUT

CAPITAL: HARTFORD
COLLEGE: TRINITY
COUNTY: TOLLAND WINDHAM
INDIAN: PEQUOT MOHEGAN NIANTIC
STATE BIRD: ROBIN
STATE FLOWER: LAUREL
STATE NICKNAME: NUTMEG
STATE TREE: OAK
TOWN: AVON BETHEL CANAAN COSCOB DARIEN MYSTIC SHARON STORRS WILTON DANBURY MERIDEN NIANTIC NORWALK NORWICH TOLL AND WINDSOR NEWHAVEN SIMSBURY WESTPORT GREENWICH RIDGEFIELD
UNIVERSITY: YALE WESLEYAN

CONNECTING BETWEEN SYNDETIC
CONNECTION Y HUB TAP TIE BOND LINK HITCH NEXUS UNION BUCKLE CLEVIS FAMILY GROUND REPORT SUTURE SWIVEL BEARING BOLSTER CONTACT DESCENT FERRULE HOLDING KINSHIP LIAISON LINKAGE RAPPORT SIAMESE SIBNESS SOCIETY AFFINITY ALLIANCE COMMERCE CONNEXUS INTIMACY JUNCTION LIGATION RELATIVE SYNDETIC RELATIONSHIP
(— BETWEEN UNIVERSES) WORMHOLE
(ELECTRICAL —) GROUND
(FISH-LINE —) LEADER
(FORKED —) BRANCH
(MECHANICAL —S) LEADOUT
(WORKING —) GEAR
CONNECTIVE IZAFAT SUTURAL JUNCTION LIGATIVE SYNDETIC VINCULAR
CONNECTOR AND
CONNING TOWER SAIL
CONNIVANCE CAHOOT CAHOOTS
CONNIVE ABET PLOT WINK BLINK CABAL ASSENT FOMENT INCITE COLLUDE
(— AT MEDICAL TREATMENT) COVER
CONNIVING FOXY
CONNOISSEUR JUDGE CRITIC EXPERT CAMEIST EPICURE GOURMET CIDERIST DILETANT LAPIDARY COGNOSCENTE MEDIEVALIST
(— OF WINES) OENOPHILE
CONNOTATION DEPTH INTENT MEANING

CONNOTE MEAN

CONNUBIAL MARITAL CONJUGAL DOMESTIC

CONQUER GET WIN BEAT BEST DOWN FIRK GAIN LICK ROUT TAME WHIP CRUSH DAUNT DEBEL EVICT DEBELL DEFEAT EVINCE HUMBLE IMPORT MASTER REDUCE SUBDUE VICTOR ACQUIRE PREVAIL SUBJECT SURPASS TRIUMPH OVERCOME OVERGANG SURMOUNT VANQUISH

CONQUEROR HERO MASTER VICTOR WINNER TRIUMPHER

CONQUEST MASTERY SCALING TRIUMPH VICTORY WINNING

CONSANGUINEOUS AKIN CARNAL KINDRED NATURAL RELATED

CONSANGUINITY BLOOD NASAB KINSHIP AFFINITY

CONSCIENCE WORD DAENA HEART INWIT SENSE SCRUPLE THOUGHT

CONSCIENTIOUS FAIR JUST EXACT RIGID EIDENT HONEST STRICT DUTIFUL UPRIGHT FAITHFUL

CONSCIENTIOUSNESS RELIGION

CONSCIOUS KEEN WARE ALIVE AWAKE AWARE JERRY GUILTY FEELING KNOWING WITTING RATIONAL SENSIBLE SENTIENT CONSCIENT
(— OF) ONTO

CONSCIOUSNESS EGO HEART SENSE SPIRIT ANOESIS FEELING THOUGHT SENTIENT AWARENESS PERCEPTION
(HALF —) DOVER
(REGAIN —) COMETO

CONSCRIPT LEVY CHOCO DRAFT ENROL ENLIST MUSTER DRAFTEE DRAUGHT RECRUIT JEANJEAN

CONSCRIPTION LEVY

CONSECRATE VOW FAIN HOLY SAIN SEAL BLESS DEIFY HEAVE SACRE ANOINT DEVOTE HALLOW ORDAIN SACRATE CONSACRE DEDICATE SANCTIFY

CONSECRATED BLEST OBLATE SACRED VOTARY VOTIVE BLESSED SACRE HALLOWED HIERATIC

CONSECRATION IHRAM SACRE SACRY SACRING DEVOTION HOLINESS

CONSECUTIVELY TOGETHER

CONSECUTIVENESS SEQUENCE

CONSENT HEAR AGREE ALLOW GRANT YIELD ACCEDE ACCORD AFFORD ASSENT BETEEM COMPLY CONCUR PERMIT APPROVE GOODWILL PERMISSION

CONSENTIENT UNANIMOUS

CONSEQUENCE AND END BORE EVENT FORCE FRUIT ISSUE SUITE WORTH BROWST CHARGE EFFECT ENTAIL FIGURE GROWTH IMPORT MOMENT REPUTE RESULT SEQUEL WEIGHT CONCERN OUTCOME PRODUCE PURPOSE SEQUELA SEQUENT BACKLASH INTEREST MISCHIEF OCCASION SEQUITUR COROLLARY OUTGROWTH CONSECTARY RAMIFICATION

(DONE IN —) PURSUANT
(HARMFUL —) EVIL
(ILL —) MISCHIEF
(PERSON OF —) HEAVY
(PL.) AFTERINGS

CONSEQUENT COMES THESIS ADJUNCT

CONSEQUENTIAL HEAVY POMPOUS COROLLARY MOMENTOUS

CONSEQUENTLY SO ERGO THEN THUS HENCE LATER PURSUANT PRESENTLY

CONSERTAL SUTURAL

CONSERVATION HUSBANDRY

CONSERVATISM BOURBONISM

CONSERVATIVE SAFE TORY FUSTY QUIET STAID FABIAN HUNKER STABLE BOURBON DIEHARD HARDHAT MODERATE UNIONIST

CONSERVATORY STOVE SCHOOL ACADEMY

CONSERVE CAN JAM SAVE GUARD GUMBO JELLY DEFEND SECURE SHIELD UPHOLD HUSBAND PROTECT SEATRON SUSTAIN MAINTAIN PRESERVE
(GRAPE —) UVATE

CONSIDER AIM BAT LET SEE CALL CAST DEEM GAUM GIVE HASH HEAR HEED HOLD MULL MUSE RATE SEEM TAKE TALE VIEW VISE WISE ALLOW BESEE COUNT ENTER ETTLE JUDGE PANSE POISE SPELL STUDY THINK VERSE VOLVE WEIGH ADVERT ADVISE BEHOLD DEBATE DEVISE DIGEST ESTEEM EXPEND FIGURE IMPUTE PONDER REASON RECKON REGARD REWARD SURVEY ACCOUNT BELIEVE BETHINK CANVASS CONSULT EXAMINE INSPECT PERPEND PREPEND REFLECT RESPECT REVOLVE SUPPOSE COGITATE ESTIMATE MEDITATE PERPENSE RUMINATE
(— FAVORABLY) CREDIT
(— PROS AND CONS) ARGUE
(— SEPARATELY) SPECIALIZE

CONSIDERABLE GAY GEY FAIR GOOD TIDY BONNY CANNY GEYAN GREAT LARGE SMART STARK GOODLY PRETTY GOODISH HEALTHY INTENSE NOTABLE SEVERAL HANDSOME POWERFUL SENSIBLE UNLITTLE

CONSIDERABLY FAR GAY GEY WELL GEYAN PRETTY SMARTLY

CONSIDERATE KIND MILD NICE GENTLE TENDER CAREFUL HEEDFUL PRUDENT SERIOUS TACTFUL DELICATE GRACIOUS ATTENTIVE

CONSIDERATENESS GRACE
(MUTUAL —) SHU

CONSIDERATION GUT GUTS SAKE COUNT PRICE STUDY TOPIC ADVICE ASPECT COMITY DEBATE ESTEEM MOMENT MOTIVE NOTICE REASON REFLEX REGARD SURVEY ACCOUNT INSIGHT PREMIUM RESPECT THOUGHT ALTRUISM COURTESY DELICACY EMINENCE

EMPHASIS GRATUITY PROSPECT SANCTION
(BASIC —) BEDROCK
(ETHICAL —) SCRUPLE
(THOUGHTFUL —) THEORIA
(UNDER —) ONTHETAPIS

CONSIDERED ADVISED DELIBERATE

CONSIDERING IF FOR SINCE SEEING

CONSIGN DOOM GIVE MAIL SEND SHIP ALLOT AWARD CHECK DIGHT REMIT SHIFT YIELD ASSIGN COMMIT DESIGN DEVOTE REMAND RESIGN ADDRESS BETEACH CONFIDE DELIVER DEPOSIT ENTRUST INTRUST BEQUEATH DELEGATE RELEGATE TRANSFER
(— FOR DESTRUCTION) ACCURSE
(— TO OBLIVION) BURY EXPUNGE
(— TO PERDITION) DAMN CONDEMN

CONSIGNEE AGENT FACTOR SHIPPER RECEIVER

CONSIGNMENT INVOICE FOREDOOM SHIPMENT
(— OF TEA) BREAK

CONSIST LIE HOLD RELY REST DWELL EXIST STAND INHERE RESIDE CONTAIN EMBRACE COMPRISE

CONSISTENCY BODY UNION DEGREE CONCENT CONCORD HARMONY KEEPING COMPAGES EVENNESS FIRMNESS SOLIDITY SYMMETRY

CONSISTENT EVEN FIRM STEADY DURABLE LOGICAL REGULAR UNIFORM COHERENT ENDURING SUITABLE COMPATIBLE SEQUACIOUS
(— WITH NATURE) KIND KINDLY
(BE —) ACCORD
(MAKE —) CLEAR

CONSISTING
(PREF.) **(— OF)** DIA
(SUFF.) **(— OF)** IC(AL)

CONSOCIES
(SUFF.) ETUM

CONSOLATION SOP FINE RELIEF SOLACE COMFORT SPIRITING

CONSOLE CALM ALLAY ANCON CHEER ORGAN TABLE SOLACE SOOTHE BRACKET CABINET COMFORT RELIEVE SUPPORT SUSTAIN CARTOUCH

CONSOLER PARACLETE

CONSOLIDATE COG MIX KNIT MASS POOL WELD BLEND CLOSE MERGE UNIFY UNITE HARDEN MINGLE SETTLE COMBINE COMPACT ANKYLOSE COALESCE COMPRESS CONDENSE ORGANIZE SOLIDIFY

CONSOLIDATED CONFLATE

CONSOLS GOSCHENS

CONSOMME MADRILENE

CONSONANCE ACCORD UNISON HARMONY DIAPASON DIAPENTE SYMPATHY SYMPHONY

CONSONANT WAW MUTE STOP DENTAL FORTIS LABIAL LETTER LIQUID SONANT UNISON LATERAL MUTABLE PALATAL PLOSIVE

SPIRANT UNIFIED ALVEOLAR ASPIRATA ASPIRATE BILABIAL EJECTIVE GEMINATE HARMONIC SUITABLE
(CONSECUTIVE —S) CLUSTER
(SMOOTH —) LENE LENIS
(TENSE AND STRONG —) FORTIS
(VOICELESS —) SURD SPIRATE

CONSORT COT AIDE ALLY JOIN MATE MOUP WIFE YOKE GROUP TROOP UNITE ACCORD ATTEND ESCORT MINGLE SPOUSE COMPANY COMRADE CONCERT DAMKINA EMPRESS HUSBAND PARTNER ACCUSTOM ASSEMBLY PRINCESS
(VISHNU'S —) LAKSHMI

CONSPECTUS LIST APERCU SURVEY OUTLINE THEATER THEORIC SPECTRUM SYNOPSIS

CONSPICUOUS BIG BOLD RANK CLEAR FAMED NOISY PLAIN STARY EXTANT FAMOUS MARKED PATENT SIGNAL BLATANT EMINENT GLARING NOTABLE OBVIOUS POINTED SALIENT SIGHTLY STARING VISIBLE APPARENT EMPHATIC FLAGRANT KENSPECK MANIFEST STRIKING PROMINENT NOTICEABLE OUTSTANDING
(— ONE) STANDOUT

CONSPIRACY COUP PLAN PLOT RING CABAL COVIN JUNTO PARTY COVINE SCHEME COMPACT COMPLOT INTRIGUE CATILINISM

CONSPIRATOR PACKER PLOTTER SCHEMER

CONSPIRE ABET PACK PLOT CABAL UNITE LEAGUE SCHEME COLLUDE COMPLOT CONJURE CONNIVE COLLOGUE CONTRIVE

CONSTABLE COP BULL PEON SLOP BEADLE BEAGLE HARMAN KAVASS KEEPER KOTWAL WARDEN BAILIFF CORONER DOZENER NUTHOOK OFFICER STALLER SUBASHI ALGUAZIL DOGBERRY TIPSTAFF CASTELLAN CATCHPOLE CATCHPOLL BORSHOLDER

CONSTANCE (FATHER OF —) FONDLOVE NONESUCH
(HUSBAND OF —) ALLA
(SON OF —) ARTHUR

CONSTANCY ZEAL ARDOR FAITH TRUTH FEALTY HONESTY LOYALTY ONENESS PURPOSE DEVOTION FIDELITY

CONSTANT K SET EVEN FIRM JUST LEAL TRUE FIXED LOYAL SOLID STILL TIGHT TRIED ITHAND STABLE STEADY CERTAIN CHRONIC DURABLE FOREVER LASTING REGULAR STAUNCH UNIFORM DEFINITE ENDURING FAITHFUL POSITIVE RESOLUTE SEDULOUS STANDING PERENNIAL
(KIND OF —) HUBBLE

CONSTANTLY AWAY EVER ALWAYS THRONG

CONSTANT NYMPH (AUTHOR OF —) KENNEDY
(CHARACTER IN —) DODD KATE CARYL LEWIS SUSAN TESSA ALBERT

SANGER TERESA ANTONIA PAULINA FLORENCE CHURCHILL SEBASTIAN

CONSTELLATION ARA CUP FLY FOX LEO APUS ARGO COLT CROW CRUX DOVE GOAT GRUS HARE HARP LION LYNX LYRA MAST PAVO PLOW SIGN SWAN TAUR URSA VELA WAIN WOLF ALTAR ARIES CAMEL CETUS CLOCK CRANE DRACO EAGLE GROUP HYDRA INDUS LEPUS LIBRA LUPUS MALUS MENSA MUSCA NORMA ORION PYXIS RAVEN TABLE VIRGO WAGON WHALE ANTLIA AQUILA AURIGA BOOTES CAELUM CANCER CARINA CORVUS CRATER CYGNUS DIPPER DORADO FORNAX GEMINI HYDRUS INDIAN LIZARD OBELUS OCTANS OKNARI PICTOR PISCES PISCIS PLOUGH PUPPIS SCALES SCUTUM TAURUS TIGRIS TOUCAN TUCANA VOLANS ALGEBAR CEPHEUS CLUSTER COLUMBA COMPASS DOLPHIN FURNACE GIRAFFE LACERTA MONARCH OETAEUS PATTERN PEACOCK PEGASUS PERSEUS PHOENIX RHOMBUS SAGITTA SCORPIO SERPENS SERPENT SEXTANS SEXTANT XIPHIAS AQUARIUS ASTERISM CHAMPION CIRCINUS CYNOSURE EQUULEUS ERIDANUS HERCULES HERDSMAN KASHYAPA QUADRANS REINDEER RETICULE SCORPION SCORPIUS SCULPTOR TRIANGLE

(— OF VEGA) LYRA

CONSTERNATION FEAR ALARM PANIC DISMAY FRIGHT HORROR TERROR TREPIDITY

CONSTIPATE BIND ASTRICT

CONSTIPATED BOUND COSTIVE STENOTIC

CONSTIPATION STENOSIS

CONSTITUENCY BOROUGH

CONSTITUENT ATOM ITEM PART PIECE VOTER DETAIL FACTOR FUSAIN MATTER MEMBER SIMPLE ELECTOR ELEMENT FEATURE TAGMEME INTEGRAL

(— OF BLOOD SERUM) OPSONIN

(— OF CLINKER) ALITE CELITE

(— OF COAL) DURAIN FUSAIN

(— OF DURAIN) ATTRITUS

(— OF MUSCLE) CREATINE

(— OF STEEL) PEARLITE

(—S OF BEER) EXTRACT

(NECESSARY —) ESSENCE

(PL.) MATTER BIOSESTON

CONSTITUTE BE FIX SET FORM MAKE ENACT ERECT FORGE FOUND SHAPE SPELL CREATE DEPUTE GRAITH ORDAIN APPOINT COMPOSE FASHION STATION COMPOUND COMPRISE

CONSTITUTION LAW SET CODE SETT BEING CANON FRAME FUERO HUMOR SETUP STATE CHARTE CRASIS CUSTOM DESIGN ESTATE HEALTH NATURE TEMPER CHARTER HABITUS SYNODAL GRONDWET GRUNDLOV HABITUDE PHYSIQUE POLITEIA

(— STATE) CONNECTICUT

(BODILY —) HABIT SPIRITS

(GERMINAL —) HEREDITY

CONSTITUTIONAL WALK HECTIC INNATE RIKKEN EXERCISE

CONSTITUTIVE FORMAL

CONSTRAIN ART PUT TIE ARCT BEND BIND CURB DOOM FAIN HALE HOLD LEAD URGE CHAIN CHECK CLASP COART CRAMP DETER DRIVE FORCE IMPEL LIMIT PRESS COERCE COMPEL EVINCE OBLIGE RAVISH SECURE STRAIN THRAST ASTRICT CONFINE CONJURE ENFORCE MANACLE OPPRESS REPRESS VIOLATE COMPRESS CONCLUDE DISTRESS OBLIGATE PERFORCE POUNDAGE RELIGATE RESTRAIN

CONSTRAINED FAIN TIED VAIN BOUND FORCED FORMAL UNEASY COACTED

CONSTRAINING UNEASY COMPELLENT

CONSTRAINT BOND CRAMP FORCE BRIDLE DURESS STRESS RESERVE STRAINT COERCION DISTRESS PRESSURE

CONSTRICT TIE BIND CURB GRIP CHOKE CRAMP LIMIT STRAP HAMPER SHRINK STRAIN STRAIT ASTRICT DEFLATE SQUEEZE STIFFEN TIGHTEN ASTRINGE COMPRESS CONDENSE CONTRACT DISTRAIN RESTRICT

CONSTRICTED STRAIT STRICT ADENOID

(— AT INTERVALS) MONILIFORM

CONSTRICTION KNOT CHOKE ISTHMUS STENOSIS THLIPSIS

CONSTRICTOR BOA ABOMA NOOSE GUAVINA

CONSTRUCT UP BIG ATOM FORM IDEA LEVY MAKE REAR BUILD CRAFT DIGHT EDIFY ERECT FRAME MODEL WEAVE BURROW DEDUCE DESIGN DEVISE FABRIC ARRANGE CARPENT COMBINE COMPILE COMPOSE CONCEPT CONFECT CONTOUR EXTRUCT FASHION CONSTRUE ENGINEER PRACTISE SLIPFORM

(— ARCH) TURN

CONSTRUCTED BUILT EDIFICATE

(CAREFULLY —) CLEVER

(HASTILY —) GIMCRACK JIMCRACK

CONSTRUCTION BOOM ALTAR FRAME FABRIC MONSTER SYNESIS APPROACH BUILDING DWELLING ERECTION

(— OF NAME) ABSTRACTION

(— SET) ERECTOR

(ABSTRACT —) STABILE

(GRAMMATICAL —) SYNESIS APPOSITION

(POINTED —) BEAK

CONSTRUCTIVE PONENT FACTIVE HELPFUL VIRTUAL CREATIVE IMPLICIT INFERRED

CONSTRUCTOR ENGINEER

CONSTRUE INFER PARSE STRUE INTEND RENDER ANALYZE

CONSTER DISSECT EXPLAIN EXPOUND RESOLVE

CONSUL SUFFECT

CONSULT LOOK SEEK TALK ADVISE CONFER EMPARL IMPARL COUNSEL RESOLVE

CONSULTANT EXPERT ADVISER COUNSEL

CONSULTATION ADVICE COUNCIL COUNSEL

CONSUL, THE (CHARACTER IN —) JOHN MAGDA SOREL

(COMPOSER OF —) MENOTTI

CONSUME EAT SUP USE BOLT BURN CHEW FANG FARE FEED FRET GULP IDLE KILL RUST TAKE TUCK WEAR DALLY DRINK FLAME LURCH RAVEN SHIFT SPEND TOOTH WASTE ABSORB BEZZLE BROWSE CANKER DEVOUR ENGAGE EXPEND FINISH IMBIBE INHALE PERISH PUNISH VANISH CORRODE DESTROY DWINDLE ENGROSS EXHAUST SWALLOW CONTRIVE SQUANDER

(— IN LARGE QUANTITY) PUNISH

(— TOTALLY) KILL

(— VORACIOUSLY) HOG

CONSUMED ALL PAU DOWN BURNT SPENT COMBUST OUTWORN

CONSUMER MOUTH

(UNPRODUCTIVE —) CATERPILLAR

CONSUMING EATING SACRED BURNING FLAMING

CONSUMMATE END FINE FULL RIPE CLOSE IDEAL SHEER ARRANT EFFECT FINISH FULFIL RATIFY ACHIEVE CONSUME CROWNED FULFILL PERFECT PERFORM ABSOLUTE COMPLETE MERIDIAN THOROUGH

CONSUMMATION CROWN PERIOD UPSHOT

CONSUMPTION USE DECAY WASTE EXPENSE WASTING PHTHISIS SPENDING

(PREF.) PHTHISIO

CONSUMPTIVE LUNGY HECTIC PREDATORY

CONTACT ABUT JOIN KISS MEET SLED CROSS TOUCH TRUCK UNION ARRIVE IMPACT SYZYGY EPHAPSE HOLDING MEETING TACTION JUNCTION TANGENCY TOUCHING

(— BY RADIO) RAISE

(— OF TELEGRAPH KEY) ANVIL

(ELECTRICAL —) HUB HUBB POINT

(EVIL —) CONTAGION

(FLEETING —) BRUSH

(FORCIBLE —) IMPACT

(3-POINT —) OSCNODE

(PREF.) HAPT(O) THIGMO

CONTAGION POX TAINT VIRUS MIASMA POISON

CONTAGIOUS TAKING NOXIOUS SMITTLE CATCHING EPIDEMIC

CONTAIN RUN HAVE HOLD KEEP STEM STOW TAKE CARRY CHECK CLOSE COVER HOUSE EMBODY ENFOLD ENSEAM HARBOR RETAIN COMPILE EMBRACE ENCLOSE INCLUDE INVOLVE RECEIVE

SUBSUME SUSTAIN COMPRISE RESTRAIN

(PREF.) CHADA

CONTAINED IN

CONTAINER BAG BOX CAN CUP HAT JAR JUG KEG LUG NIN PAN POD POT TIN TUB URN VAT BAIL BOMB CAGE CASE CASK CRIB DISH DRUM EWER FILE FLAT JACK SACK SALT SILO SINK SKIP TANK TUBE VASE VIAL ALBUM BASIN BILLY CADDY CHEST CRATE CRUET CRUSE DEWAR EMPTY FLASK GLASS GOURD POUCH SCOOP SCRAY STAND STOOP STOUP BARREL BASKET BOTTLE BUCKET BUSHEL CARBOY CARTON CASTER CASTOR COOLER CRADLE DUSTER HAMPER HATBOX HOLDER INKPOT MAILER PICNIC RABBIT RIDDLE SHAKER WITJAR AEROSOL AMPULLA BANDBOX BLADDER CAPSULE COASTER COSTREL CRISPER FEEDBOX HANAPER HOLDALL INKWELL OILDRUM PACKAGE SEEDLIP SHIPPER SNIFTER SPOONER STEEPER CANISTER DECANTER DEMIJOHN ENVELOPE HOGSHEAD HONEYPOT INHOLDEN KNAPSACK PENTAGON PUNCHEON SLIPCASE RELIQUARY POCKETBOOK

(— FOR BEER) GROWLER

(— FOR BOBBINS) BUFFALO

(— FOR BRANDY) SNIFTER

(FOR COINS) BANK

(— FOR EXPLOSIVE CHARGE) CAP

(— FOR FISH) BASS

(— FOR GOLD DUST) CHAMMY

(— FOR HOLY OIL) STOCK

(— FOR LEFTOVER FOOD) DOGGYBAG DOGGIEBAG

(— FOR PLANTS) BAND

(— HUNG FROM OBI) INRO

(— IN WHICH TO HEAT DRUGS) COOKER

(— MADE OF HOLLOW LOG) GUM

(— OF ASSAYER) CUPEL

(COFFEE —) INSET

(DESSERT —) COUPE

(DRINK —) DOP

(EARTHENWARE —) STEAN

(FIRECLAY —) SETTER

(KITCHEN —) CANISTER

(RAILROAD —S) BUNKER

(SHELVED —) CABIN

(SHIPPING —) KIT

(SNUFF —) WEASAND

(TOBACCO —) SARATOGA

(VENTILATED —) CHIP

(5-GALLON —) JERICAN JERRICAN

(PL.) CONVEYER CONVEYOR

CONTAINING IN

(SUFF.) IC(AL)

CONTAMINATE FOUL HARM SLUR SMIT SOIL STAIN SULLY TAINT BEFOUL DEBASE DEFILE INFECT INJURE POISON ATTAINT CORRUPT DEBAUCH FLYBLOW POLLUTE TARNISH VITIATE DISHONOR

CONTAMINATED DIRTY DEGRADED INFECTED

CONTAMINATION INFECTION
TAINTMENT
(— IN GLASS) STONE
CONTE TALE CRAYON
CONTEMN HATE FLOUT SCORN
SPURN REJECT SLIGHT DESPISE
DISDAIN CONTEMPT INDIGNIFY
CONTEMPLATE FACE MUSE PLAN
SCAN VIEW DEIGN STUDY THINK
WEIGH BEHOLD DESIGN PONDER
REGARD SURVEY CHERISH
PROPOSE REFLECT CONSIDER
ENVISAGE ENVISION MEDITATE
CONTEMPLATION MUSE STUDY
DHYANA MUSING PRAYER REGARD
THEORY INSIGHT MOONING
REQUEST THEORIA PETITION
RECOLLECTION
(— OF PAST) RETROSPECT
RETROSPECTION
CONTEMPLATIVE BROODY
PENSIVE THEORIC STUDIOUS
CONTEMPORANEOUS COEVAL
LIVING MODERN CURRENT
EXISTING
CONTEMPORARY EQUAL COEVAL
FELLOW CURRENT PRESENT
YEALING EXISTENT
SIMULTANEOUS
CONTEMPT PRUT SCORN SHAME
SNEER SLIGHT CONTEMN DESPECT
DESPITE DISDAIN HETHING
MOCKERY DEFIANCE DERISION
DESPISAL DISGRACE MISPRIZE
MISPRISION OPPROBRIUM
(— FOR DANGER) TEMERITY
(— OF OPPOSITION) DEFIANCE
(ONE HELD IN —) FINK
CONTEMPTIBLE LOW BASE MEAN
POOR VILE BALLY CHEAP DIRTY
DUSTY LOUSY MANGY MUCKY
PETTY POCKY RUDDY SCALD
SORRY ABJECT BLOODY CRUDDY
GRUBBY MEASLY PALTRY SCABBY
SCUMMY SCURVY SHABBY SNOTTY
SORDID YELLOW BROKING
LIGHTLY PEEVISH PELTING PITIFUL
SCALLED SCORNED SHITTEN
SLAVISH SQUALID BAUBLING
BEGGARLY FRIPPERY INFAMOUS
INFERIOR PICAYUNE PITIABLE
PRECIOUS SNEAKING UNWORTHY
WRETCHED MISBEGOTTEN
(— PERSON) CRUD
(SUFF.) (— ONE) EEN EER
CONTEMPTIBLENESS BEGGARY
CONTEMPTUOUS SLIGHT SNEERY
SNOOTY HAUGHTY LIGHTLY
SLIGHTY SPITOUS ARROGANT
FLOUTING INSOLENT SCOFFING
SCORNFUL
CONTEND TUG VIE WAR WIN CAMP
COCK COPE DEAL FRAB KEMP
PLEA RACE WAGE ARGUE BANDY
BRAWL CHIDE CLAIM FIGHT FLITE
PRESS ASSERT BATTLE BICKER
BREAST BUCKLE BUFFET BUSTLE
COMBAT DEBATE DIFFER JOSTLE
JUSTLE MEDDLE OPPOSE PINGLE
REASON STRIVE BARGAIN
COMPETE CONTEST COUNTER
DISPUTE PROPUGN QUARREL
SCUFFLE STICKLE SUSTAIN

WRESTLE CONFLICT CONTRAST
CONTRIVE MAINTAIN MILITATE
SQUABBLE STRUGGLE
(— FOR) SUPPORT
CONTENDER ATHLETE STICKLER
CONTENT PAY CALM EASE GIST
GLAD PAID RATH SATE APPAY
HAPPY HUMOR RATHE SERVE
AMOUNT CUBAGE PLEASE
APPEASE CONTENU GRATIFY
PERFECT REPLETE SATIATE
SATISFY SUFFICE WILLING
BLISSFUL CAPACITY CONTINEU
WILCWEME
(—S OF SACK) BUDGET
(—S OF STOMACH) COOKIES
(CUBICAL —) VOLUME
(ENERGY —) STRENGTH
(HEAT —) ENTHALPY
(SUPERFICIAL —S) AREA
(PL.) LINING
CONTENTED COZY FAIN VAIN QUIET
SATED CONTENT PLEASED
CHEERFUL
CONTENTION WAR BAIT BATE
CASE FEUD PLEA RIOT TIFF TOIL
BROIL CHEST CLAIM STRUT BICKER
COMBAT DEBATE ESTRIF JANGLE
STRIFE CHIDING CONTEKE
CONTEST DISCORD DISPUTE
OPINION QUARREL RIVALRY
WRANGLE ARGUMENT CONFLICT
SQUABBLE STRUGGLE VARIANCE
COLLUCTATION
(VERBAL —) WORDS
CONTENTIOUS CROSS BATEFUL
PEEVISH PERVERSE BELLICOSE
CONTENTMENT EASE BLISS
HEAVEN PLEASURE SATISFACTION
CONTERMINOUS NEXT ADJACENT
FRONTIER PROXIMAL
CONTEST GO IT BEE FIX RUN SUE
TRY VIE AGON BOUT CAMP COPE
DUEL FEUD FRAY GAME HOLD
KEMP LAKE MART PULL RACE
SHOW SPAR TIFF TILT TURN YOKE
AGONY ARGUE BROIL CLASH
DERBY EVENT FIGHT MATCH PLATE
PRIZE RODEO ROLEO SCRUB
SPORT TRIAL WAGER ACTION
ADJURE AFFRAY BATTLE BISLEY
COMBAT DEBATE DEFEND FLIGHT
OPPOSE RESIST RUBBER SEESAW
STRIFE STRIVE TUSSLE YOKING
BARGAIN BRABBLE CLASSIC
COMPETE CONTECK CONTEND
DERAIGN DISPUTE GRAPPLE
PROTEST SHUTOUT TOURNEY
WARFARE ARGUMENT CONCOURS
CONFLICT DOGFIGHT HANDICAP
LITIGATE SKIRMISH SLUGFEST
STRIVING STRUGGLE WALKAWAY
WALKOVER PANCRATIUM
PENTATHLON
(— EASILY WON) LAUGHER
(— IN WORDS) SPAR
(— NARROWLY WON) SQUEAKER
(ATHLETIC —) AGON BIATHLON
(AUTOMOBILE — ON FROZEN
LAKE) ICEKHANA
(BEAUTY —) PAGEANT
(CLOSE —) DICE
(DRAWN —) TIE DRAW STALEMATE

(MOCK —) SCIAMACHY
(MOST IMPORTANT —)
SUPERBOWL
(RACING —) DRAG
(REAPING —) KEMP
(PREF.) MACHO
(SUFF.) AGONIST(IC) MACHIA
MACHY
CONTESTANT VIER RIVAL WAGER
PLAYER AGONIST ENTRANT
SCRATCH FINALIST PROSPECT
CONTIGUITY ADJACENCY
CONFINITY IMMEDIACY
CONTIGUOUS NEAR NEXT NIGH
NEARBY TANGENT ABUTTING
ADJACENT TOUCHING
CONTINENT ASIA MASS PORE
SOBER AFRICA CHASTE EUROPE
CONTENT CAPACITY MAINLAND
MODERATE ABSTINENT
(VANISHED —) LEMURIA
CONTINGENCY BOOK CASE EVENT
CHANCE ADJUNCT CONTACT
VENTURE ACCIDENT CASUALTY
FORTUITY INCIDENT JUNCTURE
PROSPECT
CONTINGENT TROOP CASUAL
CHANCE DOUBTFUL EVENTUAL
INCHOATE POSSIBLE TOUCHING
ACCIDENTAL DELEGATION
CONTINUAL STILL HOURLY
ABIDING ENDLESS ETERNAL
LASTING REGULAR UNDYING
UNIFORM CONSTANT ENDURING
UNBROKEN
CONTINUALLY AY AYE EVER STILL
ALWAYS EVERLY HOURLY STEADY
ENDLESS ETERNAL FOREVER
MINUTELY
CONTINUANCE STAY WHEN DELAY
LEASE SEQUEL ABIDING DURANCE
LASTING ABIDANCE DURATION
STANDING SURVIVAL
CONTINUANT OPEN LIQUID
DURATIVE
CONTINUATION SEQUEL
CONTANGO DURATION
PROLONGATION PERSEVERATION
(— OF DOUBLET) BASQUE
CONTINUE BE DO ABY SUE ABYE
BIDE DURE HOLD JUMP KEEP LAST
LIVE STAY TIDE ABIDE CARRY EXIST
PERGE STICK UNITE ABEGGE
BELEVE ENDURE EXTEND PURSUE
REMAIN RESUME BELEAVE
CONNECT CONTUNE PERSIST
PROCEED PROLONG SUBSIST
SURVIVE SUSTAIN PROTRACT
(— UNALTERED) TARRY
CONTINUED STILL SERIAL CHRONIC
CONSTANT
CONTINUING ABIDING DURARI F
LASTING DURATIVE PERPETUAL
PERSISTENT OUTSTANDING
(— FOR LONG TIME) CHRONIC
(— TO BE) YET
CONTINUITY TRACT SCRIPT
COHESION SCENARIO CONTINUUM
(PREF.) SYNECHIA
CONTINUOUS RUN EVEN ANEND
EIDENT ENTIRE EYDENT STEADY
CHRONIC ENDLESS RUNNING

UNBROKEN PERENNIAL
PERPETUAL
CONTINUOUSLY AWAY EVER FAST
ANEND OUTRIGHT
CONTORT WRY BEND COIL CURL
TURN WARP GNARL SCREW TWIST
WREST CRINGE DEFORM WRITHE
DISTORT PERVERT SQUINCH
WREATHE OBVOLUTE
CONTORTED WRY WRIED KNOTTY
CRISPED KNOTTED SCREWED
WRITHEN OBVOLUTE
CONTORTION SCREW STITCH
WRITHE MURGEON WORKING
CONTOUR FORM LINE CURVE
GRAPH SHAPE SWEEP AMOEBA
FIGURE OUTLINE PROFILE
CARTOUCH CONTORNO
MANDORLA PLANFORM
TOURNURE
(— ON SHIP) HANCE
CONTRA CONTRE AGAINST
COUNTER OPPOSED
CONTRABAND HOT GOODS
ILLEGAL ILLICIT SMUGGLED
UNLAWFUL
CONTRABASS BASS OCTOBASS
CONTRACEPTIVE SHEATH MINIPILL
(ORAL —) PILL
CONTRACT GET BOND DRAW FARM
FORM HALE KNIT PACT SALE TACK
CATCH CLOSE COACT COUCH
CRAMP FEVER INCUR LEASE LIMIT
NEXUM PINCH SHRUG SNURP
CARTEL COCKLE COMMIT CRINGE
ENGAGE FUTURE GATHER HIRING
INDENT LESSEN MUTUUM
NARROW PIGNUS PLEDGE POLICY
PROMPT PUCKER REDUCE SHRIMP
SHRINK SUBLET TREATY ABRIDGE
APPALTO BARGAIN BUMMERY
CHARTER COMPACT CRIMPLE
CRUMPLE CURTAIL DEFLATE
FIDUCIA MANDATE PROMISE
SCRUNCH SHORTEN SHRIVEL
SOCIETY WRINKLE ASSIENTO
BOTTOMRY CONDENSE COVENANT
HANDFAST HARDNESS LOCATION
RESTRICT STEELBOW STRAITEN
SYNGRAPH ABBREVIATE
OBLIGATION
(— BROW) FROWN
(— INTO WRINKLES) KNIT
(BRIDGE —) SOLO AUCTION
(MARRIAGE —) KETUBA AFFIANCE
HANDFAST BETROTHAL SPONSALIA
CONTRACTED BOXY CRAMP
BOOKED ASTRICT INGROWN
INSULAR SCREWED CONTRACT
CONTRACTILITY MOTILITY
CONTRACTION HM ANT NIP TIC TIS
AINT CANT ISNT KNIT MAAM WONT
CRAMP HADNT HASNT NISUS
SPASM CRASIS GATHER INTAKE
MUSTNT SHRINK TWITCH ELISION
EPITOME WOULDNT APNEUSIS
TRACTION ABRIDGMENT
ABRIDGEMENT
(— OF HEART) SYSTOLE
(— OF SYLLABLES) SYNIZESIS
(PL.) TREPPE
CONTRACTOR KHOT BUTTY
BUILDER REMOVER SUPPLIER

CONTRADICT DENY BELIE CROSS REBUT FORBID IMPUGN NEGATE OPPOSE RECANT REFUTE THREAP COUNTER GAINSAY REVERSE WITHSAY CONTRARY DISPROVE DOWNFACE NEGATIVE OUTSTAND

CONTRADICTION CLASH DENIAL DEMENTI PARADOX WITHSAW ANTILOGY ANTIMONY ANTILOQUY
(**LUDICROUS —**) BULL

CONTRADICTORY OPPOSE ANTINOME OPPOSITE THWARTING

CONTRAPTION RIG TOOL DEVICE DOODAD GADGET JIGGER CONCERN MACHINE DOOHICKEY HOOTNANNY

CONTRARIETY DISCORD

CONTRARILY BACKWARD CRISSCROSS

CONTRARIWISE CONTRA CONTRARY

CONTRARY BALKY CROSS KICKY SNIVY AVERSE CONTRA CUSSED ORNERY SNIVEY THRAWN ADVERSE COUNTER CRABBED FROWARD HOSTILE INVERSE OPPOSED PEEVISH RESTIVE REVERSE STROPPY WAYWARD ABSONANT ANTIPODE CAPTIOUS CONTRAIR INIMICAL OPPOSITE PERVERSE PETULANT SINGULAR ABHORRENT
(**— EXPRESSION**) OXYMORON
(**— TO**) BESIDE AGAINST ATHWART
(**— TO HAPPINESS**) ILL
(**— TO REASON**) SILLY ABSONANT
(PREF.) CONTRA COUNTER DIS RETRO

CONTRAST CLASH STRIFE COMPARE CONTEND DISCORD ANTIMONY DIVISION DYNAMICS OPPOSITE

CONTRASTING
(PREF.) CONTRA

CONTRAVENE DEFY DENY HINDER OPPOSE THWART DISPUTE VIOLATE INFRINGE OBSTRUCT

CONTRAVENTION SIN VICE CRIME BREACH OFFENSE

CONTRETEMPS SLIP BONER HITCH MISHAP SCRAPE ACCIDENT INCIDENT

CONTRIBUTE AID ANTE FORK GIVE HELP MAKE TEND CAUSE ENTER GROUT PUTUP SERVE ASSIST BESTOW CONCUR CONFER DONATE PUNGLE RENDER SUPPLY TENDER ANIMATE CONDUCE FURNISH FURTHER PROVIDE THROWIN

CONTRIBUTING ACCESSORY

CONTRIBUTION BIT SUM TAX ALMS BOON GIFT SCOT SHOT ESSAY INPUT SHARE IMPOST SYMBOL ARTICLE LARGESS PAYMENT PRESENT RENEWAL WRITING DONATION EXACTION OFFERING ROMESHOT
(**CHURCH —**) TITHE
(**LITERARY —**) PAPER
(**SMALL —**) MITE

CONTRITE WORN SORRY HUMBLE RUEFUL PENITENT SORROWFUL

CONTRITION SORE SORROW PENANCE PENITENCE

CONTRIVANCE (ALSO SEE DEVICE) ART BOW FLY GIN JET JIG LEG DROP GEAR HARP JACK KITE LURE PAGE PLAN PLOT RASP REED TOOL ALARM BRAKE CARRY CHECK DOLLY DRAFT FLOAT FRAME GUIDE HICKY KNACK MIXER QUIPU SHIFT SNARE STOCK ANCHOR DAMPER DECEIT DESIGN DEVICE DOCTOR DOLLIE ENGINE FABRIC FANGLE GABION GADGET GIMBAL HANGER HARROW HEATER HICKEY HOLDER JIGGER JINKER MARKER MORTAR MUZZLE POLICY RATTLE SCHEME SLUICE SPIDER TEASEL WEIGHT WHEEZE WINDAS WRENCH BOLSTER CLEANER CLEARER CONCERN COUPLER CUNNING DINGBAT DRAUGHT FICTION FISHWAY HUMIDOR KNOCKER MACHINE PAGEANT PROJECT REDUCER ROASTER SCRAPER SHEBANG SPANNER STOPPER TOASTER TRIPPER VOLVELL ADAPTION ARTIFICE CROTCHET DUTCHMAN EUPYRION FAKEMENT FORECAST GOVERNOR INDUSTRY MOLITION OXIDATOR REGISTER RESOURCE SCISSORS SQUEEZER SUBTLETY WITCRAFT

CONTRIVE GET LAY BREW CAST DRAW FIND FIRK MAKE PLAN PLOT WORK FRAME FUDGE HATCH SHAPE STAGE WEAVE AFFORD DESIGN DEVISE DIVINE ENGINE FIGURE INVENT MANAGE SCHEME WANGLE ACHIEVE AGITATE COMMENT COMPASS CONCOCT CONJURE CONSULT CONTEND FASHION IMAGINE MACHINE PROCURE PROJECT REPAREL CONSPIRE ENGINEER FORECAST INTRIGUE PURCHASE

CONTRIVED PAT SLICK STAGED TIMBERED

CONTRIVER DAEDAL DAEDALUS ENGINEER

CONTRIVING FASHION SCHEMERY

CONTROL BIT LAP LAW MAN POT RUN CONN CURB EGIS GRIP HAND HANK HAVE HOLD REDE REIN RULE STAY SWAY WIND AEGIS BOOST CHARM CHECK COACT DAUNT DUMMY GRASP GUIDE LEASH ORDER POWER STEER SWING THEAT TREAT TUTOR VERGE WIELD BANDON BRIDLE CHARGE CLUTCH COERCE CORNER DANGER DIRECT EMPERY GOVERN HANDLE MANAGE POCKET TEMPER AMENAGE COMMAND CONDUCT CONTAIN CUSTODY FORBEAR MASTERY MONITOR QUALIFY STRINGS COACTION DOMINATE DOMINIUM IMPERIUM MODERATE REGULATE SERVOTAB POSSESSION
(**— A BULL**) MANDAR
(**— OF RESOURCES**) HUSBANDRY
(**— OVER WIFE**) MANUS
(**ABSOLUTE —**) BECK

(**FIRE —**) BLANKET
(**GET EXCLUSIVE — OF**) SEWUP
(**GOVERNMENT —**) DIRIGISM SQUADRISM
(**MANUAL —**) JOYSTICK
(**NONCLERICAL —**) LAICISM LAICITY
(**OUT OF —**) RUNAWAY
(**VOLUME —**) GAIN

CONTROLLED STEADY SERVILE CONTAINED

CONTROLLER FENCER GERENT MASTER STARTER
(**SPEED —**) GOVERNOR RHEOCRAT

CONTROLLING MASTER LEADING DOMINANT HEGEMONIC

CONTROVERSIAL ERISTIC POLEMIC

CONTROVERSIALIST ERISTIC POLEMIC DISPUTANT GLADIATOR

CONTROVERSY FLAP PLEA SPAT SUIT CHEST FUROR BATTLE COMBAT DEBATE FURORE HASSEL HASSLE HOORAH HURRAH STRIFE TUSSLE DISPUTE POLEMIC QUARREL WRANGLE ARGUMENT TRAVERSE CONTENTION
(**ART OF —**) POLEMICS

CONTROVERT DENY FACE MOOT ARGUE DEBATE DEFEND OPPOSE OPPUGN REFUTE CONTEST DISPUTE GAINSAY DISPROVE

CONTUMACIOUS UNRULY RIOTOUS CONTUMAX INSOLENT MUTINOUS PERVERSE STUBBORN

CONTUMELY ABUSE SCORN INSULT CONTECK DISDAIN REPROOF UPBRAID CONTEMPT RUDENESS

CONTUSE BEAT POUND THUMP BRUISE INJURE SQUEEZE

CONTUSION POUND BRUISE

CONUNDRUM PUN WHIM GUESS ENIGMA PUZZLE RIDDLE CONCEIT CROTCHET

CONURE ARATINGA

CONVALESCE MEND GUARISH RECOVER

CONVENANCE FORM

CONVENE SIT CALL HOLD MEET UNITE GATHER MUSTER SUMMON CONVENT CONVOKE ASSEMBLE CONVERGE

CONVENIENCE GAIN BEHOOF URINAL LEISURE COMMODITY

CONVENIENT FIT GAIN HEND NIGH HANDY HENDE READY ATHAND CLEVER FITTED PROPER SUITED USEFUL ADAPTED AVENANT COMMODE HELPFUL BECOMING EXPEDITE SUITABLE OPPORTUNE COMMODIOUS

CONVENIENTLY WELL HANDILY CLEVERLY

CONVENT ABBEY HOUSE TEKKE TEKYA CENOBY COVENT FRIARY PRIORY MEETING RECLUSE CLOISTER LAMASERY MOTHERHOUSE

CONVENTION DIET FEIS FORM MISE RULE TABU SYNOD TABOO USAGE CARTEL CAUCUS CUSTOM TREATY DECORUM MEETING ASSEMBLY ASSIENTO CONCLAVE

CONGRESS CONTRACT COVENANT PRACTICE PRECEDENT
(**LONG-ESTABLISHED —**) TRADITION
(**SET OF —S**) PROTOCOL
(**STAGE —**) ASIDE
(PL.) DECENCIES

CONVENTIONAL MORE NOMIC RIGHT TRITE USUAL DECENT FORMAL MODISH PROPER CORRECT POMPIER REGULAR ACADEMIC ACCEPTED COPYBOOK ORTHODOX CUSTOMARY
(**RIGIDLY —**) UPTIGHT

CONVENTIONALITY FORM ACADEMISM FORMALITY GRUNDYISM

CONVENTIONALIZE STYLIZE

CONVERGE JOIN MEET FOCUS CONCUR CORNER CONNIVE DESCEND APPROACH FOCALIZE

CONVERSANT ADEPT BUSIED EXPERT VERSED SKILLED FAMILIAR OCCUPIED

CONVERSATION RAP SAY CALL CHAT CHIN RUNE TALE TALK BOARD CRACK PROSE CACKLE CONFAB DEVICE GOSSIP PARLEY POWWOW SPEECH YABBER CEILIDH COMMUNE CONDUCT PALAVER PURPOSE BACKCHAT BEHAVIOR CAUSERIE CHITCHAT COLLOGUE COLLOQUY DIALOGUE GIFFGAFF HARANGUE PARLANCE QUESTION COLLOCUTION
(**— BETWEEN WHALERS**) GAM
(**LIGHT —**) SMALLTALK

CONVERSATIONALIST TALKER CAUSEUR

CONVERSE CHAT CHIN LIVE MOVE TALK DWELL SPEAK CACKLE COMMON CONFER DEVISE HOMILY PARLEY REASON COMMUNE CONVERT DISCUSS OBVERSE PROPOSE REVERSE COLLOQUE EXCHANGE OPPOSITE QUESTION

CONVERSION CHANGE EXCHANGE METRICATION PROSELYTISM
(**— INTO VAPOR**) FLASH
(**— OF IRON**) FINING

CONVERT TAW TURN WEND ALTER AMEND APPLY MAULA RENEW CHANGE DECODE DETECT DIRECT MAWALI NOVICE SHAIKH SOUPER COMMUTE CONCOCT RESOLVE RESTORE REVERSE ACTIVATE CONVERSE DISCIPLE NEOPHYTE PERSUADE PROSELYTE
(**— COTTON**) LAP
(**— INTO CASH**) NEGOTIATE
(**— INTO LEATHER**) TAN TAW
(**— INTO LIQUID**) BREW
(**— INTO MONEY**) REALIZE
(**— INTO PELLETS**) PRILL
(**— INTO SOAP**) SAPONIFY
(**— INTO STEEL**) ACIERATE
(**— INTO STONE**) LAPIDIFY
(**— INTO VAPOR**) EVAPORATE
(**— SOAP**) CLOSE
(**— TO CARBON**) CHAR
(**— TO ISLAM**) SHEIK

CONVERTER ROTARY SELECTOR

CONVERTIBLE AUTO DROPHEAD
(**— CAR**) RAGTOP

CONVERTIPLANE STOL
CONVEX BOWED ARCHED CAMBER CURVED BULGING EMBOWED GIBBOUS ROUNDED
CONVEXITY CAMBER ARCUATION
CONVEY JAG BEAR BOOK CART CEDE DEED DUCT HAVE LEAD MEAN PASS SEND SIGN TAKE TOTE WAIN WILL BRING CARRY DRIVE FETCH GRANT GUIDE HURRY STEAL ARRIVE ASSIGN CONVOY DEDUCE DELATE DEMISE DEVISE ELOIGN GIGGIT IMPART IMPORT REMOVE YMMOTE AUCTION CHANNEL CHARIOT CHARTER CONDUCT DELIVER DERRICK DISPONE DISPOSE LIGHTER RESTORE ALIENATE BEQUEATH DESCRIBE TRANSFER TRANSMIT
  (— AN ESTATE) DEMISE
  (— BY ALLUSION) IMPLY
  (— FORCIBLY) HUSTLE
  (— HORIZONTALLY) ADVECT
  (— LEGALLY) DEED GRANT LEASE DEMISE ELOIGN DISPONE
  (— NEARER) BRING
  (— SECRETLY) CRIM
CONVEYANCE BUS CAR AUTO CART DEED DRAG GIFT LOAD SLED TAXI TRAM GRANT SEDAN STAGE TAUGA THEFT TRAIN WAGON DEMISE JINGLE CHARTER CONDUCT COURIER MACHINE RATTLER TRAILER TRAJECT TRANSIT TROLLEY VECTURE VEHICLE WAFTAGE CARRIAGE CARRYING CONVEYAL DELATION FERRIAGE STEALING TRANSFER
CONVEYOR LIFT WORM DRAPER LADDER SHAKER CARRIER CREEPER HURRIER SCRAPER CAROUSEL CONVEYER ELEVATOR
CONVICT LAG CAST FIND STAR ARGUE EXILE FELON LIFER PROVE TAINT ATTAIN FORCAT LAGGER TERMER TRUSTY APPROVE ATTAINT CAPTIVE CONDEMN CULPRIT EXPIREE IMPEACH REPROVE CRIMINAL JAILBIRD PRISONER REDARGUE SENTENCE
CONVICT FISH MANINI HINALEA
CONVICTION CREDO CREED DOGMA FAITH HEART SENSE TAINT TENET BELIEF CREDIT CONCERN OPINION SENTENCE
CONVINCE SELL EVICT FETCH ASSURE EVINCE REPROVE RESOLVE SATISFY CONCLUDE
  (— OF ERROR) CONVICT
CONVINCED FIRM SOLD SURE CERTAIN ABSOLUTE POSITIVE
CONVINCING SOUND VALID COGENT POTENT EVIDENT TELLING FORCIBLE LUCULENT POWERFUL PREGNANT
CONVIVIAL GAY BOON FESTAL GENIAL JOVIAL SOCIAL FESTIVE HOLIDAY JOCULAR REVELING ANACREONTIC
CONVIVIALITY REVEL FESTIVAL MERRYMAKING
CONVOCATION DIET SYNOD CALLING COUNCIL MEETING SUMMONS ASSEMBLY CONGRESS VOCATION
CONVOKE CALL HOLD GATHER SUMMON CONVENE ASSEMBLE
CONVOLUTE COIL ROLL WIND TWIST TANGLE WRITHE CONTORT INVOLUTE OBVOLUTE
CONVOLUTED GYRATE
CONVOLUTION COIL CURL FOLD TURN WRAP GYRUS SWIRL TWINE TWIRL TWIST WHORL CUNEUS GYROMA VOLUME VOLUTION
CONVOLUTIONAL SNAKY
CONVOLVE TURN WIND TWIST ENFOLD ENWRAP INFOLD WRITHE
CONVOLVULUS BINDWEED SCAMMONY
CONVOY LEAD WAFT CARRY GUARD GUIDE PILOT TRADE WATCH ATTEND CONVEY ESCORT MANAGE CONDUCT WAFTAGE SAFEGUARD
CONVULSE ROCK STIR SHAKE EXCITE AGITATE DISTURB
CONVULSION FIT SHRUG SPASM THROE ATTACK TUMULT UPROAR CONVULSE LAUGHTER PAROXYSM COMMOTION
CONVULSIVE FITFUL EPILEPTIC
CONY DAS HARE PIKA CONEY CUNNY DAMAN DASSY GANAM HUTIA HYRAX BURBOT CONEEN DASSIE GAZABO GAZEBO RABBIT WABBER ASHKOKO BOOMDAS HYRACID KLIPDAS HYRACOID KLIPDACH
COO CROO CURR WOOT CHIRR CHIZZ CROOD MURMUR CROODLE CRUDDLE
COOEE BIRD KOEL
COOK DO FIX FRY BAKE BOIL CHEF COCT FAKE MAKE SEAR STEW BROIL CUIRE CUSIE FRIZZ GRILL POACH ROAST SCALD SHIRR STEAM SWING BRAISE CODDLE COOKIE COOPER DECOCT DIGEST PORTER SAUTEE SEETHE SIMMER ARTISTE BROILER FRIZZLE GRIDDLE PASTLER PERCOCT POTAGER PREPARE PROCESS SERVANT SMOTHER SWAMPER BAWARCHI BOBACHEE COCINERO CUSINERO GRILLADE MAGIRIST PASTERER MICROWAVE
  (— IN BOILING LIQUID) POACH
  (— IN MICROWAVE) ZAP NUKE
  (— TOO LONG) OVERDO
  (— UP) BUILD
  (BULL —) FLUNKY FLUNKEY GREASER
  (SHIP'S —) DOCTOR SLUSHY SKILLET SLUSHER
  (PREF.) MAGIRO
COOKED DONE FRIED BOILED
  (— BY BOILING) AUBLEU
  (— IN CLAY OVEN) TANDOORI
  (— IN EARTHENWARE OVEN) TANDOORI
  (— IN EARTHEWARE OVEN) TANDOORI
  (— WITH SUGAR) CANDIED
  (PREF.) COCTO
COOKEE FLUNKY HASHER FLUNKEY
COOKER CANNER HAYBOX DIGESTER
COOKERY CURY CUISINE KITCHEN MAGIRICS
COOKHOUSE GALLEY
COOKIE CAKE OREO ROCK SNAP COOKY HERMIT KIPFEL SPRITZ BISCUIT BROWNIE OATCAKE PLACENT BISCOTTO CRESCENT SEEDCAKE
  (KIND OF —) FORTUNE
COOKING COCTION
  (— UTENSIL) WOK
  (INDIAN —) TANDOORI
  (STYLE OF —) HUNAN
COOKING KIND OF —) TEXMEX
COOKROOM CUDDY
COOKWARE (KIND OF —) TEFLON
COOL AIR FAN HEP HIP ICE RAD CALM COLD DOWN KEEL AKELE ALGID ALLAY ALOOF CHILL EVENT FRESH GELID NERVY QUEEL SOBER STAID WHOLE AIRISH CALLER CHILLY PLACID QUENCH SEDATE SERENE TEMPER UNWARM COOLISH DISTANT RADICAL REFROID UNMOVED CARELESS CAUTIOUS COMPOSED MITIGATE MODERATE TRANQUIL NERVELESS POSSESSED NONCHALANT UNFLAPPABLE
  (— IN WATER) SLACK SLACKEN
  (— OF EVENING) SERENE
  (— OFF) FAN
  (BLOW ONE'S —) LOSEIT
COOLED COLD FRAPPE
COOLER PEN COLA ICER JAIL KEEL OLLA SINK POKEY ICEBOX LOCKUP PRISON SINKER KEELFAT ALCOGENE
  (WINE —) GLACIER
COOLIE CHANGAR MADRASI MAZDOOR
COOLING REFRESHING
COOLNESS COOL FROST NERVE SWALE APLOMB PHLEGM SERENITY SANGFROID
COOM CULM GAUM SMUT SOOT COOMB GRIME SLACK
COONTIE SAGO ZAMIA COMPTIE
COOP COT CUB CUP MEW PEN POT RIP CAGE COOB COTE JAIL CRAMP HUTCH BASKET CORRAL CONFINE
  (— UP) PEN IMMEW INCOUP
  (HEN —) CAVEY CAVIE BARTON
COOPER BUNGS COPER COWPER HEADER HOOPER TUBBER TUBBIE TUBMAN
COOPERATE HAND TEND AGREE COACT UNITE CONCUR COMBINE CONDUCE CONNIVE COADJUTE CONSPIRE
COOPERATION SOCIETY COURTESY TEAMWORK
COOPERATIVE COOP ARTEL SOCIAL SYNERGIC
  (RUSSIAN—) ARTEL
  (SOVIET—) ARTEL
  (SOVIET —) ARTEL
CO-OPT ABSORB
COORDINATE MESH SINE ADAPT EQUAL ADJUST ARRANGE SYNTONY ABSCISSA CLASSIFY ENSEMBLE
COORDINATION BOND SKILL HARMONY LIAISON
COORG KADAGA
COOT CUIT DUCK RAIL QUEET SMYTH BELTIE GORHEN PELICK SCOTER HENBILL LOBIPED PULLDOO LOBEFOOT RAILBIRD SWAMPHEN
COP BAG NAB ROB BANK BLOW BULL HEAD HEAP JOHN LIFT PILE TRAP TUBE ADMIT CATCH CREST FILCH MOUNT QUILL SHOCK SNARE STEAL STOCK SWIPE BOBBIN COPPIN PEELER SPIDER STRIKE CAPTURE
  (— OUT) EVADE
COPA YAYA COPITA
COPAL BOEA LOBA ANIME CONGO KAURI KAURY RESIN COWRIE DAMMAR CHAKAZI
COPE VIE WAR CAPE DUTY FACE LIFT MEET CAPPA CLOAK COVER DRESS EQUAL FIGHT MATCH NOTCH RIVAL VAULT WIELD BARTER CANOPY CHAPEL COMBAT MANTEL MUZZLE OPPOSE SEMBLE STRIKE STRIVE ANABATA CHLAMYS CONTEND CONTEST GRAPPLE MANDYAS PLUVIAL COMPLETE EXCHANGE FACTABLE SEMICOPE STRUGGLE VESTMENT
COPEHAN WINTUN
COPEPOD CALANID CAYENNE DIAPTOMID
COPIAPITE MISY MISSY IHLEITE
COPIER COPIST SCRIBE JOHNSONIAN
COPING CAP COPE FLUE SKEW CORDON CAPSTONE FACTABLE
COPING STONE TABLET TABLING
COPIOUS FREE FULL GOOD LUSH RANK RICH AMPLE LARGE FLUENT LAVISH DIFFUSE FLOWING FULSOME LENGTHY PROFUSE REPLETE TEEMING UBEROUS ABUNDANT AFFLUENT FRUITFUL GENEROUS NUMEROUS PLENTIFUL
COPIOUSNESS COPY PLENTY
COPPER AES COP BULL CENT BOBBY METAL PENNY VENUS CUPRUM PEELER VELLON BLISTER CARNELIAN
  (GILDED —) VERMEIL
  (OF —) AEN
  (PREF.) CHALC(O) CHALK(O) CUPR(I)(O)
  (SUFF.) CHALCITE
COPPERAS COPEROSE INKSTONE COQUIMBITE
COPPERHEAD REDEYE MOCCASIN
COPPERSMITH TINKERBIRD
COPPER SULFATE BLUESTONE
COPPER SULFIDE FERRETTO COVELLINE COVELLITE
COPPERY CUPREOUS
COPPICE COP BROW WOOD COPPY COPSE FIRTH FRITH GROVE COVERT FOREST GROWTH SPROUT THICKET ARBUSTUM
  (SUFF.) DRYMIUM

COPREUS (FATHER OF —) PELOPS
(HORSE OF —) ARION
(MOTHER OF —) HIPPODAMIA
COPSE CUT HAG HASP HEWT HOLT
MOTT SHAW TRIM DROKE HURST
CLEVIS SPINNY COPPICE
LOWWOOD SHACKLE SPINNEY
ARBUSTUM COPEWOOD
COPULA BAND LINK UNION
COPULATE RUT BULL LINE RIDE
COVER MOUNT SERVE TREAD
GENDER
COPY APE CALK CAST ECHO EDIT
LOAD MIME MOCK NICK TEXT
DITTO DUMMY GROSS IMAGE
MIMIC MODEL PRINT REVIE STICK
STUFF TRACE XEROX CALQUE
DOUBLE ECTYPE EFFIGY FILLER
FLIMSY FOLLOW MATTER RECORD
REFLEX SAMPLE SHADOW EDITION
EMULATE ENGROSS ESTREAT
EXTRACT IMITATE PATTERN
REDRAFT REPLICA REPRINT
RUBBING TRACING VIDIMUS
APOGRAPH AUTOTYPE EXEMPLAR
EXSCRIBE EXSCRIPT KNOCKOFF
LIKENESS MANIFOLD POROTYPE
PORTRAIT RESEMBLE SPECIMEN
MICROCOPY MINIATURE
PHOTOSTAT
(— EDITOR) SLOT
(— ILLEGALLY) PIRATE
(— IN COMPUTER) DUMP
(— OF DOCUMENT) EXTRACT
PROTOCOL
(— OF DRESS) FORD
(DUPLICATE — OF PROGRAM)
BACKUP
(ENLARGED —) MACROCOPY
(EXACT —) TENOR
(FIRST —) DRAFT
(LITERARY —) STUFF
(MAKE A — OF) CLONE
(PRINTING —) KILL BOGUS
(SMALL —) MINATURE
(UNREMUNERATIVE —) LEAN
(WORTHLESS —) BALAAM
(XEROX —) REPRO
COPYING MIMICRY INSINUATION
COPYIST COPIER PENMAN SCRIBE
COPYCAT SCRIVENER
COPYREAD EDIT SUBEDIT
COQUET TOY VAMP COPPY DALLY
FLIRT TRIFLE BLINKER CELIMENE
COQUETRY AGACERIE
COQUETTE TOYER
COQUILLE SHELL
COQUINA DONAX
CORA NAYARIT
(HUSBAND OF —) ALONZO
CORACIIFORM NONPASSERINE
CORACLE SCOW CURAGH CURRACH
CURRANE
CORAL RED PINK AKORI BLOOD
POLYP ALCYON PALULE PORITE
FUNGIAN OCULINA ACROPORE
ASTRAEAN CORALLUM FAVOSITE
POLYPITE STAGHORN TUBIPORE
ZOOPHYTE MADREPORE
MILLEPORE
CORAL BEAN SOPHORA FRIJOLILLO
CORAL-BELLS HEUCHERA
CORALBERRY BUCKBUSH

CORALFISH DOLLFISH
CORALROOT ORCHID CRAWLEY
CORAL SNAKE ELAPID ROLLER
ELAPOID SCYTALE
CORAL TREE GABGAB ERYTHRINA
CORBEIL PANNIER
CORBEL KNOT ANCON CORBET
TIMBER BRAGGER RESPOND
CARTOUCH SPRINGER
CORBELING SQUINCH
CORBIESTEP CATSTEP CROWSTEP
CORCIR CORKE ARCHIL CORKER
ORCHIL ARCHILLA
CORD AEA RIB AGAL BAND BIND
BOND FILE LACE LASH LINE ROPE
WELT BRAID CHORD FUNIS GUARD
LEASH LIGNE MATCH NERVE
OLONA TWINE TWIST BINDER
BOBBIN BRIDLE BUNGEE CATGUT
CHORDA CORDON FIADOR GIRDLE
LASHER LISERE RACHIS SENNET
STRING TENDON TOGGLE
AMENTUM BOWYANG BULLION
CORDING FUNICLE LANIARD
LANYARD MACRAME SEAMING
SEIZING SKIRREH TIEBACK
URACHUS BELLPULL CHENILLE
DRAWCORD HAIRLINE SHOELACE
WHIPCORD
(— AROUND BOWSTRING) SERVING
(— FOR PIPING) BOBBIN
(— OF CANDLENUT BARK) AEA
(CROCHETING —) CORDE
(ELASTIC —) BUNGEE
(ELECTRIC —) FLEX
(EMBROIDERY —) ARRASENE
(FACE —) RANK
(FRINGED —) LLAUTU
(HAMMOCK —S) CLEW
(HAWK'S —) CREANCE
(KIND OF —) RIP
(MASON'S —) SKIRREH
(ORNAMENTED —) AGLET AIGLET
(PARACHUTE —) SHROUD
(SACRED —) KUSTI
(SPINAL —) EON AEON NUKE
(TWISTED —) TORSADE
(PL.) PANTS
(PREF.) CHORD(O)
CORDAGE DA COIR ERUC FERU
HEMP IMBE JUTE KYAR ROPE
HAMBER SENNIT RIGGING
(LENGTH OF —) CATENARY
CORDATE HEARTED
CORDED TIED JETTED REPPED
RIBBED WELTED TWILLED
CORDELIA (SISTER OF —) REGAN
COR-DE-NUIT PASTORITA
CORDER RUFFER
CORDIAL REAL WARM CREAM
ARDENT CASSIS CLOVES DEVOUT
ELIXIR GENIAL HEARTY PASTIS
PERSICO RATAFIA ROSOLIO
SINCERE ZEALOUS ANISETTE
FRIENDLY GRACIOUS PERSICOT
VIGOROUS BENEDICTINE
(NOT —) DISTANT STANDOFF
(PL.) SWEETS
CORDIERITE IOLITE FAHLUNITE
CORDITE (INVENTOR OF —) ABEL
CORDON BLEU BENGALEE
CORDONNET CRESCENT

CORDUROOY DUROY
CORDWOOD BODYWOOD
CORE AME COB HUB NUT BONE
COKE COLK GIST KNOT NAVE PITH
BLOCK FOCUS HEART NOWSE
RUMPF SPOOL BARREL CENTER
CENTRE HEATER KERNEL MATRIX
MIDDLE NODULE POCKET STAPLE
CENTRUM CHEMISE COMPANY
CORNCOB ESSENCE NUCLEUS
FILAMENT HEARTING
(— OF COAL) STOCK
(— OF COLUMN) BELL HEART
(— OF CRICKET BALL) QUILT
(— OF LOG) PITH
(— OF MOLD) NOWEL
(EARTH'S HYPOTHETICAL —) NIFE
(WATER —) GLASSINESS
CORE ARBOR STALK
COREE CORANINE
CORELIGIONIST BROTHER
COREMIUM SYNEMA SYNNEMA
COREOPSIS TICKSEED TICKWEED
LEPTOSYNE
CORF TUB CAGE CAWF COFF CORB
SKIP CREEL BASKET DOSSER
CORFU CORCYRA KERKYRA
SCHERIA
CORGI CARDIGAN PEMBROKE
CORIANDER (— LEAVES) CILANTRO
CORIOLANUS (AUTHOR OF —)
SHAKESPEARE
(CHARACTER IN —) CAIUS TITUS
BRUTUS JUNIUS TULLUS LARTIUS
MARCIUS VALERIA AUFIDIUS
COMINIUS MENENIUS SICINIUS
VIRGILIA VOLUMNIA
CORIUM CUTIS DERMA LAYER
DERMIS
CORK BUNG PLUG FLOAT SHIVE
SUBER BOBBER BOUCHON
CRINKLE PHELLEM SOBERIN
STOPPER STOPPLE
(PREF.) PHELL(O) SUBERI
CORKED BOUCHE
CORKER LULU ONER WHIZ BEAUT
DILLY RAKER WHIZZ CUTTER
DOOZER HUMDINGER
CORKSCREW WORMER
CORKWING CONNER GOLDFINNY
CORKWOOD BALSA GUANO
HAREFOOT
CORM SET BULB SEED CORMEL
CORMUS FREESIA UINTJIE
CORMEL BULBLET
(PL.) SPAWN
CORMORANT SHAG CRANE GORMA
NORIE SCARF SCART DUIKER
DUYKER GORMAW GUANAY
SCARFE SCARTH GLUTTON
SHAGLET
CORN ZEA DANA DENT MAIS SALT
SAMP GRAIN MAIZE SPIKE WYROK
AGNAIL CALLUS CLAVUS HELOMA
INDIAN KERNEL MEALIE NOCAKE
NUBBIN POWDER WYROCK
FORMITY FRUMENT FRUMENTY
PRESERVE SAUTERNE
(— SALAD) MACHE
(— SPURREY) YARR
(CROW —) COLICROOT
(CRUSHED —) STAMP
(DECORATED EAR OF —) TIPONI

(EAR OF —) ICKER
(GUINEA —) DURRA DHURRA
(INDIAN —) MAIZE INDIAN NOCAKE
(PARCHED —) ROKEE NOCAKE
PINOLE YOKAGE GRADDAN
ROKEAGE YOKEAGE
(STRING OF —) TRACE
(UNRIPE EAR OF —) TUCKET
CORNAGE HORNGELD
CORN BREAD PONE KANKIE
BANNOCK
CORNCOB COB
CORN COCKLE GITH COCKLE
POPPLE COCKWEED HARDHEAD
MELANTHY
CORNCRACKER STATE KENTUCKY
CORNCRAKE RAIL CORNBIRD
CORN CROWFOOT JOY
GOLDWEED HELLWEED
JACKWEED
CORNEL DOGWOOD REDBRUSH
KILLIKINICK KINNIKINICK
CORNEOUS HORNLIKE KERASINE
CORNER IN GET OUT WRO BEND
CANT COIN HALK HERN JAMB
NOOK POOL TRAP TREE WICK
ANCON ANGLE BIGHT CATCH
COIGN ELBOW HERNE INGLE
JAMBE NICHE QUOIN TRUST
BOTTLE CANTLE CANTON COLLAR
CORNEL CRANNY RECESS SQUARE
OUTSIDE QUINYIE TURNING
MONOPOLY
(— IN A DRIFT) ARRAGE
(— OF EYE) CANTHUS
(— OF GUNSTOCK) TOE
(— OF MOLDBOARD) SHIN
(— OF SAIL) CLEW CLUE TACK
GOOSEWING
(CHIMNEY —) LUG
(LOWER —) CLEW CLUE
(RE-ENTRANT —) DIEDRE
(ROUNDED —) FILET FILLET
(SECRET —) CREEK
(TIGHT —) BOX
(PREF.) KERAT(O)
(— OF EYE) CANTH(O)
CORNERPIECE BUMPER CANTLE
CORNERSTONE COIN BASIS COIGN
QUOIN HEADSTONE
CORNET CONE HORN ZINK TWIST
ZINKE ZINCKE CORONET
CORNETTO CORNOPEAN
CORNETFISH FLUTEMOUTH
HEMIBRANCH
CORN-FED RUSTIC
CORNFIELD MOW
CORN FLAG LEVERS
CORNFLOWER BLUET BLAVER
BARBEAU BLUECAP BLUECUP
BLAEWORT
CORN GROMWELL SALFERN
CORNHUSK CAP
CORNHUSKER STATE NEBRASKA
CORNHUSKING SHUCKING
CORNICE CAP BAND DRIP EAVE
JOPY ANCON CROWN JOWPY
DETAIL GEISON PELMET ANTEFIX
MOLDING SURBASE ASTRAGAL
SWANNECK
(UNDER SIDE OF —) PLANCIER
(PREF.) GEISSO
CORNICHON GHERKIN

CORNICLE SIPHON SYPHON
CORNISHMAN CELT KELT
CORN MARIGOLD GOLD GOOLS BODDLE BOODLE BUDDLE GOWLAN GOLDING GOLLAND
CORN MEAL MASA SAMP ATOLE HOECAKE
CORN PARSLEY UMBEL
CORN POPPY BLAVER CANKER COCKLE COPROSE EARACHE PONCEAU REDWEED SOLDIER
CORN SALAD MACHE FETTICUS MILKGRASS
CORN SPURREY YARR
CORN STACK HOVEL
CORNSTALKS KARBI
CORNSTARCH BINDER
CORNU HORN THYROHYAL
CORNUCOPIA HORN CORNU COFFIN
CORNUS CORNIN REDBRUSH
CORN VIOLET SPECULARIA
CORN WOUNDWORT STACHYS
CORNY BANAL STALE TRITE MICKEY BUCKEYE
COROADO BORORO
CORODY CONRED
COROEBUS (FATHER OF —) MYGDON
(SLAYER OF —) DIOMEDES
COROLLA CUP BELL COROL CUPULE LIGULE PERIANTH
COROLLARY DOGMA PORISM RESULT TRUISM ADJUNCT THEOREM CONSECTARY
COROMANDEL COLCOTHAR
CORONA BUR BURR CIGAR CROWN GLORY AURORA FILLET ROSARY WREATH AUREOLE CIRCLET CORONET GARLAND LARMIER SCYPHUS
CORONAL CRONET CORONEL CROWNAL
CORONATION ABHISEKA CROWNMENT
CORONATION OF POPPAEA (CHARACTER IN —) NERONE OTTONE SENECA OTTAVIA POPPAEA DRUSILLA
(COMPOSER OF —) MONTEVERDI
CORONER ELISOR CROWNER EXAMINER SEARCHER
CORONET BAND BURR CROWN TIARA ANADEM CIRCLE CRONET DIADEM TIMBRE WREATH CHAPLET CORONAL CROWNAL CROWNET GARLAND CROWNLET
CORONIS (FATHER OF —) PHLEGYAS PHORONEUS
(HUSBAND OF —) BUTES
(LOVER OF —) APOLLO ISCHYS
(SON OF —) ASCLEPIUS
CORONOPUS CARARA
CORPORAL NYM FANO NAIG NAIK PALL FANON FANUM NAYAK PHANO BODILY EXEMPT GUNNER NAIGUE NAIQUE SINDON TINDAL
CORPORATE UNITED COMBINED
CORPORATION BODY CITY FIRM POUCH TRUST SCHOLA BOROUGH COLLEGE COMMUNE FREEDOM GUILDRY SOCIETY SPONSOR
CORPOREAL REAL HYLIC SOMAL

ACTUAL BODILY CARNAL FLESHLY SOMATIC MATERIAL PHYSICAL TANGIBLE
CORPOSANT HERMO
CORPS CORE ORDU VELITES SERAGLIO
(— DE BALLET) ENSEMBLE
(MEMBER OF WOMEN'S ARMY —) WAC
CORPSE BIER BODY CLAY DUST LICH MORT GHOST MUMMY RELIC STIFF TRUCK ZOMBI CORPUS DEADER ZOMBIE ANATOMY CADAVER CARCASS CARRION CROAKER DEADMAN FLOATER
(— WASHING) TAHARAH
(PREF.) NECR(O)
CORPSELIKE CADAVEROUS
CORPSMAN MEDIC BEARER
CORPULENCE FAT FATNESS STOUTNESS
CORPULENT FAT BEEFY BULKY BURLY FATTY GROSS HUSKY OBESE PLUMP PURSY STOUT TUBBY FLESHY GREASY PORTLY ROTUND ADIPOSE BELLIED WEIGHTY
CORPUSCLE CELL GHOST GLOBULE HEMATID HAEMATID HEMOCYTE
CORRAL PEN STY COOP ATAJO POUND TAMBO CONFINE ENCLOSE STOCKAGE SURROUND
(ELEPHANT —) KRAAL KEDDAH
CORRECT DUE FIT FIX TIC BEET BOOK EDIT JAKE JUST LEAL LEAN MARK MEND NICE OKAY SMUG TRUE AMEND CHECK CLEAN EMEND EXACT ORDER RIGHT SOUND SPILL ADJUST BETTER CHANGE DEADON INFORM PROPER PUNISH REBUKE REFORM REMEDY REPAIR REVAMP REVISE SEEMLY STRICT ADDRESS CHAPTER CHASTEN CORRIGE ELEGANT IMPROVE PERFECT PRECISE RECLAIM RECTIFY REDRESS REGULAR REPROVE RIGHTON SINCERE ACCURATE CHASTISE DEFINITE EMENDATE EQUALIZE REGULATE RIGOROUS STRAIGHT TRUTHFUL CASTIGATE
(APPROXIMATELY —) BALLPARK
(GRAMMATICALLY —) CONGRUE
(MATHEMATICALLY —) PURE
(NOT —) INEXACT
(PREF.) ORTH(O)
CORRECTABLE CORRIGIBLE
CORRECTED TRUE
(NOT —) RAW
CORRECTION YARD REFORM CENSURE FLEXURE IMPRINT REDRESS SCOURGE FUGACITY
(— IN COMPUTER PROGRAM) PATCH
CORRECTIVE SALT REMEDY
CORRECTLY JUST RIGHT ARIGHT MEETLY RIGHTLY SOUNDLY PROPERLY
CORRECTNESS TRUTH DECORUM FITNESS JUSTICE ACCURACY JUSTNESS VERACITY
CORREGIDOR, DER (CHARACTER IN —) TIO LUCAS MERCEDES

FRASQUITA CORREGIDOR
(COMPOSER OF —) WOLF
CORRELATE PARALLEL HARMONIZE
CORRELATIVE OR NOR THEN EQUAL STILL EITHER MUTUAL NEITHER ANALOGUE CONJOINT REDDITIVE
CORRESPOND FIT GEE JIBE SUIT AGREE MATCH TALLY WRITE ACCORD ANSWER CONCUR SQUARE COMPORT RESPOND COINCIDE PARALLEL QUADRATE
(— IN SOUND) ASSONATE
(— TO) ENSUE
CORRESPONDENCE MAIL TALLY ANALOGY CONSENT HARMONY KEEPING LETTERS TRAFFIC FUNCTION HOMOGENY HOMOLOGY SYMMETRY SYMPATHY SIMILARITY SIMILITUDE PARALLELISM RESEMBLANCE
(— IN SOUND) RIME RHYME
(INCOMPLETE —) ASSONANCE
(OFFICIAL —) BUMF
CORRESPONDENT NEWSMAN QUADRATE RELEVANT STRINGER SUITABLE STRINGMAN
CORRESPONDING LIKE SIMILAR PARALLEL ACCORDANT CONGRUENT
(PREF.) COUNTER
CORRESPONDINGLY SORTLY SIMILARLY
CORRIDA BULLFIGHT
CORRIDOR HALL AISLE ORIEL VISTA ARCADE COULOIR GALLERY PASSAGE COULISSE HALLCIST TRESANCE
CORRIE CIRQUE
CORRIGENDUM ERROR ERRATUM
CORRIGENDUM ERROR ERRATUM
CORROBORATE PROVE SECOND APPROVE COMFORT CONFIRM SUPPORT SUSTAIN ROBORATE
CORRODE EAT BITE BURN ETCH FRET GNAW RUST DECAY ERODE EXEDE TOUCH WASTE BEGNAW CANKER IMPAIR CONSUME GRAPHITE
CORRODING BITE RODENT ESURINE
CORROSION EROSION EMBAYMENT
CORROSIVE ACID ACRID ARDENT BITING CORSIE EATING CAUSTIC EROSIVE ESURINE FRETFUL MORDANT DIERETIC
CORRUGATE GIMP CRIMP CRISP FURROW RUMPLE CRINKLE CRUMPLE WRINKLE
CORRUGATED PLAITED WRINKLY FURROWED WRINKLED
CORRUGATION BAT FOLD GILL REED RUGA CREASE PUCKER CRINKLE WRINKLE
CORRUPT BAD ILL LOW ROT WEM BENT EVIL RANK SICK SOIL VILE ADDLE BLEND BRIBE FALSE SPOIL STAIN SULLY TAINT VENAL VENOM WEMMY AUGEAN CANKER DEBASE DEFILE FESTER IMPURE INFECT PALTER POISON PUTRID RAVISH ROTTEN SEPTIC ABUSIVE ATTAINT BEDEVIL BEGRIME BESHREW CARRION CORRUMP CROOKED DEBAUCH DEFINED DEGRADE

DEPRAVE ENVENOM FALSIFY IMMORAL PECCANT PERVERT POLLUTE PUTREFY SUBVERT TRADING VIOLATE VITIATE CONFOUND DECADENT DEPRAVED EMPOISON PERVERSE POLLUTED PRACTICE PRACTISE SINISTER VITIATED PERVERTED ADULTERATE CONTAMINATE PECKSNIFFIAN
CORRUPTED SICK
CORRUPTION DIRT SOIL VICE DECAY SPOIL TAINT JOBBERY PRAVITY SQUALOR ADULTERY BARRATRY INFECTION MALVERSATION PUTREFACTION
CORSAC ADIVE KARAGAN
CORSAGE WAIST BODICE BOUQUET CANEZOU
CORSAIR BUG CAPER PIRATE ROBBER CURSARO PICAROON ROCKFISH
CORSAIR, THE (CHARACTER IN —) SEID MEDORA CORRADO GULNARA
(COMPOSER OF —) VERDI
CORSELET LORICA THORAX ALLECRET HALECRET
CORSET BELT BUSK STAY STAYS GIRDLE LORICA SUPPORT
CORSICA (CAPITAL OF —) AJACCIO
(HARBOR OF —) BASTIA
(MOUNTAIN OF —) CINTO ROTONDO
(RIVER OF —) GOLO TARAVO GRAVONE
(TOWERLIKE STRUCTURES OF —) TORRI
(TOWN OF —) CALVI CORTE ALERIA BASTIA AJACCIO SARTENE
(VEGETATION OF —) MAQUIS
CORSICAN PINE LARCH
CORTEGE POMP SUITE TRAIN PARADE RETINUE
CORTEX BARK PEEL RIND MANTLE PALLIUM PERIBLEM PERIDIUM
CORUNDUM RUBY SAND EMERY ADAMAS ALUMINA ABRASIVE AMETHYST CORINDON SAPPHIRE BARKLYITE
(SYNTHETIC —) EMERALD
CORUSCATE BLAZE FLASH GLEAM SHINE GLANCE GLISTEN GLITTER RADIATE SPARKLE BRANDISH
CORVEE POLO
CORVINO (WIFE OF —) CELIA
CORYPHENE DORADO
CORYTHUS (FATHER OF —) ZEUS PARIS JUPITER
(SON OF —) DARDANUS
(WIFE OF —) ELECTRA
CORYZA COLD
COSAM (FATHER OF —) ELMODAM
COSA RARA, UNA (CHARACTER IN —) TITA LILLA CORRADO LISARGO GIOVANNI
(COMPOSER OF —) SOLER
COSCET COTTAR COTARIUS COTSETLE
COSETTE (MOTHER OF —) FANTINE
COSH SANDBAG
COSI FAN TUTTE (CHARACTER IN —) ALFONSO DESPINA FERRANDO DORABELLA GUGLIELMO FIORDILIGI
(COMPOSER OF —) MOZART

COSMETIC KOHL WASH CREAM FUCUS HENNA LINER PAINT PETER ROUGE BLANCH CERUSE CRAYON ENAMEL POMADE POWDER BLUSHER BRONZER GLEAMER MASCARA PANCAKE STIBIUM AMANDINE LIPSTICK STIBNITE (**— PREPARATION**) TONER

COSMIC VAST MUNDANE ORDERLY CATHOLIC INFINITE

COSMOLABE PANTACOSM

COSMOPOLITAN URBAN ECUMENIC PANDEMIC AMPHIGEAN

COSMOS EARTH GLOBE ORDER REALM WORLD FLOWER HEAVEN HARMONY UNIVERSE

COSSACK TURK TATAR ATAMAN HETMAN TARTAR ZAPOROGUE

COSSET MUD PET LAMB CARESS CODDLE CUDDLE FONDLE PAMPER TIDDLE

COSSETTE CHIP SLICE STRIP SCHNITZEL

COST SIT GAFF LOSS PAIN SOAK BASIS PRICE SPEND STAND VALUE CHARGE DAMAGE OUTLAY SCATHE EXPENSE FREIGHT REPRISE ESTIMATE SPENDING (**LOW**) LOWBALL

COSTA RICA

CAPE: ELENA VELAS BLANCO
CAPITAL: SANJOSE
COIN: COLÓN CENTIMO
DANCE: PUNTO TORITO
GULF: DULCE NICOYA PAPAGAYO
INDIAN: BORUCA GUAYMI
ISLAND: COCO
LAKE: ARENAL
MEASURE: VARA CAFIZ CAHIZ FANEGA TERCIA CAJUELA CANTARO MANZANA
MOUNTAIN: BLANCO CHIRRIPO
PENINSULA: OSA NICOYA
POINT: QUEPOS CAHUITA GALONOS LLERENA
PORT: LIMON PUNTARENAS
RIVER: POAS IRAZU MATINA SIXAOLA TENORIA TARCOLES
TOWN: CANAS LIMON VESTA BORUCA NICOYA BAGACES CARTAGO GOLFITO HEREDIA LIBERIA NEGRITA ALAJUELA COLORADO GUAPILES
VOLCANO: POAS IRAZU
WEIGHT: BAG CAJA LIBRA

COSTERMONGER COSTER HAWKER NIPPER PEARLY PEDDLER BARROWMAN

COSTIVE BOUND EMPLASTIC

COSTLINESS DEARTH DEARNESS

COSTLY DEAR FINE HIGH RICH SALT PRICY DAINTY LAVISH PRICEY SILVER COSTFUL COSTLEW GORGEOUS PLATINUM PRECIOUS PRODIGAL SPLENDID PRICELESS

COSTMARY TANSY ALECOST MAUDLIN ROSEMARY

COSTREL KEG HEAD FLASK BOTTLE COYSTREL

COSTUME RIG DRAG GARB ROBE SARI SUIT BURKA DRESS GETUP HABIT SHAPE TRUSS ATTIRE DOMINO FORMAL SETOUT TOILET APPAREL BLOOMER CLOTHES POLLERA RAIMENT SCARLET UNIFORM CHARSHAF CLOTHING ENSEMBLE TOILETTE VENETIAN (**ACADEMIC —**) GUISE (**JUDO —**) JUDOGI (**KARATE —**) GI GIE

COSTUSROOT PACHAK PUTCHOCK

COSY FEEL FEIL SNUG INTIME

COT BED HUT MAT PEN BOAT COOP COTE FOLD ABODE BOTHY CABIN COUCH COVER HOUSE STALL COTEEN CRADLE GURNEY PALLET SHEATH TANGLE CHARPAI CHARPOY COTTAGE SHELTER BEDSTEAD COTHOUSE DWELLING STRETCHER

COTERIE SET RING CABAL JUNTO MONDE CIRCLE CLIQUE GALAXY SETOUT CENACLE CIRCUIT COLLEGE PLATOON SOCIETY

COTHURNUS BOOT BUSKIN COTHURN

COTILLION GERMAN

COTINGA CHATTERER

COTO OREJON

COTTA KATHA STOLE MANTLE BLANKET SURPLICE VESTMENT

COTTAGE BOX COT HUT BACH BARI COSH CRIB SHED WALK BOTHY BOWER CABIN HOUSE HOVEL LODGE SHACK BOHAWN BOTHIE CABANA CHALET SHELTER BUNGALOW COTHOUSE SHEELING SHIELING THALTHAN (**RUSSIAN —**) DACCA

COTTAGE CHEESE SKYR SMEARCASE SMIERCASE

COTTAGER MAILER

COTTER KEY MAT PIN VEX CLOT BOWPIN COTMAN FASTEN MAILER POTTER PUCKER SHRINK TOGGLE WITHER CONGEAL COTTIER PEASANT SHRIVEL VILLEIN COTARIUS COTTAGER COTTEREL ENTANGLE FORELOCK LINCHPIN

COTTON SAK BEAT DRAB FLOG MALO PIMA AGREE BAYAL BOLLY DERRY MATTA SAKEL SURAT BROACH CODDLE COMBER DHURRY FABRIC MAARAD MALLOW NANKIN PEELER STAPLE ALGODON BENDERS BOMBACE CANTOON DHURRIE GARMENT GINNING SILESIA SUCCEED (**— SQUARE**) TZUT TZUTE (**BOLL OF —**) SNAP (**NAPPED —**) LAMBSKIN (**PAINTED —**) INDIENNE (**PIECE OF —**) SPONGE (**PRINTED —**) CHINTZ SARONG (**RAW —**) LINT BAYAL (**SILK —**) FLOSS (**STOUT —**) THICKSET (**STRIPED —**) BENGAL (**TREE —**) MACO (**TWILLED —**) JEAN SALLO SALLOO (**WAD OF —**) TAMPON (**WASTE —**) GRABBOTS (**PREF.**) BYSSI BYSSO

COTTON GRASS CANNA CANNACH DRAWLING

COTTON PLANT LAMB (**— FLOWER**) SQUARE

COTTON TREEE SIMAL

COTTONWOOD ALAMO POPLAR

COTTON-WOOL BOMBAST WADDING

COTYLEDON BUTTON PICHURIM SARCOLOBE

COUCAL PHEASANT

COUCH BED COT KIP LAY LIE HIDE LAIR LURK SOFA SUNK DIVAN INLAY LODGE PRESS SKULK SLINK SNEAK SNOOP SQUAB SQUAT UTTER BURROW CLOTHE DAYBED LITTER PALLET PLINTH SETTEE CONCEAL EXPRESS HAMMOCK OTTOMAN OVERLAY RECLINE TRANSOM RECAMIER (**NUPTIAL —**) THORE (**WOODEN —**) RUSTBANK (**PREF.**) CLIN(O) STROMATI STROMATO (**SUFF.**) STROMA

COUCH GRASS CUTCH KUTCH QUACK QUICK TWICH QUITCH SCOTCH SCUTCH STROIL QUICKEN WITHVINE

COUGAR CAT PUMA PAINTER PANTHER CARCAJOU

COUGH YEX YOX BAFF BARK HACK HOST KINK CHINK CROUP HOAST HOOSE HOOZE TISICK TUSSIS

COUGH DROP PASTIL TROCHE LOZENGE PASTILLE

COUGH SYRUP LINCTUS

COULEE DRAW GORGE GULCH COOLEY RAVINE

COULOMB WEBER

COUMA SORVA HYAHYA

COUNCIL BODY BULE DAEL DIET DUMA FONO RAAD REDE YUAN BOARD BOULE BUNGA CABAL CAPUT DIVAN DIWAN DOUMA JIRGA JUNTA JUNTO SABHA SOBOR STATE SYNOD THING JIRGAH LUKIKO MAJLIS POWWOW QUORUM SENATE SOVIET TARYBA CABILDO CABINET CHAMBER CONSULT GERUSIA HUSTING MEETING PENSION WHITLEY ASSEMBLY CONCLAVE CONGRESS FOLKMOOT FOLKMOTE HEEMRAAD HEEMRAAT MINISTRY PLACITUM RIGSRAAD CAMARILLA PARLIAMENT AMPHICTYONS (**— CHAMBER**) DIVAN (**MORMON —**) PRESIDENCY

COUNCILLOR RAT VIZIR ENDUNA INDUNA VIZIER FAIPULE SENATOR WISEMAN DECURION (**PL.**) ANZIANI

COUNSEL RAD LORE REDE RULE RUNE SILK WARD WARN AREED CHIDE DEVIL GUIDE ADVICE ADVISE CONFER LEADER ABOGADO CAUTION COUNCIL LECTURE ADMONISH ADVOCATE PRUDENCE (**JUNIOR LEGAL —**) DEVIL (**KING'S —**) SILK (**SACRED —**) TORAH

COUNSELOR RAT SAGE WITE CONSUL LAWYER MENTOR NESTOR ADVISER ADVISOR COUNSEL ECHEVIN GONZALO PROCTOR STARETS ADVOCATE ATTORNEY REDESMAN UCALEGON

COUNT ADD GAN SUM TOT BANK CAST EARL FOOT GANO GRAF NAME RELY RIME SIZE TALE TELL TOTE COMES COMPT COMTE GRAVE JUDGE RHYME SCORE TALLY WEIGH CENSUS CONSUL COUNTY DEPEND ESTEEM FIGURE IMPUTE MATTER NUMBER RECKON TOTTLE ACCOUNT ARTICLE ASCRIBE COMPUTE GANELON ADNUMBER NUMERATE SANCTION CALCULATE PALSGRAVE (**— IN BILLIARDS**) DOUBLE (**— OF A FIBER**) GRIST (**— OF SHEEP OR CATTLE**) BREAK (**— ON**) LITE RELY (**— UNIT**) WARP

COUNTABLE DISCRETE

COUNTE COMTE

COUNTENANCE AID MUG OWN RUD ABET BROW FACE GIZZ LEER MIEN PUSS SHOW VULT CHEER FAVOR FRONT GRACE ASPECT ENDURE UPHOLD VISAGE APPROVE BEARING CONDUCT ENDORSE FEATURE PROFFER SUPPORT BEFRIEND DEMEANOR FOREHEAD SANCTION SEMBLANCE (**PREF.**) PROSOP(O)

COUNTER BAR DIB LOT BANK BUCK CENT CHIP DESK DUMP EDDY FISH JACK KIST PAWN STOP CAROM CHECK FORCE HATCH JETON MERIL PIECE SHELF STALL STAND TABLE TOTER BUFFET COMBAT GEIGER ISLAND JETTON MARKER OPPOSE SQUAIL ADVERSE BUTTOCK CONTEND CURRENT FANTAIL SHAMBLE CONTRARY MAHOGANY OPPOSITE TELLTALE (**— TO**) AGAINST (**LEADEN —**) DUMP (**LUNCH —**) PLACE (**PREF.**) ANTI GAIN

COUNTERACT CHECK CANCEL OPPOSE RESIST THWART BALANCE CORRECT DESTROY NULLIFY ANTIDOTE NEGATIVE

COUNTERACTION DEADLOCK

COUNTERACTIVE REMEDY ADVERSE

COUNTERBALANCE COVER WEIGH CANCEL SETOFF BALANCE

COUNTERCLOCKWISE DIRECT DIRECTLY

COUNTERCURRENT BACKSET

COUNTEREARTH ANTICHTHON

COUNTERFEIT ACT BASE COIN COPY DAUB DUFF FAKE IDOL MOCK SHAM BELIE BOGUS DUMMY FALSE FEIGN FLASH FORGE FUDGE GAMMY MIMIC PHONY QUEER SNIDE AFFECT ASSUME CHEMIC ERSATZ FORGED PSEUDO TINSEL BASTARD CHEMICK DUFFING FALSIFY FASHION FEIGNED FORGERY

IMITANT IMITATE SIMULAR
BORROWED DEFORMED
PHANTASM POSTICHE POSTIQUE
RESEMBLE SIMILIZE SIMULATE
SPURIOUS SUPPOSED
BRUMMAGEM
(PREF.) PSEUD(O)
COUNTERFEITER COINER
JACKMAN JARKMAN SCRATCHER
COUNTERFEITERS (AUTHOR OF —)
GIDE
(CHARACTER IN —) LAURA VEDEL
ARMAND GEORGE ROBERT
BERNARD EDOUARD LILLIAN
OLIVIER VINCENT DOUVIERS
GRIFFITH MOLINIER PASSAVANT
GHERIDANISOL PROFITENDIEU
COUNTERFEITING COINING
FICTION POSTICHE POSTIQUE
COUNTERFOIL FOIL STUB CHECK
COUNTERFORT SCONCE BUTTRESS
COUNTERION GEGENION
COUNTERIRRITANT MOXA GINGER
IODINE PEPPER MUSTARD
CANTHARIS
COUNTERMAND STOP ANNUL
CANCEL FORBID RECALL REVOKE
ABOLISH RESCIND REVERSE
UNORDER ABROGATE PROHIBIT
COUNTERMOVE DEMARCHE
COUNTERMOVEMENT BACKFIRE
COUNTERPANE PANE QUILT
LIGGER BEDSPREAD
COUNTERPART COPY LIKE MATE
SPIT TWIN FETCH IMAGE MATCH
MORAL SHELL TALLY COUSIN
DOUBLE SHADOW BALANCE
COUNTER OBVERSE PENDANT
SIMILAR ANTIPART PARALLEL
RESCRIPT SIMILITUDE
(SPEECH —) A
COUNTERPOINT FOIL DESCANT
CONTRAST FABURDEN
COUNTERPOISE POISE OFFSET
BALANCE EQUALIZE MAKEWEIGHT
COUNTERPOISON ORVIETAN
COUNTERSIGN BACK MARK SEAL
SIGN SIGNAL CONFIRM ENDORSE
PASSWORD SANCTION
COUNTERSINK DISH REAM BEVEL
CHAMFER
COUNTERSTATEMENT ANSWER
COUNTERSUN ANTHELION
COUNTER-TENOR ALTO
COUNTERTENOR ALTO
COUNTERWEIGHT TARE
MAKEWEIGHT
COUNTERWORD ANIMAL COUNTER
COUNTESS OLIVIA COMTESSE
CONTESSA
COUNTING ACCOUNT
COUNTLESS INFINITE
NUMBERLESS
(PREF.) MYRI(A)(O)
COUNT OF MONTE CRISTO
(AUTHOR OF —) DUMAS
(CHARACTER IN —) FARIA ALBERT
DANTES EDMOND HAIDEE
MONDEGO MORRELL DANGLARS
MERCEDES FERDINAND VALENTINE
VILLEFORT CADEROUSSE
MAXIMILIAN

COUNTRIFIED JAY RURAL BUCOLIC
LOBBISH AGRESTIC CORNPONE
HOBNAILED
COUNTRY SOD DESH EARD HICK
HOME KITH LAND PAIS SOIL ADDLE
CLIME EARTH FAIRY FRITH MARCH
PLAGE REALM STATE TRACT
WEALD GROUND KINTRA KINTRY
NATION PEOPLE REGION STICKS
UPLAND IMAMATE KWINTRA
MONKERY MUFASAL BACKVELD
DISTRICT DOMINION ELDORADO
LANDWARD MAGAZINE MOFUSSIL
REGALITY PRINCIPALITY
(— DANCE) CLOG
(— OF ETHIOPIA) SEBA
(— OF ORIGIN) HOMELAND
(— OF PERFECTION) EUTOPIA
(— ON SEA) SEABOARD
(— STYLE) PAYSANNE
(ANCIENT —) ARAM
(BIBLICAL —) SHEBA
(CABIN —) LOBBY
(FRONTIER —) BORDER
(HOME —) BLIGHTY
(IMAGINARY —) EREWHON LILLIPUT
RURITANIA
(LIMESTONE —) KARST
(MARITIME —) MAREMMA
(MYTHICAL —) UTOPIA LEONNOYS
SVITHIOD SWITHIOD TEUTONIA
(OPEN —) BLED VELD FIELD VELDT
WEALD CAMPAIGN
(PETTY —) TOPARCHY
(ROUGH —) STICKS BOONIES
BOONDOCK BUNDOCKS
BOONDOCKS
(RURAL —) OUTBACK
(PREF.) RURI
(SUFF.) STAN
COUNTRYMAN HOB BOOR HIND
KERN TIKE CHURL CLOWN HODGE
KERNE SWAIN YOKEL GAFFER
GIBARO JIBARO GRANGER
HAYSEED LANDMAN PAESANO
PAISANO PEASANT PLOWMAN
LANDSMAN
(PL.) KITH
COUNTRY-ROCK METAL
COUNTRY-SEAT CHATEAU
COUNTRYSIDE BLED BOCAGE
MOFUSSIL
COUNTRY WIFE (AUTHOR OF —)
WYCHERLEY
(CHARACTER IN —) HORNER
ALITHEA HARCOURT SPARKISH
PINCHWIFE
COUNTY AMT LAN SEAT FYLKE
SHIRE DOMAIN PARISH BOROUGH
COMITAT NORFOLK DISTRICT
COUP BUY BLOW DEAL PLAN PLAY
COUPE FAULT SCOOP UPSET
ATTACK BARTER PUTSCH REFAIT
STRIKE STROKE CAPSIZE TRAFFIC
OVERTURN
COUP DE POING BOUCHER
HANDSTONE
COUPE CUT CABRIOLET LANDAULET
COUPED HUMETTY HUMETTEE
COUPLE DUO TIE TWO BOND CASE
DYAD JOIN LINK MATE PAIR SPAN
TEAM TWIN YOKE BRACE LEASH
MARRY TWAIN UNITE GEMINI

SPLINE SWINGE BRACKET
CONNECT COUPLER COUPLET
DOUBLET SHACKLE TWOSOME
VOLTAIC ACCOUPLE ASSEMBLE
COPULATE ACCOMPANY
(— OF HAWKS) CAST
(ROMANTIC —) ITEM
COUPLED GEMEL YOKED JOINED
WEDDED GEMELED COPULATE
GEMINATE
COUPLER LINK RING BOBBER
COPULA JANNEY LINKER SUTURE
UNITER DRAGBAR DRAWBAR
REDUCER SHACKLE SNAPPER
TIRASSE DRAGBOLT DRAWBOLT
DRAWGEAR SHACKLER
COUPLET BAIT COPLA ELEGIAC
COUPLING HUB HICKY UNION
CLUTCH HICKEY NIPPLE SHACKLE
SHACKLER
COUPON TWOFER VOUCHER
COURAGE BIEL FIRE GRIT GUTS
MIND MOOD PROW SAND SOUL
BIELD CREST HEART HONOR
MOXIE NERVE PLUCK SPUNK
VALOR DARING DAUBER METTLE
PECKER SPIRIT VIRTUE VIRTUS
BRAVERY COJONES CORAGIO
HEROISM MANHEAD MANHOOD
MANSHIP PROWESS STOMACH
VENTURE AUDACITY BOLDNESS
CORRAGIO FIRMNESS TENACITY
(— OF CONVICTION) STAMINA
(MORAL —) STRENGTH
(PREF.) THYM(O)
(SUFF.) THYMIA
COURAGEOUS BOLD GAME GOOD
TALL BRAVE GUTSY HARDY LUSTY
MANLY STOUT WIGHT DARING
GRITTY HEROIC MANFUL PLUCKY
SPUNKY CORIAUS GALLANT
SPARTAN STAUNCH VALIANT
FEARLESS GENEROUS INTREPID
VALOROUS
COURAGEOUSLY BIG BRAVELY
COURANT ROMP CAPER DANCE
LETTER CORANTO CURRENT
GAZETTE RUNNING
COURBARIL JATOBA LOCUST
GUAPINOL CUAPINOLE
COURGETTE ZUCCHINI
COURIER NEWS POST GUIDE SCOUT
KAVASS NEWING POSTER ESTAFET
ORDERLY PATAMAR POSTBOY
POSTMAN SOILAGE CICERONE
CURSITOR DRAGOMAN
HORSEMAN ORDINARY PATTAMAR
COURLAN LIMPKIN
COURONNE CROWN
COURSE FLY LAP RUN WAY BEAT
BENT FLOW GAGE GAME GANG
GATE HEAT HUNT LANE LINE LODE
MESS MODE PACE PATH RACE
RACK RAIK RAND RILL RING RINK
ROAD ROTA ROTE WENT CLASS
COURS CRUST CURRY CURVE
CYCLE DRAFT DRIFT DRIVE EMBER
GAUGE GREAT LAPSE LAYER
LEDGE MARCH MOYEN ORBIT
PLATE POINT ROUTE SENSE SITHE
SPACE STEPS SWELT SWING
TENOR TRACK TRACT TRADE TRAIL
TREND WEENT ARTERY CAREER

COPING CURSUS DROMOS
FURROW GALLOP GIRDER GUTTER
HONORS MANNER METHOD
MOTION RESACA SCHOOL SERIES
SPHERE STREAM STREET SYSTEM
TRIPOS ZODIAC AZIMUTH BEELINE
CHANNEL CIRCUIT CONDUCT
DIAULOS DRAUGHT HIGHWAY
LECTURE PASSADE PASSAGE
PATHWAY PROCESS ROUTINE
RUNNING SEMINAR SERVICE
STRETCH SUBJECT SUCCESS
TIDEWAY TRAJECT TRUNDLE
CURRENCY CURRICLE DIADROME
DISTANCE ELECTIVE PROGRESS
RECOURSE SEQUENCE STEERAGE
TENDENCY MOTORDROME
(— OF ACTION) LARK TACK TROD
VEIN DANCE CUSTOM ROUTINE
DEMARCHE
(— OF ACTIVITY) SIDELINE
(— OF A ROPE) LEAD
(— OF BOAT) LEG
(— OF BRICK) BED ROWLOCK
SCINTLE CREASING
(— OF FEEDING) DIET
(— OF KNITTING) BOUT
(— OF LIFE) GOINGS PILGRIMAGE
(— OF LIGHTNING) STREAK
(— OF LUCK) FORTUNE
(— OF MASONRY) BAHUT STILT
COPING HEADING SKEWBACK
(— OF NATURE) TAO
(— OF PROCEDURE) RULE
(— OF PROCEEDING) FORE
(— OF PURSUIT) SCENT
(— OF ROADBED) SUBCRUST
(— OF STONES) BED PLINTH
(— OF STUDY) DEBATE COLLEGE
LECTURE SEMINAR ELECTIVE
(— OF SUN) JOURNEY
(— OF TREATMENT) CURE
(— OF WALL) CORNICE
(— WITH GREYHOUNDS) GREW
(BELL-RINGING —) HUNT
(CIRCULAR —) SWEEP CHUKKAR
CHUKKER COMPASS
(COLLEGE —) PRECEPTORIAL
(CURVING —) SWING
(CUSTOMARY —) GUISE
(DOWNWARD —) DIP DECLINE
TOBOGGAN
(DUE —) TRAIN
(EASY —) PIPE
(EASY COLLEGE —) GUT
(EXACT —) BEAM
(FIRST —) ANTEPAST
(FIXED —) RUT
(FREE —) FORTH
(HONEST —) UPANDUP
(IRREGULAR —) ERROR
(LAST —) VOID
(MIDDLE —) MIDS TEMPER
(NATURAL —) RITA
(NORMAL —) WAY
(OBLIQUE —) SKEW
(OFF —) ASTRAY
(OVERHANGING —) JET
(PREDETERMINED —) DESTINY
(RACING —) RINK
(REGULAR —) ORBIT ROUTINE
(ROUNDABOUT —) DETOUR
WINDLASS

(SETTLED —) BIAS GROOVE
(SKIING —) SCHUSS
(ZIGZAG —) TACK
(PREF.) DROM(O)
COURSER HORSE RACER STEED
CUSSER CHARGER
COURSING CURSIVE
COURT BAR BID HOF SEE SUE WOO
AREA BAIL BODY CLAW FUSS GATE
GIRL LEET QUAD ROTA SEAT SEEK
SUIT TOWN WALE WARD WYND
YARD ARENA BENCH BUREO CURIA
CURRY DAIRI DIVAN FAVOR
FORUM FUERO GARTH JUDGE
PATIO SHIRE SPACE SPARK SPOON
SWEET TEMPT THING THINK
TOURN TRAIN YAMEN ADALAT
ALLURE ATRIUM BAILEY COUNTY
DARGAH DURBAR DURGAH
GEMOTE HOMAGE INVITE PALACE
PARVIS PURSUE SPLUNT SUITOR
TOLSEY ADAWLUT ADDRESS
ASSIZES ATTRACT BARMOTE
DUOVIRI EPHETAE FOREIGN
HELIAEA HUSTING JUSTICE
PARVISE RETINUE SOLICIT
TEMENOS TOURNEL AUDIENCE
BURHMOOT CHANCERY FOUJDARY
LAWCOURT MARKMOOT
MARKMOTE QUARANTY SERENADE
SESSIONS SWANMOTE TRIBUNAL
WOODMOTE PERIBOLOS
PARLIAMENT
(— FAVOR) FAWN
(— OF A HUNDRED) MALL MALLUM
MALLUS
(— OF CIRCUIT JUDGES) EYRE
(— OF FORTRESS) PEEL
(— OF MIKADO) DAIRI
(— ORDER) VACATUR
(— THE GREAT) LEVEE
(ECCLESIASTICAL —) ROTA CURIA
SYNOD COLLOQUY AUDIENCIA
(EXERCISE —) EPHEBEUM
(FORTIFIED —) BAWN
(GERMAN —) FEHM VEHM
(INNER —) PATIO
(MUSLIM —) DIVAN DIWAN
(REFORMED —) CLASIS
(SMALL —) WIND WYND CORTILE
(SUPREME —) SUDDER
(TAKE TO —) SUE
(TURKISH —) GATE
COURTEOUS FAIR HEND BUXOM
CIVIL GENTY SUAVE BONAIR
GENTLE POLITE SMOOTH URBANE
AFFABLE CORDIAL GALLANT
GENTEEL GENTILE REFINED
DEBONAIR FAMILIAR GRACIOUS
OBLIGING
COURTEOUSLY FAIR FAIRLY
GENTLY KINDLY AFFABLY
COURTEOUSNESS COMITY
COURTESAN MADAM QUAIL THAIS
WHORE COURTY GEISHA LALAGE
MADAME PLOVER AMOROSA
ASPASIA CANIDIA DELILAH
LORETTE PUCELLE DEVADASI
(PL.) DEMIMONDE
COURTESY MENSK COMITY EXTENT
GENTRY MANSHIP TASHRIF
BREEDING CALIDORE CORTEISE

ELEGANCE GENTRICE GRATUITY
URBANITY
(PL.) HONORS
COURTHOUSE CUTCHERY
KACHAHRI
COURTIER CURAN OSRIC WOOER
OSRICK COURTER IACHIMO
COURTMAN DAMOCLES POLONIUS
COURTING SUING SPLUNT
COURTLY HEND AULIC CIVIL HENDE
POLITE AULICAL ELEGANT REFINED
STATELY POLISHED DIGNIFIED
COURT-NOUE RONCET
COURTSHIP SUIT AMOUR DRURY
SPARKING
COURTYARD AREA WYND CLOSE
CURIA PATIO ATRIUM TRANCE
BALLIUM CORTILE TETRAGON
CURTILAGE
COUSIN COZ KIN AKIN HERO ALLIED
NEPHEW
COUSIN BETTE (AUTHOR OF —)
BALZAC
(CHARACTER IN —) HULOT AGATHE
CREVEL MONTES ADELINE LISBETH
HORTENSE MARNEFFE VICTORIN
CELESTINE STEINBOCK
COUSINRY KITH
COVE CO BAY DEN CAVE CHAP FILE
GILL HOLE NOOK PASS SUMP
BASIN BAYOU RIGHT CREEK INLET
ARMLET COVING FELLOW
HOLLOW RECESS VALLEY
MOLDING CALANQUE GUNKHOLE
COVENANT BIND BOND BRIS MISE
PACT TRUE AGREE BERIT BRITH
TOUCH ACCORD BERITH CARTEL
COMART CONAND ENGAGE
INDENT LEAGUE PATISE PLEDGE
TREATY BARGAIN COMPACT
CONCORD PROMISE ALLIANCE
CONTRACT DOCUMENT HANDFAST
TREATISE
COVENANTER HILLMAN TRUEBLUE
COVER DO CAP COT HAP LAP LAY
LID NAP TOP TUP WRY BIND CEIL
CLAD COAT COOM CURE DAUB
DECK FACE FADE FALL FURL GARB
GATE HEAD HEAL HEEL HIDE HILL
HOOD LATH LEAD LEAP LINE MASK
PAVE ROOF SILE SPAN TELD TICK
TIDE TILT VEIL WRAP APRON
BATHE BOARD CLOAK CLOUT
COPSE CROWN DRAPE DRESS
FENCE FLESH FLOOD GUISE
HATCH KIVER MOUNT RECTO
SCARF SERVE SHADE STREW
STUDY THEAK THEEK TOWEL
TREAD VERSO WELME WHALM
AWNING BATTER BINDER BLAZON
CANOPY CHALON CLOTHE DOUBLE
EARLAP ENAMEL ENCASE ENFOLD
ENROBE ENTIRE ENVEIL FOLDER
HACKLE IMMASK INVEST JACKET
KIRTLE MANTLE OVERGO POTLID
RUNNER SCONCE SCREEN
SHADOW SHEATH SHIELD SLEEVE
SPREAD SPRING SWATHE TOILET
TOPPER WHAUVE APPAREL
ASPHALT BANDAGE BESTREW
BLANKET CAPSULE CONCEAL
CONTECT COUVERT ELYTRON
EMBRACE ENCRUST FASCINE

HEADCAP HOUSING INCRUST
KNEECAP MANHEAD OBSCURE
OMNIBUS OVERLAY PRETEXT
SHEATHE SHELTER SHUTTER
TAMPION THIMBLE BEDCOVER
COMPRISE COVERCLE DEBRUISE
ENCLOTHE ENSCONCE HOODWINK
IMMANTLE OVERHAIL OVERSILE
OVERWEND PALLIATE PRETENCE
PRETENSE SLIPOVER SURPOOSE
(— A FIRE) BANK DAMP
(— AROUND FLOWER) CYMBA
(— BRICKS) SCOVE
(— BY EXCUSES) ALIBI PALLIATE
(— DISPERSEDLY) STREW
(— FOR ALEMBIC) HEAD
(— FOR CHAIR BACK) TIDY
(— FOR CHALICE) PALL
(— FOR DIAPER) SOAKER
(— FOR ENGINE) COWLING
(— FOR FOOD) BELL
(— FOR GUN) TAMPION
(— FOR MILITARY CAP) HAVELOCK
(— FOR PISTON) FOLLOWER
(— FOR POWDER PAN) HAMMER
(— FOR REAL PURPOSE) STALE
(— FOR WIRES) BOOTLEG
(— GROUND) HEAT
(— HEARTH) FETTLE
(— OF BALL) CARCASS
(— OF BOILER) VOMIT
(— OF COFFIN) COOM
(— OF HAWSEHOLE) BUCKLER
(— OF MATTRESS) TICK TICKING
(— OF MINE CAGE) BONNET
(— OF RIFLE MAGAZINE) GATE
(— OF SPORANGIUM) EPIGONE
(— OF VEGETATION) GROWTH
(— OPPRESSIVELY) SMOTHER
(— OVER) RAKE WELME WHELM
QUELME SHEUGH BECLOUD
OVERDECK WITHHELE OVERWHELM
(— PLANTS) BAG
(— PROTECTIVELY) SHROUD
SHEATHE
(— ROAD) BLIND
(— SOIL WITH CLAY) GAULT
(— UP) HAP BELY FOLD BELIE SALVE
SLEEK HUDDLE
(— WITH ASHES) SOIL
(— WITH BACON) BARD
(— WITH BOMBS) SATURATE
(— WITH CLAY) CLOAM
(— WITH COWL) MOB
(— WITH CRUMBS) BREAD
(— WITH DOTS) CRIBBLE
(— WITH DROPS) DAG
(— WITH EARTH) BURY HEAL INTER
(— WITH FILM) SKIM
(— WITH FLESH) INCARN
(— WITH FOAM) EMBOSS
(— WITH GOLD) GILD
(— WITH MEAL) MELVIE
(— WITH MUD) BEMUD BELUTE
(— WITH OAKUM) FOTHER
(— WITH PITCH) PAY
(— WITH PLASTER) PARGET
(— WITH SHEATH) GLOVE
(— WITH SOLDER) SPLASH
(— WITH STONE) ASHLAR
(— WITH STRAW) THATCH
(— WITH TIN) BLANCH
(— WITH TOPSOIL) KELLY

(— WITH WATER) DOUSE DOWSE
FLOOD WHELM OVERFLOW
(— WITH WAX) CERE
(— WITH WEAVING) GRAFT
(— WITH WINGS) BROOD
(BED —S) HEALING
(BEEHIVE —) QUILT
(BOOK —) CASE SIDE
(CANVAS —) TARP TARPAULIN
(GLASS —) STRIKE
(KIND OF —) MAIL
(PACK —) MANTA
(PILLOW —) CASE SHAM
(POSTAL —) ENTIRE
(POT —) BRED
(RAIN —) TARP
(SADDLE —) PILCH HOUSING
(SEED —) TESTA
(SLIDING —) BRIDGE
(TABLE —) BAIZE DUCHESSE
(WING — OF BEETLE) SHARD
(PREF.) OPERCULI
COVERAGE PROTECTION
COVERALL GOWN JUMPER
COVERED CLAD FULL SHOD TECT
BLIND MOSSY CLOSED COVERT
HIDDEN ENCASED OBTECTED
SCREENED
(— WITH CRYSTALS) DRUSY
(— WITH FEATHERS) HIRSUTE
(— WITH FOREST) HYLEAN
(— WITH HAIRS) COMATE VILLOUS
(— WITH PROTUBERANCES) HUMPY
(— WITH SCALES) SCUTATE
(— WITH SEAWEED) TANGLY
(— WITH WHITE DUST) PRUINOSE
(THINLY —) DARISH
(PREF.) CALYPT(O) CRYPT(O)
KRYPT(O)
COVERED WAGON WHITETOP
BUCKWAGON
COVERER DECKER
COVERING (ALSO SEE COVER) BOX
COT FUR HAP KEX LAG ARIL BARB
BARK BOOT CASE CAUL COAT
CUFF DECK FILM HAME HEAD
HOOD HULL HUSK KELL MASK
OVER PALL PUFF ROBE ROOF SLIP
SPAT TARP TILE TILT TRAP VEIL
APRON ARMOR BRAID BURSE
CRUST DRESS GLOBE GLOVE
HATCH QUILT SCALE SHELL SKIRT
STALL SWARD TESTA TUNIC
TWEEL WREIL ARMING ATTIRE
AWNING BANCAL BANKER CANOPY
CANVAS COVERT DRAPET EMBRYO
ENAMEL FACING FENDER GAITER
GANOIN HACKLE HATCAP HELMET
JACKET MUZZLE PELAGE SADDLE
SCREEN SHEATH SHROUD SINDON
TEGMEN VERNIX BLANKET
BUFFONT CAMISIA CAPPING
CAPSULE CEILING COATING
COWLING EARLAP ENVELOP
EXCIPLE GRATING HAPPING
HEALING HEELCAP HOUSING
MUFFLER OVERLAY PURPORT
SARPLER SHADING SHELTER
SHOEING SLIPPER TECTURE
TEGMENT VESTURE WRAPPER
ARMGUARD BLAZONRY BOARDING
CASEMENT CLEADING CLOTHING
COMPRESS COVERLET EGGSHELL

EPISPORE INDUMENT INDUSIUM MANTELET MANTLING OVERCAST PAVILION PERICARP SETATION UMBRELLA TECTORIAL PILLOWCASE
(— FOR ANTENNA) RADOME
(— FOR BENCH) BANKER
(— FOR BOXERS' HANDS) CESTUS
(— FOR CHEST) STOMACHER
(— FOR EGG) COSY
(— FOR FOREHEAD) BONGRACE
(— FOR NECK) TUCKER PARTLET
(— FOR ROOF APEX) EPI
(— FOR SHOULDERS) STOLE
(— FOR SKI) SKIN
(— FOR STIRRUP) HOOD
(— FOR TEAPOT) COSY COZY
(— OF BED) TIKE
(— OF BELL ROPE) GRIP
(— OF BIRD) INDUMENT
(— OF BOW HANDLE) ARMING
(— OF CASH SHORTAGE) LAPPING
(— OF EYEBALL) CORNEA
(— OF FEATHERS) DOWN
(— OF GILLS) OPERCULUM
(— OF MUMMY) CARTONAGE CARTONNAGE
(— OF NUTMEG) MACE
(— OF PIE) CRUST
(— OF ROOT) CALYPTRA
(— OF ROPE) SERVICE
(— OF VEGETATION) FLEECE
(— OVER DRESS) PINAFORE
(—S FOR NIPPLES) PASTIES
(— WITH IRON) ACIERAGE
(CAST —S) EXUVIAE
(CHIMNEY —) COWL
(CLOTH —) TOILET
(COARSE —) CADDOW TILLET
(DEFENSIVE —) ARMOR KICKER
(EAR —) EARLAP EARFLAP EARMUFF OREILET
(EYE —S) GOGGLES
(FLOOR —) RUG TILE CRASH CARPET LINOLEUM OILCLOTH
(FOUL —) SCUM
(HEAD —) CAP HAT WIG HAIR HIVE HOOD CURCH BONNET HELMET BIRETTA CHAPEAU CHAPERON HAVELOCK HEADRAIL TROTCOZY
(LEATHER —) GAMBADO
(LEG —) BOOT HOSE STOCK GAITER LEGGIN PEDULE KNEELET LEGGING STOCKING
(LIGHT —) GRIMING
(LINEN —) BARB
(OUTER —) BARK HIDE HULL HUSK CRUST TESTA JACKET CARAPACE
(PLANT —) PERIDERM
(PROTECTIVE —) APRON ARMOR SHELL COCOON
(SADDLE —) MOCHILA
(SEED —) PERIGONE
(SHELF —) OILCLOTH
(SLIGHT —) CYMAR
(SOFT —) DOWN
(STAGE —) HEAVENS
(STERILE —) DRAPE
(STICKY DAMP —) GLET
(THIN —) FILM SCRUFF WASHING
(PREF.) CALYPT(O) COLE STEG(O) STRATI STRATO

(SUFF.) DERM(A)(ATOUS)(IA)(IS)(Y)
(— OF PLATE) STEGE
COVERLET PANE HELER HOUSE QUILT REZAI THROW AFGHAN CADDOW CHALON COLCHA LIGGER SPREAD BLANKET BUFFALO COVERLID DAGSWAIN
COVER-SHAME SAVIN SAVINE
COVERT DEN LAY LIE SLY LAIR VERT EARTH NICHE PRIVY ASYLUM HARBOR HIDDEN LATENT MASKED MYSTIC REFUGE SECRET COVERED DEFENSE PRIVATE SHELTER TECTRIX THICKET DISGUISE INVOLVED
(PL.) CRISSUM
COVERTLY CLOSE CLOSELY
COVET ACHE ENVY PANT WANT WISH CRAVE YEARN YISSE DESIRE GRUDGE HANKER
COVETOUS AVID GAIR GARE EAGER FRUGAL GREEDY SORDID STINGY ENVIOUS GRIPPLE MISERLY DESIROUS GRASPING
COVETOUSNESS GREED MISERY AVARICE YISSING COVETISE CUPIDITY PLEONEXIA
COVEY BEVY FALL BROOD FLOCK HATCH COVERT COMPANY
COVIN BAND CREW FRAUD COVINE COMPANY CONVENE ASSEMBLY TRICKERY
COW AWE KEY NOT BEEF BOGY BOSS COWL CUSH FAZE MOIL MULL NOTT ROAN RUNT VACA ABASH ALARM BEEVE BOSSY BROCK BULLY CUSHA DAUNT DOMPT DRAPE MOGGY QUAIL SCARE SNOOL VACHA BOVINE BULLER COLLOP CRUMMY GOBLIN HAWKEY HAWKIE HEIFER MAILIE MILKER MULLEY ROTHER SUBDUE BOARDER BUGBEAR BULLOCK CRITTER CRUMMIE DEPRESS MESTENO MILCHER OVERTOP SQUELCH TERRIFY ALDERNEY AUDHUMLA BROWBEAT COWBRUTE DISPIRIT FRIGHTEN STRIPPER THREATEN
(— ABOUT 3 FEET HIGH) GYNEE
(— BEFORE CALVING) SPRINGER
(BAD-TEMPERED —) RAGER
(BARREN —) DRAPE BARRENER
(DRY —) KEY SEW
(HORNLESS —) NOT MOIL NOTT DODDY MULEY DODDIE HUMLIE MAILIE HUMBLIE POLLARD MOULLEEN
(NOTED —) ELSIE
(PART OF —) HIP JAW RIB CROP HOCK HOOF HORN KNEE LOIN NECK POLL RUMP TAIL TEAT CHEST CHINE FLANK GIRTH PLATE THIGH THURL UDDER BARREL BRIDGE DEWLAP MUZZLE SWITCH THROAT BRISKET DEWCLAW PASTERN PINBONE WITHERS FOREHEAD
(PREGNANT —) CALVER INCALVER
(WHITE-FACED —) HAWKEY HAWKIE
(YOUNG —) QUEY STIRK HEIFER
(PL.) KYE KINE DAIRY
(PREF.) VACCI(NI)(NO)

COWARD COW CUR COOF DAFF FUNK FUGIE LACHE PIKER CRAVEN FUNKER PIGEON BUZZARD CAITIFF CHICKEN COUCHER DASTARD MEACOCK NITHING PANURGE QUITTER NIDERING POLTROON RECREANT TURNBACK TURNTAIL VILLIAGO
COWARDICE DASTARDY LASHNESS POLTROONERY
COWARDLINESS PUSILLANIMITY
COWARDLY SHY ARGH FAINT LACHE TIMID AFRAID COWARD COWISH CRAVEN TURPID YELLOW CAITIFF CHICKEN GUTLESS HILDING MEACOCK FACELESS NIDERING POLTROON RECREANT SNEAKING POLTROONISH PIGEONHEARTED
COW BARN BYRE SAUR BARTH SHIPPON VACCARY
COWBIRD BECCO BUNTING CUCKOLD OXBITER COKEWOLD LAZYBIRD
COWBOY HAZER RIDER ROPER SCREW WADDY CHARRO GAUCHO GINETE HERDER JINETE WADDIE COWHAND COWHERD COWPOKE GRAZIER HERDBOY LLANERO PANIOLO PUNCHER REFUGEE VAQUERO BUCKAROO DALLYMAN JACKAROO NEATHERD NOWTHERD OUTRIDER PASTORAL RANCHERO SWINGMAN WRANGLER
COWCATCHER GUARD LASSO PILOT FENDER
COWED HANGDOG DOWNCAST
COWER HUG COUR FAWN RUCK HOVER QUAIL SHRUG SNOOL SQUAT STOOP TOADY WINCE COORIE CRINGE CROUCH HURKLE SHRINK CROODLE CRUDDLE
COWFISH TORO BECCO CUCKOLD MANATEE SIRENIA
COWHAGE KIWACH
COWHAND PEELER FLANKER STOCKMAN
COWHERB COCKLE SOAPWORT
COWHERD HERDSMAN NEATHERD
COWHOUSE BYRE SHIPPEN SHIPPON
COWL CAP COW LID SOE TUB COUL HOOD MONK MITER BONNET CUCULE CAPUCHE SCUTTLE CAPUCHIN
COW PARSNIP MADNEP CADWEED HOGWEED PIGWEED BEARWORT BUNDWEED
COWPEA SITAO FRIJOL FRIJOLE TOWCOCK BLACKEYE BLACKPEA
COWPEN CUPPEN CUPPIN
COW PILOT PINTANO
COWPOX PAPPOX KINEPOX VACCINA VACCINIA
COWRIE COWRY VENUS ZIMBI CYPRAEID
COWSHED STALL
COWSLIP PAIGLE PRIMULA SHOOTER AURICULA CYCLAMEN MARIGOLD PRIMROSE
COXA HIP HAUNCH
COXCOMB FOP NOB BUCK DUDE FOOL PRIG TOFF CLEAT DANDY

HINGE PRINCOX POPINJAY PRINCOCK
COXCOMBRY FOPPERY
COXSWAIN PATROON
COY PAL SHY ARCH COAX NICE ALOOF CHARY DECOY QUIET SQUAB STILL ALLURE CARESS DEMURE MODEST PROPER SKEIGH BASHFUL DISTANT PEEVISH STRANGE RESERVED SKITTISH VERECUND KITTENISH
COYNESS SHYNESS
COYO CHININ
COYOL COROJO COROZO
COYOTE VARMINT
(— STATE) SOUTHDAKOTA
COYPU DEGU NUTRIA
COZBI (FATHER OF —) ZUR
COZEN COG CON BILK FOOL GULL POOP CHEAT TRICK CHISEL GREASE BEGUILE DECEIVE DEFRAUD SWINDLE HOODWINK
COZENER SNAP SNECKDRAW
COZENING SIMILATE
COZIER CADGER CODGER COSIER
COZY RUG BEIN BIEN COSY EASY HOMY SAFE SNUG BIELD CANNY COMFY CUSHY HOMEY CHATTY PENTIT SECURE TOASTY COVERING FAMILIAR HOMELIKE SOCIABLE
CPU CHIP
CRAB GIN UCA BOCO JUEY MAJA ZOEA ANGER ARROW AYUYU BLUEY MAIAN MAIID MAJID RACER SANDY THIEF WINCH BUSTER CANCER GROUCH GROUSE HARPER HERMIT KABURI NIPPER PARTAN PEELER PUNGAR PUNGER RACING SCRAWL SPRITE BUCKLER BUCKLUM BURSTER CABOUCA CANCRID DECAPOD FIDDLER GRUMBLE INACHID OCYPODE PANFISH POLYPOD SHEDDER SOLDIER SPECTER SPECTRE SURIQUE ARACHNID CRABFISH DORIPPID GRAPSOID HORSEMAN IRRITATE LIMULOID LITHODID OCHIDORE OXYSTOME PAGURIAN PORTUNID RANINIAN TRAVELER WINDLASS BRACHYURA
(KIND OF —) SNOW PURSE
(MATING —) DOUBLER
(PREF.) CANCERI CANCERO CANCRI CARCIN(I)(O)
CRAB APPLE CRAB SCRAB SCROG COLING
CRABBED SOUR UGLY CABBY CRANK CROSS SURLY TESTY BITTER COPPED CROOSE CROUSE CRUSTY MOROSE RUGGED SULLEN TEETHY TRYING BOORISH CANKERY CRABBIT CRAMPED CRONISH CROOKED FRABBIT GNARLED KNOTTED OBSCURE PEEVISH CANKERED CHURLISH CONTRARY CRABBISH LIVERISH PETULANT VINEGARY
CRABBEDNESS ACRIMONY ASPERITY
CRABCATCHER CRABIER
CRABER VOLE AGOUARA
CRABGRASS DRAWK FONIO PANIC

DARNEL PANICLE CRABWEED
ELEUSINE
CRAB LOUSE CRAB MORPION
MOREPEON
CRAB PLOVER DROME
CRAB'S-EYE JEQUIRITY
CRAB TREE GRIBBLE
CRABWOOD ANDIROBA
POISONWOOD
CRACK GAG KIN POP BANG BLOW
CHAP CHIP CHOP CLAP CONE
DOKE FENT FLAW GAIG JEST JIBE
JOKE KIBE LEAK LICK QUIP REND
RIFT RIME RIVE SCAR SLAT SNAP
YERK BRACK BREAK CHARK CHECK
CHICK CHINE CHINK CLACK CLEFT
CRAKE CRAZE FLAKE FLANK FLASH
GRIKE KNACK KNICK SCORE SHAKE
SLASH SOLVE SPANG SPLIT
CLEAVE CRANNY SLITER SPIDER
SPRING BLEMISH CRACKLE
CREVICE FISSURE SLIFTER SLITHER
FRACTURE HAIRLINE STRAMASH
(— A WHIP) YERK FLANK
(— IN FLESH) KIN CHAP KIBE
(— IN FLOOR) STRAKE
(— IN INGOT) SPILL
(— IN MAST) SPRING
(— IN ROCK) GRIKE JOINT
(— IN SEA ICE) RIFTER
(— IN STEEL) CHECK SPILL
(— OPEN) SEAM
(— PETROLEUM) BURN
(— WHILE FIRING) DUNT
(FILLER FOR —S) SPACKLE
(PL.) CRAZE
(PREF.) RIMI
CRACKAJACK NAILER NAILING
CRACKBRAINED BATS CRAZY
NUTTY CRACKY ERRATIC
CRACKED BATS FLED NECKED
CHAPPED COMICAL TOUCHED
CRACKERS
CRACKER BAKE LIAR WAFER
BONBON POPPER BISCUIT
BOASTER BREAKER BURSTER
COSAQUE REDNECK SALTINE
SNAPPER
(— STATE) GEORGIA
(BOILED —S) CUSH
(BROKEN —S) DUNDERFUNK
CRACKERJACK ACE TRUMP
CRACKING CRAZE SHIVERING
(PL.) SCRAP
CRACKLE SNAP BREAK CRACK
CRISP BRUSTLE CRINKLE SPARKLE
SPUTTER CREPITATE
CRACKLING CRISP GREAVE SNAPPY
CRACKEL CRACKLE CREMANT
GREAVES CRACKNEL CRITLING
CREPITANT
(— OF PAPER) RATTLE
(PL.) SCRAPS GRIEBEN
CRACKNEL SIMNEL CRACKLING
CRACKPOT NUT CRACK ERRATIC
LUNATIC CRANKISH
CRACKSMAN YEGG BURGLAR
PETEMAN
CRADLE BED COT CRIB REST ROCK
WOMB CRATE FRAME CRECHE
MATRIX ROCKER SADDLE TROUGH
BERCEAU SHELTER BASSINET
CUNABULA

(— FOR SHIP) BED SLEE
(— FOR VATS) STILLING STILLION
(— IN ARCHERY) PURSE
(CERAMICS —) CHUM
(GRAIN —) CADAR CADER
(PL.) CHOCKS
CRADLESONG BERCEUSE
CRADLING BRACK
CRAFT ART BARK BOAT SAIL FRAUD
GUILE SKILL TRADE BARQUE
BATEAU CAUTEL DECEIT DROGER
METIER MISTER POLICE ROADER
STRUSE TALENT VESSEL ABILITY
CUNNING DROGHER MYSTERY
PANURGY SLEIGHT APTITUDE
ARTIFICE BASKETRY VOCATION
(ANTIQUATED OR CLUMSY —)
HOOKER
(CLUMSY —) ARK
(LANDING —) DUCK
(PREF.) TECHNI TECHNO
(SUFF.) TECT
CRAFTILY FOXILY
CRAFTINESS DESIGN SLEIGHT
SLYNESS
CRAFTSMAN CARL HAND CARLE
CRAFT NAVVY ARTIST WRITER
ARTISAN TOHUNGA WORKMAN
LETTERER MECHANIC ANTIFICEN
MACHINIST
CRAFTY SLY ARCH DEEP DERN FINE
FOXY NOUP SLIM WILY WISE
ADEPT COONY PAWKY SLAPE
SLEEK ADROIT ARTFUL ASTUTE
CALLID QUAINT SHREWD SOLERT
SUBTLE TRICKY CUNNING POLITIC
SLEEKIT SLEIGHT SUBTILE
VAFROUS VERSUTE VULPINE
CAPTIOUS DEXTROUS ENGINOUS
FETCHING JESUITIC SLEIGHTY
CAUTELOUS
CRAG TOR CRAW KNEE NECK ROCK
SCAR SPUR ARETE BRACK CLIFF
CLINT CRAIG HEUCH HEUGH
THROAT
(PREF.) CREMNO
CRAGGY ROUGH ABRUPT CLIFFY
CLIFTY KNOTTY PAMPER RUGGED
CRAGGED KNAGGED
CRAKE CROW RAIL ROOK RAVEN
CORNBIRD RAILBIRD
CRAKOW BEAKER CRACOWE
POULAINE
CRAM BAG MUG RAM WAD BONE
CRAP FILL GLUT LADE PACK PANG
PORR PURR STOW TRIG TUCK
URGE CROWD CRUSH DRIVE
FARCE FORCE FRANK GORGE
GRIND LEARN PRESS SCRAM
STECH STUDY STUFF TEACH
AGROTE BONEUP CROMME
PESTER STEEVE STODGE THRACK
(— WITH RICH FOOD) PAMPER
CRAMMED PANG STODGY
CHOCKFUL JAMPACKED
CRAMMER CRAM FEEDER
CRAMMING GAVAGE
CRAMP ART ARCT COOP CRIB KINK
PAIN TUCK CRICK CRIMP CROWD
DOWEL PINCH STUNT TRAMP
AGRAFE DOGTIE HAMPER HINDER
KNOTTY PESTER CONFINE

CRAMPER CRAMPET COMPRESS
CONTRACT RESTRAIN RESTRICT
CRAMPED POKY CRIMP POKEY
NIGGLY BOUNDED CRIMPED
SQUEEZY NIGGLING
CRAMPFISH TORPEDO
CRAMPING UNEASY
CRAMPON CRAMP CRAMPET
CRAMPOON
CRANBERRY BERRY CRANE ERICAD
BOGWORT PEMBINA ACROSARC
BILBERRY BOGBERRY COWBERRY
FENBERRY FOXBERRY
CROWBERRY
(— BUSH) PIMBINA
CRANBERRY TREE PEMBINA
SNOWBALL VIBURNUM
CRANE JOB GRUS HOOK SWAY
CYRUS DAVIT HERON HOIST JENNY
RAISE SARUS TITAN WADER
BROLGA COOLEN JIGGER KULANG
SAHRAS COOLUNG CRAWLER
DERRICK GOLIATH KAIKARA
WHOOPER ADJUTANT GRUIFORM
TRAVELER
(— FOR FIREPLACE) COTTREL
COTTEREL
CRANE ARM GIB JIB GIBBET
RAMHEAD COTTEREL
CRANE-FLY LONG-LEGS
CRANESBILL ALUMROOT
DOVEFOOT FLUXWEED
CRANIUM PAN HEAD CRANE CRANY
SKULL BRAINPAN
(PART OF —) INION
CRANK NUT WIT BENT SICK WALT
WEAK WHIM WIND BRACE GRUMP
LOOSE ROGUE SHAKY THROW
WALTY WINCH AILING BOLDLY
CRANKY EVENER GROUCH HANDLE
INFIRM AWKWARD BRACKET
FANATIC LUSTILY
(SOMEWHAT —) TENDER
CRANKCASE SUMP
CRANKINESS ANGULARITY
CRANKY UGLY CRAZY CRONK
CROSS LUSTY SHAKY TESTY AILING
CRANNY FIFISH INFIRM SICKLY
CROOKED GROUCHY PERVERSE
TORTUOUS
CRANNY HOLE NOOK CHINK CLEFT
CRACK CORNER CRANNEL CREVICE
FISSURE
CRANTARA TARIE
CRANTS WREATH CORANCE
GARLAND
CRAPE BAND CURL FRIZ CREPE
CRIMP DRAPE GAUZE SHROUD
MOURNING
CRAPE MYRTLE JAPONICA
ASTROMEDA
CRAPPIE BACH SHAD BATCH
CALICO CROPPIE BACHELOR
BACULERE NEWLIGHT SACAI AIT
TINMOUTH CHINKAPIN
CRAPS CRAP HAZARD
CRASH BASH FAIL FALL RACK BLAST
BURST CLOTH CRUSH FRUSH
PRANG SHOCK SMASH SOUND
FIASCO FRAGOR HURTLE FAILURE
SHATTER STENTER COLLAPSE
ICEQUAKE SPLINTER STRAMASH
(— OF THUNDER) CLAP

CRASHING ROPAND SMASHING
CRASH-LAND DITCH
CRASS RAW DULL LOUD RUDE
CRUDE DENSE GROSS ROUGH
THICK COARSE OBTUSE STUPID
CRASSNESS SQUALOR
CRATCH CRIB RACK CRITCH
MANGER GRATING
CRATE BOX CAR CASE CRIB FLAT
PLANE SERON BASKET CRADLE
ENCASE HAMPER HURDLE
CACAXTE CANASTA CARRIER
PACKAGE VEHICLE
(EMPTY —) EMPTY
CRATER CUP PIT CONE HOLE DINOS
FOVEA NICHE CELEBE HOLLOW
CALDERA
(— FORMED BY STEAM) MAAR
(LUNAR —) LINNE
(VOLCANIC —) MAAR
CRATUS (FATHER OF —) PALLAS
URANUS
(MOTHER OF —) GAEA STYX
CRAUNCH CRANCH SCRANCH
CRAVAT TIE TECK ASCOT FRONT
SCARF STOCK CHOKER GRAVAT
BANDAGE NECKTIE OVERLAY
SOUBISE CRUMPLER
CRAVE ASK BEG GAPE ITCH LONG
NEED PINE PRAY SEEK WISH
COVET GREED YEARN DESIRE
HANKER HUNGER LINGER THIRST
YAMMER BESEECH ENTREAT
IMPLORE REQUEST REQUIRE
SOLICIT APPETITE
CRAVEN AFRAID COWARD SCARED
DASTARD COWARDLY DEFEATED
OVERCOME POLTROON RECREANT
SNEAKING
CRAVING AVID ITCH WANT LETCH
DESIRE HUNGER THIRST LONGING
APPETITE LIKEROUS TICKLING
APPETENCE
(— FOR LIQUOR) DRY
(— FOR UNNATURAL FOOD) PICA
(ABNORMAL —) BULIMY BULIMIA
BOULIMIA
CRAW MAW CRAG CROP STOMACH
CRAWFISH KREEF
CRAWL LAG COON DRAG FAWN
INCH LOOP RAMP SHUG SWIM
CREEP KRAAL SLIDE SLIME SNAKE
TRAIL BUSTLE CRINGE GROVEL
SCRAWL SCRIDE CLAMBER
SLITHER SNIGGLE TRUDGEN
INCHWORM SCRABBLE
CRAWLING
(SUFF.) **(— CREATURE)** ERPETON
CRAWLY CREEPY
CRAYFISH DAD CRAB YABBY
YABBIE CAMARON CRAWDAD
LOBSTER CAMBARUS CRABFISH
CRAWFISH
CRAYON KEEL PLAN CHALK CONTE
SAUCE PASTEL PENCIL SKETCH
SANGUINE
CRAZE BUG FAD FLAW MAZE MODE
RAGE BREAK CRACK CRUSH FEVER
FUROR MANIA VOGUE DEFECT
IMPAIR MADDEN MADDLE
WEAKEN WHIMSY DERANGE
DESTROY FASHION SHATTER
WHIMSEY DISTRACT

(NEWSPAPER —) STUNT
(PREF.) MANIC
CRAZED MAD REE AMOK LOCO WILD WOOD WOWF ZANY BALMY BATTY DAFFY DOTTY GIDDY MANIC NUTTY POTTY WACKY COOCOO DOTTLE INSANE LOONEY BERSERK FANATIC LUNATIC DATELESS DELEERIT DEMENTED DERANGED POSSESSED
CRAZINESS CRAZE LUNACY DEMENTIA
CRAZY (ALSO SEE CRAZED) APE OFF REE WET BATS BUGS GAGA GYTE HITE LOCO NUTS WILD ZANY BATTY BEANY BUGGY DAFFY DIPPY DOILT DOTTY FLAKY GOOFY KOOKY LOOLY LOONY POTTY WACKO WACKY WIGGY CRANKY CUCKOO DOTTLE FLAKEY FRUITY INSANE KOOKIE LOCKET MENTAL SCATTY SCREWY WHACKO WHACKY BANANAS BONKERS CRACKED LUNATIC PEEVISH SCRANNY BUGHOUSE COCKEYED CRACKERS DERANGED HALLICET HALUCKET MESHUGGA
CREAK CRY GIG GEIG GIRG JARG RASP YIRR CHARK CHEEP CHIRK CRAIK CRANK CROAK GRIND GROAN FRATCH SCREAK SCRIKE SCROOP SKRAIK SQUEAK COMPLAIN
(— OF TIN) CRY
CREAKING JARG SCREAK SCRIKE
CREAKY ARTHRITIC
CREAM DIP BEAT BEST FOOL HEAD REAM CREME ELITE FROTH REAME SAUCE WHOMP BONBON CHOICE TRIFLE COLOGNE FATNESS EMULSION OINTMENT
(ICE —) GELATA
CREAMING MANTLING
CREAM PUFF PUFF DUCHESSE
CREAMY RICH REAMY ACREAM SMOOTH LUSCIOUS
CREASE GAW CLAM FOLD LINE LIRK RUCK RUGA SEAM BLOCK CRESS CRIMP PLAIT PLEAT PRESS SCARF SCORE FURROW SCARPA SUTURE WREATH CRUMPLE CRUNKLE WRIMPLE WRINKLE
(SERIES OF —S) BREAK
(PL.) RASCETA
CREASED CRUMPLED ACCORDION
CREASELESS (HAVING — LEGS) STOVEPIPE
CREATE COIN CREE FORM MAKE PLAN BUILD CAUSE ERECT FORGE IMPEL RAISE SETUP SHAPE WRITE AUTHOR DESIGN IMPOSE INVENT COMPACT COMPOSE CONJURE FASHION IMAGINE PRODUCE COMPOUND GENERATE CONSTRUCT
(— A DISTURBANCE) RIOT
(— CONFUSION) GARBOIL
(NEWLY -D) SUNRISE
CREATING CREANT
CREATION WORLD COSMOS EFFECT NATURE POETRY EDITION FACTURE FASHION POIESIS

PRODUCT SHAPING BERESHIT BUSINESS CREATURE UNIVERSE
(MENTAL —) FANTASY PHANTASY
(VISIONARY —) DREAM
CREATIVE FERTILE FORMFUL PLASTIC POIETIC FORGEFUL GERMINAL NATURING POMATIVE PROMETHEAN ORIGINATIVE
CREATOR MAKER AUTHOR FATHER FORMER VARUNA WORKER KHEPERA TAGALOA DESIGNER INVENTOR OPERATOR PRODUCER TANGALOA
CREATURE MAN FOOD TOOL BEAST BEING DABBA JOKER SLAVE THING TRICK WIGHT ANIMAL FELLOW MINION PERSON WRETCH CRITTER GANGREL MINIKIN MINIMUS SHAPING CRAYTHUR CREATION HELLICAT
(— OF LITTLE VALUE) SHOT
(CANNIBALISTIC —) WENDIGO WINDIGO
(CHARMING —) FAIRY
(DEFORMED —) MOONCALF
(DISORDERLY —) ROIT ROYT
(DWARF —) FAIRY GNOME
(ELFLIKE —) PERI
(EVIL —) HELLICAT
(FABLED —) LUNG SIREN MERMAN WIVERN ALBORAK MERMAID
(FRIVOLOUS —) MOTH
(LITTLE —) MITING
(MANGY —) RONION RONYON
(MANLIKE —) HOMINID HOMONID HOMINIAN
(MEAN —) LEFT
(MECHANICAL —) GOLEM
(MISERABLE —) SNAKE
(NONSENSE —) SNARK
(POOR —) EARTHWORM
(SILLY —) GOOSE
(SMALL —) ATOM GRIG BEASTIE
(SPRY —) WHIPPET
(STUNTED —) WIRL URLING WIRLING
(SUPERNATURAL —) MAN DRAGON
(TINY —) ELF ATOMY
(UNDERDEVELOPED —) SLINK
(UNDERSIZED —) DURGAN
(USELESS —) HUSHION
(VICIOUS —) DEVIL
(WICKED —) HELLICAT
(WORTHLESS —) SCULPIN SNIPJACK
(WRETCHED —) ARMINE
(3 —S OF A KIND) LEASH
(PL.) CREATION
CRECHE CRIB PUTZ MANGER NURSERY
(— FIGURES) MAGI
CREDENCE FAITH TRUST BELIEF BUFFET CREDIT CREANCE CREDENZA
CREDENTIAL VOUCHER CREDENCE
CREDENZA NICHE SHELF TABLE BUFFET SERVER CREDENCE CUPBOARD
CREDIBILITY FAITH CREDIT
CREDIBLE LIKELY CREDENT FAITHFUL PROBABLE TROWABLE PLAUSIBLE
CREDIT LOAN TICK ASSET CHALK

ENDOW FAITH HONOR IZZAT MENSK MERIT STRAP TENET TRUST BELIEF CHARGE ESTEEM IMPUTE RENOWN REPUTE TICKET WEIGHT ACCOUNT ASCRIBE BELIEVE CREANCE JAWBONE OPINION WORSHIP ACCREDIT CREDENCE HEADMARK PRESTIGE
(HOCKEY —) ASSIST
CREDITABLE HONEST CREDIBLE REPUTABLE
CREDITOR DEBTEE SHYLOCK TRUSTER ADJUDGER APPRIZER CRANSIER CREANCER
(TROUBLESOME —) DUN
CREDO FAITH
CREDULITY EASINESS
CREDULOUS FOND SIMPLE SPOONY SPOONEY BOOBYISH CREDIBLE GULLIBLE
CREED ISM LAY CULT SECT CREDO DOGMA FAITH TENET BELIEF KELIMA SYMBOL CREANCE KALIMAH TROWING DOCTRINE SYMBOLUM
(KIND OF —) NICENE
CREEK BAY CUT GEO GIO GUT POW RIA RIO RUN VLY VOE BECK BURN COVE HOPE KILL PILL RILL SLEW SLUE VLEI VLEY WASH WICK BACHE BAYOU BIGHT BOGUE BROOK CRICK DRAFT FLEET INLET ZANJA ARROYO BRANCH BREACH CANADA ESTERO SLOUGH STREAM DRAUGHT ESTUARY RIVULET ZANJONA MUSKOGEE
(AUSTRALIAN —) COWAL
(TIDE —) SLAKE
CREEK SEDGE THATCH
CREEL RIP CAUL CAWL HASK JACK KELL RACK TRAP HARSK BASKET JUNKET
(— FOR BOBBINS) BANK SKEWER
CREELER TUBER LIGGER
CREEP COON FAWN GEEK INCH NERD RAMP CRAWL CROPE DRIFT GLIDE PROWL SKULK SLINK SMOOT STEAL TRAIL CRINGE GROVEL SCRIDE SPRAWL TIPTOE WEIRDO CRAMBLE CRAMMEL SNIGGLE WEIRDIE TAURANGA
(— AS IVY) RIZZLE
(PL.) WILLIES
(PREF.) HERPETI HERPETO
CREEPER IVY JITI SHOE VINE WORM CREEP CROPE SNAKE COWAGE CRADLE IPECAC REPENT ROMPER TECOMA CLAMPER CLIMBER COWHAGE COWITCH CRAWLER REPTANT REPTILE RUNNING TRAILER FOXGLOVE GUITGUIT PICUCULE WOODBINE PERIWINKLE
CREEPING SLOW REPTANT REPTILE SERVILE SARMENTOUS SERPIGINOUS
(— OF FLESH) GREW GRUE
(PREF.) HERPET(I)(O)
(SUFF.) (— CREATURE) ERPETON
CREEPING CROWFOOT SITFAST CRAWFOOT
CREEPING JENNY MONEYWORT
CREEPING SNOWBERRY MOXA TEABERRY

CREESE KRIS STAB CHESS CRISE SWORD DAGGER
CREMATE BURN
CREMATION SUTTEE
(PLACE OF —) GHAT GHAUT
CRENEL LOOP CORNEL KERNEL CRENELET
CREOLE KRIO PATOIS CRIOLLO DIALECT HAITIAN MESTIZO
(— STATE) LOUISIANA
(ENGLISH-BASED —) SRANAN
CREON (DAUGHTER OF —) GLAUCE
(FATHER OF —) MENOECEUS
(SISTER OF —) JOCASTA HIPPONOME
CREOSOTE BUSH LARREA
CREPE CRAPE FRIZZED NACARAT PANCAKE CHIRIMEN CRINKLED WRINKLED
CREPITATE SNAP GRATE RATTLE CRACKLE
CRESCENT HORN LUNE MOON ROOL CURVE LUNAR LUNOID LUNULE MOONED SICKLE WAXAND LUNETTE DEMILUNE MENISCUS
(END OF —) CUSP HORN
(PREF.) MENISCI MENISCO
CRESCENTLIKE BICORN
CRESCENT-SHAPED MOONY LUNATE LUNATED
(PREF.) SELEN(O)
CRESCIVE WAXING GROWING INCREASING
CRESOL FROTHER
CRESPHONTES (BROTHER OF —) TEMENUS ARISTODEMUS
(FATHER OF —) ARISTOMACHUS
(SON OF —) AEPYTUS
CRESS EKER KERSE CUCKOO MADWORT CRUCIFER WHITETOP PEPPERGRASS
CRESSET TORCH BASKET BEACON SIGNAL CRISSET FLAMBEAU
CREST COP TIP TOP ACME APEX COMB EDGE HOOD KNAP PEAK RUFF SEAL TUFT CHINE CROWN PLUME RIDGE COPPLE CREASE CRISTA CUMBRE FINIAL HEIGHT HELMET SUMMIT TIMBER TIMBRE BEARING FEATHER TOPKNOT CENTROID CRESTING ECTOLOPH METALOPH PINNACLE WHITECAP
(— OF BREAKER) SEEGE
(— OF HELMET) COMB CIMIER
(— OF HILL) KNAP
(— OF MINERAL VEIN) APEX
(— OF MOUNTAIN RANGE) ARETE SAWBACK
(— OF PEACOCK) CHAPLET
(— OF RIDGE) EDGE
(— OF SNOW) CORNICE
(— ON BIRD) CROWN ECKLE COPPLE
(IMPERIAL —) KIKUMON
(WAVE —) FEATHER WHITECAP
(PREF.) CRISTI LOPH(I)(IO)(O)
(SUFF.) LOPH(US)
CRESTED COMBED MUFFED TAPPET TAPPIT COPPLED CRISATE CROWNED CRISTATE PILEATED CRISTATED
CRESTED GREBE CARGOOSE
CRESTED QUAIL COPPY

CRESTFALLEN COWED DEJECTED
CRESTING CHENEAU
CRETACEOUS CHALKY
CRETAN KEFTI MINOAN CANDIOT
CRETAN SPIKENARD PHU

CRETE
BAY: SUDA KANCA KISAMO MESARA
CAPE: BUZA LIANO SALOME SIDERO
 SPATHA STAVROS LITHINON
 SIDHEROS
CAPITAL: CANEA
GULF: KHANIA MERABELLO
MOUNTAIN: IDA DIKTE JUKTAS
 LASITHI THEODORE
NAME: CRETA KRETE CANDIA
TOWN: HAG LATO CANEA KHORA
 SITIA ZAKRO ANOYIA CANDIA
 KHANIA KISAMO RETIMO
 KISAMOS KASTELLI HERAKLION

CRETHEUS (FATHER OF —) AEOLUS
 (MOTHER OF —) ENARETE
 (SLAYER OF —) TURNUS
 (SON OF —) AESON PHERES
 AMYTHAON
 (WIFE OF —) TYRO
CRETIN IDIOT
CREUSA GLAUCE GLAUKE
 (FATHER OF —) CREON PRIAM
 ERECHTHEUS
 (HUSBAND OF —) AENEAS XUTHUS
 (MOTHER OF —) HECUBA
 PRAXITHEA
 (SLAYER OF —) MEDEA
 (SON OF —) ION DORUS ACHAEUS
 ASCANIUS
CREVALLE JACK JUREL
CREVASSE CHASM SPLIT MOULIN
 SCHRUND CLEAVAGE
 BERGSCHRUND
CREVICE KIN BORE LEAK NOOK
 PEEP SEAM VEIN BREAK CHINE
 CHINK CLEFT CRACK CREEK CUNNE
 GRIKE CRANNY STRAKE CRANNEL
 FISSURE GUNNIES KRAVERS
 OPENING SLIFTER CREVASSE
 PEEPHOLE
 (VOLCANIC —) SOLFATARA
CREW LOT MEN MOB SET BAND
 GANG GING HERD OARS SHIP
 TEAM UNIT COVIN EIGHT HANDS
 MEINY PARTY SQUAD STAFF
 COVINE MEINIE SEAMEN THRONG
 AIRCREW COMPANY FACULTY
 MANNING MEMBERS RETINUE
 EQUIPAGE
 (— OF SHEARERS) BOARD
CREWEL CRUEL CADDIS CADDICE
CRIB BED BIN BOX CAB COT CUB
 HUT KEY BOOM CRUB CURB DIVE
 JACK PONY RACK RAFT SKIN TROT
 BOOSE BOOSY CHEAT CRATE
 FRAME HOVEL STALL STEAL
 BUNKER CRATCH CRECHE CRITCH
 MANGER PIGSTY PILFER CABBAGE
 ENGLISH PURLOIN BASSINET
 CORNCRIB CRIBBAGE CRIBBING
 CRIBWORK
CRIBBER SHORER STUMPSUCKER
CRICK KINK CREEK HITCH SPASM
 TWIST
CRICKET GRIG MOLE SNOB CHANGA

 SADDLE GRYLLID TWIDDLER
 ORTHOPTERAN
 (— HIT) SLOG
 (— SCORE OF 100 RUNS) TON
 (KIND OF —) MORMON
 (PREF.) GRYLLO
CRICKETER CUT COLT PLAYER
 RABBIT GENTLEMAN
CRICKET ON THE HEARTH
 (AUTHOR OF —) DICKENS
 (CHARACTER IN —) DOT MAY JOHN
 CALEB BERTHA EDWARD PLUMMER
 FIELDING TACKLETON PERRYBINGLE
CRIER HUER CRYER BEADLE
 HERALD WAILER BELLMAN
 MUEZZIN WRAWLER OUTCRIER
CRIME ACT SIN EVIL FACT LACK
 ABUSE ARSON BLAME CAPER
 FOLLY LIBEL WRONG FALSUM
 FELONY INCEST MURDER PIACLE
 FORFEIT FORGERY MISDEED
 OFFENCE OFFENSE INIQUITY
 SABOTAGE VILLAINY
 MALEFACTION MISDEMEANOR
 (— PHRASE) DOESNTPAY
 (ORGANIZED —) GANGLAND
CRIME AND PUNISHMENT
 (AUTHOR OF —) DOSTOEVSKI
 (CHARACTER IN —) SONIA DOUNIA
 LUZHIN PORFIRY PETROVICH
 RAZUMIHIN MARMELADOV
 RASKOLNIKOV SVIDRIGAILOV
CRIMINAL BAD SORE YEGG CROOK
 FELON TOUGH APACHE BASHER
 DACOIT GUILTY GUNMAN INMATE
 KILLER NOCENT SLAYER WARGUS
 WICKED CONVICT CULPRIT
 HEINOUS HOODLUM ILLEGAL
 ILLICIT MOBSTER NOXIOUS
 SEVENER VAUTRIN CRIMEFUL
 CULPABLE GANGSTER GAOLBIRD
 HABITUAL HARDCASE JAILBIRD
 PIACULAR SCELERAT
 (HABITUAL —) RECIDIVIST
 (PETTY —) ROUNDER
 (VIOLENT —) DESPERADO
 (PL.) AMALAITA
CRIMINATE IMPEACH
CRIMP BEND CURL FOLD FRIZ POKE
 POTE WAVE WEAK CLAMP CRISP
 FLUTE FRILL FRIZZ PINCH PLAIT
 BUCKLE GOFFER RUFFLE CRIMPER
 CRIMPLE CRINKLE FRIABLE
 GAUFFER WRINKLE OBSTACLE
CRIMSON LAC RED PINK GRAIN
 BLOODY JOCKEY MAROON
 MODENA CARMINE SCARLET
 CRAMOISY CREMOSIN
 (— TIDE) BAMA
CRIMSON CLOVER NAPOLEON
CRIMSON LAKE SULTAN
CRINE HAIR
CRINED MANED
CRINGE BOW BEND CURB CURR
 DUCK FAWN JOUK BINGE COWER
 CRAWL CREEP QUAIL SNEAK
 SNOOL STOOP WINCE YIELD
 BUCKLE CROUCH GROVEL SHRINK
 SUBMIT ADULATE CRINKLE
 DISTORT SCRINGE TRUCKLE
CRINGER FLUNKEY
CRINGING ABJECT HANGDOG
 SERVILE SPANIEL

CRINKLE BEND CURL KINK TURN
 WIND CREPE CRISP PUCKER
 RIPPLE RUMPLE RUSTLE CRACKLE
 CRANKLE FRIZZLE WRINKLE
CRINKLED CRIMP CURLY BUCKLED
 ENCOMIC CRISPATE
CRINKLY CREPY CREPEY
CRINOID POLYP CRINITE CAMERATE
 COMATULA
 (BODY OF —) CROWN
CRINOLINE CRIN HOOP
CRIPPLE MAR CRIP GIMP HARM
 HURT LAME MAIM BACACH
 HOBBLE IMPAIR INJURE SCOTCH
 WEAKEN CRAPPLE CRUMPET
 DISABLE LAMETER LAMIGER
 LAMITER HANDICAP LAMESTER
 MUTIL ATE PARALYZE
 (PL.) LAMZIEKTE
CRIPPLED GIMPY LAMED COUPLED
 DISABLED
CRIPPLING MAIM MAYHEM
CRISIS FIT ACME CRUX FLAP HEAD
 JUMP PASS TURN BRUNT CARDO
 CRISE PANIC PERIL PINCH POINT
 STATE STORM TRIAL STRAIT
 DUNKIRK DECISION JUNCTURE
 MOUNTAIN
 (AUTHOR OF —) CHURCHILL
 (CHARACTER IN —) BRICE GRANT
 CARVEL COLFAX ABRAHAM
 LINCOLN STEPHEN WHIPPLE
 CLARENCE VIRGINIA
CRISP NEW COLD CURL FRIZ FROW
 HARD BRISK CLEAR CRIPS CRUMP
 CURLY FRESH FRIZZ NIPPY PITHY
 SHARP SHORT SPALT STIFF TERSE
 BITING BRIGHT CRISPY LIVELY
 SNAPPY BRACING BRITTLE
 CONCISE CRACKLY CRUNCHY
 CUTTING FRIABLE FRIZZLE
 SMOPPLE INCISIVE POTATOCHIP
CRISPED FUZZY FRIZZLY CRISPATE
CRISPINELLA (SISTER OF —)
 BEATRICE
CRISPNESS SNAP
CRISSCROSS AWRY CROSS
 NETWORK CONFUSED
CRITERION LAW NORM RULE TEST
 TYPE AXIOM CANON CHECK
 GAUGE MODEL PROOF TOUCH
 CRISIS METRIC INDICIA MEASURE
 PLUMMET STANDARD
 SHIBBOLETH
CRITIC MOME BOOER JUDGE
 MOMUS RATER CARPER CENSOR
 CORNER EXPERT PUNDIT SLATER
 SYNDIC ZOILUS STYLIST ZOILIST
 COLLATOR CRITIQUE DEBUNKER
 OVERSEER REVIEWER THONGMAN
 ARISTARCH
 AMERICAN CARY GILL KAEL KERR
 LAHR MORE SOBY TATE AIKEN
 BANGS BOGAN BREEN BROWN
 CANBY CRIST CUPPY EBERT ELSON
 FINCK FISKE GIBBS HEWES KALEM
 KAZIN KOBBE LEVIN MABIE POUND
 SIMON WHITE ALLSOP BECKER
 BROOKS CHENEY DOWNES FULLER
 GILMAN HUTTON KRASNA KRUTCH
 LEDOUX LOWELL MANTLE MILLER
 MUNSON NATHAN PARKER PHELPS
 SHALIT SISKEL SONTAG TAYLOR

 WILSON ALDRICH ANDREWS
 AVAKIAN FIEDLER GRANICK
 HUNEKER POIRIER SMAROFF
 VENDLER WHIPPLE WIMSATT
 ATKINSON BOOKSPAN CROWTHER
 HAGEDORN SAARINEN ROSENFELD
 WOOLLCOTT CHOTZINOFF
 AUSTRALIAN HUGHES TURNER
 AUSTRIAN KUH KRAUS
 CANADIAN FRYE SMITH BIRNEY
 CZECH HANSLICK
 DANISH LANGE BRANDES
 GERSTENBERG
 DUTCH BRINK BILDERDIJK
 JONCKBLOET VALCKENAER
 ENGLISH BAX FRY BELL LAMB READ
 SHAW WAIN WEST AGATE BOWRA
 DILKE ELIOT ELWIN GAUNT GOULD
 GREIN LAVES LEVIN MERES PAGET
 PATER PATES RYMER SCOTT TYNAN
 WAUGH ARNOLD BINYON COLLES
 COLVIN DENNIS EMPSON HUXLEY
 LEAVIS MORGAN PALMER RUSKIN
 SYMONS THOMAS WALKER
 WARTON AINSLIE BENTLEY
 BRADLEY COLLIER COLLINS
 FREEMAN GIFFORD GISSING
 JOHNSON KERMODE LUBBOCK
 RALEIGH SHORTER SITWELL
 STEPHEN TOYNBEE WALKLEY
 WHIBLEY BEERBOHM MARRIOTT
 SECCOMBE STEPHENS MACCARTHY
 PARTRIDGE SAINTSBURY
 SWINNERTON
 FINNISH WALTARI
 FRENCH GIDE BAYLE BAZIN BIDOU
 BLAZE DENIS GILLE TAINE CASSOU
 FAGUET FRANCE LANSON MENDES
 OZANAM SARCEY VALERY BARTHES
 BATTEUX BOURGET BREMOND
 GAUTIER MERIMEE REGNIER
 AUBIGNAC MEZIERES MONTEGUT
 VALLETTE BRUNETIERE
 APOLLINAIRE
 GERMAN BAB EYE KERR MERCK
 MUNDT OPITZ MENZEL SCHOLL
 WAAGEN LESSING NICOLAI RIBBECK
 ZARNCKE ACIDALIUS
 GREEK ELYTIS ZOILUS
 ARISTARCHUS CALLIMACHUS
 HUNGARIAN KOLCSEY
 ICELANDIC BLONDAL
 INDIAN ANAND
 IRISH BOYD DEVERE MARTYN
 ITALIAN PRAZ CECCHI OJETTI
 OVIDIO BARETTI CAPUANA
 MONTALE ZANELLA CARDUCCI
 CHIARINI ALGAROTTI DESANCTUS
 CASTELVETRO CAVALCASELLE
 MEXICAN PAZ
 NORWEGIAN WELHAVEN
 POLISH LANGE
 PORTUGUESE VASCONCELLOS
 RUSSIAN PYPIN STASOV BELINSKI
 SCOTTISH DENT MUIR ARCHER
 WILSON JEFFREY
 SPANISH CANETE
 SWEDISH SIREN LEOPOLD
 KELLGREN LEVERTIN
 SWISS BODMER
 WELSH SYMONS
CRITICAL EDGY HIGH NICE ACERB
 ACUTE VITAL CHILLY CRITIC

NASUTE SEVERE URGENT ACERBIC
ADVERSE CARPING EXIGENT
NERVOUS PARLOUS CAPTIOUS
CARDINAL CAVILING DECISIVE
EXACTING JUDICIAL PRESSING
SLASHING TICKLISH CLIMACTERIC
CRITICISM DIG RAP FIRE FLAK GAFF
SLAM BLAME KNOCK SLATE
ATTACK CRITIC REVIEW STATIC
CENSURE COMMENT DESCANT
LITCRIT PANNING QUIBBLE
SLASHER SLATING ZOILISM
BLUDGEON CRITIQUE DIATRIBE
JUDGMENT STRICTURE
(PETTY —) NITPICKING
(POINTED —) JAB
(UNJUSTIFIED —) NITPICKING
CRITICIZE HIT PAN RAP RIP CARP
CRAB FLAY FLOG RIDE SKIN SLAM
SLUR TIDE YELP BLAME BLAST
CAVIL DECRY GRIPE JUDGE KNOCK
ROAST SCORE SLASH SLATE
TRASH BERATE CRITIC REBUKE
REVIEW CENSURE COMMENT
CONDEMN CRITIZE EXAMINE
NITPICK SCARIFY BADMOUTH
CRITIQUE DENOUNCE TOMAHAWK
(— MINUTELY) NITPICK
(— SEVERELY) FLAY JUMP
(— SLASHINGLY) SLASH SLATE
CRITIQUE CRITIC REVIEW CRITICISM
CRIUS (FATHER OF —) URANUS
(MOTHER OF —) GAEA
(SON OF —) PALLAS PERSES
ASTRAEUS
CRO CROY PAYMENT
CROAK CAW DIE GASP KILL PORK
ROUP CRAKE CREAK CRONK
PLUNK QUALM QUARK SPEAK
CROAPE GRUMBLE COMPLAIN
FOREBODE
CROAKER SPOT RONCO CROCUS
RONCHO TOMCOD BUBBLER
CABEZON CORBINA CORVINA
CABEZONE HARDHEAD KINGFISH
SCIAENID
CROAKING CROAKY HOARSE
RANARIAN COAXATION
CROAT CHORWAT CHROBAT
SYRMIAN
(PL.) HRVATI HERVATI
CROATIA (ALSO SEE YUGOSLAVIA)
CAPITAL: ZAGREB
COIN: DINAR
GULF: KOTOR
LANGUAGE: CROATIAN
SERBOCROATIAN
MOUNTAIN: TROGLAV
MOUNTAIN RANGE: DINARIC
ZAGORJE
PENINSULA: ISTRIAN
PLAIN: PANNONIAN
PARAPANNONIAN
REGION: ISTRIA DALMATIA
RIVER: UNA KRKA KUPA SAVA
DRAVA CETINA
SEA: ADRIATIC
TOWN: SPLIT OSIJEK RIJEKA
WIND: BORA BURA JUGO MISTRAL
CROCARD BRABANT SCALDING
SLEEPING
CROCHET HOOK KNIT BRAID PLAIT
WEAVE CROTCHET

CROCK JAR PIG POT SMUT SOIL
SOOT STEAN STEEN STOOL
CHATTY CRITCH GOOLAH PANMUG
SMUDGE CRAGGAN TERRINE
POTSHERD
CROCKERY CHINA CLOAM DISHES
PIGGERY POTWARE CLAYWARE
CROCODILE GOA CROC GATOR
MAGAR CAYMAN GAVIAL JACARE
LIZARD MUGGER YACARE
CRAWLER CREEPER DIAPSID
REPTILE SAURIAN SERPENT
LORICATE
CROCODILE BIRD SICSAC TROCHIL
MESSMATE
CROCUS IRID LILY SAFFRON
COLCHICUM
CROFT FARM TORP CRAFT CRYPT
FIELD GARTH VAULT BLEACH
CAVERN PARROCK PIGHTLE
CROMLECH QUOIT CIRCLE DOLMEN
CROMMEL GORSEDD
CROMORNA CREMONA
KRUMHORN
CRONE HAG AUNT TROT CRONY
WITCH BELDAM RIBIBE BELDAME
CRONOS (DAUGHTER OF —) HERA
CRONY PAL CHUM BILLY GOSSY
NETOP GIMMER GOSSIP
CROOK BEND HOOK TURN WARP
CHEAT CHINK CLEEK CRANK
CROMB CROOM CRUMP CURVE
GANEF HUNCH NIBBY PEDUM
STAFF THIEF TRICK CRUMMY
INDENT TWICER CAMBUCA
CROSIER CROZIER CRUMMIE
INCURVE POTHOOK SLICKER
ARTIFICE CHISELER CRUMMOCK
SWINDLER
(— A FINGER AT) BECKON
(— IN BRANCH) KNEE
(— OF HEAD) HEEL
(SHEPHERD'S —) CROTCH KEBBIE
CROOKBACKED CROUCHIE
CROOKED CAM WRY AGEE ALOP
AWRY BENT GAME WOGH AGLEY
ASKEW BANDY BOWLY CRANK
CRUMP FALSE GLEED KINKY SNIDE
THRAW TIPSY WRONG ACROOK
AKIMBO ARTFUL ASLANT CAMMED
CAMSHO CRABBY CRAFTY CRANKY
CURVED DOGLEG HURLED
THRAWN TRICKY WEEWAW
WEEWOW ZIGZAG ASKANCE
ASQUINT CORRUPT CRABBED
CURVOUS OBLIQUE TURNING
TWISTED WINDING CAMSHACH
THRAWART TORTUOUS
(PREF.) ANKYL(O) CROM
CROOKEDNESS PRAVITY RHEBOSIS
CROOKNECK CASHAW CUSHAW
CROON HUM LOW BOOM LULL
SING WAIL CHIRM CRONY WHINE
LAMENT MURMUR TEEDLE
COMPLAIN
CROP BOB COW CUT LOP MAW SET
TOP CLIP CRAP CRAW KNAP MINE
REAP SETT SNIP STOW TRAP TRIM
WHIP FRUIT GRAZE PLANT QUIRT
SHAVE SHEAR SHIFT SWATH TILTH
TRASH BROWSE BURDEN DECERP
GATHER GEBBIE SILAGE BEARING
BURTHEN CRAPPIN CURTAIL

CUTTING HARVEST MAMMONI
MASHLUM TILLAGE GLEANING
PROFICHI TRASHIFY INGLUVIES
(— CANDLEWICK) SNUFF
(— OF A HAWK) GORGE
(— OF BIRDS) INGLUVIES
(— OF FRUIT) HANG
(— OF GRASS) LEA LEY SWATH
SWARTH SWATHE
(— OF OYSTERS) SET
(— OF POTATOES) GARDEN
(— OUT) BASSET
(— UP) EMERGE
(GREEN —S) SOILAGE
(INDIAN —) RABI KHARIF
(LARGE —) HIT
(RIDING —) ROP
(SECOND-GROWTH —) ROWEN
AFTERMATH
(PL.) FEED TILLAGE
CROPPED GOTCH SHAVED
GOTCHED
CROPPER CARVER MUCKER PURLER
GRINDER PLUMPER
CROPPING EARMARK
CROQUET ROQUE BOMBARD
CROQUETTE CECIL OYSTER
KROMESKI KROMESKY
CROSIER BAGLE CROCE CROOK
PEDUM STAFF POTENT BACULUS
CAMBUCA CROZIER PASTORAL
CROSS GO CAM CUT MIX TAU ANKH
CRUX FORD FUNK MARK PASS
ROOD SIGN SOUR SPAN TREE
WOOD ANGRY CANGY CHUFF
CORSE GAMMY GURLY IRATE
SURLY TEATY TESTY THRAW TRAVE
TRIAL YAPPY BISECT CHUFFY
CRABBY CRANKY CROUCH DENIAL
EMBLEM FRANZY GIBBET GROUTY
GRUMPY HIPPED OUTWIT PATCHY
SIGNUM SNAGGY SNASTY SNUFFY
SULLEN SYMBOL TEETHY THWART
TOUCHY WICKED WOOLLY
ATHWART BECROSS CALVARY
CRABBED CROSIER CROZIER
CRUSADE CRUSADO FRABOUS
FRETFUL FROWARD OBLIQUE
PASSAGE PATIBLE PEEVISH
PETTISH POTENCE SALTIER
SALTIRE CAMSHACH CRANTARA
CROCIATE CROISADE CROSSLET
CROTCHED CRUCIFIX DEBRUISE
DEMISANG FRAMPOLD FRATCHED
FRUMPISH OVERPASS PECTORAL
PETULANT PHRAMPEL SNAPPISH
SWASTIKA THUNDERY TRAVERSE
VEXILLUM WINDMILL
**(— BETWEEN GRAPEFRUIT AND
TANGERINE)** UGLI
(— BY PLANE) HOP
(— ONESELF) SAIN
(— OVER) SPAN TRAJECT
(DOUBLE —) BUSINESS
(KIND OF —) TAU
(MALTESE —) FIREBALL
(PREF.) CRUCI STAUR(O)
CROSSARM WISHBONE
CROSSBAR RUNG CROWN JUGUM
DRIVER TRANSOM
(— IN GATE) SWORD
(— IN SHAFT) STEMPEL STEMPLE
(— OF BALANCE) BEAM

(— OF DOOR) SLOAT
(— OF WINDOW) LOCKET
CROSSBEAM BAR BUNK SPUR
TRAVE GIRDER BOLSTER
DORMANT TRANSOM TRAVERSE
CROSSBEARER CRUCIFER
SPREADER
CROSSBILL FINCH
CROSSBOW PROD RODD BRAKE
LATCH PIECE PRODD TILLER
SLURBOW ARBALEST BALISTER
BALLISTA STEELBOW STOCKBOW
STONEBOW
(PART OF —) NUT IRON LOCK
GUARD SIGHT STOCK WEDGE
GROOVE STIRRUP TRIGGER
BOWSTRING
CROSSBREED CUR HUSKY METIS
SANGA SANGU HYBRID
CROSS CARRIER CRUCIFER
CROSSCURRENT EDDY SURGING
CROSSCUT DRIFT OFFSET TUNNEL
COUPURE
CROSSCUT SAW BRIAR
CROSSCUTTER BUCKER
CROSSE STICK
CROSSED ACROSS SQUINT
WOOFED CRUCIAL THWARTING
(PREF.) CHIASTO
CROSSER STICKER
CROSSETTE EAR ANCON ELBOW
ANCONE CROSET
CROSS-EXAMINE GRILL TARGE
CROSSEXAMINE TARGE
CROSS-EYE ESOTROPIA
CROSS-EYED SQUINT
CROSS-FERTILIZATION
ALLOGAMY PHYTOGAMY
CROSS FORM URDE URDY
CROSS-GRAINED THWART UGLY
NURLY GNARLED HICKORY
CONTRARY FRAMPOLD
CROSSHEAD YOKE
CROSSING XG PASS CROSS LACED
MIXTURE PASSAGE TRAJECT
CRUCIATE OPPOSING OVERPASS
TRAVERSE CROSSOVER
(KIND OF —) ZEBRA
(NAVE —) TRANSEPT
CROSSLIKE CRUCIAL
CROSS-LINE (— OF LETTER) SERIF
CROSSPATCH BEAR CRAB CRANK
GROUCH
CROSSPIECE BAR BAIL SPAR STEP
YOKE BEARD GLAND GRILL ROUND
STOCK PUTLOG THWART TOGGEL
TOGGLE BOLSTER TRANSOM
CROSSARM CROWFOOT FOOTRAIL
HEADRAIL TRAVERSE CHOPSTICK
(PL.) CROSSTREE
CROSS-QUESTION GRILL TARGE
TAIRGE
CROSSROAD LEET VENT WENT
WEENT CAREFOX CARFOUR
COMPITUM CROSSWAY
(PL.) TRIVIA
CROSSRUFF SAW SEESAW
CROSS-SHAPED CRUCIAL
CRUCIATE
CROSS-STAFF CROSS RADIUS
CROSIER CROZIER ARBALEST
CROSS STROKE BIND
CROSS-TEMPERED FRUMPISH

CROSSWALK ZEBRA
CROSSWISE CROSS ACROSS
ATHWART ACROSTIC DIAGONAL
OVERWART TRAVERSE WEFTWISE
CROSSWAYS
CROSSWORD (— PUZZLER)
CRUCIVERBALIST
CROSSWORT MAYWORT
MUGWEED MUGWORT
CROTALUM CROTAL CYMBAL
CROTCH FORK POLE POST CLEFT
NOTCH STAKE CRATCH CRUTCH
GRAINS CROTCHET
CROTCHET FAD TOY HOOK KINK
WHIM CRANK FANCY FREAK FIZGIG
MAGGOT VAGARY CORCHAT
CRANKUM
(HALF —) QUAVER
CROTCHETY KINKY CRANKY
SNARKY
CROUCH HUG BEND CLAP COOK
CURB DARE DROP FAWN FORM
ROOK RUCK COWER HOVER
SQUAT STOOP COORIE CRINGE
CROOCH HUDDLE HUNKER
HURKLE HURTLE SCOOCH SCOUCH
CROODLE CROWDLE SCROOCH
SCRUNCH SQUATTER
CROUCHING SQUAT CROUCHANT
CROUD SCROUGE
CROUP CRUP HIVES CRUPPER
CROUPIER DEALER TOURNEUR
CROUTON DIABLOTIN
CROW AGA CAW CRY DAW BRAG
BRAN CRAW DOWP ROOK AYLET
BOAST CRAKE CROWD EXULT
GLOAT HOODY KELLY RAVEN
VAUNT CARNAL CHOUGH CORBIE
CORVUS HOODIE KOKAKO
GORCROW GRAPNEL JACKDAW
SWAGGER ABSAROKA BALDHEAD
BLACKNEB GAVELOCK GRAYBACK
GREYBACK
(PREF.) CORACO CORVI
(SUFF.) CORAX
CROWBAR PRY SET CROW BETTY
JEMMY JIMMY LEVER SETUP
SWAPE FORCER GABLOCK
PITCHER GAVELOCK HANDSPEC
CROWBERRY HEATH HEATHER
CROWD FRY HUG JAM MOB SET
TAG TIP BIKE CRAM CRUT FARE
GANG HEAP HERD HOST JOSS
MONG PACK PAVE PILE PUSH RAFT
ROCK ROTE ROUT RUCK SERR SKIT
SLUE SORT STOW SWAD TURB
WOOD BUNCH CLOUD COHUE
COVEY CRAMP CRUSH CRWTH
DROVE FLOCK GROUP HORDE
HURRY PLUMP POSSE PRESS
ROTTA SERRY SHACK SHOAL
STECH STIVE STUFF SWARM
THREE VOLGE WEDGE BOODLE
CHORUS CLIQUE HUBBLE HUDDLE
HUSTLE IMPACT JOSTLE MITHER
MOIDER OUTFIT PESTER RABBLE
RESORT SCRUZE THRAVE THREAD
THRIMP THRONG THRUST TOURBE
TYMPAN VOLLEY BOUROCK
CHROTTA CLUSTER COMPANY
CONGEST IMPRESS JIMBANG
SCROOGE SCROUGE SQUEEZE
THICKEN THRUTCH CABOODLE

ENTHRONG FREQUENT JINGBANG
SANDWICH SATURATE VARLETRY
CONCOURSE GATHERING
MULTITUDE CLAMJAMFRY
(— ABOUT) FLOCK
(— AROUND) MOB BESIEGE
(— OUT) DISPLACE
(— TOGETHER) HUG HOTTER
HOWDER HUDDLE CLUTTER
CONTRUDE
(CONFUSED —) HURRY
(MOVING —) DROVE
(NOISY —) ROUT
(PREF.) OCHLO
CROWDED PANG CLOSE DENSE
SPISS STIFF THICK FILLED SPISSY
THRONG BUNCHED COMPACT
OPPLETE POPULAR SERRIED
STIPATE STUFFED TEEMING
NUMEROUS POPULOUS
JAMPACKED
CROWFOOT JOY PAGLE CREATE
EXOGEN PAIGLE EELWARE
GOLDCUP GOLLAND GOWLAND
BANEWORT CRAWFOOT
GOLDWEED HELLWEED
CROWING COCK
CROWN CAP TAJ TIP TOP BULL COIN
GULL HELM PALE PATE PEAK POLL
RIGO TIAR ADORN BASIL BEZEL
BEZIL CREST MITER MITRE MURAL
POLOS REGAL ROUND ROYAL
TIARA ANADEM CANTLE CIRCLE
CLIMAX CORONA DIADEM DOLLAR
FILLET INVEST LAUREL POTONG
REWARD SUMMIT TIMBER TROPHY
UPWARD VALLAR VERTEX WREATH
AUREOLE CHAPLET CORNICE
CORONAL CORONET FORETOP
GARLAND INSTALL PSCHENT
STEPHEN TONSURE CORONATE
CORONULE ENTHRONE PINNACLE
SURMOUNT TURNPIKE
(— OF CHICORY) ENDIVE
(— OF EGYPT) ATEF PSCHENT
(— OF HEAD) NOLL PATE SKULL
CANTLE POMMEL FORETOP
(— OF HILL) KNAP
(— OF LAUREL) BAY
(— OF ROCK) KRANTZ
(HALF —) GEORGE ALDERMAN
(PIECE OF —) BULL
(PLANT —) STOOL
(PREF.) CORONI CORONO
STEPHAN(O)
CROWNED CORONATE LAURELED
(— WITH ROSES) ROSATED
CROW SHRIKE MAGPIE SQUEAKER
CROW'S NEST LOOKOUT
CROZER CHUCKER
CRUCIAL KEY ACUTE PIVOT NEEDLE
SEVERE TRYING PIVOTAL SUPREME
TELLING CRITICAL DECISIVE
CRUCIAN CARP GIBEL
CRUCIBLE POT DISH ETNA SHOE
TEST CRUCE FOYER TRIAL CRUSET
HEARTH MONKEY RETORT
FURNACE CROSSLET
CRUCIFIX PAX ROOD CROSS
CRUCIFIXION RANSOM
CRUCIFY VEX HANG KILL HARRY
MORTIFY TORMENT TORTURE
CRUCIATE

CRUDE ILL RAW BALD BARE RUDE
BRUTE CRASS GREEN GROSS
HAIRY HARSH ROUGH TACKY
CALLOW COARSE DOUGHY INCULT
KUTCHA SAVAGE UNRIPE VULGAR
ARTLESS GLARING SQUALID
UNCOUTH AGRESTIC IGNORANT
IMMATURE IMPOLITE INDIGEST
PRIMITIVE
(NOT —) DELICATE
CRUDELY HARSHLY GAUCHELY
CRUDITY RUDENESS BARBARITY
CRASSNESS GAUCHERIE
ROUGHNESS
CRUEL ILL FELL GRIL GRIM HARD
BLACK BREEM BREME BRUTE
FELON HARSH RETHE SADIC STERN
WROTH BITTER BLOODY BRUTAL
DIVERS DREARY FIERCE IMMANE
SAVAGE SEVERE UNJUST UNKIND
UNMEEK UNMILD UNRIDE
WANTON WICKED BESTIAL
BOARISH BRUTISH GRIMFUL
INHUMAN NERONIC SCADDLE
SPITOUS WILROUN BARBARIC
DIABOLIC FELONOUS FIENDISH
INHUMANE PITILESS RUTHLESS
SADISTIC TYRANNIC TRUCULENT
(THOUGHTLESSLY —) WANTON
CRUELLY FELL HARD CRUEL FELLY
HARSHLY
CRUELTY RIGOR DURESS SADISM
DEVILRY DEVILTRY FELLNESS
SEVERITY
CRUET AMA JAR JUG VIAL BURET
CRUSE BOTTLE CASTER CREVET
CREWET GUTTUS AMPULLA
BURETTE URCEOLE
CRUISE SAIL TRIP JUNKET STOOGE
(— AS A PIRATE) BUSK
CRUISER SHIP VALUER VESSEL
WARSHIP ESTIMATOR
CRUISING ASEA
CRULLER WONDER OLYCOOK
OLYKOEK TWISTER DOUGHNUT
CRUMB BIT ORT MURL NIRL PIECE
LITTLE MORSEL CRIMBLE
CRUMBLE MEALOCK MURLACK
REMNANT FRAGMENT
(PL.) PANADA PANURE MOOLINGS
CRUMBLE ROT CRIM MULL MURL
MUSH BREAK BROCK CRUSH
DECAY RAVEL SLAKE SPALL SPOIL
BUCKLE MOLDER MYRTLE PERISH
SLOUGH CORRADE CRIMBLE
MOULDER COLLAPSE
(— DOWN) GRUSH
(— UNDER OVERWEIGHT) FLUSH
CRUMBLED UNDURE
(EASILY —) CRIMP BRUCKLE
CRUMBLY
CRUMBLING SAMEL SAMMEL
POWDERY
CRUMBLY NESH MURLY CRUMBY
CRUMMY FRIABLE PULVERULENT
CRUMPET CAKE MUFFIN PIKELET
CRUMPLE FOLD MOOL MUSS ROOL
WISP CRUSH SCREW BUCKLE
CREASE FURROW RAFFLE RUCKLE
RUMPLE CRIZZLE CRUNKLE
FRUMPLE SCRUNCH WRINKLE
COLLAPSE CONTRACT SCRUMPLE
CRUNCH BITE CHEW MUCH CHOMP

CRASH CRUMP CRUSH GNASH
GRIND PRESS RUNCH CRANCH
CRINCH GRANCH GROWSE
CRAUNCH SCRANCH SCRUNCH
CRUPPER CROUP CURPEL CURPIN
TAILBAND
CRUSADE WAR JEHAD JIHAD
CROISEE CAMPAIGN CROCIATE
CRUSADER PILGRIM TEMPLAR
EQUITIST REFORMER
(PL.) CROISES
**CRUSADER IN EGYPT (CHARACTER
IN —)** ADRIANO ALADINO ARMANDO
PALMIDE DORVILLE ELMIRENO
(COMPOSER OF —) MEYERBEER
CRUSH DOWT JUG JAM BEND BORE
BRAY CASE CHEW CRAM DASH
MASH MILL MULL PASH RAVE
STUB BRAKE BREAK BRIZZ CHAMP
CHECK CRASH CRAZE CREEM
CROWD FORCE FRUSH GRIND
GRUSH PRESS QUASH QUELL
SMASH SMUSH SQUAB SQUAT
STAMP TREAD UNMAN BRUISE
BURDEN CRUNCH DEFOIL DEFOUL
KNATCH KNETCH SCOTCH SCRUSH
SCRUZE SQUASH SQUISS SUBDUE
THRING THRONG THWACK
ACCABLE DECIMATE CONQUER
CONTUSE CRACKLE CRUMPLE
DEPRESS DESTROY OPPRESS
OVERRUN REPRESS SCRUNCH
SCRUNGE SHATTER SQUEEZE
SQUELCH SUCCUMB TRAMPLE
COMPRESS FORBREAK OVERCOME
SQUABASH SUPPRESS
OVERWHELM
(— BEANS) NIB
(— HAT) BONNET
(— IN) STAVE
(— ROCK) DOLLY DOLLEY DOLLIE
(— SPIRIT) BREAK
CRUSHABLE QUASHY
CRUSHED TAME BROKEN ECRASE
MUSHED CONTRITE CRUMPLED
CRUSHER NIBBER
CRUSHING FIERCE BRUISING
SMASHING SQUABASH
(SUFF.) TRIPSY
CRUST FUR PIP CAKE HULL RIND
SCAB SHELL SKULL COFFIN
CRUSTA ESCHAR GRATIN HARDEN
RONDLE SCRUFF ABAISSE CALICHE
COATING ENCRUST INCRUST
CARAPACE PELLICLE SCUTULUM
WINEBALL DURICRUST
(— IN BOILER) FUR
(— OF DIKE) SALBAND
(— OF DYKE) SALBAND
(— OF EARTH) SIAL SIMA
(— ON WINE) ARGAL ARGOL
(PIE —) HUFF COFFIN
(PL.) SORDES
CRUSTA PES
CRUSTACEAN BUG APUS CRAB
FLEA SCUD ZOEA ALIMA CARID
KRILL LOUSE PRAWN SCREW
SCROW CYPRID ENDITE ISOPOD
SHRIMP SLATER SQUILL ARTEMIA
COPEPOD CRAYLET DAPHNID
DECAPOD GRIBBLE HAYSEED
LOBSTER SQUAGGA SQUILLA
AMPHIPOD BARNACLE CIRRIPED

CRAYFISH GAMMARID LERNAEAN MONOCULE OSTRACOD PAGURIAN SQUILLID BRACHYURA PHYLLOPOD SCHIZOPOD SHELLFISH MALACOSTRACAN RHIZOCEPHALAN
(FEMALE —) HEN
CRUSTADE DARIOLE
CRUSTY CURT BLUFF BLUNT RUSTY TESTY MOROSE SULLEN CRABBED PEEVISH PETTISH STARCHY SNAPPISH
CRUTCH FORK STILT CLUTCH CRATCH CROTCH POTENT SADDLE SCATCH STADDLE
CRUX NUB GIST HALF PITH CROSS POINT PUZZLE RIDDLE PROBLEM
CRUX ANSATA ANKH
CRWTH ROTA ROTE CROWD CRUTH ROTTA ROTTE CROUTH CHROTTA
CRY HO AHA BOO CAW CRI FAD HOA HUE OLE PIP SOB YIP BAWL BELL BUMP CALL COWL CROW EVOE FALL GLAM GOWL HAIL HAWK HOOT HOWL KEEN MEWL NOTE OYES OYEZ PULE RAGE RAME RANE REEM RERD ROOP SCRY SIKE TOOT WAIL WEEP YELL YELP YOWL BARLA BLART BLORE CHEVY CLEPE CRAKE CROUP CRUNK GREDE GREET GROAN QUEAK RUMOR SHOUT SOUND TROAT UTTER VOGUE WHEWL WHINE WHULE WRAWL BARLEY BELLOW BOOHOO CHIVVY CLAMOR DEMAND ENSIGN LAMENT OUTCRY QUETHE SCREAM SHRIEK SLOGAN SNIVEL SQUALL SQUAWL SQUEAL TONGUE WIMICK YAMMER EXCLAIM FASHION HOSHANA SCREECH SPRAICH GARDYLOO PROCLAIM SCRONACH
(— ALOUD) BLART GREDE
(— AT SIGHT OF WHALE) FALL
(— DOWN) DOWNCRY BERATTLE
(— FOR TRUCE) BARLA BARLY BARLEY
(— HOARSELY) CROUP
(— LIKE ELEPHANT) BARR TRUMPET
(— LIKE PIG) WRINE
(— MOURNFULLY) YOWL
(— OF A BAT) CHIP
(— OF ABORIGINES) COOEE
(— OF BACCHANALS) EVOE
(— OF BIRD) CAW COO PEW BOOM CAWK CLANG BIRDCALL
(— OF BITTERN) BILL
(— OF CAT) MEW MEWL MIAOU MIAOW MIAUL MIAUW CALLING
(— OF CONTEMPT) BOO
(— OF DEER) BELL
(— OF DELIGHT) WHEE YIPES
(— OF DISCOVERY) EUREKA
(— OF DISGUST) PAH
(— OF ENTHUSIASM) BANZAI
(— OF GOOSE) HONK YANG
(— OF GUINEA HEN) POTRACK
(— OF HORROR) ACK
(— OF HOUND) MUTE MUSIC
(— OF JACKAL) PHEAL PHEALE PHEEAL
(— OF MOURNING) KEEN TANGI
(— OF NEWBORN CHILD) VAGITUS

(— OF RAVEN) QUALM
(— OF SHEEP) BAA BLAT BLEAT
(— OF SNIPE) SCAPE
(— OF SORROW) ULLAGONE
(— OF SURPRISE) ACK
(— OF SURRENDER) KAMERAD
(— OF WATCHMAN) WATCH
(— OUT) BAY BAWL BRAY GALE GAPE HOOT HOWL JERK SCRY BLORE CHIRM CLAIM ESCRY SHOUT HALLOO HOLLER SCREAM SHRIEK THREAP THROPE BREATHE EXCLAIM RECLAIM DISCLAIM PROCLAIM
(— TO CLEAR PASSAGE) HALL
(— TO COMBATANTS) BAILE
(— UP) CRACK
(BATTLE —) CRY ENSIGN MONTJOY GERONIMO MONTJOYE
(DERISIVE —) BOO FIE POOF POOH HUMBUG
(DISMAL —) HOWL WAIL YOWL
(DRINKING —) RIVO
(HOARSE —) CROAK
(HUNTING —) TIVY CHEVY CHIVY CHEVVY STABOY YOICKS TALLYHO TANTARA TANTIVY PILILLOO
(KIND OF —) FAR
(MAGICIAN'S —) PRESTO
(PROLONGED —) RANE
(RALLYING —) SLOGAN
(RAUCOUS —) CATCALL
(SHRILL) SKIRL SQUEAK SQUEAL SCREECH YALLOCK
(WAR —) DIN ALALA HAVOC BANZAI SLOGAN
(WORDLESS —) KEEN ULULU
CRY-BABY MARDY
CRYING PIPING URGING CLAMANT HEINOUS VAGIENT PRESSING RECREANT
(— OF HOUND) BELLING
CRYPT PIT CRAFT CROFT CROWD VAULT CAVERN GROTTO RECESS SHROUD CHAMBER FOLLICLE
CRYPTIC DARK VAGUE HIDDEN OCCULT SECRET OBSCURE ELLIPTIC MYSTICAL SIBYLLIC
CRYPTOGAM ACROGEN
CRYPTOGAMOUS AGAMIC AGAMOUS
CRYPTOGRAM CODE CRYPT CIPHER
CRYPTOGRAPH GEMATRIA
CRYPTOGRAPHER VIGENERE
CRYPTORCHID RIDGLING
CRYSTAL XL ICE DIAL DOME HARD IRIS SEED XTAL CLEAR CRANK GLASS GRAIN LUCID LUNET NICOL TABLE GLASSY LIMPID MIRROR NEEDLE PEBBLE QUARTZ TABLET ACICULA DIAMOND DIPLOID GLASSIE LUNETTE ORTHITE SPICULE TWOLING ULEXITE YAJEINE ZOISITE FIVELING FOURLING PELLUCID TRICHITE TRILLING PERIMORPH PHENOCRYST
(— FOREIGN TO ROCK) XENOCRYST
(— OF GREAT STRENGTH) WHISKER
(FINE —) BERYL
(ICE —S IN WATER) FRAZIL
(NEEDLE-SHAPED —S) RAPHIDES
(ROCK —) BRISTOL CITRINE

(TWIN —) TWIN MACLE TWINDLE TWOLING FOURLING
(PL.) DRUSE GRAIN
(PREF.) CHRYSTO
(SUFF.) BLAST(IC)(Y) HEDRON
CRYSTAL GAZE SCRY
CRYSTAL GAZER SEER SCRYER SKRYER
CRYSTALLINE PURE CRYSTAL PELLUCID
CRYSTALLITE BELONITE TRICHITE BACILLITE SCOPULITE
CRYSTALLIZE FIX FIRM JELL CANDY SUGAR NEEDLE CONGEAL SOLIDIFY
CRYSTALLOGRAPHY LEPTOLOGY
C-SHAPED SIGMATE
CTENIDIUM COMB
CTENOPHORE RIB NUDA CESTOID CYDIPPID JELLYFISH
CUADRA MANZANA
CUB FRY PEN BEAR CHIT COOP SHED TOTO STALL WHELP LIONET NOVICE CODLING REPORTER
(— SCOUT) WEBELOS

CUBA
BAY: NIPE PIGS
CAPE: CRUZ MAISI LUCRECIA
CAPITAL: HAVANA
CIGAR: HAVANA
COIN: PESO CENTAVO CUARENTA
DANCE: CONGA RUMBA DANZON RHUMBA GUARACHA PACHANGA
FALLS: TOA AGABAMA CABURNI
GULF: MEXICO ANAMARIA BATABANO
INDIAN: CARIB TAINO ARAWAK
ISLAND: PINES
ISLANDS: SABANA CAMAGUEY
MEASURE: VARA BOCOY TAREA CORDEL FANEGA
MOUNTAIN: TURQUINO
MOUNTAINS: CRISTAL MAESTRA ORGANOS TRINIDAD
PROVINCE: HAVANA ORIENTE CAMAGUEY MATANZAS
RIVER: ZAZA CAUTO
SWAMP: ZAPATA
TOWN: COLON MANES ALAMAR BAYAMO GUINES HAVANA BARACOA HOLGUIN PALMIRA ARTEMISA CAMAGUEY GUAYABAL MATANZAS SANTIAGO
TREE: JIQUE JIQUI
WEIGHT: LIBRA TERCIO

CUBAN LILY SCILLA
CUBBYHOLE CELL NOOK CUBBY
CUBE CUT DIE NOB KNOB BLOCK EIGHT SOLID TIMBO BABASCO CUBELET TESSERA BARBASCO QUADRATE TESSELLA
(— OF BREAD) CROUTON
(— OF COLORED GLASS) SMALTO
(— WITH 21 SPOTS) DIE
(MEAT —S) CABOB KABOB KEBOB
(PUZZLE —) RUBIC
(PL.) DICE
CUBIC SOLID CUBOID CUBICAL
CUBICALLY DIEWISE
CUBIC CENTIMETER FLUIGRAM
CUBICLE BAY CELL ROOM BOOTH

CABIN NICHE STALL ALCOVE CARREL CARRELL
CUBIC METER STERE
CUBIT ELL CODO HATH COVID HASTA COUDEE
CUBITUS ULNA
CUB SHARK LAMIA GALEID REQUIEM
CUCKING STOOL THEW TUMBLER TUMBREL TUMBRIL
CUCKOLD TUP HORN BECCO VULCAN WITTOL ACTAEON CORNUTE CORNUTO HORNIFY RAMHEAD COKEWOLD
CUCKOLDED FORKED UNICORN
CUCKOLDISE GRAFT
CUCKOLD-MAKING HORNING
CUCKOLDRY HORNWORK
CUCKOO ANI GAG COWK CUCK FOOL GOUK GOWK KOEL KOIL CLOCK CRAZY KOKIL SILLY COUCAL DIDRIC HUNTER KOBIRD BOOBOOK CHATAKA DIEDRIC KOWBIRD SIRKEER CHOWCHOW PICARIAN RAINBIRD RAINFOWL
(PREF.) CUCULI
CUCKOOFLOWER HEAD PAGLE SPINK CUCKOO PAIGLE HEADACHE MILKMAID
CUCKOOPINT ARUM RAMP AARON AROID BOBBIN DRAGON BUCKRAM OXBERRY MANDRAKE
CUCKOO SPIT WOODSERE
CUCULLATE COWLED HOODED COVERED
CUCUMBER CUKE PEPO GOURD CONGER CUCURB PEPINO PICKLE GHERKIN PICKLER CUCURBIT PEPONIDA PEPONIUM
(BITTER —) COLOCYNTH
(SHRIVELED —) CRUMPLING
(WILD —) SICYOS CREEPER
(PREF.) CUCUMI
CUCURBIT BODY FLASK GOURD CUCURB ALEMBIC MATRASS
CUD CHEW QUID BOLUS QUEED RUMEN CUDGEL
CUDBEAR CORK PERSIO PERSIS CUDWEED
CUD-CHEWING RUMINANT
CUDDLE HUG LAP PET CARESS COSSET FONDLE HUGGLE KIDDLE KIUTLE NESTLE PETTLE CROODLE CRUDDLE EMBRACE SMUGGLE SNOOZLE SNUGGLE CANOODLE
CUDDLESOME HUGGABLE
CUDDY ASS LOUT BRIBE CABIN DONKEY GALLEY PANTRY CUDEIGH
(BELOVED OF —) BUXOMA
CUDGEL BAT CUD BEAT CANE CLUB CRAB DRUB KENT MACE RACK RUNG TREE BASTE BATON BILLY DRIVE KEBBY KEVEL LINCH LINGE SHRUB STAFF STAVE STICK THUMP TOWEL ALPEEN BALLOW BASTON BILLET GIBBET KEBBIE LIBBET THRASH WASTER BELABOR BOURDON DRUBBER SWADDLE SWINGLE TROUNCE BLUDGEON SHILLALA THWACKER SHILLALAGH
CUDWEED ENAENA CATFOOT
CUE QU NOD TAG TIP HINT MAST TAIL WINK BRAID CLUFF PLAIT

QUEUE TWIST PROMPT SIGNAL PIGTAIL
(BILLIARD —) MACE MAST STICK
(MUSICAL —) PRESA
(PART OF —) TIP BUTT HILT JOINT POINT SHAFT BUMPER FERRULE
(SHUFFLEBOARD —) SHOVEL
(TIP OF —) LEATHER
CUFF BOX BANK BLOW GOWF SLAM SLAP SLUG SWAT TURF CLOUT FIGHT GOWFF MISER SCUFF SCUFT SMITE SOUSE BUFFET CODGER FENDER MITTEN STRIKE TURNUP COLPHEG SCUFFLE WHERRET GAUNTLET HANDBLOW HANDCUFF TURNBACK
CUIN DORADO
CUIRASS CURACE CURATE CURIET LORICA THORAX
CUIRASSIER LOBSTER
CUISINE FOOD MENU TABLE COOKERY KITCHEN
(KIND OF —) HAUTE
(SOUTHERN —) CAJUN CREOLE
CUITLATEC TECO
CUL-DE-SAC POCKET STRAIT IMPASSE
CULL OPT CAST COIL DUPE GULL PICK PIKE SIFT SORT ELECT CLEAN PLUCK ASSORT CHOOSE GARBLE GATHER REMOVE SELECT CULLING SEPARATE
CULLET SCRAP
CULLODEN MOOR
CULM COOM HAULM SLACK COOMBE REFUSE DEPOSIT
(PL.) SIRKI SIRKY
CULMINATE CLIMAX
CULMINATION END ACME APEX AUGE CULM NOON ROOF BLOOM CREST CROWN HIGHT POINT APOGEE CLIMAX CULMEN CUMBLE HEIGHT PAYOFF PERIOD SUMMIT VERTEX ZENITH BLOWOFF
CULOTTE PANTDRESS
CULOTTES GAUCHOS
CULPABILITY BLAME FAULT GUILT DEMERIT
CULPABLE FAULTY GUILTY LACHES SINFUL IMMORAL TOBLAME BLAMABLE CRIMINAL
CULPRIT FELON CONVICT CRIMINAL OFFENDER
CULT CLAN DADA SECT CREED KUKSU CHURCH CULTUS DOMNEI MANISM NUDISM RITUAL SCHOOL SHINTO AMIDISM DADAISM ICONISM MYALISM MYSTERY WORSHIP DEVILISM HUMANISM SATANISM
(— OF MALE VIRILITY) MACHISMO
(ADHERENT OF RELIGIOUS —) RASTA RASTAMAN
(SUFF.) ISM
CULTCH CUTCH STOOL SCULCH
CULTIVATE EAR HOE CROP DISC DISK FARM GROW PLOW REAR TEND TILL WORK DRESS EARTH LABOR NURSE RAISE STUDY TRAIN AFFECT FOSTER FURROW HARROW MANAGE MANURE PLOUGH RATOON SARCLE SCHOOL ACQUIRE CHERISH

CONTOUR CULTURE EDUCATE EMBRACE EXPLOIT HUSBAND IMPROVE NOURISH PREPARE SCRATCH CIVILIZE
(— FAVOR) BOOTLICK
CULTIVATED ABAD TAME CIVIL GROWN POLITE SATIVE TOILED POLITIC REFINED CULTURED ARTIFICIAL
(ARTIFICIALLY —) HOTHOUSE
CULTIVATION CROP TILTH FINISH GROWTH CULTURE TILLAGE TILTURE LABORAGE MANURAGE REFINEMENT
(— IN MANNERS) FINISH
(MENTAL —) HUMANITY
CULTIVATOR JAT KMET RYOT ILAVA SULKY FARMER GADABA HARROW ILAVAN MAMOTY MILLER RIDGER TILLER FLORIST GRUBBER HUSBAND MEADOWER ROSARIAN SCUFFLER
(— GANG) RIG
(PL.) LAETI
CULTURAL HUMANIST
CULTURE ART AGAR STAB KULLI NASCA NAZCA SHAKE SLANT SLOPE TAJIN TASTE TILTH JHUKAR KULTUR POLISH STREAK WILTON ABASHEV ANANINO AZILIAN IRANISM JHANGAR KAYENTA SOCIETY STARTER TILLAGE HUMANISM LEARNING
(ESKIMO —) DORSET
(MEXICAN —) MAZAPAN
(MIDDLEBROW —) MIDCULT
(PREF.) ETHEO
CULTURED CIVIL POLITE LETTERED
CULVERIN SLING CULVER LANTACA PELICAN SPIROLE
CULVERT FOX GOUT DRAIN SLUIT BRIDGE CONDUIT CULBERT PINNOCK PONCEAU OVERPASS
CUMBER BURDEN CUMMER SHACKLE
CUMBERSOME GOURD HEAVY CLUMSY UNRIDE AWKWARD LUGSOME ONEROUS WEIGHTY CUMBROUS UNWIELDY
CUMMER GIRL LASS WOMAN KIMMER
CUMMERBUND BAND BELT SASH
CUMMUTATIVE ABELIAN
CUMULATE HEAP GATHER COMBINE
CUMULATIVE CHAIN SUMMATIVE
CUNA CUEVA DARIEN
CUNEIFORM ULNARE WEDGED
CUNNER CANOE NIPPER WRASSE BURGALL CHOGSET GOLDNEY NIBBLER BERGGYLT BLUEFISH CORKWING GILTHEAD
CUNNING ART OLD SHY SLY WIT ARCH CUTE DEEP FAST FINE FOXY KEEN SLIM SNOD TRAP WILY WISE CANNY CRAFT DOWNY FAVEL GUILE LOOPY PAUKY PAWKY POKEY SHARP SMART ADROIT ARTFUL ASTUTE CALLID CLEVER CRAFTY DAEDAL DECEIT ENGINE FOXERY PRETTY QUAINT SHREWD SUBTLE SUPPLE TRICKY WISDOM COMPASS CRAFTLY CURIOUS

FINESSE KNOWING PARLISH PARLOUS POLITIC PRACTIC SLEIGHT SUBTILE VARMINT VULPINE CONTOISE DEXTROUS MANAGERY QUENTISE SKILLFUL SLEIGHTY STEALTHY YEPELEIC
CUNNING LITTLE VIXEN
(CHARACTER IN —) LAPAK PRIEST HARASTA TERYNKA FORESTER SHARPEARS GOLDENMANE SCHOOLMASTER
(COMPOSER OF —) JANACEK
CUNNINGLY YEPLY YEPELY
CUP AMA BOX CAN DOP MUG NOG POT TOT TUN TYG CELL DOPP HORN LOTA PECE SHOE SKEW TASS TOSS BOUSE CALIX CHARK COGUE COPPE CRUSE CYLIX DEPAS GLASS GODET GRAIL KITTY PHIAL SCALE STEIN STOOP STOUP TASSE TAZZA THECA BEAKER BICKER BUCKET BUMPER CAPPIE CHOANA COTYLA CRATER CUPULA DOBBIN EGGCUP EYECUP FALSIE FESSEL FINJAN GOBLET JICARA KOTYLE MAZARD NAGGIN NOGGIN OXHORN POTION RUMKIN TASSIE VESSEL BRIMMER CAPSULE CHALICE CHEERER CYATHUS GODDARD KYATHOS QUONIAM SCYPHUS SHERBET STIRRUP THIMBLE TRINKET VENTOSE BRIDECUP GRADUATE PANNIKIN STANDARD TJANTING
(— FOR HOLDING DIAMOND) DOP DOPP
(— FOR PERFUMES) CONCH
(— FOR YEAST) SKEP
(— IN SAUCER OF ALCOHOL) ETNA
(— OF FLOWER) BELL
(— OF TEA) DISH CUPPA SPEED OYSTER
(— ON BULLET) GASCHECK
(— WITH COVER) HANAP
(ASSAYING —) CUPEL
(CAFE —) TASSE
(DRINKING —) CAN MUG NUT TIG TUN TYG CANN HORN TASS TOSS GODET BEAKER GOBLET HOLMOS QUAICH RUMMER CHALICE GODDARD TRINKET
(FAIRY —) COOLWORT
(FILLED —) BUMPER
(IRISH —) MADDER METHER
(IRON —) CULOT MUSHROOM
(LARGE —) FACER BLACKJACK
(LEATHER —) WELL GISPIN
(LONG-HANDLED —) CYATH DIPPER CYATHUS KYATHOS
(MAPLE —) MAZER
(NAUTICAL —) THIEF
(ORNAMENTAL —) TAZZA
(PAPER —) DIXIE
(PASTRY —) DARIOLE
(PRIZE —) PEWTER
(SACRED —) GRAIL
(SHALLOW —) CYLIX TAZZA TASTER CAPSULE
(SMALL —) DOP NOG TOT DOPP TASS DOBBIN NAGGIN NOGGIN TASSIE
(SQUARE —) MADDER METHER
(STIRRUP —) BONAILIE

(WINE-TASTING —) TASTEVIN
(WOODEN —) COG COGUE CAPPER CAPPIE METHER QUAICH
(PL.) VALONIA
(PREF.) CALATHI CALICI COTYL(I)(O) CUPULI CYATH(I)(O) POCILLI SCYPH(I)(O)
(SUFF.) COTYL(LY)(OUS)
CUPBEARER HEBE SAKI CUPPER GANYMEDE
CUPBOARD CUB KAS BOLE CASE COIN SAFE AMBRY CHEST CUBBY CUDDY HUTCH PRESS ABACUS AUMBRY AWMRIE BUFFET CLOSET LARDER LOCKER PANTRY SPENCE ALMIRAH ARMOIRE CABINET DRESSER PIESAFE SKIBBET ALHACENA CREDENCE CREDENZA TROSTERA
(ARCHERY —) ASCHAM
CUPEL TEST
CUPFUL CUP CAROUSE
CUP HOLDER ZARF
CUPID DAN AMOR EROS LOVE PUTTO CHERUB AMORINO AMOURET AMORETTO
(PL.) PUTTI
CUPIDITY LUST GREED DESIRE AVARICE AVIDITY LONGING APPETITE RAPACITY
CUPOLA DOME KILN TYPE VAULT BELFRY TURRET CALOTTE FURNACE LANTERN LOOKOUT CIMBORIO COCKLOFT
(ROUND —) THOLUS
CUPOLAMAN HEATER
CUPPED GLENOID
CUPPING GLASS VENTOSE
CUPSEED NUTSEED
CUP-SHAPED PEZIZOID SCYPHATE
CUPULE CUP BOLSTER CYATHUS THUMBMARK
CUR DOG YAP FICE FIST FYCE MUTT TIKE TYKE FEIST KEOUT BRAKJE MESSAN MESSIN BOBTAIL MONGREL WHAPPET
CURABLE SANABLE
CURARE URARE URARI OORALI WOORALI
CURASSOW MITU COPPY HOCCO MITUA PAUXI
CURATE ABBE CURA AGENT VICAIRE MINISTER
CURATIVE HEALING IATRICAL PHYSICAL REMEDIAL SALUTARY SANATIVE
CURATOR KEEPER STEWARD GUARDIAN OVERSEER
CURB BIT LID CRUB FOIL KERB REIN SKID SNIP SNUB BRAKE CHECK CRIMP CURVE GUARD LEASH LIMIT MOUND ARREST BOTTLE BRIDLE COERCE COLLAR DECKLE GOVERN HAMPER STIFLE STRAIN SUBDUE THWART CONTROL CURBING INHIBIT REFRAIN REPRESS SHACKLE ATTEMPER COMPESCE MODERATE RESTRAIN RESTRICT WITHHOLD
(OFFICIAL —) LID
(WELL —) PUTEAL
CURCULIO TURK WEEVIL
CURCUMA ZEDOARY

CURD CRUD DAHI CHEESE CURDLE CASEINE CLABBER CONGEAL COAGULUM
(**— IN MILK**) ZIEGA
(**—S AND WHEY**) SLIP PINJANE
(**BEAN —**) TOFU
(**PL.**) SKYR FLEETINGS
(**PREF.**) THROMB(O)

CURDLE CAP LOP RUN SAM SET CRIM CURD EARN LEEP QUAR SAMM SOUR TURN WHIG YERN CARVE QUAIL QUARL SPOIL YEARN CAILLE LAPPER LOBBER LOPPER POSSET QUARLE CLABBER CONGEAL CRIDDLE CRUDDLE THICKEN CONDENSE

CURDLED CURDLY QUARRED SHOTTEN
(**NOT —**) UNCRUDDED

CURE DIP DRY DUN FIX BEEF BOOT CARE CORN HEAL HEED HELP JERK MEND SALT SANE SAVE AMEND BLOAT BOTEN LEECH REEST SMEEK SMOKE CHARGE CURATE KIPPER PHYSIC PRIEST RECURE REMEDY SEASON SUCCOR TEMPER WARISH BESMOKE RECOVER RESTORE THERAPY TREACLE ANTIDOTE BARBECUE CURATION GUERISON PRESERVE REVOCERY
(**— A HABIT**) BREAK
(**— BY SMOKING**) GAMMON SMUDGE
(**— FISH**) DUN ROUSE
(**— GRASS**) HAY
(**— HAY**) WIN
(**— HERRINGS**) BLOAT
(**— IN SUN**) RIZZAR
(**— SKINS**) DRESS
(**COUGH —**) SAPA SAPE

CURE-ALL BALM AVENS ELIXIR REMEDY PANACEA THERIAC

CURED SALT BLOATED

CURIO DOODAD

CURIOSITY CURIO ODDITY INTEREST
(**— OF SMALL VALUE**) GABION
(**—S OF THE CITY**) LIONS
(**PL.**) CURIOSA

CURIOUS ODD NOSY RARE SELI QUEER SELLE SELLY PRYING QUAINT SNOOPY CUNNING STRANGE UNUSUAL FREAKISH MEDDLING PECULIAR SINGULAR
(**— ONE**) PANDORA

CURL BOB BEND COIL FEAK FURL KINK LOCK PURL ROLL TUBE WAVE WIND ACKER CANON CRIMP CRISP DILDO FRILL FRIZZ QUIRL SPIRE TRESS TWIRE TWIST BERGER BUCKLE CANNON CRUCHE CURDLE FROWSE MULLET RIPPLE SPIRAL TUNNEL WRITHE CRIDDLE CRIMPLE CRINKLE CROCKET CRUDDLE EARLOCK FLEXURE FRIZZLE FROUNCE RINGLET SERPENT TENDRIL WHISKER FAVORITE LOVELOCK SQUIGGLE
(**— HAIR**) CROOK
(**— OF SMOKE**) WREATH
(**— OF WIG**) SNAKE

(**— ON FOREHEAD**) CRUCHE CROUCHE
(**— OVER**) BREAK
(**— UP**) CRUMP HUNCH SNIRL HUDDLE SHRINK SNUGGLE
(**FRINGE OF —S**) FRISETTE FRIZETTE
(**METAL —**) CHIP
(**SMALL —**) CROCK
(**PREF.**) CIRR(I)(O) CIRRH(I)(O)

CURLED CRISP FUZZY KINKY SPIRY CIRRATE COCKLED CRISPED FRIZZLY SAVOYED WREATHY CRISPATE CRUMPLED GAUFFRED GOFFERED HELICINE SCROLLED

CURLER GOFFER TEASER CRIMPER FRIZZER MULLETS

CURLEW FUTE JACK SPOW KIOEA SNIPE SPOWE WHAAP WHAUP DIKKOP MARLIN SMOKER BANKERA BUSTARD DOEBIRD BLUELEGS WHIMBREL SICKLEBILL

CURLICUE ESS CAPER CURVE CASSIS PARAPH SQUIRL FLOURISH PURLICUE SCRIGGLE SQUIGGLE

CURLING CRISP

CURLING MARK TEE

CURLING MATCH SPIEL

CURLING STONE IRON STONE LOOFIE GRANITE
(**— SPIN**) RAISE

CURL-PAPER CRACKER PAPILLOTE

CURLY WAVY CRISP CRULL OUNDY CRIMPY RIPPLED CRINKLED
(**— HAIR**) VEDDOID

CURMUDGEON CRAB CHURL HUNKS MISER GLEYDE GROUCH NIGGARD
(**LIKE A —**) CRUSTY

CURMUDGEONLY STINGY

CURRANT PASA BERRY CASSIS RAISIN RIZZAR RIZZLE CORINTH
(**PL.**) RIBES SPICE

CURRANT BUN WIG WIGG

CURRAWONG SQUEAKER STREPERA

CURRENCY CASH COIN PASS BILLS CATER MONEY SCRIP SERIES SPECIE PASSAGE WILDCAT
(**FRACTIONAL —**) SPONDULIX
(**SHELL —**) UHLLO

CURRENT NOW WAY EDDY FLOW FLUX FORD RACE RIFE TIDE VEIN WAFT ALIVE DRIFT GOING RAPID ROUST SCOUR SWIFT TENOR TESLA TREND USUAL ABROAD ACTUAL COEVAL COMMON COURSE DOUCHE DURANT FLUENT LATEST LIVING MOTION MOVING OFFSET OUTSET RECENT RIZZER RULING SLUICE STRAND STREAM TONGUE VOLANT COUNTER DRAUGHT FLOWING FRESHET GENERAL INDRAFT INSTANT PASSANT PRESENT RUNNING STICKLE THERMAL TORRENT BACKWASH CURRANCE DOWNCAST FREQUENT MILLRACE OCCURRENT PASSABLE TIDERACE TODAYISH UNDERTOW
(**— IN SPEECH**) WAIF
(**— INSTRUMENT**) AMMETER
(**AIR —**) DRAFT SHEET SPLIT BREEZE DRAUGHT DOWNCAST DOWNFLOW

(**ELECTRIC —**) STRAY
(**HOT —**) BACK
(**JAPAN —**) KUROSHIO KUROSIWO
(**KIND OF —**) RIP
(**PREVAILING —**) MAINSTREAM
(**RAPID —**) SWIFT TONGUE
(**SOUND —**) DISTORTION
(**STRONG —**) GALE ROOST ROUST
(**PREF.**) RHEO

CURRENTLY ANYMORE

CURRICULUM STREAM PROGRAM PROGRAMME

CURRISH BASE CYNICAL DOGGISH IGNOBLE SNARLING

CURRY COMB DRUB KARI CLEAN DRESS GROOM BRUISE CAJOLE CARREE POWDER PREPARE TARKEEAN
(**— FAVOR**) HUG NUT QUILL COTTON SMOOGE CUITTLE SMOODGE

CURSE BAN HEX POX BANE BLOW CUSS DAMN JINX OATH PIZE WARY BLAST BLESS CORSE SHREW SPELL SWEAR WEARY WINZE DETEST DEVOTE GOOFER GUFFER MAKUTU MALIGN MAUGER MAUGRE ACCURSE BESHREW MALISON SWEARAT ANATHEMA EXECRATE FORSPEAK MALEDICTION

CURSED DASH CUSSED DAMNED DASHED ACCURSED

CURSER WARIER

CURSING BLESSING BLASPHEMY

CURSIVE RUNNING

CURSORILY OBITER

CURSORY FAST BRIEF HASTY QUICK SHORT FITFUL ROVING SPEEDY PASSANT PASSING SHALLOW CARELESS RAMBLING

CURT BUFF RUDE TART BLUFF BLUNT BRIEF BRUSK NIPPY SHORT SQUAB TERSE ABRUPT CURTAL CUTTED SNIPPY BRUSQUE · CONCISE CRYPTIC LACONIC CAVALIER SNAPPISH SNIPPETY SUCCINCT

CURTAIL CUT LOP CLIP CROP DOCK PARE STOP ABATE ELIDE SHORT SLASH STUNT TRUNK DECURT LESSEN REDUCE ABRIDGE BOBTAIL CRACKLE SHORTEN DIMINISH MINORATE RETRENCH

CURTAILED TAIL CUTTY SHORT STUNT CURTAL BOBTAIL CONCISE ABRIDGED

CURTAIN END BOOM DROP IRIS MASK VEIL WALL BLIND DRAPE SCENE SHADE SHEET VELUM COSTER HANGER PURDAH SCREEN SHROUD CEILING CONCEAL CORTINE DRAPERY HANGING VITRAGE ASBESTOS PORTIERE TRAVERSE
(**CHURCH —**) CLOTH RIDDEL ENDOTYS ENDOTHYS
(**THEATER —**) IRON SCRIM TEASER TRAVELER TORMENTER
(**PL.**) END DEATH

CURTAIN ROD TRINGLE

CURTAIN STRETCHER SCRAY STRAINER

CURTAL CRAPE COURTAL CURTLAX

CURTSY BOB BOW DIP DOP BECK DROP JOUK KNEE CONGE HONOR CURCHY

CURUBA CASSA BANANA

CURVATED STUNT HOOKED

CURVATURE ARC PLY ARCH BENT BOOL CURL CURVE SHEER SINUS CAMBER CURVITY ADUNCITY APOPHYGE CYRTOSIS GRYPOSIS KYPHOSIS LORDOSIS
(**— OF BONE**) ARCUATION
(**— OF DECK**) SHEER
(**— OF LEGS**) RHEBOSIS
(**— OF SHOE SOLE**) SWING
(**— OF SPINE**) KYPHOSIS SCOLIOSIS
(**— OF STOMACH**) FUNDUS
(**— OF STRAKE**) SPILING

CURVE ARC BOW CUP ESS SAG ARCH BEND BOUT COME CURB FADE HOOK KNEE LINE OGEE TURN VEER WIND AMBIT BIGHT BREAK CONIC CROOK CRUMP CUBIC HELIX NONIC OGIVE PEDAL POLAR QUIRK SLICE SWEEP SWIRL TARVE TREND TWIST WITCH BOUGHT CAMBER CIRCLE DEFLEX JORDAN LITUUS SOLVUS SPIRAL SPRING TOROID WIMPLE ADIABAT BRACKET CAUSTIC CIRCUIT CISSOID COMPASS CONCAVE CONTOUR COSEISM CURVITY CYCLOID ELLIPSE ENVELOP FESTOON FLEXURE INCURVE INFLECT LIMACON PHUGOID PROFILE QUARTIC SCALLOP SINUATE SOLIDUS CARDIOID CATENARY CONCHOID DYGOGRAM ELASTICA EXTRADOS FADEAWAY INTRADOS INVOLUTE LIGATURE LIQUIDUS OPHIURID PARABOLA SINUSOID TONOGRAM TRACTRIX TROCHOID STROPHOID CATACAUSTIC
(**— DESCRIBED BY GRAPH**) GRAM
(**— IN HANDRAIL**) KNEE
(**— IN PLANKING**) HANG
(**— IN SAIL**) ROACH
(**— OF ARCH**) INTRADOS
(**— OF BALL**) DROP
(**— OF BIT**) LIBERTY
(**— OF COLUMN**) APOPHYGE
(**— OF FINGERNAIL**) GRYPOSIS
(**— OF HORSE'S NECK**) CREST
(**— OF PLANK**) SNY
(**— OF SHIP'S BOW**) FLAIR FLARE
(**— OF TIMBER**) CUP
(**— SATISFYING EQUATION**) BRANCH
(**— SPACE**) KNOT
(**— WHEN DRAWN**) COME
(**BASEBALL —**) SNAKE
(**CRICKET —**) SWERVE
(**DOUBLE —**) CIMA CYMA
(**KIND OF —**) LAFFER LEARNING PRACTICE
(**PLANE —**) ROSE STROPHOID
(**PLANE CUBIC —**) WITCH
(**VERTICAL —**) RAMP

CURVED BENT SOFT ADUNC CORBE CURVE CURVY ROUND WOUND CONVEX CURVEY GYRATE HAMATE TURNED ARCUATE ARRONDI

CONCAVE CROOKED CURVANT EMBOWED FALCATE SIGMOID ADUNCOUS ANCHORAL AQUILINE ARCIFORM CRUMPLED CYGNEOUS DECURVED EXCURVED SCROLLED ARCHIFORM
(PREF.) ANCYLO ANKYLO CAMPTO CAMPYL(O) CURVI CURVO CYRT(O) (SUFF.) CLASTIC

CURVET HOP LEAP LOPE SKIP TURN BOUND CAPER FRISK PRANK VAULT CAVORT CROUPE FROLIC GAMBOL PRANCE PANNADE CORVETTO CROUPADE

CURVING SPIRY SIMOUS TWISTY AQUILINE DRAWDOWN
(— IN) CONCAVE
(— OUTWARD) BOMBE
(DOWN —) EPINASTY
(SMOOTHLY —) FAIR

CUSH (FATHER OF —) HAM
CUSH-CUSH CARA YAMPEE
CUSHION BAG COD MAT PAD PIG BALL BANK BOSS PUFF SEAT SUNK TRIM GADDI GADHI PANEL SQUAB TRUSH BUFFER INSOLE JOCKEY MUSNUD PILLOW SACHET BOLSTER BRIOCHE COSSHEN HASSOCK KNEELER MUFFLER PILLION REPOSAL ROOTCAP CUTIDURE OREILLER PULVINAR PINCUSHION
(KIND OF —) WHOOPEE
(LACE-MAKERS —) BOTT
(PIN —) PRINCOD
(SEAT —) BANKER
(TAILOR'S —) HAM
(PREF.) PULVILLI PULVINI

CUSHIONING DUNNAGE
CUSHIONLIKE PULVINAR
CUSHION PLANT POLSTER
CUSHIONY PADDY
CUSHITIC NUBIAN
CUSHY PLUM
CUSK COD TUSK TORSK BURBOT CATFISH
CUSP APEX CONE HORN PEAK ANGLE POINT STYLE TOOTH CORNER SPINODE ENTOCONE HYPOCONE METACONE PARACONE
CUSPID CANINE
CUSPIDOR GABOON CRACHOIR SPITTOON
CUSSO KOSO KOUSSO BRAYERA BRAZERA
CUSTARD FLAN FOOL CREME FLAWN DOUCET DOWCET CHARLET PARFAIT FLUMMERY DIABLOTIN ZABAGLIONE
(— PIE) QUICHE
CUSTARD APPLE ANONA ANNONA PAWPAW CORAZON SWEETSOP
CUSTODIAN HACK GUARD BAILEE CUSTOS KEEPER SEXTON WARDEN WARDER CURATOR JANITOR CERBERUS CLAVIGER GUARDIAN CONCIERGE
CUSTODY LAP BAIL CARE HOLD KEEP WARD TRUST ARREST CHARGE SAFETY YEMSEL CONTROL DURANCE KEEPING

TUITION COMMENDA CUSTODIA HANDFAST SECURITY WARDSHIP

CUSTOM FAD LAW MOS PAD TAX URE USE WON ASAL DUTY FORM GARB MODE MORE RITE ROTE RULE THEW TOLL WONE WONT FUERO GUISE HABIT HAUNT RITUS STYLE SUNNA TRADE TREAD TRICK USAGE VOGUE BYRLAW DASTUR DHARMA GROOVE IMPOST MANNER MINHAG MONTEM PRAXIS SUNNAH USANCE COSTUME DUSTOOR DUSTOUR FASHION FORMULA HALAKAH TRIBUTE USAUNCE WARNOTH BUSINESS ENDOGAMY HABITUDE PRACTICE ASSUETUDE CONSUETUDE PRESCRIPTION
(BINDING —) LAW
(BUSINESS —) TRADE GOODWILL
(CHILDBIRTH —) COUVADE
(CHURCH —) COMITY
(CORRUPT —) ABUSE
(FESTIVAL —) HOCKING
(OUTMODED —) ARCHAISM
(PRIMITIVE —) COUVADE
(RURAL —) HEAVING
(SECRET —) SANDE
(TEMPORARY —) FAD VOGUE
(PL.) MORES MOEUR HAIKWAN FOLKLORE PROPRIETIES
CUSTOMARILY USUALLY CUSTOMLY
CUSTOMARY PER RIFE TAME USED NOMIC USUAL BEATEN COMMON SOLEMN VULGAR WONTED CLASSIC GENERAL REGULAR USITATE EVERYDAY FAMILIAR HABITUAL ORTHODOX
(NOT —) INSOLENT
CUSTOMER CHAP COVE BUYER CLIENT PATRON SUCKER ACCOUNT CALLANT CHAPMAN PATIENT SHOPPER MERCHANT PROSPECT
(PRINTER'S —) AUTHOR
(PROBABLE —) PROSPECT
(TOUGH —) HARDCASE
(PL.) CUSTOM CLIENTELE
CUSTOMHOUSE ADUANA DOGANA DOUANE
CUSTOM-MADE BESPOKE BESPOKEN
CUSTOMS OFFICER SHARK WAITER
CUT AX ADZ AXE BOB DAG DAP DIE HAG HEW KIT LOP MOW NIP RIT SAW SNY TAP ADZE BANG BITE BOLO BOLT BUZZ CHIP CHOP CLIP CROP DADO DOCK FACE FELL FILE GASH GIRD HACK HASH HEWN JERK KNAP LIMB MAKE MODE MUSH NICK OCHE PARE RACE RASH RAZE REAP SIDE SKIN SLIT SLOT SMIT SNEE SNEG SNIP SNUB STOW SUMP SWAP SWOP TAME TRIM VELL VIDE BEVEL BLOCK BREAK CANAL CANCH CARVE CHIVE CHYND CLEFT COPSE COUPE CRIMP DRESS FLICK FRAZE FRITH GOUGE GRAVE GRIDE GROOP HOWEL KITTE KNIFE LANCE LATHE MINCE NOTCH PLATE PRUNE RAZEE SABER SABRE

SCALP SCARP SCIND SCORE SEVER SHAPE SHARE SHEAR SHIVE SHRED SKICE SKISE SLASH SLICE SLICK SLISH SLIVE SNICK SPLIT STAMP SWEEP SWIPE SWISH TOUCH TWITE VOGUE WHITE ABLATE AJOURE BARBER BISECT BROACH CAMBER CHISEL CLEAVE CORNER CUTTED DIVIDE EXCISE FIGURE FLETCH FLITCH FRENCH GROOVE GULLET HACKLE HAGGLE IGNORE INCIDE INCISE INDENT LESSEN MANGLE OUTPUT RASURE REDUCE RIPPLE SCORCH SCOTCH SCRIBE SCYTHE SLIGHT SLIVER SNATHE STRAIT STREAK SULLET SWINGE TAILYE THWITE TRENCH AFFRONT CONVERT CURTAIL CUTTING DIACOPE DISCIDE DISSECT DRAWCUT ENGRAVE FASHION FRITTER HATCHET RAKEOFF SCALPEL SCISSOR SCUTTLE SECTILE TAILZEE WHITTLE DISSEVER FRACTION INCISION INCISURE INTAGLIO LACERATE MALAHACK RETRENCH THWITTLE
(— AN OPENING) BREACH
(— ASLANT) RAKE
(— AT ANGLE) CANT BEVEL
(— A THREAD) CHASE
(— AT RANDOM) SLASH
(— AWAY) COPE SLIT UNDO ABATE CONCISE
(— BACK) HEAD SPUR
(— BARK) CHIP
(— BEAM) KERF
(— CARS) LIFT
(— CHEESE) HARP
(— CLAY) ELING
(— CORNERS) SKIRT CHAMFER CHAMPHER
(— CRUST) CHIP
(— DEEPER) REENTER
(— DEEPLY) DIG SHANK
(— DIAGONALLY) CATER SLANT
(— DOWN) HEW MOW FELL STAG STUB RAZEE SCANT SCARP ABRIDGE SHORTEN RETRENCH
(— FANCY FIGURE) DASH
(— FINELY) DICE
(— FISH) SOLAY STEAK
(— FOR FODDER) CHAFF
(— GEAR TEETH) RATCH
(— GLASS) SPLIT
(— GRAIN) BAG FAG CRADLE SWINGE
(— HAIR) DOD
(— IN) INSECT INCISED
(— IN A TREE) FACE
(— IN BARK) RING
(— IN BARREL STAVE) HOWEL
(— IN CURVES) SCALLOP
(— IN EXCAVATIONS) GULLET
(— IN LARGE SLICES) WHANG
(— IN RELIEF) ENCHASE
(— IN SOFT ROCK) CAVATE
(— IN SQUARES) CHECK
(— INTO LARGE SLICES) WHANG
(— INTO SLIPS) ZEST
(— INTO STRIPS) JERK FLETCH FLITCH JULIENNE
(— INTO TREE) BOX

(— IN WHALE'S CARCASS) SCARF
(— JAGGEDLY) HACK SNAG
(— LEDGES) BENCH
(— LOGS) LUMBER
(— OFF) BOB LOP CLIP CROP DOCK KILL PARE SHUT SLIT STAG BELEE CROSS ELIDE PRUNE SCIND SEVER SHAVE SHEAR SKIVE SLIPE SPIKE COUPED DECIDE EXEMPT FORCUT RESECT SHIELD STIFLE SWATCH ABJOINT ABSCIND ABSCISE ABSCISS CURTAIL EXSCIND ISOLATE PRECIDE RESCIND AMPUTATE CLEIDOIC DESECATE RESECATE RETRENCH TRUNCATE LANDLOCKED
(— OFF BY BITS) DRIB
(— OFF END) BUTT
(— OF FISH) JOWL
(— OFF WOOL) DOD DODD
(— OF GEM) STAR BAGUET BAGUETTE
(— OF GRAIN) MELL
(— OF MEAT) ARM SEY CROP HOCK SHIN SIDE CHUCK SHANK STEAK BRISKET FORESEY ICEBONE SIRLOIN EDGEBONE FORERIBS
(— OF RIFLING) GROOVE
(— OPEN) SPLAY
(— OUT) AX DESS DINK CLICK BROACH EXCIDE EXCISE EXSECT
(— PATH) FRAY
(— SALMON) CHINE
(— SHEEP) TOMAHAWK
(— SHORT) BOB COW HOG LOP BANG CROP DOCK JIMP SNIB BOBBED CURTAL HOGGED BOBTAIL CHAPPED CONCISE SCANTLE PRESCIND
(— TENDONS) ENERVATE
(— THE THROAT) JUGULATE
(— THE WAVES) SNORE
(— THINLY) CURL
(— TO PIECES) CHOP DICE MINCE BRITTLE FRITTER
(— TO SIZE) TAIL
(— TURF) VELL
(— UNDER) KIRVE
(— UNEVENLY) CHATTER
(— UP) TUSK CARVE CHINE JOINT PRANK SPOIL TRAIN GOBBET COLLOPED
(— UP SWAN) LIFT
(— WHALE BLUBBER) LEAN FLENSE
(— WITH BACKWARD SLOPE) COOT
(— WITH DIE) DINK BLANK
(— WITH SHEARS) SHIRL
(— WITH SICKLE) BAG REAP
(COLD —S) ASSIETTE
(CREW —) BUTCH FLATTOP
(DEEP NARROW —) JAD
(FENCING —) STRAMAZON
(LARGE — OF FOOD) DODGE
(NOT —) UNCORVEN
(SHORT —) ATAJO
(SLIGHT —) SNICK SCOTCH
(THIN —) TARGET
(PREF.) SEC(O) TEMNO TOMC
(SUFF.) COPATE COPE SECT SECTED TOMA TOME TOMIC TOMOUS TOMY
CUT-AND-DRIED CANNED
CUTANEOUS DERMAL
CUTCH GAMBIR CATECHU GAMBIER

CUTE COY KEEN TWEE COONY DINKY DUCKY SHARP CLEVER PRETTY SHREWD CUNNING DARLING

CUTICLE DERM HIDE SKIN SHUCK THECA MEMBRANE PELLICLE
(— OF EGGSHELL) BLOOM

CUTLASS SWORD CURTAL DUSACK HANGER TESACK CURTAXE MACHETE SHABBLE CAMPILAN

CUTLASS FISH HIKU SAVOLA KALKVIS MACHETE HAIRTAIL

CUTLERY SILVER FLATWARE

CUTLET SCHNITZEL
(KIND OF —) PORK VEAL

CUTOVER COUPE

CUTPURSE NIP BUNG THIEF HORNTHUMB

CUTTER DIE BEEF BOAT IRON MILL PONE SLED BRAVO FACER FRAZE SLOOP SMACK BAYMAN CHERRY COLTER COTTER DOCKER EDITOR FRAZER MINCER SLEIGH SLICER CLIPPER COULTER DROMOND INCISOR RUFFIAN KNIFEMAN REVENUER SCHOKKER SHEPSTER
(— OF STONES) LAPIDARY
(BRICK —) RUBBER
(PEAT —) PINER
(WIRE —) SECATEUR

CUTTERHEAD WABBLER WOBBLER

CUTTHROAT THUG BRAVO CUTTER RUFFIAN SWORDER

CUTTHROAT TROUT MYKISS

CUTTING CUT HAG RAW SET ACID CARF CURT KEEN KERF SECT SETT SLIP TART TWIG ACUTE BLEAK CHECK CRISP EAGER EDGED GRIDE SCION SCRAP SCROW SHARP SMART BITING BITTER BORING ENTAIL GODOWN GORING JAGGED PHYTON PIPING SECANT SEVERE SNITHE BURNING CAUSTIC GRIBBLE INCISAL MORDANT NICKING OVERCUT PAINFUL PIQUANT POLLING SARMENT SATIRIC SECTION SLICING CHILLING CLEARING INCISIVE PIERCING POIGNANT QUICKSET SCATHING SCISSION SNAPPISH WOUNDING TRENCHANT
(— FOR DIRT-CAR TRACK) GULLET
(— FOR WATER) TAJO
(— FROM PLANT) SLIP SHROUD SARMENT PROPAGULE TRUNCHEON
(— OF DEER) SAY
(— OFF) AVULSION
(— OF TREES) HAG
(— SHORT) ABORTIVE
(— TOOL) HOB
(DRILL —S) MUD
(OBLIQUE —) BARBING
(SECOND —) ROWEN
(WASTE —) SELVAGE SELVEDGE
(SUFF.) THEMA THESIS TOMA TOME TOMIC TOMOUS TOMY
(— OUT) ECTOMY

CUTTLEBONE SEPIA SEPION SEPIUM GLADIUS SEPIARY

CUTTLEFISH SEPIA SHELL SQUID CUDDLE CUTTLE SCRIBE CATFISH DECAPOD INKFISH MOLLUSK

OCTOPUS SCUTTLE
(PREF.) TEUTHIS

CUVETTE POT TUB TANK BASIN BUCKET TRENCH CISTERN

CYANEE (DAUGHTER OF —) BYBLIS
(FATHER OF —) MAEANDER
(HUSBAND OF —) MILETUS
(SON OF —) CAUNUS

CYANIDE NITRILE CYANURET PRUSSIATE

CYANIPPUS (FATHER OF —) PHARAX
(WIFE OF —) LEUCONE

CYANITE SAPPARE DISTHENE

CYANOGEN PRUSSIN PRUSSINE

CYANOTYPE BLUEPRINT

CYBELE RHEA KYBELE AGDISTIS
(DAUGHTER OF —) JUNO
(FATHER OF —) URANUS
(HUSBAND OF —) SATURN
(MOTHER OF —) GAEA
(SON OF —) JUPITER NEPTUNE

CYCAD BANGA CICAD ZAMIA COONTIE CYCADITE

CYCHREUS (DAUGHTER OF —) GLAUCE
(FATHER OF —) NEPTUNE POSEIDON
(MOTHER OF —) SALAMIS

CYCLADES (ISLAND OF —) IOS KEOS DELOS MELOS NAXOS PAROS SYROS TENOS ANDROS AMORGOS KYTHNOS SANTORIN SERIPHOS

CYCLAMEN BACCHAR PRIMWORT SOWBREAD

CYCLE AGE EON ERA AEON BIKE EPOCH KALPA PEDAL PRIME ROUND SAROS SECLE WHEEL BAKTUN CIRCLE COURSE CYCLUS PERIOD BICYCLE CIRCUIT DICYCLE TRICYCLE
(— FURIOUSLY) SCORCH
(— OF TIME) ORB
(— OF WORK) ROTA JOURNEY
(— OF 3600 YEARS) SAROS
(—S CAUSED BY KARMA) SAMSARA SANSARA
(BUSINESS —) JUGLAR KITCHIN
(GO THROUGH —S) ROTATE
(KIND 0F —) CALVIN
(LUNAR —) SAROS
(ONE — PER SECOND) HERTZ
(SECONDARY —) EPICYCLE

CYCLIC CYCLAR ANNULAR CYCLICAL PERIODIC

CYCLING (— TRACK) VELODROME

CYCLIST CYCLER WHEELER WHEELMAN

CYCLOLITH CROMLECH

CYCLOMETER ODOGRAPH VIAMETER

CYCLONE GALE GUST WIND BLAST STORM BAGUIO TORNADO TWISTER TYPHOON SECONDARY NEUTERCANE

CYCLOPARAFFIN NAPHTHENE

CYCLOPEAN HUGE VAST STRONG MASSIVE COLOSSAL GIGANTIC

CYCLOPS ARGES BRONTES COPEPOD STEROPES

CYCLORAMA CYKE PANORAMA

CYCLOSIS STREAMING

CYCLOSTOME HAGFISH

CYCNUS (DAUGHTER OF —) HEMITHEA
(FATHER OF —) ARES MARS NEPTUNE POSEIDON
(MOTHER OF —) CALYCE PYRENE PELOPIA
(SON OF —) TENES
(WIFE OF —) PROCLEA PHYLONOME

CYLINDER CAN EKE GIG TIN BEAM BOMB BURR CAGE CANE DRUM LEAD MUFF PIPE PRIM ROLL SLUG TUBE WELL BLOCK CORER DRAIN FIBER FIBRE FUDGE SCREW SHELL SPOOL STELA STELE SWIFT BARREL BOBBIN BUTTON COLUMN COPPER DECKER DOFFER DUSTER FILTER GABION PISTON PLATEN ROLLER SCREEN TIPITI TUMBLE URCHIN WORKER CUTCHER SLEEVER SLUDGER SUCCULA FOLLOWER GRADUATE NEURAXIS SPARKLET
(— AROUND MOLD) COTTLE
(— FOR DANCE RHYTHM) CLAVE
(— OF STEAM WHISTLE) BELL
(— OF TISSUE) CORTEX
(— OF YARN) CAKE
(— ON LOOM) BEAM
(—S PULLED THROUGH DUCT) MANDREL
(— WITH PERFORATIONS) FLUSHER
(ARMORED —) BARBETTE
(GLASS —) MUFF
(HOLLOW —) PIPE TUBE
(MARKING —) LEAD
(NAPPING —) GIG
(RELAY —) BATON
(REVOLVING —) BEATER ROLLER
(TOOTHED —) SPROCKET
(WATERMARK —) DANDY

CYLINDRICAL ROUND TERETE TOROSE CENTRIC TUBULAR TERETIAL
(PREF.) TERETI

CYMA GOLA GULA OGEE DOUCINE MOLDING CYMATIUM

CYMA REVERSA HEEL

CYMBA YET

CYMBAL ZEL ZILL CHIME TARGET CROTALUM KYMBALON
(PAIR OF —S) HIGHHAT
(PL.) TAL BECKEN PIATTI

CYMBELINE (AUTHOR OF —) SHAKESPEARE
(CHARACTER IN —) CAIUS HELEN CLOTEN IMOGEN LUCIUS MORGAN IACHIMO PISANIO BELARIUS LEONATUS PHILARIO ARVIRAGUS CORNELIUS CYMBELINE GUIDERIUS POSTHUMUS
(SON OF —) ARVIRAGUS GUIDERIUS

CYMBIUM MELO

CYME AXIS CYMULE BOSTRYX

CYMLING SIMNEL CYMBLIN SCALLOP PATTYPAN

CYMOSE DEFINITE SYMPODIAL

CYMRY KYMRI WELSH

CYNIC SATYR TIMON DOUBTER SNEERER APEMANTUS

CYNICAL CYNIC SULLEN CURRISH DOGGISH DOGLIKE CAPTIOUS SARDONIC SNARLING JAQUESIAN

MISOGYNIC PESSIMISTIC MISANTHROPIC

CYNOCEPHALUS AANI

CYNORTES (BROTHER OF —) HYACINTHUS
(FATHER OF —) AMYCLAS
(MOTHER OF —) DIOMEDE
(SON OF —) PERIERES

CYNOSURE SHOW LODESTAR

CYPRESS CULL SABINO SIPERS FIREBALL AHUEHUETE BELVEDERE

CYPRESS SPURGE BALSAM NAPOLEON

CYPRIPEDIUM CYP DUCK NERVINE

CYPRUS	
CAPE:	GATA GRECO ANDREAS ARNAUTI ZEVGARI
CAPITAL:	NICOSIA
COIN:	PARA
MEASURE:	OKA OKE PIK CASS DONUM KOUZA GOMARI KARTOS MEDIMNO
MOUNTAIN:	TROODOS
RIVER:	PEDIAS PEDIEOS
TOWN:	POLIS CITIUM PAPHOS KYRENIA LARNACA MORPHOU NICOSIA LIMASSOL FAMAGUSTA
WEIGHT:	OKA OKE MOOSA KANTAR

CYRANO DE BERGERAC (AUTHOR OF —) ROSTAND
(CHARACTER IN —) CYRANO ROXANE VALVERT DEGUICHE CHRISTIAN

CYRENE (FATHER OF) HYPSEUS
(MOTHER OF —) CHLIDANOPE
(SON OF —) IDMON DIOMEDES ARISTAEUS

CYRILLA TITI

CYRUS KORESH

CYST BAG SAC WEN POUCH CYSTUS RANULA DERMOID HYDATID HYGROMA SACCULE VESICLE ATHEROMA DACRYOPS MUCOCELE STEATOMA

CYSTOPTERIS FILIX

CYTOKININ ZEATIN

CYTOLYSIN AMBOCEPTOR

CYTOME SPHEROME

CYTOPLASM MASSULA OOPLASM PLASMON DIASTEMA
(PREF.) PLASTO

CZAR CSAR IVAN TSAR TZAR PETER AUTOCRAT NICHOLAS

CZARDAS CSARDAS
(SECTION OF —) FRISS LASSU FRISZKA

CZECH CECH TSECH TSCEKH BOHEMIAN

CZECH REPUBLIC	
CAPITAL:	PRAHA PRAGUE
COIN:	CROWN DUCAT HALER HELLER KORUNA
DANCE:	POLKA REDOWA FURIANT
FOREST:	BOHEMIAN
FORMER NAME:	CZECHOSLAVAKIA
MEASURE:	LAN SAH MIRA KOREC LATRO STOPA MERICE STRYCH
MOUNTAIN:	SNEZKA
MOUNTAIN RANGE:	ORE GIANT

SUMAVA SUDETEN KRKONOSE
JAVORNIKY CARPATHIAN
KRUSNEHORY BILEKARPATY
PEOPLE: ROMA CZECH GYPSY
MORAVIAN
PLATEAU: BOHEMIAN
REGION: BOHEMIA MORAVIA
RIVER: MZE DYJE EGER ELBE ISER
LABE NISA ODER ODRA OHRE
OLSE OLZA OPPA BECVA OPAVA
JIZERA MOLDAU MORAVA
SAZAVA VLTAVA LUZNICE
BEROUNKA
TOWN: AS ASCH BRNO CHEB EGER
MOST ZLIN BRUNN OPAVA PLZEN
PRAHA TABOR AUSSIG BILINA
KLADNO OSTROV PILSEN VSETIN
BUDWEIS HAVIROV JIHLAVA
OLOMOAC OSTRAVA TEPLICE
TEPLITZ KARLOVYVARY

D

D DE DEE DOG DELTA
DA DUCKTAIL
DAB DAP DOB DOT DUB HIT PAT BLOW CHIT DAUB LICK LUMP PECK SPOT CLOUT DHABB DIGHT LEMON SMEAR BLOTCH EXPERT STRIKE DABSTER PORTION SPLOTCH FLATFISH FLOUNDER MARYSOLE SANDLING
DABBER BALL PROD TAMPON
DABBING PICKING
DABBLE DAB DIB MESS DALLY DIBBLE MEDDLE MUDDLE PADDLE POTTER SOSSLE SPLASH TAMPER TRIFLE DRABBLE MOISTEN PLOUTER PLUTTER SMATTER SPATTER DELIBATE SPRINKLE **(— WITH BLOOD)** ENGORE
DABBLER AMATEUR DABSTER
DABBLING PLOUTER PLOWTER
DABCHICK GREBE DIPPER DOBBER DOPPER PUFFER HENBILL DIDAPPER DOPCHICK
DACE CHUB DARE DART CYPRINID GRAYLING
DACHSHUND DACHS TECKEL BADGERER
DACOIT DAKU DAKOO ROBBER CRIMINAL
DACTYL TOE FOOT FINGER **(— AND IAMB)** FEET
DACTYLOPODITE POLLEX
DACTYLOZOOID PALPON
DACTYLUS DACTYL DIGITUS
DAD BEAT BLOW DAUD HUNK LUMP PAPA KNOCK THUMP FATHER STRIKE
DADA (FOUNDER OF —) ARP
DADAIST (— PAINTER) ARP **(— POET)** TZARA
DADDY BABBO DEDDY
DADDY LONGLEGS SPINNER LONGLEGS PHALANGID
DADO DIE GROOVE SOLIDUM
DAEDALUS (ANCESTOR OF —) ERECHTHEUS **(NEPHEW OF —)** TALUS **(SON OF —)** ICARUS
DAEMON (ALSO SEE DEMON) GHOST DAIMON PYTHON EUDAEMON MISTRESS **(PL.)** CURETES
DAFFODIL GLEN LILY DAFFY DILLY JONQUIL ASPHODEL BELLWORT CROWBELL
DAFT GAY MAD LOCO WILD ZANY BALMY BATTY CRAZY DAFFY GIDDY LOONY POTTY SILLY INSANE FOOLISH IDIOTIC IMBECILE
DAG JAG DAGG STAB SLASH DAGGLE PIERCE DAGGING DAGLOCK PRICKET

DAGAME SALAMO MADRONA LEMONWOOD
DAGGER DAG SAX DIRK ITAC KRIS SAEX SNEE SPUD STAB TANG CRISE DAGUE KATAR KREES POINT PRICK SKEAN STEEL ANLACE BODKIN COUTEL CREESE DIESIS HANGER KIRPAN KUTTAR PANADE PINKER POPPER SKHIAN STYLET BALARAO BAYONET COUTEAU DUDGEON HANDJAR KANDJAR KHANJAR OBELISK PONIARD SLASHER STABBER BASELARD PUNCHEON PUNTILLA STILETTO **(— AS CERAMICS COVER)** HILLER **(— REFERENCE MARK)** SPIT **(— WITH WAVY BLADE)** KRIS CREESE KREESE **(DOUBLE —)** DIESIS **(PART OF —)** HAFT BLADE **(SACRED —)** KIRPAN **(PREF.)** MACHAIRO
DAGOMBA DAGBANE DAGBANI
DAH DAO DOW DHAO
DAHLIA JICAMA POMPON
DAHOMEY (CAPITAL OF —) PORTONOVO **(PEOPLE OF —)** FON FONG BARIBA **(RIVER OF —)** NIGER OUEME **(TOWN IN —)** KANDI NIKKI ABOMEY OUIDAH COTONOU
DAIL ASSEMBLY
DAILY ADAY ADAYS DIARY DIURNAL QUOTIDIAN
DAINCHA NARDOO
DAINTIES EST ESTE SOCK CATES DIABLOTIN
DAINTILY CHOICELY GINGERLY MINIONLY
DAINTINESS FLUTTER DELICACY
DAINTY CATE FINE NICE RARE TEAR TWEE ACATE DAINT DENTY FRILL GENTY NAISH TREAT BONBON CHOICE COSTLY FRIAND MIGNON MINION PICKED REGALO SCARCE SPICED SUNKET CURIOUS ELEGANT FINICAL FINICKY MINIKIN REGALIA TAFFETA TAFFETY DAINTITH DAINTREL DELICACY DELICATE ETHEREAL LIKEROUS MIGNIARD TRYPHOSA **(PREF.)** ABRO HABRO
DAIRY TAMBO LACTARY VACCARY CREAMERY DEYHOUSE **(— PRODUCTS)** MILCHIGS
DAIRYMAID DEE DEY DEYWOMAN MILKMAID
DAIRYMAN AHIR MILKMAN
DAIS PACE SEAT BENCH LEWAN STAGE TABLE CANOPY ESTATE LISSOM PODIUM PULPIT SETTLE ESTRADE TERRACE TRIBUNE

CHABUTRA FOOTPACE HALFPACE HATHPACE HUSTINGS PLATFORM
DAISY BULL GOLD DANDY GOWAN OXEYE BENNET MORGAN SHASTA BONESET BOWWORT COMFREY DOGBLOW BACKWORT BONEWORT COMPOSIT HEXAFOIL KNITBACK PISSABED MOONPENNY BRUISEWORT MARGUERITE
DAISY CUTTER GRUB
DAISY FLEABANE ERIGERON SCABIOUS
DAKOTA SIOUX LAKOTA
DALE HAW DELL DENE GLEN VALE SPOUT BOTTOM DINGLE TROUGH VALLEY
DALEA PAROSELA
DALIBOR (CHARACTER IN —) BENES ZDENEK DALIBOR MAILADA **(COMPOSER OF —)** SMETANA
DALLES DELLS RAPIDS
DALLIANCE TOY CHAT PLAY TALK SPORT GOSSIP TOUSEL TOUSLE TRIFLE COLLING
DALLIER PINGLER
DALLY TOY CHAT DAFF FOOL IDLE JAKE JAUK PLAY SWAN WAIT DELAY FLIRT SPORT TARRY COQUET DABBLE DAWDLE LINGER LOITER PINGLE TRIFLE WANTON DRINGLE SLIDDER PHILANDER
DALLYING COQUETRY SISSETON
DALMATIAN COACHDOG
DALMATIC TUNICLE
DALPHON (FATHER OF —) HAMAN
DAM BAR BAY PEN REE BUND DAME HEAD POND SADD SPUR STAY STEM STOP SUDD WEIR BLOCK CAULD CHECK CHOKE GARTH MOUND POUND STANK ANICUT CAUSEY HINDER MOTHER PARENT ANNICUT BARRAGE BARRIER BURROCK MILLDAM PENHEAD RAMPIRE TAPPOON ABOIDEAU BLOCKADE GRANDDAM OBSTACLE OBSTRUCT RESTRAIN **(PART OF —)** GATE PIER POOL SILL WALL BASIN CREST OUTLET SLUICE ROADWAY TAINTOR OVERFLOW SPILLWAY POWERHOUSE
DAMAGE MAR BLOT BURN COST HARM HURT JEEL LOSS RUIN SKIN TEEN BLITZ BURST CLOUD CRACK HAVOC PRANG SPOIL WOUND WRONG BANJAX BATTER CHARGE DANGER DEFACE DEFECT HINDER IMPAIR INJURE INJURY INSULT LESION SCATHE SORROW AFFLICT DAMNIFY DEGRADE DISTURB EXPENSE FOUNDER OFFENCE OFFENSE PAYMENT SCRATCH SCUTTLE SHATTER ACCIDENT

BUSINESS DISSERVE FRACTURE FRETTING MISCHIEF SABOTAGE **(MINOR SURFACE —)** DING **(PREF.)** DAMNI
DAMAGED HURT CRAZY LESED BROKEN CRACKED INJURED
DAMAGES INTEREST HAMESUCKEN **(EXCESSIVE —)** SMART SMARTMONEY
DAMAGING HARMFUL HURTFUL SCATHING
DAMAN DAS CONY CONEY CUNNY DASSY GANAM HYRAX DASSIE WABBER ASHKOKO CHEROGRIL
DAMA PADEMELON TAMMAR WALLABY
DAMASCENED WATERED
DAMASCENE WORK KOFTGARI
DAMASK LINEN DARNEX DORNIC DORNICK VALANCE DAMASSIN DRAWLOOM
DAMAYANTI (HUSBAND OF —) NALA
DAME DINT LADY DAMIE WOMAN MATRON
DAME BLANCHE, LA (CHARACTER IN —) ANNA BROWN JENNY GEORGE DICKSON GAVESTON **(COMPOSER OF —)** BOIELDIEU
DAME'S VIOLET EVEWEED
DAMKINA (HUSBAND OF —) EA
DAMMARA AGATHIS
DAMN DEE DEM DOG RAT BLOW BURN DANG DARN DASH DING DRAT DUMB DURN BLAME BLANK BLAST BLESS CURSE FETCH TARAL WHOOP BEDAMN BUGGER DEMPNE DEVOTE GODDAM CONDEMN CONSARN DOGGONE GODDAMN GOLDARN GOLDURN CONFOUND EXECRATE
DAMNABLE RUDDY DAMNED ODIOUS ACCURSED INFERNAL
DAMNABLY DEUCED CURSEDLY DEUCEDLY
DAMNATION NATION PERDITION
DAMNATION DE FAUST (CHARACTER IN —) FAUST MARGUERITE MEPHISTOPHELES **(COMPOSER OF —)** BERLIOZ
DAMNED DEE DAMN DARN DEED DURN LOST BALLY DOOMS BLAMED BLOODY DARNED DASHED DURNED GODDAM GORMED TARNAL BLASTED BLESSED CONSARN DOGGONE ETERNAL GOLDARN GOLDURN MUCKING ACCURSED BLANKETY BLINKING DASHEDLY FREAKING INFERNAL JIGGERED
DAMO (FATHER OF —) PYTHAGORAS **(MOTHER OF —)** THEANO
DAMP DEG FOG RAW WAK WET

CLAM DANK DEWY DULL MIST
ROKY SOFT WACK BLUNT DABBY
HUMID JUICY MALMY MOCHY
MOIST MOOTH MUGGY MUNGY
MUSTY RAFTY RAINY RAWKY
SAPPY SEEPY SOBBY SOGGY
THONE WAUGH WEAKY BLIGHT
CLAMMY DAMPEN DEADEN
MUFFLE QUENCH RHEUMY
STUPOR BEDEWED DAMPISH
DEPRESS MOISTEN SQUIDGY
DEJECTED DISPIRIT HUMIDIFY
HUMIDITY MOISTURE
(— OF EVENING) SERENE
(CHOKE —) STYTHE
(PREF.) HUMI(DI)
DAMPED SORDO
DAMPEN DEG DAMP MOIL CHILL
CRAMP FREEZE SPONGE
MOISTURE
DAMPENER MULLER
DAMPER DAMP MUTE BREAD
CHECK CHECKER SORDINE
REGISTER
DAMPNESS CLAM DAMP HUMIDITY
DAMSEL GIRL MISS WENCH
MAIDEN MOPPET DAMOSEL
DAMOZEL PUCELLE DONZELLA
PRINCESS
DAMSELFISH PINTANO
DAMSELFLY NAIAD ODONATE
DAN GI DEN
(MOTHER OF —) BILHAH
DANAKIL AFAR
DANAUS ANOSIA
(BROTHER OF —) AEGYPTUS
(DAUGHTER OF —) AMYMONE
(FATHER OF —) BELUS
(MOTHER OF —) ANCHINOE
DANCE BAL ROB HOP JIG MAI SON
BALL DRAG DUET DUMP FISH
FOOT FRUG HEEL HOOF HORA
JAZZ JIVE JUBA JUKE KOLO LEAP
LOPE LOUP MASK MILL MOVE
PROM REEL SAIL SHAG SKIT STEP
BAILE BAMBA BONGO BOOGY
BRAWL CANON CAPER CAROL
CONGA DANZA DISCO ENTRY
FLING FLISK FRIKE FRISK GOPAK
HORAH LASYA LIMBO LINDY
MAMBO PAVAN POLKA RINKA
RUMBA SALLY SAMBA STOMP
SWING TANGO TRACE TREAD
TWIST VOLTA WALTZ ALTHEA
AREITO BALLET BALTER BOLERO
BOOGIE BOSTON BRANLE CANARY
CANCAN CEBELL CHACHA CORDAX
DANZON DIDDLE DREHER FADING
FORMAL FROLIC GERMAN
HORMOS MASQUE MINUET
MOBBLE MONKEY MORRIS NRITTA
PASSAY RACKET RHUMBA SHIMMY
TODDLE TRESCA TUMBLE VALETA
VELETA ANTHEMA BEGUINE
CALINDA CANTICO COURANT
CZARDAS DANSANT FADDING
FARRUCA FOOTING FOXTROT
FURLANA GAVOTTE MEASURE
MORISCO PATTERN SALTATE
SARDANA SHUFFLE TEMPETE
TRESCHE TRIPPLE VOLTIZE
ZIGANKA ANGLAISE AURRESCU

BAMBOULA BUNNYHUG
CACHUCHA CAKEWALK
CHACONNE COMPARSA COONJINE
COTILLON ENTRACTE ESTAMPIE
FANDANGO FANTASIA FLAMENCO
GALLIARD GALOPADE GUARACHA
HABANERA HEYDEGUY HORNPIPE
KOLATTAM MATELOTE MERENGUE
SALTATION SHAKEDOWN
CARMAGNOLE SCHOTTISCHE
(— ART) NATYA ORCHESIS
(— ATTENDANCE) LACKEY
LACQUEY
(— CLUMSILY) BALTER
(— DRAMA) NO NOH
(— FACE TO FACE) SET
(— FORM) PIVA
(— IN CIRCLE) JIGGER
(— METHOD) LABAN
(— NIMBLY) CANARY
(— RESEMBLING THE POLKA)
BERLIN
(— STEP) RIFF PICKUP
(— STYLE) ABHINAYA
(— SUGGESTIVELY) BUMP GRIND
(— TYPE) TANDAVA
(ACROBATIC —) ADAGIO
(AFRICAN —) SHOUT
(ARGENTINE —) CUANDO
(AUSTRIAN —) LANDLER
(BALINESE —) KEBYAR LEGONG
(BALLROOM —) SON CONGO
TWOSTEP COTILLON
(BOHEMIAN —) REDOWA FURIANT
(BRAZILIAN —) SAMBA
(CARNIVAL —) COOCH FOLIA
COOTCH
(CEREMONIAL —) AREITO CANTICO
DUTUBURI
(COQUETTISH —) PURPOSE
(COUNTRY —) HAY CLOG RANT
CONFESS LANDLER MUSETTE
ZIGANKA ANGLAISE SARABAND
(COURTSHIP —) CUECA BATUQUE
LEZGINKA
(DANISH —) SEXTUR
(FIESTA —S) AKRIEROS
(FLAMENCO —) ALEGRIAS
(FRENCH —) BAL BOREE BRAWL
GAVOT BRANLE BOURREE BOUTADE
BRANSLE GAVOTTE LAVOLTA
ALLEMANDE
(GAY —) RANT GAILLARD GALLIARD
(GESTURE —) SIVA
(GREEK —) CORDAX KORDAX
ROMAIKA SIRTAKI SIKINNIS
(GYPSY —) FARRUCA
(HAITIAN —) JUBA
(HAWAIIAN —) HULA
(HOBBYHORSE —) CALUSAR
(HOLIDAY —) PATTERN
(HUNGARIAN —) KOS
(IMPROMPTU —) BOUTADE
(INDIAN —) IRUSKA KATHAK
KANTIKOY
(IRISH —) FADING PLANXTY
(ITALIAN —) FORLANA FURLANA
BERGAMASK SALTARELLO
(JAPANESE —) BUGAKU KAGURA
(JAVANESE —) SERIMPI
(KIND OF —) TAP
(LIVELY —) JIG REEL GALOP GIGUE
POLKA RUMBA BOLERO CANARY

RHUMBA SPRING BOURREE
CORANTO FURLANA HOEDOWN
GALLIARD GALOPADE HORNPIPE
(MAORI —) HAKA
(MARTIAL —) PYRRHIC
(MEXICAN —) JARABE HUAPANGO
SANDUNGA
(MOURNFUL —) DUMP
(NORWEGIAN —) HALLING
(OLD-FASHIONED —) LOURE
PASSACAGLIA
(OLD ENGLISH —) CEBELL MORRIS
ARGEERS ANGLAISE
(PEASANT —) JOTA DANZON
BALITAO
(PERUVIAN —) CUECA KASWA
CACHUA
(POLISH —) POLACCA KUJAWIAK
POLONAISE VARSOVIENNE
(POLYNESIAN —) HULA
(PORTUGUESE —) FADO
(ROMAN —) TRIPUDIUM
(ROUND —) RAY BRAUL CAROL
WALTZ CAROLE MAXIXE
(RUSSIAN —) ZIGANKA
(RUSTIC —) HAY HEY HAYMAKER
(SPANISH —) JOTA POLO JALEO
BOLERO JARABE CHACONNE
FLAMENCO GUARACHA
MALAGUENA ZAPATEADO
SEGUIDILLA
(SPEAR —) BARIS
(SQUARE —) SQUARE ARGEERS
HOEDOWN LANCERS QUADRILLE
(STATELY —) PAVAN PAVANE
EMMELEIA SARABAND POLONAISE
(SWORD —) BACUBERT MATACHIN
(VENEZUELAN —) JOROPO
(WEDDING —) CANACUAS
(WEST INDIAN —) LIMBO
(WHIRLING —) TARANTELLA
(PREF.) CHORE(I)(O) CHORO
ORCHESO
DANCE-DRAMA NOH
(JAPANESE —) NO
DANCER PONY CLOWN PONEY
ARTIST CORNER EXOTIC HOOFER
HOPPER MAENAD APSARAS
CLOGGER DANSEUR PASCOLA
PRANCER PRANKER SAILOUR
STEPPER TODDLER BALADINE
BAYADERE DANSEUSE DEVADASI
FIGURANT MORRICER
(BALLET —) ETOILE SOLISTE
CORYPHEE
(EGYPTIAN —S) GHAWAZI
GHAWAZEE
(JAVANESE —) SERIMPI
(JAVANESE —S) BEDOYO
(MASKED —S) GAHE
(SQUARE —S) FLOOR
(SWORD —) MATACHIN
(ZUNI —S) SHALAKO
DANCE-TUNE BRAWL BRANTLE
DANCING SWING ADANCE BALLET
CHANGE FROLIC MORRIS SALTANT
SURGING STEPPING TRIPSOME
(— MANIA) TARANTISM
DANCING-GIRL ALMA ALME
ALMEH ALAMAH BAYADERE
DANDELION BLOW BLOWER
CANKER DINDLE CHICORY

HAWKBIT BLOWBALL COMPOSIT
PISSABED
(RUSSIAN —) KOKSAGYZ
DANDELION HEAD PUFF CLOCK
BUFFBALL BULLFICE BULLFIST
PUFFBALL
DANDER ANGER DUTCH SCURF
STROLL TEMPER WANDER
HACKLES PASSION SAUNTER
DANDRUFF
DANDIFIED SPRUCE BUCKISH
ADONIZED
DANDIFY ADONIZE DANDYIZE
DANDLE DANCE DIDDLE DOODLE
FADDLE FONDLE PAMPER
DANDRUFF SCURF DANDER
FURFUR PORRIGO
DANDY FOP JAY ADON BEAU BUCK
DAND DUDE FINE JAKE MAJO PRIG
TOFF TRIG YAWL BLOOD DILDO
JEMMY SWELL ADONIS MIZZEN
BUCKEEN CAPSTAN COXCOMB
ELEGANT FOPPISH JESSAMY
MACARONI MUSCADIN SAILBOAT
DANDY HORSE HOBBY DRAISINE
DANDYISHNESS SPIFF
DANDYISM BUCKISM
DANE DANSKER LOCHLIN
DUBHGALL
DANEWORT EBULUS LOCHLIN
DANEBALL DANEWEED
DEADWORT WALLWORT
DANGER FEAR RISK DOUBT PERIL
WATHE HAZARD PLIGHT EXTREME
PITFALL VENTURE DISTRESS
JEOPARDY
(— SIGNAL) RED
(MORAL —) SNARE
DANGEROUS BAD HOT ILL RUM
DEAR FOUL GRAVE NASTY RISKY
FICKLE KITTLE SCATHY SHREWD
UNSURE AWKWARD FEARFUL
PARLOUS UNCANNY DOUBTFUL
INSECURE PERILOUS UNCHANCY
BREAKNECK WANCHANCY
PRECARIOUS PESTIFEROUS
(MAKE LESS —) DEFUSE
(NOT —) CUSHY
(VERY —) TOXIC
DANGLE BOB LOP HANG LOLL
DROOP SWING DANDLE SHOGGLE
SHOOGLE SUSPEND SWINGLE
TROLLOP
DANGLER (— AFTER WOMEN)
PHILANDER
DANGLIN DANLI
DANGLING PENDANT VERSATILE
DANIEL (FATHER OF —) DAVID
(MOTHER OF —) ABIGAIL
DANK WET DAMP DONK HUMID
MADID MOIST CLAMMY COARSE
DAMPEN DANKISH DRIZZLE
WETNESS MOISTURE
DANSEUSE DANCER BALLERINA
DANUBE (— FEEDER) INN
DANZIG GDANSK
(— LIQUEUR) RATAFIA
DAPHNE (CHARACTER IN —) GAEA
APOLLO DAPHNE PENEIOS
LEUKIPPOS
(COMPOSER OF —) STRAUSS
DAPPER CHIC COOL NEAT TRIM

NATTY SNAZZY SPRUCE FINICAL FOPPISH SPARKISH

DAPPLE COVER FLECK FRECK

DAPPLED BLOCKY DOTTED POMELY FLECKED MOTTLED SPOTTED FRECKLED

DAPPLE-GREY LIARD

DARBHA KUSA KUSHA

DARDA (FATHER OF —) MAHOL

DARDANUS (CHARACTER IN —) VENUS IPHISE TEUCER ANTENOR ISMENOR DARDANUS
(COMPOSER OF —) RAMEAU
(DAUGHTER OF —) IDAEA
(FATHER OF —) ZEUS JUPITER
(MOTHER OF —) ELECTRA
(SON OF —) ILUS DEIMAS IDAEUS ERICHTHONIUS

DARE OSS DAST DEFY FACE OSER OSSE RISK BRAVE STUMP ASSUME BANTER DACKER ATTEMPT BRAVADE FASHION PRESUME VENTURE
(— NOT) DASSNT DAURNA DASSENT

DAREDEVIL MADCAP HARDYDARDY

DARING BOLD DARE DERF PERT RACY RASH WILD BRAVE HARDY MANLY NERVE PREST FELONY HEROIC COURAGE DAIROUS DAREFUL BOLDNESS DEVILISH FEARLESS STALWART

DARIOLE MADELINE

DARK DIM DUN MUM SAD WAN BASE BLAE DEEP DERK DERN DUSK EBON HARD MALE MIRK MURK BLACK BLIND BROWN CLOUD DINGY DUSKY FAINT MIRKY MURKY ROOKY SHADY SOOTY SWART UMBER UNLIT VAGUE CLOSED CLOUDY CYPRUS DIMPSY DISMAL DRUMLY GLOOMY OPAQUE SOMBER SOMBRE SWARTH WICKED APHOTIC DARKISH DUSKISH MELANIC OBSCURE PITMIRK RAYLESS STYGIAN SUNLESS SWARTHY THESTER UNCLEAR ABSTRUSE DARKLING DARKSOME GLOOMFUL GLOOMING IGNORANT LOWERING SINISTER CIMMERIAN CALIGINOUS
(PREF.) AITHO MAVRO MEL(A) MELAN(O)
(SUFF.) MELANE

DARK BEAVER PRALINE

DARK-COLORED SAD SWART SOMBER SOMBRE SWARTH SWARTHY
(PREF.) FUSCO

DARK-COMPLEXIONED BROWN MELANOUS

DARKEN DIM DUN BLUR DULL DUSK BEDIM BLIND CLOUD GLOAM GLOOM POCHE SHADE SULLY SWART UMBER DEEPEN ENDARK SHADOW BECLOUD BENIGHT BLACKEN ECLIPSE EMBROWN OBSCURE OPACATE PERPLEX SLUBBER TARNISH OVERCAST OBFUSCATE OVERSHADOW
(— HAIR) BLEND

DARKENED SABLE CLOUDY BLINDED LAMPLESS

DARKENING SCURF

DARK HORSE MOREL

DARKISH DIM

DARKLY DARK CLOSE SABLY MISTILY

DARKNESS DARK DERN DUSK MIRK MURK BLACK GLOOM NIGHT SHADE TAMAS SHADOW DIMNESS PITMIRK PRIVACY SECRECY TENEBRA GLOAMING INIQUITY MIDNIGHT TENEBRES TWILIGHT NIGRITUDE
(PLACE OF —) EREBUS
(PREF.) SCOTO TENEBRI

DARKNESS AT NOON (AUTHOR OF —) KOESTLER
(CHARACTER IN —) ARLOVA BOGRAV IVANOV GLETKIN HARELIP KIEFFER MICHAEL NICHOLAS RUBASHOV

DARLING JO JOE PET CHOU CONY DEAR DUCK LIFE LOVE NOBS PEAT ROON AROON ARUIN BULLY CHERI DEARY DUCKS LIEVE SWEET WHITE CHERIE DAUTIE DAWTIE MINION MOPPET OCHREE POPPET ACUSHLA ASTHORE BUNTING CUSHLAM DILLING MINIKIN PIGSNEY PINKENY QUERIDA STOREEN DEARLING DUMPLING FAVORITE LIEBCHEN LOVELING MACUSHLA PRECIOUS SWEETING MAVOURNIN MAVOURNEEN

DARLING PEA INDICO INDIGO

DARN DOG BLOW DERN DURN MEND PATCH BUGGER RENTER REPAIR DOGGONE

DARNED BLAME BLAMED DAGNAB DAGNAG DANGED DEUCED DURNED BLESSED BLINDING DOWNGONE

DARNEL RAY CRAP TARE WEED CHEAT CHESS DRANK DRAWK DRUNK EAVER GRASS IVRAY NEELE COCKLE EGILOPS AEGILOPS

DART JET POP BOLT BUZZ CANE CHOP COLP FLIT JOUK LEAP LICK PILE PLAN PLAY ROUT ARROW BOUND FLAME FLING FLIRT GLEAM GLINT LANCE SCAMP SCOOT SHAFT SHOOT SKITE SKIVE SPEAR SPEED SPRIT START ANCHOR BULTEN DARTLE ELANCE GLANCE LANCET LAUNCH METHOD SCHEME SPRING SQUIRT STRIKE SUMPIT THRUST JAVELIN MISSILE STRALET VERUTUM BRANDISH GAVELOCK JACULATE SPICULUM BANDERILLA
(— ABOUT) SPRINKLE
(— OF LIGHTNING) STREAK
(— OF MOLDING) ANCHOR
(— REPEATEDLY) DARTLE
(PART OF —) POINT SHAFT BARREL FLIGHT
(PREF.) JACULI TELI

DARTER SPECK

DARTING SALLY ARROWY

DARTLIKE SPICULAR

DASH DAD DAH PEP ZIP BANG BOLT CAST DING DIVE ELAN GIFT HINT HURL LASH LINE LUSH PASH PELT POSS RACE RASH RUIN RULE RUSH SHOW SLAM SOSH TICK VEIN

WHAP WHOP ABASH ARDOR BLANK BREAK CHAFE CLASH CRASH CRUSH DRIVE ECLAT FLASH FLING FRUSH KNOCK PLASH PLOUT SKITE SLASH SLOSH SMASH SPEED SPEND SPICE SPURN START STYLE SWASH SWELL TASTE THROW TOUCH TRICK BEDASH DALLOP DASHEE DOLLOP ENERGY HURTLE HYPHEN JABBLE RELISH SHIVER SPIRIT SPLASH SPRINT STRAIN STROKE THRUST ABANDON BRAVURA BREENGE COLLIDE DEPRESS DISPLAY HUNDRED IMPINGE PANACHE SHATTER SPATTER SPLOTCH TANTIVY VIRETOT CONFOUND GRATUITY SPLINTER
(— ABOUT WILDLY) GAD REEL
(— AGAINST) BEAT
(— DOWN) QUELL STRAM STRAMASH
(— IN PIECES) CRASH
(— OF LIQUID) JAW
(— OF SPIRITS) LACE LACING
(— OUT) QUELL
(— TOGETHER) COLLIDE
(— UP) FLURR
(— WITH WATER) JAW BLASH SLASH

DASHARATHA (FATHER OF —) AJA
(SON OF —) RAMA BHARATA LAKSHMANA SHATRUGHNA
(WIFE OF —) KAIKEYI SUMITRA KAUSHALYA

DASHBOARD DASH FACIA DASHER FASCIA

DASHED SWITCHED

DASHEEN TARO

DASHER DASH BEATER PLUNGER

DASHING BOLD BULLY DASHY DOGGY SHOWY SMART SPICY SWASH JABBLE SPANKY SWANKY VELOCE DOGGISH GALLANT GALLOWS LARKING STYLISH SWAGGER VARMINT SLASHING SPANKING SPIRITED

DASSIE HYRAX

DASTARD CAD SOT DAFF SNEAK COWARD CRAVEN DULLARD HILDING VILLAIN WITHING POLTROON

DASTARDLY BASE FOUL VILLAIN COWARDLY POLTROON SNEAKING

DASYLIRION SOTOL

DASYPUS TATU

DASYURE TIGER YABBI DAPPLE

DATA DOPE FILE FACTS IMPUT INPUT MATERIAL
(— RETRIEVAL SYSTEM) VIDEOTEX
(— STRUCTURE) ARRAY
(COMPUTER —) FILE PUSHDOWN
(ENTER —) READIN
(INACCURATE —) GARDAGE
(SHORT SECTION OF —) PACKET
(STORE OF —) PUSHDOWN
(USELESS —) GARBAGE

DATE DAY ERA SEE DRAG FARD FUSS DATUM EPOCH FARDH FRUIT SAIDI TRYST CUTOFF FRIEND HALAWI JUJUBE RECKON GALLANT ANTEDATE ASHARASI DEADLINE

(— BACK) TRACE RELATE
(— FIXED UPON) TERM
(— OF DEATH) OBIT
(— RIPENING) KIMRI RUTAB KHALAL
(CHINESE —) BER
(REGULAR —) STEADY

DATED GIVEN PASSE STALE OUTMODED

DATELESS STAG

DATE PLUM LOTUS SAPOTE ZAPOTE

DATHAN (FATHER OF —) ELIAB

DATING (KIND OF —) OPEN

DATOLITE BAKERITE HUMBOLDTITE

DATUM FACT ITEM GIVEN DONNEE

DATURA DUTRA STRAMONY TOGUACHA

DAUB DAB DOB MUD BALM BLOB BLOT CLAG CLAM CLAT CLAY COAT GAUM MOIL SOIL TEER CLAIK CLART CLEAM COVER DITCH FLICK PAINT SLAKE SLAUM SMEAR BEDAUB CLATCH GREASE LABBER SMUDGE SPLASH BESMEAR DRIBBLE PLASTER SCLATCH SLUBBER SPLATCH SPLOTCH SLAISTER

DAUBE LARD

DAUBED GAUMY

DAUBING DUBBING MOILING

DAUBY BLOTTY

DAUGHTER ANAC BINT DAME GIRL CHILD FILLE FILLY KIBEI REGAN ALUMNA CADETTE DOCHTER GONERIL CORDELIA
(NISEI —) SANSEI
(PANTALOON'S —) COLUMBINE
(PRIEST'S —) NIECE
(PREF.) FILI

DAUGHTER OF THE REGIMENT
(CHARACTER IN —) MARIE TONZIO SULPICE COUNTESS
(COMPOSER OF —) DONIZETTI

DAUNT AWE COW DAW ADAW DARE DAZE FAZE MATE PALL STUN TAME ABASH ACCOY AMATE BREAK CHECK DETER DOMPT QUAIL APPALL DANTON DISMAY SUBDUE CONQUER CONTROL OVERAWE REPRESS STUPEFY TERRIFY DISPIRIT OVERCOME

DAUNTED MATE

DAUNTLESS BOLD GOOD BRAVE AWELESS SPARTAN FEARLESS INTREPID

DAUNUS (DAUGHTER OF —) EUIPPE
(FATHER OF —) PILUMNUS
(MOTHER OF —) DANAE
(SON OF —) TURNUS
(WIFE OF —) VENILIA

DAVENPORT DESK SOFA COUCH DIVAN

DAVID TAFFY DAWKIN
(COMPANION OF —) JONATHAN
(DAUGHTER OF —) TAMAR
(FATHER OF —) JESSE
(SON OF —) AMNON ABSALOM
(WIFE OF —) ABIGAIL AHINOAM

DAVID COPPERFIELD (AUTHOR OF —) DICKENS
(CHARACTER IN —) HAM DICK DORA HEEP JANE MICK ROSA AGNES BETSY CLARA DAVID EMILY

JAMES MEALY TOMMY URIAH BARKIS DARTLE GRINBY STRONG WALKER CREAKLE SPENLOW WILKINS MICAWBER PEGGOTTY TRADDLES TROTWOOD MURDSTONE WICKFIELD STEERFORTH

DAVIDIST JORIST

DAVIT CRANE

DAW DA DAWN DRAB DAUNT MAGPIE DAWPATE JACKDAW SLATTERN SLUGGARD

DAWDLE LAG IDLE JAUK LOAF MOON MUCK MULL POKE TOIT DALLY DELAY DRILL KNOCK DADDLE DAIDLE DIDDLE DOODLE DRETCH FADDLE LINGER LOITER MUCKER PICKLE PIDDLE PINGLE POTTER PUTTER TANTLE TRIFLE DRIDDLE FINNICK QUIDDLE SAUNTER LALLYGAG LOLLYGAG SHAMMOCK SLUMMOCK

DAWDLER DAWDLE MUSARD LOUTHER

DAWN DAW ROW EOAN MORN BREAK CREEK LIGHT PRIME SHINE SUNUP AURORA MORROW ORIENT SPRING UPRISE DAWNING GREKING MORNING SUNRISE COCKCROW DAYBREAK (PREF.) EO EOSINO

DAWN-HORSE EOHIPPUS

DAY DA DEI ERA SUN YOM DATE DIEM DIES DIET JOUR TIME EPOCH LIGHT FRIDAY MONDAY PERIOD SUNDAY JOURNEY TUESDAY LIFETIME SATURDAY THURSDAY WEDNESDAY
(— AND NIGHT) KAI PA
(— BEFORE) EVE
(— OF BRAHMA) CALPA KALPA
(— OF JOY)) FEAST
(— OF JUDGMENT) INQUEST DOOMSDAY
(— OF ORIGIN) BIRTHDAY
(— OF REST) SABBATH
(— OF ROMAN MONTH) IDES NONES CALENDS KALENDS
(DOG —S) CANICULE
(EVERY —) ALDAY
(EVIL —S) DISMAL
(FAST —) ASHURA FASTEN
(FIRST — OF AUGUST) LAMMAS
(FIRST — OF MAY) BELTANE BEALTINE
(HOLY —) FEAST HOLIDAY
(HOT —) BROILER ROASTER SCORCHER
(LAST — OF FESTIVAL) APODOSIS
(LAST — OF YEAR) HOGMANAY
(MARKET —) NUNDINE TIANGUE
(NO FLESH —) MAIGRE
(PATRON SAINT'S —) PATTERN
(QUARTER —) TERM
(SAINT'S —) FESTA FIESTA
(TWELFTH —) EPIPHANY
(UNLUCKY —S) DISMAL
(WEEK —) FERIA
(WORK —) WARDAY
(40 —S) QUARANTINE
(5 NAMELESS —S) UAYEB
(60TH OF —) GHURRY

(8TH — AFTER FEAST) UTAS
(PREF.) HEMER(O)
(LASTING BUT —) EPHEMERO

DAYAK DYAK IBAN BAHAU DUSUN KAYAN KENYA KENYAH KELABIT

DAYBOOK BOOK DIURNAL JOURNAL

DAYBREAK DAWN MORN SUNUP DAWNING DAYDAWN DAYLIGHT (PREF.) EO EOSINO

DAYDREAM DWAM MUSE DREAM DWALM FANCY VISION FANTASY REVERIE PHANTASY

DAYDREAMER MITTY REVEUR

DAYFLOWER COHITRE

DAYLIGHT DAY LIGHT DAYSHINE (BROAD —) FAIRDAYS

DAYWORKER DILKER

DAZE FOG DAMP DARE MAZE ROCK STUN DAUNT DAVER DIZZY DOZEN GALLY SWOON ASTONY BEDAZE BEMUSE BENUMB DAZZLE DEAFEN MUDDLE STUPOR TRANCE CONFUSE PETRIFY STUPEFY TORPIFY ASTONISH BEWILDER DUMFOUND PARALYZE

DAZED MAD ASEA DAMP ASSOT DIZZY DOYLT MUZZY SILLY TOTTY WOOZY CUCKOO DOILED GROGGY ROTTEN BEMUSED DONNERT SPOILED WITLESS ASTONIED BESOTTED DITHERED DONNERED WITHERED

DAZEDLY GROGGILY

DAZZLE DARE DAZE BLEND BLIND DROWN GLAIK SHINE FULGOR ECLIPSE BEWILDER OUTSHINE SURPRISE

DAZZLED BLINDED

DAZZLING FLARE FLASH GLAIK FLASHY GARISH ADAZZLE FLARING FULGENT GLARING RADIANT DIZZYING GORGEOUS

DDT TDE DICOPHANE

DEACON ADEPT CLERIC DOCTOR LAYMAN LEVITE MASTER PHILIP MINISTER

DEACONESS WIDOW

DEACTIVATE MOTHBALL

DEAD FEY LOW AWAY BONG BUNG COLD DEAF DOWD DULL FLAT GONE MORT NUMB POKY SURE TAME ADEAD AMORT BLIND DEEDS INERT NAPOO POKEY QUIET SLAIN STARK VAPID ASLEEP BYGONE FALLEN LAPSED NAPOOH PARTED REFUSE DEADISH DEFUNCT EXACTLY EXPIRED EXTINCT INSIPID SAINTED STERILE TEDIOUS ABSOLUTE COMPLETE DECEASED DEPARTED INACTIVE LIFELESS OBSOLETE SCUPPERED
(— AT TOP) RAMPICK
(BLESSED —) SAINT
(PREF.) NECR(O)

DEAD-ARM NECROSIS

DEAD-DRUNK BLIND

DEADEN DAMP DRUG DULL DUMB KILL MULL MUTE NUMB SEAR STUN BLUNT SLAKE BENUMB DAMPEN MUFFLE OBTUND OPIATE RETARD STIFLE WEAKEN MORTIFY PETRIFY REPRESS SLUMBER

SMOTHER AMORTIZE ASTONISH ENFEEBLE
(— A SCENT) FOIL

DEAD END PLACE
(AUTHOR OF —) KINGSLEY
(CHARACTER IN —) KAY JACK DRINA TOMMY GIMPTY HILTON MARTIN BABYFACE

DEADENED DEAD DEAF SEAR SERE

DEADENING PUGGING

DEADFALL SNARE

DEADHEAD SINK BOBBER SINKER

DEADHOUSE MORGUE MORTUARY

DEAD LETTER NIX

DEADLINE DATELINE

DEADLINESS LETHALITY

DEADLOCK TIE DRAW LOGJAM IMPASSE STANDOFF STOPPAGE

DEADLY WAN DIRE FELL MORT FATAL FERAL TRUANT DEATHY FUNEST LETHAL MORTAL CAPITAL DEATHLY FATEFUL RUINOUS MORTIFIC VENOMOUS VIRULENT PESTILENT THANATOID PERNICIOUS

DEADLY CARROT DRIAS THAPSIA

DEADLY-NIGHTSHADE DWALE

DEAD NETTLE HENBIT

DEADS MULLOCK

DEAD SOULS (AUTHOR OF) GOGOL
(CHARACTER IN —) PAVEL ALEXEI PLATON KLOBUEFF KOPEYKIN MANILOFF NOZDREFF LYENITZEN PLATONOFF PLIUSHKIN SOBAKEVITCH KOSTANZHOGLO TCHITCHIKOFF TENTETNIKOFF BETRISHTCHEFF

DEAF SURD DUNCH DUNNY SORDA SORDO (PREF.) SURDI SURDO

DEAFEN DIN DORR DEAVE DEADEN

DEAFENING DEEVEY

DEAF-MUTE FENELLA SURDOMUTE

DEAFNESS ASONIA SURDITY ANACUSIA ANACUSIS COPHOSIS

DEAL GO END JOB DAIL DOLE LEND PART SALE TALE WHIZ ALLOT BOARD BROKE FETCH PLANK SERVE SEVER SHAKE SHARE SHIFT TRADE TREAT TROKE TRUCK WIELD YIELD BATTEN BESTOW DIVIDE HANDLE MEDDLE NUMBER PARCEL BARGAIN DELIVER INFLICT PIANOLA PORTION SCATTER TRUCKLE WRESTLE DISPENSE SEPARATE
(— CARDS) DRAW TALLY
(— CLANDESTINELY) TRINKET
(— DISHONESTLY) SHORTCHANGE
(— IN) SELL VEND
(— IN A TRIFLING WAY) PIDDLE
(— IN BRIDGE) BOARD
(— IN GRAIN) SWALE
(— OF CARDS) COUP SPOIL GOULASH
(— OUT) HELP METE
(— SHREWDLY) JOCKEY
(— SPARINGLY) TAPE
(— WITH) HAND COVER DIGHT TOUCH TREAT BUCKET CUSTOM DEMEAN HANDLE ENTREAT NEGOTIATE

(GOOD —) HANTLE
(GREAT —) MORT LOADS MIGHT SIGHT JUGFUL OODLES SKINFUL
(POLITICAL —) DICKER

DEALER BANK CHAP AGENT COPER BADGER BANKER BROKER CADGER EGGLER GROCER JOBBER JUNIOR MONGER SELLER TRADER BUTCHER CHAPMAN KEELMAN YOUNGER CHANDLER MERCHANT OCCUPIER OPERATOR STICKMAN TAILLEUR
(— IN CATTLE) COUPER COWPER DROVER
(— IN CHEMICALS) SALTER DRYSALTER
(— IN DRY GOODS) DRAPER
(— IN GRAIN) SWALER
(— IN OLD CLOTHES) FRIPPER
(— IN PAINTS) COLORMAN
(— IN TEXTILES) MERCER
(CARDS —) FARMER
(COAL —) COLLIER
(EXTORTIONATE —) SHAVER
(HORSE —) COPER COUPER COWPER CHANTER SCORSER
(SCRAP —) TOTTER DIDAKAI
(SLAVE —) MANGO
(STOCK —) STAG JOBBER OUTSIDER

DEALFISH VAAGMAR VAAGMAER RIBBONFISH

DEALING DOLE PRICE TRUCK TAFFIC TRADING EXCHANGE
(BUSINESS —S) TROKE
(JUST —) DOOM
(TRICKY —) BROKING
(PL.) DEAL TRAFFIC BUSINESS COMMERCE PRACTICE PRACTISE
(SUFF.) (— WITH) IC(AL)

DEAN DECAN DOYEN DEANER SENIOR VERGER PREFECT PROVOST SUBDEAN ARCHDEAN PRAEFECT

DEAR JO GRA HON JOE PET AGRA CARA CHER CHOU CONY FAIR FOND GOOD HIGH LAMB LIEF LOVE NEAR NOBS SALT ANGEL BOSOM CHARY CHERE CHERI CHUCK DEARY HONEY LOVED PRICY SWEET TIGHT CHERIE COSTLY DAUTIE DAWTIE DEARIE DEARLY POPPET PRICEY SCARCE SEVERE SQUALL TENDER WORTHY BELOVED DARLING LOVABLE PIGSNEY QUERIDA SPECIAL TOOTSIE ESPECIAL ESTEEMED GLORIOUS PRECIOUS VALUABLE
(SUFF.) (— ONE) EEN

DEARLY DEAR ALIFE DEEPLY KEENLY RICHLY HEARTILY

DEARNESS CHERTE DEARTH

DEARTH LACK WANT CHERTE FAMINE PAUCITY POVERTY DEARNESS SCARCITY SOLITUDE
(SUFF.) PENIA

DEASPIRATION PSILOSIS

DEATH DEE END BALE BANE DEAD DOOM EXIT FAIL FATE KILL MORS MORT OBIT PASS REST WINK ANKOU DECAY GRAVE GRUEL LETHE NIGHT SLEEP CHAROS CHARUS DEMISE DEPART ENDING EXITUS EXPIRY MURDER PERIOD

REAPER WAGANG ACHERON CURTAIN DECEASE FUNERAL PARTING PASSAGE QUIETUS SILENCE BIOLYSIS CASUALTY CURTAINS FATALITY NECROSIS RAWBONES THANATOS MORTALITY NOTHINGNESS
(— ANGEL) AZRAEL
(— BY BURNING) STAKE
(— BY HANGING) HALTER
(— OF TISSUE) GANGRENE
(PREF.) LETHI THANAT(O)
(SUFF.) THANASIA
DEATH ADDER ELAPID ELAPOID
DEATH-AGONY (— OF WHALE) FLURRY
DEATH CAMASS LOBELIA
DEATH INSTINCT THANATOS
DEATH IN VENICE (CHARACTER IN —) TADZIO ASCHENBACH
(COMPOSER OF —) BRITTEN
DEATHLESS ETERNAL UNDYING IMMORTAL
DEATHLESSNESS ATHANASY
DEATHLIKE CHARNEL DEATHLY GHASTLY MACABRE GHASTFUL MORIBUND MORTUOUS
DEATHLY DEAD FATAL DEADLY MORTAL GHASTLY STYGIAN DEATHFUL MORTALLY
DEATH OF A SALESMAN (AUTHOR OF —) MILLER
(CHARACTER IN —) BIFF HAPPY LINDA LOMAN WILLY
DEATH'S-HEAD SKULL
DEBACLE ROUT COLLAPSE STAMPEDE
DEBAR DENY TABU CROSS ESTOP REPEL TABOO DISBAR FORBID HINDER REFUSE BOYCOTT DEPRIVE EXCLUDE OUTSHUT PREVENT SECLUDE SUSPEND PRECLUDE PROHIBIT
DEBARK LAND GOASHORE
DEBARRED FROZEN OUTSHUT
DEBASE SINK ABASE ALLAY ALLOY AVILE DIRTY LOWER STOOP BEMEAN DEFILE DEMEAN DILUTE EMBASE IMPAIR NIDDER NITHER REDUCE REVILE VILIFY CORRUPT DEBAUCH DECLINE DEGRADE DEPRAVE PERVERT PROFANE TRADUCE VILLAIN VITIATE DEROGATE PROSTITUTE
DEBASED BASE VILE HEDGE BASTARD CORRUPT SQUALID CANKERED DEGRADED DEROGATE
DEBASEMENT TARNISH PROSTITUTION
DEBASING DOWNWARD
DEBATABLE MOOT DISPUTABLE
DEBATE AGON BEAT FRAY MOOT ARGUE FIGHT PLEAD STUDY ARGUFY COMBAT HASSEL HASSLE REASON STRIFE AGITATE CANVASS CONTEND CONTEST DISCEPT DISCUSS DISPUTE EXAMINE MOOTING PALAVER QUARREL WRANGLE ARGUMENT COLLOQUY CONSIDER CONTRARY MILITATE PARLANCE QUESTION CONTENTION
(VIGOROUS —) SETTO

DEBATER PICADOR
DEBAUCH BUM BOUT FILE SPREE TAINT WHORE DEBASE DEBOSH DEFILE GUZZLE MISUSE SEDUCE SPLORE VILIFY CORRUPT DEBOISE DEPRAVE MISLEAD POLLUTE VIOLATE DISHONOR SQUANDER STRUMPET STUPRATE
DEBAUCHED LEWD RAKELY RAKISH DEBOIST DEBOSHED RAKEHELL
DEBAUCHEE RIP RAKE ROUE HOLOUR LECHER RAKEHELL
DEBAUCHERY RIOT RAKERY DEBAUCH PRIAPISM
DEBENTURE BOND SECURITY
DEBENZOLIZE STRIP
DEBILITATE SINK
DEBILITATED WEAK SEEDY FEEBLE INFIRM SAPPED ASTHENIC
DEBILITY ATONY ADYNAMY ASTHENY LANGUOR MALAISE ADYNAMIA ASTHENIA WEAKNESS MYASTHENIA
(PREF.) ASTHEN(O)
(SUFF.) ASTHENIA
DEBIR (SLAYER OF —) JOSHUA
DEBIT DEBT LOSS CHARGE
DEBONAIR AIRY JAUNTY POLITE CAVALIER GRACEFUL GRACIOUS
DEBORA E JAELE (CHARACTER IN —) JAELE DEBORA SISERA
(COMPOSER OF —) PIZZETTI
DEBOUCH FALL MOUTH
DEBOUCHMENT EXIT INFLUX INFLUXION
DEBRIS GUCK SLAG DECAY FRUSH TRADE TRASH WASTE RAFFLE REFUSE RUBBLE RUDERA CRUMBLE ELUVIUM RUBBISH SLIDDER DETRITUS
(— AT BASE OF CLIFF) SCREE
(— IN WOOL) BUR BURR
(— OF INSECTS) FRASS
(— OF ROCKS) HEAD DRIFT SCREE TALUS ELUVIUM
(FLOATING —) LAGAM JETSAM FLOTSAM
(FLUFFY —) FLUE
(FOREST —) SLASH
DEBT DUE SIN CHIT POST DEBIT FAULT STOCK ARREARS DEBITUM JUDGMENT TRESPASS
(PL.) OBLATA WANIGAN ARREARAGE
DEBTOR OWER PEON SKIP DYVOUR DEBITOR YIELDER
DEBUT OPENING ENTRANCE
DEBUTANTE BUD DEB BELLE DEBBY INGENUE ROSEBUD
DECADENT EFFETE DECAYED HOTHOUSE OVERRIPE
DECAHYDRATE SODA
DECALOGUE WITNESS
DECAMP GUY PUT BOLT HIKE KITE ELOPE MOSEY SCOOT SCOUR SLOPE VAMOS DEPART ESCAPE LEVANT MIZZLE MORRIS POWDER VAMOSE ABSCOND DISCAMP VAMOOSE ABSQUATULATE
DECAMPING GUY
DECAN DECURION
DECANT EMIT POUR RACK UNLOAD TRANSFER

DECANTER CARAFE CARAFON URCEOLE GARDEVIN INGESTER
DECAPITATE BEHEAD DECOLLATE
DECAPITATION DECOLL HEADING
DECAPOD CRAB BUSTER
DECARBONIZE DECOKE
DECATING SPONGING
DECAY EBB ROT ROX BLET CONK DOAT DOTE DOZE FADE FAIL RUIN SEED WANE WEAR CROCK DEATH SHANK SLOOM SLOUM SPOIL WASTE BLIGHT CANKER CARIES FADING MARCOR MILDEW MOLDER MOSKER SICKEN WITHER CRUMBLE DECLINE FAILURE FORFAIR MORTIFY PUTREFY DECREASE FORDWINE
(— IN WOOD) CONK DOZE
(— OF FRUIT) BLETTING
(INCIPIENT —) BLET
(TOOTH —) CARIES
(PREF.) SAPR(O)
(TOOTH —) CARIO
DECAYED BAD DEAF DOZY ROXY FRUSH SEEDY DAISED MARCID PUTRID ROTTEN SPAKED CARIOUS RUINOUS SNAGGLED
DECAYING COLD DOTY SHABBY CARIOUS
DECEASE DIE FAIL OBIT PASS DEATH DEMISE PASSAGE
DECEASED DEAD LATE PARTED DEFUNCT EXTINCT UMWHILE DEPARTED UMQUHILE
DECEIT GAB DOLE FLUM GAFF GULL RUSE SHAM TRAP TRAY WILE ABUSE COVIN CRAFT DOLUS FRAUD GUILE SARAB SWICK SWIKE CAUTEL FELONY WOIDRE CUNNING DISSAIT FAITERY FICTION ARTIFICE COZENAGE FALSEDAD INTRIGUE SPOOFERY SUBTLETY TRICKERY TRUMPERY WILINESS
(— IN LOVE) COQUETRY
DECEITFUL JIVE RUSE BLIND BRAID FALSE GAUDY JANUS LOOPY PUNIC SLAPE SNAKY ARTFUL COVERT CRAFTY DOUBLE FICKLE HOLLOW ROTTEN TRICKY CUNNING EVASIVE FICTIVE SIRENIC SLEEKIT SLIDDER UNWREST WINDING COVINOUS GUILEFUL ILLUSIVE INDIRECT SHAMMISH TORTUOUS MENDACIOUS
DECEITFULLY DOUBLE FALSELY
DECEITFULNESS SHAM DECEIT FALSITY
DECEIVE BOB COG CON DOR FOB FUB GAB GAS GUM KID LIE BILK BRAG BUNK CRAP DUPE FAKE FLAM FOOL GAFF GULL HAVE HOAX HYPE JILT JOUK MOCK SCAM SELL SHAM SILE SNOW TURN WILE ABUSE AMUSE BLEAR BLEND BLENK BLIND BLINK BLUFF CATCH CHEAT COZEN CROSS CULLY DODGE DORRE FEINT GLEEK GLOZE HOCUS LIETO LURCH PATCH SHUCK SPOOF SWICK SWIKE TRICK TROIL TRUFF TRUMP TRYST BAFFLE BARRAT BEDOTE BEFLUM BEFOOL BETRAY BLANCH BUBBLE CAJOLE CLOINE

CLOYNE DELUDE DIVERT EUCHRE GAMMON HUMBUG ILLUDE JUGGLE MISUSE NIGGLE SUCKER TAKEIN WIMPLE BEGUILE DEFRAUD MISLEAD OVERSEE TRAITOR BEJUGGLE FLIMFLAM HOODWINK OUTREACH
DECEIVER ANGLE CHEAT HOCUS COGGER FAITOR FALSER GUILER MOCKER TRAPAN TREPAN FALSARY ILLUSOR JUGGLER SHARPER SPOOFER TRUMPER WARLOCK WERNARD IMPOSTOR LOSENGER LOTHARIO MAGICIAN TREGETOUR
DECEIVING FALSE ILLUSIVE
DECELERATE SLOW
DECENCY GRACE DECORUM HONESTY MODESTY CHASTITY
DECENNIUM DECADE
DECENT FAIR CHASTE COMELY HONEST MODEST PRETTY PROPER SEEMLY FITTING GRADELY JANNOCK SHAPELY SIGHTLY DECOROUS GRAITHLY WISELIKE
DECENTLY WHITE
DECEPTION BAM COG DOR GAG LIE DOLE FLAM FLUM GAFF GULL HOAX HYPE MAZE RIDE RUSE SELL SHAM WILE ABUSE BLIND BLUFF CHEAT COVIN CRAFT CURVE DOLUS DORRE FAVEL FRAUD GLAIK GLEEK GUILE MAGIC SHUCK SNARE SPOOF TRICK BARRAT CAUTEL DECEIT DUPERY HUMBUG JUGGLE ABUSION BLAFLUM CHICANE CUNNING EVASION FALLACY FALSERY FICTION GULLAGE GUILERY KNAVERY PRETEXT SLYNESS ARTIFICE DISGUISE FALSEDAD FLIMFLAM ILLUSION INTRIGUE PHANTASM PRESTIGE SUBTLETY TRICKERY TRUMPERY WILINESS
DECEPTIVE FLAM FALSE ARTFUL BUBBLE SIRENIC TRICKSY DELUSIVE DELUSORY FLIMFLAM ILLUSORY IMPOSING SHAMMISH UNSICKER
DECEPTIVENESS FANTASTRY
DECIBEL (10 —S) BEL
DECIDE FIX CAST DEEM HOLD RULE TELL WILL AWARD JUDGE PATCH PITCH DECERN DECISE DECREE FIGURE REWARD SETTLE ADJUDGE DERAIGN RESOLVE CONCLUDE SENTENCE
(— UPON) SET ELECT CHOOSE TERMINE
(RIGHT TO —) SAY
DECIDED FIRM FLAT MAIN FORMED SETTLED DECISIVE RESOLUTE
DECIDEDLY DIRECTLY DISTINCTLY
DECIDUA CADUCA
DECIGRAM LI
DECIMA TENTH TITHE
DECIMAL DENARY REPEATER
(— PART) MANTISSA
DECIMATE TENTH DESTROY
DECIPHER READ SOLVE CIPHER DECODE DETECT REVEAL DECRYPT DISCOVER INDICATE UNPUZZLE
DECIPHERING EPIGRAPHY

DECISION ACT END CALL DOOM FIAT GRIT ARRET AWARD CANON FAITH ISSUE PARTY PLUCK POINT ACTION CHOICE CRISIS DECREE DIKTAT RULING ACUERDO CONSULT INTERIM PRACTIC VERDICT FINALITY JUDGMENT PLACITUM SENTENCE SUFFRAGE UMPIRAGE
(— BY MAJORITY) VOTE
(— OF COURT) HOLDING ABSOLVITOR
(— OF REFEREE) TKO
(— OF UMPIRE) OUT FOUL SAFE
(EXISTENTIAL —) LEAP
(FINAL —) ISSUE
(LEGAL —) FETWA
(MUSLIM LEGAL —) FETWA
DECISIVE FATAL FINAL CRISIC PAYOFF VIRILE CRUCIAL DECIDED CRITICAL CRUSHING DECRETAL POSITIVE
DECISIVELY FINALLY
DECK FIG TOG BANK BUSK BUSS DAUB DINK FLAT HEAP PINK POOP PROW TIER TRIG ADORN ARRAY COVER DIZEN DRESS EQUIP FLOOR HATCH PRANK PRINK STORE AWNING BEDECK BETRIM BLAZON CLOTHE ENRICH FETTLE FOCSLE LAUREL APPAREL BEDIGHT BEDIZEN FEATHER FLOUNCE GEMMATE TERRACE BEAUTIFY DECORATE EMBLAZON PLATFORM FLYBRIDGE
(— OF CARDS) BOOK
(— OUT) BARB TIFF ARRAY DIZEN SPICK BEDECK DAIKER FANGLE FINIFY BEDIGHT
(HIGH —) POOP
(LOWEST —) ORLOP
DECKED CLAD BESEEN ARMORIED LAURELED
(— OUT) CLAD SPIFFED
DECKHAND BOATMAN TRIMMER BARGEMAN ROUSTABOUT
DECKHOUSE CABOOSE CAMBOOSE PILOTHOUSE
DECKLE DECKEL FEATHEREDGE
DECKMAN TRIPPER LEVERMAN
DECLAIM GALE RANT RAVE ROLL MOUTH ORATE SPEAK SPOUT BLEEZE RECITE ELOCUTE INVEIGH DENOUNCE DISCLAIM HARANGUE PERORATE SINGSONG
DECLAIMER BARD SPEECHIFIER
DECLAMATION FROTHING HARANGUE RHETORIC SPOUTING PHILIPPIC
DECLARATION BILL CALL DICK NARR TALE WORD COUNT FUERO LIBEL PAROL AVOWAL DECEIT MISERE ORACLE PAROLE PLACET SAYING EXPRESS PROMISE RESOLVE MANIFEST PLATFORM
(— IN BRIDGE) MAKE AUCTION
(— OF HOSTILITIES) DEFIANCE
(OFFICIAL —) AUTHORITY
(PUBLIC —) MANIFESTO
DECLARE BID KEN LAY SAY VOW AVER AVOW DENY MAKE READ SHOW SNUM SWAN TROW VOTE AREAD AREED BRUIT KEETH KITHE

KYTHE POSIT SNORE SOUND SPEAK STATE TRUTH VOUCH AFFIRM ALLEGE ASSERT ASSURE AUTHOR AVOUCH BLAZON COUTHE DEPONE DESCRY EXPONE HERALD INDICT NOTIFY PATEFY RELATE SPRING UPGIVE ACCLAIM BEHIGHT DISCUSS EXPRESS OUTTELL PROFESS PROTEST PUBLISH SIGNIFY TERMINE TESTIFY ANNOUNCE DENOUNCE DESCRIBE INDICATE INTIMATE MAINTAIN MANIFEST NUNCIATE PROCLAIM RENOUNCE PREDICATE
(— ARBITRARILY) GAVEL
(— A SAINT) CANONIZE
(— INVALID) ANNUL
(— PUBLICLY) CRY
(— TRUE) SOOTHE
(— UNTRUE) DENY
(— WAR) DEFY
(SOLEMNLY —) AFFY SWEAR
DECLARED AVOWED STATED
DECLARER LAWMAN VIVANT
DECLINATION BIAS DECAY SLOPE REGRET DECLINE DESCENT REFUSAL SOUTHING SWERVING
DECLINE BEG DIP EBB SAG SET BALK BEND BUST DENY DIVE DOWN DROP FADE FAIL FALL FLAG FLOP HELD SINK SLIP TURN VAIL WANE WELK BAULK CHUTE DECAY DROLL DROOP DWINE FAINT HEALD HELD LAPSE LOWER QUAIL REPEL SLACK SLOPE SLUMP SPURN STOOP STRAY TABES WAIVE DEBASE DEVALL FALTER REFUSE REJECT RENEGE SICKEN WEAKEN ATROPHY DESCEND DESCENT DETRECT DEVIATE DISAVOW DWINDLE ECLIPSE FAILURE FALLOFF FORBEAR INFLECT LETDOWN SINKAGE DECREASE DOWNBEAT DOWNTURN FOREBEAR LANGUISH MELTDOWN TOBOGGAN WITHDRAW REPUDIATE
(— IN MARKET PRICE) SPILL
(— IN POPULATION) CRASH
(ECONOMIC —) SLUMPFLATION
(INTO A STATE OF —) SOUTH
(PREF.) CLIN
DECLINING DOWN AWANE BEARISH FALLING WESTERN DECADENT
DECLIVITY BENT BREW FALL HANG SIDE SKUG CLIFF COAST DEVEX PITCH SCARP SLENT SLOPE CALADE HANGER DECLINE DESCENT HANGING DOWNHILL
DECLIVOUS PRONE SLOPING
DECOCT BOIL COOK SMELT EXCITE KINDLE REFINE EXTRACT
DECOCTION BANG OOZE SAVE BHANG APOZEM CREMOR PTISAN TISANE APOZEMA DECOCTUM
DECODE CLEAR DECRYPT
DECOHERER TAPPER
DECOLLETE LOW
DECOMPOSE ROT FOUL FRIT DECAY ATTACK DIGEST DEGRADE DISSOLVE
DECOMPOSED BAD PUTRID

DECOMPOSITION DECAY BREAKUP BIOLYSIS EXCHANGE
(DOUBLE —) METATHESIS
(SUFF.) LYSE LYSIS LYST LYTE LYTIC LYZE
DECORATE DO BIND BUSK CHIP CITE DECK EDGE FRET GAUD PINK RAIL RULE TIFF TIRE TRIM ADORN DRESS FLOCK FRILL GRAIN INLAY MENSE PANEL POKER TRAIL TRICK BEDECK BUTTON DAIKER DAMASK DECORE EMBOSS FLOWER FRESCO PARGET POUNCE PURFLE SPONGE SUBORN BECROSS CORONET ENCHASE FESTOON FURNISH GADROON GARNISH HISTORY IMPASTE INWEAVE MINIATE PERFORM BELETTER FLOURISH ORNAMENT OVERWORK TITIVATE
DECORATED GIDDY LACED AJOURE FLAMBE ORNATE ADORNED DAMASSE FROGGED INCISED WROUGHT COCKADED DISTINCT FLORETED
(— WITH PENDANTS) SCARFED
(ELABORATELY —) RICH
DECORATING LIMNERY
DECORATION KEY BUHL FALL FUSS IKAT BOULE DECOR DODAD HONOR MEDAL PRIDE BOULLE DECKER DECORE DESIGN DOODAB DOODAD FINERY FLORET FRIEZE GOTHIC NIELLO PLAQUE SETOFF TINSEL ARTWORK BARBOLA DECKING EPERGNE FLUTING GARNISH TRACERY BAYADERE DENTELLE DIAMANTE ESCALLOP FILIGREE FLOURISH FOOFARAW FRETTING FRETWORK FRIPPERY FURBELOW INTARSIA ORNAMENT
(— IN GUEST CHAMBER) XENIUM
(— OF LEAVES) VIGNETTE
(— OF MONKEYS) SINGERIE
(— TECHNIQUE) PLANGI
(BOOK-COVER —) DENTELLE
(CURVED —) OGEE
(CUTOUT —) APPLIQUE
(ENAMEL —) WUTSAI
(FESTIVE —) GALA
(INESSENTIAL —) SPINACH
(INLAID —) BUHL BOULE BOULLE
(MURAL —) TOPIA
(MUSICAL —) GRACE
(PAINTED —) ROSEMALING
(PORCELAIN —) KAKIEMON
(POTTERY —) BRODERIE
(RICH —) PARAMENT
(SCANDINAVIAN —) ROSEMALING
(TABLE —) DOILY
(WALL —) ARRAS
(WALL —S) TENTURE
(PL.) COLORS BUNTING GREENERY
DECORATIVE FANCY FIKIE
(OVERLY —) DITSY DITZY
DECORATOR PAINTER
DECOROUS CALM DONE GOOD NICE PRIM DOUCE GRAVE QUIET SOBER STAID CHASTE DECENT DEMURE MODEST POLITE PROPER SEDATE SEEMLY SERENE STEADY BECOMED FITTING ORDERLY

REGULAR SETTLED BECOMING COMPOSED MANNERLY
DECOROUSLY FITLY
DECOROUSNESS CHASTITY POLITESSE
DECORTICATE FLAY HULL HUSK PARE PEEL PILL SKIN STRIP DENUDE
DECORUM DECENCY DIGNITY FITNESS HONESTY MODESTY PROPRIETY
DECOY COY BAIT CALL GOAD LURE TOLE TOLL COACH CRIMP DRILL PLANT ROPER SHILL STALE STALL STOOL TEMPT TRAIN ALLURE BUTTON CALLER CAPPER ENTICE ENTRAP PIGEON SEDUCE TOLLER TREPAN BARNARD BERNARD DECOYER INVEIGLE SQUAWKER
(— FOR GAMBLERS) CAPPER
(— FOR SWINDLERS) BARNARD BERNARD
(AUCTIONEER'S —) BONNET BUTTON
DECREASE EBB BATE DROP FALL LOSS SINK WANE WELK WILK ABATE CROCK DECAY LAPSE SWAGE TAPER WANZE WASTE CHANGE DECESS DECREW IMPAIR LESSEN NARROW REDUCE SHRINK ATROPHY CUTDOWN DECLINE DWINDLE SHORTEN SLACKEN SUBSIDE ABLATION DECIMATE DIMINISH DOWNTURN MODERATE RETRENCH
(— IN FORCE) LAY
(— IN VOLUME) ABLATION
(— IN WIDTH) INTAKE
(— OF EFFICIENCY) FATIGUE
(— STITCHES) FASHION
DECREE ACT DIT LAW SAW SET DOOM FIAT REDE RULE WILL WITE AREAD AREED ARRET CANON EDICT ENACT FIANT GRACE HATTI IRADE JUDGE ORDER POINT SHAPE TENET UKASE WRITE ARREST ASSIZE DECERN DICTUM DIKTAT FIRMAN INDICT MODIFY ORDAIN PLACIT RECESS ADJUDGE APPOINT BESLUIT COMMAND CONSULT DECREET DICTATE DIVORCE ESCRIPT GEZERAH MANDATE SETNESS STATUTE WORKING DECISION DECRETUM JUDGMENT PLACITUM PSEPHISM RESCRIPT ROGATION SANCTION SENTENCE ORDINANCE ABSOLVITOR
(— BEFOREHAND) DESTINE
(ECCLESIASTICAL —) CANON SYNODICAL
(JUDICIAL —) AUTO
(MOHAMMEDAN —) IRADE
(OFFICIAL —) RESCRIPT
(PAPAL —) BULL DECRETAL
DECREPIT LAME WEAK UNORN BEDRID CREAKY FEEBLE INFIRM SENILE FAILING INVALID FORFAIRN
DECRY BOO CRAB SLUR LOWER ROGUE DESCRY LESSEN ASPERSE BARRACK CENSURE CONDEMN DEBAUCH DEGRADE DETRACT BELITTLE DEROGATE MINIMIZE
DECRYPT BREAK DECODE

DECURRENT DEFLUENT
DECUSSATION CHIASM CHIASMA
DEDAN (FATHER OF —) RAAMAH
JOKSHAN
(MOTHER OF —) KETURAH
DEDANS HAZARD
DEDICATE VOW VOTE DEVOW
SACRE SACRI DEVOTE DEVOVE
DIRECT HALLOW OBLATE ASCRIBE
ENTITLE CHRISTEN INSCRIBE
INTITULE SEPARATE NUNCUPATE
(— TO CHURCH) IMMOLATE
DEDICATED HOLY OBLATE SACRED
VOTIVE
DEDICATION CULT WAKF
DEVOTION
DEDUCE PUT DRAW LEAD TAKE
BRING DRIVE FETCH GUESS INFER
TRACE DEDUCT DERIVE ELICIT
EVOLVE GATHER COLLECT
EXPLAIN EXTRACT SUBSUME
CONCLUDE
DEDUCT BATE DOCK TAKE ABATE
ALLOW SHAVE DEFALK REBATE
RECOUP REDUCT REMOVE
CURTAIL SUBDUCT TAKEOUT
TRADUCE ABSTRACT DISCOUNT
SEPARATE SUBTRACT
DEDUCTION AGIO SALT CREDIT
DEDUCT REBATE BEAMAGE
DOCKAGE IMPRESS OFFTAKE
REPRISE DISCOUNT ERGOTISM
ILLATION STOPPAGE ABATEMENT
COROLLARY
(YEARLY —) REPRISE
DEDUCTIVE DOGMATIC
DEE DUANT
DEED DO ACT BILL BOOK CASE FACT
FAIT FEAT FIAT GEST HARD JEST
TURN WORK ACTUM ACTUS
BROAD CHART DOING GESTE
ISSUE SANAD THING TITLE ACTION
CONVEY ESCROW FACTUM
POTTAH REMISE SASINE SUNNUD
TAILYE CHARTER EXPLOIT FACTION
TAILZIE CHIVALRY HEIRLOOM
PARERGON PRACTICE PRACTISE
TRANSFER HARDIMENT
PERFORMANCE
(BRUTAL —) ATROCITY
(CHARITABLE —S) ALMS
(DARING —) GESTE
(EVIL —) PRANK MALEFACTION
(GOOD —) BENEFIT MITZVAH
(HEBREW —) STARR
(KIND —) FAVOR
(PART OF —) HABENDUM
(VALIANT —) VALIANCE
(WICKED —) ILL
(PL.) DOINGS SERVICE
MUNIMENTS
DEEM LET SAY SEE GIVE HOPE RECK
SEEM TELL JUDGE OPINE THINK
ESTEEM EXPECT ORDAIN RECKON
REGARD ACCOUNT ADJUDGE
BELIEVE RECOUNT RESPECT
SURMISE ANNOUNCE CONSIDER
JUDGMENT PROCLAIM
DE-EMPHASIZE DOWNPLAY
DEEMSTER DOOMSMAN
DE-ENERGIZE KILL CLEAR
DEEP LOW SAD SEA BASS BOLD
DUAT HOLL HOWE NEAL RAPT

ABYSS BROAD DEWAT GRAVE
GREAT GRUFF HEAVY OCEAN
SOUND STIFF STOOR STOUR
HOLLOW INTENT STRONG SULLEN
ABYSMAL INTENSE SERIOUS
UNMIXED ABSORBED ABSTRUSE
COMPLETE POWERFUL PROFOUND
THOROUGH RECONDITE
(— IN COLOR) RICH
(— IN THE THROAT) GRUM
(PREF.) (— SEA) BATH(O)(Y)
DEEP-DYED ENGRAINED
DEEPEN CLOUD DARKEN DREDGE
ENHANCE THICKEN HEIGHTEN
DEEPEST INMOST DEEPMOST
DEEPLY DEEP INLY ADEEP DEARLY
SOUNDLY DEVOUTLY GROUNDLY
INWARDLY
DEEP-SEA DIPSY BATHYL DIPSEY
BATHYAL
DEEP-SEATED CHRONIC DEEP
INTIMATE PROFOUND INGRAINED
DEEP-TONED STOUR
DEER ELK RED REH ROE AXIS BUCK
DAIM HART HIND MILU MUSK
OLEN PARA PUDU RUSA SHOU
SIKA STAG WILD BROCK GEMUL
MARAL MOOSE SABIR SPADE
STAIG CERVID CHITAL CHITRA
FALLOW GUEMAL HANGUL
HEARST HUEMUL PARRAH RASCAL
SAMBAR SAMBUR THAMIN
VENADA BROCKET BROWZER
CARIBOU CERVINE CERVOID
CHEETAL DEERLET FANTAIL
GUAZUTI KASTURA MUNTJAC
PLANDOK SAMBHAR THAMENG
VENISON BOBOLINK CARIACOU
CARJACOU ELAPHURE RUMINANT
(— IN 3RD YEAR) SPAY SOREL
SPAYAD SPAYARD
(— UNDER 1 YEAR) KID
(CASTRATED —) HAVIER
(FEMALE —) DOE ROE HIND
(FEMALE — IN 2ND YEAR) TEG
HEARST
(HINDQUARTERS OF —) FOUCH
FOURCHE
(MALE — IN 2ND YEAR) PRICKET
(MALE — IN 4TH YEAR) SORE
STAGGARD STAGGART
(MALE — OVER 5 YEARS) HART
STAG
(RED —) OLEN SPAY MARAL
BROCKET
(RUSINE —) AXIS
(YOUNG —) KID FAWN SPITTER
(2-YEAR OLD —) KNOBBER
(PREF.) CERVI
DEER BUSH SOAPBUSH
DEER FERN HARDFERN
DEERFLY TABANID
DEERHAIR SEDGE BULRUSH
DEERHOUND DEERDOG
BUCKHOUND
DEERSKIN BUCK DEER
DEERSLAYER (AUTHOR OF —)
COOPER
(CHARACTER IN —) HARRY HETTY
NATTY UNCAS BUMPPO HUTTER
JUDITH THOMAS CHINGACHGOOK
DEFACE MAR FOUL RUIN SCAR
ERASE SHAME SPOIL CANCEL

DAMAGE DAMASK DEFAME DEFOIL
DEFORM DEFOUL EFFACE INJURE
INJURY DESTROY DETRACT
DISTORT SLANDER DISGRACE
DISHONOR MALAHACK MUTILATE
OUTSHINE
DEFACED FOUL
DEFACING DIMINUTION
DEFALCATE DRIB DEFALK
DEFAMATION LIBEL SMEAR
DEFAME DEFAMY DEPRAVE
SCANDAL SLANDER ASPERSION
DEFAMATORY SCANDALOUS
DEFAME FOUL ABASE BELIE CLOUD
LIBEL NOISE SMEAR ACCUSE
CHARGE DEFACE DEFOIL DEFOUL
FORGAB INFAME INJURE MALIGN
REVILE SUGGIL VILIFY ASPERSE
BLACKEN BLEMISH DEBAUCH
DETRACT DIFFAME PUBLISH
SCANDAL SLANDER SPATTER
TRADUCE DISHONOR INFAMIZE
VILIPEND
DEFAMER SYCOPHANT
DEFAULT FAIL FLAW LOSS MORA
ERROR FAULT OFFEND BLEMISH
FAILURE MISTAKE NEGLECT
OFFENSE OMISSION
(— ON DEBT) LEVANT
DEFAULTER DUCK
(PL.) JANKERS
DEFEASANCE DEFEAT UNDOING
DEFEASIBLE IMPERFECT
DEFEAT ACE EAT PIP WIN BALK
BEAT BEST BOWL CAST DING
DOWN DRUB FOIL HAVE JINK KILL
LACE LICK LOSS ROUT RUIN RUSH
SINK SKIN STOP TOLL TOSS TRAP
TRIM UNDO WHAP WHIP WHOP
AVOID BREAK CHECK FACER FALSE
FLING FLOOR OUTDO PASTE
SHEND SKUNK SMITE SWAMP
THROW UPEND WASTE WHACK
WORSE WORST WRACK BAFFLE
CUMBER DEROUT EUCHRE HOSING
LARRUP MASTER MURDER
OUTGUN REBUFF STOUSH
THWACK THWART WAGGLE
WEAKEN CLOBBER CONQUER
DEPRIVE DESTROY LICKING
OVERSET PEREMPT REVERSE
SCOMFIT SETBACK SHELLAC
SNOOKER SUBVERT TROUNCE
INFRINGE IRRITATE OUTFIGHT
OVERCOME SLOSHING VANQUISH
WATERLOO OVERPOWER
OVERTHROW
(— BY INGENUITY) OUTWIT
(— COMPLETELY) SKUNK
(— DECISIVELY) EAT DRUB SACK
BLAST CLEAN FLATTEN SHELLAC
(— IN BRIDGE) SET
(— IN LAWSUIT) CAST
(DECISIVE —) CLEANUP CLEANING
PLASTERING
(INTO —) DOWN
(UTTER —) MATE ROUT DEROUT
DEFEATED DOWN LOST KAPUT
BEATEN CRAVEN WHIPPED
DEFEATIST BOLO FATALIST
DEFECT BUG FLAW LACK MAIM
MOTE TWIT VICE WANE WANT
WART BOTCH CLOUD CRAZE

ERROR FAULT MINUS MULCT
TOUCH DAMAGE DESERT HIATUS
INJURY LACUNA MALADY
MAYHEM PLIGHT VICETY VITIUM
ABSENCE BLEMISH DEMERIT
FAILING MISPICK PEELING PINHOLE
COLOBOMA CRESCENT
DRAWBACK WEAKNESS
SHORTCOMING
(— IN ARTICULATION) PSELLISM
(— IN CRYSTAL) HOLE
(— IN ENAMEL) SCAB SAGGING
SCUMMING
(— IN FABRIC) GOUT SCOB BARRE
BRACK SMASH
(— IN GLASS) KNOT TEAR STONE
WREATH THREADS
(— IN IRON) SEAM
(— IN MARBLE) TERRAS TERRACE
TERRASSE
(— IN METAL) SNAKE BLOWHOLE
(— IN PRINTING PLATE) HICKY
HICKEY
(— IN STEEL) LAP
(— IN TIMBER) LAG SHAN
COLLAPSE
(— IN YARN) SINGLING CORKSCREW
(— OF CHARACTER) HOLE SHADE
HAMARTIA
(LINT —) SPOT
(SPEECH —) BALBUTIES
CLUTTERING
(TELEVISION —) FLOPOVER
DEFECTION LETDOWN APOSTASY
DESERTION
DEFECTIVE BAD ILL EVIL FOXY LACK
LAME MANK POOR SICK BAUCH
BAUGH BLIND FALSE FLAWY
PASUL COMMON FAULTY FLAWED
MANGUE MEAGER MEAGRE
RAGGED HALTING TOMFOOL
VICIOUS DISGENIC DYSGENIC
MUTILOUS VITIATED
(— PRODUCT) LEMON
(MENTALLY —) WANTING
(PREF.) ATEL(O)
DEFECTOR APOSTATE DESERTER
FUGITIVE
DEFEND FEND HOLD KEEP SAVE
WARD WARN WEAR COVER GUARD
SHEND WATCH ASSERT FORBID
SCREEN SECURE SHIELD UPHOLD
WARISH BUCKLER BULWARK
CONTEST DERAIGN ESPOUSE
EXPOUND FLANKER JUSTIFY
PREVENT PROPUGN PROTECT
SHELTER SUPPORT WARRANT
ADVOCATE CHAMPION CONSERVE
GARRISON MAINTAIN PRESERVE
PROHIBIT SAFEGUARD
(— WITH SUCCESS) VINDICATE
DEFENDANT REA REUS ACCUSED
AVOWANT APPELLEE
DEFENDER FENDER PATRON
ADVOCATE ASSERTER ASSERTOR
CHAMPION GUARDIAN UPHOLDER
DEFENSE EGIS FORT PALE ROCK
WALL WARD WEAR AEGIS ALIBI
FENCE GRITH GUARD TOWER
ABATIS ANSWER BEHALF COVERT
FRAISE SCONCE BARRACE
BARRIER BASTION BULWARK
CONTEST COUNTER DEFENCE

DILATOR OUTWORK PARADOS RAMPART SHELTER WARDING WARRANT ADVOCACY APOLOGIA BOUNDARY FRONTIER GALAPAGO GARRISON MUNITION SECURITY SEPIMENT

DEFENSELESS BARE COLD NAKED SILLY UNARMED HELPLESS

DEFENSIBLE TENABLE JUSTIFIABLE

DEFER BOW RISE STAY WAIT DELAY DRIVE HONOR REFER REMIT STAVE TARRY TRACK WAIVE YIELD ESTEEM HUMBLE RETARD REVERE SUBMIT ADJOURN SUSPEND CONSIDER INTERMIT POSTPONE PROROGUE PROTRACT SUSPENSE

DEFERENCE VAIL COURT HONOR CRINGE ESTEEM HOMAGE REGARD RESPECT WORSHIP CIVILITY OBEISANCE

DEFERENT ECCENTRIC

DEFERENTIAL DUTIFUL OBEISANT

DEFERMENT STAY

DEFERVESCENCE LYSIS DECLINE

DEFIANCE DARE DEFI DEFY GAGE BRAVE DEFIAL CHALLENGE

DEFIANT BOLD BARDY BRAVE STOUT DARING STOCKY INSOLENT STUBBORN OBSTREPEROUS

DEFIANTLY ACOCK

DEFICIENCY FAIL LACK WANT ANOIA ERROR FAULT MINUS DEARTH DEFECT INLAIK ULLAGE ABSENCE ANOESIA BLEMISH DEFICIT FAILING FAILURE POVERTY DELETION SCARCITY SHORTAGE SHORTFALL SHORTCOMING

  (**— OF BLOOD**) ISCHEMIA

  (**— OF NERVOUS ENERGY**) ANEURIA

  (**— OF OXYGEN**) ASPHYXIA

  (**CARBON DIOXIDE —**) ACAPNIA

  (**MENTAL —**) IDIOCY AMENTIA

  (PL.) SHORTS

  (PREF.) ISCH

  (SUFF.) PENIA

DEFICIENT BAD LEAN WANE BLUNT MINUS SCANT BARREN FEEBLE MEAGER MEAGRE SCARCE SCRIMP SKIMPY BOBTAIL DISGENIC DYSGENIC INDIGENT

  (**— IN BEAUTY**) PLAIN

  (**— IN HEALTH**) INVALID

  (**— IN TURGOR**) FLACCID

  (**MENTALLY —**) SOFT

  (SUFF.) PRIVIC

DEFICIT SHORTAGE UNDERAGE

DEFILE GUT RAY ABRA BAWD BEDO FILE FOIL FOUL GATE GOWL HALS LIME MOIL MUCK PACE PASS SLIP SLOT SLUT SMUT SOIL ABUSE BERAY CLEFT CROCK DIRTY FILTH GLACK GORGE HALSE NOTCH SLACK SMEAR STAIN SULLY TAINT BEWRAY DEBASE GULLET IMBRUE INFECT RAVISH SMOUCH SMUTCH CORRUPT DEBAUCH DEPRAVE DISTAIN PASSAGE POLLUTE PROFANE SLOTTER SMATTER TARNISH VIOLATE DISHONOR MACULATE

DEFILED DIRTY IMPURE SPOTTY UNCLEAN MACULATE

DEFILEMENT MOIL SOIL SULLAGE TAINTURE

  (PREF.) MEASMATO MIASMO MYS(O)

DEFILING PIKY PITCHY

DEFINE END FIX SET MERE TERM BOUND LIMIT DECIDE CLARIFY DELIMIT EXPLAIN EXPOUND DESCRIBE DISCOVER

DEFINED FORMED STRICT

  (**SHARPLY —**) HARD

DEFINITE SET FIRM HARD SURE CLEAR FINAL FIXED SHARP FINITE FORMED LIQUID STRAIT CERTAIN EXPRESS LIMITED POINTED PRECISE DISTINCT EMPHATIC EXPLICIT LIMITING POSITIVE PUNCTUAL SPECIFIC

DEFINITELY BUT WELL FAIRLY EVERMORE

DEFINITION GLOSS CLARITY DIORISM

  (**— OF FORM**) SFUMATO

  (PREF.) ORISMO

DEFINITIVE LAST FINAL GRAND ORISTIC DEFINITE

DEFLATE EMPALE IMPALE CONTRACT

DEFLATED FLAT

DEFLATING SETDOWN

DEFLATION HANGOVER

DEFLECT CUT WRY BEND COCK SWAY WARP PARRY WREST WRING BAFFLE DETOUR DIVERT SWERVE DEVIATE DIVERGE INFLECT REFLECT REFRACT

DEFLECTION DROOP SWEEP WINDAGE

  (**— ON METER**) KICK

  (PREF.) SPHINGO

DEFLECTOR (**AIR —**) SPOILER

DEFLOWER FRAY DEFOIL DEFOUL FORLIE RAVAGE RAVISH DEFLURE DESPOIL VIOLATE UNMAIDEN UNVIRGIN

DEFORM MAR FLOW WARP GNARL DEFACE BLEMISH CONTORT DISFORM DISTORT DIFFORME DISGUISE DISHONOR MISSHAPE SHAUCHLE

DEFORMATION CREEP SPRING STRAIN FLEXURE FLOWAGE

DEFORMED GAMMY WRONG INFORM PAULIE CROOKED HIDEOUS MISBORN FORMLESS UNMACKLY MISCREATE MISCREATED

  (PREF.) CACH CAC(O)

  (SUFF.) CACE

DEFORMITY GALL VICE BLEMISH HARELIP PRAVITY CLUBFOOT CLUBHAND FLATFOOT WANSHAPE

DEFRAUD ROB BEAT BILK FAKE GULL NICK ROOK SCAM TRIM WIPE CHEAT COZEN GOUGE LURCH MULCT SLICK STICK TRICK WRONG BOODLE CHOUSE CHOWSE RIPOFF DECEIVE SKELDER SWINDLE

DEFRAY PAY BEAR AVERT COVER ABSORB EXPEND PREPAY APPEASE REQUITE SATISFY DISBURSE

DEFT FEAT GAIN NEAT TALL TRIM AGILE HANDY NATTY QUICK SLICK ADROIT EXPERT HEPPEN NIMBLE SPRACK SPRUCE DELIVER DEXTROUS SKILLFUL

DEFTEST EFTEST

DEFTLY LIGHTLY SLICKLY DELIVERLY

DEFTNESS SLEIGHT

DEFUNCT DEAD EXTINCT DECEASED DEPARTED FINISHED

DEFY BRAG DARE DEFI FACE MOCK BEARD BRAVE FLOUT STUMP TEMPT CARTEL FORBID MAUGER MAUGRE REJECT AFFRONT BRAVADE DESPISE DISDAIN OUTDARE OUTFACE CHAMPION DEFIANCE OUTSCOUT RENOUNCE CHALLENGE

DEGENERATE ROT SINK DEBADE EFFETE UNKIND DEGENER DEGRADE DEPRAVE DESCEND DEGENDER DEROGATE

  (**— IN IDLENESS**) RUST

  (**— TOWARD BARBARISM**) WILDER

DEGENERATION WALLER ATROPHY ADIPOSIS PEJORATION

DEGRADATION FALL WOHL SHAME DEMISS DECLINE DESCENT ADULTERY COMEDOWN DEPOSURE IGNOMINY ABJECTION

DEGRADE BUST SINK ABASE BREAK DECRY LOWER SHAME SHEND STOOP STRIP UNMAN DEBASE DEMEAN DEMOTE DEPOSE EMBASE HUMBLE LESSEN REDUCE VILIFY CORRUPT DECLINE DEPRESS IMBRUTE REGRADE VILLAIN DIMINISH DISGRACE DISHONOR DISMOUNT DISPLUME SUPPLANT

DEGRADED BASE BROKE SEAMY ABJECT DEMISS FALLEN SORDID DEBASED DEGREED GRIECED OUTCAST

DEGRADING BASE VILE MENIAL SHAMEFUL

  (PREF.) LY(O)

DEGRAS MOELLON

DEGREE PEG PIP POL BANK CAST DEAL FORM GREE HEAT PEEP POLL RANK RATE RUNG STEP TERM TIER CLASS GRADE GRADO GRECE GRICE HONOR LEVEL NOTCH ORDER PITCH PLACE POINT PRICK SHADE STAGE STAIR EXTENT GRIECE LENGTH MEDIUM SOEVER DESCENT DIGNITY MEASURE SAENGER STATION ACCURACY AEGROTAT QUANTITY STANDING STRENGTH

  (**— OF CLOSENESS**) FIT

  (**— OF COLOR**) SHADE

  (**— OF COMBINING POWER**) VALENCE

  (**— OF CONTRAST**) GAMMA

  (**— OF DEVIATION**) LEEWAY

  (**— OF DISTINCTION**) PHD

  (**— OF ELEVATION**) ASCENT

  (**— OF ENGAGEMENT**) DEPTH

  (**— OF EXCELLENCE**) DIGNITY

  (**— OF FLAWLESSNESS**) CLARITY

  (**— OF FORCE**) KICK

  (**— OF HEIGHT**) GRADE

  (**— OF IMPORTANCE**) CALIBER CALIBRE

  (**— OF INFESTATION**) BURDEN

  (**— OF INTOXICATION**) EDGE

  (**— OF KNOWLEDGE**) SCIENTER

  (**— OF LIGHTNESS**) VALUE

  (**— OF MIXTURE**) ALLOY

  (**— OF OPACITY**) DENSITY

  (**— OF PLENTIFULNESS**) ABUNDANCE

  (**— OF PRESTIGE**) PLACE

  (**— OF QUALITY**) VALUE

  (**— OF SLOPE**) PITCH SPLAY

  (**— OF STREAMLINING**) FAIRNESS

  (**— OF THE SOUL**) RUACH

  (**— OF WATER HARDNESS**) GRAIN

  (**— OF WHITENESS**) BLEACH

  (**CONFUSING —**) WHIRL

  (**EXCESSIVE —**) EXTREME

  (**GREATEST —**) UTMOST OPTIMUM

  (**HIGHEST —**) PINK SUMMIT SUPREME SUBLIMITY

  (**INDEFINITE —**) SEEM

  (**LEAST —**) MINIMUM

  (**MINUTE —**) DROP SHADE

  (**MUSICAL —**) SPACE SUBTONIC

  (**RABBINICAL —**) SEMICHA SEMIKAH SEMICHAH

  (**SMALL —**) ACE TAD HAIR INCH IOTA SHADOW GLIMMER

  (**SOME —**) BIT

  (**TO A GREAT —**) INSPADES

  (**TO A MODERATE —**) RATHER SORTOF

  (**UTMOST —**) MAX NTH SUM ACME HEIGHT EXTREME EXTREMITY

  (**10 —S OF LONGITUDE**) FACE

  (**15 —S**) HOUR

  (PREF.) (**OF THE THIRD ALGEBRAIC —**) CUB(I)(O)

  (SUFF.) ANCE ANT ENCE ITY NESS TY

DEGU OCTODONT

DEGUM STRIP

  (**— SILK**) SOUPLE

DEHGAN SWAT SWATI

DEHORN SNUB DISBUD

DEHWAR DEHKAN

DEHYDRATE DRY DESICCATE

DEIANIRA (**BROTHER OF —**) TYDEUS MELEAGER

  (**FATHER OF —**) OENEUS

  (**HUSBAND OF —**) HERCULES

  (**MOTHER OF —**) ALTHAEA

DEIDAMIA HIPPODAMIA

  (**FATHER OF —**) LYCOMEDES

  (**LOVER OF —**) ACHILLES

  (**SON OF —**) PYRRHUS NEOPTOLEMUS

DEIFICATION APOTHEOSIS

DEIFY GOD BEGOD DIVINE GODDIZE DIVINIFY DIVINIZE

DEIGN STOOP VOUCHSAFE

DEILEON (**BROTHER OF —**) PHLOGIUS AUTOLYCUS

  (**FATHER OF —**) DEIMACHUS

DEION (**DAUGHTER OF —**) ASTERODIA

  (**FATHER OF —**) AEOLUS

  (**MOTHER OF —**) ENARETE

  (**SON OF —**) ACTOR AENETUS CEPHALUS PHYLACUS

  (**WIFE OF —**) DIOMEDE

DEIPHOBUS (BROTHER OF —) PARIS
HECTOR
(FATHER OF —) PRIAM
(MOTHER OF —) HECUBA
(WIFE OF —) HELEN
DEIPYLE (FATHER OF —) ADRASTUS
(HUSBAND OF —) TYDEUS
(SISTER OF —) AEGIA ARGIA
(SON OF —) DIOMEDES
DEIPYLUS (FATHER OF —)
POLYMNESTOR
(MOTHER OF —) ILIONE
DEITY (ALSO SEE GOD AND
GODDESS) EA EL KA RA RE SU ABU
BEL GAD GOD RAN SHU SOL AKAL
AMEN AMON BAAL CAGN DEVA
FAUN FURY GWYN MIND MORS
RANA SIVA SOBK ALALA ALALU
AMIDA AMITA AMMON DAGAN
DAGON HAOMA HOBAL HORUS
HUBAL INUUS JANUS MIDER
MITRA MONAD SATYR SEBEK
SHIVA SIRIS SURYA ZOMBI ASHIMA
ATHTAR BATALA BUNENE CAISSA
FATHER FAUNUS IASION MARDUK
MOLOCH NIBHAZ OANNES ORISHA
ORMAZD ORMUZD RIMMON
SOMNUS SUCHOS SYLVAN
VARUNA ZOMBIE ALASTOR
FORSETE FORSETI GODDESS
GODHEAD GODLING GODSHIP
HERSHEF IAPETUS KHEPERA
MANITOU NINURTA NISROCH
PHORCUS PHORKYS RESHEPH
SETEBOS SILENUS TAGALOA
TARANIS VIRBIUS BAALPEOR
BEELPEOR BELFAGOR DEVARAJA
DIVINITY ELAGABAL GOVERNOR
HACHIMAN MELKARTH
MERODACH PICUMNUS PILUMNUS
SEILENOS SILVANUS TANGALOA
TUTELARY ZEPHYRUS ZOOMORPH
(AVENGING —) ALASTOR
(BIBLE —) ELI ABBA ELOI
(HEATHEN —) IDOL
(INFERIOR —) GODKIN GODLING
DEMIURGE PETTYGOD
(PRESIDING —) NUMEN
(SHINTO —) KAMI
(SUPREME —) HANSA
(TUTELARY —) LAR NUMEN GENIUS
(ZOROASTRIAN —) HAOMA
(PL.) CABIRI PENATES
DEJECT ABASE LOWER HUMBLE
LESSEN FLATTEN DISPIRIT
DOWNCAST
DEJECTA EGESTA
DEJECTED BAD LOW SAD DAMP
DOWN GLUM POOR SUNK AMORT
MUDDY WAPED ABASED ABATTU
DEJECT DEMISS DROOPY GLOOMY
PINING SOMBER SOMBRE
ALAMORT DUMPISH HANGDOG
HANGING HUMBLED LUMPISH
UNHAPPY DOWNCAST
DOWNWARD REPINING
WOBEGONE WRETCHED
MELANCHOLY
DEJECTEDLY HEAVILY
DEJECTION CRAB DAMP GLOOM
SLOTH DISMAY DISMALS
HUMDRUM SADNESS
MELANCHOLY

DEJEUNER LUNCH BREAKFAST
COLAZIONE COLLATION
DEKASTERE (ABBR.) DAS
DEL NABLA
DELAIAH (FATHER OF —)
MEHETABEEL
(SON OF —) SHEMAIAH

DELAWARE

CAPITAL: DOVER
COUNTY: KENT SUSSEX
NEWCASTLE
INDIAN: LENAPE
STATE BIRD: BLUEHEN
STATE FLOWER: PEACH
STATE NICKNAME: FIRST BLUEHEN
DIAMOND
STATE TREE: HOLLY
TOWN: LEWES NEWARK SMYRNA
ELSMERE CLAYMONT
WILMINGTON

DELAY LAG LET BLIN BODE HOLD
HONE LENG LING LITE MORA SIST
SLOW SLUG STAY STOP WAIT
ABIDE ABODE ALLAY BLINE CHECK
DALLY DEFER DEMUR DETER
DRIFT DWELL FRIST PAUSE REPRY
SLOTH STALL STENT STICK STINT
TARDY TARRY TRACT ARREST
ATTEND BACKEN BELATE DAWDLE
DETAIN DILATE DILUTE DRETCH
ESSOIN FUTURE HINDER HOLDUP
IMPEDE LINGER LOITER QUENCH
REMORE RETARD TAIGLE TARROW
TEMPER WEAKEN ADJOURN
ASSUAGE BARRACE CONFINE
DRUTTLE FORSLOW PROLONG
RESPECT RESPITE SLACKEN
SOJOURN DEMURRAL DILATION
FORESLOW FOURCHER HANGFIRE
HESITATE MACERATE MITIGATE
MORATION OBSTRUCT POSTPONE
PROTRACT REPRIEVE STOPPAGE
DEMURRAGE CUNCTATION
OBSTRUCTION
(— IN COUNTDOWN) HOLD
(— IN EXECUTION) REPRIEVE
(— IN EXPLOSION) HANGFIRE
(— TRIAL) TRAVERSE
(LEGAL —) DILATOR INDUCIAE
(UNDUE —) LACHES
(WITHOUT —) PRONTO
(PL.) AMBAGES
DELAYED LATE TARDY LAGGED
BELATED OVERDUE
DELAYING TRAIN DILATORY
DELECTABLE TASTY DESIROUS
PLEASING BEAUTIFUL EXQUISITE
DELECTATE PLEASE
DELEGATE NAME SEND ASSIGN
COMMIT DELATE DEPUTE DEPUTY
LEGATE NUNCIO APPOINT
CONSIGN EMPOWER ENTRUST
EMISSARY RELEGATE TRANSFER
DELEGATION MISSION DELEGACY
(ATHENIAN —) DELIA
DELETE DELE EDIT OMIT BLACK
ERASE PURGE SLASH CANCEL
CENSOR DELATE REMOVE STRIKE
DESTROY EXPUNGE STONKER
CASTRATE
DELETERIOUS BAD PRAVE

HARMFUL HURTFUL NOXIOUS
PRAVOUS DAMAGING DELETERY
PERNICIOUS
DELI (— ORDER) BLT
DELIBERATE COOL PORE RUNE
SLOW STUDY THINK VOULU
ADVISE CONFER DEBATE PONDER
REGARD ADVISED BALANCE
BETHINK CONSULT COUNCIL
COUNSEL DELIBER DELIVER
REFLECT RESOLVE STUDIED
WILLING WITTING CONSIDER
DESIGNED MEASURED MEDITATE
PERPENSE PREPENSE PROPENSE
STUDIOUS
DELIBERATELY COOLY COOLLY
APURPOSE ADVISEDLY
DELIBERATENESS MATURITY
DELIBERATION ADVICE COUNCIL
COUNSEL LEISURE THOUGHT
VISEMENT
DELICACY BIT ROE CATE EASE NORI
TACT ACATE FRILL KNACK TASTE
CAVIAR DAINTY DELICE JUNKET
LUXURY NICETY REGALO TIDBIT
FINESSE RAREBIT REGALIA
TENUITY TRINKET AIRINESS
DAINTITH DAINTREL DELICATE
KICKSHAW LEGERETE NICENESS
PLEASURE SUBTLETY
(STUFFED —) DERMA
(PL.) CATES ACATES
DELICATE SLY AIRY FINE LACY NESH
NICE SOFT TEAR TWEE ZART DELIE
DORTY ELFIN FAIRY FRAIL LIGHT
SILKY TEWLY CASHIE CHOICE
DAINTY FLIMSY GENTLE GINGER
INCONY KITTLE MINION PASTEL
PETITE PULING QUEASY SILKEN
SLIGHT SUBTLE TENDER TICKLE
TWIGGY ELEGANT EPICENE FINICAL
FRAGILE MINIKIN REFINED
SLIMMER SUBTILE SUMMERY
TAFFETA TAFFETY TENUOUS
TIFFANY WILLOWY ARANEOUS
CHARMING ETHEREAL FEATHERY
GOSSAMER GRACEFUL HOTHOUSE
LUSCIOUS MIGNIARD PINDLING
PLEASANT SENSIBLE SUMMERLY
TICKLISH UNLUSTIE
(— IN APPEARANCE) HUNGRY
(AFFECTEDLY —) ROSEWATER
(PREF.) ABRO HABRO
DELICATELY FINE SMALLY FAIRILY
MELTINGLY
DELICATESSEN DELI DELLY
GASTRONOME CHARCUTERIE
DELICIOUS TASTY YUMMY DAINTY
FRIAND DELICATE SCRUMPTIOUS
DELIGHT JOY GLEE GUST LITE LOVE
SEND TAKE BLESS BLISS CHARM
EXULT FEAST GRACE GUSTO
MIRTH REVEL SAVOR SMACK
ADMIRE ARRIDE DELICE DIVERT
LIKING PLEASE RAVISH REGALE
RELISH TICKLE DISPORT ECSTASY
ENCHANT GLADDEN GRATIFY
JOYANCE JOYANCY LECHERY
RAPTURE REJOICE DELICATE
ENTRANCE GLADNESS PLEASURE
SAVORING
(— IN) LOVE SAVOR
(PL.) DELICIAE

DELIGHTED GLAD
DELIGHTFUL NICE GREAT JAMMY
JOLLY MERRY SOOTH DREAMY
SAVORY ELYSIAN LEESOME
ADORABLE CHARMING DELICATE
DELITOUS GLORIOUS GORGEOUS
HEAVENLY LUSCIOUS
SCRUMPTIOUS
DELIMER DRENCHER
DELIMIT FIX DEFINE SUBTEND
DELIMITATION
(PREF.) HORISMO
DELIMITED MERED MEERED
DELINEATE MAP DRAW ETCH LIMN
LINE CHALK CHART FENCE IMAGE
PAINT STELL TABLE TOUCH TRACE
TRICK BLAZON CIPHER DELINE
DEPICT DESIGN DEVISE SKETCH
SURVEY DEPAINT EXPRESS
LINEATE OUTLINE PICTURE
PORTRAY DECIPHER DEFIGURE
DESCRIBE TRAVERSE
DELINEATION DRAFT DESIGN
SKETCH SURVEY DRAUGHT
(CARELESS —) PERIGRAPH
DELINQUENCY FAULT GUILT
FAILURE MISDEED OFFENSE
OMISSION
DELINQUENT CRIMINAL
(JUVENILE —) HALBSTARKER
(PL.) KALANG
DELIQUESCE MELT LIQUEFY
DISSOLVE
DELIRIOUS FEY MAD OFF REE GYTE
LIGHT MANIC INSANE RAVING
FLIGHTY FRANTIC LUNATIC
MADDING BRAINISH DELEERIT
DELIERET DERANGED FRENETIC
FRENZIED
DELIRIUM FURY MAZE MANIA
FRENZY LUNACY RAVERY RAVING
MADNESS DELIRACY IDLENESS
INSANITY
DELIRIUM TREMENS JUMP
HORRORS JIMJAMS JIMMIES
POTOMANIA
DELITESCENT LATENT
DELIVER DO HIT LAY LET RID BAIL
BORN DEAL FREE GIVE LEND REDD
SAVE SELL SEND TAKE BEKEN
BRING COUGH LIVER SERVE SPEAK
UTTER ADDICT ASSIZE ASSOIL
BETRAY COMMIT CONVEY EXEMPT
PREACH RANSOM REDEEM
RENDER RESCUE RESIGN SUCCOR
UNBIND BETEACH BITECHE
COMMEND CONSIGN DECLAIM
DICTATE OUTTAKE PRESENT
RECOVER RELEASE RELIEVE
DISPATCH EXORCISE EXORCIZE
LIBERATE
(— BALL) BOWL
(— BLOW) LEND POKE SEND
(— BLOWS ON HEAD) NOB
(— CHILD) LIGHT
(— FORCEFULLY) FASTEN
(— FORMALLY) SERVE
(— FROM EVIL SPIRIT) EXORCIZE
(— FROM SIN) SAVE
(— LECTURES) READ
(— LOGS) STOCK
(— MERCHANDISE) UTTER
(— OVER) BETAKE CONSIGN

(— RHETORICALLY) DECLAIM
(— SERMON) PREACH
(— SPEECH) ADDRESS
DELIVERANCE BOOT ESCAPE RANSOM RESCUE SAVING DELIVERY RIDDANCE SOLUTION VOIDANCE SALVATION
(FESTIVAL OF —) PURIM
DELIVERED LANDED
(— FREE) FRANCO
(PRECISELY —) FLUSH
DELIVERER SOTER SAVIOR DRAYMAN SAOSHYANT
DELIVERY FLY BAIL FLIER FLYER ISSUE LIVERY RESCUE ADDRESS AIRDROP BAILMENT SHIPMENT ACCOUCHEMENT
(— IN SPEAKING) DICTION
(— OF BALL) BOWL
(— WAGON) FLY
(MAIL —) TAPPALL TAPPAUL
(PREF.) TOCO TOKO
(SUFF.) TOCIA TOCO(US) TOKIA TOKO(US) TOKY
DELL DEN HOW DALE DEAN DENE DILL DRAB GLEN VALE SLACK SLADE TRULL WENCH DARGLE DIMBLE DINGLE RAVINE VALLEY
(PL.) DALLES
DELPHINIUM DAUPHIN DOLPHIN LARKSPUR
DELPHUS (FATHER OF —) APOLLO NEPTUNE POSEIDON
(MOTHER OF —) CELAENO MELANTHO
DELUDE BOB JIG BILK DUPE FOOL HOAX MOCK AMUSE CHEAT COZEN ELUDE EVADE GLAIK SPOOF TRICK BAFFLE BANTER BEFOOL BUBBLE CAJOLE RIDDLE ILLUDE BEGUILE DECEIVE ENCHANT MISLEAD OVERSEE BEJUGGLE HOODWINK INVEIGLE OVERSILE
DELUGE SEA FLOW FLOOD SWAMP DILUVY CATARACT INUNDATE OVERFLOW SATURATE SUBMERGE CATACLYSM
DELUNDUNG LINSANG ZINSANG VIVERRINE
DELUSION MAZE MOHA ABUSE DWALE FRAUD TRICK MIRAGE VISION CHIMERA FALLACY FANTASM PHANTOM WANHOPE ILLUSION NIHILISM PHANTASM
DELUSTER DULL
DELUXE PALACE ELEGANT ELABORATE SUMPTUOUS
DELVE DEN DIG DIP PIT CAVE DINT MINE DITCH PLUMB BRUISE BURROW EXHUME FATHOM INDENT IMPRESS EXCAVATE INSCRIBE
DEMAGNETIZE DEPERM DEPOLARIZE
DEMAGOGUE CLEON LEADER ORATOR ROUSER DEMAGOG JACOBIN SPEAKER TRIBUNE JAWSMITH OCHLOCRAT
DEMAND ASK CRY TAX USE CALL NEED RAME SALE CLAIM CRAVE DRAFT EXACT GAVEL ORDER QUERY SIGHT BEHEST CHARGE DESIRE ELICIT EXPECT SNATCH

SUMMON ARRAIGN COMMAND CONSIST DRAUGHT INQUIRE MANDATE REQUEST REQUIRE SOLICIT INSTANCE QUESTION POSTULATE SCISCITATION
(— HIGHER PRICE) GAZUMP
(— PAYMENT) DUN CALL
(— RECOGNITION) CLAIM ASSERT
(STRONG —) PRESSURE
(PL.) EXIGENCE EXIGENCY
DEMANDABLE DUE EXIGIBLE
DEMANDED COMPULSORY
DEMANDING HEFTY EXIGENT
(— ATTENTION) ACUTE
DEMANTOID EMERALD OLIVINE
DEMARCATE DELIMIT SEPARATE
DEMARCATION CELL
DEMEAN ABASE CARRY LOWER BEHAVE DEBASE DEPORT CONTAIN DEGRADE DESCEND DEROGATE MALTREAT
DEMEANOR AIR GARB MIEN PORT FRONT HABIT ACTION HAVIOR BEARING CONDUCT DISPOSE FASHION CARRIAGE PORTANCE
(COLD —) MORGUE
DEMENTED MAD NUTS BUGGY CRAZY LOONY NUTTY INSANE SKEWED FATUOUS
DEMENTIA FATUITY INSANITY
DEMERIT MARK FAULT DESERT BROWNIE
(PL.) GIG
DEMESNE MANOR PLACE REALM DOMAIN ESTATE REGION DISTRICT
DEMETER CERES MISTRESS
DEMETRIUS (BELOVED OF —) CELIA HERMIA
(MOTHER OF —) TAMORA
DEMIGOD AITU HERO KAMI YIMA ADAPA SATYR GARUDA PAGODA TRITON GODLING
(PL.) NEPHILIM
DEMIGODDESS URD NORN HEROINE
DEMILUNE RAVELIN
DEMISE WILL DEATH CONVEY DECEASE BEQUEATH
DEMISED LETTEN
DEMIT LOWER HUMBLE RESIGN ABDICATE
DEMOCRACY POPULACY COMMONALTY
DEMOCRAT DEMO DANITE HUNKER SNAPPER DEMOCRAW LOCOFOCO POPOCRAT
(CONSERVATIVE —) HARD
DEMOCRATIC LEFT POPULAR
DEMODULATE DETECT
DEMOISELLE KULM CRANE COOLEN KAIKARA
DEMOLISH RASE RAZE RUIN ABATE BREAK ELIDE LEVEL TOTAL WASTE WRECK BATTER SLIGHT DESTROY RUINATE SHATTER SUBVERT UNBUILD DOWNCAST STRAMASH PULVERIZE
DEMOLITION END FALL
DEMON ALP DEV HAG IMP NAT OKI AITU ATUA BADB BALI BHUT DEVA DOOK OGRE OKEE PUCK RAHU SURT WADE ASURA DEVIL DHOUL FIEND GENIE GHOST JUMBY LAMIA

LESHY LESIY OTKON SATAN SATYR SHEDU SURTR TAIPO WITCH ABIGOR AFREET ARIOCH BILWIS DAEMON DAIMON DAITYA GENIUS JUMBIE MAMMON PILWIZ PISACA THURSE VRITRA YAKSHA YAKSHI ASMADAI ASMODAY DEMONIO HARPIER INCUBUS PISACHA VILLAIN WARLOCK ALICHINO ASHMODAI ASMODEUS BAALPEOR BEELPEOR CURUPIRA EUDAEMON OBIDICUT SUCCUBUS WATERMAN
(— OF WOODS) LESHY LESIY LESHEY
(ARABIC —) AFRIT AFREET AFRITE EFREET
(DESERT —) SATYR
(EVIL —) SHEDU
(FEMALE —) HAG LAMIA PISACHI SUCCUBUS
(NATURE —) GENIUS
(PETTY —) IMP
(WATER —) NICKER
(PL.) DASYUS
DEMONASSA (FATHER OF —) AMPHIARAUS
(HUSBAND OF —) THERSANDER
(MOTHER OF —) ERIPHYLE
(SON OF —) TISAMENUS
DEMONIAC DEMONIC LUNATIC SATANIC DEVILISH DIABOLIC FIENDISH INFERNAL
DEMONIACAL DEMONIAC INFERNAL
DEMONICE (FATHER OF —) AGENOR
(MOTHER OF —) EPICASTE
(SON OF —) MOLUS EVENUS PHYLUS THESTIUS
DEMONSTRABLE ACTUAL
DEMONSTRATE GIVE SHOW CLEAR PROVE SPEAK EVINCE CONVICT DISPLAY PORTRAY CONVINCE INSTANCE MANIFEST
DEMONSTRATION SHOW SIGN TIME PROOF OVATION APODIXIS BALLYHOO DARSHANA MANIFEST
(— OF POWER) MANIFESTATION
(OSTENTATIOUS —) SPLURGE
DEMONSTRATIVE THAT THIS THESE THOSE EFFUSIVE EVINCIVE
DEMOPHON (FATHER OF —) CELEUS THESEUS
(MOTHER OF —) PHAEDRA METANIRA
(NURSE OF —) DEMETER
DEMORALIZE UNMAN WEAKEN CONFUSE CORRUPT DEPRAVE PERVERT
DEMORALIZING INFECTIOUS SHATTERING
DEMOTE BUMP BUST REDUCE UNRANK DEGRADE DISRATE
DEMOTIC POPULAR ENCHORIAL
DEMOTION BUMP
DEMULCENT MANNA SALEB SALEP BORAGE GINSENG EMULSION SOOTHING
DEMUR COY GIB JIB SHY BALK STAY DELAY DOUBT PAUSE QUALM STICK BOGGLE LINGER OBJECT STRAIN DEMEORE SCRUPLE STICKLE STUMBLE SUSPEND DEMURRER HESITATE SUSPENSE

DEMURE COY MIM SHY MURE PRIM GRAVE SPAKE STAID SUANT SUENT MODEST SEDATE PRENZIE PRIMSIE COMPOSED DECOROUS
DEN MEW CAVE COVE DEAN DELL DIVE GLEN HELL HOLE HOLT HUNK LAIR LAKE NEST ROOM SHED SINK BIELD CABIN CAVEA COUCH DELVE HAUNT LODGE SLADE STUDY BURROW CAVERN COVERT GROTTO HOLLOW KENNEL RAVINE SHROUD LIBRARY RETREAT SPELUNK HIDEAWAY SNUGGERY WORKROOM
(— BEAR) WASH
(— OF INIQUITY) DOMDANIEL
(DRINKING —) BOTHAN
(FOUL —) SPITAL
(GAMBLING —) DEADFALL
DENARIUS DENAR PENNY DINDER
DENATURANT PYRIDINE
DENDRITE PROCESS
DENIAL NO NAY WARN DENAY DENIER NAYSAY DEFENSE DEMENTI REFUSAL REPULSE CONTRARY NEGATION TRAVERSE
(— OF AUTHORITY) ANARCHY
(— OF REALITY) NIHILISM
(— OF TRUTH) HERESY
DENIED LOST
DENIER DINERO NEGATOR DENARIUS DINHEIRO
(HALF —) MAIL MAILLE
DENIGRATE BEFOUL CRUCIFY DEROGATE
DENIM DUNGAREE
DENIZEN CITIZEN RESIDENT
(— BY BIRTH) NATIVE
(— OF HELL) HELLION

DENMARK
CAPITAL: COPENHAGEN
CHEESE: SAMSO
COIN: ORA ORE KRONE
COUNTY: AMT FYN RIBE SORO VEJLE AARHUS MARIBO ODENSE TONDER VIBORG AALBORG RANDERS AABENRAA BORNHOLM
INLET: ISE LIM FJORD VEJLE NISSUM ODENSE HORSENS LOGSTOR MARIAGER
ISLAND: OE ALS FYN MON AARO AERO FANO FOHR MORS ROMO BAAGO FAROE LAESO SAMSO SANDO AMAGER FAEROE SEJERO SUDERO FALSTER SEELAND ZEALAND
MEASURE: ELL FOD MIL POT ALEN FAVN RODE ALBUM KANDE LINJE PAEGL TOMME ACHTEL PAEGEL SKEPPE LANDMIL OLTONDE SKEPPE VIERTEL FJERDING
PARLIAMENT: RIGSRAAD FOLKETING LANDSTING
PENINSULA: JUTLAND
POSSESSION: FAROE ICELAND GREENLAND
RIVER: ASA HOLM OMME STOR GUDEN SKIVE SUSAA VARDE GELSAA STORAA VORGOD GUDENAA LILLEAA LONBORG
SETTLERS: OSTMEN
STRAIT: KATTEGAT SKAGERRAK

TOWN: ARS HOV HALS KOGE NIBE SORO VRAA FARUM HOBRO SKIVE AARHUS DRAGOR KORSOR NYBORG ODENSE SKAGEN STRUER VIBORG AALBORG HERNING HORSENS KOLDING RANDERS ALSINORE BALLERUP GENTOFTE GLOSTRUP ROSKILDE HELSINGOR COPENHAGEN
TRIBE: DANES JUTES ANGLES CIMBRI TEUTONS
TRIBUNAL: RIGSRAD RIGSRET
WEIGHT: ES LOD ORT VOG LAST MARK PUND UNZE CARAT KVINT POUND QUINT TONDE CENTNER LISPUND QUINTIN LISPOUND SKIPPUND

DENOMINATE CALL NAME STYLE TITLE DENOTE CHRISTEN INDICATE NOMINATE
DENOMINATION CULT NAME SECT CLASS FAITH TITLE VALUE CHURCH SCHOOL SOCIETY CATEGORY
DENOMINATIONAL SECTARIAN CONFESSIONAL
DENOTATION SIGN TOKEN EXTENT NOTION SPHERE AMBITUS BREADTH REFERENCE
DENOTE GIVE MARK MEAN NAME NOTE SHOW SOUND IMPORT NOTIFY BETOKEN CONNOTE EXPRESS SIGNIFY DENOTATE DESCRIBE INDICATE
DENOUEMENT END ENVOY ISSUE PAYOFF OUTCOME SOLUTION ANAGNOSIS
DENOUNCE BAN DAMN WRAY ASCRY BASTE BLAST DECRY TAUNT ACCUSE DELATE DESCRY DETEST MENACE SCATHE ARRAIGN CONDEMN DECLAIM DECLARE UPBRAID EXECRATE PROCLAIM THREATEN OBJURGATE
DENOUNCEMENT DELATION
DENSE SAD FAST FIRM CLOSE CRASS DUNCH FOGGY GROSS HEAVY MASSY MURKY SILLY SOLID SOUND SPISS STIFF THEET THICK TIGHT WOOFY OBTUSE OPAQUE SPISSY STUPID THICKY THIGHT COMPACT CROWDED INTENSE SERRIED CONDENSE
(NOT —) TENUOUS
(PREF.) PACHY PYCN(O) PYKN(O)
DENSELY CLOSE
DENSITY FOG CANDY FASTNESS GAUSSAGE SOLIDITY
(UNIT OF —) TESLA
(PREF.) DASY
DENT BASH BURT DING DINT DOKE DUNT FAZE NICK CLOUR DELVE DINGE NOTCH STOVE TOOTH BATTER DUNTLE HALLOW INDENT BLEMISH DEPRESS
(— OF REED) SPLIT
(PL.) BEER
DENTAL POINT
DENTATE TOOTHED
DENTICLE RASP
DENTICULATE SERRATE SERRATED
DENTICULATION JAG JAGG
DENTIFRICE WASH

DENTIL DENTEL DENTELLO DENTICLE
DENTINE IVORY DENTIN
DENTIST ODONTIST OPERATOR
DENTISTRY PROSTHODONTICS
DENTURE PLATE BRIDGE
(PL.) WALLIES
DENUDE BARE SCALP SHAVE STRIP DIVEST NUDATE DESPOIL DENUDATE
DENUNCIATION BAN THREAT THUNDER ANATHEMA DIATRIBE
DENY NAY NAIT NICK NITE WARN BELIE DEBAR NITTE RENAY REPEL WERNE ABJURE DISOWN FORBID IMPUGN NAYSAY NEGATE OPPOSE REFUSE REFUTE REJECT RENEGE CONFUTE DEPRIVE DISAVOW DISPUTE FORSAKE GAINSAY PROTEST SUBLATE WITHSAY ABNEGATE DENEGATE DISALLOW DISCLAIM FORSWEAR NEGATIVE RENOUNCE TRAVERSE WITHHOLD REPUDIATE
(— ACCESS) CLOSE
(— RECOGNITION) BLINK
DEODORANT ROLLON
DEOXIDIZE REDUCE
DEOXIDIZED
(PREF.) DESOXY
DEPART GO DIE MOG OFF WAG BLOW EXIT FLIT HOOK MOVE PACK PART PASS PIKE QUIT SHED STEP VADE VARY VOID WALK WEND WITE AVOID BREAK FOUND LEAVE MOSEY SEVER SHAKE SHIFT START TRUSS AVAUNT BEGONE DECAMP DECEDE DEMISE DESIST DIVIDE PERISH RECEDE REMOVE RETIRE SKIDOO SUNDER SWERVE WANDER ABSCOND DEVIATE SKIDDOO TAKEOFF VAMOOSE DISCEDE FORSAKE RETREAT DISCOAST FAREWELL SEPARATE TRESPASS WITHDRAW
(— FROM HARBOR) SORTIE
(— FROM LIFE) DECEASE
(— IN HASTE) BREEZE
(— IN HURRY) SKIVE LAMMAS
(— SECRETLY) ABSCOND ABSQUATULATE
(— SUDDENLY) FLEE DECAMP MIZZLE
(— WITH SPEED) VAMOOSE
DEPARTED DEAD BYGONE DEFUNCT DECEASED DECEDENT
DEPARTMENT END PART OKRUG REALM AGENCY BRANCH BUREAU EXCISE MEMBER OKROOG SPHERE FOUNDRY HANAPER PORTION REVENUE SPICERY AGITPROP CHANCERY DIVISION INDUSTRY NOMARCHY PROVINCE SCULLERY
(— IN CHINA) FU
(— OF CHANCERY) HAMPER HANAPER
(— OF KNOWLEDGE) STUDY
(ACADEMIC —) FACULTY
(NEWSPAPER —) COLUMN FEATURE
(TREASURY —) CAMERA
DEPARTURE BUNK EXIT BREAK DEATH EXODE GOING LEAVE LUCKY OUTGO CHANGE CONGEE

DEPART EGRESS EXODUS HEGIRA SETOFF WAGANG WAYING DECEASE EASTING OUTGANG PARTING PARTURE RETREAT SAILING TRUNDLE WAYGATE DEPARTER FAREWELL OFFGOING REMOTION
(— FROM CORRECTNESS) ATROCITY
(— FROM SUBJECT) ASIDE
(— FROM THEME) CADENZA
(— OF SHIP) SORTIE
(CHARACTER IN —) LUISE TROTT GILFEN
(COMPOSER OF —) D'ALBERT
(EMERGENCY —) BAILOUT
(GEOLOGICAL —) ANOMALY
(SECRET —) GUY SLIP
DEPEND BANK HANG LEAN PEND RELY REST RIDE STAY TURN BUILD COUNT FOUND HINGE TRUST LIPPEN CONFIDE
DEPENDABILITY SECURITY
DEPENDABLE GOOD SURE TRIG SIKER SOLID SOUND THERE SECURE SICCAR SICKER STANCH STEADY CERTAIN STAUNCH RELIABLE SILVENDY SUREFIRE
DEPENDENCE MAINSTAY RELIANCE SERVILITY
DEPENDENCY TALUK COLONY APANAGE APPANAGE
DEPENDENT CHILD CLIENT HANGBY MINION SPONGE VASSAL FEODARY FEUDARY PRONEUR RELIANT SERVILE SPONGER SUBJECT WRAPPED BEHOLDEN CLINGING CREATURE ENCLITIC EVENTUAL FOLLOWER RETAINER
(— ON) ILLATIVE
(— ON DRUGS) HOOKED
(— PERSON) JUNKIE
(NOT —) ABSOLUTE
DEPENDING ATTENDANT
(— ON UNCERTAIN EVENTS) ALEATORY
DEPICT HUE DRAW ETCH LIMN PICT UNDO ENTER IMAGE PAINT SPEAK WRITE BLAZON SHADOW DEPAINT DISPLAY EXPRESS IMPAINT PICTURE PORTRAY DESCRIBE EMBLAZON RESEMBLE
(— IN MOSAIC) IMPAVE
(— WITH EXAGGERATION) OVERPAINT
DEPICTED DEPAINT
(— AS BROKEN) ROMPU
DEPICTION SCAN SCHEMA
(PHOTOGRAPHIC —) RENOGRAM
DEPILATION PSILOSIS
DEPILATORY RUSMA EPILATOR PELADORE PSILATRO
DEPILOUS BALD
DEPLETE DRAIN EMPTY PUNISH REDUCE UNLOAD EXHAUST BANKRUPT DIMINISH
DEPLETED WASTE BANKRUPT
DEPLETION DRAIN EROSION
DEPLORABLE SAD WOFUL WOEFUL DOLOROUS GRIEVOUS WAILSOME WRETCHED
DEPLORABLY SADLY
DEPLORE RUE MOAN SIGH WAIL

MOURN BEMOAN BEWAIL GRIEVE LAMENT REGRET COMPLAIN
DEPLOY UNFOLD DISPLAY
DEPLOYMENT FORMATION
DEPOLYMERIZE DEGRADE
DEPONE SWEAR DEPOSE TESTIFY
DEPONENT AFFIANT DEPONER EXAMINATE
DEPOPULATE RAVAGE DESOLATE DISPEOPLE
DEPORT BEAR EXILE EXPEL BANISH BEHAVE DEMEAN BEARING CONDUCT DISPORT RELEGATE
DEPORTMENT AIR GEST MIEN PORT GESTE HABIT TENUE ACTION DEPORT HAVING MANNER ADDRESS BEARING COMPORT CONDUCT GESTURE HAVANCE BREEDING CARRIAGE DEMEANOR MAINTAIN PORTANCE
DEPOSE AVER ABASE PRIVE SWEAR AFFIRM ASSERT BANISH DEPONE DIVEST REDUCE REMOVE DEGRADE DEPOSIT DESTOOL TESTIFY DETHRONE DISCROWN DISPLACE
DEPOSIT FUR LAY PUT SET ADHI BANK CAKE CAST CRUD DROP DUMP FUND HIDE HOCK PAWN BLOOM CHEST COUCH COVER DEPOT LODGE PLACE SCURF STORE TOSCA BESTOW DEPONE DEPOSE ENTOMB ESCROW FLYSCH GARNER IMPOSE INHUME PLEDGE REPOSE SALINE SCORIA SCROLL SETTLE SINTER TOPHUS ASHFALL CONSIGN HORIZON DILUVIUM FOULNESS SANDBANK PRECIPITATION
(— BALLOT) CAST
(— DRIFT-SAND) SUD
(— EGGS) BLOW SPAWN
(— FOR COPYRIGHT) ENTER
(— FROM HOT SPRINGS) SINTER
(— IN CHAMPAGNE) GRIFFE
(— IN EARTH) INTER INHUME
(— IN GUN BORE) FOULING
(— IN WINE CASK) CRUST TARTAR
(— OF DEBRIS) BRECCIA
(— OF LOAM) LOESS
(— OF ORE) BANK FLAT
(— OF PEBBLES AND SAND) BEACH CASCALHO
(— OF SALT WATER) SOAK
(— ON LEATHER) BLOOM
(— ON LEAVES) HONEYDEW
(— STOLEN ARTICLES) FENCE
(— USED AS FERTILIZER) FALUN
(ALLUVIAL —) APRON DELTA
(ARCHAEOLOGICAL —) LENS LENSE
(BANK —S) CASH
(BLACK —) STUPP
(BROKER'S —) MARGIN
(CORNEA —) ARCUS
(DEEP-SEA —) OOZE
(EARTHY —) GUHR MARL
(GEOLOGIC —) BLANKET HORIZON
(GLACIAL —) TILL DRIFT ESKAR ESKER SHEET PLACER MORAINE
(GOUTY —) TOPHUS
(GRANULAR —) SABURRA
(GRAVEL —) LEAD
(KIDNEY —) GRAVEL

(MASS OF SEDIMENTARY —S) GOBI
(MINERAL —) FLAT LODE CARBONA
(MUDDY —) SLUDGE SLUMGULLION
(POWDERY —) BERGMEHL
(SEDIMENTARY —) SILT VARVE
TURBIDITE
(SHELLY —) CRAG
(SHOAL-WATER —) CULM
(SKELETAL —) CORAL
(STOMACH —) SABURRA
(TARRY —) GUM
(VALUABLE —) VEIN
(WELDING —) TACK
(PREF.) THESO
DEPOSITARY POSITOR SEQUESTER
DEPOSITION PAD BURIAL DEPOSIT
OPINION SILTING DEPOSURE
SEDIMENT
DEPOSITORY BANK DROP SAFE
AMBRY ATTIC VAULT DEPOSIT
OSSUARY SENTINE DEPOSITO
ESCROWEE OSSARIUM
DEPOT BANK BASE GARE AURANG
AURUNG STAPLE STATION
MAGAZINE TERMINAL TERMINUS
(MISSILE —) SILO
DEPRAVE TAINT DEBASE DEFILE
INFECT MALIGN REVILE BESHREW
CORRUPT PERVERT VITIATE
DEPRAVED BAD EVIL UGLY VILE
PRAVE ROTTEN SHREWD WICKED
BESTIAL CORRUPT IMMORAL
PRAVOUS VICIOUS MISCREANT
DEPRAVITY VICE ABYSS ILLNESS
PRAVITY VILLAINY TURPITUDE
DEPRECATE PRAY INVOKE BESEECH
DEPRECATORY PEJORATIVE
DEPRECIATE FALL LACK SLUR
ABASE AVILE DECRY SLUMP
DEBASE EMBASE LESSEN MINISH
REDUCE SHRINK CHEAPEN
DEBAUCH DEGRADE DEPRAVE
DEPRESS DETRACT DISABLE
SLANDER SMALLEN BELITTLE
DEROGATE DISCOUNT DISPRIZE
DISVALUE MINIMIZE PEJORATE
VILIPEND WRITEOFF
DEPRECIATION AGIO DECRIAL
DISCOUNT
DEPREDATION PREY RAPINE
PILLAGE
DEPRESS BOW COW HIP LOW BATE
BEAR BORE DAMP DASH DENT
FALL FLAT SINK SUMP ABASE
APPAL BREAK CHILL COUCH
CRUSH FAINT LOWER SLUMP
VAPOR WEIGH APPALL DAMPEN
DEBOSS DISMAY HUMBLE INDENT
LESSEN MURDEN SADDEN SETTLE
SICKEN SLOUCH STRIKE WEAKEN
DECLINE DEGRADE DESTROY
FLATTEN OPPRESS REPRESS
BROWBEAT DIMINISH DISPIRIT
DOWNBEAR ENFEEBLE
(— STRINGS OF INSTRUMENT)
FRET
DEPRESSANT HELLEBORE
DEPRESSED LOW SAD BLUE DAMP
DULL FLAT SICK SUNK COWED
WROTH BROODY BUMMED
DISHED GLOOMY HIPPED HOLLOW
LONELY OBLATE SOMBER TRISTE
ACCABLE LETDOWN DEJECTED

DOWNCAST DOWNSOME
(— AT THE POLES) OBLATE
(ECONOMICALLY —) HARD
DEPRESSING SAD BLUE COLD
BLEAK CHILL DREAR DUSKY
MUZZY OURIE DISMAL DREARY
GLOOMY SOMBER SOMBRE
TRISTE OPPRESSIVE
DEPRESSION COL DIP EYE GAT PAN
PIT BUST CROP DAMP DELK DENT
DOKE DOWN FALL FOSS FUNK
GASH GLEN HOLL HOWE SLEW
SLOT SLUE WELL ATRIO BASIN
BLAHS BLUES BOSOM CANON
COWAL CRYPT DELVE DINGE
FOSSA FOSSE FOVEA GLOOM
GROIN NADIR NAVEL ORBIT POLJE
SALAR SCOOP SELLA SINUS
SLUMP SWALE AMPHID BLIGHT
BUCKLE CAFARD CANYON CAVITY
CRATER CUPULE DIMPLE DISMAY
FURROW GROOVE GULLEY
GUTTER INDENT LACUNA RAVINE
SAUCER SLOUGH SPLEEN VALLEY
WALLOW ALVEOLA BLOWOUT
BOGHOLE CHAGRIN CLAYPAN
CONCAVE COUNTER FOSSULA
FOSSULE FOVEOLA JIMMIES
SADNESS SALTPAN SINKAGE
SINKING VARIOLE BOTHRIUM
DOLDRUMS DOWNBEND FAINTING
FOLLICLE FOREDEEP FOSSETTE
FOSSULET PUNCTURE SINKHOLE
SOAKAWAY EPHIPPIUM
MELANCHOLY OPPRESSION
(— BEHIND COW'S SHOULDERS)
CROP
(— BETWEEN BREASTS) CLEAVAGE
(— BETWEEN HILLS) SWIRE
(— IN BOARD) SKIP
(— IN BOTTLE BOTTOM) KICK
(— IN DECK) COCKPIT
(— IN DOG'S FACE) STOP
(— IN FRUITS) EYE
(— IN GROUND) DALK DELK SOAK
SWAG WELL SWALE CHARCO
(— IN MILLSTONE) BOSOM
(— IN NILE VALLEY) KORE
(— IN RANGE) PASS
(— IN RIDGE) COL
(— IN SNOW) SITZMARK
(— IN VELD) COMITJE KOMMETJE
(— OF EAR) SCAPHA
(— OF SPIRITS) JAWFALL
(— PRONE) VAPORISH
(ARTICULAR —) GLENE
(OBLONG —) CIRCUS
(SMALL —) DENT DIMPLE LACUNA
FOLLICLE
DEPRIVATION COST LOSS MAIM
WANT MAYHEM AMOTION
MISTURE DEPRIVAL
(— OF SIGHT) DARKNESS
(SUFF.) STERESIS
DEPRIVE BAR ROB BATE DENY
DOCK EASE GELD TWIN ABATE
BENIM BREAK DEBAR EMPTY
EXUTE PREVE SPOIL STRIP WRONG
AMERCE DEFEAT DENUDE DEPOSE
DEVEST DISMAY DIVEST FAMISH
FORBAR HINDER HUSTLE REMOVE
ABRIDGE BEGUILE BEREAVE
CASHIER CURTAIL DECEIVE

DEFORCE DEPRAVE DESPOIL
DESTROY DISABLE EXHAUST
FOREBAR GUDGEON PRIVATE
UNDRESS BANKRUPT DENATURE
DESOLATE DISANNUL EVACUATE
(— BY TRICKERY) NOSE MULCT
(— FRAUDULENTLY) GUDGEON
(— OF BRILLIANCE) DEADEN
(— OF COLOR) STAIN
(— OF COURAGE) UNNERVE
(— OF FOOD) STARVE
(— OF FREEDOM) FETTER
(— OF INDIVIDUALITY) FORDIZE
(— OF LIFE) DEADEN
(— OF OFFICE) DEPOSE
(— OF PAY) DOCK
(— OF POSSESSIONS) FLAY
(— OF REASON) DEMENT
(— OF SENSATION) BENUMB
(— OF SENSE) INEBRIATE
(— OF SIGHT) SEEL
(— OF STRENGTH) ENERVATE
(— OF VIRGINITY) DEFLOWER
(— WRONGFULLY) ROB
(PREF.) **(— OF)** DE DIS
DEPRIVED REFT SANS BANKRUPT
DESOLATE
DEPTH DIP BURY DEEP DROP MOHO
ABYSS MIDST SIDTH FATHOM
HEIGHT ALTITUDE DEEPNESS
PROFOUND SOUNDING STRENGTH
PENETRATION
(— CHARGE) ASHCAN
(— OF NIGHT OR WINTER) HOLL
HOWE
(— OF SAIL) HOIST
(— OF SHIP) GAGE GAUGE
(— OF SIN) SLOUGH
(— OF SPADE) SPIT GRAFT
(— OF WATER) DRAFT DRAUGHT
(—S OF SEA) PROFOUND
(LOWEST —) GROUND
(MORAL —) ABYSS
(PL.) MUD ABYSS HEART
(PREF.) BATH(O)(Y)
DEPUTATION MISSION THEORIA
LEGATION
DEPUTE SEND ALLOT ASSIGN
DEVOTE APPOINT DELEGATE
DEPUTY AIDE VICE AGENT ENVOY
NABOB PROXY VICAR ANGELO
COMMIS CURATE DEPUTE EXARCH
FACTOR KEHAYA LEGATE MINION
ADJOINT BAILIFF ESCALUS
SUBDEAN CAIMACAM DELEGATE
ORDINARY PYLAGORE QAIMAQAM
TENIENTE VICARIAN
(— OF BISHOP) VICAR VIDAME
(BISHOP'S —) VIDAME
(PREF.) CO
DERACINATE UPROOT
DERAIL TOAD DERAILER THROWOFF
FRUSTRATE
DERANGE TURN CRAZE UNWIT
UPSET HAMPER RUFFLE CONFUSE
DERAIGN DISEASE DISTURB
PERTURB UNSHAPE DISORDER
DISPLACE UNSETTLE
DERANGED OUT GYTE CRAZY
CRAZED SKIVIE FRANTIC FURIOUS
BUGHOUSE DEMENTED DETRAQUE
INFORMAL
DERANGEMENT MANIA UPSET

FRENZY LUNACY DISEASE
MADNESS PHRENSY RUMMAGE
DELIRIUM DISORDER INSANITY
DERBY POT CADY KATY RACE
BOXER CADDY DICER KELLY SHIRE
BOWLER POTHAT BILLYCOCK
DERBY BLUE ELDERBERRY
DERELICT REMISS STREET FAILURE
BETRAYER CASTAWAY
DERELICTION FAILURE RELICTION
DERIDE BOO GECK GIBE HOOT JAPE
JEER JIBE LOUT MOCK RAZZ TWIT
DRAPE FLEER FLOUT KNACK
LAUGH RALLY SCOFF SCORN
SCOUT TAUNT EXPOSE ILLUDE
IRRIDE CATCALL LOWBELL
RIDICULE
DERIDER IRRISOR
DERISION GECK JEER MOCK HOKER
SCORN SPORT MOWING ASTEISM
MOCKERY CONTEMPT IRRISION
RIDICULE
(EXPRESS —) SNEER SNORT
DERISIVE JEERY SNIDE MOWING
SNEERY SNOOTY SATANIC
DERISORY IRRISORY SARDONIC
SCOFFING
DERIVATION ORIGIN DESCENT
PEDIGREE PARENTAGE
DERIVATIVE FURAN LININ SLOPE
ACOINE ACYLAL BORANE FURANE
INDOLE PHENOL RETENE ALKYLOL
ANALGEN DERIVED ENOLATE
FLAVONE FLUXION FULGIDE
FULVENE GERMANE SUCRATE
ALBUMOSE ANALGENE FLAVONOL
FORMAZAN HEMATINE INDAZOLE
STANNANE SECONDHAND
ADSCITITIOUS
DERIVE GET DRAW STEM TAKE
BRING CARRY DRIVE FETCH INFER
TRACE BORROW CONVEY DEDUCE
DESUME ELICIT EVOLVE GATHER
OBTAIN SPRING DESCEND
EXTRACT PROCEED RECEIVE
TRADUCE
(IMPROPERLY —) WREST
DERIVED
(SUFF.) **(— FROM)** IC(AL)
DERMA LAYER CORIUM DERMIS
KISHKE
DERMATITIS ICH ICK CASCADO
CUTITIS
DERMATOGEN PROTODERM
DERMIS CUTIS DERMA CORIUM
DERNIER LAST FINAL DARREIN
DERNIER CRI CRY KICK LATEST
NEWEST FASHION
DEROGATE ANNUL DECRY LESSEN
REPEAL DETRACT SLANDER
RESTRICT WITHDRAW
DEROGATORY BAD
DERRICK JIB RIG LIFT SPAR CRANE
DAVIT HOIST STEEVE TACKLE
ERECTER ERECTOR GALLOWS
HANGING HANGMAN STIFFLEG
JINNYWINK
DERRIS TUBA DEGUELIA
DERVISH AGIB FAKIR FAKEER
SADITE SANTON DARWESH
WHIRLER CALENDER
DESALT DEIONIZE
DESATURATE SADDEN

DESCANT SING SONG COPULA MELODY REMARK WARBLE COMMENT QUINIBLE

DESCEND DIP SYE DIVE DROP DUCK FALL SHED SINK SKIN VAIL AVALE LIGHT LOWER SQUAT STOOP SWOOP ALIGHT DERIVE DEVALL DEVAUL SETTLE DECLINE DELAPSE DEVOLVE SUBSIDE SUCCEED DISMOUNT PREPONDERATE
(— BY ROPE) RAPPEL
(— INTO HELL) HARROW

DESCENDANT SON CION GHUZ HEIR SEED SLIP CHILD GHUZZ SCION BRANCH LINEAL DESCENT AARONITE ASHERITE DAUGHTER EPIGONUS
(— OF IMMIGRANTS) BRAVA
(— OF JEW) CHUETA
(— OF MOHAMMED) EMIR
(— OF NOAH) AD
(—S OF MOHAMMED) ASHRAF
(INSIGNIFICANT —) TAG
(PL.) SEED DONMEH DUNMEH STRAIN PROGENY OFFSPRING POSTERITY
(SUFF.) ITE

DESCENDING FALL CADENT DOWNWARD
(— FROM COMMON ANCESTOR) AKIN

DESCENT JET KIN SET DIVE DOWN DROP FALL KIND VAIL BIRTH BLOOD CANCH CHUTE ISSUE PITCH SCARP SHUTE SLOPE STOCK CLEUCH CLEUGH ESCARP RAPPEL STRAIN ASSAULT DECLINE DISSENT EXTRACT FALLOUT INCLINE KINDRED LINEAGE PROGENY ANCESTRY BREEDING COMEDOWN DOWNCOME DOWNFALL DOWNGATE DOWNHILL GLISSADE INVASION PEDIGREE PARENTAGE
(— IN MOUNTAINEERING) ABSEIL
(— OF AIRPLANE) LETDOWN APPROACH
(— OF BIRD) STOOP
(— OF DEITY) AVATAR AVATARA
(— OF LIQUID) DRIBBLE
(— OF MASS) SLIDE
(— OF RIVER) LEAP
(FAMILIAR —) HAVAGE
(OVERWHELMING —) AVALANCHE
(PARACHUTE —) JUMP BAILOUT
(PLUNGING —) SPIN

DESCHAMPSIA AIRA

DESCRIBE DRAW GIVE LIMN READ TELL BLAZE IMAGE LABEL PAINT POINT STYLE WRITE DENOTE DENOTE DEPICT DEVISE DILATE RELATE REPORT SKETCH TITULE DECLARE DEPAINT DISPLAY EXPLAIN EXPRESS NARRATE OUTLINE PICTURE PORTRAY PRESENT RECOUNT STORIFY DESCRIVE INSCRIBE REHEARSE
(— A LINE) CUT
(— AS) CALL
(— BRIEFLY) KODAK
(— GRAMMATICALLY) PARSE
(— VIVIDLY) PICTURE

DESCRIBER (VIVID —) PAINTER

DESCRIBING GRAPHIC

DESCRIPTION KIN IMAGE BLAZON SKETCH SURVEY ACCOUNT DICTION DISPLAY PICTURE LANDSKIP RELATION TREATISE
(— OF A COUNTRY) FACE
(— OF VISION) AISLING
(BRIEF —) LEGEND
(RUSTIC —) IDYL IDYLL
(VIVID —) PICTURE PAINTING

DESCRY SEE SPY ESPY MAKE SCRY ASCRY SIGHT BEHOLD BETRAY DETECT REVEAL DISCERN DISPLAY DENOUNCE DESCRIBE DISCLOSE DISCOVER PERCEIVE

DESDEMONA (FATHER OF —) BRABANTIO
(HUSBAND OF —) OTHELLO

DESECRATE ABUSE DEFILE POLLUTE PROFANE VIOLATE TEMERATE UNHALLOW

DESECRATION PROFANATION

DESENSITIZE DRUG DEADEN

DESERT DUE ERG RAT RUN AREG ARID BOLT FAIL FLEE MEED SAND SERT TURN VAST DITCH GUILT LEAVE LURCH MERIT PLANT SERIR START WAIVE WASTE WORTH BARREN BETRAY DEFECT EXPOSE LONELY RENEGE REWARD SHRINK THIRST WESTEN ABANDON ABSCOND CHICKEN DEMERIT FORSAKE HORNADA OVERRUN WASTERN WASTINE DESOLATE RENOUNCE SOLITARY SOLITUDE WASTABLE
(PL.) GUILT
(PREF.) EREM(O)

DESERTED DEAD LONE WYSTY LONELY FORLORN DESOLATE FORSAKEN SOLITARY
(— WOMAN) AGUNAH

DESERTER RAT BOLTER BUGOUT APOSTATE BUSHWACK FUGITIVE RECREANT RENEGADE RUNAGATE TURNTAIL

DESERTION BUGOUT RATTERY APOSTASY

DESERT LEMON KUMQUAT

DESERVE EARN MEED RATE MERIT REPAY SERVE ASSERVE BENEFIT DEMERIT DISSERVE PROMERIT

DESERVED JUST COMING WORTHY CONDIGN

DESERVING WORTHY CONDIGN WORTHFUL ADMIRABLE MERITORIOUS

DESICCATE DRY ARID SEAR SERE DRAIN DEHYDRATE

DESICCATION XERANSIS

DESIDERATUM NEED DESIRE

DESIGN AIM END MAP CAST DRAW GOAL IDEA MARK MEAN PLAN PLAT PLOT TOOL TREE WORK ALLOT CHECK DECAL DECOR DODAD DRAFT DRIFT ETTLE FANCY MODEL MOTIF NOTAN QUILT SHAPE STAMP STUDY STYLE BOWPOT CACHET CORNER CREATE DEVICE DEVISE DOODAD DOODLE EMBLEM FIGURE FLORAL FLOWER INCUSE INTEND INTENT INVENT LAYOUT MODULE OBJECT

OBTENT PROJET SCHEME SKETCH SYSTEM VERVER ALLOVER BOSCAGE CARTOON CARVING CHASING COMPOSE CONCERT COUNSEL CROQUIS DESTINE DIAGRAM DRAUGHT ETCHING FANTASY FASHION OUTLINE PATTERN PRETEND PROJECT PROPOSE PURPORT PURPOSE REVERSE SCALLOP SLEIGHT THOUGHT APPLIQUE BAYADERE BOUGHPOT CONTRIVE CYMATION CYMATIUM ENGINEER FILIGREE FLOCKING FORECAST GRAFFITO GROOVING INTAGLIO PHANTASY PLATFORM REMARQUE SINGERIE STRIPING SUNBURST GOFFERING SCHEMATISM
(— AS TITLE PAGE) VIGNETTE
(— ON BOOK) TOOL
(— ON CARPET) MEDALLION
(— ON COIN) BEADING
(— ON FABRIC) BATIK BATTIK
(AIRCRAFT —) STEALTH
(ARTFUL —) MACHINATION
(BOOK —) FILET FILLET
(COMPUTER —) CAD
(CUP-SHAPED —) HUSK
(EMBLEMATIC —) IMPRESS
(ESSENTIAL —) BONES
(FASHION —) FORD
(OPENWORK —) POINTELLE
(OUTLINE —) KEYSTONE
(PERFORATED —) POUNCE
(SPOTTED —) SEME
(STRIPED —) STRIA STRIE
(TESSELLATED —) MOSAIC
(TEXTILE —) STRIPE HAIRLINE

DESIGNATE SET HAIL MARK MEAN NAME SHOW ELECT LABEL SPEAK STYLE TITLE ANOINT ASSIGN DENOTE DESIGN FINGER INTEND SETTLE TARGET APPOINT EARMARK ENTITLE EXPRESS SPECIFY SURNAME ALLOCATE DESCRIBE IDENTIFY INDICATE NOMINATE PRESCRIBE

DESIGNATION NAME TERM TYPE LABEL STYLE TITLE CAPTION HOMONYM ADDITION
(— OF PLACE) ADDRESS

DESIGNED PREPENSE SUPPOSED
(— FOR MALE AND FEMALE) UNISEX

DESIGNER ERTE STYLER FANCIER PLANNER PLOTTER SCHEMER STYLIST COLORIST ENGINEER MEDALIST MOSAICIST
(FASHION —) DIOR FENLI RENTA CASSINI
(PL.) COUTURE

DESIGNING ARTFUL CUNNING JESUITIC PLANNING PLOTTING SCHEMING

DESIRABLE FAIR GOOD KEEN WORTH PLUMMY AMIABLE GRADELY HEALTHY OPTABLE WELCOME WISHFUL DESIROUS ELIGIBLE ENVIABLE PLEASING SALUTARY

DESIRE HOT YEN ACHE CARE ENVY EROS FAIN HAVE HOPE HOTS ITCH KAMA KEEP LEST LIST LOAD LUST

MIND NEED PANT URGE WANT WILL WISH WIST ARDOR BOSOM BRAME COVET CRAVE FANCY GIMME GREED GROAN HEART MANGE MANIA NISUS QUEST STUDY TANHA TASTE WILNE YEARN YISSE AFFECT APPETE ASPIRE BEHEST BESOLN DEMAND DEVICE HANKER HUNGER OREXIS POTHOS PREFER TALENT THIRST UTINAM YAMMER AVARICE AVIDITY CONATUS COURAGE CRAVING EROTISM FANTASY HIMEROS HOPEFOR INKLING LONGING PASSION STOMACH VOLUNTY WILLING AMBITION APPETITE COVETISE CUPIDITY PLEASING NECESSITY
(— FOR LIFE) TANHA
(— WITH EAGERNESS) ASPIRE
(ARDENT —) THIRST
(IRRITATING —) ITCH
(SEXUAL —) HOTS PRIDE
(STRONG —) CUPIDITY SLAVERING
(UNCONTROLLABLE —) CACOETHES
(PREF.) **(SEXUAL —)** ERO EROTO
(SUFF.) OREXIA

DESIRE UNDER THE ELMS
(AUTHOR OF —) ONEILL
(CHARACTER IN —) EBEN ABBIE CABOT PUTNAM EPHRAIM

DESIROUS AVID FAIN FOND LIEF VAIN EAGER FRACK FRECK LUSTY ARDENT WILFUL ANXIOUS THIRSTY WILLFUL WILLING WISHING APPETENT COVETOUS LIKEROUS PRURIENT SPIRITED

DESIST HO LIN EASE HALT QUIT REST SIST STOP WHOA CEASE LEAVE SPARE STINT SWICK SWIKE WONDE DEPART ABANDON FORBEAR FORFEIT RESPITE SUBSIST SURCEASE
(— FROM) CUT LEAVE REMIT FORBEAR

DESK PEW AMBO SCOB BOARD DESSE TABLE BUREAU CAISSE PULPIT CONSOLE LECTERN PLUTEUS COPYDESK STANDISH VARGUENO
(KIND OF —) ROLLTOP

DESMA CLON CLONE

DESMAN MOLE SQUASH MUSKRAT ONDATRA

DESMANTHUS ACUAN

DESOLATE SAD BARE LORN RUIN SACK SOLE VAST WILD ALONE BLEAK DREAR GAUNT GUBAT OURIE STARK UNKED UNKET UNKID WASTE WASTY WYSTY BARREN DESERT DISMAL DREARY GLOOMY GOUSTY LONELY RAVAGE DESTROY FORLORN GOUSTIE HOWLING LACKING UNCOUTH WIDOWED WILSOME DEPRIVED DESERTED FORSAKEN SOLITARY WASTEFUL WOBEGONE

DESOLATION WOE RUIN GLOOM GRIEF HAVOC WASTE RAVAGE SADNESS

DESPAIR GLOOM UNHOPE WANHOPE

DESPAIRING HOPELESS
DESPERADO BRAVO BADMAN
  BANDIT RUFFIAN CRIMINAL
  RESOLUTE
DESPERATE MAD DIRE RASH
  ACHARNE DESPERT EXTREME
  FORLORN FRANTIC HEADLONG
  HOPELESS PERILOUS RECKLESS
DESPERATELY BONE
DESPICABLE BUM BASE MEAN
  ORRA VILE CHEAP DIRTY FOUTY
  SCALY ABJECT PALTRY ROTTEN
  SHABBY SORDID CAITIFF IGNOBLE
  PITIFUL REPTILE PITIABLE
  UNWORTHY WRETCHED
DESPICABLY DIRTILY
DESPISE DEFY HATE SCORN SCOUT
  SPISE SPURN DETEST FORHOO
  LOATHE SLIGHT VILIFY CONTEMN
  DESPITE DISDAIN DISPRIZE
  MISPRIZE VILIPEND
DESPITE DY VEX SPITE MALGRE
  DESPISE
DESPOIL ROB PELF PILL POLL RAID
  RAPE RUIN SKIN BOOTY HARRY
  PLUME RAVEN REAVE RIFLE SPOIL
  STRIP STRUB TRICE BEZZLE DIVEST
  FLEECE HESPEL HUSPEL RAVAGE
  RAVISH REMOVE BEREAVE
  DEPRIVE DISROBE PILLAGE
  PLUNDER UNSPOIL DEFLOWER
  DISARRAY SPOLIATE SPUILZIE
  UNCLOTHE
DESPOINA KORE PERSEPHONE
DESPONDENCY DUMP HUMP
  BLUES DUMPS GLOOM ATHYMY
  MISERY ATHUMIA ATHYMIA
  DESPAIR DESPOND
DESPONDENT SAD BLUE GLOOMY
  FORLORN DEJECTED DOWNCAST
  HOPELESS
DESPOT CZAR TSAR TZAR ANARCH
  SATRAP TYRANT AUTARCH
  MONARCH AUTOCRAT
DESPOTIC LORDLY ABSOLUTE
  DOMINANT
DESPOTISM TYRANNY AUTARCHY
  SULTANISM
DESQUAMATE PEEL
DESSERT EIS ICE PIE BABA CAKE
  FOOL SKYR SNOW VOID BETTY
  BOMBE COUPE DOLCE FRUIT
  GLACE GRUNT JELLY LACTO
  SLUMP AFTERS ECLAIR JUNKET
  MOUSSE PASTRY POSTRE SPONGE
  SWEETS TRIFLE BAKLAVA
  BANQUET PARFAIT PAVLOVA
  PUDDING SHERBET SOUFFLE
  SPUMONE STRUDEL SUPREME
  DUMPLING FLUMMERY FRUMENTY
  NAPOLEON PANDOWDY SILLABUB
  DACQUOISE ENTREMETS
  SOPAPILLA SOPAPILLA
  (BAKED —) CRISP
  (CARAMEL) FLAN
DESTINATION END GOAL PORT
  BOURN BILLET BOURNE
DESTINE DOOM EURE FATE MARK
  ALLOT SHAPE SLATE WEIRD
  DEPUTE DESIGN DEVOTE INTEND
  ORDAIN APPOINT PURPOSE
  SENTENCE
DESTINY LOT DOLE DOOM EURE

FATE SORT KARMA MOIRA STARS
WEIRD KHARMA KISMET DESTINE
FORTUNE PORTION FOREDOOM
DESTITUTE BARE NACE POOR SANS
  VOID CLEAN EMPTY NAKED NEEDY
  WASTE BEREFT DEVOID VACANT
  WASTED FORLORN LACKING
  NAUGHTY VIDUATE WANTING
  BANKRUPT BEGGARED DEFEATED
  DEPRIVED DESOLATE FORSAKEN
  HELPLESS INDIGENT INNOCENT
  VIDUATED PENNILESS
  (— OF) BUT
  (— OF FEATHERS) DEPLUMATE
  (— OF LEAVES) APHYLLOUS
  (— OF LIGHT) DARK
  (— OF TEETH) EDENTATE
  (— OF WATER) ANHYDROUS
  (SUFF.) (— OF) LESS
DESTITUTION NEED WANT FAMINE
  PENURY BEGGARY DEFAULT
  POVERTY
DESTROY BAG EAT END GUT MOW
  RID ZAP BLOW CHEW FRAP FULL
  KILL NUKE NULL RASE RAZE RUIN
  RUSH SINK SLAY SMIT STRY TINE
  UNDO VOID BREAK CRACK CRAZE
  DECAY ELIDE ERASE ERODE
  FORDO HAVOC MISDO PRANG
  QUADE QUAIL QUELL SHEND
  SHOOT SMASH SMITE SPEED
  SPEND SPILL SPLIT SPOIL STROY
  SWAMP TOTAL TRASH WASTY
  WRACK WRECK BLIGHT CANCEL
  CUMBER DEFACE DEFEAT DELETE
  DEVOID DEVOUR EFFACE FAMISH
  FOREDO MURDER PERISH QUENCH
  RANKLE RAVAGE STARVE STIFLE
  UNMAKE UNPILE UNWORK
  UPROOT UPTEAR ABOLISH
  CONSUME CORRODE DEPRIVE
  DISTURB ENECATE EXPUNGE
  FLATTEN FORFARE FORLESE
  MORTIFY NULLIFY OVERRUN
  PEREMPT RUINATE SHAMASH
  SHATTER SMOTHER SUBVERT
  TERRIFY UNBUILD WHITTLE
  AMORTIZE CONFOUND DECIMATE
  DEMOLISH DESOLATE DESTRUCT
  DISANNUL DISPLANT DISSOLVE
  FRACTURE FRAGMENT IMMOLATE
  INFRINGE MUTILATE OVERTURN
  PARALYZE SABOTAGE STRAMASH
  OBLITERATE
  (— BARK) GIRDLE
  (— BY FIRE) CONSUME
  (— COMPLETELY) RUBOUT
  (— FERTILITY) EXHAUST
  (— FOR FUN) TRASH
  (— SELF-POSSESSION) ABASH
  (— TOTALLY) SMASH SWEEP
  CUMBER SCUTTLE
  (SUFF.) CLASE CLASIA CLAST(IC)
DESTROYED FLAT BLOWN KAPUT
  KAPUTT
DESTROYER CAN HUN DEATH
  TINCAN UNDOER VANDAL VICTOR
  FLIVVER STROYER UNMAKER
  WARSHIP APOLLYON DEVOURER
  SABOTEUR
  (— OF MACHINERY) LUDDITE
  (SUFF.) CIDAL CIDE PHTHORA
DESTROYING FELL

(PREF.) ANTI
(SUFF.) CLASTIC
DESTRUCTIBLE FRAIL
DESTRUCTION BAR END HEW
  BANE DOGS DOOM FIRE LOSS
  RACK RUIN STRY TALA CRUSH
  DEATH DECAY GRAVE HAVOC
  SMASH STRIP STROY WASTE
  WRACK DEFEAT DISMAY ENDING
  EXPIRY WONDER ABADDON
  CARNAGE EROSION UNDOING
  COLLAPSE DELETION DISPOSAL
  DOWNFALL EVERSION EXCISION
  SHAMBLES SMASHERY RUINATION
  (— OF BONES) CARIES
  (— OF ENVIRONMENT) ECOCIDE
  (— OF SHIP'S PAPERS) SPOLIATION
  (CELL —) LYSIS
  (GOD OF —) SIVA
  (GRADUAL —) CORROSION
  (MALICIOUS —) SABOTAGE
  (UTTER —) PERDITION
  (SUFF.) LYSE LYSIS LYST LYTE
  LYTIC LYZE
DESTRUCTIVE FELL FATAL DEADLY
  MORTAL BALEFUL BANEFUL
  DEATHLY EXITIAL FATEFUL
  HARMFUL HUMLIKE HURTFUL
  NOISOME NOXIOUS RUINOUS
  ANERETIC DEATHFUL EXITIOUS
  WASTEFUL WRACKFUL WREAKFUL
  ANAERETIC PESTILENT
  (— TO LIFE) BIOCIDAL
DESUETUDE BREACH DISUSE
DESULTORY IDLE HASTY LOOSE
  ROVING AIMLESS CURSORY
  RAMBLING UNSTEADY WAVERING
  IRREGULAR
DETACH CUT DRAFT LOOSE SEVER
  AVULSE LOOSEN UNBIND UNGLUE
  UNWORK CRACKLE DISJOIN
  DRAUGHT ISOLATE UNHINGE
  UNRIVET UNSEIZE ABSTRACT
  DISSOLVE DISUNITE PRESCIND
  SEPARATE UNFASTEN WITHDRAW
DETACHABLE SLIP
DETACHED CUT COLD FREE ALONE
  ALOOF LOOSE DEADPAN INSULAR
  PORTATO SCIOLTO ABSTRACT
  CLINICAL DISCRETE ISOLATED
  OUTLYING SEPARATE SPICCATO
  UNBIASED IMPERSONAL
  (PREF.) APH APO
DETACHMENT POINT POSSE
  ATARAXY OUTPOST ATARAXIA
  AVULSION OUTGUARD
  (SUFF.) LYSE LYSIS LYST LYTE
  LYTIC LYZE
DETAIL CREW ITEM DODAD POINT
  ACCENT ASSIGN DOODAB
  DOODAD NICETY PARCEL RELATE
  RETAIL ACCOUNT APPOINT
  ARTICLE ITEMIZE MINUTIA
  NARRATE NULLING RESPECT
  SEVERAL SPECIFY INSTANCE
  REHEARSE SALIENCE PARTICULAR
  PARTICULARITY
  (—S OF MAP) CULTURE
  (CLIMACTIC —) BEAUTY
  (PETTY —) CHICKEN
  (SPECIFIC —S) NITTYGRITTY
  (UNIMPORTANT —S) TRIVIA
  (PL.) DOPE FROUFROU FURNITURE

DETAILED NARROW PROLIX
  CLOSEUP SPECIAL PUNCTUAL
  TIRESOME
DETAIN BAIL HOLD KEEP STAY STOP
  CHECK DELAY TARRY ARREST
  ATHOLD COLLAR HINDER RETARD
  TAIGLE IMPRISON RESTRAIN
  WITHHOLD
DETECT SEE SPY ESPY FIND NOSE
  SPOT CATCH SCENT SENSE SMOKE
  SNIFF TRACE DESCRY DIVINE
  EXPOSE REVEAL DEVELOP
  DISCERN UNCOVER DECIPHER
  DISCOVER OVERTAKE
DETECTIVE EYE TEC BULL BUSY
  DICK JACK TRAP PLANT SNOOP
  SPADE BEAGLE MOUSER RUNNER
  SHADOW SHAMUS SLEUTH TAILER
  TRACER GUMSHOE MAIGRET
  SCENTER SNOOPER SPOTTER
  TEMPLAR TRAILER BEAUMONT
  DETECTOR FLATFOOT HAWKSHAW
  HOUSEMAN OPERATOR SHERLOCK
  OPERATIVE PINKERTON
  PLAINCLOTHESMAN
  (— FICTION AWARD) EDGAR
  (— OF FICTION) LUPIN
  (— STORY) WHODUNIT
  (FICTIONAL —) CHAN LUPIN QUEEN
  TRACY VANCE CARTER HOLMES
  MARPLE POIROT CHARLES
DETECTOR ASDIC COHERER
  REAGENT SFERICS SPHERICS
  (ELECTRONIC —) SOLION
  (KIND OF —) METAL
  (LIE —) POLYGRAPH
DETENT DOG PALL PAWL CATCH
  CLICK RATCH PALLET RATCHET
DETENTION DELAY ARREST
  CAPTURE DETINUE JANKERS
  DETAINER STOPPAGE
DETER BAR FEAR BLOCK BLUFF
  CHECK DELAY DEHORT HINDER
  RETARD PREVENT TERRIFY
  DISSUADE PRECLUDE RESTRAIN
DETERGE PURGE CLEANSE
  MUNDIFY
DETERGENT SOAP SYNDET
  ABLUENT PURGING RHYPTIC
  SMECTIC SOLVENT CLEANSER
  GARDINOL
DETERIORATE GO FAIL GIVE SLIP
  SOUR WEAR DECAY ERODE SPILL
  WORST APPAIR APPERE DEBASE
  IMPAIR SICKEN WORSEN DECLINE
  PERVERT FIREFANG
DETERIORATED MUSTY
DETERIORATING DECADENT
DETERIORATION DECAY IMPAIR
  MALADY DECLINE EROSION
  FAILURE DOLDRUMS PEJORATION
DETERMINABLE FIXED DEFINITE
  DEFINABLE GAUGEABLE
DETERMINANT CYTOGENE
  JACOBIAN CIRCULANT
  WRONSKIAN PLASTOGENE
DETERMINATE CERTAIN ORISTIC
  DEFINITE RESOLUTE RESOLVED
  SPECIFIC
DETERMINATION ACT HEST WILL
  ASSAY BLANK CAUSE ADVICE
  BEARING CONSULT PURPOSE

DETERMINATION RESOLVE ANALYSIS BACKBONE BIOASSAY DECISION DIVISION FIRMNESS FORECAST JUDGMENT JUDICIAL SENTENCE VOLITION

DETERMINATIVE FINAL FORMANT SHAPING LIMITING
(MOST —) DOMINANT

DETERMINE END FIT FIX GET RUN TEST WILL ASSAY AWARD JUDGE PITCH WIELD ADJUST ASSESS ASSIGN ASSOIL CHOOSE DECERN DECIDE DECREE DEFINE DESCRY DETECT DETERM DEVISE FIGURE GOVERN PERFIX SETTLE ACCOUNT ADJUDGE ANALYZE APPOINT ARRANGE COMPUTE DELIMIT DERAIGN DISPOSE RESOLVE TERMINE COGNOSCE CONCLUDE DISCOVER PINPOINT INFLUENCE
(— FINENESS) SET SETT
(— PATERNITY) AFFILIATE
(— RATE) ASSESS
(— ROOT) EXTRACT

DETERMINED SET BENT DERN FIRM GRIM BOUND GIVEN STOUT UPSET BITTER DOGGED GRITTY INTENT MULISH STURDY DECIDED SETTLED DECISIVE FOREGONE PERVERSE RESOLUTE RESOLVED STUBBORN

DETERMINER GENE CHANCE PLASMAGENE

DETERMINING CRUCIAL

DETERMINIST JABARITE

DETEST DAMN HATE ABHOR CURSE LOATHE CONDEMN DESPISE DISLIKE DENOUNCE EXECRATE ABOMINATE

DETESTABLE FOUL HORRID ODIOUS BLASTED HATABLE HATEFUL HELLISH HIDEOUS ACCURSED DAMNABLE HATEABLE INFAMOUS INFERNAL MALEDICT ABHORRENT ABOMINABLE

DETESTATION ODIUM HATRED HORROR LOATHING ANTIPATHY

DETHRONE DEPOSE DIVEST UNCROWN

DETONATE FIRE BELCH BLAST SHOOT EXPLODE DETONIZE

DETONATION BLAST KNOCK AMBITUS PINGING PINKING

DETONATOR CAP FUSE FUZE FUSEE FUZEE SQUIB TORPEDO INITIATOR

DETOUR BYPASS CIRCUIT REROUTE DIVERSION ROUNDABOUT

DETRACT TAKE DECRY DEDUCT DEFAME DETRAY DIVERT VILIFY ASPERSE TRADUCE BELITTLE DEROGATE DIMINISH DISTRACT MINIMIZE PROTRACT SUBTRACT WITHDRAW
(— FROM) IMPEDE

DETRACTION CALUMNY SCANDAL SLANDER ZOILISM

DETRIMENT COST HARM HURT LOSS SORE WOUND DAMAGE DAMNUM DENIAL INJURY BEATING EXPENSE JACTURE DISFAVOR MISCHIEF

DETRIMENTAL ADVERSE CAPITAL HARMFUL HURTFUL LOSSFUL

DAMAGING INVIDIOUS PERNICIOUS PREJUDICIAL
(— TO HEALTH) HARD

DETRITUS OUTWASH SHINGLE SHEETWASH

DEUCALION (FATHER OF —) PROMETHEUS
(MOTHER OF —) CLYMENE
(SON OF —) HELLEN ORESTHEUS AMPHICTYON
(WIFE OF —) PYRRHA

DEUCE TWO DIANTRE DICKENS
(WILD —) FREAK

DEUCEDLY BLAME BLAMED

DEUEL (SON OF —) ELIASAPH

DEUTERIUM DIPLOGEN

DEUTEROGAMY DIGAMY

DEUTOMALA LABIUM

DEUX JOURNEES, LES
(CHARACTER IN —) ARMAND MIKELI MAZARIN
(COMPOSER OF —) CHERUBINI

DEVA DEV DEWA SURA ANGEL DEITY

DEVASTATE NUKE EXILE HARRY HAVOC WASTE DEVAST RAVAGE ATOMIZE DESTROY PILLAGE PLUNDER SCOURGE DEMOLISH

DEVASTATED WASTE

DEVASTATING DEADLY LETHAL SAVAGE CRUSHING FEROCIOUS MURDEROUS

DEVASTATION RUIN SACK EXILE HAVOC WASTE WRACK HARASS RAVAGE SACCAGE SACKAGE SACCADGE

DEVASTATOR LOCUST

DEVELOP BUD RUN BOOM COOK FORM GROW STEM TILL ARISE BREAK BREED BUILD ERECT RIPEN SHOOT APPEAR BRANCH DETECT EVOLVE EXPAND FLOWER FULFIL MATURE REVEAL UNFOLD UNFURL BLOSSOM BURGEON BURNISH EDUCATE ENLARGE EVOLUTE EXPOUND FULFILL UNCOVER DEVELOPE DISCLOSE DISCOVER DISVELOP ENGENDER GENERATE INCUBATE MANIFEST
(— A HEAD) HEART
(— BULB) BOTTOM
(— COLOR) AGE
(— CRACKS) ALLIGATOR
(— FLAVOR) BREATHE
(— WELL) COTTON

DEVELOPABLE TORSE

DEVELOPED DEEP FORWARD
(— AFTER BIRTH) ACQUIRED
(FULLY —) BOLD ADULT FLORID FORMED SUMMED
(GREATLY —) ADVANCED
(IMPERFECTLY —) ABORTIVE
(INCOMPLETELY —) SEED

DEVELOPER ELON SOUP METOL ORTOL AMIDOL GLYCIN KACHIN QUINOL BUILDER GLYCINE RODINAL

DEVELOPING
(SUFF.) PLASTIC

DEVELOPMENT WAX DRIFT EVENT HATCH ESTATE GROWTH DESCENT GENESIS PROCESS STATURE BREEDING INCREASE ONTOGENY

PEDIGREE UPGROWTH UPSPRING
(— OF SEX) DIOECISM
(FULL —) BLOW MATURITY
(HIGHEST —) BLOOM
(NORMAL —) APHANISIA
(SUBSEQUENT —) SEQUEL
(THEMATIC —) CONTINUITY
(UNEXPECTED —) ACCIDENT
(PREF.) PLASTO
(SUFF. PLASIA PLASIS PLASM(A)
(IA)(IC) PLAST(IC)(Y) PLASY

DEVI UMA KALI DURGA GAURI CHANDI SHAKTI BHAVANI BHOWANI HIMAVAT MAHADEVI HAIMAVATI
(FATHER OF —) HIMAVAT
(HUSBAND OF —) SHIVA

DEVIANT KINKY ABERRANT DIVERGENT

DEVIATE ERR RUN WRY YAW LEAN MISS VARY VEER BEVEL BREAK DRIFT LAPSE SHEER SPORT START STRAY WAIVE CHANGE DEPART DETOUR DIVERT RECEDE SQUINT SWERVE WANDER DECLINE DEFLECT DIGRESS DIVERGE INCLINE REFLECT ABERRANT ABERRATE DEROGATE
(— FROM VERTICAL) HADE

DEVIATING SKEW DEVIANT DEVIOUS ERRATIC SINUOUS ABERRANT INDIRECT

DEVIATION BOW YAW HELM JUMP SKEW TURN DRIFT LAPSE QUIRK SHEER TWIST ABRASH BATTER CHANGE DETOUR FIGURE SPREAD ANOMALY BRISURE LICENCE LICENSE ACCURACY DRIFTAGE LATITUDE SOLECISM VARIANCE ABERRATION
(— OF COLOR) ABRASH
(STANDARD —) SIGMA

DEVICE (ALSO SEE INSTRUMENT) ARM ART DIE DOG DOP EYE FAN FLY FOB GAG GIN GUN HOG JIG KEY MOP MOT PEN SET TIP TUP WAY WIT ARCH BELL BOND BOOM BUFF COIN COMB COUP DARE DOPP DRAG DRIP FAKE FIRE FLAG FORK FROG FUSE FUZE GAGE GATE GOBO GRAB GRIP GYRO HASP HAUL HEAD HECK HORN IRIS IRON JACK KEEP KITE LAMP LENS LOCK MOVE MULE MUTE NAIL PACE PAGE PAWK PLAN PLOW POKE PUMP REEL SEAL SHOE SHUT SIGN SLAY SLEY SLUR SNAP SPUD STOP STUD SUMP TOOL TRAP TRIP VICE WEIR WHIM WHIP WIND WING WOLF ALARM APRON BADGE BALUN BITCH BLOCK BREAK BRUSH CHECK CLAMP CODER COVIN CRAMP CROSS DODGE DRIER DRIFT DRIVE DRYER DUMMY FADER FANCY FLAIL FLARE FLASH FLIRT FLOAT GAUGE GLAND GORGE GRIPE GUARD GUIDE GUILE HICKY HINGE HOKUM IMAGE KAZOO KEYER LADLE LASER LATCH LEVEL LIDAR LINAC MATCH MODEM OTTER PARER PLATE PROBE PUNKA SCREW SHADE SHANK SHIFT SIEVE SIGHT SIGIL

SIREN SIZER SKATE SLAVE SLICK SLIDE SLING SONDE SPOOL SPOUT SQUIB STAMP STILL STOOL STOVE SWEEP SWELL TABLE TABUT TAMER THIEF TIMER TORCH TRUER TUNER UNION VERGE AGRAFE AIRWAY ALARUM ALINER ANCHOR ARREST BAILER BASTER BEACON BEATER BECKET BEDDER BEEPER BINDER BLOWER BOBBIN BOOMER BRIDLE BROOCH BUCKLE BUFFER BULLEN BUMPER BUNGEE BUNTER BURNER BUTTON CHARGE CIPHER COOKER DASHER DECEIT DERAIL DESIGN DIMMER DOFFER DOTTER DRIVER DROGUE DUMPER EMBLEM ENGINE EVENER FABRIC FALLER FEEDER FENDER FILLER FILTER FINDAL FINDER FORMER GADGET GLAZER GOFFER GOGGLE GRADER GRATER GRISLY GUIDER HANGER HEATER HICKEY HOLDER HOOTER INVENT JIGGER JOGGER KEEPER KICKER LAYBOY LETOFF LIFTER LOOPER MARKER MIRROR MODULE MORTAR MOTHER NAVAID NIPPLE NONIUS NOTION PACKER PEELER PICKUP PLAYER PLOUGH PORTER POTEYE PULLER PUNKAH REROLL RINGER ROCKET ROLLER ROOTER ROTULA ROUTER SACKER SADDLE SAFETY SANDER SCALER SCHEME SCREEN SEALER SEEKER SENSOR SETTER SHAKER SHIELD SIFTER SIGNAL SINKER SIPPER SLEIGH SLICER SLIDER SLIMER SLOPER SLUICE SOCKET SOLION SORTER SPACER SPRING STONER STYLUS SUCKER SWITCH TACTIC TAGGER TAPPER TELLER TEMPLE TESTER TILLER TRACER TUCKER TUNNEL TURNER WARMER WASHER WEANER WEEDER WHEEZE WINDER WINNOW WORKER ADAPTER ADJUNCT AERATOR AGRAFFE ALIGNER AUTOCUE BALANCE BECKETT BIMETAL BIMORPH BINDING BLEEDER BLEEPER BLENDER BLINKER BLOCKER BLOWOFF BLOWOUT BOOKEND BOOSTER BREAKER CALTROP CHIPPER CLAPPER COMPASS DASHPOT DISHMOP DIVISOR DRAWOFF DRESSER DRINKER EARPICK EDUCTOR EJECTOR EMPRESA EXCITER FACEBOW FASHION FETLOCK FICELLE FICTION FITMENT FIXTURE FLASHER FLIPPER FLUSHER FLYFLAP FRISKET GAUFFER GIMMICK GLASSES GRAINER GRENADE GRIDDLE GRILLER GRINDER GRIPPER GRIZZLY GROMMET GROOVER GROWLER GUDGEON GUZZLER HATCHER HELIDON IGNITER IMAGINE IMPRESA IMPRESS INFUSER INHALER IRONMAN KICKOFF KNOTTER LIGHTER MACHINE MUFFLER OOGRAPH PIGTAIL PLOTTER POINTER PRESSER RATCHET RATTLER RECEDER

REDUCER RELEASE ROASTER
ROSETTE SAMPLER SCALPER
SCANNER SCOGGAN SCRAPER
SCUPPER SERVANT SETBACK
SETOVER SETWORK SHACKLE
SHEDDER SHIFTER SHIPPER
SHOOFLY SHUTTER SHUTTLE
SINKBOX SKIMMER SLAPPER
SLEEVER SLINGER SLITTER
SLUDGER SLUSHER SNAPPER
SNIFFER SNIGGLE SNORKEL
SNUBBER SNUFFER SNUGGER
SONOVOX SOUNDER SPARGER
SPEEDER SPLICER SPOTTER
SPRAYER SQUEEZE STACKER
STAPLER STARTER STEMMER
STENTER STIRRER STOPPER
STRIKER STRIPER SUCTION
SWATTER SWEEPER SYRINGE
TAMBOUR TENDRIL TENSION
THEORIC THINNER TICKLER
TOKAMAK TREADLE TRINDLE
TRIPPER TRIPPET TUMBLER
TURNOUT TWISTER WASHOUT
WRINGER ABSORBER ADJUSTER
AQUASTAT BACKSTAY BAROSTAT
BIOMETER BLOCKING BOOTJACK
BRAILLER BREATHER BRONTEUM
BUSINESS BUSYBODY CATAPULT
CATHETER COLOPHON CONTOISE
COUPLING CROTCHET CRYOTRON
DAMPENER DEHORNER DERAILER
DIFFUSER DIRECTOR DISPOSER
DOORSTOP DROPHEAD DUPLEXER
EARPHONE EPISEMON ESPRESSO
EXPLODER FAIRLEAD FAKEMENT
FASTENER FLASHGUN FLYBRUSH
FUELIZER GASCHECK GATHERER
GIMCRACK GUNSTICK GYROSTAT
HALLMARK HANDTRAP HEADGEAR
HOLDBACK IMPROVER INKSTAND
IRENICON IRISCOPE ISOLATOR
KNOCKOUT LAUNCHER LEEBOARD
LOXOCOSM LUNARIUM
MNEMONIC MOLITION NEOSTYLE
ODOGRAPH OVERLIFT OVERRIDE
PACIFIER PARAVANE PENWIPER
PINWHEEL PULSATOR PYROSTAT
QUADRANT QUENTISE REFILTER
REHEATER REPEATER RETARDER
REVERSER SCORCHER SCOTCHER
SCRAWLER SCUTCHER SELECTOR
SHRINKER SILENCER SILVERER
SINKBOAT SMOOTHER
SNOWPLOW SNOWSHOE SPLITTER
SPREADER SPROUTER SQUEEGEE
SQUEEZER STOPWORK STRAINER
STRINGER STRIPPER STROPPER
SURFACER SWEATBOX TELETYPE
TELLTALE TERMINAL THROWOFF
THROWOUT TRAVELER TRAVERSE
TRIANGLE NEURISTOR PINSETTER
PROJECTOR STRATAGEM
MARTINGALE PERIPHERAL
PINSPOTTER ACCELERATOR
(— FOR BENDING PIPE) HICKEY
(— FOR BORING WELLS) TIGER
(— FOR CONCENTRATING ORE)
JIGGER
(— FOR PUTTING IN GEAR) STRIKER
(— IN LOOM) FEELER TEMPLE
(— ON FLAG) UNION
(— PLACED OVER CHIMNEY) JACK

(— PROTECTING DENTIST'S HAND)
THIMBLE
(— THAT CONVERTS SIGNALS)
MODEM
(— TO LOCATE AN OBJECT) LIDAR
(— TO RETAIN COFFEE GROUNDS)
GRECQUE
(ARTIFICIAL —) PROSTHESIS
(AUTOMATIC —) BRAIN
(BRAKE —) CALIPER
(CENTRIFUGAL —) CYCLONE
(CLEVER —) COUP KNACK
(COMPUTER —) WAND MOUSE
TERMINAL ACCUMULATOR
(COMPUTER CONTROL —) PADDLE
(CONVERTING —) MODEM
(CUBICAL BULB —) FLASHCUBE
(DISTINGUISHING —) SPOT
(ELECTORNIC —) MASER
(ELECTRICAL —) OVONIC
(ELECTRONIC —) DME NEURISTOR
(FILM —) MOVIOLA
(FILM EDITING —) MOVIOLA
(GAMBLING —) HOLDOUT
(GLASSBLOWER'S —) DUMMY
(HAMPERING —) HOBBLES
(HEATING —) ETNA
(HERALDIC —S) ARMS
(LISTENING —) BUG
(LITERARY —) FRAME
(MAGICIAN'S —) FAKE FEKE CRAFT
(MIXING —) CRUTCHER
(MUSIC —) HOOK
(NAVIGATIONAL —) LORAN
(OPTICAL —) NIGHTSCOPE
(PAGING —) BEEPER
(POLISHING —) WAGWAG
(PYROTECHNIC —) FOUNTAIN
(RHETORICAL —) ANAPHORA
(ROTATION —) TACH
(SHIELDING —) GOBO
(SIGHTING —) ALIDADE
(SIGNALLING —) CRICKET
(SKILLFUL —) ART
(SOUND —) PINGER
(SPEECH —) ITALICS
(SWIMMING —) SNORKEL
(THEATRICAL —) SLOAT SLOTE
(TIMEKEEPING —) HOROLOGE
(TOROIDAL —) TOKAMAK
(WATER-RAISING —) JANTU SWEEP
CHURRUS
(WEAVING —) BOAT ENGINERY
(SUFF.) STAT(IC)(ICS)
(MUSICAL —) INA INE
DEVIL DEL IMP BENG BHUT BOGY
DEIL HAZE MAHU NICK PUCK QUED
WOLF WOND ANNOY BOBBY
BOGEY BOGIE CHORT CLOOT
DEMON DEUCE EBLIS FIEND
HARRY SATAN SCRAT SHEDU
TAIPO TEASE AMAMON BELIAL
DAEMON DIABLE DIABLO HORNIE
NICKIE PESTER RAGMAN SORROW
THURSE AMAIMON ANHANGA
CLOOTIE DIANTRE DICKENS
GREMLIN LUCIFER MAHOUND
RUFFIAN SERPENT SHAITAN
TORMENT WARLOCK WENDIGO
WINDIGO APOLLYON BAALPEOR
BEELPEOR BELFAGOR CAGNAZZO
CURUPIRA DEVILING DEVILKIN
DIABOLUS MEPHISTO MISCHIEF

OBIDICUT PLOTCOCK WIRRICOW
WORRICOW WORRYCOW
BEELZEBUB
(BLUE —S) MARE
(PREF.) DIABOL(O)
DEVILFISH RAY MANTA
DEVIL-IN-A-BUSH NIGELLA
DEVILISH DARING DEUCED DEVILY
RAKISH WICKED DEMONIC
EXTREME FIENDLY HELLISH
INHUMAN SATANIC DEMONIAC
DIABOLIC FIENDISH INFERNAL
SATURNINE
DEVILISHLY DEUCED DEUCEDLY
DEVILKIN IMP
DEVIL'S CLUB FATSIA
DEVIL'S COACHHORSE DARDAOL
DEVIL'S DISCIPLE (AUTHOR OF —)
SHAW
(CHARACTER IN —) DICK ESSIE
JUDITH DUDGEON ANDERSON
BURGOYNE
DEVIL'S-MILK WARTWEED
WARTWORT
DEVIL'S-TREE DITA
DEVIOUS DEEP ERRING LOUCHE
ROVING SHIFTY SUBTLE TRICKY
OBLIQUE PLAITED VAGRANT
WINDING HAVERING INDIRECT
RAMBLING SCHEMING TORTUOUS
AMBAGIOUS MEALYMOUTHED
DEVISE AIM CAST COOK FIND GIVE
PLAN PLOT WARP WILL ARRAY
FANCY FRAME FUDGE IMAGE
LEAVE SHAPE WEAVE ADVISE
CONVEY DECOCT DESIGN DEVICE
DIVIDE DIVINE INVENT SCHEME
AGITATE APPOINT ARRANGE
BETHINK COMMENT COMPASS
CONCERT CONCOCT CONSULT
IMAGINE PREPARE PROJECT
BEQUEATH CONTRIVE
DEVISED INVENIT
DEVISER FINDER ARTIFICER
DEVISING DEVICE DEVISAL
FORGERY
DEVITALIZE DULL DEADEN
DEVITALIZED DEGENERATE
DEVITRIFIED AMBITTY
DEVOID FREE VAIN VOID EMPTY
BARREN EXPERT VACANT SINCERE
WANTING DESOLATE
(— OF) BOUT EMPTY
(— OF HELP) AIDLESS
(— OF KINDNESS) CRUEL
(— OF MERCY) BRUTAL
(— OF MIND) AMENTAL
(— OF VALUE) HOLLOW
DEVOLUTION DESCENT
DEVOLVE FALL PASS VEST RESULT
BLOSSOM SUCCEED OVERTURN
TRANSFER TRANSMIT
DEVOTE VOW ALLY AVOW DOOM
GIVE LEND TAKE TURN APPLY
DEVOW ADDICT ATTACH BESTOW
DEPUTE DESIGN DEVOVE DIRECT
EMPLOY INTEND RESIGN ADDRESS
APPOINT CONSIGN DESTINE
DEDICATE VENERATE
(— TIME) BOTHER
(— TO MISERY) ACCURSE
DEVOTED MAD HIGH TRUE LIEGE
LOYAL PIOUS ARDENT DEVOUT

DOOMED ENTIRE FERVID LOVING
OBLATE VOTARY VOTIVE ADORING
ARDUOUS JEALOUS SERIOUS
ZEALOUS ADDICTED ATTACHED
CONSTANT FAITHFUL
(— TO COUNTRY) PATRIOTIC
(— TO ENJOYMENT) APOLAUSTIC
(OVERLY —) SUPERSTITIOUS
DEVOTEE CAT FAN NUN BUFF
MONK YATI ADEPT JNANI ADDICT
BHAGAT BHAKTA DEVOTO DEVOUT
HEPCAT VOTARY VOTEEN ZEALOT
ADMIRER AMATEUR BOPPIST
BOPSTER CINEAST FANATIC
HEPSTER HIPSTER SHAVIAN
TARTUFE AMOURIST BURNSIAN
CABALIST DEVOTARY FOLLOWER
IBSENITE PARTISAN PRIAPIAN
SAVOYARD SIMPLIST TARTUFFE
VOTARESS VOTARIST ALLIGATOR
AFICIONADO
DEVOTION CULT ZEAL ARDOR PIETY
BHAKTI NOVENA ANGELUS
ARABISM CULTISM LOYALTY
PIETISM FIDELITY IDOLATRY
JEALOUSY KAVVANAH KAWWANAH
RELIGION NATIONALISM
(— OF ONESELF) VOW NARCISSISM
(— TO HUMAN WELFARE)
HUMANISM
(— TO LADIES) GALLANTRY
(FERVENT —) ADORATION
(PARENTAL —) PROGENITY
(PL.) HOLIES
(SUFF.) LATER LATRIA LATROUS
LATRY
DEVOTIONAL PIOUS SOLEMN
DEVOUR EAT JAW FRET GULP SWAP
SWOP VOUR GORGE RAVEN SCOFF
WASTE AFRETE ENGULF CONSUME
ENGORGE FRAUNCH SWALLOW
(— GREEDILY) SWILL
(RAVENOUSLY —) WOLF
(SUFF.) VORA VORE VOROUS
DEVOURER LOCUST
DEVOURING PREY EATING GREEDY
VORANT EDACIOUS
DEVOUT GOOD HOLY WARM
FROOM GODLY GRACY PIOUS
HEARTY INWARD SOLEMN
CORDIAL DEVOTED GODLIKE
PITEOUS SAINTLY SINCERE
REVERENT PIETISTIC PRAYERFUL
RELIGIOUS PIETISTICAL
SANCTIMONIOUS
(NOT —) LINK
DEVOUTNESS PIETY DEVOTION
DEW DAG RIME BLOOM FROST
TEARS MOISTEN REFRESH
MOISTURE
(— METER) PAGOSCOPE
(NIGHT —) SERENE
(PREF.) DROSO RORI
DEWBERRY MAYES
DEWDROP PEARL
DEWLAP JOWL GULLET JOLLOP
CHOLLER WATTLES
(— OF MALE MOOSE) BELL
DEWY DAMP RORY MOIST RORAL
RORIC RORID GENTLE ROSCID
DEXTERITY ART CHIC CRAFT KNACK
SKILL STROIL ABILITY ADDRESS
AGILITY APTNESS CUNNING

FINESSE SLEIGHT APTITUDE
DEFTNESS FACILITY
(— IN ARMS) CHIVALRY
DEXTEROUS APT FLY DEFT FEAT
HEND NEAT WISE ADEPT CANNY
CLEAN FEATY HANDY HAPPY
HENDE JIMMY QUICK READY
SMART TIGHT ADROIT ARTFUL
CLEVER DRAFTY CUNNING SLEIGHT
DEXTROUS HANDSOME SKILLFUL
SLEIGHTY
DEXTEROUSLY YARELY HANDILY
DEXTRAN GLUCOSAN
DEXTROROTATORY POSITIVE
DEXTRORSE EUTROPIC
DEXTROSE AME CERELOSE
DHAK DAK PALAS PULAS
DHAVA BAKLI
DHOLE KOLSUN
DHOW BUGALA LATEEN SAMBUK
SAMBOUK LATEENER
DHRITARASHTRA (BROTHER OF —)
PANDU
(FATHER OF —) VYASA
VICHITRAVIRYA
(SON OF —) DURYODHANA
(WIFE OF —) GANDHARI
DHYANA JHANA
DIABASE OPHITE DOLERITE
THOLEITE
DIABOLICAL CRUEL WICKED
DEMONIC HELLISH INHUMAN
SATANIC VIOLENT DEMONIAC
DEVILISH DIABOLIC FIENDISH
INFERNAL
DIABOLISM SATANISM
DIACETATE ACETIN
DIACONATE DEACONRY
DIACONICON PARABEMA
DIACRITIC HACEK TILDE UMLAUT
MODIFIER
DIAD DIGONAL TWOFOLD
DIADEM TAJ MIND CROWN TIARA
ANADEM CIRCLE EMBLEM FILLET
CIRCUIT CORONET HEADBAND
DIAERESIS TREMA CESURA
CAESURA DIALYSIS
DIAGNOSE ANALYZE IDENTIFY
KNOWLEDGE
DIAGONAL BIAS SLANT SLASH
COUNTER SOLIDUS VIRGULE
BENDWISE DIAGONIC
DIAGONALLY BIAS ASLOPE
BENDWAYS BENDWISE
DIAGRAM MAP PLAN PLOT TREE
CARTE CHART EPURE GRAPH
PARSE DESIGN FIGURE SCHEMA
SCHEME SYMBOL YANTRA
ISOGRAM ISOTYPE SECTION
VIAGRAM PICTOGRAM
PICTOGRAPH
(KIND OF —) FEYNMAN
DIAGRAMMATIC GRAPHIC
DIAGRAPH OE
DIAL NOB CALL FACE KNOB WATCH
DIACLE JIGGER AZIMUTH CRYSTAL
DECLINER HOROLOGE INCLINER
RECLINER
DIAL BIRD DAYAL DHYAL
DIALECT (ALSO SEE LANGUAGE) HO
KA WU GEG GIZ KHA LAI SAC TWI
AMOY CANI CANT DRAA EFIK EGBA
EPIC GEEZ GHEG GONA GUEG

IOWA ITZA KORA MANX NAMA
NORN OGAM PALI SAUK SHOR
SOGA TALK TCHI TOSK TUBA ALTAI
ARGOT ASURI ATTIC CONOY DORIC
FANTI GHEEZ GHESE HAKKA IDIOM
IONIC IOWAY IRAQI KANSA KAREL
KOINE LADIN LINGO MAZUR
MOPAN MUKRI NGOKO OGHAM
PARSI PUNIC SABIR SAXON SCOTS
SLANG TIGRE TSCHI VALVE VOGUL
ZMUDZ AEOLIC AGNEAN ASANTE
ATSINA AWADHI BADAGA BRETON
BROGUE CANTON CREOLE DEBATE
DUNGAN FAEROE FANTEE FURLAN
GASCON GULLAH GUTNIC HARARI
HARAYA IBANAG ISINAI ITAVES
JARGON KABYLE KANSAS KHAMIR
KORANA KVITSH LADAKI LADINO
LAHULI LALLAN LEDDEN LIBYAN
PARSEE PATOIS PATTER PICARD
SANTEE SCOTCH SCOUSE SHARRA
SKAGIT SPEECH SUDANI SWATOW
SYRIAC SZEKEL TAVAST TONGUE
TUSCAN YANKEE ZENAGA ACADIAN
AEOLIAN AMOYESE ANGLIAN
ASHANTI BHOTANI BHUTANI
BUNDELI CATALAN CHILULA
CHUVASH CLATSOP COCKNEY
CORNISH CUZCENO CYPRIOT
FAYUMIC FOOCHOW GEECHEE
GHEGISH GUTNISH JAIPURI
KARAITE KENTISH KITKSAN
KONKANI LADAKHI LALLAND
LEONESE LESBIAN MALTESE
MARSIAN MARWARI MERCIAN
MIDLAND MULTANI MUNDARI
OLONETS PANAYAN PRAKRIT
SAHIDIC SANPOIL SHORTZY
SOKOTRI SPOKANE SQUAXON
SWABIAN SZEKLER TIGRINA
VAUDOIS WALLOON ABANEEME
ACHMIMIC AKHMIMIC ALGERINE
ARCADIAN ASSYRIAN BASILECT
BAVARIAN BHOJPURI BISCAYAN
BOEOTIAN BOHAIRIC CLAKAMAS
COLVILLE CORSICAN CYPRIOTE
FALERIAN FALISCAN FAROEISH
FRANCIEN FRIULIAN GARHWALI
HARARESE IZCATECO KANESIAN
KARELIAN KERMANJI KICKAPOO
KINGWANA LACANDON LANGUAGE
LAWLANTS MAGHREBI MAGHRIBI
MAITHILI MANDAEAN MANDARIN
MANISIAN MAZATECO MAZURIAN
MEMPHITE NABATEAN NEENGATU
PANAYANO PEKINESE RABBINIC
SALTEAUX SOULETIN SOUTHERN
TAUNGTHU TIGRINYA TIRHUTIA
TUNISIAN VENERIAN VIENNESE
NORTHUMBRIAN
(ENGLISH — IN LIVERPOOL)
SCOUSE
(ESKIMO —) INUIT INUKTITUT
(STRANGE —) GIBBERISH
(PL.) WU ANGLIAN
DIALECTIC PILPUL
DIALOGUE ION CRITO DIALOG
EPILOG PATTER PHAEDO TIMAEUS
COLLOQUY DUOLOGUE EPILOGUE
EXCHANGE PHAEDRUS
COLLOCUTION
(—S OF BUDDHA) SUTRA SUTTA
(COMIC —) LAZZO

DIAMETER BORE GAGE GEAR MOOT
GAUGE WIDTH MODULE
(— OF BULLET) CALIBER CALIBRE
(— OF PELVIS) CONJUGATA
(— OF PUPIL) APERTURE
(— OF WIRE) GAGE GAUGE
DIAMOND GEM ICE BORT LASK PICK
ROCK ROSE BAHIA BOORT BORTZ
DORJE FANCY FIELD JAGER JEWEL
LOZEN MACLE MELEE POINT
RHOMB RIVER SANCY SPARK
STONE TABLE VAJRA ADAMAS
BOARTS CANARY CARBON JAEGER
LASQUE ORLOFF PENCIL REGENT
RONDEL SHINER TABLET
ADAMANT BRIOLET CARREAU
CRYSTAL FISHEYE INFIELD
LOZENGE PREMIER RHOMBUS
SPARKLE CORUNDUM KOHINOOR
RONDELLE SPARKLER BRIOLETTE
(— CUT TOO THIN) FISHEYE
(— MOLDER) DOP
(— STATE) DELAWARE
(— UNIT) INNING
(— USED FOR ENGRAVING) SHARP
(BLACK —) CARBONADO
(FLAT —) LASQUE
(GLAZIER'S —) QUARREL
(IMITATION —) SCHLENTER
(INFERIOR GRADE OF —) FLAT
(PASTE —) RHINESTONE
(PERFECT —) PARAGON
(PURE WHITE —) RIVER
(ROUGH —) BRAIT
(SINGLE —) SOLITAIRE
(TRANSPARENT —) CRYSTAL
(YELLOW —) CANARY
(PL.) MELANGE
DIAMOND BIRD PARDALOTE
DIAMORPHINE HEROIN
DIANA LUCINA TRIVIA ARTEMIS
(BROTHER OF —) APOLLO
(FATHER OF —) JUPITER
(MOTHER OF —) LATONA
DIANA MONKEY ROLOWAY
DIAPASON MONTRE DIAPASE
DIAPAUSE BLOCK
DIAPER FUR DIDY CLOUT DIDIE
NAPPY HIPPEN HIPPIN NAPKIN
NAPPIE DIAPERY
DIAPHANOUS CLEAR SHEER
FRAGILE DIAPHANE VAPOROUS
DIAPHONY ORGANUM TRIPHONY
DIAPHORETIC BUCCO BUCHU
BUCKU BORAGE DIAPNOIC
HIDROTIC SUDATORY SASSAFRAS
PILOCARPINE
DIAPHRAGM IRIS RIFF SLIT APRON
PHREN SKIRT WAFER DECKER
PLATEN MIDRIFF PHRAGMA
SKIRTING TRAVERSE TYMPANUM
(KIND OF —) IRIS
(PREF.) PHREN(O)
DIAPHRAGMATIC PHRENIC
DIARIST ENTERER
DIARRHEA LAX FLUX LASK GURRY
RELAX SCOUR SPRUE PURGING
SQUIRTS LIENTERY
DIARY LOG RECORD DAYBOOK
DIURNAL JOURNAL REGISTER
EPHEMERIS
DIASKEUAST EDITOR REVISER
DIASPORA GALUT GOLAH GALUTH

DIASPORE MIGRULE
DIASTASE MALT ENZYME AMYLASE
DIATOM BRITTLEWORT
ASTERIONELLA
DIATOMITE TRIPOLI
DIATONIC ACHROMATIC
DIATRIBE SATIRE SCREED
HARANGUE INVECTIVE
DIAZAPAM VALIUM
DIB DAP DIP DIBBLE DIBSTONE
DIBBLE DAP DIB DABBLE DIBBER
KIPPIN TRIFLE DIBBLER KIPPEEN
DIBRI (SON OF —) SHELOMITH
DIBS COCKAL
DICAST HELIAST JURYMAN
DICE CHOP CUBE DEES BONES
CRAPS FLATS LOWMEN REJECT
CHECKER IVORIES
(— GAME) SET RAPHE MUMCHANCE
(— HAVING FOUR SPOTS) QUATRE
(FALSE —) GOAD TATS GOURD
GRAVIERS SQUARIER STOPDICE
(HIGHEST THROW AT —)
APHRODITE
(LOADED —) TOPS DOCTOR
(LOWEST THROW AT —) AMBSACE
(PAIRED NUMBERS AT —) DUPLET
DOUBLETS
(2, 3, OR 12 ON 1ST —) MISSOUT
(PREF.) ASTRAGAL(O)
DICE-BOX RATTLE
DICE PLAYER THROWSTER
DICER HAT DERBY GAMBLER
GRAINER
DICERION DYKER
DICHASIAL BIPAROUS
DICHLORVOS DDVP
DICHONDRA LAWNLEAF
DICHOTOMY DUALITY
DICHROITE IOLITE
DICK TEC
DICKENS HECK DEUCE
(LITTLE —) IMP
DICKER ICRE SWAP DAKER BARTER
HAGGLE BARGAIN CHAFFER
EXCHANGE
DICKEY POOP WEAK DICKY FRONT
GILET SHAKY DONKEY RUMBLE
VESTEE HADDOCK PLASTRON
DICKIE SHAM DICKY FRONT SQUARE
TUCKER STARCHER
DICLINOUS IMPERFECT
DICTATE SAW SAY DITE TELL UTTER
WRITE DECREE DICTUM ENJOIN
IMPOSE INDITE OCTROY ORDAIN
SCHOOL COMMAND DELIVER
REQUIRE SUGGEST WARRANT
DICTAMEN PRESCRIBE
DICTATION DICTAMEN
DICTATOR CHAM CZAR DUCE TSAR
CAESAR PENDRAGON
DICTATORIAL BOSSY LORDLY
CZARIST POMPOUS TSARIST
ARROGANT DOGMATIC ORACULAR
POSITIVE ARBITRARY MAGISTERIAL
DICTION STYLE TERMS PHRASE
IMAGERY LANGUAGE PARLANCE
VERBIAGE
(BAD —) CACOLOGY
(SUFF.) ESE
DICTIONARY GRADUS ALVEARY
CALEPIN LEXICON GLOSSARY
WORDBOOK THESAURUS

(BRITISH —) OED
(PREF.) LEXICO
DICTUM SAY ADAGE AXIOM EDICT DECREE SAYING DICTATE EFFATUM OPINION APOTHEGM PRINCIPLE STATEMENT
DID D CAN DED DEDE DYDE
(— NOT) DIDNA DIDNT
DIDACTIC DRY PREACHY SERMONIC
DIDO ANTIC CAPER PRANK TRICK
(BROTHER OF —) PYGMALION
(FATHER OF —) BELUS
(HUSBAND OF —) SICHAEUS
(LOVER OF —) AENEAS
DIDO AND AENEAS (CHARACTER IN —) DIDO AENEAS BELINDA MERCURY
(COMPOSER OF —) PURCELL
DIE GO BED DEE DOD END HOB HUB PIP ROT SIX TAT BOSS COIN CONK CUBE DADO DEAD DICE DROP EXIT FADE FAIL FALL FINE FIVE FLIT KICK MARK MOLD PART PASS PIKE PILE SEAL TATT TINE WANE CROAK FORCE FUDGE GHOST IVORY NAPOO PATAY PRINT PUNCH QUAIL SHAPE SNUFF SOUGH SPILL STALL STAMP STOCK SWELT CHANCE DEMISE DEPART DOCTOR EXPIRE FAMISH FINISH FORCER FORMER FULLAM MATRIX MULLAR PATRIX PERISH ROLLER STARVE STRIKE TORFEL TORFLE TRANCE VANISH WITHER BLOCKER DECEASE STEPOUT SUCCUMB TESSERA INTAGLIO LANGUISH MISCARRY PUNCHEON TRESPASS TRUSSELL
(— AWAY) FAIL SWOON
(— BEFORE) PREDECEASE
(— BY HANGING) SWING
(— DOWN) FLIT SINK ABATE
(— FOR DRAWING WIRE) WHIRTLE WHORTLE
(— FOR MAKING DRAINPIPE) DOD
(— FOR MOLDING BRICK) KICK
(— FROM HUNGER) AFFAMISH
(— OF COLD) STARVE
(— OF HUNGER) STARVE
(— OF PEDESTAL) SOLIDUM
(— WITH 4 SPOTS) QUATRE
(— WITH 6 SPOTS) CISE SICE SISE SIZE
(COINING —) SICCA
(FRAUDULENT —) FULHAM FULLAM FULLOM
(HOLLOW —) GOURD
(IMPROPER —) FLAT
(LOADED —) TAT DOCTOR FULHAM HIGHMAN LANGRET
(LOWER —) BED
(REVOLVING —) DREIDEL
DIEBACK STAGHEAD EXANTHEMA
DIED DYDE OBIIT WRATE
DIEHARD TORY BLIMP
DIESIS FEINT
DIET BANT FARE FAST FOOD SEIM SEYM BOARD HOFTAG REDUCE SEIMAS VIANDS VICTUS BANTING DIETINE LANDTAG REGIMEN RIKSDAG CONGRESS KREISTAG VOLKSTAG

DIETARY LOCAL
(— LAWS) KASHRUTH
DIETER SLIMMER
DIETETICS SITOLOGY
DIETHER APIOL APIOLE DIOXANE
DIETING BANTING
DIFFER VARY RECEDE SQUARE COMPARE DISCORD DISSENT DIVERGE DISAGREE
DIFFERENCE SHED CHASM CLASH FAVOR BREACH CHANGE DIFFER ANOMALY BRISURE DISCORD DISPUTE QUALITY VARIETY DISTANCE DIVISION IMPARITY VARIANCE
(— IN ELEVATION) HEAD
(— IN EXCHANGE) AGIO
(— IN LATITUDE) SOUTHING
(— IN LONGITUDE) EASTING
(— IN PITCH) COMMA INTERVAL
(— IN PRESSURE) DRAFT DRAUGHT
(— IN WIDTH) BILGE
(— OF OPINION) DISSENT ARGUMENT
(— OF VESSEL'S DRAFT) DRAG
(ANGULAR —) EXPLEMENT
(GRADED —) GRADIENT
(MAKE A —) MATTER
(MINUTE —) SHADE
(POTENTIAL —) EMF
(PRICE —) BASIS
(SMALL —) NUANCE HAIRLINE
DIFFERENT FAR MANY SERE FRESH OTHER PARTY DIVERS SCREWY SUNDRY UNLIKE ANOTHER DISTANT DIVERSE SEVERAL STRANGE UNALIKE UNUSUAL VARIANT VARIOUS CONTRARY DISTINCT MANIFOLD SEPARATE OTHERWISE OTHERGUESS NONIDENTICAL
(NOT —) IDENTIC INDENTICAL
(VERY —) WISE
(PREF.) DIVERSI HETER(O)
DIFFERENTIA MARK LIMIT
DIFFERENTIAL FLUXION
DIFFERENTIATE APLITE DIFFER DISCERN HAPLITE CONTRAST SPECIATE
DIFFERENTIATION ANABOLY DEVIATION DICHOTOMY
(PREF.) ALL(O)
DIFFERING DIVERSE SINGULAR DIVERGENT
DIFFICULT ILL HARD WICK CRAMP CRANK GREAT HEAVY SPINY STEEP STIFF AUGEAN CRABBY CRANKY KNOTTY SEVERE STICKY STRAIT STRONG TICKLE TRAPPY UNEASY UNEATH UPHILL WENETH WICKED ARDUOUS AWKWARD BRITTLE COMPLEX CRABBED DIFFUSE LABORED NERVOUS OBSCURE PAINFUL PERPLEX PRACTIC SERIOUS STICKLE UNNETHE ABSTRACT CUMBROUS FIENDISH PUZZLING SCABROUS STRUGGLE STUBBORN TICKLISH
(— TO BEAR) BITTER
(— TO COMPREHEND) STRANGE
(— TO FOLLOW) DIRTY
(— TO GRASP) FUGITIVE
(— TO HANDLE) SPINOUS

(— TO MANAGE) SURLY STURDY
(— TO OBTAIN) CLOSE
(— TO OVERCOME) STRONG
(— TO PLEASE) CURIOUS
(— TO PRONOUNCE) BREAKJAW
(— TO RAISE) DORTY
(— TO SATISFY) CHOOSY CHOOSEY
(— TO UNDERSTAND) DEEP HIGH SUBTLE CRABBED ABSTRACT ABSTRUSE ESOTERIC
(PREF.) DYS MOGI
DIFFICULTY ADO BAR BOX ILL JAM RUB BUMP CLOG COIL HEAT JAMB KNOT LOCK NODE PAIN PINE SNAG SORE WERE CHECK DOUBT GRIEF NODUS PRESS RIGOR STAND STOUR TRADE APORIA BOGGLE BUNKER HABBLE HOBBLE PLIGHT PLUNGE RUBBER SCRAPE STRAIT TIFTER BARRIER DICKENS GORDIAN PITFALL PROBLEM SQUEEZE ASPERITY DISTRESS HARDNESS HARDSHIP OBSTACLE SEVERITY STRUGGLE
(TEMPORARY —) HICCUP
(UNEXPECTED —) SNAG
(WITH —) SCARCELY
(PREF.) (WITH —) DYS MOGI
DIFFIDENCE DOUBT MODESTY RESERVE SHYNESS DISTRUST HUMILITY TIMIDITY
DIFFIDENT SHY BLATE CHARY MODEST BASHFUL BACKWARD RESERVED RETIRING SHEEPISH
DIFFUSE FULL SHED BLEED EXUDE LARGE STREW WORDY DEFUSE DERIVE DILATE DIVIDE EXPAND EXTEND OSMOSE PROLIX SPREAD SPRING COPIOUS DIALYSE DIALYZE DIFFUND PERFUSE PERPLEX PERVADE PUBLISH RADIATE SCATTER SPARKLE SPRAWLY SPRENGE SUFFUSE VERBOSE CONFUSED DIFFUSED DIOSMOSE DISPERSE PATULENT PATULOUS SPRANGLE
(NOT —) STRICT COMPACT
DIFFUSION SPREAD OSMOSIS BLEEDING DEFUSION
DIG GET HOE JOB NIP CLAW DIKE DYKE GIRD GORE GRUB HOWK LIKE MINE MOOT PICK PION POKE PROD ROOT SINK SLAM SMUG SPIT SPUD SUMP SWOT DELVE DITCH DWELL GAULT GRAFT GRAVE LODGE POACH PROBE SNOUT SPADE START STOCK BURROW DREDGE EXHUME GRAVEL HOLLOW PLUNGE SHOVEL THRUST TUNNEL BEDELVE COSTEAN SPUDDLE UNEARTH EXCAVATE UNDERSTAND
(— IN) EAT ENTRENCH
(— OUT) SCOOP STUMP EXHUME
(— OUT CREVICES) FOSSICK
(— PEAT) SHEUGH
(— POTATOES) LIFT
(— TRENCHES) GRIP LABOR COSTEAN COSTEEN
(— UP) CAST GRUB STUB SPADE STOCK EXHUME UPGRAVE DISINTER
(— WITH NAILS) SCRAPE

(— WITH SNOUT) GROUT
(— WITH STICK) CROW
DIGAMMA VAU
DIGEST COCT CODE DEFY ENDEW ENDUE INDUE RIPEN CODIFY DECOCT DOCKET MATURE SEETHE CONCOCT EPITOME PANDECT SUMMARY CONDENSE SYLLABUS
(— OF ROMAN LAWS) PANDECTS
DIGESTION PEPSIS COCTION EUPEPSY EUPEPSIA
(SUFF.) PEPSIA PEPTIC
DIGESTIVE PEPSIN PEPTIC DIGERENT
DIGGER DIG PAL PLOW MINER BANKER BILDAR DRUDGE PLOUGH COMRADE PEATMAN PIONEER PLODDER TRENCHER
(POST HOLE —) LOY
DIGGING DIG DIKAGE DYKAGE STRIPPING
DIGHT DAB RUB DECK DINK DITE WIPE ADORN DICHT DRESS EQUIP ORDER RAISE TREAT MANAGE REPAIR WINNOW APPOINT CONSIGN PERFORM PREPARE
DIGIT TOE BYTE ONEK UNIT DOIGT POINT THUMB DACTYL FIGURE FINGER HALLUX MEDIUS NUMBER DEWCLAW DIGITAL INTEGER
(BINARY —) BIT BINIT
(EXTRA —) PREPOLLEX
(GROUP OF EIGHT BINARY —S) BYTE
(PREF.) DACTYLIO DACTYL(O)
(SUFF.) DACTYLIA DACTYLOUS
DIGITAL KEY MANUAL
DIGITATE DIGITAL FINGERED
DIGNIFIED GRAND LOFTY MANLY NOBLE REGAL STAID AUGUST LORDLY SEDATE SOLEMN COURTLY EXALTED STATELY TOGATED ELEVATED ENNOBLED MAJESTIC
DIGNIFY DUB ADORN CROWN EXALT GRACE HONOR RAISE ELEVATE ENNOBLE PROMOTE
DIGNITARY DON WIG BABA RAJA CANON RAJAH PRIEST SHERIF DIGNITY HUTUKTU PRELATE PROVOST SHEREEF ALDERMAN HUTUKHTU VESTIARY
DIGNITY DOG CHIC FACE RANK BENCH DINES HONOR IZZAT PRIDE STATE AFFAIR BARONY LAUREL REPOSE BARONRY BEARING DECORUM DUKEDOM EARLDOM FITNESS GRAVITY MAJESTY SHAHDOM STATION WORSHIP CHIVALRY EARLSHIP GRANDEUR NOBILITY
(— OF BISHOP) LAWN
(— OF CARDINAL) HAT
(— OF KING) PURPLE
(ACCIDENTAL —) JOY HAYZ
(EPISCOPAL —) MITER MITRE CATHEDRA
(PAPAL —) TIARA
(SUFF.) DOM SHIP
DIGRAPH CH OE PH RH TH RRH BIGRAM LIGATURE DIPHTHONG
DIGRESS VEER EXCUR DIVERT SWERVE WANDER DEVIATE

DIVERGE EXCURSE DISGRESS DIVAGATE

DIGRESSION ASIDE VAGARY DIGRESS ECBASIS EPISODE EXCURSE PASSAGE TANGENT DISGRESS EXCURSUS SIDESLIP PARENTHESIS
(RHETORICAL —) ECBOLE

DIKE BAR RIB BANK BUND DICE DICK DYKE GALL POND POOL DIGUE DITCH GROIN LEVEE CAUSEY CRADGE CHANNEL DIKELET POWDIKE ABOIDEAU CAUSEWAY ESTACADE SPREADER

DIKER COWAN COWEN

DIKETONE BENZIL BIACETYL DIMEDONE

DIKLAH (FATHER OF —) JOKTAN

DILACTONE LACTIDE ANEMONIN

DILAPIDATE DESTROY

DILAPIDATED BAD BEATEN CREAKY RAGGED RUINED SHABBY WRECKY CRAICHY CREACHY RUINOUS DESOLATE TATTERED WOBEGONE

DILAPIDATION RUIN DECAY DECREPITY DISREPAIR

DILATATION BULB SINUS VARIX JARBOT SPREAD AMPULLA ECTASIA ECTASIS ANEURISM DILATION MYDRIASIS
(— OF ARTERY) ANEURYSM
(— OF TRACHEA) AIRSAC
(SUFF.) ECTASIA ECTASIS

DILATE TENT DELAY PLUMP SWELL WIDEN DELATE EXPAND EXTEND SPREAD AMPLIFY BROADEN DESCANT DIFFUSE DISTEND ENLARGE INFLATE PROLONG STRETCH DISPERSE INCREASE LENGTHEN PROTRACT DISCOURSE

DILATED TURGID VARICOSE

DILATING
(SUFF.) EURYSIS

DILATOR DIOPTER DIOPTRA DIOPTRY DIVULSOR SPECULUM

DILATORY LATE SLOW SLACK SPARE TARDY FABIAN REMISS DILATOR LAGGARD LATREDE TEDIOUS BACKWARD DELAYING INACTIVE SLUGGISH

DILEMMA FIX FORK LOCK NODE BRIKE POSER CHOICE PICKLE PLUNGE CORNUTE SNIFTER JEOPARDY QUANDARY

DILETTANTE LOVER SUNDAY ADMIRER AMATEUR DABBLER DABSTER ESTHETE AESTHETE

DILIGENCE HIE CARE HEED DILLY EFFORT CAUTION HORNING BUSINESS INDUSTRY SEDULITY ASSIDUITY

DILIGENT BUSY HARD TIDY ACTIVE EIDENT ITHAND STEADY CAREFUL EARNEST HEEDFUL OPEROSE PAINFUL PATIENT WORKFUL CAUTIOUS CONSTANT LABOROUS SEDULOUS STUDIOUS

DILL ANET CALM SOYA ANISE UMBEL PICKLE SOOTHE DILLWEED

DILLIDALLY TARRY

DILLY ONER

DILLYDALLY LAG TOY LOAF DELAY DILLY STALL LOITER TRIFLE

DILOGY ECHO

DILUENT CARRIER VEHICLE

DILUTE CUT BREW FUSE LEAN THIN WEAK ALLAY BLUNT DELAY WATER RAREFY REDUCE WEAKEN WHITISH DIMINISH LENGTHEN WATERISH
(— LIQUOR) BREW SPLIT
(— WINE) GALLIZE
(VERY —) SMALL

DILUTED WASHY DILUTE REMISS

DILUTING ATTENUANT

DILUTION (— OF A SERUM) TITER

DIM DIP WAN BLUR DARK DULL FADE GRAY HAZY MIST PALE PALL VEIL BEDIM BLEAK BLEAR BLIND DUSKY DUSTY FAINT FOGGY MISTY STAIN UNLIT BEMIST BLEARY CLOUDY DARKEN DASWEN DIMPSY GLOOMY OBTUSE SHADOW TWILIT BECLOUD DARKISH DISLIMN ECLIPSE OBSCURE OPACATE SHADOWY TARNISH DARKLING OVERCAST CALIGINOUS CREPUSCULAR
(NOT —) FRESH

DIME HOG HOGG DISME TENPENCE TENPENNY
(HALF —) PICAYUNE

DIMEDON METHONE

DIMENHYDRINATE DRAMAMINE

DIMENSION BODY BULK SIZE SCOPE WIDTH ASSIZE DEGREE EXTENT HEIGHT LENGTH MOISON BREADTH PROPORTION MEASUREMENT
(COLOR —) CHROMA
(TYPE —) EM EN
(PL.) GAGE SIZE GAUGE GIRTH EXTENT SIDING MEASURE

DIMENSIONS
(PREF.) (THREE —) STERE(O)

DIMER (— IN EXCITED STATE) EXCIMER

DIMERCAPROL BAL

DIMIDIATE HALVED

DIMINISH GO CUT EBB SAP BATE BURN CHOP DAMP DROP EASE FADE FAIL FINE FRET MELT PARE PINK SINK WANE WEAR ABATE ALLAY BREAK CLOSE DRAFT DWARF ELIDE ERODE LOWER MINCE PETER SLACK SMALL TAPER DAMPEN DEBATE DECOCT DEDUCT DILUTE IMPAIR LESSEN MINISH REBATE REDUCE SLOUGH VANISH WITHER ABRIDGE ASSUAGE CORRODE CURTAIL DEGRADE DEPLETE DEPRESS DETRACT DIMINUE DRAUGHT DWINDLE FRITTER INHIBIT QUALIFY REFRACT RELIEVE TARNISH ADMINISH AMOINDER CONDENSE DECREASE DIMINUTE DISCOUNT MINORATE MITIGATE MODERATE RETRENCH
(— FRONT) PLOY

DIMINISHED SLACK ABATED GRAYED DIMINUTE

DIMINISHING TAPER CRITICAL FLAGGING
(— IN LOUDNESS) CALANDO

DIMINUTION FALL WASTE RABATE DECREASE PERDITION

DIMINUTIVE TOY WEE BABY TINY BANTY DWARF PETTY RUNTY SMALL YOUNG BANTAM LITTLE MIDGET PETITE POCKET MANIKIN MIDGETY MINIKIN SHRIMPY EXIGUOUS
(— OF BAR) SCARP CLOSET SCARPE
(SUFF.) CLE CULE CULUS EL ET ETTE KIN OCK SY ULA ULE

DIMLY DULLY DARKLY FEEBLY SHADOWY

DIMMED BLEARY CLOUDY GRAYED BLEARED

DIMMING GRAYOUT

DIMNESS DIM HAZE MIST SLUR GLOOM CALIGO DARKNESS

DIMPLE DOKE AHMADI AHMEDI RIPPLE GELASIN FOSSETTE

DIM-SIGHTED PURBLIND

DIMWIT DODO DOLT DUMMY AIRHEAD DINGDONG

DIN BUM DUN REEL RERD RIOT UTIS ALARM BABEL BRUIT CHIME CHIRM CLANG DEAVE DEEVE FRUSH NOISE RERDE ALARUM BELDER CLAMOR FRAGOR HUBBUB RACKET RANDAN RATTLE STEVEN TUMULT UPROAR CLANGOR CLATTER DISCORD TURMOIL DINGDONG TINTAMAR

DINAH (BROTHER OF —) LEVI SIMEON
(FATHER OF —) JACOB
(MOTHER OF —) LEAH

DINAR DENARE MARAVEDI

DINARZADE (SISTER OF —) SCHEHERAZADE

DINDLE RING QUIVER THRILL TINGLE TINKLE TREMOR STAGGER VIBRATE

DINE EAT SUP FARE FEAST REGALE

DINER EPICURE GOURMAND

DING DIN BEAT DANG DASH KICK PUSH RING WHIP CLANG DRIVE EXCEL FLING KNOCK PITCH POUND PUNCH THUMP STROKE THRASH THRUST

DINGE DENT DINT BATTER BRUISE TARNISH

DINGHY PRAM SKIFF DINGEY ROWBOAT SHALLOP SNOWBIRD

DINGLE DEN DALE DELL GLEN VALE DIMBLE DUMBLE HOLLOW VALLEY

DINGMAN BUMPER

DINGO WARRAGAL WARRIGAL

DINGUS GADGET DOOHICKEY

DINGY DUN DARK BLACK DIRTY DUSKY GRIMY OURIE SMOKY DINGHY FUSCOUS SUBFUSC SMIRCHED

DINING CENATION
(— HALL) MESS
(PREF.) DEIPNO

DINING ROOM TRICLINIUM

DINKA JANGHEY

DINNER DINE HALL KALE MEAL MEAT NOON BEANO FEAST DINING REPAST BANQUET PUCHERO FUNCTION
(— AT HOME) EATIN
(CEREMONIAL —) SEDER
(PERTAINING TO —) PRANDIAL
(PREF.) DEIPNO

DINOSAUR DIAPSID SAURIAN DUCKBILL NODOSAUR SAUROPOD TROODONT ORNITHISCHIAN

DINT BEAT BLOW DENT DUNT NICK CLOUR DELVE DINGE FORCE NOTCH ONSET POWER PRESS SHOCK ATTACK CHANCE EFFORT STRIKE STROKE IMPRINT EFFICACY STRIKING

DIOCESAN EPISCOPAL

DIOCESE SEE EPARCHY DISTRICT BISHOPRIC

DIODE LED KENOTRON
(— THAT EMITS LIGHT) LED
(KIND OF —) ZENER
(LIGHT-EMITTING —) LED
(TYPE OF —) ZENER

DIOLEFIN DIENE ALLENE HEXADIENE

DIOMEDES (FATHER OF —) MARS TYDEUS
(MOTHER OF —) CYRENE DEIPYLE
(WIFE OF —) AEGIALE

DION (DAUGHTER OF —) EUPHRASIA
(FATHER OF —) HIPPARINUS
(SISTER OF —) ARISTOMACHE
(SLAYER OF —) CALLIPPUS
(TEACHER OF —) PLATO
(WIFE OF —) ARETE

DIONYSUS BACCHUS BROMIOS BROMIUS LENAEUS LIKNITES

DIONYZA (HUSBAND OF —) CLEON

DIOPSIDE VIOLAN ALALITE PYROXENE

DIORITE CORSITE DIABASE ORNOITE APPINITE TONALITE

DIOSCURI ALCIS ANACES ANAKES CASTORES

DIOXIDE SILICA BINOXIDE

DIOXIN TCDD AGENTORANGE

DIP DAP DIB DOP SOP BAIL DROP DUCK DUNK LADE LAVE SINK SOAK BATHE DELVE LADLE LOWER MERSE PITCH SCOOP SLOPE SOUSE SWOOP TAINT CANDLE HOLLOW PLUNGE BAPTIZE DECLINE IMMERGE IMMERSE INCLINE MOISTEN DIPSTICK SUBMERGE GUACAMOLE
(— AND THROW) BAIL BALE
(— IN DANCING) CORTE
(— IN HOT WATER) PLOT
(— INTO) SAMPLE
(— OUT) KEACH

DIPENTENE CINENE CAJUPUTENE

DIPHOSPHATE UDP

DIPHTHONG BIVOCAL

DIPHTHONGIZED BROKEN

DIPLOIDIZE SPERMATIZE

DIPLOMA SANAD DEGREE SUNNUD CHARTER CODICIL PARCHMENT SHEEPSKIN

DIPLOMACY TACT POLICE TREATY
(KIND OF —) GUNBOAT SHUTTLE

DIPLOMAT DEAN ENVOY CONSUL ATTACHE MINISTER
(ISRAELI —) EBAN

DIPLOMATIC SUAVE FECIAL FETIAL

DIPLOPIA POLYOBA AMBIOPIA

DIPNOAN DIPNOID MUDFISH

DIPODY METER METRE DIIAMB SYZYGY

DIPPER BAIL GAWN PIET PLOW GOURD HANDY LADLE SCOOP

SPOON BUCKET DUNKER PIGGIN
PLOUGH TUNKER DUNKARD
PICKLER CALABASH
(ASTRONOMICAL —) WAGON
WAGGON
DIPPING DOOK MERSION
(SUFF.) CLINIC CLINOUS
DIPSOMANIA ENOMANIA
POTOMANIA
DIPTERAN SYRPHID
DIPTEROCARP GURJUN
DIPTERON DIPTER
DIPTEROUS BIALATE
DIRDUM BLOW BLAME DURDUM
OUTCRY REBUKE TUMULT UPROAR
SCOLDING
DIRE DERN EVIL FELL AWFUL FATAL
DEADLY DISMAL DREARY FUNEST
TRAGIC WOEFUL DIREFUL
DOLEFUL DRASTIC FEARFUL
DREADFUL FUNESTAL HORRIBLE
TERRIBLE ULTIMATE
DIRECT AIM BID CON KEN SAY SET
WIS AGYE AIRT BAIN BEAM BEND
BOSS CAST DEAD EDIT EVEN FLAT
FULL GAIN HEAD HELM HOLD
LEAD NEAR NIGH OPEN REIN SEND
SOON SWAY TELL TURN WAFT
WEND WILL WISE AIRTH APPLY
AHEAD AREED BLANK BOUND
BURLY COACH DRESS ETTLE
FLUSH FRAME FRANK GUIDA
GUIDE HIGHT INDEX LEVEL ORDER
PLUMP POINT REFER RIGHT SPEED
STEER TEACH TRAIN UTTER WEISE
WRITE ADVERT ARRECT CUSTOS
DEVOTE ENJOIN ENSIGN FASTEN
GOVERN GRAITH HANDLE HOMELY
HONEST IMPART INDITE INFORM
INTEND LINEAL MANAGE MASTER
MOSTRA REFORM SQUARE
STEADY STRECK TEMPER WITTER
ADDRESS APPOINT COMMAND
CONDUCT CONTROL CONVERT
DEICTIC DESTINE EXECUTE
EXPRESS FRONTAL GENERAL
INSTANT MARSHAL OFFICER
PRESIDE SPADISH ABSOLUTE
ADMONISH CONVERSE DEDICATE
DIRECTOR HOMESPUN IMMEDIAL
INSTRUCT INTIMATE MANUDUCE
MANUDUCT MINISTER OUTRIGHT
REGULATE STRAIGHT
(— AGAINST) LAUNCH
(— ATTENTION) ATTEND
(— BLOW) MARK
(— DOGS) BLOW
(— FALL OF TREE) GUN
(— HELMSMAN) CON CONN
(— HORSE) HUP
(— ITSELF) TENT
(— ONE'S COURSE) HIT
(— PROCEEDINGS) PRESIDE
(— SECRETLY) STEAL
(— SIDEWAYS) SKLENT
(— TO GO) ADDRESS
(— UPWARD) MOUNT
DIRECTED FAST COMPULSORY
(— BACKWARD) RETROGRADE
(— FORWARD) ANTRORSE
(— TOWARD GOAL) HORMIC
(— UPWARD) ERECT
DIRECTING AIM LEADING PRINCIPAL

DIRECTION (ALSO SEE MUSICAL
DIRECTION) AIM RUN WAY AIRT
BENT CARE DUCT EAST EGIS GATE
HAND LEFT PART ROAD RULE
WEST WORD YARD AEGIS ANGLE
COAST DRIFT EAVER KIBLA NORTH
ORDER PARTY POINT QIBLA RANGE
ROUTE SENSE SOUTH TENOR
TREND ASPECT COURSE DESIGN
ADDRESS BEARING BIDDING
CHANNEL COMMAND CONDUCT
CONTROL COUNSEL DICTATE
HEADING HELMAGE MANDATE
PRECEPT STRETCH BEARINGS
CALENDAR DELEATUR DIAGONAL
GUIDANCE STEERAGE STEERING
TENDENCY ORDINANCE
ORIENTATION PRESCRIPTION
(— IN WOOD) GRAIN
(— OF CURRENT) AXIS
(— OF FLOW) SET
(— OF ROCK CLEAVAGE) GRAIN
(— OF WIND) EYE CORNER
(— OUTWARD) BEAM
(—S FOR DELIVERY) ADDRESS
(DANCE —) CALL
(GENERAL —) RUN
(HORIZONTAL —) COURSE AZIMUTH
(MUSICAL —) SEGUE
(NEW —) TURN
(OBLIQUE —) SKEW
(OPPOSITE —) EYE COUNTER
(SINGING —) GIMEL GYMEL
(PREF.) PHORO
(SUFF.) ERLY ERN
(— TO) WARD
DIRECTIVE MEMO GUIDE DICTATE
CIRCULAR
DIRECTLY DUE BANG BOLT DEAD
FLAT GAIN JUST MEAN PLAT PLUM
SLAP SOON PLAIN PLUMB PLUNK
POINT ROUND SHEER SMACK
SOUSE SPANG STANG ARIGHT
CLEVER SIMPLY SQUARE RIGHTLY
SHEERLY OUTRIGHT PROMPTLY
SLAPDASH STRAIGHT PRESENTLY
DIRECTNESS CLARITY IMMEDIACY
DIRECTOR BOSS HEAD COACH
GUIDE PILOT STAFF ARCHON
AUTEUR BISHOP LEADER MASTER
RECTOR WARDEN CURATOR
DESKMAN MANAGER PREFECT
STARETS STERNER TRAINER
ACCENTOR DISPOSER GOVERNOR
PRAEFECT PRODUCER TETRARCH
(BALLET —) REGISSEUR
(FILM —) AUTEUR
DIRECTORY PIE BOOK
DIRGE KEEN SONG ELEGY KINAH
LINOS LINUS QINAH TANGI HEARSE
LAMENT MONODY THRENE
EPICEDE REQUIEM CORONACH
THRENODY ULLAGONE
(PREF.) THREN(O)
DIRIGIBLE BLIMP AIRSHIP
DIRK SNEE SKEAN SWORD DAGGER
SKHIAN SKIVER WHINGER
WHINIARD
DIRT FEN MUD PAY CRUD DUST
GORE GUCK MOOL MUCK NAST
SOIL SUMP CROCK EARTH FILTH
GRIME GROUT SEUCH SEUGH
TRASH FULYIE FULZIE GRAVEL

GROUND GRUNGE REFUSE
MULLOCK SLOTTER MUCKMENT
(— ON PRINTING TYPE) PICK
DIRT-COLORED SORDID
DIRTINESS GRIME JAKES
DIRTY LOW RAY BASE CLAT DIRT
FOUL MOIL MUSS SOIL WORY
BAWDY BLACK CABBY DINGY
FOGGY GRIMY GUSTY HORRY
MUDDY NASTY POUSY SOILY
SULLY BEMIRE CLARTY CLATTY
DEFILE DIRTEN FILTHY FULYIE
FULZIE GREASY GRUBBY GRUNGY
IMPURE MUSSED POUCEY REECHY
SCRIMY SLASHY SLURRY SMIRCH
SMUTTY SOILED SORDID STORMY
BEGRIME BROOKED BROOKIE
BRUCKLE CLOUDED GRUFTED
IMBROIN MUDDIED PIGGISH
RAUNCHY ROYNOUS SCRUFFY
SLOTTER SMUTCHY SQUALID
SULLIED TARNISH UNCLEAN
AMUROOUS SLOBBERY SLOTTERY
SOAPLESS
DIS BELITTLE
DISABLE OUT HOCK LAME MAIM
BREAK CHINK CROCK GRUEL UNFIT
WRECK BRUISE DISMAY UNABLE
WEAKEN CRIPPLE
(— CANNON) SPIKE
(— HORSE) NOBBLE
(— TANK) BELLY
DISABLED LAME INVALID
DISABLING BUM
DISACCHARIDE BIOSE LACTOSE
MALTOSE SUCROSE
DISACCUSTOM DISUSE
DISACKNOWLEDGE DISCLAIM
DISADVANTAGE HURT MISS RISK
LURCH WORRY DAMAGE DENIAL
INJURY STRIKE DICKENS PENALTY
UNSELTH UNSPEED DISAVAIL
DISFAVOR DRAWBACK HANDICAP
DISADVANTAGEOUS HURTFUL
INCONVENIENT
DISAFFECT DEBAUCH ALIENATE
ESTRANGE
DISAFFECTED FALSE UNTRUE
DISEASED DISLOYAL FORSWORN
PERJURED RECREANT
DISAFFECTION DECEIT MUTINY
DISEASE DISGUST DISLIKE
DISORDER HOSTILITY
DISAFFIRM DENY ANNUL REVERSE
DISCLAIM
DISAGREE VARY ARGUE CLASH
DIFFER DISCEPT DISCORD DISSENT
QUARREL CONFLICT
DISAGREEABLE BAD ILL ACID EVIL
FOUL PERT SOUR UGLY VILE
AWFUL CROSS HARSH NASTY
STIFF GREASY PUTRID ROTTEN
SNUFFY STICKY UNEASY UNGAIN
BEASTLY CHRONIC COMICAL
GHASTLY HATEFUL INGRATE
IRKSOME NAUGHTY UNLUSTY
CHISELLY KINDLESS TERRIBLE
UNGENIAL UNLIKELY UNLOVELY
UNSAVORY
DISAGREEABLENESS ILLNESS
ASPERITY
DISAGREEABLY HARSHLY
DISAGREEING ODD DISSENTIVE

DISAGREEMENT BREE CLASH
CROSS FIGHT BREACH FRATCH
DISCORD DISGUST DISPUTE
DISSENT FISSURE MISLIKE
QUARREL WRANGLE ARGUMENT
CLASHING DISTANCY DIVISION
FRICTION SQUABBLE VARIANCE
MISUNDERSTANDING
(IN —) APART
DISALLOW FORBID REJECT
CENSURE DISCLAIM DISPROVE
PROHIBIT
DISAPPEAR DIE FLY DROP FADE
FALL FLEE LIFT PASS SINK WEND
WHOP BREAK CLEAR FAINT LAPSE
SLIDE SLOPE SNUFF REMOVE
RETIRE VANISH EVANISH IMMERGE
DISSOLVE EVANESCE
(— GRADUALLY) ELY FADE DRAIN
EVANESCE
(— SUDDENLY) COOK DUCK BURST
MIZZLE
(— UNEXPECTEDLY) LEVANT
DISAPPEARANCE ECLIPSE
FADEAWAY
DISAPPOINT BALK BILK FAIL FALL
MOCK SOUR UNDO CHEAT SNAPE
BAFFLE DEFEAT DELUDE OUTWIT
THWART BEGUILE DECEIVE
DESTROY FALSIFY NULLIFY
DISPOINT
DISAPPOINTED OUTED BUMMED
THROWN SOREHEAD
DISAPPOINTING FIERCE
FALLACIOUS
DISAPPOINTMENT RUE BALK
DRAG SUCK BAULK LURCH DENIAL
DOWNER LETDOWN COMEDOWN
DISAPPROBATION ODIUM DISLIKE
DISAPPROVAL BAN BOOH HISS
VETO CATCALL CENSURE
DISFAVOR DISGRACE
(EXPRESSION OF —) TUT TUTTUT
(SHOW —) HISS
DISAPPROVE NIX GROAN REJECT
RESENT CENSURE CONDEMN
DISLIKE MISTAKE PROTEST
DISALLOW DISPROVE HARRUMPH
DISAPPROVED DISTASTED
DISAPPROVER WOWSER
DISARM SUBDUE UNSTEEL
DISARRANGE MESS MUSS
DEFORM GARBLE RUFFLE TIFFLE
UNTIDY UNTUNE CLUTTER
CONFUSE DERANGE DISTURB
RUMMAGE SLATTER TROUBLE
COCKBILL DISHEVEL DISORDER
UNSETTLE
(— TYPE) SQUABBLE
DISARRANGEMENT DISARRAY
DISARRAY MESS TASH RIFLE STRIP
CADDLE DISRAY FUFFLE HUDDLE
DESPOIL UNDIGHT DISHEVEL
DISORDER
DISARRAYED UNKEMPT
DISASSEMBLE UNDO STRIP
DEMOUNT DISMOUNT
(— CASK) SHAKE
DISASSEMBLY TAKEDOWN
TEARDOWN
DISASSOCIATE SEVER SEPARATE
DISASTER ILL WOE BALE BLOW
EVIL FATE RUIN GRIEF MISHAP

STROKE REVERSE ACCIDENT CALAMITY CASUALTY EXIGENCY FATALITY

(ONE WHO PREDICTS —) CASSANDRA

DISASTROUS BAD ILL FATAL WEARY SINISTER

DISAVOW DENY DEVOW ABJURE DISOWN RECANT REFUSE DECLINE RETRACT ABNEGATE DISCLAIM DISVOUCH RENOUNCE

DISAVOWAL DENIAL

DISBAND BREAK REDUCE REFORM ADJOURN CASHIER DISMISS RELEASE SCATTER DISSOLVE

DISBAR EXCLUDE

DISBELIEF ATHEISM SCRUPLE ACOSMISM

(EXPRESSION OF —) TUT TUTTUT

DISBELIEVE DOUBT REJECT SUSPECT DISCOUNT DISCREDIT

DISBELIEVER ATHEIST HERETIC INFIDEL

DISBURDEN RID EASE CLEAR UNLOAD DELIVER DISLOAD RELIEVE

(— BY CONFESSION) SHRIVE

DISBURSE SPEND DEFRAY EXPEND OUTLAY DEBURSE

DISC (ALSO SEE DISK) DIAL DISK GONG BLANK MEDAL PATEN PLATE QUOIT COLTER RECORD RONDEL SQUAIL COULTER DISCOID FRISBEE PLATTER ROUNDEL TROCHUS

(— FOR PRESSING HERRINGS) DAUNT

(— ON BIT) ROWEL

(— ON SPINDLE) WHORL

(— ON TAMBOURINE) JINGLE

(— ON TARGET) GONG FRISBEE ROUNDEL

(CILIATED —) VELUM

(COPPER —) ROSETTE

(FLESHY —) SARCOMA

(FLOPPY —) DISKETTE

(HOCKEY —) PUCK

(JELLYFISH —) UMBRELLA

(KIND OF —) LASER SECCHI

(POLISHING —) LAP

(TELEVISION —) SCANNER

DISCANT HOCKET

DISCARD CAST DECK DEFY JILT JUNK MOLT OMIT OUST SHED CHUCK DITCH FLING SCRAP SHUCK SLUFF THROW TRASH CHANGE DECARD DISUSE DIVEST EXCUSS REJECT SLOUGH ABANDON CASHIER DISMISS EXPUNGE FORSAKE ABDICATE JETTISON

(— IN BRIDGE) ECHO

DISCARDED DORMANT OFFCAST

DISCARDING DISPOSAL

DISCERN KEN SEE SPY WIT DEEM ESPY KNOW READ SCAN JUDGE SIGHT BEHOLD DESCRY DETECT DEVISE NOTICE PIERCE SCERNE DIGNOSCE DISCOVER PERCEIVE

(— BY SMELL) SCENT

DISCERNIBLE EVIDENT VISIBLE APPARENT MANIFEST OBSERVABLE

DISCERNING SAGE WISE NASUTE

SHREWD SUBTLE SAPIENT SAGACIOUS PERCEPTIVE PERCIPIENT PENETRATING

DISCERNMENT EYE DOOM GOUT TACT FLAIR SENSE SKILL TASTE ACUMEN INSIGHT ELECTION JUDGMENT SAGACITY SAPIENCE PERCEPTION PENETRATION

DISCHARGE AX DO AXE CAN GUN LET RUN BOLT BOOT CASS DUMP EMIT FIRE FLOW FLUX FREE GIVE KICK PASS POUR QUIT RIFF SACK SEND SHOT VENT VOID BLAST BLEED BRUSH CLEAR DRAIN EGEST EJECT EMPTY EXPEL EXUDE FRUSH GLEET GRASS ICHOR ISSUE LOOSE OZENA PURGE RHEUM SHOOT SPEED START VOMIT WHIFF YIELD ACQUIT ASSOIL BOUNCE DEFRAY EFFECT EXCERN EXEMPT EXHALE FEEDER LOCHIA OZAENA TICKET UNLADE UNLOAD ABSOLVE CASHIER DEBOUCH DEFEASE DEHISCE DELIVER DERAIGN DISBAND DISMISS EXCRETE EXHAUST MISSION PAYMENT PERFORM QUIETUS RELEASE RELIEVE SATISFY SKITTER SOLUTIO CATAPULT COMPOUND DEFECATE DESPATCH DISGORGE DISPATCH DISPLACE DISPLODE EMISSION EVACUATE MITTIMUS OUTSHOOT PERSOLVE SEPARATE SOLUTION STREAMER

(— ARROW) TWANG

(— AT RANDOM) ROVE

(— BULLET) DRIVE

(— CARGO) STRIKE

(— DEBT) MEET CLEAR ACQUIT LOOSING

(— DUTY) SERVE

(— FROM HORSE'S FOOT) FRUSH

(— FROM NOSE) RHEUM OZAENA

(— FROM RESERVOIR) HUSHING

(— FROM WOUND) SANIES

(— MATTER) WEEP

(— OF DEBT) SETOFF

(— OF GAS) FEEDER

(— OF STREAM) FALL SPOUT

(— SUDDENLY) HIKE

(BLOODY —) SHOW SANIES

(CANNON —) TIRE CANNON

(CONCENTRATED —) BARRAGE

(CONTINUOUS — OF FIREARMS) FUSILLADE

(DISHONORABLE —) BOBTAIL

(ELECTRIC —) ARC SPARK LEADER EFFLUVE STREAMER LIGHTNING

(ELECTRIC —S) STATIC

(HEAVY —) STORM

(MENSTRUAL —) PERIOD

(SIMULTANEOUS —) SALVO BROADSIDE FUSILLADE

(SUFF.) CENOSIS RRHAGIA RRHEA RRHOEA

DISCHARGED SPED SATISFIED

DISCHARGER EXCITATOR

DISCHARGING LABILE

DISCIPLE SON JOHN MARK CHELA JUDAS MURID PETER PUPIL TEACH TRAIN ANANDA DISPLE DORCAS HEARER PUNISH APOSTLE AUDITOR MATTHEW OVIDIAN

SCHOLAR SECTARY SRAVAKA STUDENT ADHERENT FOLLOWER GALENIST SECTATOR

DISCIPLINARIAN RAMROD TRAINER MARTINET

DISCIPLINARY STRICT

DISCIPLINE THEW WHIP BREAK DRILL INURE TEACH TRAIN TUTOR CHURCH ETHICS FERULA FERULE GOVERN INFORM PUNISH SEASON TAIRGE VIRTUE CHASTEN CORRECT CULTURE EDUCATE FURNACE NURTURE SCOURGE DISCIPLE DOCTRINE EXERCISE INSTRUCT LEARNING MATHESIS PEDAGOGY REGULATE RESTRAIN TEACHING TRAINING TUTORING PHILOSOPHY CASTIGATION

(CHINESE —) TAICHICHUAN

(MENTAL —) YOGA

(RELIGIOUS —) CHURCH PENANCE SADHANA

DISCIPLINED INURED STEADY

DISCLAIM DENY DEVOW WAIVE ABJURE DISOWN REFUSE DISAVOW ABDICATE ABNEGATE DISALLOW RENOUNCE

DISCLOSE OPE RIP BARE BLOW CALL KNOW OPEN TELL BREAK COUGH UNRIP UNWRY UTTER BETRAY BEWRAY DESCRY DIVINE EVOLVE EXPOSE IMPART REVEAL SHRIVE UNBURY UNCASE UNHASP UNHIDE UNLOCK UNROLL UNSEAL UNSHUT UNVEIL UNWRAP CONFESS DEVELOP DISCUSS DISPLAY DIVULGE EXHIBIT EXPLAIN PROPALE UNCLOSE UNCOVER DISCOVER INDICATE MANIFEST UNBUNDLE UNKENNEL UNSECRET UNTHATCH

(— PARTIALLY) ADUMBRATE

DISCLOSED OUT

DISCLOSURE REVEAL SHRIFT COLORING DESCRIAL DISCLOSE OVERTURE APOCALYPSE

DISCOLOR FOX BURN FADE SPOT BLACK SMOKE STAIN TINGE SMIRCH STREAK DISTAIN TARNISH BESMIRCH

DISCOLORATION CORN BLEED SCALD SPECK STAIN TINGE FOXING LIVEDO MILDEW ARGYRIA BURNING MELASMA BRONZING BROWNING CHLOASMA CYANOSIS DYSCHROA SCALDING

(— IN FISH) PINKEYE

(— OF FRUIT) SUNBURN

(— OF TURKEYS) BLUEBACK

(— ON CHOCOLATE) BLOOM

(— ON CURED FISH) RUST

(SMALL —) FRECKLE

(SUFF.) CHROIA

DISCOLORED HAW FOUL DINGY FOXED RUSTY STAINED SCORCHED USTULATE

(— BY DECAY) DOTY FOXED

DISCOMFIT MATE ROIT ABASH ABAVE AFLEY SHEND SHENT UPSET WORST BAFFLE DEFEAT FEAGUE SQUASH CONFUSE CONQUER DISTURB

DISCOMFITURE LURCH

DISCOMFORT HELL PAIN UNEASE MALAISE PURGATORY

(FEELING OF —) BLAHS

DISCOMPOSE FEEZE PERTURB

DISCONCERT BASH BOWL FAZE FUSS HACK ABASH BLANK DAUNT FEEZE PHASE UPSET WORRY BAFFLE BLENCH MISPUT PUZZLE RATTLE SQUASH CONFUSE DISTURB FLUMMOX NONPLUS PERTURB SQUELCH BROWBEAT DISORDER

DISCONCERTED BLANK ASHAMED RATTLED CONFUSED

DISCONCERTING BAFFLING

DISCONNECT UNDO SEVER DIVIDE UNDOCK UNYOKE DISJOIN DISSOLVE DISUNITE SEPARATE UNCOUPLE

DISCONNECTED LOOSE ABRUPT BROKEN CHOPPY CURSORY DECOUSU SNATCHY RAMBLING STACCATO ASYNARTETE

DISCONSOLATE SAD GLOOMY WOEFUL DOLEFUL FORLORN UNCOUTH DEJECTED DESOLATE DOWNCAST HOPELESS

DISCONTENT ENVY ENNUI DISQUIET SOURNESS

DISCONTENTED DUMPY RESTLESS MALCONTENT

DISCONTINUANCE BREAK LAPSE DEMISE CUTBACK DISUNION SHUTDOWN CESSATION

DISCONTINUE END DROP HALT QUIT STOP BREAK CEASE CLOSE LETUP DESIST DISUSE SUNDER DISRUPT SUSPEND INTERMIT SURCEASE

DISCONTINUITY JAR BREAK COMMA BREACH HIATUS

DISCONTINUOUS BROKEN DISJUNCT SALTATORY

DISCORD DIN JAR BROIL JANGLE SCHISM STRIFE DISLIKE FACTION FISSURE JARRING MISTONE CONFLICT DISTANCE DIVISION FRACTION MISCHIEF UNSAUGHT VARIANCE CACOPHONY

DISCORDANT AJAR RUDE CRONK HARSH FROWZY HOARSE JANGLY HIDEOUS JARRING SQUAWKY ABSONANT CONTRARY JANGLING SCORDATO

DISCOTHEQUE AGOGO DISCO

DISCOUNT AGIO BATTA SHAVE REBATE REDUCE DISCOMPT

DISCOURAGE CARP DAMP CHILL DAUNT DETER FROST DAMPEN DEJECT DISMAY FREEZE STIFLE DEPRESS FLATTEN INHIBIT DISPIRIT DISSUADE

DISCOURAGEMENT COLD DAMP CHILL DAUNT REBUFF LETDOWN PUTBACK

DISCOURAGING CHILL DREARY

DISCOURSE SAW CARP RANT READ TALE TALK TELL WORD DROOL FABLE ORATE PAPER SPEAK SPELL THEME TRACT TREAT COMMON DILATE EULOGY HOMILY PARLEY PREACH REASON SCREED SERMON THESIS TONGUE TREATY

ACCOUNT ADDRESS COMMENT CONTEXT DECLAIM DELIVER DESCANT DIETARY DISCANT DISCUSS DISSERT ENTREAT EXPOUND GRAMMAR LECTURE NARRATE ORATION PARABLE PRATING PRELECT PURPOSE RECITAL TALKING ARGUMENT COLLOQUY CONVERSE EXERCISE LOCUTION LOQUENCE PARLANCE SPEAKING SPELLING TRACTATE TREATISE PHILIPPIC PROLUSION
(— OF LITTLE VALUE) STUFF
(— POLICY) GLASNOST
(LAUDATORY —) PANEGYRIC
(LONG —) SCREED
(OBSCENE —) SMUT
(PROLONGED —) DIATRIBE
(RAMBLING —) RHAPSODY RIGMAROLE
(SERIOUS —) HOMILY
(SIMPLE —) PAP
(UNIMAGINATIVE —) PROSE
(PL.) EXOTERICS
(PREF.) LOG(O)
(SUFF.) LOG(ER)(IA)(IAN)(IC)(ICAL) (IST)(UE)(Y)

DISCOURTEOUS RUDE SCURVY UNCIVIL UNHENDE CAVALIER IMPOLITE UNGENTLE
DISCOURTESY CUT SLIGHT
DISCOVER RIP SEE SPY WIT ESPY FEEL FIND PICK TWIG CATCH LEARN SPELL DEFINE DESCRY DETECT DIVINE EXPOSE IMPART INVENT LOCATE OVERGO REVEAL STRIKE UNHIDE CONFESS DESCURE DEVELOP DISCERN DISCURE DISPLAY DIVULGE EXHIBIT EXPLORE UNCOVER UNEARTH CONTRIVE DECIPHER DESCRIBE DISCUREN MANIFEST UNKENNEL
DISCOVERABLE VISIBLE
DISCOVERER SPY SCOUT COLUMBUS EXPLORER INVENTOR
DISCOVERY FIND TROVE DESCRY ESPIAL STRIKE DESCRIAL
DISCREDIT FOUL SLUT DECRY DOUBT REFEL DEFACE DEFECT ASPERSE BLEMISH DESTROY IMPEACH SCANDAL SUSPECT BELITTLE DISGRACE DISHONOR DISTRUST REPROACH UNCREDIT (SUFF.) ARD ART
DISCREDITABLE BLACK UNHONEST
DISCREET SAGE WARY WISE CIVIL WITTY HUSHED POLITE SILENT CAREFUL GUARDED POLITIC PRUDENT CAUTIOUS RESERVED RETICENT
DISCREETLY SENSIBLY
DISCREPANCY VARIANCE
DISCREPANT VARIANT CONTRARY DISSONANT
DISCRETE ETERNAL DISTINCT
DISCRETION TACT OPTION WISDOM CONDUCT RETENUE COURTESY JUDGMENT PRUDENCE
DISCRETIONARY ARBITRARY
DISCRIMINATE PART SEVER SECERN DISCERN PERCEIVE SEPARATE

DISCRIMINATED DISTINCT
DISCRIMINATING GOOD NICE ACUTE SHARP ASTUTE CHOICE NASUTE SELECT CHOOSEY CRITICAL EXPLICIT
DISCRIMINATINGLY CHOICE FINELY
DISCRIMINATION EYE BIAS DOOM TACT TASTE ACUMEN AGEISM CHOICE SEXISM FINESSE RESPECT DELICACY SAPIENCE
(— AGAINST ANIMALS) SPECIESISM
(SYMBOL OF —) HANSA
DISCRIMINATIVE RESPECTIVE
DISCURSIVE ROVING CURSORY RAMBLING DESULTORY
DISCURSIVELY WIDE
DISCUS DISC DISK QUOIT DISKOS DISCOID
DISCUSS AIR MOOT RUNE TALK ARGUE BANDY COVER DANDY TRACT TREAT COMMON CONFER DEBATE DICKER EMPARL EXCUSS IMPARL PARLEY AGITATE RESPEAK CANVASS COMMENT CONSULT DESCANT DISCANT DISCEPT DISCUTE DISPUTE DISSERT EXAMINE NARRATE TRAVERSE CONJOBBLE
(— AT LENGTH) BAT
(— CASUALLY) MENTION
(— EXCITEDLY) AGITATE
(— LIGHTLY) BANDY
(— QUICKLY) SKIP
(— SECRETLY) ROUN
(— TERMS) CHAFFER
(— THOROUGHLY) EXHAUST
(— TO EXCESS) VEX
DISCUSSION MOOT DEBAT FORUM COMMON CONFAB DEBATE HASSEL HOMILY HUDDLE PARLEY TREATY BARGAIN CANVASS COMMENT COUNSEL DISCUSS DISPUTE MOOTING PALAVER PRIBBLE ARGUMENT CAUSERIE CHINFEST COLLOQUY DIATRIBE ENTREATY EXCURSUS QUESTION
(CONTROVERSIAL —) DISPUTE
(DIDACTIC —) HARANGUE
(HEATED —) FLAK
DISDAIN COY TUT DAIN DEFY PRIDE SCORN SDAIN SPURN SDEIGN SLIGHT CONTEMN DESPISE CONTEMPT
DISDAINFUL COY DIGNE PROUD SAUCY TOSSY SCORNY SLIGHT SNIFFY SNUFFY DAINFUL HAUGHTY ARROGANT DEIGNOUS PROUDFUL SCORNFUL SNIFFISH TOPLOFTY
DISDAINFULLY SMALL SNIFFILY
DISEASE BUG FLU MAL ROT AIDS BATS COTH CRUD EVIL FLAW GOUT GRIP KURU NOMA PEST PHOS SORE AGROM BATTS BEJEL BENDS CAUSE COTHE CROUP DECAY DOLOR FEVER GRIEF LUPUS PHOSS PINTA PINTO SCALL SHAKE SPRUE SURRA AINHUM ANGINA CANCER CARATE CORYZA COURAP DENGUE GRAVEL GRIPPE HERPES MALADY MORBUS PALMUS PIEDRA POPEYE SCURVY SICKEN SURRAH THRUSH UROSIS

ZOOSIS AILMENT CHOLERA COXALGY DECLINE ENDEMIC ENTASIA LANGUOR LEPROSY MALEASE MISLIKE MYCOSIS MYIASIS PATHEMA RAPHANY SCOURGE SEQUELA SERPIGO SIBBENS SORANCE SYCOSIS TETANUS XERASIA ZYMOTIC ADENOSIS ALASTRIM ATHEROMA BERIBERI COXALGIA CRIPPLER CYNANCHE DIAMONDS ENZOOTIC JAUNDICE LEUKEMIA PALUDISM PANDEMIC PELLAGRA RAPHANIA SCABBADO SHINGLES SICKNESS SMALLPOX SORRANCE STAGGERS SYPHILIS UNHEALTH XANTHOMA ZOONOSIS
(— OF ANIMALS) SURRA
(— OF ANIMALS, GENERAL) ROT CLAP CORE FIRE GOUT HUSK LICK WEED APTHA CLEFT CLING CLOSH COTHE CROOK DRUSE FARCY FLAPS NENTA NGANA PAINS SPEED SWEAT TAINT APHTHA AVIVES BROSOT CANKER CARNEY CREEPS FARCIN GARGET GRAPES LAMPAS NAGANA ROUGET SPAVIN SURRAH WOBBLE ANTHRAX BIGHEAD CALCINO CALORIC CANCEAG DOURING EARWORM EQUINIA FASHION FISTULA FOUNDER FROUNCE KETOSIS LAMPERS MURRAIN MURRINA QUITTER QUITTOR SLOBBER SOLDIER TAKOSIS BULLNOSE CRATCHES CRIPPLES FERNSICK FOOTHALT HORSEPOX HYSTERIA MAWBOUND SLOBBERS SNUFFLES THWARTER VACCINIA EPIZOOTIC
(— OF APPLES) CORK BLOTCH
(— OF BANANAS) SIGATOKA SQUIRTER
(— OF BARLEY) STRIPE
(— OF BEES) SACBROOD
(— OF BEETS) HEARTROT
(— OF BIRDS) GOUT
(— OF BLUEBERRY) BLUESTEM
(— OF CABBAGE) ANBURY CLUBROOT
(— OF CATERPILLARS) WILT FLACHERY
(— OF CATS) PANLEUCOPENIA
(— OF CATTLE) PUCK TURN BARBS BLAIN CLOSH FARCY HOOVE HOOZE SLOWS COWPOX GARGET GRAPES HAMMER HEAVES ANTHRAX BLACKLEG BLOATING
(— OF CEREALS) BRAND ERGOT
(— OF CHICKEN) PIP CORYZA
(— OF CHILDREN) PROGERIA
(— OF COTTON) HYBOSIS CYRTOSIS STENOSIS
(— OF DUCKLING) KEEL
(— OF EYES) WALL GLAUCOMA SYNECHIA TRACHOMA
(— OF FIGS) SMUT
(— OF FINGERNAILS) FLAW
(— OF FLAX) BROWNING
(— OF FOWLS) PIP CRAY ROUP GAPES SOREHEAD
(— OF GRAIN) ILIAU ICTERUS
(— OF GRAPES) COLEUR ERINOSE ROUGEAU ROUGEOT SHELLING

(— OF HAWKS) RYE CRAY CROAK CROAKS FROUNCE FILANDER
(— OF HORSES) HAW CLAP CURB MOSE MULE WEED FARCY LEUMA VIVES APHTHA SCALMA THRUSH BARBELS DOURINE QUITTOR SARCOID AZOTURIA GLANDERS HORSEPOX SCRATCHES STRANGLES
(— OF INSECTS) POLYHEDROSIS
(— OF LAMB) SWAYBACK
(— OF LETTUCE) STUNT
(— OF NARCISSUS) SMOLDER SMOULDER
(— OF ONION) SMUDGE
(— OF ORANGE) LEPROSIS
(— OF PALMS) KOLEROGA
(— OF PLANTS) SCAB NECROSIS
(— OF PLANTS, GENERAL) POX ROT BUNT CORK DROP FIRE GOUT KNOT PULP SMUT BLAST DWARF EDEMA ERGOT FLECK FLOCK GRUBS SCALD SCALE SCURF SEREH SPIKE STUNT TUKRA TWIST AUCUBA BLIGHT BLOTCH BLUING BRAUNE CALICO CANKER COLEUR GIRDLE OEDEMA OIDIUM PETECA SMUDGE STREAK STRIPE VIROSE BLISTER BLUEING BRINDLE CRINKLE DIEBACK ERINOSE EYESPOT FROGEYE HYBOSIS MEASLES PRURIGO ROSETTE SHATTER SMOLDER STIPPEN TIPBURN TOMOSIS VIRUELA WALLOON BLUESTEM BREAKING BROWNING BUCKSKIN CLUBROOT CYRTOSIS DARTROSE EXANTHEM FLYSPECK GUMMOSIS KOLEROGA LEPROSIS MELANOSE MELAXUMA POLEBURN PSOROSIS RAPHANIA SMOULDER STENOSIS VIROSITY WHIPTAIL WILDFIRE CHLOROSIS
(— OF POTATO) CURL HAYWIRE
(— OF RABBITS) SNUFFLES
(— OF RICE) BLAST SPECK
(— OF RODENTS) TULAREMIA
(— OF SHEEP) CAW COE GID MAD RAY ROT BANE BELT CORE HALT SHAB WIND BLAST BLOOD BRAXY GILLAR OVINIA PINING STURDY ANTHRAX BRADSOT DAISING RUBBERS SCRAPIE THWARTER WILDFIRE BREAKSHARE
(— OF SILKWORM) UJI CALCINO GATTINE PEBRINE FLACHERY
(— OF SUGARCANE) ILIAU SEREH EYESPOT
(— OF SWINE) GARGET
(— OF TOBACCO) ETCH CALICO BRINDLE FROGEYE
(— OF TOMATO) FERNLEAF GRAYWALL
(— OF TONGUE) AGROM
(— OF TREES) KNOT CANKER
(— OF TULIPS) SHANKING
(— OF UNKNOWN ORIGIN) AINHUM ACRODYNIA
(AGENT OF PLANT —) VIROID
(CAISSON —) CHOKES
(FATAL — OF NERVOUS SYSTEM) KURU
(FOOT-AND-MOUTH —) AFTOSA
(FUNGUS —) PECK MYCOSIS
(KIDNEY —) RIPPLE

(KIND OF —) LYME KISSING
MINAMATA
(LUNG —) CON
(MUSHROOM —) FLOCK
(PINK —) ACRODYNIA
(PLANT —) ESCA YAWS
(SKIN —) ACNE SCAB FAVUS HIVES
LEPRA MANGE PSORA RUPIA SCALL
TINEA ECZEMA LICHEN TETTER
EXORMIA PORRIGO PRURIGO
PURPURA SERPIGO VERRUGA
CHLOASMA IMPETIGO MILIARIA
MYCETOMA SHINGLES VERRUGAS
VITILIGO PEMPHIGUS
(SWELLING —) EDEMA
(VENEREAL —) BURNING SYPHILIS
(WINE —) GRAISSE
(WOOLSORTER'S —) ANTHRAX
(PREF.) MORBI NOS(O) PATH(O)
(SUFF.) IASIS ITIS NOSUS
OMATOSIS OSIS SIS
(FUNGUS —) OSIS
DISEASED BAD EVIL SICKLY
MORBOSE PECCANT VICIOUS
MORBIFIC
(PREF.) CACH CAC(O) DYS
(SUFF.) CACE
DISEMBARK LAND ALIGHT ARRIVE
DEBARK UNBARK UNBOAT
DISBOARD
DISEMBARKATION LANDING
DISEMBARRASS EXTRICATE
DISEMBODIED SEPARATE
DISBODIED FLESHLESS
DISEMBODIMENT SOUL SPIRIT
DISEMBOGUE MOUTH
DISEMBOWEL GUT HULK PAUNCH
DEBOWEL EMBOWEL GARBAGE
UNTRIPE GRALLOCH
DISEMIC DIMORIC DICHRONOUS
DISENCHANT DISMAY
DISENCHANTED SOUR
DISENCUMBER RID FREE REDD
UNCUMBER
DISENCUMBERMENT RIDDANCE
DISENGAGE FREE CLEAR EDUCE
UNTIE DETACH EVOLVE LOOSEN
CUTOVER DISGAGE RELEASE
UNRAVEL LIBERATE UNCLUTCH
DISENGAGED OFF CLEAR
DISENTANGLE CARD COMB FREE
REED TOSE TOZE CLEAR LOOSE
RAVEL TEASE EVOLVE SCUTCH
SLEAVE UNMAZE UNMESH
RESOLVE UNRAVEL UNREAVE
UNTWINE UNTWIST OUTTWINE
UNTANGLE
DISENTANGLEMENT SOLUTION
DISESTEEM UMBRAGE DISVALUE
DISFAVOR DUTCH ODIUM DISLIKE
OFFENCE OFFENSE UMBRAGE
MALGRACE
DISFIGURE MAR BLUR FOUL MAIM
SCAR TASH AGRISE DEFACE
DEFEAT DEFORM INJURE MANGLE
BLEMISH DISGRACE DISGUISE
MUTILATE
DISFIGURED FOUL DEFET DEFEIT
DEFORMED
DISFIGUREMENT SCAR BLEMISH
CATFACE DEFORMITY
DISGORGE SPEW VENT EGEST
EJECT EMPTY VOMIT

DISGRACE BLOT FOIL FOUL HISS
LACK SLUR SMIT SOIL SPOT TASH
ABASE CRIME ODIUM SCORN
SHAME SHEND SPITE STAIN TAINT
BAFFLE BEFOUL BISMER HUMBLE
INFAMY REBUKE STIGMA VILIFY
AFFRONT ATTAINT DEGRADE
OBLOQUY OFFENCE OFFENSE
REPROOF SCANDAL SLANDER
UMBRAGE CONTEMPT DISHONOR
IGNOMINY REPROACH SHENDING
UNWORTHY VILLAINY
OPPROBRIUM
(PUBLIC —) ATIMY
DISGRACEFUL MEAN SOUR FILTHY
INDIGN IGNOBLE CRIMINAL
DEFAMOUS INHONEST SHAMEFUL
DISGRUNTLED SORE PEEVISH
DISGUISE DAUB FACE HIDE LAIN
LEAN MASK VEIL BELIE CLOAK
COLOR COUCH COVER FEIGN
GLOZE GUISE SHADE VISOR VIZOR
COVERT DEFORM IMMASK
MANTLE MASQUE VIZARD
CONCEAL OBSCURE PRETEND
PURPORT COLORING DISLIKEN
MISGUISE PALLIATE PRETENCE
PRETENSE TRAVESTY UMBRELLA
SMOKEANDMIRRORS
(— INFORMATION) LAYNE
DISGUISED COVERT FUCATE
GILDED LATENT MYSTIC FEIGNED
PALLIATE TRAVESTY INCOGNITA
INCOGNITO
DISGUST IRK UGH CLOY PALL
BLECH LOATH REPEL SHOCK
STALL DEGOUT HORROR NAUSEA
OFFEND REVOLT SICKEN SCUNNER
STOMACH SURFEIT AVERSION
DISTASTE KREISTLE LOATHING
NAUSEATE SCOMFISH SICKNESS
(EXPRESSION OF —) BAH ICK ROT
RATS YECH YUCK PSHAW YECCH
PHOOEY
(INTERJECTION TO EXPRESS —)
YUK TUCK YECH YECCH
(SOUND OF —) RAZZ RASPBERRY
(WORD OF —) ICK
DISGUSTED IRK SICK IRKSOME
DISGUSTING FOUL PERT VILE
LOUSY MUCKY NASTY FILTHY
SCRIMY SICKLY BEASTLY CLOYING
FULSOME HATEFUL LOATHLY
MAWKISH NOISOME OBSCENE
SHITTEN FOULSOME LOATHFUL
NAUSEOUS SHOCKING VOMITOUS
DISH CAP CAUP CUSH DISC DISK
FOOL MEAT MOLD PLAT SOLE
BASIN BATEA COMAL DEVIL
MOULD NAPPY PATEN PINAX
PLATE SHAPE BASQUE BASSIE
BICKER BLAZER BUTTER CHAFER
CRITCH CUSCUS ENTREE FONDUE
GOSSIP LUGGIE NAPPIE OLIVES
PADDLE PANADA PATERA PATINA
PHIALE RECIPE SAUCER SUNDAE
TAMALE TUREEN BALANCE
BOBOTEE BOBOTIE CAPSULE
CEVICHE CHARGER COCOTTE
COMPORT COMPOTE CRESSET
DORMANT DOUBLER EPERGNE
PAPBOAT PATELLA PLATEAU

PLATTER RAMEKIN SCUTTLE
STIRFRY SUPREME TERRINE
TIMBALE AMATORIO CIOPPINO
CLAPDISH COQUILLE COUSCOUS
GALATINE KEDGEREE MAZARINE
POWSODDY STANDARD
ENTREMETS
(— IN PYRAMID STYLE) BUISSON
(— OF FISH) SUSHI
(— OF MEAT AND EGGPLANT)
MOUSSAKA
(— OF RAW FISH) SEVICHE
(— OF SLOPPY FOOD) SOSS
(— WITH TOAST) RAREBIT
(BAKING —) SCALLOP SCOLLOP
(BRAISED —) HASLET
(CASSEROLE —) POTAUFEU
(CHAFING —) CHAFER CHOFFER
SCALDINO
(CHEESE —) RACLETTE
(CHINESE —) LOMEIN SUBGUM
(CHOICE —) REGALE
(CONE-SHAPED —) BOMBE
(CURRIED MEAT —) VINDALOO
(EXQUISITE —) AMBROSIA
(FANCY —) SURPRISE
(FIRST —) STARTER
(FISH —) CIOPPINO
(FLAT —) ASHET COMAL CHARGER
(FRIED —) SKIRL
(HIGH-FLAVORED —) HOGO
(INDIAN —) BIRYANI BURIANI
(INDIAN — OF LEGUMES) DAL DAHL
DHAL
(IRISH —) COLCANNON
(JAPANESE —) SUSHI TEMPURA
TERIYAKI YAKITORI
(JEWISH —) CHOLENT
(LIGHT —) SOUFFLE
(MEAT —) SPIEDINO
(PASTA —) CARBONARA
(PHILIPPINE —) BURO
(PHILIPPINE FISH —) DOBO
(PIE —) COFFIN
(PILE OF —S) BUNG
(RICE —) PILAU
(ROMAN —) LANX PATERA PATINA
(SAILOR'S —) BURGOO SCOUSE
(SAUSAGE —) CHIPOLATA
(SCOTTISH —) BROSE
(SIDE —) OUTWORK
(SPANISH —) ADOBO
(SPANISH MEAT —) ADOBO
(SWEET —) JUNKET FLUMMERY
(TASTY —) MORSEL
(WARMED-UP —) RECHAUFFE
(WOODEN —) CUP CAUP BOWIE
GOGGAN LUGGIE KICKSHAW
(PL.) GARNISH BAKEWARE
FLATWARE ENTREMETS
(PREF.) LECO
DISHABILLE MOB DISARRAY
DISORDER NEGLIGEE
DISHAN (FATHER OF —) SEIR
DISHARMONY SCHISM ADHARMA
FRACTION
DISHCLOTH DISHRAG TORCHON
DISHCLOTH GOURD LOOFAH
PATOLA DISHRAG
DISHEARTEN AMATE DAUNT FAINT
DEJECT DEPRESS FLATTEN
UNHEART UNNERVE DISHEART
DISPIRIT

DISHEARTENED DULL GLUM
GLOOMY DOWNCAST DEPRESSED
DISHEARTENING GLOOMY
DESOLATE
DISHEVEL MUSS TOWSE RUFFLE
TOUSEL TOUSLE TUMBLE
TRACHLE DISARRAY DISORDER
DISHEVELED ROOKY BLOUSY
BLOWZY FROWZY TUMBLED
UNKEMPT FROWZLED SHEVELED
SLIPSHOD TATTERED
DISHON (FATHER OF —) ANAH
DISHONEST BENT FOUL LEWD
CRONK CROSS FALSE LYING
QUEER SNIDE TWISTY UNFAIR
UNJUST CORRUPT CROOKED
JACKLEG KNAVISH INDECENT
INDIRECT SHAMEFUL SINISTER
UNCHASTE UNHONEST
MENDACIOUS
DISHONESTLY DOUBLY FALSELY
DISHONESTY IMPROBITY
DISHONOR FILE FOUL ABASE
ABUSE ATIMY ODIUM SHAME
SPITE STAIN WRONG DEFAME
DEFILE DEFORM INFAMY VILIFY
DEGRADE DISTAIN OBLOQUY
SLANDER VIOLATE DISGLORY
DISGRACE DISPLUME IGNOMINY
REPROACH VILLAINY ATTAINDER
DISHONORABLE BASE FOUL MEAN
BLACK NASTY SHABBY YELLOW
DISLEAL IGNOBLE SHAMEFUL
UNHONEST UNWORTHY
DISHONORED DEFAMED
DISHPAN KEELER
DISH RACK FIDDLE
DISHWASHER SWILLER
DISILLUSION SOUR DISMAY
DISINCLINATION NILL UNLUST
UNWILL DISLIKE QUARREL
AVERSION DISTASTE
DISINCLINED LOTH LOATH AFRAID
AVERSE HESITANT
(— TO) ABOVE
DISINFECT SCRUB SEASON
CLEANSE SWEETEN
DISINFECTANT LYSOL IODINE
PHENOL CREOLIN EUGENOL
TACHIOL FUMIGANT HALAZONE
PARAFORM ANTISEPTIC
DISINFECTION ANTISEPSIS
DISINGENUOUS FALSE UNFAIR
OBLIQUE
DISINHERIT DEPRIVE DISHEIR
ABDICATE DISHERIT
DISINTEGRATE BEAT DUST MELT
BREAK DECAY ERODE GRUSH
SLAKE SPLIT MOLDER CRUMBLE
DISBAND RESOLVE SHATTER
COLLAPSE DISSOLVE SEPARATE
DISINTEGRATING ROTTEN
SCHIZOID
(SUFF.) CLASTIC
DISINTEGRATION DECAY BREAKUP
EROSION BIOLYSIS COLLAPSE
HEARTROT SOLUTION
(SUFF.) LYSE LYSIS LYST LYTE
LYTIC LYZE
DISINTER EXHUME UNBURY
UNTOMB UNGRAVE
DISINTERESTED FAIR CANDID
APATHETIC IMPARTIAL

DISJOIN PART UNDO SEVER DETACH SUNDER UNTACK UNYOKE DISSOLVE DISUNITE SEPARATE

DISJOINED BITTY SEJOINED DIAZEUTIC

DISJOINTED BITTY

DISK (ALSO SEE DISC) EYE NOB ORB PAN SAW WAX WEB BURR CHAD DIAL DISC FLAN FLAT KNOB PALM PUCK STAR TUFT CAKRA DAUNT LAMIN MEDAL PATEN PLATE ROUND SABLE SABOT SPILL TOKEN TRUCK WAFER WHEEL WHORL BEZANT BOTTOM BUCKET BUMPER BUTTON CACHET CARTON CHAKRA CONCHA CONCHO CORONA DISCUS FLOPPY GHURRY HARROW PALLET PELLET RECORD RIFFLE RONDEL SEQUIN SHEAVE SQUAIL WASHER WEIGHT ZEQUIN ACETATE BLOTTER BOBECHE CHECKER CHIPPER CLIPEUS DIOPTER DISCOID FREEBEE FRISBEE GOGGLES KNICKER MEDALET PHALERA ROSETTE SLITTER SPINNER SPOTTER TONDINO DIFFUSER EYEPIECE HOLDFAST PLANCHET RONDELLE ROUNDLET ZECCHINO (— FOR BARRELING HERRING) DAUNT
(— FOR CHEESE) FOLLOWER
(— FOR STRIKING HOURS) GHURRY
(— OF JELLYFISH) BELL
(— OF LAMELLAE) THYLAKOID
(— OF WAX) AGNUS
(— ON WOODEN ROD) SPILL
(— OPERATING SYSTEM) DOS
(BULL'S-EYE —) CARTON
(COIN-MAKING —) FLAN PLANCHET
(COMPUTER —) FLOPPY MINIFLOPPY
(CONTENTS OF —) DATA
(DOUBLE —) YOYO
(ECCENTRIC —) SHEAVE
(FLESHY —) SARCOMA
(FLOPPY —) DISKETTE
(HANDLED —) RIFFLE
(HOCKEY —) PUCK
(KIND OF —) FLOPPY
(MEDICATED —) LAMELLA
(METAL —) SLUG MEDAL
(ORNAMENTAL —) BANGLE SPANGLE
(PADDED IRON —) SPINNER
(PAPER —S) CONFETTI
(PLASTIC —) FRISBEE
(POTTER'S —) BAT
(REVOLVING —) WAFTER
(ROTATING —) SCANNER
(SOLAR —) ATEN ATON
(SUN —) ATEN CAKRA CHAKRA
(TROCHAL —) CORONA
(WINGED —) FEROHER
(PREF.) DISC(I)(O)

DISLIKE DEFY DOWN HATE LOTH LUMP MIND DERRY LOATH SPITE DETEST PHOBIA REGRET RESENT SPLEEN UNLIKE DESPISE MISLIKE QUARREL SCUNDER SCUNNER STOMACH AVERSION DESPISAL DISFAVOR DISTASTE DYSPATHY

(— OF CHILDREN) MISOPEDIA
(FOOLISH —) TOY

DISLOCATE LUX SLIP BREAK SPLAY UNSET LUXATE DISLOCK UNWREST DISJOINT DISPLACE SEPARATE

DISLOCATED SHOTTEN DISLOCATE

DISLOCATION BREAK SHIFT SLIDE THROW
(PL.) SETTLEMENTS

DISLODGE BEAT BOLT BUCK BUMP EXPEL SHAKE SHIFT SWOOP REMOVE DISROOT UNHORSE UNHOUSE UNLODGE DISHABIT
(— BY BLASTING) BRUSH
(— FROM SADDLE) THROW

DISLODGING BULLING

DISLOYAL FALSE FELON UNTRUE DISLEAL

DISLOYALTY SWICK SWIKE UNLEWTY UNTRUTH

DISMAL SAD WAN BLUE DARK DIRE DOWF DREE DULL FERY GASH GLUM GRAY GREY BLACK BLEAK DOWFF DREAR EERIE LURID MORNE OORIE OURIE SABLE SORRY SURLY SWART WASTE WISHT DREARY DREICH DREIGH GLOOMY GOUSTY LENTEN SULLEN TRISTE DIREFUL DOLEFUL FUNERAL GASHFUL GHASTLY GOUSTIE JOYLESS OMINOUS POCOSIN STYGIAN UNCOUTH UNHAPPY DESOLATE DOLESOME DOLOROUS FUNEREAL GROANFUL LONESOME NOVEMBRY SOLITARY WEARIFUL MELANCHOLY

DISMAL-LOOKING GASH WOBEGONE

DISMALLY DERNLY DIRELY

DISMANTLE RASE RAZE STRIP DIVEST STRIKE DEPRIVE DESTROY UNCLOAK DISMOUNT

DISMAY DOWL FEAR RUIN ALARM AMATE APPAL DAUNT DREAD FLUNK APPALL ASTONY CHASSE FRIGHT SUBDUE TERROR DEPRESS DEPRIVE FOUNDER HORRIFY TERRIFY AFFRIGHT CONFOUND CONSTERNATION
(INTERJECTION EXPRESSING —) OOPS WOOPS

DISMAYED ASTONIED

DISMAYING HIDEOUS

DISMEMBER LIMB MAIM PART REND SEVER MANGLE UNLIMB DISCERP DISLIMB DISSECT QUARTER DISJOINT MUTILATE

DISMISS AX AXE CAN PUT BOOT BUMP BUST CASH CAST DAFF DROP DRUM FIRE KICK OUST QUIT SACK SEND SHAB SWAP SWOP TURN VAIK VOID AMAND AMOVE BREAK BRUSH CHUCK DEMIT DIMIT DITCH EJECT EXPEL FLIRT FLUNK LOOSE SCOUT BANISH BOUNCE CHASSE CONGEE DEHIRE DISMIT DISOWN REJECT REMOVE SHELVE CASHIER DISBAND DISCARD LICENCE LICENSE TURNOFF DESELECT DISGRACE DISPATCH DISPOINT RELEGATE SETASIDE WITHDRAW
(— LIGHTLY) SNEEZEAT

DISMISSAL AX BOOT SACK BRUSH CHUCK CONGE SHAKE AVAUNT BOUNCE OUSTER KICKAXE REMOVAL DISPATCH MITTIMUS REDUNDANCY
(LARGE-SCALE —) PURGE
(UNCEREMONIOUS —) CONGE CONGEE

DISMISSED DEGOMME
(ONE WHO IS —) PUSHOUT

DISMOUNT AVALE AVOID LIGHT ALIGHT DEVOID DESCEND FLYAWAY UNHORSE UNMOUNT DISHORSE UNSTRIDE

DISOBEDIENCE CONTEMPT

DISOBEDIENT BAD FORWARD FROWARD NAUGHTY UNBUXOM UNGODLY WAYWARD MUTINOUS

DISOBEY SIT REJECT

DISOBLIGE OFFEND REFUSE AFFRONT NEGLECT

DISOBLIGING MEAN UNBAIN UNBANE

DISORDER ILL MUX PIE CRUD FLAW MESS MUSS RIOT RUFF STIR TOUT CHAOS CRACK DERAY GRIME HAVOC REVEL SNAFU UPSET TOUSE TUKRA UPSET BURBLE CHOREA DEFUSE DEGRAY HUDDLE JUMBLE LITTER MALADY MASTIC MUCKER MUDDLE RUFFLE TOUSLE TROPPO TUMULT UNTIDY WALTER AILMENT CLUTTER COBWEBS CONFUSE DERANGE DISEASE DISTURB EMBROIL FERMENT FLUTTER GARBOIL ILLNESS MISDEED MISRULE OUTRAGE PERTURB SHATTER TROUBLE UNRAVEL UNSHAPE DISARRAY DISHEVEL EPILEPSY MILIARIA MISORDER NEUROSIS ROWDYISM SICKNESS UNSETTLE COMMOTION CONFUSION POLLINOSIS
(— OF BIRDS) PIP
(— OF EYES) HIPPUS
(— OF VISION) DIPLOPIA
(— OF WINES) CASSE
(COMPLETE —) CHAOS ANARCHY
(EATING —) BULIMIA
(MENTAL —) INSANITY PARANOIA
(NERVOUS —) VAPORS
(SPEECH —) LALOPATHY
(SUFF.) (SPEECH —) PHASIA PHEMIA PHRASIA

DISORDERED ILL SICK WILD CRAZY GAUMY LIGHT MESSY UNRID BLOTTO FROUZY FROWSY FROWZY INCULT INSANE MUSSED TURBID CHAOTIC CLOUDED FORLORN TUMBLED UNGLUED UNSIDED CONFUSED DERANGED DISEASED FEVERISH FLURRIED INCHOATE SHAMBOLIC

DISORDERING CRIMP

DISORDERLY RAND RANDY ROWDY RABBLE UNRULY BUNTING LAWLESS ROARING CONFUSED FAROUCHE LARRIKIN SLIPSHOD SLOVENLY SLUTTISH SLATTERNLY

DISORGANIZE SHOCK UPSET CONFUSE CONTUSE DERANGE DISBAND DISRUPT DISORDER DISSOLVE

DISOWN DENY RENAY UNOWN REJECT DISAVOW RETRACT ABDICATE DISALLOW DISCLAIM RENOUNCE REPUDIATE

DISPARAGE LACK SLUR ABUSE DECRY LOWER TRASH DEBASE LESSEN SLIGHT BACKCAP DEBAUCH DEGRADE DEMERIT DEPRESS DETRACT DISABLE DOWNCRY IMPEACH RUBBISH RUNDOWN BELITTLE DEROGATE DIMINISH DISCOUNT DISHONOR DISPRIZE MINIMIZE MISLIKEN VILIPEND

DISPARAGEMENT DIASYRM SNIDERY WASHWAY

DISPARAGING SNIDE SLIGHTING PEJORATIVE

DISPARATE UNEQUAL SEPARATE

DISPARITY DISSENT DISTANCE IMPARITY

DISPASSIONATE CALM COOL FAIR STOIC SEDATE SERENE CLINICAL COMPOSED MODERATE

DISPATCH RID FREE KILL MAIL NOTE POST SEND SLAY WING BRIEF ENVOY FLASH HASTE HURRY SHOOT SPEED DIRECT EMPLOY HASTEN ADDRESS COMMAND DELIVER DISPEED EXPRESS HATCHET BREVIATE CELERITY CONCLUDE DESPATCH EXPEDITE TELEGRAM

DISPATCH BOAT AVISO PACKET

DISPATCHER STARTER

DISPEL FRAY SHOO CHASE ASSOIL BANISH DISCUSS SATISFY SCATTER DISPERSE

DISPENSATION LAW LILA GRACE LIVERY ECONOMY FACULTY QUIENAL TOTQUOT COVENANT DISPOSAL

DISPENSE DEAL DOLE HELP SHED WEIGH EFFUSE EXCUSE EXEMPT FOREGO MANAGE SPREAD ABSOLVE ARRANGE DISPEND DRIBBLE MINISTER
(— WITH) MISS WANT SPARE SUSPENSE

DISPENSER BOMB MANAGER STEWARD

DISPERSE DOT SOW FRAY MELT PART ROUT SHED LOOSE SCALE SEVER SKAIL STREW BAFFLE DEFEAT DILATE DISPEL FANOUT SKIVER SPARSE SPERSE SPREAD UNKNIT VANISH WINNOW DIFFUSE DISBAND DISJECT DISMISS DRIBBLE FRITTER SCATTER SHATTER SPARKLE SPARPLE SPERPLE DISSOLVE DISTRACT SEPARATE SQUANDER STAMPEDE

DISPERSEDLY PASSIM

DISPERSING SCALE
(— SHADOWS) SCIALYTIC

DISPERSION CUT FOAM STAIN SPREAD DEBACLE SCATTER DIASPORA EMULSOID SOLUTION STAMPEDE
(PREF.) LYO

DISPIRIT COW DAMP MATE MULL CHILL DAUNT DEJECT DEPRESS FLATTEN OPPRESS

DISPIRITED SAD BLUE DOWN DOWY DOWIE ABATTU ABATTUE LETDOWN SHOTTEN DOWNCAST DOWNSOME SACKLESS UNHEARTY WOBEGONE

DISPIRITING COLD BLEAK CHILL DISMAL

DISPLACE BUMP EDGE MOVE STIR BANISH DEPOSE LUXATE MISLAY REMOVE WINKLE DERANGE SWALLOW UNHINGE UNPLACE ANTEVERT DISLODGE DISPLANT MISPLACE SUPPLACE SUPPLANT UNSETTLE
(— **LATERALLY**) HEAVE

DISPLACED ATOPIC DEPAYSE

DISPLACEMENT JEE BUMP SLIP HEAVE SCEND SHIFT START CUBAGE OFFSET UPSLIP FALLING EVECTION
(— **OF FAULT**) THROW
(— **OF STAR**) ABERRATION
(**DOWNWARD** —) PTOSIS
(**OPTICAL** —) PARALLAX
(**ROCK** —) HITCH

DISPLAY ACT AIR BRAG DASH GAUD OOZE ORGY POMP SHOW SIGN STAR WEAR AGONY ARRAY BINGE BLAZE BOAST DERAY ECLAT EMOTE FLASH PRIDE SCENE SHINE SIGHT SPLAY SPORT STAGE VAUNT BLAZON DEPLOY DESCRY ESTATE EVINCE EXPOSE EXTEND FLAUNT MUSTER OSTENT OUTLAY PARADE REVEAL RUFFLE SETOUT SPLASH SPRANK SPREAD UNCASE APPROVE BALLOON BRAVERY ETALAGE EXHIBIT EXPRESS FANFARE FLUTTER GAUDERY PAGEANT PRESENT SHOWING SPLURGE TRADUCE UNCOVER BEEFCAKE BLAZONRY BOOKFAIR CEREMONY DISCLOSE DISCOVER EMBLAZON EQUIPAGE EVIDENCE EXERCISE EXPOSURE FLOURISH INDICATE MANIFEST PARAFFLE SPLENDOR TINSELRY
(— **EXCITEMENT**) FAUNCH
(— **GLARINGLY**) FLARE
(— **OF COMPUTER TASKS**) MENU
(— **OF EMOTION**) GUSH
(— **OF GOODS**) ETALAGE
(— **OF SKILL**) APPERTISE
(— **OF STRONG COLORS**) RIOT
(**BOASTFUL** —) JACTATION
(**BOISTEROUS** —) SPLURGE
(**COMPUTER VIDEO** — **OF TASKS**) MENU
(**DARING** —) BRAVURA
(**EMPTY** —) GAUD EYEWASH
(**EXCESSIVE** —) OSTENTATION
(**FLASHY** —) CLAPTRAP
(**FLORAL** —) BLOW BLANKET
(**IMPRESSIVE** —) SWELL
(**LAVISH** —) PROFUSION
(**LIGHT** —) LED
(**MOVE COMPUTER** — **UP OR DOWN**) SCROLL
(**OSTENTATIOUS** —) DOG GAUDERY SWAGGER
(**PRETENTIOUS** —) PARAFLE PARAFFLE

(**RADAR** —) SCAN
(**SHOWY** —) PYROTECHNICS

DISPLAYED SPLAY EXPANDED

DISPLEASE VEX MIFF ANGER ANNOY PIQUE MISPAY MISSET OFFEND DISLIKE DISSUIT MISLIKE PROVOKE IRRITATE

DISPLEASED MAD GLUM UNEASY UNFAIN

DISPLEASING BAD DRY PUTRID IRKSOME TEDIOUS UNLOVELY

DISPLEASURE IRE ANGER MUMPS PIQUE INJURY STRUNT UNLUST UNWILL DISLIKE OFFENSE TROUBLE UMBRAGE UNTHANK DISFAVOR DISGRACE DISTASTE

DISPORT PLAY AMUSE FRISK SPORT DIVERT FROLIC GAMBOL DISPLAY

DISPOSAL SALE BANDON CLEANUP PROPINE BESTOWAL DEVOTION DISPATCH
(— **OF DEAD**) FUNERAL
(**ARBITRARY** —) WILL
(**QUICK** —) WASHWAY

DISPOSE APT SET BEND CAST DUMP GIVE MIND TRIM YARK ARRAY BRUSH DIGHT ORDER PLACE POSIT ADJUST ATTIRE BESTOW DIGEST SETTLE TEMPER APPOINT ARRANGE DISPONE GESTURE INCLINE PREPARE RESOLVE DISPATCH REGULATE
(— **OF**) JOB SELL SCRAP FINISH HANDLE WORKOFF
(— **VARIOUSLY**) STAGGER

DISPOSED APT FIT SET SIB LIEF DIGHT GIVEN PRONE READY WRAST MINDED MINDFUL SUBJECT WILLING ADDICTED AFFECTED PREGNANT PROCLIVE PROPENSE PROTENSE TALENTED
(— **AT INTERVALS**) ALTERNATE
(— **TO ACTION**) ACTIVE
(— **TO ASSOCIATE WITH ONE GROUP**) CLANNISH
(— **TOWARD**) AFFECTED
(**FAIRLY** —) CANDID
(**FAVORABLY** —) PROPITIOUS
(**KINDLY** —) FOND
(**OPENLY** —) LOOSE
(**WELL** —) FAIN INCLINED

DISPOSITION BENT BIAS MAKE MIND MOOD RACE SORT TRIM TURN DRIVE ETHOS FRAME GRAIN HABIT HEART HUMOR SHAPE SPITE TACHE AFFECT ANIMUS DESIGN GENIUS HEALTH KIDNEY NATURE PTYXIS SPIRIT SPRITE STRIND TALENT TEMPER CONCEPT COURAGE DISPOSE FACULTY STOMACH APTITUDE ATTITUDE DISPOSAL POSTURE PERSONALITY
(— **OF DRAPERIES**) CAST
(— **OF PARTS**) SYMMETRY
(— **OF PAWNS**) SKELETON
(— **OF STRATA**) OVERLAP
(— **TO ANGER**) CHOLER
(— **TO RESIST**) DEFIANCE
(**BRIGHT** —) OPTIMISM
(**DEVILISH** —) SATANISM
(**GENEROUS** —) HEART
(**GENIAL** —) BONHOMIE
(**INHERITED** —) RACE

(**KINDLY** —) CHARITY HUMANITY
(**NATURAL** —) KIND GRAIN TARAGE INDOLES
(**ORNAMENTAL** —) DECOR
(**ULTIMATE** —) FATE

DISPOSITIONN (**FORGIVING** —) MERCY

DISPOSSESS OUST EJECT EVICT EXPEL STRIP WRONG DEPOSE DIVEST BEREAVE CASHIER DEPRIVE DISSEIZE SEPARATE

DISPOSSESSED LUMPEN

DISPOSSESSION OUSTER

DISPRAISE BLAME CENSURE

DISPROOF ELENCH REFUTE IMPROOF REPROOF

DISPROPORTIONATE UNEQUAL

DISPROVE BREAK REBUT REFEL NEGATE REFUTE CONFUTE EXPLODE IMPROVE REPROVE DISALLOW NEGATIVE REDARGUE

DISPUTABLE MOOT VAGUE UNSURE DUBIOUS FALLIBLE

DISPUTANT FENCER POLEMIC WRANGLER

DISPUTATION PARVIS PILPUL POLEMIC PROBLEM WRANGLE ARGUMENT COURSING DEBATING EXERCISE QUODLIBET

DISPUTATIOUS POLEMIC LITIGIOUS POLEMICAL

DISPUTE JAR ROW TAX CALL CHOP DENY FEUD FRAY FUSS HOLD MOOT ODDS RIOT SAKE SPAR SPAT TILT ARGUE BRAWL BROIL CABAL CHEST FLITE FLYTE HURRY PLEAD SPUTE SQUIB ARGUFY BARNEY BICKER CAMPLE CANGLE DABBER DACKER DAIKER DEBATE DIFFER FITTER FRATCH HAGGLE HASSLE IMPUGN MATTER NAGGLE SHARRY SQUALL SQUEAL THREAP BRABBLE CONTEND CONTEST DERAIGN DISCEPT DISCUSS DISSERT FACTION GAINSAY PRIBBLE QUARREL WRANGLE ARGUMENT CATFIGHT CONTRARY POLEMIZE QUESTION SKIRMISH SPARRING SPLUTTER SQUABBLE
(**POETICAL** —) FLYTING PARTIMEN

DISQUALIFY DEBAR UNFIT OUTLAW DISABLE

DISQUIET VEX FEAR FRET PAIN TOSS UNRO EXCITE UNCALM UNEASE UNREST AGITATE ANXIETY DISREST DISTURB INQUIET PERTURB SOLICIT TROUBLE TURMOIL UNPEACE UNQUIET

DISQUIETED UNEASY

DISQUIETING UGLY

DISQUIETINGLY UGLY

DISQUIETUDE CHAGRIN WANREST WANRUFE

DISRAELI DIZZY

DISREGARD BY SIT BLOW MOCK OMIT PASS WANE BELAY FLING WAIVE FORGET HUBRIS IGNORE SLIGHT UNHEED CASHIER DESPISE FORHEED LICENCE LICENSE NEGLECT OVERSEE DISCOUNT DISFAVOR DISPENSE DISVALUE EASINESS OVERHALE OVERLOOK OVERPASS UNREGARD

DISRFLISH DISLIKE DISTASTE

DISREPUTABLE LOW BASE GAMY HARD WAFF GAMEY SEAMY SEEDY SHADY TOUGH LOUCHE SHODDY RAFFISH SHAMEFUL UNHONEST

DISREPUTABLENESS BEGGARY

DISREPUTE DISFAME DISFAVOR DISHONOR REPROACH

DISRESPECT AFFRONT CONTEMPT RUDENESS

DISRESPECTFUL HARM SAUCY UNCIVIL IMPOLITE IMPUDENT INSOLENT

DISROBE STRIP CHANGE DIVEST DESPOIL UNDRESS

DISRUPT GASH REND TEAR BREAK CROSS HAMPER DISRUMP DISTRACT SONICATE
(— **WITH SOUND TREATMENT**) SONICATE

DISRUPTED BROKEN DISRUPT

DISRUPTION BREACH BREAKUP DEBACLE RUPTURE SOLUTION

DISSATISFACTION PAIN DISTASTE VEXATION
(**FEELING OF** —) BLAHS

DISSATISFIED UNEASY MALCONTENT

DISSATISFY MISPAY

DISSECT BAR ANALYZE DISJOIN SCALPEL UNPIECE

DISSECTED MATURE

DISSECTION ANATOMY ANALYSIS

DISSEMBLE ACT FOX LIE HIDE MASK CLOAK FEIGN BOGGLE SEMBLE CONCEAL DISGUISE SIMULATE SIMULIZE

DISSEMBLER SIMULAR

DISSEMBLING SLY BRAIDE IRONIC FICTION AESOPIAN IRONICAL

DISSEMINATE SOW BEAR BLAZE STREW EFFUSE SPREAD DIFFUSE PUBLISH SCATTER SPARPLE DISPERSE SEMINATE

DISSEMINATION PROPAGATION

DISSENSION JAR ODDS DEBATE STRIFE DISCORD DISLIKE DISSENT FACTION MISLIKE BROILERY DISPEACE DISTANCE DISUNION DISUNITY DIVISION FRACTION FRICTION SEDITION

DISSENT VARY DIFFER HERESY CONTEND PROTEST DISAGREE

DISSENTER HERETIC SECTARY RECUSANT SEPARATE RASKOLNIK
(**PL.**) SEPARATION

DISSENTING PANTILE

DISSEPIMENT REPLUM SEPTUM PHRAGMA

DISSERTATION ESSAY THEME TRACT DEBATE MEMOIR SCREED THESIS DESCANT LECTURE MEMOIRS EXCURSUS EXERCISE TRACTATE TREATISE
(— **ON TEA**) TSIOLOGY

DISSERVE HARM

DISSERVICE HARM DAMAGE INJURY MISCHIEF

DISSIDENT FRONDEUR

DISSIMILAR UNLIKE DIFFORM DIVERSE UNLIKEN

DISSIMILATE UNLIKEN

DISSIMULATION IRONY DECEIT

DISSIPATE BURN FRAY SPEND WASTE BANISH DISPEL EXPEND CONSUME DIFFUSE DISCUSS FRITTER RESOLVE SCAMBLE SCATTER SHATTER SWATTLE TARNISH DISPERSE DISSOLVE EMBEZZLE EVANESCE SQUANDER
DISSIPATED FAST HIGH LOST SPORTY OUTWARD RACKETY
DISSIPATION RAKERY
DISSOLUTE LAX LEWD WILD LOOSE SLACK RAKELY RAKISH SUBURB UNTIED WANTON IMMORAL LAWLESS VICIOUS DESOLATE RAKEHELL RECKLESS RESOLUTE SUBURBAN UNCURBED
DISSOLUTION END RUIN DECAY BREAKUP DECEASE DIVORCE DIALYSIS
(PREF.) LYS(I)
DISSOLVE CUT END DEFY FADE FUSE MELT SOLV THAW BREAK FLEET LOOSE SOLVE UNFIX DIGEST DISTIL RELENT SOLUTE UNBIND UNGLUE UNKNIT ADJOURN DESTROY DISBAND DISJOIN DISTILL DIVORCE LIQUEFY RESOLVE DISCANDY DISUNITE SEPARATE
(— MEAT PARTICLES) DEGLAZE
(— OUT) LEACH
(PREF.) LY(O)
DISSOLVED SOLUT REMISS SOLUTE RESOLUTE
DISSOLVING
(SUFF.) LYSE LYSIS LYST LYTE LYTIC LYZE
DISSONANCE WOLF DISCORD DIAPHONY
DISSONANT AJAR HARSH RAGGED GRATING JARRING JANGLING
DISSUADE BLUFF DETER DEHORT DIVERT RETIRE
DISTAFF ROCK FEMALE
DISTAFFINA (LOVER OF —) BOMBASTES
DISTANCE DX HOP WAY BLUE GAIT GATE LOOK PIPE SPAN STEP DEPTH DRAFT RANGE SPACE GROUND HEIGHT LENGTH SPREAD STANCE STITCH BOWSHOT BREADTH DRAUGHT FARNESS JOURNEY MILEAGE MILEWAY RESERVE STRETCH YARDAGE COLDNESS COSECANT DIAMETER FOOTSTEP HANDSPAN INTERVAL LATITUDE OFFSCAPE OUTSTRIP
(— ALONG TRACK) LEAD
(— BETWEEN BATTENS) GAG
(— BETWEEN GEAR TEETH) PITCH
(— BETWEEN MASTS) INTERVAL
(— BETWEEN RAILS) GAGE GAUGE
(— BETWEEN RIVET-HEADS) GRIP
(— BETWEEN TACKS) REACH
(— FOR PUTTING COAL) RENK
(— FROM BELLY TO BACK) BODY
(— FROM CENTER) RADIUS
(— FROM EQUATOR) HEIGHT
(— FROM LOCK FACE) BACKSET
(— FROM THE EYE) DEPTH
(— IN ADVANCE) START
(— OF ARCHERY RANGE) BUTT
(— OF BOW SHOT) CAST

(— OF GOLF BALL) CARRY
(— OF HAUL) LEAD LEADAGE
(— OF TURNING SHIP) ADVANCE
(— OF VISION) KEN
(— ON FISHHOOK) BITE
(— ON GEAR WHEEL) ADDENDUM
(— OVER WHICH WIND BLOWS) FETCH
(— UPWARDS) HEIGHT
(ANGULAR —) ANOMALY
(AT A —) LARGE
(GREAT —) INFINITY
(INTERVENING —) GAP
(PERPENDICULAR —) DROP CAMBER ALTITUDE
(REMOVE TO A —) ELOIN
(SAFE —) BERTH
(SEA —) OUTING STEAMING
(SHOOTING —) SHOOT
(SHORT —) HAIR INCH SPIT STEP SPELL BITTIE FOOTSTEP
(SHORT — AWAY) OUTBYE
(SMALL —) HAIR STEP
(UNIT OF —) LI YOJAN PARASANG
DISTANT DX COY FAR OFF AFAR AWAY BACK COLD SIDE YOND ALOOF CHILL FERNE HENCE FERREN REMOTE YONDER FARAWAY FOREIGN FROSTED REMOVED STRANGE RESERVED
(— FROM COAST) MIDLAND
(— IN TIME) EARLY
(— PART) OFFSCAPE
(MORE —) YOND YONDER ULTERIOR
(MOST —) OUTMOST OUTERMOST
(PREF.) TEL(E)(EO)
DISTASTE HATE DEGOUT UNLUST DISGUST DISLIKE MISLIKE AVERSION MISTASTE
(— FOR FOOD) APOSITIA
DISTASTEFUL ICKY SOUR YUCKY AUGEAN BITTER BEASTLY HATEFUL BRACKISH NAUSEOUS SHOCKING UNSAVORY REPUGNANT
DISTEMPER SOAK STEEP CHOLER DILUTE GARGET GARGIL GARGLE MALADY PANTAS AILMENT DISEASE ILLNESS DISORDER DYSCRASE SICKNESS UNSETTLE
(— OF COLT) STRANGLES
DISTEND BAG BLOW FILL GROW HEFT BLOAT PLUMP STRUT SWELL WIDEN DILATE EXPAND EXTEND INTEND SPREAD BALLOON ENLARGE INFLATE STRETCH
DISTENDED BIG FULL PENT TAUT TRIG WIDE BLOWN POOCH TUMID ASTRUT GRAVID BLOATED DISTENT SWOLLEN INFLATED PATULENT PATULOUS
DISTENDEDLY ASTRUT
DISTENTION BLOAT DISTENT TYMPANY
DISTHENE CYANITE KYANITE
DISTICH GLOKA PROODE COUPLET
DISTILL DROP ELIX EMIT RATE STILL DISTIL EXTILL INFUSE ALEMBIC LIMBECK TRICKLE
DISTILLATE GUNDY ROSIN BENZIN ALCOHOL BENZINE
DISTILLATION RUN DESCENT
DISTILLER ABKAR STILLER
DISTILLERY STILL JIGGER STILLERY

DISTINCT HOT FAIR FREE VIVE BREME BRISK CLEAR PLAIN SHARP VIVID PLUCKY PROPER SECRET SUNDRY ANOTHER ASUNDER DIVERSE EVIDENT LEGIBLE OBVIOUS PRECISE SCIOLTO SEVERAL SPECIAL APPARENT DISCRETE DIVIDUAL PALPABLE PECULIAR SEPARATE TRENCHANT
(— FROM) BESIDE
(NOT —) DIM OBSCURE
(PREF.) CHORI CHORIST(O) IDIO
DISTINCTION MARK NOTE RANK SHED TEST CLASS GLORY HONOR FIGURE LAUREL LUSTER LUSTRE RENOWN DIORISM QUALITY QUILLET ACCESSIT DIVISION GRANDEZA SUBTLETY REFINEMENT
(ACADEMIC —) HONORS HONOURS
(LACKING —) VANILLA
(WITHOUT —) COMMON
DISTINCTIVE RARE JUICY DIRECT PROPER SIGNAL PECULIAR PHONEMIC SEPARATE SPANKING TALENTED
DISTINCTIVENESS EMPHASIS
DISTINCTLY CLEAR REDLY FAIRLY CLEARLY
DISTINCTNESS PLUCK CLARITY SEVERALTY
(LACKING —) SMUDGY
DISTINGUISH DEEM KNOW MARK SORT BADGE JUDGE LABEL SEVER SKILL STAMP DECERN DEFINE DESCRY DEVISE DIVIDE ENSIGN SECERN SINGLE CONCERN DISCERN DESCRIBE PERCEIVE SEPARATE
DISTINGUISHED CLEAR GREAT NOTED SWELL BANNER FAMOUS GENTLE MARKED SOLEMN EMINENT INSIGNE NOTABLE SIGNATE SPECIAL TOPPING DISTINCT ESPECIAL LAUREATE RENOWNED SPLENDID CONSPICUOUS
DISTINGUISHING BETWEEN
DISTORT WRY SKEW WARP CLOUD COLOR FUDGE SCREW TWIST WREST WRING CRINGE DEFACE DEFORM DETORT GARBLE MANGLE SHEVEL WRENCH WRITHE BLUBBER CONTORT FALSIFY GRIMACE PERVERT SHACHLE SHACKLE SLANDER OUTIMAGE WIREDRAW
DISTORTED WRY AWRY BENT SKEW ASKEW CRANK SKEWED WARPED CROOKED DISTORT GNARLED LOXOTIC WRITHEN CAMSHACH DEFORMED DEGRADED STRAINED TORTIOUS PERVERTED
DISTORTING CONVULSION
DISTORTION FIB HOG SAG WOW WREST STRAIN FLUTTER GRIMACE GARBLING SKEWNESS
(— IN WOOD) WARP DIAMONDING
(FACIAL —) GRIMACE
DISTRACT MAD AMUSE CRAZE STROY BEMUSE DETRAY DIVERT HARASS INSANE MADDEN MITHER MOIDER PUZZLE TWITCH AGITATE

CONFUSE DETRACT DISTURB EMBROIL PERPLEX SCATTER BEWILDER CONFOUND FORHAILE
DISTRACTED GYTE WILD CRAZY EPERDU STRACT FRANTIC MADDING SCRANNY FRENETIC SCATTERED
DISTRACTION ALARM BLIND ALARUM ESCAPE FRENZY TUMULT ECSTASY
DISTRAIN NAM NAAM DRIVE POIND STRAIN STRESS DISTRESS POUNDAGE
DISTRAINT NAM NAAM POIND
DISTRAUGHT MAD CRAZED FRANTIC DERANGED DISTRACT DISTRAIT STRAUGHT
DISTRESS AIL ILL MAR VEX BITE CARK GNAW HURT MOAN NEED PAIN PORT PUSH TEAR TEEN AGONY ANGER ANNOY DOLOR GRATE GRIEF GRILL GRIPE LABOR PINCH PRESS SMART TRYST TWEAK WORRY WOUND WRING BARRAT DANGER DURESS GRIEVE GRUDGE HARASS HARROW LAMENT MISERY SORROW STRESS TAKING THRONG WORRIT AFFLICT ANGUISH ANXIETY CHAGRIN DAYMARE DESTROY DISEASE EXTREME HERSHIP MISEASE OPPRESS PASSION PENANCE PERPLEX STURBLE TORMENT TORTURE TRAVAIL TROUBLE UNQUERT AGGRIEVE CALAMITY DARKNESS DISTASTE DISTRAIN EXIGENCE FORHAILE PRESSURE SORENESS STRAITEN WANDRETH GRIEVANCE
DISTRESSED WRUNG DOWNGONE
DISTRESSFUL STRAIT
DISTRESSING BAD HOT SAD GRIM HARD SORE BLEAK CHARY CRUEL DIRTY SHARP BITTER SEVERE SHREWD THORNY CARKING FEARFUL GRIPING PAINFUL GRIEVOUS
DISTRIBUTE DOT SOW CAST DEAL DOLE GRID METE SEED SORT TAME ALLOT CLASS DIVVY ISSUE PLACE SHARE SHIFT SPEND ASSIGN ASSORT DEPART DEVISE DIGEST DIVIDE EXPEND IMPART PARCEL REPART SPARSE SPREAD ARRANGE DISPEND DISPOSE EROGATE PRORATE SCATTER ALLOCATE CLASSIFY DESCRIBE DISBURSE DISPENSE DISPERSE SEPARATE SPRINKLE
(— GUNFIRE) SEARCH
(— SEED) SOW SEED DRILL
(— TYPE) DISH THROW
DISTRIBUTED BALANCED DISPERSE
DISTRIBUTION DOLE SALE ARRAY DIVVY DETAIL DIVIDE PARTING DISPOSAL DIVIDEND
DISTRIBUTIVELY EACH APIECE
DISTRIBUTOR SOWER SHARER CARRIER ZANJERO
DISTRICT DO AMT GAU LAN SOC WAY WON AREA COIL FARM HUNT LEET LIWA PALE PART SIDE SLUM SOKE TEMA WARD WENE WICK

WOON AIMAK ANNEX COILA
EXURB HARSH JAGIR JEWRY
MAHAL OKRUG PAGUS PARTY
SHIRE SOKEN TALUK TEMAN
TRACT VICUS AGENCY BARRIO
BOWERY CANTON CERCLE CIRCLE
COUNTY FOREST JAGHIR MARKAZ
MEMBER MERINA OKROOG
PARAMO PARISH POLLAM REGARD
REGION SIRCAR STAPLE STREET
SYSSEL VINTRY ZILLAH CALABAR
CIRCUIT CLASSIS COMARCA
COMMUNE COUNTRY CURRAGH
DEMESNE DIOCESE ENCLAVE
FREEDOM LIBERTY MAHALLA
MALACCA MAYFAIR MELIZKI
MISSION PIMLICO PURLIEU
QUARTER SEASIDE SLUMDOM
THANAGE THEBAID UPRIVER
CHAPELRY CIMARRON DISTRITO
DIVISION FAUBOURG GILDABLE
LEGATION MACASSAR MAGAZINE
MONTANAS PRECINCT PROVINCE
REGIMENT MAGISTRACY
PREFECTURE
(— BORDERING RIVER) WATER
(— FOR GAME HUNTING)
SHOOTING
(— OF COURT) LEET
(— OF JAPAN) DO KEN
(ADMINISTRATIVE —) ZILA ZILLAH
TOWNSHIP
(BROTHEL —) STEW
(BURNED —) QUEMADO
(CHINESE —) HIEN
(COASTAL —) RIVIERA
(ECCLESIASTICAL —) SYNOD
CLASSIS DIOCESE
(HUNTING —) WALK
(ICELANDIC —) SYSSEL
(ISLE OF MAN —) SHEADING
(JUDICIAL —) CIRCUIT
(MARKED-OFF —) PALE
(MOUNTAINOUS —) HIGHLAND
(OUTER —) END
(OUTWARD —) END
(OVERCROWDED —) WARREN
(POOR —) SLUM SLUMS
(POSTAL —) RAYON
(RURAL —) WAYBACK
(RURAL —S) STICKS
(RUSSIAN —) OBLAST STANITSA
STANITZA
(TENANT —) THIRL
(THEATER —) RIALTO
(TRIBAL —) GAU
(TURKISH —) ORDU SANJAK
(PL.) GAELTACHT
DISTRUST FEAR DOUBT DREAD
STRIFE DIFFIDE SUSPECT UNFAITH
UNTRUST DEFIANCE DISFAITH
MISFAITH MISTRUST QUESTION
WANTRUST
DISTRUSTFUL SHY LEERY JEALOUS
DISTURB JEE VEX BUSY FAZE FRET
FUSS JOLT RILE ROCK ROIL STIR
TOSS ALARM ANNOY BRASH
DROVE FEEZE KNOCK PHASE
ROUSE SHAKE STEER UPSET
AFFRAY BOTHER HARASS JOSTLE
MOLEST RUFFLE SQUEAK UNCALM
UNEASE AGITATE COMMOTE
COMMOVE CONCUSS DERANGE

DISREST DRUMBLE FRAZZLE
GARBOIL INQUIET MISMAKE
PERTURB SCUFFLE SOLICIT
STURBLE TEMPEST TROUBLE
CONVULSE DISJOINT DISORDER
DISQUIET DISTRACT DISTRESS
FRIGHTEN
(— BY HANDLING) TOUCH
(— SUDDENLY) START
(— THE PEACE) RIOT INQUIET
DISTURBANCE VEX BOIL BREE CAIN
COIL DUST RIOT ROUT STIR WIND
WORK ALARM BEANO BRAWL
BROIL DERAY FUGUE FUROR
HURRY SHINE SHOCK STEER
STORM STROW STURT TOUSE
AFFRAY BOTHER BREEZE CATHRO
DESRAY FRACAS FRAISE FURORE
HUBBUB KICKUP POTHER RUCKUS
RUMBLE RUMPUS SHINDY SQUALL
STATIC TUMULT TURNUP UPROAR
BLUNDER BOBBERY BRULYIE
BRULZIE CHAGRIN CLATTER
CLUTTER DISTURB EMOTION
FERMENT GRINDER MADNESS
ROOKERY RUCTION TROUBLE
TURMOIL BROILERY BUSINESS
DISORDER FOOFARAW INCIDENT
REELRALL STRAMASH TRAVALLY
RABBLEMENT PERTURBATION
(— OF OCEAN) SEA
(ATMOSPHERIC —) STORM
GRINDER
(DIGESTIVE —) BLOAT
(MENTAL —) FRENZY PHRENSY
DELIRIUM
(SEISMIC —) SEAQUAKE
DISTURBED CRACKED INQUIET
MAKADOO TROUBLE AGITATED
FLURRIED STREAKED
DISTURBING BREAK NASTY
HAUNTING
DISUNION DIVORCE
DISUNITE RIP PART SEVER UNTIE
DETACH DIVIDE SUNDER UNKNIT
UNLIME DISBAND DISJOIN DISLINK
DISSENT DIVORCE UNRAVEL
ALIENATE DISSEVER DISSOLVE
ESTRANGE SEPARATE UNSOLDER
DISUNITY DISCORD DISUNION
DIVISION
DISUSE MISUSE OUTAGE ABANDON
DISCARD DISUSAGE MISAPPLY
DISUSED DEAD WASTE DESUETE
EXOLETE OBSOLETE
DITCH GAW RUT SAP SOW DELF
DICK DIKE DYKE FOSS GOOL GOUT
GRIP GURT HOLL LEET LODE MOAT
SEEK SICK SIKE SINK TRIG CANAL
CLAUD DELFT DELVE FENCE
FLEAM FOSSA FOSSE GRAFF
GRAFT GRAVE GRIPE GROOP
GULLY PUDGE RHEEN RHINE RIGOL
SEWER SHORE SLUNK SLUIT
SOUGH STANK STELL ZANJA
GUTTER GUZZLE HOLLOW RELAIS
SHEUCH SHEUGH TRENCH ZANJON
ABANDON ACEQUIA CHANNEL
GRINDLE GRIPPLE LATERAL
VANFOSS ZANJONA WATERING
(— AROUND ARENA) EURIPUS
(MUDDY —) LETCH
(NARROW —) RELAIS

(OPEN —) STELL
(WIDE —) SLOT
(PREF.) FOSSI
DITCH GRASS ENALID
DITCH MILLET HUREEK PASPALUM
DITCH REED SPIRE BENNEL
DITHER FLAP STEW SHAKE TIZZY
BOTHER LATHER SHIVER TROUBLE
DITI (FATHER OF —) DAKSHA
(HUSBAND OF —) KASHYAPA
DITROCHEE DIPODY
DITSY CRAZY DIZZY GIDDY INANE
SILLY SPACY WIFTY SPACEY
DITTO SAME REPEAT LIKEWISE
DITTY DIT LAY DITE DYTE POEM
SING SONG THEME VERSE SAYING
DICTATE VINETTA
DIURETIC ZEA CAVA KAVA BUCCO
BUCHU CUBEB LAPPA PICHI SABAL
NASROL DROSERA EMICTORY
FUROSOMIDE PIPSISSEWA
DIVAGATE ROVE
DIVAN SOFA OTTOMAN SOCIABLE
DIVE BAR DEN DASH DUCK DUMP
JOINT SOUSE GAINER HEADER
PLUNGE SALOON BROTHEL
RATTRAP JACKNIFE SUBMERGE
JACKKNIFE
(— DEEP) SOUND
(KIND OF —) SWAN TWIST GAINER
JACKKNIFE
(MAKE A NOSE —) PEARL
DIVER AMA LOON DUCKER PEARLER
PLUNGER PLUNGEON
(SCUBA —) AQUANAUT
(SUFF.) DYTA DYTES
DIVERGE LEAVE BRANCH DIFFER
DIVIDE RAMIFY SPREAD SQUARE
SWERVE DEVIATE DIGRESS
DIVERSE DISAGREE DIVAGATE
DIVERGENCE DIP ERROR CHANGE
SPREAD SWERVE VAGARY
CONTRAST OBLIQUITY
(UNDUE —) OUTRAGE
DIVERGENT OFF APART REMOTE
TANGENT VARIANT
(MORE —) FARTHER
DIVERS EVIL MANY CRUEL SUNDRY
SEVERAL VARIOUS PERVERSE
DIFFERING
(PREF.) PARTI PARTY
DIVERSE EVIL SERE MOTLEY
SUNDRY UNLIKE VARIED ADVERSE
SEVERAL VARIOUS DISTINCT
PERVERSE SEPARATE VARIETAL
(PREF.) PARTI PARTY POLY VARI(O)
DIVERSIFIED MOTLEY EXTENDED
DIVERSIFY DOT FRET VARY CHECK
FRECK BEGARIE CHECKER VARIATE
SPRINKLE
DIVERSION JEU GAME MASK PLAY
ALARM FEINT FRISK HOBBY SPORT
ATTACK DEDUIT DIVERT LAUGHS
SCHEME SOLACE DISPORT
PASTIME ESCAPISM PLEASURE
SIDESHOW VARIORUM
(— OF STREAM) CAPTURE
DIVERSITY CHANGE DISCORD
DISSENT VARIETY CONTRAST
(PREF.) POLY
DIVERT SWAY AMUSE BLANK RELAX
SHUNT SPORT WRING DERAIL
DERIVE DETURN SIPHON SWITCH

SYPHON TICKLE BEGUILE CELIGHT
DECEIVE DEFLECT DETRACT
DISPORT PASTIME PERVERT
REFLECT ABSTRACT DISSUADE
DISTRACT ESTRANGE RECREATE
(— ATTENTION) COVER
(— HEADWATERS) BEHEAD
(— STREAM) CAPTURE
(— WATER) FLUME
DIVERTED MERRY AMUSED
DISTRACT
DIVERTICULUM UTERUS OLEOCYST
DIVERTING DROLL AMUSING
FOOLISH PLEASANT SPORTFUL
LAUGHABLE
DIVEST BARE DOFF REFT TIRL
EMPTY EXUTE REAVE SHEAR SPOIL
STRIP DELAWN DENUDE DEPOSE
DEVEST DISMIT UNVEST BEREAVE
DEPRIVE DESPOIL DISROBE
UNCOVER UNDRESS DENATURE
DETHRONE UNCLOTHE
(— OF) ABDICATE
(— OF ARMOR) DEMAIL
(— OF VALUE) DEVALUE
DIVIDE CUT LOT CAST DEAL FORK
MERE PART RIFT SHED SLIP TEAR
ZONE BREAK CARVE CLASS CLEFT
DIVVY GAVEL JOINT SCALE SCIND
SEVER SHARE SHIFT SLICE SNACK
SPACE SPLIT SPRIT WHACK
BEPART BISECT BRANCH CANTLE
CANTON CLEAVE COTEAU DEPART
DEVISE DIFFER DOMIFY INDENT
PARCEL RAMIFY SECTOR SEJOIN
SLEAVE SUNDER ALIQUOT
ANALYZE ATOMIZE AVERAGE
BRITTEN COMPART DIFFUSE
DIREMPT DISCIDE DISPART
DISSECT DIVERGE FISSURE
FRITTER PARTAKE PRORATE
ALLOCATE CLASSIFY CROSSCUT
DISCRETE DISSEVER DISTRACT
DISUNITE FRACTION FRAGMENT
GRADUATE HEMISECT MEDISECT
SEPARATE STRATIFY UNSEEDER
(— BEEF) BLOCK
(— FILAMENTS) SLEAVE
(— INTO DISTRICTS) CANTON
(— INTO MEASURES) BAR
(— INTO PIECES) GOBBET
(— INTO 2 PARTS) HALVE BISECT
(— INTO 4 PARTS) QUARTER
(— LAND) STINT
(— NATURALLY) FALL
(— SMALL) SCANTLE
DIVIDED ENTE REFT SIDE CLEFT
FORKY SPLIT ATOMIC CLOVEN
PRONGY FISSATE FOURCHE
GYRONNY PARTITE SEPTATE
AEROLATE CAMERATE DIVIDUAL
FOURCHEE
(— BY VERTICAL LINES) PALY
(— INTO 4 PARTS) PALY
QUARTERED
(— IN TWO) FOURCHE DIMIDIATE
(— TWICE) RETAILLE
(NOT —) GLOBAL
(PREF.) CHORI(ST)(STO) FISSI PARTI
PARTY SCHIZ(O)
(SUFF.) FID FIDATE SECT SECTED
TOMOUS
DIVIDEND BONUS SHARE

DIVIDER BUNTON MERIST SEPTUM SHARER BUNTING COMPASS MULLION SEVERER DIVIDANT

DIVI-DIVI LIBIDIBI

DIVINATION OMEN SORS SORT AUGURY MANTIC SORTES AUSPICE SCRYING SORCERY GEOMANCY TAGHAIRM
(**— SCIENCE**) MANTIC
(PREF.) MANTO
(SUFF.) MANCER MANCY MANTIC

DIVINE HOLY SORT SPAE TWIG AREAD AREED ATMAN AUGUR DIVUS GODLY GUESS PIOUS DEIFIC DETECT DEVISE GODFUL HALSEN PRIEST SACRED BLESSED FORESEE GODLIKE PORTEND PREDICT PRESAGE ARIOLATE CONTRIVE FOREBODE FOREKNOW FORETELL HEAVENLY IMMORTAL MINISTER PERCEIVE UBIQUIST SPIRITUAL

DIVINER SEER AUGUR SIBYL ARUSPEX AUGURER PROPHET HARUSPEX

DIVING BELL NAUTILUS

DIVING BOARD RISE

DIVING SUIT GANGAVA

DIVINING ROD TWIG DOWSER

DIVINITY (ALSO SEE GOD AND GODDESS) JOSS LI FULI EW TIEN AHURA DEITY HYBLA NUADA NUADU NYMPH POWER ATHTAR VEDUIS GLAUCUS GODDESS GODHEAD GODSHIP HYBLAEA TARANIS VIRBIUS TEUTATES VEDIOVIS
(**— CIRCUIT BINDING**) YAPP
(PL.) CABIRI ELOHIM

DIVISIBLE SECABLE DIVIDUAL PARTIBLE
(**— BY 2**) AIM

DIVISION BAY BOX CUT DAG FU JAG LEG CHAP CLAN DOLE FARM FAUN FORK GELD GELT GORE HOLD LITU NEAT PACE PANE PART RANK RAPE RIFT CAPUT CHASM CLASS CLEFT CURIA DIGOR DIVVY DULAN DULAT FIELD FIGHT GENOS GRANT GROUP IJORE MURUT PERES REALM SHARD SHARE SUBAH TAXIS THEME TOMAN WHEEN BARONY CANTON COHORT DECADE DECURY DEGREE DIVIDE EOGAEA HAWIYA IMAHAL JHURIA PORTIO SCHISM SEASON SECTOR SUNDER VOLOST ZILLAH BREAKUP COMARCA CUSTODY DIOCESE DUALISM ENOMOTY FISSURE FURLONG HASHIYA KINGDOM KITKSAN NATUARY PARTAGE PARTING ROULADE SECTION SEGMENT SUBRACE ARPEGGIO CATEGORY CLEAVAGE DECANATE DIERESIS DISTRICT FASCICLE MEROTOMY PARGANNA PRECINCT SCISSION SCISSURE SHEDDING SQUADRON SUBCLASS
(**— BETWEEN PIERS**) BAY
(**— BETWEEN STALLS**) BAIL
(**— FOR TAXATION**) GELD
(**— IN DENMARK**) AMT
(**— IN HUNGARY**) COMITAT
(**— IN MINING BED**) CLEAVE

(**— OF ANGELS**) CHOIR
(**— OF ARMY**) BATTLE LOCHUS
(**— OF BEJA**) BISHARIN
(**— OF BOOK**) CHAPTER FASCICLE
(**— OF BUDDHIST CANON**) PITAKA
(**— OF BUILDING**) STORY STOREY
(**— OF CHAPTER**) VERSE
(**— OF CHARIOTEERS**) FACTION
(**— OF CHURCH**) AISLE
(**— OF COMPASS**) POINT
(**— OF CONTEST**) HEAT INNING
(**— OF COUNTY**) RAPE BARONY HUNDRED
(**— OF CROPLAND**) FLAT
(**— OF DISCOURSE**) HEADING
(**— OF DRAMA**) ACT SCENE
(**— OF FAMILY**) BRANCH
(**— OF FIELD**) RIG
(**— OF FOOT**) SEMEION
(**— OF FOREST**) WARD
(**— OF GEOLOGICAL TIME**) ERA EPOCH PERIOD
(**— OF GRASS**) SPRIG
(**— OF GREAT HORDE**) DULAN DULAT KANGLA KANGLI
(**— OF HEADLINE**) BANK DECK
(**— OF HERALDIC SHIELD**) POINT
(**— OF ISLE OF MAN**) SHEADING
(**— OF KENT**) LATHE
(**— OF LAND**) LAINE KONOHIKI
(**— OF LEAF**) LOBE
(**— OF LEGION**) COHORT HASTATI MANIPLE TRIARII
(**— OF LOG LINE**) KNOT
(**— OF MANCHU ARMY**) BANNER
(**— OF MANKIND**) RACE
(**— OF MEAL**) COURSE
(**— OF MUSICAL COMPOSITION**) MOVEMENT
(**— OF NIGHT**) WATCH
(**— OF ORANGE**) LITH
(**— OF PARTED HAIR**) LIST
(**— OF PEOPLE**) STREAM
(**— OF PLAY**) ACT SCENE
(**— OF POEM**) FIT DUAN CANTO STANZA STROPHE
(**— OF PROCESS**) STAGING
(**— OF ROAD**) LANE
(**— OF ROCKS**) SYSTEM
(**— OF ROSARY**) DECADE CHAPLET
(**— OF SCHOOL YEAR**) TERM SESSION
(**— OF SOCIETY**) CASTE ATOMISM
(**— OF SONG**) FIT
(**— OF STOPE**) FLOOR
(**— OF STRUCTURE**) STAGE
(**— OF SUSSEX**) RAPE
(**— OF TREF**) RANDIR
(**— OF TRIBE**) CURIA
(**— OF UTTERANCE**) COLON
(**— OF WINDOW**) DAY
(**— OF YEAR**) SEASON
(**— OF YORKSHIRE**) RIDING
(**— OF ZILLAH**) PARGANA PERGUNNAH
(**— OF ZODIAC**) SIGN DECAN
(**— OVER ISSUE**) BREACH
(**— SIGN**) OBELUS
(**ADMINISTRATIVE —**) FU LATHE CHARGE CIRCLE COUNTY EYALET CUSTODY DIOCESE TOWNSHIP
(**ANTHROPOLOGICAL —**) STOCK
(**ARMY —**) MORA

(**ASTROLOGICAL —**) FACE
(**CELL —**) MITOSIS AMITOSIS
(**ECCLESIASTICAL —**) SCHISM SOCIETY PRECINCT
(**GEOLOGICAL —**) ERA LIAS MALM BUNTER KEUPER LUDIAN SERIES LARAMIE ARNUSIAN RICHMOND
(**HINGED —**) LEAF
(**ISLE OF MAN —**) SHEADING
(**MUSICAL —**) ALLEGRO
(**NUCLEAR —**) FISSION
(**PHILIPPINE —**) ATO
(**POLICE —**) TANA THANA
(**POLITICAL —**) ATO CITY LATHE STATE COUNTY PARISH BOROUGH HUNDRED SURPLUS DISTRICT PURCHASE WAPENTAKE
(**POPULATION —**) STRATUM
(**SOCIAL —**) HORDE
(**TRIBAL —**) CLAN
(SUFF.) KINESIS

DIVITIACUS (**BROTHER OF —**) DUMNORIX

DIVORCE GET GETT AHSAN HASAN KHULA SEVER TALAK SUNDER ASUNDER DISBAND DISMISS MUBARAT UNMARRY DISSOLVE DISUNION DISUNITE SEPARATE

DIVOT CLOD TURF

DIVULGATION (**UNAUTHORIZED —**) LEAK

DIVULGE BARE CALL SHOW TELL BLURT BREAK SPILL UTTER VOICE BABBLE BEWRAY EVULGE EXPOSE IMPART REVEAL SPREAD UNFOLD PROPALE PUBLISH UNCOVER DISCLOSE DISCOVER EVULGATE PROCLAIM

DIZZINESS HILO SWIM DINUS TIEGO MEGRIM VANITY MERLIGO SCOTOMY VERTIGO SWIMMING WILLNESS

DIZZY DUNT AREEL CRAZY DITSY DITZY FAINT GIDDY LIGHT TOTTY WESTY WOOZY FICKLE STUPID FOOLISH SWIMMING UNSTEADY

DJIBOUTI (**GULF OF —**) TADJOURA

DNA (**— SEGMENT**) CISTRON
(**— SEQUENCE**) HOMEOBOX

DO D ACT DIV FAY TRY BILK BURN CHAR COME DEAL DOST MAKE PASS SUIT AVAIL BITCH CHEAT EXERT GUISE SERVE SHIFT TRICK ANSWER COMMIT NOBBLE RENDER ACHIEVE EXECUTE PERFORM PRODUCE SATISFY SUFFICE TRANSACT
(**— AWAY WITH**) BURK ABATE BURKE FORDO BANISH FOREDO ABOLISH AMOLISH CASHIER CONSUME ABROGATE DEMOLISH DISSOLVE IMBOLISH RETRENCH
(**— BUSINESS**) CHAFFER
(**— CARELESSLY**) SLIM
(**— CASUAL WORK**) GRASS
(**— FOR**) FIX GET JACK POOP SINK FETCH NAPOO DIDDLE SCUPPER
(**— IMPERFECTLY**) HUDDLE
(**— INJURY**) BANE
(**— IN SLOVENLY WAY**) SLUBBER
(**— NOT**) DONT DINNA
(**— OVER**) REVAMP REMODEL
(**— PENANCE**) SATISFY

(**— PIECEWORK**) DACKER
(**— SMARTLY**) LINK
(**— THOROUGHLY**) FLOOR
(**— WITHOUT**) LACK SPARE FORBEAR DISPENSE
(**— WRONG**) ERR SIN MISCARRY
(**— YE**) DEE

DOABLE AGIBLE

DOBLON ISABELLA

DOBRA JO JOE OCTAVE

DOCENT TUTOR TEACHER LECTURER

DOCILE CALM MEEK TALL TAME TAWIE FACILE GENTLE DOCIOUS DUCTILE DUTIFUL BIDDABLE OBEDIENT TOWARDLY

DOCK BOB CUT PEN BANG CLIP MOOR PIER QUAY RUMP SCUT BASIN SHORE WHARF CAMBER COFFER DOCKEN FIDDLE HAMBLE MARINA SORREL STRUNT BOBTAIL CURTAIL PARELLA PARELLE SHORTEN CANAIGRE PATIENCE SHIPSIDE
(**SPACE BETWEEN —S**) SLIPWAY

DOCKAGE BERTHAGE

DOCKET LIST AGENDA

DOCKMACKIE VIBURNUM

DOCKWORKER (**—S GROUP**) ILA

DOCKYARD ARSENAL
(**— WORKMAN**) MATEY

DOCTOR (ALSO SEE PHYSICIAN) DOC COOK DOPE DOSE FAKE PILL BRUJO HAKIM LEECH SUGAR TREAT CROCUS DEACON EXTERN HAIKUN HEALER INTERN MAULVI POWWOW CROAKER KORADJI TEACHER MEDICATE PHYSICIAN MANIPULATE
(**— OF CANON LAW**) JCD
(**— OF LAWS**) JD
(**— UP**) COOK FAKE EYEWASH
(**— WINE**) STUM
(**IRISH —**) OLLAV OLLAMH
(**KIND OF —**) SPIN
(**PLAY —**) FIXER
(**QUACK —**) CROCUS
(**WITCH —**) BOCOR BOKOR GOOFER GUFFER WIZARD WITCHMAN

DOCTOR'S DILEMMA (**AUTHOR OF —**) SHAW
(**CHARACTER IN —**) LOUIS RALPH CULLEN COLENSO DUBEDAT PATRICK RIDGEON WALPOLE JENNIFER BONINGTON BLENKINSOP

DOCTRINAIRE ISMY

DOCTRINAL CREEDAL

DOCTRINE ISM DOXY LEAR LORE RULE CREDO CREED DOGMA LIGHT MAXIM TABLE TENET ZOISM AHIMSA BABISM BELIEF DHARMA EGOISM EROTIC GOSPEL HOLISM MALISM MONISM NOETIC THEORY ACROAMA AMIDISM ANIMISM ARTICLE ATAVISM ATHEISM ATOMISM BAHAISM DUALISM EGOTISM EVANGEL KARAISM KRYPSIS MISHNAH NEOLOGY NOETICS OPINION PEELISM PRECEPT PROGRAM REALISM SENSISM TRIKAYA ACTIVISM AGATHISM ANALYTIC ARIANISM ARYANISM BAJANISM CHILIASM

CYNICISM DARBYISM DEVILISM DOCETISM DYNAMISM ENERGISM FATALISM FINALISM GOBINISM HEDONISM HYLOLOGY IDENTISM IDEOLOGY ISLAMISM MOLINISM NIHILISM PAJONISM PAMNESIA PEJORISM POSITION POSOLOGY PSYCHISM REGALISM RHEMATIC SIDERISM SOLIDISM SPHERICS TYPOLOGY UBIQUITY VITALISM DITHESISM MECHANISM MUTUALISM PANTHEISM PESSIMISM PLURALISM NATURALISM
(BAD —) CACODOXY
(BUDDHIST —) ANATTA ANATMAN
(CONTRARY —) HERESY
(ESOTERIC —) CABALA QABBALA CABALISM
(EVIL —) MOLOCH
(MUSLIM —) TAUHID TAWHID
(PL.) ESOTERY SCOTISM CREDENDA DONATISM LABADISM SCRIBISM
(SUFF.) ISM LOGER LOGIA(N) LOGIC(AL) LOGIST LOGUE LOGY OLOGY
DOCUMENT DOC GET BILL BOND BOOK CALL CHOP DEED FORM GETT OLLA SEAL WRIT CHART DEMIT DIMIT GRIEF LEASE PAPER PROOF SCRIP SCRIT STIFF TARGE TEACH TITLE BILLET BREVET CADJAN CAJANG CEDULA COCKET DOCKET PATENT RAGMAN SCHOOL SCRIPT SOURCE SURVEY TICKET VOLUME ARCHIVE CONDUCT DIPLOMA ELOHIST ESCRIPT EXHIBIT INQUEST LICENSE MISSIVE PLACARD PRECEPT WARRANT WAYBILL WHEREAS WRITING CITATION CONTRACT COVENANT FURLOUGH INSTRUCT MORTGAGE SCHEDULE SECURITY TRANSIRE BORDEREAU
(CONDITIONAL —) SCRIP
(COPY OF —) VIDIMUS
(COURT —) WRIT PRODUCTION
(REGISTRATION —S) LOGBOOK
(PL.) BUMF ARCHIVE ARCHIVE PALAPALA
DODAVAH (SON OF —) ELIEZER
DODDER SCAD SCALD SHAKE DODDLE DOTHER FIDEOS TOTTER TREMBLE FLAXDROP HAIRWEED HALEWEED HELLWEED MULBERRY
DODDERING OLD ANILE INANE INFIRM SENILE FOOLISH
DODDER LAUREL WOEVINE MISTLETOE
DODDIE HUMLIE
DODECANESE (— ISLAND) KOS SYME KASOS LEROS TELOS KHALKE LIPSOS PATMOS NISYROS KALYMNOS
DODGE RIG SHY BILK DUCK GAME JINK JOUK LURK RUSE AVOID CHEAT ELUDE EVADE FENCE FUDGE GLOSS LURCH PARRY PLANT SHIFT SHIRK SHUNT STALL TRICK ESCAPE FIDDLE PALTER RACKET WHEEZE DECEIVE EVASION PROFFER ARTIFICE

CROTCHET GILENYIE MALINGER SIDESTEP
DODGER FLIER FLYER SOGER HAGGLER HANDBILL
(DRAFT —) BUSHWACK
DODGING JINK
DODO (SON OF —) ELEAZAR ELHANAN
DOE DA ROE TEG FAUN HIND NANNY ALMOND BISCUIT
(— IN 1ST YEAR) FAWN
(BLUE —) FLIER FLYER
DOER ACTOR AGENT MAKER AUTHOR FACTOR FEASOR WORKER FACIENT MANAGER ATTORNEY EXECUTOR
(— OF ODD JOBS) JACK
(SUFF.) AST ATOR IST OR STER STRESS
DOES S DOTH DUSE
(— NOT) DONT DISNA DOESNT
DOFF OFF DAFF VAIL AVALE DOUSE DOWSE STRIP DIVEST REMOVE UNDRESS
DOFFER DRUM DUFFER
DOFFING CAP
DOG CUR LAB MUT PUG PUP YAP ALAN ALCO CHOW DANE FAUS GOER HUND KIYI MONG MUTT PAWL STAG TIKE TRAY TYKE ALAND ALANT ARGOS BAWTY BEDOG BESET BOUCH BOXER CALEB CANID CHIEN CORGI DERBY DODGE HOUND HUSKY LIMER PELON POOCH PUPPY RACHE RAKER RATCH SILKY SLING SPITZ STALK WHELP AFGHAN BANDOG BARBET BARKER BASSET BAWTIE BEAGLE BELTON BORZOI BOSTON BOWWOW BRIARD BUFFER CANINE COCKER COLLIE COONER DANCER DETENT DRIVER ESKIMO FINDER GUNDOG HEADER HEELER HUNTER JOWLER KELPIE KENNET MISSET POODLE RANGER RATTER SALUKI SEIZER SETTER SHADOW SHOUGH SIRIUS SUSSEX TALBOT TANUKI TOLLER TOWSER VIZSLA YAPPER YAUPER YELPER BASENJI BOARDER BULLDOG CARRIER COURSER CRAMPON CREEPER DOGGESS DROPPER GRIFFON HARRIER LURCHER MALTESE MASTIFF MONGREL OWTCHAH POINTER SCOTTIE SHARPAI SKIRTER SLEUGHI SPANIEL SPORTER STARTER TERRIER TUMBLER WHIPPET YAPSTER ABERDEEN AIREDALE ALEUTANT ALSATIAN CERBERUS COACHDOG COCKAPOO CYNHYENA DEMIWOLF DOBERMAN ELKHOUND FISSIPED FOXHOUND KEESHOND LABRADOR LANDSEER LONGTAIL MALEMUTE MALINOIS PAPILLON PEKINESE SAMOYEDE SEALYHAM SHEPHERD SIBERIAN SPRINGER TURNSPIT VERMINER WATCHDOG WATERRUG PEKINGESE POMERANIAN AFFENPINSCHER
(— OF BUSTER BROWN) TIGE
(— OF INDIA) PARIAH
(— OF LATHE) DRIVER

(— OF ORPHAN ANNIE) SANDY
(— TRAINED AS DECOY) TOLLER
(BELGIAN —) SCHIPPERKE
(BIRD —) BOLTER
(CHAINED —) BANDOG
(CHINESE —) SHARPEI SHIHTZU
(COMICS —) OTTO
(COMMON NAME FOR —) ZEKE
(CORN —) FRANKFURTER
(DECOY —) PIPER
(ESKIMO —) HUSKY SIWASH
(FAMOUS —) ASTA FALA TIGE TOTO
(FARM —) KOMONDOR
(FEMALE —) GYP SLUT BITCH DOGGESS
(FICTIONAL —) LAD TOBY SANDY
(FOXLIKE —) COLPEO
(GERMAN —) ROTTWEILER
(GUIDE —) SEEINGEYE
(HOUSE —) WAP WAPP
(HUNGARIAN —) PULI KUVASZ
(HUNTING —) ALAN BRACH RACHE RATCH ALAUND BASSET HUNTER KENNET LUCERN RACCHE SALUKI SEIZER SETTER SLOUGH COURSER DROPPER HARRIER POINTER STRIKER
(JAPANESE —) AKITA
(KIND OF —) FOO
(LAP —) MESSAN SHOUGH
(LARGE —) DANE TOWSER MASTIFF KOMONDOR
(LIKE A —) CYNIC
(LONG-EARED —) BEAGLE
(LONG-HAIRED —) ALCO SHOCK
(MONGREL —) CUR BRAKJE DEMIWOLF
(MOVIE —) ASTA LADY TOTO BENJI TRAMP CHANCE LASSIE OLDYELLER RINTINTIN
(NON-BARKING —) BASENJI
(PARTI-COLORED —) PIE PYE
(PART OF —) PAD PAW TOE ARCH BACK DOME HOCK KNEE LOIN RUMP STOP CHEEK CHEST CREST CROUP ELBOW FLEWS THIGH CARPUS DEWLAP MUZZLE STIFLE BRISKET CUSHION KNUCKLE LEATHER OCCIPUT PASTERN WITHERS FOREHEAD HEELKNOB
(PET —) MINX LAPDOG MOPPET
(POPULAR — NAME) FIDO LADY SHEP SPOT ROVER
(PRESIDENT'S —) FALA MINNIE CHECKERS
(PUG —) MOPS
(PUNCH'S —) TOBY
(RACCOON —) TANUKI
(RUNNING —) LACKEY
(SHAGGY —) RUG OWTCHAH
(SHEEP —) CUR COLLIE KELPIE BEARDIE MALINOIS SHEPHERD
(SHORT-BODIED —) PUG
(SMALL —) TOY FICE FIST DOGGY FEIST LAIKA PIPER DOGGIE AMERTOY SPANIEL PAPILLON PEKINESE
(VICIOUS —) TAEPO
(WATCH —) CUR GARM GARMR
(WELSH —) CORGI
(WILD —) ADJAG DHOLE DINGO GUARA JACKAL AGOUARA CIMARRON

(YELPING —) WAPPET
(PL.) DOGGERY
(PREF.) CYN(O)
DOGBANE KENDIR KENDYR ECHITES FLYTRAP ALSTONIA MILKWEED OLEANDER PERIWINKLE
DOGBOAT PIG
DOGCART GADDER TUMTUM BOUNDER GADABOUT
DOG COLLAR TRASH
DOG DAYS CANICULE
DOG EAR LEATHER
DOG FENNEL HOGWEED
DOGFIGHT SCRAMBLE
DOGFISH DOG HOE HUSS TOPE FLAKE HOUND HURSE MANGO TOPER BOUNCE DAGGAR GALEID MORGAY BONEDOG GABBACK SPURDOG TRIAKID GRAYFISH SEAHOUND
(PREF.) SCYLLIO SQUALI SQUALO
DOGGED DOUR SULLEN DOGGISH DOGLIKE STUBBORN OBSTINATE
DOGGEREL NOMINY TRIVIA DOGGREL SINGSONG
DOGGONE BLESSED DOWNGONE
DOGIE CALF LEPPY STRAY
DOG KEEPER FEWTERER
DOGLIKE CYNIC CYNOID DOGGED
DOGMA CREED TENET DICTUM DOCTRINE DOCUMENT
DOGMATIC THETIC PONTIFIC POSITIVE ARBITRARY CONFIDENT PONTIFICAL
DOGMATISM BOWWOW
DOGMATIST BIGOT PHILODOX
DOG POUND GREENYARD
DOG ROSE BUCKY CANKER BEDEGUAR DOGBERRY
DOG SALMON CHUM KETA MORGAY DOGFISH
DOGSBODY DRUDGE
DOGSHORE DOG DAGGER
DOG'S MERCURY SAPWORT
DOG SNAPPER JOCU
DOGSTAIL BENT
DOGSTAR SIRIUS
DOGWOOD OSIER SUMAC CORNEL CORNUS GAITER WIDBIN BARBASCO FISHWOOD
DOILY MAT TIDE TIDY NAPKIN
DOING ACT DEED FACT STIR EVENT ACTION FUNCTION PRACTIVE
(PL.) FARE GEAR
(SUFF.) ANT ENT PRACTIC PRAXIA PRAXIS
DOIT DODKIN
DO-IT-YOURSELF DIY
DOLE LOT ALMS DEAL DOOL GIFT GOAL METE PART VAIL ALLOT FRAUD GRIEF GUILE MOURN POGEY SHARE DECEIT GRIEVE RELIEF SORROW CHARITY DEALING DESTINY HANDOUT PAYMENT PORTION BOUNDARY DIMENSUM DISPENSE DIVISION GRATUITY LANDMARK PITTANCE
DOLEFUL SAD DOWY DOWIE DREAR HEAVY DISMAL DOOLFU DREARY FUNEST RUEFUL FLEBILE DOLESOME DOLOROUS FUNESTAL MOURNFUL TRAGICAL

DOLERITE DIABASE
DOLICHOTIS MARA
DOLL GAL TOY BABE BABY MOLL
ARRAY DOLLY DOLLIE KEWPIE
MAIDEN MAUMET MOPPET
MUNECA POPPET POUPEE PUPPET
KACHINA KATCINA KATCHINA
MISTRESS
(— UP) PRIMP SWANK
(PASTEBOARD —) PANTINE
(PREF.) PUPI
DOLLAR BALL BEAN BONE BUCK
CASE CLAM DURO FISH ROCK
SCAD SKIN SPOT ADOBE BERRY
DALER EAGLE PLONK PLUNK
WHEEL GOURDE PATACA
DAALDER RINGGIT SMACKER
FROGSKIN PATACOON SIMOLEON
(FIVE —S) NICKEL
(ONE MILLION —S) MEGABUCK
(SILVER —) SINKER
(SPANISH —) COB DURO COBBE
(TEN —S) DIME
(THOUSAND —S) GEE THOU GRAND
DOLLARFISH SHINER MOONFISH
STARFISH
DOLLOP GLOB
DOLL'S HOUSE (AUTHOR OF —)
IBSEN
(CHARACTER IN —) NORA RANK
HELMER LINDEN TORVALD
KROGSTAD CHRISTINA
DOLLY DRAB HOBBY PEGGY PUNCH
SWAGE MAIDEN FOLLOWER
MISTRESS SLATTERN
DOLLYMAN BUCKER
DOLLYWAY DOCK
DOLMEN SENAM TOLMEN
CROMMEL CROMLECH MEGALITH
DOLOMITE ANKERITE PEARLSPAR
DOLOR CALOR GRIEF SORROW
ANGUISH SADNESS DISTRESS
MOURNING
DOLOROUS SAD DISMAL DOLEFUL
GRIEVOUS PATHETIC
DOLPHIN INIA SUSU BOUTO WHALE
DORADO KILLER PALACH TURSIO
BOLLARD COWFISH PELLOCK
PULLOCK SNUFFER CETACEAN
MAHIMAHI MUTILATE PORPOISE
(PREF.) DELPHIN DELPHO
(SUFF.) DELPHIS
DOLPHIN STRIKER MARTINGALE
DOLT ASS OAF PUT ASSE BOZO
CALF CHUB CLOD COOF DULT
FOOL GOFF MOKE PEAK POOP
STUB BOOBY CHUMP CLUNK
DOBBY DUMMY DUNCE FUNGE
GOLEM IDIOT NUMPS PATCH
THICK BEFOOL CUDDEN DIMWIT
DOODLE DULTIE HOBBIL NITWIT
OXHEAD AIRHEAD BLUNTIE
DAWCOCK DULLARD JACKASS
SAPHEAD SCHNOOK BONEHEAD
BOSTHOON CLODPATE CLODPOLL
DUMBBELL IMBECILE LUNKHEAD
MACAROON MOONCALF
NUMSKULL LAMEBRAIN
DOLTISH DULL STUPID FOOLISH
PEAKISH SOTTISH TOMFOOL
BESOTTED BLOCKISH DOLTLIKE
DOMAIN LAND BOUND BOURN
REALM SCOPE STATE WORLD
BARONY BOURNE COUNTY
DEMAIN EMPERY EMPIRE ESTATE
SPHERE DEMESNE EARLDOM
BIRTHDOM DOMINION LORDSHIP
PROVINCE SEIGNORY STAROSTY
(— OF SULTAN) SOLDAN
(— OF THE UNCONSCIOUS)
SHADOWLAND
(MATHEMATICAL —) FIELD
(NETHER —) HELL
(TRANSCENDENT —) HEAVEN
(WOMAN'S —) DISTAFF
DOMBEYA ASSONIA
DOMBEY AND SON (AUTHOR OF
—) DICKENS
(CHARACTER IN —) GAY PAUL
EDITH CARKER CUTTLE DOMBEY
WALTER GRANGER FLORENCE
DOME CAP CIMA TYPE CROWN
VAULT COCKLE CUPOLA THOLOS
CALOTTE EDIFICE CIMBORIO
HEMIDOME
(— OVER TOMB) WELI
(BUDDHIST —) TOPE
(KIND OF —) ONION
(OBSERVATION —) BLISTER
(POINTED —) IMPERIAL
(ROUND —) THOLUS
(SNOW-CAPPED —) CALOTTE
DOMER CLASPER
DOME-SHAPED BEEHIVE
DOMESTIC HIND HOME MAID
MOZO DOMAL TABBY FAMILY
HAMEIL HAMELT HEYDUC HOMELY
HOMISH HOUSAL INLAND INMATE
INWARD MENIAL NATIVE FAMELIC
HEYDUCK ONSHORE SCALDER
SERVANT FAMILIAR HOMEBRED
HOMEMADE INTIMATE
(PL.) FOLK
DOMESTICALLY ONSHORE
DOMESTICATE TAME ENTAME
AMENAGE RECLAIM CIVILIZE
DOMESTICATED CADE TAME
GENTLE INWARD DOMESTIC
FAMILIAR
DOMICILE CRIB HOME SHED ABODE
HOUSE MENAGE DWELLING
RESIDENCE
DOMINANCE SWAY INFLUENCE
DOMINANT BOSSY CHIEF FIFTH
TENOR MASTER RULING SOVRAN
CENTRAL REGNANT SUPREME
DOMINULE SUPERIOR
PARAMOUNT OVERBEARING
PREPONDERANT
DOMINATE TOP BOSS HAVE RULE
CHARM REIGN COERCE DIRECT
GOVERN VASSAL BEWITCH
COMMAND CONTROL ENVELOP
POSSESS BESTRIDE DOMINEER
OVERRIDE OVERSWAY OVERTONE
(— THE MIND) POSSESS
(— THE WILL) MESMERIZE
DOMINATING SUPERIOR
BREATHLESS
DOMINATION EMPIRE CONTROL
STRINGS BOVARISM BOVARYSM
DOMINION POSSESSION
DOMINEER BOSS BRAG LORD RULE
BULLY FEAST REVEL TOWER
COMPEL COMMAND SWAGGER

DOMINATE OVERBEAR OVERLEAD
OVERLORD
(— OVER) RIDE HECTOR
DOMINEERING SURLY LORDLY
HAUGHTY ARROGANT DESPOTIC
MASTERLY MASTERFUL
DOMINICA (CAPITAL OF —) ROSEAU
(MOUNTAIN PEAK IN —)
MORNEDIABLOTIN
DOMINICAN JACOBIN JACOBITE
PREACHER PREDICANT

DOMINIE MASTER PASTOR
DOMINION RULE SWAY CROWN
REALM REIGN DITION DOMAIN
EMPERY EMPIRE REGNUM
CONTROL DIOCESE DYNASTY
KHANATE MASTERY POUSTIE
REGENCY CALIFATE IMPERIUM
LORDSHIP SEIGNORY SIGNORIA
SOVRANTY OBEDIENCE
(PL.) DUCHY
DOMINO DIE BONE CARD FIVE
MASK TILE BLANK JETON STONE
DOUBLE JETTON MATADOR
VENETIAN
(FIRST — PLAYED) SET
(PL.) MATATADOR MUGGINS
BONEYARD
DOMINO NOIR, LE (COMPOSER OF
—) AUBER
DOMITILLA (DAUGHTER OF —)
DOMITILLA
(HUSBAND OF —) VESPASIAN
(SON OF —) TITUS DOMITIAN
DOM PEDRO SNOOZER
DON CAPO WEAR ARRAY DRESS
ENDUE INDUE PUTON THROW
ASSUME CLOTHE INVEST ADDRESS
NOBLEMAN
DONALBAIN (FATHER OF —)
DUNCAN
DONATE GIE GIFT GIVE BESTOW
PRESENT
DONATION GIFT GRANT DONATIO
PRESENT DONATIVE BENEFACTION
(—S RECEIVED BY SINGERS) CARL
DON CARLOS (CHARACTER IN —)

EBOLI CARLOS PHILIP VALOIS
CHARLES RODRIGO ELISABETH
(COMPOSER OF —) VERDI
DONE GAR DEEN OVER BAKED
ENDED GIVEN COOKED THROUGH
FINISHED
(— AS DUTY) PERFUNCTORY
(— BY HAND) MANUAL
(— BY WORD OF MOUTH) PAROL
PAROLE
(— CARELESSLY) SCAMBLING
(— FOR) GONE SUNK KAPUT KAPUTT
FINISHED
(— IN FAITH) AF
(— IN PLAIN SIGHT) BRAZEN
(— POORLY) BOTCHY
(— THOROUGHLY) PERFECT
(— TOGETHER) CONCERTED
(— WITH) BY
(— WITHOUT DELIBERATION) SNAP
(— WRONG WAY) AWK
(TO BE —) PASS
DONEE DONATOR HERITOR
RECEIVER
DON GIOVANNI (CHARACTER IN —)
ANNA ELVIRA MASETTO OTTAVIO
ZERLINA GIOVANNI LEPORELLO
(COMPOSER OF —) MOZART
DUNJON KEEP ROCCA DUNGEON
DON JUAN (MOTHER OF —) INEZ
DONKEY ASS BUSS DONK FUSS
MOKE BURRO CHUMP CUDDY
DICKY EQUID GENET GUDDA HINNY
HORSE JENNY NEDDY BRAYER
CUDDLE DICKEY JENNET ONAGER
ASINEGO BUSSOCK FUSSOCK
JACKASS LONGEAR
CARDOPHAGUS
(MILNE —) EEYORE
DONKEY ENGINE DOCTOR DONKEY
ROADER YARDER DOLLBEER
DONNA DEL LAGO (CHARACTER IN
—) ELENA DOUGLAS GIACOMO
MALCOLM RODERICK
(COMPOSER OF —) ROSSINI
DONNA DIANA (COMPOSER OF —)
REZNICEK
DONNYBROOK MELEE
DONOR GIVER DONATOR
DO-NOTHING DONNOT DONOUGHT
FAINEANT
DON PASQUALE (CHARACTER IN
—) NORINA ERNESTO PASQUALE
SOFRONIA MALATESTA
(COMPOSER OF —) DONIZETTI
DON QUIXOTE (AUTHOR OF —)
CERVANTES
(CHARACTER IN —) PANZA PEDRO
PEREZ ALONZO DAPPLE SAMSON
SANCHO TOBOSO GUINART
QUIXOTE CARRASCO DULCINEA
NICHOLAS ROSINANTE
DONUM GIVER DEUNAM
DOODAD DODAD DOODAB
DOFUNNY TRINKET GIMCRACK
JIMCRACK
DOOHICKEY GISMO
DOOM KER LAW LOT DAMN FATE
RUIN CURSE DEATH JUDGE
ADDEEM DECREE DEVOTE STEVEN
CONDEMN DESTINE DESTINY
FORTUNE STATUTE DECISION
FOREDOOM SENTENCE

DOOMED FEY DEAD DONE LORN FATAL DAMNED FORLORN ACCURSED FINISHED
DOOM PALM DOUM
DOOMSAYER DOOMSTER DOOMSDAYER
DOOMSMAN LAWMAN
DOOMSTER JUDGE
DOOR LID DROP EXIT FOLD GATE HECK SHUT TRAP ENTRY HATCH JANUA VALVE DAMPER JIGGER PORTAL RADDLE WICKET BARRIER DOORWAY INGRESS OPENING OUTDOOR PASSAGE POSTERN ANTEPORT ENTRANCE FOREDOOR POSTICUM SERVIDOR STOPPING TRAVERSE VOMITORY
(**— IN MINE**) STOPPING
(**— OF ASH PIT**) ARCH
(**— OF MASONIC LODGE**) TILE
(**ADIT —**) STULM
(**AIRPLANE —**) CLAMSHELL
(**HALF —**) HECK HATCH
(**PART OF —**) RAIL SILL STILE LINTEL MULLION
(**ROMAN —S**) FORES
(**SLIDING —**) SHUT SHOJI FUSUMA TRAVERSE
(**STORM —**) DINGLE
(**STRONG —**) OAK
(**TRAP —**) SLOT SCRUTO VAMPIRE VAMPYRE
(**PREF.**) THYRE(O) THYRO
(**SUFF.**) THYRIS
DOORFRAME BUCK
DOORHEAD DERNER
DOORKEEPER TILER TILIA USHER DURWAN PORTER WARDEN DOORMAN JANITOR OSTIARY DOORWARD HUISSIER JANITRIX PORTRESS WISKINKY
DOOR KNOCKER HAMMER RAPPER
DOOR LATCH SNECK HAGGADAY
DOORMAN FOOTMAN HALLMAN DOORWARD
DOORMAT COCOMAT
DOORPOST DURN JAMB PIER POST ALETTE POSTEL
DOORSILL SOIL
DOORSTOP BUMPER HOLDBACK
DOORWAY DOOR EXIT PORTAL OPENING
DOOZER PIP DARB LULU BEAUT DILLY CORKER SNORTER HUMDINGER
DOOZY LULU HUMDINGER
DOPATTA UPARNA DOOPUTTY
DOPE HOP LUG BOOB DRUG GOFF GOON GOOP INFO BOOBY OPIUM PASTE STUPE HEROIN INSIDE OPIATE SKINNY LOWDOWN PREDICT STUPEFY NARCOTIC
(**— SMUGGLER**) MULE
DOPED CRONK
DOPER GREASER
DOR BEE DORR JOKE MOCK BONGO CLOCK DORRE JOKER SCOFF TRICK BEETLE DRONER BUFFOON DECEIVE MOCKERY
DORADO CUIR XIPHIAS GOLDFISH
DORALICE (HUSBAND OF —) PHODOPHIL MANDRICARDO
(**LOVER OF —**) RODOMONT

DORBEETLE DOR CLOCK DRONER BUZZARD BUMCLOCK
DORIGEN (HUSBAND OF —) ARVIRAGUS
(**LOVER OF —**) AURELIUS
DORIMENE (HUSBAND OF —) SGANARELLE
(**LOVER OF —**) DORANTE
DORINDA (HUSBAND OF —) AIMWELL
(**SISTER OF —**) MIRANDA
DORIS (BROTHER AND HUSBAND OF —) NEREUS
(**FATHER OF —**) OCEANUS
(**MOTHER OF —**) TETHYS
DORK JERK NERD DWEEB
DORMANCY TORPOR ABEYANCE
DORMANT FIXED INERT ASLEEP LATENT TORPID RESTING SLEEPER INACTIVE LATITANT SLEEPING CONNIVENT
DORMER WINDOW LUCOMB MEMBER DORMANT EYEBROW LUCARNE LUTHERN
DORMITORY DORM HALL HOUSE DORMER DORTER HOSTEL BULLPEN COLLEGE DORTOUR CUBATORY QUARTERS
DORMOUSE LOIR DRYAD LEROT GLIRID SLEEPER
(**PREF.**) GLIRI
DORNICK DONEY LINEN DARNEX DONACK DONNICK
DORPER DORSIAN
DORSAL NOTAL DORSER DOSSER NEURAL TERGAL ABAXIAL HANGING SUPERIOR POSTERIOR
(**PREF.**) OPISTH(O)
DORSUM BACK
DORUS (BROTHER OF —) LAODOCUS POLYPOETES
(**FATHER OF —**) APOLLO HELLEN XUTHUS
(**MOTHER OF —**) CREUSA ORSEIS PHTHIA
(**SLAYER OF —**) AETOLUS
DOSAGE (RADIATION —) REM REP REPP
(**SCIENCE OF —**) POSOLOGY
DOSE BOLE DOST SHOT BROMO DATIO DOSIS DRAFT STORE TREAT DATION DOCTOR DOSAGE DRENCH POTION BOOSTER BROMIDE CAPSULE DRAUGHT QUANTITY
(**— OF SUBSTANCE**) PULSE
(**DRUG —**) HIT
(**NARCOTIC —**) LOCUS BINDLE LOCUST
DOSS BOW DOS KNOT TUFT BUNCH
DOSSERET PULVINO
DOT SET CLOT DOTE LUMP MOTE PECK SPOT STAR TICK COVER DOWER DOWRY POINT PRICK PUNTO SPECK BULLET CENTER CENTRE DOTLET PERIOD STIGME TITTLE TOCHER PUNCTUM PUNCTUS SPECKLE SPOTTLE STIPPLE FLYSPECK PARTICLE SPRINKLE
(**— IN CODE**) DIT
(**— ON DICE**) PIP
(**— ON FOREHEAD**) BOTTU

(**— ON PATCH OF DIFFERENT COLOR**) ISLET
(**BLACK —**) DARTROSE
(**PL.**) LEADERS
DOTAGE DOTE FOLLY DRIVEL SENILITY TWICHILD
DOTARD DOBBY DOTER SILLY DOBBIE DOTANT SENILE DOTTREL DOTTEREL IMBECILE LIRIPIPE LIRIPOOP
DOTCHIN STEELYARD
DOTE ROT DOVE DOZE FOND LIKE LOVE TIRE ADORE DECAY ENDOW BESTOW DOTAGE DOTARD DRIVEL STUPOR IMBECILE
DOTING FON FOND GAGA DOTAGE PAWING UXORIOUS
DOTTED SEME CRIBLE SEMEED TICKED TOUCHY SPOTTED PUNCTATE SPECKLED STIPPLED STELLATED
(**— SWISS**) LAPPET
DOTTER SPOTTER
DOTTEREL DUPE GULL WIND PLOVER DOTTREL MORINEL
DOTTY TOTY CRAZY TOTTY FEEBLE SPOTTY
DOUBLE KA BOW PLY DUAL FOLD SORE TWIN CRACK DUPLE FETCH ROUND SOSIE BIFOLD BINARY BINATE DOPPIO DUPLEX MIDDLE DIPLOID DOUBLET TWOFOLD BIVALENT GEMINATE BIFARIOUS SIMILITUDE
(**— IMPRESSION**) MACKLE
(**— IN POKER**) STRADDLE
(**— MUSICAL NOTES**) AUGMENT
(**— UP**) BUCK JACKKNIFE
(**PHANTOM —**) FETCH
(**PREF.**) BI BIN(I)(O) DI(S) DIPHY DIPL(O) DISS(O) DITTO GEMINI
DOUBLE BASSOON FAGOTTONE
DOUBLE CHIN CHOLLER
DOUBLECROSS BITCH CHEAT BETRAY DECEIVE SWINDLE BUSINESS
DOUBLE-CROSSER RAT HEEL
DOUBLED GEMEL GEMINOUS
(**PREF.**) BIS
DOUBLE DAGGER DIESIS
DOUBLE-DEALING DECEIT DUPLICITY
DOUBLE FLUTE DIAULOS
DOUBLEHEADER (BASEBALL —) TWINIGHT
DOUBLENESS DUALITY PLENITUDE
(**— OF ASPECT**) POLARITY
DOUBLE-RIPPER BOBSLED BOBSLEIGH
DOUBLE-RUNNER SKATE
DOUBLET SNIFF DOUBLE DUPLET PALTOCK PLACCATE POURPOINT
DOUBLE-TALK NEWSPEAK RAZZMATAZZ
DOUBLETREE EVENER SPREADER
DOUBLING LAP FOLD HEAD LOOP
(**— OF THE BLIND**) STRADDLE
DOUBLOON ONZA
DOUBLY
(**PREF.**) BI
DOUBT FEAR WEIR DEMUR DREAD DWERE QUERY WAVER NIGGLE BALANCE DIFFIDE DUBIETY

SCRUPLE SKEPSIS SUSPECT SWITHER UMBRAGE DISTRUST DUBITATE HESITATE MISTRUST QUESTION STAGGERS MISLIPPEN
(**EXTREME —**) RACK
(**PROFESSED —**) APORIA
DOUBTER CYNIC SKEPTIC DUBITANTE
DOUBTFUL JUBUS DOUBTY UNSURE DUBIOUS FEARFUL JEALOUS PERHAPS WILSOME BOGGLISH DREADFUL JUBEROUS PERILOUS WAVERING QUESTIONABLE PROBLEMATICAL
DOUBTING DUBIOUS DUBITANT
DOUBTLESS WITTERLY
DOUCEUR TIP BONUS POURBOIRE
DOUCHE RINSE EYEWASH
DOUGH CASH DUFF FILO MASA CRUST DAIGH MONEY MOOLA PASTE PUPPY CHANGE DINERO HALLAH NOODLE PHYLLO SPONGE WAMPUM BRIOCHE CABBAGE MANDLEN TEIGLACH
(**BISCUIT —**) CAKE
(**BREAD —**) SPONGE
(**CASE OF —**) PIROGI PIEROGI
(**FERMENTING —**) LEAVEN
(**FRIED —**) SPUD
(**NOODLE —**) FARFEL FERFEL
(**PASTRY —**) PHYLLO
(**SWEET SQUARE OF —**) SOPAPILLA SOPAPILLA
DOUGHBOY YANK
DOUGHNUT NUT SINK DONUT TORUS CYMBAL SINKER BEIGNET CRULLER FATCAKE NUTCAKE OLYCOOK OLYKOEK SIMBALL TWISTER ZEPPOLE BISMARCK FASNACHT
(**SHAPED LIKE —**) TOROIDAL
DOUGHTY FELL PREU TALL BRAVE VALIANT INTREPID
DOUGHY SAD DUNCH SODDEN
DOUR DERN GLUM GRIM HARD SOUR ROUGH STERN GLOOMY MOROSE SEVERE STRONG SULLEN OMINOUS TACITURN
DOUSE BEAT BLOW DOFF DUCK QUIT STOW CEASE DOWSE RINSE SOUSE DRENCH PLUNGE SLUICE STRIKE STROKE IMMERSE DOWNPOUR
(**— WITH LIQUOR AND IGNITE**) FLAMBE
DOUZEPER ANSEIS PALADIN
DOVE DOO DOW DOZE KUKU JONAH CULVER CUSHAT JEMIMA PIGEON COLUMBA DOVELET LAUGHER NAMAQUA SLUMBER DOVELING RINGDOVE
(**— SOUND**) CURR
(**GROUND —**) ROLA
(**RING —**) TOOZOO
(**ROCK —**) SOD
(**SCALE —**) INCA
DOVECOTE DOOCOT LOUVER DOVECOT DOWCOTE PIGEONRY COLUMBARY
DOVEKIE AUK ALLE BULL ROTCH ROTGE DOVEKEY BULLBIRD DOVELIKE

DOVETAIL COG JAG JAGG MESH
MERGE TENON
DOWDINESS FRUMPERY
DOWDY POKY FRUMP MOPSY
POKEY TACKY BLOWZY SHABBY
STODGY UNTIDY FRUMPISH
SLOVENLY
DOWEL NOG PEG PIN COAK STUD
SPRIG JOGGLE PINTLE DULEDGE
DOWER DOS DOWRY ENDOW
TOCHER DOARIUM PORTION
HERITAGE MARITAGE
DOWITCHER SNIPE DRIVER
SLEEPER GRAYBACK GREYBACK
LONGBEAK
DOWN BAS EAT HUP OFF BETE CAST
COOL DOON DOWL FELL FLIX FLUE
FUZZ HILL LINT MOXA PILE SOUR
ADOWN BELOW DOWLE EIDER
FLOOR FLUFF SOUTH BEDOWN
FRIEZE LANUGO PAPPUS
CONSUME HANDOUT HILLOCK
PLUMAGE DOWNLAND
(**— AND OUT**) QUISBY
(**— AT THE HEEL**) SLIPSHOD
(**— THAT WAY**) DOWNBY DOWNBYE
(**— THE LINE**) ALONG
(**BE — WITH**) HAVE
(**BEAVER —**) FLIX
(**FAR —**) DEEP DEEPLY
(**FARTHEST —**) BOTTOMMOST
(**GO —**) SET
(**STRAIGHT —**) DOWNRIGHT
(**PREF.**) CAT(A)(O) CATH DE HYPO
KAT(A) LACHN(O) OB PTIL(O) SUB
DOWN-AND-OUT DERELICT
DOWNBEAT THESIS
DOWNCAST BAD LOW SAD DOWN
ABJECT GLOOMY HANGING
DEJECTED HOPELESS
DOWNER DRAG
DOWNFALL PIT FALL FATE RUIN
TRAP ABYSS DECAY FINISH
DESCENT ECLIPSE UNDOING
COLLAPSE DOWNCOME
FLAMEOUT TAILSPIN
(**AUTHOR OF —**) ZOLA
(**CHARACTER IN —**) JEAN WEISS
HONORE GOLIATH GUNTHER
MAURICE SILVINE FOUCHARD
MACQUART HENRIETTE LEVASSEUR
DELAHERCHE GARTLAUBEN
DOWNFEED OVERHEAD
DOWNFLOW VAIL DEFLUX
DOWNFOLD SADDLE DOWNWARP
DOWNGRADE DERATE
DOWNHILL DOWNDALE
(**SKI —**) WEDEL
DOWN-HOME CORNPONE
DOWNPOUR POUR RAIN BRASH
DOUSE DOWSE FLOOD PLASH
SPILL SPOUT DELUGE TORRENT
CATARACT AVALANCHE
DOWNRIGHT FAIR FLAT PURE RANK
BLANK BLUNT PLAIN PLUMB
PLUMP ROUND SHEER STARK
ARRANT DIRECT FAIRLY STURDY
REGULAR ABSOLUTE EVENDOWN
POSITIVE THOROUGH
DOWNSPOUT SPOUT DOWNPIPE
DOWNTAKE
DOWNSTAIRS BELOW
DOWNSTROKE DOWNBEAT

DOWNSWING DOLDRUMS
DOWNWARD ADOWN BELOW
LOWER PRONE DEORSUM
DOWNWITH
(**— ON ONE SIDE**) SIDEWAYS
(**PREF.**) BATH(O)(Y) CAT(A)(O) CATH
DOWNWIND LEEWARD
DOWNY SOFT FLUEY MOSSY NAPPY
PILAR PLUMY QUIET CALLOW
FLEDGY FLOSSY FLUFFY PILARY
PLACID COTTONY CUNNING
KNOWING SOOTHING
(**PREF.**) HEBE
DOWRY DOS DOT GIFT DOWER
SULKA DOWAGE LOBOLA LOBOLO
TALENT PORTION
DOWSE WITCH
DOXOLOGIZE LAUD
DOXOLOGY GLORIA KADDISH
DOXY WENCH HARLOT
DOYEN DEAN DOYENNE
DOZE NAP NOD ROT DARE DORM
DOTE DOVE DECAY DOVER SLEEP
SLOOM CATNAP DROWSE
MUDDLE SNOOZE DROPOFF
MEMENTO PERPLEX SLUMBER
SNOOZLE STUPEFY
DOZEN DIZZEN DOSAIN
(**FIVE —**) TALLY
(**TWO —**) THRAVE
DOZING DOGSLEEP
DRAB BOX DAW FOX SAD BLAH
DELL DRUG DULL BESOM BLEAK
DINGY DOLLY DREAR GRAVE
GRAZE HEAVY MOUSY TRULL
WENCH WHORE DREARY FRUMPY
ISABEL MALKIN POISON PUSSEL
STODGY PROSAIC PUCELLE
SUBFUSC DOLLYMOP EVERYDAY
POMPLESS
(**CHAETURA —**) DEAN
DRABBLE DRAGGLE
DRACHM DRAM
DRACO ANGUIS DRAGON
DRAFT NIP SIP CHIT DOSE DRAG
DRAM DRAW GLUT GULF GUST
ITEM LEVY PLAN PLOT SUCK SWIG
TOOT WORK BLAST CHECK DRINK
EPURE SLOCK SWILL SWIPE TAPER
WRITE DESIGN DRENCH GODOWN
MINUTE POTION PROJET REDACT
RETURN SCHEME SCROLL SKETCH
WAUCHT WAUGHT ABBOZZO
DRAUGHT DRAWING OUTLINE
PATTERN PHILTER PROJECT
BEVERAGE POTATION PROTOCOL
(**— OF AIR**) COOKE
(**— OF A VESSEL**) GAGE GAUGE
(**— OF COMPOSITION**) SCORE
(**— OFF**) SHED
(**— OF LAW**) BILL
(**— OF PATTERN**) STRIP
(**HEAVY —**) WHITTER
(**LARGE —**) SCOUR CAROUSE
(**MIDDAY —**) NOONING
(**ORIGINAL —**) PROTOCOL
(**ROUGH —**) EBAUCHE BROUILLON
SCANTLING
(**SECOND —**) REDO REWRITE
(**SLEEPING —**) DORTER
(**SMALL —**) NIP SIP SUCK TIFF TIFT
DRAFTER HORSER

DRAFTSMAN DRAWER TRACER
TIPPLER
DRAG DOG LAG TOW DRUG HALE
HONE HOOK KITE RASH SHOE SKID
SLUR TOLE TOLL TUMP CREEP
DEVIL DRAWL DRIFT FLOAT GETUP
LURRY NOWEL PLUCK RALLY
SLIDE SNAKE SWEEP TEASE TRAIL
TRAIN TRAWL TRICE DAGGLE
DOWNER DROGUE LINGER OUTFIT
REMORA SCHOOL TAIGLE TRAYNE
DRAGBAR DRAGGLE GRAPNEL
GRAPPLE SCHLEPP SKIDPAN
ARRASTRA DRAGSHOE
(**— ALONG**) LUG CRAWL SHOOL
TRAYNE TRACHLE TRAUCHLE
(**— CARELESSLY**) HIKE
(**— DOWN**) DEGRADE
(**— FEET**) SLODGE
(**— FORCIBLY**) SNAKE
(**— HOME CARCASS OF GAME**)
TUMP
(**— IN DEEP WATER**) CREEP
(**— JERKILY**) SNIG
(**— LOGS**) SKID
(**— OFF**) HARRY
(**— OUT**) DRAWL
(**PLANK —**) RUBBER
DRAGGING LEADEN
(**— DEAD BULL FROM RING**)
ARRASTRE
DRAGGLE LAG DRAIL DAGGLE
DRABBLE TRACHLE
DRAGNET FLUE TRAIN TRAWL
DRAWNET TRAINEL
DRAGON AHI LUNG WORM DRAKE
RAHAB NIDHOG VRITRA WYVERN
BASILISK DRAGONET NIDHOGGR
NITHHOGG
(**— WITH 7 HEADS**) HYDRA
(**SEA —**) QUAVIVER
(**WINGLESS —**) LINDWORM
(**PREF.**) DRACO(NT)(INTO)
DRAGONET FOX ILLECK FOXFISH
GOWDNIE GURNARD JUGULAR
SCULPIN LORICATE QUAVIVER
DRAGONFLY NAIAD ODONATE
SKIMMER LIBELLULA
DRAGON TREE DRACAENA
DRAGROPE DRAG GUSS
DRAGSTER FUELER SLINGSHOT
DRAIN DRY FRY GAN GAW SAP SEW
TOP BUZZ COUP DAIL DALE DELF
DIKE DRAG DRAW GOUT GRIP
GURT LADE LODE MILK SIKE SINK
SOAK SUFF SUMP TEEM TILE
BLEED BUNNY CANAL DELFT
DRAFT DREEN DRILL DROVE
EMPTY FLEET GROOP GULLY
LEECH RHINE SEUCH SEUGH
SEWER SHORE SIVER STANK STELL
EMULGE FILTER FURROW GUZZLE
RIGGOT SHEUCH SHEUGH SIPHON
SPONGE SWOUGH SYPHON
TRENCH TROGUE TROUGH ZANJON
ACEQUIA ALBERCA CAROUSE
CARRIER CHANNEL CULVERT
DEPLETE DRAUGHT EXHAUST
GRINDLE GRIPPLE SCUPPER
ZANJONA CANALIZE CARRIAGE
SINKHOLE SUBDRAIN THURROCK
(**— DRY**) JIB
(**— IN CHURCH**) PISCINA

(**— IN FEN**) LEAM
(**— IN MINE**) SOUGH
(**— IN STABLE**) GROOP
(**— SUGAR**) POT
(**COVERED —**) THURROCK
(**OPEN —**) SIVER STELL KENNEL
(**SMALL —**) TRONE
DRAINAGE ADIT SAUR SOCK
SULLAGE SUMPAGE
DRAINAGEWAY DRAW
DRAINER COLANDER
DRAINING SEEPAGE DRAINAGE
EMULGENT
DRAINPIPE SINK SHELL WHELM
LEADER QUELME
DRAKE STAG STAIG DRAKELET
DRAM GO NIP MITE SLUG TIFF TIFT
DRAFT DRINK SOPIE CALKER
CHASSE DRACHM JIGGER
CAULKER SNIFTER MERIDIAN
POTATION QUANTITY
(**— OF LIQUOR**) TOT SLUG SNIFTER
(**— OF SPIRITS**) NOBBLER
DRAMA RAS AUTO MIME PLAY
LEGIT OPERA COMEDY NATAKA
SCENES SOAPER TRAGIC ATELLAN
COMEDIA HISTORY PROVERB
THEATRE TRAGEDY DUODRAMA
MONODRAM OPERETTA PASTORAL
(**DANCE —**) KATHAKALI
(**JAPANESE —**) NO NOH KABUKI
(**MUSICAL —**) OPERA SAYNETE
OPERETTA
DRAMATIC WILD VIVID SCENIC
THESPIAN
(**— REPRESENTATION**) WAYANG
(**— WORK**) PREQUEL
(**HAVING LYRIC AND — QUALITIES**)
SPINTO
DRAMATIST (ALSO SEE
PLAYWRIGHT) OG ACTOR IBSENITE
DRAMSHOP GROGSHOP
DRAPE HANG PALL VEST ADORN
COVER CRAPE WEAVE CURTAIN
FESTOON HANGING VALANCE
DRAPED BEHUNG
DRAPER TAILOR LINENMAN
DRAPERY SWAG BAIZE DRAPE
SCENE CURTAIN REREDOS
VALANCE MOURNING
(**— ON BEDSTEAD**) PAND
(**PIECE OF —**) HANGING
DRAPING BLOUSE DRAPERY
DRASTIC DIRE HARSH EXTREME
RADICAL RIGOROUS
(**NOT —**) BLAND
DRAT DARN NUTS RATS PSHAW
PHOOEY RABBIT SHUCKS
DOGGONE
DRATTED BLESSED
DRAUGHT (ALSO SEE DRAFT) SLUG
WAUGHT OENOMEL
DRAUPADI (FATHER OF —)
DRUPADA
DRAVIDIAN GOND KOTA TODA
TULU ARAVA COORG GONDI
KHOND KLING MALTO ORAON
TAMIL ANDHRA BADAGA BIRHOR
BRAHUI KODAGU KURUKH TELEGU
TELUGU COLLERY DRAVIDA
TAMILIC KANARESE TAMILIAN
DRAW LUG TEE TIE TOW TUG DRAG
DUCT HALE HAUL LADE LIMN LINE

LURE PUFF PULL RAKE SPAN TILL
TIRE TOLL TREK VENT CATCH
DRAFT DRILL EDUCE ENDUE EXACT
HEAVE PAINT SKINK TRACE TRAIN
TRECK ALLURE BUCKET DEDUCE
DEPICT DERIVE DESIGN DEVISE
ELICIT ENGAGE ENTICE INDUCE
INHALE SELECT SKETCH STRIKE
ATTRACT BEGUILE CONTOUR
DETRACT DOGFALL DRAUGHT
EXTRACT INSPIRE PORTRAY
SCREEVE SCUMBLE INSCRIBE
INVEIGLE OUTBRAID STANDOFF
(— A CARD) CUT
(— AIR) BREATHE
(— ALONG) TRACK TRAIN
(— APART) REAM DIVEL DIDUCE
DIVERGE
(— ASIDE) SEDUCE
(— ASUNDER) TEAR
(— AT A PIPE) SHOOH SHAUGH
(— AWAY) ARACE DRAFT ABDUCT
ARACHE DRAUGHT ENTRAIN
ABSTRACT DISTRACT
(— AWKWARDLY) SCRAWL
(— BACK) FADE REVEL START
WINCE ARREAR RETIRE REVOKE
SHRINK CRINKLE RECLAIM RETRACT
RETREAT WITHTEE
(— BACK FROM) BLENCH FLINCH
RESILE TORFEL TORFLE DETRECT
(— BACK LIPS) GRIN
(— BOLT) SLOT
(— BY SUCTION) ASPIRATE
(— DEEP BREATH) SUSPIRE
(— DRINK) BIRL
(— EARTH AROUND) HILL
(— FIRST FURROW) FEER
(— FORTH) EDUCE EVOKE FETCH
ELICIT DEPROME EXHAUST
(— IN) PINK TRAP ENTRAP
(— IN DOTS) STIPPLE
(— OFF) BROACH
(— ON) INDUE INDUCE SOLICIT
(— ON PAVEMENT) SCREEVE
(— ON UNCOLLECTED FUNDS) KITE
(— OUT) MILK SLUB EDUCE EVOKE
EXACT SKINK TRACT ELICIT EXHALE
EXTEND EXTORT EXTRACT
(— STITCHES TIGHT) YERK
(— TIGHT) FRAP THRAP STRAIN
(— TOGETHER) COWL LACE COART
GATHER CRIMPLE
(— UP) FORM MAKE HUCKLE INKNIT
UPWALE
(— WITH FORCE) STRAIN
DRAWBACK OUT LETDOWN
TAKEOFF DISCOUNT PULLBACK
DRAWBAR DRAGBAR BULLNOSE
DRAWLINK SLIPRAIL
DRAWBRIDGE PONTLEVIS
DRAWEE ACCEPTER
DRAWER TILL LIMNER LOCKER
TILLER ENTERER INTAKER SHUTTLE
(— OF WATER) GIBEONITE
(BOTTOM —) GLORYBOX
(CASH —) TILL
(COAL —) PUTTER
(TYPEWRITER —) BED
DRAWER-DOWN KNOBBLER
DRAWER-IN ENTERER HEALDER
HEDDLER
DRAWER-OFF RACKER

DRAWERS PANTS SHORTS LININGS
PANTIES SHALWAR CALSOUNS
CALZOONS SHINTYAN PANTALETS
PANTELETS SHULWAURS
PANTALETTES
DRAWGATE SLACKER
DRAWING DRAW CHALK DRAFT
ENVOI EPURE SEPIA TUSHE
CRAYON DESIGN DETAIL FIGURE
FUSAIN SKETCH CAMAIEU
CARTOON CROQUIS DIAGRAM
DRAUGHT HAULING ISOTYPE
PULLING RETRAIT TOUSCHE
ADDUCENT CHARCOAL CROSSING
DOODLING FREEHAND FROTTAGE
HATCHING LINEWORK SANGUINE
SLUBBING SPECULUM STICKMAN
TRACTION TRANSFER TRICKING
(— ASUNDER) DIVELLENT
(— BACK) ABDUCENT
(— IN) INDRAFT
(— IN RED CHALK) SANGUINE
(— LIQUOR) BIRLING
(— OFF) DERIVATION
(— OF LOTS) BALLOT
(— OUT) BATTUE
(— TOGETHER) STYPTIC
(CHARCOAL —) FUSAIN
(COMIC —) CARTOON DROLLERY
(MARGINAL —) REMARK
(PREHISTORIC —) PICTOGRAM
PICTOGRAPH
(PREPARATORY —) SINOPIA
(SIDEWALK —) SCREEVE
(PL.) GRAFFITI
(PREF.) GRAMO
(SUFF.) GRAM
DRAWING-IN DRAW ENTERING
DRAWING-ROOM SALON
DRAWING ROOM SALON PARLOR
DRAWKNIFE SHAVE JIGGER
DRAWL DRANT DRATE DRUNT TRAIN
LOITER PROLATE
DRAWN DRAFT STREIT DRAUGHT
GRAPHIC HAGGARD
(— APART) DISTRACT
(— AWAY) ABSTRACT
(— CLOSE) STRICT
(— OFF) DRAINED
(— OUT) DREE DREICH DREIGH
EXTENDED
DRAWPLATE AGATE FLATTER
DRAWSHEET TYMPAN
DRAWSTRING LATCH STRING
DRAY CART LORRY SCOOT SLOOP
WAGON CAMION JIGGER ROLLEY
RULLEY SLOVEN WHEERY
DREAD AWE DREE FEAR FRAY FUNK
WARD WERE ANGST AWFUL
DOUBT GRISE TIMOR ADREAD
AGRISE DISMAY ESCHEW HORROR
TERROR ANXIETY DISMISS
DRIDDER REDOUBT AFFRIGHT
DREDDOUR GASTNESS MISDREAD
TERRIBLE
(SUFF.) PHOBE PHOBIA(C) PHOBIC
PHOBOUS
DREADED AWESOME BEDREAD
DREADFUL DERN DIRE AWFUL
CRUEL DISMAL GRISLY HORRID
AWESOME CAREFUL DIREFUL
DRIDDER FEARFUL GHASTLY
GRIMFUL HIDEOUS UNCOUTH

DOUBTFUL DOUBTOUS GHASTFUL
HORRIBLE HORRIFIC PERILOUS
SCAREFUL SHOCKING TERRIBLE
TERRIFIC
DREADFULLY DIRELY GRISLY
ABYSMALLY
DREADNOUGHT TANK DAREALL
WARSHIP FEARLESS
DREAM METE MOON MUSE REVE
FANCY SWEVEN VISION AISLING
AVISION CHIMERA FANTASY
IMAGINE NIRVANA REVERIE
ROMANCE CHIMAERA DAYDREAM
PHANTASM SOMNIATE
(— UP) ENVISION
(FRIGHTENING —) NIGHTMARE
(PREF.) ONEIR(O) ONIR(O)
DREAMER POET METER MUSARD
FANTAST IDEALIST PHANTAST
DREAMINESS LANGUOR
DREAMING ADREAM TRAUMEREI
DREAMTIME ALCHERA
DREAMY KEF SOFT MOONY VAGUE
POETIC FARAWAY LANGUID
MUSEFUL ONEIRIC PENSIVE
DREAMFUL FANCIFUL SOOTHING
DREAR DERN BLEAK DISMAL
GLOOMY DOLEFUL
DREARY SAD DIRE DOWY DREE
DULL FLAT GLUM BLEAK CRUEL
DOWIE DRURY OURIE WASTE
WISHT DISMAL DREICH ELENGE
GLOOMY GOUSTY LONELY
DOLEFUL GOUSTIE HOWLING
WILSOME GRIEVOUS WEARIFUL
DREDGE MOP DRAG DREG SIFT
SCOOP TRAIN DEEPEN DRUDGE
SCRAPE SPONGE TANGLE
GANGAVA SCALLOP EXCAVATE
SPRINKLE
(KIND OF —) EKMAN
(NATURALIST'S —) TANGLE
DREDGER DUSTER HEDGEHOG
DREDGING JILLING
DREGS LAG MUD CRAP FAEX LAGS
LEES SCUT SILT SUDS TAIL DRAFF
DREST DROSS DRUGS FECES
FOOTS GROUT JAUPS MAGMA
BOTTOM DRAINS DUNDER FECULA
MOTHER REFUSE SORDES
SORDOR ULLAGE DRIBBLE
GROUNDS GRUMMEL HEELTAP
OUTWALE RESIDUE RINSING
GRUMMELS REMNANTS SEDIMENT
SETTLING
(— OF LIQUOR) TAPLASH
(— OF MOLTEN GLASS) DRIBBLE
(— OF SOCIETY) WASH LEGGE
CANAILLE
(— OF TALLOW) GREAVES
DREIBUND TRIPLICE
DREIDEL TRENDEL
**DREI PINTOS, DIE (CHARACTER IN
—)** GOMEZ PINTO GASTON
AMBROSIO CLARISSA PANTALEONE
(COMPOSER OF —) MAHLER
DRENCH SOP DOSE HOSE SIND SINK
SOAK TOSH BLASH DOUSE DOWSE
DRAFT DRINK DROKE DROUK
DROWN SLOCK SLUSH SOUSE
STEEP SWILL BUCKET DELUGE
DOUCHE IMBRUE INFUSE POTION
SLUICE DRUNKEN EMBATHE

IMMERSE INDRENCH PERMEATE
SATURATE SUBMERGE
DRENCHED DRUNKEN
DRENCHER INFUSER
DRENCHING DOUSE DOWSE
DOWNPOUR
DRESS AX AXE BED DON DUB FIG
FIT HOE KIT RAG RAY RIG TOG
BARB BEGO BOWN BUSK BUSS
CLAY COAT COMB DESK DILL DINK
GALA GARB GEAR GORE GOWN
HONE HUKE KNAP MIDI MILL MINI
RAIL ROBE SUIT TIFF TIRE TRIM
TUBE TUCK VEST WEAR ADORN
ARRAY BIGAN BRAWS CLEAN
CLOTH CRUMB CRUSH CURRY
DIGHT DIZEN EQUIP FLOAT FROCK
GUISE HABIT IHRAM MAGMA
PREEN PRICK PRIMP PRINK PRUNE
SHAPE SHIFT TENUE THING TRICK
AGUISE ATTIRE ATTRAP BARBER
BETRIM BROACH CLOTHE ENROBE
FANGLE FETTLE FRAISE GRAITH
INVEST JELICK JUMPER KIRTLE
MAGPIE MULLET MUUMUU OUTFIT
PLIGHT REVEST SARONG SHEATH
SHROUD TOILET ADDRESS AFFAITE
APPAREL BANDAGE BEDIZEN
CHEMISE CLOTHES COSTUME
DALLACK DUBBING GARMENT
GARNISH HARNESS HATCHEL
RAIMENT TOGGERY VESTURE
ACCOUTER ACCOUTRE CLEADING
CLOTHING DECORATE FEATHERS
HANDMADE ORNAMENT
SUNDRESS TAILLEUR VESTMENT
EMBELLISH
(— A SKIN) WHEEL
(— DOWN) BRACE BERATE
(— ELEGANTLY) DINK
(— FISH) CALVER
(— FLAX) TED
(— FLINT) NAP KNAP
(— FOOD) SAUCE
(— FOR FELTING) CARROT
(— HAIR) TIRE TRUSS BARBER
(— HIDES) BEAM
(— HURRIEDLY) HUDDLE
(— IN FINE CLOTHES) DIKE BRANK
(— MEAT) LARD SHROUD
(— NEGLIGENTLY) MOB
(— OF OFFICE) ROBE
(— ORE) VAN
(— OVER) STOP
(— SHEEPSKINS) TAW
(— SHOWILY) PRANK
(— SMARTLY) DALLACK
(— STONE) DAB NIG DAUB DRAG
FACE GAGE HACK GAUGE NIDGE
POINT SCABBLE SCAPPLE
(— TAWDRILY) BEDIZEN
(— UNTIDILY) MAB
(— UP) BUSK DILL ADORN ARRAY
PRANK PRIMP PRINK SPICK WATER
FETTLE TOGGLE BECLOUT BEDRESS
TITIVATE
(— VULGARLY) DAUB
(— WITH CHISEL) DROVE
(— WITH SLIT SKIRT) CHEONGSAM
(— WITH TROWEL) STRIKE
(— WORN BY MAN) DRAG
(— WOUND) PANSE BANDAGE
(CIVILIAN —) MUFTI

(COAT —) SIMAR SYMAR SIMARRE
(EVENING —) FORMAL
(FESTIVE —) GALA
(HAWAIIAN —) MUUMUU
(HIGHLANDER —) FILABEG
(HOMESPUN —) RUSSET
(INCOMPLETE —) DISARRAY
(LONG —) MAXI
(LOOSE —) SACK SACQUE
(MORNING —) PEIGNOIR
(ONE-PIECE —) CAGE
(ORIENTAL —) CHEONGSAM
(PECULIAR —) LIVERY
(POPLIN —) TABINET TABBINET
(RUSSIAN NATIONAL —) SARAFAN
(SHOWY —) BRAVERY
(SLEEVELESS —) SKIMMER
(STYLE OF —) GETUP
(SUFF.) ESTHES
DRESSED CLAD DONE BOUND
BECLAD COATED COMBED
HABITED GOFFERED
(— GAILY) FRESH SPARKISH
(— IN WHITE) CANDIDATE
(LOOSELY —) DISJUNCT
(NOT —) UNDIGHT
(RICHLY —) BROCADED
(ROUGHLY —) HEWN
(SHOWILY —) BEPRANKED
(STYLISHLY —) SMART
(WELL —) BRAW GASH
DRESSER AMBRY AWMRY ROBER
TAWER BUREAU FRAMER
ENROBER MODISTE CUPBOARD
(LEATHER —) LEVANTER
(WELSH —) TRIDARN
DRESSING CAST MAYO GRAVY
BANDAGE BEATING BLANKET
IODOFORM RAVIGOTE REMOLADE
SCOLDING STUFFING MAYONNAISE
(— FOR WOUNDS) LINT SPONGE
(— OF STONE) SKIFFLING
(HAIR —) LACKER LACQUER
(KIND OF —) RANCH
DRESSING-GOWN KIMONO
PEIGNOIR
DRESSING ROOM SHIFT VESTRY
CAMARIN VESTUARY
DRESSING-TABLE LOWBOY
DRESSMAKER SEWER SEAMER
MODISTE STITCHER COUTURIER
TIREWOMAN
DRESSMAKING COUTURE
DRESS RACK FRIPPERY
DRESSY SHARP
DRIBBLE DRIB DRIP DROP CARRY
DRIVEL DRIBLET DRIPPLE DRIZZLE
SLABBER
DRIBLET CLOT PIECE
(PL.) SMALLS
DRIED SEAR SERE ADUST GIZZEN
TORRID WIZENED GIZZENED
DRIFT FAN JET SAG DENE DUNE
FORD HERD PLOT RACK SILT TIDE
TILL DRIVE DROVE FLEET FLOAT
FLOCK IOWAN SENSE SLIDE
SLOOM SLOUM TENOR TREND
BROACH COURSE DESIGN DEVICE
DRIVER OFFSET PODGER SCHEME
STREAM TUNNEL WINDLE
CURRENT DIPHEAD DRIBBLE
GALLERY HEADING IMPETUS
IMPULSE LATERAL OUTWASH

PASTURE PROCESS PURPORT
SETBOLT DILUVIUM DRIFTPIN
TENDENCY
(— LANGUIDLY) SWOON
(— OF CLOUDS) CARRY
(— OF SAND OR SNOW) WREATH
(— SIDEWISE) CRAB
(— WITH ANCHOR DOWN) CLUB
(DOWNWARD —) DROOP
(GLACIAL —) CARY TILL IOWAN
(RUBBLE —) HEAD
DRIFTER HOBO TRAMP DROVER
SWAGMAN VAGRANT
DRIFTING ADRIFT DRIFTAGE
DRIFT PLUG DUMMY
DRIFTWAY DROVE
DRIFTWOOD WAFTURE
DRILL GAD JAR JIG RIG SOW TAP
BORE CORE SPUD AUGER BORER
CHARK CHURN DECOY DREEL
PADDY THIRL TRAIN TUTOR TWIRL
WHIRL ALLURE BROACH ENTICE
FURROW JUMPER PIERCE SCHOOL
SEEDER SINKER STOPER THRILL
CHANNEL DRIFTER JANKERS
PLUGGER STARTER EXERCISE
INSTRUCT PRACTICE
(— SYSTEM) MARTINET
(MASONRY —) AIGUILLE
(WEAPONS —) MANUAL
DRILLMAN STOPER
DRINK GO ADE ALE BIB BUM FIX GIN
HUM KIR LAP MOP NOG PEG POT
RUM RYE SIP SUP TEA TOT WET
BALL BEER BEND BENO BOLL
BOSA BOZA BREW BULL BUMP
CHIA CHUG COKE COLA DRAG
DRAM FIZZ FLIP GROG HAVE HORN
JAKE LUSH MEAD MIST NIPA NOGG
PULL PURL SHOT SIND SLUG SOAK
SOMA SOPE SPOT SWIG TIFF TOOT
TOPE WHET AIRAH ASSAI BEVER
BINGE BLAND BOMBO BOOZE
BOUSE BOZAH BUBUD BUMBO
CIDER CRUSH DAISY DRAFT FLOAT
GLOGG HAOMA JULEP LAGER
MORAT NEGUS PAINT POSCA
PUNCH QUAFF ROUSE SETUP
SKINK SLING SLOCK SMACH
SMASH SMILE SMOKE SNIFF
SNORT SOPIE SOUSE SWATS
SWILL THING TOAST TODDY
VODKA WHIFF ZOMBI ABSORB
BEZZLE BRACER BRANDY BUMPER
BURTON CALKER CASIRI CATLAP
CAUDLE CHASER COFFEE COOPER
DIBBLE DRENCH EGGHOT EGGNOG
FUDDLE GIMLET GODOWN
GUGGLE GUZZLE HOOKER IMBIBE
MESCAL POSSET POTION PTISAN
RICKEY ROBROY SCREED SHANDY
SIPPLE SIRPLE SWANKY SWINGE
TACKLE TAMPOY TASTER TIPPLE
VELVET WAUCHT WAUGHT ZOMBIE
BRAGGET BRIMMER CAROUSE
CHEERER CHIRPER COBBLER
COLLINS CONSUME CORDIAL
DILUENT DRAUGHT EXHAUST
FLANNEL GUARANA GUARAPO
INHAUST MORNING NOONING
PROPOMA SHERBET SIDECAR
SNEEZER SNIFTER SUCTION
SUPPAGE SWALLOW TANKARD

TRILLIL AMARETTO APERITIF
BEVERAGE BRIDECUP BULLSHOT
CHUGALUG COCKTAIL HIGHBALL
LIBATION MAHOGANY NIGHTCAP
POTATION QUENCHER REFRESCO
RUMBARGE SANGAREE SPRITZER
SYLLABUB TEQUILA PHOSPHATE
SUNDOWNER
(— AFTER A MEAL) DIGESTIF
(— AT DRAFT) TOP
(— EXCESSIVELY) TOPE BIBLE
SOUSE BEZZLE BIBBLE TIPPLE
SWIZZLE
(— FROM FERMENTED MILK) AIRAN
KEFIR
(— GREEDILY) SLOP SWACK SWILL
GUTTLE GUZZLE
(— HEAVILY) TOOT SWINK
(— INTOXICATING LIQUOR)
IRRIGATE
(— LIQUOR) TIP DRAM SOAK BOOZE
PAINT
(— NOISILY) SLURP
(— OF BEER) BUTCHER
(— OF BEER AND BUTTERMILK)
BONNY CLABBER
(— OF BEER AND GINGERALE)
SHANDYGAFF
(— OFF) COUP
**(— OF HONEY AND MULBERRY
JUICE)** MORAT
(— OF IMMORTALITY) SOMA
(— OF INDIA) SHRAB
(— OF LIQUEUR) FRAPPE
(— OF LIQUOR) WET DRAM JOLT
SHOT SPOT TASS WHET SETUP
WHIFF CALKER JIGGER TASTER
WETTING HIGHBALL NIGHTCAP
(— OF MOLASSES) SWITCHEL
(— OF THE GODS) AMRITA NECTAR
(— OF VINEGAR AND WATER)
POSCA
(— SOCIALLY) BIRL HOBNOB
(— SPARINGLY) BLEB
(— TOAST) PLEDGE
(— TO EXCESS) SOAK
(— TO EXCITE LOVE) PHILTER
(— TO LAST DROP) BUZZ
(— UP) CRUSH EPOTE CAROUSE
EXHAUST
(— WITHOUT PAUSE) CHUGALUG
(ACID —) SOUR
(ADDITIONAL —) EIK EKE
(ALCOHOLIC —) BENO BINO MIST
NIPA BOMBO BUDGE BUMBO DRAIN
JOUGH SHRAB SLING SNORT
SNIFTER
(AUSTRALIAN —) BEAL
(BRAZILIAN —) ASSAI ASSAHY
(BUTTERMILK AND WATER —)
BLAND
(CURRANT —) CASSIS
(DIETETIC —) POSSET
(DRUGGED —) HOCUS
(FARINACEOUS —) PTISAN
(FERMENTED —) BOSA MEAD
BALCHE MUSHLA PULQUE CASSIRI
GUARAPO
(FREE —) SHOUT
(FRUIT —) SQUASH
(GREAT —) JORUM
(HALF-SIZED —) CHOTAPEG
(HEADY —) HUFFCAP

(HERBAL —) SNAPS
(HOT —) COPUS NEGUS SALOP
TODDY BISHOP EGGHOT PLOTTY
SALOOP CARDINAL
(INCLINED TO —) OUTWARD
(INSIPID —) SLUM
(INTOXICATING —) AVA GROG SUCK
BOOZE KUMISS SCOTCH DRAPPIE
PAIWARI SWIZZLE SKOKIAAN
(INTOXICATING —S) SAUCE BOTTLE
(LONG —) SWIPE HIGHBALL
(MAKE A — LAST) NURSE
(MEAN —) LAP
(MEDICINAL —) TISANE ADVOCAAT
(MIDDAY —) NOONING MERIDIAN
(MIXED —) TWIST
(NARCOTIC —) KAVA
(NON-ALCOHOLIC —) GAZOZ
COOLER
(PALM —) ASSAI
(PARTING —) BONAILIE
(POISONOUS —) DRENCH
(RUSSIAN —) QBARNE QBARNI
(SACRED —) HOMA AMRIT HAOMA
AMRITA
(SACRIFICIAL —) HOMA SOMA
(SMALL —) PEG DRAM SOPIE
DALLOP WETTING
(SOFT —) SLUSH
(SOUR —) ALEGAR
(SPANISH —) SANGRIA
(STRONG —) BUB HUM BENO SICER
FUDDLE SHICKER
(TASTELESS —) SLOP
(THIN —) SLOSH
(WEAK —) LAP BOOL BULL CATLAP
(WEST INDIES —) SANGAREE
DRINKER SOT LUSH TANK POTER
TOAST TOPER BARFLY BENDER
CUPMAN LUSHER SOAKER
SPONGE IMBIBER INTAKER
QUAFFER DRUNKARD
(EXCESSIVE — OF TEA) THEIC
(HEAVY —) JUICEHEAD
(WATER —) HYDROPOT
DRINKING BEVER DRAFT DRINKY
GUZZLE DRAUGHT POTTING
CAROUSAL POTATION
(CONTINUOUS —) BOUT
DRINKING-BOUT CAROUSE
DRIP LIP SIE SYE DROP LEAK SEGE
SILE WEEP CANAL DRILL EAVES
LABEL STILL DRIBBLE DRIPPLE
LARMIER TRICKLE TRINKLE
TRINTLE
(— WITH TINKLING SOUND) PINK
(PREF.) STALACTI(TI) STALAGMO
DRIPPING ADRIP ALEAK STAXIS
WEEPING
DRIPSTONE BAT DING LABEL
HOODMOLD
DRIVE CA CAW COT FOG HOY JOG
AUTO BANG BEAR BEAT BUTT CALL
CRAM DING DRUB DRUM FIRE FIRK
FLOG GOAD HACK HERD HUNT
HURL JASM JEHU KICK LASH MOVE
PICK PILE POSS PUSH RACK RIDE
SEND SERR SINK SLOG SPUR STAB
STUB TOOL TOUR TURN URGE
BRAWL CHASE CHECK COACT
CROWD DRIFT DROVE FEEZE FLAIL
FORCE HORSE HURRY IMPEL INFER
LODGE MOTOR PEDAL POACH

PRESS PULSE PUNCH REPEL
ROUST SHOVE SLASH SMITE
SPANK SWEEP TEASE ATTACK
BATTER BEETLE BENSEL CHARGE
COMPEL CUDGEL DEDUCE DERIVE
FERRET HAMMER HASTEN IMPACT
JARVEY JOSTLE PLUNGE PROPEL
BLUSTER ENFORCE IMPULSE
OVERTAX SETDOWN TRAVAIL
CATAPULT CONATION SHEPHERD
TENDENCY MOTIVATION
(— A BALL) LACE SEND
(— A HORSE ONWARD) WHIG
(— AIR) BLOW
(— ANIMALS) HAZE
(— AT TOP SPEED) BARREL CAREER
(— AWAY) RID FIRK HUSH SHOO
BANDY EXILE FEEZE FLEME HOOSH
REPEL SMOKE SWEEP AROINT
BANISH DEFEND DISPEL ENCHASE
DISPLACE EXORCISE
(— BACK) RUSH REBUT REPEL
CULBUT DEFEND REBATE REBUFF
RETUND REPULSE REFRINGE
(— BACK AND FORTH) TENNIS
(— BEFORE STRONG WIND) SPOON
(— BRISKLY) JUNE
(— CLOSE BEHIND WHILE RACING)
DRAFT
(— CRAZY) BUG
(— DISTRACTED) BEDEVIL
(— FORTH) ISH
(— FURIOUSLY) SCORCH
(— HARD) RAM SWEAT HACKNEY
(— HOME) CLINCH
(— HURRIEDLY) BUM BUCKET
(— IN) CRAM DINT PILE TAMP
INJECT
(— IN A PARK) TOUR
(— INTO THE GROUND) STUB
(— INTO WATER) ENEW
(— LEISURELY) TOOTLE
(— LOGS) SPLASH
(— OFF) KEEP LIFT EXCOCT
(— OFF STAGE) EXPLODE
(— ON BACK ROADS) SHUNPIKE
(— OUT) BOLT FIRE DEPEL DROWN
EJECT EXPEL KNOCK WREAK
AROINT EXTURB ABANDON
DISLODGE EXORCISE PROPULSE
(— RECKLESSLY) COWBOY
(— ROUGHLY) CHOUSE
(— RUDELY IN TRAFFIC) CUTIN
(— SLANTINGLY) TOE
(— SLOWLY) TAXI
(— TO BAY) EMBOSS
(— TO MADNESS) FRENZY
(— VIOLENTLY) THUD SMASH
HURTLE
(— WITH BLOWS) SKELP COURSE
(— WITH SHOUTS) HOY HUE
(FREE GOLF —) MULLIGAN
(RECREATIONAL —) SPIN
DRIVEL GOO BLAH DOTE DRIP
MUSH DROOL SLUSH DOTAGE
DRUDGE FOOTLE HUMBUG
MENIAL SLAVER DRIBBLE
EYEWASH MAUNDER SLABBER
TWADDLE NONSENSE SALIVATE
CODSWALLOP
DRIVELING INANE SLAVERY
FOOTLING IMBECILE SLOBBERY
BLITHERING

DRIVEPIPE POINT
DRIVER MUG HACK JEHU MUSH
WHIP DRABI URGER CABMAN
CALLER COWBOY DROVER
FLYMAN HAULER JARVEY JOCKEY
MALLET MIZZEN MUSHER PONIER
STAGER VANMAN WAINER
CATCHER COCHERO FLANKER
HACKMAN HOODLUM HURRIER
JITNEUR PHAETON SPANKER
SPEEDER SUMPTER TOPSMAN
TRUCKER WHIPMAN BANDYMAN
BULLOCKY CALESERO CAMELEER
COACHMAN DRAGSMAN
ENGINEER GALLOWAY GOADSMAN
IMPULSOR JITNEUSE MOTORMAN
OVERSEER REINSMAN TEAMSTER
WHIPSTER
(— OF ANIMALS) DROVER SKINNER
(— OF ELEPHANT) MAHOUT
(— OF OMNIBUS) PIRATE
(CAMEL —) SARWAN CAMELEER
(FAST —) JEHU SPEEDER
(FIELD —) HAYWARD
(PACK-HORSE —) SUMPTER
(SKILLFUL —) REINSMAN
(TOWPATH —) HOGGY HOGGEE
(PREF.) ELATRO
DRIVEWAY DRIVE SWEEP AVENUE
DRIFTWAY
DRIVING PELTING COACHING
SLASHING
(— ALONG) SCUD
(— OF GAME) BATTUE
(— OF WIND) GUST
(— TOGETHER) DRIFT
(— TOWARD) APPULSE
DRIZZLE DEG MUG DANK DRIP
DROW HAZE LING RAIN SMUR
STEW DRISK MISLE SMURR MIZZLE
DRISSEL SCOUTHER SPRINKLE
(— OF RAIN) SKEW
DRIZZLY SOFT DRIPPY MIZZLY
DROGUE DRAG DRUG SLEEVE
DROLL ODD RUM WRY COMIC
DROLE FUNNY MERRY QUEER
WITTY JESTER JOCOSE AMUSING
BUFFOON COMICAL JOCULAR
STRANGE WAGGISH FARCICAL
HUMOROUS
DROLLERY WIT JEST FARCE HUMOR
DROLERIE
DROMEDARY OONT CAMEL DELUL
DELOUL HAGEEN HAGEIN HYGEEN
MEHARI CAMAILE CAMELUS
DROMOND
DRONE BEE BUM HUM DRUM SLUG
SPIV DRANT DROLL IDLER SNAIL
THRUM BUMBLE BURDEN CHORUS
DRAUNT DRONEL DRONET LUBBER
BAGPIPE BUMBARD BUMBASS
HUMMING SHIRKER SLEEPER
SOLDIER SPEAKER LOITERER
SLUGGARD
DRONE BASS FOOT
DRONGO FORKTAIL
DRONING BOURDON HUMDRUM
HUMMING SINGSONG
DRONISH SLOW INDOLENT
SLUGGISH
DROOL FLAT DRIVEL SLAVER
DRIBBLE SLABBER SLOBBER
SALIVATE

DROOP FAG LOB LOP SAG BEND
DROP FADE FLAG HANG LAVE LOLL
PEAK PINE SINK SWAG WEEP WILT
DAVER DREEP DROWK FLACK
HEALD HIELD MOURN BANGLE
BLOUSE DANGLE DEPEND NUTATE
SLOUCH CURTAIN DECLINE
FLITTER LANGUISH PENDENCY
DROOPING LOP DRAG FLAG LANK
LAZY LIMP GOTCH OURIE ADROOP
DROOPY FLAGGY NUTANT SLOUCH
SOPITE GOTCHED HANGING
LANGUID NODDING POPPIED
CERNUOUS TRAILING
(— OF EARS) LAVE
(— OF EYELID) PTOSIS
DROOPY DREEPY SLIMPSY
DROP DAP DIP SIE SYE BEAD BEDE
BLOB CAST DRIB DRIP DUMP FALL
GLOB GOUT OMIT SEGE SHED SILE
SINK SPOT STOP TEAR BREAK
CLOTH DROOP FLUMP GUTTA
LAPSE LOWER MINIM PEARL
PLUMP PLUNK SLUMP STILL
SWOOP CANCEL DISTIL DRAPPY
EXTILL FUMBLE GOBBET GOUTTE
PLUNGE SINKER SLOUGH SPRINK
TUMBLE ABANDON CURTAIN
DESCENT DEWDROP DISCARD
DISMISS DISTILL DRAPPIE DRIBBLE
DRIBLET DROPLET EXPUNGE
FORSAKE GLOBULE GUTTULA
GUTTULE INCURVE LETDOWN
MELDROP PLUMMET RELEASE
SPATTER DECREASE DROPLING
(— ANCHOR) SLIP
(— ARGENT) LARME
(— AS SEEDS FROM A POD) ROSE
(— AWAY) DESERT
(— BAIT IN WATER) DAP
(— BY DROP) DROPWISE GUTTATIM
(— DOWN) VAIL
(— IN) STOP HAPPEN INSTIL INSTILL
(— INTO LIQUID) PLUMP
(— OFF) NAP NOD DOZE SNOOZE
(— OF GIN) DAFFY
(— OF SEALING-WAX) KISS
(— OUT) FLOUNCE
(ARCHITECTURAL —) GUTTA
(CHOCOLATE —) DRAGEE
(THEATRICAL —) TAB SCRIM
(UNEXPECTED —) DOYST
(PL.) GTT GUTT
(PREF.) GUTTI STAGMO STAGONO
STILLI
DROP-CURTAIN GREENY
DROP ELBOW PIERDROP
DROPLET GLOBULE
(PL.) DEW
DROPLIGHT PENDANT
DROPPER SINK BOBBER SINKER
PIPETTE
DROPPING FALL SCAT SKAT SHARD
COWSHARD
(— ABRUPTLY) BOLD
(— SHARPLY) ABRUPT
(PL.) SOIL SPOOR FLYINGS
DROPSICAL PUFFY EDEMIC
DROPSIED HYDROPIC
DROPSY EDEMA OEDEMA ASCITES
ANASARCA
DROPWORT HORSEBANE
DEADTONGUE

DROSS KISH LEES SCUM SLAG
CHAFF DREGS DRUSH SCOBS
SLACK SPRUE WASTE GARBLE
REFUSE SCORIA SCRUFF SHRUFF
SINTER CINDERS LEAVING
OFFSCUM
DROSSEL SLUT HUSSY DRAZEL
DRAZIL
DROUGHT DRYTH DROUTH THIRST
ARIDITY DRYNESS ARIDNESS
DROVE MOB SENT ATAJO CROWD
DRIFT FLOCK MANADA BOASTER
DISTURB TROUBLE DRIFTWAY
DROVER DEALER DRIVER TOPMAN
TOPSMAN WHACKER HERDSMAN
DROWN DEAFEN DRENCH STIFLE
ADRENCH DRUNKEN INDRENCH
INUNDATE OVERTONE
DROWNED ADRENT
DROWNING NOYADE
DROWSE NOD SOG DOZE DOVER
DRONE SLEEP SNOOZE SLUMBER
DROWSINESS COMA DULLNESS
LETHARGY NARCOSIS
DROWSING DORMANT
DROWSY DOZY DULL LOGY HEAVY
NODDY SLEEPY SNOOZY SOPITE
STUPID SUPINE SWOONY
DORMANT LULLING NODDING
POPPIED COMATOSE COMATOUS
OSCITANT SLUGGISH LETHARGIC
DRUB TAP WAP BANG BEAT BLOW
DRUM PAIK ARRAY CREAM CURRY
PASTE STAMP THUMP WHALE
ANOINT CUDGEL SCUTCH THRASH
BELABOR DRYBEAT SHELLAC
DRUBBING PAIK LICKING SACKING
DRUDGE DIG FAG TUG DROY DRUG
GRUB HACK MOIL PEON PLOD
SERF TOIL DROIL DRONE GRIND
SCRAT SCRUB SLAVE SWEAT
DIGGER DRIVEL ENDURE JACKAL
MOILER SCODGY SCOGIE SLAVEY
SLUDGE SUFFER GRUBBER
HACKNEY PLODDER SLAVERY
SWEATER TRACHLE DOGSBODY
DRUDGERY FAG MOIL SLOG TOIL
WORK GRIND LABOR SWEAT
SWINK FAGGERY SLAVERY
TRACHLE TURMOIL DRUDGISM
(ROUTINE —) TREADMILL
DRUG (ALSO SEE NARCOTIC) DEX
DOM HOP STP ACID ALOE ALUM
BUKU CURE DOPE DRAB DULL
HEMP LOAD MDMA NUMB SCAG
SINA BUCHU HOCUS JALAP LDOPA
LOCUS MECON NSAID OPIUM
RUTIN SALOL SENNA SPECE SPEED
SULFA TONGA TRUCK COOLER
DEWTRY DOWNER ELAVIL FINGER
HEROIN IPECAC JAMBUL LOCUST
MYOTIC NOBBLE OPIATE PEYOTE
PEYOTL PITURI POTION SIDDHI
SIMPLE SULPHA ANODYNE ASPIRIN
ATEBRIN BOTANIC CUSHION
DAMIANA DAPSONE DILATER
ECBOLIC ECSTASY ETHICAL
HASHISH JAMBOOL LIBRIUM
METOPON PHILTER PHILTRE
QUASSIA STUPEFY STYPTIC
SURAMIN ZEDOARY ADJUVANT
AROMATIC ASPIDIUM ATARAXIC
BANTHINE HYPNOTIC KOROMIKO

LAETRILE LAXATIVE MEDICATE
MEDICINE MERSALYL NARCOTIC
NEPENTHE PEMOLINE QUAALUDE
SALIVANT SEDATIVE SPECIFIC
THIAZIDE TOXICANT ZERUMBET
ATARACTIC BARBITONE
BEMEGRIDE BRETYLIUM
CAPTOPRIL CLONIDINE
COLCHICUM IBUPROFEN
MELPHALAN NIALAMIDE
SALURETIC AMANTADINE
CLOFIBRATE CLOMIPHENE
PAINKILLER
(— CAPSULE) QUAALUDE
(— CAPSULES) RED REDS
(— DOSE) HIT
**(— IN TABLET OF VARIOUS
COLORS)** RAINBOW
(— SMUGGLER) MULE
(— USER) DOPER FREAK DRUGGY
DRUGGIE ACIDHEAD JOYPOPPER
(BITUMINOUS —) MUMMY
(DEPRESSANT —) DOWNER
(FIVE DOLLAR — PACKET) NICKEL
(FREE FROM — ADDICTION) CLEAN
(INHALE A —) SNORT
(INJECT —) SKINPOP
(INJECT —S) SHOOT
(KIND OF —) SULFA ORPHAN
DESIGNER
(NONUSER OF —S) STRAIGHT
(NOT USING —S) STRAIGHT
(ONE WHO USES —S) DRUGGY
DRUGGIE
(ONE WHO USES A —) HEAD
(ONE WHO USES ILLICIT —S) FREAK
(ORAL DIURETIC —) THIAZIDE
(RENDER FREE FROM —S) DETOX
(STIMULANT —) UPPER
(STRENGTHENING —) ROBORANT
(TAKE —S ORALLY) POP
(TAKE —S THROUGH THE MOUTH)
DROP SWALLOW
(TAKE A — THROUGH THE MOUTH)
DROP
(TO INJECT —) SHOOT
(VEGETABLE —) FINGER
(PL.) DRUGGERY
(PREF.) PHARMACO
DRUGGED POPPIED
DRUGGET BAUGE BOCKING
DRUGGIST CHEMIST DRUGGER
GALLIPOT APOTHECARY
DRUGSTORE APOTHEC PHARMACY
DRUID SARONIDE
DRUM BAZ GIN GON GOO GYO
BOWL CAGE CHIH DRUB LALI
MUYU POPO QASA ROUT SKIN
SPOT TOPH TRAP ZUZU ADAPU
BONGO CONGA CRAWL DAVUL
DRONE DUGGI ENNEN EWTIE
FOUCT FURIN GUMBE GUMBY
JAIRA KENON MBIRA NAKER QABIB
REBAB SARON SHAPE SNARE
SWASH TABOR THRUM TOMBE
TUPAN ZURLA AFUCHE AMBIRA
ATABAL BAMBUS BARREL CROCUS
GAMAKA GRELOT KANOON
KEMPUL KHANSI KURTAR LIVIKA
RIGGER TABRET TAMBOR TIMBRE
TUMBLE TUMMER TYMPAN
UDAKKI ANACARA BODHRAN
BUBBLER CROAKER DAULBAZ

ENCLUME FRUSTUM GHIRBAL
GRUNTER RATTLER REDFISH
SLENTEM SNUBBER TABORIN
TAMBOUR TEMPEST TIMBREL
TUMBLER VOSHAGA ZAMBONA
BAMBOULA BARBUKKA CANISTER
CYLINDER DERBUKKA DRUMFISH
HUEHUETI HUEHUETL MAQQAREH
MOULINET MRIDANGA TYMPANUM
ABURUKUWA BRONTERON
DUMTAKTAK MRIDANGAM
PUTIPUTI ROMMELPOT
TSANATSEL CACCAVELLA
(— AS SHIP'S SIGNAL) SHAPE
(— FOR WINDING ROPE) CAGE
(— IN WINCH) GIPSY GYPSY
(— MADE FROM HOLLOW TREE)
GUMBE GUMBY
(— OF CAPSTAN) RUNDLE MOULINE
(— OF INDIA) MRIDANGA
MRIDANGAM
(— ON WINDLASS) WILDCAT
(— UP BUSINESS) HUSTLE
(— UP INTEREST) BALLYHOO
(HEATED —) DRIER DRYER
(IGOROT —) GANGSA
(KIND OF —) STEEL
(NARROW —) RIGGER
(PAIR OF —S) TABLA
(PAIR OF HINDU —S) TABLA
(REVOLVING —) GURDY BARREL
RATTLER
(SUMERIAN —) ALA ALAL
DRUMBEAT DUB FLAM RUFF TUCK
MARCH RUFFLE SHUFFLE
ASSEMBLY BERLOQUE BRELOQUE
(— SOUND) TUCK
DRUM-BELLY HOOVE
DRUMFISH SPOT CROCUS BUBBLER
CROAKER DRUMMER DRUMSLER
SCIAENID
DRUMLIN DRUM SOWBACK
DRUMMER DRUM TABOR STICKS
TABRET ROADMAN SWASHER
TAMBOUR TUMBLER DRUMSLER
SALESMAN
DRUMMING TATTOO
DRUM ROLL DIAN DIANA
DRUMS ALONG THE MOHAWK
(AUTHOR OF —) EDMONDS
(CHARACTER IN —) HON JOHN
LANA MARK YOST BRANT JURRY
NANCY WOLFF ARNOLD GAHOTA
JOSEPH MARTIN DEMOOTH
GILBERT MCLONIS SCHUYLER
MAGDELANA MCKLENNAR
DRUMSTICK LEG STICK BAGUET
TAMPON BAGUETTE
DRUNK CUT FAP FOU REE WET
GONE HIGH LUSH NASE PAID RIPE
SOSH BLIND BOOZE BOSKY CLEAR
DRINK GONZO LITUP LUMPY
LUSHY MALTY MOPPY OILED
QUEER SHICK STIFF TIGHT TIPSY
BAGGED BLOTTO BOILED BOMBED
BUZZED CANNED FLUFFY GROGGY
JAGGED LOADED LOOPED
MORTAL POTTED RIPPED SLOPPY
SODDEN SOSHED SOUSED SOZZLY
SPONGY SPRUNG STEWED STINKO
STONED TIDDLY UPPISH UPPITY
ZONKED BLOTTER BONKERS
BOTTLED CROCKED DRUNKEN

JINGLED MAUDLIN PICKLED
SCREWED SHICKER SLOPPED
SLOSHED SMASHED SOZZLED
SQUIFFY SWACKED UNSOBER
WRECKED COCKEYED GLORIOUS
MUCKIBUS PLEASANT SQUIFFED
STINKING WIPEDOUT BLITHERED
PIXILATED
DRUNKARD SOT LUSH SOAK WINO
BLOAT DIPSO DRUNK GULCH
RUMMY SOUSE TOPER BARFLY
LUSHER SOAKER SPONGE
DRUNKER FUDDLER POTSHOT
SHICKER STEWBUM TIPPLER
TOSSPOT BORACHIO HABITUAL
SWILLTUB
DRUNKEN REE WAT GONE WINY
BLIND BOUSY DROWN DRUNK
BLOTTO FLUFFY SODDEN BACCHIC
DRUCKEN PICKLED SOTTISH
WHIPCAT DRENCHED SATURATE
SQUIFFED VINOLENT WOODSERE
DRUNKENNESS BUN IVRESSE
POTSHOT METHYSIS
DRUPE TRYMA DRUPEL DRUPELET
DRUPEOLE
DRUPELET GRAIN ACINUS
DRUPE STONE NUTLET
DRUSE GEODE
DRUSILLA (BROTHER OF —)
CALIGULA
(FATHER OF —) HEROD CALIGULA
GERMANICUS
(HUSBAND OF —) FELIX AZIZUS
AUGUSTUS
(MOTHER OF —) CYPROS CAESONIA
AGRIPPINA
(SON OF —) AGRIPPA TIBERIUS
DRY EBB KEX SEC TED WIN ADRY
ARID BAKE BLOT BRUT DULL EILD
GELD HASK KEXY KILN PINE SAVE
SERE SOUR WELT WIPE AREFY
CORKY DRAIN FRUST GUESS
HASKY JUSKY MEALY PARCH
PROSY SANDY SECCO SMEEK
SWEAT VAPID WIZEN BARKEN
BARREN BIRSLE BORING CHIPPY
ENSEAR GIZZEN HISTIE JEJUNE
SCORCH STARKY AREFACT
BRUSTLE INSIPID SAHARAN
SAPLESS SICCATE SQUALID
STERILE THIRSTY TORREFY
XEROTIC BARBECUE DROUGHTY
INFUMATE TIRESOME WOODSERE
(— HERRINGS) DEESE
(— IN SUN) RIZZAR
(— OFF) TOWEL
(— OF MILK) SEW EILD
(— PARTLY) SAMMY
(— UP) SERE WELK WITHER
AREFACT FORWELK SKELLER
(— WITH SMOKE) REAST REEST
(— WOOD) BEATH SWEAT SEASON
(KIND OF —) DRIP
(NOT —) SWEET
(PREF.) DEHYDR(O) JEJUN(O)
SCLER(O) SICCI TORRE XER(O)
XER(O)
DRYAD DRYAS NYMPH CAISSA
YAKSHA YAKSHI WOODMAID
DRYER DRIER STOVE SIROCCO
DRY GOODS DRAPERY
DRYING SICCANT

DRYING RACK CRIB
DRYNESS DROUTH ARIDITY
DROUGHT SICCITY XEROSIS
XEROTES HASKNESS AREFACTION
(— OF THE HAIR) XERASIA
DRYOPE (FATHER OF —) EURYTUS
(HUSBAND OF —) ANDRAEMON
(SISTER OF —) IOLE
(SON OF —) AMPHISSUS
DUAL TWIN BINARY DOUBLE
DUALIST TWOFOLD
DUALISM DVAITA
DUALITY DUAD TWINE TWONESS
DUANT DE DEE
DUB DIB RUB ADUB BLOW CALL
NAME POOL ADORN ARRAY DRESS
STYLE THUMP CLOTHE KNIGHT
PUDDLE SMOOTH STRIKE ENTITLE
BEGINNER DRUMBEAT ORNAMENT
DUBBIN DAUBING
DUBIOUS DICKY FISHY JUBUS
DOUBTY BEARISH DOUBTFUL
DOUBTING JUBEROUS
PRECARIOUS QUESTIONABLE
(NOT —) EXPRESS
**DUCA D'ALBA, IL (CHARACTER IN
—)** AMELIA EGMONT MARCELLO
(COMPOSER OF —) DONIZETTI
DUCHY SAVOY DUCATUS DUCHERY
DUKEDOM PARMESAN
DUCK AIX BOB BOW CAN DIG DIP
DOP MIG PET WIO CHAP COLK
COOT DIVE DOGS DOGY DOKE
DUKW JOUK LADY LORD PATO
ROOK SMEE SMEW TEAL TEUK
BOOBY BUNTY CRICK DILLY
DODGE DOUSE DOWSE DUCKY
EIDER EVADE HOUND MOMMY
NODDY PADDY POKER RODGE
ROUEN SCAUP SHIRK SOUSE SPIKE
SPRIG STOOL BOBBER CALLOO
CALLOW CANARD CANNET DUCKIE
FELLOW GARROT HARELD PEKING
PERSON PLUNGE QUANDY
RUNNER SCOTER SMETHE
ANATINE BARWING BLACKIE
BOWSSEN BUMMALO CANETTE
CRACKER DABBLER DARLING
DRABBET DUCKING DUCKLET
DUNBIRD FIDDLER FLAPPER
GADWALL GEELBEC GREASER
MALLARD OLDWIFE PENTAIL
PINKEYE PINTAIL POCHARD
REDHEAD REDLEGS REDWING
SCOOTER SLEEPER SPATTER
WADDLER WIDGEON YAGUAZA
BALDPATE BLUEBILL BLUEWING
BOATBILL BULLNECK DUCKLING
DUCKWING GARGANEY GRAYBACK
GREYBACK HARDHEAD IRONHEAD
MOONBILL MORILLON PIKETAIL
REDSHANK RINGBILL RINGNECK
SHOVELER SHUFFLER SQUEALER
WIRETAIL BERGANDER
(— AT CRICKET) BLOB
(— EGGS) PIDAN
(DEAD —) GONER
(KIND OF —) PEKING SITTING
(MALE —) DRAKE
(PART OF —) EAR EYE WEB BEAN
BILL CAPE HEAD NECK RUMP TAIL
WING FLUFF SHANK BREAST
SADDLE COVERTS NOSTRIL

DUCK SHOULDER PRIMARIES
SECONDARIES
(STUFFED —) DUMPOKE
(YOUNG —) CANETON FLAPPER
FLOPPER
DUCKBILL OOTOCOID PLATYPUS
TAMBREET MONOTREME
DUCKING SOUSE
DUCKTAIL DA HAIRSTYLE
DUCKWEED GLIT GRAIN LEMNAD
LENTIL DIGMEAT DUCKMEAT
FROGFOOT
DUCT VAS MAIN PIPE TUBE VEIN
CANAL ALVEUS BUSWAY DUCTUS
MEATUS URETER CHANNEL
CONDUIT DUCTULE DUCTURE
LACTEAL LEADING PASSAGE
TRACHEA AQUEDUCT CALIDUCT
DOWNTAKE EFFERENT EMISSARY
EXHALANT GONADUCT GUIDANCE
OLEODUCT
(PREF.) RHYN(O) VAS(I)(O)
DUCTILE SOFT DOCILE FACILE
PLIANT PLASTIC PLIABLE TENSILE
FLEXIBLE TRACTILE
(PREF.) ELAST(O)
DUD TOG FLOP LEMON STUMER
STUMOR FAILURE
DUDE FOP DANDY DUDINE JOHNNY
COXCOMB JACKEEN
DUDGEON PIQUE
DUDGEON IRE RAGE ANGER PIQUE
OFFENSE
(HIGH —) IRE
DUE HAK LOT OWE BACK CENS
DEBT FAIR FARM FLAT HAKH JUST
MEED OWED TOLL DROIT ENDOW
ENDUE FATED MERIT OWING
COMING CUSTOM DESERT EXTENT
LAWFUL MATURE PROPER UNPAID
CONDIGN EXACTLY FALDFEE
FITTING JETTAGE TALLAGE
ADEQUATE DIRECTLY HEREGELD
HEREZELD RIGHTFUL SUITABLE
TRUNCAGE
DUEL TILT FENCE FIGHT AFFAIR
COMBAT DUELLO MENSUR
CONTEST MEETING CONFLICT
DUELLIZE HOLMGANG
DUELIST FIGHTER SPADASSIN
DUENNA DRAGON GRIFFIN GRIFFON
CHAPERON
DUES TOLLS DROITS CHIEFRY
INWARDS JETTAGE PAYMENT
PENSION QUAYAGE ALTARAGE
HAVENAGE SOUNDAGE THIRLAGE
WHARFAGE
DUET DUO TWO DUETTO TWOSOME
(BALLET —) ADAGIO
DUFF ALTER BRAND CHEAT FLOOR
PUDDING
DUFFER DUB MUFF SHAM CHEAT
BUFFER GEEZER HAWKER RABBIT
SHICER PEDDLER
DUG TEAT
(— UP) HOWKIT
(PREF.) ORYCTO
DUGONG SEACOW YUNGAN
COWFISH MANATEE HALICORE
MUTILATE SIRENIAN
DUGOUT ABRI BOAT BURY CAVE
BANCA BONGO BUNGO CANOE
DONGA DUNGA SHELL BAROTO

BUNKER CAYUCA CAYUCO CORIAL
TROUGH BANTING PIRAGUA
PIROGUE SHELTER BLINDAGE
LIPALIPA
DUHSHASANA (FATHER OF —)
DHRITARASHTRA
DUIKER IPITI DUYKER BLAUBOK
DUKE DUC DUX KNEZ PEER AYMON
CHIEF KNIAZ HERZOG LEADER
ORSINO AUMERLE GORLOIS
SOLINUS STEENIE HERETOGA
PROSPERO
DUKEDOM DUCHY ALBANY
DUCATUS
DULCET SWEET DULCID SIRUPY
SYRUPY SOOTHING
DULCIAN CURTAL
DULCIMER ROTA CANUN CITOLE
SANTIR CEMBALO MAGADIS
SANTOUR CYMBALOM PANTALON
SAUTERIE ZIMBALON
DULIA ADORATION
DULL DIM DOW DRY FAT LAX MAT
SAD ARID BLAH CLOD COLD DAMP
DEAD DILL DOWD DOWF DOWY
DRAB DREE DRUG DUMB FLAT
GRAY GREY LOGY MOPE MULL
POKY SLOW TAME THIN TURN
BESOT BLACK BLAND BLATE
BLEAR BLIND BLUNT BRUTE CRASS
DENSE DINGY DOWFF DOWIE
DOWLY DREAR DUBBY DUNCH
DUNNY DUSTY FISHY FOGGY
GLAZY GRAVE GROSS HEAVY
HOHUM INERT LOURD MATTE
MORON MOSSY MUDDY MUSTY
MUZZY NOOSE PLUMP POKEY
PROSE PROSY SHADE SLACK
SOGGY STARY STILL SULKY TERNE
THICK UNAPT VAPID WASTE
BARREN BLEARY BOVINE CLOUDY
DAMPEN DARKEN DEADEN DISMAL
DRAGGY DREARY DRIECH DRIGGH
DROWSY EARTHY FRIGID FRUMPY
GLASSY HEBETE JEJUNE LEADEN
LOURDY MUFFLE OBTUND OBTUSE
OPAQUE PALLID REBATE RETUND
SLEEPY SLOOMY SODDEN
SOMBER SOMBRE STODGY STOLID
STUFFY STUPID SULLEN TIMBER
TORPID TRISTE TURBID URLUCH
WOODEN ADENOID BLUNTED
CONFUSE DEADISH DISEDGE
DOLTISH DOWFART DRAINED
DULLISH DUMPISH HUMDRUM
INSIPID IRKSOME LANGUID
LUMPISH MUMPISH PEAKISH
PINHEAD PROSAIC SHEATHE
SOTTISH STUPEFY TEDIOUS
UNLUSTY VACUOUS BACKWARD
BANAUSIC BEFUDDLE BLOCKISH
BOEOTIAN BROMIDIC COMATOSE
COMATOUS DIDACTIC DISCOLOR
DULLSOME EDGELESS FRUMPISH
GAUMLESS HEBETATE INFICETE
LIFELESS LISTLESS LOURDISH
OVERCAST PLODDING SLOTTERY
SLUGGISH SOULLESS STAGNANT
TIRESOME PINHEADED
PONDEROUS SATURNINE
(— EDGE OF) ABATE
(— IN MOTION) LOGY
(— IN SPEECH) PROSY

(— SCENT) FOIL
(— WITH LIQUOR) SEETHE
(BECOME —) PALL RUST
(MENTALLY —) DOPY DOPEY
BARREN
(PREF.) AMBLY(O) BRADY
DULLARD DOLT BOOBY DUNCE
IDIOT MORON DODUNK STUPID
BROMIDE DASTARD DOLDRUM
DULBERT POTHEAD BLINKARD
DULLHEAD
DULLED EMPTY HEAVY JADED
BROKEN CLOUDY GRAYED
SODDEN STUPID BLEARED
DULLISH DIRTY
DULL-LOOKING OWLISH
DULLNESS DRAB HAZE YAWN
CLOUD TAMAS FADEUR PHLEGM
TORPOR DIMNESS DOLDRUM
DULLITY DUNCERY FATUITY
LANGUOR OPACITY DUMBNESS
HEBETUDE SLOWNESS SOPITION
VAPIDITY SEGNITUDE STOLIDITY
(— OF SIGHT) AMBLYOPIA
DULL-SPIRITED MUZZY
DULL-WITTED FOZY WITLESS
BESOTTED DONNERED
(— PERSON) MOREPORK
DULLY FLATLY HEAVILY
DULSE DILLESK DILLISK SEAWEED
DULY DUE FITLY RIGHT RITELY
PROPERLY
DUMAH (FATHER OF —) ISHMAEL
DUMB DULL MUTE STONY SILENT
STONEY STUPID IDIOTIC
(— OX) BOZO
DUMBBELL DODO DUMMY DUNCE
IDIOT HALTER AIRHEAD KNOTHEAD
DUMBFOUND DAZE STUN AMAZE
CONFUSE CONFOUND SURPRISE
DUMBFOUNDED AWED STUPENT
DUMBNESS SILENCE APHRASIA
DUMBWAITER LIFT DUMMY
DUM-DUM AIRHEAD KNUCKLEHEAD
DUMMY COPY DOLT MUTE SHAM
DUMBY FAGOT EFFIGY FAGGOT
PONTIC SHADOW SILENT
PHANTOM DUMBBELL
(SWORDSMAN'S —) PEL
DUMNORIX (BROTHER OF —)
DIVITIACUS
DUMP SUM TIP BEAT CASH COIN
COUP FALL HOLE JAIL MUSE NAIL
TOOM EMPTY HOUSE SHOOT
GRIEVE PLUNGE TIPPLE UNLOAD
BOGHOLE COUNTER DEPOSIT
REVERIE SADNESS STORAGE
(MINE —) BURROW
(PL.) SUDS MOPES SADNESS
DUMPCART DUMPER TUMBREL
TUMBRIL
DUMPER TIPMAN
DUMPLING COB CRUST KNODEL
PIROGI KNAIDEL NOCKERL PIEROGI
SPATZLE DOUGHBOY QUENELLE
SPAETZLE AGNOLOTTI
(POLISH —) PIEROGI
(RUSSIAN MEAT —S) PELMENI
PELMENY
(PL.) KLOSSE GNOCCHI
DUMPY DUNCH GROSS PUDGY
SQUAB SQUAT DUMPTY STOCKY
SQUATTY

DUN BUM TAN FORT KICK URGE
ANNOY BROWN CRAVE CROWD
DINGY FAVEL MOUND PRESS SEPIA
DUNNER LEADEN PESTER PLAGUE
DUNNISH SWARTHY
DUNCE ASS CLOD DODO DOLT
DULT GABY GONY BOBBY BOOBY
DOBBY IDIOT NINNY DULTIE
HOBBIL PEDANT DULLARD
SOPHIST NUMSKULL STUNPOLL
TOMNODDY WISEACRE
DUN-COLORED
(PREF.) PHAEO PHEO
(SUFF.) PHAEIN PHEIN
DUNDERHEAD OAF CLOD DOLT
SAPE DUNCE TURNIP GOMERIL
DUNE BAR DENE MEAL MOUND
TOWAN TWINE BARKAN BARCHAN
BARKHAN
(SAND —) DRAB SAIF SEIF
DUNG MIS CACK CHIP DOLL FIME
GORE MERD MUCK MUTE SOIL
TATH ARGAL ARGOL FECES FILTH
FUMET MIXEN SCARN SHARN
BILLET CASSON FIANTS LESSES
MANURE ORDURE SCUMBER
SCUMMER TREDDLE COWSHARD
DROPPING STALLAGE
(— AS FUEL) ARGOL CASSON
CASSONS
(— OF BEAST OF PREY) LESSES
(— OF DEER) FUMET FEWMET
(COW —) MIST UPLA COWSHARD
COWSHARN
(OTTER'S —) SPRAINTS
(SHEEP —) BUTTONS TREDDLE
TROTTERS
(PREF.) COPR(O) FIMI GUANI
GUANO MERDI SCAT(O) SCORI
SPATILO STERCO STERCOR(I)
DUNG BEETLE SCARAB
DUNGEON PIT CELL HELL HOLE
LAKE VAULT CACHOT DONJON
PRISON CONFINE OUBLIET
REVOLVER OUBLIETTE
DUNGHILL MIXEN MIDDEN MIXHILL
DUNGON DONGON SUNDARI
DUNK DIP SOP SOAK STEEP
IMMERSE MOISTEN
(— SHOT) JAM
DUNKER DIPPER TAUFER TUNKER
DUMPLER DUNKARD TUMBLER
DUNLIN STIB OXEYE PURRE STINT
DORBIE OXBIRD REDBACK
LEADBACK
DUNNAGE FARDAGE
DUODECIMO TWELVEMO
DUPE APE BAM FOB FOP MUG
BOOB COAX CONY CULL DUST
FOOL GECK GULL HOAX LAMB
ROOK SCAM TOOL CHEAT CHUMP
COKES CONEY CULLY HEALD
MOOTH MOUTH PROOF REPRO
SLANG STALE TRICK BEFOOL
BUBBLE CHOOSE CHOUSE COUSIN
DELUDE DERIDE MONKEY PIGEON
PLOVER SQUARE SUCKER TAKEIN
VICTIM BECASSE CATSPAW
CHICANE CULLION DECEIVE
GUDGEON MISLEAD SAPHEAD
SWINDLE YOUNKER DOTTEREL
HOODWINK RODERIGO DUPLICATE
DUPERY RAMP

DUPLE BINARY DOUBLE TWOFOLD
DUPLEX DOUBLE TWOFOLD
DUPLEXITY EQUIVOKE
DUPLICATE BIS COPY DUPE ALIKE
DITTO SPARE TALLY DOUBLE
FLIMSY REPEAT COUNTER
ESTREAT MISLEAD REPLICA
TWOFOLD LIKENESS
(PREF.) COUNTER
DUPLICATION DISOMATY
DUPLICATOR MIMEOGRAPH
DUPLICITY ART GUILE DECEIT
TRICKERY
DUPONDIUS BRONZE
DURABILITY WEAR FIBER FIBRE
STEEL DURANCE STAMINA
DURABLE FIRM HARD LASTY PAKKA
PUKKA STOUT STABLE STAPLE
LASTING SERVICE CONSTANT
ENDURING LIVELONG
DURABLENESS DURATION
DURAMEN HEARTWOOD
DURANCE DURANT DURESS
CUSTODY
DURANGO CARTOUCH
DURATION AGE DATE LAST LIFE
SPAN TERM TIME WHEN DUREE
KALPA SPACE LENGTH PERIOD
DURANCE LASTING INFINITE
LIFETIME STANDING
(— BREEZE) SLATCH
(— OF DWELLING) RESIDENCE
(BOUNDLESS —) INFINITE
(INFINITE —) ETERNITY
(RELATIVE —) VALUE
DURAZZO (WARD OF —) CALDORO
DURESS FORCE DANGER CRUELTY
DURANCE COERCION HARDNESS
PRESSURE
DURGA KALI CHAMUNDA
(HUSBAND OF —) SHIVA
DURIAN JAK JACK JAKFRUIT
DURING IN ON DIN AMID OVER TIME
AMONG INTRA WHILE AMIDST
WHILST WITHIN AMONGST
DURANTE PENDING ENDURING
(PREF.) DIA INTRA
DURRA DARI DURA MILO JOWAR
CHOLUM DHURRA JONDLA
SORGHUM FETERITA
DURUM WHEAT
DURYODHANA (BROTHER OF —)
PANDU
(FATHER OF —) DHRITARASHTRA
(SON OF —) LAKSHMANA
(WIFE OF —) DRAUPADI
DUSACK TESACK
DUSHYANTA (SON OF —) BHARATA
(WIFE OF —) SHAKUNTALA
DUSK DIM EVE DARK DIMPS GLOAM
GLOOM DIMMET DIMPSY DIMNESS
DUCKISH DARKNESS GLOAMING
OWLLIGHT TWILIGHT NIGHTFALL
DUSKINESS PHAEISM
DUSKY DIM DUN SAD WAN DARK
DUSK ADUSK BLACK BROWN
DINGY GRIMY MOORY TAWNY
GLOOMY PHAEIC SMUTTY
SOMBER SOMBRE SWARTH
DARKISH DARLING OBSCURE
SUBFUSC SUBFUSK SWARTHY
BLACKISH
(PREF.) PERCNO PHAEO

DUST ROW COOM DIRT FOGO
MUCK MULL PILM SMUT BRISS
CLEAN COOMB FLOUR POUCE
STIVE STOUR DREDGE FILLER
KITTEN POLLEN POWDER SMEECH
BEFLOUR EBURINE REMAINS
SAWDUST SMEDDUM TURMOIL
ANTELOPE BULLDUST PUMICITE
(— IN FLOUR MILLS) STIVE
(— IN QUARTZ MILL) SLICKENS
(BLOOD —) HEMOCONIA
(CHOKING —) POTHER
(COAL —) COOM CULM DUFF
COOMB
(COKE —) BREEZE
(COSMIC —) STARDUST
(DIAMOND —) SEASONING
(FIBER —) FLOCK
(FLAX —) POUCE POUSE
(THICK —) SMOTHER
(PREF.) CON(I)(ICO)(IDIO)(O)
(SUFF.) CONITE
DUST CLOUD STEW
DUST COVER WRAPPER
DUSTER COAT DEVIL WILLOW
ZEPHYR TORCHON DUSTCOAT
DUSTMAN GARBO
DUST-STORM DEVIL
DUST-UP TODO
DUSTY ADUST MOTTY MOTTLE
POUCEY STOURY POWDERY
UNDUSTED
DUTCH (SEE NETHERLANDS) HOGEN
HOLLAND
DUTCH FOIL ORSEDE ORSEDUE
DUTCH GOLD CLINQUANT
DUTCHMAN HANS HOGEN BLANDA
DUTCHY BELANDA DUTCHER
MYNHEER BATAVIAN
DUTCHMAN'S-BREECHES
DICENTRA
DUTCHWOMAN FROW
DUTIFUL PIOUS DOCILE LAWFUL
DEBTFUL DUTEOUS OBEDIENT
OFFICIAL REVERENT OFFICIOUS
DUTIFULNESS PIETY
DUTY DO END JOB LOT TAX CALL
CARE FYRD MUST ONUS PART
PROW ROLE TAIL TASK TOLL WIKE
CHORE DEVER ERMIN LADLE LIKIN
OUGHT PREST RIGHT STINT WIKEN
BLANCH BURDEN CHARGE COCKET
DEVOIR DHARMA EXCISE EXITUS
HERIOT IMPOSE IMPOST INGATE
OFFICE RIVAGE TARIFF AVERAGE
BAILAGE BOOMAGE FOSSAGE
FURDUNG GRANAGE INDULTO
KEELAGE LASTAGE PONTAGE
PRIMAGE ROYALTY SCAVAGE
SERVICE STATION TONNAGE
TRIBUTE TRONAGE TUNNAGE
BALLIAGE BUSINESS FUNCTION
MALIKANA MALTOLTE REDDENDO
WEIGHAGE OBLIGATION
(— FOR LEAD ORE) COPE
(— OF SPARING LIFE) AHIMSA
(CHINESE TRANSIT —) LIKIN
(CUSTOMS —) OCTROI
(FEUDAL —) HERIOT
(IMPORT —) ERMIN INDULTO
(MILITARY —) STABLES
(TIRING —) FATIGUE
(PL.) CUSTOMS INGATES ACTIVITY

DUX CHIEF LEADER SUBJECT
HERETOGA
DWALE BELLADONNA
DWARF ELF PUG URF AETA CRUT
GRIG GRUB NANA RUNT CRILE
CROWL GALAR GNOME KNURL
MIDGE PIGMY PYGMY SCRUB
STUNT TROLL ABLACH ALVISS
CONJON DROICH DURGAN
DURGEN MIDGET SHRIMP ANDVARI
ANDWARI BLASTIE CONGEON
MANIKIN OVERTOP PACOLET
WRATACK ALBERICH BELITTLE
HOMUNCIO HOMUNCLE
HUCKMUCK KNURLING MENEHUNE
NANANDER
(PL.) CERCOPES NIBLUNGS
NIBELUNGS
(PREF.) NAN(O) NANN(O)
DWARF DANDELION KRIGIA
DWARFED STUNTY STUNTED
DWARF ELDER WALLWORT
DWARFING BRACHYSM
DWARFISH FI FIN PIGMY PYGMY
GRUBBY KNURLY NANOID RUNTISH
STUNTED
DWARFISHNESS NANISM
DWARFISM NANISM ATELIOSIS
DWARF MALLOW CHEESE PELLAS
DWARF RASPBERRY PLUMBOG
DWEEB NERD
DWELL BIG COT DIG SIT WIN WON
BIDE BIGG HAFT HARP LIVE STAY
TELD WINE WONT ABIDE BIELD
BOWER BROOD BUILD DELAY
HOUSE LODGE PAUSE SHACK
STALL TARRY LINGER REMAIN
RESIDE TENANT CLIMATE COHABIT
INHABIT CONVERSE
(— IN) BIG BIGG BEDWELL INHABIT
(— IRRITATINGLY) GRATE
(— ON) HARP BROOD GLOAT
DWELLER TENANT WONNER
DENIZEN PALEMAN DOWNSMAN
HABITANT OCCUPANT RESIDENT
(— BY SEA) PARALIAN
(BUSH —) HATTER
(CAVE —) CAVEMAN TROGLODYTE
(CITY —) SLICKER
(COAST —) BUFFALO ORARIAN
(LAKE —) LACUSTRIAN
(PL.) HUTHOLD
(SUFF.) ITE
DWELLING DAR HUT INN SEE WON
CASA FARM FLAT FORT HAFT HALL
HOME NEST ROOF SLUM TENT
WIKE WONE ABODE BOWER CABIN
DOMUS HOGAN HOOCH HOTEL
HOUSE HOVEL JOINT MANSE
MOTEL PLACE CASTLE DUGOUT
DUPLEX HOMING HOOTCH
MALOCA SHANTY TEEPEE
WIGWAM WONING COTTAGE
LODGING MANSION SALTBOX
TRAILER TRIPLEX WONNING
BUILDING BUNGALOW DOMICILE
TENEMENT PENTHOUSE
RESIDENCE
(— IN UNDERWORLD) CHTHONIC
(— PLACE) HOWF HOWFF
(— WITH ANOTHER) INMATE
(ATTRACTIVE —) BOWER

(CRUDE —) SHED SHEBANG
(ESKIMO —) IGLOO
(HERMIT'S —) CELL
(LAKE —) CRANNOG PALAFITTE
(MEAN —) SHANTY
(MISERABLE —) BURROW
DOGHOLE
(NAVAJO —) HOGAN
(NEOLITHIC —) TERRAMARA
(ONE-ROOM —) CELL
(OVERCROWDED —) WARREN
(PORTABLE —) CAMPER
(RAMSHACKLE —) HUMPY
(RUDE —) BOTHY BOTHIE
(SMALL —) CRIB
(SUBTERRANEAN —) WEEM
(SWISS —) CHALET
(TEMPORARY —) BOTHY BOTHIE
(WRETCHED —) HOVEL
(PL.) HOUSING
DWINDLE FADE FAIL FINE MELT
PINE WANE DECAY DRAIN PETER
TAPER TRAIL WASTE MOLDER
SHRINK CONSUME DECLINE
FRITTER MOULDER DECREASE
DIMINISH FORDWINE
DWINDLING DOWN FLAGGING
DYAD PAIR
DYBBUK GILGUL
DYE (ALSO SEE DYESTUFF) AAL AZO
DIP LIT ANIL BLUE COLOR EMBUE
FUCUS IMBUE LOKAO STAIN
SUDAN TINCT VENOM ARCHIL
IMBRUE INFECT MADDER TINGER
ENGRAIN INTINCT LACMOID
LOGWOOD PUCCOON ZAMBESI
AMARANTH COLORANT DYESTUFF
FUGITIVE INDIGOID TINCTURE
(— FUR) FEATHER
(— NOT FAST) FUGITIVE
(BLACK —) GUAKO
(BLUE —) RUM ANIL ROOM SAXE
WOAD INDIGO METHYL ANILINE
CYANINE DICYANINE
(BROWN —) CACHOU
(GENERAL —S) NIL NILL AZINE
BROWN EOSIN GREEN DIANIL
EOSINE ISAMIN ORANGE PURPLE
VIOLET CYANINE FUCHSIN METANIL
PONCEAU PRIMULA ALIZARIN
AURANTIA CIBACRON DICYANIN
EURHODOL FUCHSINE HYPERNIC
INDULINE NIGROSIN TURNSOLE
VIRIDINE NIGROSINE SAFRANINE
(HAIR —) RASTIK
(KIND OF —) AZO SRA
(ORANGE —) KAMALA ROUCOU
(PURPLE —) CASSIUS GALLEIN
TURNSOLE
(RED —) AAL ANATO AURIN EOSIN
GRAIN HENNA RUBIN ANATTO
AURINE CERISE EOSINE RELBUN
RUBINE ALKANET ANNATTO
CORINTH CRIMSON MAGENTA
PONCEAU SAFFLOR ALIZARIN
AMARANTH BORDEAUX CORALLIN
CROCEINE
(SCARLET —) TULY GRAIN
(VIOLET —) MAUVE ARCHIL ORCHIL
LACMOID ARCHILLA
(VIOLET — SOURCE) MUREX
(YELLOW —) ARUSA FLAVIN

CHRYSIN FISETIN FLAVINE
LAWSONE WONGSHY AURAMINE
DYED INGRAIN
  (PERMANENTLY —) FAST
DYED-IN-THE-WOOL INVETERATE
DYEING TINCTION
DYEPOT JIG VAT LEAD DYEBECK
DYER LISTER TINGER TINTER
  DYESTER FIELDER SKEINER
  TAINTOR TINTIST
DYERMA ZARMA ZAREMA
DYERS' MULBERRY FUSTIC
DYERS'-WEED SOLIDAGO
DYESTUFF (ALSO SEE DYE) DYE LIT
  WELD WOAD CHICA LOKAO

WOULD ANATTO BRAZIL KAMALA
LITMUS ORCEIN RELBUN ALKANET
ARNATTO CUDBEAR DYEWARE
SAFFRON INDULINE LUTEOLIN
PITTACAL PURPURIN
DYEWEED WOODWAX
DYEWOOD FUSTET FUSTIC
  BARWOOD CAMWOOD HYPERNIC
DYING FEY DEATH MORENDO
  PARTING MORIBUND
  (— AWAY) CALANDO DILUENDO
  MANCANDO PERDENDO
  SMORZATO
DYNAMIC POTENT DRIVING KINETIC
  FORCEFUL

DYNAMITE BLAST DUALIN
  SAWDUST RENDROCK GELIGNITE
DYNAMO EXCITER TORNADO
  (PART OF —) BRUSH FIELD FRAME
  RIGGING ARMATURE COUPLING
  COMMUTATOR
DYNASTY (OR MEMBER THEREOF)
  HAN KIN SUI WEI YIN CHIN CHOU
  HSIA RACE SUNG TANG YUAN
  BUYID CHING PIAST REALM RULER
  SHANG HAFSID PRINCE SAFAVI
  SELJUK ABBASID ALMOHAD
  ARSACID ATTALID AYUBITE
  AYYUBID BOUIDES FATIMID
  HAFSITE IDRISID JAGELLO

LAKHMID MONARCH OMAYYAD
ROMANOV SAADIAN SAFAWID
SAMANID TULUNID ABBASIDE
AGHLABID AGLABITE ASMONEAN
BUWAIHID CAPETIAN CHALUKYA
DOMINION EDRISITE GOVERNOR
IDRISITE JAGIELLO LORDSHIP
SAFFARID SARGONID SASANIAN
SELEUCID SOFFARID SASSANIDE
DYSENTERY FLUX SCOUR MENISON
  TOXEMIA DIARRHEA
DYSPEPTIC CACOGASTRIC
DYSPHORIA FIDGET
DYSSODIA BOEBERA
DZIGGETAI HEMIONUS

E

E EASY ECHO
EA HEA ENKI
EACH A EA UP ALL ILK THE UCH ILKA UCHE EVERY APIECE EITHER EVERYONE
(**OF —**) ANA
EAGER HOT RAD YAN ACID AGOG AVID EDGY FAIN FELL FOND FREE GAIR HIGH KEEN RATH SOUR TARE THRO VAIN WARM WAVE YARE YERN AFIRE AGASP ANTSY BRIEF FIRST FRACK FRECK HASTY HIGRE ITCHY PRIME READY SHARP SNELL YIVER ARDENT FIERCE GREEDY HETTER INTENT STRONG TIPTOE ANXIOUS ATHIRST BRITTLE BURNING EMULOUS EXCITED FERVENT FORWARD ITCHING PROVOKE DESIROUS IRRITATE SPIRITED VIGOROUS YEARNING SOLICITOUS
(**— IN PURSUIT**) SHARP
(**— TO KNOW**) INQUISITIVE
(**VERY —**) WILD
(**WILDLY —**) CRAZY
EAGERLY FAST FELL YERN HOTLY BELIVE TIPTOE YARELY YEPELY PRESTLY HUNGRILY INTENTLY
EAGERNESS GOG ELAN GARE ZEAL ARDOR DESIRE FERVOR ARDENCY AVIDITY ALACRITY CUPIDITY DEVOTION FAINNESS FERVENCY
EAGLE AAR ERN CROW ERNE GIER TERN HARPY AQUILA DENOUT EAGLET FALCON FORMAL FORMEL RAPTOR ALLERION BATALEUR BATALEUR BEARCOOT BERGHAAN RINGTAIL
(**KIND OF —**) LEGAL
(**SEA —**) ERN ERNE PYGARG PYGARGUS
(PREF.) AET(O)
(SUFF.) AETUS
EAGLE OWL KATOGLE
EAGLESTONE AETITES
EAGLET BIRD LAIGLON
EAGLEWOOD AGAR ALOE AGILA ALOES AGALLOCH AQUILARI
EAGRE BORE WAVE AEGIR HYGRE
EANFLED (**FATHER OF —**) EADWINE
(**HUSBAND OF —**) OSWIU
EAR LUG NEB CLIP HEAR HEED HOOK LIST OBEY PLOW TILL AURIS BRACE PINNA SENSE SOUSE SOWSE SPIKE CANNON CONCHA CROSET EARLET LISTEN AURICLE HEARING SENSORY AUDIENCE PAVILION RECEPTOR
(**— OF BELL**) CANON CANNON
(**— OF CORN**) COB ICKER MEALIE NUBBIN CORNCOB
(**— OF GRAIN**) RISOM SPIKE RIZZOM
(**— OF WHEAT**) SPICA WHEATEAR

(**—S OF GRAIN**) CAPES EARHEAD
(**KIND OF —**) TREE
(**KIND OF —S**) RABBIT
(**OF THE —**) AURICULAR
(**PART OF —**) LOBE TUBE CANAL HELIX INCUS PINNA CONCHA MEATUS SCAPHA STAPES TRAGUS COCHLEA MALLEUS MEMBRANE TYMPANUM ANTIHELIX ANTITRAGUS
(**UNRIPE — OF CORN**) TUCKET
(PREF.) AUR(I) AURICULO OT(ICO) (IO)(O) SPICI SPICULI SPICULO
(**— OF CORN**) ATHERO STACHY(O)
(SUFF.) OTIC
EARACHE OTALGY OTALGIA
EAR-BONE OTOLITH
EARCOCKLE PURPLES
EARDRUM TABOR TABOUR TYMPAN MYRINGA DRUMHEAD TYMPANUM
(PREF.) TRYPAN(O) TYMPAN(O)
EARED SEAL SEALION
EARFLAP LUG EARLAP EARTAB EARMUFF
EARINE (**LOVER OF —**) AEGLAMOUR
EARL EORL GRAF JARL LORD PEER COMES NOBLE CONSUL SIWARD
(**— OF COVENTRY**) SNIPSNAPSNORUM
EARLDOM DERBY COUNTY
EARLIER ERE OLD ERST FORE ELDER SUPRA UPPER BEFORE FORMER HITHER RATHER SOONER FIRSTER FURTHER PIONEER PREMIER PREVIOUS
(PREF.) FORE PROTER(O)
(**— THAN**) PRE PRO
EARLIEST ERST FIRST ELDEST MAIDEN PIONEER PREMIER RATHEST FURTHEST PRIMROSE ABORIGINAL
(PREF.) EO
EAR LOBE LUG EARLAP
(**— PEOPLE**) OREJON
EARLY AIR ERE OLD GOOD HIGH RARE RATH SOON FORME PRIMY RATHE VERTY REARLY SUDDEN TIMELY ANCIENT BETIMES ERLICHE FORWARD YOUTHFUL MATUTINAL
(**UNDULY —**) PREMATURE
(PREF.) EO PALAE(O) PALE(O)
EARMARK BIT CROP SIGN SPLIT LUGMARK OVERBIT SLEEPER ALLOCATE OVERCROP UNDERBIT
EAR MUFF OREILET
EARN GET WIN FANG GAIN MAKE TILL VANG ADDLE ETTLE GLEAR MERIT GARNER HUSTLE OBTAIN ACHIEVE ACQUIRE CHEVISE DEMERIT DESERVE
(**— BY LABOR**) ADDLE SWINK BESWINK
EARNEST ARRA DEAR DERN HARD PAWN ARLES EAGER GRAVE

SMART SOBER STAID ARDENT ENTIRE HANSEL HEARTY INTENT SEDATE SOLEMN EMULOUS ENGAGED FERVENT FORWARD HANDSEL INTENSE SERIOUS SINCERE ZEALOUS DILIGENT EMPHATIC STUDIOUS
(**IN —**) AGOOD
EARNESTLY HARD DEARLY WISHLY WISTLY EARNEST DEVOUTLY DINGDONG ENTIRELY HEARTILY INTENTLY INWARDLY
EARNESTNESS GLOW FERVOR WARMTH GRAVITY DEVOTION DILIGENCE
EARNINGS GET MAKING ADDLINS PICKING ADDLINGS
EARPIECE BUTTON
EARPLUG STOPPLE TEMBETA EARSPOOL
EARRING DROP GRIP EARBOB EARLET PENDLE EARCLIP EARDROP PENDANT EARSCREW
(**— LOCALE**) LOBE
EARS (**KIND OF —**) RABBIT
EAR SHELL ORMER ABALONE
EARSHOT SOUND HEARING EARREACH
EARTH ERD ORB SET BALL BANK BURY BYON CLAY CLOD DIRT DUST FLAG FOLD GRIT LAND LOAM MARL MASS MEAL MOLD MOOL MUCK ROCK SOIL SORY STAR VALE YIRD ADOBE CRUMB FLOSS GLEBE GLOBE GROOT INTER LOESS MOULD REGUR TERRA TRASS UMBER WORLD CENTER CENTRE COARSE GROUND YACATA KOKOWAI MIDGARD TERRENE TIERRAS TOPSOIL TRIPOLI MAGNESIA MIDGARTH
(**— FOR RAMPART**) REMBLAI
(**— INHABITANT**) TERRAN
(**— PROVIDING OCHER**) KOKOWAI
(**— SUITABLE FOR CULTIVATION**) LAYER
(**BLACK —**) MUCK SORY KILLOW AMPELITE CHERNOZEM
(**BLUE —**) KIMBERLITE
(**BROWN —**) UMBER
(**CLAYEY —**) LAME LOAM
(**DRY —**) MOOL GROOT
(**FULLER'S —**) CRETA CIMOLITE SMECTITE
(**GEM-BEARING —**) BYON
(**HEAVY —**) BARYTA
(**LOOSE —**) CRUMB GEEST
(**MOIST —**) SLAB SLIME
(**POOR —**) RAMMEL
(**RAMMED —**) PISE
(**RED —**) RUDDLE
(**REFUSE —**) MURGEON
(**RIVER-BANK —**) GREWT

(**SMALL —**) TERRELLA
(**SOAP —**) SOAPROCK
(**STRAW-YELLOW —**) BISMITE
(**SUN-DRIED —**) SWISH
(**VITRIFIED —**) FLOSS
(**VOLCANIC —**) TRASS TARRASS
(PREF.) AGRO GE(O) TELLUR(I) TERR(A)(E)(I)
(SUFF.) GAEA GEA
EARTHEN FICT DIRTEN EARTHLY YARTHEN
EARTHENWARE PIG POT DELF CHINA CLOAM CROCK DELFT CLAYEN JASPER ASTBURY BISCUIT FAIENCE POTTERY TICKNEY BUFFWARE CROCKERY MAJOLICA TALAVERA
(**BROKEN PIECE OF —**) CROCK
EARTHINESS SALT TERREITY
EARTHKIN TERRELLA
EARTHLY LAIRY CARNAL EARTHY MORTAL EARTHEN GLEBOUS MUNDANE SECULAR TERRAIN TERRENE WORLDLY SUBLUNAR TELLURIC TEMPORAL
EARTHMAN TERRAN
EARTHNUT ARNOT ARNUT CHUFA HOGNUT JARNUT PEANUT PIGNUT HARENUT HAWKNUT TRUFFLE
EARTH PIG ERDVARK AARDVARK
EARTHQUAKE QUAKE SEISM SHAKE SHOCK TEMBLOR SEAQUAKE
(PREF.) SEISMO SISMO
(SUFF.) SEISM SEISMAL SEISMIC
EARTHSTAR GEASTER
EARTH STATION DISH
EARTHWALL TRINCHERA
EARTH WOLF AARDWOLF
EARTHWORK BANK RATH RING AGGER CASTLE SCONCE PARADOS RAMPART TERRACE
(PL.) PARADOS
EARTHWORM ESS MAD WORM ANNELID DEWWORM IPOMOEA MADDOCK ANGLEDOG BRANDLIN EACEWORM FISHWORM RAINWORM TWATCHEL BRANDLING LUMBRICID OLIGOCHATE
EARTHY GROSS SALTY WORMY CLODDY VULGAR EARTHLY TERRENE BARNYARD TERREOUS VISCERAL
EAR TICK PINOLIA
EAR TRUMPET CORNET AEROPHONE
EARWAX CERUMEN
(PREF.) CERUMINI
EARWIG GOLACH GOLOCH TOUCHBELL
EARWORM BOLLWORM
EASE CALM COSY COZY EASY REST

ABATE ALLAY KNACK LETUP PEACE QUIET RELAX SLAKE LOOSEN PACIFY REDUCE RELIEF REPOSE SAUGHT SMOOTH SOFTEN SOOTHE APPEASE ASSUAGE COMFORT CONTENT FACULTY FLUENCY FREEDOM LEISURE LIBERTY LIGHTEN RELIEVE SLACKEN SUBSIDE DIMINISH FACILITY MITIGATE MODERATE PALLIATE PLEASURE SECURITY UNBURDEN
(— GENTLY) SLIDE
(— OF A BURDEN) LIGHT
(— OFF) FLOW CHECK START SLOUGH
(APATHETIC —) INDOLENCE
(AT —) OTIOSE
(CAREFREE —) ABANDON

EASEL FRAME SUPPORT SCAFFOLD

EASEMENT EASE EASING RELIEF HERBAGE TURBARY SERVITUS WAYLEAVE

EASE-TAKING PICKTOOTH

EASIEST EFTEST

EASILY EASY EATH WELL LIGHT EATHLY GENTLY GLIBLY HANDILY LIGHTLY READILY SLIGHTLY SMOOTHLY
(PREF.) EU

EASINESS GRACE FACILITY

EASING DETENTE

EAST OST ASIA MORN LEVANT ORIENT SUNRISE EASTWARD
(— OF) FOLLOWING

EAST AFRICA (— TREE) PODO

EASTER PT PACE PASCH EOSTRE PASCHA PASQUE

EASTERN LEVANT ORTIVE AURORAL ORIENTAL

EASTERNER DUDE

EAST INDIAN (— TREE) SAL AMLA DHAK TEAK KOKAN LANSA MAHUA MOHWA NIEPA PALAS PULAS ROHAN ROHUN SALAI SIMAL

EASTLAND ESTRICHE

EASTWARD EAST EASEL EASSEL

EASY CALM COZY CRIP EATH EITH GAIN GLIB MILD RIFE SNAP SOFT CUSHY JAMMY LARGE LIGHT PLAIN PRONE ROYAL SUAVE YEZZY CASUAL COMODO FACILE FLUENT FRUITY GENTLE GENTLY SECURE SIMPLE SMOOTH UNHARD ARTLESS GRADUAL LENIENT NATURAL CAREFREE CARELESS CAVALIER EXPEDITE FAMILIAR FRIENDLY GRACEFUL HOMELIKE MODERATE TRANQUIL UNFORCED
(— IN MIND) SECURE
(— TO HANDLE) HANDSOME
(— TO SPEAK TO) AFFABLE
(— TO UNDERSTAND) PELLUCID
(— TO USE) CLEVER
(TAKE IT —) SIT LAZE

EASYGOING LAX QUIET DEGAGE

EAT FOG KAI SUP BITE CHOP CHOW DINE FARE FEED FRET GNAW GRUB HAVE HEYT MAKE PECK RUST TUCK DIGIN ERODE FEAST GRAZE MANGE MUNCH SCOFF STOKE TASTE WASTE ABSORB BEGNAW DEVOUR INGEST NIBBLE RAVAGE

CONSUME CORRODE DESTROY SWALLOW VICTUAL
(— A MEAL) GRUB
(— AS HOGS) SLUICE
(— A SNACK) NOSH
(— AWAY) GNAW ERODE RANKLE CORRODE
(— BETWEEN MEALS) NOSH
(— BIG MEAL) STOKE
(— CRUNCHINGLY) GROUZE
(— GLUTTONOUSLY) GUDGE STUFF
(— GREEDILY) GAMP GAWP SLAB SLOP TUCK CHAUM MOOCH SCARF SCOFF GOBBLE GOFFLE GUTTLE GUZZLE PIGOUT RAUNGE GLUTTON GOURMAND
(— HEARTILY) THORN
(— IN GULPS) LAB
(— MINCINGLY) PICK PICKLE PIDDLE
(— NOISILY) SLOP GULCH SLURP GUTTLE SLOTTER
(— OUT) EXEDE
(— RUDELY) TROUGH
(— SLOVENLY) SLUP MUMMICK
(— SPARINGLY) DIET NIBBLE
(— TO EXCESS) COLF BEZZLE
(— UP) DEMOLISH
(— VORACIOUSLY) CRAM WORRY
(— WITH GUSTO) SMOUSE
(— WITHOUT CHEWING) BOLT
(SUFF.) ESTES PHAG(A)(E)(IA)(ISM) (IST)(O)(OUS)(US)(Y) VORA VORE VOROUS

EATABLE FOODY COOKER EDIBLE ESCULENT

EATEN CANKERED
(HALF —) SEMESE
(PREF.) BROTO

EATER PECKER DEVOURER
(GREEDY —) GOURMAND

EATING BIT FOOD ESURINE
(— BETWEEN MEALS) TIFFIN
(— COARSE FOOD) FOUL
(— DISORDER) BULIMIA
(— INTO) CANKEROUS
(— OUT) EXESION
(PREF.) PHAG(O)

EAVES EASE EASING

EAVESDROP DARK HARKEN LISTEN HEARKEN

EAVESDROPPER COWAN EARWIG SNOOPER DRAWLATCH

EAVES TROUGH CHENEAU

EBAL (FATHER OF —) SHOBAL

EBB FAIL FALL FLAG SINK WANE ABATE DECAY RECEDE REFLOW REFLUX RETIRE TIDING DECLINE REFLOAT SUBSIDE DECREASE DIMINISH
(— AND FLOW) ESTUS AESTUS FLUIDITY

EBBING AWANE REFLUENT REFLUOUS
(— AND FLOWING) TIDAL

EBED (FATHER OF —) JONATHAN
(SON OF —) GAAL

EBER (FATHER OF —) SALAH ELPAAL

EBLIS JANN IBLIS

EBONY EBON BLACK GABON GABOON WAMARA HEBENON IRONWOOD

EBULLIENCE OVERFLOW ELEVATION

EBULLIENT BRASH FERVID YEASTY BOILING

EBULLIOSCOPE ZEOSCOPE

EBULLITION SEETHE FERMENT OUTBURST

ECAD ECOPHENE

ECCENTRIC FEY NUT ODD OFF CARD DOER NUTS CRANK DOTTY KINKY OUTRE QUEER WEIRD WIPER CRANKY LOCOED OUTISH PSYCHO SCREWY SHAGGY WEIRDO WEIRDY BIZARRE CURIOUS DEVIOUS DINGBAT ERRATIC ODDBALL STRANGE TOUCHED ABNORMAL CRACKPOT FITIFIED PECULIAR SINGULAR
(— PERSON) KOOK

ECCENTRICITY KINK FERLY ODDITY ANOMALY CROTCHET QUIDDITY
(— OF CURVE) E

ECCLESIASTES KOHELETH QOHELETH

ECCLESIASTIC ABBE ABBOT CLERK VICAR ARCHON FATHER LECTOR LEGATE PRIEST KIRKMAN PRELATE SECULAR EPISTLER SUBDEACON

ECCLESIASTICAL CHURCH CANONIC CHURCHLY CHRISTIAN SPIRITUAL

ECHELES (FATHER OF —) ACTOR
(FOSTER SON OF —) EUDORUS
(WIFE OF —) POLYMELA

ECHEVIN SCABINE SCABINUS

ECHIDNA NODIAK ANTEATER EDENTATE MONOTREME PORCUPINE
(CHILD OF —) HYDRA LADON ORTHUS SPHINX CERBERUS CHIMAERA
(FATHER OF —) PHORCYS CHRYSAOR
(MOTHER OF —) CETO CALLIRRHOE
(SLAYER OF —) ARGUS

ECHINODERM CYSTID CRINOID BLASTOID STARFISH

ECHINOPANAX FATSIA

ECHINO-SOREX GYMNURA

ECHION (FATHER OF —) MERCURY
(MOTHER OF —) ANTIANIRA
(SON OF —) PENTHEUS
(WIFE OF —) AGAVE

ECHO APE ECO BLIP RING SING CHORUS REPEAT REVERB SECOND IMITATE ITERATE RESOUND RESPEAK RESPOND REVOICE REDOUBLE RESPONSE
(— EFFECT) REVERB
(RADAR —) ANGEL
(RADIO —) ANGEL

ECLAT FAME GLORY RENOWN ACCLAIM SCANDAL APPLAUSE FACILITY PRESTIGE SPLENDOR

ECLECTIC BROAD LIBERAL

ECLIPSE DIM BIND BLOT HIDE BLIND CLOUD SHADE STAIN SULLY DARKEN DAZZLE DEFECT EXCEED OCCULT DEFAULT OBSCURE PRODIGY TRAVAIL OUTRIVAL OCCULTATION

ECLOGUE IDYL IDYLL BUCOLIC

ECOLOGIST BIONOMIST

ECOLOGY BIOLOGY BIONOMY MESOLOGY

ECONOMIC
(PREF.) EC(O) OEC(O) OIKO

ECONOMICAL WARY CHARY FENDY FRUGAL SAVING CAREFUL PRUDENT SPARING THRIFTY SCREWING

ECONOMICS PLUTONOMY

ECONOMIST HUSBAND MANAGER PHYSIOCRAT
AMERICAN DAY ELY GRAY OKUN POOR ADAMS ARROW ARROW BALCH BURNS CAREY CLARK DEWEY GRAMM HANEY HAUGE HICKS LUBIN MEYER SOLOW TOBIN WELLS WITTE YOUNG CARVER DEBREU DUNBAR DURAND ECCLES FISHER FOSTER GEORGE HADLEY HARVEY KATONA MILLIS RAGUET RIPLEY RIVLIN SPLAWN SUMNER TUCKER TURNER VEBLEN WALKER WEAVER WILLIS BULLOCK COMMONS CROWELL GARRETT JOHNSON KUZNETS TAUSSIG TUGWELL ANDERSON FRIEDMAN KEMMERER KOOPMANS LAUGHLIN LEONTIEF MITCHELL ROSOVSKY GALBRAITH HENDERSON HOLLANDER SAMUELSON MODIGLIANI WILLOUGHBY JANEWAY
AUSTRALIAN DONALD
AUSTRIAN BOHM HAYEK MISES SPANN MENGER
BELGIAN ZEELAND LEVELEYE MOLINARI
CANADIAN HOWE MAVOR ERDMAN LALONDE LEACOCK
DUTCH TINBERGEN
ENGLISH JAY COLE MILL WARD WEBB WEST HAYEK HICKS HIRST JAMES MEADE PAISH PETTY PRICE STAMP ASHLEY BARBON BAXTER COBDEN FARRER GIFFEN HOBSON JEVONS KEYNES KIRKUP LAYTON LESLIE REEVES ROGERS SALTER SENIOR SHANKS TUCKER WILSON BAGEHOT CHAPMAN CLAPHAM FAWCETT GRESHAM MALTHUS MALYNES RICARDO TOYNBEE BELLERBY MARSHALL BEVERIDGE EDGEWORTH HOLLOWOOD MACMILLAN MARTINEAU NICHOLSON OVERSTONE CUNNINGHAM
FINNISH PROCOPE
FRENCH SAY LEVY RIST BODIN GUYOT CAMBON HAUSER MONNET ALPHAND BASTIAT BLANQUI BLONDEL COURNOT FAUCHER GARNIER GOURNAY MONTYON QUESNAY SCHUMAN MIRABEAU PECQUEUR ROEDERER WOLOWSKI CHEVALIER LEVASSEUR SIEGFRIED
GERMAN RAU BONN HAHN ENGEL FUCHS HARMS JUSTI KNIES LANGE BRIEFS BUCHER CONRAD ECKERT ERHARD GESELL GOSSEN HIRSCH SERING ANDREAE DUHRING EHEBERG GERLOFF HEIMANN JASTROW LEDERER MICHELS ROSCHER HUFELAND SCHAFFLE BAMBERGER RODBERTUS SCHMOLLER FLURSCHEIM

HAXTHAUSEN HELFFERICH KESSELRING RAIFFEISEN SCHUMPETER OPPENHEIMER
GREEK ANDREADES
IRISH SMIDDY CAIRNES BASTABLE CANTILLON
ITALIAN BODIO CARLI GIOJA LORIA NITTI PELLA ROSSI BOTERO PARETO GALIANI BECCARIA GENOVESI LUZZATTI SCIALOIA CERNUSCHI PANTALEONI
NORWEGIAN FRISCH
POLISH GRABSKI WOJCIECHOWSKI
RUSSIAN BUNGE KANTOROVICH VOZNESENSKI
SCOTTISH MILL SMITH MACLEOD ANDERSON MCCULLOCH
SWEDISH OHLIN CASSEL MYRDAL
SWISS SISMONDI CHERBULIEZ
URUGUAYAN COSIO
ECONOMIZE HAIN SAVE SKIMP STINT SCRAPE SCRIMP HUSBAND UTILIZE RETRENCH
ECONOMY SPARE SAVING SYSTEM THRIFT MANAGERY PARSIMONY
ECOTONE EDGE
ECSTASY JOY BLISS POWER SWOON TRANCE DELIGHT EMOTION MADNESS RAPTURE RHAPSODY
ECSTATIC HOT RAPT PYTHIAN GLORIOUS
ECTENE IRENICON
ECTODERM EXODERM EPIBLAST
ECTOMORPHIC LINEAR ASTHENIC LEPTOSOME
ECTROPION EVERSION
ECU CROWN SCUTE SHIELD

ECUADOR
ANCIENT NAME: QUITO
CAPE: ROSA PASADO PUNTILLA
CAPITAL: QUITO
COIN: SUCRE CONDOR CENTAVO
INDIAN: CARA INCA PALTA CANELO JIVARO
ISLAND: PUNA WOLF MOCHA PINTA BALTRA CHAVES DARWIN PINZON WENMAN ISABELA
ISLANDS: COLON GALAPAGOS
LANGUAGE: JIBARO QUECHUA SPANISH
MEASURE: CUADRA FANEGA
MOUNTAIN: ANDES SANGAY CAYAMBE ANTISANA COTOPAXI
NATIVE: MONTUVIO
PROVINCE: LOJA AZUAY CANAR COLON ELORO CARCHI GUAYAS MANABI BOLIVAR LOSRIOS COTOPAXI IMBABURA
RIVER: COCA MIRA NAPO DAULE PINDO TIGRE GUAYAS TUMBES ZAMORA CURARAY PASTAZA AGUARICO BOBONAZA CONONACO NARANJAL PUTUMAYO
TOWN: JAMA LOJA MERA NAPO PUYO TENA CANAR GUANO MANTA PAJAN PINAS PIURA QUITO YAUPI AMBATO CUENCA IBARRA PUJILI TULCAN ZARUMA AZOGUES CAYAMBE GUAMOTE MACHALA PELILEO PILLARO
SALINAS BABAHOYO GUARANDA RIOBAMBA
WATERFALL: AGOYAN
WEIGHT: LIBRA

ECUMENE HEARTH
ECUMENICAL LIBERAL CATHOLIC
ECZEMA TETTER EARWORM MALANDERS
EDACITY GREED APPETITE VORACITY
EDDA SAGA
EDDISH ETCH ARRISH EEGRASS
EDDO TARO COCOYAM
EDDY CURL GULF PURL WASH WEEL WELL ACKER GURGE SHIFT SWIRL TWIRL WHIRL SWOOSH VORTEX WIRBLE BACKSET WREATHE (PREF.) DINO
EDDYING WALE
EDEMA BRAXY TUMOR DROPSY BIGHEAD HYDROPS ANASARCA SWELLING
EDEMATOUS BLOATED HYDROPIC
EDEN ADEN HEAVEN UTOPIA ARCADIA ELYSIUM PARADISE (FATHER OF —) JOAH
EDENTATA BRUTA
EDENTATE SLOTH AARDVARK ANTEATER
EDGE AGE BIT HEM JAG LIP RIM BANK BERM BRIM BROW CURB DRAW FACE KANT LIMB LIST RAND SIDE TRIM WELL WHET ARRIS BERME BEVEL BLADE BOARD BRINK CHIMB CHIME CREST EAVES FRILL KNIFE LABEL LEDGE MARGE PEARL RULER SHARP SIDLE SPLAY VERGE BORDER CANTLE DECKLE FLANGE FORAGE IMPALE LADRUM MARGIN NOSING PLANGE MARGENT NOSEOUT SELVAGE SHARPEN VANDYKE BOUNDARY EMBORDER KEENNESS MAJORITY OUTSKIRT SELVEDGE STICKING UMSTROKE
(— FORWARD) CREEP
(— IN MINING DRIFT) ARRAGE
(— OF BASKET) FOOT
(— OF BED) STOCK
(— OF BIRD'S BILL) TOMIUM
(— OF BOOK) FERRULE BACKBONE
(— OF BOOK COVER) FLAP
(— OF BRILLIANT) GIRDLE
(— OF CASK) CHIME CHINE
(— OF COAL PILE) RUN
(— OF DAM) CREST
(— OF DUMP) TOE
(— OF FABRIC) SELVAGE SELVEDGE
(— OF FLAG) HOIST
(— OF MESA) CEJA
(— OF MINERAL VEIN) APEX
(— OF ROADWAY) SHOULDER
(— OF RUDDER) BEARDING
(— OF RUFFLE) HEADING
(— OF SAIL) FOOT HEAD LEACH LEECH
(— OF SAW) SAFE
(— OF SHELL) HINGE
(— OF STRATUM) BASSET
(— OF STREAM) HAG
(— OF TOOL) BEZEL BEZIL
(— OF TOOTH) SCALPRUM

(— OF TROUSERS) CREASE
(— OF VAULT) GROIN
(— OF WOOD) WOODRIME
(—S OF COAT) LAP
(BEVELED —) CHAMFER
(CUTTING —) SHOE FRONTIER VANGUARD
(DOUBLE —) FLAT
(EMBROIDERED —) SURFLE SURPHUL
(EXTERIOR —) AMBITUS
(FRONT — OF BOOK) FACE
(HAVING IRREGULAR —) EROSE
(ORNAMENTAL —) FRILL
(RAGGED —) RAG
(ROCKY —) ARETE
(ROUGH —S) FASH
(SHARP —) ARRIS BEARD
(UNPLOWED — OF FIELD) RAND
(UNTRIMMED —) DECKLE (PREF.) AMBO
EDGED EDGY EROSE SHARP CRENATE CUTTING
(— BY ARCS) INVECTED
EDGER WHETTER STRANDER
EDGEWISE (NOT —) FLATLONG
EDGING HEM CURB EDGE LACE LIST FILET FRILL LEDGE PICOT BORDER FILLET FRINGE LIMBUS BEADING BINDING GIMPING HAMBURG COQUILLE FRILLING PUNTILLA RICKRACK SKIRTING SURROUND PASSEMENTERIE
(— TO COLLAR) PIKADELL PICCADILL PICCADILLO PICCADILLY
(GRASS —) VERGE
EDGY ANTSY EAGER FUSSY SHARP TENSE ANGULAR NERVOUS CRITICAL SNAPPISH
EDIBLE FOOD ALIBLE EATABLE ESCULENT
EDICT ACT BAN LAW BULL FIAT TYPE ARRET BANDO BULLA IRADE ORDER SANAD UKASE ASSIZE DECREE DICTUM NOTICE COMMAND EMBARGO PLACARD PROCESS PROGRAM STATUTE ECTHESIS RESCRIPT
EDIFICE DOME CHURCH TURBEH BUILDING ERECTION TETRAGON
EDIFY GROW BUILD FAVOR TEACH BENEFIT IMPROVE PROSPER CONVINCE INSTRUCT ORGANIZE
EDIFYING HIGH SAVORY ELEVATED
EDIT CUT EMEND DIRECT REDACT REVIEW REVISE ARRANGE COMPILE CORRECT PREPARE PUBLISH REWRITE COPYREAD
EDITION KIND EXTRA FINAL FIRST ISSUE PRINT STAMP ALDINE DIGLOT SOURCE AUSGABE BULLDOG HEXAPLA OCTAPLA VERSION PRINCEPS VARIORUM
(FIRST —) PRINCEPS
EDITOR AUTHOR OVERSEER REDACTOR
AMERICAN BOK DAY BOVA BOYD BURR BYRD CARY DANA DELL DUNN FARB FOSS FUNK HILL HOWE LUCE REID ROSS SHAW WARE YUST ALLEN BACON BYERS CANBY CLARK COLBY DEBOW DUBAY ELSON FENNO FODOR FOLEY GOULD

GRADY KNOTT LASCH LOCKE LYNES MABIE MOORE NILES PAINE PRATT PUSEY RENSE RIDER RUDER SHAWN SWOPE WHITE ABBOTT AIKENS ANGELL ANGOFF BALLOU BARRON BIRNIE BOWKER BOWLES CAPPER CATTON CHURCH CLARKE COWLEY DABNEY DANIEL DENNIE DUBOIS FINLEY FLOWER FORBES GILDER GIROUX HANSEN HEARST HOOPER LARSEN LAWSON LUMMIS MALONE MANTLE MARKEL MARTIN MERWIN MONROE MUNSON NATHAN PALLEN RASCOE WILLIS ALDRICH BROWLES BURNETT COUSINS DREISER EASTMAN FADIMAN FERNALD FREEMAN GANNETT HAPGOOD HAZLITT HOFFMAN HOLLAND HUBBARD JOHNSON LINCOLN LITTELL LOVEJOY LOWNDES MENCKEN NAVASKY ONASSIS STEDMAN TAGGARD VIERECK WALLACE ALLIBONE ANDERSON BARSOTTI BENJAMIN CRAWFORD DOCTOROW GINGRICH GRINNELL GRUENING HUZTABLE LIPPMANN PETERSON RUIKEYSER SEDGWICK STRUNSKY TAISHOFF THOMPSON VANDOREN WHEELOCK ALISHELER BARTHOLDT BLACKWELL DUYCKINCK KAEMPFFERT UNTERMEYER CHAMBERLAIN CROWNINSHIELD
CANADIAN MCGEE NEWMAN
ENGLISH LEE MEE FELL FENN OPIE PEEL READ RHYS RYLE TODD CRAIG GIBBS HICKS WAUGH ALLOTT BARNES BOOSEY DEANE GARVIN HAWKES HUTTON HUXLEY KELTIE SEAMAN BOWDLER BURNAND CHAPMAN DUGDALE HYAMSON KNOWLES VERRALL CHISHOLM GOLDRING MUIRHEAD PROTHERO QUENNELL RICKWORD SPEDDING BOTTOMLEY CUSHENDUN HOLINSHED HOLLOWOOD PEMBERTON RAPPOPORT MONTGOMERY
FINNISH WALTARI
FRENCH MIGNE MORTIER YRIARTE CHAUMEIX HACHETTE
GERMAN BARTH HUBER MULLER
HUNGARIAN HARSANYI
IRISH RUSSELL ALLINGHAM
ITALIAN ASCOLI
MALTESE BUTTIGIEG
PANAMANIAN ARIAS
RUSSIAN CAHAN ARBATOV BLEEKER
SCOTTISH DYCE LAING CURRIE DAVIES HERVEY SPENCE ANDERSON HASTINGS LOCKHART FINDLATER MOTHERWELL
EDITORIAL LEADER
EDO BENI BINI
EDRED (BROTHER OF —) EDMUND
(FATHER OF —) EDWARD
(MOTHER OF —) EADGIFU
EDUCATE REAR BREED TEACH TRADE TRAIN EXPAND INFORM SCHOOL DEVELOP NURTURE INSTRUCT

EDUCATED BRED CIVIL TAUGHT
TRAINED INFORMED LETTERED
LITERATE
EDUCATION CLERGY NURTURE
BREEDING LEARNING NORTELRY
PEDAGOGY TRAINING
(— GROUP) NEA
(LIBERAL —) HUMANITY
(PHYSICAL —) GYM
EDUCATOR TEACHER
  AMERICAN BOK DAY FEW GAY HAM
ILG AMES BATE BLOW BODE CASE
CHEW COLN CONE FORD FRYE HALL
HART HESS HILL HOLT HOPE HULL
HYDE KOHL LEVI LIDZ LYND LYON
MANN MAYR MOON ODUM PAGE
RAND ROOS ROOT RUGG TARR
TRUE WARD WARE WEST AARON
ADAMS ADLER AIKEN AVERY AYRES
BAKER BATES BAUGH BEARD BEERS
BEGLE BERRY BOLEY BROWN
BRYAN BYRNE CANBY CAPEN CAPPS
CHASE CLAPP CLARK COONS CROSS
CURRY DAMON DENNY DEWEY
DOBIE ELIOT EWING FLORY FRANK
FUESS GATES GAUSS GOULD
HEDGE HUBEL JAMES JENKS JONES
KNOTT KOZOL KRAPP KRAUS KUSCH
LANGE LOCKE LOWES MANLY
MEYER MEZES MINOT ORTON PATRI
PERRY POUND PUSEY RILES ROLFE
ROSSI SCOTT SHERA SMITH SMYTH
SZASZ TAUBE TEMIN TYLER UNGER
UPHAM WHITE WOLFF YOUNG
ANGELL BAGLEY BAILEY BARNES
BARZUN BASCOM BAXTER BOVARD
BOWKER BOWMAN BRIGGS
BUMPUS BUTLER CARMER CARTER
CARVER CHIANG CONANT COOPER
CORSON COUNTS CRONIN DABNEY
DAVIES DOMAGK DONHAM DRAPER
DUBOIS DURANT EURICH FERRIS
FINLEY FINNEY FOWLER GAYLEY
GEDDES GILMAN GOEBEL GRAVES
GRIMKE HADLEY HARPER HARRIS
HAWKES HAZARD HIBBEN HIGHET
HOWARD JESSUP JEWETT JUDSON
KELLER KEPPEL LANDIS LERNER
LOVETT LOWELL MARTIN MATHER
MCAFEE MEARNS MILLIS MONROE
NORTON PALMER PARKER PEFFER
PEIRCE PHELPS PORTER SARETT
SCOPES SLOANE SPARKS SPROUL
STRONG STROUP STUART THOMAS
THWING WIGGIN WILDER WRIGHT
AGASSIZ ANAGNOS ANDREWS
BABBITT BARBOUR BARNARD
BARROWS BENEZET BETHUNE
BRADLEY BRAWLEY CALKINS
CARDOZO CLAXTON COFFMAN
COLBURN COMFORT CONNELY
DENNETT DOHERTY DYKSTRA
ERSKINE FARRAND GARNETT
GARRATY GARRETT GILMORE
GOODNOW GOODWIN GOUCHER
GUMMERE HASKINS HERRICK
HOPKINS HOUSTON HUEBNER
HULBERT HULBURT JACKSON
JARDINE JOHNSON KHORANA
KIMBALL KIMPTON LEONARD
LINCOLN LINDSAY MATHEWS
MCMURRY PADOVER PATRICK

PEABODY RAYMOND RICKERT
ROLLINS SCUDDER SHUSTER
TATLOCK TAUSSIG THACHER
VANDYKE VANHISE VIERECK
VOELKER WALLACE WHEELER
WILLARD WIMSATT WOOLSEY
ZEITLIN ALDERMAN BANCROFT
BASHFORD BLANDING BREWSTER
BRITTAIN CALLAHAN CHANDLER
COMMAGER COMSTOCK COPELAND
DJERASSI FLETCHER FOERSTER
GRISWOLD HARNWELL HARRISON
HOLLOWAY HUTCHINS LANGSTON
LAWRENCE MARQUAND
MATTHEWS MCGUFFEY MCKNIGHT
PENNIMAN PHILLIPS ROBINSON
SCHURMAN SEASHORE SILLIMAN
STODDARD SUZZALLO TUTWILER
WHEELOCK WILLIAMS WOODBURN
WOODWARD ARMSTRONG
AYDELOTTE CARPENTER
CHAUVENET FAIRBANKS FAIRCHILD
GOODSPEED GRANDGENT
GREENOUGH HENDERSON
KITTREDGE LOUNSBURY PARTRIDGE
PATTERSON PENDLETON
SCHELLING SHARPLESS SPAULDING
THORNDIKE WENTWORTH
BLOOMFIELD CHADBOURNE
KILPATRICK LONGSTREET
PARRINGTON STURTEVANT
WASHINGTON GILDERSLEEVE
  ARGENTINIAN HOUSSAY
SAAVDEDRA AVELLANEDA
  AUSTRALIAN GREER HOLME
CALDWELL
  AUSTRIAN NEURATH
  BELGIAN HEYMANS LAFONTAINE
  CANADIAN ABEL GRANT OSLER
PRATT WIGLE CAPPON HUTTON
MACKAY MURRAY LEACOCK
MACLEAN MCLUHAN
  CZECH KELSEN COMENIUS
  DANISH LUND KROGH
  DUTCH ASSER DEVRIES EIJKMAN
LORENTZ ZERNIKE COUPERIUS
  ECUADORIAN ROCAFUERTE
  EGYPTIAN HUSSEIN
  ENGLISH DENT KING KLUG ALLEN
BEALE BOWRA CECIL CHAIN DYSON
ELTON FITCH GRANT KEBLE LUCAS
OGDEN PETTY ROUSE SMITH
SWANN ARNOLD BARNES CATLIN
COTTON FARMER HADDON HOGBEN
INGOLD KEYNES MORANT RAIKES
RIPMAN SADLER BAINTON BALFOUR
BALLARD COGHILL KENDREW
STARKIE WESTRUP CHAMBERS
CUNLIFFE SIDGWICK SPURGEON
MANSBRIDGE ABERCROMBIE
  FRENCH EPEE ANDLER BOUTMY
CAMPAN DORIOT FONCIN WAILLY
ABELARD BELJAME BIDAULT
BUISSON CHINARD RENAULT
BOUTROUX COMPAYRE
  GERMAN AHN ALER BAUR KERN
LAUE REIN CAMPE GRAFE LANGE
STURM CARNAP GEDIKE JENSEN
LIEBIG NATORP WITTIG ZIMMER
BECKMAN FISCHER FROEBEL
JASPERS SPEMANN DORPFELD
FOERSTER DIESTERWEG
TROTZENDORF

  HUNGARIAN BEOTHY MANNHEIM
  INDIAN HUSAIN GOKHALE
  IRISH HUNTER WALTON STARKIE
  ISRAELI SCHOLEM
  ITALIAN PEI NATTA FEDELE
DAPONTE VILLARI BELTRAMI
GALLENGA LOMBROSO MALPIGHI
MONTESSORI
  JAPANESE NAGAI SUZUKI YUKAWA
ASAKAWA NEESIMA FUKUZAWA
  MEXICAN CAMPOS
  NORWEGIAN HASSEL ONSAGER
  PORTUGUESE EGAS
  RUSSIAN BAER RUBIN
  SCOTTISH BELL BLAIR NEILL
AYTOUN DALGARNO
  SWEDISH SIREN SIEGBAHN
  SWISS HESS BLOCH PAULI GIRARD
KARRAR TOPFFER DUCOMMUN
FELLENBERG
EDUCE DRAW EVOKE ELICIT EVOLVE
EXTORT EXTRACT
EEL ELE APOD GRIG LING OPAH SNIG
TUNA APODE ELVER MORAY SIREN
APODAN CARAPO CONGER
FAUSEN MOREIA MURENE
CONGRIO KWATUMA LAMPREY
MURAENA SNIGGLE WRIGGLE
CONGEREE GYMNOTID KINGKLIP
  (KIND OF —) MORAY
  (YOUNG —) GRIG ELVER OLIVER
YELVER
  (25 —S) STICK SWARM
EELGRASS DREW WRACK ENALID
EELPOUT BARD LING POUT QUAB
BURBOT CONGER GUFFER
YOWLER LYCODOID
EELSKIN (10 —S) TIMBER
EELSPEAR PILGER
EELWORM EEL NEMA
EERIE EERY SCARY TIMID WEIRD
WISHT CREEPY DISMAL GLOOMY
GOUSTY SPOOKY AWESOME
GHOSTLY GOUSTIE MACABRE
STRANGE UNCANNY ELDRITCH
GHOULISH POKERISH
EFFACE BLOT DASH DELE RASE
RAZE WEAR ERASE CANCEL
DEFACE SPONGE STRIKE DESTROY
DISLIMN EXPUNGE NULLIFY
UNPAINT WEAROUT
EFFECT DO SEE DENT DOES FECK
HAVE PRAY PREY TEEM WORK
CAUSE CLOSE ECLAT ENACT ETTLE
EVENT FORCE FRUIT ISSUE STAMP
ACTION ENERGY GROWTH INDUCE
INTENT OBTAIN RESULT SECURE
SEQUEL STEREO UPSHOT ACHIEVE
ACQUIRE ARRANGE COMPASS
CONDUCE EMOTION EXECUTE
FULFILL IMPRESS IMPRINT
OPERATE OUTCOME PERFORM
PROCURE PRODUCE PURPORT
REALIZE CAUSATUM COMPLETE
CONCLUDE CONTRIVE FRUITAGE
CONSEQUENT
  (— OF PAST EXPERIENCE) MNEME
  (BLURRED —) FUZZ
  (COUNTERBALANCING —)
STANDOFF
  (DAZZLING —) ECLAT
  (DECORATIVE —) CHIPPING
  (ELECTRICAL —) STRAY

  (ESTHETIC —) ATMOSPHERE
  (FALSE —) FACADE
  (FINAL —) AMOUNT
  (GRANULAR —) SPECKLE
  (ILL —) EVIL
  (INTENSE —) STRESS
  (KIND OF —) BOHR GUNN COANDA
DOMINO RIPPLE DOPPLER PLACEBO
HAWTHORNE MOSSBAUER
  (MOTTLED —) SPRINKLE
  (MUSICAL —) BEND SHADING
  (OPTICAL —) PHANTASMAGORIA
  (PAINFUL —) JAR
  (PAINTING —) STIPPLE
  (PENETRATING —) SEARCH
  (PERNICIOUS —) BLAST
  (PERSONAL —S) DUNNAGE
  (SECONDARY —) OVERTONE
  (SHATTERING —) BRISANCE
  (THEATRICAL —) CURTAIN
  (TO HAVE —) MILITATE
  (TOTAL —) ENSEMBLE
  (TOXIC —S) THEISM
  (TREMOLO —) BEBUNG
  (VISIBLE —) TOUCH
  (SUFF.) ERGATE ERGY
EFFECTIVE ABLE HOME MEAN REAL
ALIVE GREAT HAPPY PITHY SIKER
SOUND VALID ACTIVE ACTUAL
CAUSAL COGENT DEADLY DIRECT
FRUITY POTENT SEVERE SICKER
SOVRAN CAPABLE FECKFUL
OPERANT TELLING VIRTUAL
ADEQUATE FORCEFUL POWERFUL
SMASHING STRIKING VIGOROUS
TRENCHANT
EFFECTIVELY NAITLY
EFFECTIVENESS AIM BANG CHIC
EDGE TEETH VOLTAGE EFFICACY
LEVERAGE
EFFECTUAL ACTUAL TOOTHY
ADEQUATE POWERFUL
MAGISTRAL
EFFECTUATE FULFIL FULFILL
COMPLETE
EFFEMINATE NICE SOFT MILKY
MISSY NELLY SAPPY SISSY BITCHY
EFFETE FEMALE LYDIAN NELLIE
NIMINY PRISSY SILKEN TENDER
WANTON WEAKLY CITIZEN
EPICENE MEACOCK WOMANLY
FEMINATE FEMININE LADYLIKE
OVERSOFT WOMANISH
EFFERENT EXODIC
EFFERVESCE FIZZ HUFF KNIT
BUBBLE SPARKLE CARBONATE
EFFERVESCENCE FRET CRACKLE
SPARKLE
EFFERVESCENT UP BRISK FIZZY
QUICK BUBBLY ABUBBLE ELASTIC
BUBBLING
EFFERVESCING BRISK
EFFETE SERE WEAK JADED PASSE
SPENT BARREN DECADENT
ETIOLATE MORIBUND OUTMODED
EFFICACIOUS VALID MIGHTY
POTENT FORCIBLE POWERFUL
SINGULAR VIGOROUS VIRTUOUS
OPERATIVE
EFFICACY DINT FECK DEVIL FORCE
GRACE MIGHT POWER DEGREE
VIRTUE POTENCY VALIDITY
OPERATION

EFFICIENCY POWER SKILL AGENCY ABILITY FACULTY DISPATCH EFFICACY PERFORMANCE

EFFICIENT ABLE GOOD SMART VALID POTENT CAPABLE FECKFUL POWERFUL SPEEDFUL

EFFIGY GUY IDOL POPE SIGN DUMMY IMAGE LIKENESS MONUMENT

EFFLORESCE GERMINATE

EFFLORESCENCE RASH BLOOM BLOSSOM ROSEOLA ANTHESIS ERUPTION WHITEWASH

EFFLUENCE ISSUE EFFLUX ELAPSE EMANATE

EFFLUVIA SCENT

EFFLUVIUM AURA ODOR MIASMA FLUXION SPECIES APORRHEA EMISSION OUTGOING EMANATION

EFFLUX OUTGO OUTFLOW EFFUSION

EFFORT JOB TRY TUG DINT FIST HUMP JUMP MINT PASS SHOT TOIL ASSAY BRUNT BURST CRACK DRIVE ESSAY FLING LABOR NISUS PAINS POWER REACH STUDY THROE TRIAL ANIMUS DEVOIR FAVORS FIZZLE FUFFLE PINGLE STRAIN STROKE THRIFT ATTEMPT CONATUS MOLIMEN NITENCY SPLURGE STRETCH TENSURE TROUBLE WORKING ENDEAVOR EXERTION GOODWILL INDUSTRY MOLITION REACHING STRIVING STRUGGLE

(— FOR ONESELF) FEND

(ABORTIVE —) FIZZLE

(AGONIZED —) THROE

(ARTICULATIVE —) ACCENT

(EARNEST —) STUDY

(EFFECTIVE —) LICK

(FINAL —) CHARETTE

(INITIAL —) ASSAY

(MAXIMUM —) BEST

(SALVATIONIST —) ATTACK

(SINGLE —) HEAT TRICE

(STRENUOUS —) HASSEL HASSLE

(UNSUCCESSFUL —) ATTEMPT CLUNKER

(UTMOST —) DEVOIR BUSINESS

(VIOLENT —) BURST STRAIN OUTRAGE STRUGGLE

EFFORTLESS EASY

EFFORTLESSNESS EASE

EFFRONTERY BROW FACE GALL BRASS FRONT BRONZE AUDACITY BOLDNESS CHUTZPAH FOREHEAD TEMERITY

EFFULGENCE BLAZE GLORY RADIANT RADIANCE SPLENDOR

EFFULGENT BRIGHT FULGENT RADIANT SHINING

EFFUSE GUSH SHED FLING EFFUND EMANATE DISPENSE

EFFUSION EFFLUX FOISON SCREED SPILTH STREAM

EFFUSIVE GOOEY GUSHY LAVISH SLOPPY GUSHING BUBBLING

EFFUSIVENESS SLOP

EFT ASK EVET NEWT LIZARD TRITON

EGAD ADAD ECOD IGAD SGAD

EGEST VOID EXCRETE ELIMINATE

EGEUS (DAUGHTER OF —) HERMIA

EGG AI ABET GOAD GOOG OEUF OVUM PROD SEED SPUR URGE CHECK HUEVO OVULE SPORE DARNER INCITE OOCYTE PEEWEE ZYGOTE ACTUATE COCKNEY COKENEY OOPLAST OOSPERM PROTOVUM

(— CASE) POD

(— CLUTCH) LAUGHTER

(— OF FISH OR LOBSTER) BERRY

(— ON) HAG ABET EDGE GOAD URGE

(— ON ONE'S FACE) EMBARRASSMENT

(— PRODUCT) ZOON

(—S OF BEES) BROOD

(—S OF SILKWORM) GRAINE

(— WITH BACON) COLLOP

(ACID —) SLOWCASE

(CRACKED —) CHECK CRACK LEAKER

(DRIED —S) AHUATLE

(DUCK —S) PIDAN

(FLY'S —) BLOW FLYBLOW

(FOSSIL —) OVULITE

(GOLDEN —S) SUNCUP

(GOOSE —) BLOB

(HAVE AN —) LAY

(HUNT BIRDS' —S) OOLOGIZE

(INFERTILE —) CLEAR

(INSECT —) NIT BLOW

(PART OF —) YOLK SHELL WHITE ALBUMEN CHALAZA MEMBRANE BLASTODISC

(SHAPED LIKE AN —) OVOID

(SHAPE LIKE AN —) OVOID

(SMALL —) OVULE OVULUM

(PL.) OVA ROE SEED EYREN SPAWN CLUTCH ETTING AHUATLE

(PREF.) OARI(O) OIDIO OO OV(I)(O)

(— CASE) OOTHEC(O)

EGG AND DART ECHINUS

EGG CAPSULE OVISAC

EGG CELL GAMETE

EGGFRUIT LUCUMA CANISTEL

EGGHEAD EINSTEIN HIGHBROW INTELLECTUAL

EGGNOG NOG CAUDLE ADVOCAAT

EGGPLANT BRINJAL SOLANUM BRINGELA EGGFRUIT

EGG-SHAPED OOID OVAL OVATE OVOID OOIDAL OBOVOID OVALOID OVIFORM

EGGSHELL SHARD CASCARON

EGG WHITE GLAIR ALBUMEN

EGG YOLK YELLOW VITELLUS

EGLAH (HUSBAND OF —) DAVID

EGLANTINE (FATHER OF —) PEPIN

(HUSBAND OF —) VALENTINE

EGO I ATTA SELF ATMAN EGOITY FYLGJA CONCEIT SUBJECT

EGOCENTRIC INSEEING

EGOISM PRIDE ONEISM VANITY CONCEIT EGOTISM OWNHOOD SELFNESS NARCISSISM

EGOIST (AUTHOR OF —) MEREDITH

(CHARACTER IN —) DALE LUCY CLARA HARRY VERNON DECRAYE CROSSJAY DARLETON LAETITIA PATTERNE WHITFORD MIDDLETON CONSTANTIA WILLOUGHBY

EGOTISM EGO PRIDE EGOISM VANITY CONCEIT EGOMANIA SELFLOVE

EGREGIOUS FINE GROSS CAPITAL EMINENT FLAGRANT PRECIOUS SHOCKING

EGREGIOUSLY BEASTLY

EGRESS EXIT ISSUE OUTGO OUTLET EXITURE OUTCOME OUTGATE PASSAGE REGRESS OUTGOING

EGRET HERON PLUME GAULIN KOTUKU AIGRETTE GAULDING

EGYPT MIZRAIM

EGYPT

BAY: FOUL

CALENDAR: AHET APAP TYBI PAYNI SHEMU THOTH CHOIAK HATHOR MECHIR MESORE PAOPHI PACHONS

CANAL: SUEZ

CAPE: BANAS RASBANAS

CAPITAL: CAIRO ELQAHIRA

CHRISTIAN: COPT COPTIC

COIN: FILS DINAR GIRSH POUND DIRHAM GUINEA JUNAYH PIASTER MILLIEME

DAM: ASWAN

DESERT: LIBYAN

GOVERNORATE: SUEZ CAIRO CANAL SINAI BAHARIYA BAHRIYAH ALEXANDRIA

GULF: AQABA

ISTHMUS: SUEZ

KING: AY IB KA ITI ITY TUT DJER DJET HUNY PAMI PEPI SETI TEOS TETI UNIS ARSES BEBTI FOUAD ITETI KEBEH KHUFU KNIAN MENES NEBKA NECHO NEFER UDIMU ZEMTI ZOSER CHEOPS DARIUS FAROUK KHAFRE NARMER RANSES SENEDJ XERXES MENKURE PHARAOH PTOLEMY RAMESES SALADIN CHEPHREN THUTMOSE

LAKE: EDKU IDKU MARYUT MOERIS MANZALA BURULLUS MAREOTIS

LAKES: BITTER

MEASURE: APT DRA HEN PIK ROB DRAA KHET ROUB THEB ABDAT ARDAB CUBIT FARDE KELEH KILAH SAHME ARTABA AURURE FEDDAN KEDDAH ROBHAH SCHENE CHORYOS DARIBAH MALOUAH ROUBOUH TOUMNAH KASSABAH KHAROUBA

MOUNTAIN: SINAI GHARIB KATHERINA

NAME: UAR

NATIVE: ARAB COPT NILOT BERBER MUSLIM NUBIAN

OASIS: SIWA DAKHLA KHARGA FARAFRA BAHARIYA

OLD CAPITAL: SAITE

PENINSULA: SINAI

PORT: TOR SUEZ ATTUR DUMYAT QUSEIR RASHID SAFAGA SALLUM ROSETTA DAMIETTA HURGHADA PORTSAID ALEXANDRIA

PROVINCE: GIZA QENA QINA ASWAN ASYUT MINYA SOHAG DUMYAT FAIYUM SAWHAJ TAHRIR ALJIZAH BEHEIRA BENISUEF DAMIETTA GHARBIYA MINUFIYA SHARQIYA

RESERVOIR: ASWAN

RIVER: NILE

RUINS: ABYDOS THEBES MEMPHIS PYRAMIDS

SUN GOD: RA RE ATUM

TOWN: NO MUT DUSH GIZA IDFU ISNA QENA SAIS SIWA SUEZ ZOAN ASWAN ASYUT BENHA BULAQ CAIRO EL TUR FAYID GIRGA GIZEH LUXOR NAKHL SALUM SOHAG TAHTA TANIS TANTA ABYDOW AKHMIN DUMYAT ELQASR HELWAN RASHID THEBES BURSAID ROSETTA ZAGAZIG BENISUEF DAMIETTA ISMAILIA

WEIGHT: KAT KET OKA OKE HEML KHAR OKIA ROTL ARTAL ARTEL DEBEN KERAT MINAE MINAS OKIEH POUND RATEL UCKIA HAMLAH KANTAR DRACHMA QUINTAL

WELL: BIRTABA

WIND: KAMSIN SIROCCO KHAMSEEN

EGYPTIAN ARAB COPT GIPPY GYPPY TASIAN PHARIAN BADARIAN MEMPHIAN

EHUD (FATHER OF —) GERA BILHAN

EIDER COLK WAMP DIVER EDDER DUCKER SHOREYER

EIDOLON ICON GHOST IMAGE IDOLUM PHANTOM LIKENESS

EIGHT ETA ECHT AUGHT CHETH OCTAD OCTET OCTAVE OGDOAD OCTONARY

(PREF.) OCT(A)(O)(U)

EIGHTEENMO OCTODECIMO

EIGHTEEN-WHEELER RIG

EIGHTFOLD OCTUPLE

EIGHTH AUGHT

(— PART OF CIRCLE) OCTANT

EIGHTH NOTE UNCA CROMA CHROMA QUAVER

EIGHTY FOURSCORE

EIGHTY-SIX EJECT

EINSTEIN BRAIN

EIRE (SEE IRELAND)

EITHER ANY EDDER ITHER OTHER WHETHER

EJACULATE BELCH BLURT EJECT FLING EXCLAIM EMISSION

EJACULATION HOW COADS ZOWIE BEGORRA CRIMINE UTTERING

(MYSTIC —) OM

EJACULATORY SPUTTERY

EJECT OUT BLOW BOOT CAST EMIT FIRE HOOF OUST SHED SPAT SPEW SPIT VOID WARP AVOID BELCH CHUCK ERUCT ERUPT EVICT EXPEL SHAKE SHOOT SPOUT SPURT VOMIT BANISH BOUNCE REJECT SQUIRT DEFORCE DISMISS EXCLUDE EXTRUDE OBTRUDE DISGORGE OUTBRAID

(— DROPS) SPUTTER

EJECTION BLOW OUSTER OUTING EVICTION

EJECTOR LIFTER EDUCTOR

EKE IMP ALSO YEKE AUGMENT ENLARGE HUSBAND STRETCH

APPENDIX INCREASE LENGTHEN LIKEWISE UNDERLAY

ELABORATE LUSH FIKIE GREAT LABOR DELUXE DRESSY ELABOR ORNATE QUAINT REFINE CURIOUS DEVELOP ENLARGE LABORED PERFECT
(OVERLY —) NIGGLING
ELABORATED WROUGHT
ELABORATELY FANCILY
ELABORATENESS FINENESS CURIOSITY
ELABORATION FINISH
(PETTY —) NIGGLING
ELAH (FATHER OF —) UZZI CALEB BAASHA
(SLAYER OF —) ZIMRI
(SON OF —) HOSHEA
ELAINE (FATHER OF —) PELLES BRANDEGORIS
(SON OF —) GALAHAD
ELAIS (FATHER OF —) ANIUS
(MOTHER OF —) DORIPPE
(SISTER OF —) OENE SPERMO
ELAMITE SUSIAN ANZANITE
ELAN DASH ZEST ARDOR DRIVE FLAIR GUSTO VERVE SPIRIT WARMTH PANACHE POTENCY
ELAND ORYX IMPOFO
ELAN VITAL ZOISM
ELAPS MICRURUS
ELAPSE GO RUN PASS ROLL SLIP GLIDE SPEND EXPIRE RUNOUT
ELAPSED PAST
ELAPSING CURRENT
ELASAH (FATHER OF —) SHAPHAN
ELASMOBRANCH PLACOID
ELASTIC QUICK GARTER RUBATO SPONGY BUOYANT SPRINGY STRETCH CHEVEREL CHEVERIL FLEXIBLE STRETCHY VOLATILE
ELASTICITY GIVE LIFE ELATER SPRING STRETCH
ELATE BYOU PUFF CHEER EXALT EXULT FLUSH LOFTY RAISE SETUP ELATED EXCITE PLEASE THRILL ELEVATE GLADDEN INFLATE SUBLIME SUCCESS ELEVATED HEIGHTEN INSPIRIT JUBILATE
ELATED RAD HIGH RADE CHUFF ELATE GIDDY HAPPY PROUD VAUDY VOGIE WLONK CHUFFY JOVIAL UPPISH UPPITY EXCITED EXULTED JOCULAR SUBLIME EUPHORIC EXULTANT GLORIOUS INFLATED JUBILANT PRIDEFUL UPLIFTED
ELATER BEETLE CRINULA SKIPJACK
ELATION JOY GLEE RUFF RUFFE BUOYANCY
ELATUS (FATHER OF —) ARCAS
(MOTHER OF —) ERATO CHRYSOPELIA
(SON OF —) CYLLEN ISCHYS PEREUS AEPYTUS STYMPHALUS
(WIFE OF —) LAODICE
ELBOW ELL BEND ANCON JOINT NUDGE SHOVE CROSET ELBUCK JOSTLE JUSTLE SPRING PIERDROP
(OUT AT THE —S) SEEDY
(PREF.) CUBITO ULNO
ELCAJA MAFURA
ELDER AIN IVA AINE WITE ELLER

OLDER PRIOR MAHANT PRIMUS SENIOR ANCIENT NEGUNDO STAROST TRAMMON ANCESTOR BOUNTREE BOURTREE CARELESS DANEWORT ELDERMAN PRESBYTER
ELDERLY AGED GRAY ALDER ANILE ELDERN SENILE BADGERLY GERIATRIC
ELDEST AYNE EIGNE OLDEST PRIMUS
ELDRICH EERIE
ELEASAH (FATHER OF —) HELEZ RAPHA
ELEAZAR (BROTHER OF —) ABIHU NADAB ITHAMAR
(FATHER OF —) AARON ELIUD MAHLI PAROSH ABINADAB PHINEHAS
(GRANDFATHER OF —) MERARI
ELECAMPANE INULA CANADA ELFWORT SCABWORT
ELECT CALL PICK VOICE ASSUME CHOOSE CHOSEN DECIDE ISRAEL PREFER SELECT
ELECTION PROXY CHOICE LECTION PRIMARY
ELECTIONEERING HUSTINGS
ELECTIVE OPTION OPTIONAL
ELECTOR VOTER ELISOR CHOOSER ELIGENT INTRANT ELECTANT
ELECTORATE PEOPLE COUNTRY
ELECTRA LAODICE
(BROTHER OF —) ORESTES
(DAUGHTER OF —) IRIS AELLO OCYPETE
(FATHER OF —) ATLAS OCEANUS AGAMEMNON
(HUSBAND OF —) PYLADES THAUMAS
(MOTHER OF —) ERATO TETHYS PLEIONE CLYTEMNESTRA
(SON OF —) IASION DARDANUS
(UNCLE OF —) MENELAUS
ELECTRIC
(PREF.) POTAM(O)
(— RAY) NARC(O)
ELECTRICIAN WIRER GAFFER JUICER BOARDMAN
ELECTRICITY JUICE POWER PYROGEN ELECTRIC GALVANISM
(GENIUS OF —) TESLA
ELECTRIFY EXCITE THRILL STARTLE
ELECTROCARDIOGRAPHIC (— EXAMINATION) STRESSTEST
ELECTROCUTE BURN EXECUTE
ELECTROCUTION CHAIR
ELECTRODE DE DEE GATE GRID ANODE PLATE DYNODE CATHODE IGNITER CROWFOOT REOPHORE
(PL.) ELEMENT
ELECTRODEPOSIT STRIKE REGULINE
ELECTROLYTE STRIKE IONOGEN
ELECTROMAGNETIC (— UNIT) OERSTED ABAMPERE
ELECTRON ION NEGATON POLARON NEGATRON POSITRON CORPUSCLE
ELECTRONIC RADIONIC
(— DEVICE) WAWAPEDAL
ELECTRONICS (— WHIZ) TECHIE
(BRANCH OF —) OVONICS
ELECTRONOGRAPHY ONSET

ELECTRON TUBE TRIODE
ELECTROPHONE MARTENOT
ELECTROPLATE SILVER
ELECTROTYPE PATCH CLICHE WORKER ELECTRO
ELECTRUM AMBER ELECTRE ORICHALC
ELECTRYON (DAUGHTER OF —) ALCMENE
(FATHER OF —) PERSEUS
(MOTHER OF —) ANDROMEDA
ELECTUARY DIASCORD LECTUARY THERIACA MITHRIDATE
ELEGANCE CHIC GARB LUXE TONE CLASP GRACE STYLE SWANK TASTE FINERY GAIETY GAYETY LUXURY NICETY POLISH COURTESY EUPHUISM FINENESS FRIPPERY GRANDEUR SPLENDOR
ELEGANT CHIC DINK FAIR FEAT FINE FIXY GENT JIMP POSH CIVIL COMPT FANCY GRAND NOBBY RITZY SHARP SLEEK SWANK SWISH CHOICE CLASSY DAINTY DELUXE DRESSY FACETE MINION POLITE PRETTY QUAINT SUPERB SWANKY URBANE VENUST CAPITAL CLEANLY COURTLY FEATISH FEATOUS GENTEEL MINIKIN REFINED SMICKER DEBONAIR DELICATE GINGERLY GRACEFUL GRAZIOSO HANDSOME POLISHED TASTEFUL CONCINNOUS
ELEGANTLY FINE TALLY FAIRLY GENTLY GINGERLY
ELEGIAC MOURNFUL EPICEDIAL
ELEGY POEM SONG DIRGE KINAH QINAH LAMENT MONODY EPICEDE
ELEKTRA (CHARACTER IN —) OREST AEGISTH ELEKTRA CHRYSOTHEMIS KLYTEMNESTRA
(COMPOSER OF —) STRAUSS
ELEMENT AIR ATOM DIAD DYAD RECT WOOF BEARD ETHER FIBER FIBRE IODIN METAL MONAD PUNCT STUFF AETHER ARTIAD COSTAL FACTOR HEPTAD LOSSER MATTER MOMENT SMITH ACTINON ADAPTER BUNCHER CARRIER CATCHER ESSENCE FEATURE ACTINIDE BACKBONE CEREBRAL EQUATION PERISSAD RUDIMENT SELECTOR THERBLIG
(— IN GRAPH) SPIKE
(— IN WAVE) DART
(— IN WORD GROUP) KOINON
(— OF ALCHEMIST) AIR FIRE EARTH WATER
(— OF EXISTENCE) DHARMA
(— OF MACHINE) HORN SPIDER
(— OF WEALTH) COMMODITY
(— ON TV SCREEN) PIXEL
(ALIEN —) ALLOY
(ARCHITECTURAL —) SLAB
(BINDING —) CEMENT
(CHARACTER —) STRAIN
(CHARACTERISTIC —) PARAMETER
(CHEMICAL —) TIN GOLD IRON LEAD NEON ZINC ARGON BORON RADON XENON BARIUM CARBON CERIUM CESIUM COBALT COPPER CURIUM ERBIUM HELIUM INDIUM IODINE MURIUM NICKEL OSMIUM OXYGEN

RADIUM SILVER SODIUM SULFUR ARSENIC BISMUTH BROMINE CADMIUM CALCIUM FERMIUM GALLIUM HAFNIUM HOLMIUM IRIDIUM KRYPTON LITHIUM MERCURY NIOBIUM RHENIUM RHODIUM SILICON TERBIUM THORIUM THULIUM URANIUM WOLFRAM YTTRIUM ACTINIDE ACTINIUM ANTIMONY ASTATINE CHLORINE CHROMIUM EUROPIUM FLUORINE FRANCIUM HYDROGEN LUTETIUM MASURIUM NITROGEN NOBELIUM NONMETAL PLATINUM POLONIUM RUBIDIUM SAMARIUM SCANDIUM SELENIUM TANTALUM THALLIUM TITANIUM TUNGSTEN VANADIUM METALLOID PALLADIUM PLUTONIUM
(COMMUNION —) GIFT
(CRIMINAL —) GANGLAND
(DECORATIVE —S) ART
(DOMINANT —) CAPSHEAF
(ELECTRIC —) IMPEDOR
(ESSENTIAL —) CORPUS
(EUCHARISTIC —S) HAGIA SPECIES
(FATAL —) BANE
(FIRST —) PRIMORDIAL
(FUNDAMENTAL —) STAMEN KEYSTONE
(GLOOMY —) PALL
(HEATING —) CALANDRIA
(HYPOTHETICAL —) CORONIUM
(IMAGE —) PIXEL
(INTERFERING —) CRIMP
(LAMP —) GLOWER
(LEADING —) HEAD
(LINGUISTIC—) SERVILE INTENSIVE
(MILITARY —) SUPPORT
(MODIFYING —) LEAVENING
(MORAL —) DAENA
(MOST IMPORTANT —) CAPSTONE
(PRIMAL —) GUNA SALT ARCHE
(PRINCIPAL —) STAPLE
(SKELETAL —) SCLERE
(STRUCTURAL —) ARCUALE
(SUPPOSED —) PROTYLE WELSIUM VICTORIUM
(SUSTAINING —) BREAD STAPLE
(TRACE —) MICRONUTRIENT
(TRANSITORY —S) SKANDHAS
(UNITING —) BOND
(UNSOUND —) ULCER
(PL.) DETAIL ALPHABET
(PREF.) **(FIRST —TH)** STOICHIO
(SUFF.) AD IUM
(CHEMICAL —) ID IDE INE IUM
ELEMENTAL PURE BASIC PRIMAL SIMPLE PRIMARY ULTIMATE PRIMITIVE
ELEMENTARY PRIMAL SIMPLE INITIAL PRIMARY INCHOATE ULTIMATE RUDIMENTARY
ELEMI ANEMI ANIME MATTI RESIN CONIMA
ELEPHANT COW BULL CALF HINE PUNK BABAR HATHI HATTY JUMBO ROGUE MUCKNA TUSKER KOOMKIE AIRAVATA LOXODONT MASTODON OLIPHANT PACHYDERM PROBOSCIDEAN
(— BOY) SABU
ELEPHANT BIRD AEPYORNIS

ELEPHANT FISH JOSEF JOSUP
JOSEPH
ELEPHANTIASIS TYRIASIS
ELEPHANTINE HUGE ENORMOUS
ELEPHANT'S-EAR TARO
ELEPHANT'S -EARS BEGONIA
ELEPHANT SHREW JUMPER
ELEUT KALMUK KALMYK KALMUCK
ELEVATE HAIN JUMP LIFT REAR
RISE EDIFY ELATE ENSKY ERECT
EXALT EXTOL GRIMP HEAVE HOIST
MOUNT RAISE TOWER REFINE
UPLIFT ADVANCE DIGNIFY
ENHANCE ENNOBLE GLORIFY
PROMOTE SUBLIME UPRAISE
HEIGHTEN INSPIRIT
ELEVATED EL FINE HIGH GREAT
LOFTY NOBLE RISEN STEEP AERIAL
AMOTUS ELATED RAISED RISING
WINGED BULLATE ELEVATO
EXALTED MOUNTED STILTED
SUBLIME MAJESTIC UPLIFTED
(— IN CHARACTER) HIGH
(NOT —) COMICAL
ELEVATION UP ARM BAND BANK
DOME DRUM GLEE HIGH HILL
HUMP LIFT RISE SPUR TOFT TOOT
UMBO AGGER BULLA GRADE
KNOLL MOUND PITCH RAISE RIDGE
SHOAL SWELL TOWER WHEAL
CONULE CRISTA HEIGHT PAPULE
UPLIFT DIGNITY FURCULA
MAJESTY UPRIGHT ALTITUDE
EMINENCE EVECTION HIGHNESS
LEVATION MOUNTAIN SWELLING
MONTICULE
(— OF CARTILAGE) ANTHELIX
(— OF CUTICLE) BLEB
(— OF SKIN) BLISTER
(— OF VOICE) ARSIS
(— ON TOOTH) STYLE
(— SEPARATING CREEKS) BUGOR
(ANGULAR —) SILLVE
(GUN —) RANDOM
(TURRET —) HOOD
(PREF.) ORO
ELEVATOR BIN CAGE LIFT SILO
HOIST BRIDGE LIFTER TEAGLE
HOISTER STACKER UPTAKER
UPLIFTER UPRAISER
(TAKE THE —) RIDEUP
ELEVEN
(PREF.) HENDEC(A) UNDEC(A)
ELEVENTH ELFT
ELF FAY HAG HOB IMP OAF PUG
DROW FANE OUPH PERI PIXY PUCK
DWARF ELFIN FAIRY GNOME
OUPHE PIGMY PIXIE ELFKIN
GOBLIN SPIRIT SPRITE URCHIN
BLASTIE BROWNIE INCUBUS
SUCCUBUS
ELFIN ELF FEY CHILD ELFIC ELFISH
URCHIN
ELFISH ELFIN ELVAN ELVISH IMPISH
URCHIN ELFLIKE TRICKSY
ELFRIDA (HUSBAND OF —) EDGAR
(SON OF —) AETHELRED
ELIA LAMB
ELIAB (BROTHER OF —) DAVID
(DAUGHTER OF —) ABIHAIL
(FATHER OF —) HELON NAHATH
(SON OF —) ABIRAM DATHAN
ELIADA (FATHER OF —) DAVID

ELIADAH (SON OF —) REZON
ELIAKIM (FATHER OF —) ABIUD
MELEA HILKIAH
(SON OF —) AZOR JONAN
ELIAM (DAUGHTER OF —)
BATHSHEBA
ELIASAPH (FATHER OF —) LAEL
ELIASHIB (FATHER OF —) BANI
ZATTU
ELICIT CALL DRAW MILK PUMP
CLAIM EDUCE EVOKE EXACT
FETCH WREST WRING DEDUCE
DEMAND ENTICE EXTORT INDUCE
EXTRACT PROVOKE SOLICIT
ELIDE OMIT SKIP ANNUL IGNORE
CURTAIL DESTROY NULLIFY
DEMOLISH SUPPRESS
ELIEZER (FATHER OF —) JORIM
MOSES BECHER ZICHRI DODAVAH
ELIGIBILITY FITNESS
ELIGIBLE FIT ACTIVE WORTHY
SUITABLE
(— IN POKER) ACTIVE
ELIMELECH (SON OF —) MAHLON
CHILION
(WIFE OF —) NAOMI
ELIMINATE FAN COMB EDIT KILL
EDUCE EXPEL PURGE SCRUB
DELETE EFFACE EXCEPT IGNORE
REMOVE SCREEN WINNOW
ABOLISH BLANKET BRACKET
DIVULGE EXCLUDE EXCRETE
RELEASE RULEOUT SCISSOR
SILENCE SUBLATE TAKEOUT
SEPARATE
ELIMINATION STRIP
ELIOENAI (FATHER OF —) NEARIAH
ELIPHAL (FATHER OF —) UR
ELIPHALET (FATHER OF —) DAVID
ELIPHAZ (FATHER OF —) ESAU
(MOTHER OF —) ADAH
(SON OF —) TEMAN
ELIPHELET (FATHER OF —) DAVID
ESHEK
ELISABETH (HUSBAND OF —)
ZACHARIAS
(SON OF —) JOHN
ELISHA (FATHER OF —) SHAPHAT
ELISHAH (FATHER OF —) JAVAN
ELISHAMA (FATHER OF —) DAVID
(SON OF —) NETHANIAH
ELISHAPHAT (FATHER OF —) ZICHRI
ELISHEBA (BROTHER OF —)
NAHSHON
(FATHER OF —) AMMINADAB
(HUSBAND OF —) AARON
ELISHUA (FATHER OF —) DAVID
ELISION SYNCOPE
**ELISIR D'AMORE (CHARACTER IN
—)** ADINA BELCORE NEMORINO
DULCAMARA
(COMPOSER OF —) DONIZETTI
ELISSA (BROTHER OF —)
PYGMALION
(FATHER OF —) BELUS METGEN
(HUSBAND OF —) ACERBAS
SYCHAEUS SICHARBAAL
(SISTER OF —) ANNA
ELITE BEST LITE PINK CREAM
CHOICE CIRCLE FLOWER GENTRY
SELECT PERFECTI
ELIUD (FATHER OF —) ACHIM
ELIXIR DAFFY AMRITA SPIRIT

AMREETA ARCANUM CORDIAL
CUREALL ESSENCE PANACEA
MEDICINE
(ALCHEMIST'S —) TINCT
ELIZAPHAN (FATHER OF —) UZZIEL
ELK ALCE DEER LAMA LOSH ALAND
ALCES ELAND LOSHE MOOSE
CERVID SAMBAR WAPITI SAMBHUR
WAMPOOSE
(— HIDE) LOSH
(YOUNG —) DEACON
ELKANAH (FATHER OF —) KORAH
(SLAYER OF —) ZICHRI
(SON OF —) SAMUEL
ELK BARK BIGBLOOM
ELL ULNA WING ELBOW ALNAGE
ADDITION
ELLIPSE OVAL
ELLIPSIS BRING ELLIPSE
ELLIPSOGRAPH TRAMMEL
ELLIPSOID CONOID ELLIPTIC
SPHEROID
ELLIPSOIDAL OVAL
ELLIPTICAL OVAL OVATE OVOID
OBLONG
ELLOBIUM AURICULA
ELM ULME ELVEN ULMUS WAHOO
MEZCAL CHEWBARK
ORLIAMWOOD
(FRUIT OF —) SAMARA
ELMODAM (FATHER OF —) ER
ELMSEED
(PREF.) SAMARI
ELNAAM (SON OF —) JERIBAI
JOSHAVIAH
ELOCUTION SPEECH DICTION
ORATORY
ELOCUTIONIST READER RECITER
ELOIGN CONVEY REMOVE
ABSCOND CONCEAL
ELON (FATHER OF —) ZEBULUN
ELONGATE EXTEND REMOVE
STRETCH LENGTHEN PROTRACT
(— RAPIDLY) SHOOT
ELONGATED LANK LONG LINEAR
OBLONG PROLATE SLENDER
HAIRLIKE PRODUCED
ELOPE DECAMP ESCAPE ABSCOND
ELOQUENCE FACUND FLUENCY
ORATORY
ELOQUENT VOCAL DISERT FACUND
FERVID FLUENT SILVER RENABLE
SPEAKING ORATORICAL
ELPAAL (BROTHER OF —) ABITUB
(FATHER OF —) SHAHARAIM
(MOTHER OF —) HUSHIM
ELPALET (FATHER OF —) DAVID

EL SALVADOR	
CAPITAL:	SANSALVADOR
COIN:	PESO COLON CENTAVO
DANCE:	PASILLO
DEPARTMENT:	LAPAZ CABANAS
	MORAZAN SONSONATE
GULF:	FONSECA
INDIAN:	PIPIL
LAKE:	GUIJA ILOPANGO
MEASURE:	VARA CAFIZ CAHIZ
	FANEGA TERCIA BOTELLA
	CAJUELA CANTARO MANZANA
POINT:	REMEDIOS
PORT:	CUTUCO ACAJUTLA
RIVER:	JIBOA LAPAZ LEMPA
RUINS:	TAZUMAL
TOWN:	CUTUCO IZALCO CORINTO
	METAPAN ACAJUTLA USULUTAN
	SONSONATE AHUACHAPAN
VOLCANO:	IZALCO
WEIGHT:	BAG CAJA LIBRA

ELSE OR ENS ENSE OTHER BESIDES
INSTEAD
ELSEWHERE ALIBI EXCEPT THENCE
(FROM —) ALIUNDE
ELUCIDATE CLEAR LUCID EXPLAIN
SIMPLIFY
ELUDE BEAT FLEE FOIL JINK MISS
MOCK SLIP AVOID DODGE EVADE
BAFFLE BEFOOL DELUDE DOUBLE
ESCAPE BEGUILE DECEIVE
HEDGEHOP
ELUSIVE EELY LUBRIC SHIFTY
SUBTLE TRICKY TWISTY EVASIVE
BAFFLING FUGITIVE SLIPPERY
ELYSIUM EDEN ANNWFN PARADISE
ELYTRON HUSK SCUTE SHARD
SHERD SHEATH
ELYTRUM SHARD TEGMEN
ELZAPHAN (FATHER OF —) UZZIEL
EM EMMA
(HALF —) EN
EMACIATED LEAN POOR EMPTY
GAUNT MEAGER PEAKED SKINNY
WASTED TABETIC WASTREL
MARASMIC SKELETAL
WANTHRIVEN
EMACIATING MARCID
EMACIATION NITON TABES MACIES
ATROPHY POVERTY ASTHENIA
MARASMUS
EMANATE FLOW ARISE EMANE
EXUDE ISSUE DERIVE EFFUSE
EXHALE OUTRAY SPRING BREATHE
OUTCOME PROCEED RADIATE
EMANATING EFFLUENT
EMANATION FUG AURA BEAM
BLAS AROMA GLORY NITON
AZILUT BREATH EFFLUX ELAPSE
EIDOLON MOFETTE OUTCOME
PROCESS SEPHIRA EMISSION
PROCESSION
(— FROM A MEDIUM) ECTOPLASM
(SENSED —) KARMA
(PL.) SCENT
EMANCIPATE FREE MANUMIT
RELEASE LIBERATE UNFETTER
EMANCIPATION FREEDOM
RELEASE
(FINAL —) NIRVANA
EMASCULATE GELD SOFTEN
EVIRATE CASTRATE ENERVATE
EMATHION (BROTHER OF —)
MEMNON
(FATHER OF —) TITHONUS
(MOTHER OF —) EOS
(SLAYER OF —) HERCULES
EMBALM BALM CERE MUMMY
SPICE BALSAM SEASON CONDITE
MUMMIFY
EMBANK BUND
EMBANKMENT BAY BAND BANK
BUND DIKE DYKE FILL QUAY ARGIN
DIGUE LEVEE MOUND REVET
SCARP BUNKER ESCARP STAITH
BACKING BANKING PARADOS
PILAPIL RAMPART RAMPIRE

SEAWALL APPROACH STRENGTH REVETMENT

EMBARGO EDICT ORDER IMBARGE BLOCKADE STOPPAGE

EMBARK BANK SAIL SHIP ENGAGE ENLIST INSHIP INVEST LAUNCH IMBARGE

EMBARRASS SET CHAW CLOG FAZE HACK LAND POSE ABASH ANNOY SHAME UPSET BOGGLE CUMBER GRAVEL HAMPER HINDER HOBBLE IMPEDE PLUNGE PUZZLE RATTLE CONFUSE ENTRIKE FLUMMOX INVOLVE NONPLUS BEWILDER CONFOUND DUMFOUND ENCUMBER ENTANGLE HANDICAP IMPESTER OBSTRUCT STRAITEN

EMBARRASSED AWKWARD FLURRIED SHEEPISH

EMBARRASSING STICKY AWKWARD HIDEOUS

EMBARRASSINGLY AWKWARDLY

EMBARRASSMENT FIX GENE LURCH SHAME STAND CADDLE CUMBER HOBBLE PUZZLE CHAGRIN NONPLUS CONFUSION

EMBASSY SAND ERRAND AMBASSY MESSAGE MISSION INBASSAT LEGATION

EMBATTLED BATTLED CRENELE BRETESSE CRENELEE

EMBAY BATHE DETAIN ENCLOSE SHELTER SUFFUSE ENCIRCLE SURROUND

EMBAYMENT FIORD FJORD

EMBDEN GOOSE

EMBED BED SET BOND IMBED LAYIN STAMP CHARGE ENGAGE EMBOWEL IMMERSE
(— **IN SAND**) DOCK

EMBEDDED INNATE ENGAGED IMMERSED

EMBELLISH GEM DECK GILD LARD TRIM ADORN DRESS FUDGE GRACE BEDECK BETRIM BLAZON EMBOSS ENRICH FIGURE FLOWER APPAREL BEDRAPE EMBLAZE GARNISH MYSTIFY VARNISH BEAUTIFY DECORATE FLOURISH ORNAMENT

EMBELLISHED FLORID GESTED ORNATE COLORED FUCUSED BROCADED SPLENDID

EMBELLISHMENT FILIP GRACE FILLIP RELISH AGREMEN GARNISH GILDING WINDING AGREMENT FLOURISH MOUNTING ORNAMENT PARERGON TRAPPING TRICKING PASSAGGIO
(**MUSICAL** —) SERIF MELISMA ROULADE ARABESQUE
(**PL.**) FIXINGS

EMBER ASH COAL AIZLE GLEED IMBER CINDER
(**RED-HOT** —**S**) BAGA

EMBEZZLE STEAL PECULATE SQUANDER

EMBEZZLEMENT THEFT PLUNDERAGE

EMBITTER SOUR BITTER CURDLE ACIDIFY ENVENOM ACERBATE EMPOISON VERJUICE

EMBITTERED SOURED ACERBATE ENFESTED

EMBLAZON LAUD ADORN EXTOL BLAZON DISPLAY EMBLAZE EXHIBIT GLORIFY

EMBLAZONED CLOUE CLOUEE CRINED CRESTED BRISTLED
(— **WITH ANTLERS**) ATTIRED
(— **WITH BEARD**) BARBED

EMBLAZONMENT HERALDRY

EMBLEM BAR ANKH ATEN LOGO MACE ORLE SEAL SIGN STAR TYPE AWARD BADGE CREST CROSS EAGLE FAVOR IMAGE TIARA TOKEN DEVICE DIADEM ENSIGN FIGURE KAHILI SABCAT SHIELD SIGNAL SYMBOL TRISUL CHARACT IMPRESA IMPRESE SCEPTER SCEPTRE ALLEGORY CADUCEUS COLOPHON INSIGNIA
(— **OF AUTHORITY**) ROD SCEPTER
(— **OF CUCKOLD**) HORN
(— **OF ENGLAND**) ROSE
(— **OF IMMORTALITY**) AMARANTH
(— **OF IRELAND**) SHAMROCK
(— **OF PIRACY**) CROSSBONES
(— **OF SCOTLAND**) THISTLE
(— **OF SOVEREIGNTY**) GLOBE
(— **OF VENGEANCE**) SWORD
(— **OF WALES**) LEEK
(**AUTOMOBILE** —) MARQUE
(**FLYER'S** —) WINGS
(**PRINTING** —) COLOPHON
(**SACRED** —) HIEROGRAM

EMBLEMATIC TYPAL FIGURAL TYPICAL SYMBOLIC

EMBLIC AMLA AULA MYROBALAN

EMBODIMENT MAP SON SELF AVATAR GENIUS EPITOME IMAGERY BODIMENT
(— **OF JUSTICE**) ARISTIDES
(— **OF PERFECTION**) FLOWER
(**VISIBLE** —) PICTURE

EMBODY BODY UNITE INBODY CONTAIN EXPRESS COALESCE ORGANIZE
(— **IN FLESH**) INCARNATE

EMBOLDEN BOLD BIELD BRAVE ERECT NERVE ASSURE BOWDEN ENHARDY HEARTEN STOMACH

EMBOLUS CLOT STYLE

EMBOSOM BOSOM FOSTER CHERISH ENCLOSE IMBOSOM SHELTER SURROUND

EMBOSS BOSS HIDE KNOB KNOT ADORN BLOCK CHASE GOFFER INDENT POUNCE ANTIQUE CONCEAL ENCLOSE EXHAUST GAUFFER INFLATE ORNAMENT

EMBOSSED BOSSED RAISED ANTIQUE CHAMPED MATELASSE

EMBOSSING CELATURE

EMBOUCHURE LIP CHOPS LIPPING

EMBOWER BOWER

EMBOWERED ARBORED

EMBRACE ARM HUG CLIP COLL FOLD LOVE NECK PLAT SIDE ZONE ADOPT BOSOM BRACE CHAIN CLASP CLING CRUSH ENARM GRASP HALCH HALSE INARM OXTER PRESS TWINE ABRAZO ACCEPT ACCOLL AMPLEX BECLIP CARESS CLINCH COMPLY CUDDLE

ENFOLD FATHOM HUDDLE INCLIP INFOLD PLIGHT SHRINE AMPLECT CHERISH CONTAIN ENCLOSE ESPOUSE INCLUDE INVOLVE ACCOLADE AMPLEXUS CANOODLE COMPLECT COMPRESS COMPRISE CONCLUDE ENCIRCLE

EMBRACING COLLING OSCULANT AMPLECTANT

EMBRASURE LOOP PORT VENT CRENEL CRENELLE PORTHOLE

EMBROCATION ARNICA EMBROCHE LINIMENT

EMBROIDER RUN TAT DARN FRET LACE BROUD COUCH FAGOT PANEL SMOCK BEWORK EMBOSS FAGGOT FRIEZE NEEDLE PURFLE STITCH SURFLE TISSUE BROIDER TAMBOUR ORNAMENT

EMBROIDERED BRODE BRODEE BROWDEN BROCADED

EMBROIDERER SPRIGGER

EMBROIDERY KANT LACE OPUS WORK BREDE ASSISI BONNAZ CREWEL EDGING HEDEBO APPAREL CHICKEN CUTWORK ORPHREY SETWORK TAMBOUR ARRASENE BRODERIE BROIDERY COUCHING FAGOTING LISTWORK PHULKARI SMOCKING TAPESTRY CREWELLERY NEEDLEPOINT

EMBROIL BROIL JUMBLE INVOLVE PERPLEX TROUBLE DISORDER DISTRACT ENTANGLE

EMBRYO GERM CADET FETUS OVULE FOETUS EMBRYON NEURULA PLANULA ACANTHOR BLASTULA GASTRULA PRINCIPE
(**PREF.**) BLAST(O)

EMBRYONIC GERMINAL

EMCEE HOST

EME AUNT YEME UNCLE FRIEND NEIGHBOR

EMEND (**ALSO SEE AMEND**) EDIT MEND ALTER AMEND BETTER REFORM REPEAL REVISE CORRECT IMPROVE RECTIFY REDRESS EMENDATE

EMERALD BERYL GREEN EMRAUD EMERANT PRASINE SMARAGD

EMERALD FISH ESMERALDA

EMERGE BOB DIP BOLT LOOM PEER RISE BREAK ERUPT EXUDE ISSUE START APPEAR BECOME PLUNGE SPRING DEBOUCH EXTRUDE
(— **FROM EGGSHELL**) HATCH ECLOSE
(— **FROM SLEEP**) AWAKE
(— **SLOWLY**) PEEK

EMERGENCE NEED BIRTH PINCH EGRESS GROWTH PRICKLE BECOMING DEBOUCHE ECLOSION EMERSION ERUPTION EXIGENCE TENTACLE
(— **FROM DARKNESS**) BREAK
(**SUDDEN** —) OUTCROP

EMERGENCY NEED PEND PUSH PINCH CRISIS STRAIT SUDDEN EMERGENT EXIGENCY JUNCTURE

EMERGENT RISING ONCOMING

EMERGING EMANANT EMERGENT

EMERITA HIPPA

EMERY EMERIL SMIRIS ABRASIVE CORUNDUM

EMETIC ALUM PICK PUKE PUKER VOMIT IPECAC EVACUANT VOMITIVE VOMITORY

EMIGRANT EMIGRE EXODIST PATARIN SETTLER COLONIST PATERINE STRANGER
(— **FROM MECCA**) COMPANION

EMIGRATE MOVE REMOVE MIGRATE

EMIGRATION EXODUS HEGIRA HEJIRA SWARMING

EMILIA (**HUSBAND OF** —) IAGO PALAMON

EMINENCE DUN NAB BALL BERG CRAG KNOT MONS MOTE NOTE POLE RANK RISE SCAR TOOT CHIEF HOYLE KNOLL PERCH STATE WHEAL WORTH ASCENT HEIGHT KRANTZ RENOWN RIDEAU STATURE ALTITUDE GRANDEUR TUBERCLE
(— **OF HAND**) SUBVOLA

EMINENT BIG ARCH HIGH CHIEF GRAND GREAT LOFTY NOBLE NOTED FAMOUS MARKED SIGNAL EXCELSE SUBLIME TOPPING GLORIOUS RENOWNED SINGULAR TOWERING PROMINENT CONSPICUOUS

EMIR AMIR AMEER NOBLE RULER LEADER PRINCE ADMIRAL GOVERNOR

EMISSARY SPY AGENT SCOUT LEGATE DELEGATE

EMISSION FUME GUST PUFF VENT ESCAPE

EMISSIVE EMITTENT EXHALANT

EMIT RUN BARK BEAM CAST DRIP GIVE GUSH HURL LASH MOVE OOZE PASS POUR REEK SEND SHED SPIT VENT VOID WARP AVOID BELCH EJECT ERUCT EXERT EXUDE FLASH FLING ISSUE UTTER YIELD DECANT DONATE EVOLVE EXHALE EXPIRE SPREAD BREATHE DISTILL EMANATE EXHAUST OUTSEND RADIATE REFLAIR ERUCTATE TRANSMIT
(— **COHERENT LIGHT**) LASE
(— **FOAM**) SPURGE
(— **FORCEFULLY**) FIRE
(— **IN PUFFS**) PLUFF
(— **LIGHT**) GLOW
(— **ODOR**) REEK STEAM
(— **OUTCRIES**) CHUNNER CHUNTER
(— **PLAY OF COLORS**) OPALESCE
(— **RAYS**) RADIATE IRRADIATE
(— **SMOKE**) SMEECH
(— **SOUND**) BUFF MOVE
(— **SPARKS**) SNAP
(— **SPITTLE**) SPAWL

EMITTING EMISSIVE SOUNDING
(**SUFF.**) (— **LIGHT**) ESCENT

EMMA (**AUTHOR OF** —) AUSTEN
(**CHARACTER IN** —) EMMA JANE BATES ELTON FRANK SMITH GEORGE MARTIN ROBERT WESTON FAIRFAX HARRIET CHURCHILL KNIGHTLEY WOODHOUSE

EMMENAGOGUE ALOE SAFFRON GROUNDSEL

EMMER SPELTZ AMELCORN

EMMET ANT ENEMY PISMIRE FORMICID

EMMOR (SON OF —) SHECHEM

EMOLLIATE SOFTEN

EMOLLIENT BALM LOTION LENIENT ICHTHYOL LENITIVE MALACTIC MOLLIENT SUPPLING

EMOLUMENT FEES WAGES INCOME PROFIT SALARY BENEFIT STIPEND
(PL.) PERK

EMOTE HAM OVERACT

EMOTION IRE LOVE ONDE PANG STIR AGONY ANGER CHORD GRIEF HEART SHAME AFFECT EFFECT MOTION RAPTUS SNIVEL SPLEEN ECSTASY FEELING PASSION VULTURE GRAMERCY MOVEMENT SURPRISE SENTIMENT
(CONTROLLING —) LEITMOTIF LEITMOTIV
(CONVULSIVE —) SPASM
(EVIL —) DEMON DAEMON
(PAINFUL —) PANG
(PERIOD OF —) CRISIS
(PREF.) THYM(O)
(SUFF.) THYMIA

EMOTIONAL MUSHY DRIPPY EMOTIVE AFFECTIVE
(OPENLY —) TOUCHYFEELY
(UNDULY —) SPOONY SPOONEY RHAPSODIC

EMOTIONLESS COLD

EMPATHY SYMPATHY

EMPEROR I IMP CZAR INCA KING TSAR AKBAR RULER TENNO CAESAR DESPOT KABAKA KAISER SULTAN BAGINDA MONARCH VIKRAMA AUGUSTUS IMPERIAL PADISHAH
(ROMAN —) GETA NERO OTHO OTTO CARUS GALBA NEROS NERVA TITUS ADRIAN CAESAR JULIAN HADRIAN CALIGULA

EMPERY DOMAIN EMPIRE EMPIRY DOMINION

EMPHASIS ANGLE ACCENT STRESS WEIGHT EMPIRISM SALIENCE

EMPHASIZE HIT CLICK PINCH PRESS RUBIN ACCENT BETONE CHARGE HARPON PLAYUP STRESS FOREGROUND

EMPHATIC LOUD STRONG EARNEST MARCATO SERIOUS ENFATICO FORCIBLE MARCANDO POSITIVE RESOUNDING

EMPHATICALLY FLATLY STRONGLY POINTEDLY

EMPHYSEMA HEAVES

EMPIRE RULE SWAY POWER REALM REIGN STATE DIADEM DOMAIN EMPERY CONTROL KINGDOM IMPERIUM
(— STATE) NEWYORK
(— STATE OF SOUTH) GEORGIA
(SELJUK —) RUM ROUM

EMPIRIC QUACK IMPOSTOR

EMPIRICAL POSITIVE

EMPIRICIST VIRTUOSO

EMPLACEMENT BATTERY GALLERY PLATFORM

EMPLOY FEE PAY USE BUSK BUSY HIRE PLOY TAKE WAGE WISE ADOPT APPLY BESET IMPLY SPEND BESTOW ENGAGE ENLIST INFOLD INVOKE OCCUPY SUPPLY CONCERN CONDUCT ENCLOSE IMPROVE INVOLVE SERVICE UTILIZE PRACTICE
(— FLATTERY) COLLOGUE
(— ONESELF ABOUT) TOSS
(— SHIFTS) CHICANE

EMPLOYED APPLIED ENGAGED

EMPLOYEE HAND HELP BOOTS CLERK FACTOR LEADER BELLBOY BOOTBOY CALLBOY CARRIER SERVANT CHASSEUR CIVILIAN FLOORMAN IMPROVER
(— PROGRAM) ESOP
(— WHO RUNS ERRANDS) GOFER GOPHER

EMPLOYER BOSS JOSS BLOKE GAFFER ENGAGER MANAGER PADRONE GOVERNOR
(SMALL —) CORK

EMPLOYMENT FEE JOB USE CALL HIRE NOTE TASK TOIL USER WORK CRAFT TRADE TREAD USAGE MISTER THRIFT CALLING PURPOSE PURSUIT SERVICE USAUNCE BUSINESS EXERCISE POSITION RETAINER VOCATION
(CASUAL —) GRASS

EMPORIUM MART SHOP BAZAR STORE BAZAAR EMPORY MARKET STAPLE MONOPOLE

EMPOWER POWER ENABLE ENTITLE DELEGATE DEPUTIZE

EMPRESS IMPX EMPERESS IMPERIAL KAISERIN

EMPTIED DRAINED

EMPTILY TOOMLY

EMPTINESS VAIN VOID INANE ANEMIA VACUUM VANITY ANAEMIA INANITY VACANCY VACUITY LEERNESS
(— OF SPIRIT) ENNUI

EMPTY DRY FAT RID TIM AIRY BARE BOSS BUZZ CANT DEAF DUMP EMPT FALL FARM FREE GLIB HOWE IDLE LEER NEAR POUR ROOM TEEM TOOM VAIN VIDE VOID ADDLE AVOID BLANK BLEED CLEAN CLEAR DRAIN EQUAL EXPEL HUSKY INANE LEERY MOUTH SCOOP SHOOT SKAIL STARK START STRIP SWAMP TINNY WINDY BARREN BUBBLE CHAFFY DEVOID GOUSTY HOLLOW JEJUNE STRIKE SWASTY UNEMPT UNLOAD VACANT VACATE DELIVER DEPLETE EXHAUST EXPRESS UNTAKEN VACUATE VACUOUS VIDUOUS DISGORGE EVACUATE EVANESCE NEGATION UNFILLED
(— AN EGG) BLOW
(PREF.) CEN(O) JEJUN(O) KEN(O)

EMPTY-HEADED VAIN DOLLISH

EMPTYING EVACUANT
(ACT OF —) KENOSIS

EMPTY-SOUNDING TOOM

EMPUSA MONSTER SPECTER SPECTRE

EMPYREAN ETHER AETHER HEAVENS EMPYREUM

EMU EMEU RHEA RATITE

EMU APPLE COLANE

EMU BUSH BERRIGAN

EMULATE APE VIE COPY EMULE EQUAL EXCEL RIVAL COMPETE IMITATE

EMULATION STRIFE CONTEST PARAGON RIVALRY

EMULATOR RIVAL

EMULOUS EMULATE ENVIOUS CORRIVAL

EMULOUSLY AVIE

EMULSIFIABLE SOLUBLE

EMULSION PAP FLUID LATEX
(SENSITIVE —) PHOTOGENE

EMU WREN STIPITURE

EN NUT

ENABLE ABLE EMPOWER ENTITLE QUALIFY INHABILE

ENACT LIVE MAKE PASS ADOPT STAGE DECREE EFFECT ORDAIN ACTUATE APPOINT PERFORM PORTRAY

ENACTMENT LAW DOOM ENACT NOVEL ASSIZE DECREE MEASURE PASSAGE STATUTE ENACTION ENACTURE

ENAMEL AMEL FLUX SLIP EMAIL GLAZE GLOSS PAINT SLUSH AUMAIL SHIPPO SMALTO DENTINE LIMOGES SCHMELZ
(KIND OF —) CANTON

ENAMOR LOVE CHARM SMITE CAPTIVE

ENAMORED FOND EPRIS EPRISE MASHED AMOROUS CHARMED SMITTEN
(VAINLY —) FOOLISH

ENARCHUS (NEPHEW OF —) MUSIDORUS
(SON OF —) PYROCLES

ENCAMP TELD TENT LODGE PITCH INCAMP LAAGER BIVOUAC LEAGUER

ENCAMPMENT CAMP DOUAR ETAPE SIEGE LAAGER BIVOUAC CASTRUM HUTMENT TOLDERIA

ENCASE CASE WRAP HOUSE SHELL INCASE ENCHASE INCLOSE SURROUND ENCAPSULE

ENCELIA INCENSO

ENCEPHALON CEREBRUM

ENCHAIN FETTER INCHAIN

ENCHANT CHARM DELUDE GLAMOR INCANT ATTRACT BECHARM BESPELL BEWITCH DELIGHT GLAMOUR BEDAZZLE ENSORCEL CAPTIVATE

ENCHANTED RAPT HAGGED CAPTIVE

ENCHANTER MAUGIS CHARMER MAGICIAN MALAGIGI ARCHIMAGE

ENCHANTING ORPHIC WIZARD HEAVENLY SPELLFUL

ENCHANTMENT HEX TAKE CHARM FAIRY MAGIC SPELL SPOKE CARACT CHANTRY DEVILRY GRAMARY SORCERY SORTIARY WITCHERY

ENCHANTRESS CIRCE FAIRY MEDEA ACRASIA URGANDA

ENCHARGE ENJOIN ENTRUST

ENCHASE INFIX ENRICH ENGRAVE

ENCHIRIDION MANUAL HANDBOOK TREATISE

ENCHORIAL NATIVE DEMOTIC DOMESTIC

ENCIPHER CODE CIPHER ENCRYPT

ENCIRCLE ORB BAND BELT BIND CLIP COIL GIRD GIRT HALO HOOP PALE RING RINK STEM WIRE ZONE BELAY BESET BRACE CLASP CROWN EMBAY EMBOW GIRTH HEDGE INORB ROUND TWINE TWIST BECLIP BEGIRD CIRCLE EMBALL ENGIRT ENLACE ENRING ENWIND FATHOM GIRDLE IMPALE SWATHE WRITHE BETREND COMPASS EMBRACE ENCLAVE ENCLOSE ENTWINE ENVIRON ENWHEEL SERPENT WREATHE CINCTURE CORSELET ENSPHERE IMMANTLE SURROUND

ENCIRCLED GIRT CINCT BELTED SUCCINCT

ENCIRCLEMENT EMBRACE

ENCIRCLING AROUND AMBIENT EMBRACE CORONARY ENCYCLIC
(PREF.) AMPLEXI

ENCLAVE INLIER
(— IN SOUTH AFRICA) BANTUSTAN

ENCLOAK MANTLE

ENCLOSE IN BAY BOX CAN HEM LAP MEW ORB PAR PEN PIN RIM BANK BUNG CAGE CASE COOP FORT GIRD HAIN HOOP PALE SPAR TINE WALL WARD WOMB YARD BOSOM BOUND BOWER BRICK CHEST CLOSE DITCH EMBAR EMBED EMBOX FENCE FRAME GARTH GRIPE HEDGE HOUSE IMBED INURN BOUGHT CARTON CASTLE CAVERN CIRCLE CORDON CORRAL EMBANK EMBOSS EMPALE EMPARK EMPLOY ENCASE ENCYST ENFOLD ENGILE ENLOCK FASTEN IMMURE IMPALE IMPARK INCASE INCLIP INHOOP INSACK INWALL JACKET PICKET POCKET SHUTIN TACKLE APPROVE CAPSULE COMPASS CONFIDE CONTAIN CURTAIN EMBOSOM EMBOWEL EMBOWER EMBRACE ENCHASE ENCLAVE ENGLOBE ENHEDGE ENVELOP HARNESS IMBOSOM IMMERSE IMPOUND INBOUND INCLUDE INFIELD PARROCK PINFOLD SHEATHE BULKHEAD COMPRISE COMPRIZE CONCLUDE CONVOLVE EMBORDER ENCIRCLE ENSHRINE ENSPHERE IMPRISON LANDLOCK PALISADE PARCLOSE SURROUND
(— IN ARMOR) EMPANOPLY
(— LOGS) CRIB

ENCLOSED BOUND CLOSED INDOOR OBTECT SHUTIN INGROWN INTERNAL

ENCLOSING LIMITARY
(PREF.) PERI

ENCLOSURE HAG HAW HOK MEW PAR PEN REE STY TYE BAWN BOMA BYTH CAGE CAVE CELL COOP DOCK FOLD HAIN HOCK HOPE KILN LIST PALE PEEL SEPT SKIT SLOT TIGH TOWN WALL WEIR

YARD ALTIS ATAJO BASIN BLIND BOOLY BOOTH BOSOM CAROL CLOSE COURT CRAWL CREEP CUBBY FENCE FRANK GARTH GOTRA HOARD KENCH KRAAL LOBBY MARAI PLECK POUND REEVE STALL STELL AVIARY BOOLEY BOXING CANCHA CARREL CORRAL COWPEN CRUIVE DRYLOT GARDEN HURDLE INTAKE KENNEL OUTSET PALING PRISON SERAIL TAMBOR TEOPAN TINING VIVARY WARREN BELLOWS BOROUGH BULLPEN CLOSURE COCKPIT EMBRACE GALLERY GONDOLA HAINING HENNERY HOUSING HUMIDOR LANTERN PADDOCK PIGHTLE PUDDOCK SEVERAL STUFFER TAMBOUR AEDICULA CASEMATE CHIPYARD CINCTURE CLAPNEST CLAUSURE CLOISTER COMPOUND DELUBRUM ENCEINTE ENCHASER PARADISE POUNDAGE PRECINCT PURPRISE SEPIMENT SERAGLIO SKIRTING STOCKADE VIVARIUM
(— ABOUT ALTAR) BEMA
(— FOR BOWLING) ALLEY
(— FOR COCKPIT) CANOPY
(— FOR FISH) CROY YAIR YARE KENCH SPILLER SPILLET
(— FOR JURY) BOX
(— FOR KNIGHTLY ENCOUNTERS) BARRACE
(— FOR LIGHT) LANTERN
(— FOR ROASTING ORE) STALL
(— OF HOUSE) BAWN
(— ON AIRPLANE) NACELLE
(— SURROUNDED BY DITCH) COP
(ELEPHANT —) KEDDAH
(OBLONG —) CIRCUS
(PORTABLE —) PLAYPEN
(POULTRY —) HENNERY
(PRIVATE SEAT —) SKYBOX
(ROOFED —) SKYBOX
(SACRED —) SECOS SEKOS
(PREF.) CLAUSTRO SEPTATO
(SUFF.) SEPTATE
ENCOLPION PANAGIA
ENCOLURE MANE
ENCOMIAST EULOGIST
ENCOMIUM ELOGE ENCOMY EULOGY PRAISE PLAUDIT TRIBUTE PANEGYRIC
ENCOMPASS BEGO BELT CLIP GIRD PALE RING SPAN WALL WRAP BELIE BERUN BESET BIGAN BRACE CLOSE CROWN ROUND BEGIRD BEGIRT CIRCLE ENGIRD BESEIGE COMPASS EMBOWEL EMBRACE ENCLOSE ENVIRON INCLUDE SUBSUME UMBESET CINCTURE ENCIRCLE ENGIRDLE PURPRISE SURROUND
(— WITH ARMS) FATHOM
ENCOMPASSED AMID BAYED AMIDST BEGIRT
ENCOMPASSING ROUND AMBIENT CINCTURE PROFOUND INCLUSIVE
ENCORE BIS AGAIN RERUN ANCORA RECALL REPEAT
ENCOUNTER BIDE BUMP COIL COPE FACE FIND KEEP MEET

MOOT RINK BRUSH CLOSE FIGHT FORCE GREET INCUR OCCUR ONSET SHOCK STOUR VENUE ACCOST AFFRAY ANSWER ASSAIL ATTACK BATTLE BREAST CAREER COMBAT JOSTLE JUSTLE OPPOSE RUFFLE ADDRESS AFFRONT CONTEST COUNTER DISPUTE HOSTING JOINING PASSAGE CONFLICT CONFRONT CONGRESS REANSWER RECONTER SKIRMISH COLLISION
(— HOSTILELY) CROSS
(HOSTILE —) CLOSE
(MILITARY —) ACTION
(PUGILISTIC —) MILL
ENCOURAGE DAW EGG ABET BACK FIRM URGE BOOST CHEER ERECT FAVOR FLUSH HEART IMPEL NERVE SERVE STEEL ADVISE ASSURE EXHORT FOMENT FOSTER HALLOO HARDEN INCITE INDUCE INVITE NUZZLE REHETE SECOND SPIRIT UPHOLD ADVANCE ANIMATE CHERISH COMFORT CONFIRM CONSOLE ENFORCE ENLIVEN FLATTER FORTIFY FORWARD HEARTEN INSPIRE PROMOTE STOMACH UPCHEER UPRAISE EMBOLDEN INSPIRIT REASSURE
ENCOURAGED BUCKED CONFIRMED
ENCOURAGEMENT BOOST FLUSH HURRAH COMFORT FOMENTO IMPETUS BLESSING SANCTION
ENCOURAGING HELPFUL FAVORING
ENCRATITE TATIAN AQUARIAN
ENCROACH JET INCH POACH IMPOSE INVADE TRENCH IMPINGE INTRUDE SHINGLE ENTRENCH INFRINGE INTRENCH TRESPASS
ENCROACHING INVASIVE
ENCROACHMENT BREACH INROAD ENCROACH INVASION
ENCRUST CAKE CANDY BARKEN BARKLE INCRUST
ENCRUSTATION SCALE
ENCRUSTED CAKED SCABROUS
ENCUMBER CLOG LOAD PACK BESET CHECK CRAMP CROWD TRASH ACCLOY BEMOIL BURDEN FELTER HAMPER HINDER IMPEDE LUMBER MITHER MOIDER RETARD SADDLE WEIGHT BEPAPER INVOLVE OPPRESS ACCUMBER ENTANGLE HANDICAP OBSTRUCT OVERCOME OVERLOAD
ENCUMBERED HEAVY CONGESTED
ENCUMBRANCE CLOG LIEN LOAD CLAIM BURDEN CHARGE CUMBER TROUBLE MORTGAGE ALBATROSS
ENCYCLICAL PASCENDI
ENCYCLOPEDIA TOME
(GAME —) HOYLE
ENCYSTED CYSTIC SACCATE SACCATED
END EN AIM DAG EAR FAG TIP BUTT CUSP DATE DOUP FACE FATE FINE FOOT GOAL HALT HEEL LAST MAIN MARK SAKE STOP TAIL TERM VIEW AMEND ANNUL ARTHA BLOCK BREAK CAUSE CEASE CLOSE

DEATH ENSUE EVENT FINIS ISSUE LIMIT LOOSE NAPOO OMEGA POINT PRICK RAISE SCOPE SCRAP SHANK START STASH THULE DECIDE DEFINE DESIGN DOMINO EFFECT EFFLUX ENDING EXITUS EXPIRE EXPIRY FINALE FINISH INTENT NAPOOH OBJECT PERIOD RESULT THIRTY UPSHOT UTMOST WINDUP ABOLISH ACHIEVE CLOSURE CURTAIN DESTROY FANTAIL FINANCE LINEMAN MEANING OUTGIVE PURPOSE REMNANT BOUNDARY COMPLETE CONCLUDE DESITION DISSOLVE FINALITY SURCEASE TERMINAL TERMINUS ULTIMATE
(— DEBATE) CLOTURE
(— OF ANTENNA) CLAVA
(— OF ANVIL) BICKIRON
(— OF ARCHERY PILE) STOPPING
(— OF ARROW) NOCK
(— OF BEEF LOIN) BUTT
(— OF BLANKET) DAGON
(— OF BONE) EPIPHYSIS
(— OF BOOM) JAW
(— OF BOW) EAR
(— OF BRICK) HEADING
(— OF BRISTLE) FLAG
(— OF BUILDING) GABLE
(— OF CAN) BREAST
(— OF CANE) FRAZE
(— OF CART) TIB
(— OF CRESCENT) HORN
(— OF EAR CANAL) AMPULLA
(— OF EGG) DOUP
(— OF EXISTENCE) DEMISE
(— OF FABRIC) FENT
(— OF FISHHOOK) SPEAR
(— OF FLAG) FLY
(— OF FROG) TOE
(— OF HALTER) CAPITULUM
(— OF HAMMER) CLAW POLL
(— OF HAMMERHEAD) PEEN
(— OF HORSE-COLLAR) GULLET
(— OF INGOT) CROP
(— OF KEEL) GRIPE
(— OF LEVER) FORK
(— OF LOAF) HEEL
(— OF MINERAL LODE) SLOVAN
(— OF MINE TUNNEL) FACE
(— OF MINING LEVEL) DEAN
(— OF MUZZLE) MUFFLE
(— OF NAIL) CLENCH
(— OF ONE'S LIFE) DOOM
(— OF PIER) CUTWATER
(— OF PIPE) TAFT SPIGOT
(— OF POCKETKNIFE HANDLE) BOLSTER
(— OF RAILROAD CAR) BEND
(— OF ROAD) ROADHEAD
(— OF ROD) FORKHEAD
(— OF SHEEP SHEARING) CUTOUT
(— OF SHIP) STERN
(— OF SPINE) ACRUMION
(— OF TENON) HAUNCH
(— OF TOOL) BUTT
(— OF UTERUS) FUNDUS
(— OF WEAVER'S THREAD) THRUM
(— OF WORLD) PRALAYA
(— OF YARD) ARM YARDARM
(— ON) ABUT
(— ON POND) FOREBAY

(—S OF RIBBONS) FATTRELS
(—S OF SATURN'S RINGS) ANSA
(— UP WITH) NET
(CANDLE —) DOUP SNUFF
(DOMINO —) ACE
(FAG —) RUMP
(HANGING —) DAG DAGGE
(JAGGED —) SHRAG
(KIND OF —) TIGHT
(LOOSE —) TAG
(NARROWED —) NEB
(NORTH — OF COMPASS NEEDLE) LILY
(POINTED —) APEX
(POSTERIOR —) BOTTOM
(REEF —S) DEADMAN
(ROPE'S —) COLT FEAZE PIGTAIL FEAZINGS
(SPECIAL —) SAKE
(TAPERING —) POINT
(TATTERED —) FRAZZLE
(ULTIMATE —) SUM TELOS
(UNPLEASANT —) GRIEF
(UPPER —) HEAD
(WARP —S) ACCIDENTAL
(PREF.) ACR(O) FINI TEL(IO)
ENDANGER DANGER HAZARD IMPERIL SCUPPER
ENDANGERED BESTED BESTEAD FRAUGHT
ENDANGERER MARPLOT
ENDEARMENT LOVE CARESS
ENDEAVOR DO AIM PUT TRY WIN BEST MINT SEEK WORK ASSAY ESSAY ETTLE EXERT OFFER STUDY TEMPT TRIAL AFFAIR ASSAIL DEVOIR EFFORT INTEND STRIFE STRIVE AFFORCE ATTEMPT CONATUS CONTEND CULTURE EMPRISE EMULATE IMITATE MOLIMEN NITENCY WORKING EXERTION PURCHASE STRUGGLE
(— TO CONCLUSION) STUDY
(BEST —) DEVOIR
(EARNESTLY —) FEND
ENDED DONE OVER PAST FINISHED
(— BY CONSONANT) CHECKED
ENDEMIC LOCAL ENDEMIAL
ENDING END CLOSE DEATH GRAVE FINALE BREAKUP FINANCE DESITION
(KIND OF —) NERVE
(MUSICAL —) CODA
(NERVE —) SPINDLE
(ROMAN —) CODA
ENDIVE CHICORY WITLOOF ESCAROLE SCARIOLE
ENDLESS ANANTA ETERNE ETERNAL FOREVER UNDYING UNENDED UNENDLY DATELESS FINELESS IMMORTAL INFINITE UNENDING
ENDMOST TIPMOST FARTHEST REMOTEST
ENDOCARP STONE PYRENA PUTAMEN
ENDOGENOUS INNATE AUTOGENIC
ENDOMORPHIC PYCNIC PYKNIC
ENDOPITE PETASMA
ENDOPLEURA TEGMEN
ENDORSE BACK SIGN ADOPT BOOST DOCKET ENDOSS SECOND APPROVE CERTIFY INDORSE

SPONSOR SUPPORT ADVOCATE SANCTION RECOMMEND

ENDORSEE HOLDER

ENDORSEMENT FIAT FORM VISA RIDER BACKING APPROVAL HECHSHER SANCTION

ENDOSPERM FARINA ALBUMEN

ENDOSPORIUM INTINE

ENDOW DOW DUE DOTE GIFT RENT VEST BLESS CROWN DOWER ENDUE EQUIP FOUND INDUE SEIZE STATE STUFF ASSIGN CLOTHE DOTATE ENABLE ENRICH ENSOUL ESTATE IMPART INVEST CHARTER ENLARGE FURNISH INSTATE APPANAGE BENEFICE BEQUEATH ENTALENT
(— WITH FORCE) DYNAMIZE

ENDOWED ABLE GIFTED FAVORED

ENDOWMENT CLAY FINE GIFT WAKF WAQF DOWER DOWRY GRACE GRANT CORPSE GENIUS TALENT APANAGE CHANTRY CHARISM FACULTY APPANAGE DOTATION PATRIMONY BENEFACTION
(NATURAL —S) BUMP DOTES TALENT
(PL.) ALTARAGE

ENDPAPER FLYLEAF

ENDPIECE BRACE CHUMP
(— OF STETHOSCOPE) BELL

ENDUE DUE ENDOW INDUE TEACH CLOTHE INVEST INSTRUCT

ENDURABLE LIVABLE BEARABLE LIVEABLE PORTABLE

ENDURANCE GAME LAST TACK PLUCK BOTTOM BEARING COMFORT DURANCE GRANITE LASTING STAMINA BEARANCE DURATION GAMENESS HARDSHIP PATIENCE STRENGTH

ENDURE GO ABY SIT VIE ABYE BEAR BIDE DREE DURE HOLD KEEP LAST TAKE TIDE WEAR ADEAR ABIDE ALLOW BROOK CARRY DRIVE POUCH SPARE STAND STICK STOUT THOLE TOUGH WIELD ABROOK ACCEPT DRUDGE HARDEN REMAIN SUFFER ABROOKE COMFORT FORBEAR PERSIST STOMACH SUPPORT SUSTAIN SWALLOW TOUGHEN UNDERGO WEARING CONTINUE FOREBEAR TOLERATE
(— LONGER) OUTLAST

ENDURING FAST SURE STOUT BIDING DURING STABLE STURDY ABIDING DURABLE ETERNAL LASTING PATIENT IMMORTAL REMANENT STUBBORN PERENNIAL

ENDWAYS ANEND ENDWISE

ENDYMION (DAUGHTER OF —) EURYDICE
(FATHER OF —) ZEUS JUPITER AETHELIUS
(MOTHER OF —) CALYCE
(SON OF —) EPEUS PAEON AETOLUS
(WIFE OF —) CROMIA ASTERODIA HYPARIPPE

ENEMA CLYSMA CLYSTER COLONIC LAVEMENT

ENEMY FOE AXIS BOYG FEID DEVIL FIEND SATAN FOEMAN HOSTILE CONTRARY OPPONENT
(— OF MANKIND) DEVIL FIEND SATAN
(PERSONAL —) HATER

ENEMY OF THE PEOPLE (AUTHOR OF —) IBSEN
(CHARACTER IN —) KIIL PETER MORTEN HORSTER HOVSTAD ASLAKSEN STOCKMANN

ENERGETIC BUSY FAST FELL HARD LIVE RASH SPRY BRISK DASHY LUSTY PITHY STOUT TIGHT VITAL YAULD ZIPPY ACTIVE HEARTY HUSTLE LIVELY SPROIL ACTIOUS ANIMOSO ARDUOUS DASHING DRIVING DYNAMIC ENERGIC FURIOUS NERVOUS PUSHFUL PUSHING VIBRANT EMPHATIC ENERGICO FORCEFUL FORCIBLE HUSTLING VIGOROUS
(— PERSON) TOWSER

ENERGETICALLY MANLY FURIOUSLY

ENERGID PROTOPLAST

ENERGIZE LIVEN EXCITE ANIMATE

ENERGIZING KINETIC VIRTUAL

ENERGY U W GO GAS PEP VIM ZIP BANG BENT BIRR DASH EDGE JASM LIFE SAKT SNAP TUCK ZING ARDOR ECLAT FORCE INPUT MOXIE NERVE OOMPH POWER STEAM VIGOR EFFORT FOISON INTAKE ORGONE OUTPUT SPIRIT SPRAWL SPRING SPROIL STARCH VIRTUE POTENCY SPIRITS ACTIVITY AMBITION DYNAMISM ENERGEIA MOTIVITY PRAKRITI STRENGTH VIVACITY
(— PEAK) NUCLEUS
(EMOTIONAL —) LIBIDO
(LIBINAL —) CATHEXIS
(LIFE —) JIVA SAKTI SHAKTI
(LIGHT —) RAD
(LOW IN —) COLD
(MENTAL —) DOCITY PSYCHURGY
(POINT OF PHYSICAL —) CHAKRA
(POTENTIAL —) ERGAL
(QUANTUM OF —) PLASMON
(RADIANT —) SOUND ACTINISM EINSTEIN
(VITAL —) HORME PANZOISM
(PREF.) (RADIANT —) PENETRO
(SOLAR —) HELI(O)

ENERVATE SAP COOK FLAG MELT SOFTEN WEAKEN MOLLIFY UNNERVE UNSINEW ENFEEBLE

ENERVATED LIMP BEDRID EFFETE LANGUID LIFELESS BEDRIDDEN

ENERVATING MUGGY DREARY

ENERVATION COLLAPSE

ENFEEBLE SAP NUMB FAINT SHAKE APPALL DEADEN FEEBLE IMPAIR SOFTEN WEAKEN DEPRESS UNSINEW AFFEEBLE ENERVATE IMBECILE UNSTRONG

ENFEEBLED FEY NUMB

ENFILADE RAKE

ENFOLD (ALSO SEE INFOLD) LAP FURL ROLL WRAP CLASP COVER DRAPE ENROL IMPLY COMPLY ENLACE ENROLL ENWIND ENWRAP

INCLIP INFOLD INWIND SHADOW SWATHE WATTLE EMBRACE ENCLOSE ENVELOP ENVIRON INCLUDE INVOLVE UMBELAP CONVOLVE

ENFORCE BULL LEVY EXACT FORCE PRESS COERCE COMPEL EFFECT FOLLOW INVOKE EXECUTE IMPLANT

ENFORCED COMPULSORY

ENFORCER EXECUTOR MUSCLEMAN

ENFRAMEMENT CARTOUCH

ENG AGMA

ENGAGE DIP WED BOOK BUSY GAGE HAVE HIRE JOIN LIST MESH RENT SIGN TAKE WAGE AGREE AMUSE CATCH ENTER LEASE PITCH TRADE TRYST ABSORB ARREST EMBARK EMPLOY ENLIST INDUCE OBLIGE OCCUPY PLEDGE PLIGHT TAKEON BESPEAK BETROTH CONCERN CONDUCE CONSUME ENGROSS IMMERSE INVOLVE PROMISE THROWIN AFFIANCE CONTRACT COVENANT ENTANGLE INTEREST INTRIGUE PERSUADE PREOCCUPY
(— ATTENTION) INTEREST
(— DEEPLY) DROWN
(— IN) GO CUT SUE HAVE JOIN LEAD PROSECUTE
(— IN ARGUMENT) BALK BAULK
(— IN COMBAT) DEBATE STRIKE
(— IN DEBATE) STONEWALL
(— IN DISCUSSION) CONTEND
(— IN PRANKS) LARK
(— IN TILT) JUST JOUST
(— OVERMUCH) TROUBLE
(— WHOLLY) ABSORB CONSUME IMMERSE
(SUFF.) (— IN) IZE

ENGAGED BENT BUSY FAST GONE HIRED ACTIVE BONDED BOOKED MESHED ASSURED BESPOKE EARNEST ENTERED PLEDGED TOKENED VERSANT ABSORBED ATTACHED EMBEDDED EMPLOYED INSERTED INTEREST INVOLVED OCCUPIED PROMISED
(— IN) ABOUT
(— IN CONTROVERSY) DISPUTANT
(MENTALLY —) VERSANT
(WARMLY —) ZEALOUS

ENGAGEMENT AVAL DATE COWLE SPURN ACTION AFFAIR BATTLE COMBAT ESCROW PLIGHT STANZA SURETY BARGAIN BOOKING DUSTING SERVICE CONFLICT RETAINER SKIRMISH WARRANTY
(— OF GEARS) MESH
(— TO MARRY) TRYST
(MILITARY —) DO SHOW
(SHORT —) RUN SNAP
(SINGLE —) GIG
(THEATRICAL —) SHOP
(WRITTEN —) COWLE

ENGAGING SOFT SAPID SWEET TAKING

ENGENDER BEGET BREED CAUSE EXCITE GENDER DEVELOP PRODUCE GENERATE INGENDER OCCASION

ENGIDU EABANI

ENGINE GAS JET SIX FOUR GOAT TANK EIGHT JINNY MOTOR OILER STEAM BANKER DIESEL DOCTOR DUDLER DUDLEY INGENE JORDAN KICKER PUFFER RADIAL RAMJET ROADER YARDER MACHINE POACHER POTCHER SKIDDER STEAMER TRACTOR TURBINE BULLGINE COMPOUND DOLLBEER EXPANDER GASOLINE IMPULSOR SCRAMJET
(— FOR HAULING LOGS) DUDLER DUDLEY
(— FOR THROWING MISSILES) GIN PETRARY SPRINGAL
(— OF TORTURE) GIN RACK
(— OF WAR) RAM SWEEP HELEPOLE
(— PART) STATOR
(AIRPLANE —) SCRAMJET
(DONKEY —) DOCTOR
(FIRE —) TUB
(JET —) ATHODYD
(KIND OF —) PLASMA WANKEL
(MILITARY —) BOAR TOWER BRICOL FABRIC TREPAN BRICOLE DONDINE PERRIER PETRARY TORMENT WARWOLF BALLISTA DONDAINE MANGONEL MARTINET SCORPION
(RAILROAD —) HOG GOAT YARDER SWITCHER
(REACTION —) THRUSTER THRUSTOR
(ROCKET —) ARCJET VERNIER
(SMOOTH RUNNING —) HUMDINGER
(TYPE OF ROTARY —) WANKEL

ENGINEER PLAN GUIDE DRIVER FANNER HOGGER MANAGE SAPPER HOGHEAD PLANNER PLOTTER CONTRIVE DESIGNER INGENIER INVENTOR MANEUVER
AMERICAN AMY BURR BUSH DORR DUNN EADS HERR HILL KRUG LAKE LEAR PECK RICE ROUS WANG ALLEN CARTY ELLET GANTT HAUPT HENCH LAMME MILLS MOORE OWENS PRATT STOUT TESLA AMDAHL ARNOLD BEATTY BOGART COFFIN CONRAD COOPER COWLES CRAVEN FERRIS GARAND GREENE HAMMER HOLLEY HOLLIS HOUDRY HUTTON JACOBY JENNEY LAMONT LITTLE MORGAN NEWELL PARKER PENDER PINCUS PORTER RUMSEY STUMPF WILSON WRIGHT BALDWIN BARRELL BEHREND CLEMSON CROCKER DEJONGH DRINKER EHRICKE FANNING FREEMAN GODFREY GRAYDON HASWELL KINEALY KINTNER KNOWLES LATROBE LEONARD PACKARD PARSONS PATRICK SERRELL STRAUSS WHIPPLE AMSTRUTZ DINKELOO EDGERTON ELLSBERG ERICSSON GOETHALS HARRISON HARTNESS HUNSAKER KENNELLY MCALPINE MODJESKI OVINGTON REYNOLDS RICHARDS ROEBLING ZWORYKIN ARMSTRONG CARPENTER GILLESPIE KETTERING STEINMETZ TRAUTWINE ZACHARIAS FARNSWORTH LETOURNEAU

LINDENTHAL RIESENBERG
STRICKLAND WORTHINGTON
ALEXANDERSON BRECKENRIDGE
AUSTRALIAN CLAPP
AUSTRIAN BIRAGO ENGERTH
MANNLICHER
CANADIAN DUMAS KLOTZ MARKLE
CHINESE KWOH
CUBAN MENOCAL
CZECH SKODA
DANISH POULSEN
DUTCH NORDEN STEVIN MUSSERT
ENGLISH FOX AIRD PAUL BAKER
BOYLE CLARK COOKE GABOR
GOOCH GROVE KEMPE MANCE
ROYCE AYRTON BRAMAH BRUNEL
CAYLEY CLARKE CUBITT DONKIN
FLOREY FOWLER HARRIS HEDGES
HINTON MCADAM WALLIS BERKLEY
BOULTON CAUTLEY CRAPPER
DUDDELL FLEMING HARTLEY
MURDOCK SIEMENS SMEATON
ANDERSON BRINDLEY BUCHANAN
CRAMPTON FERRANTI HAWKSHAW
REDMAYNE SYDENHAM
GREATHEAD GRIFFITHS HOPKINSON
ISSIGONIS WILLCOCKS WIMSHURST
HORNBLOWER TREVITHICK
BRAITHWAITE FITZMAURICE
FRENCH LAME ARCON MALUS
PRONY BERTIN CHAPPE COANDA
CUGNOT DEPREZ EIFFEL LEPLAY
MARTIN RATEAU RIQUET ALPHAND
BELIDOR BERLIER BERNARD
BIERIOT BLERIOT CLERGET GIFFARD
LEBLANC LENFANT LESSEPS
TELLIER BELGRAND PONCELET
FOURNEYRON HENNEBIQUE
GERMAN BACH BENZ KOCH OTTO
BOSCH KNORR AMMANN CRELLE
DIESEL GERBER LANGEN WANKEL
CARNALL CULMANN DAIMLER
SIEMENS FLETTNER EYTELWEIN
BAUERSFELD LILIENTHAL
BAUERNFEIND GOLDSCHMIDT
HASELWANDER
ITALIAN NERVI VINCI BUGATTI
CODAZZI FABRONI MARCONI
LATVIAN MOISSEIFF
POLISH NARUTOWICZ
RUSSIAN THEREMIN FEOKTISOV
SCOTTISH BARR BELL WATT BAIRD
CLERK ELDER EWING MCADAM
MURRAY NAPIER RANKINE TELFORD
BRUNLEES FAIRBAIRN STEVENSON
SYMINGTON
SPANISH CIERVA CANDELA
SWEDISH DALEN LAVAL POLHEM
BRINELL DAHLBERG
SWISS ILG FAVRE
ENGINEMAN HOISTER HOISTMAN
ENGINERY TIRE
ENGIRDLED CINCT
ENGLAND HOME ALBION LOGRIA
BLIGHTY BRITAIN LOEGRIA
HOMELAND

ENGLAND
AIRFORCE: RAF
BAY: TOR LYME WASH START
MOUNTS BIGBURY BIDEFORD
CARDIGAN FALMOUTH
TREMADOC WEYMOUTH

CAPITAL: LONDON
CHANNEL: SOLENT BRISTOL
ENGLISH SPITHEAD
CHANNEL ISLAND: HERM SARK
JERSEY ALDERNEY GUERNSEY
COIN: ORA RIAL RYAL ACKEY ANGEL
CROWN GROAT NOBLE PENCE
PENNY POUND SPRAT UNITE
BAWBEE FLORIN GUINEA SESKIN
TESTON ANGELET CAROLUS
HAPENNY TUPPENY FARTHING
SHILLING SIXPENCE TUPPENCE
CONSERVATIVE: TORY
COUNTY: KENT DEVON ESSEX
HANTS NOTTS SALOP WIGHT
DORSET DURHAM LONDON
SURREY SUSSEX NORFOLK
RUTLAND SUFFOLK CHESHIRE
CORNWALL SOMERSET
DANCE: MORRIS
FIRTH: SOLWAY
FOREST: ARDEN EPPING EXMOOR
DARTMOOR SHERWOOD
HEAD: SPURN BEACHY FORMBY
LIZARD CEMMAES TREVOSE
HILLS: MENDIP BRENDON CHEVIOT
MALVERN CHILTERN COTSWOLD
INVADER: DANE PICT ROMAN
SAXON NORMAN
ISLAND: HOLY LUNDY WIGHT
COQUET MERSEA THANET
TRESCO WALNEY BARDSEY
HAYLING IRELAND SHEPPEY
ANGLESEA ANGLESEY FOULNESS
HOLYHEAD
ISLANDS: FARNE SCILLY CHANNEL
KING: HAL LUD BRAN BRUT CNUT
COLE KNUT LEAR HENRY JAMES
SWEYN ALFRED BLADUD
BRUTUS CANUTE EDWARD
EGBERT GEORGE ARTEGAL
ELIDURE RICHARD WILLIAM
GORBODUC
LAKE: CONISTON
LIBERAL: WHIG
MEASURE: CUT ELL LEA MIL PIN
ROD RUN TON TUN VAT ACRE
BIND BOLL BUTT CADE COMB
COOM CRAN FOOT GILL GOAD
HAND HANK HEER HIDE INCH
LAST LINE MILE NAIL PACE PALM
PECK PINT PIPE POLE POOL ROOD
ROPE SACK SEAM SPAN TRUG
TYPP WIST YARD YOKE BODGE
CABOT CHAIN COOMB CUBIT
DIGIT FLOAT FLOOR FLUID HUTCH
JUGUM MINIM OUNCE PERCH
POINT PRIME QUART SKEIN STACK
TRUSS BARREL BOVATE BUSHEL
CRANNE FATHOM FIRKIN GALLON
HOBBET HOBBIT LEAGUE
MANENT OXGANG POTTLE
RUNLET SECOND SQUARE STRIKE
SULUNG THREAD TIERCE
AUCHLET FURLONG KENNING
QUARTER RUNDLET SEAMILE
SPINDLE TERTIAN VIRGATE
CARUCATE CHALDRON
HOGSHEAD LANDYARD
PUNCHEON QUADRANT
QUARTERN STANDARD
MOUNTAIN: PEAK SCAFELL
SKIDDAW SNOWDON

MOUNTAINS: BLACK PENNINE
SNOWDON CAMBRIAN CUMBRIAN
NAME: ALBION BRITAIN BRITANNIA
PENINSULA: PORTLAND
POINT: NAZE LYNAS MORTE SALES
DODMAN LIZARD PRAWLE
HARTLAND LANDSEND
GIBRALTAR
POLICEMAN: BOBBY COPPER
PEELER
RACE TRACK: ASCOT
RESORT: BATH BRIGHTON
BLACKPOOL
RIVER: CAM DEE DON ESK EXE LEA
NEN URE WYE AIRE AVON EDEN
LUNE NENE NIDD OUSE PENK
TAME TEES TILL TYNE WEAR YARE
ANKER COLNE DEBEN STOUR
SWALE TAMAR TAWAR TRENT
TWEED HUMBER KENNET
MERSEY RIBBLE ROTHER SEVERN
THAMES WENSUM WHARFE
WITHAM DERWENT PARRETT
WAVENEY WELLAND TORRIDGE
ROCKS: MANACLES
ROYAL HOUSE: YORK TUDOR
STUART HANOVER WINDSOR
LANCASTER PLANTAGENET
SCHOOL: ETON RUGBY HARROW
SEA: IRISH NORTH
SEAPORT: POOLE
SETTLER: JUTE PICT ANGLE SAXON
NORMAN
SOLDIER: TOMMY REDCOAT
FUSILEER
STRAIT: DOVER
TOWN: ELY BATH DEAL ETON HULL
RYDE WARE YORK BLYTH BRENT
DERBY DOVER ERITH FLINT LEEDS
RIPON TRURO WIGAN BARNET
BOLTON BOOTLE CAMDEN
DURHAM EALING EXETER HANLEY
JARROW LEYTON LONDON
OLDHAM OXFORD YEOVIL
BRISTOL BROMLEY BURNLEY
CHELSEA CROYDON ENFIELD
GRIMSBY HALIFAX HORNSEY
IPSWICH LAMBETH NEWPORT
NORWICH PRESTON SALFORD
SEAFORD WESTHAM BRADFORD
BRIGHTON CORNWALL COVENTRY
DEWSBURY HASTINGS
PLYMOUTH ROCHDALE
WALLASEY WALLSALL
GREENWICH LIVERPOOL
SHEFFIELD BIRMINGHAM
MANCHESTER
TRIBE: ICENI
UNIVERSITY: LONDON OXFORD
CAMBRIDGE
VALLEY: COOM EDEN TEES TYNE
COMBE COOMB COQUET
WEIGHT: BAG KIP TOD TON KEEL
LAST MAST MAUN BARGE FAGOT
GRAIN MAUND POUND SCORE
STAND STONE TRUSS BUSHEL
CENTAL FANGOT FIRKIN FOTHER
FOTMAL POCKET QUARTER
QUINTAL SARPLER

ENGLISH SPIN SAXON AUSTRAL
BRITISH ENGLAND SAXONISH
SOUTHRON STANDARD

(— DIALECT IN LIVERPOOL) SCOUSE
(— MIXED WITH SPANISH)
SPANGLISH
(IN —) ANGLICE
(TEACHING —) TEFL TESL TESOL
(PREF.) ANGLO
ENGLISHMAN PONGO SAXON
BRITON BRONCO GODDAM
GRINGO JOHNNY ROOINEK
MACARONI SOUTHRON
ENGLISHER
(— IN INDIA) QUIHIQUIHYE
(— IN SOUTH AFRICA) ROOTNEK
(RICH —) MILOR MILORD
ENGLISHWOMAN INGLESA
ENGORGE GLUT GORGE DEVOUR
SWALLOW
ENGRAFT INSET
ENGRAM TRACE
(— PATTERN) MEANING
ENGRAVE CUT ETCH RIST CARVE
CHASE GRAVE HATCH PRINT
SCULP CHISEL INCISE SCULPT
CRIBBLE ENCHASE EXARATE
IMPRESS IMPRINT INSCULP
STIPPLE INSCRIBE ORNAMENT
ENGRAVED GRAVEN GRAPHIC
INCISED
(PREF.) GRAPTO
ENGRAVER POINT CHASER ETCHER
GRAVER ARTISAN INSCULP
BURINIST MEDALIST SCULLION
WRIGGLER
(— OF STONES) LAPIDARY
ENGRAVING CUT PRINT SCULP
STAMP GRAVERY GRAVING
GRAVURE WOODCUT AQUATINT
DRYPOINT HATCHING INTAGLIO
LINEWORK MEZZOTINT
(PREF.) GLYPHO GLYPT(O)
ENGROSS BURY SINK SOAK AMASS
GROSS ABSORB ENGAGE ENROLL
ENWRAP OCCUPY SCROLL
COLLECT CONSUME IMMERSE
INVOLVE PREOCCUPY
ENGROSSED DEEP FULL RAPT
INTENT BEMUSED WRAPPED
ABSORBED IMMERSED
PREOCCUPIED
ENGULF GULF ABYSM ABYSS
SOUSE SWAMP WHELM ABSORB
DEVOUR INVADE QUELME SLOUGH
ENGORGE SWALLOW SUBMERGE
ENHANCE FOIL LIFT BUILD ENARM
ENDOW EXALT RAISE DEEPEN
AUGMENT ELEVATE ENLARGE
EXHANCE GREATEN IMPROVE
SHARPEN HEIGHTEN INCREASE
ENHANCEMENT SAKE
ENHYDRA LATAX
ENID (HUSBAND OF —) GERAINT
ENIGMA WHY EGMA GRIPH REBUS
PUZZLE RIDDLE SPHINX GRIPHUS
MYSTERY PROBLEM PROVERB
ENIGMATIC HUMAN MYSTIC
CRYPTIC OBSCURE ELLIPTIC
MYSTICAL ORACULAR PUZZLING
RIDDLING MYSTIFYING
PERPLEXING
ENISLE MAROON
ENJAMBMENT OVERFLOW
ENJOIN BID JOIN WILL ENIUN
ORDER CHARGE DECREE DIRECT

FORBID COMMAND DICTATE
REQUIRE ADMONISH PROHIBIT
ENJOY GO JOY FAIN HAVE LIKE
BROOK FANCY PROVE SAVOR
TASTE WIELD ADMIRE DEVOUR
GROOVE RELISH DELIGHT
(— AT LEISURE) SIP
(— ONESELF) FEAST LAUGH
ENJOYABLE GOOD FRUITY
AMIABLE BLESSED CAPITAL
GLORIOUS SAVOROUS SPLENDID
ENJOYING FRUITIVE
ENJOYMENT FUN JOY USE BANG
BASK BOOT EASE GUST KAMA
PLAY ZEST FEAST GUSTO LIKING
RELISH COMFORT DELIGHT
JOLLITY JOYANCE JOYANCY
FELICITY FRUITION PLEASURE
SKITTLES
(— FROM OTHERS' TROUBLES)
SCHADENFREUDE
ENKINDLE WARM STIRUP INCENSE
INFLAME
ENLARGE ADD EKE BORE GROW
HONE HUFF OPEN REAM ROOM
BUILD FARCE LARGE SWELL
WIDEN BIGGEN BRANCH BROACH
DIDUCE DILATE EXPAND EXTEND
FRAISE GATHER LARGEN OMNIFY
SPREAD AMPLIFY AUGMENT
DISTEND ENHANCE GREATEN
IMPROVE INGREAT MAGNIFY
STRETCH AMPLIATE CUMULATE
FLOURISH INCREASE
(— COAL MINE) SNUB
ENLARGED TUMID BLOATED
CLUBBED SWELLED SWOLLEN
AMPLIATE CAPITATE EXPANDED
EXTENDED VARICOSE
ACCRESCENT
ENLARGEMENT BULB DISC DISK
KNOP NODE CLAVA SWELL
BLOWUP BUNION GIBBER
GROWTH ACTEAD ENLARGE
FOOTING SCYPHUS STATION
ANEURYSM INCREASE SWELLING
PROPAGATION
(— IN MINE SHAFT) STATION
(— IN MUSCLE) KNOT
(— OF BONE) EXOSTOSIS
(— OF GLAND) GOITER GOITRE
(— OF GULLET) CROP
(— OF MOLD) RAPPAGE
(— OF NERVE FIBER) BOUTON
(— OF ORGAN) STRUMA
(— ON HORSE'S LEG) SPLINT
(ABNORMAL —) ANEURYSM
(BONY —) SPAVIN SPAVINE
(MORBID —) TUMOR
(PREF.) MACR(O) MEG(A)
MEGAL(O) PLETHYSMO
(SUFF.) AUXE MEGALY
ENLARGING EVASE SWELLING
(PREF.) MICR(O)
ENLIGHTEN OPEN CLEAR EDIFY
TEACH ILLUME INFORM UNSEEL
EDUCATE LIGHTEN CIVILIZE
ENKINDLE INSTRUCT
ENLIGHTENED WISE LUMINOUS
ENLIGHTENMENT BODHI LIGHT
SATORI WISDOM CULTURE
INSIGHT SAMADHI AUFKLARUNG

ENLIST DRUM JOIN LEVY SOUD
ENROL ENTER HITCH PREST
ENGAGE ENROLL INDUCT JOINUP
SIGNUP IMPRESS RECRUIT
REGISTER
(— AGAIN) REUP
ENLISTMENT LEVY HITCH PREST
LISTING
ENLIVEN DASH JAZZ WARM BRACE
BRISK CHEER PEPUP QUICK RAISE
ROUSE KITTLE REVIVE ANIMATE
COMFORT INSPIRE REFRESH
SMARTEN BRIGHTEN INSPIRIT
RECREATE
ENLIVENED MERRY
ENLIVENING GENIAL LIVELY VIVIFIC
CHIRPING
ENMESH TRAP CATCH SNARL
IMMESH ENSNARE ENTANGLE
ENMITY WAR FEUD SPITE WRAKE
ANIMUS HATRED MALICE RANCOR
STRIFE FOEHOOD AVERSION
ENNEAGON NONAGON
ENNOBLE LORD EXALT HONOR
NOBLE RAISE GENTLE UPLIFT
DIGNIFY ELEVATE GLORIFY
GREATEN NOBLIFY SUBLIME
ENNUI BORE TEDIUM ACCIDIE
BOREDOM DOLDRUM
ENOCH (FATHER OF —) CAIN JARED
(SON OF —) METHUSALEH
ENOCH ARDEN (AUTHOR OF —)
TENNYSON
(CHARACTER IN —) LEE RAY LANE
ANNIE ARDEN ENOCH MIRIAM
PHILIP
ENORMITY GRAVITY
ENORMOUS BIG GOB HUGE REAM
VAST ENORM GREAT HEROIC
MIGHTY UNRIDE IMMENSE
ABNORMAL COLOSSAL FLAGRANT
GIGANTIC WHAPPING WHOPPING
ENOS (FATHER OF —) SETH
(GRANDFATHER OF —) ADAM
(SON OF —) CAINAN
ENOUGH BAS ENOW WELL WHEN
AMPLE ASSAI BASTA BELAY
ANEUCH PLENTY APLENTY SUFFICE
ADEQUATE
(— SAID) VERBUMSAP
(HARDLY —) SKIMP
(MORE THAN —) PLENTY APLENTY
ENOUNCE STATE UTTER AFFIRM
DECLARE PROCLAIM
ENRAGE RAGE ANGER GRIEVE
MADDEN INCENSE INFLAME
STOMACH
ENRAGED MAD ASHY WODE WOOD
ANGRY IRATE LIVID SAVAGE
AGRAMED BERSERK CHOLERIC
INCENSED MADDENED
ENRAPTURE RAVISH TRANCE
ECSTASY ENCHANT ENRAVISH
ENTRANCE
ENRAPTURED RAPT ENRAPT
TRANCED ECSTATIC
ENRICH FAT BOOT FEED FRET LARD
RICH ADORN CROWN ENDOW
GUANO BATTEN FATTEN INVEST
FEATHER FORTIFY FURNISH
GUANIZE INCREASE ORNAMENT
TREASURE

(— A GAS) CARBURET
(— A MINE) SALT
(— FUEL MIXTURE) CHOKE
ENRICHED FLORID
ENRICHMENT DITATION
ENROLL BEAR JOIN LIST POLL
ENROL ENTER WRITE ATTEST
BILLET ENFOLD ENLIST INDUCT
MUSTER RECORD ASCRIBE
IMPANEL INITIATE INSCRIBE
REGISTER
ENROLLMENT LISTING REGISTRY
ENROOT ENRACE IMPLANT
ENSCONCE HIDE COVER SETTLE
CONCEAL SHELTER
ENSEMBLE CORPS DECOR WHOLE
COSTUME PANTSUIT
(— OF ARMS) ARMORY
(WOMAN'S —) PANTSUIT
ENSHEATHE EMBOSS
ENSHRINE SAINT SHRINE ENCHASE
ENTEMPLE
ENSHROUD WRAP
ENSIFORM ENSATE XIPHOID
GLADIATE
ENSIGN FLAG IAGO SIGN BADGE
COLOR SENYE AQUILA BANNER
BEACON PENNON PISTOL SIGNAL
SYMBOL ALFEREZ ANCIENT
INSIGNE DANEBROG GONFALON
ORIFLAMB PAVILION STANDARD
(—S ARMORIAL) ARMS
(IMPERIAL —) TUT
(JAPANESE —) SUNBURST
(PL.) ENSIGNRY HERALDRY
ENSILE SILO SILAGE
ENSLAVE THEW CHAIN SLAVE
THIRL ENTHRAL NESLAVE SLAVISH
ENTHRALL
ENSLAVED SLAVE THRALL
ENSLAVEMENT DULOSIS SLAVERY
ENSNARE NET WEB GIRN LACE
LIME MESH TOIL TRAP WRAP
BENET CATCH NOOSE SNARE
SNARL ALLURE ATTRAP ENGINE
ENMESH ENTOIL ENTRAP TANGLE
TREPAN BEGUILE DECEIVE
ENGLEIM SNIGGLE SPRINGE
BIRDLIME INVEIGLE OVERTAKE
SURPRISE
ENSNARL ENTANGLE
ENSPHERE INORB SPHERE
ENSTATITE BRONZITE
ENSUE FOLLOW RESULT SUCCEED
(— UPON) SUE
ENSUING NEXT SUING SEQUENT
ENSURE ASSURE INSURE SECURE
BETROTH ESPOUSE WARRANT
AFFIANCE
ENTABLATURE (PART OF —)
CORONA FRIEZE TAENIA CORNICE
CYMATIUM ARCHITRAVE
ENTADA LENS
ENTAIL TAIL INCUR IMPOSE
CONTAIN INVOLVE REQUIRE
TAILZIE
ENTAILED AYNE TAIL EIGNE
ENTAMOEBA LOSCHIA
ENTANGLE ELF LAP MAT TAT WEB
BALL CAST COLL FOUL HARL KNIT
KNOT LIME MESH MIRE TOIL WRAP
BROIL CATCH HALCH RAVEL
SNAFU SNARE SNARL TWIST

BEFOUL COMMIT COTTER ENGAGE
ENLACE ENMESH ENTRAP ENWRAP
FANKLE FELTER HAMPER HANKLE
HATTER INMAZE INMESH PESTER
PUZZLE RAFFLE RANGLE TACKLE
TAIGLE TANGLE WRAPLE CONFUSE
EMBRAKE EMBROIL ENSNARL
ENTRIKE IMBRIER INVOLVE
PERPLEX TRAMMEL BEWILDER
ENCUMBER IMPESTER INTRIGUE
STRAPPLE
ENTANGLED DEEP FOUL COTTY
TANGLY COMPLEX KNOTTED
IMPLICIT
ENTANGLEMENT WEB FOUL KNOT
TWIT HITCH BUNKER COBWEB
ENTRAIL HEDGEHOG OBSTACLE
PERPLEXITY
ENTASIS SWELL
ENTELLUS HANUMAN
ENTENTE TREATY ALLIANCE
ENTER BOX DIP SET BEAR BOOK
JOIN POST ADMIT BEGIN BOARD
BREVE ENROL GETIN INCUR PROBE
SHARE START ACCEDE APPEAR
BILLET ENGAGE ENLIST ENROLL
ENTRER INCEPT INVADE PIERCE
RECORD SPREAD INGRESS
INTRUDE COMMENCE ENCROACH
INITIATE INSCRIBE NOMINATE
REGISTER PENETRATE
(— A COMPUTER PROGRAM) LOAD
(— BY FORCE) BREAK IRRUPT
INTRUDE
(— COMPUTER PROGRAM) BOOT
(— DATA) INPUT
(— HASTILY) BULGE
(— IN ATTACK) FORCE
(— IN BOOK) ACCESS
(— IN BOOKS) ACCRUE
**(— INFORMATION INTO
COMPUTER)** WRITE
(— INTO) JOIN INTERN
(— NOISILY) STOMPIN TROMPIN
(— PROGRAM INTO COMPUTER)
LOAD
(— SLOWLY) SEEP
(— UNNOTICED) CREEP
(— UPON CAREER) INCEPT
(— UPON DUTIES) ASSUME
(— WITHOUT RIGHT) ABATE
ENTERING ENTRY INGOING
INGRESS INTRANT INCOMING
ENTEROTOXEMIA STRUCK
ENTERPRISE FIRM IRON PUSH
TOGT DRIVE ESSAY ACTION
EMPIRE SPIRIT VOYAGE ATTEMPT
EMPRISE HOLDING PROJECT
VENTURE BUSINESS CARNIVAL
GUMPTION VIRITOOT
(CRIMINAL —) JOB
(HARD —) DIFFICULTY
(REMEDIAL —) CRUSADE
(SPECULATIVE —) ADVENTURE
(UNPROFITABLE —) SINKHOLE
ENTERPRISING BOLD FORTHY
PUSHFUL PUSHING
ENTERTAIN INN BEAR BUSK EASE
FETE HAVE HOLD HOST AMUSE
ENJOY FEAST GUEST SPORT TREAT
DIVERT FROLIC GESTEN HARBOR
JUNKET RECULE REGALE RETAIN

ENTERTAIN SOLACE TICKLE ACCOURT BEGUILE CHERISH DISPORT KITCHEN CONSIDER INTEREST RECREATE
(— IN THE MIND) HAVE
(— WITHOUT CHARGE) DEFRAY

ENTERTAINED OUGHT

ENTERTAINER BHAT HOST ACTOR AMUSER ARTIST BUSKER DANCER FIDDLE HARLOT SINGER ACTRESS ARTISTE DISEUSE GLEEMAN HETAERA HOSTESS REGALER SPEAKER BEACHBOY COMEDIAN HOSTELER MAGICIAN MINSTREL
(WEST AFRICA —) GRIOT

ENTERTAINING GOOD RICH TREAT PRETTY AMUSING BEDSIDE GUESTING SPORTFUL

ENTERTAINMENT BASH BILL FARE FETE GALA GLEE PLAY SHOW BOARD CHEER FEAST GAUDY OPERA REVUE SPORT CIRCUS DIVERT DOMENT GAIETY GAYETY HOSTEL INFARE KERMIS NAUTCH SETOUT SHIVOO WATTLE BANQUET BENEFIT BUMMACK BUMMOCK BURLESK CEILIDH CONCERT COSHERY FESTINE FESTINO JOLLITY KERMESS PASTIME RIDOTTO TAMASHA CAKEWALK CARNIVAL COMMORTH DROLLERY EASEMENT ENTREATY ENTREMES FUNCTION GESTNING GESTONIE GUESTING HOGMANAY JONGLERY MUSICALE WAYZGOOSE
(BLUE —) NUDIE
(FAREWELL —) FOY
(OF INDIA —) TAMASHA
(TRIVIAL —) PAP
(VARIETY —) VODVIL VAUDEVILLE

ENTERTAINMNET (CHEAP —) HONKYTONK

ENTHALPY H

ENTHRALL SEND CHARM THIRL THRALL ENSLAVE ENTHRAL CAPTIVATE

ENTHRALLED AGOG RAPT HOOKED

ENTHRONE CROWN EXALT STALL ENSEAT THRONE THRONIZE

ENTHUSIASM BUG ELAN FIRE FURY ZEAL ZEST ZING ARDOR ESTRO FEVER FLAME FUROR HEART MANIA OOMPH VERVE FERVOR HURRAH SPIRIT WARMTH ABANDON ARDENCY AVIDITY MADNESS MUSTARD DEVOTION LYRICISM
(— IN BATTLE) EARNEST
(CONTAGIOUS —) FUROR FURORE
(EXCESSIVE —) MANIA
(LOSE —) COOL SOUR
(WILD —) DELIRIUM

ENTHUSIAST BUG FAN NUT BUFF BIGOT DEMON FREAK ROOTER VOTARY ZEALOT BOOSTER DEVOTEE EUCHITE FANATIC FANCIER GROUPIE FOLLOWER VOTARESS VOTARIST
(PHOTOGRAPHY —) SHUTTERBUG
(PL.) ARDITI

ENTHUSIASTIC GAGA KEEN NUTS WARM HAPPY NUTTY RABID ARDENT GUNGHO HEARTY STOKED CRACKED FERVENT GLOWING CRACKERS PASSIONATE
(BECOME —) FLIP
(EXCESSIVELY —) FANATIC
(VAINLY —) FOOLISH

ENTICE COG COY PUT WIN BAIT COAX DRAW DRIB LEAD LOCK LURE TICE TOLE TOLL WILE CHARM DECOY DRILL LATHE SIREN SLOCK STEAL TEMPT TRAIN TROLL TULLE ALLECT ALLURE ATTICE CAJOLE ENLURE INCITE INDUCE INVITE SEDUCE ATTRACT BEWITCH SOLICIT SUGGEST INVEIGLE PERSUADE

ENTICEMENT BAIT CORD LURE TICE

ENTICING SIREN ALLURING

ENTIRE ALL DEAD EVEN FULL HALE MEAR MERE SOLE CLEAN EVERY GROSS PLAIN QUITE ROUND SOUND STARK TOTAL TUTTO UTTER WHOLE VERSAL PERFECT PLENARY ABSOLUTE COMPLETE ENDURING GLOBULAR INTEGRAL LIVELONG OUTRIGHT TEETOTAL UNBROKEN
(NOT —) PARTIAL
(PREF.) HOL(O) INTEGRI

ENTIRELY DEAD DEIN FAIR FULL PURE CLEAN CLEAR FULLY PLAIN QUITE STARK WHOLE BODILY WHOLLY EXACTLY QUITELY THROUGH CLEVERLY ABSOLUTELY

ENTIRETY WHOLE ENTIRE TOTALITY
(PREF.) PAM PAN

ENTITLE DUB CALL NAME TERM AFFIX STYLE ENABLE CAPTION EMPOWER QUALIFY INTITULE NOMINATE

ENTITLED APPARENT ELIGIBLE

ENTITY ENS BODY FORM UNIT BEING HABIT OUSIA SPACE THING ENERGY ESSENCE INTEGER TOTALITY

ENTOMB BURY TOMB INTER INURN ENCAVE HEARSE IMMURE INHUME SHRINE

ENTOMBMENT BURIAL

ENTOMOLOGIST BUGHUNTER
AMERICAN SAY DYAR HORN BANKS BRUES RILEY FORBES HARRIS HOWARD MORGAN BURGESS PACKARD POLLARD SCHWARZ COMSTOCK COQUILLETT
DANISH FABRICIUS
DUTCH LYONNET
ENGLISH SCOTT LEFROY HAWORTH ORMEROD WESTWOOD
FRENCH FABRE AUDOUIN LATREILLE LACORDAIRE
GERMAN BRAUER
SWISS FOREL SAUSSURE

ENTOMOLOGY BUGOLOGY

ENTOMOPHTHORA EMPUSA

ENTOTROPHI DIPLURA

ENTOURAGE TRAIN COMITES RETINUE

ENTRACTE INTERACT INTERVAL INTERMEZZO

ENTRAIL BOWEL TRAIL INTRAIL
(PREF.) SPLANCHN(O)

ENTRAILS GUT GUTS DRAFT TRIPE FIBERS GIBLET HALLOW HASLET INWARD JAUDIE MUGGET PAUNCH QUARRY QUERRE UMBLES INSIDES NUMBLES CHAWDRON GRALLOCH PUDDINGS PURTENANCE
(DEER'S —) QUARRY

ENTRANCE ADIT BOCA CUSP DOOR GATE HALL PEND BOCCA CHARM DEBUT ENTER ENTRY FOYER GORGE INLET MOUTH PORCH STULM THIRL TORAN ACCESS ATRIUM ENTREE INFAIR INGANG INGATE INROAD PORTAL RAVISH TORANA TRANCE ZAGUAN DELIGHT GATEWAY HALLWAY INGOING INGRESS INITIAL INTRADO INTROIT PASSAGE POSTERN ENTRESSE FOREGATE VOMITORY PROPYLAEUM
(— TO SEWER) JAWHOLE
(— TO VALLEY) CHOPS
(ASTROLOGICAL —) CUSP
(CELLAR —) ROLLWAY
(FORCIBLE —) INROAD
(FORMAL —) DEBUT
(HARBOR —) BOCA
(HOSTILE —) INVASION
(HURRIED —) BOUT
(MINE —) EYE ADIT
(PRIVATE —) POSTERN

ENTRANCED RAPT CHARMED TRANCED ECSTATIC

ENTRANCEMENT SPELL

ENTRANCING ORPHIC

ENTRANT INTRANT STARTER BEGINNER

ENTRAP BAG EBB NET HOOK SNIB TOIL TRAP CATCH CRIMP DECOY NOOSE SNARE ALLURE AMBUSH ATTRAP CAJOLE ENGAGE ENTOIL TAIGLE TANGLE TREPAN BEGUILE ENSNARE PITFALL ENTANGLE INVEIGLE

ENTRAPMENT SETUP

ENTRAPPED (— IN SEDIMENT) CONNATE

ENTREAT ASK BEG BID SUE WOO PRAY PRIG SEEK URGE CRAVE HALSE PLEAD PRESS TREAT ADJURE APPEAL DESIRE INVOKE BESEECH CONJURE EXORATE IMPLORE PREVAIL PROCURE REQUEST SOLICIT PERSUADE PETITION

ENTREATING TREAT CRAVING

ENTREATY DO CRY PLEA SUIT APPEAL DEESIS PRAYER TREATY BESEECH BIDDING ENTREAT PURSUIT REQUEST URGENCY PETITION PLEADING

ENTRECHAT (PERFORM —S) LEAP

ENTREE ENTRY ACCESS BOUDIN OSTIUM ENTRADA INTRADA SOUFFLE ENTRANCE FRICANDO MAZARINE

ENTREMES SAINETE SAYNETE

ENTRENCH DIGIN INVADE SCONCE TRENCH ENCROACH TRESPASS

ENTRENCHED (BECOME —) DIGIN

ENTRENCHMENT CLOSURE COUPURE LODGMENT

ENTROPY S

ENTRUST ARET FIDE GIVE STOW BEKEN TRUST CHARGE COMMIT CREDIT LIPPEN ADDRESS BEHIGHT COMMEND CONFIDE CONSIGN DEPOSIT INTRUST BEQUEATH DELEGATE ENCHARGE RECOMMEND
(— TO DEPUTY) DEVIL

ENTRY ADIT HALL ITEM STET BREAK CLOSE DEBIT AUTHOR CREDIT DOCKET ENTREE PORTAL POSTEA RECORD RINGER TRANCE ENTRADA INGRESS INTRADO PASSAGE ENTRANCE ENTRESSE ENTRYWAY NOTANDUM REGISTER VOCATION
(— IN CHRONICLE) ANNAL
(— WORD) HEADWORD
(LEDGER —) POSTING

ENTWINE FOLD LACE WIND BRAID CLASP IMPLY PLASH TWINE TWIST WEAVE ENLACE INWIND ENTWIST INVOLVE SERPENT WREATHE

ENTWINED ACCOLLE BRAIDED INWOVEN ACCOLLEE

ENUMERATE POLL TELL COUNT SCORE DETAIL NUMBER RECITE RECKON RELATE COMPILE COMPUTE ITEMIZE RECOUNT ESTIMATE REHEARSE

ENUMERATION LIST TALE COUNT SCORE CENSUS ACCOUNT CATALOG RECITAL CITATION

ENUNCIATE SAY UTTER DECLARE DELIVER ENOUNCE ANNOUNCE PROCLAIM

ENUNCIATION DICTION DELIVERY
(IMPERFECT —) LALLATION

ENVELOP BUR FOG LAP LOT POD WEB BURR CASE COMA FOLD HUSK MAIL ROLL BRACE CLOUD COVER KNIFE ROUND BEGIRD BEGIRT BEMIST BINDLE CLOTHE COCOON CORONA CUPULE ENFOLD ENGIRT ENTIRE ENWRAP FARDEL FOLDER INFOLD INVEST JACKET MANTLE MUFFLE POCKET SHEATH SHROUD STIFLE SWATHE WRIXLE CALYMMA CAPSULE CHORION ENCLOSE ENVIRON INVOLVE SWADDLE SWALLOW VESTURE WRAPPER ENSPHERE ENVELOPE MANTLING PERIANTH PERIDIUM POCHETTE SURROUND WRAPPAGE
(— CLOSELY) SMOTHER
(— IN SMOKE) ENFUME
(GLASS —) BULB
(LUMINOUS —) CORONA
(NEBULOUS —) CHEVELURE
(OPEN —) JACKET
(PAY —) PACKET
(STAMPED —) ENTIRE
(VEGETABLE —) COD

ENVELOPE (— ENCLOSURE) SASE
(FRUIT —) CUPULE
(SUN'S —) CORONA
(PREF.) **(OUTER —)** PERIDI
(SUFF.) LEMMA

ENVELOPED WOMPLIT

ENVELOPING AMBIENT

ENVENOM VENOM CORRUPT VITIATE EMBITTER EMPOISON

ENVIOUS YELLOW EMULOUS JEALOUS ENVIABLE

ENVIRON HEM BEGO GIRD BIGAN LIMIT VIRON ENVIRE GIRDLE SUBURB COMPASS ENVELOP INCLOSE INVOLVE PURLIEU DISTRICT ENCIRCLE SURROUND (PL.) SKIRT UMLAND BANLIEU SUBURBS PRECINCT

ENVIRONMENT HOTBED MEDIUM MILIEU AMBIENT CONTEXT ELEMENT HABITAT SETTING TERRAIN AMBIANCE CINCTURE PRECINCT
(— OF NURTURE) LAP
(ACADEMIC —) ACADEME
(DOMESTIC —) INTERIEUR
(NORMAL —) HOME
(PREF.) EC(O) OEC(O) OIK(O)

ENVISAGE FACE CONFRONT ENVISION

ENVISION PICTURE

ENVOY AGENT ELCHI ENVOI DEPUTY ELCHEE LEGATE LENVOY NUNCIO EMBASSY TORNADA ABLEGATE LEGATION METATRON

ENVY CHAW ONDE COVET GRUDGE EMULATE BEGRUDGE GRUDGERY JEALOUSY

ENWRAP FOLD ROLL CLASP IMPLY ENFOLD INFOLD KIRTLE ENGROSS ENVELOP OBVOLVE CONVOLVE ENVELOPE INSWATHE

ENZOOTIC RABIES

ENZU SIN

ENZYME ASE ZYM ZYMO LYASE RENIN CYTASE KINASE LIGASE LIPASE LOTASE MUTASE OLEASE PAPAIN PEPSIN RENNIN UREASE ZYMASE ACYLASE ADENASE AMIDASE AMINASE AMYLASE APYRASE CASEASE CYCLASE EMULSIN ENOLASE EREPSIN FERMENT GUANASE HYDRASE INULASE LACCASE LACTASE MALTASE MYROSIN OXIDASE PECTASE PEPSINE PHYTASE PLASMIN PRUNASE TANNASE TRYPSIN ALDOLASE ARGINASE BROMELIN CATALASE CATALYST CYTOLIST DIASTASE ELASTASE EREPTASE ESTERASE FUMARASE INVERTIN LYSOZYME NUCLEASE PERMEASE PROTEASE RACEMASE SEMINASE SYNTHASE THROMBIN TRYPTASE UROKINASE
(PREF.) ZYM(O)
(SUFF.) ASE EIN EINE IN INE

EOANTHROPUS DAWNMAN

EOS MORNING
(SISTER OF —) SELENE

EPAPHUS (DAUGHTER OF —) LIBYA
(FATHER OF —) ZEUS JUPITER
(MOTHER OF —) IO
(WIFE OF —) MEMPHIS

EPAULET KNOT SWAB SWOB WING SCALE SHELL

EPENDYTES HAPLOMA

EPENTHESIS ANAPTYXIS

EPEUS (BROTHER OF —) AETOLUS
(DAUGHTER OF —) HYRMINA
(FATHER OF —) ENDYMION PANOPEUS
(WIFE OF —) ANAXIROE

EPHAH BATH
(FATHER OF —) JAHDAI MIDIAN

EPHELIS FRECKLE

EPHEMERAL BRIEF VAGUE HORARY DIURNAL FUNGOUS PASSANT PASSING EPISODAL EPISODIC FUGITIVE MUSHROOM STAYLESS MOMENTARY

EPHEMERIS DIARY TABLE RECORD ALMANAC JOURNAL CALENDAR

EPHER (FATHER OF —) EZRA MIDIAN

EPHIPPIUM SADDLE

EPHOD VAKASS
(SON OF —) HANNIEL

EPHRAIM (FATHER OF —) JOSEPH
(MOTHER OF —) ASENATH

EPHRATAH (HUSBAND OF —) CALEB
(SON OF —) HUR

EPHRON (FATHER OF —) ZOAR

EPHTHALITE HAITHAL

EPI PEAK SPIRE FINIAL PINNACLE

EPIBLAST ECTODERM

EPIC EDDA EPOS SAGA GRAND ILIAD NOBLE BYLINA EPOPEE HEROIC LUSIAD BEOWULF EPYLLION KALEVALA RAMAYANA MAHABHARATA
(SUFF.) AD

EPICALYX CALYCLE

EPICARP HUSK RIND EXOCARP

EPICENE SEXLESS

EPICURE FRIAND FEASTER GLUTTON GOURMET GOURMAND PALATIST GASTRONOME GASTRONOMER

EPICUREAN APICIAN SENSUOUS

EPIDEMIC FLU PLAGUE POPULAR PANDEMIA PANDEMIC

EPIDERMIS SKIN CUTICLE ECDERON VELAMEN

EPIDOTE SCORZA

EPIGLOTTIS FLAP WEEZLE

EPIGRAM POEM ENGLYN EPITAPH

EPIGRAMMATIC LACONIC POINTED

EPIGRAPH EPIGRAM IMPRINT

EPILEPTIC FITIFIED

EPILOGUE CLOSE FINALE APPENDIX

EPIMANIKION CUFF

EPIMETHEUS (WIFE OF —) PANDORA

EPINAOS POSTICUM

EPINEPHRINE ADRENINE

EPINICION ODE

EPIPACTIS SERAPIAS

EPIPHANY TWELFTH

EPIPHARYNX PALATE EPIGLOTTIS

EPIPHRAGM TYMPANUM

EPIPHYTE KARO EPIPHYLL

EPIPHYTOTIC EPIDEMIC

EPIRUS (KING OF —) PYRRHUS

EPISCOPACY BISHOPRIC PRELATISM

EPISCOPAL PRELATIC

EPISODE GAG EPOCH EVENT SCENE STORY AFFAIR INCIDENT SEQUENCE OCCURRENCE
(COMIC —) BURLA SIGHTGAG
(MUSICAL —) COUPLET

EPISPASTIC VESICANT

EPISPERM TESTA

EPISTAXIS NOSEBLEED

EPISTERNUM MANUBRIUM

EPISTLE CANON JAMES LETTER PISTLE MISSIVE WRITING DECRETAL

EPISTLER SUBDEACON

EPISTOLOGRAPHIC DEMOTIC

EPISTROPHE EPODE ABGESANG

EPISTYLE PLATBAND

EPITHELIUM ENDODERM

EPITHET AKAL GOOD NAME TERM LABEL SMEAR TITLE BYWORD MONETA PHRASE AGNOMEN JAPHETIC MULCIBER
(PL.) LANGUAGE

EPITOME MAP SUM FLETA DIGEST PRECIS SCHEME COMPEND PITOMIE SUMMARY SUMMULA ABSTRACT BREVIARY LANDSKIP SYLLABUS SYNOPSIS ABRIDGMENT CONSPECTUS

EPITOMIZE RESUME ABRIDGE CURTAIL ABSTRACT COMPRESS CONDENSE CONTRACT DIMINISH

EPITONIUM SCALA

EPIZOA PARASITA

EPOCH AGE ERA DATE ECCA TIME DWYKA EVENT EOCENE PERIOD CLINTON OLIGOCENE

EPONYM LIMMU ANCIENT

EPOPEUS (BROTHERS OF —) ALOIDAE
(FATHER OF —) ALOEUS POSEIDON
(MOTHER OF —) CANACE IPHIMEDIA
(WIFE OF —) ANTIOPE

EQUABLE EVEN JUST EQUAL SUANT SMOOTH STEADY UNIFORM TRANQUIL

EQUAL AEQ PAR TIE COPE EGAL EVEN FERE JUST LIKE MAKE MATE MEET PEEL PEER SAME ALIKE LEVEL MATCH PARTY RIVAL TOUCH DOUBLE EQUATE EVENLY FELLOW MARROW PARFIL ABREAST BALANCE COMPEER EMULATE EQUABLE IDENTIC PARAGON PAREGAL UNIFORM ADEQUATE EQUALIZE EVENHAND PATCHING TRANQUIL
(— A BET) SEE
(— IN MEANING) BE
(— QUANTITY) ANA
(— TO) ANOTHER
(NOT —) UNMEET UNMETE
(PREF.) AEQUI EQUI IS(O) PARI

EQUALING TO

EQUALITY PAR TIE EQUITY OWELTY PARAGE PAREIL PARITY BALANCE EGALITE EGALITY ISOTELY EQUATION EVENHAND EVENNESS FAIRNESS
(— BEFORE THE LAW) ISONOMY
(— OF ELEVATION) ISOMETRY
(—OF MEASURE) ISOMETRY
(— OF POWER) ISOCRACY
(— OF RATIOS) ANALOGY
(— STATE) WYOMING

EQUALIZATION EQUATION DISCHARGE

EQUALIZE EVEN KNOT EQUAL LEVEL EQUATE SQUARE BALANCE ADEQUATE

EQUALIZER EVENER

EQUALLY AS BOTH LIKE ONCE SAME ALIKE EGALLY EVENLY JUSTLY EMFORTH

EQUANIMITY POISE PHLEGM TEMPER BALANCE EGALITY CALMNESS EVENNESS SERENITY SANGFROID

EQUATE EQUAL BALANCE EQUALIZE

EQUATING COMPARISON

EQUATION CUBIC IDENTITY

EQUATOR LINE GIRDLE EQUINOX
(— CROSSER) POLLIWOG

EQUATORIAL GUINEA (CAPITAL OF —) MALABO
(COIN OF —) EKUELE EKPWELE
(MONEY OF —) EKUELE EKPWELE
(MONEY OF —) CENTIME
(RIVER OF —) MUNI CAMPO BENITO
(TOWN OF —) BATA NSOK SANTAISABEL

EQUES KNIGHT

EQUIDISTANT CENTRAL HALFWAY

EQUILIBRIUM POISE APLOMB BALANCE STATION EQUATION EVENHAND ISOSTASY
(— OF FLUID) LEVEL
(PREF.) STATO

EQUINE COLT FOAL MARE FILLY HORSE ZEBRA EQUOID EQUINAL HORSELY

EQUINIA MALLEUS

EQUIP ARM FIT IMP KIT RAY RIG ABLE BEAM DECK FEAT FIND GEAR GIRD GIRT HEEL REEK TRIM ARRAY DIGHT DRESS ENARM ENDOW POINT SPEED STUFF AGUISE ATTIRE BUCKLE ORDAIN OUTFIT SUBORN APPAREL APPOINT BEDIGHT FORTIFY FRAUGHT FURNISH GARNISH HARNESS PLENISH PREPARE QUALIFY ACCOUTER ACCOUTRE ACCOMPLISH
(— FOR ACTION) ARM

EQUIPAGE RIG CREW SAMAN SUITE TRAIN SUPPLY RETINUE TURNOUT UNICORN CARRIAGE

EQUIPMENT KIT FARE GEAR TIRE STOCK STUFF ATTIRE CONREY DUFFEL DUFFLE FITOUT GRAITH OUTFIT SETOUT TACKLE APPAREL BAGGAGE FITMENT HARNESS PANOPLY ARMAMENT EQUIPAGE MATERIAL MATERIEL MOUNTING SUPELLEX
(— FOR CATCHING FISH) CRAFT
(— FOR JOURNEY) FARE
(CLASSROOM —) REGALIA

EQUIPOISE POISE BALANCE

EQUIPOTENTIAL LEVEL

EQUIPPED SEEN ARMED BODEN THERE EQUIPT ARMORED INSTRUCT WEAPONED
(FULLY —) SUMMED
(INADEQUATELY —) HAYWIRE
(LIGHTLY —) EXPEDITE

EQUISETUM CANDOCK

EQUITABLE EVEN FAIR JUST EQUAL RIGHT EVENLY HONEST EQUABLE UPRIGHT BONITARY RATIONAL RIGHTFUL

EQUITY LAW EPIKY MARGIN EPIKEIA HONESTY JUSTICE EQUALITY EVENHAND FAIRNESS

EQUIVALENCE AMOUNT PARITY

EQUIVALENT KIND SAME EQUAL NODEL COUSIN UNISON ANALOGUE EVENHAND
(— IN MONEY) CHANGE
(— OF TWO BUSHELS) HUTCH
(FAIR —) VALUE
EQUIVOCAL FISHY SHADY DOUBLE FORKED DUBIOUS EVASIVE HALFWAY OBSCURE DOUBTFUL HAVERING PUZZLING SIBYLLIC
EQUIVOCATE HAW HEM LIE DODGE EVADE SHIFT BOGGLE ESCAPE PALTER TRIFLE WAFFLE WEASEL QUIBBLE SHUFFLE SCRAFFLE PUSSYFOOT PREVARICATE
EQUIVOCATION QUIP QUIRK EVASION QUIBBLE SHUFFLE EQUIVOKE
EQUIVOQUE PUN
EQUULEUS FOAL
ER (FATHER OF —) JOSE
(SON OF —) ELMODAM
ERA AGE AEON ERA TIME EPOCH STAGE PERIOD CENOZOIC PALEOZOIC PROTEROZOIC
(EMPEROR'S —) KIMIGAYO
(GEOLOGICAL —) QUATENARY
(HINDU —) SAMVAT
(MUSLIM —) HEGIRA HEJIRA
ERADICATE DELE ROOT SLAY WEED CROSS ERASE STAMP DELETE EFFACE REMOVE UNROOT UPROOT ABOLISH DESTROY EXPUNGE OUTROOT SUPPLANT
(— HAIR) EPILATE
ERADICATOR ERASER
ERAL MOINE
ERAN (GRANDFATHER OF —) EPHRAIM
ERASE BLOT DASH DELE RACE RASE RASH RAZE ANNUL PLANE CANCEL DEFACE DELETE EFFACE EXCISE REMOVE SCRAPE SPONGE DESTROY EXPUNGE OUTRAZE SCRATCH UNWRITE WEAROUT OBLITERATE
ERASER RASER RUBBER
ERASTE (LOVER OF —) JULIE LUCILLE ORPHISE
ERASURE RASURE ERASION DELETION EXCISION
ERD SHREW RANNY
ERE OR AIR SOON EARLY PRIOR BEFORE EREWHILE FORMERLY
EREBUS (FATHER OF —) CHAOS
(SISTER OF —) NOX
(SON OF —) CHARON
ERECHTHEUS (DAUGHTER OF —) CREUSA PROCRIS CHTHONIA ORITHYIA
(FATHER OF —) PANDION
(SLAYER OF —) JUPITER
(SON OF —) MERION CECROPS PANDORUS
(WIFE OF —) PRAXITHEA
ERECT BIG SET BIGG LEVY REAR RECT STEP STEY SWAY TELD AREAR BRANT BUILD DRESS EXALT FRAME MOUNT ONEND PUTUP RAISE SETUP STAND ARRECT UPLIFT UPREAR ADDRESS ATROPAL BRISTLE ELEVATE STATELY UPRAISE UPRIGHT

UPSTART STANDING STRAIGHT VERTICAL
(— HASTILY) RUNUP
(— TENT) PITCH
(NOT —) LAZY COUCHED
ERECTED UPSET
ERECTION DOME HARD FABRIC CHORDEE MACHINE
(— FOR SPECTATORS) STAND
(TEMPORARY —) SCAFFOLD
ERELONG ANON SOON
EREMITE LONER HERMIT ASCETIC RECLUSE ANCHORET
EREWHILE ERE WHILOM
EREWHON (AUTHOR OF —) BUTLER
(CHARACTER IN —) HIGGS GEORGE STRONG ZULORA CHOWBOK AROWHENA NOSNIBOR
ERG REG EROGON
(PL.) AREG
ERGINUS (FATHER OF —) CLYMENUS POSEIDON
(SON OF —) AGAMEDES TROPHONIUS
ERGO SO ARGO ARGAL HENCE
ERGOT SPUR CLAVUS ECBOLIC
(STAGE OF —) SPHACELIA
ERI (FATHER OF —) GAD
ERICHTHONIUS (FATHER OF —) VULCAN DARDANUS
(MOTHER OF —) ATTHIS
(SON OF —) PANDION
ERIDANUS (FATHER OF —) OCEANUS
(MOTHER OF —) TETHYS
ERIE WENRO
ERIGONE (FATHER OF —) ICARIUS AEGISTHUS
(MOTHER OF —) CLYTEMNESTRA
ERINYS FURY ALECTO MEGAERA
(PL.) DIRAE FURIAE SEMNAE EUMENIDES
ERIOPHORUM DRAWLING
ERIPHYLE (FATHER OF —) TALAUS
(HUSBAND OF —) AMPHIARAUS
(SON & SLAYER OF —) ALCMAEON
ERISTIC DIALECTIC
ERITREA (CAPITAL OF —) ASMARA
ERMINE VAIR VARE STOAT WEASEL ERMELIN FUTERET FUTTRAT MINIVER CLUBSTER WHITRACK WHITTRET
ERNANI (CHARACTER IN —) CARLO GOMEZ SILVA ELVIRA ERNANI
(COMPOSER OF —) VERDI
ERODE EAT ROT COMB ETCH GNAW GULL WEAR CLIFF GULLY SCOUR ABRADE DENUDE CORRODE DESTROY
ERODIUM HERONBILL
EROS AMOR KAMA CUPID AENGUS POTHOS
EROSE ERODED UNEVEN
EROSION PIPING CHIMNEY NIVATION SCOURING
(MECHANICAL —) PLANATION
ERO THE JOKER (COMPOSER OF —) GOTOVAC
EROTIC SEXY LOVING STEAMY AMATORY AMOROUS CURIOUS LESBIAN THERMAL
EROTICA CURIOSA FACETIAE

ERR MAR SIN BOOT FAIL MISS SLIP ABERR LAPSE MISGO STRAY BUNGLE FORVAY SLIPUP WANDER BLUNDER DEVIATE MISPLAY MISTAKE SCRITHE STUMBLE MISCARRY MISJUDGE
(— AT BRIDGE) RENEGE
ERRAND CHORE ENVOY JOURNEY MISSION LEGATION
(— BOY) LOBBYGOW
(RUNNER OF —S) GOFER GOPHER
ERRANT STRAY ASTRAY ERRING DEVIOUS PRICKANT
ERRATIC WILD CRAZY HUMAN LOONY QUEER WACKY CRANKY WHACKY STRANGE TANGENT VAGRANT ACROSTIC ERRABUND FITIFIED PLANETAL PLANETIC TRAVELED VAGABOND PLANETARY
ERRATUM ERROR
ERRING ASTRAY ERRANT DEVIOUS
ERRINGLY FALSE
ERRONEOUS AMISS FALSE WRONG UNTRUE ERRATIC MISTAKEN STRAYING WRONGFUL
(PREF.) PSEUD(O)
ERRONEOUSLY AWRY
ERRONEOUSNESS FALLACY
ERROR X HOB SIN BALK BUBU BULL FLUB HELL MUFF SLIP TRIP TYPO BEARD BEVUE BONER DEVIL FAULT FLUFF LAPSE SCAPE BOBBLE BOOBOO FUMBLE GARBLE HOWLER LAPSUS MISCUE NAUGHT SPHALM BLOOMER BLUNDER DEFAULT ERRATUM FALLACY FALSITY LITERAL MISPLAY MISSTEP MISTAKE OFFENSE RHUBARB SNAPPER STUMBLE DELUSION HAMARTIA MISPRINT MISSMENT SOLECISM OVERSIGHT MISPRISION
(— IN PLEADINGS) JEOFAIL
ERS VETCH KERSANNE
ERSATZ FAUX
ERSE ERSCH IRISH CELTIC GAELIC SCOTTISH
ERST ONCE FORMERLY RECENTLY
ERSTWHILE ONCE FORMER FORMERLY
ERUCT RASP BELCH
ERUCTATION BRASH
ERUDITE LEARNED CLERGIAL DIDACTIC
ERUDITION WIT LORE WISDOM LETTERS LEARNING
ERUPT BOIL SPEW BELCH BURST EJECT IRRUPT
ERUPTING ACTIVE
ERUPTION ITCH RASH REEF RUSH AGRIA BLAIN BRASH BURST RUPIA SALLY SALVO STORM BLOTCH HYDROA NIRLES ACTERID BLOWOUT ECTHYMA MORPHEA MORPHEW PUSTULE SAWFLOM SUDAMEN SYCOSIS EMPYESIS ENANTHEM EXANTHEM MALANDER OUTBREAK OUTBURST
(— ON CHIN) MENTAGRA
(CUTANEOUS —) HUMOR
(SKIN —) SPOT REDGUM TETTER
(SUFF.) ANTHEMA PHLYSIS
ERVUM LENS LENTILLA

ERYSICHTHON (FATHER OF —) CECROPS TRIOPAS
(MOTHER OF —) AGRAULOS
(SISTER OF —) IPHIMEDIA
ERYSIPELAS POX ROSE BLAST WILDFIRE
ERYTHROBLASTOSIS HYDROPSY
ERYX (FATHER OF —) BUTES
(MOTHER OF —) VENUS
(SLAYER OF —) HERCULES
ESAU EDOM
(BROTHER OF —) JACOB
(FATHER OF —) ISAAC
(LIKE —) HAIRY
(MOTHER OF —) REBEKAH
(SON OF —) JEUSH KORAH REUEL JAALAM ELIPHAZ
(WIFE OF —) ADAH BASHEMATH
ESCALADE SCALE SCALADE SCALADO ESCALADO
ESCAPADE LARK CAPER FLING PRANK SALLY SCHEME SCRAPE SPLORE RUNAWAY FREDAINE
ESCAPE FLY GUY LAM RUN BAIL BALE BEAT BLOW BOLT FLEE GATE HISS JINK JUMP LEAK MISS SHUN SKEW SLIP VENT AVOID BREAK CHAPE DODGE ELOPE ELUDE EVADE FLANK ISSUE SCAPE SHIFT SKIRT SMOKE SPILL ASTERT DECAMP ESCHEW OUTLET POWDER SQUEAK ABSCOND AVOLATE BLOWOUT ELUSION EXHAUST GETAWAY LEAKAGE MISTAKE OUTFLOW SCRITHE SQUEEZE WILDING BLOWBACK BREAKOUT ESCAPADE ESCAPAGE EXSHEATH OUTSCAPE OVERSLIP RIDDANCE WITHSLIP
(— FROM) FLY SHUN ILLUDE
(— FROM WORK) SNIB
(— LEGAL PROCESS) ABSCOND
(— NOTICE) ELUDE
(— OF FLUID) EFFUSION
(CUT OFF FROM —) HEMIN
(NARROW —) SHAVE
ESCAPEMENT SCAPE CRUTCH ESCAPE FOLIOT VIRGULE KARRUSEL
ESCARGOT SNAIL
ESCAROLE ENDIVE SCAROLA
ESCARPMENT EDGE
ESCHAR SCAB CRUST ASCHER
ESCHAROTIC CAUSTIC
ESCHEAT FALL LAPSE REVERT EXCHEAT FORFEIT
ESCHEW SHUN ABHOR AVOID FORGO ESCAPE FOREGO ABSTAIN
ESCOLAR PALU ROVET OILFISH ROVETTO MACKEREL
ESCORT MAN SEE SET TRY BEAR BEAU COND LEAD SHOW TEND WAIT BRING CARRY GUARD USHER ATTEND CONVEY CONVOY FOLLOW SQUIRE COLLECT CONDUCT CONSORT ESQUIRE GALLANT CAVALIER CHAPERON SHEPHERD SAFEGUARD
(PAID —) GIGOLO
ESCRITOIRE DESK BUREAU LECTERN
ESCULENT EDIBLE EATABLE

ESCUTCHEON CREST SHIELD
(CENTER OF —) NOMBRIL
ESHBAN (FATHER OF —) DISHON
ESHCOL (BROTHER OF —) ANER
MAMRE
(COMPANION OF —) ABRAHAM
ESKER AS OS OSE KAME ESKAR
HOGBACK
ESKIMO ITA HUSKY INUIT INNUIT
AGOMIUT AMERIND ANGAKOK
KUNMIUT OKOMIUT ORARIAN
AGLEMIUT ESQUIMAU IKOGMIUT
KIDNELIK KINIPETU MAGEMIUT
MALEMIUT NUGUMIUT SINIMIUT
(— ASSEMBLY HOUSE) KASHIM
(— CULTURE) PUNUK
(— ISLAND) ALEUT
(— TENT) TUPEK TUPIK
ESLI (FATHER OF —) NAGGE
ESOPHAGUS GULLET SWALLOW
WEASAND
(PREF.) LAEMO LEMO
ESOTERIC DEEP INNER ARCANE
MYSTIC ORPHIC SECRET PRIVATE
ABSTRUSE RAREFIED RARIFIED
ESPADON ESPADA SPADON
SPADROON
ESPALIER CORDON LATTICE
RAILING TRELLIS PALISADE
ESPARTO ALFA HALFA SPART STIPA
ATOCHA
ESPAVE CARACOLI
ESPECIAL VERY CHIEF SPECIAL
PECULIAR UNCOMMON
ESPECIALLY SUCH EXTRA RATHER
CHIEFLY OVERALL SPECIAL
ESPIAL SPY ESPY EYING SCOUT
NOTICE
ESPINAL MONTE
ESPIONAGE SPYING
ESPLANADE BUND WALK DRIVE
MAIDAN MARINA
ESPOUSAL CEREMONY SPOUSAGE
BETROTHAL
ESPOUSE WED AFFY MATE ADOPT
MARRY DEFEND ENSURE SPOUSE
BETROTH EMBRACE HUSBAND
SUPPORT ADVOCATE MAINTAIN
ESPOUSED HANDFAST
ESPRESSO COFFEE
ESPUNDIA UTA
ESPY SEE ASPY SPOT ASCRY SIGHT
WATCH BEHOLD DESCRY DETECT
LOCATE NOTICE DISCERN
OBSERVE DESCRIBE DISCOVER
ESQUIRE RADMAN ARMIGER
ESCUDERO SERGEANT
ESSAY TRY SEEK ASSAY CHRIA
OFFER PAPER PROVE TASTE
THEME TRACT TRAIL CASUAL
EFFORT MEMOIR SAILYE SATIRE
SCREED THESIS ARTICLE ATTEMPT
PROFFER VENTURE WRITING
CAUSERIE ENDEAVOR EXERCISE
EXERTION TRACTATE TREATISE
TURNOVER
(PRELIMINARY —) STUDY
ESSAYIST AMERICAN DAY MORE
VERY ADAMS GRANT WHITE YOUNG
BROOKS COFFIN FISHER GUINEY
HOLMES HUTTON KILMER KRUTCH
LOWELL EMERSON LAZARUS
SISSMAN WHIPPLE WHITMAN

WHITTER KOSINSKI REPPLIER
STRUNSKY TUCKERMAN
SCHAUFFLER
AUSTRIAN BLEI
BELGIAN MAETERLINCK
CANADIAN MACMECHAN
CZECH CAPEK
ENGLISH HUNT LAMB BACON
DRAKE MUNRO MYERS PAGET
PATER POWYS SMITH GARROD
MACHEN MARTIN SEELEY STEELE
TEMPLE ADDISON BUDGELL
CHAPONE HAYWARD HAZLITT
HEWLETT MEYNELL RALEIGH
SYMONDS CHAMBERS CONGREVE
DISRAELI NEVINSON STERLING
THOMPSON DICKINSON STEVENSON
CHESTERTON
DOBSONLEGALLIENNE
FRENCH ALAIN CAMUS ARAGON
MOUREY CHAMSON STAPFER
CHARTIER SCHOPFER MONTAIGNE
GERMAN ZWEIG FONTANF
GREEK XENOPHON
IRISH BOYD LECKY MAGEE
ITALIAN BRACCO CECCHI
MEXICAN REYES
POLISH BELCIKOWSKI
MAKUSZYNSKI
SCOTTISH SMITH WILSON CARLYLE
THOMSON STEVENSON
SWEDISH EKELUND
ESSE BEING
ESSENCE ENS NET ALMA ATAR
BASE BONE CORE CRUX DRAW
ESSE GIST GUTS KIND ODOR OTTO
PITH QUID RASA SOUL YOLK
ATTAR BASIC BASIS BEING EIDOS
FIBER FIBRE FUMET HEART JUICE
OTTAR OUSIA STUFF BOTTOM
EFFECT ENTITY FLOWER INWARD
MARROW NATURE SPRITE
ALCOHOL ELEMENT EXTRACT
FUMETTE GODHEAD INBEING
MEDULLA PERFUME RATAFIA
BERGAMOT CONCRETE ESSENTIA
(— OF BEING) SAT
(— OF FLOWERS) CONCRETE
(— OF GOD) SPIRIT DIVINITY
(— OF MEAT) BLOND
(— OF TEA) DRAW
(— OF VITAL MATTER) GLAME
(INNERMOST —) ATMAN
(UNIVERSAL —) FORM
(VITAL —) STAMINA
ESSENE ESSEE ASCETIC
ESSENTIAL KEY MUST REAL BASAL
BASIC VITAL ENTIRE FORMAL
INWARD CENTRAL CRUCIAL
NEEDFUL CARDINAL CRITICAL
INHERENT MATERIAL OBLIGATE
NECESSARY
(— TO LIFE) BIOGENOUS
(NOT —) ACCIDENTAL
(PL.) ABCS
ESSENTIALLY AUFOND
ESSONITE GARNET HYACINTH
ESTABLISH BED FIX PUT SET BASE
FAST FIRM FOOT MAKE REAR REST
ROOT SEAT BUILD DEFIX EDIFY
ENACT ERECT EVICT FOUND PLANT
PROVE RAISE SEIZE SETUP START
STATE STELL ATTEST AVOUCH

BOTTOM CEMENT CLINCH CREATE
ENROOT FASTEN FICCHE GROUND
INVENT INVEST LOCATE ORDAIN
RATIFY SETTLE STABLE VERIFY
ACCOUNT APPOINT APPROVE
CONFIRM ENSTATE INSTALL
INSTATE INSTORE POSSESS
PREEMPT SUSTAIN COLONIZE
CONSTATE CONTRACT ENSCONCE
ENTRENCH IDENTIFY INITIATE
INSTRUCT RADICATE REGULATE
STABLISH VALIDATE ASCERTAIN
(— FACT) APPROVE
(— FIRMLY) HAFT INDURATE
(— MORALS) ETHIZE
(— TRUMP) PITCH
ESTABLISHED SAD FAST FIRM
SURE LEGAL ROOTED SEATED
SICCAR STABLE STAPLE STATED
STRONG CERTAIN SETTLED
STANDING
ESTABLISHMENT HONG MILL
SHOP STAB DAIRY FORGE JOINT
PLANT POWER SALON STORE
AGENCY CAISSE CENOBY ECESIS
LAYOUT MENAGE SALOON
SCHOOL ARSENAL ATELIER
BROTHEL COENOBY CONCERN
DOWNSET FACTORY FISHERY
FOUNDRY FUNDUCK SHEBANG
AQUARIUM AVERMENT BUSINESS
CHEESERY CREAMERY ERECTION
HACIENDA
(— IN NEW HABITAT) ECESIS
(— OF COLONY) DEDUCTION
(BATHING —) THERM HAMMAM
HOTHOUSE
(DOMESTIC —) MENAGE
(DRINKING —) STUBE SALOON
BARROOM SHEBEEN
(GAMBLING —) HOUSE TRIPOT
(HORSE-BREEDING —) HARAS
(MONASTIC —) CLOISTER
(NAVAL —) DOCKYARD
(WHITE —) MAN
ESTAFETTE COURIER STAFETTE
ESTAMINET CAFE
ESTATE FEE ALOD COPY FEOD FIEF
HOME LAND POMP RANK UDAL
ACRES ALLOD DAIRA DOWER
DOWRY ESTER ESTRE ETHEL FINCA
FUNDO HABIT HOUSE MANOR
STATE TALUK VILLA ABBACY
BARONY DEMISE DOMAIN ENTAIL
GROUND LIVING MISTER QUINTA
TALUKA ALODIUM CHATEAU
COMMONS DEMESNE DIGNITY
DISPLAY FORTUNE HAVINGS
MAJORAT ALLODIUM BENEFICE
COPYHOLD DOMINION EXECUTRY
FREEHOLD HACIENDA JOINTURE
LIFEHOLD LONGACRE MESNALTY
POSITION PROPERTY SENATORY
STANDING STAROSTY PATRIMONY
PERPETUITY
(— OF REBEL) FISC FISK
(— WITH SERFS) HAM
(CATTLE —) ESTANCIA
(HINDU —) CHAK
(PORTION OF —) LEGITIM
(REAL —) FUNDUS
(PL.) AMANI

ESTEEM AIM LET USE DEEM HOLD
RATE TALE ADORE COUNT FAVOR
HONOR PRICE PRIDE STEEM THINK
VALUE WEIGH WORTH ADMIRE
CREDIT EXTIME REGARD REPUTE
REVERE TENDER WONDER
ACCOUNT CONCEIT OPINION
RESPECT SUSPECT APPRAISE
CONSIDER ESTIMATE VENERATE
ESTEEMED DEAR PRECIOUS
ESTER ADP FMN BIXIN ETHER OLEIN
SARIN TABUN BORATE CAPRIN
ERUCIN FOLATE HUMATE LAURIN
MALATE OLEATE ACETATE
ADIPATE ANISATE AZELATE
CINERIN ELAIDIN FORMATE
FUROATE GALLATE HEPARIN
INDICAN LACTATE LACTONE
LAURATE MALEATE MELLATE
NITRATE OCTOATE OXALATE
OXAMATE PECTATE PEPSIDE
PICRATE SORBATE STEARIN
SULTONE ABIETATE ACRYLATE
ARSENATE ARSENITE ARSONATE
BEHENATE BENZOATE CAFFEATE
CONGENER DIPHENAN ESTOLIDE
FLUORIDE FUCOIDIN KETIPATE
LINOLATE LINOLEIN MALONATE
MARGARIN MYRISTIN NUCLEATE
PALMITIN PIMELATE PIPERATE
RACEMATE SEBACATE SELENATE
SILICATE SINAPATE STEARATE
SUBERATE TARTRATE TOSYLATE
PYRETHRIN
(SUFF.) OATE
ESTHER (COUSIN OF —) MORDECAI
(FATHER OF —) ABIHAIL
(HUSBAND OF —) AHASUERUS
ESTHER WATERS (AUTHOR OF —)
MOORE
(CHARACTER IN —) FRED RICE
LATCH SARAH ESTHER JACKIE
PEGGIE TUCKER WATERS PARSONS
WILLIAM BARFIELD
ESTIMABLE GOOD SOLID WORTH
GENTLE HONEST WORTHY THRIFTY
VALUABLE
ESTIMATE AIM SET CALL CAST
GAGE RANK RATE READ RECK
ASSAY AUDIT CARAT CENSE
COUNT GAUGE GUESS JUDGE
MOUNT PLACE PRIZE SCALE
STOCK TALLY VALUE WEIGH
ASSESS BUDGET ESTEEM RECKON
REGARD SURVEY ACCOUNT
AVERAGE BALANCE CENSURE
COMPUTE CONCEIT MEASURE
APPRAISE CONSIDER CRITIQUE
CALCULATE
(— OF ONE'S SELF) OPINION
(— TOO HIGHLY) OVERRATE
(KIND OF —) POINT
(LOW COST —) LOWBALL
ESTIMATION AIM EYE CESS FAME
NAME ODOR PASS RATE COUNT
HONOR PRICE SIEGE VALUE
CHOICE ESTEEM REGARD REPUTE
ACCOUNT OPINION JUDGMENT
PRESTIGE
(— OF STRAIGHTNESS) BONING
(HIGH —) CONCEIT
(LOW —) DISREPUTE
ESTIMATOR RATER CRUISER

ESTOC STOCK SWORD
ESTOILE STAR ETOILE

ESTONIA
CAPITAL: TALLINN
COIN: SENT KROON ESTMARK
DIALECT: TARTU
ISLAND: DAGO MUHU OESEL SAARE
   VORMSI HIIUMAA SAAREMAA
LAKE: PEIPUS
MEASURE: TUN ELLE LIIN PANG
   SUND TOLL TOOP FADEN VERST
   SAGENE VERSTA KULIMET
   VERCHOC TONNLAND
NATIVE: ESTH AESTI
PROVINCE: SAARE
RIVER: EMA NARVA PARNU KASARI
TOWN: NARVA PARNU REVAL TARTU
   TALLINN
WEIGHT: LOOD NAEL PUUD

ESTONIAN ESTH
ESTOP BAR FILL PLUG STOP DEBAR
   PREVENT
ESTRANGE PART WEAN ALIEN
   AVERT DIVERT ALIENATE DISUNITE
   STRANGER
ESTRANGED ALIEN FRAIM FREMIT
ESTRANGEMENT STANCE
   DISTASTE
ESTRAY STRAY WANDER
ESTREAT COPY FINE EXACT
   RECORD STREET EXTRACT
   EXTREAT
ESTREPEMENT STRIP
E STRING QUINT
ESTRIOL THEELOL
ESTROGEN MESTRANOL
   TAMOXIFEN
ESTRONE THEELIN
ESTRUS HEAT SEASON
ESTUARY ARM RIA PARA WASH
   CREEK FIRTH FLEET FRITH INLET
   LIMAN ESTERO
ESURIENCE GREED HUNGER
ETCETERA ETC KTL
ETCH BITE FROST ENGRAVE
   AQUATINT INSCRIBE
ETCHED FROSTED
ETCHER POINT
ETCHING ETCH AQUATINT
ETEOCLES (BROTHER OF —)
   POLYNICES
   (FATHER OF —) OEDIPUS
   (MOTHER OF —) JOCASTA
ETERNAL ETERNE TARNAL AGELESS
   ENDLESS LASTING UNAGING
   ENDURING IMMORTAL TIMELESS
   UNCAUSED
ETERNALLY AKE EER EVER ALWAYS
   ETERNE FOREVER
ETERNITY AGE EON AEON OLAM
   GLORY FTFRNE ETERNAL
   EWIGKEIT INFINITY PERPETUITY
ETESIAN ANNUAL PERIODIC
ETHAN (FATHER OF —) KISHI MAHOL
ETHANE DIMETHYL
ETHAN FROME (AUTHOR OF —)
   WHARTON
   (CHARACTER IN —) ETHAN FROME
   ZEENA MATTIE PIERCE SILVER
   ZENOBIA
ETHANOL ISOMER

ETHBAAL (DAUGHTER OF —)
   JEZEBEL
ETHER AIR SKY APIOL ESTER PINOLE
   ANISOLE ASARONE EPOXIDE
   ETHYLIN HARMINE SAFROLE
   SESAMIN SESAMOL SOLVENT
   ACACETIN ELEMICIN EMPYREAN
   GUAIACOL PHENETOLE
ETHEREAL AERY AIRY SKYEY
   AERIAL SKYISH AIRLIKE ETHERIC
   FRAGILE SLENDER DELICATE
   HEAVENLY SUPERNAL VAPOROUS
ETHICAL ETHIC MORAL
   HONORABLE
ETHICS HEDONICS PHILOSOPHY

ETHIOPIA
ANCIENT CAPITAL: AXUM AKSUM
CAPITAL: ADDISABABA
COIN: BESA BIRR AMOLE GIRSH
   DOLLAR TALARI ASHRAFI PIASTER
DEPRESSION: DANAKIL
FALLS: TISISAT BLUENILE
ISLANDS: DAHLAK
LAKE: ABE TANA ABAYA SHOLA
   ZEWAY RUDOLF STEFANIE
LANGUAGE: GEEZ TIGRE SOMALI
   AMHARIC GALLINYA TIGRINYA
MARRIAGE: DAMOZ QURBAN
   SEMANYA
MEASURE: TAT KUBA SINJER
   SINZER FARSAKH FARSANG
MOUNTAIN: BATU GUGE GUNA
   TALO
MOUNTAINS: AHMAR CHOKE
NAME: ABYSSINIA
NATIVE: AFAR GALLA ABIGAR
   AMHARA ANNUAK HAMITE
   SEMITE SOMALI TIGRAI CUSHITE
   DANAKIL FALASHA
PORT: ASSAB MASSAWA
PRINCE: RAS
PROVINCE: BALE KEFA WELO ARUSI
   GOJAM HARER SHEWA TIGRE
   SIDAMO ERITREA
RIVER: OMO WEB BARO DAWA GILA
   ABBAI AKOBO AWASH FAFAN
   TAKKAZE
TOWN: EDD DESE GOBA GORE JIMA
   THIO ADOLA ADUWA AKSUM
   ASSAB AWASH DIMTU HARAR
   HARER JIMMA MOJJO ASMARA
   DESSYE DUNKUR GONDAR
   MAKALE MEKELE GARDULA
   MASSAWA NAKAMTI NEKEMTE
   DIREDAWA LALIBALA MUSTAHIL
VALLEY: RIFT
WATERFALL: FINCHA DALVERME
   TESISSAT
WEIGHT: KASM NATR OKET ALADA
   NETER WAKEA WOGIET
   FARASULA

ETHIOPIAN SIDI HAMITE HARARI
   AETHIOP AFRICAN CUSHITE
   FALASHA
ETHIOPIC GIZ GEEZ GHEEZ
ETHNAN (FATHER OF —) ASHUR
   (MOTHER OF —) HELAH
ETHNIC RACIAL
   (— GROUP) ACHANG
ETHNOLOGIST AMERICAN GIBBS
   HODGE LOWIE MASON SMITH

   FEWKES MOONEY MORGAN
   THOMAS BARROWS GODDARD
   HENSHAW PILLING FLETCHER
   GATSCHET GRINNELL CHURCHILL
   SCHOOLCRAFT
   AUSTRIAN MULLER LUSCHAN
   WINTERNITZ
   DANISH RASMUSSEN
   DUTCH STEINMETZ NIEUWENHUIS
   ENGLISH HADDON LATHAM
   PRICHARD
   FINNISH CASTREN
   GERMAN BOEHM FINSCH GROSSE
   KRAUSE BASTIAN GERLAND
   STEINEN FROBENIUS FRIEDERICI
   RUSSIAN KOPPEN
ETHOS MANNER
ETHYLENE ELAYL ETHENE ETHERIN
ETIOLATED DRAWN
ETIQUETTE FORM DECORUM
   MANNERS
   (— OF DRINKING TEA) CHANOYU
ETRUSCAN TUSCAN RASENNA
   ETRURIAN TYRRHENE
   (PL.) TURSENOI TYRRHENI
ETUDE STUDY
ETUI CASE ETWEE TWEEZE
   TWEEZER EQUIPAGE RETICULE
ETYMOLOGY ORIGIN DERIVATION
ETYMON RADIX
EUAECHME (DAUGHTER OF —)
   PERIBOEA
   (FATHER OF —) MEGAREUS
   (HUSBAND OF —) ALCATHOUS
EUBOEANS ABANTES
EUCALYPT GUM YATE APPLE
   BIMBIL CARBUN JARRAH MALLEE
   MYRTAL CARBEEN CUTTAIL
   MESSMAN COOLABAH IRONBARK
   MESSMATE WHITETOP YERTCHUK
EUCALYPTOLE CINEOL CINEOLE
EUCALYPTUS TUART MALLEE
   TEWART BLUEGUM EUCALYPT
   IRONBARK SUGARGUM WHIPSTICK
EUCHARIST HOUSEL MAUNDY
   SUPPER MYSTERY VIATICUM
EUCHARISTIC (— ELEMENTS) HAGIA
EUCHITE SATANIST ADELPHIAN
   MESSALIAN
EUCHRE LOVE
   (— HAND) JAMBONE JAMBOREE
EUDAEMONIA HAPPINESS
EUDOCIMUS GUARA
EUDOXIA (FATHER OF —) BAUTO
   (HUSBAND OF —) ARCADIUS
   (SON OF —) THEODOSIUS
EUGENE ONEGIN (CHARACTER IN
   —) OLGA GREMIN LARINA ONEGIN
   OLENSKY TATYANA TRIQUET
   (COMPOSER OF —) TCHAIKOVSKY
EUGENIE GRANDET (AUTHOR OF
   —) BALZAC
   (CHARACTER IN —) NANON
   CHARLES CRUCHOT EUGENIE
   GRANDET DEGRASSINS
EULALIA NETI
EULENSPIEGEL OWLGLASS
EULOGIST PRAISER LAUREATE
   PANEGYRIST
EULOGISTIC EULOGIC EPENETIC
   MAGNIFIC LAUDATORY
EULOGY PRAISE TONGUE ADDRESS

   ELOGIUM ORATION ENCOMIUM
   PANEGYRE
EUMOLPUS (FATHER OF —)
   NEPTUNE
   (MOTHER OF —) CHIONE
   (SON OF —) ISMARUS
EUNEUS (BROTHER OF —) THOAS
   (FATHER OF —) JASON
   (MOTHER OF —) HYPSIPYLE
EUNICE (SON OF —) TIMOTHEUS
EUNUCH CAPON SPORUS
   WETHER GELDING HALFMAN
   CASTRATE
EUPHAUSID SHRIMP
EUPHEMISM DEE FIB GEE GOR
   DASH GOSH GOLES GOLLY LAWKS
   DIANTRE DICKENS CODEWORD
   GRACIOUS
   (— FOR DAMN) HANG
   (— FOR MURDER) REMOVAL
EUPHEMUS (FATHER OF —)
   NEPTUNE POSEIDON
   (MOTHER OF —) EUROPA
   (SON OF —) BATTUS
EUPHONIOUS TUNEFUL
EUPHORIA BLISS ELATION
EUPHORIC GIDDY
EUPHROSYNE JOY
EUPHUISM GONGORISM
EURASIAN BURGHER FERINGI
EUREKA RED PUCE
EURIPIDES (TRAGEDY OF —)
   ELECTRA
EURO WALLAROO
EUROPA (BROTHER OF —) CILIX
   CADMUS THASUS PHINEUS
   PHOENIX
   (FATHER OF —) AGENOR
   (HUSBAND OF —) ASTERIUS
   (MOTHER OF —) TELEPHASSA
   (SON OF —) MINOS SARPEDON
   RHADAMANTHYS

EUROPE
(ALSO SEE SPECIFIC COUNTRIES)
LAKE: COMO GARDA ONEGA
   VANEM GENEVA LADOGA
   LUGANO PEIPUS VANERN ZURICH
   BALATON MALAREN SCUTARI
   VATTERN MAGGIORE CONSTANCE
   NEUCHATEL
MOUNTAIN: DOM ETNA ELBRUS
   KAZBEK LYSKAMM SHKHARA
   JUNGFRAU NADELHORN
   WEISSHORN ZUGSPITZE
   MATTERHORN
NATION: ITALY SPAIN FRANCE
   GREECE LATVIA MONACO
   NORWAY POLAND RUSSIA
   SWEDEN ALBANIA ANDORRA
   AUSTRIA BELGIUM DENMARK
   ENGLAND ESTONIA FINLAND
   GERMANY HOLLAND HUNGARY
   ICELAND IRELAND ROMANIA
   BULGARIA PORTUGAL SCOTLAND
   SLOVAKIA SLOVENIA SANMARINO
   LUXEMBOURG YUGOSLAVIA
   NETHERLANDS SOVIETUNION
   SWITZERLAND VATICANCITY
   LIECHTENSTEIN
   CZECHOSLOVAKIA
RANGE: ALPS URAL BALKAN
   KJOLEN RHODOPE SUDETEN

CAUCASUS PYRENEES APENNINES
CARPATHIAN
RIVER: PO AAR DON AARE EBRO
ELBE ODER DOURO DVINA LOIRE
RHINE RHONE SEINE TAGUS
TIBER VOLGA DANUBE
THAMES DNIEPER VISTULA
DNIESTER

EUROPEAN FRANK SAHIB BOHUNK
EUROPE FRINGE INDIAN FERINGI
TOPIWALA
(— IN INDIES) BLIJVER
(WESTERN —) FRANK
EUROPEAN BARRACUDA SPET
EUROPEAN BASS BRASSE
EUROPEAN BISON AUROCHS
EUROPEAN CLOVER ALSIKE
EUROPEAN GULL MEW
EUROPEAN HERRING SPRAT
EUROPEAN JUNIPER CADE
EUROPEAN KITE GLEDE
EUROPEAN LAVENDER ASPIC
EUROPEAN LINDEN TEIL
EUROPEAN MINT HYSSOP
EUROPEAN OAK DURMAST
EUROPEAN PERCH RUFF RUFFE
EUROPEAN POLECAT FITCHEW
EUROPEAN PORGY BESUGO
EUROPEAN RABBIT CONY
EUROPEAN SHARK TOPE
EUROPEAN SPARROW WHITECAP
EUROPEAN STARLING STARNEL
EUROPEAN SWALLOW MARTIN
EUROPEAN THRUSH MAVIS OUZEL
EUROPEAN WIDGEON WHIM
WHEWER
EUROPEAN WREN STAG
EURYANTHE (CHARACTER IN —)
ADOLAR LYSIART EGLANTINE
EURYANTHE
(COMPOSER OF —) WEBER
EURYDIA (FATHER OF —) PONTUS
(MOTHER OF —) GAEA
(SON OF —) PALLAS PERSES
ASTRAEUS
EURYNOME (DAUGHTERS OF —)
GRACES CHARITES
(FATHER OF —) CHAOS OCEANUS
EURYPTERID SERAPHIM
EURYPYLUS (FATHER OF —)
NEPTUNE TELEPHUS
(MOTHER OF —) ASTYOCHE
(SLAYER OF —) PYRRHUS
HERCULES
EURYSACES (FATHER OF —) AJAX
(MOTHER OF —) TECMESSA
EURYSTHEUS (FATHER OF —)
STHENELUS
(MOTHER OF —) NICIPPE
(SLAYER OF —) HYLLUS
EURYTUS (DAUGHTER OF —) IOLE
(FATHER OF —) ACTOR AUGEAS
MELANEUS
(MOTHER OF —) GAEA
(SLAYER OF —) HERCULES
EUTECTIC STEADITE
EUTERPE (FATHER OF —) JUPITER
(MOTHER OF —) MNEMOSYNE
EUXANTHONE PURRONE
EUXOA AGROTIS
EVACUATE PASS VENT VOID AVOID
EMPTY EXPEL STOOL VACATE

DEPRIVE EXCRETE EXHAUST
NULLIFY VACUATE PERSPIRE
EVACUATION OFFICE DUNKIRK
MEDEVAC
EVADE BEG GEE BILK DUCK FLEE
FOIL JOUK JUMP SHUN SLIP VOID
AVERT AVOID BLINK DALLY DODGE
ELUDE FENCE FLANK PARRY SHIRK
SKIRT SKIVE BAFFLE BLENCH
BYPASS COPOUT DELUDE ESCAPE
ILLUDE BEGUILE FINESSE OUTSLIP
QUIBBLE TURNOFF HEDGEHOP
LEAPFROG SIDESTEP
(— LEGAL PROCESS) ABSCOND
(— PAYMENT) BILK
(— QUESTIONS) QUIBBLE SHUFFLE
(— WORK) JOUK BLUDGE
EVADNE (FATHER OF —) PELIAS
NEPTUNE POSEIDON
(HUSBAND OF —) CAPANEUS
(MOTHER OF —) IPHIS PITANA
(SON OF —) IAMUS
EVALUATE RATE ASSESS PONDER
RECKON DISSECT APPRAISE
ESTIMATE
EVALUATION STOCK ESTIMATE
EVANDER (FATHER OF —) HERMES
(MOTHER OF —) CARMENTA
EVANESCE FADE VANISH
EVANESCENCE ANICCA
EVANESCENT FLEET EVANID
BRITTLE CURSORY EVASIVE
FRAGILE DELICATE FLEETING
FLITTING FUGITIVE STAYLESS
EVANGELICAL GOSPEL SIMEONITE
(— ACTIVITY) WARFARE
EVANGELIST LUKE MARK EVANGEL
GOSPELER SALVATIONIST
EVAPORATE DRY EXHALE AVOLATE
CONDENSE VAPORIZE
EVAPORATING (— QUICKLY)
VOLATILE
EVAPORATOR BOILER EFFECT
EVASION JINK SLIP DODGE QUIRK
SALVE SHIFT AMBAGE ESCAPE
SNATCH ELUSION OFFCOME
SHUFFLE TWISTER ARTIFICE
ESCAPISM VOIDANCE
(— OF DUTY) COMEOFF
(ARTFUL —) QUIRK
EVASIVE SLY EELY DODGY SHIFTY
SUBTLE TWISTY ELUSIVE ELUSORY
TRICKSY SLIPPERY SLIPSKIN
(TO BE —) STONEWALL
EVE DUSK EREB EREV EVEN VIGIL
SUNSET SUNDOWN
(NEW YEAR'S —) HAGMENA
HOGMANAY
EVELINA (AUTHOR OF —) BURNEY
(CHARACTER IN —) JOHN DUVAL
ARTHUR HOWARD ANVILLE
BELMONT CLEMENT EVELINA
ORVILLE VILLARS WILLOUGHBY
EVEN ALL DEN EEN TIE YET FAIR
HUNK JUST PAIR TIED TILL ALINE
CLEAN EQUAL EVERY EXACT
FLUSH GRADE HUNKY LEVEL
MATCH PLAIN RIVAL STILL SUANT
SUENT SWEET DIRECT ITSELF
PLACID SILKEN SMOOTH SQUARE
STEADY ABREAST BALANCE
EQUABLE FLATTEN REGULAR
UNIFORM UPSIDES EQUALIZE

MODERATE PARALLEL SOMUCHAS
(— NUMBERS) PAIR
(— OFF) LEVEL
(— THOUGH) IF ALTHO ALBEIT
ALTHOUGH
(MAKE —) WEIGH STEADY
(PREF.) ARTIO HOMAL(O) LEUR(O)
EVENING DEN EVE EREB EVEN SOIR
ABEND TARDE SUNSET VESPER
EVENTIDE VESPERAL
(— BEFORE PASSOVER) PARASCEVE
(— OF SONG) CEILIDH
(AT —) TEEN
(EARLY —) UNDERN
(YESTERDAY —) STREEN
EVENING PRIMROSE SUNCUP
SCABIOUS
EVENING STAR VENUS HESPER
VESPER EVESTAR HESPERUS
EVENLY FAIR PLAIN FLATLY
EQUALLY
EVENNESS EQUALITY
EVENSONG VESPERS
EVENT HAP CASE FACT FATE FEAT
TILT CASUS DOING EPOCH FRAME
ISSUE THING ACTION EFFECT
FACTUM RESULT TIDING TIMING
EPISODE FIXTURE MIRACLE
PORTENT TRAGEDY INCIDENT
OCCASION OCCURRENCE
PHENOMENON
(AMUSING —) COMEDY
(CHANCE —) ACCIDENT FORTUITY
(EXTRAORDINARY —) MIRACLE
(FORTUITOUS —) HAZARD
(GRAVE —) CALAMITY
(HAPPY —) GODSEND
(IMPORTANT —) ACE ERA
(INTRODUCTORY —) PROLOGUE
(KIND OF —) MEDIA
(PAST —S) HISTORY
(SEISMIC —) STARQUAKE
(SET OF —S) EPISODE
(SIGNIFICANT —) CRISIS
(SKI —) DOWNHILL
(SOCIAL —) BENEFIT
(SPORTING —) STAKE
(STAGED —) FRAMEUP
(SUPERNATURAL —) MIRACLE
(THEATRICAL —) DRAW
(TURNING-POINT —) LANDMARK
(UNEXPECTED —) STUNNER
ACCIDENT AFTERCLAP
(UNPLEASANT —) BUMMER
(YEARLY —) ANNUAL
EVENTFUL LIVELY NOTABLE
EVENTIDE VESPER EVENING
EVENTUAL LAST FINAL ULTIMATE
EVENTUALITY EVENT
EVENTUALLY YET FINALLY
EVENTUATE GO LEAD ISSUE
RESULT SUCCEED ULTIMATE
EVENUS (DAUGHTER OF —)
MARPESSA
(FATHER OF —) ARES MARS
EVER O AY SO AYE EER ONCE STILL
ALWAYS ETERNE FOREVER
EVERGLADE STATE FLORIDA
EVERGREEN BOX FIR IVY YEW ASIS
ATLE BAGO ILEX PINE TAWA ATLEE
BOLDO CAROB CEDAR HEATH
HOLLY LARCH SAVIN THUYA
TOYON BAUERA COIGUE DAHOON

LAUREL MASTIC SPRUCE BANKSIA
BARETTA BEBEERU BILIMBI
GOWIDDE HEMLOCK JASMINE
TARATAH BOXTHORN CALFKILL
CARAUNDA IRONWOOD TAMARISK
TILESEED
(— SHRUB) GORSE
(PL.) CHRISTMAS
EVER-INCREASING ACCRESCENT
EVERLASTING ETERNE AEONIAL
AEONIAN AGELESS AGELONG
DURABLE ENDLESS ETERNAL
FOREVER LASTING TEDIOUS
ENDURING IMMORTAL INFINITE
TIMELESS PERPETUAL
EVERLASTINGLY ALWAYS
FOREVER
EVERSION BLOWOUT BEARINGS
EVERT UPSET EVERSE SUBVERT
OVERTURN
EVERY ALL ANY ILK PER THE EACH
EVER ILKA ENTIRE EVERICH
COMPLETE
(— DAY) QD QUOTID
(— HOUR) QH
(— NIGHT) QN
(PREF.) PAM PAN
EVERYBODY ALL EACH EVERYMAN
EVERYONE
EVERYDAY USUAL HOMELY
PROSAIC ORDINARY WORKADAY
EVERY MAN IN HIS HUMOUR
(AUTHOR OF —) JONSON
(CHARACTER IN —) EDWARD KITELY
BOBADIL BRIDGET CLEMENT
KNOWELL MATTHEW WELLBRED
BRAINWORM
EVERYTHING ALL ATHING
(— TAKEN INTO ACCOUNT)
ALLINALL
(COUNTING —) INALL
EVERYWHERE PASSIM UBIQUE
ALGATES AYWHERE OVERALL
ALLWHERE
EVICT OUST EJECT EXPEL
EVICTION OUSTER
EVIDENCE CLUE MARK SHOW SIGN
TEST PROOF SCRIP SMOKE TOKEN
TRACE TRIAL ATTEST AVOUCH
BETOKE RECORD REVEAL
CHARTER EXHIBIT HEARSAY
SHOWING SUPPORT ARGUMENT
DISPROOF DOCUMENT EVICTION
INDICATE MANIFEST MONUMENT
MUNIMENT WARRANTY
ADMINICLE
(— OF DISEASE) SYMPTOM
(— OF FRESHNESS) BLOOM
(— OF RIGHT) TITLE
(— OF WRONGDOING) GOODS
(POSITIVE —) CONSTAT
(VERBAL —) PAROL
EVIDENT LOUD OPEN PERT APERT
BROAD CLEAR FRANK GROSS
NAKED PLAIN EXTANT LIQUID
PATENT WITTER EMINENT GLARING
OBVIOUS PROBATE VISIBLE
APPARENT DISTINCT FLAGRANT
LUCULENT MANIFEST PALPABLE
(PREF.) DELO
EVIL BAD DER ILL SIN BALE BASE
DIRE HARM LEWD PAPA POOR
SORE VICE VILE WICK YELL CRIME

CURSE DEVIL FELON FOLLY HYDRA
MALUM QUEDE SORRY WATHE
WRONG CANCEL DIVERS INJURY
MALIGN MENACE NAUGHT PLAGUE
ROTTEN SHREWD SINFUL UNFEEL
UNFELE UNGOOD NOXIOUS
WICKED WONDER ADVERSE
BALEFUL CORRUPT DISEASE
DIVERSE HEINOUS HURTFUL
IMMORAL MISDEED NOXIOUS
SATANIC UNHAPPY UNSOUND
VICIOUS CALAMITY DEPRAVED
DEVILISH DISASTER GANGRENE
IMPROPER INIQUITY MISCHIEF
QUEDSHIP SINISTER NEFARIOUS
(— BEING) MARE
(— OF MANY PHASES) HYDRA
(— SPIRIT) JUMBIE
(IMAGINARY —) WINDMILL
(IMPENDING —) MENACE
IMMINENCE
(SOCIAL —) SCOURGE
(SPIRITUAL —) SCAB
(PREF.) MAL(E) PONERO
EVIL-DOER VILLAIN
EVILDOER BADMASH BUDMASH
SLASHER
EVIL EYE DROCHUIL MALOCCHIO
EVINCE SHOW ARGUE PROVE
SUBDUE BREATHE CONQUER
DISPLAY EXHIBIT EVIDENCE
INDICATE MANIFEST
EVISCERATE GUT DRAW BOWEL
PAUNCH GARBAGE
EVOCATION SADHANA
EVOCATIVE REDOLENT
EVOKE FIT MOVE STIR EDUCE
AROUSE ELICIT SUMMON
EVOCATE PROVOKE SUGGEST
EVOLUTION DRIFT GROWTH
BIOGENY DIOECISM HOROTELY
MANEUVER BRADYTELY
(PL.) AEROBATICS
EVOLUTIONISM DARWINISM
EVOLVE COOK EMIT EDUCE DERIVE
UNFOLD UNROLL BLOSSOM
DEVELOP EVOLUTE CONCEIVE
UNPLIGHT
EWE KEB TEG CROCK CRONE DRAPE
SHEEP GIMMER LAMBER RACHEL
THEAVE CHILVER
(— AND LAMB) COUPLE
(OLD —) BIDDY CROCK CRONE
BIDDIE
(YOUNG —) THEAVE
EWER JUG CREW LAIR BASIN
UDDER PITCHER URCEOLE
EXACERBATE SOUR ENRAGE
FERMENT EMBITTER IRRITATE
EXACERBATION PAROXYSM
EXACT ASK DUE DEAD EVEN FINE
FLAT HAVE JUMP JUST LEVY NEAT
NICE TRUE VERY PRESS SCREW
WREAK WREST COMPEL DEMAND
ELICIT EVINCE EXTORT FORMAL
GRAITH MINUTE NARROW PROPER
SEVERE SQUARE STRAIT STRICT
CAREFUL CERTAIN COLLECT
COMMAND CORRECT ENFORCE
ESTREAT EXPRESS EXTRACT
LITERAL PARTILE PERFECT
POINTED PRECISE PRECISO
REFINED REGULAR REQUIRE

ACCURATE CRITICAL EXPLICIT
FAITHFUL RIGOROUS SPECIFIC
(— BY FINE) ESTREAT
(— SATISFACTION) AVENGE
(NOT —) PLATIC
(VERY —) RELIGIOUS
(PREF.) ORTH(O)
EXACTING NICE HARSH PICKY
STERN STIFF TIGHT SCREWY
SEVERE STRAIT STRICT ARDUOUS
EXIGENT FINICKY ONEROUS
CRITICAL IMPOSING IRONCLAD
PRESSING SCREWING PARTICULAR
PERSNICKETY
(— EXCLUSIVE DEVOTION)
JEALOUS
EXACTION FEE TAX MART GOUGE
GRIPE
(— OF PROVISIONS) CESS COYNE
COIGNY
(ANCIENT IRISH —) SOREHON
(UNDUE —) EXTORTION
EXACTITUDE RIGOR
EXACTLY DUE AMEN BANG DEAD
EVEN FLAT FLOP FULL JUMP JUST
VERY PLUMB PLUNK QUITE RIGHT
SHARP SPANG TRULY ARIGHT
EVENLY ITSELF JUSTLY NICELY
PERFECT SLAPDAB DIRECTLY
MINUTELY SMACKDAB
EXACTNESS RIGOR TRUTH NICETY
ACCURACY DELICACY DISPATCH
FIDELITY IDENTITY JUSTNESS
SAPIENCE SEVERITY PRECISION
PARTICULARITY
(FUSSY —) FIKE
EXAGGERATE GAB MORE COLOR
BOUNCE CHARGE COLOUR
EXTEND OVERDO AMPLIFY
ENHANCE ENLARGE MAGNIFY
OUTLASH ROMANCE STRETCH
INCREASE OVERDRAW OVERLASH
OVERPLAY OVERTELL OVERSTATE
OVERCHARGE
(— OPENING OF MOUTH) CHINK
EXAGGERATED CAMP SLAB TALL
COLORED FUSTIAN FABULOUS
INFLATED OVERDONE OVERSHOT
OVERWEENING
EXAGGERATING ARROGANT
EXAGGERATION BLAH REACHER
HYPERBOLE
EXALT HAUT LAUD REAR AREAR
BUILD DEIFY ELATE ENSKY ERECT
EXTOL HEAVE HEEZE HONOR
MOUNT RAISE TOWER ALTIFY
ASCEND EXHALE PREFER REFINE
THRONE UPREAR WORTHY
ADVANCE AUGMENT DIGNIFY
ELEVATE ENHANCE ENNOBLE
FEATHER GLORIFY GREATEN
INSPIRE MAGNIFY PROMOTE
SUBLIME DIVINIZE ENTHRONE
GRADUATE HEIGHTEN INHEAVEN
PEDESTAL
EXALTATION LAUD AVATAR
ANAGOGE ANAGOGY ELATION
RAPTURE ERECTION
EXALTED HAUT HIGH ELATE GRAND
LOFTY NOBLE SHEEN SKYEY
SOARY ASTRAL TIPTOE TOPFUL
HAUGHTY SUBLIME ELEVATED
EXALTATE MAGNIFIC

EXALTING HUMAN
EXAM MUG
(— ANSWER) TRUE FALSE
(— TAKER) TESTEE
(HIGH SCHOOL —) PSAT
EXAMINATION EX MAY EXAM FACE
QUIZ TEST ASSAY AUDIT BOARD
CHECK FINAL GREAT POINT PROBE
STUDY TRIAL BIOPSY EXAMEN
NOTICE REVIEW SCHOOL SEARCH
SURVEY TRIPOS AUTOPSY
BEARING CANVASS CHECKUP
DIVVERS EXAMINE HEARING
INQUEST INQUIRY MIDYEAR
OPPOSAL TUGGERY ANALYSIS
CRITIQUE DOCIMASY EXERCISE
NECROPSY PHYSICAL RESEARCH
SCANNING SCRUTINY PRACTICAL
PRELIMINARY
(BRITISH —) SLEVEL
(ELECTROCARDIOGRAPHIC —)
STRESSTEST
(PL.) HOURS
(SUFF.) SCOPE SCOPIC SCOPUS
SCOPY
EXAMINE ASK CON FAN SEE SPY
TRY BOLT CASE COMB FEEL LAIT
LINE LOOK OGLE QUIZ RIPE SCAN
SEEK SIFT TEST VIEW ASSAY AUDIT
CHECK ENTER GROPE PROBE
QUEST QUOTE SAMEN SENSE
SOUND STUDY VISIT APPOSE
BEHOLD CANDLE DEBATE PERUSE
PONDER REVIEW SCREEN SEARCH
SURVEY ANALYZE CANVASS
COLLATE DISCUSS EXPLORE
INQUIRE INSPECT OVERSEE
PALPATE RUMMAGE COGNOSCE
CONSIDER OVERHAUL TRAVERSE
(— BY TOUCH) PALPATE
(— CAREFULLY) SCAN SIFT PONDER
(— LAND) SOUM
EXAMINER POSER TRIER CENSOR
CONNER SABORA ANALYST
APPOSER AUDITOR CORONER
PROBATOR SEARCHER
EXAMPLE A CASE CAST COPY LEAD
NORM TYPE BEAUT BYSEN ESSAY
LIGHT MODEL PIECE EMBLEM
PRAXIS SAMPLE BOUNCER
LEADING LECTURE PATTERN
PURPOSE SAMPLER THEATER
CALENDAR ENSAMPLE EXEMPLAR
EXEMPLUM FORBYSEN FOREGOER
INSTANCE PARADIGM SPECIMEN
(CHOICE —) PEACH
(DISGRACEFUL —) BIZEN BYSEN
BYZEN MONSTROSITY
(EXTREME —) CAUTION
(FINEST —) PEARL
(INFERIOR —) EXCUSE
(INSTRUCTIVE —) LESSON
(NOTABLE —) MONUMENT
(OLDEST —) DOYEN
(PERFECT —) APOTHEOSIS
(STANDARD —) PROTOTYPE
(SUPERLATIVE —) BLINGER
EXANTHEMA DIEBACK ERUPTION
EXASPERATE IRE IRK MAD BAIT
GALL HEAT URGE ANNOY BLOOD
ENRAGE EXCITE NETTLE EXASPER
INFLAME PROVOKE ROUGHEN
ACERBATE IRRITATE

EXASPERATED SNAKY WROTH
SNAKEY SNAKISH ACERBATE
EXASPERATION AGRO GALL HEAT
AGGRO WRATH
EXCAVATE CUT DIG PIT HOLE
HOWK MINE MOLE MUCK PION
SINK DELVE DRILL DRIVE GRAVE
NAVVY SCOOP STOPE BURROW
DREDGE EXCAVE GULLET HOLLOW
QUARRY
EXCAVATION CUT DIG PIT HOLE
MINE REDD SINK SUMP BERRY
DELFT DELPH DITCH GRAFT GRAVE
HEUGH PILOT STOPE BURROW
CAVITY DUGOUT GROOVE TRENCH
BREAKUP CUTTING PADDOCK
TUTWORK WORKING DENEHOLE
SLUSHPIT
(TRIAL —) SONDAGE
EXCAVATOR DIG BILDAR CLEOID
DIGGER DIPPER DRIFTER HATCHET
PIONEER
EXCEED COW TOP BEST PASS
EXCEL OUTDO OUTGO BETTER
OUTRUN OUTVIE OVERDO OVERGO
ECLIPSE OUTPASS OVERRUN
OVERTAX PRECEDE SURPASS
OUTRANGE OUTREACH OUTSTRIP
OVERCOME OVERGANG OVERSTEP
OVERWEND SURMOUNT
PREPONDERATE
(— IN IMPORTANCE) OVERSHADOW
(— THE RESOURCES) BEGGAR
EXCEEDING VILE
EXCEEDINGLY ALL DONE PURE
TRES VERY AMAIN BLAME BLAMED
MASTER PROPER PURELY
AWFULLY LICKING PARLOUS
PASSING HEARTILY HEAVENLY
HORRIBLE PROPERLY
(PREF.) PRE ULTRA
EXCEL CAP COB TOP BANG BEAT
BEST DING FLOG MEND PASS STAR
BLECK OUTDO OUTGO SHINE
TRUMP BETTER EXCEED MASTER
OUTRAY OVERDO OVERGO PRECEL
ECLIPSE EMULATE OUTPEER
SURPASS OUTCLASS OUTRANGE
OUTRIVAL OUTSHINE OUTSTRIP
OVERPEER SUPERATE SURMOUNT
EXCELLENCE ARETE MERIT PRICE
VIRTU WORTH BEAUTY DESERT
HEIGHT VIRTUE DIGNITY PROWESS
GOODNESS SPLENDOR
BRILLIANCE PREROGATIVE
(— OF QUALITY) STRIKE
(MORAL —) GRACE
(PL.) SANCTITIES
EXCELLENT FAB GAY RUM BEST
BOSS BRAW COOL FINE GOOD
HEND HIGH PURE RARE RIAL SLAP
TALL TRIM ATHEL BEAUT BONNY
BONZA BRAVE BULLY BURLY
CRACK GREAT JAMMY JOLLY
LUMMY PIOUS PRIME PRIMO
SOLID SUPER SWELL TOUGH TRIED
WALLY BONNIE BONZER BOSKER
BUMPER CHEESY CHOICE CLASSY
FAMOUS FREELY GENTLE GOODLY
MELLOW PRETTY PROPER SELECT
SPIFFY TIPTOP WICKED WIZARD
WORTHY YANKEE BLIGHTY
BOSHTER CAPITAL CORKING

CURIOUS ELEGANT GALLANT
IMMENSE QUALITY SNIFTER
STAVING TOPPING CLIPPING
COLOSSAL EXIMIOUS GENEROUS
KNOCKOUT SPIFFING STUNNING
SUPERIOR VALUABLE VIRTUOUS
WAUREGAN YNGOODLY
GANGBUSTERS
(— **IN QUALITY**) FRANK
(**MOST** —) BEST
EXCELLENTLY BRAWLY CLEVER
FINELY FREELY PROUDLY DIVINELY
FAMOUSLY
EXCELLING BEST PASSANT
EXCEPT BAR BUT CEP NOR NOT
BATE BOUT OMIT ONLY SAVE
ABATE FORBY SEVER EXEMPT
FORBYE NOBBUT SAVING SCUSIN
UNLESS BARRING BESIDES
EXCLUDE OUTCEPT OUTSIDE
OUTTAKE OUTWITH RESERVE
WITHOUT FORPRISE OUTTAKEN
RESERVED
(PREF.) PRETER
EXCEPTING BATING EXCEPT SAVING
UNLESS BARRING
EXCEPTION DEMUR SALVO SAVING
DISSENT OFFENSE DEMURRER
FALLENCY FORPRISE INSTANCE
(— **TO JUROR**) CHALLENGE
(**WITHOUT** —) BARNONE
EXCEPTIONAL RARE EXEMPT
ROUSING STRANGE UNUSUAL
ABERRANT ABNORMAL ESPECIAL
SINGULAR UNCOMMON
EXCEPTIONALLY AMAZING
SPANKING
EXCERPT CITE PATCH QUOTE
SCRAP EXTRACT OFFPRINT
(— **FROM SONG**) SNATCH
EXCESS OVER PLUS RIOT FLOOD
INORD LUXUS PRIDE ACRASY
SPILTH ACRASIA BALANCE
DEBAUCH EXTREME MISRULE
NIMIETY OUTRAGE OVERAGE
OVERSET PROFUSE RIOTISE
SURFEIT SURPLUS EXCEDENT
GLUTTONY INTEREST OVERLASH
OVERMUCH OVERPLUS PLEONASM
PLETHORA PLEURISY SATURNALIA
OVERABUNDANCE
(— **OF ACTION**) OVERKILL
(— **OF LOGS**) BANK
(— **OF METAL**) FEEDHEAD
(— **OF SOLAR MONTH**) EPACT
(— **OF VOTES**) PLURALITY
(SUFF.) ARD ART
EXCESSIVE TOO OVER RANK
ENORM FANCY STEEP STIFF THICK
UNDUE DEADLY DEUCED WOUNDY
BURNING EXTREME FURIOUS
NIMIOUS OVERDUE SURFEIT
ABNORMAL CRIMINAL DEVILISH
ENORMOUS HORRIBLE INSOLENT
OVERMUCH TERRIBLE TERRIFIC
PLETHORIC
(PREF.) POLY SUR
EXCESSIVELY TOO SUPER DEADLY
OVERLY STRONG UNDULY PARLISH
PARLOUS PASSING PLAGUEY
WOUNDLY DEVILISH PLAGUILY
(PREF.) HYPER
EXCHANGE RAP SET CASH CAUP

CHOP CODE COPE COUP KULA
MART SELL SWAP SWOP BANDY
BOARD BOLSA CORSE SHIFT
STORE TRADE TROKE TRUCK
BARTER BOURSE CAMBIO CHANGE
DICKER EXCAMB MARKET NIFFER
RESALE RIALTO SCORSE SHOPPE
TOLSEL TOLZEY VALUTA WISSEL
WRIXLE BARROOM CAMBIUM
CHAFFER COMMUTE CONVERT
DEALING PERMUTE TRAFFIC
COMMERCE TRADEOFF TRUCKAGE
(— **COURTESIES**) GAM
(— **IN CHECKERS**) CUT SHOT
(— **OF BLOWS**) HANDPLAY
(— **OF PRISONERS**) CARTEL
(— **OF SYLLABLES**) ANACLASIS
(— **PREMIUM**) AGIO
(— **SMALL TALK**) CHAFFER
(— **THOUGHTS**) CONVERSE
(— **VISITS**) GAM
(**DANCE** —) CROSSOVER
(**FAIR** —) GIFFGAFF
(**FOREIGN** —) DEVISE
(**POETICAL** —) FLYTING
(**POST** —) CANTEEN
(**TELEPHONE** —) CENTRAL
(PREF.) CAMBI(O)
EXCHEQUER FISC PURSE COFFER
KHALSA CHECKER FINANCE
TREASURY
EXCIPIENT OXYMEL
EXCISE CUT TAX CROP DUTY GELD
TOLL SLASH EXCIDE EXSECT
IMPOST RESECT EXSCIND
ALCABALA RETRENCH
EXCISEMAN GAGER GAUGER
EXCISOR
EXCISION CUT ERASURE ABLATION
EXCITABLE HYPER NAPPY NERVY
NERVOUS RACKETY
EXCITATION LASH
(**CONVULSIVE** —) SHOCK
EXCITE HOT CITE FIRE HEAT HYPO
SEND SPUR STIR URGE WAKE
WHET WORK YERK ALARM AMOVE
ANGER CHAFE ELATE ERECT
FLAME FLUSH IMPEL PIQUE RAISE
ROUSE SCALD SPOOK AROUSE
AWAKEN BOTHER DAZZLE DECOCT
FLURRY FOMENT GROOVE IGNITE
INCEND INCITE INVOKE JANGLE
KINDLE LATHER PROMPT SALUTE
TICKLE TURNON UPREAR WECCHE
AGITATE ANIMATE COMMOVE
ENCHAFE FERMENT INCENSE
INFLAME PHILTER PROVOKE
QUICKEN STARTLE WHITTLE
DISQUIET ENGENDER EXCITATE
IRRITATE
(— **MIRTH**) DIVERT
EXCITED UP APE GAY HOT AGOG
GAGA GYTE PINK ABOIL AGLOW
CADGY EAGER MANIC PROUD
RANTY SKEER WIRED BLEEZY
ELATED HEATED STEAMY ATHRILL
FEVERED HAYWIRE SKEERED
WAKENED AGITATED ATWITTER
ELEVATED FEVERISH FLURRIED
FRENETIC STARTLED
OVERWROUGHT
(**EASILY** —) KITTLE
(**INTENSELY** —) MAD AMOK

EXCITEMENT ADO GOG BUZZ FUME
FUSS GLOW HEAT HWYL KICK
RUFF STIR TOSS UNCO FEEZE
FEVER FUROR KICKS LARRY MANIA
SETUP SPARK STOUR UNCOW
FRENZY SPLASH WARMTH
FERMENT FRISSON NERVISM
TAMASHA WIDDRIM BROUHAHA
DELIRIUM INTEREST RACKETRY
(**FILLED WITH** —) HECTIC
(**GREAT** —) FEVER
(**MENTAL** —) WIDDRIM
(**PLEASANT** —) SUSPENSE
(**SHOW** —) ENTHUSE
(**VIOLENT** —) GARE
EXCITING HOT HIGH KICKY ZINGY
HECTIC AGACANT BURNING
PARLOUS RACKETY ROUSING
EXCITANT EXCITIVE PATHETIC
STIRRING TERRIFIC FASHIONABLE
(— **HORROR**) DIRE DIREFUL
(**ENJOYABLY** —) ZINGY
EXCLAIM CRY HOWL BLURT ESCRY
SNORT CLAMOR OUTCRY BESPEAK
(— **IN AMAZEMENT**) OOH
(— **IN PROTEST**) RECLAIM
EXCLAMATION (ALSO SEE
INTERJECTION) O AH AI AY BO EH
EY HA HI HO LA LO MY OH OW SO
ST YO AHA AIE BAH BAM BOO FEN
FIE FOH GEE GIP GRR GUP HAI
HAW HAY HEM HEP HEY HIC HOY
HUH NOW OCH OFF OHO OUF OUT
PAH PEW POH POX ROT SEE SUZ
TCH TCK TUT UGH VOW WEE WOW
YAH YOW AHEM ALAS AVOY BUFF
DEAR DRAT EGAD EVOE FAST
GARN GOOD HAIL HECH HECK HIST
HOLA HUFF HUNH HUSH HYKE
OONS OUGH PHEW PHOO PHUT
PIFF PISH POOH PRUT PUGH RATS
RIVO SCAT SIRS SOFT SOHO TCHU
TUSH WALY WEEK WEET WELL
WHAM WHAT WHEW WHEW WHIR
WHIT WUGG YOOP YULE ALACK
BRAVO EWHOW FAINS FANCY
FAUGH FEIGH GLORY GOODY
HEIGH HELLO HOLLA HUFFA
HULLO HUMPH HUZZA JOSSA
OHONE PSHAW RIGHT SALVE
SHISH SKOAL SORRY SUGAR
TEREU WAUGH WELOO WHING
WHISK WHIST WHOOP WIRRA
WOONS CARAJO CLAMOR
ENCORE HALLOO HEYDAY
HOOTAY HURRAH INDEED OUTCRY
PERFAY QUOTHA RATHER RIGHTO
SHUCKS STEADY WALKER
WHOOSH ZOUNDS CARAMBA
DOGGONE GODSAKE HOSANNA
JEEPERS JIGGERS KERCHOO
KERWHAM NICHEVO PRITHEE
RUBBISH SALAMAT TANTIVY
THUNDER WELCOME WHOOPEE
FAREWELL WAESUCKS WELLAWAY
(— **OF DISGUST**) AUH FIE FOH PAH
UGH AUGH AVOY PHEW PISH POOT
PSHA PUGH FAUGH FEICH FEIGH
PSHAW WELOO
(— **OF DISTRESS**) AI AIE HARO
HARROW
(— **OF DOUBT**) HUM HUMPH
(— **OF IMPATIENCE**) GIP PHEW

(— **OF INCREDULITY**) AHEM INDEED
WALKER
(— **OF REPUGNANCE**) UGH
(— **OF SURPRISE**) HA OW GIP LAW
HEIN HUNH LACK LAND LAWK LORD
ODSO BABAI HEUGH LAWKS MARRY
CRIMINE CRIMINY HEAVENS
JUCKIES GORBLIMY GRAMERCY
(— **OF TRIUMPH**) AH IO GRIG HEUCH
HOOCH HURRAH
(**BIBLICAL** —) SELAH
(**IRISH** —) ARRA
(**PROFANE** —) BAN
EXCLAMATION POINT BANG
SHOUT SCREAMER
EXCLUDE BAR SHUT SINK CLOSE
DEBAR EJECT EXPEL FENCE
BANISH DISBAR EXCEPT EXEMPT
FORBAR FORBID REJECT BLANKET
DEFAULT EXPUNGE FOREBAR
FOREIGN OUTTAKE OUTWALL
REPULSE RULEOUT SECLUDE
SHUTOUT SUSPEND OSTRACIZE
(PREF.) DIS
EXCLUDED EXEMPT FOREIGN
EXCLUDING BAR BUT LESS
BARRING
EXCLUSION TABU TABOO
OSTRACISM
EXCLUSIVE ALL ONLY RARE SOLE
VERY ALONE ELECT WHOLE
NARROW SELECT CLANNISH
CLIQUISH ENTIRELY RECHERCHE
(— **OF**) BEFORE
EXCLUSIVELY ALL ONLY ALONE
SINGLY ENTIRELY
EXCOGITATE CONSIDER
EXCOMMUNICATE CURSE
UNCHURCH
EXCOMMUNICATION BAN CURSE
HEREM EXCISION
EX-CONVICT LAG LAGGER
EXCORIATE FLAY GALL SCORE
STRIP ABRADE SCATHE SCORCH
BLISTER LAMBASTE
EXCREMENT LEE CRAP DIRT DREG
DUNG FRASS JAKES SIEGE HOCKEY
ORDURE REFUSE VOIDING
CROTTELS COLLUVIES
(— **OF EARTHWORM**) CAST
(— **OF FOXES**) SCUMBER
(— **OF HARES**) CROTTELS
(— **OF INSECTS**) FRASS
(PL.) DEJECTA
(PREF.) COPR(O) MERDI
EXCRESCENCE NOB PIN WEN BURL
BURR GALL HORN KNOB KNOT
KNUR LUMP SCAB WART FUSEE
FUZEE KNURL THORN EXCESS
HURTLE MORULA NUBBLE PIMPLE
BOLSTER PUSTULE RATTAIL
SPINACH CARUNCLE EPITHEMA
TUBERCLE
(— **ON BIRD'S THROAT**) WATTLE
(— **ON HORSE'S FOOT**) FIG TWITTER
(— **ON WHALE'S HEAD**) BONNET
(**FLESHY** —) SARCOMA
(**TUBERCULOUS** —) WOLF
(PREF.) GANGLI GANGLO
EXCRETA EGESTA
EXCRETE EGEST SWEAT EXCERN
SECERN DEFECATE PERSPIRE

EXCRETION SORDES ECRISIS PERISARC

EXCRUCIATE RACK GRIND AGONIZE TORMENT TORTURE

EXCRUCIATING GRINDING

EXCULPATE FREE CLEAR REMIT ACQUIT EXCUSE PARDON ABSOLVE FORGIVE JUSTIFY RELEASE PALLIATE

EXCULPATION EXCUSE

EXCURSION DIP HOP ROW DIET RIDE SAIL SPIN TOUR TRIP ESSAY JAUNT RANGE SALLY START TRAMP AIRING CANTER CRUISE FLIGHT JUNKET OUTING PASEAR RAMBLE SASHAY VAGARY VOYAGE JOURNEY OUTLOPE OUTRIDE OUTROAD CAMPAIGN ESCAPADE

EXCURSIONIST TRIPPER

EXCUSABLE VENIAL

EXCUSE OUT FAIK PLEA ALIBI COLOR GLOSS PLANE REMIT SALVO SCUSE STORY ACQUIT ESSOIN EXEMPT PARDON REASON REFUGE SCONCE SECURE SUNYIE ABSOLVE APARDON APOLOGY CONDONE ESSOIGN EVASION EXCUSAL FORGIVE OFFCOME PRETEXT DISPENSE OCCASION OVERLOOK PALLIATE PRETENCE (CONSCIENTIOUSLY —) SCRUPLE

EXCUSS SHAKE DISCARD DISCUSS

EXECRABLE BAD CURST CURSED DAMNED HEINOUS ACCURSED DAMNABLE WRETCHED

EXECRATE BAN DAMN ABHOR CURSE DETEST DEVOTE

EXECRATION CURSE ANATHEMA MALEDICTION

EXECUTE DO ACT CUT TOP BURN DASH FILL GIVE HANG HAVE KILL OBEY PASS PLAY SLAY FRAME GANCH LYNCH SCRAG YIELD DESIGN DIRECT EFFECT FINISH FULFIL GARROT GIBBET MANAGE ACHIEVE CONDUCT ENFORCE FULFILL GAROTTE PERFORM STRETCH COMPLETE DISPATCH EXPEDITE PRACTICE PRACTISE
(— BOW) WREATHE
(— POORLY) DUB
(— SUCCESSFULLY) COMPLETE

EXECUTED GIVEN
(— EXQUISITELY) CURIOUS
(— WITH CARE) ACCURATE
(CRUDELY —) DAUBY

EXECUTION GANCH TOUCH EFFECT FACTURE GARROTE HANGING TECHNIC CARRIAGE GARROTTE PRACTICE PERFORMANCE
(— BY BURNING) STAKE
(— BY DROWNING) NOYADE
(— OF WILL) FACTUM

EXECUTIONER BURRIO HEADER TORTOR BUTCHER HANGMAN HEADMAN LOCKMAN CARNIFEX EXECUTOR HEADSMAN CRUCIFIER

EXECUTIVE ROSS DEAN EXEC MAYOR WARDEN CASHIER MANAGER PODESTA PREMIER GOVERNOR OFFICIAL
(— OFFICER) CEO

EXECUTOR DOER AGENT ALBACEA SECUTOR ENFORCER MINISTER

EXEGESIS ANAGOGE ANAGOGY MIDRASH HAGGADAH

EXEMPLAR COPY TYPE MODEL FATHER MIRROR MODULE EIDOLON EXAMPLE PARABLE PATTERN PARADIGM

EXEMPLARY LAUDABLE

EXEMPLIFICATION SOUL SAMPLE CONSTAT EXAMPLE

EXEMPLIFY SAMPLE SATISFY ENSAMPLE MODELIZE

EXEMPT EXON FREE EXEEM EXEME FRANK SEVER SPARE EXPERT FIDATE IMMUNE EXCLUDE RELEASE DISPENSE EXCEPTED PRIVILEGE
(— FROM DEATH) IMMORTAL
(PREF.) IMMUNO

EXEMPTION GRACE CHARTER FREEDOM LIBERTY SWEATER BLOODWIT IMMUNITY IMPUNITY

EXEQUATUR PLACET

EXERCISE ACT AIR DIP PLY URE USE BEAR HAVE DRILL ETUDE EXERT HALMA LATIN LONGE SWEAT AIRING BREATH CAREER EMPLOY EXERCE LESSON MANUAL PARADE PRAXIS PUSHUP SCHOOL AUFGABE BREATHE DISPLAY ENHAUNT JOGGING PROBLEM ACTIVITY EXERTION FORENSIC PALESTRA PRACTICE PRACTISE
(— AUTHORITY) COMMAND
(— CONTROL) BOSS PRESIDE
(— HORSE) BREEZE
(— POWER) RULE
(—S TO REDUCE WEIGHT) SLIMNASTICS
(ACADEMIC —) PRACTICUM
(BRIEF —) THEME
(CAVALRY —) MELEE
(DEVOTIONAL —) ANGELUS
(GYMNASTIC —) PRESSUP
(MARTIAL —) BARRIERS
(MUSICAL —) ETUDE SOLFEGE VOCALISE
(PRACTICE —) DRYRUN
(PRELIMINARY —) WARMUP PROLUSION
(PUNISHMENT —) PENSUM
(REDUCING —S) SLIMNASTICS
(RHYTHMICAL —) MEDAU
(STRONG —) INTENSION
(SYSTEM OF —) AEROBICS
(UNWARRANTED —) STRETCH
(PL.) ALLEGRO ATHLETICS

EXERT DO PLY PUT DRAW EMIT HUMP STIR DRIVE SPEND SWING BESTIR EXTEND PUTOUT REVEAL STRAIN AFFORCE ENFORCE IMPRESS CHARETTE ENDEAVOR EXERCISE
(— A SPELL) TAKE
(— POWER) ACT BEAR
(— PRESSURE) PRESS SQUEEZE
(— TRACTION) HAUL

EXERTING (— POWER) AGENT

EXERTION DINT HEFT BURST ESSAY LABOR NISUS TRIAL WHILE ACTION EFFORT MOTION PINGLE STRESS STRIFE ATTEMPT TROUBLE ENDEAVOR EXERCISE STRUGGLE
(EXCESSIVE —) STRAIN
(STRENUOUS —) HUMP

EXFOLIATE SCALE SPALL SPAWL

EXFOLIATION FURFUR

EXHALATION AURA FUME REEK STEAM BREATH EXPIRY MIASMA HALITUS MALARIA FUMOSITY MEPHITIS

EXHALE CAST EMIT REEK EXUDE STEAM WHIFF EXPIRE BREATHE FURNACE REFLAIR RESPIRE EXHALATE PERSPIRE

EXHALED SFOGATO

EXHAUST DO FAG SAP BEAT BURN COOK COWL EMIT FAIL FLAG FLOG JADE KILL MATE SOAK TIRE TUCK BLAST BREAK CLEAN DRAFT DRAIN EMPTY FORDO GRUEL LEECH PETER SHOOT SPEND SWINK WASTE WEARY ABRADE BETOIL BOTTOM BUGGER EMBOSS FINISH FOREDO HARASS HATTER OVERDO TAIGLE TUCKER BREATHE CONSUME DEPLETE DEPRIVE DRAUGHT EXTRACT FATIGUE OUTWEAR SCOURGE SURREIN TRACHLE WEAROUT DISTRESS EDUCTION EVACUATE FORSPEND FORSWINK FORWEARY OVERWEAR OVERSPEND

EXHAUSTED TAM BEAT DEAD DONE DUNG GONE WEAK WORN BLOWN EMPTY JADED SPENT STANK TIRED BARREN BEATEN BUSHED EFFETE GROGGY MARCID PLAYED TOILED TRAIKY ATTAINT DRAINED EMPTIED FORDONE FORSUNG FORWORN TEDIOUS WHACKED WORNOUT BANKRUPT CONSUMED FOREDONE FOREWORN FORFAIRN FORSPENT FOUGHTEN HARASSED OUTSPENT OVERWORN
(— OF AIR) HIGH

EXHAUSTING ARDUOUS IRKSOME PREYING

EXHAUSTION EXHAUST FATIGUE SELLOUT SOOREYN DISTRESS GONENESS HEATSTROKE PROSTRATION

EXHAUSTIVE FULL MINUTE THOROUGH

EXHIBIT AIR PEN FAIR HAVE SHEW SHOW TURN WEAR CARRY SPORT STAGE BLAZON DEMEAN EVINCE EXPOSE OPPOSE OSTEND PARADE REVEAL APPROVE CONCENE DIORAMA DISPLAY EXPRESS MONSTER PERFORM PRESENT PRODUCE PROJECT PROPOSE TRADUCE BOOKFAIR BRANDISH CONCEIVE DISCLOSE DISCOVER EMBLAZON EVIDENCE FORTHSET MANIFEST SHOWCASE
(— ALARM) GLOFF
(— DOGS) BENCH
(— IN SNARLING) GRIN

EXHIBITION EXPO FAIR SALE SHOW DROLL ENTRY SALON SIGHT ANNUAL PARADE SALARY ACADEMY DISPLAY EXHIBIT PAGEANT PENSION PRESENT SHOWING STAGERY EXERCISE PERFORMANCE
(— OF DOGS) BENCH
(— ON STAGE) STAGERY
(ART —) SALON
(POETICAL —) FLYTE
(PUBLIC —) SPECIES
(RIDING —) CAROUSEL

EXHIBITIONER SERVITOR

EXHIBITIONIST HAM FLASHER HAMFATTER

EXHIBITOR SHOWER

EXHILARANT GOOFBALL

EXHILARATE AMUSE CHEER ELATE ANIMATE ELEVATE ENLIVEN GLADDEN

EXHILARATED RAD GLAD HAPPY HEADY STOKED ELEVATED SPIRITED

EXHILARATING RACY SAPID BREEZY LIVELY

EXHILARATION GAIETY JOLLITY GLADNESS HILARITY

EXHORT URGE WARN CHARM ADHORT ADVISE CHARGE DEHORT ENGAGE INCITE PREACH CAUTION ADMONISH DISSUADE

EXHORTATION ADVICE EXHORT HOMILY COUNSEL PROPHECY PREACHMENT

EXHORTER HORTATOR PREACHER

EXHUME DIG DELVE UNBURY UNTOMB UNEARTH DISINTER EXHUMATE

EXIGENCY NEED PUSH WANT EXIGENT URGENCY JUNCTURE OCCASION PRESSURE

EXIGENT DIRE VITAL URGENT CRITICAL EXACTING PRESSING

EXIGUITY PAUCITY

EXIGUOUS MEAGER MEAGRE

EXILE EXUL POOR RUIN THIN EXPEL GALUT WREAK BANISH DEPORT GALUTH OUTLAW SCANTY WRETCH EXULATE GERSHOM OUTCAST PILGRIM REFUGEE SLENDER DIASPORA FUGITIVE OUTLAWRY RELEGATE OSTRACIZE
(PLACE OF —) ELBA

EXILED FOREIGN FUGITIVE

EXIST AM BE IS ARE LIE COME GROW LIVE MOVE PASS DWELL CONSIST SUBSIST
(— IN FULL SUPPLY) FLOW

EXISTENCE ENS ESSE LIFE SEIN BEING DASEIN ENTITY IDEATE INESSE ESSENCE IDEATUM REALITY ENERGEIA IDENTITY STANDING SURVIVAL PERSONALITY
(— AFTER DEATH) AFTERLIFE
(DULL —) DEATH
(ETERNAL —) SAT
(EVER-CHANGING —) SAMSARA SANSARA
(FIRST —) ORIGIN
(IN —) GOING AROUND EXTANT
(INDEPENDENT —) ASEITY PERSEITY
(PERMANENT —) INHERENCE
(WAKING —) JAGRATA
(PREF.) ONTO

EXISTENT HARD REAL ALIVE BEING ACTUAL EXTANT EXISTING

(— IN DIFFERENT FORMS) ALLOTROPIC

(CONTINUALLY —) STUBBORN

EXISTING GOING ACTUAL EXTANT PRESENT EXISTENT

(— IN NAME ONLY) DUMMY

(SUFF.) ANT ENT

EXIT ISH DOOR GATE VENT GOING ISSUE LEAVE EGRESS EXITUS OUTLET OUTWAY EXITION OUTGATE OUTPORT PASSAGE DEBOUCHE

(HURRIED —) BOUT

EXITE BRACT

EX LIBRIS BOOKPLATE

EXOCYCLIC IRREGULAR

EXODUS EXODY EXITUS FLIGHT HEGIRA HEJIRA EXODIUM

EXON EXEMPT

EXONERATE FREE ALIBI CLEAR ACQUIT EXCUSE EXONER UNLOAD ABSOLVE RELIEVE EXCULPATE

EXOPODITE EXOPOD SQUAMA

EXORABLE PRAYABLE

EXORBITANT STEEP UNDUE ABNORMAL

EXORCISE LAY

EXORCIST BENET

EXORDIUM PREFACE PRELUDE

EXOSKELETON CORSLET CORSELET

EXOSPORIUM EXINE EXTINE EXOSPERM

EXOSTOSIS POROMA SPLINT OSSELET RINGBONE

EXOTIC ALIEN FOREIGN STRANGE ADVENTIVE RECHERCHE

EXOTOSPORE BLAST

EXOTROPIA WALLEYE

EXPAND OPE WAX BLOW BULK FLAN FLUE FOAM GROW HUFF OPEN FARCE FLASH RETCH SPLAY SWELL WIDEN DIDUCE DILATE EXTEND INTEND SPREAD SPROUT UNFOLD UNFURL AMPLIFY BALLOON BLOSSOM BOLSTER BROADEN BURGEON DEVELOP DIFFUSE DISPAND DISPLAY DISTEND EDUCATE ENLARGE EXPANSE EXPLAIN INFLATE STRETCH DISPREAD INCREASE LENGTHEN OUTREACH

(— AS A VESSEL) FLAN

(— FEATHERS) PRIDE

(— INTO PODS) KID

EXPANDED NOWY OPEN OVERT DILATE PATENT SPREAD DILATED SWOLLEN INFLATED PATULENT PATULOUS

EXPANDER EXTENDER

EXPANDING BOSOMY

EXPANSE AREA ROOM BOSOM BURST FIELD REACH TRACT EXTENT LENGTH SPREAD COUNTRY STRETCH DISTANCE EXPANSUM SEPARATE

(— OF ICE) SHEET

(— OF SEA ICE) FIELD

(— OF SPACE) VOID

(— OF WATER) OCEAN

(BROAD —) ACRE MAIN

(FLAT —) LEVEL

(GREAT —) MAIN

(IMMEASURABLE — OF TIME) ETERNITY

(IMMENSE —) OCEAN

(INDEFINITE —) VAGUE

(UNBROKEN —) MASS

(VAST —) SEA

(WIDE —) BREADTH

EXPANSIBILITY ELATER

EXPANSION ALA BULB WING FLUSH SPLAY GROWTH SPREAD ECTASIA ECTASIS EXPANSE HASTULA ACROCYST COQUILLE DIASTOLE DILATION INCREASE SWELLING

(— IN SEEDS) ALA WING

(— OF COBRA'S NECK) HOOD

(— OF DECK) SPONSON

(— OF LEAF-BASE) SPUR

(— OF RIVER) BROAD

(— OF ROADWAY) LAYBY

(FOLIOSE —) LAMINA

(LITURGICAL —) EMBOLISM

EXPANSIVE FREE WIDE BROAD GENIAL ELASTIC LIBERAL GENEROUS SPACIOUS SWELLING

EXPATIATE DWELL DILATE EXPAND SPREAD AMPLIFY BROADEN DESCANT DIFFUSE ENLARGE SATISFY

EXPATRIATE EXILE EXPAT EXPEL BANISH OUTLAW OUTCAST

EXPATRIATION EXILE

EXPECT ASK DEEM HOPE LITE LOOK STAY TEND TROW WAIT WEEN ABIDE AWAIT THINK ATTEND DEMAND INTEND LIPPEN RECKON PRESUME REQUIRE SUPPOSE SUSPECT CALCULATE

(— CONFIDENTLY) TRUST

(— TOO MUCH) OVERWEEN

EXPECTANT AHIP ATIPTOE CHARGED HOPEFUL INCHOATE

EXPECTANTLY AGOG TIPTOE

EXPECTATION HOPE VIEW WAIT WEEN TRUST EXPECT FUTURE ESPEIRE OPINION SUPPOSE THOUGHT WEENING PROSPECT

(CONFIDENT —) TRUST

EXPECTED DUE NATURAL SUPPOSED

EXPECTORANT CINEOL STORAX CINEOLE EMETINE AMMONIAC CREOSOTE GUAIACOL TEREBENE

EXPECTORATE SPIT

EXPECTORATION EMPTYSIS

EXPEDIENCE ARTIFICE

EXPEDIENT FIT WISE ATAJO CRAFT DODGE JOKER KNACK SALVO SHIFT DEVICE RESORT STRING DODGERY POLITIC STOPGAP ARTIFICE RESOURCE DESIRABLE MAKESHIFT

EXPEDITATE LAW

EXPEDITATION LAWING

EXPEDITE HIE EASY FREE HURRY SPEED EXPEDE GREASE HASTEN QUICKEN DISPATCH

EXPEDITION CAMP FARE PLOY ROAD TREK DRAVE HASTE HURRY RANGE SCOUT TRADE SAFARI VOYAGE CARAVAN CRUSADE ENTRADA JOURNEY OUTLOPE SERVICE WARFARE WARPATH

COMMANDO HEADHUNT PROGRESS

(FISHING —) DRAVE

(HUNTING —) SAFARI

(MILITARY —) HARKA CRUSADE HOSTING JOURNEY WARPATH

EXPEDITIOUS FAST HASTY QUICK RAPID READY SHORT PROMPT SPEEDY

EXPEL CAN OUT USH BLOW BOLT DRUM DUMP FIRE OUST VOID WARP AVOID CHASE CHECK DEPEL EJECT ERUPT EVICT EXILE KNOCK SPURT BANISH BOUNCE DEBOUT DEPORT DEVOID DISBAR DISOWN OUTPUT OUTRAY REFUSE ABANDON EXCLUDE EXPULSE EXTRUDE OBTRUDE SCRATCH SECLUDE SUSPEND DISLODGE DISPLACE EVACUATE FORJUDGE

(— AIR) COUGH

(— FROM MEMBERSHIP) HAMMER

(— GAS) BELCH

(— SUDDENLY) SKIRT

(PREF.) DIS

EXPEND USE LEND SPEND SPORT WASTE WREAK DEFRAY IMPEND OCCUPY OUTLAY PONDER CONSUME DISPEND EROGATE EXHAUST OVERUSE DISBURSE SQUANDER

EXPENDITURE COST MISE OUTGO PENSE CHARGE OUTLAY EXPENSE OUTFLOW PENSION SPENDING

(— OF ENERGY) EFFORT

EXPENSE FX COST GAFF LOSS BATTA PRICE SUMPT CHARGE DAMAGE GERSUM ONCOST OUTLAY OUTSET AVERAGE OVERHEAD SUMPTURE

(— OF CARRYING) CARRIAGE

(— OF TREAT) SAM

(PL.) BATTA COSTS MISES

EXPENSIVE DEAR HIGH SALT PRICY STEEP STIFF COSTLY LAVISH PRICEY APICIAN LIBERAL THRIFTY

(— IN DIET) APICIAN

EXPERIENCE SEE TRY FEEL FIND GUST HAVE HENT HOLD KNOW LIVE TEST ASSAY EVENT PROOF PROVE SKILL TASTE TRIAL USAGE BEHOLD EXPERT FRAIST ORDEAL SAMPLE SUFFER APPROVE CALVARY CONTACT FEELING FURNACE KNOWING REALIZE SUSTAIN UNDERGO ESCAPADE

(— GOOD OR ILL FORTUNE) SPEED

(— OF INTENSE SUFFERING) CALVARY

(— WITH BITTERNESS) BEAR

(CALAMITOUS —) ADVERSITY

(DRUG —) TRIP

(ENJOYABLE —) GROOVE

(EXCITING —) TRIP

(FIRST —) TIROCINIUM

(HALLUCINATORY —) TRIP FREAKOUT

(HORRIFYING —) NIGHTMARE

(HUMILIATING —) PRATFALL

(IRRITATING —) RUB

(ORDINARY —) USE

(PAINFUL —) FIT

(PARTIAL —) GUST

(TASTE —) GUST

(TEDIOUS —) DRAG

(TRYING —) ORDEAL

(UNPLEASANT —) BUMMER MISERY

(VISIONARY —) PHANTOM

(WARNING —) LESSON

EXPERIENCED HAD MET OLD SEEN USED SALTY EXPERT SALTED TRADED ANCIENT PRACTIC THRIVEN VETERAN WEIGHED SEASONED

(— INTENSIVELY) ACUTE

(ACTUALLY —) SPECIOUS

EXPERIENTIAL EMPIRIC

EXPERIMENT SHY TRY TEST ASSAY ESSAY TRIAL ATTEMPT CONTROL

(PREF.) EMPIRICO EMPIRIO

EXPERIMENTAL SAMPLE

(NOT —) STANDARD

EXPERT ACE DAB PRO DEFT FULL GOOD GURU PERT ADEPT CRACK FLASH MAVEN MAVIN READY SHARP SWELL ADROIT ARTIST CLEVER FACILE HABILE KAHUNA MASTER MAYVIN PANDIT PERTLY QUAINT SUBTLE WIZARD ARTISTE ATTACHE CAPABLE DABSTER MEISTER PERFECT PERITUS SKILLED DEXTROUS GAINSOME SKILLFUL SPEEDFUL VIRTUOSO PROFESSED PROFICIENT

(— IN JEWISH LAW) DAYAN

(— LEVEL IN JUDO) DAN

(— ON DRIVING LOGS) LAKER

(BANK —) SHROFF

(GREAT —) ONER

(SCIENTIFIC —) BOFFIN

(PL.) PERITI

(SUFF.) ICIAN

EXPERTISE MOXIE

EXPERTNESS SAVVY SKILL FACILITY HABILITY

EXPIATE ABY SKUG ATONE AVERT ASSOIL RANSOM

EXPIATORY PIACULAR

EXPIRATION END DEATH BREATH EFFLUX ELAPSE EXPIRE EXPIRY

(SPASMODIC —) SNEEZE

EXPIRE DIE END EMIT FALL EXPEL GHOST LAPSE ELAPSE EXHALE INLAIK OUTRUN PERISH RUNOUT

EXPIRED UP DEAD EXPIATE

EXPIRING DYING

EXPIRY ISH CLOSE DEATH EFFLUX

EXPLAIN OPEN REDE SAVE SCAN UNDO WISE AREAD AREED CLEAR GLOSS GLOZE PLANE RECHE SOLVE SPEED TOUCH DEFINE EXPAND EXPLAT EXPONE REMENE RIDDLE UNFOLD ABSOLVE ACCOUNT AMPLIFY CLARIFY COMMENT CONTRUE DECLARE DEVELOP DISCUSS EXHIBIT EXPOUND JUSTIFY RESOLVE CONSTRUE DESCRIBE MANIFEST SIMPLIFY UNPLIGHT UNWONDER

(— BY HYPOTHESIS) SALVE

EXPLAINER EXPONENT

EXPLAINING EXPONENT

EXPLANATION KEY NOTE FARSE GLOSS SALVE SALVO ANSWER CAVEAT ACCOUNT APOLOGY

ADDENDUM EXEGESIS INNUENDO NOTATION SOLUTION
(PRELIMINARY —) PREFACE
EXPLETIVE ACH AND GEE BOSH EGAD GOSH OATH BEGAD MODAL BEHEAR SDEATH TUNKET DAMMISH MORBLEU GOODYEAR GRACIOUS
EXPLICATE OPEN CLEAR EXPAND UNFOLD ACCOUNT EXPLAIN
EXPLICATION CRIB ANALYSIS
EXPLICIT OPEN CLEAR EXACT FIXED PLAIN EXPRESS PRECISE ABSOLUTE DEFINITE IMPLICIT POSITIVE PUNCTUAL SPECIFIC
EXPLICITLY BARELY DIRECT FORMALLY
EXPLODE POP BLOW FIRE BELCH BLAST BURST CRUMP ERUPT GOOFF PLUFF SHOOT SQUIB SPRING BACKFIRE DETONATE DISPLODE
EXPLOIT ACT USE DEED FEAT GEST JEST MILK WORK GESTE GOUGE STUNT PERFORM SUCCESS CHIVALRY PARERGON PROPERTY
(— FINANCIALLY) RIPOFF
(— SUCCESSFULLY) PARLAY
EXPLOITATION RIPOFF
EXPLOITER KULAK
EXPLORATION SPY PROBE SEARCH EXPLORE
(— OF CAVES) SPELEOLOGY
EXPLORATORY FRONTIER PROBATIVE PROBATORY
EXPLORE DO DIP MAP SPY DIVE DRAG FEEL VIEW CHART COAST DELVE RANGE SCOUT SOUND SEARCH EXAMINE PALPATE BOTANIZE DISCOVER
(— CAVES) SPELUNK
(— FOR MINERALS) PROSPECT
EXPLORER CAVEMAN PIONEER COLUMBUS
AMERICAN BOYD BYRD COOK GRAY HALL KANE LONG PIKE BEEBE CLARK FIALA GOULD HAYES JAMES LEWIS MUSIL NILES PEARY RONNE AKELEY ASHLEY BRYANT CARVER CATLIN COLTER DELONG EKLUND GIMBEL GREELY HENSON HERVEY LUMMIS RAINEY WILKES AGASSIZ ANDREWS BALCHEN BALDWIN BURNHAM FREMONT POULTER STANLEY VERRILL WELLMAN WORKMAN BRAINARD BRIDGMAN LOCKWOOD MELVILLE SCHWATKA ELLSWORTH MACMILLAN DANENHOWER HUNTINGTON HALLIBURTON
AUSTRALIAN WILLS MAWSON STUART FORREST KENNEDY LINDSAY WILKINS BERNACCHI
AUSTRIAN HUGEL PAYER GLASER BAUMANN PAULITSCHKE
BELGIAN GERLACHE
CANADIAN MACKAY JOLLIET SIMPSON BARTLETT PALLISER IBERVILLE VINCENNES STEFANSSON
COLOMBIAN REYES
DANISH BOCK HOLM KOCH FREUCHEN MIKKELSEN RASMUSSEN
DUTCH TASMAN NIEUWENHUIS

ENGLISH BACK BASS BENT BYNG COOK EYRE BAKER BATES BRUCE DAVYS EVANS FUCHS GRANT OATES PARRY SCOTT SPEKE STURT YOUNG BAILEY BURTON CONDER GROGAN HEARNE HOWITT LANDER MAWSON OSBORN PHILBY SABINE WILSON CAMERON CHESNEY DAMPIER DEWINDT GREGORY HOLDICH JACKSON WEDDELL WHYMPER WICKHAM FLINDERS FRANKLIN GRENFELL JOHNSTON SCORESBY ALEXANDER VANCOUVER WARBURTON INGLEFIELD MCCLINTOCK SCHOMBURGK SHACKLETON LIVINGSTONE YOUNGHUSBAND
FRENCH BONIN MONTS BINGER BRAZZA CALLIE DULUTH GENTIL HAARDT ABBADIE CARTIER CRAMPEL CREVAUX FOUREAU GARNIER LASALLE NICOLET BONVALOT COUDREAU HENNEPIN MARCHAND RADISSON CAILLIAUD CHAMPLAIN IBERVILLE MARQUETTE VINCENNES
GERMAN EMIN LENZ BARTH PFEIL POGGE REISS VOGEL DECKEN FLEGEL JUNKER PETERS ROHLFS FISCHER NEUWIED NIEBUHR OVERWEG WEGENER DENHARDT FILCHNER FRANCOIS HUMBOLDT KOLDEWEY KOTZEBUE WISSMANN FEDERMANN GUSSFELDT WEYPRECHT LEICHHARDT SCHLAGINTWEIT
ICELANDIC ERICSON
IRISH BURKE SHACKLETON
ITALIAN ZENO CABOT CAGNI GESSI CASATI NOBILE ABRUZZI BELZONI CODAZZI FILIPPI PIAGGIA ALBERTIS ANTINORI BECCARIA COLUMBUS CADAMOSTO VERRAZANO SCHIAPARELLI
NEW ZEALAND HAAST HILLARY
NORWEGIAN ASTRUP NANSEN WISTING AMUNDSEN JOHANSEN SVERDRUP HEYERDAHL JOHANNESEN BORCHGREVINK
PORTUGUESE CABRAL DAGAMA CABRILLO COVILHAO MAGELLAN FERNANDES
RUSSIAN TOLL PAPANIN POTANIN WRANGEL PRZHEVALSKI BELLINGSHAUSEN
SCOTTISH RAE PARK ROSS BRUCE LAING LAIRD BAIKIE CADELL FORBES THOMSON MITCHELL MACKENZIE CLAPPERTON LIVINGSTONE
SPANISH ANZA OJEDA AYLLON BALBOA CABEZA CORTES DESOTO AGUIRRE ALARCON CORDOBA MENDOZA PIZARRO BASTIDAS CARDENAS CORONADO GRIJALVA ORELLANA VIZCAINO ESCALANTE ESTAVANICO
SWEDISH HEDIN ANDREE NATHORST PALANDER ANDERSSON NORDENSKJOLD
SWISS BODMER PICCARD MUNZINGER
EXPLOSION POP BANG BLOW

BLAST BURST CRUMP SALVO BLOWUP BOUNCE REPORT PLOSION INCIDENT OUTBURST
(FUEL —) BACKFIRE
(SLIGHT —) PLUFF
EXPLOSIVE EGG TNT MINE AMVIS AMATOL JOVITE LIMPET POWDER TETRYL TONITE TORPEX TOUCHY TRITON ABELITE AMMONAL AZOTINE DUNNITE LIGNOSE LYDDITE PLOSIVE PRIMING PUDDING SHIMOSE THORITE AMMONITE CHEDDITE DYNAMITE ECRASITE ERUPTIVE GELATINE MAXIMITE MELINITE PYROLITE ROBURITE SABULITE SAXONITE SECURITE VOLATILE RACKAROCK SAMSONITE
(— COMPOUND) TNT
(CHARGE OF —) TULIP RESPONDER
(NOT —) SOFT
EXPONENT INDEX POWER
(SUFF.) ICIAN
EXPORT OUTCARRY
(— HERRING) KLONDIKE
EXPORTATION EXPORT OUTPORT
EXPOSE AIR BARE GIVE OPEN RISK SHOW STRIP BEWRAY DEBUNK DETECT EXPONE GIBBET OBJECT OPPOSE REVEAL UNHUSK UNMASK DISPLAY EXHIBIT EXPOUND PILLORY PROPINE PUBLISH SUBJECT UNCOVER UNEARTH UNTRUSS BRANDISH DISCLOSE DISCOVER MUCKRAKE RIDICULE SATIRIZE UNCLOTHE UNSHROUD
(— FOR BLEACHING) CROFT
(— INDECENTLY) FLASH
(— ORE) HUSH
(— PLAYING CARD) BURN
(— SELF TO) WAGE
(— SUDDENLY) FLASH
(— TO AIR) AERATE
(— TO ATTENTION) PARADE
(— TO DANGER) JUMP COMMIT SUBMIT
(— TO FUMES) FUMIGATE
(— TO HAZARD) RISK
(— TO HEAT) AIR
(— TO INFAMY) GIBBET
(— TO MOISTURE) RET
(— TO RADIATION) PUMP
(— TO SCORN) PILLORY
(— TO SULFUR DIOXIDE) STOVE
(— TO SUN) INSOLATE SOLARIZE
(— TO SUN AND AIR) FIELD
EXPOSED AIRY BARE OPEN BLEAK LIABLE PUBLIC UNSAFE SUBJECT VEILLESS
(— TO) AGAINST
(— TO DANGER) INSECURE
EXPOSITION EXPO FAIR GECK SHOW ZEND TRACT APERCU EXPOSE METHOD SURVEY ACCOUNT EXPOSAL MIDRASH ANALYSIS EXEGESIS EXPOSURE EXTHESIS HAGGADAH TREATISE
(— OF FEAST) SYNAXARY
EXPOSITORY EXEGETIC
EXPOSTULATE ARGUE OBJECT DISCUSS EXAMINE PROTEST
EXPOSTULATION PROTEST
EXPOSURE ASPECT EXPOSE

EXPOSAL FLASHING FRONTAGE PROSPECT
(— OF CARDS) SPREAD
(— OF KING) CHECK
(— TO AIR) AERATE AIRING
(BODY —) FLASH
(PHOTOGRAPHIC —) SHOT
(PUBLIC —) NOTORIETY
EXPOUND OPEN REDE UNDO GLOZE SENSE TREAT DEFINE EXPONE EXPOSE COMMENT DEVELOP DISCUSS EXPLAIN EXPOSIT EXPRESS CONSTRUE SIMPLIFY PHILOSOPHIZE
(— SCRIPTURES) PROPHESY
EXPOUNDER MUFTI MULLAH SCRIBE EXPRESS EXPONENT HERMETIC
(— OF THEORY) ALFAQUI PHILOSOPHER
EXPRESS AIR BID PUT SAY CAST EMIT FAST PASS POST VENT COUCH EMOTE FRAME OPINE SPEAK STATE UTTER VOICE WIELD BROACH DEMEAN DENOTE DIRECT EVINCE IMPORT PHRASE ABREACT BREATHE DECLARE DICTATE EXPOUND EXPREME TESTIFY DEFINITE DESCRIBE DISPATCH EXPLICIT INTIMATE MANIFEST
(— APPROVAL) AGREE ACCEDE APPLAUD
(— AS LANGUAGE) LAY
(— AT LENGTH) EXPAND
(— A VIEW) OPINE
(— BY GESTURE) BECK
(— BY LAUGHTER) LAUGH
(— CONCERN) CLUCK
(— DISAPPROVAL) BOO CHIDE DECRY GROAN CATCALL
(— DISDAIN) TUT
(— EFFERVESCENTLY) CHORTLE
(— FOLLY) EXPAND
(— GRATITUDE) THANK AGGRATE
(— GRIEF) DEPLORE
(— INDIRECTLY) IMPLY
(— IN OTHER WORDS) REDUCE PARAPHRASE
(— IN WORDS) SAY DRAW SPEAK PHRASE
(— NUMERICALLY) EVALUATE
(— ONE'S FEELINGS) FLOW
(— SORROW) LAMENT COMPLAIN
(— WILLINGNESS) CONSENT
(NOT AN —) LOCAL
EXPRESSION DIT HIT SAY CAST EUGE FACE FORM MIEN POSE SHOW SIGN TERM VULT WORD ADIEU GLIFF IDIOM SNEER TOKEN VOICE BYWORD DILOGY DIVERB EFFECT FACIES ORACLE PHRASE SPEECH SYMBOL COMMENT DESCANT EPITHET EXPRESS GRIMACE ALLEGORY AUSDRUCK DANICISM FELICITY LACONISM MONOMIAL
(— IN FEW WORDS) BREVITY
(— OF ANNOYANCE) SOH
(— OF APPROVAL) EUGE PLACET
(— OF ASSENT) CONTENT
(— OF BEAUTY) ART
(— OF CHOICE) VOTE
(— OF CONTEMPT) COBLOAF

(— **OF DELIGHT**) WHEE
(— **OF DISPLEASURE**) FROWN
(— **OF DISTASTE**) FACE
(— **OF HOMAGE**) OVATION
(— **OF JOY**) GREETING
(— **OF OPINION**) EDITORIAL
(— **OF RESPECT**) DUTY
(— **OF SADNESS**) SHADE
(— **OF SCORN**) GECK
(— **OF SINGLE IDEA**) RHEME
(**APT** —) FELICITY
(**CHEMICAL** —) EQUATION
(**COMMONPLACE** —) BROMIDE
(**CORRECT** —) SUMPSIMUS
(**CURT** —) LACONIC
(**FACIAL** —) GRIN CHEER SCOWL
SMILE
(**HACKNEYED** —) CLICHE
(**HIGH-FLOWN** —) EUPHUISM
(**INCONGRUOUS** —) BULL
(**LOUD** —) CLAMOR
(**MATHEMATICAL** —) INDEX SERIES
BINOMIAL EQUATION FUNCTION
INTEGRAL
(**MOCKING** —) SCOFF
(**MOMENTARY** —) SHADE
(**PECULIAR** —) IDIOM
(**PET** —) CANT
(**PUERILE** —) BOYISM
(**SARCASTIC** —) GIBE JIBE
(**SERIOUS** —) EARNEST
(**SINCERE** —) CANDOR
(**SYMBOLIC** —) FORMULA
(**TENDER** —) LANGUISH
(**TRITE** —) CLICHE
(**UNRESTRAINED** —) EFFUSION
(**VERBAL** —) LETTER
(**VOCAL** —) TONE
(**VULGAR** —) SOLECISM
(**WISE** —) ORACLE
(**SUFF.**) LOG(ER)(IA)(IAN)(IC)(ICAL)
(IST)(UE)(Y)
EXPRESSIONLESS BLANK STONY
GLASSY LEADEN SODDEN VACANT
WOODEN TONELESS
EXPRESSIVE POETIC TONGUED
ELOQUENT EMPHATIC SPEAKING
EXPRESSIVENESS DICTION
DELICACY TOURNURE ELOQUENCE
EXPRESSLY NAMELY EXPRESS
PRESSLY FORMALLY
EXPRESSWAY FREEWAY
SPEEDWAY
EXPROBATE CENSURE UPBRAID
EXPULSION EXILE BOUNCE OUSTER
BANNIMUS EJECTION EXCISION
(— **OF SPORES**) ABJECTION
EXPUNGE BLOT DELE ERASE SLASH
CANCEL DELETE EFFACE EXCISE
SCRAPE DESTROY SCRATCH
DISPUNGE
EXPURGATE GELD PURGE
CASTRATE
EXPURGATION BOWDLERISM
EXQUISITE FOP DUDE FINE NICE
PERT PINK RARE DANDY EXACT
CHOICE DAINTY CAREFUL
ELEGANT GEMLIKE PERFECT
REFINED AFFECTED DELICATE
ETHEREAL MACARONI RECHERCHE
EXQUISITELY CHOICELY
EXSCIND CUT SEVER EXCISE
EXTANT ALIVE BEING LIVING

VISIBLE EXISTING MANIFEST
(**PREF.**) NEO
EXTEMPORE SUDDEN OFFHAND
IMPROVISO
EXTEMPORIZE ADLIB
EXTEND GO EKE LIE RUN BEAR
BUSH COME DATE DRAW GROW
LAST OPEN PASS PUSH RISE ROLL
SPAN SPIN BREDE BULGE CARRY
COVER FARCE REACH RENEW
RETCH SEIZE SHOOT STENT VERGE
WIDEN AMOUNT DEEPEN DEPLOY
DILATE EXPAND INTEND OUTLIE
SPREAD SPRING STRAIN STREAK
THRUST TRENCH AMPLIFY
BROADEN DIFFUSE DISPLAY
DISTEND ENLARGE OVERLAP
OVERRUN PORRECT PORTEND
PRODUCE PROFFER PROJECT
PROLONG PROMOTE PROTEND
RADIATE STRETCH CONTINUE
ELONGATE INCREASE LENGTHEN
OUTREACH PROROGUE PROTRACT
PROTRUDE OUTSPREAD
PROPAGATE OUTSTRETCH
(— **ACTIVITIES**) BRANCH
(— **AROUND**) GIRTH
(— **HAND**) RAX
(— **IN SPACE**) DURE
(— **IRREGULARLY**) TRAIL
(— **OVER**) SPAN COVER CROSS
CONTAIN OVERLAP OVERRIDE
(— **SAIL**) SHEET
(— **THE FRONT**) DEPLOY
(— **TO**) LINE REACH
EXTENDED FAT LONG OPEN BROAD
EXTENT SPREAD EXTENSE
LENGTHY PROLATE SPLAYED
EXPANDED INTENDED
(**PREF.**) MEG(A) MEGAL(O)
EXTENDER INERT FILLER LIGNIN
EXTENDING BROAD
(— **OVER**) ASTRIDE
EXTENSION ARM EKE ELL AREA
CAPE LIMB SCOPE POCKET SATIVA
SPHERE SPREAD BREADTH
STRETCH ADDENDUM ADDITION
DURATION INCREASE PROTENSE
(— **OF BUILDING MATERIAL**) APRON
(— **OF CREDIT**) DATING
(— **OF MINERAL VEIN**) FLAT
(— **OF RACE TRACK**) CHUTE SHUTE
(— **OF SHELL**) LAPPET
(— **OF TIME**) RESPITE
(— **OF WAGON FRAME**) THRIPPLE
(**BALLET** —) BATTEMENT
EXTENSIVE HUGE VAST WIDE
AMPLE BROAD LARGE EXTENSE
IMMENSE EXPANDED FARFLUNG
INFINITE SPACIOUS SWEEPING
EXTENT DUE RUN TAX AREA BODY
BULK DEAL GAGE LEVY PASS SIZE
WRIT AMBIT DEPTH FIELD GAUGE
LIMIT RANGE REACH SCOPE SPACE
STENT SWEEP TRACK AMOUNT
ASSIZE ATTACK DEGREE LENGTH
SPREAD STREEK ACREAGE
ASSAULT BREADTH COMPASS
CONTENT EXPANSE PURVIEW
SEIZURE STRETCH VARIETY
DISTANCE INCREASE LATITUDE
OUTREACH QUANTITY STRAIGHT
(— **OF FRONT**) FRONTAGE

(— **OF JURISDICTION**) VERGE
(— **OF LAND**) HEIGHT CONTINENT
(— **OF SPACE**) ROOM
(— **OF TIME**) SPACE
(**BROAD** —) SWEEP MAGNITUDE
(**GREATEST** —) MAX MAXIMUM
(**RELATIVE** —) SCALE
(**SOME** —) BIT
(**UNLIMITED** —) INFINITY
(**UTMOST** —) FULL
(**VAST** —) DEEP
(**VERTICAL** —) ALTITUDE
EXTENTION (— **OF LETTER**) TAIL
EXTENUATE THIN GLOZE MINCE
EXCUSE LESSEN SOOTHE WEAKEN
DIMINISH PALLIATE
EXTERIOR CRUST ECTAD ECTAL
OUTER SHELL EXTERN OUTSIDE
OUTWARD SURFACE EXOTERIC
EXTERNAL OUTLYING
(**PREF.**) OUT
EXTERMINATE WIPE EXPEL
UPROOT ABOLISH DESTROY
EXTERMINATION (**RACIAL** —)
GENOCIDE
EXTERNAL OUT OUTER EXTERN
OUTSIDE OUTWARD STRANGE
EXOTERIC EXTERIOR INCIDENT
PHYSICAL PERIPHERAL
(**PREF.**) ECT(O) OUT
EXTERNALITY OUTNESS
EXTERNALIZE OBJECTIFY
EXTERNALLY OUTWARD WITHOUT
EXTINCT DEAD BYGONE DEFUNCT
QUENCHED
(— **MAN**) KANJERA
(**PREF.**) NECR(O)
EXTINCTION DOOM FINE DEATH
EXPIRY DELETION
EXTINGUISH OUT DAMP DOUT
REDD STUB ANNUL CHOKE CRUSH
DINCH DOUSE DOWSE DROWN
QUELL REPEL SLAKE SNUFF STAMP
ASLAKE QUENCH STANCH STIFLE
ABOLISH BLANKET DESTROY
ECLIPSE EXPIATE EXTINCT
OBSCURE OPPRESS SLOCKEN
STAUNCH SUPPRESS
(— **BY CRUSHING**) DINCH
(— **CIGARETTE**) SNUB
EXTINGUISHED OUT DEAD EXTINCT
EXTINGUISHER DOUTER STAUNCH
BACKPACK QUENCHER STANCHER
EXTIRPATE DELE ROOT STUB
ERASE EXPEL STAMP STOCK
EXCISE EXTIRP UPROOT DESTROY
EXSCIND OUTROOT SUPPLANT
EXTIRPATION ROOTAGE EXCISION
EXTOL CRY FETE HYMN LAUD BLESS
CRACK EXALT KUDOS ROOSE
SPEAK EXTOLL PRAISE ADVANCE
APPLAUD COLLAUD COMMEND
ELEVATE ENHANCE GLORIFY
MAGNIFY RESOUND UPRAISE
EMBLAZON EULOGIZE PROCLAIM
EXTOLMENT PRECONY
EXTORT MILK PEEL PILL RAMP
BLEED BRIBE EDUCE EXACT FORCE
PINCH WREST WRING COMPEL
ELICIT SPONGE STRAIN WRENCH
WRITHE EXTRACT OUTWREST
EXTORTION CHOUT GOUGE
EXTORT HOLDUP SCOTAL BRIBERY

PILLAGE CHANTAGE EXACTION
RAPACITY SHAKEDOWN
EXTORTIONATE HARD CRIMINAL
GRINDING
EXTORTIONER BRIBER POLLER
SHAVER BLEEDER VAMPIRE
EXTORTIONIST POLLER
EXTRA ODD GASH MORE ORRA
OVER PLUS ADDED SPARE SPECIAL
SURPLUS SUPERIOR LAGNIAPPE
(**PREF.**) HYPER SUPER
EXTRACT DIG PRY CITE COPY DRAW
KINO KOLA MILK PULL SOAK
ANIMA BLEED CUTCH DRAFT
EDUCE ELUTE EXACT KUTCH
KYPOO QUOTE RENES RUSOT
SCRAP STEEP WRING CORTIN
CURARE DECOCT DEDUCE DERIVE
DEWTRY DISTIL ELICIT ELIXIR
EVULSE EXTORT GOBBET GUACIN
MULIUM OVARIN REMOVE RENDER
RUSWUT TRIPOS UZARON
ABORTIN AMALTAS ARCANUM
CATECHU DESCENT DISTILL
DRAUGHT ERGOTIN ESSENCE
ESTREAT EXCERPT EXHAUST
FUMARIA INTRAIT LIMBECK
MONESIA PASSEWA SUMMARY
VANILLA ACETRACT AMBRETTE
GINGERIN HYPERNIC INFUSION
LICORICE PERICOPE SEPARATE
TIKITIKI TINCTURE WITHDRAW
(— **BY BOILING**) DECOCT ELIXATE
(— **BY DIGGING**) GRUB
(— **DATA FROM COMPUTER**) READ
(— **FORCIBLY**) MULCT EVULSE
(— **FROM ACACIA**) KATH CASHOO
CATECHU
(— **FROM BERBERIS**) RUSOT
RUSWUT
(— **OF BARK**) FLUONYMIN
(— **OF GINGER**) JAKE JAKEY
(— **ONE**) STONE
(— **WITH LIQUID**) LEACH
(**ALOE** —) ORCIN ORCINOL
(**TANNING** —) AMALTAS
EXTRACTION KIN BIRTH BROOD
STOCK ORIGIN DESCENT EDITION
ESSENCE EXTRACT EXTREAT
BREEDING TINCTURE
(— **OF ROOTS**) EVOLUTION
(— **OF STEAM**) BLEEDING
EXTRACTIVE AGAR BANG BHANG
AMAROID CARAGEEN
EXTRACTOR JUICER
EXTRADITE BANISH
EXTRANEOUS ALIEN OUTER
EXOTIC FOREIGN OUTLYING
SPURIOUS
EXTRAORDINARILY BYOUS
EXTRAORDINARY ODD FREM
ONCO RARE BYOUS ENORM
SMASH DAMNED EXEMPT MIGHTY
RAGING SIGNAL AWESOME
CORKING CURIOUS HUMMING
NOTABLE SPECIAL STRANGE
UNUSUAL ABNORMAL ESPECIAL
EXIMIOUS FORINSEC FRABJOUS
SINGULAR SMASHING
UNCOMMON PHENOMINAL
PRODIGIOUS
EXTRARETINAL PAROPTIC
EXTRATERRESTRIAL ALIEN

EXTRAVAGANCE CAMP FRILL
PRIDE WASTE LUXURY EXPENSE
RAMPANCY SQUANDER UNTHRIFT
WILDNESS PROFUSION
SATURNALIA
(MENTAL —) MADNESS
EXTRAVAGANT MAD HIGH LUSH
WILD FANCY FISHY FOLLE LARGE
OUTRE COSTLY GOTHIC HEROIC
LAVISH SHRILL WANTON
BAROQUE BIZARRE COSTLEW
FANATIC FLAMING FURIOUS
NIMIOUS PROFUSE RAMPANT
VAGRANT INSOLENT PRODIGAL
RECKLESS ROMANTIC UNTHRIFT
WANDERER WASTEFUL
BOMBASTIC PROFLIGATE
EXTRAVAGANTLY LARGE
EXTRAVAGANZA FEERIE
EXTRAVAGATION VIBEX
EXTRAVASATION EFFUSION
EXTREME NTH BLUE DEEP DIRE
HIGH LAST RANK SORE VILE ACUTE
BLACK CLOSE CRUEL DENSE DIZZY
FINAL GREAT LIMIT PITCH STEEP
ULTRA UNDUE UTTER ARDENT
ARRANT BRAZEN DEADLY FAROUT
FIERCE HEROIC LENGTH MORTAL
SAVAGE SEVERE STRONG UTMOST
WOUNDY ABYSMAL DRASTIC
FEARFUL FORWARD FRANTIC
HOWLING INTENSE OUTWARD
PROFUSE RADICAL SURFEIT
VICIOUS VIOLENT ALMIGHTY
DEVILISH DREADFUL EGYPTIAN
ENORMOUS FABULOUS FARTHEST
GREATEST MERCIFUL SPENDFUL
TERRIBLE TERRIFIC ULTIMATE
EXQUISITE
(NOT —) SWEET
(TO THE —) INSPADES
(PL.) PASO
(PREF.) ACR(O) ARCH
EXTREMELY SO BIG DOG TOO WAY
BONE DEAD EVER FULL MAIN
RANK SELI THAT UNCO VERY
AWFUL BLACK BULLY BYOUS
CRAZY CRUEL EXTRA HEAPS RIGHT
SELLE SOWAN SUPER BITTER
DAMNED DEADLY DEUCED HIGHLY
MIGHTY NATION POISON SORELY
SURELY UNCOLY APLENTY
AWFULLY BOILING CRUELLY
EXTREME GALLOWS HOPPING
INNERLY SOPPING STAVING

ALMIGHTY ENORMOUS MORTALLY
PRECIOUS PROPERLY
EXTREMISM JACOBINISM
EXTREMIST CRAZY ULTRA JACOBIN
RADICAL SANSCULOTTE
EXTREMITY END TIP HEAD NEED
PUSH TAIL CLOSE LIMIT SHIFT
START VERGE BORDER FINGER
EXIGENT EXTREME ACROSTIC
ALTITUDE DISASTER JUNCTURE
OUTRANCE TERMINAL
(— OF MOON) HORN
(— OF TENDRIL) HOLDFAST
(— OF TOOTH ROOT) APEX
(HORSE'S —) POINT
(REMOTEST —) CORNER
(PREF.) ACR(O)
EXTRICATE FREE HELP WIND CLEAR
LOOSE RESCUE SQUIRM OUTWIND
EXPEDITE LIBERATE UNTANGLE
(— ONESELF) WANGLE
EXTRINSIC ALIEN EVERY FOREIGN
OUTWARD EXTERNAL OUTLYING
EXTROVERT SYNTONIC
EXTRUDE BEAR SPEW EJECT EXPEL
SHOOT PROJECT PROTRUDE
EXUBERANCE BEANS PRICE
EXCESS LUXURY PLENTY
ABANDON LAUGHTER OVERFLOW
RAMPANCY
EXUBERANT RANK BOUNCY FEISTY
LAVISH COPIOUS FERTILE
GLOWING PROFUSE RAMPANT
EFFUSIVE
EXUDATE GUM SPEW SPUE MANNA
DIKAMALI GUAIACUM HONEYDEW
SARCOCOL
EXUDATION DIP GUM LAC SAP TAR
BALM KINO COPAL PITCH RESIN
ROSIN SUDOR ULMIN CHARAS
MASTIC SANIES CHURRUS GALIPOT
MOCHRAS SPEWING BLEEDING
EXUDENCE LAITANCE MOISTURE
EXUDE GUM DRIP EMIT OOZE REEK
SPEW BLEED STILL SWEAT EXTILL
STRAIN STREAM EXUDATE
GUTTATE SCREEVE SECRETE
SWELTER PERSPIRE
EXULT JOY CROW LEAP BOAST
GLOAT GLORY INSULT SPRING
MAFFICK REJOICE TRIUMPH
EXULTANT PROUD ELATED
PRIDEFUL
EXULTATION JOY GLEE PAEAN
OVATION RAPTURE

EXULTING EXULTANT JUBILANT
EXUVIATE MOLT
EYALET VILLAYET
EYAS NESTLING
EYE O EE HE ORB SPY DISC GAZE
GLIM LAMP LOOP MIEN OEIL OGLE
SCAN UVEA VIEW GLARE GLASS
GLENE NAVEL OPTIC SENSE SHANK
SIGHT TOISE WATCH BEHOLD
COLLAR EUCONE EYELET GOGGLE
OCULAR OCULUS OILLET PEEPER
POPEYE REGARD ROLLER SHINER
STEMMA VISION WINDOW WINKER
BLINKER EUCONIC EXOCONE
EYEBALL EYEHOLE OBSERVE
OCELLUS PIERCER PIGSNEY
PINKANY PINKENY SENSORY
WITNESS LATCHING NOISETTE
OMMATEUM RECEPTOR
(— AMOROUSLY) OGLE
(— DISEASE) STYE PINKEYE
(— FORMED BY ROPE) TONGUE
(— IN BIGHT) COLLAR
(— IN EGYPTIAN SYMBOLISM)
UTA
(— MAKEUP) KOHL MASCARA
(— MOVEMENT) REM
(— OF BEAN) HILUM
(— OF CAMERA) LENS
(— OF FRUIT) NOSE
(— OF HINGE) GUDGEON
(— OF INSECT) STEMMA
(— OF POTATO) BUD
(— OF RA) SEKHET
(— SORENESS) LIPPITUDE
(BLACK —) KEEK MOUSE SHINER
(EVIL —) DROCHUIL MALOCCHIO
(JERKY — MOVEMENT) SACCADE
(KIND OF —) RIB LAZY
(METAL —) HONDA
(PART OF —) IRIS LENS FOVEA
PUPIL CORNEA MACULA SCLERA
CHAMBER CHOROID LIGAMENT
CONJUNCTIVA
(PRIVATE —) GUMSHOE
(PL.) EEN EES NIE YEN YES EYNE
LAMPS LIGHTS SEEING GOGGLES
KEEKERS GLAZIERS GLIMMERS
(PREF.) OCELLI OCUL(I)(O)
OMMA(TO) OPHTHALM(O) OPTI(CO)
OPTO
(SUFF.) OMMA OPHTHALMA
OPHTHALMUS OPIS OPS
(DEFECT OR CONDITION OF —) OPE
OPIA OPIC OPIS OPS OPY

EYEBALL EYE BALL GLASS GLOBE
(— MOVEMENT) VERGENCE
(PREF.) OPHTHALM(O)
EYEBOLT SPRIG RINGBOLT
(INTERLOCKING —S) SNIBEL
EYEBRIGHT EYEWORT EUPHRASY
EYEBROW BREE BROW EEBREE
WINBROW WRIGGLE
EYE-CATCHING BOLD
EYE-CORNER
(PREF.) CANTH(O)
EYECUP EYEGLASS
EYED
(SUFF.) OPIS OPS
EYEGLASS QUIZ NIPPER MONOCLE
EYEGLASSES GLIMS SPECS LENSES
GLASSES LORGNON NIPPERS
BIFOCALS
EYEHOLE EYELET EYEPIT
EYELASH BREE LASH CILIUM
WINKER EYEBREE
(LOSS OF —S) MADAROSIS
(PL.) CILIA EAVES
(PREF.) CILI(I)(O)
EYELET MAIL PINK OELET AGRAFE
OILLET POUNCE AGRAFFE CRINGLE
GROMMET PEEPHOLE
EYELID HAW LID BREE WINDOW
EYEBREE PALPEBRA
(PL.) EAVES
(PREF.) BLEPHAR(O) CILI(I)(O)
(SUFF.) BLEPHARON CIL
EYEPIECE OCULAR EYEGLASS
(— OF TELESCOPE) POWER
EYESHADE VISOR OPAQUE
EYESHOT RANGE REACH EYESIGHT
EYESIGHT VIEW LIGHT SIGHT
EYE SOCKET ORBIT
EYESORE DESIGHT
EYESPOT EYEDOT STIGMA
EYEHOLE OCELLUS EYEPOINT
EYESTALK STIPES
EYETOOTH CUSPID DOGTOOTH
EYEWASH COLLYRIE EYEWATER
COLLYRIUM
EYING ESPIAL
EYOT AIT EIGHT ISLET
EYRE AIR ITER
EZBAI (SON OF —) NAARAI
EZBON (FATHER OF —) GAD BELA
EZEKIEL (FATHER OF —) BUZI
EZER (FATHER OF —) EPHRAIM
(SON OF —) HUSHAH
EZRA (SON OF —) EPHER
EZRI (FATHER OF —) CHELUB

F

F EF FF EFF FOX DIGAMMA FOXTROT

FABA VICIA

FABLE MYTH TALE FEIGN STORY LEGEND TRIFLE FICTION PARABLE POETIZE UNTRUTH ALLEGORY APOLOGUE FABULATE FABULIZE
(**— OF GOLD COAST**) NANCY
(**MORAL —**) EMBLEM
(PREF.) MYTHO

FABRIC ABA BAN ACCA CORD DUCK GOLD GROS HAIR HUCK IKAT SILK SUSI TAPA TARS TUKE BATIK CHECK CREPE DHOTI DOBBY DYNEL FANCY GAZAR MOIRE NINON PRINT RUMAL SCRIM SPLIT STUFF SUPER SURAH SURAT TABBY TAMMY TARSE TERRY TEWKE TULLE TWEED TWILL UNION VICHY VOILE WEAVE WIGAN WOVEN AGARIC ALACHA BENGAL BROCHE BYSSUS CAFFOY CARPET COTTON CREPON CYPRUS DACRON DAMASK DIAPER DOBBIE EPONGE ESTRON FLEECE HARDEN LAPPET LUSTER LUSTRE MARBLE MASHRU MURREY PLISSE POODLE SENNIT STRIPE TAMINY TANJIB TARTAN TRICOT TUSSAH VELURE VELVET WADMAL WINCEY ZENANA ACETATE ALEPINE ALLOVER BANDALA BANDING BELTING BEWPERS BINDING BUCKRAM CANILLE CHALLIS CHEKMAK CHIFFON CYPRESS DAMASSE DOESKIN DRABBET EDIFICE ELASTIC EPINGLE FACONNE FISHNET FUSTIAN MIXTURE MORELLA ORGANZA PAISLEY PLUMBET RASCHEL SAYETTE SEGATHY SILESIA SUITING TABARET TABINET TAFFETA TEXTILE TIFFANY VESSETS AGABANEE BARRACAN BOCASINE BOURETTE BROCATEL CAMELINE CANNELLE CASEMENT CHAMBRAY CRETONNE DIAMANTE DUCHESSE FIBRANNE HAIRLINE HANDMADE HARATEEN JACQUARD KNITTING LUSTRINE MATERIAL METALLIC MOLESKIN OSNABURG SHANTUNG SHIRTING SICILIAN SKIRTING SWANSKIN TAPESTRY TARLATAN VALENCIA POINTELLE VELVETEEN
(**— CLOSURE**) VELCRO
(**— CONTAINING GOLD OR SILVER THREAD**) ACCA TASH TASS KINCOB
(**— FOR STIFFENING**) WIGAN
(**— OF TWO OR MORE MATERIALS**) UNION
(**— RESEMBLING TOWELING**) AGARIC
(**— WITH INWOVEN SCENES**) ARRAS

(**ABSORBENT —**) HUCK
(**BROCADED —**) LAMF LAMPAS
(**CARPET —**) DURRIE
(**COARSE —**) TAT BAFT CRASH HAIRE DUFFEL RATINE STAMIN BAGGING BOCKING DRABBET SACKING STAMMEL DAGSWAIN FIBRANNE
(**CORDED —**) REP PIQUE DUCAPE POPLIN OTTOMAN BENGALINE
(**COTTON —**) CREA DUCK JEAN LENO LINO SUSI BAIZE BASIN DENIM DRILL RUMAL SUPER SWISS VICHY WIGAN BURRAH CALICO CANVAS CATGUT CHILLO CHINTZ COUTIL COVERT DIMITY MADRAS MUSLIN PENANG SATEEN BLANKET BUSTIAN CANTOON DAMASSE ETAMINE FLANNEL GALATEA GINGHAM HICKORY HOLLAND JACONET ORGANDY ORLEANS PERCALE TICKING BOCASINE BUCKSKIN COTELINE COUTILLE CRETONNE DRILLING DUNGAREE INDIENNE SHEETING SULKALINE MARSEILLES
(**CURTAIN —**) NINON
(**DECORATED —**) DIAMANTE
(**DELICATE —**) HUSI JUSI
(**DURABLE —**) SCRIM SERGE
(**ELASTIC —**) GORING ELASTIC
(**EMBOSSED —**) CLOKY CLOQUE
(**EMBROIDERED —**) BALDAQUIN
(**FIGURED —**) BROCADE BROCATEL
(**FINE —**) PIMA SILK SUSI LINEN DIMITY MERINO MOHAIR BATISTE PERCALE
(**GAUZELIKE —**) BAREGE GOSSAMER
(**GLAZED —**) CIRE
(**GLOSSY —**) SATIN GLORIA SATEEN PERCALINE
(**GOAT'S-HAIR —**) ABA TIBET
(**HEAVY —**) GROS CRASH DENIM DRILL BURLAP CATGUT FRIEZE LINENE TOBINE WHITNEY
(**JUTE —**) BALINE BURLAP
(**KNITTED —**) SUEDE BOUCLE JERSEY TRICOT CHIFFON
(**LIGHTWEIGHT —**) GLORIA BUNTING DELAINE FORTISAN PARAMATTA SEERSUCKER
(**LINEN —**) HARN SINDON BEWPERS BUCKRAM CAMBRIC DRABBET HOLLAND NACARAT CRETONNE
(**METALLIC —**) LAME
(**MOTTLED —**) CHINE
(**MOURNING —**) ALMA
(**MUSLIN —**) TANJIB
(**NYLON —**) VELCRO
(**OPEN-WEAVE —**) LENO
(**OPENWORK —**) LACE SKIPDENT

(**ORNAMENTAL —**) GIMP LACE LAMPAS GALLOON
(**PEBBLY-SURFACED —**) ARMURE
(**PILED —**) TERRY BOLIVIA KRIMMER CHENILLE
(**PRINTED —**) BATIK CALICO ALLOVER PERCALE TOURNAY
(**RAFFIA —**) RABANNA
(**RIBBED —**) CORD GROS PIQUE COTELE FAILLE SOLEIL DROGUET CORDUROY MAROCAIN MOGADORE WHIPCORD
(**RICH —**) SAMITE SATEEN
(**ROUGH —**) TERRY HOPSACK HOMESPUN
(**SATIN —**) CAMLET ETOILE CHARMEUSE
(**SHEER —**) LAWN NINON SHEER SWISS BAREGE DIMITY BATISTE SOUFFLE VALENCE GOSSAMER MOUSSELINE MARQUISETTE
(**SHORT-NAPPED —**) RAS
(**SILK —**) ACCA ALMA FUGI FUJI GROS IKAT MOFF RASH ATLAS CARDE NINON PEKIN RAJAH RUMAL SATIN SHIKH SURAH TIRAZ ARMURE BROCHE CAMACA CHAPPE CREPON DIAPER DUCAPE FAILLE KHAIKI MANTUA PONGEE SAMITE SENDAL ALACHAH ALAMODE BROCADE EPINGLE GROGRAM SARSNET SCHAPPE YESTING BARATHEA DOUPPIONI EOLIENNE IMPERIAL ORMUZINE SARCENET SARSENET SHAGREEN SIAMOISE MARCELINE MESSALINE BROCATELLE
(**SOFT-NAPPED —**) PANNE DUVETYN
(**SOFT SILK —**) KASHA BARATHEA
(**STRIPED —**) ABA STRIPE BAYADERE MERALINE
(**THIN —**) CRISP GAUZE VOILE PONGEE TAMISE HERNANI MARABOU ORGANZA PERSIAN
(**TWILLED —**) REP SAY DENIM KASHA SERGE SURAH COUTIL RUSSEL BOLIVIA ESTAMIN FLANNEL ZANELLA CAMELINE CASHMERE CORDUROY DIAGONAL MARCELLA SHALLOON VENETIAN
(**UNBLEACHED —**) DRABBET
(**UNGLAZED —**) CRETONNE
(**UPHOLSTERY —**) FRISE FRIEZE BROCATEL MOQUETTE
(**VELVETY —**) TRIPE DUVETYN
(**VINYL —**) NAUGAHYDE
(**VINYL-COATED —**) NAUGAHYDE
(**WATERPROOF —**) MACINTOSH MACKINTOSH
(**WOOLEN —**) REPP BAIZE DOILY OSSET SERGE TAMIS TWEED BUFFIN BURNET COTTON DJERSA DUFFEL FRISCA MANTLE MOREEN MOTLEY PERPET SAXONY SHAYAK SHODDY

STAMIN TAMISE VICUNA WADMAL WITNEY BATISTE BOCKING BOLIVIA CHEVIOT CHEYNEY CRYSTAL DELAINE DRUGGET FRISADO HEATHER RATTEEN STAMMEL ALGERINE BATSWING BURBERRY CASHMERE CATALOON CHIVERET HARATEEN LAMBSKIN PRUNELLA RATTINET SHALLOON SHETLAND WOOLENET ZIBELINE
(**WORSTED —**) TABBY COBURG ESTAMIN ETAMINE SAGATHY BARATHEA
(**WOVEN —**) LENO TWEED TWILL SOLBIL TISSUE GROGRAM TEXTURE VALENCIA

FABRICATE COIN COOK FAKE FORM MAKE MINT VAMP WARP BUILD FORGE FRAME FRUMP WEAVE DEVISE FANGLE INVENT CONCOCT FASHION IMAGINE PRODUCE CONTRIVE
(**— CLOTH**) DRAPE
(**— PAPER**) CONVERT

FABRICATION LIE WEB TRIFLE CHIMERA FICTION FINGURE FORGERY UNTRUTH BASKETRY PRETENSE
(PL.) INVENTARY

FABRICATOR LIAR COINER FORGER

FABULIST LIAR AESOP FABLER

FABULOUS FAB FEIGNED MYTHICAL ROMANTIC

FACADE FACE FRONT FUCUS FRONTAL FRONTLET
(**— FEATURE**) CEDILLA

FACE JIB MAP MUG NEB PAN BIDE CHIV CLAD COPE DARE DEFY DIAL GIZZ HEAD LEER LINE MASK MEET MOUE MUNS PHIZ PUSS SIDE ABIDE BEARD BRAVE BRICK BRUNT CASTE CHECK CHEER COVER FACET FAVOR FRONT GUARD INDEX REVET STAND STONE VISOR VIZOR ASPECT BRAZEN FACADE FACIES KISSER MAZARD MUZZLE OPPOSE PHIZOG VENEER VISAGE AFFRONT BAZOOKA COMMAND DIGLYPH FASHION FEATURE GRIMACE GRUNTLE PROPOSE RESPECT REVERSE SURFACE UPRIGHT CONFRONT ENVISAGE EXTRADOS FEATURES FROGFACE FRONTAGE FRONTIER PROSPECT SEMBLANT PERPENDICULAR
(**— DOWN**) DEFACE
(**— IN DEFIANCE**) AFFRONT
(**— OF ANIMAL**) MASK
(**— OF CUBE**) SQUARE
(**— OF CUTTING TOOL**) BEZEL BEZIL
(**— OF GLACIER**) SNOUT
(**— OF PEDIMENT**) TYMPANUM
(**— OF STEAM HAMMER**) TUP

(— OF STUMP) SCARF SCARPH
(— ON DOOR KNOCKER) MASCARON
(— ONE'S DANCING PARTNER) SET
(— THE EAST) ORIENTATE
(— TO FACE) AFRONT BEFORE FACIAL DIRECTLY
(— WITH MARBLE) PIN
(— WITH MASONRY) REVET
(— WITH PLASTER) STUCCO
(— WITH STONE) BATCH
(CLOCK —) DIAL TABLE WATCH
(CRYSTAL —) PINAKOU
(CURVED —) EXTRADOS INTRADOS
(DIE —) ACE
(FANTASTIC —) ANTIC
(HALF DOMINO —) END
(HAVING SHORT BROAD —) LATERAL
(INNER —) CONCAVE
(MADE-UP —) MOP
(MINING —) BANK BREAST FOREHEAD LONGWALL
(MOCKING —) MOE MOWE
(QUARRY —) HEUGH
(ROCK —) CLIFF
(UPPER —) BROW
(WRY —) MOUTH GRIMACE
(PREF.) FACIO PROSOP(O)
FACE-ARBOR KNIFE
FACED
(SUFF.) PROSOPOUS
FACE GUARD FRONTAL
FACEMAN HAGGER WINNER
FACEPLATE FRONT DOGPLATE
FACER BUMPER DRIFTER TANKARD
FACET PANE STAR BEZEL CULET PHASE COLLET STEMMA FACETTE LOZENGE TEMPLET
FACETIAE CURIOSA
FACETIOUS FUNNY MERRY SMART WITTY FACETE JOCOSE JOCULAR HUMOROUS POLISHED
FACIAL
(PREF.) FACIO
FACIENT DOER
FACILE PAT ABLE EASY GLIB QUICK READY EXPERT FLUENT GENTLE AFFABLE DUCTILE LENIENT
FACILITATE AID EASE HELP FAVOR SPEED ASSIST GREASE EXPEDITE
FACILITY ART EASE FEEL HELP ECLAT KNACK SKILL ADDRESS COMMAND FREEDOM PROWESS EASINESS
(PL.) ADDITIONS
FACING DADO HARL FRONT HARLE LAPEL LINER PANEL SKIRT BEFORE TOWARD VENEER AGAINST FORNENT SURFACE BLACKING CAMPSHOT CONFRONT COVERING FACEWORK FORNENST OPPOSITE PITCHING
(— AGAINST GLACIER) STOSS
(— AHEAD) FULL
(— APEX) ACROSCOPIC
(— AUDIENCE OBLIQUELY) EFFACE AFFRONTY
(— EACH OTHER) AFFRONTE AFFRONTY
(— FOR WALLS) CASE
(— FROM GLACIER) STOSS
(— INWARD) INTRORSE
(— OF BODICE) VEST

(— OUTWARDS) EXTRORSE
(PREF.) OB
FACSIMILE FAX COPY IMAGE MODEL REPLICA AUTOTYPE
FACT CASE DEED FAIT DATUM EVENT SOOTH TRUTH DONNEE EFFECT FACTUM VERITY COMPERT FORMULA GENERAL INDICIA KEYNOTE LOWDOWN REALITY PARTICULAR
(CONCLUSIVE —) CRUSHER
(DECISIVE —) CLINCHER
(FUNDAMENTAL —) KEYNOTE
(OBVIOUS —) TRUISM
(TRUE —S) STRENGTH
(PL.) DATA FEAT
FACTION BLOC NERI PART SECT SIDE WING CABAL JUNTO PARTY BRIGUE CLIQUE SCHISM BIANCHI DISPUTE PINFOLD QUARREL INTRIGUE SPLINTER
(— OF SECEDERS) CAVE
(PARTY —) STASIS
FACTITIOUS SHAM WHIPPED KRITRIMA
FACTOR GEN DOER GENE ITEM AGENT ALLEL CAUSE MAKER ALLELE AUTHOR CENTER DETAIL BAILIFF CONTROL COUCHER CUSHION ELEMENT ENTROPY FACTRIX ISOLATE STEWARD ADHERENT AUMILDAR COFACTOR DOMINANT EQUATION GOMASHTA INCIDENT INCITANT PARAMETER
(—S IN EVOLUTION) ANTICHANCE
(CYTOPLASMIC —) KAPPA
(DECISIVE —) CAPSTONE
(ECOLOGICAL —) INFLUENT
(ENVIRONMENTAL —) GEOGEN
(HEREDITY —) GENE INSTINCT
(HINDERING —) CRIMP
(INTELLIGENCE —) G
(MATHEMATICAL —) ROOT
(PERSONALITY —) SURGENCY
(RESTRICTIVE —) BARRIER
(UNFORSEEN —) JOKER
FACTORY HONG MILL SHOP PLANT USINE AURANG AURUNG FABRIC SUGARY CANNERY HATTERY HOSIERY OFICINA SOAPERY BUILDING COMPTOIR FABRIQUE FILATURE HACIENDA OFFICINA STAMPERY WORKSHOP MANUFACTORY
FACTOTUM SIRCAR FAMULUS COMPRADOR
(INDIAN —) SIRCAR SIRKAR
FACTUAL HARD REAL TRUE ACTUAL BEDROCK EARTHLY EMPIRIC LITERAL PROSAIC
(INSUFFICIENTLY —) ABSTRACT
FACTUALLY INSOOTH
FACULTY ART WIT BOOM BUMP EASE GIFT WILL FANCY POWER SENSE TASTE BREATH BUDDHI GIFTIE SEEING TALENT ABILITY COLLEGE COUNSEL HABITUS APTITUDE CAPACITY FELICITY
(— FOR DETECTING) NOSE
(— OF EXPRESSION) LANGUAGE
(CRITICAL —) JUDGMENT
(MENTAL —) HEADPIECE

(POETIC OR CREATIVE —) IDEALITY PRINCIPLE
(REASONING —) DISCOURSE
(PL.) INDULTS
FAD BUG CULT FIKE RAGE WHIM CRAZE FANCU HOBBY FOIBLE MAGGOT CROCHET FASHION WRINKLE
FADDISH TRENDY
FADDIST CRANK
FADE DIE DIM DOW FLY WAN BRIT CAST FATE FLAT GIVE PALE PEAK PINE PINK VADE WELK WILK WILT BLANK DAVER DECAY FLEET PASSE PETER QUAIL SWING SWOON DARKLE PERISH VANISH WITHER DECLINE INSIPID LIGHTEN DIMINISH DISCOLOR DISSOLVE EVANESCE LANGUISH
(— AWAY) DOW BREAK FLEET WALLOW
FADED PASSE SHABBY EXOLETE SHOPWORN
FADELESS AMARANTIN
FADGE FAY FIT SUIT
FADING FUGITIVE MANCANDO SWINGING
FAERIE QUEENE (AUTHOR OF —) SPENSER
(CHARACTER IN —) UNA GUYON IRENE TALUS ACRASY AMORET ARTHUR DUESSA TIMIAS ASTRAEA MALEGER ARTEGALL CALIDORE GLORIANA ORGOGLIO RADIGUND ARCHIMAGO BELPHOEBE BRITOMART FLORIMELL GRANTORTO SCUDAMOUR
FAFNIR (FATHER OF —) HREIDMAR
(SLAYER OF —) SIGURD
FAG FLAG JADE TIRE TOIL DROOP WEARY DRUDGE HARASS MENIAL EXHAUST FATIGUE FRAZZLE
FAG-END LAG BUTT
FAGGED TASKIT
FAGGOT BROSNA CHUMPA FAGALD
FAGOT KID BUNT PILE PIMP BAVIN FADGE NICKY NITCH FAGGOT KNITCH GARBAGE
FAIL GO CUT EBB ERR PIP BANK BOMB BUST CONK FALL FLAG FLOP FOLD LACK LOSE MISS SINK SKEW SPIN WANE APPAL BREAK BURST CRACK FAULT FLUFF FLUKE FLUNK PETER QUAIL SLAKE SMASH SPILL VAILE APPALL BETRAY COPOUT DEFAIL DEFECT DESERT FALTER FIZZLE REPINE WINDER BACKOUT DECLINE DEFAULT EXHAUST FALSIFY FINKOUT FLICKER FLUMMOX FOUNDER MISFARE MISGIVE SCANTLE LANGUISH
(— AT) FLUB
(— IN DUTY) LAPSE
(— IN EARLY STAGES) ABORT
(— IN HEALTH) SINK BREAK
(— IN SPIRIT) QUAIL
(— IN STUDIES) BILGE
(— ON RIFLE RANGE) BOLO
(— TO ADVANCE) STICK
(— TO FOLLOW SUIT) RENIG RENEGE
(— TO GAIN ALTITUDE) MUSH

(— TO GROW) MISS
(— TO NOTICE) OVERLOOK
(— TO PERFORM) CHOKE
FAILING BAD ILL BLOT FAULT FOIBLE SENILE BLEMISH FAILURE FRAILTY ABORTIVE WEAKNESS
(NEVER —) PERENNIAL
FAILURE DUD BALK BOMB BUST FAIL FLOP FLUB FOIL LACK LOSS MISS MUFF TRIP BAULK BILGE CRASH DECAY ERROR FAULT FLUKE FLUNK FROST GRIEF GUILT LAPSE LEMON PLUCK SMASH BRODIE BUMMER FIASCO FIZZLE OUTAGE STUMER STUMOR TURKEY BLOOMER CROPPER DEBACLE DECLINE DEFAULT FLIVVER FLUMMOX NEGLECT STUMBLE ABORTION COLLAPSE DISASTER FAILANCE FLOPEROO OMISSION
(— OF DAM) BLOW
(— OF FIREARM) STOPPAGE
(— OF MILK SECRETION) AGALAXY AGALAXIA
(— OF MUSCLE) ACHALASIA
(— OF PAVEMENT) BLOWUP
(— OF PRIMER) HANGFIRE
(— OF VITALITY) DELIQUIUM
(— TO MEET) GAPE
(— TO NOTICE) OVERSIGHT
(— TO PLAY) GO
(— TO RAISE OAR) CRAB
(COMPUTER —) CRASH
(FLAT —) DUD
(POWER —) OUTAGE
(RIDICULOUS —) FIASCO
FAIN FOND GLAD LIEF EAGER PLEASED WILLING DESIROUS INCLINED
FAINEANT IDLE LAZY LOAFER
FAINT GO DIM LOW WAN WAW COLD CONK COOL DARK PALE PALL SOFT THIN WEAK LIGHT QUEAL QUEER SHADY SWELT SWOON TIMID WAUFF WAUGH WERSH EVANID FEEBLE REMISS REMOTE SICKLY WAMBLY FEIGNED FORGONE LANGUID OBSCURE SWITHER SYNCOPE WEARISH COWARDLY DELICATE LANGUISH LISTLESS SLUGGISH TIMOROUS
(— FROM HEAT) SWELTER
(— FROM HUNGER) LEERY
(— OF SCENT) COLD WAUGH
FAINTHEARTED TIMID COWARD CRAVEN COWARDLY UNHEARTY
FAINTHEARTEDNESS QUALM
FAINTING AFAINT SYNCOPE DELIQUIUM
(— SPELL) DROW DWAM DWALM
FAINTLY DIMLY FAINT SMALL
FAINTNESS TENUITY GONENESS WEAKNESS
FAINT-VOICED INWARD
FAIR GAY GEY MOP BEAU BELL CALM EVEN FINE GAFF GALA GOOD HEND JUST MART PLAY TIDE TIDY BAZAR BLOND CLEAN CLEAR EQUAL FERIA HENDE LARGE RIGHT ROUND SHEER TRYST WHITE AONACH BAZAAR

BLONDE CANDID COMELY DECENT DINKUM HONEST KERMIS PRETTY SERENE SQUARE EXHIBIT JANNOCK KERMESS STATUTE BOOKFAIR DISTINCT FESTIVAL HORNFAIR MIDDLING RATIONAL STRAIGHT UNBIASED EQUITABLE OBJECTIVE REASONABLE
(— AND CALM) SETTLED
(— AND SQUARE) DINKUM
(HINDU —) MELA
(VILLAGE —) WALK
FAIR-DEALING HONEST
FAIRER SHIPWRIGHT
FAIRING SPAT SPINNER FAIRLING
FAIR-LEAD WAPP
FAIRLY WELL GAILY GAYLY GEYAN EVENLY JUSTLY MEANLY HANDILY PLAINLY RIGHTLY MIDDLING PROPERLY SUITABLY
FAIRNESS FAIR CANDOR EQUITY HONESTY JUSTICE EQUALITY EVENNESS FAIRHEAD FAIRHOOD
FAIRWAY HOLE WATERWAY
(ANGLED —) DOGLEG
FAIR-WEATHER SUNSHINE
FAIRY ELF FAY FEE HOB IMP FAIN PERI PIXY PUCK SHEE VILA OUPHE PECHT PIXIE SIDHE WIGHT COURIL FAERIE HATHOR KEWPIE SPIRIT SPRITE YAKSHA YAKSHI ARGANTE BANSHEE ORIANDA SHEOGUE SYLPHID URGANDA FOLLETTO MELUSINA
(— QUEEN) MAB
(IRISH —) SHEE SIDHE
(TRICKSY —) PUCK
(PL.) GENTRY
FAIRY BELL FOXGLOVE
FAIRYFOLK SHEE SIDHE
FAIRYLAND ANNWN ANNWFN FEERIE ELFLAND
FAITH DIN FAY FOY LAW LAY VAY FACK FAIX FEGS SLAM TROW CERTY CREED HAITH STOCK TOUCH TROTH TRUST TRUTH BELIEF CERTIE CREDIT GOSPEL CREANCE FACKINS AFFIANCE RELIANCE RELIGION
(BAD —) DUPLICITY
(MUSLIM —) CRESCENT
(RELIGIOUS —) SRADH SRADDHA SHRADDHA
(SHOW OF GOOD —) GESTURE
(PREF.) FIDE(I) PISTIO PISTO
FAITHFUL FAST FEAL FIRM GOOD JUST LEAL LIKE REAL TRIG TRUE FALSE HEMAN LIEGE LOYAL PIOUS SOOTH SWEER TIGHT TREST TRIED AEFALD ARDENT ENTIRE FIDELE HONEST LAWFUL PISTIC STANCH STEADY TRUSTY DEVOTED SINCERE STAUNCH ACCURATE CONSTANT RESOLUTE SPEAKING RELIGIOUS
FAITHFULNESS HSIN FEALTY VERITY LOYALTY FIDELITY TRUENESS
FAITHFUL SHEPHERDESS
(AUTHOR OF —) FLETCHER
(CHARACTER IN —) CHLOE ALEXIS AMORET CLORIN THENOT DAPHNIS PERIGOT AMARILLIS

FAITHLESS FALSE PUNIC FICKLE HOLLOW ROTTEN UNJUST UNTRUE ATHEIST APOSTATE DELUSIVE DISLOYAL SHIFTING UNSTABLE NIDDERING PERFIDIOUS
FAITHLESSNESS FALSITY PERFIDY UNTRUTH
FAKE DUD DUFF DUPE FEKE HOAX HOKE SHAM BOGUS CHEAT FALSE FEIGN FLAKE FRAUD FUDGE PHONY WANGLE DUFFING FALSIFY FURBISH GUNDECK PRETEND SWINDLE SIMULATE SPURIOUS ADULTERINE
(— OF STOWED ROPE) FLEET
(— OUT OF POSITION) JUKE
(FOOTBALL —) JUKE
(PREF.) PSEUD(O)
FAKER FAKIR QUACK HUMBUG CAMELOT PEDDLER
(— OF ART) TRUQUEUR
FAKIR FAKIH FAQUIR DERVISH
FALCHION FALX
FALCON EYAS HAWK SORE BESRA HOBBY SAKER STOOP GENTLE JAGGER JUGGER LANNER LUGGAR LUGGER MERLIN MUSKET PREYER RAPTOR SHAHIN TERCEL KESTREL SAKERET BERIGORA BOCKEREL FALCONET PEREGRIN SOREHAWK
(— BOARD) HACK
(— IN FIRST YEAR) SORE SOREHAWK
(FEMALE —) FORMAL FORMEL LANNER
(MALE —) TASSEL TERCEL SAKERET
(SMALL —) HOBBY MERLIN KESTREL
(WHITE —) ICELANDER
FALCONER HAWKER OSTREGER
FALCONRY HAWKING
FALDSTOOL ORATORY
FALL GO EBB SAG SYF TIP BACK BAND COME COUP DIVE DRIP DROP DUNT FLOP HANG PICK PLOP RASH RUIN RUSE SHED SILE SINK SLIP SWAK SWAP SWAY SWOP TILT WHAP WHOP ABATE CHUTE CLOIT CRASH DROOP HANCE INCUR JABOT LAPSE LIGHT LODGE PITCH PLUMB PLUMP RAPID SAULT SHAKE SHOOT SKITE SLIPE SLUMP SPILL SQUAB SQUAT THROW TRACE TWINE ALIGHT AUTUMN BRODIE DEVALL DOUNCE DRYSNE FOOTER HAPPEN HEADER JOUNCE PERISH PLUNGE RECEDE SEASON SLOUGH STREEK STRIKE TOPPLE TUMBLE CASCADE CROPPER CROWNER DECLINE DEGRADE DEPRESS DESCEND DEVOLVE DRIBBLE ESCHEAT ILLAPSE PLUMMET RELAPSE RETREAT SQUELCH STUMBLE SUBSIDE CATARACT COLLAPSE COMMENCE DECREASE DOWNCOME PRECIPITATE
(— ABRUPTLY) DUMP
(— APART) BREAK SHIVER COLLAPSE DISUNITE
(— AWAY) DEFECT
(— BACK) RECEDE RESORT

(— BEHIND) LAG
(— DIZZILY) SPIN
(— DOWN) CAVE FLOP SWAP SLUMP REVERSE SWITHER
(— DUE) ACCRUE BEFALL
(— FAST) HOP
(— FLAT) PLAT FLIVVER
(— FOR) BITE
(— FORWARD) PECK PITCH PROLAPSE
(— FROM A HORSE) PURL VOLUNTARY
(— FROM SURFBOARD) WIPEOUT
(— FROM UNDERMINING) CALVE
(— FROM VIRTUE) LAPSE
(— GRADUALLY) EBB SAG
(— GUY) GOAT CHUMP SCAPEGOAT
(— HEAVILY) DING LUMP SOSS CLOIT CLYTE GULCH PLOUT PLUMP SOUSE SWACK THROW
(— ILL) TRAIK
(— IN) CAVE FOUNDER
(— IN DROPS) DRIP STILL DRIBBLE
(— IN FLURRIES) SPIT
(— IN FOLDS) BLOUSE
(— IN RIVER) SAULT
(— INTO) STRIKE
(— INTO ERROR) SLIP STUMBLE
(— INTO FAINT) DWAM DWALM
(— INTO RUIN) DECAY
(— INTO SLUMBER) DROWSE
(— INTO TRAP) DECOY
(— INTO WATER) DOP
(— IN WITH) INCUR
(— OF DEW) SEREIN SERENE
(— OFF) RATE SLIP SLACK
(— OF RAIN) SKIFF SKIFT ONDING SHOWER
(— OF SNOW) SKIFF SKIFT ONCOME SCOUTHER SNOWFALL
(— OF WICKETS) ROT
(— ON BACK) BACKER
(— ON SUCCESSIVE DAYS) CONCUR
(— ON THE NOSE) NOSER
(— OUT) BREAK LIGHT FORTUNE QUARREL
(— PRONE) GRABBLE
(— RAPIDLY) SKID
(— SHORT) DROP FAIL FAULT
(— SLOWLY) SETTLE
(— SUDDENLY) BOLT PLOP SLUMP
(— THROWING HORSE AND RIDER) CRUMPLER
(— TO NOTHING) DISSOLVE
(— TO PIECES) BUCKLE CRUMBLE
(— UPON) WARP
(— VIOLENTLY) BEAT
(BAD —) BUSTER
(HEAVY —) PASH POUR SWAG BLASH CLOIT GULCH SKELP SOUSE SQUAT MUCKER
(INCOMPLETE WRESTLING —) FOIL
(SOFT —) SCLAFF
(SUDDEN —) HANCE SQUAT SQUASH TAILSPIN
FALLACIOUS SLY WILY ABSURD CRAFTY UNTRUE DELUSIVE GUILEFUL ILLUSORY
FALLACY IDOL ERROR FALLAX IDOLUM SOPHISM EQUIVOKE ILLUSION
(PL.) IDOLA

FALLEN DOWN FAUN FLAT SHED LAPSED DECLASSE
(— IN) SUNKEN
FALLER GILL FLATHEAD
FALLFISH CHUB DACE CORPORAL
FALLGUY PATSY
FALL HERRING TAILOR
FALLIBLE HUMAN ERRANT ERRABLE
FALLING SIT CADENT CAVING PROLAPSE WINDFALL
(— BACK) ESCHEAT
(— BEHIND) LAG
(— DOWN) RUIN
(— IN FOLDS) FLOWING
(— IN RUINS) DERELICT
(— INTO) INFALL
(— OFF) CADUCE LEEWAY CADUCOUS
(— OF MINE ROOF) SIT
(— OF RAIN) SPIT
(— ON SOMETHING) INCIDENT
(— OUT) DIFFICULTY
(— SHORT) DEFICIT
(PREF.) CADUCI
(SUFF.) PTOMA PTOSIS
FALLOPIAN TUBE TUBAL
(PREF.) FALL(O)
FALLOVER OSTREGER
FALLOW LEA PALE HOBBY BARREN VALEWE
(PREF.) POLI(O)
FALLOW DEER DAMINE DAPPLE
FALLOWING ARDER
FALSE DEAD FAKE FLAM SHAM BOGUS FAUSE LYING PASTE PHONY WRONG FICKLE HOLLOW LUTHER PSEUDO UNTRUE ASSUMED BASTARD CROOKED FEIGNED APOSTATE DISLOYAL ILLUSIVE RECREANT RENEGADE SPECTRAL SPURIOUS MENDACIOUS
(PREF.) PSEUD(O)
FALSE BEACHDROPS PINESAP
FALSE CRAWLEY PINEDROPS
FALSE FOXGLOVE FEVERWEED
FALSE HELLEBORE EARTHGALL
FALSEHOOD COG FIB LIE BUNG CRAM FLAM TALE CRACK ERROR FABLE STORY FALSET UNFACT YANKER CRAMMER CRETISM FALSAGE FALSERY FALSITY FIBBERY FICTION LEASING PERFIDY PHANTOM ROMANCE UNTRUTH FALSHEDE ROORBACK STRAPPER
FALSE MERMAID FLOERKEA LIMNANTH
FALSENESS SHAM DECEIT
FALSE WINTERGREEN PYROLA
FALSEWORK CENTERING
FALSIES CHEATERS
FALSIFIER LIAR FALSER FORGER FALSARY
FALSIFY LIE COOK FAKE WARP ABUSE BELIE FEINT FORGE BETRAY DOCTOR FIDDLE WANGLE GUNDECK VIOLATE EMBEZZLE MISREPRESENT
FALSITY LIE ERROR VANITY UNTRUTH INVERITY
FALSTAFF (CHARACTER IN —) MEG FORD JOHN PAGE ALICE BROOK

CAIUS FENTON QUICKLY FALSTAFF NANNETTA
(COMPOSER OF —) VERDI
FALTER FAIL HALT LIMP PAUSE WAVER BOGGLE FLINCH TOTTER FRIBBLE STAMMER STUMBLE TREMBLE HESITATE
FALTERING HINK HALTING
FALX FALCULA
FAME BAY CRY LOSE NAME STAR WORD BRUIT ECLAT GLORY HONOR KUDOS PRICE RUMOR VOICE ESTEEM LAUREL RENOWN REPORT REPUTE TONGUE HEARSAY STARDOM WORSHIP
(HALL OF —) OF (SEE HALL FAME)
(ILL —) OPPROBRIUM
FAMED RIFE KNOWN NOTED EMINENT RENOMEE RENOWNED
FAMEUSE APPLE
FAMILIAR FLY BAKA BOKO BOLD COZY EASY FREE FULL HOMY TAME TOSH CLOSE CONNU GREAT HOMEY KNOWN PRIVY THICK USUAL ATHOME BEATEN CHUMMY COMMON ENTIRE FOLKSY GERMAN HOMELY INWARD KENNED STRAIT THRONG VERSED AFFABLE FAMULAR FOLKSEY POPULAR FREQUENT HABITUAL INTIMATE SOCIABLE STANDARD
(— FEELING) DEJAVU
(— WITH) KNOWING
(MAKE —) POST
(PRESUMPTUOUSLY —) INSOLENT
FAMILIARITY HABIT FREEDOM LIBERTY PRIVACY PRIVITY TRAFFIC HABITUDE INTIMACY CONSUETUDE
FAMILIARIZE HAFT VERSE ACCUSTOM ACQUAINT FREQUENT
FAMILIARLY HOMELY
FAMILY ILK KIN AIGA CLAN GING KIND LINE NAME RACE TEAM TRIP CINEL CLASS FLESH GOTRA GROUP HOUSE MEINY STIRP STOCK CLETCH FAIMLY PARAGE STEMMA STIRPS STRAIN ZEGRIS DYNASTY KINDRED LINEAGE ORLEANS PROGENY CATEGORY FIRESIDE
(COSMOPOLITAN —) FELIDAE FABACEAE
(FIRST —) FF
(LANGUAGE —) CHON BANTU CLICK COCHE CUNAN KADAI STOCK AIMARA ATALAN AYMARA CHOLON GILIAK HUARPE LENCAN SERIAN URALIC BOTOYAN CADDOAN CARIBAN CATIBAN CHINOOK CHOLONA CHUMASH COPEHAN ESSELEN KARTHLI KARTVEL KERESAN SHASTAN ATAKAPAN CHANGOAN
(LARGE —) QUIVERFUL
(ONE-PARAMETER —) PENCIL
(RAISE A —) PARENT
(SUPER —) APINA APOIDEA
FAMINE LACK PINE WOLF DEARTH HUNGER SCARCITY
FAMISH KILL STARVE DESTROY ENFAMISH
FAMOUS MERE BREME FAMED GRAND NOBLE NOTED FAMOSE

NAMELY EMINENT NAMABLE NOTABLE RENOWNED
FAMULUS WAGNER SERVANT
FAN ONE RUN VAN BEAT BLOW BUFF COOL WASH DELTA PUNKA WHIFF BASKET BLOWER CHAMAR COLMAR FANNER FLABEL FLIGHT PUNKAH ROOTER SHOVEL SPREAD VENTOY WINNOW ADMIRER DEVOTEE FLABRUM FLYFLAP MPANGWE PAHOUIN WHISKER EVENTAIL FOLLOWER RHIPIDION
(— FOR BLOWER) WAFTER
(— OF ROCK GROUP) GROUPIE
(ALLUVIAL —) CONE APRON DELTA
(FEMALE — OF ROCK MUSICIAN) GROUPIE
(FOOTBALL —) GRIDDER
(JAZZ —) CAT
(WINNOWING —) SAIL LIKNON
(PL.) FOLLOWING
(PREF.) FLABELLI RHIPI(D)(DO)
FANALOKA FOSSA FOUSSA
FANATIC MAD NUT BIGOT CRAZY FIEND RABID ULTRA ZEALOT DEVOTEE FURIOSO PHANTIC PULAHAN PULIJAN BABAYLAN FRENETIC
(TYPE OF —) PURIST
FANATICAL RABID ULTRA EXTREME FURIOUS
FANCIED UNREAL DREAMED AFFECTED
FANCIFUL ODD ANTIC FAIRY IDEAL QUEER VIEWY DREAMY QUAINT UNREAL BIZARRE CURIOUS FANCIED LAPUTAN STRANGE WHIMSIC CHIMERIC FANCICAL FILIGREE NOTIONAL ROMANTIC VAPAROUS WHIMSICAL
FANCY BEE FAD GIG IDEA ITEM LIKE LOVE MAZE TROW WEEN WHIM BRAID BRAIN DREAM FREAK GUESS HUMOR SHINE AFFECT BEGUIN FANGLE FIGURE FLOSSY IDEATE LIKING MAGGOT MEGRIM NOTION ORNATE SHINDY VAGARY VISION WHIMSY CAPRICE CHIMERA CONCEIT CONCEPT CROCHET FANCIED FANCIFY FANTASY PROPOSE ROMANCE SUSPECT THOUGHT WRINKLE CHIMAERA CONCEIVE CROTCHET DAYDREAM ILLUSION PHANTASM PHANTASY
(FOOLISH —) CHIMERA CHIMAERA
(PASSING —) FIKE
(PERVERSE —) CROTCHET
(WILD —) TOY MAZE
(PL.) DREAMERY
FANDANGO MURCIANA
FANE FLAG BANNER FANACLE
FANFARE TUSCH HOOPLA HOORAY HURRAH TUCKET TANTARA FANFARON FLOURISH
FANFARONADE BLUSTER FANFARE SWAGGER BOASTING
FANFLOWER TACCADA
FANG FAN EARN FALX TAKE TANG TUSK VANG BEGIN PRONG SEIZE SNARE TOOTH ASSUME OBTAIN PANGWE CAPTURE PAHOUIN PROCURE

FANON CAPE ORALE PHANO FANNEL MANIPLE
FAN PALM YARAY ERYTHEA FANTREE TALIPOT
FAN-SHAPED FLABELLATE ALARY RHIPIDATE
FANTAIL COMET SHAKER WAGTAIL
FAN-TAN PARLIAMENT
FANTASIA FANTASY QUODLIBET
FANTASTIC ODD WILD ANTIC LUCIO OUTRE QUEER ABSURD GOTHIC ROCOCO TOYISH UNREAL ANTICAL BAROQUE BIZARRE WHIMSIC FANCIFUL FREAKISH ROMANTIC SINGULAR
(— PERSON) KICKSHAW
FANTASY IDEA MYTH DREAM FANCY DESIRE VISION CAPRICE CHIMERA PHANTOM ROMANCE CHIMAERA PHANTASM PHANTASY
(FUTURISTIC —) SPACEOPERA
FANTINE (DAUGHTER OF —) COSETTE
FAR AWAY LONG MUCH ROOM SIDE WELL WIDE CLEAN SIZES WIDEN REMOTE DISTANT FARAWAY ROOMWARD
(— AND AWAY) STREETS
(— OFF) OUTBYE
(— ON) ADVANCED
(— OUT) RAD WOW RADICAL
(— UP) HIGH
(SO —) ASYET UPTONOW
(PREF.) TEL(E) TELOTERO
FARAMONDO (COMPOSER OF —) HANDEL
FARCE MIME DROLL EXODE FORCE STUFF COMEDY GARLIC SOTTIE EXODIUM MOCKERY TEMACHA BURLETTA DROLLERY FARCETTA
(RELATING TO —) ATELLAN
FARCEUR WAG JOKER FORCER
FARCICAL BUFFO COMIC DROLL ATELLAN
FARCTATE STUFFED
FARCY FARCIN EQUINIA FASHION
FARE DO GO EAT TRY COME DIET FEND FOOD PATH RATE TIME TOLL WEND CHEER CHEFE CHIVE FRAME GOING LIGHT PRICE SPEED TABLE TOKEN TRACK VIAND COMMON FARING FETTLE HAPPEN TRAVEL CARFARE JOURNEY MAKEOUT PASSAGE PROCEED PROSPER WAFTAGE WAYFARE FERRYAGE PROGRESS
(— FOR FERRY) NAULUM FERRYAGE
(— WELL) SPEED
(COARSE —) HAWEBAKE
(USUAL —) ORDINARY
FAREWELL AVE BYE CIAO TATA VALE ADIEU ADIOS ALOHA CONGE FINAL LEAVE BYEBYE CHEERO SOLONG BONALLY CHEERIO GOODBYE LEAVING LULLABY PARTING
FAREWELL TO ARMS (AUTHOR OF —) HEMINGWAY
(CHARACTER IN —) HENRY BARKLEY RINALDI FREDERIC CATHERINE
FARFETCHED FARFET FORCED DEVIOUS STRAINED EXQUISITE

FAR-FETCHED (NOT —) NATURAL
FAR-FLUNG EXTENDED
FAR FROM THE MADDING CROWD (AUTHOR OF —) HARDY
(CHARACTER IN —) OAK TROY FANNY ROBIN GABRIEL BOLDWOOD EVERDENE BATHSHEBA
FARIDUN (FATHER OF —) ABTIN
(MOTHER OF —) FIRANAK
(SON OF —) TUR IRAJ SALM
FARINA MEAL FLOUR FARINE POLLEN STARCH
FARKLEBERRY BLUET
FARL PARLY FARREL
FARM FEU PEN CROP TACK TILL TORP TOWN WALK CROFT DAIRY EMPTY FIRMA HARAS MAINS MILPA PLACE RANCH RANGE STEAD BARTON BOWERY CHACRA ESTATE FURROW GRANGE RANCHO TYDDEN TYDDYN CLEANSE HENNERY KOLKHOZ MAILING POTRERO POULTRY SOVKHOS VACCARY ESTANCIA HACIENDA HATCHERY LABORING LOCATION STEADING TOWNSHIP
(— OUT) DIMIT ARRENT
(AUSTRALIAN —) STATION
(COLLECTIVE —) ARTEL KIBBUTZ KOLKHOZ
(COMMUNAL —) KVUTZA KVUTZAH
(DAIRY —) WICK
(KIND OF — AS ASYLUM) FUNNY
(LARGE —) RANCH BARTON
(RENTED —) MAILING
(SMALL —) CHACRA
(STOCK —) ESTANCIA
(STUD —) STUD HARAS
(WEST INDIAN —) PEN
FARMER HOB MEO CARL FARM HOBB KHOT KYLE RUBE RYOT TATE AILLT AUMIL BOWER CARLE CEILE CLOWN COLON HODGE KISAN COCKIE GROWER HOGMAN JIBARO TILLER YEOMAN BUCOLIC BUSHMAN BYWONER COTTIER CROFTER GRANGER HAYSEED HUSBAND LANDMAN METAYER PLANTER PLOWMAN RANCHER SCULLOG TILLMAN TRUCKER AGRONOME COCKATOO PRODUCER PUBLICAN RURALIST SELECTOR AGRONOMIST
(AUSTRALIAN —) SELECTOR
(NORWEGIAN —) BONDER
(POOR —) PIKE
(PROSPEROUS —) KULAK
(SMALL —) BOOR COCKIE
(TENANT —) AILLT GEBUR SIRDAR COLONUS SHAREMAN SHARECROPPER
FARMHAND HAND HELP
FARMHOLD CROFT
FARMHOUSE FARM TOWN ONSET GRANGE QUINTA CASERIO ONSTEAD STEADING
FARMING SOIL FARMERY HUSBANDRY
(— SYSTEM) NOTILL METAYAGE
FARMLAND ACREAGE
FARMSTEAD TOWN WICK STEAD FARMERY ONSTEAD

FARMYARD WERF CLOSE BARTON RICKYARD
FARO MONTE STUSS TIGER PHARAOH
(— CARD) SODA
FARO BANK TIGER
FAR-OFF DISTANT
FAR-OUT RAD GONZO KINKY
FARRAGO OLIO
FAR-REACHING GREAT FARGOING
FARRIER SHOER SMITH MARSHAL
FARROW PIG ROW RAKE DRAPE LITTER
FARSEEING ORACULAR
FARSIGHTED SHREWD SIGHTY
FARTHER YOND AHEAD STILL LONGER FURTHER REMOTER THITHER
FARTHEST ULTIMA ENDMOST EXTREME FARMOST LONGEST OUTMOST DOWNMOST FURTHEST REMOTEST ULTIMATE
FARTHING RAG GRIG JACK QUAD FADGE FERLING QUARTER QUADRANS QUADRANT
(HALF —) CUE
(THREE —S) GILL
FARTHINGALE FERDEGEW VERTUGAL
FASCIA BAND SASH FACIA FILLET BANDAGE MOLDING LIGATURE PLATBAND
FASCICLE BUNDLE PHALANGE
FASCICULUS HEFT BUNDLE COLUMN TRACTUS
FASCINATE DARE CHARM RIVET SEIZE WITCH ALLURE ENAMOR ATTRACT BEWITCH ENCHANT ENGROSS GLAMOUR PHILTER PHILTRE ENSORCEL ENTRANCE INTEREST INTRIGUE SIRENIZE CAPTIVATE
FASCINATED HOOKED BESOTTED
FASCINATING NUTTY ORPHIC TAKING SIRENIC CHARMING FETCHING MESMERIC
FASCINATION CHARM SPELL WITCHERY
FASCINE FAGOT FAGGOT SAUCISSE
FASCIOLA DISTOMA DISTOMUM
FASCIOLE SEMITA
FASCIST BLACK FASCISTA
FASHION GO CRY CUT FAD LAT TON WAY CHIC FEAT FORM GARB GATE KICK MAKE MODE MOLD RAGE RATE SORT TURN TWIG WEAR WISE BUILD CRAZE FEIGN FORGE FRAME GUISE MODEL MOULD SHAPE STYLE TASTE VOGUE WEAVE AGUISE ASSIZE BUSTLE CAMBER CREATE CUSTOM DESIGN FANGLE INVENT MANNER METHOD TAILOR ALAMODE COMPOSE IMAGERY PORTRAY QUALITY CONTRIVE
(LATEST —) KICK
(OF PAST —) RETRO
(PREVAILING —) CRY
(SPECIAL —) TOUCH
FASHIONABLE HIP CHIC GOGO LATE PINK POSH TONY DASHY DOGGY DOSSY NOBBY RITZY SMART SWELL SWISH VOGUE GIGOLO JAUNTY MODISH TIMISH TONISH TRENDY DASHING GALLANT GENTEEL STYLISH SWAGGER BELGRAVIAN
(NOT —) DEMODE
FASHIONABLY SMARTLY
FASHIONED HUED CARVED SHAPED WROUGHT FEATURED
FASHIONING FINGENT
FASHION PLATE SWELL
FASSAITE PYRGOM
FAST HOT HUT COLD FIRM HARD LENT SOON SURE WIDE AGILE APACE BRISK CHEAP FIXED FLASH FLEET HASTY QUICK RAPID ROUND SADLY STUCK SWIFT TIGHT TOSTO CARENE ESTHER FASTLY LIVELY SECURE SPEEDY SPORTY STABLE STARVE ABIDING EXPRESS HOTSHOT HURRIED PROVISO RASPING SETTLED SIKERLY STATION TAANITH ENDURING FAITHFUL SPINNING SPORTING WIKIWIKI
(— DAY) ASHURA
(DANGEROUSLY —) BREAKNECK
(MUSLIM —) MOHARRAM
(SUFF.) (MAKING —) PEXIA PEXIS PEXY
FAST-DYED INGRAIN
FASTEN BAR DOG FAY FIX GAD GIB KEY LAG PEN PIN SEW TAG TIE YOT BELT BEND BIND BITT BOLT BRAD CLIP FRET GIRD GIRT GLUE GRIP HANG HANK HASP HOOK HOOP HORN KILT KNIT KNOT LACE LASH LINK LOCK MOOR NAIL ROPE SEAL SNIB SOUD SPAN SPAR STAY WELD WIRE AFFIX ANNEX BELAY BIGHT BRACE CABLE CATCH CHAIN CHOCK CINCH CLAMP CLASP CLING COPSE CRAMP DEFIX GIRTH HALSH HITCH INFIX LATCH PASTE RIVET SCREW SEIZE SLOUR SNECK STEEK STICK STRAP TRUSS WITHE ANCHOR ATTACH BATTEN BUCKLE BUTTON CEMENT CLINCH COTTER COUPLE ENGAGE ENTAIL FATHER GARTER HAMPER HANKLE INKNOT PICKET SECURE SKEWER SOLDER STAPLE STITCH STRAIN TETHER BRACKET CONFINE CONNECT EMBRACE GRAPPLE GROMMET PADLOCK BARNACLE FORELOCK INTERTIE OBLIGATE TRANSFIX
(— ABOUT) THRAP
(— ANCHOR) SCOW
(— A SAIL) CROSS
(— AS SPURS) SPEND
(— IN) EMBAR
(— PROMPTLY) CLAP
(— THE LEGS) HOBBLE
(— TO) TAG
(— TOGETHER) COAPT SEIZE SPLICE CONNECT
(— WINGS ON) IMP
(— WITH A GIRTH) WARRICK
(— WITH NOTCHES) GAIN
(PREF.) HAPT(O)
FASTENED FAST SHUT BOUND FIXED BOUNDEN
(PREF.) (— TOGETHER) SYNAPTO

FASTENER BAR GIB GIN NUT PIN AGAL BOLT DOME FAST FROG HASP LOCK NAIL SNAP STUD TACK CATCH CLAMP CLASP LATCH RIVET SCREW SPIKE STRAP TATCH THONG BUCKLE BUTTON HATPIN STAPLE ZIPPER FIXATOR LATCHET PADLOCK SNAPPER TENDRIL FASTNESS STAYLACE
FASTENING TEE TIE FROG HASP SEAL SNAP SNIB STAY TACK TACHE BUCKLE CLINCH LACING MUZZLE STRIKE TINGLE BINDING CLOSURE LATCHET MOUSING PINNING SEIZING FORELOCK KNITTING
(— FOR HAWK'S WING) BRAIL
(— OF COPE) MORSE
(— ON HARPOON IRON) HITCH
(HOOK AND LOOP —) AGRAFE AGRAFFE
(PL.) GRIPES
(PREF.) DESM(A)(IDI)(IDIO)(O)
(SUFF.) PEXIA PEXIS PEXY
FAST-GOING CLIPPING
FASTIDIOUS FINE NEAT NICE CHARY DONCY FEEST FUSSY NAISH NATTY PAWKY PICKY CHOICE CHOICY CHOOSY DAINTY DONSIE MOROSE PICKED QUAINT QUEASY SPRUCE CHOOSEY CURIOUS ELEGANT FINICAL FINICKY HAUGHTY PICKING REFINED TAFFETA TAFFETY CRITICAL DELICATE EXACTING GINGERLY OVERNICE PICKSOME PRECIOUS SCORNFUL SQUEAMISH PARTICULAR PERSNICKETY SCRUMPTIOUS
(NOT —) GROSS
(OVERLY —) SAUCY
FASTIDIOUSNESS DAINTY NICETY DELICACY
FASTIGIATE CONIC
FASTING RAMADAN
(PREF.) NEST(I)
FAST-MOVING SUDDEN
FASTNESS FORT CASTLE CITADEL RETREAT FORTRESS
FAST-WORKING HOTSHOT
FAT GHI OIL TUB FOZY GHEE GRAS LARD LIPA MORT RICH SAIM SUET ADEPS BEEFY BROSY CETIN CHUFF COCUM ESTER FLECK FLICK FOGGY GROSS JUICY KEDGE KOKUM LARDY LIPID LIPIN LUSTY OBESE PLUMP PODGY PORKY PUDDY PUDGY PURSY SAAME SPICK SQUAB STOUT SUMEN THICK WASTY AXUNGE BLOWSY CHOATY CHUBBY CHUFFY DEGRAS FATTED FINISH FLESHY GREASE LIPIDE LIPOID PLUFFY PORTLY PUBBLE PUNCHY PYKNIC ROTUND STOCKY STUFFY TALLOW UCUUBA ADIPOSE BLOATED BLUBBER CEROTIN FATNESS FERTILE FLESHLY FULSOME LANOLIN OPULENT PINGUID PURSIVE REPLETE STEARIN EXTENDED FRUITFUL MARROWED MURUMURU PALMITIN UNCTUOUS
(— AROUND WHALE'S NECK) KENT
(— MEAT) SPECK

(— OF HIPPOPOTAMUS) SPECK
(— PERSON) SQUAB
(ANIMAL —) GLOR SAIM SUET ADEPS GLORE GREASE TALLOW
(CHEW THE —) GAB JAW YAK
(FLOATING —) FLOT
(LARD —) FLARE FLECK FLICK
(LOW IN —S) SPA
(LUMP OF —) KEECH
(LUMPY —) CELLULITE
(NATURAL —) ESTER
(POULTRY —) SCHMALZ SCHMALTZ
(SOLID —) LARD KIKUEL STEARIN
(PREF.) ADIP(O) LIP(O) LIPAR(O) PI(O) PIA(R)(RO) PINGUE PINGUI SEBI STEAR(O) STEAT(O)
FATAL FEY DIRE MORT FERAL VITAL DEADLY DISMAL DOOMED FUNEST LETHAL MORTAL TRAGIC CAPITAL DEATHLY EXITIAL FATEFUL KILLING OMINOUS RUINOUS UNSONSY BASILISK DESTINED EXITIOUS FUNESTAL MORTIFIC
FATALITY DOOM ACCIDENT CALAMITY DISASTER
FATA MORGANA MIRAGE
FAT-BELLIED GUTTY
FATE DIE END KER LOT CAST DOLE DOOM EURE NORN RUIN SORT STAR CAVEL EVENT GRACE KARMA MOIRA MORTA WEIRD WHATE WRITE ANANKE CHANCE KISMET DESTINY FORTUNE OUTCOME PORTION DOWNFALL FATALITY
(INEXORABLE —) HEAVEN
(PREF.) FATI
FATED DUE FEY FATAL DOOMED DECREED DESTINED
FATEFUL FATAL FATED DEADLY DOOMFUL OMINOUS DOOMLIKE
FATES CLOTHO MOERAE PARCAE ATROPOS LACHESIS
(ONE OF —) URD NONA PARCA SKULD CLOTHO DECUMA ATROPOS LACHESIS VERDANDE
FATHEAD REDFISH
FATHEADED FOZY
FATHEADEDNESS FOZINESS
FATHER BU DA PA ABU AMA DAD POP TAT ABBA ABOU AMBA ANBA ATEF BABA BAPU DADA PAPA PERE SIRE ADOPT BABBO BEGET DADDY FRIAR PADRE PATER VADER PARENT PRIEST SUBORN ELKANAH GENITOR TATINEK BEAUPERE GENERATE GOVERNOR PATRIARCH PATERFAMILIAS
(CHURCH —) APOLOGIST
(SEMIDIVINE —) PITRI
(SIDE OF —) AGNATE
(PL.) PP
(PREF.) PARRI PATR(I)(IO)(O)
FATHER GORIOT (AUTHOR OF —) BALZAC
(CHARACTER IN —) EUGENE GORIOT VAUTRIN DELPHINE ANASTASIE DERESTAUD TAILLEFER VICTORINE DENUCINGEN DEBEAUSEANT DERASTIGNAC
FATHERLAND KITH HOMELAND
FATHER-LASHER GUNDIE COTTOID SCULPIN BULLHEAD LORICATE
FATHERLESS ORBATE SIRELESS

FATHERS AND SONS (AUTHOR OF —) TURGENEV
(CHARACTER IN —) KATYA PAVEL ARKADY VASILY NIKOLAI BAZAROFF FENICHKA KIRSANOFF ODINTZOFF SITNIKOFF
FATHOM BRACE BRASS DELVE FADME PLUMB SOLVE SOUND TOUCH BOTTOM MEASURE PLUMMET
FATIGUE FAG HAG TEU BEAT BORE COOK JADE TASH TIRE TRAY SPEND STALL TARRY THRIE TRAIK TRASH WEARY HARASS OVERDO TAIGLE TUCKER EXHAUST LANGUOR TRACHLE FATIGATE VEXATION
(FLIGHT —) AERONEUROSIS
FATIGUED BEAT GONE JADED TIRED WEARY TASKIT OUTWORN WEARIED FATIGATE HARASSED OVERDONE TUCKERED
FATIGUING HARD IRKSOME
FATLIKE LIPOID
FATNESS BLOOM GREASE
FATTEN FAT BEEF LARD SOIL BRAWN FARCE FLESH FRANK PROVE SMEAR STALL BATTEN BATTLE ENRICH FINISH TALLOW THRIVE PINGUEFY SAGINATE
FATTENING FRANK BATTEL BATTABLE
FATTY SUETY BACONY GREASY ADIPOSE ADIPOUS FATLIKE PINGUID SEBIFIC STEARIC LIPAROID LIPAROUS UNCTUOUS ALIPHATIC
(PREF.) LIPAR(O)
FATUITY INANITY
FATUOUS DOPY GAGA DOPEY INANE SILLY SIMPLE STUPID UNREAL FATUATE FOOLISH IDIOTIC WITLESS DEMENTED ILLUSORY IMBECILE
FAUCES JAWS
FAUCET BIB TAP BIBB COCK QUILL SPOUT VALVE CUTOFF DOSSIL DOZZLE OFFLET SPIGOT BIBCOCK HYDRANT PETCOCK TURNCOCK
(WOODEN —) HORSE
FAUGH BAH FOH VAH
FAUJDAR PHOUSDAR
FAULT BUG RUB SIN BEAM CLAG COUP DEBT FAIL FLAW FLUB GALL HOLE LACK LAST MOLE SAKE SLIP SPOT VICE WANT WITE ABUSE AMISS BLAME BREAK CULPA ERROR FLUFF GUILT LAPSE SCAPE SHIFT SLIDE SWICK TACHE BLOTCH DEFECT FOIBLE RUNNER THRUST VICETY VITIUM BLEMISH BLISTER BLUNDER DEFAULT DEMERIT EYELAST FAILING FAILURE FRAILTY MISTAKE NEGLECT OFFENSE FAULTING PECCANCY WEAKNESS
(— IN BADMINTON) SLING
(AT —) CULPABLE
(MINING —) COUP LEAP CHECK HITCH
(TRIFLING —) PECCADILLO
(PL.) FAULTAGE
FAULTFINDER MOMUS CARPER

CHIDER CRITIC MOMIST CAPTION KNOCKER NAGSTER
FAULTFINDING CARPING CAPTIOUS CRITICAL
FAULTILY BADLY
FAULTLESS PURE CLEAN RIGHT CORRECT PERFECT PRECISE FLAWLESS
FAULTY BAD ILL SICK AMISS UNFIT WRONG FLAWED FAULTED PECCANT VICIOUS BLAMABLE CULPABLE SPURIOUS
(PREF.) DYS PARA
FAUN SATYR WOODMAN WOODWOSE
FAUNA ANIMALS FAUNULA FAUNULE ZOOLOGY
(FOSSIL —) BIOCHRON
FAUSSEBRAIE VAMURE VAUMURE
FAUST (AUTHOR OF —) GOETHE
(CHARACTER IN —) FAUST HELEN SIEBEL WAGNER GRETCHEN VALENTINE HOMUNCULUS MARGUERITE MEPHISTOPHELES
(COMPOSER OF —) GOUNOD
FAUX PAS GAFF SLIP BONER ERROR GAFFE BLOOMER FLOATER MISSTEP MISTAKE SNAPPER
FAVOLA D'ORFEO (CHARACTER IN —) PLUTO APOLLO CHARON ORPHEUS MESSENGER PROSERPINA
(COMPOSER OF —) MONTEVERDI
FAVOR AID FOR ORE PRO BOON ESTE FACE GREE HEAR HELP LIKE MAKE BLESS BRIBE GRACE LEAVE MENSK SERVE SPARE SPEED THANK TREAT ASSIST ERRAND ESTEEM FAVOUR LETTER NOTICE PENCEL UPHOLD ADVANCE AGGRACE BENEFIT ENFAVOR FEATURE FORWARD GRATIFY INDULGE RESPECT SUPPORT ADVOCACY BEFRIEND COURTESY FAVORIZE GOODWILL KINDNESS RESEMBLE SYMPATHY ACCEPTANCE
FAVORABLE HOT BOON FAIR FREE GOOD HIGH KIND ROSY TIDY CIVIL CLEAR HAPPY LARGE MERRY TRINE WILLY WILLY BENIGN DEXTER GENIAL GOLDEN KINDLY TOWARD BENEFIC EXALTED OPTIMAL POPULAR PRESENT FAVONIAN FRIENDLY GRACIOUS PLEASING PROPENSE SPEEDFUL TOWARDLY BENIGNANT PROPITIOUS PROSPEROUS
(— TO PURCHASER) KEEN
(NOT —) INFAUST
FAVORABLY FAIR WELL HIGHLY
FAVORED WELL FAURD HAPPY FAURED GIFTED BLESSED FAVOURED
FAVORER FAUTOR FRIEND FAVORITE
FAVORING FAVONIAN
(PREF.) PRO
(SUFF.) ABLE IBLE
FAVORITE BOY PET POT DEAR PEAT CHALK GREAT INGLE WHITE MINION DARLING FANCIED MINIKIN

POPULAR SPECIAL GRACIOSO WHITEBOY
FAVORITE, LA (CHARACTER IN —) GUSMAN ALFONSO LEONORA FERNANDO
(COMPOSER OF —) DONIZETTI
FAVORITISM BIAS FAVOR NEPOTISM
FAVUS TILE WHITECOMB
FAWN COG BUCK CLAW DEER FAON JOUK ROOT COWER CRAWL CREEP GLOZE HONEY SMARM TOADY WHELP CRINGE CROUCH GROVEL KOWTOW SHRINK SLAVER ADULATE CROODLE CRUDDLE FLATTER FLETHER HANGDOG SERVILE SPANIEL TOADEAT TRUCKLE WHEATEN BOOTLICK
(— UPON) SUCK SMOOGE ADULATE
FAWN-COLORED CERVINE
FAWNIA (LOVER OF —) DORASTUS
FAWNING SLEEK CRINGE GREASE MENIAL SLEEKY SMARMY SUPPLE FLETHER GLOZING HANGDOG SERVILE SPANIEL FLATTERY
FAWNSKIN NEBRIS
FAY ELF FEY FAIRY FEIGH
FAZE DAUNT FEEZE PHASE WORRY
FEALTY FEE FEWTE HOMAGE LOYALTY SERVICE TREWAGE FIDELITY
FEAR UG AWE DREE FLAY FUNK WARD ALARM DOUBT DREAD JELLY PANIC AFFRAY ALARUM DANGER DISMAY FRIGHT HORROR PHOBIA TERROR ANXIETY SUSPECT AFFRIGHT DISQUIET DISTRUST EERINESS MISDOUBT VENERATE
(— OF CROSSING STREETS) DROMOPHOBIA
(— OF DRAFTS) AEROPHOBIA
(— OF FALLING) BATHOPHOBIA HYPSOPHOBIA
(— OF HOME SURROUNDINGS) ECOPHOBIA
(— OF OPEN PLACES) AGORAPHOBIA
(— OF THUNDER) ASTRAPHOBIA
(INTERJECTION TO EXPRESS —) YIKES
(IRRATIONAL —) PARANOIA
(PREF.) PHOB(O)
(SUFF.) PHOBE PHOBIA(C) PHOBIC PHOBOUS
FEARFUL ARGH DIRE AWFUL FERLY PAVID TIMID WINDY WROTH AFRAID COWISH FRIGHTY GHASTLY NERVOUS PANICKY WORRIED CAUTIOUS DOUBTFUL DREADFUL GREWSOME GRUESOME HORRIBLE HORRIFIC PARANOID SHOCKING SKITTISH TERRIBLE TERRIFIC TIMOROUS
(PREF.) DEIN(O) DIN(O)
FEARLESS BOLD BRAVE DARING HEROIC AWELESS IMPAVID INTREPID
FEASIBLE FIT LIKELY POSSIBLE PROBABLE SUITABLE
FEAST (ALSO SEE FESTIVAL) EAT FOY PIG SUP DINE FARM FETE LUAU MEAL TUCK UTAS AZYME CHEER CHOES CITUA DIRGY FESTA

FESTY GAUDY REVEL TREAT ARTHEL AVERIL BRIDAL DEVOUR DINNER DOUBLE INFARE ISODIA JUNKET MAUNDY REGALE REPAST SIMPLE SMOUSE SPREAD AHAAINA BANQUET BRIDALE DELIGHT FESTINO GRATIFY GREGORY LAMBALE LEMURIA SHEVUOS SYNAXIS ANALEPSY CAROUSAL DOMINEER EPIPHANY FESTIVAL GESTNING GESTONIE HANUKKAH KOIMESIS PASSOVER POTLATCH SHABUOTH VESTALIA
(— BEFORE JOURNEY) FOY
(— OF BOOTHS) SUCCOS SUKKOTH
(— OF LANTERNS) HON
(— OF LOTS) PURIM
(— OF WEEKS) SHEVUOS SHABUOTH
(— PLACE) IDGAH
(DRINKING —) BANQUET
(FUNERAL —) ARVAL ARVEL DIRGY DIRGIE DREDGIE
(HARVEST —) BUSK
(JEWISH —) SENDAH
(LOVE —) AGAPE
(RELIGIOUS —) CANAO KANYAW PENTECOST
(VILLAGE —) TANSY
(PREF.) DAPI FESTI FESTO HEORTO
(SUFF.) (— DAY) MAS
FEASTER CONVIVE
FEASTING FEAST CARNIVAL
FEAT ACT KIP DEED FATE GEST WORK GESTE SPLIT STUNT TRICK CRADDY CUTOFF EXPLOIT MASTERY MIRACLE WORSHIP DEXTROUS PERFORMANCE
(— IN SURFING) SPINNER QUASIMODO
(ACROBATIC —) SPLITS
(CRICKETER'S —) DOUBLE
(EASY —) PICNIC
(EFFECTIVE —) STROKE
(TUMBLING —) SCISSORS
(PL.) DAGS
FEATHER BOO PEN TAB DECK DOWN FLAG HERL SETA STUB VANE ADORN AXIAL PENNA PINNA PLUMA PLUME QUILL REMEX CLOTHE COVERT CRINET FLEDGE FLETCH FLIGHT HACKLE MANUAL PINION SARCEL SICKLE SQUAMA TIPPET TONGUE AXILLAR BRISTLE FLEMISH IMPLUME PRIMARY RECTRIX REMICLE STIPULE TECTRIX TERTIAL TOPPING AXILLARY SCAPULAR STREAMER TERTIARY
(BRISTLELIKE —) VIBRISSA
(HAWK'S —S) BRAIL BRAILS
(HORSE —) SPEAR
(NECK —) HACKLE
(NEW —) STIPULE
(OSTRICH TAIL —) BOO
(PINION —) SARCEL
(PRIMARY —) MANUAL
(TAIL —) SICKLE RECTRIX
(YELLOW —S) HULU
(PL.) GIG BOOT CAPE DOWN FLUE MAIL BRAIL CRISSUM CUSHION FLIGHTS PLUMAGE REMIGES SPURIAE

(PREF.) PENNAT(I)(O) PENNI PENNO
PINN(I)(O) PINNAT(I)(O) PLUMI
PTER(O) PTIL(O)
(SUFF.) PENNATE PENNINE PTILE
PTILUS

FEATHER BED TYE
FEATHER CLOAK AHUULA TEMIAK
FEATHERED FLEDGE FLEDGY
PLUMED PENNATE PINNATE
FLIGHTED
(PREF.) PTENO
(SUFF.) PINNATE
FEATHERHEAD FOOL
FEATHERING STOCKING
FEATHER KEY FIN STOP SPLINE
FEATHER
FEATHER-LEGGED COOTY COOTIE
FEATHERLIKE PINNATE
FEATHERY LIGHT PLUMY FLEDGY
FLUFFY PLUMOSE PLUMEOUS
FEATLY NEATLY FOOTINGLY
FEATURE WAY FACE ITEM NOTE
STAR BREAK FAVOR GRACE MOTIF
TOKEN TRACT TRAIT TREAT
ASPECT CACHET FAVOUR SPLASH
AMENITY OUTLINE HALLMARK
SALIENCE
(— OF WORD FORM) ASPECT
(ATTRACTIVE —) AMENITY
(DETERMINING —) LIMIT
(DISTINGUISHING —) TRAIT STROKE
HALLMARK
(ESSENTIAL —) CHARACTER
(FATAL —) BANE
(LINGUISTIC —) ISOGLOSS
SURVIVAL
(MAIN —) CRUX
(MOST COGENT —) BEAUTY
(OBJECTIONABLE —) DISCOUNT
DRAWBACK
(SALIENT —) MOTIF
(TOPOGRAPHIC —) ARC
(TOPOGRAPHIC —S) LIE
(PL.) LAY FACE CONTOUR FASHION
GEOLOGY RETRAIT
FEAZE FRAY FAIZE ROUGHEN
FEBRIFUGE PEREIRA ANGOSTURA
FEBRILE PYRETIC FEVERISH
FECES DRAST HOCKEY ORDURE
(PREF.) COPR(O)
FECKLESS WEAK FEEBLE
FECULENCE DREG
FECULENT DREGGY
FECUND FERTILE FRUITFUL
PROLIFIC
FED FAT MEATED
FEDERATION BUND CROM UNION
LEAGUE NATION COUNCIL
ALLIANCE FEDERACY TRIALISM
FEDORA (CHARACTER IN —) LORIS
FEDORA IPANOV ROMANOV
(COMPOSER OF —) GIORDANO
FEE FEU DUES DUTY FEAL FEUL FIEF
FIER HIRE RATE WAGE CAULP
EXTRA HANSE PRICE RIGHT
ALNAGE AMOBER BARONY
CHARGE DASTUR EMPLOY EXCISE
REWARD SALARY SHEKEL
BUOYAGE DASTURI DUMPAGE
DUSTOOR FALDAGE FIRNAGE
FURNAGE GAOLAGE GARNISH
GRATIFY GUIDAGE HALLAGE
HOUSAGE JAILAGE MULTURE

PAYMENT PINLOCK PREFINE
STIPEND STORAGE TALLAGE
TRIBUTE VANTAGE BOOTHAGE
BOUNTITH CHUMMAGE EXACTION
FAREWELL GRATUITY MALIKANA
POUNDAGE REREFIEF RETAINER
SHIPPAGE WHARFAGE
(— TO LANDOWNER) TERRAGE
(— TO TEACHER) MINERVAL
(CUSTOMARY —) DASTUR
(CUSTOMS —) LOT
(ENTRANCE —) HANSA HANSE
INCOME
(GRINDING —) THIRLAGE
(INITIATION —) FOOTING
(INSTALLATION —) FOOTING
(PHYSICIAN'S —) SOSTRUM
(ROAD —) PIKE
(UNAUTHORIZED —) GARNISH
(PL.) EXHIBITS
FEEBLE LOW WAN FLUE LAME
MEAN PALE POOR PUNY SOFT
WEAK DONCY DOTTY FAINT SEELY
SILLY SOBER UNORN WANKY
WASHY WERSH WONKY CADUKE
DEBILE DONSIE DOTAGE FAINTY
FLABBY FLIMSY FOIBLE INFIRM
PAULIE PUISNE SCANTY SEMMIT
SICKLY SIMPLE TANGLE UNFIRM
WANKLE WEANLY DWAIBLY
DWEEBLE FRAGILE INVALID
LANGUID QUEECHY RICKETY
SAPLESS SHILPIT SLENDER
SLIMPSY THREADY UNWIELD
UNWREST WEARISH DECREPIT
DROGHLIN FEATLESS IMBECILE
IMPOTENT INFERIOR LUSTLESS
MALADIVE RESOLUTE SACKLESS
THEWLESS THOWLESS UNSTRONG
UNWIELDY WATERISH YIELDING
NERVELESS
FEEBLE-MINDED ANILE DOTTY
DOTTLE FOOLISH MORONIC
WANTING IMBECILE
FEEBLENESS DOTAGE FEEBLE
POVERTY CADUCITY DEBILITY
WEAKNESS
FEED EAT HAY BAIT BEET BRAN
CROP DIET DINE FILL FOOD GLUT
GRUB MEAL MEAT OATS SATE
AGIST FLESH FLUSH GORGE GRASS
GRAZE NURSE SERVE STOKE TABLE
BATTLE BROWSE FODDER FOSTER
INFEED NOODLE REFETE REPAST
SUCKLE SUPPLY BLOWOUT
FURNISH GRATIFY HERBAGE
INDULGE KEEPING NOURISH
NURTURE PASTURE PROVENT
SATIATE SATISFY SUBSIST SURFEIT
SUSTAIN VICTUAL PROVENDER
(— ABUNDANTLY) STOKE
(— ANIMAL) SORT SERVE
(— AT NIGHT) SUP
(— CATTLE) SOIL
(— FOR CATTLE) FODDER STOVER
TACKLE
(— FORCIBLY) CRAM
(— GLUTTONOUSLY) BATTEN
(— GREEN FOOD TO CATTLE) SOIL
(— HIGH) FRANK
(— IN STUBBLE) SHACK
(— ON FLIES) SMUT
(— RAVENOUSLY) FRAUNCH

(— STOCK) FOG SOIL SOILING
(— TO REPLETION) ENGORGE
(— TO THE FULL) SATIATE
(— WELL) BATTLE
(GROUND —) CHOP
(HORSE'S —) OATS
(POULTRY —) SCRATCH
(RED —) HAYSEED
(STOCK —) BRAN
(WHALE —) GRIT
(PREF.) THREP(SO)
FEEDBOARD DECK
FEEDER HOGGER HOPPER PECKER
STOCKER
(YARN —) CARRIER
FEEDHEAD RISER FEEDER
SINKHEAD
FEEDING RELIEF FOLDAGE
PANNAGE
(— GROUND FOR FISH) MEADOW
(— THROUGH TUBE) GAVAGE
(FREE-CHOICE —) CAFETERIA
(IMPROPER —) MISDIET
(PREF.) PHAG(O)
FEEL FIND PALP GROPE SENSE
THINK TOUCH FIMBLE FINGER
HANDLE RESENT EXAMINE
EXPLORE FEELING SENSATE
PERCEIVE
(— ACUTELY) SUFFER
(— AVERSION FOR) HATE LOATHE
(— CHILLY) CREEM
(— COMPASSION) PITY YEARN
(— DEJECTION) REPINE
(— FEAR) UG GRUE UGGE TREMBLE
(— GRIEF) GRIEVE DEPLORE
(— HAPPY OR BETTER) LIGHT
(— NAUSEA) WAMBLE
(— OF CLOTH) HAND
(— ONE'S WAY) GROPE FUMBLE
GRAMMEL
(— OUT) SOUND
(— PAIN) URN
(— REPUGNANCE) ABHOR
(— SHAME) BLUSH
(— WANT OF) MISS
FEELER DRAW KITE PALP SNIFF
PALPUS TACTOR ANTENNA
SMELLER PROPOSAL TENTACLE
(PREF.) ANTENNI
FEELING AURA FEEL PITY TACT VIBE
VIEW CHEER HEART HUMOR
SENSE SORGE TOUCH VIBES
AFFECT CEMENT MORALE
CONSENT EMOTION OPINION
PASSION VELUNGE ATTITUDE
SENTIENT SENSATION
PRESENTIMENT
(— ILL) HOWISH
(— MIRTH) JOCUND
(— OF ACCORD) SYMPATHY
(— OF AMUSEMENT) CHARGE
(— OF ANTIPATHY) ALLERGY
(— OF ANXIETY) ANGST
(— OF CONTEMPT) DISDAIN
(— OF DISGUST) UG
(— OF DOUBT) SCRUPLE
(— OF HAVING SEEN BEFORE)
DEJAVU
(— OF HORROR) CREEP CREEPS
(— OF HOSTILITY) ANIMUS
(— OF JOY) GLOAT
(— OF LOSS) REGRET

(— OF NAUSEA) WAMBLE
(— OF OPPOSITION) KICK
(— OF PLEASURE) THRILL
(— OF RESENTMENT) GRUDGE
(— OF ROMANCE) STARDUST
(— OF UNEASINESS) MALAISE
(— OF WARMTH) GLOW
(— OF WEARINESS) ENNUI
(— OF WELL-BEING) EUPHORIA
(— PRODUCED BY DRUG) RUSH
(ACTIVE —) SWANKY
(ANGERED —) DUDGEON
(AWKWARD —) LUBBER
(BODILY —) TABET
(BRISTLING —) GOOSEFLESH
(COMPASSIONATE —) REMORSE
(CONCEITED —) SWELLING
(EXALTED —) ECSTASY
(FAMILIAR —) DEJAVU
(HUMILIATING —) SHAME
(ILL —) HARDNESS
(INMOST —S) HEART
(INTUITIVE —) HUNCH
(KINDLY) GOODWILL
(LOW-BORN —) LOON
(MISCHIEVOUS —) SPALPEEN
(OFFENDED —) PET
(PALTRY —) SQUIB
(PLEASANT —) BUZZ
(RAGGED —) SNUDGE
(RAKISH —) RAFF
(REPRESSION OF —) STOICISM
(SCURVY —) SCALD
(SHOCKED —) SCANDAL
(SICKLY —) QUALM
(STRONG —) STAB
(STRONG, POSITIVE —) SOUL
(TENDEREST —S) QUICK
(TRIFLING —) TOMFOOL
(UNKIND —) ILLWILL
(PL.) HEART WITHERS
(PREF.) SENSI
(SUFF.) PATH(IA)(IC)(Y)
FEEN, DIE (CHARACTER IN —) ADA
GROMA ARINDAL
(COMPOSER OF —) WAGNER
FEET DOGS TONGS STAMPS
WALKERS GUNBOATS TRILBIES
PETTITOES
(— WASHING) MAUNDY
(BOARD —) FOOTAGE
(LARGE —) GUFFINS
(PREF.) PED(I)
(SUFF.) PEDE
(MEASURE OF —) METER
FEIGN ACT FAKE MINT MOCK SEEM
SHAM VEYN AVOID FABLE FALSE
FORGE PAINT PUTON SHAPE SHIRK
AFFECT ASSUME GAMMON INVENT
POSSUM CONCEAL FALSIFY
FASHION IMAGINE POETIZE
PRETEND ROMANCE DISGUISE
SIMULATE
(— ASSENT) COLLOGUE
(— IGNORANCE) CONNIVE
(— ILLNESS) MALINGER
FEIGNED SHAM FALSE FEINT
POETIC PSEUDO SHADOW
ASSUMED COLORED FICTIVE
PAINTED FABULOUS FICTIOUS
SIMULATE SUPPOSED
(PREF.) PSEUD(O)

FEIGNING FICTION FORGERY SIMULATION
FEIJOA ANDRE
FEINT FAKE MINT RUSE APPEL FAINT SHIFT SPOOF TRICK FALSIFY FEIGNED FEINTER FINCTURE PRETENSE REVIRADO
FELDSPAR ALBITE AMBITE GNEISS CELSIAN SYENITE ADULARIA ANDESINE FELSPATH PERTHITE PETUNTZE SANIDINE SUNSTONE MOONSTONE
FELICIA AGATHAEA
FELICITATE HUG BLESS MACARIZE
FELICITOUS FIT HAPPY
FELICITOUSLY HAPPILY
FELICITY JOY BLISS SONSE HEAVEN
FELINE CATTISH
FELL CUR FEN HEW COSH DOWN DROP FALL HIDE HILL MOOR PELT RUIN SKIN VERY CRUEL EAGER FIELD GRASS GREAT SHARP DEADLY FIERCE FLEECE INTENT MIGHTY SAVAGE SHREWD TUMBLE BRUTISH CRASHED DOUGHTY HIDEOUS INHUMAN STRETCH TUMBLED MOUNTAIN SPIRITED VIGOROUS
(**— A TREE**) HEW LODGE
FELLER GIDEON
FELLING FALL CUTTING
FELLOE BOD FELF FALLY
FELLOW S BO BOY BUB COD DON EGG FOX GUY JOE LAD MAC MAN MUN NUT WAG WAT YOB BALL BEAN BEAU BIRD BOZO BUFF CARL CHAL CHAP COOT COVE CUSS DEAN DICK DUCK DUDE DULL GENT GILL GINK HIND HUSK JACK JAKE JOHN LOON MATE NABS PEER PRIG SNAP BILLY BIMBO BLOKE BROCK BUDDY BULLY CARLE CHIEL COVEY CULLY FRUIT GROOM GUEST JOKER MATCH PARTY SCOUT SKATE SLAVE SPORT SPRIG SWIPE BEGGAR BILLIE BIRKIE BOHUNK BOOGER BUDDIE BUFFER BUGGER BUSTER CALLAN CHIELD CODGER CUFFIN CUTTER FELLER FOOTER FOUTER FOUTRA GALOOT GAZABO GEEZER HOMBRE JASPER JOCKEY JOHNNY JOSSER KIPPER PERSON SHAVER SINNER SIRRAH SISTER SOCIUS TURNIP BASTARD BROTHER CALLANT CHAPPIE COMRADE CULLIES CULLION CUSTRON KNOCKER PARTNER SCROYLE SNOOZER BLIGHTER CONFRERE DOTTEREL MERCHANT NEIGHBOR SYNODITE
(**AWKWARD —**) JAY OAF CLUB GAWK CLOWN LOOBY GALOOT SLOUCH
(**BASE —**) CARL CARLE CULLION
(**BASHFUL —**) SHEEP
(**BOLD —**) HEARTY
(**BRUTAL —**) CLUBFIST
(**CLOWNISH —**) COOF BAYARD LOBLOLLY
(**CLUMSY —**) BOOB FILE CAMEL FARMER LUBBER PALOOKA
(**COMMON —**) JACK LOUT

(**CONCEITED —**) JEMMY DALTEEN PRINCOX
(**CONTEMPTIBLE —**) DOG SCUT SMAIL SNAKE RABBIT SMATCH PEASANT
(**CONTENTIOUS —**) SQUARER
(**CORPULENT —**) POMPION
(**COUNTRY —**) JAKE JASPER
(**CRUDE —**) STIFF
(**DASHING —**) BUCK BLADE
(**DASTARDLY —**) HOUND
(**DECEITFUL —**) KNAVE
(**DESPICABLE —**) FOUTER FOUTRA HANGDOG SMATCHET
(**DIRTY —**) SCAB BROCK
(**DISAGREEABLE —**) GLEYDE
(**DISSOLUTE —**) RAKE ROUE RAKEHELL
(**DROLL —**) CARD
(**DROWSY —**) LUNGIS
(**DRUNKEN —**) BORACHIO
(**DULL —**) BUFF DRIP FOGY CHUFF SUMPH LUNGIS HUMDRUM
(**ENERGETIC —**) HUSTLER
(**FAT —**) HIND GULCH GLUTTON
(**FIERCE-LOOKING —**) KILLBUCK
(**FINE —**) BAWCOCK
(**FOOLISH —**) SOP GABY GOFF ZANY GANDER JACKSON WIDGEON
(**GAY —**) GALLIARD
(**GOOD —**) BRICK BULLY TRUMP HEARTY TROJAN
(**GOOD-FOR-NOTHING —**) JACKEEN
(**GREEDY —**) SLOTE
(**IDLE —**) FANION FOOTER STOCAH LOLLARD SKULKER
(**IGNORANT —**) GOBBIN
(**ILLBRED —**) LARRIKIN
(**IMPERTINENT —**) JACK WHISK
(**INSIGNIFICANT —**) SQUIB
(**JOLLY —**) VAVASOR VAVASOUR
(**LAZY —**) BUM LUSK TOOL LENTO
(**LOW —**) RAG WAFF SWEEP LIMMER VARLET MECHANIC WHORESON
(**LUBBERLY —**) HULK
(**MEAN —**) CAD DOG BOOR BOUCH BUCKO CAVEL CHURL SCURF RASCAL CULLION BEZONIAN COISTREL COISTRIL SNEAKSBY SPALPEEN STINKARD
(**NIGGARDLY —**) SNUDGE
(**NOISY —**) MOUTH
(**OLD —**) GLYDE GAFFER GEEZER
(**OLD-FASHIONED —**) FOGY
(**OVERBEARING —**) GRIMSIR
(**PROSAIC —**) PRUNE
(**PUNY —**) SMAIK
(**QUARRELSOME —**) HECTOR
(**QUEER OLD —**) CODGER GEEZER
(**RESIDENTIAL —**) DON
(**ROGUISH —**) DOG
(**RUDE —**) BOOR JACK ROUGH
(**SHABBY —**) SHAB SQUEEF
(**SHEEPISH —**) SUMPH
(**SHIFTLESS —**) PROG SHACK PROGGER
(**SHREWD —**) COLT
(**SILLY —**) TOT GUMP ZANY SHEEP SMAIK BUFFER DOTTEREL MUSHHEAD
(**SIMPLE —**) DOODLE

(**SLOVENLY —**) SLUTE
(**SLY —**) FOX COON
(**SNEAKING —**) SNUDGE
(**SORDID —**) HUNKS
(**SOUTH AFRICAN —**) KEREL
(**SPIRITED —**) BRICK
(**SPORTY —**) PLAYBOY
(**STRANGE —**) CODGER
(**STRAPPING —**) SWANKY SWANKIE
(**STUPID —**) ASS BOOB CLOD COOF DAFF DOLT GUMP HASH MUFF SIMP BOOBY CUDDY DUNCE MORON STIRK BAYARD BUFFER FARMER FOOZLE GANDER ASINOCO DOWFART HUMDRUM CLODPATE CLODPOLE CLODPOLL CODSHEAD SOCKHEAD
(**STURDY —**) HUSKY
(**SULLEN —**) GLUMP
(**SURLY —**) CHUFF CHOUGH
(**TEDIOUS —**) FOOZLE
(**TRICKISH —**) HUMBUG
(**TRICKY —**) ROOK GREEK KNAVE SCAMP DODGER RASCAL
(**UNCIVIL —**) RUDESBY
(**UNCOUTH —**) JAKE KEMP TIKE
(**VILE —**) RAT SKUNK
(**VULGAR —**) TIGER
(**WORTHLESS —**) BUM CUR DOG HASH PROG RAFF WAFF JAVEL ROGUE SCAMP SHOAT SNAKE STUMER BROTHEL BUDMASH PROGGER VAURIEN TARTARET
(**WRETCHED —**) DEVIL DOGBOLT
(**YOUNG —**) BILLY BUCKO CADIE CADDIE
(PREF.) CO
(SUFF.) ENGRO
FELLOWMAN BROTHER NEIGHBOR
FELLOWSHIP GUILD HAUNT UNION FAMILY COMPANY ALLIANCE SODALITY
(**CHRISTIAN —**) KOINONIA
FELLY RIM FELF FELLOE KEENLY CRUELLY BITTERLY FIERCELY SAVAGELY TERRIBLY
FELO-DE-SE SUICIDE
FELON WILD CRUEL FETLOW FIERCE WICKED CONVICT CULPRIT PANARIS VILLAIN WHITLOW PHLEGMON RUNROUND MALEFACTOR
FELONY ARSON CRIME OFFENSE
FELT JIG PLAIT FILTER NUMNAH SENSED SOLEIL VELOUR DOUBLER FELTING PANNOSE
(**— INTENSIVELY**) ACUTE
(**— THROUGH SENSES**) SENSATE
(**DEEPLY —**) CORDIAL INTENSE
(**PERSONALLY —**) CONSCIOUS
(PL.) CLOTHING
(PREF.) PIL(O)
FELTWORK NEUROPIL
FEMALE DOE EWE HEN HER SHE SOW DAME GIRL GYNE LADY MORT ADULT JENNY SMOCK SQUAW WOMAN WAHINE WEAKLY DISTAFF FEMINAL WOMANLY DAUGHTER FEMININE GYNAECIC LADYLIKE WOMANISH PETTICOAT
(**— ANCESTOR**) TAPROOT
(**IMPERFECT —**) FREEMARTIN

(**PARTHOGENETIC —**) AMAZON
(PREF.) FEMINO GYN(AE)(AECO) (AEO)(ANDRO)(E)(ECO)(EO)(O) THELY
(SUFF.) ESS ETTE GYN(E)(IST)(OUS) INE TRIX
FEMININE FAIR SOFT WEAK WOMAN FEMALE TENDER WAHINE FEMINAL WOMANLY WOMANISH PETTICOAT
(SUFF.) ENNE INA INE
FEMININE WILES (**CHARACTER IN —**) BELLINA LEONORA FILANDRO GIAMPOLO ROMUALDO
(**COMPOSER OF —**) CIMAROSA
FEMININITY MUSLIN FEMINITY MULIEBRITY
FEMME FATALE VAMP SIREN
FEMORAL CRURAL
(PREF.) CRURO
FEMUR THIGH
FEN BOG CARR FAIN FELL FOWL MERE MOOR WASH BROAD FAINS MARSH SNIPE SWAMP VENTS MORASS MUSKEG QUAGMIRE
FENCE BAR HAW HAY BANK DIKE DUEL DYKE HAHA HAIN PALE PLAY RAIL STUB WALL WEIR WIRE BEARD DODGE FRITH GUARD HEDGE MOUND PALIS STICK STUMP DETENT FENDER FRAISE GLANCE HURDLE LEADER PALING PICKET RADDLE RASPER SCHERM SCRIME TIMBER BARRIER BULWARK CYCLONE DEFENSE ENCLOSE FENCING FENSURE IMPALER PASSAGE RAILING SWAGMAN BACKSTOP ENCHASER ENCLOSER GRAFFAGE HOARDING PALISADE PALISADO SEPIMENT SKIRMISH BRANDRETH BRANDRITH
(**— AROUND BULLRING**) BARRERA
(**— AROUND MACHINERY**) BRATTICE
(**— CLOSING DITCH**) WOLF
(**— OF LOCK**) STUB
(**— OF LOGS**) GLANCE
(**CATTLE —**) OXER WIPE SKERM SCHERM
(**FISH —**) WEIR KIDDLE LEADER
(**METAL —**) RAIL RAILING
(PREF.) HERCO PHRAGMO SEPTATO
(SUFF.) SEPTATE
FENCER DUELIST IMPALER PARRIER PROVOST SCRIMER SWORDER FOILSMAN BACKSWORD
FENCE RAIL DRAWBAR
FENCE SECTION PANE
FENCE-SITTER MUGWUMP
FENCING WIRE FENCE PALING ESCRIME PASSAGE SCIENCE SWORDING
(**— THRUST**) PASSADO
(**JAPANESE —**) KENDO
FEND WARD PARRY SHIRK DEFEND FORBID RESIST SUPPORT
FENDER SKID WING CAMEL GUARD SKATE BUFFER BUMPER SHIELD DOLPHIN PUDDING BOWGRACE MUDGUARD SPLASHER
(**— FOR FIREPLACE**) CURB KERB
(**— NEAR HOLE**) TELLTALE

(ROPE —) PUDDENING
(SHIP'S —) SKID
FENDER SKID GLANCER
FENESTRA FORAMEN
FENGHUANG FUM PHOENIX
FENKS FRITTERS
FENMAN WEBFOOT
FENNEC ZERDA
FENNEL ANIS DILL HEMP SOYA
FERULE FINKEL COWBANE
HOGWEED SPINGEL FINOCHIO
FLORENCE CAROSELLA
FENNER ZERDA
FENRIS (FATHER OF —) LOKI
(MOTHER OF —) ANGURBODA
(SISTER OF —) HEL
(SLAYER OF —) VIDAR
FENSTER WINDOW
FENUGREEK BAUMIER MELLILOT
(SEEDS OF —) HELBEH
FERAL WILD BRUTAL DEADLY
FERINE SAVAGE BESTIAL
UNTAMED FUNEREAL UNBROKEN
FER-DE-LANCE BONETAIL
JARARACA
FERMATA HOLD PAUSE TENOR
CORONA
FERMENT FRY LOB ZYM BARM
BREW FRET HEAT SOUR TURN
WORK ZYME FEVER SWEAT YEAST
DANDER ENZYME FLOWER
FOMENT SEETHE SIMMER TUMULT
UPROAR AGITATE QUICKEN
TURMOIL DISORDER
(— IN SALIVA) PTYALIN
(DIGESTIVE —) TRYPSIN
(PREF.) ZYM(O)
(SUFF.) ZYME
FERMENTATION SWEAT CUVAGE
FERMENT MOWBURN WORKING
ZYMOSIS
FERMENTED SOD HARD
(IMPROPERLY —) FOXY
FERMENTING BARMY WORKING
FERN HEII NITO PULU TARA WEKI
BRAKE DUGAL EKAHA FROND
NARDO PITAU PONGA ULUHI
WHEKI AMAMAU DOODIA NARDOO
OSMUND PTERIS ACROGEN
ATERACH BOGFERN BRACKEN
OSMUNDA SYNANGE WOODSIA
ADIANTUM ASPIDIUM BAROMETZ
BUCKHORN BUNGWALL CETERACH
DAVALLIA DENDRITE FERNWORT
FILICITE GOLDBACK HARDFERN
KOLOKOLO MOONWORT
MULEWORT PARAREKA PILLWORT
POLYPODY SPOROGEN STAGHORN
MAIDENHAIR
(KIND OF —) MALE
(PART OF —) AXIS CASE LEAF STEM
BLADE FROND PINNA STIPE TOOTH
MIDRIB RACHIS LEAFLET PETIOLE
PINNULE SUBLEAFLET
(PL.) FILICES
(PREF.) PTERID(O)
(SUFF.) PTERIS
FERN LEAF FROND CROSIER
FERNLIKE FERNY PTEROID
FEROCIOUS ILL FELL GRIM RUDE
WILD BRUTE CRUEL FERAL
BLOODY BRUTAL FEROCE FIERCE
GOTHIC RAGING SAVAGE ACHARNE

INHUMAN OMINOUS VIOLENT
WOLFISH PITILESS RAVENOUS
RUTHLESS TARTARLY
FEROCITY FERITY SAVAGERY
VIOLENCE ACHARNEMENT
FERRARA ANDREW
FERRET HOB MONK TAPE PADOU
MONACH WEASEL POLECAT
(— OUT) FOSSICK
(FEMALE —) GIL GILL JILL BITCH
(MALE —) HOB HOBB
FERRIAGE WAFTAGE
FERRIC OXIDE CROCUS
FERROCYANIDE PRUSSIATE
FERROTYPE GLAZE TINTYPE
FERROUS SIDEROUS
FERRULE CAP TIP CUFF RING SHOE
VIRL COLLET PULLEY RUNNER
VERREL VIROLE ARMGARN
BUSHING CRAMPET
FERRY FORD PASS PONT SCOW
PASSAGE TRAJECT TRANECT
TRANSFER
FERRYBOAT BAC PONT SCOW
FERRY
FERRYMAN CHARON FERRIER
WATERMAN
FERTILE FAT GOOD RANK RICH
GLEBY ARABLE BATFUL BATTLE
FECUND HEARTY STRONG
TEEMING ABUNDANT BATTABLE
FRUITFUL GENEROUS PREGNANT
PROLIFIC SPAWNING
FERTILITY HEART FATNESS
(PATRON OF —) YAKSHA
FERTILIZATION ENDOGAMY
POROGAMY
FERTILIZE FAT DUNG FISH LIME
MARL CHALK BATTEN ENRICH
FRUCTIFY
FERTILIZER FAT MARL GUANO
HUMUS ALINIT FLOATS MANURE
POLLEN POTASH CARRIER
COMPOTE HUMOGEN KAINITE
NITRATE TANKAGE AMMONITE
CINEREAL NITROGEN
FERULA NARTHEX
FERULE ROD RULER COLLET
FENNEL FERULA PALMER
FERVENCY WARMTH CANDENCY
FERVENT HOT KEEN WARM EAGER
FIERY ARDENT BITTER FERVID
FIERCE INWARD RAGING SAVAGE
BOILING BURNING GLOWING
INTENSE PECTORAL ROMANTIC
VEHEMENT RELIGIOUS
FERVID HOT ARDENT TROPIC
BOILING BURNING FERVENT
GLOWING ZEALOUS UNCTUOUS
VEHEMENT
FERVOR FIRE HEAT HWYL RAGE
SOUL ZEAL ARDOR SPIRIT
WARMTH PASSION CANDENCY
DEVOTION STRENGTH VIOLENCE
(— IN PRAYER) KAVVANAH
KAWWANAH
FESCUE VESTER
FESS BAR BAND PERT DANCE
HUMET
(DIMINUTIVE —) TRANGLE
FEST GALA
FESTAL GAY GALA GAUDY FESTIVE
FESTUAL FEASTFUL

FESTER ROT BEAL RANK SCAR
RANKLE PUSTULE PUTREFY
FESTERING RANK FRETTY
FESTIVAL (ALSO SEE FEAST) ALE
BON PWE BUSK FAIR FEIS FETE
GALA HOLI MELA PUJA TIDE UTAS
WAKE DELIA FEAST FERIA FESTA
GAUDY HALOA PURIM REVEL
ROUSE SEDAR ADONIA BAIRAM
BRIDAL CARNEA DEWALI DIASIA
DIPALA FIESTA HOHLEE HUFFLE
KERMIS KWANZA LAMMAS LENAEA
OPALIA PONGOL POOJAH POSADA
SUCCOS AGONIUM AGRANIA
BANQUET BELTANE DASAHRA
EQUIRIA FESTIAL HILARIA
KERMESS KWANZAN MATSURI
PALILIA SUKKOTH THIASOS
TOXCATL UPHELYA VINALIA
AGRIONIA AIANTEIA APATURIA
ATHENAEA BEALTINE BRUMALIA
CARNIVAL COTYTTIA DASAHARA
DIIPOLIA DIONYSIA DUSSERAH
ENCAENIA FASNACHT FLORALIA
HANUKKAH HIGHTIDE KALENDAE
LUPERCAL MARYMASS MATRALIA
MITHRIAC MUHARRAM MUNYCHIA
NATIVITY NEOMENIA POTLATCH
STAMPEDE TAARGELIA
SATURNALIA
(FALL —) OCTOBERFEST
(HIGHLAND —) MOD
(MUSICAL —) EISTEDDFOD
(PL.) MOED VOTA
(SUFF.) MAS
FESTIVE GAY GALA JOLLY FESTAL
GENIAL JOYOUS FEASTLY HOLIDAY
JOCULAR CONVIVAL FEASTFUL
MIRTHFUL SPORTIVE CONVIVIAL
(— TIME) TET
FESTIVITY GALA GAUD UTAS UTIS
BEANO FEAST MIRTH RANDY
REVEL GAIETY GAYETY SPLORE
HOLIDAY JOLLITY JOYANCE
PATTERN FESTIVAL FUNCTION
MERRIMENT MERRYMAKING
(RIOTOUS —) RAG
FESTOON SWAG TRIM WREATH
GARLAND DECORATE
(PL.) ENCARPUS
FETCH FET FESH GASP GIVE SHAG
TACK TAKE TEEM WAIN BRING
SWEEP TRICK DOUBLE STROKE
WRAITH ACHIEVE ATTRACT
ARTIFICE FETCHING INTEREST
FETCHED FOSH
FETCHING SWEET CRAFTY
CUNNING ALLURING PLEASING
SCHEMING
FETE FAIR GALA FEAST HONOR
ROAST BAZAAR FIESTA HOLIDAY
FETID OLID RANK MUSTY PUTID
ROTTEN VIROSE NOISOME
SANIOUS MALODOROUS
FETIDLY FOULLY
FETISH OBI IDOL JUJU OBIA ZEME
ZEMI ZOGO ANITO ASCON CHARM
GUACA HUACA OBEAH OBIAH
TOTEM AMULET FETICH GRIGRI
NAGUAL VOODOO SHINTAI
SORCERY FETISHRY GREEGREE
TALISMAN
FETLOCK COOT FOOTLOCK

FETTER BAND BEND BOLT BOND
FIND GYVE IRON SPAN BASIL
BEWET BILBO CHAIN SLANG
SWATH ANKLET GARTER HALTER
HAMPER HOBBLE HOPPLE IMPEDE
LANGEL RACKAN SWATHE CLINKER
CONFINE ENCHAIN ENSLAVE
FETLOCK GARNISH MANACLE
SHACKLE SPANCEL TRAMMEL
RESTRAIN
(PL.) IRONS LINKS DARBIES
GARNISH GARTERS
FETTERBUSH PIPESTEM PIPEWOOD
FETTLE BEAT DECK FUSS MULL TIDY
TWIG VEIN DRESS GROOM WHACK
YARAK GIRDLE REPAIR SETTLE
STRIKE ARRANGE BANDAGE
FEATHER HARNESS
FETTLER BILLYER NOBBLER
FETTLING FIX FETTLE FIXING
FETUS BIRTH CHILD YOUNG
AMELUS BREECH EMBRYO
FOETUS ABORTUS CYCLOPS
FEATURE AMORPHUS
(PREF.) EMBRY(O) FETI FETO FOETI
FOETO
FEUD FIEF FRAY BROIL AFFRAY
ENMITY FEODUM FEUDUM STRIFE
CONTEST DISPUTE QUARREL
VENDETTA
FEUDATORY FIEF VASSAL
ZAMINDAR ZEMINDAR
FEUILLE MORTE PHILAMOT
FEVER AGUE FIRE ARDOR CAUMA
DANDY LEUMA OCTAN CAUSUS
DENGUE FEBRIS HECTIC SEPTAN
SEXTAN SODOKU TYPHIA TYPHUS
VOMITO AMAKEBE FERMENT
FEVERET HELODES HOTNESS
MALARIA PINKEYE PYREXIA
QUARTAN TERTIAN TYPHOID
SYNOCHUS TERTIANA TYPHINIA
CALENTURE
(— OF HORSE) WEED SCALMA
(— OF PERU) VERRUGA
(— OF SHEEP) BRAXY
(BRAIN —) PHRENITIS
(HAY —) RHINITIS
(KIND OF —) LASSA
(MALARIAL —) TAP
(MARSH —) HELODES
(SPLENIC —) ANTHRAX
(TEXAS —) TRISTEZA
(WITHOUT —) APYRETIC
(YELLOW —) VOMITO
(PREF.) FEBRI PYR(ET)(ETO)
(SUFF.) PYRA
FEVERED DISEASED
FEVERFEW MAYWEED MUGWORT
PELLITORY
FEVERISH HOT FIERY FEVERY
HECTIC EXCITED FEBRILE FRANTIC
RESTLESS
FEVERLESS APYREXIA
FEVERROOT GENSON
FEVER TREE BITTERBARK
FEVERWEED FITWEED
FEVERWORT BONESET
FEW LIT CURN LESS SOME SCANT
THREE WHEEN WHONE CURRAN
PICKLE SPOTTY LIMITED SEVERAL
EXIGUOUS
(PREF.) OLIG(O) PAUCI

FEWER LESS
(PREF.) MI(O)
FEWNESS PAUCITY
FEY DEAD CRAZY DYING ELFIN
FATAL DOOMED TOUCHED
UNLUCKY PIXILATED
FEZ TARBOOSH
FIADOR THEODORE
FIANCE TRUST SPOUSE FIANCEE
PROMISE AFFIANCE INTENDED
FIASCO CRASH FLASK FROST FIZZLE
FAILURE DISASTER
FIAT EDICT ORDER UKASE DECREE
COMMAND DECISION SANCTION
FIB LIE YED FLAW WHID SLANT
STORY FITTEN PUMMEL SKLENT
TARADIDDLE
FIBBER LIAR
FIBER TAL ADAD BASS BAST COIR
ERUC FERU FLAX HARL HEMP
IMBE JUTE LINE PITA SILK SUNN
TULA ABACA AGUST AZLON CAJUN
CAROA CHOEL ERIZO FIBRE GRAIN
HARLE ISOTE ISTLE IXTLE IZOTE
KAPOK KENAF KITUL LYCRA MESTA
MURVA OAKUM RAMIE RAPHE
SIMAL SISAL STRAW TERAP TOSSA
TUCUM VIVER AMIRAY ARAMID
ARGHAN BINDER BUNTAL BURITI
CABUYA CATENA DACRON EMBIRA
FIBRIL FIMBLE HINOKI KANAFF
KENDIR KOHEMP MUCUNA NYTRIL
RAFFIA SALAGO STAPLE STRAND
STRING SUTURE THREAD TUCUMA
TURURI VINYON YACHAN ZAPUPE
ACETATE ACRYLIC ANONANG
ARAMINA BASSINE CANTALA
CASCARA CHANDUL CHINGMA
COQUITA ESPARTO FILASSE
FUNICLE GEBANGA GRAVATA
GUAXIMA GUMIHAN HUARIZO
KERATTO KITTOOL MOCMAIN
PALMITE PANGANE PAUKPAN
POCHOTE SABUTAN CANAPINA
CURRATOW FILAMENT HARAKEKE
HENEQUEN PIASSAVA TOQUILLA
TRONADOR
(— FROM PEACOCK FEATHERS)
MARL
(— OF PALM) DOH LIF ERUC COYOL
COROZO GOMUTI KITTUL COQUITA
GEBANGA
(—S OF FLAX) HARE
(CLUSTER OF —S) NEP
(COARSE —) KEMP
(COCONUT —) COIR KYAR
(COTTON —) LINT STAPLE
(FLAX —) TOW
(KNOT OF —) NOIL
(MANUFACTURED —) DYNEL
ORLON ESTRON ACRILAN SPANDEX
(MATTED —) SHAG
(MINERAL —) ASBESTOS
(MUSCLE —) RHABDIUM
(NERVE —) EFFERENT DEPRESSOR
(PULVERIZED —) FLOCK
(SILKY —) PULU KAPOK KUMBI
YACHAN CASTULI
(TEXTILE —) SPANDEX
(TWISTED —S) STRAND
(WASTE —) FLY GOUT
(WASTE —S) FLOSS
(WOODY —) BAST GRAIN SCUTCH

(PL.) FUZZ KERATTO
(PREF.) FIBRO IN(O)
FIBRIL AXONEME DESMOSE
MYONEME MYOPHAN
FIBRILS
(SUFF.)
(NETWORK —) SPONGIA(E)(N)
SPONGIUM
FIBRIN GLUTEN MYOSIN
FIBROCARTILAGE FABELLA
MENISCUS
FIBROID DESMOID
FIBROMA INOMA FIBROID
FIBROUS FIBROSE STRINGY
NEMALINE
FIBULA LACE CLASP BROOCH
BUCKLE PERONE SPLINT
(PREF.) PERONEO PERONO
FICHE FILMCARD
FICKLE GERY DIZZY FALSE GIDDY
LIGHT UNSAD HARLOT KITTLE
MOBILE PUZZLE SHIFTY VOLAGE
WANKLE WANKLY CASALTY
CASELTY FLATTER MOONISH
MOVABLE MUTABLE VAINFUL
VARIANT VOLUBLE GOSSAMER
MOVEABLE SKITTISH STIRRING
UNSTABLE UNSTEADY VARIABLE
VOLATILE WAVERING
FICKLENESS CHANGE LEVITY
EASINESS FICKLETY VARIANCE
FICO FIG FIGO TANTI
FICTILE FIGULINE
FICTION BAM TALE FABLE FALSE
NOVEL ROMAN STORY DECEIT
DEVICE FABULA FITTEN LEGEND
COINAGE FANTASY FIGMENT
FORGERY MARCHEN NOVELRY
ROMANCE ROMANZA KAILYARD
PHANTASY PRETENCE PRETENSE
(CRIME —) NOIR
FICTITIOUS MADE BOGUS DUMMY
FALSE PHONY FABLED POETIC
ASSUMED FEIGNED PHANTOM
FABULOUS FICTIOUS MYTHICAL
ROMANTIC SIMULATE SPURIOUS
LEGENDARY
(PREF.) PSEUD(O)
FICUS PYRULA
FID PRICK NORMAN PRICKER
SPLICER
FIDDLE BOW BOX GIG SAW VIOL
CHEAT CROWD GEIGE GIGUE
GUDOK CHORUS DIDDLE FITHEL
POTTER TRIFLE URHEEN VIOLIN
CHROTTA SARANGI SWINDLE
HUMSTRUM
(— STRING) THAIRM
(— WITH) TWIDDLE
(BASS —) GUTBUCKET
(OLD —) REBEC
FIDDLER CRAB VIOLER VIOLIN
CROWDER SCRAPER SIXPENCE
FIDDLER CRAB RACER FIDDLER
OCYPODE SOLDIER
FIDDLESTICKS POOH PSHAW
FIDDLE
FIDELIO (CHARACTER IN —) ROCCO
FIDELIO LEONORE PIZARRO
JACQUINO FLORESTAN MARZELLINE
(COMPOSER OF —) BEETHOVEN
FIDELITY TRUE ARDOR FAITH PIETY
TROTH TRUTH FEALTY HONESTY

LOYALTY ADHESION DEVOTION
RELIGION VERACITY CONSTANCY
FIDGET MOP FIKE FIRK FUSS ROIL
FIDGE FITCH HOTCH SHRUB
SHRUG WORRY BREVIT FIGGLE
FISSLE FISTLE FRIDGE FUSSER
HIRSEL JIFFLE JIGGET NESTLE
NIBBLE NIGGLE TIDDLE TRIFLE
VIGGLE WORRIT NERVOUS
RESTLESS TWITCHEL
(— ABOUT TRIFLES) SPOFFLE
(STATE OF —) FANTAD FANTOD
(PL.) JUMPS
FIDGETY ANTSY FIKIE FUSSY ITEMY
FEISTY FIGENT FLISKY KITTLE
UNEASY RESTIVE TWITCHY
RESTLESS
FIDUCIARY TRUSTEE TRUSTFUL
FIE SISS FAUGH
FIEF FEE HAN FEUD FEOFF TIMAR
ZIAMET SATSUMA SUBFIEF
BENEFICE
(— HOLDER) TIMARIOT
FIELD LEA LOT ACRE AGER AREA
BENT CAMP FELL FLAT HADE INAM
LAND LIST MEAD PALE PARK PLAY
RAND TOWN WONG BRECK
CAMPO CHAMP CLOUR CROFT
EARTH GLEBE INNAM LAYER MILPA
NILPA PADDY RANGE ROWEN
SAWAH TILTH VELDE ARRISH
CAMPUS CAREER CHAMPE
DOMAIN FURROW GARDEN
GROUND MACHAR MATTER
MEADOW PADANG PINGLE SHIELD
SPHERE CHARMEL COMPASS
CULTURE DIAMOND FERRING
GARSTON INFIELD MOWLAND
NEWTAKE PADDOCK PARROCK
PIGHTLE PURVIEW QUILLET
TERRAIN THWAITE TILLAGE
CLEARING PROVINCE
(— ADJOINING HOUSE) CROFT
(— AT CRICKET) SCOUT
(— OF ACTIVITY) GAME ARENA
BARONY SPHERE TERRAIN
(— OF BATTLE) PLAIN
(— OF BLOODSHED) ACELDAMA
AKELDAMA
(— OF CONTROL) DOMAIN
(— OF ENDEAVOR) BUSINESS
(— OF SNOW) NEVE SNOWPACK
(— OF STUDY) MAJOR GROUND
(— ON WHICH GRASS IS GROWN)
MEAD MEADOW
**(— SOWN FOR TWO SUCCESSIVE
YEARS)** HOOK
(ENCLOSED —) AGER TOWN CLOSE
CROFT
(FOOTBALL —) GRIDIRON
(FRUITFUL —) CHARMEL
(GRASSY —) LEA PEN GARSTON
(HOP —) HOPYARD
(KIND OF —) SKEW
(LAVA —) PEDREGAL
(LITTLE-KNOWN —) BYWAY
(NEW GOLD —) RUSH
(PLOWED —) FURROW
(RICE —) SAWAH
(SMALL —) HAW CLOSE CROFT
PADDOCK
(SPORTS —) ARENA PITCH

(STUBBLE —) HIRSH ROWEN
ARRISH GRATTEN GRATTON
(TILTING —) LISTS
(TOBACCO —) VEGA
(UNEXPLOITED —) FRONTIER
(UNPLOWED EDGE OF —) RAND
(PL.) FIELDEN
(PREF.) AGRI AGRO ARVI CAMPI
FIELD BALM SHEEPMINT
FIELD CAMOMILE OXEYE
FIELDER GLOVEMAN
(CRICKET —) SLIP COVER FIELD
GULLY POINT SCOUT GULLEY
INFIELDER
FIELDFARE FELT JACK REDLEG
FELLFARE HILLBIRD JACKBIRD
REDSHANK SNOWBIRD VELTFARE
FIELDING (— ABILITY) GLOVE
FIELD MADDER SPURWORT
FIELD MOUSE VOLE MIGALE
FIELDPIECE GUN AMUSETTE
GALLOPER
FIELD SCABIOUS BLUECAP
FIELDWORK LUNET REDAN
LUNETTE REDOUBT
FIEND FEN FOE PUG FEND FYND
DEMON DEVIL ENEMY SATAN
TRULL WIZARD SHAITAN SUCCUBA
TITIVIL BARBASON SUCCUBUS
FIENDISH CRUEL WICKED DEMONIC
FIENDLY SATANIC DEMONIAC
DEVILISH DIABOLIC INFERNAL
FIERCE ILL BOLD FELL GRIM KEEN
RUDE THRO WILD WOOD ASPER
BREME CRUEL EAGER FELON
HATEL ORPED RETHE SHARP
SMART STARK STERN STOUR
STOUT WROTH ARDENT FEROCE
GOTHIC HETTER IMMANE LUPINE
RAGING RUGGED SAVAGE STURDY
UNMEEK UNMILD WICKED
BRUTISH FERVENT FURIOSO
FURIOUS GRIMFUL INHUMAN
MANKIND RABIOUS RAMPANT
SCADDLE VICIOUS VIOLENT
STERNFUL TIGERISH
(PREF.) LABRO
FIERCE-EYED WALLEYED
FIERCELY FELL HARD FELLY FIERCE
FIERCENESS FURY FEROCITY
FIERY HOT RED ADUST FIRED QUICK
SHARP ARDENT FLASHY IGNITE
BURNING FERVENT FLAMING
FURIOUS GLOWING HOTHEAD
IGNEOUS PARCHED PEPPERY
VIOLENT ADUSTIVE CHOLERIC
FEVERISH FRAMPOLD INFLAMED
PHRAMPEL SPIRITED SPITFIRE
VEHEMENT
FIERY ANGEL (CHARACTER IN —)
RENATA AGRIPPA HEINRICH
RUPPRECHT MEPHISTOPHELES
(COMPOSER OF —) PROKOFIEV
FIERY RED SANDIX
FIERY-TEMPERED SPUNKY
FIESTA FETE FERIA PARTY HOLIDAY
(— COSTUME) POLLERA
FIFE STICK PIFERO PIFFERO
FIFTEEN FIVE
(PREF.) PENTADEC(A)
FIFTEENTH DOUBLETTE
FIFTH QUINT QUINTIN HEMIOLIA
(— ABOVE TONIC) DOMINANT

(PERFECT —) HEMIOLA HEMIOLIA
(PREF.) QUINT(I)
FIFTY (— YEAR ANNIVERSARY)
JUBILEE
FIFTY-FIFTY EVEN
FIG RIG FICO ARRAY BREBA DRESS
ELEME ELEMI PIPAL SABRA TANTI
BALETE BALITI FOUTER FOUTRA
GINGER LOBFIG PEEPUL TRIFLE
FURBISH GONDANG SICONUS
SYCONUS WARINGIN
(— CROP) MAMME
(PREF.) FICI SYCO
FIG BASKET CABAS
FIGHT BOX MIX WAP WAR WIN BEAT
BEFF BLUE BOUT CAMP CLEM
COCK COPE COWP CRAB CUFF
DUEL DUKE FLOG FRAY LAKE MEET
MELL MILL SHOW SLUG SPAR TILT
WAGE YOKE BANDY BRAWL CLASH
FIELD FLOLT HURRY JOUST MATCH
MELEE MIXUP RAMMY SCRAP
SETTO SHINE SPURN STOUR
TOUSE AFFAIR AFFRAY BARNEY
BATTLE BICKER BLOWUP COMBAT
DEBATE FEUCHT FRACAS FRAISE
HASSLE IMPUGN MEDDLE OPPOSE
RELUCT REPUGN RESIST RIPPIT
RUFFLE SHOWER STOUSH STRIFE
STRIKE STRIVE TOUSEL TURNUP
BARGAIN BRABBLE CONTEND
CONTEST COUNTER JOURNEY
QUARREL RUCTION SIMULTY
TUILYIE WARFARE CONFLICT
DOGFIGHT DUOMACHY FINISHER
GUNFIGHT MILITATE SKIRMISH
SLUGFEST SQUABBLE STRUGGLE
TIRRIVEE TIRRWIRR TRAVERSE
(— AGAINST) BUCK OPPUGN
(— BETWEEN TWO) DUEL
DUOMACHY
(— FOR) SERVE CHAMPION
(— WITH CLUB) TIMBER
(FIST —) RIPPIT TURNUP
(GANG —) RUMBLE
(SEA —) NAUMACHY
(STREET —) HABBLE RUMBLE
(SUFF.) MACHIA MACHY
FIGHTER PUG VAMP BOXER COCKER
BATTLER DUELIST SLUGGER
SOLDIER WARRIOR ANDABATA
BARRATER BARRATOR CHAMPION
GUERILLA PUGILIST SCRAPPER
(FIRE —) EXEMPT HOTSHOT
(GUERILLA —) MAQUIS
BUSHWHACKER
(GUERILLA —S) MUJAMIDEEN
FIGHTING BLOW ACTION AFFRAY
DEBATE WARLIKE CONFLICT
MILITANT
(— WITH SHADOW) SCIAMACHY
FIGHTING FISH PLAKAT
**FIGLIA DI JORIO, LA (CHARACTER
IN —)** MILA ALIGI LAZARO
(COMPOSER OF —) PIZZETTI
FIG MARIGOLD SAMH MESEM
FICOID FOXCHOP FICOIDAL
ICEPLANT
FIGMENT IDEA FICTION
FIGPECKER BECCAFICO
FIGURATE FLORID FIGURAL
FIGURED FIGURATO

FIGURATION FORM SHAPE DESIGN
OUTLINE
FIGURATIVE FLORID FIGURAL
FIGURED FLOWERY TYPICAL
ALLUSIVE TROPICAL
FIGURE FIG HUE VOL BOSH DOLL
FORM IDEA SIGN STAR ANGLE
ANTIC DATUM DIGIT FLIRT FRAME
IMAGE MAGOT MOTIF SHAPE
SPADE SPRIG AUMAIL BABOON
CHANGE CIPHER COCKUP CUTOUT
DEVICE EFFIGY EMBLEM ENTAIL
FIGGER GOOGOL INCUSE NUMBER
PERSON SCHEME SYMBOL TAILLE
TATTOO CHASSIS CHEVRON
CHIFFER CHIFFRE COMPUTE
CONTOUR DRAWING GESTALT
IMPRESS NUMERAL OUTLINE
STATURE DIHEDRAL FIGURATE
GRAFFITO HEXAGRAM LIKENESS
SEMBLANT MARIONETTE
(— FORMED BY INTERSECTING
LINES) KNOT
(— IN PRAYER) ORANT
(— IN WOOD GRAIN) BURL FLAKE
(— MADE OF CORN) KNACK
(— MADE OF 3 LINES) TRIGRAM
TRIANGLE
(— OF SPEECH) IMAGE IRONY
TROPE APORIA CLIMAX FLOWER
SCHEME SIMILE VISION ZEUGMA
ANALOGY IMAGERY CHIASMUS
DIALLAGE METAPHOR METONYMY
OXYMORON SYLLEPSIS ABSCISSION
(— OUT) SUS DOPE SUSS BOTTOM
(—S OF SPEECH) COLORS
(— UP) ITEM
(— USED AS COLUMN) ATLAS
TELAMON CARYATID
(— USED AS MAGIC SYMBOL)
PENTACLE
(ANATOMICAL —) ECORCHE
(ARTIFICIAL —) GOLEM
(BIBLICAL —) ANGEL CHERUB
(BIZARRE —) GROTESQUE
(CARVED —) GLYPH FIGURINE
(CENTRAL —) HERO
(CIRCULAR —) HOOP
(CLAY —) HANIWA
(COMIC —) BILLIKEN
(CONSPICUOUS —) MARK
(CRESCENT-SHAPED —) LUNE
(DANCE —) SWING TRACE SQUARE
PURPOSE ASSEMBLE PROMENADE
(DOMINANT —) CAPTAIN
(DUMMY —) MANNEQUIN
(FEMALE —) ORANTE
(FOLDED PAPER —) FLEXAGON
(GEOMETRICAL —) BODY CONE
CUBE LUNE PRISM RHOMB SOLID
CIRCLE GNOMON ISAGON ISOGON
OBLONG SECTOR SPHERE SQUARE
DIAGRAM ELLIPSE LOZENGE
PELCOID POLYGON RHOMBUS
SECTION HEXAFOIL SPHEROID
TRIANGLE RECTANGLE
POLYHEDRON PARALLELOGRAM
(GREEK —) KOUROS
(GROTESQUE —) MAGOT BABOON
MAXIMON
(HAVING FULL ROUNDED —)
ZAFTIG ZOFTIG
(IDEAL —) EIDOLON

(IMAGINARY —) BOGEYMAN
(IMPORTANT —) PANJANDRUM
(INCISED —) INTAGLIO
(JAPANESE — ON GRAVE) HANIWA
(MATH —) SINE COSINE
(MUMMYLIKE —) USHABTI
(MUSICAL —) IDEA LICK OSTINATO
(ODD —) MAUMET
(OVAL —) SWASH ELLIPSE
(PAPER —) FLEXAGON
(PREHISTORIC —) CHACMOL
CHACMOOL
(QUADRILLE —) POULE
(QUEER —) GIG
(RHETORICAL —) COLOR COLOUR
(RHYTHMIC —) SNAP
(SCULPTURED —) CANEPHOR
(SHADOW —) SKIAGRAM
(SKATING —) SPIRAL BRACKET
COUNTER
(SPINDLE-SHAPED —) FUSEE FUZEE
(STUFFED —) DUMMY
(SYLLOGISTIC —) SCHEMA
(SYMBOLIC —) MORAL EMBLEM
(TAILOR'S —) MANNEQ
MANNEQUIN
(TRIANGULAR —) TRIQUET
(UNDRAPED —) NUDE
(WINGED —) ANGEL EIDOLON
(WORSHIPPING —) ORANT
(PL.) DATA SPILING
(PREF.) EID(O)
(SUFF.) HEDRON
FIGURED FIGURY FACONNE
FIGUREHEAD DUMMY FRONT
SCROLL
FIGURINE TANAGRA CRIOPHORE
FIGWORT BARTSIA PILEWORT
PAULOWNIA PENSTEMON
BLUEHEARTS

FIJI

BAY: MBYA NATEWA NGALOA
SAVUSAVU
CAPITAL: SUVA
EASTERN GROUP: LAU
ISLAND: ELD KIA ONO AIWA KIOA
KORO MALI NGAU VIWA WAIA
AGATA MANGO MOALA NAIAU
RAMBI MAMOLO MATUKU
MBENGA MBULIA NAIRAI NAVITI
NGAMEA OVALAU TOTOYA
YASAWA YENDUA KAMBARA
KANDAVU LAKEMBA TAVEUNI
VITILEVU
MOUNTAIN: NARARU MONAVATU
NIECE OR NEPHEW: VASU
POINT: VUYA
TOWN: BA MAU MBA MOMI NADI
REWA SUVA TUVU NANDI THUVU
ETUMBA LABASA NALOTO
NAMOLI NARATA NASALA
NAVOLA SAGARA LAUTOKA
VATUKOULA

FIJIAN VITIAN
FILAGO GIFOLA
FILAMENT BRIN DOWL HAIR HARL
NEMA PILE SILK CHIVE CHORD
FIBER FIBRE FILUM TWIRE CIRRUS
ELATER HEATER MANTLE STRAND
THREAD CIRRHUS FIMBRIA
FLIMMER RHIZOID TEXTILE

PARANEMA PHACELLA STERIGMA
PARAPHYSIS
(— MATERIAL) TUNGSTEN
(— OF FEATHER) BARB DOWL
DOWLE
(— OF MINERAL) STRINGER
(— OF SILK) BRIN
(—S OF FLAX OR HEMP) HARL
(TWISTED —S) STRAND
(PL.) HACKLE
FILAMENTOUS BYSSOID STRINGY
HAIRLIKE
FILANDERS BACKWORM
FILARIASIS MUMU
FILBERT HAZEL COBNUT HAZELNUT
(SIEVE OF —S) PRICKLE
FILCH BOB FUB NIM ROB BEAT DRIB
FAKE PILK PRIG SMUG SNIP FETCH
LURCH PILCH SNAKE SNEAK STEAL
CLOYNE PILFER SMOUCH STRIKE
CABBAGE PURLOIN
FILE BOX ROW BARB DECK LINE LIST
RANK RASP RATE RISP ROLL SLIP
STUB EMERY ENTER FLOAT FOUND
GRAIL INDEX LABEL MILL TRACK
TRAIN ACCUSE ANSWER BEFOUL
CARLET DEFILE FILACE RASCAL
RUBBER STRING TOPPER ARCHIVE
ARRANGE CHOILER CONDEMN
DOSSIER EXHIBIT GRAILLE
QUANNET TICKLER DRAWFILE
(— DOWN SAW TEETH) JOINT
(— OFF) DEFILE
(— OF SIX SOLDIERS) ROT
(— USED BY COMBMAKERS) GRAIL
TOPPER GRAILER GRAILLE
(— WITH COURT OF LAW) BOX
(COARSE —) RAPE
(CURVED —) RIFFLER
(KIND OF —) INDIAN
FILE BOX SOLANDER
FILEFISH LIJA UNIE TURBOT
UNICORN BALISTID FOOLFISH
PLECTOGNATH
FILET DEBONE
FILIAL PIUS SONLY
FILIBUSTER FLIBUTOR STONEWALL
FILIGREED LACED
FILING RASION LIMATION
(PL.) LEMEL SCOBS LIMAIL
FILIPENDULA ULMARIA
FILIPINO MORO KALINGA KANKANAI
FILL EKE HIT PAD BUNG CLOY CRAM
FEED GLUT HOLD LADE LINE MEET
PANG QUAR SATE STOP TEEM
BELLY BLOAT BULGE CHOKE
ESTOP FLOCK GORGE KEDGE
PITCH PRIME STORE STUFF
CHARGE FULFIL INFUSE OCCUPY
QUERRE SUPPLY AGGRADE
DISTEND ENLARGE EXECUTE
FILLING FRAUGHT FULFILL
IMPLETE INFLATE INVOLVE
PERFECT PERFORM PERVADE
PLENISH SATIATE SATISFY
SUFFUSE COMPLETE COMPOUND
FREQUENT PERMEATE
(— COMPLETELY) SATURATE
(— CUP TO BRIM) BRIM CROWN
BUMPER
(— FULL) FARCE STUFF
(— HORSES' TEETH) BISHOP

(— IN) NOG KILL STOP SLUSH INFILL BALLAST
(— IN CHINKS) LIP
(— INTERSTICES) BLIND
(— IN WITH RUBBLE) HEART
(— LEATHER WITH OIL) FAT
(— OUT) BUNCH SWELL
(— THE BASES) LOAD
(— TO EXCESS) CROWD FLOOD CONGEST SURFEIT
(— TO OVERFLOWING) FLOW THWACK
(— UP) STOP BRICK CHOKE CLOSE ESTOP STOAK FULFIL IMPACT STODGE PLENISH
(— UP HOLE) STIFLE
(— WITH) SWILL
(— WITH ALE) RACK
(— WITH ANXIETY) ALARM ALARUM
(— WITH CARGO) STOW
(— WITH CLAY) CAT PUG
(— WITH FEAR) APPAL APPALL
(— WITH HORROR) ABHOR
(— WITH LIGHT) GLUT
(— WITH LIQUOR) TUN SKINK
(— WITH METAL) BACK
(— WITH MORTAR) GROUT
(— WITH ODORS) EMBALM
(— WITH RUBBISH) BASH
(— WITH TERROR) AMAZE
(ONE'S —) SLITHERS
FILLED BIG ALIVE FLUSH QUICK SATED SOLID GRAVID LOADED CROWDED HAUNTED IMPLETE OPPLETE REPLETE SWOLLEN FREQUENT INSTINCT POPULOUS
(— OUT) BOLD FULL
(— TO EXCESS) FLOWN
(— WITH AIR) INFLATED
(— WITH EXCITEMENT) ABUZZ
(— WITH FEAR) AFRAID
(— WITH INTERSTICES) AREOLAR
(— WITH MOISTURE) FAT
(— WITH PRIDE) YNPRIDID
FILLER GARA BOGUS SILEX SILKA SQUIB BALAAM LIGNIN FILLING LOADING WRAPPER
(— FOR CRACKS) SPACKLE
(QUILT —) BATT BATTING
FILLET BAND BONE GIRT LIST ORLE ORLO SOLE TAPE AMPYX CROWN FACET FILET GORGE LABEL LEDGE MITER MITRE QUIRK SCROD SNOOD STRAP STRIA TIARA VITTA ANADEM BENDEL BINDER CIMBIA COMBLE CORONA DIADEM FASCIA INFULA LISTEL NORSEL POTONG QUADRA REGLET REGULA RIBBON ROLLER TAENIA TURBAN TURBOT ANNULET BANDAGE BANDEAU CLOISON CORONET EYEBROW FACETTE FRONTAL GARLAND LAMBEAU MOLDING TRESSON TRINGLE BANDELET CINCTURE FRONTLET HAIRLACE HEADBAND PLATBAND TRESSOUR TRESSURE UNDERCUT
(— OF HERRING) ROLLMOP
(BEEF —) TOURNEDOS
(PREF.) TAENI(A)(O)
FILLIFORM CATENOID
FILL-IN MODESTY
FILLING GOB FILL MODE PLUG

WEFT WOOF INLAY STUFF FILLER STOPPING STUFFING FIBERFILL
(— OF COLUMN FLUTES) CABLING
(— OF GAPS) CONFAB
(— UP) CLOSURE RIPIENO
(BASKET —) SLEW
(DENTAL —) INLAY
(SILK —) SHIKII
FILLIP BLOW FLIP SNAP SPUR TOSS URGE FILIP FLASH FLIRT FLISK IMPEL BUFFET INCITE MOMENT PROJECT STIMULATE
(— ON THE NOSE) SNITCH
FILLY COLT FOAL GIRL
FILM H BRAT HAZE HULL KELL MIST SCUM SKIM SKIN VEIL WEFT BLEAR COVER FLAKE FLICK GLAZE LAYER MYLAR PEARL PLATE SCALE SHOOT SHORT BUBBLE MOTHER PATINA SCRUFF CUTICLE FEATURE PHILOME TAFFETA TOPICAL TRAILER BEESWING FIRECOAT NEGATIVE PELLICLE MICROFILM MONOLAYER
(— OF AIR) PLASTRON
(— OF ICE) VERGLAS
(— OF OIL) SLICK
(— OF OXIDE) TARNISH
(— OF TARTAR) SCALE PLAQUE
(— ON COPPER) PATINA
(— ON PORRIDGE) BRAT
(— ON TEETH) PLAQUE
(— ON WINE) BEESWING
(— OVER EYE) WEB
(— OVER THE EYES) WEB
(DISCARDED —) OUTTAKE
(ORIGINAL —) MASTER
(POLYESTER —) MYLAR
(X-RAY —) BITEWING
FILMING (REALISTIC —) VIDEOVERITE
FILMY FINE HAZY GAUZY MISTY SHEER WISPY CLOUDY CLOUDED TIFFANY FILMLIKE GOSSAMER
FILOSOFO DI CAMPAGNA, IL
(CHARACTER IN —) NARDO EUGENIA LESBINA RINALDO TRITEMIO
(COMPOSER OF —) GALUPPI
FILTER CLAY RAPE SEEP SIFT SILE DRAIN SEITZ SIEVE BOUGIE CANDLE COLATE CONTEX LAUTER MEDIUM PURIFY REFINE STRAIN BAGHOUSE COLATURE FILTRATE INFILTER STRAINER
FILTERER CLARIFIER
FILTH FEN KET DIRT DUNG GORE MUCK NAST SLUT SOIL SUDS ADDLE BILGE DRECK GLEAM GLEET JAKES POUCE SWILL DEFILE FULYIE FULZIE IMMUND ORDURE SORDES SORDOR VERMIN SLOTTER SQUALOR SULLAGE FOULNESS MUCKMENT SNOTTERY WORTHING COLLUVIES
(PREF.) COPR(O)
FILTHINESS MUCOR SQUALOR SULLAGE CENOSITY
FILTHY LOW FOUL MIRY VILE BAWDY DIRTY DROVY DUNGY GROSS LAIRY MUCKY NASTY AUGEAN BAWDRY CRUMBY CRUMMY CRUSTY DIRTEN

IMMUND IMPURE SORDID BEASTLY BESTIAL HOGGISH OBSCENE PIGGISH SQUALID UNCLEAN ORDUROUS SLUTTISH
FILTRATE MALLEIN
FILTRATION BAGGING COLATURE
(KIND OF —) GEL
FIN ARM RAG RIB ANAL BURR FANG HAND KEEL SAIL FLASH PINNA CAUDAL FINLET ACANTHA FEATHER FLIPPER PINNULE VENTRAL FORELIMB PECTORAL
(BOMB —) VANE
(PREF.) PTER(O) PTERYG(O)
FINAGLE CHEAT TRICK REVOKE DECEIVE FENAGLE
FINAL LAST UTTER FINIAL LATTER RUNOFF ULTIMA UTMOST DARREIN DERNIER EXTREME FINALIS OUTMOST PARTING SUPREME ABSOLUTE DECISIVE DECRETAL DEFINITE EVENTUAL FAREWELL ULTIMATE
(— STANZA) ENVOI
(NOT —) NISI
FINALE END CODA FINIS ENDING WRAPUP CLOSING
FINALITY END ERGO
FINALLY YET LAST AFINE ATLAST LASTLY
FINANCE TAX BACK BANK FUND GOODS REVENUE TAXATION TREASURE
FINANCIAL FISCAL MONETARY PECUNIARY
FINANCIER BANIAN BANYAN MONEYMAN
(AUTHOR OF —) DREISER
(CHARACTER IN —) FRANK HENRY AILEEN BUTLER EDWARD SEMPLE STENER LILLIAN WINGATE COWPERWOOD
FINBACK WHALE FINNER GIBBAR FINFISH RORQUAL JUBARTAS
FINCH FINK MORO PAPE JUNCO SERIN TERIN BURION CANARY CITRIL LINNET PALILA SISKIN TOWHEE BUNTING CHEWINK PEEWEEP REDHEAD REDPOLL SENEGAL SPARROW TANAGER WAXBILL AMADAVAT COMBASOU FIRETAIL GOULDIAN GROSBEAK HAWFINCH LONGSPUR SNOWBIRD BRAMBLING SEEDEATER
(— FLOCK) CHARM
(SOUTH AMERICAN —) REDSISKIN
FIND GET RUG MEET VAIL CATCH INVENT LOCATE STRIKE ADJUDGE FINDING DISCOVER SCROUNGE
(— FAULT) CARP BARGE BLAME CAVIL GRONT KNOCK PINCH SCOLD NATTER ARRAIGN
(— GUILTY) ATTAINT CONVICT
(— OUT) AFIND CHECK ESSAY LEARN SPELL TROVE DETECT CONTRIVE DECIPHER DISCOVER
(— REFUGE) BIEL BIELD
(— SOLUTION) SOLVE
(— THE SUM) SUMMATE
(— TIME) EEM
FINDER SIGHT SEEKER FOUNDER
FINDING TROVER INQUEST VERDICT
(POLICE —) MO

FINE AOK CRO GAY RUM TAX BEIN BIEN BOTE BRAW CAIN CROP DIRE ERIC FAIR GENT GOOD HUNK JAKE LEVY MOOI NEAT NICE PURE RARE SEPT SLAP TALL TEAR TINE TRIM ABWAB BONNY BRAVE BULLY CHECK DAISY DANDY DELIE DUCKY FRAIL GAUDY GRAND GREAT HUNKY ISSUE KELTY MULCT NIFTY NOBLE RORTY SHARP SHEER SMALL SPALE SWANK SWEET SWELL UNLAW WALLY WHITE AMENDE AMERCE BONNIE BONZER BRAWLY BRIGHT CHEESY CHOICE CLEVER COSTLY CRAFTY DAINTY FACETE FINISH FLUTED GERSUM HERIOT HUNGRY INCONY MELLOW ORNATE PEACHY PRETTY PROPER QUAINT RANSOM SARAAD SCONCE SERENE SILKEN SLIGHT SPIFFY TENDER CLARIFY CONDEMN CORKING CREANCE CUNNING ELEGANT ESTREAT FERDWIT FINICAL FORFEIT FRAGILE GALANAS GALLANT GALLOWS GRADELY GRASSUM IMMENSE MARCHET MERCHET MURDRUM ORFGILD PENALTY PERFECT REFINED SCUTAGE STAVING TENUOUS TOPPING VALIANT WERGILD ABSOLUTE BLOODWIT BUDGEREE CAVALIER CLINKING DELICATE DUSTLIKE FLITWITE FOOTGELD HANDSOME LASHLITE MARITAGE PENALIZE PESHKASH PINPOINT PLEASANT SKILLFUL SPLENDID SUPERIOR WARDWITE WIRESPUN COPACETIC MAGNIFICENT
(— AGAINST SERVANTS) CHECK
(— FOR KILLING) BOTE
(— IN LIEU OF FLOGGING) HIDE
(BLOOD —) ERIC WITE
(FEUDAL —) RELIEF
(OSTENTATIOUSLY —) GAUDY
(PRINTING OFFICE —) SOLACE
(VERY —) BUNKUM SPLENDID
(PL.) SILT FLOUR
(PREF.) LEPT(O)
FINE-DRAW RANTER
FINE-LOOKING SPICY WALLY SPIFFY
FINELY FINE GAILY GAYLY WALLY BRAGLY RARELY SMALLY BRAVELY SMICKLY SWEETLY
FINENESS ALLOY GRAIN TRICK DENIER FINERY PURITY THREAD EXILITY FINESSE DELICACY
(— AS RECKONED BY CARATS) TITLE
(— OF FABRIC) CUT GAGE GAUGE
(— OF METAL) STANDARD
(— OF PITCH) COUNTS
FINERY GAUD WALY ARRAY BRAWS WALLY BAUBLE BAWDRY BEAUTY FEGARY GAIETY GAYETY TAWDRY BRAVERY GAUDERY REGALIA BEAUETRY ELEGANCE FINENESS FOFARRAW FOLDEROL FOOFARAW FRIPPERY ORNAMENT RIBANDRY
(TAWDRY —) FRIPPERY
FINESPUN HAIR THIN TWITTERY

FINESSE ART TACT CHEAT SKILL TRICK PURITY SERENE CUNNING ARTIFICE DELICACY SUBTLETY THINNESS
FINE-TUNE TWEAK
FINFOOT SUNBIRD
FINGER TOY PAUT PLAY DIGIT INDEX PINKY DACTYL HANDLE MEDDLE MEDIUS PADDLE PILFER PINKIE POLLEX ANNULAR DIGITAL MINIMUM MINIMUS PURLOIN DIGITIZE THRIMBLE
(— IDLY) TWIDDLE
(— INFECTION) FELON
(CROOK A — AT) BECKON
(FORE —) INDEX
(LITTLE —) PINKY PINKIE PIRLIE MINIMUS AURICULAR
(RING —) ANNULAR RINGMAN ANNULARY
(THIRD —) RINGMAN
(PL.) HOOKS
(PREF.) DACTYL(IO)(O) DIGITI DIGITO
(SUFF.) DACTYLIA DACTYLOUS
FINGERFLOWER FOXGLOVE
FINGERING DOIGTE
FINGERLING PARR TROUTLET
FINGERNAIL DIGGER
(RELATING TO —) ONYCHOID
(SUFF.) ONYCHA ONYCHES ONYCHIA ONYCHIUM ONYCHUS ONYX
FINGERPRINT DAB ARCH LOOP WHORL LATENT
FINGERPRINTING (KIND OF —) DNA
FINGERROOT FOXGLOVE
FINGERSTALL COT
FINIAL EPI NOB TEE TOP CROP KNOB KNOP KNOT BUNCH CREST CROWN FINAL POPPY PRICKET ORNAMENT PINNACLE
FINICAL NICE FUSSY CHOOSY DAINTY DAPPER JAUNTY PRETTY PRISSY SPRUCE CHOOSEY FINICKY FINIKIN FOPPISH MINCING PERJINK PICKING SMICKER DELICATE
FINICALLY SMICKLY GINGERLY
FINICKY NICE DINKY FIKEY FIKIE PRISSY FINICAL FINIKIN PRECISE
FINISH DO DIE END CHAR EDGE FACE FILL OVER PASS SINK SNUG STOP BLOOM BOUND CEASE CHARE CHEVE CLOSE CROWN ENDUP FEEZE GLACE GLAZE LIMIT SPEED UPPER BOTTOM BUSHEL FULFIL FULLDO PLISSE POLISH SETTLE WINDUP ABSOLVE ACHIEVE DEPETER EXECUTE FLUTING FULFILL PERFECT SURFACE COMPLETE CONCLUDE DEPRETER DRESSING FINALIZE FROSTING TERMINAL
(— CAREFULLY) NEATEN
(— CLOTH) BURL CONVERT
(— FILMING) WRAP
(— METAL) PLANISH
(— OFF) DASH CRUSH ABSOLVE ACCOMPLISH
(— OF FABRIC) CIRE HOLLAND
(— OF PAPER) STIPPLE
(— STONE) COMB BOAST DROVE
(— WITH A SEAM) FELL

(— WORK) FLOOR
(CALENDERED —) CHASING
(DULL —) MAT MATTE
(GLAZED —) GLACE LACKER LACQUER
(PHOTO —) MAT MATT MATTE
(STUCCO —) SPATTER
(SUPERFICIAL —) BLAZONRY
FINISHED BY DID OER PAU ARCH DONE DOWN FINE GONE OVER PAST PURE RIPE SHOT ENDED EXACT KAPUT NAPOO ROUND CLOSED NAPOOH ORNATE PERFECT REFINED ROUNDED STOPPED THROUGH BANKRUPT CLIMAXED GOFFERED LUSTERED POLISHED
(— IN NATURAL COLOR) FAIR
(— WITH NAP) BRUSHED
(ABSOLUTELY —) SUNK
(HIGHLY —) SUAVE
(IMPERFECTLY —) RUDE
FINISHER EYER ENDER CORKER GAFFER BEETLER CEMENTER ENAMELER SOCKDOLOGER
FINISHING GNUGLIING
FINITE LIMITED
FINK (PLAY THE —) RATON

FINLET PINNULE
FINN FIOUN INGER OSTIAK OSTYAK TAVAST INGRIAN CHEREMIS INGERMAN SWEKOMAN
(PL.) SUOMI
FINNISH
(PREF.) FENNO

FINNOCK HERLING
FINTA GIARDINIERA, LA
(CHARACTER IN —) ONESTI ANCHISE ARMINDA BELFIORE SANDRINA SERPETTA VIOLANTE
(COMPOSER OF —) MOZART
FIORD FJORD INLET
FIORIN KNOTGRASS
FIORITURA ORNAMENT
FIPPLE FLUTE RECORDER
FIR VER LARCH SAPIN BAUMIER LASHORN PINABETE
FIR CLUB MOSS FOXFEET
FIRE CAN FEU LOW AGNI APOY BALE BRIO BURN HEAT KILN LOWE POOP SACK SWAP SWOP ZEAL ARDOR ARSON BLAST BLAZE BREAK BURST EMPTY FEVER GLEED INGLE LIGHT LOGHE LOOSE LOUGH PLUFF SERVE SHOOT SQUIB STOKE AROUSE ENGHLE EXCITE FERVOR IGNITE INCITE KINDLE SMUDGE SPIRIT SPLEEN VULCAN ANIMATE BONFIRE BURNING BURNOUT CHIMNEY DISMISS EMITTER EXPLODE FURNACE GLIMMER INFLAME INSPIRE SMOLDER BACKFIRE BALEFIRE CAMPFIRE DETONATE HELLFIRE ILLUMINE IRRITATE NEEDFIRE SMOULDER VIVACITY PORCELAINIZE
(— A REVOLVER) FAN
(— ON) AFIRE
(— THE CHARGE) HIT
(— TWO ROUNDS) DOUBLE
(— UPON) GUN SPRAY
(BALL OF —) DYNAMO
(CROSS —) GANTLET GAUNTLET
(DAMPENED —) SMOTHER
(FOREST —) BREAK
(LITTLE —) SPONK SPUNK
(MASSED —) ARTILLERY
(PEAT —) GREESAGH
(RUNNING-OUT —) DANDY
(SIGNAL —) BALE BEACON BALEFIRE
(PREF.) EMPYRO IGNEO IGNI PHLOGO PYR(ET)(ETO)(ITI)(O)
(SUFF.) PYRA
FIRE ALARM FIREBOX
FIREARM ARM GUN IRON SHOT TUBE FIRER ORGAN PIECE RIFLE JEZAIL MAGNUM MAUSER MUSKET PISTOL POPPER BOMBARD CARBINE CURRIER DEMIHAG HANDGUN PINFIRE SHOOTER SPANNER ARQUEBUS BROWNING CULVERIN EXPELLER EXPLODER PETRONEL REVOLVER
(PL.) HARDWARE ARTILLERY
FIRE ARROW MALLEOLUS
FIREBACK REREDOS MACARTNEY
FIREBALL BOLIDE
FIRE BEETLE COCUYO CUCUYO ELATER ELATERID
FIREBOAT PALANDER
FIREBRAND BLAZE BRAND BLEERY BOUTEFEU RABBLEROUSER
FIREBRICK QUARLE
(PL.) GROG
FIREBUG BUG ARSONIST
FIRE CARRIER PORTFIRE

FIRECLAY THILL
FIRE COVER CURFEW CURPHEW
FIRECRACKER DEVIL SQUIB BANGER PETARD SALUTE CRACKER SNAPPER FIREWORK WHIZBANG
FIRE-CURED DARK
FIREDAMP GAS FOULNESS WILDFIRE
FIREDART PHALARICA
FIREDOG DOG IRON ANDIRON
FIRE ENGINE RIG TUB MANUAL
FIRE EXTINGUISHER SQUIRT EXTINCTOR
FIRE FIGHTER EXEMPT HOTSHOT
FIREFLY CUCUYO FIREBUG GLOWFLY LAMPFLY FIREWORM GLOWWORM LAMPYRID
FIREGUARD FENDER
FIRELINE GUTTER
FIRELOCK FUSEE FUZEE SPANNER
FIREMAN VAMP FIRER FUELER STOKER TEASER TIZEUR FIREBOY HOSEMAN BAKEHEAD FURNACER
FIREPLACE FOCUS POGON FORGE FOYER GRATE INGLE TISAR HEARTH CHIMNEY CHEMINEE
(— AND CHIMNEY) STACK
(— STONE) MANTEL
(PORTABLE —) BARBECUE BARBEQUE
FIREPLUG PLUG HYDRANT
FIRER STOKER BLASTER
FIRESIDE SMOKE HEARTH
FIRESTAND HASTER HASTENER
FIRE THORN PYRACANTH
FIREWEED FIRETOP ROSEBAY PILEWEED PILEWORT
FIREWOOD FIRE LENA SLAB WOOD CHUNK FAGOT BILLET BILLOT ELDING FIRING TALWOOD FIREBOTE TALLWOOD TALSHIDE
FIREWORK JET SUN GERB DEVIL GERBE PEEOY SAXON SHELL SQUIB WHEEL FIZGIG MAROON PETARD ROCKET SALUTE SHOWER TRACER CASCADE SERPENT SPARKER TORPEDO VOLCANO FOUNTAIN SPARKLER GIRANDOLE
(PL.) FUN FIRE
FIRE WORSHIPPER PARSI GHEBER GHEBRE PARSEE
FIRING FIRE FUEL COUGH SALVO BURNING DRUMFIRE
FIRKIN VESSEL
FIRM HUI PAT BUFF FAST HARD IRON NASH SURE TAUT TRIG TRIM CHAMP CORKY CRISP DENSE FIRMA FIXED HARDY HOUSE LOYAL RIGID SOLID SOUND STARK STIFF STITH STOUT SWITH TIGHT TOUGH CEMENT HARDEN HEARTY SECURE SETTLE SICCAR SICKER SINEWY STABLE STANCH STEADY STEEVE STOLID STRONG STURDY TRUSTY ADAMANT CERTAIN COMPACT COMPANY CONCERN CONFIRM CONTEXT DECIDED DURABLE STAUNCH UNMOVED CONSTANT FAITHFUL FIDUCIAL OBDURATE RESOLUTE SUBSTANT UNSHAKEN

(— BUT EASILY CUT) SEMISOFT
(NOT —) FUZZY
(PREF.) PAGIO
FIRMAMENT SKY DEEP POLE
CARRY ETHER CANOPY HEAVEN
EXPANSE EMPYREAN EMPYREUM
EXPANSUM
FIRMLY BUFF FAST FIRM HARD
SADLY STARK TIGHT HARDLY
SQUARE SURELY SOLIDLY
SECURELY STRONGLY
FIRMNESS BODY GRIT IRON ETHAN
PROOF FIXURE COURAGE FIRMITY
GRANITE BACKBONE DECISION
FASTNESS SECURITY SOLIDITY
STRENGTH TENACITY
(— OF CHARACTER) SAND
(— OF PURPOSE) RESOLVE
FIRN NEVE
FIRST ERST FUST GULE HEAD HIGH
MAIN AHEAD ALPHA CHIEF FORME
NIEVE PRIMA PRIME PRIMO
MAIDEN PRIMAL PRIMUS VIRGIN
FIRSTLY HIGHEST INITIAL LEADING
PREMIER PRIMARY EARLIEST
FOREHAND FOREMOST FORMERLY
ORIGINAL PARAVANT PREMIERE
PRINCEPS
(— PRIZE) BLUE
(— SERGEANT) TOP
(— STATE) DELAWARE
(PREF.) PRIMI PRIMO PROT(O)
(— IN TIME) ARCH
FIRSTBORN AYNE EIGNE ELDEST
FIRST-CLASS PUCKA GAY TOP
BOSS POSH FLASH PRIME PUKKA
BUNKUM STUNNING
FIRST-FRUITS ANNATES
FIRSTHAND DIRECT PRIMARY
ORIGINAL
FIRST-RATE AOK SLAPUP TIPTOP
BOSS BRAG GOOD JAKE MAIN
SLAP BULLY DANDY LUMMY PRIME
SLEEK SLICK SUPER SWELL
BONSER BONZER BOSKER CHEESY
FAMOUS TIPTOP BLIGHTY
BOSHTER CAPITAL SKOOKUM
STELLAR TOPPING CHAMPION
CLINKING CLIPPING TOPNOTCH
FIRTH ARM KYLE FRITH INLET
COPPICE ESTUARY
FISCAL BURSAL MONETARY
FISH AU ID AKU AWA AYU BIB CAT
COD DAB DAP DIB EEL FIN GAR GIG
GOO HEN IDE IHI JIG JUG ORF RAY
SAR TAI UKU BANK BARB BASS
BLAY BOCE BOGA CARP CAST
CERO CHUB CHUG CHUM CLOD
CRAB CUSK DACE DORY DRAG
DRAW DRUM ERSE FUGU GADE
GHOL GOBY GRIG HAKE HIND
HUCH HUSO JACK JUNK LINE LING
LOTE MADO MERO MOLA OPAH
PEAL PEGA PIKE POOR POUT PRIM
QUAB RAIL RUDD RUFF SCAD
SCUP SEER SHAD SOLE SPET SPIN
SPOT TILE TORO TUNA ULUA
ACARA AHOLE AKULE ANGLE
ATULE BEGTI BETTA BINNY BLAIN
BLEAK BOLTI BOLTY BREAM BULLY
BULTI CABIO CATLA CHIRO CISCO
COBIA CONEY DANIO DORAB
DOREE DRAIL DRIFT DRIVE ELOPS

ERIZO FLOAT FLUKE FOGAS FRIAR
GADID GRUNT GUPPY HILSA
HUCHO JUREL KILLY LAKER LANCE
MANTA MIDGE MINIM MORAY
OTTER PERCH PIABA PLATY PORGY
POWAN POWER REINA ROACH
SAIDE SARGO SAURY SEINE SHARK
SKATE SMELT SNOEK SNOOK
SPRAT SQUID SULEA SWEEP
TENCH TETRA TRABU TRAWL
TROLL TROUT TUNNY UMBRA
VIUVA VORAZ WAHOO WHIFF
AIMARA ALEVIN ANABAS ANGLER
BARBEL BARBER BENNET BICHIR
BISKOP BLENNY BONITO BOWFIN
BUMPER BURBOT CALLOP CANDIL
CAPLIN CARANX CARIBE COELHO
COTTID CREOLE CUCHIA CUNNER
DARTER DASSIE DENTEX FISHET
GANOID GINNEL GULPER GUNNEL
HAMLET HAPUKU HILSAH HUSSAR
INANGA KOKOPU LAUNCE LEDGER
LIGGER LOUVAR MAIGRE MARLIN
MEDAKA MENISE MILTER MINNOW
MOLLIE MOLOID MULLET NONNAT
PHOEBE PLAICE POMPON PUFFER
PUNECA REDFIN REMORA ROBALO
ROUGHY RUNNER SABALO SALELE
SALEMA SALMON SAPSAP SARDEL
SAUGER SAUREL SERRAN SHINER
SIERRA SIMARA SPARID SUCKER
TAILER TAIMEN TANDAN TARPON
TAUTOG TESTAR TETARD TINOSA
TOMCOD TURBOT VENDIS WALLER
WEAVER WIRRAH WRASSE ZINGEL
ALEWIFE ALFIONA ANCHOVY
BACALAO BARBUDO BATFISH
BEARDIE BERGYLT BERYCID
BOXFISH BRAGGLE BUFFALO
BUMMALO CABEZON CANDIRU
CAPELIN CAPLING CATFISH
CAVALLA CAVALLY CHIMERA
CHROMID CICHLID CLUPEID
CONVICT CORVINA COWFISH
CRAPPIE CROAKER CTENOID
CUTLIPS CYCLOID DRABBLE
DREPANE DRUMMER EELPOUT
ESCOLAR FATHEAD FINFISH
GALJOEN GEELBEC GEELBEK
GOBIOID GOGGLER GOLDEYE
GOURAMI GRAYSBY GROUPER
GRUNION GRUNTER GUAPENA
GUAVINA GUDGEON GULARIS
GURNARD GWYNIAD HADDOCK
HAGFISH HALIBUT HARMOOT
HERRING HINALEA HOGFISH
HOUTING ICEFISH ICHTHUS
INCONNU JAWFISH JEWFISH
JUGULAR LABROID LAGARTO
LONGFIN MACHETE MAHSEER
MAYFISH MOJARRA MOONEYE
MORWONG OARFISH OLDWIFE
OQUASSA PEGASUS PIGFOOT
PINTADO PIRANHA POISSON
POLLACK POMFRET POMPANO
PUPFISH RASBORA RONQUIL
SANCORD SARDINE SAUROID
SAVELHA SCARLET SCALARE
SCAROID SCHELLY SCULPIN
SENNETT SEVRUGA SILURUS
SLEEPER SMUTTER SNAPPER
SOLDIER SPAWNER STERLET
SUNFISH TELEOST TOMTATE

TOPKNOT TORPEDO TUBFISH
UMBRANA UNICORN VENDACE
VIAJACA WAREHOU WAUBEEN
WHAPUKA WHAPUKU WHITING
ALBACORE ALFONSIN APOGONID
ARAPAIMA ATHERINE BAITFISH
BALISTID BIGMOUTH BILLFISH
BLENNOID BLUEBACK BLUEFISH
BOARFISH BONEFISH BRISLING
BROTULID BULLHEAD CACKEREL
CANCHITO CARANGID CARANGIN
CARDINAL CATALINA CATALUFA
CHANCITO CHIMAERA CHOANATE
CHROMIDE CORACINE CREVALLE
CREVALLY CROSSOPT CYPRINID
DEALFISH DIPNEUST DITREMID
DONCELLA DRAGONET DRUMFISH
DUMBFISH ECHENEID ELEOTRID
EPISCATE FALLFISH FILEFISH
FLAGFISH FLATFISH FLATHEAD
FLOUNDER FOOLFISH FROGFISH
FUNDULUS GAMBUSIA GEELBECK
GILTHEAD GOATFISH GOLDFISH
GRAINING GRAYFISH GRAYLING
GREYSKIN HAIRFISH HALFBEAK
HANDFISH HANDLINE HAPLOMID
HARDHEAD HARDTAIL HOMOCERC
HORNFISH HORSEMAN JACKFISH
JUMPROCK KABELJOU KARMOUTH
KELPFISH KINGFISH LADYFISH
LUMPFISH MACKEREL MENHADEN
MILKFISH MOONFISH PICKEREL
PILCHARD PIRARUCU PORKFISH
QUERIMAN ROBALITO ROCKFISH
ROCKLING ROSEFISH SAILFISH
SALANGID SANDFISH SANDGOBY
SCIAENID SCOMBRID SCOTSMAN
SEERFISH SKILFISH SKIPJACK
SOAPFISH STUDFISH STURGEON
TALLYWAG TARWHINE TERAGLIN
TILEFISH TOADFISH TREEFISH
TREVALLY WARMOUTH WEAKFISH
WHISTLER WRYMOUTH
QUILLBACK SCORPAENO
NEEDLEFISH SHEEPSHEAD
SHOVELHEAD SHOVELNOSE
SILVERSIDES MOUTHBREEDER
(— BROTH) DASHI
(— BY TROLLING) DRAIL
(— FOR EELS) GRIG SNIGGLE
(— FOR SALMON) SNIGGER
(— LIGHTLY) DAP
(— NETTED) LIFT
(— NOT UNDERSIZED) COUNT
KEEPER
(— PRODUCT) SURIMI
(— TAPE) SNAKE
(— THROUGH ICE) CHUG
(— UNDERWATER) GOGGLE
(— WITH HANDS) GUMP GUDDLE
(AQUARIUM —) GUPPY RASBORA
(BAKED —) COULIBIAC
(BLIND —) PINKFISH
(CURED —) DUNFISH
(DISH OF RAW —) SEVICHE
(FABLED —) MAH
(FEMALE —) RAUN SPAWNER
(FIGHTING —) PLAKAT
(FRIED —) ESCABECHE
(HAWAIIAN —) AU
(HERALDIC —) CHABOT
(INDIAN —) ROHU

(NUMBER OF —) SCHOOL
(OLD —) MOSSBACK
(PART OF —) EYE FIN JAW ANUS
CHEEK NARIS SCALE MAXILLA
MANDIBLE OPERCULUM
PREMAXILLA
(PULPED —) POMACE
(PUREE OF —) BRANDADE
(QUANTITY OF —) MAZE
(RAW —) SASHIMI
(REFUSE —) CHUM SHACK
(SALTED —) COR
(SMALL —) TIDDLER
(SMOKED —) FUMADO
(SPLIT —) KLIPFISH
(STEWED —) MATELOTE
(THIN —) RACER
(YOUNG —) FRY ALEVIN
(25 LBS. OF —) STICK
(PREF.) ICHTHY(O) ISCI
(SUFF.) CHROMIS ICHTHYS
FISH BASKET POT CAUL CREEL
SLATH
FISH BOX TRUNK
FISH BRINER COBBERER
FISH CLEANER GILLER
FISH DRESSER IDLER
FISHER MART EELER PEKAN SABLE
SOBOL TAIRA TAYRA MARTEN
SEINER WEJACK MARTRIX
TRAWLER TROLLER
(SPONGE —) HOOKER
FISHERMAN (ALSO SEE ANGLER)
TOTY EELER ANGLER GIGMAN
GILLER KEDGER MAIMUL SEINER
WORMER ADMIRAL DORYMAN
DRAGMAN DRIFTER PRAWNER
RODSTER SHANKER SMELTER
STRIKER TRAWLER TROTTER
TROWMAN PETERMAN PISCATOR
SEASONER SHRIMPER
FISHERY FISHING PISCARY SEALERY
FISHGARTH WEIR
FISHHOOK FLY GIG HOOK LARI
ANGLE DRAIL KIRBY LARIN SLEEK
ANGULE SPROAT KENDALL
ABERDEEN BARBLESS CARLISLE
LIMERICK
(PART OF —) EYE GAP BARB BEND
POINT SHANK
(PL.) PULLDEVIL
FISHING PIKING ANGLING BANKING
BASSING GRAINING SNOEKING
(— TOOL) OVERSHOT
FISHING GROUNDS HAAF
FISHING ROD GAD
FISHING TACKLE TEW LEDGER
FISHLINE GIMP TROT SNELL TRAWL
DIPSEY LIGGER BOULTER
GANGION OUTLINE SETLINE
TRIMMER HAIRLINE TROTLINE
FISH LOUSE GISLER
FISHMONGER PESSONER
FISH NEST REDD
FISHNET FLUE SEINE SETNET
FISHPOND STEW VIVER PISCINA
VIVARIUM
FISHPOUND MADRAGUE
FISH SPEAR GRANES WASTER
LEISTER
FISHTAIL SKID UROSOME
FISHWAY PASS RACEWAY
FISHY DULL FUNNY GLASSY VACANT

FISSION BREAKING CLEAVAGE CLEAVING GAMOGENY SCISSION

FISSURE GAP CHAP CONE FLAW GOOL GULL LEAK LOCH LODE REFT RENT RIFT RIMA RIME SEAM SLIT TEAR VEIN VENT CHASM CHINE CHINK CLEFT CRACK FLAKE GRIKE PIPER PORTA SHAKE SPLIT ZYGON CLEAVE CRANNY DIVIDE LESION RICTUS RIMULA SPRING SULCUS BLEMISH CREVICE FISSURA MOFETTE OPENING SWALLET APERTURE BLOWHOLE CLEAVAGE COLOBOMA CREVASSE INCISURE QUEBRADA SCISSURA TRAVERSE
(— **IN BUILDING STONE**) DRY
(— **IN HEEL**) GAUG
(— **IN LIMESTONE**) GRIKE
(— **IN MAST**) SPRING
(— **IN PLATEAU**) ABRA
(— **OF LIVER**) PORTA
(**UNDERGROUND —**) SWALLET SWALLOW
(PL.) RHAGADES
(PREF.) RHAGAD(I)
(SUFF.) SCHISIS SCHIST

FISSURED RIMATE CHAPPED CLEFTED FISSATE

FIST JOB PUD DUKE NAVE NEIF NIEF FOIST GRASP INDEX NIEVE CLENCH CLUTCH DADDLE EFFORT MAULER MAULEY PINKER STRIKE ATTEMPT CLUBFIST FISTNOTE PUFFBALL TIGHTWAD

FISTFIGHT SETTO TURNUP

FISTICUFF BOX NEVEL FISTIFY

FISTULA EGILOPS
(PREF.) SYRING(O)

FISTULOUS TUBULAR

FIT GO APT FAY GEE JAG PAN RIG SET SIT ABLE AGUE BOUT FEAT FURY GOOD HARD KINK MEET MEGH PANG RIPE SORT SUIT TRIM TURN WELL WHIM ADAPT ADEPT APPLY BESIT CHINK CLICK DIGNE EXIES FADGE FANCY FITLY FRAME FRISK FUROR HAPPY ICTUS MATCH PITCH QUEME QUIRK READY RIGHT SERVE SPASM SPELL START STOUR SWOON TALLY ACCESS ADJUST ANSWER ATTACK BECOME BEHOVE BESORT DUEFUL FINISH FITTEN HABILE HEPPEN LIABLE PROPER SEASON SEEMLY SPLEEN SQUARE STREAK STROKE STRONG SUITED WORTHY ADAPTED BEHOOVE CAPABLE CONCENT CONDIGN CONFORM CORRECT DESPAIR FASHION FITTING HEALTHY PREPARE QUALIFY SEIZURE TANTRUM WIDDRIM ADEQUATE BECOMING DOVETAIL ELIGIBLE GLOOMING IDONEOUS OUTBREAK PAROXYSM PASSABLE SUITABLE SYNCOPES
(— **CLOSELY**) FAY CHOCK
(— **CORNER TO CORNER**) BUTT
(— **FOR THE GALLOWS**) WIDDIFOW
(— **IN**) GO NESTLE
(— **INTO SOCKET**) FANG
(— **LOOSELY**) SLOP
(— **NAUTICALLY**) RIG

(— **OF ANGER**) WAX FRAP FUME HUFF RAGE SNIT TIFF FLING RAVERY SPLEEN
(— **OF DEPRESSION**) HUMP
(— **OF ILL HUMOR**) DOD PET TIG FUNK POUT TOUT GRUMPS
(— **OF ILLNESS**) DROW TOUT FLING
(— **OF ILL TEMPER**) MAD TANTRUM
(— **OF LAUGHTER**) GIRD KINK
(— **OF NERVOUSNESS**) TWITCHET
(— **OF RESENTMENT**) PIQUE SNUFF
(— **OF SHIVERING**) AGUE GROOSE
(— **OF STUBBORNNESS**) REEST
(— **OF SULKS**) GEE STRUM
(— **OF SULLENNESS**) DOD
(— **OF TEMPER**) WAX BAIT BIRSE HISSY PADDY TETCH GROUCH SPLEEN SQUALL BRAINGE
(— **OF WEEPING**) CRY
(— **OF YAWNING**) GAPE
(— **ONE WITHIN ANOTHER**) NEST
(— **OUT**) ARM RIG BUSK BEFIT EQUIP ASTORE CLOTHE OUTFIT APPAREL APPOINT FURNISH HABILLE ACCOUTER
(— **RIFLE BARREL**) BED
(— **TIGHTLY**) STUFF
(— **TO BE DRUNK**) SORBILE
(— **TOGETHER**) MESH NEST COAPT JOINT COHERE ASSEMBLE
(— **UP**) RIG
(— **WITH COMPACTNESS**) BOX
(— **WITH FETTERS**) GARNISH
(**FAINTING —**) SWOON SYNCOPE
(**RITUALLY —**) KOSHER
(PL.) LUNES
(SUFF.) ABLE IBLE

FITCH LINER

FITFUL GERY CATCHY GERFUL GLEAMY CURSORY FLIGHTY RESTLESS UNSTABLE VARIABLE SPASMODIC

FITLY FIT PAT DULY FEATLY GLADLY MEETLY TIDELY APROPOS HAPPILY PROPERLY SUITABLY

FITNESS FORM APTNESS DECENCY DECORUM DIGNITY APTITUDE CAPACITY IDONEITY JUSTNESS PROPERTY CONGRUITY

FITTED APT ABLE ADAPT KEYED SUITED ADAPTED ENGAGED ADJUSTED ASSORTED ELIGIBLE

FITTER TUBER GASMAN

FITTING TO APT CAP DUE LUG PAT BUTT FAIR FEAT FORK HARP JUMP JUST KIND MEET CLEAT HAPPY QUEME WORTH BECOME CLENCH CLEVIS LEADER PROPER SADDLE SEEMLY WASHER ADAPTER CONGRUE PENDANT SERVING SHACKLE SUCTION TACTFUL CONDULET DECOROUS GRACEFUL RIGHTFUL SUITABLE RECEPTACLE
(— **FOR MILL-STONE**) RIND RYND
(— **TIGHTLY**) CLOSE
(**GREASE —**) ZERK
(**LIGHT —**) PLUG LUMINAIRE
(**PIPE —**) CROSS ELBOW
(PL.) BRASS COVER REPAREL FITMENTS

FITZGERALD ELLA

FIVE CINQ FUNF CINQUE EPSILON QUINQUE

(— **CENTS**) JITNEY NICKEL
(— **HUNDRED DOLLARS, POUNDS**) MONKEY
(— **IN CRAPS**) PHOEBE
(— **OF TRUMPS**) PEDRO
(— **YEARS**) LUSTRUM
(**GAME CALLED —S**) HANDBALL
(**TWO —S**) QUINAS
(PREF.) CINQUE LEPT(O) PEN(T)(TA)
(TH) QUINQU(E)

FIVES BALL SNACK

FIVESTONES SNOBS

FIX BOX JAM PEG PIN SET CLEW CLUE FAST FIRM GAFF GLUE HOLD HOLE JAMB LOCK MEND MOOR NAIL PICK RELY SEAL SPOT STAY AFFIX ALLOT DEFIX FOUND GRAFT GRAVE IMBED INFIX LIMIT PLACE PLANT POINT POSIT SEIZE STATE STEEK STELL STICK TRYST ADJUST ANCHOR ARREST ASSIGN ASSIZE ATTACH CEMENT CLINCH DEFINE ENROOT ENTAIL FASTEN FICCHE FIXATE FREEZE GROUND IMPALE REPAIR REVAMP SETTLE SQUARE TEMPER APPOINT ARRANGE CALCIFY CONFIRM DELIMIT DESTINE DILEMMA GRAPPLE IMPLANT IMPRESS IMPRINT PREPARE STATION PINPOINT RENOVATE TRANSFIX
(— **A FIGHT**) RIG
(— **A MAST**) STEP
(— **AMOUNT**) AFFEER
(— **ATTENTION**) NAIL
(— **DEEPLY**) GRAVE
(— **FIRMLY**) SEAL FREEZE IMPACT INCUBE RAMPIRE
(— **IMMOVABLY**) RIVET
(— **IN AMAZEMENT**) PETRIFY
(— **IN MUD**) MIRE
(— **IN POSITION**) SHIP
(— **PRICE**) ASSIZE CHARGE SETTLE
(— **THE MIND**) INTEND
(— **UP**) CLEW CLUE
(— **UPON**) CHAP AFFIX
(— **WORK OF ART**) REDO
(**GAMBLING —**) RIG STCK

FIXATION TIC FETICH FETISH
(SUFF.) PAGUS PEXIA PEXIS PEXY

FIXATIVE FIXER SKATOLE AMBRETTE EUDESMOL HYRACEUM LABDANUM

FIXED PAT PUT SAD SET SOT FAST FIRM FLAT HARD GIVEN SIKER STAID UPSET FINITE FROZEN INTENT MENDED SICKER STABLE STATED STEADY STRONG CERTAIN DORMANT EMPIGHT HABITED LIMITED SETTLED SITFAST STATARY STATIVE STELLED ACCURATE ARRANGED ATTACHED CONSTANT DEFINITE EXPLICIT FASTENED IMMOBILE IRONCLAD MOVELESS RESIDENT RESOLUTE STANDING STUBBORN
(**NOT —**) FLUID SHIFTY MOVABLE FUGITIVE INSECURE MOVEABLE
(PREF.) APLANO

FIXEDLY SAD FAST FIRM FIXLY INTENTLY

FIXEDNESS FASTNESS

FIXER HYPO PATCH

FIXTURE ANNEX EVENT GUARD FAUCET SHIELD BRACKET CREEPER KNOCKER THIMBLE
(**LIGHTING —**) SCONCE
(**STORE —**) GONDOLA

FIZZING FIZZY GASSING

FIZZLE FLOP FUSS BARNEY FAILURE FLIVVER
(— **OUT**) DIE

FLABBINESS MYATONIA

FLABBY LAX FOZY LASH LIMP WEAK BAGGY FLASH FOGGY FRUSH SAPPY WOOZY CASHIE DOUGHY FEEBLE FLAGGY FLAPPY LIMBER QUAGGY WATERY FLACCID YIELDING

FLABELLUM RHIPIDION

FLACCID LIMP WOOZY FLABBY FLAGGY EMARCID FLACKED YIELDING

FLAG FAG LAG SAG SOD FAIL FANE FLAT HOOK IRIS JACK JADE LECK PINE TIRE TURF WAFT WAIF WILT CREST DROOP FAINT FLAKE SEDGE SLAKE UNION VEXIL WHEFT WHIFF BANNER BOUGEE BURGEE COLORS CORNET EMBLEM ENSIGN FANION GUIDON LEVERS PENCEL PENNON SIGNAL TABARD WIMPLE ANCIENT BEEWORT CALAMUS CATTAIL CURTAIN DECLINE DRAPEAU FANACLE LABARUM PENDANT PENNANT SCOURGE BANDEROL BRATTACH GONFALON HANDFLAG LANGUISH PAVILION STANDARD STREAMER TRICOLOR VEXILLUM WATCHMAN
(— **CORNER**) UNION
(— **OF DENMARK**) DANEBROG
(— **OF TRANSVAAL**) VIERKLEUR
(— **OF TRUCE**) KARTEL
(— **OF U.S.**) GRIDIRON
(— **ON LANCE**) PAVON
(**BLUE — WITH WHITE SQUARE**) PETER
(**CAVALRY —**) STANDARD
(**KNOTTED —**) WAFT
(**PIRATE —**) ROGER BLACKJACK
(**SERPENT-LIKE —**) DRACO ANGUIS
(**SHIP'S —**) DUSTER
(**TURKISH —**) ALEM
(**WATER —**) SAG
(PL.) BUNTING

FLAG BEARER GUIDON ANCIENT

FLAGELLANT WHIPPER SCOURGER
(PL.) ALBI

FLAGELLATE MONAS NOCTILUCA

FLAGELLUM WHIP CILIUM RUNNER KONSEAL WHIPLASH
(PREF.) BLEPHAR(O) MASTIG(O)
(SUFF.) KONT

FLAGEOLET PIPE ZUFOLO BASAREE LARIGOT SIBILUS ZUFFOLO MONAULOS

FLAGGING WEAK LANGUID

FLAGITIOUS WICKED CORRUPT HEINOUS CRIMINAL FLAGRANT GRIEVOUS

FLAGON GUN STOUP BOTTLE VESSEL FLACKET FLAGONET REHOBOAM

FLAGRANT BAD RED RANK GROSS ODIOUS STRONG WANTON

WICKED BLATANT GLARING
HATEFUL HEINOUS SCARLET
VIOLENT SHAMEFUL

FLAGSHIP FLAG ADMIRAL

FLAGSTONE FLAG LECK SLAB
FAVUS

FLAIL BEAT FLOG WHIP DRASH
FRAIL THRAIL THRASH THRESH
SWINGLE SWIPPLE STRICKLE
THRESHEL

FLAIR RAY BENT ELAN NOSE ODOR
SMELL VERVE GENIUS TALENT
LEANING PANACHE

FLAKE CHIP FILM FLAG FLAW RACK
SNOW FLANK FLECK FLOCK LAMIN
SCALE SLATE SPALL SPAWL STRIP
APHTHA HURDLE LAMINA PALING
FLAUGHT SHAVING FLOCCULE
FRAGMENT
(— OF DIRT) SMUT
(— OF METAL) FLITTER
(— OF SNOW) FLAG
(— OF SOOT) STRANGER
(PREF.) LEPID(O)
(SUFF.) LEPIS

FLAKY SCALY WACKY OFFBEAT
SHIVERY

FLAMBE JUBILEE

FLAMBEAU TORCH

FLAMBOYANCE BLARE PANACHE

FLAMBOYANT BAROCK FLORID
GARISH ORNATE BAROQUE
BUCKEYE FLAMING GORGEOUS

FLAME LOW FIRE GLOW LOWE
LUNT ARDOR BLAZE FLARE FLASH
GLARE GLEED INGLE LIGHT
RESEPH TONGUE BURNING
FLAMELET INKINDLE
(ACETYLENE —) CALCIUM
(SMALL —) SPUNK FLAMELET
FLAMMULE
(PL.) GLEED

FLAME SCARLET FLORENTINE

FLAME TREE KURRAJONG

FLAMING LIVE AFIRE FIERY FLAMY
VIVID AFLARE ARDENT BLAZING
BURNING FLARING FLAGRANT

FLAMMA, LA (CHARACTER IN —)
AGNES CERVIA BASILIO DONELLO
SILVANA
(COMPOSER OF —) RESPIGHI

FLAN PLANCHET

FLANGE BEAD BOSS BEZEL COLLAR
COLLET FLANCH SHROUD
FEATHER DUCKBILL FOLLOWER
(— OF GIRDER) BOOM
(WITHOUT —) BALD

FLANGER FLAYER GOUGER

FLANK LEER LISK SIDE WING CHEEK
SKIRT THIGH BORDER FLITCH
(— OF ARCH) HANCH HAUNCH
(PL.) ILIA
(PREF.) LAPAR(O)

FLANNEL LANA DOMETT SAXONY
STAMIN RUBBISH WHITTLE
MOLLETON NONSENSE SWANSKIN

FLAP ADO FAN LUG ROB TAB TAG
TAP WAP BATE BEAT BLOW CLAP
FLIP FLOG FLOP GILL LOBE LOMA
SLAM SLAT WAFF WELT ALARM
APRON FLACK FLAFF FLICK BALLUP
BANGLE LAPPET LIBBET STRIKE
TONGUE WAFFLE WALLOP

WINNOW AILERON BLINDER
CLICKET FLACKER FLAPPET
FLICKER FLOUNCE FLUTTER
SWINDLE VALANCE AVENTAIL
BACKFLAP COATTAIL CODPIECE
TURNOVER AGITATION
COMMOTION CONFUSION
(— OF BOOTEE) FLY
(— OF GARMENT) LAP
(— OF HAT OR CAP) VALANCE
(— OF HINGE) LEAF
(— ON HOLSTER) FLOUNCE
(— ON SADDLE) SKIRT JOCKEY
(— VIOLENTLY) FLOG SLAT
(CARDIAC —) CUSP
(FLESHY —) GILL
(MUD —) BOOT
(TROUSERS' —) FALL

FLAPPER FLAP WING FLOPPER
SNICKET

FLAPPING WAFF WHUTTER

FLARE BELL FLUE BLAZE FLAME
FLASH FLECK FUSEE LIGHT SPIRT
TORCH FLANCH SIGNAL SPREAD
FLICKER TRUMPET OUTBURST
(— ON SHIPBOARD) DUCK
(— UP) ERUPT KINDLE
(RAILROAD —) FUSEE
(PL.) TROUSERS

FLARING BELL FLUE EVASE GAUDY
AFLARE FLIPPY FLAMING GLARING
SWAGGER BOUFFANT DAZZLING

FLASH DOT BEAT DASH LAIT LAMP
LASH LEAM POOL RUSH SHOT
STAB WINK BLASH BLAZE BURST
FLAME FLARE FLOSH FLUFF GLADE
GLAIK GLEAM GLENT GLINT GLITZ
LEVIN MARSH SPARK STEAM
BOTTLE FILLIP GLANCE QUIVER
REPORT BLUETTE FLAUGHT
FOULDRE GLIMMER GLIMPSE
GLISTEN GLITTER INSTANT
LIGHTEN QUICKEN SHIMMER
SPARKLE TWINKLE BULLETIN
SPLINTER SUNBURST CORUSCATE
SCINTILLATION
(— FORTH) OUTRAY
(HOT —) FLUSHING
(NEWS —) FUDGE

FLASHBACK THROWBACK

FLASHING CURB FLASH STEEP
ARDENT BRIGHT FLASHY
FORWARD LAMPING SHINING
CREASING METEORIC SLASHING
SNAPPING

FLASHLIGHT BUG GLIM FLASH
TORCH PENLITE PENLIGHT

FLASHY GAY FLAT GAUD LOUD
BAVIN FIERY GAUDY NOBBY
SHOWY SLEEK ZOOTY FLOSSY
FROTHY GARISH SLANGY SPORTY
STUNTY INSIPID RAFFISH TINHORN
DAZZLING FLASHING SPORTING
TIGERISH VEHEMENT

FLASK BOX PIG BODY HEAD HELM
JACK OLPE SNAP BETTY BULGE
DEWAR FRAME GIRBA GOURD
BOTTLE FIASCO FLACON GUTTUS
HELMET LAGENA AMPULLA
BOMBOLA CANTEEN FLASKET
MATRASS TICKLER WARBURG
CHRISMAL CUCURBIT

(POCKET —) TICKLER
(PREF.) OLPIDI

FLAT DEAD DOWD DULL EVEN FADE
FLUE PLAT SLOB TAME ABODE
AFLAT BANAL BLAND BLUNT
DUSTY HAUGH LEVEL MOLLE
MUSTY PLAIN PLANE PRONE
ROOMS SEBKA SLAKE VAPID
WALSH AGRUFE BORING CALLOW
DREARY FLASHY JEJUNE LEADEN
PLANAR QUATCH SEBKHA SILENT
SIMOUS DECIDED FLIPPER INSIPID
INSULSE PLATOID PROSAIC
SHILPIT TABULAR UNIFORM
DIRECTLY LIFELESS TENEMENT
UNBROKEN WATERISH
CHAMPAIGN POINTLESS
PROSTRATE
(— AND CIRCULAR) DISCOID
(— AND SHORT) CAMUS CAMUSE
(— IN MUSIC) BEMOL MOLLE
(— OF SWORD) PLAT
(MUD —) SLOB SLAKE CORCASS
(NOT —) BRISK
(SALT —) SALINA
(THEATRICAL —) JOG
(PREF.) PLAN(I) PLAT(Y)

FLATBOAT ARK SCOW PULLBOAT

FLATCAR FLAT IDLER LORRY
(ON A —) PIGGYBACK

FLATFISH DAB RAY BUTT DACE KITE
SLIP SOLE TONG BREAM BRILL
FLUKE QUIFF RHINA WHIFF ACEDIA
CARTER PLAICE TURBOT HALIBUT
SUNFISH TORPEDO FLOUNDER
MARYSOLE

FLATHEAD SALISH

FLATIRON IRON GOOSE STEEL
SADIRON

FLATLY
(PREF.) PLANO

FLATNESS BATHOS SILENCE
EVENNESS KURTOSIS
(— OF NOSE) SIMITY

FLAT-NOSED CAMUS

FLATTEN BEAT COMB DECK EVEN
PLAT CRUSH GRADE LEVEL PLUSH
SPLAT BEETLE CLINCH DEJECT
SMOOTH SPREAD SQUASH
DEPRESS EXPLAIN PANCAKE
PLANISH SUBSIDE SURBASE
COMPRESS DISPIRIT

FLATTENED ECRASE OBLATE
DILATED PLANATE TABULAR

FLATTER BULL CLAW COAX DAUB
FAGE FUME PALP SOAP WORD
CHARM FLOAT GLOZE HONEY
PAINT ROOSE SLEEK SMALM
BECOME BUTTER CAJOLE CRINGE
FICKLE FLEECH FRAISE GLAVER
KITTLE PEPPER PHRASE SAWDER
SLAVER SMOOGE SOOTHE STROKE
ADULATE BEGUILE BEHONEY
BLARNEY FLETHER FLUTTER
INCENSE PALAVER SOOTHER
SWEETEN WHEEDLE BESLAVER
BLANDISH BOOTLICK COLLOGUE

FLATTERER FLOIT COGGER DAUBER
EARWIG GLOZER JENKINS
PRONEUR SOOTHER BOOTLICK
CLAWBACK COURTIER DAMOCLES
INCENSER LOSENGER SLAVERER
SMOOTHER

FLATTERING SOAPY SMARMY
SMOOTH BUTTERY CANDIED
COURTLY GLAVERING

FLATTERY BULL BUNK DAUB FLUM
MUSH SOAP FRAIK GLOZE SALVE
TAFFY BUTTER CARNEY FLEECH
GREASE PHRASE SAWDER SLAVER
BLARNEY DAUBING EYEWASH
FAWNING FLETHER INCENSE
PALAVER CAJOLERY ADULATION

FLATULENCE WIND VAPOR

FLATULENT GASSY WINDY TURGID
POMPOUS VENTOSE FLATUOUS
INFLATED

FLATWARE SILVER

FLATWORM ACOEL FLUKE
PLATODE RADIATE POLYCLAD

FLAUNT BOSH SHOW WAVE BOAST
SKYRE STOUT VAUNT PARADE
DISPLAY FLUTTER TRAIPSE
BRANDISH FLOURISH

FLAUNTING GAUDY PURPLE SKYRIN
FLAGGERY

FLAVONE CHROMONE

FLAVOR GAMY GOUT MASK ODOR
RASA SALT TANG ZEST AROMA
ASSAI CURRY DEVIL SAPID SAPOR
SAUCE SAVOR SCENT SMACK
SPICE TASTE TINGE ASARUM
ASSAHY INFUSE RANCIO RELISH
SEASON TARAGE FLAVOUR
PERFUME SUPTION VARIETY
HAUTGOUT PIQUANCY
(DEVELOP —) BREATHE
(DISTINCTIVE —) TACK SMACK
(HIGH —) HOGO
(SHARP —) TWANG
(SPECIAL —) GUST
(UNPLEASANT —) TACK

FLAVORED SPICY TINCT SPICED

FLAVORFUL SAPID SAVOROUS

FLAVORING DIP MOCHA ALMOND
CASSIS VANILLA MIREPOIS

FLAVORLESS BLAND STALE SILENT
WATERISH

FLAW BUG FIB GAP LIE MAR RUB
WEM BANE BLOT CHIP FLEE GALL
HOLE RASE RIFT SPOT WIND
BOTCH BRACK BURST CHICK CLEFT
CRACK CRAZE FAULT FLAKE
PLUME SPECK BLOTCH BREACH
DEFECT FOIBLE LACUNA LESION
BLEMISH BLISTER DEFAULT
EYELAST FEATHER FISSURE
NULLIFY SUNSPOT VIOLATE
WHITLOW FRACTURE FRAGMENT
GENDARME WINDFLAW
(— IN CASTING) BUCKLE
(— IN CLOTH) BRACK
(— IN DIAMOND) GENDARME
(— IN MARBLE) TERRACE
(— IN METAL) SNAKE
(— IN PRECIOUS STONE) FEATHER
(— IN STEEL) STAR
(— IN STONE) DRY
(— IN WICK) THIEF
(MORAL —) SMIRCH

FLAWED CRACKED

FLAWLESS CLEAN SOUND PERFECT

FLAX LIN POB TOW CARD FLIX HARL
LINE LINT ROCK GRAIN HURDS
BREADS BYSSUS KORARI PEANUT

PEBBLE SCUTCH LINSEED
FLAXWORT HARAKEKE
(— DISEASE) PASMO
(PREPARE —) RET
(PREF.) BYSSI BYSSO LINO
FLAXEN FLAXY BLONDE
FLAXWEED TOADFLAX
FLAY SKIN SCULP STRIP FLEECE
UNCASE CENSURE PILLAGE
REPROVE SCARIFY
FLEA LOP SCUD FLECH FLECK PULEX
TUNGA CHEGRE CHIGOE VERMIN
PULICID SANDBOY
(— INFESTED) PULICOSE
(PREF.) PULI
FLEABANE SKEVISH SCABIOUS
WHITETOP
FLEA BEETLE THRIPS
FLEAM BEVEL
FLEAWORT CAMMOCK FLEASEED
PSYLLIUM
FLECHE SPIRE SPIRELET
FLECK FLAKE FREAK DAPPLE FLEECE
POUNCE STREAK STIPPLE
**FLEDERMAUS, DIE (CHARACTER IN
—)** ADELE FALKE FRANK ALFRED
ORLOFSKY ROSALINDE EISENSTEIN
(COMPOSER OF —) STRAUSS
FLEDGED FLUSH FLIGGED
FLEDGLING SQUAB NESTER
FLIGGER BIRDLING
FLEE FLY LAM RUN BOLT FLEG LOUP
SCUR SHUN TURN ELOPE ELUDE
SKIRR SPEED DECAMP ESCAPE
RUNOFF VANISH ABANDON
ABSCOND FORSAKE SCAMPER
LIBERATE SKEDADDLE
(SUFF.) FUGAL FUGE
FLEECE JIB KET TEG BUCK CAST
FELL GAFF MORT PLOT ROOK SKIN
TEGG TEGS CHEAT FLICK PASHM
PLOAT SHAVE SHEAR SHEEP
SWEAT PASHIM PIGEON PUSHUM
TOISON SHEARING
(— OF MEDIUM GRADE) SUPER
(POOREST PART OF —) ABB
FLEEING FUGIENT HOTFOOT
RUNNING FUGITIVE
FLEER GIBE JIBE LEER FLIRE FLOUT
SCOFF SNEER
FLEET BAY FAST FLIT NAVY SAIL
SKIM SWIM CREEK DRAIN DRIFT
EVAND FLOAT FLOTA HASTY INLET
POWER QUICK RAPID SWIFT
ARGOSY ARMADA FLIGHT HASTEN
NIMBLE SPEEDY CARAVAN
COMPANY FLOTILLA NAVARCHY
WARCRAFT
FLEETING BRIEF BUBBLE CADUCE
FLYING VOLAGE CURSIVE FLIGHTY
PASSING POSTING SHADOWY
VOLATIC CADUCOUS FUGITIVE
VOLATILE
FLESH KIN BEEF BODY FELL GAME
LAMB LIRE MEAT RACE WEED
SLATE STOCK FAMILY MUSCLE
SEASON CARNAGE KINDRED
MANKIND NATURAL HUMANITY
MOONLIGHT
(— ABOUT CHIN AND JAWS) GILL
(— OF CALF) SLINK
(— OF GOAT) CHEVON
(— OF KID) CABRITO

(— OF SHEEP) TRAIK
(— ON LOWER JAW) CHOLLER
(— OUT) CLOTHE
(— UNDER SKIN) FELL
(ANIMAL —) BRAWN
(DEAD —) MURRAIN
(HORSE —) JACK
(LIFELESS —) MUMMY
(PUTREFYING —) CARRION
(SUN-DRIED —) TAPA
(SUPERFLUOUS —) LUMBER
(PREF.) CARNI CRE(O) CREATO
KRE(O) SARC(O)
(SUFF.) SARC
FLESHBRUSH STRIGIL
FLESH-COLORED SARCOLINE
FLESH-EATING CARNAL
CARNIVOROUS
FLESHER LINING
FLESHINESS FULLNESS
CORPULENCE
FLESHLESS LENTEN
FLESHLY CARNAL FLESHY SENSUAL
SARKICAL
FLESHY FAT BEEFY LUSTY OBESE
PLUMP PULPY STOUT ANIMAL
BODILY BRAWNY CARNAL
BUNTING CARNOSE SARCOUS
CARNEOUS
FLETCH WING FLIGHT
FLEUR-DE-LIS LIS LYS LILY LUCY
FLEUR
FLEX BEND
FLEXED PENCHE
FLEXIBILITY WHIP FLUIDITY
FLEXIBLE ACDC LIMP LUSH SOFT
BUXOM LIMSY LITHE WANDY
WITHY FLOPPY LIMBER LITHER
PLIANT SUPPLE DUCTILE ELASTIC
FINGENT FLEXILE FLEXIVE
LISSOME PLIABLE SPRINGY
WILLOWY WINDING WRIGGLE
BENDSOME YIELDING
(PREF.) CAMPTO
FLEXURE ARCH BEND BENT CURL
FOLD CURVE TWIST SIGMOID
WINDING
FLICK PIC FILM FLIP CLICK FLACK
FLANK FLECK FLIRT FLISK MOVIE
CINEMA
(SKIN —) NUDIE
(PL.) CINEMA
FLICKER FAIL FLIT LICK WINK BLINK
FLAME FLARE FLICK FLUNK WAVER
BICKER FITTER SHIVER YUCKER
BLINTER FLIMMER FLITTER
FLUTTER SKIMMER TREMBLE
TWINKLE WHIFFLE FLICHTER
HIGHHOLE
FLICKERING FLICKY FLUTTER
LAMBENT FLEXUOUS UNSTEADY
FLICKERTAIL STATE
NORTHDAKOTA
FLIER ACE BIRD KIWI FLYER PILOT
AIRMAN AVIATOR LEAFLET
CIRCULAR PAMPHLET
FLIGHT FLY GUY HOP LAM BOLT
BUNK LAKE PAIR ROUT WING
CHEVY FLOCK GLIDE GRICE SCRAP
VOLEE CHIVVY EXODUS FUGACY
HEGIRA HEJIRA JOYHOP SPIRAL
BOUQUET EVASION FLAUGHT

FLYOVER MIGRATE MISSION
SCAMPER STEPWAY REGIFUGE
STAMPEDE SWARMING
(— APPROVAL) AOK
(— OF BALL) HOOK DRIVE SLICE
(— OF BIRDS) VOLARY VOLERY
VOLLEY
(— OF FANCY) SALLY
(— OF GEESE) SKEIN
(— OF SNIPE) WISP
(— OF STEPS) RISE TRAP GRECE
PITCH SCALE STOOP PERRON
STAIRS STEPWAY STAIRWAY
(— OF WILD FOWL) SKEIN
(— OF WOODCOCK) RODING
(ABORTIVE —) ABORT
(HASTY —) TIFT
(HAWK'S —) CAREER
(HIGH —) TOWER
(IN —) ALOFT
(LATE NIGHT —) REDEYE
(SUDDEN —) START STAMPEDE
(UNAUTHORIZED —) BUGOUT
(UPWARD —) SOAR
(PREF.) AERO
(SUFF.) FUGAL FUGE PHOBE
PHOBI(A)(AC)(C) PHOBUS
FLIGHTY ANILE BARMY GIDDY LIGHT
SWIFT FITFUL GARISH UNFIRM
VOLAGE WHISKY FLYAWAY
FOOLISH GIGGISH MOONISH
ROCKETY FLEETING FREAKISH
HELLICAT SKIPPING VOLATILE
(— PERSON) TRIVVET
FLIMFLAM CON
FLIMSINESS INANITY
FLIMSY LIMP THIN VAIN WEAK FRAIL
GAUDY JERRY FEEBLE PALTRY
SLEAZY SLIGHT SLIMSY HAYWIRE
SHALLOW TENUOUS TIFFANY
GIMCRACK GOSSAMER JIMCRACK
TWITTERY
FLINCH SHY FUNK GAME JARG
BLUNK BUDGE FEIGN QUAIL
SHUNT START WINCE WONDE
BLANCH BLENCH FALTER FLENSE
RECOIL SHRINK SCRINGE
SCUNNER SQUINCH
FLINCHER VELLINCH
FLINDER FLITTER SMITHERS
FLINDERSIA SILKWOOD
FLINDOSA CUDGERIE
FLING SHY BUZZ CAST DART DASH
DING EMIT FLAP FLEG GIBE HURL
KICK LASH PECK PICK SLAT TOSS
WARP BRAID CHEAT DANCE FLIRT
LANCE PITCH SHOOT SLING SNEER
SWING THROW WHANG BAFFLE
EFFUSE HURTLE LAUNCH PLUNGE
REBUFF SPIRIT ENFORCE FLOUNCE
REPULSE SARCASM SCATTER
SWINDLE SHYLANCE SPANGHEW
(— HEADLONG) RUINATE
(— MISSILES) CHUNK
(— UPWARD) HAUNCH
(HIGHLAND —) WALLOCH
FLINT CORE BLANK CHERT MISER
SILEX EOLITH QUARTZ REJECT
ESLABON FURISON SCRAPER
GRATTOIR GUNFLINT
(PREF.) SILICEO SILICI SILICO
FLINTINESS HEART

FLINTLOCK FUSEE FUSIL FUZEE
MUSKET SPANNER FIRELOCK
MIQUELET SNAPHAAN
FLINTWOOD WHITETOP
FLIP SKY TAP FLAP SNAP TOSS TRIP
FLANK FLICK FLIRT GOAPE SLIRT
SMART FILLIP FLITCH GOGAGA
LIMBER NIMBLE PLIANT PROPEL
(— OUT) GOAPE
FLIP-FLOP SANDAL REVERSAL
FLIPPANT AIRY FLIP GLIB FLUENT
LIMBER NIMBLE
FLIPPER ARM FIN PAW HAND SWELL
PADDLE FLAPPER SPRINGER
FLIRT TOY FIKE FLIP MASH TICK
VAMP FLICK ROVER SLIRT JILLET
MASHER TRIFLE GALLANT PICKEER
TWINKLE COQUETTE PHILANDER
FLIRTATION FIKE PASSADE
COQUETRY PHILANDER
FLIT DART FLOW SCUD FLECK FLEET
FLICK FLIRT FLOAT FLURR HOVER
QUICK SCOOT SKIFF SWIFT NIMBLE
FLICKER FLUTTER
FLITCH FLICK GAMMON
LONGWOOD MIDDLING
FLOAT BOB FLY KIT SEA BOOM
BUOY CORK DRAG FLOW FLUX
HAWK HONE HOVE LIVE PONT
RAFT RIDE SAIL SCOW SOAR SWIM
TILT WAFT WAVE BALSA BLADE
CAMEL DERBY DRIFT DRIVE FLEET
FLOOD FLUSH GRAIL HOVER
LADLE QUILL SHOAD SWOON
BILLOW BOBBER BUCKET BUNGEY
CANNEL DOBBER PADDLE PONTON
RADEAU STREEL TOPPER CAISSON
DRINGLE FLATTER FLOTTER
FRESHEN OROPESA PAGEANT
PLANKER PLUMMET PONTOON
SLICKER LEVITATE PICKOVER
(— AIMLESSLY) DRIFT
(— DELIGHTFULLY) COWD
(— FOR HERRING NET) BOWL
(— FOR RING BUOY) LEMON
(— LOGS) DRIVE
(— OF REEDS) KELEK LIGGER
(— PAST) GLACE
(— PROPERLY) WATCH
(CANOE —) AMA
(FISHLINE —) BOB CORK BOBBER
DOBBER TRIMMER
(PLASTERER'S —) DARBY
FLOATBOARD BLADE FLOAT LADLE
FLOATER STIFF
FLOATING FREE WAFT AWASH
LOOSE ADRIFT AFLOAT FLYING
NATANT BUOYANT FLYAWAY
PENDENT DRIFTING FLUITANT
SHIFTING UNFUNDED
FLOCCILATION TILMUS
FLOCK MOB POD BAND BANK BEVY
FOLD GAME GANG HERD MANY
PACK ROUT SAIL SORT TEAM TRIP
WISP BROOD BUNCH CHARM
COVEY CROWD DRIFT DROVE
FLAKE FLECK GROUP PLUMP
SEDGE SHOAL SWARM TRIBE
TROOP COVERT FLIGHT GAGGLE
HIRSEL MANADA MEINIE RAFTER
SCHOOL SCURRY VOLERY
COMPANY GOOSERY THICKEN
PADDLING

(— OF BIRDS) POD BANK HERD TEAM WISP BROWN COVEY SEDGE SIEGE TRIBE FLIGHT VOLERY
(— OF BITTERNS) SEDGE SIEGE
(— OF DUCKS) PADDLING
(— OF FINCHES) CHARM CHIRM
(— OF GEESE) SKEIN GAGGLE
(— OF HERONS) SEDGE SIEGE
(— OF LARKS) EXALTATION
(— OF LIONS) PRIDE
(— OF MALLARDS) SORD SUTE
(— OF NIGHTINGALES) WATCH
(— OF PARTRIDGE) COVEY
(— OF PEACOCKS) MUSTER
(— OF PIGEONS) KIT LOFT
(— OF PLOVER) WING
(— OF ROOKS) ROOKERY
(— OF SANDPIPERS) FLING
(— OF SHEEP) FOLD HIRSEL
(— OF SHELDRAKE) DOPPING
(— OF SNIPE) WISP
(— OF SWANS) BANK GAME MARK
(— OF TURTLE-DOVES) DOLE
(— OF WIDGEONS) COMPANY
(— OF WILDFOWL) SCRY SKEIN
(— TOGETHER) RAFT
(SMALL —) SPRING
(PREF.) (— OF WOOL) FLOCCI
FLOCKING REPAIR
FLOE PAN
FLOG CAT TAN TAW BEAT CANE CHOP HIDE LASH LICK LUMP TOCO WALE WARM WELK WHIP YANK BIRCH EXCEL FIGHT FLAIL HORSE KNOUT LINGE QUILT SAUCE SKEEG SWISH WHANG BREECH COTTON LARRUP LATHER STRIKE SWITCH THRASH WALLOP WATTLE BALEISE BELABOR COWHIDE SCOURGE SJAMBOK TROUNCE CARTWHIP CHAWBUCK SLAISTER URTICATE VAPULATE
(— WATER) SCRINGE
FLOGGER HORSING SWISHER
FLOGGING TOCO TOKO TANNING BIRCHING WHIPPING
FLOOD SEA BORE BUOY FLOW FLUX POUR TIDE EAGRE FLOAT FLUSH SPATE SWAMP SWILL WATER DELUGE EXCESS RAVINE SLUICE SPLASH DEBACLE FLOTTER FRESHET NIAGARA TORRENT ALLUVION CATARACT INUNDATE OVERFLOW SURROUND
FLOODED AWASH AFLOAT
FLOODGATE CLOW DRAG GOLE HATCH SLUICE STAUNCH CATARACT PENSTOCK
FLOODING UP PROUD FLOWAGE DILUVIAL FLOATING
FLOODLIGHT OLIVET
FLOODPLAIN BENCH DAMBO
FLOOR BECK DECK DROP FLAT LAND LOFT PAVE SEAT BOARD FLOAT GRASS PIANO PIECE SOLAR STAGE STORY BELFRY FLIGHT GROUND SOLLAR PLANCHE BARBECUE FLOORING HALFPACE PAVEMENT SUBFLOOR
(— OF COAL MINE) SOLE THILL
(— OF COAL SEAM) SILL
(— OF FORGE) HEARTH
(— OF GLASS FURNACE) SIEGE

(— OF OCEAN) SEABED
(— OF SPORTS RING) CANVAS
(— OF WOOLSHED) BOARD
(FOREST —) SEEDBED
(GROUND —) TERRENO BASEMENT
(OPENWORK —S) GRATINGS
(RAISED —) LEEWAN HALFPACE
(THEATRE —) GALLERY
(THRESHING —) MOWSTEAD
(UPPER —) LOFT
FLOORBOARD FOOTLING
(BOAT'S —) BURDEN
(BOAT'S —S) BURDEN
FLOORING STAGE PARQUET TERRAZZO
(— FOR STACK) RICKSTAND
FLOORMAN CALLBOY
FLOP DOG BOMB SWOP WHOP SQUAB BUMMER TURKEY FAILURE TRAGEDY
FLORA CYBELE FLORULA
(— AND FAUNA) BIOTA
FLORAL TREE LEAF
FLORENCE FLASK BETTY
FLORENCE IRIS ORRIS TREOS
FLORESTAN (WIFE OF —) LEONORA
FLORID FINE HIGH BUXOM FRESH RUDDY ORNATE ROCOCO RUBIED ASIATIC FLOWERY TAFFETA BLOOMING FIGURATE RUBICUND SANGUINE SPLENDID VIGOROUS

FLORIDA

BAY: BISCAYNE APALACHEE WACCASASSA
CAPITAL: TALLAHASSEE
COLLEGE: ROLLINS
COUNTY: BAY LEE DADE GULF LEON POLK BAKER DIXIE HARDEE HENDRY NASSAU ORANGE ALACHUA BREVARD BROWARD MANATEE OSCEOLA VOLUSIA PINELLAS SARASOTA
INDIAN: AIS OCALE UTINA CALUSA CHATOT POTANO TIMUCUA SEMINOLE
ISLANDS: KEYS
KEY: WEST LARGO BISCAYNE
LAKE: DORA APOPKA HARNEY JESSUP NEWNAN LEDWITH ARBUCKLE KISSIMMEE OKEECHOBEE
NATIVE: CONCH CRACKER
RIVER: BANANA INDIAN AUCILLA MANATEE SCAMBIA SUWANEE OCHLAWAHA
STATE BIRD: MOCKINGBIRD
STATE NICKNAME: SUNSHINE
STATE TREE: PALMETTO
TOWN: TICE COCOA MIAMI OCALA TAMPA ORLANDO PALATKA SEBRING TAMARAC SARASOTA PENSACOLA
UNIVERSITY: STETSON
WETLANDS: GLADES

FLORIDIAN CRACKER
FLORIMEL (HUSBAND OF —) MARINEL
FLORIN GULDEN
FLORIPES (BROTHER OF —) FIERABRAS
(HUSBAND OF —) GUY

FLOSS FLUFF SKEIN WASTE CADDIS SLEAVE CADDICE
FLOSSER FANNER
FLOSS-SILK TREE SAMOHU
FLOTSAM JETSAM WILSAM WAFTURE WAVESON DRIFTAGE FLOATAGE
FLOUNCE FLAP HUFF SKIT SLAM FLING FRILL RUCHE PEPLUM RIPPLE ROBING ROUNCE RUFFLE VOLANT FALBALA FALBELO FROUNCE RUCHING FLOUNDER FURBELOW STRUGGLE
FLOUNDER DAB GAD BUTT KEEL POLE ROLL TOSS BREAM FLUKE SLOSH WITCH WRELE GADOID GROVEL MEGRIM MUDDLE PLAICE TOLTER TURBOT WALLOP WALLOW WARSLE BLUNDER FLASKER FLOUNCE PLOUNCE STUMBLE SUNFISH TOPKNOT VAAGMAR ANACANTH FLATFISH FOOLFISH PLUNTHER SANDLING
FLOUR AMYL ATTA DUST CONES HOVIS BINDER CLEARS FARINA FLOWER PATENT POLLEN SICKEN TSAMBA WHITES BOXINGS BRAVURA CRIBBLE CANAILLE
(— OF MALT) SMEDDUM
(COARSE —) THIRD CHISEL BOXINGS CRIBBLE
(COVER WITH —) DREDGE
(FINE —) CONES SUJEE
(LOW-GRADE —) TAIL
(PARTICLE OF —) CHOP
(POTATO —) FROW
(UNSORTED —) ATTA
(PREF.) ALEURO
FLOURISH TAG WAG BOOM BRAG FUSS GROW LICK RIOT RISE SHOW TUCK WAVE ADORN BLOOM BOAST CHEVE GLOSS QUIRK REIGN SHAKE SWASH SWING SWISH TUSCH VAUNT CATTER PARADE PARAPH QUAVER SQUIRL THRIVE BLOSSOM BURGEON CADENZA DISPLAY ENLARGE FANFARE GAMBADE GAMBADO PASSAGE PROSPER ROULADE SUCCEED TRIUMPH WAMPISH ARPEGGIO BRANDISH CURLICUE INCREASE ORNAMENT SKIRMISH
(— OF BAGPIPE) WARBLER
(— OF TRUMPET) MORT SENNET TUCKET
FLOURISHING FAR FRIM FRUM PERT GREEN PALMY PEART VITAL BLOOMY FLORID GOLDEN FLORENT HEALTHY VERNANT THRIVING VEGETOUS PROSPEROUS
FLOURY MEALY
FLOUT BOB GIBE JEER JERK JIBE LOUT MOCK FLEER FLITE FRUMP SCOFF SCOMM SCORN SCOUT SNEER TAUNT DERIDE INSULT BETONGUE
FLOW GO EBB ERN JET PUT RUN SET SUE BORE COMB FLIT FLUX FUSE GUSH HALE LAVA LAVE MELT PASS POUR RAIL ROLL SEND SHED SILE SLIP SOAK SWIG TAIL TEEM TIDE WELL AVALE DRAIN DRIFT EAGRE EXUDE FLEAM FLEET

FLOAT FLOOD FLUSH FRESH GLIDE ISSUE QUELL RIVER SCOOT SLIDE SPEND SPILL SPURT SWILL TRILL ABOUND AFFLUX COURSE CURSUS DELUGE GUGGLE GUTTER POPPLE RECEDE RINDLE SPRING STREAM CURRENT DEVOLVE DISTILL DRIBBLE EMANATE FLOWAGE FLUTTER FLUXION ILLAPSE INDRAFT MEANDER SPURTLE TRINKLE TRINTLE ALLUVION BACKWASH CURRANCE CURRENCY DOWNFLOW EMISSION FOUNTAIN GOWITHIT INUNDATE
(— AGAINST) LAP LAVE BATHE
(— BACK) EBB
(— BEYOND BANKS) DEBORD SURROUND
(— DOWN) AVALE
(— IN) INFLOW INFLOOD
(— IN RILLS) DRILL
(— IN RIVULETS) GUTTER
(— IN SPURTS) SALTATION
(— INTERMITTENTLY) HEAD
(— NOISILY) BICKER
(— OF AIR) SIDEWASH
(— OF ELECTRICITY) BOLT OSCILLATION
(— OF LANGUAGE) STRAIN
(— OF METAL) CREEP
(— OF RADIO SIGNAL) BEAM
(— OF SOUNDS) CADENCE
(— OUT) EMIT ISSUE EFFUSE SPREAD EXHAUST RESOLVE
(— OVER) BERUN
(— SLOWLY) SEEP EXUDE GLEET
(— TOGETHER) CONCUR CONFLOW
(— WITH) FLEET
(CONTINUOUS —) LAPSE
(COPIOUS —) HALE RIVER
(LAVA —) COULE COULEE
(RHYTHMICAL —) LILT
(STRONG —) TORRENT
(TIDAL —) BORE AEGIR EAGER EAGRE
(PREF.) RHEO RHYSI
(SUFF.) FLUENCE FLUENT FLUOUS FLUX RRHAGIA RRHEA RRHOEA
FLOWER (ALSO SEE PLANT AND HERB) BUD GAY BEST BLOW FLAG IRIS IXIA PINK POLE POSY ROSE ARROW ASTER BLOOM BLUET BREAK DAISY ELITE FANCY FLOOR GOWAN LILAC PANSY PHLOX TRUSS TULIP TUTTY AZALIA CHOICE CORYMB CROCUS CYMULE DAHLIA DATURA FLORET MAYPOP ORCHID SCILLA SEASON SHOWER SINGLE STEVIA UNFOLD AMELLUS ANEMONE ARBUTUS BLETHIA BLOSSOM BOSTRYX CAMPANA DEVELOP ESSENCE FLEURET FLOSCLE GAZANIA GENTIAN GERBERA IPOMOEA PETUNIA PICOTEE TORENIA BELAMOUR CAMELLIA CYCLAMEN DAFFODIL DIANTHUS GARDENIA GERANIUM HEPATICA HIBISCUS HYACINTH PRIMROSE SNOWDROP SPARAXIS
(— FOR BUTTONHOLE) BOUTONNIERE
(— STATE) FLORIDA

(— WITH 6 SEGMENTS) SEXFOIL
(ART OF — ARRANGING) IKEBANA
(AXIS OF —) CYME SPIKE UMBEL
CORYMB MIASMA RACEME
(COTTON —) SQUARE
(DEFORMED —) BULLHEAD
(DOUBLE —) BURSTER
(DRIED —S) BRAYERA
(GLOWING —) TORCH
(IMAGINARY —) AMARANTH
(PART OF —) OVARY PETAL SEPAL
STALK STYLE ANTHER CARDEL
PISTIL STAMEN STIGMA PEDICEL
FILAMENT PEDUNCLE PERIANTH
RECEPTACLE
(SHOWY —) ORCHIS
(STRIPED —) BIZARRE
(UNFADING —) AMARANTH
(PL.) SPRAY BOUQUET
(PREF.) ANTH(O) FLORI
(SUFF.) ANTHEMA ANTHEMUM
ANTHERA ANTHEROUS ANTHERY
ANTHES ANTHOUS ANTHUS
FLORAL FLOROUS
FLOWER-BED KNOT BORDER
FLOWER-BUD CAPER CLOVE
FLOWERFLY SYRPHID
FLOWERHEAD CALATHUS
FLOWERING AFLOWER FLOWERY
ANTHESIS BLOOMING
FLOWERING GLUME LEMMA
FLOWERLESS ANANTHOUS
FLOWER-LIKE ANTHOID
FLOWER-OF-AN-HOUR SHOOFLY
FLOWER-PECKER KAKAWAHIE
FLOWERPOT POT CACHEPOT
FLOWERY BLOWN BLOOMY FLORID
POSIED FLORENT PRIMROSE
FLOWING FAIR FLUX LAVE SIDE
AFLOW FLOAT FLUID FLUOR QUICK
TIDAL AFFLUX DEFLUX FLUENT
FUSILE LIVING COPIOUS CURRENT
CURSIVE EMANANT FLUXING
FLUXION FLUXIVE RUNNING
SLIDING STREAMY DEFLUENT
DILUENDO FLUVIOSE
(— AT LOW SPEED) SLACK
(— BACK) EBB
(— IN) INFLUX INFLUENT INFLUXION
(— OF GLAZE) STREAMING
(— OF TIDE) FLOOD
(— OUT) ELAPSE EFFLUENT
(— SMOOTHLY) VOLUBLE
PROFLUENT
(— TOGETHER) CONFLUX
(PREF.) (— OUT) EFFLUVIO
FLOWOFF RUNOFF
FLU (TYPE OF —) ASIAN
FLUB BOOT ERRATUM
FLUCAN SELVAGE SELVEDGE
FLUCTUATE SWAY VARY VEER
YOYO FLEET SWING WAVER
BALANCE VIBRATE WAMPISH
UNDULATE UNSTEADY VACILLATE
FLUCTUATING WAVY HECTIC
LABILE RUBATO ERRATIC FLUXIVE
WAYWARD UNSTABLE UNSTEADY
FLUCTUATION CYCLE FADING
JIGGLE FLICKER FLUTTER VIBRATO
OSCILLATION
(— IN LAKES) SEICHE
(— OF LAKE SURFACE) SEICHE
FLUE NET BARB DOWN OPEN PIPE

THIN VENT FLARE FLUFF FLUKE
TEWEL FUNNEL TUNNEL UPTAKE
CHIMNEY OUTTAKE PASSAGE
DOWNTAKE
FLUE-CURED BRIGHT
FLUENCY SKILL
FLUENT GASH GLIB FLUID READY
FACILE LIQUID SMOOTH STREAM
COPIOUS CURRENT FLOWING
FLUIDIC RENABLE VERBOSE
VOLUBLE ELOQUENT FLIPPANT
FLUFF FUG FLUE FUZZ LINT OOZE
PUFF BEARD ERROR FLOSH FLOSS
WHEEL MISTAKE
FLUFFING WHEELING
FLUFFY SOFT DOWNY DRUNK FILMY
FLUEY FUZZY LIGHT LINTEN
PLUFFY FEATHERY UNSTEADY
(NOT —) CLOSE
FLUID INK SAP MASS RASA BLOOD
FLUOR HUMOR JUICE LATEX
SERUM SPERM SWEAT WATER
FLUENT LIQUID WATERY COOLANT
FLOWING FLUIBLE FLUXILE
GASEOUS SYNOVIA EMULSION
FLOATING FLUXIBLE FORESHOT
PERSPERATION
(ANIMAL —) SERUM
(BODY —) CHYLE
(EAR —) PERILYMPH
(EGYPTIAN PRIMEVAL —) NU NUN
(ELECTRIC —) VRIL
(ETHEREAL —) ICHOR
(LIVER —) BILE
(LUBRICATING —) SYNOVIA
(MAMMARY —) MILK
(PLANT —) SERO
(SLIMY —) MUCUS
(SOLDERING —) FAKE
(SUPPURATION —) PUS
(THICK VISCOUS —) GRUME
(WATERY —) LYE SANIES SEROSITY
(WORKING —) AIR
(PREF.) SERO
FLUIDITY LENGTH
(— UNIT) RHE
FLUKE FLUE PALM BLADE GRASP
SCALE PLAICE DISTOME PLATODE
SCRATCH FLATWORM FLOUNDER
BILHARZIA
(— OF ANCHOR) HOOK KILLICK
(— OF WHALE'S TAIL) BLADE
FLUME CHUTE DITCH SHUTE SLUICE
FLUMMERY SOWENS WASHBREW
FLUMMOX ABASH ADDLE
CONFOUND EMBARRASS
DISCONCERT
FLUNK BUST FAIL SKEW SPIN
FLICKER
FLUNKY SNOB TOADY COOKEE
JEAMES LACKEY FOOTMAN
SERVANT STEWARD
FLUORESCENCE BLOOM
FLUORESCENT PSYCHEDELIC
FLUORINE PHTOR PHTHOR
FLUORITE CAND FLUX FLUOR
FLURRY ADO FIT FACT FRET GUST
PIRR SPIT STIR TEAR HASTE SKIFF
SKIRL BOTHER BUSTLE SCURRY
SQUALL CONFUSE FLUSKER
FLUSTER FLUTTER FOOSTER
SWITHER WHITHER SPITTING
FLUSH JET EVEN GLOW HUSH JUMP

POOL ROSE BLOOM BLUSH COLOR
ELATE FLASH FLUSK FRESH KNOCK
LEVEL RAISE ROUGE SCOUR START
VIGOR AFLUSH EXCITE HECTIC
LAVISH MANTLE MORASS REDDEN
RUDDLE SLUICE SPRING THRILL
ANIMATE BOBTAIL CRIMSON
SUFFUSE ABUNDANT AFFLUENT
PRODIGAL ROSINESS
(— GAME) SERVE
(— IN SKY) SUNGLOW
(NOT —) FLAT
FLUSHED RED ROSY BEAMY FIERY
FLOWN FLORID FLUSHY HECTIC
CRIMSON RUBICUND
FLUSTER PAVIE SHAKE BOTHER
FLURRY FUDDLE MUDDLE POTHER
RATTLE CONFUSE FLUSKER
FOOSTER SWITHER BEFUDDLE
FLOWSTER FLUSTRUM
FLUTE NAY FIFE FUYE PIPE AULOS
CRIMP CUENA PUNGI QUENA STICK
STYKE TIBIA TWILL CANNEL
DOUCET FLAUTO GEWGAW
GOFFER POOGYE ZUFOLO
CHAMFER DIAULOS FLAMFEW
FLUTING GAUFFER HEMIOPE
MAGADIS MATALAN PICCOLO
SIBILUS SIFFLOT TONETTE
TRANGAM WHISTLE ZUFFOLO
FLAUTINO MONAULOS RECORDER
(— OF A COLUMN) STRIGA
CHANNEL
(— STOP) VENTAGE
(CHINESE —) TCHE
(EAST INDIAN —) MATALAN
(EUNUCH —) KAZOO
(JAPANESE —) FUYE SHAKUHACHI
(LYDIAN —) MAGADIS
(MOSLEM —) NAY
(PHOENICIAN —) GINGRAS
(PL.) NEHILOTH
(PREF.) AUL(O)
FLUTED QUILLED
FLUTEMOUTH CORNETFISH
FLUTE PLAYER AULETE FLUTER
FLUTIST TIBICEN TOOTLER
AULETRIS FLAUTIST
FLUTING STRIX FULLER GADROON
STRIGIL COULISSE QUILLING
FLUTTER BAT FAN FUG BATE BLOW
BUZZ FLAP FLIT FLOW FLUE OOZE
PLAY WAFF WAVE FLACK FLAFF
FLARE FLECK FLICK FLOSS FLURR
HOVER PULSE SHAKE WAVER
BANGLE FLAUNT FLURRY RUFFLE
SWIVET TREMOR WAFFLE WALLOP
WINNOW FLACKER FLAFFER
FLASKER FLATTER FLAUGHT
FLICKER FLITTER FLUSKER
SKIMMER WAGTAIL WHIFFLE
FLICHTER SQUATTER VOLITATE
(IN A —) PITAPAT
FLUTTERING AWING FLITTY
WHUTTER AFLUTTER FLICKERY
FLUTTERINGLY PITAPAT
FLUTTER-TONGUING GROWL
FLUX FLOW FUSE LASK MELT
BORAX FLOAT FLOOD ISSUE RESIN
ROSIN SMEAR SMELT FUSION
CURRENT EURIPUS FLOWING
LEAKAGE OUTFLOW
(— UNIT) WEBER MAXWELL

FLY BEE FAG FAN GAD HOP RUN
FIRK FLEA FLEE FLEG FLIT FRIT
GNAT KITE KIVU LASH LEAP MELT
RACK RAKE SAIL SCUD SMUT SOAR
SOLO WHEW WHIR WHIZ WIND
WING ZIMB AGILE ALERT EMPID
FLEET FLIER FLOAT FLURR FLUSH
FLYER GLIDE LATCH MIDGE
MUSCA OXFLY PERLA PHORA
PILOT POPUP QUICK SEDGE SHARP
SKIRL SKIRR STOUR WHAME
WHIRR ZEBUB ASILID AVIATE
BANGLE BLOWER BOTFLY BREEZE
DAYFLY ESCAPE FLIGHT FLYBOY
GADFLY GORFLY JARFLY LEPTID
MEDFLY MOTUCA NIMBLE
PALMER PHORID PUNKIE RANDON
ROBBER SEPSID SEROOT SPRING
TIPULA TSETSE VANISH VERMIN
WINNOW AVIGATE AVOLATE
BROMMER CANOPID CHALCID
CONOPID FORMATE GRANNOM
KNOWING LOVEBUG ORTALID
PYRALIS SCIARID TYRPHID
AIRPLANE BIBIONID BRACONID
COACHMAN DIPTERAN DROPPING
EPHYDRID EULOPHID GLOSSINA
HORSEFLY HOUSEFLY RUBYTAIL
SIMULIID TACHINID TATUKIRA
VOLITATE
(— AFTER GAME) RAKE
(— AIMLESSLY) BANGLE
(— ALOFT) SOAR TOWER
(— AWAY) CARRY
(— CLUMSILY) FLIGHTER
(— ERRATICALLY) GAD
(— INTO RAGE) FUFF RARE
(— LOW) DICE DRAG HEDGEHOP
(— NEAR THE GROUND) ACCOST
(— OUT) EXPIRE
(— RAPIDLY) SCUR SKIRR
(— TOO HIGH) SCUD
(— WIDE) MISS
(BITING —) PIUM
(FISHING —) BEE DUN OAK BUZZ
GNAT HARL HERL SMUT WASP ZULU
ABBEY ALDER BAKER FAIRY NYMPH
SEDGE BADGER BOBFLY CADDIS
CAHILL CANARY CLARET DOCTOR
HACKLE MILLER ORIOLE WILLOW
BABCOCK BUTCHER CADDICE
COLONEL DROPPER DUBBING
GRANNOM HUZZARD SPINNER
WATCHED WATCHET BUCKTAIL
CATSKILL COACHMAN FERGUSON
GOVERNOR STREAMER WOODRUFF
WRENTAIL
(KIND OF —) FACE
(MAY —) DUN DRAKE
(POP —) BLOOP BLOOPER
(SHEEP —) FAG KED
(STONE —) SALLY
(PREF.) MUSCI MYI(O)
(SUFF.) MYI(A)(O)
FLYBLOWN BLOWN STRUCK
FLYBOAT FLUTE FLIGHT
FLYCATCHER TODY PEWEE PEWIT
CHEBEC COBWEB MILLER PEEWEE
PHOEBE PIPIRI RAFTER TYRANT
YETAPA ELEPAIO FANTAIL GRIGNET
GRINDER PITIRRI TOMFOOL
TYRANNI BEAMBIRD FIREBALL
FIREBIRD FLYEATER FORKTAIL

GERYGONE KINGBIRD KISKADEE PITANGUA WALLBIRD SCISSORTAIL

FLYER (FLEXIBLE —) SLED

FLY, FISHING (PART OF —) EYE TAG BODY BUTT HEAD HORN TAIL WING CHEEK JOINT HACKLE RIBBING TOPPING

FLYING AWING FLIGHT VOLANT WAVING FLOTANT VOLATIC AVIATION FLOATING
(— MANEUVER) LUFBERY
(— TAIL DOWN) CABRE
(STUDY OF — OBJECTS) UFOLOGY

FLYING DUTCHMAN, THE
(CHARACTER IN —) ERIK SENTA DALAND
(COMPOSER OF —) WAGNER

FLYING FISH SKIPPER VOLADOR

FLYING FOX KALONG PTEROPID

FLYING GURNARD ANGLER BATFISH LATCHET LOPHIID VOLADOR

FLYING LEMUR COBEGO COLUGO KUBONG

FLYING MACHINE AVIATOR AEROSTAT

FLYING PHALANGER CUSCUS SQUIRREL

FLYING SAUCER UFO

FLYING SQUIRREL TAGUAN ASSAPAN

FLYMAN LOFTMAN

FLYSCH MACIGNO

FLYWHEEL FLY FLIER FLYER WHORL WHARVE

FOAL CADE COLT FILLY PODDY SLEEPER

FOAM FOB SUD BARM BEES BOIL FUME HEAD KNIT REAM SCUD SCUM SUDS WORK CREAM FROST FROTH SPUME YEAST BUBBLE FLOWER FLURRY FREATH IMBOST LATHER SEETHE BLUBBER DESPUME MELDROP
(PREF.) APHR(O) SPUMI

FOAMING AFOAM NAPPY YEASTY SPUMOUS MANTLING SPUMANTE

FOAMY BARMY BEADY SPUMY SUDSY FROTHY SPUMOSE

FOB FUB SPUNG POCKET

FOCAL POINT OMPHALOS

FOCUS AIM FIX PUT POINT PURSE TRAIN CENTER CLIMAX DIRECT FASTEN FIXATE HEARTH TEMPLE NUCLEUS CONVERGE FOCALIZE GANGLION

FODDER HAY FEED FOOD SOIL VERT GOOMA MANGE VETCH EATAGE FORAGE FOTHER PODDER SILAGE STOVER FARRAGE PODWARE PROVAND BROWSING ENSILAGE ROUGHAGE

FODDERCAGE TUMBREL

FODDERER FOGGER

FOE ENEMY FIEND RIVAL FOEMAN HOSTILE OPPOSER OPPONENT WRANGLER
(STUBBORN —) WRANGLER

FOG FF DAG RAG DAMP DAZE HAAR HAZE MIST MOKE MOSS MURK PRIG RACK ROKE SMOG SMUR SOUP BEDIM BRUME CLOUD GRASS HUMOR MUDDY SMIRR

SPRAY STOUR VAPOR MUDDLE NEBULA SALMON STUPOR FOGGAGE OBSCURE POGONIP SMOTHER BEWILDER MOISTURE
(— OF THE NILE) QOBAR
(FROZEN —) BARBER
(LIGHT —) GAUZE
(SEA —) HAAR HARR

FOGBOW DOG FOGDOG SEADOG MISTBOW FOGEATER

FOGDOG DOG STUBB FOGBOW SEADOG FOGEATER

FOGGINESS CLOUDING

FOGGY DIM DULL HAZY MIRK MOKY MURK ROKY DENSE DIRTY GROSS MISKY MISTY MURKY ROOKY ROUKY SPEWY CLOUDY GREASY GROGGY MARSHY MILKEN SMURRY BRUMOUS MUDDLED OBSCURE CONFUSED NUBILOUS VAPOROUS

FOGHORN SIREN TYFON RIPPER MEGAFOG

FOG-SIGNAL DIAPHONE

FOGY DODO FOGEY DUFFER FOGRAM FOOZLE STODGER MOSSBACK

FOGYISH MUSTY

FOIBLE VICE FAULT FERLY FEEBLE FAILING FRAILTY WEAKNESS

FOIL BACK BALK EPEE FILE FOIN SOIL TAIN BLADE BLANK BLUNT CHEAT ELUDE EVADE FALSE STAIN STUMP SWORD TRACK TRAIL BAFFLE BLENCH BOGGLE CHATON DEFEAT DEFILE FLORET OFFSET OUTWIT STIGMA STOOGE THWART BEGUILE FAILURE FOILING FOLIATE LAMETTA PAILLON POLLUTE REPULSE STONKER TRAMPLE DISGRACE
(— STRIPS) WINDOW
(FENCING —) EPEE BLUNT FLORET FLEURET
(PART OF —) END TIP BELL GRIP HILT BLADE FORTE GUARD POINT BUTTON FOIBLE HANDLE POMMEL MOUNTING
(POINTED —) TANG
(TIN —) TAIN

FOIST WISH FUDGE FATHER SUBORN FOISTER SHOEHORN

FOLD BOW FLY LAP PEN PLY SET WAP BEND COTE CREW CRUE DART FAIL FALX FAUN FELD FLAP FURL HANK HOOD LIRK LOOP RUCK RUGA SWAG TUCK WRAP BREAK CLASP CRIMP CRISP CROZE DRAPE FAULD FLIPE FLOCK FLYPE FRILL GROIN LAYER PARMA PINCH PLAIT PLEAT PLICA PRANK QUILL SINUS YIELD BOUGHT BUCKLE COLLOP CREASE CRISTA CUTTLE DEWLAP DIAPIR DOUBLE ENFOLD FORNIX FRENUM FURDLE GATHER GUSSET HURDLE INFOLD LABIUM LAPPET MANTLE PIPING PLIGHT PUCKER RIMPLE RUMPLE WIMPLE CAPSIZE CRINKLE CRUMPLE EMBRACE ENVELOP FLEXION FLEXURE PINFOLD PLACATE PLICATE REVERSE ROLLING ROULEAU TURNING VALVULA

CRIMPING FLECTION FLITFOLD QUILLING SCAPULET SPLENIUM SURROUND PLICATION REPLICATE REFLECTION
(— CLOTH) RAG
(— DOWN) COLLAPSE
(— FOR CATTLE) BAWN
(— IN HOOD) SHOVE
(— INWARD) CRIMP
(— OF MEMBRANE) CRISTA
(— OF SKIN) APRON DEWLAP SHEATH OMENTUM FORESKIN MESENTERY
(— ROCKS) DEFORM
(—S OF TOGA) SINUS
(CARDIAC —) CUSP
(GEOLOGICAL —) DIAPIR CLOSURE EXOCLINE SYNCLINE MONOCLINE
(LOOSE —) LAPPET
(RESTRAINING —) FRENUM FRAENUM
(SCOTTISH —) CAT
(SHEEP —) REEVE
(PREF.) PLEXI PLICATO PLICI PTYCH(O) SINU(ATO) VALVI VALVO
(SUFF.) FARIOUS PLEX PLICATE PLOID
(COVERING —) STEGE STEGITE

FOLDAGE SOC SOKE

FOLDED SHUT DOUBLE FANLIKE PLICATE PLICATED REFLEXED WREATHED
(— AND WAVED) GYROSE
(PREF.) PLICATO

FOLDER KIT BOOK FILE FOLD ATLAS COVER FOLIO BINDER CLEANER HANDOUT LEAFLET STROKER PAMPHLET

FOLDING KNOT
(— OF LEAF) PTYXIS
(— PAPER) ORIGAMI

FOLDOUT GATEFOLD

FOLIACEOUS LEAFY PHYLLOID

FOLIAGE HERB SHADE GREENS LEAVES SHROUD BOSCAGE GILLERY LEAFAGE LEAFERY UMBRAGE FRONDAGE GREENERY
(CARVED —) KNOT

FOLIATED SPATHIC

FOLIATION SEXFOIL TREFOIL CINQFOIL SEPTFOIL

FOLIC ACID PGA

FOLIO CASE ATLAS FOLIUM

FOLK SOULS DAIONE PEOPLE
(— TALES) LORE
(FAIRY —) SHEE SIDHE
(STRANGE —) FRAIM FREMD
(PL.) GENTRY

FOLKLORE (IMITATION —) FAKELORE

FOLKSONG SON TONADA VOLKSLIED

FOLKSY HOMY HOMEY HOMESPUN

FOLKTALE DROLL FABULA MARCHEN

FOLLETTO DUSIO

FOLLICLE CRYPT LACUNA OVISAC CONCEPTACLE

FOLLOW GO PAD SUE TAG COME COPY HUNT NEXT OBEY SEEK SHAG TAIL TAKE TOUT ADOPT AFTER CHASE DODGE ENSUE SNAKE SPOOR TRACE TRACK TRAIL

TREAD ADHERE ATTEND DANGLE FOLLER OCCUPY PURSUE RESULT SECOND SHADOW SUIVEZ TAGGLE HOTFOOT IMITATE OBSERVE PROFESS REPLACE SUCCEED VALOUWE PRACTICE SUPPLANT
(— A COURSE) RUN
(— A POINTER'S LEAD) BACK
(— CLOSELY) TAILGATE
(— HOSTILELY) DOG
(— INSIDIOUSLY) DOG
(— IN SUCCESSION) VARY
(— SCENT) ROAD CARRY
(— SLAVISHLY) ECHO
(— SLOWLY) DRAGGLE
(— THROUGH) PRESS
(— TRACK) SLEUTH
(— UP) SUE ATTEND
(— UPON) WAIT

FOLLOWER FAN IST SON APER BEAU ZANY ADEPT CHELA GILLY BILDAR COHORT DRIVEN ENSUER GILLIE GUDGET KNIGHT LACKEY SEQUEL SUITOR SULTER VOTARY ACACIAN ACOLYTE CARRIER DEVOTEE EPIGONE FLATTER GRIFTER POLIGAR PURSUER RETINUE SECTARY SEQUENT SPANIEL SUPPOST TRAILER ADHERENT DISCIPLE FAITHFUL FAVORITE HENCHMAN MYRMIDON OBSERVER OFFSIDER PARTISAN RETAINER SECTATOR SERVITOR SATELLITE PURSUIVANT
(— OF ART) BOHEMIAN
(— OF CELEBRITY) GROUPIE
(CAMP —) BUMMER GUDGET LASCAR
(CRANE —) SPOTTER
(SERVILE —) SLAVE LACKEY ANTHONY
(PL.) FOLK SECTA SEQUACES
(SUFF.) ITE

FOLLOWING LAST NEXT SECT SUIT AFTER FIRST INTOW SUANT TRACE TRAIN BEHIND SEQUEL ENSUANT ENSUING SEQUENT AUDIENCE BUSINESS SECUNDUM SEGUENDO TRAILING VOCATION

FOLLOW-UP FOLO

FOLLY ATE SIN RAGE LAPSE MORIA SOTIE BETISE DOTAGE LUNACY NICETY WANWIT DAFFERY DAFFING FOOLERY FOPPERY IDIOTCY MADNESS MISTAKE SOTTAGE UNSKILL LEWDNESS FOOLHEAD IDLENESS LEWDNESS MOROLOGY NONSENSE RASHNESS SURQUIDY UNTHRIFT UNWISDOM WILLNESS WOODNESS SIMPLICITY

FOMALHAUT DIFDA DIPHDA

FOMENT SOW ABET BREW SPUR ROUSE STUPE AROUSE EXCITE INCITE AGITATE FERMENT INSPIRE

FOND TID DAFT DEAR DOTE FAIN FOOL FUND KIND VAIN WEAK CRAZY SILLY STOCK STORE ARDENT BEFOOL CARESS CHOICE DEARLY DOTING FONDLE FONDLY LOVING SIMPLE TENDER AMATORY AMOROUS BEGUILE BROWDEN FONDISH FOOLISH INSIPID

PARTIAL DESIROUS ENAMORED
SANGUINE TRIFLING UXORIOUS
(FOOLISHLY —) SPOON SPOONY
(PREF.) (— OF) PHIL(O)
(SUFF.) (— OF) PHIL(A)(AE)(E)(OUS)
(US)

FONDLE PET BABY BILL CLAP COAX
DAUT DAWT FOND NECK TICK
WALY DAUNT INGLE NURSE WALLY
CARESS COCKER CODDLE COSSET
CUDDLE CUTTER DANDLE GENTLE
KITTLE MUZZLE PAMPER SLAVER
STROKE TANTLE TIDDLE CHERISH
FLATTER SMUGGLE TWATTLE
BLANDISH CANOODLE

FONDLING NINNY NURSLING

FONDLY DEAR FOND DEARLY
FOOLISH

FONDNESS GRA LOVE FANCY
FOLLY TASTE DOTAGE NOTION
FEELING DEARNESS WEAKNESS
(— FOR WOMEN) PHILOGYNY
(SUFF.) (— FOR) ITIS

FONS (FATHER OF —) JANUS
(MOTHER OF —) JUTURNA

FONT BILL FUND PILA BASIN FOUNT
SOURCE SPRING LAVACRE PISCINA
BENITIER DELUBRUM

FONTANEL MOLD MOULD
FENESTRA

FOOD BIT KAI PAP SAP BAIT BITE
BUNK CARB CATE CHIH CHOP
CHOW CRAM DIET DISH EATS FARE
FARM FUEL GEAR GRUB HASH
JOCK KAIL KALE MEAT NOSH PECK
PLAT PROG SALT SOCK STEW TACK
TOKE TUCK BREAD BROMA CARBO
CHEER CHUCK FLUFF FORAY GRILL
SCAFF SCOFF SCRAN TABLE THING
TOMMY TREAT TRIPE APPAST
BUTTER DODGER DOINGS EATING
FODDER FOSTER LIVING MAIGRE
MORSEL MUKTUK PABLUM
PANADA PANADE REFETE STOVER
SUNKET TACKLE TUCKER VIANDS
VIVERS WRAITH ALIMENT FAUSTER
HANDOUT INGESTA KEEPING
KITCHEN NURTURE PABULUM
PASTURE PECKAGE PROVANT
PULTURE EATABLES FLUMMERY
GRUBBERY NUTRIENT PEMMICAN
PROVIANT TRENCHER VICTUALS
PROVENDER NOURISHMENT
(— AND DRINK) BOUGE CHEER
LOWANCE
(— AND LIQUOR) GEAR
(— AND LODGING) FOUND
EASEMENT
(— BANNED DURING PASSOVER)
HAMETZ CHAMETZ
(— EATEN AS RELISH) KITCHEN
(— EATEN BETWEEN MEALS)
BAGGING
(— FOR ANIMALS) FODDER FORAGE
(— FOR CATTLE) BROWSE TACKLE
(— FROM KELP) KOMBU
(— IN SLICES) LEACH
(— IN STOCK) LARDER
(— NOT RITUALLY CLEAN)
TEREPHAH
(— OF DUCK EGGS) BALUT
(— OF RUMINANTS) CUD

(— OF THE GODS) AMRITA
AMREETA AMBROSIA
(— OF WHALE) KRILL
(— OF WORKMEN) TOMMY
(— ON TABLE AT ONE TIME) MESS
(— PRESERVATIVE) TINFOIL
(— TO BE CONSUMED ELSEWHERE)
TAKEOUT CARRYOUT
(ASIAN —) TEMPEH
(ASIATIC —) TEMPEH
(BABY —) PAP
(BEE —) CANDY
(BREAKFAST —) GRANOLA
(CHINESE —) DIMSUM
(COOKED —) CURY BAKEMEAT
(DAILY —) TUCKER
(EXTRA —) GASH
(FILLING —) STODGE
(FLAVORLESS —) HOGWASH
(GROUND —) DUST
(HAWAIIAN —) POI
(HEAVENLY —) MANNA
(INDIGESTIBLE —) STODGE
(JAPANESE —) TERIYAKI
(KIND OF —) JUNK FINGER
(LIQUID —) LAP SLOP SOUP GRUEL
LEBAN LEBEN SUPPING
(LUXURIOUS —) CATE CATES
JUNKET
(MADE OF SEVERAL —S) PANACHE
(MIRACULOUS —) MANNA
(RICH —) CHEER
(SEMILIQUID —) SWILL
(SLICED —) PIZZA
(SNACK —) MUNCHIES
(SOFT —) PAP
(STARCHY —) AMYLOID
(TAPIOCA-LIKE —) SALEP
(WATERY —) SLIPSLOP
(WRAPPED —) TAMALE
(PREF.) SITIO SITO TROPH(O)
(SUFF.) PHAGA PHAGE PHAGIA
PHAGOUS PHAGUS PHAGY
TROPHIA TROPHIC TROPHY
(WANT OF —) ATROPHIA

FOODLESS JEJUNE VICTLESS

FOODSTUFF TRADE CEREAL
COOKABLE

FOOFARAW ADO FUSS TODO FRILL
BOTHER

FOOL APE ASS BAM BOB COD CON
DAW DOR FON FOP FOX FUN GIG
KID MUG NIT NUP POT RIG SAP
SOT TOY BULL BUTT CAKE CHUB
CLOT COLT DINK DOLT DUPE FOND
FUTZ GECK GOER GOFF GOOP
GOWK GYPE HARE HAVE HOIT
JAPE JEST JOKE JOSH MOME
MUCK NIZY POOP RACA RACH
SIMP TONY TOOT TWIT YOYO ZANY
ASINO BLIND BLUFF BUFFO
CHUMP CLOWN DALLY FUNGE
GALAH GLAIK GOOSE GREEN
HORSE IDIOT KNAVE MORON
NINNY NIZEY NODDY PATCH PATSY
SAMMY SCREW SILLY SNIPE
SPOOF STICK STIFF STIRK TOMMY
TRICK BUFFLE COUSIN CUCKOO
CUDDEN DELUDE DIMWIT DISARD
DOTARD DOTTLE FOLEYE FOOTER
GAMMON JESTER MOTLEY
MUCKER MUSARD NIDGET NIMSHI
NINCOM NUPSON SAWNEY

SHMUCK STRING TAMPER WITTOL
ASINEGO BECASSE BUFFOON
CHARLEY CHARLIE COXCOMB
DAGONET DECEIVE DIZZARD
FATHEAD FOOLISH FRIBBLE
GOMERAL GOMERIL HAVERAL
JACKASS LACKWIT MADLING
MISLEAD NATURAL OMADAWN
PINHEAD PLAYBOY SCHMUCK
STOOKIE TOMFOOL WANTWIT
WITLING ABDERITE BADINAGE
DRIVELER FONDLING HOODWINK
IMBECILE MONUMENT
OMADHAUN TOMNODDY
BAMBOOZLE NINCOMPOOP
LIGHTWEIGHT
(— AROUND) FUTZ JIVE SKYLARK
LALLYGAG
(— AWAY) FRIBBLE
(BORN —) MOONCALF
(LEARNED —) MOROSOPH
(NATURAL —) INNOCENT
(PL.) FOOLERY

FOOLERY GAME FOLLY BARNEY
MOTLEY BAUBLERY

FOOLHARDY RASH BRASH
FOOLATUM

FOOLISH FAT SOT BETE DAFT DUMB
FOND FOOL GAGA GYPE IDLE
MADE NICE RASH SOFT VAIN VOID
WEAK ZANY BALMY BARMY BATTY
BOGGY BUGGY DILLY DIPPY DIZZY
DOILT EMPTY FONNE GAWKY
GOOFY GOOSY INANE INEPT JERKY
LOONY NODDY POTTY SAPPY
SAWNY SCREW SEELY SILLY
YAPPY ABSURD CUDDEN DOTISH
DOTTLE FONDLY GLAKED GOTHAM
GOWKIT HARISH INSANE MOMISH
MOPISH SHANNY SIMPLE SLIGHT
SOFTLY SPOONY STOLID STULTY
STUPID TAWPIE UNWISE VACANT
ASININE DAMFOOL DOLTISH
ETOURDI FANGLED FATUOUS
FLIGHTY FOLLIAL FOPPISH GLAIKIT
GOOSISH GULLISH IDIOTIC
PEEVISH PUERILE SOTTISH
TOMFOOL UNWITTY WANTWIT
WITLESS ABDERIAN FOOTLING
FOPPERLY HEADLESS HEEDLESS
HIGHLAND IMBECILE SENSELESS
(PREF.) STULT(I)

FOOLISHLY IDLY FONDLY SIMPLE
SIMPLY

FOOLISHNESS JAZZ PUNK FOLLY
BARNEY BUNKUM FADDLE LEVITY
LUNACY RUBBLE VANITY FATUITY
PORANGI BUNCOMBE FONDNESS
INSANITY TOMMYROT ABSURDITY
SAPPINESS

FOOT FIT PAT PAW PEG PES BASE
COOT FUSS GOER HEEL HOOF PIED
SOLE TAIL BASIS PIECE BOTTOM
CLUTCH GAMMON PATTEN
PODIUM RHYTHM TOOTSY TRILBY
WALKER FOOTING GAMBONE
MEASURE METREME PEDICEL
TOOTSIE FOREFOOT
(— OF ANIMAL) PAD PAW HOOF
TROTTER
(— OF APE) HAND
(— OF INSECT) TARSUS
(— OF WINE GLASS) MULE

(CHINESE —) CHEK CHIH
(DOUBLE —) DIPODY
(HALF —) SEMIPED
(HOLLOW OF —) VOLA
(LARGE AWKWARD —) CAVE
(METRIC —) IAMB BASIS DIAMB
IONIC PAEAN CHOREE DACTYL
DIIAMB IAMBUS SYZYGY ANAPEST
BACCHIC PYRRHIC SPONDEE
TROCHEE ANAPAEST BACCHIUS
CHORIAMB DOCHMIUS EPITRITE
MOLOSSUS TRIBRACH TRIMACER
(STEWED OX —) COWHEEL
(TUBE —) SUCKER
(WEB —) FOURCHETTE
(PREF.) PED(I)(O) PEDATI PEDICULO
PEZO POD(O)
(SUFF.) PED(F) POD(A)(AL)(E)(IA)
(IUM)(OUS) PUS

FOOTAGE SETUP

FOOTBALL GRID HURLY ROUGE
FOOTER HURLING LEATHER
PIGSKIN KICKBALL
(— FORMATION) SHOTGUN
WISHBONE
(— LINEMAN) NOSEGUARD
(— LINE SHIFTING) STUNT
(— PASS PATTERN) FLY
(— PATTERN) FLY
(— PLAY) DRAW DELAY SWING
KEEPER AUDIBLE REVERSE
ROLLOUT SCRAMBLE
(— PLAYER) HUFF LANE RICE
BROWN DITKA ELWAY FOUTS SMITH
STARR YOUNG AIKMAN BLOUNT
BUTKUS CSONKA DEACON DUDLEY
GRANGE GREENE MARINO NAMATH
NEVERS PAYTON SAYERS SHARPE
TAYLOR THOMAS THORPE TITTLE
UNITAS DONOVAN DORSETT
FLANKER GIFFORD HORNUNG
MONSTER MONTANA RIGGINS
SIMPSON BRADSHAW SLOTBACK
STAUBACH JURGENSEN
NOSEGUARD TARKENTON
HIRSCHSHELL
(— RECEIVER) WIDEOUT
(— TEAM) JETS RAMS BEARS BILLS
COLTS LIONS BROWNS CHIEFS
EAGLES GIANTS OILERS SAINTS
BENGALS BRONCOS COWBOYS
FALCONS PACKERS RAIDERS
VIKINGS CHARGERS DOLPHINS
PATRIOTS REDSKINS SEAHAWKS
STEELERS CARDINALS BUCCANEERS
FORTYNINERS
(AUSTRALIAN —) RULES
(KIND OF —) CAMP
(KIND OF — PASS) SPOT SCREEN
(RUSH ON — PLAYER) BLITZ
(SHORT PASS IN —) FLARE

FOOTBOARD CRAMPET CRAMPIT

FOOTBOY PAGE PEDES

FOOTBRIDGE PLANK LIGGER
FOOTLOG

FOOTED FITTIT PEDATE
(SUFF.) PEDE PODOUS

FOOTFALL PAD STEP TREAD
FOOTSTEP

FOOTGEAR PATTEN FOOTWEAR

FOOTHILL SLOPE

FOOTHOLD TIP HACK STEP
FOOTING TOEHOLD BEACHHEAD

FOOTING PAR FOOT TROD BASIS EARTH TRACK HEADING PIECING TOEHOLD FOOTHOLD
FOOTLESS APODAL
FOOTLIGHTS FOOTS FLOATS LIGHTS
FOOTLIKE PEDATE
FOOTMAN SKIP FLUNKY JEAMES LACKEY VARLET DOORMAN FOOTPAD BOTTOMER CHASSEUR HIRCARRA WAGONMAN
FOOTNOTE IBID IBIDEM
FOOTPACE MAT DAIS CARPET HALFPACE PREDELLA
FOOTPAD PAD WHYO PADDER ROBBER FOOTMAN PADFOOT SCOURER LANDRAKER
FOOTPATH LANE TROD JETTY SENDA TRAIL FOOTWAY HIGHWAY PARAPET RAMPIRE SIDEWALK TROTTOIR
(— TO A PASTURE) DRUNG
(RAISED —) CLAPPER
FOOTPICK CASCROM
FOOTPIECE STEP
FOOTPRINT PAD PUG STEP TROD PRICK SPOOR TRACE TRACK TRADE TREAD FOOTING ICHNITE PUGMARK VESTIGE FOOTMARK
(DEER'S —S) SLOT
(HARE'S —) PRICK
(OTTER'S —) SEAL
(PREF.) ICHN(O)
FOOTREST COASTER HASSOCK STIRRUP
(— OF SPADE) TRAMP
FOOTROPE HORSE
FOOTROT HALT
FOOTS SEDIMENT
FOOTSCRAPING SAND
FOOT-SOLDIER KERN PEON KERNE
(PL.) INFANTRY
FOOTSORENESS SURBATE
FOOTSTALK STRIG PODIUM PEDICEL PETIOLE PEDUNCLE
(PREF.) PEDICULO
FOOTSTEP PAD STEP TROD CLAMP VESTIGE FOOTBEAT FORESTEP
(PREF.) ICHN(O)
FOOTSTOOL TUT LOVE MORA STOOL BUFFET SAMBLE CRICKET HASSOCK OTTOMAN FOOTREST
FOOT-WASHING NIPTER
FOOTWAY PATH CATWALK FOOTPATH
(— ALONGSIDE BRIDGE) BANQUETTE
FOOTWEAR CLOG FEET
FOOTYBALL (— PLAYER) SCATBACK
FOP TO ADON BEAU BUCK DUDE DUPE FOOL KNUT PRIG TOFF DANDY FLASH PUPPY MASHER MOPPET VANITY COXCOMB JESSAMY GIMCRACK MACARONI MACAROON MUSCADIN POPINJAY SKIPJACK
FOPPISH APISH DANDY FOPPY SAPPY SILLY DAPPER PRETTY SPRUCE STUPID BEAUISH BUCKISH FANGLED FINICAL FOOLISH DANDYISH SKIPJACK
FOR P IN TO PRO TIL VER TILL SINCE

FORWHY BECAUSE FORNENT
FAVORING
(— A LONG TIME) YORE
(— CASH) SPOT
(— EXAMPLE) EG VG
(— FEAR THAT) LEST
(— INSTANCE) AS SAY
(— THE EMERGENCY) PRN
(— THE MOST PART) FECKLY GENERALLY
(— TIME BEING) ACTUALLY
(PREF.) PRO
FORAGE ERS OAT RYE CORN GUAR MAST PROG RAID ETAPE FORAY BREVIT RUSSUD ZACATE GOITCHO HAYLAGE PICKEER BOOTHALE SCROUNGE
(— PLANT) ERS
FORAGE-CAP KEPI
FORAGER OUTRIDER
FORAMEN PORE EXOSTOME METAPORE TROCHLEA
FORAMINIFER NUMMULITE
FORAY RAID MELEE CREAGH FURROW INROAD MARAUD RAVAGE RAZZIA SORTIE CHAPPOW HERSHIP PILLAGE SPREAGH SPREATH
FORBEAR LET BEAR HELP HOLD SHUN SIRE AVOID FORGO SPARE WAIVE DEPORT DESIST ENDURE PARENT RETAIN ABSTAIN DECLINE REFRAIN RESPITE ANCESTOR FOREBEAR WITHDRAW
(— PROSECUTION) COMPOUND
(— TO SPEAK) OVERGO
FORBEARANCE MERCY LENITY NONACT PARDON QUARTER MILDNESS PATIENCE
FORBEARING CLEMENT LENIENT PATIENT MERCIFUL TOLERANT
FORBID BAN BAR NIX DEFY DENY FEND TABU VETO WARN DEBAR TABOO BANISH DEFEND ENJOIN IMPEDE OPPOSE REFUSE SHIELD FORFEND FORWARN GAINSAY INHIBIT WITHSAY DISALLOW FORSPEAK PRECLUDE PROHIBIT PROSCRIBE
(— ENTRANCE) SHUT
FORBIDDANCE BAN VETO FORBODE
FORBIDDEN TABU TABOO BANNED DENIED VERBOTEN
(— AS FOOD) TREF TREFA
(SOMETHING —) NONO
FORBIDDING DOUR GRIM HARD BLACK GAUNT STERN FIERCE GLASSY GLOOMY GRISLY ODIOUS STRICT FORBODE GRIZZLY REPULSIVE
(— CLOSED MEETINGS) SUNSHINE
FORCE GAR GAS GUT HAP JAM LID VIM VIS ZIP BANG REAR BEAT BEND BIRR BODY CLIP CRAM DINT DOOM DRAG EDGE FECK FOSS GRIP GUTS HEAD JAMB JINX MAIN MAKE MANA SNAP SOCK ABATE AGENT ARDOR BRAWL BRING BRUSH CLAMP COACT CRAFT CROWD CRUSH DEMON DRAFT DRIVE EXACT EXERT FOHAT GAVEL IMPEL KARMA MIGHT PAINT PEISE

POACH POINT POWER PRESS PRIZE PUNCH REPEL SHEAR SHOVE SINEW STEAM STUFF THROW WAKAN WREST CHARGE COERCE COMPEL CUDGEL DURESS EFFECT EFFORT ENERGY EXTORT HIJACK HOTBED IMPACT IMPOSE JOSTLE MUSCLE OBLIGE POWDER RAVISH SHAKTI STRAIN STRESS WRENCH ABILITY AFFORCE BLUSTER CASCADE COGENCE COGENCY CONCUSS DRAUGHT DYNAMIC IMPETUS IMPRESS IMPULSE LASHKAR OPPRESS REQUIRE SQUEEZE TORMENT VIOLATE WAKANDA ACTIVITY ADHESION AFFINITY BULLDOZE COACTION COERCION DYNAMISM EFFICACY HOTHOUSE MOMENTUM PRESSURE STRENGTH VALIDITY VIOLENCE VIRILITY NECESSITATE
(— AIR UPON) BLOW
(— AN ENTRANCE) RANDOM THRUST
(— APART) SUNDER DISPART
(— BACK) REPEL RAMBARRE
(— BY THREAT) SWAGGER
(— DOWN) CLEW CLUE DETRUDE DISMOUNT
(— IN) INJECT INTRUDE
(— OPEN) BURST JIMMY SPORT RANFORCE
(— OUT) SPEW EJECT ERUPT EVICT EXPEL KNOCK WRING EXTUND EXPRESS
(— PASSAGE) SQUEEZE
(— TO MOVE) STICTION
(— WAY) CROWD WREST WRING
(— WITH LEGAL AUTHORITY) POSSE
(AIR —) LUFTWAFFE
(ALLEGED —) OD
(ARMED —) CREW HEAD POWER CONREY ARMAMENT BATTALIA
(CONCENTRATED —) PITH
(CONFINING —) LID
(CONSTRAINING —) STRESS
(COSMIC —) EVIL
(CREATIVE —) NATURE
(DRIVING —) STEAM SWINGE
(EVOLUTIONARY —) BATHMISM
(EXPLOSIVE —) MEGATON
(HYPOTHETICAL —) FORTUNE
(KIND OF —) LORENTZ
(LACK OF — TO DEFEAT) UNDERKILL
(LIFE —) SHAKTI
(MAIN —) BRUNT
(MILITANT —) SWORD
(MILITARY —) FYRD LEGION WERING BAYONET OCCUPATION ESTABLISHMENT
(MOVING —) SOLICITATION
(NAVAL —) FLEET
(PHYSICAL —) NERVE
(PREPONDERATING —) SWAY
(PROTECTIVE —) CONVOY
(RELIGIOUS —) SANCTITY
(SACRED —) KAMI
(SPIRITUAL —) SOUL
(UNRESTRAINED —) FURY
(UPWARD —) BUOYANCY

(PL.) ARMY WILL COLORS
(SUFF.) **(UNIT OF —)** DYNE
FORCED LABORED ENFORCED FALSETTO SARDONIC SPURIOUS STRAINED SFORZANDO
FORCEFUL RUDE GREAT GUTSY PITHY STIFF STOUT MIGHTY PUNCHY STRONG VIRILE DYNAMIC STHENIC VIOLENT BRUISING ELOQUENT EMPHATIC ENFATICO FORCIBLE VIGOROUS TRENCHANT
FORCEFULNESS PUNCH EMPHASIS
FORCEMEAT FARCE BOUDIN GODIVEAU QUENELLE STUFFING
FORCEPS DOG FURCA TONGS TENAIL BULLDOG CLAMMER PINCERS PINSONS RONGEUR CROWBILL DENTAGRA PINCETTE VULSELLA TENACULUM
(PREF.) FORCI LABID(O)
FORCIBLE VIVE STOUT VALID COGENT MIGHTY POTENT STRONG FORCIVE NERVOUS VIOLENT WEIGHTY EMPHATIC FORCEFUL POWERFUL PREGNANT PUISSANT VEHEMENT VIGOROUS
FORCIBLY AMAIN SADLY HARDLY MAINLY HEAVILY STRONGLY
FORD PASS RACK RIFT WADE WATH DRIFT STREAM CURRENT FORDING PASSAGE PASSING CROSSING
(PAVED —) STEAN STEENING
FORE VAN WAY AFORE AHEAD FRONT PRIOR FORMER FURTHER
FOREARM CUBIT CUBITAL CUBITUS
FOREBEAR ANCESTOR
FOREBODE BODE GIVE OMEN ABODE AUGUR CROAK BETIDE DIVINE BETOKEN MISBODE OMINATE PORTEND PREDICT PRESAGE FORETELL
(— EVIL) CROAK
FOREBODING OMEN BLACK FATAL AUGURY BODING DISMAL GLOOMY ANXIETY BALEFUL BANEFUL DRUTHER OMINOUS PRESAGE BODEMENT SINISTER ABODEMENT PROGNOSTICATION
FOREBODINGLY DIRELY
FOREBRAIN CEREBRUM PROENCEPHALON
FORECAST BODE CAST SCHEME CAUTION FORESEE FORESET PREDICT FOREDEEM FOREDOOM FORETELL PROPHESY ADUMBRATE PREVISION PROGNOSIS PREDICTION PROGNOSTICATION
FORECASTER SEER ORACLE PROPHET
FORECASTLE FOCSLE ISLAND
FORECOURT VESTIBULE
FOREDOOM JINX DESTINY
FOREFACE CUSHION
FOREFATHER AYEL SIRE ELDER PITRI PARENT ANCESTOR FOREBEAR PROGENITOR PRIMOGENITOR
FOREFINGER INDEX
FOREFOOT PAW PUD GRIPE
FOREFOOTING MANGANA
FOREFRONT VAN FRONT VAVARD
FOREGO FORGO WAIVE ESCHEW ABSTAIN NEGLECT PRECEDE

REFRAIN ABNEGATE DISPENSE RENOUNCE

FOREGOING PAST ABOVE ANTERIOR PREVIOUS PRECEDING

FOREGROUND PROSCENIUM

FOREHEAD BROW FRONS FRONT FRONTLET SINCIPUT

(— **INDENTATION**) STOP

(— **MARK**) KUMKUM

(**HIGH** —) LEPTENE

(PREF.) FRONTI FRONTO METOPO

FOREHEARTH SETTLER

FOREIGN UNCO ALIEN FREMD WELSH ALANGE EXILED EXOTIC FRENCH REMOTE UNKIND DISTANT ECDEMIC EPIGENE EXCLUDE FRAMMIT HEATHEN OUTBORN OUTLAND OUTWARD STRANGE BARBARIC EPIGENIC EXTERIOR EXTERNAL FORINSEC OVERSEAS PEREGRIN STRANGER BARBAROUS OUTLANDISH TRAMONTANE

(— **TO**) DEHORS

(**ONE ATTRACTED TO** — **THINGS**) XENOPHILE

(PREF.) ALIENI EXOTO

FOREIGNER ALIEN HAOLE ALLTUD GRINGO PAKEHA GREENER OUTBORN OUTLAND PARDESI ETRANGER OUTSIDER PEREGRIN PORTUGEE STRANGER MLECHCHHA OUTLANDER

(— **IN JAPAN**) GAIJIN

(— **LIVING IN CHINA**) TAIPAN

(PREF.) XEN(O)

(SUFF.) XENE XENOUS XENY

FOREIGN-LOOKING EXOTIC

FOREKNOW DIVINE FORESEE FOREWIT

FOREKNOWLEDGE PRESAGE

FORELEG GAMB

FORELOCK TOP BANG QUIFF COTTER TOUPET FORETOP TOPPING FORBRUSH

FOREMAN BOSS BULL CORK JOSS LUNA PUSH CHIEF DOGGY BUNTER GAFFER GANGER LEADER RAMROD SIRDAR TENTER CAPATAZ CAPORAL CAPTAIN FOUNDER HEADMAN MANAGER MANDOOR OVERMAN SHOOFLY SKIDDER STEWARD FOREHAND GANGSMAN OVERSEER

(— **OF JURY**) CHANCELLOR

FOREMOST TOP HEAD HIGH MAIN CHIEF FIRST FORME FRONT GRAND BANNER FORMER LEADING RANKING SUPREME VANMOST CHAMPION

(— **PART**) VAWARD

FOREORDAIN FATE SLATE DESTINE FORESAY PREDOOM FORECAST

FOREORDINATION FATE

FOREPART FRONT FOREHEAD

(— **OF FACE**) CHAP

(— **OF HEAD**) SINCIPUT

(— **OF HORSE'S HEAD**) CHANFRIN

(— **OF SHIP**) STEM FORWARD CUTWATER ENTRANCE

FOREPOLE LATH SPILE SPILING

FORERUN HERALD OUTRUN PRECEDE PRELUDE ANNOUNCE FORESHOT

FORERUNNER OMEN SIGN USHER AUGURY HERALD ANCESTOR FOREGOER FOURRIER OUTRIDER PRODROME MESSENGER PRECURSOR

FORERUNNING PRECURSE

FORESADDLE RACK

FORESEE SEE READ DIVINE PURVEY PREVISE PROVIDE ENVISAGE ENVISION FORECAST FOREKNOW PROSPECT PREFIGURE

FORESHADOW HINT FIGURE HERALD BESPEAK FORERUN PATTERN PRELUDE PRESAGE UMBRATE FORETYPE ADUMBRATE

FORESHORE HARD SHORE HARDWAY SEASHORE

FORESHOW BODE ABODE AUGUR BETOKEN PORTEND SIGNIFY FORETELL PROPHESY

FORESIGHT FEAR VISION FOREWIT PRESAGE FORECAST FORELOOK PROSPECT PRUDENCE

(**LACKING** —) MYOPIC

FORESIGHTED CAGY CAGEY CANNY

FOREST BUSH GAPO MATA RUKH WOLD WOOD FIRTH GLADE GUBAT MATTA MATTO MONTE SYLVA TAIGA WASTE WEALD JUNGLE TIMBER BOSCAGE CALYDON COPPICE CAATINGA WOODLAND

(— **CITY**) PORTLAND SAVANNAH CLEVELAND

(— **FOR DEER**) FIRTH

(**DENSE** —) JUNGLE

(**IMMENSE** —) MONTANA

(**RAIN** —) SELVA

(**RIVERSIDE** —) GAPO

(**SHAKESPEAREAN** —) ARDEN

(**SIBERIAN** —) URMAN

(**STUNTED** —) CAATINGA KRUMMHOLZ

(PREF.) HYL(O) SILVI SYLVI

FORESTAGE APRON

FORESTALL BEAT HELP AVERT DETER LURCH STALL DEVANCE FORERUN OBVIATE PREVENE PREVENT FORSTEAL STAVEOFF ANTICIPATE

FORESTALLER KIDDER GROSSER

FORESTAYSAIL JUMBO

FORESTER FOSTER WALKER MONTERO TINEMAN TREEMAN WOODMAN WOODSMAN

FORETASTE GUST HANSEL TEASER EARNEST HANDSEL ANTEPAST PROSPECT PRELIBATION

FORETELL BODE ERST READ SPAE AUGUR INSEE WEIRD WRITE DIVINE HALSEN HERALD BESPEAK FORESAY PORTEND PREDICT PRESAGE ANNOUNCE FOREBODE FORECAST FORESHOW PROPHESY SOOTHSAY

FORETELLING PROPHECY

FORETHOUGHT CAUTION FORECAST PREPENSE PRUDENCE

FORETOKEN OMEN AUGUR PORTEND PROMISE FORECAST FORESHOW FORESIGN

FOREVER AY AKE AYE EVER ETERN ALWAYS ETERNE ENDLESS ETERNITY EVERMORE

FOREWARN WEIRD PREMONISH

FOREWARNING HINT PORTENT PREMONITION

FOREWING PRIMARY

FOREWORD PROEM PREFACE PREAMBLE

FORFEIT WED FINE LOSE TINE WITE CHEAT CRIME DEDIT FORGO LAPSE FOREGO SCONCE DEFAULT ESCHEAT FORWORK PENALTY FORFAULT

FORFEITURE FINE BLIND MULCT TINSEL ESCHEAT FORFEIT PENALTY

FORGE FOGE MINT TILT WELL CLICK FALSE FEIGN SMITH STOVE HAMMER SMITHY STEADY STITCH STITHY SWINGE CHAFERY FALSIFY FASHION BLOOMERY

FORGED BOGUS SPURIOUS

FORGER SMITH FALSER FALSARY LEVERMAN

FORGERY SHAM FALSUM FICTION BLOOMERY

FORGET LOSE OMIT WANT FLUFF BILEVE UNKNOW UNMIND NEGLECT OVERLOOK

FORGETFUL FLAKY SPACY OBLIVIOUS

FORGETFULNESS SWIM FLUFF LETHE AMNESIA AMNESTY OBLIVION

(PREF.) LETHO

FORGET-ME-NOT MYOSOTE

FORGETTING

(PREF.) LETHO

FORGING HOOP CLICK JACKET

FORGIVE REMIT SPARE ASSOIL EXCUSE PARDON ABSOLVE CONDONE OVERLOOK

FORGIVENESS GRACE PARDON FORGIFT

FORGIVING GRACE HUMANE CLEMENT MERCIFUL MAGNANIMOUS

FORGOTTEN DERELICT UNMINDED

FORINT FLORIN

FORK CROC EVIL HOOK TANG TINE CLEFT CLOFF FURCA GLACK GRAIN GRAIP PRONG TWIST BISECT BRANCH CLITCH CROTCH DIVIDE FEEDER GAFFLE HACKER OFFSET TWISEL BIPRONG FOURCHE FRUGGIN HAYFORK TOASTER CROTCHET EQUULEUS GRAINING PITCHFORK

(— **OF BODY**) SHARE

(— **OF PENNON**) FANON

(— **OF WINDPIPE**) BRONCHUS

(— **OVER**) PAYOUT

(**FISHING** —) SPEAR

(**MEAT** —) TORMENTOR

(**THATCHER'S** —) GROM

(**TUNING** —) DIAPASON

(PREF.) FURCI

FORKED BIFID FORKY FURCAL PRONGY DIVIDED FURCATE LITUATE BIFORKED BIRAMOUS BRANCHED FOURCHEE SUBBIFID

FORKING STAR

FORLORN LORN LOST REFT ALONE ABJECT FORFAIRN FORSAKEN HELPLESS HOPELESS PITIABLE WITLOSEN

FORM AME DIG FIG HEW HUE SET BLEE BODY CASE CAST CAUL DOME FLOW GARB IDEA KERN KITE MAKE MODE MOLD PLAN RITE SEAT THEW TURN BENCH BLANK BLOCK BOARD BUILD BUNCH CHART CHECK CRUSH DUMMY EIDOS ERECT FORGE FORMA FORME FRAME GALBE GUISE IMAGE MATCH MEUSE MODEL SHAPE SPELL STAMP THROW USAGE ADJUST CHALAN COUPON CREATE CUSTOM DEVISE DOCKET FIGURE FILLER HANGER INVENT MANNER REMOVE RITUAL SCHEMA SCHOOL SPONGE STRIKE SYSTEM TAILLE AGENDUM ARRANGE COMPOSE CONFECT CONTOUR DEVELOP FASHION FEATURE FORMULA GESTALT IMPANEL INVOICE LITURGY MAKEDOM OUTLINE PATTERN PORTRAY PORTURE PRODUCE PROFILE SPECIES STATURE BILLHEAD CEREMONY COMPOUND CONCEIVE CONTRIVE FORMWORK INSTRUCT LIKENESS MODALITY ORGANIZE SEMBLANCE

(— **A HEAD**) POME

(— **A NETWORK**) PLEX

(— **A RING**) ENVIRON

(— **ASSUMED AFTER DEATH**) KAMARUPA

(— **BRANCHES**) BREAK

(— **BY CUTTING OFF**) ABJOINT

(— **CONNECTION**) ALLY

(— **FOR BELL FOUNDING**) SWEEP

(— **FOR CONCRETE**) BOXING

(— **FOR HOLDING BARREL**) SQUAW

(— **FOR MOLD**) JACKET

(— **FOR PRESSING VENEERS**) CAUL

(— **FRUIT**) KNIT

(— **INTO A CHAIN**) CATENATE

(— **INTO BALL**) CONGLOBE

(— **INTO RINGLETS**) CRISP

(— **LEATHER**) CRIMP

(— **MOUND**) TUMP

(— **OF GOVERNMENT**) ESTATE KINGSHIP

(— **OF PREDICATION**) CATEGORY

(— **POLITICAL SUCCESSION**) CAVE

(— **WITH PLASTER**) RUN

(— **YARN INTO THREAD**) CABLE

(**ANCESTRAL** —) BLASTAEA STEMFORM

(**CEREMONIAL** —) RITE

(**CONVENTIONAL** —) AMENITY

(**DEXTROROTATORY** —) CAMPHOR

(**DISPLAY** —) MANNEQUIN

(**IMPERFECT** —) SEMIFORM

(**IRREGULAR** —) PSEUDOMORPH

(**ISOMETRIC** —) DIPLOID

(**LINGUISTIC** —) FOSSIL GERUND

(**LITERARY** —) KNACK

(**LITURGICAL** —) SERVICE

(**LYRICAL** —) SESTINA

(**MUSICAL** —) RAGA SUITE

(**POETIC** —) CINQUAIN

(**POINTED** —) ANGLE

(**SCHOOL** —) SHELL

(**SHOE** —) LAST FILLER

(**SHORTENED** —) ABBREVIATION

(**SONG** —) BAR

(SPECTRAL —) SHADOW
(SPEECH —) LEXEME IDIOLECT
(SPIRAL OR CIRCULAR —) GYRE
(STRUCTURE —) MORPHOLOGY
(TOP —) GROOVE
(VERB —) FUTURE CONATIVE DEFINITE DURATIVE
(VERSE —) EPODE BALLAD PANTUM SONNET KYRIELLE LIMERICK
(VISIBLE —) RUPA
(WILD —) AGRIOTYPE
(WORD —) ETYMON ANOMALY
(PREF.) IDO MORPH(O) PLASMATO
(SUFF.) FY GEN(E)(ESIA)(ESIS)(ETIC)(IC)(IN)(OUS)(Y) IFY MORPH(A)(AE)(IC)(ISM)(OSIS)(OTIC)(OUS)(Y) PLASIA PLASIS PLASM(A)(IA)(IC) PLAST(IC)(Y) PLASY
(HAVING — OF) IC(AL)
(IN THE — OF) OID(AL)
FORMAL DRY SET BOOK PRIM BUDGE CHILL COURT EXACT STIFF SOCIAL SOLEMN STOCKY ANGULAR BOOKISH LOGICAL NOMINAL ORDERLY OUTWARD PRECISE REGULAR SOLWARD STARCHY STATELY STILTED ABSTRACT ACADEMIC AFFECTED ELEVATED FORMULAR OFFICIAL PUNCTUAL STARCHED WHITETIE
FORMALDEHYDE FORMAL MONOSE HARDENER METHANAL
FORMALISM ACADEMISM
FORMALIST PEDANT SCHOLASTIC
FORMALISTIC COURT ACADEMIC
FORMALITY FORM POMP SASINE STARCH BUCKRAM DECENCY WIGGERY CEREMONY PHARISAISM
FORMALIZE STIFFEN
FORMALLY FORMLY STARCHLY
FORMAT SIZE GETUP SHAPE STYLE
FORMATION FORM RANK SPUR BIOME FLIGHT GROWTH HARROW MASSIF SPREAD POTENCE BOTRYOID
(— ENCLOSING MINE WORKING) GROUND
(— ENCOUNTERED IN DRILLING) STRAY
(— OF BRAIN) FORNIX
(— OF BRANCHES) CANOPY
(— OF CRYSTAL) SHOOT
(— OF JOINT) ANKYLOSIS
(— OF PLANES) JAVELIN
(— OF SCAR) ULOSIS
(— OF WILDFOWL) WEDGE
(— ON TOAD) SPADE
(— RESEMBLING ICICLE) STIRIA
(BATTLE —) HERSE
(BRAIN —) FORNIX
(CLOUD —) NUBECULA
(DANCE —) SET
(DIAGONAL —) HARROW
(DRIPSTONE —) COLUMN
(ECOLOGICAL —) BIOME
(FLIGHT —) SQUADRON
(FOOTBALL —) SHOTGUN WISHBONE
(GEOLOGIC —) BOEL CULM CHICO STRAY MARKER MEDINA CURTAIN MANLIUS MATAWAN POTOMAC TERRAIN AQUIFUGE FERNANDO

KOOTANIE KOOTENAI LOCKPORT TOPATOPA YORKTOWN
(GLACIAL —) ARETE
(HABIT —) FIXATION
(INDENTED —) CLEFT
(INFANTRY —) TERTIA ECHELON
(LAND —) BOOTHEEL
(MILITARY —) SNAIL FLIGHT
(MORBID —) GROWTH
(NAVAL —) SCREEN
(POINTED —) BEAK
(THICKET —) MAQUIS
(PREF.) PLASTO
(SUFF.) GENESIA GENESIS OSIS POEIA POESIS POIESIS POIETIC
FORMATIVE CREANT PLASTIC DEMIURGIC
(SUFF.) POEIA POESIS POIESIS POIETIC
FORMED BUILT BOOKIT DECIDED MATURED SETTLED WROUGHT TIMBERED
(— AT BASE OF MOUNTAIN) PIEDMONT
(— INTO STEPS) GRADY
(— ON SURFACE OF EARTH) EPIGENE
(IMPERFECTLY —) ABORTIVE
(STURDILY —) BUXOM
(PREF.) APO PLASTO
FORMEE PATE PATTEE
FORMER DIE OLD ERER ERST FERN FORE LATE ONCE PAST ELDER FORME GAUGE GUIDE MAKER OTHER PRIOR BYGONE RATHER WHILOM ANCIENT ANOTHER CREATOR EARLIER FIRSTER FURTHER ONETIME PRIDIAN QUONDAM TEMPLET UMWHILE PRETERIT PREVIOUS PRISTINE SOMETIME STRICKLE UMQUHILE PRECEDING
(PREF.) PROTER(O)
FORMERLY ERE NEE OLD ERST FORE ONCE THEN YORE GRAVE WHILOM WHILST ONETIME QUONDAM SOMETIME UMQUHILE
FORMIDABLE MEAN STOUR FEARFUL ALARMING DREADFUL MENACING TERRIBLE FEROCIOUS REDOUBTABLE
(— PERSON) TARTAR
FORMING
(SUFF.) GENIC GEROUS
FORMLESS ARUPA DOUGHY ANIDIAN CHAOTIC DEFORMED INDIGEST
FORMOSA (SEE TAIWAN)
FORMULA LAW MIX DATE FIAT FORM RULE CANON CREED DHIKR GRAPH INDEX LURRY KEKULE MANTRA METHOD RECIPE THEORY RECEIPT APOLYSIS CLAUSULE DOXOLOGY EXORCISM
(— OF FAITH) KELIMA
(MAGICAL —) CARACT
(OFFICIAL —) PROTOCOL
(WORD —) PATERNOSTER
(PL.) RAKA RAKAH
FORMULARY SYMBOL
FORMULATE PUT CAST DRAW

FRAME DEVISE CAPSULE COMPOSE FORMULE PLATFORM
FORMULATED STATED WRITTEN
FORMULATION (— OF A TRUTH) COUNT CREED DOGMA APHORISM APOTHEGM DOCTRINE
(SUFF.) **(SYSTEMATIC —)** ICS
FORMWORK SHUTTERING
FORNIX VAULT PSALIS
FORSAKE DENY DROP FLEE QUIT SHUN ABAND AVOID FORGO LEAVE WAIVE DEFECT DEPART DESERT FOREGO FORHOO FORLET REFUSE REJECT ABANDON DISCARD FORLESE DESOLATE FORHOOIE RENOUNCE WITHDRAW
FORSAKEN LORN FORLORN DESERTED DESOLATE LASSLORN
FORSETE (FATHER OF —) BALDER
FORSOOTH EVEN MARRY QUOTH
FORSWEAR DENY ABJURE REJECT ABANDON PERJURE ABNEGATE MANSWEAR RENOUNCE
FORSYTE SAGA (AUTHOR OF —) GALSWORTHY
(CHARACTER IN —) JON VAL JUNE MONT FLEUR HOLLY IRENE JOLLY MONTY DARTIE JOLYON PHILIP SOAMES ANNETTE FORSYTE LAMOTTE MICHAEL PROFOND PROSPER SWITHIN TIMOTHY BOSINNEY WINIFRED
FORT PA DUN LIS PAH LISS PEEL SHEE SPUR WORK COTTA REDAN SIDHE CASTLE SANGAR SCHERM SCONCE STRONG BASTION BULWARK CITADEL CLOSURE REDOUBT BASTILLE CASTILLO FASTHOLD FASTNESS FORTRESS MARTELLO PRESIDIO
(FAIRY —) LIS LIOS LISS SHEE SIDHE
(HILL —) RATH
(MAORI —) PA PAH
(RUINS OF —) ZIMBABWE
(SMALL —) GURRY FORTIN BASTIDE FORTLET FORCELET
FORTE FORT LOUD STARK METIER STRONG EMINENCY STRENGTH
FORTESCUE COBBLER SCORPION
FORTH OUT AWAY FURTH
(PREF.) E OUT
FORTHCOMING PROXIMATE
FORTHRIGHT BALD BURLY GUTTY CANDID
FORTHRIGHTLY FRANKLY
FORTHRIGHTNESS CANDOR PLUMPNESS
FORTHWITH EFT NOW ANON AWAY BEDENE DIRECT BETIMES FORTHON DIRECTLY
FORTIFICATION BAWN BOMA FORT MOAT WALL REDAN TOWER ABATIS CASHEL CASTLE GLACIS LAAGER BASTION BULWARK CITADEL DEFENCE DEFENSE PARAPET PILLBOX RAMPART RAVELIN REDOUBT FORTRESS MUNITION RONDELLE STRENGTH
(LINE OF —S) TROCHA
(PART OF —) BERM MOAT ANGLE DITCH FLANK GORGE SCARP SLOPE COVERT ESCARP GLACIS PARADE BASTION CURTAIN PARAPET

RAMPART SALIENT TENAILLE BANQUETTE TERREPLEIN COUNTERSCARP
FORTIFIED ARMED CONFIRMED
FORTIFY ARM MAN BANK FORT LINE WALL WARD FENCE SPIKE STANK BATTLE IMMURE MUNIFY MUNITE BULWARK COMFORT DEFENSE GARNISH RAMPIRE BASTILLE EMBATTLE FORTRESS RAMFORCE STOCKADE
FORTITUDE GRIT GUTS SAND FIBER FIBRE HEART NERVE PLUCK METTLE BRAVERY COURAGE HEROISM STAMINA BACKBONE PATIENCE STRENGTH
(AUTHOR OF —) WALPOLE
(CHARACTER IN —) TAN HANZ NORA BOBBY BRANT CLARE JERRY PETER ZANTI EMILIO LAUNCE GALLEON JERRARD MONOGUE STEPHEN ZACHARY BROCKETT ROSSITER WESTCOTT CARDILLAC GOTTFRIED AITCHINSON
FORTNIGHT (HALF A —) WEEK
FORTNIGHTLY BIWEEKLY
FORTRESS (ALSO SEE FORT) BURG KEEP KASBA PIECE PLACE ROCCA CASBAH CASTLE ALCAZAR BARRIER BOROUGH CASTRUM CHATEAU CITADEL KREMLIN ZWINGER ALCAZAVA BASTILLE FASTNESS STRENGTH
(AUTHOR OF —) WALPOLE
(CHARACTER IN —) ADAM JOHN KRAFT PARIS ROGUE BENJIE CAESAR JUDITH REUBEN TEMPLE UHLAND WALTER HERRIES SUNWOOD JENNIFER MARGARET ELIZABETH GOLIGHTLY CHRISTABEL
(NORTH AFRICAN —) KABBAH
FORTUITOUS CASUAL CHANCE RANDOM FORTUIT FORTUNEL
FORTUITY LUCK CHANCE
FORTUNATE EDI FAT HAP SRI GOOD SHRI WELL CANNY FAUST HAPPY LUCKY RIGHT WHITE DEXTER EUROUS BLESSED FAVORED WEIRDLY GRACIOUS
FORTUNATELY FAIR HAPPILY
FORTUNE DIE HAP LOT URE BAHI DOOM FALL FARE FATE HAIL LUCK PILE SEEL STAR EVENT GRACE ISSUE LINES SONSE SPEED WEIRD WHATE CHANCE ESTATE MISHAP RICHES WEALTH DESTINY SUCCESS THEEDOM VENTURE ACCIDENT CASUALTY FELICITY STOCKING
(GOOD —) SELE SONSE SPEED THRIFT FURTHER GOODHAP BONCHIEF FELICITY
(ILL —) DOOM THRAW
(PREF.) TYCH(O)
FORTUNES OF RICHARD MAHONY (AUTHOR OF —) RICHARDSON
(CHARACTER IN —) TOM JOHN LUCY MARY ZARA CUFFY OCOCK POLLY SARAH LALLIE MAHONY RICHARD TURNHAM CUTHBERT
FORTUNE-TELLER SEER SIBYL

SYBIL SPAEMAN SORTIARY SPAEWIFE
(PL.) CHALDAEI

FORTY DAYS OF MUSA DAGH
(AUTHOR OF —) WERFEL
(CHARACTER IN —) TER HAIK MARIS SARKIS BEREKET GABRIEL STEPHAN GONZAGUE HAIGASUN HULIETTE KILIKIAN BAGRADIAN NOKHUDIAN

FORUM COURT PLATFORM
TRIBUNAL

FORWARD ON TO AID BOG BUG GAY ABET BAIN BOLD FORE FREE HELP PERT SEND SHIP STEP AHEAD ALONG AVANT BARDY BRASH CAGER EAGER FAVOR FORTH FRACK FRECK FRONT HASTY PAWKY PUSHY RANDY READY RELAY REMIT SAUCY SERVE SPACK ULTRA AFFORD ARDENT AVAUNT BEFORE BRIGHT COMING DEVANT FORRIT FORTHY HASTEN NUZZLE ONWARD PROMPT REMAIL ROUDAS SECOND TOWARD ADVANCE BETIMES EARNEST EXTREME FURTHER PROMOTE PUSHING RADICAL SOLICIT ADELANTE ARROGANT FROMWARD IMMODEST IMPUDENT MALAPERT ONCOMING PERVERSE PETULANT TELLSOME TOWARDLY TRANSMIT OBTRUSIVE
(MOST —) HEADMOST
(PREF.) ANTE
(LEANING —) PRONO

FORWARDNESS IMMODESTY
FOR WHOM THE BELL TOLLS
(AUTHOR OF —) HEMINGWAY
(CHARACTER IN —) MARIA PABLO PILAR JORDAN ROBERT ANSELMO

FORZA DEL DESTINO, LA
(CHARACTER IN —) CARLO ALVARO LEONORA CALATRAVA
(COMPOSER OF —) VERDI

FOSSA FOSS FOVEA GALET TRENCH VALLIS FOSSULA FOSSETTE

FOSSE DITCH GRAFF

FOSSIL CYCAD CYSTID DOLITE EOZOON FUCOID ICHITE PINITE AMBRITE BLASTID CHAMITE CRINITE ICHNITE JUNCITE LITUITE NEREITE OVULITE REMANIE TYLOPOD ZOOLITE ZOOLITH AISTOPOD AMMONITE ANCODONT ASTROITE BACULITE BALANITE BIOCHRON BLASTOID BUFONITE CALAMITE CERATITE CONCHITE CONODONT ECHINITE EOHIPPUS FAVOSITE FILICITE FUSULINA GEDANITE GYROLITH MIMOSITE PEUCITES POLYPITE SALIGRAM SCAPHITE SERAPHIM SPONGOID SYNAPSID TARSIOID CARPOLITE TRILOBITE OSTRACODERM
(PREF.) NECR(O) ORYCT(O)
(SUFF.) LITE LITH(IC) LITIC

FOSSILIZE PETRIFY

FOSTER REAR NURSE COCKER HARBOR NUZZLE SUCKLE CHERISH DEPOSIT EMBOSOM GRATIFY INDULGE NOURISH NOURSLE NURTURE BEFRIEND CULTIVATE

FOSTERAGE NURSERY

FOSTER-CHILD DALT DAULT
FOSTERED (ARTIFICALLY —)
SPOONFED

FOSTERER NORRY

FOUL BAD BASE EVIL HORY RANK ROIL VILE BAWDY BLACK DIRTY DITCH FUNKY GRIMY GURRY HORRY KETTY LOUSY MUDDY MUSTY NASTY RUSTY SULLY WEEDY CLARTY DEFAME DIRTEN DREGGY FILTHY GREASY IMPURE MALIGN ODIOUS PUTRID ROTTEN SOILED SORDID UNFAIR VIROSE ABUSIVE BEASTLY DEFACED FULSOME HATEFUL ILLEGAL IMBROIN NOISOME OBSCENE PROFANE SLOTTER SMEARED SQUALID TETROUS UNCLEAN VICIOUS AMURCOUS ENTANGLE FECULENT INDECENT MEPHITIC SLOTTERY STAGNANT STINKING TRAUCHLE WRETCHED
(— UP) ERR BOTCH
(BASKETBALL —) HACK

FOULMOUTHED RIBALD ROUDAS
ABUSIVE OBSCENE PROFANE

FOULNESS FEDITY PRAVITY
(— OF MOUTH) SABURRA

FOUL-SMELLING FUNKY

FOUL-UP SNAFU

FOUMART POLECAT

FOUND FIX TRY YET BASE CAST REST STAY BEGIN BOARD BUILD ENDOW ERECT PLANT SETUP START ATTACH BOTTOM DEPART GROUND INVENT EQUIPPED PRACTICE PROVIDED SUPPLIED

FOUNDATION BED BASE BODY FIRM FOND FUND GIST ROOT SILL SOLE BASIS FOUND STOCK STOOL ANLAGE BOTTOM CRADLE GROUND LEGACY MATRIX PODIUM RIPRAP BEDDING BEDROCK CHANTRY COLLEGE MORTISE PINNING RADICAL ROADBED SUBBASE WARRANT BACKBONE DONATION MATTRESS MIREPOIX PEDESTAL PLATFORM STANDARD UNDERLAY
(— FOR WIG) CAUL
(— OF BASKET) SLATH SLARTH
(FLOATING —) CRIB
(LACE —) RESEAU
(PRECARIOUS —) STILT

FOUNDATIONER GOWNBOY
COLLEGER

FOUNDATION-STOP DIAPASON
FOUNDED FUSILE
FOUNDER FAIL IMAM SINK AUTHOR CASTER DYNAST EPONYM HELLEN YETTER AFOUNDE STUMBLE BELLETER MISCARRY LAMINITIS PATRIARCH
(— OF COLONY) OECIST OIKIST

FOUNDLING WAIF ORPHAN
FOUNT FONS FONT SOURCE
FOUNTAIN URN AQUA FOND HEAD KELD PANT PILA SYKE WELL DIRCE FOUNT GURGE QUELL SURGE ORIGIN PHIALE PIRENE SOURCE SPRING BUBBLER CONDUIT SPRUDEL AGANIPPE SALMACIS UPSPRING WELLHEAD

(— ON SHIP) SCUTTLEBUTT
(INK —) DUCT
(SODA —) SPA
(PREF.) PEGO
(SUFF.) CRENE

FOUNTAINHEAD ORIGIN SOURCE
FOUNTAIN PEN STICK STYLO
FOUR MESS CATER DELTA DALETH FEOWER TETRAD QUARTET QUATRAL MURNIVAL QUADRATE
(— OF ANYTHING) GUNDA
(— OF TRUMPS) TIDDY
(— TIMES A DAY) QD QID
(— YEAR PERIOD) PYTHIAD
(GROUP OF —) TETRAD
(PREF.) QUADR(I)(U) QUADRATO QUATER TESSARA TETR(A)
(— ATOMS OF HYDROGEN) TETRAZ(O)
(— TIMES) QUATER TETRAKIS
(HAVING — PARTS) TETR(A)

FOURCHETTE FORGET SIDEWALL
WISHBONE

FOURFOLD FOURBLE QUATERN
FOUR HORSEMEN OF APOCALYPSE (AUTHOR OF —)
IBANEZ
(CHARACTER IN —) JULIO CHICHI MARCELO DESNOYER HARTROTT

FOURIERISM SOCIALISM
FOUR-O'CLOCK FRIARBIRD
FOURPENNY BIT JOE FLAG JOEY GROAT

FOURSQUARE FRANK
FOURTEENER SEPTENAR
FOURTH DELTA QUART FARDEL FORPIT FERLING QUARTER QUADRANT
(— HOUR) SEXT
(— OF BAHMANI EMPIRE) TARAF
(— OF CAKE) FARL FARLE
(— OF YEAR) RAITH
(AUGMENTED —) TRITONE
(PREF.) QUART(I) TETART(O)

FOUSSA CIVET GALET
FOVEOLA VARIOLE
FOWL HEN RED COCK GAME GRIG JAVA ROCK SLIP BIDDY CHUCK CLUCK COPPY DUMPY MALAY MANOC MARAN SILKY ANCONA ASHURA BANTAM BRAHMA CAMBAR COCHIN HOUDAN LAMONA LEGBAR POLISH REDCAP SULTAN SUSSEX BUFFBAR CAMPINE CHICKEN CORNISH DORKING FRIZZLE HAMBURG LEGHORN MINORCA OKLABAR POULTRY ROOSTER SPANISH SUMATRA COCKEREL CUBALAYA DELAWARE DUCKWING DUNGHILL GAMECOCK LANGSHAN SHANGHAI SHOWBIRD VOLAILLE
(AGGREGATION OF —) RAFT
(CASTRATED —) CAPETTE
(CRESTED —) TOPKNOT
(GUINEA —) KEET COMEBACK
(MALE —) STAG
(STUFFED —) FARCI
(TAILLESS —) RUMKIN
(5-TOED —) SILKY SILKIE

FOWLER BIRDMAN
FOWLING-PIECE SHOTGUN
FOX DOG KIT PUG TOD ASSE FOOL

STAG WILD ADIVE BRANT CAAMA SWIFT TRICK VIXEN ZORRO ARCTIC BAGMAN CANDUC COLFOX CORSAC FENNEC LOWRIE OUTWIT RENARD RUSSEL BEGUILE CHARLEY CHARLIE KARAGAN REYNARD STUPEFY VULPINE CUSTOMER MUSKWAKI OUTAGAMI PLATINUM
(KIND OF —) KIT

FOX-AND-GEESE MERELS
FOXGLOVE POPPY POPDOCK THIMBLE FLAPDOCK POPGLOVE
FOX GRAPE ISABELLA LABRUSCA
FOXHOUND WALKER
FOX HUNTER PINK
FOX-LIKE ALOPECOID
FOXTAIL CAUDA CHAPE COUGH KNEED TWITCH SETARIA GAMELOTE

FOXY SLY WILY COONY SHREWD CUNNING VULPINE DEXTROUS

FOYER HALL LOBBY ANTEROOM
FRACAS BOUT BRAWL MELEE MUSIC BICKER RUMPUS SHINDY UPROAR QUARREL SHINDIG FRACTION INCIDENT

FRACTION DIT CUT PYO FLUX PART BREAK PIECE SCRAP BREACH LITTLE MOIETY DECIMAL GLUTOSE WETNESS
(— OF RADIATION) ALBEDO
(NAPHTHA —) LIGROIN
(PREF.) MER(I)(O)
(SUFF.) MER(E)(IC)(OUS)(Y)

FRACTIONAL ALIQUOT FRACTED PARTIAL

FRACTIOUS MEAN UGLY CROSS UNRULY CRABBED PEEVISH WASPISH PERVERSE SNAPPISH

FRACTURE BUST FLAW REND BILGE BREAK CLEFT CRACK FAULT JOINT BREACH DEFORM HACKLE DIACOPE FISSURE RUPTURE DIACLASE FRACTION
(PREF.) RHEGMA RHEGNO
(SUFF.) CLASE RHEXIS RRHEXIS

FRACTURED SPLIT BROKEN
FRACTURING SLIP STRAIN FAILURE
FRA DIAVOLO (CHARACTER IN —)
PAMELA DIAVOLO LORENZO ZERLINA COCKBURN
(COMPOSER OF —) AUBER

FRAGILE FINE FROW WEAK FRAIL FROWY LIGHT SWACK FEEBLE FROUGH INFIRM SLIGHT TENDER BRICKLE BRITTLE FROUGHY SLENDER TIFFANY DELICATE EGGSHELL ETHEREAL FRACTILE SLATTERY BREAKABLE

FRAGILITY DELICACY
FRAGMENT BIT END ORT ATOM BLAD CHIP DRIB FLAW GROT MOIT MOTE PART RUMP SHED SNIP WISP ANGLE BLAUD BRACK BREAK BROKE CATCH CHUNK CLOUT CRUMB FRUST GIGOT PIECE RELIC SCRAP SHARD SHERD SHIVE SHRED SPALL SPELL SPLIT CANTLE FARDEL FILING GOBBET MORSEL REMAIN SCREED SHIVER SIPPET SLIVER CANTLET EXCERPT FLINDER FLITTER FRITTER FRUSTUM

MACERAL MAMMOCK REMANIE
REMNANT SEGMENT SHATTER
SHAVING SNIPPET AVULSION
CHIPPING DETRITUS FRACTION
OARTICLE POTSHERD SCANTLET
SKERRICK SPLINTER
(— CUT OFF) CANTLE
(— OF BONE) SEQUESTER
SEQUESTRUM
(— OF BRICK) BRICKBAT
(— OF DIAMOND) CLEAVAGE
(— OF ICE) CALF
(— OF LAVA) FAVILLA LAPILLUS
(— OF MELODY) LAY
(— OF ROCK) CRAG CLAST
AUTOLITH LAPILLUS
(— OF SAIL) HULLOCK
(— OF SOD) TAB
(— OF STONE) SCABBLING
(— OF UNFINISHED WORK) TORSO
(— OF VEIN MATERIAL) SHOAD
SHODE
(—S OF CLOUD) SCUD
(—S OF DIAMOND) BORT
(—S OF SAND) FINES
(CAST IRON —) POTLEG
(ICE —S) BRASH
(JAGGED —) BROCK
(LITERARY —) ANALECTA
(LITERARY —S) ANALECTA
(MASS OF —S) BRASH
(PLANT —) SHIVE
(SHELL —S) SHRAPNEL
(WOODY —S FOUND IN FOOD)
CHAD
(PL.) BRASH FRUSH SCRAPS
CINDERS FITTERS GUBBINS
SMATTER FLINDERS LEFTOVER
SMITHERS SMITHEREENS
FRAGMENTAL CLASTIC
FRAGMENTARY HASHY SNIPPY
SCRAPPY DIVIDUAL
FRAGRANCE BALM ODOR AROMA
SCENT SMELL SWEET BREATH
FLAVOR FRAGOR BOUQUET
INCENSE PERFUME SUAVITY
FRAGRANT NOSY RICH BALMY
OLENT SPICY SWEET SAVORY
SPICED ODORANT ODOROUS
PERFUMY SCENTED AROMATIC
FLAGRANT NECTARED ODORIFIC
REDOLENT
FRAIL FINE POOR PUNY WEAK
CRAZY REEDY SEELY SILLY BASKET
BROTEL CROCKY FLIMSY INFIRM
SICKLY SINGLE SLIGHT SLIMSY
SQUEAL TICKLE TOPNET BRITTLE
BRUCKLE FRAGILE SLENDER
SLIMPSY UNHARDY DELICATE
PINDLING
FRAILTY FAULT FOIBLE INVENT
FAILING DELICACY WEAKNESS
(HUMAN —) ADAM
FRAMBESIA PIAN YAWS BUBAS
MORULA
FRAME BED BIN BOW BOX FLY GYM
MAT SET BAIL BEAM BIER BUCK
BULK BUNK CANT CASE CAUM
CELL CLAM CRIB CURB DESK DRAG
FORM FROG GATE GILL HACK
HARP HECK JACK MOLD PORT
RACK SASH SLEY SOLE STEP AIRER
ANGLE BANJO BLADE BLIND

BLOCK BUILD CADRE CHASE
CLEAT CRATE CROOK DRAFT
EASEL FLAKE FLASK FLEAK FLOAT
GRATE HERSE HORSE MOUNT
OXBOW PERCH PRESS SCRAY
SETUP SHAPE STAND STATE STEAD
STOCK STOOL TRAIL BARROW
BATTEN BINDER BUCCAN BUCKET
CASING CHEVAL COFFIN CRADLE
CRATCH CRUTCH DECKLE DREDGE
FABRIC FENDER GANTRY GRILLE
HANGER HARROW HOTBED
HURDLE PERSON PILLAR QUADRA
REDACT REEDER SCREEN SETTLE
SLEDGE SPIDER SQUARE STAPLE
TANGLE TENTER TESTER ARMRACK
BREAKER CABINET CARRIER
CASEBOX CHASSIS COAMING
COASTER CRAMPON CRIMPER
DRAUGHT DROSSER FASHION
FRAMING FRISKET GALLOWS
GARLAND GATEWAY GIGTREE
GRATING HAYRACK HOUSING
ICEBOAT MACHINE MONTURE
OXBRAKE PORTRAY SETTING
STADDLE TRANSOM TRESTLE
TRIBBLE BARBECUE BOWGRACE
CARRIAGE CASEMENT CONCEIVE
CONTRIVE DOORCASE GRAFFAGE
GRIDIRON GRILLAGE HALBERDS
HOGFRAME PLOWHEAD RAILROAD
RECEIVER RETAINER SKELETON
THRIPPLE TRIANGLE TURNPIKE
BRANDRITH OUTRIGGER
(— FOR ARCH) COOM COOMB
(— FOR BEEHIVE) SECTION
(— FOR CANDLES) HEARSE
(— FOR CARRYING STRAW) KNAPE
(— FOR CASK) GANTRY STALDER
(— FOR CATCHING FISH) HATCH
(— FOR CLOTHES DRYING) AIRER
(— FOR CONFINING HORSE) TRAVE
TRAVAIL
(— FOR COW'S HEAD) BAIL
(— FOR DRYING FISH) HACK HAIK
(— FOR DRYING SKINS) HERSE
(— FOR FISHING LINE) CADAR
CADER
(— FOR GLAZING LEATHER) BUCK
(— FOR HAWKS) CADGE
(— FOR HONEYCOMB) SECTION
(— FOR KILLING PIGS) CREEL
(— FOR LENS) BOW
(— FOR ROLLER BEARINGS) CAGE
(— FOR SMOKING MEAT) BOUCAN
BUCCAN
(— FOR STACK) HAYRACK STADDLE
(— FOR WASHING ORE) BUDDLE
(— OF A VESSEL) HULL
(— OF MIND) HAZE SPITE SPIRIT
TEMPER FEELING POSTURE
(— OF PIER) JETTY
(— OF SAW) HUSK
(— OF SPINNING MULE) SQUARE
(— OF STRAW) SIME
(— OF TINWORK) MARQUITO
(— ON STAGE) CEILING
(— TO CATCH STARFISH) TANGLE
(— TO CLEAN SHIP'S BOTTOM)
HOG
(— TO DRY CLOTHES) AIRER
(— WHICH JOINS) YOKE
(BELL —) SWEEP

(BOBBIN —) BANK
(CARRIAGE —) BRAKE BREAK
(CLOTHES —) AIRER
(COUNTING —) ABACUS
(DIVING —) LUNET LUNETTE
(EMBROIDERY —) TENT TABORET
TAMBOUR
(FISHING —) DREDGE
(GLAZIER'S —) FRAIL
(HARNESS —) HEALD
(LOOM —) SLAY SLEY LATHE
BATTEN SLEIGH
(MINING —) APRON
(PHOTOGRAPHY —) BUTTERFLY
(PORTABLE —) BIER CACAXTE
(PRINTING —) CHASE PRESS
(SHIP'S —) CANT
(SLUBBING —) BILLY
(STRETCHING —) TENT SLEDGE
TENTER
(TANNING —) BEAM
(WINDOW —) CHESS
(2-WHEELED —) GILL
(PL.) PROFILE
FRAMED NATE NATED ENGAGED
FRAMEWORK BED BENT BIER BONE
BUCK BULK CAGE CRIB DURN GRID
RACK SASH BONES CADRE CHUTE
COPSE CREEL FLAKE SHELL STOCK
BELFRY BRIDGE BUSTLE CABANE
CASING CRADLE DESIGN FABRIC
GOCART GUARDS HARROW
HEARSE REBATO SHIELD STROMA
WATTLE CABINET CARCASS
CLIMBER COMMODE DERRICK
FRAMING FULCRUM JACKBOX
LATTICE PANNIER REBATER
RETABLE STADDLE TRESTLE
BARBECUE BEDSTEAD BULKHEAD
CARRIAGE CRADLING CRIBWORK
GRIDIRON GRILLAGE OSSATURE
SCAFFOLD SHELVING SHOWCASE
SKELETON TEMPLATE
(— AROUND HATCHWAY) FIDDLEY
(— FOR BUILDING SHIP) STOCKS
(— FOR CORNSTACK) HOVEL
(— FOR PEAL OF BELLS) CAGE
(— OF REFERENCE) SCHEMA
(— TO EXPAND SKIRTS) BUSTLE
PANNIER
(EMPTY —) HUSK
(FOLDING —) SCREEN
(SCULPTOR'S —) ARMATURE
FRAMING CURB LEAD BELFRY
ARMATURE BEDPLATE
**FRAMLEY PARSONAGE (AUTHOR
OF —)** TROLLOPE
(CHARACTER IN —) LUCY MARK
FANNY SMITH LUFTON THORNE
CRAWLEY ROBARTS SOWERBY
DUNSTABLE
FRANC LEU LEY
FRANCE
(PREF.) GALLO

FRANCE
BAY: BISCAY ARACHON
CAPE: HAGUE
CAPITAL: PARIS
CHEESE: BLEU BRIE BONBEL
BOURSIN MUNSTER CAMEMBERT
MARCILLAT ROQUEFORT
COIN: ECU SOL SOU GROS AGNEL

BLANC BLANK FRANC LIARD LIVRE
LOUIS OBOLE SAIGA SCUTE
BLANCA BLANCO DENIER DIZAIN
TESTON AGNEAUX CENTIME
TESTOON CAVALIER NAPOLEON
DANCE: GAVOT BRANLE CANARY
CANCAN BOUTADE GAVOTTE
DEPARTMENT: AIN LOT VAR AUBE
AUDE CHER EURE GARD GERS
JURA NORD OISE ORNE TARN
AISNE INDRE ISERE LOIRE RHONE
YONNE ARIEGE CANTAL CREUSE
LOZERE NIEVRE CORREZE
GIRONDE MOSELLE
DIVISION, ANCIENT: ARLES PERCHE
NEUSTRIA AQUITAINE AQUITANIA
DYNASTY: CAPET VALOIS BOURBON
ORLEANS CAPETIAN
MEROVINGIAN
FOOD: PATE CREPE CANAPE
MOUSSE QUICHE BRIOCHE
SOUFFLE ESCARGOT PIPERADE
POTAUFEU TOURNEDO
ISLAND: RE YEU CITE CORSE GROIX
HYERE OLERON USHANT CORSICA
KING: ODO EUDES PEPIN CLOVIS
LOTHAIR
LAKE: ANNECY CAZAUX
MEASURE: POT SAC AUNE LINE
MINE MUID PIED VELT ARPEN
CARAT LIEUE LIGNE MINOT
PERCH PINTE POINT POUCE TOISE
VELTE ARPENT HEMINE LEAGUE
QUARTE SETIER CHOPINE
HEMINEE POISSON SEPTIER
BOISSEAU QUARTAUT ROQUILLE
QUARTERON
MILITARY ACADEMY: STCYR
SAINTCYR
MOUNTAIN: PUY DORE BLANC
CINTO FOREZ PELAT COTEDOR
MOUNIER VENTOUX VIGNEMALE
CHAMBEYRON
MOUNTAIN RANGE: ALPS ECRINS
VOSGES CEVENNES PYRENEES
MARITIMES
NAME: GAUL GAULE GALLIA
NATIONAL ANTHEM: MARSEILLAISE
NATIVE: CELT GAUL FRANK BASQUE
BRETON GASCON NORMAN
PICARD CATALAN GALLOIS
LORRAIN FRANCIEN LIGURIAN
PROVENCAL BURGUNDIAN
PORT: CAEN BREST CALAIS TOULON
LEHAVRE BORDEAUX
CHERBOURG DUNKERQUE
MARSEILLE
PROTESTANT: HUGUENOT
PROVINCE: FOIX ANJOU AUNIS
BEARN ALSACE ARTOIS COMTAT
POITOU AUVERGNE BRETAGNE
BRITTANY LIMOUSIN LORRAINE
PROVENCE TOURAINE
RACE TRACK: AUTEUIL
LONGCHAMPS
REPUBLIC CALENDAR: NIVOSE
FLOREAL VENTOSE BRUMAIRE
FERVIDOR FRIMAIRE GERMINAL
MESSIDOR PLUVIOSE PRAIRIAL
FRUCTIDOR THERMIDOR
VENDEMIAIRE
RESORT: PAU NICE CANNES
MENTON RIVIERA

RIVER: AIN ILL LOT LUY LYS VAR
AIRE AUBE AUDE CHER DRAC
EURE GARD GERS LOIR OISE
ORNE TARN VIRE ADOUR AISNE
AULNE DROME INDRE ISERE
LOIRE MARNE MEUSE RHONE
RISLE SAONE SEINE SELLE
SOMME VIAUR YONNE ALLIER
ARIEGE ESCAUT SAMBRE SCARPE
VEZERE VIENNE DURANCE
GARONNE GIRONDE MAYENNE
MOSELLE CHARENTE DORDOGNE
STOCK EXCHANGE: BOURSE
STRAIT: BONIFACIO
TOWN: AY EU AIX DAX GEX PAU
AGDE AGEN ALBI ALES AUBY
AUCH BRON CAEN LAON LOOS
METZ NICE OPPY ORLY RIOM
SENS SETE STLO TOUL UZES
VAUX VIMY VIRE ARLES ARRAS
BLOIS BREST DIJON DINAN DOUAI
ERNEE LAVAL LILLE LISLE LYONS
NANCY NERAC NESLE NIMES
ORNES PARIS REIMS ROUEN
SEDAN TOURS TULLE VICHY
AMIENS ANGERS CALAIS LEMANS
LONGWY NANTES PANTIN
RENNES RHEIMS SARLAT SENLIS
SEVRES TARARE TARBES TOULON
TROYES TULLUM VALOIS VERDUN
BAREGES CASTRES LIMOGES
ORLEANS ROUBAIX VALENCE
BORDEAUX CLERMONT
GRENOBLE MULHOUSE
ROCHELLE TOULOUSE
MARSEILLE STRASBOURG
TRIBE: REMI AEDUI ARVERNI
SALUVII ALLOBROGES
VERSE FORM: LAI ALBA AUBADE
RONDEL BALLADE DESCORT
RONDEAU VIRELAI VIRELAY
WATERFALL: GAVARNIE
WEIGHT: GROS MARC ONCE CARAT
LIVRE POUND TONNE TONNEAU
ESTERLIN
WIND: MISTRAL
WINE: MACON MEDOC GRAVES
CHABLIS POMEROL BORDEAUX
BURGUNDY MUSCADET
SAUTERNE CHAMPAGNE
WINE DISTRICT: MEDOC ALSACE
BORDEAUX BURGUNDY
CHAMPAGNE

FRANCESCA DA RIMINI
(CHARACTER IN —) PAOLO
FRANCESCA GIANCIOTTO
MALATESTINO
(COMPOSER OF) ZANDONAI
FRANCHISE SOC SOKE VOTE CHASE
FERRY HONOR INFANG CHARTER
FREEDOM LIBERTY CONTRACT
FREELAGE SUFFRAGE TENEMENT
FRANCISCAN MINOR MINORITE
FRANCOLIN COQUI TETUR TITAR
REDWING PHEASANT
FRANCOPHILE GALLOMAN
FRANGIBLE BRITTLE
FRANGIPANI SHAKEWOOD
FRANK FREE OPEN RANK BLUFF
BLUNT BURLY LUSTY NAIVE PLAIN
BRAZEN CANDID DIRECT FORTHY
HONEST SALIAN ARTLESS

GENUINE LIBERAL PROFUSE
SINCERE CAREFREE CAVALIER
GENEROUS OUTFRONT STRAIGHT
VIGOROUS OUTSPOKEN
FOURSQUARE OPENHEARTED
PLAINSPOKEN
FRANKENSTEIN (AUTHOR OF —)
SHELLEY
(CHARACTER IN —) HENRY ROBERT
VICTOR WALTON CLERVAL JUSTINE
WILLIAM ELIZABETH FRANKENSTEIN
FRANKFURTER DOG HOTDOG
REDHOT CORNDOG
FRANKINCENSE THUS OLIBAN
OLIBANUM
FRANKLY FREELY OPENLY PLAINLY
CANDIDLY
FRANKNESS CANDOR FREEDOM
OPENNESS
FRANKPLEDGE BORROW FRIBORG
FRANSERIA RAGWEED
FRANTIC MAD WOOD RABID
INSANE MANIAC FURIOUS LUNATIC
VIOLENT DERANGED FEVERISH
FRENETIC FRENZIED MANIACAL
FRAPPE ICE GRANITE
FRATERCULA MORMON
FRATERNAL BROTHERLY
DIZYGOTIC NONIDENTICAL
FRATERNITY FRAT FRARY HOUSE
ORDER FRATRY QUALITY SOCIETY
SODALITY
FRATERNIZE FRAT COTTON
FRAUD GYP DOLE FAKE GAFF GAUD
GULL JAPE JUNT LURK RUSE SHAM
SKIN WILE CHEAT COVIN CRAFT
DOLUS FAKER FAVEL GLAIK GUILE
HOCUS LURCH SHARK SHIFT
SHUCK SWICK SWIKE TRICK
BROGUE DECEIT FIDDLE FULLAM
HUMBUG INTAKE STUMER
WRENCH FLIVVER KNAVERY
ROGUERY STUMOUR SWINDLE
BOODLING COZENAGE IMPOSTER
OPERATOR SUBTLETY TRUMPERY
FRAUDULENT SKIN WILY CRONK
COGGED CRAFTY QUACKY
ABUSIVE CROOKED CUNNING
KNAVISH CHEATING COVINOUS
FRAUDFUL GUILEFUL QUACKISH
SINISTER SPURIOUS
FRAXINELLA DITTANY RUEWORT
FRAY FRET BROIL BROOM FEAZE
MELEE RAVEL AFFRAY BUSTLE
CHAUVE FRIDGE TIFFLE CONTEST
FRAZZLE
FRAYED WORN FLAGGY RAVELED
RAVELLY
FRAZER FINNER
FREAK FIRK FLAM WHIM FANCY
HUMOR LUSUS MAVEN MOODS
SCAPE SPORT HIPPIE MEGRIM
SPLEEN WHIMSY CAPRICE
CROTCHET ESCAPADE FLIMFLAM
WHIMWHAM MONSTROSITY
(CRAZY —S) LUNES
FREAKISH FREAKY BIZARRE
FLIGHTY MAGGOTY WHIMSIC
CRANKISH
FRECKLE CHIT EPHELIS FRECKEN
LENTIGO SUNSPOT HEATSPOT
FERNTICLE FERNTICKLE
FRECKLED FRECKLY FLECKLED

FREE LAX LET MOD RID BOLD EASE
LISS OPEN PERT REDD SHED SHUT
CLEAN CLEAR FLUID FRANK LARGE
LISSE LOOSE READY SCOUR SLAKE
SPARE UNTIE ACQUIT DEGAGE
DEVOID EXEMPT FACILE FLUENT
FREELY GRATIS IMMUNE LOOSEN
SOLUTE UNSLIP VACANT VAGILE
CLEANSE DELIVER GRIVOIS
INEXACT LASKING LIBERAL
MANUMIT RELEASE SCIOLTO
UNBOUND UNBOWED UNSLAVE
UNTWIST WELCOME WILLING
ABSOLUTE AUTARKIC BUCKSHEE
EASINESS EXPEDITE FACILITY
FREEHAND GRIVOISE INDIGENT
LAXATIVE LIBERATE UNBRIDLE
FOOTLOOSE
(— AND EASY) GLIB CAVALIER
FAMILIAR
(— BROOK OF WEEDS) RODE
(— FROM) EX REDD DEVOID
DISPATCH
(— FROM ACCUSATION) SACKLESS
(— FROM ACIDITY) DULCIFY
(— FROM AMBIGUITY) HOMELY
DECIDED
(FROM ANXIETY) CONTENT
(— FROM ARTIFICIAL) ARTLESS
(— FROM BIAS) CANDID
(— FROM CARE) EASY CARELESS
(— FROM CHARGE) FDD PURGE
FRANCO
(— FROM CONSTRAINT) CASUAL
(— FROM DEDUCTIONS) NET
(— FROM DEFECT) HAIL HALE
SOUND
(— FROM DIRT) BRIGHT
(— FROM DOUBT) RESOLVE
(— FROM DRUG ADDICTION) CLEAN
(— FROM ELECTRICAL CHARGE)
DEAD
(— FROM ERROR) LEAL SOUND
CORRECT ACCURATE
(— FROM EVIL) RESCUE
(— FROM EXTREMES) EQUABLE
(— FROM FLAWS) GOOD
(— FROM FROST) FRESH
(— FROM IMPURITIES) FINE DRESS
DEFECATE DEPURATE
(— FROM KNOTS) ENODE ENODATE
(— FROM MARKS) BLANK
(— FROM MICROORGANISMS)
ASEPTIC STERILE
(— FROM OBLIGATION) ACQUIT
EXCUSE
(— FROM PENALTY) ABSOLVE
(— FROM RESTRAINT) ABANDONED
(— FROM STONES) CHESSOM
(— FROM WHITE) SATURATE
(— OF DIFFICULTIES) AFLOAT
(— OF FAT) ENSEAM
(— OF OVERTONES) PURE
(— OF TAR) WRECK
(— ONE'S SELF) SOLVE
(— PLUNGER) ARM
(— THROW AREA) KEYHOLE
(PREF.) ELEUTHER(O) IMMUNO
LIBRO
(— FROM) DE
FREEBASE COCAINE
FREEBOARD QUICKSIDE

FREEBOOTER TORY RIDER ROVER
THIEF PIRATE RAIDER BRIGAND
CATERAN CORSAIR PINDARI
PILLAGER RAPPAREE SNAPHANCE
FREEBORN INGENUOUS
FREEDMAN LEYSING TITYRUS
(PL.) LAET
FREEDOM RUN EASE FRITH LARGE
UHURU ACCESS STREET APATHIA
BREADTH LEISURE LIBERTY
LICENCE LICENSE RELEASE
AUTONOMY FREELAGE FREENESS
IMMUNITY IMPUNITY LARGESSE
WITHGATE
(— FROM BIAS) CANDOR
(— FROM CALAMITY) WELFARE
(— FROM CONSTRAINT) ABANDON
(— FROM DANGER) SECURITY
(— FROM ERROR) ACCURACY
(— FROM GUILT) SHRIVE
(— FROM MIXTURE) PURITY
(— FROM NOISE) QUIET
(OF ACCESS) ENTREE
(— OF ACTION) SWINGE LATITUDE
(— OF MOVEMENT) RANGE
(— OF SPEECH) PARISIA
(— TO PROCEED) HEAD
(— TO RETURN) RECOURSE
(CARELESS —) ABANDON
(LIMITED —) PLAY
(PREF.) ELEUTHER(O)
FREEHOLD BARONY REALTY
FREEHOLDER SWAIN BONDER
YEOMAN FRANKLIN
FREEING LIVERY ACQUITAL
FREE LANCE ROUTIER
FREELY FREE LIEF LARGE LARGELY
READILY HEARTILY
FREEMAN BUR AIRE BARON CEORL
HAULD BONDER CITIZEN FRANKLIN
ROTURIER
(POOR —) THETE
FREEMASON FRATER MORGAN
NOACHITE
(ONE NOT A —) COWAN
FREESTONE HAZEL
(— STATE) CONNECTICUT
FREETHINKER INFIDEL SKEPTIC
AGNOSTIC
FREEZE ICE RIME CATCH CHILL
FROST CURDLE FRAPPE HARDEN
STARVE STEEVE CONGEAL
GLACIATE
FREEZING COLD FREEZY FRIGID
FROSTY GLACIAL ICECOLD
CRYONICS GELATION
(PREF.) CRY(O) KRY(O)
FREIGHT COST LOAD CARGO
GOODS ASTRAY BURDEN LADING
FRAUGHT HOTSHOT PLUNDER
PORTAGE TRUCKAGE
(— CAR) TRUCK
FREISCHUTZ, DER (CHARACTER IN
—) MAX CUNO AGATHE HERMIT
KASPAR SAMIEL AENNCHEN
(COMPOSER OF —) WEBER
FREMD FRAIM FRAMMIT
FRENCH CREOLE FRANCO GALLIC
GALLIAN GALLICAN
(— MIXED WITH ENGLISH)
FRANGLAIS
(CANADIAN —) JOUAL
(PREF.) FRANCO GALLO

FRENCH GUIANA (CAPE OF —) ORANGE
  (CAPITAL OF —) CAYENNE
  (RIVER OF —) MARONI
  (TOWN OF —) MANA KOUROU
FRENCH HONEYSUCKLE SULLA
FRENCH LAVENDER STECHADOS
FRENCH MULBERRY SOURBUSH
FRENCH NUDE ALESAN
FRENCH REPUBLIC MARIANNA MARIANNE
FRENCH SUDAN (SEE MALI)
FRENCHWOMAN GRISETTE
FRENULUM TENDON
FRENUM BRIDLE FRAENUM FRENULUM VINCULUM
FRENZIED MAD AMOK MUST RABID RAMAGE BERSERK FANATIC FRANTIC MADDING FRENETIC FURIBUND POSSESSED
FRENZY AMOK FURY GERE MOON MUST RAGE AMUCK FUROR MANIA MUSTH FURORE RAVING MADNESS OESTRUS SWIVVET DELIRIUM INSANITY
FREQUENCY HERTZ PITCH CREBRITY
FREQUENT USE BANG KEEP HAUNT HOWFF OFTEN THICK AFFECT COMMON HOURLY INFEST RESORT ENHAUNT OFTTIME CREBROUS FAMILIAR PRACTICE ACCUSTOMED
  (PREF.) SYCHNO
FREQUENTLY OFT OFTEN HOURLY UNSELDOM
FRESH GAY HOT NEW WET FLIP GOOD RACY SMUG WARM BRISK CRISP GREEN MOIST QUICK RUDDY SASSY SMART SOUND SWEET VIVID CALLER CALVER FLORID LIVELY MAIDEN REDHOT STRONG UNUSED VERNAL VIRENT VIRGIN ANOTHER NOUVEAU UNFADED VERDANT NOUVELLE ORIGINAL SPANKING YOUTHFUL
  (NOT —) PALE STALE
  (PREF.) CENO
  (SUFF.) CENE
FRESHEN PERK BRACE FRESH RENEW BREEZE CALLER REVIVE CHOUNCE PEARTEN REFRESH SWEETEN FRENCHEN
FRESHENER BRACER
FRESHET TIDE FLOOD FRESH SPATE TORNADO
FRESHMAN FOX BEJAN FROSH BEJANT GREENY PENNAL FRESHER
  (GERMAN —) PENNAL
FRESHNESS DEW SASS VERD NOVELTY VERDURE VIRIDITY ORIGINALITY
FRET DIK NAG ORP RUB RUX VEX CARK FASH FRAY FUSS GALL GNAW RAGE STEW YIRM CHAFE CRAKE CRISP FLISK GRATE PIQUE WORRY WREAK ABRADE CORSIE CRYSAL HARASS MUCKLE NETTLE PLAGUE REPINE RIPPLE RUFFLE CHRYSAL GRECQUE GRIZZLE MEANDER SCRUPLE SQUINNY ALIGREEK IRRITATE

FRETFUL CROSS GIRNY ORPIT TEATY TEENY TESTY FRETTY PENCEY SULLEN TATCHY TWISTY FRECKET PEEVISH PETTISH SPLEENY CAPTIOUS CRANKOUS FRETSOME FROPPISH PETULANT PINDLING QUERULOUS
FRETTED FRETTY MAGGED
FRETTING FRET EATING
FREY FREYR YNGVI
  (FATHER OF —) NJORD
  (SISTER OF —) FREYA
FREYA (BROTHER OF —) FREY
  (FATHER OF —) NJORD
  (HUSBAND OF —) ODIN
FRIABLE CRIMP CRISP CRUMP FLAKY FRUSH MEALY SHORT CRUMBY CRUMMY FLUFFY PUTRID CHESSOM CRUMBLY MOLDERY POWDERY RESOLUTE ROTTENLY SHATTERY
  (NOT —) SAD
FRIAR FRATE FREER MINIM MINOR BHIKKU FRATER GELONG GOSAIN LISTER BHIKSHU JACOBIN LIMITER SERVITE BREVIGER CAPUCHIN JACOBITE MINORIST MINORITE PREACHER AUGUSTINE CARMELITE CORDELIER MENDICANT BENEDICTINE
FRIARBIRD COLDONG PIMLICO MONKBIRD
FRIAR SKATE DOCTOR
FRICANDEAU GRENADINE
FRICASSEE POTPIE
FRICATIVE BUZZ HISS OPEN YOGH DURATIVE
FRICTION BUZZ DRAG HISS CHAFE WINDAGE
  (PREF.) TRIBO
  (SUFF.) TRIPSIS
FRICTIONLESS SMOOTH
FRIED FRIT SAUTE
FRIEDCAKE WONDER CRULLER FATCAKE DOUGHNUT
FRIEND AME AMI AMY BOR CAD EME PAX AMIE BHAI CHUM NABS OPPO PARD WINE AMIGA AMIGO BRICK BUDDY INGLE NETOP TROUT AIKANE BELAMY COBBER COUSIN CUMMER GOSSIP INWARD KIMMER PRINCE QUAKER ACHATES COMRADE SOCIETY COCKMATE COMPADRE DEMOPHIL FEDERATE HICKSITE INTIMADO INTIMATE TILLICUM CATERCOUSIN
  (— OF BRIDEGROOM) PARANYMPH
  (—S NOT SPEAKING) CUTS
  (BOSOM —) CONFIDANT
  (CLOSE —) PRIVY COBBER COMPADRE
  (DIVINE —) SOCIUS
  (FAMILIAR —) CRONY GREMIAL SPECIAL
  (GIRL —) DOXY DRAG DONEY DOXIE STEADY
  (INTIMATE FEMALE —) CUMMER
  (PRIVATE —) PRIVADO
  (WOMAN —) GIMMER
  (PL.) FOLK KITH SOCE FOLKS SOCIETY
FRIENDLESS FORLORN

FRIENDLINESS AMITY AFFINITY BONHOMIE GOODWILL
FRIENDLY COSH EASY GOOD HOLD HOMY KIND TOSH CADGY CHIEF COUTH GREAT HOMEY MATEY THICK AMICAL CHATTY CHUMMY FOLKSY FORTHY HOMELY KINDLY SMOOTH AFFABLE AMIABLE AMICOUS COUTHIE AMICABLE HOMELIKE INTIMATE SOCIABLE NEIGHBORLY
FRIENDSHIP PAX AMITY AMOUR
FRIEZE KELT FRISE CUSHION FALDING FRISADO FRIEZING
FRIGATE ZABRA
FRIGATE BIRD IOA IWA ALCATRAS
FRIGATE MACKEREL BONITO TASSARD
FRIGG FREA FRIJA
FRIGGA (HUSBAND OF —) ODIN
  (SON OF —) BALDER
FRIGHT COW BOOF FEAR FLEG FRAY ALARM GHAST GLIFF GLOFF PANIC SCARE AFFRAY GASTER GLIFFY SCHRIK TERROR STARTLE SWITHER FRIGHTEN GASTNESS GLIFFING
FRIGHTEN AWE COW FLY SHY SOB BAZE BREE DARE DOSS FEAR FLEG FLEY FRAY FUNK HARE HAZE SHOO AFEAR AFLEY ALARM APPAL BLUFF GALLY GHOST GLIFF HAZEN SCARE SHORE SPOOK AFFRAY ALARUM APPALL BOGGLE BOOGER COWARD FLAITE FLIGHT FRIGHT GALLEY GALLOW AFFREUX FRECKEN SCARIFY STARTLE TERRIFY AFFRIGHT MISTRYST
  (— BIRDS) KEEP
  (PREF.) TERRI TERRORI
FRIGHTENED RAD EERY FRIT GAST EERIE GHAST WINDY AFEARD AFRAID AGHAST SCARED SCAREY STURTIN GHASTFUL
  (EASILY —) TIMID SKITTISH
FRIGHTENING EERY DREAD EERIE GOURY HAIRY FRIGHTY GHASTLY SHIVERY DREADFUL FEARSOME FLEYSOME
FRIGHTFUL WAN DIRE GRIM UGLY AWFUL FERLY HORRID UGSOME AFFREUX DIREFUL FEARFUL GASHFUL GHASTLY HIDEOUS ALARMING DREADFUL ELDRITCH FEARSOME GHASTFUL HORRIBLE HORRIFIC TERRIBLE TERRIFIC
FRIGID DRY ICY COLD BLEAK FISHY ARCTIC FROSTY FROZEN WINTRY GLACIAL FREEZING SIBERIAN
FRIGIDITY GLARE
FRILL DIDO PURL JABOT RUCHE RUFFLE ARMILLA FLOUNCE SPINACH SPINAGE CHITLING CRIMPING FRILLERY FURBELOW
  (— OF HAIR) APRON
  (PL.) PUFFERY FOOFARAW FRILLERY
FRILLINESS CHICHI
FRILLING RUCHE ROUCHE SWEEPER
FRILLY CHICHI
FRINGE WLO EDGE GILL LOMA RUFF WELT BEARD THRUM BORDER

EDGING MARGIN PELMET TASSEL BULLION CREPINE EYELASH FEATHER FIMBRIA MACRAME SELVAGE TRAILER VALANCE WHISKER CILIELLA FRISETTE INDUSIUM PENUMBRA SELVEDGE TRIMMING
  (— OF TEETH) PERISTOME
  (SOFT —S) THRUM
  (PL.) ZIZITH TZITZIS TZITZIT
  (PREF.) CROSS(O) FIMBRI(O) LACINI THYSAN(O)
FRINGED JUBATE CILIATE LACINIATE
FRINGEFOOT UMA
FRINGEPOD LACEPOD
FRINGETAIL VEILTAIL
FRINGE TREE SHAVINGS
FRIPPERY FLIPPERY TRINKUMS
  (PL.) GAUDERY
FRISK COLT FISK PLAY ROLL SKIP WHID BOUND CAPER SKICE CAREER CAVORT CURVET FRISCO FROLIC TITTUP WANTON FRISCAL FRISKLE
FRISKY GAY PERT FRISK CROUSE FEISTY KIPPER LIVELY WANTON BUCKISH COLTISH JIGGISH PLAYFUL SKITTISH SPORTIVE
FRISON KNUB
FRIT FRETT CALCINE
FRITTER FOOL FRIT TEAR BOLLO DRILL WASTE BANGLE DRIVEL LOUNGE BEIGNET DRIBBLE FLITTER SLATTERN
FRIVOLITY LEVITY FRIBBLE INANITY ITEMING FUTILITY NONSENSE NUGACITY
FRIVOLOUS GAY DAFT VAIN GIDDY INANE LIGHT PETTY SILLY WASHY FLIMSY FRILLY FRIVOL FROTHY FUTILE TOYISH YEASTY FATUOUS FRIBBLE LIGHTLY NIDGETY SHALLOW TRIVIAL GIMCRACK JIMCRACK SKITTISH TRIFLING
FRIVOLOUSNESS FUTILITY
FRIZZ FRIZ CREPE FRIZE FRIZZLE FROUNCE
FRIZZED CRISPY
FRIZZLE CRAPE CREPE
FRIZZLY FUZZY CRIMPY FRIZZY
FRIZZY FUZZY CRIMPY FRIZZLY
FROCK DUD JAM GOWN JUMP SLIP SLOP WRAP LAMMY SMOCK TRUSS TUNIC CLERIC JERSEY LAMMIE MANTLE ROCHET SUKKENYE
FROCK COAT CRISPIN
FROG PAD POD KICK FROSH FROSK FROUD PADDO PADDY RANID RONCO ANURAN PEEPER TOGGLE CHARLIE CRAWLER CREEPER CROAKER CUSHION FRESHER FROGLET PADDOCK POODDOCK QUILKIN BULLFROG FERREIRO FROGGING PLATANNA REPLACER
  (— IN LOOM) HEATER
  (— OF HORSE'S HOOF) FRUSH CUSHION
  (TREE —) HYLA NOTOTREMA
  (PREF.) BATRACH(O) RANI
FROG CRAB RANININA

FROGFISH ANGLER SLIMER TOADFISH
FROGGER CHASER TRAILER ZOOGLER
FROGGY RANARIAN
FROGHOPPER HOPPER CERCOPID
FROGMOUTH MOPOKE MOREPORK PODARGUE
FROGS (AUTHOR OF —) ARISTOPHANES
(CHARACTER IN —) AEACUS CHARON BACCHUS DIONYSUS HERCULES XANTHIAS AESCHYLUS EURIPIDES
(SUFF.) BATRACH(O)(US)
FROLIC BUM GAY RIG BLOW COLT GAME GELL HAZE JINK LAKE LARK ORGY PLAY PLOY RANT REEK ROMP TEAR CAPER FREAK FRISK MERRY PRANK RANDY ROUSE SALLY SPORT SPREE BUSTER CAVORT CURVET FRATCH GAMBOL PLISKY POWWOW PRANCE ROLLIX SHINDY SPLORE VAGARY WANTON DISPORT GAMMOCK MARLOCK PLISKIE ROLLICK SCAMPER SKYLARK SPANIEL STASHIE WASSAIL CAROUSAL JAMBOREE
FROLICSOME GAY DAFT ROID ANTIC BUXOM CADGY FRISK GILPY LARKY FRISKY LIVELY WANTON ANTICAL JOCULAR LARKING LARKISH PLAYFUL WAGGISH ESPIEGLE FRISKFUL FROLICKY GAMESOME LARKSOME PRANKISH SPORTFUL SPORTIVE
FROLICSOMENESS HEYDAY
FROM A AB DE EX OF FAE FRA FRO VAN VON ASOF THROM AGAINST
(— A DISTANCE) ALOOF
(— BEGINNING TO END) THROUGH
(— ELSEWHERE) ALIUNDE
(— OFF) AFFA
(— SIDE TO SIDE) OVER CROSS ATHWART
(— THIS PLACE) HENCE
(— THIS TIME) HENCE
(PREF.) AP APH APO
FROND FERN TRESS CROSIER FRONDLET
FRONT BOW VAN BROW FACE FORE HEAD PROW THIN AFORE VAUNT BEFORE DEVANT FACADE FACING FORMER OPPOSE SECTOR VAWARD ADVANCE FORWARD FRONTAL FURTHER OBVERSE PALATAL PREFACE RESPECT SLENDER FOREHEAD FOREMOST FOREPART FORESIDE FRONTAGE
(— OF ASTROLABE) WOMBSIDE
(— OF BARN) FOREBAY
(— OF BIRD'S NECK) GUTTUR
(— OF BODY) GROUF
(— OF HEAD) VISAGE FORETOP
(— OF HELMET) VENTAIL
(— OF SHIRT) BOSOM
(— OF WATERWHEEL BUCKET) START
(— UPON) AFFRONT
(PREF.) ANTER(O) PRO
(IN —) FORE PRO(S)(SO)
(IN — OF) ANTE ANTER(O) PRAE PRE

FRONTAL PALL FRONT SINDON TABULA FRONTON METOPIC FRONTLET SUFFRONT
(ALTAR —) TABULA
FRONTIER BOUND COAST FRONT MARCH BORDER BARRIER FRONTURE OUTLYING
(FORTIFIED —) LIMES
FRONTING OBVIOUS
FRONTISPIECE FRONT UNWAN FRONTIS
FRONTLET TIARA FRONTAL CHAMFRON
FRONT PAGE (AUTHOR OF —) HECHT MACARTHUR
(CHARACTER IN —) EARL BURNS GRANT HILDY PEGGY WALTER HARTMAN JOHNSON WILLIAMS
FRONTPIECE GORE
FROST ICE COLD HOAR RIME RIND
(GROUND —) PERMA
(PREF.) CRYMO PAGO RHIGO
(HOAR —) PACHNO
FROSTED GLACE PRUINOSE
FROSTING ICING DIVINITY
FROSTWEED ROCKROSE
FROSTY ICY COLD RIMY CHILL CRISP FRORE GELID GLARY HUNCH BOREAL FRIGID FROREN CHILLING INIMICAL PRUINOUS
(NOT —) OPEN
FROTH FOB BARM FOAM HEAD REAM SCUM SUDS WORK CREAM SPUME YEAST FLOWER FREATH LATHER SPURGE
FROTHER CREOSOTE
FROTHING HUMMING MANTLING
FROTHY BARMY FOAMY LIGHT REAMY SPEWY SPUMY SUDSY FLASHY YEASTY SPUMOSE SPUMOUS WHIPPED SPUMANTE
FROWARD RANK CROSS AWKWARD PEEVISH WAYWARD CONTRARY FROPPISH PERVERSE PETULANT PROTERVE SHREWISH UNTOWARD
FROWN GLUM LOUR GLOOM GLOUT GLUMP LOWER SCOWL GLOWER GLUNCH FROUNCE FRONTLET
FROWNING GLUM GLUNCH
FROWZY BLOUSY BLOWSY BLOWZY RAFFISH FROWZLED SCABROUS SLOVENLY
FROZEN FAST FIXED FRORE FRORY GELID GLARY FRAPPE FROREN GLACIAL
FRUCTIFICATION CONK AECIDIUM BASIDIUM APOTHECIUM
FRUCTOSE ACROSE
FRUGAL EASY MILD CANNY CHARY ROMAN SCANT SPARE MEAGER SAVING SCANTY SCARCE SCOTCH SKIMPY CAREFUL PRUDENT SCRIMPY SLENDER SPARING THRIFTY PROVIDENT PARSIMONIOUS
FRUGALITY SPARE THRIFT ECONOMY PARCITY MANAGERY
FRUGALLY HARD CHARILY SAVINGLY
FRUIT BEL FIG HAW UVA AKEE ATTA BAEL BITO COYO DATE DIKA DROP GEAN JACK LIME NOOP PEAR

PLUM POME SEED SLOE SNAP SORB AKENE ANISE APPLE BERRY CLING COUMA DRUPE GENIP GOURD GRAPE GUAVA HAZEL ILAMA LEMON LIMON MANGO MELON OLIVE PAPAW PEACH RIPER SORVA TRYMA ACHENE ACINUS ALMOND BANANA BUTTON CEDRON CEREZA CHERRY CITRON CITRUS COBNUT COCHAL COCONA DAMSON DURIAN EMBLIC EMBOLO GUARRI JUJUBE KEEPER LEGUME LONGAN LOQUAT MAMMEE MARANG MAYPOP MUYUSA NARRAS ORANGE PAPAYA PAWPAW PELLAS POMATO RESULT SAPOTA SQUASH UVALHA WAMPEE WESTME ZAPOTE APRICOT ATEMOYA AVOCADO AZAROLE BILIMBI BLOATER CARAWAY CHAYOTE CHECKER CIRUELA COCONUT CURRANT DESSERT GEEBUNG GENIPAP GHERKIN KUMQUAT MURCOTT PIGFACE PRODUCT RIPENER SERVICE SHALLON SOROSIS SOURSOP TANGELO ACHENIUM BAYBERRY BELLERIC BILBERRY CALABASH CANISTEL CAPSICUM CARDAMUM CITRANGE COCOPLUM CUCUMBER DEWBERRY DOGBERRY EGGFRUIT FOLLICLE FRUITAGE FRUITERY FRUITLET GOLKAKRA INKBERRY LIMEQUAT OSOBERRY PIEPRINT PODOCARP RAMBUTAN SEBESTEN SEEDBALL SHADDOCK SWEETSOP SYCONIUM CARYOPSIS CHERIMOYA NECTARINE PINEAPPLE SAPODILLA TAMARILLO CHERIMOYER CLEMENTINE MANGOSTEEN
(— LIKE APPLE) MEDLAR
(— OF CACTUS) SABRA
(— OF CAPER) CAPOT
(— OF CITRON) ETROG ETHROG
(— OF HEMLOCK) CONIUM
(— OF OAK) ACORN
(— OF PALM) SALAK PUPUNHA
(— OF ROSE) HEP HIP BUTTON
(— ON TREES) HANG
(—S COOKED IN SYRUP) COMPOTE
(AGGREGATE —) ETAERIO DRUPETUM HETAERIO
(ASTRINGENT —) GAB GAUB CHEBULE
(AVOCADO-LIKE —) ANAY
(CANDIED —) CONSERVE
(CARMINATIVE —) BADIAN
(COILED —) STROMBUS
(COLLECTIVE —) SYNCARP
(COMPOUND —) SYNCARP
(DRIED —) PASA CUBEB MUMMY SABAL OREJON CAPSULE EMBELIA
(EARLY —) PRIMEUR HASTINGS
(FALLEN —) SHEDDER WINDFALL
(FIRST —S) ANNATES BIKKURIM PRIMICES
(FLESHY —) SYCONIUM SARCOCARP
(FUZZY —) KIWI
(GOURD —) PEPO

(GRAPEFRUIT-LIKE —) SUHA
(GRAPELIKE —) WAMPEE
(HAWTHORN —) PEGGLE
(IMPERFECT —) SPECH NUBBIN
(MASHED —) FOOL
(MEDICINAL —) DRUPE AIWAIN AJOWAN EMBELIA
(ONE-SEEDED —) AKENE ACHENE
(PALMYRA —) PUNATOO
(PLUMLIKE —) CARISSA CIRUELA
(PRESERVED —) SUCCADE CONFITURE
(PRICKLY —) HEDGEHOG
(SELF-FERTILIZED —) AUTOCARP
(SLICED DRIED —) SNITS SNITZ SCHNITZ
(SPURGE —) TAMPOE
(SUPERIOR —) TOPPER
(UNRIPE OAK —) CAMATA
(WINGED —) SAMARA
(WOODY —) XYLOCARP
(PREF.) CARP(O) FRUCTI FRUGI
(BEAK-LIKE —) RYNCO
(SUFF.) CARP(OUS)(US)(Y)
FRUIT BAT KALONG
FRUIT-BEARING FERTILE
FRUIT DOVE KUKU
FRUITFUL FAT FOODY BATTEL FECUND FRUITY GRAVID FERTILE TEEMFUL UBEROUS ABUNDANT CHILDING FRUITIVE PREGNANT PROLIFIC PLENTEOUS
FRUITFULNESS UBERTY FATNESS
FRUITGROWER FRUITIST
FRUITLESS DRY GELD VAIN ADDLE BARREN FUTILE STERILE USELESS ABORTIVE BOOTLESS
FRUIT PIGEON KUKU LUPE KUKUPA MANUMA MANUTAGI
FRUIT ROT BLET
FRUIT STONE COB PYRENE PUTAMEN
(PREF.) PYREN(O)
FRUMP JUDY
FRUSTRATE BALK BEAT BILK CRAB DASH DISH FOIL LAME BAULK BLANK BLOCK CHECK CROSS ELUDE SMEAR THRAW WRECK BAFFLE BLIGHT BUGGER DEFEAT DELUDE DERAIL KIBOSH OUTWIT SCOTCH THWART ANIENTE DECEIVE FALSIFY PREVENT CONFOUND INFRINGE STULTIFY
FRUSTRATED DISHED MANQUE
FRUSTRATER MARPLOT
FRUSTRATING BOOTLESS
FRUSTRATION FOIL SUCK DEFEAT FIASCO
FRUSTRUM GUTTA
FRUSTULE TESTULE HYPOTHECA
FRY SILE BROOD FRIZZ KRILL SAUTE FRIZZLE GREYFISH
(HANGTOWN —) OMELET
(KIND OF —) HANGTOWN
FRYER FRIER FRIZZER SPRINGER
FRYING PAN FRYPAN SPIDER CREEPER SKILLET
FUCHSIA CORREA KONINI FUCHSIN EARDROPS
FUCHSIN ROSEINE SOLFERINO
FUCHSINE RUBIN RUBINE MAGENTA ROSANILINE

FUDDLE FUZZLE FLUSTER
FUDDLED FAP REE DOPY BOSKY
DOPEY SWASH TIPSY WOOZY
MAUDLIN TOSTICATED
(— WITH MALT LIQUOR) SWIPEY
FUDGE HUNCH SNUDGE PENUCHE
DIVINITY
FUEL GAS OIL POB COAL COKE FIRE
PEAT UPLA ARGOL AVGAS ACETOL
BUNKER ELDING FIRING NAPALM
SHRUFF TIMBER COALITE
GASOHOL PABULUM SYNTHOL
FIREBOOT FIREBOTE GASOGENE
GAZOGENE TRIPTANE
(GAS —) ETHANE
(JELLED —) NAPALM
(ROCKET —) BORANE HYDYNE
FUGITIVE HOT FLEME FLYER FUGIE
SCAMP OUTLAW FLEEING
LAMSTER REFUGEE RUNAWAY
FLEETING RUNAGATE UNSTABLE
(PL.) MANZAS
FUGUE FUGA RICERCAR
(— THEME) DUX
(PART OF —) STRETTA
FULA PEUL PEUHL FELLANI FELLATA
FULANI PEUL PEUHL
FULCRUM BAIT GLUT
(— FOR OAR) ROWLOCK
FULFILL FILL FULL KEEP MEET
HONOR ANSWER COMPLY FULFIL
REDEEM ACHIEVE PERFORM
SATISFY COMPLETE COMPLISH
ACCOMPLISH
(— A TERM) EXPIRE
FULFILLMENT PASS EFFECT
FUNCTION PERFORMANCE
(— OF GOD'S WILL) KINGDOM
(IMAGINARY —) FANTASY
FULGURATION BLICK
FULL BAD BIG FAT FOW COOL DEEP
FAIR GOOD JUST PANG RANK TRIG
TUCK AMPLE AWASH BROAD
CLEAR FLUSH LARGE LUCKY PIENO
PLAIN PLENY ROUND SATED SOLID
TIGHT TOTAL WHOLE ENTIRE
GOGGLE HONEST STRONG BAPTIZE
BRIMFUL COPIOUS DESTROY
DIFFUSE FULFILL FULSOME
LIBERAL OROTUND PERFORM
PLENARY REPLETE TEEMING
TRAMPLE WEALTHY ABSOLUTE
ADEQUATE BOUFFANT BRIMMING
CHOCKFUL COMPLETE EXTENDED
FREQUENT PREGNANT RESONANT
THOROUGH
(— CLOTH OR YARN) WALK
(— OF AIR) LIGHT
(— OF BLANKS) LACUNOSE
(— OF CHINKS) RIMOSE
(— OF DELAY) MOROSE
(— OF DEVILTRY) HEMPY HEMPIE
(— OF DIRT) FOUL
(— OF EGGS) GRAVID
(— OF ENERGY) STOUT SWANK
(— OF ENTHUSIASM) RARING
(— OF ERRORS) FOUL
(— OF FLAWS) CRAZY
(— OF FUN) FROLIC
(— OF HAPPINESS) SUNSHINY
(— OF INTEREST) AGOG
(— OF IRON) SIDEROSE

(— OF LIFE) SPUNKY ANIMATE
(— OF LOOPS) KINKY
(— OF MATTER FOR THOUGHT)
MEATY
(— OF PROMISE) PREGNANT
(— OF RUSHES) SPRITTY
(— OF SAND) ARENOSE
(— OF SLEEP) SOPOROSE
(— OF SMALL OPENINGS) POROUS
(— OF SPIRIT) GENEROUS
(— OF VIGOR) FLUSH GREEN LUSTY
ANIMATED SPIRITED
(— OF ZEST) RACY
(NOT —) SCANT
(VERY —) SKELPING
(PREF.) PLENI PLERO
(SUFF.) (— OF) IOUS OSE OUS
FULL-BLOODED PLETHORIC
FULL-BLOWN JUICY
FULLBODIED FAT LOFTY HEARTY
ROBUST
FULL-BOSOMED BUXOM
FULLER GAG HARDY HARDIE
ROLLER TUCKER WALKER
BLOCKER CREASER THICKER
CLOTHIER
FULL-FACED AFFRONTE AFFRONTY
FULL-FLAVORED BOLD RACY
FULL-FLEDGED ALLOUT ENTIRE
SUMMED
FULL-GROWN ADULT RIPE GROWN
MATURE SEEDED
FULL-LENGTH UNCUT
FULLLNESS (— OF TONE) VOLUME
FULLNESS BODY FLAIR FLARE
FULTH PLENUM FULNESS
PLEROMA SATIETY
FULL-SOUNDING ROUND
SONOROUS
FULLY ALL DOWN EVEN INLY WELL
AMPLY LARGE ENOUGH FAIRLY
THRICE WHOLLY CLEARLY
LARGELY UTTERLY CLEVERLY
ENTIRELY INWARDLY MATURELY
FULMAR HAG NELLY NODDY
HAGDON NELLIE MALDUCK
MALMOCK STINKER MALLEMUCK
FULMINATE BLOW RAIL FULMINE
FULSOME FAT SUAVE FOULSOME
FUMARIC BOLETIC LICHENIC
FUMAROLE HORNITO
FUMBLE BOOT DROP MUFF MULL
PIRL BOBBLE BOGGLE FAFFLE
MUMBLE PRODDLE MISFIELD
THRUMBLE
FUMBLER STUMER BUNGLER
STUMOUR
FUMBLING HALTING
FUME FUFF RAGE REEK STEW
EWDER SMOKE STIFE STORM
VAPOR SEETHE SNUFFLE
FUMIGATE
(— A CASK) STUM
FUMID SMOKY SMOKEY
FUMIGATE SMEEK SMOKE PASTIL
CYANIDE PASTILLE
FUMIGATION GASSING
FUMIGATOR AERATOR
FUMITORY FUMARIA FUMEROOT
FUMEWORT
FUN GIG GAME GELL JEST JOKE
LAKE PLAY BORAK BOURD HUMOR
KICKS MIRTH MUSIC SPORT

FROLIC GAIETY GAYETY DAFFERY
DAFFING GAMMOCK WHOOPEE
(MAKE — OF) JAPE RIDE
(UNRESTRAINED —) HELL
FUNCTION ACT JOB MAP RUN USE
DUTY FORM ROLE WORK POWER
ACTION AGENCY MATRIX MISTER
OFFICE SQUASH CONCEPT
FACULTY ISOLATE MAPPING
OPERATE PERFORM SERVICE
WORKING ACTIVITY BUSINESS
MINISTRY PROVINCE
(— EFFECTIVELY) AVAIL
(—S OF JUDGES) ERMINE
(APPARENT —) STUDY
(CHEMICAL —) PARACHOR
(CLERICAL —) DIET
(ECCLESIASTICAL —) DIET
(ESSENTIAL —) DHARMA
(LAVISH —) WINGDING
(MATHEMATICAL —) DEL FORM
METRIC INVERSE QUARTIC
(SPECIAL —) CEREMONY
(USEFUL —) PURPOSE
(WORD —) DEIXIS
(SUFF.) CY URE
FUNCTIONAL DYNAMIC
FUNCTIONARY BEADLE FLUNKY
CAPTAIN FLUNKEY CHAPRASI
FUNCTIONING ALIVE AFLOAT
FUNCTIONLESS OTIOSE
FUND BOX BANK FOND MASS
CHEST KITTY MOUNT SLUSH
STOCK STORE ESCROW CHALUKA
JACKPOT RESERVE HALUKKAH
PECULIUM
(COMMON —) POT POOL
(POLITICAL —S) BARREL
(RESERVE —) REST
(PL.) CAJA PURSE COFFER
FUNDAMENT NOCK TAIL BOTTOM
FUNDUS
FUNDAMENTAL NET BASE BASAL
BASIC KLANG PRIME VITAL
BOTTOM PRIMAL SIMPLE BASILAR
BEDROCK ORGANIC PRIMARY
RADICAL ABSOLUTE CARDINAL
ORIGINAL RUDIMENT SUBSTRAT
ULTIMATE PRIMORDIAL
RUDIMENTARY
(PL.) ABCS NITTYGRITTY
FUNDAMENTALLY AUFOND
FUNDUS FORNIX
FUNERAL TANGI BURIAL EXEQUY
BURYING CORTEGE FUNEBRE
FUNERARY MORTUARY
FUNERAL DIRECTOR BLACKMAN
FUNEREAL BLACK FERAL DISMAL
SOLEMN FUNEBRE FUNERAL
DIRGEFUL EXEQUIAL MOURNFUL
SEPULCHRAL
FUNGI MYCOFLORA
FUNGICIDE MANEB NABAM ZINEB
CAPTAN FERBAM CALOMEL
BORDEAUX DICHLONE
FUNGOID MYCOID FUNGOUS
FUNGOSO (FATHER OF —) SORDIDO
FUNGUS BUNT MOLD SMUT BLACK
BRAND ERGOT FUNGE HYPHO
MOREL MOULD PHOMA SPUNK
SWARD TRUFF VALSA VERPI
AGARIC BOLETE FUNGAL MILDEW
OIDIUM AMANITA BOLETUS

CHYTRID FUNGOID GEASTER
LEPIOTA TRUFFLE AECIDIUM
CLATHRUS CORNBELL EUMYCETE
FUSARIUM HELVELLA MUCEDINE
MUSHROOM OOMYCETE
OTOMYCES PHALLOID POLYPORE
PUFFBALL RHIZOPUS SAPROGEN
SPOROGEN TREMELLA TUCKAHOE
STINKHORN NEUROSPORA
PENICILLIUM
(KIND OF —) PORE
(PLANT —) UREDO
(UNICELLULAR —) BEES EAST
YEAST
(PREF.) AGARICI BASIDIO HYDNO
MYC(ET)(ETO)(O)
(SUFF.) MYCES MYCET(O)
MYCETE(S) MYCOSIS
(— DISEASE) OSIS
FUNK FUNG NESH
FUNKY HIP FOUL PANICKY
FUNNEL CAST STACK TEWEL TRUNK
FILLER FUMMEL HOPPER SIPHON
SYPHON TUNNEL TUNNER
TRUMPET TUNDISH HYPONOME
WINDSAIL
(UNDERGROUND —) SWALLET
SWALLOW
(PREF.) CHOAN(O)
(SUFF.) CHOANITE CHOANITIC
FUNNY ODD GOOD COMIC DROLL
MERRY QUEER COMICAL JOCULAR
RISIBLE STRANGE HUMOROUS
(VERY —) SPLITTING SIDESPLITTING
FUR FOX BEAR CALF COON FLIX
FLUE FOIN GRAY GREY GRIS MINK
PEAN PELF PELL PILE SEAL VAIR
BUDGE COYPU CROSS FITCH FLICK
GENET GRISE OTTER PAHMI SABLE
SCARF SHUBA BADGER BEAVER
COUGAR DESMAN ERMINE FISHER
GALYAC JACKET MARTIN NUTRIA
PELAGE POTENT RABBIT SPRING
SUSLIK TANUKI CALABER CARACAL
FITCHET FITCHEW FURRURE
MINIVER TOPCOAT CACOMIXL
ERMINOIS KOLINSKI
(— OF LAMBSKIN AND WOOL)
BUDGE
(— OF SABLE) ZIBELINE
(— RESEMBLING PERSIAN LAMB)
KRIMMER
(BEAVER —) WOOM CASTOR
(GRAY —) GRAY GREY GRIS GRISE
CRIMMER LETTICE
(HERALDIC —) PEAN
(LAMB —) CARACUL KARAKUL
(NUMBER OF — SKINS) TIMBER
TIMMER
(RABBIT —) CONY SCUT CONEY
FLICK LAPIN HATTER SUSLIK
SEALINE SOUSLIK ERMILINE
(SQUIRREL —) SISEL CALABAR
(SQUIRREL OR MARTIN —) AMICE
POPEL
(STONE MARTEN'S —) FOIN
(PL.) PELTRY FURRIERY
(PREF.) DORA
FURBEARER PLATINUM
FURBELOW DIDO FRILL FALBALA
FURBISH DO FIG RUB FAKE FINE
VAMP CLEAN SCOUR FINIFY

POLISH BURNISH VARNISH RENOVATE

FURCATE FORKY BRANCH FURCAL

FURCULA SPRING FURCULUM

FURCULUM WISHBONE

FURFOOZ GRENELLE

FURIES DIRAE ALECTO ERINYS ERINYES MEGAERA ERINNYES TISIPHONE

FURIOUS MAD GRIM WOOD YOND ANGRY BRAIN GIDDY IRATE LIVID RABID SHARP FIERCE FURIAL FURIED INSANE RENISH STORMY ACHARNE FRANTIC HOPPING MADDING MANKIND PELTING RAGEOUS REDWOOD RUSHING TEARING VIOLENT FRENZIED MAENADIC TOWERING VEHEMENT VESUVIAN WRATHFUL

FURIOUSLY CRAZY ANGERLY TEARING

FURL FOLD HAND ROLL STOW WRAP FRESE TRUSS FARDEL FURDLE TAKEIN

FURLED IN

FURLONG SHOT STADE

FURLOUGH LEAVE BLIGHTY

FURNACE ARC KILN OVEN TANK BENCH CUPEL DRIER DRYER FORGE MOUTH TISAR BURNER CALCAR COCKLE CUPOLA HEATER ATHANOR CHAFERY CRESSET FIREPOT PUDDLER ROASTER BESSEMER BLOOMERY CALCINER CHAUFFER FIREWORK IRONCLAD LIMEKILN PRODUCER REFINERY TRYWORKS

(**— DOOR)** TWEEL

(**ALMOND —)** ALMAN

(**ARC —)** HEROULT

(**GLASS-HEATING —)** TISAR

(**PLUMBER'S —)** DEVIL

(**PORTABLE —)** DANDY CRESSET

FURNACEMAN BUSTLER DROSSER SMELTER IMPROVER REHEATER

FURNISH ARM SOW DECK FEAT FEED FILL FRET FRUB GIVE LEND TRIM VEST ARRAY BESEE ENDOW EQUIP FRAME INDUE PITCH POINT SERVE SPEED STOCK STORE STUFF

AFFORD GRAITH INSURE INVEST OUTFIT RENDER SUPPLY ADVANCE APPAREL APPOINT BRACKET GARNISH INSTORE PERFORM PLENISH PRESENT PRODUCE PROVIDE SUFFICE ACCOUTER DECORATE FRUBBISH MINISTER ACCOMMODATE

(**— ABUNDANTLY)** FREQUENT

(**— ANALYSIS)** ACCOUNT

(**— FULLY)** CHARGE

(**— REFRESHMENT)** EASE

(**— WITH)** BESEE

(**— WITH DRINK)** BIRL BYRL

(**— WITH MEALS)** BOARD

(**— WITH NEW PARTS)** RETROFIT

(**— WITH POWER)** QUALIFY

(**— WITH STEEP SLOPE)** ESCARP

(**— WITH STRENGTH)** MAN

(**— WITH TROOPS)** GARRISON

(**— WITH WINGS)** IMP

FURNISHED ARMED BODEN GARNI

(**COMFORTABLY —)** BEIN

FURNISHING ADVANCE FITMENT

(**PL.)** STUFF BAGGAGE PENATES

FURNITURE ADAM BUHL TIRE SAMAN STOOL STUFF GRAITH FITMENT INSIGHT MEUBLES MOVABLE EQUIPAGE ORNAMENT SUPELLEX TACKLING

(**— PIECE)** ETAGERE

(**CHEAP —)** BORAX

(**SHIP'S —)** HARNESS

(**STORED —)** LUMBER

(**STYLE OF —)** SHERATON

FURORE FUROR BROUHAHA

FURRED PURED LOADED

FURRING PACKING

FURROW FUR GAP GAW RIB RUT FURR GRIP HINT LINE PLOW RAIN RILL ROUT RUCK SEAM SULK CHASE DRAIN DRILL EARTH FIELD RIGOL SCORE SEUGH STRIA GROOVE GUTTER INDENT SULCUS SUTURE TRENCH BREAKER CHAMFER CHANNEL CRUMPLE FEERING PLOWING QUILLET SCRATCH WINDROW WRINKLE CARRIAGE NOTAULIX THOROUGH VALLECULA

(**PREF.)** AULAC(O) HOLC(O) LIRELLI SULCI SULCO

FURROWED SEAMED EXARATE FURROWY SULCATE TRENCHED

FURROWING KNOT DRESS

FURRY SHAGGY

FUR SEAL URSAL

FURTHER MO AID YET ALSO HELP YOND ADDED AGAIN FRESH SPEED SUPRA BEYOND EXTEND SECOND ADVANCE DEVELOP FARTHER FORWARD PROMOTE MOREOVER REMANENT ULTERIOR

FURTHERMORE BESIDES FURTHER OVERMORE

FURTIVE SLY PRIVY CLAMMY SECRET SHIFTY SNEAKY HANGDOG MEACHING MYSTICAL SNEAKING STEALTHY THIEVISH CLANDESTINE

FURTIVELY SLILY SLYLY SIDELINS

FURTIVENESS STEALTH

FURUNCLE BOIL

FURY HAG IRE MAD WAX BURN RAGE ANGER BRETH DREAD FUROR IRISH RIGOR WRATH ALECTO BELDAM CHOLER FRENZY FURORE MADNESS MEGAERA WIDDRIM DELIRIUM FEROCITY VIOLENCE WOODNESS TISIPHONE

FURZE FUN FUZZ LING ULEX WHIN GORSE WHINCOW

FUSE RUN CAKE FLOW FLUX FRIT FUZE MELT WELD BLEND FOUND FUSEE FUZEE QUILL SMELT SQUIB SWAGE TRAIN UNITE MINGLE SPITTER COALESCE CONCRETE CONFLATE COPULATE PORTFIRE SAUCISSE COLLIQUATE

FUSED CONNATE

FUSEE FUZEE SPINDLE VESUVIAN VESUVIUS

FUSELAGE BODY

(**— MEMBER)** LONGERON

FUSIFORM FUSATE SPINDLE

FUSIL (DIVIDED INTO —S) PLUMETE

FUSION ZYG FLUX UNION FUSURE CHIASMA FLUXION CYTOGAMY MITAPSIS PLASMOGAMY

(**PREF.)** ZYG(O)(OTO)

(**SUFF.)** APSIS

FUSS DO ADO ROW TEW COIL FAFF FIKE FIRK FIZZ FRET ROUT SONG STIR TIME TODO TOUSE TOWSE TRADE WHAUP BOTHER CADDLE DIRDUM FANTAD FETTLE FISSLE FISTLE FIZZLE FRAISE FUFFLE FUSTLE HOORAY HURRAH PHRASE POTHER RACKET SETOUT STROTH TURNUP FOOSTER FRIGGLE FUSSIFY NAUNTLE POOTHER SPUFFLE SPUTTER TAMASHA BUSINESS FOOFARAW SCRONACH

FUSSBUDGET PRIG

FUSSBUDGETY CROFTISH

FUSSINESS DAINTY FADDLE FIKERY FOOSTER

FUSSING BOTHER

FUSSY BUSY FIKY FIXY DITSY DITZY FUDGY PICKY CHICHI FIDDLY FIDFAD PROSSY SPOFFY SPRUCE STICKY FIDGETY NIGGLING NOTIONAL SPOFFISH SQUEAMISH PERSNICKETY

FUSTET ZANTE FUSTIC

FUSTIAN RANT HOLMES PILLOW BOMBAST TWADDLE CORDUROY MOLESKIN

FUSTIC LIME MORA FUSTET DYEWOOD AMARILLO

FUSTINESS FOIST FROWST

FUSTY FOIST MOLDY MUSTY FOISTY RANCID FROWSTY MALODOROUS

FUTILE IDLE TOOM VAIN OTIOSE USELESS BOOTLESS FECKLESS FOOTLESS FUTILOUS HELPLESS NUGATORY

FUTILITY VANITY NUGACITY VAINESSE

FUTTAH WHATA

FUTURE TOBE LATER SKULD AVENIR COMING ONWARD OPTION TOCOME TOWARD L AVENIR FUTURITY ONCOMING

(**— TIME)** MANANA

FUZZ LINTERS

FUZZY LINTY LOUSY MUZZY WOOLY WOOLLY

FYTTE PASSUS

G

G GEE GOLF GEORGE
GA AKRA ACCRA INKRA
GAAL (FATHER OF —) EBED
GAB GOB YAP BLAB CHIN CHINFEST
GABBLE WAB CANK CHAT CONK
JAVER BABBLE GAGGLE HABBLE
PATTER RABBLE TATTER
YABBLE CLATTER JAUNDER
TWADDLE TWITTER SLIPSLOP
SLUMMOCK
GABBRO BOJITE NORITE EUCRITE
GABION KISH KEESH BASKET
WALING CORBEIL
GABLE GAVEL GOFOL DETAIL
DORMER GABLET KENNEL
MEMBER PINION AILERON
PEDIMENT
GABON (CAPITAL OF —) LIBREVILLE
(LAKE OF —) ANENGUE AZINGUO
(MOUNTAIN OF —) MPELE
IBOUNDJI
(NATIVE OF —) FANG ADOUMA
ECHIRA OKANDE
(RIVER OF —) ABANGA IVINDA
OGOOUE NGOUNIE
(TOWN OF —) OYEM BONGO
KANGO MITZIC OMVANE MAKOKOU
GABOON OKOUME
GABRIELINO TOBIKHAR
GAD GAR RUN FISK GAUD JAZZ
RAKE JINKET GADLING TRAIPSE
VIRETOT
(— ABOUT) HAIK ROLL STRAM
GALLANT TROLLOP
(BROTHER OF —) ASHER
(FATHER OF —) JACOB
(MOTHER OF —) ZILPAH
GADABOUT GAD GOER GADDER
TRAIPSE
GADDI (FATHER OF —) SUSI
GADFLY GAD CLEG GLEG BRIZE
CLEGG STOUT WHAME BOTFLY
BREEZE GADBEE OESTRID
TABANID HORSEFLY
(PREF.) ESTRA ESTRI ESTRO
OESTR(I)
GADGET DODAD GISMO GIZMO
HICKY DINGUS DOODAD GILGUY
HICKEY JIGGER JIMJAM WIDGET
CONCERN DOFUNNY GIMMICK
WHATNOT BUSINESS DOHICKEY
GIMCRACK JIMCRACK
HOOTNANNY CONTRAPTION
THINGAMAJIG WHANGDOODLE
(PL.) GIBBLES GUBBINS GADGETRY
GADI (SON OF —) MENAHEM
GADUS MORRHUA
GADWALL RODGE VOLANT
GADWELL REDWING SHUTTLE
GAEL CELT KELT SCOT GOIDEL
GAEDHEAL
GAELIC ERSE IRISH
GAFF CLIP SPAR SPUR YARD GAFFLE

GABLOCK GAFFLET SLASHER
GAVELOCK
(— MACKEREL) GAMBEER
GAFFE SLIP
GAFFER STAGEHAND
GAG YAK YUK BOFF GEGG JOKE
PONG SCOB YOCK YUCK HEAVE
KEVEL SCOBE AGUAJI MUZZLE
WHEEZE
(KIND OF —) SIGHT
GAGA (GO —) FLIP
GAGARIN YURI
GAGE (ALSO SEE GAUGE) LAY PAWN
WAGE GAUGE JEDGE NORMA
WAGER FEELER PLEDGE SPIDER
SCANTLE STANDARD UDOMETER
GAHAM (FATHER OF —) NAHOR
(MOTHER OF —) REUMAH
GAHERIS (MOTHER OF —)
MORGANSE
GAIETY JOY GALA JEST RANT
CHEER MIRTH BAWDRY FROLIC
GAYETY LEVITY BAUDERY BEGONIA
DAFFERY DAFFING GAYNESS
JOLLITY JOYANCE ROLLICK
BUOYANCY FESTIVAL HILARITY
VIVACITY
(NOISY —) RACKET
GAILY GAY GAYLY BRAVELY LIGHTLY
GAIN BAG DAP GET NET POT WIN
BEAR BOOT DRAW GROW HAVE
LAND MAKE PELF SACK TILL
ADDLE BOOTY CATCH LATCH
LUCRE REACH SCORE ARRIVE
ATTAIN CHIEVE DERIVE GATHER
INCOME OBTAIN PROFIT RACKUP
STRAIN CAPTURE CONQUER
EMBRACE GAYMENT GETTING
HARVEST POSSESS PROCURE
REALIZE VANTAGE WINNING
CLEANING CONQUEST PURCHASE
PERQUISITE
(— ADMISSION) ENTER
(— ADVANTAGE) GLEEK
(— ASCENDANCY) PREVAIL
(— BY EXTORTION) SQUEEZE
(— BY FORTUNE) DRAW HAZARD
(— COMMAND OF) MASTER
(— IN FAVOR) PROPITIATE
(— KNOWLEDGE) EDIFY LEARN
(— OVER) ENGAGE
(— UNDERSTANDING) SMOKE
(— WITHOUT DEDUCTION) CLEAR
(DISHONEST —) MEED
(ESTIMATED —) ESTEEM
(ILL-GOTTEN —) PELF BOODLE
(ILLICIT —) SPLOSH
(MATERIAL —) PUDDING
(UNEXPECTED —) BUNCE
(PL.) PICKING PLUNDER
GANANCIAS
GAINFUL LUCROUS GAINSOME
GAINSAY DENY FORBID IMPUGN

OPPOSE REFUTE RESIST DISPUTE
RECLAIM WITHSAY AGAINSAY
CONTRAVENE
GAIT BAT JOG GANG LOPE PACE
RACK SKIP STEP TROT VOLT WALK
AMBLE AUBIN GOING STALK TRAIN
ALLURE CANTER GALLOP LOUNGE
SLOUCH SWINGE TODDLE
WADDLE WALLOW WAMBLE
WOBBLE DOGTROT HICKORY
PIAFFER SAUNTER SCUTTLE
SHAMBLE SHUFFLE WALKING
WAUCHLE
(— OF ILL-BROKEN HORSE) CHACK
(DEFECTIVE —) WINDING
(LIMPING —) HIRPLE
(UNGAINLY —) SLOUCH
(UNSTEADY —) STAGGER
(4-BEAT —) AMBLE
GAITER SPAT VAMP STRAD BONNET
BRAGAS COCKER GASKIN GUETRE
HOGGER HUGGER LEGGIN PUTTEE
GAMBADE GAMBADO LEGGING
STARTUP BOOTIKIN CUTTIKIN
SPATTERDASH
(PL.) UPPERS GASKINS GAMASHES
GRAMOCHES
GAIZE MALMSTONE
GAJO GORGIO
GALABIA ROBE
GALACTITE MILKSTONE
GALACTOSIDE IDEIN IDAEIN
GALAGO LEMUR LEMUROID
GALAHAD (MOTHER OF —) ELAINE
GALAL (FATHER OF —) ASAPH
JEDUTHUN
GALANAS GAINES
GALAOR (BROTHER OF —) AMADIS
GALATEA (DAUGHTER OF —)
LEUCIPPUS
(FATHER OF —) NEREUS
(HUSBAND OF —) PYGMALION
(LOVER OF —) ACIS
(MOTHER OF —) DORIS
(SON OF —) PAPHUS METHARME
GALAX COLTSFOOT
GALAXY NEBULA SPIRAL
(KIND OF —) SEYFERT
(PREF.) GALACT(O)
GALBANUM FERULA GALBAN
ALBETAD
GALCHA PAMIR
GALE BLOW GELL HELM WIND
GAGEL PERRY STOUR BUSTER
EASTER BAYBUSH BURSTER
GALEAGE TEMPEST FLEAWOOD
GALEWORT NORWESTER
(KIND OF —) NEAR
GALEA MITRA HELMET
GALGA INGUSH
GALIBI CARIBI KALINA
GALINGALE CYPRESS WANHORN
CHINAROOT

GALIPOT BARRAS GALLIPOT
TACAMAHAC
GALJOEN BLACKFISH
GALL GA GAW BAIT FELL FRET
NERVE WRING ANBURY COCKLE
HARASS HUTZPA ANBERRY
BEDEGAR CHUTZPA GALLNUT
HUTZPAH KNOPPER NUTGALL
BEDEGUAR CECIDIUM CHUTZPAH
FLEASEED IRRITATE OAKBERRY
SEEDGALL SPURGALL TACAHOUT
(SAND —) SALT NATRON SANDIVER
(PL.) PURPLES
(PREF.) CHOL(E)(O)
(SUFF.) CHOLIA CHOLY
GALLANT GAY BEAU PROW BLADE
BRAVE BULLY CIVIL JOLLY LOVER
NOBLE PREUX SHOWY SPARK
SWAIN DONZEL ESCORT HEROIC
POLITE RUTTER SPARKY SQUIRE
SUITOR AMATORY AMORIST
AMOROSO AMOROUS CONDUCT
GALANTE GREGORY SPARKER
STATELY TOPPING YOUNKER
BELAMOUR CAVALIER CICISBEO
FEMALIST GALLIARD HANDSOME
POLISHED
GALLANTRY GAME DRURY DRUERY
BRAVERY COURAGE PROWESS
CHIVALRY PARAMOUR
GALLBERRY INKBERRY
GALLED RAW
GALLEON CARAC CARRACK
GALLOON
GALLERY POY SAP COOP GODS
JUBE LOFT PAWN ALURE BOYAU
ORIEL PRADO ARCADE BURROW
DEDANS NARROW PIAZZA SCHOOL
SOLLAR SUBWAY TUNNEL
BALCONY GALERIE HEADWAY
MIRADOR TERRACE VERANDA
BARTISAN BRATTICE CANTORIA
CORRIDOR HOARDING PARADISE
PERAMBLE SCAFFOLD TRAVERSE
VERANDAH BLINDSTORY
(— IN BAZAAR) PAWN
(— IN HOUSE OF COMMONS)
VENTILATOR
(— MADE BY INSECT) MINE
(— OF FORT) CASEMATE
(CHURCH —) JUBE LAFT LOFT
(MINE —) BORD BROW SLOVAN
(MINSTREL'S —) ORIEL
(OPEN —) LOGGIA
(UNDERGROUND —) HYPOGEE
HYPOGEUM
GALLEY FUST CUDDY DRAKE FOIST
STICK BIREME GALIOT HEARTH
ZYGITE BASTARD CABOOSE
DROMOND GALLIOT HEXERIS
KITCHEN LYMPHAD TRIREME
UNIREME CAMBOOSE COOKROOM
CROMSTER GALLEASS RAMBERGE

(**— BOTTOM**) SLICE
(**CHIEFTAIN'S —**) BIRLING BIRLINN
(**PHILIPPINE —**) CALAN
(**VIKING —**) AESC DRAKE
GALLEY SLAVE FORSADO
SFORZATO
GALLFLY CYNIPID
GALLIMAUFRY HASH OLIO
GALLINACEOUS RASORIAL
GALLINAE RASORES
GALLINAZO VIRU VULTURE
GALLING BITTER
GALLINULE COOT KORA MOHO
RAIL GORHEN PUKEKO SKITTY
MOORHEN STANKIE SULTANA
DABCHICK HYACINTH MANUALII
RAILBIRD RICEBIRD SWAMPHEN
GALLIVANT KITE ROAM ROVE
GALLANT
GALLNUT
(**PREF.**) CECIDIO CEDIDO
GALLON GAWN CONGIUS
(**— OF ORE**) DISH
(**EIGHTH —**) OCTARIUS
(**HALF —**) POTTLE
(**128 —S**) LEAGUER
GALLOON ORRIS
GALLOP FOG RUN AUBIN PRICK
CANTER CAREER COURSE TITTUP
WALLOP TANTIVY
GALLOWS NUB CRAP DROP FORK
TREE BOUGH CHEAT FURCA
WIDDY GIBBET WOODIE DERRICK
FORCHES JUSTICE POTENCE
STIFLER WARYTREE
GALLOWS BIRD HEMPY WIDDY
HEMPIE HEMPSEED WIDDIFOW
CRACKROPE
GALOOT OAF
GALOSH ARCTIC ZIPPER EXCLUDER
OVERSHOE
GALUTH GOLUS GOLAHI
GALVANIC VOLTAIC
GALVANIZE ZINC ZINCIFY
SHERADISE
GALVANOMETER DETECTOR
REOMETER
GAMBADO BOOT ANTIC CAPER
GAITER LEGGING
GAMBESON WAMBAIS
GAMBIA (**CAPITAL OF —**) BANJUL
(**COIN OF —**) BUTUT DALASI
(**LANGUAGE OF —**) JOLA WOLOF
FULANI MALINKE
(**MONEY OF —**) DALASI
(**NATIVE OF —**) JOLA PEUL WOLOF
DIOLAS FULANI MANDINGO
SERAHULI
(**TOWN OF —**) KAUUR MANSA
FATOTO BINTANG BRIKAMA
KUNTAUR
GAMBIA POD BABLOH
GAMBIER CATECHU
GAMBIT PLOY MANEUVER
GAMBLE BET DICE GAFF GAME NICK
PLAY PUNT RISK SPORT STAKE
WAGER CHANCE GAMMON
HAZARD PLUNGE FLUTTER
(**— AGAINST**) BUCK
GAMBLER PIKER SPORT CARROW
DEALER PLAYER PUNTER HUSTLER
PLAYMAN PLUNGER SLICKER

THROWER BLACKLEG GAMESTER
HAZARDER
GAMBLER, THE (**CHARACTER IN —**)
ALEXEY BLANCHE PAULINE
(**COMPOSER OF —**) PROKOFIEV
GAMBLING GAMING HAZARDRY
(**— CHARGE**) VIG VIGORISH
(**— DEVICE**) PACHINKO
GAMBLING HOUSE HELL TRIPOT
GAMBO GOOSE SPURWING
GAMBOL HOP PLAY ROMP CAPER
FRISK KEVEL PRANK CAREER
CAVORT FROLIC PRANCE
GAMBADO CAPRIOLE
GAMBREL ROOF CAMMOCK
SPREADER
GAME COB FUN JEU JIG GAMY LAKE
MAIL PLAY DANCE DOZEN GAMEY
PARTY SPIEL SPORT WATHE
BATTUE DOZENS MORRIS QUARRY
RAMSCH VENERY JENKINS
KNICKER BREATHER FIGHTING
FOREGAME FRONTENIS
(**— CALLED FIVES**) HANDBALL
(**— EASILY WON**) LAUGHER
(**— FOR FISHERMEN**) SKISH
(**— LIKE HANDBALL**) FIVES
(**LIKE HOCKEY**) DODDART
(**— NARROWLY WON**) SQUEAKER
(**— OF CAT**) BILLET
(**— OF FIVE HUNDRED**) EUCHRE
(**— OF FOOTBALL**) BOWL CAMP
(**— OF FORFEITS**) KEN
(**— OF HOCKEY**) BANDY SHINNY
(**— OF INSULTS**) DOZENS
(**— OF MARBLES**) TAW BOWL
BONCE GULLY KEEPS KNUCKS
MIGGLES
(**— OF MENTAL SKILL**) GO CHESS
CHECKERS
(**— OF NINEPINS**) KAILS KAYLES
(**— OF PRISONER'S BASE**) CHEVY
CHIVVY
(**— WITH BOOMERANG**) BRIST
(**— WITH COUNTERS**) DUMPS
GOOSE
(**— WITH SHUTTLECOCK**) TAHYING
(**BACKGAMMON —**) HIT IRISH
(**BALL —**) CAT TUT SNOB CATCH
RUGBY SOCCER SQUASH TENNIS
CRICKET KNAPPAN ONEOCAT
BASEBALL FOOTBALL HANDBALL
SLUGFEST SOFTBALL BROOMBALL
(**BASQUE —**) JAI
(**CALL THE —**) UMP
(**CARD —**) AS HOC LOO MAW NAP
PAM PIT PUT SET BRAG CENT FARO
FISH FROG GRAB JASS LANT PINK
POOL POPE POST RUFF SANT SKAT
SLAM SNAP SOLO STUD VINT BEAST
BUNCO BUNKO CARDS CARIE CHICO
CINCH COMET CRIMP DECOY GILET
GLEEK GRAND LEAST MONTE
NODDY OMBER OMBRE PEDRO
PITCH POKER PRIME RUMMY SCOPA
SLAMM STOPS STUSS TRUMP
WHIST BANKER BASSET BIRKIE
BOODLE BOSTON BRIDGE CASINO
CHEMMY COMMIT ECARTE EIGHTS
EUCHRE FARMER FLINCH HEARTS
HOWELL LOADUM PANFIL PIQUET
QUINZE RAMSCH ROUNCE SLOUGH

SMUDGE SPIDER TOURNE AUCTION
AUTHORS BELOTTE BEZIQUE
CANASTA CASSINO CAYENNE
CHICAGO COONCAN GARBAGE
HUNDRED JACKPOT PLAFOND
PONTOON PRIMERO REVERSI
SCOPONE SETBACK TRIUMPH
VINGTUN VITESSE BACCARAT
BASEBALL BRISCOLA COMMERCE
CONQUIAN CONTRACT CRIBBAGE
FREAKPOT HANDICAP IMPERIAL
NAPOLEON PATIENCE PENCHANT
PENNEECH PINOCHLE SHOWDOWN
SKINBALL SKINNING SLAPJACK
TREDILLE TRESILLO VERQUERE
VIDERUFF
(**CARNIVAL —**) HOOPLA
(**CHILDREN'S —**) TAG DIBS JACKS
KICKBALL PEEKABOO
(**CONFIDENCE —**) RAMP SCAM
STING MURPHY BIGMITT
(**COURSE —**) GOLF
(**COURT —**) PELOTA SQUASH
TENNIS HANDBALL
(**DICE —**) FARE TRAY BINGO CRAPS
NOVUM RAPHE HAZARD BARBUDI
ADDITION BARBOTTE CAMEROON
HOOLIGAN
(**DRAWN —**) SPOIL REFAIT
(**DRINKING —**) HIJINKS
(**EGYPTIAN —**) SENT SENIT
(**FOLLOW THE —**) HUNT
(**GAMBLING —**) EO TAN FARO HAND
KENO PICO BOULE CRAPS MACAO
MONTE POKER PROPS RONDO
STUSS BRELAN HAZARD RONDEAU
ROULETTE
(**GENERAL —**) HEI HIT HOB NIM TAG
TAW TIG BALL BASE BULL BUNT
BUZZ CENT DIBS DUCK FARE GOLF
HOLE JOWL KENO MALL PALM
POLO POOL SLAM SNOB TICK
BANDY BINGO BONCE BOULE
CHESS CHUBA CHUNK CLOSH
DARTS DOLOS FIVES GOOSE HALMA
HOUSE IRISH JACKS LOTTO LURCH
NOVUM NULLO PITCH PUSSY
RUGBY SALTA SALVO SCRUB TOUCH
TROCO WHOOP BEAVER BEETLE
CAROMS CHIVVY CHUNKY CLUMPS
COBNUT COCKAL COOTIE CRAMBO
FEEDER GOBANG GRACES HAZARD
HOOPLA HUBBUB JEREED KAYLES
MERELE PACHIS PELOTA PLUMPS
RAGMAN RINGER SEESAW SHINNY
SIPPIO SKILLO STICKS TENNIS
TIGTAG TIPCAT TIVOLI TRIGON
TRUCKS BALLOON BEANBAG
BEEBALL BOWLING COBBLER
CONKERS CROQUET CURLING
DIABOLO DODDART DOUBLES
DREIDEL ENDBALL GOGGANS
HANGMAN HURLBAT LOGGATS
MAHJONG MATADOR MUGGINS
NETBALL PALLONE PASSAGE
PEEVERS PUSHPIN QUINTET
RINGTAW SARDINE SQUAILS
STATUES TENPINS TOMBOLA
ANAGRAMS BALKLINE BASEBALL
CHARADES CHECKERS CHOUETTE
DOMINOES DOUBLETS DRAUGHTS
DUCKPINS FIVEPINS FOOTBALL
FORFEITS GIVEAWAY HARDHEAD

KICKBALL KORFBALL LEAPFROG
NINEPINS PARCHESI PEEKABOO
PETANQUE PURPOSES PUSHBALL
PYRAMIDS RINGTOSS ROULETTE
ROUNDERS SCRABBLE SKITTLES
STOBBALL STOWBALL TRAPBALL
VERQUERE PARCHEESI PHILOPENA
SHUFFLEBOARD
(**GUESSING —**) LOVE MORA
CANUTE
(**INDIAN —**) CHUNKY HUBBUB
(**INFERIOR —**) CHECK
(**JAPANESE —**) GO
(**KIND OF —**) VIDEO
(**MEXICAN —**) FRONTENIS
(**NUMBERS —**) BUG
(**OUTDOOR —**) GOLF POLO HURLY
ROQUE RUGBY SOCCER CROQUET
HURLING BASEBALL FOOTBALL
LACROSSE
(**PROGRESSIVE —**) DRIVE
(**PUZZLE —**) GLAIK
(**QUIZZING —**) TRIVIA
(**REHEATED —**) SALMI SALMIS
(**SWINDLING —**) BUNCO BUNKO
(**SWISS —**) JASS
(**THREE BOWLING —S**) SERIES
(**TRAPSHOOTING —**) SCOOT
(**VIDEO —**) ATARI
(**WAR —**) BARRIERS
(**WORD —**) GHOST HANGMAN
ANAGRAMS
(**PL.**) LUDI
GAMECOCK STAG STAIG
GAMEKEEPER GAMIE KEEPER
WALKER WARNER VENERER
WARRENER
GAMESTER DICER PLAYER
GAMBLER PLAYMAN SHARPER
HAZARDER TABLEMAN
GAMETE OVUM SPERM OOCYTE
ZYGOTE GAMETOID OOGAMETE
OOSPHERE
GAMETOCYTE GAMONT CRESCENT
GONOCYTE
GAMETOPHYTE GERMLING
GAMIN TAD ARAB URCHIN
GAVROCHE
GAMMA AGMA
GAMMON BAM
GAMP ORRIS UMBRELLA
GAMUT GAMME RANGE SCALE
SERIES COMPASS DIAGRAM
GANDAREWA (**SLAYER OF —**)
KERESASPA
GANDER STEG STAIG GANNER
(**— AND GEESE**) SET
GANDHARI (**HUSBAND OF —**)
DHRITARASHTRA
GANEF RASCAL
GANESA GUNPUT GANAPATI
GANG MOB SET BAND BUND CORE
CREW GING PACK PAIR PUSH TEAM
BATCH BUNCH GROUP HORDE
SPELL SQUAD CHIURM COFFLE
GAGGLE LAYOUT MOHOCK
SCHOOL COMPANY
(**— MEMBER**) WHYO
(**— MEMBER**) SKINHEAD
(**— OF CONVICTS**) PUSH
(**— OF FISHHOOKS**) PULLDEVIL
(**— OF MINERS**) CORE
(**— OF WITCHES**) COVEN

(GROUP OF —S) MAFIA
(ROWDY —) TRIBULATION
GANGBUSTERS SOCKO
GANGLING GAWKY RANGY GANGLY
GANGLION TUMOR CEREBRUM
GANGPLANK BROW GANGWAY
GANGRENE NOMA CANKER
GANGER SPHACEL NECROSIS
MORTIFICATION
(PREF.) NECR(O) SPHACELO
GANGSTER HOOD PUNK WHYO
APACHE BANDIT COWBOY
GUNMAN GUNSEL CHOPPER
GANGUE MATRIX LODESTUFF
VEINSTONE
GANGWAY BROW ROAD SLIP
LOGWAY TUNNEL CATWALK
COULOIR GATEWAY
GANJA GUNJAH CANNABIS
GANNET BOOBY GAUNT SOLAN
PIQUERO SEAFOWL ALCATRAS
GANTRYMAN DROPMAN
GANYMEDE (BROTHER OF —) ILUS
ASSARACUS
(FATHER OF —) TROS
(MOTHER OF —) CALLIRRHOE
GAOLER (ALSO SEE JAILER) ADAM
ALCAIDE
GAP SAG FLAW GAPE GOWL GULF
MUSE NICK SLAP SLOP WANT
BREAK BRECK CHASM CHAUM
CHAWN CLOVE FRITH MEUSE
MUSET NOTCH SHARD SHERD
VUIDE BREACH GULLET HIATUS
LACUNA SPREAD THROAT
VACUUM CLOSING OPENING
VACANCY VACUITY APERTURE
DIASTEMA ENTREFER INTERVAL
MULTIGAP QUEBRADA
(— IN BANK OF STREAM) GAT
(— IN FENCE) SLAP
(— IN FOOTBALL LINE) SLOT
(— IN MEMORY) AMNESIA
(— IN TURF) BUNKER
(— SERVING AS PASS) COL
(VOCAL CORD —) RIMA
(PREF.) CHASMO
GAPER COMBER
GAPING GALP AGAPE HIANT
CHAPPY CHASMA GAWISH
MOUTHED RINGENT ADENOIDAL
GAR HOUND SNOOK AGUJON
CHERNA GARFISH GARPIKE
BILLFISH GOREFISH GURDFISH
HORNBEAK HORNFISH HORNKECK
LONGJAWS LONGNOSE
GARAGE HANGAR LOCKUP SIDING
GARRIDGE
(ROW OF —S) MEWS
GARAM MASALA SPICES
GARAVANCE CARAUNA GARBANZO
GARB (ALSO SEE APPAREL AND
DRESS) COWL GEAR TOGA VEST
DRESS GUISE HABIT STOLA
APPAREL CLOTHES COSTUME
RAIMENT GLADRAGS
(LIGHT —) STRIP
(MUSLIM —) IHRAM

(PARTICOLORED —) MOTLEY
(PLAY —) ROMPERS
(RED —) SCARLET
(SPECIAL —) REGALIA
(UNIVERSITY —) ACADEMICALS
GARBAGE GASH SLOP OFFAL
TRASH WASTE GIBLET REFUSE
SCRAPS
(— IN — OUT) GIGO
(— IN, — OUT) GIGO
GARBAGEMAN DUSTMAN
GARBLE GELD JUMBLE MANGLE
DISTORT GARBLING MUTILATE
MISREPRESENT
GARDANT AFFRONTE
GARDEN HAW EDEN KNOT TILL
YARD ARBOR GARTH CIRCLE
POMACY POMARY QUINTA
ROSARY SHAMBA VERGER VIHARA
ACADEMY HERBARY OLITORY
ORCHARD ROCKERY TOPIARY
CHINAMPA FLORETUM HORTYARD
KALEYARD LEIGHTON PARADISE
PARTERRE POTAGERE ROSARIUM
CULTIVATE
(— CITY) CHICAGO
(— PLOT) ERF
(— STATE) NEWJERSEY
(BEER —) BRASSERIE
(SECLUDED —) PLEASANCE
(PREF.) HORT(I) TOPI
(SUFF.) ETUM
GARDENER MALI PONICA TILLER
CROPPER PLANNER BOSTANGI
GARDEN HELIOTROPE VALERIAN
GARDENIA TIARA
GARDENING TOPIARY
GARDEN ROCKET RUGOLA
ARUGULA EVEWEED
GARDEN-VARIETY AVERAGE
GARDEN WARBLER JACK HAYBIRD
BECAFICO FAUVETTE FIGEATER
GARFISH (SEE GAR)
GARGAMELLE (SON OF —)
GARGANTUA
GARGANEY TEAL CRICK
GARGANTUA AND PANTAGRUEL
(AUTHOR OF —) RABELAIS
(CHARACTER IN —) JOHN BRIDE
BACBUC TRIPPE BADEBEC PANURGE
ANARCHUS JOBERLIN GARGANTUA
TRIBOULET GARGAMELLE
GRANGOSIER HOLOFERNES
PANTAGRUEL PICROCHOLE
PONOCRATES ENTOMMEURES
TROUILLOGAN RAMINAGROBIS
GARGANTUAN HUGE VAST GIANT
HOMERIC TITANIC ENORMOUS
GIGANTIC HOMERIAN
GARGET MASTITIS
GARGLE GURGLE COLLUTORY
GARGOYLE BOSS
GARIBALDI GOLDFISH
GARISH GAUDY GIDDY SHOWY
CRIANT GLARING
GARISHNESS GLARE
GARLAND BAY LEI CROWN TORAN
VITTA ANADEM CORONA CRANTS
ROSARY WREATH CHAPLET
CORANCE CORONAL FESTOON
(PREF.) STEMMATI STEPHAN(O)
GARLIC AJO MOLY RAMP CHIVE
PORET ALLIUM PORRET RAMSON

GARMENT GI DUD TOG BACK BRAT
COAT GOWN PELL PELT RAIL ROBE
SARI SARK SHAG SILK SLIP SLOP
SULU VEST WEED ABAYA BUREL
BURKA CENTO CLOAK CLOTH
COTTE CYMAR DRESS FROCK
HABIT HAORI JOSEY JUPON KHAKI
MANGA NABOB SHAWL SHIFT
SHIRT SIMAR SKIRT STOLE WRIEL
ALPACA ATTIRE BARROW BLOUSE
BOUBOU BURKHA CAFTAN
CAMLET CAPOTE CHAMMA
COTTON CYCLAS ERMINE EXOMIS
FECKET HUIPIL JACKET JERSEY
JUMPER KERSEY KIRTLE MOHAIR
MOTLEY SARONG SHORTY
SHROUD STROUD TAMEIN ZIZITH
AMICTUS BLOUSON BROIGNE
BUNTING CAMBLET CASSOCK
CHIRIPA CRAWLER CUCULLA
CULOTTE DOUBLET FALDING
FLOCKET GROGRAM PALETOT
PELISSE RAIMENT SHORTIE
SURCOAT SWEATER VESTURE
WRAPPER BATHROBE BODYSUIT
CAMELINE CAPUCHIN CHAUSSES
COLOBIUM CORSELET COVERALL
DEERSKIN EPIBLEMA GAMBESON
GUERNSEY HIMATION INDUMENT
PADUASOY PULLOVER SCAPULAR
SEALSKIN SLIPOVER SNOWSUIT
VESTMENT WEARABLE PETTICOAT
REDINGOTE STROUDING
(— OF DERVISH) KHIRKAH
(— OF HERALD) TABARD
(— OF HIGH PRIEST) EPHOD
(— OF PATCHES) CENTO
(ARAB —) ABA
(ARABIAN —) ABA
(BABY'S —) BARROW CRAWLER
CREEPER
(BADLY-MADE —) DRECK
(BLUE —) MAZARINE
(BURIAL —) SHROUD
(COARSE —) BRAT STROUD
(DEFENSIVE —) JACK BROIGNE
GAMBESON
(ECCLESIASTICAL —) STOLE
RHASON ROCHET CASSOCK
(ECCLIASTICAL —) FANON ORALE
CHASUBLE
(ETHIOPIAN —) CHAMMA
(HINDU —) SARI SAREE
(INFANT'S —) BARRY BARROW
DIAPER BUNTING SLEEPER
PANTYWAIST
(INQUISITION —) SANBENITO
(JAPANESE —) HAORI
(LEATHER —) BUFF
(LINEN —) LINE
(LONG —) JIBBA KANZU STOLE
JIBBEH MANDYAS PELISSE
HIMATION
(MALAY —) SARONG
(MEDIEVAL —) ROCHET CHAUSSES
DALMATIC GAMBESON
(MONK'S —) SCAPULAR
(MOURNING —) SABLE
(ONE-PIECE —) BODYSUIT
JUMPSUIT
(ONE-PIECE WOMAN'S —) CATSUIT
(OUTER —) BRAT COAT GOWN HAIK
HYKE SLOP WRAP FROCK HAORI

NABOB PALLA PILCH SMOCK
DOLMAN ROCHET CHEMISE
GALABIA PALETOT SURCOAT
SWEATER HIMATION OVERSLOP
(PADDED —) TRUSS
(PENITENTIAL —) CILICE
(PULLOVER —) DASHIKI
(RED —) SCARLET
(ROMAN —) TOGA
(SLEEVELESS —) ABA CAPE COWL
VEST MANTLE CUCULLA GANDURAH
(SQUARE —) KAROSS
(SYRIAN —) ABAYA
(THIN —) GOSSAMER
(TIGHT-FITTING —) HOSE COTTE
TRICOT LEOTARD
(WOMAN'S —) IZAR BURKA CYMAR
NABOB SIMAR BURKHA CHITON
JOSEPH PEPLOS PEPLUM VISITE
BLOUSON BURNOUS
(PL.) GEAR COSTUME GARNISH
FLANNELS
(PREF.) RHACO
GARNER REAP MOPUP STORE
GATHER IMBARN COLLECT
GARNET YAG YIG GRENAT PYROPE
ANTHRAX GRANATE OLIVINE
VERMEIL ESSONITE MELANITE
ROSOLITE YANOLITE CARBUNCLE
RHODOLITE UVAROVITE
(SYNTHETIC —) YAG
(YTTRIUM IRON —) YIG
GARNISH LARD TRIM ADORN
DRESS EQUIP MENSE STICK
FURNISH PARSLEY TOPPING
CHUMMAGE DECORATE DUXELLES
ORNAMENT
GARNISHED GARNI
(— WITH GRAPES) VERONIQUE
(— WITH VEGETABLES)
BOUQUETIERE
GARNISHEE CHECK FACTOR
GARNISH
GARRET ATTIC SOLAR SOLLAR
MANSARD COCKLOFT
GARRISON WARD STUFF PRESIDY
WARNISON
GARROTE STRANGLE
GARRULITY POLYLOGY
GARRULOUS GABBY TALKY WORDY
BABBLY TONGUY VOLUBLE
GARTER GARTEN LEGLET ELASTIC
STRAPPLE
GARTH CORTILE OUTGARTH
GARUM LIQUAMEN
GAS DAMP XENON FLATUS GENAPP
LEAVEN OXYGEN PETROL EXHAUST
KRYPTON PROPANE YPERITE
AFTERGAS ETHERION FIREDAMP
HYDROGEN STANNANE VESICANT
(— CONSTANT) R
(— FUEL) ETHANE
(COLORLESS —) OXAN OXANE
KETENE GERMANE STIBINE
SILICANE
(EXPLOSIVE —) METHYLAMINE
(KIND OF —) NERVE
(MARSH —) METHANE
(NERVE —) SARIN
(NONCOMBUSTIBLE —) INERT
(POISONOUS —) ARSINE ADAMSITE
AQUINITE CYANOGEN PHOSGENE
BRETONITE PHOSPHINE

(RADIOACTIVE —) THORON
(TEAR —) ACROLEIN
(VOLCANIC —) MOFETTE
(PREF.) MANO PNEUM(O)(ON)
(ONO) PNEUMA PNEUMAT(O)
(CONTAINING —) PYOPNEUMO
(PRESENCE OF —) PHYS(O)
(SUFF.) **(INERT —)** ON
GAS-BURNER BUNSEN
GASCONADE BRAG CROW BOAST
BLUSTER
GASEOUS AERIFORM GASIFORM
VOLATILE
GASH CUT CHOP LASH BLASH
CHIMP GANCH GRIDE SCORE
SLASH SLISH SCOTCH SLUICE
TRENCH INCISION INCISURE
(— A FISH) RIM
GASKET LUTE CASKET GASKIN
GROMMET SCISSIL
GASKIN BRAGAS
GASOLINE AVGAS JUICE PETROL
BENZINE NATURAL
GASP FOB BLOW GAPE KINK PANK
PANT CHINK CROAK FETCH
THRATCH
GASPING CHINK
GASTEROPOD WHELK STROMB
UNICORN PTEROPOD
GASTRONOME EPICURE
GASTROPOD SLUG DRILL HARPA
OLIVA SNAIL BUCKIE NERITE
ABALONE MOLLUSK TOXIFER
UNIVALVE VELUTINA PULMONATE
PROSOBRANCH
GAT HEATER
GATAM (FATHER OF —) ELIPHAZ
GATE BAR BAR JET HEAD LIFT PORT
SASH SI AP TAKE YATE YETT ENTRY
HATCH JANUA PURSE SALLY
SPRAY STICK TORAN ENAJIM
ESCAPE FENDER FUNNEL HARROW
INGATE LIGGAT PADDLE PORTAL
RUNNER TIMBER TORANA WICKET
ZAGUAN BARRIER CLICKET
FIVEBAR GATEWAY LIDGATE
POSTERN SHUTTER ABOIDEAU
ANTEPORT DECUMANA ENTRANCE
FOREGATE GURDWARA PENSTOCK
TOLLGATE TOWNGATE TRIMTRAM
TURNPIKE ELECTRODE
(— OF CASTLE) BAR
(— OF DRYDOCK) CAISSON
(BACK —) POSTERN
(COMPUTER —) AND
(CUSTOMS —) BARRIER
(IRRIGATION —) CHECK TAPON
TAPPOON
(LICH —) SCALLAGE TRIMTRAM
(RUNNING —) FUNNEL
(SAW —) FRAME
(SAWMILL —) SASH
(SLALOM —S) HAIRPIN
(SLUICE —) HATCH VALVE
(TEMPLE —) VIMANA
(TIDE —) ABOIDEAU ABOITEAU
(WATER —) SLUICE
(PREF.) PYL(E)
GATEADO DIOMATE
GATEHOUSE BAR LODGE
GATEKEEPER WARDEN CERBERUS
GATEWARD PORTITOR STILEMAN
GATEMAN GUARD

GATEPOST DURN HARR HEEL PIER
POST SHAFT POSTEL
GATEWAY DAR DOOR GATE LOKE
PORT TORU PYLON TORAN TORII
BARWAY GOPURA TORANA
PROPYLON
(COMPUTER —) PORT
GATHER GET LEK POD WIN BAND
BREW CLAN CLOT CROP CULL
FURL HERD HIVE HOST PICK REAP
RELY TUCK AMASS BANGE BROOM
BUNCH FLOCK GLEAN GUESS
INFER LEASE PLUCK RAISE SWEEP
ACCRUE COMPEL CORRAL DECERP
DERIVE GARNER HUDDLE HUSTLE
IMBARN MUSTER RAMASS SCRAPE
CLUSTER COLLATE COLLECT
COMPILE CONGEST CONVENE
CONVOKE HARVEST RAMMASS
RECRUIT ASSEMBLE CUMULATE
SHEPHERD
(— AS ARMY) HOST
(— BY SCRAPING) SCRATCH
(— GRAPES) VINDEMIATE
(— GRASS SEED) STRIP
(— HEADWAY) SET
(— HERBS) SIMPLE
(— IN A HEAP) HATTER
(— IN RAGS) TAT
(— SEWING) GAGE GAUGE
(— UP) KILT
(SUFF.) LEGE
GATHERED KILTED CUMULATE
GATHERER GEDDER TUCKER
RUFFLER CHICLERO PLICATOR
PUCKERER
GATHERING BEE HUI LED LEK SUM
FAIR FEST KNOT SING SIVA LEVEE
SHINE TRYST AFFLUX INDABA
MUDDLE PLISSE POWWOW
RUELLE SMOKER COLLECT
COMMERS COMPANY FUNFEST
HARVEST HOSTING HUSKING
JOLLITY KLATSCH MEETING
MOOTING NYMPHAL ROCKING
TURNOUT ASSEMBLY CONCLAVE
FUNCTION JAMBOREE PANIONIA
POTATION RECOURSE SINGSONG
SOCIABLE STAMPEDE
(— FOR DANCING) FANDANGO
(— OF ANIMALS) DRIVE
(— OF ARMED MEN) HOSTING
(— OF CLOTH) SHIRR SHIRRING
(— OF FILM) CISSING
(— OF SCOUTS) CAMPOREE
JAMBOREE
(— OF TEAM) HUDDLE
(— OF WITCHES) COVEN
(— OF WOMEN) HENPARTY
(— PLACE) LESCHE
(BASUTO —) PITSO
(FORMAL —) HALL
(RELIGIOUS —) SHOUT
(SOCIAL —) BEE FRY BAKE BALL
CLUB DRUM STAG WINE BAILE
BINGE BINGO DANCE MIXER SHIVOO
SMOKER CANTICO COTERIE
KLATSCH SHINDIG SQUEEZE
BARBECUE CAMPFIRE CLAMBAKE
TALKFEST RECEPTION SYMPOSIUM
(STUDENTS' —) KOMMERS
(THREE-DAY —) CURSILLO
(SUFF.) **(FESTIVE —)** FEST

GAU BANT
GAUCHE CLUMSY AWKWARD
GAUD GAY GAUDY FANGLE VANITY
TRINKET
GAUDINESS GLARE GLITTER
GAUDY GAY LOUD CHEAP FLARY
SHOWY VAUDY BRAZEN FLASHY
FLIMSY FLORID GARISH GAWISH
SKYRIN TAWDRY TINSEL BRANKIE
CHINTZY FLARING GAUDISH
GLARING BRUMMAGEM
MERETRICIOUS
GAUGE (ALSO SEE GAGE) BORE
GAGE MOOT PLUG SIZE TRAM
GADGE NORMA RANGE DENTIN
FEELER FORMER GABARI DEPTHEN
TEMPLET TRAMMEL ESTIMATE
INDICANT MEASURER STANDARD
SURFACER TEMPLATE
MANOMETER
(— FOR SLATES) SCANTLE
(RAIN —) UDOMETER
GAUGER SURVEYOR
GAUL GALLIA
(PL.) PICTONES
GAULISH
(PREF.) GALLO
GAUNT BONY GRIM LANK LEAN
SLIM THIN PINED SPARE THIRL
BARREN HAGGED HOLLOW
MEAGER MEAGRE SHELLY SKINNY
HAGGARD SCRAWNY SLENDER
DESOLATE RAWBONED
CADAVEROUS
GAUNTLET TOP CUFF GLOVE
GANTLET GAINPAIN GANTLOPE
GAUR BISON SELADANG
GAUZE LISSE MARLI MARLY UMPI F
CYPRUS CYPRESS TIFFANY
CARBASUS
GAUZY FILMY
GAVE GIN GUV YAF YAFE
GAVEL HAMMER GAVELAGE
GAVIAL NAKOO LIZARD GHARIAL
LORICATE
GAVOTTE MUSETTE
GAWK GAWKY GAWNEY LUMPKIN
RAMMACK
GAWKY GOWKIT ANGULAR
AWKWARD GAWKISH
GAY MAD AIRY BOON DAFT GLAD
GLEG HIGH RORY TRIM WILD
BONNY BUXOM GAUDY JOLLY
LIGHT MERRY NITID RIANT RORTY
SUNNY VAUDY WLONK ALEGER
BLITHE CHEERY FLASHY FRISKY
FROLIC GARISH JOCUND JOVIAL
JOYFUL JOYOUS KIPPER LIVELY
SOCIAL SPORTY WANTON
BOBBISH CHIPPER FESTIVE
GALLANT GIOJOSO GLEEFUL
LARKING RACKETY SMICKER
SMILING TITTUPY WINSOME
CAVALIER DEBONAIR FROHLICH
GAMESOME PLEASANT PRIMROSE
SPARKISH SPLENDID SPORTIVE
GAY-FEATHER LIATRIS
GAYUMART (SLAYER OF —)
ANGROMAINYUS
(SON OF —) SIYAMAK
GAYWINGS MAYWINGS
GAZE EYE PRY CAPE GAPE GOUK
GOWK LEER LOOK MOON OGLE

PEER PORE SCAN TOOT GLAIK
GLARE GLOAT GLORE SIGHT STARE
TWIRE VISIE WLITE ASPECT
GLOWER REGARD AFTEREYE
GAZELLE AHU GOA ADMI AOUL
CORA DAMA MOHR ADDRA ARIEL
KORIN MHORR DZEREN GROUSE
ALGAZEL CHIKARA CORINNE
DIBATAG TABITHA CHINKARA
GAZELLE HOUND SALUKI
GAZETTE COURANT JOURNAL
(— OF CRIMES) HUE
GAZEZ (FATHER OF —) CALEB
HARAN
(MOTHER OF —) EPHAH
GE TAPUYAN
GEAN MERRY MURIE MURRY
GUIGNE GASKINS
GEAR KIT SPUR TACK TRIM IDLER
TOOTH FOURTH GRAITH HYPOID
PINION TACKLE CLOBBER GEARING
HARNESS REVERSE RIGGING
SEGMENT TRILOBE BACKPACK
HEADGEAR OVERDRIVE
(— OF DIVER) ARMOR
(CAR —) LOW HIGH FIRST SECOND
REVERSE
(CHAFING —) SCOTCHMAN
(DEFENSIVE —) ARMORY
(RUNNING —) CARRIAGE
(TRANSMISSION —) HIGH FIRST
SPEED FOURTH SECOND REVERSE
GEARED GIRT
GEARWHEEL UNILOBE WABBLER
WOBBLER
GEB KEB SEB
GEBER (FATHER OF —) URI
GECKO FANFOOT TARENTE
GEKKONID LACERTID
GEDALIAH (FATHER OF —) AHIKAM
(SLAYER OF —) ISHMAEL
GEE WOW GOSH GOLLY JEFFERS
GEELBEC SALMON TERAGLIN
GEEPOUND SLUG
GEESE SET
GEEZER COOT
GEIGER TREE ALOEWOOD
SEBESTEN
GEL JELL JELLY LIVER GELATE
ALCOGEL
GELATIN AGAR GLUE COLLIN
GLUTIN GLUTOID HAITSAI NORGINE
ISINGLASS
GELATINOUS COLLOID MUCULENT
COLLOIDAL JELLYLIKE
GELD LIB GELT ALTER CASTRATE
GELDING HORSE SPADE SPADO
GEM GIM JADE ONYX OPAL RUBY
SARD AGATE BERYL BIJOU CAMEO
JAZEL JEWEL PEARL SPARK STONE
TOPAZ ZIMME AMULET BAGUET
CRUSTA GARNET IOLITE JASPER
PEBBLE PYROPE RONDEL ZIRCON
ASTERIA CITRINE DIAMOND
DOUBLET EMERALD JACINTH
KUNZITE ONEGITE PERIDOT
SPARKLE ACHROITE AMATRICE
AMETHYST BAGUETTE HYACINTH
INTAGLIO MARQUISE ORIENTAL
RONDELLE SAPPHIRE SARDONYX
HIDDENITE MOONSTONE
RUBICELLE

(— CARVED IN RELIEF) CAMEO INTAGLIO
(— ENGRAVED WITH CHARM) ABRAXAS
(— OF IMPERFECT BRILLIANCY) LOUPE
(— REFLECTING LIGHT IN 6 RAYS) ASTERIA
(— STATE) IDAHO
(— SURFACE) BEZEL FACET
(IMITATION —) PASTE
(MYTHICAL —) CARBUNCLE
(TRANSPARENT —) IOLITE
(UNCUT —) ROUGH CABOCHON
GEMALLI (SON OF —) AMMIEL
GEMARIAH (FATHER OF —) HILKIAH SHAPHAN
(SON OF —) MICHAIAH
GEMMA BUD GEMMULE SOREDIUM
GEMMULE SPORE BROODSAC
GEMMY EMERALD
GEMSBOK ORYX KOKAMA GEMSBUCK
GEMSTONE JADE STAR CHEVEE PYROPE SPINEL EMERALD FISHEYE CROSSCUT HYALITHE MORGANITE TANZANITE
(PART OF —) BEZEL CROWN CULET FACET TABLE GIRDLE PAVILION
(SYNTHETIC —) YAG
GENA CHEEK
GENDER SEX KIND CLASS FEMININE
GENE GEN ALLEL ALLELE AMORPH FACTOR LETHAL PRIMER CYTOGENE MODIFIER POLYGENE RECESSIVE
(— MATERIAL) DNA
(GROUP OF —S) OPERON
(SET OF —S) HAPLOTYPE
GENEALOGY PEDIGREE
GENERAL (ALSO SEE SOLDIER) MAIN MOST BROAD GROSS ATAMAN COMMON HETMAN PUBLIC VULGAR CURRENT GENERIC MARSHAL SUMMARY AUFIDIUS CANIDIUS CATHOLIC ECUMENIC ENCYCLIC OVERHEAD PANDEMIC PUFIDIUS STRATEGE BRIGADIER
(PL.) DIADOCHI
(PREF.) CAEN(O) CEN(O) COEN(O) PAN
GENERALITY CREDO GENERALE
GENERALIZATION LAW AXIOM BROMIDE
GENERALIZE WIDEN EXTEND SPREAD BROADEN
GENERALIZED GROSS GLOBAL
GENERALLY ASARULE BROADLY LARGELY OVERALL ROUNDLY MOSTWHAT
GENERALSHIP STRATEGY
GENERATE MAKE SIRE TEEM BEGET BREED IMPEL SPAWN STEAM CREATE FATHER GENDER IMPOSE KITTLE DEVELOP INBREED PRODUCE ENGENDER
(— PUS) DIGEST
GENERATION AGE KIND TIME WORLD STRAIN STRIND DESCENT DIPLOID GETTING KINDRED GAMOBIUM GENITURE SAECULUM

THEOGONY TRIPLOID UPSPRING OFFSPRING
(FUTURE —S) POSTERITY
(SPONTANEOUS —) ABIOGENESIS
(SUFF.) GON(E)(IDIUM)(IMO)(IUM)(Y)
GENERATIVE GENIAL GAMETIC GENESIC GENETIC SEEDFUL SEMINAL PROLIFIC
GENERATOR KIPP BUZZER DYNAMO RULING ELEMENT DIPHASER GENERANT OSCILLATOR
GENEROSITY GRACE LARGE BOUNTY GENTRY BREADTH FREEDOM HONESTY COURTESY GOODNESS KINDNESS LARGESSE
GENEROUS BIG FREE OPEN SOFT FRANK HEFTY LARGE NOBLE LIBERAL GRACIOUS HANDSOME INSORDID LARGEOUS MAGNIFIC OPENHANDED
GENEROUSLY LUCKY MANLY KINDLY FRANKLY
GENESIS BIRTH ORIGIN BERESHIT GENETICS
GENET BERBE CIVET DAPPLE VIVERRINE
GENEVA GIN
GENIAL BEIN BIEN WARM DOUCE SONSY DOULCE FORTHY FURTHY HEARTY KINDLY MELLOW MENTAL CHEERFUL GRACIOUS PLEASANT
GENIALITY BONHOMIE
GENICULATE KNEED ELBOWED
GENIE GENIUS HATHOR SANDMAN
GENII XIN JANN
GENIN BUFAGIN
GENIP GINEP JAGUA IRONWOOD
GENIPAP LANA GENIP JAGUA GUENEPE
GENISTA FURZE RETAMA
GENITAL SECRET
(PL.) HARNESS PRIVITY GENITURE
GENITALS
(PREF.) EDE(O)
GENIUS KA FIRE GIFT HAPI KALI TURN ANGEL BRAIN DEMON GENIO KNACK NUMEN DAEMON INGENY INGINE TALENT WIZARD DUSTMAN DUAMUTEF EINSTEIN FRAVASHI PENCHANT SILVANUS
(— OF LANGUAGE) IDIOM
GENOA GEANE
GENOTYPE BIOTYPE LOGOTYPE
GENOUILLERE KNEELET
GENRE EPIC KIND SORT TYPE CLASS STYLE FABLIAU SPECIES CATEGORY
GENS CLAN HOUSE
GENSERIC (BROTHER OF —) GONDERIC GONTHARIS
(FATHER OF —) GODIGISDUS
GENTEEL NICE GENTY GENTIL JAUNTY POLITE STYLISH GRACEFUL
GENTIAN BIT FELWORT AGUEWEED GALLWEED BALDMONEY PENNYWORT
GENTILE ARIAN ARYAN HEATHEN
GENTILITY COUTH POLISH CIVILITY GENTRICE NICENESS
GENTLE MOY CALM DEFT DEWY FAIR HEND KIND MEEK MILD MURE NESH SLOW SOFT SOOT TAME

BLAND CANNY LIGHT LITHE MILKY QUIET SMALL SOBER SWEET BENIGN BONAIR CADISH DOCILE FACILE LYDIAN MODEST PLACID REMISS SILKEN SILVER SOFTLY TENDER AFFABLE AMABILE CLEMENT GRADUAL SOAKING SUBDUED DEBONAIR DELICATE DOVELIKE EGGSHELL LAMBLIKE LENITIVE MAIDENLY MANSUETE MODERATE PEACEFUL SARCENET TOWARDLY TRANQUIL
(— AS OF THE WIND) LOOM
GENTLEFOLK GENTRY GENTILITY
GENTLEMAN NIB SIR BABU GENT TOFF BABOO CURIO DORAY SAHIB SENOR GEMMAN MILORD SENHOR SIGNOR YONKER BRAVERY GALLANT GENTMAN MYNHEER CAVALIER MIRABELL SEIGNEUR SEIGNIOR SQUIREEN
(— COMMONER) HAT
(— TRAINING FOR KNIGHTHOOD) DONZEL
(— WITHOUT FORTUNE) STALKO
(COUNTRY —) SQUIRE
(GIPSY —) RYE
(MALAY —) TUAN
(MILITARY —) CADET
(POOR —) BUCKEEN
(WOULD-BE —) SHONEEN
(PL.) HERREN CHIVALRY
GENTLEMAN-AT-ARMS PENSIONER
GENTLEMANLY JAUNTY
GENTLENESS FLESH LENITY AMENITY DOUCEUR CLEMENCY KINDNESS MANSUETUDE
GENTLY SOFT CANNY SOAVE EASILY FAIRLY LIGHTLY EASYLIKE PRETTILY TENDERLY
GENTRY COUNTY GENTRICE SQUIRAGE SZLACHTA
GENUBATH (FATHER OF —) HADAD
GENUFLECTION VENIE KNEELING
GENUINE ECHT GOOD LEAL PURE REAL TRUE VRAI PLAIN PUKKA SOLID ACTUAL ARRANT DINKUM DIRECT HONEST KOSHER PISTIC CURRENT GERMANE GRADELY SINCERE VERIDIC GRAITHLY STERLING RIGHTEOUS
(NOT —) TIN SHAM BOGUS PLASTIC PRETENDED
(SEEMINGLY —) COLORABLE
(SUFF.) (NOT —) ASTER
GENUINENESS VERIDITY
GENUS KIND CLASS ANALOG GENDER GENERAL
(— OF ALGAE) DASYA FUCUS BANGIA CHORDA CODIUM HYPNEA NOSTOC PADINA DIATOMA LEMANEA LIAGORA PTILOTA VALONIA ZYGNEMA ANABAENA BRYOPSIS CAULERPA CERAMIUM CHONDRUS CONFERVA CUTLERIA DICTYOTA DUMONTIA GELIDIUM GOMONTIA HALIMEDA LERAMIUM LESSONIA NEMALION OOCYSTIS PALMELLA PORPHYRA STRIARIA TAONURUS ULOTHRIX
(— OF AMOEBA) CHAOS
(— OF AMPHIBIAN) HYLA RANA

SIREN PROTEUS AMPHIUMA NECTURUS
(— OF ANT) ATTA ECITON LASIUS PONERA TERMES FORMICA PHEIDOLE TAPINOMA
(— OF ANTELOPE) ORYX KOBUS BUBALIS GAZELLA MADOQUA REDUNCA ANTILOPE EGOCERUS
(— OF APE) PAN PONGO SIMIA
(— OF APHID) ADELGES CHERMES
(— OF ARACHNID) ACARUS GALEODES
(— OF ARMADILLO) DASYPUS XENURUS
(— OF ASCIDIAN) CIONA MOLGULA BOLTENIA PYROSOMA
(— OF ASCLEPIAD) STAPELIA
(— OF AUK) ALCA ALLE
(— OF BABOON) PAPIO
(— OF BACTERIA) VIBRIO EIMERIA ERWINIA GAFFKYA PROTEUS SARCINA BACILLUS BRUCELLA SERRATIA SHIGELLA YERSINIA BORDETELLA
(— OF BADGER) MELES ARCTONYX HELICTIS
(— OF BAMBOO) DENDROCALAMUS
(— OF BARNACLE) LEPAS BALANUS ELMINIUS
(— OF BASIDIOMYCETE) BOVISTA
(— OF BAT) EUDERMA PETALIA DESMODUS DIPHYLLA MOLOSSUS MORMOOPS NOCTILIO NYCTERIS PLECOTUS PTEROPUS VAMPYRUM
(— OF BEAN) ABRUS
(— OF BEAR) URSUS EUARCTOS MELURSUS
(— OF BEAVER) CASTOR
(— OF BEE) APIA APIS BOMBUS ANDRENA TRIGONA COLLETES HALICTUS MELIPONA
(— OF BEETLE) AMARA FIDIA HISPA LAMIA LARIA LYTTA MELOE SAGRA ALTICA ASILUS CLERUS ELATER LYCTUS PTINUS SILPHA ACILIUS ADELOPS AGRILUS ANOBIUM ANOMALA BRUCHUS CARABUS CASSIDA EPITRIX PRIONUS SAPERDA SITARIS ADORETUS AGRIOTES APHODIUS CALOSOMA CATORAMA CYBISTER DYNASTES DYTISCUS EPICAUTA EUMOLPUS HARPALUS LAMPYRIS MEGASOMA PASSALUS POPILLIA SCOLYTUS SPHINDUS TENEBRIO DERMESTES
(— OF BIRD) ARA ALCA APUS CRAX CREX GYPS JYNX MIRO MITU MOHO OTIS PICA RHEA SULA TYTO XEMA AJAJA ANOUS ANSER ARDEA ARGUS ASTUR BUCCO FALCO GAVIA GOURA GUARA GYGIS IRENA JUNCO LARUS LERWA LOXIA MIMUS MITUA MUNIA PIPRA PITTA SITTA TODUS UPUPA VIDUA VIREO ALAUDA ALCEDO ANHIMA ANTHUS AQUILA BONASA BRANTA CAPITO CIRCUS COLIUS CORVUS DACELO ELANUS FULICA GALLUS JACANA LANIUS LEIPOA LIMOSA MARECA MENURA MEROPS MILVUS MONASA NESTOR NUMIDA PASSER PASTOR PERDIX PERNIS PROGNE QUELEA RALLUS SAPPHO SCOPUS SIALIA SPINUS

STERNA SYLVIA TETRAO TRERON
TRINGA TROGON TURDUS TURNIX
VULTUR ANHINGA APTERYX
ARTAMUS BUCEROS CACICUS
CAPELLA CARIAMA CERTHIA
CHIONIS CICONIA CINCLUS COLINUS
COLUMBA COTINGA CUCULUS
ELAENIA GALBULA GARRUPA
HALCYON HIRUNDO IBYCTER
ICTERUS KAKATOE LAGOPUS
LOPHURA LYRURUS MALURUS
MANACUS MESITES MILVAGO
MOMOTUS ORIOLUS PANDION
PAROTIA PIRANGA PITYLUS
PLAUTUS PLOCEUS PORZANA
REGULUS SEIURUS SERINUS
STURNUS TANAGRA TIMALIA
TOTANUS XENICUS ZENAIDA
ACCENTOR ACCIPTER ACREDULA
AFROPAVO AGELAIUS AMIZILIA
BOTAURUS BUCORVUS BURHINUS
CHAETURA COLUMBUS CORACIAS
COTURNIX DELICHON DIATRYMA
DINORNIS DIOMEDEA DREPANIS
EMBERIZA EUPHONIA EURYPYGA
FULMARUS GARRULUS GEOSPIZA
GERYGONE GLAREOLA GRALLINA
GYPAETUS IONORNIS LUSCINIA
MACHETES MYCTERIA NEOPHRON
NOTORNIS NUMENIUS OREORTYX
PENELOPE PHAETHON PITANGUS
PLATALEA PLEGADIS PODARGUS
PRIONOPS PRUNELLA PUFFINUS
RUPICOLA SALTATOR SAXICOLA
SCOLOPAX SPEOTYTO SPIZELLA
STRUTHIO TRAGOPAN TYRANNUS
(— OF BIVALVES) MYA PINNA
ANOMIA MACTRA NUCULA ETHERIA
MYTILUS PANDORA COLUMBUS
HINNITES PISIDIUM SAXICAVA
TRIDACNA XYLOTRYA SPHAERIUM
(— OF BOWFIN) AMIA
(— OF BRACHIOPOD) ATRYPA
CRANIA ATHYRIS DISCINA SPIRIFER
(— OF BRYOPHYTE) RICCIA
(— OF BRYOZOAN) BUGULA
ESCHARA FLUSTRA RETEPORA
(— OF BUG) ANASA CIMEX EMESA
CORIXA TINGIS
(— OF BUTTERFLY) CALIGO COLIAS
DANAUS MORPHO PIERIS THECLA
EURYMUS JUNONIA KALLIMA
LYCAENA PAPILIO STRYMON
VANESSA ARGYNNIS HESPERIA
LEMONIAS MELITAEA SPEYERIA
(— OF CABBAGE) COS
(— OF CACTUS) CEREUS NOPALEA
OPUNTIA HARRISIA
(— OF CANTELOUPE) CUCUMIS
(— OF CAT) FELIS ACINONYX
HEMIGALE
(— OF CATTLE) BOS NEAT TAURUS
(— OF CEPHALOPOD) SEPIA
SPIRULA
(— OF CETACEAN) INIA
(— OF CHINK) LACUNA
(— OF CHIPMUNK) EUTAMIAS
(— OF CILIATE) COLPODA
CHILODON EUPLOTES
(— OF CIVET) FOSSA PAGUMA
(— OF CLAM) ENSIS GEMMA SOLEN
SPISULA
(— OF COCKLE) CHIONE

(— OF COCKROACH) BLATTA
(— OF CODFISH) GADUS
(— OF CORAL) ASTREA FUNGIA
MAENDRA OCULINA PORITES
ACROPORA TUBIPORA
(— OF CRAB) UCA MAIA BIRGUS
CANCER GRAPSUS OCYPODE
PAGURUS LITHODES PORTUNUS
(— OF CRANE) GRUS
(— OF CRAYFISH) CAMBARUS
(— OF CRICKET) ACHETA GRYLLUS
(— OF CRUSTACEAN) APUS HIPPA
JASUS LIGIA MYSIS CYPRIS LIGYDA
SELLUS TRIOPS ARGULUS ARTEMIA
ASTACUS BOPYRUS CALAPPA
CHELURA DAPHNIA EMERITA
HOMARUS IDOTHEA LERNAEA
NEBALIA SQUILLA CAPRELLA
ESTHERIA GAMMARUS LEUCIFER
LIMNETIS LIMNORIA NEPHROPS
PHRONIMA
(— OF CTENOPHORE) BEROE
CESTUM
(— OF CUCUMBER) CUCUMIS
(— OF CURASSOW) CRAX
(— OF DEER) AXIS DAMA PUDU
RUSA CERVUS MAZAMA MOSCHUS
RUCERVUS
(— OF DIATOM) DIATOMA SYNEDRA
MERIDION NAVICULA
(— OF DODO) DIDUS
(— OF DOG) CUON CANIS LYCAON
(— OF DORMOUSE) GLIS
(— OF DRAGONFLY) AESCHNA
(— OF DUCK) AIX ANAS AYTHYA
MERGUS NYROCA NETTION
SPATULA CLANGULA FULIGULA
(— OF EAGLE) AQUILA
(— OF ECHINODERM) ASTERIAS
(— OF EDENTATE) MANIS
(— OF EEL) CONGER ECHIDNA
MURAENA ANGUILLA GYMNOTUS
MORINGUA
(— OF FERN) FILIX TODEA ANEMIA
AZOLLA DOODIA CYATHEA ISOETES
ONOCLEA OSMUNDA PELLAEA
WOODSIA ADIANTUM ASPIDIUM
ATHYRIUM BLECHNUM CETERACH
CIBOTIUM CLEMATIS DAVALLIA
LYGODIUM MARATTIA SALVINIA
SCHIZAEA VITTARIA
(— OF FIREFLY) LAMPYRIS
(— OF FISH) AMIA ESOX HURO LOTA
MOLA RAJA ZEUS ALOSA BADIS
BERYX BETTA DORAS ELOPS GADUS
GOBIO HUCHO LATES MANTA
MUGIL PERCA SALMO SARDA
SOLEA UMBRA ALBULA ANABAS
APOGON BAIGRE BARBUS BELONE
CARANX CLUPEA COTTUS DIODON
GERRES GOBIUS HUDSON KUHLIA
LABRUS LATRIS MOBULA MYXINE
NOMEUS PAGRUS PSETTA REMORA
SCARUS SPARUS TRIGLA TRUTTA
TURSIO WEEVER ABRAMIS
ALOPHAS ALOPIAS ARACANA
ASPREDO BROTULA CARAPUS
CLARIAS DREPANE ECHIDNA
GARRUPA GIRELLA GYMNORA
LEPOMIS LIMANDA LUCANIA
LYCODES OSMERUS PEGASUS
PRISTIS SCIAENA SCOMBER
SEPIOLA SERIOLA SIGANUS

SILLAGO SILURUS SPHYRNA
SQUALUS SYNODUS THUNNUS
TORPEDO TOXOTES TRIODON
XIPHIAS ZOARCES AMEIURUS
ANABLEPS ANGUILLA ARAPAIMA
ASTYANAX ATHERINA BALISTES
BODIANUS CARANGUS CHIMAERA
CLADODUS CTENODUS CYPRINUS
DAPEDIUS DIPLODUS DIPTERUS
DOROSOMA ECHENEIS ETRUMEUS
FUNDULUS GADOPSIS GALAXIAS
GAMBUSIA GOBIESOX HAEMULON
ICOSTEUS KYPHOSUS LEBISTES
LUTIANUS MEGALOPS MORMYRUS
MUSTELUS NOTROPIS OPHIDION
PALOMETA PANTODON PHOCAENA
POLYODON PYGIDIUM SERRANUS
SQUATINA COREGONUS
MYCTOPHUM
(— OF FLAGELLATE) COCOS
GONIUM OPHION SYNURA VOLVOX
ATTALEA CARYOTA EUGLENA
GIARDIA BORASSUS CERATIUM
EUDORINA HEXAMITA HYDRURUS
(— OF FLEA) PULEX BOSMINA
(— OF FLY) DACUS MUSCA MYMAR
PERLA PHORA ASILUS CEPHUS
FANNIA PIMPLA RHYSSA SCIARA
TIPULA CALIROA CHALCIS DIOPSIS
EPHYDRA HYLEMYA MIASTOR
ORTALIS OSCINIS PANORPA
TACHINA THEREVA ACROCERA
AGROMYZA ANOMALON APHIDIUS
BORBORUS CHELONUS CHRYSOPA
CHRYSOPS GLOSSINA PSYCHODA
SCHEDIUS SIMULIUM STOMOXYS
(— OF FLYING SQUIRREL) BELOMYS
(— OF FOSSIL) AMPYX ERYON
ADAPIS ATRYPA BAIERA ERYOPS
GEIKIA HYENIA KLUKIA MAMMUT
OLENUS ORTHIS RHYNIA ANDRIAS
ANTHCON APTIANA ASAPHUS
DICERAS EXOGYRA GANODUS
HAMITES HYBODUS KNORRIA
LESKEYA LESLEYA LOXOMMA
MESONYX MOROPUS MYLODON
OTOZOUM PHACOPS PHIOMIA
PROAVIS PROETUS WALCHIA
AGLASPIS AGNOSTUS AMYNODON
APHELOPS ARCHELON BIRKENIA
BRONTOPS CALIPPUS CALYMENE
CAYTONIA CERATOPS CLYMENIA
CTENODUS DAPEDIUS DEINODON
DIATRYMA DINOHYUS DIPLODUS
DIPTERUS ENCHODUS ENCRINUS
EODISCUS EOHIPPUS EOSAURUS
EUSMILUS GORDONIA GRYPHAEA
HALLOPUS HELIGMUS ILLAENUS
LANARKIA LEBACHIA LECROSIA
LEGUATIA LESTODON LITUITES
MACLUREA MARRELLA METOPIAS
OLDHAMIA PLACODUS PORTHEUS
RUTIODON SMILODON SPIRIFER
STEGODON STEGOMUS TAONURUS
THELODUS XIPHODON ZAMICRUS
CONULARIA
(— OF FOX) ALOPEX VULPES
UROCYON
(— OF FROG) RANA ANURA
HYLODES
(— OF FUNGUS) FOMES IRPEX
PHOMA TUBER VALSA VERPA
ALBUGO BREMIA CAEOMA EMPUSA

FUMAGO HYDNUM ISARIA OIDIUM
PEZIZA TORULA ZYTHIA ACRASIA
ACRASIN AMANITA BOLETUS
CANDIDA CHALARA CYATHUS
ELSINOE ERYSIBE FABRAEA
GEASTER LEPIOTA MONILIA
NECTRIA OZONIUM PACHYMA
PYTHIUM RHIZINA RUSSULA
SIMBLUM STEREUM STICTIS
STILBUM TYPHULA XYLARIA
ACHORION AECIDIUM AGARICUS
BOTRYTIS CALVATIA CLATHRUS
CLAVARIA COLLYBIA COPRINUS
CORYNEUM CYPHELLA CYTTARIA
DAEDALEA DIPLODIA ENDOTHIA
ENTOLOMA ENTYLOMA ERYSIPHE
EXOASCUS FUSARIUM GEASTRUM
GNOMONIA GRAPHIUM HELOTIUM
HELVELLA LENZITES MERULIUS
MYCOGONE PAXILLUS PHOLIOTA
PUCCINIA RHIZOPUS RHYTISMA
SEPTORIA SORDARIA SPICARIA
TAPHRINA TERFEZIA TRAMETES
TREMELLA TROCHILA USTILAGO
USTULINA VENTURIA CORDICEPS
(— OF GALLFLY) CYNIPS
(— OF GASTROPOD) FICUS HARPA
LIMAX OLIVA EBURNA PATELLA
TENEBRA SCYLLAEA STROMBUS
(— OF GEESE) CHEN ANSER
NETTAPUS
(— OF GNAT) SCIARA
(— OF GOAT) IBEX CAPRA
OREAMNOS
(— OF GRASS) POA ZEA AIRA COIX
AVENA BRIZA ORYZA STIPA APLUDA
ARUNDO BROMUS ELYMUS
HOLCUS LOLIUM LYGEUM MELICA
MILIUM NARDUS PHLEUM SECALE
UNIOLA ZOYSIA BAMBUSA
BUCHLOE CHLORIS CYNODON
FESTUCA HILARIA HORDEUM
LAGURUS LEERSIA MELINIS
MOLINIA PANICUM SETARIA
SORGHUM ZIZANIA AEGILOPS
AGROSTIS ARISTIDA AXONOPUS
BULBILIS CENCHRUS DACTYLIS
ELEUSINE GLYCERIA GYNERIUM
IMPERATA PASPALUM PHALARIS
SPARTINA SPINIFEX TRISETUM
TRITICUM
(— OF GRASSHOPPER) LOCUSTA
(— OF GUAN) CRAX
(— OF GULL) XEMA LARUS
(— OF HAWK) BUTEO CIRCUS
(— OF HERB) GYP IVA AMMI ARUM
BETA GEUM GLAX HEBE LENS
MEUM MUSA OLAX RUTA SIDA
SIUM ADOXA AJUGA APIOS APIUM
CALLA CANNA CAREX CARUM CICER
DALEA DRABA ERUCA ERVUM FEDIA
GALAX GAURA GILIA GLAUX HOSTA
INULA LAPPA LAVIA LAYIA LEMNA
LINUM LOASA LOTUS LUFFA MADIA
MALVA NAPEA PANAX PARIS PHACA
PHLOX PILEA RHEUM RHOEO RUBIA
SEDUM TACCA URENA VICIA VIGNA
VINCA VIOLA ZIZIA ACAENA ACNIDA
ACORUS ACTAEA ADONIS ALISMA
ALLIUM ALSINE AMOMUM ANOGRA
ARABIS ARALIA ARNICA ASARUM
ATROPA BACOPA BAERIA BASSIA
BELLIS BIDENS BLITUM BLUMEA

BORAGO CAKILE CALTHA CASSIA
CELSIA CICUTA CISTUS CLEOME
CNICUS COLEUS CONIUM COPTIS
COSMOS CRAMBE CREPIS CRINUM
CROCUS CROTON CUNILA CYNARA
DAHLIA DATURA DAUCUS DIODIA
DONDIA ECHIUM ELODEA ELODES
EMILIA EUCLEA FILAGO GALEGA
GALIUM GIFOLA GYNURA ISATIS
ISMENE KOCHIA KRIGIA KUHNIA
LAMIUM LECHEA LUZULA MALOPE
MENTHA MIMOSA MONTIA
MUCUNA MUILLA NERINE NERIUM
NESLIA ONONIS OTHAKE OXALIS
PICRIS PISTIA PYROLA RESEDA
RESTIO RHEXIA RIVINA RUPPIA
SAGINA SALVIA SCILLA SESBAN
SESELI STEVIA SUAEDA THALIA
TULIPA VIORNA ZINNIA ABRONIA
ADLUMIA AETHUSA ALEGRIA
ALETRIS ALKANNA ALPINIA
ALTHAEA ALYSSUM AMORPHA
AMSONIA ANCHUSA ANEMONE
ANETHUM ANYCHIA APHANES
ARACHIS ARCTIUM ARNEBIA
ARUNCUS BABIANA BARTSIA
BEGONIA BOEBERA BUTOMUS
CACALIA CAJANUS CALYPSO
CARLINA CELOSIA CHELONE
CIRCAEA CIRSIUM CLARKIA
COMARUM CROOMIA CURCUMA
CUSCUTA CYTINUS DATISCA
DECODON DERINGA DIASCIA
DROSERA ELATINE EOMECON
EPISCIA ERODIUM FELICIA FICARIA
FRASERA FREESIA FUMARIA
GAZANIA GERBERA GLECOMA
GLYCINE GUNNERA HALENIA
HECHTIA HEDEOMA HOMERIA
HUGELIA HYPOXIS IRESINE JASIONE
KICKXIA KNAUTIA KOELLIA LACTUCA
LAPPULA LAPSANA LEWISIA LIATRIS
LINARIA LINNAEA LOGANIA LOPEZIA
LUNARIA LUPINUS LYCHNIS
LYTHRUM MARANTA MEDEOLA
MIMULUS MITELLA MOLLUGO
MONESES MUSCARI NEMESIA
NIGELLA OTHONNA PAEONIA
PAPAVER PAVONIA PEGANUM
PETUNIA PLUCHEA PRIMULA
RORIPPA ROTALIA RUELLIA
SALSOLA SAMOLUS SCANDIX
SENECIO SESAMUM SHORTIA
SILYBUM SINAPIS SOLANUM
SONCHUS STACHYS STATICE
SUCCISA SWERTIA TAGETES
TALINUM TELLIMA THAPSIA
THESIUM THLASPI THURNIA
TORENIA TORILIS TOVARIA TRILISA
URGINEA VALLOTA VERBENA
ZEBRINA ACALYPHA ACANTHUS
ACHILLEA ACONITUM AGALINIS
AGERATUM ALLIARIA ALLIONIA
ALOCASIA AMBROSIA AMMOBIUM
ANDRYALA ANGELICA ANTHEMIS
ANTICLEA APOCYNUM ARCTOTIS
ARENARIA ARGEMONE ARISAEMA
ASPERULA ATRIPLEX BAPTISIA
BARBAREA BARTONIA BERGENIA
BERTEROA BETONICA BISTORTA
BOLTONIA BORRERIA BRASSICA
BRUNONIA BUCHNERA CALATHEA
CAMASSIA CAMELINA CANNABIS

CAPSICUM CERINTHE CLEMATIS
COCHARUS COLLOMIA COLUMNEA
COMANDRA COOPERIA CRASSULA
CUBELIUM DENTARIA DIANTHUS
DICENTRA DIPSACUS DISPORUM
DYSSODIA ECHINOPS EPIFAGUS
ERANTHIS EREMURUS ERIGENIA
ERIGERON ERYNGIUM ERYSIMUM
EUCHARIS EUTHAMIA FITTONIA
FLAVERIA FLOERKEA FRAGARIA
GALACTIA GENTIANA GERARDIA
GESNERIA GILLENIA GLAUCIUM
GLECHOMA GLORIOSA GLOXINIA
GOODENIA GRATIOLA GUZMANIA
HELENIUM HELONIAS HEPATICA
HESPERIS HEUCHERA HIBISCUS
HIPPURIS HOSACKIA HOTTONIA
HUDSONIA HYDROLES HYSSOPUS
IONIDIUM ISNARDIA JATROPHA
JUSSIAEA JUSTICIA KNEIFFIA
KOHLERIA LAPORTEA LAVATERA
LEONOTIS LEONURUS LEPIDIUM
LEPTILON LIMONIUM LOPHIOLA
LYCOPSIS MACLEAYA MANFREDA
MANTISIA MEDICAGO MEIBOMIA
MYOSOTIS MYOSURUS OBOLARIA
OENANTHE OPOPANAX ORONTIUM
PAROSELA PHACELIA PHORMIUM
PHYMOSIA PHYSALIS PHYSARIA
PLANTAGO PLUMBAGO POLYGALA
POLYMNIA POTERIUM PRUNELLA
PSORALEA RAPHANUS RHAGODIA
SABBATIA SAMBUCUS SANICULA
SARCODES SAROTHRA SATUREIA
SCABIOSA SCOLYMUS SESBANIA
SESUVIUM SEYMERIA SIDALCEA
SILPHIUM SOLIDAGO SPERGULA
SPIGELIA SPINACIA STOKESIA
TAENIDIA THASPIUM TIARELLA
TRIBULUS TRILLIUM TROLLIUS
TUECRIUM UVULARIA VACCARIA
VALERIAN VANELLUS VERATRUM
VERNONIA VERONICA VISCARIA
WATSONIA XANTHIUM RUDBECKIA
(— **OF HERON**) ARDEA EGRETTA
(— **OF HORSE**) EQUUS CALIPPUS
EOHIPPUS
(— **OF HYDROZOAN**) DIPHYES
PHYSALIA
(— **OF HYENA**) HYAENA CROCUTA
(— **OF INSECT**) NEPA APHIS EMESA
JAPYX SIREX BOREUS CICADA
COCCUS CORIXA EMPUSA ICERYA
KERMES MANTIS PHASMA PODURA
SIALIS THRIPS CHALCIS FORMICA
FULGORA LEPISMA ORYSSUS
RANATRA STYLOPS VEDALIA
BACILLUS CAMPODEA EPHEMERA
LABIDURA LACCIFER LECANIUM
LYONETIA MACHILIS MANTISPA
NERTHRUS REDUVIUS
(— **OF ISOPOD**) IDOTEA IDOTHEA
CIROLANA
(— **OF JAY**) GARRULUS
(— **OF JELLYFISH**) CYANEA AURELIA
AEQUOREA
(— **OF JERBOA**) DIPUS
(— **OF KELP**) AGARUM
(— **OF LANGUR**) SIMIAS
(— **OF LEAFHOPPER**) AGALLIA
EMPOASCA
(— **OF LEECH**) HIRUDO HAEMOPIS
(— **OF LEMUR**) INDRI GALAGO

(— **OF LIANA**) BAUHINIA
(— **OF LICE**) APHIS PSYLLA
ARGULUS ONISCUS BOVICOLA
ERIOSOMA GONIODES LIPEURUS
(— **OF LICHEN**) CORA USNEA STICTA
EVERNIA GRAPHIS LECIDEA
LOBARIA PHYSCIA CETRARIA
CLADONIA LECANORA PARMELIA
ROCCELLA STRIGULA
(— **OF LILY**) CAMAS CAMASS
QUAMASH
(— **OF LIMPET**) ACMAEA
(— **OF LIZARD**) UTA AGAMA DRACO
GEKKO AMEIVA ANGUIS ANOLIS
IGUANA EUMECES LACERTA
PYGOPUS SCINCUS ACONTIAS
CHIROTES COLEONYX LYGOSOMA
RHINEURA
(— **OF LOCUST**) TETRIX TETTIX
(— **OF MACAW**) ARA
(— **OF MAMMAL**) BOS SUS HOMO
LAMA ALCES BISON CAPRA TAYRA
DUGONG FRISON AELURUS
AILURUS BUBALUS GALIDIA
GYMNURA LINSANG OTOCYON
AUCHENIA CYCLOPES CYNOGALE
SURICATA TRAGULUS
(— **OF MAPLE**) ACER
(— **OF MARSUPIAL**) DASYURUS
MACROPUS POTOROUS TARSIPES
(— **OF MARTEN**) MARTES MUSTELA
(— **OF MEDUSA**) SARSIA GERYONIA
(— **OF MICROSPORIDIAN**) GLUGEA
(— **OF MILDEW**) ERYSIPHE
UNCINULA
(— **OF MILLIPEDE**) JULUS
(— **OF MINT**) ICIMUM NEPETA
MELISSA PERILLA PHLOMIS
ORIGANUM
(— **OF MITE**) ACARUS ACERIA
LEPTUS DEMODEX ACARAPIS
(— **OF MOLD**) MUCOR FULIGO
MELIOLA
(— **OF MOLE**) TALPA SCALOPS
SCALOPUS
(— **OF MOLLUSK**) ARCA DOTO LEDA
LIMA CHAMA DONAX EOLIS FICUS
HARPA LIMAX MUREX OLIVA VENUS
AEOLIS ANOMIA BANKIA CASSIS
CHITON LEPTON LUCINA OSTREA
PECTEN PHOLAS PYRULA SEMELE
TEREDO TETHYS ACTAEON ASTARTE
ATLANTA CARDITA CARDIUM
CYPRAEA CYPRINA DOSINIA
ETHERIA EXOGYRA LINGULA
TELLINA BUCCINUM GRYPHAEA
HALIOTIS LIMACINA LUTRARIA
MODIOLUS NAUTILUS PINCTADA
SCYLLAEA STROMBUS
(— **OF MONGOOSE**) GALIDIA
(— **OF MONKEY**) AOTES AOTUS
CEBUS ATELES MACACA CACAJAO
COLOBUS NASALIS SAIMIRI
PITHECIA
(— **OF MOOSE**) ALCES
(— **OF MOSQUITO**) AEDES CULEX
STEGOMYIA
(— **OF MOSS**) BRYUM CHILO EUXOA
MNIUM SAMIA SESIA TINEA ACTIAS
ALYPIA ARCTIA BOMBYX COSSUS
DATANA HYPNUM LESKEA PLUSIA
PSYCHE SPHINX THYRIS URANIA
AGROTIS ALABAMA APATELA

ARCHIPS ATTACUS BARBULA
CRAMBUS FUNARIA GRIMMIA
PHASCUM PRONUBA PYRALIS
SESAMIA TORTRIX ZEUZERA
ZYGAENA ANDREAEA CATOCALA
DAWSONIA DIATRAEA DICRANUM
ENDROMIS EPHESTIA EUPREPIA
GALLERIA GELECHIA HEPIALUS
PLUTELLA PRODENIA PYRAUSTA
SATURNIA SPHAGNUM THUIDIUM
(— **OF MOTH**) CHILO ABRAXAS
(— **OF MOUSE**) MUS APODEMUS
(— **OF MUSKMELON**) CUCUMIS
(— **OF MUSKRAT**) FIBER ONDATRA
(— **OF NARWHAL**) MONODON
(— **OF NEMATODE**) ACUARIA
ALAIMUS ANGUINA NECATOR
(— **OF NUDIBRANCH**) GLAUCUS
(— **OF OATS**) AVENA
(— **OF OPOSSUM**) MARMOSA
(— **OF ORCHID**) DISA VANDA BLETIA
LAELIA PHAJUS ACINETA AERIDES
ANGULOA BRASSIA CORDULA
EUCOSIA IBIDIUM ISOTRIA LIPARIS
LISTERA MALAXIS POGONIA
VANILLA ANGRECUM ARETHUSA
BLETILLA CALANTHE CATTLEYA
CYTHEREA FISSIPES GOODYERA
MILTONIA ONCIDIUM PERAMIUM
SERAPIAS SOBRALIA TRIPHORA
(— **OF OSTRICH**) STRUTHIO
(— **OF OTTER**) LUTRA
(— **OF OWL**) BUBO NINOX STRIX
KETUPA NYCTEA AEGOLIUS
SPEOTYTO
(— **OF OXEN**) BIBOS
(— **OF OYSTER**) OSTREA AVICULA
(— **OF PALM**) NIPA ARECA ASSAI
COCOS HOWEA SABAL ARENGA
ELAEIS INODES KENTIA RAPHIA
RHAPIS ATTALEA BACTRIS
CALAMUS CARYOTA CORYPHA
ERYTHEA EUTERPE GEONOMA
LATANIA LICUALA PHOENIX
SERENOA THRINAX BORASSUS
HYPHAENE IRIARTEA LODOICEA
MAURITIA
(— **OF PARASITE**) STRIGA CUSCOTA
CUSCUTA HYDNORA OLPIDIUM
CASSYTHIA
(— **OF PARRAKEET**) ARATINGA
(— **OF PARROT**) NESTER AMAZONA
KAKATOE
(— **OF PEACOCK**) PAVO
(— **OF PENGUIN**) EUDYPTES
(— **OF PHALANGER**) DROMICIA
(— **OF PIGEON**) GOURA DUCULA
COLUMBA
(— **OF PLANT**) ALOE ARUM COLA
DION FABA IRIS IXIA PUYA SOJA
ADOXA AGAVE ASTER BATIS CANNA
CHARA DIOON DRYAS INULA NAIAS
PIPER RUMEX TRAPA TYPHA XYRIS
YUCCA ZILLA ABROMA ACACIA
AIZOON ALBUCA ANANAS CACTUS
CUPHEA DATURA EXACUM FERULA
IBERIS JAMBOS JUNCUS LICHEN
LILIUM MAYACA MORAEA NUPHAR
PHRYMA RICCIA SILENE SMILAX
STRIGA URTICA VISCUM ALONSOA
ASTILBE BALLOTA CABOMBA
CUCUMIS CYPERUS DIONAEA
DROSERA ENCELIA EPACRIS

EPIGAEA EURYALE FAGELIA
GLYCINE GODETIA HELXINE
HOOKERA ISOETES ISOLOMA
KARATAS LYCOPUS MANIHOT
MONARDA NELUMBO NITELLA
RAOULIA RICINUS STEMONA
SYRINGA TRIURUS TURNERA
WOLFFIA WYETHIA ZOSTERA
ABUTILON ACANTHUS ADIANTUM
ANABASIS ANTHYLIS BRASENIA
BRODIAEA BROMELIA CALADIUM
CAPSICUM CYCLAMEN FORCRAEA
FURCRAEA GALTONIA GASTERIA
GERANIUM LATHRAEA LATHYRUS
MARSILEA MONSTERA NYMPHAEA
PANDANUS PEDALIUM PELVETIA
PERESKIA SAURURUS SPARAXIS
THEVETIA TIGRIDIA TRITONIA
VELLOZIA VICTORIA ZINGIBER
(— **OF POLYZOAN**) LEPRALIA
LOXOSOMA
(— **OF POPLAR**) ALAMO
(— **OF PORCUPINE**) COENDOU
HYSTRIX
(— **OF PORPOISE**) INIA PHOCAENA
(— **OF PRAWN**) PALAEMON
(— **OF PROTOZOAN**) BODO HYDRA
MONAS ADELEA AMOEBA ACINETA
ARCELLA EIMERIA STENTOR
DIDINIUM EUGLYPHA ISOSPORA
UROGLENA
(— **OF RABBIT**) LEPUS
(— **OF RACCOON**) OLINGO
(— **OF RAT**) ANISOMYS
(— **OF REPTILE**) SPHENOGON
(— **OF RHIZOPOD**) AMOEBA
GROMIA LAGENA HATTERIA
PELOMYXA
(— **OF RODENT**) MUS CAVIA DIPUS
LEPUS ZAPUS GEOMYS LEMMUS
SPALAX CYNOMYS DINOMYS
ECHIMYS LEGGADA MERINES
NESOKIA ZYZOMYS ALACTAGA
ARVICOLA CAPROMYS CITELLUS
CRICETUS HAPLODON HYDROMYS
LAGIDIUM MICROTUS MYOTALPA
ORYZOMYS
(— **OF ROTIFER**) HYDATINA
PEDALION
(— **OF RUST**) UREDO HEMILEIA
UROMYCES
(— **OF SALAMANDER**) ANDRIAS
EURYCEA SIREDON TRITURUS
(— **OF SCALE**) KERMES LECANIUM
(— **OF SCALLOP**) HINNITES
(— **OF SCORPION**) BUTHUS
SCORPIO CHELIFER
(— **OF SEA ANEMONE**) MINYAS
ACTINIA
(— **OF SEACOW**) RHYTINA
(— **OF SEA FAN**) GORGONIA
(— **OF SEAL**) PHOCA HYDRURGA
MIROUNGA ZALOPHUS
(— **OF SEA OTTER**) ENHYDRA
(— **OF SEA SLUG**) ELYSIA
(— **OF SEA URCHIN**) ARBACIA
CIDARIS DIADEMA ECHINUS
(— **OF SEAWEED**) ULVA FUCUS
ALARIA LAMINARIA RHODYMENIA
(— **OF SEDGE**) FUIRENA SCIRPUS
SCLERIA SCHOENUS
(— **OF SHARK**) LAMNA GALEUS
ISURUS ACRODUS ALOPIAS

SPHYRNA SQUALUS CLADODUS
MENASPIS SQUATINA
(— **OF SHEEP**) OVIS
(— **OF SHELL**) PUPA LAMBIS
EXOGYRA LATIRUS MALLEUS
TROCHUS HAMINOEA MACLUREA
OLIVELLA TRIGONIA UMBRELLA
(— **OF SHREW**) SOREX BLARINA
(— **OF SHRIMP**) CRAGO CRANGON
(— **OF SHRUB**) IVA ACER BIXA BRYA
HOYA ILEX INGA ITEA MABA OLEA
RHUS ROSA SIDA THEA ULEX ALNUS
ANONA BIOTA BUTEA BUXUS CATHA
DALEA DIRCA ERICA EURYA FICUS
HAKEA IXORA LEDUM MALUS
OCHNA PADUS RIBES RUBUS SABIA
SALIX TAXUS THUJA TREMA UNONA
URENA VITEX ABELIA ACAENA
ADELIA ALHAGI AMYRIS ANNONA
ARALIA ARONIA AUCUBA AZALEA
BAPHIA BAUERA BETULA BLUMEA
BYBLIS CANTUA CASSIA CELTIS
CERCIS CISTUS CITRUS CLEOME
CLUSIA COFFEA CORDIA COREMA
CORNUS CORREA CROTON DAPHNE
DATURA DERRIS DIOSMA DONDIA
DRIMYS ECHIUM EVODIA FATSIA
FEIJOA GARRYA GNETUM GREWIA
GUAREA KALMIA KERRIA LANNEA
LIPPIA LITSEA LUCUMA LYCIUM
MIMOSA MYRCIA MYRICA MYRTUS
OCOTEA OLINIA OPILIA PENAEA
PERSEA PIERIS PROTEA PTELEA
PUNICA QUIINA RAMONA RANDIA
ROCHEA ROYENA RUSCUS SALVIA
SAPIUM SCHIMA SELAGO SESBAN
SORBUS STEVIA STYRAX SUAEDA
TECOMA AECULUS AMORPHA
ARBUTUS ARDISIA ARMERIA
ASIMINA ASSONIA BANKSIA
BAROSMA BENZOIN BORONIA
BUMELIA BURSERA CALLUNA
CARISSA CASASIA CERASUS
CESTRUM CLETHRA CNEORUM
COLUTEA CORYLUS COTINUS
CUNONIA CYRILLA CYTISUS DEUTZIA
DOMBEYA DURANTA EHRETIA
ENCELIA EPACRIS EPHEDRA
EUCHLEA EUGENIA EURSERA
FABIANA FUCHSIA GENISTA
GMELINA GYMINDA HAMELIA
HOVENIA KARATAS LAGETTA
LANTANA MAHONIA MERATIA
MONIMIA MORINDA MUTISIA
MYRRHIS NANDINA NEMESIA
OLEARIA OTHONNA PAVETTA
PAVONIA PENTZIA PIMELEA PISONIA
PURSHIA QUASSIA QUERCUS
RAPANEA REMIJIA RHAMNUS
RHODORA ROBINIA ROMNEYA
RUELLIA SALSOLA SENECIO
SKIMMIA SOLANUM SOPHORA
SPIRAEA SURIANA SYRINGA
TAMARIX TELOPEA XIMENIA
XYLOPIA XYLOSMA ZELKOVA
ACALYPHA ALANGIUM ALSTONIA
ANAGYRIS ATRIPLEX BALOGHIA
BAUHINIA BERBERIS BORRERIA
BUCKLEYA BUDDLEIA CAMELLIA
CAPPARIS CAPSICUM CARAGANA
CASSIOPE CASTANEA CODIAEUM
COLLETIA CONDALIA CONNARUS
COPROSMA CORIARIA CRATAEVA

DAVIESIA DENDRIUM DILLENIA
DODONAEA DOVYALIS DRACAENA
DUBOISIA EMPETRUM EUONYMUS
EUPTELEA EXOSTEMA FRAXINUS
GALACTIA GOODENIA GORDONIA
GUAIACUM HIBISCUS HIRTELLA
IONIDIUM JASMINUM JATROPHA
JUSTICIA KNIGHTIA KRAMERIA
LABURNUM LAVATERA LAWSONIA
LEONOTIS MAGNOLIA MAYTENUS
MICHELIA MYOPORUM NOTELAEA
PALIURUS PAROSELA PHILESIA
PHOTINIA PHYMOSIA PLUMIERA
POLYGALA POTERIUM PROSOPIS
PSORALEA RHAGODIA ROLLINIA
RORIDULA RUSSELIA SAMBUCUS
SATUREIA SAURAUIA SESBANIA
SOLANDRA SORBARIA SPARTIUM
TABEBUIA TORRUBIA TRECULIA
VARRONIA VERNONIA VERONICA
VIBURNUM VOCHYSIA WITHANIA
ZIZYPHUS MENZIESIA
(— **OF SILKWORM**) BOMBYX
(— **OF SKUNK**) MEPHITIS
(— **OF SLOTH**) BRADYPUS
(— **OF SLUG**) DOTO ARION DORIS
LIMAX ELYSIA GLAUCUS
(— **OF SNAIL**) HUA PILA CONUS
FUSUS GALBA HELIX MITRA OVULA
PHYSA THAIS TURBO CERION
EULIMA NATICA NERITA RISSOA
TRITON ANCYLUS BITTIUM BULINUS
BUSYCON CYMBIUM LATIRUS
LITIOPA LYMNARA MELANIA
MODULUS PURPURA RANELLA
VALVATA VERTIGO VITRINA ZONITES
ACHATINA ALOCINMA ELLOBIUM
FOSSARIA GYRAULUS HELICINA
HELISOMA JANTHINA KATAYAMA
LITORINA NERITINA OLEACINA
SUCCINEA
(— **OF SNAKE**) BOA ERYX NAIA
NAJA ASPIS BITIS BOIGA ECHIS
ELAPS CAUSUS DABOIA ELAPHE
HURRIA ILYSIA LIGUUS NATRIX
PYTHON VIPERA ATHERIS BOAEDON
COLUBER ECHIDNA MEHELYA
OPHIDIA ZAMENIS BOTHROPS
BUNGARUS CERBERUS CROTALUS
DEMANSIA EUNECTES FARANCIA
LACHESIS MICRURUS STORERIA
TYPHLOPS
(— **OF SPIDER**) ARANEA LYCOSA
MYGALE AGALENA ARGIOPE
ATTIDAE NEPHILA PHOLCUS
LINYPHIA ULOBORUS
(— **OF SPIROCHETE**) BORRELIA
(— **OF SPONGE**) SYCON GEODIA
SCYPHA ASCETTA CHALINA GRANTIA
SPONGIA SYCETTA LEUCETTA
(— **OF SPOROZOAN**) NOSEMA
(— **OF SQUID**) LOLIGO SEPIOLA
(— **OF SQUIRREL**) SCIURUS
(— **OF SUBSHRUB**) LECHEA
ARMERIA ASCYRUM BEGONIA
FELICIA ATRIPLEX COLUMNEA
(— **OF SWAN**) OLOR CYGNUS
(— **OF TAKIN**) BUDORCAS
(— **OF TAPEWORM**) BERTIA LIGULA
DAVAINEA HARRISIA
(— **OF TAYRA**) GALERA GALICTIS
(— **OF TELEDU**) MYDAUS
(— **OF TERN**) GYGIS STERNA

(— **OF THISTLE**) CNICUS CARDUUS
(— **OF TICK**) ARGAS ARGUS IXODES
HYALOMMA
(— **OF TOAD**) BUFO HYLA PIPA
ALYTES XENOPUS ASCAPHUS
(— **OF TREE**) ACER BIXA BRYA COLA
HURA ILEX INGA MABA OLAX OLEA
RHUS THEA ABIES AEGLE ALNUS
ANIBA BIOTA BUTEA BUXUS CARYA
CEIBA CYCAS DURIO EURYA FAGUS
FICUS HAKEA HEVEA HOPEA IXORA
KHAYA LARIX MALUS MELIA MESUA
MORUS NYSSA OCHNA PADUS
PICEA PINUS PYRUS SALIX TAXUS
THUJA TILIA TOONA TREMA TSUGA
ULMUS UNONA VITEX XYLIA
ABROMA ACHRAS AKANIA AMOMIS
AMYRIS ANDIRA ANNONA ARALIA
AUCUBA AZALEA BAPHIA BETULA
BOMBAX CANTUA CARAPA CARICA
CASSIA CEDRUS CELTIS CERCIS
CITRUS CLUSIA COFFEA CORDIA
CORNUS DATURA DRIMYS EPERUA
EPERVA EUCLEA EVODIA FEIJOA
GARRYA GENIPA GINKGO GNETUM
GREWIA GUAREA IDESIA ILLIPE
LAURUS LITCHI LITSEA LUCUMA
LYCIUM MAMMEA MIMOSA MYRCIA
MYRICA OCOTEA OLNEYA OSTRYA
OWENIA PAPPEA PARITI PERSEA
PRUNUS PTELEA QUIINA RANDIA
ROYENA SAPIUM SAPOTA SCHIMA
SENCIO SESBAN SHOREA SIMABA
SORBUS STYRAX TECOMA AGATHIS
ARBUTUS ARDISIA ASIMINA
ASSONIA BANKSIA BUMELIA
BURSERA CANANGA CANELLA
CASASIA CATALPA CEDRELA
CERASUS CLETHRA COPAIVA
CORYLUS COTINUS CUNONIA
CUPANIA CYDONIA CYRILLA
DOMBEYA ECHINUS EHRETIA
EPACRIS EUGENIA FERONIA
GMELINA GUAZUMA GYMINDA
HAGENIA HALESIA HICORIA
HOVENIA HUMIRIA JUGLANS
KADELIA KOKOONA LAGETTA
LICANIA LINGOUM MACLURA
MICONIA MORINDA MORINGA
MURRAYA OCHROMA OLEARIA
PANGIUM PIMENTA PISONIA
PLANERA POPULUS PROTIUM
PSIDIUM QUASSIA QUERCUS
RAPANEA REMIJIA RHAMNUS
ROBINIA SCHINUS SENECIO
SEQUOIA SLOANEA SOLANUM
SOPHORA SURIANA SYRINGA
TAMARIX TECTONA TELOPEA
TORREYA TROPHIS VATERIA
XIMENIA XYLOPIA XYLOSMA
ZELKOVA AESCULUS ALANGIUM
ALBIZZIA ALSTONIA ANTIARIS
AVERRHOA BALANOPS BALOGHIA
BAUHINIA BRABEJUM BROSIMUM
BUDDLEIA CABRALEA CAMELLIA
CANARIUM CAPPARIS CARAGANA
CARPINUS CARYOCAR CASEARIA
CASTANEA CASTILLA CECROPIA
CINCHONA CODIAEUM CONDALIA
CYBISTAX DILLENIA DIPTERYX
DODONAEA DOVYALIS DRACAENA
DUBOISIA EUCOMMIA EUONYMUS
EUPTELEA EXOSTEMA FITZROYA

FRAXINUS FUNTUMIA GARCINIA
GARDENIA GORDONIA GUAIACUM
HIBISCUS HIRTELLA HOMALIUM
HYMENAEA ILLICIUM JATROPHA
KANDELIA KNIGHTIA LABURNUM
LAPORTEA LAVATERA LECYTHIS
LEUCAENA LYSILOMA MAGNOLIA
MALLOTUS MAYTENUS MESPILUS
MICHELIA MIMUSOPS MYOPORUM
NOTELAEA PHOTINIA PISCIDIA
PISTACIA PLATANUS PLUMIERA
PONCIRUS PROSOPIS QUILLAJA
RAVENALA ROLLINIA SAMADERA
SAMBUCUS SANTALUM SAPINDUS
SAURAUIA SESBANIA SIMARUBA
SPONDIAS SWARTZIA TABEBUIA
TAXODIUM TORRUBIA TRECULIA
VARRONIA VERONICA VIBURNUM
VIRGILIA VOCHYSIA
(— OF TUNICATE) SALPA ASCIDIA
DOLIOLUM
(— OF TURTLE) EMYS AMYDA
CHELUS CHELYS CARETTA CHELONE
CLEMMYS TESTUDO TRIONYX
ARCHELON CHELONIA CHELYDRA
PELUSIOS
(— OF TWINER) STEMONA
(— OF UNIVALVE) DOLIUM
(— OF VINE) ROSA ABRUS ABUTA
PISUM TAMUS UNONA VIGNA VITIS
AKEBIA CISSUS COBAEA DERRIS
ENTADA HEDERA MUCUNA PETREA
POTHOS SICANA SICYOS SOLLYA
VIORNA ARAUJIA BASELLA
BOMAREA BRYONIA ECHITES
EMBELIA EPACRIS FALCATA
HUMULUS IPOMOEA MIKANIA
PISONIA SECHIUM UNCARIA
ZANONIA ANAMIRTA ATRAGENE
BIGNONIA CLEMATIS COCCULUS
DEGUELIA DOLICHOS EUONYMUS
JASMINUM KENNEDYA PANDOREA
PUERARIA SECAMONE SERJANIA
TACSONIA WISTARIA
(— OF WALRUS) ODOBENUS
(— OF WASP) SPHEX VESPA
BEMBEX CYNIPS SCOLIA TIPHIA
CHRYSIS EUMENES MASARIS
MUTILLA ANDRICUS CHLORION
ODYNERUS POLISTES POMPILUS
SPHECIUS
(— OF WEASEL) MUSTELA
(— OF WEED) CAPSELLA
(— OF WEEVIL) APION HYPERA
SITONA CLEONUS CALANDRA
CALENDRA CURCULIO
(— OF WHALE) CETE ARETA KOGIA
BALAENA ORCINUS ZIPHIUS
PHYSETER
(— OF WOLVERINE) GULO
(— OF WORM) DERO SPIO ALARIA
EUNICE KERRIA MERMIS NEREIS
SYLLIS ACHAETA ACHOLOE ASCARIS
DUGESIA EISENIA FILARIA GLYCERA
GORDIUS HESIONE LEODICE
POLYNOE SABELLA SAGITTA
SERPULA SETARIA SPIRURA TUBIFEX
ARABELLA ASCAROPS BIPALIUM
BONELLIA COOPERIA DOCHMIUS
ECHIURUS FASCIOLA GEOPLANA
PHORONIS SPADELLA SUBULURA
SYNGAMUS SYPHACIA

(— OF ZORIL) ICTONYX
(PREF.) GEN(O)
(SUFF.) IA
GEODE DRUSE
GEOGRAPHER AMERICAN BAKER
DAVIS GUYOT RONNE ATWOOD
BOWMAN BRYANT SEMPLE
DAVIDSON HUTCHINS MITCHELL
ROBINSON GROSVENOR
HUNTINGTON
ARAB BAKRI
AUSTRIAN KORISTKA PAULITSCHKE
CANADIAN PALLISER
DUTCH BLAEU
EGYPTIAN PTOLEMY
ENGLISH BEKE PEEL KEANE
BEAZLEY EVEREST HAKLUYT
MARKHAM RENNELL THOMPSON
GREENOUGH MACKINDER
FRESHFIELD
FRENCH JOMARD RECLUS VALLOT
ANVILLE DELISLE DEMANGEON
GERMAN BEHM KOHL BANSE
PENCK VOGEL ANDREE BEHAIM
CLUVER RATZEL RITTER APIANUS
EBELING GERLAND HETTNER
KIEPERT KRUMMEL PESCHEL
SCHONER BERGHAUS BRUCKNER
BUSCHING DRYGALSKI PETERMANN
RICHTHOFEN CHRISTALLER
GREEK SCYLAX STRABO MARINUS
PYTHEAS DIONYSIUS PAUSANIAS
ERATOSTHENES
HUNGARIAN TELEKI
ICELANDIC THORODDSEN
ITALIAN BALBI CODAZZI AMORETTI
MARSIGLI
POLISH LELEWEL
PORTUGUESE CORDEIRO
RUSSIAN SEMENOV GERASIMOV
KROPOTKIN SHOKALSKI
PRZHEVALSKY
SCOTTISH MILL BROWN JOHNSTON
SPANISH COSA
SWEDISH HEDIN
GEOLOGIST AMERICAN DALY DANA
HALL KEMP KING REID TARR CROSS
GUYOT HAGUE HOBBS LEITH
MCGEE ORTON SCOTT SMITH
SPURR WHITE ARNOLD ATWOOD
BAYLEY DUTTON EMMONS FOSTER
HAYDEN HOLMES IRVING JAGGAR
LAWSON LESLEY MARCOU MATHER
MENARD POWELL SHALER UPJOHN
WRIGHT BALLARD BARRELL
BRANNER GILBERT HOLLICK
IDDINGS JOHNSON MACLURE
MERRILL PIRSSON RANSOME
RUSSELL TALMAGE VANHISE
WHITNEY WRATHER LEVERETT
MASURSKY MITCHELL NEWBERRY
PUMPELLY SILLIMAN WINCHELL
HITCHCOCK JOHANNSEN
SALISBURY TWENHOFEL
CHAMBERLIN LOUDERBACK
WASHINGTON
AUSTRALIAN DAVID MAWSON
AUSTRIAN BECKE HAUER SUESS
HAIDINGER HOCHSTETTER
MOJSISOVICS
BELGIAN RENARD
CANADIAN BELL ADAMS LOGAN
DAWSON TYRRELL WALLACE

DANISH KOCH
DUTCH TROMP
ENGLISH BELT TATE FUCHS JUKES
LYELL SMITH SORBY ANSTED
BONNEY CLARKE FORBES HOLMES
MAWSON SCROPE DAWKINS
GREGORY HOLLAND MANTELL
BUCKLAND LYDEKKER PHILLIPS
SEDGWICK GREENOUGH
MURCHISON PRESTWICH
STRICKLAND
FRENCH FOUQUE ARCHIAC
DAUBREE DELESSE BARRANDE
BEAUMONT BERTRAND DOLOMIEU
DUFRENOY LAPPARENT
GERMAN BUCH ABICH COHEN
DECHEN ROEMER WERNER ZITTEL
ALBERTI BISCHOF CREDNER GEINITZ
LEONHARD QUENSTEDT
KEYSERLING ROSENBUSCH
ICELANDIC THORODDSEN
IRISH OLDHAM
ITALIAN MERCALLI
NEW ZEALAND HAAST
NORWEGIAN BROGGER KJERULF
RUSSIAN OBRUCHEV
SCOTTISH HALL CROLL LYELL
GEIKIE HUTTON MILLER RAMSAY
OGLIVIE PLAYFAIR MACCULLOCH
SWEDISH ANTEVS TORELL
HISINGER NATHORST
NORDENSKJOLD
SWISS HEIM DELUC
GEOMETRIC CUBIST CUBISTIC
(— TERM) SECANT
GEOMETRY EUCLID SPHERICS
(KIND OF —) SOLID
GEOPHAGY PICA

GEORGIA

CAPITAL: ATLANTA
COLLEGE: SPELMAN MOREHOUSE
COUNTY: BIBB CLAY COBB COOK
HALL TIFT WARE BANKS BRYAN
BUTTS DOOLY EARLY FLOYD
GRADY PEACH RABUN TROUP
WORTH COFFEE COWETA DEKALB
ECHOLS ELBERT FANNIN FULTON
JASPER LANIER OCONEE TWIGGS
WILKES CATOOSA LAURENS
LUMPKIN GWINNETT MUSCOGEE
INDIAN: GUALE YUCHI CHIAHA
OCONEE YAMASEE
LAKE: LANIER MARTIN HARDING
NOTTELY BANKHEAD HARTWELL
SINCLAIR
MOUNTAIN: STONE KENNESAW
NATIVE: CRACKER
PRESIDENT: CARTER
RIVER: PEA FLINT ETOWAH OCONEE
PIGEON CONECUH SATILLA
ALTAMAHA OCMULGEE
STATE BIRD: THRASHER
STATE NICKNAME: PEACH
STATE TREE: LIVEOAK
TOWN: JESUP MACON JASPER
OCILLA AUGUSTA CONYERS
DECATUR ELLIJAY GRIFFIN
VIDALIA MARIETTA MOULTRIE
SAVANNAH VALDOSTA
WAYCROSS
UNIVERSITY: EMORY GATECH
MERCER

GEORGIA (ALSO SEE RUSSIA)
CAPITAL: TIFLIS TBILISI
COIN: RUBLE
LANGUAGE: KARTVELIAN
MOUNTAIN: USHBA SHKHARA
TETNULD DIDIABULI RUSTAVELI
MOUNTAIN RANGE: LIKHI KARTLI
LOMISI LIKHSKY MESKHET
CAUCASUS LOMISSKY MESKHETI
KARTLIYSKY KARTALINIAN
PEOPLE: GORJ OSSET GEORGIAN
KARTVELI SAKARTVELO
PLAIN: KARTLI COLCHIS KOLKHIDA
KARTALINIAN
RIVER: KURA RIONI INGURI KODORI
MTKVARI
TOWN: GORI POTI BATUMI KUTAISI
RUSTAVI SUKHUMI KHASHURI
MTSKHETA
VOLCANO: KAZBEK MKINVARI

GEORGIAN ADZHAR CRACKER
GEORGIA PINE LONGLEAF
GEPHYREAN STARWORM
GER STRANGER
GERAINT (WIFE OF —) ENID
GERANIUM DOVEFOOT FLUXWEED
SHAMEFACE
GERANIUM LAKE SPARK NACARAT
GERANIUM PINK BERMUDA
GERBIL JIRD
GERIANOL ISOLATE
GERM BUG CHIT SEED SPARK
SPAWN SPERM GERMEN
GERMULE MICROBE SEMINAL
RUDIMENT SEEDLING SEMINARY
SEMINIUM
(— CELL) GONE
(PREF.) BLAST(O) SPERM(A)(ATI)
(ATIO)(ATO)(I)(IO)(O)
(SUFF.) BLAST(IC)(Y) SPERM(A)(AE)
(AL)(IA)(IC)(OUS)(UM)(Y)
GERMAN BALT HANS ALMAN HEINE
JERRY ALMAIN DUTCHY HEINIE
TEUTON TEDESCO COTILLON
GERMANIC TUDESQUE
(PREF.) TEUTO
GERMANDER POLY BETONY
FOXTAIL SOVENEZ SCORDIUM
GERMANE GERMAN APROPOS
RELEVANT PERTINENT
GERMANIC GOTHIC GOTHONIC
TEUTONIC
GERMAN MEASLES ROSEOLA
RUBELLA
GERMAN SHEPHERD ALSATIAN
GERMAN SILVER ALBATA

GERMANY
ANCIENT: ALMAIN ALMAINE
ANCIENT TRIBESMAN: JUTE
TEUTON VISIGOTH OSTROGOTH
CANAL: KIEL WESER LUDWIG
CAPITAL: BERLIN
CHEESE: MUENSTER TILSITER
LIMBURGER
COAL REGION: RUHR SAAR SARRE
COIN: MARK KRONE TALER GULDEN
KRONEN THALER PFENNIG
GROSCHEN
DIALECT: KOLSCH KOELSCH
BALTISCH HESSISCH

DYNASTY: HOHENSTAUFEN
HOHENZOLLERN
FOOD: WURST KNODEL SPATZLE
STRUDEL MARZIPAN ROULADEN
HANSEATIC CITY: KOLN LUBECK
COLOGNE HAMBURG LUEBECK
ISLAND: USEDOM WOLLIN
FEHMARN FRISIAN
LAKE: DUMMER WURMSEE
AMMERSEE BODENSEE
CHIEMSEE MURITZEE
CONSTANCE
LANGUAGE: DEUTSCH
MEASURE: AAM IMI OHM FASS
FUSS LAST RUTE SACK STAB
CARAT EIMER KANNE KETTE LINIE
MAASS METZE RUTHE SIMRI
MASSEL MORGEN OXHOFT
SEIDEL STRICH JUCHART KLAFTER
TAGWERK SCHEFFEL SCHOPPEN
STUBCHEN VIERLING
MONEY: NOTGELD OSTMARK
MOUNTAIN: FELDBERG WATZMANN
MOUNTAIN RANGE: ORE ALPS
HARZ RHON HARDT HUNSRUCK
NAME: REICH ASHKENAZ GERMANIA
DEUTSCHLAND
NATIVE: GOTH SAXON TEUTON
PORT: EMDEN BREMEN HAMBURG
ROSTOCK STETTIN
RESORT: EMS BADEN AACHEN
RIVER: ALZ EMS INN EDER EGER
ELBE ISAR LAHN LECH MAIN
NAAB NAHE ODER OKER REMS
RUHR SAAR SIEG ALLER DONAU
EIDER FULDA HAVEL HUNTE ILLER
LEINE LIPPE MOSEL MULDE
PEENE REGEN RHEIN RHINE
SAALE SAUER SPREE UCKER
VECHT WERRA WESER DANUBE
ELSTER KOCHER NECKAR NEISSE
RANDOW TAUBER WARNOW
ALTMUHL JEETZEL PEGNITZ
SALZACH UNSTRUT
STATE: BADEN HESSE LIPPE
BAYERN BREMEN HESSEN
SAXONY BAVARIA HAMBURG
PRUSSIA SAARLAND BRUNSWICK
TOWN: AUE EMS HOF ULM BONN
GERA GOCH HAAR HAMM JENA
KIEL KOLN LAHR SUHL AALEN
AHLEN EMDEN ESSEN FURTH
GOTHA HAGEN HALLE HERNE
MAINZ MOLLN NEUSS PIRNA
TRIER AACHEN ALTENA ALTONA
BARMEN BERLIN BREMEN
CASSEL DACHAU DESSAU ERFURT
KASSEL LINDEN LUBECK MUNICH
PLAUEN TREVES BAMBERG
BRESLAU COBLENZ COLOGNE
COTTBUS CREFELD DRESDEN
GORLITZ HAMBURG HANOVER
LEIPZIG MAYENCE MUNCHEN
MUNSTER POTSDAM ROSTOCK
SPANDAU ZWICKAU AUGSBURG
CHEMNITZ DORTMUND
DUISBURG FREIBURG LIEGNITZ
MANNHEIM NURNBERG
SCHWERIN WURSELEN
WURZBURG DARMSTADT
KARLSRUHE MAGDEBURG
NUREMBERG OSNABRUCK
STUTTGART WUPPERTAL

DUSSELDORF HEIDELBERG
OBERHAUSEN
UNIVERSITY TOWN: FREIBURG
HEIDELBERG
WEIGHT: LOT GRAN LOTE LOTH
UNZE LOTHE PFUND STEIN
PRUNDE DRACHMA ZENTNER
VIERLING
WINE: MOSELLE RIESLING

GERMFREE AXENIC
GERMICIDE KRELOS MERBROMIN
GERMINABLE PREGNANT
GERMINATE BUD HIT CHIP CHIT
GERM SHOOT SPIRE SPRIT BRAIRD
SPROUT STRIKE PULLULATE
GERMINATION CATCH
GERSHOM (FATHER OF —) LEVI
MOSES
(MOTHER OF —) ZIPPORAH
GERSHWIN IRA GEORGE
GERYON (DOG OF —) ORTHUS
(FATHER OF —) CHRYSAOR
(MOTHER OF —) CALLIRRHOE
(SLAYER OF —) HERCULES
GESAN TAPUYAN CHAVANTE
GESHAM (FATHER OF —) JAHDAI
GESTATION GOING BREEDING
PREGNANCY
GESTE DEED
GESTICULATE GESTURE
GESTURE CUT FIG BECK BERE GEST
SIGN FILIP GESTE HONOR SANNA
ACTION BECKON BREATH CUTOFF
FILLIP MOTION SALUTE SIGNAL
CURTSEY FASHION FLICKER
MURGEON ACCOLADE CEREMONY
(— OF DERISION) SNOOK
(— OF DOUBT) SHRUG
(— OF SALUTATION) SALAAM
(AFFECTED —) GAATCH
(HAND —) MUDRA
(HINDU —) NAMASTE
(OBSCENE —) BIRD
(OSTENTATIOUS —) POMP
(THREATENING —) MINT
(USELESS —) FUTILITY
GET COP DIG GIT WIN EARN FALL
GAIN GRAB HAVE HENT TAKE TILL
AFONG ANNEX CATCH COVER
FETCH LATCH DERIVE OBTAIN
PUZZLE SECURE ACQUIRE
CAPTURE COMPARE CONQUER
PROCURE PRODUCE RECEIVE
PERCEIVE
(— ABOARD) FLIP
(— ABOUT) BEGO NAVIGATE
(— ALONG) DO GEE FARE FEND
AGREE FADGE FODGE SPEED
FETTLE
(— AROUND) BYPASS COMPASS
FINESSE FLUMMER OUTFLANK
(— AT) ACCESS ATTAIN
(— AWAY) LAM RYNT SLIP EVADE
CHEESE ESCAPE
(— BACK) REDEEM RETIRE
RECOVER
(— BETTER OF) WAX BEST DING
DOWN DAUNT FLING SHEND SHENT
STICK STING JOCKEY OVERGO
RECOVER OVERCOME SURMOUNT
(— BY ARTIFICE) WIND
(— BY ASKING) KICK

(— BY CUNNING) WHIZZLE
(— BY EXTORTION) GRATE
(— BY FLATTERY) COG
(— CLEAR OF) STRIP
(— DISHONESTLY) FIRK
(— DOWN) ALIGHT
(— DRUNK) SOUSE
(— IN RETURN) REAP
(— LOST) STRAY TRAIK
(— ON) AGE FARE BOARD CHEFE
CHEVE FRAME MOUNT SHIFT
EXPLOIT
(— ON WELL) LIKE
(— OUT) LEAK SCRAM CHEESE
OUTWIN VOETSAK
(— PACT) BEAT HURDLE
(— POSSESSION) CARRY
(— READY) GET BOUN PARE RANK
BOWNE BRACE FRAME FETTLE
ORDAIN APPAREL
(— RID) CAST DISH DUMP FREE
JUNK SHAB TOSS ERASE SHAKE
SHIFT SHOOT SLOUGH UNLOAD
DELIVER DISCARD EXTRUDE
DISPATCH DISSOLVE
(— SURREPTITIOUSLY) SNEAK
(— THE POINT) SAVVY
(— TO BOTTOM OF) FATHOM
(— UNDER CONTROL) RAIM
(— UNDER WAY) ROLL
(— UP) ARISE HUDDUP UPRISE
HAIRPIN
(PREF.) (— OFF) DE
GETA SABOT
GETHER (FATHER OF —) ARAM
GETHSEMANE (LOCALE OF —)
OLIVET
GETTING (— ON) TOWARD
(— OUT OF BED) LEVEE
GET-TOGETHER DO DRINK
HOBNOB BAMROCHE POTLATCH
GET-UP ATTIRE
GETUP SETOUT
GEWGAW DIE TOY WALY KNACK
WALLY BAUBLE FANGLE FEGARY
JIGGER FLAMFEW TRANGAM
TRINKET FOLDEROL GIMCRACK
JIMCRACK TRIMTRAM
GEYSER BORE JETTER

GHANA

CAPITAL: ACCRA
COIN: PESEWA
DAM: AKOSOMBO
LAKE: VOLTA BOSUMTWI
LANGUAGE: GA EWE TWI FANTI
HAUSA DAGBANI DAGOMBA
MONEY: CEDI NEWCEDI
MOUNTAIN: AFADJATO
NATIVE: GA EWE AHAFO BRONG
FANTI ASHANTI DAGOMBA
MAMPRUSI
REGION: VOLTA ASHANTI
BRONGAHAFO
RIVER: OTI PRA DAKA TANO
AFRAM VOLTA ANKOBRA
KULPAWN
TOWN: HO WA ODA AXIM FIAN
KETA TALA TEMA ACCRA BAWKU
ENCHI LAWRA LEGON SAMPA
YAPEI DUNKWA KARAGA KPANDU
KUMASI NSAWAM OBUASI
SWEDRU TAMALE TARKWA

WASIPE ANTUBIA DAMONGO
MAMPONG PRESTEA SEKONDI
SUNYANI WINNEBA AKOSOMBO
KINTAMPO TAKORADI
WIND: HARMATTAN

GHARRY SHIGRAM
GHASTLY WAN GASH GRIM PALE
BLATE GHAST LURID UNKET UNKID
DISMAL GOUSTY GRISLY PALLID
CHARNEL DEATHLY FEARFUL
GASHFUL GRIZZLY GRUGOUS
HIDEOUS MACABRE DREADFUL
GRUESOME HORRIBLE SHOCKING
TERRIBLE
GHAWAZI BARAMIKA
GHAZEL ODE POEM
GHERKIN CUCUMBER CORNICHON
GHETTO JEWRY JUDAISM
GHIBELLINE WAIBLING
GHOST HAG KER BHUT HANT JUBA
WAFF BUGAN CADDY DUFFY
DUPPY FETCH GAIST GUEST HAUNT
JUMBY LARVA PRETA SHADE
SPOOK UMBRA CHUREL IDOLON
SOWLTH SPIRIT SPRITE TAISCH
ANTAEUS ANTAIOS BOGGART
BUGGANE GYTRASH PHANTOM
SPECTER SPECTRE VAMPIRE
BARGHEST GUYTRASH PHANTASM
REVENANT
(PREF.) SPECTRO SPOOKO
GHOSTFISH WRYMOUTH
GHOSTLY EERY EERIE GOUSTY
SHADOWY UNCANNY WEIRDLY
CHTHONIC GHASTFUL SPECTRAL
GHOST MOTH SWIFT HEPIALID
GHOSTS (AUTHOR OF —) IBSEN
(CHARACTER IN —) HELEN JACOB
ALVING OSWALD REGINA MANDERS
ENGSTRAND
GHOST-WRITER SPOOK
GHOULISH SATANIC
GHUZ OGHUZ
GI DOGFACE SOLDIER
GIAI NHANG
**GIANNI SCHICCHI (CHARACTER IN
—)** BUOSO DONATI LAURETTA
RINUCCIO SCHICCHI
(COMPOSER OF —) PUCCINI
GIANT ORC ANAK ETEN HUGE OGRE
OTUS WATE YMER YMIR AFRIT
BALOR CACUS HYMIR JOTUN
MIMAS MIMER THRYM TITAN
TROLL AFREET ALBION FAFNIR
GIGANT GOEMOT PALLAS THJAZI
THURSE TITYUS WARLOW
ANTAEUS CYCLOPS GOLIATH
WARLOCK ASCOPART BELLERUS
COLBRAND GIGANTIC GOEMAGOT
GOGMAGOG MASTODON
MORGANTE ORGOGLIO TYPHOEUS
PROCRUSTES
(1-EYED —) CYCLOPS
(100-EYED —) ARGUS
(100-HANDED —) GYGES COTTUS
BRIAREUS
(1000-ARMED —) BANA
(PL.) ANAK ANAKIM COTTUS
ALOADAE REPHAIM NEPHILIM
ZAMZUMMIM
(PREF.) GIGANT(I)(O)
GIANTESS NORN ARGANTE

GIANT FULMAR NELLY STINKER STINKPOT
GIANT GRASS OTATE
GIANT HERON GOLIATH
GIANTISM ACROMEGALY
GIANTLIKE CYCLOPIC CYCLOPEAN CYCLOPIAN
GIANT LILY FIGUE MAGUEY
GIANT PUFFBALL FUZZ FUZZBALL
GIANTS IN THE EARTH (AUTHOR OF —) ROLVAAG
　(CHARACTER IN —) OLE PER ANNA HANS OLSA BERET HANSA PEDER
GIARDIA LAMBLIA
GIB JIB SHOE DEMUR SLIPPER
GIBBAR GIBBERT JUBARTAS
GIBBER CHAT CHATTER
GIBBERISH GREEK JABBER JARGON CHOCTAW ABRACADABRA
GIBBET STOB TREE CROOK JEBAT GALLOWS POTENCE EQUULEUS
GIBBON LAR WAWA UNGKA WUYEN CAMPER HULOCK HOOLOCK SIAMANG HYLOBATE
GIBBOUS CONVEX HULCHY HUMPED SACCATE
GIBE (ALSO SEE JIBE) BOB RUB GIRD JAPE JEST JIBE PROG QUIB QUIP SKIT WIPE FLEER FLING FLIRT FRUMP GLEEK KNACK SCOFF SCOMM SCORN SLANT SNEER DERIDE GLANCE HECKLE BROCARD SARCASM RIDICULE
GIBING SNASH
GID DUNT GIDDY STURDY GOGGLES POTHERY VERTIGO
GIDDALTI (FATHER OF —) HEMAN
GIDDINESS LUNACY SOORAWN
GIDDY GAGA AREEL BARMY DITSY DITZY GLAKY INANE LIGHT SILLY SPACY WESTY GIGLET GLAKED GOWKED GOWKIT SHANNY STURDY VOLAGE GLAIKET LARKING HALUCKET HELLICAT SKIPPING
GIDDY-HEADED HELLICAT
GIDEON (FATHER OF —) JOASH
GIDEONI (SON OF —) ABIDAN
GIFT BOX FOY QUO SOP BENT BOON DASH ENAM MEED SAND BONUS BRIBE CAULP CUDDY DONUM FLAIR GRANT KNACK TOKEN BEFANA CADEAU DASHEE DONARY GENIUS GERSUM GIFTIE GIVING HANSEL LEGACY RECADO REGALO TALENT XENIUM APTNESS BEFFANA BENEFIT CHARISM CHARITY DEODATE DONATIO DOUCEUR ETRENNE FACULTY FAIRING GIFTURE HANDSEL PRESENT PROPINE REGALIO SUBSIDY TASHRIF TRIBUTE AMATORIO APTITUDE BENEFICE BESTOWAL BLESSING COURTESY DONATION DONATIVE GARRISON GIVEAWAY GRATUITY MORTUARY OBLATION OFFERING POTLATCH SPORTULA BENEFACTION REMEMBRANCE PHILANTHROPY PRESENTATION
　(— FROM HUSBAND TO WIFE) ARRAS
　(— OF GOD) GRACE

　(— OF MONEY) POUCH GARNISH BAKSHISH BAKSHEESH
　(— OF NATURE) DOWER DOWRY
　(— RECEIVER) DONEE
　(— TO GOD) DEODATE
　(— TO ROMAN PEOPLE) CONGIARY
(CHARITABLE —) ALMS ENAM PITTANCE
(COMPULSORY —) SIXENIA
(LIBERAL —) LARGESSE
(NATURAL —) TALENT
(NEW YEAR'S EVE —) ETRENNE HAGMENA HOGMANAY
(SPIRITUAL —) CHARISM CHARISMA
(PL.) OBLATA MISSILES
GIFTBOOK ANNUAL KEEPSAKE
GIG RUN TUB MOZE BANDY BUGGY CHAIR GIGGE CHAISE CLATCH DENNET WHISKY CALESIN TILBURY STANHOPE ENGAGEMENT
GIGANTIC HUGE GIANT MAMMOTH TITANIC COLOSSAL ENORMOUS GIGANTAL ATLANTEAN MONSTROUS BROBDINGNAGIAN
GIGGER TEASELER
GIGGLE TEHEE KECKLE NICKER TEEHEE TITTER SNICKER TWITTER
GIGLET JIG
GIL BLAS
GIL BLAS (AUTHOR OF —) LESAGE
　(CHARACTER IN —) GIL BLAS LEWIS PEREZ AURORA MENCIA SCIPIO ANTONIA ARSENIA ROLANDO ALPHONSO DOROTHEA FABRICIO MATTHIAS OLIVAREZ SANGRADO
GILD GILT BEGILD ENGILD ORFGILD
GILDED GILT AURATE INAURATE
GILDER TRACER
GILEAD (FATHER OF —) MACHIR
　(SON OF —) JEPHTHAH
GILGAMESH IZDUBAR
GILL JILL QUAD GHYLL PLICA GILLIE LAMELLA BRANCHIA QUADRANT
　(—S OF BIVALVE) BEARD
　(PL.) GINNERS CHOLLERS BRANCHIAE
　(SUFF.) BRANCH(IA)(IATE)
GILLAR PITTO
GILLIE GILLY HENCHMAN
GILLS
　(PREF.) BRANCHI(O)
GILLYFLOWER STOCK GILVER GELOFRE GILLIVER
GILT SOW
GILTHEAD CONNER MELANURE
GIMBAL GEMEL JEMBLE
GIMCRACK QUIP BAUBLE FIZGIG GEWGAW JIMJAM TRIFLE TRANGAM TRINKET JIMCRACK WHIMWHAM
GIMLET SCREW WIMBLE PIERCEL PIERCER
GIMMICK GAFF SHTIK SHTICK SCHTICK
GIMP TAR ORRIS GUIMPE GIMPING
GIN MAX CRAB GRIN LACE RUIN TAPE TRAP CLEAN JACKY SNARE SNARL DIDDLE GENEVA JAMBER JAMMER SPRINGE TITTERY TWANKAY EYEWATER HOLLANDS SCHIEDAM SCHNAPPS
　(— AND TREACLE) MAHOGANY

(BAD —) RUIN
(DROP OF —) DAFFY
GINATH (SON OF —) TIBNI
GINGER PEPPER RATOON AROMATIC ZINZIBER COLTSFOOT
GINGERBREAD SPICE PARKIN PEPPERCAKE
GINGERLY GINGER WARILY CHARILY EDGINGLY
GINGERROOT HAND RACE
　(PL.) ASARUM
GINGHAM CHAMBRAY
GINKGO ICHO
GINSENG SANG FATIL PANAX ARALIA IVYWORT REDBERRY
GIOCONDA, LA (CHARACTER IN —) ENZO CIECA LAURA ALVISE BARNABA GIOCONDA GRIMALDO
　(COMPOSER OF —) PONCHIELLI
GIRAFFE OONT CAMEL DAPPLE KAMEEL SERAPH CAMAILE RUMINANT
GIRASOL OPAL
GIRD BELT BIND GIRR GIRT HASP YERK CLOSE SCOFF ENGIRD ENRING FASTEN GIRDLE SECURE ACCINGE ENVIRON CINCTURE SURROUND
GIRDER BEAM GIRD GIRT GIRTH TABLE TRUSS BINDER SUMMER WARREN GIRDING TWISTER BUCKSTAY STRINGER
GIRDING CINCTURE
GIRDLE OBI ZON BARK BELT CEST GIRD HOOP SASH ZONA ZONE CEINT GIRTH MITER PATTE SARPE WAIST BODICE CESTUS CINGLE CIRCLE MOOCHA TISSUE ZODIAC ZONULA ZOSTER BALDRIC BALTEUS CENTRUM CENTURE COMPASS GIRDING SHINGLE CEINTURE CINCTURE CINGULUM SURROUND
　(— FOR HELMET) TISSUE
　(— OF CASSOCK) SURCINGLE
　(— OF DIATOM) HOOP
(BRIDE'S —) CEST CESTUS
(LITTLE —) ZONULE ZONELET
(ROYAL —) MALO
(SACRED —) KUSTI
(PREF.) ZON(I)(O) ZOSTERI ZOSTERO
(SUFF.) PLEURA
GIRDLED RUNG
GIRL BIT GAL HER KIT POP SHE SIS TIB TID TIT BABE BABY BINT BIRD CHIT DAME DEEM DELL GILL JANE JILL JUDY LASS MARY MOPS MORT PERI PUSS SLUT WREN BEAST BUNNY FILLY FLUFF GUIDE KITTY LUBRA QUEAN SISSY SKIRT TIDDY TITTY TOOTS TRULL BURDIE CALICO CLINER CUMMER DALAGA DAMSEL DEEMIE FEMALE FIZGIG GEISHA GIRLIE LASSIE LOVELY MAGGIE NUMBER PIGEON SHEILA SISTER SUBDEB TOMATO CAMILLA COLLEEN CRUMPET DAMOSEL MADCHEN MAUTHER TENDREL BONNIBEL FARMETTE FEMININE GRISETTE MUCHACHA
　(— NOT YET 13) PRETEEN

　(— OF MEXICAN DESCENT) CHICANA
(AGILE —) YANKER
(AWKWARD —) HOIT
(BEATIFIED —) BEATA
(BEAUTIFUL —) PERI BELLE
(BOISTEROUS —) GILPY GILPEY
(BOLD —) HOIDEN HOYDEN
(CAMP FIRE —) ARTISAN
(CHORUS —) CHORINE CORYPHEE
(CLUMSY —) TAUPIE TAWPIE
(COUNTRY —) MEG JOAN
(DANCING —) ALMA DASI ALMAH KISANG KISAENG BAYADERE DEVADASI
(DANCING —S) GHAWAZI
(DEAR —) PEAT
(DUMPY —) CUTTY
(FLIGHTY —) GOOSECAP
(FLIRTATIOUS —) JADE JILLET
(FLOWER —) NYDIA
(FORWARD —) STRAP
(FROLICSOME —) GILPY
(GANGSTER'S —) MOLL
(GIDDY —) GIG GIGLET GIGLOT JILLET
(GREEK —) HAIDEE
(GYPSY —) GITANA
(HIRED —) BIDDY BIDDIE
(IMPUDENT —) STRAP
(JAPANESE —) GEISHA
(LITTLE —) SIS COOKY SISSY COOKIE LASSOCK
(MISCHIEVOUS —) CUTTY HUSSY
(MODEST —) BLUSHET
(NAIVE —) INGENUE
(NON-JEWISH —) SHIKSE SHICKSA
(PERT —) MINX HUSSY
(PRETTY —) PRIM BUNNY
(PRETTY—) BUNNY
(PRETTY —) CUTEY CUTIE
(ROMPING —) STAG TOMBOY
(SAUCY —) SNIP
(SEDUCTIVE —) LOLITA
(SERVANT —) SLUT
(SHIFTLESS —) MYSTERY
(SILLY —) SKIT
(SINGING —) ALMA ALMEH
(SLENDER —) SYLPH
(SMALL —) PINAFORE
(SPIRITED —) FILLY
(UNATTRACTIVE —) FRUMP
(UNMARRIED —) MOUSME TOWDIE MUSUMEE MADEMOISELLE
(WANTON —) GIG FILLOCK
(WILD —) BLOWZE
(WORKING —) ORISETTE
(WORTHLESS —) HUSSY
(YOUNG —) BUD MODER TITTY MAIDEN MOTHER BAGGAGE COLLEEN FLAPPER GIRLEEN ROSEBUD
　(PL.) GIRLERY GIRLHOOD
　(PREF.) PUPI
GIRLFRIEND LADY STEADY
　(GANGSTER'S —) MOLL
GIRL OF THE GOLDEN WEST
　(CHARACTER IN —) DICK JACK RANCE MINNIE JOHNSON RAMERREZ
　(COMPOSER OF —) PUCCINI
GIRT CINCT
GIRTH GIRD GIRT TAPE CINCH

GARTH GIRSE GRETH WANTY CINGLE WARROK COMPASS GIRDING SHINGLE WEBBING

GIST JET NET NUB SUM CHAT CORE GITE KNOT MEAT PITH GREAT HEART JOIST POINT SENSE BURDEN KERNEL ESSENCE PURPORT SUMMARY STRENGTH

GITH MELANTHY

GIVE ADD GIE HOB TIP BEAR DEAL DOLE HAND METE SELL TAKE WEVE WHIP YEVE ALLOW AWARD COUGH GRANT REFER YIELD ACCORD AFFORD BESTOW CONFER DEMISE DOTATE FASTEN IMPART IMPOSE IMPUTE RENDER SUPPLY CONSIGN DELIVER FORGIVE FURNISH PRESENT PROPINE BEQUEATH DISPENSE
(— A BOOST) BOLSTER
(— ADHERENCE) ASSENT
(ADMITTANCE) ACCEPT
(— ADVICE) READ ADVISE
(— AN ACCOUNT) TELL RELATE REPORT
(— AND TAKE) GIFFGAFF
(— ANYTHING NAUSEOUS TO) DOSE
(— A PLACE TO) SITUATE
(— APPROVAL) CONSENT
(— A REASON) ACCOUNT
(— A REMEDY) MINISTER
(— AS CONCESSION) YETTE
(— AS EXPLANATION) ASSIGN
(— ASSURANCE) EFFRONT
(— ATTENTION TO) HEED
(— AUTHORITY) ENABLE EMPOWER ACCREDIT
(— AWAY) PART
(— BACK) REFUND RETURN RESTORE
(— BIRTH) KIT BEAR BORN DROP FIND MAKE BEGET BREED ISSUE WORLD FARROW KINDLE LITTER DELIVER FRESHEN
(— BY WILL) DEVISE
(— CARE) NURSE
(— CLAIM TO) REMISE
(— COUNSEL) AREAD AREED
(— CREDIT FOR) FRIST
(— CURRENCY TO) PASS
(— EAR) HARK HARKEN LISTEN HEARKEN
(— EXPRESSION TO) EMOTE FRAME VOICE
(— FORM) CUT
(— FORTH) WARP YIELD AFFORD CONCEIVE
(— GROUND) RETIRE
(— HEED) LOOK ATTEND
(— IN) BOW RELENT CONCEDE COLLAPSE
(— IN EXCHANGE) SWAP SWOP
(— INFORMATION) WARN
(— IN MARRIAGE) BESTOW SPOUSE
(— INSTRUCTION) LEAR
(— NAME TO) BAPTIZE
(— NOTICE) WARN HERALD APPRISE PUBLISH ANNOUNCE INTIMATE
(— NOTICE TO APPEAR) GARNISH
(— OBLIQUE EDGE) CANT
(— OFF) EMIT SEND SHED EXUDE

FLING DIVIDE EFFUSE EVOLVE EXHALE EXPIRE EXCRETE SEPARATE
(— ONE'S SELF OVER TO) ADDICT
(— ONE'S WORD) PROMISE
(— OUT) BOOM LEAK EXUDE ISSUE PETAL EVOLVE EMANATE OUTGIVE
(— OVER) LIN
(— PAIN) AGGRIEVE
(— PLACE) VAIL BACCARE
(— PLEDGE) GAGE
(— PROMINENCE TO) FEATURE
(— RELUCTANTLY) BEGRUDGE
(— SATISFACTION) ABY ABYE ABEGGE
(— SPARINGLY) INCH
(— STRENGTH TO) NERVE
(— SUPPORT) ASSIST ANIMATE
(— TEMPORARILY) LEND
(— TIP) TOUT
(— TONGUE) CRY YEARN
(— UP) PUT BURY DROP PART CHUCK DEMIT DEVOW FORGO LEAVE RAISE REMIT SHOOT SPARE SPEND WAIVE ABJURE ADDICT BETRAY DESERT DEVOTE FOREGO MIZZLE REFUSE RELENT RENDER RESIGN VACATE ABANDON DEPOSIT DESPAIR FLUMMOX FORBEAR FORGIVE REFRAIN RELEASE ABDICATE RENOUNCE
(— VENT TO) EMIT ISSUE DISCHARGE
(— VOICE) BOLT ACCENT
(— WARNING) ALERT
(— WAY) GO FAIL FOLD KEEL MOVE SINK VAIL BREAK BUDGE BURST FAINT SLAKE YIELD BUCKLE FALTER RELENT SWERVE FOUNDER RECLAIM SUCCUMB
(WITNESS) DEPOSE

GIVE-AND-TAKE SWAP

GIVEN APT DONEE NATHAN PROMPT
(— TO) ALL AFTER
(SUFF.) **(— TO)** ABLE IBLE LEW

GIVER DONOR
(— OF ALMS) ALMONER
(— OF LIFE) APHETA
(NAME —) EPONYM

GIVING DOLE BOUNTY DATION REMISE
(— BY WILL) TESTATION
(— HELP) ADJUTANT
(— MILK) FRESH
(— NO MILK) YELD YELL
(— TROUBLE) CUMBROUS

GIZMO DOODAD GADGET
GIZZARD CROP GIGERIUM
GIZZARD SHAD SKIPJACK
GLABROUS BALD SMOOTH GLABRATE LEVIGATE
GLACIAL (— FORMATION) ARETE
GLACIARIUM RINK
GLACIATE ICE
GLACIATION MINDEL
(— STAGE) RISS WURM
GLACIER BRAE ICECAP STREAM CALOTTE ICEBERG PIEDMONT
(FACING A —) STOSS
(FACING AGAINST —) STOSS
(PREF.) GLACIO
GLACIOLOGY CRYOLOGY
GLACIS ESPLANADE

GLAD GAY FAIN LIEF VAIN CANTY HAPPY PROUD BLITHE FESTUS GLADLY JOCUND JOYFUL JOYOUS GLADFUL GLEEFUL JOCULAR ANIMATED CHEERFUL CHEERING FESTIVAL GLADSOME PLEASING
GLADDEN JOY GLAD BLESS BLISS CHEER EXULT MIRTH BLITHE COMFORT GLADIFY LIGHTEN REJOICE
(PREF.) TERP(I)(SI)
GLADE LAWN LAUND SLADE SHRADD SUNGLADE SUNSCALD
(PREF.) NEMO
GLADIATOR THRAX RETIARY SAMNITE SECUTOR ANDABATA
GLADIOLUS GLAD IRID LILY LEVERS LILIUM GLADIOLA
GLADLY GLAD LIEF FAINLY LIEFLY LOVELY HAPPILY
GLADNESS JOY GLAD GLEE BLISS MIRTH BLITHE FAINNESS GLADSHIP PLEASURE
GLADSOME BLITHE
GLAGA KASA KUSA TALTHIB
GLAMOR SCRY UTIS OOMPH PIZAZZ BRABBLE PIZZAZZ BALLYHOO
GLAMORIZE POT GLORIFY
GLAMOROUS GLAM EXOTIC ALLURING CHARMING
GLAMOUR HALO PAZAZZ PIZAZZ PIZZAZZ PRESTIGE
GLANCE EYE RAY SEE BEAM CAST GLIM LEER PEEK SCRY SKEG VIEW WINK BLENK BLINK BLUSH CAROM FLASH GLEEK GLENT GLIDE GLIFF GLINT GLISK GRAZE PRINK SCREW SIGHT SKIME SLANT SQUIZ TWIRE APERCU ASPECT CARROM GANDER REGARD SCANCE STRIKE VISION EYEBEAM EYESHOT FYFWINK GLIMPSE BELAMOUR GLIFFING OEILLADE
(— OFF) GLACE
(— THROUGH) SAMPLE
(LOVE —) AMORET
(MELANCHOLY —) DOWNCAST
(SHARP —) DART
(SIDELONG —) SHEW SLENT SKLENT
(SLY —) GLEG GLIME GLOAT
GLAND MILT NOIX SETA CLYER CRYPT GONAD LIVER MAMMA ACINUS BREAST KERNEL THYMUS TONSIL ADRENAL CRUMENA NECTARY PAROTID PAROTIS TEARPIT THYROID CONARIUM ENDOCRIN FOLLICLE FOLLOWER GANGLION GLANDULA GLANDULE HOOFWORM PROSTATE SCIRRHUS SPERMARY TESTICLE
(PREF.) ADEN(O) SCIRRH(O)
(SUFF.) ADEN SCIRRHUS
GLANDERS FARCY MALLEUS
GLANDULAR EARTHY INNATE SEXUAL ADENOID PHYSICAL ADENOIDAL
GLANS NUT GLAND
GLARE BEAT GAZE BLARE BLAZE BLOOM FLAME GLAZE STARE GLITTER ICEBLINK RADIANCE
GLARING HARD RANK GLARY

AGLARE GARISH BURNING FLARING STARING FLAGRANT
GLASGOW (NATIVE OF —) GLASWEGIAN
GLASS CUP VER CALX FLAT FLUX FRIT JENA MOIL PONY VITA CHARK FACER FLINT GLAZE STOOP STOUP VERRE VITRE CALGON CEMENT CULLET RUMMER SPECKS VITRUM ALEYARD BIFOCAL BRIMMER CHIRPER CRYSTAL PERLITE SCHMELZ TALLBOY VITRITE FROSTING OBSIDIAN SCHOPPEN PERSPECTIVE
(— IN STATE OF FUSION) METAL
(— OF A MIRROR) STONE
(— OF BEER) BREW
(— OF BRANDY) SNEAKER
(— OF SPIRITS) CHASSE
(— OF WHISKY) KELTY RUBDOWN
(— OF WINE) APERITIF
(— STICKING TO PUNTY) COLLET
(BEER —) SHELL SEIDEL PILSNER PILSENER
(BELL-SHAPED —) CUP CLOCHE
(BURNING —) SUNGLASS
(CHEVAL —) PSYCHE
(COLORED —) SMALT SMALTO TINTER SCHMELZ
(COLORED —S) GOGGLES
(CUPPING —) VENTOSE
(CURVED —) LENS
(DESSERT —) COUPE
(DRINKING —) GOBLET RUMKIN PILSNER PIMLICO SCUTTLE TUMBLER SCHOONER
(EUROPEAN ORNAMENTAL —) PELOTON
(EXAMINATION —) SLIDE
(FULL —) BUMPER
(FUSIBLE —) FLUX
(HALF —) SPLIT
(ICE CREAM) SLIDER
(KIND OF —) CUSTARD CRANBERRY
(LEAD —) STRASS
(LIQUEUR —) PONY PONEY
(LIQUOR —) GUN
(MAGNIFYING —) LOUPE
(MASS OF MOLTEN —) PARISON
(METEORITIC —) TEKTITE MOLDAVITE
(OPALESCENT —) OPALINE
(OPAQUE —) HYALITHE
(ORNAMENTAL —) PELOTON
(PIECE OF —) PANE
(PIECE OF HOT —) BIT
(PULVERIZED —) FROSTING
(REFUSE —) CALX CULLET
(RUBY —) SCHMELZE
(RUSSIAN —) CHARK
(SHERBET —) SUPREME
(SHERRY —) COPITA
(SMOKED —) SHADE
(STAINED —) VITRAIL
(TALL —) RUMMER
(THIN —) MOUSSELINE
(VOLCANIC —) PUMICE PERLITE
(WINDOW —) PANE
(WINE —) FLUTE
(PL.) SHELLS
(PREF.) HYAL(O) VITR(EO)(I)(O)
GLASSBLOWER MUMBLER
GLASS CRAB SPECTER SPECTRE

GLASSES EYEWEAR
(TINTED —) SHADES
GLASSHOUSE STOVE HOTHOUSE
GLASS-LIKE VITRIC
GLASS MENAGERIE (AUTHOR OF
—) WILLIAMS
(CHARACTER IN —) TOM JAMES
LAURA AMANDA OCONNOR
GLASSWARE AGATA AURENE
BURMESE FAVRILE OPALINE
STEUBEN VITRICS AMBERINA
CORALENE
GLASSWORK GLAZING GLAZIERY
GLASSWORKER GANGMAN
GLAZIER SNAPPER GLASSMAN
SERVITOR
GLASSWORT KALI KELPWORT
SALTWORT SAMPHIRE
GLASSY GLIB FILMY GLAZY GLAZEN
GLASSEN HYALINE HYALOID
VITREAL VITREOUS
(PREF.) HYAL(O)
GLAUCE (FATHER OF —) CREON
(HUSBAND OF —) JASON
GLAUCUS (FATHER OF —) MINOS
ANTHEDON SISYPHUS
HIPPOLOCHUS
(MOTHER OF —) MEROPE PASIPHAE
GLAZE DIP LEAD SIZE SLIP GLASS
SLEET SMEAR ENAMEL QUARRY
CELADON COPERTA EELSKIN
GLASSEN GLAZING GLIDDER
COUVERTE TIGEREYE
(— OF ICE) GLARE
(POTTERY —) SMEAR
GLAZED FILMY GLACE GLASSEN
GLOSSED
GLAZED WARE GLOST
GLAZIER PUTTIER
(TOOL OF —) SPRIG LADKIN
GLEAM RAY BEAM GLOW LEAM
WAFT WINK BLENK BLINK BLUSH
FLASH GLAIK GLEEN GLENT GLINT
GLISK GLIST GLOSE SHINE SKIME
SPUNK STARE STEEM TWIRE
GLANCE SCANCE FOULDRE
GLIMMER GLITTER SHIMMER
CORUSCATE SCINTILLA
(— FAINTLY) SHIMMER
(— OF LIGHT) LEAM PINK GLAIK
SCANCE
(FAINT —) SCAD
GLEAMING FAW GLOW CLEAR
GLINT STEEP ABLAZE BRIGHT
GLEAMY ADAZZLE SHINING
GLOOMING
GLEAN CULL EARN REAP LEASE
DEDUCE GATHER COLLECT
SCRINGE
GLEANER STIBBLER
GLEANING CROP GATHERING
(LITERARY —S) ANALECTA
ANALECTS
GLEBE SOD CLOD LAND SOIL
TERMON KIRKTOWN
GLEE GLY JOY SONG MIRTH SPORT
GAIETY DELIGHT ELATION
WASSAIL HILARITY MADRIGAL
GLEEFUL GAY MERRY JOYOUS
JOCULAR GLEESOME
GLEEMAN SONGMAN MINSTREL
GLEN DEN GILL GLYN GRIFF HEUCH

HEUGH KLOOF SLACK SLADE
TEMPE CANADA DINGLE POCKET
GLIADIN GLUTIN PROLAMIN
GLIB PAT FLIP SLICK CASUAL
GLOSSY OFFHAND RENABLE
SHALLOW VOLUBLE FLIPPANT
GLIBLY SLICK
GLIBNESS UNCTION
GLIDE GO SKI FLOW SAIL SILE SKIM
SLIP SLUR SOAR SWIM COAST
CREEP DANCE FLEET GLACE
GRAZE LAPSE MERGE PLANE
SCOOP SHIRL SKATE SKIFF SKIRR
SKITE SLADE SLEEK SLICK SLIDE
SLIPE STEAL GLANCE GLIDER
SASHAY SNOOVE ILLAPSE SCRIEVE
SCRITHE SKITTER SLITHER
AIRPLANE GLISSADE VOLPLANE
SEMIVOWEL
(— AWAY) ELAPSE
(— BY) PASS FLEET
(— IN) ILLAPSE
(— OFF) EXIT
(MUSICAL —) PORTAMENTO
GLIDER BIPLANE SCOOTER
PARAWING SAILPLANE
(KIND OF —) HANG
GLIDING LAPSE TRAIL SLIDING
(— OF THE VOICE) DRAG
(— OVER) LAMBENT
GLIMMER FIRE GLIM GLOW IDEA
LEAM STIM BLINK FLASH GLEAM
GLOOM STIME SIMPER BLINTER
FLIMMER GLIMPSE GLITTER
SHIMMER SPARKLE TWINKLE
SUNBLINK
GLIMMERING GHOST AGLIMMER
GLOOMING
GLIMPSE ESPY IDEA WAFF WAFT
BLINK BLUSH FLASH GLIFF GLINT
GLISK SIGHT STIME TINGE TRACE
WHIFF GLANCE GLEDGE LUSTER
SCANCE GLIMMER INKLING
(BRIEF —) APERCU
(FLEETING —) SHIM SNATCH
GLINT PEEP FLASH GLEAM GLENT
GLANCE SPARKLE
GLIS MYOXUS
GLISSANDO GLISS SMEAR
GLISSADE
GLISTEN FLASH GLISK GLISS GLIST
SHINE GLISTER GLITTER SHIMMER
SPANGLE SPARKLE RUTILATE
GLISTENING SHINY AGLISTEN
GLITCH FLAW SNAG
GLITTER FLASH GLARE GLEAM
GLEIT GLINT GLITZ GLORE SHEEN
SHINE SKYRE STARE BICKER
LUSTER SCANCE GLIMMER
GLISTEN GLISTER SKINKLE
SPANGLE SPARKLE TWINKLE
BRANDISH RADIANCE RUTILATE
CORUSCATE
(FALSE —) GILT
GLITTERING GEMMY SHEEN SHINY
STEEP FULGID SPANGLY AGLITTER
GLITTERY RUTILANT BRILLIANT
CLINQUANT
GLOAMING EVE DUSK GLOAM
GLOOMING TWILIGHT
GLOAT GAZE GLUT TIRE EXULT
PREEN
GLOBAL PLANETARY

GLOBE ORB BALL BOWL CLEW
CLUE POME AGGER GEOID MONDE
MOUND ROUND SPHERE
COMPASS GEORAMA GLOBULE
GRENADE AQUARIUM ROUNDURE
GLOBEFISH FUGU TOBY TOADO
ATINGA BOTETE PUFFER BLAASOP
BURFISH OOPUHUE BLOWFISH
GLOBEFLOWER BOLT GOLLAND
GOWLAND CORCHORUS
GLOBE THISTLE ECHINOPS
GLOBOSE COCCOID COCCOUS
CAPITATE GLOBULAR
GLOBULAR GLOBED ROTUND
GLOBATE GLOBOSE GLOBICAL
GLOBULE BEAD BLOB DROP GLOB
PEARL BUBBLE BUTTON REGULUS
GLOBULET SPHERULE
(— OF TAPIOCA) FISHEYE
GLOBULIN MAYSIN MYOSIN VIGNIN
ARACHIN CORYLIN EDESTIN
LEGUMIN TUBERIN VICILIN
ANTIBODY BIOLOGIC EXCELSIN
GLYCININ MUSCULIN ORYZENIN
GLOCKENSPIEL BELL LYRA
CARILLON
GLOMERULE GLOME FASCICLE
GLOOM DAMP DUSK MURK CLOUD
DREAR FROWN SOMBER DESPAIR
DIMNESS GLOOMTH SADNESS
DARKNESS MIDNIGHT
GLOOMINESS DUMPS
GLOOMY DUN SAD WAN BLUE
COLD DARK DOUR DREE DULL
EERY GLUM MIRK MURK ADUSK
ADUST BLACK BROWN DOWFF
DREAR DUSKY EERIE FERAL
GUMLY HEAVY LURID MOODY
MORNE MUDDY MUNGY MUSTY
MUZZY ROOKY SABLE SORRY
STERN SULKY SURLY SWART TRIST
CLOUDY DISMAL DREARY DREICH
DROOPY DRUMLY GLUMMY
MOROSE SOLEMN SOMBER
SULLEN TETRIC THRAWN
OBSCURE STYGIAN THESTER
DARKSOME DESOLATE DOLESOME
DOWNBEAT DOWNCAST
FUNEREAL GLOOMING LOWERING
OVERCAST TRISTFUL PESSIMISTIC
GLORIA HALO GLORY AUREOLE
GLORIFICATION AVATAR
GLORIFY HERY LAUD BLESS DEIFY
EXALT EXTOL HERSE HONOR
PRIDE WURTH ENHALO KUDIZE
PRAISE CLARIFY ELEVATE
MAGNIFY DIVINIZE EMBLAZON
EULOGIZE PROCLAIM STELLIFY
GLORIOLE HALO AUREOLE
GLORIOUS SRI DEAR DERE MERE
SHRI GRAND PROUD BRIGHT
EMINENT RENOWNED
GLORY JOY ORE SUN FACE FAME
GLOR HALO HORN BLAZE BOAST
EXULT HONOR KUDOS PRIDE
WULDER AUREOLA CLARITY
GARLAND GLORIFY RADIANCE
SPLENDOR WORTHING
GLORY-PEA KOWHAI KAKABEAK
KAKABILL KOWHAI
GLOSS GILL COLOR DUNCE GLASS
GLAZE GLOZE JAPAN SHEEN SHINE
BLANCH LUSTER LUSTRE POSTIL

REMARK VENEER BURNISH
EXPOUND VARNISH FLOURISH
PALLIATE POLITURE WHITEWASH
(— OVER) FARD HUSH SALVE SLEEK
SOOTHE
GLOSSA LINGUA
GLOSSARY GLOSS CLAVIS
GLOSSIPHONIA CLEPSINE
GLOSSY GLOZE NITID SHINY SILKY
SLEEK SLICK SATINY SMOOTH
GLOVE KID CUFF GAGE MITT COFFE
BERLIN MITTEN CHEVRON
DANNOCK GANTLET GOMUKHI
GAUNTLET
(— FOR RUBBING SKIN) STRIGIL
(BISHOP'S —) GWANTUS
(BODY OF —) TRANK
(BOXING —) MUFFLE
(HEDGER'S —) DANNOCK
(HUSKING —) HUSKER
(PART OF —) THUMB TRANK
GUSSET BINDING FOURCHETTE
GLOVEMAKER DOMER GLOVER
CLASPER FINGERER
GLOVER TRANKER
GLOW ARC LOW AURA BURN FIRE
LEAM LOOM LOWE BLAZE BLOOM
BLUSH FLAME FLASH FLUSH
GLAZE GLEAM GLEED GLORY
GLOSS GLOZE SHINE STEAM
CORONA KINDLE WARMTH
FLUSTER LIGHTEN
(— OF PASSION) ESTUS AESTUS
(— WITH INTENSE HEAT) IGNITE
GLOWER GAZE GLOW GLARE
GLOOM GLORE SCOWL
GLOWING HOT RED LIVE ROSY
WARM AGLOW FIERY LIGHT QUICK
RUDDY VIVID ABLAZE ARDENT
ORIENT BURNING CANDENT
FERVENT RADIANT SHINING
FLAGRANT RUTILANT
GLOWWORM FIREFLY FIREWORM
GLOWBIRD LAMPYRID
GLOZE FAWN PAINT SMOOTH
FLATTERY
GLUCINUM BERYLLIUM
GLUCOSE AME GLYCOSE
DEXTROSE
GLUCOSIDE GEIN APIIN RUTIN
TUTIN ADONIN BINDER CORNIN
DURRIN FRAXIN FUSTIN IRIDIN
PICEIN UZARIN ACACIIN ARBUTIN
DAPHNIN DIOSMIN ESCULIN
ESTEVIN GITALIN GITONIN GITOXIN
HEDERIN HELECIN INDICAN
LOGANIN LOTUSIN LUPININ
OUABAIN POPULIN ROBININ
SALICIN TABACIN TEUCRIN
ADONIDIN CARTHAME ERICOLIN
GENISTIN GOSSYPIN MORINDIN
NARINGIN PARIGLIN PARILLIN
PRUNASIN QUINOVIN SAPONINE
SCILLAIN SINIGRIN SYRINGIN
THEVETIN VERNONIN VIBURNIN
VICIANIN
GLUE PAD EPOXY MOUNT STICK
BEGLEW CEMENT FUNORI
FUNORIN STICKER STICKUM
TAUROCOL
(BEE —) PROPOLIS
(WEAK —) SIZE

(PREF.) COLL(A)(O)(OIDIO)(OIDO) GLOEO
(SUFF.) COLL GLIA GLOEA

GLUE-LIKE
(PREF.)
(— **SUBSTANCE**) GLI

GLUEY GLUISH STICKY STRINGY VISCOUS ADHESIVE

GLUM CLUM DOUR GRUM SURLY GLOOMY GLUMPY MOROSE SULLEN DEJECTED

GLUMALES POALES

GLUME PILE FLIGHT
(**FLOWERING** —) LEMMA
(PL.) CHAFF

GLUSIDE SACCHARIN

GLUT CLOY FILL GULP QUAT SATE CHOKE DRAFT GORGE BATTEN ENGLUT EXCESS MARROW PAMPER PAUNCH ENGORGE GLUTTON SATIATE SURFEIT SWALLOW OVERFEED SAGINATE SATURATE

GLUTEAL NATAL

GLUTELIN AVENINE ORYZENIN

GLUTENIN AVENIN ZYMOME ZYMOMIN

GLUTINOUS ROPY SIZY ROPEY SLIMY TOUGH STICKY VISCID
(PREF.) GLOEO GLOIO

GLUTTED QUAT GORGED SATIATED

GLUTTER VEER

GLUTTON HOG PIG GLUT GORB GUTS GULCH MIKER GLOTUM HELLUO MACCUS EPICURE GUTLING LURCHER MOOCHER RAVENER SWILLER CARCAJOU DRABMAN GOURMAND GULLYGUT
(**STUPID** —) GRUB

GLUTTONIZE BIZLE BEZZLE

GLUTTONOUS GREEDY GLUTTON HOGGISH GOURMAND

GLUTTONY GULE EDACITY SURFEIT

GLYCERIDE BUTYRIN

GLYCINE SOJA

GLYCOL CARBOWAX

GLYCOPROTEIN MUCIN MUCOID

GLYCOSIDE APIIN CROCIN ACACIIN CYMARIN DIGOXIN GITALIN GITOXIN HEDERIN HYPERIN LOGANIN LOTUSIN SAPONIN ALDESIDE ANDROSIN ANTIARIN HOLOSIDE KETOSIDE

GLYPTOLOGIST JEWELLER

GNARL NOB KNOB KNUR KNARL KNURR SNIRL WARRE DEFORM

GNARLED GNARLY KNARRY KNOTTY CRABBED KNOTTED KNURLED

GNASH TUSK CHAMP CRASH GANCH GRASH GRATE KNASH

GNAT KNAW SMUT MIDGE PUNKY STOUT KNATTE SCIARA SCIARID SCINIPH BLACKFLY DIPTERAN GNATLING
(PREF.) CULIC(I)

GNATCATCHER SYLVIID

GNATHION MENTON

GNAW EAT NAB BITE FRET TIRE CHELE GNARL MOUSE SHEAR ARRODE BEFRET BEGNAW CANKER CHAVEL NATTLE NIGGLE ROUNGE CHIMBLE CHUMBLE CORRODE

GNAWED
(PREF.) BROTO

GNAWING EATING RODENT FRETFUL ARROSION ROSORIAL

GNOME NIS ADAGE NISSE PECHT PYGMY KOBOLD VAKSHA YAKSHI GNOMIDE GREMLIN HODEKEN ERDGEIST

GNOMON COCK INDEX STILE STYLE FESCUE STYLUS

GNOSTIC CLEVER SHREWD KNOWING PERATES EBIONITE MANDAEAN SEVERIAN SIMONIAN SIMONITE

GNU KOKOON BRINDLE

GO BE DO ACT GAE HOP ISH LAY NIM PEP TEE WAG BANG BEAR BING BOWN BUSK DRAW FAND FARE FOND GANG HARK HAUL HUMP MOVE QUIT RAIK ROAM ROLL SEEK SHOT SILE SLAP SNAP STAB STEP TAKE TEEM TOUR WADE WANE WEAR WEND WEVE WIND WISE WORK YEAD YEDE AMBLE BOUND CARRY CHEVE DEMON DRESS FETCH FRAME HAUNT KNOCK LEAVE MOSEY PLUCK REACH SCRAM SHAKE SLOPE SPEED TOUCH TRACE TRACK TRENE TRINE TRUSS WHIZZ YONGE BECOME BETAKE CHIEVE CRUISE DEPART EXTEND QUATCH QUETCH REPAIR RESORT RESULT RETIRE SASHAY STRAKE STRIKE TODDLE TRAVEL WEAKEN JOURNEY SCRITHE DIMINISH WITHDRAW
(— **ABOUT**) JET BEGO BIGAN
(— **ABOUT DEJECTEDLY**) PEAK
(— **ABOUT GOSSIPING**) COURANT
(— **AHEAD**) HOLD
(— **AIMLESSLY**) ERR BUMMLE
(— **ALONG**) PATH
(— **ALONG WITH**) ACCOMPANY
(— **AROUND**) SKIRT BYPASS CIRCUE COMPASS ENCOMPASS
(— **ASHORE**) LAND
(— **ASTRAY**) ERR MAR WRY MANG WILL MISGO DELIRE FORVAY MISWEND DEROGATE MISCARRY
(— **AWAY**) AGO HOP OFF BEAT BUNK HIKE NASH PART SHOO VADE CLEAR HENCE IMSHI LEAVE SCRAM SHIFT BEGONE BUGGER DEPART REMOVE VACATE SKIDDOO ELONGATE
(— **AWAY AT ONCE**) SCRAM
(— **BACK**) RECEDE RETURN REGRESS RETRACE
(— **BACK IN TIME**) MOUNT
(— **BAD**) SOUR
(— **BEFORE**) LEAD FOREGO PRECEDE ANTECEDE PREAMBLE
(— **BEYOND**) SURPASS FOREPASS
(— **BRISKLY**) JUNE
(— **BROKE**) BUST
(— **BY**) PASS
(— **BY WATER**) SAIL
(— **COURTING**) WENCH
(— **DOGGEDLY**) PLUG
(— **DOWN**) SET SINK VAIL DROOP SOUND DESCEND
(— **EASILY**) AMBLE

(— **ERRATICALLY**) KICK
(— **FAST**) HURRY SPLIT BARREL BEELINE
(— **FOR**) ATTEMPT
(— **FORTH**) AGO DEPART FORTHGO
(— **FORWARD**) HUP HUPP ADVANCE AGGRESS PROCEED
(— **FOWLING**) AUCUPATE
(— **FURTIVELY**) SLINK SNEAK STEAL
(— **HANG**) SNICK
(— **HEAVILY**) LOB LAMPER
(— **IN**) ENTER INGRESS
(— **IN A HURRY**) SCUFFLE
(— **IN CROWDS**) PILE
(— **IN HASTE**) LEN LAMMAS
(— **IN PURSUIT**) SUE
(— **IN SEARCH**) QUEST
(— **INTO BUSINESS**) EMBARK
(— **IT ALONE**) SOLO
(— **LAME**) FOUNDER
(— **LEISURELY**) BUMMEL JIGGET JIGGIT
(— **LIGHTLY**) TIPTOE
(— **MAD**) CRAZE MADDLE
(— **NEAR**) APPROACH
(— **NOISILY**) LARUM
(— **OFF**) MOG DISCHARGE
(— **ON**) DO GARN LAST PASS PERGE FURTHER PROCEED
(— **ON BOARD**) BOARD EMBARK ENTRAIN
(— **ON FOOT**) SHANK
(— **ON TO SAY**) ADD
(— **OUT**) EXIT ISSUE SLOCK EGRESS EXEUNT QUENCH SORTIE
(— **OVER**) KNEE REVOLT SURPASS OVERGANG
(— **OVER AGAIN**) RENEW REVISE RETRACE
(— **PROSPEROUSLY**) COTTON
(— **QUICKLY**) BOP GET HIE BUZZ LAMP PIKE SCAT SPEED
(— **RAPIDLY**) LAMP SPLIT
(— **SHARES**) SNACK
(— **SIDEWAYS**) SIDLE
(— **SLOWLY**) CRAWL CREEP
(— **SLUGGISHLY**) SHACK
(— **SMOOTHLY**) SLIP SKATE
(— **STEALTHILY**) SHIRK SLINK SNEAK GUMSHOE
(— **SUDDENLY**) CLAP SCOOT
(— **SWIFTLY**) SKISE STRIP HIGHBALL
(— **THE ROUNDS**) PATROL
(— **THROUGH**) SUFFER
(— **THROUGHOUT**) COAST
(— **THROUGH WATER**) SQUATTER
(— **TO BED**) KIP DOSS FLOP SNUG
(— **TO EXCESS**) DEBORD
(— **TO HARBOR**) VERT
(— **TOO FAR**) OUTREACH
(— **TO PIECES**) SNURP
(— **TO SCHOOL**) SCOLEY
(— **TO SLEEP**) HUSHABY
(— **TO WAR**) RISE
(— **UP**) CLIMB AMOUNT ASCEND
(— **WEARILY**) HAGGLE
(— **WELL**) COOK
(— **WITH**) ASSENTTO
(— **WITH EFFORT**) HIKE
(— **WITH IT**) FLOW
(— **WRONG**) MISS FAULT CURDLE MISFARE BACKFIRE

GOAD EGG GAD GIG HAG BAIT BROD BROG DARE EDGE GAUD LASH MOVE PROD SPUR URGE WHIP YERK ANKUS HARRY IMPEL PIQUE PRICK PROGG PUNGE STING VALET INCITE NEEDLE OXGOAD ANKUSHA HOTFOOT INFLAME PROVOKE IRRITATE SLAPJACK STIMULUS

GOADMAN GADMAN GAUDSMAN GOADSTER

GOAL BYE DEN END BASE BUTT DOLE DOOL HAIL HALE MARK METE PORT BOURN FINIS IDEAL SCOOP SCOPE SCORE STING DESIGN OBJECT SIGHTS DESTINY HORIZON TERMINUS OBJECTIVE
(— **IN GAMES**) HUNK
(**FIELD** —) BASKET
(**REMOTE** —) THULE
(**UNATTAINABLE** —) STAR

GO-ASHORE KOHUA

GOAT BOK TUR IBEX TAHR BEDEN BILLY BOVID EVECK SEROW ALPINE ANGORA AOUDAD CAPRID CHAMAL JEMLAH MAZAME NUBIAN PASANG SAANEN WETHER CHAMOIS AEGAGRUS CAPRIPED MARKHOOR BOUQUETIN
(**DOMESTIC** —) HIRCUS
(**FEMALE** —) DOE NANNY DOELING
(**MALE** —) BUCK BUCKLING
(**YOUNG** —) KID KIDDY TICCHEN GOATLING
(PREF.) AEG(I)(O) CAPRI EGO

GOAT ANTELOPE GORAL SEROW GOORAL

GOAT CHEESE CHEVRE

GOATEE TUFT

GOATFISH MOANO

GOATHERD DAMON

GOAT-LIKE CAPRINE GOATISH HIRCINE

GOAT MOTH COSSID

GOATSBEARD ROSACEAN

GOATSKIN CRUST CASTOR CHEVRETTE

GOATSUCKER PUCK PEWKE POTOO EVEJAR BULLBAT DORHAWK GRINDER SPINNER DOORHAWK EVECHURR NIGHTJAR PAURAQUE

GOB TAR CLOT GOAF SALT SWAB SWOB WASTE GOBBET SWABBY

GOBBET BIT CHUNK MORSEL

GOBBLE MOP BOLT SLOP EATUP GOFFLE GORBLE

GOBBLEDYGOOK PEDAGESE BAFFLEGAB

GO-BETWEEN AGENT BAWD FIXER MEANS BROKER DEALER PANDAR CONTACT MEDIATOR

GOBLET TASS DINOS GLASS HANAP POKAL SKULL STOOP STOUP BEAKER BUMPER HOLMOS RUMKIN CHALICE SCYPHUS SNIFTER TALLBOY JEROBOAM STANDARD STEMWARE
(PREF.) CALICI

GOBLIN (ALSO SEE HOBGOBLIN) COW HAG NIS PUG BHUT BOGY MARE PUCK BOGEY NISSE OUPHE POOKA BODACH BOGGLE BOOGER CHUREL EMPUSA FOLIOT SPRITE BOGGARD BOGGART BROWNIE

BUGBEAR KNOCKER PADFOOT
BARGHEST BOGEYMAN FOLLETTO

GOBY MAPO BULLY BIGHEAD
CHALACO GOBIOID GUAVINA
GUDGEON MUDFISH BULLHEAD
PINKFISH SANDGOBY

GOCART SULKY WALKER STROLLER

GOD (ALSO SEE DEITY) AS EA EL ER
RA VE ANU BEL BES COG DAD DES
DEV DIS DOD EAR GAR GAW GEB
GOG GOL GOM GUM ING KEB LAR
LOK MEN MIN ODD ORO SEB SUN
TEM TYR ULL UTU VAN AITU AMEN
AMON ARES ASUR ATEO ATUA
ATYS BAAL BEER BRAN BURE
CHAC COCK DEUS DEVA DIEU ESUS
FONS FREY GAWD GOSH HAPI
HOLY HOTH INTI JOVE KANE KING
LIFE LLEU LOKE LOKI LOVE LUGH
MARS MIND NABU NEBO NUDD
ODIN PTAH SHEN SHIN SOMA
SOUL TANE THOR TIKI ULLR UTUG
VAYU XIPE YAMA ZEUS ARAWN
ASHUR ASURA ATTES ATTIS
COMUS DAGDA DEITY DEOTA
DUVEL DYAUS DYLAN EBISU
ELOAH FREYR GHOST GOLES
GOLLY GRAVE GUACA HESUS
HIEMS HORUS HOTHR HUACA
HYMEN INDRA JUDGE KINGU
LADON LIBER LLUDD MAKER
MENTU MIDER MOMUS NJORD
NUMEN PALES PICUS SILEN TAMUZ
THOTH TINIA TRUTH TYCHE URASH
WAKEA WODIN WOTAN ZOMBI
ADITYA ADONAI ADONAY ANSHAR
ANUBIS APOLLO ASEITY AUTHOR
CHAMOS CONSUS DEVATA
DHARMA ELATHA ELOHIM FATHER
FAUNUS GANESA HEAVEN HERMES
HOENIR MEZTLI MILCOM MITHRA
NEREUS NERGAL OSIRIS PATRON
PENEUS PLUTUS PUSHAN SESHAT
SOCIUS SOURCE SPIRIT SUTEKH
SYLENE TAAROA TAMMUZ TARTAK
TERAPH TRITON TRIVIA VARUNA
VEDUIS VERITY VISHNU VULCAN
WISDOM YAKSHA YAKSHI ZOMBIE
ABRAXAS ADRANUS ALPHEUS
ANTEROS BELENUS CHEMOSH
DAIKOKU DELLING ETERNAL
GODHEAD HANUMAN IAPETUS
JEHOVAH JUPITER KANALOA
MERCURY MITHRAS MUTINUS
NEPTUNE NJORTHR PROTEUS
PRYDERI REMPHAN ROBIGUS
SAVITAR SERAPIS TRIGLAV
VATICAN VEJOVIS ZAGREUS
ALMIGHTY ASTRAEUS BISHAMON
CAMAXTLI DEMIURGE DEVOTION
DIVINITY GUCUMATZ INFINITE
JIUROJIN KUKULKAN MIXCOATL
MORPHEUS POSEIDON SABAZIOS
SUMMANUS TANGAROA
TERMINUS TUTELARY VEDIOVIS
ZEPHYRUS OMNIPOTENT
(**— OF AGRICULTURE**) PICUS URASH
FAUNUS AMAETHON NINGIRSU
(**— OF ARTS**) SIVA
(**— OF ATMOSPHERE**) HADAD
(**— OF BOUNDARIES**) TERMINUS
(**— OF COMMERCE**) MERCURY
(**— OF CORN**) CAT

(**— OF DAY**) HORUS
(**— OF DESTRUCTION**) SIVA
(**— OF EARTH**) BEL GEB KEB SEB
DAGAN
(**— OF EVIL**) SET FOMOR FOMORIAN
ZERNEBOCK
(**— OF FERTILITY**) SHANGO
(**— OF FIRE**) AGNI GIRRU NUSKU
RUDRA VULCAN
(**— OF FLOCKS**) PAN
(**— OF HAPPINESS**) HOTEI JUROJIN
(**— OF HEAVENS**) ANU JUMALA
(**— OF HOUSEHOLD**) LARES
PENATES
(**— OF JUSTICE**) FORSETE FORSETI
(**— OF LEARNING**) IMHOTEP
(**— OF LOVE**) AMOR ARES EROS
KAMA BHAGA CUPID AENGUS
(**— OF MOCKERY**) MOMUS
(**— OF MOON**) SIN ENZU NANNAR
(**— OF NATURE**) MARSYAS
(**— OF POETRY**) BRAGE BRAGI
(**— OF RAIN**) PARJANYA
(**— OF REGENERATION**) SIVA
(**— OF RIDICULE**) MOMUS
(**— OF SEA**) LER VAN AEGIR DYAUS
NEPTUNE PROTEUS PALAEMON
POSEIDON
(**— OF SKY**) ANU GWYDION
(**— OF SLEEP**) HYPNOS HYPNUS
MORPHEUS
(**— OF SOUTHEAST WIND**) EURUS
(**— OF STORM**) ZU ADAD ADDA
ADDU MARUT RUDRA TESHUP
(**— OF SUN**) RA RE SHU SOL TEM
TUM UTU AMON ATEN ATMU ATUM
BAAL LLEU UTUG SAMAS SEKER
SURYA APOLLO HELIOS SOKARI
KHEPERA PHOEBUS SHAMASH
PHAETHON TONATIUH
(**— OF THUNDER**) THOR DONAR
PERUN PERKUN PEROUN SHANGO
TLALOC HURAKAN TARANIS
(**— OF UNDERWORLD**) DIS BRAN
GWYN YAMA HADES ORCUS PLUTO
(**— OF VEGETATION**) ATYS ATTIS
(**— OF WAR**) ER IRA ORO TIU TYR
ARES COEL IRRA MARS MENT ODIN
THOR MONTU NINIB MEXITL
SKANDA CAMULUS MEXITLI
NINURTA ENYALIUS NINGIRSU
QUIRINUS
(**— OF WEALTH**) BHAGA KUBERA
KUVERA PLUTUS
(**— OF WIND**) ADAD ADDA ADDU
VAYU MARUT AEOLUS BOREAS
EECATL
(**— OF WISDOM**) TAT THOTH
(**— WILLING**) DV
(**ANCIENT GREEK —**) CHAOS
(**BLIND —**) HOTH HOTHR
(**EGYPTIAN — OF MUSIC**) BES
(**FALSE —**) BAAL IDOL MAUMET
(**FEMALE —**) GODDESS
(**HAWAIIAN —**) AUMAKUA
(**HOUSEHOLD —**) PENATE
(**IMMORTAL —**) AKAL
(**INFERIOR —**) PANISK
(**NORSE —**) AESIR
(**PAGAN —**) DEMON
(**RAM-HEADED —**) AMON KHNUM
KHNEMU
(**TIMELESS —**) AKAL

(**TUTELARY —**) LAR
(**UNKNOWN —**) KA
(**WOOD —**) SILEN SILENUS
(**PL.**) DI DII KAMI AESIR IGIGI
SUPERI PANTHEON TRIMURTI
(**PREF.**) DEI DEO THE(O)

GODDESS (ALSO SEE DEITY) AI NU
ANA ANU ATE AYA DEA DON NUT
OPS UNI VAC ANTA BADB BODB
CACA DANA DANU ERIS ERUA FRIA
HELA HERA JORD JUNO MAIA
MEDB NIKE NINA NONA NORN
PELE SAGA SATI TARA UPIS ALLAT
AMENT ANATH ANTUM ARURU
BAUBO CERES CHLOE DEESS
DIANA DIANE DIRGA DOLMA
DOMNU EPONA FREYA FRIGG
HYBLA IAMBE ISTAR KOTYS MAEVE
NANAI NINTU PAKHT PALES PARCA
SALUS SEDNA SKADI TANIT TYCHE
USHAS VENUS VESTA ADEONA
AESTAS ANATUM ANUKIT APHAIA
ATHENA BELILI BENDIS BOOPIS
BRIGIT CYBELE CYRENE EOSTRE
FRIGGA GEFJON HELENA HESTIA
HYGEIA INNINA KISHAR LIBERA
MOTHER NINGAL PEITHO PHOBOS
POMONA PRORSA RUMINA
SEKHET SELENE SEMELE SKATHI
SOTHIS TANITH TEFNUT TRIVIA
URANIA VACUNA YDGRUN
ANAHITA ANAITIS ARTEMIS
ASHERAH DEMETER DERCETO
FERONIA FJORGYN GALATER
GODHEAD KOTYTTO LARENTA
LARUNDA MAJAGGA MAJESTA
MINERVA MORNING MORRIGU
MYLITTA NEKHEBT NEMESIS
PALATUA PARBATI PARVATI
SALACIA ADRASTEA AGLAUROS
ANGERONA BELISAMA CARMENTA
CENTEOTL COCAMAMA DESPOINA
DICTYNNA GULLVEIG MORRIGAN
NEPHTHYS PARBUTTY PRAKRITI
RHIANNON SEFEKHET THOUERIS
VICTORIA
(**— IN CHARIOT**) SELENE
(**— OF AGRICULTURE**) BAU OPS
DEMETER CENTEOTL
(**— OF AIR**) AURA
(**— OF BEAUTY**) VENUS LAKSHMI
(**— OF BURIAL**) LIBITINA
(**— OF CHILDBIRTH**) LEVANA LUCINA
(**— OF DAWN**) EOS USAS USHAS
AURORA MATUTA
(**— OF DEW**) HERSE
(**— OF DISCORD**) ATE ERIS
(**— OF EARTH**) GE LUA SEB ERDA
GAEA GAIA TARI ARURU DIONE
JORTH TERRA SEMELE TELLUS
THEMIS DAMKINA PERCHTA
(**— OF FATE**) NONA NORN MOIRA
(**— OF FERTILITY**) MA ISIS MAMA
NERTHUS
(**— OF FLOWERS**) FLORA CHLORIS
(**— OF FORTUNE**) TYCHE FORTUNA
(**— OF GRAIN**) CERES
(**— OF HEALING**) EIR GULA
(**— OF HEALTH**) DAMIA HYGEIA
VALETUDO
(**— OF HEARTH**) VESTA HESTIA
(**— OF HISTORY**) SAGA
(**— OF HOPE**) SPES

(**— OF INFATUATION**) ATE
(**— OF JUSTICE**) DIKE MAAT THEMIS
ASTRAEA NEMESIS JUSTITIA
(**— OF LEGISLATION**) EUNOMIA
(**— OF LOVE**) ATHOR FREYA VENUS
FREYJA HATHOR
(**— OF LUCK**) FORTUNA
(**— OF MAGIC**) HECATE
(**— OF MARRIAGE**) HERA
(**— OF MATERNITY**) APET
(**— OF MERCY**) KWANNON
(**— OF MOON**) SELENE
(**— OF MOTHERHOOD**) ISIS
(**— OF NIGHT**) NOX NYX
(**— OF OCEAN**) NINA
(**— OF OVENS**) FORNAX
(**— OF PEACE**) PAX IRENE NERTHUS
(**— OF PLEASURE**) BES
(**— OF PLENTY**) OPS
(**— OF RAINBOW**) IRIS
(**— OF SEASONS**) DIKE HORA
(**— OF THE DEAD**) HEL HELA
(**— OF THE HUNT**) DIANA VACUNA
ARTEMIS
(**— OF THE MOON**) LUNA MOON
DIANA SELENA SELENE TANITH
ARTEMIS
(**— OF THE SEA**) INO RAN DORIS
BRANWEN EURYNOME
(**— OF TRUTH**) MAAT
(**— OF VEGETATION**) OPS CERES
COTYS COTYTTO
(**— OF VENGEANCE**) ARA NEMESIS
(**— OF VICTORY**) NIKE
(**— OF WAR**) ENYO ANATH ANATU
ANUNIT BELLONA
(**— OF WATER**) ANAHITA
(**— OF WEALTH**) LAKSHMI
(**— OF WISDOM**) ATHENA MINERVA
(**— OF YOUTH**) HEBE JUVENTAS
(**COW-HEADED —**) ISIS
(**ESKIMO —**) SEDNA
(**FERTILITY —**) ASTARTE
(**MARRIAGE —**) VOR
(**PRESIDING —**) QUEEN
(**SUBORDINATE —**) DEMIURGE
(**THUNDER-SMITTEN —**) SEMELE
KERAUNIA
(**3-HEADED —**) HECATE
(**PL.**) HORAE MATRIS POINAE
ASYNJUR

GO-DEVIL SLED WEIGHT HANDCAR
SCRAPER CULTIVATOR TRAVOIS
ALLIGATOR

GODFATHER GOSSIP GODPAPA
PADRINO SPONSOR GODPHERE

GODHEAD DEITY GODHOOD
DIVINITY

GODLESS WICKED ATHEIST
IMPIOUS PROFANE UNGODLY

GODLESSNESS ATHEISM

GODLIKE DEIFIC DIVINE IMMORTAL
OLYMPIAN

GODLINESS PIETISM SANCTITY

GODLING DEVATA GENIUS GODKIN
GODLET PANISC DEMIGOD
PANISCUS

GODLY HOLY WISE PIOUS DEVOUT
GRACIOUS

GODMOTHER CUMMER GOSSIP
SPONSOR GODMAMMA MARRAINE

GODOWN WAREHOUSE

GODPARENT SPONSOR

GOD'S S
GODSON FILLEUL GODCHILD
GOD TREE CEIBA
GODWIT PICK PRINE BARKER
MARLIN SCAMMEL YARWHIP
RINGTAIL SHRIEKER SPOTRUMP
YARDKEEP YARWHELP
GOFFER QUILL FULLER GAUFFER
GOG (FATHER OF —) SHEMAIAH
GO-GETTER HUSTLER
GOGGLER SCAD
GOGLET COOJA SERAI MONKEY
SURAHI GURGLET SURAHEE
GOING FARE GAIT BOUND AGOING
WAYING PASSADO SLEDDING
(— ABOUT) AROUND
(— BEYOND OTHERS) ULTRA
(— IN) INEUNT INFARE INGOING
(— ON) FARE AGATE TOWARD
(— OUT) EGRESS
(— UP) ANABASIS
(GET —) BEGIN
(SUFF.) GRESS
GOITER WEN GLANS GOITRE
STRUMA BRONCHOCELE
GOITERED ANTELOPE ZENU
GOITROUS STRUMOUS
GOLD OR ORO RED SOL DORE GILT
GUILT ALTUN AURUM GUILD METAL
OCHER OCHRE RIDGE SHINY
GOLDEN OBRIZE ORMOLU
YELLOW BULLION SPANKER
(— PIECE) TALI
(GREENISH —) AENEUS AENEOUS
(IMITATION —) PINCHBECK
(PREF.) AUR(I) AUREO CHRYS(O)
ORI
GOLDBEATER (TOOL OF —) WAGON
GOLDBRICK LOAF SHIRK SLACKER
GOLDCREST MOON TIDLEY
MUDDLER TROCHIL
**GOLD DUST (PENNY'S WORTH OF
—)** PESEWA
GOLDEN RED DORE GOLD BLEST
DURRY GOLDY SUNNY AUREAL
BLONDE GILDEN GILTEN AUREATE
AUREOUS HALCYON AURULENT
DEAURATE
(— STATE) CALIFORNIA
GOLDEN-AGER RETIREE
GOLDEN ASS (AUTHOR OF —)
APULEIUS
(CHARACTER IN —) ISIS MILO FOTIS
LUCIUS CHARITES PAMPHILE
SOCRATES BYRRHAENA
LEPOLEMUS THRASILLUS
ARISTOMENES
GOLDEN BOWL (AUTHOR OF —)
JAMES
(CHARACTER IN —) ADAM STANT
MAGGIE VERVER AMERIGO
CHARLOTTE
GOLDEN CHAIN LABURNUM
GOLDEN CLUB TAWKEE TAWKIN
TUCKAHOE
GOLDEN EAGLE RINGTAIL
GOLDENEYE CUR GARROT
COBHEAD GOWDNIE BULLHEAD
IRONHEAD MORILLON WHIFFLER
WHISTLER
GOLDEN LION TAMARIN
MARMOSET
GOLDEN ORIOLE PIROL WITWALL

GOLDEN PLOVER KOLEA
FROGSKIN SQUEALER WHISTLER
GOLDEN RAGWORT LIFEROOT
GOLDENROD BONEWORT
SOLIDAGO JIMMYWEED
GOLDENSEAL EYEBALM EYEROOT
ICEROOT PUCCOON
GOLDEN SHINER CHUB DACE
WINDFISH
GOLDFINCH JACK FINCH GOLDY
GOWDY CANARY REDCAP
FLAXBIRD GRAYPATE
GOLDFINNY CONNER GOLDNEY
CORKWING
GOLDFISH FUNA MOOR COMET
CALICO FANTAIL CYPRINID
VEILTAIL
GOLD-LEAF ORMOLU
GOLD-OF-PLEASURE FLAX
MADWORT OILSEED
GOLDSINNY CONNER CORKWING
GOLDSMITH SONAR AURIFEX
ENGLISH HILLIARD
FRENCH MEISSONIER
GERMAN JAMNITZER
ITALIAN LEONI ROBBIA
WELSH MYDDELTON
GOLF (— CLUB) IRON WOOD BAFFY
CLEEK MASHY SPOON WEDGE
BULGER DRIVER MASHIE PUTTER
BRASSIE MIDIRON NIBLICK
(— COURSE) GREEN LINKS
(— PLAYER) BALL BERG KING KITE
VARE BRAID FALDO FLOYD HAGEN
HOGAN IRWIN JONES LOCKE LOPEZ
MILLS PRICE RAWLS SMITH SNEAD
STACY SUGGS ALCOTT CAPONI
CARNER GEDDES HAYNIE HILTON
LANGER MALLON MILLER MORRIS
NELSON PALMER PLAYER VARDON
WATSON WRIGHT BERNING
BRADLEY COUPLES DEMARET
INKSTER SARAZEN SHEEHAN
THOMSON TREVINO ZOELLER
ANDERSON NICKLAUS ZAHARIAS
WHITWORTH BALLESTEROS
(— SCORE) ACE PAR BOGEY EAGLE
BIRDIE
(— STROKE) BAFF CHIP HOOK PUTT
DRIVE PITCH SLICE
(FREE SHOT IN —) MULLIGAN
(PUTTING TENSION IN —) YIPS
(SHORT — PUTT) GIMME TAPIN
GOLFER TEER
GOLLY GEE WOW GOSH JEEPERS
GOMER (FATHER OF —) JAPHETH
(HUSBAND OF —) HOSEA
GOMUTI EJOO IROK ARENG KITTUL
SAGWIRE SAGOWEER
GONAD OVARY GERMEN
GONCALO ALVES KINGWOOD
GONDOLA GON BARGE GUNDALOW
(— GUIDE) POLER
GONE AWAY LOST NAPOO USEDUP
(— BY) AGO DONE PAST AGONE
PASSE BEHIND BYGONE
(— OUT OF USE) EXTINCT
(— TO PIECES) HAYWIRE
GONERIL (SISTER OF —) REGAN
**GONE WITH THE WIND (AUTHOR
OF —)** MITCHELL
(CHARACTER IN —) FRANK OHARA
RHETT ASHLEY BUTLER WILKES

CHARLES KENNEDY MELANIE
HAMILTON SCARLETT
GONG BELL CLOCK GANGSA
DOORBELL
(SERIES OF —S) BONANG
GONGORISM CULTISM
GONOPHORE MEDUSOID
SPOROSAC
GOO GUCK GUNK TRIPE
GOOD BAD BON GAY TOP TRY ABLE
BEAU BEIN BIEN BOON BRAW FINE
GAIN HEND NICE NOTE PROW
SAKE BONNE BONNY BONUM
BRAVE BULLY CANNY FRESH
GWEED JELLY KAPAI PAKKA PUKKA
SEELY SOUND VALID BENIGN
BRAWLY BUCKRA DIVINE EXPERT
FACTOR FORBYE HONEST MABUTI
PRETTY PROFIT PROPER WEALTH
BENEFIT COPIOUS CORKING
FAIRISH FORTHBY GODLIKE
GRADELY HELPFUL LIBERAL
SNIFTER STAVING TRAINED
UPRIGHT BUDGEREE GRAITHLY
INTEREST LAUDABLE PLEASING
SALUTARY SKILLFUL SUITABLE
(— FOR NOTHING) NAPOO NAUGHT
(ESPECIALLY —) RARE
(EXCEPTIONALLY —) SLAMBANG
(EXTREMELY —) SLICK
(FAIRLY —) TIDY MIDDLING
(HOLD —) BEAR
(INFINITELY —) HOLY
(MARVELOUSLY —) FANTABULOUS
(MIGHTY —) SKOOKUM
(NO —) DUFF VOID NAPOO NAPOOH
VOIDED
(PRETTY —) FAIR TIDY
(RELATIVELY —) SMOOTH
(STRIKINGLY —) RATTLING
(SUPERLATIVELY —) BRAG
BEAUTIFUL
(SUPREMELY —) IMMENSE
GORGEOUS
(SURPASSINGLY —) SUPERIOR
(VERY —) HOT TOP DANDY DICTY
GRAND NIFTY BONZER BOSHTA
BOSKER BOSHTER NAILING
SPLENDID SWINGING
(PREF.) AGATH(O) BENI EU
GOOD-BYE CIAO LATER BY BYE
TATA
GOODBYE TATA
GOOD-BYE ADDIO ADIEU
GOODBYE ADIEU
GOOD-BYE ADIOS
GOODBYE ADIOS
GOOD-BYE LULLABY FAREWELL
SAYONARA
GOODBYE (IMPOLITE —) SCRAM
**GOOD COMPANIONS (AUTHOR OF
—)** PRIESTLEY
(CHARACTER IN —) DEAN HUGH
NUNN ELSIE INIGO JERRY JIMMY
SUSIE TRANT JESIAH OAKROYD
ELIZABETH JOLLIFANT LONGSTAFF
MCFARLANE JERNINGHAM
GOOD EARTH (AUTHOR OF —)
BUCK
(CHARACTER IN —) LIU LUNG NUNG
OLAN PEAR WANG CHING HWANG
LOTUS
GOOD-FOR-NAUGHT LOSEL

GOOD-FOR-NOTHING STIFF
VAURIEN BUM ORRA SLIM SLINK
DONNOT KEFFEL RIBALD STUMER
BRETHEL FUSTIAN SCROYLE
SHOTTEN SKEEZIX SKELLUM
SKYBALD VAURIEN WOSBIRD
VAGABOND
GOOD FRIDAY PARASCEVE
GOOD-HUMORED SONSY
GOOD-KING-HENRY BLITE
ALLGOOD MARKERY MERCURY
CHENOPOD
GOOD-LOOKING BRAW FAIR FOXY
MOOI BONNY GAWSY COMELY
PRETTY SEEMLY EYESOME
GRADELY WINSOME GOODLIKE
HANDSOME STUNNING
GOODLY BOON PROPER GOODLIKE
GOOD-NATURED SONSY CLEVER
AMIABLE
GOODNESS BONTE BONUM MENSK
PROOF BONITY BOUNTY SATTVA
VIRTUE KINDNESS
GOODS FEE BONA GEAR KIND PELF
CARGO STUFF TRADE WORLD
WRACK ADVANCE CAPITAL
CHATTEL EFFECTS FINANCE
HAVINGS INSIGHT TRAFFIC
CHATTELY HIGGLERY PROPERTY
(— BARTERED) DICKER
(— CAST OVERBOARD) JETSAM
(— SUNK IN SEA) LAGAN LIGAN
LAGEND
(DRY —) DRAPERY
(HOUSEHOLD —) INSIGHT
(IMPERFECT —) FENT
(INFERIOR —) BRACK
(PIECE —) CUTTANEE
(SECONDHAND —) BROKERY
(SLOW-SELLING —) JOBS
(STOLEN — THROWN AWAY) WAIF
(SURPLUS —) OVERAGE
(VALUABLE —) SWAG
GOOD-SIZED TIDY HEFTY GAWSIE
GOOD-TASTING DAINTY
GOODWIFE GOODY VROUW
GOODWILL GREE PHILANTHROPY
GOODY-GOODY PI MOLLYCODDLE
GOOEY CLARTY
GOOF SAP BOOB FLUB BONER
GOOFER
GOOFBALL DOOFUS
GOOGLY BOSEY WRONGUN
GOOK SLIME
GOON HOOD THUG GORILLA
MUSCLEMAN
GOOSANDER JACKSAW RANTOCK
GOOSE ELK OIE LAMA NENE ROUT
ANSER BRANT BRENT EMDEN
HANSA HOBBY ROMAN SOLAN
WAVEY CAGMAG CANADA
EMBDEN GALOOT GANDER
GOSLET HISSER HONKER SOLAND
AFRICAN BLACKIE BUSTARD
GAGGLER GOSLING GRAYLAG
GREASER GREYLAG OUTARDE
WIDGEON BALDHEAD BARGOOSE
BARNACLE BERNICLE SPURWING
TOULOUSE
(— GENUS) ANSER
(MYTHICAL —) GANZA
(PART OF —) BOW EAR EYE TOE
WEB BEAN BILL CAPE FOOT KEEL

RUMP WING FLUFF SHANK BREAST COVERT DEWLAP SADDLE FEATHER NOSTRIL SHOULDER SECONDARY (PREF.) CHEN(O)

GOOSEBERRY BLOB FABE FAPE POHA BRAGAS GOBLIN GOZILL GROZER DOWNING GASKINS GROZART CARBERRY CATBERRY DOGBERRY EATBERRY FEABERRY GOOSEGOG HOUGHTON INDUSTRY KIWIFRUIT (PL.) THAPES

GOOSE EGG DUCK

GOOSEFOOT BLITE ORACH BASSIA KOCHIA ORACHE QUINOA ALLSEED PIGWEED

GOOSEGIRL GOSSARD

GOOSE GRASS HERIF HARIFFE CLEAVERS

GOOSEHERD GOZZARD GOOSEBOY

GOOSENECK LAMP ROOSTER

GOPHER TUZA GAUFFRE GEOMYID MUNGOFA QUACHIL SALAMICH TUCOTUCO (— STATE) MINNESOTA

GOPHER BALL HOMER

GOPHERMAN SWAMPER

GOPHERWOOD FUSTIC

GORBODUC (SON OF —) FERREX PORREX

GORDIUS (SON OF —) MIDAS

GORE CLY CLOY GARE HIKE HIPE HOOK HORN PICK PIKE SHOT CRUOR GODET STICK GORING GUSSET

GOREVAN AUBURN

GORGE GAP JAM FILL GASH GAUM GLUT JAMB KHOR RENT SATE BREAK CAJON CANON CHASM CHINE CLUSE DRAFT FARCE FLUME GULLY GURGE KLOOF PONGO POUCH STECH STRID STUFF TANGI CANYON DEFILE NULLAH PIGOUT RAVINE STODGE STRAIT THROAT COULOIR DATIATE DRAUGHT ENGORGE SATIATE SLABBER BARRANCA QUEBRADA

GORGED ACCOLLE

GORGEOUS VAIN GRAND SHOWY COSTLY DAZZLING GLORIOUS SPLENDID

GORGERIN NECK NECKING

GORGIBUS (DAUGHTER OF —) CELIE

GORGING STODGE

GORGON HAG MEDUSA STHENO EURYALE (MOTHER OF —S) CETO

GORGOPHONE (FATHER OF —) PERSEUS (HUSBAND OF —) OEBALUS PERIERES (MOTHER OF —) ANDROMEDA (SON OF —) ICARIUS APHAREUS LEUCIPPUS TYNDAREUS

GORILLA APE GOON THUG PIGMY PYGMY

GORING CORNUPETE

GORMANDIZE STECH STEGH GUTTLE

GORMANDIZER HELLUO GLUTTON

GORSE ULEX WHIN FURZE GORST

GORY BLOODY

GOSHAWK GOS ASTUR TERCEL

GOSLING GULL

GOSPEL SPELL DHARMA EVANGEL KERUGMA KERYGMA SYNOPTIC (— OF REDEMPTION) CROSS (PL.) TEXT

GOSSAMER MOUSEWEB STARDUST

GOSSIP EME GAB GUP PIE WAG AUNT BLAB BUZZ CANT CLAT CONK COZE DIRT DISH NEWS TALK CAUSE CLACK CLASH CLYPE COOSE CRACK FERLY FRUMP GOSSY SIEVE YENTA BABBLE CACKLE CADDLE CALLET CAMPER CLAVER CUMMER FERLIE JANGLE KIMMER NORATE TATTLE TITTLE CLATTER COMPERE GOSTHER HASHGOB NASHGAB SCANDAL TATTLER TRATTLE CAUSERIE CHITCHAT GOSSIPRY QUIDNUNC SCHMOOZE NEWSMONGER SCUTTLEBUTT (MALICIOUS —) SCANDAL (OUTPOURING OF —) EARFUL

GOSSIPY BUZZY NEWSY CHATTY

GOTH GOTHIAN SUIOGOTH VISIGOTH

GOTHAM ABDERA

GOTHAMITE ABDERITE

GOTHIC OGIVAL

GOTTERDAMMERUNG (CHARACTER IN —) HAGEN GUNTHER GUTRUNE SIEGFRIED WALTRAUTE BRUNNHILDE (COMPOSER OF —) WAGNER

GOUGE DIG PUG BENT SCUFF CHISEL EXTORT FLUKAN GOUGER HOLLOW SCRIBE FLOOKAN SCORPER SELVAGE SELVEDGE STICKING (— OUT) BULLDOZE (V-TYPE —) VEINER

GOUGER CHISELLER

GOURD MATE PEPO LUFFA ABOBRA JICARA PATOLA ANGURIA DISHRAG HECHIMA CALABASH CUCURBIT PEPONIDA PEPONIUM

GOURMAND EATER EPICURE GLUTTON GORMAND

GOURMET PALATE EPICURE GOURMAND

GOUT GUT CLOT DROP SPLASH PODAGRA PODAGRY CHIRAGRA ARTHRITIS (— IN HAND) CHIRAGRA (SUFF.) AGRA

GOUTTE DROP ICICLE

GOUTWEED AXWEED ASHWEED ACHEWEED AISEWEED BOLEWORT GOATWEED GOUTWORT

GOUTY PODAGRAL PODAGRIC

GOVERN RUN WIN CURB KING LEAD REDE REIN RULE SWAY WALD WARD WIND YEME GUIDE JUDGE REGLE STEER TREAT WIELD BRIDLE DIRECT MANAGE ORDAIN POLICE POLICY TEMPER COMMAND CONDUCT CONTROL PRESIDE REFRAIN DISPENSE DOMINATE IMPERATE MODERATE OVERRULE OVERSWAY POLICIZE REGULATE RESTRAIN

GOVERNED BENT

GOVERNESS ABBESS DUENNA FRAULEIN MISTRESS MADEMOISELLE

GOVERNING REGENT REGITIVE

GOVERNMENT GATE LAND RULE KREIS METRO POWER STATE STEER DURBAR HAVANA POLICY RULING CABINET CZARISM DIARCHY DYARCHY RECTION REGENCY REGIMEN TSARISM CIVILITY ENDARCHY GOBIERNO HEGEMONY ISOCRACY ISOCRYME KINGSHIP STEERING ABSOLUTISM (— BY FEW) OLIGARCHY (— BY GOD) THEONOMY (— BY MANY) POLYARCHY (— BY MOB) OCHLOCRACY (— BY SMALL CLASS) OLIGARCHY (— BY THREE) TRIARCHY (— BY WEALTHY) PLUTOCRACY (— BY WOMEN) GYNARCHY GYNOCRACY (— BY 10) DECARCHY (— BY 2) DIARCHY DUARCHY (— NOTE) TBOND (— OF CEYLON) DISSAVA (— OF TURKEY) GATE PORTE (ARBITRARY —) ABSOLUTISM (BAD —) MISRULE (CHURCH —) PRELACY (INDIAN —) CIRCAR SIRCAR (ITALIAN —) QUIRINAL (MALAYSIAN —) KOMPENI (MOROCCAN —) MAGHZEN MAKHZAN (REGIONAL —) METRO (RUSSIAN —) KREMLIN (SWAHILI —) SERKALI (TURKISH —) PORTE (PREF.) CRATO (WITHOUT —) ANARCH(O) (SUFF.) ARCH ARCHIC ARCHY CRACY CRAT(IC)

GOVERNMENTAL ARCHICAL

GOVERNOR BAN BEY DEY EARL KAID LORD NAIK TUTU VALI BANUS CLEON DEWAN DIWAN HAKIM NABOB NAZIM PACHA PASHA SHEIK SUBAH TUPAN AUTHOR DYNAST GRIEVE LEGATE MOODIR MYOWUN NAIGUE NAIQUE PATESI PENLOP RECTOR REGENT SACHEM SATRAP SHEIKH SHERIF TUCHUN WARDEN CATAPAN DAROGHA LEONATO PODESTA RECTRIX SERKALI SHEREEF TOPARCH TSUNGTU VICEROY WIELDER AUTOCRAT BURGRAVE ETHNARCH HOSPODAR LANDVOGT MISTRESS PENTARCH RESIDENT SUBAHDAR TETRARCH CASTELLAN PRESIDENT PROCONSUL (— OF ALGIERS) DEY DISAWA (— OF BURMA) WUN WOON (— OF EGYPT) MUDIR (— OF FORTRESS) ALCAIDE ALCAYDE (— OF SHIRE) ALDERMAN (— OF TAMMANY) SACHEM (BYZANTINE —) EXARCH CATAPAN (CEYLON —) DISAWA (GERMAN —) LANDVOGT (GREEK —) ETHNARCH

(JAPANESE —) SHOGUN TYCOON (PAPAL —) LEGATE (ROMAN —) TETRARCH (SELJUK —) ATABEG ATABEK (SPARTAN —) HARMOST (TURKISH —) BEY WALI MUDIR KEHAYA

GOVERNOR-GENERAL VALI

GOWDIE SCULPIN

GOWK CUCKOO

GOWN GOR SAC GITE GORE HUKE JAMA RAIL SACK SILK TOGA BANIA DRESS FROCK GOUND HABIT JAMAH MANTO TABBY TOOSH BANIAN BANIYA CAFTAN CAMISE CANDYS CHITON JESUIT JOHNNY KIMONO KIRTLE KITTEL LEVITE MANTUA ARISARD CASSOCK GARMENT JOHNNIE SLAMKIN SULTANA SULTANE WRAPPER CAMISOLE GANDOURA MAZARINE PEIGNOIR (HAWAIIAN —) MOLOKU MUUMUU

GOYA CURRANT

GOYIM GENTES

GRAB NAB NAP RAP GLAM GOPE GLAUM SCRAB CLUTCH COLLAR CRATCH DIPPER NIPPER NOBBLE SNATCH CRAPPLE GRABBLE GRAPNEL GRAPPLE NIPPERS

GRAB BAG LUCKYDIP

GRABBY ARID

GRABEN TROUGH

GRABWEED BISHOPWEED

GRACE EST ORE BEAT ESTE GARB HELD SWAY ADORN COULE FAVOR HONOR MENSE MENSK MERCY POISE SLIDE THANK VENUS BEAUTY BECOME BEDECK CHARIS POLISH RELISH THALIA AGGRACE CHARISM COMMEND DIGNITY FINESSE GRATIFY MELISMA MORDENT BACKFALL BEAUTIFY BLESSING DECORATE EASINESS ELEGANCE FELICITY GRATUITY LEVATION ORNAMENT (— OF FORM) FLOW SWAY TOURNURE

GRACEFUL AIRY FEAT GENT BONNY GENTY GRATE COMELY FEATLY FELINE FLUENT GAINLY QUAINT SEEMLY SILKEN VENUST ELEGANT FITTING GENTEEL GRACILE SYLPHID WILLOWY CHARMING DELICATE GRACIOUS LEGGIERO MACEVOLE SWANLIKE SYLPHISH (PREF.) ABRO HABRO

GRACEFULLY FAIR FEATLY HAPPILY LEGGIERO

GRACEFULNESS JOLLITY ELEGANCE

GRACELESS AWKWARD

GRACES CHARITES

GRACIOUS GOOD HEND HOLD KIND MILD CIVIL GODLY HAPPY LUCKY SUAVE WINLY BENIGN GENIAL GENTLE GOODLY KINDLY AFFABLE CORDIAL WINSOME BENEDICT DEBONAIR GENEROUS HANDSOME MERCIFUL PLEASING SOCIABLE BENIGNANT

GRACIOUSLY FAIR SWEETLY

GRACIOUSNESS GRACE MENSK
FACILITY GRATUITY
GRACKLE BEO DAW JACKDAW
BOATTAIL TINKLING TROOPIAL
GRADATION HUE CLINE ABLAUT
CLIMAX NUANCE GEOCLINE
STRENGTH
GRADE CUT BANK CHOP EVEN
FORM MARK RANK SIZE STEP
GLIDE LEVEL ORDER PLANE SCORE
SIEGE STAGE ASCENT DEGREE
RATING STAPLE TRIAGE FAILURE
INCLINE INSPECT DEMISANG
GRADIENT GRADUATE MERIDIAN
STANDARD
(— DOWN) FAULT
(— LUMBER) SURVEY
(— OF BEEF) GOOD CUTTER
(— OF LIFE) PLANE
(— OF LUMBER) CULL
(— OF OAK) WAINSCOT
(— OF OFFICER) CORNET
(— ROAD) IMPROVE
(—S ONE THROUGH TWELVE) ELHI
(—S 1 THROUGH 12) ELHI
(ABLAUT —) GUNA
(DESIGNED FOR USE IN —S 1-12)
ELHI
(POOR —) DEF
(SUPERIOR —) SUPER
(THIRD —) FAIR
GRADER PLANER CLASSER
SCRAPER
GRADIENT GRADE LAPSE SLOPE
ASCENT INCLINE DOWNHILL
(SUFF.) CLINAL CLINE
GRADIN GRADINO PREDELLA
GRADUAL EASY FLAT SLOW GRAIL
GENTLE LENTOUS STEPWISE
PIECEMEAL
GRADUALLY GENTLY EDGINGLY
GRADUATIM INCHMEAL PIECEMEAL
GRADUATE ALUM GRAD GRADE
ALUMNA DIVIDE FELLOW
ALUMNUS GRADATE BACHELOR
(EISTEDDFOD —) OVATE
GRADUATED SCALAR MEASURED
GRADUATION CLICK
GRAFT BUD IMP PIE CION WORK
GRAFF GRAVY INEYE SCION
BOODLE INARCH PAYOLA SPLICE
ENGRAFT IMPLANT JOBBERY
SQUEEZE TOPWORK APPROACH
BOODLING GRAFTING INSITION
GRAFTED ENTE
GRAFTER BOODLER
GRAFTING GRAFTAGE INSITION
(PREF.) GREFFO
GRAIL CUP GRAAL CHALICE
SANGRAAL
GRAIN JOT RUN RYE WAY CORN
CURN DANA KERN PILE RICE SAND
SEED WALE WOOD EMMER FIBER
FIBRE FUNDI GAVEL GLEBE GRIST
PANIC SCRAP SPARK STUFF TRACE
WHEAT ANNONA BARLEY BRAINS
CEREAL CURRAN GROATS KERNEL
FRUMENT GRANULE PANICLE
VICTUAL GRAINING PARTICLE
STRAIGHT SWEEPAGE
(— FOR MUSH) KASHA
(— FROM MASH TUN) DRAINS

(— LEFT AFTER HARVEST) GAVEL
SHACK
(— MEASURE) THRAVE
(— OF BOARD) BEAT
(— OF CORN) PICKLE
(— OF GOLD) PIPPIN
(— OF WOOD) BATE
(—S OF PARADISE) MALAGUETTA
(CHAFF OF —) BRAN
(COARSE —) THIRD
(COARSELY GROUND —) MEAL
GRITS KIBBLE
(DAMAGED —) SALVAGE
(EAR OF —) SPIKE RISSOM RIZZON
(GERMINATED —) MALT
(GROUND —) GRIST
(HANDFUL OF —) REAP
(HULLED —) GRITS GROUT GROATS
SHELLING
(HUSKED —) SHEALING SHILLING
(MILLET —) CUSCUS
(MIXED —) MASLIN
(MIXED —S) DREDGE
(PARCHED —) GRADDAN
(REFUSE —) SHAG DRAFF
(SACRIFICIAL —) ADOR
(SHOCK OF —) COP
(STACK OF —) HOVEL
(STORED —) MOW
(STREAKED —) ROEY
(PL.) PICKLES RAGGING
(PREF.) CHONDR(I)(IO)(O) COCC(O)
GRANI GRANUL(I)(O) SITIO SITO
(SUFF.) COCCAL COCCIC
GRAIN BEETLE CADELLE
GRAINER DICER BOARDER
GRAINSMAN THROWER
DRAFFMAN
GRAIN SORGHUM DURRA SHALLU
GRAM KHESARI
(MILLIONTH —) GAMMA
GRAMMAR DONAT SYNTAX
GRAMARY PRISCIAN
(TYPE OF —) TAGMEMIC
GRAMMARIAN PRISCIAN
GRAMPUS ORC ORCA COWFISH
DOLPHIN SPRINGER
GRANARY GOLA GUNJ SILO GOLAH
GUNGE LATHE GARNER GIRNEL
GRANGE HORREUM RESERVE
CORNLOFT GRAINERY
GRAND OLD AIRY BRAW EPIC MAIN
TALL CHIEF GREAT LOFTY NOBLE
PIANO PROUD SHOWY SWELL
WLONK ANDEAN AUGUST COSMIC
EPICAL FAMOUS GLOBAL KINGLY
LORDLY SIGHTY SUPERB SWANKY
EXALTER IMMENSE STATELY
SUBLIME COSMICAL FOREMOST
GLORIOUS GORGEOUS IMPOSING
MAJESTIC SPLENDID MAGNIFICENT
(PREF.) BEL
GRAND CANYON STATE ARIZONA
GRANDCHILD OE OY OYE
(GREAT —) IEROE
GRANDDAUGHTER NIECE
GRANDEE DON GRAND OMRAH
BASHAW GRANDO MAGNATE
GRANDEUR POMP STATE ESTATE
FIGURE PARADE MAJESTY
ELEGANCE GRANDEZA HAUTESSE
NOBILITY SPLENDOR VASTNESS
GRANDFATHER AIEL NONO BOBBY

GRAMP ATAVUS GRAMPS BELSIRE
GRANDAD GRANDPA GRANDFER
GUIDSIRE
(GREAT —) NONO
(GREAT-GREAT-GREAT —)
QUATRAYLE
GRAND HOTEL (AUTHOR OF —)
BAUM
(CHARACTER IN —) ANNA OTTO
FLAMM GAIGERN PREYSING
ELISAVETA FLAEMMCHEN
KRINGELEIN GRUSINSKAYA
OTTERNSCHLAG
GRANDILOQUENT TALL HEROIC
TURGID BOMBAST MAGNIFIC
RHETORICAL
GRANDIOSE GRAND COSMIC
TURGID SUBLIME COSMICAL
IMPERIAL
GRANDISSIMUS (AUTHOR OF —)
CABLE
(CHARACTER IN —) KEENE AURORA
HONORE JOSEPH PALMYRE
AGRICOLA CLOTILDE FUSILIER
NANCANOU FROWENFIELD
GRANDISSIMUS
GRANDMOTHER GRAM GRAN
NANA LUCKY NANNY GRANNY
GUDAME LUCKIE BELDAME
NOKOMIS BABUSHKA GRANDAME
GRANDMOTHERS (AUTHOR OF —)
WESTCOTT
(CHARACTER IN —) JIM EVAN ROSE
ALWYN FLORA HENRY NANCY
RALPH TOWER CANNON SERENA
LEANDER MARIANNE
GRANDPARENT TUTU TUPUNA
(OF —S) AVAL
GRAND SLAM VOLE
GRANDSON NEPHEW NEPOTE
GRANITE MOYITE RUNITE GREISEN
SYENITE ALASKITE RAPAKIVI
PEGMATITE
(— STATE) NEWHAMPSHIRE
(DECOMPOSED —) GROWAN
(PREF.) PEGMATO SYENO
GRANITEWARE GRAYWARE
GRANNY TUTU BABUSHKA
GRANT AID FEU BOOK BOON CEDE
ENAM GALE GIFT GIVE HEAR LEND
LOAN MISE SEND STOW YARK
ADMIT ALLOT ALLOW AWARD
BONUS CHART COWLE FLOAT
FUERO LEASE SEIZE SPARE TITHE
YETTE YIELD ACCEDE ACCORD
AFFORD ASSENT BESTOW BETAKE
BETEEM BOUNTY CONFER DESIGN
EXTEND FIRMAN IMPART JAGEER
NOVATE OCTROI PATENT PERMIT
REMISE ADJUDGE APPOINT
COLLATE CONCEDE CONSENT
DISPONE INDULGE LICENSE
PRESENT PROMISE SUBSIDY
TRIBUTE APPANAGE BESTOWAL
CONTRACT DONATION EXCHANGE
MONOPOLY PITTANCE TRANSFER
CONCESSION ACKNOWLEDGE
(— AS PROPER) ACCORD
(— FOR EXPENSES) SUPPLY
(— IN REMISSION) PARDON
(— OF LAND) FEU ENAM GALE PATA
SASAN CASATE

(— PERMISSION) ALLOW DISPENSE
(— RELIEF) FORGIVE
(— TIME) FRIST
(INDIAN —) ENAM COWLE SASAN
JAGEER JAGHIR
(PL.) PORK
GRANTING IF ALTHO REMISE
ALTHOUGH ACCORDANCE
GRANTOR LESSOR
GRANULAR CORN OPEN GRAINY
GRANULATE CORN KERN GRAIN
SUGAR
GRANULATED CORN GRANULAR
GRANULATION SUGARING
GRANULE GRIT GRANUM LUCULE
NODULE BIOBLAST GONIDIUM
GRANULET
(— IN PROTOPLASM) PLASTID
(ALTMANN'S —S) BIOPLAST
(ICE —S) FRAZIL
(SUFF.) PLAST
GRAPE UVA EDEN VINE BERRY
GRAIN PINOT TOKAY ACINUS
AGAWAM ISABEL MALAGA
MONICA MUSCAT RAISIN VERDEA
WORDEN CATAWBA CONCORD
HAMBURG MALMSEY MISSION
NIAGARA SULTANA CABERNET
DELAWARE GRAPELET HANEPOOT
ISABELLA LABRUSCA MALVASIA
MORILLON MOUNTAIN MUSCATEL
NUCULANE RIESLING SLIPSKIN
SYLVANER THOMPSON VINIFERA
MUSCADINE
(GARNISHED WITH —S) VERONIQUE
(PREPARED WITH —S) VERONIQUE
(PL.) RAPE UVAE
(PREF.) ACINI UVI UVULO
GRAPEFRUIT POMELO POMOLO
POMMELO TORONJA SHADDOCK
POMPELMOUS POMPELMOOSE
GRAPE HYACINTH MUSK
GRAPE JUICE MUST SAPA STUM
GRAPENUTS TERRAPIN
GRAPEROOT BERBERIS
GRAPES
(PREF.)
(BUNCH OF —) BOTRY(O)
STAPHYL(O)
**GRAPES OF WRATH (AUTHOR OF
—)** STEINBECK
(CHARACTER IN —) AL JIM TOM
JOAD NOAH ROSE CASEY MULEY
CONNIE GRAVES RUTHIE WINFIELD
GRAPESTONE
(PREF.) ACINI
GRAPEVINE
(PREF.) AMPEL(O)
GRAPH CHART CURVE OGIVE TRACE
CONTOUR DIAGRAM PROFILE
ISOPLETH
(BOTTOMS OF —S) XAXES
(KIND OF —) FEYNMAN
GRAPHIC PICTORIAL PICTURESQUE
GRAPHITE WAD KISH LEAD WADD
KEESH PENCIL PLUMBAGO
MODERATOR
GRAPNEL CROW DRAG GRAB
CREEP CREEPER GRABBLE
GRAPPLE SNIGGER GRABHOOK
GRAPPLE DOG CLOSE GRASP GRIPE
LATCH BUCKLE CLINCH GRABBLE

GRAPNEL GRIPPLE SNIGGER SNIGGLE WRESTLE
(— QUARRY) BIND
GRAPPLING IRON CLIP DRAG CLASP CRAMP CORVUS CRAMPER CRAMPON CREEPER GRAPNEL GRAPPLE HARPAGO
GRAPTOLITHA XYLINA
GRASP HUG NAP SEE CLAM CLAW CLUM FAKE FANG FIST GLAM GRAB GRIP HAND HENT HOLD SNAP SPAN TAKE VICE CATCH CINCH CLAMP CLASP CLAUT CLEUK GRIPE GROPE LATCH SAVVY SEIZE SENSE SHAKE SPEND CLENCH CLINCH CLUTCH COLLAR FATHOM GOUPEN RUMBLE SNATCH CLAUGHT COMPASS ENCLOSE GRAPPLE GRIPPLE SMITTLE CONCEIVE HANDFAST HOLDFAST
(— FULLY) SWALLOW
(— MENTALLY) ENVISAGE
(— OF REALITY) EPIPHANY
(PREF.) CHADA
GRASPING HARD NIPPY SNACK GRABBY GREEDY GRIPPY HAVING TAKING BROKING MISERLY PUGGING COVETOUS HANDGRIP AVARICIOUS
GRASS BON FAG FOG POA RAY BENT COIX DISS DOOB GAMA HERB ICHU KANS KUSA MUNJ MUSK RAGI TARE TORE USAR ANKEE BARIT BROME COGON COUCH CROFT DRAWK DRINN FLAWN FUNDI GARSE GIRSE GLAGA GRAMA HARIF HAVER HICHU ILLUK KOGON KUSHA KWEEK MELIC MUHLY PANIC QUILA REESK ROOSA SEREH SPIRE STIPA SUDAN ZORRA BARLEY BHABAR BHARTI DARNEL EMOLOA FESCUE FIORIN GLUMAL KIKUYU QUITCH RAGGEE REDTOP RIPGUT SCUTCH TOETOE TWITCH ZACATE AMOURET CANNACH DOGFOOT ESPARTO EULALIA FESTUCA FINETOP FOXTAIL GALLETA GOLDEYE HERBAGE HORDEUM JARAGUA MATWEED MUSCOVY PANICLE PASTURE PIGROOT SETARIA SORGHUM TIMOTHY TOCUSSO TUSSOCK VETIVER ZACATON AEGILOPS BLUESTEM BROWNTOP CALFKILL CAMALOTE CELERITY COCKSPUR DOGSTAIL DRAWLING DROPSEED EELGRASS ELEUSINE FINEBENT GAMELOTE MANGRASS MATGRASS PASPALUM SANDBURR SANDSPUR SANDSTAY SPANIARD SPARTINA SPINIFEX SWEEPAGE TEOSINTE WHITETOP MARIJUANA
(— AMONG GRAIN) DRAWK
(— FOR STOCK) EATAGE
(— FOR THATCHING) BANGO
(— ON BORDER OF FIELD) RAND
(— READY FOR REAPING) SWATH SWATHE
(— USED FOR MAKING PAPER) ESPARTO

(AROMATIC —) KHUS CUSCUS KHUSKHUS
(BEACH —) STAR
(BERMUDA —) DOOB SCUTCH
(CEREAL —) SORGO SORGHUM
(COARSE —) FAG RISP TATH COGON REESK LALANG SNIDDLE
(COUCH —) CUTCH KWEEK QUITCH SCUTCH STROIL SQUITCH
(CURED —) HAY
(DEAD —) FOG FOGGAGE
(DITCH —) ENALID
(GOOSE —) CLIVERS CLEAVERS
(KIND OF —) COUCH QUACK
(MEADOW —) POA
(NUT —) COCO COCOA
(ORCHARD —) DOGFOOT
(PART OF —) AWN TIP APEX CULM LEAF NODE ROOT STEM BLADE BRACT GLUME SHOOT FLORET FLOWER LIGULE SHEATH TILLER PEDICEL RHIZOME SPIKELET
(PASTURE —) TORE GRAMMA
(POVERTY —) HEATH
(QUAKING —) SHAKER
(REED —) CARRIZO
(REEDLIKE —) BENT DISS
(STORED FORAGE —) HAYLAGE
(SUDAN —) GARAWI
(SWEET —) SORGO
(PREF.) CHORTO GRAMIN(I)(O) HERBI
GRASS-EATING
(PREF.) POE
GRASSERIE JAUNDICE
GRASSHOPPER GRIG CICADA HOPPER QUAKER SAWYER TETTIX ACRIDID CRICKET KATYDID SKIPPER ACRIDIAN LANGOSTA
GRASSLAND HAM LEA RAKH VELD VELDT BOTTOM MEADOW PATANA LEYLAND PASTURE SAVANNA
(ARGENTINE —) CAMPO
(RUSSIAN —) STEPPES
(SWAMPY —) EVERGLADE
(TRACT OF —) PRAIRIE
(PL.) SCHIH
GRASS PEA LANG KHESARI
GRASSQUIT QUAT QUIT CIVITE
GRASS TREE BLACKBOY
GRASSY HERBY
GRATE JAR FRET GRIT RASP CHARK CHIRK DANDY DEVIL GRIDE GRIND RANGE STOVE ABRADE CHAFER SCRAPE SCREAR SCREEK SCROOP GRATING MANGRATE
(FALSE —) DANDY
GRATEFUL KIND SAPID WELCOME THANKFUL
GRATEFULNESS GRATUITY
GRATER RISP
GRATIANO (BROTHER OF —) BRABANTIO
(WIFE OF —) NERISSA
GRATIFICATION GLUT GUST LUXURY RELISH REWARD SATIETY DELICACY GRATUITY PLEASURE TICKLING SATISFACTION
GRATIFIED GLAD PROUD CHARMED CONTENT PLEASED
GRATIFY PAY BABY FEED LUST SATE AMUSE FEAST FLESH GRACE HUMOR MIRTH QUEME SAVOR

SERVE SETUP STILL WREAK ARRIDE FOSTER OBLIGE PAMPER PLEASE REGALE SALUTE TICKLE AGGRATE CONTENT DELIGHT FLATTER GLADDEN INDULGE SATISFY PLEASURE
(— THE PALATE) SEASON
GRATIFYING GOOD COMELY DELICATE GRATEFUL
GRATING GRID HACK HARP HECK JACK RACK CRATE CRUDE GRILL HARSH RANGE RASPY TRAIL BAFFLE CRATCH GITTER GRILLE HOARSE RUGGED WICKET BAFFLER ECHELLE ECHELON BABRACOT CATAPULT GRIDIRON METALLIC SCRANNEL STRIDENT PORTCULLIS
(— OVER DRAIN) SIVER SYVER
GRATIS FREE FREELY BUCKSHEE
GRATITUDE THANK THANKS GRATUITY
GRATUITOUS FREE WANTON BASELESS NEEDLESS
GRATUITY FEE TIP BOON DASH VAIL PILON SPIFF SPILL BOUNTY CUMSHAW DASTURI DOUCEUR PRESENT PRIMAGE BAKHSHISH BONAMANO BUCKSHEE COURTESY DUSTOORI GRATUITO REAPDOLE BAKHSHISH BAKSHEESH PERQUISITE
(CHRISTMAS —) BOX
(GAMBLER'S —) TOKE
(PL.) LARGESSE
GRAVE BED DRY LOW PIT SAD URN BALK BASS BIER CELL CIST DEEP DELF FOSS GRIT HIGH HOME KIST LAIR LAKE MOLD MOOL RUDE SADE SAGE TOMB URNA DELFT FOSSE GRAFF GROVE HEAVY MOULD SHEOL SOBER STAID STIFF SUANT VAULT BURIAL DEMURE GRIEVE HEARSE SEDATE SEVERE SOLEMN SOMBER SOMBRE STEADY AUSTERE EARNEST FUNERAL PITHOLE SERIOSO SERIOUS SOBERLY CATONIAN DECOROUS MATRONAL SERMONIC SATURNINE
GRAVECLOTHES LINEN CEREMENTS
GRAVEDIGGER RATEL BEDRAL BURIER FOSSOR PITMAN BEDERAL
GRAVEL GRIT ARENA GEEST GRAIL CHESIL RANGLE SAMMEL SHILLA BALLAST CALICHE CHANNEL RATCHEL SHINGLE STANNER BLINDING
(— AND SAND) DOBBIN
(— DEPOSIT) LEAD
(— IN KIDNEYS) ARENA
(LOOSE —) SLITHER
(SCREENED —) HOGGINS
(PREF.) CROCO
GRAVELLY HASKY CHISELLY GLAREOUS
GRAVELY SADLY DEEPLY
GRAVE MOUND TUMULUS
GRAVER BURIN STYLE PLASTIC SCORPER
GRAVESTONE BAUTA PLANK STELA

STELE STONE TABLE CIPPUS JUMPER THROUGH
GRAVEYARD CEMETERY
GRAVID HEAVY WOMBED PREGNANT
GRAVIMETER DOODLEBUG
GRAVITATIONAL UNIT SLUG
GRAVITY WEIGHT DIGNITY EARNEST SOBRIETY
(KIND OF —) ZERO
GRAVY JUS SOP BREE FOND LEAR BLANC BUNCE JIPPER
GRAY ASH BAT FOG ASHY BEAR BLAE BLUE DOVE DUSK GREY GRIS GULL HOAR IRON LEAD SALT ACIER CAMEL CRANE HOARY LYART MOUSE STEEL WHITE CASTOR CINDER DENVER FROSTY FRUSTY GREIGE GRISLY ISABEL LEADEN NICKEL NUTRIA PEWTER QUAKER STRING BLUNKET CRUISER GRANITE GRIZARD GRIZZLE GRIZZLY HUELESS MURINUS NEUTRAL PELICAN PILGRIM SARKARA SPARROW ALUMINUM BLONCKET CHARCOAL CINEREAL CINEROUS EVENGLOW FELDGRAU PLATINUM PLYMOUTH
(BROWNISH —) TAUPE
(DARKEST —) BLACK
(GOOSE —) LAMA
(MOLE —) TAUPE
(MOTH —) SHEEPSKIN
(STREAKED WITH —) LYARD
(VIOLET —) GRIDELIN
(PREF.) GLAUC(O) POLI(O)
GRAYBACK DOWITCH GRAYCOAT GREYBACK
GRAYBEARD OLDSTER
GRAY CRANE COOLEN COOLUNG
GRAY DRAB ACIER
GRAYISH NEUTRAL
GRAYLING PINK OMBRE UMBER HERRING UMBRANA BLUEFISH SALMONID
GRAYNESS CANITIES
GRAY PARROT JAKO
GRAYSBY CONY CONEY
GRAY WHALE RIPSACK GRAYBACK HARDHEAD
GRAZE BITE CROP FEED SCUR SKIM AGIST BRUSH GRASS GRIDE RANGE SCAMP SCUFF SHAVE SKIFF SKIRR STOCK BROWSE CREASE FODDER GLANCE RIPPLE SCRAPE SCRAZE PASTURE
GRAZIER PASTURER SQUATTER TREKBOER
GRAZING BIT FEED GRASS COLLOP RASANT FOLDING PASCUAGE
GREASE COOM SAIM SEAM ADEPS BLECK COOMB SMEAR SPICK ARMING AXUNGE CREESH ENSEAM LIQUOR POMATE ALEMITE SAINDOUX
(— IN HARD CAKES) SEAK
(— UP) LARD
(PIG'S —) MORT
(WOOL —) YOK DEGRAS LANOLIN
(PREF.) SEBI
GREASE-HEELS GRAPES
GREASER DOPER
GREASEWOOD CHICO CHEMIZO

GREASY FAT GLET OILY RICH FATTY PORKY YOLKY SMEARY TRAINY CREESHY PINGUID TALLOWY UNCTUOUS

GREAT BAD BIG FAR FAT FIT OLD RAD BARO COOL DEEP DREE FELL FINE GONE GURT HUGE KEEN MAIN MUCH RIAL SOME TALL UNCO VAST VILE AMPLE BURRA CHIEF DANDY FELON GRAND LARGE MEKIL STOUR SUPER SWEET SWELL TOUGH YEDER FIERCE GAPING HEROIC MICKLE NATION STRONG SUPERB CAPITAL EMINENT EXTREME GALLOWS HOWLING IMMENSE INTENSE STAVING TITANIC VIOLENT VOLUMED ALMIGHTY CRACKING ELEVATED ENORMOUS FAVORITE GALACTIC GALAXIAN GIGANTIC HORRIBLE INFINITE PRECIOUS TERRIFIC MONSTROUS MAGNIFICENT
(— LAND) ALASKA
(IMMEASURABLY —) ABYSMAL
(TOO —) OVERDUE
(VERY —) MAIN VARE AWFUL STEEP ARDENT DEADLY IMMANE INGENT MORTAL EXTREME FRANTIC GHASTLY HOWLING SUBLIME DREADFUL MOUNTAIN MONUMENTAL
(PREF.) ARCH MAGN(I) MAHA MEG(A) MEGAL(O)
(HOW —) QUANTI
(SUFF.) MEGALY
GREAT AUK PENGUIN PINWING GAREFOWL
GREAT BARRIER (— ISLAND) OTEA
GREAT BRITAIN (SEE ENGLAND)
GREATCOAT GREGO JEMMY JOSEPH POSTEEN OVERCOAT
GREAT DANE BEARHOUND
GREATER SUPERIOR
(PREF.) MEIZO
GREATER STITCHWORT HEAD SNAPPER HEADACHE SNAPJACK SNAPWORT
GREATER YELLOWLEGS YELPER
GREATEST UTMOST EXTREME MAXIMAL
(— EXTENT) MAX MAXIMUM
(— POSSIBLE) ALL SUPREME
GREAT EXPECTATIONS (AUTHOR OF —) DICKENS
(CHARACTER IN —) JOE PIP ABEL BIDDY DOLGE SARAH ORLICK PHILIP PIRRIP POCKET PROVIS BENTLEY DRUMMLE ESTELLA GARGERY HERBERT JAGGERS MATTHEW HAVISHAM MAGWITCH COMPEYSON PUMBLECHOOK
GREAT GATSBY (AUTHOR OF —) FITZGERALD
(CHARACTER IN —) JAY TOM NICK BAKER DAISY MCKEE GATSBY GEORGE JORDAN MYRTLE WILSON BUCHANAN CARRAWAY CATHERINE WOLFSHIEM
GREAT-GRANDCHILD IEROE
GREAT GRANDFATHER NONO BESAIEL GRANDSIR

GREAT LAKE ERIE HURON ONTARIO MICHIGAN SUPERIOR
GREATLY FAR MUY FELL MUCH AMAIN SWITH FINELY MAINLY STRONG SWYTHE SWEETLY WOUNDLY MIGHTILY
GREAT MOLE RAT ZEMMI ZEMNI
GREATNESS FORCE GRANDEUR GRANDEZA MUCHNESS
GREAT RAGWEED KINGHEAD
GREAT TITMOUSE SHARPSAW
GREAVE JAMB JAMBE JAMBEAU (PL.) CRAP HOSE GRAVES
GREBE LEAD LOON DIVER GAUNT WITCH DIPPER DOBBER DUCKER FINFOOT HENBILL PYGOPOD ARSEFOOT CARGOOSE DABCHICK DIDAPPER GRUIFORM
GRECE GRICE DEGREE GRISSEN

GREECE

ANCIENT LOCATIONS: ELIS DORIS PYLOS ACHAEA ACTIUM ATTICA DELPHI EPIRUS HELLAS LOCRIS PHOCIS SPARTA THEBES TIRYNS BOEOTIA CORINTH EPEIROS LACONIA MACEDON MEGARIS MYCENAE PAESTUM
ARMY UNIT: TAXIS
BAY: ELEUSIS CALAMIC HVRELLION
CAPE: KRIOS MALEA SPADA AKRITAS MATAPAN SIDEROS DREPANON GRAMBYSA TAINARON
CAPITAL: ATHENS ATHENAI
COIN: OBOL HECTE DIOBOL LEPTON STATER DRACHMA DIOBOLON
COLUMN: DORIC IONIC CORINTHIAN
DANCE: PYRRHIC ROMAIKA
DIALECT: COAN ATTIC DORIC ELEAN EOLIC IONIC AEOLIC MELIAN THERAN ACHAEAN ARCADIAN
DISTRICT: ARTA ELIS CANEA CHIOS CORFU CRETE DRAMA EVROS KHIOS PELLA SAMOS ZANTE ACHAEA ACHAIA ATTICA EPIRUS EUBOEA KILKIS KNANIA KOZANE LARISA LESBOS LEUKAS PHOCIS PIERIA SERRAI THRACE XANTHE AETOLIA ARCADIA ARGOLIS BOEOTIA CORINTH KAVALLA LACONIA LARISSA LASETHI MTATHOS PREVEZA RHODOPE CYCLADES IOANNINA KARDITSA KASTORIA MAGNESIA MESSENIA PHLORINA RETHYMNE SALONIKA THESSALY TRIKKALA MACEDONIA
GULF: VOLOS ATHENS MESARA PATRAI PATRAS ARGOLIS CORINTH KAVALLA KNANION LACONIA LEPANTO MESSINI RENDINA SARONIC STRIMON MESSENIA SALONIKA SINGITIC THERMAIC TORONAIC
HOME OF GODS: OLYMPUS
ISLAND: DIA IOS KEA KOS NIO CEOS KEOS MILO SYME SYRA CHIOS CORFU CRETE DELOS KASOS KHIOS LEROS MELOS MILOS NAXOS PAROS PAXOI PAXOS PSARA RODOS SAMOS SARIA SYROS TELOS TENOS THERA THIRA TINOS ZANTE ANAPHE

ANDROS CANDIA CERIGO CHALKE EUBOEA EVVOIA GAVDOS IKARIA ITHACA ITHAKI LEMNOS LESBOS LEUKAS LEVKAS PATMOS RHENEA RHODES SIFNOS SKYROS THASOS AMORGOS CIMOLUS CYTHERA KERKYRA KIMOLOS KYTHERA KYTHNOS LEVITHA MYKONOS NISYROS SALAMIS SIPHNOS KALYMNOS MYTILENE SANTORIN SERIPHOS
ISLANDS: IONIAN CYCLADES SPORADES DODECANESE STROPHADES
LAKE: KARLA VOLVE COPAIS KOPAIS PRESPA TOPOLIA KASTORIA TACHINOS VISTONIS
LETTER: MU NU PI XI CHI ETA PHI PSI RHO TAU BETA IOTA ZETA ALPHA DELTA GAMMA KAPPA OMEGA SIGMA THETA LAMBDA EPSILON OMICRON UPSILON
MARKET PLACE: AGORA
MEASURE: PIK BEMA PIKI POUS BARIL CADOS CHOUS CUBIT DIGIT MARIS PEKHE PODOS PYGON XYLON ACAENA BACHEL BACILE BARILE COTULA DICHAS GRAMME HEMINA KOILON ORGYIA PALAME PECHYO DOHENE AMPHORA CHENICA CHOENIX CYATHOS DIAULOS HEKTEUS METRETA STADION STADIUM STREMMA CONDYLOS DAKTYLOS DEKAPODE DOLICHOS MEDIMNOS METRETES PALAISTE PLETHRON PLETHRUM SPITHAME STATHMOS
MOUNTAIN: IDA IDHI OSSA ATHOS PAROS ELIKON PARNON PELION PILION WITSCH HELICON OLYMPUS VUNANON KHAONOVO SMOLIKAS TAYGETOS PARNASSUS
MOUNTAINS: OETA OTHRYS PINDUS RODOPI RHODOPE HYMETTOS TAYGETUS
NAME: ELLAS HELLAS
PENINSULA: ACTE AKTE AKTI MOREA SITHONIA PELOPONNESE
PORT: SYRA CORFU PYLOS SYROS VOLOS MEGARA PATRAI PATRAS KAVALLA KERKYRA PIRAEUS SALONIKA
RIVER: IRI ARDA ARTA AURO AXIOS DOONA EVROS LERNA ALFIOS NESTOS PENEUS PINIOS STRUMA VARDAR ALPHEUS EUROTAS EVROTAS ILISSOS PENEIOS ROUFIAS SARANTA STRIMON ACHELOUS AKHELOOS ALIAKMON KEPHISOS RHOUPHIA
RUINS: DELOS PELLA SAMOS CORINTH ELEUSIS ELEVSIS ACROPOLIS
SEA: CRETE AEGEAN IONIAN MIRTOON
STATE: PHOCIS
TOWN: IOS KEA KOS ARTA ELIS KYME PETA SYME YDRA ADREA AGYIA ARGOS CANEA CHIOS CORFU DRAMA KARYA MELOS NAXOS NEMEA PELLA POROS PSARI PYLOS PYRGI SAMOS

SYROS TENOS VAMOS VATHY VOLOS VYRON ZANTE ACTIUM ATHENS CANDIA DAPHNI DELPHI EDESSA ITHACA JANINA KOZANE LARISA MEGARA NIKHIA PATRAS RHODES SERRAI SERRES SPARTA THEBES TIRYNS XANTHE ATHENAI CORINTH ELEUSIS KERKYRA LARISSA MYCENAE PIRAEUS IOANNINA KOMOTINE MARATHON PHARSALA SALONIKA TRIKKALA PERISTERI
VALLEY: NEMEA
VERNACULAR: DEMOTIC
WEIGHT: MNA OKA OKE MINA OBOL LITRA LIVRE MANEH POUND DIOBOL DRAMME KANTAR OBOLOS OBOLUS STATER TALENT CHALCON CHALQUE DRACHMA DIOBOLON TALANTON
WOMEN: THYIAD

GREED AVARICE AVIDITY HOGGERY CUPIDITY RAPACITY
GREEDINESS AVARICE AVIDITY GULOSITY
GREEDY AVID GAIR GORB YELP AVIDE EAGER GUTTY YIVER GRABBY GUNDIE KITISH STINGY GLUTTON GRIFFLE HOODOCK MISERLY PIGGISH COVETOUS ESURIENT GRASPING RAVENOUS LICKERISH
(PREF.) LICHNO
GREEK GREW ATTIC HADJI KOINE METIC ARGIVE IONIAN KLEPHT ACHAEAN ACHAIAN AEOLIAN GRECIAN GRIFFON HELLENE GRECANIC HELLADIC HELLENIC ITALIOTE SICELIOT
(— RESISTANCE GROUP) EDES ELAS
(MODERN —) ROMAIC
(PREF.) GRAECO GRECO HELLENO
GREEN (ALSO SEE COLOR) NEW RAW LEEK NILE VERD VERT CRUDE FRESH LODEN NAIVE CALLOW VIRENT NOUVEAU SINOPLE UNFIRED VERDANT BAYBERRY IMMATURE NOUVELLE VAGABOND VIRIDIAN WEDGWOOD WOODLAND UNTRAINED
(— MOUNTAIN STATE) VERMONT
(COOKED —S) SALAD
(GRAYISH —) RESEDA
(KIND OF —) MOSS KELLY PARIS
(NILE —) BOA
(PALE —) ALOE ALOES
(YELLOWISH —) GLAUZY ABSINTHE GLAUCOUS
(PREF.) CHLOR(O) PRASEO PRASO VERD(O) VIRID(I)
GREEN AMARANTH REDROOT
GREENBACK NOTE FROGSKIN
(PL.) GREEN LETTUCE
GREEN BAY TREE (AUTHOR OF —) BROMFIELD
(CHARACTER IN —) CYON LILY ELLEN GIGON IRENE JULIA SHANE HATTIE WILLIE HARRISON KRYLENKO TOLLIVER
GREENBRIER SMILAX SARSAPARILLA

GREEN CORMORANT SHAG
GREENERY VERDURE
GREENFISH BLUEFISH
GREENHEART BIBIRU BEBEERU
GREEN HERON KIALEE
GREENHORN JAY MUG YAP JAKE
  PUTT TYRO IKONA GREENY ROOKIE
  SUCKER INNOCENT SOFTHORN
  (— ON WHALER) WAISTER
GREENHOUSE STOVE GREENERY
  HOTHOUSE ORANGERY
  COOLHOUSE
GREENISH BERYL SANIOUS
GREENISH-YELLOW RESEDA

GREENLAND
AIR BASE: THULE
BAY: DISKO BAFFIN MELVILLE
CAPE: JAAL GRIVEL WALKER
  BISMARCK BREWSTER FAREWELL
  LOWENORN
CAPITAL: GODTHAAB
DISCOVERER: ERIC
MOUNTAIN: FOREL PAYER
  KHARDYU GUNNBJORN
STRAIT: DAVIS DENMARK
TOWN: ETAH NORD THULE UMANAK
  GODHAVN IVIGTUT GODTHAAB
  JULIANEHAB EGEDESMINDE
  SUKKERTOPPEN HOLSTEINSBORG

GREENLING TROUT BOREGAT
  BODIERON LORICATE ROCKFISH
GREEN MANSIONS (AUTHOR OF
  —) HUDSON
  (CHARACTER IN —) ABEL RIMA
  NUFLO
GREEN MONKEY GUENON
GREENNESS VERD VERT VERDURE
  VERDANCY VIRIDITY
GREEN ONION RARERIPE
GREEN PIKE JACK
GREENROOM FOYER
GREENSHANK TATTLER
GREENSTONE POUNAMU
GREEN SUNFISH REDEYE
GREENWEED WOODWAX
GREEN WOODPECKER ECCLE
  SPRITE YAFFLE YOCKEL YUKKEL
  HEWHALL HEWHOLE SNAPPER
  SPEIGHT YAFFLER POPINJAY
  WOODHACK WOODWALL
GREET CRY JOY CROW HAIL HALSE
  ACCOST HERALD SALAAM SALUTE
  ADDRESS RECEIVE WELCOME
GREETING HOW CIAO HIYA ALOHA
  GREET HELLO HOWDY KOMBO
  ACCOST CHEERO SALAAM SALUTE
  SHALOM ADDRESS CHEERIO
  COMMEND SLAINTE WELCOME
  REMEMBRANCE
GREGARIOUS GREGAL SOCIAL
GREGE NUTRIA
GRENADA (CAPITAL OF —)
  STGEORGES
  (ISLAND OF —) CARRIACOU
GRENADE EGG TROMBE GRENADO
  FIREBALL PINEAPPLE
GRENADIER RATTAIL WHIPTAIL
GRENADINE FLORENCE
GRENDEL (SLAYER OF —) BEOWULF
GREREN (— LIGHT) GOAHEAD
GRETCHEN (BELOVED OF —) FAUST

GRETTIR THE STRONG (AUTHOR
  OF —) UNKNOWN
  (CHARACTER IN —) ATLI GEST
  GLAM GRIM JARL ANGLE BJORN
  EINAR ASMUND ILLUGI OGMUND
  OXMAIN SKEGGI STEINN THORIR
  DROMUND GRETTIR MAKSSON
  HALLMUND LONGHAIR REDBEARD
  SNAEKOLL STEINVOR THORFINN
  THORGILS SLOWCOACH
  THORBJORN THORSTEINN
GREY (SEE GRAY)
GREYHOUND GREW SALUKI
  BANJARA SAPLING TUMBLER
  WHIPPET
GREYISH BEIGE
GRID BOUCAN BUCCAN GRIDDLE
  GRIDIRON
  (CIRCULAR —) DISC DISK
GRIDDLE COMAL GRILL GIRDLE
  GRILLE BRANDER
GRIDDLE CAKE AREPA LATKE
  CHAPATTY CORNCAKE FLAPJACK
  SLAPJACK
GRIDIRON GRID GRILL TRAIL
  BRANDER BROILER GRIDDLE
GRIEF VEX WOE CARE DILL DOLE
  DOOL DREE HARM HURT MOAN
  MOOD PAIN RUTH SORE TEEN TINE
  AGONY DOLOR GRAME RUING
  TRIAL WRONG BARRAT DESIRE
  MISHAP REGRET SORROW
  STOUND WONDER ANGUISH
  CHAGRIN EMOTION FAILURE
  OFFENSE SADNESS THOUGHT
  TROUBLE WAESUCK WAYMENT
  DISASTER DISTRESS HARDSHIP
  (— STEM) KELLY
  (SECRET —) CANKER
  (PREF.) DOLORI LYPO
GRIESEN ZWITTER
GRIEVANCE BEEF GRIEF PEEVE
  BURDEN BYGONE GRAVAMEN
  HARDSHIP
GRIEVE VEX CARE DOLE DUMP
  EARN ERME HONE HURT PAIN PINE
  SIGH WAIL GRAME GRIPE MOURN
  SORRY WOUND YEARN ATHINK
  CORSIE LAMENT REPINE SORROW
  AFFLICT CHAGRIN CONDOLE
  GRIZZLE TROUBLE WAYMENT
  COMPLAIN DISTRESS
GRIEVED WOE GRAME SORRY
GRIEVING SORRY
GRIEVOUS SAD DEAR DEEP DERF
  HARD SORE CHARY DIRTY GRIEF
  HEAVY SORRY WEARY BITTER
  DREARY SEVERE SHREWD
  CAREFUL HEINOUS WEIGHTY
  DOLOROUS ATROCIOUS
GRIEVOUSLY DERNLY FOULLY
  SORELY HEAVILY
GRIFFE SPUR
GRIFFIN GRIPE GRYPHON EPIMACUS
GRILL ASK REJA BRACE BROIL DEVIL
  TRAIL AFFLICT BROILER GRILLADE
GRILLE FACE REJA HAZARD
GRILLROOM GROOM
GRILSE PEAL SEWIN FINNAC
  GRAWLS BOTCHER FORKTAIL
GRIM DOUR GASH SOUR BLEAK
  CRUEL GAUNT STERN GRIMLY
  GRISLY HORRID SEVERE SULLEN

  TORVID GHASTLY GRIZZLY
  HIDEOUS MACABRE TORVOUS
  PITILESS RUTHLESS
GRIMACE MOP MOW MUG POT
  FACE GIRN IRPE MOUE MUMP YIRN
  FLEER MOUTH SNEER SNOOT
  GIMBLE SHEYLE STITCH MURGEON
  SIMAGRE
GRIMALKIN CAT HAG MOLL CRONE
  WITCH BELDAM HARRIDAN
GRIME DIRT SMUT COLLY SMOUCH
  SMUTCH
GRIMME COQUETOON
GRIMNESS TORVITY
GRIMP CLIMB
GRIMY DINGY GRUBBY STAINED
  SCABROUS
GRIN DRAD GIRN MUMP FLEER
  RISUS SNEER SIMPER GRIZZLE
GRIND DIG SAP BONE BRAY CHEW
  FILE GRUN MILL MULL MUZZ
  SMUG SWOT CRUSH FLOAT FLOUR
  GRATE GRIDE GRIST QUERN
  CRUNCH DRUDGE POWDER
  EMERIZE GRISTLE SWOTTER
  LEVIGATE
  (— COARSELY) KIBBLE
  (— DIAMONDS) SKIVE
  (— SMALL) BRAY
  (— TEETH) GNASH GRATE GRINT
  GRISBET
  (— TO POWDER) TRITURATE
  (— WITH WATER) PUG
GRINDER SUB HERO CRASH HOAGY
  MOLAR HOAGIE MULLER BRUISER
  TORPEDO PEPPERMILL
GRINDING BREAK MOLAR
  ABRASION
  (— OF CORN) MULTURE
  (— OF MEAL) BREAK GRIST
  (— OF TEETH) BRUXISM
  (PL.) SWARF
GRINDSTONE MANO PAVER STONE
GRIP BITE BURR CLIP FANG FIST
  HOLD HOLT TAKE VICE CHOKE
  CINCH CLAMP CLASP GRASP GRIPE
  PINCH SALLY SEIZE BARREL
  CLINCH CLUTCH CRADLE FREEZE
  EMBRACE HANDBAG HOLDING
  SEIZURE ADHESION FOOTLOCK
  HANDFAST HANDGRIP HANDHOLD
  STAGEHAND
  (— OF A SWORD) FUSEAU
  (— OF BELL ROPE) SALLY
  (— TO A SPAR) DOG
GRIPE BEEF CARP CRAB FRIB BITCH
  CREATE GROUSE HOLLER KVETCH
  NATTER SNATCH GRIZZLE
  COMPLAIN
GRIPER GRIZZLER
GRIPES TORMINA
GRIPING GRIPPLE PINCHING
GRIPPER TALON KEEPER NIPPER
GRIPPING STONY STONEY
GRIQUA BASTARD BASTAARD
GRIS-GRIS AMULETS
GRISKINISSA (HUSBAND OF —)
  ARTAXAMINOUS
GRISLY GRIM GHASTLY GRIZZLY
  HIDEOUS GRUESOME
GRISON HURON GALICTIS
GRIST PABULUM
GRISTLE CARTILAGE

GRIT SAND GRIND PLUCK SPUNK
  BOTTOM BRAVERY DECISION
  GRITROCK RUBSTONE
  (— FROM AXLE) SWARF
  (PL.) CUTLINGS
GRITH MUND GYRTH
GRITTY SANDY SHARP GRISTY
  CHISELLY SABULINE SABULOUS
GRIVET TOTA WAAG GEUNON
  NISNAS
GRIZZLE ROAN
GRIZZLED GRISLY STREAKED
GRIZZLY BEAR (— STATE)
  CALIFORNIA
GROAN MOAN ROME GRANK
  GRUNT STECH COMPLAIN
GROANER PUN JOKE
GROAT BIT FLAG GILL HARP
GROATS
  (PREF.) ATHERO
GROCER SPICER EPICIER PEPPERER
GROCERY BODEGA PULPERIA
GROG RUMBO TEMPER CHAMOTTE
GROGGERY SHANTY GROGSHOP
GROGGY SHAKY UNSTEADY
  WAVERING
GROGSHOP SHANTY DOGGERY
  GROGGERY
GROIN LISK PIER SHARE CLITCH
  INGUEN GRUNZIE
  (PREF.) INGUIN(O)
GROMMET RING BECKET COLLAR
  EYELET CRINGLE GARLAND
GROMWELL PUCCOON REDROOT
  SALFERN GRAYMILL
GROOM LAD MAFU NEAT SYCE
  CURRY DRESS MAFOO PREEN
  PRIMP STRAP SWIPE TIGER
  BARBER BATMAN FETTLE FOGGER
  GUINEA MEHTAR OSTLER
  HOSTLER MARSHAL COISTREL
  COISTRIL GROOMLET STRAPPER
GROOMING TOILETTE
GROOVE RUT BEAD DADO GAIN
  KERF LUCE NOCK PORT RAKE SLOT
  CANAL CHASE CROZE FLUTE
  FOSSA GLYPH GORGE GOUGE
  GUIDE JOINT QUIRK REGAL RIFLE
  RIGOL SCARF SCORE STRIA
  SWAGE CREASE CULLIS FULLER
  FURROW GUTTER KEYWAY
  RABBET RAGGLE RAGLET REBATE
  RIFFLE RUNNER SCROBE SULCUS
  THROAT TRENCH CHAMFER
  CHANNEL GARLAND KEYHOLE
  PLOWING SULCATE BOTHRIUM
  GROOVING PHILTRUM CANNELURE
  VALLECULA
  (— FOR SLIDING DOOR) REGLE
  (— IN AUGER) POD
  (— IN COLUMN) FLUTE
  (— IN HORSE'S TOOTH) MARK
  (— IN MASONRY) RAGGLE
  (— IN SLUICE) RIFFLE
  (— IN STAVES) CROZE
  (— IN STONE) JAD
  (— IN TIRE) SIPE
  (— OF RECORD) TRACK
  (— ON UPPER LIP) PHILTRUM
  (— ON WEEVIL) SCROBE
  (— ON WHALE) SCARF
  (—S ON ROCK) LAPIES
  (— UNDER COPING) GORGE

(JOINER'S —) SEAM
(RECTANGULAR —) REGLET
GROOVED FLUTED MILLED
EXARATE SULCATE
GROOVER FLUTER
GROOVY IN HIP RAD COOL FAROUT
SMOOTH STRIATE
GROPE CLAM CLAW FEEL POKE
RIPE GLAUM GRAIP FUMBLE
GUDDLE GRABBLE GRAPPLE
GROPPLE GRUBBLE SCRABBLE
(— AWKWARDLY) FUMBLE
GROSBEAK FINCH HAWFINCH
GROSGRAIN ROYALE
GROSS FAT DULL FOUL LUMP RANK
BROAD CRASS FOGGY GREAT
GUTTY LARGE MACRO SLUMP
THICK WHOLE ANIMAL COARSE
EARTHY FILTHY GREASY SORDID
STRONG BLOATED FULSOME
CLODDISH FLAGRANT INDECENT
SLUTTISH
GROSSO MATAPAN
GROTESQUE ANTIC WOOZY
ROCOCO BAROQUE BIZARRE
CROTESCO FANCIFUL
GROTTO CAVE GROT ANTRE SPEOS
CAVERN LUPERCAL
GROUCH BEAN CHAD SULK CRANK
GROUSE SOURBALL SOURPUSS
GROUND SEW SOD SUE BASE CLOD
DIRT FOLD FOND GIST LAND MOLD
REST ROOT SOIL STAY WOLD
EARTH FIELD FIRTH FOUND
MOULD PLACE SCORE SOLUM
TRAIN TUTOR VENUE CREASE
MATTER REASON SMACKED
FORELAND INITIATE
(— AT TOP OF SHAFT) BANK
(— COVERED WITH RUBBLE) TITI
(— FOR COMPLAINT) BEEF
(— OF FLAG) FIELD
(— OF LACE) FOND
(— OVERLYING TIN DEPOSIT)
BURDEN
(BOGGY —) SOG CARR SNAPE
(BROKEN —) HAG
(BURYING —) CEMETERY
(CAMPING —) AUTOCAMP
(COLLEGE —S) CAMPUS
(DUMPING —) TIP TOOM
(FALLOW —) BRISE
(FEEDING —) HAUNT
(FIRM-HOLDING —) LANDFANG
(FISHING —) HAAF
(FROZEN —) TJAELE
(GRASSY —) LAWN CLOWRE
(GRAZING —) HERDWICK
(HARD —) HARDPAN
(HUNTING —) CHASE
(LOW —) INCH SWALE TALAO
(MIDDLE —) LIMBO
(MUDDY —) SLOB
(NEW ENCLOSED —) TINING
(ORIGINAL —) URGRUND
(PARADE —) MAIDAN
(PASTURE —) HIRSEL
(RECREATION —) PARK
(RISING —) HURST HYRST
(SLOPING —) CLEVE
(SOLID —) HILL
(SPONGY —) BOG
(SWAMPY —) PUXY CRIPPLE

(UNCULTIVATED —) JUNGLE
(UNUSED —) AREA
(WET WASTE —) MOOR REESK
(PL.) GROUT STOCK
(PREF.) CHAMAE CHAME GE(O)
PEDO SOLI
(ON THE —) HUMI
GROUND BEETLE CARABID
GROUND COVER AJUGA VETCH
MYRTLE
GROUNDER COMEBACKER
GROUND HEMLOCK SHINWOOD
GROUND HOG MARMOT
GROUND IVY GILL HEWE HOVE JILL
YARROW ALEHOOF CATFOOT
GAGROOT MILFOIL TUNHOOF
FOALFOOT
GROUNDLESS IDLE FALSE
BASELESS
GROUNDLINE SETLINE
GROUNDMAN GRUNT
GROUNDMASS PASTE CEMENT
MATRIX
GROUNDNUT GOBBE PEANUT
PIGNUT
GROUND PINE FOXTAIL STAGHORN
GROUNDS RATIONALE
GROUNDSEL SIMSON DOGBUSH
SENCION SENECIO BINDWEED
BIRDSEED
GROUNDSMAN CURATOR
GROUND SQUIRREL GOPHER
GRINNY SUSLIK MEERKAT SCIURID
SOUSLIK SCIURINE
GROUND THRUSH PITTA
GROUNDWORK BASE FOND FUND
BASIS BOTTOM FUNDUS
GROUP MOB SET BAND BEVY BODY
CREW DECK FOLD GANG KNOT
PAIR RING SECT SORT STEW TEAM
TREE ARRAY BATCH BREED BUNCH
CASTE CLASS CLUMP COVEY FIRCA
FLOCK GENUS GLOBE PLUMP
RADHA SKULK SQUAD STACK
TALLY WHEEN CIRCLE CLUTCH
COHORT FAMILY GRUPPO PARCEL
RUBRIC AGGROUP BATTERY
BOILING BOUROCK BRACKET
CLASSIS CLUSTER COLLEGE
COMMUNE COMPANY CONSORT
FELLOWS FLUTTER QUOTITY
SECTION SEVERAL SOCIETY
ALLIANCE CATEGORY CLASSIFY
DIVISION FAISCEAU FLOTILLA
GROUPING
(— HIRED TO APPLAUD) CLAQUE
(— OF ANGELS) FLIGHT
(— OF ARTIFACTS) CACHE
(— OF ATOMS) CLUSTER RADICAL
(— OF BADGERS) CETE
(— OF BLOOD CELLS) NEME
(— OF BUILDINGS) BLOCK CLUSTER
(— OF CASTINGS) SPRAY
(— OF CATS) CLOWDER
(— OF CELLS) GLAND ISLET LAURA
CENTER CORONA EPITHEM
SEMILUNE
(— OF CHIMNEYS) STACK
(— OF COMMUTERS) VANPOOL
(— OF COMPUTER JOBS) BATCH
(— OF CRAFTSMEN) ARTEL
(— OF DECOYS) STOOL
(— OF DEITIES) CABEIRI

(— OF DIALECTS) AEOLIC
(— OF EELS) SWARM
(— OF EIGHT) OCTAD OCTET
OCTETTE
(— OF EIGHT BINARY DIGITS) BYTE
(— OF FAMILIES) FINE
(— OF FIVE) PENTAD CINQUAIN
(— OF FOUR) MESS QUARTET
(— OF FRIENDS) BUNCH
(— OF FURNISHINGS) ENSEMBLE
(— OF HAITIANS) COMBITE
COUMBITE
(— OF HORSEMEN) QUADRILLE
(— OF HOUSES) BOROUGH
(— OF HUTS) BUSTI KRAAL BUSTEE
(— OF ILLUSTRIOUS PERSONS)
PANTHEON
(— OF INDIAN STATES) AGENCY
(— OF ISOGLOSSES) BUNDLE
(— OF KINDRED) SIOL
(— OF KINSMEN) AHL
(— OF KITTENS) KENDLE KINDLE
(— OF LAYMEN) COFRADIA
(— OF LIONS) PRIDE
(— OF LISTENERS) AUDIENCE
(— OF MARTENS) RICHESSE
(— OF MILITARY VEHICLES)
DEADLINE
(— OF MOLDINGS) DANCETTE
(— OF NERVE CELLS) GANGLIA
(— OF NINE) ENNEAD NONARY
(— OF NUCLEONS) SHELL
(— OF OFFSPRING) CLUTCH
(— OF ORGANISMS) FORM STRAIN
(— OF PARACHUTISTS) STICK
(— OF PERSONS) BAG CLUB KNOT
SWAD CROWD DROVE CIRCLE
GAGGLE KENNEL
(— OF RETORTS) BENCH SETTING
(— OF RUFFIANS) PUSH
(— OF SCHOLARS) ULAMA
(— OF SCULPTURE) MORTORIO
(— OF SEVEN) HEPTAD SEPTET
HEBDOMAD
(— OF SIX) HEXAD SENARY
(— OF SLAVES) COFFLE
(— OF SOILS) LATERITE
(— OF SOLDIERS) DRAFT COHORT
(— OF STARS) ASTERISM
(— OF STRATIFIED BEDS) FACIES
(— OF STUDENTS) SEMINAR
(— OF SYLLABLES) FOOT
(— OF SYMBOLS) FORMULA
(— OF SYMPTOMS) SYNDROME
(— OF TAXA) CLADE
(— OF TEN) DECADE DENARY
(— OF TENTS) CAMP CANVAS
(— OF THEATERS) CIRCUIT
(— OF THREE) TRIO GLEEK TRIAD
TRINE TROIKA
(— OF TRAITS) COMPLEX
(— OF TROUT) HOVER
(— OF VERSES) SYSTEM
(— OF WEAPONS) NEST
(— OF WINGS) RUFFLE
(— OF WIRES) DROP
(— OF WORDS) ACCENT GENITIVE
(— OF 10 NOTES) DECUPLET
(— OF 100) SENATE
(— OF 1000) CHILIAD
(— OF 12) DOZEN
(— OF 2 VOWELS) DIGRAM
DIGRAPH

(— OF 40 THREADS) BEER BIER
(— OF 60 PIECES) SHOCK
(— TO RAISE CAMPAIGN MONEY)
PAC
(ASSISTANCE —) AINI
(ATHLETIC —) TEAM
(ATOMIC —) LIGAND
(AUTHORITATIVE —) CONCLAVE
(AVANT-GARDE —) UNDERGROUND
(CONFUSED —) SNARL
(CORE —) CADRE
(CRIME SYNDICATE —) FAMILY
(ECOLOGICAL —) GUILD
(ETHNIC —) LI ACHANG BALAHI
BATTAK ETHNOS CHINGPAW
(ETHNOLOGICAL —) ISLAND
(EXCLUSIVE —) ELECT
(EXPERT —) PANEL
(FAMILY —) GWELY
(GREEK RESISTANCE —) EDES ELAS
(HARMONIOUS —) DOVECOTE
(INTIMATE —) COTERIE
(KINSHIP —) SUSU
(LANGUAGE —) ATALAN
(LARGE —) PASSEL
(LINKED —) NEXUS
(LIVELY —) GALA
(MEMBER OF COMMANDO —)
FEDAYEE
(NON-MOSLEM —) MILLET
(PAGAN —) BATAK BATANGAN
(PERFORMING —) COMBO TROUPE
ENSEMBLE
(PHILOSOPHICAL —) CENACLE
(POLITICAL —) BLOC PARTY FASCIO
COMMONS MACHINE
(SEGREGATED —) GHETTO
(SMALL —) PLUMP
(SOCIAL —) KITH SEPT TRIBE
FAMILY INGROUP
(WEALTHY SOCIAL —) JETSET
(PREF.) (CULTURAL —) ETHNO
(SUFF.) AD ET OME SOME
GROUPED AGMINATE
GROUPER GAG HIND MERO GUASA
HAMEL SCAMP AGUAJI BONACI
CHERNA GROPER HAMLET
WARSAW BACALAO GARLOPA
GARRUPA GOURAMI JEWFISH
REDFISH LAPULAPU REDBELLY
ROCKFISH SCIRENGA SERRANID
(KIND OF —) WARSAW
(YOUNG —) SNAPPER
GROUPING KIND ARRAY BATTERY
KINDRED DIVISION GROUPAGE
SODALITY SYNTAGMA
(— OF POTTERY) SERIES
GROUSE CRAB BITCH GANGA GRIPE
PEEVE GORHEN GROUCH HOOTER
ATTAGEN CHEEPER GAZELLE
GORCOCK PINTAIL COMPLAIN
MOORBIRD MOORFOWL
PARTRIDGE PTARMIGAN
(YOUNG —) POULT SQUEALER
GROUT GROOT LARRY SLUSH
GROUTING
GROUTER GUNITER
GROVE CAMP HEWT HOLT MOTT
SHAW TOFT TOPE WONG ALTIS
BLUFF COPSE GLADE HURST
HYRST GARDEN GREAVE GROVET
ISLAND OLIVET SCROBE SPRING
ACADEMY ARBORET BOSCAGE

COPPICE SPINNEY THICKET WOODING SERINGAL WODELEIE
(— OF ALDERS) CARR
(— OF MANGO TREES) TOPE
(— OF OAKS) ENCINAL
(— OF OSIERS) HOLT
(— OF SUGAR MAPLES) CAMP
(SACRED —) ALTIS SARNA
(SMALL —) SHAW
(PREF.) NAEMOR
(SUFF.) ETUM
GROVEL FAWN ROLL CREEP CRINGE TUMBLE WALLOW WELTER GRABBLE FLOUNDER
GROVELING PRONE WORMY ABJECT HANGDOG REPTILE
GROW AGE BUD GET HIT ICH WAX BOLL COME CROP ECHE ITCH MAKE RISE SEED THEE THRO WEAR EDIFY ISSUE PLANT PROVE RAISE SHOOT SWELL ACCRUE BATTEN BECOME DOUBLE EXPAND EXTEND GATHER SPRING SPROUT THRIVE AUGMENT BROADEN BURGEON DEVELOP DISTEND ENLARGE IMPROVE NOURISH ADOLESCE FLOURISH HEIGHTEN INCREASE MUSHROOM THRODDEN PROLIFERATE
(— ANGRY) STIVER
(— BETTER) IMPROVE
(— COLD) QUENCH
(— DARK) GLOAM GLOOM NIGHT DARKEN DARKLE
(— FAINT) DIE APPAL APPALL
(— FAT) FEED BATTEN
(— IN LENGTH) ELONGATE
(— IRREGULARLY) SCRAMBLE
(— LESS) ABATE SLAKE ASSUAGE DECREASE
(— LIGHT) DAWN
(— LOUDER) SWELL
(— LUXURIANTLY) THRIVE
(— MAD) WOOD
(— MILD) GIVE
(— OLD) AGE OLD SENESCE
(— OVER) INVADE
(— PLUMP) PLIM
(— RAPIDLY) SNOWBALL
(— RICH) FATTEN
(— SOUND) HEAL
(— SPIRITLESS) FLAG
(— STILL) HUSH
(— STRONG) FORTIFY STORKEN
(— THIN) PEAK
(— TOGETHER) JOIN KNIT ACCRETE CONCREW COOSIFY COALESCE
(— TO HEAD) CABBAGE
(— TO STALK) SPINDLE
(— UNDER GLASS) GLASS
(— UNTIDILY) STRAGGLE
(— UP) STEM ACCRUE
(— WEAK) FAINT
(PREF.) **(— TOGETHER)** SYMPHY(O)
GROWING GROWY ONGOING CRESCENT CRESCIVE ACCRESCENT
(— ANGRY) IRASCENT
(— IN AIR) AERIAL
(— IN CLUSTERS) RACEMOSE
(— IN GRAIN FIELDS) SEGETAL
(— IN HEAPS) ACERVATE
(— IN MEADOW) PRATAL
(— IN PAIRS) BINATE

(— IN RUBBISH) RUDERAL
(— IN WATER) AQUATIC
(— ON A STEM) CAULINE
(— OUT) ENATE
(— RAPIDLY) BOOMING
(— THICKLY) HOUSY
(— VIGOROUSLY) THRIFTY
(— WILD) SAVAGE AGRARIAN AGRESTAL
(GOOD FOR —) ARABLE
(SUFF.) PLASIA PLASIS PLASM(A)
(IA)(IC) PLAST(IC)(Y) PLASY
(— IN OR ON) COLE COLINE COLOUS
GROWL YAR GNAR GURL GURR NARR RASE ROIN ROME WIRR YARR YIRR GARRE GNARL GNARR GROIN SNARL GOLLAR HABBLE GRUMBLE MAUNDER
GROWLER CLARENCE
GROWLING GROIN SURLY
GROWN THRIVEN
(— COLD) DEAD
(— FROM SEED) MAIDEN
(— HIGH) LOGGY
(— TOGETHER) ADNATE ACCRETE
(FULL —) GREAT MATURE
(WELL —) THRODDY
GROWN-UP ADULT GROWN MATURE
GROWTH FUR WAX BUSH COAT CORN FILM GROW JUBA RISE SPUR SUIT DUVET FLUSH GUMMA MAQUI STAND STOCK STOOL SWELL BUTTON CALLUS CANCER CLAVUS EATAGE EPULIS FRINGE FUNGUS LANUGO SCREEN SPROUT TYLOSE UPCOME WASTME AUXESIS BRACKEN COPPICE ERINEUM FUNGOID MACCHIE SARCOID STATURE TYLOSIS BEARDING CARUNCLE ENDOGENY INCREASE SETATION SWELLING UPSPRING ACCRETION
(— IN EYE) FILM
(— OF BEARD) DOWN
(— OF HAIR) SUIT
(— OF HORN) BUTTON SPIDER
(— OF PLANKTON) BLOOM
(— OF SHOOTS) STOOL
(— OF TREES) MOTTE BOSQUE BOSCAGE COPPICE SHINNERY
(— ON HORSE'S LEG) FUSEE FUZEE
(— ON VESSEL'S BOTTOM) GARR
(ABUNDANT —) FLUSH
(CANCEROUS —) WOLF
(DENSE —) BRUSH FOREST SHINNERY
(DOWNY —) LANUGO
(GREEN —) GREENTH
(HARD —) STONE
(LUXURIANT —) FLOURISH
(ROUGH —) STUBBLE
(RUDIMENTARY —) STUB STUMP
(SIDE —) SPRIG
(SPARSE —) SCRAGGLE
(SUPERFICIAL —) MILDEW
(TRANSPARENT —) DRUSE
(VIGOROUS —) THRIFT
(WOODY —) BURL
(2ND — OF GRASS) FOG
(PREF.) AUXANO AUXO
(SUFF.) PHYTA PHYTE(S) PHYTIC

PHYTUM PLASTY TROPHIA TROPHIC TROPHY
(INHIBITION OF —) STASIA STASIS
GROWTH OF THE SOIL (AUTHOR OF —) HAMSUN
(CHARACTER IN —) AXEL ISAK BREDE INGER OLINE OLSEN STROM BARBRO SIVERT ARONSEN ELESEUS REBECCA GEISSLER LEOPOLDINE
GRROVE (— ALONGSIDE MOLDING) QUIRK
GRUB BOB DIG CHOW EATS HUHU MOIL MOOT ROOT ROUT STUB WORM CHUCK GROUT MATHE SCRAN SNOUT WROTE ASSART ESSART GRUGRU MAGGOT MUZZLE ROOTLE NEASCUS PIGROOT FLAGWORM GRUBWORM MUCKWORM SKINWORM
GRUBBY TIRED
GRUBROOT STARWORT
GRUDGE DOWN ENVY DERRY PEEVE SCORE SPITE ANIMUS GROUCH GRUNCH GRUTCH MALICE MALIGN SPLEEN DESPITE EYELAST SIMULTY
GRUDGING JEALOUSY
GRUEL SLOP BLEERY BURGOO CAUDLE CONGEE CROWDY SKILLY SOFKEE BROCHAN CROWDIE LOBLOLLY WANGRACE
GRUESOME UGLY GRISLY GROOLY HORRID SORDID FEARFUL GHASTLY HIDEOUS MACABRE
GRUFF BLUFF ROUGH SURLY CLUMSE SULLEN AUSTERE BEARING BRUSQUE CLUMPST
(PL.) TAILINGS
GRUIFORMES GRALLAE
GRUMBLE CARP GIRN GREX HONE KREX ROIN BLEAT BROCK CROAK DRUNT GROIN GROWL GRUMP GRUNT MUNGE GROUCH GROUSE GRUDGE GRUNCH MUMBLE MUNGER MURMUR MUTTER NOLLER PEENGE REPINE RUMBLE SQUEAL TARROW YAMMER CHANNER CHUNNER CHUNTER GNATTER GRIZZLE GRUNTLE MAUNDER MURGEON QUADDLE SWAGGER COMPLAIN
GRUMBLER GROUCH QUADDLE GROGNARD
GRUMBLING BITCH DRUNT GRIPE GROIN GRUDGE MURMUR MURGEON
GRUMP SULK GRUMBLE COMPLAIN
GRUMPY ILL CROSS DUMPY SURLY GLUMPY GLUMPISH GRUMPISH
GRUNGY DUMPY
GRUNION SMELT
GRUNT OINK BURRO GROIN HUMPH RONCO SARGO GRUMPH RONCHO BURRITO CROAKER GRUNTER GRUNTLE PIGFISH PINFISH TOMTATE KNORHAAN KOORHAAN PORKFISH REDMOUTH RONCADOR
GUACHARO FATBIRD OILBIRD
GUAICURU CADUVEO
GUAM (BAY OF —) AGAT YLIG CETTI AJAYAN UMATAC

(CAPITAL OF —) AGANA
(HARBOR OF —) APRA
(ISLAND OF —) CABRAS
(MOUNTAIN OF —) TENJO LAMLAM
(PENINSULA OF —) OROTE
(TOWN OF —) UPI ARRA ASAN TOTO YONA AGANA LUPOG MAGUA MERIZO UMATAC MALOLOS
GUAMA INGA PACAY
GUAN JACU ORTALIS PHEASANT
GUANA CHANE
GUANABANA SOURSOP
GUANACO LLAMA
GUANCHE CANARIAN
GUANO OSITE
GUAPENA SERRAN SERRANA AGUAVINA
GUARANTEE (ALSO SEE GUARANTY) BAIL BAND SEAL CINCH COVER ASSURE AVOUCH ENGAGE ENSURE INSURE RATIFY SECURE SURETY CAUTION CERTIFY HOSTAGE WARRANT AWARRANT GUARANTY PRESTATE SECURITY WARRANTY
GUARANTEED ASSURED CERTIFIED FOOLPROOF
GUARANTOR ENGAGER GRANTOR GUARAND SPONSOR GUARANTY
GUARANTY (ALSO SEE GUARANTEE) ANDI AVAL PAWN SEAL CAUTIO PLEDGE WARRANT SECURITY WARRANTY
GUARD BOW LEG NIT PAD SEE CARE CURB HERD HOLD KEEP KNOW LOOK REDE SAVE STOP STUB TENT TILE WAIT WEAR WERE WITE YEME ASKAR AWARD BLESS BLOCK CHECK COVER FENCE FORAY HEDGE HINGE PILOT SCREW SKIRT TUTOR WAKEN WATCH SKIRR BANTAY BASKET BRACER BRIDLE BUMPER BUTTON CONVOY DEFEND DRAGON ESCORT FENDER GHAFIR GUNMAN JAILER KAVASS KEEPER MIDDLE POLICE SCREEN SECURE SENTRY SHIELD SHROUD WAITER WARDER YEMING BULWARK CHERISH ESGUARD FRONTAL GHAFFIR GHATWAL GUARDER KEEPING PANDOUR PRESIDY PROTECT SOULACK TRABANT WARDAGE WARRANT CHAPERON DEFENDER GARRISON MUDGUARD OUTGUARD PEDESTAL PILOTMAN PRESERVE SECURITY SENTINEL SHEPHERD SPLASHER WARDSMAN WATCHMAN
(— ON FOIL) BUTTON
(— WHILE IN TRANSIT) RIDE
(AXLE —) HOUSING
(COACH —) SHOOTER
(CONSULAR —) KAVASS
(IMPERIAL —) BOSTANGI BOSTANJI
(KEYHOLE —) LAPPET
(LET DOWN —) NAP
(MOUNTED —) SHOMER
(NECK —) CAMAIL
(ON —) AWARE EXCUBANT
(PRISON —) HACK SCREW CHASER JAILER
(STIRRUP —) TAPADERA

(SWORD —) BOW TSUBA
(WRIST —) BRACER
(PL.) HEAVIES
GUARDED WARY IMMUNE MANNED
GUARDEDLY GINGERLY
GUARDHOUSE BRIG CLINK
BULLPEN HOOSEGOW
GUARDIAN HERD ANGEL ARGUS
TUTOR YEMER CUSTOS KEEPER
MIMING PASTOR PATRON SHOMER
WARDEN CORONER CURATOR
GARDANT GARDEEN GRIFFIN
BARTHOLO BELLERUS CERBERUS
CREANCER DEFENDER ECKEHART
FRAVASHI GOVERNOR GUARDANT
PROTUTOR TUTELARY
(— OF GARDENS) PRIAPUS
(— OF HOME) SIF
(WORLD —) LOKAPAI A MAHARAJA
(PL.) SELLI SELLOI
GUARDIANSHIP WARD TUTELA
CUSTODY KEEPING TUITION
WARDAGE WARDING CUSTODIA
GUARDAGE TUTELAGE WARDENRY
WARDSHIP
GUARDROOM WARDROOM
GUARDSMAN GUARDEE
GUASA MERO

<table>
<tr><td colspan="2" align="center">GUATEMALA</td></tr>
<tr><td>CAPITAL:</td><td>GUATEMALA</td></tr>
<tr><td>COIN:</td><td>PESO CENTAVO QUETZAL</td></tr>
<tr><td>DANCE:</td><td>ELSON GUARIMBA</td></tr>
<tr><td>DEPARTMENT:</td><td>PETEN IZABAL
JALAPA QUICHE SOLOLA ZACAPA
JUTIAPA ESCUINTLA</td></tr>
<tr><td>GULF:</td><td>HONDURAS</td></tr>
<tr><td>INDIAN:</td><td>MAM CHOL ITZA IXIL MAYA
XINCA CARIBE QUICHE POKOMAM</td></tr>
<tr><td>LAKE:</td><td>DULCE GUIJA PETEN IZABAL
ATITLAN</td></tr>
<tr><td>MEASURE:</td><td>VARA CUARTA FANEGA
TERCIA CAJUELA MANZANA</td></tr>
<tr><td>MOUNTAIN:</td><td>AGUA FUEGO PACAYA
TACANA ATITLAN TOLIMAN
TAJAMULCO</td></tr>
<tr><td>PORT:</td><td>OCOS BARRIOS LIVINGSTON</td></tr>
<tr><td>RIVER:</td><td>AZUL BRAVO DULCE LAPAZ
BELIZE CHIXOY NEGINO PASION
SAMALA CHIAPAS MOTAGUA
SARSTUN POLOCHIC</td></tr>
<tr><td>RUINS:</td><td>TIKAL</td></tr>
<tr><td>TOWN:</td><td>OCOS COBAN VIEJA CHAHAL
CHISEC CUILCO FLORES IZTAPA
JALAPA SALAMA SOLOLA TACANA
TECPAN YALOCH ZACAPA
ANTIGUA CUILAPA JUTIAPA
SANJOSE PROGRESO</td></tr>
<tr><td>VOLCANO:</td><td>AGUA FUEGO PACAYA
TACANA ATITLAN TAJUMULCO</td></tr>
<tr><td>WEIGHT:</td><td>CAJA LIBRA</td></tr>
</table>

GUAVA ARACA MYRTAL GUAYABA
GUAYABO GOIABADA
GUAYCURU MBAYA
GUDDLE GUMP NOODLE HANDFISH
GUDGEON PIN QUAB CHALDER
TRUNNION
GUDRUN (FATHER OF —) HETEL
(HUSBAND OF —) ATLI
GUELDER-ROSE GAITER OPULUS
DOGWOOD WHITTEN DOGBERRY
SNOWBALL VIBURNUM

GUENDOLEN (HUSBAND OF —)
LOCRINE
GUENON GRIVET NISNAS VERVET
TALAPOIN TALLAPOI MOUSTACHE
GUEREZA COLOBIN COLOBUS
GUERILLA (VIETNAMESE —)
VIETCONG
GUERRILLA COWBOY GORILLA
JAYHAWK SKINNER BUSHWACK
FELLAGHA KOMITAJI
GUERRILLERO KOMITAJI
GUESS AIM CALL HARP REDE SHOT
WEEN AREAD COUNT ETTLE FANCY
INFER TWANG DEVISE DIVINE
RECKON IMAGINE SURMISE
SUSPECT
(— CORRECTLY) TOUCH
(WILD —) STAB
GUEST COME GOER HOST DINER
INVITEE VISITOR SYMPHILE
VISITANT
(— AT RANCH) DUDE
(UNINVITED —) SHADOW
(PL.) LEVEE COMPANY
(PREF.) XEN(O)
(SUFF.) XENE XENOUS XENY
GUEST-HOUSE GASTHOF
GUESTHOUSE BANDB
GUFA KUFA GOOFAH KUPHAR
GUFFAW GAFF ROAR HEEHAW
GUIDANCE AIM DUCT EGIS AEGIS
STEER CONDUCT GUIDAGE
HELMAGE LEADING WISSING
AUSPICES ENGINERY REGIMENT
STEERAGE
GUIDE GUY LAY PIR TIP AIRT BEAD
CURB GAGE GATE LEAD PASS REIN
RULE SWAY WISE CARRY CHARM
DRESS FRAME GAUGE LIGHT
MAHDI MOROC PILOT STEER
TEACH WEISE ADAI ID BARKER
BEACON BEDWAY CONVOY DIRECT
ESCORT FORMER GILLIE GOVERN
INFORM LEADER MANAGE
MENTOR POPPET CONDUCE
CONDUCT COURIER GHILLIE
INSPIRE MARSHAL MERCURY
PIONEER SHIKARI STERNER
TRACKER CALENDAR CICERONE
DIRECTOR DRAGOMAN ENGINEER
FAIRLEAD LODESMAN PEDESTAL
POLESTAR PRACTICO REPEATER
SHIKAREE SIGNPOST
(— ON GUN) SIGHT
(MORAL —) LABARUM
(RAILWAY —) ABC BRADSHAW
(SPIRITUAL —) PIR GURU BISHOP
DIVINE
(TRAFFIC —) MUSHROOM
(SUFF.) AGOGUE AGOGY
GUIDEBOOK ABC GUIDE WAYBOOK
BAEDEKER HANDBOOK
ROADBOOK
GUIDELINE SLUG DIRECTIVE
PARAMETER
GUIDEPOST GUIDE PARSON
WAYMARK WAYPOST SIGNPOST
GUIDERIUS (FATHER OF —)
CYMBELINE
GUIDEWAY SLAY SLEY SLEIGH
SLIDEWAY SWANNECK
GUIDING POLAR BEHIND HOMING
LEADING

GUIDO (WIFE OF —) ALERIA
GUILD HUI GILD HOEY HONG YELD
CRAFT HANSA HANSE GREMIO
GUIDRY SCHOLA BASOCHE
COLLEGE COMPANY MYSTERY
(CHINESE —) TONG
GUILE DOLE WILE CHEAT CRAFT
FRAUD TRAIN CAUTEL DECEIT
HUMBUG CUNNING FALLACY
ARTIFICE
GUILELESS PLAIN CANDID HONEST
ARTLESS ONEFOLD IGNORANT
INNOCENT SACKLESS UNNOOKED
GUILLEMOT AUK COOT LARY LAVY
LOOM QUET TURR URIA ARRIE
CUTTY FROWL MURRE SCOUT
TOIST TYSTE GRYLLE LUNGIE
MAGGIE MARROT SCRABE TINKER
DOVEKEY DOVEKIE SEACOOT
SKIDDAW TARROCK WILLOCK
PUFFINET ROCKBIRD SCUTTOCK
SPRATTER
GUILT SIN SAKE WITE BLAME CULPA
FAULT PIACLE PLIGHT NOCENCE
OFFENSE HAMARTIA INIQUITY
GUILTLESS FREE PURE CLEAN
UNSAKED INNOCENT SACKLESS
GUILTY FAULTY NOCENT WICKED
CONREAL HANODOO NOXIOUS
PECCANT BLAMEFUL CRIMINAL
CULPABLE GUILTFUL
(— OF ERROR) LAPSED
GUINEA MEG BEAN QUID QUEED
GEORGE SHINER GEORDIE
(HALF —) SMELT

<table>
<tr><td colspan="2" align="center">GUINEA</td></tr>
<tr><td>CAPE:</td><td>VERGA</td></tr>
<tr><td>CAPITAL:</td><td>CONAKRY</td></tr>
<tr><td>COIN:</td><td>FRANC</td></tr>
<tr><td>ISLAND:</td><td>TOMBO TRISTAO</td></tr>
<tr><td>ISLAND GROUP:</td><td>LOS</td></tr>
<tr><td>MEASURE:</td><td>JACKTAN</td></tr>
<tr><td>MONEY:</td><td>SYLI CAURI</td></tr>
<tr><td>MOUNTAIN:</td><td>TAMGUE</td></tr>
<tr><td>MOUNTAINS:</td><td>LOMA NIMBA</td></tr>
<tr><td>NATIVE:</td><td>SUSU TOMA KISSI FULANI
GUERZI MALINKE KOURANKE
LANDUMAN</td></tr>
<tr><td>RIVER:</td><td>NIGER BAFING FALEME
SENEGAL KONKOURE TINKISSO</td></tr>
<tr><td>TOWN:</td><td>BOKE FRIA KADE LABE
BENTY BEYLA COYAH KOULE
MAMOU DABOLA DALABA
DOUAKO FABALA KANKAN KINDIA
BOFOSSO CONAKRY DUBREKA
FARANAH KONFARA KOUMBIA
OUASSOU SIGUIRI KEROUANE</td></tr>
<tr><td>WEIGHT:</td><td>AKEY PISO UZAN BENDA
SERON QUINTO AGUIRAGE</td></tr>
</table>

GUINEA-BISSAU (ARCHIPELAGO OF
—) BIJAGOS
(CAPITAL OF —) BISSAU
(RIVER OF —) GEBA CACHEU
MANSOA CORUBAL
GUINEA FOWL KEEL KEET PEARL
MEBACK GALEENY PINTADO
COMEBACK GALLINEY
(SOUND OF —) POTRACK
GUINEA GRASS PANIC PANICLE
SACATON ZACATON GAMELOTE
GUINEA PEPPER PIMENTO

GUINEA PIG CAVY
(MALE —) BOAR BUCK
GUINEA RUSH ADRUE
GUISE HUE FORM GARB COLOR
COVER SHAPE MANNER PERSON
APPAREL CLOTHES GUISARD
LIKENESS
GUISER MUMMER
GUITAR AX AXE BOX KIT PIPA
DOBRO JAMON KITAR SITAR TIPLE
CUATRO GIMBRI KITTAR SANCHO
SATTAR CITHERN CITTERN
MACHETE UKULELE CHARANGO
CHITARRA BOTTLENECK
(ACOUSTIC —) DOBRO
(JAPANESE —) SAMISEN SHAMISEN
(KIND OF —) FOLK PEDALSTEEL
(PART OF —) KEY NUT PEG BASE
BODY BONE FRET HEAD HEEL HOLE
NECK BRACE GUARD WAIST BRIDGE
SADDLE STRING ROSETTE
FINGERBOARD
GUITARFISH RAY BATOID PURAQUE
GUITGUIT PITPIT
GULANCHA GILO GILOE
GULCH COULE GULLY SLUIT
CANYON COULEE RAVINE
GULDEN FLORIN GUILDER
(100,000 —) TUN
GULES MARS RUBY TORTEAU
GULF SINE CHAOS GULPH VORAGE
VORAGO
(BOTTOMLESS —) ABYSM ABYSS
GULFWEED SARGASSO
GULL COB COX MEW COBB CONY
COOT CULL DUPE FOOL GOLL LARI
MALL PINT PIRR SELL SKUA XEME
ALLAN ALLEN ANNET BOSUN
CHEAT CHUMP COBBE COKES
CROCK CULLY HOODY JAGER
LARID LARUS PEWIT SCULL SMELT
YAGER BONXIE BUBBLE CHOUSE
COUSIN JOCKEY PEEWIT PIGEON
SIMPLE TEASER TULIAC VICTIM
WAGGEL WHILLY CROCKER
DECEIVE MEDRICK PICKMAW
POPELER SCAURIE SEABIRD
SEAFOWL SWARBIE TARROCK
TRUMPIE BLACKCAP DIRTBIRD
DOTTEREL DUNGBIRD SEEDBIRD
(LIKE A —) LAROID
(YOUNG —) SCAURY SCAURIE
GULLET MAW GULE LANE GORGE
GARGLE PECHAN THROAT
KEACORN STOMACH SWALLOW
WEASAND GURGULIO
(PREF.) ESOPHAG(O) LAEMO LEMO
RUMENO
GULLIBLE GOOFY GREEN SIMPLE
CULLIBLE
GULLIVER GRILDRIG
GULLY BOX GEO GUT DRAW GULL
RAIK RAKE SICK SIKE DONGA
DRAFT GOYLE GULCH SLAKE SLUIT
ZANJA ARROYO GULLET GULLEY
GUTTER NULLAH RAVINE SHEUCH
SHEUGH CHIMNEY COULOIR
DRAUGHT BARRANCA
GULLYWASHER TORRENT
CLOUDBURST
GULP BOLT GAUP GLUT GULL POOP
SOPE SWIG GULCH QUILT SLOSH

SWIPE ENGLUT GLUTCH GOBBLE GOLLOP PAUNCH SLABBER SWALLOW SWATTLE SLUMMOCK
(— NOISILY) SLORP

GUM ASA AMRA BLOB FILL GOOM LOAD TUNO ALGIN AMAPA BABUL CUMAY DHAVA ACAJOU ANGICO BALATA BARRAS CHICLE KARAYA TOUART TUPELO CARANNA CARAUNA CHICLET GINGIVA GUMWOOD PERRIER BORRACHA CARABEEN DEXTRINE DRESSING FEVERGUM CALENDULIN
(ACACIA —) GEDDA
(AROMATIC —) MYRRH
(ASTRINGENT —) KINO
(CHEWING —) WAX CHICLE
(FRAGRANT —) BUMBO
(KIND OF —) ESTER XANTHAN
(PERSIAN —) SARCOCOLLA
(RED —) JARRAH
(UNGRADED —) SORTS
(WOOD —) XYLAN
(PL.) ULA
(PREF.) COMMI GUMMI GUTTI

GUM ARABIC KIKAR ACACIA ACACIN

GUMBO MUD OKRA

GUMBOIL PARULIS

GUMBO-LIMBO JOBO BIRCH GOMART MASTIC NEGRITO ALMACIGO ARCHIPIN

GUMDROP GUM JUJUBE

GUMMER BIDDY BIDDIE SCRAPER SCUFFER SCUFFLER SCUPPLER

GUMMY GLUEY CLAGGY MASTIC GUMMOUS

GUMPTION GRIT NOUS NERVE PLUCK SENSE SPUNK SPRAWL

GUMS
(PREF.) GINGIV(O) ULEMO ULO

GUMSHOE TEC

GUM SUCCORY HOGBITE

GUM TREE KARI KARRI TOOART TOUART TUPELO EUCALYPT

GUMWEED GRINDELIA SUNFLOWER

GUN GAT POP BREN HAKE PIAT ROER STEN TUBE BARIL FIFTY FIRER FUSEE FUZEE RAKER REWET RIFLE ARCHIE BERTHA CANNON CHASER CULVER DUCKER HEATER INCHER JEZAIL MINNIE QUAKER RANDOM ROSCOE SPIGOT SWIVEL TUPARA CALIVER FIREARM HACKBUT HANDGUN JINGALL LANTACA MUZZLER AMUSETTE ARQUEBUS CHAUCHAT CULVERIN FIRELOCK GALLOPER OERLIKON PEDERERO REVOLVER SHAGBUSH STERLING TROMBONE
(—FOR DISCHARGING STONES) PERRIER
(AFGHAN —) JEZAIL

(BOAT —) BASE
(KIND OF —) ZIP BURP RIOT STUN HIRED
(LOWER-DECK —) BARKER
(MACHINE —) CHOPPER GATLING
(SPRING —) STEL
(TOP —) ACE
(TOY —) SPARKLER
(TYPE OF —) BURP BOFORS
(PL.) FLAK CHASE ARTILLERY

GUNA RAJAS TAMAS SATTVA

GUNBOAT SKIP BARCA GONDOLA TINCLAD

GUN CARRIAGE PANEL MADRIER GALLOPER

GUNCREWMAN PLUGMAN

GUNDOBAD (BROTHER OF —) GODOMAR CHILPERIC GODEGISEL
(FATHER OF —) GUNDIOCH

GUNDOG POINTER

GUNFLINT STONE

GUNI (FATHER OF —) NAPHTALI

GUNITE SHOTCRETE

GUNK GOO

GUNLOCK ROWET FIRELOCK

GUNMAN HOOD GUNSEL GUNSMAN TORPEDO ENFORCER GANGSTER

GUNNEL BLENNY SWORDICK

GUNNER GUN POPPER FIREMAN SHOOTER ENGINEER

GUNNY TAT BURLAP BAGGING SACKING

GUNNYSACK CORNSACK

GUNPOWDER SULFUR SULPHUR
(— SIZE) PEBBLE

GUNSHOT REPORT

GUNSIGHT VISIE HAUSSE

GUNSTOCK BLANK TIPSTOCK

GUNSTONE OGRESS PELLET

GUNTHER (SISTER OF —) KRIEMHILD
(WIFE OF —) BRUNEHILDE

GUNTRAM (BROTHER OF —) SIGEBERT CHARIBERT CHILPERIC
(CHARACTER IN —) ROBERT GUNTRAM FREIHILD FRIEHOLD
(COMPOSER OF —) STRAUSS
(FATHER OF —) CLOTAIRE

GUNWALE GUNNEL PORTOISE

GUNZ SCANIAN

GUPPY MILLIONS BELLYFISH

GUR GOOR KHAUR JAGGERY VOLTAIC

GURGE EDDY SWIRL

GURGLE GLOX GLUG BRAWL CLUNK QUARK SLOSH BICKER BUBBLE BULLER BURBLE GOLLER GUGGLE RUCKLE

GURGLINGLY TRILLIL

GURJUN YANG

GURNARD CUR TUB PIPER ELLECK ROCHET BATFISH CAPTAIN

GRUNTER LATCHET SOLDIER TRIGLID TUBFISH VOLADOR HARDHEAD KNORHAAN LORICATE

GURO KWENI

GURU MENTOR

GUSH JET BOIL FLOW FOAM HUSH RAIL SLOP WALM BELCH SLUSH SMALM SMARM SPATE SPIRT SPURT STOUR SWOSH BURBLE PHRASE SWOOSH WALLOW WHOOSH SLOBBER
(SENTIMENTAL —) SLOSH

GUSHING SLOPPY SMARMY EFFUSIVE

GUSSET GORE INSET MITER MITRE QUIRK PIECETTE

GUST BUB FLAN GALE GUSH WAFF WAFT WIND BLAST FRESH SLANT FLURRY HUFFLE SQUALL FLAUGHT WILLIWAW WINDFLAW WINDBLAST
(— OF RAIN) SKIT
(— OF WIND) FLAM FLAN FUFF GALE GUSH PIRR SCUD TIFT BERRY BLAST BLORE FLAFF THODE SQUALL WINDFLAW

GUSTATION TASTE

GUSTO GUST ZEST VERVE RELISH UNCTION

GUSTY DIRTY PUFFY BLASHY BLASTY FRETFUL GUSTFUL SQUALLY

GUT GIB BOWEL CECUM CLEAN CAECUM CATGUT HOLLOW STRING ELISION GRALLOCH VISCERAL
(FISH —) GIP GILL
(TWISTED —) THARM THERM
(PL.) MOXIE BOWELS COJONES PUDDING ENTRAILS

GUTHRIE ARLO

GUTSY BALLSY PLUCKY SPUNKY

GUTTA SOH DROP PUAN SIAK SUSU DUJAN GERIP SANGE SUNDIK CAMPANA JANGKAR SEMARUM TRENAIL TRUNNEL HANGKANG KETAPANG

GUTTER GRIP REAN SIKE GRIPE GULLY RIGOL SIVER SPOUT SWEAL BOTTOM CANNEL CULLIS GROOVE GUZZLE KENNEL RIGGOT RUNNEL STRAND TROUGH VENNEL CHANNEL CHENEAU GRIZZLE
(— OF STREET) KENNEL
(MINING —) BOTTOM HASSING
(ROOF —) RONE
(PL.) LIMBERS

GUTTERMAN SWAMPER

GUTTURAL GRUM BURRY HARSH THICK

GUY BOD CAT EGG JOE NUT BIRD BOZO DUDE GENT GINK HUSK JACK JOHN STUD BLOKE CABLE COOKY JOKER SCOUT SPOOF STIFF

BUFFER COOKIE FELLOW GAZABO GAZEBO GAZOOK GILGUY HOMBRE JASPER JIGGER MALKIN MAUMET MAWKIN KNOCKER BLIGHTER
(FALL —) GOAT CHUMP SCAPEGOAT

GUYANA (CAPITAL OF —) GEORGETOWN
(RIVER OF —) CUYUNI BERBICE DEMERARA MAZARUNI ESSEQUIBO
(TOWN OF —) ITUNI BILOKU ISSANO MACKENZIE
(WATERFALL IN —) MARINA KAIETEUR

GUY MANNERING (AUTHOR OF —) SCOTT
(CHARACTER IN —) GUY MEG LUCY BROWN DANDY HARRY JULIA BERTRAM DINMONT GLOSSIN SAMPSON MANNERING MERRILIES ELLANGOWAN HATTERAICK

GUY ROPE STAY VANG

GUZ GAZ GEZ ZAR ZER GUDGE

GUZERAT KANKREJ

GUZZLE BUM GUM SOT TUN BEND GULL SLOSH SWILL GOOZLE GUDDLE SWATTLE SWIZZLE CHUGALUG

GUZZLER BENDER

GWYNIAD SCHELLY

GYASCUTUS PROCK

GYLE BEER GAIL BREWING

GYMKHANA AUTOCROSS

GYMNASIUM GYM PALESTRA TURNHALL PALAESTRA

GYMNAST SOKOL BENDER TURNER ACROBAT TUMBLER
(FAMOUS —) KORBUT

GYMNASTIC (— SOCIETY) SOKOL

GYNOECIUM BRUSH APOCARP

GYNOPHORE PODOGYN

GYPSUM GYP GYPS YESO GESSO LUDIAN PARGET GYPSITE SATINITE SELENITE ALABASTER

GYPSY FAW ROM CALO APTAL CAIRD GIPSY ROMNI BOSHAS GITANO ROMANY TINKER AZUCENA CZIGANY MOONMAN TINKLER TZIGANE ZINCALO ZINGARO BOHEMIAN EGYPTIAN FLAMENCO ZIGEUNER
(MALE —) ROM
(NON —) GORGIO
(SEA —) BAJAU
(PL.) ROMANESE

GYRATE GYRE SPIN TURN TWIRL WHIRL CURVET INGYRE ROTATE REVOLVE SQUIRREL

GYRATION PRECESSION

GYRATORY GIDDY GYRAL

GYRFALCON JERKIN

GYRON GIRON ESQUIRE

GYROSE SINUATE

GYVE FETTER

H

H ETA HOW AITCH HOTEL ASPIRATE
HABERDASHER OUTFITTER
HABERDASHERY TOGGERY
HABERGEON HAUBERK
HABILIMENT GARB HABIT APPAREL
 RAIMENT CLOTHING
 (PL.) CLOTHES EQUIPAGE
HABILITATE ENABLE
HABIT LAW PAD SET USE WON
 COAT GARB GATE SUIT THEW
 WONT FROCK HAUNT JONES
 TACHE TRADE TRICK USAGE
 CUSTOM GROOVE MANNER
 PRAXIS TALENT CLOTHES
 FOLKWAY HABITUS WONTING
 CROTCHET HABITUDE PHYSIQUE
 PRACTICE PRACTISE ASSUETUDE
 CONSUETUDE
 (— OF GRINDING TEETH) BRUXISM
 (BAD —) HANK VICE MISTETCH
 CACOETHES
 (CHARACTERISTIC —) TRICK
 (DEPRAVED —) CACHEXY CACHEXIA
 (MONASTIC —) SCHEMA
 (SPEECH —S) ACCENT
 (PL.) DAPS
 (PREF.) HEXICO
HABITABLE BIGLY LIVABLE
HABITAT ECE HOME RANGE PATRIA
 STATION LOCALITY
 (NATURAL —) ELEMENT
 (PREF.) EC(O) OEC(O) OIKO
HABITATION HOLD TELD TENT
 ABODE BIELD HABIT HOUSE
 BIDING WONING DOMICILE
 DWELLING PANTHEON TENEMENT
 RESIDENCE
 (— SITE) YACATA
 (COMMUNIAL —) PUEBLO
 (QUIET —) SHADE
 (UNDERGROUND —) HOLE
HABITUAL USUAL COMMON
 HECTIC CHRONIC REGULAR
 FREQUENT ORDINARY
HABITUATE USE HOWF ENURE
 FLESH HABIT INURE ADDICT
 SEASON HACKNEY ACCUSTOM
 ACQUAINT OCCASION
HABITUATED WONT SEASONED
 ACCUSTOMED
HABITUDE HABIT SCHESIS
HABITUE DENIZEN COURTIER
HABRONEMIASIS BURSATI
 BURSATTEE
HACEK WEDGE
HACHALIAH (SON OF —) NEHEMIAH
HACK CAB HAG HEW BOLO CHIP
 HAKE DEVIL HATCH CABBIE
 DRUDGE FIACRE HACKLE HAGGLE
 HODMAN JOBBER MANGLE
 SCOTCH HACKNEY MATTOCK
 VETTURA MUTILATE
 (LITERARY —) GRUB DEVIL

HACKBERRY EGGBERRY HACKTREE
 HAGBERRY ONEBERRY
HACKBUT HAGBUT DEMIHAG
 HACKBUSH
HACK GHARRI SHIGRAM
HACKLE COMB RUFF HECKLE
 NAPPER RUFFER HATCHEL
 ROUGHER
HACKNEY HACK MIDGE NODDY
HACKNEY CARRIAGE MIDGE
 FIACRE JARVEY VETTURA
HACKNEYED HACK WORN BANAL
 HOARY STALE TRITE CANNED
 CLICHE COMMON FOREWORN
 TIMEWORN
HAD D HED HEDDE
 (— NOT) HADNA HADNT
HADAD (FATHER OF —) ISHMAEL
HADADEZER (FATHER OF —) REHOB
HADDOCK GADE GADID SCROD
 DICKEY HADDIE
 (DRIED —) CRAIL RIZZAR SPELDING
 SPELDRIN
HADE UNDERLIE
HADES DIS PIT ADES HELL AIDES
 ORCUS PLUTO SHEOL SHADES
 TARTAR ACHERON AIDONEUS
 TARTARUS
 (FATHER OF —) SATURN
 (GODDESS OF —) HEKATE
 (RIVER IN —) STYX LETHE
 (RIVER OF —) STYX
 (WIFE OF —) PROSERPINA
HADORAM (FATHER OF —) TOU
 JOKTAN
HAECCEITY THISNESS
HAEMON (FATHER OF —) CREON
 PELASGUS
 (SON OF —) THESSALUS
HAEMUS (FATHER OF —) BOREAS
 (MOTHER OF —) ORITHYIA
 (SON OF —) HEBRUS
 (WIFE OF —) RHODOPE
HAFF LAGOON
HAFNIUM CELTIUM
HAFT HEFT HOVE HELVE DUDGEON
HAFTER HANDLER
HAG ATE MARE CRONE REBEC
 RUDAS SHREW SIBYL VECKE
 WITCH BELDAM HECATE ROUDAS
 BELDAME HAGGARD HELLCAT
 HARRIDAN
HAGAR (MISTRESS OF —) SARAH
 (SON OF —) ISHMAEL
HAGBOAT HOGGET HOGGIE
HAGFISH HAG BORER VECKE
 MYZONT SUCKER PLACOID
 MYXINOID
HAGGARD PALE THIN GAUNT
 WISHT HAGGED
HAGGI (FATHER OF —) GAD
HAGGITH (HUSBAND OF —) DAVID
 (SON OF —) ADONIJAH

HAGGLE CHOP PRIG DODGE
 BADGER BANTER BOGGLE DICKER
 HACKER HIGGLE HUCKLE NAGGLE
 NIFFER PALTER SCOTCH THREEP
 BARGAIN CHAFFER HUCKSTER
HAGGLER DODGER
HAGGLING BARGAIN CHAFFER
HAGIOGRAPHA KETUBIM
HAGIOSCOPE SQUINT SQUINCH
HAIDA SKITTAGET
HAIL AVE HOY HALE GREET SALVE
 SPEAK STORM ACCOST BAYETE
 HAGGLE HALLOO HERALD SALUTE
 ACCLAIM
 (SOFT —) GRESIL GRAUPEL
 (PREF.) CHALAZI CHALAZO
HAILSTONE STONE
HAINAI IONI
HAIR FAX JAG RIB WIG BARB CROP
 FLUE GLIB HEAD KEMP PELF PILE
 SETA WIRE BEARD CRIMP CRINE
 FRIZZ FRONT PILUS QUIFF ANGORA
 BRILLS BRUTUS CRINET FIBRIL
 FROWZE MERKIN SETULA THATCH
 TRAGUS CULOTTE ELFLOCK
 GLOCHS TOPKNOT WHISKER
 CAPILLUS COLLETER PALPOCIL
 TENTACLE TRICHODE TRICHOME
 VIBRISSA
 (— BROWN) ARGALI
 (— OF ANIMALS) FUR PELF
 (— OF HORSES OR COWS) CERDA
 (— OF TERRIER) FALL
 (— ON HORSE'S HOOF) CRONET
 (— ON LEAF) GLAND
 (— ON TEMPLES) HAFFET HAFFIT
 (— ON THIGHS) CULOTTE
 (— OVER EYES) BROW GLIB
 EYELASH
 (BARBED —) GLOCHIS
 (BRAID OF —) QUEUE PIGTAIL
 (BUNDLE OF —) LEECH
 (CAMEL'S —) DEER
 (COARSE —) KEMP BRISTLE
 (CURLED —) FRIZZ
 (CUTDOWN —) STUMPS
 (FALSE —) WIG JANE FRONT
 PERUKE
 (FRIZZED —) FROWZE
 (GRAY —) GRIZZLE
 (LOCK OF —) TUZ FEAK TATE FLOCK
 TRESS
 (LONG HEAVY —) MANE
 (LOOSE —) COMBINGS
 (MATTED —) SHAG ELFLOCK
 (MOP OF —) MANE SHOCK TOUSLE
 (NOSE —) VIBRISSA
 (PERSON WITH SHORT —)
 SKINHEAD
 (PLANT —) COLLETER
 (ROOT —) FIBRIL
 (SNARL OF —) TANGLE
 (SOFT —) DOWN LANUGO

 (STINGING —) STING STIMULUS
 (STINGING —S) COWHAGE
 (STRAIGHTEN —) CONK
 (STRAY LOCK OF —) TAG
 (STYLE —) CORNROW
 (TREAT —) CONK
 (TUFT OF —) PLUME KROBYLOS
 (WAVING LOCK OF —) WIMPLER
 (WHITE —) SNOW SNOWS
 (PL.) SETAE COWAGE COWHAGE
 HACKLES
 (PREF.) CAPILLI CHAET(I)(O) CHETO
 COME COMI CRINI HIRSUTO
 LACHN(O) PIL(I)(O) TRICH(O)
 TRICHINO VILLI
 (SUFF.) CHAETA CHAETES
 CHAETUS COMA THRICHOUS THRIX
 TRICHA TRICH(I)(A) TRICHY
HAIRBREADTH HERMELE WHISKER
HAIR BROWN QUAIL
HAIRBRUSH TOILETRY
HAIRCLOTH HAIR CILICE
HAIRCUT BOB CUT CROP BUTCH
 SHINGLE DUCKTAIL
HAIRDO AFRO COIF BEEHIVE
 FRISURE PAGEBOY
HAIRDRESSER WAVER FRISEUR
 COIFFEUR
HAIRDRESSING FRISURE
 BANDOLINE
HAIR FRAME PALISADE
HAIRINESS PILOSISM PILOSITY
HAIRLESS BALD PELON CALLOW
 ATRICHIC DEPILOUS GLABROUS
 (— PERSON) PILGARLIC
HAIRLIKE PILIFORM TRICHOID
HAIRLINE WHISKER
HAIRNET KELL SNOOD
HAIRPIECE MERKIN POSTICHE
HAIRPIN ACUS BODKIN SKEWER
HAIRSPLITTING FINE PILPUL
HAIRSTYLE DA AFRO CONK SHAG
 UPDO BINGLE MOHAWK
 CORNROW PAGEBOY DUCKTAIL
 PONYTAIL DREADLOCKS
HAIRWORM GORDIID GORDIOID
HAIRY FAXED MOSEY PILAR ROUGH
 COMATE COMOUS PILARY PILINE
 PILOSE CRINITE CRINOSE HIRSUTE
 PILEOUS VILLOUS UNSHAVEN
 (PREF.) DASI DASY HEBE

LAKE: SAUMATRE
MAGIC: OBI OBEAH
MOUNTAIN: NORD CAHOS NOIRES
   LAHOTTE LASELLE TROUDEAU
NATIONAL HERO: OGE
PLAIN: NORD CAYES JACMEL
   LEOGANE ARCAHAIE CULDESAC
   GONAIVES
PRIEST: BOCOR HOUNGAN
RELIGION: OBEAH
RIVER: GUAYAMOUC ARTIBONITE
SPIRIT: LOA BAKA BOKO
TOWN: AQUIN CAYES FURCY LIMBE
   HINCHE JACMEL JEREMIE
   LEOGANE SALTROU GONAIVES
   KENSCOFF

HAKAM CACAM HAHAM CHOCHEM
   KHAKHAM
HAKE GADE HAIK LING GADOID
   CODLING HADDOCK WHITING
   ANACANTH QUODLING
HAKENKREUZLER SWASTIKA
HALBERD BILL PIKE GLAIVE GLEAVE
   POLEARM PARTISAN
   (PART OF —) BEAK BUTT BLADE
   SPIKE
HALBERDIER DRABANT
HALCYON CALM ALCYON GOLDEN
HALE FIT YELL FRACK FRECK TRAIL
   ROBUST STRONG HEALTHY
   VIGOROUS
HALER HELLER
HALF M ARF ELF DEMI HAUF HOVE
   SEMI SIDE MEDIO HALFEN HALFLY
   MOIETY MEDIETY
   (— AND —) ONE
   (— GALLON) POTTLE
   (— OF BLADE) FORTE
   (— OF DRAW) BRACKET
   (— OF EM) EN
   (— OF INNING) BOTTOM
   (— OF MOLD) VALVE
   (FRUIT —S) SLABS
   (PREF.) DEMI HEMI SAM SEMI
   (ONE AND A —) SESQUI
HALFBACK (OFFENSIVE —)
   SLOTBACK
HALFBEAK GAR IHI BALAO PIPER
   BALLYHOO
HALF-BLOOD DEMISANG
HALF BOOT PAC BUSKIN BOTTINE
HALF-BREED BREED METIF METIS
   SAMBO MUSTEE RAMONA
   CABOCLO MESTIZO METISSE
   DEMISANG HARRATIN MIXBLOOD
HALF-CASTE TOPAZ TOPASS
HALF-CONSCIOUSNESS DOVER
HALF-CRAZY FIFISH
HALF CROWN GEORGE ALDERMAN
HALF-DEAD ALAMORT
HALF DENIER MAILE MAILLE
HALF DOBRA PECA
HALF-DRUNK MAUDLIN
HALF-EATEN SEMESE
HALF-FARTHING CUE MITE MINUTE
HALF-GABLE AILERON
HALF GAINER ISANDER
HALF-GROWN HALFLIN
HALF-GUINEA SMELT
HALF-HEARTED LUKEWARM
HALFHEARTED TEPID
HALF HITCH ROLLING

HALF MASK LOUP DOMINO
HALF-MOON LUNETTE DEMILUNE
HALF NOTE MINIM
HALFPENCE GROCERY
HALFPENNY OB MAG MEG DUMP
   GRAY GREY MAIK MAIL MAKE
   MEKE OBOL SOUSE STAMP
   BAUBEE BAWBEE MAILLE
   HAPENNY PATRICK STUIVER
   (COUNTERFEIT —) RAP GRAY
   (IRISH —) PATRICK
   (THICK —) DUMP
HALF-PIKE SPONTON DEMIPIKE
   SPONTOON
HALF-PINT CUP JACK CUPFUL
HALF REST SOSPIRO
HALF SOLE TAP
HALF STEP CHROMA
HALFTONE DROPOUT
HALF TURN DEMIVOLT
HALF-WIT ASS DOLT DUNCE
   HAVEREL TOMFOOL STAUMREL
   UNDERWIT
HALF-WITTED SOFT DOTTY SIMPLE
   HALUCKET IMBECILE STAUMREL
HALF-YEARLY BIANNUAL
HALIBUT BUT BUTT FLITCH TURBOT
   FLATFISH
HALIFAX BALLYHACK
HALIOTIS ABALONE
HALIRRHOTHIUS (FATHER OF —)
   NEPTUNE
   (MOTHER OF —) EURYTE
   (SLAYER OF —) MARS
HALL HA AULA HELL HAWL IWAN SALA
   AIWAN ATRIO BALAI BURSA CURIA
   DIVAN ENTRY FOYER HOUSE
   OECUS SALLE SALON ATRIUM
   CAMERA DURBAR EXEDRA
   GARDEN LESCHE SALOON SCHOOL
   SENATE TOLSEY TRANCE APADANA
   CHAMBER DANCERY GALLERY
   HALLWAY KURHAUS KURSAAL
   MEGARON PASSAGE VINGOLF
   ANTEROOM ARCHEION ASSEMBLY
   BASILICA CHOULTRY COLISEUM
   CORRIDOR FOREHALL HASTROND
   HOSPITAL RAADZAAL TOLBOOTH
   VALHALLA
   (— FOR PERFORMANCES) ODEON
   ODEUM
   (— OF JUSTICE) COURT
   (— WITH STATUES) VALHALLA
   (DINING —) MESS COMMON
   REFECTORY
   (LECTURE —) SCHOLA
   (MISSION —) CITADEL
   (MUSIC —) GAFF
   (TOWN —) CABILDO RATHAUS
   TRIBUNAL
   (UNIVERSITY —) BURSA
HALLMARK CROWN TRAIT
   SHOPMARK
HALL OF FAME (AVIATION —) ELY
   SIX BYRD LAHM LEAR LINK LUKE
   MOSS POST RYAN WADE EAKER
   GLENN LEMAY PIPER REEVE
   ARNOLD BOEING CESSNA FOKKER
   HUGHES LEVIER MARTIN ROGERS
   SPAATZ SPERRY TOWERS TRIPPE
   TURNER WALDEN WRIGHT YAEGER
   CHANUTE EARHART GRUMMAN
   LANGLEY LOENING SHEPARD

   TWINING MITCHELL NORTHROP
   SIKORSKY ARMSTRONG LINDBERGH
   MCDONNELL RICKENBACKER
   (BASEBALL —) OTT COBB DEAN
   FORD FOXX HOYT KELL KLEM MACK
   MAYS MIZE RUTH WYNN AARON
   BANKS BERRA COMBS EVERS FRICK
   GOMEZ GROVE HAFEY KINER
   LEMON LOPEZ LYONS PAIGE PLANK
   RUSIE SPAHN TERRY VANCE WALSH
   WANER WHEAT YOUNG ALSTON
   CHANCE CRONIN CUYLER FELLER
   FRISCH GEHRIG GOSLIN KALINE
   KOUFAX LAJOIE LANDIS MANTLE
   MANUSH MCGRAW MUSIAL RICKEY
   SISLER TINKER WAGNER WILSON
   WRIGHT YAWKEY APPLING AVERILL
   BURKETT HORNSBY HUBBARD
   HUGGINS JOHNSON PENNOCK
   RUFFING SIMMONS SPEAKER
   STENGEL TRAYNOR BOUDREAU
   COMISKEY DIMAGGIO GRIFFITH
   MACPHAIL MARICHAL MCCARTHY
   ROBINSON WILLIAMS COVELESKI
   BRICKHOUSE MARANVILLE
   (BASKETBALL —) GALE GOLA PAGE
   REED WEST COUSY FULKS GREER
   HAGAN HYATT LUCAS MIKAN ARIZIN
   BARLOW BAYLOR COOPER FOSTER
   HANSON HOLMAN KRAUSE
   MURPHY PETTIT PHILIP RAMSEY
   ROOSMA SEDRAN TWYMAN
   WOODEN BECKMAN BRADLEY
   BRENNAN DEHNERT GRUENIG
   KURLAND POLLARD SCHAYES
   SCHMIDT SHARMAN WACHTER
   BORGMANN ENDACOTT LAPCHICK
   LUISETTI MACAULEY SCHOMMER
   MCCRACKEN STEINMETZ VANDIVIER
   DEBERNARDI DEBUSSCHERE
   (BUSINESS —) FORD HAAS LUCE
   OCHS VAIL GARST HEINZ ROUSE
   SLOAN BATTEN DISNEY DORIOT
   DUPONT HILTON KAISER LASKER
   MELLON MORGAN OGILVY PENNEY
   SCHIFF SCHWAB EASTMAN
   SARNOFF WHITNEY CARNEGIE
   FRANKLIN MCCORMICK
   VANDERBILT ROCKEFELLER
   WESTINGHOUSE WEYERHAEUSER
   (FOOTBALL —) MIX RAY BELL HEIN
   HUFF LARY MARA OTTO FEARS
   GROZA GUYON HALAS HAYES
   LAYNE LILLY LYMAN MUSSO NEALE
   RINGO ROYAL BADGRO BLANDA
   BUTKUS GRANGE HINKLE KINARD
   MATSON MCAFEE ROONEY THORPE
   TITTLE TRIPPI UNITAS ALWORTH
   GILLMAN LUCKMAN MILLNER
   LOMBARDI MITCHELL WARFIELD
   JURGENSEN PARSEGHIAN
   (GOLF —) BERG FORD HOPE BOROS
   BURKE DUTRA EVANS HAGEN
   HOGAN JONES SHUTE SMITH
   SNEAD ARMOUR COOPER DIEGEL
   GHEZZI LITTLE NELSON OUIMET
   PALMER PICARD RUNYAN TRAVIS
   DEMARET GULDAHL HARBERT
   MANGRUM REVOLTA SARAZEN
   ZAHARIAS DEVICENZO
   (THEATER —) DREW KERR BROOK
   HECHT KELLY SIMON PRINCE
   DUNNOCK CHAMPION KINGSLEY

   LANSBURY MCARTHUR MEREDITH
   SONDHEIM STRASBERG
   YOUNGMANS BLOOMGARDEN
HALLOO HO HOO LOO ALEW BAWL
   LURE WHOOP ACCOST TALLYHO
HALLOW BLESS HALWE DEDICATE
   SANCTIFY
HALLOWED HOLY SACRED
   BLESSED
HALLSTAND HATRACK
HALLUCINATION DWALE
   ACOASMA ACOUASM ACOUSMA
   FANTASY PHONEME DELUSION
   ILLUSION PHANTASY ZOOSCOPY
HALLUCINOGEN ACID
HALLUX TALON
HALLWAY ENTRY FOYER TRANCE
HALMA HOPPITY
HALMALILLE PETWOOD
HALO DOG BURR GLOR NIMB
   GLORY SHINE AREOLA CIRCLE
   CORONA GLORIA NIMBUS SUNDOG
   AREOLET AUREOLE BOROUGH
   CINCTURE
HALOHESH (SON OF —) SHALLUM
HALT HO HOP ALTO BAIT BALK
   HOLD LIMP SKID STAY STOP TRIP
   WAIT BAULK BLOCK BREAK CEASE
   CHECK HILCH HITCH STAND STICK
   ARREST BARLEY FREEZE PULLUP
   SCOTCH STANCE CONTAIN
   CRIPPLE STATION STOPPAGE
   (— GAME) CALL
   (— TO DOGS) TOHO
   (REFRESHMENT —) DRIVEIN
HALTER EVIL SOLE BRANK NOOSE
   TRASH WANTY WIDDY WITHE
   POISER CAUSSON CAVESON
   JAQUIMA POINTEL BALANCER
   NECKLACE HACKAMORE
HALTING BODE LAME ZOPPA
   CRIPPLE LIMPING
HALVE BISECT DIVIDE DIMIDIATE
   (PL.) HALVERS
HALVING HAPLOSIS
HAM PIG EMOTE GAMMON JAMBON
   JARRET PESTLE GAMBONE
   PROSCIUTTO
   (— IT UP) EMOTE
   (BROTHER OF —) SHEM JAPHET
   (FATHER OF —) NOAH
   (PICNIC —) CALA CALI
   (SON OF —) CUSH PHUT CANAAN
   MIZRAIM
   (PL.) HUNKERS
HAMATUM UNCIFORM
HAMBURGER WIMPY
HAMESUCKEN HAMFARE
HAMITE BORAN BORANA DANAKIL
   DANKALI
HAMLET KOM BURG DORP TOON
   TOWN TREF VILL ALDEA CASAL
   HAMEL SITIO STEAD THORP VICUS
   ALDEIA BUSTEE THORPE CLACHAN
   KAMPONG KIRKTON KIRKTOWN
   (AUTHOR OF —) SHAKESPEARE
   (CHARACTER IN —) OSRIC HAMLET
   HORATIO LAERTES OPHELIA
   BERNARDO CLAUDIUS GERTRUDE
   POLONIUS REYNALDO CORNELIUS
   FRANCISCO MARCELLUS
   VOLTIMAND FORTINBRAS
   ROSENCRANTZ GUILDENSTERN

HAMMEDATHA (SON OF —) HAMAN
HAMMER AX AXE BIT DOG PEG SET
CALL COCK DROP HORN MALL
MASH MAUL MELL SETT TILT CAVIL
KEVEL KNOCK MADGE POUND
SMITE THUMP BEETLE BUCKER
CLOYER DRIVER FALLER FULLER
MALLET MARTEL NOPPER OLIVER
PLEXOR SCUTCH SLEDGE TACKER
TILTER KNAPPER KNOCKER
MALLEUS PLESSOR STRIKER
CRANDALL MALLEATE MJOLLNIR
SCUTCHER TREMBLER
   (— FOR DRESSING STONE) KEVEL
   (— OF GUNLOCK) DOG COCK
   DOGHEAD
   (— OUT) ANVIL
   (BRICKLAYER'S —) SCOTCH SCUTCH
   SCUTCHER
   (FLATTEN BY —) PEEN
   (LEADEN —) MADGE
   (MINER'S —) BULLY
   (PART OF —) BELL CLAW FACE GRIP
   HEAD NECK PEEN POLL CHEEK
   HANDLE
   (PAVING —) REEL
   (PERCUSSION —) PLEXOR PLESSOR
   (PNEUMATIC —) GUN BUSTER
   (POINTED —) PICK
   (SLATE-CUTTER'S —) SAX
   (STEAM —) IMPACTER IMPACTOR
   (THOR'S —) MJOLNIR MJOLLNIR
   (TUNING —) KEY
   (WAR —) MARTEL
HAMMERED BEATEN WROUGHT
HAMMERHEAD PEEN UMBRE
CORNUDA UMBRETTE
HAMMERKOP UMBER UMBRETTE
HAMMERLOCK BAR ARMLOCK
HAMMERMAN STRIKER
HAMMOCK SACK HUMMOCK
   (— CARRIED BY BEARERS) DANDY
   (— SLUNG ON POLE) MACHILA
   (WOODEN —) KATEL KARTEL
HAMMOLEKETH (BROTHER OF —)
   GILEAD
   (FATHER OF —) MACHIR
HAMPER BIN COT MAR PED TUB
BEAT BIND CLOG CURB FLAT HURT
LOAD SLOW TUCK BLOCK CABIN
CRAMP CRATE MAUND RUSKY
SERON BASKET BURDEN FETTER
HALTER HINDER HOBBLE HOPPLE
IMPEDE TANGLE BUFFALO
CONFINE HANAPER MANACLE
PANNIER PERPLEX SHACKLE
TRAMMEL ENCUMBER ENTANGLE
OBSTRUCT RESTRAIN RESTRICT
STRAITEN
HAMPERING STIFLING DIFFICULT
HAMSTER CRICETID
HAMSTRING HOX HOCK LAME
HOUGH IMPEDE ENERVATE
HAMUL (FATHER OF —) PHAREZ
HAMUTAL (FATHER OF —)
   JEREMIAH
   (HUSBAND OF —) JOSIAH
   (SON OF —) JEHOAHAZ ZEDEKIAH
HANAMEEL (COUSIN OF —)
   JEREMIAH
   (FATHER OF —) SHALLUM
HANAN (FATHER OF —) AZEL
ZACCUR MAACHAH IGDALIAH

HANANI (FATHER OF —) HEMAN
   (SON OF —) JEHU
HANANIAH (FATHER OF —) AZUR
BEBAI HEMAN ZERUBBABEL
   (GRANDSON OF —) IRIJAH
   (SON OF —) ZEDEKIAH
HANAPER HAMPER
HAND M CAT DAB FAM FIN HAN
PAW PUD CLAW DEAL DUKE GIVE
GOLL HALF JACK LOOF MAIN
MANO MITT PART PASS SPAN
CAMAY CLAUT CLEUK FLUSH
GLAUM GRASP GRIPE INDEX
MANUS NIEVE POWER SHARE
STIFF STOCK BRIDGE CLUNCH
CLUTCH DADDLE DOUBLE FAMBLE
GOWPEN HANDLE MAULEY MINNIE
STAGER WORKER CLAWKER
FAMELEN FLAPPER FLIPPER
POINTER WORKMAN GRAPPLER
MORTMAIN
   (— COUNTING ZERO) BACCARA
   BACCARAT
   (— DOWN) DEVOLVE TRADUCE
   BEQUEATH TRANSMIT
   (— GESTURES) MUDRA
   (— IN POKER) FULL SKIP BLAZE
   FLUSH SKEET TIGER BICYCLE
   JACKPOT SKIPPER IMMORTAL
   STRAIGHT
   (— IN WHIST) MORT TENACE
   (— ON) BUCK SPREAD
   (— ON HIP) AKIMBO
   (— OVER) GIVE REACH BETEACH
   BITECHE DELIVER
   (— UP STRAW) SERVE
   (— WITH 5 HIGHEST TRUMPS)
   JAMBOREE
   (AT —) NEAR CLOSE
   (BABY'S —) SPUD
   (BIG AND UNGAINLY —) MAIG
   (BRIDGE —) BID DUMMY DOUBLE
   CHICANE LAYDOWN
   (CLENCHED —) FIST
   (COLD —S) SHOWDOWN
   (CURSIVE —) CIVILITE
   (DECK —) HAWSEMAN
   (DUMMY —) BOARD
   (ELDEST —) EDGE SENIOR
   (EUCHRE —) JAMBONE
   (EXTRA — IN LOO) MISS
   (FRENCH —) COULEE
   (GRASPING —) CLAUT
   (GREEN —) FARMER JACKEROO
   (LEFT —) SINISTRA
   (LONE —) JAMBONE
   (PART OF —) PAD BALL HEEL PALM
   DIGIT INDEX THUMB WRIST CARPUS
   CREASE FINGER PINKIE THENAR
   MINIMUS BRACELET LIFELINE
   FINGERTIP FOREFINGER
   HYPOTHENAR TRANSVERSE
   (PERSIAN —) SHIKASTA
   (POKER —S) BOARD
   (RANCH —) COWBOY
   (REEL —) SPINDLER
   (RIGHT —) DEXTER
   (ROUND —) RONDE
   (SECTION —) SNIPE
   (SKILLFUL —) DAB
   (SLAPPING OF RIGHT —) HIGHFIVE
   (SPARE — IN CARDS) CAT
   JAMBOREE

   (UNSKILLED —) DABSTER
   (UPPER —) BULGE EMINENCE
   (WEAK CARD —) BUST
   (PREF.) CHEIR(O) CHIR(O) MANI
   MANU PALMATI PALMI
   (SUFF.) CHEIRIA CHIRIA
HANDBAG BAG CABA NEIF CABAS
PURSE SATCHEL ENVELOPE
GRIPSACK POCHETTE RETICULE
POCKETBOOK
HANDBALL PALM
HANDBARROW BIER HANDY TRUCK
BARROW
HANDBELL SKELLAT TANTONY
HANDBILL BILL FLIER FLYER LIBEL
DODGER
HANDBOOK VADY GRADUS
MANUAL BAEDEKER
HANDBOW STONEBOW
HANDCAR DRAG
HANDCART PRAM DANDY HURLY
TRUCK GOCART TROLLY TROLLEY
HANDCUFF CUFF STAY LINKER
NIPPER STAYER MANACLE
TRAMMEL WRISTER BRACELET
HANDBOLT HANDLOCK LIGAMENT
SNITCHER WRISTLET
   (PL.) IRONS SNAPS DARBIES
   NIPPERS
HANDEDNESS
   (SUFF.) CHEIRIA CHIRIA
HANDER-IN INGIVER
HANDFUL M MAN GRIP LOCK WISP
YELM CLAUT GRIPE LITCH GOUPIN
GOWPEN HANTLE YAFFLE FISTFUL
MANIPLE
   (— OF GRAIN) RIP REAP SINGLE
   SONGLE
   (— OF LEAVES) PATRIN
   (DOUBLE —) GOWPEN
   (LAST — OF HARVEST) KIRN
   (SMALL —) PUGIL
**HANDFUL OF DUST (AUTHOR OF
   —)** WAUGH
   (CHARACTER IN —) JOCK JOHN
   LAST TODD TONY BEAVER BRENDA
   MENZIES MESSINGER
HANDGRIP TUFFING
HANDGUN GAT HAKE ROSCOE
CALIVER HANDARM ARQUEBUS
REVOLVER ARQUEBUSE
HANDICAP START BURDEN DENIAL
HAMPER HINDER IMPEDE STRIKE
PENALTY ENCUMBER PENALIZE
   (SPORTS —) BISQUE
HANDICAPPED CRIMP CRIMPED
HANDICRAFT MYSTERY ARTIFICE
MECHANIC HANDCRAFT
HANDICRAFTSMAN ARTISAN
HANDILY HANDY GAINLY
HANDINESS YARAGE
HANDING (— OVER) TRADITION
HANDIWORK MACHINE
   (SAILOR'S —) SCRIMSHAW
HANDKERCHIEF WIPE CLOUT
FOGLE HANKY ROMAL STOOK
WIPER HANKIE MADRAS NAPKIN
SUDARY TIGNON BANDANA
BELCHER FOULARD KERCHER
MANIPLE ORARIUM SNEEZER
BANDANNA KERCHIEF MOCKETER
MONTEITH MOUCHOIR SUDARIUM
VERNACLE VERONICA

HANDLE BOW EAR FAN LUG NIB
NOB PAD PIN PLY USE ANSA BAIL
BALE BOOL BUTT CROP FEEL FIST
GAUM GRIP HAFT HALE HAND
HANK HILT KILP KNOB LIFT RAPE
RUNG STOP GRASP GRIPE GROPE
HELVE MOUNT SHAFT SPOKE STAIL
STALE START STEAL STELE STOCK
SWING TREAT WIELD BECKET
FETTLE FINGER FUSEAU HANGER
LIFTER MANAGE MANURE
POMMEL ROUNCE TILLER
CONDUCT DUDGEON WOOLDER
BEERPULL BELLPULL BITSTALK
BITSTOCK DISPENSE HANDGRIP
HANDHOLD HANDLING MOPSTICK
STAGHORN PENHOLDER
MANIPULATE
   (— AWKWARDLY) FUMBLE
   THUMBLE
   (— BADLY) ILLGUIDE
   (— CLUMSILY) PAW FUMBLE
   (— IMPROPERLY) GAUM
   (— MODISHLY) GALLANT
   (— OF AXE) HELVE
   (— OF BENCH PLANE) TOAT TOTE
   (— OF CANNON) MANIGLION
   (— OF DAGGER) DUDGEON
   (— OF KETTLE) BAIL
   (— OF LADLE) SHANK
   (— OF OAR) GRASP
   (— OF PLOW) HALE STAFF START
   STILT PLOWTAIL
   (— OF PRINTING PRESS) ROUNCE
   (— OF RAKE) STALE
   (— OF SCYTHE) TACK SNATH SNEAD
   THOLE SNATHE SNEATH
   (— OF SPOON) STEM
   (— OF SWORD) HAFT HILT
   (— OF WHIP) CROP
   (— RECKLESSLY) FOOL
   (— ROUGHLY) MALL MAUL TOWSE
   MUZZLE GRABBLE MANHANDLE
   (— VIOLENTLY) BOUNCE
   (CRANK —) WINK
   (CROSSBOW —) TILLER
   (CURVED —) BOOL BOUL
   (DETACHABLE —) KILP
   (LIFTING — OF GUN) DOLPHIN
   (PUMP —) BRAKE SWIPE
   (ROPE —) SHACKLE
   (WOODEN —) TREE
   (PL.) HALES
HANDLED (EASILY —) BANTAM
HANDLER DOCKHAND
   (AIRPLANE —) AIREDALE
   (SUFF.) STER STRESS
HANDLEY CROSS (AUTHOR OF —)
   SURTEES
   (CHARACTER IN —) JOHN PIGG
   HARDY MELLO BELINDA BRAMBER
   DOLEFUL MICHAEL SWIZZLE
   JORROCKS FLEECEALL
   BARNINGTON
HANDLING USE CONTROL
   (SEVERE —) KILLING
   (SKILLFUL —) CONDUCT
   (UNSKILLFUL —) BUNGLING
HANDMAID ANCILLA
HAND-MILL QUERN PEPPERMILL
HANDOUT DOWN
HANDRAIL BAR RAIL MANROPE

BANISTER EASEMENT MOPSTICK TOADBACK
HANDSAW STADDA
HANDSHAKE SHAKE SHRUG
HAND-SHAPED PALMATE
HANDSOME BRAW FAIR FINE MOOI NICE PERT TALL BONNY FETIS FITTY FUSOM LUSTY ADONIC BRAWLY CLEVER COMELY FARAND GOODLY HEPPEN LIKELY PROPER SEEMLY ADONIAN AVENANT ELEGANT FEATISH FEATOUS FEWSOME GALLANT LIBERAL SMICKER GOODLIKE STUNNING VENEREAN WEELFARD
HANDSOMELY FAIRLY HANDSOME
HANDSTONE MANO
HAND STRAP TOGGEL TOGGLE
HANDSTROKE TALLY
HANDWORK MACRAME TOOLING
HANDWRITING PAW FIST HAND WRITE DUCTUS NESHKI NIGGLE SCRIPT SCRIVE BATARDE WRITING BACKHAND HANDWRIT
(**ARABIC —**) NESKI NASKHI NESHKI
(**BAD —**) CACOGRAPHY
(**CRAMPED —**) NIGGLE
HANDY DAB DEFT GAIN NEAT WEME JEMMY LUSTY QUEME READY TIGHT ADROIT CLEVER HEPPEN KNACKY DEXTROUS EXPEDITE HANDSOME SKILLFUL
HANDYMAN MOZO JUMPER GREASER SWAMPER
HANG NUB TOP CRAP DRAG FALL HANK KILT PEND TREE TUCK DRAPE DROOP HOVER KETCH NOOSE SCRAG STRAP SWING TRINE TRUSS TWIST ANHANG APPEND DANGLE DEPEND GIBBET HALTER IMPEND SLOUCH STRING TALTER DOGGONE HANGING LANTERN STRETCH SUSPEND
(**— ABOUT**) DRING HOVER
(**— AROUND**) KNOCK HANKER LOITER SLINGE
(**— BACK**) LAG BOGGLE
(**— BEHIND**) PLOD
(**— CRIMINAL**) STRAP TOTTER
(**— DOWN**) DIP LOP LAVE DROOP DEPEND FESTOON PROPEND
(**— HEAVILY**) SWAG
(**— IN POSITION**) SET
(**— IN SUSPENSE**) POISE
(**— LOOSELY**) BAG SAG FLAG FLOW LOLL BANGLE DANGLE PAGGLE
(**— OF GARMENT**) SET
(**— ONE'S HEAD**) SLINK
(**— ON THE LINE**) DRIPDRY
(**— OUT**) LILL
(**— OVER**) HOVER WAUVE IMPEND WHAUVE
(**— PICTURE NEAR CEILING**) SKY
(**— SOGGILY**) TROLLOP
(**— VERTICALLY**) PLUMB
(**— WITH TAPESTRY**) TAPIS
(PREF.) CREMO
HANGAR DOCK GARAGE AIRDOCK
HANGER PASSIVE SHABBLE BASELARD WHINYARD
(**— FOR CARCASSES**) STANG
(**COAT —**) SHOULDER
(**CRANK —**) BRACKET

(**LACE-MAKING —**) WORKER
(**SWORD —**) CARRIAGE
HANGER-ON BUR CAD BURR SPIV LEECH TOADY CLIENT HANGBY HEELER LACKEY SPONGE LACQUEY PENDING PARASITE
(**— OF CELEBRITY**) GROUPIE
HANGING FLAG HEMP TURN ARRAS BAGGY DRAPE SWING CELURE DORSEL DOSSER DERRICK DRAPERY PENDENT PENSILE ANTEPORT HANGMENT PARAMENT
(**— LOOSE**) LOPPY BAGGED
(**— LOW**) SIDE
(**— THREATENINGLY**) IMMINENT
(**ALTAR —**) FRONTAL
(**LIMPLY —**) FLAGGY SLIMPSY
(**WALL —**) CEILING DRAPERY TENTURE KAKEMONO
(PL.) TAPIT TAPPET DRAPERY PARAMENT
HANGMAN KETCH HANGER HANGIE TOPMAN DERRICK GREGORY TOPSMAN VERDUGO CARNIFEX SCRAGGER
(**HALTER OF —**) TOW
HANGMAN'S DAY FRIDAY
HANGNAIL AGNAIL
HANGOUT NEST HAUNT JOINT SCATTER
HANGOVER HOLDOVER RESIDUUM KATZENJAMMER
HANG-UP BAG
HANIEL (FATHER OF —) ULLA
HANK HASP SKEIN BOBBIN SELVAGEE
(**— OF FLAX**) HEAD
(**— OF TWINE**) RAN
(**— OF YARN**) SLIP
HANKER HANK ITCH LONG YEARN LINGER
HANKERING ITCH HANKER
HANKUL ENMUN ONMUN
HANNAH (HUSBAND OF —) ELKANAH
(**SON OF —**) SAMUEL
HANNIEL (FATHER OF —) EPHOD
HANOCH (FATHER OF —) REUBEN
HANS BRINKER (AUTHOR OF —) DODGE
(**CHARACTER IN —**) HANS RAFF GLECK HILDA GRETEL BOEKMAN BRINKER MEVROUW
HANSOM CAB SHOFUL SHOWFUL
HANUMAN ENTELLUS
HANUN (FATHER OF —) NAHASH ZALAPH
HAP REDE CHANCE FORTUNE HAPPING
HAPHAZARD CASUAL CHANCE CHANCY RANDOM BUCKEYE SCRATCH CARELESS SCRAMBLY SLAPDASH TUMULTUARY
HAPHAZARDLY ANYHOW SLAPDASH
HAPLESS POOR UNLUCKY
HAPLY HAPS HAPPILY
HAPPEN BE DO GO HAP COME COOK FALL FARE GIVE LUCK PASS RISE TIDE TIME BREAK EVENE EVENT LIGHT OCCUR SHAPE ARRIVE BECOME BEFALL BETIDE

CHANCE TUMBLE FORTUNE STUMBLE SUCCEED BECHANCE OVERCOME
(**— AGAIN**) RECUR
(**— TOGETHER**) CONCUR
HAPPENING HAP FACT EVENT THING CHANCE TIDING TIMING INCIDENT OCCASION OCCURRENCE
(**ACTUAL —**) FACT
(**UNCANNY —**) WEIRD
(**UNEXPECTED —**) ACCIDENT
HAPPILY FAIN FITLY GLADLY JOYOUSLY
HAPPINESS JOY WIN GLEE SELE SONS WEAL BLISS GLORY MIRTH SOOTH FELICE WEALTH DELIGHT ECSTASY FELICIA RAPTURE UTILITY FELICITY GLADNESS HILARITY
(**PLACE OF —**) CAMELOT
HAPPY FIT COSH FAIN GLAD GLEG SELI WELY BONNY FAUST FELIX LIGHT LUCKY MERRY PROUD SEELY SONSY SUNNY WHITE BLITHE BONNIE BRIGHT JOYFUL COMICAL GLEEFUL HALCYON JOCULAR PERFECT SEELFUL WEALFUL WEIRDLY BLISSFUL CAREFREE DISPOSED FROHLICH GRACIOUS SUNSHINE
(PREF.) FELICI
HARA-KIRI SEPPUKU
HARALD (FATHER OF KING —) OLAF
HARAN (BROTHER OF —) ABRAHAM
(**DAUGHTER OF —**) ISCAH MILCAH
(**FATHER OF —**) CALEB TERAH
(**MOTHER OF —**) EPHAH
(**SON OF —**) LOT
HARANGUE RANT ORATE SPOUT CONCIO PATTER SCREED SERMON SPEECH SPRITZ TIRADE ADDRESS DECLAIM EARBASH DIATRIBE PERORATE
HARASS FAG GIG HAG HOX MAG NAG RAG TAW VEX BAIT CARK FRAB FRET GALL GNAW HAKE HALE HARE HAZE HOCK JADE PAIL PUSH RIDE SEEK TIRE TOIL TOSS WORK ANNOY BESET BULLY CHAFE CHASE CHEVY CHIVY CURSE FLISK GRIND GRIPE HARRY HOUND HURRY PRESS TARGE TEASE TRASH WEARY WORRY BADGER BOTHER CHIVVY CHOUSE CUMBER FERRET HASSLE HATTER HECKLE HECTOR HESPEL HOORAY HURRAH INFEST MOLEST MURDER OBSESS PESTER PINGLE PLAGUE POTHER PURSUE AFFLICT AGITATE BEDEVIL DRAGOON HAGRIDE HARRAGE OPPRESS PERPLEX PROVOKE TERRIFY TORMENT TRAVAIL TROUBLE TURMOIL BULLYRAG DISTRACT DISTRESS EXERCISE FORHAILE IRRITATE SPURGALL SUPPRESS PERSECUTE
(**— MENTALLY**) GRUDGE
HARASSED BESTEAD HARRIED HAUNTED
(**— BY**) BEFORE
HARASSING WARM
HARBINGER OMEN ANGEL USHER

HERALD FORAGER FORAYER FURRIER OUTRIDER PRODROME
(**— OF SUMMER**) SWALLOW
HARBOR REE BEAR DOCK HOLD PIER PORT BASIN BAYOU CHUCK CREEK HAVEN HITHE SLADE BREACH BUNDER COTHON FOSTER REFUGE OUTPORT PORTLET SEAPORT SHELTER CARENAGE ENHARBOR SHIPRADE
(**— A CRIMINAL**) RESET
(**SUBMARINE —**) PEN
HARBOR SEAL DOTANT DOTARD RANGER SEALCH TANGFISH
HARD DRY FIT ILL COLD DEAR DOUR DURE FAST FIRM IRON MEAN NASH OPEN CHAMP CLOSE CORKY HARSH HORNY ROCKY SMART SNELL SOLID SOUND STEEL STERN STIFF STONY STOOR STOUT TIGHT BOARDY BRAWNY COARSE FLINTY GLASSY KITTLE KNOBBY KNOTTY ROBUST RUGGED SEVERE STARKY STINGY STRICT STRONG STURDY UNEATH UNNETH WOODEN ADAMANT ARDUOUS AUSTERE CALLOUS HARDWAY HORNISH ONEROUS SUBDURE CORNEOUS DILIGENT HARDBACK HARDENED IRONHARD OBDURATE PETROSAL RIGOROUS SCLEROID SCLEROSE TOILSOME
(**— BY**) FORBY FORTHBY
(**— TO BEAR**) FIERCE
(**— TO MANAGE**) SALTY
(**— TO PLEASE**) FINICKY CONCEITY
(**— TO REACH**) CUMBROUS
(**— TO READ**) BLIND
(**— TO SATISFY**) EXIGENT EXIGEANT
(**— TO SELL**) STICKY
(**— TO UNDERSTAND**) DIFFUSE
(PREF.) DURO SCLER(O) STERE(O)
HARD-BILL SEEDEATER
HARD-BITTEN GNARLED
HARDEN SET TAW BAKE BEEK CAKE FIRM HARN KERN SEAR BRAZE ENURE FLESH INURE SETUP STEEL STONE BRONZE ENDURE FREEZE OBDURE OSSIFY POTASH SEASON TEMPER CALCIFY EMBRAWN PETRIFY STIFFEN THICKEN CONCRETE ENHARDEN INDURATE SOLIDIFY
(**— QUILL**) DUTCH
(**CASE —**) STEEL
HARDENED DRAW HARD LOST SALTED CALLOUS COCTILE CRUSTED FIBROUS INDURATE OBDURATE
HARDENING SET POROMA SCLEROMA OSSIFICATION
(**— OF TISSUES**) SCLEREMA SCLERIASIS
HARDHACK SPIREA IRONBUSH WHITECAP
HARDHEAD LION BOCHE
HARDHEARTED STERN STONY OBDURATE
HARDICANUTE (FATHER OF —) CANUTE
(**HALF-BROTHER OF —**) HAROLD
(**MOTHER OF —**) EMMA

HARDIHOOD PLUCK COURAGE AUDACITY

HARDLY ILL SCANT BARELY RARELY SCARCE UNEATH SCARCELY

HARDNESS SEG GRAIN PROOF RIGOR STEEL DURESS DURITY ADAMANT HARDSHIP SEVERITY SOLIDITY
  (— OF CHARACTER) HEART
  (— SCALE) MOHS

HARD-OF-HEARING DULL DUNCH DEAFISH

HARDPAN PAN CLAYPAN MOORPAN MOORBAND ORTSTEIN

HARDSCRABBLE ARID

HARDSHIP HARD GRIEF PINCH RIGOR STOUR THRONG UNWEAL SQUEEZE ASPERITY HARDNESS
  (PL.) EXTREMES

HARDTACK PANTILE
  (— AND MOLASSES) BURGOO

HARD TIMES (AUTHOR OF —) DICKENS
  (CHARACTER IN —) JUPE JAMES SISSY JOSIAH LOUISA SLEARY THOMAS SPARSIT STEPHEN GRAGRIND BLACKPOOL BOUNDERBY HARTHOUSE MCCHOAKUMCHILD

HARDWARE TRIM IRONWARE
  (COMPUTER —) MONITOR

HARDWOOD ASH HARD BREAKAX LEAFWOOD

HARDWORKING EIDENT

HARDY DOUR HARD WIRY LUSTY MANLY STOUR STOUT TOUGH GARDEN INURED RUGGED STURDY SPARTAN STUBBED GAILLARD GALLIARD STUBBORN

HARE PUG WAT BAWD CONY PUSS SCUT BAWTY CUTTY LEPUS PUSSY MALKIN MAUKIN BELGIAN LEPORID POUSSIE VENISON BAUDRONS KLIPHAAS LEPURINE
  (— IN FIRST YEAR) LEVERET
  (— TRACK) PRICK
  (FEMALE —) DOE
  (GREAT —) MANABOZHO
  (KIND OF —) VARYING SNOWSHOE
  (LITTLE CHIEF —) CONY PIKA
  (MALE —) BUCK
  (PATAGONIAN —) MARA
  (SIBERIAN —) TOLAL
  (PL.) FLICK
  (PREF.) LAG(O) LEPORI

HAREBELL BLAWORT THIMBLE BLAEWORT BLUEBELL

HAREBRAINED GIDDY WINDY

HARELIP LAGOSTOMA

HAREM SERAI ZENANA ANDERUN HAREMLIK SERAGLIO
  (ROOM IN —) ODA ODAH

HAREPH (FATHER OF —) CALEB
  (SON OF —) BETHGADER

HARE'S-EAR MODESTY BUPLEVER

HARHAIAH (SON OF —) UZZIEL

HARIJAN PANCHAMA

HARK (— BACK) HOICKS

HARL WHIRL

HARLEQUIN DUCK SQUEALER
  (FEMALE —) LADY
  (MALE —) LORD

HARLOT PUG DRAB LOON SLUT HIREN PAGAN QUEAN RAHAB STRAP TWEAK WHORE RIBALD TOMBOY DELILAH MERMAID WAGTAIL MERETRIX MISWOMAN STRUMPET
  (PREF.) PORN(O)

HARLOTRY PUTAGE BITCHERY

HARM NEY NOY NYE WEM ARME BALE BANE DERE HURT SCAT SORE TEEN WERD ABUSE ANNOY GRAME HERME LOATH QUALM SHEND SPOIL TOUCH WATHE WEMMY WOUGH WOUND WRAKE WREAK WRONG DAMAGE DAMNUM DANGER GRIEVE INJURE INJURY SCATHE SORROW WONDER DESPITE DISEASE FORFEIT IMPEACH TROUBLE UNQUERT BUSINESS DISAVAIL DISSERVE ENDAMAGE MISCHIEF NOCUMENT NUISANCE
  (— REPUTATION) DEFAME
  (DO —) ENVY
  (PREF.) NOCI

HARMFUL BAD EVIL HARM NASTY NOXAL NOCENT NOCIVE NOYFUL UNSELY BANEFUL HURTFUL NOISOME NOXIOUS DAMAGING INIMICAL SINISTER PERNICIOUS

HARMFULNESS VICE MALICE

HARMINE BANISTERINE

HARMLESS SAFE SELI TAME CANNY SEELY SILLY WHITE DOVISH FEARLESS HURTLESS INNOCENT SACKLESS UNHARMED
  (MAKE —) DEFANG

HARMONIA (DAUGHTER OF —) INO AGAVE SEMELE AUTONOE
  (FATHER OF —) MARS
  (HUSBAND OF —) CADMUS
  (MOTHER OF —) VENUS
  (SON OF —) POLYDORUS

HARMONIC OVERTONE

HARMONICA HARP EUPHON SYRINX AEOLINE PANPIPE ARMONICA ZAMPOGNA MOUTHORGAN

HARMONIOUS HAPPY SWEET COSMIC SILKEN UNITED MUSICAL SPHERAL TUNEFUL BALANCED CHARMING HARMONIC PEACEFUL ACCORDING CONCINNOUS CONCORDANT
  (— RELATIONSHIP) SYNC
  (PREF.) SYMPHO

HARMONITE RAPPIST RAPPITE

HARMONIUM ORGAN VOCALION

HARMONIZE GO FIT GEE KEY JIBE SORT TUNE AGREE ATONE BLEND CHORD GROUP HITCH RHYME ACCORD ASSORT ATTUNE COTTON COMPORT CONCENT CONCORD CONSORT ORDINATE ACCOMMODATE

HARMONIZING HENOTIC

HARMONY SUIT TUNE CHIME CHORD UNITY ACCORD ATTUNE COSMOS HEAVEN MELODY UNISON BALANCE CONCENT CONCERT CONCORD CONSENT CONSORT KEEPING RAPPORT DIAPASON FABURDEN SYMPATHY SYMPHONY CONGRUITY
  (— OF COLORS) TONE

HARNEPHER (FATHER OF —) ZOPHAH

HARNESS TUG GEAR HAME LEAF REIN YOKE BRACE CROWN DRAFT FRONT GEARS SLING TRACE COLLAR FETTLE GULLET INSPAN TACKLE DRAUGHT GEARING GIGTREE LORMERY SIMBLOT TOGGERY DRAWGEAR ENCLOSER HEADGEAR TACKLING TURNBACK
  (— FOR LOOM) LEAF HEALD MOUNTING
  (— FOR PULLING GUNS) BRICOLE
  (DECORATIVE —) CAPARISON
  (PART OF —) BIT REIN GIRTH TRACE COLLAR BLINDER CRUPPER BELLYBAND BREECHING CHECKREIN
  (WEAVING —) HEADLE HEDDLE

HARNESSED ANTELOPE GUIB GUIBA BOSCHBOK BUSHBUCK

HARNESS MAKER KNACKER WHITTAW

HAROLD I HAREFOOT

HARP ARPA FORK LYRE VINA NABLA NANGA HARPER SABECA CHROTTA DECHORD SAMBUKE AUTOHARP CLARSACH
  (— ON) RUBIN
  (CELTIC —) TELYN CLARSACH
  (FINNISH —) KANTELA KANTELE
  (ICELANDIC —) LANGSPIL
  (JAPANESE —) KOTO
  (JEW'S —) TRUMP
  (PART OF —) BASE BODY FOOT NECK BOARD PEDAL PILLAR STRING
  (PERSIAN —) SANG
  (TRIANGULAR —) TRIGON TRIGONON

HARPER MINSTREL

HARPOON IRON FIZGIG GRAINS FISHGIG HARPAGO STRIKER HARPAGON

HARPOONED FAST

HARPOONER STRIKER

HARP SEAL HARP BEATER SADDLER

HARPSICHORD SPINET CEMBALO CLAVIER CLAVECIN HASPICOL

HARPY HAG AELLO CELAENO OCYPETE PODARGE

HARQUEBUS HAGBUT CALIVER HACKBUT ARQUEBUS

HARQUEBUSIER CARABIN

HARRIDAN HAG

HARRIER HAWK KAHU BEAGLE FALLER MILLER PUTTOCK HARROWER

HARROW COG CHIP DISC DISK DRAG HARO TINE BRAKE BREAK HERSE DREDGE DRUDGE FALLOW LADDER SPADER CUTAWAY LACERATE OXHARROW

HARROWED HAGGARD

HARROWING TINE TINING TEARING
  (— OF HELL) ANASTASIS

HARRY DUN HAG BRACE CHIVEY CHIVVY FERRET HARASS CRUCIFY

HARSH ILL ACID BULL DOUR FOUL HARD HASH HASK IRON RUDE SOUR ACERB ACRID ASPER BRUTE CRONK CRUDE GRILL GRUFF HEAVY HUSKY RASPY ROUGH ROUND RUVID SHARP SNELL STARK STERN STIFF STOUR STOUT BRUTAL COARSE FLINTY GRAVEL GRISLY HOARSE RAGGED RASPED RUGGED SEVERE SHREWD STURDY SULLEN TETRIC UNKIND UNRIDE AUSTERE CRABBED RASPING RAUCOUS SQUAWKY VIOLENT ABRASIVE ACERBATE ASPERATE ASPEROUS CATONIAN CLASHING DRACONIC GRAVELLY GRINDING GUTTURAL JANGLING OBDURATE RIGOROUS SCABROUS SCRANNEL STRIDENT STROUNGE STUBBORN TETRICAL UNGENTLE UNKINDLY
  (— OF VOICE) STEER

HARSHLY HARD HARSH SHORTLY

HARSHNESS WOLF RIGOR DURESS CATOISM CRUDITY CRUELTY DUREZZA RAUCITY ACERBITY ACRIMONY ASPERITY FELLNESS HARDNESS HASKNESS MORDANCY SEVERITY

HART SPADE VENISON

HARTEBEEST ASSE TORA TORI BUBAL CAAMA KAAMA KONZE LECAMA BUBALIS CONGONI KONGONI SASSABY

HART'S-TONGUE LONGLEAF

HARUM (SON OF —) AHARHEL

HARUMAPH (SON OF —) JEDAIAH

HARUSPEX SEER ARUSPEX ARUSPICE EXTISPEX

HARUZ (DAUGHTER OF —) MESHULLEMETH

HARVEST IN WIN CROP HEAP PICK RABI REAP SLED SNAP FOISON GATHER HAIRST RUBBEE UPROOT COMBINE GRABBLE INGATHER SHEARING
  (— OF GRAPES) VENDAGE

HARVESTER COMBINE

HARVEST FISH WHITING MOONFISH STARFISH

HARVEST HOME KIRN MELL HOCKEY HORKEY

HARVESTING SLEDDING

HARVESTMAN CARTER CARTARE

HARY JANOS (COMPOSER OF —) KODALY

HAS S AS HATH
  (— NOT) NAS AINT

HASADIAH (FATHER OF —) ZERUBBABEL

HAS-BEEN WUZZER

HASH RAPE MINCE HACHIS MUDDLE RAGOUT

HASHABIAH (COMPANION OF —) EZRA
  (FATHER OF —) BUNNI KEMUEL JEDUTHUN MATTANIAH

HASHABNIAH (SON OF —) HATTUSH

HASHISH HEMP ASSIS CHARAS

HASHUBAH (FATHER OF —) ZERUBBABEL

HASID ASSIDEAN

HASKALAH (FOLLOWER OF —) MASKIL

HASP COP HAPS COPSE SPRENT

HASSAR DORAD

HASSOCK TUT BOSS PESS POUF TOIT TRUSH BUFFET TUFFET

HASTE HIE POST RACE RAGE RAPE CHASE FEVER HASTY HURRY SPEED BUSTLE FLURRY SWIVET DISPATCH RAPIDITY STROTHER PRECIPITATION
(HEADLONG —) SPURN
(IN —) HOTFOOT
(IN GREAT —) AMAIN
(WITH —) EXPRESS

HASTEN HIE RAP RUN BUSK DUST FIRK PELL PLAT POST RACE RAPE RUSH SPUR URGE CATCH CHASE DRIVE FLEET HASTE HURRY PRESS PREST SLATE SPEED STEER EXPEDE SCURRY STREAK SWITHE ADVANCE FORWARD HACKNEY HOTFOOT PREVENT QUICKEN SLITHER SWIFTEN WITHHIE DISPATCH EXPEDITE ACCELERATE
(— AWAY) FLEE SHERRY SQUIRR

HASTILY HOTLY RAPELY RASHLY FOOTHOT HOTFOOT HYINGLY HEADLONG

HASTY FAST RAPE RASH BRASH FLEET QUICK FLYING RAPELY CURSORY HOTHEAD HURRIED PEPPERY TEARING HASTEFUL HEADLONG SUBITANE
(TACTLESSLY —) BRASH

HAT DIP FEZ LID NAB ATTE BAKU CADY COIF DISC DISK FELT FLAT HIVE HOOD KNAB MOAB SLOP TILE TOPI BEANY BENJY BENNY BERET BOXER CADDI CORDY DERBY DICER GIBUS JERRY KELLY MILAN MITER MITRE SHAKO SHELL TARAI TERAI TOPEE TOQUE TRUSH ABACOT BEANIE BEAVER BOATER BOWLER BRETON BUMPER CADDIE CASQUE CLAQUE CLOCHE COCKUP COIFFE FEDORA GALERO HELMET PANAMA PILEUS RAFFIA SAILOR SHOVEL SLOUCH TITFER TOPPER TURBAN VIGONE BANDEAU BANGKOK BLOOMER BRIMMER BYCOKET CATSKIN CAUBEEN CHAPEAU FANTAIL HATTING HATTOCK HOMBURG LEGHORN PETASOS PILLBOX PLATEAU PLATTER SALACOT SCRAPER SHALLOW SKIMMER SMASHER STETSON TARBUSH TRICORN BONGRACE CAPELINE GOSSAMER HEADGEAR JIPIJAPA MONTABYN MUSHROOM NABCHEAT RAMILIES REHOBOAM ROUNDLET SOMBRERO TARBOOSH TARBOUCH BORSALINO
(— BLOCKER) ROPER
(— MAKER) MODISTE MILLINER
(— OF MERCURY) PETASUS
(BEAVER —) CASTOR
(CARDINAL'S —) GALERO
(CLERGYMAN'S —) SHOVEL
(COCKED —) BICORNE RAMILIE SCRAPER
(COWBOY —) STETSON
(FABRIC —) TOQUE
(FELT —) DERBY JERRY TARAI TERAI ALPINE BOWLER TRILBY BILLYCOCK
(FLAT-TOP —) TAM
(HARD —) LABORER
(HIGH —) KYL PLUG TILE TOPPER

(IRON —) GOSSAN GOZZAN
(KIND OF —) COSSACK PORKPIE
(MILITARY —) BUSBY BEARSKIN
(OILSKIN —) SQUAM
(OPERA —) GIBUS CLAQUE
(PART OF —) BOW BRIM CROWN PINCH LINING BINDING HATBAND SWEATBAND
(PITH —) TOPI TOPEE
(RED —) GALERO
(SILK —) KYL BEAVER SHINER CATSKIN
(STIFF —) TILE DERBY KELLY BOATER BOWLER SAILOR
(STOVEPIPE —) CAROLINE
(STRAW —) BAKU FLAT HOOD KADY KATY TOYO BENJY BENNY CADDY STRAW BASHER BOATER PANAMA LEGHORN
(TOP —) PLUG TOPPER
(UNBLOCKED —) CONE
(WATERPROOF —) TARPAULIN
(WIDE-BRIMMED —) FLAT BENJY TARAI SMASHER SUNDOWN
(3-CORNERED —) TRICORN

HATBAND BAND WEED WEEPER
HAT BRIM LEAF TARFE TURNUP
HATCH HECK BREED BROOD CLECK CLOCK COVEY GUICHET UNSHELL DISCLOSE INCUBATE
HATCHED (NEWLY —) SQUAB
HATCHERY CHICKERY
HATCHET MOGO HACHE GWEEON THIXLE CLEAVER FRANCISC TOMAHAWK
(PREF.) SECURI
HATCHING CLETCH BREEDING ECLISION
HATCHWAY HATCH SCUTTLE
HATE FIRE TEEN ABHOR SPITE DETEST HATRED LOATHE UNLOVE DESPITE
HATEFUL FOUL LOTH BLACK CURST DIRTY HATEL LOATH CURSED ODIOUS HEINOUS HIDEOUS ACCURSED FLAGRANT ABOMINABLE
HATER ULYSSES
HATH MOOLUM
HATHATH (FATHER OF —) OTHNIEL
HATING
(PREF.) MIS(O)
HAT MONEY TAMPANG
HAT-PLANT SOLA
HATRED DOSA ENVY HATE HELL ONDE HATE ODIUM SPITE ENMITY RANCOR AVERSION ABHORRENCE
(— OF CHILDREN) MISOPEDIA
(— OF MARRIAGE) MISOGAMY
(— OF MEN) MISANDRY MISANTHROPY
(— OF NEW IDEAS) MISCAINEA
(— OF REASONING) MISOLOGY
(— OF WOMEN) MISOGYNY
(PREF.) MIS(O)
HATTER GADGER HURRER
HATTUSH (FATHER OF —) HASHABNIAH
HAUBERK BYRNIE
HAUGHTILY BIGLY
HAUGHTINESS AIR PRIDE HEIGHT MORGUE ORGUIL DISDAIN HAUTEUR STOMACH HAUTESSE

HAUGHTY DAIN HIGH RANK STAY DIGNE DORTY HUFFY LOFTY LUSTY POTTY PROUD STOUT SURLY TAUNT FEISTY FIERCE HAUGHT QUAINT SNOOTY UPPISH DISTANT HAUTAIN HONTISH PAUGHTY STATELY SUBLIME ARROGANT CAVALIER DEIGNOUS FASTUOUS GLORIOUS IMPERIAL INSOLENT ORGULOUS PRIDEFUL SCORNFUL SNIFFISH SUPERIOR TOPLOFTY PEREMPTORY

HAUL KEP LUG RUG TEW TOW TUG CART DRAG DRAW DRAY HALE HURL JUNK PULL SKID TAKE TOTE TRAM BOUSE DRAVE HEAVE LIGHT ROUSE SNAKE TOUSE TOWSE TRACT TRICE TRAVOY DRAUGHT SCHLEPP CORDELLE HANDBANK
(— AFT) TALLY
(— DOWN) STRIKE
(— IN) GATHER
(— LOGS) TODE SLOOP SWAMP SIWASH HANDBANK
(— OF FISH) TACK DRAVE
(— OF NET) LIFT
(— SAIL) BUNT CLEW CLUE
(— SHIP) SPRING
(— TO DECK) BOARD
(— UP AND FASTEN) TRICE
(— WITH TACKLE) BOUSE
HAULAGE DOOK
HAULAGEWAY GANGWAY
HAULING HALE CARTAGE
HAUNCH HIP HOOK HUCK HANCE HUCKLE
(PL.) GRUG HUNKERS
HAUNT DEN HANT HOME HOWF KEEP NEST WALK GHOST HOWFF SPOOK STALK INFEST KENNEL OBSESS OUTLAY PURSUE REPAIR PURLIEU FREQUENT PRACTICE
(— OF ANIMALS) LIE HOME
(FAMILIAR —) SLAIT
HAUNTED SPOOKY
HAUNTING BESETTING
HAUSTELLATE GLOSSATE
HAUSTORIUM SINK SINKER SUCKER
HAUTBOY OBOE WAIT
HAUTEUR PRIDE HEIGHT MORGUE
HAVE A AN OF OWN HOLD BOAST ENJOY OUGHT WIELD POSSESS
(— ON) WEAR
HAVEN ARK HOPE PIER PORT HITHE HARBOR HAVENET
HAVILAH (FATHER OF —) CUSH JOKTAN
HAVING
(SUFF.) IOUS OSE OUS
HAVOC HOB HELL RUIN WASTE RAVAGE
HAW HOI HECK SLOE WIND WYND BOOTS PEGGLE ALISIER

<table>
<tr><td colspan="2" align="center">**HAWAII**</td></tr>
<tr><td>**BAY:**</td><td>POHUE HALAWA KIHOLO MAMALA KAMOHIO KANEOHE WAIAGUA KAWAIHAE MAUNALUA</td></tr>
<tr><td>**BEACH:**</td><td>WAIKIKI</td></tr>
<tr><td>**CAPITAL:**</td><td>HONOLULU</td></tr>
<tr><td>**CHANNEL:**</td><td>AUA KAIWI KALOHI PAILOLO</td></tr>
<tr><td>**COUNTY:**</td><td>MAUI KAUAI HAWAII HONOLULU</td></tr>
<tr><td>**CRATER:**</td><td>KILAUEA</td></tr>
<tr><td>**DESERT:**</td><td>KAU</td></tr>
<tr><td>**DISTRICT:**</td><td>KONA PUNA</td></tr>
<tr><td>**FISH:**</td><td>ULUA AKULE MOANO</td></tr>
<tr><td>**FORMER NAME:**</td><td>SANDWICH</td></tr>
<tr><td>**HARBOR:**</td><td>PEARL</td></tr>
<tr><td>**HEAD:**</td><td>DIAMOND</td></tr>
<tr><td>**ISLAND:**</td><td>MAUI OAHU KAUAI KAULA LANAI NIIHAU MOLOKAI</td></tr>
<tr><td>**MOUNTAIN:**</td><td>KAALA KOHALA KAMAKOU MAUNAKEA LANAIHALE</td></tr>
<tr><td>**MOUNTAIN RANGE:**</td><td>KOHALA KOOLAU WAIANAE</td></tr>
<tr><td>**NATIVE:**</td><td>KANAKA</td></tr>
<tr><td>**STATE BIRD:**</td><td>NENE GOOSE</td></tr>
<tr><td>**STATE FLOWER:**</td><td>HIBISCUS</td></tr>
<tr><td>**STATE NICKNAME:**</td><td>ALOHA</td></tr>
<tr><td>**STATE TREE:**</td><td>CANDLENUT</td></tr>
<tr><td>**TOWN:**</td><td>EWA AIEA HANA HILO LAIE PAIA KAPAA KEAAU LIHUE MAILI KAILUA KEKAHA PAHALA HONOKAA KAHULUI KANEOHE WAHIAWA WAIANAE WAILUKU HONOLULU PAPAIKOU</td></tr>
<tr><td>**TREE:**</td><td>KOA NAIO WILIWILI</td></tr>
<tr><td>**VALLEY:**</td><td>MANOA</td></tr>
<tr><td>**VOLCANO:**</td><td>KILAUEA HUALALAI MAUNAKEA MAUNALOA</td></tr>
</table>

HAWAIIAN KANAKA KAMAAINA
HAWFINCH KATE GROSBEAK
HAWK IO EYAS KITE SELL ALLAN BATER BUTEO CADGE EYESS HOICK HOUGH REACH RIVER STOOP BAWREL FALCON FOOTER HIGGLE KEELIE MERLIN MUSKET OSPREY PALLET PEDDLE RAMAGE RAPTOR RIFLER SHIKRA VERMIN BUZZARD GOSHAWK HAGGARD HARRIER HERONER KESTREL LENTNER STANIEL SWOOPER BRANCHER CARACARA HARROWER LENTINER PASSAGER ROUGHLEG SPARHAWK TALENTER TARTARET MORTARBOARD
(— FIGHT) CRAB
(CAGE FOR —S) MEW
(COUPLE OF —S) CAST
(CROP OF —) GORGE
(FEMALE —) FORMAL FORMEL
(MALE —) JACK TASSEL TERCEL
(SMALL —) ELANET
(UNTAMED —) HAGGARD
(YOUNG —) EYAS NIAS BOWET BOWESS BRANCHER
(PREF.) HIERACO
HAWKER CRIER CRYER BADGER CADGER COSTER DUFFER JOWTER PEDDER PETHER CAMELOT CHAPMAN HIGGLER MERCURY PEDDLER CRATEMAN GLASSMAN HUCKSTER
HAWKEYE STATE IOWA
HAWKING FALCONRY
HAWKMOTH SPHINX
HAWK PARROT HIA
HAWKWEED DINDLE BUGLOSS FIREWEED OXTONGUE
HAWSE BAG JACKASS
HAWSER FAST WARP HEADLINE

HAWTHORN HAW MAY QUICK THORN AIGLET MAYBUSH COCKSPUR MAYBLOOM MAYTHORN QUICKSET
(FRUIT OF —) HAZEL PEGGLE
HAY HEI RIP MATH RAKH RISP FETTLE STOVER WINDLIN SWEEPAGE
(— CUT FINE) CHAFF
(— PUT IN BARN) END
(— SPREADER) TEDDER
(BUNDLE OF —) TRUSS
(PILE OF —) TUMBLE
(ROW OF —) WINDROW
(SECOND-GROWTH —) EDDISH
(SMALL LOAD OF —) HURRY
(SMALL PIECE OF —) TATE
HAYCOCK MOW COIL HOVEL QUILE SHOCK DOODLE HIPPLE LAPCOCK HAYSHOCK
HAYFIELD PARK RAKH MOWING
HAYFORK PIKE PICKEL
HAYLOFT LOFT TALLET SCAFFOLD
HAYMAKER PICKMAN
HAYMOW GOAF HAYLOFT OVERDEN OVERHEAD
HAYRACK HECK HAYRIG THRIPPLE
HAYSTACK COB PIKE RICK HOVEL HAYRICK STACKAGE
HAYSUCK FYSOGE
HAY SWEEP BUCK
HAYWARD MEADSMAN
HAZAN CANTOR CHAZZAN
HAZARD DIE LAY LOT JUMP PAWN RISK WAGE JENNY LOSER PERIL CHANCE DANGER NIFFER BALANCE IMPERIL VENTURE ENDANGER JEOPARDY SANDTRAP
(BILLIARDS —) INOFF
(GOLF —) TRAP BUNKER
(ROAD —) ESS
HAZARDOUS NICE NASTY RISKY CHANCY QUEASY RISQUE UNSAFE UNSURE PARLOUS PERILOUS
HAZARDOUSLY CHANCILY
HAZE FOG URE FILM GLIN MIST REEK SMOG TRUB DEVIL GAUZE HAZLE SMEETH
(— AND SMOKE) SMAZE
HAZEL AGLET AIGLET COBNUT MUFFIN FILBERT HAZELNUT NOISETTE
(— FOR THATCHING) SPRAYS
HAZEL HOE PULASKI
HAZELNUT NIT HAZEL FILBERT
HAZEL TREE AVELLANO
HAZILY DIMLY
HAZINESS HAZE GRAYOUT
HAZO (FATHER OF —) NAHOR
(MOTHER OF —) MILCAH
HAZY DIM ABLUR FOGGY MISTY MUZZY SMOKY THICK VAGUE BLURRY CLOUDY DREAMY OBSCURE SMUISTY NEBULOUS
(NOT —) OPEN
HE A E HI HO HEH HEY HIM HYE SHE ESSO ILLE THON CESTUI
(— DIED) OB
(— GAVE AND DEDICATED) DDD
(— MADE) F FEC
(— PAINTED IT) PNXT
(— READS) LEG
(— WAS NOT FOUND) NEI

HEAD BIT BUT COP DON FAT MIR NAB NOB PEN POW TOP BEAN BOSS CAPE COCO CONK COSP CROP DATU DEAN DOME HELM JOLE JOWL KAID KNOB LEAD LOAF MAKE MASK NOLL PASH PATE POLL RAIS TETE TURN YEAD ALDER ATTIC BLADE BLOCK BONCE CHIEF CHUMP CROWN DATTO MAZER ONION RISER SCALP SHODE SKULL START TIBBY TROPE BELFRY BLANCH CABEZA CENTER CHAULE COBBRA COCKER DAROGA EXARCH GARRET GATHER HEADER KAISER MAHANT MAZARD NAPPER NODDLE PALLET RUBRIC SCONCE CAPITAL CAPTAIN COCONUT COSTARD COSTREL COXCOMB CRUMPET CUPHEAD GENARCH HEADING HEGUMEN NUCLEUS PRELATE TOPKNOT CALABASH CEPHALON DECURION DIRECTOR DUFFADAR FOUNTAIN HEADLINE INITIATE PHYLARCH POINTING TOPPIECE CAPERNOITIE
(— IN PARTICULAR DIRECTION) STEM
(— OF ABBEY) ABBOT
(— OF ALEMBIC) MITER MITRE
(— OF BEAR, WOLF OR BOAR) HURE
(— OF CABBAGE) LOAF
(— OF CEREAL) EAR
(— OF CHAIR) MAKER
(— OF CLOVER) COB SUCKER
(— OF COLUMN) CHAPITER
(— OF COMET) COMA
(— OF CONVENT) ABBESS SUPERIOR
(— OF CRIME SYNDICATE) CAPO
(— OF DANDELION) BLOWBALL
(— OF DRILL BRACE) CUSHION
(— OFF AGAIN) RESUME
(— OF FAMILY) ALDER COARB COMARB GOODMAN
(— OF FISH) JOWL
(— OF GANG) TINDAL
(— OF GOVERNMENT) MUKHTAR
(— OF GRAIN) ICKER
(— OF GUILD) ALDERMAN
(— OF HAIR) SUIT CRINE FLEECE CHEVELURE
(— OF HARPOON) BOMB
(— OF HERRING) COB
(— OF INSTITUTION) WARDEN
(— OF JEWISH ACADEMY) GAON
(— OF LANCE) MORNE MOURNE
(— OF LOOM) JACQUARD
(— OF MONASTERY) HEGUMEN
(— OF MUSHROOM) BUTTON
(— OF MUSICAL INSTRUMENT) SCROLL
(— OF NUNNERY) DAME
(— OF ORDER) MURSHID
(— OF PROJECTILE) OGIVE
(— OF RING) CHATON
(— OF RIVET) BULLHEAD FLATHEAD SNAPHEAD
(— OF SEPT) COARB COMARB
(— OF STATE) CAUDILLO PRINCEPS
(— OF TAPEWORM) SCOLEX
(— OF TREE) COMA
(— OF 10 MONKS) DEAN
(— ON) SQUARE

(— PREMATURELY) BUTTON
(— USED AS TARGET) SARACEN
(— WRAP) SNOOD
(ACADEMIC —) DEAN
(BAKED SHEEP'S —) JAMES JEMMY
(BALD —) PILGARLIC
(BARBED —) FLUKE
(DRAGON'S —) RAHU
(EMPTY —) MONAD
(FLOWER —) DAISY ARNICA BUTTON PINBALL
(FLOWER —S) CURD ANTHEMIS
(FROM — TO FOOT) CANAPE
(LATHE —) POPPET
(NAIL —) ROSEHEAD
(POPPY —) POST
(PRINTED —) BOXHEAD
(SEED — OF FLAX) HOPPE
(SHRUNKEN —) TSANTSA
(PL.) GEONIM
(PREF.) CEPHAL(O) CORY(PH)(PHO) CRANIO
(SUFF.) CEPHALIC CEPHALOUS CEPHALUS CEPHALY PATE
HEADACHE HEAD SODA BUSTHEAD HEADWARK MIGRAINE CEPHALALGY
HEADBAND MITER MITRE VITTA CARCAN DIADEM TAENIA CIRCLET GARLAND CARCANET FOOTBAND STEPHANE
HEADBOROUGH VERGES
HEADCAP SETHEAD CAPELINE
HEADCLOTH ROMAL RUMAL
HEADDRESS FLY TOP TOY APEX COIF FRET HEAD HORN KELL PARE POUF TETE TIRE TOUR AEGIS AMPYX CROWN GABLE LAUTU PASTE POLOS PSHEM SHAKO TIARA TOWER VITTA ALMUCE ATTIRE ATTOUR BONNET CASQUE CORNET FAILLE HENNIN KENNEL KULLAH MORCAP PINNER TIRING TUINGA BANDORE COMMODE FLANDAN MORTIER PSCHENT STEEPLE TABLITA THERESE TRESSON TUTULUS BILIMENT BINNOGUE BYCOCKET CAPRIOLE COIFFURE HEADGEAR HEADTIRE KAFFIYEH MASKETTE STEPHANE TRESSURE
(— OF DOGES) TOQUE
(— OF GODS) MODIUS
(— OF POPE) REGNUM
(— WITH LONG LAPPET) PINNER
(HIGH —) TOWER STEEPLE FONTANGE
(MEDIEVAL —) BARB
(WIDOW'S —) BANDORE
HEADED KNOTTED
(— OUT) RIZZOMED
(SUFF.) PATED
HEADER BINDER BONDER NOBBER SADDLE KNOBBER HEADSMAN STRETMAN
HEADFAST HEADROPE
HEADFIRST HEADLONG
HEADFOREMOST TOPSAIL
HEADFRAME POPPET GALLOWS
HEADGEAR (ALSO SEE HEADDRESS) HIVE PASTE BONNET BRIDLE HEADWEAR

HEADHUNTER LAKHER TAIYAL ATAIYAL QUIANGAN
HEADING END HEAD STOW LEMMA PILOT TROPE WICKET CAPTION DIPHEAD HEADILY STENTON WITCHET FOREHAND STENTING
(MASTHEAD —) EDITOR
HEADLAND KOP PEN RAS BILL CAPE HEAD MULL NASE NAZE NESS NOOK NOUP PEAK SCAW THRUM FORELAND PROMONTORY
HEADLESS ACEPHALOUS
(PREF.) ACEPHALO
HEADLINE HEAD STAR LABEL BANNER CAPTION DROPLINE SCREAMER STREAMER SCAREMONGER
HEADLONG FULL RANK AHEAD HASTY PRONE STEEP SUDDEN RAMSTAM TANTIVY GADARENE HEADLING RECKLESS PRECIPITATE
HEADMAN BAAS JARL CHIEF DATTO MALIK PATEL POMBO VIDAN ATAMAN CABEZA HETMAN INDUNA LOWDAH LULUAI POTAIL TOPMAN KOMARCH ALDERMAN CABOCEER CAPITANO HEADSMAN KONOHIKI MALGUZAR MOKADDAM PENGHULU PRINCEPS STAROSTA TENIENTE
HEADMASTER HEAD RECTOR REGENT PRECEPTOR
HEADMOST FOREMOST
HEADNOTE SYLLABUS
HEADPHONE
(PL.) CANS
HEADPIECE CAP POT BASKET CASQUE HELMET PALLET TESTER TREMOR BASINET BRASSET CASQUET CHAMFRON TESTIERE
HEADPIN KINGPIN
HEADQUARTERS BASE DEPOT YAMEN AGENCY FONDACO EXCHANGE BATTALION
(MILITARY —) SHAKO PENTAGON
HEADROPE BALK BAULK HEADLINE
HEADSET PHONES
HEADSHIP CHIEFTY
(SPIRITUAL —) KHALIFAT
HEADSPACE OUTAGE
HEADSTALL HALTER BRADOON BRIDOON JAQUIMA
HEADSTOCK POPPET
HEADSTONE STELE
HEADSTRONG RASH COBBY RACKLE STOCKY UNRULY HOTSPUR RAMSTAM VIOLENT WAYWARD PERVERSE STUBBORN
HEADWAITER CAPTAIN
HEADWAY WAY DENT SEAWAY WAYGATE HEADROOM
HEADWORD ENTRY
HEADY BOLD WINY NAPPY HUFFCAP
HEAL CURE HALE KNIT MEND SAIN AMEND COVER LEECH SALVE SOUND WHOLE PHYSIC RECURE SUPPLE TEMPER WARISH CLEANSE GUARISH RECOVER REDRESS RESTORE MEDICATE
(— OVER) INCARN
HEALD CAMB DUPE HAVEL
HEALED WHOLE
HEALER CURER ALTHEA SHAMAN

HEALER POWWOWER PRACTITIONER
(SUFF.) IATRIST
HEALING IATRIC POWWOW
BALSAMIC CURATION IATRICAL
SANATION
(PREF.) IATR(O)
(SUFF.) IATRIA IATRIC(S) IATRIST
IATRY
HEALTH SAP HAIL HEAL SONS
QUART SALEW LIKING PLEDGE
SALUTE SANITY EUCRASY SLAINTE
EUCRASIA TONICITY VALETUDE
VALIDITY GESUNDHEIT
(— **ORGANIZATION**) HMO
(**GOOD** —) PROST PLIGHT PROSIT
VERDURE GESUNDHEIT
(**ILL** —) SICKNESS
(**NORMAL** —) USUAL
(**RESTORE CONDITION OF** —)
REHAB
(PREF.) HYGE(I) HYGI SALUTI
HEALTHFUL HEALTHY HYGIENIC
SALUTARY SANATORY SANITARY
HEALTHY FIT FIER FIRM HALE IRON
SAFE SANE SANO TIDY WELL
BONNY HODDY QUART SOUND
STOUT VALID ENTIRE HEARTY
ROBUST BOUNCING LAUDABLE
SALUTARY SANITARY VEGETOUS
VIGOROUS
(PREF.) SANI
HEALTHY-LOOKING BONNY
BONNIE
HEAP COP CUB HOT MOW PIE SOW
TON BALE BING BULK DECK DESS
HILL HOTT LEET PILE POKE POOK
RAFF REEK RUCK SESS TASS TUMP
AMASS CLAMP CLUMP COUCH
CROWD SHOCK SORUS STACK
WOPSE BURROW HIPPLE HOTTER
ISLAND JALOPY MEILER OODLES
QUARRY RICKLE RUCKLE SCRAPE
SORITE TOORIE BOUROCK
CUMULUS ENDORSE HAYCOCK
HAYRICK HURROCK TOOROCK
TUMMELS WINDROW BASURALE
CONGERIES ACCUMULATE
ACCUMULATION
(— **HAY**) UNCOCK
(— **OF DEAD BODIES**) CARNAGE
(— **OF GAME**) QUARRY
(— **OF GRAIN**) BING
(— **OF MORTAR**) BINK
(— **OF ORE**) PANEL MONTON
(— **OF PRODUCE**) BURY CLAMP
(— **OF REFUSE**) BURROW BASURAL
(— **OF RUBBISH**) GAGING
(— **OF SILVER ORE**) TORTA
(— **OF SLAIN**) CARNAGE
(— **OF STONES**) AHU MAN CAIRN
SCRAE SCREE HURROCK MONTJOY
(— **OF VEGETABLES**) HOG
(— **REPROACHES**) KICK
(— **TOGETHER**) AGGEST HOWDER
LUMBER CUMULATE
(— **UP**) HILL SACK AGGEST
ACERVATE AGGERATE OVERHEAP
(**COMBUSTIBLE** —) PYRE
(**MANURE** —) HOTT MIXEN
(**PROMISCUOUS** —) RAFF
(**STONE** —) CAIRN
(PREF.) CUMULI CUMULO SOREDI
SORI SORO THOMO

HEAPED COCKED ACERVATE
CUMULATE
HEAR EAR LIST OYES OYEZ LEARN
LITHE HARKEN LISTEN HEARKEN
(— **CONFESSION**) SHRIVE
(— **DIRECTLY**) IMPINGE
(PREF.) ACOU(O) AUDIO
HEARD AUDIBLE
(**EASILY** —) CLEAR
(**VAGUELY** —) RUMOROUS
HEARER AUDIENT AUDITOR
HEARING EAR LIST OYER AUDIT
SOUND ASSIZE AUDIENCE
AUDITION
(**DISORDERED** —) PARACUSIS
(PREF.) ACOU(O)
(SUFF.) ACOUSIA ACOUSIS ACUSIA
ACUSIS
HEARKEN HARK HEAR HEED LIST
TEND LITHE ATTEND HARKEN
INTEND
HEARSAY REPORT ACCOUNT
HEARSE HACK CATAFALCO
HEART AB COR ANGI CORE GIST
HATI PUMP RAAN SOUL YOLK
ANGIO BOSOM BOWEL CHEER
JARTA QUICK BREAST CENTER
CENTRE DEPTHS HASLET MIDDLE
NATURE TICKER VISCUS COURAGE
EMOTION ESSENCE FEELING
(— **OF DIXIE**) ALABAMA
(— **OF ROTTEN TREE**) DADDOCK
(**DEAR** —) DILIS
(PREF.) ANGI ANGIO CARDI(A)(O)
CORDI PHREN(O)
(**AROUND THE** —) PERICARDI(O)
(SUFF.) CARDIA CARDIUM
HEARTACHE SORROW
HEARTBEAT STROKE
(SUFF.) CROTIC
HEARTBREAK HOUSE (**AUTHOR OF**
—) SHAW
(**CHARACTER IN** —) DUNN ELLIE
MANGAN HESIONE MAZZINI
HUSHABYE SHOTOVER UTTERWORD
HEARTBURN PYROSIS
HEART CHERRY GASKINS
HEARTEN BIELD CHEER HEART
SPIRIT EMBOLDEN INSPIRIT
HEARTFELT DEAR DEEP REAL TRUE
INFELT INWARD CORDIAL GENUINE
SINCERE
HEARTH EARD SOLE TEST ASTRE
CUPEL EARTH FOCUS FOGON
FOYER INGLE SMOKE CHIMNEY
(— **GODDESS**) VESTA
HEARTH-MONEY FUMAGE
HEARTILY INLY AGOOD DEARLY
FREELY WARMLY SHEERLY
DINGDONG INWARDLY STRONGLY
HEARTINESS GOODWILL
HEARTLESS SARDONIC
HEARTLESSNESS CYNICISM
HEART OF MIDLOTHIAN (**AUTHOR**
OF —) SCOTT
(**CHARACTER IN** —) MEG JOHN
DAVID DEANS EFFIE MADGE BUTLER
GEORGE JEANIE REUBEN GEORDIE
PORTEUS STAUNTON ROBERTSON
MURDOCKSON
HEARTSEASE PANSY
HEARTSICK (**BE** —) ACHE
HEARTSORE ACHING

HEARTTHROB DUNT FLAME
HEARTWOOD ALOES HEART SAPAN
SPINE GUAYAB BUBINGA
DURAMEN TRUEWOOD
HEARTY REAL WARM BUXOM
COBBY FRECK HEAVY STOUT
DEVOUT ENTIRE ROBUST STANCH
BOBBISH CORDIAL EARNEST
HEALTHY RAFFING SINCERE
HEARTFUL VIGOROUS
BOISTEROUS
HEAT HET HOT RUT SUN TAP BOIL
FIRE GLOW SALT WARM ARDOR
BEATH BROIL CALOR CAUMA
CHAFE FEVER PRIDE PROUD STECH
TEPOR TRIAL ACHAFE ANNEAL
DEGREE DIGEST FERVOR HEATEN
IGNITE SCORCH SEASON SIZZLE
SPARGE WARMTH CALCINE
CALORIC ENCHAFE FERMENT
FLUSTER INCENSE INFERNO
PASSION SWELTER UPERIZE
CALIDITY PRESSURE MICROWAVE
(— **GENTLY**) SOAK
(— **OF BATTLE**) PRESS
(— **SCRAP IRON**) BUSHEL
(— **SWEETEN, AND SPICE**) MULL
(— **TOBACCO**) SAP
(**ROWING** —) REPECHAGE
(**SCORCHING** —) EWDER
(**TRIAL** —) REPECHAGE
(PREF.) CALORI PYR(O)
THERM(ATO)(O)
(**BURNING** —) KAUMO
(**MODIFIED BY** —) COCTO
(SUFF.) THERM(Y)
HEATED WARM FIERCE STEAMY
HEATER GAT GUN FIRE COCKLE
PISTOL SMOKER CHAFFER
CHOFFER LATROBE
(**WATER** —) BOILER
HEATH BENT YETH BESOM BRIAR
BRIER ERICA ERICAD COMMONS
HEATHER RHODORA CRAKEBERRY
(PREF.) ERICO
HEATHCOCK GROUSE
HEATHEN AKKUM PAGAN ETHNIC
PAYNIM GENTILE PROFANE
SARACEN GENTILIC
HEATHENISM ODINISM OTHINISM
PAGANISM
HEATHER BENT GRIG LING BROOM
ERICA HEATH HADDER
HEATHERY LINGY
HEATH PEA CARMELE
HEATING BAKEOUT BURNING
HEATLESS ATHERMIC
HEAVE GAG BUNG HEFT HOVE KECK
LIFE QUAP FETCH HOIST SCEND
SURGE BUCKLE KECKLE POPPLE
ESTUATE
HEAVEN SKY HIGH ABOVE BLISS
DYAUS ETHER GLORY ASGARD
CANAAN HIMMEL SVARGA
SWARGA URANUS WELKIN
KINGDOM OLYMPUS DEVALOKA
EMPYREAL EMPYREAN PARADISE
SVARLOKA VALHALLA
(**12TH PART OF** —) HOUSE
(PL.) ARCH LIFT LANGI HEIGHT
REGION SPHERE ELEMENT
TENGERE EMPYREAN KAMALOKA
(PREF.) URAN(I)(O) URANOSO

HEAVENLY ABOVE DIVINE ANGELIC
BLESSED URANIAN ETHEREAL
OLYMPIAN AMBROSIAL
HEAVEN'S MY DESTINATION
(**AUTHOR OF** —) WILDER
(**CHARACTER IN** —) BAT HERB
BRUSH COREY EFRIM LOUIE MCCOY
BURKIN CROFUT GEORGE JESSIE
MARGIE MORRIE DOREMUS
QUEENIE ROBERTA BLODGETT
ELIZABETH
HEAVENWARD ZIONWARD
HEAVER COALY DANNER HEFTER
HEAVILY SOSS CLOIT CLYTE HEAVY
PLUMP SADLY SOUSE SWACK
HEAVINESS DOLE HEFT GLOOM
POISE WEIGHT GRAVITY
(— **OF MIND**) GLOOM
HEAVING HEFT SWELL
HEAVY FAT HOT SAD CLIT DEEP
DOWF DULL HARD BEEFY BURLY
DENSE DOWFF DUNCH GRAVE
GREAT GROSS HEFTY HOGGY STIFF
THARF THERF THICK WROTH
CHARGE CLUMPY CLUMSY
COSMIC DOUGHY DRAGGY HEARTY
LEADEN LIVERY LOGGER SODDEN
STODGY STRONG STUPID
WOODEN INSIPID LABORED
LIVERED LUMPING MASSIVE
ONEROUS OUTSIZE PESANTE
WEIGHTY CUMBROUS GRIEVOUS
PERSANTE PREGNANT THUMPING
PONDEROUS SATURNINE
(— **LOOKING**) HORSY
(PREF.) BARY GRAVI HADR(O)
HEAVY-FOOTED SOGGY LEADEN
INFICETE
HEBDOMAD WEEK
HEBDOMADARY WEEKLY
HEBE (**FATHER OF** —) JUPITER
(**HUSBAND OF** —) HERCULES
(**MOTHER OF** —) JUNO
HEBER (**GRANDFATHER OF** —)
ASHER
(**SON OF** —) SOCHO
(**WIFE OF** —) JAEL
HEBREW RABBINIC
HEBRIDES (**ISLAND OF** —) IONA
HARRIS
(**ISLAND OF** —) MULL SKYE ULST
BARRA ISLAY LEWIS
HEBRON (**FATHER OF** —) KOHATH
HECATE TRIVIA
(**FATHER OF** —) PERSES
(**MOTHER OF** —) ASTERIA
HECKELPHONE OBOE HAUTBOY
HECKLE BAIT GIBE HACK RAZZ
HARRY BADGER DERIDE HARASS
HECTOR NEEDLE HATCHEL
HECTIC ETIK SEPTIC HECTIVE
FEVERISH FRENETIC FRENZIED
HECTOLITER VAT
(5.82 —**S**) LEAGUER
HECTOR BAIT HUFF BULLY HARRY
TEASE WORRY HARASS HECKLE
BLUSTER BRAVADO BROWBEAT
(**FATHER OF** —) PRIAM
(**MOTHER OF** —) HECUBA
(**SLAYER OF** —) ACHILLES
(**WIFE OF** —) ANDROMACHE
HECUBA (**DAUGHTER OF** —)
POLYXENA

(FATHER OF —) DYMAS CISSEUS
(HUSBAND OF —) PRIAM
(SON OF —) PARIS HECTOR HELENUS POLYDORUS
HEDDA GABLER (AUTHOR OF —) IBSEN
(CHARACTER IN —) THEA BRACK DIANA HEDDA EILERT GABLER GEORGE TESMAN ELVSTED JULIANA LOVBERG
HEDDLE CAMB DOUP HAVEL HEALD
(PL.) CAAM
HEDGE BAR HAW HAY HYE OXER SAVE BEARD EDDER FENCE FRITH FUDGE HOVER MOUND QUICK COPPER FRIGHT RADDLE ENCLOSE QUICKSET RUFFMANS SEPIMENT SURROUND THICKSET
(PREF.) SEPI SEPTATO
(SUFF.) SEPTATE
HEDGE BINDWEED CREEPER HELLWEED WOODBINE
HEDGEHOG ORCHEN TENREC URCHIN ECHINUS ERICIUS YLESPIL HEDGEPIG HERISSON
HEDGE LAUREL TARATA
HEDGE MUSTARD BANKWEED FLUXWEED
HEDGE NETTLE STACHYS
HEDGE PARSLEY HOGWEED
HEDGE-PRIEST PATRICO
HEDGE SPARROW DICKY DONEY DICKEY EYSOGE PHILIP CHANTER DUNNOCK HAYSUCK PINNOCK TITLING ACCENTOR
HEDGEWOOD LAYER
HEED EAR CARK COME CURE GAUM HEAR KEEP LOOK MIND NOTE OBEY RECK TEND TENT VISE WARE YEME AWAIT TASTE VALUE ATTEND INTENT NOTICE REGARD REMARK REWARD CAUTION OBSERVE RESPECT SUSPECT THOUGHT OBSERVATION
HEEDFUL WARE ATTENT DILIGENT VIGILANT REGARDFUL
(ANXIOUSLY —) JEALOUS
HEEDFULNESS CARE CAUTION
HEEDLESS DEAF RASH BLIND DIZZY GIDDY BLITHE REMISS UNWARY LANGUID UNHEEDY CARELESS LISTLESS MINDLESS RECKLESS WISTLESS NEGLECTFUL
HEEDLESSLY BLIND HEADLONG
HEEL CAD TIP BUTT CALX FROG JERK HIELD LOUSE SPIKE TALON DOTTLE BUDMASH INCLINE BOOTHEEL
(— IN) SHOUGH
(— OF GATE) HARR
(— OF HORSESHOE) SPONGE
(— OF SWORD BLADE) TALON RICASSO
(— OVER) SEEL TILT CAREEN
(PREF.) CALCANEO TAL(I)(O)
HEEL BEVEL RAND
HEELING ALIST
HEEL PLATE SHOD CLEAT
HEELTAPS LEES DREGS
HEFT WEIGHT
HEFTY HEAVY
HE-GOAT
(PREF.) HIRCO

HEIFER IO QUI QUEE QUEY QUOY BULLER STOCKER
(— IN 2ND YEAR) STIRK
(YEARLING —) BURLING
HEIGH-HO HECH
HEIGHT SUM ACME ALTO APEX FELL HIGH LOFT MOTE PINK TUNE CREST HICHT STATE ALTURE INCHES SUMMIT CEILING COMMAND HEIGHTH STATURE SUPREME ALTITUDE EMINENCE HAUTESSE SIDENESS VERTICAL ACROPOLIS
(— OF AMBITION) EVEREST
(— OF EXALTATION) RUFF RUFFE
(— OF EXCELLENCE) TIPTOP
(— OF FASHION) GO
(— OF INSPIRATION) ESTRO
(— OF PERFECTION) PRIME
(— OF PROSPERITY) GLORY
(— OF ROOM) STUD STUDDING
(— OF SAIL) HOIST
(GREATEST —) NOON SUMMIT ZENITH
(ROCKY —) KNOT
(PREF.) ACR(O) BATHO BATHY BATO HYPS(I)(O)
HEIGHTEN ENDOW EXALT FORCE RAISE ACCENT BOLSTER ELEVATE ENHANCE SUBLIME ESCALATE
(— FLAVOR) PETUNE
HEINOUS SWART CRYING WICKED SCARLET FLAGRANT GRIEVOUS ATROCIOUS
HEIR SCION SPRIG COHEIR HERITOR LEGATEE APPARENT PARCENER
(— APPARENT) ATHELING ETHELING
(CELTIC —) TANIST
(CELTIC CHIEF'S —) TANIST
(FEMALE —) DISTAFF
(PREF.) HEREDI HEREDO
HEIRESS BEGUM PORTIA FORTUNE HERITRIX
HEIRLOOM
(PL.) CIMELIA
HEL (FATHER OF —) LOKI
(MOTHER OF —) ANGURBODA
HELAH (HUSBAND OF —) ASHUR
(SON OF —) TEKOA
HELEB (FATHER OF —) BAANAH
HELEK (FATHER OF —) GILEAD
HELEN (PURSUER OF —) PARIS
HELENUS (FATHER OF —) PRIAM
(MOTHER OF —) HECUBA
(SON OF —) CESTRINUS
(WIFE OF —) ANDROMACHE
HELEZ (FATHER OF —) AZARIAH
HELI (SON OF —) JOSEPH
HELIANTHEMUM SUNROSE
HELICAL SPIRAL
HELICAON (FATHER OF —) ANTENOR
(MOTHER OF —) THEANO
(WIFE OF —) LAODICE
HELICOPTER HOVER COPTER CHOPPER MEDEVAC WINDMILL WHIRLYBIRD
(— TO REMOVE CASUALTIES) DUSTOFF
(ARMED —) GUNSHIP
(MOVE LIKE A —) HOVER
HELIOGRAPH (USE A —) SIGNAL
HELIOPOLIS ON

HELIOS HYPERION PHAETHON
(DAUGHTER OF —) CIRCE PASIPHAE
(FATHER OF —) HYPERION
(MOTHER OF —) THEIA
(SISTER OF —) EOS SELENE
(SON OF —) AEETES PHAETHON
HELIOSIS SUNBURN
HELIOTROPE HELIO BENNET SETWALL GIRASOLE TURNSOLE VALERIAN
HELIPORT SKYPORT
HELIX COIL SPIRAL
HELIXIN HEDERIN
HELL PIT POT HECK PAIN ABYSS AVICI BLAZE DEUCE HADES SHEOL BLAZES NARAKA TARTAR TOPHET TUNKET ABADDON GEHENNA HELLBOX INFERNO TORMENT TARTARUS BARATHRUM PERDITION PANDEMONIUM
(RIVER IN —) STYX LETHE
(PREF.) TARTARO
HELLBENDER TWEEG MENOPOME
HELLE (BROTHER OF —) PHRIXUS
(FATHER OF —) ATHAMAS
(MOTHER OF —) NEPHELE
HELLEBORE POKE BUGBANE ITCHWEED LINGWORT LUNGWORT NOSEWORT POKEROOT VERATRUM EARTHGALL
HELLEN (FATHER OF —) DEUCALION
(MOTHER OF —) PYRRHA
(SON OF —) DORUS AEOLUS XUTHUS
(WIFE OF —) ORSEIS
HELLER HALER HALFER
HELLERI SWORDTAIL
HELL-FIRE BRIMSTONE
HELLGRAMMITE DOBSON SIALID CLIPPER CRAWLER SPRAWLER
HELLION TERROR
HELLISH HELLY AVERNAL SATANIC STYGIAN DEVILISH INFERNAL TOPHETIC
HELLKITE FIEND
HELLO CIAO HALLO HILLO HULLO HILLOA CHINCHIN
HELM KEY STEER STERN TIMON HELMET TIMBER STEERAGE
HELMET CAP POT CASK HELM HOOD ARMET CREST GALEA MAZER MOUND BARBEL BEAVER CASQUE CASTLE GALERA HEAUME MORION PALLET SALADE SALLET TESTER BASINET CASQUET GALERUM GALERUS AVENTAIL BURGANET BURGONET HEADGEAR KNAPSCAP SCHAPSKA SKULLCAP TARNHELM TESTIERE KNAPSKULL
(— PART) VENTAIL
(CRASH —) SKIDLID
(PITH —) TOPI TOPEE
(PREF.) GALEI
HELMET-SHAPED GALEATE
HELMSMAN PILOT STEER GLAUCUS TIMONEER
HELON (SON OF —) ELIAB
HELP AID BOT ABET AMOI BACK BOOT CAST LIFT STOP AVAIL BOOST FAVOR FRITH HEEZE RESET SPEED START STEAD YELDE ASSIST HELPER RELIEF REMEDY SECOND SUCCOR UPTAKE BENEFIT

BESPEED BESTEAD CHEVISE COMFORT FORWARD FURTHER HELPING IMPROVE PRESIDY PROMOTE REDRESS RELIEVE SUPPORT SUSTAIN ADJUMENT BEFRIEND SUFFRAGE
(— FORWARD) FRANK FURTHER
(— IN GROWTH) NOURISH
(— ON) ADVANCE
(— ONWARD) FORWARD
(— OUT) FIRK
(HIRED —) LABOR
HELPER AID CAD FOAL HELP MATE PAGE ANSAR AIDANT BARBOY COOKEE DIENER FLUNKY JUMPER NIPPER TENTER WAITER ADJOINT ADJUNCT ADJUTOR ANCILLA CASHBOY GALOPIN SUMPMAN SWAMPER HELPMATE OFFSIDER SCULLION TROUNCER
(— IN GLASSWORKS) SNAPPER
(BLACKSMITH'S —) STRIKER
(CHIMNEY SWEEP'S —) CHUMMY
(COOK'S —) SLUSHY
(COOPER'S —) TUBBIE
(HORSESHOER'S —) FLOORMAN
(LEGAL —) PARACLETE
(PICKPOCKET'S —) BULKER
(YOUNG —) FOAL
HELPFUL GOOD AIDANT AIDFUL HELPLY SECOND SPEEDY USEFUL ADJUVANT HELPSOME OBLIGING SINGULAR SERVICEABLE
HELPING HELP ORDER AIDANT PORTION SERVING ADJUTORY ADJUVANT
(SECOND —) FOLLOW
HELPLESS NUMB SILLY ABJECT UNABLE AIDLESS FORLORN FECKLESS HAVELESS REDELESS
HELPLESSNESS ADYNAMIA
HELTER-SKELTER TAGRAG PELLMELL
HELVE HELM SHAFT
HELVE HAMMER OLIVER
HEM HUM WLO FELL SLIP WELT HEDGE SPLAY PURFLE TURNUP HEMMING TURNING SURROUND
(— AND HAW) HAVER
(— GLOVE) WRIST
(— IN) BOX LAP GIRD BEBAY BESET IMPALE BESIEGE COMPASS ENCLOSE ENVIRON STRAITEN SURROUND
(— IN FISH) EBB
(— OF SAIL) TABLING
(— OF TROUSERS) CUFF
(PREF.) LIMBI
HEMAM (BROTHER OF —) HORI
(FATHER OF —) LOTAN
HEMAN (FATHER OF —) JOEL ZERAH
(GRANDFATHER OF —) SAMUEL
HEMATITE ORE OLIGIST SANGUINE
HEMDAN (FATHER OF —) DISHON
HEMICRANIA MIGRAINE
HEMIEPES ENOPLION
HEMIMORPHITE CALAMINE
HEMIOLIC SESCUPLE
HEMISTICH SECTION
HEMITHEA (BROTHER OF —) TENES
(FATHER OF —) CYCNUS
(MOTHER OF —) PROCLEA

HEMLOCK BUNK CASH KELK BENNET CICUTA COWBANE DEATHIN SHINWOOD
HEMOPHILIAC BLEEDER
HEMORRHAGE STAXIS APOPLEXY BLEEDING HEMOPTOE PETECHIA
HEMOSTATIC RHATANY ERIGERON
HEMP IFE KEF KIF TOW BANG CARL POOA RINE SANA SUNN ABACA BHANG DACHA DAGGA FIQUE GANJA HURDS MURVA RAMIE SABZI SISAL AMBARY CABUYA FIMBLE LIAMBA NALITA SINAWA AMYROOT CABULLA GAGROOT NIYANDA PANGANE PITEIRA SOSQUIL BIRDSEED CANNABIS CHUCKING LOCOWEED NECKWEED NEPENTHE MARIJUANA
(KIND OF —) ALOE
(REFUSE —) HARDS HURDS
(PREF.) CANNABI
HEMP AGRIMONY EUPATORY HEMPWEED
HEMPEN NOGGEN
HEMP NETTLE IRONWORT
HEMPWEED BONESET DUCKBLIND
HEN FOWL BIDDY CHUCK LAYER BROODY MABYER PULLET SULTAN CLOCKER HOVERER PARTLET LANGSHAN
(— THAT HAS NOT LAID) TOWDIE
(— WITH CHICKENS) CLUCK
(— WITH SHORT LEGS) GRIG
(BROODY —) SITTER
(FATHER OF —) ZEPHANIAH
(FATTENED —) POULARD
(MUD —) COOT
(1-YEAR-OLD —) YEAROCK
HENBANE HEBENON CHENILLE
HENCE AWAY ERGO HYNE THUS AVAUNT HETHEN HEREOUT
HENCEFORTH YET ERGO HENCE
HENCHMAN FELLOW SATRAP SERVANT FOLLOWER RETAINER UNDERLING
HEN COOP CAVY CAVIE
HENGEST (BROTHER OF —) HORSA
(KINGDOM FOUNDED BY —) KENT
(SON OF —) AESC
HEN HARRIER FALLER KATABELLA
(IMMATURE —) RINGTAIL
(MALE —) MILLER
HENHOUSE ROOST
HENNA MENDY ALCANNA ALHENNA CAMPHIRE
HENNIN STEEPLE
HENPECK NAG
HENRY QUAD HAWKIN SECOHM HEINRICH QUADRANT
HENRY ESMOND (AUTHOR OF —) THACKERAY
(CHARACTER IN —) HOLT FRANK HENRY JAMES MOHUN ESMOND RACHEL STUART BEATRIX FRANCIS
HENRY IV-PART I (AUTHOR OF —) SHAKESPEARE
(CHARACTER IN —) JOHN OWEN PETO BLUNT HENRY PERCY POINS EDMUND SCROOP THOMAS VERNON WALTER DOUGLAS HOTSPUR MICHAEL QUICKLY RICHARD BARDOLPH FALSTAFF GADSHILL MORTIMER ARCHIBALD

GLENDOWER LANCASTER WESTMORELAND
HENRY IV-PART II (AUTHOR OF —) SHAKESPEARE
(CHARACTER IN —) DAVY DOLL FANG JOHN PETO WART BLUNT GOWER HENRY POINS RUMOR SNARE FEEBLE MORTON MOULDY PISTOL SCROOP SHADOW SURREY THOMAS MOWBRAY QUICKLY SHALLOW SILENCE TRAVERS WARWICK BARDOLPH BULLCALF CLARENCE FALSTAFF HARCOURT HASTINGS HUMPHREY COLEVILLE LANCASTER TEARSHEET WESTMORELAND NORTHUMBERLAND
HENRY V (AUTHOR OF —) SHAKESPEARE
(CHARACTER IN —) NYM GREY JAMY YORK ALICE BATES COURT GOWER HENRY LEWIS EXETER ISABEL PISTOL SCROOP THOMAS BEDFORD BOURBON CHARLES MONTJOY ORLEANS WARWICK BARDOLPH BURGUNDY FLUELLEN GRANDPRE RAMBURES WILLIAMS ERPINGHAM KATHARINE MACMORRIS SALISBURY GLOUCESTER WESTMORELAND
HENRY VIII (AUTHOR OF —) SHAKESPEARE
(CHARACTER IN —) ANNE VAUX BUTTS DENNY HENRY SANDS BULLEN LOVELL SURREY THOMAS WOLSEY ANTHONY BRANDON CRANMER NORFOLK SUFFOLK CAMPEIUS CAPUCIUS CROMWELL GARDINER GRIFFITH NICHOLAS PATIENCE GUILDFORD KATHARINE BUCKINGHAM ABERGAVENNY
HENRY VI-PART I (AUTHOR OF —) SHAKESPEARE
(CHARACTER IN —) JOAN JOHN LUCY HENRY BASSET EDMUND TALBOT THOMAS VERNON ALENCON BEDFORD CHARLES RICHARD SUFFOLK WARWICK WILLIAM BEAUFORT BURGUNDY FASTOLFE GARGRAVE MARGARET MORTIMER REIGNIER GLANSDALE LAPUCELLE SALISBURY WOODVILLE GLOUCESTER PLANTAGENET
HENRY VI-PART II (AUTHOR OF —) SHAKESPEARE
(CHARACTER IN —) SAY CADE DICK HUME IDEN JACK JOHN VAUX BEVIS GOFFE HENRY PETER SMITH EDWARD GEORGE HORNER SCALES ELEANOR HOLLAND MATTHEW MICHAEL RICHARD SIMPCOX STANLEY SUFFOLK WARWICK BEAUFORT CLIFFORD HUMPHREY JOURDAIN MARGARET SOMERSET STAFFORD ALEXANDER SALISBURY SOUTHWELL BUCKINGHAM BOLINGBROKE PLANTAGENET
HENRY VI-PART III (AUTHOR OF —) SHAKESPEARE
(CHARACTER IN —) BONA HUGH JOHN HENRY LEWIS MARCH EDMUND EDWARD EXETER GEORGE OXFORD RIVERS BOURBON

NORFOLK RICHARD RUTLAND STANLEY WARWICK CLIFFORD HASTINGS MARGARET MONTAGUE MORTIMER PEMBROKE SOMERSET STAFFORD MONTGOMERY PLANTAGENET WESTMORELAND NORTHUMBERLAND
HEP (NOT —) ICKY
HEPATICA AI TRINITY
HEPATITIS FAVISM JAUNDICE
HEPHAESTUS LEMNIAN
(FATHER OF —) ZEUS
(MOTHER OF —) HERA
(WIFE OF —) CHARIS
HEPHZIBAH (HUSBAND OF —) HEZEKIAH
(SON OF —) MANASSEH
HER A ARE SHE HARE HERS HURE
HERA JUNO
(FATHER OF —) CRONOS KRONOS
(HUSBAND OF —) ZEUS
HERALD BODE LYON USHER BEADLE DECLARE FORERUN PREFACE STENTOR USHERIN BLAZONER PRECURSE PROCLAIM ROTHESAY MESSENGER
HERALDIC FECIAL FETIAL
HERALDRY ARMORY
HERB ANU APE PIA RUE UDO WAD ALOE ANET ANYU ARUM COUS DILL HEMP IRID LEEK MINT MOLY POLY RAPE RUTA SAGE SOLA WOAD WORT YAMP YARB AVENS AWIWI BLITE BRUSH CANNA CHIVE CREAT CROUT DAGGA DAISY DRABA GALAX GAURA GILIA GRASS HOSTA LOASA LUFFA MEDIC MUNGO NANCY ORACH SEDGE SEDUM SENNA SOLAH STOCK SULLA TANSY THYME ZIZIA ALLIUM ARALIA ARNICA AXSEED BAGPOD BAMBAN BANANA BLINKS BORAGE CANCER CATGUT CATNIP CENIZO CICELY CISTUS CLOVER COCASH COLEUS CONIUM COWISH COWPEA CRAMBE ELODEA ENDIVE ERYNGO FENNEL GALAXY GINGER HARMEL HYSSOP KOCHIA KRIGIA KRIGLA LOOFAH LOVAGE RAMTIL RATTLE ROBERT SESAME SESELI SHEVRI WASABI ABRONIA ALPINIA ALTHAEA ALYSSUM AMORPHA AMSONIA ANCHUSA ANEMONE ANGELON ARACHIS BABIANA BABROOT BARTSIA BIRDEYE BLINKER BONESET BUGSEED BUGWEED CHICORY CUDWEED CULVERS DEWDROP DYEWEED EPISCIA ERODIUM FREESIA FROGBIT FUMMORY GERBERA GINSENG GOITCHO GOSMORE GOUAREE GUAYULE GUNNERA HARMALA HEDEOMA HENBANE HERBLET IRESINE ISOLOMA JONQUIL LABIATE LEWISIA LINNAEA MARANTA MIMULUS MUDWEED MUDWORT MULLEIN MUSTARD NAILROD NEMESIA NIEVETA PAVONIA PETUNIA PINESAP PINWEED PUCHERA ROSELLE SAFFLOR SALSIFY SEEDBOX SKIRRET SOWBANE SPIGNEL STACHYS ABELMOSK

ABELMUSK ACANTHUS ACONITUM AGERATUM ALOCASIA ALUMROOT AMBROSIA AMMOBIUM ANGELICA ARGEMONE ASPHODEL BEDSTRAW CALATHEA CAPEWEED CARELESS CENTAURY CHENILLE COLLOMIA COSTMARY COWWHEAT CRASSULA CROMWELL DANEWEED DEERWEED DROPWORT ECHINOPS EGGPLANT EREMURUS ERIGERON EUCHARIS FEVERFEW FLEABANE FOWLFOOT GAYWINGS GERARDIA GESNERAD GESNERIA GHETCHOO GLOXINIA GOATROOT GUZMANIA HAREBELL HEPATICA HEUCHERA HIBISCUS HOLEWORT HONEWORT HOROKAKA HUDSONIA IRONWEED LICORICE LOCOWEED MANDRAKE MANFREDA MANYROOT MARDOWRT MARJORAM MARTYNIA MURRNONG PHACELIA PINKROOT PLUMBAGO POKEWEED SACALINE SAINFOIN SALICORN SAMPHIRE SANDBURR SCABIOUS SHINLEAF SMALLAGE SNOWDROP SOAPROOT SOAPWORT STAPELIA SUNDROPS TETRIFOL TOCALOTE WOODRUFF MONEYWORT PUSSYTOES RUDBECKIA SAXIFRAGE SPIKENARD NASTURTIUM PENNYCRESS PERIWINKLE SARRACENIA
(— COUNTERACTING POISON) CANCER
(— OTHER THAN GRASS) FORB
(AROMATIC —) MINT ANISE CLARY CATNIP CAAPEBA CHERVIL DITTANY
(BIENNIAL —) LEEK PARSLEY ANGELICA
(BULBOUS —) LILY CANNA ALLIUM CRINUM GARLIC NERINE SQUILL BABIANA SHALLOT DOGTOOTH SLANGKOP
(FABULOUS —) MOLY PANAX PANACE
(FLOATING —) FROGBIT
(FORAGE —) FITCHES GOITCHO
(MEDITERRANEAN —) CRAMBE
(MYTHICAL —) MOLY
(POISONOUS —) CONIUM HEMLOCK MONKSHOOD
(PL.) POTAGERIE
HERBAGE HAY BITE GRASS GRAZE PICHI ADONIS SACATE ZACATE GRAZING
HERB EVE IVA IVY
HERB GRACE RUE
HERBICIDE IPE DIQUAT DIURON SILVEX DALAPEN DALAPON LINURON MONURON ATRAZINE PARAQUAT PICLORAM PROPANIL SIMAZINE
HERB IMPIOUS DOWNWEED HOARWORT
HERB PARIS TRUE ONEBERRY TRUELOVE
HERB ROBERT JENNY ROBIN ROBERT
HERCULEAN HUGE
HERCULES ERCLES ALCIDES HERSHEF OETAEUS OVILLUS HERAKLES

(BROTHER OF —) IPHICLES
(CAPTIVE OF —) IOLE
(FATHER OF —) JUPITER
(MOTHER OF —) ALCMENA
(WIFE OF —) HEBE MEGARA
DEIANIRA
HERCULES ALLHEAL OPOPANAX
HERCULES-CLUB ARALIA IVYWORT
RUEWORT SHOTBUSH
HERD BOW CAM MOB BAND CREW
GAME GANG HEAD RACE ROUT
RUCK TAIL TEAM TRIP DROVE
FLOCK HEARD TROOP CAVIYA
CHOUSE HIRSEL HUDDLE MANADA
MEINIE REMUDA SPREAD THRAVE
CREAGHT RANGALE SHEPHERD
(— CATTLE) TAIL WRANGLE
(— OF CATTLE) FLOTE
(— OF COLTS) RAG
(— OF HORSES) RACE HARAS
HARRAS REMUDA
(— OF SEALS) PATCH
(— OF WHALES) GAM
(— OF WILD SWINE) SOUNDER
HERDBOY BOUCHAL
HERDER DROVER FEEDER HERDBOY
HERDSMAN AMOS SENN GAUCHO
HERDER LOOKER PASTOR
HERDBOY LLANERO THYRSIS
VAQUERO BEASTMAN DAMOETAS
GARTHMAN NEATHERD PASTORAL
PASTURER RANCHERO SWANHERD
WRANGLER
HERE ICI ADSUM READY WHERE
HEREAT HITHER PRESENT
(— AND THERE) ABOUT ABROAD
AROUND PASSIM SPARSIM
HEREAFTER BEYOND
HEREDITAMENT LAND
HEREDITARY INBORN INNATE
KINDLY LINEAL PATERNAL
HEREDITY (— UNIT) RNA
HEREIN WITHIN
HERESY DOCETISM KETZEREI
MISBELIEF
HERETIC BUGGER KETZER ZINDIQ
LOLLARD PATARIN PROFANE
SECTARY JUDAIZER MISCREANT
SABELLIUS MISBELIEVER
(PL.) ACEPHALI
HERETICAL HERETIC HETERODOX
MISCREANT
HERETO HITHER
HERETOFORE ERST BEFORE
ERENOW EREWHILE FORMERLY
HEREWARD THE WAKE (AUTHOR
OF —) KINGSLEY
(CHARACTER IN —) BRAND GODIVA
MARTIN WILLIAM ALFTRUDA
HEREWARD TORFRIDA LIGHTFOOT
HERITAGE DESCENT HEIRDOM
HEIRSHIP PATRIMONY
HERMA MERCURY
HERMAPHRODITE MOPH SCRAT
ANDROGYNOUS
HERMAPHRODITIC BISEXED
BISEXUAL MONOECIOUS
HERMAPHRODITISM GYNANDRY
HERMAPHRODITUS (FATHER OF —)
MERCURY
(MOTHER OF —) VENUS
HERMENEGILD (FATHER OF —)
LEOVIGILD

HERMES MERCURY AGORAIOS
CYLLENIUS
(FATHER OF —) ZEUS
(MOTHER OF —) MAIA
HERMIA (BELOVED OF —) LYSANDER
(FATHER OF —) EGEUS
HERMIONE (FATHER OF —)
MENELAUS
(HUSBAND OF —) PYRRHUS
(MOTHER OF —) HELEN
HERMIT ARME MUNI HANIF MINIM
ANCHOR SANTON SULLEN ASCETIC
EREMITE RECLUSE TAPASVI
ANCHORET MARABOUT SOLITARY
HERMITAGE ASHRAM ASHRAMA
RECLUSE
HERNIA BURST RAMEX BREACH
RUPTURE MEROCELE
(SUFF.) CELE COELE COELUS
HERO CID KIM RAB AJAX EGIL IDAS
KAMI MAUI NALA NATA OFFA RINK
YIMA ADAPA BERNE DEBON ETANA
FAUST GHAZI HODER HOTHR
IRAYA KIPPS MARKO ORSON
TASSO TIMON VOTAN EGMONT
FIGARO GIDEON GOLIAS HEROIC
IASION IOLAUS MAUGIS MINYAS
OSSIAN PELHAM PENROD RIENZI
ROLAND RUSTAM SIGURD TARZAN
USHEEN VATHEK ALCESTE
BOGATYR DEMIGOD FAUSTUS
GLUSKAP GRINDER INGOMAR
JAMSHID MACBETH MANRICO
MARMION MAZEPPA ORLANDO
OTHELLO PALADIN RAFFLES
TANCRED THALABA THESEUS
TROILUS ULYSSES VOLPONE
WERTHER WIDSITH WIELAND
ACADEMUS ARGONAUT
CHAMPION FANSHAWE FERUMBAS
FRITHJOF GAEDHEAL GILGAMES
I AMMIKIN MALAGIGI MORGANTE
OROONOKO PALMERIN PARSIFAL
PERICLES RASSELAS RODOMONT
SUPERMAN TRISTRAM WAVERLEY
(LOVER OF —) LEANDER
(TRIBAL —) JUDGE
HERODIAS (BROTHER OF —)
AGRIPPA
(FATHER OF —) ARISTOBULUS
(HUSBAND OF —) HEROD
HEROIC EPIC FELL GREAT NOBLE
EPICAL FEATLY EXTREME GALLANT
VALIANT FEARLESS HEROICAL
HOMERIAN INTREPID SPLENDID
HEROIN JUNK SCAG SKAG SNOW
HORSE JONES SMACK STUFF
HEROINE AIDA EMMA MIMI RUTH
JULIE MEDEA NORMA SEDNA
THAIS ESTHER FEDORA GUDRUN
HELENA JUDITH JULIET MARTHA
MIGNON PAMELA PHEDRE
RAMONA ROMOLA SALOME SILVIA
TRILBY UNDINE ERMINIA EVELINA
GALATEA GINEVRA GRAINNE
HEROESS MONIMIA SHIRLEY
ZENOBIA ZULEIKA ATALANTA
ISABELLA MARGARET PATIENCE
POMPILIA ROSMUNDA SOFRONIA
HEROISM VALOR BRAVERY
COURAGE PROWESS
HERON QUA POKE SOCO CRAIG
CRANE EGRET FRANK HERNE

PADDY QUAWK YABOA AIGRET
GAULIN KIALEE KOTUKU QUAKER
SQUAWK BITTERN CRABIER
GOLIATH HANDSAW QUABIRD
SQUACCO BOATBILL GAULDING
HERONSEW UMBRETTE
(— FLOCK) SIEGE
HERON'S-BILL ERODIUM
HERPES DARTRE TETTER
HERPES ZOSTER ZONA SHINGLES
HERRING ALEC BRIT CHUB SHAD
SILD BLOAT CAPON CISCO DORAB
HILSA MARAY MATIE SPRAT
KIPPER POLLAN TAILOR ANCHOVY
BLOATER CLUPEID NAILROD
ROLLMOP SHADINE BLUEBACK
BRISLING BUCKLING CROPSHIN
GRAYBACK QUODDIES SCUDDAWN
STRADINE
(— SEASON) DRAVE
(— UNIT) LAST MAZE
(FEMALE —) RAUN
(LAKE —) KIYI CISCO
(RED —) CAPON SOLDIER
(SMOKED —) BLOATER
(YOUNG —) COB BRIT SILD GILE
SILL SOIL WILE BRITT COBBE MATIE
SPRAT SARDINE SPERLING
(2, 3 OR 4 —S) WARP
HERS HERN SHISN
HERSE (FATHER OF —) CECROPS
(SISTER OF —) AGRAULOS
(SON OF —) CEPHALUS
HERSELF HI HER SELF ITSELF
HERSEY (— LOCALE) ADANO
HERSHEF ARSAPHES
HESHVAN BUL CHESHVAN
HESIONE (FATHER OF —)
LAOMEDON
(HUSBAND OF —) TELAMON
(RESCUER OF —) HERCULES
HESITANCY HANG
(— IN SPEECH) BALBUTIES
HESITANT SHY CAGY CHARY
GROPING HALTING RETICENT
SUSPENSE
(NOT —) FACILE
HESITATE COY HEM BALK STAY
STOP CHECK CRANE DEMUR
DOUBT FORCE PAUSE STALL
STAND STICK SUSSY WAVER
BOGGLE FALTER HANKER LINGER
MAMMER RELUCT SCOTCH
TARROW TARTLE BALANCE
PROFFER SCRUPLE STAGGER
STAMMER SWITHER THRIMBLE
(— IN SPEAKING) HACKER
HESITATING JUBUS HALTING
BACKWARD DOUBTFUL JUBEROUS
TIMOROSO
HESITATION HANG HINK WAND
PAUSE STAND STICK SUSSY
SWITHER
(SPEECH —) STAMMER
HESPERUS VESPER
HESRON (FATHER OF —) REUBEN
HESSIAN BURLAP
HESTIA (FATHER OF —) KRONOS
(MOTHER OF —) RHEA
HETAERA LAIS THAIS PHRYNE
MISTRESS
HETER-
(PREF.) XEN(O)

HETERODOX HERETIC SINISTRAL
HETERODOXY HERESY CACODOXY
HETEROGENEOUS MIXED MOTLEY
UNLIKE DIVERSE PIEBALD
ASSORTED
HETEROMYS SACCOMYS
HETEROSEXUAL STRAIGHT
HETEROTROPHIC HOLOZOIC
HETEROXENOUS INDIRECT
HETEROZYGOUS CROSS SPLIT
IMPURE
HETMAN ATAMAN
HEW CUT HAG CHIP SNAG STUB
SHRED SLICE
(— OUT) CARVE
(— STONE) CHAR
HEWER JOEY GETTER GIDEON
FACEMAN
HE WHO GETS SLAPPED (AUTHOR
OF —) ANDREYEV
(CHARACTER IN —) ALFRED ZINIDA
BENZANO BRIQUET JACKSON
MANCINI REGNARD CONSUELO
HEX WITCH VOODOO WHAMMY
HEXAGON SEXANGLE
HEXAGONAL HEX DIMETRIC
HEXAGRAM PENTACLE
HEXAMETER MIURUS RHOPALIC
(DACTYLIC —) EPOS HEROIC
HEXOBARBITAL EVIPAL
HEXOSAN MANNAN GLUCOSAN
MANNOSAN
HEYDAY MAY HIGHDAY
HEY PRESTO SUDDENLY
HEZEKIAH (FATHER OF —) AHAZ
NEARIAH
(MOTHER OF —) ABI
HEZION (SON OF —) TABRIMON
HEZRON (FATHER OF —) PHAREZ
REUBEN
HIATUS GAP BREAK CHASM
BREACH HIATAL LACUNA
HIBERNATE SHACK WINTER
SLUMBER
HIBERNATING LATITANT
HIBERNIA EIRE ERIN IRELAND
JUVERNA
HIBERNIAN IRISHMAN IVERNIAN
HIBISCUS ROSELLE
HICCUP YEX YOX HICK HOCKET
HOQUET SINGULTUS
HICK BOOR HIND JAKE BACON
BUSHMAN CORNBALL
CHAWBACON
HICKORY NOGAL PIGNUT BULLNUT
SHAGBARK
HICKORY NUT TRYMA PIGNUT
BULLNUT KISKITOM
HICKWALL ECCLE HECKLE HICKWAY
HID LATENT
HIDDEN HID SHY DEEP DERN LOST
TECT BLIND CLOSE DOGGO DUSKY
PERDU PRIVY ARCANE BURIED
COVERT INNATE LATENT MASKED
MYSTIC OCCULT SECRET VEILED
BOSOMED CLOUDED COVERED
CRYPTIC OBSCURE RECLUSE
SUBTILE ABDITIVE ABSTRUSE
CRYPTOUS HIDEAWAY PALLIATE
SCREENED SECLUDED SNEAKING
CRYPTICAL RECONDITE
(PREF.) CRYPT(O) KRYPT(O)

HIDE HOD WRY BUFF BURY CASE CROP DARK DERN FELL FELT HILL HOOD JOUK LEAN MASK PELL PELT SCAB SKIN SKUG SNUG STOW VEIL WELL BELIE BELLY BLIND CACHE CLOAK CLOUD COUCH COVER DITCH EARTH FLANK GLOSS LAYNE LOSHE MANSE PLANT SHADE SPOIL STASH STEER TAPIS BURROW BUSHEL CASATE EMBOSS ENCASE ENCAVE ENWOMB FOREST HUDDLE IMBOSK LIELOW MANENT PELAGE SCREEN SHADOW SHIELD SHROUD ABSCOND CONCEAL COWHIDE EMBOWEL FLAUGHT OBCLUDE OVERLAY SECLUDE SECRETE SPREADY TAPPICE CARUCATE DISGUISE ENSCONCE HIDELAND HOODWINK PALLIATE PLOWLAND SQUIRREL SUPPRESS CLANDESTINE
(— AS AN EEL) MUD
(— IN WOODS) WOOD BUSHWACK
(— UNDER) BUSHEL
(CALF'S —) DEACON
(DRESSED —)S LEATHER
(HALF OF —) BEND
(HAVING SOFT —) MELLOW
(SHEEP'S —) SLAT
(TANNED —) CROP
(THICKEST —S) BACKS
(UNDRESSED —) KIP
(PL.) JUFTI JUFTS
(PREF.) DERM(AT)(ATO)(O) DORA
(SUFF.) DERM(A)(ATOUS)(IA)(IS)(Y)
HIDE-AND-GO-SEEK BOGLE WHOOP BOGGLE
HIDEAWAY MEW LAIR SHANGRILA
HIDEBOUND BORNE NARROW BIGOTED
HIDEOUS FELL GASH GRIM UGLY AWFUL TOADY DEFORM GRIMLY GRISLY HORRID ODIOUS OGRISH GHASTLY DEFORMED DREADFUL FIENDISH GRUESOME HORRIBLE SHOCKING TERRIBLE MONSTROUS
HIDEOUSLY FOULLY
HIDING DERN MICHING SECRECY ABDITIVE HIDEAWAY
HIDING-PLACE CACHE
HIEMAL WINTRY
HIERACIUM DINALE HAWKWEED
HIERARCHY SATRAPY
HIEROGLYPH CIPHER
(PL.) SIGNARY
HIEROPHANT PRIEST
HIGGLE HUCK HAGGLE
HIGH UP ALT AIRY DEAR HAUT MAIN MUCH RANK TALL ACUTE ALOFT BRENT CHIEF CLOSE DRUNK FIRST GREAT HAUTE LOFTY MERRY NOBLE SHARP SPACY STEEP BOMBED COSTLY RIPPED SHRILL SPACEY STONED ZONKED EMINENT EXALTED HAUGHTY STICKLE SUBLIME TOPPING VIOLENT ELEVATED FOREMOST PIERCING TOWERING WIPEDOUT SPACEDOUT
(— AND MIGHTY) HOGEN
(— IN CHROMA) STRONG
(— IN PITCH) ALT ACUTE
(— IN RANK) MUCH
(— ON DRUGS) STONED
(— PITCH) ORTHIAN
(BE —) FLY
(MOST —) SERENE
(PRETTY —) STIFFISH
(VERY —) TAUNT RAREFIED RARIFIED
(PREF.) ALTI HYPS(I)(O)
(ON —) HYPS(I)(O)
HIGHBORN NOBLE GENEROUS
HIGHBOY TALLBOY
HIGHBRED SOFT REFINED
HIGHBROW EGGHEAD
HIGH-CLASS CLASSY UPSTAGE
HIGH-CLIMBER TOPPER
HIGH-COLORED BLOWSY BLOWZY
HIGH-CROWNED COPATAIN
HIGHER OVER ABOVE SENIOR SUPERIOR
(PREF.) SUPER(O) SUPRA
HIGHEST ACE TOP HEXT FIRST EXTREME MAXIMAL SUPREME BUNEMOST HIGHMOST OVERMOST
(— IN DEGREE) LAST
HIGHFALUTIN PAUGHTY
HIGH-FED BEANY
HIGH-FLAVORED GAMY
HIGH-FLOWN TALL TUMID
HIGH-HANDED BOSSY CAVALIER
HIGH-HAT SNOOT
HIGHLAND RAND CERRO
HIGHLANDER GAEL TARTAN NAINSEL PLAIDMAN REDSHANK TREWSMAN UPLANDER
(PL.) TREWS TARTAN
HIGHLIGHT ADORN HEIGHTEN PINPOINT SALIENCE
HIGHLY THRICE
HIGH-MINDED HAUGHT
HIGHNESS ALTESSE ALTEZZA ALTITUDE
(— OF PRICE) DEARTH
HIGH-PITCHED ACUTE PROUD PIPING TREBLE ORTHIAN SHRIEKY
HIGH-POWERED INTENSE MAGNUM
HIGH-PRICED DEAR
HIGH-RIGGER TOPPER
HIGH-SOUNDING BIG BOMBAST MAGNIFIC SONORANT SONOROUS SOUNDING
HIGH-SPIRITED METTLED CRANK FIERY FIERCE LIVELY GALLANT GINGERY RAMPANT CAVALIER VASCULAR
HIGH-SPIRITEDNESS SPLEEN
HIGH-STRUNG HYPER TENSE NERVOUS
HIGHTAIL (— IT) LEAVE SCRAM
HIGH-TONED TONY DICTY DICKTY
HIGHWAY VIA WAY BELT ITER PATH PIKE ROAD TOBY BOLOS ARTERY CAUSEY COURSE RUMPAD SKYWAY STREET BELTWAY CALZADA FREEWAY RAMPIRE THRUWAY ARTERIAL AUTOBAHN BROADWAY CAUSEWAY CHAUSSEE HIGHROAD MOTORWAY SPEEDWAY
(— ROBBERY) TOBY
(LOCATED OFF THE —) DEVIOUS

(PART OF —) EXIT GORE LANE LOOP RAMP ACCESS BRIDGE ISLAND MEDIAN DIVIDER ROADWAY JUNCTION OVERPASS SHOULDER UNDERPASS INTERSECTION
HIGHWAYMAN PAD RIDER SCAMP BANDIT CUTTER PADDER RODMAN BRIGAND FOOTPAD LADRONE PRANCER RODSMAN TOBYMAN BIDSTAND DAMASTES HIGHTOBY HIJACKER LANCEMAN OUTRIDER BANDOLERO
HIGH-WROUGHT INTENSE
HIKE UP MUSH WALK MARCH RAISE TRAMP RAMBLE ADVANCE INCREASE
HILARIOUS MAD RORTY JOVIAL JOCULAR RAUGHTY CHIRPING GLORIOUS
HILARITY GIG JOY GLEE LAUGH MIRTH GAIETY GAYETY DEVILRY JOLLITY WHOOPEE MERRIMENT
HILKIAH (FATHER OF —) AMZI HOSAH
(SON OF —) ELIAKIM GEMARIAH JEREMIAH
HILL BEN DEN DUN HOE HOW KOP LOW PUY TOR VAN ALTO BANK BERG BRAE BULT BUMP COTE DAGH DENE DOWN DRUM FELL HIGH HONE KNAP LOMA LUMP MESA MOOR MOTE NOUP PAHA TOFT ZION BARGH BUTTE CERRO CLIFF COAST HEUGH KNOCK KNOLL KOPJE MORRO MOUND MOUNT STILL SWELL TELLE WATCH ASCENT BARROW BEACON COBBLE COLLIS COPPLE CUESTA HEIGHT HEUVEL LOMITA SPRUNT STRONE CAELIAN CAPITOL COLLINE DRUMLIN HILLOCK NUNATAK PICACHO SOWBACK VIMINAL AREOPAGY CATOCTIN DRUMLOID FOOTHILL MONTICLE QUIRINAL MONADNOCK
(— OF SAND) DENE DUNE
(— OF STRATIFIED DRIFT) KAME
(— UP) MOLD
(ARABIAN —) TEL
(BROAD-TOPPED —) LOMA
(CONICAL —) LAW PAP PINGO
(CRAGGY —) TOR
(FORTIFIED —) RATH
(HIGH —) BEN
(ISOLATED —) HUM TOFT BARGH BUTTE
(LAST —) STRONE
(LOW —) HOW BAND DENE WOLD KOPPIE SOWBACK
(NIPPLELIKE —) PAP
(NORTH AFRICAN —) JEBEL DJEBEL
(RESIDUAL —) CATOCTIN
(ROUNDED —) DODD HONE MAMELON
(SAND —) DENE
(SHARP-POINTED —) KIP KIPP PIKE
(SMALL —) KNAP KNOLL KOPJE KOPPIE HILLOCK MOLEHILL
(STEEP —) BREW BROW STILL
(STONY —) ROACH
(SUGAR-LOAF —) SPITZKOP
(WOODED —) HOLT HURST
(PREF.) BUNO

HILLARY (CONQUEST OF —) EVEREST
HILLBILLY HOEDOWN
HILL-FORT RATH
HILLOCK HOW LOW NOB BOSS BULT DOWN KAME KNAP KNOB TERP TOFT TUMP BERRY HEAVE HURST KNOCK KNOLL KOPJE MOUND TOMAN BARROW BURROW COPPET HILLET HUMMOCK MAMELON TUMMOCK TUMULUS MOLEHILL
HILLSIDE BENT BRAE COTE EDGE CLEVE FALDA SLADE SLOPE FELLSIDE SIDEHILL
HILLTOP DOD NAB PIKE RISE KNOLL
HILLY KNOBBY
HILT HAFT BASKET POIGNET HANDGRIP
(— OF DAGGER) DUDGEON
(PART OF —) BOW CUT GRIP RING GUARD BUTTON POMMEL CAPSTAN LANGUET QUILLON RICASSO CROSSPIECE COUNTERGUARD
HILUM EYE SCAR HILUS PORTA NUCLEUS CICATRIX
HIM A EN HE HEM HIN LUI MUN
HIMATION PALLION PALLIUM
HIMERUS (FATHER OF —) LACEDAEMON
(MOTHER OF —) TAYGETE
(SISTER OF —) CLEODICE
HIMSELF HIM IPSE SELF HISSEL ITSELF HERSELF HISSELF
HIND ROE CONY HINE HINT CONEY HEARST HINDER VENISON CABRILLA
HIND-BODY ABDOMEN
HINDBRAIN RHOMBENCEPHALON
HINDER BAR DAM KEP LET MAR ROB CLOG HELP SLOW SLUG STAY STOP TENT WARN AFTER BLOCK CHEAT CHECK CHOKE CRAMP DEBAR DELAY DETER EMBAR ESTOP HEDGE SLOTH STYMY THROW TRASH ARREST CUMBER DETAIN FORBID FORLET HAMPER HARASS HINNER IMPEDE IMPEND INJURE RETARD RETRAL SCOTCH TAIGLE UNHELP ABSTAIN DEPRIVE FORELAY IMPEACH INHIBIT OCCLUDE PREVENT TRACHLE ENCUMBER HANDICAP IMPEDITE OBSTRUCT PRECLUDE PROHIBIT POSTICOUS
(PREF.) POSTERO
HINDERED FOUL
HINDERER LETTER
HINDERMOST LAG ACHTER
HINDQUARTER HIND HAUNCH
(HALF —) LEG
(PL.) FOUCH CRUPPER HAUNCHES
HINDRANCE BAR LET RUB BALK CURB REIN SLUG SNAG STAY STOP BLOCK CHECK DELAY HITCH TRASH ARREST CUMBER DENIAL HINDER OBJECT REMORA UNHELP SHACKLE UNSPEED DISCOUNT DRAWBACK HOLDBACK OBSTACLE PULLBACK
HINDU BABU BABOO SUDRA BABHAN BANIAN BANYAN GENTOO JAJMAN KALWAR KHATRI NAYADI

SHUDRA THAKUR VAISYA
MUSAHAR VAIRAGI
(— ASCETIC) SADHU
(— ASSOCIATION) SANGH
(— CASTE) TELI VARNA
(— CUSTOM) SATI SUTTEE
(— ENERGY) SAKTI SHAKTI
(— IDOL) SWAMI
(— INTERJECTION) OM AUM
(— PHILOSOPHY) YOGA VEDANTA
(— PRACTICE) PURDAH
(— RITE) PUJA POOJA
(— SAGE) RSI RISHI
(— SCRIPTURE) VEDA
(— SECT) SIKH
(— VARNA MEMBER) SUDRA
(— WORSHIPER) SAKTA
(— WRITING) VEDA
(— WRITINGS) SMRTI TANTRA
(TWICE-BORN —) KSATRIYA
HINDUSTANI URDU HINDI OORDOO
DAKHINI
HINDWING BALANCER
HINGE RUN BAND BUTT FLAP HARR
TRIM TURN CARDO CROOK GEMEL
JOINT MOUNT NODUS SKELL
SKEWL TWIST DEPEND GARNET
GEMMEL GIMMER HANGLE
JIMMER SNIREL CHARNEL
COXCOMB FULCRUM HOLDBACK
(— OF BIVALVE SHELL) CARDO
(— OF HELMET) CHARNEL
(— TOGETHER) SCISSOR
(HALF OF —) FLAP
(PHILATELIC —) STICKER
(PREF.) GINGLYMO
HINGED SWING
(SUFF.) POMATOUS
HINNY BURDON JUNNEL JENNET
HINT CUE TIP ASTE ITEM MINT TANG
WIND WINK CHEEP IMPLY INFER
POINT SPELL STEER TOUCH TRACE
WHIFF ALLUDE BREATH GLANCE
OFFICE SMATCH TIPOFF WHEEZE
INKLING LEADING MEMENTO
POINTER SUGGEST UMBRAGE
WHISPER WRINKLE ALLUSION
INDICATE INNUENDO INTIMATE
TELLTALE
(HUNT —) CLUE
HINTERLAND BLED BACKLAND
HIP HEP MOD COXA HUCK FUNKY
PITCH SHOOP HAUNCH HUCKLE
TRENDY TUNEDIN HIPBERRY
TURNEDON
(— JOINT) COXA THURL
(— OF ROSE) BERRY CHOOP SHOOP
(— OF TARGET) SPOT
(PREF.) COX(O) ISCHI(O) OSPHY(O)
HIPBONE FINBONE PINBONE
EDGEBONE SIDEBONE
HIPPARCHUS (BROTHER OF —)
HIPPIAS
(FATHER OF —) PISISTRATUS
HIPPARETE (BROTHER OF —)
CALLIAS
(FATHER OF —) HIPPONICUS
(HUSBAND OF —) ALCINIADES
HIPPEUS KNIGHT
HIPPIE FREAK
HIPPOCAMPUS ERGOT HIPPO
SEAHORSE

HIPPOCOON (BROTHER OF —)
TYNDAREUS
(FATHER OF —) OEBALUS
(MOTHER OF —) GORGOPHONE
(SLAYER OF —) HERCULES
HIPPODAMIA (FATHER OF —)
ADRASTUS OENOMAUS
(HUSBAND OF —) PELOPS
PEIRITHOUS
(SON OF —) ATREUS TROEZEN
PITTHEUS THYESTES
HIPPOLYTUS (FATHER OF —)
THESEUS
(MOTHER OF —) HIPPOLYTE
(STEPMOTHER OF —) PHAEDRA
HIPPOMENES (FATHER OF —)
MEGAREUS
(MOTHER OF —) MEROPE
(WIFE OF —) ATALANTA
HIPPONACTEAN SCAZON
HIPPOPOTAMUS HIPPO ZEEKOE
BEHEMOTH BUNODONT
HIPPOTHOE (FATHER OF —)
MESTOR
(MOTHER OF —) LYSIDICE
(SON OF —) TAPHIUS
HIPPOTRAGUS OZANNA
EGOCERUS
HIPSTER HEPCAT
HIRAH (COMPANION OF —) JUDAH
HIRE FEE JOB HAVE MEED RENT
SIGN WAGE LEASE PREST WAGES
EMPLOY ENGAGE RETAIN SALARY
TAKEON BESPEAK CHARTER
CONDUCE CONDUCT FREIGHT
STIPEND
(— CATTLE) TACK
HIRED PAID TEEKA TICCA WAGED
HIRELING HACK VENAL HACKNEY
MYRMIDON WAGELING
MERCENARY PENSIONER
PENSIONARY
HIRSUTE HAIRY PILOSE SHAGGY
TRESSY
HIS S AS ES IS HISN
HISPID STRIGOSE STRIGOUS
HISS BLOW FUFF HISH HIZZ QUIZ
SISS SIZZ GOOSE WHISS FISSLE
FIZZLE SIFFLE WHOOSH WHISTLE
SIBILATE
(— OF SWORD) SOUGH
HISSING BIRD AFFLATUS SIBILANT
HIST PEACE
HISTONE GLOBIN
HISTORIAN MORONI STORIER
ANNALIST
AMERICAN FAY FOX GAY NYE BEER
BOYD DODD FEIS FISH GARD HART
KANE MAYS SHEA ZINN ADAMS
AMORY BEARD BEMIS CURTI ELSON
FORCE GIBBS GROSS HAZEN HORAN
LEECH MAHAN MARTY MCGEE
MOORE MUNRO MYERS SMITH
STONE UNGER USHER WROTH
ABBOTT ARENDT BARBER BARZUN
BECKER BEESLY BOURNE BOWERS
BRAUER FISHER GREENE HANSEN
LATANE LOWELL MALONE MOTLEY
MUZZEY NEVINS OWSLEY PATTEE
PAXSON REEVES RHODES ROSZAK
SLOANE SPARKS STILES TOLAND
TURNER WINSOR ANDREWS
BASSETT CHAPMAN CHEYNEY

CHIDSEY CLELAND DUNNING
GARRATY GAYARRE HEADLEY
HULBERT JAMESON LEARNED
LENGYEL LOVEJOY MCELROY
MORISON PADOVER PALFREY
PARKMAN RIDPATH SCHMITT
SHANNON TICKNOR TUCHMAN
VANLOON VANTYNE BANCROFT
BETTMANN BOTSFORD BRODHEAD
CHANNING COMMAGER COOLIDGE
HILDRETH JOHNSTON MCMASTER
PENNIMAN PHILLIPS PRESCOTT
ROBINSON STEPHENS THWAITES
TRUMBULL BEVERIDGE
GROSVENOR MACDONALD
PRIESTLEY STEVENSON
KUYKENDALL MCLAUGHLIN
WESTERMANN OBERHOLTZER
ROSTOVTZEFF SCHLESINGER
ARGENTINIAN FUNES LOPEZ MITRE
CARBIA
AUSTRIAN BIBI SRBIK ARNETH
LORENZ HORMAYR LOSERTH
MENGHIN PRIBRAM ASCHBACH
HELLWALD WURZBACH SCHREIBER
BELGIAN JUSTE HYMANS GACHARD
HASSELT LAURENT PIRENNE
CANADIAN BEGG BRYCE WRONG
BIBAUD DENISON GARNEAU
BOURINOT CASGRAIN
CHINESE PANKU
COLOMBIAN ACOSTA RESTREPO
CZECH GOLL PALACKY
DANISH HOLM ALLEN BARFOD
AAGESEN AAGESON BRANDES
MOLBECH WORSAAE PEDERSEN
HAMMERICH NEERGAARD
DUTCH BOR BLOK GEYL FRUIN
HOOFT JAPIKSE BARLEAUS
HUIZINGA
ENGLISH COXE DYER HALL HYDE
MUIR OMAN PAUL ROSE STOW
TOUT WARD ACTON BIRCH BROWN
CARTE DAVIS DIXON DORAN DOYLE
EDMER FIRTH FYFFE GOOCH GREEN
GROTE GUEST HELPS INNES MERES
PARIS SMITH TERRY TOOKE WELLS
BARKER BUCKLE BURNET CAMDEN
COLOMB CREASY DUTTON FINLAY
FISHER FROUDE GIBBON GILDAS
HALLAM MILMAN PETRIE POWELL
ROSCOE SEELEY STRYPE STUBBS
TAWNEY TURNER WARNER WILSON
BEAZLEY BOULGER COULTON
DOUGLAS FORSTER FREEMAN
HASSALL HAYWARD KNOLLES
LANGTON LINGARD MITFORD
POLLARD RALEIGH SYMONDS
TOYNBEE ADOLPHUS CHADWICK
GAIRDNER GARDINER GUEDALLA
KINGLAKE MACAULAY MAITLAND
MARRIOTT OLDMIXON PALGRAVE
PHILLIPS PROTHERO STRACHEY
ARMSTRONG KINGSFORD
ROBERTSON TEMPERLEY
TREVELYAN HAVERFIELD
FINNISH FORSMAN
FRENCH FAY SEE DROZ FAIN THOU
DURUY FILON FLACH GEBD GLOTZ
GOYAU MABLY MONOD NAUDE
RENAN SOREL AULARD BALUZE
BEMONT BONNET DANIEL DAUDET
GERARD GILSON GUIZOT HAUSER

MARTIN MASSON MATTER MIGNET
OZANAM ROMIER THIERS VANDAL
VERTOT ZELLER BARANTE BLONDEL
CHENIER CHERUEL COMINES
FAGNIEZ FAURIEL JULLIAN
LAGORCE LANFREY LAVISSE
LERMINA MADELIN MEZERAY
PFISTER RAMBAUD THIERRY
DEBIDOUR DUCHESNE GODEFROY
HANOTAUX LUCHAIRE MICHELET
PARFAICT RULHIERE BEAUCOURT
BONNEMERE BOURGEOIS
HERICAULT LAMARTINE SEIGNOBOS
SIEGFRIED TILLEMONT DESJARDINS
GUIGNEBERT ROHRBACHER
CHANTELAUZE
GERMAN DAHN HEHN KAPP KOCH
LENZ NIEM ALZOG FALKE JAFFE
KLOPP KOSER LUDEN MEYER
MOSER PERTZ RANKE RIEHL SYBEL
VEHSE VOGEL VOIGT WAITZ WEBER
ZEUSS ABELIN BELOCH BOHMER
HEEREN HEIDEN KUGLER MENZEL
ONCKEN PREUSS QUIDDE RITTER
SICKEL WUTTKE ANDREAS
DROYSEN DUMMLER ECKHART
FISCHER FORSTER HAEBLER
HELMOLT HETTNER KEUTGEN
LEHMANN LINDNER NOTTECK
NUVILLE SCHAFER SCHMIDT
SCHULTE BRESSLAU DELBRUCK
DONNIGES FLEMMING GALLETTI
GERVINUS HOETZSCH HOFFMANN
KAUFMANN KROMAYER LEDEBOUR
SCHLOZER FREIDRICH LAMPRECHT
SCHIEMANN SCHMOLLER
SLEIDANUS ARCHENHOLZ
BAUMGARTEN BIEDERMANN
HIRSCHFELD LAPPENBERG
MARHEINEKE POSCHINGER
TREITSCHKE ZIMMERMANN
BRANDENBURG FALLMERAYER
GARDTHAUSEN GREGOROVIUS
SECKENDORFF
GREEK DURIS GREEN ARRIAN
STRABO BIKELAS EPHORUS
LAMBROS SOZOMEN TIMEAUS
DEXIPPUS EUSEBIUS HERODIAN
POLYBIUS XENOPHON CRATIPPUS
DIONYSIUS HERODOTUS
HESYCHIUS PHILISTUS TIMAGENES
ANAXIMENES CLITARCHUS
HELLANICUS HIERONYMUS
PHYLARCHUS THEOPOMPUS
THUCYDIDES ARISTOBULUS
MEGASTHENES OLYMPIODORUS
AGATHARCHIDES
HEBREW JOSEPHUS
HUNGARIAN FEJER TOLDY PAULER
TELEKI FESSLER FRAKNOI MAILATH
MANNHEIM MARCZALI SZILAGYI
ICELANDIC SNORRI
IRISH BURY LECKY CHESNEY
GILBERT WADDING
ITALIAN AMARI CANTU VOLPE
CANALE CIAMPI DENINA EMILIO
FEDELE GIOVIO NOVATI VASARI
ACCOLTI FERRERO VILLANI VILLARI
AMMIRATO CIBRARIO GIANNONE
MOLMENTI MURATORI BERTOLINI
LIUTPRAND SALVEMINI
GUICCIARDINI

MEXICAN ALAMAN PEREYRA CLAVIJERO BUSTAMANTE
NORWEGIAN KOHT LANGE MUNCH DIETRICHSON
PERUVIAN ULLOA
POLISH KUBALA BIELSKI CHODZKO DIUGOSZ LELEWEL SZUJSKI ASKENAZY JABLONSKI BOBRZYNSKI KUCHARZEWSKI
PORTUGUESE GOES MELO LOPES BARROS CASTANHEDA
ROMAN CATO LIVY NEPOS CORDUS FLORUS TROGUS SALLUST TACITUS APPIANUS VALERIUS EUTROPIUS SUETONIUS FENESTELLA
RUMANIAN IORGA KOGALNICEANU
RUSSIAN KAVELIN POGODIN BRUCKNER KARAMZIN MILYUKOV SOLOVIEV TURGENEV VENGEROV DRUZHININ POKROVSKI HRUSHEVSKY KOSTOMAROV
SCOTTISH MILL BOECE BROWN LAING BURTON TYTLER CARLYLE GILLIES NEILSON SPALDING BOBERTSON MACKINTOSH MACPHERSON
SPANISH AVILA LOPEZ XEREZ PINELO PULGAR TORENO DESCLOT GOMARRA HERRERA MARIANA MONCADA FERRERAS LAFUENTE MENENDEZ SEPULVEDA MONTESINOS
SWEDISH DALIN BESKOW GEIJER CARLSON FRYXELL FORSSELL MESSENIUS
SWISS KOPP BLUMER GELZER MULLER STUMPF TSCHUDI SISMONDI GAGLIARDI BURCKHARDT
HISTORICAL GENETIC
HISTORIOGRAPHER SCALD SKALD
HISTORY STORY ANNALS LEGEND RECORD SURVEY ACCOUNT ANCESTRY PROPHECY RELATION
(— OF EXPERIENCES) MEMOIRS
(— OF JAPAN) KOJIKI
(LIFE —) COURSE
(MUSE OF —) CLIO
(PAST —) RECORD
(PERIOD OF JAPANESE —) HEIAN
(PREVIOUS —) BACKGROUND
(TRIBAL —) PHYLOGENY
HISTRION ACTOR
HISTRIONIC ACTORY ACTORISH ACTRESSY
HIT BAT BOP BOX DOT GET HAT JOB PEG PIP WOW BASH BEAN BEAT BELT BIFF BLOW BOFF BONK BUST CHOP CONK DONG FOUR GOLD NAIL PINK POKE PUCK PUNT RUFF SLAM SLAP SLUG SOCK SWAT SWIP TAKE TANK TWAT WART WIPE ANGLE BOFFO CHECK CLOUT CLUNK CROWN FIVER FLICK GOUFF KNOCK PASTE POTCH PRANG PUNTA PUNTO SCORE SLASH SLOSH SMASH SMITE SNICK SOCKO SWIPE TAINT TOUCH VENUE ATTAIN DOUBLE FOURER HURTLE SCLAFF STRIKE VOLLEY ATTAINT BOFFOLA CONNECT MUZZLER SANDBAG SHELLAC WHERRET BLUDGEON BOUNDARY LENGTHER STRICKEN

(— A KEY) STRIKE
(— BALL) CUR FLY DINK DRIVE SHOOL SKITE SNICK
(— BUNT) DRAG
(— GAME) STOP
(— GENTLY) BABY
(— GLANCINGLY) TIP
(— GOLF BALL) CAN BLAST EXPLODE
(— HARD) DUMP SLOG SLUG PASTE SKELP SOUSE DEVVEL STOUSH STONKER
(— IN BOXING) LEADOFF
(— IN FACE) CLOCK
(— IN FIELD HOCKEY) CORNER
(— IN TILTING) TAINT
(— IT OFF) CLICK
(— LIGHTLY) KISS
(— ON BULL'S-EYE) GOLD
(— POORLY) DUB
(— SHARPLY) CLIP
(— SUDDENLY) ZAP
(— TOGETHER) CLASH
(— UPON) FIND
(— WITH FOOT) KICK SPURN
(BASE —) BINGLE DOUBLE SAFETY SINGLE TRIPLE SCRATCH SMOTHER
(BOXING —) SLUG PUNCH
(CRICKET —) SLOG BOUNDARY
(EASILY —) SITTING
(FENCING —) HAI HAY VENUE
(SHARP —) LICK
(SMASH —) SOCKEROO
(SOLID —) LINEDRIVE
HITCH JET TUG WED HALT HIKE ITCH KNOT LIFT PULL CATCH HOTCH SPELL TRACE FASTEN HIRSLE INSPAN MAGNUS SHUFFLE CONTRETEMPS
(— IN ROPE) CATSPAW
(NOSE —) BOZAL
HITCHHIKE HOP THUMB
HITCHHIKER PICKUP
HITCHING KNOT SHRUG
HITHER HERE
HITHERTO YET BEFORE
HITLERITE NAZI
HIT-OR-MISS CASUAL CHANCE HOBNOB CARELESS
HITTER SWATTER
HITTING BATTING SLOGGING
HITTITE HATTI KHATTI TABALIAN
HIVE GUM BIKE SKEP PYCHE STAND STATE STOCK SWARM APIARY ALVEARY BEEHIVE SWARMER
(— PLACED OVER ANOTHER) SUPER
HIVES CROUP UREDO
HLORRITHI THOR THORR
HOAGIE TORPEDO
HOAR GRAY RIME HOARY
HOARD HEAM KEEP POSE SAVE AMASS HUTCH MISER STASH STOCK COFFER MAGPIE MUCKER STOUTH GENIZAH HUSBAND SQUIRREL TREASURE
(— OF SAVINGS) STOCKING
(SECRET —) POSE
(THIEF'S —) PLANT
HOARDER MUCKER STORER HUSBAND
HOARFROST RAG HOAR RIME RIND
HOARINESS HOAR ROOP MUCOR

HOARSE RAW FOGGY GRUFF HEAZY HUSKY RAWKY ROKEY ROUGH ROUPY STOUR CROAKY CROUPY RASPED ROUPIT GRATING RAUCOUS
HOARSENESS FROG ROUP QUACK RAUCITY HASKNESS BARYPHONIA
HOARY AGED GRAY GREY HOAR WHITE FROSTY ANCIENT HOARISH INCANOUS
HOATZIN ANNA HANA HOACTZIN
HOAX BAM COD FUN GAG HUM KID RAG RIG BILK DUPE FAKE GAFF GEGG GUNK JOSH QUIZ RAMP RUSE SELL SHAM SKIT CHEAT FRAUD GREEN SHAVE SPOOF TRICK WINDY CANARD DIDDLE HUMBUG STRING BLAFLUM DECEIVE FLIVVER ARTIFICE
HOB HUB PUNCH MATRIX
HOBAB (BROTHER-IN-LAW OF —) MOSES
HOBBER LEANER
HOBBLE GIMP LOCK SPAN BUNCH HILCH HITCH STILT STUMP HABBLE HIRPLE HOPPLE LANGLE LANKET TOLTER CRAMBLE CRAMMEL CRIPPLE SHACKLE SHAFFLE SPANCEL STAGGER TRAMMEL SIDELINE
HOBBLEBUSH DOGWOOD
HOBBLING LAME
HOBBY BUG FAD HOBBLER PASTIME AVOCATION
HOBBYHORSE HOBBY PLAYMARE
HOBBYIST BUG
HOBGOBLIN (ALSO SEE GOBLIN) COW HAG HOB PUG BOGY PUCK BOGEY BUCCA BUGAN POKER SCRAT SPOOK BOODIE BOWSIE EMPUSA SPOORN BUGABOO RAWHEAD BOGGLEBO COLTPIXY POPLEMAN PUCKEREL WORRICOW
HOBNAIL HOB HUB PUNCH TACKET
HOBNAILED TACKETY
HOBO BO BOE BUM STIFF TRAMP VAGRANT VAGABOND SUNDOWNER
HOCK HAM HOX HEEL ANKLE HOUGH HUXEN SINEW SKINK IMPAWN JARRET CAMBREL GAMBREL HOCKSHIN SUFFRAGO
HOCKEY HURLY HORKEY HURLEY SHINNY CAMMOCK HURLBAT
(— DISK) PUCK
(— PLAYER) DYE ORR ROY HALL HOWE HULL BUCYK DIONE MOORE SHORE CLARKE COWLEY DRYDEN DURNAN GOULET HARVEY MALONE MIKITO MORENZ PILATE PLANTE POLVIN ULLMAN VACHON BOURQUE GRETZKY LAFLEUR LEMIEUX MESSIER RATELLE SAWCHUK WORSLEY CHEEVERS CONACHER ESPOSITO SCHRINER THOMPSON TROTTIER LAROCOQUE MAHOVLICH PERREAULT DELVECCHIO
(— STAR) ORR
(— TEAM) JETS BLUES KINGS BRUINS DEVILS FLAMES FLYERS OILERS SABRES SHARKS CANUCKS RANGERS WHALERS CAPITALS

PENGUINS REDWINGS SENATORS CANADIENS ISLANDERS LIGHTNING NORDIQUES BLACKHAWKS MAPLELEAFS NORTHSTARS
(AREA IN FRONT OF — GOAL) CREASE
(ILLEGAL CHECK IN —) SPEARING
(INFRACTION IN —) SPEARING
HOCKEY STICK HOOKY HURLY STICK BULGER SHINNY CAMBUCA CAMMOCK DODDART HURLBAT
HOCUS-POCUS CANTRIP JUGGLERY FAKERY HUMBUG FLIMFLAM QUACKERY
HOD TRAY
(FATHER OF —) ZOPHAH
HODAVIAH (FATHER OF —) HASSENUAH
HOD CARRIER PADDY
HODESH (HUSBAND OF —) SHAHARAIM
HODGEPODGE CHOW HASH MESS OLIO RAFF SALAD BOLLIX JUSSEL MAGPIE MEDLEY MELANGE CHIVAREE CHOWCHOW HOTCHPOT KEDGEREE MISHMASH PASTICHE PORRIDGE SCRAMPUM PATCHWORK
HODOMETER VIAMETER
HOE BROD CHIP CLAT HACK HOWE SHIM CLAUT LARRY THIRD CHONTA HACKER PAIDLE PECKER SARCLE GRUBBER PULASKI SCRAPER SCUFFLE GRIFFAUN STRADDLER
(— HANDLE) STAIL
(HORSE —) NIDGET NIGGET
(PART OF —) BLADE SHANK HANDLE FERRULE
HOECAKE CORNCAKE
HOG BEN SOW BOAR GALT GILT PORK DUROC GRUNT SHOAT BARROW HOGGET HOGGIE OINKER PORKER PORKET YORKER BACONER BUTCHER GRUNTER HOGLING MONTANA BABIRUSA BUNODONT HEREFORD LANDRACE VICTORIA RAZORBACK
(KIND OF —) ROAD
(PREF.) SUI
HOGAN ABODE LODGE TEPEE DWELLING
HOGBACK RIDGE FLATIRON HOGFRAME
HOGCHOKER SOLE
HOGFISH CAPITAN LADYFISH LORICATE SCORPION
HOGGER HUGGER HOGHEAD
HOGGISHNESS GRILL GRYLL
HOGLAH (FATHER OF —) ZELOPHEHAD
HOGNOSE SNAKE ADDER FLATHEAD
HOG PLUM AMRA JOBO
HOGSHEAD CASK CARDEL
HOG'S-MEAT TOSTON HOGWEED
HOG-TIE HAMPER
HOGWASH SLOP DRAFF SWASH SWILL PIGWASH
HOIST FID HEFT KILT LIFT SWAY SWIG WHIM WHIP CRANE ERECT HEAVE HEEZE HEIST HOICK HOOSH HORSE RAISE WEIGH JAMMER

LAUNCH LIFTER TUGGER WHIMSY DERRICK
(— A LOG) CANNON
(— ANCHOR) CAT
(— FISH) BRAIL
(— FLUKES) FISH FANCHER
HOISTED (— TIGHT) ATRIP
HOISTMAN CAGEMAN
HOKUM BLAA BLAH HOKE JUNK
HOLD HOD OWN BULK DEEM FEEL FILL GAOL GAUM GIVE GRIT HANK HAVE HELD HEND HILT HOLE HOLT HOOK JAIL KEEP LOCK NAIL RELY SOFT STOW AFONG AHOLD AHOLT BELAY CARRY CINCH CLAMP CLING GRASP GRIPE LATCH LEASE PAUSE POISE ROCCA STORE WOULD ADHERE ADSORB ARREST CLUTCH DETAIN HANDLE INTERN MANURE OCCUPY REGARD REPUTE RETAIN ADJUDGE CAPTURE CLAUGHT CONFINE CONTAIN ENCLOSE FERMATA GRAPPLE HOLDING RECEIVE SEIZURE SUBSIST SUSPEND COMPRISE FOOTHOLD FOREHOLD HANDFAST HANDHOLD HEADLOCK HOLDFAST PURCHASE THURROCK
(A BELIEF) SUPPOSE
(— AS PRECIOUS) TREASURE
(— AS TRUE) ACCEPT
(— AT BAY) DOMPT
(— BACK) STAY STOP WELL BELAY LAYNE STINT BOGGLE DETAIN FLINCH HINDER RETIRE SHRINK CONTAIN DETRACT FORBEAR INHIBIT RECLAIM REFRAIN REPRESS SLACKEN HESITATE RESTRAIN SUPPRESS WITHDRAW
(— BACK ON LEASH) TRASH
(— CLOSELY) CRADLE CUDDLE
(— CONSULTATION) ADVISE
(— CORONER'S INQUEST) CROWN
(— DEAR) CHERISH
(— DOWN) PINION CONTAIN
(— FAST) FIX RAIL RIVE CLING SNARL CLENCH CLINCH SECURE STABLE
(— FIRMLY) CLIP INSIST
(— FORTH) ORATE SPIEL
(— FROM) ABSTAIN
(— GOOD) APPLY SERVE
(— IN CHECK) REIN GOVERN REPRESS COMPESCE
(— IN CONTEMPT) SMILE DISPRIZE
(— IN PLACE) ANCHOR
(— OF PLASTER) KEY
(— ON COURSE) STEM FETCH STAND
(— ON FINAL NOTE) TENOR
(— ON SHORE) LANDFAST
(— OUT) DREE LAST STAY OFFER EXTEND PROTEND STRETCH SUSTAIN
(— PROTECTIVELY) LAP
(— TIGHTLY) CLIP STICK
(— TOGETHER) BOND COHERE CONSIST
(— UP) ROB BEAR HALT STAY ERECT HEIST IMPEDE UPHOLD RUMPADE SUPPORT SUSTAIN TRADUCE
(— UP BY LEADING STRINGS) DADE
(— UP TO CONTEMPT) FLEER

(— UP TO PUBLIC NOTICE) GIBBET
(SHIP'S —) HOLE HOLL FISHHOLD
(WRESTLING —) CROTCH NELSON KEYLOCK CHANCERY HEADLOCK SCISSORS SIDEHOLD
(PREF.) CHADA
HOLDBACK DAM
HOLDER WYE HAVER STOCK DIPPER SOCKET CRACKER CASSETTE JAGIRDAR
(— FOR CARRYING GLASS) FRAIL
(— FOR COIL) SPOOL
(— FOR CUP) ZARF
(— FOR FLOWERS) FROG JARDINIERE
(— FOR FOOD) COZY COSEY
(— FOR TOOLS) TURRET
(— FOR WHIP) BUCKET
(— OF BENEFICE) ABBE
(— OF GRANT) ENAMDAR
(ALLOTMENT —) CLERUCH
(CANDLE —) SPIDER GIRANDOLE
(FLOWER —) FROG
(LAMP —) BODY
(TAPE —) CASSETTE
(PL.) GRIPPERS
(PREF.) PORTE
HOLDFAST CLINCH HAPTERON
HOLDIKEN HADDIN
HOLDING HAL COPY COTE HOLD TAKE GRASP HONOR HADDIN POFFLE TENANT TENURE TENANCY COMMENDA
(— DIFFERENT OPINIONS) APART
(— FAST) IRON
(— OF LAND) ROOM
(— OF OFFICE) OCCUPATION
(— OF SECURITIES) CARRY
(PL.) FLOCKS PROPERTY
HOLDUP HEIST STICKUP
HOLE CAN CUP EYE GAP PIT TAP BORE BURY LEAK MAIL MUSE PECK PINK POCK PUKA WANT CHINK DITCH FLOSS FOSSE MEUSE SINUS SLACK SPRUE SQUAT TEWEL THIRL THURL BURROW CAVITY CENTER CENTRE CRANNY CRATER EYELET HOLLOW LACUNA OBTAIN OILLET PIERCE POCKET POUNCE WEEPER BLOWOUT BOGHOLE BOTHROS DIBHOLE EYEHOLE KEYHOLE MORTICE MORTISE OILHOLE OPENING PINHOLE POTHOLE SCUTTLE SWALLET VENTAGE ACCEPTER APERTURE BLOWHOLE BOREHOLE COALHOLE CRABHOLE FUMAROLE HANDHOLE KNOCKOUT KNOTHOLE OVERTURE PEEPHOLE POSTHOLE PUNCTURE WELLHOLE WINDHOLE PERTUSION PERFORATION
(— CAUSED BY LEAK) GIME
(— FOR MOLTEN METAL) SUMP
(— FOR WIRE) HUB HUBB
(— IN BANK OF STREAM) GAT
(— IN GARMENT) FRACK
(— IN GUILLOTINE) LUNET LUNETTE
(— IN HEDGE) SMEUSE
(— IN HOLE) BOTHOLE
(— IN KEEL) LIMBER RUFFLE
(— IN KIVA) SIPAPU
(— IN ONE STROKE) ACE
(— IN STREAM BED) DUMP

(— INTO MOLD) GEAT SPRUE
(— IN WIND INSTRUMENT) LILL
(— THREE BELOW PAR) ALBATROSS
(AIR —) SPIRACLE
(BREATHING —) SUSPIRAL
(DEEP —) POT GOURD
(FOX —) KENNEL
(FULL OF —S) POROSE
(GOLF —) CUP DOGLEG
(KIND OF —) OZONE
(MELON —) GILGAI
(RABBIT —) CLAPPER
(SAND —) BUNKER
(SINK —) SOAKAWAY
(SPY —) JUDAS
(TO —) GOBBLE HAZARD
(VOLCANIC —) FUMAROLE
(VOLCANIC STEAM —S) SOFFIONI
(WATER —) DUB CHARCO
(WELL-LIKE —) CASCAN
(PREF.) TREMATO TROGLO
HOLIDAY HOL PLAY TIDE WAKE FERIE FESTA MERRY FIESTA JOVIAL FESTIVE HALEDAY PLAYDAY YEARDAY PASSOVER SHABUOTH WAYGOOSE
(EASTERN —) TET
(HALF —) REMEDY
(PL.) FERIA
HOLINESS PIETY HALIDOM SANCTITY SANCTIMONY
HOLLA SOLA
HOLLAND (ALSO SEE NETHERLANDS) FROGLAND
HOLLANDAISE GULASH GOULASH
HOLLAND BLUE ORION
HOLLANDER DUTCHMAN
HOLLANDS GIN GENEVA
HOLLER HALLO HOLLO HALLOO KYOODLE
HOLLO SOLA
HOLLOW DEN DIP KEX BOSS BOWL CAVE COMB COOM COVE DALK DELL DENT DINT DISH DOCK DOKE FOLD GORE HOLE HOLL HOWE IDLE KEXY KHUD SINK SLOT THIN VAIN VOID WAME BASIN BIGHT CAVUM CHASE CLEFT CUPPY DELVE DOWFF EMPTY FALSE FOSSA GAUNT GOYLE GULCH GULLY HEUCH LAIGH NOTCH SCOOP SINUS SLOCK SWAMP WOMBY ARMPIT BULLAN CAVITY CORRIE DIMPLE HOLLER INDENT KETTLE MATRIX POCKET RECESS SOCKET SUNKEN VACANT WALLOW BOXLIKE CONCAVE UNSOUND VACUITY CAVITARY CHELIDON CORELESS CRUCIBLE FISTULAR FOSSETTE NOTCHING SPECIOUS
(— AMONG HILLS) SWAG SLOCK
(— BETWEEN BREASTS) SLOT CLEAVAGE
(— BETWEEN WAVES) TROUGH
(— IN COIL OF CABLE) TIER
(— IN HILL) COOM CLASH COMBE COOMB CORRIE
(— IN SNOW) IGLOO
(— IN TILE) KEY
(— OF ARM) LEAD ARMPIT
(— OF EAR) ALVEARY
(— OF EYEBALL) ORBIT ORBITA

(— OF FOOT) VOLA
(— OF HANDS) GOUPEN GOWPEN
(— OF HORSE'S TOOTH) MARK
(— OF KNEE) HAM
(— OF ROOF) VALLEY
(— OUT) CUT DIG BORE HOWK KERF CAVERN EXCISE
(LONG —) GROOVE
(NOT —) SOLID FARCTATE
(PASSING —) CRESCENT
(ROUND —) CIRQUE
(SECLUDED —) GLEN
(SPRINGY —) GAW
(WOODED —) GULLY
(PREF.) CAEL(I)(O) CAVI CAVO CEL(O) COEL(I)(O) (SUFF.)** COELOUS COELUS
HOLLOWED HOWKIT CONCAVE SPOUTED
HOLLOW-EYED HAGGARD
HOLLOWNESS VANITY INANITY VACUITY CONCAVITY
HOLLY HOLM HULL ILEX MATE DAHOON HOLLIN HULVER TOLLON YAUPON CATBERRY INKBERRY MILKMAID
HOLLYHOCK HOCK ALTHEA MALLOW
HOLM AIT ISLET ISLAND BOTTOMS
HOLM-OAK ILEX
HOLOFERNES (SLAYER OF —) JUDITH
HOLOTHURIAN TREPANG
HOLY SRI SHRI HUACA SAINT SANTO DEVOUT DIVINE SACRAL SACRED BLESSED PERFECT SAINTLY SINLESS BLISSFUL INNOCENT REVEREND SPIRITUAL SANCTIMONIOUS
(— MAN) SADHU
(— OF HOLIES) ADYT ADYTUM
(ALL —) PANAGIA
(PREF.) HAGI(O) HIERATICO HIER(O) HOSIO SANCTI SANCTO SEMNO (SUFF.)** HIERIC
HOLY BASIL TULCE TOOLSY
HOLY SPIRIT PARACLETE
HOLY STONE BEAR BIBLE
HOLY WOOD LIGNUM
HOMAGE FEE COURT HONOR YMAGE FEALTY MANRED INCENSE LOYALTY MANRENT MANSHIP OVATION SERVICE TREWAGE EMINENCE OBEISANCE
(PAY —) GENUFLECT
(PAY — TO) KNEEL
(SUPREME —) LATRIA
HOME BYE DEN HAM BASE CASA HAME HUNK WIKE ABODE ASTRE BEING DOMUS FOYER HAUNT SMOKE HEARTH HEIMAT BLIGHTY SHELTER DOMICILE FIRESIDE ROOFTREE
(— FOR THE POOR) HOSPICE
(— OF REFUGE) HOSPICE
(— OF THE BLESSED) GIMLE
(AT THE — OF) CHEZ
(FUNERAL —) CHAPEL
(HARVEST —) KERN KIRN MELL HOCKEY
(IN THE — OF) CHEZ
(KIND OF —) MOTOR

(NURSING —) CLINIC
(REST —) FARM HOSTEL
(PREF.) (RETURN —) NOST(O)
HOMELAND HAVAIKI BANTUSTAN
HOMELESS ROOFLESS VAGABOND
HOMELIKE HOMEY HAMEIL HAMILT
   HOMISH HOMESOME
HOMELINESS YEOMANRY
HOMELY FOUL UGLY PLAIN
   DUDGEN RUGGED PLAINLY
   EVERYDAY FAMILIAR HOMELIKE
HOME PLATE RUBBER
HOMER KOR CHOMER
HOME RUN SWAT SWOT BLAST
   DINGER
HOMESICKNESS HEIMWEH
   NOSTALGIA
HOMESPUN KERSEY RUSSET
   RAPLOCH
HOMESTEAD TOFT TREF ONSET
   PLACE WORTH GRANGE TYDDYN
   FARMERY ONSTEAD STEADING
HOMESTEADER NESTER
HOMETHRUST HAI HAY
HOMEWORK PREP
HOMICIDE DEATH MORTH KILLING
HOMILETIC KERYSTIC
HOMILY PRONE OMELIE POSTIL
   SERMON
HOMINY SAMP NASAUMP
HOMOEOMERY GERM SEED
   (PL.) SPERMATA
HOMOGENEITY SAMENESS
HOMOGENEOUS LIKE SOLID
   GLOBAL SIMPLE COMPACT
   MASSIVE SIMILAR
   (PREF.) HOL(O) IS(O)
HOMOGENOUS ENTIRE
HOMOLOGUE CYANINE HOMOTYPE
   (PREF.) NOR
HOMOPHONY MONODY
HOMORGANIC COGNATE
HOMOSEXUAL GAY FLIT
   (— WOMAN) LESBIAN
   (FEMALE —) DIKE DYKE
HOMOZYGOUS PURE ISOGENIC

HONDURAS

CAPITAL: TEGUCIGALPA
COIN: PESO CENTAVO LEMPIRA
DEPARTMENT: YORO COLON
   COPAN VALLE OLANCHO
GULF: FONSECA
INDIAN: MAYA PAYA SUMO ULVA
   CARIB LENCA PIPIL TAUIRA
   JICAQUE MISKITO MOSQUITO
ISLAND: ROATAN
ISLANDS: BAY BAHIA
LAKE: CRIBA YOJOA BREWER
MEASURE: VARA MILLA MECATE
   TERCIA CAJUELA MANZANA
MOUNTAINS: PIJA AGALTA
   CELAQUE
PORT: LACEIBA TRUJILLO
RIVER: COCO SICO ULUA AGUAN
   LEMPA NEGRO TINTO WANKS
   PATUCA SULACO GUAYAPE
   OLANCHO SEGOVIA SANTIAGO
RUINS: TENAMPUA
TOWN: TELA YORO COPAN LAPAZ
   ROATAN GRACIAS LACEIBA
   TRUJILLO YUSCARAN JUTICALPA
WEIGHT: CAJA LIBRA

HONE HO STROP STROKE STRICKLE
HONEST FAIR GOOD JAKE TRUE
   AFALD FRANK LEGIT ROUND
   SOUND WHITE CANDID DEXTER
   DINKUM ENTIRE PROPER RUSTIC
   SINGLE SQUARE SINCERE UPRIGHT
   RIGHTFUL STRAIGHT
   (BARELY —) SHARP
HONESTLY TRULY DINKUM HONEST
   INDEED SINGLY SQUARE
   SQUARELY
HONESTY FAITH HONOR SATIN
   CANDOR EQUITY LUNARY REALTY
   VERITY JUSTICE LUNARIA PROBITY
   BOLBONAC FAIRNESS FIDELITY
   MOONWORT SATINPOD
   YEOMANRY
HONEY MEL MELL HINNY
   HONEYBUN
   (— BEVERAGE) MULSE
   (COLOR OF —) AMBER
   (ROSE-FLAVORED —) RODOMEL
   (PREF.) MELI(TTO) MELL(I)
HONEYBEE (ALSO SEE BEE) BEE
   GYNE KING DRANE DRONE QUEEN
   DINGAR DRONER EGATES CYPRIAN
   DEBORAH DESERET KOOTCHA
   MELISSA STINGER ACULEATE
   ANGELITO
HONEY BUZZARD PERN
HONEYCOMB COMB FRAME
   WAXCOMB
   (PREF.) CERIO FAVI
HONEYCOMBED FAVOSE
   FAVEOLATE
HONEYCREEPER IIWI MAMO
   PALILA DREPANID GUITGUIT
HONEYDEW MANNA MILDEW
HONEY EATER OO IAO TUI MOHO
   MINER TENUI MANUAO MAOMAO
   ROSTER BELLBIRD WURRALUH
HONEYED SWEET HYBLAN SUGARY
   SUGARED HYBLAEAN LUSCIOUS
HONEY GUIDE MOROC
HONEY MESQUITE ALGAROBA
   HONEYPOD
HONEY PLANT HOYA HUAJILLO
HONEY-STONE MELLITE
HONEYSUCKLE VINE SUCKLE
   WEIGELA BINDWEED SUCKLING
   WOODBINE

HONG KONG

BAY: SHEKO REPULSE
CAPITAL: VICTORIA
COIN: CENT DOLLAR
DISTRICT: WANCHAI
GARDENS: TIGERBALM
ISLAND: LANTAO
MOUNTAIN: CASTLE VICTORIA
PENINSULA: KOWLOON
TOWN: KOWLOON

HONING (— DEVICE) OILSTONE
HONK KONK YANG CRONK
HONKER GOOSE
HONOR BAY ORE CLIO FAME FETE
   HORN KUDO LAUD ADORE CROWN
   GLORY GRACE HERRY IZZAT
   MENSE MENSK SPEAK TREAT
   CREDIT DECORE ENHALO ESTEEM
   HOMAGE HONOUR LAUREL PRAISE
   REVERE SALUTE WORTHY DIGNITY

   EMBLAZE GLORIFY HONESTY
   MANSHIP RESPECT WORSHIP
   ACCOLADE DECORATE GRANDEZA
   TASHREEF
   (PL.) ACES
   (PREF.) TIMO
HONORABLE DEAR FREE GOOD
   DIGNE NOBLE OPIME WHITE
   GENTLE HONEST HONORA LORDLY
   SQUARE UPRIGHT GENEROUS
   HANDSOME HONORARY
HONORABLENESS HONESTY
HONORABLY GENTLY
HONORARIUM SALARY DOUCEUR
   ALTARAGE HONORARY
HONORED GOOD FAMOUS LAUREL
   LAURELED PRESTIGIOUS
HONORIFIC MAGNIFIC
HOOD HOW COIF COWL GOON
   HEAD HUDE JACK AMICE ALMUCE
   BIGGIN BONNET BURLET CALASH
   CAMAIL CANOPY CAPOTE CUTOFF
   DOMINO FUNNEL MANTLE RAFFIA
   BANGKOK BASHLYK CALOTTE
   CAPUCHE MOBSTER BLINDAGE
   CALYPTRA CAPUCCIO CAPUTIUM
   CHAPERON CUCULLUS FOOLSCAP
   GANGSTER LIRIPIPE LIRIPOOP
   MAZARINE TROTCOZY NITHSDALE
   (— AND CAPE COMBINED)
   FALDETTA
   (— FOR EVENING WEAR) CAPELINE
   (— OF BOILER) VOMIT
   (— OF CARRIAGE) HEAD
   (— OF MAIL) COIF CAMAIL COIFFE
   (— OF REFRACTORY MATERIAL)
   MANTLE
   (— OF VEHICLE) TOP CAPOTE
   (— ON CUPBOARD) TREMOR
   (— ON HORSES) BLINKER
   (— OVER DOOR) MARQUISE
   (— OVER SIGNAL LIGHT) VISOR
   (LENS —) SUNSHADE
   (MONK'S —) COWL
   (STIRRUP —) TAPADERO
   (STRAW —) JAVA
   (WOMAN'S —) SURTOUT VOLUPER
HOODED COWLED GALEATE
   CUCULLATE
HOODED CROW HOODIE
   GRAYBACK GREYBACK
HOODED MERGANSER SMEW
   SNOWL SPIKE TADPOLE TOWHEAD
   MOSSHEAD
HOODED SEAL WIG HOOD
   HOODCAP
HOODLUM YOB HOOD LOUT PUNK
   BADDY YOBBO YOKEL BADDIE
   SKOLLY LURCHER HOOLIGAN
   LARRIKIN
HOODOO JINX
HOODWINK MOP DUPE FOOL SEEL
   BLEAR BLIND BLUFF CHEAT
   BAFFLE CLOYNE DELUDE
   GAMMON WIMPLE AVEUGLE
   BEGUILE BLINKER DECEIVE
   MISLEAD INVEIGLE
HOOEY BUSHWAH
HOOF CLOOF CLOOT COFFIN
   UNGUIS UNGULA CLOOTIE
   HOOFLET FOREHOOF
   (PREF.) UNGULI
HOOFED UNGULATE

HOO-HA ADO
HOOK DOG GAB JIG PEW TUG CLIP
   DRAG FLAG GAFF HAKE HUCK KILP
   MEAK NOCK PEVY PRIN PUGH SETT
   SKID STAY TACK CATCH CHAPE
   CLEEK CLICK CRAMP CROME
   CROOK DRAIL HAMUS ONCIN
   PEAVY PREEN SARPE SPOON
   TACHE UNCUS BECKET DETENT
   HANGLE HINGLE PINTLE TENTER
   AGRAFFE GAMBREL GRUNTER
   HAMULUS HITCHER HOOKLET
   KNUCKLE NUTHOOK PELICAN
   PENNANT PINHOOK POTHOOK
   RAMHEAD SNIGGLE SPERKET
   UNCINUS BOATHOOK CROTCHET
   GRABHOOK PORTHOOK PULLBACK
   VULSELLA WEEDHOOK
   (— FISH) FOUL HANG SNAG DRAIL
   HITCH STRIKE SNIGGLE FISHHOOK
   (— FOR BACON) COMB
   (— FOR KETTLE) KILP HANGLE
   TRAMMEL
   (— FOR POT) DRACKEN POTHOOK
   SLOWRIE
   (— FOR TWISTING HEMP) WHIRL
   WHIRLER
   (BENCH —) JACK
   (BOAT —) HITCHER
   (BOXING —) CROSS
   (BUTCHER'S —) GAFF
   (COUPLING —) JIGGER
   (KIND OF —) MOUTH
   (LONG-HANDLED —) HOCK MEAK
   (MUSICAL —) FLAG PENNANT
   (PRUNING —) SARPE CALABOZO
   (REAPING —) HINK TWIBILL
   (SAFETY —) CLEVIS
   (SKIDDING —S) GRAB
   (2 —S FASTENED AT SHANKS)
   DOUBLES
HOOKAH KALIAN CHILLUM
   NARGHILE
HOOKED ADUNC UNCATE UNCOUS
   ADUNCAL FALCATE HAMATED
   HAMULAR ADUNCATE ADUNCOUS
   AQUILINE HAMIFORM UNCINATE
HOOKEDNESS ADUNCITY
HOOKER-OUT STICKMAN
HOOK-SHAPED ANKYROID
HOOKUP CIRCUIT
HOOKWORM STRONGYL
HOOLIGAN ROUGH ROWDY TOUGH
   APACHE GOONDA LARRIKIN
   (SOUTH AFRICAN —) TSOTSI
   (PL.) AMALAITA
HOOP RIB BAIL BAND BOND BOOL
   CLIP GIRD GIRR PASS RING TIRE
   GARTH GIRTH FRETTE HOOPLE
   LAGGIN WICKET CIRCLET GARLAND
   TROCHUS TRUNDLE
   (— FOR A SPAR) BANGLE
   (— FOR BARREL) BAND GIRD GIRTH
   (— FOR LAMPSHADE) HARP
   (— FOR ORE BUCKET) CLEVIS
   (— FOR WINNOWING GRAIN)
   WEIGHT
   (— NET) TRUNK
   (— OF WHEEL) STRAKE
   (— TO STRENGTHEN GUN) FRETTE
   (HALF —) BAIL BALE
HOOPED RUNG
HOOPLA FANFARE

HOOPOE HOOP UPUPA WHOOP IRRISOR DUNGBIRD PICARIAN
HOOPSKIRT TUBTAIL
HOOP SNAKE WAMPUM
HOOPSTER CAGER
HOOSE HUSK
HOOSEGOW JUG JAIL POKY POKEY
HOOSIER SCHOOLMASTER
  (AUTHOR OF —) EGGLESTON
  (CHARACTER IN —) BUD PETE JONES MEANS RALPH SMALL WHITE HANNAH MARTHA SANDER SHOCKY WALTER HAWKINS JOHNSON MATILDA PEARSON THOMSON
HOOSIER STATE INDIANA
HOOT CURR WHOO WHOOP WHOOT EXPLODE ULULATE
  (— OF REPROACH) FIE
HOOVE BLOAT
HOOVER VACUUM
HOP HIP NIP FLIP JUMP LEAP BOUND HITCH SWINE FLIERS GAMBOL SPRING TITTUP CROWHOP HOPBIND HOPVINE LUPULUS SKIPPER
HOPBUSH AKE AKEAKE
HOP CLOVER SHAMROCK SUCKLING
HOPE WON DEEM SPES TROW COMBE THINK TRUST DESIRE EXPECT PERDUE ESPEIRE THOUGHT SPERANZA VELLEITY
  (VAIN —) PIPE WANHOPE
HOPEFUL FOND BUOYANT SANGUINE WENLICHE
HOPEFULNESS OPTIMISM
HOPELESS DULL ALLUP ABJECT FORLORN DOWNCAST
HOPELESSNESS ANOMIE DESPAIR
HOPHNI (BROTHER OF —) PHINEHAS
  (FATHER OF —) ELI
HOP HORNBEAM DEERWOOD HARDHACK IRONWOOD
HOPI MOKI MOQUI
HOP-LIKE LUPULINE
HOPPER CURB JACK BUNKER CLOSET HAPPER MACARONI
HOPPLE HOBBLE PASTERN SIDELANG
HOPS SHATTER
  (— BETWEEN 2 AND 4 YEARS) OLDS
HOPSCOTCH POTSY HOPPERS PALLALL PEEVERS
HOP TREE RUEWORT WINGSEED
HORDE ARMY CAMP CLAN PACK CROWD GROUP SWARM LEGION THRONG
  (INNER —) BUKEYEF
HOREHOUND HENBIT MARVEL WONDER MARRUBE
HORI (FATHER OF —) LOTAN
  (SON OF —) SHAPHAT
HORIZON LAYER VERGE COMPASS FINITOR ORTERDE SKYLINE
HORIZONTAL LEVEL LINEAR NAIANT ACLINAL STRAIGHT
HORIZONTALLY FLATLY BARWAYS BARWISE ENDLONG FESSWAYS FESSWISE
HORMIGO QUIRA
HORMONE HGH ACTH KININ CORTIN LUTEIN EQUILIN ESTRIOL ESTRONE GASTRIN INSULIN RELAXIN STEROID THEELIN THEELOL ANDROGEN ECDYSONE ENDOCRIN ESTROGEN FLORIGEN GALACTIN LACTOGEN OESTRIOL SECRETIN CORTISONE
  (PITUITARY —) ACTH
HORN BEAK BATON BUGLE CONCH CORNO CORNU SHOOT ANTLER CLAXON KLAXON OXHORN TOOTER ALPHORN ALTHORN ANTENNA BUFFALO CLARONE FOGHORN HELICON HUTCHET OUTHORN PRICKET SHOPHAR UNICORN BEAKIRON BUCKHORN CLAVICOR CORNICLE OLIPHANT SLUGHORN STAGHORN WALDHORN NOISEMAKER
  (— NOTE) MORT
  (— OF COW) SCUR
  (— OF CRESCENT MOON) CUSP
  (— OF DILEMMA) PIKE
  (— OF DRINK) SLOSH
  (— OF YOUNG STAG) BUNCH
  (BUDDING —) SHOOT
  (DRINKING —) RHYTON
  (ENGLISH —) CA
  (FRENCH —) CORNO
  (GREY —) COLUMN
  (HUNTER'S —) HUTCHET WALDHORN
  (INSECT'S —) ANTENNA
  (IVORY —) OLIFANT
  (RAM'S —) SHOPHAR SHOFAR
  (RUDIMENTARY —) SLUG
  (STUNTED —) SCUR
  (PREF.) CORNEO CORNI CORNU
  (SUFF.) CERA(S) CEROS CEROUS CERUS CORN
HORNBEAM HARDBEAM HARDHACK HORNWOOD IRONWOOD
HORNBILL TOCK CALAO TOUCAN BUCEROS HOMURAI BROMVOEL PICARIAN YEARBIRD
HORNBLENDE SIDERITE
HORNED FORKED CORNUTE
  (PREF.) CERA CERVI CORNEO CORNI CORNU
HORNED DACE CHUB
HORNED POUT CATFISH
HORNED SCREAMER ANHIMA KAMACHI KAMICHI UNICORN
HORNED VIPER WAMPUM CERASTES
HORNET VESPA VESPID STINGER
HORNGELD CORNAGE
HORNLESS NAT NOT MOIL POLL DODDY MULEY POLEY DODDED HUMBLE HUMMEL MAILIE MULLEY POLLED ACEROUS
HORNPIPE MATELOTE
HORN POPPY SQUATMORE
HORNSTONE CHERT KERALITE
HORNSWOGGLE DUPE
HORNTAIL SIREX ORYSSID UROCERID WOODWORM
HORNWORT COONTAIL HORNWEED
HORNWRACK SEAMAT
HORNY WAUKIT CALLOUS CERATOID CORNEOUS KERASINE KERATOID
HORNYHEAD CHUB

HOROSCOPE SCOPE THEME FIGURE GENESIS NATIVITY
HORRIBLE DIRE GRIM UGLY AWFUL BLACK GREAT GRISLY HORRID GEARFUL GHASTLY HIDEOUS HORRENT UNSLOGH DREADFUL GRUESOME HORRIFIC SHOCKING TERRIBLE MONSTROUS
HORRID GRIM UGLY AWFUL ROUGH RUGGED SNUFFY UGSOME WICKED HIDEOUS DREADFUL GRUESOME HORRIBLE SHOCKING
HORRIFIC FEARFUL
HORRIFIED AGHAST GHASTLY HORRENT
HORRIFY APPAL AGRISE DISMAY ENHORROR
HORROR FEAR DREAD TERROR CONSTERNATION
  (PL.) JIMJAMS
HORRORS CREEPS
HORSA (BROTHER OF —) HENGIST
HORS D'OEUVRE CANAPE RELISH OUTWORK ZAKUSKA
  (PL.) ASSIETTE
HORS D'OEUVRE TAPA
HORSE BAY COB CUT DUN GEE GRI NAG PAD POT RIP TIT ARAB AVER BARB DOON GOER GROG HACK HAND HOSS JADE MARE MOKE PRAD PROD QUAD RACK RIDE ROAN ROIL SKIN STUD TEAM TURK WEED YAWD ZAIN AIVER ARION ARVAK BEAST BIDET BLACK BROCK CAPLE CAPUL CHUNK CLYDE CREAM CROCK DUMMY EQUID FAVEL GLYDE GRANI HAIRY HOBBY MILER MOREL PACER PINTO PIPER POLER PUNCH RACER ROGUE RUNSY SCREW SHIER SHIRE SKATE SOMER STEED STIFF TACKY WALER WIDGE ALEZAN AMBLER BANKER BOLTER BRONCO BRUMBY BUCKER BUSSER CABBER CALICO CASTER CHASER CHEVAL COLLOP CURTAL CUSSER DAPPLE DOBBIN DRIVER ENTIRE EQUINE FENCER FILLER GANGER GARRON GLEYDE GRULLA HUNTER JUMPER KEFFEL LEADER MAIDEN MORGAN NUBIAN ORLOFF OUTLAW PELTER PLATER POSTER PULLER RACKER ROARER ROUNCY RUNNER SAVAGE SORREL STAGER TARPAN TRACER TURKEY VANNER WARPER WEAVER ALSVINN ALSVITH ARABIAN BARBARY BELGIAN BOARDER CABALLO CHARGER CLICKER CLIPPER COACHER COCOTTE COURSER CRIBBER CRIOLLA CRITTER DRAFTER FLEMISH GALATHE GELDING GIGSTER GRUNTER HACKNEY KNACKER LEEFANG MONTURE MUSTANG NEIGHER PACOLET PALFREY PIEBALD PRANCER PRANKER RATTLER REESTER REFUSER REMOUNT RUNAWAY SADDLER SLEDDER SLEEPER SPANKER STAGGIE STEPPER SUFFOLK SUMPTER TRAPPER TRESTLE TROOPER TROTTER WHEELER ARDENNES BATHORSE

BUCKSKIN CHESTNUT CHEVALET COCKTAIL COLICKER CREATURE CYLLAROS DEMISANG DESTRIER EOHIPPUS FOOTROPE FRIPPERY GALLOPER GALLOWAY HRIMFAXI KADISCHI MACHINER OUTSIDER PALOMINO RIDGLING ROADSTER SKEWBALD STALLION STIBBLER TRIPPLER WHISTLER YARRAMAN CLYDESDALE
  (— ACT) MANAGE
  (— ANCESTOR) EOHIPPUS
  (— CERTAIN NOT TO WIN) STIFF
  (— ESTABLISHMENT) HARAS
  (— LOSING FIXED RACE) STUMER STUMOUR
  (— OF ACHILLES) XANTHUS
  (— OF ALEXANDER THE GREAT) BUCEPHALUS
  (— OF CALIGULA) INCITATUS
  (— OF DALE EVANS) BUTTERMILK
  (— OF DICK TURPIN) BLACKBESS
  (— OF DON QUIXOTE) ROSINANTE
  (— OF DUKE OF WELLINGTON) COPENHAGEN
  (— OF GENERAL CUSTER) COMANCHE
  (— OF GENERAL SHERMAN) RIENZI
  (— OF LONE RANGER) SILVER
  (— OF MOHAMMED) ALBORAK
  (— OF NAPOLEON) MORENGO
  (— OF ORLANDO) VEGLIANTINO
  (— OF RINALDO) BAYARD
  (— OF ROBERT E. LEE) TRAVELLER
  (— OF ROY ROGERS) TRIGGER
  (— OF SIGURD) GRANI
  (— OF STONEWALL JACKSON) LITTLESORREL
  (— OF TEX RITTER) WHITEFLASH
  (— OF TOM MIX) TONY
  (— OF ULYSSES GRANT) CINCINNATI
  (— OF UNIFORM DARK COLOR) ZAIN
  (— OF WILL ROGERS) SOAPSUDS BOOTLEGGER
  (— RACE) WALKOVER
  (—S RUNNING BEHIND) RUCK
  (— THAT WON'T START) STICK
  (ARABIAN —) ARAB KOHL ARABIAN
  (BALKY —) JIB JIBBER
  (BREED OF —) SHETLAND APPALOOSA PERCHERON CLYDESDALE LIPPIZANER
  (BROKEN-DOWN —) JADE CROCK SCREW DURGAN GARRAN
  (CALICO —) PINTO
  (CASTRATED —) GELDING
  (CLUMSY —) STAMMEL
  (DECREPIT —) SKATE GLEYDE
  (DRAFT —) HAIRY PUNCH SHIRE BEETEWK BELGIAN SUFFOLK PERCHERON
  (DROVE OF —S) ATAJO
  (EASY-PACED —) PAD
  (FALLOW —) FAVEL
  (FAMILY —) DOBBIN
  (FAMOUS —) SILVER TRIGGER
  (FAST —) GANGER
  (FEMALE —) MARE FILLY
  (FLEMISH —) ROIL
  (GOLD —) PALOMINO
  (GRAY —) SCHIMMEL

(HIGH-SPIRITED —) STEPPER
(IMAGINARY —) AULLAY
(IMMUNIZED —) BLEEDER
(INFERIOR —) PLUG CAYUSE PLATER
(JUMPING —) LEPPER
(MALE —) STALLION
(NEAR —) HAND
(OLD —) JADE PLUG PROD YAUD AIVER CROCK
(PACK —) BIDET SUMPTER
(PART OF —) EAR EYE JAW RIB FACE HOCK HOOF KNEE LOIN MANE NECK NOSE POLL TAIL BELLY CHEEK CROUP ELBOW FLANK MOUTH THIGH BREAST CANNON GASKIN HAUNCH STIFLE BUTTOCK CORONET FETLOCK FOREARM NOSTRIL PASTERN WITHERS FOREHEAD FORELOCK SHOULDER THROATLATCH
(PIEBALD —) CALICO
(RANGE —) CAYUSE
(ROAN —) SCHIMMEL
(SADDLE —) MOUNT
(SHAFT —) SHAFTER THILLER
(SHAGGY —) ALTAI
(SLUGGISH —) HOG
(SMALL —) NAG TIT BIDET GENET HOBBY CANUCK JENNET GALLOWAY
(STOCKY —) COB
(TEAM OF —S) CARTWARE
(TEAM OF 3 —S WITH LEADER) UNICORN
(TRICK —) SIMON
(TV —) MRED
(UNBROKEN —) BRONCO
(VICIOUS —) LADINO
(WILD —) BRONC FUZZY BRUMBY KUMRAH OUTLAW TARPAN JUGHEAD BANGTAIL FUZZTAIL WARRIGAL
(WINGED —) PEGASUS
(WORN-OUT —) HACK GARRAN KNACKER CROWBAIT
(WORTHLESS —) JADE SHACK KEFFEL
(YOUNG —) TIT COLT FOAL STAG STOT STAGGIE
(2-YEAR OLD —) TWINTER
(3 —S ABREAST) TROIKA
(3 —S ONE BEHIND ANOTHER) RANDEM
(4 —S ABREAST) QUADRIGA
(PL.) MANADA STABLE UNICORN
(PREF.) HIPP(O)
(SUFF.) HIPPUS
HORSE BALM KNOBWEED KNOTROOT RICHWEED
HORSE BLANKET RUG MANTA
HORSE BOY TRACER
HORSE CHESTNUT CONKER
HORSE-CLOTH MANTA
HORSECLOTH HOUSE HOUSING
HORSE DEALER COPER CHANTER COURSER
HORSE-EYE JACK XUREL
HORSE FENNEL SESELI
HORSEFLESH JACK
HORSEFLY BOT GAD CLEG CLEGG STOUT BOTFLY BREEZE GADBEE GADFLY BULLDOG DEERFLY TABANID

HORSEHAIR SETON
HORSELAUGH GUFFAW
HORSELEECH ALUKAH
HORSELOAD SEAM
HORSE MACKEREL TUNNY SAUREL
HORSEMAN RIDER CHARRO COWBOY HUSSAR KNIGHT RUTTER COURIER PICADOR PRICKER CAVALIER GALLOPER
(PL.) HORSE CAVALRY
HORSEMANSHIP CAVALRY
HORSEMINT RIGNUM
HORSE MUSHROOM WHITECAP
HORSE NETTLE SOLANUM
HORSEPLAY HIJINKS
(PANTOMIME —) RALLY
HORSEPOWER SOUP
HORSEPOX GREASE
HORSE-RACE DERBY
HORSE-RADISH MAROR MOROR REDCOLL
HORSE-RADISH TREE BEN BEHN BEHEN
HORSESHOE TIP SHOE PLATE HOBBER LUNETTE
HORSETAIL TAIL PRELE TOADPIPE
HORSETAIL LICHEN TREEHAIR
HORSETAIL TREE AGOHO AGOJO
HORSEWEED COCASH COWTAIL HOGWEED FIREWEED SCABIOUS
HORSEWHIP BEAT CHABOUK
HORTATORY EMOTIVE
HORTICULTURIST (ALSO SEE BOTANIST)
HORUS SEPT SOPT SEPTI HORMAKHU
(FATHER OF —) OSIRIS
(MOTHER OF —) ISIS
HOSACKIA ACMISPON
HOSE LINE VAMP HOSEN GASKIN BROGUES BULLION HOSIERY CHAUSSES HANDLINE HOSEPIPE
HOSEA OSEE
(FATHER OF —) BEERI
HOSHAIAH (SON OF —) AZARIAH JEZANIAH
HOSHEA (FATHER OF —) NUN AZAZIAH
HOSIERY HOSE KNEESOCK KNITWEAR
(— WORKER) LOOPER
HOSPICE IMARET DIACONIA HOSPITAL
HOSPITABLE DOUCE CLEVER DOULCE SOCIAL CORDIAL FRIENDLY
HOSPITAL BEDLAM CRECHE SPITAL COLLEGE LAZARET PESTHOUSE POLYCLINIC
(— AREA) ICU
(— WARD) ICU
(MENTAL —) SNAKEPIT
(MOVABLE —) AMBULANCE
(PRIVATE —) HOME
HOSPITALITY SALT MENSE XENODOCHY
HOSPODAR VOIVOD GOSPODAR
HOST SUM ARMY FYRD WARE CROWD EMCEE HORDE JASON MAKER POWER SWARM WERED LEGION LODGER NATION THRONG BALEBOS COMPANY FYRDUNG

SACRING VIANDER LANDLORD PARTICLE MULTITUDE
(— OF INVADERS) HERE
(EUCHARISTIC —) LAMB SACRING
(PL.) SABAOTH
(SUFF.) XENOUS XENY
HOSTA NIOBE FUNKIA
HOSTAGE BORROW PLEDGE SURETY RANSOMER
HOSTEL INN ENTRY HOSTAGE KINGDOM HOSPITAL
HOSTELRY AUBERGE PARADOR
HOSTESS TAUPO LANDLADY CHATELAINE
HOSTILE FOE HARD UGLY ALIEN BLACK ENEMY FREMT HATEL STOUT DEADLY FRIGID INFEST ADVERSE ASOCIAL FIENDLY OPPOSED UNQUERT WARLIKE CONTRARY INIMICAL OPPOSITE
HOSTILITY WAR FEID FEUD HATE ANIMUS ENMITY HATRED RANCOR SCHISM DAGGERS RUPTURE
(PL.) WAR ARMS ARMOR WARFARE
HOSTLER NAGMAN OSTLER HORSEBOY
HOT WARM ADUST CALID EAGER FIERY ARDENT CALIDO ESTIVE FERVID IGNITE STOLEN SULTRY TORRID ANIMOSE ANIMOUS BOILING BURNING CANDENT FERVENT PEPPERY THERMAL CALIENTE CAYENNED FEVERISH SEETHING SIZZLING GANGBUSTERS
(— WATER) SOUP
HOTBED BED NEST HOTHOUSE
HOT-BLOODED VASCULAR
HOTBOX SMOKER STINKER
HOTDOG DOG FRANK WEENIE WEINER WIENER WIENIE FRANKFURTER
(— KIND OF PERSON) FIREBRAND
HOTEL INN SPA DIGS FLOP FONDA HOUSE HYDRO HOSTEL HOTTLE POSADA FLEABAG FONDACO FUNDUCK GASTHOF HOSTELRY
(— AT AIRPORT) AIRTEL
(— NEAR AIRPORT) AIRTEL
(WATERSIDE —) BOATEL
HOTELKEEPER HOTELIER
HOTHAM (FATHER OF —) HEBER
HOTHAN (SON OF —) SHAMA JEHIEL
HOT-HEADED BRAINISH MADBRAIN
HOTHIR (FATHER OF —) HEMAN
HOTHOUSE STEW STOVE PINERY FRUITERY
HOT ROD DRAGSTER
HOTSHOT HONCHO
HOT-TEMPERED PEPPERY CHOLERIC SPITFIRE
HOTTENTOT NAMA TOTTY HOTNOT KOKANA WITBOOI QUAEQUAE
(PL.) BALAO BALAWU
HOUND DOG PIE BAIT HARL HUNT MUTE BESET BRACE BRACH ENTRY HARRY LEASH LIMER SLATE AFGHAN BASSET BEAGLE CANINE HARASS HUNTER JOWLER LEAMER LUCERN SLEUTH TUFTER CURTISE ENTRADA GELLERT REDBONE SKIRTER BARUKHZY BLUETICK BRATCHET COURSING FOXHOUND

(BITCH —) BRACH
(CRY OF —) MUSIC
(EXTINCT —) TALBOT
(KIND OF —) BIZAN IBIZAN
(RELAY OF —S) VANLAY
(SLEUTH —) TALBOT
(SPECTRAL —) SHUCK
(PL.) RACHES
HOUND'S-TONGUE TORYWEED
HOUR URE TIDE TIME CURFEW GHURRY
(CANONICAL —) NONE SEXT PRIME TERCE MATINS TIERCE ORTHROS VESPERS COMPLINE EVENSONG
(HALF —) BELL
(KILOWATT —) KELVIN
(KIND OF —) HAPPY
(LAST —S) DEATHBED
(STUDY —) PREP
(6 —S) QUADRANT
(PREF.) HORO
HOURGLASS (PART OF —) BULB SAND FRAME WAIST
HOURLY HORAL HORARY
HOUSE BOX KEN CASA CRIB DOME DUMP FIRM FLET HALL HELL HOLE HOME RACE ROOF STOW ABODE ADOBE AERIE BAHAY BANDA COVER DACHA DOMUS HOOCH HOOSE JACAL LODGE MEESE PLACE STAGE WHARE BESTOW BIGGIN BOTTLE CAMARA CASITA CASTLE CHEMIS CLOTHE DUPLEX FAMILY HEARTH HOOTCH MAISON PALACE PARISH SINGLE STABLE WIGWAM BASTIDE BIGGING CABOOSE CASSINE EUDEMON FAZENDA HOGGERY HOUSING MESUAGE QUARTER SHELTER AEDICULA BARADARI BUNGALOW DOMICILE DOVECOTE DWELLING HACIENDA MEDSTEAD MESSUAGE TENEMENT NOVITIATE
(— AND LAND) DEMESNE
(— AND 5 ACRES) COTE
(— FOR DOGS) KENNEL
(— FOR WOMEN) HAREM
(— IN BOROUGH) HAW
(— OF A MARABOUT) KOUBA
(— OF CORRECTION) BRIDEWELL
(— OF ILL-FAME) KIP
(— OF KNIGHTS TEMPLARS) PRECEPTORY
(— OF LEGISLATURE) SEANAD CHAMBER ASSEMBLY
(— OF PARLIAMENT) COMMONS LAGTING REICHSTAG
(— OF PROSTITUTION) CRIB BAGNIO BORDEL
(— OF REFUGE) MAGDALEN MAGDALENE
(— OF THIEVES) KEN
(— OF WORSHIP) BETHEL CHURCH
(— WITH TRIANGULAR FRONT) AFRAME
(APARTMENT —) INSULA
(ASTROLOGICAL —) ANGLE
(AUSTRALIAN —) HUMPY
(CHANGE —) DRY
(CHAPTER —) CABILDO
(CHEAP EATING —) SLAPBANG
(CLAY —) ADOBE TEMBE
(COACH —) REMISE

(COMMUNAL —) MORONG
(COUNTRY —) PEN DACHA CASINO GRANGE QUINTA BASTIDE CHATEAU
(COW —) VACCARY
(DAIRY —) WICK
(DISREPUTABLE —) KEN
(EATING —) COOKSHOP
(EMPTY —) SQUAT
(ESKIMO —) IGLU IGLOO TOPEK KASHGA KASHIMA
(FIJI —) BURE
(FORTIFIED —) GARRISON
(FULL —) SRO
(GAMBLING —) BANK HELL RIDOTTO
(GOVERNMENT —) KONAK
(GREEK —) FRAT SORORITY FRATERNITY
(GRINDING —) HULL
(GROUP OF —S) CLUSTER
(HAWAIIAN —) HALE
(LODGING —) INN KIP HOST ENTRY HOTEL HOSTEL
(LOG —) TILT
(MANOR —) HAM HALL COURT PLACE SCHLOSS SEIGNEURY
(MERCANTILE —) HONG
(PLANETARY —) TOWER
(POULTRY —) ARK HENNERY
(PUBLIC —) INN PUB HOWF HOWFF JOINT HOSTEL SHANTY CANTEEN POTSHOP SNUGGERY
(RANCH —) HUT
(RELIGIOUS —) CELL CONVENT KELLION MONASTERY PRESBYTERY
(RENTED —) LET
(REST —) DAK KHAN SERAI
(RETREAT —) CENACLE
(ROOMING —) DOSS FLOP FLEABAG
(ROYAL —) AERIE
(SENATE —) CURIA
(SMALL —) COT HUT BACH CELL CABIN HOVEL SHACK CASITA COTTAGE MAISONETTE
(SOD —) SODDY
(STILT —) CHIKEE CHICKEE
(SUMMER —) TRELLIS
(TENEMENT —) LAND CHAWL
(THATCHED —) BANDA
(TOY —) COBHOUSE
(TURKISH —) KONAK
(TYPE OF —) PREFAB
(PREF.) DOMI ECO OECO OIKO STEG(O)
(SUFF.) OECA OECIA STEGE STEGITE
HOUSEBOAT BARGE HOUSER WANGAN WANIGAN DAHABEAH
HOUSEBREAKER MILL JACOB MILLKEN
HOUSEBREAKING CRACK
HOUSECARL THINGMAN
HOUSECOAT DUSTER
HOUSED (— IN) PUTUPAT
(NOT —) OUTLER
HOUSEFINCH BURION LINNET REDHEAD
HOUSEHOLD HIRED HOUSE FAMILY HOUSAL MEINIE MENAGE FIRESIDE MAINPAST
(— GOD) LAR
(PREF.) EC(O) OEC(O) OIKO
HOUSEHOLDER ASTRER

GOODMAN GUIDMAN NAUKRAR FRANKLIN
HOUSEKEEPER HUSSY MATRON
HOUSELEEK JUBARB AYEGREEN HOMEWORT SENGREEN SILGREEN
HOUSEMATE DOMESTIC
HOUSE OF MIRTH (AUTHOR OF —) WHARTON
(CHARACTER IN —) GUS BART JUDY LILY GRYCE PERCY SIMON BERTHA DORSET GEORGE SELDEN TRENOR LAURENCE PENISTON ROSEDALE
HOUSE OF SEVEN GABLES
(AUTHOR OF —) HAWTHORNE
(CHARACTER IN —) MAULE PHOEBE VENNER JAFFREY CLIFFORD HEPZIBAH HOLGRAVE PYNCHEON
HOUSEWARMING INFARE
HOUSEWIFE DAME FRAU FROW WIFE HUSSY VROUW BUSHWIFE HAUSFRAU
(MEAN —) NIP
HOUSEY-HOUSEY BINGO
HOUSING BOX BASE CASE DRUM TRAP BANJO BLIMP GLOBE HOUSE KIOSK BARREL RADOME SHIELD HOUSAGE SHELTER DOGHOUSE PADCLOTH PECTORAL PEDESTAL SHABRACK
(HORSE'S —) BASE
(PLASTIC —) RADOME
(RADAR —) BLISTER
(PL.) HOLSTERS
HOVA IMERINA
HOVEL HUT COSH CREW CRIB CRUE HELM HULK HULL BOTHY CHOZA HUTCH LODGE BOTHIE BURROW CRUIVE PONDOK
HOVELER HOBBLER HUFFLER
HOVEN BLOATING
HOVER BAIT FLIT HANG HOVE LOOM BROOD POISE FLUTTER HOVEREN
HOW AS FOO HOO HOWE HOWEER HOWEVER QUOMODO WHEREBY
HOWDAH TOWER AMBARI AMBAREE
HOWEVER BUT THO YET ONLY HOWSO STILL THOUGH
HOW GREEN WAS MY VALLEY
(AUTHOR OF —) LLEWELLYN
(CHARACTER IN —) HUW BETA DAVY IVOR OWEN EVANS IANTO GWILYM IESTYN MARGED MORGAN BRONWEN ANGHARAD GRUFFYDD
HOWITZER HOWITZ LICORN UNICORN
HOWITZER SHELL OBUS
HOWL BAY WAP WOW BAWL GOWL GURL HURL RAVE WAUL WAWL YAWL YOLL YOUT YOWL TIGER WHEWL WRAWL BEHOWL STEVEN ULULATE
(— VOCIFEROUSLY) TONGUE
HOWLER BONER ERROR ARAGUATO
HOWLER MONKEY MONO ARABA HOWLER GUARIBA GUEREBA STENTOR ALOUATTE
HOWLING ULULANT
HOY TJALK BILANDER CRUMSTER
HOYDEN MEG BLOWZE RIGSBY TOMBOY
HREIDMAR (SON OF —) REGIN FAFNER FAFNIR

H-SHAPED ZYGAL
HUAMUCHIL INGA
HUAVE WABI HUABI
HUB HOB BOSS NAVE STOCK CENTER CENTRE FAUCET HUBBLE SOCKET SPIDER OMPHALOS
(— AND SPOKES) SPEECH
HUBBLE UPROAR TELESCOPE
HUBBLE-BUBBLE CALEAN KALIAN CALAHAN
HUBBUB ADO DIN COIL FLAP STIR CLAMOR FRAISE HUBBLE RABBLE RACKET TUMULT BOBBERY CLUTTER BROUHAHA HUBBABOO ROWDYDOW SPLATTER
HUCHEN HUSO
HUCHNOM TATU
HUCKLEBERRY HURT ERICAD CRACKERS
HUCKLEBERRY FINN (AUTHOR OF —) TWAIN CLEMENS
(CHARACTER IN —) JIM TOM DUKE FINN HUCK JANE KING POLLY SALLY SUSAN WILKS JOANNA PHELPS SAWYER WATSON DOUGLAS GRANGERFORD SHEPHERDSON
HUCKSTER BADGER CADGER KIDDER HAGGLER KIDDIER TRUCKER OUTRIDER
HUDDLE RUCK HUNCH CRINGE CROUCH FUMBLE HOWDER HURTLE SCRUMP SHRIMP SHRINK CROODLE SCRINCH SCROOCH SCRUNCH SHUFFLE
HUDIBRAS (AUTHOR OF —) BUTLER
(CHARACTER IN —) RALPHO CROWDERO HUDIBRAS SIDROPHEL
HUE RUD BLEE BLUE COND CYAN CHLOR COLOR GREEN LEMON SHOUT TAINT TINCT CHROMA
(DULL —) DRAB
(SOMBER —) DARK
HUELESS GRAY GREY
HUFF DOD PET BLOW RUFF TIFF DRUNT SNUFF OFFENSE
(— AND PUFF) PANT
HUFFY FUFFY SHIRTY
HUG CLIP COLL COUL MOLD CREEM CRUSH HALSE PRESS CUDDLE HUDDLE HUGGLE STRAIN CHERISH EMBRACE SQUEEZE
HUGE BIG FELL MAIN VAST ENORM GIANT GREAT JUMBO LARGE STOUR HEROIC IMMANE BANGING BUMPING DECUMAN HIDEOUS IMMENSE MASSIVE MONSTER TITANIC COLOSSAL ENORMOUS GALACTIC GIGANTIC MOUNTAIN PYTHONIC SLASHING SWAPPING THUMPING HUMONGOUS THWACKING MOUNTAINOUS
HUGENESS ENORMITY
HUGUENOT CAMISARD
HUGUENOTS, LES (COMPOSER OF —) MEYERBEER
HUISACHE WABI AROMO CASSIE POPINAC OPOPANAX
HUL (FATHER OF —) ARAM
(GRANDFATHER OF —) SHEM
HULDAH (HUSBAND OF —) SHALLUM
HULK CHOP HULL CORSE

HULL HUD POD BODY BULK HULK HUSK PILL BURSE CASCO SWELL
(— OF COTTON BOLL) BUR BURR
(— OF SHIP) BODY HULK BOTTOM
(PART OF —) BEAM DECK KEEL RAIL BATTEN RABBET CEILING FUTTOCK KEELSON GARBOARD PLANKING STRINGER WATERWAY STANCHION SHELFPIECE SPIRKETING
HULLABALOO DIN FLAP FUROR MANIA CLAMOR HUBBUB RACKET BROUHAHA
HUM BUM BLUR BRUM BUZZ HUSS TUNE CHIRM CROON DRONE FEIGN SOUGH SOWFF THRUM HUMBLE TEEDLE FREDDON TRUMPET BOMBINATE
(— OF VOICES) CHIRM
HUMAN BEING BIPED MANLY FINITE FLESHY HUMANE MORTAL MANNISH HOMININE HUMANIST
(— BEING) CYBORG
(— LINKED TO SPACE ENVIRONMENT) CYBORG
(BIONIC — BEING) CYBORG
(PREF.) HOMI HOMIN(I)
HUMAN BEING MAN WIGHT MORTAL PERSON ADAMITE CREATURE RATIONAL
(PREF.) ANTHROP(O)
HUMAN COMEDY (AUTHOR OF —) SAROYAN
(CHARACTER IN —) BESS MARY ARENA HOMER KATEY TOBEY ACKLEY GEORGE GROGAN HUBERT LIONEL MARCUS THOMAS BYFIELD ULYSSES MACAULEY SPANGLER
HUMANE CIVIL KINDLY TENDER MERGIFUL
HUMANELY MANLY
HUMANITARIAN (ALSO SEE PHILANTHROPIST) PUBLIC PHILANTHROPIC
HUMANITY FLESH MENSK WORLD MANHEAD MANHOOD MANSHIP SPECIES ADAMHOOD HUMANISM KINDNESS LENITUDE
HUMBLE LOW BASE HOWE MEAN MEEK MILD MURE POOR TAME VAIL ABASE ABATE BUXOM DEMIT DIMIT LOWER LOWLY PLAIN SILLY SMALL SOBER WORMY ATTERR DEJECT DEMEAN DEMISS EMBASE HONEST MASTER MODEST REDUCE SIMPLE SLIGHT UNPUFF AFFLICT DEGRADE DEMPSY FOOLISH IGNOBLE MORTIFY OBSCURE CONTRITE DISGRACE
(— ONESELF) STOOP GROVEL
HUMBLED SMALL ABASED DEJECTED
HUMBLENESS HUMILITY
HUMBLER INFERIOR
HUMBLING SETDOWN ABJECTION
HUMBLY SIMPLE
HUMBUG BOO FIE GAS GUM HUM KID BOSH BUNK FLAM GAFF GAME GUFF JAZZ SHAM CHEAT FRAUD FUDGE GULE JOLLY SPOOF SPOOK TRICK BARNEY BLAGUE BUNKUM GAMMON BLARNEY EYEWASH FLUMMER HOGWASH VERNEUK BUNCOMBE FLIMFLAM

FLUMMERY HUCKMUCK IMPOSTER NONSENSE
(SORT OF —) BEE
HUMDINGER ACE PIP DARB LULU ONER BEAUT DILLY DOOZY CORKER DINGER HUMMER SNORTER RIPSNORTER
HUMDRUM IRKSOME PROSAIC BOURGEOIS
HUMERAL VEIL
HUMERUS ARM
HUMID WET DAMP DANK MOIST SOGGY STICKY SULTRY WETTISH HUMOROUS
HUMIDITY
(PREF.) HYGR(O)
HUMILIATE ABASE ABASH SCALP SHAME NIDDER NITHER DEGRADE MORTIFY PUTDOWN UNPLUME DISGRACE
HUMILIATED SMALL ASHAMED
HUMILIATION DUST COMEDOWN DISGRACE
HUMILITY MODESTY MEEKNESS MILDNESS
HUMIN MELANIN
HUMMEL FALTER
HUMMING AHUM BROOL SINGING
HUMMINGBIRD RUBY STAR MANGO SYLPH TENUI TOPAZ AMAZON COQUET HERMIT HUMMER ROSTER SAPPHO COLIBRI EMERALD HUMBIRD JACOBIN RAINBOW SNOWCAP TROCHIL WARRIOR CALLIOPE COQUETTE FIRETAIL FROUFROU MIMOTYPE PICARIAN SAPPHIRE WHITETIP
HUMMOCK HUMP KNOLL CHENIER HAMMOCK TUSSOCK
HUMOR CUE PIN TID WIT BABY BILE CANT COAX MOOD TIFF VEIN WHIM FRAME IRONY TUTOR MEGRIM PAMPER PHLEGM SANIES SOOTHE SPLEEN SPRITE TEMPER FOOLING GRATIFY INDULGE VITREUM VITRINA ARCHNESS DISHUMOR DROLLERY EYEWATER FUMOSITY SANGUINE VITREOUS
(BAD —) BATS THROW
(ILL —) BILE DUDGEON
(KIND OF —) WRY
(QUIET —) DRYNESS
(SLIMY —) HIPPOMANES
(WATERY —) ICHOR
HUMORIST JOKER FUNSTER FUNMAKER FUNNYMAN
AMERICAN NYE LEAF SHAW WARD LEWIS SHUTE SMITH LELAND LOOMIS MASSON ROGERS MARQUIS THOMSON PERELMAN STREETER SULLIVAN SHILLABER
AUSTRIAN SAPHIR
CANADIAN LEACOCK
ENGLISH PAIN WARD SEAMAN
FRENCH RABELAIS
GERMAN RICHTER
IRISH MAHONY
HUMOROUS DROLL FUNNY PAWKY QUEER JOCOSE COMICAL GIOCOSO PLAYFUL WAGGISH PLEASANT SARDONIC
HUMP BOSS HUNK BULGE BUNCH

CROUP CRUMP HULCH HUNCH GIBBER GIBBUS HUMMIE GIBBOUS
(— ACROSS ROAD) RAMP
(PREF.) HYB(O)
HUMPBACK LORD CRUMP PUNCH WHALE KYPHOSIS
HUMPBACKED HUMPED HUMPTY GIBBOSE GIBBOUS
(PREF.) CYPH(O) HYB(O)
HUMPBACKED SALMON HADDO HOLIA
HUMPED HULCH HUMPY HUTCH HUMPTY HUNCHY BUNCHED
HUMPHRY CLINKER (AUTHOR OF —) SMOLLETT
(CHARACTER IN —) JERRY LYDIA GEORGE WILSON BRAMBLE CLINKER HUMPHRY JENKINS MATTHEW MELFORD OBADIAH TABITHA DENNISON WINIFRED LISMAHAGO
HUMUS MOR MOLD MULL HUMIN MOULD
HUN AVAR BOCHE BULGAR MAGYAR VANDAL
(KING OF —S) ATLI ETZEL ATTILA
(KING OF THE —S) ATLI ETZEL ATTILA
HUNCH HUMP HUNK HULCH HUNCHET SCRUNCH
HUNCHBACK URCHIN HUMPBACK
HUNCHBACK OF NOTRE DAME (AUTHOR OF —) HUGO
(CHARACTER IN —) CLAUDE FROLLO PHOEBUS ESMERALDA GRINGOIRE QUASIMODO CHATEAUPERS
HUNDRED RHO CENT CENTUM HUNDER HUNNER CANTRED CANTREF CENTARY
(— THOUSAND) LAC LAKH
(NINE —) SAN SAMPI
(ONE — DOLLARS) BILL
(5 —) D
(PREF.) CENT(I) HECATO HECATOM HECATON HECT(O)
HUNDREDFOLD CENTUPLE
HUNDRED-HANDED BRIAREAN
HUNDREDTH CENTESIMAL
(— OF INCH) POINT
(— OF RIGHT ANGLE) GRAD GRADE
HUNDREDWEIGHT CENT CENTAL CENTENA CENTNER HUNDRED QUINTAL
HUNGARIAN HUN KUMAN MAGYAR
(PREF.) UGRO

HUNGARY

CANAL: SIO SARVIZ
CAPITAL: BUDAPEST
COIN: GARA BALAS FILLER FORINT KORONA
COUNTY: VAS PEST ZALA BEKES FEJER HEVES TOLNA NOGRAD SOMOGY BARANYA
DANCE: CZARDAS
DYNASTY: ARPAD ANGEVIN
FOREST: BAKONY
GYPSY: SZIGANE TZIGANE
KING: BELA GEZA IMRE ARPAD ISTVAN KALMAN MATTHIAS
LAKE: FERTO BALATON VELENCE BLATENSEE

MEASURE: AKO HOLD JOCH YOKE ANTAL ITCZE MAROK METZE HUVELYK MERFOLD
MONEY: PENGO
MOUNTAIN: KEKES BAKONY MECSEK BORZSONY KORISHEGY
MOUNTAIN RANGE: BUKK MATRA MECSEK CARPATHIAN
MUSICAL INSTRUMENT: TAROGATO
NATIVE: HUN SERB CROAT GYPSY MAGYAR SLOVAK UGRIAN
PLAIN: PUSZTA
REGIME: KADAR
RIVER: DUNA MURA RAAB RABA SAJO ZALA BODVA DRAVA DRAVE IPOLY KAPOS KOROS MAROS RABCA TARNA TISZA DANUBE HENRAD POPRAD SZAMOS THEISS ZAGYVA VISTULA BERRETYO
TOWN: ABA ACS OZD VAC BUDA EGER GYOR MAKO PAPA PECS PEST TATA ZIRC KOMLO CEGLED MOHACS SOPRON SZEGED DBRECEN MISKOLC SZENTES DEBRECEN SZEGEDIN
WEIGHT: VAMFONT VAMMAZSA
WINE: EGER TOKAJ TOKAY SZEKSZARD

HUNGER BELL CLEM WANT ACORIA DESIRE FAMINE CRAVING APPETITE
(— PANGS) MUNCHIES
HUNGRY YAP HOWE KEEN LEER YAUP EAGER EMPTY THIRL UNFED HOLLOW JEJUNE PECKISH YAPPISH ANHUNGRY ESURIENT
HUNK DAD DAUD JUNK STUD ADONIS MOUNTAIN
(— OF BREAD) TOMMY
HUNKY STUDLY MUSCULAR ATTRACTIVE
HUNKY-DORY JIMDANDY
HUNT DOG GUN JAG MOB RUN GREW JACK LARK PUMP SEAL SEEK SHOP CHASE CHEVY DRIVE HOUND REVAY STALK TRACK TRAIL BATTUE BEAGLE BREVIT CHEVVY COURSE FALCON FERRET SEARCH SHIKAR VANLAY ENCHASE AUCUPATE PIGSTICK SCROUNGE VENATION
(— BIG GAME) GHOOM
(— DEER) FLOAT
(— DOWN) QUARRY
(— DUCKS) TOLL
(— FOX) CUB
(— HINT) CLUE
(— WITH HAWK) FLY
(— WITH SPEAR) STICK
HUNTER GUN HUNT PINK JAGER BIRDER CHASER GUNNER JAEGER NIMROD THERON ACTAEON BUSHMAN CATCHER COURSER MONTERO SHIKARI SHOOTER SKIRTER STALKER TRAILER VENERER CEPHALUS CHASSEUR FIELDMAN HUNTSMAN TRAILMAN
(— ON SNOW) CRUSTER
(BUFFALO —) CIBOLERO
(MYTHOLOGICAL —) GWYN ORION
(RING OF —S) TINCHEL TINCHILL
HUNTING DRAG HANK AHUNT

WATHE SHIKAR VENERY CUBBING GUNNING BEAGLING PURCHASE SHOOTING SURROUND VENATION
(— SIGNAL) SEEK
HUNTRESS DIANA
HUNTSMAN WHIP HUNTER JAEGER ACTAEON CATCHER COURSER MONTERO SCARLET VENATOR VENERER CHASSEUR
HUPHAM (FATHER OF —) BENJAMIN
HUR (GRANDSON OF —) BEZALEEL
(SON OF —) REPHAIAH
HURAM (FATHER OF —) BELA
HURDLE TRAY FLAKE FRITH PANEL STALE STICK DOUBLE RADDLE SLEDGE WATTLE
HURDS TOW
HURDY-GURDY LIRA ROTA LANTUM VIELLE SAMBUKE HUMSTRUM SYMPHONY
HURI (SON OF —) ABIHAIL
HURL BUM BUN CAST CLOD DASH DUST FIRE PASH PELT PICK SLAT SOAK SOCK DRIVE FLING HEAVE LANCE PITCH SLING SMITE SPANG SWING THIRL THROW WHIRL LAUNCH THRILL HURLBAT SWITHER WHITHER JACULATE PRECIPITATE
HURLY-BURLY HURL RACKET UPROAR
HURRAH HAIL HUZZA HOORAY HURRAY BRAVISSIMO
HURRICANE BAGUIO PRESTER FURACANA FURICANE WILDWIND
HURRIED HASTY RAPID THRONG HASTEFUL SNATCHED
HURRY ADO FOG HIE NIP RAP RUB RUN BUSK DASH DUST HUMP PELL PLAT POST RAPE RESE RUSH STIR TEAR TIFT TROT URGE WHIR CHASE CROWD HASTE HYPER LURRY MOSEY PRESS SESSA SKIRT SPEED STAVE STOUR WHIRL BUCKET BUNDLE BUSTLE HASTEN HUSTLE POWDER STROTH TATTER WHORRY HOTFOOT QUICKEN SCUDDLE SKELTER SLITHER WHITHER DISPATCH EXPEDITE SPLUTTER ACCELERATE
(— ABOUT) SCOUR
(— A HORSE) SPUR
(— AWAY) FLEE BUNCH SCREW SKIRT
(— CLUMSILY) TAVE TEAVE
(— NOISILY) SPLUTTER
(— OFF) DUST
(— UP) BUSK
(GO IN A —) ZOOM
HURRYING FLUSTER
HURT CUT HOT NOY DERE FIKE GALL HARM PAIN SCAT ABUSE BLAME GRIEF GRIPE PINCH SORRY SPITE THORN WATHE WOUND BRUISE DAMAGE GRIEVE IMPAIR INJURE INJURY LESION MIFFED MITTLE PAINED PUNISH SCATHE STRAIN STROKE WINGED AFFLICT HURTING OFFENCE OFFENSE SCADDLE MISCHIEF NUISANCE
(— EASILY) FROISSE
(— FEELINGS) CUT TOUCH

(— REPUTATION) LIBEL
(— SEVERELY) KILL
(EASILY —) GINGER
(PREF.) NOCI
HURTFUL BAD ILL EVIL MALIGN
NOCENT NOCIVE NOUGHT
SHREWD TAKING BALEFUL
BANEFUL HARMFUL MALEFIC
NOCUOUS NOXIOUS SCADDLE
UNQUERT GRIEVOUS HURTSOME
SCATHFUL
HURTLE HURL FLING THIRL
HUSBAND EKE MAN WER BOND
CHAP FERE KEEP LORD MAKE
MATE SAVE SIRE BARON CHURL
HOARD HUBBY MATCH STORE
MANAGE MASTER MISTER SPOUSE
CONSORT GOODMAN GUIDMAN
HENPECK PARTNER CONSERVE
(— OF ADULTRESS) CUCKOLD
(— OF SQUAW) SANNUP
(AFFIANCED —) FUTURE
(SUPPLEMENTARY —) PIRRAURU
(PL.) PUNALUA
(PREF.) MARITI
HUSBANDMAN BOND BOOR CARL
CLOWN COLON RUSTIC TILLER
ACREMAN HUSBAND PLOWMAN
TILLMAN AGRICOLE
HUSBANDRY GAINER GAINOR
THRIFT ECONOMY MANAGERY
HUSH SH HSH MUM PAX HESH
HOOT LULL BURKE SHUSH STILL
WHISH WHIST WHUSH HUDDLE
BESTILL HUSHABY SILENCE
HUSHED QUIET STILL GENTLE
WHISHT
HUSHIM (HUSBAND OF —)
SHAHARAIM
HUSK BUR COD HUD KEX SID ARIL
BARK BURR COAT COSH HOSE
HUCK HULK PILL SEED SHIV SKIN
HOOSE SCALE SHACK SHALE
SHAUP SHELL SHILL SHOOD
SHUCK SHUDE COLDER DEHUSK
FLIGHT SLOUGH BOLSTER
CARCASS CASCARA
(— OF NUT) SHACK BOLSTER
(— OF OATS) SHUD SHOOD FLIGHT
(CORN —) HOJA
(PL.) BHUSA CHAFF BHOOSA
HULKAGE SHELLING
(PREF.) LEMMO LEPO LOPO
SILIQUI
(SUFF.) LEMMA
HUSKY HUSK CODDY FOGGY THICK
FURRED BUIRDLY HULKING
BOUNCING SIBERIAN
HUSSITE TABORITE
HUSSY MINX SLUT BESOM CUTTY
GIPSY GYPSY MADAM STRAP
HIZZIE LIMMER DROSSEL
HUSTINGS BEMA
HUSTLE FAN PEG HUMP JUMP
BLITZ SKELP BUCKET BUNDLE
BUSTLE JOSTLE RABBLE RUSTLE
SCUFTER
HUSTLECAP PINCH
HUSTLER HUSTLE PEELER BUSTLER
FIREBALL
HUT COE COT BARI BUTT COSH
COTE CREW CRIB HALE HULK HULL

ISBA IZBA SHED SKEO TENT TILT
BASHA BENAB BOHIO BOOTH
BOTHY CABIN CHAWL CHOZA
HOOCH HOVEL HUMPY HUTCH
JACAL KRAAL LODGE SCALE SETER
SHACK SHIEL TOLDO TOPEK
WHARE WURLY BOHAWN BOTHAN
CANABA CHALET GUNYAH GUNYEH
HOOTCH MIAMIA PONDOK
RANCHO REFUGE SAETER SCONCE
SHANTY SHELTY WIGWAM WIKIUP
BALAGAN BARRACK BOUROCK
CAMALIG COTTAGE GOONDIE
HUDDOCK HUTMENT SHEBANG
YAKUTAT BARABARA CHANTIER
RONDAWEL SHIELING THOL THAN
TUGURIUM
(— FOR TEMPORARY USE) CORF
(— IN VIETNAM) HOOCH HOOTCH
(— OVER MINING SHAFT) COE
(ABORIGINAL —) MIMI WURLY
GUNYAH MIAMIA WURLEY GOONDIE
(FISHERMAN'S —) SKEO SKIO
(HEATED —) HOTHOUSE
(HERMIT'S —) CELL
(KIND OF —) NISSEN
(NAVAJO —) HOGAN
(POULTRY —) IGLOO
(RITUAL —) SUCCAH SUKKAH
(SAMOYED —) CHUM
(SENTRY —) BOX
(SIBERIAN —) JURT
(SOUTH AFRICAN —) STRUIS
(PREF.) CALIO
HUTCH ARK BUDDLE RABBITRY
HUTIA UTIA JUTIA PILORI
HUZ (FATHER OF —) NAHOR
HUZZAH SHOUT
HWYL FERVOR EXCITEMENT
HYACINTH LILY MUSK LILIUM
CROWTOE FLOATER GREGGLE
JACINTH BLUEBELL CROWFOOT
HAREBELL JACOUNCE
HYACINTH BEAN LABLAB
BONAVIST BONNYVIS DOLICHOS
HYACINTHUS (FATHER OF —)
AMYCLAS
(MOTHER OF —) DIOMEDE
HYALITE OPAL
HYALOGEN NEOSSIN
HYBRID DZO ZHO MULE ZOBO
CROSS GRADE HINNY LIGER
COYDOG GALYAK MOSAIC MULISH
SPLAKE TURKEN BASTARD
BIGENER CATTALO JERSIAN
MONGREL PLUMCOT ZEBRASS
ZEBRULA ZEBURRO CARIDEER
CITRANGE KAFERITA LIMEQUAT
ZEBRINNY
(PREF.) NOTH(O)
HYBRIDIZE CROSS
HYDRA POLYP
HYDRANT CHUCK FIREPLUG
(PART OF —) NUT CHAIN BARREL
BONNET STANDPIPE CONNECTION
HYDRANTH SIPHON SYPHON
HYDRATE SLAKE
HYDRAULIC
(PREF.) HYDR(I)(O)
HYDRAZINE DIAMIDE
HYDRAZOATE AZIDE
HYDRIA KALPIS

HYDROCARBON ARENE CUMOL
FREON GUTTA IDRYL INDAN IRENE
TOLAN XYLOL ALKANE ALKYNE
ALLENE BUTANE BUTYNE CARANE
CETANE CETENE CYMENE DECANE
ETHANE ETHENE HEXINE INDANE
INDENE MELENE NONENE OCTANE
OCTENE OCTINE PICENE PINENE
PYRENE RETENE TOLANE TOLUOL
XYLENE AMYLENE AZULENE
BENZENE CHOLANE CYCLENE
DECALIN ETHERIN FULVENE
HEPTANE HEPTENE HEPTYNE
LYCOPIN MUCKITE MYRCENE
OLEFINE PENTINE PENTYNE
PHYTANE PROPANE STYRENE
TETROLE TOLUENE BIPHENYL
CADALENE CADINENE CAMPHANE
CARBURAN CEROTENE CETYLENE
CHRYSENE CORONENE CUMULENE
DECYLENE DIOLEFIN DIPHENYL
DOCOSANE DYSODILE EICOSANE
ETHYLENE EUDALENE FLUORENE
HEXYLENE ILLIPENE ISOPRENE
LYCOPENE MENTHENE NONYLENE
OCTYLENE PARAFFIN PRISTANE
PYRACENE RUTYLENE SABINENE
SQUALENE STILBENE
(SUFF.) YLENE
HYDROCHLORIC ACID
(SUFF.) CHLORHYDRIA
HYDROCYANIC PRUSSIC
HYDRODAMALIS RHYTINA
HYDROEXTRACTOR BUZZER
WHIZZER
HYDROFLUORIC PHTHORIC
HYDROFOIL FOIL
HYDROGEN HYDRO PROTIUM
(HEAVY —) DIPLOGEN
HYDROGRAPHER AMERICAN
MAURY MITCHELL
ENGLISH SMYTH MURRAY
GERMAN NEUMAYER
NORWEGIAN SVERDRUP
HYDROHEMATITE TURGITE
HYDROID POLYP OBELIA ACALEPH
ZOOPHYTE
HYDROLEA NAMA
HYDROMEL ALOJA
HYDROMETER SPINDLE
HYDROPERITONEUM ASCITES
HYDROPHOBIA LYSSA RABIES
HYDROPHOBIC LYSSIC
HYDROPHYLLIUM BRACT
HYDROPLANE SKIM GLIDER
HYDROXIDE ALKALI HYDRATE
HYDRIDE
HYDROXYL
(SUFF.)
(CONTAINING —) OLIC
HYDROZINCITE CALAMINE
HYENA HINE DABUH SIMIR HYAENID
HYGIENIC SANITARY
HYGRODEIK PAGOSCOPE
HYLAS (FATHER OF —) THIODAMAS
(LOVER OF —) DRYOPE
(MOTHER OF —) MENODICE
HYLLUS (FATHER OF —) HERCULES
(MOTHER OF —) DEIANIRA
(SLAYER OF —) ECHEMUS
(WIFE OF —) IOLE
HYLOZOIST PHYSICIST

HYMEN CHERRY BRIDEGOD
MAIDENHEAD
HYMENIUM THECIUM
HYMENOCALLIS ISMENE
HYMN ODE FUGE LAUD SING DIRGE
GATHA PAEAN PSALM YASHT
YMPNE ANTHEM CARVAL CHORAL
HIMENE HIRMOS MANTRA ORPHIC
THEODY VESPER CHORALE
EXULTET HEIRMOS INTROIT
CANTICLE CATHISMA DOXOLOGY
ENCOMIUM PSALMODY
SEQUENCE TRISAGION TROPARION
(— COLLECTION) MENAION
(MEXICAN —) ALABADO
(VEDIC —) MANTRA
(PL.) HYMNODY
HYMNAL HYMNARY HYMNBOOK
HYPATIA (AUTHOR OF —) KINGSLEY
(CHARACTER IN —) AMAL MIRIAM
AUFUGUS HYPATIA ORESTES
PELAGIA RAPHAEL VICTORIA
HERACLIAN PHILAMMON
HYPE EXCITE PROMOTE PUFFERY
INCREASE
HYPER EXCITABLE
HYPERACTIVE MANIC
HYPERBOLE AUXESIS
HYPERCORACOID RADIAL
SCAPULA
HYPERCRITICAL NICE CAPTIOUS
CRITICAL
HYPERDULIA ADORATION
HYPEREMIA RUBOR
HYPEREMIC CONGESTED
HYPERENOR (BROTHER OF —)
EUPHORBUS POLYDAMAS
(FATHER OF —) PANTHOUS
(MOTHER OF —) PHRONTIS
(SLAYER OF —) MENELAUS
HYPERICUM TUTSAN
HYPERION (DAUGHTER OF —)
AURORA
(FATHER OF —) URANUS
(MOTHER OF —) GAEA
(WIFE OF —) THEA
HYPERON BARYON
HYPEROPIC FARSIGHTED
HYPERSENSITIVITY ATOPY
ALLERGY
HYPHA STOLON
HYPHEN BAND
(PL.) LEADERS
HYPNOTIC AMYTAL BROMAL
CHLORAL SECONAL BARBITAL
NARCEINE SOPORIFIC
HYPNOTISM DEVIL BRAIDISM
HYPNOSIS MESMERISM
HYPNOTIST OPERATOR SVENGALI
HYPO FIXER
HYPOBLAST ENDODERM
HYPODERM
HYPOCHONDRIA HIP HYP HYPO
MEGRIM
HYPOCHONDRIAC ARGAN HIPPY
HIPPIST ATRABILIAR
HYPOCOTYL RADICLE TIGELLA
TIGELLUS
HYPOCRISY SHAM POPEHOLY
PHARISAISM
HYPOCRITE CANT BIGOT CHEAT
FACER FRAUD BLIFIL CAFARD

HUMBUG MUCKER MAWWORM SIMULAR CHADBAND DECEIVER TARTUFFE
HYPOCRITICAL FALSE SLAPE DOUBLE CANTING PLASTER POPEHOLY SPECIOUS
HYPOCYCLOID ASTROID
HYPODERMIS SKIN
HYPOPHARYNX LINGUA LABIELLA
HYPOSTASIS PERSON

HYPOSTATIZE ENTIFY
HYPOSTOME MANUBRIUM
HYPOTENUSE SUBTENSE
HYPOTHESIS SYSTEM THEORY PREMISE WEGENER SUPPOSAL POSTULATE
HYPOTHETICAL IDEAL
HYPOTRACHELIUM GORGERIN
HYPSEUS (DAUGHTER OF —) CYRENE

(FATHER OF —) PENEUS
(MOTHER OF —) CREUSA
(WIFE OF —) CHLIDANOPE
HYPTIS OREGANO
HYRAX DAS CONY CONEY DAMAN WABUR DASSIE WABBER ASHKOKO KLIPDAS HYRACOID
HYRMINA (FATHER OF —) EPEUS
(HUSBAND OF —) PHORBAS
(SON OF —) ACTOR

HYRNETHO (BROTHER OF —) AGELAUS CALLIAS EURYPYLUS
(FATHER OF —) TEMENUS
(HUSBAND OF —) DEIPHONTES
HYSTERIA MOTHER NERVES PIBLOKTO TARASSIS
(PRONE TO —) VAPORISH
(RELIGIOUS —) LATA
HYSTERICAL FRANTIC NERVOUS SHRIEKY

I

I A Y HI HY CHE ICH ISS SHE ITEM
UTCH INDIA UTCHY
(— AM) ISE CHAM ICHAM
(— HAD) CHAD
(— WILL) CHILL ICHULLE
(— WOULD) CHUD
IALEMUS (FATHER OF —) APOLLO
(MOTHER OF —) CALLIOPE
IALMENUS (BROTHER OF —)
ASCALAPHUS
(FATHER OF —) ARES APOLLO
(MOTHER OF —) ASTYOCHE
CALLIOPE
IAMB IAMBIC IAMBUS
(— AND DACTYL) FEET
(DOUBLE —) DIIAMB
IAMUS (FATHER OF —) APOLLO
(MOTHER OF —) EVADNE
IAPETUS (FATHER OF —) URANUS
(MOTHER OF —) GAEA
(SON OF —) ATLAS MENOETIUS
(WIFE OF —) ASIA CLYMENE
IAPYGIANS MESSAPII
IAPYX (BROTHER OF —) DAUNIUS
PEUCETIUS
(FATHER OF —) LYCAON DAEDALUS
IASION (BROTHER OF —) DARDANUS
(FATHER OF —) ZEUS JUPITER
(LOVER OF —) CERES DEMETER
(MOTHER OF —) ELECTRA
(SON OF —) PLUTUS
IATROCHEMICAL SPAGYRIC
IATROCHEMISTRY SPAGYRIC
IBANAG CAGAYAN
IBEX KYL TEK TUR ZAC GOAT RAIL
BEDEN EVECK IZARD JAELA EVICKE
SAKEEN
IBHAR (FATHER OF —) DAVID
IBIS GUARA GANNET HADADA
JABIRU TURKEY CICONIID
IRONHEAD
IBNEIAH (FATHER OF —) JEROHAM
ICARIUS (BROTHER OF —)
TYNDAREUS
(DAUGHTER OF —) ERIGONE
PENELOPE
(FAITHFUL DOG OF —) MOERA
(FATHER OF —) OEBALUS
(MOTHER OF —) GORGOPHONE
ICARUS (FATHER OF —) DAEDALUS
(MOTHER OF —) NAUCRATE
ICE YS GEAL FROST GLACE CRYSTAL
VERGLAS
(— IN ROUGH BLOCKS) RUBBLE
(ANCHOR —) FRAZIL
(DRIFTING FRAGMENT OF —) PAN
CALF
(GROUND —) FRAZIL
(PATCH OF —) RONE
(PINNACLE OF —) SERAC
(RIDGE OF —) HAMMOCK
HUMMOCK
(SEA —) GLACON SLUDGE

(SHORE —) FAST
(SLUSHY —) SISH
(SOFT —) SLOB LOLLY
(THIN NEW —) DISH PANCAKE
(THIN OR FLOATING —) FLOE GRUE
BRASH
(WATER —) SHERBET
(PREF.) CRYSTALL(I)(O) GLACI(O)
(SUFF.) CRYST
ICE AX PIOLET
ICEBERG BERG GROWLER
FLOEBERG
(OFFSHOOT OF —) CALF
ICEBOAT SKEETER
ICE CREAM BISK CREAM GLACE
AUFAIT BISQUE NOUGAT TASTER
SPUMONI TORTONI
(— BETWEEN WAFERS) SLIDER
(— MOLD) BOMBE
(— TREAT) MALT
ICE CREAM CONE CORNET
ICED COLD GLACE FRAPPE
ICEFISH SALANGID
ICE FLOE PAN
ICEHOUSE IGLU IGLOO
(— WORKER) AIRMAN

ICELAND
BALLAD: RIMUR
BAY: FAXA HUNA
CAPITAL: REIKJAVIK REYKJAVIK
COIN: AURAR EYRIR KRONA
DISH: SKYR SVIO BLOOMOR
HAROFISK
EPIC: EDDA SAGA
FIRST SETTLER: ARNARSON
FJORD: BREIDHA
GEYSER: GRYLA
GIANT: ATLI
GLACIER: HOFSJOKULL
LANGJOKULL VATNAJOKULL
HERO: BELE ERIC LEIF SIGUROSSON
LAKE: MYVATN THORISVATN
MEASURE: SET ALIN LINA ALMUD
TURMA ALMENN ALMUDE FERFET
POTTUR FATHMUR FERALIN
FERMILA OLTUNNA SJOMILA
MOUNTAIN: JOKUL
PARLIAMENT: ALTHING
REPUBLIC: LYOVELDIO
RIVER: HVITA JOKULSA THJORSA
TOWN: AKRANES AKUREYRI
KEFLAVIK KOPAVOGUR
VOLCANIC ISLAND: SURTSEY
VOLCANO: LAKI ASKJA HEKLA
ELDFELL
WATERFALL: GULL DETTI GULLFOSS
DETTIFOSS
WEIGHT: PUND POUND

ICE-STONE CRYOLITE
ICHABOD (FATHER OF —) PHINEHAS
(GRANDFATHER OF —) ELI

ICHNEUMON URVA NYMSS
MEERKAT VANSIRE
ICHOROUS GLEETY
ICHTHYOSIS FISHSKIN
ICHU HICHU STIPA
ICICLE ICARY ICKLE YOKEL TANGLE
SHOGGLE SHOOGLE COCKBELL
ICINESS GLARE
ICING ICE PIPING ALCORZA
FROSTING MERINGUE
ICON IKON EIKON IMAGE DEESIS
ICONOCLAST DEBUNKER
ICONOSTASIS DIASTYLE
ICTEROHEMATURIA CARCEAG
ICTONYX ZORILLA
ICTUS ACCENT STRESS DOWNBEAT
ICY GELID BOREAL FRIGID WINTRY
GLACIAL
ID ES OBE GARDON SYPHILID

IDAHO
CAPITAL: BOISE
COUNTY: ADA GEM BUTTE CAMAS
LATAH LEMHI POWER TETON
BLAINE BONNER CARNAS CASSIA
JEROME OWYHEE BENEWAH
KOOTENAI
DAM: OXBOW BROWNLEE
INDIAN: BANNOCK KALISPEL
NEZPERCE SHOSHONI
LAKE: BEAR GRAYS PRIEST
MOUNTAIN: RYAN BORAH RHODES
TAYLOR BIGBALDY BLUENOSE
MOUNTAIN RANGE: CABINET
SELKIRK
NICKNAME: GEM
RIVER: SNAKE LOCHSA SALMON
PAYETTE
SPRINGS: SODA HOOPER LAVAHOT
STATE BIRD: BLUEBIRD
STATE FLOWER: SYRINGA
TOWN: ARCO BUHL MALAD NAMPA
BURLEY DRIGGS DUBOIS
MOSCOW WEISER CASCADE
CHALLIS ORIFINO REXBURG
POCATELLO

IDAS (BROTHER OF —) LYNCEUS
(FATHER OF —) APHAREUS
(MOTHER OF —) ARENE
(WIFE OF —) MARPESSA
IDDO (FATHER OF —) ZECHARIAH
(SON OF —) AHINADAB
IDE ORFE
IDEA EGG GIG KINK EIDOS IMAGE
THING ANONYM DHARMA ECTYPE
FIGURE INTENT NOTICE NOTION
RECEPT THREAP THROPE BEGRIFF
CONCEIT CONCEPT GIMMICK
GLIMPSE MAROTTE OPINION
PROJECT SPECIES SURMISE
THOUGHT GIMCRACK NOTIONAL
BRAINCHILD PRECONCEPTION

(—S OF LITTLE VALUE) STUFF
(CENTRAL —) ARGUMENT
(COMMONPLACE —) SHIBBOLETH
(CONSERVATIVE —S) FOGYISM
(DOMINANT —) CLOU
(DULL STUPID —S) STODGE
(FAINT —) GLIMMER
(FALSE —) FALLACY
(FANTASTIC —) VAPOR MAGGOT
(FAVORITE —) HORSE
(FIXED —) TICK
(FUNDAMENTAL —) KEYNOTE
(GENERAL —) HANG
(IRRATIONAL —) FOLLY
(MAIN —) POINT
(MUSICAL —) SENTENCE
(ODD —) FREAK
(OVERWORKED —) CLICHE
(PLATONIC —) ESSENCE
(RECURRING —) BURDEN
(STALE —S) BILGE
(SUPERSTITIOUS —) FREIT
(TRANSCENDENT —) FORM
(TRITE —) PABLUM PABULUM
(PL.) EIDE THOUGHT
(PREF.) IDEO
IDEAL ISM IDEA DREAM AERIAL
BEAUTY DOMNEI DREAMY EDENIC
MENTAL UNREAL PATTERN
PERFECT UTOPIAN ABSTRACT
FANCIFUL IDEALITY NOTIONAL
QUADRATE ORIFLAMME
(— OF BEAUTY) KALON
IDEALISM IDEOLOGY
IDEALIST IDEIST UTOPIAN FICHTEAN
UTOPIAST
IDEALIZE PLATONIZE
IDEALIZED POETICAL
IDENTICAL LIKE SAME SELF VERY
ALIKE EQUAL METOO EVENLY
PROPER CORRECT IDENTIC
NUMERIC SELFSAME
IDENTIFIABLE NAMEABLE
IDENTIFICATION IDENT DOCUMENT
EQUATION RECOGNITION
(— METHOD) DNA
IDENTIFIED SIGNATE
IDENTIFIER LINK BIRDER
IDENTIFY PEG TAB MARK NAME
RANK SPOT IDENT PLACE TALLY
FINGER DISCERN DIAGNOSE
PINPOINT
(— WITH) ENTER
IDENTITY SEITY UNITY IPSEITY
ONENESS EQUALITY SAMENESS
(— OF PITCH) UNISON
(PERSONAL —) SEITY
IDEOGRAPH CHARACTER
(PL.) KANJI
IDEOGRAPHIC REAL
IDEOLOGICAL MENTAL
IDEOLOGY ISM
IDIOBLAST SPHERE IDIOSOME

IDIOCY ANOIA ANOESIA FATUITY IDIOTRY MOROSIS IDIOTISM
IDIOM CANT ARGOT JUANG DORISM IFUGAO JARGON MEDISM SPEECH AEOLISM ANOMALY GRECISM PAHLAVI PEHLEVI TURKISM DANICISM DORICISM IDIOTISM IONICISM LANGUAGE LOCALISM PARLANCE RURALISM
IDIOMORPHIC EUHEDRAL
IDIOPHONE RATTLE
IDIOSOME SPHERE
IDIOSYNCRASY TIC WAY QUIRK IDIASM RUMNESS
IDIOT FON OAF SOT DAFF DOLT FOOL AMENT BOOBY DUNCE FONNE CRETIN HOBBIL NIDGET NIDIOT DINGBAT DULLARD NATURAL OMADAWN PINHEAD IMBECILE INNOCENT SLAVERER
(AUTHOR OF —) DOSTOEVSKI
(CHARACTER IN —) LEF GANYA AGLAYA PARFEN MYSHKIN NATASYA EPANCHIN ROGOZHIN FILIPOVNA ARDALIONOVITCH
IDIOTIC DAFT DOPY ZANY IDIOT FATUOUS FOOLISH WANTWIT IMBECILE
IDLE COLD DEAD HACK HAKE HANG HULL JAUK LAKE LAZE LAZY LUSK MUZZ ORRA SOFT SORN TICK VAIN VOID DALLY EMPTY ORROW SHOOL SLIVE THOKE WASTE COOTER DAIDLE DANDER DREAMY FOOTER GAMMER LOUNGY OTIANT OTIOSE SLIMSY TEETER TIDDIE TIFFLE TRIFLE TRUANT UNUSED VACANT DRONISH IDLEFUL IDLESET LOAFING SAUNTER SHACKLE SLUMBER SLUTHER UNLUSTY VACUOUS WHIFFLE BASELESS BOOTLESS FAINEANT INACTIVE INDOLENT SHAMMOCK SLAISTER SLOTHFUL TRIFLING WORKLESS
(TO BE —) SLOTH
IDLENESS LAZE RUST SLOTH IDLETY IDLESET IDLESSE IGNAVIA VACANCY VACUITY FLANERIE IDLEHOOD INACTION
(— PERSONIFED) LAURENCE LAWRENCE
(LIVE IN —) MAROON
IDLER BUM GAUM HAKE JAUK KERN LOON DRONE BADAUD BUMBLE DONNOT IDLEBY LUBBER PLAYER QUISBY RODNEY STALKO TRUANT BLELLUM BUCKEEN DAWDLER FAITOUR FRANION IDLESBY LOLLARD LOUNGER LOUTHER LURDANE SLOUNGE TRIFLER DOLITTLE FAINEANT IDLESHIP LAYABOUT LAZARONE UNWORKER WHIFFLER
IDLE WHEEL IDLER RUNNER
IDLY TOOMLY VAGUELY
IDMON (DAUGHTER OF —) ARACHNE
(FATHER OF —) APOLLO
(MOTHER OF —) CYRENE ASTERIA
IDOCRASE EGERAN CYPRINE VESUVIAN
IDOL GOD BAAL ICON JOSS LION TIKI WOOD ZEMI ANITO BESAN

EIKON GUACA HOBAL HUACA IMAGE STOCK SWAMI IDOLET IDOLUM MAMMET MAUMET MINION PAGODA POPPET PUPPET TERAPH EIDOLON MAHOMET BAPHOMET MAUMETRY PANTHEUM
(HEATHEN —) DEVIL
(PREF.) EIDOLO IDOLO
IDOLATER AKKUM PAGAN BAALIST BAALITE HEATHEN IDOLIST
IDOLATROUS PAGAN IDOLISH
IDOLATRY BAALISM IMAGERY ADULTERY MAUMETRY
IDOLIZE GOD IDOL ADORE ADMIRE WORSHIP
IDUMAEAN EDOMITE
IDUN (HUSBAND OF —) BRAGI
IDYIA (DAUGHTER OF —) MEDEA
(FATHER OF —) OCEANUS
(HUSBAND OF —) AEETES
(MOTHER OF —) TETHYS
(SON OF —) APSYRTUS
IDYL IDYLL BUCOLIC ECLOGUE
IDYLLIC HALCYON PASTORAL THEOCRITEAN
IDYLLS OF THE KING (AUTHOR OF —) TENNYSON
(CHARACTER IN —) BORS ENID BALAN BALIN ISOLT ARTHUR ELAINE GARETH GAWAIN MERLIN MODRED VIVIEN ETTARRE GALAHAD GERAINT LYNETTE PELLEAS BEDIVERE LANCELOT TRISTRAM GUINEVERE PERCIVALE
IF AN AND GIF GIN THO GEVE IFFEN INCASE SOBEIT THOUGH PROVIDED
(— EVER) ONCE
(— NOT) BUT ELSE NISI
(PREF.) **(AS —)** QUASI
IF WINTER COMES (AUTHOR OF —) HUTCHINSON
(CHARACTER IN —) MARK NONA EFFIE MABEL PERCH SABRE TYBAR BRIGHT FARGUS HAROLD FORTUNE TWYNING
IGAL (FATHER OF —) JOSEPH NATHAN
IGDALIAH (SON OF —) HANAN
IGEAL (FATHER OF —) SHEMAIAH
IGERNA (HUSBAND OF —) UTHER GORLOIS
(SON OF —) ARTHUR
IGNEOUS PLUTONIC
(SOURCE OF — ROCK) MAGMA
(PREF.) PLUTONO
IGNIS FATUUS WISP SPUNKIE WILDFIRE
IGNITE TIND FLASH LIGHT SHOOT SPARK ILLUME KINDLE CALCINE LIGHTEN
IGNITED LIVING BURNING
(CAUSE TO BECOME —) RETROFIRE
IGNITER PUNK SPARKER
IGNITION FIRE LIGHTING
IGNOBLE LOW BASE MEAN VILE ABJECT GRUBBY SORDID CURRISH SERVILE UNNOBLE BASEBORN SHAMEFUL
IGNOBLY BASELY
IGNOMINIOUS BASE VILE INFAMOUS SHAMEFUL

IGNOMINY SHAME REBUKE SCANDAL DISGRACE DISHONOR
IGNORAMUS IDIOT IGNARO SIMPLE AMHAAREZ
IGNORANCE IRONY TAMAS AGNOSY AVIDYA AVIJJA BETISE NICETY RUDITY UNSKILL DARKNESS IDIOTISM NESCIENCE
(BOLD —) BAYARD
(FEIGNED —) IRONY
(PREF.) AGNOIO
IGNORANT LAY DARK NICE RUDE VAIN GREEN GROSS SILLY INGRAM SIMPLE ARTLESS REDNECK SECULAR UNAWARE UNCOUTH UNKNOWN IMPERITE INNOCENT INSCIENT INSCIOUS NESCIENT UNTAUGHT BENIGHTED
(— OF EVIL) INNOCENT
IGNORANTLY SIMPLY
IGNORE BALK BLOW OMIT SINK SNUB VAIN BAULK BLINK ELIDE BYPASS MISKEN SLIGHT DESPISE MISKNOW NEGLECT TUNEOUT CONFOUND OVERJUMP OVERLEAP OVERLOOK OVERPASS
IGOROT BONTOK NABALOI KANKANAI
IGUANA GUANA GUANO LEGUAN
IGUVINE UMBRIAN
IJO DJO BONI BONNY
IKKESH (SON OF —) IRA
ILAIRA (FATHER OF —) LEUCIPPUS
(HUSBAND OF —) CASTOR
(MOTHER OF —) PHILODICE
(SISTER OF —) PHOEBE
ILEUM
(PREF.) ILEO
ILEUS MISERERE
ILIA RHEA
(FATHER OF —) NUMITOR
(SON OF —) REMUS ROMULUS
ILIAD (AUTHOR OF —) HOMER
(CHARACTER IN —) AIAS HELEN PARIS PRIAM ATHENA HECTOR NESTOR ACHILLES DIOMEDES MENELAUS ODYSSEUS PANDARUS AGAMEMNON APHRODITE PATROCLUS ANDROMACHE
ILIONE (BROTHER OF —) POLYDORUS
(FATHER OF —) PRIAM
(HUSBAND OF —) POLYMNESTOR
(MOTHER OF —) HECUBA
(SON OF —) DEIPYLUS
ILIUM TROY
ILK KIN KIDNEY
ILL BAD EVIL ILLY SICK AEGER CRONK CROOK DONCY FUNNY WISHT GROGGY INJURY POORLY SICKLY UNWELL SICKISH VICIOUS MISCHIEF PHYSICAL
(— AT EASE) ASHAMED AWKWARD FAROUCHE
(PREF.) MAL(E) MIS
ILL-ADVISED FOOLISH
ILL-BALANCED LOPSIDED
ILL-BEHAVED UNTHEWED
ILL-BEING ILLTH
ILL-BODING DIRE DISMAL
ILL-BRED HOYDEN CADDISH CHURLISH PLEBEIAN MISLEARED

ILL-CHOSEN UNSORTED
ILL-CONSIDERED HASTY
ILL-DEFINED BLIND VAGUE MONGREL
ILL-DRESSED FRUMPY FRUMPISH
ILLEGAL BLACK LAWLESS UNLAWFUL WRONGOUS ADULTERINE
(NOT —) COLD
ILLEGALITY NONO UNLAW
ILLEGIBLE BLIND
ILLEGITIMACY BASTARDY
ILLEGITIMATE BASE BASTARD BOOTLEG NATURAL NOTHOUS MISBEGOT NAMELESS UNLAWFUL WRONGFUL MISBEGOTTEN
(PREF.) NOTH(O)
ILL-FATED UNHAPPY UNSONCY UNCHANCY
ILL-FAVORED UGLY UNSONCY
ILL-FEELING PIQUE
ILL-FORMED SCRAWLY INFORMED
ILL HUMOR TID BILE DRUNT GRUMP THRAW FANTEE SPLEEN DUDGEON FANTIGUE
ILL-HUMORED FOUL GLUM CROOK DUDDY GRUMPY MOROSE STUFFY SULLEN CROOKED FRETFUL PEEVISH
ILLIBERAL LITTLE NARROW INSULAR BANAUSIC GRUDGING
ILLICIT SLY BLACK ILLEGAL UNLAWFUL
ILLIMITABLE INFINITE

ILLINOIS

CAPITAL: SPRINGFIELD
COLLEGE: AURORA EUREKA OLIVET QUINCY SHIMER
COUNTY: BOND CASS COOK KANE OGLE COLES MACON BUREAU DUPAGE GRUNDY HARDIN MASSAC PEORIA IROQUOIS MACOUPIN SANGAMON
FRENCH SETTLEMENT: CAHOKIA
HILLS: SHAWNEE
INDIAN: FOX SAUK
LAKE: MICHIGAN
NICKNAME: SUCKER PRAIRIE
PRESIDENT: REAGAN
RIVER: OHIO ROCK WABASH ELKHORN MACKINAW SANGAMON
STATE BIRD: CARDINAL
STATE FLOWER: VIOLET
STATE TREE: OAK
TOWN: PANA ALEDO ALTON CAIRO CARMI DIXON FLORA LACON OLNEY PARIS PEKIN ALBION CANTON EUREKA GALENA HARDIN HAVANA HERRIN JOLIET NORMAL OTTAWA PEORIA QUINCY SKOKIE URBANA VIENNA CHICAGO DECATUR GENESEO MENDOTA NOKOMIS TAMPICO KANKAKEE ROCKFORD

ILLINOISIAN SUCKER
ILLIPE BASSIA VIDORICUM
ILLITERATE UNREAD IGNORANT MUSELESS UNTAUGHT
ILL-MADE AWKWARD
ILL-NATURED SHREWD CRABBED

SHREWISH ACID UGLY NASTY SURLY CRABBY SNARLY SULLEN THWART CANKERY PEEVISH

ILLNESS DROW TOUT BRASH CHILL TRAIK MORBUS PLUNGE DISEASE SICKNESS

(IMAGINARY —) HYPOCHONDRIA

(MENTAL —) MANIA MONOMANIA

(MINOR —) HURRY

(MOMENTARY —) DROW

(SUDDEN —) WEED SWEAM

ILL-NOURISHED SHELLY

ILLOGICAL MAD SPURIOUS

ILL-OMENED OBSCENE DISMAL UNLUCKY

ILL-SHAPED WEEDY

ILL-SMELLING FUSTY STINKING

ILL-TEMPERED SURLY ILL FESS MEAN PUXY ACRID CHUFF NURLY RATTY CAMMED CHUFFY CURSED GIRNIE SHRILL SNAGGY RAMPANT ROPABLE VICIOUS CAMSHACH LUNGEOUS SHREWISH VIXENISH MALODOROUS

ILL-TREAT FOB HOIN MISDO AFFRONT

ILLUMINATE FIRE LIMN CLEAR LIGHT ENLIMN ILLUME KINDLE RESHINE CLARIFY EMBLAZE LIGHTEN MINIATE RADIATE EMBRIGHT FLOURISH ILLUMINE LUMINATE

(— FAINTLY) TWILIGHT

ILLUMINATED FIRELIT

ILLUMINATION E GLIM GLORY LIGHT SHINE LIGHTING LUMINARY

(— INCREASE) WOMP

(— UNIT) PHOT

(MANUSCRIPT —) MINIATURE

ILLUMINE SUN FIRE LAMP CLEAR LUMINE ENLIGHT

ILL-USAGE ABUSE

ILLUSION MAYA DEATH DREAM ERROR FAIRY FANCY FLESH TRICK MATTER CHIMERA ELUSION FALLACY FICTION MOCKERY PHANTOM RAINBOW ZOLLNER DELUSION PHANTASM PRESTIGE

ILLUSIVE PHANTOM

ILLUSORY FALSE EVANID FATUOUS PHANTOM TRICKSY APPARENT ILLUSIVE SPECTRAL

ILLUSTRATE INSTANCE

ILLUSTRATION CUT GAY ICON IKON SHOW SPOT INSET FIGURE COMPARE DISIMILE EXEMPLUM INSTANCE VIGNETTE

ILLUSTRATIVE CLASSIC

ILLUSTRATOR ERTE

ILLUSTRIOUS GRAND NOBLE NOTED SHEEN BRIGHT CANDID HEROIC EMINENT EXALTED GLORIED SHINING GLORIOUS HEROICAL LUCULENT MAGNIFIC PRECLARE RENOWNED SPLENDID STARLIKE BRILLIANT REDOUBTABLE

(MOST —) ILMO ILLMO

ILL WILL SPITE ENMITY GRUDGE MALICE MAUGER MAUGRE RANCOR DESPITE AMBITION

ILL-WISHER FOE

ILUS (FATHER OF —) TROS

(MOTHER OF —) CALLIRRHOF

(SON OF —) LAOMEDON

ILVAITE YENITE LIEVRITE

ILYSIA TORTRIX

IMAGE DAP GOD MAP FORM ICON IDOL IKON JOSS MAKE SEAL SIGN SPIT TIKI AGNUS DITTO EPHOD FANCY HERMA IMAGO MEDAL MORAL PAINT PRINT SAMMY SANTO SHAPE SIGIL SWAMI SWAMY TOTEM AGALMA ALRAUN EFFIGY EMBLEM FIGURE MAUMET MODULE POPPET RECEPT REFLEX SHRINE SPHINX STATUE SVAMIN TERAPH VISAGE WEEPER EIDOLON EXPRESS FANTASY GODLING IMAGERY KATCINA PICTURE PROPOSE CONCEIVE DAIBUTSU OPTOGRAM PORTRAIT SURPRINT ZOOMORPH SEMBLANCE SIMILITUDE SIMULACRUM RESEMBLANCE

(— IN CHINESE COSTUME) MANDARIN

(OF CHRIST) SUDARIUM

(— OF DEITY) SWAMI GODKIN SVAMIN GODLING

(— OF SAINT) BULTO SAINT SANTO GEORGE SANTON

(— OF WOOD) XOANON

(— RECALLED BY MEMORY) IDEA

(CULT —) JOSS

(FALSE —) GHOST GHOSTING

(GOOD-LUCK —) ALRAUN ALRUNA

(HEAVENLY —) FRAVASHI

(LINGERING —) SHADE

(MENTAL —) FANCY IMAGO RECEPT CONCEPT FANTASY SPECIES PHANTASM

(RADAR —) BLIP

(REFLECTED —) SHADOW SPECIES

(SEQUENCE OF —S) REVERIE

(VAGUE —S) FRINGE

(PL.) IMAGERY TERAPHIM

(PREF.) EID(O)(OLO) EIKON(O) ICON(O) IDOLO IKON(O) TYP(I)(O)

IMAGERY ICONISM

IMAGINARY IDEAL AERIAL FEIGNED FICTIVE SHADOWY CHIMERAL CHIMERIC FANCIFUL FICTIOUS MYTHICAL NOTIONAL QUIXOTIC ROMANTIC SCENICAL VISIONAL BARMECIDE

IMAGINATION CHIC BRAIN FANCY FLAME NOTION FANTASY PROJECT THOUGHT

(DROLL —) HUMOR

IMAGINATIVE FORMFUL CREATIVE FANCIFUL POETICAL

IMAGINE SEE WIS REDE WEEN DREAM FANCY FEIGN FRAME GUESS IMAGE THINK DEVISE FIGURE IDEATE INVENT RECKON COMPASS CONCEIT CONJURE FANCIFY FANTASY FEATURE PICTURE PORTRAY PROJECT PROPOSE SUPPOSE SURMISE SUSPECT CONCEIVE DAYDREAM JEALOUSE

IMAGINED FANCIED SUPPOSED

IMAGINER FANCIER

IMAGINING FICTION PHANTOM

IMAGO MOTH

IMAM IMAUM MAHDI

IMBALANCE DRIVE DYSCRASIA

IMBECILE MAD DOTE FOOL AMENT ANILE DAFFY IDIOT CRANKY DOTARD DOTING DOTISH CONGEON FATUOUS

IMBECILITY AMENTIA FATUITY

IMBIBE DRINK SMACK ABSORB SPONGE INHAUST SWALLOW IRRIGATE

(— NOISILY) SLURP

IMBIBING SUCTION

IMBIBITORY SPONGY

IMBRIUS (FATHER OF —) MENTOR

(SLAYER OF —) AJAX

(WIFE OF —) MEDESICASTE

IMBRUE EMBREW INSTEEP

IMBUE SOAK STEW COLOR CROWN EMBUE ENDUE INDUE SCENT STEEP TINCT ENSOUL IMBIBE INFUSE LEAVEN SEASON ANIMATE INGRAIN INSENSE INSTILL SATURATE TINCTURE INOCULATE

IMBUED INSTINCT REDOLENT

IMHOTEP (FATHER OF —) PTAH

(MOTHER OF —) SEKHMET

IMIDE LACTIM SACCHARIN

IMITATE APE COPY ECHO MIME MOCK ZANY ENGUE FORGE IMAGE MIMIC AFFECT ANSWER FOLLOW PARROT SEMBLE COPYCAT EMULATE PAGEANT PATTERN PASTICHE RESEMBLE SIMULATE

(— WITH RECORDED SOUND) LIPSYNC LIPSYNCH

(PREF.) MIMO

IMITATION COPY FAKE FAUX SHAM DUMMY IMAGE MIMIC ALPACA ANSWER BUMPER ECTYPE SHADOW CAMBLET FOULARD IMITANT MIMESIS MOCKAGE MOCKERY CHENILLE PARROTRY PASTICHE POSTIQUE

(OF COIN) COUNTER

(BURLESQUE) TRAVESTY

(COTTON —) CAMBRIC

(EXAGGERATED —) BURLESQUE

(UNSUBSTANTIAL —) GHOST

(PREF.) NE

(SUFF.) EEN ETTE

IMITATIVE ARTY MIMIC ARTFUL ECHOIC SHODDY MIMETIC SIMULAR SLAVISH APATETIC EPIGONAL

IMITATOR APE MIME ZANY MIMIC COPIER COPYIST EPIGONE EMULATOR EPIGONUS HOMERIST

(SUFF.) MIMUS

IMMACULATE CLEAN CANDID CHASTE BLOTLESS PRISTINE SPOTLESS UNSOILED

IMMANENCE INBEING

IMMATERIAL MENTAL SLIGHT ETHEREAL FORMLESS SEPARATE TRIFLING

IMMATURE RAW CRUDE GREEN SAPPY SMALL VEALY YOUNG BOYISH CALLOW JEJUNE LARVAL NEANIC TENDER GIRLISH HALFLIN IMPUBIC LADDISH NOUVEAU PUERILE UNBAKED JUVENILE NEPIONIC UNWEANED SHIRTTAIL

IMMATURITY NONAGE

IMMEASURABLE UNTOLD ABYSMAL INFINITE

IMMEDIACY HERE

IMMEDIATE CLOSE DIRECT MODERN PARATE SUDDEN INSTANT PRESENT PROXIMAL SYNECTIC POSTHASTE

IMMEDIATELY PDQ TIT ANON ASAP AWAY FAST JUST ONCE SOON PLUMB RIGHT ASTITE DIRECT PRESTO PRONTO SUBITO DIRECTLY HEREUPON OUTRIGHT STRAIGHT

IMMEDIATENESS INSTANCY

IMMEMORIAL DATELESS

IMMENSE HUGE VAST GIANT GRAND GREAT LARGE UNMEET UNRIDE TITANIC ENORMOUS GIGANTIC INFINITE SLASHING WHOOPING PLANETARY

IMMENSELY ALOT EVER

IMMENSITY VAST IMMANE IMMENSE ENORMITY GRANDEUR HUGENESS

IMMERSE DIP SINK SOAK COVER DOUSE MERGE MERSE SOUSE STEEP DRENCH PLUNGE BAPTIZE BOWSSEN DEMERGE EMBATHE ENSTEEP IMMERGE DISSOLVE

IMMERSED DEEP INNATE

IMMERSION DIP DUNKING MERSION

IMMERSIONIST DIPPER

IMMIGRANT LAG BALT ISSEI JIMMY METIC POMMY GUINEA HALUTZ CHALUTZ INCOMER PILGRIM COMELING

IMMINENCE INSTANCY

IMMINENT TOWARD PENDING PROXIMATE

IMMIX BLEND

IMMOBILE FIXED INERT STILL FROZEN DORMANT GLACIAL TRANCED MOVELESS

(PREF.) ANKYL(O)

IMMOBILIZATION FUSION FIXATION

IMMOBILIZE PIN FREEZE SPLINT STIFFEN

IMMOBILIZED STIFF

IMMODERATE FREE DIZZY UNDUE LAVISH UNMETH EXTREME OVERWEENING

IMMODERATENESS EXCESS

IMMODEST FREE BRAZEN OBSCENE INDECENT PETULANT UNCHASTE SHAMELESS

(NOT —) DELICATE

IMMORAL BAD ILL EVIL IDLE LOOSE WRONG WANTON CORRUPT VICIOUS CULPABLE DEPRAVED INDECENT SLIPPERY

IMMORTAL DIVINE ENDLESS ETERNAL GODLIKE UNDYING ENDURING UNDEADLY

IMMORTALITY AMRITA ATHANASY ETERNITY

IMMOVABLE PAT SET FAST FIRM FIXED RIGID ADAMANT SITFAST CONSTANT IMMOBILE IMMOTIVE OBDURATE

IMMUNE FREE SALTED REFRACTORY

IMMUNITY SOC CHARTER FREEDOM LIBERTY WOODGELD PROTECTION

IMMUNOGLOBULIN IGA IGE IGM UGG

IMMURE MURE WALL CONFINE CLOISTER IMPRISON

IMMUTABILITY ONENESS

IMMUTABLE ETERNAL

IMNAH (FATHER OF —) ASHER

IMOGEN (FATHER OF —) CYMBELINE
(HUSBAND OF —) POSTHUMUS

IMP PUG BRAT LIMB DEMON TERROR URCHIN DEVILET DEVILING DEVILKIN FOLLETTO
(PRINTING-HOUSE —) RALPH

IMPACT HIT JAR BEAT BITE BLOW BUMP DASH DUSH JOLT SLAM BRUNT CLASH FEEZE PEISE POISE PULSE SHOCK SKITE GLANCE STROKE CONTACT IMPULSE COLLISION
(— OF VALUES ON YOUTH) YOUTHQUAKE
(HAVING STRONG —) GUT

IMPAIR MAR BLOT HARM HURT MAIM MANK SOUR WEAR ALLOY CLOUD CRACK CRAZE DECAY ERODE QUAIL SPOIL TAINT ACRAZE DAMAGE DEADEN DEFACE HINDER INJURE LABEFY LESSEN REDUCE SICKEN WEAKEN WORSEN BLEMISH CRIPPLE DISABLE IMPEACH REFRACT SHATTER STRETCH VITIATE DECREASE ENFEEBLE IMBECILE IMPERISH INFRINGE LABEFACT
(— BY INACTIVITY) RUST
(— ESSENTIALLY) RUIN
(— GRADUALLY) WASTE

IMPAIRED HURT STALE CROCKY FLYBLOWN
(— BY AGE) FUSTY
(— IN TONE) BREATHY
(HEARING —) DEAF
(SPEECH —) APHASIC
(PREF.) DYS

IMPAIRMENT ALLAY FAULT SPOIL DOTAGE IMPAIR INJURY LESION BEATING DEFICIT DISEASE EROSION WEARING AKINESIA PAIRMENT
(— OF CONSCIOUSNESS) ABSENCE

IMPALA PALLA PALLAH REDBUCK ROOIBOK ROODEBOK ROOYEBOK

IMPALE BAIT SPIT GANCH GANSH SPEAR SPIKE STAKE STICK STING SKIVER TRANSFIX

IMPALPABLE ELUSIVE

IMPART GIVE SEND SHED TELL BREAK DRILL SHARE YIELD BESTOW COMMON CONFER CONVEY DIRECT IMPUTE INSTIL PARTEN REVEAL DELIVER DIVULGE PURPORT DISCOVER INSTRUCT INTIMATE
(— KNOWLEDGE) TEACH INFORM
(— SECRETS) CONFIDE
(— TONE) TONE
(— ZEST) ANIMATE

IMPARTIAL EVEN FAIR JUST EQUAL LEVEL CANDID NEUTER UNBIASED

IMPARTIALITY CANDOR EQUITY EQUACITY EVENNESS

IMPARTIALLY FAIRLY EQUALLY

IMPASSABLE WICKED INVIOUS PASSLESS ROADLESS TRACKLESS

IMPASSE LOGJAM DEADLOCK

IMPASSION COMMOVE

IMPASSIONED ARDENT FERVID FERVENT FEVERISH PERFERVID

IMPASSIVE STOIC FROZEN STOLID PASSIVE STOICAL APATHETIC PHLEGMATIC

IMPASSIVENESS APATHY MORGUE STOICISM

IMPATIENT HOT ANTSY EAGER HASTY SHARP TESTY FRETFUL PEEVISH RESTIVE TIDIOSE CHOLERIC PETULANT

IMPATIENTLY HASTILY

IMPEACH CALL ACCUSE CHARGE INDICT ARRAIGN CENSURE IMPLEAD TRAVERSE

IMPEACHMENT APPEAL

IMPECCABLE SINLESS

IMPECUNIOUS POOR

IMPEDE BOG DAM GUM JAM LET MAR CLOG GRAB JAMB KILL SLUG SNAG ANNOY BLOCK CHECK CHOKE DELAY EMBAR ESTOP HITCH SLOTH SPOKE BAFFLE FETTER FORBID FORSET HAMPER HARASS HINDER HOBBLE PESTER RETARD STYMIE IMPEACH PREVENT SHACKLE ENCUMBER HANDICAP OBSTRUCT PRECLUDE

IMPEDED FOGBOUND

IMPEDIMENT BAR RUB CLOG SNAG STOP BLEAR BLOCK HITCH SPOKE STICK BURDEN RUBBER SCOTCH BLINDER EMBARGO OBSTACLE OBSTANCY
(— IN SPEECH) HAAR HALT

IMPEDIMENTA STUFF

IMPEDING CATCH HEAVY FOULING

IMPEL PAT PUT BEAR BEAT CALL CAST GOAD HURL MOVE SEND URGE WHIP CARRY DRIVE FEEZE FORCE KNOCK PRESS PRICK PULSE COMPEL EXCITE INCITE INDUCE PROPEL ACTUATE DESTINE INSPIRE INSTINCT MOTIVATE
(— TO GREATER SPEED) GATHER

IMPELLER RUNNER

IMPEND BREW HANG DEPEND OVERHANG

IMPENDING TOWARD PENDENT PENDING IMMINENT MENACING

IMPENETRABLE HARD DENSE MURKY PROOF THICK AIRTIGHT HARDENED

IMPENITENT OBDURATE

IMPERATIVE AMUST VITAL PRESSING MASTERFUL

IMPERCEPTIBLE OCCULT SUBTLE

IMPERFECT ILL HALF POOR AMISS BLIND FUZZY ROUGH BOTCHY FAULTY PLATIC ATELENE STICKIT UNWHOLE VICIOUS INPARFIT MUTILOUS
(PREF.) ATEL(O)

IMPERFECTED INCHOATE

IMPERFECTION BUG RUB WEN FLAW KINK MOLE SLUR VICE WART ERROR FAULT BLOTCH DEFECT FOIBLE BLEMISH CRUDITY DEFAULT DEMERIT FAILING FRAILTY WEAKNESS
(— IN BOTTLE) HEELTAP
(— IN GLASS) STRIA STREAK
(— IN LEATHER) FRIEZE
(— IN SILK) CORKSCREW
(— IN WICK) THIEF WASTER

IMPERFECTIVE ATELIC

IMPERFECTLY ILL HALF AMISS ROUGHLY

IMPERFORATION ATRESIA

IMPERIAL TUFT ROYAL KINGLY PURPLE MAJESTIC

IMPERIALIST KHAKI CAESAR CAESAREAN

IMPERIL RISK EXPONE EMPERIL ENDANGER JEOPARDY

IMPERIOUS BOSSY SURLY LORDLY HAUGHTY DESPOTIC IMPERIAL MASTERLY PRESSING MASTERFUL

IMPERISHABLE ETERNAL UNDYING ENDURING IMMORTAL

IMPERMANENCE ANICCA

IMPERMANENT FLEETING

IMPERMEABLE AIRTIGHT

IMPERSONAL COLD DEADPAN INHUMAN ABSTRACT

IMPERSONALITY UNSELF

IMPERSONATE POSE TYPIFY PERSONIFY

IMPERSONATION GENIUS

IMPERSONATOR APER ACTOR MIMIC CACHINA KACHINA KATCINA

IMPERTINENCE PAWK SNASH AUDACITY

IMPERTINENT GAY FREE PERT RUDE FRESH SASSY SAUCY PUSHING IMPERENT IMPUDENT OBTRUSIVE OFFICIOUS MEDDLESOME

IMPERTURBABILITY ATARAXY ATARAXIA SANGFROID

IMPERTURBABLE COOL PLACID GLACIAL TRANQUIL UNFLAPPABLE

IMPERVIOUS DEAD GASTIGHT HARDENED HERMETIC MOTHPROOF
(— TO HEAT) ADIATHERMIC
(— TO LIGHT) OPAQUE
(SUFF.) PROOF

IMPETUOSITY BIRR ELAN FURY HASTE WRATH FOUGUE POWDER RANDOM SPLEEN

IMPETUOUS HOT RAMP RASH RUDE BRASH EAGER FIERY FRECK HASTY HEADY SHARP ARDENT BROTHE FIERCE FLASHY LAVISH RACKLE STRONG BUCKISH FURIOUS HOTHEAD HOTSPUR RAMSTAM VIOLENT BRAINISH EMPRESSE HEADLONG SLAPDASH VEHEMENT PRECIPITATE

IMPETUS BIRR FARD SEND DRIFT GRACE SWING YMPET BENSEL IMPACT POWDER RAVINE SWINGE SWOUGH IMPULSE MOMENTUM

IMPIGNORATE PAWN

IMPINGE FALL IMPACT ASSAULT CROSSCUT ENCROACH

IMPINGEMENT IMPACT

IMPIOUS UNHOLY ATHEIST ATHEOUS GODLESS UNGODLY DOWNWEED HOARWORT NEFANDOUS NEFARIOUS

IMPISH IMPY ELFISH PUCKISH WARLOCK

IMPLACABLE STOUT DEADLY MORTAL

IMPLACABLY FATALLY

IMPLANT FIX IMP SET SOW HAFT ROOT GRAFT INFIX INLAY ENRACE ENROOT FASTEN INFUSE INSTIL ENFORCE ENGRAFT IMPRESS INSPIRE ENTRENCH INSTINCT

IMPLANTED INBORN INSITE

IMPLEMENT (ALSO SEE TOOL) AX AXE BAT CARD DISC DISK FORK GRAB HACK HONE HOOK LOOM PLOW SPUD SPUR TOOL CROOK DRILL FLINT LANCE SCRUB SHEAR SLICK SPADE SPOON STEEL STICK TRIER AMGARN BEAMER BLADER BROACH COLLAR COOLER DIBBLE DREDGE DRIVER DUSTER EOLITH FLAKER FLUTER HACKER HARROW INVOKE LADDER LIPPER LUNATE MARKER MEALER PACKER PADDLE PALLET PESTLE PLOUGH RIMMER SCREEN SCYTHE SEATER SEEDER SERVER SHEARS SHOVEL SICKLE SLICER SMOOTH BREAKER CHOPPER CLEANER CLEAVER ENFORCE FLESHER FLYFLAP GAROTTE GRUBBER HARPOON HUSTLER KNAPPER MATTOCK NUTPICK SKIMMER SLABBER SLASHER SLEEKER SLICKER SPATTLE SPATULA SPITTLE SPURTLE STAMPER STICKER SWATHER UTENSIL AGITATOR BUSHWACK MEASURER SCUTCHER SEARCHER SHREDDER SKETCHER SPLITTER SPREADER STRIPPER TERRACER THWACKER TOLLIKER TRANCHET TWEEZERS WARKLOOM WORKLOOM NUTCRACKER
(— FOR CUTTING CHEESE) HARP
(— FOR HANGING POT) HALE
(—S OF HUSBANDRY) WAINAGE
(— TO PREVENT MALT FROM OVERFLOWING) STROM
(ANCIENT —) POINT SLICE AMGARN EOLITH NEOLITH RACLOIR PALEOLITH
(BAKER'S —) PEEL
(CLIMBING —) CREEPER
(ESKIMO —) ULU
(GARDENING —) HOE RAKE SEEDER SICKLE
(HEDGING —) TRAMP
(IRRIGATION —) CROWDER
(LOGGING —) TODE
(POTTER'S —) PALLET SPATTLE
(PREHISTORIC —) CELT FLAKER
(SHOVEL-LIKE —) SCOOP
(SOLDERING —) DOCTOR
(TORTURE —) ENGINE
(UPROOTING —) MAKE
(WINNOWING —) FAN
(PL.) GEAR CUTLERY GAINAGE FLAUGHTS
(SUFF.) LABE

IMPLEMENTATION PERFORMANCE
IMPLICATE DIP ENWRAP CONCERN
EMBROIL INCLUDE INVOLVE
IMPLICATION CLAIM IMPLIAL
INNUENDO
IMPLICIT COVERT
IMPLIED TACIT IMPLICIT
IMPLORATION PETITION
IMPLORE ASK BEG CRY PRAY
CHARM CRAVE PLEAD INVOKE
OBTEST BESEECH CONJURE
ENTREAT SOLICIT PETITION
IMPLOSION INRUSH
IMPLY HINT ARGUE CARRY COUCH
INFER EMPLOY ENTAIL IMPORT
INDUCE CONNOTE CONTAIN
INCLUDE INVOLVE PRESUME
SIGNIFY SUGGEST SUPPOSE
PREDICATE
IMPOLITE RUDE UNCIVIL
IMPOLITENESS CRUDITY
IMPONDERABLE FRIGORIC
IMPORT SAY WIT BEAR BODY GIST
TOUR DRIFT FORCE IMPLY MORAL
SCOPE SENSE SOUND SPELL
TENOR VALOR AMOUNT CHARGE
DENOTE INGATE INTENT MATTER
SPIRIT BETOKEN MEANING
PRETEND SIGNIFY CARRIAGE
INDICATE
(PL.) INWARDS
IMPORTANCE BORE MARK PITH
FORCE POISE WORTH CHARGE
IMPORT MATTER MOMENT
REMARK STRESS STROKE WEIGHT
ACCOUNT ESSENCE GRAVITY
VALENCY EMPHASIS MAGNITUDE
SIGNIFICANCE
**IMPORTANCE OF BEING
EARNEST (AUTHOR OF —)** WILDE
(CHARACTER IN —) JACK ALGIE
PRISM CECILY EARNEST ALGERNON
WORTHING BRACKNELL
GWENDOLEN MONCRIEFF
IMPORTANT BIG KEY DEAR DREE
HIGH MAIN REAL GRAVE GREAT
HEAVY MAJOR GAPING MIGHTY
NEEDLE STRONG URGENT VALOUR
CAPITAL CENTRAL CRUCIAL
EMINENT MATTERY PIVOTAL
SERIOUS WEIGHTY EVENTFUL
MATERIAL PRESSING MOMENTOUS
OVERBEARING SIGNIFICANT
(— PERSON) LION
(HIGHLY —) VITAL
(MOST —) TOP ULTIMATE
(MOST — ONE OF GROUP)
FLAGSHIP
IMPORTER MILLINER
IMPORTUNATE URGENT INSTANT
DEVILING EXIGEANT PRESSING
IMPORTUNE BEG WOO BEAT BONE
PREY PRIG TOUT URGE PRESS
TEASE BESEECH BESIEGE INSTANT
SOLICIT TERRIFY INSTANCE
IMPORTUNITY BRASS URGENCY
IMPOSE LAY SET TOP CLAP GIVE
LEVY MUMP POLE SORN ABUSE
APPLY CLAMP INPUT STAMP
TRUMP BURDEN CHARGE ENJOIN
ENTAIL FASTEN FATHER IMPONE
IMPUTE BLAFLUM DICTATE INFLICT
IRROGATE

(— UPON) FOB GAG HUM LAY DUPE
SELL CULLY TRAIL BLUDGE DELUDE
EXCISE HUMBUG NUZZLE CULLION
DECEIVE HOODWINK
IMPOSED BOUNDEN
IMPOSING BIG EPIC BUDGE BURLY
GRAND HEFTY NOBLE PROUD
AUGUST EPICAL FEUDAL PORTLY
HAUGHTY POMPOUS STATELY
HANDSOME MAGNIFIC SONORANT
SONOROUS
(— UPON) PRACTICE PRACTISE
IMPOSITION BAM COD HUM LEVY
SELL TAIL GOUGE IMPOT CHOUSE
GAMMON INTAKE TAILLE IMPOSAL
ARTIFICE IMPOSURE
(MILITARY —) CESS
(SCHOOL —) PENSUM
IMPOSSIBLE OUT HOPELESS
IMPOST LAY TAX CAST LEVY TAIL
TASK TOLL ABWAB ANNALE
AVANIA EXCISE GABELLE
POUNAMU TALLAGE TONNAGE
TRIBUTE CHAPTREL SPRINGER
(PL.) CUSTOMS
IMPOSTOR FOB FAKE GULL IDOL
CHEAT FAKER FRAUD GOUGE
QUACK BUNYIP FOURBE HUMBUG
MUMPER EMPIRIC FAITOUR
PROSTOR DISSEMBLER PHANTOM
IMPOSTURE BAM GAG FAKE HOAX
SHAM CHEAT FRAUD TRICK DECEIT
HUMBUG JUGGLE ARTIFICE
DELUSION JUGGLERY
IMPOTENCE ACRATIA UNMIGHT
WEAKNESS
(— THROUGH MAGIC) LIGATURE
IMPOTENCY UNWELTH
IMPOTENT WEAK FRIGID PAULIE
UNABLE STERILE UNMIGHTY
IMPOUND FIND POIND POUND
INTERN PINFOLD
IMPOVERISH NILL CLOUD BEGGAR
IMPOOR SICKEN DEPLETE
DEPRESS EMPOVER BANKRUPT
POVERISH PAUPERIZE
IMPOVERISHED POOR OBOLARY
BANKRUPT INDIGENT
IMPRACTICAL CRAZY FECKLESS
IMPRECATE WISH SWEAR
IMPRECATION DASH OATH PIZE
WISH BLAME CURSE DAMME
DAMMIT CONSARN ANATHEMA
IMPREGNABILITY STRENGTH
IMPREGNABLE FAST PROOF
IMPREGNATE BIG HOP DOPE FILL
LIME MILT BREED IMBUE STOCK
STUFF TINCT AERATE CHARGE
INFORM INFUSE LEAVEN SEASON
SETTLE ASPHALT ENVENOM
IMPREGN CHROMATE CONCEIVE
CREOSOTE FRICTION FRUCTIFY
GRAPHITE MEDICATE PERMEATE
SATURATE SILICATE TINCTURE
(SUFF.) **(— WITH)** URET(UM)
IMPREGNATED BRED COATED
IMPRESS FIX BITE COIN DING DINT
ETCH GRAB MARK AFFIX BRAND
CLAMP CRIMP DRIVE GRAVE GRILL
INFIX PRESS PRINT REACH SEIZE
STAMP STEAD WRITE AFFECT
ENSEAL FASTEN INCUSE INDENT
SALUTE STRIKE ANTIQUE ENGRAVE

ENSTAMP IMPLANT IMPREST
IMPRINT INSENSE AUTOTYPE
INSCRIBE NEGATIVE
(— CONSIDERABLY) WOW
(— DEEPLY) DELVE ENGRAVE
(— SUDDENLY) SMITE
(— VERY MUCH) SLAY
(— WITH FEAR) AFFRIGHT
(FAIL TO —) UNDERWHELM
IMPRESSED AGOG BLIND ANTIQUE
INDENTED
IMPRESSIBLE WAXY
IMPRESSION CUT HIT AURA CAST
CHOP DENT DINT IDEA MARK
MOLD SEAL STEP STIR FANCY
GOUGE IMAGE MOULD PRINT
STAMP STATE ECTYPE EFFECT
ENGRAM FIGURE INCUSE OFFSET
SIGNET SPLASH STRIKE EOPHYTE
ETCHING FANTASY IMPRESS
MOULAGE OPINION SEALING
SQUEEZE STENCIL TOOLING
BLANKING ENGRAMMA NEGATIVE
PRESSION PRESSURE STAMPAGE
TOOLMARK PHOTOGENE
(— OF DIE) CLICHE
(— ON COIN) CROSS
(— WITHOUT INK) ALBINO
(AUDITORY —) SOUND
(DOUBLE —) MACKLE MACULE
(GENERAL —) REPUTE
(IMMEDIATE —) APERCU
(LATER —) REPRINT
(LUMINOUS —) PHOSPHENE
(MAKE AN — ON) GRAB
(MENTAL —) GRAVING
(STRONG —) HUNCH
(TRANSITORY —) SNAPSHOT
(VIVID —) SPLASH
(PREF.) TYP(H)(O)
(SUFF.) TYPAL TYPE TYPIC TYPY
IMPRESSIONABLE SOFT WAXY
WAXEN TENDER PLASTIC PASSIBLE
IMPRESSIONIST LUMINIST
IMPRESSIVE BIG FAT EPIC AWFUL
GRAND NOBLE PROUD SOCKO
EPICAL SOLEMN PESANTE
STATELY TEARING TELLING
WEIGHTY FORCIBLE IMPOSING
SMASHING SONORANT SONOROUS
STUNNING MAGNIFICENT
IMPRESSIVENESS WEIGHT
IMPREST LOAN
IMPRIMATUR SEAL LICENSE
APPROVAL SANCTION
IMPRINT DINT ETCH MARK SIGN
STEP PRESS STAMP CUTOFF
FASTEN STRIKE ENGRAVE
ENSTAMP IMPRESS APREYNTE
COLOPHON EPIGRAPH PRESSION
PRESSURE STAMPAGE
(— ON CHEEK) FASTEN
(PUBLISHER'S —) COLOPHON
IMPRISON JUG LAG NUN BOND
GAOL HULK JAIL QUOD SEAL SHOP
WARD CROWD EMBAR GRATE
COMMIT IMMURE JIGGER PRISON
SLOUGH CONFINE INTOWER
BASTILLE
IMPRISONED FAST
IMPRISONMENT BAND BOND
ARREST CHAINS DURESS PRISON
CUSTODY DURANCE

IMPROBABLE FISHY UNLIKE
UNLIKELY
IMPROMPTU GLIB MAGGOT
SUDDEN OFFHAND
IMPROPER BAD PAH PAW AMISS
LARGE SPICY UNDUE UNFELE
UNJUST ILLICIT INDECENT
PERVERSE TORTIOUS UNSEEMLY
WRONGOUS MALODOROUS
IMPROPERLY AMISS
IMPROPRIETY SOLECISM
IMPROVE FIX BEET GAIN GOOD
GROW HELP MEND AMEND EDIFY
EMEND GRADE MOISE SMART
TOUCH BETTER ENRICH PROFIT
ADVANCE BENEFIT CORRECT
CULTURE ELEVATE PERFECT
PROMOTE RECTIFY UPGRADE
UPSWING
(— APPEARANCE OF HORSE)
BISHOP
(— APPEARANCE OF TEA) FACE
(— CONDUCTIVITY) AGE
IMPROVED BETTER
IMPROVEMENT AMENDS PICKUP
POLICY PROFIT REFORM REDRESS
UPSWING
IMPROVIDENT PRODIGAL
WASTEFUL
(— PERSON) MICAWBER
IMPROVISATION THEME CALYPSO
IMPROVISE JAM COOK FAKE PONG
VAMP WING ADLIB FANTASY
(— MUSICALLY) JAM FAKE NOODLE
(— NONSENSE SYLLABLES) SCAT
IMPRUDENCE FOLLY
IMPRUDENT FESS RASH FALSE
UNWARY FOOLISH RECKLESS
IMPUDENCE GALL BRASS CHEEK
MOUTH NERVE SLACK BRONZE
PUPPYISM
IMPUDENT BOLD COXY FACY RUDE
DANTY DANDY BRASH FRESH
GALLY LIPPY SASSY SAUCY
BRASSY BRAZEN CHEEKY STOCKY
BIGGETY CHUNKED FORWARD
GALLOWS PERKING INSOLENT
MALAPERT AUDACIOUS
BAREFACED
IMPUDENTLY COOLY COOLLY
FRESHLY
IMPUGN DENY FALSE DISPUTE
IMPEACH
IMPULSE FIT BIAS RESE SEND URGE
DRIVE NISUS SPEND START DESIRE
MOTIVE SIGNAL SPLEEN YETZER
CALLING CONATUS IMPETUS
INSTINCT MOVEMENT STIRRING
(— CARRIER) AXON
(BLIND —) ATE
(ELECTRICAL —) KICK
(SPONTANEOUS —) ACCORD
(SUDDEN —) SPLEEN
(SUPERNATURAL —) AFFLATUS
(PREF.) OSMO
IMPULSION SWING IMPULSE
IMPULSIVE QUICK FITFUL
HEADLONG IMPETUOUS
IMPURE DRY FOUL LEWD GROSS
HORRY MUDDY FILTHY TURBID
UNPURE MONGREL SCABBED
UNCLEAN VICIOUS INDECENT
MACULATE PRURIENT MACULATED

IMPURITY CRUD DONOR DROSS DOPANT FEDITY ACCEPTER ACCEPTOR FOULNESS
(— IN LINT) SHALE
(— IN MINERAL) GANG GANGUE
(PL.) SCUM GARBLE SLUMMAGE
IMPUTABLE OWING
IMPUTATION SCANDAL
IMPUTE LAY PUT RET ARET EVEN WITE COUNT REFER ARRECT CHARGE FASTEN IMPOSE OBJECT RECKON REPUTE ASCRIBE ENTITLE IMPEACH
IN A I N Y AT TO BAJO INBY INTO UPON ALONG INTIL ATHOME
(— ACCORDANCE) AFTER
(— ADDITION) EKE TOO ALSO ABOVE AGAIN ALONG FORBY STILL BEYOND BESIDES FARTHER FURTHER MOREOVER OVERPLUS THERETIL
(— ADVANCE) AHEAD FORTH BEFORE
(— A FAINT) AWAY
(— ANY CASE) EVER HOWEVER
(— A SERIES) SERIATIM
(— A STATE OF ACTION) ENERGIC
(— BEHALF OF) PRO
(— CASE THAT) AUNTERS
(— CIRCULATION) ABROAD
(— CONNECTION WITH) FORNENT FERNINST
(— EARNEST) AGOOD
(— EXCESS OF) OVER
(— FACT) SOOTH TRULY INDEED ITSELF MERELY VERILY ACTUALLY VERAMENT
(— FAITH) IVADS EFECKS YFACKS
(— FRONT) FORE AFACE FORNE AGAINST PARAVANT
(— FULL) ALONG
(— GOOD SEASON) BETIMES
(— GOOD SPIRITS) BOBBISH
(— GRACEFUL MANNER) ADAGIO
(— JEST) AGAME
(— NO MANNER) NOWISE NAEGATES
(— ONE DIRECTION) ANON
(— ORDER) FOR ATAUNT ATAUNTO
(— PLACE OF) FOR WITH INSTEAD
(— POSSESSION) WITHIN
(— PROGRESS) AFOOT TOWARD
(— PROPER MANNER) DULY
(— RESPECT TO) ANENT
(— RETURN FOR) AGAINST
(— ROTATION) ABOUT
(— SO FAR AS) AS QUA
(— SOLE CONTROL) ABSOLUTE
(— SOOTH) PARFEY PERFAY
(— SPITE OF) FOR ALTHO MALGRE AGAINST DESPITE MALGRADO
(— SUSPENSE) PENDING
(— THE DOING OF) WITH
(— THE FIELD) ABROAD
(— THE FIRST PLACE) IMP IMPRIMIS
(— THE FUTURE) HENCE
(— THE MORNING) MANE
(— THE REAR) AREAR ASTERN
(— THE REGIONS OF UNBELIEVERS) IPI
(— THE SAME PLACE) IBID IBIDEM
(— THE SAME WAY) AS
(— TOWARD) INOWER

(— TRUTH) MARRY SOOTH CERTES INDEED VERILY SOOTHLY FORSOOTH
(— VAIN) WASTELY
(— VIEW OF THE FACT THAT) SEEING
(— WHAT MANNER) HOW QUOMODO
(NOT —) OUT
(PREF.) A IL IM IN INTRO IR
INABILITY (— TO FEED) APHAGIA
(— TO MASTICATE) AMASESIS
(— TO SPEAK) ALOGIA ANEPIA DUMBNESS
(— TO WALK) ABASIA
(— TO WRITE) AGRAPHIA
INACCESSIBILITY FASTNESS
INACCESSIBLE COY REMOTE UNGAIN WICKED SHADOWY
INACCURATE SOUR FALSE LOOSE FAULTY UNJUST INEXACT IMPROPER SLIPSHOD
INACHUS (DAUGHTER OF —) IO
(FATHER OF —) OCEANUS
(MOTHER OF —) TETHYS
(SON OF —) PHORONEUS
INACTION RUST
INACTIVATE MOTHBALL
INACTIVE LAX DEAD DRUG FLAT IDLE LAZY MESO SLOW HEAVY INERT NOBLE SLACK SULKY ASLEEP SEDENT STATIC SUPINE TORPID CESSANT DORMANT PASSIVE RESTIVE COMATOSE COMATOUS DEEDLESS DILATORY FAINEANT SLOTHFUL SLUGGISH THEWLESS THOWLESS QUIESCENT
INACTIVITY SLOTH ANERGY TORPOR ANERGIA ABEYANCE IDLENESS CESSATION SEGNITUDE
INADEQUACY DEFECT FRAILTY SCARCITY
INADEQUATE BAD BARE POOR THIN INEPT SCANT SHORT SLACK FEEBLE STRAIT FOOLISH INVALID SLENDER HIGHLAND INFERIOR MISERABLE
(PREF.) MAL
INADEQUATELY BADLY SLACK SLACKLY
INADVERTENCE LAPSUS
INADVERTENT CARELESS
INAJA JAGUA
INALIENABLE INHERENT
INAMORATA AMORADO AMORETTO
INANE DITSY DITZY DIZZY EMPTY GIDDY JERKY SILLY VAPID JEJUNE VACANT FATUOUS FOOLISH INSIPID PUERILE VACUOUS IMBECILE SLIPSLOP TRIFLING SENSELESS
INANGA MINNOW
INANIMATE DEAD DULL BRUTE INERT DEADLY STOLID STUPID LIFELESS
INANIMITY CONSENSUS
INANITY FATUITY VACUITY
INAPPLICABLE SPURIOUS
INAPPROPRIATE INEPT UNAPT UNDUE FOREIGN UNHAPPY
(SOMETHING —) CAMP

INAPT UNHAPPY BACKWARD FOOTLESS MALAPROPOS
INARTICULATA LYOPOMA
INARTICULATE DUMB LAME THICK
INARTISTIC CRUDE ARTLESS
INATTENTION ABSENCE NEGLECT APROSEXIA
INATTENTIVE DEAF SLACK ABSENT REMISS SUPINE DREAMSY UNTENTY CARELESS DISTRAIT HEEDLESS MINDLESS
INAUDIBLE SECRET
INAUDIBLY INWARDLY SECRETLY
INAUGURATE AUGUR BEGIN SETUP HANDSEL INITIATE
INAUGURATION HANDSEL
INAUSPICIOUS BAD ILL EVIL FOUL ADVERSE OBSCENE OMINOUS UNHAPPY UNLUCKY SINISTER
INAUTHENTIC SPURIOUS
INBORN GENIAL INBRED INNATE NATIVE CONNATE NATURAL HABITUAL INHERENT
INBRED INBORN INNATE
INBREED SELF
INBREEDING ENDOGAMY
INCA INGUA OREJON
INCALCULABLE UNTOLD SUMLESS UNKNOWN
INCA MAGIC FLOWER CANTUT CANTUTA
INCANDESCENCE GLOW
INCANDESCENT BRIGHT
INCANTATION CHARM DAWUT SPELL CARMEN FETISH MANTRA SHAZAM CANTION CHANTRY GREEGREE
INCAPABLE DEAD NUMB UNABLE HANDLESS
INCAPACITATE NAPOO UNFIT NOBBLE UNABLE DISABLE
INCAPACITATED FLAT DISABLED STRICKEN
INCARCERATE JAIL IMMURE CONFINE IMPRISON
INCARNATE BODIED EMBODY CARNATE ENFLESH HUMANIFY PERSONIFY
INCARNATION RAMA IMAGE ADVENT AVATAR GENIUS MNEVIS TERTON HUTUKTU EPIPHANY PERSONIFICATION
INCAUTIOUS RASH UNWARY UNCHARY UNTENTY CAREFREE RECKLESS
INCENDIARY FIREBUG ARSONIST BOUTEFEU
INCENSE CENSE INFLAME KETURAH PROVOKE IRRITATE THYMIAMA
(— INGREDIENT) ONYCHA
(— VESSEL) SHIP
(PREF.) THURI
INCENSE-BOAT NAVICULA
INCENSED RAW HETUP IRATE RILED WROTH WRATHFUL
INCENTIVE BROD GOAD SPUR PRICK MOTIVE IMPETUS IMPULSE INCITIVE STIMULUS MOTIVATION
INCEPTION ORIGIN ANCESTRY
INCESSANT STEADY ENDLESS CONSTANT
INCESSANTLY FOREVER

INCH UNCH PRIME UNCIA
(ABOUT 7 —S) FISTMELE
(100TH OF —) POINT
(4 —S) HANDFUL
(48TH OF —) IRON
(9 —S) SPAN
INCHOATE FORMLESS
INCIDENT GO EVENT LIABLE CAUTION EPISODE PASSAGE SUBJECT ACCIDENT CASUALTY OCCASION OCCURRENCE
(AMUSING —) BAR BREAK
(LITERARY —) BIT
INCIDENTAL BY BYE SIDE STRAY CASUAL EPISODIC GLANCING INCIDENT OCCURRENT
INCIDENTALLY BYHAND OBITER APROPOS BYTHEWAY
INCINERATE COMBUST CREMATE
INCINERATOR BURNER SALAMANDER
INCIPIENCE BUD
INCIPIENT INITIAL GERMINAL INCHOATE
INCISE CHOP RASE LANCE INCIDE CHANNEL ENGRAVE
INCISION CUT GASH SLIT SNIP ISSUE SCORE BROACH SCOTCH STREAK CUTDOWN DIACOPE APLOTOMY CECOTOMY COLOTOMY CULDOTOMY
(SUFF.) TOMY
INCISIVE ACID KEEN CRISP SHARP BITING BRUTAL CUTTING ACULEATE PIERCING TRENCHANT
INCISIVENESS MORDANCY
INCISOR CUTTER NIPPER GATHERER
INCITE EGG HIE HOY PUT SIC TAR ABET BEET BUZZ EDGE FIRE GOAD LASH MOVE PROD SICK SNIP SPUR STIR URGE WHET AWAKE CHIRK EGGON IMPEL PRICK PROKE SPARK SPURN STING TEMPT AROUSE BESTIR ENTICE EXCITE EXHORT FILLIP FOMENT HALLOO INDUCE KINDLE NETTLE PROMPT UPSTIR URGEON ACTUATE ANIMATE COMMOVE INCENSE INSPIRE PROMOVE PROVOKE QUICKEN SOLICIT INCITATE MOTIVATE
(— SECRETLY) SUBORN
(— TO ATTACK) SET HIRR SOOL
INCITEMENT GOAD PROD SPUR STING MOTIVE EGGMENT STIRRING
(— OF LITIGATION) BARRATRY
INCITER FEEDER MONITOR INCENSOR INCENTOR
INCLEMENCY RIGOR CRUELTY TYRANNY ASPERITY HARDNESS SEVERITY
INCLEMENT RAW HARD RUDE SOUR GURLY STARK COARSE RUGGED SEVERE UNFINE UNKINDLY
(NOT —) OPEN CIVIL
INCLINATION DIP GEE MAW PLY SET BENT BIAS BROO CANT CARE DRAG DRAW EDGE FALL GUST HANG LEAN LIKE LIST LOVE LUST MIND SLEW TURN VEIN WILL BEVEL BOSOM DRAFT DRIFT FANCY GRAIN HABIT HIELD HUMOR KNACK LURCH PITCH POISE SLANT

SLOPE STUDY SWING TASTE THEAT
TREND AFFECT ANIMUS ANLAGE
ASCENT DESIRE DEVICE GATHER
GENIUS INTENT LIKING MOTION
NOTION PONDUS RELISH SQUINT
TALENT YETZER APTNESS
CONATUS COURAGE CURRENT
DESCENT DRAUGHT FANTASY
INKLING LEANING STOMACH
VERSANT WILLING APPETITE
APTITUDE CLINAMEN DEVOTION
GRADIENT PENCHANT TENDENCY
VELLEITY VERGENCY WOULDING
PROCLIVITY PROPENSITY
(— DOWNWARD) DIP DESCENT
HANGING
(— FROM VERTICAL) RAKE
(— OF OARSMAN'S BODY)
LAYBACK
(INWARD —) BATTER
(PLEASUREFUL —) RELISH
(PREDOMINATE —) STRENGTH
INCLINE APT BOW DIP KIP TIP WRY
BEAR BEND BIAS BREW CANT
CAST DOCK DOOK DOOR DROP
GIVE HANG HEEL HELD HILL LEAN
LIKE LIST PECK PEND RAKE SEEL
STAY SWAY TILT TURN BEVEL
CLIMB CLINE DROOP FLECT HIELD
JINNY OFFER PITCH SHAPE SLANT
SLOPE SOUND VERGE AFFECT
GLACIS INTEND SHELVE STEEVE
UPBROW DECLINE DESCEND
GANGWAY PROPEND PROCLINE
PROCLIVE
(— SKI) EDGE
(PREF.) CLIN(O)
INCLINED APT FIT SIB BENT CANT
FAIN LIEF RIFE VAIN ALIST ARAKE
ATILT GIVEN LEANT PRONE READY
ASLOPE COUCHE MINDED PROMPT
SLOPED SUPINE FORWARD
HANGING OBLIQUE PRONATE
STUDIED AFFECTED DISPOSED
ENCLITIC PREGNANT PROPENSE
SIDELING TALENTED
(— TO DRINK) BIBULOUS
(— TO LEARN) WALTY
(READILY —) PROMPT
INCLINING HILLY SHELVY SLOPING
CERNUOUS PROPENSE SIDELING
(SUFF.) CLINIC CLINOUS
INCLUDE ADD LAP HAVE TAKE
ANNEX COUCH COVER IMPLY
EMPLOY ENSEAM RECKON
BELOUKE COLLECT CONNOTE
CONTAIN EMBRACE IMMERSE
INVOLVE RECOUNT SUBSUME
COMPRISE CONCLUDE
(— IN LIST) ENGROSS
INCLUDING TO CUM
(— EVERYTHING) OVERALL
INCLUSIVE GRAND CAPABLE
CATHOLIC
INCLUSIVELY BROADLY
INCLUSUS RECLUSE
INCOHERENT FUZZY BROKEN
RAVING INCHOATE
INCOHERENTLY IDLY
INCOMBUSTIBLE APYROUS
ASBESTIC
INCOME GAIN PORT RENT RENTE
LIVING PEWAGE PEWING PROFIT

SALARY FACULTY INTRADO
INTRATE PRODUCE REVENUE
STIPEND INTEREST PROCEEDS
POCKETBOOK
(— OF BENEFICE) ANNAT
(ANNUAL —) RENTE
(FRENCH —) RENTE
(UNFORESEEN —) GRAVY
INCOMMENSURATE UNEQUAL
INCOMMODE VEX ANNOY MOLEST
PLAGUE TROUBLE DISQUIET
INCOMPARABLE ALONE
INCOMPATIBILITY SOLECISM
ANTIPATHY
INCOMPATIBLE ALIEN REPUGNANT
INCOMPETENT INEPT UNFIT
SLOUCH UNABLE UNMEET
FECKLESS HANDLESS HELPLESS
SPLITTER
INCOMPLETE WANE BLIND ROUGH
BROKEN UNDONE DIVIDED
LACKING PARTIAL SKETCHY
IMMATURE INCHOATE SEGMENTAL
(GRAMMATICALLY —) PENDANT
(PREF.) ATEL(O) DEMI SEMI
INCOMPLETELY BADLY HALVES
INCOMPOSITE PRIME
INCOMPREHENSIBILITY
ACATALEPSY
INCOMPREHENSIBLE PARTIAL
COCKEYED
INCONCLUSIVE FUZZY
INCONGRUITY JAR ANOMALY
SOLECISM
INCONGRUOUS ALIEN ABSURD
ANOMALOUS
INCONNU CONY NELMA CONNIE
SHEEFISH
INCONSEQUENTIAL NUGATORY
INCONSIDERABLE WEAK LIGHT
PETTY LITTLE
INCONSIDERATE RASH UNKIND
ASOCIAL RECKLESS
INCONSISTENCY HOLE
INCONSISTENT ALIEN REPUGNANT
INCONSPICUOUS OBSCURE
INCONSTANCY CHANGE LEVITY
INCONSTANT FICKLE BRUCKLE
FLUXILE MOONISH MUTABLE
PROTEAN SLIDING VARIOUS
FLUXIBLE METEORIC MOVEABLE
STRUMPET VARIABLE CHAMELEON
MERCURIAL VERSATILE
INCONTESTABLE SURE CLEAN
CERTAIN POSITIVE
INCONTINENCE ENURESIS
INCONTINENT LOOSE LAXATIVE
INCONTROVERTIBLE GRAND
INCONVENIENCE FASH BOTHER
CUMBER STRESS SQUEEZE
DISQUIET
INCONVENIENT UNKED CLUMSY
UNBANE UNGAIN AWKWARD
UNHANDY ANNOYING UNCHANCY
UNTOWARD
INCOORDINATION ASTASIA
INCORPORATE MIX FOLD FUSE
JOIN ANNEX KNEAD MERGE UNITE
ABSORB EMBODY ENGRAIN
ENTRAIN INWEAVE INCORPSE
(— IN WALL) ENGAGE
INCORPOREAL AERY BODILESS
ASOMATOUS

INCORRECT BAD ILL OFF FALSE
WRONG PECCANT UNRIGHT
UNSOUND VICIOUS PERVERSE
(PREF.) CAC(O)
INCORRIGIBLE HARD
INCORRUPTIBLE IMMORTAL
INCREASE UP ADD EIK EKE IMP
WAX BUMP ECHE GAIN GROW
HELP HIKE HYPE ITCH JACK JUMP
MEND MORE MUCH PLUS PUSH
RISE SOAR THEE THRO BOOST
BUILD BULGE CLIMB CROWD
FLUSH FRESH GOOSE HEAVE
LARGE RAISE SPURT SWELL
ACCENT ACCESS ACCRUE BETTER
BIGGEN CHANGE CREASE DEEPEN
DOUBLE EXPAND EXTEND EXTENT
GATHER GROWTH PUMPUP
SPREAD SPRING UPTICK ADVANCE
AMPLIFY AUCTION AUGMENT
AUXESIS BALLOON DISTEND
ELEVATE ENGROSS ENHANCE
ENLARGE GREATEN IMPROVE
INFLATE MAGNIFY STEEPEN
SURCRUE ACCRESCE ADDITION
COMPOUND ESCALATE FLOURISH
HEIGHTEN LENGTHEN MAJORATE
MAXIMATE MAXIMIZE MULTIPLY
THRODDEN PROPAGATE
PROLIFERATE
(— ACCORDING TO RATIO)
SCALEUP
(— AT USURY) OCKER
(— GREATLY) ACCUMULATE
(— HEAT OF KILN) RUSTLE GLISTER
(— IN BUSINESS) UPBEAT
(— IN PAY) FOGY FOGIE
(— IN SIZE) AUXESIS
(— IN STRENGTH) FRESHEN
(— KNOWLEDGE) ENRICH
(— OF DEPTH) OVERFALL
(— OF LOUDNESS) CRESCENDO
(— OF POWER) SURGE
(— OF WEALTH) THRIFT
(— POWER) SOUP
(— PRICE BY BIDDING) CANT
(— RAPIDLY) SOAR MUSHROOM
(— SPEED) JAZZ GOOSE
ACCELERATE
(— STITCHES) FASHION
(— SUDDENLY) LEAP
(PRICE —) RIST
(SALARY —) FLOWON
(SHORT-TERM —) BOOMLET
(TEMPORARY —) BULGE
(PREF.) AUXO
(SUFF.) AUXE OSIS
INCREASING GROWING CRESCENT
CRESCIVE DILATANT SWELLING
CUMULATIVE
(— RAPIDLY) BOOMING
INCREDIBLE TALL STEEP DAMNED
FABULOUS COCKAMAMY
COCKAMAMIE
INCREDULITY UNBELIEF
INCREDULOUS INFIDEL
INCREMENT DOSE DELTA
INCREASE
INCRIMINATE ACCUSE
INCRUST FOUL
INCRUSTATION CRUD MOSS
CRUST SCALE TARTAR FOULING
FURRING

INCUBATE SIT BROOD CLOCK
COVER HATCH
INCUBATION PASSAGE
INCUBATOR FURNACE HATCHER
COUVEUSE ISOLETTE
INCUBUS DUSE MARE DUSIO
NIGHTMARE
INCULCATE BREED INFIX INCULK
INFUSE IMPLANT IMPRESS INSTILL
INCULCATED BRED
INCUMBENT COARB BEARER
INCUR RUN BEAR GAIN WAGE
CONTRACT
INCURABLE BOOTLESS HOPELESS
INCURRENT INHALANT
INCURSION RAID ROAD FORAY
INFALL INROAD RAZZIA DESCENT
HOSTING INBREAK INCURSE
ANABASIS INVASION
INCUS AMBOS ANVIL
INDEBTED LIABLE DEBTFUL
BEHOLDEN
INDEBTEDNESS DEBT SCORE
INDECENCY IMPURITY PRIAPISM
RIBALDRY
INDECENT PAW BLUE FOUL LEWD
RANK BAWDY GROSS NASTY
SAUCY GREASY IMPURE PAWPAW
SMUTTY CURIOUS GRIVOIS
IMMORAL OBSCENE IMMODEST
IMPROPER SHAMEFUL UNCOMELY
INDECENTLY DIRTY
INDECISION DEMUR DOUBT MAYBE
POISE SWITHER
(PSYCHOTIC —) ABULIA
INDECISIVE DRAWN HALTING
(BE —) TEETER
INDECISIVENESS SUSPENSE
INDECOROUS RUDE COARSE
FORWARD UNCIVIL IMMODEST
IMPOLITE IMPROPER INDECENT
UNSEEMLY UNTOWARD
GRACELESS TASTELESS
INDEED SO ARU NAY TOO WIS YEA
AWAT DEED EVEN IWIS JUST SURE
MARRY QUOTH TIENS ATWEEL
ITSELF PARDIE SURELY FAITHLY
FRANKLY FORSOOTH
VERAMENT
INDEFATIGABLE TIRELESS
INDEFENSIBLE INVALID
INDEFINABLE NAMELESS
INDEFINITE HAZY FUZZY GROSS
LOOSE VAGUE DIVERS INEXACT
AORISTIC NUBILOUS
INDEFINITELY IN
INDELIBLE FAST FIXED
INDELICATE RAW FREE WARM
BROAD GROSS ROUGH COARSE
GREASY IMPOLITE IMPROPER
UNSEEMLY
INDEMNIFICATION RELIEF
INDEMNIFY PAY REPAY RECOUP
SATISFY WARRANT
INDENT JAG BRIT DENT GIMP MUSH
NICK CHASE DELVE NOTCH STAMP
TOOTH WHEEL BRUISE CRENEL
ENGRAIL GAUFFER
INDENTATION CHOP DENT DINT
DOKE FOIL KINK SCAR BOSOM
BULGE CLEFT CRENA DINGE
NOTCH SINUS DIMPLE FURROW

GROOVE INDENT RECESS IMPRESS
CRENELLE TOOTHING
(— IN BOTTLE) KICK
(— IN DOG'S FACE) STOP
(— IN SHELL) EYE
INDENTED WAVED CRENATE
NOTCHED SINUATE
INDENTURE BIND INDENT
ESCALLOP SYNGRAPH
INDEPENDENCE AUTARKY
FREEDOM AUTARCHY
(— OF GOD) ASEITY ASEITAS
(POLITICAL —) SWARAJ
INDEPENDENT FREE PROUD
SEEKER BIGGITY DIVIDED
MUGWUMP SECTARY ABSOLUTE
PECULIAR POSITIVE SEPARATE
(STATISTICALLY —) ORTHOGONAL
(PREF.) SELF
INDEPENDENTLY APART
INDESCRIBABLE TERMLESS
INEFFABLE
INDETERMINATE AORISTIC
FORMLESS INFINITE
INDEX PIE FIST HAND ARNETH
ELENCH PIGNET TONGUE POINTER
ALPHABET EXPONENT REGISTER
(COMPUTER —) KWIC KWOC

INDIA
ANCIENT NAME: BHARAT
CAPE: COMORIN
CAPITAL: NEWDELHI
CASTE: JAT MAL AHIR GOLA JATI
MALI DHOBI SANSI SUDRA VARNA
DACOIT DHANUK LOHANA VAISYA
AGARWAL BRAHMAN DHANGAR
COAST: MALABAR
COIN: LAC PIE ANNA FELS LAKH PICE
TARA ABIDI CRORE PAISA RUPEE
COLLEGE: TOL
DESERT: THAR
DISTRICT: SIBI NASIK PATNA SIMLA
ZILLAH MALABAR NELLORE
MOFUSSIL
GULF: KUTCH CAMBAY MANNAR
ISLAND: CHILKA
LAKE: WULAR CHILKA COLAIR
DHEBAR SAMBAHR
LANGUAGE: URDU HINDI TAMIL
TELUGU SANSKRIT
MEASURE: ADY DHA GAZ GUZ JOW
KOS LAN SER BYEE COSS DAIN
DHAN HATH JAOB KUNK MOOT
PARA RAIK RATI SEIT TAUN TENG
TOLA AMUNA BIGHA CAHAR
COVID CROSA DANDA DRONA
GARCE GIREH HASTA PALLY
PARAH RATTI SALAY YOJAN
ADHAKA ANGULA COVIDO
CUDAVA CUMBHA GEERAH
LAMANY MOOLUM MUSHTI
PALGAT PARRAH ROPANI TIPREE
UNGLEE YOJANA ADOULIE
DHANUSH GAVYUTI KHAHOON
NIRANGA PRASTHA VITASTI
OKTHABAH
MOUNTAIN: MERU GHATS KAMET
MASTUJ TANKSE KALAHOI
SIWALIK VINDHYA SULEIMAN
MOUNTAIN RANGE: SATPURA
VINDHYA ARAVALLI HIMALAYA
NATIVE: TODA HINDU TAMIL

PROVINCE: HAR ASSAM BIHAR
ANDHRA BENGAL KERALA
MADRAS MYSORE ORISSA
PUNJAB GUJARAT HARYANA
KASHMIR MANIPUR
REGION: MALABAR
RIVER: AI DOR SON TEL KOSI KUSI
NIRA REHR SIND BETWA BHIMA
DAMOH GOGRA INDUS JAWAI
RAPTI SANKH SONAR TAPTI
TUNGA CHENAB GANGES KISTNA
PENNER SUTLEJ WARDHA
CAUVERY CHAMBAL IRAWADI
KRISHNA NARMADA NARMEDA
HEMAVATI HYDASPES MAHANADI
NERBUDDA VINDHYAS
SEAPORT: DAMAN BOMBAY
COCHIN MADRAS CALCUTTA
STATE: ASSAM BIHAR KERALA
MYSORE ORISSA PUNJAB
GUJARAT MANIPUR
STRAIT: PALK
TERRITORY: DIU GOA DAMAN
MINICOY AMINDIVI
TOWN: DIU AGRA DAMA GAYA
PUNA REWA ADONI AKOLA
ALWAR ARCOT BHERA DACCA
DATIA DELHI GIROT KALPI PATAN
PATNA POONA SALEM SIMLA
SURAT TEHRI AJMERE AMBALA
BARELI BARODA BHOPAL
BOMBAY CHAMBA COCHIN
DUMDUM HOWRAH INDORE
JAIPUR KANPUR LAHORE MADIRA
MADRAS MADURA MEERUT
MULTAN MUTTRA MYSORE
NAGPUR RAMPUR UJJAIN
ALIGARH BENARES BIKANER
CALICUT CAWNPUR DINAPUR
GWALIOR JODHPUR KARACHI
KURNOOL LASWARI LUCKNOW
RANGOON RANGPUR AMRITSAR
BHATINDA BHATPARA CALCUTTA
DINAPORE JABALPUR KOLHAPUR
MANDALAY MIRZAPUR PESHAWAR
SHOLAPUR SRINAGAR VARANASI
TRIBE: AO GOR BHIL BADAGA
SHERANI
WATERFALL: JOG GOKAK CAUVERY
WEIGHT: MOD PAI SER VIS DHAN
DRUM KONA MYAT PALA PANK
PICE RAIK RATI RUAY SEER TANK
TOLA YAVA ADPAD BAHAR CANDY
CATTY HUBBA MASHA MAUND
PALLY POUAH RATTI RETTI RUTEE
TICAL TICUL TIKAL ABUCCO
DHURRA KARSHA CHITTAK
PEIKTHA

INDIAN LO RED ROJO INJUN TAWNY
ABNAKI INDISH REDMAN BHARATI
HOSTILE NAIKPOD REDSKIN
LONGHAIR MUSKOGEE
PENOBSCOT SHAHAPTIAN
NARRAGANSET
(— LEADER) NEHRU
(AMERICAN —) AIS AUK FOX HOH
KAW OTO REE SAC SIA UTE WEA ZIA
ADAI COOS CREE CROW DOEG ERIE
EYAK HANO HOPI HUPA IOWA KATO
KOSO MOKI MONO OTOE OTTO
PIMA PIRO SAUK TANO TAOS TEWA
TIOU TOAG UTAH WACO YUMA ZUNI

ACOMA ALSEA BANAK BIDAI CADDO
CHAUI COMOX CONOY COREE
CREEK HANIS HOOPA HUECO
HURON JEMEZ KANIA KANSA KAROK
KERES KIOWA KOROA KUSAN
LENCA LIPAN MAKAH MANSO
MIAMI MINGO MODOC MOQUI
NAMBE OMAHA OSAGE OSTIC
OZARK PECOS PINAL PIUTE PONCA
SAMBO SARSI SEWEE SIOUX SITKA
SKIDI SLAVE SNAKE SOOKE TETON
TEXAS TIGUA TONTO TWANA TYIGH
UINTA UNAMI WAPPO WASCO
WASHO WIYOT YAMEL YAZOO
YUCHI YUROK AGAWAM AHTENA
APACHE ATSINA ATUAMI AVOYEL
BILOXI CALUSA CAYUGA CAYUSE
CHATOT CHERAW CHETCO COOSUC
CUPENO DAKOTA DIGGER EYEISH
FARAON GILENO HAINAI HAISLA
ISLETA KAIBAB KAINAH KANSAS
KICHAI KOSIMO KUITSH LAGUNA
LENAPE MANDAN MAUMEE
MAYEYE METOAC MICMAC MIKMAK
MOHAVE MOHAWK MUNSEE
NASHUA NATICK NAUSET NAVAHO
NAVAJO NEUTER NOOTKA OGLALA
ONEIDA OREJON OTTAWA PAIUTE
PAPAJO PATWIN PAWNEE PEORIA
PEQUOD PEQUOT PIEGAN PODUNK
PUEBLO QUAPAW QUERES RIKARI
SALISH SAMISH SANTEE SAPONI
SATSOP SENECA SHASTA SILETZ
SIOUAN SIWASH SKAGIT SOKOKI
SUMASS SUMDUM SUTAIO SYLVID
TAPOSA TENINO TOHOME TOLOWA
TONGAS TUNICA TUTELO UMPQUA
WALAPI WAPATO WATALA
WAXHAW WEANOC WIKENO
WINTUN YAKIMA YAMASI ZUNIAN
ABENAKI ALABAMA ALIBAMU
AMERIND ANDARKO ANDASTE
ARIKARA ATAKAPA AYAHUCA
BANNOCK CAHOKIA CALOOSA
CATAWBA CHILCAT CHILULA
CHINOOK CHOCTAW CHUMASH
CHUMAWI CIBECUE CLALLAM
CLATSOP COCHITI COLCINE
COWLITZ DEADOSE DHEGIHA
DWAMISH ESSELEN GOSHUTE
HELLELT HIDATSA HUCHNOM
HUICHOL INGALIK JUANENO
KANAWHA KLAMATH KOASATI
KOHUANA KOPRINO KUNESTE
KUTCHIN KUTENAI LUISENO
MASHPEE MASKOKI MOHEGAN
MOHICAN MONACAN MONSONI
MONTAUK MOUSONI NANAIMO
NASCAPI NATCHEZ NIANTIC
NIMKISH NIPMUCK OJIBWAY
PACIFID PADUCAH PAMLICO
PICURUS QUAITSO SALINAN
SANETCH SANPOIL SERRANO
SHAPTAN SHAWANO SHAWNEE
SIKSIKA SIUSLAW SONGISH
SPOKANE SQUAXON STIKINE
TAMAROA TESUQUE TIMUCUA
TLINGIT TONKAWA TUALATI TULALIP
TUTUTNI UGARONO WAILAKI
WALPAPI WAMESIT WANAPUM
WASHAKI WEWENOC WHILKUT
WICHITA WISHOSK WITUMKI
WYANDOT YANKTON YAQUINA

YAVAPAI YOJUANE YONKALA
ABSAROKA ACHOMAWI ACHUMAWI
ALGONKIN AMERICAN AMOSKEAG
APALACHI ARIVAIPA ARKANSAS
ASTAKIWI ATFALATI ATSUGEWI
CAHINNIO CAHUILLA CANARSIE
CHAWASHA CHEHALIS CHEMAKUM
CHEROKEE CHEYENNE CHIMAKUM
CHOPTANK CHOWANOC CLACKAMA
COLUMBIA COLVILLE COMANCHE
COQUILLE COYOTERO DELAWARE
DIEGUENO ETCHIMIN FLATHEAD
HITCHITI HUNKPAPA ILLINOIS
IROQUOIS KALISPEL KAWAIISU
KICKAPOO KIKATSIK KLASKINO
KLIKITAT KONOMIHU LAMANITE
MALECITE MASCOTIN MENOMINI
MIKASUKI MINITARI MISSOURI
MOGOLLON MUSCOGEE MUSKWAKI
NEHANTIC NESPELIM NOTTOWAY
OKINAGAN ONONDAGA PAMUNKEY
PANAMINT PATUXENT PAVIOTSO
PENACOOK PISHQUOW POWHATAN
PUYALLUP QUATSINO QUERECHO
QUILEUTE QUINAULT ROCKAWAY
SAHAPTIN SAULTEUR SAVANNAH
SEMINOLE SHIVWITS SHOSHONE
SIHASAPA SINGSING SINKIUSE
SINKYONE SINTSINK SISSETON
SOUHEGAN SQUAMISH SQUEDUNK
TLAKLUIT TOBIKHAR TOPINISH
TSIHALIS TUSHEPAW TUSKEGEE
UMATILLA WABANAKI WACHUSET
WAHPETON WETUMPKA YAHUSKIN
YAMACRAW DOUSTIONI SQUAWTITS
(BRAZILIAN —) BUGRE
(CANADIAN —) DENE COMOX
HAIDA SLAVE TINNE DOGRIB HAISLA
LASSIK MICMAC SARSEE BEOTHUK
GOASILA KHOTANA KOYUKON
CHISEDEC COWICHAN HEILTSUK
KIMSQUIT KWAKIUTL LILLOOET
SALTEAUX SHUSHWAP
(FEMALE —) SQUAW KLOOCH
(MALE —) BUCK SANNUP SIWASH
(MEXICAN —) MAM OVA CHOL
CORA JOVA MAYA MAYO ROTO SERI
TECA TECO XOVA AZTEC CHIZO
CHORA HUABI HUAVE KAMIA
NAHUA OPATA OTOMI YAQUI
ZOQUE CAHITA CHOCHO CONCHO
EUDEVE KILIWI NEVOME OTONIA
PAKAWA TARASC TOLTEC ZOTZIL
ACOLHUA AKWAALA AMISHGO
CHATINO CHINCHA CHINIPA
CHONTAL COTONAM COUHIMI
GUASAVE HUASTEC HUAXTEC
MAZATEC MISTECA MIXTECA
NAYARIT SINALOA TEGUIMA
TEHUECO TEPANEC TEPEHUA
TZENTAL TZOTZIL ZACATEC
ZAPOTEC CHANABAL CHAPANEC
CHUCHONA COLOTLAN COMANITO
CONICARI GUASAPAR HUASTECO
IRRITILA JACALTEC JANAMBRE
LACANDON LAGUNERO TARUMARI
TECPANEC TEXCOCAN TEZCUCAN
TOTONACO TZAPOTEC YUCATECO
(OTHER —) GE ITE ONA URO URU
YAO AGAZ ANDE ANTA ANTI AUCA
BABU CAME CANA CARA CHUJ
COTO CUNA DENE DIAU DUIT INCA
ITEN ITZA IXIL MOJO MOXO MURA

MUSO MUZO PEBA PIRO RAMA
TAMA TAPE TATU TOBA TRIO TUPI
TUPY ULUA ULVA ACROA ARARA
ARAUA ARUAC AUETO BAURE BETOI
BRAVO BUGRE CAITE CAMPA
CANCA CARIB CHANE CHIMU CHITA
CHOCO CHOKO CHOLA CHOLO
CHONO COCTO COLAN CUEVA DIRIA
GUANA GUATO HUARI JAVAH KASKA
LENCA MOCOA MOZCA OPATA
OYANA PALTA PAMPA PASSE PETEN
PINTO PIOJE PIOXE PIPIL POKAN
POKOM QUITU SENCI SIUSI SMOOS
TAINO UAUPE UMAUA VEJOZ
WAURA XINCA YAGUA YAMEO
YUNCA YUNGA AGUANO AIMARA
AKAVAI AKAWAI AMORUA ANDOKE
ANTISI APANTO APARAI APIACA
ARAWAK AROACO ATORAI AYMARA
BABINE BANIVA BETOYA BORORO
BRIBRI BRUNKA CAHETE CAIGUA
CANCHI CANELO CARAHO CARAJA
CARAYA CARIRI CAUQUI CAVINA
CAYAPA CHAIMA CHARCA CHAYMA
CHICHA CHISCA CHOCOI CHORTI
COCAMA COCOMA COCORA
COFANE COLIMA COTOXO CUCAMA
CULINO CUMANA DOGRIB DORASK
GALIBI GOYANA GUAIMI GUAQUE
GUAYMI HUARPE HUBADO IGNERI
INCERI IXIAMA JIVARO JUCUNA
JUMANA JURUNA KARAYA KEKCHI
KUCHIN LENGUA LUCAYO MACUSI
MAKUSI MANGUE MANIVA MIRANA
MUYSCA NAHANE NASCAN
OMAGUA OTOMAC PAPAGO
PKOMAM PURUHA QUICHE SABUJA
SACCHA SALIBA SALIVA SAMUCU
SEKANE SETIBO SIPIBO SUERRE
TACANA TAGISH TAHAMI TAMOYO
TAPAJO TAPUYA TARUMA TEGUNA
TICUNA TIMOTE TOTORO TUCANO
TUNEBO UIRINA UITOTO VILELA
WAIWAI WITOTO WOOLWA YAHGAN
YAHUNA YARURO YURUNA ZAPARA
ACHAGUA ACKAWOI AKAMNIK
ANDAQUI ANGAITE APALAII
APINAGE ARECUNA ARHUACO
BEOTHUK BILQULA CACHIBO
CAINGUA CALIANA CAMACAN
CARANGA CARIBAN CARIBEE
CARRIER CASHIBO CHARRUA
CHIBCHA CHIMANE CHIMILA
CHIRINO CHONCHO CHOROTE
CHUMULU CHUNCHO CHURAPA
CHUROYA CIBONEY CJACOGO
COROADO FRENTON FUEGIAN
GITKSAN GOAHIVO GOAJIRA
GUAHIVO GUARANI GUARANY
GUARAYO GUARRAU GUARUAN
GUATUSO GUETARE HUANUCO
HUATUSO ITONAMA JACUNDA
JICAQUE KALIANA KOPRINO
KULIANA LUCAYAN MAIPURE
MISKITO MONGOYO MORCOTE
NICARAO PAMPERO PAYAGUA
PEDRAZA PIARROA POKOMAM
PUELCHE PUQUINA QUECHUA
QUEKCHI RANQUEL SARIGUE
SATIENO SHUSWAP SINSIGA
SIRIONE TAHLTAN TALUCHE
TALUHET TAMANAC TARIANA

TARRABA TAYRONA TELEMBI
TIMBIRA TIRRIBI TSONECA
UARAYCU UCAYALE VOYAVAI
WOYAWAY YUSTAGA ZUTUHIL
AGUARUNA AHOUSAHT AKIYENIK
ALACALUF AMAHUACA APOLISTA
ARAQUAJU AWISHIRA BOTOCUDO
CAINGANG CALINAGO CANAMARY
CANOEIRO CAQUETIO CARIBISI
CARIJONA CARIPUNA CAYUBABA
CHAMBOIA CHANDALA CHAVANTE
CHIQUITO CHIRIANA COLORADO
COMIAKIN CONCHUCU CORABECA
CUSTENAU GUAYAQUI GUAYCURU
JAVITERO KANHOBAL KLASKINO
LOROKOTO MACARANI MAYORUNA
MISSKITO MOSQUITO NIQUIRAN
OCHOZOMA OROTINAN PACAVARA
PALENQUE PARUKUTU PINALENO
POIGUARA POKONCHI POPOLOCO
POTYUARA PUPULUCA QUATSINO
QUERENDY QUIMBAYA SHIRIANA
SNONOWAS SUBTIABA TADOUSAC
TAPACURA TENAKTAK TOCOBAGA
TOROMONA TSATTINE TUMUPASA
UAREKENA URUKUENA USPANTEC
YURUCARE
(SOUTH AFRICAN   ) COOLY
COOLIE
(SPANISH-AMERICAN —) CHOLO

INDIANA
CAPITAL: INDIANAPOLIS
COLLEGE: BALL BETHEL DEPAUW
    GOSHEN MARIAN PURDUE
    WABASH
COUNTY: JAY CASS CLAY KNOX
    OWEN PIKE RUSH VIGO BOONE
    FLOYD WELLS JASPER TIPTON
    DAVIESS PULASKI
INDIAN: MIAMI HAWNEE
LAKE: MONROE MANITOU
    WAWASEE MICHIGAN
NATIVE: HOOSIER
RIVER: OHIO WHITE WABASH
STATE BIRD: CARDINAL
STATE FLOWER: PEONY
STATE TREE: TULIP
TOWN: GARY PERU PAOLI VEVAY
    ALBION ANGOLA BRAZIL GOSHEN
    JASPER KOKOMO MUNCIE
    SHOALS WABASH

INDIAN BEECH KURUNJ
INDIAN BREAD TUCKAHOE
INDIAN CORN KANGA MAIZE
    CHOLUM JAGONG MEALIES
INDIAN FIG SABRA
INDIAN FISH FLATFISH
INDIAN GOOSEBERRY EMBLIC
INDIAN HEMP KEF KIF SANA DAGGA
    SABZI AMYROOT DOGBANE
INDIANIAN HOOSIER
INDIAN JALAP TURPETH
INDIAN LICORICE JEQUIRITY
INDIAN MADDER MUNJEET
INDIAN MALLOW SIDA DAGGA
    PIEPRINT
INDIAN MILLET JONDLA
INDIAN MULBERRY AL AAL ACH
    ALROOT
INDIAN PIPE FITROOT EYEBRIGHT
    WAXFLOWER

INDIAN POKE ITCHWEED
    HELLEBORE
INDIAN RED BOLE
INDIAN SHOT ALIIPOE
INDIAN TOBACCO GAGROOT
    LOBELIA PUKEWEED SOURBUSH
INDIAN YELLOW PIOURY PURREE
INDIA-RUBBER BUNGEE BUNGIE
INDIC (— LANGUAGE) URDU VEDIC
INDICATE RUN SAY BODY CITE HINT
    LOOK MAKE MARK READ SHOW
    ARGUE INDEX INFER POINT PROVE
    SPEAK ALLUDE ATTEST BETRAY
    DENOTE DESIGN EVINCE FINGER
    IMPORT NOTIFY REVEAL BESPEAK
    BETOKEN CONNOTE DECLARE
    DISPLAY POINTTO PORTEND
    SIGNIFY SPECIFY ADMONISH
    ANNOUNCE DECIPHER DISCLOSE
    EVIDENCE MANIFEST OUTPOINT
    REGISTER SIGNALIZE
    (— BY SOUNDING) STRIKE
    (— WILLINGNESS) AGREE
INDICATION BECK CLEW CLUE HINT
    LEAD MARK NOTE SHOW SIGN
    CURVE INDEX PROOF SCENT
    TOKEN AUGURY BEACON INDICE
    REMARK SAMPLE SIGNAL AUSPICE
    MENTION PROFFER SYMPTOM
    ALLUSION ARGUMENT EVIDENCE
    MONITION MONUMENT NOTATION
    SIGNANCE TELLTALE
    (— OF APPROVAL) CACHET
    (— OF CONTROL) COLLAR
    (— OF LIGHT) AUREOLE
    (— OF OFFICE) SEAL
    (— OF SOMETHING TO COME)
    PROGNOSTIC PROGNOSTICATION
    (INFALLIBLE —) ORACLE
    (OBSCURE —) SHADOW
    (VAGUE —) GLIMMER
    (PL.) INDICIA
INDICATOR PIN HAND OMEN SIGN
    FLOAT INDEX LITMUS SHOWER
    STYLUS TARGET LACMOID
    POINTER DETECTOR TELLTALE
    (— LIGHT ON COMPUTER) CURSOR
    (— OF BALANCE) COCK
    (— OF HOUR) GNOMON
    (DIRECTION —) FLASHER
    (ECONOMIC —) LAGGER LEADER
    (ELECTRONIC — TUBE) NIXIE
INDICIA POSTAGE
INDICT DITE CRIME PANEL ACCUSE
    ATTACH CHARGE INDITE ARRAIGN
    ARTICLE IMPEACH TROUNCE
    WARRANT
INDICTMENT CHARGE DITTAY
INDIFFERENCE APATHY PHLEGM
    ATARAXY DISDAIN ATARAXIA
    COLDNESS EASINESS FROIDEUR
    STOICISM
INDIFFERENT COLD COOL DEAD
    DRAM EASY SOSO ALOOF BLASE
    EQUAL HOHUM SOBER STOIC
    CASUAL DEGAGE FRIGID SUPINE
    CALLOUS LANGUID NEUTRAL
    DETACHED LISTLESS LUKEWARM
    MEDIOCRE RECKLESS SUPERIOR
    UPSITTEN APATHETIC
INDIFFERENTIST POLITIC
INDIFFERENTLY DRYLY HUMDRUM

INDIGENCE NEED WANT PENURY
    BEGGARY POVERTY TENUITY
INDIGENE ENDEMIC
INDIGENOUS DESI NATIVE
    DOMESTIC HOMEBORN
    ABORIGINAL
INDIGENT POOR NEEDY BEGGARLY
    HAVELESS
INDIGESTIBLE STUDGY
INDIGESTION APEPSY APEPSIA
    DYSPEPSY
INDIGNANT ANGRY WROTH
    ANNOYED UPTIGHT INCENSED
INDIGNATION IRE RAGE ANGER
    WRATH DESPITE DISDAIN
    DUDGEON JEALOUSY
INDIGNITY CUT SLUR SCORN
    INSULT SLIGHT AFFRONT OFFENCE
    CONTUMELY
INDIGO ANIL NILL SHOOFLY
    (PREF.) INDI(CO)
INDIRECT SLY SIDE DEVIOUS
    OBLIQUE CIRCULAR GLANCING
    OVERHEAD OVERWART SIDELONG
    SIDEWAYS SIDEWISE
    ROUNDABOUT
    (— WAY) AMBAGE
INDIRECTION CIRCUITY
INDIRECTLY ROUND SECONDHAND
INDIRECTNESS OBLIQUITY
INDISCREET RASH HASTY SILLY
    WITLESS CARELESS HEEDLESS
INDISCRETION FOLLY LAPSE
    FREDAINE
INDISCRIMINATE MIXED MINGLED
    SWEEPING PROMISCUOUS
INDISCRIMINATELY PELLMELL
INDISPENSABLE CENTRAL
    NEEDFUL CRITICAL
INDISPOSED ILL MEAN SICK ILLISH
    UNWELL
INDISPOSITION AIL BRASH
    MALADY AILMENT SICKNESS
    (— TO MOTION) INERTIA
INDISPUTABLE SURE CERTAIN
    EVIDENT MANIFEST POSITIVE
    APODICTIC
INDISTINCT DIM DARK DULL HAZY
    FAINT FUZZY INNER LIGHT MISTY
    MUDDY SHADY THICK VAGUE
    BLEARY CLOUDY DREAMY INWARD
    SLURRY WOOLLY BLEARED
    BLURRED OBSCURE SHADOWY
    UNCLEAR NEBULOUS
    (— IN SOUND) NEUTRAL
    (— IN UTTERANCE) CHOKING
INDISTINCTNESS BLUR
    CONFUSION
INDITE PEN DITE DRAW
INDIVIDUAL GEE MAN ONE HEAD
    SORT UNIT BEING MONAD THING
    PROPER SINGLE SPIRIT VERSAL
    APOMICT ATAVISM AZYGOTE
    BIONTIC DIPLOID EIDETIC ISOLATE
    MONADIC NUMERIC SEVERAL
    SPECIAL EVERYONE IDENTITY
    SEPARATE SINGULAR SOLITARY
    SPECIMEN PERSONAGE
    (COLOR-BLIND —) MONOCHROMAT
    (COUNTRIFIED —) HOBNAIL
    (DESPICABLE —) HEEL
    (DULL —) BOEOTIAN
    (FOOLISH —) SOP

(HAUGHTY —) POT
(IDENTICAL —) CLONE
(IMMATURE —) ADULTOID
(IMPUDENT —) BOLDFACE
(INDEPENDENT —) MAVERICK
(IRRITABLE —) SNAPPER
(LEADING —) KEY
(MOSAIC —) GYNANDER
(MUTANT —) SALTANT
(PHYSIOLOGICAL —) BION
(PROSAIC —) PHILISTINE
(ROUGH-LOOKING —) BOHUNK
(SKILLED —) ADEPT
(SLOVENLY —) GROBIAN
(STUPID —) HOBBIL
(TRICKY —) BILK
(UNDERSIZED —) KIT KITT
(WINGED —) ALATE
(YOUNG —) KID
(PL.) FRY
INDIVIDUALITY KA SEITY QUALITY
　SELFDOM HECCEITY IDENTITY
　SELFHOOD
INDIVIDUALIZE ATOMIZE
INDIVIDUALLY APART APIECE
　SINGLY PROPERLY
INDIVIDUATION AHANKARA
INDIVISIBLE PUNCTUAL
INDO-CHINESE SERIFORM
INDOCTRINATE BRIEF INSTRUCT
INDO-EUROPEAN ARIAN ARYAN
　JAPHETIC
INDOLE KETOLE
INDOLENCE SLOTH LANGUOR
　IDLESHIP MUSARDRY SLUGGING
　(— PERSONIFIED) LAURENCE
　LAWRENCE
INDOLENT IDLE LAZY FAINT INERT
　SWEER DROWSY OTIOSE SUPINE
　DRONISH LANGUID WILSOME
　FAINEANT INACTIVE LISTLESS
　LOUNGING SLOTHFUL SLUGGISH
　PICKTOOTH
INDO-MALAYAN (— TREE) SUPA

INDONESIA

CAPITAL: DJAKARTA
COIN: RUPIAH
GULF: BONE TOLO TOMINI
ISLAND: ALOR BALI BURU JAVA
　CERAM IRIAN SUMBA WETAR
　BAWEAN BORNEO BUTUNG
　FLORES KOMODO LOMBOK
　MADURA PELENG CELEBES
　SALAJAR SUMATRA SUMBAWA
　SULAWESI
ISLAND GROUP: ARRU EWAB
　SUNDA BANJAK NATUNA
　ANAMBAS MOLUCCA TABELAN
　SABALANA
LAKE: RANAU TOWUTI
LANGUAGE: BAHASA MALAYAN
MOUNTAIN: BULU NIUT RAJA
　DEMPO MURJO NIAPA LEUSER
　SLAMET MENJAPA OGOAMAS
　SAMOSIR KATOPASA KERINTJI
　MAHAMERU RINDJANI TALAKMAU
MOUNTAINS: MULLER BARISAN
　QUARLES SCHWANER
NATIVE: BUGI
PROVINCE: RIAU ATJEH DJAMBI
　MALUKU LAMPUNG BENGKULU
RIVER: HARI MUSI DIGUL KAJAN

　PAWAN BARITO KAMPAR KAPUAS
　MAHAKAM
SEA: JAVA BANDA CERAM TIMOR
　FLORES ARAFURA CELEBES
STRAIT: SUNDA LOMBOK
　MAKASSAR
TOWN: PALU MEDAN MALANG
　MANADO BANDUNG KENDARI
　MAKASAR SEMARANG SURABAJA
　PALEMBANG SURAKARTA
VOLCANO: GEDE AGUNG DEMPO
　RAUNG MARAPI MERAPI SINILA
　SLAMET SUNDORO TAMBORA
　KERINTJE RINDJANI
WEIGHT: CATTY OUNCE THAIL

INDONESIAN NESIOT SADANG
INDOORS WITHIN
INDRA SAKKA SAKRA
INDRI BABACOOTE
INDUBITABLE SURE EVIDENT
　APPARENT MANIFEST UNIVOCAL
INDUCE GET DRAW LEAD MOVE
　URGE WORK ARGUE BRIBE BRING
　CAUSE IMPEL INFER TEMPT WEIGH
　ADDICT ADJURE ALLURE ENGAGE
　ENTICE IMPORT INCITE INVITE
　OBTAIN REDUCE SEDUCE SUBORN
　ACTUATE PREVAIL PROCURE
　PROVOKE SOLICIT MOTIVATE
　PERSUADE WIREDRAW
　(— BY BRIBERY) FIX
INDUCEMENT BAIT MOTIVE
　REASON FEATURE PERSUASION
INDUCT STALL INSTAL KNIGHT
　INITIATE
INDUCTANCE HENRY
INDUCTION EPAGOGE
INDULGE PET BABY CADE CANT
　FEED GLUT ALLOW HUMOR JOLLY
　SPOIL TUTOR WALLY WREAK
　COCKER FOSTER PAMPER PETTLE
　DEBAUCH GRATIFY
　(— IN PRIDE) PRIDE
　(— ONESELF) WALLOW WANTON
　(— TO EXCESS) PAMPER DEBAUCH
　SURFEIT
INDULGED CADE
INDULGENCE LAW BINGE FAVOR
　FOLLY MERCY SPREE EXCESS
　INDULT PARDON PATENT JUBILEE
　QUIENAL SURFEIT COURTESY
　DELICACY EASINESS GLUTTONY
　POCULARY
　(FREE —) SWING
　(SEXUAL —) LECHERY
INDULGENT FOND GOOD MEEK
　MILD SPOONY LENIENT TOLERANT
INDURATE HARDEN INDURE
INDURATED SCLEROID SCLEROUS
INDURATION SCLEROMA
INDUSTRIOUS BUSY DEEDY EIDENT
　STEADY OPEROSE PAINFUL
　DILIGENT SEDULOUS VIRTUOUS
　WORKSOME
INDUSTRY TOIL LABOR SCREEN
　VIRTUE CERAMICS SEDULITY
INDWELLING IMMANENT INHERENT
INE (WIFE OF —) AETHELBURH
INEBRIATE SOUSE EBRIATED
INEBRIATED DRUNK DRINKY
INEFFACEABLE INBURNT INDELIBLE
INEFFECTIVE DUD WEAK CLUMSY

　DREEPY FLABBY FUTILE FLACCID
　HALTING STERILE BUMBLING
INEFFECTIVELY ILL BADLY FEEBLY
INEFFECTUAL WAN DEAD IDLE
　TAME VAIN VOID JERKY FUTILE
　SPINDLY USELESS BOOTLESS
　FAINEANT FIDDLING NUGATORY
INEFFICIENT ILL LAME POOR
　CLUMSY DOLESS ROTTEN UNABLE
　SLOUCHY USELESS FECKLESS
　HANDLESS
INELASTIC DEAD
INELEGANT RUDE HOYDEN
　AWKWARD
INELOQUENT WANMOL
INEPT DORKY INAPT ABSURD
　AWKWARD FOOTLESS MALADROIT
INEPTITUDE PIFFLE
INEQUAL ROUGH
INEQUALITY ODDS CAHOT WHELK
　ANOMALY EVECTION IMPARITY
　NUTATION
　(— OF SURFACE) WAVE
INEQUITABLE HARD
INERADICABLE LASTING INDELIBLE
　PERMANENT
INERT DEAD DULL LAZY SLOW
　HEAVY NOBLE SULKY LEADEN
　SODDEN STUPID SUPINE TORPID
　PASSIVE INACTIVE INDOLENT
　LIFELESS SLOTHFUL SLUGGISH
　STAGNANT THEWLESS THOWLESS
INERTIA TAMAS
INESCAPABLE DEAD NECESSARY
INESTIMABLE SUMLESS PRICELESS
INEVITABILITY FINALITY
INEVITABLE DUE SURE DIRECT
　CERTAIN FATEFUL FOREGONE
INEXACT FREE ROUGH CLOUDY
INEXHAUSTIBLE INFINITE
INEXORABLE STERN STONY STRICT
　RIGOROUS
INEXPEDIENCY IMPOLICY
INEXPEDIENT UNWISE
INEXPENSIVE LOW CHEAP
　DIMESTORE REASONABLE
INEXPERIENCED RAW PUNY CRUDE
　FRESH YOUNG UNSEEN KITLING
　STRANGE INEXPERT INSOLENT
　PRENTICE UNTRADED
INEXPERT ILL RUDE CRUDE GREEN
　SIMPLE
INEXPLICABLE FELL
INFALLIBLE FAILSAFE SUREFIRE
　UNERRING FOOLPROOF
INFAMOUS BASE RUDDY BLOODY
　NOTOUR ODIOUS BLEEDING
　FLAGRANT NIDERING SHAMEFUL
　NEFARIOUS OPPROBRIOUS
INFAMY STAIN BAFFLE DEFAME
　SHONDE DISHONOR IGNOMINY
　OPPROBRIM OPPROBRIUM
INFANCY CRADLE BABYHOOD
INFANT BABE BABY TINY WEAN
　CHILD MINOR PREMIE CHRISOM
　MILKSOP PREEMIE BALDLING
　BANTLING
　(NAKED —) SCUDDY
　(NEWLY-BORN —) NEONATUS
　(VORACIOUS —) KILLCROP
INFANTILE BABYISH
INFANTRY FOOT FANTERIE
　FOOTFOLK

INFANTRYMAN GI ASKAR ZOUAVE
　DOGFACE DRAGOON DOUGHBOY
　PIOUPIOU SOREFOOT
　VOETGANGER
INFATUATE FOOL ASSOT BESOT
INFATUATED MAD FOND GAGA
　GONE ASSOT CRAZY DOTTY
　ENTETE ENGOUEE FOOLISH
　BESOTTED
INFATUATION ATE PASH RAVE
　CRUSH FOLLY BEGUIN
　(TRANSIENT —) CRAZE
　(SUFF.) (— FOR) MANE MANIA(C)
　(— WITH) ITIS
INFECT SMIT TAINT CANKER DEFILE
　EMPEST ENTACH INFEST POISON
　CORRUPT DISEASE POLLUTE
　SMITTLE CONTAMINATE
INFECTED SEPTIC FUNGUSED
　(NOT —) BLAND
INFECTION COLD DOSE SMIT
　FELON TAINT FUNGUS
INFECTIOUS TAKING SMITTLE
　CATCHING SMITABLE SMITTING
　VIRULENT
INFEFTMENT SASINE
INFER DRAW PICK READ TAKE
　EDUCE GUESS JUDGE ALLEGE
　DECIDE DEDUCE DEDUCT DERIVE
　DIVINE GATHER INDUCE REASON
　COLLECT INCLUDE PRESUME
　SURMISE CONCLUDE CONSTRUE
INFERENCE EDUCT SEQUEL
　ANALOGY SEQUELA ILLATION
　SEQUENCE SEQUITUR
　OBSERVATION PRESUMPTION
INFERIOR BAD BUM DOG ILL JAY
　LOW OFF SAD EVIL LESS MEAN
　POOR PUNK SLIM SOUR WAFF
　BASER BAUCH BELOW CHEAP
　DOGGY GROSS LOUSY LOWER
　PETTY PLAIN SCALY SCRUB TACKY
　TATTY WORRY BEHIND CAGMAG
　COARSE COMMON CRAPPY
　FEEBLE FEMALE IMPURE LESSER
　MEASLY PALTRY PEDARY PUISNE
　PUISNY ROTTEN SECOND SHABBY
　SHODDY WOODEN BADDISH
　CRIPPLE HUMBLER NAGGISH
　POPULAR SCRUBBY SUBJECT
　ABNORMAL ANTERIOR DEROGATE
　ORDINARY PARAVAIL TERRIBLE
　(PREF.) DEMI INFRA SUB
　(SUFF.) ASTER EEN
　(— ONE) LING
INFERIORITY LESSNESS MEANNESS
INFERNAL BLACK AVERNAL
　BLASTED ETERNAL HELLISH
　SATANIC SHEOLIC STYGIAN
　CHTHONIC DAMNABLE DEVILISH
　PLUTONIC PLUTONIAN
INFERTILE DEAD DEAF DOUR LEAN
　POOR THIN CLEAR EFFETE STERILE
INFEST COE VEX BESET INFECT
　PESTER PLAGUE OVERRUN
　TORMENT
INFESTATION SCALE PLAGUE
　STRIKE MYIASIS LOAIASIS
　PEDICULOSIS
INFESTED MITY BLOWN BROOD
　BUGGY FLUKY FLUKED GRUBBY
　HAUNTED FLYBLOWN
INFIDEL DEIST KAFIR GIAOUR

PAYNIM ATHEIST SARACEN SKEPTIC AGNOSTIC MISCREANT MISBELIEVER
INFIDELITY PERFIDY ADULTERY TRAHISON
INFIELD CARPET INTOWN DIAMOND
INFILTRATE FILTER CRETIFY COLONIZE
INFILTRATION SEEPAGE ADIPOSIS SATURATION
INFINITE CHAOS COSMIC ENDLESS ETERNAL IMMENSE
INFINITENESS ETERNITY
INFINITESIMAL PUNCTUAL
INFINITIVE SUPINE VERBID
  (**FRENCH —**) ETRE
INFINITY OLAM ANANTA ETERNITY
INFIRM LAME WEAK ANILE CRAZY CRONK SHAKY CRANKY FEEBLE SICKLY UNFIRM UNSURE CASALTY CRAICHY DOWLESS DWAIBLE FRAGILE INVALID SAPLESS UNFEARY DODDERED FIRMLESS INSECURE RESOLUTE UNSTRONG
INFIRMARY SICKBAY
INFIRMITY WOE CRAZE DOTAGE FOIBLE UNHEAL DISEASE FAILING FRAILTY UNMIGHT DEBILITY SICKNESS WEAKNESS
INFIX INLAY INSET ENGRAVE IMPLANT INGRAIN
INFIXED INHERENT
INFLAME RAW BURN FIRE GOAD HEAT STIR ANGER BLAIN FLAME SCALD SHAME AROUSE ENAMOR EXCITE FESTER IGNITE INCEND KINDLE MADDEN RANKLE EMBRASE FLUSTER INCENSE ESCHAUFE
  (**— WITH LOVE**) ENAMOR
INFLAMED RED ANGRY FIERY ABLAZE FRETTY HEATED TORRID FLAGRANT
INFLAMMABLE FIERY ARDENT TOUCHY PICEOUS TINDERY
INFLAMMATION ACNE FIRE ANGER FELON GLEET SCALD SEBEL AGNAIL ANCOME BLIGHT CANKER DEFLUX GREASE IRITIS CATARRH CECITIS CHAFING COLITIS COXITIS FISTULA GONITIS ILEITIS QUITTOR SUNBURN ADENITIS ANGIITIS AORTITIS BURSITIS CHILITIS CYCLITIS CYSTITIS SHINGLES
  (**SUFF.**) ITIS
INFLATE HOVE HUFF KITE PLIM PUFF BLOAT BOLNE HEAVE SWELL DILATE EMBOSS EXPAND HUFFLE INBLOW PLIMPUP TUMEFY BLADDER BOMBAST DISTEND FORBLOW OUTSWELL SUFFLATE
INFLATED TRIG BLOWN FLOWN GASSY PUFFY TUMID TURGID BOMBAST BULLATE FUSTIAN OROTUND STILTED SWOLLEN TURGENT BLADDERY OUTBLOWN TOPLOFTY TUMOROUS VANITOUS BOMBASTIC OVERBLOWN PLETHORIC
INFLATION FLATUS CADENCE TYMPANY
INFLECT COMPARE DECLINE
INFLECTION SIGN TONE ARSIS

ACCENT FLEXION LATINISM MODULATION
INFLECTIONAL FORMAL
INFLEXIBILITY ACAMPSIA
INFLEXIBLE ACID DOUR FIRM HARD IRON EAGER SOLID STERN STIFF STONY STOUR SEVERE STRICT STUFFY ADAMANT RESTIVE GRANITIC IRONCLAD OBDURATE PREFRACT RESOLUTE RIGOROUS STIFFISH STUBBORN ADAMANTINE
INFLICT DO ADD PUT SET GIVE SEND INFER YIELD IMPOSE RAMROD STRIKE
  (**— CHASTISEMENT**) WREAK
  (**— HURT**) BRUISE
  (**— INJURY**) AGGRIEVE
  (**— PAIN**) LAY CHASTISE
INFLICTION (**— OF PUNISHMENT**) AUTODAFE
INFLORESCENCE CHAT CYME AMENT ARROW BRUSH SPIKE UMBEL CORYMB FLOWER RACEME SPADIX TASSEL BOSTRYX PANICLE THYRSIS CYATHIUM FASCICLE NUCAMENT
INFLOW INSET AFFLUX INCOME INFLUX INCOURSE
INFLOWING AFFLUENT
INFLUENCE IN WIN BEND BIAS COAX DRAG DRAW HAND HANK HEFT LEAD MOVE PULL PUSH RULE SUCK SWAY BRIBE CHARM CLOUT COLOR ENACT FORCE GRACE IMPEL JUICE MOYEN POWER REACH SPELL VAPOR VOGUE WEIGH AFFECT ALLURE CREDIT EFFECT GOVERN IMPORT INDUCE INFLOW INFLUX MOTIVE OBSESS PONDUS SALUTE SHADOW STROKE WEIGHT ACTUATE ATTINGE ATTRACT BEARING BEWITCH BLARNEY BOSSDOM CAPTURE CONCUSS CONTROL DISPUTE ENCHANT GRAVITY IMPRINT INCLINE INSPIRE MASTERY SUASION TENDRIL DOMINION HEGEMONY INTEREST LEVERAGE MEDICINE PRESTIGE SANCTION STRENGTH CAPTIVATE
  (**— BY GIFTS**) GREASE
  (**— BY THREATS**) INTIMIDATE
  (**— CORRUPTLY**) BRIBE
  (**— FOR DESTRUCTION**) MAELSTROM
  (**— OF GODS**) MANA
  (**— OF PERSONALITY**) MAGNETISM
  (**— OF THE STARS**) BLAS
  (**— UNREASONABLY**) OBSESS
  (**ATTEMPT TO —**) JAWBONE
  (**BENIGN —**) UNCTION
  (**CONSTRAINING —**) STRESS PRESSURE
  (**CONTROLLING —**) SWAY
  (**CORRUPTING —**) SMOUCH SMUTCH
  (**DEPRESSING —**) CHILL
  (**DIABOLICAL —**) DEVILDOM
  (**DISRUPTIVE —**) GREMLIN
  (**DOMINANT —**) GENIUS STREAM
  (**DULLING —**) DAMPER
  (**ELEVATING —**) LIFT
  (**HARMFUL —**) UPAS GRUDGE

  (**INJURIOUS —**) RUST
  (**MALEVOLENT —**) DISASTER
  (**MALIGN —**) TAKING
  (**PERNICIOUS —**) BALE BLAST
  (**SINISTER —**) MALICE
  (**SOOTHING —**) SALVE
  (**SPIRITUAL —**) NUMEN
  (**SURROUNDING —**) AIR AMBIENCE
  (**UNDER — OF ALCOHOL OR DRUGS**) ZONKED
INFLUENCING INFUSIVE
INFLUENTIAL BIG GRAVE POWERFUL
INFLUENZA FLU LEUMA GRIPPE PINKEYE
INFLUX STORM INCOME INFLOW INRUSH ILLAPSE
  (**— IN A MINE**) COURSE
  (**— OF TIDE**) INSET
INFOLD WRAP IMPLY TWINE EMPLOY INWRAP ENVELOP INVOLVE CONVOLVE
INFORM KEN BEEF BLOW FINK NOSE POST SHOP SHOW TELL WARN WISE LEARN PEACH ADVISE ASSURE DELATE DETECT NOTIFY PREACH SNITCH WITTER APPRISE EDUCATE IMPEACH INSENSE PARTAKE POSSESS RESOLVE SIGNIFY SUGGEST ACQUAINT DENOUNCE INFORMED INSTRUCT SPARSILE
  (**— AGAINST**) SHOP RUMBLE DENOUNCE
INFORMAL BREEZY CASUAL CHATTY COMMON FOLKSY TWEEDY INTIMATE SLIPSHOD SOCIABLE NEGLIGENT OFFICIOUS
INFORMANT AUTHOR INFORMER SQUEALER SYCOPHANT
INFORMATION AIR GEN OIL WIT CLEW CLUE DOPE INFO LORE NEWS NOTE TALE WIRE WORD DATUM GRIFF SCOOP SKILL ADVICE INSIDE LIGHTS NOTICE APPRISE PEMICAN READOUT TIDINGS WITTING BRIEFING NOTITION PEMMICAN
  (**— ON VIDEO SCREEN**) DISPLAY
  (**BODY OF —**) DIGEST
  (**CONDENSED —**) PEMICAN PEMMICAN
  (**INCIDENTAL —**) SIDELIGHT
  (**SECRET —**) ARCANUM
  (**SUFF.**) ANA IANA
INFORMED UP HEP WISE AWARE WITTY KNOWING LEARNED
  (**WELL —**) UPON
INFORMER FINK NARK NOSE PIMP SPIV STAG RUSTY SNEAK SPLIT BEAGLE CANARY FINGER SETTER SNITCH TELLER DELATOR STOOLIE TANQUAM APPROVER PROMOTER SQUAWKER SQUEAKER SQUEALER TELLTALE SYCOPHANT WHISTLEBLOWER
INFORTUNE MARS SATURN
INFRACTION BREACH OFFENCE TRESPASS
  (**— IN HOCKEY**) SPEARING
INFRARED ULTRARED
INFREQUENCY SELDOMCY

INFREQUENT RARE SELDOM FUGITIVE SPORADIC UNCOMMON
INFRINGE IMPOSE INVADE TRENCH IMPINGE INFRACT INTRUDE ENCROACH REFRINGE TRESPASS
INFRINGEMENT FOUL BREACH TRESPASS VIOLENCE
INFRINGER PIRATE
INFULA FANON LABEL LAPPET HEADBAND
INFUNDIBULUM FUNNEL PAVILION
INFURIATE ENRAGE ENFELON
INFUSE DRAW MASK IMBUE IMMIT SPOIL STEEP AERATE AERIFY IMMISS INFLOW INFORM INFUND INVEST LEAVEN BREATHE DISTILL ENGRAIN IMPLANT INFOUND INSPIRE INSTILL SUFFUSE SATURATE
  (**— TEA**) TRACK
  (**— WITH HATRED**) TURN
INFUSED SHOT
INFUSION SHADE CARDIN INCOME TISANE HORDEATE
  (**— OF MALT**) WORT GROUT
  (**BITTER —**) RUE
INFUSORIAN LEPOCYTE
INGA GUAVA
INGATE GATE LEDGE TEDGE
INGATHERING HARVEST
INGENIOUS SLY CUTE FAST FEAT FINE ACUTE SHARP SMART WITTY ADROIT BRAINY CLEVER CRAFTY DAEDAL GIFTED KNACKY PRETTY QUAINT SUBTLE CUNNING POLITIC SKILLFUL
INGENUITY ART WIT ENGINE ADDRESS COMPASS ARTIFICE CONTOISE INDUSTRY QUENTISE
INGENUOSITY NAIVETE
INGENUOUS FREE FRANK NAIVE PLAIN CANDID HONEST SUBTLE ARTLESS NATURAL SINCERE INNOCENT
INGENUOUSNESS NAIVETE
INGEST EAT INCEPT ENGLOBE SWALLOW
INGESTION SLURP
INGOT GAD SOW WEDGE LINGOT NIGGOT CROPHEAD
  (**— OF BRASS**) STRIP
  (**— OF SILVER**) SHOE TING SCHUYT
  (**SILVER —**) SYCEE
  (**SILVER —S**) SYCEE
  (**SOAKING —S**) HEAT
INGRAIN GRAIN INFUSE ENFLESH
INGRAINED INWORN
INGRATE SNAKE
INGRATIATE FLATTER
INGRATIATING BLAND SILKY SLEEK SLICK SOAPY SILKEN SMOOTH
INGRATITUDE UNTHANK
INGREDIENT FACTOR AMALGAM BINDING ELEMENT ADJUVANT
  (**ACTIVE —**) ANIMA
  (**FUNDAMENTAL —**) BASIS
  (**FUSIBLE —**) BOND
  (**MAIN —**) BASE
  (**SALVE —**) ALOE
INGRESS ENTRY ENTRANCE
INGROWTH APODEMA
INGUEN GROIN

INHABIT BIG WIN WON COVER DWELL HABIT OCCUPY BEDWELL INDWELL POSSESS POPULATE
INHABITANT INMATE BURGHER CITIZEN DENIZEN DWELLER PEOPLER BORDERER CONFINER DEMESMAN HABITANT INCOLANT INHOLDER
  (**— OF ALASKA**) SOURDOUGH
  (**— OF BORDER REGION**) MARCHER
  (**— OF CITY**) CIT CITIZEN
  (**— OF EXTREME NORTH**) HYPERBOREAN
  (**— OF INDIA**) BHARATA
  (**— OF JUNGLE**) JUNGLI
  (**— OF MAINE**) DOWNEASTER
  (**— OF MOON**) LUNARIAN
  (**— OF SWISS ALPS**) GRISON
  (**— OF TORRID ZONE**) ASCIAN
  (**— OF VIRGINIA**) COOHEE
  (**— OF WISCONSIN**) BADGER
  (**EARTH —**) TERRAN
  (**OLDEST —**) PATRIARCH
  (**PL.**) SIDE WARE
  (**SUFF.**) COLA ITE OT OTE
INHABITING
  (**SUFF.**) COLE COLINE COLOUS
INHALATION SNUFF BREATH
  (**PREF.**) ANEM(O)
INHALE DRAW TAKE SMOKE SNIFF SNUFF ATTRACT BREATHE INHAUST INSPIRE RESPIRE ASPIRATE
  (**— A DRUG**) SNORT
  (**PREF.**) INSPIRO
INHALER SNIFTER
INHARMONIOUS ABSURD RUGGED ABSONANT
INHERE CONSIST INEXIST
INHERENCE INBEING
INHERENT KIND INBORN INNATE INWARD NATIVE PROPER INGENIT NATURAL HABITUAL IMMANENT INTEGRAL INTERNAL RESIDENT
INHERIT HEIR SUCCEED
INHERITANCE KIND ENTAIL HEIRDOM HEIRSHIP HEREDITY HERITAGE LANDFALL VACANTIA
  (**— OF CATTLE**) KIND
  (**PARTICULATE —**) MENDELISM
INHERITED INBORN INNATE CONGENITAL
  (**SUFF.**) CLINOUS CLINY
INHIBIT COOP CURB SNUB CRIMP DETER FORBID STIFLE SUPPRESS
INHIBITED COLD
INHIBITION AKINESIS
INHIBITOR PARGYLINE PHENELZINE
INHIBITORY COLYTIC
INHOSPITABLE STERN DESERT
INHUMAN FELL CRUEL BRUTAL FIERCE IMMANE SAVAGE BESTIAL MANLESS DEVILISH KINDLESS
INHUMANE WANTON
INHUMANITY CRUELTY
INHUME BURY INTER ENTOMB
INIMICAL BAD FROSTY HOSTILE
  (**— TO LIFE**) ANTIBIOTIC
INIQUITOUS ILL DARK WRONG SINFUL WICKED NEFARIOUS
INIQUITY SIN EVIL VICE CRIME GUILT DARKNESS MISCHIEF

INITIAL LETTER VIRGIN ASPIREE PRINCIPAL
  (**INTERWOVEN —S**) CIPHER
  (**PL.**) PERFINS
INITIALLY ATFIRST
INITIATE HEAD MYST OPEN ADEPT ADMIT BEGIN BREAK ENTER EPOPT FOUND START GROUND INDUCE INDUCT INVENT LAUNCH MYSTES ORPHIC BAPTIZE INSTALL INSTATE OPERATE ORPHEAN SYMMIST YTIGGER COMMENCE ESOTERIC INCHOATE ORIGINATE
INITIATION DIKSHA OPENING ENTRANCE
  (**— OF GROWTH**) BUDBREAK
INITIATIVE PEP LEAD GETUP ACTION AMBITION GUMPTION OVERTURE
INJECT DRIVE IMMIT
  (**— DRUG**) SKINPOP
  (**— DRUGS**) SHOOT MAINLINE
INJECTION JAG HYPO SHOT BOOSTER CLYSTER INSERTION
INJUDICIOUS UNWISE
INJUDICIOUSNESS ACRISY
INJUNCTION HEST BEHEST CHARGE IMPOSE RUBRIC BIDDING DICTATE EXPRESS MANDATE PRECEPT
INJURE DO GAS ILL MAR BURN CHEW DERE ENVY GALL HARM HURT MAUL TEAR TEEN WERD ABUSE BLAST CRAZE DIRTY MISDO RIFLE SCALD SHEND SMITE SPOIL STEER WOUND WRONG BRUISE DAMAGE DEFACE DEFECT DEPAIR GRIEVE HINDER IMPAIR INJURY MANGLE NOBBLE PUNISH RANKLE SCATHE SCOTCH STRAIN AFFLICT AFFRONT CONTUSE DAMNIFY DESPITE FORWORK MISBEDE TERRIFY AGGRIEVE DISASTER DISSERVE FORSLACK IMPERISH INTERESS MISCHIEF MISGUIDE MUTILATE PREJUDGE SPURGALL
  (**— BY ASPERSION**) SPATTER
  (**— BY FALSE REPORT**) SLANDER
  (**— BY GLANCE OF BASILISK**) STRIKE
  (**— BY TREADING UPON**) FITTER
  (**— SCENT**) STAIN
  (**— SERIOUSLY**) DO KILL SPOIL
  (**— SLIGHTLY**) ANNOY
  (**— THE BACK**) CHINK
  (**— WITH GRENADE**) FRAG
  (**DELIBERATELY —**) FRAG
  (**SEVERELY —**) WASTE
INJURED HURT LESED BLASTED
  (**EASILY —**) NICE
INJURIOUS BAD ILL EVIL NOCENT NOYANT NOYFUL SHREWD ABUSIVE HARMFUL HURTFUL NOXIOUS SCADDLE DAMAGING GRIEVOUS SINISTER TORTIOUS TORTUOUS WRACKFUL WRONGFUL PERNICIOUS
INJURIOUSLY HEAVILY
INJURY ILL JAM MAR BALE BANE BURN EVIL HARM HURT JEEL LOSS RUIN SCAT TEEN TORT WITE ABUSE BLAME CHAFE CRUSH GRIEF SCALD SCORE SPITE SPOIL

TOUCH WATHE WRACK WRONG BREACH BRUISE DAMAGE DANGER IMPAIR LESION SCATHE STRAIN STROKE TRAUMA BEATING DESPITE EXPENSE OFFENSE OUTRAGE PAYMENT SCADDLE SCRATCH SORANCE BUSINESS CASUALTY CREPANCE INTEREST MISCHIEF NUISANCE
  (**— OF HORSES**) TREAD CREPANCE
  (**— OF PLANTS**) SUNSCALD
  (**— TO REPUTATION**) SCANDAL
  (**CHIEF —**) FOCUS
  (**MALICIOUS —**) REVENGE
  (**SERIOUS —**) MAYHEM
INJUSTICE WRONG INJURY INJURIA UNRIGHT HARDSHIP INEQUITY
  (**GROSS —**) INIQUITY
INK BEAT SIGN COLOR ARNEMENT ATRAMENT
  (**DISPENSER OF —**) SQUID
  (**KIND OF —**) RED INDIA
  (**PRINTER'S —**) CYAN
INK-BALL DABBER PUMPET
INKER SLOSHER
INKING PAD TOMPION
INKLE SPINEL
INKLING HOE HINT ITEM SCENT GLIMMER GLIMPSE UMBRAGE
INKSTAND STANDISH
INKWELL FOUNT INKSTAND
INKY BLACK ATRAMENTOUS
INLAID PIQUE CONTISE
  (**— DECORATION**) BUHL BOULE BOULLE
  (**— WORK**) KOFTGARI
INLAND MAUKA INMORE INWARD MIDLAND INGHEL
INLAY PICK PIKE COUCH HATCH INLET PIQUE SPELL CRUSTA ENAMEL IMPAVE INDENT NIELLO TARSIA ENCHASE ENCRUST INCRUST COMMESSO
INLAYING TARKASHI
INLET ARM BAY CUT GEO RIA VOE COVE DOCK HOPE MERE SLEW WICK BAYOU BRACE CHUCK CREEK FIORD FJORD FLEET HAVEN LOGAN LOUGH STOMA ESTERO HARBOR INFALL SLOUGH TONGUE DOGHOLE INDRAFT SUCTION CALANQUE SEAPOOSE
  (**— OF THE SEA**) EA
  (**MUDDY —**) SUMP
  (**REGULATED —**) SLUICE
  (**TIDAL —**) GAP
INLIER WINDOW
INLYING INNERLY
INMATE FISH LODGER TENANT BEADSMAN DOMESTIC PRISONER
  (**BEDLAM —**) ABRAMMAN ABRAHAMMAN
  (**RELIGIOUS —**) NOVICE
INMOST SECRET RETIRED
INN PUB KHAN STOP VENT ANGEL BANDB FONDA HOTEL MESON SERAI TAMBO VENTA CABACK HARBOR HOSTEL HOSTRY IMARET POSADA PUBLIC SHANTY TABARD ALBERGE AUBERGE BOLICHE CAFENEH CAFENET FONDACO FONDOUK HOSTAGE LOCANDA OSTERIA SOJOURN SURAHEE

CHOULTRY GASTHAUS HOSTELRY ORDINARY SERAGLIO WAYHOUSE ROADHOUSE
  (**KIND OF —**) MOTOR
INNARDS GIZZARD INWARDS STUFFING
INNATE BORN KIND INBORN INBRED CONNATE INGRAIN NATURAL INHERENT INSTINCT
  (**— QUALITY**) LARGESS
INNER BEN ENTAL INSIDE INWARD INWITH MENTAL INTERIOR INTERNAL PECTORAL
  (**— LIGHT**) SEED
  (**PREF.**) ENT(O) ESO
  (**— PARTS OF BODY**) BATHY
INNER MONGOLIA (**CAPITAL OF —**) HOHHOT HUHEHOT
INNERMOST UPPER INMOST MIDMOST INTIMATE
INNERVATE AROUSE
INNINA ISHTAR
INNING END HAND HEAD FRAME
  (**PL.**) KNOCK WICKET
INNKEEPER HOST DUENA TAPPER VENTER GOODMAN HOSTESS HOSTLER PADRONE BONIFACE HOSTELER
  (**PL.**) CAUPONES
INNOCENCE BLUET WHITE CANDOR PURITY SIMPLICITY
INNOCENT SOT DEWY FREE NAIF PURE CANNY CLEAR NAIVE SEELY SILLY WHITE CHASTE DOVISH HONEST SIMPLE CHRISOM LAMBKIN UPRIGHT ARCADIAN HARMLESS IGNORANT PASTORAL PRIMROSE SACKLESS UNGUILTY ZACCHEUS
INNOCUOUS HARMLESS INNOCENT
INNOVATE NOVELIZE
INNOVATION NOVEL NOVELTY
INNOVATOR HERETIC
INNUENDO HINT SLUR SLIPE
INNUMERABLE MYRIAD NUMBERLESS
INO (**BROTHER OF —**) POLYDORUS
  (**FATHER OF —**) CADMUS
  (**HUSBAND OF —**) ATHAMAS
  (**MOTHER OF —**) HARMONIA
  (**SISTER OF —**) AGAVE SEMELE AUTONOE
  (**SON OF —**) LEARCHUS PALAEMON MELICERTES
INOCULATE SEED PLANT INFUSE ENGRAFT EQUINATE
INOCULATION JAG
INOCULUM STAB STREAK
IN-OFF JENNY
INOFFENSIVE HARMLESS
INOPERATIVE OFF DEAD RESTY SILENT NUGATORY
INOPPORTUNE UNTIMELY
INORDINATE WILD UNDUE ENORMOUS
INORGANIC MINERAL
INOSITOL DAMBOSE
INPOURING INFLUX
INQUEST CROWN QUEST ASSIZE OFFICE INQUIRY
INQUIET UNEASY
INQUILINE GUEST
INQUIRE ASK AXE SEEK QUERY

SPERE DEMAND FRAYNE SEARCH EXAMINE HEARKEN QUESTION

INQUIRER ASKER QUERENT

INQUIRY PROBE QUERY THANK TRIAL DEMAND EXAMEN TRACER DOCIMASY QUESTION RESEARCH SCRUTINY SPEERING

INQUISITION CUSTOM INQUIRY QUAESTIO

INQUISITIVE NOSY PEERY PRYING CURIOUS MEDDLING QUIZZICAL

INROAD RAID BREACH INBREAK INVASION

INSALUBRIOUS NOXIOUS

INSANE MAD WUD DAFT NUTS WILD WOOD BALMY BATTY BUGGY CRAZY DIPPY MANIC QUEER WRONG CRANKY LOCOED SCREWY FLIGHTY FRANTIC FURIOUS LUNATIC WITLESS BUGHOUSE DEMENTED DERANGED DISTRACT
(— ONE) MANIAC

INSANITY RAGE CRACK CRAZE FOLIE MANIA FRENZY LUNACY MADNESS VESANIA DELIRIUM DEMENTIA WOODNESS ACROMANIA PSYCHOSIS

INSATIABLE GREEDY VORACIOUS

INSCRIBE DELVE ENTER WRITE BLAZON DOCKET ENDOSS INDITE LEGEND LETTER SCRIBE SCRIVE SCROLL ASCRIBE ENDORSE ENGROSS DEDICATE DESCRIBE EMBLAZON ENSCROLL INTITULE

INSCRIBED INWRIT WRITTEN DESCRIPT

INSCRIPTION HEAD ELOGY CACHET LEGEND LETTER ELOGIUM EPIGRAM EPITAPH MENTION TITULUS WRITING COLOPHON EPIGRAPH GRAFFITO INSCRIPT SCRIBING
(— ON ROCK) PETROGLYPH
(— ON TOMBSTONE) ELOGE ELOGIUM
(3-LETTER —) TRIGRAM

INSCRUTABLE EQUIVOCAL MYSTERIOUS

INSECT ANT BEE BUG DOR DUN ELF FLY NIT ANER FLEA GNAT GOGO GYNE MOTH PELA PEST PUPA SPIT WASP WETA ZIMB APHID APHIS BICHO BORER FLYER GOGGA GUEST IMAGO LOUSE MINER ROACH SCALE BEETLE BLIGHT CALLOW CICADA CIXIID EARWIG EMBIID HAWKER HOPPER INSTAR MANTIS NITTER PODURA PSOCID SAPPER SAWFLY THRIPS VERMIN WALKER WEEVIL ATTACUS BLATTID BOATMAN BRUMMER BUZZARD CRAWLER CREEPER CRICKET CYNIPID DEALATE DRUMMER EARWORM FIREBUG FIREFLY GALLFLY GIRDLER GRAYFLY HEXAPOD JAPYGID KATYDID PHASMID SANDBOY SCINIPH SKIPPER SPECTRE STAINER STYLOPS TERMITE VAGRANT WEBWORM ALDERFLY ALKERMES BLACKFLY BRACONID DIPTERAN FIREBRAT FULGORID GLOWWORM HOMOPTER

HORNTAIL LACEWING LECANIUM MEALYBUG PRONYMPH SEMIPUPA SEXUPARA SPHECOID STINKBUG STYLOPID SYMPHILE
(— STAGE) PUPA IMAGO LARVA
(IMMATURE —) NYMPH
(LOWEST —S) AMETABOLA
(PART OF —) EYE CLAW COXA WING FEMUR TIBIA CERCUS LABRUM PALPUS TARSUS THORAX ABDOMEN ANTENNA OCELLUS MANDIBLE SPIRACLE OVIPOSTOR PROTHORAX TYMPANIUM MESOTHORAX METATHORAX OVIPOSITER TROCHANTER
(PL.) HEXAPODA
(PREF.) ENTOM(O)
(SUFF.) CORIS

INSECTICIDE DDD DDT DIP EPN CUBE FLIT MINEX MIREX NALED SEVIN TIMBO ALDRIN DERRIS ENDRIN RONNEL CALOMEL ISODRIN LINDANE MENAZON OVICIDE PHORATE CARBARYL CHLORDAN CULICIDE DIELDRIN FENTHION NICOTINE ROTENONE SCHRADAN ANTRYCIDE MALATHION PARATHION PYRETHRUM

INSECTIVORE MOLE SHREW AGOUTA DESMAN TENREC MOONRAT ALAMIQUI

INSECURE DICKY EEMIS LOOSE SHAKY INFIRM TICKLE UNFAST UNSAFE UNSURE CASALTY

INSECURITY DANGER

INSEMINATE BREED

INSENSATE SURD FATUOUS

INSENSIBILITY DAMP APATHY STUPOR TORPOR

INSENSIBLE DEAD DULL LOST NUMB BRUTE DENSE MARBLE OBTUSE SEARED STUPID WOODEN DATELESS APATHETIC

INSENSITIVE DEAD BLUNT CRASS STONY OBTUSE STUPID BOORISH

INSEPARABLE WRAPPED

INSERT SLIP SPUD STOP BOTCH DICKY ENROL ENTER FUDGE IMMIT INFER INFIX INLET INSET SETIN STUFF COLLET GUSSET INWORK INWEAVE GATEFOLD INTROMIT SANDWICH SLASHING SUBTRUDE THROWOUT
(— IN SHOE) CUSHION
(— STONE CHIPS) PIN
(— SURREPTITIOUSLY) FOIST
(SKIRT —) GORE

INSERTION FLOWER BEADING
(TAPERED —) MITER MITRE

INSET GODET INSERT
(DRESS —) MOTIF

INSHEATHE EMBOSS

INSIDE IN BEN ATHIN INBYE INNER INWITH KEYHOLE INTERIOR
(— OF ANGLE BAR) BOSOM
(— OF OUTER EAR) BUR BURR
(PREF.) END(O)

INSIDIOUS SLY SNARY COVERT SUBTLE GUILEFUL

INSIGHT KEN SIGHT APERCU THEORY NOSTRIL

INSIGNIA TYPE BADGE ORDER SIGNS COLLAR GEORGE CADUCEUS COMMENDA HERALDRY OPINICUS PONTIFICALS
(HERALDIC —) ARMOR
(MILITARY —) EAGLE

INSIGNIFICANCE NOTHINGNESS

INSIGNIFICANT NULL POOR PUNY DINKY FOOTY PETIT PETTY POTTY SCRUB SMALL HUMBLE NAUGHT PALTRY PUISNE SIMPLE SLIGHT FOOLISH NAUGHTY NIFLING NOMINAL PELTING PIMPING SCRUBBY TENUOUS TRIVIAL BAUBLING INFERIOR PEDDLING PITIABLE SNIPPING TRIFLING TRIPENNY

INSINCERE FALSE DOUBLE HOLLOW FEIGNED LIPDEEP ARTIFICIAL

INSINCERITY ARTIFICE DISGUISE

INSINUATE HINT MINT WIND CRAWL SCREW TWIST ALLUDE GLANCE INFUSE INSTIL WRITHE IMPLANT INNUATE

INSINUATING SNIDE SILKEN SMARMY

INSINUATION HINT INKLING

INSIPID DRY WAW BLAH DEAD FADE FLAT FOND FOZY LASH TAME BANAL BAUCH BLAND FLASH INANE PROSY STALE VAPID WALSH WAUGH FLASHY FRIGID JEJUNE SWASHY THREEP WAIRSH WALLOW EXOLETE FATUOUS INSULSE MAWKISH PROSAIC SAPLESS SHILPIT WEARISH WEERISH LIFELESS UNSAVORY WATERISH

INSIST AVER PRESS ASSERT THREAP CONSIST
(— PEEVISHLY) CRAIK
(— UPON) SOLICIT

INSISTENCE URGENCY INSTANCY

INSISTENT LOUD ADAMANT INSTANT EMPHATIC FRENZIED IMPOSING

INSISTER STICKLER

INSOLE CUSHION SLIPSOLE

INSOLENCE GUM LIP SASS CHEEK MOUTH PRIDE SNASH HUBRIS DISDAIN AUDACITY SURQUIDY CONTUMELY PETULANCE

INSOLENT FACY PERT RUDE WISE BARDY BRASH LUSTY PROUD CHEEKY LORDLY WANTON ABUSIVE DEFIANT PAUGHTY ARROGANT IMPUDENT PETULANT SCORNFUL AUDACIOUS

INSOLUBLE HOPELESS

INSOLVENT BANKRUPT

INSOMNIA AHYPNIA AGRYPNIA

INSOUCIANT CAVALIER

INSPECT SEE SUS VET CASE ESPY LOOK SUSS BRACK CHECK SIGHT VISIT INLOOK PERUSE SURVEY EXAMINE OVERSEE CONSIDER OVERLOOK OVERVIEW
(— CASUALLY) BROWSE
(— COINS) SHROFF
(— MERCHANDISE IN BALTIC) BRACK
(— TROOPS) REVIEW

INSPECTION EYE PRY VIEW CHECK SIGHT REVIEW SURVEY BEDIKAH CHECKUP INSIGHT INSPECT PERUSAL VIDIMUS OVERHAUL OVERVIEW SCRUTINY
(— OF CLOTH) ALNAGE
(— OF TROOPS) REVIEW
(KIT —) RAGFAIR

INSPECTOR SAYER SNOOP BISHOP CENSOR CONNER JUMPER LOOKER VIEWER GRAINER MOOCHER PERCHER SAMPLER SNOOPER VEADORE EXAMINER SEARCHER
(— OF COAL) KEEKER
(— OF COTTON LOOMS) TACKLER
(— OF ELECTRIC LAMPS) AGER
(ECCLESIASTICAL —) EXARCH

INSPIRATION FIRE SIGH POESY ANIMUS SPIRIT SPRITE IMPULSE MADNESS PEGASUS AFFLATUS AGANIPPE INFLATUS
(— IN ORATORY) HWYL
(ORATORICAL —) HWYL

INSPIRE FIRE MOVE CHEER ELATE EXALT SPARK BEACON INBLOW INCUSS INDUCE INFORM INFUSE KINDLE PROMPT ACTUATE ANIMATE EMBRAVE ENFORCE ENLIVEN HEARTEN IMPLANT PREMOVE QUICKEN SUGGEST CATALYZE ENTALENT INSPIRIT MOTIVATE SUFFLATE

INSPIRED AWED VATIC AFFLATED DAEMONIC ENTHEATE VISIONED

INSPIRER SOUL

INSPIRING INFUSIVE SPLENDID STIRRING
(— AWE) FORMIDABLE

INSPIRIT CHEER ELATE HEART ROUSE SPIRIT ANIMATE QUERIGH COMFORT ENLIVEN HEARTEN INSPIRE QUICKEN ALACRIFY

INSPISSATE STIFFEN THICKEN

INSPISSATED STIFF THICK

INSTABILITY ANOMY ANOMIE SLIDDER FLUIDITY

INSTALL SEAT CHAIR STALL INDUCT INVEST ENSTOOL POSSESS ENTHRONE INITIATE

INSTALLATION INDUCTION
(— OF MINISTER) INFARE
(FLOATING —) PLATFORM
(MILITARY —) GARRISON

INSTALLMENT KIST SERIAL EARNEST CONTRACT
(— OF SERIAL) HEFT
(— OF WAGES) COMPO
(— SELLER) TALLYMAN
(FIRST —) HANDSEL
(NEXT —) SEQUEL

INSTALMENT (— OF EPIC) RHAPSODY
(— OF SERIAL) HEFT

INSTANCE SEC CASE PINK SAMPLE EXAMPLE PURPOSE ENSAMPLE EXEMPLAR
(EXTREME —) CAPSHEAF

INSTANT POP SEC HINT WHIP WINK BLICK CLINK CRACK FLASH GLENT GLIFF GLISK JIFFY POINT SHAKE SOUND START TRICE WHIFF WIGHT

BREATH FLIFFY MINUTE MOMENT SECOND PRESENT CLIFFING
(PRECISE —) TIME
INSTANTANEOUS PRESTO DIRECTLY
INSTANTANEOUSLY OUTRIGHT
INSTANTLY SLAP SWITH PRONTO SWITHE DIRECTLY MOMENTLY
INSTAR STAGE
INSTEAD EITHER
(PREF.) ANTI PRO
INSTEP WRIST TARSUS
(PREF.) PEDI(O)
INSTIGATE EGG ABET GOAD MOVE SPUR URGE IMPEL SETON ATTICE ENTICE EXCITE FOMENT INCITE INDUCE INVOKE PROMPT SPIRIT SUBORN ACTUATE INCENSE INSTINCT
INSTIGATION MOTION MOTIVE EGGMENT INSTANCE INSTINCT
INSTIGATOR AUTHOR MOTIVE SOURCE MONITOR
INSTILL GRAFT INFIX IMPART INFUSE INSTIL BREATHE IMPLANT
INSTINCT KIND FILLED NATURE CHARGED IMPULSE CAPACITY TENDENCY
INSTINCTIVE INNATE NATURAL INHERENT ORIGINAL
INSTITUTE BEGIN BRING ERECT FOUND RAISE START STUDY FOMENT INVENT KINDLE ORDAIN ACTIVATE
(— MEMBER) PIARIST
INSTITUTION BANK CAMP FOLD CLINIC FRIARY SCHOOL ACADEMY CHARITY COLLEGE GALLERY JUBILEE LIBRARY SHELTER STATION VERITAS SEMINARY ORPHANAGE OBSERVATORY PENITENTIARY
(— FOR HOMELESS CHILDREN) PROTECTORY
(— FOR INSANE) ASYLUM
(CHARITABLE —) SPITTLE DEACONRY HOSPITAL
(DRUIDICAL —) GORSEDD
INSTRUCT KEN REAR SHOW WISE BREED COACH DRILL EDIFY ENDUE GUIDE TEACH TRAIN CHARGE DIRECT GROUND INDUCE INFORM LESSON PREACH REFORM SCHOOL COMMAND EDUCATE INSENSE POSSESS ADMONISH DOCUMENT
(— BEFOREHAND) PRIME
INSTRUCTED SCIENCED
INSTRUCTION LORE ADVICE ASSIZE CHARGE LESSON COUNSEL PRECEPT TUITION WISSING COACHING DOCTRINE DOCUMENT MONITION PEDAGOGY PROPHECY TEACHING TUTELAGE
(COMPUTER —) MACRO
(DIVINE —) LAW
(SACRED —) TORAH
(SERIES OF COMPUTER —S) LOOP
(PL.) BRIEF BRIEFING
INSTRUCTIVE DOCENT DIDACTIC
INSTRUCTOR DON SOAK SCREW TUTOR MENTOR REGENT ACHARYA

CRAMMER MONITOR TEACHER BEACHBOY CHAIRMAN ELDERMAN
(RELIGIOUS —) SWAMI
INSTRUMENT (ALSO SEE MUSICAL INSTRUMENT) DEED TOOL WRIT AGENT SLANG THEME FACTUM OCTANT TEREBRA UTENSIL SYNGRAPH
(— FOR ACQUIRING KNOWLEDGE) ORGANON
(— NOT UNDER SEAL) PAROL
(— OF DESTRUCTION) SWORD
(— OF DIVINATION) EPHOD
(— OF TORTURE) BOOT RACK BRAKE BRANK FURCA GADGE WHEEL TUMBREL BARNACLE SQUEEZER SCARPINES PILLIWINKS
(—S OF WAR) ENGINERY
(CALCULATING —) ABACUS
(DETECTING —) SQUID
(FINANCIAL —) ITEM
(KEYBOARD —) MELLOTRON
(LEGAL —) DEED GRANT FACTUM SASINE SCRIPT CHARTER CODICIL DUPLICATE
(METEOROLOGICAL —) LIDAR
(NAUTICAL —) OCTANT
(NAVIGATIONAL —) LORAN TELERAN
(NEGOTIABLE —) HUNDI HOONDEE
(OFFICIAL —) SLANG
(PREHISTORIC —) CELT
(SCIENTIFIC —) HELIOSTAT
(SCIENTIFIC OR OTHER —) AWL FAN HOE KEY MET RAX SAX BROG CLAM COMB DIAL DRAG FILE FORK GAGE HOOK PALM PLOW RACK RING SPAR ARMIL BEVEL BLADE BRACE BRAKE CHAIN CLAMP CORER DATER DOLLY DRILL FLAIL FLOAT FLUKE GAUGE GLASS INDEX KNIFE LADLE LEVER METER MISER PILOT RAZOR SCALE SCOPE SLATE SLICE SLING SPADE SPEAR SPRAY STAMP STEEL SWIFT THROW TONGS TUNER WHISK ABACUS BEATER BEETLE BODKIN BRIDGE CHOWRY CIRCLE DOUCHE ENGINE ERASER FERULE FOLDER GRATER LEAPER MORTAR NEEDLE PALLET PESTLE PICKER PLOUGH PULLER PUMPER RAMMER RASPER RATTLE RUBBER SCALER SCORER SCRIBE SCUTCH SCYTHE SHEARS SQUARE SQUIRT STADIA STRAIK STROBE STYLET STYLUS TACKLE TICKER WIMBLE ALIDADE BELLOWS BREAKER CADRANS CLEAVER COMPASS DIOPTER DOLABRA DOUBLER FISTUCA GRAFTER GRAINER GRAPPLE HATCHET LAYOVER MASSEUR MEASURE OOMETER OOSCOPE PAVIOUR PRICKER PRINTER PYROPEN QUADRAT SCRAPER SEXTANT SHOCKER SHUTTLE SLITTER SOUNDER SPLAYER SPRAYER STRIGIL SUNDIAL SWINGLE TRAMMEL TRIMMER WHISTLE ANALEMMA ATOMIZER BARNACLE BIRDCALL BLOWPIPE BUTTERIS CALLIPER COALRAKE DECAPPER DETECTOR DIAGRAPH DIPMETER

DIVIDERS EQUULEUS ERGMETER EXPLORER FATHOMER GEOPHONE HOROLOGE IMPINGER IRISCOPE ISOGRAPH ISOSCOPE JOVILABE MESOLABE MHOMETER ODOMETER OHMMETER PHOTOMER QUADRANT RECORDER RINGHEAD RUMMAGER SCISSORS SEARCHER SQUEEGEE STILETTO STRICKLE TJANTING TRIANGLE VELLINCH VIAGRAPH YAWMETER
(SURGICAL OR MEDICAL —) GAG HOOK SPUD FLEAM PROBE SCALA SCOOP SNARE SOUND STAFF STYLE BILABE BOUGIE BROACH GORGET LANCET SEEKER TREPAN TROCAR UNGULA VECTIS XYSTER AGRAFFE AIRDENT DILATER FORCEPS HARPOON LEVATOR LIGATOR MYOTOME PELICAN PLUGGER RONGEUR SCALPEL SOUNDER SYRINGE TRACTOR TRILABE TURNKEY ANOSCOPE AURILAVE AXOMETER BISTOURY DIRECTOR DIVULSOR ECRASEUR ELEVATOR EXSECTOR HEMOSTAT KERATOME MYOGRAPH SPECULUM TREPHINE
(VOID —) NULLITY
(PREF.) **(POINTED —)** SCOLO
(WIND —) AEOLO
(SUFF.) LABE METER METR(E)(O)(Y) STAT(IC)
(MUSICAL —) INA
(SURGICAL REMOVAL —) ECTOME
INSTRUMENTAL MEDIATE ORGANIC SERVILE SERVIENT MINISTERIAL
INSTRUMENTALIST KLEZMER SIDEMAN
(SUPPLEMENTARY —) RIPIENO RIPIENIST
INSTRUMENTALITY HAND MEANS AGENCY MEDIUM CHANNEL COUNCIL MINISTRY
(— FOR ACQUISITION OF KNOWLEDGE) ORGANON
(NAVAL —S) BEACH
INSUBORDINATE FACTIOUS MUTINOUS UNWIELDY
INSUBORDINATION MUTINY
INSUBSTANTIAL AIRY PUNY INANE WISPY FROTHY POROUS SLENDER SPECTRAL VAPOROUS INTANGIGLE
INSUBSTANTIALITY FRAILTY
INSUFFICIENCY PAUCITY
(PREF.) OLIG(O)
INSUFFICIENT POOR WANE SHORT SCANTY
INSUFFICIENTLY BARELY FEEBLY THINLY
INSULATE ISLE DEADEN ISLAND ISOLATE
INSULATION LAGGING ISOLATION
INSULATOR NOB KNOB CLEAT TAPLET VITRITE MEGOHMIT STANDOFF
(PL.) STRING
INSULT CAG FIG JOEY RUMP SLAM SLAP SLUR ABUSE CHECK FLOUT FRUMP SLANG INJURE INJURY OFFEND OUTRAY RUFFLE SCRAPE ABUSION AFFRONT OFFENCE

OUTRAGE BRICKBAT DISHONOR CONTUMELY
INSULTING RUDE ABUSIVE ARROGANT INSOLENT
INSULTINGLY FOULLY
INSURANCE LINE CHOMAGE COVERAGE INDEMNITY
(— AGENT) TWISTER
(UNEMPLOYMENT —) DOLE POGEY
INSURE COVER ASSURE ENSURE FURNISH
INSURER ABANDONEE
INSURGENT REBEL RISER CHOUAN OAKBOY TAIPING BARRABAS CAMISARD STEELBOY
INSURRECTION RIST MUTINY REVOLT UPROAR OUTBREAK SEDITION UPRISING REBELLION
INSURRECTO GUGU
INTACT SOUND WHOLE ENTIRE MAIDEN
(PREF.) INTEGRI
INTAGLIO ENTAIL DIAGLYPH
(PART OF —) INCAVO
INTAKE (AIRCRAFT ENGINE —) AIRSCOOP
INTANGIBLE VAGUE SUBTLE AERIFORM SLIPPERY
INTEGER SUM NORM TOTITIVE
INTEGRAL FLUX NEEDFUL
INTEGRANT ELEMENT
INTEGRATE FUSE PIECE COMBINE FULFILL ORGANIZE
INTEGRATED FUSED INTEGRAL
INTEGRATION BALANCE HARMONY
INTEGRITY HONOR TRUTH HONESTY JUSTICE PROBITY CHASTITY STRENGTH SINCERITY
INTEGUMENT KEX ARIL PILL SKIN TESTA TUNIC SWATHE CUTICLE ENVELOP EPIDERM EXODERM PRIMINE TUNICLE VELAMEN EPISPERM PERISARC SCABBARD SECUNDINE
(PREF.) SCYT(O)
(SUFF.) DERM(A)(ATOUS)(IA)(IS)(Y)
INTELLECT MIND NOUS HEART INWIT MAHAT SKILL BRAINS NOTICE REASON SPIRITS THINKING
(HIGHEST —) NOUS
INTELLECTUAL BLUE GAON IDEAL BOOKSY MENTAL NOETIC SOPHIC BRAHMIN EGGHEAD GNOSTIC CEREBRAL HIGHBROW LONGHAIR SOPHICAL DIANOETIC SPIRITUAL
(PL.) EGGMASS
INTELLIGENCE AIR CIT SAT CHIT KNOW MIND NEWS NOTE NOUS WORD AGIEL SAVVY SENSE SMART ADVICE BRAINS ESPRIT INGENY NOTICE PSYCHE SMARTS WITTING MENTALITY
(— IN EGYPTIAN LORE) CHU
(— OF PLANET JUPITER) JOPHIEL
(LACKING —) VACUOUS
(LIVELY —) WIT
INTELLIGENT APT GASH PERT ACUTE ALERT SHARP SMART SPACK AKAMAI BRAINY BRIGHT CLEVER MENTAL SHREWD SPRACK WITFUL KNOWING INFORMED LUMINOUS RATIONAL SKILLFUL
(— GROUP) MENTA

INTELLIGENTSIA CLERISY

INTELLIGIBLE CLEAR PLAIN
LUMINOUS PELLUCID PERVIOUS
REVELANT PERCEIVABLE

INTELLIGIBLY SIMPLY

INTEMPERANCE ACRASY EXCESS
ACRASIA OUTRAGE

INTEMPERATE SHRILL SURFEIT
(NOT —) SWEET

INTEND GO AIM FIX CAST MEAN
MIND MINT PLAN PLOT TEND
ALLOT ALLOW ETTLE TIGHT
ATTEND DESIGN RECKON SETOUT
BEHIGHT DESTINE FORELAY
PRETEND PROPOSE PURPORT
PURPOSE FOREMIND MEDITATE
PRETENSE

INTENDED ON FIANCEE SUPPOSED

INTENSE HOT ACID COLD DEEP
HARD HIGH KEEN BLANK DENSE
GREAT HEAVY QUICK SHARP TENSE
VIVID ARDENT BRAZEN FIERCE
INTENT PITCHY SEVERE STRONG
BURNING CHARGED CHRONIC
CUTTING EXTREME FERVENT
FRANTIC FURIOUS VICIOUS
VIOLENT EGYPTIAN GRIEVOUS
POWERFUL PROFOUND SEETHING
TERRIFIC VEHEMENT
(VIOLENTLY —) RABID

INTENSELY VERY STIFF HIGHLY
ACUTELY CURSEDLY FERVIDLY
MORTALLY SHREWDLY

INTENSIFICATION
(PREF.) DE

INTENSIFIED ACUTE

INTENSIFY RISE URGE EXALT RAISE
ACCENT DEEPEN HEATUP BOLSTER
ENFORCE ENHANCE IMPROVE
INFLAME MAGNIFY SHARPEN
THICKEN CONDENSE HEIGHTEN
INCREASE REDOUBLE

INTENSION INTENT MEANING

INTENSITY EDGE HEAT ARDOR
DEPTH DRIVE FEVER FIELD VIGOR
ACCENT DEGREE DOSAGE FERVOR
FRENZY STRESS CURRENT
FEROCITY STRENGTH VIOLENCE
(— OF DISEASE) ACUITY
(— OF EMOTION) ARDENCY

INTENSIVE HARD HIGH EXTENDED

INTENSIVELY HARD SOLIDLY

INTENT SET DEEP DOLE FELL HENT
MIND RAPT TENT BEADY CAUSE
DRIFT ETTLE FIXED HEART PRICK
SCOPE TENOR TENSE EFFECT
SPIRIT COUNSEL INTENSE
PRESENT PURPOSE STUDIED
WISTFUL
(CRIMINAL —) DOLE
(EVIL —) DOLUS

INTENTION AIM END GOAL HENT
MIND VIEW WILL HEART SCOPE
ANIMUS ATTENT DESIGN DEVICE
EFFECT INTENT OBJECT REGARD
COUNSEL COURAGE EARNEST
FORESET MEANING PROPOSE
PURPORT PURPOSE SUPPOSE
THOUGHT PRETENSE OBJECTIVE
(CRIMINAL —) DOLE

INTENTIONAL SET WILLFUL
WILLING WITTING INTENDED

INTENTLY BUSILY WISHLY EAGERLY
FIXEDLY

INTER BURY EARTH ENTER GRAVE
PLANT ENTOMB INHUME INEARTH

INTERACTION COUPLING

INTERAGENT MEDIUM MIDDLER

INTERBREED CROSS

INTERBREEDING APOGAMY
MIXTURE PANMIXY CROSSING

INTERCALATE INSERT

INTERCALATION EMBOLISM

INTERCEPT KEP HEAD KEEP STOP
CATCH NORMAL ABSCISS
TRAMMEL GAINCOPE INTERPEL
RETRENCH

INTERCEPTION CUTOFF

INTERCESSION MOYEN DIPTYCH
PLEADING

INTERCESSOR MEANS PLEADER
ADVOCATE MEDIATOR

INTERCHANGE CHANGE ANAGRAM
COMMUTE PASSAGE PERMUTE
COMMERCE EXCHANGE
(— OF OPINION) COUNSEL
(— OF WORDS) SPEECH
(PREF.) TRANS

INTERCHANGEABLE FUNGIBLE

INTERCHANGED CROSS

INTERCOLUMNIATION EUSTYLE
SYSTYLE DIASTYLE

INTERCOMMUNICATION LIAISON

INTERCONNECTED SYNDETIC

INTERCONNECTION BONDING

INTERCOURSE GAM DEAL MANG
MONG TRADE TRUCK TURGY
BAWDRY HOBNOB NEGOCE
COITION DEALING MIXTURE
QUARTER SOCIETY TRAFFIC
BUSINESS COMMERCE CONVERSE
RECOURSE RELATIONS

INTERDICT BAN TABU DEBAR
TABOO FORBID UTRUBI INHIBIT
PROHIBIT SUPPRESS

INTERDICTION VETO

INTEREST BUG DIP FAD USE BENT
GOOD HAND HOLD PART CLOSE
COLOR DRIVE FAVOR FETCH
GAVEL HOBBY RENTE RIGHT STAKE
STUDY USAGE USURA USURY
BEHALF ENGAGE EQUITY ESTATE
FAENUS FERVOR FINGER INCOME
USANCE ATTRACT CONCERN
RESPECT USAUNCE CONTANGO
INCREASE VIGORISH
(— OF HUSBAND) CURTESY
(— ON LAND) CLOSE
(— PAID TO MONEYLENDER) VIG
VIGORISH
(ACTIVE —) SYMPATHY
(EXORBITANT —) JUICE
(LEGAL —) EASEMENT
(POLITICAL —) FENCE
(SECURITY —) LIEN
(SPECIAL —) MEAT ANGLE

INTERESTED HIPPED ENGAGED
SERIOUS CONCERNED
(— IN) INTO
(UNEASILY —) PRURIENT

INTERESTING FRUITY CURIOUS
PIQUANT STORIED ABSORBING

INTERFACE PORT
(COMPUTER —) PORT

INTERFERE CUT MAKE ANNOY
BLOCK CHECK HITCH POACH
BAFFLE HAMPER HINDER HOBBLE
IMPEDE MEDDLE STRIKE TAMPER
INTRUDE INTROMIT
(— SLIGHTLY) BRUSH
(— WITH) AIL JOLT MESS CROSS
HECKLE BLANKET DISTURB

INTERFERENCE BALK CHOKE
THUMP HINDER JOSTLE MEDDLE
CONFLICT FREINAGE

INTERFERING CUT

INTERFEROMETER ETALON

INTERFLUVE DOAB

INTERGROWTH PERTHITE

INTERIM BREAK VACANCY

INTERIOR BEN BELLY BOSOM
INNER ENTIRE INLAND INWARD
INWITH MIDDLE GIZZARD
ENTRAILS INTERNAL
(— OF CUPOLA) CALOTTE
(— OF TEMPLE) CELLA
(— OF VESSEL) HOLD
(— PART) MANTLE

INTERJECT POKE ENTER SQUIB
INJECT THRUST

INTERJECTION (ALSO SEE OATH)
AW FR HA LO BAH BOO COO FIE
GAD GEE GIP GUP HAH HAY HEH
HEY HOY HUH LAW OOH POW
WOW AHEM AHOY ALAS ANAN
BOOH CHUT CIAO DAMN DEAR
EGAD EVOE FORE GOSH HAHA
HAIL HECH HECK HEHE HEIL HELL
HOLA JOVE ODSO OOPS OUCH
OYEZ PISH POOH POSH RATS
SHOO WELL WHEW ADIOS ALACK
ARRAH BASTA BEDAD BRAVO
BULLY FAITH FANCY FAUGH GOLLY
GOODY HALLO HEIGH HOLLA
HUZZA MAFEY MARRY MERCY
MUSHA OHONE PROST PSHAW
RIGHT SUGAR TENEZ ZOWIE
ATWEEL BARLEY CRIKEY CRIPES
EUREKA HARROW JIMINY OUTCRY
PHOOEY PROSIT RIGHTO SHUCKS
YIPPEE BEGORRA CARAMBA
CRIMINE HEAVENS BEGORRAH
GADZOOKS LACKADAY
(— EXPRESSING APOLOGY) OOPS
WOOPS
(— INDICATING DISMAY) UHOH
(— OF AGREEMENT) UHHUH
(— OF NEGATION) UHUH
(— TO EXPRESS DISGUST) YUK
YECH YUCK YECCH
(— TO EXPRESS FEAR) YIKES
(— TO EXPRESS PLEASURE)
YUMYUM
(BIBLICAL —) SELAH

INTERLACE LACE WARP BRAID
WEAVE ENLACE PLEACH WATTLE
ENTRAIL INWEAVE WREATHE

INTERLACED BRACED FRETTED
PLEACHED

INTERLACEMENT KNOT

INTERLACING RETE TWINY

INTERLINING DOUBLER

INTERLOCK KNIT LOCK MESH PITCH
ENGAGE FINGER TANGLE
DOVETAIL

INTERLOPE INTRUDE

INTERLUDE JIG JEST LETUP
COMEDY VERSET TEMACHA

TRIUMPH ANTIMASK ENTRACTE
ENTREMES RITORNEL VERSETTE
PARENTHESIS
(OPERATIC —) RITORNELLO
(QUIET —) LACUNA
(ROMANTIC —) IDYL IDYLL

INTERMEDDLER STRANGER

INTERMEDDLING GESTION

INTERMEDIARY MEAN AGENT
MOYENER MEDIATOR TRAMPLER
MIDDLEMAN

INTERMEDIATE MEAN MESNE
FILLER ISATIN MEDIAL MEDIUM
MIDDLE NEUTRAL MIDDLING
(PREF.) MEDI MES(O)

INTERMEDIATOR BROKER

INTERMENT BURIAL BURYING
DEPOSIT HUMATION

INTERMINABLE ETERNAL INFINITE
TIMELESS UNENDING

INTERMINGLE MIX BRAID
COALESCE IMMINGLE INTERMIT
INTERMIX

INTERMINGLED AMONG AMONGST

INTERMINGLING
(SUFF.) MIXIS

INTERMISSION REST WAIT BREAK
DWELL PAUSE DEVALL RECESS
NOONING RELACHE RESPITE
INTERVAL SURCEASE VACATION
(— OF FEVER) APYREXIA
(— OF PAIN) SABBATH

INTERMISSIVE CESSANT

INTERMIT CEASE DEFER DEVAUL
SUSPEND

INTERMITTENT BROKEN FITFUL
PERIODIC

INTERMIX BLEND MEDLEY MINGLE

INTERMIXTURE CROSS INTIMACY

INTERNAL INLY INNER ENTIRE
INLAND INNATE INSIDE INWARD
DOMESTIC
(PREF.) INTRA

INTERNALLY INLY INSIDE INWARD
INWARDLY

INTERNET (CONNECTED TO —)
ONLINE

INTERNODE ROSETTE

INTERPELLATION FLOWER

INTERPENETRATED SHOT

INTERPLAY AUSPICE

INTERPOLATE FARCE FARSE FOIST
FUDGE INSERT THRUST

INTERPOLATION GAG FARSE
(ACTOR'S —) GAG

INTERPOLATOR DIASKEUAST

INTERPOSE BAR CHOP POKE
DEMUR OBJECT STRIKE THRUST
THWART MEDIATE STICKLE

INTERPRET MAKE OPEN READ SCAN
TAKE AREAD AREED FANCY GLOSS
GLOZE RECHE DEFINE DIVINE
INTEND CLARIFY COMMENT
DECLARE ENGLISH EXPLAIN
EXPOUND CONSTRUE DECIPHER
SIMPLIFY

INTERPRETATION REDE GLOSS
SENSE GOSPEL STRAIN ANAGOGE
BARAITA COMMENT DOBHASH
EPIKEIA MEANING READING
CABALISM EXEGESIS INNUENDO
MOONSHEE SOLARISM SOLUTION

INTERPRETER BROKER DUBASH

MUNSHI UNDOER EXEGETE
LATINER MUNCHEE CABALIST
DRAGOMAN EXPONENT LINKSTER
TRUCHMAN
(— OF DREAMS) ONEIROCRITIC
(— OF SCRIPTURE) TROPIST
(PL.) HAHAM SELLI SELLOI
CHOCHEM HAKAMIM
INTERRELATED INTIMATE
INTERRELATIONSHIP ACCORD
LIAISON COMMERCE
INTERROGATE ASK GRILL TARGE
DEBRIEF EXAMINE INQUIRE
INTERROGATION EROTESIS
QUESTION
INTERROGATORY EROTETIC
INTERRUPT CUT MAR NIP CHOP
STOP TAKE BREAK CHECK CRACK
EMBAR ARREST DERAIL DERANGE
DISRUPT FORBREAK INTERMIT
INTERPEL OBSTRUCT
INTERRUPTED BROKEN CHOPPY
SNATCHY
INTERRUPTER BUZZER
INTERRUPTION BLIP CESS JUMP
STOP BLOCK BREAK CHECK DWELL
LAPSE PAUSE BREACH HIATUS
HOCKET HOQUET ISLAND OUTAGE
CAESURA CUTBACK DIASTEM
BLOCKING BREAKAGE SOLUTION
STOPOVER
(— OF SOUND) BLIP BLEEP
(WITHOUT —) FLUSH
INTERRUPTER TIKKER BREAKER
CHOPPER RHEOTOME
INTERSECT CUT CROSS BISECT
INCISE CROSSCUT
INTERSECTING SECANT CRUCIAL
COMPITAL
INTERSECTION LEET CHINE CROSS
CURVE CHIASMA CROSSING
CROSSWAY JUNCTION
INTERSESSION WINTERIM
INTERSEXUAL EPICENE
INTERSEXUALITY GYNANDRY
INTERSPACE SPACE POCKET
INTERSPERSE DOT SALT SHED
MEDDLE THREAD CHECKER
INTERSOW SPRINKLE
INTERSTICE GAP PORE SEAM CHINK
GRATE SPACE AREOLA AREOLE
RIFFLE CELLULE VACUITY
(PL.) CANCELLI
INTERSTRATIFY INTERBED
INTERTWINE KNIT LACE WARP
PLAIT TWINE FELTER TANGLE
WAMPLE WARPLE WRITHE
ENSNARL COMPLECT IMPLEACH
INTERTEX
INTERTWINED INWOUND
INTERTWIST RADDLE
INTERVAL GAP LAG CENT GULF
REST SAND SEXT SPOT STEP
BLANK BREAK COMMA CYCLE
FIFTH LAPSE PRIME QUINT SIXTH
SPACE SWING TENTH THIRD
BREACH DECIMA DEGREE DIESIS
DITONE FOURTH MERLON SECOND
SLATCH SYSTEM ADVANCE
DIASTEM DISCORD HEADWAY
HEMIOLA INTERIM PASTIME
RESPITE SCHISMA SETTIMO
STADIUM TRITONE DIAPASON

DIAPENTE DISTANCE ELEVENTH
ENTRACTE FONTANEL INTERACT
MICROTONE PARENTHESIS
(— BETWEEN FINGERS) SUBVOLA
(— BETWEEN ROPE STRANDS)
CONTLINE
(— OF BRIGHTNESS) FLICKER
(— OF CALM) LULL
(— OF EASE) REPRIEVE
(— OF FAIR WEATHER) SLATCH
(— OF HARSH WEATHER) SNAP
(— OF ROPE STRANDS) CONTLINE
(— OF SEMITONE) APOTOME
(— OF TIME) WINDOW
(AT REGULAR —S) SPACED
(MUSICAL —) TONE FIFTH NINTH
SIXTH TENTH THIRD FOURTH
OCTAVE SECOND UNISON SEVENTH
TRITONE MEANTONE
(REST —) SOB
(SHORT —) STREAK
(TIME —) HEADWAY
INTERVALE BOTTOM
INTERVENE CHOP STEP STRIKE
MEDIATE OBVIATE STICKLE
INTERCUR
INTERVENING MESNE MIDDLE
MEDIANT
(PREF.) INTER
INTERVIEW BUZZ CONTACT
AUDIENCE CONGRESS
INTERWEAVE MAT PLAT CRISP
PLAIT PLASH PLEACH RADDLE
TANGLE WATTLE ENTWINE
TEXTURE TRELLIS COMPLECT
ENTANGLE IMPLEACH INTERTEX
INTERWEAVING BREDE CROWN
INTIMATE
(— OF INITIALS) CIPHER
INTERWOVEN INWOVEN IMPLICIT
INTIMATE
(— WITH COLORS) PIRNIT
INTESTINAL INNER ENTERAL
ENTERIC SPLANCHNIC
INTESTINE GUT ROPE BOWEL
INNER THARM INWARD MIDDLE
THAIRM
(PORTION OF —) JEJUNUM
(PL.) VISCUS INGANGS CHITLINS
(PREF.) COL(O) ENTER(O)
INTHROW RIDGE
INTIMACY LIAISON PRIVACY
AFFINITY CHUMMERY GOSSIPRY
INTRIGUE MUTUALITY
(UNDUE —) LIBERTY
INTIMATE PAL SIB BOON GRIT HINT
HOME HOMY KIND NEAR NEXT
PACK TOSH BOSOM CHIEF CLOSE
GREAT HOMEY PALLY PRIVY THICK
ALLUDE ENTIRE FRIEND HOMELY
INTIME INWARD NOTICE SECRET
STRAIT STRICT THRANG THRONG
CHAMBER CLOSEUP GREMIAL
INNERLY INNUATE KEYHOLE
PRIVADO PRIVATE SIGNIFY SPECIAL
SUGGEST UPCLOSE COCKMATE
ESPECIAL FAMILIAR FREQUENT
FRIENDLY INDICATE INTIMADO
(INGRATIATINGLY —) PALSY
(MOST —) MIDMOST
(PL.) FOLKS
INTIMATELY INLY NEAR TOSH WELL
COZILY CLOSELY INWARDLY

INTIMATION CUE HINT ITEM WARN
WIND SCENT NOTICE OFFICE
GLIMMER INKLING CIRCULAR
INNUENDO MONITION
INTIMIDATE COW HAZE ABASH
BULLY COWER DAUNT DETER
PSYCH HECTOR PSYCHE TERRIFY
BROWBEAT BULLDOZE BULLYRAG
FRIGHTEN
INTO IN INTIL WITHIN
(PREF.) IL IM IN INTRO IR
INTOLERABLY PLAGUY
INTOLERANCE BIGOTRY
INTOLERANT CLOSED BIGOTED
INTONATION FALL CHANT ITALICS
(LOCAL —) TWANG
(MONOTONOUS —) SINGSONG
INTONE CANT SING TONE CHANT
CHAUNT ENTUNE MODULATE
CANTILLATE
INTOXICANT BOZA HASH BHANG
CHARAS MESCAL PEYOTE
COCAINE HASHISH HASHEESH
MARIJUANA
INTOXICATE FOX TIP TOX CORN
FLAW GOOF SOAK TODDY FUDDLE
MUDDLE SOZZLE SPRING TIPSIFY
DISGUISE OVERTAKE SPRINKLE
INTOXICATED CUT FAP LIT WET
HIGH LUSH RIPE SHOT SOSH TOFT
TOSY BOSKY BUFFY DRUNK FRESH
FRIED FUNNY HEADY LACED
NAPPY PIPED TIGHT BLOTTO
BOILED GROGGY LOADED LOOPED
MELLOW PIPPED QUAINT SCREWY
SKEWED SLEWED SLOPPY
SODDEN SOSHED SOZZLE STEWED
TANKED UPPISH UPPITY WASTED
ZONKED EBRIATE EXALTED
FLECKED JINGLED POTSHOT
SCREWED SLOPPED SMASHED
SPIFFED SQUIFFY UNSOBER
WRECKED BESOTTED COCKEYED
DELEERIT ELEVATED OVERSEEN
OVERSHOT PLEASANT SQUIFFED
TEMULENT TOXICATE WIPEDOUT
INTOXICATING HARD HEADY
STARK HUFFCAP
INTOXICATION WINE FUDDLE
IVRESSE LOCOISM DISGUISE
EBRIOSITY TEMULENCE
(— OF ANIMALS) DUNZIEKTE
INTRACTABLE BAD HARD SALTY
STACK SURLY FIERCE KITTLE
SULLEN THWART UNRULY
CRABBED HAGGARD RESTIVE
ROPABLE WAYWARD CHURLISH
INDOCILE MUTINOUS OBDURATE
PERVERSE SHREWISH
INTRADA ENTREE
INTRADOS SOFFIT
INTRANSITIVE NEUTER
INTREPID BOLD BRAVE HARDY
HEROIC PRETTY SAVAGE DOUGHTY
VALIANT RESOLUTE
INTREPIDITY GAME VALOR
COURAGE
INTRICACY KNOT INTRIGUE
INTRICATE HARD MAZY BLIND
DAEDAL IMPLEX KNOBBY KNOTTY
SUBTLE TANGLY TRICKY COMPLEX
CRABBED CURIOUS GORDIAN
PERPLEX PUZZLED SINUOUS

INVOLUTE INVOLVED
ANFRACTUOUS
(ARTIFICIALLY —) CONTRIVED
INTRIGUE PLOT ANGLE CABAL
CLOAK STORY AFFAIR AMOUNT
BRIGUE DECEIT SCHEME CONNIVE
FACTION FINAGLE JOBBERY
TRINKET TRINKLE ARTIFICE
CHEATING COLLOGUE PRACTICE
PRACTISE STRATEGY TRIPOTER
INTRIGUER JESUIT SCHEMER
DESIGNER TRINKETER
INTRIGUING EXCITING SCHEMING
INTRINSIC REAL TRUE INBORN
INBRED INNATE INWARD NATIVE
GENUINE NATURAL ABSOLUTE
IMMANENT INHERENT INTERNAL
INTIMATE
INTRINSICALLY PERSE PROPERLY
INTRODUCE READ DEBUT ENTER
FRONT IMMIT INFER PLANT START
USHER BROACH HERALD INDUCE
INDUCT INFUSE INJECT INSERT
INVECT INVOKE LAUNCH PREFER
FORERUN IMPLANT INSTILL
INVEIGH PRECEDE PREFACE
PRELUDE PRESENT SHUFFLE
SPONSOR TROTOUT ACQUAINT
INNOVATE INTROMIT WIREDRAW
(— AIR INTO) AERATE
(— AS FIRST ACT) INITIATE
(— FROM WITHOUT) IMPORT
(— SURREPTITIOUSLY) FOIST
INTRODUCTION LASSU PROEM
PRONE INTRADA INTROIT ISAGOGE
MENTION PREFACE ENTRANCE
EXORDIUM PREAMBLE PROLOGUE
PRELUSION
(— INTO STOMACH) GAVAGE
(— OF DRAMA) PROTASIS
(— OF NEW PRODUCT) ROLLOUT
(— OF NOVELTY) CHANGE
(MUSICAL —) INTRO INTRADA
OVERTURE
(SUFF.) PHORESIS
INTRODUCTORY EXORDIAL
ISAGOGIC LIMINARY PROTATIC
SYSTATIC PRELUSIVE
PRELIMINARY
INTROIT REQUIEM
INTRORSE ANTICAL
INTROSPECTION INLOOK REFLEX
INTRUDE JET ABATE BARGE CRASH
POACH BOTHER CHISEL INGYRE
INJECT INVADE IRRUPT THRUST
AGGRESS OBTRUDE ENCROACH
INFRINGE TRESPASS
INTRUDER INTRUS INCOMER
INVADER STRANGER
INTRUSION INVASION
INTRUSIVE NOSY FRESH NOSEY
SPURIOUS
(PREF.) XEN(O)
INTUITION HUNCH PRESAGE
INSTINCT
INTUITIONIST EIDETIC
INULIN ALANTIN
INUNDATE FLOW DROWN FLOOD
INUND SWAMP DELUGE
OVERFLOW SUBMERGE
SURROUND
INUNDATED AWASH
INUNDATION FLOW FLOOD SPATE

WATER DELUGE ALLUVIO FRESHET
ALLUVION FLOODAGE OVERFLOW
INURE URE BREAK ENURE STEEL
HARDEN SCHOOL SEASON
ACCUSTOM INDURATE
ACCLIMATIZE
INVADE ASSAIL INTRUDE
ENCROACH INTRENCH TRESPASS
INVADER HUN PICT
INVADING INGRUENT
INVAGINATION GULLET
INVALID BAD BUM NULL CHRONIC
NUGATORY
INVALIDATE UNDO AVOID BREAK
CANCEL INFIRM IMPROVE INVALID
VITIATE
INVALUABLE COSTLY PRECIOUS
PRICELESS
INVARIABLE STEADY UNIFORM
CONSTANT
INVARIABLENESS ONENESS
INVARIABLY EVER ALWAYS
INVASION RAID INROAD DESCENT
INBREAK INJURIA
(— BY BACTERIA) SEPSIS
INVECTIVE ABUSE HOKER SATIRE
RAILING DIATRIBE REPROACH
INVEIGH RANT INVECT DECLAIM
DENOUNCE
INVEIGLE COAX ROPE WILE CHARM
DECOY SNARE ALLURE ENTICE
SEDUCE
INVENT COIN FIND FORM MINT
VAMP FEIGN FRAME FRUMP
CREATE DESIGN DEVISE IDEATE
CONCOCT CONJURE CONTRIVE
DISCOVER
INVENTED MADE
INVENTION FANCY DEVICE FINDAL
NOTION FANTASY FICTION
FIGMENT FORGERY WITCRAFT
(DRAMATIC —) IBSENISM
INVENTIVE ADROIT FERTILE
CREATIVE MECHANIC ORIGINAL
PREGNANT
INVENTIVENESS WIT ARTIFICE
INVENTOR TALOS COINER FINDER
FRAMER MINTER CREATOR
MINTMAN ENGINEER ARTIFICER
AMERICAN HOE LEE BELL COLT
EADS FELT GRAY HALL HOWE HUNT
IVES LAND LINK LOWE MOOG OLDS
OTIS PAGE READ VAIL WOOD
ADAMS ALLEN BLAKE BOWIE
BROWN COWEN DAVIS DOLBY
EARLE ELLIS EVANS FIELD FITCH
GIBBS HYATT LEWYT LIBBY LOCKE
MCKAY MOODY MOREY MORSE
NOYES PERKY PRATT PUPIN RUBIC
TESLA WHITE BENDIX BISELL BITTER
BORDEN BORTON BOYDEN BOYKIN
CAHILL CHURCH CLYMER CURTIS
DURYEA EDISON FARBER FOLMER
FRENCH FULTON GARAND GAYLEY
GORDON GORRIE HAMLIN HAYNES
HORGAN HOUDRY HUGHES HUSSEY
JANNEY JATVIK JUDSON KALMUS
LOOMIS PITNEY PORTER SAXTON
SHOLES SINGER SPANEL SPERRY
TIMKEN TUPPER WARING WESSON
WILCOX WILSON WRIGHT ACHESON
APPLEBY BABBITT BETHELL

BIGELOW BRADLEY CARRIER
CORLISS CURTISS EASTMAN
GATLING GODFREY HAMMOND
HOLLAND JACUZZI JENKINS
KNOWLES LANSTON PERKINS
PULLMAN SCHICCK SELLERS
STEVENS TAINTER THURBER
WHITNEY ZAMBONI BACHRACH
BERLINER BIRDSEYE BOGARDUS
BUSHNELL DAHLGREN DEFOREST
ELLSBERG ERICSSON EVINRUDE
GILLETTE GOODYEAR HALSTEAD
WATERMAN ABPLANALP
BURROUGHS BUTTERICK
DRAWBAUGH HONEYWELL
HOTCHKISS INGERSOLL
MCCORMICK HENREGHOFF
WESTINGHOUSE
AUSTRIAN PORSCHE KEMPELEN
WELSBACH
BELGIAN SAX BAEKELAND
CANADIAN ABBOTT FESSENDEN
CHINESE TSAI
DUTCH BORDEN COSTER DREBBEL
ENGLISH KAY MOON WATT DUNNE
MAXIM MILLS SMITH AYRTON
BRAMAH BRUNEL DONKIN GURNEY
HOLDEN LISTER PITMAN WALLIS
BABBAGE BESEMER BUDDING
BURGESS DELARUE GAUDENS
MORI AND MURDOCK SIEMANS
STARLEY CROMPTON OUGHTRED
STURGEON ACKERMANN
APPLEGATH ARKWRIGHT
ARMSTRONG HEATHCOAT
WHITWORTH CARTWRIGHT
HARGREAVES STEPHENSON
TREVITHICK WHEATSTONE
FRENCH LYOT COANDA FOUCHE
GIRARD LENOIR MONIER PROGIN
LAENNEC LUMIERE CHRETIEN
LONGCHRIL DELCALLE JACQUARD
CHASSEPOT CHARDONNET
MONTGOLFIER
GERMAN FOCKE BUNSEN DIESEL
DREYSE MAUSER WANKEL DAIMLER
SIEMENS FLETTNER BAUERSFELD
GREEK CTESIBIUS ARCHIMEDES
IRISH BRENNAN
ITALIAN MARCONI
NORWEGIAN KRAG
SCOTTISH GED BARR WATT BAIRD
DUNLOP MILLER GREGORY
NEILSON TWADDELL MACINTOSH
SYMINGTON
SWEDISH DALEN NOBEL POLHEM
SWISS ZWICKY PICCARD SCHWEPPE
VETTERLI
INVENTORY BILL LIST STOCK
ACCOUNT INVOICE TERRIER
ANAGRAPH DATABASE REGISTER
SCHEDULE
INVERSE
(PREF.) OB
INVERSION WALDEN CHIASMUS
ENTROPION
(— OF STITCHES) PURL
INVERT CANT TURN REVERT
REVERSE
INVERTASE SUCRASE
INVERTEBRATE INSECT MOLLUSC
MOLLUSK
INVERTED AWKWARD

INVEST DON DUB PUT BELT FUND
GARB GIFT GIRD GIRT GOWN LOCK
SINK VEST WRAP BELAY BLOCK
ENDOW ENDUE FEOFF INDUE
CLOTHE EMBODY ENROBE FORSET
OCCUPY ORDAIN BESIEGE
COMPASS ENFEOFF ENVELOP
INSTATE OBSERVE BENEFICE
BLOCKADE SURROUND
(— IN ARMOR) EMPANOPLY
(— ONESELF) COVER ASSUME
(— WITH) INFEFT
(— WITH AUTHORITY) SCEPTER
ACCREDIT
(— WITH ENERGY) CATHECT
(— WITH HONOR) DIGNIFY
(— WITH SOVEREIGN DIGNITY)
ENTHRONE
(SUFF.) (— WITH ATTRIBUTES OF)
FY IFY
INVESTED GARTERED
(— WITH AUTHORITY) REGENT
INVESTIGATE SPY SUS SIFT SUSS
CHECK PROBE SOUND STUDY
EXCUSS FATHOM SEARCH
DISCUSS EXAMINE EXPLORE
INQUIRE INDAGATE SCRUTATE
(— QUICKLY) SKIP
INVESTIGATION CHECK PROBE
TRIAL EXAMEN PILPUL SEARCH
DELVING INQUEST INQUIRY
LEGWORK ZETETIC ANALYSIS
QUESTION RESEARCH SCRUTINY
SOUNDING
INVESTIGATOR SNOOP TRIER
SLEUTH GUMSHOE SPOTTER
FIELDMAN
(NARCOTICS —) NARC NARK
(PRIVATE —) SHAMUS
INVESTING AMBIENT
INVESTITURE VESTURE INDUMENT
INVESTMENT DOG FLIER CUTICLE
CATHEXIS PANNICLE
(— OF TOWN) SIEGE
(RISKY —) SPECULATION
INVETERATE BLACK SWORN
ROOTED CHRONIC HARDENED
INVIDIOUS ENVIOUS HATEFUL
INVIGORATE PEP BRACE CHEER
RAISE RENEW VIGOR VIVIFY
COMFORT ENFORCE ENLIVEN
FORTIFY INNERVE INSINEW
REFRESH INSPIRIT
INVIGORATING BRISK CRISP FRESH
TONIC VITAL HEARTY LIVELY
BRACING CORDIAL VEGETANT
INVIOLABILITY SANCTITY
INVIOLABLE SACRED SECURE
STYGIAN
INVIOLATE SACRED
INVISIBLE HID BLIND SECRET
UNSEEN VIEWLESS SIGHTLESS
(PREF.) APHAN(O) CRYPT(O)
KRYPT(O)
INVITATION BID CALL CARD INVITE
BIDDING CALLING
(— TO CONTEND) DARE
(— TO RIDE) GETIN GETON HOPIN
HOPON CLIMBON
INVITE ASK BID WOO BEAR CALL
LURE PRAY TOLL CLEPE COURT
LATHE TEMPT TRYST ALLURE

DESIRE ENTICE INDITE ATTRACT
CONVITE PROVOKE REQUEST
SOLICIT
INVITING ADORABLE HOMELIKE
INVOCATION WISH DAWUT NANDI
BISMILLAH
INVOICE BILL BRIEF CHALAN
FACTURE MANIFEST BORDEREAU
INVOKE WISH CLEPE EVOKE APPEAL
ATTEST OBTEST CONJURE
ENTREAT PROVOKE SOLICIT
INVOCATE
(— EVIL) BESHREW IMPRECATE
INVOLUCRE HULL HUSK CUPULE
CALYCLE CALYCULE EPICALYX
INVOLUNTARY FORCED REFLEX
HELPLESS
INVOLUTE INVOLVED
INVOLUTED SCREWY
INVOLUTION ATRESIA
INVOLVE DIP LAP MIX MIRE WRAP
BROIL CARRY COUCH IMPLY
RAVEL DIRECT EMPLOY ENGAGE
ENTAIL HANKLE INWRAP TANGLE
COMPORT CONCERN CONNOTE
EMBRACE EMBROIL ENSNARE
ENTWINE ENVIRON IMMERSE
INCLUDE ENCUMBER ENTANGLE
INTEREST
(— IN DIFFICULTY) STEAD
INVOLVED IN DEEP GONE INTO
BLIND KNOTTY COMPLEX
ENGAGED PLAITED IMPLICIT
INVOLUTE CONCERNED
ANFRACTUOUS
INWARD ENTAD INNER INWITH
BENWARD INNERLY HOMEFELT
INTRINSIC
(PREF.) IL IM IN INTRO IR OB
INWICK INRING
IO (BROTHER OF —) PHORONEUS
(FATHER OF —) INACHUS
(SON OF —) EPAPHUS
IODINE (SOURCE OF —) KELP
(PREF.)
(REMOVAL OF —) DESIODO
IOLAUS (COMPANION OF —)
HERCULES
(FATHER OF —) IPHICLES
(MOTHER OF —) AUTOMEDUSA
(WIFE OF —) MEGARA
IOLE (FATHER OF —) EURYTUS
(HUSBAND OF —) HYLLUS
IOLITE IBERITE PELIOMA
ION ACID ADION ANION CATION
ISOMER KATION LIGAND AMPHION
HYDRION OXONIUM SPECIES
ZWITTERION
(— DURATION) LIFETIME
(FATHER OF —) XUTHUS
(MOTHER OF —) CREUSA
(SON OF —) GELEON ARGADES
HOPLETES AEGICORES
(PREF.) IONTO
(SUFF.) (CHARGED —) ONIUM
IONIA (GULF OF —) ARTA
IONIAN (— ISLAND) CORFU
IONIZATION BURST
IOPHON (FATHER OF —) SOCRATES
(MOTHER OF —) NICOSTRATE
IOTA JOT TAD WHIT GHOST TITTLE
SCRUPLE SCINTILLA
IOU SCRIP MARKER

IOWA
CAPITAL: DESMOINES
COLLEGE: COE DORDT LORAS CORNELL PARSONS GRINNELL WARTBURG
COUNTY: IDA LEE SAC CASS LINN PAGE POLK TAMA ADAIR BOONE CEDAR EMMET FLOYD LUCAS SIOUX BREMER KEOKUK OBRIEN DUBUQUE KOSSUTH MAHASKA OSCEOLA
LAKE: CLEAR STORM SPIRIT
NICKNAME: HAWKEYE
PRESIDENT: HOOVER
RIVER: CEDAR SKUNK BIGSIOUX MISSOURI
STATE BIRD: GOLDFINCH
STATE FLOWER: WILDROSE
STATE TREE: OAK
TOWN: ADEL AMES LEON ALBIA MASON ONAWA OSAGE PERRY SIOUX ALGONA ELDORA KEOKUK LEMARS MARION SIBLEY VINTON ANAMOSA OTTUMWA WATERLOO DAVENPORT

IOWAN HAWKEYE
IPECAC ITOUBOU
IPHIANASSA (FATHER OF —) PROETIUS
(HUSBAND OF —) BIAS
(MOTHER OF —) ANTIA
IPHICLUS (BROTHER OF —) HERCULES
(FATHER OF —) PHYLACUS AMPHITRYON
(MOTHER OF —) ALCMENA
(SON OF —) PODARCES PROTESILAUS
(WIFE OF —) CLYMENE
IPHIDAMAS (FATHER OF —) ANTENOR
(MOTHER OF —) THEANO
(SLAYER OF —) AGAMEMNON
IPHIGENIA (BROTHER OF —) ORESTES
(FATHER OF —) AGAMEMNON
(MOTHER OF —) CLYTEMNESTRA
(SISTER OF —) ELECTRA
IPHIMEDIA (HUSBAND OF —) ALOEUS
(SON OF —) OTUS EPHIALTES
IPHINOE (FATHER OF —) PROETUS
(MOTHER OF —) ANTIA
(SISTER OF —) LYSIPPE IPHIANASSA
IPHIS (FATHER OF —) LIGDUS
(MOTHER OF —) TELETHUSA
(WIFE OF —) IANTHE
IPHITUS (BROTHER OF —) CLYTIUS
(FATHER OF —) EURYTUS
(SISTER OF —) IOLE
(SLAYER OF —) HERCULES
IPIL VESI
IPOMOEA NIL NILL BATATAS MANROOT TURBITH TURPETH SCAMMONY
IPSEITY SELFHOOD
IRA (FATHER OF —) IKKESH
IRACUND IREFUL
IRAD (FATHER OF —) ENOCH
(GRANDFATHER OF —) CAIN
(SON OF —) MEHUJAEL

IRAN
CAPE: HALILEH
CAPITAL: TEHRAN TEHERAN
COIN: PUL ASAR CRAN LARI RIAL BISTI DARIC DINAR LARIN SHAHI TOMAN STATER ASHRAFI KASBEKE PAHLAVI
DESERT: KERMAN
FORMER NAME: PERSIA
GOVERNORSHIP: ILAM YAZD SEMNAN ZANJAN HAMADAN LORESTAN
LAKE: NIRIS NIRIZ TASHT TUZLU URMIA SAHWEH SISTAN MAHARLU NEMEKSER URUMIYEH
LANGUAGE: ZEND PAHLAVI
MEASURE: GAZ GUZ MOV ZAR ZER CANE FOOT GAREH JERIB KAFIZ MAKUK QASAB ARTABA CHARAC CHEBEL GARIBA GHALVA OUROUB CAPICHA CHENICA FARSAKH FARSANG MANSION MISHARA PAIMANEH PARASANG SABBITHA STATHMOS
MOUNTAIN: CUSH KUSH HINDU KHOSF ARARAT HAMUNT BINALUD KHORMUJ SABALAN DEMAVEND
MOUNTAIN RANGE: ELBURZ SIAHAN ZAGROS JAGATAL
PEOPLE: LUR KURD MEDE SART KAJAR MUKRI PERSE TAJIK HADJEMI PERSIAN
PORT: JASK BUSHIRE PAHLEVI
PROVINCE: FARS GILAN KERMAN TEHRAN ESFAHAN KHORASAN KORDESTAN
RIVER: MAND MUND SHUR ARAKS JAGIN KARUN RABCH SEFID BAMPUR GORGAN HALIRI TIGRIS KARKHEH MASHKEL SAFIDRUD ZAYENDEH EUPHRATES
STRAIT: HORMUZ
TOWN: FAO KOM QUM AMOL ARAK SARI YAZD AHWAZ KHVOY NIRIZ RASHT RESHT ABADAN DEZFUL GORGAN KASVIN KERMAN MASHAD MESHED SHIRAZ TABRIZ TAURIS HAMADAN ISFAHAN SANANDAJ
WEIGHT: SER DRAM DUNG ROTL SANG SEER ABBAS ARTEL MAUND PINAR RATEL BATMAN DIRHEM GANDUM KARWAR MISCAL NAKHOD NIMMAN ABBASSI TCHEIREK

IRANIAN TAT SART GALCHA SHUGNI BACTRIAN BARTANGI
(— SOVEREIGN) SHAH

IRAQ
CAPITAL: BAGDAD BAGHDAD
COIN: DINAR DIRHAM
DISTRICT: BASRA KURDISTAN
FORMER NAME: MESOPOTAMIA
MOUNTAINS: ZARGOS KURDISTAN
OASIS: MANIYA
PEOPLE: ARAB KURD
PORT: FAO BASRA
RIVER: ZAB TIGRIS EUPHRATES

TOWN: ANA HIT AFAQ AMARA BAIJI BASRA ERBIL HILLA MOSUL NAJAF HILLAH KIRKUK TIKRIT KARBALA

IRASCIBILITY BILE CHOLER
IRASCIBLE WARM ANGRY CROSS FIERY GASSY HASTY IRATE SHARP TECHY TESTY CRANKY CRUSTY IREFUL ORNERY SPUNKY TETCHY TOUCHY ANGULAR BILIOUS FRETFUL IRACUND PEEVISH TINDERY TOUSTIE WASPISH CAPTIOUS CHOLERIC PETULANT SNAPPISH STOMACHY
IRATE MAD SORE ANGRY HEATED CHOLERIC WRATHFUL
IRE FURY ANGER STEAM WRATH
IREFUL ANGRY HETUP JEALOUS

IRELAND
BAY: MAL CLEW SLIGO BANTRY DINGLE GALWAY TRALEE DONEGAL DUNDALK KILLALA BLACKSOD DROGHEDA
CAPE: CLEAR
CAPITAL: TARA DUBLIN BELFAST
COIN: RAP REAL
COUNTY: CORK DOWN LEIX MAYO CAVAN CLARE KERRY LOUTH MEATH SLIGO ANTRIM ARMAGH CARLOW GALWAY OFFALY TYRONE ULSTER DONEGAL KILDARE LEITRIM WEXFORD WICKLOW KILKENNY LIMERICK MONAGHAN FERMANAGH LONDONDERRY
ISLAND: ARAN TORY SALTEE RATHLIN
LAKE: DOO KEY REE TAY CONN DERG ERNE MASK CARRA GOWNA LEANE RAMOR BODERG COOTER ENNELL DROMORE OUGHTER SHEELIN
MEASURE: MILE BANDLE
MONEY: PUNT
MOUNTAIN: OX CAHA ANTRIM GALTEE KEEPER MOURNE MULREA DONEGAL ERRIGAL KENNEDY KIPPURE WICKLOW LEINSTER
MOUNTAIN RANGE: GALTY STACKS COMERAGH
OTHER NAME: EIRE ERIN BANBA IERNE IRENA ULSTER BOGLAND HIBERNIA INISFAIL
PEOPLE: CELT ERSE GAEL CELTIC HIBERNIAN
PERTAINING TO: CELTIC GAELIC
POINT: CAHORE CARNSORE
PORT: COBH
PROVINCE: ULSTER MUNSTER CONNACHT LEINSTER CONNAUGHT
RIVER: LEE BANN DEEL ERNE NORE SUIR BOYNE CLARE FEALE FLESK FOYLE LAUNE BANDON BARROW LIFFEY KENMARE MUNSTER SHANNON
TOWN: CORK NAAS TRIM ADARE CAVAN ENNIS OMAGH SLIGO ARMAGH CARLOW DUBLIN GALWAY LURGAN TRALEE LIMERICK TIPPERARY

IRENE (FATHER OF —) JUPITER
(MOTHER OF —) THEMIS
IRENIC CALM HENOTIC PEACEFUL
IRENICA AITESIS
IRI (FATHER OF —) BELA
IRIDESCENCE LUSTER LUSTRE REFLET
(— ON METAL) TARNISH
IRIDESCENT SHOT IRISED IRIDINE IRISATE OPALINE PAVONINE
IRIS EYE SET FLAG LILY LUCE LUCY SEGG AZURE IREOS ORRIS SEDGE FLAGON LEVERS LILIAL LILIUM SHADOW SUNBOW ALCAZAR BABIANA FLAGGER GLADDON FLAGLEAF
(FATHER OF —) THAUMAS
(MOTHER OF —) ELECTRA
(PREF.) IRIDICO IRIDIO IRID(O)
IRISH ERSE EIRANN IRISHRY MILESIAN HIBERNIAN
(— KING) RIG
(ILLITERATE —) KEELMAN
(MEMBER OF — REPUBLICAN ARMY) PROVO
(PREF.) HIBERNO
IRISHMAN MAC PAT CELT GAEL KELT SCOT GREEK IRISH PADDY YREIS TEAGUE GRECIAN IRISHER MILESIAN ORANGEMAN
(LEARNED —) OLLAMH
IRISH MOSS SLOKE CHONDRUS
IRISHWOMAN HARP
IRK BORE ITCH ANNOY WEARY BOTHER
IRKSOME DULL WARM WEARY HUMDRUM OPEROSE PAINFUL TEDIOUS ANNOYING TIRESOME
IRKSOMENESS TEDIUM
IROKO ODUM ODOOM MUVULE KAMBALA
IRON BIT DOG IRE AIRN MARS WIRE ANGLE ANVIL BASIL BRAND DRAIL DRIFT FLOSS HORSE NEGRO PRESS SPIKE STEEL WAVER ANCONY BEATER CALKER CAUTER FERRUM GAGGER GOFFER JAGGER OSMUND CAUTERY COBIRON CRAMPER FERRITE FURISON GAMBREL GAUFFER PRICKER SADIRON FLATIRON TRICOUNI
(— FOR CLOSING STAVES) HORSE
(— FOR STRIKING COINS) PILE
(— OF MILLSTONE) RIND RYND
(— ORE) LIMNITE
(— PIECES) POTLEG
(— PLATE) TRAMP
(— SHORTAGE) ANEMIA
(— SUPPORTING SPIT) COBIRON
(— TO SUPPORT BEAM) TORSEL
(ANGLE —) LATH STIFFENER
(BASKETWORK —) BEATER
(BOOM —) WITHE WYTHE
(BRANDING —) BURN
(CAST —) METAL YETLIN SPIEGEL YETLING PROMETAL SEMISTEEL
(CLIMBING —) GAFF SPUR CREEPER
(CRUDE CASTING OF —) PIG
(DRIVING —) CLEEK
(GLASSBLOWING —) BAIT

(GOLF —) WEDGE JIGGER MASHIE MIDIRON NIBLICK
(GRAPPLING —) CRAMPON CRAMPOON
(HATTER'S —) SLUG
(LEG —S) SLANGS
(MASS OF WROUGHT —) BLOOM
(METEORIC —) SIDERITE
(PASTY —) SPONGE
(PIG —) SPIEGEL KENTLEDGE
(PRIMING —) DRIFT
(PUDDLING —) RABBLE
(RUSSIAN —) SABLE
(SHEET —) TERNE
(SOLDERING —) COPPER
(SPECULAR —) HEMATITE
(TAILOR'S —) GOOSE
(TAMPING —) DRIVER
(8 PIGS OF CAST —) FODDER
(PL.) GARTERS
(PREF.) FERRI FERRO SIDER(O)
(SUFF.) SIDERITE
IRONBARK MUGGA
IRON BROWN NEGRO
IRONCLAD ARMORED IRONSIDE
IRON, GOLF (PART OF —) TOE FACE GRIP HEAD HEEL NECK NOSE SOLE HOSEL SHAFT
IRON GRAY BAT
IRON HAT GOSSAN
IRONIC DRY WRY ACERB ACERBIC SATIRIC SARCASTIC
IRONICAL BLAND CRUEL PAWKY
IRON-LIKE MARTIAL
IRON MAN TALUS
IRONMONGERY HARDWARE
IRON-OXIDE RED TARRAGONA
IRONSMITH FERRER
IRONSTONE DOGGER SIDERITE
IRONWEED FLATTOP VERNONIA WINGSTEM
IRONWOOD TITI COLIMA MOPANE MOPANI PURIRI WAMARA CYRILLA JOEWOOD AXMASTER BURNWOOD FIREWOOD
IRONWORKER LOHAR MOSCHI
IRONWORT SIDERITE
IRONY SATIRE ASTEISM SARCASM RIDICULE
IROQUOIS HURON MINGO CAYUGA MENGWE
IRRADIATE XRAY EMBEAM
IRRATIONAL MAD REE SURD WILD BRUTE SILLY ABSURD RAVING STUPID BESTIAL FOOLISH
IRRECONCILABLE HOSTILE FRONDEUR
IRREDUCIBLE BASIC
IRREGULAR ODD DUMB WILD BUMPY EROSE FANCY MIXED WOPSY ATYPIC CATCHY FITFUL PATCHY RAGGED RUGGED SPOTTY UNEVEN UNLIKE WEEWAW ANAXIAL ATACTIC BAROQUE CATERAN CRABBED CROOKED CURSORY DEVIOUS DIFFORM ERRATIC FRECKET MUTABLE SCRAWLY SNATCHY UNEQUAL WAYWARD ABNORMAL ATYPICAL DOGGEREL INFORMAL PINDARIC SCRAGGLY SCRAMBLY UNLAWFUL UNSTABLE UNSTEADY VARIABLE

AMORPHOUS SCRAMBLING PROMISCUOUS
(— IN SHAPE) BAROQUE
(HAVING — EDGE) EROSE
(PREF.) AMETR(O) ANOM ANOMAL(O)
IRREGULARITY SNAG DEFECT RUFFLE ANOMALY ACCIDENT
(— IN YARN) SLUB SNICK
IRREGULARLY UNDULY
IRRELEVANT INEPT
IRRELIGIOUS PAGAN WICKED HEATHEN IMPIOUS PROFANE SENSUAL
IRREMEDIABLE HELPLESS HOPELESS
IRREPROACHABLE SPOTLESS
IRRESISTIBLE KILLING MESMERIC OPPOSELESS
IRRESISTIBLY FATALLY
IRRESOLUTE FICKLE INFIRM UNSURE WANKLE DOUBTFUL UNSTABLE
IRRESPONSIBLE WILDCAT CAREFREE FECKLESS SKITTISH
IRRESPONSIVE LEADEN
IRRETRIEVABLE HOPELESS
IRREVERENCE IMPIETY
IRREVERENT ATHEIST AWELESS IMPIOUS PROFANE
IRREVOCABLE DEAD
IRREVOCABLY FATALLY FINALLY
IRRIGATE FLOAT WATER SYRINGE
IRRIGATION KAREZ
IRRIGATOR FLOATER
IRRITABILITY BATE NERVES SPLEEN ERETHISM SORENESS VAGOTONY SENSITIVITY
IRRITABLE BAD EDGY BIRSY CROOK FIERY FUSSY HASTY HUFFY JUMPY MUSTY NAGGY RASPY TESTY TETTY TILTY TOITY CRANKY GROWLY NETTLY PATCHY SNUFFY SPUNKY STOCKY TEETHY TETCHY TOUCHY BILIOUS CRABBED FRATCHY FRETFUL HORNETY HUFFISH KICKISH PECKISH PEEVISH SPLEENY TEDIOUS TWITCHY WASPISH CHOLERIC LIVERISH PETULANT SNAPPING SNAPPISH STOMACHY SPLENETIC
IRRITANT PHOSGENE
IRRITATE BUG EAT GET IRE IRK NAG RUB TAR TEW TRY VEX BURN CRAB FIRE FRET GALL GOAD GRIG GRIT ITCH NARK RASP RILE ROIL SOUR TEEN ANGER ANNOY CHAFE EAGER FRUMP GRATE GRILL GRIPE PEEVE PIQUE STING TARRY ABRADE BOTHER FRIDGE GRAVEL HARASS HECTOR NETTLE PUTOUT RUFFLE AFFRONT INCENSE INFLAME NERVOUS PROVOKE STOMACH ACERBATE
IRRITATED RILY SORE HUFFY RAGGY MUFFED SHIRTY EMPORTE FRATCHED SOREHEAD
(EASILY —) TESTY
IRRITATING ACRID HARSH PESTY CORSIE ELVISH GRAVEL FRETFUL GALLING IRKSOME PUNGENT RASPING ANNOYING FRETSOME GRAVELLY NETTLING SCRATCHY

SPITEFUL STINGING TIRESOME MADDENING NETTLESOME
IRRITATION AGRO FRET TEEN AGGRO BIRSE PIQUE STEAM NEEDLE RUFFLE TEMPER WARMTH ANTPRICK FLEABITE PINPRICK VEXATION
IRRUPTION BREAK INROAD INBREAK INBURST ERUPTION INVASION
IRU (FATHER OF —) CALEB
IS S YS BEES
(— NOT) NIS AINT ISNT
ISAAC (FATHER OF —) ABRAHAM
(MOTHER OF —) SARAH
(SON OF —) ESAU JACOB
(WIFE OF —) REBEKAH
ISABELLA (BROTHER OF —) CLAUDIO
(HUSBAND OF —) BIRON VILLEROY VINCENTIO
(LOVER OF —) ZERBINO
(SLAYER OF —) RODOMONT
ISABELLE (GUARDIAN OF —) SGANARELLE
(HUSBAND OF —) VALERE
ISAIAH ESAY ESAIAS
(FATHER OF —) AMOZ
ISANDER (BROTHER OF —) HIPPOLOCHUS
(FATHER OF —) BELLEROPHON
(SISTER OF —) LAODAMIA
ISCAH (BROTHER OF —) LOT
(FATHER OF —) HARAN
(SISTER OF —) MILCAH
ISCHEMIA ANEMIA
ISCHIAL SCIATIC
ISEULT (FATHER OF —) HOEL ANGUISH
(HUSBAND OF —) MARK
(LOVER OF —) TRISTAN
ISFENDIYAR (BROTHER OF —) BISHUTAN
(FATHER OF —) GUSHTASP
(SLAYER OF —) RUSTAM
(SON OF —) BAHMAN
ISHBAK (FATHER OF —) ABRAHAM
(MOTHER OF —) KETURAH
ISHBOSHETH (FATHER OF —) SAUL
ISHI (SON OF —) ZOHETH
ISHIAH (FATHER OF —) IZRAHIAH
ISHMAEL (FATHER OF —) ABRAHAM JEHOHANAN NETHANIAH
(MOTHER OF —) HAGAR
(SON OF —) ZEBADIAH
ISHMAIAH (FATHER OF —) OBADIAH
ISHPINGO CINNAMON
ISHSHAKKU PATESI
ISHTAR NINNI
ISHUAH (FATHER OF —) ASHER
ISHUI (FATHER OF —) SAUL
(MOTHER OF —) AHINOAM
ISINGLASS AGAR LEAF MICA PIPE KANTEN CARLOCK
ISIS (BROTHER OF —) OSIRIS
(FATHER OF —) SATURN
(MOTHER OF —) RHEA
ISLAM ABBASID
(— CALL TO PRAYER) AZAN
ISLAMIC (— CUSTOM) SUNNA
ISLAND CAY ILE CALF CAYO HOLM INCH ISLE JAVA POLO ENNIS MALTA MAYDA AVALON ITHACA

OGYGIA REFUGE RIALTO CIPANGO JAMAICA MADEIRA TOWHEAD BLEFUSCU CALAURIA DOMINICA GUERNSEY LILLIPUT LUGGNAGG
(— IN EVERGLADES) HAMMOCK
(— OF REIL) INSULA
(ARTIFICIAL —) CRANNOG
(CORAL —) ATOLL
(FABLED —) MERU UTOPIA
(FLOATING —) HOVER
(FLYING —) LAPUTA
(FORTIFIED —) CRANNOG
(LEGENDARY —) BRAZIL OBRAZIL
(LITTLE —) AIT KAY KEY ISLET
(LOW —) KEY
(ROCKY —) SKERRY
(SANDY —) BEACH BARRIER
(SMALL —) CAY EYET EYOT ISLE ISLET NUBBLE SANDKEY
(PREF.) NESO
ISLANDER KANAKA ISLEMAN INSULARY
ISLE CAY IZLE ISLET SKERRY
ISLET OE AIT CAY KEY EYOT HAFT HOLM ILOT MOTU ROCK ISLOT STACK NUBBLE
ISMENE (FATHER OF —) OEDIPUS
(MOTHER OF —) JOCASTA
(SISTER OF —) ANTIGONE
ISOBAR MEIOBAR MESOBAR PLEIOBAR
ISOGRAM ISOPLETH
ISOLATE SPORE ENISLE ISLAND DISSECT SECLUDE COLONIZE INSULATE PRESCIND SEPARATE SEQUESTER
ISOLATED LONE POCKET UNIQUE OUTLYING SOLITARY STRANDED SECESSIVE
ISOLATION HERMITRY LONENESS SOLITUDE SEQUESTER
ISOMER PYRAN TOSYL XYLENE ETHANOL CUMIDINE DECOSANE DODECANE CARBOLINE
ISOMERIC ISO ALLO
ISOMETRIC ALLO CUBIC REGULAR TESSULAR
ISOPLETH GEOTHERM
ISOPOD SLATER ASELLUS BOPYRID GRIBBLE EPICARID
ISOTOPE MUON IONIUM THORON ACTINON CARRIER PROTIUM TRITIUM
ISOTYPE COTYPE SYNTYPE
ISPAGHUL SPOGEL
ISPAHAN HERAT HERATI

ISRAEL
CAPITAL: JERUSALEM
COIN: AGORA AGURA POUND PRUTA PRUTAH SHEKEL
COLLECTIVE FARM: KIBBUTZ
DESERT: NEGEV
FORMER NAME: CANAAN PALESTINE
GULF: AQABA
LAKE: HULEH TIBERIAS
MEASURE: CAB HIN KOR LOG BATH EPHA EZBA OMER REED SEAH CUBIT EPHAH HOMER KANEH QANEH
MOUNT: TABOR
MOUNTAIN: NAFH SAGI HARIF

MERON RAMON ATZMON CARMEL
PLAIN: ESDRAELON
RIVER: FARIA MALIK SOREQ JORDAN QISHON SARIDA YARKON LAKHISH
SEA: DEAD GALILEE
SEAPORT: EILAT ELATH ASHDOD TELAVIV
TOWN: ACRE RAMA EILAT HAIFA HOLON JAFFA JENIN JOPPA RAMLE SAFAD BATYAM HEBRON NABLUS JERICHO NATANYA TELAVIV TULKARM NAZARETH

ISRAELI SABRA
(— AIRPORT) LOD
(— STUDY CENTER) ULPAN
ISRAELITE JEW SAINT HEBREW JACOBITE
(PL.) ZION
ISSUE END ISH COME EMIT FALL FLOW GIVE GUSH HEAD MISE REEK TERM VENT ARISE COUNT EVENT FRUIT LOOSE OUTGO SETON SOURD UTTER EFFECT EFFUSE EGRESS EMERGE ESCAPE EXITUS MUTTON RESULT SEQUEL SETTER SPRING UPPING BALLOON DEBOUCH DESCENT DRIZZLE EMANATE ESSENCE EXSURGE OUTCOME PROCEED PROGENY REDOUND REFLAIR SUCCESS EXPEDITE FONTANEL INCREASE ISSUANCE KINDLING OUTGOING
(— AND ORDER) BID
(— SLOWLY) EXUDE
(— SPASMODICALLY) BELCH
(— SUDDENLY) SALLY
(— WITH FORCE) SPOUT
(BOND —) CONSOL
(FAVORABLE —) SPEED FORTUNE
(FINAL —) FATE UPSHOT UTMOST
(NEW —) REMAKE
(NUMEROUS —) SPAWN
(REAL —) CRUX
ISSUED OUT
ISSUING EMANANT JESSANT MANATION
ISTHMUS BALK STRAIT TARBET
ISTLE PITA IXTLE JUAMAVE GUAPILLA
IT HE HIT MUN ESSO TAGGER
(— FOLLOWS) SEQ SEQU
(— HAS BEEN SWORN) JURAT
ITALIAN ITALIC AUSONIAN MACARONI
ITALIANA IN ALGIERI, L'
(CHARACTER IN —) ELVIRA TADDEO LINDPRO ISABELLA MUSTAPHA
(COMPOSER OF —) ROSSINI
ITALITE VESBITE
ITALY AUSONIA HESPERIA SATURNIA

ITALY
CAPE: TESTA CIRCEO LICOSA LINARO COLONNE FALCONE PASSERO RIZZUTO SANVITO TEULADA VATICANO
CAPITAL: ROMA ROME

CHEESE: ROMANO FONTINA RICOTTA BELPAESE PARMESAN TALEGGIO
COIN: LIRA LIRE TARI GRANO PAOLI PAOLO SCUDO SOLDO DANARO DENARO DUCATO SEQUIN TESTONE ZECCHINO
FAMILY: ASTI ESTE AMATI CENCE DORIA BORGIA MEDICI SFORZA
FOOD: PASTA PIZZA SCAMPI GNOCCHI LASAGNE POLENTA RAVIOLI RISOTTO SPUMONI TORTONI CAPONATA LINGUINE MACARONI PEPERONI
GULF: GAETA GENOA OROSEI SALERNO TARANTO CAGLIARI ORISTANO
ISLAND: ELBA LERO CAPRI LEROS PONZA GIGLIO ISCHIA LINOSA SALINA SICILY USTICA ALICUDI ASINARA CAPRAIA GORGONA LEVANZO PANAREA PIANOSA SICILIA VULCANO FILICUDI SARDINIA
ISLANDS: EGADI LIPARI TUSCAN PELAGIE PONTINE TREMITI
LAKE: COMO ISEO NEMI GARDA ALBANO LESINA LUGANO VARANO BOLSENA PERUGIA MAGGIORE BRACCIANO
MEASURE: PIE ORNA CANNA PALMA PALMO PIEDE PUNTO SALMA STAIO STERO BARILE MIGLIE MIGLIO MOGGIO RUBBIO TAVOLA TOMOLO BOCCALE BRACCIO SECCHIO GIORNATA POLONICK QUADRATO
MOUNTAIN: ETNA ROSA VISO AMARO BLANC CORNO SOMMA CIMONE BERNINA VESUVIUS
MOUNTAIN RANGE: ALPS ORTLES APENNINES MARITIMES
NATIVE: ITALO LATIN OSCAN ROMAN SABINE TIRANO TUSCAN LOMBARD SIENESE LIGURIAN VENETIAN
NATIVE:) PISAN PISANO
PASS: FREJUS BERNINA BRENNER SPLUGEN
PORT: BARI POLA ZARA GENOA TRANI ZADAR RIMINI SALERNO TRIESTE
PROVINCE: ASTI COMO ENNA PISA AOSTA CUNEO FORLI LECCE NUORO PARMA PAVIA RIETI SIENA UDINE FOGGIA MATERA MODENA PADOVA RAGUSA TRENTO VERONA BRESCIA PISTOIA SASSARI VITERBO
REGION: CARSO APULIA LATIUM MARCHE MOLISE PUGLIA SICILY UMBRIA ABRUZZI LIGURIA TUSCANY VENETIA CALABRIA CAMPANIA LOMBARDY PIEMONTE SARDINIA
RESORT: LIDO SANREMO TAORMINA
RIVER: PO ADDA AGRI ANIO ARNO LIRI NERA RENO SELE TARO ADIGE CRATI MANNU OGLIO PARMA PIAVE SALSO STURA

TIBER TIRSO ANIENE BELICE MINCIO OFANTO PANARO RAPIDO SANGRO SIMETO TANARO TEVERE TICINO BIFERNO BRADANO CHIENTI METAURO MONTONE OMBRONE PESCARA RUBICON SECCHIA TREBBIA VOLTURNO
SEA: IONIAN ADRIATIC LIGURIAN
STRAIT: MESSINA OTRANTO BONIFACIO
TOWN: BRA RHO ACRI ALBA ASTI BARI COMO DEGO ELEA ENNA ESTE FANO GELA IESI LODI NARO NOLA PISA POLA ROMA ROME ACQUI ANZIO AOSTA ASOLA AVOLA CAPUA CUNEO EBOLI FIUME FORLI GENOA IMOLA LECCE LUCCA MASSA MILAN MONZA OSTIA PADUA PARMA PAVIA RIETI SIENA TEANO TRENT TURIN UDINE VELIA ALCAMO AMALFI ANCONA ANDRIA AREZZO CEFALU FAENZA FOGGIA GENOVA MANTUA MESTRE MILANO MODENA NAPLES NAPOLI NOVARA RIVOLI SPEZIA TRENTO VARESE VENICE VERONA BERGAMO BOLOGNA BOLZANO BRESCIA CARRARA CASERTA CATANIA COSENZA CREMONA FERRARA FIRENZE GORIZIA IMPERIA LEGHORN LIVORNO MARSALA MESSINA PALERMO PERUGIA PISTOIA POMPEII RAVENNA TARANTO TRIESTE BRINDISI CAGLIARI FLORENCE PIACENZA SORRENTO SYRACUSE
VOLCANO: ETNA SOMMA VULCANO VESUVIUS STROMBOLI
WATERFALL: FRUA TOCE
WEIGHT: CARAT LIBRA ONCIA POUND CARATO DENARO LIBBRA OTTAVA
WINE: SOAVE CHIANTI MARSALA ORVIETO

ITCH EWK EACH REEF RIFF YEUK YEWK YUKE PSORA TICKLE ITCHING SCABIES PRURITUS CACOETHES VANILLISM
(PREF.) ACARI ACARO PSOR(O)
ITCHING ITCHY YEUKY PRURIENT PRURITUS URTICANT
ITCHY SCRATCHY
ITEM ANA JOB TOT ENTRY PIECE POINT THING DETAIL PARCEL ARTICLE SEVERAL PARTICULAR
(— IN SERIES) COURSE
(— OF PROPERTY) CHATTEL
(— OF VALUE) ASSET
(APPENDED —) ADDENDUM
(CHOICE —) PLUM
(COLLECTOR'S —) SPOIL
(DECORATIVE —) CONCEIT
(DESIRED —S) WISHLIST
(LUXURY —) BOUTIQUE
(NEWS —) FACTOID DISPATCH
(OFF-BRAND —) GENERIC
(UNPUBLISHED —S) ANECDOTE
(VALUELESS —) BEAN
(PL.) CHECKAGE

ITEMIZE DETAIL
ITERATE ECHO REPEAT REITERATE
ITERATION PLEONASM
ITHIEL (FATHER OF —) JESAIAH
ITHRA (SON OF —) AMASA
(WIFE OF —) ABIGAIL
ITHRAN (FATHER OF —) DISHON
ITHREAM (FATHER OF —) DAVID
(MOTHER OF —) EGLAH
ITHURIEL'S-SPEAR GRASSNUT
ITINERANT ERRANT ROADMAN RUNNING AMBULANT STROLLER STROLLING PERIPATETIC
ITINERARY DIET JOURNAL WAYBILL
(— OF ROYAL PROGRESS) GEST
ITINERATION EYRE
ITS HIS
ITSELF IT HERSELF
ITSY-BITSY WEE
ITTAI (FATHER OF —) RIBAI
ITYS (FATHER OF —) TEREUS
(MOTHER OF —) PROCNE
ITZA PETEN
IULUS ASCANIUS
IVANHOE (AUTHOR OF —) SCOTT
(CHARACTER IN —) JOHN BRIAN GIRTH ISAAC LUCAS ROBIN WAMBA CEDRIC ROWENA ULRICA MAURICE REBECCA RICHARD WILFRED REGINALD BEAUMANOIR
IVATAN BATAN
IVORY EBURE DENTINE ELEPHANT
(DUST OF —) EBURINE
(WALRUS —) RIBZUBA RIBAZUBA
IVORY BLACK ABAISER

IVORY COAST
CAPE: PALMAS
CAPITAL: ABIDJAN
DAM: BANDAMA
LANGUAGE: DIOULA
MOUNTAIN: NIMBA
PEOPLE: ABE AKAN ATLE KOUA KROU MANDE ABOURE LAGOON MALINKE VOLTAIC
RIVER: KOMOE BANDAMA CAVALLY SASSANDRA
TOWN: MAN DALOA TABOU BOUAKE GAGNOA KORHOGO SASSANDRA

IVORY GULL SNOWBIRD
IVORY NUT ANTA TAGUA JARINA
IVORY PALM TAGUA COROJO COROZO
IVORY TREE PALAY
IVY TOD GILL HOVE IVIN JILL PICRY ARALIA HEDERA HIBBIN ALEHOOF ARALIAD IVYWORT BINDWEED FOALFOOT
(— LEAGUER) ELI
(PREF.) HEDERI
IWW WOBBLY
IXION (FATHER OF —) PHLEGYAS
(SISTER OF —) CORONIS
(WIFE OF —) DIA
IYNX (FATHER OF —) PAN
(MOTHER OF —) ECHO
IZHAR (FATHER OF —) KOHATH
IZMIR SMYRNA

J

J JAY JIG JULIETT

JAALAM (FATHER OF —) ESAU

JAAL GOAT BEDEN JAELA

JAASIEL (FATHER OF —) ABNER

JAAZANIAH (FATHER OF —) AZUR SHAPHAN JEREMIAH

JAB GAG GIG JAG JOB POKE STAB STICK

JABAL (BROTHER OF —) JUBAL
  (FATHER OF —) LAMECH
  (MOTHER OF —) ADAH

JABBER YAP CHAT YACK JAVER BURBLE GABBER GABBLE JOBBER NATTER YABBER YATTER CHATTER

JABESH (SON OF —) SHALLUM

JABIRU STORK CICONIID

JABOT RUFFLE

JACANA PARRA

JACARANDA BROWN DATE TALLYHO

JACARE CAIMAN CAYMAN

JACHIN (FATHER OF —) SIMEON

JACINTH LIGURE

JACK DIB FLAG JACA CRICK DICKY KNAVE NANCA COLORS KATHAL SCALET SETTER WENZEL MATADOR BLOCKING JACKFISH POLIGNAL SOURJACK TURNSPIT UPLIFTER
  (— IN BOWLS) BABY MARK KITTY MASTER MISTRESS
  (— IN CARDS) PAM PUR TOM BOWER CNAFE KITTY KNAPE KNAVE MAKER KNIGHT VARLET WENZEL VARLETTO
  (— OF CLUBS) PAM NODDY BRAGGER MATADOR
  (— OF SAME SUIT) NOB
  (— OF TRUMPS) TOM JASS JASZ BOWER HONOR PLAYBOY
  (PIANO —) HOPPER STICKER SAUTEREAU
  (ROASTING —) TURNSPIT
  (SPINNING —) BEAT

JACKAL DIEB JACK KOLA THOS CANID CANINE DRAGON SILVER THOOID SIACALLE

JACKAROO RINGNECK

JACKASS JACK

JACKASS FISH MORWONG TERAKIHI

JACK BEAN OVERLOOK

JACK CREVALLE TORO

JACKDAW DAW KAE JACK SHELL CADDOW CARDER CHOUGH KADDER CADESSE DAWCOCK DAWPATE GRACKLE

JACKER SLIPMAN TORCHER

JACKET SAC COAT ETON JACK JUMP JUPE SACK VEST ACTON COVER DICKY JUPON PARKA POLKA SHRUG WAMUS BANIAN BASQUE BIETLE BLAZER BOLERO CARACO CORSET DOLMAN FECKET GANSEY JERKIN JERSEY JUMPER RAILLY REEFER SACQUE SADDLE SLEEVE SLIVER SONTAG TABARD TEMIAK WAMPUS WARMUS ZOUAVE BEDGOWN CANEZOU LOUNGER NORFOLK PALETOT PALTOCK PEACOAT RISTORI SPENCER SURCOAT SWEATER CAMISOLE CARDIGAN CHAQUETA HANSELIN JIRKINET MACKINAW OVERSLOP PENELOPE SEALSKIN CARMAGNOLE ROUNDABOUT WINDBREAKER WINDCHEATER
  (— FOR TURKEY) APRON
  (— LINED WITH STEEL) PLACCATE
  (— OF BOOK) DUSTCOVER
  (— OF INDIA) BANIAN BANIYA
  (— UNDER ARMOR) ACTON TRUSS HAQUETON
  (CROCHETED —) SONTAG
  (DINNER —) TUXEDO
  (ETON —) BUMFREEZER
  (HOODED —) GREGO ANORAK GRIEKO
  (HUSSAR'S —) PELISSE
  (KIND OF —) MAO NEHRU SAFARI
  (LADY'S —) BRUNSWICK
  (LIFE —) MAEWEST
  (LOOSE —) VAREUSE
  (MALAY —) DAJU BADJU KABAYA
  (MILITARY —) TUNIC
  (PART OF —) FOB HEM DART FLAP SEAM VENT GORGE LAPEL BUTTON COLLAR INSEAM PIPING POCKET REVERS SLEEVE ARMHOLE OUTSEAM BUTTONHOLE
  (PEASANT'S —) SAYON
  (UNDRESS MILITARY —) SHELL
  (WORK —) BAWNEEN

JACKFRUIT JACA KATHAL SOURJACK

JACKHAMMER SINKER PLUGGER

JACKKNIFE DIVE JACK PIKE BARLOW

JACKMAN SHELLMAN

JACK-OF-ALL-TRADES DOCTOR TINKER GIMCRACK

JACK-PUDDING ZANY CLOWN BUFFOON

JACKS DIBS

JACKSCREW CRICK

JACKSMELT PEIXEREY

JACKSNIPE GID JED JACK PEERT SCAPE SNIPE SNIGHT CHOROOK CREAKER JUDCOCK SQUATTER

JACKSTAY JACK HORSE PARREL JACKROD RAILWAY

JACKSTRAW SPILIKIN

JACK TREE NANGKA

JACOB ISRAEL
  (BROTHER OF —) ESAU
  (DAUGHTER OF —) RACHEL DEBORAH
  (FATHER OF —) ISAAC
  (MOTHER OF —) REBEKAH
  (SON OF —) ACER LEVI ASHOR JOSEPH

JACOB'S LADDER POLEMONIUM

JACQUARD FACONNE

JADA (BROTHER OF —) SHAMMAI
  (FATHER OF —) ONAM

JADE YU DUN TIT HACK JAUD MINX PLUG SLUT TIRE HUSSY QUEAN TRASH BEJADE HARASS RANNEL AXSTONE HILDING POUNAMU
  (DIRTY —) SLAISTER

JADED BLASE FORGONE SHOPWORN DISJASKIT

JADEITE YU

JAEGER LARI SKUA ALLAN BOSUN LABID SHOOL BONXIE TEAGER TULIAC TRUMPIE DIRTBIRD DUNGBIRD

JAEL (HUSBAND OF —) HEBER
  (VICTIM OF —) SISERA

JAFFIER (WIFE OF —) BELVIDERA

JAG BUN JOG BARB GIMP JAUG LOAD SOSH TOOT SKATE TOOTH INDENT

JAGELLO (WIFE OF —) HEDWIG

JAGGED JAGGY HACKLY RAGGED RUGGED SCRAGGY SHAGGED SNAGGED INDENTED SCRAGGLY TATTERED

JAGGERY GUR GOON GOUR KHAUR KHAJUR KITTUL

JAGUAR CAT OUNCE TIGER PANTHER UTURUNCU

JAHANGIR (FATHER OF —) AKBAR

JAHATH (FATHER OF —) LIBNI SHIMEI SHELOMOTH

JAHAZIAH (FATHER OF —) TIKVAH

JAHAZIEL (FATHER OF —) HEBRON ZECHARIAH

JAHDO (FATHER OF —) BUZ
  (SON OF —) JESHISHAI

JAHLEEL (FATHER OF —) ZEBULUN

JAHZEEL (FATHER OF —) NAPHTALI

JAI ALAI PELOTA
  (— BASKET) CESTA
  (— COURT) FRONTON

JAIL CAN GIB JUG PEN BOOB CAGE COOP CRIB DUMP GAOL HELL HOLD HOLE KEEP LAKE LOCK NICK SLAM STIR WARD CHOKY CLINK GRATE KITTY LIMBO LODGE POKEY TENCH TRONK BUCKET CARCEL COOLER ENJAIL JIGGER LIMBUS LOCKUP TOLZEY FREEZER FURNACE GEHENNA KIDCOTE PINFOLD SLAMMER TOLLERY BASTILLE CALABOZO HOOSEGOW IMPRISON MILLDOLL TOLLHALL BRIDEWELL CALABOOSE
  (— TERM) JOLT

JAILBIRD CON LAG TERMER PRISONER

JAILER ADAM GAOLER KEEPER WARDEN ALCAIDE TURNKEY INCLUDER

JAIR (FATHER OF —) KISH
  (SON OF —) ELHANAN MORDECAI

JAKAN (FATHER OF —) EZER

JAKE FINE HICK FELLOW

JAKES AJAX GONG

JALAP MECHOACAN

JALON (FATHER OF —) EZRA

JALOPY HEAP BUGGY CRATE CLUNKER

JAM DIP CRAM JAMB BLOCK CHOKE CROWD CRUSH JEELY STICK JEELIE KONFYT THRONG JACKPOT PRESERVE MARMALADE
  (— FOR LACK OF LUBRICATION) SEIZE
  (TRAFFIC —) GRIDLOCK

JAMAICA (CAPITAL OF —) KINGSTON
  (RELIGIOUS ADHERENT OF —) RASTA RASTAMAN
  (RIVER OF —) BLACK COBRE MINHO
  (TOWN OF —) MAYPEN PORTANTONIO SPANISHTOWN

JAMAICA COBNUT OUABE PIGNUT

JAMAICA DOGWOOD BABASCO BARBASCO FISHWOOD

JAMAICAN (— MUSIC) SKA

JAMAICAN RAINBIRD TOMFOOL

JAMAICA VERVAIN GERVAO

JAMAICIN BERBERINE

JAMB DURN ALETTE HAUNCH REVEAL DOORPOST
  (PL.) COVING

JAMBOREE BASH

JAMES JEM JIM JIMMY SEAMAS SHAMUS
  (BROTHER OF —) JOHN JESUS JOSES
  (COUSIN OF —) JESUS
  (FATHER OF —) CLOPAS
  (MOTHER OF —) MARY SALOME

JAMIN (FATHER OF —) RAM SIMEON

JAMMAICA PEPPER ALLSPICE

JANAKA (DAUGHTER OF —) SITA

JANAMEJAYA (FATHER OF —) PARIKSHIT

JANE EYRE (AUTHOR OF —) BRONTE
  (CHARACTER IN —) EYRE JANE JOHN MARY REED ADELE DIANA ELIZA GRACE POOLE BERTHA BESSIE EDWARD ELLIOT INGRAM LEAVEN RIVERS TEMPLE VARENS BLANCHE FAIRFAX GEORGIANA ROCHESTER

JANGLE CLAM SQUABBLE

JANGLING HARSH JANGLY AJANGLE

JANISSARY CREOLE RABIRUBIA

JANITOR DURWAN PORTER
  SERVITOR
JANIZARY SOLAK SOLACH
JANNA (FATHER OF —) JOSEPH
  (SON OF —) MELCHI
JANSENIST RIGORIST
JANUARY ENERO
  (— IN SPANISH) ENERO
JANUS IANUS BIFRONT
JAOB JOW
JAPAN NIPPON YAMATO CIPANGO

JAPAN
ABORIGINE: AINU
BAY: ISE MUTSU OTARU ARIAKE
  ATSUMI SENDAI SURUGA
  TOYAMA WAKASA UCHIURA
CAPE: TOI ESAN MINO NOMA SHIO
  SOYA SUZU ERIMO KYOGA RURUI
  MUROTO NOJIMA TODOGA
  SHIRIYA ASHIZURI SHAKOTAN
CAPITAL: TOKIO TOKYO
COIN: BU RIN SEN YEN OBAN
  KOBAN OBANG TEMPO ICHEBU
  ITZEBU KOBANG
FORMER CAPITAL: EDO
ISLAND: IKI SADO AWAJI BONIN
  HONDO KURIL REBUN HONSHU
  KIUSHU KURILE KYUSHU RYUKYU
  CIPANGO LOOCHOO RISHIRI
  SKIKOKU HOKKAIDO IKISHIMA
  OKIGUNTO OKUSHIRI TSUSHIMA
  YAKUJIMA
ISLAND GROUP: OKI GOTO BONIN
  VOLCANO
LAKE: OMI BIWA TOYA TOWADA
  CHUZENJI KUTCHAWA SHIKOTSU
  INAWASHIRO
MEASURE: BU JO SE BOO CHO KEN
  TAN HIRO SHAKU TSUBO
MOUNTAIN: ZAO FUJI ASAHI
  ASAMA YESSO ASOSAN ENASAN
  HIUCHI KIUSIU YARIGA FUJISAN
  HAKUSAN KUJUSAN TOKACHI
  FUJIYAMA
PORT: UBE OTARU YAHATA YAWATA
PREFECTURE: MIE GIFU NARA OITA
  SAGA AICHI AKITA CHIBA EHIME
  FUKUI GUMMA HYOGO IWATE
  KOCHI KYOTO SHIGA AOMORI
  KAGAWA MIYAGI NAGANO
  TOYAMA NIIGATA OKINAWA
  SAITAMA TOTTORI NAGASAKI
  WAKAYAMA YAMAGATA
  TOKUSHIMA
SEA: SUO AMAKUSA
STRAIT: KII BUNGO OSUMI NEMURO
  TANEGA TOKARA TSUGARU
  TSUSHIMA
STREET: GINZA
TOWN: OME TSU GIFU KOBE KURA
  MITO NAHA NARA OITA OTSU
  SAGA UEDA AKITA ATAMI CHIBA
  FUKUI KIOTO KOCHI NIKKO OSAKA
  OTARU SAKAI UJINA URAWA
  CHOSHI MATSUE NAGOYA
  SASEBO SENDAI TAKADA TOYAMA
  FUKUOKA NIIGATA OKAYAMA
  OKAZAKI SAPPORO HAKODATE
  KAMAKURA KANAZAWA
  KAWASAKI KUMAMOTO
  NAGASAKI YOKOHAMA
  YOKOSUKA HIROSHIMA

VOLCANO: ASO USU FUJI ASAMA
  ASOSAN HAKUSAN FUJIYAMA
WATERFALL: KEGON
WEIGHT: MO FUN KIN KON RIN SHI
  KATI KWAN NIYO CARAT CATTY
  MOMME PICUL KWAMME
  HIYAKKIN

JAPAN CEDAR SUGI
JAPANESE JAP JAPONIC
  (— ART OF SELF-DEFENSE) AIKADO
  (— CONGLOMERATE) ZAIBATSU
  (— STYLE OF PAINTING) YAMATO
  (ABORIGINAL —) AINU
  (OF — CULTURAL PERIOD) YAYOI
  (PERIOD OF — HISTORY) HEIAN
JAPANESE APRICOT UME
JAPANESE CHERRY SAKURA
JAPANESE DEER SIKA
JAPANESE GELATIN AGAR
JAPANESE IRIS SHADOW
JAPANESE PERSIMMON KAKI
JAPANESE PLUM KELSEY
JAPANESE PORGIE TAI
JAPANESE QUINCE JAPONICA
JAPANESE VELVET BIRODO
JAPE GAUD JOKE BEGUNK
JAPHETH (BROTHER OF —) HAM
  SHEM
  (FATHER OF —) NOAH
  (SON OF —) JAVAN
JAPHIA (FATHER OF —) DAVID
JAPONICA ASTILBE
JAQUENETTA (LOVER OF —)
  ARMADO
JAR TUN CELL JANG JARG JOLT
  JURR OLLA BANGA BOCAL CADUS
  CRUSE KADOS SHOCK DOLIUM
  HUSTLE HYDRIA IMPACT JUDDER
  KALPIS PANKIN PINATA PITHOS
  TINAJA CANOPUS CONCUSS
  POTICHE PSYKTER STAMNOS
  TERRINE MARTABAN STINKPOT
  (— FOR LIQUOR) GREYBEARD
  (— VIOLENTLY) STAVE
  (BELL —) CLOCHE
  (BULGING —) OLLA
  (EARTHENWARE —) CAN NAN
  CROCK GAMLA PIPKIN PITHOS
  TERRINE
  (PHYSICIST'S —) LEYDEN
  (POROUS —) GURGLET
  (SQUAT —) KORO
  (STONE —) STEEN STONE CROPPA
  (STRAWBERRY —) PLANTER
  (WATER —) KANG BANGA CHATTI
  CHATTY GUMLAH HYDRIA
  (2-HANDLED —) AMPHORA
  (PREF.) DOLIO URCEI
JARASANDHA (FATHER OF —)
  BRIHADRATHA
  (SLAYER OF —) BHIMA
JARDINIERE POT
JARED (SON OF —) ENOCH
JARGON CANT JIVE RANE SLUM
  ARGOT IDIOM LINGO SLANG
  LINGUA LINSEY PATOIS PATTER
  PIDGIN SHELTA SIWASH CHINOOK
  CHOCTAW DIALECT JARGOON
  PALAVER BARRIKIN KEDGEREE
  PARLANCE POLYGLOT SCHMOOZE
  SHOPTALK GOBBLEDEGOOK
  GOBBLEDYGOOK GOGGLEDEGOOK

  (— OF TINKERS) KENNICK
  (THIEVES' —) FLASH
  (TINKER'S —) KENNICK
  (UNINTELLIGIBLE —) BARAGOUIN
JARHA (MASTER OF —) SHESHAN
JARIB (FATHER OF —) SIMEON
JARRING JARG RUDE SOUR HARSH
  ROUGH DARING STRIDENT
JASHUB (FATHER OF —) BANI
  ISSACHAR
JASMINE BELA MALATI PIKAKE
  JESSAMY WOODBINE
JASON (VESSEL OF —) ARGO
  (WIFE OF —) MEDEA
JASPER JASPIS MORLOP DIASPER
  BASANITE CREOLITE WEDGWOOD
JATAYU (FATHER OF —) GARUDA
  (SLAYER OF —) RAVANA
JAUNDICE AURIGO GULSACH
  ICTERUS JANDERS YELLOWS
  JAUNDERS GRASSERIE
  (PREF.) ICTER(O)
JAUNDICED ICTERODE
JAUNT TRIP SALLY JAUNCE VAGARY
  JOURNEY
JAUNTILY AIRILY BOUNCILY
JAUNTING CAR SIDECAR
  OUTSIDER
JAUNTY PERK PERT TRIM COCKY
  PERKY SASSY DAPPER JANTEE
  SHANTY FINICAL PERKING
  DEBONAIR

JAVA
INDONESIAN NAME: DJAWA
ISLAND: BALI LOMBOK MADURA
MEASURE: PAAL
MOUNTAIN: GEDE MURJO RAOENG
  SEMERU SLAMET SEMEROE
  SOEMBING
PORT: BATAVIA SURABAJA
  TJILATJAP
RIVER: SOLO LIWUNG BRANTAS
TOWN: BOGOR DESSA KEDIRI
  MALANG BANDUNG BATAVIA
  JAKARTA SEMARANG
  SURABAJA
WEIGHT: POND TALI

JAVA ALMOND PILI CANARI
  KANARI TALISAY
JAVA COTTON KAPOK
JAVA HEAD (AUTHOR OF —)
  HERGESHEIMER
  (CHARACTER IN —) TAOU YUEN
  RHODA EDWARD GERRIT JEREMY
  NETTIE VOLLAR AMMIDON
  DUNSACK WILLIAM
JAVAN (FATHER OF —) JAPHETH
JAVANESE KRAMA KROMO
JAVANESE SKUNK TELEDU
JAVA PLUM DUHAT JAMBUL
  LOMBOY JAMBOOL
JAVA SPARROW MUNIA PADDY
  RICEBIRD
JAVELIN COLP DART PILE ACLYS
  PILUM SPEAR JAREED LANCET
  ASSAGAI HARPOON HURLBAT
  JAVELOT ACONTIUM GAVELOCK
JAW JIB BEAK CHAP CHAW CHOP
  JOWL WANG ANVIL CHAFT CHEEK
  CHOKE SCOLD CHAWLE FEELER
  JAWBONE MAXILLA MANDIBLE

  (— OF FORCEPS) BEAK
  (— OF SPIDER) FANG
  (— OF VISE) CHAP
  (—S OF BIRD) BILL
  (FALSE —) CLAMP
  **(RECEDING NOSE AND
  UNDERSHOT —)** LAYBACK
  (PL.) MAW BITS THROAT
  (PREF.) **(UNDER —)** GENYO
  (SUFF.) GNATHA(E) GNATHI(A)(C)
  (SM) GNATHOUS GNATHUS
JAWBONE JOWL WANG MAXILLA
  CHAWBONE
  (PREF.) MAXILLI MAXILLO
JAWBREAKING CRACKJAW
JAY JAYPIET SIRGANG BLUECOAT
  MEATBIRD
JAYHAWK RAID
JAYHAWKER KANSAN
JAZERANT GESSERON
JAZZ BOP HYPE JIVE BEBOP
  HOTCHA RICKYTICK
  (— DATE) GIG
JEALOUS YELLOW EMULOUS
  ENVIOUS
JEALOUSY ENVY YELLOWS
  EMULATION ZELOTYPIA
JEAN FROCKING
**JEAN-CHRISTOPHE (AUTHOR OF
  —)** ROLLAND
  (CHARACTER IN —) ADA JEAN
  GRAZIA KRAFFT LOUISA MICHEL
  COLETTE LORCHEN OLIVIER
  STEVENS MELCHIOR GRUNEBAUM
JEANPAULIA BAIERA
JEATERAI (FATHER OF —) ZERAH
JECHOLIAH (HUSBAND OF —)
  AMAZIAH
  (SON OF —) UZZIAH AZARIAH
JEDAIAH (FATHER OF —)
  HARUMAPH
JEDIAEL (FATHER OF —) SHIMRI
  MESHELEMIAH
JEDIDAH (HUSBAND OF —) AMON
  (SON OF —) JOSIAH
JEEP PEEP SEEP BANTAM
JEER BOB BOO MOB GECK GIBE
  GIRD JAPE JEST JIBE MOCK SKIT
  WIPE FLIRT FLOUT FLUTE FLYTE
  FRUMP GLAIK LAUGH SCOFF
  SCOMM SNEER TAUNT CHIACK
  DERIDE BARRACK RIDICULE
JEERING BIRD FLOUT DERISIVE
JEEVES VALET
JEHALELEL (SON OF —) AZARIAH
JEHIEL (BROTHER OF —) JEHORAM
  (FATHER OF —) HOTHAN
  HACHMONI JEHOSHAPHAT
  (SON OF —) GIBEON OBADIAH
  SHECHANIAH
JEHIZKIAH (FATHER OF —)
  SHALLUM
JEHOADDAN (HUSBAND OF —)
  JOASH
  (SON OF —) AMAZIAH
JEHOAHAZ (FATHER OF —) JEHU
  JOSIAH JEHORAM
  (SON OF —) JEHOASH
JEHOASH (FATHER OF —) AHAZIAH
  JEHOAHAZ
JEHOHANAN (SON OF —) ISHMAEL
JEHOIACHIN (FATHER OF —)
  JEHOIAKIM

JEHOIADA (FATHER OF —) PASEACH
(SON OF —) BENAIAH
(WIFE OF —) JEHOSHEBA
JEHOIAKIM (FATHER OF —) JOSIAH
(SON OF —) JEHOIACHIN
JEHONADAB (FATHER OF —)
RECHAB
JEHONATHAN (FATHER OF —)
UZZIAH
JEHORAM (BROTHER OF —)
AHAZIAH
(FATHER OF —) AHAB
JEHOSHAPHAT
(SLAYER OF —) JEHU
(WIFE OF —) ATHALIAH
JEHOSHAPHAT (FATHER OF —) ASA
AHILUD NIMSHI PARUAH
(SON OF —) JEHU JEHORAM
JEHOSHEBA (FATHER OF —) JORAM
(HUSBAND OF —) JEHOIADA
(SON OF —) JOASH
JEHOVAH JAH LORD JAHVE
YAHWEH
(— WITNESS) PIONEER
JEHOZABAD (FATHER OF —)
OBEDEDOM
(MOTHER OF —) SHOMER SHIMRITH
JEHOZADAK (FATHER OF —)
SERAIAH
(SON OF —) JEDIDIAH
JEHU (FATHER OF —) HANANI
JOSIBIAH JEHOSHAPHAT
(SON OF —) JEHOAHAZ
(VICTIM OF —) JEHORAM
JEHUDI (FATHER OF —) NETHANIAH
JEHUSH (FATHER OF —) ESHEK
JEJUNE DRY ARID MEAGER INSIPID
JEKAMIAH (FATHER OF —)
SHALLUM
JELL COME FIRM
(INCENDIARY —) NAPALM
JELLY GEAL JEEL JELL GELEE
CULLIS JUJUBE ALCOGEL FISNOGA
GELATIN JELLIFY FLUMMERY
HYDROGEL QUIDDANY
MARMALADE
(AGAR-AGAR —) KANTEN
(CALF'S-FOOT —) SULZE
(FRUIT —) ROB
(INFLAMMABLE —) NAPALM
(MEAT —) ASPIC
(PREF.) GELATI
JELLYFISH JELLY QUARL CARVEL
MEDUSA ACALEPH AURELIA
BLUBBER MEDUSAN SLOBBER
SUNFISH SCYPHULA SEACROSS
STROBILA SEANETTLE
(PART OF —) ARM BELL MOUTH
MARGIN STOMACH TENTACLE
UMBRELLA MANUBRIUM
(PREF.) MEDUSI
JELLYLIKE SLABBY
JEMIMA (FATHER OF —) JOB
JEMMY BETTY JIMMY
JEMUEL (FATHER OF —) SIMEON
JENNET ASS
JENNY ASS MULE BETTY JINNY
JEOPARDIZE STAKE EXPOSE
HAZARD IMPERIL ENDANGER
JEOPARDY RISK PERIL DANGER
HAZARD
JEPHTHAH (FATHER OF —) GILEAD
JEPHUNNEH (SON OF —) CALEB

JEQUIRITY BEAN EYEN RUTTEE
JERAH (FATHER OF —) JOKTAN
JERAHMEEL (FATHER OF —) MAHLI
HEZRON HAMMELECH
JERBOA GERBIL JUMPER
JERED (FATHER OF —) MAHALALEEL
(SON OF —) ENOCH
JEREED TZIRID
JEREMIAD LAMENT TRAGEDY
JEREMIAH (DAUGHTER OF —)
HAMUTAL
(FATHER OF —) HILKIAH
(SON OF —) JAZANIAH
JEREMOTH (SON OF —) ELAM
HEMAN MUSHI ZATTU
JERIMOTH (DAUGHTER OF —)
MAHALATH
(FATHER OF —) BELA DAVID HEMAN
MUSHI AZRIEL BECHER
JERIOTH (HUSBAND OF —) CALEB
JERK BOB GAG JET NUD TIT BOUT
CANT DINK DORK FIRK GIRD HIKE
JERT JIRT JOLT JOUK KICK NERD
PECK PUTZ SNAP SNIG YANK YERK
BRAID CHUCK DWEEB FLIRT HITCH
HOICK SCHMO SLIRT SNAKE
SPANG SPASM SURGE TWEAK
TWICK FILLIP JIGGER SCHMOE
SHMUCK SWITCH TWITCH
WRENCH FLOUNCE SACCADE
SADSACK SCHMUCK SPANGHEW
SCHLEMIEL
JERKED MEAT TASAJO
JERKILY HITCHILY
JERKIN SAYON JACKET
JERKY NERVY SHARP CHOPPY
ELBOIC FLICKY FLINGY HITCHY
JIGGETY CHOPPING PALMODIC
RATCHETY SACCADIC
JEROBOAM REHOBOAM
(FATHER OF —) JOASH NEBAT
(WIFE OF —) ANO
JEROHAM (FATHER OF —) PASHUR
(SON OF —) ADAIAH AZAREEL
AZARIAH ELKANAH IBNEIAH
JERSEY FROCK SHIRT GANSEY
TRICOT ZEPHYR MAILLOT SINGLET
CAMISOLE GUERNSEY
JERUSALEM ZION ARIEL SOLYMA
AHOLIBAH
JERUSALEM ARTICHOKE TUBER
CANADA GIRASOL
JERUSALEM CHERRY SOLANUM
**JERUSALEM DELIVERED (AUTHOR
OF —)** TASSO
(CHARACTER IN —) HUGH OTHO
SWENO ARMIDA OLINDO ALADINE
ERMINIA GODFREY RINALDO
TANCRED ARGANTES BOUILLON
CLORINDA SOLIMANO SOPHRONIA
JERUSALEM OAK AMBROSIA
JERUSALEM SAGE PHLOMIS
SAGELEAF
JERUSALEM THORN CASCOL
RETAMA
JERUSHA (FATHER OF —) ZADOK
(HUSBAND OF —) UZZIAH
JESAIAH (BROTHER OF —) PELATIAH
(FATHER OF —) HANANIAH
JESHAIAH (FATHER OF —)
JEDUTHUN REHABIAH
(MOTHER OF —) ATHALIAH

JESHARELAH (FATHER OF —)
ASAPH
JESHER (FATHER OF —) CALEB
(MOTHER OF —) AZUBAH
JESIAH (FATHER OF —) UZZIEL
JESSAMINE JASMINE WOODBINE
JESSE (FATHER OF —) OBED
(SON OF —) DAVID
JESSICA (FATHER OF —) SHYLOCK
(HUSBAND OF —) LORENZO
JEST BAR BOG COD COG FUN GAB
JOE TAX BULL GAME GAUD GIRD
JAPE JOKE JOSH PLAY QUIP QUIZ
RAIL SKIT BOURD BREAK CHAFF
CLOWN DROLL FLIRT GESTE GLEEK
SPORT THING BANTER GLANCE
JAPERY RAILLY TRIFLE DICTERY
GAMMOCK JOLLITY WAGGERY
DROLLERY RAILLERY
(— SPITEFULLY) SLENT
JESTER FOOL MIME BUFFO CLOWN
DROLL IDIOT JAPER JOKER PATCH
WAMBA DISOUR MOTLEY YORICK
BADCHAN BOURDER BUFFOON
DIZZARD DROLLER JOCULAR
JUGGLER PICADOR SCOFFER
SCOGGIN TOMTRAM MERRYMAN
OWLGLASS PLEASANT RAILLEUR
TRINCULO
JESTING DROLL JAPERY SCOPTIC
WAGGISH
(COARSE —) RIBALDRY
(RUDELY —) INFICETE
JESUI (FATHER OF —) ASHER
JESUIT PAULIST TERTIAN IGNATIAN
LOYOLITE
JESUS GEE GIS IHC IHS JHS YHS
JESU WISDOM
(SAYINGS OF —) AGRAPHA
JET SST BOLT NOIR TAIL TANG
BREAK DUMBY DUMMY JETTO
SALLY SCOOT SPOUT SPRAY
SPURT AIRBUS CANDLE DELUGE
DOUCHE GAGATE SQUIRT FANTAIL
JETTEAU SPATTER SPURTER
FOUNTAIN SOFFIONE UPSPRING
(— OF FLAME) TONGUE
(— OF METAL) BREAK
(— OF VOLCANIC STEAM) STUFA
(KIND OF —) JUMP LEAR PLASMA
(SMALL —) SQUIB
(SUBSONIC —) AIRBUS
JET-BLACK BUGLE
JETHER (FATHER OF —) EZRA JADA
GIDEON
(SON-IN-LAW OF —) MOSES
(SON OF —) AMASA
JETHRO (DAUGHTER OF —)
ZIPPORAH
(SON-IN-LAW OF —) MOSES
JETTING SALIENT
JETTISON DUMP DITCH JETSAM
JETTY JET PEN DIKE PIER GROIN
JUTTY BRIDGE OVERHANG
JEUSH (FATHER OF —) ESAU BILHAN
REHOBOAM
(MOTHER OF —) AHOLIBAMAH
JEW SAINT ESSENE JUDEAN LITVAK
SEMITE SMOUCH SMOUSE TOBIAD
BARABAS GRECIAN KARAITE
MARRANO APIKOROS CONVERSO
GALICIAN JUDAHITE LANDSMAN
SEPHARDI

(—S OUT OF ISRAEL) DIASPORA
(BALKAN —) LADINO
JEWEL GEM JOY DROP OUCH BIJOU
REGAL STONE BROOCH GEORGE
TRIFLE CRAPAUD GARLAND
POUNDER
(MATCHING SET OF —S) PARURE
(PL.) BULSE PERRIE
JEWELER GEMMARY LAPIDARY
JEWELRY ICE JUNK OUCH PARURE
COLLARET LAPIDARY
(CHEAP — MATERIAL) OROIDE
(MOCK —) LOGIE
(PIECE OF —) GAUD
JEWELS OF THE MADONNA
(CHARACTER IN —) GENNARO
MALIELLA RAFFAELE
(COMPOSER OF —) WOLLFERRARI
JEWELWEED CEROLINE EARJEWEL
SNAPWEED
JEWFISH MERO GUASA WARSAW
PERCOID JUNEFISH MULLOWAY
SERRANID
JEWISH JUDAIC SEMITIC
(— BODY) VAAD
(— COMMUNITY) KEHILLAH
(— QUARTER) MELLAH
(— SCHOOL) ALJAMA
(PREF.) JUDEO JUDEO
JEW OF MALTA (AUTHOR OF —)
MARLOWE
(CHARACTER IN —) JACOMO
MARTIN ABIGAIL BARABAS MATHIAS
CALYMATH ITHAMORE LODOWICK
BELLAMIRA BERNARDINE
JEWRY GHETTO JUDAISM
JEW'S-HARP HARP TROMP TRUMP
GEWGAW FLAMFEW TRANGAM
GUIMBARD
JEW'S MALLOW DESI
JEZANIAH (FATHER OF —)
HOSHAIAH
JEZEBEL GILLIVER
(FATHER OF —) ETHBAAL
(HUSBAND OF —) AHAB
(SLAYER OF —) JEHU
JEZER (FATHER OF —) NAPHTALI
JEZOAR (FATHER OF —) ASHER
(MOTHER OF —) HELAH
JEZREEL (FATHER OF —) HOSEA
JIB GIB BALK BAULK DEMUR GIGUE
STICK GIBBET SPITFIRE
JIBE (ALSO SEE GIBE) FIT GEE KAY
GAFF GIBE JAPE JERK MOCK SKIT
AGREE FLIRD MARCH SNACK
SQUARE THRUST
JIBSAM (FATHER OF —) TOLA
JIDLAPH (FATHER OF —) NAHOR
JIFFY SEC JIFF BRAID FLISK WHIFF
GLIFFY GLIFFING
JIG BUCK FRISK GIGUE SQUID
GARLIC JIGGER JIGGET JITTER
LOCATOR
(— FOR WASHING ORE) HUTCH
(FISHING —) PILK
JIGGER SHOT DANDY PIQUE
DOODAD GADGET JIGMAN
VATMAN CHIGGER
JIGGLE DIDDLE JUGGLE TEETER
JIHAD WAR JEHAD STRIFE CRUSADE
JILT GUNK KICK SACK BEGOWK
BEGUNK MITTEN

JIMMY PRY OPEN BETTY JAMES
JEMMY
JIMNA (FATHER OF —) ASHER
JIMSONWEED DATURA DEWTRY
JIMSON FIREWEED STRAMONY
JINGLE TUNE CHIME CHINK CLINK
DINGLE RICKLE TINKLE CHINKLE
CLERIHEW DINGDONG JINGLING
(MEANINGLESS —) SPORT
JINGLING SMIT JANGLE RIGADIG
TINKLING
JINGO WARRIOR WARMONGER
JINGOISM CHAUVINISM
JINKER WHIM
JINN DJIN JANN AFRIT EBLIS GENIE
AFREET DJINNI SHAITAN
(PL.) JINNI
JINNI MARID AFREET ALUKAH
GENIUS YAKSHA YAKSHI JINNIYEH
JINRIKIMAN KURUMAYA
JINRIKISHA GOCART KURUMA
RICKSHAW
JINX HEX JONAH HOODOO
WHAMMY
JIPIJAPA CHIDRA PANAMA
PALMILLA TOQUILLA
JITTERBUG TRUCKING
JITTERY EDGY JUMPY TENSE
SPOOKY AJITTER ILLATEASE
JIVARO JIBARO SHUARA XIBARO
JIVE BOP ROCK
JIVER HEPCAT
JOAB (BROTHER OF —) ASAHEL
ABISHAI
(MOTHER OF —) ZERUIAH
(SLAYER OF —) BENAIAH
(UNCLE OF —) DAVID
(VICTIM OF —) ABNER
JOAH (FATHER OF —) ASAPH JOAHAZ
ZIMMAH OBEDEDOM
(SON OF —) EDEN
JOAHAZ (SON OF —) JOAH
JOAN JUG JONE
(— OF ARC) PUCELLE
JOANNA (FATHER OF —) RHESA
(HUSBAND OF —) CHUZA
JOASH (FATHER OF —) AHAB
BECHER AHAZIAH SHEMAAH
JEHOAHAZ
(SON OF —) GIDEON
(VICTIM OF —) ZECHARIAH
JOB LAY TUT CHAR CRIB FIST SHOP
TURN BERTH CHORE FIRST PLACE
BILLET HOBJOB HUSTLE JOBSITE
SWEATER BUSINESS POSITION
(EASY —) BLUDGE
(FATHER OF —) ISSACHAR
(HIGH-PAYING EASY —) PLUM
(KIND OF —) NOSE
(SMALL —) CHORE JOBBLE
JOBAB (FATHER OF —) JOKTAN
JOBBER BRAGER DEALER FLUNKY
BROGGER COURSER
JOB'S TEARS COIX ADLAI ADLAY
JOCHEBED (HUSBAND OF —)
AMRAM
(SON OF —) AARON MOSES
JOCKEY JOCK RIDER ROPER
WASTER CHANTER EQUISON
TURFITE SKIPJACK
(— FOR POSITION) DICE
(DISC —) DEEJAY

JOCOSE JOCO LEPID JOCULAR
PLAYFUL
JOCOTE MOMBIN
JOCOTE DE MICO BARBAS
JOCULAR GAY AIRY GLAD JOKY
DROLL FUNNY HAPPY JOLLY
MERRY WITTY BLITHE ELATED
JAPISH JOCOSE JOCUND JOKISH
JOVIAL JOYFUL JOYOUS LIVELY
BUOYANT COMICAL FESTIVE
GLEEFUL PLAYFUL WAGGISH
ANIMATED CHEERFUL DEBONAIR
GLADSOME HUMOROUS
JOCATORY JOKESOME LAUGHING
MIRTHFUL BURLESQUE
JOCULARITY FUN WAGGERY
JOCUND BUDGE MERRY JOCANT
JOCULAR
JOE JO
(HALF —) JOANNES JOHANNES
JOED (FATHER OF —) PEDAIAH
JOEL (BROTHER OF —) NATHAN
(FATHER OF —) NEBO SAMUEL
ZICHRI PEDAIAH PETHUEL IZRAHIAH
(SON OF —) HEMAN
JOELAH (FATHER OF —) JEROHAM
JOE-PYE WEED EUPATORY
JOEWOOD JOEBUSH BARBASCO
IRONWOOD
JOG BOB HOD JAG JIG JOT MOG
KICK LOPE POKE SHOG SPUD STIR
TROT WHIG DUNCH HOTCH MOSEY
NUDGE TWEAK DIDDLE JITTER
JOGGLE JUNDIE
(— ALONG) FADGE FODGE
(— AWKWARDLY) DODGE
(— WITH ELBOW) DUNCH
JOGGER LOPER LAYBOY RUNNER
JOGGLE HOTCH JUGGLE SHOGGLE
SHOOGLE
JOGLI (SON OF —) BUKKI
JOHA (FATHER OF —) BERIAH
JOHANAN (FATHER OF —) JOSIAH
KAREAH TOBIAH AZARIAH ELIOENAI
HAKKATAN
(SON OF —) AZARIAH
JOHANNES JOE PECA
JOHN IAN JEAN JOCK JONE JUAN
SEAN JOHANN SEAGHAN
GIOVANNI
(BROTHER OF —) JAMES
(FATHER OF —) ZEBEDEE
ZACHARIAS
(MOTHER OF —) SALOME
ELISABETH
**JOHN BROWN'S BODY (AUTHOR
OF —)** BENET
(CHARACTER IN —) CLAY JACK
LUCY LUKE DUPRE SALLY SOPHY
SPADE VILAS ELLYAT MELORA
SHIPPY WINGATE WEATHERBY
BRECKINRIDGE
JOHNNYCAKE CORNCAKE
JOIADA (FATHER OF —) ELIASHIB
JOIAKIM (FATHER OF —) JESHUA
JOIN ADD COP FAY MIX OUP PAN
TAG TIE UNY ALLY COPE FAIR FUSE
GAIN GLUE KNIT LINK MEET MELL
SEAM SOUD TAIL TEAM YOKE
ANNEX BLEND ENTER FRANK
GRAFT JOINT MERGE TENON UNITE
WRING ACCEDE ADJECT ADJOIN
ASSIST ATTACH CEMENT COCKET

COMMIT CONCUR ENGAGE INDENT
JOGGLE MARROW MINGLE PIECEN
RELATE RELIDE SPLICE STITCH
STRIKE COMBINE CONJOIN
CONNECT CONTACT INJOINT
JOINING MORTISE SHACKLE
ACCOUPLE COALESCE COMPOUND
COPULATE DOVETAIL JUNCTION
ACCOMPANY COMPAGINATE
(— BATTLE) JOUST ENGAGE
(— BY SEWING) STITCH SUTURE
(— CLOSELY) FAY AFFY WELD
GRAFT
(— IN COMBAT) BUCKLE
(— IN MARRIAGE) WED TACK HITCH
COUPLE
(— MECHANICALLY) DOCK
(— THE PARTS OF) PIECE
(— TOGETHER) CLOSE COAPT
FRANK HITCH COUPLE ENGLUE
ENJOIN ASSEMBLE COAGMENT
COALESCE
(— UP) ACCEDE
(PREF.) ARTIO
JOINED JOINT ALLIED DIRECT
SEAMED ACCOLLE ADJUNCT
APPINED EMBOITE ADJUGATE
COMBINED CONJUNCT COPULATE
INTEGRAL
(PREF.) GAM(ETO)(O) ZEUCTO
ZEUGLO
JOINER SNUG WRIGHT JOINTER
JOINING BAR JOIN SEAM BRIDE
CLOSE SPLICE BETWEEN JOINDER
ADDITION JUNCTION JUNCTIVE
JUNCTURE SYNECTIC
JOINT BED HAR HIP JAY BUTT COXA
FISH HEAD HELL HOCK JOIN KNEE
LITH LOCK SEAL SEAM TUCK
ANKLE BRAZE BUILD CARDO
CHASE ELBOW MITER MITRE
PLACE SCAPE SCARF SPALD UNION
UNITE WRIST BOXING COMMON
HAUNCH MUTUAL SCARPH SPLICE
STIFLE SUTURE TOGGLE UNITER
ARTHRON ARTICLE COGGING
DIGITAL FETLOCK FLEXURE
ISCHIUM JOINING KNUCKLE
SCATTER SHIPLAP SIAMESE
CONJOINT CONJUNCT COUPLING
DIACLASE DOVETAIL FLASHING
JOINTURE JUNCTURE SUBJOINT
SUFFRAGO TROCHOID VARIATOR
(— ABOVE HOCK) STIFLE
(— OF APPENDAGE) SEGMENT
(— OF BIRD'S WING) FLEXURE
(— OF FLAIL) CAPEL
(—OF INSECT LEG) PHALANX
(— OF MEAT) BARON SADDLE
(— OF SHIP) CHASE
(— OF STEM) NODE
(ANKLE —) COOT
(ELBOW —) NOOP
(FLEXIBLE —) HINGE
(GROOVED —) RABBET
(HIP —) COXA THURL
(MASONRY —) JOGGLE
(MINING —) CLEAT SLINE
(QUARRYING —) CUTTER
(SCARF —) BOXING
(THE —) STIR PRISON
(UNIVERSAL —) CARDAN

(VERTICAL —) BUILD
(WHEEL-LIKE —) TROCHITE
(PREF.) ARTHR(O) ARTI CO
CONDYL(O) HARMO HOM(O)
JOINTED ARTHROUS
JOINTED CHARLOCK KRAUT
RUNCH
JOINTER JOINER SKIMMER
JOINT FIR EPHEDRA
JOINT GRASS PASPALUM
JOINTLY
(PREF.) CO COL COM CON COR
JOINTURE DOWER
JOIST GEEST LEDGE BRIDGE RAGLIN
DORMANT SLEEPER CARRIAGE
(PL.) PIGGIN JOISTING
JOJOBA PIGNUT SHEEPNUT
JOKE BAR DOR FUN GAB GAG GIG
JOE KID ROT WIT YAK YUK FOOL
GAFF GAME GAUD GEGG JAPE
JEST JOSH LICE NOTE QUIP QUIZ
TYPE YOCK YUCK BREAK CRACK
FLIRT GLEEK GRIND LAUGH PRANK
RALLY SPORT TRICK BANTER
JAPERY PLISKY WHEEZE JOKELET
WAGGERY CHESTNUT
(— COLLECTION) ANA
(PRACTICAL —) BAR FUN GAG RIG
HOAX REAK SHAVIE HOTFOOT
(STALE —) GROANER CHESTNUT
(PL.) JAPERY
JOKER BUG DOR WAG CARD
CLOWN GRIND SLAVE FARCER
FOOLER GAGGER JOKIST FARCEUR
GIMMICK FUNNYMAN HUMORIST
JOKESTER
JOKESTER WAG WIT
JOKIM (FATHER OF —) SHELAH
JOKING JOSH BANTER JOCOSE
(PRACTICAL —) GAME
JOKSHAN (FATHER OF —) ABRAHAM
(MOTHER OF —) KETURAH
(SON OF —) DEDAN SHEBA
JOKTAN (FATHER OF —) EBER
JOLLIFICATION RAG RANT BEANO
JOLLY SINDIG
JOLLITY MIRTH GAIETY HILARITY
JOLLITRY
JOLLY GAY KID BOON BUXOM
GAWSY MERRY RORTY SONSY
WALLY BLITHE CROUSE JOVIAL
STRING JOCULAR RAUGHTY
DISPOSED
JOLLY BOAT YAWL DANDY
JOLT JAR JET JIG JOG JOT JUT BELT
BUMP DIRD DIRL HIKE JOWL JUMP
KICK SHOG JAUNT HOTTER IMPACT
JOGGLE JOSTLE JOUNCE JUMBLE
JOLTING JERKY BUMPITY HOTTERY
JONA (SON OF —) PETER
JONADAB (COUSIN OF —) AMNON
(FATHER OF —) SHIMEAH
(UNCLE OF —) DAVID
JONAH JINX JONAS HOODOO
(FATHER OF —) AMITTAI
JONAN (FATHER OF —) ELIAKIM
JONATHAN (BROTHER OF —)
JOHANAN
(COMPANION OF —) DAVID
(FATHER OF —) SAUL ASAHEL
JOIADA KAREAH ABIATHAR
(SON OF —) MEPHIBOSHETH

JONES HABIT HEROIN ADDICTION
(ARCHITECT —) INIGO
JONQUIL JONK LILY DAFFODIL
JORAM (FATHER OF —) TOI AHAB
JEHOSHAPHAT

JORDAN
CAPITAL: AMMAN
COIN: DINAR
GULF: AQABA
MOUNTAIN: BUKKA DABAB ATAIBA
MUBRAK
REGION: PEREA BASHAN PERAEA
RIVER: HOR JORDAN YARMUK
TOWN: AQABA ARIHA IRBID KARAK
ZARQA ZERKE NABLUS JERICHO

JORIM (FATHER OF —) MATTHAT
JOSE (FATHER OF —) ELIEZER
JOSEPH JOSEY GIUSEPPE
(FATHER OF —) HELI JACOB JUDAH
MATTATHIAS
(MOTHER OF —) RACHEL
(SON OF —) IGAL JESUS
(WIFE OF —) MARY ASENATH
JOSEPH ANDREWS (AUTHOR OF
—) FIELDING
(CHARACTER IN —) ADAMS BOOBY
FANNY PETER JOSEPH PAMELA
POUNCE THOMAS WILSON
ANDREWS GOODWILL SLIPSLOP
JOSEPHINE BLUSH PHENY
JOSEPH VANCE (AUTHOR OF —)
DEMORGAN
(CHARACTER IN —) JOE BONY
JANEY NOLLY SIBYL VANCE JOSEPH
LOSSIE THORPE VIOLET BEPPINO
DESPREZ PHEENER RANDALL
SPENCER PERCEVAL CHRISTOPHER
MACALLISTER
JOSES (BROTHER OF —) JESUS
(FATHER OF —) ELIEZER
JOSH GUY KID RIB JEST JOKE CHAFF
STRING
JOSHAVIAH (FATHER OF —)
ELNAAM
JOSHBEKASHAH (FATHER OF —)
HEMAN
JOSHI JOTI JOTISARU
JOSHUA JESUS
(FATHER OF —) NUN JOZADAK
JOSIAH (FATHER OF —) AMON
ZEPHANIAH
(MOTHER OF —) JEDIDAH
JOSIBIAH (SON OF —) JEHU
JOSTLE JOG JOLT JOSS PUSH SHOG
CROWD ELBOW HUNCH JUNDY
SHOVE HURTLE HUSTLE JOGGLE
JUNDIE JUSTLE SHOULDER
JOSTLING SCRAMBLE
JOT ACE DOT ATOM IOTA MARK
MITE TARE WHIT GRAIN MINIM
POINT TWINT WIGHT TITTLE
SCRUPLE SMIDGEN SYLLABLE
(— DOWN) NICK
JOTHAM (FATHER OF —) GIDEON
UZZIAH
(MOTHER OF —) JERUSHAH
JOTTING TOT
JOTUNN GEIRROTH
JOUNCE HIKE JOLT JAUNT
JOURNAL TOE BOOK DIARY PAPER
BLAZER SERIAL DAYBOOK

DIURNAL GAZETTE GUDGEON
JOURNEY CASHBOOK NOCTUARY
TRUNNION
(SEA —) LOGBOOK
JOURNAL BEARING RHODING
JOURNALISM NEWSWRITING
JOURNALIST SCRIBE WRITER
BYLINER DIARIAN
AMERICAN BLY DIX NEW BAER
BAUM CAIN CAPA CERF CHEW
COBB CONY CROW DALY DANA
DREW EDEL EDGE GELB HOWE HUIE
HUNT IDOE KENT LOEB MOTT OTIS
OWEN PAGE PAUL PECK POST PRAY
PYLE RAAB REED REID ROSS SANN
SNOW WALN WEBB WEED WIND
ADAMS ALSOP BACHE BAKER
BEACH BEALS BEEBE BENET BRANN
BROUN CANBY CREEL DUANE
EARLY ELSER FISKE FLYNN GREEN
GUILD HABER HARTE HOPPE HOUSE
IRWIN JAMES KEOGH KROCK LAHEY
LASKY LEWIS LOCKE MCCOY
MEANS MOLEY MOORE MORSE
NOVAK NOYES OGDEN OHARA
OMARR PAINE PIATT POORE PRIME
QUINN RALPH REEDY ROWAN
ROYKO SAXON SCALI SIDEY SOBOL
STONE STOWE SWING SWOPE
TIEDE TOWLE TWAIN UPTON UTLEY
WALSH WHITE WILLE YOUNG ZEVIN
ALLSOP ASBURY BAILEY BIERCE
BIRNIE BISHOP BLIVEN BONSAL
BOWERS BOWLES BUGBEE
BURMAN CAPUTO CHILDS CROUSE
DECTER FOWLER GILDER GILMER
GODWIN GRAHAM GRAVES GREENE
HAMILL HARSCH HARVEY HASKIN
HATTON HERSEY HICKOK HOWARD
HOWELL KEIHAN KENNAN KNEBEL
LAFFAN LAWSON LELAND LUBELL
MANNES MANTLE MARDEN MEDILL
MILLER MILLIS MOLLOY MORRIS
MORTON MOWRER NELSON
NEWELL PEGLER REDMAN RESTON
RIDDER RUNYON SAFIRE SAVAGE
SEAMAN SEATON SELDES SHIRER
STREIT TAYLOR TERKEL TILTON
TOLAND TUCKER TURNER WALKER
WALTER WARMAN WIESEL WILCOX
WILSON YARMON ANTHONY
AXTHELM BARRETT BIGELOW
BOMBECK BRENNAN BULLARD
CARROLL CONNIFF DANIELS
DREIFUS EASTMAN EDWARDS
FARRELL FEARING FISCHER
FREEMAN FRENEAU GALLICO
GARRETT GERVASI GIBBONS
GREELEY GUNTHER HALLOCK
HASSARD HELOISE KENDALL
LOSSING MANNING MARQUIS
MELONEY OCONNOR OURSLER
OVERTON POLLARD PRINGLE
RANDALL RAYMOND REDPATH
RITCHIE RUSSELL SANBORN
SERVISS SMALLEY STANTON
VANLOON VEILLER VILLARD
WELLMAN WHEELER WOLFERT
YARDLEY BROWNELL BUCHWALD
CREELMAN JOHNSTON LAWRENCE
LIPPMANN MCINTYRE MCKELWAY
MEREDITH PULITZER ROBINSON
STARRETT STEFFENS STILLMAN

STODDARD SULLIVAN THOMPSON
TOWNSEND WESTCOTT WHITLOCK
WILLIAMS BENEFIELD BERNSTEIN
MACDONALD MARCOSSON
MCCORMICK MOREHOUSE
PATTERSON WATTERSON
WOOLLCOTT CHAMBERLIN
WEITZENKORN
ARGENTINIAN AVELLANEDA
AUSTRALIAN DONALD WARNER
FAWKNER PATERSON MOOREHEAD
AUSTRIAN BAHR SEIDL HEVESI
SAPHIR CASTELLI
BRAZILIAN BANDEIRA
CANADIAN LAUT RYAN BROWN
DAFOE BOWELL BRIAND DUNTON
HEWITT RASKIN PAASSEN WHITMAN
DECELLES SINCLAIR FRECHETTE
CZECH CAPEK NERUDA HAVLICEK
DANISH PALUDAN JORGENSEN
GOLDSCHMIDT
DUTCH SCHIMMEL
ENGLISH LOW MEE BELL FOOT
FYFE GORE HARE LANE LUCY MAIS
SALA SIMS TOYE ARRAN BANKS
BLAKE COTES CROWE DIGFY
DORAN GIBBS LEMON LEVIN LEWIS
LOCKE MIALL MOULT SCOTT SHIEL
STEAD STEED WERTH ARKELL
ARNOLD BAINES BANGOR BARKER
BEGBIE BENIIAM BOADEN BROOKS
BUCKLE CANTON CASTLE CHIROL
DARWIN DILLON DIVINE FORBES
GARVIN GIBBON HANNAY MACKAY
MANNIN MAYHEW MORLEY
MURRAY NORMAN REEVES SQUIRE
TRAILL WATSON BENTLEY BOLITHO
BURGESS BYWATER CARLILE
CHORLEY COBBETT DURANTY
ENNEVER GILLOTT HAMMOND
HASKELL HERBERT HORABIN
LEHMANN MEYNELL MITFORD
ROBERTS SHORTER SPENDER
STANLEY WALLACE BAERLEIN
CARSWELL CHISHOLM COCKBURN
COURTNEY FLETCHER HOBHOUSE
LAWRENCE LOCKHART MONTAGUE
MORRISON ROBINSON SLOCOMBE
STEEVENS STRACHEY TOWNSEND
WOODFALL BLANCHARD
COLERIDGE COLQUHOUN
CRANKSHAW GREENWOOD
LESTRANGE MACDONELL
MONYPENNY THORNBURY
BALLANTYNE BRAILSFORD
CHATTERTON CHESTERTON
FONBLANQUE HUDDLESTON
MASSINGHAM THURSFIELD
HOLLINGSHEAD
FRENCH BLUM KARR MACE PUJO
BULOZ CAPUS CLAIR DUPUY GOSSE
GRIMM HAMEL HAVES HERVE
MEYER MILLE SOREL STEEG VERON
BABEUF BERTIN BODARD CARNOT
CARREL DAUDET DELORD DUCAMP
FONTAN FRERON GOZLAN HEBERT
LEROUX MAZADE NISARD PICHON
ROMIER SARCEY SCHWOB UZANNE
BRISSOT CARRERE CHARMES
GENOUDE HAUREAU LARBAUD
LINGUET MATHIEU MICHAUD
MIRBEAU NALECHE RECOULY
REINACH REYBAUD SCHERER

SIMONDS TABOUIS TILLIER VIARDOT
CALMETTE CLARETIE DUJARDIN
GIRARDIN GUEROULT JOUVENEL
MAZELINE NEFFTZER PELLETAN
PERTINAX PROUDHON QUILLARD
RENAUDOT RIVAROLI VEUILLOT
BAINVILLE CAILLAVET CAVAIGNAC
DESCHAMPS MIRECOURT
ROCHEFORT SAUERWEIN
VACQUERIE BARTHELEMY
DESMOULINS LACRETELLE
MONTLOSIER TASCHEREAU
TAILLANDIER MONTALEMBERT
GERMAN LONS BUSCH GIDAL
THOMA BECKER DREYER EISNER
GEROLD GORRES GROSSE GUBITZ
HARDEN ZENGER BARTELS
FRANZOS GUTZKOW HAMMANN
KALISCH MARTENS BERNHARD
FRAENKEL ROHRBACH LIEBNECHT
SCHUCKING STREICHER
BEUMELBURG POSCHINGER
HUNGARIAN BAJZA HERZL BALAZS
HUSZAR MORICZ RAKOSI
INDIAN ABBAS MEHTA
IRISH BELL LYND WEST CONNOR
LESLIE OBRIEN OKELLY PIGOTT
DESMOND OCONNOR ROLLESTON
ITALIAN NENNI ANCONA MONETA
PALLACI MORAVIA BATTISTI
ALBERTINI FEDERZONI
JAPANESE HEARN INUKAI
FUKUZAWA KAWAKAMI
NEW ZEALAND BALLANCE
NORWEGIAN FINNE VINJE BRATTELI
PARAGUAYAN BENITEZ
PERUVIAN CANDAMO
RUSSIAN KATKOV SHUKOV
CHERNOV NOVIKOV DOBROLYUBOV
SCOTTISH BELL DENT REID BLACK
CALER MUNRO FORBES CHALMERS
CARRUTHERS
SOUTH AFRICAN WOODS
SWEDISH MYRDAL THORILD
STRANDBERG
SWISS DROZ FAZY MEYER MURET
GIROUD DUCOMMUN
WELSH EVANS CUDLIPP
JOURNEY BE GO JOG RUN WAY
DIET EYRE FARE FORE GAIT GANG
GATE HIKE JUMP RACE RAIK RIDE
ROAD STEP TOUR TREK TRIP TURN
WENT BROAD COVER DRIVE JAUNT
REISE SITHE TRAIK TRAIL TURUS
WEENT COMINO ERRAND FLIGHT
HEGIRA JUNKET TRAVEL VAGARY
EMBASSY ENTRADA EXCURSE
JORNADA JOURNAL MEANDER
PASSAGE STRETCH TRAVAIL
TROUNCE WALKING WAYFARE
GODSPEED PROGRESS
PILGRIMAGE
(— BY SEA) VOYAGE
(— DOWNSTREAM) DESCEND
(DAY'S —) DIET
(DESERT —) JORNADA
(FATIGUING —) TRAIK
(LONG —) TREK
(PART OF —) LEG
(TEDIOUS —) TRANCE
(PL.) PERIPATETICS
JOURNEYING CRUISE
JOURNEYMAN YEOMAN

JOUST PLAY TILT JOSTLE JUSTLE TOURNEY

JOUSTER TILTER

JOVIAL GAY BOON JOVY BULLY JOLLY MERRY GENIAL HEARTY MELLOW WANTON BACCHIC HOLIDAY JOCULAR CONVIVIAL RANTIPOLE

JOVIALITY JOLLITY ROLLICK HILARITY

JOWL CHOW CHAULE
(PL.) CHOPS

JOY JO WIN GLEE LIST PLAY BLISS CHEER DREAM EXULT MIRTH REVEL GAIETY HEYDAY DELIGHT ECSTASY ELATION JOYANCE RAPTURE REVELRY FELICITY GLADNESS HILARITY PLEASURE

JOYFUL GAY GLAD BEAMY JOLLY BLITHE FESTUS JOCUND JOVIAL JOYANT JOYOUS GAUDFUL GLADFUL GLEEFUL JOCULAR GLADSOME

JOYFULLY FAIN FAINLY GLADLY JOYOUSLY

JOYLESS DESOLATE LUSTLESS UNBLITHE

JOYOUS GAY GLAD JOLLY MERRY YOUSE BLITHE JOVIAL FESTIVE GIOJOSO GLEEFUL JOCULAR SMILING FRABJOUS FROHLICH SUNSHINY

JOYOUSNESS HILARITY

JOYRIDE SPIN

JOY STICK CONTROL

JOZABAD (FATHER OF —) JESHUA

JOZACHAR (VICTIM OF —) JOASH

JUBAL (FATHER OF —) LAMECH
(MOTHER OF —) ADAH

JUBILANT ELATED JOYFUL EXULTANT

JUBILATION JOY JOYANCE JUBILEE

JUDA (FATHER OF —) JOSEPH HANANIAH
(MOTHER OF —) JOANNA

JUDAH (FATHER OF —) JACOB
(MOTHER OF —) LEAH
(SON OF —) ONAN

JUDAHITE JEW

JUDAISM JEWISM HEBRAISM

JUDAS TREE CERCIS

JUDEA JEWRY

JUDEO-SPANISH JUDESMO JUDEZMO LADINO

JUDE THE OBSCURE (AUTHOR OF —) HARDY
(CHARACTER IN —) SUE DONN JUDE FAWLEY RICHARD ARABELLA DRUSILLA BRIDEHEAD PHILLOTSON

JUDGE (ALSO SEE JURIST) DAN JUS SEE WIG CADI CAID CAZY DEEM DOOM HOLD IMAM JUEZ JURY KAZI QADI RATE RULE SCAN AWARD COUNT COURT DAYAN GAUGE HAKIM INFER JUDEX MINOS OPINE PUNEE TRIER WEIGH BREHON CENSOR CRITIC DANIEL DECERN DEEMER DICAST DOOMER INTEND JUDGER JURIST OPINER PUISNE SAMSON SAMUEL SETTLE SQUIRE ACCOUNT ADJUDGE ALCALDE ARBITER BENCHER BRIDOYE CENSURE DISCERN FLAGMAN FOUJDAR HELIAST JURYMAN JUSTICE MUNSIFF PODESTA REFEREE SCABINE SHAMGAR SUPPOSE APPRAISE CENTENAR CONCLUDE CONSIDER DEEMSTER DEMPSTER DIRECTOR DOOMSMAN DOOMSTER ESTIMATE FOREDEEM JEPHTHAH JUDGMENT JUDICATE LINESMAN MINISTER MITTIMUS ORDINARY QUAESTOR RECORDER REGICIDE SCABINUS STRADICO
(— OF UNDERWORLD) AEACUS
(PREF.) KRIT(O)

JUDGMENT ACT EYE BOOK DEEM DOME DOOM REDE VIEW ARRET AWARD FANCY JUISE SENSE SIGHT SKILL TASTE ADVICE ASSIZE DECREE ESTEEM JUWISE OUSTER STEVEN ACCOUNT CENSURE CONCEIT HOLDING OPINION THOUGHT VERDICT WITTING DECISION ESTIMATE JUDICIAL JUDICIUM SAGACITY SAPIENCE SENTENCE THINKING PREJUDICE OBSERVATION
(PREF.) GNOMO

JUDICATORY SYNOD

JUDICIOUS SAGE WISE POLITIC PRUDENT CRITICAL JUDICIAL MODERATE SENSEFUL SENSIBLE WISELIKE

JUDITH (FATHER OF —) BEERI
(HUSBAND OF —) ESAU

JUDITH PARIS (AUTHOR OF —) WALPOLE
(CHARACTER IN —) ADAM EMMA JOHN CARDS DAVID PARIS STANE JUDITH REUBEN WALTER WARREN DOROTHY FRANCIS GAUNTRY GEORGES HERRIES SUNWOOD WILLIAM FORESTER JENNIFER CHRISTABEL FERNYHIRST

JUDO (— EXERCISES) KATA
(— LEVEL) DAN
(— PRACTICE) RANDORI
(— SCHOOL) DOJO
(EXPERT LEVEL IN —) DAN
(EXPERT LEVEL OF —) DAN

JUG CAN EWER JACK JUST OLLA ASCUS ASKOS BUIRE GAMLA GOTCH JORUM JUBBE STEAN BOGGLE CROUKE GOGLET PITCHER CRUISKEN LECYTHUS LEKYTHOS OENOCHOE PROCHOOS
(— FOR BEER) GROWLER
(— WITH SPOUT) BUIRE DOLLIN
(ALE —) TOBY
(BEER —) BOCK
(BULGING —) GOTCH
(CREAM —) POURER POURIE
(LEATHER —) JACK BOMBARD
(ONE-HANDLED —) URCEUS
(SPOUTLESS —) OLPE

JUGATED BAJOIRE

JUGGERNAUT IDOL

JUGGLE TRICK BAFFLE FUMBLE CONJURE SHUFFLE

JUGGLER HARLOT CONJURER JONGLEUR TREGETOUR

JUGGLERY GUILE HANKYPANKY HOCUSPOCUS LEGERDEMAIN

JUGHEAD SAP

JUGLONE NUCIN

JUGULARES DERIPIA

JUGUM FIBULA JUGULUM

JUICE JUS SEW BREE BROO FOND OOZE PULL SUCK ANIMA BLOND BLOOD CLOUT GRAVY HUMOR LASER MOBBY PERRY CASIRI CREMOR JIPPER LIQUOR SUCCUS CAMBIUM AGUAMIEL HYPOCIST VERJUICE INFLUENCE
(— OF COCONUT) MILK
(— OF TREE) SAP LYCIUM JELUTONG
(— OF UNRIPE FRUIT) OMPHACY
(APPLE —) CIDER
(CANE —) SLING
(CASSAVA —) CASSAREEP CASSARIPE
(CONCENTRATED —) SIRUP SYRUP
(DRIED —) ALOE KINO
(ETHEREAL —) ICHOR
(FERMENTED —) SURA GRAPE
(FRUIT —) ROB ROHOB
(GRAPE —) MUST SAPA STUM
(INSPISSATED —) HYPOCIST
(INTOXICATING —) SOMA
(LETTUCE —) THRIDACE
(MEAT —) BLOND
(POPPY —) CHICK MECONIUM
(TOBACCO —) AMBEER AMBIER
(VITAL —) SAP
(PL.) ESSENCE HUMIDITY
(PREF.) CHYL(I)(O) MYRO OPO
(SUFF.) CIDAL CIDE

JUICY FAT FRIM FRUM NAISH SAPPY FRUITY SUCCOSE WATERISH

JUJUBE BER ELB TSAO LOTUS LOTEBUSH LOTEWOOD ZIZYPHUS

JUKEBOX PICCOLO NICKELODEON

JULIUS CAESAR (AUTHOR OF —) SHAKESPEARE
(CHARACTER IN —) CATO CASCA CINNA CLITO PORTA VARRO BRUTUS CAESAR CICERO CIMBER DECIUS JULIUS LUCIUS MARCUS STRATO CASSIUS FLAVIUS LEPIDUS MESSALA PUBLIUS ANTONIUS CLAUDIUS LIGARIUS LUCILIUS MARULLUS METELLUS OCTAVIUS PINDARUS POPILIUS TITINIUS CALPURNIA DARDANIUS TREBONIUS VOLUMNIUS ARTEMIDORUS

JUMBLE PI PIE ROG HASH MESS MUSS RAFF BOTCH BOLLIX BUMBLE FUDDLE GARBLE HUDDLE JABBLE JUMPER JUNGLE MEDLEY MOMBLE MUDDLE PALTER RAFFLE WELTER WUZZLE CLUTTER CONFUSE EMBROIL GOULASH SHUFFLE DISORDER MISHMASH PASTICHE RHAPSODY SMACHRIE
(— OF SOUNDS) LURRY

JUMBLED CRAZY HASHY JUMBLY MEDLEY HUDDLING MACARONIC

JUMP HOP LEP NIP DART JETE LEAP LUTZ SKIP SKIT STEN STOT TUMB BOUND CAPER FENCE HALMA SALTO SAULT SPANG SPEND START STOIT VAULT DOUBLE FOOTER HURDLE INSULT LAUNCH SPRING SPRUNT STARRE WALLOP CISEAUX CROWHOP SALTATE SKYLARK BALLONNE
(— ABOUT) SKIT CAPER
(— FROM AIRCRAFT) BAIL BALE
(— IN FENCING) BALESTRA
(— ON HORSEBACK) LARK
(— ON SKATES) AXEL SALCHOW
(— TO CONCLUSION) SALTUS
(ELECTRICAL —) ARC
(PL.) ALLEGRO

JUMPER LAMMY SWAGE BARKER LEPPER HANDYMAN

JUMPING SALIENT SALTANT

JUMPING-JACK PANTINE

JUMPING JACK PANTINE

JUMPY ITCHY NERVOUS

JUNCO SNOWBIRD

JUNCTION HIP FROG JOIN NODE SEAM CLOSE CROWN RAPHE UNION FILLET INFALL CONTACT JOINING MEETING UNITION ABUTMENT JUNCTURE CONSERTION
(— OF EARTH AND SKY) HORIZON
(— OF STREAMS) GRAINS
(— OF THREADS) FELL STOP
(— ON TOOTH) CERVIX
(ROAD —) TOLL

JUNCTURE PASS SEAM PINCH CRISIS STRAIT ARTICLE BRACKET JOINING OPHRYON EXIGENCY JOINTAGE JOINTURE OCCASION QUANDARY

JUNEBERRY SHADBLOW SHADBUSH SERVICEBERRY

JUNE BUG DOR BUZZARD DUMCLOCK

JUNGLE BUSH RUKH SHOLA BOONDOCK
(AUTHOR OF —) SINCLAIR
(CHARACTER IN —) ONA JACK DUANE JONAS CONNOR JURGIS MARIJA RUDKUS ANTANAS ELZBIETA STANISLOVAS

JUNGLE BENDY WEENONG

JUNGLE BOOK (AUTHOR OF —) KIPLING
(CHARACTER IN —) KAA KHAN AKELA BALOO HATHI SHERE BULDEO MESSUA MOWGLI TABAQUI BAGHEERA BANDARLOG

JUNIOR PUNY CADET YOUNG PUISNE YOUNGER

JUNIPER CADE EZEL GORSE GORST RETEM SAVIN SABINE

JUNK CRAM GEAR GOOK TOPE DRECK REFUSE SCULCH DISCARD PLUNDER TONGKANG
(WORTHLESS —) SLUM

JUNKET TRIP KNACK JINKET SAFARI

JUNKMAN TATTER SCRAPMAN SCAVENGER

JUNO MONETA PRONUBA

**JUNO AND THE PAYCOCK
(AUTHOR OF —)** OCASEY
(CHARACTER IN —) JACK JUNO MARY BOYLE JERRY JOXER DEVINE JOHNNY BENTHAM CHARLIE TANCRED

JUNTO CABAL

JUPITER JOVE STATOR FORTUNE MUSHTARI TERMINUS

(SATELLITE OF —) LEDA
(PREF.) JOVI ZENO
JUPITER'S BEARD JOUBARB
SENGREEN
JUR LWO LUOH
JUREL RUNNER CREVALLE
HARDTAIL
JURGEN (AUTHOR OF —) CABELL
(CHARACTER IN —) LISA HELEN
JURGEN MERLIN SEREDA ANAITIS
CHLORIS DESIREE DOLORES
DOROTHY KOSHCHEI GUENEVERE
JURIDIC LEGAL
JURISDICTION SOC BAIL SOKE
FUERO HONOR REALM VERGE
ABBACY BANDON BEYLIK DANGER
DIWANI RIDING SPHERE DEANERY
DEWANEE DROSTDY EMIRATE
FOUDRIE KHANATE BAILIERY
CHAPELRY FOUJDARY LIGEANCE
PASHALIC PROVINCE
(— OF BISHOP) SEE
(COERCIVE —) SWORD
(MORMON —) KEYS
(REMOVE FROM —) ELOIN
(SUFF.) DOM
JURISPRUDENCE LAW BYRLAW
REPORTS
JURIST JUDGE MUFTI BREHON
LAWYER DOTTORE
AMERICAN DAY JAY LEE BEAN
BOND BORK DANA DANE DYER
GOFF GRAY HALL HAND HUNT KENT
NOTT POPE REED RUSK SHAW TAFT
TAIT WARE ZANE ADAMS BETTS
BLACK BLAIR BROWN CASEY CHASE
DAVIS DAWES DUANE EATON FIELD
FREAR GRIER LAMAR LIMAN LOGAN
MIKVA MOODY MOORE PAINE
RANDA SMITH STONE STORY TANEY
TYLER WAITE WAYNE WEARE WHITE
WYTHE YATES BAYLOR BREWER
BURGER BURTON BUTLER BYRNES
CATRON CLARKE COOLEY CRATER
CURTIS DANIEL DARROW DONLON
DULLES FOLGER FORTAS FULLER
GASTON GIBSON HARLAN HOLMES
HUDSON HUGHES JEROME KENYON
LANDIS LOWELL LURTON MARTIN
MEDINA MILLER MINTON MORRIS
MURPHY NELSON PARKER PECORA
PETERS PITNEY POWELL SCALIA
SEWALL SHIRAS SIRICA STRONG
SUMNER SWAYNE UPSHUR VINSON
WARREN WILBUR BALDWIN
BRADLEY CARDOZO CLAYTON
CUSHING DOUGLAS DRAYTON
GRIFFIN JACKSON JOHNSON
JUSTICE LINDSEY MCKENNA
PARSONS ROBERTS SANBORN
SANFORD SHERMAN STEVENS

STOWELL TRIMBLE VOELKER
WHARTON WHEATON ANDERSON
BLACKMUN BRANDEIS CLIFFORD
GOLDBERG GRISWOLD GROSSCUP
KIRCHWAY LAWRENCE MACVEAGH
MARSHALL MATTHEWS MCKINLEY
MITCHELL PENFIELD ROSENMAN
RUTLEDGE SEDGWICK STAFFORD
WALWORTH WOODBURY
ELLSWORTH GREENLEAF
GROESBECK HOPKINSON
PENDLETON REHNQUIST
SHARSWOOD UNDERWOOD
WHITTAKER YOUNGDAHL
BLATCHFORD CELEBREZZE
MCREYNOLDS POINDEXTER
TROWBRIDGE WASHINGTON
FRANKFURTER VANDEVANTER
ARGENTINIAN CALVO DRAGO
ALBERDI QUESADA CASTILLO
AUSTRIAN GROSS UNGER GLASER
ZELLER REDLICH LAMMASCH
RINTELEN SCHMERLING
BELGIAN NYS PICARD LAURENT
DESCAMPS GERLACHE
BOLIVIAN SILES SAAVEDRA
BRAZILIAN PESSOA BARBOSA
BARROSO PECANHA
CANADIAN CARON JETTE ARMOUR
DAVIES MULOCK STUART DOHERTY
LACOSTE FOURNIER HAULTAIN
NEWCOMBE RICHARDS ROBINSON
THOMPSON HALIBURTON
FITZPATRICK
CHILEAN EGANA DONOSO
COSTA RICAN CARRILLO
CUBAN URRUTIA
CZECH HACHA
DUTCH GEER ASSER LODER
GROTIUS OPZOOMER
BYNKERSHOEK
ENGLISH MAY AMOS GAVE COKE
HALE HOLT KING REID ANSON
BOWEN BRYCE GROVE HURST
IMPEY JAMES MAINE PRATT SCOTT
TWISS VINER ABBOTT ATKYNS
AUSTIN BARNES CARSON DAVIES
FINLAY GATLEY HENLEY HEWART
HUGHES MERSEY NORTON PALMER
SANKEY SELDEN AMULREE
BRACTON DARLING DENNING
GODFREY HOLLAND JENKINS
MOULTON PLOWDEN RUSSELL
WIDGERY CAMPBELL CHALMERS
HAILSHAM JEFFREYS CALDECOTE
FORTESCUE HERSCHELL LITTLETON
OPPENHEIM BLACKSTONE
FITZHERBERT
FRENCH ADAM GIDE MOLE DOMAT
FLACH WEISS CASSIN COCHIN
DEMETZ DONEAU DUGUIT GOHIER

HOTMAN MERLIN PITHOU DECAZES
HENAULT LECONTE NOGARET
RENAULT CUJACIUS DUMOULIN
GODEFROY PASQUIER PORTALIS
AGUESSEAU BEAUMANOIR
EPREMESNIL LAFERRIERE
GERMAN UZ BAR FALK GANS HUGO
KAHL POST WACH ZORN CROME
FRANK HANEL KRAUS MOSER
SPAHN TEMME WITTE AEGIDI
AHRENS FICKER GERBER GNEIST
HITZIG KELSEN LABAND MEZGER
PREUSS BOCKING COCCEJI
GOLDAST GOSCHEL HEFFTER
KOSTLIN RICHTER THIBAUT
WICHERT ANCILLON DERNBURG
EICHRODT FISCHART GEFFCKEN
HABERLIN HEDEMANN HUFELAND
ALTHUSIUS EBERMAYER
FEUERBACH HINSCHIUS
KIRCHMANN PUFENDORF
HEINECCIUS KOHLRAUSCH
GOLDSCHMIDT KANTOROWICZ
MITTERMAIER HOLTZENDORFF
GREEK POLITES
INDIAN SAPRU
IRISH BALL MORRIS OHAGAN
MACNEILL ODALAIGH FITZGIBBON
ITALIAN AZO FIORE ROCCO
ACCORSO ALCIATI CARRARA
GRAVINA MANCINI ORLANDO
TANUCCI BARTOLUS BULGARUS
GAROFALO IRNERIUS ANZILOTTI
ROMAGNOSI FILANGIERI
PIERANTONI
JAPANESE ADACHI
MEXICAN IGLESIAS
NEW ZEALAND STOUT BULLER
MANING
NORWEGIAN FALSEN HAGERUP
PANAMANIAN PORRAS
PARAGUAYAN BAEZ
PERUVIAN CORNEJO
ROMAN GAIUS LABEO CELSUS
FRONTO PAULUS ULPIAN SABINUS
SALVIUS PAPINIAN PROCULUS
SCAEVOLA SULPICIUS TRIBONIAN
MODESTINUS GREGORIANUS
RUSSIAN KAVELIN MARTENS
MUROMTSEV MEYENDORFF
VINOGRADOFF POBEDONOSTSEV
SCOTTISH HOME CRAIG FORBES
ERSKINE GIFFORD JEFFREY
LORIMER BROUGHAM
SPANISH GALVEZ PINELO AGUSTIN
SWEDISH UNDEN
SWISS DUBS MUSY HILTY HUBER
LARDY MEILI BLUMER DELOLME
URUGUAYAN BRUM
JUROR JURAT ASSIZER JURYMAN
CENTUMVIR

JURY ARRAY PANEL QUEST ASSIZE
JURATA COUNTRY EMPANEL
INQUEST
(— COUNTY) VISNE
JURYMAN DICAST JURIST ASSIZER
JURY-RIGGED HAYWIRE
JUST ALL DUE EVEN FAIR FLOP LEAL
MERE ONLY TRUE EQUAL FIRST
LEVEL NOBUT ROUND VALID
ZADOC CANDID GIUSTO HONEST
JUSTIN JUSTUS MERELY SQUARE
EQUABLE LEESOME MERITED
UPRIGHT ACCURATE LIEFSOME
RATIONAL RIGHTFUL SKILLFUL
UNBIASED
(— AS) AFTER
(— HOVE CLEAR) ATRIP
(— IN TIME) SONICA
(ONLY —) HARDLY SCARCELY
JUSTAUCORPS JUSTICO
JUSTICE LAW DOOM RIGHT SKILL
DHARMA EQUITY REASON
HONESTY SHALLOW SILENCE
DEEMSTER JUDGMENT JUSTITIA
JUSTNESS RECORDER
(— OF PEACE) BEAK SQUIRE
(AUTHOR OF —) GALSWORTHY
(CHARACTER IN —) HOW RUTH
DAVIS FROME JAMES FALDER
WALTER CLEAVER COKESON
WILLIAM HONEYWILL
(RETRIBUTIVE —) NEMESIS
(PREF.) DICAEO
JUSTIFIABLY FAIRLY
JUSTIFICATION CALL COLOR
EXCUSE APOLOGY DEFENCE
WARRANT APOLOGIA
JUSTIFIED FAIR JUST
JUSTIFY AVOW CLEAR PROVE
SALVE DEFEND EXCUSE HONEST
DERAIGN EXPLAIN RECTIFY
SUPPORT WARRANT DARRAIGN
MAINTAIN SANCTION UNDERPIN
VINDICATE
JUST-IN-TIME KANBAN
JUSTLY WELL TRULY EVENLY
FAIRLY EQUALLY HANDILY
SQUARELY
JUSTNESS SQUARE FITNESS
JUSTICE ACCURACY
JUSTUS JESUS
JUT HANG BULGE JETTY JUTTY
BEETLE EXTEND IMPEND EXTRUDE
JUTE PAT DESI PAUT DAISEE
ARAMINA CHINGMA
JUTTING HANGING
JUVENILE TEEN YOUNG JEJUNE
PUERILE YOUTHFUL
JUXTAPOSED ADJACENT
JUXTAPOSITION BALANCE
CONTACT CONTRAST NEARNESS

K

K KA KAY KILO KING
KAABA CAABA ALCAABA
KABAYA BADJU CABIE
KABELJOU KOB
KABISTAN KUBA
KABOB KEBOB SHASLIK
KABUKALLI CUPIUBA
KACHA (FATHER OF —) BRIHASPATI
KACHARI BODO
KACHIN SINGFO SINGPO CHINGPAW
KADAGA COORG
KADAMBARI (FATHER OF —)
  CHITRARATHA
  (MOTHER OF —) MADIRA
KAFFIR KATI XOSA FINGO TEMBU
  CAFFRE INFIDEL TAMBUKI WAIGULI
  (— BOY) UMFAAN
KAGU GRUIFORM
KAHODA (SON OF —) ASHTAVAKRA
KAIKAWAKA CEDAR
KAIKAWUS (FATHER OF —)
  KAIQUBAD
  (WIFE OF —) SAUDABAH
KAIKEYI (HUSBAND OF —)
  DASHARATHA
  (SON OF —) BHARATA
KAIKHUSRAU (FATHER OF —)
  SYAWAUSH
  (MOTHER OF —) FARANGIS
KAINGIN SWIDDEN
KAKI TRIUMPH
KAKU (GRANDFATHER OF —) ZOHAK
  (SLAYER OF —) MINUCHIHR
KALAPOOIAN LAKMIUT
KALE COLE KAIL COLLARD SPROUTS
  BORECOLE
KALEVALA (AUTHOR OF —)
  UNKNOWN
  (CHARACTER IN —) KULLERVO
  ILMARINEN VAINAMOINEN
  LEMMINKAINEN
KALI (HUSBAND OF —) SIVA SHIVA
KALMASHAPADA (FATHER OF —)
  SUDASA
KALMUCK ELEUT UIRAD KHOSHOT
KALPA EON AEON
KALUMPIT ANAGEP
KAMA (DAUGHTER OF —) TRISHA
  (FATHER OF —) DHARMA
  (MOTHER OF —) LAKSHMI
  SHRADDHA
  (SON OF —) ANIRUDDHA
  (WIFE OF —) RATI PRITI
KAMAHI BIRCH TOWAI
KAMALA WURRUS ROTTLERA
KAME AS ESKAR ESKER
KAMICHI SCREAMER
KAMPUCHEA (SEE CAMBODIA)
KANA IROFA IROHA
KANGAROO ROO EURO BILBI
  FLIER FLYER TUNGO BOOMER
  FOSTER WOILIE DIDELPH
  POTOROO WALLABY BETTONGA

BOONGARY FILANDER FORESTER
  WALLAROO
  (FEMALE —) DOE GIN
  (YOUNG —) JOEY
KANGAROO APPLE GUNYANG
  POROPORO
KANGAROO RAT JERBOA
  BETTONG POTOROO
KANHOBAL CONOB
KANKANAI IGOROT
KANS KUSA GLAGA KUSHA GLAGAH
KANSA (FATHER OF —) UGRASENA
  (SLAYER OF —) KRISHNA
KANSAN JAYHAWK

KANSAS
CAPITAL: TOPEKA
COLLEGE: BAKER TABOR BETHANY
  STERLING WASHBURN
COUNTY: ELK GOVE LINN LYON
  NESS RENO GEARY PRATT ROOKS
  TREGO BARTON COFFEY NEMAHA
  NEOSHO BOURBON LABETTE
  ATCHISON
FORT: RILEY SCOTT
INDIAN: KANSA KIOWA PAWNEE
  WICHITA COMANCHE
LAKE: CHENEY KIRWIN NEOSHO
  MILFORD
MOUNTAIN: SUNFLOWER
NATIVE: JAYHAWK
NICKNAME: JAYHAWKER
  SUNFLOWER
PRESIDENT: EISENHOWER
RIVER: SALINE SOLOMON
  ARKANSAS MISSOURI
STATE BIRD: MEADOWLARK
STATE FLOWER: SUNFLOWER
STATE TREE: COTTONWOOD
TOWN: ALMA GOVE HAYS IOLA
  COLBY DODGE HOXIE LAKIN
  LEOTI SEDAN LARNED SALINA
  ABILENE CHANUTE LIBERAL
  ULYSSES WICHITA

KAOLIANG SORGHUM
KAOLIN PIPECLAY
KAPOK CEIBO FLOSS
KARAISM ANANISM
KARAKA KOPI
KARA KIRGHIZ BURUT BOUROUT
KARATAS PITA
KARATE (— SCHOOL) DOJO
  (EXPERT LEVEL IN —) DAN
  (EXPERT LEVEL OF —) DAN
  (KOREAN —) TAEQUONDU
KAREN SGAU SGAW
KARENNI PADAUNG
KARMA FATE
  (BAD —) DEMERIT
KARNA (FATHER OF —) SURYA
  (MOTHER OF —) KUNTI PRITHA
  (SLAYER OF —) ARJUNA

KARTTIKEYA (FATHER OF —) RUDRA
  SHIVA
KASKA NAHANE
KAT KHAT QUAT CAFTA
KATE KAI
KATHERINE (HUSBAND OF —)
  PETRUCHIO
KAUNAS KOVNO
KAURI COWRIE BERAIROU
KAUSHALYA (HUSBAND OF —)
  DASHARATHA
  (SON OF —) RAMA
KAVA AVA AWA YAQONA KAVAKAVA
  YANGGONA
KAW AKHA
KAYANUSH (BROTHER OF —)
  FARIDUN PURMAYAH

KAZAKHSTAN (ALSO SEE RUSSIA)
CAPITAL: ALMATY ALMAATA
COIN: RUBLE
DESERT: BARSUKI KARAKUM
  KYZYLKUM
LAKE: ALAKOL TENGIZ ZAYSAN
  BALKHASH SILETITENIZ
  SELETYTENGIZ
LANGUAGE: KAZAKH KIPCHAK
  QIPCHAQ
MOUNTAIN: KHANTENGRI
MOUNTAIN RANGE: ALTAI ULUTAU
  TIENSHAN CHINGIZTAU
  DZUNGARIAN TARBAGATAY
NAME: KAZAK KAZAKH
PENINSULA: MANGYSHLAK
PLATEAU: USTYURT
RIVER: URAL YAIK ISHIM TOBOL
  IRTYSH SYRDARYA
SEA: ARAL CASPIAN
TOWN: OMSK YAIK RUDNY URALSK
  ALMAATA TROITSK CHIMKENT
  ORENBURG KARAGANDA
  QARAGHANDY PETROPAVLOVSK
  SEMIPALATINSK
VALLEY: FERGANA

KAZOO BAZOO GAZOO ZARAH
  HEWGAG MIRLITON
KEEL FIN BACK SEEL BARGE CARINA
  CRISTA RADDLE SERRULA
  (— OF BIRD'S MANDIBLE) GONYS
  (AFTERPART OF —) SKAG SKEG
  (PREF.) CARINI
KEELBILL ANI
KEELBIRD ANI
KEEN DRY FLY GAY SHY YAP ACID
  DEAR FINE GAIR GLEG HIGH HOWL
  NUTS PERT TART TEEN WAIL
  WARM WILD ACUTE ALERT BREME
  BRIEF BRISK EAGER QUICK SHARP
  SMART SNELL SPICY VIVID ARGUTE
  ASTUTE BITTER CAOINE GREEDY
  LIVELY SEVERE SHREWD SHRILL
  CUNNING HAWKING MORDANT

PARLISH PARLOUS PUNGENT
  SERIOUS THIRSTY OBSERVANT
  SAGACIOUS TRENCHANT
  PERSPICACIOUS
  (PREF.) OXY
KEENER HOWLER
KEENLY KEEN FELLY DEARLY
  ACUTELY
KEENNESS EDGE ACUITY ACUMEN
  PUNGENCY
  (— OF SIGHT) ACIES
KEEN-SCENTED NASUTE
  NOSEWISE
KEEN-SIGHTED EAGLE
KEEP HUG HAVE HOLD SALT SAVE
  STOW WAIT WITE BLESS ROCCA
  WITIE COFFER DETAIN REDUIT
  CONFINE CONTAIN DEFORCE
  HUSBAND KEEPING OBSERVE
  RESERVE WARRANT CONSERVE
  MAINTAIN PRESERVE RESTRAIN
  WITHHOLD
  (— ABREAST) FOLLOW
  (— A COURSE) CAPE
  (— AFLOAT) BUOY
  (— AN EYE ON) STAG
  (— APART) DOTTLE ISOLATE
  SEPARATE
  (— A SMALL SHOP) CRAME
  (— ASUNDER) PART
  (— AT A DISTANCE) ESTRANGE
  (— AWAY) ABSENT
  (— AWAY FROM) ABHOR AVOID
  (— A WOUND OPEN) TENT
  (— BACK) DAM HAP ROB STAY
  ARREAR DETAIN RETARD RESERVE
  (— COMPANY WITH) GANG MOOP
  CONSORT
  (— FOR SALE) STOCK
  (— FREE) ESCHEW
  (— FROM BOILING OVER) KEEL
  (— FROM BURNING) REDD
  (— GUARD) SENTINEL
  (— HIDDEN) HOARD SECRETE
  (— IN) CAGE
  (— IN CIRCULATION) WIND
  (— IN EXCITEMENT) ALARM
  ALARUM
  (— IN MIND) RETAIN
  (— IN ORDER) TARGE
  (— IN STOCK) CARRY
  (— IN THE TRACK) GATHER
  (— OFF) FEND WEAR EXPEL FENCE
  SHIELD
  (— OUT) BAR EXPEL
  (— POSSESSION) HARBOR
  (— SCORELESS) BLANK
  (— SECRET) HUSH WHIST
  (— STRAIGHT) DIRECT
  (— TABS ON) FINGER
  (— TIME) GO
  (— TOGETHER) WHIP
  (— TO ONESELF) BOSOM

(— UNTIL YEAR OLD) HOG
(— UP) SUBSIST SUSTAIN CONTINUE
(— WAITING) DELAY
(— WARM) STIVE STOVE FOSTER
(— WATCH) BARK TOUT WAIT
BEWAKE
(PREF.) SOZ(O)
(— OFF) ALEXI
KEEPER NAB KEEP SCREW TUTOR
YEMER CUSTOS GAOLER JAILER
LIFTER LOOKER PARKER PASTOR
RAHDAR RANGER WARDEN BAILIFF
CURATOR GEARMAN PIKEMAN
PROVOST BEARWARD DEERHERD
DOLLYMAN ELDERMAN FEWTERER
GUARDANT GUARDIAN
HOUNDMAN TRAITEUR WARRENER
(— OF CATTLE) HAYWARD
(— OF DOGS) FEWTERER
(— OF ELEPHANT) MAHOUT
(— OF INN) PUBLICAN
(— OF LOCK) NAB
(— OF PRISON) GAOLER JAILER
WARDEN ALCAIDE PROVOST
(DOOR —) DURWAN
KEEPING CARE WARD TRUST
CHARGE CUSTODY STORAGE
DETAINER
KEEPSAKE DRURY TOKEN
GIFTBOOK SOUVENIR
KEEVE TUB VAT KIEVE
KEG CAG PIN TUB CADE CASK KNAG
WOOD ANKER BARRICO COSTREL
KELOID SCAR
KELP KILP LEAG VAREC WRACK
GIRDLE SEAWEED BELLWARE
KELPIE NIX BARB
KELT SLAT LIGGER
KENAF DA GOMBO MESTA AMBARI
KANAFF PAPOULA STOKROOS
KENILWORTH (AUTHOR OF —)
SCOTT
(CHARACTER IN —) AMY HUGH
TONY GILES JANET SMITH ALASCO
DICKIE DUDLEY EDMUND FOSTER
SLUDGE SUSSEX VARNEY WALTER
GOSLING MICHAEL RALEIGH
RICHARD ROBSART WAYLAND
DOBOOBIE ELIZABETH LAMBOURNE
LEICESTER TRESSILIAN
FLIBBERTIGIBBET
KENNEL STALL VENERY VENISON
DOGHOUSE
KENO HOUSE
KENTISH (— UNIT) YOKE

KENTUCKY
CAPITAL: FRANKFORT
COLLEGE: BEREA ASBURY CENTRE
BRESCIA URSULINE
COUNTY: BATH BELL BOYD HART
TODD ADAIR BOYLE TRIGG WOLFE
ESTILL MENIFEE MAGOFFIN
INDIAN: SHAWNEE CHEROKEE
IROQUOIS
LAKE: CUMBERLAND
RIVER: DIX OHIO SALT BARREN
STATE BIRD: CARDINAL
STATE FLOWER: GOLDENROD
STATE NICKNAME: BLUEGRASS
STATE TREE: TULIP
TOWN: INEZ BEREA CADIZ DIXON
HYDEN MCKEE PARIS CORBIN
HARLAN HAZARD GLASGOW
GREENUP PADUCAH DANVILLE
COVINGTON LEXINGTON
OWENSBORO

KENYA
BAY: FORMOSA
CAPITAL: NAIROBI
COIN: SHILLING
LAKE: MAGADI RUDOLF NAIVASHA
VICTORIA
LANGUAGE: LUO KIKUYU SWAHILI
MEASURE: WARI
MOUNTAIN: ELGON KENYA KULAL
NYIRU MATIAN LOGONOT
PEOPLE: LUO MERU BANTU KAMBA
KISII LUHYA MASAI NANDI KIKUYU
OGADEN BALUHYA HAMITIC
HILOTIC TURKANA KIPSIGIS
RIVER: LAK ATHI TANA KEIRO
TURKWELL
TOWN: MERU KITUI NAROK KIPINI
KISUMU MOYALE NAKURU
NAYUKI ELDORET MALINDI
MOMBASA

KERATIN HORN
KERCHIEF CURCH DORAG ROMAL
RUMAL ANALAV CYPRUS MADRAS
NAPKIN PEPLUM CYPRESS
KERCHER PANUELO THERESE
BABUSHKA BANDANNA HEADRAIL
KAFFIYEH KINGSMAN
KERESAPA (BROTHER OF —)
URVAKHSHAYA
(FATHER OF —) THRITA
KERF CARF SKAFF GROOVE
UNDERCUT
KERI QRI KERE
KERMANSHAH COCONUT
KERMES GRAIN
KERNEL NUT BUNT CORE KERN
MEAT PITH BERRY GOODY GROAT
ACINUS ALMOND CARNEL PICKLE
NUCLEUS PICHURIM
(CORN —S) HOMINY
(UNHUSKED —S) CAPES
(PL.) NIXTAMAL
(PREF.) CARY(O) KARY(O)
KEROGEN SAPROPEL
KEROSINE PARAFFIN
KERSENNEH ERS ERVIL
KERSEY WASHER ORDINARY
KESTREL FANNER KEELIE STANIEL
STANNEL STANYEL STANCHEL
WINDHOVER
KETA CHUM
KETCH SAIC
KETONE IRONE ACETOL ARMONE
CARONE CARVOL COTOIN HEXONE
IONONE QUINOL ACETOIN
ACETONE ACYLOIN BENZOIN
CAMPHOR CARVONE DYPNONE
FLAVONE JASMONE MUSCONE
PHORONE SHOGAOL THUJONE
ACRIDONE ANTHRONE BAECKEOL
BUTANONE BUTYRONE CHALCONE
CHALKONE CHROMONE DEGUELIN
EXALIONE FENCHONE MENTHONE
PROPIONE PULEGONE ROTENONE
STEARONE TAGETONE THIENONE
VALERONE XANTHONE

KETTLE LEAD STEW DIXIE BOILER
CANNER FESSEL MARMIT MASLIN
TRIPOD VESSEL CALDRON SKILLET
STEWPOT CALABASH FLAMBEAU
KETTLEDRUM NAKER ATABAL
KETTLE TIMBAL TYMBAL TIMBALE
TYMPANY
KEVEL CAVEL HAMMER KNAPPER
KEWPIE DOLL
KEX KECKSY
KEY CAY KAY CLEW CLUE CRIB FLAT
ISLE JACK KING NOTE PLUG PONY
BASAL DITAL INDEX SCREW TASTO
WREST BUTTON CHIAVE CIPHER
CLAVIS COTTER OPENER SAMARA
SPLINE WINDER DIGITAL LANGUET
PASSKEY SPEAKER LATCHKEY
TONALITY
(— FOR TUNING HARP) WREST
(— OF KEYBOARD INSTRUMENT)
CHIP MANUAL
(— OF LIFE) ANKH
(— OF ORGAN) TASTO DIGITAL
(— OF PIANO) IVORY NATURAL
(— OF SPINET) CHIP
(— ON WOODWIND INSTRUMENT)
LANGUET SPEAKER
(—S OF CARILLON) CLAVECIN
(— UP) STRING
(ARITHMETICAL —) ADDITIVE
(ASH —) PIGEON
(FALSE —) GLUT
(FEATHER —) FIN STOP SPLINE
FEATHER
(KIND OF —) CHURCH
(PART OF —) BOW BLADE WARDING
SHOULDER SERRATION
(SKELETON —) GILT TWIRLER
(TELEGRAPH —) BUG TAPPER
(WHITE —) NATURAL
(PREF.) CLAVI CLEID(O) CLEIST(O)
(SUFF.) CLEISIS CLISIS
KEYBOARD MANUAL CELESTA
CELESTE CLAVIER PEDALIER
(PRACTICE —) DUMBPIANO
(TYPEWRITER —) QWERTY
(PREF.) CLAVI
KEY-DESK CONSOLE
KEYHOLE KEY SLOT LOCKHOLE
KEYNOTE A B D E KEY MESE TONIC
FINALIS
KEYSTONE KEY QUOIN VERTEX
SAGITTA VOUSSOIR
(— STATE) PENNSYLVANIA
KEYWAY SPLINE KEYSLOT
KEZIA (FATHER OF —) JOB
KHA KA KHMU KACHE LAMET
KHALAT SEERPAW
KHAN CAN CHAM HAWN SERAI
TACON CHAGAN KHAKAN
KHAS-KURA NEPALI PAHARI
PARBATI GORKHALI
KHATTISH HATTIC
KHEDIVE QUITEVE
KHELLIN VISAMMIN
KHOTANA KOYUKON
KHUSKHUS CUSCUS VETIVER
KIANG ONAGER CHIGETAI
HEMIONUS
KIBBLE GIG KETTLE
KIBBLER CRACKER
KICK BOOT FICK FLEG FLIG FOOT
FUNK HEEL HOOF LASH PORR

POTE PUNT RUSH SHIN TRIP TURF
YERK ANGLE BUNCH FLING KEVEL
PAUSE PUNCH SCENE SKELP
SPANG SPURN CHARGE CORNER
FITTER KICKER KICKUP OBJECT
SPIRAL VOLLEY DROPOUT
FOUETTE KICKOFF DROPKICK
PLACEKICK
(— ABOUT) SPARTLE
(— AS A HORSE) FLING WINCE
(— AT GOAL) SHOOT
(— HEELS UP) SPURN
(— IN) ANTEUP
(— ON SHINS) HACK SHINNER
(— OUT) SPUR
(— OVER) CATCH
(BALLET —) BRUSH
(KIND OF —) SQUIB
(SOCCER —) CORNER
(SWIMMING —) THRASH
KICKBACK RECOIL
KICKER TEDDER WINCER
KICKOFF (BEFORE —) PREGAME
KICKSHAW TIDBIT TITBIT
KID COD FUN POD RIB TUB FAWN
FOOL GOAT JIVE JOKE JOSH
CHAFF CHILD FAGOT HORSE JOLLY
KIDDY SPOOF TEASE KIDLET
SQUIRT DECEIVE EANLING FATLING
TICCHEN YOUNGER CHEVEREL
YEANLING
(UNDRESSED —) SUEDE
(WHIZ —) BRAIN GENIUS EINSTEIN
KIDDING JOKE SPOOFERY
KIDNAP STEAL ABDUCT HIJACK
PANYAR SPIRIT
KIDNAPER PLAGIARY SNATCHER
SPIRITER
KIDNAPING SNATCH PLAGIUM
PLAGIARY
KIDNAPPED (AUTHOR OF —)
STEVENSON
(CHARACTER IN —) ALAN BRECK
COLIN DAVID RIACH SHUAN
BALFOUR RANSOME CAMPBELL
EBENEZER HOSEASON RANKEILLOR
KIDNEY NEAR NEER REIN TYPE
CLASS NEPHRON
(PL.) REINS ROGNONS
(PREF.) NEPHR(O) RENI RENO
(SUFF.) NEPHRITIS NEPHROSIS
KIDNEY BEAN FRIJOLE
(PL.) FASELS
KIER KEEVE PUFFER
KIESELGUHR DOPE GUHR
KILL DO BAG END GET ICE MOW OFF
OUT PIP ZAP BANE BOLO COOK
COOL DOIN DOWN FELL MORT
NECK SLAY TAME WING BLAST
BRAIN CROAK CULLE FETCH
FORDO GANCH MISDO NAPOO
QUELL SABER SCRAG SHOOT
SMITE SNUFF SPEED SPEND SPILL
SPOIL STALL STICK SWELT SWORD
WASTE CORPSE DEADEN DIDDLE
FAMISH FINISH HANDLE IMPALE
MARTYR MURDER POISON
RUBOUT STARVE UNLIVE ACHIEVE
BUTCHER DESTROY EXECUTE
FLATTEN HATCHET KILLING
MORTIFY SMOTHER STONKER
SUICIDE DEATHIFY DISPATCH

DISSOLVE IMMOLATE JUGULATE
STILETTO
(— ANIMALS) CONTROL
(— BY STONING) LAPIDATE
(— BY SUBMERSION) STIFLE
(— CALF AFTER BIRTH) DEACON
(— CATTLE) PITH
(— EVERY TENTH) DECIMATE
(— GAME) SATCHEL
(— OFF) ENECATE
(— SMALL GAME) BARK
(— TIME) GOOF
(— WITH GRENADE) FRAG
(DELIBERATELY —) FRAG
KILLDEER PLOVER KILLDEE
DEERKILL
KILLED KILT WINGED SKITTLED
(FRESHLY —) GREEN
KILLER GUN BRAVO GUNMAN
SLAYER TORPEDO MURDERER
THRESHER
(SUFF.) CIDAL CIDE
KILLER WHALE ORCA DOLPHIN
GRAMPUS
KILLIFISH KELLY KILLY MINNOW
COBBLER GUDGEON MAYFISH
MUDFISH PANCHAX FUNDULUS
ROCKFISH SACALAIT STUDFISH
SWAMPINE MUMMICHOG
KILLING FELL KILL MORT QUELL
TUANT MURDER CLEANUP
HANGING CLEANING DISPATCH
FELICIDE HOMICIDE
MANSLAUGHTER
(MERCY —) EUTHANASIA
KILLJOY NARK GLOOM LEMON
GRINCH SOURPUSS
KILN BING KEEL LEHR OAST CULLE
DRIER GLAZE STOVE TILER COCKLE
CUPOLA TILERY FURNACE
CALCINER LIMEKILN
KILOGRAM (— OF MARIJUANA) KEY
(— OF MARIJUANA OR HEROIN)
KEY
(— OF NARCOTIC) KEY
(907 —S) NETTON
KILOMETER LI CLICK KLICK
KILORAD KRAD
KILOWATT-HOUR KELVIN
KILT QUELT PIUPIU FILIBEG PHILIBEG
PETTICOAT
KILTER SKEET
KIM (AUTHOR OF —) KIPLING
(CHARACTER IN —) ALI KIM OHARA
ARTHUR HURREE LURGAN MAHBUB
BENNETT KIMBALL CREIGHTON
MOOKERJEE
KIN SIB KATI KITH CATTY CUNNE
FLESH FAMILY AFFINITY RELATION
KIND ILK KIN LOT BOON CAST FAIR
FORM GOOD HAIR HEND LIKE
MAKE MEEK MILD MODE MOLD
NICE RATE SELY SOFT SORT SUIT
TRIM TYPE WING BREED BROOD
CLASS GENRE GENUS GESTE
ORDER SPICE STAMP BENIGN
BLITHE FACILE GENDER GENTLE
GOODLY HUMANE KIDNEY KINDLY
MANNER MISTER NATURE SPEECE
STRAIN STRIPE TENDER CLEMENT
EDITION FASHION FEATHER
FLESHLY LENIENT QUALITY
REGIMEN SPECIAL SPECIES

SPECKLE FRIENDLY GENEROUS
MANSUETE OBLIGING BENIGNANT
INDULGENT OFFICIOUS
PERSUASION
(— OF) A
(— OF PEOPLE) FOLK
(DIFFERENT IN —) DIVERS
(DISTINCTIVE —) BRAND
(OF EVERY —) ALKIN
(PREF.) GEN(O)
KINDLE BEET BLOW FIRE LUNT
MOVE TAKE TEND TIND FLAME
LIGHT QUICK SPARK SPUNK
ACCEND ALIGHT DECOCT ENFIRE
EXCITE IGNITE ILLUME EMBLAZE
ESPRISE INCENSE INFLAME
SOLICIT KINDLING
KINDLINESS CANDOR
KINDLING FIRE BAVIN FAGOT TWIGS
TINDER IGNITION
KINDLY FAIR GAIN KIND NESH
AGREE COUTH HENDE NAISH
BENIGN BLITHE COUTHY GENIAL
HOMELY AMIABLE BENEFIC
INNERLY FAVOROUS GENEROUS
GRACIOUS QUEMEFUL TOWARDLY
KINDNESS LOVE ALOHA FAVOR
BOUNTY CANDOR LENITY BENEFIT
SERVICE CLEMENCY EASINESS
GOODNESS HUMANITY LENITUDE
MILDNESS
KIND OF
(SUFF.) EE
KINDRED KIN SIB KIND KITH BLOOD
FLESH HOUSE FAMILY KOBONG
NATION STRIND COGNATE KINFOLK
KINSMEN RELATED SIBSHIP
AFFINITY COGNATION CONGENIAL
CONGENEROUS
KINE KYE COWS CATTLE
KINETIC ACTUAL
(— POTENTIAL) L
KING RI SO ASA BAN DAM LOT LUD
PUL REX REY RIG ROY AGAG AMON
ATLI BALI BELI BIJA BORS BRAN
BRES CRAL CZAR JEHU KRAL LEIR
MARK NUDD NUMA OMRI OTTO
PHUL RAJA RIAL SIRE TSAR TZAR
WANG YIMA ARDRI BALOR BELUS
CONOR CREON DAGDA DAHAK
EGLON ETZEL GYGES HEROD
HIRAM HOGNI HOSEA IPHIS IXION
JOASH LAIUS LLUDD LYCUS
MESHA MIDAS MINOS NADAB
NEGUS NORSE NUADA PEKAH
PRIAM RAJAH SAMMY SWAMI
ZIMRI ZOHAK AEOLUS AGENOR
AILILL ALARIC ALBOIN ALONSO
ALOROS ARIOCH BLADUD CODRUS
DIOMED DUNCAN ELATHA FINGAL
FRODHI FROTHI GOEMOT INKOSI
KABAKA LEMUEL LYCAON
MEMNON MINYAS NESTOR
NODONS OENEUS OGYGES PELEUS
PELIAS SAUGHT SHESHA SVAMIN
TEUCER URIENS UZZIAH VASUKI
ADMETUS AHAZIAH AMAIMON
AMYCLAS ANGEVIN ARDRIGH
ARTEGAL ATHAMAS BAGINDA
BELINUS BUSIRIS CACIQUE
CEPHEUS CROESUS ELIDURE
EPAPHUS EPOPEUS ETHBAAL
EURYTUS GUNTHER HYGELAC

INACHUS JAMSHID JEHOASH
JEHORAM KINGLET LAERTES
LATINUS LEONTES MENAHEM
MONARCH PANDION PHINEUS
POLYBUS REGULUS ROMULUS
ROYALET SMERDIS SOLOMON
VOLSUNG ACRISIUS ADRASTUS
AEGYPTUS ALBERICH AMRAPHEL
ASNAPPER BAHMANID BRENNIUS
CLAUDIUS COPHETUA ELDORADO
ETEOCLES ETHELRED GILGAMES
GOEMAGOT GOGMAGOG
GORBODUC HEZEKIAH HROTHGAR
JEHOAHAZ JEROBOAM KINGLING
LAOMEDON LISUARTE MANASSEH
MELIADUS MENELAUS ODYSSEUS
ORCHAMUS OSNAPPAR OVERKING
PADISHAH PEKAHIAH PENTHEUS
RAMESSID REHOBOAM RODERICK
RODOMONT ROITELET SARPEDON
SHEPHERD SISYPHUS TANTALUS
GILGAMESH
(— AND QUEEN OF TRUMPS) BELLA
(— CHANGED TO WOLF) LYCAON
(— OF ARMS) GARTER NORROY
(— OF BEASTS) LION
(— OF DWARFS) ALBERICH
(— OF FAIRIES) OBERON
(— OF JUDAH) ASA
(— OF TRUMPS) HONOR
(— WITH 10 WIVES) HEROD
(IRISH —) RI RIG ARDRI ARDRIGH
(NEIGHBOR OF —) QUEEN BISHOP
(POLYNESIAN —) ALII ARII ARIKI
(PREF.) REGI
KING ARTHUR (MOTHER OF —)
IGRAINE
KINGBIRD PIPIRI PETCHARY
KINGBOLT KING KINGPIN MAINPIN
KING CRAB LIMULID LIMULUS
PANFISH
KINGDOM WEI ELAM REALM REIGN
WORLD ESTATE MONERA MORVEN
REGION REGNUM SAXONY
MITANNI
(ANCIENT IONIAN —) EPIRUS
KINGFISH BARB CERO HAKE HAKU
MINK OPAH TOMCOD CHENFISH
SCIAENID TOMMYCOD
KINGFISHER HALCYON PODITTI
TOROTORO
KING JOHN (AUTHOR OF —)
SHAKESPEARE
(CHARACTER IN —) JOHN BIGOT
ESSEX HENRY JAMES LEWIS MELUN
PETER ARTHUR BLANCH ELINOR
GURNEY HUBERT PHILIP ROBERT
DEBURGH LYMOGES BRETAGNE
PANDULPH PEMBROKE CHATILLON
CONSTANCE SALISBURY
FAULCONBRIDGE
KING LEAR (AUTHOR OF —)
SHAKESPEARE
(CHARACTER IN —) KENT LEAR
CURAN EDGAR REGAN ALBANY
EDMUND OSWALD GONERIL
BURGUNDY CORDELIA CORNWALL
GLOUCESTER
KINGLET REGULI
KINGLY REGAL ROYAL REGNAL
BASILIC IMPERIAL MAJESTIC
PRINCELY

KING-OF-ARMS NORROY
KING PARAKEET WELLAT
KINGPIN TOPBANANA
KING'S EVIL CRUELS CREWELS
CRUELLS
KING'S HENCHMAN, THE
(CHARACTER IN —) EADGAR
AELFRIDA AETHELWOLD
(COMPOSER OF —) TAYLOR
KINGSHIP STOOL THRONE
KINGDOM ROYALTY DEVARAJA
KINGHOOD
KING SOLOMON'S MINES
(AUTHOR OF —) HAGGARD
(CHARACTER IN —) GOOD JOHN
JOSE ALLAN HENRY KHIVA TWALA
CURTIS GAGOOL GEORGE IGNOSI
UMBOPA FOULATA SCRAGGA
INFADOOS SILVESTRE VENTVOGEL
QUATERMAIN
KING'S PEACE GRITH
KING'S ROW (AUTHOR OF —)
BELLAMANN
(CHARACTER IN —) DRAKE ELISE
JAMIE NOLAN RANDY RENEE
TOWER CASSIE GORDON LOUISE
MCHUGH PARRIS SANDOR PERDOFF
MONAGHAN CASSANDRA
WAKEFIELD
KING'S SCHOLAR TUG
KING VULTURE PAP PAPA
KININ KALLIDIN
KINK NIB SNICK BUCKLE DOGLEG
KINKLE
(— IN ROPE) GRIND
KINKAJOU POTTO HEYRAT
APOROSO
KINKING FLUTING
KINKY NAPPY ENCOMIC KINKLED
KINO BIJA BIJASAL
KINSHIP SIB BLOOD NASAB STOOL
ENATION KINDRED SIBNESS
SIBSHIP AFFINITY AGNATION
RELATION PROPINQUITY
KINSMAN KIN SIB ALLY BLOOD
AFFINE AGNATE COUSIN FRIEND
BROTHER GOTRAJA KINDRED
WINEMAY BANDHAVA RELATION
RELATIVE COLLATERAL
KINSWOMAN SISTER KINDRED
RELATIVE
KIOSK STALL STAND
KIP SKIP GRASSER KIPSKIN UPSTART
KIRGHIZ QYRGHYZ
KIRGIZ (MOUNTAIN RANGE IN —)
ALAI
KIRIBATI (CAPITAL OF —) TARAWA
BAIRIKI
(FORMER NAME OF —)
GILBERTISLANDS
(ISLAND OF —) BERU MAKIN
ABAIANG ABEMAMA NONOUTI
TABITEUEA
KIRN MELL
KISH (FATHER OF —) JEHIEL
(SON OF —) SAUL
KISMET FATE
KISS BA LIP NEB BASS BUSS PECK
PREE MOUTH POGUE SLAKE
SMACK BEKISS CARESS SALUTE
SLAVER SMOOCH SMOUCH
OSCULATE
(— OF PEACE) PAX

(— WETLY) SLOBBER
(STOLEN —) SMOORICH
KISSING LIPWORK
KIT CHIT DUFFEL KITTEN OUTFIT
POCHETTE
(LUMBERMAN'S —) TURKEY
(MESS —) CANTEEN
KITCHEN BUT GALLEY CABOOSE
CUISINE KITCHIE COOKROOM
(— CONTAINER) CANISTER
(SHIP'S —) CABOOSE
KITCHEN-GARDEN OLITORY
KITE LAP CHIL CYTE HAWK GLEDE
CHILLA DRACHE DRAGON ELANET
FALCON PREYER SENTRY MILVINE
PUDDOCK PUTTOCK FORKTAIL
HELLKITE
KITH COUSINRY
KITTEN KIT KITTY KITTLE CATLING
KITLING
KITTIWAKE GULL WAEG ANNET
KITTY PICKUP HACKLET TARROCK
TIRRLIE
KITTY CAT POT BADRANS
BAUDRONS
KIVA ESTUFA
KIWI APTERYX
(BROWN —) ROA
KLAMATH WEED AMBER
(GOATWEED)
KLANG PHONE
KLIPSPRINGER KAINSI KLIPBOK
KLONDIKE CANFIELD SOLITAIRE
KLUTZ BOOB
KNACK ART FEAT FEEL GATE GIFT
HANG CATCH QUIRK SKILL TRICK
TALENT SLEIGHT WRINKLE
INSTINCT
(— FOR DISCOVERY) NOSE
KNACKER CLAPPER
(PL.) BONES
KNAPSACK WALLET MOCHILA
MUSETTE SNAPBAG SNAPSACK
KNAPWEED SWEEP BLUETOP
FLATTOP BALLWEED BELLWEED
BOLEWEED BULLWEED
BUNDWEED CENTAURY
CLUBWEED CROPWEED
HARDHEAD IRONHEAD IRONWEED
KNOTWEED MATFELON
KNAVE BOY ELF LAD NOB PAM PUR
TOM JACK BOWER CHEAT DROLE
MAKER NODDY ROGUE TIGER
VIPER COQUIN FRIPON HARLOT
KNIGHT PICARO RASCAL VARLET
WENZEL CAMOOCH CUSTREL
PEASANT VILLAIN BEZONIAN
COISTREL SWINDLER VARLETTO
(— OF CLUBS) PAM
KNAVERY ROPERY CATZERIE
PATCHERY RASCALITY
KNAVISH ROGUISH SCAMPISH
KNAWEL KNOTWEED KNOTWORT
KNEAD ELT TEW MOLD POST BRAKE
STOCK PETRIE MASSAGE
(— HIDES) STOCK
KNEADING (— MACHINE) BRAKE
KNEADING-TROUGH HUTCH
KNEE GENU HOCK CROOK KNAPPER
SLEEPER SUFFRAGO
(— HOLLOW) HAM
(— OF COMPOSING STICK) SLIDE
(PREF.) GENU GONY

KNEECAP CAP ROTULA PATELLA
(PL.) MARROWBONES
KNEE-JERK AUTOMATIC
KNEEL SIT KNEE COUCH SHIKO
KOWTOW
KNEELER SPRINGER
KNEELING SHIKO BENDED
KNEEPAN ROTULA PATELLA
KNELL BELL RING TOLL KNOLL
STROKE
KNICKERBOCKERS PLUSFOURS
KNICKKNACK TOY CURIO KNACK
TRICK GEWGAW NOTION PRETTY
BIBELOT GIMCRACK TCHOTCHKE
KNICKNACK CURIO
KNIFE DAH DIE PIN SAX ULU BOLO
BUCK MOON SAEX SHIM SHIV
SNEE SPUD TANG BOWIE BURIN
CHIVE CUTTO FACON GULLY KNIVE
KUKRI PANGA SHANK SHAVE
SKEAN SLICE BARLOW BARONG
CAMPIT CARVER COLTER COUTEL
CUTTLE CUTTOE DAGGER DOCTOR
JIGGER PANADE PARANG PAVADE
PORKER PULLER RIMMER SICKLE
SLICER TREVET TRIVAT WORKER
BREAKER CATLING CHOPPER
COUTEAU FIPENNY KIOTOME
MACHETE PALETTE SCALPEL
SEVERER SKINNER SLASHER
SNICKER STICKER SUNDANG
TICKLER WHITTLE BELDUQUE
BILLHOOK CALABOZO JOCTELEG
SERPETTE THWITTLE YATAGHAN
SNICKERSNEE
(— FOR BREAKING FLAX) BEATER
(— FOR LEATHER) PIN
(— FOR RUBBER DOUGH) DOCTOR
(BLACKSMITH'S —) BUTTERIS
(BOWIE —) TOOTHPICK
(BURMESE —) DAH DAO DOW
(CURRIER'S —) CLEANER
(ENGRAVER'S —) CRADLE
(ESKIMO —) ULU
(MORO —) BARONG
(PART OF —) NEB TIP WEB BACK
EDGE HEEL HILT BLADE CHOIL
GUARD POINT RIVET FULLER
HANDLE POMMEL BOLSTER
QUILLON ROCASSO
(SHOEMAKER'S —) BUTT
(SURGICAL —) LANCET CATLING
SCALPEL BISTOURY EXSECTOR
(TANNER'S —) GRAINER
(WHALER'S —) SPADE
KNIFE-PLEATED KILTED
KNIGHT N DUB ELF SIR ADUB GANO
TULK EQUES EQUIS HORSE LANCE
RIDER THANE TOLKE CABALL
ERRANT KEMPER PENCEL RITTER
ROGERO GENILON PALADIN
YOUNKER ALMANZOR BACHELOR
BANNERET CAVALIER COLVILLE
GANELONE IRONCLAD ISENBRAS
PALMERIN RUGGIERO
(— IN CHESS) HORSE
(— OF ROUND TABLE) GAN KAY
BORS OWEN GARETH GAWAIN
MODRED CARADOC CRADOCK
GALAHAD GANELON EGLAMORE
LANCELOT PALMERIN PERCIVAL
TRISTRAM
(BOASTFUL —) KAY

(CARPET —) DAMMARET
(MERCENARY —) FREELANCE
(NEIGHBOR OF —) ROOK BISHOP
(ROMAN —) MAECENAS
KNIGHT-ERRANT KEMPER PALADIN
KNIGHTHOOD CAVALRY
KNIGHTS (AUTHOR OF —)
ARISTOPHANES
(CHARACTER IN —) CLEON DEMUS
NICIAS AGORACRITUS
DEMOSTHENES
KNIPHOFIA TRITOMA
KNIT SET BIND KNOT PLAIT PURSE
UNITE WEAVE COMPACT CONNECT
WRINKLE CONTRACT
(— STOCKINGS) SHANK
(KIND OF —) WEFT
KNITTED FLAT WOVEN
KNITTING PURL
(— OF BONES) POROSIS
KNITTING LOOP STEEK
KNITTING NEEDLE WIRE
KNOB BOB BUR NOB NUB BEAD
BOLL BOSS BURR CLUB DENT
HEAD HEEL KNOP KNOT KNUB LIFT
NODE NOOP PULL SNUG STUD
TORE BERRY BULLA BUNCH FORTE
GEMMA KNURL NATCH ONION
PLOOK PLUKE BUTTON CROCHE
EMBOSS NOBBLE NUBBLE PIMPLE
PISTON POMMEL FERRULE
HORNTIP KNOBBLE BELLPULL
DOORKNOB DRAWSTOP
OMPHALOS
(— OF HAIR) TOORIE
(— OF ROCK) BUHR BURR KNUCKLE
(— ON BILL OF SWAN) BERRY
(— ON BUTT OF CANNON) GRAPE
(— ON CHAIR) POMMEL
(— ON DEER'S ANTLER) OFFER
CROCHE
(— ON ROPE) MOUSE
(TY —) VOL
(PREF.) CONDYL(O) TYL(O)
KNOBBED NODOSE TOROSE
BULLATE TUBEROUS TYLOTATE
KNOBBY GOUTY NODAL KNOTTY
TOROSE WHELKY GOUTISH
KNOBBLY SCRAGGED
KNOCK CON DAD HIT JOW JUT POP
PUN RAP WAP BANG BASH BEAT
BUMP CALL CHAP CHOP DASH
DAUD DING DUMP DUNT HACK
JOLT JOWL KNAP NOCK NOIT PINK
PLUG POLT POSS PUSH ROUT
SLAM SLAY SNOP TANK TIRL WHAP
WHOP CLOUR CLUMP KNOIT
POUND SMITE SNOCK STAVE
STRAM THUMP BOUNCE DUNTLE
KNATCH KNETCH STOTER
CANVASS PINKING
(— ABOUT) RUMBLE
(— DOWN) MOW DROP DUMP FELL
FLOOR GRASS LEVEL SMITE SOUSE
HURTLE RAFFLE UNPILE
CLOTHESLINE
(— FOR A LOOP) FLOOR
(— OFF) SECURE
(— ON HEAD) MAZER MAZARD
(— OUT) OUT SAP CONK COOL
KAYO FLATTEN STIFFEN
(— UNCONSCIOUS) COLDCOCK

(— WITH THE HORNS) DISH
(IGNITION —) PING
KNOCKER CROW RISP HAMMER
WHACKER
(DOOR —) CROW HAMMER RAPPER
KNOCK-KNEED VARUS VALGUS
KNOCKOFF COPY
KNOCKOUT KO KAYO CRUSHER
NOBBLER
(PRETENDED —) DIVE
KNOLL NOB HIGH KNAP KNOB
KNOW TOFT HEAVE HURST HYRST
MOUND SHOAL COPPLE BOUROCK
HUMMOCK
KNOP NOB KNOB KNOSP KNAPPE
KNOT BOB BOW BUN FAG NIB NOB
NUB PIN TIE BEND BURL BURR
CHOU CLOD CLOT CLUB HARL KILL
KNAG KNAR KNOB NODE NOIL
NURL SLUG SNUB TRUE WAFT
WALL BUNCH CLOVE CROWN
DUNNE GNARL GNARR HALCH
HALSH HATCH HITCH KNURL
MOUSE NODUS NOEUD SNARL
SNICK SWIRL TWIST WARRE
BOUGHT BUTTON CLINCH CROCHE
FINIAL GRANNY MASCLE SORTIE
TANGLE BOWKNOT BOWLINE
CHIGNON COCKADE GORDIAN
MAYBIRD CICISBEO DRAWKNOT
GRAYBACK KNITTING SLIPKNOT
TRUELOVE CLOVEHITCH
SHEEPSHANK
(— IN CLOTH) FAG NEP BURL
(— IN COTTON FIBERS) NEP
(— IN SIGNAL FLAG) WAFT WEFT
WHEFT
(— IN WOOD) NUR PIN BURL BURR
KNAG KNAR KNUR NURR SNUB
GNARL KNAUR KNURL KNURR
(— IN YARN) SLUG SNICK
(— OF HAIR) BOB BUN COB PUG
CLUB KNURL CHIGNON
(— OF RIBBONS) FAVOR
(EMBROIDERY —) PICOT
(KIND OF —) LOVER LOVERS
(LOVE —) AMORET
(ORNAMENTAL —) BOW
(SHOULDER —) WING
(WALL —) WALE
(PREF.) NODI
KNOTGRASS LIGNUM HOGWEED
PIGWEED BINDWEED BIRDWEED
DOORWEED KNOTWEED
KNOTWORT PINKWEED POLYGONY
WIREWEED
KNOTTED KNIT NOUE TIED NOWED
NODOSE SWIRLY CRABBED
NODATED SCRAGGY
KNOTTY HARD CRAMP GOUTY
NODAL COMMON CRAGGY
GNARLY KNAGGY KNOBBY KNURRY
NODOSE NODOUS COMPLEX
GNARLED GOUTISH JOINTED
KNARRED KNOTTED SCABROUS
KNOTWEED LIGNUM ALLSEED
HOGWEED JUMPSEED POLYGONY
POLYGONUM
KNOW CAN CON KEN WIS WIT WOT
CITE HAVE SABE WEET WIST WOTH
SAVVY SKILL COGNIZE
(— NOT) NOOT
(—S NOT) NOTE

(DID NOT —) KENDNA
(DO NOT —) KENNA
KNOWABLE SENSABLE
KNOW-HOW CRAFT MOXIE SMART
SMARTS SAVVY SKILL
KNOWING FLY HEP HIP SLY FOXY
GASH INON ONTO SPRY WISE
AWARE CANNY DOWNY JERRY
LEERY SPACK WITTY EXPERT
SCIENT SCIOUS SHREWD WITFUL
WITTER GNOSTIC SAPIENT
WISEDUP
(— SUPERFICIALLY) SCIOLOUS
(SUFF.) GNOSIA GNOSIS GNOSTIC
GNOSY
KNOWINGLY CANNILY SCIENTER
SHREWDLY WITTERLY
KNOW-IT-ALL MAVIN SAVANT
KNOWLEDGE CAN WIT BOOK KITH
KNOW LAIR LEAR LORE NOTE
INWIT JNANA SAVVY SKILL VIDYA
ADVICE AVIDYA CLERGY GNOSIS
NOESIS NOTICE WISDOM CUNNING
DIANOIA HEARING KNOWING
MEANING SCIENCE WITTING
DAYLIGHT DOCTRINE EPISTEME
LEARNING LETTRURE NOTITION
PRUDENCE SAPIENCE SCIENTIA
COGNIZANCE
(— OF ALL THINGS) OMNISCIENCE
(— OF SPIRITUAL TRUTH) GNOSIS
(ABSOLUTE —) PANSOPHY
(EXPERT —) SKILL
(FAMILIAR —) HANG
(GENERAL —) GROUNDING
(INWARD —) INWIT
(LATER —) AFTERWIT
(MYSTERIOUS —) ARCANUM
(PIECEMEAL —) SMATTER
(PRACTICAL —) INSIGHT
(PRIVATE —) PRIVITY
(PUBLIC —) LIGHT
(SLICK —) ANGLE
(SLIGHT —) INKLING SMATTER
(SPIRITUAL —) GNOSIS
(SUPERFICIAL —) SCIOLISM
(SUPERIOR —) MASTERY
(SUPREME —) PRAJNA
(SYSTEMATIZED —) SCIENCE
(UNIVERSAL —) PANSOPHY
(PREF.) EPISTEMO GNOSIO
(SUFF.) GNOSIA GNOSIS GNOSTIC
GNOSY ICS SOPH(ER)(IC)(IST)(Y)
KNOWLEDGEABLE KNOWING
SKILLED STUDIED

KNOWN EVER COUTH COMMON
(ACTUALLY —) SPECIOUS
(ALSO — AS) AKA
(GENERALLY —) PUBLIC
(LITTLE —) FAMELESS
(NOT —) DARK SILENT
(OTHERWISE — AS) ALIAS
(PUBLICLY —) EXOTERIC
(UNMISTAKABLY —) STATED
(WIDELY —) COMMON
KNOW-NOTHING SAM
KNUCKLE KNUCK JARRET
(PREF.) CONDYL(O)
KNUCKLEBONE DIB DOLOS TALUS
COCKAL SHACKLE
KNUCKLEHEAD SAP DUMDUM
KNURL MILL NULL DWARF SNARL
KNURLING NULLING REEDING
KNULLING
KOALA BEAR BAALU BALOO SLOTH
KOOLAH WOMBAT CARBORA
PHALANGER
KOANGA (CHARACTER IN —) JOSE
PEREZ SIMON KOANGA PALMYRA
MARTINEZ
(COMPOSER OF —) DELIUS
KOBOLD NIS GNOME NISSE
HODEKEN HUTCHEN
KOEL KOIL KOKIL RAINBIRD
KOHATH (FATHER OF —) LEVI
(SISTER OF —) JOCHEBED
KOHL COHOL ALCOHOL
KOHLRABI BROMATIUM
KOKAN LAMPATIA
KOKO LEBBEK
KOKOON GNU
KOKUM GARCINIA
KOKUMIN BAN
KOLA COLA BICHY GOORANUT
KOLAIAH (SON OF —) AHAB
KOMATIC SLED
KOMATIK SLED
KOMBU KOBU KAMBOU CHAKOBU
KOMMETJE WALLOW COMITJE
KONAK YALI
KOOK NITWIT DINGBAT DINGALING
KOOKABURRA KOOKA JACKASS
KOOKY CRAZY OFFBEAT
KOPECK KAPEIKA
KORAH (FATHER OF —) ESAU IZHAR
ELIPHAZ
(MOTHER OF —) AHOLIBAMAH
KORAKAN RAGI RAGGI RAGGY
KORAN KITAB QURAN ALCORAN
(SECTION OF —) SURA SURAH

KORE DESPOINA
(FATHER OF —) IMNAH
KOREA (SEE NORTH KOREA OR
SOUTH KOREA)
KOREC MIRA
KORINA LIMBA
KOS COAN
KOSHER (NOT —) TREF
KOSIN KOUSSIN TAENNIN BRAYERIN
KOSO PANAMINT
KOULAN GOUR
KOVANSHCHINA (CHARACTER IN
—) ENNA IVAN MARFA ANDREY
DOSIFEY GOLITSYN KHOVANSKY
(COMPOSER OF —) MUSSORGSKY
KOWHAI GOAI PELU LOCUST
SOPHORA
KOWTOW KNEEL SHIKO
KOYUKON TENA KHOTANA
KRAAL CRAW MANYATTA
ZIMBABWE
KRAIT ADDER KORAIT BUNGARUM
KRATER KELEBE
KRAUNHIA WISTARIA
KREIS CIRCLE
KREUTZER SONATA (AUTHOR OF
—) TOLSTOY
(CHARACTER IN —) LIZA VASYLA
POZDNISHEF TRUKHASHEVSKY
KRIEMHILD (BROTHER OF —)
GERNOT GUNTHER GISELHER
(FATHER OF —) GIBICH
(HUSBAND OF —) ATTILA SIEGFRIED
KRIS CREASE CREESE DAGGER
KRISHNA VASUDEVA
(BROTHER OF —) BALARAMA
(FATHER OF —) VASUDEVA
(FOSTER FATHER OF —) NANDA
(FOSTER MOTHER OF —) YASHODA
(MOTHER OF —) DEVAKI
(UNCLE OF —) KANSA
KRISTIN LAVRANSDATTER
(AUTHOR OF —) UNDSET
(CHARACTER IN —) ULF IVAR GAUTE
MUNAN SIMON SKULE ERLEND
JOFRID NAAKVE AASHILD HALVARD
KRISTIN LAVRANS RAMBORG
ULVHILD BJORGULF JARDTRUD
NIKULAUS RAGNFRID ANDRESSON
BJORGULFSON IVARSDATTER
LAVRANSDATTER
KRONE CROWN CORONA
KRU KROOBOY KROOMAN
KRUMMHORN CREMONA
CROMORNE

KSHATRIYA THAKUR
KUA MAKUA MAKWA
KUBA BUSHONGO KABISTAN
KUDZU VINE KOHEMP
KUI KHONDI
KU KLUXER KLUXER KLUCKER
KLANSMAN
KUKURUKU IKPERE
KULANAPAN POMO
KUMAN POLOVTZY
KUMBUK ARJAN ARJUN
KUMMEL ALLASCH
KUMQUAT NAGAMI
KUNTI (FATHER OF —) PANDU
SHURA
(SON OF —) BHIMA KARNA ARJUNA
YUDHISHTHIRA
KURRAJONG CALOOL LACEBARK
KURUKH ORAON
KUSA DARBHA
KUSHAIAH (SON OF —) ETHAN
KUSIMANSEL MANGUE
KUTCHIN LOUCHEUX
KUWAIT (— NATIVE) ARAB
(CAPITAL OF —) ALKUWAIT
(OIL FIELD OF —) WAFRA BAHRAH
BURGAN SABRIYA MINAGISH
RAUDHATAIN
(OTHER NAME OF —) KOWEIT
KUWEIT
(TOWN OF —) MAGWA AHMADI
HAWALLI ABDULLAH FAHAHEEL
KVASS ALE BEER QUASH
KWENI GURO
KYANITE DISTHENE
KYOODLE YAP
KYPHOSIS HUMPBACK

KYRGYZSTAN (ALSO SEE RUSSIA)
CAPITAL: FRUNZE BISHKEK PISHPEK
COIN: SOM
LAKE: ISSYKKUL
MOUNTAIN: VICTORY KHANTENGRI
MOUNTAIN RANGE: ALAY KIRGIZ
ZAALAY CHATKAL FERGANA
TIENSHAN TRANSALAY
KOKSHAALTAU KUNGEYALATAU
TERSKEYALATAU
NAME: KYRGYZ KIRGHIZIA KIRGIZIYA
RIVER: CHU NARYN SYRDARYA
TOWN: OSH TOKMAK BISHKEK
KYZYLKIYA PREZHEVALSK
VALLEY: CHU TALAS FERGANA

KYURINISH LESGHIN LEZGHIAN

L

L EL LIMA FIFTY
LAADAH (FATHER OF —) SHELAH
  (GRANDFATHER OF —) JUDAH
LAADAN (FATHER OF —) GERSHOM
LAAGER LEEGTE LEAGUER
LABAN (DAUGHTER OF —) LEAH
  RACHEL
  (FATHER OF —) BETHUEL
  (SISTER OF —) REBEKAH
LABDACUS (FATHER OF —)
  POLYDORUS
  (MOTHER OF —) NYCTEIS
  (SON OF —) LAIUS
LABDANUM MYRRH
LABEL TAG BILL FILE MARK FICHE
  STAMP TALLY TITLE DIRECT
  DOCKET TICKET ENDSEAL
  LAMBEAU STICKER
  (ON SUIT OF CLOTHES) ETIQUET
LABELLUM LIP LABEL PETAL
  (PART OF —) HYPOCHIL
LABIAL ROUND
LABIATE HOREHOUND
LABIUM LIP LABRUM
LABOR ADO FAG TUG WIN CARK
  MOIL TASK TAVE TILL TOIL WORK
  BEGAR DELVE GRAFT GRIND
  HEAVE PAINS SWEAT SWINK TEAVE
  TREAD WHILE YAKKA CORVEE
  DRUDGE EFFORT HAMMER STRIVE
  BULLOCK FATIGUE MANUARY
  OFIFICE PROCURE SERVICE
  SLAVERY TRAVAIL TROUBLE
  TURMOIL BUSINESS DRUDGERY
  EXERTION GROANING INDUSTRY
  LABORAGE STRUGGLE
  (— ARDUOUSLY) BILDER
  (— HARD) THRASH THRIPPLE
  (— LEADER) DEBS
  (— UNDER) SUFFER
  (DAY'S —) DARG JOURNEY
  (DIFFICULT —) DYSTOCIA
  (EXCESSIVE —) STRAIN
  (FORCED —) BEGAR CORVEE
  (HARD —) HARD BULLWORK
  (HIRED —) TOGT
  (IMPOSED —) TASKAGE
  (MENTAL —) HEADWORK
  (ROUTINE —) SCUTWORK
  (SEVERE —) AGON
  (UNPAID —) CORVEE
LABORATORY LAB SHOP KITCHEN
  OFFICINA WORKSHOP PHYTOTRON
LABOR CAMP GULAG
LABORED HEAVY FORCED SWEATY
  STRAINED
LABORER (ALSO SEE WORKER AND
  WORKMAN) BOY BHAR ESNE HIND
  JACK JOEY MOZO PEON TOTY
  BAGDI CHURL GUASO HUNKY
  NAVVY PALLI PINER STIFF BALAHI
  BEGARI BOHUNK COALER COOLIE
  DAYMAN DILKER DOCKER FELLAH

FLUNKY FOGGER HEAVER
HODMAN HOLEYA JIBARO LUMPER
RAFTER TASKER WAYMAN
WORKER BRACERO BYWONER
CREWMAN DAYSMAN DIGGORY
DIRGLER DRAINER DVORNIK
GRECIAN HARDHAT HOBBLER
MANUARY MAZDOOR PICKMAN
PIONEER PIPEMAN PLOWMAN
SANDHOG SCOURER SHIPPER
SMASHER SOUGHER SPALLER
STOCKER SWINKER TOTYMAN
WORKMAN BIJWONER CHAINMAN
COTTAGER DOLLYMAN
FARMHAND FLOORMAN
GANGSMAN HOLDSMAN
SPADEMAN SPALPEEN STRAPPER
TIDESMAN ROUSTABOUT
(DOCK —) SEAGULL
(INEXPERIENCED —) GREENER
(LOWLY —) GRUNT
LABORIOUS HARD HEAVY STIFF
  TOUGH SWEATY UPHILL ARDUOUS
  OPEROSE SLAVISH TOILFUL
  DILIGENT LABOROUS TOILSOME
LABRADOR TEA LEDUM GOWIDDIE
LABRYS AX AXE
LABURNUM AWBER
LABYRINTH MAZE CIRCUIT
  MEANDER
LABYRINTHINE TORTUOUS
  BYZANTINE
LAC LACCA LACQUER
LACE VAL BEAT BEST FOND GOTA
  LASH PEAK FILET LACIS LIVEN
  ORRIS POINT SCREW SPRIG
  WEAVE BLONDE CADDIS CORDON
  DEFEAT EDGING GRILLE LACING
  LASHER THRASH TUCKER VENISE
  ALENCON ALLOVER BULLION
  CURRAGH CUTWORK FOOTING
  GALLOON GUIPURE HONITON
  LATCHET MACRAME MALINES
  MECHLIN MELANGE NANDUTI
  TAMBOUR TATTING TORCHON
  TROLLEY ARGENTAN BOBBINET
  BONEWORK BOOTLACE BRUSSELS
  DENTELLE ILLUSION LACEWORK
  LIMERICK PEARLING STAYLACE
  COLBERTINE NEEDLEPOINT
  (— EDGING) PUNTILLA
  (— IN PLACE OF COLLAR) RUCHE
  (— MAKER) TWISTHAND
  (— PATTERN) TOILE
  (KIND OF —) CLUNY
  (KNOTTED —) TATTING
LACEBARK LAGETTO DAGUILLA
  LACEWOOD
LACE BUG TINGITID
LACEDAEMON (DAUGHTER OF —)
  CLEODICE
  (FATHER OF —) ZEUS JUPITER
  (MOTHER OF —) TAYGETE

  (SON OF —) HIMERUS
  (WIFE OF —) SPARTA
LACERATE REND TEAR GANCH
  ENGORE HARROW MANGLE
  SCARIFY FRACTURE
LACERATION RIP TEAR WOUND
LACERTA LIZARD
LACEWING NEUROPTERAN
LACEWOOD SYCAMORE
LACEWORK DENTELLE
LACHRYMOSE SAD TEARY WEEPY
  MAUDLIN
LACINARIA LIATRIS
LACING LACET LINGEL ECHELLE
  LANGUET
  (RAWHIDE —S) BABICHE
LACINIATION DAG
LACK FAIL LANK LIKE LOSS MAIM
  MISS NEED VOID WANE WANT
  FAULT MINUS DEARTH DEFECT
  INLAIR ABSENCE BLEMISH
  DEFAULT FAILURE PAUCITY
  REQUIRE VACANCY SCARCITY
  SOLITUDE WANTROKE
  (— CONFIDENCE) DOUBT
  (— FAITH) DIFFIDE
  (— HARMONY) DISAGREE
  (— OF APPETITE) ANOREXIA
  (— OF CLARITY) DARKNESS
  (— OF CONFIDENCE) MISTRUST
  (— OF COORDINATION) ASYNERGY
  DYSERGIA
  (— OF DEVELOPMENT) AGENESIS
  (— OF EARNESTNESS) ITEMING
  (— OF EFFUSIVENESS) RESERVE
  (— OF EMOTION) APATHY
  (— OF ENERGY) ATONY ANERGY
  ATONIA
  (— OF FLAVOR) SILENCE
  (— OF FORESIGHT) MYOPIA
  (— OF HARMONY) DISCORD
  DISUNITY
  (— OF INTENTION) ACCIDENT
  (— OF INVOLVEMENT) DISTANCE
  (— OF ORDER) ATAXY ATAXIA
  DISARRAY
  (— OF PATRIOTISM) INCIVISM
  (— OF REFINEMENT) CRUDITY
  (— OF SENSE) FOLLY
  (— OF SENSE OF SMELL) ANOSMIA
  (— OF STEADINESS) LEVITY
  (— OF SYMPATHY) DYSPATHY
  (— OF VIGOR) LANGUOR
  (— OF VITALITY) ANEMIA
  ADYNAMIA
  (— OF WIND) CALM
  (— OF WORTH) IMMERIT
  (— STRENGTH) DROOP
LACKADAISICAL LANGUID
  LISTLESS
LACKEY SKIP SLAVE LAPDOG
  LACQUEY STAFFIER
LACKING BUT SHY BARE FREE SANS

WANT ALACK GNEDE MINUS
SHORT ABSENT BARREN DEVOID
WITHIN WANTING DESOLATE
INDIGENT
(PREF.) LONCH(O)
LACKLUSTER DULL FISHY CLOUDY
  GLASSY
LACONIA (CAPITAL OF —) SPARTA
LACONIAN SPARTAN
LACONIC CURT SHORT CONCISE
  POINTED SPARTAN SUCCINCT
LA CORUNA GROIN
LACQUER LAC DOPE DUCO JAPAN
  CHATON LACKER URUSHI VARNISH
LACRIMAL
  (PREF.) DACRY(O)
LACTATION (— PERIOD) NOTE
LACTONE CUMARIN LIMONIN
  MECONIN DIKETENE
LACTOSCOPE PIOSCOPE
LACUNA GAP BREAK HIATUS
LACUSTRINE LAKISH
LAD BOY BUB MAN BOYO CARL
  CHAP DICK HIND JOCK LOON LOUN
  SNAP BILLY BUCKO CADDY CHIEL
  GROOM YOUTH BURSCH CADDIE
  CALLAN FELLOW LADDIE LADKIN
  MANNIE NIPPER SHAVER CALLANT
  MUCHACHO SPRINGER STRIPLING
  (AWKWARD —) GROMET GRUMMET
  (MISCHIEVOUS —) GAMIN
  (MY —) AVICK
  (SERVING —) GILLIE GOSSOON
LADDER STY STEE JACOB SCALE
  AERIAL BANGOR ESCAPE PULEYN
  GANGWAY POLEYNE POMPIER
  (— IN HOSE) RUN
  (— TO LOFT) TRAP
  (FIREMAN'S —) STICK
  (FISH —) FISHWAY
  (JACOB'S —) CHARITY
  (REVOLVING —) POTENCE
  (ROPE —) ETRIER
LADDER-LIKE SCALAR
LADDIE JOCKEY LATHIE LADDOCK
  LADDIKIE
LADE BAIL LAVE LADEN TRUSS
  BURDEN ONLOAD FRAUGHT
  (— INTO COOLER) STRIKE
LADEN HEAVY BELAST LOADED
  FRAUGHT FREIGHT GESTANT
LA-DI-DA TOOTOO EXTREME
LADING LOAD CARGO BURDEN
  FREIGHT
LADINO SPANIOL
LADLE DIP JET GAWN SKEP CLATH
  CYATH KEACH STOOP DIPPER
  LADING CUVETTE CYATHUS
  KYATHOS POTSTICK
  (— FOR MOLTEN METAL) SHANK
  (— OUT SOUP) SLEECH
  (— WITH HANDLES) CYATH SHANK
  CYATHUS KYATHOS SKIPPET

(BRINE —) LOOT
(LARGE —) SCOOP
(PREF.) ARYTENO
LADRONE TULISAN LATHERIN
LADY BIBI BURD DAMA DAME RANI
DONNA HANUM BEEBEE DOMINO
FEMALE KADINE KHANUM RAWNIE
SAHIBA SENORA LADYKIN
MADONNA SENHORA BELAMOUR
SINEBADA
(— OF HIGH RANK) BEGUM
(— OF HOUSE) GOODWIFE
(BEAUTIFUL —) CLEAR
(LEADING —) PREMIERE
(TURKISH —) KHANUM
(YOUNG —) DEB MISS DAMSEL
MAIDEN DAMOZEL DEBUTANTE
(PL.) LADYHOOD
LADYBUG VEDALIA
LADYFISH WRASSE PUDIANO
BONEFISH BONYFISH DONCELLA
LADYISH TENPOUNDER
LADYLIKE FEMALE
LADYLOVE LADY DELIA MINION
MISTRESS
LADY'S-COMB NEEDLES
LADY'S-MANTLE DEWCUP
PADELION
LADY'S-SLIPPER DUCK YELLOW
NERVINE YELLOWS UMBILROOT
(PREF.) CYPRI CYPRO
LADY'S-SMOCK SPINK
LADY WINDERMERE'S FAN
(AUTHOR OF —) WILDE
(CHARACTER IN —) LORTON
ERLYNNE AUGUSTUS MARGARET
DARLINGTON WINDERMERE
LAEL (SON OF —) ELIASAPH
LAERTES (FATHER OF —) ARCESIUS
(MOTHER OF —) CHALCOMEDUSA
(SON OF —) ULYSSES
(WIFE OF —) ANTICLEA
LAG DRAG DRAW SLOG DELAY
TRAIL HOCKER LAGGER LINGER
LOITER STRING DRIDDLE LAGGING
(— IN PRODUCTION) SLIPPAGE
(KIND OF —) JET
LAGGARD SLOW TARDY LAGGER
TORTOISE
LAGGING TARDY JACKET DEADING
LAGGARD CLEADING DRAWLING
FOREPOLE
LAGNIAPPE TIP GIFT BONUS EXTRA
PILON PRESENT
LAGOMORPH HARE PIKA RABBIT
LAGOON HAFF POOL BAYOU LIMAN
LAGUNA SALINA
LAHAD (FATHER OF —) JAHATH
LAHMI (BROTHER OF —) GOLIATH
LAID (— ACROSS WALL) INBOND
(— DOWN) THETIC THETICAL
(— WASTE) BARE
LAIR DEN LAY FORM HOLD SHED
COUCH EARTH HAUNT LODGE
MEUSE SQUAT HARBOR KENNEL
SPELUNK
(— OF FOX) KENNEL
(— OF OTTER) HOLT HOVER
(— OF WILD BOAR) SOUNDER
LAISH (SON OF —) PHALTIEL
LAISSE TIRADE
LAITY FOLK LAYMEN PEOPLE

LAIUS (FATHER OF —) LABDACUS
(SON OF —) OEDIPUS
(WIFE OF —) JOCASTA
LAKE LAY SEA VLY BAHR JAIL JHIL
LAGO LLYN LOCH MERE MOAT
SHOR TANK TARN VLEI VLEY
BAYOU CHOTT JHEEL LERNA
LIMAN LOUGH SPARK TUBIG
LAGOON NYANZA STROND
ANCYLUS CARMINE LAKELET
TURLOUGH
(CASHEW —) AUBURN
(DRY —) PLAYA
(FENNY —) BROAD
(MOUNTAIN —) TARN
(RELATING TO —S) LIMNAL
(SALT —) SHOT CHOTT SHOTT
SALINA SALINE
(SHALLOW —) PLAYA
(SMALL —) GURGES MARIGOT
(TEMPORARY —) PINAG
(YELLOW —) PINK
(PREF.) LIMN(I)(O)
(SUFF.) LIMNION
LAKE CARP DRUM LAKER
LAKE-DWELLING CRANNOG
LAKE HERRING KIYI CISCO
GRAYBACK
LAKE TROUT POGY TOGUE
LAKE WHITEFISH POLLAN
LAKME (CHARACTER IN —) LAKME
GERALD NILAKANTHA
(COMPOSER OF —) DELIBES
LAKSHMANA (FATHER OF —)
DURYODHANA
(SLAYER OF —) ABHIMANYU
LAKSHMI SRI SHREE
(HUSBAND OF —) VISHNU
LALAPALOOZA ONER
LAMA ELK AUCHENIA
LAMB BUM PET PUR CADE DEAR
DUPE ELIA LOME SOCK YEAN
AGNUS PESAH PODDY AGNEAU
COSSET HIEDER LAMBIE LAMKIN
PESACH SUCKER WASTER WEANER
CHILVER EANLING FATLING
HOGLING PASCHAL PERSIAN
RUFFIAN TWAGGER BAAHLING
LAMBING PASSOVER YEANLING
(— AND WHEAT) KIBBE
(SCYTHIAN —) BAROMETZ
(SHOULDER OF —) BANJO
(SIDE OF —) CONCERTINA
LAMBASTE BEAT WHIP CREAM
SCOLD SCORE CENSURE
SQUABASH
LAMBENT BRIGHT RADIANT
LAMBREQUIN MANTLING
LAMBSKIN LAMB BAGDAD
BAGHDAD SALZFELLE
LAMB'S QUARTERS MUCKWEED
LAMB'S WOOL WASSAIL
LAME BUM GAME HALT LAHN
GAMMY GIMPY GRAVEL TINSEL
CRIPPLE CRIPPLY HALTING
HIPHALT GORGERIN SPAVINED
(— A HORSE) STUB NOBBLE
(— WITH HORSESHOE NAIL)
ACCLOY
LAMEBRAIN CLOD KNUCKLEHEAD
LAMECH (DAUGHTER OF —)
NAAMAH

(SON OF —) NOAH JABAL JUBAL
TUBALCAIN
(WIFE OF —) ADAH ZILLAH
LAMELLA PLICA FOLIUM FORNIX
LAMELLAR SPATHIC
LAMELLIBRANCH PELECYPOD
LAMENESS HALT
LAMENT CRY WEY CARE DOLE
HONE HOWL KEEN MEAN MOAN
PINE SIGH TEAR WAIL WALY WEEP
CROON DUMKA GREET KINAH
MOURN PLAIN QINAH BEHOWL
BEMOAN BEWAIL BEWEEP
COMMOS KOMMOS PLAINT
REGRET REPINE SORROW
SQUAWK THREAP YAMMER
BEMOURN CONDOLE DEPLORE
EJULATE ELEGIZE GRIZZLE
REGRATE THRENOS WAYMENT
COMPLAIN CORONACH MOURNING
THRENODY ULLAGONE WELLAWAY
LAMENTABLE YEMER FUNEST
RUEFUL DOLEFUL PITIFUL PITIABLE
PLAINFUL YAMMERLY
LAMENTATION KEEN MOAN WAIL
DOLOR LINOS RUING TANGI
LAMENT PLAINT REGRET SORROW
THRENE PLANGOR TRAGEDY
WAYMENT WILLAWA CORONACH
MOURNING PATHETIC WAILMENT
WELLAWAY LAMENTING
LAMINA FILM LAME LAMP LEAF
OBEX BLADE FLAKE LAMIN PLATE
SCALE SHELL TABLE FOLIUM
CAPSULE
LAMINATE LEAFY FLAGGY
LAMINATED BUILT FOLIATE
TABULAR
LAMINATION SLABBING
LAMINITIS FOUNDER
LAMMAS DAY GULE TERM
LAMMERGEIER AREND OSSIFRAGE
LAMP ARC EYE SEE DAVY GLIM INKY
JACK SLUT ALDIS ARGAND ASTRAL
BULLET HELION LAMPAD TARGET
ILLUMER LAMPION LAMPLET
LANTERN LUCERNE LUCIGEN
SUNLAMP SUNSPOT AEOLIGHT
CIRCLINE GASLIGHT SIDELAMP
TORCHERE PHOTOFLASH
PHOTOFLOOD
(— FOR FIREPLACE) KYLE
(CHIMNEYLESS —) TORCH
(DARKROOM —) SAFELIGHT
(IRON —) CRUSIE
(KIND OF —) POLE
(MAKESHIFT —) BITCH
(NIGHT —) VEILLEUSE
(PART OF —) CAP CORD HARP
SHELL FINIAL NIPPLE SOCKET
SWITCH WASHER NECKWING
(SAFETY —) DAVY GEORDIE
(STAGE —S) BATTEN
(TYPE OF —) GOOSENECK
(4-CORNERED —) CHILL
(PL.) CLUSTER
(PREF.) LYCHNO
LAMPBLACK LINK SOOT
LAMPETIA (FATHER OF —) APOLLO
HELIOS
(MOTHER OF —) NEAERA
(SISTER OF —) PHAETHUSA

LAMP HOLDER HUSK
LAMPLIGHTER LEERIE
LAMPOON PIPE SKIT GESTE LIBEL
SQUIB IAMBIC SATIRE BERHYME
PASQUIN COCKALAN RIDICULE
SATIRIZE PASQUINADE
LAMPOONER PASQUIL PASQUIN
LAMPREY EEL PRIDE LAMPER
MYZONT RAMPER SAYNAY SUCKER
LAMPERN
LAMP RING CRIC
LAMPSHADE GLOBE
(PART OF —) RIB RING SHADE
SPIDER
LAMPSTAND TORCHERE
LAMPWARE (— STYLE) TOLE
LAMPWICK MATCH
LANATE WOOLY LANOSE WOOLLY
LANCE PIC CANE DART SHAFT
SPEAR STAFF BROACH ELANCE
GLAIVE GLEAVE LANCET ROCKET
LANCELET SPICULUM
(KING ARTHUR'S —) RON
LANCE GUARD VAMPLATE
LANCE HEAD MORNE SOCKET
LANCELET AMPHIOXUS
LANCER LANCE SOWAR UHLAN
LANCE REST QUEUE FEWTER
LANCET FLEAM FLEEM LANCELET
LANCEWOOD YAYA CIGUA CANELA
YARIYARI
LAND ERD ERF NOD RIB AGER DIRT
FOLD GALE GISH GORE JODO
MARK SITE SOIL EARTH EJIDO
ETHEL FIELD GLEBE JUGER PLANT
SHORE SOLUM ALIGHT ASSART
FUNDUS GROUND COMMONS
COUNTRY DEMESNE ELLASAR
HOLDING LANDING LIBRATE
QUILLET TERRENE ALLODIAL
BOOKLAND COMMONTY
FARMLAND FLEYLAND FOLKLAND
POMERIUM PRAEDIUM
(— A PLANE) GREASE
(— BETWEEN FURROWS) SELION
(— BETWEEN RIVERS) DOAB
(— BORDERING SEA) SHORE
(— CLEARING) KAINGIN
(— CONVERTED TO TILLAGE)
TWAITE THWAITE
**(— HAVING VALUE OF POUND PER
YEAR)** LIBRATE
(— IN CONACRE) MOCK
(— IN GRASS) LAYER
(— LEFT FALLOW) ARDER
(— MEASURE) RIG
(— OF BLISS) GOKURAKU
(— OF GIANTS) UTGARTHAR
(— OF MANSION) DEMESNE
(— OF OPPORTUNITY) ARKANSAS
(— OF PLENTY) GOSHEN
(— OF REGION) MOLD MOULD
(— PLOWED IN A DAY) JORNADA
(— RECOVERED FROM SEA) INTAKE
INNINGS
(— REGULARLY FLOODED) SALTING
(— SURROUNDED BY WASTE)
HOPE
(— UNIT) URE KIPUKA MECATE
MORGEN MANZANA VIRGATE
(ALLUVIAL —) BATTURE
(ANCESTRAL —) ETHEL
(ARABLE —) LEA LEY LAINE

(ARID —) DESERT STEPPE
(BOTTOM —) SLASH CALLOW STRATH
(CHURCH —) GLEBE TERMON
(CHURCH —S) CROSS
(CLEAR —) BUSHHOG
(CLEARED —) ASSART
(COMMON —) EJIDO EXIDO STRAY
(CONTINENTAL —) MAIN
(CULTIVATED —) FARM ARADA TILTH CULTURE FEERING WAINAGE LABORAGE METAIRIE
(ENCLOSED —) CLOSE INTAKE
(FREEHOLD —) MULK
(GRAVELLY —) GEEST GRAVES
(GRAZING —) GRASS HIRSEL HIRSLE FEEDING
(HEATHY —) ROSLAND
(HERITABLE —) ODAL UDAL
(IMAGINARY —) FAERIE COCKAYNE LILLIPUT
(LEASED —) TACK
(LONG STRIP OF —) SLANG SPONG
(LOW —) BOG FEN GALL INKS CARSE BOTTOM
(LOW RICH —) CARSE
(NATIVE —) SOD KITH BLIGHTY BIRTHDOM HOMELAND
(OBDURATE —) TILL
(ON —) ASHORE
(PARCEL OF —) FEU LOT MOCK
(PASTURE —) HA ALP FEED HOGA WALK GRASS VELDT LEASON SCATHOLD SCATLAND
(PLATEAU —) HIGHVELD
(PLOWED —) ARADA FALLOW FURROW BREAKING
(PRIVATE —) SEVERAL
(PROMISED —) CANAAN
(PURE —) JODO SUKHAVATI
(RECLAIMED —) POLDER THWAITE
(REGROWN —) HOOKLAND
(ROUGH —) BRAKE
(SAVANNAH —S) LALANG
(SCRUBBY —) SCROG SCROGS
(SMALL PARCEL OF —) SUERTE
(SWAMPY —) WOODSERE
(TIMBER —S) STICKS
(WASTE —) HEATH
(WESTERN —) HESPERIA
(WET —) SOAK SWAMP SWANG
(WOODED —S) STICKS
(PL.) ACRES SUCKEN LAENDER NOVALIA
(PREF.) CHERSO CHOR(O)
(SUFF.) GAEA GEA
LANDBOOK TERRIER
LAND-CRAB HORSEMAN
LANDED PRAEDIAL
LANDFORM CUSP CUESTA
LANDHOLDER LAIRD COSCET TALUKDAR
LANDHOLDING BARONY
LANDING BANK VTOL YARD STAITH LANDAGE ARRIVAGE FOOTPACE HALFPACE LANDFALL
(— IN WATER) SPLASHDOWN
(ABRUPT —) PANCAKE
(BOAT —) SLIP
(CRASH —) PRANG
(SMOOTH —) GREASER
LANDING PLACE GHAT HARD SCALE PALACE ARRIVAGE

LANDING STAGE MEAR STAGE STAIR STAITH STELLING
LANDLADY WIFE DUENA PADRONA GOODWIFE
LAND-LOCK EMBAY
LANDLOCK EMBAY
LAND-LOCKED MEDITERRANEAN
LANDLORD HOST LEASER LESSOR GOODMAN PADRONE ZAMINDAR
LANDMARK COPA DOLE DOOL MARK MERE BAKEN BOUND CAIRN MARCH MEITH SENAL CIPPUS SEAMARK
LANDMASS BULGE
LANDOWNER THANE BONDER SQUIRE CACIQUE EFFENDI FREEMAN BHUMIDAR FRANKLIN ZAMINDAR
(PL.) GAMORI GEOMOROI
LANDSCAPE VIEW BOCAGE PAYSAGE SCENERY LANDSKIP
LANDSLIDE SLUMP LANDFALL LANDSLIP
LANDSLIP SLIDE
LANDSMAL MAL NYNORSK
LAND SPRING LAVANT
LANDVOGT BAILIFF
LANE GUT WAY GANG LOAN LOKE PASS RACE VEIN WIND WYND ALLEY CHASE DRANG DRONG ENTRY BORFEN VENNEL LANEWAY LOANING TWITTEN DRIFTWAY
(AIR TRAFFIC —) CORRIDOR
(FREE-THROW —) PAINT
(NARROW —) CHAR CHARE TEWER BOREEN RUELLE
(OCEAN —) SEAWAY
LANGOUSTINE PRAWN
LANGUAGE (ALSO SEE DIALECT) BAT KWA LIP CHIB CODE LEED RUNE TALK TESO LEDEN LINGO SLANG VEDIC LANGUE LINGUA SPEECH TONGUE YABBER ACCENTS CABLESE DIALECT IDIOLECT LEGALESE PARLANCE PILIPINO
(— AKIN TO SHAN) THAI
(— COMBINATION) SPANGLISH
(— ENDING) ESE
(— FAMILY) URALIC
(— IN SURINAME) SRANAN
(— THAT CONDEMNS) ABUSE
(— VARIETY) BASILECT
(ARTIFICIAL —) RO IDO NEO ARULO NOVIAL VOLAPUK ESPERANTO
(BANTU —) TSWANA KIRUNDI UMBUNDU TSHILUBA
(BIBLICAL —) ARAMAIC
(COMPUTER —) ADA BAL RPG ALGOL BASIC COBOL PROLOG SNOBOL FORTRAN
(ENGLISH WITH YIDDISH —) YINGLISH
(FIGURATIVE —) IMAGERY
(FLORID —) SILLABUB
(FOOLISH —) STUFF FLUMMERY
(FOUL —) SMUT ORDURE
(GYPSY —) CALO
(IMPUDENT —) SNASH
(INCOMPREHENSIBLE —) CHOCTAW
(INDO-ARYAN —) SINHALA
(INTERNATIONAL —) ANGLIC
(KIND OF —) MACHINE

(LATIN —) GRAMMAR HUMANITY
(NONSENSICAL —) BANTER
(OBSCENE —) BAWDY BAWDRY
(OF — OR BEHAVIOR) ETIC
(OF — STRUCTURE) EMIC
(OF A —) EMIC
(ORDINARY —) PROSE
(OVERPRETENTIOUS —) BOMBAST
(PERT —) SAUCE
(PIDGIN —) SABIR CAVITENO FANAKALO
(PLAIN —) CLEAR
(PROPAGANDISTIC —) NEWSPEAK
(SECRET —) ARGOT
(SHOWY —) FLUBDUB
(SIGN —) ASL AMESIAN
(SLEAZY —) SMARM
(SPECIFIC —) GA GE HO MO VU AIS AKA ATA EDO EFE EPE EVE EWE FAN FON FOX FUL GEG HET ICA IJO ILA KAI KAU KOL KOT KRU KUI LAB LAI LAZ MON MRU SIA TWI UDI YAO ZIA AFAR AGAO AGAU AGNI AHOM AINU AKAN AKIM ALUR AMBO ANDI ANTA ARUA AVAR BARI BEJA BIAK BODO BONI BORA BUBE BUGI BULU CARA CHAM CHIN CHOL CHUJ COOS CORA COTO CREE CROW CUNA DENE DOBU D'YAK EFIK EKOI ERIE EYAK FANG FIJI FULA FUNG GARO GEEZ GHEG GOLA GOLD HARE HEHE HOPI HOVA HULA HUPA IBAN IDJO IJAW IXIL KADU KAFA KAMI KAVI KAWI KELE KOCH KOMI KONO KOTA KUKI KURI LAHU LAKH LAPP LASI LATI LAZI LESU LETT LUBA MANX MAYA MOLE MORO NAGA NAMA NIAS NIUE NUBA NUPE OGOR PALA PALI PEGU PEUL PUME RAMA SAHO SERB SERI SGAW SHAN SIUS SORB SULU SUMO SUMU SUSU TAAL TIAM TIDU TINO TODA TOII TUPI TUPY VEPS VOTE XOSA ZULU ALEUT ALSEA ARAUA AUETO AZTEC BAJAU BALTI BANTU BASSA BATAK BATTA BAURE BEMBA BHILI BICOL BILIN BONNY CAMPA CARIB CAYUA CHANE CHIMU CHOCO CHOPE COFAN COIBA COMAN CUEVA CUMAN CUNZA CZECH DAFLA DAYAK DIERI DINKA DUALA DUTCH DYULA EMPEO FANTI FINGO FUNJI GAFAT GALLA GANDA GETAN GETIC GOLDI GONDI GREBO GREEK GUAMO GUATO GURMA GYPSY HABAB HAIDA HAIKH HATSA HAUSA HINDI HUABI HUARI HURON HUSKY HYLAM IGALA ILOKO IRAYA IRISH JAKUN JATKI JUANG JUTIC KABYL KAMBA KAMIA KANDH KAREN KAROK KHASI KHMER KHOND KHUZI KIOWA KISSI KIWAI KONIE KOLIS KONDE KONGO KORKU KORWA KOTAR KUMUK KUMYK KUSAN KWOMA LAMBA LAMUT LANGO LATIN LENCA LENDU LHOKE LHOTA LIMBA LIMBU LUIAN LUNDA MAGHI MAHRA MAHRI MALAY MALTO MAORI MAZUR MBUBA MEDIC MENDI MIKIR MODOC MOSSI MUONG MURMI MURUT NAHUA NOGAI NORSE NYORO ORAON

ORIYA OROMO OSAGE OSCAN PALAU PAMIR PELEW PEUHL PLATT PUNIC RONGA SAKAI SAMAL SANTO SAXON SCOTS SERER SHILH SHINA SHONA SICEL SIKEL SLAVE SOTHO SOYOT SUOMI SWAZI TAINO TAMIL TELEI TONGA TURKI UDISH UIGUR URIYA UZBEK VOGUL WAYAO WELSH WOLOF YAKUT YUNCA ZERMA ABIPON ABKHAS ACAWAI ACHOLI ADIGHE ADZHAR AFGHAN AHTENA ALTAIC ANDAKI ANDHRA ANDOKE ANGAMI APACHE APANTO APIACA ARABIC ARANDA ARAONA ARAWAK ARUNTA ATAROI AVANTI AYMARA BAGOBO BAHASA BAITSI BAKELE BANIVA BASQUE BASUTO BEAVER BHOTIA BHUMIJ BIHARI BILAAN BILOXI BOIUNK BONTOC BORORO BRAHUI BRETON BRIBRI BUKAUA BULGAR BURIAT CAGABA CANITA CARAJA CARIAN CARIRI CAUQUI CAVINA CAYAPA CAYUGA CAYUSE CEBUAN CHAGGA CHAIMA CHANGO CHOCHO CHOKWE COCAMA CONIBO COPTIC CREOLE DAKOTA DANISH DOGRIB DYERMA ESKIMO EUDEVE FRENCH FULANI FULNIO FUTUNA GADDAN GALCHA GALIBI GATHIC GENTOO GERMAN GILAKI GILIAK GILYAK GOTHIC GUAIMI GUETAR GUINAU GULLAH GURIAN HAINAN HANTIK HARARI HATTIC HEBREW HERERO HIBITO IBANAG IBIBIO IFUGAO IGNERI IGOROT INDIAN INDOIS INNUIT INUPIK ISINAI ISLETA IVATAN KABARD KACHIN KAFFIR KAIBAL KALMUK KAMASS KANAKA KANURI KATIRI KEKCHI KHALKA KHAMTI KHARIA KHOWAR KIKUYU KILIWA KODAGA KODAQU KOIARI KOIDAL KOLAMI KOREAN KONYAK KOTIAK KPELLE KUNAMA KURNAI KURUKH KYURIN LADINO LAGUNA LAHNDA LAHULI LENAPE LEPCHA LIBYAN LIUKIU LIVIAN LUSHAI LUVIAN LUWIAN LYCIAN LYDIAN MAGAHI MAGYAR MANCHU MANOBO MBONDO MBUNDA MEDIAN MEGREL MICMAC MINOAN MISHMI MISIMA MOHAWK MONTES MUYSCA MYSIAN NEPALI NEWARI NINGPO NOOTKA NUBIAN NYANJA OJIBWA ONEIDA OORIVA OSTIAK OTOMAC OVAMPO PAHARI PAIUTE PALAIC PAPAGO PAPUAN PASHTO PAZAND POLISH PUSHTO PUSHTU RASHTI REJANG ROMANY SAFINE SAKIAN SALISH SAMOAN SANGIL SANGIR SARCEE SASSAK SAVARA SEDANG SEKANI SELKUP SELUNG SEMANG SENECA SENUFO SESUTO SHARRA SHASTA SILETZ SINDHI SLOVAK SOMALI SONRAI SUBIYA SURHAI SUSIAN TARTAR TAVGHI TELEGU TELEUT TETTUM THONGA TIPURA TUNGUS VANNIC VOTYAK YANKEE YARURA YORUBA ZAREMA ABENAKI ACHAGUA AEQUIAN AKWAALA AKWAPIM ALABAMA ALTAIAN AMANAYE AMHARIC

AMORITE AMUESHA APINAYE
ARAMAIC ARAPAHO ARAUCAN
ARECUNA ARGOBBA ARICARA
ARMORIC ASHANTI ASURINI
ATACAMA ATAKAPA AUSTRAL
AVESTAN AXUMITE BAGHELI
BAGIRMI BAINING BAKONGO
BALANTE BALUCHI BAMBARA
BANGALA BANNACK BASHKIR
BENGALI BEOTHUK BERBERI
BHOTIYA BHUTANI BOSNIAN
BRITISH BULANDA BUNDELI
BUNYORO BURMESE BUSHMAN
CALIANA CALINGA CARRIER
CASHIBO CATALAN CATAWBA
CAWAHIB CHACOBO CHARRUA
CHATINO CHEBERO CHECHEN
CHIBCHA CHIMILA CHINOOK
CHIRINO CHIWERE CHONTAL
CHOROTI CHUKCHI CHUMASH
CHUROYA CHUVASH CIBONEY
CIMBRIC CLALLAM COCHIMI
CORNISH COTONAM COWLITZ
CYMRAEG DAGBANE DAGOMBA
DANAKIL DANKALI DARGHIN
DEUTSCH DHEGIHA DRAVIDA
ENGLISH ESCUARA ESSELEN
EUSKERA FINNISH FLEMISH
FOOCHOW FRIESIC FRISIAN
GAULISH GOAJIRO GUAHIBO
GUARANI GUAYAKI GURUNSI
GYARUNG HAITIAN HANUNOC
HIDATSA HITTITE HUASTEC
HUCHNOM HUICHOL HURRIAN
IBERIAN ILOKANO ILONGOT INGALIK
IPURINA ITALIAN ITELMES ITONAMA
JACUNDA JAGATAI KAKHYEN
KALINGA KALMUCK KAMASIN
KANAUJI KANNADA KASHUBE
KASSITE KIKONGO KIPCHAK KIRANTI
KIRGHIZ KIRUNDI KLAMATH KOASATI
KONKANI KOYUKON KUBACHI
KULAMAN KURDISH KUTCHIN
KUTENAI LAMPONG LATVIAN
LESGHIN LINGALA LOATUKO
LUGANDA MAGADHI MAHICAN
MALINKE MALTESE MAPUCHE
MARATHI MASKOKI MERCIAN
MEXICAN MINAEAN MINGREL
MISKITO MITANNI MOABITE
MOCHICA MONUMBO MORATTY
MORISCO NAHUATL NICOBAR
OJIBWAY OSMANLI OSSETIC
PAHLAVI PALAUNG PANJABI
PARBATE PERMIAK PERMIAN
PERSIAN PICTISH PRAKRIT PUNJABI
PUQUINA QUECHUA QUERCHI
SABAEAN SALINAN SAMBALI
SAMNANI SAMNITE SAMOYED
SANDAWE SANTALI SANTANA
SEMITIC SERBIAN SHAWANO
SHAWNEE SHILLUH SHIPIBO
SHUSWAP SIAMESE SIRIONO
SIUSLAW SOGDIAN SONGHAI
SONGISH SORBIAN SPANIOL
SPANISH STIKINE SUBANUN
SVANISH SWAHILI SWEDISH
TAGALOG TIBETAN TUAMOTU
TURKISH UMBRIAN UMBUNDU
VISAYAN WALLOON WENDISH
YENISEI YIDDISH ZABERMA
ZONGORA ABANEEME ACHINESE
ACHUMAWI AKKADIAN AKSUMITE

ALACALUF ALBANIAN ALFURESE
AMAHUACA AMERICAN AMMONITE
ANGOLESE ANNAMESE ANZANIAN
APALACHI ARMENIAN ASSAMESE
ASSYRIAN ATJINESE AWISHIRA
BACTRIAN BALINESE BARBACOA
BECHUANA BHOJPURI BISCAYAN
BOSNISCI I BOTOCUDO CAIIUILLA
CAINGANG CANARESE CANOEIRO
CAQUETIO CARELIAN CARIJONA
CAYUBABA CHALDEAN CHAMORRO
CHEHALIS CHEMAKUM CHEYENNE
CHINGPAW CHIQUITO CHITRALI
COCONUCA COLUMBIA COMANCHE
CORAVECA CROATIAN CUSTENAU
DELAWARE DIEGUENO CHARRUA
ELAMITIC ETHIOPIC ETRUSCAN
FALISBAN FORMOSAN FRANKISH
FULFULDE GALICIAN GALLEGAN
GEORGIAN GERMANIC GORKHALI
GUAICURU GUJARATI HADENDOA
HAWAIIAN HITCHITI ILLINOIS
ILLYRIAN IROQUOIS JAPANESE
JAVANESE KANARESE KANAWARI
KANKANAI KASHMIRI KASUBIAN
KERMANJI KIMBUNDU KOLARIAN
LANDSMAL LANUVIAN LIGURIAN
LIHYANIC LILLOOET LIVONIAN
LUSATIAN MADURESE MAHRATTI
MAKASSAR MALAGASY MANDINGO
MARSHALL MASOVIAN MAYATHAN
MAZOVIAN MONGOLIC MUSKOGEE
NUMIDIAN NYAMWEZI ONONDAGA
OSSETIAN PAMPANGO PHRYGIAN
PILIPINO POLABIAN PORTUGAL
PRUSSIAN RABBINIC ROMANIAN
SABELLIC SANSKRIT SAWAIORI
SCOTTISH SCYTHIAN SEBUNDOY
SEECHELT SHAMBALA SHIRIANA
SHOSHONE SICILIAN SKIPETAR
SLAVONIC SOUTHRON SQUAMISH
SUBARIAN SUBTIABA SUMATRAN
SUMERIAN TAHITIAN TALMUDIC
TAMASHEK THRACIAN TURCOMAN
VENETIAN VOLSCIAN WOGULIAN
YUGOSLAV YUKAGHIR CANAANITE
MONGOLIAN
(STRONG —) FRENCH
(SWAHILI —) KISWAHILI
(UNCLEAN —) SEWERAGE
(UNIVERSAL —) PASILALY
(WELSH —) CYMRAEG
(PL.) BALTIC FINNIC MAHORI
SEMITIC SUDANIC ILLYRIAN
(PREF.) GLOSS(O) GLOTT(I)(O) KI
(SUFF.) ESE GLOT
LANGUE D'OC LEMOSI LIMOSI
LANGUET LANGUID LANGUAGE
LANGUID WAN LANK DOWIE FAINT
DREAMY FEEBLE SICKLY SUPINE
TORPID CARELESS FLAGGING
HEEDLESS INDOLENT LISTLESS
SLUGGISH
LANGUISH DIE FADE FALL FLAG
PINE WILT DROOP DWINE FAINT
QUAIL SWOON SICKEN WITHER
DECLINE
LANGUISHING FADE SICK LANGUID
LOVESICK
LANGUOR KEF KIF BLAHS ENNUI
MALAISE DEBILITY LASSITUDE
LANGUR DOUC MAHA LOTONG
LUTONG SIMPAI WANDEROO

LANK LEAN THIN GAUNT LANKY
SLANK MEAGER MEAGRE SCRANKY
SLUNKEN
LANKY LEAN RENKY SLINK GANGLY
GANGLING
LANOLIN LANUM DEGRAS
LANSEH DUKU LANSA LANZON
LANTANA OREGANO
LANTERN (ALSO SEE LAMP) BUAT
BOUET BOWET CROWN DARKY
LIGHT CUPOLA LOUVER PHAROS
SCONCE THOLUS CIMBORIO
LANTHORN LUMINARIA
(— ON ROOF) FEMEREIL
(DARK —) DARKY ABSCONCE
ABSCONSA
(ELEVATED —) PHAROS
(OPTICAL —) EPISCOPE
LANTERN FISH INIOME
LANTERN FLOUNDER MEGRIM
LANTERN FLY FULGORID
LANTERN PINION RUNDLE
TRUNDLE
LANYARD CORD WAPP GILGUY
LANIARD BACKROPE
LAODAMIA (BROTHER OF —)
ISANDER HIPPOLOCHUS
(FATHER OF —) ACASTUS
BELLEROPHON
(HUSBAND OF —) PROTESILAUS
(MOTHER OF —) HIPPOLYTE
(SLAYER OF —) ARTEMIS
(SON OF —) SARPEDON
LAODICE (FATHER OF —) PRIAM
(HUSBAND OF —) HELICAON
(MOTHER OF —) HECUBA
LAOIGHIS LEIX
LAOMEDON (DAUGHTER OF —)
HESIONE
(FATHER OF —) ILUS
(MOTHER OF —) EURYDICE
(SON OF —) PRIAM CLYTIUS

LAOS
CAPITAL: VIENTIANE
COIN: KIP
MEASURE: BAK
MOUNTAIN: BIA LAI LOI SAN COPI
KHAT ATWAT KHOUNG TIUBIA
PEOPLE: LU KHA LAO MEO YAO
THAI
RIVER: NOI DONE KHONG MEKONG
NAMHOU SEBANG
TOWN: NAPE PAKSE XIENG PAKLAY
THAKHEK SAVANNAKHET
LUANGPRABANG
WATERFALL: MEKONG

LAP LEP LIP BARM FOLD GORE LICK
SLAP SLOD SOSS SUCK WASH
WELT SKIVE LAPPER LAPPET
LICKUP SHOVEL INTERLAP
(— IN STEEL) SPILL
(— OF STRAKES) LAND
(KIND OF —) PACE
(LOSE A —) RISE ARISE STAND
LAPACHOL TECOMIN
LAPBOARD PANEL
LAPDOG MESSAN MESSET SHOUGH
LAPEL LAPPET REVERE REVERS
LAPIDARY STONER GEMMARY
LAPIDIST
LAPIDOTH (WIFE OF —) DEBORAH

LAPILLUS RAPILLO
(PL.) CINDER
LAPIS LAZULI AZURE
LAP-JOINTED CLINCH
LAPP LAPPISH LAPPONIC
LAPPED FOLIATED
LAPPET LAP PAN BARBE FANON
LABEL CORNET INFULA PINNER
(PREF.) LACINI
LAPSE DROP FADE FALL HALT SLIP
ERROR FAULT FOLLY SPACE TRACT
EFFLUX HIATUS LAPSUS DELAPSE
ESCHEAT FAILURE PASSAGE
PROCESS RELAPSE RESOLVE
SLIDING ABEYANCE CADUCITY
(— INTO WRONGDOING) STUMBLE
(— OF MEMORY) BLACKOUT
(MENTAL —) ABERRATION
(PL.) LACHES
LAPSED CADUCOUS
LAPSING CADUCOUS
LAPSTRAKE CLINCH
LAPTOP PORTABLE
LAPWING WEEP WYPE PEWIT
PEEWEE PEEWIT PLOVER TIRWIT
HORNPIE PEEWEEP PIEWIPE
TEUCHIT FLOPWING PEESWEEP
TEEWHAAP TERUTERU
LARBOARD PORT BABURD
LARCENY THEFT FELONY ROBBERY
BURGLARY STEALAGE
LARCH ALERCE LARICK SPRUCE
JUNIPER EPINETTE TAMARACK
LARD MORT ENARM ADEPS DAUBE
ENARM FLARE FLECK FLICK
AXUNGE ENLARD INLARD NEUTRAL
SAINDOUX
LARDED PIQUE CADUCE CADUCOUS
LARDER CAVE PANTRY SPENCE
BUTTERY LARDINER
LARGE BIG BULL DEEP FEAT GOOD
LONG MAIN ROOM TALL AMPLE
BULKY BURLY GRAND GREAT
GROSS HUSKY JOLLY LARGY
MACRO MAXIM RENKY ROUND
SMART SPACY WALLY GAWSIE
GOODLY HEROIC MAXIMA STRONG
TRABAL BOWERLY CAPITAL
COPIOUS FAIRISH FEARFUL
HEALTHY HULKING LASKING
LIBERAL MASSIVE OUTSIZE
SIZABLE BOUNCING CHOPPING
OUTSIZED PLUMPING SENSIBLE
SWACKING
(— AND HOLLOW) CAVAL
(— AND ROUND) SIDE
(— IN DIAMETER) STOUT
(APPALLINGLY —) HIDEOUS
(EXTRA —) MAXI
(EXTREMELY —) GIANT DECUMAN
GIGANTIC
(FAIRLY —) SMART
(INDEFINITELY —) NTH INFINITE
(MODERATELY —) FAIR TIDY PRETTY
(UNUSUALLY —) HEAVY SKELPIN
SKELPING
(VERY —) HUGE JUMBO ROYAL
BOXCAR BUMPER INGENT NATION
GOLIATH INTENSE BEHEMOTH
SLAPPING SPANKING SWINGING
WHACKING HUMONGOUS
(PREF.) MACR(O) MEGA MEGAL(O)
(HOW —) QUANTI

LARGE-FOOTED MEGAPOD
LARGE-FRAMED ROOMY
LARGE-LETTERED UNCIAL
LARGELY BIG HARD BIGLY
LARGENESS BULK MICKLE
BREADTH FREEDOM GIANTISM
LARGEOUR
LARGE-SCALE EPIC
LARGEST BEST MAXIMUS
LARIA BRUCHUS
LARIAT ROPE LASSO NOOSE RIATA
CABESTRO
LARK GAME ROMP ANTIC PRANK
FROLIC PEEWEE SCHEME
GAMMOCK LAVROCK LAYROCK
SKYLARK CALANDER LAVEROCK
LARKA KOLS HO
LARKSPUR LOCOWEED
LARNITE BELITE
LARRIGAN PAC
LARRIKIN NUT ROWDY HOODLUM
LARVA BOT BLOW BOTT CRAB
GRUB HUHU SLUG TURK WOLF
WORM ALIMA ASCON BARDY
BRUKE ERUCA LEECH OTTER
REDIA SYCON CORBIE COSSID
DRAGON EPHYRA GRUGRU
HOPPER LEPTUS LEUCON LOOPER
MAGGOT MEASLE PEDLAR TORCEL
WABBLE WORMIL WOUBIT
ATROCHA BUDWORM CADELLE
CREEPER DIPORPA FIGWORM
FLYBLOW GORDIAN HYDATID
HYPOPUS PEDDLER PLANULA
PLUTEUS PREPUPA VELIGER
WIGGLER ACTINULA ANTIZOEA
ARMYWORM BOLLWORM
BOMBYCID BOOKWORM
CASEWORM CERCARIA COENURUS
CYRTOPIA DEUTOVUM
DROPWORM EPHYRULA
FIREWORM FURCILIA GEOMETER
GILTTAIL GLOWWORM
GNATWORM LEAFTIER LEAFWORM
MEALWORM MUCKWORM
NAUPLIUS PILIDIUM ROOTWORM
SCYPHULA SEMIPUPA SILKWORM
SKINWORM SPANWORM
SPRAWLER STAGWORM
SUBIMAGO TORNARIA VERMICLE
WASPLING WIREWORM
WOODGRUB WOODWORM
LARVACEA ATREMATA COPELATA
LARVAL NEPIONIC
LARYNGITIS CROUP
LARYNX
(PREF.) LARYNG(O)
LASCIVIOUS LEWD NICE SALT
HORNY RANDY LUBRIC WANTON
BLISSOM FLESHLY GOATISH
PAPHIAN PRURIENT SALACIOUS
LASCIVIOUSNESS LECHERY
ASELGEIA LUXURITY LUBRICITY
LASERWORT SILPHIUM
LASH CUT BEAT FIRK FLOG JERK
LACE WELT WHIP WIRE YERK
LEASE LEASH SCORE SKEEG SLASH
THONG TRICE WHALE CANVAS
CILIUM LAINER LAUNCH STRIPE
SWINGE SWITCH FLYFLAP
KURBASH SCOURGE
(— BOWSPRIT) GAMMON

(— OUT) THRASH
(— TOGETHER) RACK
LASHER THONGMAN
LASHING YARK YERK GAMMON
LISTING MOUSING SEIZING
SLATING FRAPPING
(PL.) OODLES OODLINS SLITHERS
LASS TIB GILL PRIM TRULL DAMSEL
KUMMER LASSIE DAMOZEL
LASSIKY TENDREL MUCHACHA
(COUNTRY —) JENNY
LASSITUDE BLAHS COPOS STUPOR
LANGUOR MALAISE LETHARGY
LASSO LASH LAZO ROPE RIATA
LARIAT CABESTRO
LAST ABY LAG DURE GOON HOLD
KEEP RIDE SAVE ABIDE FINAL
SERVE ABEGGE ENDURE LATEST
LATTER REMAIN ULTIMA UTMOST
DARREIN DERNIER EXTREME
PERDURE SUPREME CONTINUE
EVENTUAL HINDMOST LATEMOST
REARMOST TERMINAL ULTIMATE
AFTERMOST
(— BUT ONE) PENULT
(— OUT) SPIN STAY
(AT —) FINALLY
(THE —) OMEGA
(PREF.) ESCHATO POSTREMO
ULTIMO
LAST DAYS OF POMPEII (AUTHOR
OF —) BULWER LYTTON
(CHARACTER IN —) IONE BURBO
JULIA NYDIA DIOMED ARBACES
CLODIUS GLAUCUS SALLUST
APAECIDES
LASTING FIXED LASTY DURANT
DURING STABLE ABIDING DURABLE
DUREFUL CONSTANT ENDURING
LIVELONG REMANENT STANDING
(— FOR LONG PERIOD) AEONIC
AEONIAL
(— FOR ONE DAY) DIARY DIURNAL
LASTINGNESS STAY DURATION
LAST OF THE MOHICANS
(AUTHOR OF —) COOPER
(CHARACTER IN —) CORA WEBB
ALICE DAVID GAMUT MAGUA
MUNRO NATTY UNCAS BUMPPO
DUNCAN HAWKEYE HEYWARD
MONTCALM CHINGACHGOOK
LAST PURITAN (AUTHOR OF —)
SANTAYANA
(CHARACTER IN —) JIM IRMA ROSE
ALDEN BOBBY EDITH MARIO PETER
WEYER BOWLER OLIVER DARNLEY
HARRIET SCHLOTE BUMSTEAD
LAST SUPPER CENA COENA
MAUNDY
LAT STAMBHA
LATCH FLY PIN HASP RISP SHUT
CATCH CHAIR CLICK CLINK SNECK
SNICK KEEPER CLICKET
LATCHET DAG TAB SANDAL
LANGUET
LATCHING LASKET
LATCHKEY CLICKET PASSKEY
LATE LAG NEW DEEP RIPE SLOW
TARDY RECENT TARDIVE UMWHILE
ADVANCED LATEWARD SOMETIME
UMWHILE
(— COMER) CUNCTATOR
(— IN DEVELOPING) SEROTINOUS

LATE GEORGE APLEY (AUTHOR OF
—) MARQUAND
(CHARACTER IN —) JOHN MARY
APLEY AMELIA GEORGE ELEANOR
HORATIO MONAHAN OREILLY
WILLIAM WILLING BOSWORTH
PRENTISS CATHARINE
LATELY LATE ALATE NEWLY
LA TENE MARNEAN
LATENT HIDDEN MASKED ABEYANT
DORMANT PASSIVE LATITANT
QUIESCENT
(PREF.) CRYPT(O) KRYPT(O)
LATER POI SIN ANON POST SYNE
AFTER ELDER NEWER BEHIND
FUTURE LATTER PUISNE ANOTHER
INFERIOR UMQUHILE
(PREF.) HYSTERO INFRA META
POST
LATERAL SIDE
(PREF.) PLEUR(O)
LATERALLY SIDELONG
LATERITE CABOOK KUNKUR
LATEST LAST LATTER FARTHEST
FURTHEST
LATEX GUTTA SORVA ANTIAR
SENAMBY
LATH BAT LAG SLAT SPAIL SPALE
SPELL SWALE REEPER SPLENT
SPLINT STOOTH LATHING
FOREPOLE LATHWORK
LATHE LAY SLEY TURN LAITH
THROW BEATER WISKET
(— FOR CYLINDERS) BROAD
(— OF LOOM) LAY
(TURNING —) THROW
(WATCHMAKER'S —) TURN TURNS
MANDREL
LATHER FOAM SUDS FROTH
FREATH SAPPLES
LATHERED SOAPY
LATIGO STRAP
LATIN ROMAN HISPERIC LATINITY
SCATTERMOUCH
(— COMPOSITION) VULGUS
LATIN-AMERICAN LATIN LADINO
LATINO HISPANIC
LATINUS (DAUGHTER OF —) LAVINIA
(FATHER OF —) FAUNUS
(SON-IN-LAW OF —) AENEAS
(WIFE OF —) AMATA
LATITUDE SCOPE SPACE WIDTH
EXTENT HEIGHT
(HELIOCENTRIC —) LIMIT
LATONA (DAUGHTER OF —) DIANA
(FATHER OF —) COEUS
(MOTHER OF —) PHOEBE
(SON OF —) APOLLO
LATRIA ADORATION
LATRINE BOG REAR PRIVY TOILET
BOGGARD
LATTER LAST FINAL RECENT
SECOND PRESENT
(— PORTION) AUTUMN
LATTICE MESA GRATE HERSE
TWINE GRILLE PINJRA UMBREL
GRATING CANCELLI
(— OF POINTS) SATIN
(MOVING —) APRON
(PREF.) CLATHR
LATTICED CLATHRATE
LATTICE PLANT LACELEAF

LATTICEWORK ARBOR GRATE
GRATING ESPALIER TUKUTUKU

LAUAN KALUNTI
LAUD EXTOL PRAISE ADVANCE
APPLAUD COMMEND GLORIFY
MAGNIFY EMBLAZON EULOGIZE
MACARIZE
LAUDATION PUFF EULOGY PRAISE
PANEGYRIC
LAUDATORY SNEER EPENETIC
PRAISING
LAUDER ESTEE
LAUGH YAK YUK GAFF YOCK YUCK
CHUCK FLEER LEUGH RISUS
ARRIDE NICKER TITTER CHORTLE
GRIZZLE SNICKER SNIGGER
SNIRTLE TWITTER LAUGHTER
(— CONTEMPTUOUSLY) SNORT
DERIDE
(— GLEEFULLY) CHECKLE
(— HYSTERICALLY) CHECKLE
(— IN AFFECTED MANNER) GIGGLE
(— IN COARSE MANNER) FLEER
GUFFAW
(— LIKE HEN) CACKLE
(— LOUDLY) GAFF GUFFAW
(— MOCKINGLY) FLEER
(— OUT LOUD) CRACKUP
(— QUIETLY) GULE SMUDGE
CHUCKLE SNIRTLE
(BELLY —) BOFF BOFFOLA
(LOUD —) GAUSTER
LAUGHABLE ODD RICH COMIC
DROLL FUNNY MERRY QUEER
WITTY AMUSING COMICAL RISIBLE
STRANGE WAGGISH FARCICAL
HUMOROUS LAUGHING PLEASANT
SPORTIVE RIDICULOUS
LAUGHING RIANT RIDENT IRRISION
MIRTHFUL
(— MATTER) MOWS
LAUGHING GULL PEWIT
LAUGHING JACKASS
KOOKABURRA
LAUGHING OWL WEKAU WHEKAU
LAUGHINGSTOCK GUY BUTT JEST
JOKE SONG SPORT DERISION
RIDICULE
LAUGHTER JOKE MIRTH RISUS
SNIRT CACKLE LAWTER SPLEEN
HILARITY RISIBILITY
(HYSTERICAL —) CACHINNATION

(VULGAR —) HAWHAW
(PREF.) GELOTO
LAUNCE LANT LANCE SMELT AMMODYTE SANDLING
LAUNCH PUT BURST DRIVE LANCE ELANCE STRIKE BAPTIZE PINNACE PROMOTE STEAMER TELSTAR VIBRATE CATAPULT
(— HOSTILELY) DIRECT
LAUNCHER (ROCKET —) BAZOOKA
LAUNCHING BLASTOFF
LAUNDER TYE WASH TRUNK SLUICE STRAKE LAUNDRY
LAUNDRESS TRILBY LAVENDER
LAUNDRY WASH BAGWASH LAVATORY WASHATERIA WASHETERIA
(PUBLIC —) STEAMIE
LAUREL BAY IVY LAURY UNITE WICKY DAPHNE KALMIA MALLET MYRTLE CAJEPUT IVYWOOD WOEVINE BREWSTER CALFKILL
(GROUND —) ARBUTUS
LAUREL OAK ACAJOU
LAURIC PICHURIC
LAURUSTINE VIBURNUM
LAUSUS (FATHER OF —) NUMITOR MEZENTIUS
(SISTER OF —) ILIA
(SLAYER OF —) AMULIUS
LAUTVERSCHIEBUNG SHIFT
LAVA AA ASHES SPINE COULEE LATITE SCORIA VERITE FAVILLA LAPILLO MALPAIS ASPERITE ORENDITE PAHOEHOE
(MUD —) MOYA LAHAR
(SCORIACEOUS —) AA SLAG
(SLAGGY —) SCORIA
LAVABO LAVATORY
LAVAGE LAVATION LAVEMENT
LAVALAVA SULU
LAVAN KALUNTI
LAVATORY LOO BASIN CHALET CLOSET LAVABO OFFICE LATRINE LAVETTE WASHROOM CLOAKROOM
LAVE LIP WASH BATHE SPLASH
LAVENDER BEHN ASPIC BEHEN SPICK SPIKE INKROOT LAVANDIN STICHADO
LAVENGRO (AUTHOR OF —) BORROW
(CHARACTER IN —) JOHN MOLL ARDRY HERNE PETER ISOPEL JASPER BERNERS FRANCIS LEONORA TAGGART LAVENGRO SAPENGRO SLINGSBY WILLIAMS WINIFRED PETULENGRO
LAVER SION SLAKE SLOKE LOUTER PHIALE AMANORI CISTERN CANTHARUS
LAVINIA (FATHER OF —) LATINUS
(HUSBAND OF —) AENEAS
(MOTHER OF —) AMATA
LAVISH FREE LASH LUSH FLUSH LARGE SPEND SPORT WASTE COSTLY WANTON COPIOUS OPULENT PROFUSE GENEROUS LUCULLAN PRODIGAL SQUANDER WASTEFUL REDUNDANT MUNIFICENT
LAVISHNESS WASTE FINERY LAVISH

LAW ACT FAS IUS JUS LAY LEX ADAT DOOM JURE RULE CANON DROIT NOMOS TORAH BYELAW BYRLAW DECREE DHARMA EQUITY BROCARD DANELAW DERECHO HALACHA HALAKAH JUSTICE PRECEPT SETNESS STATUTE JUDGMENT JUDICIAL ROGATION STATEWAY TANISTRY ORDINANCE
(—S OF MANU) SUTRA SUTTA
(— VIOLATOR) SCOFFLAW
(BEDOUIN —) THAR
(DIETARY —S) KASHRUTH
(ELEMENTARY —) BROCARD
(EQUAL —) ISONOMY
(ISLAMIC —) ADA BAI ADAT SHERI SHARIA SHERIAT
(JEWISH —) MISHNA MISHNAH
(KIND OF —) LEASH
(MARRIAGE —) LEVIRATE
(MOSAIC —) TORAH
(OPPOSING —) ANTINOMY
(PROPOSED —) BILL
(UNIVERSAL —) HEAVEN
(PL.) LORS
(PREF.) JURIS LEGI LEGO NOM(O) THESMO
(SUFF.) LEGE NOMY
LAW-ABIDING LAWFUL
LAWBREAKER FELON HOUGHER
LAWFUL DUE JUST LEAL TRUE VERY LEGAL LEGIT LICIT LOYAL VALID KINDLY LEEFUL ENNOMIC LEESOME INNOCENT LIEFSOME RIGHTFUL
LAWGIVER MINOS MOSES SOLON LAWYER LAWMAKER
LAWLESS LEWD UNRULY ILLEGAL MOBBISH ANARCHIC
LAWLESSNESS ANOMY ANOMIE ANARCHY
LAWMAKER LEGIFER
LAWN ARBOR GRASS LINON SWARD UMPLE CYPRUS BATISTE QUINTIN TIFFANY
LAWSUIT LIS CASE SAKE SECTA ACTION BRABBLE
LAWYER (ALSO SEE JURIST) JET PEAT AVOUE PATCH SHARK BREHON JURIST LAWMAN LEGIST SQUIRE WRITER COUNSEL MUKHTAR TEMPLAR DEFENDER LEGISTER TRAMPLER BARRISTER MOUTHPIECE PETTIFOGGER
(PALTRY —) PETTIFOGGER
(UNSCRUPULOUS —) SHYSTER
LAX DULL FREE LASH LAZY LINK SLOW SWAG WIDE LARGE LOOSE RELAX SLACK TARDY REMISS BACKWARD INACTIVE DISSOLUTE NEGLIGENT
LAXATIVE LAX LASK CASCARA APERIENT HYDROMEL LAPACTIC RELAXANT SOLUTIVE TARAXACUM
LAXITY LASCHETY LATITUDE
LAY LIE SET CLAP LAIC LEWD SLEY SONG WAGE BIGHT CIVIL COUCH DITTY LATHE LEDGE QUIET STAKE STILL COMMON HAZARD IMPOSE IMPUTE MELODY APPEASE ASCRIBE LAYDOWN POPULAR SECULAR SIRVENTE TEMPORAL

(— ASIDE) DOFF DOWN DUMP SHUCK DEPOSE DIVEST DEPOSIT PIGEONHOLE
(— AWAY) STORE
(— BARE) BARE NAKE TIRL TIRVE DENUDE DETECT OPPOSE UNCOVER DENUDATE
(— CLAIM) ASSERT BESPEAK ARROGATE
(— CROSSWISE) COB
(— DOWN) ABDICATE PRESCRIBE
(— EGGS) BLOW WARP LEDGE OVIPOSIT
(— FLAT) SQUAT ADPRESS
(— HOLD OF) FANG GRIP HENT TAKE GRIPE LATCH ATHOLD ATTACH COLLAR COMPRISE
(— IN) EMBED
(— IN BIGHTS) JAG
(— IN COIL) FLEMISH
(— IN PLEATS) FOLD
(— IT ON) COAT
(— LOW) STREW STRIKE
(— OFF) FORE IDLE STOP
(— OF LOOM) BEATER
(— ON) APPLY INFLICT
(— OPEN) BREAK CHINE EXPOSE UNMASK
(— OUT) FRAY PLAT ARRAY RANGE SPELD SPEND BEWARE DESIGN EXTEND SPREAD STREAK STREEK CHECKER DEVELOP STRETCH CONTRIVE
(— PRONE) LEVEL
(— RUBBLEWORK) SNECK
(— SIEGE) INVEST
(— SMOOTH) EVEN
(— SNARE FOR RABBITS) HAY
(— STONE) PAVE
(— STRAIGHT) COMB
(— TYPE) CASE
(— UP) HEAP HIVE ADDLE HOARD HUTCH STOCK TREASURE
(— WASTE) PEEL WEST HARRY HAVOC HARASS RAVAGE DESTROY DESOLATE FORWASTE
LAYABOUT IDLER
LAYBOY JOGGER
LAYDOWN LAYOUT SPREAD
LAYER BED FLY HEN LAY BARK CAKE COAT DASS FACE FILM FLAP FOLD LAIR LOFT RIND SEAM SKIN WEFT ZONA CHESS COUCH COVER CRUST CUTIS FLAKE FLASH LEDGE SCALE CARPET COURSE FASCIA FILLER FOLIUM INTINE LAMINA LISSOM STREAK BLANKET COATING CUTICLE EPICARP FEATHER FLAVEDO GANGMAN INLAYER LAMELLA PACKING PHELLEM PROPAGO PROVINE STRATUM SUBCOAT SUPPORT ECTOCYST ECTOSARC ENDOCYST ENDODERM EPIBLAST EPIBLEMA EPISPORE EPITHECA INTERBED MOLLISOL PERIOPLE PERISARC SUBCRUST PERIPLAST PHELLODERM
(— IN FUNGI) HYMENIUM
(— OF ATMOSPHERE) MESOSPHERE OZONOSPHERE
(— OF BLOOD VESSEL) EXTIMA EXTERNA

(— OF CELLS) EXINE CORTEX EXTINE CAMBIUM PHELLEM TAPETUM PERICYCLE
(— OF CLAY) GLEY VARVE SELVAGE SELVEDGE
(— OF CONCRETE) RAFT
(— OF EARTH) SPIT
(— OF EYE) RETINA
(— OF FAT) LEAF FINISH
(— OF FELT) BAT BATT
(— OF FIBER) LAP
(— OF FINE MATERIAL) CUSHION
(— OF FOREST GROWTH) SUBSTORY OVERSTORY
(— OF FUEL) FIREBED
(— OF GLASS) CASING
(— OF IRIS) UVEA
(— OF MEAT) SPINE
(— OF MORTAR) SCREED
(— OF NERVE FIBERS) ALVEUS
(— OF ORGANIC MATTER) FLOOR
(— OF PLASMA) BUFFCOAT
(— OF ROCK) CAP SHELF SHELL SLATE FOLIUM SEPTUM BLISTER SKULLCAP
(— OF ROOTS) SOLE
(— OF SEDIMENT) WARP
(— OF SHALE) BONE
(— OF SHEEPSKIN) FLESHER
(— OF SHOE HEEL) LIFT
(— OF SILT) VARVE
(— OF SKIN) DERM DERMA EPIDERM
(— OF SOIL) SOLUM CALLOW CASING HARDPAN HORIZON
(— OF STONES) DASS DESS
(— OF TANBARK) HAT
(— OF TISSUE) BED DARTOS FASCIA SEROSA ELASTICA EPIBLEMA PERIDERM
(— OF TOBACCO LEAVES) HANGER
(— OF TURF) FLAW KERF
(— OF WHITE MATTER) CAPSULE
(— OF WOOD) CORE
(BONY —) LAMELLA CEMENTUM
(BOTTOM —) BEDDING
(FLAT —) BED FLAP FLAKE
(FROZEN —) PERMAFROST
(GERM —) MESODERM
(IMPERVIOUS —) LINING
(OUTER —) HUSK
(THIN —) SCRAPE
(UNDERLYING —) SUBSTRATUM
(UPPER —) SURFACE
(PREF.) LAMELLI LAMIN(I) PTYCH(O) STRATI
(SUFF.) CLINAL CLINE LAMIN
(— OF SKIN) DERMIS
(GERM —) BLAST(IC)(Y)
LAYERING LAP GOOTEE STOOLING
LAYMAN LAIC CLERK IDIOT DEACON SECULAR DEFENSOR EXHORTER EXOTERIC FAMILIAR STRANGER WORLDMAN
LAYOFF FURLOUGH
LAYOUT MISE DUMMY SETOUT
(— OF CARDS) TABLEAU
LAZARETTO SPITAL SPITTLE
LAZARUS (SISTER OF —) MARY MARTHA
(SISTER OF —) MARTHA
LAZINESS LAZE SLOTH SLOUCH OISIVITY

LAZULITE SIDERITE

LAZY ARGH IDLE LASS DOXIE DRONY FAINT INERT LINGY LUSKY RESTY SLOAN SLOTH CLUMSY LIMPSY LURDAN LUTHER ORNERY SWEERT TRAILY CLUMPST DRONISH LUSKISH PEAKISH SLIVING DROGHLIN FAINEANT FECKLESS INDOLENT LITHERLY OSCITANT SLOTHFUL SLUGGARD THOWLESS TRIFLING SHIFTLESS

LAZY EYE AMBLYOPIA

LEA LAY GRASS LAYER LAYLAND LEALAND

LEACH TAP LETCH SOFTEN

LEAD GO TEE VAN WIN BEAR DADE GIVE GROW HAVE HEAD HERD LEED SLIP TAKE TEEM WORK BLAZE BOUND BRING CARRY GREBE GUIDE MAYNE PILOT PRESA SOUND START TRAIN TREAT CONVEY DEDUCE DIRECT ESCORT INDUCE INDUCT LEADER SATURN BEGUILE CAPTAIN CONDUCE CONDUCT LEADING MARSHAL PIGTAIL PIONEER PLUMBUM PLUMMET LEADSMAN MANUDUCE MANUDUCT SQUIRREL

(— A BAND) BATON
(— AND SUPPORT) DADE
(— ASIDE) CHAR SINGLE
(— ASTRAY) ERR MANG TURN WARP BEFOOL BETRAY ENTICE WANDER WILDER DEBAUCH MISLEAD MISWEND PERVERT SOLICIT TRADUCE BEWILDER INVEIGLE MISGUIDE
(— AWAY) CHAR ABDUCT DIVERGE
(— BACK) REDUCT
(— FORCIBLY) ESCORT
(— IN CARD GAME) SNEAK WHITECHAPEL
(— IN RACE) LAP
(— IN SINGING) PRECENT
(— INTO ERROR) ABUSE DELUDE
(— MONOXIDE) MASSICOT
(— ON) TRAIL
(— PASSIVE EXISTENCE) VEGETATE
(— POISONING) PLUMBISM
(BLACK —) WAD WADD GRAPHITE
(COLOR —) PLOMB
(DEEP-SEA —) DIPSY DIPSEY
(MOCK —) BLENDE
(OVERLAPPING —) DRIP
(PLUMBING —) BLUEY
(SYMBOL FOR —) PB
(WHITE —) KREMS CERUSE
(PREF.) GALENO MOLYBD(O) PLUMB(I)(O)
(SUFF.) AGOGUE AGOGY

LEAD-COLORED WAN BLAE

LEADEN HEAVY INERT PLUMBEAN

LEADER BO BOH COB DUX HOB MIR CAST COCK DUCE DUKE HEAD HOBB JEFE NAIG NAIK OMDA SOUL TYEE CHIEF DOYEN ELDER FIRST MAHDI MOSES OMDEH PILOT SEYID TRACE ARCHON CALIPH DESPOT HEADER HONCHO RECTOR SAYYID TYCOON ACREMAN ADVISER CAPTAIN CONDUCT DEMAGOG DRUNGAR FOREMAN FUEHRER INDUCER PRIMATE ACCENTOR CAUDILLO DIRECTOR FUGLEMAN HEADSMAN HERETOGA LODESMAN PANDARUS STRATEGE AYATOLLAH PENDRAGON PROTAGONIST

(— OF ARMY) VAIVODE VOIVODE
(— OF DACOITS) BOH
(— OF FLOCK) PATRIARCH
(— OF GUISERS) SKUDLER
(— OF MINING GANG) CORPORAL
(— OF MUTINEERS) ELECTO
(— OF REVOLT) ANARCH
(BAND —) BATONEER
(CHOIR —) CANTOR PRECENTOR
(CHORUS —) CHORAGUS
(COSSACK —) ATAMAN HETMAN
(FASCIST —) RAS
(HOLY —) MAHATMA
(INTELLECTUAL —) BRAIN
(MINING —) CORPORAL
(MOB —) MOBOCRAT
(MUSLIM —) MAHDI
(POLITICAL —) SACHEM
(PRAYER —) IMAM
(RELIGIOUS —) AGA AGHA LAMA SHEIKH
(SCOUT —) AKELA SIXER
(SPIRITUAL —) GURU SADDIK GUARDIAN
(TAMMANY —) SACHEM
(SUFF.) ARCH ARCHIC ARCHY

LEADERSHIP LEAD AEGIS MANRED CONDUCT IMAMATE LEADING MANRENT CHIEFDOM GUIDANCE HEADSHIP HEGEMONY

(— BY TALENTED) MERITOCRACY

LEADING BIG BEST COCK DUCT HEAD LEAD MAIN AHEAD CHIEF FIRST BANNER PREMIER STELLAR GUIDANCE PROMINENT

(— OUTWARD) EMISSARY
(— TO NOTHING) IDLE

LEAD MONOXIDE MASSICOT

LEADSMAN SOUNDER

LEADWORK PLUMBAGE PLUMBING

LEADWORT CROWTOE PLUMBAGO

LEAF PAD BACK BARB BUYO FLAG FLAP FOIL FOLD GEAR PAGE PALM STUB BLADE BLANK FLIER FLYER FOLIO FROND GRASS GUARD LEAVE SCALE SEPAL SIGHT SPILL TEPAL BONNET CADJAN CARPEL COUPON FOLIUM FRAISE FULZIE NEEDLE PEPPER DAMIANA FOLDOUT HARNESS LEAFLET TREFOIL WITNESS PHYLLADE PHYLLOME MICROPHYLL

(— FAT) FLICK
(— FROM AXIL) BRACT
(— OF BOOK) PAGE FOLIO INSET PLATE FLYLEAF
(— OF CALYX) BARB
(— OF CORN) HUSK
(— OF COROLLA) PETAL
(— OF DOOR) VALVE
(— OF HEDDLES) GEAR
(— OF PALM) FAN OLA PAN CHIP OLLA FROND LATANIER
(— OF SPRING) BACK
(—S OF CORIANDER) CILANTRO
(BETEL —) PAN SIRIH
(BIBLE —) COSTMARY
(DEAD —) FLAG

(EXTRA —) INSERT
(HOLLOW —) PHYLLODE
(PART OF —) RIB TIP APEX BASE LOBE STEM VEIN BLADE SINUS LAMINA MARGIN MIDRIB PETIOLE LEAFSTALK
(RUDIMENTARY —) CATAPHYLL
(SPRING —) WRAPPER
(STRAWBERRY —) FRAISE
(THIN —) LAMELLA
(TOBACCO —) LUGS STRIP CUTTER WRAPPER
(WASTE GOLD —) SKEWING
(PREF.) FOLI(O) PETAL(I)(O) PHYLL(I)(O)
(SUFF.) FOLIATE FOLIOUS PETALOUS PHYLL(A)(OUS)(UM)(Y)

LEAFAGE FOLIAGE

LEAFHOPPER HOPPER JASSID THRIPS HOMOPTER

LEAFLET FLIER PINNA TRACT MAILER FOLIOLE STUFFER

(—S DROPPED FROM AIR) BUMF
(PAIR OF —S) JUGUM
(PL.) SENNA CAROBA

LEAFLIKE PHYLLINE

LEAFMOLD KOLINSKY

LEAFSTALK HAFT CHARD PETIOLE

LEAFY GREEN LEAVY FOLIATE FOLIOSE FRONDOSE

LEAGUE BOND BUND BANDY BOARD GUEUX HANSA PARTY UNION WHEEL CIRCUIT COMPACT ALLIANCE SYSTASIS COALITION

(— OF NATIONS) GENEVA
(BUSH —S) STICKS
(MINOR —) BUSHES

LEAGUED FEDERATE

LEAH (DAUGHTER OF —) DINAH
(FATHER OF —) LABAN
(HUSBAND OF —) JACOB
(SISTER OF —) RACHEL
(SON OF —) LEVI JUDAH REUBEN SIMEON ZEBULUN ISSACHAR

LEAK BLAB BLOW SEEP WEEP GEYZE SPUNK INLEAK SIGGER SPRING ZIGGER LEAKAGE MELTERS SCREEVE

(— IN ELECTRIC CIRCUIT) FAULT

LEAKAGE ESCAPE SEEPAGE

(— OF ELECTRICITY) CREEPAGE
(— OF GAS) SLIP
(— OF WIND) RUNNING

LEAKING ALEAK DRIBBLE NAILSICK

LEAKY LEAK UNTIGHT GIZZENED

LEAL FAITHFUL

LEAN BEAR BEND BONY HANG HEEL LANK PEND POOR PRIN RACY RELY REST SEEL STAY SWAY THIN TOOM EMPTY GAUNT HIELD LANKY LEANY SLANK SOUND SPARE STOOP HOLLOW MEAGER RECUMB SKINNY SPRING UPLEAN ANGULAR FATLESS HAGGARD INCLINE SCRAGGY SCRAWNY SLUNKEN STRINGY MACILENT SCRAGGED SCRANNEL

(— FOR SUPPORT) ABUT
(— FORWARD) PROCLINE
(— OVER) WHAUVE
(PREF.) CLIN(O)

LEANDER (LOVE OF —) HERO

LEANDRE (FATHER OF —) GERONTE
(LOVER OF —) LUCINDE

LEANER HOBBER

LEANING AGEE BIAS DRIFT FLAIR TREND PENCHE HANGING ACCLINAL ENCLITIC FROMWARD PROPENSE PROCLIVITY PROPENSITY

(— BACKWARD) SUPINE
(STRONG —) GENIUS PENCHANT

LEANNESS LANK POVERTY SPARENESS

LEAN-TO SHED LINTER OUTSHOT SKILLION

LEAP FLY HOP POP BEND DART DIVE FALL GIVE JUMP LOPE LOUP RAMP RISE SKIT WIND BOUND BREAK CAPER DANCE EXULT FLIER FLYER FRISK LUNGE PRIME SALTO SAULT SCOPE SCOUP SPANG STEND VAULT BOUNCE BREACH CURVET INSULT LAUNCH SPRENT SPRING SPRUNT WALLOP REBOUND SALTARY SALTATE SUBSULT BUCKJUMP LEAPFROG SPANGHEW UPSPRING

(— BACK) RESULT SPRUNT
(— FOR JOY) EXULT
(— IN DANCING) STOT
(— LIGHTLY) SKIP
(— OF HORSE) CURVET BALOTADE CAPRIOLE CROUPADE
(— OF WHALE) BREACH
(— OUT) SALLY
(— OVER) FREE OVER SKIP CLEAR HURDLE
(— UPON) ASSAIL POUNCE
(BALLET —) FISH JETE ASSEMBLE CABRIOLE FISHDIVE ELEVATION ENTRECHAT
(FENCING —) VOLT VOLTE
(FROLICSOME —) CAPER
(SKATING —) AXEL
(SUICIDAL —) BRODIE
(PL.) ALLEGRO
(PREF.) SCIRTO

LEAPING GAMBOL SPRING RAMPANT SALIENT SALTANT

LEAR (DAUGHTER OF —) REGAN

LEARCHUS (BROTHER OF —) MELICERTA
(FATHER OF —) ATHAMAS
(MOTHER OF —) INO

LEARN DO CON GET SEE WIT ARAL FIND HAVE HEAR LEAR LERE EDIFY GLEAN STUDY RECORD REALIZE RECEIVE DISCOVER ASCERTAIN

(— FROM EXPERIENCE) ASSAY

LEARNED BLUE SEEN LERED LORED DUCTUS BOOKISH CLERKLY CUNNING ERUDITE STUDIED TUITIVE ACADEMIC CLERGIAL LETTERED OVERSEEN POLYMATH PROFOUND SCIENCED

(— GROUP) LITERATI
(— MAN) OLLAV
(AFFECTEDLY —) INKHORN
(SOMETHING TO BE —) LIRIPIPE

LEARNEDLY CLERKLY

LEARNER PUPIL NOVICE SCHOLAR TRAINEE PRENTICE ABECEDARIAN
(LATE —) OPSIMATH

LEARNING ART WIT BOOK LEIR

LERE LORE CLERGY WISDOM APPRISE CUNNING GRAMMAR INSIGHT LETTERS WISTING BOOKLEAR BOOKLORE DOCTRINE HUMANISM LETTRURE MATHESIS PEDANTRY
(— LATE IN LIFE) OPSIMATHY
(SUFF.) MATHY

LEASE FEU FEW LET SET FARM HIRE RENT TACK COWLE DIMIT FIRMA LISSE DEMISE POTTAH RENTAL ASSEDAT CHARTER SETTING BACKTACK SUBLEASE
(— AGAIN) SUBLET

LEASEHOLDER LIVIER

LEASH LEAD LYME SLIP LEASE TRASH COUPLE STRING SWINGE
(— OF HOUNDS) HARL
(DOG —) SLIP TRASH TIRRET
(HAWK'S —) LOYN LUNE TIRRET CREANCE

LEASING LOCATIO

LEAST LEST MINIMAL MINIMUM MINIMUS
(AT —) HURE

LEAST FLYCATCHER CHEBEC

LEAST SANDPIPER PEEP OXEYE STINT

LEATHER ELK KID BEND BOCK BUFF CALF CAPE HIDE NAPA ROAN SEAL ADUST ALUTA BALAT FLANK NIGER RETAN SUEDE BULGAR CASTOR CHAMMY CHROME LIZARD ORIOLE OXHIDE PEBBLE RUSSET SHAMMY SKIVER TURKEY BELTING BUFFING CANEPIN CHAMOIS COWHIDE COWSKIN DEGRAIN DOGSKIN DONGOLA HEADCAP HOGSKIN KIDSKIN MURRAIN PANCAKE PECCARY PERSIAN SAFFIAN ANTELOPE BUCKSKIN BULLNECK CABRETTA CALFSKIN CAPESKIN CHEVEREL COLTSKIN CORDOBAN CORDWAIN DEERSKIN GOATSKIN KANGAROO LAMBSKIN SHAGREEN SHEEPSKIN
(— FOR DRESSING FLAX) RIBSKIN
(— FROM SHEEPSKIN) ROAN
(— SHREDS) MOSLINGS
(— STRIP) RAND
(ARABIAN —) MOCHA
(ARTIFICIAL —) KERATOL PEGAMOID
(BOARDED —) BOX
(BOOKBINDING —) ROAN
(CORDOVAN —) CORDOBAN CORDWAIN
(GOAT —) MOROCCO MAROQUIN
(GRAINED —) ROAN
(KIND OF —) NAPA
(MOROCCO —) LEVANT MAROQUIN
(PATCH OF —) CLOUT
(PRUSSIAN —) SPRUCE
(RUSSIAN —) YUFT BULGAR RUSSIA JUCHTEN
(SHEEPSKIN —) BOCK BUCK NAPA MOCHA
(SOFT —) OOZE ALUTA
(SUPERIOR —) BUFF
(THICK —) BUTT
(UNTANNED —) RAWHIDE
(WASH —) LOSH LOSHE
(PREF.) SCYT(O)

LEATHERBACK LUTH
LEATHERFISH LIJA FOOLFISH
LEATHERJACKET FILEFISH ZAPATERO
LEATHERLEAF CASSANDRA
LEATHERNECK GYRENE MARINE
LEATHERWOOD DIRCA WICOPY BURNWOOD FIREWOOD IRONWOOD LEADWOOD ROPEBARK
LEATHERWORKER TAWER BEDDER CHAMAR MADIGA FLUFFER CHUCKLER
LEAVE GO GET LET BUNK DROP FADE FLEE HOOK LEAF PART QUIT VADE VOID WALK AVOID CONGE FAVOR FORGO GOOUT GRACE SHOVE SPLIT WAIVE BUGGER BUGOFF DEPART DESERT DEVOID FORLET PERMIT RETIRE SECEDE STRAND VACATE FORLEIT FORLESE FORSAKE LARGESS LIBERTY LICENSE FAREWELL PATIENCE UNTENANT PERMISSION SABBATICAL
(— ALONE) FORBEAR DESOLATE
(— BEHIND) LET PLANT DISTANCE OUTSTRIP
(— BRIGHT TRAIL) STREAM
(— BY WILL) BEQUEATH
(— COVER) BREAK
(— HASTILY) SCUR SKIP SKIRR
(— HURRIEDLY) CUT BLOW BOLT FLEE JUMP SCAT SKIP
(— IN ISOLATION) MAROON
(— IN SAFEKEEPING) CHECK
(— NOTHING TO BE DESIRED) SATISFY
(— OF ABSENCE) ABSIT EXEAT LIBERTY FURLOUGH
(— OFF) CEASE DEVAL PETER BILEVE CHEESE DESIST SURCEASE
(— OUT) BATE OMIT SKIP SLIP ELIDE
(— PORT) SAIL CLEAR
(— QUICKLY) SCREW
(— SECRETLY) STEAL
(— SUDDENLY) KITE
(— UNDONE) PRETERMIT
LEAVED
(SUFF.) PHYLLOUS
LEAVEN ZYM ZYMO RAISE YEAST INFUSE RAISING SOURING
(PREF.) ZYM(O)
LEAVENING EMPTINGS
LEAVES PATRIN FOLIAGE LEAFAGE LEAFERY
(— OF BAOBAB TREE) LALO
(— OF ORCHID) FAHAM
(— OF TOBACCO) LEAF FLYINGS SECONDS
(— ON STEM AFTER WITHERING) INDUVIAE
(— USED AS STYPTIC) MATICO
(— USED FOR TEA) MANUKA
(BOILED — OF POTHERB) CHARD
(DRIED —) LAUHALA
(FALLEN —) DUFF
(MEDICINAL —) COCA FILE BUCCO BUCKU FARFARA FUMARIA
(PALM —) ATAP ATTAP CADJAN CAJANG
(TEA —) SOUCHONG
(WITHERED —) PININGS

(SUFF.) **(HAVING —)** CLEMA PHYLLOUS
(NUMBER OF —) MO
LEAVE-TAKING VALE ADIEU CONGEE PARTING WAYGANG FAREWELL WAYGOING
LEAVING BIT ORT TAG
(PL.) RAFF SNUFF REFUGE RESIDUE RESIDUUM
(PREF.) LIPO

┌─────────────────────────────────┐
LEBANON
CAPITAL: BEIRUT BEYROUTH
COIN: LIVRE PIASTRE
MOUNTAIN: ARUBA HERMON SANNINE KENISSEH
PLAIN: ELBIKA
RIVER: JOZ LYCOS DAMOUR LITANI HASBANI LEONTES ORONTES KASEMIEH
SEAPORT: TYRE SAIDA SIDON BEIRUT
TOWN: SUR TYRE ALEIH HALBA SAIDA SIDON ZAHLE JUNIYE ZAHLAH QARTABA TRIPOLI MERJUYUN
VALLEY: BEQAA
└─────────────────────────────────┘

LEBBEK KOKO KOKKO SIRIS
LEBKUCHEN LEKACH
LECHER GOAT LECH LETCH LUXUR SATYR PALLIARD
LECHEROUS LEWD SALT PRIME RANDY WANTON BOARISH CODDING GOATISH LUSTFUL SATYRIC LIKEROUS SCABROUS SPORTIVE STUPROUS SALACIOUS
(PREF.) LUBRI
LECHERY LUXURY
LECTERN DESK EAGLE LUTRIN LATERAN LATTERIN
LECTION GOSPEL EPISTLE READING PERICOPE PROPHECY
LECTIONARY LEGEND
LECTOR LISTER READER
LECTURE JOBE CREED FORUM HOMILY LECTOR LESSON SERMON ADDRESS EARBASH HEARING PRELECT READING JOBATION ORDINARY
LECTURER DOCENT LECTOR READER DRYASDUST
LED (EASILY) DUCTILE
LEDA (DAUGHTER OF —) HELEN CLYTEMNESTRA
(FATHER OF —) THESTIUS
(HUSBAND OF —) TYNDAREUS
(SON OF —) CASTOR POLLUX
LEDGE BEAD BERM DESS LINE STEP ALTAR BENCH CLINT LINCH SHELF SNOUT BEARER OFFSET SETTLE STANCE CHANNEL LEDGING RETABLE
(— BEHIND ALTAR) GRADIN GRADINE
(FIRESIDE —) STOCK
LEDGEMAN BREAKER
LEDGER BOOK SLAB LIEGER JOURNAL OVERLIER
LEDGER BOARD RIBBON
LEE LEW LEEWARD
LEECH GILL HARPY LEACH APODAN SANGSUE BDELLOID HELMINTH

(PREF.) BDELL(A) HIRUDINI
(SUFF.) BDELLA
LEEK FOUAT ALLIUM PORRET SCALLION SENGREEN ROCAMBOLE
(— COLORED) PRASINE
(PREF.) PRASEO PRASO
LEEK GREEN RESEDA
LEER LEAR LOOK OGLE FLEER LEERY SKIME SMIRK TWIRE
LEERFISH GARRICK
LEES LAGS ADDLE DRAFF DREGS DROSS GROUT AMURCA BOTTOM DUNDER MOTHER SORDOR ULLAGE GROUNDS EMPTINGS SEDIMENT WINEDRAF
LEEWAN SOFA DIVAN
LEEWARD DOWNWIND
LEEWARD ISLANDS (ISLAND OF —) KURE ARUBA NEVIS NIHOA LAYSON MIDWAY NECKER ANTIGUA MONTSERRAT
LEEWAY ROOM ROPE DRIFT
LEFT G CAR KAY GAWK NEAR PORT OTHER TOWARD DESERTED SINISTER
(— BEHIND) RELICT
(— EYE) OL OS
(— HELPLESS) STRANDED
(— OVER) ODD ORRA REMAINDER
(BE — ON BASE) DIE
(TURN —) HAW
(PREF.) LAEV(O) LEV(O) SINISTR(O)
LEFT HAND MG MS SM SIN GAUCHE
(— PAGE) VERSO
LEFTHANDED CAR GAUCHE AWKWARD DUBIOUS OBLIQUE KITHOGUE SOUTHPAW
LEFT-HANDER SOUTHPAW
LEFTIST RAD RADICAL
LEFTOVER END ORT REMNANT SURPLUS REMAINDER
(— YARN) THRUMS
(TOBACCO —) TOPPER
(PL.) SCRAN ANALECTS
LEG ARM GAM PEG PIN CRUS GAMB JAMB LIMB TRAM BOUGH GAMBE JAMBE REACH SHANK STICK STUMP BENDER GAMBON GAMMON LEGLET MOGGAN OVIGER PESTLE PLANTA PROLEG WALKER FORELEG TRESTLE FORELIMB
(— OF CRUSTACEAN) PODITE
(— OF HAWK) ARM
(— OF LAMB) GIGOT WABBLER WOBBLER
(— OF TABLE) BALUSTER
(— OF WHEELBARROW) STILT
(—S OF ARTIFICIAL FLY) HACKLE
(— USED FOR FOOD) PESTLE
(ARTIFICIAL —) PYLON
(FURNITURE —) CABRIOLE
(HAVING CREASELESS —S) STOVEPIPE
(LAST —) HOMESTRETCH
(MILK —) WEED
(TROUSER —) SLOP
(WIRE —S) SLING
(WOODEN —) PEG STUMP TIMBER
(PL.) PROPS TONGS STAMPS STICKS

(PREF.) SCEL(O)

(SUFF.) SCELES

(LOWER —) CNEMA CNEMIA CNEMIC CNEMUS

LEGACY ENTAIL LEGATE BEQUEST HERITAGE WINDFALL

LEGAL LEAL LICIT SOUND VALID LAWFUL SQUARE JURIDIC RIGHTFUL

(DOING — WORK) PROBONO

LEGALISM NOMISM SCRIBISM

LEGALISTIC COURT

LEGATE ENVOY DEPUTY EXARCH LEGATUS CONSULAR LEGATARY PANDULPH

LEGATION MISSION

LEGATO SMOOTH

LEGEND EDDA MYTH POSY SAGA TALE FABLE STORY TITLE THREAP CAPTION CUTLINE HAGGADA

(MAP —) KEY

(PREF.) MYTHO

LEGENDARY FABLED FICTIOUS

LEGERDEMAIN JUGGLERY PRESTIDIGITATION

LEGERDEMAINIST JUGGLER

LEGGING SPAT COCKER BOTTINE GAMBADO JAMBEAU BALATONG BOOTIKIN CHIVARRA

(LEATHER —) STRAD

(PL.) CHAPS SHANKS BROGUES COGGERS GAMASHES LEATHERS OVERALLS

LEGIBLE FAIR READABLE

(NOT —) OBSCURE

LEGION HOST TERZO TERZIO

LEGIONARY ANT DRIVER FORAGER

LEGISLATION DYSNOMY LAWMAKING

LEGISLATOR SOLON LAWGIVER LAWMAKER

LEGISLATURE DIET COURT THING LAGTING RIKSDAG LANDRATH RIGSRAAD

LEGITIMATE JUST TRUE VERY LEGAL LEGIT LOYAL HONEST KINDLY KOSHER LAWFUL REABLE SQUARE NATURAL LEGITIME

LEGITIMATELY FAIRLY MULIERLY

LEGPIECE JAMBEAU

LEGUME DAL POD URD DAHL DHAL GUAR PULSE LENTIL LOMENT PEANUT PODDER COCHLEA LEGUMEN PODWARE SOYBEAN STROMBUS

LEHUA OHIA

LEIPOA LOWAN MEGAPOD PHEASANT

LEISHMANIASIS UTA ESPUNDIA

LEISTER SPEAR WASTER

LEISURE TIME TOOM VOID OTIUM RESPITE VACANCY VACATION

LEISURELY SLOW SOODLY TIMELY TOOMLY GRADUAL PICKTOOTH

LELEX (FATHER OF —) NEPTUNE POSEIDON

(MOTHER OF —) LIBYA

(SON OF —) MYLES

LEMAN UNDERPUT

LEMMING CRICETID

LEMMUS MYODES

LEMNISCUS FILET FILLET LAQUEUS

LEMON DOG DUD CEDRA CHLOR LEMONY CEDRATE FAILURE KUMQUAT

LEMONADE COOLER

LEMON GRASS TANGLAD

LEMON SOLE MARYSOLE

LEMON VERBENA ALOYSIA

LEMUR LORI MAKI VARI AVAHI INDRI KOKAM LORIS POTTO SIFAC ADAPID AYEAYE COBEGO COLUGO GALAGO KUBONG MACACO MAHOLI MONKEY SIFAKA APOSORO MEERKAT NATTOCK PRIMATE SEMIAPE TARSIER AMPONGUE BABAKOTO MONGOOSE PRIMATAL TARSIOID

LEND OCKER PREST SECOND ADVANCE IMPREST

(— AT INTEREST) GAVEL

(— ITSELF) ALLOY

LENDING (— AGENCY) MOUNT

LENGTH LUG DREE TOWT PITCH SCOPE SIDTH COURSE EXTENT TOWGHT FOOTAGE DISTANCE LEGITUDE SIDENESS

(— ATHWARTSHIP) ABURTON

(— OF BRIDGE) BAY

(— OF CABLE) SCOPE SHACKLE

(— OF CHAIN) SHOT

(— OF CLOTH) CUT BOLT YARD

(— OF FIBER) STAPLE

(— OF FISHING LINE) CAST

(— OF GEAR TOOTH) FACE

(— OF HAIR) KNOT

(— OF HAIR IN FISHING LINE) IMP

(— OF LIFE) LONGEVITY

(— OF LINE) LOYN

(— OF METAL) SHAPE

(— OF MOUTH) GAPE

(— OF NET) LEAD

(— OF PISTON STROKE) TRAVEL

(— OF ROPE) DRIFT SPOKE BRIDLE COURSE STOPPER

(— OF SERVICE) STANDING

(— OF SHOEMAKER'S THREAD) END

(— OF SOUND) QUANTITY

(— OF THREAD) STITCH

(— OF TILE) GAUGE

(— OF TIMBER) BALK FLITCH

(— OF TIME) DURATION

(— OF TRIP) GATE

(— OF WALL) PANE

(— OF WINDMILL ARM) WHIP

(— OF YARN) KNOT TAPE CHASE SKEIN

(— UNIT) FERMI

(— OF ORGAN PIPE) FOOTAGE

(AT FULL —) ALONG

(CONTINUOUS —) STRETCH

(FOCAL —) FOCUS

(PROJECTING —) SPONSON

(UNIT OF —) PIC PIK ROD FOOT INCH KILO PIKE REED VARA WRAP YARD FERMI METER SHAKU POLLEX FURLONG PLETHRON

(UTMOST —) EXTREME

(PREF.) MEC(O)

LENGTHEN EKE LONG DILATE EXPAND EXTEND LENGTH AMPLIFY DISTEND PRODUCE PROLONG STRETCH ELONGATE INCREASE PROTRACT

(— BY INTERPOLATION) FARSE

LENGTHENING HOLD ECTASIS DIASTOLE

LENGTHWISE ALONG ALENGTH ENDLONG ENDWAYS ENDWISE VERTICAL

LENGTHY LONG LARGE PROLIX LONGFUL EXTENDED

LENIENCY FAVOR MERCY LENITY CHARITY CLEMENCY LENIENCE

LENIENT LAX EASY KIND MILD SOFT FACILE GENTLE HUMANE LENITIVE

LENITIVE MILD MITIGANT SEDATIVE

LENITY MERCY HUMANITY KINDNESS LENITUDE

LENO GAUZE

LENS EYE CROWN GLASS OPTIC FLASER PEBBLE READER APLANAT BIFOCAL CONCAVE CONTACT DOUBLET ACHROMAT EYEGLASS EYEPIECE HYPERGON LENTICLE LUNETTES MENISCUS MAGNIFIER PANTOSCOPE

(JEWELER'S —) LOUPE

(KIND OF —) FRESNEL

(WITHOUT —) APHAKIA

(PREF.) PHAC(O)

LENT CAREME IMPREST

LENTICULAR PHACOID

LENTIGO FRECKLE

LENTIL LENS LINT TILL LENTILE LENTICLE

(PREF.) PHAC(O)

LEOFRIC (FATHER OF —) LEOFWINE

(WIFE OF —) GODIVA

LEONORE (GUARDIAN OF —) ARISTE

(SISTER OF —) ISABELLE

LEONTOCEBUS MIDAS

LEOPARD PARD TIGER PARDAL WAGATI LIBBARD PAINTER PANTHER PARDALE CATAMOUNT

(SNOW —) IRBIS OUNCE

LEOVIGILD (SON OF —) ERMENEGILD

(WIFE OF —) GOISWINTHA

LEPCHA RONG RONGPA

LEPER LAZAR MESEL LAZARUS

LEPIDOMELANE ANNITE

LEPIDOPTERA GLOSSATA

LEPIDOPTERIST AURELIAN

LEPIDOSIS SCALING

LEPRECHAUN ELF SPRITE LURACAN

LEPROSY LEPRA MESEL SCALL ALPHOS LAZARY MESELRY

LEPROUS MESELY MESELED

LEPTON MITE MUON

LEPTOSPIROSIS JAUNDICE

LERP LAAP

LESBIAN FEM DIKE DYKE FEMME EROTIC SAPPHIC TRIBADE SAPPHIST

LESBIANISM SAPPHISM

LESION PIT GALL HIVE SORE CRATER ESCHAR LEPRID ANTHRAX CHANCRE FISSURE LEPROMA BEESTING ERUPTION LEUKEMID TERTIARY

LESOTHO (MONEY OF —) LOTI MALOTI

LESPEDEZA SERICEA

LESS FEW MIN MENO FEWER MINOR LESSER SMALLER WANTING

(— BY A COMMA) MINOR

(PREF.) HYPO MEIO MIMIO MIO

(— THAN NORMAL) HYPO

LESSEE FARMER TERMOR HUURDER TACKSMAN

LESSEN CUT EBB BATE DOCK EASE FAIK FRET KILL LESS SINK WANE ABATE BREAK LOWER MINCE SMALL TAPER BUFFER DEADEN DEJECT IMPAIR INLESS MINIFY MINISH NARROW REBATE REDUCE WEAKEN AMENUSE ASSUAGE CURTAIL DEPLETE DEPRESS ELEVATE LIGHTEN RELIEVE SHORTEN CONTRACT DECREASE DEROGATE DIMINISH DISCOUNT EMBEZZLE MITIGATE MODERATE PALLIATE

(— FORCE) GELD

(— IN VALUE) SHRINK CHEAPEN

(— SENSITIVITY) DULL

(— STRENGTH) WEAR

(— TENSION) RELAX

(— VELOCITY) DEADEN

LESSENING LETUP PERDITION

(— OF PRISON TERM) REMISSION

(— PAIN) PAREGORIC

LESSER PETIT MINUTE SMALLER INFERIOR

(PREF.) MINI MI(O)

(SUFF.) (— ONE) ET ETTE

LESSER CELANDINE PILEWORT

LESSON TAX LEAR TASK STUDY EXAMPLE LECTURE PRECEPT READING DOCUMENT LIRIPOOP RECITATION

(DIFFICULT —) SOAK

(TORAH —) PARASHAH

LESSOR SETTER

LEST UNLESS ANANTER ANAUNTERS

LET LAT SET HIRE ALLOW LEASE LEAVE LETTEN PERMIT SUFFER TENANT

(— BAIT BOB) DIB

(— BECOME KNOWN) SPILL

(— BURN) BISHOP

(— CONTINUE) DRILL

(— DOWN) VAIL DEMIT DIMIT LOWER STOOP STRIKE SUBMIT

(— DOWN ROCK FACE) ABSEIL

(— FALL) DROP VAIL AVALE AWALE DEPOSE

(— FLY) PEG BOLT FIRE WING

(— GO) DROP FAIK QUIT DEMIT BILEVE DEMISE DISMIT UNHAND DISCARD UNSEIZE

(— HIM TAKE) SUM

(— IN) IMMIT INLET IMMISS ADHIBIT

(— IT BE REPEATED) REPET
(— IT STAND) STET
(— KNOW) ACQUAINT
(— LAND) GAVEL
(— LOOSE) FREE SLIP LIBERATE
(— OUT) BLAB TEAM WAGE ALTER BREAK SPILL ARRENT BROACH
(— SLIP) BALK BAULK CHECK FOREGO
(— UP) EBB EASE ABATE
LETDOWN DRAG DOWNER HANGOVER
LETHAL FATAL DEADLY MORTAL
LETHARGIC LOGY INERT DROWSY SLEEPY TORPID DORMANT PASSIVE COMATOSE COMATOUS SLUGGISH SLUMBROUS
LETHARGY COMA LOGY SLOTH STUPOR TORPOR SLUMBER HEBETUDE INACTION SOPITION
(FEELING OF —) BLAHS
LETO LATONA
LETT BALT
LETTER EF EL EM EN EX HE MU NU PE PI XI AIN AYN BEE CEE CHI DAK DEE EDH ESS ETA ETH GEE HET JAY KAY LIL MEM NUN PEE PHI PSI RHO SIN TAU TAV TAW TEE VEE WAW YOD YOK ZED ZEE ALEF ALIF AYIN BETA BETH BILL BULL CHIT DEAD HETH IOTA KAPH RESH SHIN SORT TETH YODH YOGH ZETA AITCH ALEPH ALPHA BLIND BREVE CAPON DELTA DEMIT FAVOR GAMMA GIMEL GRAPH KAPPA KNOWN KOPPA OMEGA SADHE SIGMA STAVE STIFF THETA ZAYIN ACCENT ADVICE ANSWER BILLET CADJAN CARTEL CHARTA COCKUP DALETH FAVVER ITALIC LAMBDA LAMEDH MEDIAL SAMEKH SCRIPT SIGLUM SUNNUD SYMBOL VERSAL CODICIL COLLINS CONTROL DIGAMMA DIPLOMA EPISTLE EPSILON KAREETA MISSIVE OMICRON SPECIAL UPSILON AEROGRAM ASCENDER ENCYCLIC MONITORY NUNDINAL PASTORAL
(— OF DEFIANCE) CARTEL
(— OF PERMISSION) EXEAT
(—S DIMISSORY) APOSTOLI
(—S OF MARQUE) MART
(ANGLO-SAXON —) EDH ETH THORN
(AUTHORIZING —) BREVE
(BEGGING —) SCREEVE
(BLACK —) GOTHIC
(BREAD AND BUTTER —) COLLINS
(CAPITAL —) CAP UNCIAL CAPITAL FACTOTUM MAJUSCULE
(FRIENDLY —) SCREED
(INITIAL —) BLOOMER
(LOVE —) POULET
(LOWERCASE —) MINISCULE
(OBSOLETE —) EPISEMON
(OFFICIAL —) BRIEF
(PAPAL —) BULL TOME BREVE ENCYCLIC
(PRIVATE —) BOOK
(SHORT —) CHIT LINE NOTE BILLET LETTERET
(SILENT —) MUTE
(SMUGGLED —) KITE

(SUBSCRIPT —) SUBFIX
(WORD —) LOGOGRAM
(PL.) MAIL APOSTOLI
(PREF.) EPISTOLO
LETTER BOX APARTADO
LETTER CARRIER CORREO MAILMAN POSTMAN
LETTERER SKETCHER
LETTERING FAC WRITE INCUSE CALLIGRAPHY
(— ON TV SCREEN) CRAWL
(TV —) CRAWL
LETTERPRESS TEXT CAPTION
LETTING FIRMA LOCATIO
LETTING-OUT DROPPING
LETTISH LATVIAN
LETTUCE COS BIBB GRASS SALAD KARPAS SALLET ICEBERG ROMAINE FIREWEED MILKWEED
LETUP (WITH NO —) ONEND
LETUSHIM (FATHER OF —) DEDAN
LEUCIPPE (BROTHER OF —) CALCHAS
(FATHER OF —) MINYAS THESTOR
(SISTER OF —) THEONOE
(SON OF —) TEUTHRAS
LEUCIPPUS (BROTHER OF —) APHAREUS
(DAUGHTER OF —) PHOEBE HILAIRA
(FATHER OF —) OENOMAUS PERIERES
(MOTHER OF —) GORGOPHONE
(WIFE OF —) PHILODICE
LEUCITE LENAD
LEUCITITE ITALITE SPERONE ALBANITE CECILITE
LEUCOCYTE POLY NEOCYTE HEMAMEBA MONOCYTE OXYPHILE
LEUCOMA ALBUGO WALLEYE
LEUCORRHEA WHITES
LEUCOTHEA (FATHER OF —) ORCHAMUS
(MOTHER OF —) EURYNOME
LEUKEMIA CHLOROMA LEUKOSIS
LEVANT EASTERN WORMSEED
LEVANTINE SCATTERMOUCH
LEVEE DIKE DYKE WALL WEIR DURBAR STOPBANK
LEVEL BONE EVEN FAIR FLAT GLAD LUTE PLAT RAZE SHIM VIAL COUCH EQUAL FLUSH GRADE PLAIN PLANE POINT SLICK SOLID CHARGE DOUBLE EVENLY FIELDY NIVEAU SLIGHT SMOOTH STRIKE TUNNEL FLATTEN GALLERY GANGWAY REGULAR DEMOLISH LEVELLER SUBGRADE
(— AFTER PLOWING) BUSH
(— AND SCATTER) GELD
(— A RAFTER) EDGE
(— OFF) HAMMER BULLDOZE
(— OF SOCIETY) STRATUM
(— OF STAGE) STUDY
(— PLACE) PLANILLA
(COMMON —) PAR
(ENERGY —) SINGLET
(EXPERT — OF KARATE) DAN
(EYE —) EYELINE
(HIGHER —S) BRASS
(HIGHEST —) SUMMIT
(LOWEST —) FLOOR BOTTOM HARDPAN

(MINING —) KIP HEAD GALLERY GANGWAY
(NOT ON THE —) ALOP
(ON THE —) TRUE
(STRATIGRAPHIC —) HORIZON
(TOP —) HIGH CEILING
(PREF.) PLAN(I)
LEVELED BENT
LEVELER DIGGER
(PL.) ACEPHALI
LEVELING EGALITE EGALITY
LEVER KEY PRY BEAM GAUL HOOK HORN JACK SWAY TREE BRAKE FLAIL FLIRT HELVE PEDAL PINCH PLUTO PRIZE SPOON STANG STANK SWIPE THROW BINDER CLUTCH COUPER DETENT FEELER GAFFLE HAMMER HEAVER HOPPER LOWDER PORTER ROCKER TAPPET TILLER BALANCE BOOTLEG CROWBAR POINTER RAMHEAD SHIPPER SWINGLE TREADLE TRIGGER TUMBLER BACKFALL GAVELOCK SELECTOR THROTTLE
(— ARM) NIGGER
(— FOR CROSSBOW) GAFFLE GARROT
(— FOR TURNING RUDDER) HELM TILLER
(— IN KNITTING MACHINE) JACK
(— IN TIMEPIECE) PALLET
(— LIKE CANTHOOK) PEAVY PEAVIE
(— OF GIN) START
(CONTROL —) JOYSTICK
(GEARSHIFT —) STICK
(LUMBERMAN 'S —) PEAVY PEAVIE
(ORGAN —) BACKFALL KNEESTOP KNEESWELL
(SPINNING —) BOOTLEG
(SPOKELIKE —) SWINGLE
(THROTTLE —) GUN
(WEAVING —) LAM LAMM SWELL BINDER TIPPLER
LEVERAGE PRY PRIZE
LEVI (FATHER OF —) JACOB ALPHAEUS
(MOTHER OF —) LEAH
(SON OF —) KOHATH MERARI GERSHON
LEVIGATE DUST
LEVITATE RISE FLOAT
LEVITY FOLLY HUMOR GAIETY FLIPPANCY WHIFFLERY
LEVOROTATORY LAEVO LEVOGYRE NEGATIVE
LEVY CUT TAX CESS MISE REAR LEVEL RAISE ASSESS EXTEND EXTENT IMPOSE IMPOST UPTAKE IMPRESS TRIBUTE DISTRAIN DISTRESS SHIPPAGE
(— A TAX) GELD GELT TAIL STENT
(— DISTRESS) DRIVE
(IRISH —) MART
LEVYING EXACTION
LEWD NICE BAWDY FOLLY PRIME RANDY HARLOT IMPURE LACHES LUBRIC RAKISH WANTON HIRCINE LEERING LUSTFUL OBSCENE RAMMISH RIGGISH SCARLET SENSUAL WHORISH PRURIENT SLUTTISH UNCHASTE SALACIOUS

LEWDNESS FOLLY RAKERY LECHERY HARLOTRY PUTANISM LUBRICITY SCULDUDDERY
LEXICOGRAPHER AMERICAN GOVE ALLEN EVANS GOULD CARHART MATHEWS WEBSTER WHEELER BARNHART BARTLETT WORCESTER
BRAZILIAN MORAES
ENGLISH WYLD COLES DYCHE ROGET SCOTT SMITH BAILEY BLOUNT CRAGIE FARMER FLORIO FOWLER MURRAY ONIONS WALKER BRADLEY CAWDREY JOHNSON MINSHEU WITHALS BULLOKAR COCKERAM COTGRAVE AINSWORTH COCKERELL PARTRIDGE STORMONTH RICHARDSON
FRENCH LITTRE ROBERT BEAUJAN GODEFROY LAROUSSE FURETIERE
GERMAN ERMAN MURET SACHS FLUGEL SCHNEIDER
GREEK POLLUX SUIDAS PAMPHILUS
ICELANDIC BLONDAL
ITALIAN CESARI CALENUS FANFANI FACCIOLATI FORCELLINI
NEW ZEALAND PARTRIDGE
POLISH LINDE
SCOTTISH GRANT MURRAY OGILVY
LEXICON CALEPIN WORDBOOK
LIABILITY DEBT DEBIT CHARGE TRIBUTE OBLIGATION
LIABLE APT ABLE OPEN GUILTY EXPOSED OBVIOUS ONEROUS SUBJECT AMENABLE INCIDENT
(— TO MISCHANCE) RISKY
(— TO SIN) PECCABLE
(NOT —) EXEMPT IMMUNE
(SUFF.) ABLE IBLE
LIAISON BOND AFFAIR AFFAIRE LINKING INTIMACY INTRIGUE
LIANA CIPO BEJUCO GUARANA BUSHROPE
LIANG TAEL
LIAR LEAR ANANIAS BOUNCER CRACKER CRAMMER PROCTOR WARLOCK WERNARD FABULIST
LIBATION AMBROSIA
LIBEL DEFAME MALIGN VILIFY SLANDER
LIBELOUS FAMOUS SCANDALOUS
LIBER PHLOEM
LIBERAL WET FAIR FREE GOOD OPEN WHIG BROAD FRANK LARGE NOBLE SOLUTE JANNOCK PROFUSE ADVANCED CATHOLIC GENEROUS HANDSOME LARGEOUS PRODIGAL SEPARATE MUNIFICENT
(CANADIAN —) GRIT
(NOT —) CHARY SPARE
LIBERAL ARTS MUSES
LIBERALITY LARGE BOUNTY BREADTH CHARITY FREEDOM HONESTY LARGESS
LIBERALLY LARGE BROADLY
LIBERATE FREE QUIT FRITH REMIT UNGYVE UNWRAP DELIVER MANUMIT RELEASE UNSLAVE UNFETTER UNTHRALL
LIBERATION LIB FREEDOM RELEASE DELIVERY KAIVALYA DISCHARGE
(— OF SPORE) ABSCISSION

LIBERIA
CAPITAL: MONROVIA
CUSTOM: SANDE
HILLS: BOMI
MEASURE: KUBA
MOUNTAIN: UNI NIETE NIMBA WUTIVI
MOUNTAINS: BONG SATRO
PEOPLE: GI KRU KWA VAI VEI GOLA KROO KROU TOMA BASSA GIBBI GISSI GREBO KPELLE KROOBY KRUMAN KROOBOY MANDINGO
RIVER: CESS LOFA MANO LOFFA MANNA MORRO CESTOS DOUOBE STJOHN STPAUL CAVALLY SANPEDRO
TOWN: GANTA GRIBO REBBO HARPER ZORZOR NANAKRU TAPPITA BUCHANAN MARSHALL SASSTOWN

LIBERTINE ROUE PUNKER PANURGE STRIKER LOTHARIO LOVELACE STRINGER
LIBERTY MAY SOC EASE LARGE LEAVE SCOPE ACCESS LEEWAY SCOUTH STREET FREEDOM LARGESS LICENSE WITHGANG
(**— OF ACTION**) PLAY SWING
(**— OF CHOICE**) FREEWILL
(**— OF ENTRANCE**) INGRESS
(**— OF GOING OUT**) ISH
(**— OF TURNING PIGS INTO FIELDS**) SHACK
(**— TO BUY AND SELL**) TOLL
(**— TO HUNT**) CHASE
(**AT —**) FREE IDLE
(**PARTIAL — OF HAWK**) HACK
(**SEXUAL —**) INTIMACY
(**UNDUE —**) HEAD
LIBERTY CAP PILLEUS
LIBIDINIZATION EGOISM
LIBIDINOUS FLESHY FLESHLY
LIBNI (FATHER OF —) MAHLI GERSHON
LIBRA AS PONDUS
LIBRARIAN AMERICAN COLE DANA HILL HUNT KOCH LANE DEWEY EAMES EVANS GREEN MUDGE POOLE SHERA SMITH WROTH CUTTER FOLSOM HUMMEL JEWETT MEARNS PUTNAM WINSOR CARLSON EDMANDS MUMFORD SONNECK VANNAME WELLMAN BARTLETT BOSTWICK COGSWELL HAVILAND MACLEISH SAUNDERS SPOFFORD HENDERSON YARMOLINSKY
CANADIAN READY
ENGLISH BOND COXE DIBDIN LARKIN PANIZZI PATMORE THOMPSON
FRENCH DUPUY OMONT BONNECHOSE TASCHEREAU
GERMAN EBERT BURGER
PERUVIAN ULLOA
SPANISH MACHADO
LIBRARY DEN AMBRY BIBLE MUSEUM BHANDAR BOOKERY ATHENEUM
LIBRETTO BOOK WORD TESTO TEXTBOOK

LIBYA
ALPHABET: TIFINAGH
CAPITAL: BENGASI BENGAZI TRIPOLI
COIN: DIRHAM
DESERT: FEZZAN MURZUK MURZUCH
GULF: SIDRA SIRTE
MEASURE: SAA BOZZE DONUM JABIA TEMAN BARILE MISURA MATTARO
MOUNTAIN: BETTE
OASIS: JALO KUFRA SEBHA FEZZAN GIOFRA TAZERBO GIARABUB
SEAPORT: HOMS DERNA SIDRI TOBRUK BENGAZI
TOWN: BRAK DERJ HOMS BARKA DERNA SEBHA SIDRI UBARI ZAWIA ELMARJ GARIAN MURZUQ REMADA TOBRUK MISURATA
WEIGHT: KELE UCKIA GORRAF TERMINO KHAROUBA

LICE CREEPERS
(**FISH —**) EPIZOA
LICENSE TAG CHOP GALE HEAD EXEAT LEAVE SLANG SWING BANDON CAROON FIRMAN INDULT PATENT PERMIT READER TICKET CAROOME CERTIFY CROTTLE FACULTY FREEDOM INDULTO LIBERTY LICENCE PLACARD WARRANT ESCAMBIO IMMUNITY MORTMAIN PASSPORT TEZKIRAH
(**— FOR CART**) CAROOME
(**— PLATE**) NUMBER
(**PEDDLER'S —**) SLANG
LICENTIOUS GAY LAX FREE LEWD WILD FRANK LARGE LOOSE FILTHY RIBALD UNRULY WANTON CYPRIAN FLESHLY IMMORAL LAWLESS LIBERAL UNYOKED
LICENTIOUSNESS DIRT LICENSE
LICHEN RAG MOSS MANNA USNEA ARCHIL CORKIR KORKIR ORCHIL CROTTAL CROTTLE CUDBEAR EVERNIA OAKMOSS PARELLA ARCHILLA CAPEWEED LECANORA LUNGWORT PARMELIA ROCKHAIR TREEHAIR WARTWORT
LICIT LEGAL LAWFUL LEEFUL
LICK LAP LIKE SUCK MOUTH SLAKE CONQUER
LICKER-IN TUMBLE
LICKING LAMBENT GRUELING
LICKSPITTLE LACKEY
LICORICE POMFRET SWEETROOT
LICORICE PILL CACHOU
LICYMNIUS (FATHER OF —) ELECTRYON
(**MOTHER OF —**) MIDEA
(**SISTER OF —**) ALCMENA
(**SLAYER OF —**) TLEPOLEMUS
(**WIFE OF —**) PERIMEDE
LID DIP BRED DECK TYMP COVER BRIDLE EYELID POTLID CLAPPER CLICKET CLOSURE SCUTTLE SHUTTER COVERCLE OPERCULUM
(**SUFF.**) POMATOUS
LIE FIB GAB KIP LAY LIG LIN SIT YED CRAM FALL FLAW LIGG REST RIDE WHID DEVIL DWELL FABLE FEIGN

LEASE STAND STORY BOUNCE FITTEN PALTER RAPPER RESIDE SPRAWL VANITY YANKER BOUNCER CONSIST CRACKER CRAMMER CRUMPER FALSITY GRABBLE LEASING PLUMPER TWISTER UNTRUTH WHACKER WHISKER WHOPPER MENDACITY TARADIDDLE PREVARICATE
(**— AHEAD**) AWAIT
(**— ALONGSIDE**) ACCOST
(**— AROUND**) COMPASS
(**— AT ANCHOR**) HOVE
(**— AT FULL LENGTH**) STRETCH
(**— CONCEALED**) DARKLE
(**— CONTIGUOUS**) CONFINE
(**— DETECTOR**) POLYGRAPH
(**— DORMANT**) SLEEP
(**— DOWN**) LEAN COUCH CHARGE
(**— FLAT ON BELLY**) GROVEL
(**— HEAD TO WIND**) TRY
(**— HIDDEN**) LURK MICHE TAPPISH
(**— IN AMBUSH**) HUGGER
(**— IN BED**) KIP THOKE
(**— IN WAIT**) AWAIT LOWER AMBUSH FORELAY
(**— IN WATER**) DOUSE DROWN
(**— LOW**) TAPPICE
(**— NEXT TO**) ADJOIN
(**— OPPOSITE TO**) SUBTEND
(**— OVER**) COVER
(**— PRONE**) GROVEL GRABBLE
(**— PROSTRATE**) STREEK
(**— QUIET**) SNUDGE
(**— SNUG**) CUDDLE
(**— UNEVENLY**) SAG
(**— WITH SAILS FURLED**) HULL
(**BIG —**) CAULKER
(**IMPUDENT —**) BOUNCE
(**MONSTROUS —**) STRAMMER
(**PREF.**) (**— LIID**) LANTHIAN(O) LANTHO

LIECHTENSTEIN
CAPITAL: VADUZ
CASTLE: GUTEMBURG
MOUNTAIN: RHATIKON
RIVER: RHINE SAMINA
ROMAN NAME: RHAETIA
TOWN: HAAG BALZER SCHAAN NENDELN
TRIBE: ALAMANNI

LIED BALLAD
LIEF DEAR LEAVE LEEVE LIEVE FREELY GLADLY BELOVED
LIEN MORTGAGE
LIEU STEAD
LIEUTENANT LUFF ZANY LOUEY JAYGEE KEHAYA CAIMAKAM QAIMAQAM TENIENTE WOODVILE SHAVETAIL
(**— JUNIOR GRADE**) JAYGEE
LIFE IT VIE ZOE HIDE JIVA PUFF SNAP TUCK VALE ANIMA BEING BLOOD DEMON HEART LIFER QUICK SWEAT BIOSIS BREATH CANDLE COURSE ENERGY SPIRIT SPRITE LIFELET LIFEWAY VITALITY VIVACITY
(**— AFTER DEATH**) FUTURITY
(**— IN HEAVEN**) GLORY
(**— IN SOCIETY**) SAMSARA SANSARA

(**— OF FURNACE LINING**) CAMPAIGN
(**— OF THE SEA**) HALIBIOS
(**ACADEMIC —**) ACADEMIA
(**ANIMAL —**) FLESH
(**ANIMAL AND PLANT —**) BIOS BIOTA BIOLOGY EDAPHON
(**CLOISTERED —**) VEIL
(**EARLY —**) YOUTH
(**ETERNAL —**) GRACE
(**HOME —**) DOMESTICITY
(**INTELLECTUAL —**) JIVATMA
(**LOCAL —**) BIOTA
(**MONASTIC —**) CLOISTER
(**MORAL —**) DAENA
(**MOSS —**) BRYOLOGY
(**PLANT —**) BIOS BIOTA FLORA BOTANY
(**PUBLIC —**) WORLD
(**ROBUST —**) JUICE
(**SIGN OF —**) PULSE
(**SINGLE —**) CELIBACY
(**TERRESTRIAL —**) GEOBIOS
(**WAY OF —**) BAG SCENE FASTLANE
(**WITHOUT —**) AZOIC
(**PREF.**) BI(O) EMBIO PSYCH(O) VIT(A)(O)
(**NOT —**) ABIO
(**SUFF.**) BIA BIONT BIOSIS BIOTIC BIOUS BIUM BIUS BY PSYCHE
LIFE BELT SAFETY
LIFEBLOOD BLOOD SWEAT
LIFE-FORCE KUNDALINI
(**YOGI —**) KUNDALINI
LIFE FOR THE TSAR, A
(**CHARACTER IN —**) SOBININ SUSANIN ANTONIDA
(**COMPOSER OF —**) GLINKA
LIFELESS ARID BLAH DEAD DULL FLAT AMORT HEAVY INERT VAPID ANEMIC TORPID SAPLESS DESOLATE GRIPLESS INACTIVE
(**PREF.**) ABIO
LIFELESSLY DEADLY INERTLY
LIFELESSNESS ANEMIA
LIFELIKE VIVE QUICK EIDETIC NATURAL ANIMATED SPEAKING
LIFE PRESERVER FLOAT NEDDY
LIFESAVER HERO
LIFETIME AGE DAY WORLD LIVING LIFEDAY DURATION LIFELONG
(**— OF FLOWER**) ANTHESIS
LIFE WITH FATHER (AUTHOR OF —) DAY
(**CHARACTER IN —**) DELIA GULICK CLARENCE MARGARET
LIFEWORK (ARTIST'S —) OEUVRE
LIFT WIN BOOM BUOY CAST COCK HEFT JACK REAR TOSS WEVE ARSIS BOOST BREAK ELATE HEAVE HITCH HOICK HOIST HOOSH MOUNT PRESS RAISE SPOUT STEAL WEIGH BUCKET CLEECH SNATCH TAKEUP ELEVATE ENHANCE HEELTAP NAUNTLE BOOKLIFT CHAIRWAY ELEVATOR LEVITATE
(**— HAT**) DOFF
(**— IN PAWNSHOP**) SPOUT
(**— IN VEHICLE**) SETDOWN
(**— IN WEIGHT LIFTING**) SQUAT
(**— OF WAVE**) SCEND
(**— OF WEIGHTS**) SNATCH

(— **ONESELF**) SOAR
(— **QUICKLY**) PERK
(— **UP**) HOVE CRANE ERECT EXALT EXTOL HORSE WEIGH ADVANCE ELEVATE NAUNTLE
(— **WITH BLOCK AND TACKLE**) BOUSE
(**KIND OF** —) SKI
(**SKI** —) GONDOLA
LIFTED ARRECT SUBLIME
LIFTER GAGGER SERVER HOISTER HOISTMAN
LIFTING HIKE UPTAKE
LIFT VALVE POPPET
LIGAMENT BAND BOND ARTERY FRENUM PAXWAX STRING ZONULE ARMILLA LIGATURE
(PREF.) DESM(A)(IDI)(IDIO)(O) SYNDESM(O)
LIGAMENTOUS DESMOID
LIGATE BAR
LIGATURE ASH CLAM PLICA DIGRAM PNEUMA STIGMA BANDAGE DIGRAPH FUNICLE LIGAMENT LIGATION
(— **OE**) ASH
LIGGER TRIMMER
LIGHT BUG DAY GAY HAP LAW SHY SUN AIRY EASY FAIR FALL FINE FIRE FLIT FLUX GLIM LAMP LEET LUNT MILD SLUT SOFT BAVIN BLAZE CORKY FANAL FILMY FLAME FLEET FUFFY LEGER LOUGH MERRY PITCH QUICK SHEER SPILL WHITE BEACON BRIGHT CHAFFY FLOATY FLOSSY FLUFFY FROTHY GENTLE HAPPEN ILLUME KINDLE LANCET LUSTER LUSTRE MARKER PASTEL PHAROS SIGNAL SLUSHY STINGY STRIKE STROBE SUTTLE VOLAGE BENGOLA BUOYANT CRESSET FRAGILE GLITTER LAMBENT SFOGATO SMITHER SUMMERY TORTAYS TRIVIAL UNGRAVE BACKFIRE DAYLIGHT DELICATE DIAPHANE ELECTRIC EXPEDITE FEATHERY GASLIGHT GOSSAMER LEGGIERO LUMINARY PALOUSER SUNLIGHT SUNSHINE
(— **AND BRILLIANT**) LAMBENT
(— **AND FIRE ON HORSE'S MANE**) HAG
(— **AND FREE**) FLYAWAY
(— **AND QUICK**) VOLANT
(— **CANDLES**) TOLLY
(— **DISPLAY**) LED
(— **FROM NIGHT SKY**) AIRGLOW
(— **IN WINDOW**) LANCET
(— **OF MORNING**) AURORA
(— **ON TV SCREEN**) SNOW
(— **UP**) FLASH GLOZE ILLUME RELUME GLORIFY
(— **UPON**) STRIKE
(**BRIGHT** —) GLARE GLEAM
(**BURST OF** —) FLASH
(**CIRCLE OF** —) HALO NIMBUS
(**EMIT** —) LASE
(**EMIT COHERENT** —) LASE
(**FAINT** —) GLIMMER SCARROW
(**FEEBLE** —) TAPER GLIMMER
(**FITFUL** —) SHIMMER
(**GREEN** —) GOAHEAD
(**HARBOR** —) BUG

(**INDICATOR** —) BEZEL
(**INDICATOR — ON SCREEN**) CURSOR
(**INNER** —) SEED
(**KIND OF** —) KLEIG KLIEG
(**LASER — EMITTER**) LIDAR
(**NEBULOUS** —) CHEVELURE
(**NEW** —) SEPARATE
(**NIGHT** —) MORTAR
(**PARKING** —**S**) DIMMERS
(**PATCH OF** —) CURSOR
(**PERSIAN GOD OF** —) MITHRAS
(**REFLECTED** —) SKYME
(**SHIP'S** —) FANAL
(**SMALL** —) TAPER
(**STUDIO** —) KLIEG
(**TRAFFIC** —) BLINKER
(**WAVERING** —) FLICKER
(PL.) BUFF
(PREF.) LUCI LUMIN(I)(O) PHOS PHOT(O)
LIGHT-COLORED BLONDE
LIGHTED LUMINOUS
LIGHTEN ALAY CLEAR LEVIN LIGHT RAISE ALLEGE BLEACH ENCLEAR FOULDRE MOLLIFY SWEETEN THUNDER LEVIGATE
LIGHTENING BREAK
(— **OF HAIR**) FROSTING
LIGHTER KEEL SCOW ACCON BARGE CASCO PRAAM WHERRY DROGHER GABBARD GONDOLA PONTOON CHOPBOAT
LIGHTERMAN KEELER KEELMAN
LIGHT-FOOTED SPRY
LIGHT-GREEN
(PREF.) CHLOR(O)
LIGHT-HEADED IDLE BARMY LIGHT LIVELY CARRIED GLAIKET SKITTISH
LIGHT-HEARTED GAY GLAD GIDDY BUOYANT WINSOME CAREFREE DEBONAIR VOLATILE
LIGHTHEARTEDNESS BUOYANCY
LIGHTHOUSE FANAL LIGHT MINAR BEACON PHAROS LANTERN
(PREF.) PHARO
LIGHT IN AUGUST (**AUTHOR OF** —) FAULKNER
(**CHARACTER IN** —) DOC JOE GAIL LENA ALLEN BROWN BURCH BYRON GROVE HINES LUCAS BOBBIE BURDEN JOANNA EUPHEUS CHRISTMAS HIGHTOWER
LIGHTLESS APHOTIC
(PREF.) APHOTO
LIGHTLY LIGHT AIRILY FAIRILY HOVERLY LEGGIERO SLIGHTLY
LIGHT-MINDED BLITHE ETOURDI
LIGHTNESS CHEER VALUE GAIETY LEVITY AIRINESS BUOYANCY LEGERETE LEGERITY
(— **OF MOVEMENT**) BALLON
LIGHTNING BOLT FIRE LAIT LEVIN FULMEN METEOR FOULDRE SULPHUR THUNDER FIREBALL FIREBOLT WILDFIRE
LIGHT-O'-LOVE COCOTTE LEVERET
LIGHT-TEXTURED FOZY
LIGHTWOOD FATWOOD
LIGIA LIGYDA
LIGNEOUS WOODY XYLOID
LIGNIN LIGNOSE XYLOGEN

LIGNITE JET
LIGNUM VITAE GUAYACAN POCKWOOD
LIGROIN BENZINE CANADOL
LIGULA LANGUET
LIGULE STRAP LIGULA
LIKE AS ALA DIG DOTE LIST LOVE ALIKE ENJOY EQUAL FANCY SAVOR TASTE ADMIRE AFFECT BELIKE LIKELY MATTER PLEASE SEMBLE SIMILE THEWAY CONCEIT SIMILAR SEMBLANT SUITABLE SEMBLABLE
(— **A GLAND**) ADEMOSE ADENOUS
(— **BETTER**) PREFER
(— **HAIR**) CRINITE
(**VERY** —) SIAMESE
(PREF.) HOME(O) HOMOE HOMOI SYM
(SUFF.) AR EOUS ESQUE IC(AL) INE IS ISH ISTIC LY ODE OID(AL) SOME
LIKELIHOOD APTNESS
LIKELY APT FAIR LIKE READY LIABLE PROOFY SEEMLY GRADELY SMITTLE APPARENT FEASIBLE POSSIBLE PROBABLE PROSPECTIVE
(**MOST** —) BELIKE
LIKEN EVEN LIKE REMENE SEMBLE COMPARE ASSEMBLE CREDIBLE RESEMBLE SIMILIZE
LIKENESS DAP BLEE ICON IDOL MAKE SECT BLUSH DUMMY GLIFF IMAGE MORAL SHAPE EFFIGY FIGURE STATUE ANALOGY KINSHIP PATTERN PICTURE RETRAIT EQUALITY HOMOLOGY PARALLEL PORTRAIT SEMBLANCE SIMILARITY
(— **OF ORIGIN**) ISOGENY
(**DISTORTED** —) CARICATURE
(**PERFECT** —) SPIT
LIKENING SIMILE
LIKEWISE EKE TOO ALSO ITEM EITHER EQUALLY LIKEWAYS
(— **NOT**) NOR
LIKHI (**FATHER OF** —) SHEMIDAH
LIKING GOO GRA PAY GOUT GUST LIKE LIST LUST FANCY FLAIR GUSTO HEART SHINE SKILL SMACK TASTE THEAT SWALLOW AFFINITY APPETITE FONDNESS PENCHANT
(**ECCENTRIC** —) FOIBLE
(**MENTAL** —) PALATE
(SUFF.) (— **FOR**) PHIL(A)(AE)(E)(IA) (ISM)(IST)(OUS)(US)
LIKUTA
(PL.) MAKUTA
LILAC LILAS MAUVE LAYLOCK
LILACIN SYRINGIN
LILIOM (**AUTHOR OF** —) MOLNAR
(**CHARACTER IN** —) WOLF JULIE MARIE FICSUR LILIOM LOUISE MUSKAT LINZMAN HOLLUNDER
LILLIPUTIAN TINY
LILY ALOE IXIA KELP SEGO AZTEC CALLA CLOTE AUGUST LILIUM VALLEY COCUISA MONOCOT ASPHODEL LILYWORT MARTAGON NENUPHAR
(**AFRICAN** —) AGAPANTHUS
(**CLIMBING** —) GLORIOSA
(**PALM** —) TI
(**SEA** —) CRINOID
(**WATER** —) CANDOCK CAMALOTE

(PREF.) LIRIO
(SUFF.) CRINUS
LILY OF THE VALLEY LILIUM MUGGET MUGUET MUGWET LILYWORT SHINLEAF
LIMA BEAN HABA LIMA
LIMB ARM LEG CLAW FOOT KNOT LITH TRAM WING ARTUS BOUGH SPALD SPAUL SWAMP BRANCH MEMBER PODITE FEATURE FLIPPER FORCEPS PLEOPOD NECTOPOD
(PREF.) MEL
(SUFF.) (**CONDITION OF** —) MELIA
LIMBA AFARA FRAKE
LIMBER BAIN FLIP LIMP LUSH AGILE LINGY LITHE LISSOM SEMMIT SUPPLE SWANKY BRUSHER BRUTTER KNOTTER LIMMOCK PLIABLE FLEXIBLE FLIPPANT
LIME CALX LIMA CEDRA CEDRAT CHUNAM CITRON FUSTIC
(— **IN BRICK**) BOND
(**KIND OF** —) KEY
(**WILD** —) COLIMA
(PREF.) CAL(AREO)(I)(IO)(O)
LIMEN THRESHOLD
LIMESTONE CAM HUM CALP CAUK CAUM LIAS LYAS MALM CHALK POROS ROACH CLUNCH KUNKUR MARBLE OOLITE CIPOLIN SCAGLIA DOLOMITE PISOLITE TRAVERTINE
(— **REGION**) KARST
(**DECOMPOSED** —) ROTTENSTONE
LIME TREE LIME TEIL LINDEN
LIMEY TAR
LIMIT CAP END FIX BIND BUTT FINE HOLD LINE LIST MARK MERE PALE TAIL BLOCK BOUND COAST GAUGE HEDGE SCANT STENT STINT VERGE BORDER BOURNE DEFINE EFFLUX EXTENT FINISH FINITE HAMPER LENGTH MODIFY NARROW PALING SCRIMP TROPIC UPSHOT ASTRICT CLOSURE COMPASS CONFINE CONTENT HORIZON MAXIMUM MEASURE OUTSIDE BOUNDARY CONTRACT DEADLINE IMPRISON LIMITARY LIMITATE OUTGOING OUTREACH RESTRAIN RESTRICT SOLSTICE TERMINUS PARAMETER
(— **EFFECT**) ALLAY
(— **IN A FOREST**) BAIL
(— **MOTION**) HOLD
(— **OF STATUTE**) PURVIEW
(— **OF VISION AT SEA**) KENNING
(**EXTREME** —) HEIGHT
(**LOWER** —) FLOOR
(**TAKE TO THE** —) TAX
(**UPPER** —) CEILING
(**UTTER** —) EXTREME
(PL.) AMBIT CANCELS ENVIRONS PERIMETER
(PREF.) ORI
LIMITATION TAIL FRAME STINT DENIAL CLOTURE RESERVE
(— **OF DEBATE**) CLOTURE
(— **OF INHERITANCE**) TAIL
(— **OF WANTS**) STOICISM
(PL.) SWADDLE
LIMITED MILD TAIL BORNE BRIEF SHORT SMALL FINITE NARROW STINTY STRAIT BOUNDED SPECIAL

CONFINED DEFINITE LIMITARY PAROCHIAL SECTARIAN MEASURABLE PROVINCIAL RESTRICTED

(**— IN APPEAL**) CHICHI

(**— IN SCOPE**) MODERATE

LIMITING DEFINITE ADJECTIVE EXCLUSIVE

(**— LINE**) RUBICON

LIMITS (**NEAR OUTER — OF PLAY**) DEEP

LIMMA DIESIS

LIMMU EPONYM

LIMO (**KIND OF —**) STRETCH

LIMON (**BROTHER OF —**) SCEPHRUS

(**FATHER OF —**) TEGEATES

(**MOTHER OF —**) MAERA

LIMONENE CINENE CARVENE CITRENE

LIMONITE BOGORE BOGIRON PEAIRON

LIMONIUM STATICE

LIMOUSINE LIMO BERLIN SALOON SUBURBAN

LIMP HIP HOP CLOP GIMP HALT HIMP HOIT SOFT THIN HENCH HILCH HITCH LINGY LOOSE LOPPY SLAMP STILT FLABBY FLIMSY HAMBLE HIMPLE HIRPLE HOBBLE LENNOW LIMBER LIMPSY FLACCID LIMMOCK SHAFFLE UNSMART DRAGGLED DROOPING CLAUDICATION

LIMPET CHINK OPIHI SHELL ACMAEA LIMPIN FLIDDER

LIMPID PURE CLEAR LUCID BRIGHT CRYSTAL PELLUCID

LIMPING HALT LAME GIMPY LIMPY ZOPPA HALTING

LIMPLY LANKLY

LINAGE SPACE

LINALOOL LICAREOL

LINCHPIN FORELOCK

LINCOLN (**IN-LAW OF —**) TODD

LINCTUS LOOCH LOHOCH LOHOCK

LINDEN LIN LIME LYNE TEIL TILIA TILLET LINWOOD BASSWOOD DADDYNUT WOODLIND

LINE BAR BOX FIX RAY ROW TAW BOFF CASE CEIL COLA CRIB DASH FACE FILE GAME GAPE LACE LARD LATH LEAD LING MAIN MARK RACE RANK RULE STOP TAUM WHIP AGONE FAINT FEINT FLEET HATCH LIGNE LINEA METER RANGE SCORE SPIEL STRIA TOUCH TRACE TRAIL TRAIN TWIST BINDER CABURN CEVIAN CREASE DEGREE DOUBLE EARING GASKET ISOBAR ISOHEL ISOPAG ISOTAC METIER NETTLE SECANT SECOND SPRING STREAK STRING STRIPE AZIMUTH BABBITT CATLINE CONTOUR CREANCE ENVELOP GUNLINE HIPLINE ISOCHOR ISOGRAM ISOHYET ISONEPH ISORITH ISOSTER ISOTOME KNITTLE MARLINE NACARAT SCRATCH WINDROW BALKLINE BISECTOR BOUNDARY BUSINESS CHAMPAIN DATELINE DEADLINE DIAGONAL DIAMETER DRAGLINE DRUMLINE FISHBACK

GANTLINE GEODESIC GIRTLINE HAIRLINE HANDLINE HEXAPODY ISOGLOSS ISOGONIC ISOPHANE ISOPHENE ISOPLERE ISOTHERE ISOTHERM LANDWIRE LIFELINE MARTINET SLIPBAND STRINGER SUBCLONE SUBSTILE SUBSTYLE UPSTROKE PERPENDICULAR

(**— AROUND STAMP**) FRAME

(**— AS CENTER FOR REVOLVING**) AXIS

(**— HEARTH**) FIX FETTLE

(**— IN GLASS**) STRING

(**— IN HAT**) HEADLINE

(**— MINESHAFT**) TUB

(**— OF ACTION**) LAY

(**— OF BATTLE**) FRONT

(**— OF BUSINESS**) WAY

(**— OF CELLS**) ANNULUS

(**— OF CLIFFS**) SCARP BREAKS

(**— OF COLOR**) SLASH STREAK

(**— OF DANCERS**) CHAIN

(**— OF DESCENT**) SIDE STEM STIRP STOCK PHYLUM STRAIN ANCESTRY BREEDING

(**— OF DETERMINANT**) COLUMN

(**— OF DEVELOPMENT**) STREET

(**— OF DEVOLUTION**) ENTAIL

(**— OF FAMILY**) STEM

(**— OF FIBERS**) CHRYSAL

(**— OF FIRE HOSE**) LEAD

(**— OF FLOTATION**) BEARINGS

(**— OF FORTIFICATION**) LIMES ENCEINTE

(**— OF HAY**) WAKE WALLOW

(**— OF HEALTH**) HEPATICA

(**— OF HIGH TIDE**) LANDWASH

(**— OF HOUSES**) BLOCK

(**— OF INTERSECTION**) GROIN BUTTOCK

(**— OF JUNCTION**) MEET SEAM

(**— OF LIGHTNING**) STREAK

(**— OF MERCHANDISE**) NAMEPLATE

(**— OF MERCURY**) HEPATICA

(**— OF PERSONS**) QUEUE CORDON STICKLE

(**— OF PORES**) HATCHING

(**— OF SOLDIERS**) RAY FILE RANK WAVE CORDON

(**— OF STITCHING**) BASTING

(**— OF TACK**) PITCH

(**— OF TALK**) SPIEL

(**— OF TIMBERS**) BOOM STOCKADE

(**— OF TREES**) SCREEN

(**— OF TYPE**) SLUG KICKER

(**— OF UNION**) SUTURE

(**— ON A LETTER**) SERIF

(**— ON BOOK COVER**) BAND

(**— ON COAT**) GORGE

(**— ON DOLPHIN**) STOP

(**— ON HIGHWAY**) BARRIER

(**— ON WEATHER MAP**) ISOBAR

(**— THAT CUTS ANOTHER**) SECANT

(**— TO BIND CABLES**) CABURN

(**— TO FASTEN SAIL**) EARING GASKET

(**— TO RAISE FLAG**) LANIARD LANYARD

(**— TO START RACE**) TRIG

(**— TOUCHING ARC**) TANGENT

(**— UP**) LAY QUEUE

(**— WITH BRICKS**) GINGE

(**— WITH PANELLING**) WAINSCOT

(**— WITH STONES**) STEEN STEYN

(**— WITH TIMBER**) CRIB

(**ANCHOR —**) RODING

(**BEARING —**) CUT

(**BOTTOM —**) NET

(**BOUNDARY —**) MERE FENCE BORDER ISOGLOSS

(**BOUNDING —**) SIDE BOUNDARY PERIMETER

(**BRIEF —**) ITEM

(**COASTAL —**) SEAMARK

(**CONNECTING —**) LIGATURE

(**CONTINUOUS —**) STRETCH

(**CONTOUR —**) ISOBASE ISOCHASM ISOTHERM

(**CURVED —**) ARC SLUR SWEEP

(**CUTTING —**) SECANT

(**DEMARCATION —**) BOMBLINE

(**DIAGONAL —**) BIAS

(**DIVIDING —**) EDGE MIDRIB DIVISION FRONTIER

(**ELECTRIC —**) HIGHLINE

(**ENCIRCLING —**) RIM

(**FACIAL —**) TRAIT

(**FINISHING —**) TAPE WIRE

(**FISHING —**) TOME TROT FLEET SNELL SNOOD LEADER LEDGER NORSEL BACKING BOULTER OUTLINE SPILLER SPILLET TRIMMER BLOWLINE CORKLINE FISHLINE SNAGLINE TROTLINE

(**HORIZONTAL —**) LEVEL

(**IMAGINARY —**) AGONE HINGE GROOVE ISOBAR ISOGAM ISOHEL ISOPAG HORIZON ISOBASE ISOBATH ISOGRIV ISOHYET ISOLINE ISOTACH ISOBRONT ISOCHASM ISOCHEIM ISOCHLOR ISOCHORE ISOCRYME ISOGLOSS ISOPHOTE ISOPLETH ISOSTERE ISOTHERM

(**INCISED —**) SCORE

(**INCLINED —**) CANT

(**LIMITING —**) RUBICON

(**LONGITUDINAL —**) MERIDIAN

(**MEDIAN —**) RAPHE

(**METRICAL —**) EIGHT STAFF STICH DIMETER SAPPHIC STICHOS MONOMETER OCTAMETER PENTAMETER

(**MINESHAFT —**) BRATTICE

(**MUSICAL —**) ACCOLADE

(**NAUTICAL —**) EARING LACING GESWARP MARLINE PAINTER RATLINE DOWNHAUL MESSENGER

(**ONE-TENTH OF —**) GRY

(**PERPENDICULAR —**) CATHETUS

(**PLOTTED —**) ADIABAT

(**RADIATING —**) BEAM

(**RAILROAD —**) STEM STUB

(**RAISED —**) RIDGE

(**SPECTRUM —**) GHOST DOUBLET SINGLET TRIPLET MULTIPLET

(**STARTING —**) SCRATCH

(**STRAIGHT —**) CHORD BEELINE STRAIGHT

(**SUPPLY —**) AIRLIFT UMBILICAL

(**SURVEYING —**) WAD BASE CHAIN

(**THEATRICAL —S**) FAT

(**THIN —**) THREAD

(**TOW —**) CORDELLE

(**TRANSPORTATION —**) FEEDER CARRIER

(**WAVY —**) SQUIGGLE

(**ZIGZAG —**) DANCETTE

(**42 —S**) LENGTH

(**PREF.**) LINEO STICHO

(**SUFF.**) STICH(OUS)

(**STRAIGHT —**) TRIX

LINEAGE GET KIN KIND RACE TEAM BIRTH BLOOD SPACE STIRP STOCK FAMILY HAVAGE NATION PARAGE SOURCE SPRING STRAIN DESCENT KINDRED PROGENY SUCCESS ANCESTRY PEDIGREE PARENTAGE

LINEAL DIRECT

LINEAMENT LINE TRACT TRAIT FEATURE

LINEAR RUNNING

LINECUT ZINCO

LINED MASONED

LINEMAN END GUARD CENTER TACKLE FORWARD WIREMAN CHAINMAN

LINEN LIN BUCK LAWN CRASH IRISH TOILE BARRAS DAMASK DIAPER NAPERY RAINES SENDAL BATISTE DORNICK HOLLAND LOCKRAM TABLING BARANDOS OSNABURG PLATILLA

(**— CLOSET**) LOCKER

(**— FOR SHIRTS**) SARKING

(**— TO COVER CHALICE**) PALL

(**CHINESE —**) KOMPOW

(**COARSE —**) HARN BARRAS

(**FINE —**) LAKE LAWN BYSSUS DAMASK DIAPER RAINES

(**HOUSEHOLD —**) NAPERY TABLING

(**SCRAPED —**) LINT

(**SHADE OF —**) ECRU

(**SPANISH —**) CREA

(**TWILLED —**) SILESIA

(**PREF.**) BYSSI BYSSO LINO

LINER SHIP BASKET SCRIBER STEAMER

LINES
(**PREF.**)

(**TWO CROSSED —**) CHIASMO CHIASTO

LINET (**BROTHER OF —**) LIONES

(**HUSBAND OF —**) GARETH

LINEUP SHOWUP

LING BURBOT DRIZZLE STOKVIS

LINGA DILDO

LINGCOD CULTUS

LINGER LAG HANG HOVE LING STAY CLING DALLY DELAY DEMUR DWELL HAUNT HOVER PAUSE TARRY DRETCH HANKER LOITER TAIGLE TARROW DRINGLE

LINGERER LUNGIS LAGGARD

LINGERIE FRILLIES PRETTIES

LINGERING SLOW DELAY MOROSE TARDANT DRAGGING

LINGO BAT CANT JARGON LINGUA PATTER DIALECT

LINGUA GLOSSA TONGUE

LINGUAL GLOSSAL

LINGUIST (**ALSO SEE PHILOLOGIST**)

LINGUISTIC GLOTTIC

LINGUISTICS GRAMMAR PHILOLOGY

LINIMENT EIK EMBROCHE OPODELDOC

LININ PLASTIN

LINING FUR BACK COAT BAIZE BRASS FACING PANNEL BABBITT

BUSHING CEILING FURRING
FURRURE THIMBLE TINNING
TUBBING CLEADING DOUBLING
DOUBLURE FIREBACK SHEETING
UNDERLAY WAINSCOT PERCALINE
(— FOR ROOF) SARKING
(— FOR WALL) FIRRING FURRING
(— FOR WELL) STEENING STEYNING
(— OF BEARING) JEWEL
(— OF CYLINDER) BUSH
(— OF FURNACE) BASQUE
FIREBACK
(— OF HAT) TIP CAUL
(— OF SMELTING LADLE) SCULL
(MINESHAFT —) CRIB
(WOODEN —) LAG BRATTICE
(SUFF.) PLEURA
LINK JAR TIE TOW JOIN KNIT LUNT
SHUT YOKE CLEEK COMMA NEXUS
COPULA COUPLE FASTEN FETTER
TOUGHT CODETTA CONNECT
COUPLER ENCHAIN INVOLVE
LIAISON SHACKLE CATENATE
IDENTIFY VINCULUM COLLIGATE
(— ARMS) CLEEK
(— FOR TWO COMPUTERS BY
PHONE) MODEM
(— IN NETWORK) LEG
(COMPOUND —) SWIVEL
(WOODEN —) LAG
LINKAGE BOND CELL COUPLING
LINKWORK
LINKED CONNEX CATENATE
INTEGRAL
LINKING HOOKUP ANNECTANT
(— DEVICE) LINCHPIN
LINKMAN LINKBOY LIGHTMAN
LINKS MACHAIR
(BOGGY —) MACHAIR
LINNET FINCH TWITE LENARD LINTIE
REDPOLL REDFINCH
LINSANG CIVET ZINSANG
LINSEED LINGET
LINSEY-WOOLSEY WINCEY
LINT FLY FLUE FLICK CADDIS
CADDICE CHARPIE CARBASUS
(SCRAPED —) XYSTUS
LINTEL CAP CLAVY HANCE CLAVEL
DARNER SUMMER SQUINCH·
TRANSOM BRESSUMMER
(— OF FIREPLACE) MANTEL
LINUS (BROTHER OF —) ORPHEUS
(FATHER OF —) APOLLO OEAGRUS
ISMENIUS
(MOTHER OF —) CALLIOPE
PSAMATHE
LION CAT LLEW MORNE SHEDU
SIMBA LIONEL LIONET LEOPARD
(MOUNTAIN —) PUMA COUGAR
(PREF.) LEON LEONT(O)
LION MONKEY LEONCITO
LION-TAILED MONKEY MACACO
MACAQUE WANDEROO
LIP BLOB BRIM EDGE MASK PUSS
SASS APRON CHOPS GROIN
MOUTH SPOUT TUTEL LABIUM
LABRUM ROUTER CHILOMA
LABELLUM UNDERLIP
(— DISEASE) PERLECHE
(— OF BELL) SKIRT
(— OF COROLLA) GALEA
(— OF FLOWER) HELM
(— OF ORCHID) SLIPPER

(— OF PITCHER) BEAK
(— OF VESSEL) SPOUT
(—S OF MOOSE) MUFFLE
(CHAD WOMAN WITH DISTENDED
—S) UBANGI
(FLAT —) APRON
(LOWER —) JIB FIPPLE
(PL.) LABRAS CUSHION
(PREF.) CHEIL(O) CHIL(O)
(SUFF.) CHIL(IA)(O)(US)
LIPARITE RHYOLITE
LIPASE PIALYN
LIPIDE FAT CERIDE ADIPOID STERIDE
TETHELIN
LIPLIKE LABIAL
LIPOCHROME LUTEIN
LIPOID FAT ADIPOSE
LIPOMA STEATOMA
LIPOPROTEIN HDL LPL
(PLASMA —) VLDL
LIPPED LABIATE
LIPPIA WRIGHT ALOYSIA
LIP PLUG LABRET TEMETA
LIPPY STIMPART
LIPS
(PREF.) LABIO
LIQUEFACTION (— OF GEL)
SOLATION
LIQUEFIED FUSILE POTATE REMISS
RESOLVED
LIQUEFY RUN FUSE MELT RELENT
LIQUATE DISSOLVE ELIQUATE
LIQUEUR EAU OUZO RAKI AURUM
CREME NOYAU CHASSE GENEPI
KUMMEL PASTIS PERNOD RACKEE
STREGA ANESONE CORDIAL
CURACAO PERSICO RATAFIA
RATIFIA ABSINTHE ADVOCAAT
ALKERMES AMARETTO ANGELICA
ANISETTE CALVADOS MANDARIN
PRUNELLE VESPETRO
MARASCHINO BENEDICTINE
(PL.) EAUX
LIQUID AQUA BREE BLASH DRINK
FLUID LEACH MOIST ACETAL
FLUENT FURANE AEROSOL
BUCKING CINEOLE EYEWASH
FLOWAGE VINASSE BLACKING
EFFLUENT EFFUSION EXCITANT
FURFURAN LEACHATE LIBATION
SOLUTION
(— AFTER SALT CRYSTALLIZATION)
BITTERN
(— IN CELL) EXCITANT
(— UNIT) TUN CHENG SHENG SHING
POTTLE MUTCHKIN PUNCHEON
(ACID-RESISTANT —) GROUND
(COLORING —) HENNA
(COOKING —) BREE BROO BROTH
STOCK
(DISABLING —) MACE
(DISTILLED —) SPIRIT
(FILTHY —) ADDLE
(INSULATING —) ASKAREL
(MAY BE —) ASSETS
(OILY —) ANILINE CHLORAL
PICAMAR CARDANOL CREOSOTE
(PERFUMED —) COLLEN COLOGNE
(REFUSE —) SCOURAGE
(REFUSE —S) SEWAGE
(SIZING —) GLAIK
(STERILIZED —) JOHNIN
(STINKING —) CACODYL

(SYRUPY —) HONEY
(TANNING —) LIME
(THICK —) DOPE GLOP SIRUP SYRUP
(THICK, STICKY —) GLOP
(VISCOUS —) TAR SCHRADAN
(VOLATILE —) ETHER ALCOHOL
DILUENT LIGROIN
(WEAK —) BLASH SLIPSLOP
(PREF.) LATICI
LIQUIDATE SINK SLAY SETTLE
LIQUIDATION CLEANUP
LIQUOR ALE BUB DEW GAS LAP OKE
PAD POT RUM SUP TAP WET BEER
BREE FIRE FIZZ GEAR GROG LUSH
PURL SUCK SWIG TAPE TIFF
BOGUS BUDGE CEBUR DRINK
GLASS HOOCH JUICE KEFIR
MOBBY NAPPY PERRY PISCO
SAUCE SHRAB SHRUB SICER SKINK
STICK BOTTLE CASSIS CHICHA
DIDDLE DOCTOR FOGRAM FUDDLE
GATTER GENEVA GUZZLE HYDROL
KIRSCH MAOTAI MASTIC MESCAL
POTTLE ROTGUT SAMSHU STRUNT
TIPPLE WHISKY BITTERN BRACKET
BRAGGET GROCERY PHLEGMA
SPUNKIE SUCTION TAPLASH
TEQUILA WAIPIRO WHISKEY
ABSINTHE BRAGWORT EYEWATER
HYDROMEL MEDICINE OKOLEHAO
POTATION RUMBOOZE FIREWATER
(— CABINET) TANTALUS
(— CASE) GARDEVIN
(— FROM MUST) ARROPE
(— FROM PEARS) PERRY PERRIE
(— FROM WOOL-SCOURING) SUD
SUDS
(— MIXED WITH WINE) DOCTOR
(— SALE) ABKARI
(— TAKEN IN SODA WATER)
CINDER
(ACID —) VERJUICE
(ALCOHOLIC —) GIN ARAK HOOCH
ARRACK BRANDY SAMSHU AQUAVIT
BITTERS SNOOTFUL
(ALCOHOLIC —S) ARDENT
(BITTER —) TIRE
(CHEAP —) SMOKE
(COLORLESS —) GLYCID GLYCOL
GLYCIDOL GUAIACOL
(CRAB APPLE —) WHERRY
(DISTILLED —) DEW SOTOL GRAPPA
PHLEGM SCHNAPPS
(DRUGGED —) HOCUS
(HARD —) BOOZE
(INTOXICATING —) GROG LOAD
LUSH TAPE BUDGE GUZZLE KUMISS
HASHISH MOONSHINE
(MALT —) ALE BUB BEER STOUT
ENTIRE PORTER STINGO
(MOTHER —) HYDROL BITTERN
(POT —) BREWIS
(RICE —) SAMSHU
(SPIRITUOUS —) DEW GROG
MOBBY STRUNT WAIPIRO
KAOLIANG
(STRAIGHT —) SHORT
(STRONG —) RUG TUBA VINO
HOGAN RUMBO STINGO
(TAN —) OOZE
(TANNING —) LAYAWAY TAILING
(WATERED —) BLASH
(WEAK —) BULL SLIPSLOP

LIRA LIRE ZWANZIGER
(ONE-TWENTIETH —) SOLDO
LIRIPIPE TIPPET
LISSOME LITHE LIMBER NIMBLE
SUPPLE SVELTE FLEXIBLE
LIST TIP BILL FILE HEEL LEET NOTE
POLL ROLL ROON ROTA SWAG
BRIEF CANON CISTS INDEX PANEL
SCORE SCRIP SCROW SLATE
AGENDA CENSUS COLUMN DETAIL
DOCKET ERRATA HUDDLE LEGEND
PURREL RAGGER RAGMAN
RECORD ROSTER SCREED SCROLL
SERIES CATALOG CITATOR
COMPILE DIPTYCH ITEMIZE
LISTING NOTITIA WAYBILL
CALENDAR CINCTURE HANDLIST
PLATBAND REGISTER SCHEDULE
SYNONYMY TITULARY
(— OF BOOKS) CANON
(— OF CANDIDATES) LEET SLATE
TERNA
(— OF CAPABILITIES) REPERTOIRE
(— OF CHURCH DATES) ORDO
(— OF CONTESTANTS) DRAW
SEEDING
(— OF CRIMINAL CONVICTIONS)
RECORD
(— OF DISEASES) NOSOLOGY
(— OF INGREDIENTS) FORMULA
(— OF JURORS) TALES
(— OF MAP SYMBOLS) LEGEND
(— OF PASSERS WITHOUT
HONORS) GULF
(— OF RATES) TARIFF
(— OF SAINTS) CANON
(— OF SECURITIES) PORTFOLIO
(— OF THEATRICAL PARTS) CAST
(COMPUTER —) MENU
(GENEALOGICAL —) BEGATS
(IMPRESSIVE —) ARRAY
(LEGAL —) TABLEAU
(LONG —) LITANY
(MAKE A —) CATALOG
(OBITUARY —) NECROLOGY
(PRAYER —) BEADROLL
(WINE —) CARD
(PL.) CAREER BARRACE
LISTEL QUADRA
LISTEN HARK HEAR LIST TEND
TENEZ ATTEND HARKEN INTEND
WHISPER
(— TO) DIG EAR HARK HEAR CATCH
ATTEND
LISTENER AUDITOR OTACUST
LISTENING PRICK AUDIENT
HEARING
(— DEVICE) BUG
(PREF.) ACOU
LISTER SULKY RIDGER
LISTERA OPHRYS
LISTING AGEE ITEM FRAME PARADE
LASHING
(— OF JURORS) ARRAY
LISTLESS DOPY DULL WOFF DOWFF
FAINT MOONY DONSIE SUPINE
LANGUID UNLISTY UNLUSTY
CARELESS INDOLENT THOWLESS
TONELESS UNHEARTY
LISTLESSLY DAVIELY
LISTLESSNESS ACEDIA APATHY
UNLUST VACUITY

LISUARTE (DAUGHTER OF —) ORIANA
(FATHER OF —) ESPLANDIAN
LITANY AITESIS ROGATION
LITE LOCAL LOWCAL
LITERAL VERBAL TEXTUAL
LITERALLY SIMPLY
LITERARY BLUE BOOKISH LITERATE
(— MATERIAL) KITSCH
(— WORK) PREQUEL
(SUFF.) (— STYLE) ESE
LITERATE LETTERED
LITERATI CLERISY
LITERATURE FICTION LETTERS CLAPTRAP
(— CLANDESTINELY DISTRIBUTED) SAMIZDAT
(CLANDESTINE —) SAMIZDAT
(EROTIC —) EROTOLOGY
(OBSCENE —) SCATOLOGY
(RUSSIAN SUPPRESSED —) SAMIZDAT
(SACRED —) VEDA SRUTI
(WISDOM —) CHOKMAH HOKHMAH
LITHE BAIN SPRY WIRY SWACK CLEVER LIMBER LISSOM SILKEN SUPPLE SVELTE WANDLE LISSOME FLEXIBLE

LITHUANIA
CAPITAL: VILNA WILNA VILNIUS
COIN: LIT LITAS MARKA CENTAS FENNIG OSTMARK AUKSINAS SKATIKAS
FORMER CAPITAL: KOVNO KAUNAS
NAME: LITVA LIETUVA
PEOPLE: BALT LETT ZHMUD LITVAK YATVYAG
RIVER: NEMAN NERIS RUSNE VENTA DUBYSA LIELUPE NEMUNAS PREGOLYA
TOWN: MEMEL VILNA JIFI GAVA VILNIUS KAPSUKAS KLAIPEDA SIAULIAI

LITHUANIAN BALT ZHMUD
LITIGANT SUER SUITOR
LITIGATE LAW PLEAD CONTEST
LITIGATION LAW LIS MOOT SUIT LAWING PLEADING PLEASHIP
LITMUS LAKMUS TURNSOLE
LITOTES MEIOSIS
LITTER DIG PIG BIER RAFF REDD BREED CABIN CLECK DOOLY DRECK HAULM MULCH SEDAN TRASH DOOLIE FARROW GOCART KINDLE KITTEN MAHMAL REFUSE CLUTTER LETTIGA LOUSTER MAMMOCK NORIMON RUBBISH RUMMAGE SCAMBLE BRANCARD CARRIAGE KINDLING MUNCHEEL PAVILION STRETCHER
(— FOR LIVESTOCK) BEDDING
(— OF PIGS) FAR FARE FARROW
(— ON PACK ANIMAL) CACOLET
(CAMEL —) KAJAWAH
(FOREST —) DUFF
(MOLE —) CACOLET
(SENT TO MECCA) MAHMAL
LITTERBUG SLOB
LITTERED FOUL
LITTLE FEW LIL PEU WEE CURN LITE POCO TINY VEEN CHOTA CRUMB SMALL TASTE WHONE BITTIE DAPPER LEETLE MINUTE PETITE PICKLE PUSILL KENNING MODICUM THOUGHT FRACTION SNIPPING
(— BY LITTLE) EDGINGLY INCHMEAL
(— LESS THAN) ABOUT
(— MUSICALLY) POCO
(— ONE) RUNT BUTCHA POPPET
(A —) SOMEWHAT
(INDEFINITELY —) NTH
(PREF.) OLIG(O) PARVI PAUCI PUSILL(I) STEN(O)
(SUFF.) ISK KIN STENOSIS ULE
(— ONE) CLE ELLA ETTE IE ILLA
LITTLE DEMON (AUTHOR OF —) SOLOGUB
(CHARACTER IN —) SASHA LIUDMILA PYLNIKOV PEREDONOV RUSTILOVA NEDOTYKOMKA
LITTLE DORRIT (AUTHOR OF —) DICKENS
(CHARACTER IN —) AMY JOHN CASBY FANNY FLORA ARTHUR DORRIT EDWARD PANCKS CHIVERY CLENNAM MEAGLES WILLIAM BLANDOIS PLORNISH BARNACLES
LITTLE MINISTER (AUTHOR OF —) BARRIE
(CHARACTER IN —) DOW ROB ADAM GAVIN MICAH NANNY BABBIE OGILVY DISHART MCQUEEN RINTOUL WEBSTER MARGARET
LITTLENESS ATOMITY
LITTLE WOMEN (AUTHOR OF —) ALCOTT
(CHARACTER IN —) JO AMY MEG BETH DEMI JOHN BHAER DAISY FRITZ KIRKE MARCH BROOKE CARROL LAURIF MARMEE LAURENCE THEODORE
LITTORAL COAST
LITURGY FORM RITE ABODAH MAARIB MINHAG NEILAH MINCHAH MYSTERY HIERURGY SHAHARIT
LIVE BE USE WIN KEEP LEAD STAY ALERT ALIVE DWELL EXIST GREEN HABIT LEEVE QUICK SHACK VITAL HARBOR LIVELY LIVING REMAIN RESIDE BREATHE INHABIT SUBSIST CONTINUE CONVERSE VIGOROUS
(— AT ANOTHER'S EXPENSE) COSHER
(— BY BEGGING) CADGE SKELDER
(— BY STRATAGEMS) SHARK
(— FROM DAY TO DAY) EKE
(— IN CONTINENCE) CONTAIN
(— IN LUXURY) STATE
(— IN PEACE) COEXIST
(— IN SAME PLACE) STALL
(— ON) SURVIVE
(— RIOTOUSLY) JET
(— TEMPORARILY) CAMP
(— THROUGH) PASS TIDE
(— TOGETHER) AGREE COHABIT
(— WELL) BATTEN
LIVE-BOX CAR
LIVE-FOREVER LULANG ORPINE
LIVELIHOOD BEING BREAD LIVING LIFEHOOD
LIVELINESS PEP BRIO FIRE FIZZ LIFE PUNCH SPUNK BOUNCE ESPRIT GAIETY SPIRIT ENTRAIN SPARKLE ACTIVITY VITALITY VIVACITY
LIVELONG LEELANG ENDURING
LIVELY GAY TID AIRY BRAG CANT FAST FESS GLEG KECK LIVE PERT RACY SPRY TAIT TRIG VITE VIVE WARM YARE AGILE ALERT ALIVE BONNY BRISK BUXOM CANTY CHIRK COBBY CORKY CRISP DESTO FRESH FRISK JAZZY KEDGE KINKY MERRY PAWKY PEART PEPPY POKEY RUDDY SASSY SMART VIVID WHICK ACTIVE BLITHE BOUNCY BRIGHT CHEERY CHIRPY COCKET CROOSE CROUSE DAPPER FIERCE FRISCH GINGER JOCUND KIPPER LIVING NIMBLE QUIVER SEMMIT SPARKY SPRACK TROTTY VEGETE WHISKY WIMBLE ALLEGRO ANIMATE ANIMOSE BOBBISH BUCKISH BUOYANT GIGGISH GIOCOSO JOCULAR KINETIC LEBHAFT POINTED ROUSING SPIRITY SPRINGY TITTUMY TITTUPY WINCING ANIMATED BOUNCING CHIRRUPY FRISKFUL FRISKING GALLIARD SANGUINE SKITTISH SMACKING SPANKING SPIRITED SPORTIVE STEERING STIRRING TRIPSOME VEGETOUS VOLATILE SPARKLING
(— PERSON) SWINGER
(BE —) SWING
(TO BE —) SWING
LIVEN LACE CHEER ANIMATE
LIVE OAK ENCINA
LIVER MAW FOIE HEPAR VISCUS PUDDING
(— ATROPHY) LUPINOSIS
(— OF LOBSTER) TOMALLEY
(PREF.) HEPATICO HEPAT(O)
LIVER-COLORED HEPATIC
LIVERPOOL (NATIVE OF —) SCOUSE SCOUSER LIVERPUDLIAN
LIVERWORT HEPATICA MOSSWORT
LIVERY SUIT CLOTH LIVRE UNIFORM CLOTHING
LIVESTOCK FEE WARE STOCK STORE STUFF CHATTEL BESTIALS FATSTOCK
LIVE WIRE HUSTLER
LIVID HAW WAN BLAE BLUE
LIVING KEEP ALIVE BEING BREAD GOING QUICK VITAL WHICK AROUND LIVELY VIABLE ZOETIC ANIMATE SUPPORT ANIMATED BENEFICE
(— IN THE WORLD) SECULAR
(— IN WAVES) LOTIC
(— NEAR THE GROUND) EPIGEAN
(— ON BANKS OF STREAMS) RIPAL RIPARIAN
(— THING) QUICK
(BARE —) CRUST
(ECCLESIASTICAL —) BENEFICE
(PREF.) ONT(O) VIVI
(— ORGANISMS) BIO
(SUFF.) (— IN OR ON) COLE COLINE COLOUS
LIVING-ROOM PARLOR
LIVRE FRANC
LIXIVIATE LEACH
LIXIVIUM LYE

LIZARD DAB EFT GOH UMA UTA DABB GILA IBIT SEPS TEGU TEJU URAN AGAMA ANOLE BLUEY DRACO GECKO GUANO SKINK SNAKE SWIFT TEIID TOKAY TWEEG VARAN AMEIVA ANGUID ARBALO DRAGON GOANNA HARDIM IGUANA LACERT LEGUAN MOLOCH TEIOID WORRAL ZONURE BUMMALO CAUDATE CHEECHA DIAPSID MONITOR REPTILE SAURIAN SCINCID SCINCUS TUATARA TUCKTOO BASILISK KAKARIKI MOKAMOKA SCINCOID SCORPION SLOWWORM TEGUEXIN WHIPTAIL ZONUROID CHAMELEON CHUCKWALLA PLEURODONT
(PREF.) LACERTI SAUR(O)
(SUFF.) SAUR(A)(IA)(IAN)(US)
LIZARD FISH ULAE INIOME SOAPFISH SPEARING
LLAMA ALPACA VICUNA GUANACO
LLUDD NUDD
LO SEE ECCE
LOACH DOJO BEARDIE MUDFISH
LOAD BUN JAG LUG TON BUCK CARK CRAM DECK DRAW FILL HAUL LADE LAST LUMP PACK RAKE SEAM STEM STOW TOTE TURN BARTH CARGO DRAFT PITCH PRIME STACK TRUSS TURSE BURDEN CHARGE COMBLE DEMAND FODDER FOTHER HAMPER LADING LOADEN THRACK WEIGHT BALLAST CARLOAD DERRICK DRAUGHT ENDORSE FRAUGHT FREIGHT ONERATE OPPRESS BACKPACK CARRIAGE ENCUMBER HEADLOAD SHIPLOAD PLANELOAD
(— A DIE FOR CHEATING) COG
(— FABRICS) WEIGHT
(— OF COAL) KEEL
(— OF HAY OR CORN) HURRY
(— OF LAMBS) DECK
(— OF LOGS) PEAKER BUNKLOAD
(— OF WOOL) TOD
(— ON BACK) ENDORSE INDORSE
(— SHIP) STEM
(— TO CAPACITY) SATURATE
(— TO EXCESS) ENCUMBER
(ELECTRIC —) DEMAND
(EXCESSIVE —) SURCHARGE
(HORSE —) SEAM SUMAGE
(LAST — OF GRAIN) WINTER
(SMALL —) JAG JAGG JOBBLE
(PL.) BUSHEL
LOADER CHARGER
LOADING LADING MARGIN ARRASTRE
(— PLACE) PIER
LOADSTONE MAGNET SIDERITE LODESTONE
LOAF BAP BUM COB AZYM HACK HAKE HULL LAKE MIKE SLIM SORN BANGE BREAD BRICK DRING MOUCH SHOOL SLIVE SLOSH BLUDGE BROGUE CADDLE DIDDLE GEORGE HALLAH RODNEY SLINGE WASTEL HOOSIER MANCHET SHACKLE SLOUNGE SOLDIER OBLATION PANHAGIA QUARTERN SHAMMOCK

(— AROUND) HULL HOWFF SLOSH RODNEY GOLDBRICK
(— OF BREAD) COB BATON FADGE MICHE TOMMY HALLAH TAMMIE
(BROWN —) GEORGE
(KIND OF —) DELI
(ROUND —) BUN COBURG
(SMALL —) BAP COB NACKET
(SUGAR —) TITLER
LOAFER BUM CAD YOB BEAT GRUB STIFF BUMBLE BUMMER CADGER KEELIE SLOUCH SLOVEN BLUDGER COASTER FAITOUR HOODLUM SLINKER SOLDIER COBERGER HOOLIGAN LARRIKIN LAYABOUT SEASONER
LOAFING IDLE MIKE
LOAM RAB LAME MALM MARL SLIP LOESS REGUR CLEDGE
LOAMY MELLOW
LOAN DHAN LEND LENT PREST CREDIT DONATE MUTUUM ADVANCE FIXTURE IMPREST
LOANBLEND HYBRID
LOATH LOTH LAITH LEATH SWEER DAINTY BACKWARD
LOATHE UG HATE SHUN ABHOR LAITH WLATE AGRISE DETEST DESPISE SCUNDER SCUNNER NAUSEATE
LOATHING NAUSEA REVOLT DISGUST SCUNNER
LOATHLY LAIDLY
LOATHSOME FOUL UGLY VILE POCKY LAIDLY UNLIEF HATEFUL LOATHLY MAWKISH OBSCENE TETROUS WLATFUL DEFORMED NAUSEOUS WLATSOME NEFANDOUS ABOMINABLE
LOB ARC
LOBBY HALL FOYER NARTHEX PASSAGE TAMBOUR ANTEROOM COULISSE
LOBBYIST PROMOTER
LOBE ALA FIN LAP AXIS LIST MALA ALULA EXITE FIBER FIBRE FLUKE GALEA LOBUS THECA TOOTH UVULA EARLAP FILLET FOLIUM GLOSSA INSULA LAPPET LIGULE LOBING MANTLE VANNUS VERMIS AROLIUM AURICLE HEMAPOD LACINIA LOBULUS AMYGDALA EPICHILE GLABELLA LABELLUM PALPIFER PHYLLOID SQUAMULE
(— OF ANTHER) THECA
(— OF LEAF) LACINIA PINNULA PINNULE SEGMENT
(— OF WHALE'S TAIL) FLUKE
(PREF.) (— OF BRAIN) LEUC(O)
LOBED CUT LOMATINE
(SUFF.) FID FIDATE
LOBLOLLY LOUT MIRE PINE GRUEL
LOBSTER CRAY HOMARD DECAPOD SHEDDER CRAWFISH CRAYFISH LANGOSTA MACRURAN
(— ENCLOSURE) CRAWL
(— LESS THAN 10 INCHES LONG) JOE
(FEMALE —) HEN
(NORWAY —) SCAMPO
(SMALL —) PAWK NANCY
(UNDERSIZED —) SHORT

LOBSTER POT COY CRAIL CREEL TRUNK FISHPOT
LOBULARIA KONIGA
LO-CAL LITE
LOCAL HOME NATIVE LIMITED TOPICAL VICINAL REGIONAL EPICHORIC
(NOT) AZONIC
(PREF.) TOP(O)
LOCALE AREA SITE LOCAL PLACE SCENE
LOCALITY SPA HAND PLAT SPOT LOCUS PLACE POINT SITIO SITUS STEAD HABITAT LATITUDE POSITURE SITUATION
(BARREN —) GALL
(BEAUTIFUL —) XANADU
(GUARDED —) POST
LOCALIZE SITUATE POSITION
LOCATE SITE SPOT PITCH PLACE BESTOW BILLET SETTLE SITUATE PINPOINT
(— AT INTERVALS) SPOT
(— WATER) DIVINE
LOCATED SET FIXED SEATED SITUATED
(— OFF THE HIGHWAY) DEVIOUS
LOCATING SYSTEM SOFAR
LOCATION FALL HOME PLOT SEAT PLACE SITUS WHERE UBIETY AMENITY STATION HOMESITE STANDING
(ESSENTIAL —) EYE
(FOREST —) CHANCE
(GEOGRAPHIC —) SEAT
(MINING —) MYNPACHT
(NATURAL —) HABITAT
(SUFF.) TOPE TOPY
LOCH LOUGH LOCHAN
LOCK COT KEY FEAK FRIB HOLD TRIM YALE CHUBB CLASP SASSE TRESS DUBBEH ENLOCK LUCKEN DAGLOCK EARLOCK KEYLOCK PINLOCK SPANNER DEADLOCK FORELOCK
(— IMPROPERLY) BIND
(— IN RIVER) SASSE
(— OF HAIR) COT TAG TUZ COTT CURL FEAK TATE FLAKE FLOCK FLUKE QUIFF TRESS TANGLE COWLICK EARLOCK FRIZZLE SERPENT WIMPLER FORELOCK SIDELOCK
(— OF WOOL) TAG COTT FRIB FLOCK STAPLE HASLOCK
(— UP) JAIL STOW ENCAGE CABINET
(CANAL —) COFFER CHAMBER
(DIRTY —) FRIB
(MATTED —) COT COTT DAGLOCK
(MUSKET —) ROWET
(PART OF —) REWET STRIKE
(WHEEL —) REWET
LOCKED FAST LUCKEN
LOCKER HUTCH ASCHAM
LOCKERMAN NIBBLER SCOTCHER SNIBBLER
LOCKET BRELOQUE
LOCKJAW TETANUS TRISMUS
LOCKNUT JAMNUT KEEPER
LOCKOUT SHUTOUT
LOCKS MOP
LOCKSMITH LOCKYER
LOCKUP JUG BRIG GAOL JAIL LOCK

LOGS STIR CHOKY CLINK TRONK COOLER HOOSEGOW ROUNDHOUSE
LOCOMOTION FLYING LATION
LOCOMOTIVE HOG PIG PUG BOGY GOAT HOGG MULE SHAG TANK BOGIE DINKY DUMMY MOGUL PILOT DIESEL DOCTOR DOLLIE DONKEY ENGINE LOADER PUSHER SMOKER YARDER BOBTAIL BOOSTER SHUNTER STEAMER CALLIOPE CHOOCHOO COMPOUND DOLLBEER
(— WITHOUT CARS) WILDCAT
(EXTRA —) HELPER
(PART OF —) CAB ROD BELL DOME HOSE LAMP STEP BRACE HINGE PILOT TRUCK BOILER JACKET TENDER COUPLER SANDBOX WHISTLE CYLINDER HANDRAIL INJECTOR SANDPIPE HEADLIGHT RESERVOIR DRIVEWHEEL SMOKESTACK
LOCOMOTOR ATAXIA TABES
LOCOWEED LOCO LEGUME PEAVINE CRAZYWEED
LOCRINE (DAUGHTER OF —) SABRINA
(FATHER OF —) BRUTE BRUTUS
LOCULUS THECA
LOCUS PLACE EVOLUTE SURFACE SYNAPSE CONCHOID ENVELOPE HOROPTER
LOCUST WETA BRUKE CICAD HONEY ACACIA CICADA QUAKER SKIPPER TETRIGID VOETGANGER
LOCUST TREE CAROB ACACIA LOCUST ROBINIA ALGAROBA
LODE LEAD REEF VEIN LEDGE COURSE FEEDER QUARRY SCOVAN COUNTER
LODOLETTA (CHARACTER IN —) ANTONIO FLAMMEN LODOLETTA
(COMPOSER OF —) MASCAGNI
LODESTONE MAGNET SIDERITE TERRELLA
LODGE DIG HUT INN LIE BEAT CAMP HOST KEEP ROOM STAY STOW TENT BOWER CABIN COUCH COURT GROVE GUEST HOGAN HOTEL HOUSE HOWFF LAYER LOGIS STICK TARRY ALIGHT BESTOW BILLET BURROW COSHER GESTEN GRANGE HOSTEL RESIDE SETTLE BARRACK LODGING QUARTER SOJOURN EMBOLIZE HARBINGE
(— AND EAT) COSHER
(— FOR SAFEKEEPING) DEPOSIT
(— IN COURT) BOX
(DRUID —) GROVE
(LOCAL —) COURT
(SPORTSMAN'S —) SHEAL
LODGEPOLE PINE TAMARACK
LODGER INMATE ROOMER TENANT
LODGING BED CRIB FERM GIST HAFT HOST NEST GEAST LOGIS HARBOR HOSTEL LIVERY HOSPICE HOUSING COUCHANT GUESTING
(— FOR SOLDIERS) CASERN
(— OF MARABOUT) KOUBA
(CHEAP —) DOSS
(TEMPORARY —) SHELTER

(VILE —) KENNEL
(PL.) PAD DIGS DIGGINGS
LODGINGHOUSE INN KIP GITE STOP HOTEL LOGIA LOCANDA PENSION HOSTELRY
LODICULE SQUAMULA SQUAMULE
LOESS LIMON
LOFT BALK FLAT GOLF JUBE LAFT ATTIC SOLAR GARRET SOLLAR HAYLOFT COCKLOFT SCAFFOLD TRAVERSE
(— GOLF BALL) PITCH
(HAY —) TALLET TALLIT
LOFTIEST SUPREME
LOFTINESS PRIDE HEIGHT DIGNITY MAJESTY EMINENCE GRANDEUR HIGHNESS CELSITUDE
(— OF SPIRIT) MAGNANIMITY
LOFTSMAN LINESMAN
LOFTY AIRY HIGH LOFT TALL BRENT ELATE GRAND GREAT NOBLE PROUD SKYEY STEEP WINGY AERIAL ANDEAN HAUGHT TOPFUL TOWERY UPWARD WINGED ANDESIC ARDUOUS EMINENT EXCELSE HAUGHTY SUBLIME ARROGANT ELEVATED GENEROUS MAJESTIC OLYMPIAN TOWERING
LOG NOG BUNK CLOG DRAG SKID CHOCK CHUCK CHUNK PIECE STICK STOCK BATTEN BILLET PEAKER PEELER SADDLE SAWLOG BACKLOG DAYBOOK DEADMAN DEGRADE JOURNAL LOGBOOK DEADHEAD
(— AS ANCHOR) DEADMAN
(— AS RAFTER) VIGA
(— BINDING A RAFT) SWIFTER
(— CAR) BUNK
(— FASTENED TO TRAP) DRAG
(— SUPPORTING MINE ROOF) NOG
(— WITHOUT BARK) BUCKSKIN
(— WITH SPIKES IN END) DEADENER
(ENCLOSED —S) BOOM
(FLOATING —S) DRIVE
(LOAD OF —S) PEAKER
(PILE OF —S) DECK ROLLWAY
(SAWED —) BOULE
(SLABBED —) CANT
(SMALL —) LOGGET
(SPLIT —) PUNCHEON
(STRIPPED —) BATTEN
(SUNKEN —) DEADHEAD
LOGANIN MELIATIN
LOGARITHM DENSITY
(— SYMBOL) PF PH PK RH
(NEGATIVE —) PH
LOGBOOK LOG JOURNAL
LOGE BOX BOOTH LODGE STALL
LOGGER RIDER BOWMAN DECKER FALLER GOPHER HOOKER LIMBER MARKER SCORER CHOPPER FROGGER GRABBER SPOTTER CATTYMAN
LOGGIA LODGE BALCONY MIRADOR
LOGIC NYAYA LOGICS CANONIC WITCRAFT
(— OF DISCOVERY) HEURETIC
LOGICAL SANE RAISONNE RATIONAL
LOGISTILLA (SISTER OF —) ALCINA MORGANA

LOGMAN CHASER CHOPPER
LOGO LABEL EMBLEM
LOGOGRAM IDEOGRAM
LOGOMACHY (ONE ENGAGED IN —) DEBATER
LOGOS WORD
LOGOTYPE SIG
LOG PERCH DARTER HOGFISH ROCKFISH
LOGROLLING BIRLING
(**— TOURNAMENT**) ROLEO
LOGWOOD BRAZIL ADMIRAL DYEWOOD BLUEWOOD HYPERNIC CAMPEACHY
LOGY DROWSY GROGGY
LOHAN RAKAN
LOHENGRIN (CHARACTER IN —) ELSA HENRY ORTRUD FREDERICK GOTTFRIED LOHENGRIN TELRAMUND
(**COMPOSER OF —**) WAGNER
(**FATHER OF —**) PARSIFAL
(**WIFE OF —**) ELSA
LOIN LEER LISK ALOYAU LUNYIE
(**— STEAK**) FILET FILLET TOURNEDOS
(**PORK —**) GRISKIN
(**2 UNCUT —S**) BARON
(**PL.**) REINS FILLET SADDLE
(**PREF.**) LUMB(O) OSPHY(O)
LOINCLOTH IZAR MALO MARO DHOTI LUNGI PAGNE PAREU MOOCHA PANUNG DHOOTIE
LOIS (DAUGHTER OF —) EUNICE
(**GRANDSON OF —**) TIMOTHY
LOITER LAG CLUG FOOL HAKE HANG HAWM HAZE HOVE LOUT MIKE MUCK SLUG COOSE DELAY DRAWL KNOCK MOUCH SHOOL SIDLE TARRY COOTER DAWDLE LAGGER LINGER MUCKER STRAKE TAIGLE PROJECT SHAFFLE LALLYGAG LOLLYGAG SCOWBANK SLAMMOCK SLUMMOCK HANGAROUND
LOITERER DRONE IDLER LAGGER LAGGARD LURCHER
LOITERING SLIMSY LAGGARD
LOKAPALA MAHARAJA
LOKI (DAUGHTER OF —) HEL
(**FATHER OF —**) FARBAUTI
(**MOTHER OF —**) NAL LAUFEY ANGRBODHA
(**SLAYER OF —**) HEIMDALL
(**WIFE OF —**) SIGYN ANGURBODA
LOLITA NYMPHET
LOLL FUG IDLE LAZE LOUT FROWST LOLLUP LOUNGE SOZZLE SPRAWL RECLINE SCAMBLE SCOWBANK
LOLLAPALOOZA LULU ONER
LOLLIPOP LOLLY SUCKER SUCKABOB
LOLO NOSU
LONDON SMOKE COCKAGNE
(**— DISTRICT**) SOHO CHEAPSIDE
(**BRIDGE IN —**) TOWER ALBERT PUTNEY CHELSEA WATERLOO
(**DISTRICT OF —**) SOHO ACTON ADELPHI ALSATIA BRIXTON CHELSEA MAYFAIR
(**MONUMENT IN —**) GOG MAGOG NELSON CENOTAPH VICTORIA
(**RIVER OF —**) THAMES

(**STREET OF —**) BOND FLEET CANNON SAVILE DOWNING WARDOUR HAYMARKET
(**SUBURB OF —**) KEW FINCHLEY
LONDONER FLATCAP
LONE LANE SOLE ALONE APART SINGLE SOLITARY
(**— STAR STATE**) TEXAS
LONELINESS ONENESS VACANCY SOLITUDE
LONELY LORN ONLY SOLE VAST ALONE UNKET UNKID WISHT ALANGE DEAFLY SULLEN DEAVELY FORLORN LONEFUL SOLEYNE DESOLATE SECLUDED SOLITARY
(**PREF.**) EREM(O)
LONESOME ALONE DOLEY LONELY LANESOME SOLITARY
LONG HO DIE FAR FIT YEN ACHE DREE HANK HONE ITCH LANG SIDE TALL WILN WISH YAWN CRAVE DREAM GREEN LANGA MOURN STARK WEARY YEARN ARIGUE ASPIRE DESIRE DREICH HANKER HUNGER LINGER LONGUS PROLIX STOUND THIRST LENGTHY TEDIOUS WEILANG GEMINATE INFINITE
(**— AGO**) FERN LANGSYNE
(**— AND SLENDER**) REEDY SQUINNY
(**— AND UNIFORM IN WIDTH**) LINEAR
(**— FOR**) CARE HONE COVET CRAVE TASTE ASPIRE DESIRE SUSPIRE
(**— RESTLESSLY**) ITCH
(**— SINCE**) YORE
(**EXTRA —**) MAXI
(**TEDIOUSLY —**) MORTAL
(**PREF.**) DOLICH(O) LONGI LONGO MACR(O) MEC(O)
LONG-BILLED CURLEW SMOKER
LONGBOAT GLOOD
LONG-BODIED RACY RANGY
LONGERON SPAR
LONGEVITY VIVACITY
(**— CHARACTER**) SHOU
LONGING YEN ENVY ITCH LUST PINE WISH BRAME YEARN DESIRE HANKER TALENT THIRST ATHIRST CRAVING THIRSTY WILLING WISHFUL WISTFUL APPETENT APPETITE CUPIDITY HOMESICK PRURIENT
LONGINGLY WISTLY
LONGITUDE (PLANET'S —) EPOCH
LONGITUDINALLY ENDLONG
LONG-LASTING CHRONIC
LONG-LEGGED RANGY
LONGLEGS STILT
LONGLINE BULTOW
LONG-LIVED LONGEVE MACROBIAN
LONGSHOREMAN DOCKER HOBBLER WHARFIE DOCKHAND STEVEDORE ROUSTABOUT
LONG-STANDING OLD
LONG-SUFFERING MEEK PATIENT ENDURING PATIENCE
LONG-TAILED MACRURAL
LONG-TAILED WHIDAH REDBILL
LONG TOM SKIPPER
LONG-WINDED PROLIX PROSAIC
LOOK LA LO AIR EYE KEN SEE SPY CAST GAWK GAZE GIVE GLOM

HEED KEEK LATE LUCK MARK MIEN POKE SEEM SWAP VIEW WAIT ACIES BLUSH DEKKO FAVOR FLASH GLEAM GLEER GLIFF GLINT SCREW SIGHT SQUIZ VIZZY WLITE APPEAR ASPECT EYEFUL GANDER GLANCE REGARD REWARD VISION EYESHOT EYEWINK INSIGHT SEEMING DISCOVER LANGUISH OEILLADE
(**— ABOUT**) BELOOK SPECTATE
(**— AFTER**) TENT ATTEND FATHER FETTLE PROCURE
(**— AMOROUSLY**) SMICKER
(**— ASKANCE**) GLIM LEER SKEW BAGGE GLENT GLEDGE SKLENT
(**— AT**) DIG SEE GLOM LAMP VIEW VISE GLISK ADVISE BEHOLD REGARD REWARD CONSIDER SPECTATE
(**— BACK**) RETROSPECT
(**— CLOSELY**) PRY ESPY SCAN
(**— CROSS-EYED**) SHEYLE
(**— DOWN UPON**) SNOB DESPISE
(**— DULLY**) BLEAR
(**— EVERYWHERE**) COMB
(**— FIXEDLY**) GAZE KYKE GLORE STARE
(**— FOR**) SPY FOND SEEK AWAIT GROPE EXPECT PROPOSE RESPECT
(**— FORWARD**) EXPECT FORESEE ENVISAGE ENVISION
(**— GLANCINGLY**) BLINK
(**— GLOOMY**) SCOWL
(**— IN SNEAKING MANNER**) SNOOP
(**— INTENTLY**) GLOSE VISIE GLOWER EYEBALL
(**— INTO**) SOUND SEARCH
(**— JOYOUS**) SMILE
(**— LIKE**) IMITATE
(**— OBLIQUELY**) GLIME GOGGLE SQUINT
(**— OF DERISION**) FLEER
(**— OF PLANETS**) ASPECTS
(**— ON**) SPECTATE
(**— OUT**) FEND MIND CHEESE JIGGERS OUTLOOK
(**— OVER**) SCAN TOISE BROWSE SURVEY EXAMINE
(**— SEARCHINGLY**) COMB PEER PORE TOOT
(**— SLYLY**) PEEP GLINK
(**— SOUR**) GLUNCH
(**— STEADFASTLY**) GLOAT
(**— SULKY**) LUMP
(**— SULLEN**) LOUR LOWER
(**— TO**) RESPECT
(**— UPON AS**) ACCOUNT
(**— WILDLY**) GLOP WAUL WHAWL
(**— WITH FAVOR**) SMILE
(**AMOROUS —**) SMICKER
(**ANGRY —**) SCOWL
(**BRIEF —**) GLIM GLINT GLIMPSE
(**CLOSE —**) VISIE
(**LOVING —**) BELGARD
(**OBLIQUE —**) SQUINT
(**QUICK —**) SCRY GLENT
(**SEARCHING —**) SCRUTINY
(**SEVERE —**) FROWN
(**SIDELONG —**) GLEE GLIME
(**SLY —**) GLEG GLIME TWIRE
(**SULLEN —**) GLOOM GLOUT GLUNCH
(**TENDER —**) LANGUISH

(**WANTON —**) LEER
(**PL.**) DAPS
(**PREF.**) (**— THROUGH**) PERSPECTO
LOOKER BEAUTY HERDSMAN SEARCHER
LOOKER-ON BEHOLDER
LOOK HOMEWARD ANGEL
(**AUTHOR OF —**) WOLFE
(**CHARACTER IN —**) BEN GANT LUKE DAISY ELIZA HELEN JAMES LAURA EUGENE GROVER OLIVER LEONARD MARGARET
LOOKING (**— ASKANCE**) SQUINT
(**— BACKWARD**) REVIEW RETROSPECT
(**— OBLIQUELY**) SQUINT
(**— UP**) ROSY
LOOKING BACKWARD (AUTHOR OF —) BELLAMY
(**CHARACTER IN —**) WEST EDITH LEETE JULIAN BARTLETT PILLSBURY
LOOKOUT HUER TOUT SCOUT WATCH BANTAY CONNER TOOTER FUNERAL OUTLOOK ATALAYAN BANTAYAN BARTIZAN COCKATOO PROSPECT TOWERMAN WATCHOUT OBSERVATORY
LOOM BEAM BULK HULK LEEM DOBBY FRAME GLOOM BEETLE DODDIE DRAWLOOM HANDLOOM JACQUARD OVERPICK
(**— ATTACHMENT**) LAPPET
(**PREF.**) HIST(O)
LOOM AXLE ROCKTREE
LOOM BAR EASER DAGGER
LOOMFIXER TACKLER
LOOM HARNESS LEAF HEADLE SIMBLOT MOUNTING
LOON DIVER IMBER WABBY COBBLE DUCKER GUNNER WHABBY PYGOPOD
LOONY MAD DAFT CRAZY INSANE WEIRDO FOOLISH
LOOP BOW EYE LUG NOB TAB TAG ANSA BEND COIL FAKE HANK KINK KNOB KNOP LEAF LINK LOUP PURL BIGHT BRIDE CHAPE COQUE GUIDE KINCH LACET LATCH NOOSE PEARL PICOT SHANK STRAP TERRY WITHY BECKET BILLET BUCKLE FOLIUM HANGER HOLDER KEEPER KINKLE PARRAL SPIRAL STAPLE STITCH TWITCH COCKEYE COUPURE CRINGLE CRUPPER GROMMET KNUCKLE LATCHET SEGMENT ANTINODE COURONNE
(**— AND THIMBLES**) CLEW CLUE
(**— BY ICESKATER**) SPOON
(**— FOR HOISTING**) SLING
(**— FOR REINS**) TERRET TERRIT
(**— FOR REMOVING TUMORS**) SNARE
(**— IN KNITTING**) STEEK
(**— IN MINER'S ROPE**) SLUG
(**— IN NEEDLEWORK**) BRIDE
(**— OF INTESTINES**) KNUCKLE
(**— OF IRON**) OOLLY
(**— OF ROPE**) FAKE BIGHT FLAKE KINCH NOOSE ANCHOR BECKET PARRAL SNORTER SNOTTER
(**— OF SCABBARD**) FROG
(**— OF TUBING**) SCROLL
(**— ON ARMOR**) VERVELLE

(**— ON SAIL**) LASKET
(**— ON SPINNING FRAME**) BAND
(**— ON SWORD BELT**) HANGER
(**HANGING —**) FESTOON
(**HARNESS —**) COCKEYE
(**HEDDLE —**) DOUP
(**KIND OF —**) LIPPES
(**ORNAMENTAL —**) PICOT
(**SHOULDER —**) EPAULET
(**SURGICAL —**) CURET CURETTE
(**TIGHT —**) KINK KINKLE
(**TWISTED —**) KINK
(**PREF.**) FUNDI
LOOPER INCHWORM SPANWORM
LOOPHOLE LOOP CATCH CHINK
MEUSE EYELET OILLET WICKET
BARBICAN PORTHOLE
LOOSE GAY LAX EASY EMIT FREE
GLAD LASH LIMP OPEN SOFT
UNDO WIDE WILD BAGGY CRANK
FRANK LARGE DISH RELAX SLACK
UNTIE VAGUE WASHY ADRIFT
FLUFFY LIMBER SLOPPY SOLUTE
SPORTY SUBURB UNBIND UNGIRT
UNLASH UNTIED WOBBLY
ABSOLVE CHESSOM FLYAWAY
IMMORAL MOVABLE RELAXED
SETFREE SHOGGLY STRINGY
UNBOUND UNHITCH UNTIGHT
DIFFUSED DISCINCT FLOATING
INSECURE LAXATIVE SHATTERY
UNSTABLE
(**— AN ANCHOR**) TRIP
(**— ARROW**) BOLT
(**MORALLY —**) FRANK
(**PREF.**) LAXI
LOOSE-JOINTED LANKY SHACKLY
LOOSELY SLACK LARGELY SLACKLY
LOOSEN LAX BREAK SLACK UNTIE
LAXATE LIMBER UNBEND RESOLVE
SLACKEN UNGRIPE UNLOOSE
UNSCREW DISHEVEL UNSTRING
(**— ANCHOR**) TRIP
(**— ROCK**) GAD
LOOSENESS SLACK LAXITY
LATITUDE
(**PREF.**) LYO
LOOSENING START SOLUTIVE
SOLUTORY
(**PREF.**) LYS(I)
LOOSESTRIFE KILLWEED
PEATWEED PEATWOOD
PRIMWORT
LOOSING
(**SUFF.**) LYSE LYSIS LYST LYTE
LYTIC LYZE
LOOT SACK SWAG BOOTY HARRY
SPOIL STEAL THEFT BOODLE
MARAUD HERSHIP PILLAGE
PLUNDER SNAFFLE
LOOTING SACK
LOP DOD LAP CLIP DODD OCHE
SNED SNIG SNIP TRIM SHRAG
SHRED SHRUB STUMP TRASH
TWINE SHROUD SNATHE TRASHIFY
TRUNCATE
(**— OFF**) COW DOD CROP DODD
HEAD SNAG SNED PRUNE SHRED
TRUNK DEFALK AMPUTATE
LOPE SHAG
LOPPED
(**PREF.**)
(**— OFF**) TRUNCATO

LOPPER CLABBER
LOPPINGS SHROUD
LOQUACIOUS GABBY FUTILE
SPEECHFUL
LOQUACITY PRATE PRATTLE
FUTILITY
LOQUAT BIWA NISPERO
LORAL FRENAL
LORD BEL DAM DEN DON GOD HER
LOR MAR SID SIR DION DOMN
EROS HERR LAUK LOSH NAIK SIRE
TUAN ANGUS ARAWN BARON
LAFEU LIEGE LUDDY NIGEL OMRAH
RABBI SAHIB SWAMI THANE
DOMINE DUMAIN KYRIOS PRABHU
SAYYID SIGNOR TANIST THAKUR
CAMILLO CERIMON JACQUES
JEHOVAH MARCHER OGTIERN
VAVASOR BHAGAVAT DESPOTES
DRIGHTEN GRANDPRE LORDLING
MARGRAVE OVERLORD PALATINE
SEIGNEUR SEIGNIOR SUPERIOR
SUZERAIN THALIARD
(**— OF DARKNESS**) HYLE
(**— OF UNIVERSE**) ORMAZD
ORMUZD
(**— OF WORLD**) LOKINDRA
(**FEUDAL —**) DAUPHIN VAVASOR
SUZERAIN
(**JAPANESE —**) KAMI
(**JUDAIC —**) ADONAI
(**MUSLIM —**) OMRAH
LORD CHANCELLOR WOOLPACK
LORD JIM (**AUTHOR OF —**) CONRAD
(**CHARACTER IN —**) JIM DAIN
BROWN STEIN WARIS MARLOW
DORAMIN
LORDLINESS PRIDE
LORDLY PROUD SUPERB
ARROGANT DESPOTIC
LORDOSIS SWAYBACK
LORDSHIP NAVY DYNASTY
ERECTION SEIGNORY SIGNORIA
LORE LEAR LORUM MASTAX
LEARNING
LORGNETTE STARER
LORICA LORIC SHEATH SHIELD
LORIKEET PARROT WARRIN
CORELLA WEROOLE
LORIS KOKAM LEMUR SLOTH
LEMUROID
LORN ALONE
LORNA DOONE (**AUTHOR OF —**)
BLACKMORE
(**CHARACTER IN —**) FRY TOM ALAN
JOHN RIDD ANNIE DOONE DUGAL
ENSOR LORNA CARVER FAGGUS
JEREMY REUBEN BRANDIR
STICKLES HUCKABACK
LORRY RIG DRAG RULLY TRUCK
CAMION ROLLEY TIPPER
JAGANNATH JUGGERNAUT
LORY LOORY CORELLA LORIKEET
LOSE LET TIN AMIT DROP TINE
WANT FORGO LAPSE LEASE TRAIL
GAMBLE MISLAY FORBEAR
FORFEIT FORLESE SLATTER
(**— AT CARDS**) BUST
(**— BET**) WRONG
(**— BRILLIANCE**) FAINT
(**— BY DEATH**) BURY
(**— BY GAMING**) GAME
(**— BY STUPIDITY**) BLUNDER

(**— CONTROL**) BLOW CRACK
(**— COURAGE**) DREEP TAINT
(**— DELIBERATELY**) THROW
(**— FLAVOR**) FOZE APPAL APPALL
(**— FORCE**) COLLAPSE
(**— FRESHNESS**) FADE WILT WITHER
(**— HEART**) JADE FAINT QUAIL
COLLAPSE
(**— HOPE**) DESPAIR DESPOND
(**— IT**) SNAP
(**— LUSTER**) TARNISH
(**— MOISTURE**) GUTTATE
(**— NERVE**) CHICKEN
(**— OFFICE**) FALL
(**— ONE'S BREATH**) CHINK
(**— ONE'S WAY**) STRAY
(**— ONE'S SKILL**) SLIP
(**— POWER**) FAIL DISSOLVE
(**— SELF-POSSESSION**) ABASH
(**— SPIRIT**) JADE
(**— STRENGTH**) GO FADE FAIL PALL
WEAKEN LANGUISH
(**— SUPPORT**) ERODE
(**— UNDER HORIZON**) SINK
(**— VISION**) DAZZLE
(**— WARMTH**) COOL CONGEAL
(**— WEIGHT**) ENSEAM
(**— ZEAL**) QUENCH
LOSER ALSORAN
LOSING (**BEGIN — STREAK**) GOCOLD
LOSS ACE BATH COST HARM LEAK
LOST MISS LAPSE QUALM WASTE
BURIAL DAMAGE DAMNUM
DEFEAT INJURY TINSEL AVERAGE
DEBACLE DEFICIT EXPENSE
JACTURE LEAKAGE LEESING
MISTURE REPRISE AMISSION
BREAKAGE CLEANING MISSMENT
PERDITION SACRIFICE
(**— BY EVAPORATION**) ULLAGE
(**— BY SIFTING**) ULLAGE
(**— IN WORKING**) SLIPPAGE
(**— OF ABILITIES**) COLLAPSE
(**— OF ABILITY TO WRITE**)
AGRAPHIA
(**— OF ACTIVITY**) AKINESIA
(**— OF APPETITE**) ASITIA ANOREXIA
(**— OF BRILLIANCY**) ECLIPSE
(**— OF CARGO**) AVERAGE
(**— OF CONSCIOUSNESS**) SWOON
ABSENCE APOPLEXY BLACKOUT
FAINTING
(**— OF ELASTICITY**) SET
(**— OF ELECTRICITY**) EFFLUVE
(**— OF EXPRESSION**) AMIMIA
(**— OF FEELING**) APOPLEXY
ANESTHESIA ANAESTHESIA
(**— OF FORTUNE**) RUIN DECAY
(**— OF GOOD NAME**) IGNOMINY
(**— OF GOODS**) SHRINKAGE
(**— OF HAIR**) DEFLUX ALOPECIA
PTILOSIS
(**— OF HONOR**) ATIMY
(**— OF HOPE**) DESPAIR
(**— OF MEMORY**) AMNESIA
BLACKOUT
(**— OF PRESTIGE**) DISHONOR
(**— OF SCENT**) CHECK
(**— OF SENSE OF SMELL**) ANOSMIA
(**— OF SIGHT**) ANOPSY ANOPSIA
(**— OF SIZE**) WANE
(**— OF SOUND**) APOCOPE SYNCOPE
APHERESIS

(**— OF SPEECH**) ALALIA APHASIA
APHONIA
(**— OF VOICE**) ANAUDIA APHONIA
(**— OF VOWEL**) APHESIS
(**— OF WILL POWER**) ABULIA
(**AT A —**) ASEA
(**CONTRACT —**) LESION
(**TAKE A — ON**) EAT
(**SUFF.**) ZEMIA
LOST ASEA GONE LORN TINT ATSEA
STRAY WASTE ASTRAY BUSHED
HIDDEN NAUGHT FORFEIT
FORLORN MISSING CONFUSED
OBSCURED BENIGHTED
(**— IN THOUGHT**) PREOCCUPIED
LOST HORIZON (**AUTHOR OF —**)
HILTON
(**CHARACTER IN —**) HUGH BRIAC
CHANG HENRY CONWAY LOTSEN
BARNARD CHARLES ROBERTA
BRINKLOW MALLISON PERRAULT
RUTHERFORD
LOST LADY (**AUTHOR OF —**) CATHER
(**CHARACTER IN —**) IVY BLUM NIEL
FRANK OGDEN PETERS HERBERT
ELLINGER POMMEROY CONSTANCE
FORRESTER
LOT BAG CUT HAP PEW CHOP CROP
DEAL DOLE DOOM DRAW FALL
FATE HEAP PACK PART PILE REDE
SKIT SLEW SLUE SORS SORT
BATCH BLOCK BREAK BUNCH
CAVEL FIELD GRACE GRIST GROSS
LINES SHARE SHOOT SIGHT SITHE
STAND TEEMS TROOP WEIRD
AMOUNT BARREL BOODLE
BUNDLE CHANCE DICKER FARDEL
HANGUP OODLES PARCEL TICHEL
BOILING DESTINY FEEDLOT
FORTUNE OODLINS PORTION
SANDLOT BACKYARD CABOODLE
JINGBANG MOUTHFUL RIMPTION
WOODLAND
(**— OF PERSONS**) BOODLE
(**— OF TEA**) BREAK
(**— OF 60 PIECES**) SHOCK
(**BUILDING —**) ERF
(**BURIAL —**) LAIR
(**FATHER OF —**) HARAN
(**GREAT —**) SWAG
(**MISCELLANEOUS —**) RAFT
(**SISTER OF —**) ISCAH MILCAH
(**UNCLE OF —**) ABRAHAM
(**VACANT —**) COMMON COMMONS
(**PREF.**) CLERO SORTI
LOTAN (**FATHER OF —**) SEIR
LOTION WASH EYEWASH
EYEWATER LAVATORY
(**HAND — INGREDIENT**) ALOE
LOTOPHAGUS EATER
LOTS MANY HEAPS TEEMS BUSHEL
HODFUL
LOTTERY AMBO LOTTO SWEEP
TERNO RAFFLE TOMBOLA
LOTTO KENO BINGO TOMBOLA
(**— GAME**) HOUSE
LOTUS LOTE LOTOS PADMA
NELUMBO WANKAPIN
(**SACRED —**) PADMA
LOTUS TREE SADR ZIZYPHUS
LOUCHEUX KUTCHIN
LOUD HARD HIGH MAIN CRUDE

FORTE GAUDY GREAT HEAVY
SHOWY STARK STOUR WIGHT
BRASSY BRAZEN COARSE CRIANT
FLASHY GARISH HOARSE VULGAR
BLATANT CLAMANT HAUTAIN
VIOLENT BIGMOUTH FRENZIED
PIERCING SLAMBANG STREPENT
STRIDENT VEHEMENT STREPITANT
(NOT —) LOW SOFT
(RATHER —) MEZZOFORTE
LOUDHAILER BULLHORN
LOUDLY BOST ALOUD FORTE STARK
LOUDNESS STRESS SONORITY
MAGNITUDE
(— UNIT) PHON SONE
(UNIT OF —) PHON
LOUDSPEAKER WOOFER SPEAKER
TWEETER BULLHORN SQUAWKER
LOUD-SPOKEN RANDY
LOUIS LUIGI LODOWIC

LOUISIANA
CAPITAL: BATONROUGE
COLLEGE: LSU TULANE DILLARD
GRAMBLING
COUNTY: CADDO ACADIA PARISH
TENSAS LAFOURCHE
CULTURE: TCHEFUNCTE
DIALECT: CREOLE
FESTIVAL: MARDIGRAS
INDIAN: ADAI WASHA ATAKAPA
LAKE: IATT CLEAR LARTO BORGNE
SALINE DARBONNE MAUREPAS
MOUNTAIN: DRISKILL
NATIVE: CAJUN CREOLE ACADIAN
NICKNAME: CREOLE PELICAN
PARISH: WINN CADDO ACADIA
IBERIA SABINE TENSAS ORLEANS
RAPIDES OUACHITA CALCASIEU
RIVER: RED AMITE BOEUF SABINE
TENSAS OUACHITA
STATE BIRD: PELICAN
STATE FLOWER: MAGNOLIA
STATE TREE: CYPRESS
STREAM: BAYOU
TOWN: JENA MANY HOMER HOUMA
EDGARD GRETNA MINDEN
MONROE RUSTON BASTROP
VIDALIA BOGALUSA TALLULAH
NEWORLEANS

LOUISIANIAN CAJUN ACADIAN
LOUNGE HAWM LOAF LOLL SORN
SOSS BANGE TRAIK DACKER
FROUST FROWST GLIDER LOLLUP
LOPPET RIZZLE SLINGE SOZZLE
LAMMOCK SAUNTER SLOUNGE
LOUNGER IDLER SLOUNGER
LOUPE LENS
LOUR FROWN
LOUSE BOB BUG SOW CRAB
CRUMB BOOGER BRAULA COOTIE
GISLER PALMER SISTEN VERMIN
MORPION PUCERON GRAYBACK
(FISH —) GISLER ARGULUS
(PLANT —) APHID APHIS
(WOOD —) SOW ISOPOD SLATER
(YOUNG —) NIT
(PREF.) ONISCI PEDICUL(I)(O)
LOUSEWORT RATTLE SNAFFLES
LOUSINESS PEDICULOSIS
LOUSY SEEDY CRAPPY CRUMMY
PEDICULOUS

LOUT HOB LOB LUG YOB BOOR
CHUB COOF GAUM GAWK HOOD
JAKE LOON NOWT SWAB SWAD
BOOBY CHUMP CUDDY GNOFF
LOOBY LOURD ROBIN THRUM
WHAUP YAHOO YOBBO YOKEL
BOHUNK CLUNCH GOBBIN
HOBLOB LOURDY LUBBER LUNGIS
SLOUCH TRIPAL BUMPKIN
GROBIAN HALLION HAWBUCK
HOODLUM LOBCOCK PALOOKA
LOBLOLLY
(COUNTRY —) KERN BUMPKIN
LOUTISH SWAB HULKY SLOOMY
BOORISH HULKING VILLAIN
BOEOTIAN CLOWNISH
LOUVER SLAT LOUVRE LUFFER
DIFFUSER FEMERELL
(PL.) SHUTTER
LOVABLE AMABEL CUDDLY
AMIABLE ADORABLE DOVELIKE
LOVESOME ENDEARING
LOVABLENESS DEARNESS
LOVAGE SMELLAGE
LOVE GRA LOO AMOR EROS KAMA
LIKE ALOHA AMOUR CUPID DRURY
FANCY HEART MINNE AFFECT
TENDRE CHARITY EMBRACE
FEELING PASSION DEVOTION
KINDNESS LOVEHOOD PARAMOUR
(— IN RETURN) REDAME
(— OF COUNTRY) PATRIOTISM
(— OF CRUELTY) SADISM
(— OF MANKIND) PHILANTHROPY
(— OF MARVELOUS) TERATISM
(— OF THE ARTS) VIRTU
(— OF WOMEN) PHILOGYNY
(— TO EXCESS) IDOLIZE
(— TOWARD DEITY) BHAKTI
(ARDENT —) PASSION
(CHRISTIAN —) CHARITY
(EXCESSIVE —) IDOLATRY
(INTENSE —) FIRE
(MY —) MACHREE
(NATURAL —) STORGE
(SELF-GIVING —) AGAPE
(SENTIMENTALLY IN —) SPOONY
(UNLAWFUL —) LEMANRY
(PREF.) ERO(TO)
(SUFF.) PHIL(A)(AE)(E)(IA)(ISM)(IST)
(OUS)(US)
LOVED DEAR BELOVED
(MUCH —) SWEET
LOVE-DRUG DAGGA
LOVE FEAST AGAPE
LOVE KNOT AMORET
LOVELINESS BEAUTY
LOVELOCK EARLOCK
LOVELY DREAMY LOVING TENDER
AMIABLE AMOROUS ADORABLE
LOVESOME
LOVEMAKING AMOUR
LOVER GRA LAD MAN BEAU CHAP
AMANT AMOUR DRURY LEMAN
ROMEO SPARK SWAIN AMADIS
AMANTE MARROW MINION
SQUIRE ADMIRER AMORIST
AMOROSO CELADON GALLANT
PATRIOT SPARKER SPECIAL
SPRUNNY AMORETTO BELAMOUR
CASANOVA CICISBEO PARAMOUR
STREPHON INAMORATO

(— BOY) ROMEO
(MODEL —) LEILAH
(SILLY —) SPOON
LOVE SEAT CAUSEUSE
LOVE'S LABOR'S LOST **(AUTHOR**
OF —) SHAKESPEARE
(CHARACTER IN —) DULL MOTH
BOYET MARIA ARMADO DUMAIN
ADRIANO BEROWNE COSTARD
MERCADE ROSALINE FERDINAND
KATHERINE NATHANIEL
HOLOFERNES JAQUENETTA
LONGAVILLE
LOVING DEAR FOND TENDER
AMATORY AMOROUS
(PREF.) PHIL(O)
(SUFF.) PHIL(A)(AE)(E)(OUS)(US)
LOW BAS BOO LAW MOO BASE
BASS KEEN MEAN NEAP OPEN
ORRA ROUT SLOW VILE WEAK
BLORE DIRTY GROSS HEDGE LAICH
PUTID SHORT SMALL SNIDE THIRD
CALLOW EARTHY FILTHY GENTLE
GRUBBY HARLOT HUMBLE
LIMMER MENIAL ORNERY RASCAL
RIBALD SECRET SHABBY SILKEN
TURPID VULGAR BESTIAL IGNOBLE
RAFFISH REPTILE SLAVISH
SUBMISS HOLSTEIN SOUTERLY
(— AS OF A VOWEL) OPEN
(— DOWN) SIDE
(— IN LIGHTNESS) DULL
(— IN PERCEPTION) CRUDE
(— IN PITCH) GRAVE
(— IN PRICE) MODERATE
(— IN QUALITY) HEDGE
(— IN SATURATION) GRAYISH
(— IN SPIRITS) BLUE DOWN
GLOOMY DOWNCAST
(— IN TONE) SOFT SUBMISS
(— IN WATER) RACE
(— NUMBERS) MANQUE
(— POINT) TROUGH
(IMMEASURABLY —) ABYSMAL
(PREF.) CHAMAE CHAME TAPIN(O)
LOW-BORN PLEBEAN VILLAIN
PLEBEIAN
LOWBORN WAFF
LOWBRED BASTARD PLEBEIAN
LOWCAL LITE
LOW-DOWN BUCKASS
LOWER CUT DIP LOW BASE BATE
DOWN DROP DUCK FELL SINK VAIL
ABASE ABATE ALLOY AVALE
BELOW BLAME COUCH COWER
DECRY DEMIT DOUSE FROWN
GLOOM LEVEL SCOWL STOOP
BEMEAN DEBASE DEJECT DEMEAN
EMBASE GLOWER HUMBLE
JUNIOR LESSEN MODIFY NETHER
REDUCE SETTLE STRIKE SUBDUE
SUBMIT BENEATH DECLASS
DEGRADE DEPRESS SHORTEN
DIMINISH DOWNWARD INFERIOR
MODERATE
(— BANNER) VAIL
(— BY HALF STEP) FLAT
(— IN ESTEEM) CHEAPEN
DEROGATE
(— IN PITCH) FLAT SHADE
(— ONESELF) SINK BEMEAN
DESCEND
(— PRICES) BEAR

(— SAIL) AMAIN
(— SLIGHTLY) SHADE
(— THE HEAD) STOOP
(PREF.) BATH(O)(Y) CATO INFERO
INFRA NERTERO
(— IN STATUS) INFRA
(MAKE —) DE
LOWERING DIP DUCK DOWLY
HEAVY LAPSE BEETLE SULLEN
PEJORATION
(— OF BODY) FONDU
(— OF LAND) ABLATION
LOWEST LAST LEAST EXTREME
LOWMOST PRIMARY PARAVAIL
NETHERMOST
(— CLASS) LAG
(— POSSIBLE) KNOWDOWN
LOWING MUGIENT
LOWLAND LAICH POLDER LALLAND
DOWNLAND
(— BESIDE RIVER) INKS
(BARREN —) LANDES
LOWLANDER SAXON ZHMUD
SASSENACH
LOWLIER LESS
LOWLIFE SCUM AMEBA
LOWLINESS **(— OF MIND)** HUMILITY
LOWLY LOW BASE SILLY HUMBLE
BASEBORN
LOW-LYING CALLOW LALLAN
INFERIAL SUBJECTED
LOW-MINDED BASE MEAN
LOWNESS LOWTH
(— OF PITCH) GRAVITY
(— OF SPIRITS) GLOOM SPLEEN
MEGRIMS
LOW-PITCHED GRUFF
LOW-SPIRITED HIPPED DEJECTED
LOW SUNDAY QUASIMODO
LOX **(PARTNER OF —)** BAGEL
LOY SLICK
LOYAL FAST REAL FIRM HOLD LEAL
REAL TRUE LIEGE PIOUS SOUND
ARDENT HEARTY LAWFUL SECRET
STANCH CONSTANT FAITHFUL
STALWART YEOMANLY
(BE — TO) OBEY
(REMAIN —) STANDBY
LOYALIST TORY
LOYALLY SURELY
LOYALTY ARDOR FAITH FEALTY
HOMAGE LEALTY REALTY SPIRIT
REALITY DEVOTION FIDELITY
CONSTANCY NATIONALISM
LOZENGE TAB JUBE COIGN QUOIN
CACHOU JUJUBE MASCLE PASTIL
QUARRY ROTULA RUSTRE TABLET
TABULE TROCHE CREMULE
DIAMOND TABELLA PASTILLE
ROSEDROP
(— OF CEMENT) WAFER
LOZI ROZI BAROTSE
LSD ACID
LUBBER LOUT SWAB LOOBY
SLOUCH LOBCOCK LILBURNE
LUBBERLY AWKWARD
LUBRICANT DOPE GREASE
AQUADAG UNGUENT
LUBRICATE OIL DOPE GLIB GREASE
LUBRIFY
LUBRICATOR OILER OILCAN
LUCARNE LUCOMBE
LUCE GED

LUCENT BRIGHT LUCIBLE
LUCERNE LEGUME ALFALFA
LUCIA DI LAMMERMOOR
 (CHARACTER IN —) LUCY EDGAR
 HENRY ARTHUR ASHTON BUCKLOW
 RAVENSWOOD
 (COMPOSER OF —) DONIZETTI
LUCIANA (SISTER OF —) ADRIANA
LUCID SANE CLEAR AERIAL BRIGHT
 LIMPID CRYSTAL DILUCID
 LITERATE LUCULENT LUMINOUS
LUCIDITY SANITY CLARITY
LUCIFER DEVIL MATCH PHOSPHOR
LUCK HAP CESS EURE SONS SPIN
 GRACE ISSUE CHANCE THRIFT
 FORTUNE HANDSEL SUCCESS
 VENTURE HAMINGJA
 (BAD —) ACE DOLE DEUCE
 HOODOO UNLUCK AMBSACE
 MISCHANCE
 (BAD — TO YOU) YLAHAYLL
 (GOOD —) HAP SONCE SONSE
 FORTUNE THEEDOM
 (ILL —) UNHAP DIRDUM DISGRACE
 MISHANTER
 (RELATING TO —) ALEATORY
 (STROKE OF —) MANNA
 (UNEXPECTED —) BUNCE
LUCKILY HAPPILY
LUCKY HOT CANNY HAPPY JAMMY
 SEELY SONSY CHANCY LUCKLY
 LUCKFUL ONAROLL GRACIOUS
 PROVIDENTIAL
LUCRATIVE FAT GOOD GAINFUL
LUCRE GELT SWAG DROSS MOOLA
LUCREZIA BORGIA (CHARACTER IN
 —) ALFONSO GENNARO LUCREZIA
 (COMPOSER OF —) DONIZETTI
LUD (FATHER OF —) SHEM
LUDICROUS AWFUL COMIC DROLL
 ABSURD COMICAL FOOLISH
 HIDEOUS RISIBLE FARCICAL
 BURLESQUE
LUDO UCKERS
LUFF DERRICK
LUFFA LOOFAH SPONGE
LUG EAR HUG TUG WAG SNUG SPUD
 TOTE ZULU PATCH WALTZ SCHLEP
LUGE SLED
LUGGAGE BAGS SWAG TRAPS
 HATBOX BAGGAGE CARRYON
 TRUSSERY
 (AIRPLANE —) CARRYON
LUGGAGE-CARRIER GRID
LUGGAGE CASE IMPERIAL
LUGGAR JAGGAR JUGGER LAGGAR
LUGGER CAT TOUP ZULU FIFIE
LUGUBRIOUS BLACK TEARY
 BALEFUL DOLEFUL DOLOROUS
 LACHRYMOSE
LUGWORM LOB LUG LOBWORM
 SANDWORM
LUIGINO TEMIN
LUISA MILLER (CHARACTER IN —)
 WURM LUISA MILLER WALTER
 RODOLFO FREDERICA
 (COMPOSER OF —) VERDI
LUKEWARM LEW LUKE TEPID
 WLACH
LULL CALM DRUG FODE HUSH ROCK
 CROON HUSHO LETUP SLACK
 STILL LACUNA SOPITE HUSHABY
 HUSHEEN

LULLABY LULL BALOO BALOW
 LULLAY HUSHABY HUSHEEN
 ROCKABY
LULLING DROWSY CIRCEAN
LULU PIP DARB ONER BEAUT DOOZY
 CORKER DOOZER SNORTER
 HUMDINGER
LUMBER BURR DEAL RAFF NANMU
 STOCK STRIP CUMBER FINISH
 FLITCH RAFFLE REFUSE SAMCHU
 SHORTS TIMBER DEGRADE
 DUNNAGE GUMWOOD RUMMAGE
 TRUNDLE STEPPING
 (INFERIOR —) SAPS SCOOT
LUMBERING AWKWARD LUMBERLY
 LUMBROUS
LUMBERJACK JACK AXMAN
 LOGGER TOPPER TIMBERER
 (COMPETITION FOR —S) ROLEO
LUMBERMAN PINER DOGGER
 SCORER CHOPPER GIRDLER
 TIMBERER
LUMINAIRE LAMP
LUMINANCE HELIOS
LUMINARY STAR LIGHT CANDLE
 PLANET
LUMINESCENCE FLAME
LUMINOSITY FIRE GLOW LIGHT
 VALUE
LUMINOUS LIGHT LUCID SHINY
 BRIGHT LUMINANT
LUMMOX BOZO GALOOT LOBSTER
 PALOOKA
LUMP BAT BOB COB CUB DAB DAD
 FID GOB JOB LOB NIB NOB NUB
 WAD BLOB BURL CLAG CLAM
 CLOT COOL COWL DUNT GLOB
 JUNK KNOB KNOT NIRL PONE
 SWAD TOKE BLOOM BUNCH
 CHUCK CHUNK CLAUT CLUMP
 CLUNK GLEBE HUNCH KNOLL
 KNURL MOUSE SLUMP STONE
 WEDGE WODGE CLUNCH DOLLOP
 GOBBET HUBBLE HUDDLE LUMPET
 NUBBLE NUGGET CLUMPER
 CLUNTER PUMPKNOT
 (— IN CLOTH) BURL
 (— IN GLASS) YOLK
 (— OF BLACK LEAD) SOP
 (— OF BLOOD) CLOD
 (— OF CLAY) BAT
 (— OF COAL) NUBBLING
 (— OF DOUGH) DIP
 (— OF FAT) KEECH
 (— OF GLASS) BLOOM
 (— OF IRON) OOLLY
 (— OF LAVA) BOMB
 (— OF LINT) SLUG
 (— OF MEAT) OLIVE
 (— OF METAL) MASS SLUG
 (— OF ORE) ROCK HARDHEAD
 (— OF RUBBER) THIMBLE
 (— OF SALT) SALTCAT
 (— OF WOOD) CHUMP
 (— OF YEAST) BEE
 (— ON HORSE'S BACK) SITFAST
 (— ON SKIN) MILIUM
 (LARGE —) BLAD DOLL HUNK
 (LITTLE —) NODULE KNOBBLE
 (ROUNDED —) CLOT
 (PREF.) THROMB(O)
LUMPFISH GROSS PADDLE SUCKER

LUMPISH STODGY CHUCKLE
LUMPSUCKER PADLE PADDLE
 SEAOWL
LUMPY GOBBY CHUNKY CLOGGY
 CLUNCH COBBLY STODGY
 BUNCHED NODULAR NODULOSE
LUNACY MOON FOLLY MADNESS
 DELIRIUM INSANITY
LUNARIA SATINPOD
LUNARY VOLVELLE
LUNATIC NUT GELT LOONY WACKO
 BEDLAM MADMAN MANIAC
 WEIRDO CRAZOID FANATIC
 FRANTIC CRACKPOT MOONLING
 MOONSICK MOONSTRUCK
 MOONSTRICKEN
LUNCH CUT BAIT CRIB TIFF BEVER
 PIECE SNACK BRUNCH NACKET
 TIFFIN UNDERN BAGGING ELEVENS
 DEJEUNER DRINKING ELEVENER
 LUNCHEON NUNCHEON
 COLLATION
 (— ORDER) BLT
 (DAIRY —) CREMERIE
 (MINER'S —) SNAP
LUNCHEON CRIB LUNCH STULL
 TIFFIN DEJEUNE DINETTE
 NOONMEAT
LUNCHROOM EATERY
LUNETTE OUTWORK
LUNG PULMO DRAGON LONGUE
 (PREF.) PNEO PNEUM(A)(ATO)(O)
 (ON)(ONO) PULMO PULMON(I)
LUNGE FOIN PASS SPAR POINT
 VENUE CHARGE ALLONGE
LUNGFISH CYCLOID DIPNOAN
 MUDFISH SIRENOID
LUNGS LIGHTS VISCUS BELLOWS
 (PERTAINING TO —) PULMONIC
LUNKHEAD DOLT DOPE JUGHEAD
LUNULE ALBEDO
LUO DHOLUO
LUPIN ARSINE
LUPINE SUNDIAL
LURCH JOLL STOT SWAG PITCH
 STOIT CAREEN STOITER STUMBLE
 SWAGGER
 (LEAVE IN THE —) DITCH
LURCHING DRUNKEN ROLLING
LURE CON JAY BAIT HOOK ROPE
 TOLL WISE DECOY DRILL FEINT
 SLOCK SNARE SNOOK SPOON
 SQUID STALE TEMPT TROLL
 ALLURE CAPPER CLARET ENTICE
 ENTRAP RABATE SEDUCE TREPAN
 VELURE ATTRACT GUDGEON
 INVEIGH PHANTOM PITFALL
 WOBBLER BUCKTAIL INVEIGLE
 LUREMENT
 (— INTO GAMBLING) HUSTLE
 (— OF CARRION) TRAIN
 (— WILDFOWL) STOOL
LURI ALUR
LURID RED PURPLE SULTRY
 CRIMSON GHASTLY
LURK DARE LOUT COUCH LOWER
 SKULK SLINK SNEAK AMBUSH
 DARKLE
LURKING LURKY GRASSANT
 LATITANT
LUSCIOUS FOND RICH SWEET
 CREAMY DULCET DELICATE

LUSH SOT RICH DRUNK GREEN
 LUSTY MOIST TOPER SAVORY
 FERTILE OPULENT PROFUSE
 THRIVING
LUST HELL ITCH KAMA BLOOD
 PRIDE DESIRE LIBIDO LIKING
 LUXURY NICETY PASSION
 COVETISE CUPIDITY CARNALITY
 (SUFF.) LAGNIA
LUSTER NAIF GLASS GLINT GLOSS
 SHEEN SHINE WATER LUSTRE
 POLISH REFLET BURNISH GLIMPSE
 GLISTER LUSTRUM NITENCY
 FULGENCE LUSTRATE RADIANCY
 SPLENDOR
 (— OF FIBER) BLOOM
 (BRONZE-LIKE —) SCHILLER
LUSTERLESS MAT WAN DEAD DULL
 FISHY STARY
LUSTFUL HOT GAMY GOLE LEWD
 RANK SALT CADGY LUSTY PRIME
 RANDY RUTTY WANTON BEASTLY
 CODDING FLESHLY FULSOME
 GOATISH JEALOUS RAMMISH
 RUTTISH LIKEROUS SALACIOUS
LUSTFULNESS SATYRISM
LUSTILY CRANK HOTLY
LUSTING ITCHY
LUSTRATION ABHISEKA
LUSTROUS CLEAR DOGGY NITID
 BRIGHT GLOSSY ORIENT SHEENY
 SILKEN SILVER SHINING SPLENDID
LUSTY BRAG CANT BURLY CRANK
 FLUSH FRACK FRANK FRECK
 GUTSY HARDY JUICY RANDY STIFF
 STOUT GAWSIE ROBUST STURDY
 LUSTFUL LUSTICK BOUNCING
 PHYSICAL SKELPING SPORTIVE
 VIGOROUS
LUTE TAR BIWA LAUD DOMRA
 NABIA NABLE REBAB REBEC
 SAROD CITOLE ENLUTE LORICA
 LUTING SCREED VIELLE ANGELOT
 BANDORE DICHORD DYPHONE
 MANDOLA MANDORE MINIKIN
 PANDORE THEORBO VIHUELA
 ANGELICA ARCHLUTE PENORCON
 TAMBOURA TEMPLATE TRICHORD
LUTER DAUBER PASTER
LUTJANID JEWFISH

LUXEMBOURG		
CAPITAL: LUXEMBOURG
HIGHEST POINT: BURGPLATZ
LOWLAND: BONPAYS GUTLAND
MEASURE: FUDER
MOUNTAIN RANGE: ARDENNES
PLATEAU: ARDENNES
RIVER: OUR SURE SAUER ALZETTE
 MOSELLE
TOWN: BOUS EICH ROODT WILTZ
 PETANGE VIANDEN DIEKIRCH
 DUDELANGE ETTELBRUCK
 DIFFERDANGE

LUXURIANT GOLE LUSH RANK RICH
 FRANK PROUD LAVISH WANTON
 OPULENT PROFUSE RAMPANT
 TEEMING PAMPERED PRODIGAL
LUXURIANTLY FATLY
LUXURIATE BASK REVEL FROWST
 WALLOW WANTON
LUXURIOUS HIGH LUSH NICE POSH

RANK SOFT GAUDY PLUSH SWANK
CAPUAN DELUXE GILDED PALACE
SILKEN SWANKY WANTON APICIAN
ELEGANT DELICATE LUCULLAN
PRODIGAL REGALADO SENSUOUS
TRYPHENA TRYPHOSA
SUMPTUOUS
LUXURIOUSLY HIGH DELUXE
LUXURY FRILL FINERY OUTRAGE
DELICACY ELEGANCE PLEASURE
RICHNESS PRINCELINESS
LUXURY-LOVING DELICATE
LUZON (— VOLCANO) TAAL
LYCANTHROPE WEREWOLF
LYCAON (DAUGHTER OF —)
CALLISTO
(FATHER OF —) PELASGUS
LYCEUM PLATFORM
LYCHNIS FIREBALL NONESUCH
LYCIUM RUSOT
LYCOPODIUM MOSS FOXTAIL
CROWFOOT STAGHORN

LYCURGUS (BROTHER OF —)
POLYDECTES
(FATHER OF —) DRYAS EUNOMUS
(SON OF —) OPHELTES
LYCUS (BROTHER OF —) AEGEUS
PALLAS IPHINOE
(FATHER OF —) PANDION
(MOTHER OF —) PYLIA
(WIFE OF —) DIRCE
LYDIA MAEONIA
LYE LEY BOUK BUCK STRAKE
LESSIVE LIXIVIUM SOAPLEES
LYING FLAT FALSE LEASE CRETISM
LEASING MENTERY ACCUBATION
MENDACIOUS
(— APART) DISSITE
(— AT BASE OF MOUNTAINS)
PIEDMONT
(— CLOSE) QUAT
(— DOWN) DOWN LODGED
CUMBENT DORMANT
COUCHANT

(— HID) LATITANT
(— IDLE) INACTIVE
(— ON BACK) SUPINE
(— ON FACE) PRONE PROCUMBENT
(— ON GROUND) REPENT REPTANT
(— OPEN) PATENT
(— OVER) JACENT
(— UNDER GRASS) LEA
LYING-IN INLYING CHILDBED
GROANING
LYMPH CHYLE VIRUS
(PREF.) CHYL(O)
(SUFF.) CHYLIA
LYMPHAD GALLEY
LYMPHANGITIS WEED FILLING
LYMPHATIC LACTEAL
LYMPHOGRANULOMA BUBO
LYMPHOMATOSIS FISHEYE
LYNCEUS (BROTHER OF —) IDAS
(FATHER OF —) AEGYPTUS
APHAREUS
(WIFE OF —) HYPERMNESTRA

LYNCH HANG DEWITT
LYNX LOSSE OUNCE PISHU BOBCAT
GORKUN LUCERN CARACAL
LUCIVEE WILDCAT CARCAJOU
LYRE ASOR HARP LYRA SHELL
CHELYS KINNOR KISSAR TRIGON
CITHARA TESTUDO BARBITON
PHORMINX TRICHORD TRIGONON
LYREBIRD LYRETAIL PHEASANT
LYRIC LAY LIED HOKKU LAEAN
MELIC GHAZEL TENSON CANCION
CHANSON DESCORT MADRIGAL
(HAVING — AND DRAMATIC
QUALITIES) SPINTO
(LOVE —) ALBA
(PL.) SONG
LYRICAL ODIC MELIC
LYSIPPE (FATHER OF —) PROETUS
(HUSBAND OF —) MELAMPUS
(MOTHER OF —) ANTIA
(SISTER OF —) IPHINOE IPHINASSA
LYTTA WORM

M

M EM EMMA MIKE METRO
  (WRONG USE OF —) MYTACISM
M-1 GARAND
MAACAH (HUSBAND OF —) DAVID
  (SON OF —) ABSALOM
MAACHAH (FATHER OF —) NAHOR
  URIEL TALMAI
  (HUSBAND OF —) JEHIEL MACHIR
  REHOBOAM
  (MOTHER OF —) REUMAH
  (SON OF —) HANAN ABIJAH ACHISH
  ABSALOM SHEPHATIAH
MAADAI (FATHER OF —) BANI
MA'AM MARM MISTRESS
MAARIB ARBIT ARBITH
MAASEIAH (FATHER OF —) ADAIAH
  BARUCH SHALLUM
  (SON OF —) AZARIAH ZEDEKIAH
  ZEPHANIAH
MAATH (FATHER OF —) MATTATHIAS
MAAZ (FATHER OF —) RAM
MACA ENIMAGA
MACABRE SICK SCARY HORRIBLE
MACACA PITHECUS
MACADAMIZE METAL
MACAO (CHINESE NAME OF —)
  AOMEN
  (ISLAND OF —) TAIPA COLOANE
MACAQUE KRA BROH BRUH
  MACAC TOQUE MACHIN MONKEY
  RHESUS RILAWA WANDEROO
MACARIA (FATHER OF —) HERCULES
  (MOTHER OF —) DEIANIRA
MACARIZE LAUD
MACARONI FOP DANDY DITALI
MACARONIC SKEW
MACAROON AMARETTO
MACAW ARA ARARA PARROT
  MARACAN ARACANGA COCKATOO
MACAW-TREE MACOYA
  MACAHUBA
MACBETH (AUTHOR OF —)
  SHAKESPEARE
  (CHARACTER IN —) ROSS ANGUS
  BANQUO DUNCAN HECATE LENNOX
  SEYTON SIWARD FLEANCE
  MACBETH MACDUFF MALCOLM
  MENTEITH CAITHNESS
  DONALBAIN
MACE CROC MALL MAUL POKER
  VERGE MALLET SPARTH CATTAIL
  (PART OF —) HEAD HILT SPIKE
  FLANGE HANDLE
  (REED —) DOD DODD
  (ROYAL —) SCEPTER SCEPTRE
MACE-BEARER BEADLE VERGER
  MACEMAN
MACERATE RET SOUR STEEP
MACHAON (BROTHER OF —)
  PODALIRIUS
  (FATHER OF —) AESCULAPIUS
  (MOTHER OF —) CORONIS
MACHETE BOLO GULOC PANGA

PARANG CURTAXE CUTLASH
CUTLASS
MACHI (COMPANION OF —) CALEB
  JOSHUA
  (SON OF —) GEUEL
MACHIAVELLIAN CRAFTY CUNNING
  GUILEFUL
MACHINATE TAMPER
MACHINATION ARTIFICE INTRIGUE
  SCHEMERY
MACHINE (ALSO SEE DEVICE AND
  ENGINE) GIN HOG JIG SAW AGER
  BABY COMB GEAR JACK LIFT MULE
  PUMP RASP TRAY WHIM WINK
  ADDER AWNER BALER BENCH
  BILLY BOARD BRAKE BREAK
  COPER CRANE DEVIL EDGER ERNIE
  FRAME FUDGE FUGAL JENNY
  JERRY JOLLY LATHE LAYER METER
  MIXER MOWER NAVVY RAKER
  RESAW ROVER SCREW SETUP
  SHEEN SIZER STAMP SULKY TRONE
  VINER WILLY BARKER BEADER
  BEAMER BEATER BEETLE BENDER
  BILLER BINDER BOLTER BUCKLE
  BUMPER BUTTER CANTER CAPPER
  CARDER CONCHE COOLER
  CREWER DECKER DOFFER DONKEY
  DRAPER DREDGE DUSTER ENGINE
  FLAKER FOLDER FOOTER FORMER
  GADDER GAPPER GLAZER GRADER
  GRATER GUMMER HEADER
  HEMMER HOBBER HOGGER
  HOOPER HULLER HUSKER IRONER
  JIGGER JORDAN KICKER LEGGER
  LIFTER LINTER LOGGER MAILER
  MANGLE MILLER MITRER NAPPER
  NETTER NIBBER NIPPER PACKER
  PEGGER PINNER PLATER PUMPER
  RIPPER ROSSER ROTARY ROUTER
  SANDER SCUTCH SEALER SEAMER
  SHAKER SHAPER SHAVER SINGER
  SKIVER SLICER SORTER SPACER
  STOCKS STOKER TEDDER TENTER
  TWINER VANNER WASHER
  WELDER WILLOW ABRADER
  AUTOMAT AVIATOR BACKHOE
  BATCHER BELLOWS BLENDER
  BLUNGER BOTTLER BRANNER
  BREAKER CANDROY CAPSTAN
  CHIPPER COMBINE CRUSHER
  DIBBLER DRESSER EMULSOR
  ENCODER ENROBER ERECTOR
  EXOSTRA FLANGER FLOSSER
  FREEZER GARNETT GLASSER
  GRAINER GRINDER GROOVER
  GROUTER HUMIDOR IRONMAN
  JOINTER KNITTER KNOTTER
  MACHINA MANGLER MATCHER
  MITERER PERRIER PLODDER
  PLUCKER POTCHER PRINTER
  QUILLER REPRESS RIVETER
  ROASTER SAMMIER SCALPER

SHEARER SHEETER SIROCCO
SLABBER SLASHER SLITTER
SLOTTER SLUBBER SLUGGER
SMASHER SPALLER SPEEDER
SPINNER SPONGER SPOOLER
SPRAYER STACKER STAMPER
STAPLER STEAMER STEMMER
STICKER TENONER TEREBRA
TOOTHER TRAMPER TREATER
TRIMMER TRUSSER TWILLER
TWISTER TYPOBAR WHIPPER
WHIZZER AERIFIER AIRCRAFT
BROACHER CALENDER CANCELER
CARTONER CLINCHER COLLATOR
COMPRESS DUNGBECK ELEPHANT
EXPLODER EXTRUDER FILATORY
FINISHER FLYWINCH FORKLIFT
GATHERER HARDENER HAYMAKER
HERCULES HUMMELER IMPACTER
KILLIFER MORTISER MOULINET
ODOGRAPH OROGRAPH PROFILER
PULSATOR SCHIFFLI SCUTCHER
SHREDDER SOFTENER SPLITTER
SPREADER SPRIGGER SQUEEZER
STITCHER STRANDER STRIPPER
SURFACER TEMPERER THREADER
THRESHER THROSTLE TRAVELER
TRISPAST TUNNELER UPSETTER
WINNOWER ADDRESSER
(ANCIENT MILITARY —) BALISTA
BALLISTA
(BETTING —) PARIMUTUEL
(POLITICAL —) APPARAT
(STAGE —) PAGEANT
MACHINE-GUN POMPOM
  MITRAILLEUSE
MACHINE GUN STINGER
  CHAUCHAT
MACHINERY MINT TOPCAP
  SUCCULA APPARATUS
MACHINE SHOP TURNERY
MACHINIST FRILLER THINNER
  MACHINER
MACHIR (FATHER OF —) AMMIEL
  MANASSEH
MACHISMO MACHO
MACHNADEBAI (FATHER OF —)
  BANI
MACKEREL CERO CHAD PETO SCAD
  TINK BLINK OPELU SNOEK TUNNY
  BONITO SAUREL TINKER BLINKER
  BLOATER SCOMBER TASSARD
  ALBACORE HARDHEAD SCOMBRID
  SEERFISH
  (— ABOUT 8 OR 9 INCHES) TINK
  TINKER
  (KING —) CERO
  (PICKLED —) SCALPEEN
  (POOR BONY —) SLINK SLINKER
  (SNAKE —) ESCOLAR
  (YOUNG —) SPIKE
  (PREF.) SCOMBRI
MACKLE SLUR SHAKE MACULA

MACROGAMETE OVUM
MACROSCOPIC GROSS
MACROSPECIES LINNEON
MAD FEY AWAY GITE GYTE HYTE
  WOOD YOND ANGRY BATTY BRAIN
  CRAZY DIPPY FOLLE MANIC RABID
  WACKO WACKY BEDLAM FRENZY
  INSANE MANIAC WOODEN
  BERSERK BONKERS FANATIC
  FRANTIC FURIOUS LUNATIC
  MADDING MADDOCK MANKIND
  REDWOOD WITLESS DELIRANT
  DEMENTED DISTRACT INFORMAL
  MANIACAL MINDLESS RAVENING
  POSSESSED
  (GET —) SEERED

> **MADAGASCAR**
> **CAPITAL:** ANTANANARIVO
> **FORMER NAME:**
>   MALAGASYREPUBLIC
> **ISLAND GROUP:** ALDABRA
> **LAKE:** ITASY ALAOTRA
> **MEASURE:** GANTANG
> **NATIVE:** HOVA SAKALAVA
> **PEOPLE:** HOVA COTIER MARINA
> **RIVER:** IKOPA MANIA SOFIA
>   MANGOKY MANGORO ONYLAHY
> **TOWN:** IHOSY MANJA TULEAR
>   MAJANGA NOSSIBE TSIVORY
>   TAMATAVE ANTISIRABE

MADAI (FATHER OF —) JAPHET
MADAM MEM MUM BAWD MAAM
  PANI DONNA MADAME SENORA
  SENHORA SIGNORA GOODWIFE
  MISTRESS SINEBADA
MADAMA BUTTERFLY
  (CHARACTER IN —) SUZUKI
  CIOCIOSAN PINKERTON SHARPLESS
  (COMPOSER OF —) PUCCINI
MADAME BOVARY (AUTHOR OF —)
  FLAUBERT
  (CHARACTER IN —) EMMA LEON
  BOVARY DUPUIS HOMAIS CHARLES
  HELOISE ROUAULT LHEUREUX
  RODOLPHE BOULANGER
MADAR YERCUM
MADCAP RASH
MADDEN ENRAGE INCENSE
  INFLAME DISTRACT
MADDENED ENRAGED FRENZIED
MADDER GAMENE LIZARY ALIZARI
  GARANCE MUNJEET TANAGRA
  GARANCIN SPURWORT
  WOODRUFF
MAD-DOG SKULLCAP MADWEED
  HOODWORT
MADE SET BUILT COMPACT
  PREPARED TIMBERED
  (— FLUID BY HEAT) FUSILE
  (— LATELY) NEW
  (— OF DISSIMILAR PARTS) MIXED

(**— OF FLAX**) LINEN
(**— OF GRAIN**) OATEN CEREAL
(**— OF IVORY**) EBURNEAN
(**— OF SILVER**) ARGENT
(**— OF STONE**) STONEN
(**— OF TWIGS**) VIRGAL
(**— SHORT**) CURTAL
(**— TART**) EUCHRED
(**— TO ORDER**) BESPOKEN
(**— TRANSLUCENT**) AJOURE
(**— UP**) ACCRETE
(**— WITH CEDAR**) CEDARN
(**CUNNINGLY —**) SLY
(PREF.) (**— OF**) DIA
(SUFF.) (**— OF**) INE
MADE-BEAVER SKIN CASTOR
MADEIRA ISLANDS (**ISLAND OF —**)
GRANDE DEZERTE
(**TOWN OF —**) FUNCHAL
(**WINE OF —**) BUAL TINTA MALMSEY
SERCIAL VERDELHO
MADELON POLIXENE
MADHGOUSE SCRUM
MADHOUSE ASYLUM BEDLAM
MADHUCA BASSIA ILLIPE
MADLY WOOD CRAZY
MADMAN GELT WACKO BEDLAM
MANIAC CRAZOID FURIOSO
LUNATIC WOODMAN
MADNESS MAD FURY MOON
WOOD FOLIE FOLLY FUROR MANIA
BEDLAM FRENZY LUNACY
DEWANEE ECSTASY MOONERY
WIDDRIM DELIRIUM DEMENTIA
PIBLOKTO WILLNESS WOODNESS
WOODSHIP
(PREF.) LYSSO MANIC
(SUFF.) MANE MANIA(C)
MADONNA LADY VIRGIN
MADREPORE FUNGID
MADRIGAL ENSALADA
MADRONA LAUREL MANZANITA
MADTOM TADPOLE
MADWORT ALYSSUM BUGLOSS
MAENAD FROW BASSARID
BACCHANTE
(PL.) BACCHAE
MAFIA MOB GANG CLIQUE
MAFIC FEMIC
MAFURA ROKA ELCAJA
MAGANI BAGANI
MAGAZINE MAG BOOK DRUM FLAT
IGLOO SLICK STORE RETORT
ALMACEN JOURNAL CASSETTE
(**BLACKWOOD'S —**) MAGA
(**FASHION —**) ELLE
(**OLD MUSIC —**) ETUDE
(**SCIENCE FICTION —**) FANZINE
MAGDALEN MAUDLIN
MAGGOT MAD GRUB MAWK WORM
METHE GENTLE WARBLE WORMIL
MADDOCK SKIPPER MUCKWORM
MAGGOTY MAWKISH
MAGIC JUJU MAYA RUNE CRAFT
FAIRY GOETY SPELL TURGY
GOETIC TREGET VOODOO
ALCHEMY CANTRIP CONJURY
DEVILRY GLAMOUR GRAMARY
MAGICAL SORCERY BRUJERIA
HECATEAN WIZARDRY
NECROMANCY
(**BLACK —**) GOETY GOETIC
MALEFICE

(**PERSONAL —**) CHARISM
CHARISMA
(**WHITE —**) TURGY
MAGICAL WIZARD WONDER
HERMETIC NUMINOUS THEURGIC
MAGIC FLUTE, THE (**CHARACTER IN
—**) PAMINA TAMINO PAPAGENA
PAPAGENO SARASTRO
MONOSTATOS
(**COMPOSER OF —**) MOZART
MAGICIAN MAGE BOKOR MAGUS
UTHER CUNJAH GOETIC GOOFER
GUFFER MAGIAN MERLIN WABENO
WIZARD CHARMER GWYDION
KOSCHEI WARLOCK WIELARE
WISEMAN CONJURER FETISHER
SORCERER THEURGIC TROLLMAN
ARCHIMAGE
MAGIC MOUNTAIN (**AUTHOR OF
—**) MANN
(**CHARACTER IN —**) HANS NAPHTA
BEHRENS CASTORP CAUCHAT
CLAVDIA JOACHIM ZIEMSSEN
KROKOWSKI PEEPERKORN
SETTEMBRINI
MAGISTERIAL LOFTY PROUD
AUGUST CURULE LORDLY
HAUGHTY STATELY ARROGANT
DOGMATIC
MAGISTERY MASTERY
MAGISTRACY AMT PRYTANY
MAGISTRATE BEAK FOUD EPHOR
JUDGE JURAT MAYOR PRIOR
REEVE AMTMAN ARCHON AVOYER
BAILIE BAILLI CENSOR CONSUL
FISCAL KOTWAL SYNDIC ALCALDE
BAILIFF BURGESS DUUMVIR
ECHEVIN EPHORUS JUSTICE
NOMARCH PODESTA PRAETOR
PREFECT PROVOST STEWARD
SUFFETE TRIBUNE ALABARCH
ALDERMAN CAPITOUL DEFENSOR
DEMIURGE DICTATOR GOVERNOR
MITTIMUS PHYLARCH PRYTANIS
RECORDER STRADICO STRATEGE
HUNDREDER CORREGIDOR
(**— IN CHANNEL ISLANDS**) JURAT
(**— OF ANCIENT ROME**) EDILE
AEDILE
(**— OF INDIA**) COTWAL KOTWAL
(**— OF MECCA**) SHERIF SHEREEF
(**— OF VENICE AND GENOA**) DOGE
(**MOHAMMEDAN —**) CADI CADY
SHERIF
(**SCOTCH —**) PROVOST STEWARD
MAGMA ICHOR
MAGMATIC JUVENILE
MAGNANIMITY HEIGHT FREEDOM
MAGNANIMOUS BIG FREE GREAT
LARGE LOFTY NOBLE HEROIC
EXALTED GENEROUS
MAGNATE BARON MOGUL TITAN
BASHAW TYCOON
MAGNESIA PULVIL
MAGNET FIELD ADAMAS MAGNES
ADAMANT SOLENOID TERRELLA
LODESTONE
MAGNETIC (**— FIELD MEASURER**)
SQUID
MAGNETISM IT DEVIL OOMPH
MAGNETITE LOADSTONE
LODESTONE
MAGNETIZE TOUCH SATURATE

MAGNETOMETER DOODLEBUG
MAGNIFICATION POWER
MAGNIFICENCE GITE POMP FLARE
GLORY STATE PARADE JOLLITY
ROYALTY GRANDEUR SPLENDOR
MAGNIFICENT RIAL GRAND NOBLE
PROUD ROYAL AUGUST LAVISH
IMMENSE POMPOUS STATELY
SUBLIME GLORIOUS GORGEOUS
MAGNIFIC PALATIAL PRINCELY
SPLENDID
MAGNIFICENT OBSESSION
(**AUTHOR OF —**) DOUGLAS
(**CHARACTER IN —**) BRENT HELEN
JOYCE NANCY WAYNE DAWSON
HUDSON ROBERT ASHFORD
MERRICK
MAGNIFY LAUD BLESS ERECT
EXALT PRAISE ADVANCE DISTEND
ENLARGE GLORIFY GREATEN
INCREASE MAXIMIZE MULTIPLY
MAGNIFYING
(PREF.) MICR(O)
MAGNIFYING GLASS LOUPE
READER
MAGNILOQUENT TURGID
BOMBAST
MAGNITUDE BULK MASS SIZE
DATUM LEVEL SOLID EXTENT
FIGURE PERIOD EXTREME
CONSTANT FUNCTION INFINITE
MAGNOLIA YULAN BIGBLOOM
CUCUMBER MAURICIO
(**— STATE**) MISSISSIPPI
MAGOG (**FATHER OF —**) JAPHETH
MAGPIE MAG PIE PIET PYAT CISSA
KOTRI MADGE NINUT MARGET
NANPIE PIANET PIEMAG SIRGANG
HAGISTER MARGARET PHEASANT
PIENANNY CHATTERBOX
MAGPIE LARK PEEWEE GRALLINA
MAGPIE ROBIN DAYAL DHYAL
MAGUEY AGAVE MESCAL CANTALA
MAGYAR SZEKEL SZEKLER
MAHALAH (**MOTHER OF —**)
HAMMOLEKETH
(**UNCLE OF —**) GILEAD
MAHALATH (**FATHER OF —**)
ISHMAEL JERIMOTH
(**HUSBAND OF —**) ESAU
REHOBOAM
MAHALI (**FATHER OF —**) MERARI
MAHATMA SAGE ARHAT
MAHAZIOTH (**FATHER OF —**)
HEMAN
MAH-JONGG WOO
MAHLAH (**FATHER OF —**)
ZELOPHEHAD
MAHLI (**FATHER OF —**) MUSHI
MERARI
MAHLON (**DAUGHTER OF —**) NAOMI
(**SON OF —**) ELIMELECH
(**WIFE OF —**) RUTH
MAHOE EMAJAGUA
MAHOGANY SIPO ALMON CAOBA
CEDAR ROHAN ACAJOU AGUANO
SAPELE THITKA ALBARCO AVODIRE
BAYWOOD GUNNUNG MADEIRA
RATTEEN TABASCO BANGALAY
HARDTACK TANGUILE
(**INDIAN —**) TOON
(**PHILIPPINE —**) BAGTIKAN
MAHONIA ASHBERRY ODOSTEMON

MAHOUND MACON
MAHUA FULWA MOWHA MOWRA
MADHUCA PHULWARA
MAHUANG EPHEDRA
MAHWA ILLIPE ILLUPI
MAIA (**FATHER OF —**) ATLAS
(**MOTHER OF —**) PLEIONE
(**SON OF —**) MERCURY
MAID MAY AYAH GIRL LASS MEDE
SLUT CHINA WENCH WOMAN
MAIDEN SLAVEY TWEENY VIRGIN
ANCILLA GENERAL MAIDKIN
PHYLLIS PUCELLE WENCHEL
BONIBELL BRANGANE HANDMAID
SUIVANTE TIREMAID
(**— IN WAITING**) DAMSEL DAMOZEL
(**— OF-ALL-WORK**) SLAVEY
GENERAL
(**— OF HONOR**) MARIE
(**KIND OF —**) METER
(**KITCHEN —**) SCOGIE
(**LADY'S —**) AYAH ABIGAIL
TIREMAID
(**NURSE —**) BONNE
(**OLD —**) TABBY SPINSTER
(**WAITING —**) ABIGAIL SUIVANTE
MAIDEN MAY BIRD BURD DAME
GIRL MAID DALAGA DAMSEL
FROKIN MEISJE COLLEEN CYDIPPE
DAMOZEL MADCHEN DAUGHTER
(**— WITH BASKET ON HEAD**)
CANEPHOR
(**MOUNT IDA —**) OREAD
(**MUSLIM —**) HURI HOURI
(**WEAVING —**) ARACHNE
(PREF.) PARTHENO
MAIDENHAIR GINGKO ADIANTUM
MAIDENLY VIRGIN GIRLISH
VIRGINAL
MAIDEN PINK SPINK DIANTHUS
MAIDSERVANT LASS BIDDY BONNE
SKIVVY ANCILLA LISETTE
MAIEUTIC HEBAMIC
MAIGRE BAR SCIAENID WEAKFISH
MAIL BAG DAK HOOD POST ARMOR
MATTER AIRMAIL JACKPOT
MAILBAG ORDINAR POSTAGE
POSTBAG SEAPOST TAPPALL
ORDINARY
(**IMPROPERLY ADDRESSED —**) NIX
NIXY NIXIE
(**JUNK —**) CATALOG
(**KIND OF —**) HATE VOICE
MAILBAG BAG POUCH POSTBAG
MAILBOX POST PILLAR POSTBOX
MAILLECHORT ARGENTON
MAILLOT SWIMSUIT
MAILMAN POSTMAN BREVIGER
MAIM LAME BREAK TRUNK HAMBLE
MANGLE MAYHEM SCOTCH
CRIPPLE MUTILATE TRUNCATE
(**— AN ANIMAL**) LAW MANK
MAIMED GAMMY SPAVINED
(PREF.) PERO
MAIMING MAYHEM
MAIN HIGH LINE MOST CHIEF
GRAND GREAT OCEAN PRIME
SHEER MIGHTY CAPITAL LEADING
CARDINAL FOREMOST

MAINE
CAPITAL: AUGUSTA
COLLEGE: BATES COLBY BOWDOIN

COUNTY: KNOX WALDO KENNEBEC AROOSTOOK PENOBSCOT SAGADAHOC PISCATAQUIS
INDIAN: ABNAKI
LAKE: GRAND SEBEC SEBAGO RANGELEY SCHOODIC MOOSEHEAD CHESUNCOOK
MOUNTAIN: BIGELOW CADILLAC KATAHDIN
NATIVE: MANIAC
RIVER: SACO KENNEBEC AROOSTOOK KENNEBAGO PENOBSCOT
STATE BIRD: CHICKADEE
STATE FLOWER: PINECONE
STATE NICKNAME: LUMBER PINETREE
STATE TREE: PINE
TOWN: BATH ORONO AUBURN BANGOR BELFAST HOULTON KITTERY MACHIAS BOOTHBAY LEWISTON OGUNQUIT PORTLAND SKOWHEGAN

MAINLAND
(PREF.) EPEIRO
MAINLY BROADLY CHIEFLY LARGELY
MAINSTAY KEY ATLAS SINEW STOOP PILLAR BACKBONE RELIANCE
MAIN STREET (AUTHOR OF —) LEWIS
(CHARACTER IN —) ERIK HUGH WILL CAROL MILFORD VALBORG KENNICOTT
MAINTAIN AVER AVOW BEAR FEND FIND HOLD KEEP LAST SAVE ADOPT ARGUE CARRY CLAIM ESCOT SALVE ADHERE ALLEGE ASSERT AVOUCH DEFEND INTEND RETAIN THREAP UPHOLD UPKEEP CONFIRM CONTEND DECLARE DISPUTE JUSTIFY NOURISH SUBSIST SUPPORT SUSTAIN CONTINUE PRESERVE
(— AS TRUE) AVOUCH SOOTHE
(— POSITION) STALL
(— SOLEMNLY) VOW
(— WITHOUT REASON) ARROGATE
MAINTAINER FOUNDER RETAINER
MAINTENANCE KEEP LIVING UPKEEP ALIMONY CUSTODY FINDING KEEPING PREBEND SERVICE
(— OF POPULATION) BALANCE
MAITHILI TIRHUTIA
MAIZE CORN GRAIN CEREAL INDIAN JAGONG STAPLE MEALIES DJAGOONG
(— CRUSHED WITH PESTLE) STAMP
MAJAGUA HAU BARU BOLA MAHO MOJO BURAO GUANA MAHOE PURAU BALIBAGO CORKWOOD EMAJAGUA
MAJESTIC HIGH AWFUL GRAND LOFTY REGAL ROYAL AUGUST KINGLY SUPERB STATELY SUBLIME ELEVATED IMPERIAL MAESTOSO SPLENDID
MAJESTY DIGNITY AUGUSTUS GRANDEUR KINGSHIP
MAJOON BANG BHANG

MAJOR BEY DUR DURUM SHARP CAPITAL GREATER MAGGIORE
MAJOR BARBARA (AUTHOR OF —) SHAW
(CHARACTER IN —) LOMAX SARAH CUSINS BARBARA CHARLES STEPHEN ADOLPHUS BRITOMART UNDERSHAFT
MAJORCA (SEAPORT IN —) PALMA
MAJORITY BODY BULK FECK MOST CORPSE SUBSTANCE
(ABSOLUTE —) QUORUM
MAJOR LEAGUE BIGS
MAKARAKA IDDIO
MAKARI KOTOKO
MAKE DO CUT GAR LET MAY FORM GIVE LEVY BRAND BUILD CAUSE COVER FETCH FORGE FRAME SEIZE SHAPE STAMP AUTHOR COBBLE CREATE GRAITH INDUCE RENDER CONFECT FASHION IMAGERY IWURCHE PERFORM PRODUCE CONTRIVE GENERATE
(— A BLUNDER) GOOF
(— ACKNOWLEDGMENT) CONFESS
(— ACTIVE) ENERGIZE
(— A DIFFERENCE) SKILL
(— A DRINK LAST) NURSE
(— ADVANCES) SOLICIT IMPORTUNE
(— AGAIN) RENEW
(— AMENDS) ABYE ATONE ABEGGE ANSWER REDEEM EXPIATE REDRESS
(— A MESS OF) PIE
(— ANGRY) GRAMY WRATH
(— A RUG) HOOK
(— AS PROFIT) GROSS
(— ATTRACTIVE) GILD
(— A VISIT) COSHER
(— AWAY WITH) ABOLISH EMBEZZLE
(— BARE) STRIP DENUDE
(— BELIEVE) LET PRETEND
(— BETTER) AMEND HEIGHTEN
(— BLUE) HIP
(— BRIGHT) ENGILD ILLUME CLARIFY
(— BRISK) PERK
(— BROWN) TAN
(— BY STAMPING) MINT
(— CANDLE) DIP DRAW
(— CERTAIN) ASSURE ENSURE
(— CHANNEL IN) THROAT
(— CHEERFUL) SOLACE
(— CHOICE) OPT CHOOSE SELECT
(— CLAMMY) ENGLEIM
(— CLEAR) DECLARE DEVELOP DISCUSS EXHIBIT EXPOUND LIGHTEN DESCRIBE
(— COLD) REFREID
(— COMPLETE) SPHERE
(— CONSPICUOUS) ENNOBLE
(— CONTENT) SATISFY
(— CULTIVABLE) EMPOLDER
(— CUT PRIOR TO LAYERING) TONGUE
(— DEMANDS) POSTULATE
(— DESTITUTE) BEREAVE
(— DIFFERENT) ALTER CHANGE
(— DIRTY) MOIL GRIME
(— DISPLAY OF) AFFECT DISCOVER

(— DRUNK) FOX SOUSE FUDDLE SOZZLE
(— DRY) HAZLE HAZZLE
(— EARLIER) ADVANCE
(— EFFERVESCENT) AERATE
(— EFFIGY) GUY
(— EFFORT) PUSH
(— END OF) SNIB FETCH
(— ENDURING) ANNEAL
(— EQUAL) WEIGH EQUATE
(— EVEN) GLAZE LEVEL WEIGH SQUARE
(— FACES) GIMBLE MURGEON
(— FALSE PRETENSES) SHAM
(— FAST) FIX BAIL FAST GIRD KNIT MAKE STOP BELAY HITCH BUCKLE FASTEN SECURE
(— FAT) BATTEN
(— FIRM) FIX BRACE FASTEN
(— FIT) APTATE STRIKE
(— FOOLISH) DAFF GREEN NUGIFY STULTIFY
(— FOOL OF) DOR BORE DOLT DORRE BEGOWK DOODLE
(— FOOTSORE) SURBATE
(— FOR) HEAD
(— FROTHY) MILL
(— FULL) FARCE FULFILL
(— FUN OF) GUY KID GAFF JAPE JEST JOSH RIDE DROLL GLAIK SCOUT SMOKE
(— FUSS OVER NOTHING) FAFF
(— GLAD) FAIN
(— GLASS) FOUND
(— GLOSSY) SLEEK
(— GLOW) FURNACE
(— GOLDEN) ENDORE
(— GOOD) ABET SUPPLY RESTORE SUPPORT RETRIEVE
(— GRINDING NOISE) GRINCH
(— GURGLING SOUND) CROOL
(— HAPPY) BLESS ENJOY REFORM BEATIFY SATISFY FELICIFY
(— HARD) TAW STEEL ENDURE HORNIFY
(— HARDY) FASTEN
(— HEADWAY) STEM WALK ENFORCE
(— HEALTHY) SANIFY
(— HELPLESS) STAGGER
(— HOLY) BLESS SACRE HALLOW SANCTIFY
(— HORSE SEEM YOUNGER) BISHOP
(— ILL) MORBIFY
(— IMMOBILE) FREEZE
(— IMPACT) ASSAIL
(— INCURSION) HARRY
(— INSIGNIFICANT) MICRIFY
(— INTO BUNDLE) FARDEL
(— INTO LAW) ENACT
(— INVALID) DAMASK
(— JOINT) SYPHER
(— KNOWN) BID OUT GIVE WISE AREAD BEKEN BREAK KITHE SOUND SPEAK BEWRAY BROACH COUTHE DENOTE DESCRY EXPOSE INFORM REVEAL SPREAD CONFESS DECLARE DELIVER DIVULGE PUBLISH SIGNIFY UNCOVER ANNOUNCE DECIPHER DISCLOSE DISCOVER INDICATE PROCLAIM PROMULGE
(— LESS) MINISH

(— LESS DENSE) THIN RAREFY
(— LESS SEVERE) MITIGATE
(— LIABLE) DANGER
(— LOVE) WOO COURT SPOON GALLANT
(— LUKEWARM) WLECCHE
(— LUSTERLESS) FLATTEN
(— MANIFEST) EVINCE EXPLAIN
(— MELANCHOLY) HYP
(— MELODIOUS) ATTUNE
(— MELODY) DREAM
(— MENTION) SPEAK
(— MERRY) JET GAUD CHEER SPORT FROLIC SHROVE DISPORT REHAYTE
(— METALLIC SOUND) CHINK
(— MISTAKE) ERR BOOB GOOF
(— MONOTONOUS NOISE) DRONE
(— MORAL) ETHICIZE
(— MUCH OF) DAWT DANDLE
(— MURMURING NOISE) BUM
(— NEAT) FEAT SMUG TIDY GROOM
(— NEST) TIMBER
(— NEW AGAIN) RENOVATE
(— NONMAGNETIC) DEGAUSS
(— NUMB) DAZE ETHERIZE
(— OFF) BAG BOLT HOOK ANNEX HEIST MOSEY SLOPE SPIRIT SCARPER
(— ONE) UNE
(— ONE'S WAY) AIRT BORE TRADE PLY FRAME
(— OPEN) AIR PATEFY
(— OUT) FARE FILL GLEAN SKILL DISCERN DECIPHER
(— OVER) TURN ALIEN CHANGE RECOCT DELIVER REFORGE
(— PALE) CHALK
(— PLEASANT) SWEETEN
(— POIGNANT) SAUCE
(— PREGNANT) ENWOMB
(— PROGRESS) GAIN STEM GATHER
(— PROUD) WLENCH
(— PUBLIC) BLOW BLAZE BREAK BLAZON DELATE DIVULGE FANFARE PUBLISH BULLETIN
(— QUIET) ALLAY QUIET APPEASE
(— RATTLING NOISE) TIRL
(— READY) DO BUN GET BOUN BOWN BUSK YARK BELAY BOWNE DRESS PREST PRIME FETTLE GRAITH ADDRESS APPAREL DISPOSE PREPARE
(— RECORD OF) REFER
(— REFERENCE) MENTION
(— RESISTANCE) REBEL
(— RESOLUTE) STEEL
(— RETURN FOR) REQUITE
(— RICH) FREIGHT IMBURSE
(— ROSY) FLUSH
(— RUSTLING SOUND) FISSLE FISTLE
(— RUTTING CRY) FREAM
(— SCANTY LIVING) EKE
(— SERIES OF NOTES) TINKLE
(— SHIFT) SCAMBLE
(— SIGN OF CROSS) BLESS
(— SMALL) MICRIFY BELITTLE
(— SMALLER) MINIFY COMPRESS
(— SMOOTH) SLAB GLAZE SLEEK GENTLE HAMMER SCRAPE LEVIGATE
(— SOFT) NESH GENTLE

(— **SOGGY**) SOP
(— **SOUR**) FOX WIND
(— **SPIRITLESS**) MOPE
(— **SPORT OF**) LARK
(— **SPRUCE**) PERK SMARTEN
(— **STRAIGHT**) ADDRESS
(— **STRONG**) STEEL FASTEN
FORTIFY
(— **STUPID**) MOIDER STULTIFY
(— **SUITABLE**) ADAPT
(— **SURE**) SEE INSURE
(— **THIN**) EMACIATE
(— **TIDY**) RED REDD
(— **TIPSY**) FLUSTER
(— **TRANSITION TO**) MODULATE
(— **TRIM**) SMUG
(— **UNEVEN**) RUFFLE RUMPLE
(— **UP**) UP COOK FORM SPELL
INDITE SETTLE ANALYZE COMPACT
COMPOSE COMPUTE CONCOCT
CONFECT FASHION COMPOUND
COMPRISE DISPENSE
(— **UP ACCOUNTS**) BREVE
(— **USELESS**) SPIKE SPOIL
(— **USE OF**) FEE BUSK APPLY AVAIL
BROOK SERVE SPEND EMPLOY
EXECUTE IMPROVE UTILIZE
(— **VIBRANT SOUND**) CHIRR
(— **VOID**) ABATE ANNUL
(— **WAR**) WARRAY
(— **WET**) DRAGGLE
(— **WHISTLING NOISE**) WHEW
(— **WHITE**) BLANCH BLEACH
CANDIFY
(— **WORSE**) IMPAIR PEJORATE
(PREF.) POETICO POETO
(SUFF.) EN FECT FEIT FIC(AL)(ATE)
(ATION)(ATIVE)(ATOR)(ATORY)(E)
(ENCE)(ENT)(IAL)(IARY)(IENT) FIER
FIQUE FY IFY POEIA POESIS
POIESIS POIETIC
MAKE-BELIEVE BORAK DUMMY
ASSUMED PRETENCE
MAKER DOER JACK KNAVE SMITH
FACTOR FORGER FORMER
WORKER WRIGHT CREATOR
DECLARER OPERATOR
(— **OF ARROWS**) FLETCHER
(— **OF BARRELS**) COOPER
(— **OF POTS**) POTTER
(— **OF SADDLETREES**) FUSTER
(— **OF SONGS**) BULBUL
(— **OF TALLOW**) CHANDLER
(**DRIP-COFFEE** —) MACCHINETTA
(SUFF.) STER STRESS
MAKESHIFT JURY RUDE JERRY
TOUSY BEWITH CUTCHA KUTCHA
APOLOGY JACKLEG STOPGAP
RESOURCE TIMENOGUY
MAKEUP FACE BUILD GETUP HABIT
PAINT ROUGE SETUP SHAPE
FACIES FORMAT ANATOMY
CONSIST FEATURE EYELINER
PHYSIQUE TRAVESTY MAQUILLAGE
MAKING FACT
(SUFF.) FACIENT FACT(ION)(IVE)
(ORY) FIC FICATION
MALABAR BAY
MALABAR ALMOND KAMANI
ALMENDRO
MALACCA CANE
MALACEAE POMACEAE PYRACEAE
MALADJUSTMENT SCAR

MALADROIT ILL INEPT AWKWARD
UNHANDY BUNGLING
MALADY AMOK EVIL MORB CAUSE
GRIEF ONCOME AILMENT DISEASE
ILLNESS DISORDER MISCHIEF
SICKNESS
(SUFF.) (— **ARISING FROM**) ITIS
MALAGASY LEMURIAN
MALAGASY REPUBLIC (SEE
MADAGASCAR)
MALAGIGI (**COUSIN OF** —) RINALDO
MALAISE UNEASE
MALAPROPISM SLIPSLOP
MALAR JUGAL
MALARIA AGUE MIASMA SHAKES
QUARTAN PALUDISM
(— **PARASITE**) VIVAX
MALARIAL PALUDAL PALUDOSE
PALUDOUS

MALAWI
CAPITAL: LILONGWE
COIN: KWACHA TAMBALA
FORMER CAPITAL: ZOMBA
FORMER NAME: NYASALAND
HIGHLANDS: SHIRE
LAKE: NYASA
LANGUAGE: YAO CEWA BANTU
NGONI TONGA NYANJA TUMBUKA
MOUNTAIN: MLANJE
PEOPLE: YAO BANTU CHEWA
NGURU NYANJA
RIVER: SHIRE
TOWN: DOWA CHOLO MZUZU
NCHEU ZOMBA KARONGA
BLANTYRE LILONGWE
VALLEY: RIFT

MALAY AMOK ASIL AMUCK BAJAU
ILOCO JAKUN MANOBO ILOKANO
MALAYAN (— **TREE**) TERAP
MALAY APPLE OHIA JAMBU KAVIKA

MALAYSIA
CAPITAL: KUALALUMPUR
COIN: SEN TRA TRAH RINGGIT
ISLAND: ARU GOA KAI OBI OMA
ALOR BALI GAGA JAVA MUNA
MURU SULU AMBON BANDA
BOHOL BUTON CERAM LUZON
MISOL PANAY SANGI SUMBA
TIMOR WETAR BANGKA BOEFON
BOEROE BORNEO BUTUNG
FLORES LOMBOK MADURA
PELENG SANGIR TALAUR WAIGEU
AMBOINA CELEBES JAMDENA
MINDORO MOROTAI PALAWAN
SALAJAR SALWATI SUMATRA
SUMBAWA BELITONG DJAILOLO
TANIMBAR
ISTHMUS: KRA
LANGUAGE: TAGALOG
MONEY: DOLLAR RINGGIT
MOUNTAIN: BULU NIUT RAJA
MURJO NIAPA LEUSER SLAMET
BINAIJA RINDJANI
PEOPLE: ATA BAJAU SEMANG
BISAYAN TAGALOG VISAYAN
RIVER: KUTAI PERAK BARITO
PAHANG
STATE: KEDAH PERAK SABAH
JOHORE PAHANG PENANG PERLIS
MALACCA SARAWAK

TOWN: IPOH DAVAO ILOILO
KANGAR KUPANG MANADO
KUANTAN KUCHING MALACCA
SANDAKAN SEREMBAN
WEIGHT: TAEL WANG TAMPANG

MALCHAM (**FATHER OF** —)
SHAHARAHIM
(**MOTHER OF** —) HODESH
MALCHIAH (**FATHER OF** —) HARIM
PAROSH RECHAB
MALCHIEL (**FATHER OF** —) BERIAH
MALCHIRAM (**FATHER OF** —)
JEHOIACHIN
MALCHISHUA (**FATHER OF** —) SAUL
MALCONTENT FRONDEUR
MALDIVES (**CAPITAL OF** —) MALE
(**MONEY OF** —) LAARI RUFIYAA
RUFIYAN
MALE HE DOG HIM MAN TOM BUCK
BULL COCK JACK ADULT MANLY
SPEAR JOHNNY MANFUL MASCLE
VIRILE LALAQUI MANKIND
MANLIKE MANNISH PURUSHA
(— **OF ANIMALS**) TOM BUCK BULL
JACK STUD STALLION
(**EFFEMINATE** —) NANCE
(**GELDED** —) GALT
(**SWAGGERING**) GREASER
(**YOUNG** —) GROOM
(PREF.) ANDR(O)
(SUFF.) ANDRIA ANDROUS ANDRY
MALECITE ETCHEMIN
MALEDICTION BAN WISH CURSE
MALISON ANATHEMA
MALEFACTOR BADDY FELON
BADDIE CULPRIT CRIMINAL
EVILDOER
MALEFIC TAKING
MALEFICENT BALEFUL
MALELEEL (**FATHER OF**) CAINAN
MALEO MEGAPOD
MALE ORCHIS CUCKOO CROWTOE
CULLION PURPLES RAGWORT
CROWFOOT
MALEVOLENCE SPITE ENMITY
GRUDGE HATRED MALICE RANCOR
SPLEEN MALIGNITY
MALEVOLENT ILL EVIL FELL
MALIGN HATEFUL HOSTILE
SPITEFUL RANCOROUS
MALFEASANCE MISCONDUCT
MALPRACTICE
MALFORMATION CURL ERROR
HEMITERY MONSTROSITY
(— **OF CARNATION**) TWITTER
(— **OF FRUIT**) CATFACE
MALFORMED SHAMBLE
MALFUNCTION GLITCH

MALI
ANCIENT CITY: TIMBUKTU
CAPITAL: BAMAKO
FORMER NAME: FRENCHSUDAN
LAKE: DO DEBO GAROU KORAROU
LANGUAGE: DOGON DYULA
MANDE MARKA PEULH
BAMBARA MALINKE SENOUFO
SONGHAI
MOUNTAIN: MINA MANDING
PEOPLE: MOOR PEUL TUAREG
BAMBARA MALINKE SONGHAI
SENOUFO

RIVER: BANI BAGOE BAKOY NIGER
BAOULE AZAOUAK SENEGAL
TOWN: GAO SAN KATI KITA NARA
BAMBA KAYES MOPTI NIONO
NIORO SEGOU SIKASSO

MALICE DOLE ENVY HAIN PIQUE
SPITE VENOM VIRUS ENMITY
GRUDGE RANCOR SPLEEN DESPITE
AMBITION MALIGNITY
MALEVOLENCE
MALICIOUS SHREW SNIDE TEENY
BITTER DOGGED MALIGN WANTON
HATEFUL HEINOUS LEERING
SPITOUS VICIOUS CANKERED
NARQUOIS SINISTER SPITEFUL
VENOMOUS VIPEROUS
MALIGN ILL FOUL ABUSE LIBEL
WRONG BEWRAY DEFAME REVILE
VILIFY ASPERSE DEPRAVE
HURTFUL SLANDER TRADUCE
BLASPHEME
MALIGNANCY FEROCITY
MALIGNANT EVIL ATTRY BLACK
FELON FERAL SWART ATTERY
MALIGN BALEFUL ENVIOUS
HATEFUL HELLISH PEEVISH
REPTILE VICIOUS WARLOCK
CANKERED SHREWISH SPITEFUL
VENOMOUS VIPEROUS
VIRULENT WRATHFUL
RANCOROUS
(**NOT** —) BENIGN INNOCENT
MALIGNITY GALL LIVER VENOM
VIRUS HATRED MALICE RANCOR
DESPITE
MALINGER MIKE DODGE SHIRK
SKULK
MALINGERER SCONCER
MALL MART WALK ALLEE
(**SHOPPING** —) GALLERIA
MALLARD TWISTER
(**FLOCK OF** —S) SORD SUTE
PADDLING
MALLEABLE MILD SOFT DUCTILE
PLASTIC BATTABLE
MALLEIN MORVIN
MALLEMUCK MOLLIE MALMARSH
MALLET MALL MAUL MELL GAVEL
BEATER BEETLE DRIVER HAMMER
DRESSER FLOGGER STRIKER
PLOWMELL
(— **FOR BREAKING CLODS**) BILDER
(**CURRIER'S** —) MACE
(**HATTER'S** —) BEATER
(**PAVER'S** —) TUP
(PREF.) MALLEI MALLEO SPHYRA
MALLEUS HAMMER OSSICLE
PLECTRUM
MALLOTHI (**FATHER OF** —) HEMAN
MALLOW MAW DOCK HOCK ALTEA
KOKIO MALVA MAUVE TAUPE
CHEESE ESCOBA GEMAUVE
ABUTILON PIEPRINT
MALLUCH (**FATHER OF** —) DANI
MALMSEY MALVASIA MALVOISIE
MALNUTRITION CACHEXY
CACHEXIA CACOTROPHY
MALODOROUS GAMY HIGH NOSY
OLID RANK FETID SMELLY VIROSE
VIROUS NOISOME
MALPRACTICE (**UNDERHAND** —S)
SKULDUGGERY

MALT WORT
　(GROUND —) GRIST
　(REMAINS OF —) DRAFF
MALTA (ANCIENT NAME OF —)
　MELITA
　(CAPITAL OF —) VALLETTA
　(ISLAND OF —) GOZO COMINO
　(MONEY OF —) LIRA
　(TOWN OF —) QORMI RABAT
　HAMRUN SLIEMA XAGHRA ZABBAR
　BIRKIRKARA
MALTASE GLUCASE
MALTESE CROSS (LIKE A —) PATE
　PATEE PATTEE
MALTHA BREA
MALTHOUSE MALTING
MALTOSE AMYLON
MALTREAT MAUL ABUSE DIGHT
　DEFOUL DEMEAN HESPIL HUSPEL
　MISUSE THREAT BEDEVIL
　MISGUIDE MANHANDLE
MALTREATMENT ABUSE
MALVA DOCK MALLOW
MAMAMU MU
MAMBA COBRA ELAPOID
MAMMA MA MOM MAMA WIFE
　MOMMA WOMAN MOTHER
MAMMAL OX ASS BAT CAT COW
　DOG FOX PIG YAK BEAR BOAR
　COON DEER GOAT HARE LION
　LYNX MINK MOLE PUMA SEAL
　ZEBU BEAST BISON CAMEL COATI
　COYPU GENET HORSE HYENA
　LEMUR LLAMA MOOSE OKAPI
　OTTER PANDA RATEL SABLE
　SHEEP SHREW SKUNK SLOTH
　SWINE TAPIR TIGER WHALE ZORIL
　ALPACA ANIMAL BADGER COUGAR
　CULPEO DESMAN DUGONG FISHER
　FOUSSA GOPHER GRISON JAGUAR
　MARTEN MONKEY OCELOT
　OLINGO TENREC VICUNA WALRUS
　WOMBAT BUFFALO CARIBOU
　DOLPHIN ECHIDNA GIRAFFE
　GLUTTON GUANACO HIPPOID
　HUANACO MANATEE OPOSSUM
　PECCARY POLECAT PRIMATE
　RACCOON SUCKLER SURICAT
　TARSIER TYLOPOD WILDCAT
　AARDVARK AARDWOLF ANTELOPE
　BANXRING CACOMIXL CREODONT
　ELEPHANT FALANAKA HEDGEHOG
　KINKAJOU MAMMIFER PANGOLIN
　PINNIPED REINDEER SQUIRREL
　PRONGHORN RHINOCEROS
　(EXTINCT —) STEGODONT
MAMMALIA MASTOZOA
MAMMEE ABRICO ABRICOT
MAMMILLA PAP TEAT NIPPLE
MAMMOTH HUGE LARGE GIGANTIC
MAMRE (BROTHER OF —) ANER
　ESHCOL
MAN BO HE BOY GEE GUY HIM LAD
　TAO WAT WER BUCK CHAL CHAP
　COVE DICK EARL GENT GOME
　HOMO JACK JONG MALE RINK
　TULK BERNE BIMBO BIPED BLOKE
　CHURL COVEY CULLY FORCE
　FREKE GROOM GUEST HEART
　HOMME HORSE JOKER SEGGE
　SWAIN WIGHT BIMANE CHIELD
　CUFFIN FELLOW HOMBRE MANTZU

WEPMAN BIMANUS HOMONID
KINSMAN MANKIND
　(— AFFECTING FOREIGN WAYS)
MACARONI
　(— DRESSED AS WOMAN) BESSY
MALINCHE
　(— IN DEBT) DYVOUR
　(— IN GAMES) PIECE
　(— IN PRIVATE STATION) IDIOT
　(— IN TUG-OF-WAR) ANCHOR
　(— LEADING 12TH NIGHT) BEAN
　(— OF ALL WORK) MOZO
　(— OF AUTHORITY) AGHA SEIGNIOR
　(— OF BEAUTY) APOLLO
　(— OF BRASS) TALOS
　(— OF COURAGE) LION
　(— OF GREAT WEALTH) NABOB
　(— OF HIGH RANK) CHAM KHAN
THAKUR GRANDEE
　(— OF POWER) MAGNATE
　(— OF SUBSTANCE) IDLEMAN
　(— OF THE COMMON PEOPLE) JACK
　(— OF VIGOR) WYE
　(— OF VIOLENCE) RABIATOR
　(— OF WAR) ANDREW CARAVEL
CRUISER
　(— TO MAN) SINGLE
　(ARTIFICIAL —) GOLEM
　(ATTRACTIVE —) FOX HUNK
　(BACKGAMMON —) BLOT BUILDER
　(BALD —) PILGARLIC
　(BEST —) BRIDEMAN PARANYMPH
　(BIG —) COB BRUISER MUGWUMP
　(BLESSED —) BEATUS
　(BRISK —) SPARK
　(CASTRATED —) SPADO EUNUCH
　(CHIEF —) FOREMAN OPTIMATE
　(CHURLISH —) NABAL BODACH
　(CLEANING —) BUSBOY
　(COMMON —) CARL STREET
YEOMAN
　(COVETOUS —) HUNKS
　(CRAFTY —) FOX
　(CRUEL —) OGRE BRUTE
　(DISAGREEABLE —) GLEYDE
　(DISCREET —) PRUDHOMME
　(DISLIKED —) CUT
　(DISSOLUTE —) RAKE
　(ECCENTRIC —) GEEZER
　(EDUCATED —) EFFENDI
　(EFFEMINATE —) DILDO FAIRY
NANCE PUNCE SISSY JESSIE
COCKNEY MEACOCK MIDWIFE
MILKSOP ANDROGYN
MOLLYCODDLE
　(END —) BONES BRAKE
　(ENLISTED —) GI SNIPE AIDMAN
AIRMAN KEEPER STORES ARMORER
STRIKER SONARMAN
　(ENTIRE —) EGO
　(EXTINCT —) TEPEXPAN
　(FAITHFUL —) TRUEMAN
　(FANCY —) PONCE
　(FASHIONABLE —) TOUPET
ELEGANT FOPLING GALLANT
　(FIRST —) ASK ADAM ASKR TIKI
FOREMAN
　(FLASHILY-DRESSED —) LAIR
　(FOPPISH —) BLOOD
　(FREE —) LIBER
　(GRAY-HAIRED —) GRIZZLE
　(GREAT —) VAVASOR
　(HARDHEARTED —) KNARK

　(HAUGHTY —) BASHAW
　(HOLDUP —) FOOTPAD
　(HOLY —) SADHU SAINT SANNYASI
　(HONORS —) WRANGLER
　(IDEAL —) SUPERMAN
　(IMMORAL —) REP
　(INEFFECTUAL —) DUFFER
　(INSANE —) FURIOSO
　(LADY'S —) FOPLING DAMMARET
　(LAME —) BACACH
　(LEARNED —) ULEMA LAMDAN
OLLAMH PUNDIT SAVANT SOPHIST
　(LECHEROUS —) SATYR
　(LEWD —) BROTHEL
　(LIAISON —) COURIER
　(LITERARY —) GIGADIBS
　(LITTLE —) MANNET SHRIMP
MANNIKIN
　(LUSTFUL —) GOAT
　(MAINTENANCE —) CAMPMAN
　(MARRIED —) HUSBAND BENEDICT
　(MECHANICAL —) ROBOT
　(MEDICINE —) PEAI DOCTOR
SHAMAN ANGAKOK
　(MEEK —) MOSES
　(MIGHTY —) SAMSON
　(ODD-JOB —) JOEY
　(OLD —) HAG OLD BOOL CUFF GAFF
CRONE DOBBY UNCLE BODACH
DUFFER FATHER GAFFER NESTOR
GERONTE STARETS ECKEHART
VELYARDE PATRIARCH
　(OLD-CLOTHES —) POCO
　(ONE-ARMED —) WINGY
　(ONE-EYED —) ARIMASP
　(ONE-FOOTED —) MONOPODE
　(OVERFASTIDIOUS —) DUDE
　(PARTY —) SIDESMAN
　(POOR —) PAUPER
　(PRIMITIVE —) URMENSCH
　(PRINCIPAL —) HERO TOPARCH
　(RASH —) HOTSPUR
　(RICH —) DIVES NABOB CROESUS
　(RIGHT-HAND —) HENCHMAN
　(RIGHTEOUS —) SADDIK
　(SERVING —) GARCON
　(SOUND-EFFECTS —) CRAWK
　(STERN —) GRIMSIRE
　(STRAIGHT —) STOOGE
　(STRONG —) KWASIND
　(STRONG-ARM —) HOOD GORILLA
　(STUPID —) SUBMAN
　(SWAGGERING YOUNG —)
GREASER
　(THICKSET —) GRUB KNAR SPUD
　(TOUGH —) KNAR
　(UNEMPLOYED —) BATLAN
　(UNKNOWN —) INCOGNITO
　(UTILITY —) JUMPER
　(VICIOUS —) YAHOO
　(WEAK —) WIMP
　(WELL-BUILT —) HUNK
　(WHITE —) BOSTON BUCKRA
PAKEHA CACHILA
　(WHITE — LIVING WITH ABORIGINE)
COMBO
　(WILD —) WOODMAN WOODWOSE
　(WISE —) NAB HAKAM MAGUS
.SABIO SOLON SOPHY NESTOR
WIZARD SOLOMON TOHUNGA
　(WIZENED —) GNOME
　(WOMANISH —) JENNY
　(WRETCHED —) CAITIFF

　(YOUNG —) BOY LAD JONG PUNK
YOUTH BOCHUR DAMSEL EPHEBE
KNIGHT BOUCHAL BUCKEEN
YOUNKER BOYCHICK COCKEREL
SPRINGAL
　(PREF.) ANDR(O) ANTHROP(O)
HOMI(NI)
　(SUFF.) ANDRIA ANDROUS ANDRY
ENGRO VIR(ATE)
MAN-ABOUT-TOWN JOHNNY
CLUBMAN FLANEUR
MANABOZHO MICHABOU
WINABOJO
MANACLE BAND BOND DARBY
HAMPER TIRRET SHACKLE
HANDCUFF HANDLOCK
(PL.) IRONS CHAINS
MANAGE DO GET MAN RUN BEAR
BOSS COPE CURB FEND HACK
HOLD KEEP LEAD MAKE RULE
TEND TOOL WIND WORK BROOK
CARRY DIGHT FORTH FRAME
GUIDE MAYNE ORDER SHIFT
SPEND STEER SWING WIELD
CONVEY DEMEAN DEVISE DIRECT
FETTLE GOVERN HANDLE INTEND
MANURE TEMPER AGITATE
CONDUCT DISPOSE EXECUTE
FINAGLE HUSBAND MINSTER
OFFICER OPERATE SOLICIT
STEWARD CONTRIVE ENGINEER
NEGOTIATE
　(— AWKWARDLY) FOOZLE
　(— CLUMSILY) KEVEL
　(— SKILLFULLY) MANIPULATE
　(— SUCCESSFULLY) HACK
　(— TO BEAR) AFFORD
　(— WITH CARE) NURSE
MANAGEABLE EASY YARE BANTAM
DOCILE WIELDY DUCTILE FLEXIBLE
YIELDING
MANAGEMENT CARE HEEL WORK
CHARGE CONDUCT CONTROL
ECONOMY GESTION RUNNING
CARRIAGE DEMEANOR ENGINERY
MANAGERY MANEUVER REGIMENT
STEERAGE STEERING
　(DELICATE —) NICETY
　(DOMESTIC —) MENAGE
HUSBANDRY
　(GOOD —) EUTAXY
　(SKILLFUL —) PRACTICE PRACTISE
MANAGER BOSS DOER EXEC
AGENT DAROGA DEPUTY PURSER
SYNDIC AMILDAR CURATOR
ERENACH HUSBAND STEWARD
WIELDER AUMILDAR DIRECTOR
DISPOSER ENGINEER HERENACH
INSTITOR
　(— OF ENTERTAINERS) ROADIE
　(— OF FARM) HIND GRIEVE
　(ASSISTANT —) CAPORAL
　(MINE —) CAPTAIN
　(POLITICAL —) FUGLEMAN
　(STAGE —) REGISSEUR
　(SUFF.) EER
MANAHATH (FATHER OF —)
SHOBAL
MANAKIN PIPRA
MAN-AT-ARMS KNIGHT
MANATEE DUGONG SEACOW
COWFISH HOGFISH MERMAID
LAMANTIN MUTILATE SIRENIAN

MANBARKLAK JARANA KAKARAL
MANCALA WARI
MANCHE (— CAPITAL) STLO
MANCHU SHERRY
MANCHURIA (CHINESE NAME FOR —) MANCHOW
  (PENINSULA OF —) LIAOTUNG
  (PROVINCE OF —) JILIN LIAONING HEILONGJIANG
  (RIVER OF —) AMUR LIAO YALU ARGUN USSURI SUNGARI
MANDAEAN SABAEAN
MANDANE (FATHER OF —) ASTYAGES
  (HUSBAND OF —) CAMBYSES
  (SON OF —) CYRUS
MANDARIN TOWKAY CHINESE
MANDARIN ORANGE SATSUMA
MANDATE BREVE ORDER BEHEST CHARGE DECREE FIRMAN BIDDING COMMAND PRECEPT PROCESS MANDAMUS MANDATUM WARRANTY
  (— OF GOD) JUDGMENT
MANDATORY OBLIGATORY
MANDIBLE BEAK JOWL SETA RAMUS JAWBONE GNATHITE
  (— PART) MALA
MANDINGO MANDE MALINKE WANGARA
MANDOLIN OUD MANDORA
MANDRAKE ALRAUN DUDAIM
MANDREL ROD BALL STUD SLEEVE CHEMISE SPINDLE TRIBLET
MANDRICARDO (BELOVED OF —) ANGELICA
  (FATHER OF —) AGRICAN
  (SLAYER OF —) ORLANDO
MANDRILL MAIMON MORMON
MANE JUBA MONE CREST PITRI ENCOLURE
MAN-EATER
  (PL.) ANTHROPOPHAGI REQUIN REQUIEM
MANEGE TRAIN
MANEUVER PLAY TURN WISE GAMBIT JOCKEY MANURE PESADE VRILLE FINAGLE FINESSE ARTIFICE DEMARCHE ENGINEER EXERCISE STRATEGY WINDLASS
  (— GENTLY) EASE
  (— IN AUTO RACING) SLINGSHOT
  (— IN SPACE) DOCK
  (— IN SURFING) CUTBACK
  (— OF MOTORCYCLE OR BICYCLE) WHEELIE
  (AERIAL —) BUNT LOOP SPIN FISHTAIL WINGOVER
  (BICYCLE —) WHEELIE
  (BULLFIGHTING —) VERONICA
  (ILLEGAL —) GAME
  (KIND OF —) HEIMLICH VALSALVA
  (ROADWAY —) UTURN
  (ROCK-CLIMBING —) LAYBACK
  (SKIING —) SNOWPLOW
  (VEHICLE —) WHEELIE
  (WRESTLING —) ESCAPE BUTTOCK
MANEUVERABLE YAR YARE
MANEUVERING FINESSE FLANKING FOOTWORK
MANEUVRE (DRESSAGE —) PESADE
MANGE ITCH REEF SCAB CANKER DARTARS SCABIES

MANGER BIN BUNK CRIB HECK STALL CRATCH
MANGLE MAR HACK IRON MOUTH BRUISE GARBLE HACKLE IRONER MAGGLE MURDER MAMMOCK LACERATE MUTILATE
MANGO DIKA AMHAR AMINI BAUNO AMCHOOR CARABAO PAHUTAN
  (POINT OF —) NAK
MANGOSTEEN SANTOL GARCINIA
MANGROVE BACAO GORAN MANGLE MYRTAL BACAUAN CERIOPS COURIDA HANGALAI LANGARAI
MANGUE CHOLUTECA CHOROTEGA
MANGY SCABBY ROINISH SCABETIC
MANHANDLE MAUL MESS ROUGH SCRAG WORKOVER
MANHATTAN ROBROY
MANHATTAN TRANSFER
  (AUTHOR OF —) DOSPASSOS
  (CHARACTER IN —) BUD GUS JOE HERF JOHN RUTH STAN CONGO ELLEN EMERY EMILE HARRY JIMMY SUSIE GEORGE MCNIEL NELLIE OKEEFE PRYNNE BALDWIN HARLAND MERIVALE PEARLINE THATCHER GOLDWEISER OGLETHORPE
MANHOOD ADAMHOOD
MANIA RAGE CRAZE FUROR FRENZY DELIRIUM HYSTERIA INSANITY CACOETHES
MANIAC KILLER MADMAN FANATIC LUNATIC
  (KIND OF —) EGO
MANIFEST HAVE NUDE OPEN RIFE SENE SHOW APERT CLEAR FRANK GROSS KITHE NAKED OVERT PLAIN PROVE SPEAK SUTEL ARRANT ATTEST COUTHE EVINCE EXTANT ORAITH LIQUID OSTEND PATENT PHANIC APPROVE BETOKEN CONFESS DECLARE EVIDENT EXHIBIT EXPRESS OBVIOUS SIGNIFY VISIBLE APPARENT DISCLOSE DISCOVER INDICATE PALPABLE PROCLAIM
  (NOT —) LATENT
  (PREF.) PHANER(O) PHANTA(SMO) PHANTO
MANIFESTATION ACT SON BEAM COMA SIGN GLINT AVATAR COMING EFFECT OSTENT ADVANCE DISPLAY EXPRESS OUTSIDE SHOWING EPIPHANY MANIFEST
  (BARELY PERCEPTIBLE —) SCINTIL
  (BRIEF —) GLEAM
  (DIVINE —) SPIRIT SHEKINAH
  (HORRIBLE —) CHIMAERA
  (MORAL —) SOUL
  (VAGUE —) GLIMMER
  (SUFF.) PHANE PHANOUS PHANT PHANY
MANIFESTLY WITTERLY
MANIFESTO PLACARD
MANIFOLD MANY TURRET VARIOUS FELEFOLD MANYFOLD MULTIPLE MULTIPLEX REPLICATE
  (SUFF.) PLOID
MANIKIN ECORCHE PANTINE

PHANTOM HOMUNCIO HOMUNCLE MANNIKIN
MANILA HEMP ABACA
MANIOC CASSAVA CATELLA MANDIOCA
MANIPLE BAND FANON ORALE FANNEL COMPANY HANDFUL SUDARIUM
MANIPULATE COG RIG COAX COOK DIAL FAKE HAND STIR TOOL CROOK HUMOR KNEAD SHAPE TREAT WIELD CHIVVY GOVERN HANDLE JOCKEY MANAGE WANGLE MASSAGE SHUFFLE
  (— BY DECEPTIVE MEANS) RIG
  (— DISHONESTLY) RIG SHUFFLE
  (— FRAUDULENTLY) FIDDLE
MANIPULATION PASS JUGGLERY MANAGERY
MANITO ORENDA POKUNT MANITOU TAMANOAS
MANITOBA (CAPITAL OF —) WINNIPEG
  (RIVER OF —) RED SEAL SWAN NELSON ROSEAU SOURIS PEMBINA CHURCHILL SASKACHEWAN
  (TOWN OF —) CARMAN BRANDON DAUPHIN KILLARNEY SWANRIVER
MANKIND MAN FLESH SHEEP WORLD BIMANA SPECIES HUMANITY UNIVERSE MORTALITY
MANLIKE MALE MANLY MANNISH HOMINOID
MANLINESS ARETE VIRTUS MANSHIP
MANLY BOLD MALE HARDY MANNY DARING VIRILE MANLIKE
MAN-MADE SYNTHETIC UNNATURAL CULTURAL SYNTHETIC
MANNA TREHALA WINDFALL
MANNER AIR BAT JET LAT WAY FORM GAET GARB GATE KIND MAKE MIEN MODE RATE SORT THEW TOUR WISE WONE GUISE LATES SHAPE STYLE TENUE TRICK COURSE CUSTOM METHOD MISTER STRAIN ADDRESS AMENITY FASHION QUALITY QUOMODO CARAPACE DEMEANOR LANGUAGE
  (— OF APPROACH) ABORD
  (— OF DOING) ACTION
  (— OF HANDLING) HAND
  (— OF MAKING ANYTHING) FACTURE
  (— OF PERFORMING) HAND
  (— OF SITTING) ASANA
  (— OF SPEAKING) SLUR SOUGH ACCENT GRAMMAR PARLANCE
  (— OF SWIMMING) STROKE
  (— OF WALKING) STEP
  (AFFECTED —) AIR
  (AMUSING —) DROLLERY
  (ARROGANT —) BRAG HAUTEUR
  (CHARACTERISTIC —) TOUCH
  (EMOTIONAL —) STRAIN
  (FORBIDDING —) SHELL
  (FORMAL —) STARCH
  (GRAND —) PANACHE
  (HABITUAL —) SONG
  (LIVELY —) JAZZ
  (OUTWARD —) TOUR FRONT

  (RESTRAINED —) RESERVE
  (SECRET —) STEALTH
  (SMOOTH —) JAPAN
  (SWAGGERING —) SIDE PANACHE
  (UNUSUAL —) SINGULARITY
  (USUAL —) HABIT
  (PL.) ADDRESS CORNERS HAVINGS BREEDING
  (SUFF.) WISE
  (AFTER THE — OF) FASHION
  (IN A —) LY
  (IN THE — OF) IC(AL)
MANNERED CUTE CUTESY MORATE THEWED
MANNERISM TIC POSE TRICK IDIASM
  (EXAGGERATED —) CAMP
  (PL.) DAPS
MANNERLY CIVIL POLITE
MANNERS MORES HAVANCE HAVINGS PSANDQS BEAUETRY BREEDING
MANNITOL MANNITE PUNICIN
MANOAH (SON OF —) SAMSON
MAN-OF-WAR CARAVEL
MAN-OF-WAR FISH PASTOR
MANON (CHARACTER IN —) MANON GRIEUX LESCAUT BRETIGNY
  (COMPOSER OF —) MASSENET
MANON LESCAUT (CHARACTER IN —) MANON GRIEUX GERONTE
  (COMPOSER OF —) PUCCINI
MANOR HAM HOF BURY HALL TOWN VILL BARONY ESTATE COMMOTE MANSION LORDSHIP TOWNSHIP
MANPOWER BRAWN LABOR
MANROOT IPOMOEA
MANROPE LIMMER
MANSERVANT (ALSO SEE SERVANT) LAD MOZO GROOM VALET ANDREW BUTLER TEABOY
MANSFIELD PARK (AUTHOR OF —) AUSTEN
  (CHARACTER IN —) TOM MARY WARD FANNY HENRY JULIA MARIA PRICE YATES EDMUND NORRIS THOMAS BERTRAM CRAWFORD RUSHWORTH
MANSION DOME SEAT HOTEL HOUSE MANSE SIEGE TOWER CASTLE HARBOR HOSTEL CHATEAU
  (— OF THE MOON) ALNATH
MANSLAUGHTER BLOOD FELONY HOMICIDE
MANTEL CLAVY CLAVEL
MANTELET MANTA MANTLE MANTLET GALAPAGO
MANTELPIECE BRACE PAREL CLAVEL MANTEL MANTLING
MANTICORE MONTEGRE
MANTIS CAGN RACER REARER MANTOID PROPHET
MANTIS CRAB SQUILLA
MANTIS SHRIMP SQUILL
MANTLE CAPA HOSE PALL REAM ROBE CLOAK CREAM FROCK JABUL LAMBA PALLA TUNIC CAMAIL CAPOTE KHIRKA KIRTLE ROCHET SLAVIN SOLMAN TABARD CHLAMYS CHRISOM CHUDDAR FERIDJI MANTEAU PAENULA

PALLIUM SLEEVES WHITTLE WRAPPER BARRACAN CHRYSOME MANTELET REGOLITH RICINIUM STOCKING
(PREF.) CHLAMYD(O) PHARO
MANTLEROCK REGOLITH
MANTO (DAUGHTER OF —) TISIPHONE
(FATHER OF —) HERCULES TIRESIAS
(HUSBAND OF —) RHACIUS
(SON OF —) OCNUS MOPSUS AMPHILOCHUS
MANTRA OM DHARANI GAYATRI MANTRAM SAVITRI
MANTUA MANTY SEMAR
MANTZU MIAOTZE
MANUAL VADY COACH GREAT TUTOR PORTAS CAMBIST CEMBALO DIDACHE MANUARY BOMBARDE HANDBOOK KEYBOARD ORDINARY PORTHORS SYNOPSIS
(MAGICIAN'S —) GRIMOIRE
(NAVIGATION —) BOWDITCH
MANUAO IAO
MANUBRIUM HYPOSTOME
MANUFACTORY ARSENAL
MANUFACTURE COIN FAKE MAKE FORGE PERFORM PRODUCE WORKING BOOKWORK
(— OF LIQUOR OR DRUGS) ABKARI
(ILLEGAL —) COINING
MANUFACTURED STORE
MANUFACTURER BRAND MAKER WRIGHT DISKERY SPINNER SUPPLIER
(ORIGINAL EQUIPMENT —) OEM
MANUMIT FREE DELIVER RELEASE LIBERATE
MANURE HOT MIG DUNG LIME MUCK SAUR SOIL TATH FECES GUANO MIXEN FULZIE SEASON SLEECH COMPOST FOLDING GOODING POUDRET DRESSING WORTHING
MANURED BONED
MANUS HAND
MANUSCRIPT CODEX FLIMSY MATTER SCRIPT UNCIAL CURSIVE PANDECT PAPYRUS PINTURA WITNESS EXEMPLAR PARCHMENT
MANX CAT RUMPY
MANX SHEARWATER CREW PUFFIN SCRABE SCRABER
MANY TEN ALOT FELE LOTS MUCH SERE SLEW FORTY GREAT MAINT MOULT SCADS OODLES TWENTY ENDLESS JILLION SEVERAL VARIOUS BEAUCOUP MANIFOLD COUNTLESS
(BEING —) NUMEROUS
(GOOD —) HANTLE
(GREAT —) MORT RAFF SWITH
(PREF.) MULT(I) PLURI POLY
(HOW —) POSO QUOT
MANYATTA KRAAL
MANY-COLORED POLYCHROME BONT
MANY-HANDED BRIAREAN
MANYPLIES FARDEL OMASUM MANIFOLD PSATERIUM
MANYROOT RUELLIA
MANY-SIDED VERSATILE VARIOUS

MAO NEHRU
MAOCH (SON OF —) ACHISH
MAORI (— IMAGE) TIKI
(— LAW) UTU
(— VILLAGE) PA PAH KAINGA
(NOT —) PAKEMA
MAP KEY CARD DICE PLAT PLOT CARTE CENTO CHART DRAFT INSET QUART STILL DRAUGHT GRAPHIC CARTGRAM GATEFOLD PLATFORM CARTOGRAM
(— OF HEAVENS) HOROSCOPE
(CELESTIAL —) PLANISPHERE
(PREF.) CARTO CHARTO
MAPAU MAPLE MATIPO TARATA PIRIPIRI
MAPLE MAZER DOGWOOD SYCAMORE WINGSEED
(FLOWERING —) ABUTILON
(GROVE OF —) SAPBUSH
MAQUILLAGE MAKEUP
MAR BLOT SCAR SMIT SNIP BLOOM BOTCH SHEND SPILL SPOIL BLOTCH DEFACE DEFEAT DEFORM EFFACE IMPAIR INJURE MANGLE BLEMISH DISGRACE
MARABOU STORK ARGALA MORABIT ADJUTANT
MARANAO LANAO
MARASMUS MARCOR ATHREPSIA
MARAUD RAID DACOIT PICKEER PILLAGE
MARAUDER TORY BANDIT BUMMER LOOTIE PIRATE CATERAN LADRONE
(PL.) BLACKS
MARAUDING BANDITRY OUTRIDING
MARBLE MIB MIG PEA POT TAW ALLY BOOL BOWL DUCK DUMP MARL AGATE AGGIE ALLEY BONCE COMMY IMMIE IVORY LINER PUREY RANCE DOGGLE MARMOR STEELY CARRARA CIPOLIN GLASSIE GRIOTTE KNICKER PARAGON PITCHER SHOOTER BROCATEL DOLOMITE KNUCKLER
(— WORKER'S TOOL) BURIN
(BLACK —) JET
(IMITATION —) SCAGLIOLA
(SIENA —) BROCATELLO
(PL.) TAW BOWLS PLUMPS HUNDRED
MARBLED MIRLY
MARCH FILE HIKE LIDE MARK MUSH SLOG ROUTE TRACE TRINE TROOP WALTZ DEFILE DOUBLE PARADE REVIEW DEBOUCH STRETCH FOOTSLOG PROGRESS
(— BEHIND) COVER
(— IN FRONT OF) LEAD
(— OBLIQUELY) INCLINE
(DAY'S —) ETAPE
(START OF —) HUP
(PL.) FRONTIER
MARCHING (— UP) ANABASIS
MARCHIONESS MARCHESA MARQUISE
MARCOT GOOTE
MARCOTTAGE GOOTEE
MARE SEA YAD YADE YAUD GILLIE GILLOT GRASNI HUNTRESS
MARE'S-TAIL HIPPURID

MARGARET MEG META MARGET MARGOT GRETCHEN
MARGARINE BUTTERINE
MARGATE PORGY
MARGAY TIGER
MARGIN HEM RIM VAT BANK BRIM BROW CURB EDGE FOLD HAIR INCH LIMB LIST RAND BRINK EAVES MARGE VERGE BORDER FRINGE LABRUM LACING CUSHION DRAUGHT MARGENT SELVAGE HAIRLINE
(— OF CARAPACE) DOUBLURE
(— OF CIRCLE) LIMB
(— OF LIP) PROLABIUM
(— OF PAGE) BACK
(— OF SAFETY) LEEWAY
(— OF SEA) STRAND
(— OF SHELL) LABRUM LIMBUS
(— OF SUPERIORITY) LEAD
(— OF WING) TERMEN
(—S OF HERD) SWING
(NARROW —) ACE NECK WHISKER
(SEA —) COAST
MARGOSA NIM NEEM NEEMBA
MARGRAVE RUDIGER MARKGRAF
MARIA (FATHER OF —) OCTAVIO PETROBIUS
(HUSBAND OF —) PETRUCHIO
MARIANA SILYBUM
MARIGOLD GOLD GULL SAMH AZTEC BOOTS GOLDE GOOLS HELIO BACLIN BUDDLE GOLDCUP GOLDING GOLLAND KINGCUP MARYBUD TAGETES
MARIJUANA BOO POT HERB WEED DAGGA GANJA GRASS GANJAH MOOCAH CANNABIS CARNABIS LOCOWEED MARYJANE PANAMARED SINSEMILLA
(BUTT OF — CIGARETTE) ROACH
(CHEMICAL IN —) THC
(KILOGRAM OF —) KEY
(ONE OUNCE OF —) LID
(ONE WHO SMOKES —) POTHEAD
(ONE WHO TAKES —) POTHEAD
(OUNCE OF —) CAN LID
(PUFF ON — CIGARETTE) TOKE
MARINA DOCK BASIN BOATEL
MARINADE SOUSE
MARINE JOLLY GALOOT GULPIN GYRENE TOPMAN MARINAL HALIMOUS MARITIME NAUTICAL AEQUOREAL THALASSIC THALASSIAN
(PREF.) ENALI(O) THALASS(O) THALASSI(O) THALATTO
MARINER MARINE SAILOR SEALER SEAMAN BUSCARLE SEAFARER WARRENER
(PL.) SEAFOLK
MARINHEIRO ACAJOU
MARIONETTE PUPPY POPPET PUPPET
MARITAL INTIMATE HUSBANDLY
MARITIME MARINE HALIMOUS NAUTICAL
MARJORAM ORIGAN ORIGANE AMARACUS
MARK AIM END HOB HUB MOT POP BELT BLOT BUOY BUTT CHOP CLIP DELE DINT FAZE FIST GOAL KEEL LINE MIND NOTE RIST SCAR SEAR

SIGN SMOT SMUT SPOT TEND TEXT TICK VIRE WAND WIND BADGE BOTTU BRAND BREVE CHANT CHECK CLOUD DATUM DITTO DRAFT FLECK FRANK GHOST GRADE HACEK HILUM KNIFE LABEL MARCH MARCO MEITH NOKTA POINT PRINT PROOF ROVER SCART SCOPE SCORE SCUFF SPOOR STAMP SWIRL TOKEN TOUCH TRACE TRACK TRACT WATCH WHITE ACCENT ALPIEU BEACON BESPOT BLOTCH BUTTON CARACT DAGGER DAPPLE DENOTE DIRECT INDICE LETTER MARKER NOTICE OBJECT SMUTCH STREAK STRIKE STROKE SUCKER SYMBOL TARGET UPSHOT WICKER WITTER BETOKEN CEDILLA CHARBON COCKSHY DEMERIT DIAMOND DRAUGHT EROTEME EXCUDIT FINMARK IMPRESS IMPRINT INSIGNE KENMARK SCARIFY SERRATE SIGNARY SPECKLE STRIATE SYMPTOM VESTIGE WAYMARK BRACELET CROWFOOT DATEMARK DIASTOLE DISPUNCT EVIDENCE FOOTMARK FOOTSTEP IDENTIFY IDEOGRAM MONUMENT NOTATION
(— A BIRD) BAND
(— AFTER ASSAY) TOUCH
(— AS PAID) RECEIPT
(— AS SPURIOUS) ATHETIZE
(— BOUNDS) STAKE
(— BY BURNING) CHAR
(— BY CUTTING) SCRIBE
(— BY PLOWING) STRIKE
(— CROSSWISE) CRANK
(— DENOTING CORRUPT PASSAGE) OBELUS
(— DIRECTIONS) ADDRESS
(— IN ARCHERY) CLOUT HOYLE ROVER WHITE
(— IN BOOK) PRESSMARK
(— IN CANON) LEAD
(— IN CURLING) TEE COCK
(— INDICATING CONTRACTION) CORONIS
(— INDICATING DIRECTION) ARROW
(— IN QUOITS) MOT
(— OF ACKNOWLEDGEMENT) ACCOLADE
(— OF CADENCY) MARTLET
(— OF CONDEMNATION) THETA
(— OF DISGRACE) STAIN STIGMA
(— OF DISHONOR) ABATEMENT
(— OF DISTINCTION) BELT
(— OF ESTEEM) LAUREL GARLAND
(— OFF) DIVIDE STRIKE SUBTEND
(— OFF LAND) FEER PHEER
(— OF OFFICE) SEAL
(— OF OWNERSHIP) SWANMARK
(— OF PURITY) HALLMARK
(— OF RANK) PIP
(— OF REFERENCE) OBELISK
(— OF SERVITUDE) YOKE
(— OF SIGNATURE) CROSS
(— OF SUPERIORITY) BELL
(— OF WEAVER) KEEL
(— ON ANIMAL'S FACE) BLAZE STRIPE
(— ON CHART) VIGIA
(— ON DICE) PIP

(— ON EXAM) PASS
(— ON FEATHER) BAR SPANGLE
(— ON FOREHEAD) KUMKUM
(— ON PENNSYLVANIA BARNS) HEXAFOOS
(— ON SHEEP) SMIT BUIST
(— ON SHIP) SURMARK
(— ON SKIN) PLOT CREASE
(— ON STAMP) CONTROL
(— OUT) RUN CANCEL DELINE AIRMARK APPOINT COMPART DESCRIBE
(— OVER GERMAN VOWEL) UMLAUT
(— OVER LETTER N) TILDE
(— OVER LONG VOWELS) MACRON
(— RIGS) FEER
(— SHEEP OR CATTLE) BASTE BUIST DEWLAP
(— TIME) BEAT COUNT
(— TO BE ATTAINED) BOGEY BOGIE
(— TO GUIDE VESSELS) MYTH
(— TO SCARE DEER) SHEWEL
(— TRANSVERSELY) LADDER
(— UNDER LETTER C) CEDILLA
(— UNDER SIGNATURE) PARAPH
(— WITH LINES) HATCH CAMLET
(— WITH POINTED ROLLER) GRILL
(— WITH RED) RUBRICATE
(— WITH RIDGES) RIB
(— WITH STRIPES) WALE STREAM
(— WITH TAR) BASTE
(ACCENT —) VERGE
(ANGULAR —) HOOK
(AVERAGE —) CEE
(BALLOT —) SCRATCH
(BOUNDARY —) DOOL MEAR MERE TERM WIKE MEITH STAKE LANDMARK
(CADENCY —) BRISURE
(CANCELLATION —) DUMPER KILLER
(CIRCULAR —) SEAL
(CON MAN'S —) DUPE
(CURLY —) TWIDDLE
(DIACRITICAL —) TIL BREVE GRAVE HACEK TILDE MACRON TITTLE
(DIRTY —) SMIRCH
(DISTINCTIVE —) BADGE INDICIA
(DISTINGUISHING —) ITEM COCARDE EARMARK INSIGNE
(DOUBLE-DAGGER —) DIESIS
(EASY —) YAP SMELT PIGEON
(EIGHTH —) URE
(EXACT —) NICK
(EXCLAMATION —) SCREAMER
(IDENTIFICATION —) MOLE CREST SPLIT SIGNET WATTLE EARMARK KENMARK LUGMARK COLOPHON
(LOW-WATER —) DATUM
(MAGICAL —) SIGIL
(MERIDIAN —) MIRE
(MUSICAL —) PRESA CORONA
(NAVIGATION —) PERCH
(PARAGRAPH —) PILCROW
(POOR —) DEE
(PRINTER'S —) PARALLEL
(PROOFREADER'S —) STET CARET DELE
(PUNCTUATION —) DASH STOP BRACE BREVE COLON COMMA HYPHEN PERIOD BRACKET DIERESIS

ELLIPSIS DIACRITIC SEMICOLON PARENTHESIS
(RANDOM —) ROVER
(RED —) HICKEY
(SCORING —) TALLY
(SECTARIAN —) BOTTU TILAKA
(SERVICE —) COMSAT
(SKATE —) CUSP
(SMALL ROUND —) DOT
(SURVEYOR'S —) PICKET
(TRAMP'S —) MONICA MONNIKER
(WHITE —) RACHE
(PL.) POINTING
(PREF.) STIGONO
MARKED FAR GREAT SCORED SEVERE SPOTTY COLORED EMINENT MARCATO POINTED SCARRED SPECKED SPOTTED
(— BY COLORED RINGS) AREOLATE
(— BY FURROWS) RIVOSE
(— BY INTELLIGENCE) ABLE
(— BY PROSTRATION) ALGID
(— BY REFINEMENT) ELEGANT
(— BY RIDGES) SERRIED
(— BY SHREWDNESS) ADROIT
(— BY SIMILARITY) AKIN
(— BY SIMPLICITY) ATTIC
(— BY WAVY LINES) GYROSE
(— OUT) DISTINCT
(— UP) FOUL
(— WITH BANDS) ZONATE
(— WITH SMALLPOX) FRETTEN
(— WITH SPOTS OR LINES) NOTATE
(— WITH WHITE) BAUSOND
(EXTREMELY —) INTENSE
MARKEDLY BYOUS
MARKER HOB HUB IOU DOLE FLAG MARK SPAD STUMP TYPER BUTTON GUIDON HOBBLE HUBBLE TABBER DAYMARK SCRIBER
(BRIDGE —) PYLON
(STONE —) STELE
MARKET CURB GUNJ MART PORT SALE SOOK SOUK VEND VENT CHEAP CROSS GUNGE HALLE PASAR PRICE TRONE TRYST BAZAAR BOURSE MERCAT OUTLET PARIAN RIALTO STAPLE POULTRY CHEAPING DEBOUCHE EMPORIUM EXCHANGE MACELLUM
(CATTLE —) TRISTE
(KIND OF —) BEAR BULL FLEA OPENAIR
(MEAT —) SHAMBLES
(OLD CLOTHES —) RAGFAIR
MARKETABLE SUK SUQ SOUK STAPLE SALABLE VENDIBLE
MARKET-DAY NUNDINE
MARKETING (SYSTEM OF —) ADMASS
MARKETPLACE SUK SUQ SAUK SOOK SOUK TRON AGORA CHAWK CHOWK HALLE PLAZA BAZAAR RIALTO EMPORIUM
MARKET-TOWN BORGO
MARKING EYE HOOD COLLAR CLOUDING SCARRING SCRIBING
(— OF WOOD) CURL GRAIN
(— ON FEATHER) SPANGLE
(— ON MARS) CANAL
(—S ON STEEL) DAMASK
(ANIMAL —) SADDLE SHIELD

(CATTLE —) JINGLEBOB
(CRESCENT-SHAPED —) LUNULA LUNULE
(DROP-SHAPED —) GUTTA
(POSTAL —) INDICIA OVERPRINT
(RINGLIKE —) ANNULUS
(STRIPED —) STRAKE
MARKKA FINMARK
MARKSMAN SHOT MARKER PLUFFER SHOOTER SHOTMAN SHOOTIST
MARL MALM MARLITE
MARLI MARIE
MARLIN AU AGUJA
MARLINESPIKE FID JAEGER PRICKER STABBER
MARMALADE CHEESE SQUISH CODINIAC
MARMALADE TREE CHICO MAMEY MAMMIE SAPOTE ZAPOTE
MARMOSET MICO TITI SAGOIN JACCHUS OUITITI QUIRCAL SAIMIRI TAMARIN WISTITI ORABASSU
MARMOT BOBAC PAHMI GOPHER SUSLIK SCIURID SIFFLEUR WHISTLER
MARMOTA ARCTOMYS
MAROON AZTEC ENISLE PICNIC STRAND CIMARRON
MARQUEE TENT CANOPY MARQUISE
MARQUETRY INLAY
MARQUISE NAVETTE
MARQUISETTE LENO
MARRAM SEAREED MATGRASS MATWWEED
MARRANOS ANUSIM
MARRED CUPPY SCABBY SLURRED SPECKED
MARRIAGE MUTA DAIVA HYMEN KARAO UNION BEENAH BRIDAL BUCKLE SPLICE SPOUSE EXOGAMY NUPTIAL PUNALUA SPOUSAL WEDDING WEDLOCK CONUBIUM LEVIRATE OPSIGAMY
(— AFTER DEATH OF FIRST SPOUSE) DIGAMY
(— AT ADVANCED AGE) OPSIGAMY
(— BELOW POSITION) HYPOGAMY
(— CONTRACT) KETUBAH
(— OUTSIDE FAMILY) EXOGAMY
(— PORTION) TOCHER
(— VOW) IDO
(— WITH AN INFERIOR) MESALLIANCE
(— WITHIN GROUP) ENDOGAMY
(COMMUNAL —) HETAIRISM
(SECOND —) BIGAMY
(PREF.) GAMO
(SUFF.) GAM(AE)(IST)(OUS)(Y) GAMETE
MARRIAGEABLE NUBILE
MARRIED COVERT WEDDED ESPOUSED
(NOT —) SOLE
MARROW KEEST MARIE MERCH MERGH MEDULLA
(PREF.) MEDULLI MYELINO MYEL(O) MYELO
(SUFF.) MYELIA MYELITIS
MARRY TIE WED FAST WIFE WIVE CLEEK HITCH MATCH BUCKLE CROTCH ENSURE MARROW SPLICE

HUSBAND NUPTIAL WEDLOCK DESPOUSE
(— OFF) BESTOW
(— UNSUITABLY) MISYOKE
(PREF.) GAMETO GAMO
(SUFF.) GAM(AE)(IST)(OUS)(Y) GAMETE
MARS ARES MAMERS MARMAR MAVORS MASPITER TEUTATES
(FATHER OF —) JUPITER
(MOTHER OF —) JUNO
(SON OF —) REMUS ROMULUS
(PREF.) AREO
MARSH BOG FEN HAG CARR DANK FELL FLAM FLAT HOPE JHIL MASH MIRE OOZE QUAG ROSS SOIL SUDS TARN VLEI VLEY WASH WHAM FLASH GLADE JHEEL LIMAN SLACK SLASH SLUMP SWAMP MORASS PALUDE PUDDLE CIENAGA CORCASS POCOSIN PONTINE QUAGMIRE STROTHER TURLOUGH
(SALT —) SALT SEBKA SALINA SALINE
(PREF.) ELO HELO LIMN(I)(O) PALUDI
MARSHAL ARRAY ORDER MUSTER PARADE JERONIMO MARECHAL MOBILIZE
(— FACTS) HASH
MARSHALL ISLANDS (CAPITAL:) MAJURO
(COIN:) DOLLAR
(ISLAND:) JALUIT MAJURO ENIWETOK KWAJALEIN
(LANGUAGE:) ENGLISH JAPANESE MARSHALLESE
(PEOPLE:) MARSHALLESE
MARSH BOG QUAG
MARSHBUCK CITUTUNGA
MARSH ELDER JACKO
MARSH FEVER HELODES
MARSH GAS METHANE
MARSH HARRIER PUDDOCK PUTTOCK
MARSHLAND MAREMMA
MARSHMALLOW MALLOW WYMOTE
MARSH MARIGOLD BOOTS CAPER CRAZY GOOLS DRAGON GAMOND GOWLAN COWSLIP ELKSLIP GOLDCUP KINGCOB KINGCUP MARYBUD DRUNKARD
MARSH PENNYWORT PENNYROT WATERCUP
MARSH PINK SABBATIA
MARSH TEA LEDUM
MARSH TREFOIL BUCKBEAN
MARSH WREN LONGBILL
MARSHY BOGGY FOGGY MOORY MOSSY PONDY SNAPY SPEWY CALLOW MARISH PLASHY QUAGGY QUASHY SLUMPY HELODES MOORISH PALUDAL QUEACHY PALUDINE WATERISH
MARSILEA NARDOO
MARSUPIAL KOALA QUOLL CUSCUS POSSUM QUOKKA WOMBAT BETTONG DASYURE OPOSSUM POTOROO KANGAROO BANDICOOT PETAURIST

MARSUPIUM POUCH
MART STAPLE EMPORIUM
MARTEN FOIN PEKAN SABLE SOBOL FISHER MARTRIX MUSTELID MUSTELIN
(GROUP OF —S) RICHESSE
(SUFF.) ICTIS
MARTENSITE SORBITE
MARTHA (BROTHER OF —) LAZARUS
(CHARACTER IN —) JULIA NANCY LIONEL MARTHA HARRIET PLONKETT
(COMPOSER OF —) FLOTOW
(SISTER OF —) MARY
MARTIAL BELLIC WARLIKE WARRIOR BELLICAL MILITARY
(— ART) TAEKWONDO
MARTIAL ARTS BUDO JUDO KENDO AIKIDO KARATE JUJITSU
(— SCHOOL) DOJO
(— TRAINEE) NINJA
(PERSON TRAINED IN —) NINJA KARATE KUNGFU
MARTIN MARTLET SWALLOW MARTINET
MARTIN CHUZZLEWIT (AUTHOR OF —) DICKENS
(CHARACTER IN —) GAMP MARK MARY SETH JONAS MERCY SARAH GRAHAM MARTIN TAPLEY ANTHONY CHARITY PECKSNIFF CHUZZLEWIT
MARTINI GIBSON
(KIND OF —) VODKA
MARTINMAS TERM
MARTYR STEPHEN WITNESS SUFFERER
MARTYRDOM MARTYRY PASSION
MARVEL MARL MUSE FERLY SELLY ADMIRE WONDER MAGNALE MIRACLE MONSTER PORTENT PRODIGY SELCOUTH ADMIRATION
MARVELOUS FAB SUPER SUPERB EPATANT MIRIFIC STRANGE FABULOUS WONDROUS MIRACULOUS
MARVY RAD COOL
MARX BROTHERS (ONE OF —) CHICO HARPO ZEPPO GROUCHO
MARY MOLL POLL MAMIE MAURA MOLLY MIRIAM MARILLA
MARY JANE MARIJUANA

MARYLAND
BATTLESITE: ANTIETAM
CAPITAL: ANNAPOLIS
COLLEGE: HOOD GOUCHER STJOHNS
COUNTY: KENT CECIL TALBOT CALVERT HARFORD ALLEGANY SOMERSET
INDIAN: CONOY NANTICOKE
LAKE: PRETTYBOY
MOUNTAIN: BACKBONE
NATIVE: WESORT TERRAPIN
NICKNAME: COCKADE OLDLINE
RIVER: CHESTER POTOMAC CHOPTANK PATUXENT
STATE BIRD: ORIOLE
STATE TREE: OAK
TOWN: BELAIR DENTON EASTON ELKTON TOWSON LAPLATA ABERDEEN BETHESDA POCOMOKE BALTIMORE

MARYSOLE CARTER LEADER CARTARE
MARZIPAN MARCHPANE
(— BASE) ALMOND
MASAI WAKWAFI WAKWAVI
MASCEZEL (BROTHER OF —) GILDO
MASCOT BILLIKEN
MASCULINE MALE BUTCH DOGGY MACHO RUDAS VIRILE LALAQUI MANLIKE
(EXAGGERATEDLY —) MACHO
(PREF.) ANDR(O) MASCULO
(SUFF.) ANDRIA ANDROUS ANDRY
MASCULINITY (EXAGGERATED —) MACHISMO
(EXAGGERATED AWARENESS OF —) MACHISMO
MASH PAP BEER CHAP MASA MASK MESH SLOP CHAMP CREEM SMASH SMUSH MUDDLE STILLAGE
(FATHER OF —) ARAM
MASHED CHAPPED DAUPHINE
MASHER FLIRT BEETLE
MASJID MOSQUE
MASK FACE HIDE JEST LOUP SLUR VEIL BLOCK BLOOP CLOAK COVER GRILL GUISE LARVE POINT VIZOR DOMINO GRILLE MUZZLE SCREEN VEILER VIZARD BECLOUD CONCEAL CURTAIN MASKOID ANTEMASK DEFILADE DISGUISE MASCARON PRETENSE
(— OUT) CROP
(GAS —) CANARY
(HALF —) LOO LOUP DOMINO
(KIND OF —) SKI
(PHOTOGRAPHIC —) MATTE
(PL.) AREITO
MASKED LARVATED VIZARDED
MASKED BALL (CHARACTER IN —) HORN ANGRI AMELIA RENATO TOMASI ULRICA ARMANDO RIBBING SAMUELE ARVIDSON GUSTAVUS RICCARDO ANCKERSTROEM
(COMPOSER OF —) VERDI
MASKER GUISARD MASQUER
MASKING MUMMERY MUMMING COLORING
MASKLIKE PERSONATE
MASLIN MESTLEN MASHLOCH MUNGCORN MASSELGEM
MASNADIERI, I (CHARACTER IN —) CARLO AMALIA FRANCESCO MASSIMILIAN
(COMPOSER OF —) VERDI
MASON LAYER BUILDER MASONER COMACINE KNOBBLER LAMMIKIN SCUTCHER
MASONRY ASHLAR MANTLE RUSTIC BACKING BLOCAGE MOELLON NOGGING ISODOMUM QUOINING ROCKWORK EMPLECTON RUBBLEWORK
(UNDRESSED —) RAGWORK
MASQUE MASK COMUS DEVICE ANTIMASK DISGUISE
MASQUER REX
MASQUERADE BALL MASK GUISE DOMINO MASQUE PARADE MASKERY DISGUISE
MASQUERADER RAGSHAG
MASQUERADING CARNIVAL

MASS BAT BED GOB SOP TOD WAD BODY BULK CLOD GOUT HEAP HEFT KNOT LEAD LUMP MOLE OBIT STOW SWAD AMASS BATCH BLOOM CLAMP CLASH CLUMP CROWD CRUST DIRGE GLOBE GORGE GROSS MATTE MISSA PRESS SLUMP SOLID SPIRE STONE WODGE COMMON GOBBET NUGGET PROPER VOLUME WEIGHT BOUROCK CONGEST DENSITY MASKINS MESKINS MYSTERY REQUIEM SALOMON CALAPITE CONGERIE ENDOSOME FLOCCULE MOUNTAIN MYCETOMA SOULMASS ACCUMULATION
(— IN THE WHITE NILE) SUDD
(— OF BACTERIA) SLIME BAREGINE SYMPLASM
(— OF BLOSSOMS) BLOW
(— OF BLUBBER) MELON
(— OF BRANCHES) SPRAY
(— OF BUBBLES) FOAM
(— OF BUSHES) SHAG
(— OF CARPELS) SOREMA
(— OF CELLS) COMB CANCER MORULA CUMULUS STALACE PULVINUS
(— OF CLOUDS) BANK
(— OF COAL) JUD
(— OF COLORS) BLOB
(— OF COTTON) FUSSOCK
(— OF CURED RUBBER) LOAF
(— OF DEBRIS) SLIDE
(— OF DOUGH) DUMPLING
(— OF FIBERS) KAPOK
(— OF FILAMENTS) FLOCCUS MYCELIUM
(— OF FILTH) GORE
(— OF FRAGMENTS) BRASH
(— OF GAS) PROMINENCE
(— OF GOLD) BONANZA
(— OF HAIR) GLIB TOUPET
(— OF HYPHAE) MEDULLA
(— OF ICE) BERG CALF FLOE FLAKE PATCH ICICLE STURIS GROWLER ICEBERG FLOEBERG
(— OF INSECTS) CACHE
(— OF IRON) BALL BLOB CORE BLOOM INDUCTOR
(— OF LAVA) BOMB SPINE
(— OF LEAVES) FOLIAGE
(— OF LIMESTONE) HUM
(— OF LOOSE BOULDERS) CLATTER
(— OF METAL) SOW INGOT BUTTON
(— OF MOLTEN GLASS) GOB BLOOM GATHER PARISON
(— OF MUD) CLASH
(— OF ORE) BACK SLUG BUNNY SQUAT REGULUS
(— OF PEOPLE) CROWD HORDE
(— OF POMACE) CHEESE
(— OF ROCK) DOME NECK HORSE LEDGE NAPPE SCALP SNOUT INLIER SARSEN BOULDER FOOTWALL
(— OF SAND) PAAR
(— OF SOAP) CURD
(— OF SPORES) SORUS
(— OF SUGAR) FONDANT
(— OF SUGAR CRYSTALS) STRIKE
(— OF TISSUE) COLLAR GANGLION NUCELLUS

(— OF TREES) THICKET
(— OF WATER) HEAD
(— OF YARN) COP BALLOON
(— OF YOLK) LATEBRA
(— OVERHANGING) CORNICE
(—S OF DRIFTWOOD) EMBARRAS
(— TOGETHER) HUDDLE
(ALPINE —) FLYSCH
(AMORPHOUS —) JUMBLE SYMPLASM
(BILLOWY —) CLOUD
(BUSHY —) SHOCK
(COMPACT —) BRIQUET
(CONCENTRATION OF MOON —) MASCON
(CONFUSED —) COT JUMBLE JUNGLE PILEUP CLUTTER RUMMAGE SHUFFLE
(DISORDERLY —) SCRAMBLE
(EGG —) BUNION CULTCH SPONGE
(FATTY —) BEAN HEADSKIN
(FECAL —) SCYBALUM
(FLATTISH —) DAB
(FLUFFY —) PUFF
(FLUID —) FLUOR
(GLASSY —) SLAG
(GLOBULAR —) MOORBALL
(INDISTINCT —) SMUDGE
(IRREGULAR —) CUB
(LIVING —) BLASTEMA
(MOIST —) PULP
(MOUNTAIN —) OROGEN
(NUCLEAR —) SHIELD
(OVERSPREADING —) PALL
(PART OF —) INTROIT
(PEAR-SHAPED —) BOULE
(POROUS —) FILTER
(PROJECTING —) BOSS
(PULPY —) SQUELCH
(RECTANGULAR —) BRICK
(ROOT —) SOLE
(ROUNDED —) COB NOB KNOB BOLUS KUGEL BULLET RONDLE
(SEDIMENTARY —) GOBI
(SHAPED —) PAT LOAF
(SHAPELESS —) JELLY
(SLIPPERY —) SIND SLUD SLUDDER
(SLUSHY —) POSH
(SOFT —) MASH MOXA MUMMY
(STICKY —) CLAG
(SWOLLEN —) CERE
(TANGLED — OF HAIR) MOP KNURL
(TUFTY —) FLOC
(UNCTUOUS —) LANOLIN
(UNIT OF —) DALTON
(UPRIGHT —) COLUMN
(PL.) MEINY MEINIE TRENTAL POPULACE
(PREF.) ONCO
(SUFF.) IUM OME
MASSA (FATHER OF —) ISHMAEL

MASSACHUSETTS
CAPE: ANN COD
CAPITAL: BOSTON
COLLEGE: SMITH AMHERST SIMMONS WHEATON WILLIAMS RADCLIFFE WELLESLEY
COUNTY: DUKES ESSEX BRISTOL NORFOLK SUFFOLK BERKSHIRE NANTUCKET BARNSTABLE
INDIAN: NAUSET POCOMTUC
ISLAND: DUKES NANTUCKET

LAKE: ONOTA QUABBIN ROHUNTA WEBSTER
MOUNTAIN: BRODIE POTTER ALANDER EVERETT GREYLOCK
MOUNTAIN RANGE: BERKSHIRE
POND: WALDEN
PRESIDENT: BUSH KENNEDY
RIVER: NASHUA CHARLES CONCORD QUABOAG TAUNTON CHICOPEE DEERFIELD MERRIMACK
STATE BIRD: CHICKADEE
STATE FLOWER: MAYFLOWER
STATE NICKNAME: BAY OLDBAY OLDCOLONY
STATE TREE: ELM
TOWN: AYER LYNN OTIS ATHOL BARRE LENOX AGAWAM DEDHAM GROTON LOWELL NAHANT NATICK REVERE SAUGUS WOBURN HOLYOKE IPSWICH PEABODY TAUNTON BROCKTON CHICOPEE COHASSET SCITUATE UXBRIDGE YARMOUTH CAMBRIDGE NANTUCKET WORCESTER PITTSFIELD SPRINGFIELD
UNIVERSITY: CLARK TUFTS HARVARD BRANDEIS

MASSACRE SLAY POGROM CARNAGE SCUPPER WIPEOUT BUTCHERY SLAUGHTER
MASSAGE ROLF WISP KNEAD FACIAL MODIFY PETRIE SHAMPOO SHIATSU TRIPSIS BLANDISH LOMILOMI ANATRIPSIS MANIPULATE
(— OF DEEP MUSCLES) ROLFING
(— WITH FINGERS) SHIATSU SHIHTZU
(MUSCLE —) ROLF ROLFING
(ONE WHO —S) ROLFER
MASSAGER MASSEUR VIBRATOR
MASSECUITE GUR FILLMASS
MASSED DENSE
MASSENA QUAIL COPPY
MASSIVE BIG BEAMY BULKY GROSS HEAVY LUSTY MASSY SOUND STERN STRONG HEALTHY HULKING VOLUMED TIMBERED MONUMENTAL
MAST BUCK MAIN POLE SPAR OVEST STICK STING DRIVER JIGGER MIZZEN ARTEMON ASHERAH MASTAGE PANNAGE SPANKER FOREMAST JURYMAST MAINMAST SHIPMAST MIZZENMAST
(FALLEN —) SHACK
(SIXTH —) DRIVER
MASTAX TROPHI
MASTER DON HER JOE MAS RAB SAB SIR ARCH BAAS BEAK BEST BOSS COCK FACE HERR JOSS KING LORD MIAN SIRE TUAN BWANA LEARN MARSE MASSA RABBI SAHIB SWAMI SWAMY SWELL BRIDLE BUCKRA CASTER DEACON DOMINE HUMBLE MAITRE PATRON RECTOR RHETOR SIRCAR WAFTER CAPTAIN CONQUER DOMINIE DOMINUS EFFENDI MAESTRO NAKHODA OGTIERN PADRONE RABBONI AMAISTER BARGEMAN BEMASTER KINGFISH LANDLORD MAGISTER OVERCOME SLOOPMAN SURMOUNT VANQUISH
(— OF CEREMONIES) EMCEE VERGER COMPERE CHAIRMAN
(— OF CRAFT) KAHUNA
(— OF HOUSEHOLD) BALABOS GOODMAN
(— OF REVELS) ALYTARCH
(— OF WHALER) SPOUTER
(FENCING —) LANISTA
(INFERIOR —) KNIFER
(PREF.) ARCH
MASTER-AT-ARMS JAUNTY JAUNTIE
MASTER BUILDER (AUTHOR OF —) IBSEN
(CHARACTER IN —) ALINE HILDA BROVIK RAGNAR SOLNESS
MASTERFUL BOSSY LORDLY VIRILE HAUGHTY ARROGANT MAGERFUL PEREMPTORY
MASTER OF BALLANTRAE (AUTHOR OF —) STEVENSON
(CHARACTER IN —) CHEW DASS BALLY BURKE HENRY JAMES TEACH ALISON DURRIE GRAEME FRANCIS SECUNDRA MACKELLAR DURRISDEER
MASTERPIECE GEM TOPPIECE
MASTERSTROKE COUP
MASTERY GREE GRIP GRIPE COMMAND MAISTRY OVERHAND
MASTHEAD FLAG HIGHTOP
MASTICATE GUM CHAW CHEW
MASTICATORY PAN BUYO
MASTIC BULLY JOCUM JOCUMA
MASTIC TREE ACOMA AUSUBO COCUYO COCULLO LENTISK
MASTIFF ALAN MASTY BANDOG TIEDOG
MASTIGONEME FLIMMER
MASTITIS CLAP WEED GARGET
MAST TREE ASAK
MASTURBATE ABUSE
MASTURBATION ONANISM FROTTAGE
MASTWOOD POON KAMANI
MAT COT RUG TOD BASS FLAT FLET FOOT HAIR MOSS NIPA PACE RAFT SHAG TAUT DOILY KILIM TATTY COTTER FELTER FOOTER PAUNCH PETATE TARGET TATAMI THATCH COASTER CUSHION DOORMAT KAITAKA MATTING FOOTPACE FROSTING MATTRESS SPANDREL
(— BORDER) TANIKO
(BOWLING —) FOOTER
(FIBER —) IE BASS
(PALM-LEAF —) YAPA
(PICTURE-FRAME —) FLAT
(POLYNESIAN —) LAUHALA
(SCOURING —) BEAR
(TABLECLOTH —) GARDNAP
(PL.) DUNNAGE
MATACHIN BOUFFON
MATACO CORONADO
MATADOR MAT ESPADA CAPEADOR
(— MOVEMENT) PASE
MATCH GO CAP VIE BOUT COPE EVEN FERE LUNT MAKE MATE MEET MILL MOTE PAIR PEEL PEER SIDE SUIT AGREE AMATE EQUAL FIRER FUSEE FUZEE MOUSE PARTY RIVAL SPUNK TALLY VENUE VESTA ASSORT BESORT CANCEL COMMIT FELLOW KIPPIN MARROW QUADER RUBBER SAMPLE SWATCH COMPEER EXAMPLE IGNITER ILLUMER KINDLER KIPPEEN LIGHTER LUCIFER PARAGON PAREGAL PATTERN PENDANT SINGLES APPROACH BONSPIEL BREATHER CONGREVE EUPYRION FOURSOME INFLAMER LOCOFOCO PARALLEL PORTFIRE REANSWER VESUVIAN VESUVIUS SEMIFINAL PREMINIARY QUARTERFINAL
(— AT DICE) MAIN
(— FOR FIRING CANNON) MOUSE
(— IN POKER) SEE CALL
(BOXING —) SPAR FIGHT PRELIM SLUGFEST
(CURLING —) SPIEL BONSPIEL
(DANCING —) KANTIKEY
(DISHONEST —) CROSS
(GOLF —) NASSAU FOURSOME
(LARGE-HEADED —) FUZEE
(SCOLDING —) FLYTE FLYTING
(SHOOTING —) TIR SHOOT
(SLOW —) LUNT SMIFT SQUIB
(TILTING —) CAROUSEL CARROUSEL
(UNEQUAL —) DISPARAGE
(WORTHY —) ROLAND
(PL.) LIGHTS
MATCHED INSYNC ASSORTED
MATCHING MARROW SUITABLE
(NOT —) ODD
MATCHLESS ALONE UNIQUE NONESUCH PEERLESS
MATCHMAKER SHADCHEN
MATE CAWK FERE METE PAIR PEER BILLY BREED BUDDY BULLY CHINA CLASP CULLY DICKY MATCH PARTY TALLY YERBA BUNKIE COBBER FELLOW FUTURE MARROW PAREIL SPOUSE BROTHER COMPEER COMRADE CONSORT HUSBAND PARAGON NEIGHBOR PIRRAURA
(— WELL) NICK
(BOATSWAIN'S —) BUFFER
(GUNNER'S —) LADY
(SECOND —) DICKY
MATERIAL FINE MOLD COMPO GAUZE GOUGE HYLIC METAL MOULD PASTE PLASS STUFF THING TRADE BORROW CARNAL CYANUS FABRIC GRAITH HOGGIN MATTER PAPREG PUBLIC THINGY APPAREL FOOTING SUBJECT TEXTILE UNIDEAL WEIGHTY ADDITIVE CORPORAL ECONOMIC EQUIPAGE RELEVANT SENSIBLE SNOODING TANGIBLE THINGISH OBJECTIVE PHENOMENAL
(— ELIMINATED) CULLAGE
(— FOR FERMENTING) GUILE
(— FOR OYSTER BEDS) CULCH CULTCH
(— IN GRAIN) DOCKAGE
(— IN MAKING CEMENT) ADDITION
(— IN NEEDLEWORK) INKLE
(— OF CORDED SILK) CRYSTAL
(— OF SCREENINGS) HOGGIN HOGGING
(— REMOVED BY SAW CUT) KERF
(—S FOR MAKING GLASS) FRIT
(— USED IN WAXING) BALL
(— WEIGHED) DRAFT DRAUGHT
(ABSORBENT —) DOPE
(ALLUVIAL —) SHINGLE
(ANCIENT —) MURRA MURRHA
(ARTISTIC —) KITSCH
(BAGGING —) HOPSACK
(BITUMINOUS —) KEROGEN
(BONY —) COSMINE
(BUILDING —) LATH ADOBE BRICK STAFF SWISH TABBY TAPIA SILLAR CONCRETE
(BUILDING —S) TIGNUM
(CLAY —) TAPIA
(CLAYEY —) GOUGE
(COLORING —) TINCTION
(COMBUSTIBLE —) KINDLING
(CONSTRUCTION —) BREEZE
(CORE —) NIFE
(CUSHIONING —) AIRFOAM
(DEPOSITED —) FOOTS
(DIAMOND —) BORT
(DOWNY —) FLUE
(DRESS —) FOULE VOILE PEELING COTILLON FOULENNE
(DYEING —) SUMAC SUMACH
(EMBOSSED —) CLOQUE
(EMROIDERY —) ARRASENE
(EXCAVATED —) SPOIL
(FACING —) ENAMEL
(FILLING —) FIBERFILL
(FISSIONABLE —) STUFF
(FOUNDATION —) UNDERLAY
(GLUTINOUS —) GELATIN
(GRANULAR —) BASIS
(HARD —) CARBIDE
(HEAT-RESISTANT —) ALSIFILM
(ILLUSTRATIVE —) ART
(INSECTICIDAL —) SCABRIN
(INSULATING —) KERITE PECITE BLANKET LAGGING OKONITE MEGOTALC
(LEFTOVER —S) ARISINGS
(LOOSE —) SAND GRAVEL DETRITUS
(MINING REFUSE —) ATTLE
(MINUTE —) SESTON
(MOLDING —) PREPREG
(NUTRITIVE —) FUEL
(OPAQUE —) MASK
(ORGANIC —) EXINITE
(PAPER-THIN —) FOIL
(PATCHING —) BOTCH
(PETRIFIED —) GEMSTONE
(POLISHING —) RABAT
(POWDERED —) FINES
(PRIMORDIAL —) BLASTEMA
(RAW —) STOCK STAPLE
(REFRACTORY —) GROG BULLDOG CASTABLE
(RESIDUAL —) CEMENT
(RESOURCE —) SWIPE
(REVERSIBLE —) DAMASK
(SEDIMENTARY —) SILT
(SILK —) HONAN PEKIN FOULARD SARCENET
(SLIMY —) GLIT SWARF
(SMOKING —) KEF KIF
(STIFF —) CANVAS

(STIFFENING —) BOXING
(TANNING —) BADAN SYNTAN
(THIN SLICE OF —) WAFER
(TILE-STRENGTHENING —) WEB
(TRASHY —) SLUSH
(TWEEDY —) HOMESPUN
(TYPE-HIGH —) BEARER
(UNPUBLISHED —) INEDITA
(UNSOLICITED —) SLUSH
(UPHOLSTERY —) LAMPAS
(VOLCANIC —) EJECTA TEPHRA
(WATERPROOF —) KERATOL
(WORTHLESS —) GARBLE
(WOVEN —) LAPPET
(PL.) STOCK STUFF
(PREF.) HYL(O)
(SUFF.) **(PLASTIC —)** PLASM(A)
MATERIALISM HYLISM SOMATISM
(DIALECTICAL —) DIAMAT
MATERIALISTIC SENSATE SENSUAL
BANAUSIC
MATERIALIZE REIFY DESCEND
MATER LECTIONIS GRAPHY
MATERNITY WARD NATUARY
MATGRASS NARD MATWEED
MATH MUTH MONASTERY
(KIND OF —) NEW
MATHEMATICIAN ALGORIST
GEOMETER
AMERICAN SEE FINE WEST WEYL
AIKEN BEGLE BROWN FISKE GIBBS
GODEL HARDY MASON MOORE
MUSES POLYA SMITH YOUNG
CAJORI HOPPER KASNER KEYSER
LEHMER LOOMIS MILLER NEWTON
OSGOOD PEIRCE RUNKLE VEBLEN
WIENER DICKSON GODFREY
METZLER NEUMANN SAFFORD
BANNEKER BIRKHOFF BOWDITCH
COOLIDGE FRANKLIN WELCHMAN
MURNAGHAN HUNTINGTON
VONNEUMANN WILCZYNSKI
RITTENHOUSE
AUSTRIAN HAGEN DOPPLER
PURBACH
BELGIAN LEMAITRE
BRAZILIAN GUSMAO
DUTCH BLAEU VLACQ CEULEN
STEVIN HUYGENS SNELLIUS
GRAVESANDE MUSSCHENBROEK
EGYPTIAN HYPATIA PTOLEMY
ENGLISH DEE LAMB MUIR PELL
ALLEN BONDI BOOLE COTES DIRAC
ELLIS HARDY JEANS MURIS ROUTH
SHARP SMITH WALES ATWOOD
BARLOW BARNES BARROW BRIGGS
CAYLEY COCKLE DARWIN DIGGES
GUNTER HADLEY HUTTON KELVIN
LARMOR NEWTON ROBINS STOKES
TAYLOR WALLIS WEDDLE BABBAGE
DODGSON HARRIOT LUBBOCK
MAKEHAM MASERES PEACOCK
RECORDE RUSSELL WHEWELL
WHISTON CLIFFORD GLAISHER
GOMPERTZ LEYBOURN MACMAHON
OUGHTRED RAYLEIGH BRONOWSKI
DUNSTABLE GREENHILL
NICHOLSON TODHUNTER
WHITEHEAD WHITTAKER
WOODHOUSE CODDINGTON
GELLIBRAND SACROBOSCO
SAUNDERSON

FRENCH BIOT FINE LAME LEVY
BORDA BOREL CHEZY COMTE
LEROY MONGE PRONY RAMUS
STURM VIETE BEAUNE BEZOUT
BOSSUT CAUCHY FERMAT FERNEL
GALOIS JORDAN MOIGNO PASCAL
PICARD BOUGUER BROCARD
CHARLES CHASLES CHUQUET
COURNOT DARBOUX FOURIER
GERMAIN GOURSAT HERMITE
KOENIGS LACROIX LAPLACE
POINSOT POISSON PUISEUX
VERNIER ALEMBERT BERTRAND
CLAIRAUT CORIOLIS DEMOIVRE
GERGONNE HACHETTE HADAMARD
LAGRANGE LAGUERRE LEBESGUE
LEGENDRE MERSENNE MONTUCIA
PAINLEVE POINCARE PONCELET
ROBERVAL BRIANCHON
CONDORCET DESARGUES
DESCARTES LIOUVILLE
BURCKHARDT DEPARCIEUX
MAUPERTUIS
GERMAN GAUSS HESSE KLEIN
MAYER MISES PASCH PFAFF RUNGE
WOLFF BALMER CANTOR JACOBI
KUMMER MOBIUS MULLER STIFEL
APIANUS CLEBSCH FRIESEN
HILBERT KASTNER LAMBERT
LEIBNIZ PLUCKER RIEMANN
WIDMANN ARONHOLD BLASCHKE
CLAUSIUS DEDEKIND DROBISCH
LEIBNITZ MERCATOR RHATICUS
SCHOTTKY SCHUBERT DIRICHLET
GRASSMANN KRONECKER
LINDEMANN BIEBERBACH
EISENSTEIN HINDENBURG
PRINGSHEIM TSCHIRNHAUS
WEIERSTRASS KONIGSBERGER
GREEK CONON EUCLID PAPPUS
DIOCLES PTOLEMY ANTIPHON
AUTOLYCUS OENOPIDES
SOSIGENES APOLLONIUS
ARCHIMEDES DIOPHANTUS
PYTHAGORAS DINOSTRATUS
HUNGARIAN BOLYAI
INDIAN ARYABHATA RAMANUJAN
IRISH BALL KELVIN SALMON
HAMILTON BROUNCKER
ITALIAN CEVA BALDI FRISI PEANO
AGNESI GRANDI CARDANO
CREMONA GALILEO PACIOLI
RICCATI BELTRAMI BRIOSCHI
CAMPANUS MALFATTI BOSCOVICH
CAVALIERI FIBONACCI TARTAGLIA
BELLAVITIS MASCHERONI
TORRICELLI
JAPANESE SEKI
NORWEGIAN LIE ABEL STORMER
GULDBERG
POLISH BARTEL CIOLEK WRONSKI
PORTUGUESE NUNES
RUSSIAN KRYLOV LIAPUNOV
CHEBYSHEV KOLMOGOROV
KOVALEVSKI LOBACHEVSKI
SCOTTISH TAIT IVORY KEILL LESLIE
NAPIER BURGESS FORSYTH
GREGORY MAXWELL PLAYFAIR
STIRLING
SWISS EULER AMSLER CRAMER
GULDIN BYRGIUS STEINER
BERNOULLI CHRISTOFFEL
MATHEMATICS MATHESIS

MATING NICK COUPLE DIALLEL
BREEDING HOMOGAMY PANMIXIA
(RANDOM —) PANGAMY
MATRASS BOLTHEAD CUCURBIT
MATRED (DAUGHTER OF —)
MEHETABEL
(FATHER OF —) MEZAHAB
MATRIMONIAL MARITAL NUPTIAL
SPOUSAL CONJUGAL
MATRIMONIO SEGRETO, IL
(CHARACTER IN —) FIDALMA
PAOLINO CAROLINA ELISETTA
GERONIMO ROBINSON
(COMPOSER OF —) CIMAROSA
MATRIMONY WEDLOCK MARRIAGE
MATRIMONY VINE JASMINE
JESSAMY BOXTHORN
MATRIX PI BED MAT SORT PLASM
SHELL SLIDE DYADIC MASTER
MOTHER STRIKE STROMA
CALYMMA FORMULA MATRICE
PATTERN PROPLASM
MATRON DAME
MATTAN (SON OF —) SHEPHATIAH
MATTANIAH (FATHER OF —) BANI
ELAM HEMAN ZATTU
(SON OF —) ZACCUR
MATTE SLURRY REGULUS
MATTED COTTY FELTY PINNY
FELTED TAGGED TAUTED WAUKIT
STRINGY FELTLIKE CESPITOSE
MATTENAI (FATHER OF —) JOIARIB
MATTER BIT RES BONE CASE GEAR
HYLE ITEM RECK WHAT AMPER
FORCE PARTY SKILL STUFF THEME
TOPIC AFFAIR ARGUFY BEHALF
DITTAY IMPORT ARTICLE CONCERN
MATERIA SHEBANG SIGNIFY
SUBJECT BUSINESS COMETHER
MATERIAL
(— ADDED TO BOOK) APPENDIX
(— AROUND THE TEETH) TOPHUS
(— CONSTITUTING PERFUME)
ESSENCE
(— DISCHARGED) FLUX
(— EJECTED) CAST
(— FOR PRINTING) COPY
(— IN DISPUTE) ISSUE
(— OF BUSINESS) SHAURI
(— OF CHANCE) LOTTERY
(— OF CONCERN) FUNERAL
(— OF CONSCIENCE) REMORSE
(— OF DISCOURSE) SUBJECT
(— OF FACT) SENSE
(— OF INTEREST) GRIST
(— OF NO IMPORTANCE) TOY
(— TO) CONCERN
(ALLUVIAL —) GEEST
(BRAIN —) ALBA
(CARTILAGINOUS —) GRISTLE
(COLORING —) DYE COLOR CROCK
EOSIN MORIN PIURI ALNEIN ANATTO
BUTEIN FUSTIC INDIGO ORCEIN
PIOURY ANNATTO CARMINE
CASTORY CUDBEAR LIGULIN
OENOLIN PIGMENT PUNICIN
TURACIN XANTHIN ALGOCYAN
ALIZARIN BRAZILIN FUSTERIC
LAPACHOL SCOPARIN TINCTION
TINCTURE
(CORRUPT —) PUS ATTER
(DECAYED ORGANIC —) DUFF
(DECAYING —) DUFF

(DIFFICULT —) PROBLEM
(DISCHARGED —) EXUDATE
(ESSENTIAL —) POINT
(EXPLANATORY —) HAGGADA
(FATTY —) SEBUM
(FECAL —) SIEGE
(FILTHY —) GUNK
(FOREIGN —) SOIL DROSS
(FOUL —) FILTH SORDES
(FRONT —) FOREWORD
(GELATINOUS —) BREAK SPAWN
(GRAY —) GLIOSA CINEREA
(HYPOTHETICAL —) PROTYLE
(INANIMATE —) AJIVA
(INDECENT —) STUFF
(INFECTIOUS —) MIASMA
(INFLAMMABLE —) TINDER
(MINERAL —) FLOAT FLOATS
(NERVE —) CINEREA
(POTENTIAL —) PRAKRITI
(PRIMARY —) PRADHANA
(PRINTED —) BOX DISPLAY
(PRIVATE —) SECLUSION
(PULVERIZED —) ATTRITUS
(READING —) BODY
(SLIMY —) GLAIR
(SMALL —) MINUTIA
(SOFT —) PASH
(SUBJECT —) SCOPE CONTENT
(SUPPURATIVE —) PUS
(TRIVIAL —) JOKE
(TYPESET —) CHASE
(WASTE —) DIRT DRAFF DROSS
RAMMEL SEWAGE EXCRETA
(WORTHLESS —) SLAG CHAFF
GANGUE GARBAGE
(WRITTEN —) SCRIVE
(PL.) HARNESS SQUARES
(PREF.) HYL(O)
(SUFF.) **(COLORING —)** PHYLL
MATTER-OF-FACT THINGY
PROSAIC PROSAICAL DRY PROSE
LITERAL PROSAIC
MATTER-OF-FACTNESS PROSE
MATTHAN (GRANDSON OF —)
JOSEPH
MATTHEW (FATHER OF —)
ALPHAEUS
MATTING MAT TAT BAST BEAR
BUMP SIRKI TATTY SAWALI TATAMI
COCOMAT RABANNA
MATTOCK MAT BILL HACK MATAX
PICKAX TUBBAL TWIBIL GRUBBER
MATTRESS BED MAT TICK DIVAN
FUTON QUILT RESAI REZAI PALLET
BISCUIT MATRACE PAILLASSE
PALLIASSE
(INFLATABLE —) LILO
MATURATE MATTER
MATURE AGE OLD BOLD FULL GRAY
RIPE ADULT MANLY RIPEN SHOOT
ACCRUE AUTUMN DECOCT DIGEST
MELLOW SEASON SEEDED
CONCOCT DEVELOP FURNISH
PERFECT PROVECT MATURATE
(PREF.) TEL(E)(O)
MATURED ADULT GROWN FORMED
HEADED MELLOW SEEDED
HOMOGAMY
(SEXUALLY —) HIGH
MATURING (— EARLY) RATHRIPE
MATURITY AGE RIPENESS

MATWEED NARD NARDUS
MATZOTH MATZOS AFIKOMEN
MAUDLIN BEERY MOIST FUDDLED
MAUDLINISM BATHOS
MAUL FAN PAW TUG MALL MELL
GAVEL GLAUM BEATER BEETLE
BEMAUL MUZZLE SCAMBLE
MAUND MAO MEIN MAHAN
MAUNDER HAVER
MAUNDY NIPTER MANDATE
MAURITANIA (CAPITAL OF —)
NOUAKCHOTT
(COIN OF —) KHOUM
(MONEY OF —) OUGUIYA
(RIVER OF —) SENEGAL
(TOWN OF —) ATAR NEMA AGMAR
KAEDI OUJAF
MAURITANIAN MOOR
MAURITIUS (CAPITAL OF —)
PORTLOUIS
(CHANNEL OF —) QUOIN
(ISLAND OF —) AGALEGA GABRIEL
RODRIGUEZ
(RIVER OF —) GRAND POSTE
REMPART
(TOWN OF —) VACOAS TRIOLET
CUREPIPE SOUILLAC
MAUSOLEUM MOLE TOMB SHRINE
TURBEH DARADARI
MAUVE MALLOW PURPLE MAUVINE
MAVEN ADEPT EXPERT
MAVERICK STRAY
MAW MAA CRAW CROP GORGE
CROPPY THROAT
MAWKISH CUTE SAPPY SOPPY
SOUPY WALSH DRIPPY SICKLY
VANILLA
MAXILLA SETA GNATHITE
CULTELLUS
MAXILLIPED JAWFOOT GNATHITE
MAXIM SAW SAY DICT ITEM NORM
RULE TEXT WORD ADAGE AXIOM
GNOME LARGE MOTTO DICTUM
SAYING SYMBOL BROCARD
DICTATE IMPRESA PRECEPT
PROVERB APHORISM APOTHEGM
DOCTRINE MORALISM PROTASIS
SENTENCE
(PL.) LOGIA
MAXIMUM FULL MOST PEAK CREST
EXTREME OUTSIDE SUMMARY
ULTIMATE
MAXIXE CARIOCA
MAXWELL LINE WEBER
MAY CAN MUN MOTE MOWE MUST
PRIME SHALL HEYDAY HAWTHORN
SYCAMORE
(3D OF —) RUDMASDAY
MAYA PRAKRITI
MAYAN COCOM
(— CALENDAR PERIOD) UAYEB
UINAL
(— GOD) CHAC CHAAC
MAYAPPLE MANDRAKE
MAYBE MEBBE HAPPEN PERHAPS
POSSIBLY
MAY DAY BELTANE
MAYFISH ROCKFISH
MAYFLOWER ARBUTUS
MAYFLY DUN DOON DRAKE NAIAD
DAYFLY SPINNER EPHEMERA
MAYHEM FELONY

MAYONNAISE MAYO GOULASH
DRESSING
(GARLIC —) AIOLI
MAYOR MAIRE BAILIFF DEMARCH
PODESTA PROVOST HIZZONER
PALATINE
(BULGARIAN —) KMET
(IRISH —) SOVRAN SOVEREIGN
(SPANISH —) ALCALDE
MAYOR OF CASTERBRIDGE
(AUTHOR OF —) HARDY
(CHARACTER IN —) JOPP SUSAN
DONALD NEWSON FARFRAE
LESUEUR LUCETTA MICHAEL
RICHARD HENCHARD ELIZABETH
TEMPLEMAN
MAYORSHIP CHAIR
MAYPOLE SHAFT
MAYPOP MAYCOCK MARACOCK
MAYWEED BALDER COTULA
MATHER HOGWEED COMPOSIT
DILLWEED
MAZE JUNGLE WARREN CONFUSE
BEWILDER LABYRINTH
MAZEPPA (CHARACTER IN —)
MARIA ANDREY MAZEPPA
KOCHUBEY
(COMPOSER OF —) TCHAIKOVSKY
MAZUMA (ALSO SEE MONEY)
LUCRE
MCCOY QUILL
ME I MA US MOI
MEAD MEATHE BRAGGET
HYDROMEL METHEGLIN
MEADOW LEA ABEL MEAD VEGA
WISH WONG FIELD GRASS LEASE
MARSH SWALE WARTH CALLOW
PARAMO SAETER SMOOTH
POTRERO THWAITE CHINAMPA
(ARTIFICIAL —) CHINAMPA
(FLOODED —) SALTING
(IRISH —) BAAN
(LOW —) ING INCH INGE HAUGH
CALLOW
(NORWEGIAN —) SAETER
(PREF.) PRATI
(SUFF.) ING
MEADOW CROWFOOT FROGWORT
MEADOW GRASS POA
MEADOWLAND ALP MOWING
MOWLAND
MEADOWLARK ACORN MEDLAR
MEADOW MOUSE VOLE
MEADOW PEA COWPEA
MEADOW PIPIT WEKEEN CHEEPER
TIETICK TITLING LINGBIRD
TWITLARK
MEADOW SAFFRON UPSTART
COLCHICUM
MEADOW SAXIFRAGE SESELI
MEADOWSWEET SPIREA
MEADWORT
MEAGER BALD BARE LANK LEAN
NICE POOR THIN GAUNT NAKED
SCANT SILLY SKIMP SOBER SPARE
JEJUNE LEEPIT LENTEN MEAGRE
NARROW PILLED SCANTY SLIGHT
SPARSE STINGY SCRAGGY
SCRANNY SCRIMPY SCRUBBY
SLENDER SPARING STARVED
STERILE MARGINAL SCRANNEL
SCRATCHY MISERABLE

MEAGERLY BARELY SPARELY
SPARINGLY
MEAGERNESS ECONOMY EXILITY
TENUITY SPARENESS
MEAL AMYL ATTA BAKE CENA
CHOW FARM FEED HASH KAIL
MEAT MONG NOSH TUCK COENA
FLOUR MANGE SCOFF BUFFET
COMIDA DINNER FARINA MANGER
POLLEN REPAST SPREAD SQUARE
SUPPER UNDERN BLOWOUT
COOKOUT CRIBBLE MELTITH
NAGMAAL NOONING SETDOWN
ALMUERZO CORNMEAL EVENMETE
MEALTIDE ORDINARY TRENCHER
(— AND WATER) DRAMMOCK
(— FROM CASSAVA ROOT) FARINE
FARINHA
(— FROM ORCHID ROOT) SALEP
(— GROUND BY HAND) GRADDAN
(— OF FELLOWSHIP) AGAPE
(— STIRRED WITH MILK) STUROCH
(ACORN —) RACAHOUT
(AFTERNOON —) TEA
(CEREMONIAL —) SEDER
(COARSE —) GRIT GROUT KIBBLE
CRIBBLE GURGEONS
(COLLEGE —) HALL
(CORN —) MASA ATOLE NOCAKE
(ELABORATE —) FEAST BANQUET
(EXCESSIVE —) SURFEIT
(FIRST —) ALMUERZO
(FULL —) GORGE
(HASTY —) SNAP CHACK
(HEARTY —) AIT
(HEAVY —) TIGHTENER
(IMPROMPTU —) BITE CHECK
(LIGHT —) BAIT BEVER CHACK
CHECK FOURS NUNCHEON
(MIDDAY —) NOON
(MORNING —) BRUNCH
(PERTAINING TO —) PRANDIAL
(PURIM —) SEUDAH
(SCANTY —) PICK
(SMALL —) SNAP MORSEL
(SOLITARY —) SULLEN
(UNSORTED —) ATTA
(PL.) TUCKER
(PREF.) ATHERO
MEALTIDE MELTITH
MEALTIME CHOW MELTETH
MEALY FLOURY FARINOSE
PERONATE
MEALYBUG COCCID
MEAN LOW BASE CLAM HARD LEAN
MIDS NICE POKY POOR SLIM VILE
AGENT ARGUE DINGY DIRTY DUSTY
FOOTY GRIMY KETTY LOUSY
MANGY MESNE MEZZO MIDST
MINGY MOYEN MUCKY NASTY
PETIT PETTY RATTY RUNTY SCALD
SCALL SCALY SCRUB SEEDY SILLY
SMALL SNIDE SNIVY SORRY
SOUND SPELL ABJECT BADASS
BEMEAN COMMON DENOTE
DESIGN DIRTEN FEEBLE FROWZY
FRUGAL GRUBBY HUMBLE
HUNGRY IMPORT INSECT INTEND
LEADEN LITTLE MEASLY MEDIAL
MEDIUM MENIAL MIDDLE
NARROW ORNERY PALTRY PEANUT
PILLED POKING RASCAL SCABBY
SCREWY SCUMMY SCURVY

SHABBY SLIGHT SNIFTY SNIPPY
SORDID SQUALL STRAIT TEMPER
YELLOW AVERAGE CAITIFF
CHANNEL CHETIVE COMICAL
CONNOTE HACKNEY HATEFUL
HILDING IGNOBLE MESQUIN
MISERLY MOTETUS OBSCURE
PEAKING PELTING PIGGISH
PIMPING PITIFUL PORTEND
REPTILE ROINISH SCABBED
SHABBED SIGNIFY VICIOUS
BEGGARLY CHURLISH DOGGEREL
MEDIOCRE MIDDLING NIGGLING
PICAYUNE PITIABLE RASCALLY
RIFFRAFF SHAMEFUL SNEAKING
TWOPENNY WRETCHED
MEANDER ROVE WIND STRAY
TWINE CIRCLE WIMPLE WINDLE
SERPENT WINDING STRAGGLE
MEANING WIT HANG DRIFT SENSE
SOUND IMPORT INTENT SEMEME
PURPORT PURPOSE CARRIAGE
INNUENDO SENTENCE STRENGTH
REFERENCE SIGNIFICANCE
(BASIC —) EFFECT
(DOUBLE —) WHIM EQUIVOKE
(ESSENTIAL —) CORE CONTENT
(IMPLIED —) EMPHASIS
(LITERAL —) LETTER
(MANIFEST —) FACE
(PRECISE —) VALUE
(REAL —) SPIRIT
(SECONDARY —) OVERTONE
(SECRET —) HEART
(SENSE THE — OF) READ
(SIGNIFICANT —) PITH
(SUBTLE —) OVERTONE
MEANINGFUL RICH PREGNANT
MEANINGFULNESS BODY
MEANINGLESS BANAL EMPTY
ABSURD FECKLESS SENSELESS
(— LETTER OR CODE) NULL
MEANLY POORLY SLIGHT
COMMONLY
MEANNESS BEGGARY
MEANS MIDS AGENT DRIVE MESNE
MOYEN PURSE THEME AGENCY
AVENUE ENGINE MATTER MIDDES
POCKET STRING WRENCH
BALANCE BENEFIT DEMESNE
FACULTY FASHION QUOMODO
COURTESY
(— OF ACCESS) DOOR AVENUE
(— OF COMMUNICATION) CANAL
COMMERCE
(— OF DEFENSE) HORN HEDGE
SHIELD BULWARK
(— OF ENTRANCE) INGRESS
(— OF ESCAPE) CHINK SCAPE
FLIGHT
(— OF ESTIMATE) GAGE GAUGE
(— OF INFLUENCING) HOLD
(— OF LIVING) ALIMONY
(— OF OFFENSE) ARM
(— OF PROTECTION) SAFETY
(— OF SECURITY) WALL
(— OF SUPPORT) HOLD ALIMENT
SUPPORT
(— OF TESTING) CHECK
(— TO END) FULCRUM
(ARTIFICIAL —) MACHINE
(BY THIS —) HEREBY

MEANSPIRITED POOR SUPINE CURRISH BANAUSIC RECREANT
MEANTIME MEAN WHILE WHILES INTERIM
MEANTONE TERTIAN
MEANWHILE WHILST INTERIM MEANTIME
MEANY BRUTE
MEASLES RUBEOLA MORBILLI
(**BLACK —**) ESCA APOPLEXY
MEASURE (ALSO SEE UNIT AND WEIGHT) AR BU EM EN HO KO LI MO RI SE TU AAM ARE AUM BAG CAB CHO DRA ELL FAT FEN FIT FOU FUN GAD GAZ GUZ HIN HOB IMI KAB KAN KIP KOR KOS LEA LOG LUG MAU MIL MOY PIK RIG RIN ROD SAA SHO TON TUN VAT VOG WEY ACRE ALMA AUNE BARN BATH BEKA BOLL BOUW BUTT CADE CENT CHIH COOM COSS DEPA DOSE DRAA DRAM DYNE EPHA EPHI FALL FANG FOOT FULL GAGE GERA GILL GIRT GOAD GRAM GREX HAND HATT HIDE HOOP HOUR IMMI PIK ROG KNOT KOKU LAST MEAL METE MILE MUID NAIL NOOK OMER PACE PINT PIPE POLL RATE REAM RIME ROOD ROPE ROTL SAAH SACK SALM SEAH SEAM SIZE SKEP SPAN STEP TAKT TAPE TIME TRAM TRUG TSUN VARA WIST YARD ALMUD AMBER ANKER ARDAB ARDEB ARURA BEKAH BIGHA BLANK BODGE BRASS CABAN CABLE CABOT CANDY CARAT CARGA CATTY CAVAN CHAIN CHANG CHING CLOVE COOMB CRANS CUBIT CUMAL CUNIT DENUM DEPOH DIGIT DRAFT DUNAM DUNUM EPHAH GAUGE GERAH GIRTH HOMER HUTCH JUGER LABOR LAGEN LIANG LIBRA LIGNE LIPPY LITER LITRE MEITH METER METRE MINIM MODEL OUNCE PEISE PERCH PLANK POUND QUIRE RASER RHYME SALMA SCALE SCORE SHAKU SHENG SHING SIEVE SLEEP STACK STERE STONE STOOP STOUP THERM TOISE TOVET TRACE VERST YOJAN APATAN ARCHIN ARPENT ARSHIN ASSIZE BARREL BATMAN BEMETE BOVATE BUNDLE BUSHEL CANADA CANTAR CHOMER CHOPIN COLLOP COUDEE COVIDO CUERDA DAVACH DAVOCH DECARE DEGREE DENIER DIPODY DIRHAM DRACHM ENGLER EXTENT FANEGA FATHOM FEDDAN FINGER FIRKIN FIRLOT FLAGON FODDER FORPET FOTHER GALLON GRAMME HALEBI HIDAGE KISHEN LEAGUE MICRON MODIUS MODULE MOGGIO MORGEN NUMBER OITAVA OUROUB OXHIDE QANTAR REASON SAZHEN SETIER SQUARE STERAD STRIKE SULUNG TERMIN THRAVE WINDLE YOJANA ADOULIE AMPHORA ANAPEST ARSHINE BATTUTA BRACCIO BREADTH CADENCE CALIPER CALORIE CENTARE CENTNER

CENTRAD CHITTAK COMPASS CONGIUS CONTAIN DECIARE DIOPTER DRACHMA DRAUGHT ENTROPY FARSAKH FARSANG FRUNDEL FURLONG HECTARE HEMINEE KILIARE NOCKTAT QUARTAN QUARTER SCHEPEL SCRUPLE SECCHIO SKEPFUL SKIPPLE SPANGLE SPINDLE STADION STADIUM TERTIAN VIRGATE ALQUEIRE CAPACITY CARUCATE CENTIARE CHETVERT CRANNOCK DACTYLIC DECAGRAM DECIGRAM DESIATIN DIAPASON HOGSHEAD INNOCENT LANDYARD METEWAND MUTCHKIN PARASANG PLOWGANG PLOWGATE SCHOONER SCHOPPEN STANDARD PRECAUTION
(**— DEPTH**) SOUND
(**— FOR DRINKS**) JIGGER
(**— FOR FISH**) COT VOG CRAN LAST DRAFT HAMPER DRAUGHT
(**— FOR SHELLFISH**) WASH
(**— OF BEER**) HANDLE
(**— OF BUTTER**) SPAN
(**— OF CHAFF**) FAN
(**— OF COAL**) TEN CORF KEEL CHALDER CHALDRON
(**— OF DEVELOPMENT**) AGE
(**— OF DIAMONDS**) BULSE
(**— OF DISCREPANCY**) LEEWAY
(**— OF EELS**) BIND STICK
(**— OF EFFICIENCY**) DUTY
(**— OF FURS**) MANTLE
(**— OF GRAIN**) MOY COOP
(**— OF HERRINGS**) MEASE
(**— OF HORSE**) HAND
(**— OF LIQUOR**) FIFTH
(**— OF MEDICINE**) DOSE DROP
(**— OF MERCURY**) FLASK
(**— OF MINING CLAIMS**) MERE
(**— OF OUTER SPACE**) PARSEC
(**— OF PEAS**) COP
(**— OF RAISINS**) FRAIL
(**— OF ROTATION**) ANGLE
(**— OF SILK**) DRAMMAGE
(**— OF STRAW**) KEMPLE
(**— OF SUPERIORITY**) LEAD
(**— OF TIMBER**) TON STANDARD
(**— OF WAR**) BLOCKADE
(**— OF WATCHES**) LIGNE
(**— OF WATERCRESS**) HAND
(**— OF WEIGHT FOR ARROWS**) SHILLING
(**— OF WHISKY**) CRUISKEN CRUISKEEN
(**— OF WOOD**) CORD STACK STERE
(**— OF WOOL FINENESS**) BLOOD
(**— OF WORK**) POOL
(**— OF YARN**) LEA RAP CLEW HEER THREAD SPANGLE SPINDLE
(**— OUT**) BATCH
(**ANGULAR —**) ARC
(**COERCIVE —**) SANCTION
(**COUNTERFEIT —**) SLANG
(**DANCE —**) TRACE
(**DUE —**) MANNER
(**FULL —**) SATIETY COMPLEMENT
(**LIQUID —**) CUP GILL PINT MINIM QUART GALLON
(**OLD LIQUID —**) TIERCE
(**PHARMACISTS'S —**) MINIM

(**QUANTITATIVE —**) MAGNITUDE
(**ROAD —**) SCHENE
(**RUSSIAN —**) VERST SAGENE
(**SANCTIONED —**) STANDARD
(**SIAMESE —**) NIOU
(**TAKE —S**) ACT
(PREF.) METR(O)
(SUFF.) METER METR(E)(O)(Y)
(**BY A SPECIFIED —**) MEAL
MEASURED NUMEROUS
MEASURE FOR MEASURE
(**AUTHOR OF —**) SHAKESPEARE
(**CHARACTER IN —**) ELBOW FROTH LUCIO PETER ANGELO JULIET POMPEY THOMAS CLAUDIO ESCALUS MARIANA VARRIUS ABHORSON ISABELLA OVERDONE FRANCISCA VINCENTIO BARNARDINE
MEASURELESS ENDLESS INFINITE
MEASUREMENT GAGE DEPTH GAUGE LEVEL MEITH METAGE DIALING MEASURE SOUNDING
(**— BY LINES**) STICHOMETRY
(**— FOR TAXATION**) HIDE HIDAGE
(**— OF CLOTH**) ALNAGE
(**— OF FINENESS**) SET SETT
(**CIRCULAR —**) RADIAN
(**EARTH —**) GEODESY
(**LUMBER —**) LAST
(**TIME —**) HOROMETRY
MEASURER METER
(**— OF LAND**) SURVEYOR
MEASURING
(SUFF.) METRY
MEASURING-ROD METEWAND METEYARD METESTICK
MEAT BEEF FISH FOOD LAMB LEAN LIFT PORK FLESH STEAK VIFDA VIVDA BUCCAN CAGMAG CONFIT FLEECE MATTER NUTTON TARGET PECKAGE
(**— AND FISH**) LAULAU
(**— COOKED ON SKEWERS**) SATE HASLET HASSLET
(**— COOKED WITH SKEWERS**) SASSATIE
(**— DRIED IN SUN**) JERKY CHARQUI PEMMICAN
(**— OF CONCH**) SCUNGILI
(**— OF KID**) CAPRETTO
(**— ON SKEWERS**) YAKITORI
(**— WITH VEGETABLES**) STEW MULLIGAN
(**BOILED —**) SOD SODDEN BOUILLI
(**BROILED —**) GRISKIN GRILLADE
(**BUFFALO —**) FLEECE
(**CANNED —**) SPAM
(**CHOPPED —**) BURGER
(**COCONUT —**) COPRA
(**CURED —**) HAM
(**CUT OF —**) ARM
(**DRIED —**) MUMMY
(**FAT —**) SPECK
(**FROZEN —**) FRIGO
(**INFERIOR —**) CAGMAG STICKING
(**JERKED —**) BILTONG CHARQUI
(**KIND OF —**) MINCE
(**LEAN —**) MUSCLE
(**MINCED —**) CHUET JIGOTE RISSOLE SANDERS
(**POTTED —**) RILLETT
(**RABBIT —**) LAPAN

(**RAGOUT OF —**) HARICOT
(**ROAST —**) BREDE CABOB
(**ROLLED —**) BIRD
(**SALTED —**) JUNK MART
(**SIDE —**) SOWBELLY
(**SLICED —**) CARPACCIO
(**SLICE OF —**) BRACIOLA BRACIOLE
(**SMALL PIECES OF —**) SATAY
(**SMOKED —**) BUCCAN
(**THIN SLICES OF —**) PICCATA
MEAT CURER BATHMAN
MEATHEADED DENSE
MEAT HOOK GAMBREL
MEAT JELLY ASPIC
MEATLESS PARVE LENTEN PAREVE
MEAT PIE PASTY
MEATUS BUR BURR ALVEARY
MEATY PITHY
MECATE MCCARTY
MECHANIC JOINER WRIGHT ARTISAN FELTMAN SHOPMAN WORKMAN BANAUSIC OPERATIVE
MECHANICAL FROZEN INHUMAN METALLIC AUTOMATIC
(**NOT —**) HORMIC
MECHANICALLY BLINDLY
MECHANISM FAN BOND FEED GEAR KITE LIFT MOTE APRON CATCH CROWD FORCE ORGAN SHAKE SLIDE SPARK STEER ACTION BOTTOM CUTOFF INFEED MOTION SICKLE STRIKE AUTOVAC BUILDER CHANNEL CONTROL EJECTOR GIGBACK GRIPPER GUNLOCK HOLDOUT SETTING TRIPPER ACTUATOR ELEVATOR KINETICS RACKWORK ROLAMITE SELECTOR SETWORKS SIGNALER STEERING STOPWORK THROWOUT
(**— OF HEREDITY**) PANGENESIS
MECHANIZE DESKILL AUTOMATE
MECHLIN MALINES
MECONIN OPIANYL
MEDAL GOLD GONG STAR AWARD MODEL STAMP PLAQUE SILVER MEDALET OSCELLA VERNICLE MEDALLION
(PL.) EXONUMIA
MEDALLION CAMEO TONDO PADUAN PATERA PANHAGIA
MEDAN (**FATHER OF —**) ABRAHAM
(**MOTHER OF —**) KETURAH
MEDDLE TIG FOOL MELL MESS MIRD NOSE POKE TOUCH DABBLE FIDDLE FINGER HECKLE POTTER PUTTER TAMPER TANGLE TINKER
(**— IRRESPONSIBLY**) TRIFLE
MEDDLER SNOOP YENTA SNOOPER BUSYBODY KIBITZER STICKLER STIFFLER BUTTINSKY
MEDDLESOME NOSY FRESH NEBBY
MEDDLING BUSY
MEDEA (**AUNT OF —**) CIRCE
(**BROTHER OF —**) ABSYRTUS APSYRTUS
(**FATHER OF —**) AEETES
(**HUSBAND OF —**) JASON AEGEUS
(**MOTHER OF —**) IDYIA
(**SISTER OF —**) CHALCOPE CHALCIOPE
MEDIA ELASTICA
(**ONE OF THE —**) PRESS RADIO TELEVISION

MEDIAL MEDIAN MEDIUM MIDDLE AVERGAGE

MEDIAN MEDIAL MESIAL AVERAGE MIDLINE
(— **STRIP**) MALL TERRACE

MEDIANT THIRD

MEDIATE MEAN REFEREE INTERCEDE

MEDIATING MIDDLE MIDWAY

MEDIATOR MEANS MEDIUM DAYSMAN MIDDLER PLACATER STICKLER MODERATOR

MEDIC DOC HOP DOCTOR NONESUCH SHAMROCK

MEDICAL IATRIC PHYSIC IATRICAL PAEONIAN
(— **WORK**) ALMONING
(PREF.) (— **TREATMENT**) IATR(O)

MEDICAMENT REMEDY SMEGMA FRONTAL EPULOTIC

MEDICINAL IATRIC PHYSIC MEDICAL THERIAL PHYSICAL SALUTARY THERICAL OFFICINAL

MEDICINE DRUG MUTI PEAI DROPS GRUEL STEEL STUFF TONIC TRADE AMULET ECLEGM ELIXIR MAGUAL PHYSIC POWDER REMEDY SIMPLE ALOETIC ANODYNE ANTACID CORDIAL HEPATIC LUCHDOM MIXTURE NERVINE OPORICE PLACEBO POROTIC PYROTIC SPLENIC AROMATIC DIAPENTE DIGESTER DRUGGERY EARDROPS ECCRITIC EMULGENT LAXATIVE LEECHDOM LENITIVE LOBLOLLY PECTORAL PHARMACY PULMONIC RELAXANT SEDATIVE SPECIFIC STOMATIC CATHARTIC PURGATIVE PRESCRIPTION
(— **BOTTLE**) VIAL PHIAL
(**AMOUNT OF** —) DOSAGE
(**CHINESE** —) SENSO
(**COLD** —) CONTAC
(**QUACK** —) NOSTRUM
(**SHIP'S** —) LOBLOLLY
(**SYSTEM OF** —) AYURVEDA
(**UNIVERSAL** —) PANACEA
(PL.) GALIANES
(PREF.) IAMATO IATRO PHARMACO

MEDICINE MAN PEAI DOCTOR KAHUNA PIACHE POWWOW SHAMAN SINGER ANGEKOK TOHUNGA CONTRARY POWWOWER

MEDICK SNAIL

MEDIEVAL OLD GOTHIC

MEDIOCRE BUSH HACK MEAN SUCH MEDIUM AVERAGE INFERIOR MIDDLING MODERATE PASSABLE

MEDITATE CAST CHEW MUSE BROOD GLOAT STUDY THINK WEIGH PONDER RECORD BETHINK COMMENT IMAGINE PREPEND REFLECT REVOLVE COGITATE CONSIDER PURPENSE RUMINATE

MEDITATION MOYEN STUDY THINK ZAZEN DHYANA MUSING REVERIE THOUGHT HIGGAION
(**PLACE OF** —) ZENDO

MEDITATIVE MUSING MUSEFUL PENSIVE RUMINANT

MEDITERRANEAN MIDLAND

MEDIUM BATH EVEN LENS MEAN ETHER JUICE MIDST MOYEN ORGAN BALIAN BISTER BISTRE DIGEST MIDDLE MIDWAY ORACLE SLUDGE TEMPER PSYCHIC VEHICLE MEDIOCRE SHOWCASE CONTINUUM
(— **FOR DISCUSSION**) PLATFORM
(— **OF DIVINE REVELATION**) ORACLE
(— **OF EXCHANGE**) CURRENCY
(— **OF EXPRESSION**) VOICE
(— **OF TRANSMISSION**) AIR AIRWAVE
(**CULTURE** —) AGAR STAB BROTH HYRAX SLANT CULTURE BOUILLON
(**ENVELOPING** —) SWATH
(**PAINTING** —) TEMPERA
(**PLANT GROWTH** —) PERLITE
(**REFINING** —) ALEMBIC

MEDIUM, THE (**CHARACTER IN** —) FLORA MONICA
(**COMPOSER OF** —) MENOTTI

MEDLAR MESPIL LAZAROLE

MEDLEY OLIO BABEL REVUE JUMBLE CHIVARI CLANGOR FARRAGO GOULASH MELANGE MIXTURE BROUHAHA KEDGEREE MACARONI MISHMASH RHAPSODY SLAMPAMP VARIORUM CHARIVARI MACEDOINE
(— **OF TUNES**) QUODLIBET

MEDOC WINE LAFITTE

MEDREGAL BONITO

MEDULLA PITH MARROW

MEDULLA OBLONGATA BULB

MEDUSA JELLY QUARL GORGON BLUBBER GERYONID
(**FATHER OF** —) PHORCYS
(**MOTHER OF** —) CETO
(**SLAYER OF** —) PERSEUS
(PL.) BRACT

MEEK LOW DAFT MURE LOWLY GENTLE HUMBLE NEBBISH PACIFIC LAMBLIKE YIELDING

MEEKNESS MANSUETUDE

MEERSCHAUM PIPE GRAVEL KIEFEKIL SEPIOLITE

MEET FIT KEP SEE COPE FACE FILL HENT NOSE ABIDE CLOSE CROSS FRONT GREET INCUR OCCUR PIECE TOUCH ANSWER BATTLE BEMEET COMBAT CONCUR FULFIL INVENT SEMBLE CONTACT CONTEST CONVENE CONVENT COUNCIL FULFILL RUNINTO SATISFY ASSEMBLE CONFRONT CONVERGE GAINCOPE
(— **A BET**) SEE
(— **A NEED**) SUFFICE
(— **AT END**) BUTT
(— **FACE TO FACE**) AFFRONT
(— **FORCIBLY**) SMITE
(— **SQUARELY**) ENVISAGE
(— **VIOLENTLY**) CHECK HURTLE
(— **WITH**) GET SEE BUMP FIND STRIKE
(**ATHLETIC** —) GALA GYMKHANA

MEETING MOD FEIS MOOT CLOSE FORUM SABHA SHINE STOUR SYNOD TRYST ACCESS AUMAGA CAUCUS CHAPEL CLINIC HUDDLE POWWOW SEANCE CABINET CHAPTER COLLEGE CONTACT CONVENT COUNCIL JOLLITY MOOTING OCCURSE REVIVAL SEMINAR SITTING SYNAXIS ASSEMBLY CONGRESS CONSULTA DELEGACY ECCLESIA EXERCISE JUNCTION OSCULANT TERTULIA WARDMOTE CONCOURSE COLLOQUIUM
(— **FULLY ATTENDED**) PLENUM
(— **OF BARDS**) GORSEDD
(— **OF NEIGHBORS**) HUSKING
(— **OF SCHOLARS**) LEVY
(— **OF WITCHES**) ESBAT SABBAT SABBATH
(— **OF WORSHIPERS**) SERVICE
(— **STANDARDS**) FIT
(**ANGLO-SAXON** —) GEMOTE
(**APPOINTED** —) RENDEVOUS
(**ENDWISE** —) ABUTMENT
(**EVENING** —) SOIREE
(**FORBIDDING CLOSED** —S) SUNSHINE
(**GENERAL** —) PRIME
(**NOT** —) PARALLEL
(**POLITICAL** —) CAUCUS
(**PRIVATE** —) CONCLAVE
(**RACE** —) REGATTA
(**SECRET** —) CABAL CONSULT CONCLAVE
(**SOCIAL** —) CLUB JOLLY HORNOR
(**SPORTS** —) GYMKHANA
(**TOWN** —) TUNMOOT

MEETINGHOUSE MORADA

MEETING PLACE AMBALAM CENACLE TINWALD

MEGALOMANIAC MONARCHO

MEGAPHONE VAMPHORN

MEGAPODE MALEO LEIPOA

MEGARA (**FATHER OF** —) CREON
(**HUSBAND OF** —) HERCULES

MEGAREUS (**FATHER OF** —) HIPPOMENES
(**MOTHER OF** —) OENOPE
(**SON OF** —) EUIPPUS
(**WIFE OF** —) IPHINOE

MEGILP GUMPTION

MEGINNING (— **OF ACTIVITY**) DAYONE

MEHETABEL (**HUSBAND OF** —) HADAD
(**MOTHER OF** —) MATRED

MEHIR (**FATHER OF** —) CHELUB

MEHTAR BUNGY BHUNGI

MEHUJAEL (**FATHER OF** —) IRAD

MEIOSIS LITOTES REDUCTION

MEISTERSINGER VON NURNBERG, DI (**CHARACTER IN** —) EVA HANS VEIT DAVID FRITZ SACHS POGNER KOTHNER WALTHER STOLZING MAGDALENE BECKMESSER
(**COMPOSER OF** —) WAGNER

MELAMPUS SEER
(**BROTHER OF** —) BIAS
(**FATHER OF** —) AMYTHAON
(**MOTHER OF** —) IDOMENE
(**SON OF** —) MANTIUS ANTIPHATES
(**WIFE OF** —) LYSIPPE

MELANCHOLIA ATHYMY ATHYMIA SADNESS

MELANCHOLIC HYPPISH

MELANCHOLY WO LOW SAD WOE BLUE DRAM DULL DUMP MARE ADUST BLUES DEARN DOWIE DREAR DUSKY GLOOM SORRY WISHT GLOOMY SOMBER SOMBRE SORROW SPLEEN SULLEN YELLOW CHAGRIN DOLEFUL DUMPISH ELEGIAC SADNESS SPLEENY THOUGHT ATRABILE LIVERISH TRISTFUL

MELANESIAN DOBUAN KANAGA KANAKA EFATESE

MELANGE OLIO GOMBO GUMBO SMORGASBORD

MELANIPPUS (**FATHER OF** —) THESEUS HICETAON
(**LOVER OF** —) COMAETHO
(**MOTHER OF** —) PERIGUNE
(**SON OF** —) IOXUS

MELANISM PHAEISM

MELANTERITE INKSTONE

MELANTIUS (**SISTER OF** —) EVADNE

MELATOPE EYE

MELCHI (**FATHER OF** —) ADDI JANNA

MELCHIAH (**SON OF** —) PASHUR

MELD SET SAMBA SPREAD BOLIVIA DECLARE

MELEA (**FATHER OF** —) MENAN

MELEAGER (**FATHER OF** —) OENEUS
(**MOTHER OF** —) ALTHAEA

MELECH (**FATHER OF** —) MICAH

MELEE BRAWL MEDLEY RUMBLE DOGFIGHT PELLMELL WINGDING

MELIA (**FATHER OF** —) OCEANUS
(**SON OF** —) ISMENUS TENERUS AEGIALEUS PHORONEUS

MELIBOEA (**FATHER OF** —) AMPHION
(**HUSBAND OF** —) NELEUS
(**MOTHER OF** —) NIOBE

MELIORATE MITIGATE

MELISMA JUBILUS

MELL KIRN

MELLIFLUOUS SUGARED HYBLAEAN

MELLOW AGE OMY HAZE LUSH MALM PLUM RICH RIPE SOFT FRUSH RIPEN FLUTED GOLDEN MATURE

MELLOWED BEERY

MELODIOUS SOFT SOOT TUNY SWEET TUNED ARIOSO DULCET MELODIC MUSICAL SIRENIC SONGFUL TUNABLE TUNEFUL CANOROUS CHARMING NUMEROUS SOUNDFUL
(**EXCESSIVELY** —) SIRUPY SYRUPY

MELODRAMA HAM SOAP TANK

MELODY AIR HUM LAY ARIA LILT NOTE TUNE CANTO CHANT CHARM DREAD MELOS MIRTH NIGUN CANTUS CHORAL GHAZEL MONODY NIGGUN STROKE CANZONA CANZONE CHORALE DESCANT HARMONY MEASURE MELISMA PLANXTY ROSALIA CARILLON CAVATINA DIAPASON VOCALISE
(— **COMPASS**) AMBITUS
(**MOURNFUL** —) DUMP
(**PASTORAL** —) MUSETTE
(**SIMPLE** —) PLAINSONG
(**SYNAGOGAL** —S) CHAZANUT HAZANUTH

MELON PEPO GOURD MANGO CASABA CITRON DUDAIM

MAYCOCK CUCURBIT HONEYDEW PEPONIDA PEPONIUM
(KIND OF —) CRANSHAW CRENSHAW
MELT FLY RIN RUN BLOW FADE FLOW FLUX FUSE THAW DEICE FOUND LEACH SMELT SWEAL SWELT TOUCH GUTTER RELENT SOFTEN DISTILL FORMELT RESOLVE DISCANDY DISSOLVE ELIQUATE COLLIQUATE
(— AWAY) SWEAL
(— DOWN) RENDER
(— IRREGULARLY) DROZE
MELTED RUN FONDU FUSED FUSILE
MELTING SOFT FUSILE FUSION
MELTWATER OUTWASH
MELVILLE (BOOK BY —) OMOO
MEMBER LIMB LITH PART BRANCH FELLOW FILLET GIRDER SOCIUS AMANIST COMPART ERANIST FAIRING ALBRIGHT AULARIAN BRIDLING
(— OF ANSAR) HELPER
(— OF BALLET) FIGURANT
(— OF BAND) SIDEMAN
(— OF BODYGUARD) HUSCARL
(— OF BROTHERHOOD) ESSENE SENUSSI
(— OF CHURCH) BROTHER PARISHIONER
(— OF CLAN) CHILD CALEBITE
(— OF CLERGY) DEFENSOR
(— OF COAST GUARD) SPAR
(— OF COUNCIL) CONSUL HEEMRAAD
(— OF COURT) DICAST EPHETE
(— OF CREW) HAND IDLER LAYER DRIVER STROKE BOWSMAN FORETOP BRAKEMAN SHAREMAN
(— OF CULT) ANGEL AMIDIST
(— OF FACULTY) COUNSEL LECTURER
(— OF FAMILY) FETII
(— OF FRATERNAL ORDER) ELK SHRINER FORESTER KIWANIAN
(— OF FRATERNITY) GREEK
(— OF FRENCH ACADEMY) IMMORTAL
(— OF GANG) HENCHMAN
(— OF GENTRY) SEIGNEUR
(— OF GIRL SCOUTS) BROWNIE
(— OF GREEK ARMY) EVZONE
(— OF GUILD) COMACINE HOASTMAN
(— OF HOUSEHOLD) FAMILIAR
(— OF HUNTING PARTY) STANDER
(— OF INN OF COURT) ANCIENT BENCHER
(— OF IRISH REPUBLICAN ARMY) PROVO
(— OF ITALIAN ARMY) ALPINO
(— OF KNOW-NOTHING PARTY) SAM
(— OF LEGISLATURE) SOLON DEPUTY DELEGATE
(— OF LITERARY GROUP) FELIBRE
(— OF LOWEST CLASS) LUMPEN
(— OF MIDDLE CLASS) BURGHER
(— OF PARLIAMENT) CONTENT THINGMAN
(— OF PRIMROSE LEAGUE) KNIGHT
(— OF RELIGIOUS ORDER) DAME

FRIAR EUDIST FRAILE FRATER HERMIT JESUIT SISTER ALEXIAN BEGUINE BRINSER DERVISH HUSSITE SEPARTE SERVANT SERVITE CENOBITE EXORCIST HUMANIST PENITENT SALESIAN THEATINE
(— OF RETINUE) SEQUEL SEQUENT
(— OF RUSSIAN ARISTOCRACY) BOIAR BOYAR BOYARD
(— OF SAME GENUS) CONGENER
(— OF SECRET ORGANIZATION) DEMOLAY
(— OF SECRET SOCIETY) BOXER DANITE
(— OF SECT) BABI SHIA BABEE DRUSE HASID KHOJA SHIAH AUDIAN BEREAN BRAHMO CATHAR DIPPER DOPPER IBADHI JUMPER KHLYST SHIITE SMARTA WAHABI AISSAWA AJIVIKA AUDAEAN CAINITE CHASSID DREAMER EMPIRIC EUCHITE IBADITE ISAWIYA ISMAILI RAPPIST SENUSSI SEVENER AQUARIAN CALIXTIN DARBYITE DUKHOBOR EBIONITE FAMILIST GLASSITE LABADIST MANDAEAN SADDUCEE SEVERIAN SHAFIITE SIMONIAN STUNDIST
(— OF STAFF) ATTACHE
(— OF STATE) CITIZEN
(— OF STOCK EXCHANGE) BOARDMAN
(— OF TEAM) SPARE BOBBER KICKER
(— OF TRIBE) LEVITE JUDAHITE LAMANITE
(— OF UPPER CLASS) EFFENDI
(— OF VARNA) SUDRA SHUDRA
(— OF WHITE RACE) HAOLE
(— OF WINDOW) APRON
(— OF YOUTH GANG) HOMEBOY
(—S OF CLASS) FRY
(—S OF PROFESSION) FACULTY
(—S OF SECT) SKOPTSY
(—S OF TRIBUNAL) ACUERDO
(ARCHITECTURAL —) FAN ARCH FLAT SILL SPAN GABLE SOCLE STILE STILT CORBEL FASCIA CONSOLE CORNICE
(CHURCH —) GREEK LATIN DANITE DUNKER KIRKER TUNKER AZYMITE BAPTIST BEGHARD BROTHER DUNKARD KIRKMAN SECEDER ARMENIAN BRYANITE CATHOLIC DISCIPLE DOWIEITE JACOBITE
(CHURCH —S) FAITHFUL
(EVERY —) ALL
(FEEBLEST —) WRIG
(FULL —) GREMIAL
(OLDEST —) FATHER
(OVERHANGING —) BRACKET
(POLITICAL —) CADET ENDEK SHIRT GUELPH HUNKER LEADER APRISTA LEFTIST LIBERAL ABHORRER BUCKTAIL DEMOCRAT HERODIAN LABORITE
(PROJECTING —) TENON
(SECRET —) CRYPTO
(SENIOR —) DOYEN
(TENSION —) HANGER
(TERMINAL —) TOE
(SUFF.) AD CRAT

(— OF A CLASS) ANDER MER(E)(IC) (IS)(OUS)(Y)
MEMBERS
(SUFF.)
(— OF THE FAMILY) IDAE
(— OF THE SUBFAMILY OF) INAE
MEMBERSHIP SEAT GARTER GUILDRY
MEMBRANE RIM WEB CAUL COAT DURA FELL HEAD TELA GALEA HYMEN VELUM AMNION AMNIOS EXTINE INTINE MENINX MOTHER MUCOSA PLEURA RETINA SEPTUM SEROSA TIMBAL TUNICA TYMPAN BLANKET CAPSULE CHORION CHOROID CUTICLE DECIDUA EPICYTE HYALOID OOLEMMA PERIOST PUTAMEN STRATUM VELAMEN ECTODERM ENDOCYST ENVELOPE EPENDYMA EPISPORE EXOLEMMA INDUSIUM INTEXINE LABELLUM PATAGIUM PELLICLE STRIFFEN ALLANTOIS PERIPLAST PERIOSTEUM PERITONEUM
(— OF BRAIN) MATER
(— OF EGG) POTAMEN
(— OF EYE) SCLERA SCLEROTIC
(— OF GRAIN) INTINE
(— OF ORANGE) ZEST
(NICTITATING —) HAW
(TYMPANIC —) TYMPAN MYRINGA DRUMHEAD DRUMSKIN
(PL.) ADNEXA ANNEXA MENINGES
(PREF.) CHORI(O) HYMEN(O) MENING(O) MYRINGO VEL(I)
(SUFF.) YMENITIS
MEMBRANOUS HUSKY SKINNY HYMENOID SCARIOSE SCARIOUS
MEMENTO RELIC TOKEN MEMORY TROPHY KEEPSAKE REMINDER SOUVENIR
MEMINNA PEESOREH
MEMNON (FATHER OF —) TITHONUS
(MOTHER OF —) AURORA
(SLAYER OF —) ACHILLES
MEMOIR ELOGE RECORD HISTORY MEMORIAL
MEMORABLE GRAND SIGNAL CLASSIC NOTABLE MEMORIAL NAMEABLE NOTEWORTHY
MEMORANDA (SET OF —) TICKLER
MEMORANDUM BILL CHIT MEMO NOTE SLIP BRIEF JURAT CAHIER CIPHER DOCKET MEMOIR MINUTE TICKET JOTTING MEMORIAL NOTANDUM PROTOCOL BORDEREAU DIRECTIVE
MEMORIAL AHU AGALMA CAHIER FACTUM MEMOIR MEMORY RECORD TROPHY DENKMAL MEMENTO MENTION EBENEZER MONUMENT REMEMBRANCE
MEMORIZE LEARN MANDATE REMEMBER
MEMORY MIND EPROM HEART IMAGE STORE RECALL RECORD MEMENTO STORAGE MEMORIAL SOUVENIR
(— CHIP) DRAM
(— ON COMPUTER CHIP) RAM ROM
(— SUBDIVISION) PAGE
(BAD —) FORGETTERY

(COMPUTER —) RAM ROM PAGE CACHE STACK SCRATCHPAD
(MECHANICAL —) ROTE
(OF POOR —) FLUFFY
(PAINFUL —) SCAR
(PROGRAMMABLE —) EPROM
(SMALL COMPUTER —) SCRATCHPAD
(STORED COMPUTER —) FIRMWARE
(PREF.) MNEM(I)(O)
(SUFF.) MNESIA(C) MNESIS MNETIC
MEN THEY ORANG INNUIT MANHEAD MANHOOD MANKIND MENFOLK HUMANITY
(BLESSED —) BEATI
MENACE BOAST IMPEND THREAT BOGEYMAN MINATORY THREATEN
MENACING STOUT SURLY FIERCE TOWARD MINATORY MINACIOUS
MENAHEM (FATHER OF —) GADI
(VICTIM OF —) SHALLUM
MEN-AT-ARMS CHIVALRY
MEND DO FIX BEET DARN HEAL HELP KNIT STOP TINK AMEND CLOUT EMEND GRAFT MOISE PATCH COBBLE DOCTOR FETTLE RANTER REFORM REPAIR SOLDER SPETCH TINKLE IMPROVE INWEAVE REDRESS RIGHTLE
(— BY ADDING FEATHERS) IMP
(— CLUMSILY) BOTCH
(— MEN'S CLOTHES) BUSHEL
MENDACIOUS FALSE DISHONEST
MENDACITY LYING DECEIT FALSITY UNTRUTH
MENDER TINKER KETTLER BEATSTER
MENDICANCY BEGGARY
MENDICANT NAGA DANDI FAKIR FRIAR UDASI BEGGAR BHIKKU FAKEER FRATER GOSAIN AJIVIKA BAIRAGI EUCHITE VAIRAGI PANDARAM SANNYASI PASSIONIST
MENDING COBBLE
MENEL NELL
MENELAUS (BROTHER OF —) AGAMEMNON
(FATHER OF —) ATREUS PLISTHENES
(MOTHER OF —) AEROPE
(SISTER OF —) ANAXIBIA
(WIFE OF —) HELEN
MENHADEN POGY PORGY BUNKER CHEBOG SHINER ALEWIFE BUGFISH BUGHEAD CLUPEID ELLFISH FATBACK OLDWIFE SAVELHA SHADINE WHITING BONYFISH HARDHEAD
MENHIR BOUTA GORSEDD PEULVAN CATSTONE HAGIOLITH
MENIAL FAG BASE LOON PAGE KNAVE DRIVEL HARLOT POTBOY VARLET SERVILE SLAVISH BANAUSIC SCULLION SERVITOR
MENILITE OPAL
MENISCOID CRESCENT
MENNONITE HOOKER AMISHMAN AMMANITE HUTERITE
MENOETIUS (BROTHER OF —) ATLAS PROMETHEUS
(FATHER OF —) ACTOR

(MOTHER OF —) AEGINA
(SON OF —) PATROCLUS
MENOPAUSE CLIMAX
MENSTRUATE FLOW
MENSTRUATING SICK
MENSTRUATION FLOW CURSE
FLUOR CRAMPS PERIOD COURSES
(FIRST —) MENARCHE
(PREF.) MENO
(SUFF.) (— CONDITION) MENIA
MENSTRUUM SOLVENT
MENTAL IDEAL GENIAL INWARD
MINDLY PHRENIC PSYCHIC
CEREBRAL
MENTALITY MIND SENSE ACUMEN
REASON SPIRIT PSYCHISM
MENTHA LABIATE
MENTHANE TERPANE
MENTHOL CAMPHOR
MENTION CALL CITE HINT MIND
MING MINT NAME CHEEP CLEPE
SPEAK TOUCH MEMBER NOTICE
SPEECH MEANING SPECIFY
SUGGEST CITATION INSTANCE
MEMORATE REHEARSE
REMEMBER REFERENCE
REPETITION
(— BY NAME) NEMN NEMME
NEMPNE
(— CASUALLY) DROP
(— FIRST) PROMISE
(— PUBLICLY) PLUG
(HONORABLE —) ACCESSIT
MENTOR GURU TEACHER CICERONE
MENTUM PERULA
MENU CARD CARTE
(COMPUTER —) DISPLAY
MEONOTHAI (FATHER OF —)
OTHNIEL
MEPACRINE ATABRIN ATABRINE
MEPERIDINE DEMEROL
MEPHIBOSHETH (BROTHER OF —)
ARMONI
(FATHER OF —) SAUL JONATHAN
(MOTHER OF —) RIZPAH
(SON OF —) MICHA
MEPHISTOPHELIAN SATANIC
MEPROBAMATE MILTOWN
MERAB (FATHER OF —) SAUL
(HUSBAND OF —) ADRIEL
MERARI (FATHER OF —) LEVI
MERCAPTAN THIOL
MERCEDARIAN NOLASCAN
RANSOMER
MERCENARY HACK VENAL JACKAL
HESSIAN PINDARI HIRELING
WAGELING
MERCER SILKMAN
MERCERIZE SCHREINER
MERCHANDISE LINE CARGO CHEAP
GOODS STUFF WARES ARTWARE
CHAFFER SHIPPER TRAFFIC
CHAFFERY SALEWARE
(CHEAP SHODDY —) BORAX
(RETURNED —) COMEBACK
MERCHANT ARAB SETH SETT TELI
WALLA BADGER BANIAN DEALER
FACTOR KITELY NEPMAN RETAIL
SELLER TAIPAN TRADER ANTONIO
CHAPMAN GOLADAR HANSARD
HOWADJI CHANDLER HUCKSTER
MARCHAND POVINDAH
SOUDAGAR STOREMAN

(COAL —) HOASTMAN
(GRAIN —) LAMBADI
(GREAT —) TAIPAN
(HINDU —) BUNIA BUNNIA
(WINE —) VINTNER
**MERCHANT OF VENICE (AUTHOR
OF —)** SHAKESPEARE
(CHARACTER IN —) GOBBO TUBAL
PORTIA ANTONIO JESSICA LORENZO
NERISSA SALANIO SALERIO
SHYLOCK BASSANIO GRATIANO
LEONARDO SALARINO STEPHANO
BALTHASAR LAUNCELOT
MERCIFUL KIND MILD HUMANE
RUEFUL TENDER CLEMENT
LENIENT MILDFUL PITIFUL
SPARING GRACIOUS QUEMEFUL
MERCILESS GRIM CRUEL SHARP
BLOODY FIERCE SAVAGE WANTON
PITILESS
MERCURY HG AZOCH AZOTH
DRAGON HERMES SPIRIT CHIBRIT
MARKERY TEUTATES QUICKSILVER
(FATHER OF —) JUPITER
(MOTHER OF —) MAIA
MERCY LAW ORE HORE PITY RUTH
GRACE GRITH BLITHE LENITY
CHARITY QUARTER CLEMENCY
LENIENCY COMPASSION
(— TO ANTAGONIST) QUARTER
(PREF.) MISERI
MERE BARE NUDE ONLY PURE PUTE
SOLE VERY NAKED SHEER SINGLE
(PREF.) PSIL(O)
MEREL PIN
MERELY BUT JUST ONLY BARELY
PURELY SIMPLY SINGLY SOLELY
ALONELY UTTERLY ENTIRELY
SCARCELY
MEREMOTH (FATHER OF —) BANI
URIAH
MERETRICIOUS CHEAP GAUDY
GILDED TAWDRY PUNKISH
MERGANSER SMEE SMEW HARLE
SNOWL SPIKE HERALD SAWNEB
WEASER BRACKET GARBILL
JACKSAW RANTOCK SAWBILL
TADPOLE TOWHEAD TWEEZER
WHEEZER EARLDUCK MOSSHEAD
SHELDRAKE
MERGE FUSE JOIN MELD SINK
BLEND ENTER GLIDE UNIFY UNITE
VERGE MINGLE COALESCE
COMMERGE CONFLATE LIQUESCE
MERGING BLEND FUSION
MERICARP COCCUS
**MERIDIAN (THOSE LIVING UNDER
SAME —)** ANTOECI
MERIDIONAL NOON NOONTIDE
MERINGUE KISS
MERINO DELAINE
MERISTEM PERIBLEM
MERIT DUE EARN MEED PUNY
BROOK FOUND THANK WORTH
DESERT PRAISE VIRTUE WRIHTE
DEMERIT DESERVE PUDDING
(— CONSIDERATION) COUNT
(POSSESSING —) WORTHY
MERITED JUST
(NOT —) INDIGN
MERITOCRACY ELITE
MERITORIOUS CAPITAL MERITORY
THANKFUL VALOROUS

MERL BLACKIE
MERLIN (MISTRESS OF —) VIVIAN
VIVIEN
MERLON COP
MERMAID ARIEL NIXIE SIREN
MERROW MERWOMAN
MERMAN SEAMAN MANFISH
MERODACH (FATHER OF —) EA
(WIFE OF —) ZARPANIT
MEROPE (BROTHER OF —)
PHAETHON
(FATHER OF —) ATLAS OENOPION
PANDAREUS CRESPHONTES
(HUSBAND OF —) POLYBUS
SISYPHUS POLYPHONTES
(MOTHER OF —) PLEIONE
CYPSELUS HARMOTHOE
(SISTER OF —) AEDON CLEOTHERA
(SON OF —) AEPYTUS
MEROPODITE FEMUR MEROS
MEROZOITE AGAMETE
MERRILY GAILY GAMELY LIGHTLY
LUSTICK JOYOUSLY
MERRIMENT FUN JOY GALE GLEE
JEST UTAS DERAY MIRTH FROLIC
SPLEEN DAFFERY DAFFING
FESTIVE JOLLITY WAGGERY
HILARITY
MERRY GAY BOON CANT GLAD
GOLE BONNY BUXOM CADGY
CRANK DROLL JOLLY LIGHT LUSTY
MURRY SUNNY VOGIE VOKIE
BLITHE COCKET FROLIC JOCANT
JOCOSE JOCUND JOVIAL JOYOUS
LIVELY FEASTLY GLEEFUL HOLIDAY
JOCULAR LUSTICK RAFFING
WINSOME CHIRPING DISPOSED
FESTIVAL GAMESOME GLEESOME
LAUGHING PLEASANT SPANKING
SPORTFUL SPORTIVE CONVIVIAL
(RIOTOUSLY —) SATURNALIAN
(UNREASONABLY —) DAFT
MERRY-ANDREW AIRY ZANY ANTIC
DROLL JESTER BUFFOON
MERRY-GO-ROUND CAROUSEL
TURNABOUT ROUNDABOUT
MERRYMAKING ALE MAY RAG KIRN
PLOY REVEL GAIETY JUNKET
RACKET SPLORE WHOOPEE
CARNIVAL FESTIVITY
MERRYTHOUGHT WISHBONE
MERRY WIDOW (CHARACTER IN —)
ZETA HANNA MIRKO DANILO
GLAWARI
(COMPOSER OF —) LEHAR
MERRY WIVES OF WINDSOR
(AUTHOR OF —) SHAKESPEARE
(CHARACTER IN —) NYM ANNE
FORD HUGH JOHN PAGE CAIUS
EVANS ROBIN RUGBY FENTON
PISTOL SIMPLE QUICKLY SHALLOW
SLENDER WILLIAM BARDOLPH
FALSTAFF
MERUS PALM
MESA HILL LOMA BENCH MESILLA
PLATEAU TERRACE CARTOUCH
MESADENIA CACALIA
MESCAL PEYOTE PEYOTL WOKOWI
MEXICAL CHALLOTE
MESCALERO FARAON
MESECH (FATHER OF —) JAPHET
MESENTERY CROW RUFFLE
MESH NET MASK MOKE CHAIN

PITCH SHALE ACCRUE ENGAGE
MASCLE SCREEN INTERLOCK
SCREENING
(— IMPROPERLY) BUTT
(IN —) DIRECT
MESHA (FATHER OF —) CALEB
SHAHARAIM
(MOTHER OF —) HODESH
MESHED ENGAGED
MESHEZABEEL (FATHER OF —)
ZERAH
(SON OF —) PETHAHIAH
MESHILLEMOTH (FATHER OF —)
IMMER
MESHULLAM (FATHER OF —)
BERECHIAH BESODEIAH
ZERUBBABEL
(SON OF —) SALLU
MESHULLEMETH (FATHER OF —)
HARUZ
(HUSBAND OF —) MANASSEH
(SON OF —) AMON
MESOCARP FLESH
MESOMORPHIC SOMAL SOMATIC
ATHLETIC
MESON RHO KAON MUON PION
OMEGA BARYTRON MESOTRON
MESOPODIUM PETIOLE
MESOPOTAMIA (— REGION)
SUMER
(TREE OF —) HOMA
MESOTONIC TERTIAN MEANTONE
MESQUITE HONEY KEAWE PACAY
CASHAW ALGAROBA HONEYPOD
IRONWOOD MOSQUITO
MESS JAG JAM MIX MUX PIE SOP
CLAT FIST HASH JAMB MUCK
MULL MUSS SLUB SOSS STEW
SUSS BOTCH CAUCH JAKES STREW
SWILL BOLLIX BUNGLE CADDLE
CLATCH JUMBLE MUCKER PICKLE
PUDDLE SOZZLE TUMBLE
EYESORE MAMMOCK MULLOCK
SCAMBLE SLOTTER COUSCOUS
DISORDER LOBLOLLY SHAMBLES
SLAISTER
(— AROUND) JUKE
(— OF FOOD) SAND
(— OVER) ABUSE
(GREASY —) GAUM
(SLOPPY —) SLOBBER SLAISTER
(WATERY —) SLOSH
MESSAGE CHIT MODE SAND SEND
WIRE WORD RUMOR TELEX
BREVET CIPHER ERRAND GOSPEL
LETTER SCROLL BLINKER
BODWORD DEPECHE EMBASSY
MISSION SENDING TIDINGS
AEROGRAM CREDENCE DISPATCH
GRAFFITO MAILGRAM VOICEMAIL
(— BY FLAGS) HOIST
(— FROM GOD) ANGEL
(CHRISTIAN —) EVANGEL
(CIPHER —) SCYTALE
(COMPLIMENTARY —) RECADO
(INDICATING — IS RECEIVED)
WILCO
(SECRET —) PRIVATE
(SEND —) TELEX
(SEQUENCE OF —S) QUEUE
MESSALIAN EUCHITE
MESSENE (FATHER OF —) TRIOPAS
(HUSBAND OF —) POLYCAON

MESSENGER BODE PEON POST SAND SEND TOTY VAUX ANGEL ENVOY MUMMU VISOR BEADLE BROKER BUNENE CHIAUS HERALD LEGATE NUNCIO PIGEON RUNNER APOSTLE CARRIER CASHBOY CONTACT COURANT COURIER EXPRESS FORAGER FORAYER MALACHI MERCURY MESSAGE MISSIVE NAMTARU PATAMAR TOTYMAN TROTTER TRUMPET EMISSARY FOREGOER HIRCARRA LOBBYGOW NUNCIATE ORDINARY PORTATOR APPARITOR
(— OF APSU AND TIAMAT) MUMMU
(— OF GOD) ANGEL
(— OF SHAMASH) BUNENE
(— OF THE GODS) HERMES MERCURY
(MOUNTED —) COSSID ESTAFET
(RELIGIOUS —) APOSTLE
(UNDERWORLD —) NAMTARU
MESSIAH CHRIST WOVOKA
(MUSLIM —) MAHDI
MESSINESS YUCK
MESSMATE YUBA
MESSUAGE HAW TOFT MEESE MIDSTEAD
MESSY GOOEY SLOPPY SOZZLY STICKY
MESTIZO CHOLO LADINO CURIBOCA MAMELUCO
MESTOR (DAUGHTER OF —) HIPPOTHOE
(FATHER OF —) PERSEUS
(MOTHER OF —) ANDROMEDA
(WIFE OF —) LYSIDICE
METAL ORE TIN BODY DIET GOLD IRON LEAD ZINC BARIUM CESIUM CHROME COBALT COPPER INDIUM LATTIN NICKEL ORMOLU OSMIUM RADIUM SILVER SODIUM BISMUTH CADMIUM CALCIUM HAFNIUM IRIDIUM LITHIUM MERCURY RHENIUM RHODIUM THORIUM TUTANIA URANIUM YTTRIUM ALUMINUM ANTIMONY CHROMIUM DEADHEAD PLATINUM RUBIDIUM SCANDIUM TANTALUM TINCTURE TITANIUM TUNGSTEN VANADIUM
(— IN MASS) BULLION
(— IN PLATES) LATTEN
(— IN SHEETS) LEAF PLATE
(— STRIP) SPLINE
(BABBITT —) LINING
(BASE —) BILLON
(COARSE —) MATTE
(DECORATED —) TOLE
(GROUND —) BRONZING
(HEAVIEST —) OSMIUM
(IMPURE MASS OF —) REGULUS
(LIGHTEST —) LITHIUM
(LIQUID —) MERCURY
(MASS OF —) INGOT
(MOLTEN —) TAP SQUIRT
(OLD POT —) POTIN
(ORNAMENTED —) NIELLO
(PERFORATED —) STENCIL
(PIECE OF CRUDE —) SLUG
(POINTED —) NAIL
(POROUS —) SPONGE

(PRECIOUS —) ORE GOLD PLATE SILVER PLATINUM
(SEMIFINISHED —) SEMIS
(SHEET —) LATTEN DOUBLES KALAMEIN
(TYPE —) QUAD QUADRAT
(UNREFINED —) PIGIRON
(WASTE —) GATE SPRUE
METALLIC HARD THIN TINNY
METALLOPHONE SARON
(BALINESE —) GANGSA
METALLURGIST AMERICAN HUNT HOLLEY PETERS SHIMER
ENGLISH PERCY MUSHET THOMAS HADFIELD
FRENCH HEROULT
METALOPHONE (BALINESE —) GANGSA
METALWARE TOLE LORMERY GRAYWARE PONTYPOOL
METALWORK ZOGAN
METALWORKER BARMAN FOONER FORKMAN FOUNDER SUDSMAN
METAMERE SOMITE SEGMENT MEROSOME
METAMERIC SEGMENTAL
METAMORPHIC
(PREF.) BLAST(O)
METAMORPHOSE TURN SHAPE INDENIZE TRANSMEW
METAMORPHOSIS METABOLE PETALODY PHYLLODY SEPALODY
(SUFF.) ODY
METANIRA (HUSBAND OF —) CELEUS
(SON OF —) DEMOPHON TRIPTOLEMUS
METAPHOR IMAGE TROPE FIGURE KENNING
METAPHORICAL FIGURAL FIGURATE TROPICAL
METASTOMA LABIUM
METATE QUERL
METE DEAL DOLE GIVE ALLOT AWARD MATCH SERVE MEASURE APPORTION
METEMPSYCHOSIS SAMSARA
METEOR STAR ARGID CETID COMID DRAKE LUPID LYRID URSID ANTLID AUGUST BOLIDE BOOTID CORVID CYGNID DRAGON HYDRID LEONID LIBRID LYNCID LYRAID PHASMA PISCID TAURID AQUARID AQUILID ARIETID AURIGID CAMELID CANCRID CEPHEID CORONID GEMINID MEATURE ORIONID PEGASID PERSEID POLARID PRODIGY COLUMBID CRATERID DRACONID ERIDANID FIREBALL FORNAXID HERCULID LACERTID SAGITTID SCORPIID SHOTSTAR TOUCANID VIRGINID
(SUFF.) ID
METEORITE BAETYL BOLIDE ANDRITE ATAXITE EUCRITE AEROLITE AEROLITH BAETULUS BAETYLUS IREOLITE SIDERITE SKYSTONE
METEOROLOGIST AMERICAN EDDY ESPY WARD ROTCH FERREL MARVIN CLAYTON REDFIELD CARPENTER
AUSTRIAN FALB HANN PERNTER

ENGLISH REID SHAW DINES GALTON GLAISHER
FRENCH MOREUX PELTIER
GERMAN DOVE FICKER WEGENER BRUCKNER NEUMAYER
NORWEGIAN MOHN SVERDRUP
RUSSIAN TILLO
SCOTTISH MILL BUCHAN
SWEDISH MALMGREN
SWISS WILD DELUC
METEOROLOGY AEROLOGY
METER IONIC METRE SEVEN ALCAIC RHYTHM CADENCE GAYATRI MEASURE SUBMETER VIAMETER YAWMETER
(CUBIC —) STERE
(MILLIONTH OF —) MICRON
(NETHERLANDS —) ELL
(SQUARE —) ARE CENTIARE
(VEDIC —) GAYATRI
(10,000 —S) GREX
(10 CUBIC —S) DEKASTERE
METHADONE AMIDONE
METHANE FORMENE
METHANOL WOODINE CARBINOL
METHAQUALINE QUAALUDE
METHEGLIN MEAD
METHOD ART WAY DART FORM GARB GATE KINK LINE MIDS MODE REDE RULE SORT ORDER STYLE TRACK USAGE COURSE ENGINE MANNER STEREO SYSTEM FASHION PROCESS TACTICS WRINKLE ADJUVANT STANDARD
(— OF ANGLING) HARLING
(— OF APPEALING) DHARNA DHURNA
(— OF COLORING TEA) FACING
(— OF CONSTRUCTION) JACAL
(— OF CULTIVATION) JUM JOOM STUMPING
(— OF DIETING) BANTING
(— OF DISTILLATION) DESCENT
(— OF ELECTION) SCRUTINY
(— OF FATTENING POULTRY) GAVAGE
(— OF INDUCTION) CANON
(— OF INSTRUCTION) SCHOOL
(— OF INVESTIGATION) ORGANON ORGANUM
(— OF MILKING) NIEVLING
(— OF MURAL DECORATION) KHASI
(— OF PROCEDURE) GAME
(— OF SELECTING POPE) SCRUTINY
(— OF TRACKING) DOVAP
(— OF TREATMENT) SCOPE
(CLEVER —) KINK KINKLE
(FIXED —) FORMULA
(MEDICAL —) CUSHION
(OUTMODED —) ARCHAISM
(PAINTING —) GOUACHE
(PRINTING —) AQUATONE
(SCIENTIFIC —) BACONISM
(SURVEYING —) STADIA
(USUAL —) COURSE PRACTICE
METHODICAL TRIG EXACT FORMAL SEVERE ORDERLY REGULAR ORDINARY ORDINATE
METHODIST JUMPER WESLEYAN SWADDLING
METHODIZE ORDER REGULATE

METHODOLOGY TECHNIC
METHUSAEL (FATHER OF —) MEHUJAEL
(SON OF —) LAMECH
METHUSELAH (FATHER OF —) ENOCH
METHYLAL FORMAL
METICULOUS FUSSY NARROW STICKY CAREFUL FINICAL FINICKY PARTICULAR
METION (BROTHER OF —) CECROPS
(FATHER OF —) ERECHTHEUS
(MOTHER OF —) PRAXITHEA
METONYM SYNONYM
METRICAL MEASURED
(— QUANTITY) MATRA
METRICS PROSODY
METRONOME (PART OF —) BOX KEY CASE PIVOT SCALE SHAFT WEIGHT PENDULUM
METROPOLIS CITY SEAT CAPITAL
METROPOLITAN EPARCH EXARCH
METTLE PITH SAUL PRIDE SPUNK GINGER SPIRIT COURAGE SMEDDUM
METTLESOME FIERY PROUD SKEIGH SPUNKY STUFFY FLIGHTY GINGERY SPIRITED
MEUSE
(PREF.)
(RIVER —) MOSA
MEW PEN WOW CAGE CAST COOP GULL MEWL MOLT SHED MEUTE MIAOU MIAOW SEAGULL HIDEAWAY INTERMEW SEEDBIRD CONFINEMENT
MEWER WRAWLER
MEWL WRAWL
MEWS ALLEY COURT STREET STABLES
MEXICAN AZTEC
(AMERICAN OF — DESCENT) CHICANO
MEXICAN-AMERICAN PACHUCO
MEXICAN ELM MEZCAL
MEXICAN ONYX TECALI
MEXICAN PERSIMMON CHAPOTE
MEXICAN POPPY ARGEMONE
MEXICAN TEA BASOTE APASOTE FISHWEED WORMSEED

MEXICO
CAPITAL: MEXICOCITY
COIN: PESO TLAC ADOBE CLACO TLACO AZTECA CENTAVO PIASTER
LAKE: CHAPALA
MEASURE: PIE VARA ALMUD BARIL JARRA LABOR LEGUA LINEA SITIO FANEGA PULGADA
MOUNTAIN: BUFA BLANCO CUPULA PEROTE ORIZABA
PENINSULA: BAJA YUCATAN
PEOPLE: MAM CHOL CORA MAYA MIXE PIMA SERI TECO XOVA AZTEC NAHUA OPATA OTOMI ZOQUE EUDEVE MIXTEC TOLTEC NAYARIT TEPANEC TOTONAC ZACATEC ZAPOTEC TEZCUCAN TOTONACO ZACATECO
RIVER: BRAVO LERMA BALSAS GRANDE PANUCO TABASCO GRIJALVA SANTIAGO
STATE: LEON NUEVO COLIMA

OAXACA SONORA CHIAPAS
DURANGO HIDALGO NAYARIT
SINALOA TABASCO YUCATAN
CAMPECHE QUINTANA VERACRUZ
TOWN: LEON LAPAZ TEPIC ARIZPE
COLIMA JALAPA JUAREZ MERIDA
OAXACA PARRAL POTOSI PUEBLA
CANANEA DURANGO GUAYMAS
MORELIA ORIZABA PACHUCA
TAMPICO TORREON CULIACAN
ENSENADA MAZATLAN
MONCLOVA SALTILLO TLAXCALA
VERACRUZ
VOLCANO: COLIMA TOLUCA
JORULLO PARICUTIN
POPOCATEPETL
WEIGHT: BAG ONZA CARGA LIBRA
MARCO ADARME ARROBA
OCHAVA TERCIO QUINTAL

MEZAHAB (DAUGHTER OF —)
MATRED
MEZEREON DAPHNE
MEZZANINE ENTRESOL
MIAO HMONG
MIAROLITIC DRUSY
MIASMA REEK MALARIA MAREMMA
MIB MIGGLE
MIBSAM (FATHER OF —) SIMEON
ISHMAEL
MICA DAZE TALC GLIST SLUDE
BIOTITE GLIMMER ALURGITE
FUCHSITE PHENGITE MUSCOVITE
PHLOGOPITE
MICAH (FATHER OF —) UZZIEL
MERIBBAAL
(SON OF —) ABDON
MICAH CLARKE (AUTHOR OF —)
DOYLE
(CHARACTER IN —) JACOB MICAH
SAXON CLANCY CLARKE GERVAS
JOSEPH REUBEN DECIMUS
STEPHEN LOCKARBY MONMOUTH
TIMEWELL
MICAIAH (FATHER OF —) IMLAH
MICE (BREEDING PLACE FOR —)
MURARIUM
MICHA (FATHER OF —)
MEPHIBOSHETH
(SON OF —) MATTANIAH
MICHAEL MIKE MICKY MICHEL
MIGUEL
(FATHER OF —) IZRAHIAH
JEHOSHAPHAT
(SLAYER OF —) JEHORAM
(SON OF —) OMRI SETHUR
MICHAH (FATHER OF —) UZZIEL
MICHAIAH (FATHER OF —) URIEL
GEMARIAH
(HUSBAND OF —) REHOBOAM
(SON OF —) ABIJAH
MICHAL (FATHER OF —) SAUL
(HUSBAND OF —) DAVID PHALTI

MICHIGAN
BAY: SAGINAW THUNDER
KEWEENAW STURGEON
CAPITAL: LANSING
COLLEGE: ALMA WAYNE ADRIAN
ALBION CALVIN OLIVET OWOSSO
OAKLAND
COUNTY: BAY CASS IRON LUCE
CLARE DELTA IONIA IOSCO
ALCONA OCEANA OGEMAW
OSCODA OTSEGO GOGEBIC
OSCEOLA TUSCOLA KALKASKA
INDIAN: OTTAWA
LAKE: BURT TORCH HOUGHTON
MOUNTAIN: CURWOOD
NATIVE: WOLVERINE
NICKNAME: LAKE WOLVERINE
RIVER: CASS BRULE HURON
DETROIT SAGINAW STCLAIR
ESCANABA MONTREAL
MENOMINEE
STATE BIRD: ROBIN
STATE FLOWER: APPLEBLOSSOM
STRAIT: MACKINAC
TOWN: MIO ALMA CARO HART
FLINT IONIA LANSE ADRIAN
ALPENA BADAXE OWOSSO
PAWPAW WARREN DETROIT
LANSING LIVONIA PONTIAC
SAGINAW ANNARBOR CADILLAC
ESCANABA KALKASKA MANISTEE
MUNISING MUSKEGON
CHEBOYGAN KALAMAZOO

MICIPSA (FATHER OF —) MASINISSA
MICONIA TAMONEA
MICOPLASMA PPLO
MICROBAR BARYE
MICROBE GERM
MICROBIOLOGIST AMERICAN
NATHAN
FRENCH LWOFF
SWISS ARBER
MICROCEPHALIC PINHEAD
MICROFICHE FICHE FILMCARD
MICROFILM COM
(SHEET OF —) FICHE
MICROMETER MU BIFILAR
(— CALIPER) MIKF
MICRON MU
MICRONESIA (CAPITAL:) PALIKIR
(COIN:) DOLLAR
(ISLAND:) KOSRAE ULITHI WOLEAI
POHNPEI MORTLOCK
(PEOPLE:) TRUKESE POHNPEIAN
(STATE:) YAP CHUNK KOSRAE
POHNPEI
(TOWN:) TOL WENU
MICRONESIAN KANAGA NAURUAN
(— ISLAND) NUI GUAM ROTA TRUK
MAKIN NAURU WOTHO MAJURO
MICROORGANISM BUG GERM
AZOFIER BUTYRIC MICROBE
BACILLUS MYCOPLASMA
MICROPHONE BUG MIKE
PARABOLA
(KIND OF —) LAVALIERE
(REMOVE CONCEALED —) DEBUG
(SHIELD FOR —) GOBO
MICROPYLE FORAMEN
MICROSCOPE GLASS SCOPE
(PART OF —) ARM BASE CLIP KNOB
LENS LIMB TUBE STAGE FILTER
HOLDER APERTURE EYEPIECE
CONDENSER DIAPHRAGM
NOSEPIECE OBJECTIVE
ADJUSTMENT
MICROSCOPIC SMALL MINUTE
**MICROSECOND (HUNDREDTH OF
—)** SHAKE
MICROSPECIES JORDANON
MICROSPOROPHYLL STAMEN

MICROTONE SRUTI SHRUTI
MICROTUS ARVICOLA
MICROWAVE ZAP NUKE
MIDBRAIN MESENCEPHALON
MIDDAY NOON UNDERN MIDNOON
NOONDAY MERIDIAN NOONTIME
MIDDEN BASURAL SAMBAQUI
MIDDLE MEDIO MESNE NAVEL
CENTER MEDIAL MEDIAN MESIAL
CENTRAL MEDIATE MEDILLE
(— OF SAIL) BUNT
(— OF SHIP) WAIST
(— OF WINTER) HOLL HOWE
(— WAY) VIAMEDIA
(PREF.) MEDI(O) MES(O) MESIO
MEZZO
MIDDLE-AGED MIDDLING
MIDDLE EAST (— NATIVE) WOG
MIDDLEMAN BUTTY BROKER
DEALER FOGGER JOBBER LUMPER
BUMAREE BUMMAREE BUTTYMAN
HUCKSTER REGRATER
MIDDLEMARCH (AUTHOR OF —)
ELIOT
(CHARACTER IN —) FRED TYKE WILL
CALEB CELIA GARTH JAMES RIGGS
VINCY BROOKE EDWARD JOSHUA
CHETTAM LYDGATE RAFFLES
TERTIUS CASAUBON DOROTHEA
LADISLAW NICHOLAS ROSAMOND
BULSTRODE FEATHERSTONE
MIDDLER PLATEMAN
MIDDLETONE HALFTONE
MIDDLING FAIR MEAN SOSO
NEUTRAL MEDIOCRE MEETERLY
(PL.) DUNST FARINA SHARPS
SIZINGS SEMOLINA WEATINGS
MIDGE GNAT SMUT PUNKY MIDGET
MINGIE PUNKIE WEEVIL
MIDIAN (FATHER OF —) ABRAHAM
(MOTHER OF —) KETURAH
MIDMOST
(PREF.) MESATI
MIDNIGHT NOON NOONTIDE
MIDPOINT BASION PORION
STOMION GNATHION
MIDRIB COSTA SHAFT MIDVEIN
(— OF LEAF) PEN
MIDRIFF APRON SKIRT
(PREF.) PHREN(O)
MIDSHIPMAN WART MIDDY PLEBE
REEFER SNOTTY OLDSTER
MIDST DEPTH CENTER MIDDLE
MIDWARD
(PREF.) **(IN THE —)** INTER
MIDSUMMER DAY JOHNSMAS
MIDSUMMER NIGHT'S DREAM
(AUTHOR OF —) SHAKESPEARE
(CHARACTER IN —) MOTH PUCK
SNUG EGEUS FLUTE SNOUT
BOTTOM COBWEB HELENA HERMIA
OBERON QUINCE THESEUS TITANIA
LYSANDER DEMETRIUS HIPPOLYTA
STARVELING MUSTARDSEED
PHILOSTRATE PEASEBLOSSOM
MIDWAY MEDIO GAYWAY HALFWAY
MIDWIFE BABA DHAI GAMP HOWDY
LUCKY COMMER CUMMER
GRANNY HOWDIE KIMMER LUCINA
LUCKIE GRANNIE HEBAMME
MIEN AIR BROW PORT VULT ALLURE
ASPECT DEMEAN MANNER OSTENT
BEARING DEMEANOR PORTANCE

MIFF TICKOFF
MIFFED IRKED
MIG MIB DUCK
MIGHT ARM BULK MOTE FORCE
MOUND POWER SHOULD
STRENGTH
(PREF.) CRATO
MIGHTILY HEFTILY
MIGHTINESS (HIGH —) HOGEN
MIGHTY FELL HIGH KEEN MAIN
MUCH RANK RICH VAST FELON
GREAT HEFTY STERN STOOR
POTENT STRONG VIOLENT
ENORMOUS FORCEFUL POWERFUL
PUISSANT SAMSONIC
(PREF.) DEIN(O) DIN(O) MEG(A)(AL)
(ALO)
MIGNON (CHARACTER IN —)
MIGNON MEISTER SPERATA
WILHELM LOTHARIO
(COMPOSER OF —) THOMAS
MIGNONETTE WELD WOLD
RESEDA LUTEOLA
MIGRAINE MEGRIM
MIGRANT MOVER
MIGRATE RUN FLIT TREK DRIFT
FLIGHT COLONIZE
MIGRATION TREK EXODUS FLIGHT
EELFARE EMOTION PASSAGE
DIASPORA
MIGRATORY PEREGRINE
(NOT —) RESIDENT SEDENTARY
MIKADO DAIRI
MIKIR ARLENG
MIKLOTH (FATHER OF —) JEHIEL
(MOTHER OF —) MAACHAH
MILCAH (FATHER OF —) HARAN
ZELOPHEHAD
(HUSBAND OF —) NAHOR
MILD LEW MOY CALM COLD EASY
FAIR LENT MEEK NESH PLUM SOFT
TAME WARM BALMY BLAND
BUXOM GREEN LIGHT LITHE
MELCH MELSH MILKY NAISH
QUIET BENIGN FACILE GENIAL
GENTLE HUMBLE KINDLY REMISS
SMOOTH AFFABLE AMIABLE
CLEMENT LENIENT SARSNET
VELVETY BENEDICT DOVELIKE
FAVONIAN LENITIVE MERCIFUL
SARCENET SARSENET SOOTHING
TRANQUIL
(— CLOSELY) JIB
(PREF.) LENI
MILDEW OIDIUM
MILDLY FEEBLY GENTLY
MILDNESS MILD LENITY SUAVITY
CLEMENCY HUMILITY KINDNESS
MILE (GO —S) DEGREE
(NAUTICAL —) KNOT KAIRI
(ONE-EIGHTH —) FURLONG
(SEA —) NAUT
(SIXTY —S) DEGREE
(THIRD —) LI
(3 —S) HOUR LEAGUE
MILESTONE MILLIARY
MILETUS (FATHER OF —) APOLLO
(MOTHER OF —) ARIA DEIONE
(SON OF —) BYBLIS CAUNUS
(WIFE OF —) CYANEE
MILFOIL AHARTALAV
MILIEU CLIMATE TERRAIN
AMBIENCE

MILITANT WARRISH FIGHTING
  (ONE WITH — ATTITUDE) HAWK
MILITARISTIC PRUSSIAN
MILITARY MARTIAL WARLIKE
  MILITANT SOLDIERY
  (— OBJECTS) MILITARIA
  (— POST) THANA
  (— SCIENCE) LOGISTICS
MILITIA FYRD ARRAY MILICE
MILITIAMAN CHOCO UHLAN
  LUMPER TRAINER FENCIBLE
  SHIRTMAN
  (TURKISH —) TIMARIOT
MILK COW LAC FUZZ LAIT PAIL SKIM
  BLEED JUICE MILCH MULCT
  BOTTLE ELICIT RAMMEL STROKE
  SUCKLE EXPLOIT
  (— CLOSELY) JIB
  (— DRY) STRIP
  (— OUT) EMULGE
  (— PAN) LEAD
  (— PRODUCT) KHOA
  (— SICKNESS) TIRES
  (BREAST —) SUCK DIDDY
  (COW'S —) MESS
  (CURDLED —) SKYR TYRE TAYER
  LOPPER CLABBER TATMJOLK
  (FERMENTED —) KUMISS MATZOON
  (NEW —) RAMMEL
  (PINT OF —) PINTA
  (SOUR —) SKYR WHIG BONNY
  BLEEZE BLINKY CLABBER JOCOQUE
  (WATERY —) BLASH
  (PREF.) GALACT(O) LACT(I)(O)
  (SUFF.) GALACTIA
MILK CART KIT PRAM BUNGEY
MILKFISH AWA BANGOS SABALO
  SAVOLA BANDENG SABALOTE
MILKING (— PARLOR) BAIL
  (— TIME) MEAL
MILKLESS PARVE PAREVE
MILKMAN KITTER CHALKER
MILK PAIL TRUG LEGLEN
MILK SHAKE FRAPPE
MILK SNAKE ADDER
MILKSOP SOP MOLLY SISSY
  COCKNEY MEACOCK
MILK-SUGAR LACTOSE
MILKWEED ANGLEPOD
MILKWOOD MELKHOUT
MILKWORT SENECA SENEGA
  CENTAURY GAYWINGS POLYGALA
MILKY MILCHY LACTARY LACTEAL
  OPALOID LACTEOUS
MILKY WAY GALAXY
  (PREF.) GALACT(O)
MILL FULL MILN REED STAR BREAK
  FLOUR KNURL QUERN CHERRY
  FANNER STAMPS BLOOMER
  MOLINET PUGMILL SMUTTER
  ARRASTRA ARRASTRE BUHRMILL
  SPINNERY TRAPICHE WALKMILL
  (CHOCOLATE —) MOLINET
  (FULLING —) STOCKS
  (SHINGLING —) FORGE
  (SUGAR —) CENTRAL TRAPICHE
  (PREF.) MOLARI MYL(O)
MILLBOARD TARBOARD
MILLDAM WEIR WARREN WARRANT
MILLED GRAINED
MILLENARIAN CHILIAST
MILLENIUM CHILIAD

MILLER MILLMAN STOCKER
  MULTURER NILLWARD
MILLER'S-THUMB BLOB CULL
  CABOT CHABOT COTTOID
  MUDDLER BULLHEAD
MILLET BUDA KODA KOUS MOHA
  ARZUN BAJRA CHENA CUMBU
  DUKHN DURRA GRAIN HIRSE
  KODRA MILLY PANIC PROSO TENAI
  WHISK BAJREE DHURRA HUREEK
  JONDLA JOWARI MILIUM RAGGEE
  DAGASSA PANICLE ZABURRO
  BIRDSEED KADIKANE
  (PREF.) MILIO
MILLHAND CROPMAN
MILLIGRAM (200 —S) CARAT
MILLILITER MIL
MILLIMETER LI
  (THOUSANDTH OF —) MICRON
MILLINER ARTISTE MODISTE
MILLING GRAINING
MILLION CONTO QUENT
  (THOUSAND —S) GILLION MILLIARD
  (10 —) CRORE
  (1000 —) MILLIARD
  (PL.) GUPPY
  (PREF.) MEGA
MILLIONTH
  (PREF.)
  (ONE —) MICR(O)
MILLIPEDE JULID POLYPOD
  DIPLOPOD PILLWORM RINGWORM
  WIREWORM
MILLISECOND SIGMA
MILL ON THE FLOSS (AUTHOR OF
  —) ELIOT
  (CHARACTER IN —) BOB TOM KENN
  LUCY DEANE GLEGG GUEST JAKIN
  WAKEM MAGGIE PHILIP PULLET
  STEPHEN STELLING TULLIVER
MILLPOND DAM MILLDAM
  BINNACLE MILLPOOL
MILLRACE LADE LEAD LEAT
  FOREBAY TAILRACE MILLSTREAM
MILLRYND INK
MILLSTONE RYND STONE BEDDER
  LEDGER LIGGER RUNNER
  (LOWER —) METATE
  (UPPER —) MANO
  (PL.) RUN
MILLSTREAM DAM LADE FLEAM
MILLWORKER DOGGER
MILO SORGHUM
MILPA LADANG
MILQUETOAST CASPAR
MILT MILK SEED SPLEEN
MILTONIST DIVORCER
MIMAS (FATHER OF —) THEANO
  (MOTHER OF —) AMYCUS
  (SLAYER OF —) MEZENTIUS
MIME ACTOR MIMER MIMIC
  (PL.) MIMIAMBI
MIMEOGRAPH RONEO
MIMIC APE HIT COPY ECHO MIME
  MINT MOCK ECHOER MOCKER
  MONKEY BUFFOON COPYCAT
  IMITATE PAGEANT
  (PREF.) MIM(EO)(O)
MIMICKING TAKEOFF SIMULANT
  IMITATIVE
MIMICRY APERY MIMESIS
  MOCKAGE MOCKERY

MIMOSA AROMA ACACIA CASSIE
  ALBIZZIA HUISACHE TURMERIC
MINCE CHOP SHEAR FINICK
MINCED HACHE
MINCEMEAT GIGOT MINCE
MINCING NIMINY FINICAL MINIKIN
  MIGNIARD SKIPJACK
MINCINGLY FINE GINGERLY
MIND CIT CHIT HEAD HEED LOAF
  MOOD NOTE NOUS OBEY RECK
  SOUL BESEE BRAIN PHREN SENSE
  SKULL WATCH ANIMUS MATTER
  NOTICE PSYCHE REGARD
  COURAGE SENSORY SUBJECT
  THINKER THOUGHT
  (CONSCIOUS —) SENTIENT
  (INFINITE —) GOD
  (RIGHT FRAME OF —) TUNE
  (STATE OF —) BAG
  (YEAR'S —) MINNING
  (PREF.) MENTI NOO PHREN(O)
  PSYCH(O)
  (SUFF.) (CONDITION OF —) THYMIA
MINDFUL HEEDY MINDLY HEEDFUL
  OBSERVANT
MIND READER MENTALIST
MINE BAL DIG PIT DELF HOLE HUEL
  MEUM BARGH DELFT DELPH
  METAL STOPE WHEAL COYOTE
  GOPHER GROOVE RESCUE
  BONANZA BORASCA COALPIT
  MINERAL OPENCUT TORPEDO
  GOLCONDA MYNPACHT PROSPECT
  (— BY BLASTING) SHOOT
  (— IRREGULARLY) GOPHER
  (— PASSAGE) SLUM
  (COAL —) ROB COALPIT COLLIERY
  (KIND OF —) CLAYMORE
  (MILITARY —) FOUGADE FOUGASSE
  CAMOUFLET
  (OLD —) GWAG
  (RICH —) GOLCONDA
  (TIN —) STANNARY
  (UNPRODUCTIVE —) DUFFER
  SHICER BORASCA
MINER PECK PICK PYKE BARER
  DOGGY ARTIST BUCKER CUTTER
  DAMMER DELVER DIGGER GANGER
  GETTER HAGGER JUMPER MATTER
  PELTER REEFER SNIPER STOPER
  TINNER TOPMAN VANNER COLLIER
  CRUTTER DIRGLER FEIGHER
  GEORDIE GROOVER HITCHER
  HUTCHER LEADMAN PICKMAN
  PIKEMAN PIONEER PLUGMAN
  ROCKMAN SNUBBER ENTRYMAN
  HEADSMAN STRIPPER WINZEMAN
  (— WHO WORKS ALONE) HATTER
MINERAL JET GEET HOST MINE
  SPAR TALC BERYL BLOOM EARTH
  EMERY FLUOR GLEBE GUEST
  LENAD SQUAT TRONA ACMITE
  ALAITE AUGITE BARITE BARYTE
  BLENDE CASTOR CERITE COCKLE
  CURITE DAVYNE EGERAN EHLITE
  ERRITE GALENA GARNET GLANCE
  GYPSUM HALITE HAUYNE HELVIN
  HUMITE ILLITE IOLITE LABITE
  MIXITE NATRON NOSEAN NOSITE
  PINITE RUTILE SALITE SILICA
  SPHENE SPINEL ADAMINE
  ADAMITE ADELITE ALTAITE
  ALUMITE ALUNITE AMOSITE

  ANATASE APATITE ATOPITE
  AXINITE AZORITE AZULITE AZURITE
  BAUXITE BAZZITE BELLITE BIOTITE
  BISMITE BITYITE BOHMITE BOLEITE
  BORNITE BRUCITE CALCITE
  CELSIAN CYANITE DIAMOND
  DICKITE DUFTITE EDENITE EPIDOTE
  ERIKITE ERINITE EUCLASE FLOKITE
  GAGEITE GAHNITE GEDRITE
  GLADITE GOTHITE GUMMITE
  HELVITE HESSITE HOPEITE
  HOWLITE HULSITE IHLEITE ILVAITE
  INESITE INYOITE ISERITE JADEITE
  JARLITE JOSEITE KEMPITE KERNITE
  KOPPITE KOTOITE KYANITE
  LANGITE LARNITE LAURITE
  LAUTITE LEHIITE LEIFITE LEONITE
  LEPTITE LEUCITE LOWEITE
  MARTITE MELLITE MULLITE
  OKENITE OLIVINE PALAITE
  PENNINE PETZITE PYRITES RATHITE
  REALGAR RETZIAN RHAGITE
  RINKITE ROMEITE ROSSITE
  SENAITE SODDITE SVABITE SYLVITE
  THORITE TURGITE ULEXITE
  UTAHITE UVANITE VAUXITE
  VOGLITE VRBAITE WARBITE
  WIIKITE ZEOLITE ZINCITE ZOISITE
  ZORGITE ZUNYITE AIKINITE
  ALLANITE ALLUVIAL ALUNOGEN
  AMBONITE ANAUXITE ANCYLITE
  ANDORITE ANKERITE ARIEGITE
  ARMENITE ARTINITE ASBOLITE
  AUGELITE AUTUNITE AWARUITE
  BADENITE BAKERITE BARARITE
  BARYLITE BAVENITE BETAFITE
  BEYERITE BILINITE BIXBYITE
  BLAKEITE BLOEDITE BOOTHITE
  BORACITE BOWENITE BRAGGITE
  BRAUNITE BRAVOITE BROMLITE
  BRONZITE BROOKITE BRUSHITE
  CALCSPAR CARBOCER CEROLITE
  CHIOLITE CHLORITE CHROMITE
  CIMOLITE CINNABAR CLEVEITE
  COHENITE COLUSITE COOKEITE
  COSALITE CREEDITE CROCOITE
  CRYOLITE DANALITE DAPHNITE
  DATOLITE DELTAITE DENDRITE
  DIALLAGE DIASPORE DIGENITE
  DIOPSIDE DIOPTASE DIXENITE
  DOLOMITE DYSODILE EGUEIITE
  ELIASITE ELPIDITE EMBOLITE
  ENARGITE EPSOMITE ERIONITE
  EUCOLITE EULYTINE EULYTITE
  EUXENITE EVANSITE FASSAITE
  FAYALITE FELDSPAR FERSMITE
  FIBROITE FLINKITE FLUORITE
  FOOTEITE FUCHSITE FUSINITE
  GEMSTONE GENTHITE GIBBSITE
  GINORITE GOETHITE GOYAZITE
  GRIPHITE GROTHINE GROUTITE
  GYROLITE HANKSITE HANUSITE
  HARTTITE HATCHITE HAUERITE
  HAUYNITE HEMATITE HOMILITE
  HUGELITE IDOCRASE INDERITE
  IODYRITE JALPAITE JAROSITE
  JEZEKITE KALINITE KAMACITE
  KASOLITE KEHOEITE KLEINITE
  KOKTAITE KOLSKITE KRAUSITE
  LAGONITE LAVENITE LAZULITE
  LAZURITE LEVYNITE LEWISITE
  LIMONITE LINARITE LOMONITE
  LOWIGITE MARSHITE MEIONITE

MELILITE MELONITE MESITITE
MESOLITE MIERSITE MIMETITE
MISENITE MOLYSITE MONAZITE
NADORITE NASONITE NEPOUITE
NOCERITE NOSELITE OXAMMITE
PEGANITE PETALITE PIMELITE
PINNOITE PISANITE PODOLITE
PORODINE PRICEITE PRIORITE
RINNEITE ROSELITE SAGENITE
SALEEITE SALESITE SAPONITE
SASSOLIN SCAWTITE SHANDITE
SHARPITE SHORTITE SIDERITE
SMALTITE SMITHITE SODALITE
SPADAITE SPURRITE STANNITE
STIRNITE STILBITE STOLZITE
STRUVITE STURTITE SZMIKITE
TAGILITE TANGEITE TEALLITE
TENORITE TILASITE TITANITE
TRIPLITE TROILITE TYROLITE
TYSONITE URANOTIL VEGASITE
VOLTAITE VOLTZITE WEHRLITE
WEISSITE WELLSITE WILKFITF
WURTZITE XENOLITE XENOTIME
YENTNITE ZARATITE MILLERITE
MUSCOVITE NEPHELINE NICCOLITE
PHENACITE TANZANITE WILLEMITE
STISLIOVITE
(BLACK —) JET GEET CERINE YENITE
KNOPITE NIOBITE ALLANITE
GRAPHITE HIELMITE ILMENITE
ONOFRITE MAGNETITE SAMARSKITE
(BLUE —) MOLYBDENITE
(BRIGHT —) BLENDE
(BROWN —) CERINE EGERAN
GUILDITE JAROSITE
(FIBROUS —) ASBESTOS
(GRAY-WHITE —) TRONA HOPEITE
(GREEN —) AMESITE GALINITE
ILESITE PRASINE PREHNITE
SMECTITE
(MOTTLED —) SERPENTINE
(ORANGE —) SANDIX
(RADIATED —) ASTROITE
(RADIOACTIVE —) CURITE
(RARE —) CYMRITE EUCLASE
TYCHITE BARYLITE
(RED —) GARNET RHODOCHROSITE
(SOFT —) TALC KERMES
(TRANSPARENT —) MICA POLLUX
ABRAZITE SODALITE
(WHITE —) BARITE HOWLITE
STILBITE
(YELLOW —) TOPAZ PYRITES
PENTLANDITE
(YELLOWISH-GREEN —) EPIDOTE
ECDEMITE
(PREF.) ORYCT(O)
(SUFF.) CLASE INE ITE LITE LITH(IC)
LITIC XENE
MINERALOGIST AMERICAN HUNT
KUNZ BRUSH KRAUS EGLESTON
WHITLOCK CLEAVELAND
AUSTRIAN BORN BECKE WULFEN
HAIDINGER TSCHERMAK
ENGLISH BROOKE CLARKE GREGOR
MILLER PHILLIPS
FRENCH HAUY ROME DAUBREE
FRIEDEL LACROIX LAUMONT
DOLOMIEU DUFRENOY
BRONGNIART
GERMAN MOHS COHEN RASPE

DECHEN KOBELL WERNER ZIRKEL
KARSTEN NEUMANN AGRICOLA
LEONHARD QUENSTEDT
ITALIAN SELLA BRUGNATELLI
RUSSIAN FERSMAN
SWEDISH GAHN HISINGER
SEFSTROM CRONSTEDT
BLOMSTRAND
MINERAL TAR MALTHA
MINERAL WATER SELTZER
MINERVA MENFRA
MINESWEEPER ALGERINE
MINGLE MIX FUSE JOIN MELL
MOLD MONG MOOL ADMIX BLEND
MERGE TWINE COMMIX FELTER
HUDDLE JUMBLE MEDDLE
MEDLEY COMBINE COALESCE
CONFOUND
(PREF.) MISCE
MINGLED FUSED MIXED MEDLEY
CONFUSED PELLMELL
(PREF.) MYXTI
MINGLING MIX PELLMELL
(— OF VOWELS) CRASIS
(PREF.) MIXO
(SUFF.) MIXIS
MINIATURE BABY SMALL LITTLE
POCKET MINIKIN
MINIM HALFNOTE
MINIMAL BASAL LIMINAL
MARGINAL
MINIMIZE DECRY MINCE LESSEN
MINIFY SMOOTH SCISSOR
BELITTLE DISCOUNT
MINIMUM BARE BEDROCK
(— OF CAPITAL) SHOESTRING
(— OF VISION) STIME STYME
MINING WORK MINERY SPATTER
GROOVING
(KIND OF —) PLACER
MINION PEAT SATAN MIGNON
DARLING MINIKIN CREATURE
SATELLITE
MINIONETTE EMERALD
MINISTER PRIG AGENT CLERK
DEWAN ELDER ENVOY HAMAN
PADRE VIZIR ATABEG DEACON
DIVINE GALLAH HELPER PANDER
PARSON PASTOR PESHWA PRIEST
VIZIER BROTHER DOMINIE OFFICER
PESHKAR PREFECT PALATINE
PREACHER SECRETARY
(— OF FINANCE) DEWAN
(— TO) TEND SERVE INTEND
(— TO PASSIONS) PANDER
(— WITHOUT SETTLEMENT)
STIBBLER
(PRIME —) PADRONE
(WAR —) SERASKIER
MINISTRANT
(PL.) SELLI SELLOI
MINISTRATION SERVICE
TENDANCE
MINISTRY SERVICE
MINIUM SANDIX
MINIVER LASSET
MINK FAG HURON NORSE VISON
JACKASH KOLINSKY MUSTELIN
PLATINUM

MINNESOTA
CAPITAL: STPAUL
COLLEGE: BETHEL STOLAF WINONA

BEMIDJI HAMLINE AUGSBURG
CARLETON
COUNTY: LYON PINE TODD ANOKA
MOWER AITKIN DAKOTA ISANTI
ITASCA MCLEOD NOBLES
ROSEAU WASECA WILKIN
CHISAGO WABASHA CROWWING
HENNEPIN OTTERTAIL
INDIAN: SIOUX OJIBWA CHIPPEWA
LAKE: LEECH ITASCA BEMIDJI
SUPERIOR
MOUNTAIN: EAGLE MISQUAH
MOUNTAIN RANGE: CUYUNA
MESABI MISQUAH
NICKNAME: NORTHSTAR
RIVER: SAUK RAINY STCROIX
STATE BIRD: LOON
STATE TREE: REDPINE
TOWN: ADA ELY MORA ANOKA
EDINA FOLEY AUSTIN CHASKA
DULUTH MILACA NEWULM
WADENA WASECA WINONA
BEMIDJI FOSSTON HIBBING
IVANHOE MANKATO BRAINERD
PIPESTONE

MINNESOTAN GOPHER
MINNOW PINK BANNY GUPPY HITCH
MINIM MINNY RAGGIE MENNON
DOGFISH FATHEAD GULARIS
PHANTOM PINHEAD PINKEEN
BONYTAIL CYPRINID FLATHEAD
GAMBUSIA MOONFISH SATINFIN
(PL.) MENISE
MINOR FLAT LESS MOLL WARD
PETIT PETTY INFANT LESSER
SLIGHT
(PERIOD OF BEING A —) NONAGE
MINORESS CLARE CLARISSE
MINORITY FEW NONAGE INFANCY
MINOS (DAUGHTER OF —) ARIADNE
PHAEDRA
(FATHER OF —) JUPITER LYCASTUS
(MOTHER OF —) EUROPA
(SLAYER OF —) COCALUS
(SON OF —) ANDROGEOS
DEUCALION
(WIFE OF —) PASIPHAE
MINSTER CHADBAND
MINSTREL BARD LUTER BADHAN
HARPER JOCKEY BADCHAN
GLEEMAN JOCULAR PARDHAN
PIERROT SONGMAN JONGLEUR
MINSTRELSY GLEE DREAM
MINT NEW COIN NANA SAGE AJUGA
BASIL ORGAN THYME HYSSOP
SAVORY STRIKE ALLHEAL BALLOTA
CAPMINT LABIATE MONARDA
OLITORY OREGANO PERILLA
PHLOMIS POTHERB STACHYS
BERGAMOT CALAMINT IRONWORT
LAMPWICK LAVENDER MARJORAM
SAGELEAF SELFHEAL SKULLCAP
PATCHOULI PATCHOULY
PENNYROYAL PEPPERMINT
MINTER MONEYER
MINTING COINING
MINUCHIHR (DAUGHTER OF —)
NAUDAR
(FATHER OF —) IRAJ
MINUET MINAWAY
MINUS LESS WANTING
MINUTE FINE NICE TINY CLOSE

MINIM PRIME SMALL ATOMIC
MOMENT NARROW INSTANT
SCRUPLE DETAILED
(LAST —) DEADLINE
(ORIGINAL —) PROTOCOL
(24 —S) GHURRY
(PL.) ACTA
MINX JADE PEAT SLUT SNIP HUSSY
HUZZY LIMMER SNICKET
MIRACLE SIGN ANOMY MARVEL
WONDER PRODIGY THEURGY
(SITE OF —) CANA
(PREF.) THAUMA(TO)
MIRACLE PLAY GUARY
MIRACULOUS MARVELOUS
(NOT —) NATURAL
MIRAGE SERAB CHIMERA FLYAWAY
LOOMING ILLUSION TOWERING
MIRANDA (FATHER OF —)
PROSPERO
(LOVER OF —) FERDINAND
MIRE BOG DUB CLAY GLAR LAIR
MOIL SLOB SLUB SLUE SLUR
ADDLE CLART EMBOG FANGO
GLAUR LATCH SEUGH SLAKE
SLOSH SLUSH SQUAD STALL
SLOUGH SLUDGE SLUTCH
CLABBER GUTTERS SLUBBER
LOBLOLLY WORTHING
MIREILLE (CHARACTER IN —)
RAMON OURRIAS VINCENT
MIREILLE
(COMPOSER OF —) GOUNOD
MIRIAM (BROTHER OF —) MOSES
MIRITI PALM ITA BURITI MORICHE
MIRLITON KAZOO
MIRO TOMTIT
MIRROR APE FLAT BERYL GLASS
IMAGE STEEL STONE PEEPER
PSYCHE REFLEX SHINER SHOWER
CONCAVE HORIZON REFLECT
DIAGONAL SPECULUM
(— BETWEEN WINDOWS)
PIERGLASS
(PREF.) CATOPTRO
MIRTH GLEE CHEER DREAM SPORT
GAIETY BAUDERY DISPORT
JOLLITY HILARITY
(CONTEMPTUOUS —) SPORT
(VIOLENT —) SPLEEN
MIRTHFUL CADGY MERRY RIANT
FESTIVE GLEEFUL JOCULAR
DISPOSED LAUGHFUL CONVIVIAL
MIRY OOZY PUXY LAIRY MUCKY
SLAKY CLAGGY CLASHY LUTOSE
MIRISH POACHY SLABBY GUTTERY
SLOUGHY
MISADVENTURE GRIEF ACCIDENT
CALAMITY CASUALTY DISASTER
MISHANTER
MISANTHROPE CYNIC HATER
TIMON
(AUTHOR OF —) MOLIERE
(CHARACTER IN —) ORONTE
ALCESTE ARSINOE ELIANTE
CELIMENE PHILINTE
MISANTHROPIC CYNICAL
MISANTHROPY CYNICISM
TIMONISM
MISAPPLIED ABUSIVE
MISAPPLY ABUSE CROOK WREST
DISUSE MISUSE
MISAPPREHEND MISTAKE

MISAPPREHENSION ILLUSION
MISBECOME MISSIT MISSEEM
MISBEHAVE MISUSE MISBEAR
　MISFARE MISHAVE MISLEAD
　MISGUIDE
MISBEHAVIOR MALVERSATION
MISBELIEF MISCREED
MISCALCULATE DUTCH MISCAST
　MISCOUNT
MISCALL BECALL MISNAME
MISCARRIAGE FAIL MISHAP
　FAILURE ABORTION
　(PREF.) ECTRO
MISCARRY FAIL WARP ABORT
　MISGO FOUNDER MISFARE
　MISGIVE BACKFIRE
MISCARRYING ABORTIVE
MISCELLANEOUS CHOW ORRA
　SUNDRY ASSORTED CHOWCHOW
MISCELLANY ANA VARIA MEDLEY
　WHATNOT CHOWCHOW GIFTBOOK
MISCHANCE CALAMITY CASUALTY
　DISASTER
MISCHIEF HOB ILL BALE BANE EVIL
　HARM HURT JEEL WRACK INJURY
　MURCHY SORROW WONDER
　DEVILRY KNAVERY MALICHO
　SCADDLE DEVILTRY MALLECHO
MISCHIEF-MAKING URCHIN
MISCHIEVOUS BAD SLY ARCH IDLE
　PIXY ROYT ELFIN HEMPY PIXIE
　ROYET ELFISH ELVISH GALLUS
　HEMPIE IMPISH NOCENT NOYANT
　SHREWD SULLEN WICKED
　GALLOWS HARMFUL KNAVISH
　LARKISH MOCKING NAUGHTY
　PARLISH PLISKIE PUCKISH
　ROGUISH SCADDLE UNHAPPY
　UNLUCKY WAGGISH LITHERLY
　LUNGEOUS SPORTIVE SPRITISH
　VENOMOUS WANSONSY
MISCHIEVOUSNESS ROGUERY
MISCONCEPTION DELUSION
　ILLUSION
MISCONDUCT CULPA DOLUS
　OFFENCE OFFENSE DISORDER
　MALFEASANCE
MISCONSTRUCTION STRAIN
MISCONSTRUE MISJUDGE
MISCREANT KNAVE
MISDEED ILL MISS SLIP AMISS
　UNWORK DEFAULT FORFEIT
　OFFENCE OFFENSE DISORDER
　(CATCH A —) DETECT
MISDEMEANOR SIN CRIME FAULT
　DELICT OFFENCE OFFENSE
　DISORDER
MISDIRECT PERVERT MISGUIDE
MISER CUFF SKIN CHUFF CHURL
　FLINT GRIPE HAYNE HUNKS NABAL
　PIKER SCRAT SCRIB CODGER
　HUDDLE NIPPER PELTER SCRIMP
　SNUDGE WRETCH DRYFIST
　GOBSECK NIGGARD SCRAPER
　SCROOGE CHINCHER GATHERER
　HAPTERON HARPAGON HOLDFAST
　MUCKERER MUCKWORM
　PINCHGUT CURMUDGEON
MISERABLE WOE EVIL GRAY PUNK
　SOUR DAWNY DEENY DUSTY
　MISER WOFUL YEMER ABJECT
　CHETIF CRUMBY CRUMMY ELENGE

FEEBLE PRETTY UNSELY WOEFUL
　BALEFUL FORLORN PITIFUL
　SCRUFFY UNHAPPY WANSOME
　FORSAKEN PITIABLE SCRANNEL
　UNTHENDE WRETCHED
MISERABLES, LES (AUTHOR OF —)
　HUGO
　(CHARACTER IN —) JEAN JAVERT
　MARIUS COSETTE EPONINE FANTINE
　VALJEAN JONDRETTE MADELEINE
　PONTMERCY THENARDIER
　FAUCHELEVANT
MISERERE SUBSELLA
MISERLINESS AVARICE MISERISM
　SNUDGERY TENACITY
MISERLY WOE GARE MEAN NEAR
　GRIPPY KNIVEY STINGY CHINCHE
　PELTING WANSITH SCRAPING
　SNUDGERY
MISERY WO WOE BALE RUTH
　GNEDE GRAME WREAK THREAT
　ANGUISH MISEASE TRAGEDY
　CALAMITY DISTRESS WANDRETH
　WOWENING
MISFIRE SKIP SNAP
MISFORTUNE ILL BLOW DOLE
　DREE EVIL HARM RUTH TEEN
　CROSS CURSE HYDRA SCATH
　TRAIK DAMAGE DIRDUM MISERY
　MISHAP RUBBER SCATHE SORROW
　UNHEAL UNLUCK WANHAP
　WROATH AMBSACE MALHEUR
　MISCARE MISFALL MISFATE
　MISLUCK REVERSE TRAGEDY
　TROUBLE UNSELTH UNSPEED
　CALAMITY DISASTER DISGRACE
　DISTRESS MISCHIEF ADVERSITY
　MISCHANCE
MISGIVING DOUBT QUALM
MISGOVERN MISRULE
MISGUIDED WET
MISHAEL (BROTHER OF —)
　ELIZAPHAN
　(FATHER OF —) UZZIEL
MISHAM (FATHER OF —) ELPAAL
MISHANDLE BUNGLE
MISHAP SLIP GRIEF SHUNT SITHE
　UNHAP WANHAP FORTUNE
　MISTIDE ACCIDENT CASUALTY
　MISCHIEF PRATFALL
　(MINOR —) GLITCH
MISHEARING OTOSIS
MISHIT DUFF
MISHMA (BROTHER OF —) MIBSAM
　(FATHER OF —) ISHMAEL
MISHMASH OLIO BOTCH GOULASH
MISINFORM MIZZLE
MISINTERPRET WARP WREST
　WRITHE MISREAD PERVERT
　MISCOUNT
MISJUDGE MISDEEM MISWERN
MISLAY LOSE DISPLACE MISPLACE
MISLEAD COG ERR BUNK DUPE
　GULL HOAX HYPE JIVE BLUFF
　CHEAT FALSE SHUCK BETRAY
　DELUDE SEDUCE WILDER
　CONFUSE DEBAUCH DECEIVE
　MISLEAR INVEIGLE MISGUIDE
　BAMBOOZLE
MISLEADING JIVE BLIND FALSE
　CIRCEAN TORTIOUS
MISMANAGE MULL BLUNK

BLUNDER MISLEAD MISRULE
　ILLGUIDE MISGUIDE
MISOGYNIC CYNICAL
MISPLACE MISLAY MISPUT MISSET
　DISPLACE
MISPLACED LOST MALPOSED
MISPLAY BLOW DUFF ERROR FLUFF
　FUMBLE
MISPRINT LITERAL
MISPRONOUNCE MISCALL
　STUMBLE
MISQUOTE GIVE
MISREPRESENT SKEW ABUSE
　BELIE COLOR MISUSE DISTORT
　FALSIFY SLANDER MISCOLOR
MISREPRESENTATION FRAUD
　CALUMNY DAUBERY GARBLING
MISS ERR HIP SHE FAIL LACK LOSE
　SKIP SLIP SNAB FORGO HANUM
　MISSY PANNA SKIRT DESIRE
　KUMARI FRAULEIN MISTRESS
　OVERLOOK OVERSLIP SENORITA
　(CLOSE —) SHAVE
　(NARROW —) SHAVE
MISSEL BIRD MAVIS SHIRL DRAINE
　JAYPIE MISTLE SHRITE SYCOCK
　CHERCOCK
MISSHAPE DEFORM
MISSHAPEN UGLY BLOWN
　DEFORM THRAWN DEFORMED
　UNSHAPED MALFORMED
　(PREF.) DYSMORPHO
MISSILE ABM GUN SAM BALL BIRD
　BOLT DART MIRV NIKE SHOT
　PLUMB SHAFT STONE BULLET
　EXOCET ROCKET SEEKER
　BOMBARD FIREPOT GRENADE
　MISSIVE OUTCAST PROJECT
　AERODART BRICKBAT MINUTEMAN
　PROJECTILE SIDEWINDER
　(— DEPOT) SILO
　(ANTIBALLISTIC —) ABM
　(BALLISTIC —) ICBM ATLAS
　(DEFECTIVE —) DUD
　(SURFACE-TO-AIR —) SAM
　(PL.) MITRAILLE
　(PREF.) TELI
MISSING LACK WANT ABSENT
　WANTING
　(— OF CUE) FLUFF
　(PREF.) E
MISSION SAND TASK CHARGE
　ERRAND SORTIE VISITA MESSAGE
　BUSINESS DEVOTION LEGATION
　NUNCIATURE
　(— OF MERCY) RESCUE
MISSIONARY APOSTLE COLPORTER

MISSISSIPPI	
CAPITAL:	JACKSON
COLLEGE:	RUST ALCORN BELHAVEN
	MILLSAPS TOUGALOO
COUNTY:	TATE HINDS JONES
	LAMAR LEAKE PERRY YAZOO
	ALCORN ATTALA COPIAH JASPER
	PANOLA TIPPAH TUNICA
	CHOCTAW NESHOBA NOXUBEE
	ITAWAMBA YALOBUSHA
INDIAN:	TIOU BILOXI TUNICA
	CHOCTAW NATCHEZ CHICKASAW
LAKE:	ENID SARDIS BARNETT
	GRENADA OKATIBBEE
MOUNTAIN:	WOODALL

NATIVE:	MUDCAT TADPOLE
NICKNAME:	BAYOU MAGNOLIA
RIVER:	LEAF PEARL YAZOO
	BIGBLACK
STATE BIRD:	MOCKINGBIRD
STATE FLOWER:	MAGNOLIA
STATE TREE:	MAGNOLIA
TOWN:	IUKA MARKS BILOXI LAUREL
	PURVIS TUNICA TUPELO WINONA
	BELZONI CORINTH GRENADA
	NATCHEZ WIGGINS GULFPORT
	MERIDIAN KOSCIUSKO

MISSIVE NOTE BILLET LETTER
　EPISTLE MESSAGE MISSILE
MISSLE BUS

MISSOURI	
CAPITAL:	JEFFERSONCITY
COLLEGE:	AVILA DRURY TARKIO
	LINCOLN WEBSTER STEPHENS
COUNTY:	RAY COLE DENT IRON
	LINN ADAIR BARRY HENRY
	MACON RALLS TANEY GRUNDY
	PETTIS PLATTE DAVIESS
	NODAWAY
INDIAN:	OSAGE
LAKE:	OZARKS TABLEROCK
MOUNTAIN:	TAUMSAUK
NATIVE:	PUKE PIKER
NICKNAME:	SHOWME BULLION
PLATEAU:	OZARK
PRESIDENT:	TRUMAN
RIVER:	OSAGE
STATE BIRD:	BLUEBIRD
STATE FLOWER:	HAWTHORN
STATE TREE:	DOGWOOD
TOWN:	AVA EDINA ELDON HAYTI
	LAMAR MACON MILAN ROLLA
	BUTLER GALENA KAHOKA
	NEOSHO POTOSI BETHANY
	BOLIVAR CAMERON LEBANON
	MOBERLY PALMYRA SEDALIA
	STLOUIS HANNIBAL SIKESTON

MISSPEAK ERR
MISSTATEMENT ERRATUM
MISSTEP TRIP
MIST DAG FOG MUG URE DAMP
　DRIP DROW FILM HAAR HAZE
　MOKE RACK ROKE SCUD SMUR
　BRUME CLOUD DRISK GAUZE
　STEAM MIZZLE NEBULE SEREIN
　SERENE SMEETH
　(COLD —) DROW BERBER
　(DRIZZLING —) SMUR DRISK SMIRR
　SMURR
　(SMOKY —) SMOG
　(WHITE —) HAG
　(PL.) SMOKES
　(PREF.) NEBULI NIMBI
MISTAKE ERR BALK GAFF GOOF
　MISS SLIP TRIP ERROR FAULT
　FLUFF GAFFE LAPSE BARNEY
　BOBBLE ESCAPE MISCUE SLIPUP
　STUMER BLOOMER BLOOPER
　BLUNDER CONFUSE DEFAULT
　JEOFAIL STUMOUR WRONGER
　CONFOUND MISPRINT MISPRISE
　(CLERICAL —) TYPO
　(STUPID —) BUBU BONER CLANGER
　(PL.) ERRATA
MISTAKEN WET WRONG ASTRAY

VICIOUS OVERSEEN OVERSHOT
TORTIOUS
(NOT —) RIGHT
MISTER DON REB HERR SENOR
SENHOR SIGNOR GOODMAN
SIGNIOR GOVERNOR MONSIEUR
MISTFLOWER EUPATORY
MISTILY FOGGILY
MISTINESS FILM HAZE
MISTLETOE MISSEL ALLHEAL
GADBUSH
MISTREAT BANG ABUSE SHAFT
BATTER SAVAGE VIOLATE
MISTRESS MRS PUG TOY AMIE BIBI
DAME DOLL DOXY LADY MISS
PURE AMIGA AMOUR DOLLY
DONNA DUENA FANCY LEMAN
LUCKY MADAM NANCY WOMAN
BEEBEE MINION MISSIS MISSUS
NEAERA PARNEL SAHIBA SENORA
TACKLE WAHINE BEDMATE
DELILAH HERSELF HETAERA
KITTOCK LEVERET METREZA
PADRONA SENHORA SIGNORA
SULTANA CAMPASPE DESPOINA
DULCINEA FARMWIFE GOODWIFE
GUDEWIFE HAUSFRAU LADYLOVE
LANDLADY MIGNIARD PARAMOUR
PECULIAR SINFRADA TIMANDRA
COURTESAN INAMORATA
(— OF CEREMONIES) FEMCEE
MISTRUST MISTROW SURMISE
DISTRUST JEALOUSE JEALOUSY
MISDOUBT
MISTY HAZY MOKY BLEAR DAGGY
FILMY FOGGY MISKY MOCHY
MOOTH MURKY RAWKY ROKEY
ROUKY BLURRY CLOUDY GREASY
MIZZLY SMURRY STEAMY
BRUMOUS OBSCURE NEBULOUS
NUBILOUS VAPOROUS
MISUNDERSTAND MISKNOW
MISTAKE
MISUNDERSTANDING
MALENTENDU
MISUSE ABUSE ABUSION PERVERT
MALTREAT
MITE BIT ATOM CENT DITE DRAM
ATOMY BICHO SPECK ACARID
ACARUS CHIGOE LEPTUS MINUTE
SMIDGE ACARIAN BDELLID
CHIGGER DEMODEX SMIDGEN
ARACHNID DIBRANCH FARTHING
HANDWORM ORIBATID SANDMITE
(TEXAS CITRUS —) SPIDER
(PREF.) ACAR(I)(O)
MITER MITRE TIMBER TIMBRE
MITERWORT COOLWORT
MITICIDE ACARICIDE
PHOSPHAMIDON
MITIGATE BALM COOL EASE HELP
ABATE ALLAY DELAY MEASE
RELAX REMIT SLAKE ASLAKE
LENIFY LESSEN MODIFY PACIFY
SOFTEN SOOTHE SUCCOR TEMPER
ASSUAGE COMMUTE CUSHION
ELEVATE MOLLIFY QUALIFY
RELEASE RELIEVE SWEETEN
PALLIATE ALLEVIATE
(— PAIN) PLASTER
MITIGATING LENITIVE
MITIGATION REMORSE
MITOCHONDRION SARCOSOME

MITT MUFF
MITTEN BOOT CUFF MITT MUFF
LOOFIE MUFFLE NIPPER MUFFLER
MIX BOX BEAT CARD DASH FUSE
JOIN KNIT MELL MENG MESS STIR
ADMIX ALLOY BLEND BRAID IMMIX
KNEAD MISCE TWINE BLUNGE
CAUDLE COMMIX CRUTCH GARBLE
JUMBLE MEDDLE MEDLEY MINGLE
MUDDLE PERMIX STODGE TEMPER
WUZZLE BLUNDER SHUFFLE
SWIZZLE CONFOUND LEVIGATE
SCRAMBLE
(— AND STIR WHEN WET) PUG
(— AT RANDOM) SHUFFLE
(— CONFUSEDLY) BROIL
(— FLOCKS) BOX
(— LIQUORS) BREW
(— PLASTER) GAGE GAUGE
(— TEA) BULK
(— WINE) PART
(— WITH WHITE) LOAD
(— WITH YEAST) BARM
(— WOOL OF DIFFERENT COLORS)
TUM
(CONCRETE —) SOUP
(LIQUOR —) SODA QUININE
SELTZER
MIXABLE MISCIBLE
MIXED CHOW IMPURE MEDLEY
MOTLEY PIEBALD STREAKY
CHOWCHOW
(— BLOOD) MESTIZO
(— CHALICE) KRASIS
(— UP) HAYWIRE
(NOT —) SINCERE
(PREF.) MIXO
MIXER HOG BANBURY MUDDLER
PICKLER
(CEMENT —) BOXMAN
(CONCRETE —) PAVER
(FOOD —) BEATER
MIXTURE AIR MIX BODY BREW
DASH FEED HASH MANG MELD
MONG MULL OLIO PUER SOUP
STEW ALGIN ALLOY BLEND BLENT
BROMO DOUGH GUMBO SALAD
STUFF FOURRE GARBLE GUNITE
LIGNIN MASLIN MEDLEY MELLAY
MINGLE MOTLEY TEMPER
AMALGAM COMPOST CUSTARD
FARRAGO FILICIN FORMULA
GOULASH HEADING KOGASIN
MELANGE MISTION MISTURA
MIXTION MONGREL OLLAPOD
RECEIPT TIMBALE ALKYLATE
BLENDURE DRAMMOCK
EMULSION POSSODIE POWSOWDY
SOLUTION MACEDOINE
MENAGERIE MISCELLANY
SALMAGUNDI SMORGASBORD
(— ADDED TO WINE) DOSAGE
(— ATTRACTIVE TO PIGEONS)
SALTCAT
(— FOR CAKE) BATTER
(— FOR DRESSING LEATHER)
DUBBIN DUBBING
(— OF ALE AND OATMEAL) STOORY
(— OF ALKALOIDS) ADONIDIN
JABORINE
(— OF BARKS) TONGA
(— OF CEMENT AND STONE)
BUMICKY

(— OF CLAY AND CHALK) MALM
(— OF CLAY AND ROCK) BODY
(— OF CLAY AND SAND) LOAM
(— OF DRUGS) SPECIES
(— OF ELEMENTS) DIDYMIUM
(— OF FEEDS) MASH
(— OF IMPURE ARSENIDES) SPEISS
(— OF OATS AND BARLEY) DREDGE
(— OF PRINCIPLES) EUONYMIN
(— OF PROTEINS) CROTIN
(— OF SALTS) SOYATE
(— OF SAND AND STONES) CHAD
(— OF SAWDUST AND GLUE)
BADIGEON
(— OF SHALE AND SANDSTONE)
HAZLE
(— OF SLAG AND ORE) BROWSE
(— OF VINEGAR AND HONEY)
OXYMEL
(— OF VITAMINS) BIOS
(— OF WHITE AND BLACK) GRIZZLE
(— OF WINE, HONEY AND SPICES)
CLARY
(— TO ADULTERATE LIQUORS)
FLASH
(— TO DOCTOR WINE) GEROPIGA
(— TO WHITEN BREAD) HARDS
(— USED AS A FERMENT) BUB
(— USED AT SEDER) HAROSET
CHAROSES
(ACUTE —) ACUTA
(AERIFORM —) GAS
(CARVER'S —) COMPO
(CAULKING —) BLARE
(CHEMICAL —) SYNGAS
(CLAY —) COB SLIP
(COATING —) COLOR
(CONFUSED —) MESS CHAOS
FUDDLE SOZZLE
(CRUMBLY —) STREUSEL
(EXPLOSIVE —) DUALIN FIREDAMP
(FOOD —) FILLING
(FREEZING —) CRYOGEN
(GILDING —) ASSIETTE
(HYDROCARBON —) ABIETENE
(ITALIAN CONDIMENT —) TAMARA
(JUMBLED —) BOTCH PASTICHE
(MECHANICS' —) PUTTY
(PLASTIC CEMENT —) CLOY
(PRESERVATIVE —) STUFF
(SEASONED —) STUFFING
(SMOKING —) CHARAS CHURRUS
(TANNING —) PURE
(THICKENING —) ROUX
(UNPALATABLE —) DRAMMOCK
(WATERY —) SLURRY
(WELDING —) THERMIT
(SUFF.) CRASE CRASIS CRASY
MIZZAH (FATHER OF —) REUEL
(GRANDFATHER OF —) ESAU
MIZZEN DANDY
MIZZONITE DIPYRE
MKS UNIT JOULE
MNEMONIC MEMORIAL
MOAN HONE MOON REEM WAIL
CROON GROAN MOURN MUNGE
QUIRK SOUGH MUNGER
MOANING SOUGH DIRGEFUL
MOAT FOSS DITCH FOSSE GRAFF
RUNDEL
MOB CREW GANG HERD RAFF ROUT
COHUE CROWD HURRY MAFIA
PLEBE PLEBS MOBILE RABBLE

TUMULT VOULGE DOGGERY
CANAILLE RIFFRAFF VARLETRY
CLAMJAFRY
(PREF.) OCHLO
MOBCAP MOB
MOBILE THIN FLUID ROVING
MOVEABLE
(— ARTIST) CALDER
(FREELY —) THIN
MOBSTER HOODLUM
MOBY DICK (AUTHOR OF —)
MELVILLE
(CHARACTER IN —) AHAB STUBB
ISHMAEL FEDALLAH QUEEQUEG
STARBUCK
MOCCASIN PAC CONGO TEGUA
SHOEPACK
(— WITH LEGS) LARRIGAN
(PL.) SHANKS
MOCCASIN FLOWER NERVINE
MOCHA BARK
MOCHICA YUNCA
MOCHILA MACHEER KNAPSACK
MOCK DO BOB DOR GAB MOW
COPY DEFY GECK GIBE GIRD JAPE
JEER JEST JIBE PLAY QUIZ BOURD
DORRE ELUDE FLEER FLIRT FLOUT
FRUMP HOKER KNACK MIMIC
RALLY SCOFF SCORN SCOUT
SLEER SPORT TAUNT DEMOCK
DELUDE DERIDE ILLUDE NIGGLE
IMITATE MURGEON RIDICULE
MOCKER MOWER GIRDER
BOURDER FLOUTER SCORNER
RAILLEUR
MOCKERNUT BULLNUT
MOCKERY DOR GAB MOW GLEE
JEER BOURD DORRE FARCE FLOUT
GLAIK SCOFF SPORT BISMER
HETHING LUDIBRY MOCKADO
MOCKAGE DERISION ILLUSION
RIDICULE SCOFFERY
(GOD OF —) MOMUS
MOCKING GAB ACID SPORT
SCOPTIC IRRISORY NARQUOIS
SARDONIC TRUMPERY
MOCKINGBIRD MIMUS MOWER
MOCKER
MOCK ORANGE SYRINGA
PHILADELPHUS
MOCOA COCHE
MOD HEP HIP YEYE TRENDY
MODE CUT JET TON WAY FORM
GATE MOOD RAGA TONE TWIG
WISE FERIO FINAL GENUS MODUS
STATE STYLE VOGUE ACTING
BAROCO CESARE COURSE DATISI
FAKOFO FANGLE FESAPO MANNER
METHOD BAMALIP CALEMES
CAMENES DABITIS DARAPTI
DIBATIS DIMARIS DIMATIS DISAMIS
FAPESMO FASHION FERISON
FESTINO CELARENT DOKMAROK
FELAPTON FRESISON TONALITY
(— OF BEHAVIOR) THEW HABITUDE
(— OF BEING) CATEGORY
(— OF CONDUCT) LAW
(— OF DRESS) HABIT TENUE
(— OF DRESSING HAIR) MADONNA
(— OF EXPRESSION) IRONY
(— OF MORAL ACTION) CONDUCT
(— OF PARTITIONING) CANT

(— OF PROCEDURE) ORDER SYSTEM
(— OF RULE) REGIME
(— OF SPEECH) ACCENT LATINISM PARLANCE
(— OF STANDING) STANCE
(— OF STRUCTURE) BUILD
(PREVAILING —) GARB
(TEMPORARY —) VOGUE
MODEL WAX COPY FORM MOLD NORM CANON DUMMY IDEAL LIGHT MOULD NORMA SHAPE DESIGN FUGLER GABARI MODULE PRAXIS SOURCE BOZZETO DIORAMA EXAMPLE GABARIT MODULET PARAGON PATTERN PICTURE SAMPLER CALENDAR ENSAMPLE EXEMPLAR EXEMPLUM FORMULAR FUGLEMAN MAQUETTE MODELLER MODULIZE PARADIGM PROPLASM SPECIMEN TYPORAMA MANNEQUIN PLANETARIUM
(— MATERIAL) BALSA
(— OF EARTH) TERRELLA
(— OF FOOT) CAST
(— OF HUMAN BODY) FORM MANIKIN
(— OF PERFECTION) PARAGON
(— OF SOLAR SYSTEM) ORRERY
(— OF STATUE) ESQUISSE
(INFERIOR —) JALOPPY
(MATHEMATICAL —) SPACE
(PRELIMINARY —) MAQUETTE PROPLASM
(PREF.) TYP(I)(O)
MODERATE BATE COOL CURB EASE EASY EVEN MEEK SOFT ABATE ALLAY ALLOY LIGHT LOWER MEZZO MODER REMIT SLACK SLAKE SOBER SWEET ARREST BRIDLE DECENT GENTLE LESSEN MEANLY MIDWAY MODEST MODIFY REMISS SEASON SOFTEN SUBMIT TEMPER CENTRAL CHASTEN CONTROL SLACKEN ATTEMPER CENTRIST MEETERLY MIDDLING MITIGATE MODERATO ORDINATE PALLIATE PASSABLE CONTINENT ABSTEMIOUS MEASURABLE REASONABLE
(— IN BURNING) SOFT
(— OF THE WIND) LOOM
MODERATELY GEY FAIR MEAN MEANLY MEETLY PRETTY MIDWISE MEETERLY MIDDLING
MODERATENESS CLEMENCY MODICITY
MODERATION MEAN STAY MINCE SPARE MANNER MEDIUM REASON COMPASS MEDIETY MODESTY SOBRIETY ABATEMENT IMMODESTY
MODERATO MASSIG
MODERATOR ANCHOR ANCHORMAN
MODERN NEW LATE RECENT NEOTERIC SPACEAGE
MODERNE ARTDECO
MODEST COY MIM SHY DEFT MURE NICE PURE SNUG BLATE DOUCE LOWLY QUIET SMALL CHASTE

DEMURE HUMBLE PUDENT SIMPLE VIRGIN CLERKLY PUDICAL DISCREET MAIDENLY PUDIBUND RESERVED RETIRING SHAMEFUL VERECUND VIRTUOUS
MODESTY AIDOS PUDOR NICETY DECENCY PUDENCY SHYNESS CHASTITY FOREHEAD HUMILITY PUDICITY
MODICUM DROP BREAK SPICE PENNORTH SCANTLING SEMBLANCE PENNYWORTH
MODIFICATION BOB ECAD FORM SALT CHANGE ENGRAM FACIES SANDHI SINGLE UMLAUT ENGRAMMA
(— OF A REMEDY) TINCTION
(GLOTTAL —) STOP
MODIFIED VARIANT
MODIFY EDIT VARY ALTER AMEND HEDGE TOUCH BUFFER CHANGE DOCTOR MASTER TEMPER ARABIZE COMPARE FASHION MASSAGE QUALIFY ATTEMPER DENATURE GRADUATE MODERATE FAUCALIZE
(— ARTICULATION) COLOR
(— COLOR) TONE
MODILLION ANCON MODEL TRUSS CARTOUCH
MODISH CHIC MODY SOIGNE TIMISH TONISH STYLISH
MODISHNESS CHIC
MODRED (FATHER OF —) ARTHUR
(MOTHER OF —) MARGAWSE
MODULATE SINK INFLECT QUALIFY
MODULATION ACCENT CHANGE CADENCE BUNCHING PASSAGIO
MODULE LEM UNIT COMPONENT
(KIND OF —) LUNAR
(LUNAR EXCURSION —) BUG LED
MOGUL NABOB NAWAB RULER VICEROY PADISHAH
MOHAIR MOIRE
MOHAMMED MAHOMET MAHOUND MUDEJAR PROPHET
(SITE OF — TOMB) MEDINA
(UNCLE OF —) ABBAS
MOHAMMEDAN MOSLEM PAYNIM MAHOMET
MOHAMMEDANISM TURBAN TURKERY MAUMETRY
MOHAWK NICKER
MOHR MHORR GAZELLE
MOHUR MOOR AHMEDI
MOIETY MEDIETY
MOIST WET DAMP DANK DEWY NESH UVID DABBY GIVEY GREEN HUMID JUICY MADID MOCHY SAMMY SAPPY SLACK SOAKY SOCKY SPEWY SWACK WASHY WEEPY CLAMMY MOISTY STICKY WETTISH HUMOROUS MUCULENT
(PREF.) HUMI(DI) HYGR(O) UDO
MOISTEN DIP WET DAMP MOIL BASTE BATHE BEDEW JUICE LATCH LEACH STEEP WOKIE DABBLE DAMPEN HUMECT HUMIFY IMBRUE MADEFY SPARGE TEMPER HUMIDIFY IRRIGATE IRRORATE
(— LEATHER) SAM SAMMY

MOISTURE DEW WET BREE DAMP DANK ROKE HUMOR MOIST WATER PHLEGM AQUOSITY HUMIDITY
(— DEFICIENT) XERIC
(— FROM SKIN) SWEAT
(— IN STONE) SAP
(— ON BEARD) BARBER
(CONDENSED —) BREATH
(REMOVE CONDENSED —) DEFOG
(PREF.) HUMI(DI) HYGR(O) UDO
MOJARRA SHAD PATAO
MOKI MOGUEY MOKIHI
MOKSHA MUKTI
MOLAR WANG FORMAL MOLARY GRINDER
(PREF.) MYL(O)
MOLASSES DIP LICK CLAGGUM THERIAC TREACLE LONGLICK
(PREF.) MELASSI
MOLD DIE FEN PIG PLY SOW CALM CAST CURB FORM MULL MUST SOIL TRAP BLOCK CHAPE CHILL FRAME INGOT MODEL MOULD MUCOR PLASM PRINT SHAPE SHARE STENT STINT VALVE COFFIN GABARI INFORM LINGET MATRIX SQUARE BASTARD FASHION FESTOON MATRICE RILLETT SANDBOX SKILLET TEMPLET COQUILLE FUMAGINE HOODMOLD PROPLASM TEMPLATE WHISKERS PENICILLIUM
(— FOR METAL) SOW SKILLET
(— OF ASPIC) DARIOLE
(— OF SHIP) SWEEP
(— THAT ATTACKS HOPS) FEN
(CHEESE —) CHESSEL
(SLIME —) MYCETOZOAN MYXOMYCETE
(PREF.) PLASM(ATO)(O)
(SUFF.) PLASIA PLASIS PLASM(A) (IA)(IC) PLAST(IC)(Y) PLASY
MOLDAVITE TEKTITE
MOLDBOARD REEST
(— SURFACE) WREST
MOLDED FICTILE
MOLDER ROT MURL DECAY ERODE CAPPER MANGLE MOSKER FIGURER PLASTER PLASTIC
MOLDINESS MUST FINEW MUCOR VINEW
MOLDING BEAD COVE CYMA DADO GULA KEEL LIST OGEE OVAL CABLE FILET GORGE LABEL LEDGE ROVER STAFF BANDLE BASTON BILLET CASING COLLAR CONGEE COVING FILLET LISTEL MULLER REGLET SQUARE ZIGZAG ANNULET BEADING CABLING CHAPLET CORNICE DOUCINE ECHINUS EYEBROW FINGENT HIPMOLD LOZENGE MOULAGE NECKING SURBASE TONDINO TRINGLE ASTRAGAL BAGUETTE BANDELET CASEMATE CASEMENT CINCTURE CYMATION CYMATIUM DANCETTE DOGTOOTH FUSAROLE HOODMOLD KNURLING MOULDING NAILHEAD NECKMOLD ARCHIVOLT BOLECTION
(CONCAVE —) GORGE CONGEE SCOTIA CAVETTO
(CONVEX —) REED CABLE OVOLO

THUMB TORUS BASTON REEDING ASTRAGAL FUSAROLE
(OGEE —) TALON
(OUTSIDE —) BACKBAND
(PL.) TORI LEDGMENT

MOLDOVA (ALSO SEE RUSSIA)
CAPITAL: CHISINAU KISHINEV
COIN: RUBLE
MOUNTAIN: VYSOKAYA BALANESTI
NAME: MOLDAVIA BESSARABIA
PLAIN: BUGEAC
RIVER: PRUT DANUBE IALPUG COGALNIC DNIESTER
STEPPE: BALTI
TOWN: BALTI TIRASPOL

MOLDY FUSTY HOARY MUCID MUGGY MUSTY VINNY FOISTY MOULDY FOUGHTY
MOLE COB UNT COBB MAIL OONT PIER PILE TAPE WANT JUTTY MOODY NEVUS TALPA TAUPE ANICUT MOUDIE HYDATID SLEEPER TALPOID MOLDWARP MOONCALF SORICOID STARNOSE UROPSILE ZANDMOLE
(PREF.) TALPI
MOLE CRICKET CHANGA
MOLECULE ACID ATOM BASE AMMINE CHIRAL DIPOLE HEXANE HYDROL LIGAND PRIMER HYDRONE SPECIES TEMPLATE OCTAPEPTIDE
(CLUSTER OF —) CAP
(PROTEIN —) BIOGEN
MOLEHILL TUMP HOYLE WANTHILL
MOLE RAT SEMNI ZEMMI ZOKOR SLEPEZ SPALACID ZANDMOLE
MOLEST GALL HAUNT TEASE BOTHER HARASS HECKLE INFEST PESTER MISLEST TROUBLE
MOLID (FATHER OF —) ABISHUR
(MOTHER OF —) ABIHAIL
MOLL FLANDERS (AUTHOR OF —) DEFOE
(CHARACTER IN —) MOLL JEMMY ROBIN FLANDERS
MOLLIFIER SLAVE
MOLLIFY HUSH ALLAY RELAX ADULCE GENTLE PACIFY RELENT SOFTEN SOOTHE TEMPER ASSUAGE DULCIFY SWEETEN ATTEMPER MITIGATE UNRUFFLE
MOLLIFYING MILD SUPPLING
MOLLUSK ARK CLAM CONE PIPI SPAT BORER CHAMA CHANK CHINK CLAMP CONCH COWRY DORIS DRILL MUREX PINNA SNAIL VENUS AEOLID BAILER BUBBLE CERION CHITON COCKLE COURIE DOLIUM JINGLE LEPTON LIMPET MUSSEL NERITA OYSTER PECTEN PHOLAD PURPLE SEMELE STROMB ABALONE ADMIRAL ASTARTE BIVALVE CARDITA DECAPOD JUNONIA MOLLUSC PIDDOCK SALPIAN SCALLOP TOHEROA TREPANG TROPHON DUCKFOOT FIGSHELL HALIOTIS NAUTILUS PTEROPOD SAXICAVA STROMBUS UNIVALVE VERMETUS SHELLFISH NUDIBRANCH PERIWINKLE

(— TRIBE) NAIADES
(LARVAL —) VELIGER
(YOUNG —) SPAT
MOLLYCODDLE BABY MOLLY
WANTON INDULGE MILKSOP
MOLOSSUS (FATHER OF —)
PYRRHUS
(MOTHER OF —) ANDROMACHE
MOLT MEW CAST MUTE SHED
MOULT DISCARD EXUVIATE
INTERMEW
MOLTEN FUSED
MOLTING BROKEN ECDYSIS
MOLUCCAS (ISLAND OF —) ARU KAI
OBI BURU LETI SULA AMBON BABAR
BANDA CERAM WETAR BATJAN
TIDORE MOROTAI TERNATE
TANIMBAR HALMAHERA
MOLUS (BROTHER OF —) EVENUS
(DAUGHTER OF —) MOLIONE
(FATHER OF —) ARES MARS
(MOTHER OF —) DEMONICE
MOLYBDENUM (EXCESS OF —)
TEART
MOMBIN JOCOTE
MOMENT MO GIRD HINT SAND TICK
AVAIL BLINK BRAID CLINK CRACK
GLIFF GLISK JIFFY SHAKE SNIFT
SPURT STOUN TRICE VALUE FILLIP
GLIFFY MINUTE PERIOD SECOND
STOUND WEIGHT YAWING ARTICLE
INSTANT INSTANCE MOMENTUM
TWINKLING
(— FOR LEGERDEMAIN ACTION)
TEMPS
(— OF STRESS) CRISE
(APPROPRIATE —) PLACE
(CRITICAL —) BIT INCH CORNER
(DECISIVE —) CRISIS
(EXACT —) BIT POINT
(OPPORTUNE —) KAIROS
(PRECISE —) NICK
(SCHEDULED —) TIME
MOMENTARY MOMENTAL
TRANSIENT
MOMENTOUS FELL GRAVE
EPOCHAL FATEFUL WEIGHTY
EVENTFUL PREGNANT
MOMENTOUSNESS GRAVITY
MOMENTUM WAY FORCE SPEED
IMPETUS
MON PEGUAN TALAING
MONACO (NATIVE OF —)
MONEGASQUE

<table>
<tr><td colspan="2" align="center">MONACO</td></tr>
<tr><td>ANCIENT NAME:</td><td>MONOECUS</td></tr>
<tr><td>CAPITAL:</td><td>MONACO MONACOVILLE</td></tr>
<tr><td>DYNASTY:</td><td>GRIMALDI</td></tr>
<tr><td>LANGUAGE:</td><td>FRENCH</td></tr>
<tr><td>PEOPLE:</td><td>MONEGASQUES</td></tr>
<tr><td>PRINCE:</td><td>LOUIS ALBERT HONORE ANTOINE CHARLES RAINIER FLORESTAN</td></tr>
<tr><td>RIVER:</td><td>VESUBIE</td></tr>
<tr><td>SECTION:</td><td>MONTECARLO LACONDAMINE MONACOVILLE</td></tr>
</table>

MONAD ATOM JIVA AMEBA HENAD
MONAS
MONADIC UNARY
MONADNOCK BARABOO
MONARCH KING QUEEN DANAID

DIADEM PRINCE DANAINE
EMPEROR AUTOCRAT
MONARCHIAN PRAXEAN
MONARCHICAL KINGLY
MONARCHY KINGDOM
MONASTERY WAT ABBEY BADIA
LAURA RIBAT TEKKE TEKYA FRIARY
MANDRA VIHARA BONZERY
CERTOSA CONVENT KHANKAH
MINSTER MONKERY CLOISTER
LAMASERY
(ALGERIAN —) RIBAT
(BUDDHIST —) TERA KYAUNG
BONZERY LAMASERY
(CARTHUSIAN —) CERTOSA
(HINDU —) MATH
(MOSLEM —) TEKKE TEKYA
KHANKAH
(PREF.) MANDRI
(SUFF.) MINSTER
MONASTIC MONKLY MONKISH
ABBATIAL CENOBIAN MONACHAL
MONASTICISM MONKERY
MONKISM
MONDAY LUNDI
MONETARY EXPLICIT PECUNIARY
NUMISMATIC
MONEY (ALSO SEE COIN) AES BOX
DIB FAT FEE FEI GET OOF ORO SAP
TIN WAD BUCK CASH COAT COIN
COLE CRAP CUSH DUBS DUST
FUND GATE GELT GILT GOLD HOOT
JACK JAKE KALE LOOT LOUR MALI
MINT MOSS MUCK PELF ROLL
SALT SAND SHAG SOAP SWAG
BEANS BLUNT BRASH BRASS
BREAD BUNCE BUNTS CHINK
CHIPS CLINK DARBY DIMES
DOUGH DUMPS FUNDS GREEN
GRIGS IMPUT LOLLY LUCRE
MEANS MOOLA MOPUS UCHER
PURSE RHINO ROCKS ROWDY
SCADS SHINY SMASH SPUDS STIFF
STUFF SUGAR ARGENT BARATO
BARREL BOODLE CHANGE CLINYIE
DANARO DINERO DOREMI FARLEU
FARLEY FEUAGE FLIMSY FUMAGE
GRAITH HANSEL KELTER MAZUMA
POCKET SHEKEL SILLER SILVER
SPENSE SPLOSH STAMPS STEVEN
STUMPY TALENT WAMPUM
WISSEL ADVANCE CABBAGE
CHATTEL CHINKER COUNTER
CRACKER CRUSADE DEPOSIT
FALDAGE GUNNAGE OOFTISH
SCRATCH SPANKER SPECIES
STOCKER CRIMPAGE CURRENCY
DEMIMARK INCOMING INTEREST
SPENDING STERLING STOCKING
XERAPHIN SPONDULIX
WAMPUMPEAG SPONDULICKS
WHEREWITHAL
(— BET) COMEBACK
(— DUE) DEVOIRS
(— FOR LIQUOR) WHIP
(— HOLDER) TILL
(— LENT) LUMBER
(— MANAGER) GUNSLINGER
(— OF ACCOUNT) ECU ORA
(— PAID TO BIND BARGAIN) ARLES
(— TAKEN IN) DRAWING
(ADDITIONAL —) BONUS
(AVAILABLE —) CAPITAL

(BAD —) SMASH
(BAR —) BONK TANG
(BASE —) SHICE
(BRIBE —) SOAP BOODLE
(COINED —) SPECIE
(COUNTERFEIT —) BOGUS QUEER
BOODLE DUFFER SHOWFUL
SLITHER
(EARNEST —) ARLES ARRHA
DEPOSIT HANDSEL HANDGELD
HANDSALE
(EXPENSE —) DIET
(EXTORTED —) PROTECTION
(FERRY —) NAULUM
(HARD —) SPECIE
(HAT —) TAMPANG
(HAVING NO —) FLYBLOWN
(INVESTED —) STOCK
(KIND OF —) NEAR
(LARGE SUM OF —) NUT
(NEAR —) ASSETS
(ON THE —) EXACTLY
(PAPER —) BUCK GREEN SCRIP
CABBAGE CURRENCY FROGSKIN
(PASSAGE —) SHIPHIRE
(PLEDGE —) EARNEST
(PRIZE —) PEWTER
(PROTECTION —) ICE
(PUSH —) SPIFF
(READY —) CASH DARBY PREST
READY STUFF STUMPY
(REFUNDED —) DRAWBACK
(SHELL —) PEAG HAWOK WAKIKI
WAMPUM
(SILVER —) SYCEE
(SMALL SUM OF —) SPILL
(STANDARD BANK —) BANCO
(SUBSISTENCE —) BATTA
(SYSTEM OF — TRANSFER) GIRO
(TRAVELLING —) VIATICUM
(WIRE —) LARI LARIN LARREE
(10 DOLLARS IN —) SAWBUCK
MONEYBAG FOLLIS
MONEY BELT ZONE
MONEY BOX TILL CHEST PIRLIE
MONEY-CHANGER SARAF SHROFF
CAMBIST ARGENTER
MONEY-CHANGING AGIO
AGIOTAGE AGIO
MONEY DRAWER TILL SHUTTLE
MONEYED RICH WEALTHY
MONEYLENDER BANYA CHETTY
USURER LOMBARD MAHAJAN
MARWARI SHYLOCK BUMMAREE
MONEYMAKING BANAUSIC
MONEYWORT MANG MYRTLE
PRIMWORT
MONGER DEALER
MONGOL HUN KALKA BALKAR
BURIAT DAGHUR SHARRA BERBERI
KALMUCK KHALKHA SILINGAL
(PL.) HU
MONGOLIA (CAPITAL OF —)
ULANBATOR ULAANBAATAR
(DESERT OF —) GOBI
(MONEY OF —) MONGO TUGHRIK
(RIVER OF —) ORHON DZAVHAN
KERULEN SELENGE
(TOWN OF —) ONON MUREN
DARHAN BULAGAN CHOIREN
TAMTSAK ULANBATOR
CHOYBALSAN

MONGOOSE MUNG URVA CIVET
MUNGO MONGOE MEERKAT
VANSIRE
MONGREL CUR DOG FICE FIST
MUTT CROSS FEIST LIMER POOCH
SCRUB HYBRID PYEDOG BASTARD
CURRISH PIEBALD DOGGEREL
MONIKER NAME ALIAS
MONILIALES HYPHO
MONIMIA (GUARDIAN OF —)
ACASTO
(HUSBAND OF —) CASTALIO
(LOVER OF —) POLYDORE
MONISM HENISM ONEISM
MONITION TUITION
MONITOR CRT MARKER MENTOR
LANTERN PREFECT
MONITOR LIZARD IBID IBIT URAN
VARAN WARAL GOANNA WORRAL
MONITOR KABARAGOYA
MONK BO FRA COWL LAMA MARO
ARHAT BONZE CLERK FRATE FRIAR
PADRE YAHAN ARAHAT BHIKKU
CULDEE GALLAH GETSUL GOSAIN
MONACH SANTON VOTARY
CALOYER CLUNIAC GALLACH
JACOBIN STARETS STUDITE
ATHONITE BACHELOR BASILIAN
MARABOUT MONASTIC OLIVETAN
SANNYASI TALAPOIN TRAPPIST
BALDICOOT CELESTINE THELEMITE
BERNARDINE CISTERCIAN
(CHIEF —) ABBOT
(PL.) AGAPETI ACOEMETI
MONKEY APE CAY KRA PUG SAI TUP
BEGA BROH BRUH DOUC KAHA
MONA MONK MONO SAKI SIME
TITI TOTA WAAG ZATI ARABA
CEBID DIANA JACKO JOCKO
KAHAU MUNGA QATAS RATAS
PONGO PUGGY SAJOU TOQUE
UNGKA BANDAR COAITA COUXIA
GRISON GRIVET GUENON HOWLER
LANGUR MACACO MARTEN MIRIKI
MONACH NISNAS OLINGO OUBARI
PINCHE RILAWA SAMIRI SIMIAN
SIMPAI TEETEE VERVET WARINE
WEEPER WISTIT BHUNDER
COLOBIN GUARIBA GUEREZA
HANUMAN KALASIE LUNGOOR
MACAQUE MEERKAT MOUSTOC
OUAKARI PRIMATE ROLOWAY
SAIMIRI SAPAJOU STENTOR
TAMARIN ARAGUATO CAIARARA
CAPUCHIN DURUKULI ENTELLUS
LEONCITO MANGABEY MARMOSET
MARTINET MUSTACHE ORABASSU
PRIMATAL TALAPOIN TCHINCOU
WANDEROO BRACHYURA
MALBROUCK
(HOWLER —) ALOUATTA
(KIND OF —) GREASE VERVET
COLOBUS
(LIKE A —) PUGGISH
(PREF.) PITHEC(O)
MONKEY BREAD BAOBAB
ADANSONIA
MONKEY FLOWER MIMULUS
MONKEYPOT LECYTH KAKARALI
LECYTHIS SAPUCAIA
MONKEY PUZZLE BUNYA PINON
PINION

MONKEYSHINE DIDO SINGERIE
(PL.) HORSE
MONKFISH MONK LOTTE RHINA
SQUATINA
MONKISH CENOBIAN MONASTIC
MONK PARROT LORO
MONKSHOOD ATIS ACONITE
ACONITUM NAPELLUS
MOUSEBANE
MONO MONACHI
MONOACETATE ACETIN
MONOCARPELLARY SIMPLE
MONOCHORD MAGAS MAGADIS
UNICHORD
MONOCHROME CAMAIEU
MONOTINT
MONOCLE QUIZ LORGNON
EYEGLASS
MONOCLINOUS PERFECT
MONOECISM SYNOECY SYNOEKY
MONOGRAM IHS JHS YHS CIPHER
HERALD CHRISMON
(**LITERARY —**) GBS RLS TSE
MONOGRAPH STUDY MEMOIR
BULLETIN DISCOURSE
MONOLITH MENHIR PILLAR
(**CIRCLE OF —S**) CROMLECH
MONOLITHIC GLOBAL
MONOLOGIST DISEUSE
MONOLOGUE MONOLOGY
SOLILOQUY
MONONUCLEOTIDE AMP
MONOPHTHONGAL PURE
MONOPHTHONGIZE SMOOTH
MONOPHYSITE AGNOETE AGNOITE
JACOBITE
(PL.) ACEPHALI
MONOPLANE TAUBE PARASOL
MONOPODE SKIAPOD
MONOPOLIZE LURCH ABSORB
CONSUME ENGROSS
MONOPOLY REGIE TRUST CARTEL
APPALTO
(**GOVERNMENT —**) REGIE
MONOSACCHARIDE OSE DIOSE
HEXOSE KETOSE MONOSE
GLYCOSE HEPTOSE PENTOSE
PYRANOSE
MONOTONOUS ARID DEAD DULL
FLAT WASTE DREARY SAMELY
SODDEN ADENOID HUMDRUM
INSIPID IRKSOME ONENOTE
TEDIOUS BORESOME DRUDGING
SAMESOME SINGSONG UNVARIED
VEGETABLE
MONOTONY DRAB DRYNESS
HUMDRUM DULLNESS SAMENESS
MONOTREME ECHIDNA DUCKBILL
MONOXENOUS DIRECT
MONSIEUR BEAUCAIRE (**AUTHOR
OF —**) TARKINGTON
(**CHARACTER IN —**) BEAU MARY
NASH VALOIS CARLISLE MIREPOIX
PHILLIPE MOLYNEAUX WINTERSET
CHATEAURIEN
MONSOON VARSHA
MONSTER OGRE BILCH LARVA
MORMO RAHAB TERAS UNMAN
ELLOPS GERYON MAKARA SHRIMP
TYPHON BICORNE CHIMERA
CYCLOPS DIDYMUS DIPYGUS
ECHIDNA GRENDEL GRIFFIN
GRIFFON PRODIGY SLAPPER

UNBEAST WARLOCK JANICEPS
LINDWORM MOONCALF
TARASQUE TYPHOEUS UROMELUS
LEVIATHAN
(**— WITH 100 EYES**) ARGUS
(**— WITH 100 HANDS**) BRIAREUS
(**FABULOUS —**) OGRE KRAKEN
WIVERN TANIWHA
(**FEMALE —**) HARPY LAMIA SCYLLA
(**HALF-BULL HALF-MAN —**)
MINOTAUR
(**HERALDIC —**) SATYRAL
(**IMAGINARY —**) CHIMERA
(**INVISIBLE —**) BUNYIP
(**LOCH —**) NESS NESSIE
(**MAN-DEVOURING —**) OGRE LAMIA
(**MYTHICAL —**) HARPY SCYLLA
SPHINX CHIMERA WARLOCK
MINOTAUR
(**SEA —**) ORC BELUE PHOCA
KRAKEN PISTRIX ZIFFIUS
WASSERMAN
(**SUPERNATURAL —**) LARVA
(**TWO-BODIED —**) DISOMUS
(**WATER —**) NICKER
(**9-HEADED —**) HYDRA
(PREF.) TERAT(O)
(SUFF.) PAGUS
MONSTRANCE SUN
MONSTROSITY FREAK DIPYGUS
MONSTER ABORTION IMMANITY
MOONCALF TERATISM
(SUFF.) DYMUS
MONSTROUS VAST ENORM GIANT
FIENDLY FLAMING HIDEOUS
TITANIC BEHEMOTH COLOSSAL
DEFORMED ENORMOUS
FLAGRANT GIGANTIC PYTHONIC
SLAPPING NEFARIOUS
PRODIGIOUS
MONTAGNARD SEKANI

MONTANA

CAPITAL: HELENA
COLLEGE: CARROLL
COUNTY: HILL TETON TOOLE
CARBON CUSTER FERGUS
MCCONE WIBAUX BIGHORN
PONDERA RAVALLI CHOUTEAU
FLATHEAD MISSOULA
INDIAN: CROW ATSINA SALISH
ARAPAHO KUTENAI SIKSIKA
SHOSHONE
LAKE: HEBGEN FLATHEAD
FORTPECK MEDICINE
MOUNTAIN: AJAX BALDY COWAN
SPHINX TORREY GRANITE
HILGARD TRAPPER GALLATIN
PENTAGON SNOWSHOE
MOUNTAIN RANGE: CRAZY LEWIS
POCKY BIGBELT
NICKNAME: BIGSKY MOUNTAIN
TREASURE
RIVER: MILK TONGUE KOOTENAI
MISSOURI
STATE BIRD: MEADOWLARK
STATE FLOWER: BITTERROOT
TOWN: BUTTE HAVRE MALTA TERRY
CIRCLE CONRAD HARDIN HELENA
HYSHAM SCOBEY BOZEMAN
CHINOOK CHOTEAU EKALAKA
FORSYTH GLASGOW ROUNDUP
BILLINGS MISSOULA

MONTANIST PHRYGIAN

MONTENEGRO

CAPITAL: CETINJE
COIN: PARA FLORIN PERPERA
LAKE: SCUTARI SHKODER
MOUNTAIN: DURMITOR
NAME: ZETA ILLYRIA CRNAGORA
TSERNAGORA
PORT: BAR ULCINJ ANTIVARI
DULCIGNO
RIVER: IBAR ZETA DRINA MORACA
TOWN: NIKSIC CETINJE TITOGRAD
PODGORICA

MONTEZUMA AZTEC
MONTH AB AV BUL MAY PUS SOL
ZIF ZIW ABIB ADAR AHET AOUT
APAP ASIN ELUL IYAR JETH JULY
JUNE KUAR MAGH MOON TYBI
AGHAN APRIL ASARH CHAIT
ENERO IYYAR MAIUS MARCH
NISAN PAYNI RABIA RAJAB SAFAR
SAWAN SEBAT SHVAT SIVAN
SIWAN TEBET THOTH TIZRI UINAL
AUGUST BHADON CHOIAK
JUMADA JUNIUS KARTIK KISLEV
KISLEW KISLEY MECHIR MESORE
NISSAN NIVOSE PAOPHI PHAGUN
SAPHAR SHABAN SHABAT SHEVAT
TAMMUZ TEBETH TISHRI VEADAR
ABAGHAN APRILIS BAISAKH
BYSACKI CHAITRA CHISLEV
ETHANIM FLOREAL HESHVAN
JANUARY MARTIUS OCTOBER
PACHONS PHALGUN RAMADAN
SARAWAN SHAABAN SHAWWAL
THAMMUZ VENTOSE BRUMAIRE
DECEMBER DULKAADA FEBRUARY
FERVIDOR FRIMAIRE GAMELION
GERMINAL MESSIDOR MUHARRAM
NOVEMBER PLUVIOSE POSEIDON
PRAIRIAL SEXTILIS ZULKADAH
SEPTEMBER
(**— OF ISLAMIC YEAR**) RABI SAFAR
(**IN NEXT —**) PROXIMO
(**IN PRECEDING —**) ULTIMO
(**PRESENT —**) INSTANT
(**SIX —S**) SEMESTER
(**SYNODIC —**) LUNATION
(PREF.) MENO
(SUFF.) MESTER
MONTHLY MENSAL
MONTMORILLONITE SMECTITE
MONUMENT VAT WAT LECH TOMB
CROSS STONE TABUT TITLE BILITH
DOLMEN HEARSE HEROON
MEMORY RECORD TROPHY
ARCHIVE CHAITYA CHHATRI
CHORTEN DENKMAL FUNERAL
TRILITH BILITHON CENOTAPH
MEMORIAL MONOLITH
TROPAION
(**— IN CHURCH**) SACELLUM
(**— OF BALEARIC ISLANDS**)
TALAYOT
(**— OF BALEARIC ISLES**) TALAYOT
(**— OF HEAPED STONES**) CAIRN
(**— WITHIN CHURCH**) SACELLUM
(**PILLARLIKE —**) SHAFT STELA STELE
MONUMENTAL EPIC
MOO LOW
MOOCH BUM CADGE SPONGE

MOOCHER MIKER CADGER
GRAFTER SKELDER SPONGER
FREELOADER
MOOD CUE FIT TID MIND TIFF TIFT
TONE TUNE VEIN WHIM DEVIL
FRAME FREAK HEART HUMOR
SPITE PLIGHT SPIRIT SPLEEN
SPRITE STRAIN TALENT TEMPER
CAPRICE FANTASY FEATHER
JUSSIVE ATTITUDE OPTATIVE
(**— IN LOGIC**) BARBARA
(**— OF BAD TEMPER**) MAD DORTS
(**— OF DEPRESSION**) FUNK
LETDOWN
(**CROSS —**) FRUMPS
(**FRIVOLOUS —**) JEST
(**GROUCHY —**) DODS
(**IRRITABLE —**) GRIZZLE
(**PENSIVE —**) MELANCHOLY
(**SULKY —**) PET
(**SULLEN —**) STRUNT SULLENS
MOODY SAD GLUM SULKY BROODY
GLOOMY MOROSE SULLEN
MOODISH PENSIVE
MOOLA DOUGH
MOOLAH GELT MONEY
MOON BUAT LAMP LUNA MAHI
DIANA LUNET LUCINA PHOEBE
CHANDRA CYNTHIA LEWANNA
LUNETTE MOONLET FOGEATER
MENISCUS SATELLES
(**AREA ON —**) MARE TERRA
(**FULL —**) PLENILUNE
(**LARGE MASS ON —**) MASCON
(**NEW —**) PRIME
(**PART OF COURSE OF —**) MANSION
(**SING TO THE —**) BAY
(**WANING —**) WANIAND
(PREF.) LUNI MENI SELEN(I)(O)
MOON AND SIXPENCE (**AUTHOR
OF —**) MAUGHAM
(**CHARACTER IN —**) AMY ATA DIRK
TIARE BLANCHE CHARLES COUTRAS
STROEVE STRICKLAND
MOONBLIND LUNATIC
MOONEYE HIODONT
MOONEYE CISCO BLOATER
MOON-EYED LUNATIC
MOONFISH OPAH SUNFISH
JOROBADO
MOONFLOWER ACHETE
MOONLIGHT FLESH MOONGLOW
MOONRAT GYMNURE
MOONSET MOONDOWN
MOONFALL
MOONSHINE BREW MOON SHINE
SHINNY BOOTLEG BLOCKADE
MOONSTONE (**AUTHOR OF —**)
COLLINS
(**CHARACTER IN —**) CUFF EZRA
JOHN BLAKE BRUFF CANDY LUKER
RACHEL GABRIEL GODFREY
ROSANNA FRANKLIN JENNINGS
SPEARMAN VERINDER ABLEWHITE
BETTEREDGE HERNCASTLE
MURTHWAITE
MOONSTRUCK MAD LOONY
LUNATIC
MOONWORT LUNARY HONESTY
MOOR FEN BENT FELL MOSS POST
BEACH BERTH HOVEL TURCO
COMONTE MARRANO MOGRABI

MOORMAN MORESCO MORISCO
COMMONTY
(INFERTILE —) LANDE
MOOR COCK GORCOCK MUIRCOCK
MOORED GIRT
MOORING DOCK MOORAGE
MOORLAND ROSLAND OUTFIELD
MOOSE BELL ELAND CERVID
ORIGNAL
(YOUNG —) CALF
MOOSEWOOD DIRCA
MOOT MUTE STIR PORTMOOT
MOP BOB SOP SWAB MALKIN
MERKIN MOPPET SCOVEL
(— FOR CLEANING CANNON)
MERKIN
(— OF HAIR) TOUSLE
(BAKER'S —) MALKIN MAWKIN
MOPANE IRONWOOD
MOPE MOON MUMP PEAK POUT
SULK BOODY BROOD GLOOM
MOPING FUSTY DUMPISH
MOPOKE FROGMOUTH
MOPSUS SEER
(FATHER OF —) AMPYCUS RHACIUS
(MOTHER OF —) MANTO CHLORIS
MORA LOVE TIME LIMMA SEMEION
MORAL TAG PURE CIVIL ETHIC
EPIMYTH ETHICAL UPRIGHT
HONORARY
(MAN OF —S) AESOP
(PL.) THEW
MORALIST ETHICIAN
MORALISTIC DIDACTIC
MORALITY MORALS VIRTUE
MORALIZING PI
MORASS BOG FEN FLOW MOSS
ROSS SUMP FLUSH MARSH SLACK
POLDER SLOUGH QUAGMIRE
MORAY PUSI ELGIN HAMLET
MURAENA
MORBID SICK MORBOSE PECCANT
MORDANT HANDLE SPIRIT CAUSTIC
STRIKER SCATHING
MORDECAI (FATHER OF —) JAIR
(WARD OF —) ESTHER
MORE MO MAE PIU OTHER HELDER
(— OR LESS) HALFWAY
(— THAN) BUT OVER ABOVE RISING
PLUSQUAM
(— THAN ADEQUATE) AMPLE
(— THAN ENOUGH) TOO
(— THAN HALF) BETTER
(— THAN ONE) SEVERAL
(— THAN ONE OR TWO) SUNDRY
(— THAN SUFFICIENT) ABUNDANT
(— THAN THIS) YEA
(LITTLE —) ADVANTAGE
(ONE —) ANOTHER
(PREF.) MALLO PLEIO PLEO PLIO
(— THAN) PLU SUPER
MOREEN TABBY
MOREL HELVELLA MORIGLIO
MORELLO MOREL GRIOTTE
MULBERRY
MOREOVER EFT EKE TOO ALSO
MORE AGAIN EITHER BESIDES
FARTHER FURTHER THERETO
LIKEWISE OVERMORE
MOREPORK OWL PEHO RURU
MOPOKE MOPEHAWK
MORGUE LIBRARY MORTUARY
MORION CABASSET

MORMON COHAB SAINT DANITE
PATRIARCH
(— STATE) UTAH
MORMONE CALCITONIN
MORNING GAY MORN MATIN
MORROW UNDERN COCKCROW
MORNTIME
(IN THE —) MANE
MORNING GLORY NIL KOALI
TWINER GAYBINE IPOMOEA
MANROOT PILIKAI BINDWEED
SCAMMONY MOONFLOWER
(— GROWING AMONG GRAIN)
BEAR
MORNING-GOWN PEIGNOIR
MORNING STAR VENUS DAYSTAR
LUCIFER MERCURY BARTONIA
MORO LUTAO SAMAL YAKAN
ILLANO JOLOANO MARANAO
MOROCCO MAROQUIN

MOROCCO
CAPE: NUN NOUN
CAPITAL: RABAT
COIN: OKIA RIAL OKIEH DIRHAM
  MOUZOUNA
DISTRICT: ERRIF
FRENCH NAME: MAROC
MEASURE: KALA SAAH FANEGA
  IZENBI TOMINI
MOUNTAIN: TOUBKAL
MOUNTAIN RANGE: RIF ATLAS
PEOPLE: MOOR BERBER KABYLE
  MOSLEM MUSLIM
PORT: SAFI CEUTA RABAT SAFFI
  AGADIR TETUAN LARACHE
  MAZAGAN MELILLA MOGADOR
  TANGIER
PROVINCE: CEUTA MELILLA
RIVER: DRA SOUS WADI SEBOU
  TENSIFT MOULOUYA
TOWN: FES FEZ SAFI OUJDA RABAT
  AGADIR MEKNES KENITRA
  TANGIER TETOUAN MARRAKECH
  CASABLANCA
WEIGHT: ROTL ARTAL ARTEL GERBE
  RATEL KINTAR QUINTAL

MORON FOOL AMENT IMBECILE
MORONITY MOROSIS
MOROSE SAD ACID GLUM GRUM
SOUR MOODY RUSTY SURLY
CRUSTY GLOOMY SEVERE STINGY
SULLEN CRABBED CROOKED
PEEVISH STROUNGE SATURNINE
SPLENETIC
MOROSELY CRUSTILY
MOROSENESS ASPERITY
MORPHEME BASE ETYMON
COGNATE
MORPHINE SNOW
MORPHOLOGICAL FORMAL
MORRIS MILL MERELS
MORSE WALRUS
MORSEL BIT NIG ORT TIT BITE GNAP
SNAP SCRAN TIDBIT BUCKONE
MORCEAU NOISETTE PARTICLE
SKERRICK
(— OF CHEESE) TRIP
(— OF CHOCOLATE) BUD
(— OF SEASONED MEAT) GOBBET
(CHOICE —) TIDBIT TITBIT
(PREF.) PSOMO

MORTAL BEING DYING FATAL
HUMAN VITAL DEADLY FINITE
LETHAL BRITTLE DEATHLY
DEATHFUL
(FIRST —) YAMA
MORTALITY FLESH MURRAIN
MORTALLY DEADLY FATALLY
MORTAR DAB COMPO DAGGA
GROUT LARRY ROYAL SORKI
SWISH CANNON CEMENT HOLMOS
MINNIE POTGUN BEDDING
COEHORN DAUBING PERRIER
POUNDER PUGGING SOORKEE
(— AND PESTLE) DOLLY DOLLIE
(— EXTRUDED BETWEEN LATHS)
KEY
(— FOR ROCKETS) TROMBE
(— FOR SALUTES) CHAMBER
(— MADE WITH STRAW) BAUGE
(ANTISUBMARINE —) SQUID
(INFERIOR —) SLIME
(SMALL —) HOBIT ROYAL TINKER
(THIN —) LARRY
MORTARBOARD CATERCAP
TRENCHER
MORTAR BOAT PALANDER
MORTGAGE DIP LAY BOND LIEN
ENGAGE MONKEY OBLIGE WADSET
WEDDEED THIRLAGE
(KIND OF —) ARM
MORTGAGOR REVERSER
MORTIFICATION ENVY SHAME
SPITE CHAGRIN GANGRENE
NECROSIS VEXATION
MORTIFIED ASHAMED
MORTIFY ABASE ABASH SHAME
SPITE DEMEAN HUMBLE CHAGRIN
CRUCIFY MACERATE
MORTISE GAIN COCKET
(SIDE OF —) CHEEK
MORTUARY MORGUE FUNERARY
SAWLSHOT SEPULCHRAL
MORWONG TARAKIHI
MOSAIC BUHL BOULE INLAY
AUCUBA BOULLE EMBLEM MUSIVE
SCREEN FRISOLEE INTARSIA
TERRAZZO
(— PIECE) SMALTO TESSARA
(POTATO —) CRINKLE
(WOOD —) TARSIA INTARSIA
MOSCOW (NATIVE OF —)
MOSCOVITE
MOSEL (— FEEDER) SAAR
MOSES (BROTHER OF —) AARON
MOSEY ROAM ANKLE SAUNTER
MOSLEM MOOR HADJI HAFIZ HANIF
ISLAM MALAY SALAR PAYNIM
SHIITE TURBAN ISLAMIC
MOORMAN SANGGIL SARACEN
ISLAMITE SANGUILE
(— SCHOLAR) ALIM ULAMA ULEMA
(— SECT) SUNNI
MOSQUE JAMI MOSCH DURGAH
MASJID MESKED
MOSQUITO GNAT AEDES CULICID
GAMBIAE SKEETER ANOPHELE
DIPTERAN
(PREF.) CULIC(I) EMPID(O)
MOSS FOG MNIUM USNEA HYPNUM
MUSKEG AEROGEN FOXFEET
GULAMAN HAIRCAP PILIGAN
TORTULA CROWFOOT MOSSWORT
SPHAGNUM STAGHORN

(— HANGING FROM TREE) WEEPER
(PL.) MUSCI
(PREF.) BRY(O) MUSC(I)(O)
SPHAGNI SPHAGNO
MOSSBUNKER MENHADEN
MOSSHORN STEER
MOSSI MOLE MORE
MOSSI-GURUNSI GUR
MOSS PINK PHLOX
MOSSTROOPER RIDER
MOSSY OLD FOGGY HOARY
MUSCCSE
MOST BEST MOSTLY FARTHEST
(PREF.) PLEISTO
MOSTLY MOST FECKLY CHIEFLY
MOSTDEAL
MOT JEST ZINGER
MOTE ATOM ATOMY FESCUE
MOATHILL
(PL.) DUST
MOTEL COURT
MOTH IO GEM NUN PUG DART
HAWK LUNA MOTE PAGE ACREA
APPLE ATLAS EGGAR EGGER
FLAME GAMMA IMAGO MORMO
PISKY PLUME SAMIA SWIFT THORN
USHER WITCH ANTLER BAGONG
BUGONG BURNET COSSID DAGGER
DATANA HERALD HUMMER
JUGATE LACKEY LAPPET MILLER
MOODER MUSLIN PLUSIA PRALID
QUAKER RUSTIC SPHINX THISBE
TINEID TISSUE TUSSUR VENEER
ARCTIAN ARCTIID BAGWORM
BUDWORM CRAMBID CRININE
DELTOID DRINKER EMERALD
EMPEROR EUCLEID FESTOON
FIGWORM FOOTMAN FRENATE
HOOKTIP NOCTUID PEGASUS
PSYCHID PYRALIS SLICKER
STINGER SYLINID TINEOLA
TORTRIX TUSSOCK URANIID
VAPORER ZYGENID AEGERIID
ARMYWORM ROMRYCID
CATOCALA CECROPIA CINNABAR
COCHYLIS FISHTAIL FORESTER
GEOMETER GOLDTAIL GRISETTE
HAWKMOTH HEPIALID KNOTHORN
MOTHWORM PHYCITID PLUTELLA
SPHINGID SPRAWLER WAINSCOT
SATURNIID PALMERWORM
(— BREEDER) AURELIAN
(VERY SMALL —) MICRO
(PREF.) PHALAENO SETO
MOTH BALL REPELLER
MOTHER INA MOM DAME MAMA
MERE MADRE MAMMA MAMMY
MATER MINNY MODUR MITHER
MULIER MUTTER VENTER
GENETRIX
(— OF GOD) THEOTOKOS
(— OF THE GODS) RHEA
(DIVINE —) MATRIGAN
(GREAT —) AGDISTIS
(NOURISHING — OF MAN) CYBELE
(OF THE SAME —) UTERINE
(SEVEN —S) MATRIS
(SIDE OF —) ENATE
(PREF.) MADRE MATR(I)(O) METRO
MOTHERLAND COUNTRY
MOTHERLY MATERNAL MATRONAL
MOTHER-OF-PEARL NACRE PEARL
ABALONE

MOTIF SPRIG DESIGN DEVICE MOTIVE SCALLOP APPLIQUE MORESQUE

MOTILE ZO ZOO

MOTION WAY FARD FEED GIRD MOVE SIGN WHID HURRY PAVIE APPORT MOMENT MOTIVE TRAVEL UNREST IMPULSE ACTIVITY MOVEMENT OVERTURE
(— ASEA) SCEND
(— OF AIR) AIRFLOW
(— OF CONTEMPT) FICO
(— OF HORSE) AIR
(— TO) ALLATIVE
(ABRUPT —) CHOP
(BACKWARD —) STERNWAY
(CAM —) COULIER
(CIRCULAR —) GYRE COMPASS
(CONFUSED —) GURGE
(DANCE —) CAPER
(DIZZY —) SWIMBEL
(EXPRESSIVE —) GESTURE
(FORWARD —) HEADWAY
(GLIDING —) SWIM SKITTER
(HASTY —) WAFF
(HEAVING —) ESTUS AESTUS
(HURRIED —) HUSTLE
(ILLEGAL —) BALK BAULK
(IRREGULAR —) SWAG
(JERKING —) BOB LIPE JIGGLE
(LATERAL —) DRIFT
(QUIVERING —) TREMOR
(RAPID —) SCOUR BRATTLE
(REARING —) PESADE
(RECIPROCATING —) SEESAW
(ROCKING —) SHOOGLE
(ROTARY —) SWAY BACKSPIN SIDESPIN
(SHOWY —) FANFARE
(SIDEWAYS —) CRAB
(SLOW —) CRAWL
(SPINNING —) ENGLISH
(SUNWISE —) DEASIL
(SWEEPING —) WHISK
(SWIMMING —) FLUTTER
(TREMULOUS —) SHAKE
(UNDULATING —) WAVE
(UNSTEADY —) WABBLE WOBBLE
(UPWARD —) HEAVE
(VIGOROUS —) SKELP
(VIOLENT —) JERK RAPT BENSEL
(WAVERING —) SHAKE
(WAVING —) WAFF
(WHIRLING —) SWIRL
(PREF.) CIN(E)(EMATO)(EMO)(ET) (ETO) KIN(E)(EMATO)(EMO)(ET)(ETO) KINESI MOTI MOTO PHORO
(SUFF.) CINESIA KINESIA KINESIS KINETIC

MOTIONLESS DEAD ASLEEP STATIC IMMOBILE STAGNANT STIRLESS

MOTION PICTURE PIC CINE FILM FLICK MOVIE BIOPIC CINEMA TALKIE CHEAPIE SMELLIE FLICKERS TELEFILM PHOTODRAMA
(PL.) SILENTS
(PREF.) CINE(MATO)(MO)(T)(TO)

MOTIVATE PROPEL ACTUATE ANIMATE INSPIRE

MOTIVATED COVERT

MOTIVATION DRIVE

MOTIVE GOAD SAKE SPUR CAUSE MOTIF SCORE ACTUAL DESIRE OBJECT REASON REGARD SPRING ATTACCO IMPULSE PATTERN RESPECT RINCEAU SUBJECT INSTANCE STIMULUS
(— FOR OBEDIENCE) SANCTION
(ALLEGED —) PRETEXT
(CHIEF —) MAINSPRING
(PRINCIPAL —) MAINSPRING

MOTLEY MIXED MEDLEY RAGTAG MOTTLED PIEBALD UNKEMPT
(PREF.) PARTI PARTY

MOTMOT HOUTOU SAWBILL PICARIAN

MOTOR AUTO TOOT TOUR MOVER ENGINE BOOSTER ROTATOR TURBINE EFFERENT OUTBOARD

MOTORBIKE MOPED

MOTORBOAT KICKER LAUNCH AUTOBOAT RUNABOUT HYDROFOIL

MOTORCAR LIMO COUPE MOTOR SEDAN JALOPY FLIVVER JALOPPY STEAMER CABRIOLET DOODLEBUG LIMOUSINE KNOCKABOUT
(MINIATURE —) KART
(MINIATURE — FOR RACING) KART
(RACING —) KART

MOTORCYCLE BIKE CYCLE MOPED MOTOR STEED TRICAR CHOPPER AUTOETTE DIRTBIKE MINIBIKE TRICYCLE PIPSQUEAK
(PART OF —) HORN SEAT TANK TIRE BRAKE GUARD LEVER LIGHT VALVE WHEEL CLUTCH FENDER SADDLE SIGNAL CALIPER EXHAUST MUFFLER TOOLBOX HANDGRIP THROTTLE GEARSHIFT TAILLIGHT TENSIONER CARBURETOR TACHOMETER SPEEDOMETER
(SMALL —) MINIBIKE

MOTORIST AUTOIST
(SELFISH —) ROADHOG

MOTORMAN CARMAN WATTMAN TROLLYMAN

MOTORTRUCK DRAY LORRY CAMION BOBTAIL FLATBED

MOTTLE CHECK TABBY SPONGE

MOTTLED JAZZ PIED CHINE PINTO TABBY CALICO MARLED MOTLEY RUMINATE SPLASHED

MOTTO MOT LOGO WORD ADAGE AXIOM POESY CACHET DEVICE EUREKA LEGEND REASON IMPRESA EPIGRAPH
(— IN A RING) POSY
(— OF CALIFORNIA) EUREKA
(— OF MAINE) DIRIGO

MOUE FACE

MOUFLON MUSIMON

MOULDER CRUMBLE

MOULDING (HOLLOW —) SCOTIA
(ZIGZAG —) DANCETTE

MOULIN CHIMNEY

MOUND AHU COP HOW LAW LOW BALK BANK BOSS BUND BUTT GOAL HILL HUMP KNOW MOLE POME TELL TEPE TERP TUFT TUMP AGGER BERRY DHERI ESKAR ESKER KNOLL MONDE MOTTE MOUNT PINGO RAISE STUPA TOMAN BARROW CAUSEY MEILER RIDEAU ANTHILL BOUROCK HILLOCK MAMELON BACKSTOP BARBETTE SNOWBANK TEOCALLI
(— ABOUT A PLANT) TUMP
(— FOR MEMORIAL) CAIRN
(— IN BUILDING MATERIAL) DIMPLE
(— OF DETRITUS) WASH
(— OF ICE) DOME
(— OF WOOD TO BE CHARRED) MEILER
(ANCIENT —) TEL TELL
(BURIAL —) LAW LOW TOR TOLA BERRY GUACA HUACA BARROW KURGAN TUMULUS
(FORTIFIED —) DUN
(GLACIAL —) KAME
(KING'S —) POME
(MILITARY —) BARBETTE
(PALISADED —) MOTTE
(VOLCANIC —) HORNITO
(PREF.) BUNO

MOUND BIRD MEGAPODE

MOUNT BEN STY BACK HEAD RIDE RISE SCAN ARISE BIPOD BOARD CLIMB GETON HEAVE HINGE SCALE SPEEL SPIRE SWARM ASCEND ASPIRE BREAST MORIAH CHARGER COLLINE HAIRPIN HARNESS BESTRIDE MOUNTAIN MOUNTING MOUNTURE SURMOUNT
(— A HORSE) FORK LIGHT WORTH
(— BY STEPS) SCAN
(— HIGH) SOAR
(— NEAR TROY) IDA
(— ON PIN) STICK
(— ON WINGS) SOAR
(— UP) ACCRUE
(— UP TO) RUNTO
(STEREOTYPE —) CORE

MOUNTAIN BEN KOP BERG CIMA DAGH FELL KLIP KNOB MONS MONT NEBO PICO PIKE JEBEL MOUNT RANGE BARROW BUNDOC GILEAD GUNONG HEIGHT PISGAH HELICON MONTURE NUNATAK MONADNOCK
(— INHABITED BY SPIRIT) GUACA HUACA
(— MASS) OROGEN
(— PASS) GHAT GHAUT
(— STATE) MONTANA
(— TRACT) DUAR
(AT BASE OF —) PIEDMONT
(BUDDHIST SACRED —) OMEI
(FABLED —) KAF MERU
(GREEK —) OSSA PELION HELICON OLYMPUS MENALUS
(HIGH —) ALP
(ROUND —) REEK
(SMALL —) NOB KNOB BUTTE
(SNOW —) JOKUL
(SUBMARINE —) GUYOT SEAMOUNT
(PREF.) MONTI ORE(O) ORI ORO

MOUNTAIN ASH SORB SORBUS DOGBERRY MOZEMIZE ROUNTREE WINETREE

MOUNTAIN BEAVER SEWELLEL

MOUNTAIN BINDWEED SOLDANEL

MOUNTAIN CAP SCALP

MOUNTAIN CLIMBER CRAGSMAN

MOUNTAIN CRANBERRY FOXBERRY

MOUNTAINEER WASIR WAZIR HEIDUC HAYDUCK HILLMAN ORESTES MONTESCO TIERSMAN
(PL.) GUTI GUTIANS

MOUNTAIN GOAT IBEX MAZAME

MOUNTAIN LAUREL IVY HEATH ERICAD KALMIS LAUREL IVYWOOD CALFKILL
(THICKET OF —) SLICK

MOUNTAIN LINNET TWITE

MOUNTAIN LION PUMA COUGAR

MOUNTAIN MAHOE EMAJAGUA

MOUNTAIN MISERY TARWEED

MOUNTAINOUS RANGY ALPINE VICIOUS

MOUNTAIN PARSLEY FLUELLEN

MOUNTAIN RANGE KAF QAF TIER SIERRA SAWBACK DINDYMUS

MOUNTAIN SICKNESS VETA

MOUNTAINSIDE FELLSIDE

MOUNTAINTOP MAN DOME

MOUNTAIN WOOD ROCKWOOD

MOUNTEBANK ANTIC BALADIN BALADINE IMPOSTOR OPERATOR

MOUNTED CARDED SADDLE ASTRIDE EASELED EQUITANT

MOUNT ETNA MONGIBEL

MOUNTING MOUNT SCAPE ASCENT FLIGHT MONTANT SOAKING ASPIRANT INCABLOC MOUNTURE
(— OF GEM) CHASE
(STYLE OF —) SETTING

MOURN DOLE KEEN SIGH WAIL PLAIN BEWAIL GRIEVE LAMENT SORROW GRIZZLE

MOURNER WAILER WEEPER
(HIRED —) SALLIE SAULIE
(PROFESSIONAL —) MUTE BLACK KEENER

MOURNFUL SAD BLACK MINOR SORRY WEEPY RUEFUL TRISTE DERNFUL FUNEBRE SIGHFUL WAILFUL DEJECTED DIRGEFUL ELEGIOUS FUNEREAL MAESTIVE MESTFULL PLANTFUL YEARNFUL PLAINTIVE

MOURNING DOLOR SHIVA DISMAL SORROW WIDOWED
(— CLOTH) RADZIMIR

MOURNING BECOMES ELECTRA
(AUTHOR OF —) ONEILL
(CHARACTER IN —) ADAM EZRA ORIN BRANT DAVID HAZEL NILES PETER MANNON LAVINIA CHRISTINE

MOUSE MURINE MYGALE RODENT SHINER VERMIN ARVICOLE CRICETID MYOMORPH
(COMPUTER —) TRACKBALL
(LIKE A —) MURIFORM
(MEADOW —) VOLE
(STRIPED —) KUSU
(PREF.) MURI MY(O) SMINTHO
(SUFF.) MYS

MOUSEBIRD COLY

MOUSE-COLORED DUN

MOUSE DEER PLANDOK

MOUSE GRAY SAKKARA SPARROW

MOUSELIKE MURINE

MOUSETRAP TIPE

MOUSING KEEPER

MOUSY DRAB

MOUTH OS GAB GAM GOB JIB MUG MUN NEB ORF ROW YAP BEAK BEAL BOCA HEAD MUSS PUSS

SHOP TRAP YAWN BAZOO BOCCA BRACE CHOPS CODON STOMA TUTEL GEBBIE KISSER MUZZLE RABBLE RICTUS SUCKER THROAT CLAPPER FLUMMER ORIFICE OSTIOLE STOMACH LORRIKER PAVILLON
(— AND THROAT) COPPER WHISTLE
(— OF CANYON) ABRA
(— OF GLASS FURNACE) BOCCA
(— OF HARBOR) BOCA
(— OF PERITHECIUM) OSTIOLE
(— OF RIVER) BEAL BOCA LADE ENTRY FIRTH INFLUX OSTIUM ESTUARY OSTIARY OUTFALL
(— OF SHAFT) BRACE
(— OF TRUMPET) BELL CODON PAVILLON
(— PARTS OF ARTHROPOD) TROPHI
(AWAY FROM —) ABORAL
(KILN —) KILNEYE KILNHOLE
(SORE — OF SHEEP) ECTHYMA
(TOWARD —) ORAD
(TOWARD THE —) ORAD
(WRY —) MURGEON
(PL.) ORA
(PREF.) BUCCO ORI ORO OSCULI STOM(A)(AT)(ATO)(O)
(SUFF.) STOMA(TA)(TE)(TOUS) STOME STOMI(A) STOMOUS STOMUM STOMY

MOUTHFUL GAG GOB SUP GNAP SWIG GOLEE GOBBET
MOUTH-ORGAN HARP HARMONICA
MOUTHPART BILL
MOUTHPIECE BAR BEAK BOCAL MOUTH FIPPLE SYRINX PROPHET
(— OF BAGPIPE) MUSE
(— OF OTHERS) FUGUEMAN
(— OF PIPE) STEM
MOUTHWASH GARGLE COLLUTORIUM
MOUTH-WATERING SALIVANT
MOVABLE FREE LOOSE MOBILE PORTABLE REMUABLE
(PL.) MEUBLES
MOVE GO ACT AWE FIG GEE GET WAG BOOM BORE BUCK BUMP CALL DRAW FIRK FLIT GOAD HEAT KNEE MAKE PIRL ROLL SILE SPUR STEP STIR SWAY WORK ANKLE BLITZ BUDGE CARRY CAUSE CROWD DRAFT HEAVE IMPEL LIGHT MARCH MUDGE QUECH REMUE ROUSE SHAKE SHIFT TOUCH GAMBIT HANDLE HUSTLE INCITE INDUCE KINDLE MOTION PROMPT QUITCH REMBLE SASHAY STRAKE ACTUATE AGITATE ANIMATE DISTURB DRAUGHT FLUTTER INSPIRE MIGRATE PROVOKE AMBULATE BULLDOZE CATAPULT DEMARCHE DISLODGE DISPLACE MOTIVATE
(— ABOUT) ROLL WEND DISPACE SHUFFLE CONVERSE LOCOMOTE
(— ACROSS) THWART
(— ACROSS SCREEN) CRAWL SCROLL
(— ACTIVELY) YANK
(— AIMLESSLY) GAD POKE BOGUE
(— ALONG) SHOG

(— APART) ABDUCT SPREAD
(— A RESOLUTION) FIRST
(— ASIDE) SKEW
(— AS IN STUPOR) DAVER
(— ASUNDER) SINGLE
(— AT TOP SPEED) LICK
(— AWAY) CUT MOG DECAMP RECEDE
(— AWKWARDLY) HODGE HIRSEL LARRUP SHAMBLE SLUMMOCK
(— BACK) FADE ARSLE RECUR RECEDE RETIRE RETREAT
(— BACKWARD AND FORWARD) GIG SWAY DARTLE DIDDLE SHUFFLE SHUTTLE
(— BOOM OR SAIL) JIB
(— BRISKLY) FAN HALE STIR FRICK FRIKE FRISK KNOCK SQUIRT TRANCE TRAVEL WHIPPET
(— BY FITS AND STARTS) JIFFLE
(— BY JERKS) HITCH JIGGET JIGGLE JINKLE
(— BY SMALL SHOCKS) JOG
(— BY WHEELS) ROLL TRUNDLE
(— CHESS PIECE) DEVELOP
(— CLUMSILY) HOIT JOLL PAUT BARGE KEVEL HIRSEL LUMBER TOLTER GALUMPH STUMBLE
(— COMPUTER VIDEO DISPLAY) SCROLL
(— DIAGONALLY) CATER
(— DOWN) SILE STOOP DECLINE DESCEND
(— FORCIBLY) SHOVE
(— FORWARD) BREAK ADVANCE PROGREDE
(— FROM SIDE TO SIDE) WAG
(— FURTIVELY) LEER GLIDE SLINK SLIVE SNEAK STEAL
(— GRADUALLY) EDGE
(— GRATINGLY) SCRAPE
(— HAPHAZARDLY) BUCKET
(— HASTILY) SCUR SKIRR
(— HAUGHTILY) SWOOP
(— HEAVILY) LUG LUMP FLUMP LUMBER
(— IN AGITATION) SEETHE
(— IN AWKWARD MANNER) GANGLE
(— IN CIRCLES) MILL PURL
(— IN MARBLES) FULK
(— IN ON) NEAR
(— IN RIPPLES) CURL
(— IN SHAMBLE) SHUFFLE
(— IN SHUFFLING MANNER) MOSEY
(— IN SMALL DEGREES) INCH
(— INWARDLY) ENMOVE
(— IN WATER) SQUELCH
(— IN WAVES) LAP CRINKLE
(— JERKILY) JAG BUCK FLIP KICK FLIRT BUCKET TWITCH
(— LANGUIDLY) MAUNDER
(— LAZILY) HULK
(— LEISURELY) AMBLE
(— LIGHTLY) BRUSH FLUFF
(— LOOSELY) SLOP
(— NERVOUSLY) DITHER
(— NIMBLY) KILT LINK WHIP DANCE
(— OFF) FIRK RYNT MOSEY MORRIS
(— ON) MOG VAMP AVAUNT SUCCEED WHIGFARE
(— OUT) BLOW
(— OUT OF SIGHT) SINK

(— QUICKLY) BOB FIG CLIP DUCK FIRK FLAX FLIT GIRD JINK KITE SCUR WHAP WHEW WHID WHOP YANK FLASH GLENT SKEET SKIRR SKITE SPANK SQUIB STAVE STOUR THROW NIDDLE STRIKE WALLOP SKIMMER
(— QUIETLY) SLIP
(— RAPIDLY) BANG BOLT BUZZ HEEL HURL SKIR THUD CHASE GLINT SCOUR CAREER GIGGIT HURTLE WHIRRY AGITATE CLATTER HIGHTAIL
(— RESTLESSLY) FIG GAD FIKE ITCH CHURN SQUIB JIFFLE KELTER
(— SHAKILY) HOTTER
(— SIDEWAYS) SKID SLEW SLUE
(— SIDEWISE) CRAB EDGE SIDLE SLENT
(— SINUOUSLY) WRIGGLE
(— SLOWLY) LAG MOG INCH PANT PAUT SLUG BOGUE CRAWL CREEP DRAWL FUDGE SHLEP SLOOM SNAIL HAGGLE LINGER SCHLEP SCHLEPP TRINTLE
(— SMOOTHLY) SLIP DRIFT FLOAT GLIDE SLEEK GLISSADE
(— SPIRALLY) GYRATE
(— STEADILY) FORGE
(— STEALTHILY) GLIDE SLINK SMOOT SNAKE
(— STIFFLY) CHAMBLE CRAMMEL
(— SUDDENLY) BOLT LASH YERK GLENT START FLOUNCE STARTLE
(— SWIFTLY) CUT FLY BOOM HARE LEAP RAKE SCUD SPIN BREEZE COURSE WUTHER SWIFTEN
(— THROUGH AIR) FLY
(— TO AND FRO) FAN FLOP DODGE SHAKE WIGWAG AGITATE
(— TO ANOTHER PLACE) ADJOURN
(— TO LEEWARD) DRIVE
(— TREMULOUSLY) WAPPER
(— TRIPPINGLY) WALTZ WAPPER
(— UNEASILY) FIDGET
(— UNSTEADILY) BICKER BUMBLE FALTER HOBBLE WABBLE WAMBLE WELTER WOBBLE BLUNDER STAGGER STUMBLE
(— UP AND DOWN) BOB HOWD SEESAW TEETER
(— UPWARD) ARISE ASCEND GRADUATE
(— VESSEL) KEDGE
(— VIGOROUSLY) FLOG STRAY
(— VIOLENTLY) DASH FLOG HURL LASH LEAP SWASH AGITATE COMMOVE
(— WAVERINGLY) FLEET
(— WEAKLY) FLAG
(— WITH BEATING MOTION) FLAP
(— WITH EFFORT) ACHE WADE
(— WITH LEAPS) SKIP SPRING
(— WITH NOISY ACTIVITY) BUSTLE
(— WITH POMP) SWEEP
(— WITH SHORT TURNS) ZIGZAG
(CHESS —) KEY COOK NECK PLOY GAMBIT KEYMOVE
(STRATEGIC —) TACK
(SUCCESSFUL —) SCORE
(SUDDEN —) GAMBADE
MOVED MOSSO ANIMATE FRANTIC INSTINCT

(— BY LOVE) AMOROUS
(EASILY —) FLESHLY SKINLESS
MOVEMENT EDDY MOTO PLAY STIR CARRY CAUSE FLICK FLISK FLOAT FRONT GESTE MUDGE TREND UKIYO ACTION CURSUS ENTREE MOMENT MOTION PIAFFE SPRAWL STROKE CURRENT FURIANT GAMBADO GESTURE KINESIS PIAFFER UKIYOYE BUSINESS CHARTISM FEMINISM FUTURISM HASKALAH STIRRING PERIPATETICS
(— BY ORGANISMS) TAXIS
(— FOR POLITICAL UNION) ENOSIS
(— FROM POINT TO POINT) PASSAGE
(— IN BULLFIGHT) SUERTE
(— OF AIR) SPIRIT
(— OF CHORUS) STROPHE
(— OF CLOUDS) CARRY
(— OF COMPUTER BITS) SHIFT
(— OF EYES) NYSTAGMUS
(— OF HAND) PASS
(— OF HORSE) LEVADE PIAFFE
(— OF LEG) STEP
(— OF LOOM) MOUSING
(— OF NEEDLE) STITCH
(— OF PLANTS) NUTATION
(— OF PROTOPLASM) CYCLOSIS
(— OF QUADRILLE) TRENISE
(— OF ROPE) SURGE
(— OF SHIP) STERNWAY
(— OF SHUTTLE) SHOOT
(— OF TIDE) LAKIE
(— OF TROOPS) LIFT
(— OF WATER) BOBBLE
(— TO AND FRO) SHUTTLE
(— TOWARD GOAL) STRIDE
(AGITATED —) WORKING
(ART —) CUBISM
(AVANT-GARDE —) UNDERGROUND
(BACKWARD —) BACKUP BACKLASH BACKWASH
(BALLET —) PLIE BATTU FRAPPE FOUETTE FLICFLAC
(BOBBING —) BOBBLE
(BODILY —) ACTION
(BOWEL —) LAXATION
(BOWING —) LEG
(BOXING —) SPAR
(BRISK —) SNAP
(BROWNIAN —) PEDESIS
(CAVALRY —) CARACOLE
(CIRCULAR —) CYCLING
(CLEVER —) PAW
(CONFUSED —) MILLING
(CONVULSIVE —) SPASM
(DANCE —) FRIS BRISE CLOSE GIGUE GLIDE LASSU SPIRAL BATTERIE
(DARTING —) FLIRT
(DECISIVE —) UPCOME
(DOWNWARD —) DECLINE
(DROLL —) GAMBADE GAMBADO
(ENLIGHTENMENT —) HASKALAH
(EXPANSION —) BOOM
(EYE —) REM SACCADE
(FANTASTIC —) GAMBADO
(FENCING —) VOLT
(FLAPPING —) FLAFF
(FLUCTUATING —) PLAY

(FORWARD —) SWEEP ADVANCE PROGRESS INCESSION PROCESSION
(FROLICKING —) FRISK GAMBOL
(GRADUAL —) CREEPISM
(GRAZING —) SKIFF
(GREEK UNDERGROUND —) EAM
(GYMNASTIC —) KIP SWING DISMOUNT
(HUMOROUS —) BURLA
(IMPATIENT —) FLOUNCE
(INCIPIENT —) MINT
(INDEPENDENCE —) SWADESHI
(INVOLUNTARY —) REFLEX
(JAPANESE ART —) YAMATO YAMATOE
(JERKING —S) BALLISM
(JERKY —) SNATCH
(JERKY EYE —) SACCADE
(LATERAL —) LEEWAY
(MASS —) STAMPEDE
(MASSAGE —) SCIAGE
(MILITARY —) BOUND MANEUVRE
(MUSICAL —) AIR DUET BURLA DUMKA LARGO ADAGIO ENTREE FINALE PRESTO ANDANTE PRELUDE SCHERZO POSTLUDE SARABAND SYMPHONY ALLEMANDE INTERMEZZO
(NOISELESS —) WHID
(OBLIQUE —) GLANCE
(OSCILLATING —) HUNT
(PAINTING —) FAUVISM TACHISM TACHISME VORTICISM
(POETRY —) IMAGISM
(POLITICAL —) LEFTISM GAULLISM
(QUADRILLE —) POULE
(QUICK —) PAW DART WHID WHIP YERK GLENT SHAKE GLANCE
(RATIONALISTIC —) DEISM
(REELING —) STAGGER
(RELIGIOUS —) JOCISM BABIISM PIETISM STUNDISM
(RETROGRADE —) SLIP CREEP
(RETURN —) BACKHAUL
(RHYTHMIC —) DANCE
(ROCKING —) HOWD
(ROWING —) HOICK
(SKATING —) MOHAWK CHOCTAW
(SKILLED —) SUERTE
(SNATCHING —) CLUTCH
(SPASMODIC —) JUMP HICCUP SPRUNT HICCOUGH
(SPRINGY —) LILT
(STAGGERING —) WAMBLE
(STEALTHY —) SLINK
(SUDDEN —) HITCH SPANG START FLICKER
(SWAYING —) SWAG
(SWEEPING —) SWINGE
(SWIFT —) SWOOSH
(TERRORIST —) NIHILISM
(THEOLOGICAL —) ARIANISM
(TUMULTUOUS —) HORROR EMOTION
(TURNING —) CARACOLE
(UNEXPECTED —) LUNGE
(UNSTEADY —) WABBLE WOBBLE
(UP AND DOWN —) SEESAW
(UPWARD —) BULGE SCEND
(UPWARD — OF VESSEL) SCEND
(WALKING —) AMBLE
(WATCH —) EBAUCHE BAGUETTE
(WAVING —) WAFT

(ZIGZAG —) TACK MEANDER
(PREF.) KINESI KINETO KIN(O)
(SUFF.) CINESIA KINESIA KINESIS KINETIC
MOVEMENTS
(SUFF.)
(PERFORMANCE OF —) PRACTIC PRAXIA PRAXIS
MOVER MOTIVE CLIPPER
(KIND OF —) PEOPLE
MOVIE (ALSO SEE MOTION PICTURE) PIC FILM FLICK BIOPIC FLICKS SLEEPER MELODRAMA
(— WITH BLOODSHED) SHOOTEMUP
(ANIMATED —) TOON CARTOON
(BIOGRAPHICAL —) BIOPIC
(CRIME —) FILMNOIR
(SUCCESSFUL —) MEGAHIT
(PL.) PICTURES
MOVIES (DEVOTEE OF —) CINEPHILE
MOVING WAY HIGH ASTIR GOING QUICK AFLOAT MOVENT ANIMATE CURRENT AMBULANT FLITTING PATHETIC POIGNANT TOUCHING AFFECTING
(— ABOUT) AROUND AMBULANT
(— AIMLESSLY) ERRANT
(— BACKWARDS) CRAB
(— DOWN LINE) ACTIVE
(— FORWARD) ADVANCE
(— HAPHAZARDLY) AFLOAT
(— IN MANY DIRECTIONS) DIFFUSE
(— JERKILY) ATWITCH
(— RAPIDLY) STICKLE SKELPING
(— SLOWLY) SOFT GLACIAL TEDIOUS
(— TO AND FRO) AGITATED
(NOT —) STICKY STABILE
MOVINGLY PATETICO
MOW CUT BARB GOAF SKIM TASS CRADLE SCYTHE SICKLE DESECATE
(— BEANS) THROAT
(— FOR STORING GRAIN) TOSS
(— OF CORN) CANSH
(HAY —) TASS
MOWER MEADER
(FOREMOST —) LORD
MOWING MATH MOWTH SHEAR
(SECOND —) AFTERMATH
MOXIE GALL SPIRIT
MOZA (FATHER OF —) CALEB ZIMRI
MOZAMBIQUE (CAPE OF —) DELGADO
(CAPITAL OF —) MAPUTO
(LAKE OF —) CHUALI NHAVARRE
(MONEY OF —) METICAL
(RIVER OF —) SAVE MSALU RUVUMA LIMPOPO LUGENDA ZAMBEZI
(TOWN OF —) MAUA TETE BEIRA MAPAI ZUMBO CHEMBA MANICA NAMAPA PAFURI CHIMOIO NAMPULA
MOZZETTA CAMAIL
MR HERR SIGNOR SIGNIOR SIGNORE
MR MIDSHIPMAN EASY (AUTHOR OF —) MARRYAT
(CHARACTER IN —) EASY JACK AGNES MESTY WILSON REBIERA GASCOIGNE MIDDLETON
MRS MME FRAU MISS PANI

HANOUM SENORA SENHORA SIGNORA GOODWIFE
MRS DALLOWAY (AUTHOR OF —) WOOLF
(CHARACTER IN —) PETER SALLY SETON SMITH WALSH HOLMES KALMAN WILLIAM BRADSHAW CLARISSA DALLOWAY SEPTIMUS
MRS WARREN'S PROFESSION
(AUTHOR OF —) SHAW
(CHARACTER IN —) FRANK PRAED VIVIE CROFTS GEORGE SAMUEL WARREN GARDNER
MUCH FAR FELE MICH REAL WELL GREAT HEAPS MOLTO MOULT SIZES MICKLE MUCHLY ABUNDANT BEAUCOUP MUCHWHAT
(— CALLED FOR) LEEFTAIL
(PRETTY —) GAILY GAYLY
(SO —) ALL SUCH TANTO INSOMUCH
(TOO —) TROP TROPPO
(VERY —) ALL BADLY GREAT HEAPS LOADS SWITHE SWYTHE APLENTY GEYLIES GREATLY
(PREF.) ERI MULT(I) POLY SYCHNO
(HOW —) POSO QUANTI
MUCH ADO ABOUT NOTHING
(AUTHOR OF —) SHAKESPEARE
(CHARACTER IN —) HERO JOHN PEDRO URSULA VERGES ANTONIO CLAUDIO CONRADE FRANCIS LEONATO BEATRICE BENEDICK BORACHIO DOGBERRY MARGARET BALTHASAR
MUCILAGE GUM MUCUS MUCAGO
MUCILAGINOUS MALACOID
MUCK CACK SOIL
MUCOID BLENNOID
MUCUS SNOT MUCOR BUBBLE MUCAGO PHLEGM SNIVEL PITUITE
(PREF.) BLENN(I)(O) MUC(I)(O)(OSO) MYX(O)
(SUFF.) MYXA
MUD DAB FEN CLAY DIRT DUBS FANC GLAR LAIR MIRE MOIL SAUR SIND SLAB SLEW SLOB SLOP SLUB SLUD SLUE SLUR SUMP CLART FANGO GLAUR GUMBO SLAKE SLIME SLOSH SLUSH SPOSH SQUAD WAISE PELOID SLOUGH SLUDGE CLABBER GUTTERS MURGEON SLOBBER SLODDER SLUDDER SLUTHER SULLAGE
(LACUSTRINE —) GYTTJA
(LIQUID —) SLUSH
(OF DRIED —) CUTCHA
(THIN —) SLUR
(PREF.) LIMI LIMO PEL(O) TELMAT(O)
MUDAR AK AKUND ASHUR MADOR YERCUM AKMUDDAR
MUDCAP ADOBE
MUD CAT FLATHEAD
MUDCAT STATE MISSISSIPPI
MUDDLE MIX BALL DOZE HASH MASH MESS MULL MUZZ SOSS ADDLE SNAFU BEMUSE BURBLE FANKLE FOITER FUDDLE HUDDLE JUMBLE MAFFLE MIZZLE MOFFLE MUCKER POTHER PUDDLE TANGLE BECLOUD BEDEVIL BLUNDER CONFUSE EMBROIL FLUSTER

POOTHER STUPEFY BEFUDDLE BEWILDER CONFOUND DISORDER FLIUNDER
MUDDLED ADDLE BEERY FOGGY FUZZY MUSED MUZZY DRUMLY GROGGY BESOTTED CONFUSED
MUDDY DEEP FOUL GLET OOZY ROIL SICK DIRTY DROVY DUBBY GUMLY ROILY SLAKY CLAGGY CLARTY CLASHY DREGGY DROUMY DRUMLY GROUTY LIMOUS PUDDLY SALLOW SLABBY SLOBBY SLOPPY SLUBBY SLUDGY TURBID CLATCHY GUTTERY MUDDIFY MUDDISH SLOUGHY CLABBERY LUTULENT SLOBBERY
(— BY STIRRING) STUDDLE
MUDFISH BOWFIN KOMTOK
MUDFLAT PLAYA
MUDFLOW LAHAR MUDSPATE
MUDGUARD WING CUTTOO SPLASHER
MUDHOLE PULK SLOUGH LOBLOLLY
MUD MINNOW DOGFISH MUDFISH
MUD PUPPY DOGFISH
MUERMO ULMO
MUEZZIN CRIER
MUFF ERR BLOW BOBBLE MUFFLE SNUFFKIN
MUFFIN COB GEM SINK COBBE HAZEL SINKER MANCHET PIKELET POPOVER
MUFFLE MOB MOP PAD DAMP DULL MUTE NOSE WRAP BUMBLE DEADEN MUZZLE SHROUD STIFLE ENVELOP
(— A BELL) CLAM
(— THE HEAD) MOBLE
MUFFLED DEAD DEAF DULL CLOSE THICK HOLLOW INWARD MOBBED WRAPPED
MUFFLER SCARF MUFFLE SILENCER
MUFTI JURIST CIVVIES
MUG TOT BOCK CANN FACE PUNK THUG STEIN KISSER NOGGIN PEWTER SCONCE SEIDEL CANETTE GODDARD TANKARD BLACKPOT PANNIKIN SCHOPPEN
(ALE —) TOBY
(LIQUOR —) CAN GUN
(TWO-HANDLED —) SCONCE
MUGGER GOA HAM
MUGGING YOKING
MUGGINS SNIFF
MUGGY FOZY MUNGY PUGGY STICKY MUGGISH PUTHERY
MUGWORT BULWAND MUGWEED
MUISCA CHIBCHA
MUISHOND ZORIL ZORILLE
MULATTO PARDO GRIFFE GRIQUA GRIFFIN TERCERON
MULBERRY AL AAL ACH AUTE KOZO MORE WAUKE ALROOT MURREY MORELLO SOURBUSH SYCAMINE
(PREF.) MOR(I)
MULBERRY FIG SYCAMORE
MULCT ROB FINE CHECK AMERCE SCONCE FORFEIT PENALTY
MULE BUCKER HYBRID ACEMILA IRONMAN JARHEAD JUGHEAD RATTAIL SUMPTER CENCERRO HARDTAIL QUADROON QUATERON

(DROVE OF —S) ATAJO MULADA
(MOHAMMED'S —) ALBORAK
MULE ARMADILLO MULITA
MULE DRIVER SKINNER
MULE SHOE PLANCHE
MULETEER ASSMAN ARRIERO
MULE TRAIN (— DRIVER) WAGONER
MULISH BALKY STUPID STUBBORN
OBSTINATE
MULL CHAW BOSOM STUDY FETTLE
MULMUL PONDER STEATIN
COGITATE MEDITATE
MULLAH ULAMA ULEMA
MULLEIN TORCH AGLEAF ICELEAF
DOVEWEED FELTWORT FOXGLOVE
HAGTAPER LUNGWORT VERBASCO
MULLER DAMPENER
MULLET BOBO LISA LIZA BOURI
GARAU KANAE MOLET HARDER
MULLOID GOATFISH MUGILOID
SPRINGER
(UNPIERCED —) STAR
MULLIGRUBS COLIC
MULLION MONIAL
MULLOWAY JEWFISH KINGFISH
SCIAENID
MULTICOLORED PIED CALICO
MULTIFARIOUS MANIFOLD
MULTIFARIOUSNESS VARIETY
MULTIFORM DIVERSE
MULTILINGUAL POLYGLOT
MULTIPLE DECUPLE PARALLEL
SEPTUPLE MULTIPLEX
MULTIPLICAND FACIEND
MULTIPLICATION INCREASE
DUPLATION
MULTIPLICITY MULTEITY
MULTIPLIER FACIENT COFACTOR
MULTIPLY VIE BREED LAYER
DOUBLE INVOLVE ENGENDER
INCREASE MANIFOLD PROPAGATE
PROLIFERATE
(— BY ITSELF) SQUARE
MULTIPLYING
(PREF.) POLY
MULTITUDE SEA ARMY CRAM HEAP
HIVE HOST ROUT RUCK CLOUD
CROWD FLOTE MEINY POWER
SHOAL SWARM HIRSEL HOTTER
LEGION MAMPUS MEINIE NATION
THRONG SMOTHER PLURALITY
(PL.) FLOCKS
MULTITUDINOUS LEGION MYRIAD
MANIFOLD NUMEROUS
MULTIVALENT POLYAD
MULTURE THIRL THIRLAGE
MUM CLUM DARK MUMMER
MUMBLE CHEW MOUP MUMP
BROCK CHELE MOUTH CHAVEL
FAFFLE FUMBLE HOTTER HUMMER
MAFFLE MOFFLE PALTER
DRUMBLE FLUMMER GRUMBLE
(— PEEVISHLY) WITTER
MUMBLER MAFFLER
MUMBLETY-PEG KNIFE
MUMMER ACTOR GUISER GUISARD
MUMMERY MORRIS HODENING
PUPPETRY
MUMMICHOG MUDFISH
MUMMY CONGO MUMMIA SKELET
(PREF.) MOMIO
MUMMY BROWN BAY SNUFF
TAMARACK

MUMMY CASE SLEDGE
MUMPS BRANKS PAROTITIS
MUNCH CHEW NOSH CHUMP
MANGE MUNGE
MUND GRITH
MUNDA KOLARIAN
MUNDANE WORLD EARTHLY
FLESHLY SECULAR TERRENE
SUBSOLAR
MUNG BEAN MUG GRAM MONGOE
BALATONG
MUNIA MAYA PADDA
MUNICIPAL TOWN CIVIL
MUNICIPALITY CITY TOWN
CABILDO
MUNIFICENCE BOUNTY ROYALTY
LARGESSE
MUNIFICENT ROYAL LIBERAL
MUNIFIC PROFUSE MAGNIFIC
PRINCELY OPENHANDED
MUNITION
(PL.) ARMAMENT ORDNANCE
MUNJ MOONJA MANJEET
(CULMS OF —) SIRKI SIRKY
MUNTIACUS CERVULUS
MUNTJAC KAKAR RATWA KIDANG
MURAL TOPIA FRESCO
MURCIA (RIVER OF —) SEGURA
(TOWN OF —) MULA LORCA
TOTANA
MURDER HIT OFF BANE KILL SLAY
BLOOD BURKE DEATH SCRAG
FELONY RUBOUT KILLING
MURDRUM MURTHER THUGGEE
HOMICIDE MASSACRE THUGGERY
THUGGISM PATRICIDE
(FEATURING —) SNUFF
(PREMEDITATED —) HIT
MURDERER BANE CAIN KILLER
ASSASSIN
MURDER IN THE CATHEDRAL
(COMPOSER OF —) PIZZETTI
MURDEROUS FELL GORY CRUEL
FELON BLOODY CARNAL SAVAGE
DEATHFUL SANGUINARY
MURKINESS HAZE GLOOM
MURKY DARK BLACK DIRTY MIRKY
MUDDY CLOUDY PUDDLY
MURMUR COO HUM BRUM BURR
CLUM CURR HUZZ MUSE BRAWL
BROOL GRANK INKLE MOURN
RUMOR SOUCH SOUGH BABBLE
BURBLE GRUDGE GRUTCH
HUMMER MUTTER PIPPLE REPINE
RUMBLE CROODLE MURGEON
WHIMPER WHISPER WHITTER
COMPLAIN
(— AGREEABLY) CHIRM
(— AMOROUSLY) COO
(— OF PAIN) MOAN
(— OF STREAM) PURL
(CONFUSED —) BABBLE
(DEEP —) BROOL
MURMURING BUZZ BRABBLE
MURGEON RUMOROUS
MURRAH SURTI
MURRAIN PLAGUE
MURRAL DALAG
MURRE TINK ARRIE LUNGIE STRANY
TINKER ROCKBIRD
MURREY SANGUINE
MUSA SABA

MUSANG POWCAT POLECAT
MUSCA FLY
MUSCADINE BULLACE
SCUPPERNONG
MUSCAT (SEE OMAN)
MUSCLE EYE PEC BOWR LIRE THEW
FLESH MOUSE PSOAS SINEW
BENDER BICEPS CORACO FLEXOR
LACERT PENNON RECTUS SOLEUS
TENSOR AGONIST AMBIENS
CANINUS DELTOID DILATOR
ERECTOR EVERTOR FLECTOR
GLUTEUS ILIACUS LEVATOR
MUSCLE NASALIS OBLIQUE
ROTATOR SCALENE SCALLOP
TRICEPS VAGINAL ABDUCTOR
ADDUCTOR ADJUSTER ANCONEUS
ARRECTOR ATOLLENT BIVENTER
DIDUCTOR EXTENSOR GEMELLUS
GRACILIS INVERTOR MASSETER
MENTALIS OBLIQUUS OMOHYOID
OPPONENS PALMARIS PATHETIC
PECTORAL PERONEUS PROCERUS
PRONATOR RETENTOR SCALENUS
SERRATUS SPINALIS SPLENIUS
TEMPORAL TIBIALIS HAMSTRING
OBTURATOR SARTORIUS
(— MASSAGE) ROLF ROLFING
(HAVING LUMPY —S) LOADED
(THIGH —) HAMSTRING
(PL.) BRAWN THEWS
(PREF.) INO MUSCUL(O) NERVI
NERVO
(SUFF.) EUS MYA MYARIA
MUSCLE-BOUND (NOT —) SPRY
MUSCLE SUGAR INOSITE INOSITOL
MUSCOVITE MICA
MUSCOVY DUCK PATO SCOVY
MUSCULAR ROPY HEFTY HUSKY
THEWY BRAWNY ROBUST SINEWY
STRONG TOROSE NERVOUS
ATHLETIC
MUSCULATURE DETRUSOR
(SUFF.) **(HAVING —)** MYA MYARIA
MUSE CLIO DUMP MESE MULL
NETE REVE AMUSE AOIDE DREAM
ERATO MNEME STUDY THINK
HYPATE MELETE PONDER THALIA
URANIA EUTERPE REFLECT
CALLIOPE COGITATE CONSIDER
MEDITATE POLYMNIA RUMINATE
MELPOMENE POLYHYMNIA
TERPSICHORE
(— OF ASTRONOMY) URANIA
(— OF COMEDY) THALIA
**(— OF EPIC POETRY AND
ELOQUENCE)** CALLIOPE
(— OF HISTORY) CLIO
(— OF LOVE POETRY) ERATO
(— OF MIMIC ART) POLYHYMNIA
(— OF POETRY AND DANCE)
TERPSICHORE
(— OF THE FLUTE) EUTERPE
(— OF TRAGEDY) MELPOMENE
(PL.) PIERIDES
MUSETTE OBOE
MUSEUM MOMA MUSEE PRADO
LOUVRE
(— IN NEW YORK CITY) MET MOMA
FRICK CLOISTERS GUGGENHEIM
(— PIECE) RELIC
(PREF.) MUSEO

MUSH SAMP KASHA SLUSH
MUSHER SEPAWN SOFKEE
POLENTA SAGAMITE SCRAPPLE
(LIKE —) SOGGY
MUSHI (FATHER OF —) MERARI
MUSHROOM FAT CEPE FLAT GROW
DEATH ENOKI MITRA MOREL
AGARIC BEAVER BUTTON FUNGUS
AMANITA BLEWITS BOLETUS
BROILER LEPIOTA SHITAKE
MUSHRUMP SHIITAKE WHITECAP
ENOKIDAKE CHAMPIGNON
SHAGGYMANE CHANTERELLE
TEONANACATL
(— HUNTER) MYCOPHILE
(PART OF —) CAP GILL RING STEM
STALK STIPE VOLVA PILEUS
ANNULUS MYCELIUM
(PREF.) MYC(O) MYCET(O)
MUSHY SOFT SOPPY
MUSIC RAG DRAG FUNK GLEE JAZZ
NOME ROCK BEBOP CANOR CHIME
DREAM GIMEL GYMEL MURKY
NOISE SWING DREHER FUSION
MUSICA DESCANT FORLANA
LANCERS LANDLER MUSICAL
MUSICRY FALSETTO FANDANGO
GUARACHA
(— FOR ENTRANCE) ENTREE
(— OF LOUISIANA) ZYDECO
(— OF SOUTHERN LOUISIANA)
ZODICO ZYDECO
(— OF WEST INDIES) REGGAE
(— SUNG IN UNISON) PLAINSONG
(BACKGROUND —) MUZAK
(BAGPIPE —) PIBROCH
(CALYPSO —) GOOMBAY
(CHURCH —) ANTIPHON ANTIPHONY
(CONCERTED —) ENSEMBLE
(COUNTRY —) BLUEGRASS
(DANCE —) DISCO
(EVENING —) DREAM SERENA
(IDENTIFYING —) SIG
(INDIAN —) RAGA
(JAMAICAN —) SKA REGGAE
(JAPANESE COURT —) GAGAKU
(JAZZ —) SKIFFLE
(JAZZ OR FOLK —) SKIFFLE
(KIND OF —) POP RAP SOUL
TEXMEX COUNTRY JAZZROCK
SOFTROCK TECHNOPOP
(LATIN-AMERICAN —) SALSA
(LIVELY —) GALOP FURLANA
(MOD —) RAP
(MORNING —) AUBADE
(NEGRO —) SOUL
(NIGHT —) TAPS
(OLD — MAGAZINE) ETUDE
(PASSAGE OF —) MORCEAU
(PATTERN OF HINDU —) RAGA TALA
(PIECE OF —) ARIA HYMN MASS
TRIO ALBUM ETUDE FUGUE MOTET
OPERA RONDO SONATA ARIETTA
CANTATA CHORALE PRELUDE
QUARTET CONCERTO ENSEMBLE
MADRIGAL NOCTURNE OPERETTA
ORATORIO RHAPSODY SONATINA
SYMPHONY SIMPHONIA
(PIPED —) MUZAK
(PLAY — WELL) COOK
(RECORDED BACKGROUND —)
MUZAK
(RESOUNDING —) HIGGAION

(ROCK —) PUNK BIGBEAT BUBBLEGUM
(ROUGH —) CHARIVARI
(SAD —) MESTO
(SENTIMENTAL —) SCHMALZ SCHMALTZ
(STACCATO —) SECCO
(SYNCOPATED —) RAGTIME
(TYPE OF —) SERIAL SERIALISM MINIMALISM
(UNSOPHISTICATED —) FUNK
(VOCAL STYLE OF —) DOWOP DOOWOP
(WEST INDIAN —) REGGAE
(WRITE —) NOTATE COMPOSE
(ZULU —) KWELA
MUSICAL LYRIC SWEET LIQUID LYRICAL TUNABLE TUNEFUL CANOROUS HARMONIC NUMEROUS
(— CLOSING) CODA
(— DIRECTION) BIS PIU ADUE ARCO BRIO FINE MENO MUTA POCO ANIME ASSAI DOLCE GRAVE GUSTO LARGO LENTO MEZZO MOLTO MOSSO OSSIA PRIMO SECCO SEGNO SEGUE SOPRA TACET TEMPO TUTTI ADAGIO ARIOSO DOPPIO FREDDO MARCIA PRESTO RUBATO SEMPRE SIMILE SUBITO TENUTO TROPPO VELOCE VIVACE AGITATO ALLEGRO AMABILE ANIMATO ATTACCA FURIOSO GIOCOSO MARCATO MORENDO PIETOSO SORDINO TREMOLO DOLOROSO MAESTOSO MODERATO SALTANDO SEMPLICE SPICCATO CRESCENDO GLISSANDO OBBLIGATO SOSTENUTO SPIRITOSO
(SUFF.) **(— DEVICE)** INA INE
(— INSTRUMENT) INA
MUSICAL INSTRUMENT AX AXE GLY GUE KIN OUD QIN TAR UKE ZEL ALTO ASOR BELL CRUT DRUM GLEE GLEW GORA HARP HORN KORA KOTO LIRA LUTE LYRE OBOE ROTE SANG SAWM TAAR TUBA VINA VIOL ANVIL AULOS BANJO BLOCK BUGLE CELLO CHENG CRWTH CUICA DOMRA FLUTE GORAH GOURA GUDOK GUIRO GUSLA GUSLE KAZOO MBIRA NABLA ORGAN RAMKI REBAB REBEC ROCTA RUANA SAROD SHAWM SHELL SHENG TARAU TELYN TRUMP VEENA VIOLA ZANZE ZINKE BALAFO BONANG CABASA CITOLE CORNET CROUTH CYMBAL DOUCET FIDDLE GENDER GLARIN GUITAR GUSLEE JARANA RAPPEL REBECK RIBIBE SABECA SANCHO SANTIR SPINET TABRET TREBLE TYMPAN URHEEN VIOLET VIOLIN ZITHER ALTHORN ANGELOT ANKLONG ARGHOOL BAGPIPE BANDORE BANDURA BASSOON BAZOOKA CELESTA CHEKKER CHIKARA CITHARA CLARINA CLAVIEN CLAVIOL DICHORD DOLCIAN DOLCINO DULCIAN FISTULA FLUTINA GAMELIN GITTERN HELICON KANTELE

MAGADIS MARIMBA OCARINA PANDURA PIBCORN RACKETT SAMISEN SARANGI SARINDA SAXHORN SERPENT SISTRUM SORDONO THEORBO TRUMPET UKULELE URANION VIHUELA ADIAPHON AKALIMBA AUTOHARP AUTOPHON BARBITON BERIMBAU BOUSOUKI BOUZOUKI CALLIOPE CASTANET CLARINET CORNPIPE CRESCENT DULCIMER DYOPHONE EUPHONON FIDICULA FLAUTINO HORNPIPE HUMSTRUM KRUMHORN LAPIDEON MARTENOT MELODION NEGINOTH NEHILOTH PENORCON PHONIKON PSALTERY SCHWEGEL SERINGHI SOURDINE SYMPHONY TAMBOURA TAROGATO TRIANGLE TRICHORD TROMBONE VIRGINAL ZAMBOMBA ACCORDION BOMBARDON SAXOPHONE DIDGERIDOO DIDJERIDOO MELLOPHONE PEDALSTEEL TETRACHORD VIBRAPHONE
(AFRICAN —) KORA MBIRA
(ANCIENT —) ASOR LUTE LYRE CRWTH REBEC
(BALINESE —) GANGSA
(STRINGED — OF INDIA) SARANGI
(PL.) BRASS FAMILY STRINGS PERCUSSION
MUSICALITY HARMONY
MUSIC HALL GAFF MELODEON
MUSICIAN BARD WAIT ASAPH LINOS VIOLA BOPPER BUSKER MUSICO PLAYER VIOLER VIOLIN BANDMAN BOPSTER CELLIST GAMBIST ORPHEUS TWANGER VIOLIST KORAHITE MARIACHI MINSTREL MUSICKER THRUMMER TWANGLER CITYBILLY MINNESINGER
(FOLK —) FOLKY FOLKIE
(JOB OF —) GIG
(NOISY —) RANTER
(WEST AFRICA —) GRIOT
(WEST AFRICAN —) GRIOT
(WORK AS —) GIG
(PL.) ENSEMBLE WAITSMEN
MUSING PENSIVE MUSARDRY
MUSK MOOST CATTAIL MIMULUS AMBRETTE FIXATIVE
(PREF.) MOSCHI
MUSK DEER CERVID KASTURA
MUSKEG BOG FEN
MUSKELLUNGE LONGE MUSKIE
MUSKET FUSIL FUZIL MATCH DRAGON JINGAL BUNDOOK CALIVER ENFIELD GINGALL BANDHOOK BISCAYAN BISCAYEN CULVERIN ESCOPETA SNAPHAAN TOPHAIKE MATCHLOCK
MUSKET BALL GOLI
MUSKETEER FUSILEER STRELITZ
(THREE —S) ATHOS ARAMIS PORTHOS
MUSKET FORK GAFFLE
MUSK MALLOW ABFI MOSK
MUSKMELON MANGO ATAMON WUNGEE SPANSPEK CANTALOUPE
MUSKOGEE CREEK SEMINOLE

MUSK OX OVIBOS
(WOOL OF UNDERCOAT OF —) QIVIUT
MUSKRAT SQUASH ONDATRA MUSQUASH
MUSK SHREW SONDELI
MUSK TURTLE STINKER STINKPOT
MUSKWOOD CAOBA
MUSKY MOSCHATE
MUSLIM LAZ ALIM SIDI SWAT TURK ARAIN HAFIZ IBADHI KAZAKH TURBAN ABBADID AYYUBID BAGIRMI BASHKIR IBADITE KHAKSAR MUDEJAR SUNNITE ALAOUITE ISLAMIST ISLAMITE QADARITE SIFATITE
(— BEADS) TASBIH
(— BROTHERHOOD) TARIQA
(— CALL TO PRAYER) AZAN
(— CHIEF) RAIS REIS
(— DOCTRINE) TAWHID
(— FOUNDATION) WAKF WAQF
(— JUDGE) CAID QAID
(— LEADER) MAM
(— MYSTIC) SUFI
(— OFFICIAL) OMRAH
(— PLAY) TAZIA
(— PRACTICE) PURDAH
(— PRINCIPLE) TAQIYA
(— SCHOLARS) ULAMA ULEMA
(— SECT) SUNNI WAHHABI MURJIITE
(— TOMB) TABUT
(— TREE) TUBA
(— WOMAN OF RANK) BEGUM
(EDUCATED —) MULLAH
(PL.) SHIA SHIAH SUNNI
MUSLIN BAN MULL DORIA SWISS GURRAH MULMUL SHALEE SHILLA TANJIB BETEELA FACTORY JAMDANI ORGANDY STENTER COTELINE SEERHAND TARLATAN
(PL.) COSSAS
MUSQUASH MUSKRAT ONDATRA
MUSS FUFFLE RUMPLE GLOMMOX UNDRESS
MUSSEL CLAM UNIO NAIAD ANODON JINGLE LACERT MUCKET PALOUR BIVALVE GLOCHID MYTILID UNIONID BULLHEAD DEERHORN
(PREF.) CONCH(O) MYTILI MYTILO
MUSSELCRACKER BISKOP
MUSSULMAN MOSLEM
MUST BIT BUD BUT MAN MAY MUN BOOD MAUN MOTE SAPA STUM DULCE GOTTA OUGHT SHALL
(— BE TAKEN) SUM
(— NOT) MAUNNA
MUSTACHE WALRUS VALANCE WHISKER
MUSTACHE MONKEY MOUSTOC
MUSTANG PONY BRONCO SPHINX
MUSTARD ZEST CRESS SENVY SINEWY AWLWORT CADLOCK KEDLOCK SINAPIS CHADLOCK CHARLOCK FLIXWEED AUBRIETIA
(— PLANT) WASABI
(PREF.) SIN
MUSTARD GAS YPERITE
MUSTARD PLASTER SINAPISM
MUSTELUS GALEUS
MUSTER LEVY ENROL RAISE SPUNK

GATHER HOSTING MARSHAL RECRUIT
(— OUT) DEMOB
MUSTINESS FUST MUST
MUSTY HOAR FUNKY FUSTY HOARY MOLDY MUCID RAFTY VINNY FOISTY FROWZY RANCID FOUGHTY FROWSTY CORWEBBY
MUTABLE FICKLE MUTATORY VARIABLE
MUTATE SPORT
MUTATION SHIFT SPORT CHANGE MUANCE SILKIE ANAGRAM VARIANT SALTATION
(VOWEL —) UMLAUT
MUTE PAD DUMB ECHO LENE SURD BLACK MEDIA WHIST DAMPER MUFFLE SILENT STIFLE TENUIS SORDINE SOURDINE
(— AT FUNERAL) SALLIE
(— FOR TRUMPET) DERBY
MUTED DULL SORDO STILL DISCREET SOURDINE
MUTENESS SILENCE DUMBNESS
MUTILATE MAR HACK MAIM BREAK GARBLE HAMBLE INJURE MANGLE MARTYR MITTLE CONCISE CASTRATE EMBEZZLE
(— AN ANIMAL) LAW
MUTILATION STRIP CONCISION
MUTINEER PANDY MUTINADO
MUTINOUS UNRULY
MUTINY REVOLT STRIFE REBELLION
MUTINY ON THE BOUNTY
(AUTHOR OF —) HALL NORDHOFF
(CHARACTER IN —) BYAM BLIGH PEGGY ROGER GEORGE ROBERT TEHANI BURKITT ELLISON MAIMITI STEWART TINKLER WILLIAM FLETCHER MILLWARD MORRISON MUSPRATT CHRISTIAN
MUTISM ALALIA
MUTTER CROOL MOTRE HOTTER HUMMER MUMBLE MURMUR PATTER THROAT CHANNER CHUNNER CHUNTER GRUMBLE MAUNDER TOOTMOOT MUSSITATE
MUTTERING GROWL
MUTTON BRAXY VIFDA VIVDA MOUTON BRAXIES
(LEG OF —) CABOB WABBLER WOBBLER
MUTTONBIRD OII
MUTTONFISH SAMA ABALONE EELPOUT MOJARRA
MUTTONHEAD DOLT
MUTUAL COMMON RECIPROCAL
(PREF.) CO INTER
MUZZLE GAG NOSE MOUTH SNOUT FOREFACE GUNPOINT
(— FOR FERRET) COPE
(— OF CANNON) CHOPS
MUZZLE-LOADER CAPLOCK MUZZLER
MYALGIA COURBATURE
MYALL YARRAN WARRIGAL

MYANMAR
BAY: BENGAL HUNTER HEANZAY
CAPITAL: RANGOON
DIVISION: PEGU MAGWE ARAKAN KARENNI SAGAING MANDALAY IRRAWADDY TENASSERIM

FORMER CAPITAL: AVA
GULF: MARTABAN
MEASURE: LY DHA GON LAN MAU
NGU SAO TAO TAT BYEE DAIN
PHAN SEIT TAUN TENG THAT
SALAY SHITA THUOC LAMANY
PALGAT TRUONG CHAIVAI
OKTHABAH
MONEY: KYAT
MOUNTAIN: POPA NATTAUNG
SARAMATI VICTORIA
MOUNTAINS: CHIN NAGA DAWNA
KACHIN KARENNI PEGUYOMA
NATIVE: AO VU WA AOR LAI LAO
MON PYU TAI CHIN KADU KUKI
LOLO MIAO NAGA SEMA SGAU
SGAW SHAN THAI KAREN KHMER
LHOTA BIRMAN BURMAN KACHIN
RENGMA PALAUNG ARAKANESE
PLATEAU: SHAN
PORT: AKYAB BASSEIN HENZADA
MOULMEIN
RIVER: HKA NMAI PEGU MEKONG
SALWIN SHWELI KALADAN
MALIKHA MYITNGE SALWEEN
SITTANG CHINDWIN INDAWGYI
IRRAWADDY
SEA: ANDAMAN
TOWN: YE AVA PEGU AKYAB

BHAMO KARBE KATHA MINBU
PAPUN PROME TAVOY HSENWI
HSIPAW LASHIO MAYMYO
MONYWA SHWEBO BASSEIN
HENZADA PAKOKKU RANGOON
MANDALAY MOULMEIN
WEIGHT: TA CAN MAT MOO PAI VIS
BINH DONG KYAT RUAY VISS
BAHAR BEHAR CANDY TICAL
TICUL ABUCCO PEIKTHA

MY ANTONIA (AUTHOR OF —)
CATHER
(CHARACTER IN —) JIM JAKE LENA
OTTO WICK ANTON CUZAK FUCHS
LARRY BURDEN CUTTER ANTONIA
DONOVAN HARLING LINGARD
MARPOLE AMBROSCH SHIMERDA
MYCELIUM SPAWN MYCELE
TAPESIUM
MYCTERIA TANTALUS
MY DEAR MACHREE
MYDRIATIC PHENYLEPHRINE
MYIASIS STRIKE
MYNA APER MINA MYNAH GRACKLE
MYNES (BROTHER OF —)
EPISTROPHUS
(FATHER OF —) EVENUS
(WIFE OF —) BRISEIS

MYOCOMMA FLAKE
MYRIAD HOST TOMAN COUNTLESS
MYRIAPOD JULID POLYPOD
PAUROPOD MILLIPEDE
MYRRH STACTE
MYRRHA (SON OF —) ADONIS
MYRTLE MYRT LILAC BALTIC
JAROOL ARRAYAN JAPONICA
RAMARAMA
MYSELF SELF MYSEN HERSELF
MYSID SHRIMP
MYSOST PRIMOST
**MYSTERIES OF PARIS (AUTHOR OF
—)** SUE
(CHARACTER IN —) FLEUR SARAH
CICELY MURPHY WALTER FERRAND
GEORGES JACQUES RODOLPH
CHOUETTE CLEMENCE HARVILLE
POLIDORI MACGREGOR
RIGOLETTE
MYSTERIES OF UDOLPHO
(AUTHOR OF —) RADCLIFFE
(CHARACTER IN —) EMILY DUPONT
MORANO MONTONI LUDOVICO
STAUBERT VILLEFORT LAURENTINI
VALANCOURT
MYSTERIOUS DIM DARK DEEP
EERY SELI EERIE SABLE WAKON
ARCANE EXOTIC MYSTIC OCCULT

SECRET CRYPTIC PUCKISH
UNCANNY UNCOUTH ABSTRUSE
ESOTERIC NUMINOUS SIBYLLIC
CRYPTICAL
MYSTERIOUSLY DARKLY EERILY
HEIMLICH
MYSTERY MIST RUNE CABALA
ENIGMA SECRET ARCANUM
PROBLEM SECRECY
(— STORY) WHODUNIT
(— WRITER FIRST NAME) ERLE
ELLERY
(RELIGIOUS —) SACRAMENT
(PREF.) MYST(ERI)(ERIO)(ICO)
MYSTIC SUFI OCCULT ORPHIC
SECRET EPOPTIC ESOTERIC
MYSTICAL MISTY MYSTIC
ANAGOGIC TELESTIC
MYSTICALLY GHOSTLY
MYSTICISM CABALA SUFIISM
MYSTIFY BEAT BEFOG BOTHER
MUDDLE PUZZLE BECLOUD
CONFUSE BEWILDER
MYSTIQUE AIR AURA
MYTH SAGA FABLE LEGEND
MYTHOS ALLEGORY
MYTHICAL FABLED FABULOUS
FICTIOUS
MYTHOMANIAC LIAR

N EN NU NAN NOVEMBER
NAAM (FATHER OF —) CALEB
NAAMAH (BROTHER OF —)
TUBALCAIN
  (FATHER OF —) LAMECH
  (MOTHER OF —) ZILLAH
  (SON OF —) REHOBOAM
NAARAH (HUSBAND OF —) ASHUR
NAASSENE OPHITE
NAB HAT NIB GRAB HEAD KNAB NAIL
CATCH SEIZE ARREST CLUTCH
COLLAR NIBBLE NOBBLE SNATCH
CAPTURE APPREHEND
NABAL (WIFE OF —) ABIGAIL
NABALOI IBALOI IGOROT
NABK NUBK NABAK NEBUK NABBUK
NEBACK NEBBUK NEBBUCK
NABOB DIVES NAWAB NOBOB
DEPUTY VICEROY GOVERNOR
PLUTOCRAT
  (— DEPUTY) NAWAB
  (PL.) NABOBRY
NACELLE CAR BOAT BASKET
CHASSIS COCKPIT SHELTER
NACHSCHLAG SPRINGER
AFTERNOTE
NACKET BOY CAKE LUNCH NOCKET
NACRE PEARL SHELLFISH
NADAB (FATHER OF —) AARON
SHAMMAI
  (MOTHER OF —) ELISHEBA
NADIR BATHOS BEDROCK
  (OPPOSED TO —) ZENITH
NAG CUT RAG TIT BAIT CARP FRAB
FRET FUSS GNAW JADE MOKE PLUG
PONY PROD RIDE SNAG TWIT YAFF
ANNOY COBRA HOBBY HORSE
SCOLD SKATE SNAKE STEED TEASE
BADGER BERATE BOTHER DOBBIN
GARRAN GLEYDE HAGGLE HARASS
HECKLE HECTOR KEFFEL PADNAG
PESTER PLAGUE ROUNCY
WANTON HACKNEY HENPECK
TORMENT DINGDONG HARANGUE
IRRITATE PARAMOUR CATAMARAN
  (AMBLING —) HOBBY
NAGA SEMA COBRA KABUI LHOTA
SNAKE
NAGGING NIGGLING
NAGKASSAR SURIGA
NAGOR TOHI ANTELOPE REEDBUCK
NAHANE KASKA
NAHATH (FATHER OF —) ZOPHAI
NAHBI (FATHER OF —) VOPHSI
NAHOOR SHA SNA SHEEP URIAL
BHARAL OORIAL
NAHOR (BROTHER OF —) HARAN
ABRAHAM
  (FATHER OF —) SERUG
  (SON OF —) TERAH
  (WIFE OF —) MILCAH
NAHSON (FATHER OF —)
AMMINADAB

(SISTER OF —) ELISHEBA
  (SON OF —) SALMON
NAHUATL AZTEC CAZCAN MEXICA
NAHUM ELKOSHITE
NAIAD NAIS NYMPH MUSSEL
HYDRIAD
NAIF BABE
NAIL CUT FIX HOB NAB PIN TEN
BOSS BRAD BRAG BROD CLAW
CLOY DUMP HOOF PILE SLUG
SPAD STUB STUD TACK TRAP AFFIX
CATCH CLOUT DRIVE GROPE PLATE
SCALE SEIZE SPEED SPICK SPIKE
SPRIG TALON BULLEN CLENCH
CLINCH COOLER CORKER DETAIN
FASTEN GARRON HAMMER
SECURE SINKER TACKET TENTER
TINGLE UNGUIS UNGULA CAPTURE
CLINKER FASTENER HOLDFAST
ROSEHEAD SPARABLE SPIKELET
TENPENNY TRICOUNI
  (— BITING) ONYCHOPHAGIA
  (— GROWTH) ONYCHAUXIS
  (— OBLIQUELY) TOE
  (HEADLESS —) SPRIG
  (HOOKED —) TENTER TENTERHOOK
  (INGROWN —) ONYXIS ACRONYX
  (MARKING —) SPAD SPEED
  (OLD HORSESHOE —) STUB
  (SHOEMAKER'S —) CLOUT
SPARABLE
  (TOED —) TOSHNAIL
  (PREF.) GOMPHO HELO ONYCH(O)
UNGUI
  (SUFF.) ONYCHA ONYCHES
ONYCHIA ONYCHIUM ONYCHUS
ONYX
NAILROD STICKWEED
NAIVE OPEN RACY FRANK GREEN
CANDID JEJUNE SIMPLE ARTLESS
NATURAL CHILDISH INNOCENT
UNTAUGHT WIDEEYED CHILDLIKE
GUILELESS INGENUOUS PRIMITIVE
UNTUTORED UNWORLDLY
  (— GIRL) INGENUE
NAIVETE GREENNESS SIMPLICITY
NAKED BALD BARE MERE NUDE
OPEN CLEAR EXACT PLAIN STARK
ADAMIC BARREN CUERPO SCUDDY
SIMPLE EXPOSED LITERAL
OBVIOUS MANIFEST STARKERS
STRIPPED SMOCKLESS
UNADORNED UNCLOTHED
UNCOVERED
  (PREF.) GYMN(O) NUDI
NAKED OAT PILLAS PILCORN
PILKINS
NAKEDWOOD MABI SNAKEWOOD
NAKHI MOSO MOSSO
NAKONG SITUTUNGA
NAMAYCUSH CREE FISH LAKER
LONGE LUNGE TOGUE TROUT
LONGUE SISCOWET

NAMBY-PAMBY WET INANE SILLY
VAPID CODDLE INSIPID KEEPSAKE
NAME DUB FIX NOM SET CALL CITE
FAME NAIL NOMB NOUN READ
TERM ALIAS CLAIM CLEPE COUNT
ETHIC NEVEN NOMEN POINT
QUOTE STYLE TITLE ACCUSE
ADDUCE APPEAL GOSSIP MONICA
REPUTE SELECT ALLONYM
APPOINT BEHIGHT DECLARE
ENTITLE EPITHET MENTION
MONIKER SPECIFY VOCABLE
CATEGORY CHRISTEN COGNOMEN
IDENTIFY IDENTITY INDICATE
MONICKER NOMINATE
ENUMERATE PATRONYMIC
NOMENCLATURE
  (— OF NEWSPAPER) MASTHEAD
  (— OF PLACE) TOPONYM
  (— TABLET) FACIA
  (— WRITTEN BACKWARDS)
ANANYM
  (ADDED —) AGNAME AGNOMEN
  (ALTERNATIVE —) BUNCH
  (ANCESTOR'S —) EPONYM
  (ANOTHER —) ALIAS
  (ASSUMED —) PEN ALIAS
ONOMASTIC PSEUDONYM
SOBRIQUET
  (BAD —) CACONYM
  (DAY —) AHAU
  (DERIVATION OF —) EPONYMY
  (FAMILIAR —) NICKNAME
  (FAMILY —) SURNAME
  (FIRST —) FORENAME PRAENOMEN
  (GENERIC —) PRAENOMEN
  (GOOD —) HONOR CREDIT
  (PEN —) PSEUDONYM
  (POPULAR DOG —) FIDO LADY SHEP
SPOT ROVER
  (REGISTERED —) AFFIX
  (TECHNICAL —) ONYM
  (UNSUITABLE —) MISNOMER
  (WELL-SUITED —) EUONYM
  (PREF.) NOMEN ONOMATO
  (SUFF.) NOMEN NYM ONYM
NAMED DIT CITED HIGHT NEMPT
DUBBED YCLEPT ONYMOUS
YCLEPED
NAMELESS BAS
  (— ONE) WHO
NAMELY FOR VIZ SCIL NOTED
TOWIT FAMOUS SCILICET
NAMEPLATE MASTHEAD
  (AUTOMOBILE —) MARQUE
NAMESAKE EPONYM JUNIOR
HOMONYM
NAMIBIA (BAY OF —) WALVIS
  (CAPITAL OF —) WINDHOEK
  (DESERT OF —) KALAHARI
  (PEOPLE OF —) NAMAS BANTUS
BUSHMEN HEREROS OVAMBOS
NANA (AUTHOR OF —) ZOLA

(CHARACTER IN —) NANA ROSE
HUGON LOUIS SATIN FONTAN
GEORGE HECTOR MIGNON MUFFAT
SABINE XAVIER ESTELLE STEINER
BEUVILLE DAGUENET FAUCHERY
PHILIPPE DECHOUARD
NANDI BANANDE MUNANDI KIPSIKIS
NANDU RHEA
NANISM DWARFISM
NANNAR SIN
NANNY GOAT NURSE
  (ORIENTAL —) AMAH
NANTICOKE TOAG
NAOMI MARA
  (DAUGHTER-IN-LAW OF —) RUTH
NAOS CELLA SHRINE TEMPLE
NAP GIG KIP NOD RAS CALK CAMP
DOWN DOZE FUZZ LINT OOZE PICK
PILE RUFF SHAG WINK COVER
DOVER FLUFF GRASP SEIZE SLEEK
SLEEP STEAL CATNAP DROWSE
SIESTA SNOOZE DROPOFF
EMERIZE RECLINE SLUMBER
  (TO RAISE —) TEASE
NAPE NOD CUFF NECK NUKE POLL
NUCHA NUQUE SCRAG SCUFT
SCURF NODDLE SCRUFF TURNIP
NIDDICK
  (PREF.) NUCH(I)
NAPERY LINEN DAMASK DOILIES
NAPKINS
NAPHTALITE ENAN AHIRA
NAPHTHA NEFTE PETROLEUM
NAPKIN CLOTH DOILY TOWEL
DIAPER NAPERY KERCHIEF
SUDATORY HANDCLOTH
SERVIETTE
NAPLES BISCUIT LADYFINGER
NAPLESS BARE HARD
NAPOLELEON (AIDE TO —) NEY
NAPOLEON (— III) LOUIS
BOUSTRAPA
  (BATTLE OF —) ULM ACRE JENA
WATERLOO
  (BIRTHPLACE OF —) CORSICA
  (BROTHER-IN-LAW OF —) MURAT
  (GAME LIKE —) PAM
  (ISLAND OF —) ELBA HELENA
CORSICA
  (MARSHALL OF —) NEY
  (MOTHER OF —) HORTENSE
  (PLACE OF VICTORY FOR —) LODI
LIGNY
NAPPE DECKE
NAPPY ALE DISH DOWNY HEADY
KINKY WOOLY LIQUOR SHAGGY
STRONG WOOLLY COTTONY
FOAMING VILLOUS
NARC TMAN
NARCISSUS LILY PLANT CRINUM
EGOIST FLOWER LILIUM JONQUIL
POLYANTHUS
  (FATHER OF —) CEPHISSUS

(LOVED BY —) ECHO
(MOTHER OF —) LIRIOPE
(TRUMPET —) DAFFODIL
NARCOTIC (ALSO SEE DRUG) KAT KEF BANG DOPE DRUG HEMP JUNK BHANG DAGGA ETHER OPIUM HEROIN OPIATE ANODYNE COCAINE CODEINE HASHISH METOPON NARCEIN HYPNOTIC MORPHINE TAKROURI DIACODION MARIJUANA SOPORIFIC CHLORODYNE
(— AGENT) GAZER
(— DOSE) LOCUS
(— ORGANIZATION) DEA
(— OVERDOSE) OD
(— PLANT) DUTRA MANDRAKE
(INJECT —) SHOOTUP
(SALE OF —S) SCORE
(SMALL AMOUNT OF —) SNIFTER
(PL.) JUNK STUFF
NARCOTICS JUNK HEROIN
NARCOTINE OPIANE
NARD SPICE ANOINT RHIZOME MUSKROOT SPIKENARD
NARDOO ARDOO NARDU CLOVER
NARGIL COCONUT
NARGILEH PIPE HOOKA HOOKAH NARGHILE
NARK SPY VEX NOTE ANNOY TEASE OBSERVE INFORMER IRRITATE
NARRA NAGA ASANA APALIT
NARRATE SPIN TELL BRUIT STATE STORY DEPICT DETAIL DEVISE RECITE RELATE REPORT DISCUSS RECOUNT STORIFY DESCRIBE REHEARSE
NARRATION TALE FABLE STORY DETAIL ACCOUNT HAGGADA RECITAL SYNAXAR ALLEGORY DELIVERY DIEGESIS HAGGADAH
NARRATIVE EPIC JOKE MYTH SAGA TALE CONTE DRAMA FABLE PROSE STORY COMEDY JATAKA LEGEND ACCOUNT EPISODE HISTORY MEMOIRS MIDRASH NOVELLA PARABLE RECITAL ALLEGORY ANECDOTE APOLOGUE ARETALOGY HAGIOLOGY
(— OF VOYAGE) PERIPLUS
(— POEM) EPIC EPOS SAGA
(BRIEF —) ANECDOTE
(PL.) ACTA EXEMPLA
NARRATOR TESTO TELLER RELATOR SAGAMAN TALESMAN RACONTEUR
NARROW JERK LEAN MEAN NEAR POKY SLIT TRUE BORNE CLOSE CRAMP PINCH RIGID SCANT SHARP SMALL SOUND TAPER ANGUST BIASED LINEAR LITTLE MEAGER STRAIT STRICT TWITCH BIGOTED ERICOID LIMITED PRIMARY SLENDER THRIFTY CONDENSE CONTRACT PAROCHIAL PROVINCIAL
(— DOWN) CONFINE
(— DOWN STAVES) BUCK
(— INLET) RIA
(— IN OUTLOOK) SUBURBAN
(— IN PRINCIPLE) STRAITLACED
(NOT —) CATHOLIC
(VERY —) HAIRBREADTH

(PREF.) AUGUSTI DOLICH(O) STEN(O)
(SUFF.) STENOSIS
NARROWED LISTED INSWEPT CONTRACT ANGUSTATE
NARROWING CAP CHOKE INTAKE STENOSIS
NARROWLY WIDE STRAITLY
NARROW-MINDED REDNECK BORNE PETTY
NARROWNESS BIAS BIGOTRY LOCALISM PAROCHIALISM
NARSINGA TRUMPET
NARTHECIUM ABAMA
NARTHEX HALL STOA ENTRY FOYER LOBBY PORCH PORTICO PRONAOS VESTIBULE
NARWHAL MONODON
NASAB NUSUB KINSHIP
NASAL NOSY NARINE RHINAL TWANGY ADENOID STRINGY
(PREF.) NASIO RHIN(O)
NASCENCY BIRTH ORIGIN GENESIS BEGINNING
NASEBERRY SAPODILLA
NASHGAB OAF GOSSIP
NASI OFFICER PATRIARCH
NASICORN RHINOCEROS
NASTIKA ATHEIST
NASTURTIUM CAPUCINE NOSEWORT RADICULA STURSHUM STURTION
NASTY BAD PAH FOUL MEAN UGLY DIRTY SNIDE FILTHY HORRID ODIOUS RIBALD SCUZZY BAGGAGE BEASTLY DEFILED HARMFUL OBSCENE SQUALID UNCLEAN INDECENT NAUSEOUS SPITEFUL STITEFUL DANGEROUS MALICIOUS OFFENSIVE
NAT NOT DEMON SPIRIT
NATA (WIFE OF —) NANA
NATAL INBORN INNATE NATIVE GLUTEAL CONGENIAL
NATAL BROWN MAHAL
NATAL PLUM AMATUNGULA
NATANT AFLOAT FLOATING SWIMMING
NATATORIUM BATH POOL
NATCHEZ STINKER STINKARD
NATION BENI FOLK GEAT HOST LAND LEDE RACE VOLK AEDUI CASTE CLASS FANTE FANTI REALM STATE TRIBE FANTEE GEATAS PEOPLE WAGOGO ARVERNI COUNTRY SOCIETY LANGUAGE COMMUNITY MANDATORY MINISTATE MULTITUDE
(— SYMBOL) FLAG CREST
(HEBREW —) JACOB
(LARGE —) COLOSSUS
(PREF.) ETHN(O)
NATIONAL CITIZEN FEDERAL GENTILE GENTILIC
(— DEMOCRACY) ENDEX
NATIONALISM JINGOISM PHYLETISM
NATIONALIST CHINA (SEE TAIWAN)
NATIONALITY FLAG
NATIVE (ALSO SEE PEOPLE AND TRIBE) ABO ITE RAW SON TAO

BORN FREE GOOK HOME KIND LIVE NEIF WILD INNER NATAL PUNTI EPIROT GENIAL INBORN INNATE KINDLY MOTHER NORMAL SIMPLE VIRGIN CITIZEN DENIZEN DZUNGAR ENDEMIC GENUINE NATURAL PAISANO POLISTA DOMESTIC GRASSCUT HABITUAL HOMEBORN HOMEMADE INHERENT LANDSMAN ORIGINAL PRIMEVAL PRISTINE RESIDENT YAMMADJI ABORIGINE CONGENIAL INGRAINED INHERITED INTRINSIC ORIGINARY TAWNYMOOR ABORIGINAL
(— BEAR) KOALA
(— BEECH) FLINDOSA
(— MINERAL) LIVE
(— OF ALBANIA) SKIPETAR
(— OF ANJOU) ANGEVIN
(— OF BENGAL) KOL
(— OF CANADA) HABITANT
(— OF CHINA) CELESTIAL
(— OF FENS) SLODGER
(— OF FLORIDA KEYS) CONK CONCH
(— OF GALLOWAY) GALWEGIAN GALLOVIDIAN
(— OF GLASGOW) GLASWEGIAN
(— OF ILLINOIS) SUCKER
(— OF IRELAND) BOGTROTTER
(— OF LIVERPOOL) SCOUSE
(— OF LONDON) COCKNEY
(— OF LOW CLASS) TAO
(— OF MADAGASCAR) HOVA
(— OF MALAYA) INFIEL
(— OF MANCHESTER) MANCUNIAN
(— OF MARITIME PROVINCES) BLUENOSE
(— OF N. CAROLINA) TARHEEL
(— OF NEW GUINEA) BOONG
(— OF NEW SOUTH WALES) CORNSTALK
(— OF PHILIPPINES) GUGU
(— OF SCOTLAND) GEORDIE
(— OF SOUTHERN ILLINOIS) EGYPTIAN
(— OF TYNESIDE) GEORDIE
(— OF W. AUSTRALIA) GROPER
(— PLANT) INDIGINE
(— WHO TEACHES) CATECHIST
(BORN AND BRED AS A —) CREOLE
(FREE —) TIMAWA
(UNCIVILIZED —) MYALL
(SUFF.) ESE ITE OT OTE
(— OF) ER IER YER
NATIVE SON (AUTHOR OF —) WRIGHT
(CHARACTER IN —) JAN MAX MARY BORIS MEARS BESSIE BIGGER DALTON ERLONE THOMAS BRITTEN BUCKLEY
NATIVITY BIRTH JATAKA GENESIS GENITURE HOROSCOPE
NATTERJACK NEWT TOAD
NATTY CHIC NEAT POSH TIDY TRIG TRIM NIFTY SMART SPICY DAPPER JAUNTY SPIFFY SPRUCE FOPPISH VARMINT
NATURAL RAW AFRO BORN EASY FOOL HOME KIND OPEN RACY REAL WILD NAIVE USUAL CANCEL CASUAL COMMON CONJON

CRETIN DIRECT EARTHY HOMELY INBORN INBRED INNATE KINDLY MOTHER NATIVE NORMAL PHYSIC ARTLESS GENUINE QUADRUM REGULAR INHERENT LIFELIKE ORDINARY PHYSICAL UNCOINED PRIMITIVE REALISTIC UNASSUMED UNFEIGNED
(— LOGARITHM) LN
(— TALENT) DOWER FLAIR
(NOT —) DYED AFFECTED
(PREF.) PHYSICO PHYSI(O)
NATURALIST AMERICAN LEA COPE DALL LONG MUIR SNOW WARD FLAGG HYATT LEIDY LUCAS MASON ORTON PEALE SETON TEALE ABBOTT AKELEY BARTON DELONG FOSSEY GODMAN HOLDER MORTON NELSON PORTER SAVAGE STORER WALKER WILKES WILSON AGASSIZ ANDREWS BACHMAN BUCKLEY DITMARS FUERTES GIBBONS HOLLAND HOLLING MERRIAM PEATTIE SCUDDER WALCOTT COOLIDGE HALDEMAN HOLBROOK JENNINGS SCHWATKA BURROUGHS INGERSOLL SUBLETETE RAFINESQUE SCHOOLCRAFT
AUSTRALIAN BANFIELD
DANISH BERGSOE WINSLOW
DUTCH CAMPER HOEVEN HOMBERG SWAMMERDAM LEEUWENHOEK
ENGLISH RAY BELL BAKER BANKS BATES BRADY FORBE GOSSE LEACH NORTH BAILEY DARWIN HUDSON SLOANE BORLASE CATESBY DUGMORE EDWARDS NEEDHAM PENNANT WALLACE BRODERIP BURCHELL LYDEKKER STEBBING SWAINSON BOWERBANK JEFFERIES CARRUTHERS TEGETMEIER WILLIAMSON ATTENBOROUGH
FRENCH BELON CHENU BUFFON CUVIER BAILLON DAUBENY DUMERIL GERVAIS LAMARCK LESUEUR ORBIGNY PEIRESC POUCHET POUPART REAUMUR ADDANSON AUDEBERT BONPLAND DESHAYES LACEPEDE RONDELET CASTELNAU DAUBENTON BROUSSONETT
GERMAN OKEN WIED JAGER LIBAU SEITZ MULLER PALLAS MARTIUS NEUWIED SCHWANN SIEBOLD STELLER CHAMISSO ERXLEBEN HUMBOLDT JUNGHUHN SCHUBERT EHRENBERG KIELMEYER BURMEISTER KEYSERLING TREVIRANUS ESCHSCHOLTZ SOEMMERRING SCHLAGINTWEIT
ITALIAN REDI RISSO BONELLI BROCCHI FABRONI FONTANA SCOPOLI AMORETTI MARSIGLI ALDROVANDI SPALLANZANI VALLISNIERI
NORWEGIAN ASBJORNSEN
RUSSIAN EICHWALD FEDCHENKO CHIKHACHEV
SCOTTISH BROWN BAIKIE FORBES HERDMAN JARDINE THOMSON RICHARDSON MACGILLIVRAY

SPANISH COBO AZARA MUTIS
SWEDISH ARTEDI FORSKAL ZETTERSTEDT
SWISS HEER HUBER BONNET GESNER AGASSIZ TSCHUDI SAUSSURE TREMBLEY CLAPAREDE POURTALES RUTIMEYER
NATURALIZE ADAPT ADOPT ACCUSTOM ACCLIMATE ENDENIZEN HABITUATE
NATURALLY SN NATCH KINDLY GENIALLY
NATURALNESS EASE NAIVETE
NATURE ILK BENT BIOS CAST CLAY FORM HAIR KIND MAKE MOOD RACE SORT TRIM TYPE COLOR OUSIA SHAPE STATE TENOR ANIMAL DHARMA FIGURE HEAVEN KIDNEY PHYSIS STRIPE ESSENCE FEATHER INBEING QUALITY SPECIES PRAKRITI UNIVERSE CHARACTER QUALIFICATION
(— DIVINITY) NYMPH
(— GOD) PAN
(— GODDESS) CYBELE ARTEMIS
(— OF GOD) DIVINITY
(— PRINT) PHYTOGRAPH
(— SPIRIT) NAT
(— WORSHIP) PHYSIOLATRY
(APPARENT —) STUDY
(BY ITS VERY —) IPSOFACTO
(CONCEALED —) LATENCY
(COURSE OF —) TAO
(DIVINE —) DEITY
(EMOTIONAL —) HEART
(ESSENTIAL —) ESSE FORM GENIUS
(GOOD —) BONHOMIE
(HUMAN —) FLESH MANHEAD MANKIND
(INHERENT —) GENIUS
(INNER —) SOUL
(INTRINSIC —) BOTTOM
(MORAL —) ETHNOS
(OF THE SAME —) HOMOGENEOUS
(ORGANIC —) BIOS
(PERT. TO —) COSMO
(ROUGH —) SPINOSITY
(SENSUAL —) BLOOD
(SPECIAL —) IDIOM
(SPIRITUAL —) INTERNAL
(TRIFLING —) FRIVOLITY
(TRUE —) ESSE PROPRIETY
(TRUE — OF THINGS) WHERE
(ULTIMATE —) ESSENCE
(UNREGENERATE —) ADAM
(PREF.) PHYSI(O)
(SUFF.) **(HAVING — OF)** IC ICAL
(OF — OF) EOUS
NATURIST NUDIST
NAUGHT NIL EVIL ZERO AUGHT NAGHT OUGHT CIPHER NOUGHT WICKED NOTHING USELESS WORTHLESS
NAUGHTY BAD PAW SAD EVIL WRONG PAWPAW SHREWD WICKED OBSCENE WAYWARD IMPROPER
NAUPATHIA SEASICKNESS
NAURU (CAPITAL OF —) YAREN
(DISTRICT OF —) BOE EWA AIWO IJUW BAITI BUADA NIBOK UABOE

YAREN ANABAR ANETAN MENENG ANIBARE
(FORMER NAME OF —) PLEASANTISLAND
(TOWN OF —) ANNA ORRO ANABAR RONAWI YANGOR
NAUSEA PALL QUALM DISGUST NAUSITY LOATHING SICKNESS ANTIPATHY DIZZINESS
NAUSEATE TURN TWIST WLATE REVOLT SICKEN DISGUST SCUNNER STOMACH DISTASTE SCOMFISH
NAUSEATED ILL SICKISH QUALMISH SQUEAMISH
NAUSEATING NASTY WAUGH QUEASY BILIOUS FULSOME BRACKISH STAWSOME LOATHSOME REVOLTING SICKENING
NAUSEOUS NASTY FULSOME OFFENSIVE
NAUSICAA (FATHER OF —) ALCINOUS
(MOTHER OF —) ARETE
NAUSITHOUS (FATHER OF —) NEPTUNE POSEIDON
(MOTHER OF —) PERIBOEA
(SON OF —) ALCINOUS
NAUTICAL (ALSO SEE NAVIGATION) NAVAL MARINE NAUTIC MARINAL OCEANIC TARRISH MARITIME NAVIGABLE
(— FLAG) CORNET PENNON
NAUTILUS MOLLUSK ARGONAUT ARGONAUTA
(— COMMANDER) NEMO
NAVAHO DINE NAVAJO LONGHAIR
(— GROUP) OUTFIT
(— RITE) WAY
NAVAL SEA MARINE NAUTICAL NAVIGABLE
(— DEPOT) BASE
(— FORCE) NAVY FLEET ARMADA SQUADRON
(— JAIL) BRIG
NAVAL OFFICER AMERICAN ROE CONE DALE DYER HART HULL HUSE KING LAND LEVY LUCE MAYO SIMS ALLEN AMMEN BARRY BEALE CAPPS CLARK DAVIS DEWEY DUERK EVANS FISKE FITCH FOOTE GRANT JONES LEAHY LEARY MAHAN MAURY PERRY PRATT ROWAN STARK WALKE BARNEY BENSON BIDDLE BREESE CARNEY CONNER EBERLE GREENE HALSEY HEWITT HOWELL KEARNY KIMMEL KNIGHT MCCAIN MOORER MORRIS NIMITZ PALMER PORTER RODMAN SCHLEY SEMMES TALBOT TOWERS TUCKER WILKES WORDEN BRISTOL BULLOCH CHESTER CUSHING DALGREN DECATUR ELLIOTT GLEAVES GRAVELY GRIDLEY HOLLINS HOPKINS KIMBALL KINKAID MOFFETT NIBLACK SCHENCK SIGSBEE STEWART TRUXTUN WHIPPLE WILLSON WINSLOW YARNELL ZUMWALT BUCHANAN CAPERTON CHADWICK CHAUNCEY FARRAGUT GHORMLEY INGRAHAM LAWRENCE PAULDING PERCIVAL

RICKOVER ROBINSON ROUSSEAU SHUBRICK SPRUANCE STANDLEY STIRLING THATCHER GLASSFORD PILLSBURY SCHROEDER SELFRIDGE BAINBRIDGE GREENSLADE MACDONOUGH WAINWRIGHT GOLDSBOROUGH
BELGIAN GERLACHE
BRAZILIAN MELLO
CANADIAN GARNEAU
DANISH HOLM JUEL AMRDUP ADELAER
DUTCH TROMP RUYTER ALMONDE DEWINTER HELFRICH
ENGLISH BALL BYNG HOOD HOPE HOWE LUCE MEUX ALLIN ANSON BAYLY BLAKE BLIGH BOYLE BROKE DRAKE EVANS FOLEY HARDY HAWKE KEYES LEAKE LYONS NOBLE PARRY TRYON AYLMER AYSCUE BEATTY BENBOW BOWERS BURNEY CARDEN COFFIN COLOMB FENNER FISHER FRASER GORDON HALSEY HERVEY HORNBY JERRAM LAWSON LAYTON LITTLE MADDEN MONSON NELSON OSBORN PARKER RODNEY SYFRET VERNON WILSON ADDISON BARCLAY BEDFORD BELCHER CRADOCK DOUGLAS GAMBIER HARWOOD HAWKINS JACKSON MCCLURE MORESBY NASMITH SEYMOUR ANDERSON BEAUFORT BOSCAWEN BROTHERS COCHRANE JELLICOE TRELAWNY TYRWHITT BACKHOUSE BERESFORD CALLAGHAN CHATFIELD COLLINSON FREMANTLE GRENVILLE NARBROUGH NICHOLSON CODRINGTON CUNNINGHAM SOMERVILLE TROUBRIDGE FITZMAURICE MOUNTBATTEN
FRENCH BART LOTI BELLOT DARLAN FORBIN GRASSE COURBET DUPERRE ESTAING FARRERE GUICHEN MOUCHEZ CORBIERE FLEURIAS FLEURIEU MUSELIER NOAILLES CASABIANCA
GERMAN SPEE KONIG HIPPER MULLER RAEDER BEHNCKE CANARIS CAPELLE DOENITZ LUCKNER TIRPITZ JACHMANN LANGSDORFF
GREEK KANARES MIAOULES
HUNGARIAN HORTHY
ITALIAN DORIA LAURIA JACCHINO RICCARDI
JAPANESE ITO KATO TOGO URIU KONDO OKADA SAITO YONAI NAGANO NOMURA FUCHIDA SHIMADA YOSHIDA KAMIMURA SUETSUGU
NORWEGIAN TORDENSKJOLD
PERUVIAN GRAU
PORTUGUESE CASTRO
RUSSIAN GREIG KOLCHAK MAKAROV ALEKSEEV APRAKSIN GORSHKOV KUZNETSOV BELLINGHAUSEN
SCOTTISH BARTON
SPANISH ULLOA GRAVINA MENENDEZ
SWEDISH LINDMAN EHRENSVARD

NAVARRAISE, LA (CHARACTER IN —) ANITA ARAQUIL GARRIDO ZUCCARAGA
(COMPOSER OF —) MASSENET
NAVE HOB HUB NEF APSE BODY FIST PACE AISLE NATHE NIEVE CENTER
NAVEL NOMBRIL OMPHALOS UMBILICUS
(PREF.) OMPHAL(O) UMBILI(CI)
(SUFF.) OMPHALUS
NAVIGABLE BOATABLE PORTABLE
NAVIGATE KEEL SAIL DRIVE GUIDE SKIFF STEER AVIATE COURSE CRUISE DIRECT MANAGE TRAVEL CONDUCT CONTROL JOURNEY OPERATE TRAVERSE ASTROGATE
NAVIGATION HOMING VOYAGE NAUTICS PASSAGE SAILING TRAFFIC CABOTAGE SHIPPING
(— MEASURE) TON KNOT SEAM FATHOM
(— SYSTEM) LORAN TACAN SHORAN
(SYSTEM OF —) DACCA DECCA
NAVIGATOR FLYER NAVVY PILOT AIRMAN AVIATOR COPILOT LABORER AERONAUT SEAFARER SPACEMAN NEPTUNIAN NEPTUNIST
DANISH BERING
DUTCH BERING HARTOG BARENTS HOUTMAN LEMAIRE HEEMSKERK
ENGLISH FOX COOK ADAMS BYRON DIXON DRAKE BAFFIN BARLOW BUTTON CLERKE HUDSON SOMERS WALLIS BARLOWE GILBERT GOSNOLD RALEIGH WEDDELL CAVENDISH FROBISHER LANCASTER VANCOUVER CHANCELLOR WILLOUGHBY
FRENCH CARTIER BETHENCOURT BOUGAINVILLE
GERMAN BEHAIM KOTZEBUE
GREEK EUDOXUS PYTHEAS
ICELANDIC ERICSON
ITALIAN ZENO CABOT VESPUCCI
NORWEGIAN ERIC
PORTUGUESE CAM DIAS DIAZ GAMA CUNHA ZARCO CABRAL DAGAMA GARCIA QUEIROS GILIANES MAGELLAN FERNANDES
RUSSIAN LUTKE GOLOVNIN KRUSENSTERN
SPANISH CANO GALI NINO SOLIS PINZON TORRES BERMUDEZ FERNANDEZ
NAVITE BASALT
NAVVY HAND WORKER LABORER NAVIGATOR
NAVY FLEET SHIPFERD
(— BOARD) ADMIRALTY
(— OFFICER) CPO AIDE MATE BOSUN CHIEF ENSIGN ADMIRAL ARMORER CAPTAIN COMMANDER COMMODORE
(— RADIO OPERATOR) SPARKS
(— VESSEL) PT SUB CARRIER CRUISER FLATTOP DESTROYER SUBMARINE TRANSPORT
NAWAB NABOB RULER VICEROY
NAY NO NAI NEI NOT DENY EVEN

NYET FLUTE NEVER DENIAL REFUSE REFUSAL NEGATIVE
NAZARD STOP NASAT
NAZE NASE HEADLAND
NAZI BROWN HITLERITE
(— SYMBOL) FYLFOT SWASTIKA
NAZIM VICEROY GOVERNOR
NEAERA (DAUGHTER OF —) AUGE EVADNE LAMPETIS PHAETHUSA
(FATHER OF —) PEREUS
(HUSBAND OF —) ALEUS STRYMON
(SON OF —) CEPHEUS LYCURGUS AMPHIDAMAS
NEANDERTHAL CAVEMAN
NEANIC IMMATURE YOUTHFUL
NEAR AD AT BY IN GIN KIN NAR AKIN BAIN DEAR FAST GAIN HARD HEND INBY MEAN NEXT NIGH ABOUT ANEAR ANENT ASIDE CLOSE EWEST FORBY HANDY HENDE JUXTA MATCH NUDGE ROUND SHORT TOUCH ALMOST AROUND BESIDE CLIMAX HEREBY NARROW STINGY TOWARD WITHIN ADVANCE AGAINST FORTHBY SIMILAR THRIFTY VICINAL ADJACENT APPROACH IMMINENT INTIMATE CONTIGUOUS
(— AKIN) GERMANE
(— POINT) PP
(— THE BEGINNING) EARLY FORMER
(— THE EQUATOR) LOW
(— THE MOUTH) ADORAL
(— THE SURFACE) EBB FLEET
(— THE WIND) HIGH AHOLD
(CONVENIENTLY —) HANDSOME
(PREF.) AC AD AF AG AL AP AS AT BY ENGY FPH FPI JUXTA PERI PLESI(O) PROS
NEARBY AROUND GAINLY LOCALLY ADJACENT
(ONES —) THESE
NEARER HITHER
(— FRANCE) CISALPINE
(— ROME) CISALPINE
(— THE REAR) AFTER
(PREF.) **(— IN TIME)** CIS CITRA
NEAREST NEXT EWEST CLOSEST NEARMOST PROCHAIN PROXIMAL IMMEDIATE PROXIMATE
(— THE STERN) AFTERMOST
(PREF.) PROXIMO
NEARIAH (FATHER OF —) ISHI SHEMAIAH
NEARLY GAIN JUST LIKE MOST MUCH ABOUT CLOSE ALMOST FECKLY WELLNIGH VIRTUALLY PRACTICALLY
NEARNESS AFFINITY VICINITY PROPINQUITY
NEARSIGHTED MYOPIC PURBLIND
NEAT GIM NET COSH COWS DEFT DINK FEAT FEEL FEIL GENT JIMP MACK NICE OXEN PRIM PURE SMUG SNOD SNUG TIDY TOSH TRIG TRIM BULLS CLEAN CLEAR COMPT CRISP DINKY DONCY DONSY DOUCE EXACT FEATY FETIS GENTY JEMMY NATTY NIFTY PREST QUEME SMART SMIRK SPICK TERSE TIGHT ADROIT BOVINE CATTLE CLEVER DAINTY DAPPER

DIMBER DONSIE HEPPEN MINION POLITE QUAINT SPANDY SPRUCE BANDBOX CONCISE FEATOUS ORDERLY PERJINK PRECISE REFINED SHAPELY TRICKSY UNMIXED MENSEFUL SKILLFUL STRAIGHT TASTEFUL DEXTEROUS SHIPSHAPE UNDILUTED WHOLESOME
NEATLY SNUG DEFTLY FAIRLY FEATLY SMARTLY SPRUCELY
NEATNESS MENSE DEFTNESS ELEGANCE SPRUCERY
NEATNIK (NOT A —) SLOB
NEB EAR NIB TIP BEAK BILL NOSE POINT SNOUT
NEBAIOTH (FATHER OF —) ISHMAEL
NEBAT (SON OF —) JEROBOAM
NEBO (FATHER OF —) MARDUK MERODACH
(WIFE OF —) TASHMET

NEBRASKA

CAPITAL: LINCOLN
COLLEGE: DANA DOANE DUCHESNE HASTINGS
COUNTY: GAGE LOUP OTOE DEUEL DUNDY KEITH SARPY CHERRY COLFAX FURNAS HOOKER NEMAHA VALLEY BUFFALO ANTELOPE BOXBUTTE KEYAPAHA
INDIAN: OTO OMAHA PONCA PAWNEE
PRESIDENT: FORD
RIVER: LOGAN DISMAL PLATTE ELKHORN NIOBRARA
STATE BIRD: MEADOWLARK
STATE FLOWER: GOLDENROD
STATE NICKNAME: BLACKWATER CORNHUSKER TREEPLANTERS
STATE TREE: ELM
TOWN: ORD ALMA COZAD OMAHA PONCA TRYON WAHOO GERING MULLEN NELIGH PENDER TEKAMAH OGALLALA REDCLOUD THEDFORD
UNIVERSITY: CREIGHTON

NEBRIS FAWNSKIN
NEBULA SKY CRAB SPOT VAPOR BALAXY GALAXY SPIRAL PLANETARY
NEBULIZE ATOMIZE
NEBULOUS DIM DARK HAZY FOGGY MISTY MUDDY VAGUE WISPY CLOUDY MYSTIC TURBID CLOUDED EVASIVE SHADOWY UNCLEAR DREAMLIKE
NECESSARILY NEEDS NEEDLY PERFORCE
NECESSARY NEEDY PRIVY VITAL FRIEND TOILET KINSMAN NEEDFUL FORCIBLE INTEGRAL OBLIGATE BEHOVEFUL ESSENTIAL INTRINSIC (PL.) ALIMENT MISTERS
NECESSITATE FORCE IMPEL COMPEL DEMAND ENTAIL OBLIGE REQUIRE CONSTRAIN
NECESSITY USE CALL DUTY FATE FOOD LACK MUST NEED TASK WANT DRINK ANANKE BEHOOF BESOIN MISTER MUSCLE NEEDBE

URGENCY PERFORCE REQUIREMENT
(— OF MOVING) ZUGZWANG
(BY —) PRESENTLY
(OF —) PERFORCE
(PL.) BREAD
(PREF.) DEONTO
NECK COL NUB PET CAPE CRAG CROP HALS KISS WAKE BEARD CHOKE CRAIG HALSE SCRAG SPOON SWIRE TRAIL BEHEAD CARESS CERVIX COLLET COLLUM FONDLE STRAIT CHANNEL EMBRACE ISTHMUS SQUEEZE TUBULUS LALLYGAG
(— ARTERY) CAROTID
(— MUSCLE) SCALENUS
(— OF BOTTLE) THROTTLE
(— OF LAMB) TARGET
(— OF VOLCANO) CORE
(BACK OF —) NOD NAPE NUCH NUQUE SCRUFF NIDDICK
(BOW —) HAWSE
(PERT. TO —) JUGULAR CERVICAL
(RED —) ROOINEK
(PREF.) CERVIC(I)(O) COLLI DER(O) TRACHEL(O)
(SUFF.) DERUS
NECK AND NECK TIE EVEN CLOSE
NECKBAND BAND COLLAR COLLET SHIRTBAND
NECKCLOTH BOA TIE RUFF AMICE CHOKE SCARF STOLE CHOKER CRAVAT BURDASH NECKTIE PANUELO STARCHER BARCELONA SOLITAIRE STEINKIRK
NECKERCHIEF GIMP RAIL FOGLE BELCHER FOULARD NECKLET KERCHIEF NECKATEE NECKCLOTH NECKENGER
NECKING COLLAR GORGERIN
NECKLACE BEE LEI TORC BEADS CHAIN NOOSE CARCAN CHOKER COLLAR GORGET SANKHA TAWDRY TORQUE BALDRIC CHAPLET RIVIERE SAUTOIR LAVALIER NEGLIGEE ESCLAVAGE
(PREF.) MONILI
NECKLET (FEATHER —) MARABOU MARABOUT
NECKLINE COWL SCOOP
NECK RUFF FRAISE QUELLIO
NECKTIE BOW TIE ASCOT SCARF CHOKER CRAVAT GRAVAT OVERLAY
(— PARTY) HANGING LYNCHING
(PART OF —) EDGE SEAM TACK APRON SHELL FACING MARGIN POCKET HEMMING TIPPING NECKBAND INTERLINING
(STRING —) BOLO
(WOMAN'S —) TAWDRY
NECKWEAR ASCOT
NECROMANCER GOETIC MAGICIAN
NECROMANCY GOETY MAGIC GRAMARY SORCERY WIZARDRY EGROMANCY
NECROPOLIS CEMETERY
NECROPSY AUTOPSY
NECROSIS MORTIFICATION
NECTAR HONEY AMRITA AMBROSIA
NECTAR BIRD EATER HONEY SUNBIRD

NECTARINE PEACH BRUNION NECTRON NECTARIN
NECTARY SPUR GLAND NECTARIUM
NEDABIAH (FATHER OF —) JECONIAH
NEDDER ADDER
NEDDY HORSE DONKEY
NEE BORN
NEED ASK NUD LACK TAKE THAR WANT CRAVE DRIVE THARF BEHOOF BEHOVE BESOIN DEMAND DESIRE EGENCE MISTER STRAIT BEHOOVE NEEDHAM POVERTY REQUIRE URGENCY DISTRESS EXIGENCY MISCHIEF EMERGENCE EXTREMITY NECESSITY
NEEDED NECESSARY
NEEDFIRE WILDFIRE
NEEDFUL VITAL INTEGRAL ESSENTIAL NECESSARY REQUISITE
NEEDLE RIB SEW VEX YEN ACUS DARN GOAD TIER WIRE ANNOY BLUNT POINT SHARP SPIKE STRAW STYLE BODKIN DARNER HECKLE STYLUS OBELISK PRICKER PROVOKE SPICULE TUMBLER
(— HOLE) EYE
(— SORTER) HANDER
(OOMD. FORM) ACU
(PART OF —) EYE HOLE CROWN POINT SHANK
(PINE —) SPILL
(PINE —S) PININGS
(SHAPED LIKE A —) ACEROSE
(PL.) TWINKLES
(PREF.) ACU RAPHI RAPHIDI
NEEDLE BUG NEPID RANATRA
NEEDLEBUSH URY PINBUSH
NEEDLEFISH GAR SNOOK AGUJON BELONID LONGJAW
NEEDLE GUN RIFLE DREYSE
NEEDLELIKE ACUATE ACERATE ACEROSE ACEROUS ACIFORM ACICULAR BELONOID SPLINTERY
NEEDLEMAN TAILOR
NEEDLE-POINTED ACEROSE
NEEDLESHAPED ACIFORM ACETIOUS
NEEDLESS AMOK
NEEDLESTONE NATROLITE
NEEDLEWORK SEWING SAMPLER SEAMING TATTING KNITTING WOOLWORK HEMSTITCH INSERTION STITCHERY EMBROIDERY STITCHCRAFT
NEEDY BARE POOR INDIGENT NEEDSOME HUNGARIAN PENNILESS PENURIOUS NECESSITOUS
NEEP NEPE TURNIP
NE'ER-DO-WELL LOSER BUM PELF SKELLUM SCHLEMIEL SHIFTLESS WORTHLESS RAPSCALLION
NEFANDOUS IMPIOUS EXECRABLE
NEFARIOUS BAD WICKED HEINOUS IMPIOUS FLAGRANT HORRIBLE INFAMOUS ATROCIOUS
NEFERT (HUSBAND OF —) AMENEMHAT
NEGATE DENY SUBLATE
NEGATION NAY NOT EMPTY DENIAL REFUSAL ANNULMENT NONENTITY
(PREF.) DIS

NEGATIVE NA NE NO CON NAE NAY NIT NIX NON NOR NOT NUL DENY FILM VETO MINUS NEVER NAYWARD STAMPER APOPHATIC PRIVATIVE
(— PREFIX) IL IM IN IR UN DIS NON
(— PRINCIPLE) YIN
(PHOTOGRAPHIC —) CLICHE
(PREF.) INEQUI
NEGATOR NAYSAYER OPPONENT
NEGLECT DEBT FAIL HANG OMIT SHUN SLIP FAULT FORGO SHIRK SLOTH WAIVE BYPASS CESSER FOREGO FORGET IGNORE LACHES LOITER PERMIT SLIGHT DEFAULT DISOBEY FAILURE OVERSEE RESPECT FORSLACK OMISSION OVERLOOK OVERSLIP RECKLESS DISREGARD MISLIPPEN OVERSIGHT PRETERMIT MISPRISION
(— OF DUTY) INCIVISM
NEGLECTED TACKY SHABBY UNDONE DORMANT OBSOLETE
NEGLECTFUL LAX REMISS CARELESS DERELICT HEEDLESS RECKLESS DISSOLUTE NEGLIGENT
NEGLIGEE ROBE MANTEAU MATINEE UNDRESS PEIGNOIR NIGHTGOWN DISHABILLE
NEGLIGENCE CULPA LACHES DEFAULT LASCHETY DISREGARD OVERSIGHT
NEGLIGENT LAX LASH SOFT SLACK CASUAL OVERLY REMISS CARELESS DERELICT DISCINCT RECKLESS SLOVENLY YEMELESS DISSOLUTE NEGLECTFUL
NEGLIGIBLE FAT
NEGOTIATE DEAL SELL BROKE FLOAT TREAT TROKE TRUCK TRYST ADVISE ASSIGN CONFER DICKER DIRECT MANAGE PARLEY SETTLE ARRANGE BARGAIN CHAFFER CONDUCT CONSULT DISCUSS ENTREAT CONCLUDE ENTREATY TRANSACT TRANSFER TEMPORIZE
NEGOTIATION DEAL DICKER PARLEY TREATY PASSAGE ENTREATY PRACTICE
NEGRITO ATA ATI ITA AETA AKKA BATWA BLACK KARON SEMANG TAPIRO ABENLEN BAMBUTE
NEGRITUDE SOUL
NEGRO FON JUR LUO LWO SUK AKIM ALUR BENI BINI BONI EGBA FONG IRON MADI MOKE NUBA NUPE SIDI BENIN BLACK BONGO CUFFY DINKA DJUKA FULUP FUZZY HATSA MUNGO SEPIA SEREC SMOKE TEMNE GULLAH HUBSHI AKWAPIM DAHOMAN GEECHEE QUASHIE SANDAWE SHELLUH SHILLUK BECHUANA ETHIOPIAN MANGBATTU
(— BLOOD) TARBRUSH
(GOLD COAST —) GA FANTI
(LIBERIAN —) KRU VAI VEI GREBO ICROO KRUMAN KROOBOY
(MALE —) BUCK
(OLD —) UNCLE
NEHEMIAH (ADVERSARY OF —) TOBIAH
(FATHER OF —) AZBUK HACHALIAH

NEHUSHTA (FATHER OF —) ELNATHAN
(HUSBAND OF —) JEHOIAKIM
(SON OF —) JEHOIACHIN
NEIGH NIE NVE WHI HINNY NICKER WHINNY WIGHER WHICKER
NEIGHBOR BOR ADJOIN BORDER FELLOW NEIPER ACCOLENT BORDERER CONFINER UCALEGON
(PL.) KITH CONFINES
(SUFF.) GETON
NEIGHBORHOOD WAY AREA HAND ZONE VENUE BARRIO LOCALE REGION PURLIEU SECTION DISTRICT ENVIRONS PRESENCE PROCINCT VICINAGE VICINITY BAILIWICK COMMUNITY PROXIMITY TERRITORY VOISINAGE
(SQUALID —) SLUM
NEIGHBORING NIGH NEARBY CONFINE VICINAL ACCOLENT ADJACENT
NEIGHBORLY FOLKSY FOLKSEY AMICABLE
NEITHER NOT NATHER NITHER NOWDER
(— RIGHT NOR WRONG) ADIAPHOROUS
NELEUS (BROTHER OF —) PELIAS
(DAUGHTER OF —) PERO
(FATHER OF —) NEPTUNE
(MOTHER OF —) TYRO
(SON OF —) NESTOR
(WIFE OF —) CHLORIS
NELLORE ONGOLE
NEMA EELWORM FILAMENT NEMATODE ROUNDWORM
NEMATOCYST CNIDA DESMONEME PENETRANT
NEMATODE EELWORM ROUNDWORM
NEMESIS BANE FATE UPIS AGENT AVENGER PENALTY
NEMUEL (BROTHER OF —) ABIRAM DATHAN
(FATHER OF —) ELIAB SIMEON
NENTSI SAMOYED SAMOYEDE
NEOPHYTE TYRO EPOPT NOVICE ROOKIE AMATEUR CONVERT BEGINNER PROSELYTE YOUNGLING
NEOPLASM TUMOR GROWTH TUMOUR SARCOMA NEWGROWTH
NEOTERIC NEW LATE FRESH NOVEL MODERN RECENT
NEP KNOT CATNIP CATMINT CLUSTER

NEPAL
CAPITAL: KATMANDU KATHMANDU
COIN: MOHAR RUPEE
MOUNTAIN: EVEREST
MOUNTAIN RANGE: HIMALAYA
NATIVE: KHA AOUL LIMBU MURMI NEWAR GURKHA GORKHALI
RIVER: KALI KOSI MUGU SETI BABAI BHERI RAPTI SARDA GANDAK KARNALI NARAYANI
TOWN: ILAM MUGU GALWA JUMLA PATAN BIRGANJ POKHARA BHADGAON LALITPUR BHAKTAPUR BIRATNAGAR

NEPENTHE DRUG PLANT POTION ANODYNE
NEPHEG (FATHER OF —) DAVID IZHAR
NEPHELE (DAUGHTER OF —) HELLE
(HUSBAND OF —) ATHAMAS
(SON OF —) LEUCON PHRIXUS
NEPHELINE LENAD MINERAL SOMMITE ELEOLITE
NEPHEW OY OYE NEVE VASU NEFFY NEVOY NIECE NEPOTE BENVOLIO
NEPHRIC RENAL
NEPHRITE YU JADE AXSTONE POUNAMU TREMOLITE
NEPTUNE LER PAN SEA GREEN OCEAN PLATE SEAGOD
(BROTHER OF —) PLUTO JUPITER
(CONSORT OF —) SALACIA
(DISCOVERER OF —) GALLE
(EMBLEM OF —) TRIDENT
(FATHER OF —) SATURN
(MOTHER OF —) RHEA
(SISTER OF —) JUNO
NER (NEPHEW OF —) SAUL
(SON OF —) ABNER
NERD CLOD DINK DORK DRIP JERK WONK DWEEB TWERP
(COMPUTER —) WEENIE
NEREID NYMPH NEREIS THALIA THETIS CYMODOCE
NEREIDES (FATHER OF —) NEREUS
(MOTHER OF —) DORIS
NERGAL (BROTHER OF —) NINAZU
(FATHER OF —) ENLIL
(MOTHER OF —) NINLIL
NERI (FATHER OF —) MELCHI
(SON OF —) SALATHIEL
NERIAH (FATHER OF —) MAASEIAH
(SON OF —) BARUCH SERAIAH
NERISSA (HUSBAND OF —) GRATIANO
NERO TYRANT FIDDLER
(MOTHER OF —) AGRIPPINA
(SUCCESSOR TO —) GALBA
(VICTIM OF —) LUCAN SENECA
(WIFE OF —) OCTAVIA
NERONE (CHARACTER IN —) MAGO NERO SIMON FANUEL RUBRIA ASTERIA
(COMPOSER OF —) BOITO
NERVE RIB BEND CORD GALL GRIT GUTS LINE SAND VEIN BALLS BRASS CHEEK CHORD CRUST PLUCK PUDIC SINEW SPUNK STEEL TENON VAGUS VIGOR APLOMB COSTAL DARING DENTAL ENERGY FACIAL HUTZPA LUMBAR RADIAL SACRAL STRING AXILLAR CHUTZPA COELIAC COURAGE HUTZPAH SAPHENA SCIATIC SPINDLE ABDUCENS AUDACITY BOLDNESS CERVICAL CHUTZPAH COOLNESS EFFERENT EMBOLDEN GUMPTION STRENGTH TEMERITY AUTONOMIC ENCOURAGE EYESTRING ACCELERATOR
(— CELL) ANAXON NEURON DIAXONE DENDRAXON
(— CENTER) BRAIN CORTEX PLEXUS
(— CONNECTOR) SYNAPSE
(— FIBERS) PONS
(— NETWORK) RETIA PLEXUS
(— SLEEP) NEURO HYPNOTISM

(TYPE OF AFFERENT —) EXCITOR
**(PL.) HORRORS JITTERS
(PREF.) NEUR(I)(O)
(SUFF.) NEURA(L) NEURE NEURIA NEURIC
NERVE CELL DIAXON
NERVELESS DEAD WEAK BRAVE INERT UNNERVED FOOLHARDY POWERLESS
NERVOUS EDGY TOEY ANTSY FUSSY GOOSY HYPER JUMPY TENSE TIMID WINDY WIRED FIDGET SINEWY SPOOKY TOUCHY UNEASY FEARFUL FRETFUL JITTERY RESTIVE SCADDLE NEUROTIC TIMOROUS EXCITABLE SENSITIVE TREMULOUS TWITTERLY
(— MALADY) APHASIA NEURITIS
(— SEIZURE) TIC ANEURIA
NERVURE RIB COSTA NERVE NEURON CUBITAL
NERVY BOLD RASH JERKY PUSHY BRAZEN SINEWY STRONG FORWARD JITTERY IMPUDENT INTREPID VIGOROUS EXCITABLE
NESS RAS CAPE SKAW SUFFIX HEADLAND
NEST BED DEN EST JUG WEB AERY BIKE BINK DRAY DREY EYRY HOME LAIR NIDE REDD SHED TRAP ABODE AERIE BROOD EYRIE HAUNT HOUSE NIDUS SWARM CLUTCH COLONY CUDDLE HOTBED NIDIFY RESORT WURLEY CABINET LODGING RETREAT VESPIARY WITHYPOT LARVARIUM PENDULINE RESIDENCE TERMITARY
(— OF ANIMALS) BED
(— OF ANT) FORMICARY
(— OF BOXES) INRO
(— OF EGGS) CLUTCH
(SQUIRREL'S —) CAGE DRAY DREY
(PREF.) CALIO NIDI OECO
(SUFF.) OECA OECIA
NESTER FLEDGLING
NESTLE JUG LAP LIE PET NEST SNUG FITIN NICHE SPOON BURROW CUDDLE FIDGET NUZZLE PETTLE SETTLE SNUDGE CHERISH SHELTER SNUGGLE SNUZZLE
NESTLING BABY BIRD EYAS NEST POULT SQUAB CUDDLE RETREAT BIRDLING NIDULATE FLEDGLING
NEST OF GENTLEFOLK (AUTHOR OF —) TURGENEV
(CHARACTER IN —) LIZA FYODOR PANSHIN VARVARA KALITINE PAVLOVNA LAVRETSKY
NESTOR SAGE SOLON LEADER ADVISER ADVISOR COUNSELOR PATRIARCH
(FATHER OF —) NELEUS
(MOTHER OF —) CHLORIS
(SON OF —) ANTILOCHUS
(WIFE OF —) ANAXIBIA EURYDICE
NESTORIAN WISE
NET BAG GIN HAY LAM POT WEB CAUL FLAG FLAN FLEW FLUE FYKE GAIN HAAF KELL LACE LAUN LAWN LEAD LEAP MESH MOKE NEAT PURE RETE SALE SEAN TOIL TRAP TRIM WEIR BRAIL CATCH CLEAN

CLEAR DRIFT GAUZE LACIS PITCH POUND SCOOP SEINE SEIZE SNARE SNOOD TRAWL TRINK TULLE YIELD BAGNET BASKET BRIGHT COBWEB ENMESH ENTRAP FABRIC GROUND LEADER MALINE MASILE PANTER PROFIT RAFFLE SAGENE SAPIAO TOWNET TUNNEL DRAGNET ENSNARE FLYTAIL LAMPARA MALINES NETWORK PROTECT RETICLE RINSING SCRINGE SHELTER SPILLER STALKER TRAINEL TRAMMEL MESHWORK SALAMBAO BUCKSTALL RETICULUM
(PREF.) DICTY(O) DIKTYO(N) RETI RETINO

NETHANEEL (BROTHER OF —) DAVID
(FATHER OF —) ZUAR JESSE OBEDEDOM
(SON OF —) SHEMAIAH

NETHANIAH (FATHER OF —) ASAPH ELISHAMA
(SON OF —) JEHUDI ISHMAEL

NETHER DOWN BELOW LOWER UNDER NEDDER DOWNWARD INFERIOR INFERNAL

NETHERLANDS

CANAL: ORANJE JULIANA DRENTSCH
CAPITAL: AMSTERDAM
CHEESE: EDAM GOUDA LEYDEN
COIN: CENT DOIT RYDER FLORIN GULDEN STIVER DUCATON ESCALIN GUILDER STOOTER
ISLAND: TEXEL MARKEN AMELAND VLIELAND
MEASURE: EL AAM AHM AUM ELL KAN MUD VAT ZAK DUIM LOOD MIJL ROOD ROPE VOET ANKER CARAT ROEDE STOOP WISSE BUNDER KOPPEN LEGGER MAATJE MUDDLE MUTSJE STREEP SCHEPEL MINGELEN OKSHOOFD STEEKKAN
NAME: HOLLAND
NATIVE: DUTCH DUTCHMAN
PROVINCE: DRENTHE LIMBURG UTRECHT ZEELAND FRIESLAND GRONINGEN GELDERLAND OVERIJSSEL
RIVER: EEMS LECK MAAS WAAL YSEL DONGE HUNSE YSSEL DINTEL DOMMEL KROMME MEAUSE SCHELDT
TOWN: EDE ASSEN BREDA HAGUE AALTEN ARNHEM LEIDEN ZWOLLE HAARLEM TILBURG UTRECHT AALSMEER ENSCHEDE NIJMEGEN AMSTERDAM EINDHOVEN GRONINGEN ROTTERDAM
WEIGHT: ONS LAST LOOD POND BAHAR GREIN KORREL WICHTJE ESTERLIN

NETHERWORLD HADES SHADES
NETLIKE MESHY NETTY RETIARY RETICULAR
NETTING BAR CAUL LING MESH TULLE SCREEN DEEPING FISHNET FOOTING BOBBINET WIREWORK

NETTLE VEX FRET LINE ANNOY CNIDA ETTLE PEEVE PIQUE STING HENBIT ORTIGA RUFFLE SPLICE URTICA AFFRONT BLUBBER BLUETOP KNITTLE PROVOKE STINGER IRRITATE CLOWNHEAL GLIDEWORT PELLITORY SMARTWEED
(— RASH) HIVES UREDO URTICARIA
(— TREE) LOTUS GYMPIE
(WHITE DEAD —) ARCHANGEL
(PREF.) CNID(O)

NETTLERASH HIVES

NETWORK WEB CAUL FRET GRID KELL MAZE MESH MOKE RETE CHAIN LACIS BRIDGE COBWEB CRADLE PLEXUS RESEAU SAGENE SYSTEM DRAGNET DIPLEXER GRIDIRON KNITTING WATTLING RETICULUM
(— OF BLOOD VESSELS) RETE TOMENTUM
(— OF CRACKS) CRACKLE
(— OF LINES) RETICLE
(— OF REFRACTORY MATERIALS) MANTLE
(— ON MAP) GRATICULE
(COMPUTER —) LAN
(NUCLEAR —) SKEIN
(PL.) RETIA

NEUME PES VIRGA CLIVIS PNEUMA PODATUS PUNCTUM VIRGULA CLIMACUS QUILISMA SEQUENCE TORCULUS SCANDICUS

NEURAL DORSAL NERVAL NEURIC
NEURALGIA SCIATICA COSTALGIA
NEURILEMMA
(PREF.) LEMMO
NEURITE AXON AXONE
NEURITIS SCIATICA
NEUROGLIAL
(PREF.) GLI(O)
NEUROLOGIST AMERICAN BEARD DERCUM PRINCE COLLINS CORNING MERRITT MITCHELL
AUSTRIAN FREUD
ENGLISH ASH GOWERS JACKSON
FRENCH RAYMOND DEJERINE
GERMAN NISSL GUDDEN MOBIUS ALZHEIMER
ITALIAN GOLGI
PORTUGUESE MONIZ
SCOTTISH FERRIER
NEUROTIC DRUG NERVOUS
(— CONDITION) LATAH
NEUTRAL GRAY INERT SWEET AMORAL MIDDLING NEGATIVE UNBIASED COLORLESS IMPARTIAL
(— IN COLOR) SOBER
(OPTICALLY —) INACTIVE
NEUTRALIZE KILL ANNUL BLUNT ERASE CANCEL ABOLISH BALANCE CORRECT DESTROY NULLIFY VITIATE NEGATIVE OVERRIDE SATURATE FRUSTRATE
NEUTRINO LEPTON

NEVADA

CAPITAL: CARSONCITY
COUNTY: NYE ELKO LANDER STOREY WASHOE MINERAL PERSHING
INDIAN: WASHO PAIUTE

LAKE: MUD MEAD RUBY TAHOE WALKER PYRAMID WINNEMUCCA
PEAK: BOUNDARY
RIVER: REESE TRUCKEE HUMBOLDT
STATE BIRD: BLUEBIRD
STATE FLOWER: SAGEBRUSH
STATE NICKNAME: SILVER SAGEBRUSH
STATE TREE: ASPEN
TOWN: ELY ELKO RENO EUREKA FALLON NELLIS PIOCHE SPARKS TONOPAH LASVEGAS LOVELOCK

NEVE ICE FIRN SNOW NEPHEW GLACIER
NEVER NAY NIE NOT NARY NARRA NIVER NOWHEN
NEVER-NEVER DREAMLAND
NEVERTHELESS BUT YET STILL ALWISE THOUGH ALGATES HOWBEIT HOWEVER WHETHER NATHELESS NONETHELESS
NEVUS MOLE SPOT TUMOR NAEVUS SPIDER SPILUS FRECKLE LENTIGO SPILOMA BIRTHMARK
NEW HOT NEO NEU RAW LATE MINT NOVA FRESH GREEN MOIST NOVEL YOUNG MODERN RECENT REDHOT UNUSED VIRGIN ANOTHER FOREIGN STRANGE UNTRIED UPSTART INITIATE NEOTERIC ORIGINAL YOUTHFUL BEGINNING
(— BUT YET OLD) NOVANTIQUE
(BRAND —) SPICK
(COMB. FORM) NEO
(LOVE OF WHAT IS —) NEOPHILIA
(PREF.) CAEN(O) CEN(O) NE(O) NOV(I)(O)
(SUFF.) CENE
NEWBORN YEANLING
NEW BRUNSWICK (CAPITAL OF —) FREDERICTON
(COUNTY OF —) KINGS QUEENS SUNBURY MADAWASKA
(MOUNTAIN OF —) CARLETON
(TOWN OF —) BURTON MONCTON BATHURST GAGETOWN
NEW CALEDONIA (— BIRD) KAGU
(CAPITAL OF —) NOUMEA
(ISLAND OF —) HUON BELEP DEPINS LOYALTY WALPOLE
(SEAPORT OF —) NOUMEA
NEWCASTLE GOTHAM
NEWCOMER CADET SETTLER COMELING FRESHMAN JACKEROO MALIHINI RINGNECK GREENHORN IMMIGRANT KIMBERLIN
(— IN EAST) GRIFFIN GRIFFON
NEWCOMES (AUTHOR OF —) THACKERAY
(CHARACTER IN —) ANN KEW JOHN BRIAN CLARA CLIVE ETHEL JAMES ROSEY ALFRED BARNES BINNIE HOBSON RIDLEY THOMAS NEWCOME PULLEYN FARINTOSH MACKENZIE
NEW DEAL (— AGENCY) CCC NRA NYA TVA WPA
NEWEL POST VICE SPINDLE
NEW ENGLAND (— INHABITANT) YANK YANKEE JONATHAN
(— SETTLER) PILGRIM PURITAN
NEW-FANGLED UPSTART

NEWFANGLED MODERN
NEWFOUNDLAND (— CAPE) RAY RACE BAULD
(— HOUSE) TILT
(— INHABITANT) OUTPORTER
(CAPITAL OF —) STJOHNS
(ISLAND OF —) BELL FOGO GROAIS MIQUELON
(RIVER OF —) GANDER HUMBER EXPLOITS
(TOWN OF —) GANDER HOWLEY WABANA CORNERBROOK

NEW GUINEA

BAY: ORO MILNE HOLNICOTE GOODENOUGH COLLINGWOOD
CAPITAL: PORTMORESBY
COIN: KINA
GULF: HUON PAPUA
ISLAND: BUKA MANUS MUSSAU
ISLAND GROUP: CRETIN NINIGO SAINSON SOLOMON
MONEY: KINA TOEA
MOUNTAIN: ALBERT VICTORIA
NATIVE: ARAU BOONG KARON PAPUAN
PORT: LAE DARU WEWAK MADANG
RIVER: FLY HAMU SEPIK KIKORI PURARI AMBERNO
TOWN: LAE WAU DARU SORON AITAPE KIKORI RABAUL SAMARAI

NEW HAMPSHIRE

CAPITAL: CONCORD
COLLEGE: DARTMOUTH
COUNTY: COOS BELKNAP GRAFTON MERRIMACK
LAKE: SQUAM OSSIPEE SUNAPEE UMBABOG WINNIPESAUKEE
MOUNTAIN: MORIAH PAUGUS WAUMBEK CHOCORUA MONADNOCK
MOUNTAIN RANGE: WHITE
NOTCH: CRAWFORD FRANCONIA
PRESIDENT: PIERCE
RIVER: SACO ISRAEL BELLAMY SOUHEGAN MERRIMACK PISCATAQUA
STATE NICKNAME: GRANITE
TOWN: DOVER KEENE EXETER NASHUA HANOVER LACONIA OSSIPEE

NEW HEBRIDES (CAPITAL OF —) VILA
(ISLAND OF —) EPI TANA EFATE MAEWO MABRIM MALEKULA

NEW JERSEY

CAPITAL: TRENTON
COLLEGE: UPSALA
COUNTY: ESSEX OCEAN SALEM UNION BERGEN CAMDEN MERCER MORRIS SUSSEX WARREN PASSAIC MONMOUTH
INDIAN: DELAWARE
PRESIDENT: CLEVELAND
RIVER: DENNIS HAYNES MANTUA RAMAPO MULLICA PASSAIC RARITAN COHANSEY TUCKAHOE
STATE BIRD: GOLDFINCH
STATE FLOWER: VIOLET

STATE NICKNAME: GARDEN
STATE TREE: REDOAK
TOWN: LODI SALEM CAMDEN
NEWARK NEWTON NUTLEY
RAHWAY TOTOWA BAYONNE
CLIFTON HOBOKEN HOHOKUS
MATAWAN NETCONG ORADELL
PARAMUS PASSAIC TEANECK
TENAFLY TRENTON WYCKOFF
CARTERET FREEHOLD METUCHEN
PATERSON SECAUCUS
WATCHUNG HACKENSACK
UNIVERSITY: RUTGERS PRINCETON

NEWLY ANEW AGAIN AFRESH
LATELY FRESHLY NEWLINS
RECENTLY
NEWMARKET MICHIGAN
SARATOGA GRABOUCHE

NEW MEXICO
CAPITAL: SANTAFE
COUNTY: LEA EDDY LUNA MORA
QUAY TAOS OTERO CATRON
CHAVES DEBACA HIDALGO
SOCORRO VALENCIA
CULTURE: MIMBRES
INDIAN: SIA TANO TEWA TIWA ZUNI
JEMEZ PECOS APACHE NAVAHO
NAVAJO PUEBLO
MOUNTAIN: WHEELER
RIVER: UTE GILA PECOS SANJOSE
STATE BIRD: ROADRUNNER
STATE FLOWER: YUCCA
STATE NICKNAME: SUNSHINE
LANDOFENCHANTMENT
STATE TREE: PINON PINYON
TOWN: JAL MORA AZTEC BELEN
RATON CLOVIS DEMING
GALLUP GRANTS ARTESIA
SANTAFE SOCORRO CARLSBAD
LASVEGAS TUCUMCARI
ALAMOGORDO

NEWNESS NOVITY
NEWS BUZZ DOPE UNCA UNKO
WORD CLASH FERLY ADVICE
BUDGET CRACKS FERLIE GOSPEL
NOTICE REPORT EVANGEL
KHUBBER TIDINGS WITTING
NOUVELLE KNOWLEDGE
SPEERINGS
(— AGENCY) AP UP DNB INS UPI
TASS ANETA DOMEI REUTERS
(— BEAT) SCOOP
(— INTERRUPTION) UPDATE
(— ITEM) FACTOID
NEWSBOY NEWSY CAMELOT
CARRIER PAPERBOY
NEWSCASTER ANCHORMAN
NEWSMONGER GOSSIP TATTLER
NOVELANT NOVELIST QUIDNUNC
REPORTER
NEWSPAPER RAG NEWS DAILY
ORGAN PAPER PRESS SHEET
TIMES ARRIBA HERALD SERIAL
SUNDAY COURANT DIURNAL
GAZETTE JOURNAL MERCURY
TABLOID TRIBUNE NEWSPRINT
(— EDITION) EXTRA FINAL
(— SECTION) ROTO METRO
(— USED BY PICKPOCKET) STIFF
(FEEBLE —) SQUEAK

(SECTION OF —) ROTO
(PL.) PRESS
NEWSPAPERMAN HEARST
PRESSMAN
NEWSPERSON REPORTER
NEWSSTAND BOOTH KIOSK STALL
STAND BOOKSTALL
NEWSWORTHY NEWSY
NEWT ASK EFT ESK EVET EBBET
EFFET LIZARD TRITON AXOLOTL
CRAWLER CREEPER REPTILE
MANKEEPER
NEW YEAR'S DAY NAURUZ
NOROOSE NOWROZE
NEW YEAR'S EVE HAGMENA
HOGMANAY

NEW YORK
AVENUE: PARK FIFTH MADISON
FLATBUSH
BAY: JAMAICA PECONIC MORICHES
BOROUGH: BRONX KINGS QUEENS
BROOKLYN MANHATTAN
BUILDING: RCA PANAM CHRYSLER
FLATIRON
CANAL: ERIE GOWANUS
CAPITAL: ALBANY
COLLEGE: BARD CCNY IONA PACE
FINCH UNION HUNTER VASSAR
WAGNER ADELPHI BARNARD
CANISIUS HAMILTON SKIDMORE
COUNTY: ERIE BRONX ESSEX KINGS
TIOGA WAYNE YATES BROOME
CAYUGA NASSAU ONEIDA
OSWEGO OTSEGO PUTNAM
QUEENS SENECA ULSTER
CHEMUNG GENESEE NIAGARA
STEUBEN SUFFOLK CHENANGO
DUTCHESS HERKIMER
ONONDAGA RICHMOND
ROCKLAND SARATOGA SCHUYLER
INDIAN: CAYUGA MOHAWK ONEIDA
SENECA MOHICAN MONTAUK
IROQUOIS ONONDAGA
ISLAND: FIRE LONG ELLIS STATEN
FISHERS LIBERTY SHELTER
GOVERNORS MANHATTAN
LAKE: ERIE CAYUGA GEORGE
ONEIDA OTISCO OTSEGO
OWASCO PLACID SENECA
CONESUS HONEOYE ONTARIO
SARANAC SCHROON SUCCESS
SARATOGA
MOUNTAIN: BEAR MARCY
MOUNTAINS: TACONIC CATSKILL
ADIRONDACK
NICKNAME: EMPIRE GOTHAM
PRESIDENT: FILLMORE VANBUREN
ROOSEVELT
PRISON: TOMBS ATTICA SINGSING
RIVER: TIOGA HARLEM HOOSIC
HUDSON MOHAWK OSWEGO
GENESEE NIAGARA
SQUARE: TIMES UNION HERALD
MADISON
STATE BIRD: BLUEBIRD
STATE FLOWER: ROSE
STATE NICKNAME: EMPIRE
EXCELSIOR
STATE TREE: SUGARMAPLE
STREET: WALL BOWERY
BROADWAY
SUBWAY: BMT IND IRT LEX

TOWN: RYE OVID ROME DELHI
ILION ISLIP NYACK OLEAN
OWEGO UTICA ATTICA AUBURN
CARMEL COHOES ELMIRA
GOSHEN ITHACA MALONE
ONEIDA OSWEGO TAPPAN
WARSAW ARDSLEY BABYLON
BATAVIA BUFFALO CONGERS
ENDWELL GENESEO HEWLETT
MAHOPAC MASSENA MERRICK
MINEOLA MONTAUK ONEONTA
PENNYAN POTSDAM SUFFERN
SYOSSET WANTAGH HANNIBAL
YONKERS BETHPAGE CATSKILL
HERKIMER KINGSTON OSSINING
SYRACUSE TUCKAHOE
ROCHESTER
UNIVERSITY: LIU NYU ADELPHI
COLGATE CORNELL FORDHAM
HOFSTRA YESHIVA COLUMBIA
WATERFALL: NIAGARA

NEW YORK CITY (BOROUGH OF —)
BRONX QUEENS BROOKLYN
MANHATTAN STATENISLAND
(COUNTY OF —) BRONX KINGS
QUEENS RICHMOND
(ISLAND OF —) WARD ELLIS
RANDALL WELFARE
(PARK OF —) GRANT BRYANT
BATTERY CENTRAL
(SUBWAY OF —) BMT IND IRT

NEW ZEALAND
BAY: OHUA HAWKE LYALL AWARUA
CLOUDY GOLDEN FITZROY
PEGASUS POVERTY RANGAUNU
CAPE: EGMONT FAREWELL
PALLISER
CAPITAL: WELLINGTON
GULF: HAURAKI
ISLAND: OTEA STEWART PUKETUTU
LAKE: OHAU HAWEA TAUPO PUKAKI
PUPUKE TEANAU TEKAPO
WANAKA BRUNNER ROTORUA
WAKATIPU
MOUNTAIN: COOK FLAT OWEN
CHOPE LYALL MITRE OTARI
EGMONT STOKES AORANGI
PIHANGA TUTAMOE TYNDALL
ASPIRING EARNSLAW
NATIVE: ATI ARAWA MAORI
RINGATU
PENINSULA: MAHIA OTAGO
RIVER: MOKAU ORETI WAIPA
CLUTHA TAIERI TAMAKI WAIHOU
WAIROA MATAURA WAIKATO
WAITAKI CLARENCE MANAWATU
WANGANUI RANGITIKEI
STRAIT: COOK FOVEAUX
TOWN: LEUIN ORETI OTAKI TAUPO
CLUTHA FOXTON NAPIER NELSON
OAMARU PICTON TIMARU
DUNEDIN MANUKAU RAETIHI
ROTORUA AUCKLAND HAMILTON
KAWAKAWA CHRISTCHURCH
VOLCANO: RUAPEHU NGAURUHOE
TONGARIRO
WATERFALL: BOWEN HELENA
STIRLING SUTHERLAND

NEW ZEALANDER KIWI ENZED
DIGGER

NEXT POI NEAR SYNE THEN UNTO
WISE AFTER EWEST FIRST LATER
NEIST RIGHT BESIDE COMING
SECOND TIDDER TOTHER CLOSEST
NEAREST DIRECTLY PROCHAIN
PROCHEIN UPCOMING ADJOINING
IMMEDIATE
(— AFTER) THEN FOLLOWING
(— IN ORDER) EKA
(— MONTH) PROXIMO
(— OF KIN) GOEL
(— TO LAST) PENULT
(PREF.) (— IN ORDER) EKA
NEXUS TIE BOND LINK CHAIN
NGAIO KIO KAIO NAIO TREE
NHANG GIAI
NIAM-NIAM ZANDE AZANDE
AZANDI ZANDEH AZANDEH
BABUNGERA
NIB NEB PEN BEAK BILL KINK TEAT
POINT PRONG SCORER
NIBBLE EAT NAB NIB NIP BITE GNAW
KNAB KNAP MOOP MOUP NOSH
PECK PICK CHAMP GNARL MOUSE
PIECE SHEAR ARRODE BROWSE
CHAVEL NATTLE PICKLE PILFER
CHIMBLE GNABBLE GNATTER
KNABBLE SNAGGLE
NIBELUNGENLIED (AUTHOR OF —)
UNKNOWN
(CHARACTER IN —) UTA ETZEL
HAGEN IRING GERNOT HUNOLD
LUDGER BLOEDEL GUNTHER
ORTLIEB BRUNHILD DANKWART
DIETRICH GISELHER KRIEMHILD
SIEGFRIED HILDEBRAND
NIBLICK BLASTER
NICANOR (WIFE OF —) CLEOPATRA

NICARAGUA
CAPITAL: MANAGUA
COIN: PESO CENTAVO CORDOBA
DEPARTMENT: LEON BOACO RIVAS
CARAZO ESTELI MADRIZ MASAYA
ZELAYA MANAGUA
ISLAND: OMETEPE
LAKE: MANAGUA
MEASURE: VARA CAHIZ MILLA
SUERTE TERCIA CAJUELA
ESTADAL MANZANA
MOUNTAIN: MADERA MOGOTON
PORT: CORINTO
RIVER: COCO TUMA WANKS
GRANDE ESCONDIDO
TOWN: LEON BOACO RIVAS
MASAYA OCOTAL SOMOTO
GRANADA MANAGUA
JINOTEGA MATAGALPA
CHINANDEGA
WEIGHT: BAG CAJA TONELADA

NICCOLITE ARITE KUPFERNICKEL
NICE APT FIT FEAT FINE GOOD JUMP
KIND NEAT NYCE PURE TRIM
CANNY EXACT FUSSY NIECE SWEET
BONITA BONITO DAINTY GENTIL
MINUTE PEACHY QUAINT QUEASY
SPICED STRICT SUBTLE TICKLE
CORRECT ELEGANT FINICAL
GENTEEL MINCING PERJINK
PICKING PRECISE PRUDISH
REFINED DECOROUS DELICATE
EXACTING PLEASANT PLEASING

TICKLISH PARTICULAR SCRUMPTIOUS

(TOO —) SUPERFINE

(PREF.) **(PERTAINING TO —)** NICENO

NICELY JUMP

NICETY HAIR QUIDDIT DELICACY JUSTNESS QUIDDITY CRITICISM CURIOSITY PRECISION

(PL.) PERJINKITIES

NICHE BAY WRO APSE CANT COVE NOOK SLOT AMBRY HERNE HOVEL NIECE NITCH PLACE ALCOVE ANCONA BOXING COVERT CRANNY EXEDRA GROOVE MIHRAB RECESS RINCON EDICULE HOUSING RETREAT ROUNDEL AEDICULA CREDENCE TOKONOMA HABITACLE PIGEONHOLE TABERNACLE

NICHOLAS NICKLEBY (AUTHOR OF —) DICKENS

(CHARACTER IN —) BRAY HAWK KATE FRANK GRIDE NOGGS RALPH SMIKE NEWMAN SQUEERS VINCENT CRUMMLES MADELINE MULBERRY NICHOLAS NICKLEBY WACKFORD CHEERYBLE MANTALINI

NICIPPE (FATHER OF —) PELOPS

(HUSBAND OF —) STHENELUS

(MOTHER OF —) HIPPODAMIA

(SON OF —) EURYSTHEUS

NICK CUT JAG MAR NAG NOB CHIP DENT DINT HACK NACK SLAP SLIT CHEAT CHICK GOUGE NITCH NOTCH PRICK SCORE SLACK SNICK TALLY TRICK ARREST RECORD DEFRAUD

(— OF TIME) GODSPEED

NICKEL JIT COIN JITNEY NIMBUS

(ALLOY OF —) INVAR KONEL MONEL

(CONTAINING —) NICCOLIC

(SYMBOL OF —) NI

(WOODEN —) SLUG

NICKELODEON JUKEBOX

NICKEL-SILVER PAKFONG PAKTONG PACKFONG

NICKER NEIGHER

NICKNAME DUB TAG DOEG NICK ALIAS AGNAME BYNAME BYWORD HANDLE MONICA TONAME AGNOMEN CRACKER EKENAME MISNAME MONIKER NICKERY COGNOMEN MONARCHO MONIKER TARTUFFE SOBRIQUET

NICKNAMING PROSONOMASIA

NICOMEDE (HALF-BROTHER OF —) ATTALE

(STEPMOTHER OF —) ARSINOE

NICOSTRATA (FATHER OF —) LADON

(HUSBAND OF —) ECHENUS

(SON OF —) EVANDER

NICOSTRATUS (BROTHER OF —) MEGAPENTHES

(FATHER OF —) MENELAUS

(MOTHER OF —) HELEN

NICOTINIC ACID NIACIN

NICTATE WINK BLINK CLOSE TWINK TWINKLE NICTITATE

NIDDICK NAPE

NIDE NID NEST BROOD LITTER

NIDGE NIG SHAKE QUIVER

NIDGET HOE FOOL IDIOT

NIDIFY NEST

NIDOR ODOR AROMA SAVOR SCENT SMELL

NIDUS NEST

NIECE OY OYE NEPHEW

NIELLO TULA

NIEPA NIOTA KARINGHOTA

NIEVE FIST HAND NEIF SERF NATIVE

NIFTY FINE GOOD KEEN SMART STYLISH

NIGER JOLIBA KWORRA RAMTIL

(CAPITAL OF —) NIAMEY

(MOUTH OF —) NUN

(NATIVE OF —) PEUL HAUSA DJERMA FULANI SONGHA TOUBOU TUAREG

(OASIS IN —) KAOUAR

(REGION OF —) AIR

(RIVER OF —) DILLIA

(TOWN OF —) SAY GAYA TERA BAGAM FACHI GOURE MADAMA MARADI TAHOUA ZINDER

NIGGARD CARL CHURL CLOSE MISER NIGON PIKER SCART TIGHT NIGGER SCRIMP SCRUNT STINGY CHINCHE DRYFIST NITHING SCROOGE PINCHGUT PUCKFIST SCRIMPER EARTHWORM PINCHBECK PINCHFIST PUCKFOIST SKINFLINT PINCHPENNY

NIGGARDLY MEAN CLOSE NIRLY STINT NARROW NIDING NIGHLY NIRLED SCANTY SCREWY SKIMPY SORDID STINGY STRAIT CHINCHE COSTIVE MISERLY NITHING PENURIOUS PARSIMONIOUS

NIGGERFISH CONY HIND CONEY GROUPER GUATIVERE

NIGGLE DOUBT

NIGGLER NITPICKER

NIGGLING PETTY PICAYUNE

NIGH AT NEAR ANEAR ANIGH CLOSE ALMOST NEARLY ADJACENT

NIGHT PM EVE DARK NUIT SOIR DARKY DEATH NACHT NOCHE SLEEP DARKMANS DARKNESS

(— AND DAY) NYCHTHEMERON

(CHILDREN OF —) ERINYS FURIES ERINNYES

(COMB. FORM) NYCTI

(DEPTH OF —) HOLL

(GODDESS OF —) NOX NYX

(LAST —) YESTREEN

(NORSE —) NATT NOTT

(PERT. TO —) NOCTURNAL

(STAY OUT ALL —) PERNOCTATE

(PREF.) NOCT(I)(O) NYCT(I)(O)

NIGHT APE DURUKULI

NIGHT BELL (CHARACTER IN —) ENRICO SERAFINA PISTACCHIO

(COMPOSER OF —) DONIZETTI

NIGHT BLINDNESS NYCTALOPIA

NIGHTCAP HOW COWL DOWD HOUVE PIRNY BIGGIN PIRNIE DORMEUSE SUNDOWNER

NIGHTCLUB CAFE CLUB SPOT AGOGO BOITE DISCO BISTRO NITERY CABARET DANCERY NIGHTERY

NIGHTDRESS SLOP WILYCOAT WYLIECOAT

NIGHTFALL EEN EVE DARK DUSK EVEN SHUTTING TWILIGHT

(OCCURRING AT —) ACRONICAL

NIGHTGOWN SLOP TOOSH NIGHTY BEDGOWN NIGHTIE WYLIECOAT

NIGHTHAWK PISK CUIEJO BULLBAT

NIGHTINGALE JUG BULBUL FLORENCE PHILOMEL ROSSIGNOL

(— SOUND) JUG

(SWEDISH —) LIND JENNY

(PL.) WATCH

NIGHTJAR PUCK POTOO EVEJAR DENHAWK SPINNER WHEELER MOREPORK POORWILL NIGHTHAWK

NIGHT LAMP VEILLEUSE

NIGHTMARE ALP HAG MARA MESS DREAM FANCY FIEND VISION INCUBUS CACODEMON CAUCHEMAR EPHIALTES

(— CAUSER) MARE

NIGHTMARE ABBEY (AUTHOR OF —) PEACOCK

(CHARACTER IN —) EMILY FATOUT FLOSKY GLOWRY STELLA TOOBAD CELINDA CYPRESS ASTERIAS LISTLESS SCYTHROP GIROUETTE MARIONETTA CHRISTOPHER

NIGHTSHADE HERB DWALE MOREL TOMATO HENBANE MORELLE PETUNIA SANDBUR SOLANUM MANDRAKE TROMPILLO

NIGHT'S LODGING (AUTHOR OF —) GORKY

(CHARACTER IN —) LUKA BARON PEPEL SAHTIN BUBNOFF NATASHA ALYOSCHKA KVASCHNYA KOSTILIOFF WASSILISSA

NIGHT WATCHMAN CHARLEY CHARLIE

NIGHTWEAR PJS JAMMIES PAJAMAS

NIHIL NIL NICHIL NOTHING

NIHILIST ANARCHIST SOCIALIST

NIKE VICTORY

(BROTHER OF —) BIA ZELUS CRATOS

(FATHER OF —) PALLAS

(MOTHER OF —) STYX

NIL ZERO NILGAI IPOMOEA NOTHING

NILE GREEN BOA

NILGAI NIL NYLGAU ANTELOPE NEELGHAU

NIMBLE FLY DEFT FLIP FLIT GLEG LISH SPRY SWAK YALD YARE AGILE BRISK FLEET LIGHT NIPPY QUICK SWACK TRICK WIGHT YAULD ACTIVE ADROIT CLEVER FEIRIE LIMBER LISSOM LIVELY PROMPT QUIVER SPRACK SUPPLE VOLANT WANDLE DELIVER LISSOME SWIPPER FLIPPANT TRIPPING CITIGRADE SENSITIVE SPRIGHTLY (PREF.) PRESTI

NIMBLENESS HASTE AGILITY SLEIGHT LEGERITY DEXTERITY LIGHTNESS

NIMBLE-WITTED VOLABLE

NIMBUS AURA HALO NIMB CLOUD GLORY SHINE VAPOR GLORIA AUREOLA AUREOLE

NIMIETY EXCESS

NINAZU (BROTHER OF —) NERGAL

(FATHER OF —) ENLIL

(MOTHER OF —) NINLIL

NINCOMPOOP ASS BOOB DOLT FOOL POOP NINNY NINCOM WITLING BLOCKHEAD SIMPLETON

NINE IX NIE NYE TEAM COMET POTHOOK

(— A.M.) UNDERN MIDMORN

(— ANGLED FIGURE) NONAGON

(— DAYS DEVOTION) NOVENA

(— FOLD) NONUPLE

(— HEADED MONSTER) HYDRA

(— HUNDRED) SAN

(— INCHES) SPAN

(— OF CLUBS OR DIAMONDS) COMET

(— OF DIAMONDS) BRAGGER

(— OF TRUMPS) DIX MENEL SANCHO

(— YEAR CYCLE) JUGLAR

(GROUP OF —) ENNEAD
(MUSIC FOR —) NONET
(PREF.) ENNE(A) NON(A) NOVEM
NOVEN
NINEBARK ROSACEAN SEVENBARK
NINEHOLES BUMBLEPUPPY
NINEPIN KAIL SQUAIL SKITTLE
SKITTLES
(PL.) BOWLS KEELS KAYLES
NINEPEGS
NINETEENTH LARIGOT
NINETIETH NONAGESIMAL
NINETY KOPPA
NINEVEH (FOUNDER OF —) NINUS
NINE WORLDS HEL ASGARD
ALFHEIM MIDGARD NIFLHEIM
VANAHEIM JOTUNNHEIM
MUSPELLSHEIM SVARTALFAHEIM
NINLIL (HUSBAND OF —) ENLIL
(SON OF —) NERGAL NINAZU
NINNI ISHTAR
NINNY DOLT FOOL LOUT DUNCE
GOOSE IDIOT NONNY PATCH
SAMMY SPOON FONDLE NOODLE
SAPHEAD FONDLING BLOCKHEAD
NIDDICOCK PEAKGOOSE
SIMPLETON
NINON SHEER
NINSUN (SON OF —) GILGAMESH
NINTH (EVERY —) NONAN ENNEATIC
(PREF.) NON(A)
NINTU (DAUGHTER OF —) UTTU
(HUSBAND OF —) ENKI
(SON OF —) NINSAR
NINURTA (FATHER OF —) ENLIL
NINUS (FATHER OF —) BELUS
(SON OF —) NINYAS
(WIFE OF —) SEMIRAMIS
NIOBATE TODDITE SIPYLITE
COLUMBATE
NIOBE HERB HOSTA FUNKIA
(BROTHER OF —) PELOPS
(FATHER OF —) TANTALUS
(HUSBAND OF —) AMPHION
(SISTER-IN-LAW OF —) AEDON
NIOBIC COLUMBIC
NIOBIUM COLUMBIUM
NIP CUT SIP VEX BITE BUMP CLIP
DRAM GIVE KNIP NIPE PECK SNUB
TANG TAUT TUCK BLAST CHEAT
CHECK CHILL CLAMP DRAFT FROST
PINCH SEIZE SEVER SNAPE SNEAP
THIEF BENUMB BLIGHT CATNIP
TIPPLE TWITCH WITHER SARCASM
SQUEEZE WETTING COMPRESS
FROSTBITE VELLICATE
NIPA PALM ATAP ATTAP DRINK
NIPPER BOY LAD CLAW CRAB GRAB
HAND BITER CHELA MISER THIEF
CUNNER URCHIN GRIPPER INCISOR
BRAKEMAN
NIPPERS DOG NIP BITS NIPS TONGS
GRATER PLIERS TURKIS FORCEPS
PINCERS OSTEOTOME
NIPPLE BUD DUG PAP TIT BEAN
TEAT DIDDY DUMMY SPEAN
NIBBLE PILLAR MAMILLA PAPILLA
THELIUM
(— POINT) THELION
(PREF.) EPITHELI(O) MAMM(I)(ILLI)
MAST(O) PAPILLI PAPILLO THEL(O)
NIPPLEWORT BALLOGAN
WARTWEED WARTWORT

NIPPY BOLD SHARP
NIREUS (FATHER OF —) CHAROPUS
(MOTHER OF —) AGLAIA
(SLAYER OF —) EURYPYLUS
NIRVANA EDEN EMPTINESS
NIS NIX NISSE GOBLIN KOBOLD
BROWNIE
NISAN ABIB
NISEI (— SON OR DAUGHTER)
SANSEI
NISUS POWER EFFORT IMPULSE
ENDEAVOR
(DAUGHTER OF —) SCYLLA
(FATHER OF —) PANDION
HYRTACUS
(MOTHER OF —) IDA
NITER NITRE PETER PETRE POTASH
SALTPETER
NITHER BLAST DEBASE SHIVER
TREMBLE
NITID GAY BRIGHT GLOSSY SPRUCE
SHINING LUSTROUS NITIDOUS
NITO AGSAM
NITON RADON
NITRATE SALT ESTER COTTON
AZOTATE
(PREF.) NITR(O)
NITRIC AZOTIC
NITRIDE BORAZON
NITRITE AZOTITE
NITROGEN GAS AZOTE ALKALIGEN
(PREF.) AZ(O)
NITROGLYCERIN TNT SOUP NITRO
SIRUP SYRUP GLONOIN GLONOINE
NITWIT DAW NIT BOOB DINK DOLT
DOPE KOOK DRONGO DINGBAT
DIZZARD DINGALING SIMPLETON
NIX NO HARD NECK NICKER
NOBODY SPIRIT SPRITE UNDINE
NOTHING
NJAVE ADJAB DIAVE
NJORD (DAUGHTER OF —) FREYA
(SON OF —) FREY
(WIFE OF —) SKADHI
NO NA NE NAE NAH NAW NAY NIT
NIX NUL BAAL BAIL BALE NEIN
NONE NYET NAPOO AIKONA
NAPOOH NOGAKU
(— MORE) NAPOO
(— ONE) NIX NEMO
(— POINTS IN TENNIS) LOVE
(PREF.) NULLI
NOADIAH (FATHER OF —) BINNUI
NOAH NOE
(DOVE OF —) COLUMBA
(FATHER OF —) LAMECH
ZELOPHEHAD
(GRANDFATHER OF —)
METHUSALEH
(GRANDSON OF —) ARAM MAGOG
(GREAT-GRANDSON OF —) HUL
(MEXICAN —) COXCOX
(RAVEN OF —) CORVUS
(SON OF —) HAM SEM SHEM
JAPHETH
(WINE CUP OF —) CRATER
NOB NAB BLOW HEAD NAVE KNAVE
SWELL HANDLE TIPTOPPER
NOBEL PRIZE (— IN CHEMISTRY)
LEE BERG BERG CECH CRAM HAHN
HOFF KLUG KUHN LEHN OLAH TODD
UREY ALDER ASTON BOSCH BROWN
COREY CURIE DEBYE DIELS EIGEN

ERNST FLORY FUKUI HABER HUBER
KARLE LIBBY NATTA PREGL SMITH
SODDY SYNGE TAUBE TAUBE
ALTMAN CALVIN HARDEN HASSEL
KARRER LELOIR MARCUS MICHEL
MULLIS NERNST PERUTZ PRELOG
RAMSAY SANGER SANGER SUMNER
WERNER WITTIG BERGIUS BUCHNER
GIAUQUE GILBERT GILBERT
HOFFMAN KENDREW KENICHI
MOISSAN NORRISH ONSAGER
OSTWALD POLANYI RUZICKA
SEABORG SEMENOV WALLACH
WIELAND WINDAUS HAUPTMAN
LANGMUIR MITCHELL MULLIKEN
PEDERSON TISELIUS HERSCHBACH
MERRIFIELD DEISENHOFER
(— IN ECONOMICS) FOGEL MILLER
DOUGLASS
(— IN ECONOMICS) ARROW KLEIN
KLEIN LEWIS OHLIN SIMON SIMON
SOLOW STONE TOBIN TOBIN ALLAIS
DEBREU DEBREU FRISCH MYRDAL
SHARPE KUZNETS SCHULTZ
SCHULTZ STIGLER STIGLER
BUCHANAN FRIEDMAN HAAVELMO
LEONTIEF MARKOWITZ MODIGLIANI
(— IN LITERATURE) PAZ BOLL BUCK
COLA GIDE MANN SHAW AGNON
BUNIN CAMUS ELIOT HESSE HEYSE
LEWIS PERSE SACHS SIMON YEATS
ANDRIC BELLOW ELYTIS ELYTIS
EUCKEN FRANCE MAFOUZ MILOSZ
MILOSZ NERUDA ONEILL SARTRE
SINGER SINGER TAGORE BECKETT
BRODSKY CANETTI CENETTI
GOLDING GIDE KIPLING
LAXNESS MARQUEZ MAURIAC
MISTRAL MONTALE ROLLAND
RUSSELL SEIFERT SOYINKA
WALCOTT BJORNSON CARDUCCI
FAULKNER GORDIMER LAGERLOF
MORRISON CHURCHILL
HEMINGWAY PASTERNAK
STEINBECK LAGERKVIST
MAETERLINCK
(— IN MEDICINE) DAM CORI DALE
HESS KATZ KOCH ROSS ROUS VANE
WALD ARBER BLACK BLOCH BOVET
BROWN BUMET CHAIN COHEN
CRICK CURIE DOISY ELION EULER
GOLGI HENCH HUBEL HUBEL JERNE
KREBS KREBS KROGH LOEWI LURIA
LYNEN MINOT MONIZ MONOD
NEHER OCHOA SHARP SNELL SNELL
TATUM YALOW BARANY BEADLE
BEKESY BISHOP BORDET CARREL
CLAUDE DOMAGK ECCLES ENDERS
FISHER FLOREY GASSER GILMAN
GRANIT HOLLEY HUXLEY KOCHER
KOHLER KOSSEL LORENZ MURRAY
PALADE PAVLOV RICHET SPERRY
SPERRY THOMAS VARMUS WIESEL
WIESEL AXELROD BEHRING
DAUSETT FIBIGER HERSHEY
HODGKIN KHORANA LAVERAN
NATHANS NICOLLE ROBERTS
RODBELL SAKMANN SCHALLY
THELLER DELBRUCK MILSTEIN
TONEGAWA BERGSTROM
GOLDSTEIN HITCHINGS
BENACERRAF MCCLINTOCK

MCCLINTOCK MONTALCINI
SAMUELSSON
(— IN PEACE) ORR THO HULL KING
MOTT PIRE ROOT SATO TUTU ASSER
BAJER BALCH BEGIN DAWES FRIED
GOBAT LANGE PASSY SADAT
ADDAMS ANGELL BRANDT BRIAND
BUNCHE BUTLER CASSIN CREMER
DUNANT MENCHU MONETA
MYRDAL NANSEN QUIDDE ROBLES
WALESA WALESA WIESEL WILSON
BORLAUG BUISSON DEKLERK
JOUHAUX KELLOGG LUTHULI
MANDELA PAULING RENAULT
SANCHEZ THERESA BRANTING
CORRIGAN ESQUIVEL ESQUIVEL
SAKHAROV GORBACHEV KISSINGER
ROOSEVELT SODERBLOM
SCHWEITZER HAMMARSKJOLD
AUMGSANSUUKYI
(— IN PHYSICS) LEE BOHR BORN
HESS LAMB LAUE MEER MOTT NEEL
RABI RYLE TAMM TING WIEN YANG
BASOV BETHE BLOCH BOTHE
BRAGG BRAUN CURIE DALEN DIRAC
ESAKI FERMI FITCH GABOR HERTZ
HULSE KUSCH PAULI RUSKA SEGRE
SHULL ALFVEN BARKLA BINNIG
CRONIN CRONIN FOWLER FOWLER
GENNES GLASER HEWISH LANDAU
MULLER PERRIN PLANCK RAMSEY
ROHRER RUBBIA STRUTT TAYLOR
TAYLOR TOWNES WIGNER WILSON
YUKAWA BARDEEN BEDNORZ
CHARPAK DEHMELT GELLMAN
GLAEVER GLASHOW KAPITSA
KENDALL LORENTZ MARCONI
RICHTER SHAWLOW EINSTEIN
FRIEDMAN KLITZING LEDERMAN
ROENTGEN SCHWARTZ SIEGBAHN
BROCKHOUSE BLOEMBERGEN
STEINBERGER CHANDRASEKHAR
CHANDRASEKHAR
NOBILITY RANK ELITE GRACE
GENTRY STATUS DIGNITY
KWAZOKU PEERAGE QUALITY
STATION BARONAGE SZLACHTA
ELEVATION
(MEMBER OF TATAR —) MURZA
(ROMAN —) RAMNES
NOBLE DON ALII DOGE DUKE EARL
EDEL EPIC FAME FREE GENT GOOD
GRAF HIGH JARL JUST KAMI KUGE
LORD PEER PURE RIAL ARIKI
ATHEL BARON BROAD BURLY
COUNT DUCAL ERECT ETHEL
FURST GRAND GREAT HIRAM
KHASS LOFTY MANLY MORAL
MURZA PROUD ROYAL STATE
AUGUST COUSIN DAIMIO EPICAL
FLAITH GENTLE GESITH HAUGHT
HEROIC JUNKER KINGLY LORDLY
LUCUMO MANFUL SIRDAR SUPERB
THAKUR WORTHY YONKER
ACERBAS CACIQUE GALLANT
GLAUCUS GLORIED GRANDEE
HIDALGO LIBERAL MAGNATE
MARQUIS PATRICK STAROST
STATELY STEWARD SUBLIME
TOISECH VOLPONE PANGLIMA
PRINCELY
(MINOR —) VIDAME
NOBLEMAN DUKE EARL EMIR LORD

PEER SOUL BARON COUNT ORLOV
PARIS THANE COUSIN MILORD
ORLOFF THAKUR YONKER
GRANDEE HIDALGO MAGNATE
MARQUIS STAROST VOLPONE
YOUNKER ADELIGER ALDERMAN
ALMAVIVA BELARIUS MARCHESE
MARQUESS LANDGRAVE
MAGNIFICO

NOBLE-MINDED MANFUL LIBERAL

NOBLENESS HONOR DIGNITY
(— OF BIRTH) EUGENY

NOBLEWOMAN LADY MILADY
DUCHESS PEERESS BARONESS
COUNTESS

NOBODY NIX NEMO NONE NADIE
NOMAN SCRUB SCARAB NOTHING
JACKSTRAW

NOCENT GUILTY HARMFUL
HURTFUL NOXIOUS CRIMINAL

NOCTURNAL NIGHT NOXIAL
NIGHTLY NIGHTISH MOONSHINE
(— ANIMAL) COON POSSUM
OPOSSUM
(— BIRD) OWL
(— CARNIVORE) RATEL
(— MAMMAL) BAT LEMUR
(— SIGNS) ZODIAC

NOCTURNE LULLABY UHTSONG
PAINTING SERENADE

NOD OK BOB BOW ERR NAP NID NIP
BECK BEND DOZE NAPE SIGN SLIP
SWAY WINK DROOP LAPSE ASSENT
BECKON DODDLE DROWSE
NODDLE NUTATE SALUTE SIGNIFY
(— OFF) DOZE

NODDING DROWSY NUTANT
ANNUENT CERNUOUS DROOPING
NUTATION

NODDLE HEAD PATE BRAIN SKULL

NODDY AUK FOOL JACK NOIO TERN
KNAVE NINNY DROWSY FULMAR
NOODLE SLEEPY HACKNEY
TOMNODDY SIMPLETON

NODE BOW BUMP KNOB KNOT
LUMP PLOT JOINT NODUS POINT
TUMOR BULBIL NODULE DILEMMA
GRANULE KNUCKLE FOLLICLE
PHYTOMER SWELLING TUBERCLE
(— OF GRASS) KNOT
(— OF POEM) PLOT
(— OF STEM) JOINT

NODULE BOB AUGE BUMP KNOT
LUMP MASS NODE YOLK FLINT
GEODE PHYMA MILIUM BLISTER
CATHEAD GRANULE LEPROMA
NABLOCK SARCOID AMYGDALE
AMYGDULE COALBALL TUBERCLE
WHITEHEAD
(— OF FLINT) CORE
(CHALCEDONY —) ENHYDROS
(PL.) BEADING

NOEL XMAS CAROL NOWEL NATALIS
CHRISTMAS

NOGAH (FATHER OF —) DAVID

NOGGIN ALE CUP MUG NOG PEG
PIN BEAN GILL HEAD PAIL PATE
DRINK GOGGAN NAGGIN NOODLE

NO-GOODNIK SCALAWAG

NOHAH (FATHER OF —) BENJAMIN

NOIL FIBER PINION

NOISE (ALSO SEE SOUND) ADO AIR
BUM DIN GIG HUM POP ROW

BANG BOOM BRAY BUMP BURR
CLAM COIL HOOT KLOP MUSH
PEAL RALE RASH REEL RERD ROTE
ROUT SLAM ZING ALARM BABEL
BLARE BLAST BLOOP BRAWL
BRUIT BURLE CHANG CHIRM CLICK
DREAM GRASS JERRY KNOCK
LARRY LARUM LEDEN PLASH
QUONK REERE RERDE RUMOR
SLORP SNORE SOUND STEER
SWISH WHANG BICKER CACKLE
CLAMOR DUNDER GOBBLE GOSSIP
HUBBUB NORATE OUTCRY
PUDDER RACKET RANTAN RATTLE
REPORT SPLASH SQUAWK STEVEN
STRIFE TUMULT UPROAR BLUSTER
BRATTLE CLITTER CLUTTER
CRACKLE ORATION SCANDAL
SPATTER STREPOR STRIDOR
FLICFLAC QUONKING TINTAMAR
CONFUSION
(— OF DISAPPROVAL) RASPBERRY
(EARTHQUAKE —) BRONTIDES
(ELECTRIC —) GRASS
(EXPLOSIVE —) REPORT
(LOUD —) THUNDER
(RESOUNDING —) WHAM WHANG
(SCRAPING —) SCROOP
(PREF.) (— OF FALLING OBJECT)
KER

NOISELESS QUIET STILL SWEET
TACIT SILENT APHONIC CATLIKE

NOISEMAKER BELL HORN GRAGER
RATTLE CLAPPER SQUEAKER

NOISETTE HAZEL HAZELNUT

NOISING (— ABROAD) AIR

NOISOME FOUL OLID RANK FETID
NASTY PUTRID RANCID HARMFUL
HURTFUL NOXIOUS NUISOME
ODOROUS STINKING OFFENSIVE
MALODOROUS

NOISY LOUD CLASHY CREAKY
BLATANT DINSOME FRANTIC
MOILING RACKETY RIOTOUS
ROUTOUS BRAWLING CLATTERY
SONOROUS STREPENT HILARIOUS
RATTLEBAG SCAMBLING
BOISTEROUS

NOLL HEAD NODDLE NOODLE

NOMA CANKER

NOMAD ARAB BEJA LURI MOOR
SAKA SHUA ALANI GYPSY IGDYR
JAREG ROVER SHUWA NOMADE
ROAMER ROVING SEMITE SLUBBI
TUAREG BAZIGAR BEDOUIN
SARACEN SCENITE SHORTZY
SHUKRIA SOLUBBI TOUAREG
KABABISH SCYTHIAN SHINWARI
AMALEKITE MIGRATORY
PEREGRINE
(— PEOPLE) ALANI
(ETHIOPIAN —) GALLA
(PL.) AKHLAME

NOMADIC ERRATIC VAGRANT
VAGABOND FOOTLOOSE
ITINERANT

NOMBRIL NAVEL

NOM DE PLUME PENNAME
TELONISM PSEUDONYM

NOME ELIS NOMOS MELODY
NOMARCHY PROVINCE

NOMENCLATURE LIST NAME TERM

ONYMY NAMING GLOSSARY
REGISTER CATALOGUE

NOMINAL PAR BASIC PAPER
FORMAL SLIGHT UNREAL TITULAR
TRIVIAL PLATONIC TRIFLING
(— RECOGNIZANCE) DOE

NOMINATE CALL LEET NAME ELECT
NEVEN SLATE SELECT APPOINT
ENTITLE PRESENT PROPOSE
SPECIFY DESIGNATE POSTULATE

NOMINY SPEECH RIGMAROLE

NONAGE NEANT INFANCY
MINORITY PUPILAGE

NONAGENARIAN OLDSTER

NONAGREEMENT DISSENT

NON-ALCOHOLIC SMALL

NO NAME (AUTHOR OF —) COLLINS
(CHARACTER IN —) NOEL CLARE
FRANK GARTH KIRKE NORAH
ANDREW GEORGE WRAGGE
BARTRAM BYGRAVE LECOUNT
MAGDALEN VANSTONE

NON-ARAB SHANGALLA

NONASPIRATE LENE

NONBELIEVER PAGAN ATHEIST
AGNOSTIC

NONCE NANES NONES NOANCE
PRESENT PURPOSE OCCASION

NONCHALANT COOL GLID ALOOF
CASUAL JAUNTY CARELESS
DEBONAIR NEGLIGENT

NON-CHRISTIAN PAYNIM INFIDEL

NONCITIZEN TENSOR PEREGRINUS

NONCLERICAL LAY LAIC

NONCOMBUSTIBLE APYROUS

NONCOMMITTAL NEUTRAL

NONCONFORMIST REBEL
NONCON BEATNIK DEVIANT
FANATIC HERETIC SECTARY
BOHEMIAN RECUSANT DISSENTER
(— IN ART) FAUVE

NONCONFORMITY HERESY
ADHARMA DISSENT NEGLECT
REFUSAL RECUSANCE RECUSANCY

NONCONTINUOUS DISCRETE

NON-CONVERGENCE ABERRATION

NONDESCRIPT BLAH DRAB DULL

NONDISCLOSURE FRAUD

NONDO LOVAGE ANGELICO

NONDUALISM ADVAITA

NONE NO UN NAE NIN ZIP NANE
NARY NEEN NONES
(PREF.) NULLI

NONEGO NOTSELF

NONELASTIC BROAD

NONENTITY ZERO AUGHT CIPHER
NOBODY NOUGHT NOTHING
NULLITY NEGATION

NONESSENTIAL CASUAL FRILLY
UNNEEDED EXTRINSIC
(— IN RELIGION) ADIAPHORON

NONESUCH APPLE MODEL
PARAGON PATTERN PARADIGM
MATCHLESS NONPAREIL
UNRIVALED

NON-EXISTENCE ABSENCE
NOTHING

NONEXISTENT NULL NAPOOH
NOUGHT NONBEING BARMECIDE
(PRACTICALLY —) FAT
(PREF.) NULLI

NONFEASANCE BREACH

NON GRATA UNWELCOME

NONGYPSY GAJO

NONINJURY AHIMSA

NON-JEW GOI GOY

NONJUROR USAGER

NON-LATIN SAXON

NONLEGATO DETACHE DETACHED

NON-MOSLEM GENTILE

NONMOTILE
(PREF.) APLANO

NONNASAL ORAL

NO-NO TABU TABOO

NONPAREIL BEST ONER POPE TYPE
PARAGON PERFECT SUPREME
UNEQUAL NONESUCH PEERLESS
UNRIVALED

NONPAYMENT DISHONOR

NONPLUS SET FAZE POSE STOP
BLANK FLOOR POSER STICK
STUMP TRUMP BAFFLE GRAVEL
PUZZLE RATTLE CONFUSE MYSTIFY
PERPLEX STAGGER QUANDARY
DULCARNON EMBARRASS

NONPLUSSED BLANK FOOLISH

NONPOISONOUS SAFE EDIBLE

NON-POLYNESIAN PAKEHA

NONPROFESSIONAL BUM LAY
LAIC AMATEUR

NONSENSE BAH GAS GUP PAH ROT
BILK BLAA BLAH BOSH BUFF BULL
BUNK COCK CRAP FLAM FLUM
GAFF GOOK GUFF JIVE JUNK PISH
POOH PUNK TOSH BALLS BEANS
BILGE BLASH DROOL FOLLY
FUDGE HAVER HOOEY NERTS
SPOOF STITE STUFF TRASH TRIPE
WAHOO BABBLE BETISE BLAGUE
BUNKUM DRIVEL FADDLE FOLDER
FOOTLE IDIOCY KIBOSH LINSEY
MALARK NAVERS PIFFLE RUBBLE
SQUISH TRIVIA BLARNEY BLATHER
EYEWASH FARRAGO FLANNEL
INANITY LOCKRAM MALARKY
RHUBARB RUBBISH TOSHERY
TRIFLES TWADDLE BUNCOMBE
CLAPTRAP COBBLERS DISHWASH
FALDEROL FLIMFLAM FLUMMERY
GALBANUM MACARONI
MOROLOGY PISHPOSH PISHTOSH
SKITTLES SPLUTTER TOMMYROT
TRUMPERY ABSURDITY FRIVOLITY
MOONSHINE POPPYCOCK
SILLINESS BALDERDASH
CODSWALLOP JABBERWOCK
TARADIDDLE JABBERWOCKY
GOBBLEDYGOOK
(— CREATURE) GOOP SHOO SNARK
SHIMOO
(SENTIMENTAL —) SLAVER

NONSENSICAL ABSURD

NONSURFER HODAD

NONUSER (— OF DRUGS) STRAIGHT

NON-VIOLENCE AHIMSA

NOODLE BEAN FOOL HEAD NIZY
NOLL PATE MOONY NINNY NIZEY
NODDY PASTA PASTE SAMMY
BOODLE GUDDLE NODDLE
NOGGIN DAWCOCK LOKSHEN
NOGHEAD NOUILLE BLOCKHEAD
SIMPLETON CAPERNOITIE
(— DISH) PANSIT RAVIOLI KREPLACH
(JAPANESE — SOUP) RAMEN
(STUPID —) BOODLE

(PL.) MEIN FARFEL FERFEL LASAGNA LASAGNE LOKSHEN FETTUCINI

NOOK IN BAY OUT WRO CANT COVE GLEN HERN HOLE NALK NUCK NUIK ANGLE HALKE HERNE NEUCK NICHE ALCOVE CANTLE CORNER CRANNY RECESS CREVICE NOOKERY RETREAT
(**FIREPLACE —**) INGLE

NOON M APEX DINE NOWN SEXT DINNER MIDDAY UNDERN MIDNOON MERIDIAN

NOONDAY (**— REST**) NAP SIESTA MERIDIAN

NOOSE TIE TOW BOND DULL FANK GIRN HEMP LACE LOOP ROPE TRAP BIGHT CATCH GRANE HITCH HONDA KINCH LASSO LATCH LEASH SNARE SNARL WIDDY CAUDLE CHOKER CLINCH ENTRAP HALTER LARIAT SPRING TETHER TIPPET TWITCH CHOCKER ENSNARE EXECUTE LANIARD LANYARD SPRINGE NECKLACE SQUEEZER TWITCHEL
(**— FOR HAULING LOG**) CHOKER CHOCKER
(**— FOR SNARING FISH**) DULL
(**— IN A CORD**) KINCH
(**HANGMAN'S —**) SQUEEZER

NOOTKA AHT AHOUSAHT MOATCAHT MOOACHAHT

NORATE NOISE RUMOR GOSSIP

NORAX (**FATHER OF —**) HERMES MERCURY
(**MOTHER OF —**) ERYTHEA

NORDIC ARIAN ARYAN

NORI AMANORI

NORITE GABBRO OLIGOSITE

NORM PAR MODE RULE TYPE CANON GAUGE MODEL NORMA DHARMA MEDIAN AVERAGE MODULUS PATTERN STANDARD TEMPLATE

NORMA MOLD RULE GAUGE MODEL SQUARE PATTERN TEMPLET STANDARD TEMPLATE
(**CHARACTER IN —**) NORMA ADALGISA POLLIONE
(**COMPOSER OF —**) BELLINI

NORMAL PAR FULL HOME JUST MEAN SANE WISE CLEAR ERECT USUAL FORMAL NATIVE SCHOOL AVERAGE NATURAL NEUTRAL REGULAR TYPICAL ORDINARY STANDARD CUSTOMARY

NORMANDY (**BEACH IN —**) OMAHA
(**CAPITAL OF —**) ROUEN
(**RIVER IN —**) EURE ORNE SEINE

NORN FATE URTH WURD WYRD NORNA SKULD URDHR URTHR VERDHANDI VERTHANDI

NORSE ICELANDIC

NORSEL BAND LINE ORSEL FILLET NOSSEL ORSELLER

NORTH SEPTENTRION
(PREF.) ARCT(O)

NORTH AMERICA
(ALSO SEE SPECIFIC COUNTRIES)
ISLAND: LONG BANKS PARRY BAFFIN BERMUDA VICTORIA ANTICOSTI ELLESMERE GREENLAND NEWFOUNDLAND
LAKE: ERIE HURON NIPIGON ONTARIO MANITOBA MICHIGAN REINDEER SUPERIOR WINNIPEG ATHABASCA NETTILING
MOUNTAIN: WOOD LOGAN WALSH ROBSON STEELE TOLUCA LUCANIA PARICUTIN TAJUMULCO POPOCATEPETL
NATION: CANADA MEXICO UNITEDSTATES
RIVER: GILA MILK JAMES LIARD OSAGE PEACE PEARL PECOS SNAKE YUKON BALSAS BRAZOS FRASER HUDSON MOBILE NEOSHO PANUCO PLATTE POWDER SABINE TANANA KLAMATH KOYUKUK POTOMAC SUSITNA CIMARRON COLUMBIA DELAWARE MISSOURI NIOBRARA PENOBSCOT PORCUPINE RIOGRANDE STLAWRENCE MISSISSIPPI

NORTH CAROLINA
CAPE: FEAR LOOKOUT HATTERAS
CAPITAL: RALEIGH
COLLEGE: ELON CATAWBA DAVIDSON
COUNTY: ASHE DARE HOKE HYDE NASH PITT WAKE AVERY DAVIE GATES ROWAN SURRY BERTIE BLADEN CRAVEN ONSLOW YADKIN YANCEY CATAWBA PAMLICO CURRITUCK
INDIAN: ENO COREE CHERAW MORATOK PAMLICO CHOWANOC HATTERAS
MOUNTAIN: HARRIS MITCHELL
PRESIDENT: POLK JOHNSON
RIVER: HAW TAR NEUSE CHOWAN LUMBER PEEDEE YADKIN ROANOKE
SOUND: BOGUE CROATAN PAMLICO
STATE BIRD: CARDINAL
STATE FLOWER: DOGWOOD
STATE NICKNAME: TARHEEL OLDNORTH TURPENTINE
STATE TREE: PINE
TOWN: BOONE SYLVA BURGAW DOBSON DURHAM LENOIR SHELBY SPARTA EDENTON HICKORY ROXBORO TARBORO GASTONIA CHARLOTTE
UNIVERSITY: DUKE

NORTH DAKOTA
CAPITAL: BISMARCK
COLLEGE: JAMESTOWN
COUNTY: DUNN EDDY SLOPE STARK WELLS DICKEY DIVIDE GRIGGS KIDDER OLIVER TRAILL PEMBINA ROLETTE
INDIAN: MANDAN ARIKARA HIDATSA
MOUNTAIN: WHITEBUTTE
RIVER: RUSH CEDAR HEART JAMES SOURIS DESLACS SHEYENNE WILDRICE
STATE BIRD: MEADOWLARK
STATE FLOWER: PRAIRIEROSE

STATE NICKNAME: SIOUX FLICKERTAIL
STATE TREE: ELM
TOWN: MOTT CANDO FARGO MINOT ROLLA AMIDON LAKOTA LINTON MOHALL BOWBELLS NAPOLEON

NORTHERN PIKE ARCTIC BOREAL NORLAND NORTHEN
(**— BEAR**) POLAR RUSSIA
(**— CONSTELLATION**) URSA ANDROMEDA

NORTH KOREA
CAPITAL: PYONGYANG
COIN: JUN WON CHUN HWAN
PROVINCE: CHAGANG KANGWON TANGGANG
RIVER: NAM YALU IMJIN TUMEN TAEDONG
TOWN: HAEJU HEIJO KEIJO ANDONG ANTUNG HYESAN JUSHIN POCHON SAINNI WONSAN HAMHUNG HUICHON HUNGNAM KAESONG KANGGYE SARIWON SINUIJU CHONGJIN

NORTHMAN DANE
NORTH STAR STATE MINNESOTA
NORTHWEST TERRITORY
(**CAPITAL OF —**) YELLOWKNIFE
(**DISTRICT OF —**) FRANKLIN KEEWATIN MACKENZIE
(**RIVER OF —**) BACK KAZAN DUBAWNT COPPERMINE
(**TOWN OF —**) RAE INUVIK DISCOVERY SNOWDRIFT

NORWAY LEVANGER
CAPE: NORDKYN NORDKAPP
CAPITAL: OSLO
COIN: ORE KRONE
COUNTY: AMT OSLO FYLKE TROMS BERGEN TROMSO FINMARK HEDMARK OPPLAND OSTFOLD NORDLAND ROGALAND TELEMARK VESTFOLD
DANCE: GANGAR HALLING SPRINGAR SPRINGLEIK
FJORD: OSLO SOGNE HARDANGER TRONDHEIM
INLET: IS KOB RAN ALST ANDS BOKN NORD OFOT SALT SUNN TYRI VEST FIORD FJORD FOLDA LAKSE SOGNE BJORNA HADSEL HORTENS TRONDHEIM
ISLAND: VEGA BOMLO DONNA FROYA HITRA HOPEN SENJA SMOLA ALSTEN AVEROY BOUVET HINNOY KARMOY KVALOY SOLUND SOROYA VANNOY GURSKOY LOFOTEN MAGEROY SEILAND JANMAYEN SVALBARD RINGVASSOY
LAKE: ALTE ISTER MJOSA SNASA FEMUND ROSTAVN TUNNSJO ROSTVATN
MEASURE: FOT MAL POT ALEN MAAL KANDE FATHOM SKIEPPE
MOUNTAIN: SOGNE KJOLEN NUMEDAL BLODFJEL SNOHETTA TELEMARK USTETIND JOTUNHEIM

PARLIAMENT: LAGTING STORTING ODELSTING
PLATEAU: DOURE FJELD HARDANGER
RIVER: OI ENA ALTA OTRA RANA TANA BARDU BEGNA GLAMA LAGEN ORKLA OTTER RAUMA REIBA GLOMMA LOUGEN NAMSEN PASVIK DRAMSELVA
TOWN: GOL NES BODO MOSS ODDA OSLO VOSS BJORT FLORO HAMAR MOLDE SKIEN SKJAK BERGEN HORTEN LARVIK NARVIK ALESUND ARENDAL DRAMMEN SANDNES STAVANGER
WATERFALL: VETTI SKYKJE VORING
WEIGHT: LOD MARK PUND SKAALPUND BISMERPUND

NORWEGIAN (**FORM OF —**) BOKMAL
(**LITERARY FORM OF —**) NYNORSK
NOSE CAP NEB NIZ PRY PUG SPY BEAK BOKO CONK NASE GROIN LORUM NASUS SCENT SMELL SNIFF SNOOP SNOOT SNOUT TRUNK BEEZER CYRANO DETECT GNOMON MUFFLE MUZZLE NOZZLE PECKER ROOKIE SEARCH SNITCH SOCKET ADVANCE PERFUME SMELLER DISCOVER INFORMER OLFACTOR PERCEIVE PROBOSCIS SCHNOZZLE
(**— A LOG**) SNIPE
(**— BAG**) MORRAL
(**— CARTILAGE**) SEPTUM
(**— DISEASE**) OZENA OZOENA
(**— DIVE**) VRILLE
(**— FLUTE**) PUNGI POOGYE
(**— INFLAMMATION**) CORYZA RHINITIS
(**— MEDICINE**) ERRHINE
(**— OF AIRPLANE**) PROW
(**— OF ANIMAL**) GROIN
(**— OPENING**) NARE
(**— OUT**) EDGE
(**— PARTITION**) VOMER
(**— PIECE**) NASAL
(**— RING**) PIRN
(**BLUNT —**) SNUB
(**FLAT —**) PUG SNUB
(PREF.) NAS(I)(O) NASUTI RHIN(O)
(SUFF.) RHINA RHINE RHINIA RHINOUS RHINUS RRHINE RRHINIA
NOSEBAND BOSAL MUSROL CAVESSON
NOSEBLEED EPISTAXIS RHINORRHAGIA
NOSEGAY BOB ODOR POSY POESY SCENT TUTTY BOUQUET CORSAGE PERFUME
NOSH SNACK
NOSINESS CURIOSITY
NOSING CURB
NOSTALGIA LONGING YEARNING
NOSTALGIC RETRO ELEGIAC OLDTIMEY ELEGIACAL
(**FASHIONABLY —**) RETRO
NOSTOLOGY GERIATRICS
NOSTRADAMUS SEER PROPHET PHYSICIAN
NOSTRIL ALA NARE NARIS THIRL THRILL BLOWHOLE
(**PERT. TO —**) NARIAL NARINE

(PL.) NARES NARIS SNUFFERS
(PREF.) NARI
NOSTRUM ELIXIR SECRET
NOSU LOLO
NOSY BEAKY PRYING CURIOUS
FRAGRANT INTRUSIVE
NOT NA NE NAE NAY NOR PAS BAAL
BAIL BALE NICHT SHORN SORRA
NOUGHT POLLED SHAVEN NEITHER
HORNLESS NEGATIVE
(— ANY) NO NUL NANE NARY NONE
NAIRY NOKIN STEAD
(— AT ALL) NEVER LITTLE NOWAYS
NOWHIT NOWISE
(— FINAL) NISI
(— THE SAME) OTHER ANOTHER
DIFFERENT
(— TO BE REPEATED) NR
(— WANTED) DETROP
SUPERFLUOUS
(ALMOST —) SCARCELY
(COULD —) NOTE
(PREFIX MEANING —) IL IM IN IR UN
NON
(PREF.) A ANTI DIS E IL IM IN IR
NON UM UN
NOTABLE VIP FINE FABLED
FAMOUS GIFTED NOTARY SIGNAL
UNIQUE EMINENT STORIED
SUBLIME DISTINCT ESPECIAL
EVENTFUL HISTORIC MEMORABLE
NOTORIOUS NOTEWORTHY
NOTARY NOTAR GRAFFER GREFFIER
NOTEBOOK OBSERVER OFFICIAL
SCRIVENER
NOTARY PUBLIC TABELLION
NOTATION HOLD MEMO NOTE
ENTRY SYSTEM MARKING
(— OF DANCING) ORCHESOGRAPHY
(MUSICAL —) TABLATURE
(PHONETIC —) ROMIC
NOTATOR NOTER RECORDER
NOTCH CUT DAG DAP GAP HAG JAG
JOG PEG COPE DENT DINT GAIN
GIMP KERF MUSH NICK NOCK SLAP
SLOT SNIP STEP WARD CRENA
GABEL GRADE HILUM SCORE
SHARD SHERD SWICK TALLY
CRENEL CROTCH DEFILE DEGREE
HOLLOW INDENT JOGGLE RAFFLE
RECORD SCOTCH CRENATE
GUDGEON SERRATE INCISION
UNDERCUT
(— BETWEEN HILLS) SLAP
(— ON VERTEBRAE) HYPANTRUM
(— TO FELL TREE) UNDERCUT
NOTCHED EROSE JAGGY RAGULE
RAGULY SERRATE CRENATED
SERRATED
NOTE BON DOG IOU JOT KEY SEE
TEN UNE BILL CARD CENT CHIT
ESPY FAME FLAT GOOD HEED
MARK MEMO NAME NOIT SIGN
SOLE SONG TENT TONE TUNE VIEW
CHECK FIVER GLOZE LABEL PRICK
SHORT SIXTH SOUND STIFF TENTH
TOKEN TRAIT TWANG ATTEND
BILLET DEGREE EXCUSE FIGURA
FLIMSY LETTER MELODY MINUTE
NOTICE POLICY RECORD REGARD
REMARK RENOWN REPORT
SECOND STRAIN TENNER BETOKEN
COMMENT DISCORD MESSAGE

MISSIVE NATURAL OBSERVE
PUNCTUS REDBACK ANNOTATE
BLUEBACK BRADBURY BREVIATE
DISPATCH EMINENCE MARGINAL
PERCEIVE POSTFACE TREASURY
GREENBACK POSTSCRIPT
(— FROM TRAIN) BUTTERFLY
(— OF ASSAULT) WARISON
(— OF HUMOR) TRAIT
(— OF SCALE) DO FA LA MI RE SI SO
TI UT ARE SOL
(— OF SNIPE) SCAPE
(— OF WARNING) WATCHWORD
(— ON SHOPHAR) TEKIAH
(—S ON HUNTING HORN) SEEK
(— TO RECALL DOG) FORLOIN
(ALTERED —) ACCIDENTAL
(BANK —S) CABBAGE
(BASS —) DRONE
(BIRD'S —) JUG CHIRP
(BUGLE —) MOT
(EDITOR'S —) STET
(EIGHTH —) UNCA QUAVER
(EMBELLISHING —) ORNAMENT
(ESCAPE —) ECHAPPEE
(EXPLANATORY —) ANAGRAPH
SCHOLIUM ANNOTATION
(FUNDAMENTAL —) ROOT
(GRACE —) NACHSCHLAG
(HALF —) MINIM
(HARSH —) BLOB
(HIGH-PITCHED —) BEEP
(HIGHEST —) ELA
(LEADING —) SUBTONIC
(LONG —) LARGE
(LOVE —) POULET
(LOWEST —) KEY GAMUT
(MARGINAL —) TOT QUOTE POSTIL
APOSTIL
(MUSICAL —) ALT RAY HALF MESE
MIND BREVE GAMUT SHARP TONIC
WHOLE EIGHTH ALAMIRE MEDIANT
PUNCTUS QUARTER CROTCHET
DOMINANT LICHANOS PARAMESE
SUBTONIC PIZZICATO
SUBDOMINANT APPOGGIATURA
(NONHARMONIC —) CAMBIATA
(POUND —) BRADBURY
(PROMISSORY —) DOG GOOD
HUNDI CEDULA ASSIGNAT
(QUARTER —) CROTCHET
SEMIMINIM
(SIXTEENTH —) DEMIQUAVER
SEMIQUAVER
(SIXTY-FOURTH —)
HEMIDEMISEMIQUAVER
(THIRTY-SECOND —) SUBSEMIFUSA
DEMISEMIQUAVER
(TREASURY —) TBILL
(TWO —S) DUPLET
(WARBLING —) CHIRL
(WHOLE —) SEMIBREVE
(WRONG —) CLINKER
(100-POUND —) CENTURY
(PL.) ANA GAMUT STRAIN
NUMBERS TIRALEE MARGINALIA
NOTEBOOK LOG DIARY NOTARY
RECORD STREET JOURNAL
NOTECASE WALLET POCKETBOOK
NOTED COUTH FAMED GREAT
NAMELY EMINENT INSIGNE
RENOWNED DISTINGUE
NOTEPAPER BOUDOIR

NOTEWORTHY BIG SOLEMN
EMINENT NOTABLE SALIENT
SPECIAL BODACIOUS MEMORABLE
OBSERVABLE
NOTHING NIL NIX ZIP FREE LUKE
NADA NILL RIEN WIND ZERO
AUGHT BLANK NIHIL SQUAT ZILCH
CIPHER NAUGHT NOBODY NOUGHT
TRIFLE NULLITY SCRATCH USELESS
BAGATELLE DIDDLYSQUAT
(— BUT) ALL
(— DOING) NAPOO NAPOOH
(— MORE THAN) MERE
(— OTHER THAN) ONLY
NOTHINGNESS NOT NADA ZERO
NOUGHT VACUITY NIHILITY
NOTICE AD BAN SEE SPY CALL ESPY
GAUM GOME HEED IDEA KEEP
MARK MIND NEWS NOTE PIPE RIDE
SIGN SPOT TWIG ALARM AWAIT
COUNT EDICT FLOAT NOTAM
ORDER QUOTE ADVICE ALLUDE
BILLET ESPIAL NOTION PERMIT
READER REGARD REMARK
REWARD AFFICHE ARTICLE
DISCERN MENTION OBSERVE
PLACARD PROGRAM WARNING
BULLETIN MONITION PERCEIVE
WITTERING
(— UNEXPECTEDLY) CATCH
(ADVANCE —) HERALDRY
PREMONITION
(COMMENDATORY —) PUFF BLURB
(DEATH —) OBIT OBITUARY
(FAVORABLE —) RAVE
(FINAL —) OBIT OBITUARY
(LEGAL —) CAVEAT
(MARRIAGE —) BANS BANNS
(OFFICIAL —) EDICT SUMMONS
BULLETIN CITATION
(PUBLIC —) BAN EDICT BULLETIN
SPOTLIGHT
NOTICEABLE CRUDE GROSS
FLASHY MARKED SIGNAL EVIDENT
NOTABLE POINTED SALIENT
HANDSOME PALPABLE STRIKING
OBTRUSIVE PROMINENT
CONSPICUOUS OUTSTANDING
(UNDESIRABLY —) CONSPICUOUS
NOTIFICATION DRUM NOTE AVISO
NOTICE SUMMONS
(PUBLIC —) SIGN
NOTIFY ALL BID CRY JOG CITE PAGE
TELL WARN ADVISE INFORM
NOTICE SIGNAL APPRISE DECLARE
FRUTIFY PUBLISH ACQUAINT
INTIMATE
NOTION BEE GEE BUZZ IDEA IDEE
KINK MAZE OMEN VIEW WHIM
FANCY FREIT IMAGE SENSE THING
WARES BELIEF CEMENT DESIRE
DONNEE GADGET MAGGOT NOTICE
THEORY VAGARY WHIMSY
BROMIDE CONCEIT CONCEPT
FANTASY INKLING MAROTTE
OPINION THOUGHT WHIMSEY
WRINKLE CATEGORY FOLKLORE
PHANTASY SUPPOSAL
WHIMWHAM INTENTION
SENTIMENT WHIRLIGIG
(FALSE —) IDOL
(FANCIFUL —) VAPOR REVERY
REVERIE

(FIXED —) TICK
(FOOLISH —) VAPOR VAPOUR
(PUERILE —) BOYISM
(SUPERSTITIOUS —) FREET FREIT
(VISIONARY —) ABSTRACTION
(WRONG —) FALLACY
(PL.) SMALLS SMALLWARE
NOTORIETY FAME ECLAT GLORY
HONOR RUMOR RENOWN REPUTE
PUBLICITY
NOTORIOUS BIG KNOWN ARRANT
COMMON CRYING FAMOUS
NOTARY STRONG EVIDENT
NOTABLE NOTOIRE APPARENT
FLAGRANT INFAMOUS MANIFEST
EGREGIOUS
NOTORNIS TAKAHE
NOTUS (BROTHER OF —) EURUS
BOREAS ZEPHYRUS
(FATHER OF —) AEOLUS ASTRAEUS
(MOTHER OF —) EOS
NOTWITHSTANDING BUT FOR THO
YET EVEN WITH ASIDE ALGATE
MAUGER MAUGRE THOUGH
AGAINST ALGATES DESPITE
HOWBEIT HOWEVER ALTHOUGH
NATHLESS WHATRECK
NOUGAT NUT CANDY NUTSHELL
NOUGHT BAD NIL NOT NOWT ZERO
NOCHT WRONG NOTHING USELESS
WORTHLESS
NOUMENAL ONTAL ONTIC
NOUN MANE WORD THING SUPINE
NOMINAL CONSTRUCT INCREASER
(INDECLINABLE —) APTOTE
(KIND OF —) COMMON PROPER
DIPTOTE REGULAR TRIPTOTE
MONOPTOTE
(QUOTATION —) HYPOSTASIS
(VERBAL —) GERUND
NOURISH AID FEED FOOD GROW
BREED NORSH NURSE TRAIN
BATTLE BREAST FOISON FOSTER
NORICE REFETE SUCCOR SUCKLE
SUPPLY CHERISH DEVELOP
EDUCATE NURTURE NUTRIFY
PROVIDE SUPPORT SUSTAIN
MAINTAIN CULTIVATE REPLENISH
STIMULATE
(PREF.) NUTRI
NOURISHING ALMA RICH ALIBLE
BATTLE HEARTY STRONG
NUTRIENT ALIMENTAL HEALTHFUL
NUTRITIVE WHOLESOME
NUTRITIOUS
NOURISHMENT DIET FARE FETE
FOOD KEEP MEAT MANNA FOISON
FOSTER ALIMENT PABULUM
PASTURE NUTRIMENT REFECTION
(— FOR MIND) PABULUM
(PREF.) THREPSO
NOURONIHAR (FATHER OF —)
FAKREDDIN
(LOVER OF —) VATHEK
NOUS MIND REASON ALERTNESS
INTELLECT
NOUVEAU RICHE PARVENU
UPSTART
NOVA SCOTIA (CAPITAL OF —)
HALIFAX
(COUNTY OF —) DIGBY HANTS
PICTOU
(STRAIT OF —) CANSO

(TOWN OF —) TRURO PICTOU SYDNEY ARICHAT BADDECK DARTMOUTH

NOVA SCOTIAN ACADIAN BLUENOSE

NOVEL HOT NEW BOOK EPIC RARE FRESH PROSE RECIT ROMAN STORY DARING RECENT SERIAL THRILL FICTION ROMANCE STRANGE UNUSUAL NEOTERIC ORIGINAL THRILLER UNCOMMON NARRATIVE PAPERBACK
(BRIEF —) CONTE
(PREF.) CAEN(O) CEN(O)

NOVELIST (ALSO SEE AUTHOR)

NOVELTY FAD NEWEL RENEW CHANGE NEWNESS PRIMEUR WRINKLE CURIOSITY FRESHNESS

NOVEMBER 1 SAMUIN SAMHAIN

NOVEMBER 11 MARTINMAS

NOVICE DUB HAM BOOT COLT PUNK PUNY TIRO TYRO CHELA GOYIN PUPIL ROOKY YOUTH DRONGO RABBIT ROOKIE TYRONE ACOLYTE AMATEUR CONVERT GRIFFIN LEARNER STARTER STUDENT YOUNKER BACHELOR BEGINNER FRESHMAN INEXPERT NEOPHYTE ARCHARIOS GREENHORN NOVITIATE TENDERFOOT ABECEDARIAN
(MILITARY —) CADET

NOVITIATE FUCHS NOVICERY PROBATION

NOW NOO YET ARAH HERE AHORA ARRAH NONCE SINCE TODAY EVENOO EXTANT ANYMORE CURRENT INSTANT PRESENT FORTHWITH PRESENTLY
(— AND THEN) SOMETIMES STOUNDMEAL
(BUT —) ERSTWHILE
(FROM — ON) EVERMORE
(JUST —) ENOW FRESH

NOWADAYS ANYMORE

NOWEL DRAG

NOX NYX
(BROTHER OF —) EREBUS
(FATHER OF —) CHAOS

NOXIOUS BAD ILL EVIL FETID DEADLY NOCENT NOYOUS PUTRID BALEFUL BANEFUL DAMPISH HARMFUL HURTFUL NOCUOUS NOISOME SCADDLE TEDIOUS VICIOUS INFAMOUS VIRULENT INJURIOUS MIASMATIC OFFENSIVE PESTILENT POISONOUS PERNICIOUS
(— AIR) MALARIA
(MORALLY —) UNWHOLESOME

NOZZE DI FIGARO, LE (CHARACTER IN —) FIGARO BARTOLO BASILIO SUSANNA ROSINA CHERUBINO MARCELLINA
(COMPOSER OF —) MOZART

NOZZLE BIB JET TIP BEAK BIBB NOSE ROSE VENT GIANT SNOUT SPOUT TWEER GROVEL OUTLET MONITOR NIAGARA ORIFICE SHUTOFF ADJUTAGE ROSEHEAD VERMOREL NOSEPIECE

(BLAST FURNACE —) TUYERE
(MINING —) GIANT

NUANCE SHADE NICETY FINESSE GRADATION VARIATION

NUB EAR HUB JAB JAG KEY NOB CORE CRUX GIST HANG KNOB KNOT KNUB LUMP NECK PITH SNAG HEART NUDGE POINT KERNEL NUBBIN EXECUTE

NUBBIN EAR STUB STUMP

NUBIA WRAP CLOUD SCARF

NUBIAN NUBA BARABRA HADENDOA
(— MUSICAL INST.) SISTRUM

NUBILOUS FOGGY MISTY VAGUE CLOUDY OBSCURE

NUCHA NAPE NECK NUKE NUCHE

NUCLEAR ELEMENTARY

NUCLEATE SEED

NUCLEOLUS
(PREF.) PYREN(O)

NUCLEON MESON BARYON MESOTRON

NUCLEOSIDE VICINE INOSINE CYTIDINE ADENOSINE

NUCLEOTIDE GTP
(SEQUENCE OF —S) EXON

NUCLEUS HUB CELL CORE GERM KERN PITH ROOT SEED CADRE FOCUS HEART MIDST SPERM UMBRA CENTER COLONY DEUTON KARYON KERNEL MIDDLE ISOTOPE NIDULUS HABENULA MEROCYTE MESOPLAST
(— OF ATOM) DEUTERON
(— OF CELL) KARYON
(— OF STARCH GRAIN) HILUM
(— OF SUNSPOT) UMBRA
(ATOMIC —) SPECIES
(CELL —) SYNCARYON HEMIKARYON
(PREF.) **(— OF CELL)** CARY(O) KARY(O)

NUCLIDE ISOTONE

NUDE BARE LOOSE MODEL NAKED SEASAN STATUE UNCLAD DENUDED EXPOSED PICTURE PAINTING STARKERS STRIPPED UNDRESSED
(FRENCH —) ALESAN
(NOT —) DECENT
(RUN —) STREAK

NUDGE JOG NOG NUB WAG GOAD JOLT KNUB LUMP PEST POKE POTE PROD PUSH BLOCK CHUCK DUNCH ELBOW

NUDIBRANCH SEASLUG

NUDISM NATURISM GYMNOSOPHY

NUDIST ADAMITE NUDIFIER GYMNOSOPH

NUDITY SCUD

NUDNICK PEST

NUDNIK PEST

NUGATORY IDLE NULL VAIN EMPTY PETTY FUTILE HOLLOW INVALID TRIVIAL USELESS TRIFLING FRUSTRATE WORTHLESS

NUGGET EYE LOB GOLD HUNK LUMP MASS SLUG PRILL YELLOW

NUISANCE BANE BORE EVIL HARM HURT PAIN PEST STING INJURY PLAGUE TERROR VEXATION ANNOYANCE

NUKE ZAP DESTROY DEVASTATE

NULL NIL VOID EMPTY INEPT IRRITE INVALID NULLIFY USELESS VACUOUS NUGATORY FRUSTRATE

NULLAH GORGE GULLY NULLA NALLAH RAVINE

NULLIFY BEAT FLAW LAME NULL UNDO VETO VOID ABATE ANNUL ELIDE ERASE LAPSE CANCEL DEFEAT NEGATE OFFSET REPEAL REVOKE ABOLISH COUNTER DESTROY ABROGATE EVACUATE STULTIFY FRUSTRATE

NULLIFYING DIRIMENT

NULLITY NIHILITY

NUMB DEAD DRUG DULL STUN DAZED FUNNY STONY ASLEEP BENUMB CLUMSY DEADEN STUPID TORPID STUNNED STUPEFY ENFEEBLE HEBETATE HELPLESS RIGESCENT TABETLESS

NUMBED ASLEEP

NUMBER SUM BAND BODY COPY CURN DRAW FECK HERD HOST LOTS MAIN MANY MESS MORT SLEW SURD TALE TELL COUNT DATUM DIGIT FOLIE GRIST GROUP INDEX ISSUE SCADS SCORE STAND TOTAL WHOLE ADDEND AMOUNT BUNDLE CIPHER ENCORE FACTOR FIGURE FILLER HIRSEL MYRIAD POLICY RECKON SCALAR TICHEL CHIFFER COMPUTE DECIMAL DIVISOR FOLIATE INTEGER NUMERIC SEVERAL CARDINAL FRACTION NUMERATE QUANTITY CALCULATE MAGNITUDE MULTITUDE MULTIPLIER MULTIPLICAND
(— BETWEEN 4 AND 10) MAIN
(— OF ARROWS) END
(— OF ATOMS) CHAIN
(— OF BEASTS) HERD
(— OF BOMBS) STICK
(— OF BRICKS) CLAMP
(— OF CATTLE) SOUM
(— OF FUR SKINS) TIMBER
(— OF HANKS OF YARN TO POUND) COUNT
(— OF HAWKS) CAST
(— OF HONEYBEES) CLUSTER
(— OF LINKED MINES) GIRANDOLA GIRANDOLE
(— OF NEEDLES) GAGE GAUGE
(— OF PERSONS) STABLE
(— OF POEMS) EPOS
(— OF SHEARERS) BOARD
(— OF TEA CHESTS) BREAK
(— OF THREADS PER INCH) PITCH
(— OF TRICKS) BOOK
(— OF WORDS) FOLIO
(—S GAME) BUG
(— THROWN IN CRAPS) POINT
(BALLET —) ENTREE
(CARDINAL —) ONE TWO ALEF ALEPH THREE
(CHOSEN —) FEW
(COMPLEX —) IMAGINARY
(CONSIDERABLE —) WHEEN HATFUL FISTFUL
(DESCRIBABLE —) SCALAR
(EXCESS —) ADVANTAGE
(EXCESSIVE —) SPATE

(EXTRA —) ENCORE
(GOLDEN —) PRIME
(GOOD —) THRAVE THREAVE
(GREAT —) LAC HEAP HOST LAKH MORT BREAK HIRST MEINY POWER SHOAL SIGHT SWARM LEGION MYRIAD INFINITE INFINITY THOUSAND MULTITUDE MULTIPLICITY
(GREAT —S) FLOCKS
(GREATER —) MO
(INDEFINITE —) LAC STEEN SUNDRY THRAVE JILLION SEVERAL THREAVE UMPTEEN
(IRRATIONAL —) SURD
(LARGE —) ARMY FECK HERD HOST LUMP PECK SLEW ARRAY CROWD FORCE POWER SCADS SHEAF SPATE STACK STORE WORLD GALLON GOOGOL HIRSEL HIRSLE LEGION MELDER BILLION JILLION PLURALITY
(LARGE —S) STRENGTH
(LEAF —) FOLIO
(LEAST WHOLE —) UNIT
(ODD —S) IMPAIR
(OF ANIMALS) PACK
(OPPOSITE —) COUSIN
(ORDINAL —) FIRST THIRD SECOND
(PUT ON SERIAL —) FOLIO
(SMALL —) FEW CURN CURRAN HANDFUL PAUCITY SPATTER
(SUNSCREEN —) SPF
(TOTAL —) AMOUNT
(VAST —) HORDE
(WHOLE —) ALL DIGIT INTEGER
(ZERO —) NOTHING
(PL.) STRENGTH
(PREF.) ARITHMETICO ARITHM(O) LOGARITHMO NUMERO
(SUFF.) ARITHM PLY
(— TERMINATION) TEEN
(— THAT FILLS) FUL FULL
(ORDINAL —) ETH

NUMBERED MENE

NUMBERING TALE COUNT FOLIATION

NUMBERLESS MYRIAD

NUMBERS
(PREF.)
(ODD —) PERISSO

NUMBFISH TORPEDO

NUMBING WARELESS

NUMBLES UMBLES INNARDS NOMBLES VISCERA ENTRAILS

NUMBNESS STUPOR TORPOR STUPIDITY
(PREF.) NARC(O)

NUMBSKULL OAF

NUMEN DEITY GENIUS SPIRIT VESTAL DIVINITY

NUMERAL (ALSO SEE NUMBER) SUM WORD DIGIT CIPHER FIGURE LETTER CHAPTER NUMERIC
(— STYLE) ROMAN ARABIC
(CLOCK —) CHAPTER

NUMERATIVE PEN SEGREGATIVE

NUMERICAL SCALAR

NUMEROUS BIG LOTS MAIN MANY RANK RIFE GREAT LARGE STOUR DIVERS GALORE LEGION MYRIAD SUNDRY UNRIDE COPIOUS

CROWDED ENDLESS FEARFUL FERTILE PROFUSE SEVERAL TEEMING UMPTEEN ABUNDANT FREQUENT MANIFOLD MULTIPLE POPULOUS THRONGED EXTENSIVE MULTIFOLD NUMBERFUL PLENTIFUL **(— AND POWERFUL)** MAIN
(MODERATELY —) FAIR
(VERY —) EXCESSIVE
(PREF.) MYRI

NUMIDIA (BIRD OF —) DEMOISELLE
(CITY OF —) HIPPO
(KING OF —) JUGURTHA

NUMITOR (GRANDSON OF —)
REMUS ROMULUS

NUMSKULL NUM DAFF DOLT FLAT BOOBY DUNCE LACKWIT BONEHEAD BLOCKHEAD LAMEBRAIN NUMBSKULL

NUN BIRD SMEW CLARE CLERK MONIAL PIGEON SISTER TERESA VESTAL VOWESS CLUNIAC CONFINE DEANESS DEVOTEE EXTERNE MINCHEN MONKESS RECLUSE TEATINE THEATIN BASILIAN CHAPLAIN CLARISSE PRIORESS TITMOUSE URBANIST URSULINE VISITANT VOTARESS ANGELICAL CARMELITE LORETTINE PRIESTESS RELIGEUSE TRAPPISTINE
(— BIRD) MONASE TITMOUSE
(— HEADDRESS) WIMPLE
(— HOOD) FAILLE
(— MOTH) TUSSOCK
(— ORDER) MARIST TRAPPIST DOMINICAN LORETTINE
(CHIEF —) ABBA ABBESS MOTHER
(LATIN —) VESTA
(SON OF —) JOSHUA

NUNCIATE NUNCIO ANNOUNCER MESSENGER

NUNCIO ENVOY NUNCE LEGATE NUNTIUS DELEGATE MESSENGER

NUNCUPATE DECLARE DEDICATE INSCRIBE PROCLAIM DESIGNATE PRONOUNCE

NUNCUPATIVE ORAL SPOKEN UNWRITTEN

NUNNERY ABBEY NUNRY CONVENT CLOISTER MINCHERY
(HEAD OF —) ABBESS

NUPSON FOOL SIMPLETON

NUPTIAL BRIDAL GENIAL THORAL MARITAL WEDDING ESPOUSAL HYMENEAL MARRIAGE
(PL.) SPOUSAL WEDDING

ESPOUSAL HYMENEALS WIFETHING

NUQUE NAPE NECK

NURISTANI KAFIRI

NURSE LPN SIP AMAH AYAH BABA CARE DHAI FEED NANA NUSS REAR SUCK TEND BONNE MAMMY NANNY NORSH ATTEND BAYMAN CRADLE FOMENT FOSTER GRANNY KEEPER NANNIE NORICE NUZZLE SISTER SITTER SUCKLE UMFAAN CHERISH FURTHER NOURISH NURTURE PROMOTE CULTIVATE ENCOURAGE NURSEMAID
(— A GRIEVANCE) SULK
(— OF HIAWATHA) NOKOMIS
(— OF ULYSSES) EURYCLEA
(— OF ZEUS) AMALTHEA CYNOSURA
(— SHARK) GATA
(GULLIVER'S —) GLUMDALCLITCH
(WET —) DHAI DHOLL

NURSEMAID AYAH BONNE

NURSERY RACE CRECHE HOTBED BROODER FOSTERAGE

NURSLING BABY NORRY NURRY FOSTER FOUNDLING
(PREF.) THREMMATO

NURTURE CARE DIET FEED FOOD REAR TEND BREED NURSE TRAIN COCKER CRADLE FOSTER NUZZLE CHERISH EDUCATE SUPPORT BREEDING NORTELRY TRAINING EDUCATION ESTABLISH NUTRIMENT
(PREF.) TROPH(O)

NUSAIRI ANSARIE

NUT ACA BEN BUR COB GUY JOU NIT TAP ANTA BURR COLA CORE DOLT FOOL FROG HEAD KOLA LORE MAST NITE PILI PITH SEED TASK ACORN BETEL BONGA BUNGA CRANK FLAKE FRUIT GLANS HAZEL HICAN JUVIA PECAN TRYMA ALMOND BONDUC BRAZIL CASHEW FELLOW HICCAN ILLIPE KERNEL PEANUT PIGNON PINION PYRENE CASTANA FILBERT HICKORY PROBLEM APPLENUT BEECHNUT BREADNUT CHESTNUT GOORANUT LARRIKIN CAPOTASTO CHINKAPIN ECCENTRIC MACADAMIA PHILOPENA
(— COAL) ANTHRACITE
(— GRASS) SEDGE
(— OF VIOLIN BOW) FROG
(— PINE) PIGNON PINOON PIGNOLIA
(CASHEW —) SEDGE ANACARD

(CONSORT OF —) GEB KEB SET
(DAUGHTER OF —) ISIS NEPHTHYS
(FALLEN —S) SHACK
(KIND OF —) PEA
(PALM —) BETEL LICHI BABASSU COCOANUT COQUILLA
(PERT. TO —) NUCAL
(RIPE —) LEAMER
(RUSH —) CHUFA
(SON OF —) RA OSIRIS
(PL.) MASTAGE
(PREF.) CARY(O) KARY(O) NUCI

NUT-BEARING NUCIFEROUS

NUTCRACKER XENOPS CRACKER PILLORY MEATBIRD NUTCRACK NUTHATCH NUCIFRAGA NUTPECKER

NUTHATCH SITTA TOMTIT XENOPS JARBIRD SITTINE TITMOUSE NUTJOBBER

NUTHOOK BEADLE CONSTABLE

NUTLET NUCULE PYRENA PYRENE GYROLITH

NUTMEG SEED TREE SPICE BEAVER CALABASH NOTEMIGGE NOTEMUGGE
(— COVERING) MACE
(— STATE) CONNECTICUT
(PREF.) MYRISTIC(I)

NUTRIA FUR COYPU GREGE NEUTRIA RAGONDIN

NUTRIENT STARTER
(PLANT —S) SIDEDRESS
(PL.) FOOD HEMOTROPHE

NUTRIMENT DIET FOOD KEEP VIANDS ALIMENT PABULUM SUPPORT NOURISHMENT

NUTRITION EUTROPHY TROPHISM
(IMPERFECT —) DYSTROPHY DYSTROPHIA
(PREF.) TROPH(O)
(SUFF.) TROPHIA TROPHIC TROPHY

NUTRITIOUS BATTLE BAITTLE TROPHIC

NUTRITIVE ALIBLE

NUTS KEEN BALMY BUGGY CRAZY INSANE ENTHUSIASTIC

NUT-SHAPED NUCIFORM

NUTSHELL SHELL INCLUDER

NUTTY BATS GAGA LOCO NUTS RACY ZANY BATTY BUGGY CRAZY QUEER SPICY FRUITY LOVING SPRUCE AMOROUS FOOLISH PIQUANT ZESTFUL DEMENTED PLEASANT ECCENTRIC FLAVORFUL

NUX VOMICA SNAKEWOOD

NUZZLE DIG PET ROOT NURSE SNUFF BURROW CARESS FONDLE

FOSTER NESTLE NUDDLE NURTURE SNOOZLE SNUGGLE SNUZZLE

NYCTEUS (BROTHER OF —) LYCUS
(DAUGHTER OF —) ANTIOPE
(FATHER OF —) HYRIEUS
(MOTHER OF —) CLONIA

NYE EYAS NEST NIDE BROOD FLOCK

NYLON
(PL.) HOSIERY

NYMPH FLY GIRL MAIA MITE MUSE PINK PIXY PUPA TICK AEGLE DRYAD HOURI LARVA NAIAD NIXIE OREAD SIREN SYLPH BYBLIS CYRENE DAMSEL DAPHNE HELICE HESTIA KELPIE MAIDEN NEREID SPRITE SYRINX UNDINE CORYCIA ERYTHEA HESPERA LIRIOPE OCEANID CALLISTO CYNOSURA EURYDICE MARPESSA PROSOPON BUTTERFLY HAMADRYAD
(— BELOVED BY PAN) SYRINX
(— BELOVED OF NARCISSUS) ECHO
(— CHANGED TO BEAR) CALLISTO
(— OF FOUNTAIN) EGERIA SALMACIS
(— OF HILLS) OREAD
(— OF MEADOWS) LIMONIAD
(— OF MESSINA STRAIT) SCYLLA
(— OF MT. IDA) OENONE
(CITY —) POLIAD
(LAKE —) NAIAD LIMNIAD
(OCEAN —) SIREN GALATEA OCEANID SEAMAID
(QUEEN OF —S) MAB
(RIVER —) NAIS NAIAD
(SEA —) MERROW NEREID CALYPSO GALATEA MERMAID
(WATER —) NAIS EGERIA LURLEI UNDINE APSARAS HYDRIAD JUTURNA RUSALKA EPHYDRIAD
(WOOD —) DRYAD NAPEA ARETHUSA
(PL.) HYADS THRIAI CAMENAE
(PREF.) NYMPHO

NYMPHAEA CASTALY CASTALIA

NYMPHET LOLITA

NYMPHOMANIAC (BOVINE —) BULLER

NYNORSK LANDSMAL LANDSMAAL

NYROCA AYTHYA

NYSSA TUPELO

NYSTAGMUS TIC WINK

NYX NOX NIGHT
(— PERSONIFIED) NIGHT
(BROTHER OF —) EREBUS
(DAUGHTER OF —) DAY ERIS LIGHT
(HUSBAND OF —) CHAOS
(SON OF —) CHARON

O HO OH OCH ZERO CIPHER
OMICRON

OAF AUF BOOR CLOD DOLT FOOL
LOUT CLOWN DUNCE IDIOT KLUTZ
OUPHE YOKEL MUCKER NASHGAB
PALOOKA POMPION BLOCKHEAD
FOUNDLING SCHLEMIEL
SIMPLETON

OAHU (— BAY) KAHANA
(— BIRD) JIBI

OAK CLUB CORK HOLM ILEX BRAVE
BRIAR EMORY HOLLY ROBLE
ROBUR ACAJOU BAREEN CERRIS
ENCINA KERMES STRONG TOUMEY
VALOMA AMBROSE BELLOTA
BELLOTE DURMAST EGILOPS
KELLOGG PALAYAN TURTOSA
BEEFWOOD BLUEJACK CHAMPION
CHAPARRO FLITTERN WAINSCOT
BLACKJACK CHINKAPIN
QUERCITRON
(— BARK) CRUT
(— FRUIT) MAST ACORN CAMATA
BELLOTE
(JERUSALEM —) AMBROSE
(WHITE —) ROBLE
(YOUNG —) FLITTERN
(PREF.) DRY(O) QUERCI

OAKUM OCCAM

OAKWOOD MESA

OAR AIR BOW PLY ROW PALM PEEL
POLE ALOOF BLADE ROWER
SCULL SPOON SWAPE SWEEP
YULOH PADDLE PALLET PROPEL
OARSMAN PROPELLER
(— BLADE) PALM PEEL WASH
(— FULCRUM) LOCK THOLE
OARLOCK ROWLOCK
(BOW —) GOUGER
(HANDLE OF —) GRASP
(INBOARD PORTION OF —) LOOM
(PART OF —) GRIP LOOM BLADE
SHAFT
(STERN —) SCULL SKULL
(PREF.) COPE(O) REMI

OARLOCK LOCK THOLE ROWLOCK

OARS CREW

OARSMAN OAR REMEX ROWER
BOWMAN STROKE BENCHER
SCULLER WATERMAN

OASIS BAR OJO SPA MERV SIWA
WADI WADY SPRING

OAST HOST KILN OVEN COCKLE
OASTHOUSE

OAT AIT WOT FEED FOOD PIPE
POEM SKEG SONG AUCHT CHEAT
GRAIN HAVER PEARL ANGORA
EGILOPS
(— HUSK) SHOOD FLIGHT
(— RENT) AVENAGE
(EDIBLE PORTION OF —) GROATS
(FALSE WILD —S) FATUOID
(HUSKED —) SHEALING

(NAKED —) PILLAS PILCORN
(UNTHRASHED —) OATHAY
(WILD —S) HAVERGRASS
(PL.) CORN GRAIN HAVER GROUTS
PROVENDER WHITECORN

OATCAKE CAPER HAVERCAKE
SOURBREAD

OATEN AITEN

OATH OD ADS BAN DAD DOD GAD
GAR GOL GOR GUM ODD SAM
VOW BOND CRUM CUSS DARN
DRAT ECOD EGAD GEEZ GOSH
HECK JEEZ JING NIGS OONS SANG
SLID SLUD WORD BEDAD BEGAD
BEGOB BLIMY CURSE DAMME
DEUCE GOLLY HOKEY MORDU
PARDY SACRE SFOOT SLIFE SNIGS
SWEAR YERRA ADSBUD APPEAL
CRACKY CRIKEY CRIPES CRUMBS
FEALTY JABERS JERNIE NEAKES
PARDIE PLEDGE RAPPER SBLOOD
SLIGHT STRUTH ZOUNDS
BEGORRA BEGORRY BEJESUS
BYRLADY CORBLEU GADSLID
GEEWHIZ GEEWIZZ JEEPERS
JIMMINY MORBLEU ODSFISH
ODZOOKS PROMISE THUNDER
ANATHEMA BEJABERS BODYKINS
CRICKETY GADZOOKS JURAMENT
PITIKINS SANCTION SEREMENT
SNIGGERS SPLUTTER AFFIDAVIT
BEJABBERS BLASPHEMY
DODGASTED EXPLETIVE
PROFANITY SACRAMENT SLIDIKINS
SWEARWORD

OATMEAL OATS STODGE YELLOW
POTTAGE DRAMMOCK PORRIDGE
(— BREAD) ANACK JANNACK
(— CAKE) PONE SCONE

OATS (MIXED ROLLED —) GRANOLA
(PREF.) AVENO

OBADIAH ABDIAS
(FATHER OF —) AZEL JEHIEL
SHEMAIAH
(SON OF —) ISHMAIAH

OBAL (FATHER OF —) JOKTAN

OBCLUDE HIDE OCCLUDE

OBDURATE FIRM HARD BALKY
HARSH INERT ROCKY ROUGH
STARK STONY DOGGED INURED
MULISH RUGGED SEVERE STURDY
SULLEN ADAMANT CALLOUS
HARDENED PERVERSE STUBBORN
IMPASSIVE UNBENDING

OBEAH OBI OBIA CHARM FETISH
VOODOO

OBECHE ARERE AYOUS SAMBA

OBED (FATHER OF —) BOAZ JARHA
SHEMAIAH
(MOTHER OF —) RUTH
(SON OF —) JESSE AZARIAH

OBEDEDOM (FATHER OF —)
JEDUTHUN

OBEDIENCE ORDER FEALTY
CONTROL SERVICE DOCILITY
OBEISANCE

OBEDIENT BENT RULY TALL TAME
BUXOM DOCILE PLIANT DEVOTED
DUTEOUS DUTIFUL HEEDFUL
MINDFUL ORDERLY SUBJECT
AMENABLE BIDDABLE YIELDING
ATTENTIVE OBSERVING SERVIABLE
TRACTABLE
(— TO THE HELM) HANDY

OBEDIENTIARY PRIOR

OBEDIENT PLANT DRAGONHEAD

OBEISANCE BOW LEG JOUK BINGE
CONGE HONOR SALAM CONGEE
CRINGE CURTSY FEALTY HOMAGE
SALAAM CURTSEY DEFERENCE
HUMBLESSO REFERENCE

OBELISK MARK PYLON SHAFT
DAGGER GUGLIA GUGLIO NEEDLE
OBELUS PILLAR AGUGLIA
MONUMENT HAGIOLITH

OBELUS DAGGER OBELISK

OBERON KING POEM FAIRY OPERA
SATELLITE
(CHARACTER IN —) HUON PUCK
FATIMA OBERON TITANIA
SHERASMIN
(COMPOSER OF —) WEBER
(WIFE OF —) TITANIA

OBESE FAT FOZY BEEFY PLUMP
PUDGY PUFFY PURSY STOUT
FLESHY PORTLY PYKNIC ROTUND
TURGID ADIPOSE PORCINE
PURSIVE BLUBBERY LIPAROUS
CORPULENT

OBESITY FAT FATNESS LIPOSIS
ADIPOSIS FOZINESS ADIPOSITY

OBEY EAR HEAR HEED MIND DEFER
YIELD COMPLY FOLLOW OBEISH
SUBMIT CONFORM EXECUTE
OBSERVE OBTEMPER
(— HELM) STEER

OBFUSCATE DIM BEFOG CLOUD
DARKEN MUDDLE OBFUSK
CONFUSE MYSTIFY OBSCURE
PERPLEX STUPEFY BEWILDER

OBI OBE SASH CHARM OBEAH
FETICH FETISH GIRDLE

OBIT MASS REST DEATH NOTICE
OBITAL DECEASE RELEASE
SERVICE OBITUARY NECROLOGY
OBSEQUIES

OBITUARY NECROLOGY

OBJECT AIM END TAP BALK BEEF
CARE CARP FINE GOAL IDEA ITEM
KICK MAIN MIND PASS SAKE WHAT
ARGUE CAVIL DEMUR GRIPE PINCH
POINT SCOPE SIGHT TELOS THING
AFFAIR DESIGN EMBLEM ENTITY
FIGURE GADGET INTENT MATTER
MOTIVE OPPOSE TARGET ARTICLE
DINGBAT DISLIKE DISSENT

MEANING PROTEST PURPOSE
QUARREL REALITY RECLAIM
NOUMENON TENDENCY
CHALLENGE INTENTION
SPECTACLE
(— HAVING FLAWS) SPOIL
(— OF ABHORRENCE) ANATHEMA
(— OF AMBITION) MAIN
(— OF ART) VASE CURIO VIRTU
ANTIQUE BIBELOT FIGURINE
(— OF CONTEMPT) SCORN
(— OF CRITICISM) BUTT
(— OF DERISION) SCOFF
(— OF DEVOTION) IDOL TOTEM
FETISH
(— OF DISGUST) UG
(— OF DREAD) BOGY BOGEY BOGIE
BOGGIE BUGBEAR
(— OF INTEREST) SIGHT
(— OF KNOWLEDGE) SCIBILE
(— OF LAUGHTER) JEST
(— OF LOATHING) SCUNNER
(— OF LOVE) FLAME
(— OF PILGRIMAGE) CAABA
KAABAH
(— OF PRIDE) GLORY
(— OF PURSUIT) SHADOW
(— OF RELIANCE) STAY
(— OF REVERENCE) MANITO
(— OF RIDICULE) FUN GAME
(— OF SCORN) GECK SCOFF
BYWORD HISSING DERISION
(— OF TERROR) BUG BUGABOO
BUGBEAR
(— OF THOUGHT) CONSTRUCT
(— OF WONDER) ADMIRATION
(— OF WORSHIP) GOD IDOL JUJU
MUMBOJUMBO
(— TO BE TILTED AT) QUINTAIN
(ALLURING —) DELILAH
(BELOVED —) MINION DARLING
MISTRESS
(BIZARRE —) GROTESQUE
(BULKY —) WODGE
(CELESTIAL —) QUASAR
(CONICAL —) ACORN
(CONSPICUOUS —) LANDMARK
(CONTAMINATED —S) FOMITES
(CURVED —) BELLY
(CYLINDRICAL —) BOLE
(DECORATIVE —) BIBELOT
(DESIRABLE —) GRAIL
(FACTORY-MADE —S) ARTWORK
(FLAT —) DISCUS
(HEAVY —) WEIGHT
(MINUTE —) ATOM MITE
(PALTRY —) TRINKET
(POINTED —) SPIKE
(ROUND —) COB RONDEL TRINDLE
TRUNDLE
(SACRED —) URIM ZOGO GUACA
HUACA SHRINE CHURINGA
(SILLY —) INANITY

(SMALL —) PIRLIE
(STRANGE —S) CURIOSA
(STUDY OF FLYING —S) UFOLOGY
(TEACHING —S) REALIA
(TRANSCENDENTAL —) ENTITY
(TRIVIAL —) GUBBINS
(ULTIMATE —) TELOS
(UNIDENTIFIED FLYING —) BOGEY
(VILE —S) SCUM
(WORTHLESS —) SPLINTER
(PREF.) **(FILTHY OR DIRTY —)** RHYPARO RHYPO
OBJECTION OB BAR BUT BEEF CRAB FUSS KICK CAVIL DEMUR DOUBT BOGGLE CHESON NIGGLE QUARREL QUIBBLE SCRUPLE DEMURRAL QUESTION CHALLENGE CRITICISM EXCEPTION
OBJECTIONABLE VILE AWFUL HORRID GHASTLY UNLUSTY UNLIKELY FRIGHTFUL OBNOXIOUS OFFENSIVE
(BE —) SUCK
OBJECTIVE AIM END FAIR GAME GOAL HOME REAL SAKE OUTER ACTUAL AMORAL ANIMUS DESIGN MOTIVE TARGET THRUST PURPOSE DETACHED TANGIBLE UNBIASED DIRECTION INTENTION POSITIVAL QUAESITUM ULTIMATUM
OBJECTOR (CONSCIENTIOUS —) CONCHY CONCHIE
OBJETS D'ART VIRTU
OBJURGATE BAN JAW DAMN RAIL ABUSE CHIDE CURSE DECRY BERATE REBUKE REPROVE UPBRAID VITUPER EXECRATE CASTIGATE
OBLATE MONK OFFER DEDICATE MONASTIC
OBLATION CORBAN OFLETE SACRED CHARITY ANAPHORA DEVOTION OFFERING SACRIFICE
OBLIGATE COMMIT STRICT
OBLIGATED BOUND LIABLE BEHOLDEN
OBLIGATION DUE IOU TIE VOW BAIL BAND BOND CALL DEBT DUTY KNOT LOAD LOAN MUST NOTE OATH ONUS SEAL CHECK OUGHT SCORE ARREAR BURDEN CHARGE CONSOL CORVEE CUSTOM FEALTY PLEDGE ANNUITY BONDAGE PROMISE TRIBUTE CONTRACT HYPOTHEC SECURITY WARRANTY AGREEMENT LIABILITY
(— NOT TO MARRY) CELIBACY
(— TO RENDER RENT) CUSTOM
(— TO SECRECY) SEAL
(LABOR —) CORVEE
(MORAL —) BOND DUTY
(PL.) STRINGS
OBLIGATORY BINDING BOUNDEN FORCIBLE IMPOSING LIGATORY INCUMBENT MANDATORY
OBLIGE PUT HOLD PAWN DRIVE FAVOR FORCE COMPEL ENGAGE PLEASE GRATIFY REQUIRE CONCLUDE MORTGAGE OBLIGATE CONSTRAIN ACCOMMODATE
OBLIGED FAIN BOUND DEBTED BOUNDEN DEBTFUL FAVORED PLEASED PLEDGED BEHOLDEN

GRATEFUL OBSTRICT BEHOLDING OBLIGATED
OBLIGING KIND BUXOM CIVIL CLEVER TOWARD AMIABLE FAVOROUS AGREEABLE COURTEOUS FAVORABLE OFFICIOUS
OBLIQUE AWRY BIAS SIDE SKEW ASKEW BEVEL CROSS SLANT ASLANT ASWASH LOUCHE SQUINT THWART ASKANCE AWKWARD CROOKED EMBELIF EVASIVE SCALENE SIDLING SLOPING DIAGONAL INCLINED INDIRECT SIDELONG SIDEWAYS SIDEWISE SLANTING TORTUOUS INDICULAR UNDERHAND
(— IN MINING) CLINIC
(— STROKE) SLASH SOLIDUS
(— WORK) SWASHWORK
(PREF.) LECHRI(O) LOX(O) PLAGI(O)
OBLIQUELY AGEE AWRY BIAS AGLEE ASIDE ASKEW AWASH SLANT SLOPE ASLANT ASWASH ASKANCE ASQUINT EMBELIF BIASWISE SIDELONG SIDEWAYS SIDEWISE
OBLIQUITY BIAS DIRT SWEEP DIRTINESS
OBLITERATE INK BLOT DELE RASE RAZE WIPE ANNUL BLACK COVER ERASE SMEAR CANCEL DELETE EFFACE SPONGE ABOLISH DESTROY EXPUNGE OUTRAZE SCRATCH OVERSCORE
OBLITERATION BLOT RASURE ERASURE NEGATION SYNIZESIS
OBLIVION LETHE LIMBO PARDON AMNESTY NIRVANA SILENCE OUBLIANCE
OBLIVIOUS AMORT BLISSFUL HEEDLESS OBLIVIAL FORGETFUL
OBLONG CHITON EVELONG AVELONGE EVENLONG ELONGATED
(ROUNDED —) ELLIPSE
OBLOQUY ABUSE BLAME ODIUM INFAMY CALUMNY CENSURE REPROOF CONTEMPT DISGRACE DISHONOR OBLIQUE
OBNOXIOUS FOUL PERT VILE CURST CURSED FAULTY HORRID LIABLE ODIOUS RANCID SEPTIC HATEFUL INVIDIOUS OFFENSIVE REPUGNANT VERMINOUS
(— PERSON) CREEP
OBOE PIPE REED WAIT AULOS SHAWM SURNAI SURNAY HAUTBOY MUSETTE PIFFERO CHIRIMIA HAUTBOIS SCHALMEY SZOPELKA CHALUMEAU HECKELPHONE
(— DI CACCIA) TENOROON FAGOTTINO
(BASS —) RACKETT
(PREF.) AUL(O)
OBOLE MAIL MAILLE
OBSCENE PAW FOUL LEWD NAST BAWDY GROSS NASTY ROCKY COARSE FILTHY IMPURE RIBALD SMUTTY VULGAR XRATED KNAVISH PROFANE RAUNCHY IMMODEST

INDECENT LOATHSOME OFFENSIVE REPULSIVE SALACIOUS
(— CULT) AISCHROLATREIA
OBSCENITY DIRT FILTH RIBALDRY SCULDUDDERY
(PREF.) COPR(O)
OBSCURATION COVER ECLIPSE
OBSCURE DIM FOG BLOT BLUR DARK DEEP HARD HART HAZY HIDE PALE SLUR VEIL BEDIM BEFOG BLACK BLANK BLEND BLIND CLOUD COVER DUSKY FAINT FOGGY GLOOM INNER LOWLY MIRKY MISTY MUDDY MURKY SHADE SMEAR STAIN VAGUE BEMIST CLOUDY DARKEN DARKLE DEADEN DELUDE GLOOMY HUMBLE MYSTIC OCCULT OPAQUE REMOTE SHADOW SOMBER SUBTLE BECLOUD BENIGHT CLOUDED CONCEAL CONFUSE CRABBED CRYPTIC ECLIPSE ENCRUST ENVELOP OBLIQUE OVERLAY OVERTOP SHADOWY SLUBBER TARNISH UNCLEAR UNKNOWN UNNOTED ABSTRUSE DARKLING DISGUISE DOUBTFUL FAMELESS MYSTICAL NAMELESS NUBILOUS OBSTRUSE ORACULAR OVERSILE CALIGINOUS
(MAKE —) BECLOUD
(PREF.) APHAN(O)
OBSCURED HAZY HIDDEN BLINDED CLOUDED DUSKISH DARKSOME DISGUISED INFUSCATE
OBSCURITY FOG MIST CLOUD GLOOM SHADE CALIGO SHADOW DIMNESS OPACITY PRIVACY SILENCE DARKNESS TENEBRES BLINDNESS SECLUSION
(DELIBERATE —) OBLIQUITY
(PL.) MURLEMEWES
OBSECRATE BEG PRAY BESEECH ENTREAT PETITION
OBSEQUIES MASS OBIT PYRE WAKE RITES SERVICE FUNERALS
OBSEQUIOUS SLICK MENIAL SUPPLE COURTLY DEVOTED DUTEOUS DUTIFUL FAWNING SERVILE SLAVISH VERNILE CRINGING OBEDIENT OBEISANT TOADYING ASSIDUOUS ATTENTIVE COMPLIANT
(— PERSON) LIMBERHAM
OBSEQUY RITE EXEQUY RITUAL FUNERAL CEREMONY
OBSERVANCE ACT FORM RITE RULE FREET HONOR CUSTOM REGARD KEEPING CEREMONY PRACTICE ADHERENCE ATTENTION DEFERENCE INDICTION SOLEMNITY
(— OF PROPRIETIES) DECORUM BREEDING ETIQUETTE
(RELIGIOUS —) NOVENA SACRAMENT
(REVERENTIAL —) PUJA
(SUPERSTITIOUS —) FREET FREIT
(PL.) FUNERAL CEREMONY
OBSERVANT ALERT EYEFUL CAREFUL HEEDFUL MINDFUL DILIGENT VIGILANT WATCHFUL REGARDFUL PERCEPTIVE
OBSERVATION EYE SPY HEED IDEA

NOTE RAOB VIEW SIGHT WATCH ESPIAL LOGION NOTICE REGARD REMARK AUSPICE AUTOPSY COMMENT CONTACT DESCANT OPINION EYESIGHT GAZEMENT SCHOLION SCHOLIUM ASSERTION ATTENTION ESPIONAGE COGNIZANCE PERCEPTION
(— BY BALLOON) PIBAL
(BASED ON —) EYEBALL
(ECOLOGICAL —S) ANNUATION
(PRELIMINARY —) PROEM
(STALE —) GROANER
OBSERVATIONISM SCHAULUST
OBSERVATORY LICK TOWER LOOKOUT PALOMAR
OBSERVE LO EYE SEE SPY ESPY HEED HOLD KEEP LOOK MAKF MARK MIND NARK NOTA NOTE OBEY SPOT TENT TOUT TWIG VIEW WAIT YEME ABIDE QUOTE SMOKE STUDY UTTER WATCH ADHERE ADVERT ATHOLD BEHOLD DETECT DEVISE FOLLOW NOTICE NOTIFY REGARD REMARK SURVEY COMMENT DISCERN EXPRESS MENTION PROFESS RESPECT WITNESS PERCEIVE PRESERVE SPECTATE ADVERTISE CELEBRATE SOLEMNIZE
(— CLOSELY) SMOKE
(— DULLY) BLEAR
(— FOOTBALL POSITION) KEY
(— OPPOSING POSITION) KEY
OBSERVER O BIRDER CORNER WATCHER AUDIENCE INFORMER ONLOOKER BYSTANDER SCRUTATOR SPECTATOR
OBSESS RIDE BESET HAUNT HARASS INVEST OBSEDE BESIEGE HAGRIDE POSSESS PREOCCUPY
OBSESSED CRAZY DOTTY HAPPY HIPPED BESOTTED
OBSESSION TIC CRAZE MANIA SIEGE MAGGOT ECSTASY FIXATION IDEEFIXE
(SUFF.) **(— WITH)** ITIS
OBSIDIAN CORE LAVA IZTLE IZTLI LAPIS
OBSOLETE OLD DEAD PAST DATED PASSE BYGONE EFFETE ABOLETE ANCIENT ARCHAIC CLASSIC DISUSED EFFACED EXTINCT OUTWORN OUTDATED OUTMODED OVERWORN DISCARDED
OBSTACLE BAR DAM LET BOYG BUMP DRAG HUMP JUMP OBEX SNAG STAY STOP BLOCK CHECK CLAMP CRIMP FENCE HITCH HYDRA SPOKE STICK STILE ABATIS BUNKER FRAISE HOCKET HURDLE LOGJAM OBJECT RETARD ANSTOSS BARRIER CHICANE FIVEBAR STOPPER BLOCKADE MOLEHILL BARRICADE CONDITION HINDRANCE ROADBLOCK TURNAGAIN
(— TO VIRTUE) SLANDER
(GOLF —) HAZARD
(INSURMOUNTABLE —) IMPASSE
OBSTETRICIAN ACCOUCHEUR
OBSTETRICS TOCOLOGY TOKOLOGY MAIEUTICS MIDWIFERY

OBSTINACY BRASS CONTUMACY
OBSTINATE SET SOT DOUR FIRM
SULY BALKY FIXED ROWDY RUSTY
STIFF STOUT TOUGH ASSISH
CUSSED DOGGED KNOBBY MULISH
STEEVE STUFFY STUPID STURDY
SULLEN THRAWN UNRULY ASININE
BULLISH CRABBED FROWARD
PEEVISH RESTIVE WILLFUL
CROTCHED OBDURATE PERVERSE
PREFRACT RECUSANT RENITENT
STOMACHY STUBBORN
FORERIGHT PIGHEADED
STONEWALL TENACIOUS
(— IN THE WRONG) PERVERSE
(— ONE) MULE
(NOT —) SUPPLE
OBSTREPEROUS LOUD WILD
NOISY RORTY UNRULY RAUGHTY
CLAMOROUS
OBSTRUCT BAR DAM DIT GAG JAM
CLOG COOP CRAB DITT FILL FOUL
JAMB STOP TRIG TRIP BESET
BLANK BLOCK CHAIN CHECK
CHOKE CROSS DELAY HEDGE
THROW ARREST CUMBER FORBAR
HAMPER HOBBLE IMPEDE OPPOSE
PESTER RETARD STIFLE THWART
WAYLAY WINDER BARRIER
FORELAY OCCLUDE BLOCKADE
EMBOLIZE ENCUMBER FLOUNDER
OBTURATE OPPILATE BARRICADE
EMBARRASS INCOMMODE
OBSTRUCTION BAR DAM GAG LET
RUB BOOM BUMP CLOG SLUG
SNAG STAY STOP BLOCK CHOKE
GORCE HITCH SPOKE HAMPER
TAPPEN THWART BARRACE
BARRAGE BARRIER BLINDER
CHOKAGE EMBOLISM OBSTACLE
STOPPAGE AMBUSCADE
EMPHRAXIS OCCLUSION
(— IN OILWELL) BRIDGE
(— IN RIVER) GORGE
(— IN TEAT) SPIDER
(— IN VALVE) GAG
(— OF BLOOD VESSEL) EMBOLISM
(— OF PINE LEAVES) TAPPEN
(— OF TONE) VEIL
(INNER —) LOAD
(LEGISLATIVE —) STONEWALL
FILIBUSTER
OBTAIN BEG BUM BUY EKE GET PAN
WIN EARN FANG FIND GAIN HENT
REAP ANNEX CADGE CATCH ETTLE
REACH AREACH ARECHE ARRIVE
ATTAIN BORROW DERIVE EXPEDE
SECURE SPONGE ACHIEVE
ACQUIRE CAPTURE CHEVISE
COMPASS DEMERIT EXTRACT
POSSESS PREVAIL PROCURE
RECEIVE SUCCEED PURCHASE
SCROUNGE
(— BY CHANCE) DRAW
(— BY HEAT) EXCOCT
(— BY REQUEST) IMPETRATE
(— BY THREAT) EXTORT
(— CONTROL) ENGROSS
(— DISHONESTLY) CROOK SHARP
FLEECE NOBBLE SKELDER
(— MONEY FROM) BLEED
(— PERMISSION) CLEAR

OBTAINABLE GOING GETTABLE
AVAILABLE DERIVABLE
SECURABLE
OBTAINED (— AT SCENE OF CRIME)
LATENT
(— DIRECTLY) FIRSTHAND
(WRONGFULLY —) HOT EXTORTED
OBTEST PLEAD
OBTRUDE DIN JET SORN EJECT
EXPEL GLARE FLAUNT IMPOSE
MEDDLE THRUST INTRUDE
INTERFERE
OBTRUSIVE FRESH PUSHY GARISH
BLATANT FORWARD PUSHING
BUMPTIOUS INTRUSIVE
OBTUND DULL BLUNT QUELL
DEADEN
OBTURATOR MUSHROOM
OBTUSE DIM DULL BLINK BLUNT
CRASS DENSE THICK BOVINE
OPAQUE STUPID STUBBED
BOEOTIAN HEBETATE PURBLIND
(NOT —) ACUTE
OBVERSE FACE FRONT CONVERSE
(— OF COIN) MAN HEAD
OBVIATE PREVENT PRECLUDE
FORESTALL
OBVIOUS LOUD OPEN BROAD
CLEAR CRUDE FRANK GROSS
NAKED OVERT PLAIN SLICK STARK
LIABLE PATENT BLATANT EVIDENT
EXPOSED GLARING SHALLOW
SUBJECT VISIBLE APPARENT
DISTINCT MANIFEST PALPABLE
BAREFACED PROMINENT
(NOT —) DEEP INNER ARCANE
HIDDEN MASKED OCCULT SECRET
SUBTLE DELICATE DOUBTFUL
PROFOUND INEVIDENT
OBVIOUSNESS PATENCY
OBVOLUTE CONTORTED
OVERLAPPING
OCA OKA TUBER OXALIS SORREL
SOURSOP
OCARINA CAMOTE
OCCASION SEL BOUT CALL GIVE
HINT NEED SELE SITH TIDE TIME
TURN BREAK BREED CASUS CAUSE
CHARE EVENT INFER NONCE RAISE
SITHE SLANT STOUR WHILE YIELD
AFFAIR AUTHOR CHANCE COURSE
EXCUSE PERIOD REASON STOUND
CHESOUN INSPIRE OPENING
PRETEXT QUARREL CEREMONY
ENGENDER EXIGENCY FUNCTION
INCIDENT INSTANCE CONDITION
ENCHEASON HAPPENING
(— GRIEF) GRIEVE
(— OF EXCITEMENT) ALARM
ALARUM
(DEFINITE —) TIDE
(EXCITING —) BLAST
(FAVORABLE —) ADVANTAGE
(FESTIVE —) UTAS BEANO HOLIDAY
SHINDIG BEANFEAST
MERRYMAKING
(HAPPY —) SIMHAH SIMCHAH
(SOCIAL —) COFFEE
(SPECIAL —) CEREMONY
OCCASIONAL ODD ORRA STRAY
ANTRIN CASUAL DAIMEN SCARCE
POPPING EPISODIC FUGITIVE
SPORADIC IRREGULAR

OCCASIONALLY EVERY ATTIMES
BETIMES SOMETIME SOMETIMES
OCCASIVE SETTING WESTWARD
OCCIDENTAL WEST PONENT
WESTERN HESPERIAN WESTERNER
OCCLUDE SHUT SORB CLOSE
ABSORB OBSTRUCT
OCCLUSAL MORSAL
OCCLUSION CORONARY
ARTICULATION
(SUFF.) CLEISIS CLISIS
OCCULT MAGIC ARCANE HIDDEN
LATENT MYSTIC SECRET VOODOO
ALCHEMY CRYPTIC ECLIPSE
UNKNOWN ESOTERIC MYSTICAL
SIBYLLIC CONCEALED RECONDITE
SIBYLLINE
(— SCIENCE) ESOTERICS
(PREF.) CRYPT(O) KRYPT(O)
OCCULTATION ECLIPSE
OCCULTISM MAGIC CABALA
MYSTERY
OCCUPANCY POSSESSION
OCCUPANT HOLDER INMATE
RENTER TENANT CITIZEN DWELLER
RESIDENT INCUMBENT
(— OF THEATER GALLERY) GOD
(SUFF.) ITE
OCCUPATION ART JOB LAY USE
CALL GAME LINE NOTE PLOY TOIL
WORK BERTH CRAFT GRAFT TRADE
BILLET CAREER EMPLOY METIER
RACKET SPHERE TENURE THRIFT
CALLING CONCERN CONTROL
MYSTERY PURSUIT QUALITY
SERVICE ACTIVITY BUSINESS
FUNCTION INDUSTRY INVASION
PLUMBING VOCATION
(— OF MIND) ABSORPTION
(PLEASURABLE —) RECREATIO
(PROFITABLE —) THRIFT
(SUBORDINATE —) HOBBY
AVOCATION
(TEDIOUS —) DRAG
OCCUPIED BUSY FULL HELD KEPT
RAPT TOOK INUSE ACTIVE INTENT
ENGAGED ABSORBED CAPTURED
(— WITH) INTO
(FULLY —) ENGROSSED
(NOT —) IDLE
OCCUPY LIE SIT USE BUSY FILL
HAVE HOLD KEEP TAKE WARM
AMUSE BELAY BESET DWELL
ABSORB BETAKE EMPLOY ENGAGE
EXPEND FULFIL OBTAIN TENANT
COHABIT CONCERN CONTAIN
ENGROSS ENTREAT IMPROVE
INHABIT INVOLVE OVERSIT
PERVADE POSSESS SWALLOW
DISSOLVE GARRISON INTEREST
POPULATE POURPRISE
(— AS SUBSTITUTE) SUPPLY
(— ILLEGALLY) JUMP
(— ONESELF) TIRE TRADE ENTREAT
(— QUARTERS) CAMP
(— THOUGHTS) OBSESS
OCCUR BE GO COME COOK FALL
GIVE MAKE MEET PASS RISE SORT
ARISE BREAK CLASH EXIST INCUR
LIGHT APPEAR ARRIVE BEFALL
BETIDE CHANCE HAPPEN PROCEED
TRANSPIRE

(— AGAIN) RECUR REPEAT
(— BY CHANCE) LIGHT
(— TO) CROSS ENTER STRIKE
OCCURRENCE GO HAP CASE FACT
ITEM NOTE REDE EVENT WEIRD
EPISODE PASSAGE INCIDENT
JUNCTURE OCCASION ENCOUNTER
FREQUENCE HAPPENING
(CHANCE —) ADVENTURE
CONTINGENT
(COMMON —) USE FREQUENCY
(FREQUENT —) COMMUNITY
(HALLUCINATORY —) FREAKOUT
(SIMULTANEOUS —) SYNCHRONY
COINCIDENCE
(SUDDEN —) ZAP STROKE OUTCROP
(SUPERNATURAL —) MIRACLE
(UNEXPECTED —) SUDDEN
BLIZZARD BOMBSHELL
(UNFORTUNATE —) CASUALTY
(UNUSUAL —) ODDITY
OCCURRING (— AT NIGHTFALL)
ACRONICAL
(— AT REGULAR INTERVALS)
HORAL
(— AT TWILIGHT) CREPUSCULAR
(— BY TURN) ALTERNATE
(— CASUALLY) SPORADIC
(— EVERY EIGHT DAYS) OCTAN
(— EVERY FOURTH YEAR)
PENTETERIC
(— FREQUENTLY) COMMON
(— INFREQUENTLY) OCCASIONAL
(— IN USUAL PLACE) ENTOPIC
(SELDOM —) RARE INFREQUENT
OCEAN SEA BLUE BRIM DEEP MAIN
POND BRINE DRINK ARCTIC INDIAN
EXPANSE NEPTUNE PACIFIC
ATLANTIC ANTARCTIC
(— FLOATING MATTER) ALGAE
LAGAN FLOTSAM
(— ROUTE) LANE
(— SPRAY) IRONWOOD
CREAMCUPS
(— SWELL) SEA
(DEEP PART OF —) HADAL
(OF THE DEEP —) HADAL
(ON THE —) ASEA
(PERTAINING TO — DEPTHS) HADAL
(RELATING TO — BELOW 6000
METERS) HADAL
(PL.) ALOT
OCEANIA MALAYA AUSTRALIA
MELANESIA POLYNESIA
(REPUBLIC IN —) FIJI
(SACRED OBJECT OF —) ZOGO
OCEANIC NAVAL MARINE PELAGIC
NAUTICAL AEQUOREAL
OCEANOGRAPHER (ALSO SEE
HYDROGRAPHER)
OCEANUS TITAN
(DAUGHTER OF —) DORIS OCEANID
EURYNOME
(FATHER OF —) URANUS OURANOS
(MOTHER OF —) GAEA GAIA
(SISTER OF —) TETHYS
(SON OF —) NEREUS
(WIFE OF —) TETHYS
OCELLUS EYE EYELET STEMMA
EYESPOT
OCELOT CAT TOGER LEOPARD
WILDCAT
OCHER RUD SIL KEEL OAKER OCHRE

TIVER ABRAUM RADDLE ALMAGRA TANGIER
(BLACK —) WAD WADD
(RED —) RUD KEEL TIVER ABRAUM REDDLE RUBRIC RUDDLE KOKOWAI
(YELLOW —) SIL SPRUCE
OCOTILLO COACHWHIP CANDLEWOOD
OCRAN (SON OF —) PAGIEL
OCREA OCHREA SHEATH
OCTAHEDROID HYPERCUBE TESSERACT
OCTAVE UTAS UTIS EIGHT EIGHTH OTTAVA EIGHTVO HUITAIN DIAPASON SHEMINITH
(— FLUTE) FLAUTINO
(— OF THE SEVENTH) FOURTEENTH
(— SINGING) MAGADIZE
(DIMINISHED —) SEMIDIAPASON
(FATHER OF —) ARGANTE
(TRIPLE —) TRIDIAPASON
OCTAVIA (BROTHER OF —) AUGUSTUS
(HUSBAND OF —) ANTONY
OCTAVO EIGHTS
OCTET OCTAVE OCTUOR HUITAIN OTTETTO
OCTOPUS HEE POLYP POULP PREKE SQUID CUTTLE CATFISH POLYPOD POLYPUS SCUTTLE DIBRANCH OCTOPEAN DEVILFISH
(— ARM) TENTACLE
(AUTHOR OF —) NORRIS
(CHARACTER IN —) DYKE TREE HILMA LYMAN HOOVEN MAGNUS SARRIA BEHRMAN CARAHER DELANEY DERRICK PRESLEY RUGGLES VANAMEE ANNIXTER SHELGRIM CEDARQUIST GENSLINGER
(SECRETION OF —) INK
OCTOROON METIS MESTEE MUSTEE MESTIZO METISSE OCTAROON
OCTROI TAX GRANT PRIVILEGE
OCTUPLE EIGHTFOLD
OCUBY RUM
OCULAR OPTIC VISUAL OCULARY OPTICAL ORBITAL EYEPIECE
OCULUS MUNDI OPAL
OCYRRHOE (FATHER OF —) CHIRON
(MOTHER OF —) CHARICLO
ODD AUK AWK OUT RUM FELL LEFT LONE ORRA RARE ANTIC CRAZY DIPPY DITSY DROLL EERIE EXTRA FLAKY FUNKY FUNNY IMPAR KINKY OUTRE QUEER SPACY UNKET UNKID WEIRD FLAKEY FREAKY IMPAIR QUAINT SINGLE SPACEY UNEVEN UNIQUE AZYGOUS BAROQUE BIZARRE COMICAL CURIOUS ERRATIC STRANGE UNEQUAL UNUSUAL FANCIFUL FREAKISH PECULIAR SINGULAR UNPAIRED BURLESQUE ECCENTRIC FANTASTIC GROTESQUE LAUGHABLE SQUIRRELY UNMATCHED WHIMSICAL
(— JOBMAN) JOEY
(PREF.) AZYGO IMPARI
ODDBALL GEEK KOOK SPOOK WEIRDO DINGBAT CRACKPOT

ODDITY GIG QUIP JIMJAM ANOMALY RUMNESS QUIZZITY PECULIARITY
(PL.) PURLICUES
ODDMAN UMPIRE ARBITER FLOATER REFEREE
ODDS BISK EDGE CHALK PRICE BISQUE DISCORD DISPUTE QUARREL HANDICAP VARIANCE ADVANTAGE DISPARITY
(— AND ENDS) ORTS STEW BROTT REFUSE SCRAPS GIBLETS SECONDS FEWTRILS REMNANTS SHAKINGS ETCETERAS FRAGMENTS
(AT —) ACROSS
(EXTRAVAGANT —) POUNDAGE
(FAVORABLE —) PERCENTAGE
ODE HYMN POEM SONG LYRIC PAEAN PSALM GHAZEL MONODY ODELET CANZONA CANZONE EPICEDE CANTICLE PALINODE PINDARIC SERENATA STASIMON EPICEDIUM EPINICION PARABASIS
(— OF LAMENTATION) THRENE THRENODY
ODED (SON OF —) AZARIAH
ODENATHUS (WIFE OF —) ZENOBIA
ODEON HALL ODEUM GALLERY THEATER
ODIN OTHIN WODAN WODEN WOTAN
(BROTHER OF —) VE VILI
(CREATED BY —) ASK EMBLA
(DAUGHTER-IN-LAW OF —) NANNA
(DESCENDANT OF —) SCYLD
(FATHER OF —) BOR BORR
(HALL OF —) VALHALLA
(HORSE OF —) SLEIPNER SLEIPNIR
(MANSION OF —) GLADSHEIM
(MOTHER OF —) BESTLA
(PALACE OF —) SYN
(RAVEN OF —) HUGIN MUNIN
(RING OF —) DRAUPNIR
(SHIP OF —) NAGLFAR SKIDBLADNIR
(SON OF —) TYR THOR VALI BALDR BALDER
(SPEAR OF —) GUNGNIR
(SWORD OF —) GRAM
(THRONE OF —) HLIDSKJALF
(WIFE OF —) FRIA RIND FRIGG RINDR FRIGGA
(WOLF OF —) GERI FREKI
ODIOUS FOUL LOTH UGLY VILE LOATH INFAND ODIBLE HATABLE HATEFUL HEINOUS HIDEOUS DAMNABLE FLAGRANT INFAMOUS ABHORRENT INVIDIOUS OBNOXIOUS OFFENSIVE REPUGNANT
ODIUM HATRED STIGMA DISLIKE AVERSION DISFAVOR DISGRACE DISHONOR ANTIPATHY
(PUBLIC —) ENVY
ODOACER (FATHER OF —) EDECON
ODOMETER ODOGRAPH VIAMETER WAYWISER HODOMETER PEDOMETER
ODONTALGIA TOOTHACHE
ODOR AIR FUME FUNK NOSE OLID TANG WAFF WAFT AROMA EWDER FETOR FLAIR FUMET NIDOR SCENT SMACK SMELL SNUFF SPICE STINK BREATH FLAVOR FOETOR HODURE

REPUTE STENCH BOUQUET ESSENCE FUMETTE NOSEGAY PERFUME VERDURE PUNGENCE EFFLUVIUM EMPYREUMA FRAGRANCE REDOLENCE
(— FROM FLOWERS) FUME
(— OF GAME) FUMET
(— OF HAY) NOSE
(BAD —) EWDER FROWST STENCH
(DISGUSTING —) STINK
(FOUL —) FIST MEPHITIS
(FRESH —) YMUR
(PUNGENT —) SPICE
(SPICY —) BALM
(STUDY OF —S) OSMICS
(UNPLEASANT —) PONG
(PREF.) OSM(O)
(SUFF.) OSMA OSPHRESIA
ODORIFEROUS BALMY OLENT ODOROUS FRAGRANT
ODOROUS FOUL BALMY OLENT SMELLY NOISOME ODORANT AROMATIC FRAGRANT NIDOROSE NIDOROUS PERFUMED REDOLENT SCENTFUL SMELLFUL
ODYSSEUS ULYSSES
(ADVISER OF —) ATHENA
(DOG OF —) ARGOS
(FATHER OF —) LAERTES SISYPHUS
(FRIEND OF —) MENTOR
(ISLAND OF —) ITHACA
(SON OF —) TELEGONUS TELEMACHUS
(WIFE OF —) PENELOPE
ODYSSEY (AUTHOR OF —) HOMER
(CHARACTER IN —) ARETE CIRCE HELEN AEOLUS NESTOR EUMAEUS ALCINOUS MENELAUS NAUSICAA ODYSSEUS PENELOPE DEMODOCUS EURYCLEIA TEIRESIAS POLYPHEMUS TELEMACHUS
OEAX (BROTHER OF —) PALAMEDES
(FATHER OF —) NAUPLIUS
(MOTHER OF —) CLYMENE
OEBALUS (FATHER OF —) TELON
(SON OF —) ICARIUS HIPPOCOON TYNDAREUS
(WIFE OF —) GORGOPHONE
OECIST OEKIST COLONIZER
OEDIPUS OEDIPAL
(BROTHER-IN-LAW OF —) CREON
(DAUGHTER OF —) ISMENE ANTIGONE
(FATHER OF —) LAIUS
(FOSTER MOTHER OF —) PERIBOEA
(MOTHER OF —) JOCASTA
(SON OF —) ETEOCLES POLYNICES
(WIFE OF —) JOCASTA
OEIL-DE-BOEUF OCULUS
OEILLADE OGLE ELIAD EYLIAD GLANCE ILLIAD
OENEUS (DAUGHTER OF —) GORGE DEIANIRA
(FATHER OF —) PORTHEUS
(SON OF —) TOXEUS TYDEUS MELEAGER
(WIFE OF —) ALTHAEA
OENOCHOE JUG EWER OLPE PROCHOOS
OENOMAUS (DAUGHTER OF —) HIPPODAMIA
(FATHER OF —) ARES MARS
(MOTHER OF —) STEROPE

(SON OF —) LEUCIPPUS DYSPONTEUS HIPPODAMUS
OENOMETER VINOMETER
OENONE (FATHER OF —) CEBREN
(LOVER OF —) PARIS
(SON OF —) CORYTHUS
OENOPION (DAUGHTER OF —) MEROPE
(FATHER OF —) DIONYSUS
(WIFE OF —) HELICE
OESTRID FLY
(— LARVA) BOT
OESTRUS RUT FURY HEAT STING DESIRE ESTRUS FRENZY IMPULSE STIMULUS
OEUVRE OPUS WORK
OF A O BY DE OFF VAN VON FROM HAVE TILL WITH ABOUT
(— AGE) AE
(— ALL) AVA ALDER ALLER
(— COURSE) NATCH
(— DEATH) M
(— EACH) ANA PER SING
(— THIS DAY) HODIERNAL
(— THIS MONTH) HM
(SUFF.) AL AR ILE INE ISH ISTIC ITIC ITIOUS ORIOUS ORY
OFF BY AFF FAR ODD WET AFAR AGEE AWAY DOFF DOWN GONE LESS ALONG ASIDE RIGHT WONKY WRONG ABSENT CUCKOO DEPART REMOTE DISTANT FURTHER REMOVED SEAWARD TAINTED ABNORMAL OPPOSITE
(— GUARD) TARDY
(— THE PATH) ASTRAY
(— THE SUBJECT) AFIELD
(— THE WIND) ROOM ROOMWARD
(FAR —) DISTANT
(PREF.) AP APH APO DE
OFFAL GURRY WASTE REFUSE CARRION DOGMEAT GARBAGE LEAVING RUBBISH GRALLOCH
(— OF FISH) GURRY STOSH
(MILLING —S) GRIT
OFFBEAT ODD FLAKY
OFF-BEAT KOOKY
OFFBEAT KOOKY SPACY WACKY WEIRD KOOKIE SPACEY
OFFBREAK GOOGLY
OFF-CENTER ECCENTRIC EXCENTRIC
OFF-COLOR BLUE RISQUE SUGGESTIVE
OFFENCE (— AGAINST STATE) SEDITION
OFFEND CAG ERR PET SIN VEX GALL HARM HUFF HURT MIFF RASP RASS ABUSE ANGER ANNOY GRATE GRILL PIQUE SHOCK SPITE TOUCH WRONG AGUILT ATTACK GRIEVE INJURE INSULT NETTLE REVOLT AFFRONT DEFAULT DISDAIN MORTIFY OUTRAGE PROVOKE REGRATE STOMACH UMBRAGE VIOLATE CONFRONT DISTASTE IRRITATE TRESPASS DISOBLIGE DISPLEASE
OFFENDED HUFF MIFF SORE AVERTED FROISSE INJURED INSULTED
OFFENDER SINNER CULPRIT

MISDOER PECCANT HABITUAL
OFFENDANT
(FIRST —) STAR
OFFENDING PECCANT
OFFENSE PET SIN HUFF LACK SLIP
WITE ABUSE CRIME ERROR FAULT
GRIEF GUILT MALUM PIQUE SNUFF
ATTACK BIGAMY DELICT FELONY
PIACLE PRITCH REATUS STRUNT
AFFRONT DEFAULT DEMERIT
DUDGEON LARCENY MISDEED
OUTRAGE SCANDAL UMBRAGE
PECCANCY TRESPASS EXTORTION
INDECORUM INDIGNITY
THEFTBOTE
(— AGAINST LAW) MALUM DELICT
DELICTUM
(— AGAINST MORALITY) EVIL
CRIME
(SLIGHT —) PECCADILLO
OFFENSIVE BAD ACID EVIL FOUL
HARD UGLY BILGY CRUDE DIRTY
FETID GROSS NASTY SLIMY YUCKY
COARSE FROWZY GARISH HORRID
RANCID RIBALD ROTTEN ABUSIVE
BEASTLY FULSOME HATEFUL
HIDEOUS NOISOME PECCANT
RASPING SCARLET DREADFUL
INVADING MEPHITIC SHOCKING
STINKING UNSAVORY LOATHSOME
OBNOXIOUS REPUGNANT
REVOLTING SCANDALOUS
(— SIGHT) EYESORE
OFFENSIVENESS ODIUM
OFFER GO BID PUT BODE GIVE
HAND LEND PLEA POSE SHOW
TAKE TEND DEFER HEAVE PARTY
SHORE START ADDUCE AFFORD
ALLEGE DELATE INJECT OBLATE
OPPOSE PREFER SUBMIT SUPPLY
TENDER ADVANCE BIDDING
COMMEND EXHIBIT PRESENT
PROFFER PROPINE PROPOSE
SUGGEST OVERTURE PROPOSAL
VOLUNTEER
(— A STAKE) SET
(— EXCUSE) ALIBI
(— FOR SALE) HAWK EXPOSE
(— INDUCEMENT) INVITE
(— IN EXCUSE) PLEAD
(— IN OPPOSITION) OBJECT
(— IN SACRIFICE) IMMOLATE
(— OF MARRIAGE) PROPOSAL
(— PROOF) APPROVE
(— PUBLICLY) JACTITATE
(— RESISTANCE) FEND
(— TO VERIFY) AVER
(— UP) APPEAL
(LAST —) ULTIMATUM
(PUBLIC —) SALE
(SOLEMN —) PLEDGE
(UNACCEPTED —) POLLICITATION
OFFERING BID ALMS BALI DALI
DEAL GIFT HOST SOMA DOLLY
ENTRY CORBAN NUZZER OFLETE
PIACLE PRESENT RETABLO
TRIBUTE ANATHEMA DEVOTION
DONATION LIBATION OBLATION
PESHKASH PIACULUM SACRIFICE
(— TO GOD) CORBAN DEODATE
(— TO HOUSEHOLD DEITIES) BALI
(EUCHARISTIC —) ANAPHORA
(PEACE —S) PACIFICS

(RELIGIOUS —) OBLATION
(SACRIFICIAL —) HOLOCAUST
(THEATRICAL —) FLUFF
(PL.) HIERA ALTARAGE INFERIAE
OFF-GLIDE EXIT VOCULE DETENTE
OFFHAND AIRY CURT GLIB SOON
ADLIB BLUSH HASTY ABRUPT
BREEZY CASUAL BRUSQUE
READILY CARELESS CAVALIER
GLANCING INFORMAL EXTEMPORE
IMPROMPTU UNSTUDIED
OFFICE HAT JOB SEE BOMA DUTY
NONE PART POST ROLE ROOM
SHOP TASK TOGA WIKE WORK
PLACE STINT TRUST WIKEN YAMEN
ABBACY AGENCY BUREAU CHARGE
DAFTAR DIWANI DUFTER METIER
MISTER BULLPEN CAMARIN
CENTRAL DEWANEE DROSTDY
EDILITY MYSTERY SERVICE
STATION SURGERY AEDILITY
CAPACITY CUTCHERY ENSIGNCY
FUNCTION KINGSHIP MINISTRY
POSITION PROVINCE WOOLPACK
BAILIWICK BANKSHALL SITUATION
(— BOY) CHOKRA
(— CHIEF) BOSS MANAGER
(— OF BISHOP) LAWN
(— OF JUDGE) BENCH ERMINE
(— OF PROFESSOR) CHAIR
(— OF ROMAN CURIA) DATARY
DATARIA
(— OF RULER) REGENCY
(— OF THE DEAD) DIRGE
(— WORKER) CLERK STENO TYPIST
SECRETARY
(BRANCH —) WING
(CASHIER'S —) CAISSE
(CLERICAL —) CASSOCK
(DIVINE —) AKOLUTHIA
(ECCLESIASTICAL —) FROCK
BENEFICE EXORCIST
(HIGH —) DIGNITY
(LITURGICAL —) SEXT SERVICE
(MAGISTRATE'S —) KACHAHRI
(MORNING —) ORTHRON ORTHROS
(NAVAL —) BEACH
(PAY —) WANIGAN
(POLICE —) NICK
(PRIESTLY —) SACERDOCY
(PRINTING —) CHAPEL IMPRIMERY
(RECORD —) CHANCERY
(RESIGN AN —) DEMIT
(TIMEKEEPER'S —) PENNYHOLE
(SUFF.) ATE CY DOM SHIP URE
OFFICEHOLDER IN WINNER
OFFICIAL PLACEMAN
OFFICER (ALSO SEE OFFICIAL) COP
TAB AIDE EXEC EXON FLAG HOLD
NASI SWAB VOGT AGENT CHIEF
CRIER DEWAN DIWAN GRAND
GRAVE GROOM JURAT SEWER
TAXOR USHER ALCADE BEADLE
BEAGLE BEDRAL BUTLER CENSOR
DEPUTY DIRECT ENSIGN GAILLI
GEREFA HERALD KOTWAL
LAWMAN LICTOR MANAGE
ORATOR PARNAS REDTAB SYNDIC
TINDAL ADJOINT AGISTOR
ALNAGER ASSIZER BAILIFF
COMMAND CONDUCT CORONER
DUUMVIR EPAULET FEDERAL
FEODARY GAVELER GENERAL

JEMADAR KLEAGLE LOBSTER
MUSTANG NAPERER PANTLER
PATROON REGIDOR SANCTUM
SCHEPEN SHERIFF SPEAKER
STEWARD WHIPPER WOODMAN
ADJUTANT ALDERMAN ALGUACIL
ANDREEVE BANNERET CHAFFWAX
COFFERER CURSITOR DOORWARD
FORESTER GOVERNOR GRASSMAN
MERESMAN MINISTER PALATINE
PURVEYOR QUESTEUR REPORTER
TIPSTAFF VISCOUNT WOODWARD
CONSTABLE DIKEGRAVE
FINANCIER INTENDANT
MODERATOR PAYMASTER
SCHOOLMAN TAHSILDAR
(— OF CHURCH) ABBOT ELDER
DEACON SEXTON ANTISTES
DEFENSOR LAMPADARY SACRISTAN
(— OF COURT) MACER MASTER
BAILIFF FEODARY FILACER
CURSITOR DEMPSTER EXAMINER
SERGEANT ASSOCIATE
BYRLAWMAN SURROGATE
(— OF FORESTS) AGISTER AGISTOR
(— OF KING'S STABLES) AVENER
(— OF TABLE) SEWER
(BARDIC —) DRUID
(CAVALRY —) CORNET
(CHIEF —) NASI DEWAN DAROGA
PARNAS PRESIDENT
(CHIEF EXECUTIVE —) CEO
(CHURCH —) SEXTON
(COLLEGE —) RECTOR
(COURT —) REEVE SUMMONER
(CUSTOMS —) GAGER SHARK
GAUGER JERQUER DOUANIER
SEARCHER SURVEYOR TIDESMAN
(FOREST —) RANGER
(GREEK —) STRATEGOS STRATEGUS
(JAPANESE —) SHIKKEN
(KIND OF —) PETTY
(LAW —) GANGBUSTER
(MASONIC —) EAST KING DEACON
STEWARD
(MILITARY —) NAIG NAIK COMES
MAJOR SUBAH ENSIGN NAIQUE
RANKER SARDAR SIRDAR CAPTAIN
COLONEL GENERAL JEMADAR
MARSHAL SUBADAR WARRANT
COMMANDER RABSHAKEH
SHAVETAIL
(MINOR —) CHINOVNIK
(MONASTERY —) CELLARER
(MUNICIPAL —) SCHOUT VARLET
(NAVAL —) CPO EXON MATE SWAB
BOSUN ENSIGN PURSER YEOMAN
ADMIRAL CAPTAIN MUSTANG
SPOTTER YOUNKER COXSWAIN
SUNDOWNER MIDSHIPMAN
(PAPAL —) DATARY
(POLICE —) COP PIG PEON RURAL
COPPER EXEMPT JAVERT KOTWAL
ROZZER RUNNER SBIRRO ALYTARCH
SEARCHER THANADAR DETECTIVE
ROUNDSMAN
(PRESIDING —) CHAIRONE
CHAIRPERSON
(PRISON —) SCREW WARDER
(PUBLIC —) JUDGE FISCAL NOTARY
PODESTA
(ROMAN —) LICTOR

(SHERIFF'S —) FANG BEAGLE
BAILIFF BULLDOG HUISSIER
(SHIP'S —) MATE FANTOD
(STAFF —) TAB AIDE REDTAB
ADJUTANT
(TOLL —) SCAVAGER
(TURKISH —) AGA AGHA MUTE VIZIR
VIZIER BIMBASHI BINBASHI
(UNIVERSITY —) DEAN REGENT
PROVOST
(WARRANT —) MACHINIST
(PL.) BRAID BRASS STAFF
OFFICIAL (ALSO SEE OFFICER) AGA
BEG DEY VIP AMIN BOSS KUAN
KWAN TRUE AGENT AHONG
AMALA AMBAN AMEEN AMLAH
CLERK EDILE EPHOR GYANI HAJIB
HOMER JURAT LIMMU LINER
MAYOR NAZIR OMRAH REEVE
SAHIB AEDILE ARCHON ATABEG
BASHAW CENSOR CONSUL
EPARCH EPONYM FISCAL FORMAL
GABBAI GRIEVE HAZZAN HERALD
LAWMAN MASTER NOTARY PANDIT
PREVOT RABMAG SATRAP SCRIBE
SEALER SINGER TAOTAI TAOYIN
TRONER VERGER WARDEN
WEDANA ALMONER APOSTLE
ASIARCH BURGESS CERTAIN
JEMADAR LANDRAT MARSHAL
MOORMAN PRISTAW REFEREE
STALLAR STARTER SUBASHI
VAIVODE ALDERMAN APPROVED
CARDINAL CELLARER CUSTOMER
DOGBERRY GOVERNOR LINESMAN
MANDARIN PROVIDER PRYTANIS
VESTIARY VISCOUNT WHIFFLER
EXECUTIVE MAJORDOMO
OMBUDSMAN SELECTMAN
MAGISTRATE
(— APPROVAL) VISA VISE
(— DECREE) WRIT UKASE
(— OF CARTHAGE) SUFFETE
(BLUNDERING —) DOGBERRY
(EISTEDDFOD —) DRUID
(GAME —) REF UMP SCORER
UMPIRE REFEREE
(MUSLIM —) OMRAH
(PALACE —) PALADIN
(POMPOUS —) BUMBLE
(PRETENTIOUS —) PANJANDRUM
(UNIVERSITY —) PROCTOR
(PL.) KEYS PHAR OMLAH
OFFICIATE ACT FILL SERVE SUPPLY
PERFORM CELEBRATE
OFFICIATOR DEICIDE
OFFICIOUS BUSY COOL PERT
SAUCY FORMAL FORTHY PUSHING
ARROGANT IMPUDENT INFORMAL
MEDDLING OFFICIAL INBEARING
PRAGMATIC
OFFING OFF FUTURE PICTURE
OFFISH CLAMMY UPSTAGE
OFFSCOURINGS MUD SCURF
OFF-SEASON LAYOFF
OFFSET SLAB STEP ALTAR CRIMP
ERASE POISE CANCEL CONTRA
JOGGLE REDEEM SETOFF
BALANCE COUNTER LATERAL
RETREAT SETBACK PROPAGULE
(— ON BULB) SPLIT
OFFSHOOT GET PUP ROD SON LIMB
SPUR BOUGH ISSUE SCION SHOOT

SPRIG BRANCH FILIAL GROWTH MEMBER OFFSET SPROUT ADJUNCT APOPHYSIS FILIATION OUTGROWTH RAMIFICATION
(— OF LAKE) BAYOU
(— OF RELIGIOUS ORDER) REFORM
OFFSHORE DEEPWATER
OFFSPRING BOY FRY IMP KID KIN SON BRAT BURD CHIT HEIR SEED SLIP BIRTH BREED BROOD CHILD FRUIT ISSUE SCION SPAWN BEGATS DUSTEE EMBRYO FOSTER GRIQUA JUMART PROLES RESULT STRAIN STRIND MORISCO NISHADA OUTCOME PRODUCE PRODUCT PROGENY YOUNGER CHILDREN DAUGHTER DEMISANG GENITURE INCREASE KINDLING BAIRNTEAM MUSTAFINA
(— OF EUROPEAN-INDIAN) MAMELUCO
(— OF FAIRIES) CHANGELING
(— OF NEGRO AND MULATTO) GRIFFE
(— OF STALLION AND ASS) HINNY FUNNEL
(— OF WITCH) HAGSEED HOLDIKEN
(MYTHICAL —) JUMART
(PREMATURE) CASTLING
(WITHOUT) ATOKAL ATOKOUS
(PREF.) GEN(O) GON(O) PAEDO PEDO PROLI
(SUFF.) ITE TOKOUS
OFF-THE-RACK READYMADE
OF HUMAN BONDAGE (AUTHOR OF —) MAUGHAM
(CHARACTER IN —) CAREY EMILY ERLIN FANNY NORAH PRICE SALLY WEEKS LAWSON LOUISA NESBIT PHILIP ROGERS THORPE ATHELNY CLUTTON HAYWARD MILDRED WILLIAM CRONSHAW WILKINSON
OFICINA WORKS OFFICE FACTORY
OFLETE WAFER OBLATION OFFERING
OF MICE AND MEN (AUTHOR OF —) STEINBECK
(CHARACTER IN —) SLIM CANDY SMALL CROOKS CURLEY GEORGE LENNIE MILTON
OFTEN OFT AFTEN OFTLY COMMON EFTSOONS FREQUENT REPEATED
(VERY —) CONTINUALLY
OF TIME AND THE RIVER (AUTHOR OF —) WOLFE
(CHARACTER IN —) ANN GANT JOEL WANG BASCOM ELINOR EUGENE PIERCE ROBERT WEAVER COULSON FRANCIS HATCHER MORNAYE PENTLAND
OGDOAD EIGHT OCTOAD OGDOAS OCTONARY
OGEE (ALSO SEE MOLDING) CYMA GULA TALON MOLDING
OGIVAL HEATER
OGLE EYE GAZE LEER LOOK MASH STARE GLANCE EXAMINE MARLOCK SMICKER OEILLADE
OGRE ORC BOYG BRUTE DEMON FIEND GHOUL GIANT HUGON TYRANT YAKSHA BUGABOO BUGBEAR MONSTER WINDIGO
OGRESS PELLET GUNSTONE

OGTIERN LORD MASTER
OGYGIAN ANCIENT PRIMEVAL
OH OU OW ACH OUCH

OHIO
CAPITAL: COLUMBUS
COLLEGE: KENT HIRAM KENYON XAVIER ANTIOCH OBERLIN DEFIANCE
COUNTY: ERIE PIKE ROSS DARKE MIAMI STARK GALLIA HARDIN SUMMIT LICKING CUYAHOGA HAMILTON
INDIAN TRIBE: ERIE WYANDOT
NATIVE: BUCKEYE
NICKNAME: BUCKEYE
PRESIDENT: TAFT GRANT HAYES HARDING GARFIELD HARRISON MCKINLEY
RIVER: MIAMI MAUMEE SCIOTO CUYAHOGA MUSKINGUM
STATE BIRD: CARDINAL
STATE FLOWER: CARNATION
STATE TREE: BUCKEYE
TOWN: ADA ENON LIMA TROY ADENA AKRON BEREA CADIZ NILES XENIA CANTON DAYTON ELYRIA LORAIN MENTOR TOLEDO CHARDON COLUMBUS SANDUSKY CLEVELAND

OIL BEN FAT ILE ULE BALM CHIA DIKA FUEL ZEST BRIBE CRUDE JUICE OLEUM SMEAR STOCK TRAIN ULYIE ULZIE ACEITE ANOINT BINDER BUTTER CARDOL CHRISM CREESH EUPION GREASE LIQUOR SAFROL SMOOTH ZACHUN CEDRIUM ESSENCE LANOLIN MYRRHOL PHLOROL RETINOL VETIVER BERGAMOT COUMARAN ERIGERON GINGEROL PHTHALAN SDRAVETS TETRALIN CARVACROL LUBRICATE PETROLEUM
(— BEETLE) MELOE MELOID
(— CAKE) SEEDCAKE
(— CAN) OILER
(— CASK) RIER
(— FROM ORANGE FLOWERS) NEROLI
(— FROM RESIN) RETINOL
(— IN PAINTS) TUNG
(— LAMP) LUCIGEN
(— OF TURPENTINE) CAMPHENE CAMPHINE
(— PALM) OILBERRY
(— PAN) SUMP
(— PLANT) SESAME
(— ROCK) SHALE LIMESTONE
(— TREE) EBOE POON TUNG MAHWA
(— VESSEL) DRUM OLPE CRUET CRUSE TANKER CRESSET
(— WELL) DUSTER GASSER GUSHER WILDCAT
(AROMATIC —) SPIKENARD
(BUTTER —) GHEE
(COAL —) PHOTOGEN
(CONSECRATED —) CHRISM
(FISH —) GURRY
(FIXED —) COCUM KOKAM KOKUM
(FLOWER —) ABSOLUTE
(FRAGRANT —) ATAR NARD OTTO

ATTAR OTTAR CAFFEOL BERGAMOT CAFFEONE GERANIOL
(FUEL —) DERV
(INFERIOR —) MIDDLING
(KIND OF —) CASTOR
(KIND OF COOKING —) CORN COPRA OLIVE
(LINSEED —) CARRON LINOLEUM
(MINERAL —) NAPHTHA KEROSENE
(ORANGE —) NEROLI
(ORANGE-FLOWER —) NEROLI
(PINE —) FROTHER
(PUNGENT —) CAJUPUT
(REMAINING FUEL —) RESID
(RESIDUAL —) RESID
(SESAME —) GINGILI SIRITCH
(SOLID —) KIKUEL
(VEGETABLE —) MACASSAR
(VULCANIZED —) FACTICE
(WHALE —) SPERM TRAIN
(WOOL —) YOLK
(PREF.) ELAEO ELAIO ELEO OLEI OLEO
OILBIRD FATBIRD GUACHARO
OIL CAKE POONAC RESIDUE
OILFISH ESCOLAR
OILILY SLEEK
OILSEED TIL TEEL SESAME LINSEED RAPESEED
OILSKIN OIL OILER SQUAM OILCASE OILCOAT SLICKER
OILSTONE HONE SHALE WHETSTONE
OIL WELL GUSHER
OILY FAT GLIB LIMY BLAND FATTY LOEIC OLEIC SLEEK SOAPY SUAVE GREASY OILISH OLEOSE OLEOUS SMARMY SMOOTH SUPPLE PINGUID SERVILE SLIPPERY UNCTUOUS COMPLIANT PLAUSIBLE
(PREF.) LIPAR(O)
OINTMENT UNG BALM MULL NARD PASTE SALVE SMEAR BALSAM CERATE CEROMA CHARGE CHRISM GREASE POMADE REMEDY UNGUENT EYESALVE POPULEON REMOLADE SPIKENARD WHITFIELD
(— OF GODS) AMBROSIA
OJIBWAY CHIPPEWA SAULTEUR CHIPPEWAY
OKA OCHA OQUE OQUI OCQUE
OKAPI GIRAFFINE
OKAY OK YES HUNK OKEH HUNKY APPROVE CORRECT SANCTION AUTHORIZE SAYTHEWORD
(JAPANESE —) HAI
OKIA OKET OUNCE
OKINAWA (CAPITAL OF —) NAHA

OKLAHOMA
CAPITAL: OKLAHOMACITY
COLLEGE: CAMERON LANGSTON PHILLIPS
COUNTY: KAY COAL LOVE ADAIR ATOKA CADDO GREER OSAGE ALFALFA OKFUSKEE OKMULGEE
INDIAN TRIBE: WACO WICHITA TAWAKONI
LAKE: EUFAULA OOLOGAH
MOUNTAINS: OUACHITA
NATIVE: OKIE SOONER
NICKNAME: SOONER

RIVER: RED GRAND WASHITA ARKANSAS CANADIAN CIMARRON
STATE FLOWER: MISTLETOE
STATE TREE: REDBUD
TOWN: ADA JAY ALVA ENID HUGO ALTUS MIAMI PONCA TULSA ELRENO GUYMON IDABEL LAWTON MADILL TALOGA VINITA ANTLERS SAPULPA SHAWNEE ANADARKO FORTSILL MUSKOGEE

OKRA GOBO OKRO BAMIA BENDY GOBBO GOMBO GUBBO GUMBO OCHRA BENDEE MALLOW BANDAKA BANDICOY BANDIKAI
OLD AGY ELD AGED AULD COLD WOLD YALD ANILE HOARY MOSSY STALE WOULD EFFETE FORMER FOROLD INFIRM MATURE SENILE SHABBY VETUST AGEABLE ANCIENT ANTIQUE ARCHAIC ELDERLY FORWORN OGYGIAN UMWHILE DECREPIT MEDIEVAL OBSOLETE DODDERING GERIATRIC HACKNEYED SENESCENT VENERABLE
(— AND MELLOW) CRUSTY
(— BAILEY) GAOL JAIL PRISON
(— CLOTHESMAN) POCO
(— FAITHFUL) GEYSER
(— HAND) LONGTIMER
(— MAID) SPINSTER THORNBACK
(— MAN) ANTIQUITY WHITEBEARD
(— SOD) EIRE ERIN IRELAND
(— SQUAW) DIVER HOUND MOMMY CALLOO CALLOW COWEEN DUCKER QUANDY OLDWIFE SCOLDER COCKAWEE LONGTAIL SHARPTAIL SOUTHERLY
(— WOMAN) HAG CRONE GAMMER
(BEING LESS THAN 13 YEARS —) PRETEEN
(GROWING —) SENESCENT
(OF —) WHILOM ERSTWHILE
(PREF.) PALAE(O) PALAI(O) PALE(O) SENI
(— AGE) GER(I)(O) GERATO GERONT(O) PRESBY(O)
(— MAN) GER(I)(O) GERONT(O) PRESBY(O)
OLD AND THE YOUNG (AUTHOR OF —) PIRANDELLO
(CHARACTER IN —) COSTA MAURO SALVO SELMI AURITI GIULIO AURELIO CORRADO MORTARA ROBERTO CAPOLINO DIANELLA FLAMINIO GERLANDO IPPOLITO NICOLETTA LAURENTANO
OLD BAY STATE MASSACHUSETTS
OLD CURIOSITY SHOP (AUTHOR OF —) DICKENS
(CHARACTER IN —) KIT DICK FRED NELL BRASS QUILP SARAH CODLIN JARLEY MARTON THOMAS BARBARA NUBBLES SAMPSON SWIVELLER CHRISTOPHER
OLD DOMINION STATE VIRGINIA
OLDEN ANTIQUE
OLDER MORE ALDER ELDER SENIOR ANCESTOR
OLDEST
(PREF.) EO
OLD-FASHIONED MOSSY RETRO

CORNBALL SCHMALTZY NEANDERTHAL CORNY DOWDY FUSTY PASSE FOGRAM FOGRUM QUAINT STODGY ANCIENT ANTIQUE ARCHAIC ARRIERE ELDERLY VINTAGE FRUMPISH OBSOLETE CRINOLINE PRIMITIVE RINKYDINK OLDFANGLED
(FASHIONABLY —) RETRO
OLD FRANKLIN STATE TENNESSEE
OLD LINE STATE MARYLAND
OLD MAID (AUTHOR OF —)
WHARTON
(CHARACTER IN —) JOE TINA DELIA JAMES LOVELL CLEMENT RALSTON SPENDER CHARLOTTE
OLD MORTALITY (AUTHOR OF —)
SCOTT
(CHARACTER IN —) JOHN BASIL EDITH HENRY JENNY MAUSE CUDDIE MORTON BALFOUR FRANCIS GRAHAME OLIFANT BOTHWELL DENNISON EVANDALE HEADRIGG MARGARET BELLENDEN CLAVERHOUSE
OLD-TIMER SOURDOUGH
OLD WIVES' TALE (AUTHOR OF —)
BENNETT
(CHARACTER IN —) JOHN CYRIL POVEY BAINES CHIRAC GERALD SAMUEL SCALES SOPHIA HARRIET FAUCAULT CONSTANCE CRITCHLOW
OLD-WOMANISH ANILE
OLEANDER LAUREL NERIUM DOGBANE ROSEBAY
OLEFIN ALKENE
OLEIC RAPIC RAPINIC
OLEORESIN GUM ANIME APIOL ELEMI TOLUS BALSAM GURJUN IRIDIN COPAIBA GALIPOT LABDANUM TACAMAHAC
OLFACTION NOSE SMELL OSMESIS SMELLING ESPHRESIS
OLIGARCHIC FEUDAL
OLIGARCHY KREMLIN
OLIGOCLASE SUNSTONE
OLIMPIA (HUSBAND OF —) BIRENO OBERTO
OLINDO (HUSBAND OF —)
SOFRONIA
(SAVIOR OF —) CLORINDA
OLIO STEW MEDLEY FARRAGO MELANGE MIXTURE MISHMASH MACEDOINE PASTICCIO POTPOURRI
OLIPHANT HORN ELEPHANT
OLIPRANCE ROMP SHOW FROLIC JOLLITY
OLIVE OLEA MORON BRUNET LIERRE OLIVER OXHORN PIMOLA RESEDA BAROUNI CITRINE MISSION MORILLON OLEASTER
(— FLY) DACUS
(AMERICAN —) DEVILWOOD
(OVERRIPE —) DRUPE
(PREF.) DRUPI
(—OIL) ELAEO ELAIO ELEO
OLIVER NOLL HAMMER HOLLIPER
(BROTHER OF —) ORLANDO
(WIFE OF —) CELIA
OLIVER TWIST (AUTHOR OF —)
DICKENS
(CHARACTER IN —) BILL JACK NOAH

ROSE TOBY BATES FAGIN HARRY MONKS NANCY SALLY SIKES TWIST BEDWIN BUMBLE CORNEY EDWARD MAYLIE OLIVER CHARLEY CRACKIT DAWKINS GRIMWIG LEEFORD BROWNLOW CLAYPOLE LOSBERNE SOWERBERRY
OLIVET PEARL
OLIVIA (HUSBAND OF —) SEBASTIAN
OLIVINE PERIDOT
OLLA JAR JUG OLE POT OLAY PUCHERA PUCHERO
OLLA PODRIDA HASH OLIO MEDLEY POTPOURRI
OLM PROTEUS SALAMANDER
OLOGY ISM SCIENCE
OLYMPIAN CELESTIAL
OLYMPIAS (FATHER OF —)
NEOPTOLEMUS
(HUSBAND OF —) PHILIP
(SLAYER OF —) CASSANDER
(SON OF —) ALEXANDER
OLYNTHUS ASCULA
OMAGUA CAMBEVA
OMAH SASQUATCH
OMAN (CAPITAL OF —) MASQAT
MUSCAT
(LANGUAGE OF —) ARABIC
BALUCHI
(MOUNTAIN OF —) SHAM HAFIT HARIM NAKHL TAYIN AKHDAR
(NATIVE OF —) ADNAN QAHTAN BALUCHI
(TOWN IN —) SUR NIGWA MASQAT MATRAH SALALAH
OMAR (FATHER OF —) ELIPHAZ
OMASUM BOOK BOUK BIBLE FARDEL MANYPLIES
OMBER SOLO UMBRE HOMBRE MEDIATOR QUADRILLE
OMEGA END LAST
OMELET AMLET AMELET FOOYUNG FOOYOUNG FRITTATA
OMEN BODE LUCK SIGN ABODE AUGUR BODER FREET FREIT GUEST TOKEN WEIRD WHATE AUGURY HANDEL HANSEL AUSPICE PORTENT PRESAGE PRODIGY WARNING CEREMONY FOREBODE SOOTHSAY HARBINGER
OMENTUM WEB CAUL ZIRBUS EPIPLOON
OMINOUS DIRE DOUR GRIM BLACK DOOMY FATAL BODING DISMAL SHREWD AUGURAL BALEFUL BANEFUL BODEFUL DIREFUL DOOMFUL FATEFUL MENACING SINISTER THUNDERY PROPHETIC PORTENTOUS
OMISSION OUT BALK BAULK CHASM SALTUS DEFAULT ELISION FAILURE MISPICK NEGLECT SILENCE PASSOVER OVERSIGHT
(— OF A LETTER) APOCOPE
(— OF SYLLABLES) SYNCOPE
(TACIT —) SILENCE
OMIT CUT LET BALK BATE DROP EDIT KILL MISS PASS SKIP SLIP ABATE ELIDE OBMIT SPARE BELEVE CANCEL DELETE EXCEPT FORGET IGNORE DISCARD EXPUNGE NEGLECT DISCOUNT

OVERLEAP OVERLOOK OVERSKIP OVERSLIP DISREGARD PRETERMIT
OMITTED VIDE
OMMATIDIUM FACET FACETTE
OMNIBUS BUS BUSS BARGE HERDIC JOGGER PIRATE AUTOBUS MOTORBUS KITTEREEN
OMNIPOTENT GOD ABLE DEITY GREAT ARRANT MIGHTY ALMIGHTY POWERFUL UNEQUALED UNLIMITED
OMNIPRESENCE UBIQUITY
OMNISCIENT WISE LEARNED POWERFUL PANSOPHIC
OMOPLATE SCAPULA
OMPHALE (FATHER OF —)
IARDANUS
(HUSBAND OF —) TMOLUS
(SON OF —) TANTALUS
OMPHALOS HUB BOSS KNOB NAVEL CENTER UMBILICUS
OMRI (FATHER OF —) BECHER MICHAEL
(SON OF —) AHAB
ON O AN IN TO LIT ONE SUR ATOP AWAY OVER UPON ABOUT ABOVE AHEAD ALONG ANENT ABOARD WITHIN FORWARD
(— ACCOUNT OF) IN FOR
(— A HATCH) ABROOD
(— ALL SIDES) ABOUT AROUND
(— AND ON) EVER FOREVER TEDIOUS
(— EARTH) BELOW
(— END) TOGETHER
(— FOOT) UP AFOOT TOWARD FOOTBACK
(— HAND) ALONG
(— HIGH) ALOFT
(— THE CONTRARY) BUT RATHER
(— THE MOVE) AFOOT
(— THE OTHER HAND) BUT AGAIN HOWEVER ALTHOUGH
(— THE OTHER SIDE) OVER ACROSS
(— THE WAY) AWAY AGATE
(— TIME) PROMPT
(— TOP OF) ATOP ABOVE ALOFT
(— WHAT ACCOUNT) WHY
(FATHER OF —) PELETH
(PREF.) IL IM IN IR SUPER
ONAGER ASS GOUR KULAN KOULAN ONAGRA ALACRAN CATAPULT SCORPION
ONAM (FATHER OF —) SHOBAL JERAHMEEL
(MOTHER OF —) ATARAH
ONAN (FATHER OF —) JUDAH
ONCE ANE EEN ERST AINCE ONCET WHILE YANCE FORMER WHILOM QUONDAM UMWHILE FORMERLY SOMETIME UMQUHILE WHENEVER ERSTWHILE
(— MORE) YET ANEW AGAIN ENCORE ITERUM
(AT —) PRESTO
ONDATRA FIBER
ONE J AE AN HE UN ACE AIN ANE ANY EIN MAN OON TAE UNA UNE WON YAE YAN YEN YIN YOU SAME SOLE SOME TANE TEAN THIS TONE TOON UNAL UNIT WHON WONE ALONE ALPHA UNITY WOONE ABOARD FELLOW PERSON SINGLE

UNIQUE UNITED CERTAIN NUMERAL PRONOUN SIMPLUM UNBROKEN SINGLETON UNDIVIDED UNMARRIED
(— AFTER ANOTHER) ABOUT TANDEM SERIALLY SERIATIM
(— BORN A SERF) NEIF NEIFE
(— BY ONE) APIECE SINGLY OVERHEAD
(— CONDEMNED WRONGFULLY) CALAS
(— CURIOUS TO KNOW ALL) QUIDNUNC
(— DETESTED) WARLING
(— DEVOTED TO PARTICULAR ART) IST
(— EASILY TRICKED) CULLY
(— ENGAGED IN MARAUDING) LOOTIE
(— ENROLLED IN ARMY) DRAFTEE
(— FOLLOWED BY 100 ZEROES) GOOGOL
(— GIVEN TO DEVILTRY) HELLION
(— HELD IN CONTEMPT) FINK
(— HIGHEST IN RANK) SUPREME
(— INSTRUCTED IN SECRET SYSTEM) EPOPT
(— LATE) SERO
(— MANAGING ENTERTAINERS ON ROAD) ROADIE
(— NOT A REGULAR MASON) COWAN
(— OF PAIR) FELLOW DOUBLET
(— OF TRIPLETS) TRILLING
(— OVERZEALOUS) HYPER
(— SENT FORTH) APOSTLE
(—S NEARBY) THESE
(— TENTH) TITHE
(— THAT IRKS OR ANNOYS) PAIN
(— THAT UNDERGOES CHANGE) MUTANT
(— THOUSAND) MIL
(— TWENTY-FOURTH) CARAT
(— UNKNOWN) QUIDAM
(— VERSED IN LITERATURE) SAVANT
(— WHO BRINGS MEAT TO TABLE) DAPIFER
(— WHO DISPLAYS FASTIDIOUSNESS) EPICURE
(— WHO DOCTORS SOMETHING) COOK
(— WHO EXCELS) ACE
(— WHO FABRICATES) SMITH
(— WHO FOLLOWS ARMY) SUTLER
(— WHO FORSAKES FAITH) APOSTATE
(— WHO FRUSTRATES PLAN) MARPLOT
(— WHO HAS ATTAINED PERFECTION) SIDDHA
(— WHO IS AWAY) ABSENTEE
(— WHO IS DISMISSED) PUSHOUT
(— WHO IS STRANGE OR ECCENTRIC) WEIRDO
(— WHO LOADS SHIP) BUNKER
(— WHO MAKES LIVING BY TRICKERY) CADGER
(— WHO MANAGES) GERENT
(— WHO REGULATES GUN) TRAINER
(— WHO REMOVES NUISANCE) ABATOR

(— WHO REPRESENTS NEWEST) NEO

(— WHOSE MIND IS IMPAIRED BY AGE) DOTARD

(— WHO TESTS) CONNER

(— WHO USES DRUGS) DRUGGY DRUGGIE

(— WHO WANTS TO BE SOMEONE ELSE) WANNABE

(— WITH FIRST-HAND INFORMATION) INSIDER

(APPEALING —) GAS

(BLESSED —) BHAGAVAT

(CONSPICUOUS —) STANDOUT

(EVIL —) WOND SHAITAN SHEITAN

(EXTRAORDINARY —) DOOZY DOOZER

(LITTLE —) BUTCHA PICKANINNY

(LOVED —) MINION

(MOST IMPORTANT —) FLAGSHIP

(NOT —) NARY

(SUPERIOR —) LAMA

(SWEET —) HONEYCOMB

(TIMELESS —) AKAL

(TIRESOME —) DRIP

(PREF.) HENO MON(O) UNI

(— AND A HALF TIMES) SESQUI

(— AND THE SAME) HOM(O)

(— ANOTHER) ALLELO

(— BILLIONTH) NANO

(— MILLIONTH) MICR(O)

(— TRILLIONTH) PICO

(SAME —) AUT(O) AUTH(I)

(SUFF.) (— BELONGING) AN EAN IAN

(— BELONGING TO) IE ING

(— BELONGING TO A GROUP) ID

(— BELONGING TO A LINE) ID

(— HAVING) ANDER

(— HAVING TO DO WITH) IE

(— OCCUPATIONALLY CONNECTED WITH) ER IER YER

(— OF A KIND) ING

(— OF A QUALITY) IE

(— SKILLED) AN EAN IAN

(— THAT ADVOCATES A DOCTRINE) IST

(— THAT DABBLES) IST

(— THAT DOES) ER IER YER

(— THAT HAS) ER IER YER

(— THAT MAKES) IST

(— THAT OPERATES) IST

(— THAT PERFORMS) ER IER IST YER

(— THAT PRACTICES) IST

(— THAT PRODUCES) ER IER IST YER

(— THAT SPECIALIZES) IST

(— THAT STUDIES) IST

(— THAT YIELDS) ER IER YER

(LESSER —) IDIUM

(LITTLE —) IE

(SMALL —) IDIUM IUM

ONEGITE AMETHYST GEMSTONE

ONE-LINER JEST JOKE

ONENESS UNION UNITY CONCORD ONEHOOD UNICITY UNITUDE IDENTITY SAMENESS AGREEMENT

ONE-NIGHT STAND GIG

ONE-NOTE MONOTONOUS

ONE-RAYED MONACT

ONEROUS HARD HEAVY ARDUOUS

ONEROSE WEIGHTY EXACTING GRIEVOUS LABORIOUS

ONESELF
(PREF.) SUI
(BY, FOR, PERT. TO —) AUT(O) AUTH(I)

ONE-SIDED ECCENTRIC UNILATERAL

ONETIME FORMER FORMERLY ERSTWHILE

ONFALL ONSET ATTACK ASSAULT

ON-GLIDE TENSION ENTRANCE

ONION BOLL CEPA LEEK LILY SYBO CIBOL INGAN PEARL ALLIUM LILIUM PORRET BERMUDA CEBOLLA HOLLEKE PICKLER SHALLOT AYEGREEN RARERIPE SCALLION VALENCIA
(ROPE OF —S) REEVE
(SEASONED WITH —S) LYONNAISE
(SPRING —) SYBO CIBOL SYBOE SYBOW
(STRING OF —S) TRACE

ONKOS TOPKNOT

ONLOOKER BOOK EYER GAZER WITNESS AUDIENCE BEHOLDER OVERSEER BYSTANDER SPECTATOR

ONLY ALL BUT JUST LONE MERE ONCE SAVE SOLE AFALD ALONE ARRAH FIRST MERED NOBUT OLEPY ANERLY BARELY MERELY NOBBUT SIMPLE SINGLE SINGLY SOLELY ALLENARLY EXCEPTING
(— THIS) MERE
(BEING —) SIMPLE

ONMUN HANGUL HANKUL

ONOMATOPOEIA
(PREF.) KE(R)

ONOMATOPOEIC ECHOIC IMSONIC MIMETIC IMITATIVE

ONRUSH BIRR SHAKE ATTACK TIDEWAY

ONSET DASH DINT FALL FARD RESE RUSH BRAID BREAK BRUNT FAIRD FRUSH START STORM STOUR VENUE ACCESS AFFRET ATTACK CHARGE COURGE IMPACT INSULT ONDING ONFALL POWDER THRUST ASSAULT BRATTLE BEGINNING ENCOUNTER ONSLAUGHT

ONSETTER CAGER HITCHER

ONSLAUGHT LASH BLAST ONSET ATTACK ASSAULT DESCENT SISERARA SALIAUNCE

ONSTEAD ONSET FARMHOUSE HOMESTEAD

ONTARIO (CANAL IN —) TRENT RIDEAU
(CAPITAL OF —) TORONTO
(LAKE IN —) SIMCOE
(TOWN IN —) EMO GALT LONDON OTTAWA WINDSOR HAMILTON KINGSTON KITCHENER

ONTO ATOP ABOARD

ONTOGENY DEVELOPMENT

ONTOLOGY METAPHYSICS

ONUS DUTY LOAD BLAME BURDEN CHARGE WEIGHT INCUBUS

ONWARD AWAY AHEAD ALONG FORTH UPWARD FORTHON FORWARD TOWARDS FORERIGHT

ONYX ONIX NICOLO TECALI ONYCHIN JASPONYX SARDONYX
(MEXICAN —) ALABASTER

OOCYTE PROGAMETE GAMETOCYTE

OODLES HEAP LOTS MANY TONS RAFTS SCADS SLEWS LASHINGS SLITHERS ABUNDANCE

OOGONIUM NUCULE OOCYST OOGONE

OOLAK WOLLOCK

OOLITE PISOLITE ROESTONE

OOLONG TEA

OOMPH PEP VIGOR ENERGY

OOPAK TEA

OORALI CURARE

OORIAL SHA SHEEP URIAL

OOTHECA OVISAC

OOZE OZ BOG MUD SEW SOP DRIP EMIT LEAK MIRE SEEP SLEW SLOB SLUE WEEP EXUDE GLEET MARSH SLIME SWEAT WEEZE EXHALE SICKER SLEECH SLOUGH SLUDGE SQUASH SQUDGE STRAIN SCREEVE TEICHER TRANSUDE PERCOLATE
(— OUT) SEW SPEW SPUE
(PREF.) STACTO

OOZING WEEPY SQUDGY SEEPAGE SPEWING WEEPING

OOZY OASY SEEPY WASHY SLEECHY ULIGINOUS

OPACATE DIM DARKEN

OPACITY BODY
(— OF CORNEA) ONYX NEBULA LEUCOMA

OPAH CRAVO SUNFISH KINGFISH MARIPOSA MOONFISH

OPAL GEM NOBLE RESIN FIORITE GIRASOL HYALITE ISOPYRE GIRASOLE JASPOPAL MENILITE SEMIOPAL CACHOLONG GEYSERITE

OPALESCENT OPALED OPAL INF IRISATED

OPALEYE GREENFISH

OPAQUE DIM DARK DULL DENSE MUDDY SHADY THICK VAGUE OBTUSE STUPID CLOUDED OBSCURE ABSTRUSE EYESHADE

OPEN GO CAP DUP LAX OPE AIRY AJAR BARE FAIR FLUE FREE GIVE NEAR PERT UNDO VIDE AGAPE APERT BEGIN BLOWN BREAK BROAD BURST CHINK CLEAR CRACK FLARE FRANK FRESH JIMMY LANCE LOOSE MUSHY NAKED OVERT PLAIN RELAX SPALD SPLAT SPLAY START UNBAR UNPEG UNTIE UNZIP APPERT CANDID DIRECT ENTAME EXPAND EXPOSE FACIAL FORTHY GAPING HONEST LIABLE OUVERT PATENT PUBLIC SINGLE SPREAD UNBOLT UNDRAW UNFOLD UNFURL UNGLUE UNLOCK UNROLL UNSEAL UNSHUT UNSPAR UNSTOP UNTINE UNWINK UNWRAP VACANT ARTLESS BLOSSOM DISPART FIELDEN OBVIOUS OUTLINE SINCERE THROUGH UNCLOSE UNHINGE APPARENT COMMENCE DISCLOSE EXPLICIT EXTENDED INITIATE MANIFEST OUTFRONT PERVIOUS RESERATE UNFASTEN CHAMPAIGN OSTENSIBLE
(— AIR) ALFRESCO
(— AND CLEANSE) WILLOW
(— A VEIN) BROACH
(— CLOTH) SCUTCH
(— COUNTRY) VELDT WEALD
(— EYES OR LIPS) SEVER
(— THE WAY) INVITE PIONEER
(— TO PURSUIT) FAIR
(— UP) START DEVELOP DISPART DISCLOSE
(— VIOLENTLY) SPORT
(— WIDE) YAWN EXPAND STRETCH
(— WIDELY) GAPE
(BARELY —) AJAR
(FULLY —) WIDE AGAPE YAWNING
(HALF —) MID AJAR
(SLIGHLY —) AJAR
(TOO —) OVERBARISH

OPENBILL OPENBEAK

OPENED APPAUME ECHAPPE

OPENER KEY KNOB LATCH SESAME APERIENT
(— IN POKER) PAIR JACKS
(FURROW —) SHOE STUBRUNNER
(OYSTER —) HUSKER

OPENHANDED FREE LIBERAL GENEROUS RECEPTIVE

OPENING OS CUT EYE GAP YAT ANUS BOLE BORE DAWN DOOR DROP FENT FLUE GATE HOLE LOOP PASS PORE PORT PYLA RIFT RIMA SLAP SLIT SLOT SPAN VENT VOID YAWN YEAT BLEED BRACK BREAK CHASM CHINK CLEFT CROSS DEBUT GRILL HILUM INLET LIGHT MOUTH SCOOT SINUS START THIRL WIDTH ADITUS AVENUE BREACH CASING CHANCE GRILLE HIATUS INTAKE LACUNA MEATUS OILLET OUTLET PORTAL SLUICE SPREAD AIRPORT CREVASS CREVICE DISPLAY FISSURE ORIFICE OUTCAST SWALLET APERIENT APERTURE BUNGHOLE CREVASSE ENTRANCE OVERTURE PLUGHOLE SCISSURE TEASEHOLE
(— BELOW PENTHOUSE) GALLERY
(— FOR ESCAPE) MUSE MEUSE
(— FOR SLEEVE) SCYE
(— FROM SEA) INDRAFT
(— IN ANTHER) STOMIUM
(— IN DECK) SCUTTLE
(— IN EARTH) GROTTO CHIMNEY
(— IN EARTH) MOFETTE
(— IN EARTH) SWALLOW
(— IN FLOOR OR ROOF) HATCH SKYLIGHT
(— IN GARMENT) FENT ARMHOLE
(— IN LOCK TUMBLER) GATING
(— IN MINE) EYE ADIT RAISE SHAFT WINZE WINNING
(— IN MOLD) POUR
(— IN PICTURE FRAME) SIGHT
(— IN PILLAR OF COAL) JENKIN JUNKING
(— IN ROCK) GRIKE
(— IN SALMON TRAP) SLAP
(— IN SEA CAVE) GLOUP
(— IN SKIRT) PLACKET
(— IN SPONGE) APOPYLE
(— IN STAGE) DIP

(— IN TENNIS COURTS) GRILLE HAZARD GALLERY
(— IN TROUSERS) SPARE
(— IN VAULT) LUNET LUNETTE
(— IN WALL) BOLE DREAMHOLE
(— OF BALL) PROMENADE
(— OF BUD) ANTHESIS
(— OF EAR) BUR BURR
(— OF ESOPHAGUS) CARDIA
(— OF EYE) PUPIL
(— OF GEYSER) CRATER
(— OF HOCKEY GAME) BULLY
(— OF PRAIRIE) BAY
(— OF SHELL) GAPE
(— OF SKIRT) SPARE
(— OF STOMACH) PYLORUS
(— THROUGH BULWARKS) GANGWAY GUNPORT SCUPPER
(— TO ASH PIT) GLUT
(— WIDE) DEHISCENT
(— WITH LID) SCUTTLE
(— WITHOUT TREES) BLANK
(ARCHED —) ALCOVE ARCADE
(CHECKERS —) ALMA DYKE FIFE CROSS CENTER SOUTER BRISTOL GLASGOW PAISLEY WHILTER DEFIANCE SWITCHER
(CHESS —) DEBUT GAMBIT DEFENCE DEFENSE
(EROSIONAL —) FENSTER
(FISTULOUS —) SYRINX
(FUNNELLIKE —) CHOANA
(GRILL —) GUICHET
(JAR —) PITHOIGIA
(MOUTHLIKE —) STOMA OSTIUM
(NARROW —) VISTA
(SMALL —) PORE SLOT CHINK STOMA CRANNY EYELET LACUNA CATHOLE CREVICE DOGHOLE FORAMEN GUICHET PINHOLE QUARREL FENESTRA
(WINDOWLIKE —) SPLITE FENESTRA
(PREF.) APERTO CHASMO TREMATO
(SUFF.) PORA PORE PYL(E) STOMA(TA)(TE)(TOUS) STOME STOMI(A) STOMOUS STOMUM STOMY TREMA(TA)

OPENLY BARELY FREELY BROADLY FRANKLY PUBLICE ROUNDLY STRAIGHT
OPEN-MINDED LIBERAL
OPENMOUTHED GAPING GREEDY RAVENOUS CLAMOROUS
OPENNESS CANDOR FREEDOM PATENCY DAYLIGHT FRANKNESS ROUNDNESS
OPENWORK LATTICE TRACERY CAGEWORK FILIGREE FRETTING FRETWORK
OPEN-WORKED AJOURISE
OPERA AIDA FAUST LAKME MANON NORMA THAIS TOSCA BOHEME CARMEN DAPHNE ERNANI LOUISE MIGNON OTELLO RIENZI SALOME ELEKTRA FIDELIO BURLETTA FALSTAFF IOLANTHE LOKACOLO PARSIFAL TRAVIATA WALKYRIE LOHENGRIN PAGLIACCI RHEINGOLD RIGOLETTO SIEGFRIED TROVATORE
(— DIVISION) SCENA

(— GLASS) GLASS JUMELLE LORGNET LORGNETTE
(— HAT) GIBUS CLAQUE
(— SONG) ARIA
(— STAR) DIVA
(COMIC —) BUFFA BURLETTA
(HORSE —) WESTERN
(KIND OF —) SOAP
(SOAP —) SUDSER
(SPANISH —) ZARZUELA
(TV OR RADIO —) SOAP
(16TH CENTURY —) PASTORALE
OPERA GLASSES JUMELLE LORGNETTE
OPERANT EFFICIENT OPERATIVE
OPERATE GO ACT CUT MAN RUN PUSH TAKE WORK DRIVE MULES STEER AFFECT EFFECT MANAGE CONDUCT PROCEED FUNCTION
(— BY HAND) MANIPULATE
(— GUNS) SERVE
(— MINE) FLUSH
(— MOTOR VEHICLE) VROOM
(— RADIO) BLOOP
(CAUSE TO —) POWERUP
OPERATIC LYRIC
OPERATING GOING ATWORK
(FULLY —) AFLOAT
OPERATION DEED PLAY BLAST ACTION AGENCY EFFECT OSTOMY VIRTUE PROCESS CREATION EXERCISE FACELIFT FUNCTION PRACTICE EXECUTION INFLUENCE PROCESSUS
(ARITHMETIC —) PROOF
(FRAUDULENT —) SCAM
(MILITARY —S) CAMPAIGN
(REGULAR —S) ECONOMY
(SURGICAL —) CECOPEXY
(UNDERCOVER —) STING
(SUFF.) (— FOR OPENING) STOMY
OPERATIONAL LIVE
OPERATIONS
(SUFF.) ICS
OPERATIVE EYE HAND ARTIST LIVING ARTISAN OUVRIER MECHANIC DETECTIVE EFFECTIVE
OPERATOR DEL DOER AGENT BAKER DEWER NABLA PILOT QUACK BEAMER BILLER BOLTER BUMPER BUSMAN CAPPER DEALER DEGGER DRIVER DUNGER DYADIC GAGGER JOCKEY KICKER RAGGER TRADER AVIATOR BREAKER CENTRAL CHEESER DENTIST FACIENT GLASSER JOGGLER MANAGER OPERANT SURGEON IDENTITY MOTORMAN CONDUCTOR
(INFERIOR —) PLUG
(LOGICAL —) NOT
(RADIO —) HAM CBER SPARKS SPARKER
(TRUCK —) GIPSY GYPSY
(SUFF.) STER STRESS
OPERCULUM LID FLAP ONYCHA OPERCLE APTYCHUS COVERING EYESTONE MANDIBLE
OPERETTA ZARZUELA
OPEROSE BUSY IRKSOME DILIGENT LABORIOUS
OPHELIA (BROTHER OF —) LAERTES
(FATHER OF —) POLONIUS

OPHELTES (FATHER OF —) LYCURGUS
(NURSE OF —) HYPSIPYLE
OPHIDIAN ASP EEL SNAKE CONGER REPTILE SERPENT
OPHIR (FATHER OF —) JOKTAN
OPHITE CAINIAN CAINITE
OPHIUROID ARGUS SANDSTAR
OPHRAH (FATHER OF —) MEONOTHAI
OPHTHALMOLOGIST OCULIST
OPIATE DOPE DRUG HEMP DWALE OPIUM DEADEN ANODINE HYPNOTIC NARCOTIC SEDATIVE DORMITARY PAREGORIC SOPORIFIC
OPIFICER OPIFEX WORKMAN ARTIFICER
OPINE DEEM JUDGE THINK PONDER BELIEVE SUPPOSE OPINIATE
OPINION CRY EYE MOT BOOK DOXY FAME IDEA MIND VIEW WEEN DOGMA FANCY FUTWA GUESS HEART INPUT SENSE SIGHT TENET THINK VARDI VARDY VOICE ADVICE ASSENT BELIEF DEVICE DICTUM ESTEEM GROUND NOTION REPUTE SCHISM CENSURE CONCEIT CONCEPT CONSENT COUNSEL DIANOIA FEELING HOLDING MEASURE SEEMING THINKSO THOUGHT TROWING VERDICT DECISION DOCTRINE JUDGMENT SUFFRAGE PREJUDICE SENTIMENT PERSUASION
(COLLECTION OF —S) SYMPOSIUM
(EXAGGERATED —) BIGHEAD
(EXPRESSION OF —) VOTE
(FAVORABLE —) BROO ESTEEM
(MOHAMMEDAN —) FUTWA
(SET OF PROFESSED —S) CREDO
(UNORTHODOX —) HERESY
(WRONG —) CACODOXY
(PREF.) DOXO
(SUFF.) DOX(Y)
OPINIONATED DOGMATIC CONCEITED OBSTINATE PRAGMATIC
OPINIONATIVE ENTETE
O PIONEERS (AUTHOR OF —) CATHER
(CHARACTER IN —) LOU CARL EMIL IVAR FRANK MARIE OSCAR AMEDEE BERGSON SHABATA TOVESKY ALEXANDRA LINDSTRUM
OPIUM HOP MUD DOPE DRUG OPIE POST CHANDU CHANDOO MECONIUM TOXICANT
(— ALKALOID) CODEIN CODEINE MORPHINE NARCOTIN NARCOTINE PAPAVERIN
(— POPPY) NEPENTHE
(OF —) THEBAIC
(RESIDUE IN — PIPE) YENSHEE
(TINCTURE OF —) LAUDANUM
(PREF.) MECON(O) OPIO
OPIUMISM THEBAISM
OPOSSUM QUICA YAPOK POSSUM YAPOCK MARMOSE OYAPOCK SARIGUE VULPINE MARSUPIAL PHILANDER TACUACINE
(— SHRIMP) MYSID MYSOID
(FAMOUS —) POGO

OPPONENT FOE ANTI ENEMY PARTY RIVAL ALOGIAN NEMESIS OPPOSER ADVERSARY ASSAILANT
(— OF GOV CLINTON) BUCKTAIL
(— OF WAR) PEACENIK
(BOORISH —) BOEOTIAN
(FORMIDABLE —) TIGER
(IMAGINARY —) WINDMILL
OPPORTUNE FIT PAT HAPPY LUCKY READY TIMELY APROPOS FITTING TIMEFUL SUITABLE FAVORABLE
OPPORTUNELY TIMELY APROPOS HAPPILY
OPPORTUNIST CREEPER
OPPORTUNISTIC SHUFFLING
OPPORTUNITY GO MAY OPE SEL EASE HENT MEAN MINT ROOM SELE SHOT TIDE TIME SIGHT SLANT SPACE ACCESS CHANCE SEASON SQUEAK LEISURE OPENING RESPITE VANTAGE APPROACH FACILITY OCCASION ADVANTAGE
(— FOR ACTION) OPENING
(— OF ACTIVITY) SCOPE
(— TO PROCEED) WAY
(FAVORABLE —) SHOW TIME
OPPOSE PIT VIE WAR BUCK COPE DEFY FACE HEAD MEET NOSE STEM WARN WEAR ARGUE BLOCK CHECK CLASH CROSS FIGHT FRONT OCCUR REBEL REBUT REPEL BATTLE BREAST COMBAT DEFEND NAYSAY OBJECT OBTEND OPPUGN REPUGN RESIST THWART WITHER CONTEST COUNTER GAINSAY OBVIATE REVERSE WITHSET CONFLICT CONFRONT CONTRARY CONTRAST FRONTIER OBSTRUCT TRAVERSE ENCOUNTER WITHSTAND ANTAGONIZE
(— BY ARGUMENT) REBUT
(— ONE IN AUTHORITY) REBEL DEFORCE
OPPOSED ANTI ALIEN AVERSE ADVERSE AGAINST COUNTER HOSTILE CONTRARY ABHORRENT ANTARCTIC REPUGNANT
(PERSISTENTLY —) RENITENT
OPPOSER GAINSAYER
OPPOSING RENITENT RELUCTANT
(PREF.) COUNTER
OPPOSITE TO ANENT POLAR ACROSS ANENST AVERSE FACING WITHER ADVERSE COUNTER FORNENT INVERSE OBVIOUS REVERSE ANTIPODE CONTRARY CONTRAST CONVERSE ANTIPODAL REPUGNANT RECIPROCAL
(— MIDDLE OF SHIP'S SIDE) ABEAM
(— OF TRUTH) DEVIL
(— THE ALTAR) WEST
(— THE SUN) ANTISOLAR
(PREF.) ANTI ENANTIO
(DO THE —) DIS
OPPOSITION CON FLAK ATILT CLASH FLACK STOUR STATIC SYZYGY THWART DISCORD TENSION CLASHING CONTRAST DISTANCE OBSTACLE POLARITY ANIMOSITY COLLISION HOSTILITY RENITENCY
(— TO GOD) ANTITHEISM

(ELECTRICAL —) IMPEDANCE
(PREF.) (IN —) CONTRA
OPPRESS SIT HOLD LADE LOAD
PEIS RACK RAPE RIDE SWAY THEW
CROWD CRUSH GRIND GRIPE
HEAVY PEISE POISE PRESS WEIGH
WRONG BETOIL BURDEN DEFOIL
DEFOUL EXTORT HARASS
HARROW NIDDER NITHER RAVISH
SUBDUE THREAT AFFLICT DEPRESS
INGRATE OVERLAY REPRESS
SQUEEZE TRAMPLE CONFRONT
DISTRESS ENCUMBER PRESSURE
SUPPRESS OVERPOWER
OVERTHROW OVERWEIGH
OVERWHELM
(— WITH DREAD) HAGRIDE
(— WITH HEAT) SWELTER
OPPRESSED SERVILE
OPPRESSION ROD GRIPE PRESS
BURDEN THRALL MIZRAIM
DULLNESS PRESSURE EXTORTION
GRIEVANCE LASSITUDE
OPPRESSIVE HOT DIRE DOWY
HARD CLOSE DOWIE FAINT HARSH
HEAVY BITTER LEADEN SCREWY
SEVERE SMUDGY SULTRY TORRID
URGENT WEIGHT ONEROUS
SLAVISH GRIEVOUS GRINDING
RIGOROUS
OPPRESSIVELY STRAIT
OPPRESSIVENESS LANGUOR
OPPRESSOR CSAR CZAR NERO
TSAR TZAR EGLON TYRANT
INCUBUS
OPPROBRIUM ENVY ABUSE ODIUM
SCORN SHAME INFAMY INSULT
CALUMNY DISDAIN OFFENSE
SCANDAL DISGRACE DISHONOR
REPROACH CONTUMELY
OPS (ASSOCIATE OF —) CONSUS
(CONSORT OF —) SATURN
(DAUGHTER OF —) CERES
(FESTIVAL OF —) OPALIA
(PERSONIFICATION OF —) FAUNA
TERRA TELLUS
OPT CULL PICK WISH ELECT
CHOOSE DECIDE OPTATE SELECT
(— ABRUPTLY) PLUMP
OPTIC EYE OCULAR VISUAL
OPTICAL VISIBLE
(— APPARATUS) LENS GLASS
ALIDAD ALIDADE OPTOMETER
PERISCOPE TELESCOPE
(— DEVICE ON RIFLE) SNIPERSCOPE
OPTIMIST POLLYANNA UTOPIANIST
OPTIMISTIC GLAD ROSY SUNNY
JOYOUS UPBEAT BULLISH
HOPEFUL ROSEATE EUPEPTIC
SANGUINE EXPECTANT
OPTION UP CALL DOWN CHOICE
SPREAD REFUSAL STRADDLE
PRIVILEGE
OPTIONAL ELECTIVE VOLUNTARY
PERMISSIVE
OPULENCE LUXE
OPULENT FAT LUSH RICH WELI
AMPLE FLUSH PLUSH SHOWY
LAVISH MONEYED PROFUSE
WEALTHY ABUNDANT AFFLUENT
LUXURIANT PLENTIFUL
SUMPTUOUS

OPUS WORK ETUDE STUDY
(OVERLABORED —) LUCUBRATION
OQUASSA QUASKY
OR NE ARE AUT ERE ORE GOLD
OSSIA OTHER TOPAZ EITHER
YELLOW
ORACHE SALTBUSH GREASEWOOD
ORACLE SEER TRIP SIBYL TRIPOD
TRIPOS DIVINER AUTOPHONE
ORACULAR OTIC VATIC ORPHIC
DELPHIC VATICAL DELPHIAN
PYTHONIC PROPHETIC
ORAL ALOUD PAROL VOCAL
BUCCAL PAROLE SONANT SPOKEN
VERBAL UTTERED UNWRITTEN
NONCUPATIVE
ORALE FANON
ORANGE KING MOCK CERES CHILE
CHILI CHINO FLAME GENIP HEDGE
JAFFA NAVEL OSAGE TENNE
AURORA BODOCK BRAZIL COPPER
MIKADO NAVAHO SUNTAN TEMPLE
TITIAN UVALHA COWSLIP FLORIDA
LEATHER MACLURA NARTJIE
PAPRIKA PONCEAU PUMPKIN
RANGPUR SEVILLE TANGELO
TANGIER BERGAMOT BIGARADE
CHINOTTI CLAYBANK FLAMINGO
HONEYDEW JACINTHE MANDARIN
MARATHON MOROCCAN
POMANDER SUNBURST VALENCIA
BUCCANEER CARNELIAN
PERSIMMON TANGERINE
(— BLOSSOM INGREDIENT) GIN
(— GRASS) KNITWEED PINEWEED
(— HAWKWEED) FIREWEED
HIERACIUM
(— MEMBRANE) ZEST
(— MILKWORT) CANDYWEED
(— PIECE) LITH SEGMENT
(— ROCKFISH) FLIOMA
(— SEED) PIP
(— TREE) SATSUMA
(BROWNISH —) SPICE
(LARGE —) KING
(MOCK —) SERINGA
(OSAGE —) HEDGE BODOCK
(SOUR —) CURACAO BIGARADE
CHINOTTO
(SWEET —) CHINA CHINO
(YELLOW —) SAFFRON
ORANGEBIRD TANAGER
ORANGE HAWKWEED
PAINTBRUSH
ORANGELEAF KARAMU
ORANGEMAN MARKSMAN
ORANGEWOOD OSAGE
ORANG LAUT BAJAU
ORANGUTAN APE MIAS ORANG
PONGO SATYR SATIRE SATURY
PRIMATE SALTIER SATYRUS
WOODMAN WOODSMAN
ORAON KURUKH
ORARION STOLE
ORATE PLEAD SPEAK SPIEL SPOUT
ADDRESS DECLAIM LECTURE
BLOVIATE HARANGUE DISCOURSE
SPEECHIFY
ORATION EULOGY HESPED
SERMON ADDRESS CONCION
HARANGUE SUASORIA OLYNTHIAC
PANEGYRIC PHILIPPIC
(— OF CICERO) PHILIPPIC

(FUNERAL —) ELOGE ELOGY
MONODY ELOGIUM ENCOMIUM
ORATOR RHETOR DEMAGOG
SPEAKER STUMPER CICERONE
BOANERGES DEMAGOGUE
PLAINTIFF SPOKESMAN
ORATORICAL ELOQUENT
RHETORICAL
ORATORIO ELIJAH RORATORIO
ORATORY CHAPEL SACRARY
ORACULUM SPEAKING ELOCUTION
ELOQUENCE PROSEUCHE
(EXAGGERATED —) RHETORIC
ORB EYE SUN BALL MOON STAR
EARTH GLOBE MOUND ORBIT
CIRCLE PLANET SPHERE CIRCUIT
ENCLOSE ENCIRCLE SURROUND
FIRMAMENT
ORBED LUNAR ROUND GLOBATE
ORBIT AUGE PATH APSIS CYCLE
TRACK CIRCLE SOCKET SPHERE
CIRCUIT ELLIPSE EYEHOLE
ECCENTRIC
(POINT IN —) APSIS APOGEE EPIGEE
SYZYGY PERIGEE
ORC OGRE ORCA GIANT WHALE
GRAMPUS
ORCHARD HOLT TOPE ARBOR
GROVE ARBOUR GARDEN HUERTA
OLIVET VERGER ARBUSTUM
FRUITERY PEACHERY POMARIUM
SUGARBUSH
(— GRASS) DOGFOOT COCKSFOOT
ORCHESTRA BAND GROUP CHAPEL
CAPELLE CONSORT GAMELAN
KAPELLE ENSEMBLE GAMELANG
SYMPHONY SINFONIETTA
PHILHARMONIC
(— BELLS) GLOCKENSPIEL
(— CIRCLE) PARQUET PARTERRE
(SECTION OF —) BRASS WINDS
WOODS STRINGS WOODWINDS
PERCUSSION
ORCHESTRATE SCORE ARRANGE
COMPOSE
ORCHESTRION HARMONICON
APOLLONICON
ORCHID FAAM FAHAM PETAL
VANDA CYMBID DUFOIL LAELIA
PURPLE AERIDES ANGULOA
BOATLIP CALYPSO CULLION
FLYWORT LYCASTE POGONIA
VANILLA ARETHUSA CALANTHE
DENDROBE GYNANDER LABELLUM
ONCIDIUM RAMSHEAD SATYRION
CORALROOT HABENARIA
PUTTYROOT TWAYBLADE
SNAKEMOUTH
(KIND OF —) VANDA
ORCHIS CROWTOE CROWFOOT
CRAKEFEET
ORDAIN LAW PUT DEEM DOOM
LOOK MAKE SEND WILL WITE
ALLOT ENACT JAPAN ORDER
SHAPE WIELD WRITE DECREE
PRIEST ADJUDGE APPOINT
ARRANGE BEHIGHT COMMAND
DESTINE DICTATE FORTUNE
INSTALL PREPARE PRESCRIBE
ORDEAL FIRE GAFF TEST AGONY
TRIAL CALVARY GAUNTLET
(— TREE) AKAZGA TANGHIN
TANGUIN

**ORDEAL OF RICHARD FEVEREL
(AUTHOR OF —)** MEREDITH
(CHARACTER IN —) TOM LUCY
BERRY CLARE MOUNT ADRIAN
AUSTIN BLAIZE CAROLA HARLEY
RIPTON FEVEREL RICHARD
BAKEWELL THOMPSON GRANDISON
DESBOROUGH MONTFALCON
ORDER BAN BID ILK RAY SAY TAX
BOON CALL CASE CHIT FIAT FORM
ORDO RANK RULE SAND SECT
STOP SUIT TELL TIFF TRIM WILL
WORD ALIGN ARRAY CHIME CLASS
DIGHT EDICT GENUS GRADE GUIDE
HAVOC PRESS QUIET RANGE SHIFT
STATE TABO WHACK ASSIGN
AVAUNT BEHEST BILLET CEDULA
CHARGE COSMOS CURFEW
DECREE DEGREE DEMAND DIKTAT
DIRECT ENJOIN FIRMAN FOLLOW
GRAITH HOOKUM INDENT KILTER
MANAGE METHOD NATURE
ORDAIN POLICE POTENT SERIES
SETTLE SYNTAX SYSTEM ADJUDGE
ARRANGE BESPEAK BIDDING
BOOKING COMMAND COMPOSE
DISPOSE EMBARGO FLOATER
MANDATE PRECEPT PROCESS
SOCIETY CATEGORY KODASHIM
METHODIZE ORDINANCE
PRESCRIBE
(— BACK) REMAND
(— OF ANGELS) CHOIR QUIRE
MIGHTS THRONES DOMINIONS
PRINCIPALITIES
(— OF BATTLE) BATTALIA
(— OF BELLS) CHANGE
(— OF COURT) SIST VACATUR
(— OF CRUSTACEANS) ISOPODA
(OFF) TURN
(— OF HOLY BEINGS) HIERARCHY
(— OF SUCCESSION) SEQUENCE
(— OF WORSHIP) AGODUM
(— TOBACCO LEAF) CASE
(— TO LEVY MONEY) PRECEPT
(— TO RETURN) RECALL
(CIVIL —) EUNOMY
(COSMIC —) TAO RITA
(GOOD —) EUTAXY
(IN —) SOAS
(KIND OF —) GAG
(KNIGHTHOOD —) DANNEBROG
(LACKING —) AMISS MESSY MUSSY
ROUGH CHAOTIC UNKEMPT
CONFUSED
(LEGAL —) SIST STET WRIT
DAYWRIT SUMMONS SENTENCE
SUBPOENA
(LOWER — OF MAN) ALALUS
(MARCHING —S) ROUTE
(MINOR CHURCH —) BENET
(MONASTIC —) SAMGHA SANGHA
ACOEMETI
(PROPER —) TRAIN
(RECURRENT —) ROTATION
(TAKE —S) WAITRESS
(TRAIN —) FLIMSY
(TURKISH —) MEDJIDIE
(UNIVERSAL —) KIND
(WRITTEN —) CHECK DRAFT BILLET
DRAUGHT
(PREF.) (REVERSE —) OB

(SUFF.) TACTIC TAXIS TAXY
(— OF ANIMALS) INI
ORDERED BANDBOX BESPOKE
REGULAR SCRAPED COHERENT
(WELL —) TRIM
ORDERLINESS METHOD SYSTEM
CLARITY DECORUM
ORDERLY AIDE DULY NEAT PEON
RULY SNOD TIDY TRIM CRISP
SOWAR SUWAR BATMAN BURSCH
COSMIC FORMAL MODEST
ORDENE GRADELY REGULAR
SHAPELY DECOROUS GALLOPER
GRAITHLY OBEDIENT PEACEABLE
SHIPSHAPE
ORDINANCE LAW DOOM FIAT RITE
BYLAW EDICT ASSIZE DECREE
RECESS CONTROL MANDATE
SETNESS STATUTE WORKING
DECRETUM JUDICIAL REGIMENT
TAKKANAH DIRECTION
ORDINANT DIHELY DIHELIOS
DIHELIUM
ORDINARY LAY LOW SOS BEND
FESS LALA MEAN PALE PALL RUCK
BANAL CHIEF CROSS NOMIC PLAIN
PROSE USUAL CANTON COMMON
FILLET FLANCH MODERN NORMAL
PAIRLE SIMPLE VULGAR AVERAGE
MUNDANE NATURAL PROSAIC
ROUTINE SALTIRE SAUTIER TRIVIAL
VANILLA VULGATE EVERYDAY
FAMILIAR HABITUAL MEDIOCRE
MIDDLING PLEBEIAN RUMTYTOO
WORKADAY QUOTIDIAN
SHAKEFORK
ORDINATE ORDER ORDAIN
APPOINT ORDERLY REGULAR
MODERATE TEMPERATE
ORDNANCE LAW ARMS GUNS
ARMOR ORGUE FALCON MINION
PETARD PEDRERO RABINET
SERPENT WEAPONS BASILISK
PETERERO ARTILLERY
ORDO ORDER ALMANAC DIRECTORY
ORDURE
(PREF.) SCAT(O) SCORI
ORE (ALSO SEE MINERAL) TIN CHAT
DISH DRAG FELL GOLD IRON LEAD
MINE POST PULP ROCK CRAZE
CRUDE FAVOR GLORY GRACE
HONOR MANTO MERCY METAL
PRILL COPPER CUPRITE FLOATER
RESPECT SEAWEED SMEDDUM
URANITE CLEMENCY KNOCKING
CARBONATE REVERENCE
(— CRUSHER) DOLLY
(— DEPOSIT) LODE SCRIN BONANZA
(— LAYER) SEAM STOPE
(— LOADING PLATFORM) PLAT
(— MASS) SQUAT
(— NOT DRESSED) WORK
(— WITH STONE ADHERING) CHAT
CHATS
(BEST —) CROP
(BROKEN —) DIRT
(CONCENTRATED —) MIDDLINGS
(COPPER —) BORNITE HORNITE
ATACAMITE MALACHITE
(CRUDE —) HEADS
(CRUSHED —) PULP SCHLICH
(CUBE —) SIDERITE
(EARTHY-LOOKING —) PACO

(HORSEFLESH —) BORNITE
(IMPURE —) SPEISS HALVANS
(IRON —) OCHER OCHRE MINION
IRONMAN LIMNITE MINETTE
OLIGIST TURGITE HEMATITE
LIMONITE SIDERITE TACONITE
BLACKBAND JACUTINGA
(LEAD —) BOOZE GALENA
ARQUIFOUX
(LUMP OF —) HARDHEAD
(MANGANESE —) WAD WADD
(MERCURY —) GRANZA CINNABAR
(SOLID —) RIB
(TIN —) ROWS CRAZE SCOVE WHITS
FLORAN TINSTUFF
(URANIUM —) COFFINITE
(WORTHLESS —) SLAG DROSS
MATTE
(ZINC —) SMITHSONITE
OREAD PERI NYMPH

OREGON

CAPITAL: SALEM
COLLEGE: REED PACIFIC LINFIELD
PORTLAND WILLAMETTE
COUNTY: LINN CROOK CURRY
WASCO CLATSOP KLAMATH
MALHEUR WALLOWA YAMHILL
UMATILLA
INDIAN: ALSEA MODOC WASCO
CAYUSE CHETCO KUITSH TENINO
KLAMATH TAKELMA YAQUINA
LAKE: ABERT WALDO CRATER
HARNEY MCNARY KLAMATH
MALHEUR
MOUNTAIN: HOOD WALKER
WILSON ELKHORN GRIZZLY
JACKASS RAINIER TIDBITS
MOUNTAIN RANGE: BLUE COAST
CASCADE
RIVER: ROGUE IMNAHA OWYHEE
POWDER UMPQUA BLITZEN
KLAMATH SILVIES COLUMBIA
DESCHUTES
STATE BIRD: MEADOWLARK
STATE FLOWER: GRAPE
STATE NICKNAME: BEAVER SUNSET
WEBFOOT VALENTINE
STATE TREE: FIR
TOWN: BEND MORO VALE NYSSA
CONDON EUGENE FOSSIL
MADRAS ASTORIA HEPPNER
COQUILLE PORTLAND CORVALLIS

OREGON TRAIL (AUTHOR OF —)
PARKMAN
(CHARACTER IN —) SHAW HENRY
QUINCY FRANCIS PARKMAN
CHATILLON DESLAURIERS
OREN (FATHER OF —) JERAHMEEL
ORE-PRODUCING QUICK
ORESTES (COMPANION OF —)
PYLADES
(FATHER OF —) AGAMEMNON
(FRIEND OF —) PYLADES
(MOTHER OF —) CLYTEMNESTRA
(SISTER OF —) ELECTRA IPHIGENIA
(WIFE OF —) HERMIONE
ORGAN CUP GILL LIMB PART CHELA
FLOAT GREAT HEART MEANS
PAPER REGAL SERRA ELATER
FEEDER FEELER HAPTOR MEDIUM
SPLEEN SUCKER CLASPER

CONSOLE JOURNAL ARMATURE
EFFECTOR ISOGRAFT MAGAZINE
MELODEON MELODICA
MYCETOME OOGONIUM
EQUIPMENT HARMONIUM
NEWSPAPER PORTATIVE
(— GALLERY) LOFT
(— OF HEARING) EAR
(— OF SCORPION) PECTEN
(— OF SENSE) SENSE SENSORY
(— OF SIGHT) EYE
(— OF SILKWORM) FILATOR
(— OF SPIDER) CRIBELLUM
SPINNERET
(— OF TOUCH) TACTOR TACTUS
(— PIPE) REED FLUTE SCHWEGEL
(— STOP) ECHO HARP OBOE SEXT
TUBA VIOL ACUTA DOLCE FLUTE
GAMBA ORAGE QUINT TENTH VIOLA
BIFARA CURTAL CYMBAL DECIMA
DULCET FUGARA GEDACT NASARD
OCTAVE SCHARF TIERCE TROMBA
BASSOON BOMBARD BOURDON
CELESTE CLARION CREMONA
DOLCIAN DOUBLET DULCIAN
FAGOTTO GEDECKT MELODIA
PICCOLO POSAUNE SERPENT
TERTIAN TRUMPET TWELFTH
VIOLINA BOMBARDE CARILLON
CLARINET DIAPASON DIAPHONE
DULCIANA GEMSHORN REGISTER
TENOROON TROMBONE
WALDHORN BOMBARDON
CORNOPEAN DOUBLETTE
HARMONICA PRINCIPAL
SAXOPHONE CLARABELLA
(— VIBRATO) TREMOLO
(ADHESIVE —) SUCKER
(BRISTLELIKE —) SETA
(CHINESE —) SANG CHENG
(CIRCUS —) CALLIOPE
(HAND —) SERINETTE
(INTROMITTENT —) VERGE
(KIND OF —) REED
(OLFACTORY —) NOSE
(PLANT'S —) HOLDFAST
(PORTABLE —) REGAL
(RESPIRATORY —) LUNG
(SMALL —) REGAL
(STINGING —) NEMATOCYST
(SWIMMING —) OAR CTENE
(VOCAL — OF BIRDS) SYRINX
(WASTE —) KIDNEY
(PREF.) (INTERNAL —) VISCER(I)(O)
ORGANELLE LYSOSOME
ORGANIC VITAL INBORN NATURAL
INHERENT
ORGANISM WOG BODY ECAD
GERM GUEST PLANT AEROBE
ANIMAL EMBRYO SYSTEM
DIPLONT DISEASE MACHINE
PLANONT SUSCEPT HEMAMEBA
PATHOGEN PLANKTER MESOPHILE
POLYMORPH
(— CHARACTERISTIC) MIXIS
(COLD-BLOODED —) POIKILOTHERM
(COMPOUND —) STOCK
(FOSSIL —) EOZOON
(MINUTE —) AMEBA MONAD SPORE
(MODIFIED —) ECAD
(PELAGIC —S) NEKTON
(POLITICAL —) LEVIATHAN
(SIMPLE —) MONAD

(SMALL AIRBORNE —S)
AEROPLANKTON
(PL.) BENTHON BENTHOS
HAYSEED NEUSTON PLEUSTON
(PREF.) BIO ONT(O)
(SUFF.) ACEAN ONT PHORA
(SIMPLE —) MONAS
ORGANIZATION ART DIG ITO CLUD
FIRM KLAN CADRE FIDAC FORUM
HOUSE MAFIA SETUP AUMAGA
CHURCH OUTFIT SURVEY SYSTEM
CHARITY COMPANY CONCERN
DEMOLAY ECONOMY GIDEONS
MENORAH SOCIETY CONGRESS
PATRONAGE STRUCTURE
(— OF ACTORS) COMPANY
(— OF DEALERS) AUCTION
(— OF EXPERIENCE) SCHEMA
(— WITH MANY BRANCHES)
OCTOPUS
(ARMY —) LANDSTORM
(AUXILIARY —) AID SYNODICAL
(COLLEGE —) FRAT ALUMNA
ALUMNI ALUMNUS SORORITY
(COMMUNIST —) COMECON
(HARMONIOUS —)
ORCHESTRATION
(HEALTH —) HMO
(JEWISH —) ITO MENORAH
(MARDI GRAS —) KREWE
(MUSICAL —) BAND COMBO
CAPELLE KAPELLE ENSEMBLE
ORCHESTRA
(POLICE —) GESTAPO
(POLITICAL —) PARTY VEREIN
HETAERIA HETAIRIA APPARATUS
(SAMOAN —) AUMAGA
(SECRET —) WOW BPOE ELKS
MOOSE MASONS MIDEWIN
(SOCIAL —) POLICE
(WAR VETERANS —) AVC DAV GAR
SAR VFW FIDAC AMVETS
(WOMEN'S —) DAR WAF WRC
WCTU SORORITY
(YOUTH —) KOMSOMOL
ORGANIZE FORM EDIFY FOUND
MODEL ORDER RALLY DESIGN
EMBODY ARRANGE MODULIZE
REGIMENT UNIONIZE BLUEPRINT
INSTITUTE INTEGRATE STRUCTURE
COORDINATE
ORGANIZED FORMED ORGANIC
TOGETHER
(BADLY —) INCONDITE
ORGANIZER PROMOTER
ORGANZA GAZAR
ORGIASTIC BACCHIC SATURNALIAN
ORGY LARK RITE ROMP BINGE
REVEL SPREE FROLIC SHINDY
REVELRY WASSAIL CAROUSAL
CEREMONY SATURNALIA
(PL.) ORGIACS DEBAUCHERIES
ORIANA (FATHER OF —) LISUARTE
(HUSBAND OF —) MIRABEL
(LOVER OF —) AMADIS
ORIBI OUREBI ANTELOPE BLEEKBOK
PALEBUCK
ORIEL BAY CHAPEL DORMER
RECESS WINDOW BALCONY
GALLERY MIRADOR PORTICO
CORRIDOR
ORIENT DAWN EAST ADAPT BUILD
PEARL PLACE SHEEN ADJUST

LEVANT LOCATE LUSTER RISING GLOWING INCLINE RADIANT SUNRISE LUSTROUS SPARKLING

ORIENTAL ASIAN PEARL BRIGHT INDIAN ORTIVE RISING EASTERN SHINING INDOGEAN LUSTROUS PELLUCID PRECIOUS BRILLIANT LEVANTINE

ORIENTATION ASPECT PHORIA STRIKE COLORING LOCALITY

ORIFICE BUNG HOLE PORE PORT VENT INLET MOUTH STOMA TREMA BLOWER CAVITY OUTLET RICTUS SIPHON THROAT CHIMNEY EARHOLE FORAMEN OPENING OSCULUM OSTIOLE APERTURE FUMAROLE INTROITUS
(— IN VOLCANIC REGION) FUMAROLE
(— OF INFUNDIBULUM) LURA
(BREATHING —) SPIRACLE
(VOLCANIC —) BLOWER
(PREF.) TREMATO
(— OF STOMACH) PYLOR(O)
(SUFF.) PYL(E) TREMA(TA)

ORIGANUM ORGANY MARJORAM ORGAMENT

ORIGILLE (FATHER OF —) MONODANTE
(LOVER OF —) GRIFONE
(SISTER OF —) BRANDIMARTE

ORIGIN NEE GERM KIND RISE ROOT SEED BIRTH CAUSE RADIX START STOCK FATHER GROWTH NATURE PARENT SOURCE SPRING EDITION GENESIS LINEAGE UPSTART NASCENCE UPSPRING BEGINNING INCEPTION OFFSPRING PARENTAGE PROVENANCE
(— ON EARTH) EPIGENE
(FOREIGN —) ECDEMIC
(POINT OF —) POLE
(PREF.) (ANCIENT —) PALAE(O) PALAI(O) PALE(O)
(SUFF.) GENY

ORIGINAL NEW HOME SEED FIRST FRESH NOVEL PRIME STOCK FONTAL MASTER MOTHER NATIVE PRIMAL PRIMER SAMPLE PIONEER PRIMARY RADICAL SEMINAL CREATION NASCENCY PRISTINE AUTHENTIC AUTOGRAPH BEGINNING INVENTIVE OFFSPRING PRIMITIVE
(NOT —) DERIVED
(PREF.) ARCH(AE)(AEO)(E)(EO)(I)

ORIGINALITY INGENUITY

ORIGINATE COIN COME DATE GROW HEAD MAKE MOVE OPEN REAR RISE SIRE ARISE BEGIN BIRTH BREED CAUSE ENDOW FOUND HATCH RAISE START AUTHOR CREATE DERIVE DESIGN DEVISE FATHER INVENT PARENT SPRING CAUSATE DESCEND EMANATE PIONEER PROCEED PRODUCE COMMENCE CONCEIVE CONTRIVE DISCOVER GENERATE INITIATE INSTITUTE

ORIGINATION MAKING DESCENT GENESIS BREEDING ORIGINAL COSMOGONY ETYMOLOGY

ORIGINATOR AUTHOR FATHER

CREATOR INVENTOR GENERATOR PROGENITOR

ORIOLE PIROL BUNYAH LARIOT LORIOT CACIQUE FIGBIRD PEABIRD FIREBIRD GOLDBIRD HANGBIRD HANGNEST TROUPIAL

ORION RIGEL ALGEBAR
(BELT OF —) ELLWAND
(FATHER OF —) HYRIEUS POSEIDON
(GUIDE OF —) CEDALION
(HOUND OF —) ARATUS
(SLAYER OF —) ARTEMIS

ORITHYIA (DAUGHTER OF —) CHIONE CLEOPATRA
(FATHER OF —) ERECHTHEUS
(MOTHER OF —) PRAXITHEA
(SON OF —) ZETES CALAIS

ORKNEY ISLANDS (CAPITAL OF —) KIRKWALL
(ISLAND OF —) HOY POMONA ROUSAY SANDAY STRONSAY

ORLANDO (BELOVED OF —) ROSALIND

ORLE ORLET BORDER FILLET WREATH BEARING CHAPLET TRESSURE

ORLOP DECK ARLOUP

ORMENUS (FATHER OF —) CERCAPHUS
(SON OF —) AMYNTOR

ORMER ARALONE

ORMOLU GILT GOLD ALLOY BRASS VARNISH

ORNAMENT BOB DUB FLY FOB GAY JOY PIN POT TAG TEE TOY URN BALL BOSS CURL CUSP DICE ETCH FALL FRET FROG GAUD GEAR HUSK KNOP LEAF NULL OUCH RULE STAR TOOL TRIM WALY WING ADORN BRAID BULLA CHASE CROSS CROWN DECOR EXORN FUSEE GRACE GUTTA HELIX HONOR INLAY KNOSP LUNET MENSK MENSO OVOID PATCH POPPY PRUNT SPANG SPRAY SPRIG STALK TRAIL TRICK WALLY AMULET ANKLET ATTIRE BEDAUB BEDECK BILLET BRANCH BROOCH BUTTON CIMIER COLLAR DIAPER DOODAD EDGING EMBOSS ENRICH FALLAL FINERY FLORET FLOWER GORGET INSERT LABRET LUNULA NIELLO OFFSET PAMPRE PARURE PATERA ROCOCO ROSACE RUNTEE SETOFF TABLET TAHALI TEMPLE TIRADE AGREMEN AKROTER AMALAKA BIBELOT BUCRANE CIRCLET COCARDE CORBEIL CROCKET DIGLYPH EARPLUG ECHINUS EMBLEMA ENGRAVE ENHANCE FRIGGER FURNISH GADROON GARNISH NETSUKE RINCEAU ROSETTE SEXFOIL STRIGIL TORSADE TREFOIL TRINKET ACCOLADE ANAGLYPH APPLIQUE BRELOQUE DECORATE FLOURISH GIMCRACK LAVALIER MORESQUE NOSERING PALMETTE ROCAILLE SUNBURST SWASTIKA POPPYHEAD
(— FOR HEAD) MIND TARGET
(— ON CHAIR) SPLAT
(— ON GLASS) PRUNT

(— ON SHIP) BADGE APLUSTRE
(ARCHITECTURAL —) GUTTA
(CHILD'S —) GAY
(CLAW-LIKE —) GRIFFE
(CRYSTAL —) SPAR
(DRESS —) FROG LACE JABOT SEQUIN SPANGLE
(EXTRAVAGANT —) GROTESQUE
(FANTASTIC —) ANTIC
(GLITTERING —) SPANG
(HAIR —) POMPOM TETTIX
(HEAD —) TIARA TEMPLE
(HORSE COLLAR —) HOUNCE
(JAPANESE —) NETSUKE
(JEWELRY —) RONDEL
(LIP —) LABRET
(MATCHING SET OF —S) PARURE
(MUSICAL —) TURN MORDENT BACKFALL PRALLTRILLER
(PENDANT —) BOB BULLA ANADEM BANGLE TASSEL EARRING LAVALIER
(ROCK-CRYSTAL —) ALMOND
(ROOF —) ANTEFIX
(ROOFING —) ANTEFIX
(SCROLL—) ROCAILLE
(SHIP-SHAPED —) NEF
(SHOULDER —) EPAULET
(SPIRAL —) SCROLL
(STOCKING —) CLOCK
(SUPERFLUOUS —) FRILL FURBELOW
(TAWDRY —) GINGERBREAD
(PL.) FIGGERY KNAVERY AGREMENS

ORNAMENTAL FANCY CHICHI FRILLY LILYTURF BLUEBEARD NASTURTIUM SEMPERVIVUM

ORNAMENTATION BOSS FOIL ACORN DECOR ADORNO BABERY CHICHI CILERY DICING BARBOLA CUSPING ECHELLE LACWORK STYLING ACANTHUS APPLIQUE FROUFROU HEADWORK PURFLING ROCAILLE STAFFAGE TRESSURE
(CHEAP —) TINSEL
(EXTRAVAGANT —) ROCOCO
(MUSICAL —) GRUPPO GRUPPETTO SCHLEIFER

ORNAMENTED FIGURY FOILED ORNATE TAWDRY ADORNED FLOUNCY FROSTED TREFLEE WROUGHT GOFFERED SINNOWED ELABORATE STELLATED

ORNAMNET (NECK —) GORGET
(WATCHCHAIN —) BRELOQUE

ORNATE GAY FINE FANCY FUSSY GIDDY SHOWY DRESSY FLORID FLOSSY PURPLE SUPERB AUREATE BAROQUE FLOWERY TAFFETA MANDARIN OVERRIPE SPLENDID ELABORATE UNNATURAL
(EXTREMELY —) GIDDY

ORNERY CONTRARY

ORNITHOLOGIST AUDUBON BIRDMAN
AMERICAN CORY OBER ARBIB BEEBE COUES MINER STONE BAILEY BREWER BUTLER CASSIN KEELER MILLER STROUD TORREY WILSON XANTUS AUDUBON BRASHER CHAPMAN FORBUSH FUERTES HENSHAW NUTTALL RIDGWAY SHUFELDT TOWNSEND

CANADIAN NASH
ENGLISH DIXON GOULD CLARKE LATHAM SHARPE HOSKING KIRKMAN
FRENCH LEVAILLANT
GERMAN NAUMANN REICHENOW KLEINSCHMIDT
INDIAN ALI
NEW ZEALAND BULLER

OROMO GALLA

OROONOKO (WIFE OF —) IMOINDA

OROTUND FULL CLEAR SHOWY MELLOW STRONG POMPOUS RESONANT SONOROUS BOMBASTIC

ORP FRET WEEP

ORPAH (HUSBAND OF —) CHILION
(SISTER-IN-LAW OF —) RUTH

ORPHAN PIP WAIF WARD FOUNDLING STEPCHILD

ORPHANED ORBATE

ORPHEUS (BIRTHPLACE OF —) PIERIA
(FATHER OF —) APOLLO OEAGRUS
(MOTHER OF —) CALLIOPE
(WIFE OF —) EURYDICE

ORPHREY BAND BORDER

ORPIMENT ORPIN HARTAL SPIRIT ARSENIC HARTAIL ZARNICH

ORPINE SEDUM LIVELONG BAGLEAVES EVERGREEN

ORRA ODD IDLE ORROW WORTHLESS

ORRIS GIMP IRIS LACE BRAID ORRICE GALLOON

ORSINO (WIFE OF —) VIOLA

ORT BIT END TAG CRUMB SCRAP MORSEL REFUSE TRIFLE LEAVING REMNANT FRAGMENT LEFTOVER

ORTHOCLASE ADULARIA AMAZONITE

ORTHODOX GOOD GREEK SOUND USUAL PROPER CANONIC CORRECT ACCEPTED CATHOLIC STANDARD CUSTOMARY

ORTHODOXY PIETY TRUTH SOUNDNESS

ORTHOGRAPHY WRITING

ORTHOPTERON WALKER

ORTNIT (BROTHER OF —) WOLFDIETRICH

ORTOLAN BIRD RAIL SORA BUNTING BOBOLINK WHEATEAR

ORTSTEIN HARDPAN

ORYX BEISA PASANG PASENG GAZELLE GEMSBOK ANTELOPE LEUCORYX

OS BONE ESKAR ESKER MOUTH OPENING ORIFICE

OSAGE ORANGE HEDGE OSAGE BODOCK BOWWOOD

OSCILLATE LOG WAG HUNT ROCK SWAY VARY SQUEG SWING WAVER WEAVE SHIMMY FEATHER VIBRATE FLUCTUATE

OSCILLATION HOWL WAVE SHOCK SEICHE SHIMMY SQUEAL FLUTTER LIBRATION VIBRATION
(— OF EARTH'S AXIS) NUTATION
(SUDDEN —) SURGE

OSCULATE BUSS KISS

OSCULATION TACNODE

OSCULATORY PAX

OSIER ROD WAND EDDER SALIX
SKEIN SPLIT WITHY BASKET
SALLOW WICKER WILLOW
DOGWOOD WILGERS REDBRUSH
(— CAGE) TUMBREL
(— WILLOW) TWIGWITHY
OSIRIS HERSHEF UNNEFER
(BROTHER OF —) SET SETH
(CROWN OF —) ATEF
(FATHER OF —) GEB KEB SEB
(MOTHER OF —) NUT
(SISTER OF —) ISIS
(SON OF —) HORUS ANUBIS
(WIFE OF —) ISIS
OSMANLI TURK TURKISH
OSPREY GLED HAWK OSSI GLEDE
PYGARG BALBUSARD OSSIFRAGE
OSSATURE SKELETON OSSEMENTS
OSSE DARE ATTEMPT PRESAGE
PROMISE VENTURE PROPHESY
RECOMMEND UTTERANCE
OSSEOUS BONE BONY SPINY LITHIC
OSTEAL
OSSIAN (FATHER OF —) FINN
OSSICLE BONE INCUS ADORAL
STAPES ALVEOLE BONELET
MALLEUS SCUTELLA
OSSIFICATION OSTOSIS UROSTEON
METOSTEON SIDEBONES
OSSIFIED SCLEROUS
OSSUARY URN TOMB GRAVE VAULT
OSSARIUM
OSTEND SHOW REVEAL EXHIBIT
MANIFEST
OSTENSIBLE NOMINAL SEEMING
APPARENT SPECIOUS
OSTENT AIR MIEN SIGN TOKEN
DISPLAY PORTENT
OSTENTATION DOG POMP PUFF
SHOW CLASS ECLAT FLARE GLITZ
PRIDE STRUT SWANK VAUNT
PARADE VANITY DISPLAY FLUTTER
PAGEANT PORTENT PRESAGE
FLOURISH FRIPPERY PRETENCE
PRETENSE SHOWINESS
SPECTACLE
OSTENTATIOUS ARTY LOUD VAIN
GAUDY SHOWY SWANK FLASHY
SPORTY SWANKY TURGID FLAUNTY
GLARING OBVIOUS POMPOUS
SPLASHY SPLURGY FASTUOUS
ELABORATE
OSTERIA INN TAVERN
OSTIOLE PORE MOUTH STOMA
OPENING ORIFICE APERTURE
OSTRACISM TABU TABOO
PETALISM
OSTRACIZE BAN BAR CUT SNUB
EXILE BANISH PUNISH REJECT
ABOLISH BOYCOTT CENSURE
EXCLUDE BLACKBALL PROSCRIBE
OSTRACON SHELL FRAGMENT
POTSHERD
OSTRICH EMU RHEA NANDU
BREVIPEN STRUCION
(— FEATHER) BOO
(JERKED —) BILTONG
(PREF.) STRUTHI(O)(ONI)
OSTYAK KHANTY
OSWALD (FATHER OF —)
ETHELFRITH
(SLAYER OF —) PENDA
OSWEGO TEA BALM

OTAHEITE TAHITI
(— APPLE) HEVI MACUPA MACUPI
OTALGIA EARACHE
OTARIOID SEAL SEALION
OTHELLO MOOR
(AUTHOR OF —) SHAKESPEARE
(CHARACTER IN —) IAGO BIANCA
CASSIO EMILIA MONTANO OTHELLO
GRATIANO LODOVICO RODERICO
BRABANTIO DESDEMONA
(ENSIGN OF —) IAGO
(FRIEND OF —) IAGO
(LIEUTENANT OF —) CASSIO
(WIFE OF —) DESDEMONA
OTHER HE MO HER HIM ELSE MORE
OTRA ALTER FORMER NOTHER
SECOND TIDDER TOTHER ALTERUM
FURTHER DISTINCT DIFFERENT
(— THAN) SAVE
(PL.) LAVE REST LUTRA
(PREF.) ALL(O) HETER(O)
OTHERNESS ALTERITY
OTHERS THEM THEY
OTHERWISE OR NOT ELSE ENSE
ALIAS SECUS ALITER EXCEPT
BESIDES ELSEHOW ELSEWAYS
OTHERWORDLY FEY SPACY
OTHERWORLDLY EERIE
OTHNI (BROTHER OF —) CALEB
(FATHER OF —) KENAZ SHEMAIAH
(WIFE OF —) ACHSAH
OTIC AURAL AUDITORY ORACULAR
AURICULAR
OTIONIA (FATHER OF —)
ERECHTHEUS
(MOTHER OF —) PRAXITHEA
(SISTER OF —) PANDORA
PROTOGONIA
OTIOSE IDLE LAZY VAIN ALOOF
FUTILE OTIANT REMOTE STERILE
USELESS INACTIVE INDOLENT
REPOSING
OTOLITH SAGITTA LAPILLUS
OTOSTEON
OTOLOGIST AURIST
OTTAVINO PICCOLO
OTTER DOG FUR PUP FISH NAIR
PELT BITCH HURON LOUTRE
SIMUNG TACKLE ANNATTO
PERIQUE MAMPALON MUSTELIN
PARAVANE
(— TAIL) POLE
(DEN OF — S) HOLT
(SEA —) KALAN
OTTOMAN (ALSO SEE TURKEY)
POUF SEAT SOFA TURK COUCH
DIVAN SQUAB STOOL FABRIC
OTHMAN POUFFE SULTANE
FOOTSTOOL
(— COURT) PORTE
(— GOVERNOR) PASHA
(— LEADER) OSMAN
(— PROVINCE) VILAYET
(— STANDARD) ALEM
(— SUBJECT) RAIA RAYAH
OUABE HOGNUT
OUAKARI ACARI UKARI MONKEY
UAKARI
OUBLIETTE DUNGEON
OUCH OH OW ADORN BEZEL CLASP
JEWEL NOUCH BROOCH FIBULA
NOUCHE BRACELET NECKLACE
ORNAMENT

OUGHT BIT BUD BUT MOW BOOD
BOOT MOTE MUST ZERO SHALL
BELONG CIPHER NAUGHT NOUGHT
SHOULD BEHOOVE
OUISTITI WISTITI MARMOSET
OUNCE URE OKET OKIA ONCA ONCE
ONZA OKIEH UNCIA CHEETAH
LEOPARD WILDCAT
(CHINESE —) LIANG
(EIGHT —S) CUPFUL
(HALF —) SEMUNCIA
(ONE-16TH OF —) DRAM
(ONE-20TH OF —) EASTERLING
(ONE-8TH OF —) DRAM
OUPHE ELF OOF OUF GOBLIN
OUR UR ORE URE WER WIR HORE
NOTRE UNSER
(— LORD) NS
(— SAVIOR) NSIC
(PREF.) NOSTRI
OURICURY LICURI LICURY
CABECUDO
**OUR MUTUAL FRIEND (AUTHOR
OF —)** DICKENS
(CHARACTER IN —) JOHN WEGG
WREN BELLA BETTY FANNY HEXAM
JENNY JESSE SILAS BOFFIN EUGENE
HARMON HIDGEN JULIUS LIZZIE
WILFER BRADLEY CHARLEY
CLEAVER HANDFORD WRAYBURN
HEADSTONE HENRIETTA
NICODEMUS ROKESMITH
OURSELVES USSELF USSELS
USSELVEN
OUR TOWN (AUTHOR OF —) WILDER
(CHARACTER IN —) JOE WEBB
EMILY GIBBS HOWIE SIMON WALLY
GEORGE CROWELL NEWSOME
REBECCA STIMSON GORUSLOWSKI
OUSIA NATURE ESSENCE
SUBSTANCE
OUST BAR BUMP FIRE SACK CHUCK
EJECT EVICT EXPEL BANISH
DEBOUT REMOVE CASHIER
DISCARD DISMISS SUSPEND
DISSEIZE FORJUDGE ELIMINATE
OUSTING AMOTION
OUT EX AWAY DOWN HORS DATED
FORTH ABSENT BEGONE ISSUED
OOTWITH OUTWARD EXTERNAL
PUBLISHED
(— AT ELBOWS) SCRUFFY
(— LOUD) BOST
(— OF) EX FROM DEHORS OUTWITH
(— OF BREATH) BLOWN
(— OF COMMISSION) BUNG
(— OF DATE) OLD DOWDY PASSE
OUTWORN TIMEWORN OVERDATED
(— OF DOORS) ABROAD FOREIGN
THEREOUT
(— OF EXISTENCE) AWAY
(— OF KILTER) ALOP AWRY CRANK
BROKEN
(— OF ONE'S MIND) FEY DAFT
DELEERIT
(— OF ORDER) AMISS KAPUT
FAULTY DEFICIENT
(— OF PLACE) AMISS INEPT
(— OF PLAY) DEAD FOUL
(— OF SIGHT) DOGGO INVISIBLE
(— OF SORTS) CROOK CROSS
HUMPY NOHOW SEEDY ROTTEN
COMICAL PEEVISH

(— OF THE WAY) BY BYE ASIDE
BLIND CLEAR CLOSE AFIELD
GEASON REMOTE
(— OF THIS LIFE) HYNE
(— OF TUNE) FALSE SCORDATO
(FARTHER —) UTTER
(NOT —) SAFE
(PREF.) E ECT(O) EXO PRO
(— OF) EC
OUTAGE VENT ULLAGE HEADSPACE
OUT-AND-OUT RANK STARK
PATENT REGULAR TEETOTAL
THOROUGH GROSS PLUMB SHEER
SWORN UTTER ARRANT DIRECT
WHOLLY REGULAR ABSOLUTE
COMPLETE CRASHING OUTRIGHT
OUTBID OVERCALL
OUTBREAK FIT ROW RASH RIOT
BURST SALLY EMEUTE PLAGUE
REVOLT RUCKUS TUMULT UPROAR
BOUTADE OUTCROP RUCTION
BLIZZARD ERUPTION OUTBURST
EXPLOSION
(— OF DISEASE) PANDEMIC
(— OF EMOTIONALISM) HYSTERIA
(— OF SELF-INDULGENCE) LOOSE
(— OF TEMPER) MOORBURN
(REVOLUTIONARY —) PUTSCH
(SUDDEN —) SPURT
(VIOLENT —) STORM
OUTBUILDING BARN SHED LODGE
PRIVY BARTON GARAGE HEMMEL
LEANTO OUTHOUSE SKEELING
SKILLING BACKHOUSE
OUTBURST BOUT CROW FLAW
FUME GALE GUST RAGE TEAR TIFF
AGONY BLAST BLAZE BLURT
BREAK BRUNT BURST FLARE
FLASH GEARE SALLY SPATE START
STORM ACCESS BLOWER BLOWUP
ESCAPE FANTAD FANTOD GOLLER
TIRADE TUMULT VOLLEY
BLOWOUT BOUTADE OUTCROP
PASSION TANTRUM TORRENT
ERUPTION EXPLOSION
(— OF ANGER) FIT GERE GEARE
TATTER
(— OF APPLAUSE) OVATION
(— OF BIRD) SONG
(— OF FEELING) PASSION
(— OF ORATORY) SQUIRT
(— OF SPEECH) STRAIN
(— OF TEMPER) FUFF TIFF
BLOWOUT
(— OF WORDS) VOLLEY
(SPACE —) SUPERNOVA
OUTCAST EXILE LEPER RONIN
SHREW ABJECT PARIAH WRETCH
AOUTLET ISHMAEL MISSILE
OUTWALE CASTAWAY CHANDALA
REJECTED VAGABOND DIALONIAN
(HOMELESS —) ARAB
(JAPANESE —) ETA RONIN
(PYRENEES —) CAGOT
OUTCOME END OUT FATE TERM
CLOSE EDUCT EVENT HATCH ISSUE
LOOSE PROOF UPSET BROWST
EFFECT EXITUS OUTLET PERIOD
RESULT SEQUEL UPSHOT
EMANATE PROGENY SUCCESS
FATALITY AFTERMATH
(UNPREDICTABLE —) CRAPSHOOT

OUTCROP CROP REEF LEDGE BASSET INLIER BLOSSOM BLOWOUT OUTBREAK OUTBURST
OUTCROPPING BULT SCABROCK
OUTCRY CAW CRY HUE YIP BAWL BRAY DITE GAFF HOWL REAM ROAR SCRY UTAS YARM YELL ALARM BOAST DITTY NOISE OUTAS SHOUT STINK WHAUP BELLOW CLAMOR HOLLER RACKET SCREAM SHRIEK STEVEN TUMULT CALLING EXCLAIM PROTEST SCREECH SHILLOO COMPLAINT PHILLILEW
(PUBLIC —) STINK
OUTDATED PASSE CRINOLINE
OUTDISTANCE DROP SKIN OUTGO SURPASS OUTSTRIP
OUTDO CAP COB COP COW POT TOP BANG BEAT BEST BURN FLOG WHIP EXCEL OUTGO REVIE TRUMP WORSE DEFEAT EXCEED OUTACT NONPLUS OUTPACE SURPASS OUTMATCH OUTSHINE OVERCOME
OUTDOOR OPENAIR
OUTDOORS FORTH OUTBY OUTBYE OUTSIDE
OUTER BUT OVER ALIEN ECTAD ECTAL UPPER UTTER FOREIGN OUTSIDE OUTWARD EXTERIOR EXTERNAL FORINSEC
(PREF.) ECTO EPH EPI EXO
OUTER MONGOLIA (SEE MONGOLIA)
(COIN OF—) MONGO TUGRIK
OUTERMOST FINAL UTTER UTMOST EVEREST EXTREME OUTWARD FARTHEST REMOTEST
OUTFACE DEFY RESIST SUBDUE CONFRONT OVERCOME
OUTFIELDER GARDENER OUTSCOUT
(THROW BY —) PEG
OUTFIT KIT RIG TOG DRAG GANG GARB REAR REEK SUIT TEAM UNIT DRESS EQUIP GETUP HABIT TROUP ATTIRE CONREY DUFFEL FITOUT LAYOUT CLOTHES FURNISH SHEBANG EQUIPAGE FURNITURE GRUBSTAKE
(BRIDE'S —) TROUSSEAU
(CHINESE —) SAMFU SAMFOO
(INFANT'S —) LAYETTE
(SEWING —) HOUSEWIIFE
(SPARE —) CHANGE
OUTFLANK OUTWING OVERWING
OUTFLOW FLUX DRAIN ISSUE OUTGO EFFLUX ESCAPE SPRING OUTPOUR
(SEWAGE —) EFFLUENT
OUTGO EXIT EXCEL ISSUE OUTDO EFFLUX EGRESS EXCEED OUTLAY OUTLET OUTRUN OUTCOME PRODUCT SURPASS OUTSTRIP
OUTGROWTH ALA BUD JAG ARIL FOOT HAIR LEAF MOSS SPUR CLAMP FRUIT HILUM HYPHA SCALE SPINE ACULEA COCKLE CUPULE FIBRIL ENATION FEATHER ISIDIUM VERRUCA APPENDIX CARUNCLE EPIDERMA FLOCCULE HAPTERON INDUSIUM OFFSHOOT CARBUNCLE EMERGENCE

FLOCCULUS PROPAGULE ROSTELLUM OSTEOPHYTE
(PLANTS —) OVULE
OUTGUESS PSYCH PSYCHE
OUTHOUSE SHED SKEO BIFFY LODGE PRIVY BIGGIN LINHAY OUTHUT LATRINE SKEELING SKILLION
(PL.) STEADING
OUTING OUT SKIP STAY TRIP JUNKET PICNIC COOKOUT HOLIDAY CLAMBAKE VACATION WAYGOOSE EXCURSION WAYZGOOSE
OUTLANDER ALIEN PARDESI
OUTLANDISH ALIEN KINKY OUTRE EXOTIC REMOTE BIZARRE FOREIGN STRANGE UNCOUTH PECULIAR BARBAROUS FANTASTIC GROTESQUE UNEARTHLY
(AMUSINGLY —) CAMPY
OUTLAST ELAPSE SURVIVE OVERBIDE
OUTLAW BAN BAR CACO HORN TORY EXILE EXLEX FLEME RONIN ARRANT BADMAN BANDIT BANISH BRUMBY COWBOY DACOIT UNLEDE BANDIDO ISHMAEL FUGITATE FUGITIVE PROHIBIT PROSCRIBE PROSCRIPT
(IRISH —) WOODKERN
(JAPANESE —) RONIN
(PL.) MANZAS
OUTLAWED ILLEGAL ILLICIT LAWLESS
OUTLAWRY BAN EXILE UTLAGARY
OUTLAY COST MISE OUTGO EXPENSE PENSION
OUTLET BORE DRIP EXIT VENT ISSUE EGRESS ESCAPE EXITUS FUNNEL OUTAGE OPENING FLUMEDUCT OVERFLOW SINKHOLE AVOIDANCE
(— FOR COASTAL SWAMP) BAYOU
(— FOR SMOKE) FEMERALL
(— OF CARBURETOR) BARREL
(— OF SPRING) EYE
(AIR —) GRILL GRILLE
(ELECTRIC —) POINT
(REGULATED —) SLUICE
(RETAIL —) MINILAB
OUTLIER KLIP KLIPPE
OUTLINE MAP BOSH EDGE ETCH FLOW FORM LINE PLAN PLAT BRIEF CHALK CHART DRAFT FRAME MODEL SHAPE TRACE AGENDA APERCU DESIGN DOODLE FIGURE FILLET LAYOUT SCHEMA SCHEME SCROLL SKETCH SURVEY CAPSULE CONTOUR CROQUIS DIAGRAM DRAUGHT ELEMENT EXTRACT FEATURE GABARIT ISOTYPE PROFILE SUMMARY CONTORNO DESCRIBE ESQUISSE SKELETON SYLLABUS SYNOPSIS DELINEATE GUIDELINE TREATMENT
(— HASTILY) SPLASH
(— OF ANIMAL'S BODY) UNDERLINE
(— OF A SCIENCE) GRUNDRISS
(— OF COLUMN) ENTASIS
(— OF PLAY) SCENARIO
(— SHARPLY) ITALICIZE

(CURVING —) SWING
(DOUBLE —) FRINGE
(SHADOWY —) GHOST
OUTLIVE OUTLAST OUTWEAR SURVIVE OVERBIDE
OUTLOOK MIND VIEW FRONK FRONT VISTA ASPECT CLIMATE LOOKOUT PURVIEW FRONTAGE OUTSIGHT PROSPECT MENTALITY
(BRASH —) FACE
(MEDICAL —) PROGNOSIS
(SELF-CONFIDENT —) SWAGGER
OUTLYING OUTBY FORANE OUTBYE OUTLAND
OUTMANEUVER HAVE OUTPLAY
OUTMODED COLD DATED KAPUT PASSE RUSTY BYGONE EFFETE ANTIQUE ELDERLY VINTAGE OBSOLETE
OUT-OF-DATE RINKYDINK
OUT-OF-DOOR GIPSY GYPSY
OUTPLAY HAVE
OUTPOST STATION FOREPOST OUTGUARD
OUTPOURING FLOW GALE GUSH FLOOD RIVER SPATE EARFUL LAVISH STREAM OUTFLOW TORRENT FUSILLADE
OUTPUT CUT GET CROP MAKE EXPEL GRIST POWER YIELD ENERGY UPCOME TURNOUT
(IRRELEVANT —) NOISE
OUTRAGE RAPE ABUSE INSULT OFFEND RAVISH ABUSION AFFRONT OFFENSE VIOLATE VIOLENCE INDIGNITY
OUTRAGEOUS ENORM GROSS OUTRE DAMNED UNHOLY HEINOUS OBSCENE UNGODLY FLAGRANT INFERNAL SHAMEFUL SHOCKING ATROCIOUS DESPERATE MONSTROUS
OUTRANK CAMP PREFER SURPASS
OUTRE ODD BIZARRE STRANGE ECCENTRIC
OUTREACH CHEAT EXCEED EXTEND OUTWIT SEARCH DECEIVE SURPASS OVERREACH
OUTRIDER HAYDUK HEIDUK HEYDUCK
(PL.) SWING
OUTRIGGER BOOM PROA BUMKIN RIGGER SPIDER
OUTRIGHT RUN BALD CLEAN TOTAL WHOLE DIRECT ENTIRE OPENLY WHOLLY ABSOLUTE COMPLETE DIRECTLY ENTIRELY
OUTRIVAL WIN EXCEL OUTDO DEFEAT ECLIPSE SURPASS
OUTRUN BEAT COTE NICK PASS OUTGO EXCEED ATRENNE FORERUN OUTFOOT PREVENT
OUTRUSH GUST
OUTSET START OFFSET SETOUT BEGINNING THRESHOLD
OUTSHED SKIPPER
OUTSHINE BLIND EXCEL OUTDO STAIN DAZZLE DEFACE DISTAIN SURPASS OVERSHINE
OUTSIDE BUT OUT BOUT FREE RIND OUTBY UTTER AFIELD OUTFACE SURFACE EXTERIOR EXTERNAL

(— BOUNDS) ALOGICAL
(— OF) BESIDE
(— OF COCOON) FLOSS
(COMB. FORM) ECTO
(JUST —) FRINGE
(MERE —) SHELL
(PREF.) EC ECT(O) EXO EXTERO EXTRA EXTRO
OUTSIDER ALIEN OUTMAN BOUNDER ISHMAEL CIVILIAN EXOTERIC STRANGER EXTRANEAN FOREIGNER PHILISTER
(PL.) OUSTITI
OUTSKIRTS SIDE SKIRTS PURLIEU SUBURBS ENVIRONS PURLIEUS OUTSHIFTS
OUTSMART SLICK
OUTSPOKEN BOLD FREE LOUD APERT BLUFF BLUNT BROAD FRANK NAKED PLAIN ROUND VOCAL CANDID DIRECT ARTLESS EXPRESS EXPLICIT
(ROBUSTLY —) RABELAISIAN
OUTSTANDING ACE BIG ARCH RARE SOME AMONG FAMED NOTED SMASH SOCKO BANNER FAMOUS GIFTED HEROIC MARKED SIGNAL SNAZZY UNPAID EMINENT PALMARY SALIENT STELLAR SUBLIME SUPREME TOPPING FABULOUS INSPIRED PREMIERE SEASONED SKELPING SLAMBANG SMACKING STANDOUT TOWERING BEAUTIFUL PRINCIPAL PROMINENT UNSETTLED MONUMENTAL NOTICEABLE PREEMINENT
OUTSTAY TARRY
OUTSTRETCHED STENT EXPANDED EXTENDED
OUTSTRIP CAP TOP WIN BEST COTE LEAD LOSE PASS EXCEL OUTDO STRIP EXCEED OUTRUN DEVANCE SURPASS DISTANCE OVERCOME TRANSCEND
OUTVIE SURPASS OUTSTRIP
OUTWARD ECTAD OUTER OVERT DERMAD EXODIC EXTERN FORMAL EXTREME VISIBLE APPARENT EXTERIOR EXTERNAL OBSOLETE OUTFORTH EXTRINSIC
(GROWING —) ENATE
OUTWARDS BUT OVER
OUTWEIGH WEIGH OUTPOISE OVERBEAR OVERSHADE PREPONDERATE
OUTWIT FOX POT BALK BEST DISH FOIL HAVE BLOCK CHECK CROSS ELUDE BAFFLE EUCHRE FICKLE JOCKEY OVERGO THWART STONKER OUTGUESS OUTSHARP CROSSBITE OVERREACH CIRCUMVENT
OUTWORK BRAY JETTY FLECHE TENAIL BULWARK RAVELIN BARBICAN HORNWORK TENAILLE HORSESHOE
OUTWORKER BONDAGER
OUTWORN WAPPENED
OUZEL PIET AMSEL COLLY OUSEL OWZEL DIPPER THRUSH WHISTLER
OVAL O ELLIPSE STADIUM VESICAL VULVATE AVELONGE NUMMULAR VULVIFORM

OVARY CORAL GONAD GERMEN OARIUM OOPHORON (PREF.) OOPHOR(O) OV(I) OVARI(O) OVATO

OVATION HAND APPLAUSE

OVEN OON UMU KILN LEAR LEER LEHR OAST BAKER BENCH GLAZE GLOOM HANGI KOHUA TANUH TILER CALCAR MUFFLE CABOOSE FURNACE KITCHEN TANDOOR
(— **FORK**) FRUGGAN FRUGGIN
(— **MOP**) SCOVEL

OVENBIRD BAKER FURNER HORNERO TEACHER ACCENTOR

OVER BY BYE OER TOO ALSO ANEW ATOP BACK DEAD DONE GONE PAST UPON ABOVE AGAIN ALOFT ATOUR ATURN CLEAR ENDED EXTRA VAULT ABROAD ACROSS AROUND BEYOND DESSUS EXCESS UPWARD SURPLUS THROUGH FINISHED
(— **AGAINST**) FORNENT
(— **AND ABOVE**) ATOP ATOUR BESIDES
(**ALL** —) NAPOO NAPOOH SURTOUT
(**PREFIX**) SUR SUPER SUPRA
(PREF.) EPH EPI HYPER OB PERI SUPER SUR

OVERABUNDANCE WASTE EXCESS SURPLUS PLETHORA

OVERABUNDANT LUXURIANT

OVERACT HAM EMOTE OUTDO BURLESQUE

OVERACTING HAM

OVERADORNED FLORID

OVERALL (**BABY'S** —) CRAWLER

OVERALLS SLIP CHAPS JEANS TONGS DENIMS

OVERANXIETY WORRY

OVERARCH COVE

OVERAWE COW ABASH BULLY DAUNT BUFFALO CONCUSS BROWBEAT

OVERBEARING HIGH PROUD LORDLY OVERLY HAUGHTY ARROGANT BULLYING DOGMATIC INSOLENT PRUSSIAN SNOBBISH IMPERIOUS MASTERFUL

OVERBLOUSE SHELL

OVERBLOWN RECHERCHE

OVERBURDEN COVER HOIST PESTER CONGEST OVERLAY ENCUMBER STRIPPING SURCHARGE

OVERBUSY FUSSY PRAGMATIC

OVERCAREFUL METICULOUS

OVERCAST DIM SEW BIND DARK DULL GLUM GREY WHIP CLOUD HEAVY SERGE CLOUDY DARKEN GLOOMY LOWERY CLOUDED NUBILOUS

OVERCHARGE GYP RUSH SOAK CROWD GOUGE STICK STING BURDEN EXCISE OPPRESS EXTORTION

OVERCOAT MINO BENNY GREGO JEMMY SHUBA BANGUP CAPOTE RAGLAN SLIPON TABARD TOPPER ULSTER PALETOT SPENCER SURTOUT TOPCOAT BALMACAN BENJAMIN COONSKIN TAGLIONI COTHAMORE GREATCOAT INVERNESS

OVERCOATING DUFFEL DUFFLE

OVERCOME DO AWE GET MOW WAR WIN BEAT BEST DING LICK LOCK MATE POOP SACK SUNK TAME WAUR CHARM CRUCH DAUNT DROUK DROWN FORDO MOPUP STILL STOOP THROW APPALL BEATEN BUSHED CRAVEN DEFEAT EXCEED EXPUGN FOREDO HURDLE MASTER MOIDER OUTRAY PLUNGE SUBDUE VICTOR CONFUTE CONQUER DEPRESS ENFORCE RECOVER SMOTHER CONVINCE OUTSTRIP SUPERATE SURMOUNT SURPRISE PROSTRATE
(— **DIFFICULTIES**) SWIM
(— **WITH FATIGUE**) FORDO FOREDO
(— **WITH WEARINESS**) HEAVY
(**BE** — **BY HEAT**) SWELTER
(**EASILY** —) WEAK

OVERCONFIDENT SECURE POSITIVE

OVERCROWD PESTER CONGEST SURCHARGE

OVERDAINTY TAFFETA

OVERDECORATED GARISH

OVERDEVELOPED GAUDY

OVERDO EXCEED EXHAUST FATIGUE PERCOCT OVERCOOK OVERWORK BURLESQUE

OVERDONE FUSTIAN EXUBERANT

OVERDOSE OD SICKENER

OVERDRESS SAC SACK DIZEN SACQUE POLONAISE

OVERDRESSED FLOSSY

OVERDRIED SLEEPY

OVERDUE BACK LATE TARDY UNPAID ARREARS BELATED DELAYED EXCESSIVE

OVEREAGER ANTSY FEVERISH FEVEROUS

OVEREAT GORGE SLOFF SATIATE GOURMAND

OVERELABORATE NIGGLE LABORED

OVEREMPHATIC MOUTHY

OVERENRICHED OPULENT

OVEREXACT PRECISE

OVEREXCITED HIGH
(**GET** —) GOAPE

OVEREXERT TORLE STRAIN TORFEL OVERPLY

OVEREXPOSURE (— **TO SUN**) HELIOSIS

OVERFASTIDIOUS SPRUCE

OVERFED RANK FULSOME

OVERFEED CRAM

OVERFLOW REE COME FLUX REAM SLOP SWIM TEEM VENT BRIME FLOAT FLOOD SPATE SPILL ABOUND DEBORD OUTLET SPILTH OVERRUN REDOUND BOILOVER EXUNDATE INUNDATE OUTSWELL SUBMERGE CATACLYSM
(— **FROM MOLD**) SPEW SPUE

OVERFLOWING FLOW AWASH FLOAT DELAVY DELUGE ALLUVIO COPIOUS FRESHET PROFUSE INUNDANT EXUBERANT LANDFLOOD SUPERFLUX

OVERFRIENDLY PALSY PALSYWALSY

OVERGARMENT SMOCK BLOUSE DUSTER

OVERGROWN FOZY RANK GAWKY BRANCHY FULSOME SPRATTY SPRITTY

OVERHAND WHIP

OVERHANG JUT BEND EAVE RAKE BULGE JETTY BEETLE SHELVE TOPPLE FANTAIL OVERLAP PROJECT SUSPEND

OVERHANGING BEETLE SHELVY HANGING PENDENT PENSILE BEETLING IMMINENT OBUMBRANT PENTHOUSE PRECIPITOUS

OVERHASTY RASH

OVERHAUL EXAMINE OVERHAIL RENOVATE FOREREACH

OVERHEAD COST ABOVE ALOFT BURDEN ONCOST UPKEEP EXPENSE OVERTOP

OVERHEARTY ROBUST

OVERHEAT PARBOIL SCOUTHER

OVERINDULGE PAMPER DEBAUCH

OVERINFUSE STEW

OVERLAP LAP RIDE SYPHER SHINGLE IMBRICATE INTERSECT

OVERLAPPING JUGATE RIDING EQUITANT OBVOLUTE IMBRICATE
(— **IN FUGUE**) STRETTA STRETTO

OVERLAVISH BAROQUE

OVERLAY CAP LAP CEIL COAT WHIP APPLY COUCH COVER GLAZE PATCH PLATE CEMENT CRAVAT SPREAD STUCCO VENEER ENCRUST OPPRESS OVERLIE SMOTHER APPLIQUE TEMPLATE
(— **WITH GOLD**) BEAT GILD

OVERLOAD CRAM GLUT STUFF SWAMP CHARGE ENCUMBER SURCHARGE

OVERLOADED PLETHORIC PLETHOROUS

OVERLOOK BALK MISS OMIT PASS SKIP SLIP WINK BLINK ELIDE FORGO ACQUIT EXCUSE FOREGO FORGET IGNORE MANAGE OVERGO ABSOLVE COMMAND CONDONE FORGIVE INSPECT MISKNOW NEGLECT CONFOUND DOMINATE DISREGARD DISSEMBLE

OVERLOOKER GAITER

OVERLOOKING (**INTENTIONAL** —) AMNESTY

OVERLORD LIEGE DESPOT ISWARA SATRAP TYRANT ISHVARA SUZERAIN TYRANNIZE

OVERLY CAP TOO

OVERLYING JESSANT BROCHANT INCUMBENT

OVERMAN CHIEF LEADER ARBITER FOREMAN REFEREE OVERSEER SUPERMAN

OVERMANTLE (— **TREATMENT**) TRUMEAU

OVERMASTER GET

OVERMATCH BEST DEFEAT EXCEED SURPASS VANQUISH

OVERMODEST PRIM PRUDISH

OVERMUCH TOO EXCESS SURPLUS EXCESSIVE
(PREF.) HYPER

OVERNICE FEAT FUSS SAUCY DAINTY QUAINT SPRUCE FINICKY PRECISE DENTICAL PRECIOUS SQUEAMISH

OVERPAINT CLOBBER
(— **ENAMEL**) CLOBBER

OVERPLAY HAM

OVERPOWER AWE BEAT ROUT RUSH CRUSH DROWN QUELL SWAMP WHELM COMPEL DEFEAT DELUGE ENGULF MASTER OVERGO SUBDUE WRIXLE CONQUER CONTROL OPPRESS REPRESS CONVINCE OUTSCOUT SCUMFISH SURPRISE
(— **WITH HEAT**) SWELT
(— **WITH LIGHT**) DAZZLE

OVERPOWERING DIRE FIERCE KILLING DAZZLING STUNNING DESPERATE MONSTROUS

OVERPRAISE FLATTER OVERSELL

OVERPRECISE MIM PRISSY FINICKY CLERKISH NIGGLING PRECIEUSE

OVERREACH DO POT DUPE GRAB CHEAT COZEN CHOILE GREASE NOBBLE OUTWIT OVERGO DECEIVE

OVERREADY FORWARD

OVERREFINED QUAINT PRECIOUS

OVERRIDE SUPERSEDE

OVERRIPE FRACID SQUSHY SQUUSHY

OVERRIPENESS SEED

OVERRULE NIX VETO GOVERN ABROGATE OVERCOME

OVERRULING GREAT PREDOMINANT

OVERRUN TEEM BESET CRUSH SWARM DELUGE EXCEED INFEST INVADE OVERGO RAVAGE SPREAD DESTROY

OVERSEAS OUTREMER

OVERSEE TEND WATCH DIRECT HANDLE MANAGE SURVEY EXAMINE INSPECT NEGLECT DISREGARD SUPERVISE

OVERSEER BAAS BOSS CORK JOSS EPHOR GRAVE REEVE BISHOP CENSOR DRIVER GAFFER GRIEVE KEEKER MIRDHA TINDAL WARDEN BAILIFF CAPATAZ CAPORAL CURATOR FOREMAN HEADMAN KANGANI MANAGER MANDOER MAYORAL OVERMAN PRISTAW TAPSMAN BANKSMAN CHAPRASI DECURION MARTINET SURVEYOR VILLICUS
(— **OF MACHINERY**) TENTOR
(— **OF MINE**) CAPTAIN
(**SPIRITUAL** —) PASTOR PRIEST

OVERSENSITIVE TICKLISH

OVERSENTIMENTAL SOFT SLOPPY

OVERSHADOW DIM CLOUD COVER DWARF SHADE TOWER DARKEN EFFACE ECLIPSE OBSCURE UMBRAGE UPSTAGE BESCREEN DOMINATE OVERCAST

OVERSHOE GUM BOOT GUME ARCTIC GAITER GALOSH GOLOSH PATTEN RUBBER SANDAL FLAPPER EXCLUDER FOOTHOLD PANTOFLE

OVERSIGHT EYE CARE HOLE SLIP ERROR FAULT GAFFE LAPSE

WATCH CHARGE BLUNDER CONTROL JEOFAIL MISTAKE OMISSION TUTELAGE DIRECTION **(LEGAL —)** JEOFAIL
OVERSKIRT PEPLUM PANNIER
OVERSMART FLIP
OVERSOFT QUASHY
OVERSPREAD FOG CAST CLOT DECK PALL BATHE BREDE CLOUD COVER SMEAR STREW CLOTHE DELUGE DOODLE INDUCE SCATTER SUFFUSE BESPREAD
OVERSTATE MAGNIFY EXAGGERATE
OVERSTEP PASS EXCEED SURPASS TRANSGRESS
OVERSTEPPING FOOTFAULT
OVERSTIMULATED HYPER
OVERSTOCK SURCHARGE
OVERSTRAINED EPITONIC
OVERSUPPLIED RANK
OVERSUPPLY GLUT
OVERT OPEN PATENT PUBLIC OBVIOUS APPARENT MANIFEST
OVERTAKE PASS ATAKE CATCH ATTAIN BEFALL DETECT ENSNARE OVERHIE FOREHENT OVERHAUL **(— BY DARKNESS)** BENIGHT
OVERTASK DRIVE
OVERTAX HOIST EXCEED STRAIN STRESS
OVERTHROW TIP CAST DASH DOWN FALL FELL FOIL FOLD HURL RAZE ROUT RUIN RUSH WALT WEND ALLAY CRUSH EVERT FLING LEVEL QUASH UPSET WORST WRACK WRECK DEFEAT DEJECT DEPOSE REPUTE SLIGHT TOPPLE TUMBLE UNSEAT WRITHE AFFLICT CONQUER CONVELL DESTROY DISMISS RUINATE SUBVERT UNDOING UNHORSE WHEMMLE CONFOUND DEMOLISH OVERCOME OVERTURN REVERSAL SUPPLANT VANQUISH CHECKMATE CONFUSION OVERWHELM **(— BY TRIPPING)** CHIP
OVERTONE PARTIAL HARMONIC
OVERTOP COW OVERREACH
OVERTURE OFFER PROEM ADVANCE OPENING PRELUDE APERTURE PROPOSAL SINFONIA VORSPIEL **(INDECENT —)** ASSAULT
OVERTURN TIP CAVE COUP KEEL TILT WALT WELT TERVE THROW

UPEND UPSET WELME WHALM WHELM SLIGHT TIPPLE TOPPLE WELTER CAPSIZE DESTROY PERVERT REVERSE SUBVERT WHEMMLE **(— A WATCHMAN)** BOX
OVERWEENING MISPROUD PRESUMPTUOUS
OVERWEIGHT OUTGANG
OVERWHELM BOWL BURY SINK SLAY AMAZE COVER CRUSH DROOK DROUK DROWN FLOOD FLOOR SEIZE SPATE SWAMP CUMBER DEFEAT DELUGE ENGULF OBRUTE PLUNGE QUELME QUENCH ASTOUND BESIEGE BOMBARD CONFUTE CONQUER ENGROSS FLATTEN IMMERSE INFLOOD OPPRESS SMOTHER ASTONISH DISTRESS DOMINATE INUNDATE OVERCOME SUBMERGE AVALANCHE
OVERWHELMED ACCABLE
OVERWORK HOIN TIRE TOIL SWEAT STRAIN SURMENAGE
OVINE OVIN OVILE SHEEP SHEEPLIKE
OVIPOSITOR TEREBRA
OVOID OVATE OBOVOID
OVOLO OVAL THUMB BOLTEL
OVULE EGG NIT GERM SEED EMBRYO OVULUM GEMMULE SEEDLET
OVUM EGG OVAL SEED SPORE OOSPERM OOSPHERE
OWAIA TREE BOBO
OWE DUE OWN REST AUGHT OUGHT SHALL POSSESS ATTRIBUTE
OWED DUE
OWER DEBTOR
OWING INTHEHOLL
OWL ULE BUBO LULU MOMO RURU SURN TYTO UTUM JENNY MADGE NINOX PADGE SCOPS STRIX TAWNY WEKAU AZIOLA HOOTER HOWLET KETUPA MUCARO RAPTOR STRICH VERMIN WHEKAU BOOBOOK HARFANG KATOGLE WAPACUT WOOLERT BILLYWIX COQUIMBO MOREPORK **(— CALL)** HOOT **(CRY OF —)** HOOT WHOO TUWHIT TUWHOO **(LIKE AN —)** STRIGINE **(YOUNG —)** UTUM OWLET **(PREF.)** STRIGI

OWL PARROT KAKAPO
OWN AIN OWE AVOW FESS HAVE HOLD HOWE MEET NAIN SELF ADMIT AUGHT OUGHT MASTER CONCEDE CONFESS POSSESS PROSPER ACKNOWLEDGE **(PREF.) (ONE'S —)** IDIO
OWNER BEL MALIK WALLA HOLDER DOMINUS HERITOR ODALLER PROPRIETOR **(— OF ESTATE)** ALIRD **(— OF FISHING PLANT)** PLANTER **(— OF SLAVES)** PATRON **(— OF YACHT)** AFTERGUARD **(PLANTATION —)** COLON **(SHEEP —)** NABAL
OWNERSHIP ODAL UDAL AUGHT TITLE CORNER SEIZIN SEIZURE SEVERAL TENANCY DOMINIUM PROPERTY COMMUNITY POSSESSION
OX YAK ANOA AVER BEEF BUFF BULL GAUR MUSK NAWT NEAT NEWT NOWT OWSE REEM RUNT STOT URUS ZEBU AIVER BISON BUGLE GAYAL SANGA STEER TOLLY TSINE BOVINE MITHAN ROTHER BANTENG BUFFALO KOUPREY TWINTER SELADANG TALLOWER **(CAMBODIAN —)** KOUPREY KOUPROH **(HORNLESS —)** MOIL **(KIND OF —)** MUSK **(SMALL —)** RUNT **(TAME —)** COACH **(WILD —)** URE ANOA BUFF GAUR REEM URUS BISON BUGLE BANTIN BANTENG BUFFALO SELADANG **(YEARLING —)** STIRK **(YOUNG —)** STOT **(PREF.)** BOVI BU
OXBLOOD KAZAK COPTIC KAZAKH
OXBOW INCIDENT (AUTHOR OF —) CLARK **(CHARACTER IN —)** GIL DREW ROSE CANBY CROFT GRIER JOYCE MAPEN TYLER CARTER DAVIES DONALD GERALD MARTIN OSGOOD RISLEY TETLEY FARNLEY KINKAID
OXEN NOWT OWSEN CATTLE
OXEYE BOCE GOLD ASTER CLOUD DAISY GOLDE DUNLIN PLOVER TARPON
OXFOOT (STEWED —) COWHEEL

OXFORD DOWN SHOE CLOTH OXONIAN SLIPPER
OXGANG OSKEN BOVATE OXGATE OXLAND PLOWGANG
OXIDATION RUST
OXIDATIVE AEROBIC
OXIDE EARTH FLOSS CADMIA HAFNIA MOILES ZAFFER CALCINE GUMMITE KERNITE LIMONITE DJALMAITE **(— OF CALCIUM)** LIME **(— OF IRON)** RUST COLCOTHAR MAGNETITE
OXLIP PAGLE PAIGLE PRIMULA MILKMAID PRIMROSE PRIMWORT
OXSHOE CUE
OXYGEN GAS OZONE OXYGENIUM **(LIQUID —)** LOX **(PREF.)** OXO
OXYGENATE AERATE VENTILATE
OXYGENATOR GILL
OYSTER COPIS COUNT PINNA PLANT SHELL COTUIT HUITRE NATIVE REEFER BIVALVE MOLLUSK PANDORE RATTLER SHARPER BLUEPOINT GREENGILL LYNNHAVEN **(— BED)** PARK STEW LAYER SCALP CLAIRE SCALFE OYSTERAGE **(— CATCHER)** OLIVE PYNOT TIRMA KROCKET PIANNET REDBILL SCOLDER SHELDER PILWILLET SKELDRAKE **(— CRAB)** PINNOTERE **(— FOSSIL)** OSTRACITE **(— MEASURE)** WASH **(— PLANT)** SALSIFY **(— SHELL)** HUSK TEST SHUCK **(— SMALLER THAN QUARTER)** BLISTER **(— SOLD BY POUND)** COUNT **(IRISH —)** POWLDOODY **(ROCK —)** CHAMA **(VEGETABLE —)** SALSIFY **(YOUNG —)** SET SPAT **(2,3, OR 4 —S)** WARP **(PREF.)** OSTRE(I)(O)
OYSTER CATCHER SEAPIE
OYSTERFISH TAUTOG TOADFISH
OZARK STATE MISSOURI
OZEM (BROTHER OF —) DAVID **(FATHER OF —)** JESSE
OZNI (FATHER OF —) GAD
OZOCERITE MALTHA NEFTGIL
OZONE AIR

P

P PAPA PETER
PA DAD PAW FORT PAPA DADDY FATHER VILLAGE STOCKADE
PABULUM FOOD FUEL PROG CEREAL ALIMENT SUPPORT NUTRIMENT
PAC BOOT SHOE MOCCASIN
PACA CAPA CAVY LAVA LABBA AGOUTI RODENT
PACE FIG PAD RIP WAY BEMA CLIP GAIT LOPE PASS PELT RACK RATE STEP TEAR TROT WALK AMBLE BRAWL CANTO SLINK SPACE SPEED STEEK SWING TEMPO TRACE TREAD CANTER GALLOP STRAIT STRIDE CHANNEL CHAPTER DOGTROT MEASURE PASSAGE SCUTTLE
(**FAST —**) ROMP
(**RAPID —**) CLIP CRACKER
(**SLOW —**) JOG CRAWL CREEP
(PL.) MANAGE
PACER HORSE AMBLER SPANKER TRIPPLER
PACHISI LUDO UCKERS PARCHESI
PACHYDERM BABAR HIPPO RHINO ELEPHANT
PACIFIC CALM MEEK MILD IRENE IRENIC PLACID SERENE PEACEFUL TRANQUIL PEACEABLE
(**— ISLAND PINE**) IE KOU IEIE LEHUA
PACIFIER DUMMY COMFORTER
PACIFIST BOLO
PACIFY PAY CALM EASE LULL STAY ABATE ALLAY AMESE MEASE PEASE QUELL QUIET STILL PECIFY SERENE SETTLE SOFTEN SOOTHE APPEASE ASSUAGE MOLLIFY PLACATE QUALIFY STICKLE MITIGATE ALLEVIATE RECONCILE
PACK JAM PUN WAD BALE CADE CRAM DECK FILL GANG JAMB LADE LOAD PAIR ROUT STOW SWAG TAMP TOTE TUCK COUCH CRAME CROWD DRESS FLOCK HORDE SKULK SOMER STEVE STORE STUFF TRUSS BARREL BODDLE BOODLE BUDGET BUNDLE CARTON DUFFLE EMBALE ENCASE FARDEL HAMPER IMPACT PARCEL STEEVE THWACK TURKEY WALLET PANNIER PORTAGE RUMMAGE SUMPTER KNAPSACK
(**— ANIMAL**) ASS MULE BURRO CAMEL HORSE LLAMA DONKEY PACKER
(**— BUILDER**) GOBBER
(**— JURY**) WATER
(**— LOOSELY**) HOVER
(**— OF BEARS**) SLOTH
(**— OF CARDS**) STOCK
(**— OF DOGS**) CRY KENNEL
(**— OFF**) WAG SHANK TURSE

(**— OF FOXES**) GROUP SKULK
(**— OF HOUNDS**) CRY HUNT MUTE
(**— ROAD**) PACKWAY
(**— TIGHTLY**) STIVE
PACKAGE PAD BALE BOLT PAIR DUMMY TRUSS BINDLE BUNDLE PACKET PARCEL SAMPLE SEROON DORLACH
(**— OF CIGARETTES**) DECK
(**— OF GOLDBEATER'S SKINS**) SHODER
(**— OF LEAF**) BOOK
(**— OF PEPPERS**) ROBBIN
(**— OF STAMPS**) KILOWARE
(**— OF VELLUM**) KUTCH
(**— OF VENEER**) FLITCH
(**— OF WOOL**) BAG PAD BUTT FADGE
(**YARN**) CONE CHEESE
PACKAGING (**— MATERIAL**) SARAN
PACKED THICK THRONGED CONGESTED SPOONWISE
PACKER BALER LINER ROPER CANNER
PACKET BOAT BOOK DECK ROLL SCREW BUNDLE PARCEL SACHET
(**— OF A DRUG**) BAG
(**— OF VELLUM**) CUTCH KUTCH
(**FIVE DOLLAR DRUG —**) NICKEL
PACKHORSE SOMER JAGGER PACKER SUMPTER
PACKHORSEMAN JAGGER
PACKING CUP RAGS GAUZE PAPER STRAW WASTE GASKET GROMMET STOWAGE STOPPING
(**— MATERIAL**) BALINE GASKET
(**CLAY —**) LUTE
(**SEND —**) EXPEL
PACKINGHOUSE MEATWORKS
PACKMAN HAWKER
PACKSACK KYACK
PACKSADDLE BAT BARDEL APAREJO
PACT MISE ACCORD CARTEL PACTUM TREATY BARGAIN COMPACT LOCARNO ALLIANCE CONTRACT COVENANT AGREEMENT CONCORDAT
PAD MAT WAD WAY BLAD BOSS DIGS FROG LURE MUTE PATH PUFF ROAD ROLL SHOE WALK WASE BLOCK INKER PERCH PILCH QUILT STENT STINT STUFF TABBY TRAMP BASKET BUFFER BUSTLE DAUBER HOLDER JOCKEY NUMNAH PADDLE PADNAG PANNEL PILLOW SPONGE TABLET TRUDGE VELURE WREATH BOLSTER BOMBAST CUSHION FOOTPAD PILLION SASHOON
(**— FOR HORSE'S BACK**) SADDLE
(**— IN CRIB**) BUMPER
(**— OF ROPE**) PUDDING PUDDENING

(**— OF STRAW**) SUNK WASE
(**— ON HORSE'S FOOT**) FROG
(**— WORN AT THE WAIST**) TOURNURE
(**BOXER'S —**) GUMSHIELD
(**ETCHER'S —**) DABBER
(**FENCING —**) PLASTRON
(**HAIR —**) RAT MOUSE TOQUE
(**INKING —**) INKER TOMPION
(**KIND OF —**) TOUCH
(**MEDICAL —**) PLEDGET
(**PERFUMED —**) SACHET
(**POLISHING —**) RUBBER VELOUR VELOURS
(**POOR —**) HUT SHACK
(**PROTECTIVE —**) SHIELD
(**SADDLE —**) PANEL PILLOW PILLION
(PREF.) TYL(O)
PADADE CALLITHUMP
PADAUK CORAIL
PADDER MANGLE
PADDING TABBY CADDIS BOLSTER BOMBAST BUSHING CADDICE FILLING PACKING ROBBERY WADDING MAHOITRE STUFFING
PADDLE OAR ROW SPUD WADE ALOOF CANOE SLICE SPANK BUCKET DABBLE PETTLE PUNISH STRIKE THRASH TODDLE SPANKER SPURTLE LUMPFISH
(**— BOX**) WHEELHOUSE
(**— FOR FLOUR**) SLICK
(**TAILOR'S —**) BEATER
PADDLEBOAT PEDALO
PADDLEFISH GANOID DUCKBILL STURGEON POLYODONT SPADEFISH SPOONBILL
PADDOCK LOT FROG PARK CLOSE FIELD SLEDGE GARSTON LOANING BIRDCAGE
PADDYMELON QUOKKA PADMELON
PADISHAH SULTAN PADASHA POTSHAW
PADLOCK LOCK FASTEN SECURE CLOSING FASTENER HORSELOCK
(**— LINK**) SHACKLE
PADRE MONK CLERIC FATHER PRIEST CHAPLAIN
PADRONA LANDLADY MISTRESS
PADRONE BOSS CHIEF MASTER PATRON LANDLORD INNKEEPER
PAEAN ODE HYMN SONG PRAISE OUTBURST TRIUMPHAL
PAGAN ATA BUID BATAK BUKID APAYAO BAGOBO BANGON BILAAN BONTOC ETHNIC PAYNIM SABIAN ALANGAN DUMAGAT GENTILE HEATHEN INFIDEL SARACEN SUBANUN UNGODLY IDOLATOR
(**— OF INDIA**) GENTOO
PAGANDOM PAYNIM
PAGE BOY CALL LEAF MOTH SIDE

CHILD FACER FOLIO GROOM SHEET DONZEL ERRATA SUMMON VARLET BUTTONS CALLBOY FUNNIES PAVISER SERVANT CHASSEUR HENCHMAN ICHOGLAN
(**— BOTTOM**) TAIL
(**BLANK —S**) CANCEL
(**FACING —S**) SPREAD
(**LADY'S —**) ESCUDERO
(**LAST FEW —S**) BACK
(**LEFTHAND —**) VERSO
(**NEWSPAPER —**) OPED
(**RIGHTHAND —**) RECTO OUTPAGE
(**TITLE —**) TITLE UNWAN RUBRIC
(PL.) ODDMENTS
PAGEANT JEST POMP SHOW ANTIC PARADE RIDING TABLEAU TAMASHA TRIUMPH AQUACADE CAVALCADE SPECTACLE WATERWORK
PAGEANTRY POMP PARADE HERALDRY SPLENDOR
PAGER BEEPER
PAGIEL (**FATHER OF —**) OCRAN
PAGLIACCI (**CHARACTER IN —**) BEPPE CANIO NEDDA TONIO SILVIO
(**COMPOSER OF —**) LEONCAVALLO
PAGODA PON TAA HOON WATT TEMPLE VARELLA
(**PART OF —**) TEE ROOF TOPE STUPA FINIAL BALCONY
PAHOUIN FAN FANG
PAHUTAN PAHO
PAID EVEN RESOLUTE
(**— IN COIN**) DRY
(**— IN FULL**) SATISFIED
PAIL CAN COG PAN SOA SOE BEAT BOWK GAWN MEAL STOP TRUG BOWIE COGUE CRUCK DANDY ESHIN SKEEL STOOP BLICKY BUCKET COGGIE HARASS KETTLE LEGLEN NOGGIN PIGGIN SITULA THRASH COLLOCK
(**MILK —**) KIT SOE TRUG ESHIN LEGLEN
(**ON WHEELS**) DANDY
(**PART OF —**) EAR RIM BODY CURL HANDLE
(**POTTERY —**) SEAU
(**SMALL —**) KIT BLICKY BLICKIE
(**WOODEN —**) COG COGUE LUGGIE PIGGIN
PAIN GYP ACHE AGRA BALE CARE CARK DOLE FRET GRUE HARM HURT PANG SITE SORE TEEN TINE WARK AGONY BEANS CRAMP DOLOR GRIEF GRIPE PINCH PINSE SCALD SMART STING STOUN THRAW THROE WOUND WRING BARRAT GRIEVE MISERY SHOWER STITCH TWINGE AFFLICT ALGESIS ANGUISH EARACHE HURTING MYALGIA OFFENCE PENALTY

TORTURE TRAVAIL TROUBLE
AGGRIEVE DISTRESS FLEABITE
(— **IN BACK**) NOTALGIA SCIATICA
(— **IN HAND**) CHIRAGRA
(— **IN SIDE**) STEEK
(— **IN THE NECK**) PEST
(— **OF MIND**) AGONY
(— **RELIEVER**) OPIATE ANODYNE
ASPIRIN TYLENOL
(**FILL WITH —**) YEARN
(**SHARP —**) WRING
(**STOMACH —**) GRIPES GNAWING
(**WRENCHING —**) TORSION
(PL.) FASH LABOR WHILE EFFORT
TROUBLE
(PREF.) ALG(IO)(O) DOLORI NOCI
PENO
(SUFF.) AGRA ALGIA ALGIC ODYNE
ODYNIA
PAINFUL BAD ILL DIRE EVIL FELL
SAIR SORE SOUR TART ANGRY
CRUEL SHARP SORRY BITTER
STICKY TENDER THORNY BALEFUL
GRIPING HURTFUL IRKSOME
LABORED PENIBLE PUNGENT
EXACTING TERRIBLE TORTUOUS
DIFFICULT HARROWING
(PREF.) MOGI
PAINLESS EASY
PAINSTAKING BUSY LOVING
NARROW CAREFUL PENIBLE
DILIGENT EXACTING STUDIOUS
ASSIDUOUS ELABORATE
PAINT BICE BLOT COAT DAUB DRAW
FARD GAUD LIMN PENT PICT SOIL
COLOR FEIGN FUCUS GRAIN
ROUGE STAIN BEDAUB DAZZLE
DEPICT ENAMEL FRESCO OPAQUE
SHADOW SKETCH BESMEAR
PORTRAY PRETEND SCUMBLE
AIRBRUSH DECORATE DEPEINCT
DESCRIBE DISGUISE URFIRNIS
CALCIMINE
(— **A PIPE**) SOIL
(— **FACE OR BODY**) FUCUS PARGET
(— **HASTILY**) SQUIGGLE
(— **IN DOTS**) STIPPLE
(— **SKETCHILY**) SPLASH
(— **THROUGH PATTERN**) STENCIL
(— **WITH COSMETICS**) POP POT
FARD
(PREF.) PICTO
PAINTBRUSH WICKAWEE
NOSEBLEED
(**PART OF —**) HAIR CRIMP HANDLE
BRISTLE FERRULE
PAINTED PINTO FUCATE PASTOSE
PINTADO FUCOIDAL GOFFERED
(— **BEAUTY**) VANESSA
(— **BUNTING**) POP NONPAREIL
(— **CUP**) WICKAWEE PAINTBRUSH
(— **WAKE-ROBIN**) SARA
PAINTER BRUSH FAUVE ARTIST
DAUBER PICTOR PANTHER SIGNIST
SIGNMAN WORKMAN BRUSHMAN
LUMINIST MURALIST NAZARENE
STIPPLER DECORATOR TACTILIST
(PL.) ECLECTICS
AMERICAN AHL COX GAG LOW MAX
RAY RIX AMES BAER BEAL COLE
DABO DANA DEHN DINE DOVE GRAY
HART HAYS HELD HOWE HURD
KOCH KOST LOEB LUKS NEAL NEEL

PAGE PETO POOR REID THON UFER
WEIR WEST WOOD ABBEY AGATE
AIKEN ALDIS AVERY BACON BAKER
BARSE BEARD BEAUX BETTS BOGGS
BROOK BROWN BRUSH BUNCE
CHASE CHILD CRANE CURRY DAVIS
DEWEY EATON ENNIS FIENE FLAGG
FOOTE GILES GOLUB GORDY GORKY
GRANT GROLL GROSZ HEALY HENRI
HICKS HOMER INMAN IPSEN JONES
LAHEY LUCAS MARSH MINOR
MOORE MORAN MYERS ODGEN
OKADA PEALE PERRY POONS
POORE RYDER SHINN SLOAN SMITH
SOYER TRYON UPTON WALDO
WAUGH WEBER WEEKS WHITE
WOOLF WYANT WYETH YOUNG
BENSON BENTON BLYTHE BOGERT
BOHROD BOUCHE BROWNE
CADMUS CHAPIN CHURCH COLMAN
COOPER COPLEY COTTON CRANCH
CURRAN DANIEL DANNAT DAVIES
DEARTH DECAMP DEMUTH DEWING
DUNLAP DURAND DURRIE EAKINS
FERRIS FISCHL FORBES FOSTER
FOWLER GUERIN HAGGIN HARVEY
HASSAM HAYDEN HEATON HERTER
HOPPER INGHAM INNESS JARVIS
JOUETT KINNEY KNATHS KNIGHT
LAWSON LEUTZE LEVINE LOOMIS
MARTIN MAURER MAYHEW MEIERE
MILLER MOSLER MURPHY NEAGLE
NOLAND NOURSE OAKLEY PARTON
PEARCE PIPPIN POWELL QUIDOR
RIVERS ROTHKO SAMPLE SAVAGE
SINGER STELLA STUART SYMONS
TANGUY TANNER TAUBES TURNER
VEDDER WARHOL WRIGHT ZORACH
ADDISON ALLSTON AUDUBON
BANVARD BELLOWS BINGHAM
BRINLEY CAMERON CARLSON
CARROLL CASSATT CHAPMAN
CHRISTY CORBINO COUDERT
CROPSEY DOUGHTY EDWARDS
ELLIOTT FASSETT FREEMAN
GARNSEY GIFFORD GRIFFIN
GROPPER HARDING HARNETT
HIBBARD HIGGINS HUBBARD
HUBBELL JOHNSON KARFIOL
KENDALL KENSETT LAFARGE
LATHROP MACEWEN MATHEWS
MCENTEE METCALF MUNSELL
NAEGELE OKEEFFE OLITSKI PARRISH
PEIXOTO PROCTOR RATTNER
SAMARAS SCUDDER SIMMONS
SMIBERT SPENCER STIMSON
TWOMBLY TWORKOV WATROUS
WIGGINS ALAJALOV ATCHISON
BARTLETT BECKWITH BICKNELL
BILLINGS BOUGHTON BRACKMAN
BRADFORD BREVOORT BRIDGMAN
CORNWELL COSTIGAN DUVENECK
FAULKNER HAMILTON HARRISON
HOVENDEN HUTCHENS JOHANSEN
KRONBERG LOCKWOOD MATTESON
MELCHERS PHILLIPS REINHART
RICHARDS ROCKWELL ROSSITER
SHATTUCK SPEICHER TRUMBULL
WHISTLER WILMARTH WOODBURY
ALEXANDER ARMSTRONG
BEMELMANS BERDANIER
BERNSTEIN BIERSTADT BITTINGER
BLAKELOCK DAUGHERTY

DEKOONING HALLOWELL
HAWTHORNE KUNIYOSHI
REMINGTON ROTHERMEL
SCHREIBER TWACHTMAN
VANDERLYN WENTWORTH
BLASHFIELD BURCHFIELD
CLINEDINST EILSHEMIUS
FARNSWORTH HIRSHFIELD
HUNTINGTON MACCAMERON
WHITTREDGE BERNINGHAUS
DELLENBAUGH PRENDERGAST
BLUMENSCHEIN BRECKENRIDGE
DAINGERFIELD CROWNINSHIELD
ARGENTINIAN CENTURION
AUSTRIAN ALT KLIMT EHRLICH
FUHRICH AMERLING HAUSMANN
DANHAUSER DEFREGGER
KOKOSCHKA FRIEDLANDER
PETTENKOFEN
BELGIAN CLAYS ENSOR FOLON
NAVEZ VIGNE BEIFVE KEYSER
WIERTZ GALLAIT GUFFENS LALAING
PAUWELS STEVENS WAPPERS
WAUTERS WILLEMS BAERTSON
LAERMANS MAGRITTE BROUCKERE
EVENEPOEL TONGERLOO
BRAEKELEER CHAMPAIGNE
VERBOECKHOVEN
BRAZILIAN VOLPI
CANADIAN AZIZ CARR COTE KANE
MILNE FORBES HARRIS LISMER
OBRIEN VARLEY WALKER WATSON
BORDUAS KURELEK MORRICE
COLVILLE
CHILEAN MATTA
CHINESE SHUBUN
COLOMBIAN BOTERO
CZECH KUPKA MANES MUCHA
BROZIK
DANISH JUEL BLOCH CARLSEN
DAISGAARD MARSTRAND
WIEGHORST WILLUMSEN
ZAHRTMANN ABILDGAARD
ECKERSBERG
DUTCH BOL DOU BECK BEGA CORT
CUYP GOES GOGH HAAS HALS
HEDA HEEM KALF LAAR LELY LOOY
MAES MEER NEER AELST APPEL
BAUER BOSCH BOUTS BRUYN
CODDE DAVID GOYEN HELST
HOOCH KETEL MARIS METSU NEEFS
OVENS STEEN VELDE VROOM WITTE
BACKER DECKER EGMONT ESCHER
FLINCK GELDER HEYDEN KESSEL
KEYSER MANDER MESDAG MIERIS
MULIER OSTADE POTTER RUYSCH
SCOREL TOOROP WEENIX AERTSEN
AERTZEN ASSELYN BERCHEM
BEYEREN CRABETH DOUFFET
HOBBEMA ISRAELS KONINCK
LASTMAN LIEVENS LOMBARD
PATINIR POURBUS VANGOGH
VERMEER WYNANTS AGRICOLA
DOESBURG DUJARDIN EECKHOUT
GOLTZIUS HUYSMANS JONGKIND
KOEKKOEK LAIRESSE MOREELSE
RUYSDAEL TERBORCH BLOEMAERT
CORNELISZ FABRITIUS HOEFNAGEL
HONTHORST HOUBRAKEN
MIEREVELT MONDRIAAN
MOUCHERON REMBRANDT
STEENWILK WOUWERMAN
BACKHUYSEN BERCKHEYDE

CAMPHUYSEN EVERDINGEN
GESELSCHAP LINGELBACH
BREKELENKAM HONDECOETER
POELENBURGH TERBRUGGHEN
HOOGSTRAETEN
ENGLISH COX EGG FRY BIRD BONE
COLE COPE EAST ETTY EVES GILL
HAAG HOOK HUNT JOHN LEAR
NASH OPIE SWAN TAIT WARD WEIR
BLAKE BROCK BROWN CRANE
CROME CUNEO DAVIS DOYLE FRITH
FURSE LEWIS LOWRY LUCAS
MOORE ORPEN STARK STEER
STONE TONKS UWINS WATTS
WELLS ABBOTT ASHTON BARKER
BOXALL BROOKS BROWNE CARTER
CHALON COATES COOPER COSWAY
COTMAN COWPER COZENS CROFTS
DEWINT DOBSON FILDES GIRTIN
GLOVER HACKER HAYDON HOLMES
KNIGHT LAVERY LAWSON LEADER
MARTIN MAYTER MCEVOY MULLER
NEWTON OLIVER OULESS ROMNEY
SEVERN SMIRKE STUART STUBBS
TURNER VARLEY WALKER ANSDELL
BAYLISS BEECHEY BOMBERG
CALVERT CAMERON CLAUSEN
COLLIER DANIELL DICKSEE GILBERT
GUEVARA HERBERT HODGSON
HOGARTH HOLIDAY HOLROYD
LINNELL MILLAIS MORLAND
POYNTER RIVIERE RUSSELL
SOLOMON ZOFFANY ARMITAGE
ATKINSON AUMONIER BEAUMONT
BRANGWYN CALDERON CALLCOTT
CORBOULD CRESWICK EASTLAKE
FIELDING HILLIARD LANDSEER
LEIGHTON MUNNINGS REDGRAVE
REYNOLDS RICHMOND RICKETTS
ROSSETTI STOTHARD TOPOLSKI
WATERLOW WHISTLER AMSHEWITZ
BEARDSLEY BONINGTON
BOURGEOIS COLLINSON
CONSTABLE GREENAWAY
NORTHCOTE STANFIELD THORNHILL
BROCKHURST KENNINGTON
WATERHOUSE WOOLDRIDGE
ROTHENSTEIN GAINSBOROUGH
FINNISH EDELFELT
FLEMISH VOS BLES BRIL EYCK GOES
BALEN CLAUS CLEVE COXIE ORLEY
CAMPIN COQUES CRAYER MABUSE
MASSYS RUBENS WEYDEN
BLOEMEN BREUGEL BROUWER
BRUGHEL CANDIDO TENIERS
VANDYCK VANEYCK BRUEGHEL
CHRISTUS CRAESBEECK
FRENCH ZO ARP BIDA CAIN DORE
DUFY ETEX GROS HEIM HUET LAMI
TROY BIARD CAZIN CHERY CORNU
COROT DAVID DEGAS DENIS DOYEN
DUPRE FRERE JONAS LEGER LHOTE
MANET MONET MOROT PATER
PUVIS REDON STAEL VEBER VOUET
BAUDRY BERARD BERAUD BOILLY
BONNAT BONVIN BOUDIN BOUTON
BRAQUE BRETON BUFFET CALLOT
CARREY CARZOU CHABAS CHERET
CHERON CLOUET CORMON COTTET
COUDER COUSIN COYPEL DAUBAN
DERAIN DONGEN DOUCET DUBUFE
FAVORY FORAIN FORBIN FRIESZ
GERARD GEROME GERVEX GIGOUX

GRANET GREUZE GUERIN HEBERT
HELION HENNER INGRES LAHIRE
LATOUR LEBLON LEBRUN LELEUX
LEPINE LORJOU MARTIN MERSON
MILLET MIRBEL MOREAU MULLER
RENOIR SEURAT SIGNAC STELLA
TISSOT TROYON VANLOO VERNET
VIBERT WEERTS BALTHUS BARRIAS
BESNARD BONHEUR BONNARD
BOUCHER BOUCHOR BOURDON
CABANEL CEZANNE CHARDIN
CHARLOT COGNIET COURBET
COUTURE DAMERON DORIGNY
DROUAIS DUCHAMP FERRIER
FLANDIN FOUQUET GARNIER
GAUGUIN GENDRON GLEIZES
HARTUNG HEDOUIN HERSENT
JEANRON LAFOSSE LANCRET
LANSYER LAURENS LEBOURG
LEGRAND LEHMANN LEMOYNE
LESUEUR LORRAIN MAIGNAN
MARQUET MATISSE MICHAUX
MIGNARD MORISOT NATTIER
PICABIA POUSSIN PRUDHON
RESTOUT ROUAULT SOUTINE
UTRILLO VALADON WATTEAU
BELLANGE BERCHERE CARRIERE
CHARTRAN CONSTANT DAGUERRE
DALAUNAY DAUBIGNY DESCAMPS
DETAILLE DROLLING ESPAGNAT
FLANDRIN GALIMARD JOUVENET
KLINGSOR LANDELLE LATOUCHE
LEFEBVRE LENEPVEU LEPRINCE
OZENFANT PARROCEL PISSARRO
ROUSSEAU SCHEFFER STEINLEN
VUILLARD WILLETTE BOULANGER
CHATILLON CHENAVARD
COUBERTIN DEBUCOURT
DEHODENCQ DELABORDE
DELACROIX DELAROCHE
DESPORTES FALGUIERE
FRAGONARD GERICAULT
GLEISPACH GUILLEMET HENNIQUIN
LAURENCIN METZINGER SCHUSSELE
BARTHOLOME BOUGUEREAU
BOULLONGNE BRASCASSAT
CHASSERIAU DESBROSSES
GUILLAUMET GUILLAUMIN
HARPIGNIES JACQUEMART
MEISSONIER BRACQUEMOND
CARMONTELLE LARGILLIERE
DESVALLIERES LOUTHERBOURG
GERMAN DIX MAX ADAM DIEZ HESS
JANK LENZ MARC MARR SOHN
UHDE VEIT ANTES BEGAS BEHAM
BINCK BRUYN DURER EBERS EMELE
ERNST FOLTZ FRIES FUGER GRAFF
GROSZ HOFER KNAUS KUEHL LEIBL
MACKE MENGS MEYER MUCKE
NEHER NOLDE OESER PECHT PENCZ
STUCK THOMA VOGEL BECKER
BRACHT BRAITH BUHLER BURGER
EBERLE ECHTER FITGER FRIESE
GEBLER GUSSOW HECKEL HENSEL
HERLIN HERTEL HEYDEN HUBNER
KELLER KOBELL KRAFFT KRUGER
LANGER LOFFTZ MAREES MENZEL
MULLER RETHEL WERNER
BALDUNG BARTELS BLECHEN
CORINTH CRANACH FLICKEL
GENELLI HOFMANN HOLBEIN
KLINGER KOPSICH KRELING
LENBACH LESSING LINDNER

LOCHNER PRELLER RICHTER
SCHWIND STEUBEN AGRICOLA
AMBERGER BECKMANN CARSTENS
DETTMANN FIORILLO GEBHARDT
GRUTZNER HABERLIN HENDRICH
KAULBACH KIRCHNER KOLLWITZ
KUGELGEN KULMBACH ROTTMANN
SCHIRMER SCHNEYER ZEITBLOM
ACHENBACH AINMILLER
ALTDORFER BENDEMANN
BLEIBTREU BURGKMAIR CORNELIUS
ELSHEIMER ENGELHARD FRIEDRICH
GRUNEWALD HABERMANN
KNACKFUSS KRIEGHOFF
MEYERHEIM MODERSOHN
PASSAVANT TISCHBEIN
ALDEGREVER BAUMEISTER
CAMPHAUSEN HECKENDORF
HILDEBRAND SCHONGAUER
SCHROEDTER WOHLGEMUTH
ZIMMERMANN CHODOWIECKI
HASENCLEVER HILDEBRANDT
HUCHTENBERG MORGENSTERN
SCHRAUDOLPH LINDENSCHMIT
ROTTENHAMMER WINTERHALTER
GREEK GYSIS AETION NICIAS ZEUXIS
APELLES PAUSIAS EUPOMPUS
ARISTIDES EUPHRANOR
MELANTHUS PAMPHILUS
TIMANTHES AGATHARCUS
PARRHASIUS POLYGNOTUS
PROTOGENES SPYROPOULOS
GUATEMALAN MERIDA
HUNGARIAN LOTZ ZICHY VADASZ
WAGNER SZINYEI MUNKACSY
IRISH BARRY DANBY BURTON
FORBES LAVERY PETRIE MACLISE
COSTELLO MULREADY ODOHERTY
ISRAELI AGAM RUBIN
ITALIAN CHIA FETI MOLA RENI
ROSA TURA VAGA BACCI BALLA
CAFFI CAMPI CARPI CARRA COSSA
COSTA DANTI DOLCI FERRI FETTI
FOPPA GATTI GENGA IORIS LIPPI
LOTTO LUINI MELZI PALMA PENNI
PIERO PISIS PRETI RICCI SANTI
SARTO SPADA VANNI VINCI ABBATE
ALBANI ALLORI AVANZO BATONI
CALCAR CESARI CIARDI COSIMO
CRESPI FRANCO GAULLI GIOTTO
GUUIDO MORONI NITTIS PASINI
PISANO PREDIS RICCIO ROMANO
SACCHI SIRONI SODOMA SOLARI
SUARDI TITIAN VASARI VERRIO
AMIGONI APPIANI BARBARI
BAROCCI BARTOLI BASSANO
BELLINI BERNINI BOLDINI BRUMIDI
CENNINI CHIRICO CIGNANI
CORTONA FALCONE FRANCIA
GIORGIO GOZZOLI MARATTI
MARTINI MORELLI MUZIANO
OGGIONO PALIZZI PERUZZI
RAPHAEL ROBERTI STROZZI TIBALDI
TIEPOLO UCCELLO VECELLI
ZUCCARO BACICCIO BAGLIONI
BARBIERE BOCCIONI BONFIGLI
CAGLIARI CARDUCCI CARRIERA
CASANOVA CASTELLO CIPRIANI
COGHETTI CORENZIO GRIMALDI
MAGNASCO MAINARDI MANTEGNA
MICHETTI MONTAGNA POCCETTI
PONTORMO SALVIATI SEVERINI
UBERTINI VAROTARI VERONESE

VIVARINI ASPERTINI BECCAFUMI
CAMUCCINI CANTARINI CAVALLINI
CORREGGIO FRANCESCA GHISLANDI
MAZZOLINO PIAZZETTA SCHIAVONE
SEGANTINI BELTRAFFIO
BOCCACCINO BORGOGNONE
BOTTICELLI CAMPAGNOLA
CARAVAGGIO LORENZETTI
MODIGLIANI PROCACCINI
SIGNORELLI SQUAREIONE
TINTORETTO VERROCCHIO
ZUCCARELLI ANGUISCIOLA
CASTIGLIONE GENTILESCHI
PRIMATICCIO ALBERTINELLI
BALDOVINETTI FRANCESCHINI
MICHELANGELO PARMIGIANINO
PINTURICCHIO
JAPANESE KANO OKYO BUSON
IWASA KORIN SAITO SOSEN TORII
GOSHUN KOETSU KYOSAI SESSHU
JAKUCHU JOSETSU SOTATSU
UTAMARO HARUNOBU KIYOMASU
KIYONAGA KIYONOBU MORONOBU
TOYOKUNI HIROSHEGE KIYOMITSU
TSUNETAKA
LITHUANIAN SOUTINE
MEXICAN CANTU MERIDA OROZCO
RIVERA TAMAYO SIQUEIROS
CASTELLANOS
NORWEGIAN DAHL GUDE KROHG
MUNCH LERCHE MUNTHE SINDING
FEARNLEY WERENSKIOLD
POLISH BENDA GERSON MATEJKO
GROTTGER CHELMINSKI
MARCOUSSIS WYSPIANSKI
PORTUGUESE FONSECA
RUSSIAN BAKST REPIN BENOIS
BERMAN GRABAR BURLIUK
CHAGALL ROERICH LARIONOV
LEVITSKI MALEVICH CHELISHEV
KANDINSKI LISSITZKY RODCHENKO
AIVAZOVSKI BOGOLYUBOV
BASHKIRTSEV VERESHCHAGIN
SCOTTISH BONE DYCE FAED HILL
ALLAN DAVIE GRANT PATON SCOTT
AIKMAN ARCHER BARKER BROUGH
DUNCAN GEDDES GORDON
GRAHAM HARVEY LAUDER LEITCH
MANSON MURRAY PETTIE RAMSAY
WILKIE DOUGLAS GUTHRIE
LORIMER MACBETH NASMYTH
RAEBURN THOMSON CHALMERS
MACTAGGART MACWHIRTER
ORCHARDSON
SPANISH ARCO CANO DALI GOYA
GRIS MAZO MIRO MOYA SERT
GRECO HAMEN MACIP CEREZO
COELLO PAREJA RIBERA RINCON
VARGAS ALVAREZ HERRERA IRIARTE
MADRAZO MORALES MURILLO
ORRENTE PACHECO PICASSO
RIBALTA ZULOAGA CESPEDES
PRADILLA ZAMACOIS ZURBARAN
VELASQUEZ ZUBIAURRE
BERRUGUETE
SWEDISH DAHL ZORN BERGH
ROSLIN LARSSON FAGERLIN
LUNDGREN HELLQUIST JOSEPHSON
LILJEFORS
SWISS KLEE LIPS MIND WITZ ASPER
DIDAY ITTEN MEYER BODMER
CALAME FUSELI GLEYRE HODLER
MANUEL BOCKLIN BUCHSER

DISTELI LIOTARD PETITOT VAUTIER
KAUFFMANN
WELSH JOHN
PAINTING ART OIL PAT DAUB PATA
DRAFT MURAL PIECE TABLE
WATER CANVAS CROUTE FRESCO
MINERY TITIAN BODEGON
CAMAIEU CARTOON COMBINE
DAUBING GRADINO GRAPHIC
HISTORY PAYSAGE FROTTAGE
PREDELLA SEAPIECE SYMPHONY
AQUARELLE MINIATURE
TABLATURE
(— EQUIPMENT) OIL BRUSH EASEL
PAINT CANVAS PALLET
(— IN COLLOIDAL MEDIUM)
TEMPERA
(— OF EVERYDAY LIFE) GENRE
(— OF FOLIAGE) BOSCAGE
(— ON PLASTER) SECCO FRESCO
(— ON VELVET) THEOREM
(— SCHOOL) ASHCAN
(— WITH OPAQUE COLORS)
GOUACHE
(ACTION —) TACHISM
(CIRCULAR —) TONDO
(EGG —) TEMPERA
(JAPANESE INK —) SUMIE
(JAPANESE STYLE OF —) YAMATO
(PREHISTORIC —) PICTOGRAM
PICTOGRAPH
(RELIGIOUS —) PIETA TANKA
(SCENIC —) SCAPE
(SMALL —) TABLET
(TEMPERA —) SECCO
(THREE PANEL —) TRIPTYCH
(PL.) GENRE
(SUFF.) CHROMY
PAIR DUO TWO ZYG CASE DIAD
DUAD DUAL DYAD MATE SIDE
SPAN TEAM TWIN YOKE BRACE
MARRY MATCH TWAIN UNITE
COUPLE GEMINI COUPLET
DOUBLET JUMELLE TWOSOME
(— OF FILMS) BIPACK
(— OF HORSES) SPAN
(— OF MILLSTONES) RUN
(— OF SHOTS) BRACKET
(— OF TONGS) GRAMPUS GRAPPLE
(— OF WINGS) SHEARS
(— ROYAL) PARIAL
(KIND OF —) COOPER
(ONE OF —) IMPAIR NEIGHBOR
(ONE OF A —) MATE
(PL.) GEMELS
(PREF.) GEMINI ZYG(O)(OTO)
(SUFF.) ZYGOUS
PAIRED GEMEL MATED JUGATE
ZYGOUS JUMELLE
PAISLEY PRINT SHAWL DESIGN
FABRIC
PAIUTE DIGGER
PAJAMAS JAMMIES SHALWAR
SLEEPER
PAKHT (HUSBAND OF —) PTAH

PAKISTAN	
BAY:	SOYMIANI
CANAL:	NARA ROHRI
CAPE:	FASTA JADDI JIWANI
CAPITAL:	ISLAMABAD
COIN:	ANNA PAISA RUPEE
DAM:	TARBELA

LANGUAGE: URDU PUSHTU SINDHI BALUCHI BENGALI PUNJABI
MOUNTAIN: TIRICHMIR
MOUNTAIN RANGE: MAKRAN KIRTHAR HIMALAYA SULAIMAN
NATIVE: BENGAL PATHAN SINDHI BALUCHI PUNJABI
PORT: CHALNA KARACHI
PROVINCE: SIND PUNJAB
RIVER: NAL BADO RAVI ZHOB DASHT INDUS CHENAB GANGES JAMUNA JHELUM KUNDAR PORALI
STATE: DIR SWAT KALAT KHARAN CHITRAL KHAIRPUR
TOWN: DACCA CHALNA KHULNA LAHORE MULTAN QUETTA KARACHI SIALKOT LYALLPUR PESHAWAR SARGODHA
WEIGHT: SEER TOLA MAUND

PAKTONG TUTENAG
PAL BO ALLY CHUM JACK PARD BILLY BUDDY BUTTY CHINA CRONY LOUKE COBBER COPAIN DIGGER FRIEND COMRADE PARTNER COMPANION
PALACE SALE CHIGI COURT SERAI STEAD CASTLE ELYSEE LOUVRE PALAIS ALCAZAR EDIFICE LATERAN MANSION PALAZZO TRIANON VATICAN ZWINGER BASILICA SERAGLIO WHITEHALL
 (— OF SATAN) PANDEMONIUM
 (FAIRY —) SHEE SIDHE
PALADIN HERO PEER ANSEIS ASTOLF KNIGHT CHAMPION DOUZEPER
PALAL (FATHER OF —) UZAI
PALAMEDES (BROTHER OF —) OEAX SFORZA ACHILLES
 (FATHER OF —) NAUPLIUS
 (MOTHER OF —) CLYMENE
 (SLAYER OF —) CORINDA
PALAMON (RIVAL OF —) ARCITE
 (WIFE OF —) EMELYE
PALANQUIN JAUN JUAN KAGE KAGO DANDI DOOLI DOOLY PALKI SEDAN DOOLIE LITTER PALKEE TONJON NORIMON
PALATABLE SAPID SPICY TASTY DAINTY SAVORY MOREISH DELICATE LUSCIOUS PLEASING SAPOROUS AGREEABLE DELICIOUS TOOTHSOME
PALATAL SOFT FRONT VELAR GUTTURAL
PALATALIZED MOUILLE
PALATE TASTE VELUM RELISH GOURMET URANISCUS
 (SOFT —) UVULA
 (PREF.) URAN(O)(OSO)
PALATIAL LARGE ORNATE STATELY SPLENDID
PALATINE CAPE OFFICER PALADIN PALATIAL
PALAVER GASH SLUM TALK CAJOLE DEBATE GLAVER JARGON PARLEY CHATTER FLATTER WHEEDLE CAJOLERY FLATTERY
PALE DIM WAN ASHY BLOC FADE GREY GULL LILY PALL SICK THIN WHEY ASHEN BLAKE BLATE BLEAK CLOSE FAINT FENCE GREEN LIGHT LINEN LIVID LURID MEALY STAKE STICK VERGE WHITE ANEMIC BLANCH CHALKY CHANGE DOUGHY FALLOW FEEBLE PALLID PASTEL PICKET REGION REMISS SICKLY SILVER WATERY WHITEN DEFENSE GHASTLY HAGGARD INSIPID OBSCURE SHILPIT DELICATE WATERISH
 (— BY COMPARISON) STAIN
 (IN —) HAURIENT
 (PREF.) LIRO PALLIDI POLI(O)
PALEA PALET SQUAMELLA
PALENESS WAN PALLOR ACHROMA
PALEONTOLOGIST AMERICAN HAY GABB HALL LULL MEEK BERRY GOULD MARSH CLARKE FOSTER GRABAU HORNER OSBORN BEECHER GREGORY MERRIAM WALCOTT KNOWLTON SPRINGER WILLIAMS SCHUCHERT WACHSMUTH WILLISTON
 AUSTRIAN SUESS HOERNES MOJSISOVICS ETTINGSHAUSEN
 ENGLISH TATE CAUTLEY MANTELL DAVIDSON WOODWARD BOWERBANK PARKINSON
 FRENCH DOULE GAUDRY LARTET BARRANDE TEILHARD
 GERMAN ZITTEL BEYRICH QUENSTEDT
 SCOTTISH FALCONER
 SOUTH AFRICAN BROOM
PALESTINE (SEE ISRAEL)
 (CITY OF ANCIENT —) DAN
PALETOT COAT JACKET OVERCOAT GREATCOAT
PALFREY HORSE PALFRY
PALIMPSEST TABLET PARCHMENT
PALINDROMIC SOTADIC SOTADEAN
PALING PALE FENCE FLAKE LIMIT PALIS STAKE PICKET FENCING BLENCHING
PALISADE HAY BOMA PALE PEEL CLIFF FENCE RIMER STAKE FRAISE HURDIS PICKET BARRIER ENCLOSE FORTIFY HURDIES STACKET TAMBOUR ESPALIER
 (MILITARY —) CIPPUS
 (PL.) BAIL BARRIER
PALL FOG BORE CLOY PALE SATE CLOAK CLOTH FAINT QUALM STALE WEARY MANTLE NAUSEA SHROUD DISGUST SATIATE ANIMETTA MORTCLOTH
PALLET BED COT PAD COUCH QUILT PADDLE BLANKET MATTRESS PLANCHER
PALLIARD BEGGAR LECHER RASCAL VAGABOND
PALLIATE EASE HIDE MASK VEIL ABATE CLOAK COLOR COVER GLOSS GLOZE LITHE BLANCH LESSEN REDUCE SMOOTH SOFTEN SOOTHE CONCEAL CUSHION SHELTER DISGUISE MITIGATE
PALLID WAN ASHY PALE PALY BLEAK MEALY WASHY WAXEN WHITE SALLOW GHASTLY BLOODLESS COLORLESS INNOCUOUS
PALL-MALL MAIL

PALLOR ASH WAN PALE ASHES PALENESS
PALLU (FATHER OF —) REUBEN
 (SON OF —) ELIAB
PALM ADY DOM ITA ATAP BRAB BURI BUSU COCO DATE DOUM FLAT HIDE JARA KOKO LOOF NIOG NIPA PAWN SAGO SLIP TARA ARCHA ARECA ARENG ASSAI ATTAP BONGA BUNGA CARRY COCOA COYOL CURUA DATIL FOIST HOWEA INAJA JAGUA LOULU MACAW MERUS NIKAU RATAN SABAL SALAK TECUM TUCUM UNAMO YAGUA YARAY ANAHAO ASSAHY BACABA BURITI CHONTA COHUNE COROJO COROZO GEBANG GOMUTI GRUGRU JAMBEE JUPATI KENTIA KITTUL LAWYER LONTAR NIBONG PACAYA RAFFIA ROTANG THENAR TOOROO TROPHY APRICOT BABASSU BACTRIS CARANDA CONCEAL COQUITO ERYTHEA GEONOMA MORICHE PALMYRA PUPUNHA SAGWIRE TALIPOT TROOLIE URUCURI JACITARA LATANIER MACAHUBA PIASSAVA
 (— FERN) PONJA
 (— FOOD) NUT COCO DATE NIPA SAGO SURA ASSAI TAREE TODDY COCONUT
 (— JUICE) SURA
 (— LEAF) OLA OLLA CAJAN FROND
 (— LILY) TI
 (— OFF) COG FOB TOP SHAB FOIST TRUMP
 (— OF HAND) FLAT LOOF VOLA TABLE THENAR
 (— OUT) APPAUME
 (BETEL —) ARECA BONGA PUGUA PINANG
 (CLIMBING —) RATTAN
 (FEATHER —) HOWEA GOMUTI URUCURI
 (KIND OF —) SAGO
 (SLAPPING OF —S) SKIN
 (SPINY —) PEACH GRIGRI GRUGRU
 (PREF.) CYCAD(I)(O) PALMATO PALMI PALPI PALPO
PALMARY CHIEF PALMAR SUPERIOR
PALMATE FLAT BROAD LOBED WEBBED
PALMER LOUSE FERULE STROLL TRAVEL VOTARY WANDER FOISTER PILGRIM
PALMETTO CABBAGE PALMITO BIGTHATCH
 (— STATE) SOUTHCAROLINA
PALMISTRY CHIROMANCY
PALMODIC JERKY
PALMYRA BRAB TALA LONTAR RONIER TADMOR BASSINE
 (QUEEN OF —) ZENOBIA
PALP FEEL TOUCH CAJOLE FEELER HANDLE PALPUS FLATTER TENTACLE
PALPABLE BALD RANK PLAIN PATENT AUDIBLE EVIDENT OBVIOUS TACTILE APPARENT DISTINCT MANIFEST TANGIBLE CORPOREAL

PALPATE FEEL
PALPATION THROB TOUCH WALLOP DIPPING PITAPAT
PALPEBRA EYELID
PALPITATE PANT QUAP THROB FLACKER FLICKER FLUTTER PULSATE
PALPITATION BEAT DUNT PANT FLICKER FLUTTER PULSATION SALTATION THROBBING
 (— OF HEART) THUMB
PALSIED SHAKY SHAKING PARALYZED TOTTERING TREMBLING TREMULOUS
PALSY PARLESIE PARALYSIS
PALTER FIB LIE BABBLE HAGGLE MUMBLE PARLEY TRIFLE BARGAIN CHAFFER CHATTER QUIBBLE SHAFFLE
PALTIEL (FATHER OF —) AZZAN
PALTRY BALD BARE BASE MEAN ORRA PUNY SCAB VILE WAFF CHEAP FOOTY MINOR PETTY SCALD SCALL SCRUB SILLY TRASH CHETIF FLIMSY JITNEY SHABBY SLIGHT TRASHY WOEFUL HILDING PELTING PIMPING PITEOUS PITIFUL ROYNISH RUBBISH SCABBED SCRUBBY TRIVIAL PICAYUNE PICKLING PIDDLING TRIFLING
PALUDAL MARSHY
PAMELA (AUTHOR OF —) RICHARDSON
 (BROTHER OF —) PHILOCLEA
 (CHARACTER IN —) JACOB DAVERS JERVIS JEWKES PAMELA ANDREWS SWYNFORD
 (FATHER OF —) BASILIUS
PAMPA PLAIN PRAIRIE
PAMPAS (— CAT) KODKOD PAJERO
 (— DEER) MAZAME
PAMPER PET BABY CRAM DELT GLUT POMP HUMOR SPOIL TUTOR WALLY CARESS COCKER CODDLE COSHER COSSET CUDDLE CUITER DANDLE FONDLE MAUNGE POSSET TIDDLE CHERISH COCKNEY FORWEAN GRATIFY INDULGE SATIATE SMOODGE SAGINATE
PAMPHLET JACK LEAD FLIER QUIRE SHEET TRACT FOLDER BOOKLET CATALOG LEAFLET NOVELET BROCHURE CHAPBOOK CIRCULAR WORKBOOK CATALOGUE NEWSLETTER
PAN FIT TAB VLY MELL PART PRIG VLEI WASH AGREE BASIN BATEA COVER GRAND ROAST SHEET UNITE CENSER FRACHE LAPPET PANKIN PATINA SPIDER VESSEL CRANIUM CREAMER HARDPAN PORTION ROASTER SKILLET SUBSOIL PANNIKIN RIDICULE
 (— FOR COALS) BRAZIER
 (— OF BALANCE) BOWL BASIN SCALEPAN
 (— WITH 3 FEET) POSNET
 (EARTHENWARE —) PANCHEON
 (EVAPORATING —) ROOM COVER TACHE SALTPAN
 (FRYING —) GRIDDLE
 (GOD —) FAUNUS

(IRON —) YET FRACHE
(LONG-HANDLED —) PINGLE
(MILK —) LEAD
(OIL —) SUMP
(PREF.) PATELLI PATELLO
PANACEA CURE BEZOAR ELIXIR
REMEDY SOLACE CUREALL
GINSENG HEALALL NEPENTHE
CATHOLICON
PANACHE STYLE

PANAMA

CAPITAL: PANAMA
COIN: BALBOA
COUNTY: DARIEN HERRERA
CROP: ABACA CACAO
GULF: DARIEN SANBLAS CHIRIQUI
  MOSQUITO
ISLAND: COIBA
LAKE: GATUN
MEASURE: CELEMIN
MOUNTAIN: CHICO GANDI
  COLUMAN SANTIAGO
MOUNTAIN RANGE: VERAGUA
PENINSULA: AZUERO
PORT: CRISTOBAL
PROVINCE: COCLE COLON CHIRIQUI
  VERAGUAS
RIVER: CHEPO SAMBU TUIRA
  BAYANO PANUGO CHAGRES
TOWN: COLON DAVID AZUERO
  BALBOA PANAMA PENONOME
  SANTIAGO
TREE: YAYA MARIA QUIRA ALFAJE
  CATIVO

PANAMA HAT JIPIJAPA
PANAMINT KOSO
PANCAKE BLIN FLAM AREPA CREPE
FADGE FLAWN KISRA LEFSE TOURT
BLINTZ FRAISE FROISE CRUMPET
FLAPPER FLIPPER FRITTER
HOTCAKE PIKELET CORNCAKE
FLAPJACK FLIPJACK
(PL.) LEFSEN
PANCREAS BUR NUT
PAND PAWN DRAPERY
PANDA WA WAH BEARCAT
PANDAREUS (DAUGHTER OF —)
AEDON MEROPE CLEOTHERA
(FATHER OF —) MEROPS
(WIFE OF —) HARMOTHOE
PANDARUS (BROTHER OF —) BITIAS
(FATHER OF —) LYCAON ALCANOR
PANDAVA BHIMA
PANDECT COMPENDIUM
PANDEMONIUM DIN HELL CHAOS
NOISE BEDLAM TUMULT UPROAR
DISORDER CONFUSION
PANDER BAWD PIMP BULLY CATER
BROKER MICHER PURVEY RUFFIAN
WHISKIN PROCURER BAWDSTROT
PANDION (BROTHER OF —)
PLEXIPPUS
(DAUGHTER OF —) PROCNE
PHILOMELA
(FATHER OF —) CECROPS PHINEUS
ERICHTHONIUS
(MOTHER OF —) CLEOPATRA
(SON OF —) BUTES LYCUS NISUS
AEGEUS PALLAS ERECHTHEUS
(WIFE OF —) PYLIA
PANDORA BANDORE

(BROTHER OF —) PROMETHEUS
(HUSBAND OF —) EPIMETHEUS
PANDOWDY PIE DESSERT
PANDU (BROTHER OF —)
DURYODHANA
(FATHER OF —) DHRITARASHTRA
PANE GLASS GLAZE LOZEN PANEL
QUIRK SHEET SHOCK SLASH
QUARRY QUARREL SECTION
PORTLIGHT
PANEGYRIC ELOGE ELOGY EULOGY
PRAISE ORATION TRIBUTE
ENCOMIUM LAUDATION
PANEL FIN PAN JURY SKIN BOARD
GROUP LABEL TABLE ABACUS
ASSIZE COFFER HURDLE MIRROR
PADDLE PILLOW ROSACE TABLET
TYMPAN CAISSON CONSOLE
FLIPPER LACUNAR DECORATE
MANDORLA MEDALLION
(— IN FENCE) LOOP
(— IN GARMENT) LAP STEAK
(CIRCULAR —) ROUNDEL
(GAUZE —) SCRIM
(GLAZED —) LAYLIGHT
(LEGAL —) ARRAY
(REAR — ON STATION WAGON)
LIFTGATE
(RECESSED —) ORB COFFER
LACUNAR
(SUNKEN —) CAISSON CASSOON
(3-PART —) TRIPTYCH
PANELLING WAINSCOT
PANFISH SCUP
PANG ACHE CRAM FILL GIRD PAIN
STAB TANG AGONY PINCH PRONG
SPASM STANG STOUN STUFF
THROB THROE SHOWER STOUND
TWINGE ANGUISH TRAVAIL
(PL.) GNAWINGS
PANGLOSS (PUPIL OF —) CANDIDE
PANGOLIN MANID MANIS
ANTEATER EDENTATE TANGILIN
PANGS MUNCHIES
(HUNGER —) MUNCHIES
PANGWE FAN FANG
PANHANDLE BEG CADGE SKELB
SKILDER
(— STATE) WV WVA
PANIC FEAR FRAY FUNK WILD
ALARM AMAZE CHAOS SCARE
FRIGHT SCHRIK TERROR SWITHER
CONSTERNATION
PANICKY FUNKY ALARMED
PANICLE JUBA WHISK ANTHELA
PANNIER BAG PED SERON BASKET
CAJAVA CURAGH DORSEL DORSER
DOSSAL DOSSER PANTRY CORBEIL
CURRACK KAJAWAH KEDJAVE
PANOPE (FATHER OF —) NEREUS
(MOTHER OF —) DORIS
PANOPEUS (BROTHER OF —)
CRISUS
(COMPANION OF —) AMPHITRYON
(DAUGHTER OF —) AEGLE
(FATHER OF —) PHOCUS
(MOTHER OF —) ASTERIA
PANOPLY POMP ARMOR ARRAY
UNIFORM
PANORAMA VIEW RANGE SCENE
SWEEP VISTA NEORAMA PICTURE
SCENERY CYCLORAMA
POLYORAMA

PANPIPE SICU SIKU QUILL ANTARA
SYRINX ZAMPOGNA
PANSY FANCY PENSE VIOLA KISSES
PENSEE VIOLET TRINITY
FANTASQUE HEARTEASE
(PREF.) VIOL
PANT FAB ACHE BEAT BLOW FUFF
GAPE GASP HECH LONG PANK
PECH PEGH PINE PIPE PUFF TIFT
FLAFF HEAVE QUIRK STECH SUGGE
THROB YEARN ANHELE ASPIRE
FRIESE PANTLE PULSATE
PANTAGRUEL (COMPANION OF —)
PANURGE
(FATHER OF —) GARGANTUA
(MOTHER OF —) BADEBEC
PANTALOONS PANTS TROUSERS
PANTDRESS CULOTTE
PANTHEA (HUSBAND OF —)
ABRADATUS
PANTHEIST AMALRICIAN
PANTHEON AESIR TEMPLE
ROTUNDA VALHALL VALHALLA
PANTHER CAT PARD PUMA
COUGAR JAGUAR LEOPARD
PAINTER PANTILE
(KIND OF —) GRAY
PANTIES SCANTIES
PANTILE TILE IMBREX BISCUIT
HARDTACK
PANTING ANHELOSE ANHELOUS
PANTOGRAPH EIDOGRAPH
POLYGRAPH
PANTOMIME PLAY PANTO
DUMBSHOW
PANTOMIMIST MUMMER
PANTRY CAVE STUE AMBRY COVEY
CUDDY CLOSET LARDER SPENCE
BUTLERY BUTTERY PANNIER
PANTLER SERVERY SPICERY
CUPBOARD
PANTS CORDS JEANS LEVIS BRIEFS
SLACKS DRAWERS JODHPUR
BREECHES BRITCHES KICKSIES
KNICKERS SNUGGIES TROUSERS
(— THAT REACH TO MID-CALF)
CLAMDIGGER
(— WITH WIDE BOTTOMS) BELLS
(KIND OF —) TAP CAPRI
(LEATHER —) CHAPS LEDERHOSEN
(WIDE-LEGGED —) PALAZZO
PANUELO COLLAR RUFFLE
KERCHIEF NECKCLOTH
PANURGE (COMPANION OF —)
PANTAGRUEL
PANZER TANK
PAOLO (LOVER OF —) FRANCESCA
PAP DUG TIT POBS TEAT NIPPLE
EMULSION FLUMMERY
PAPA PA DAD PAP PAW POP SIN
BABA EVIL DADDY LOVER PAPPY
BABOON FATHER POTATO PRIEST
HUSBAND VULTURE
PAPAL (ALSO SEE POPE) POPAL
PAPANE POPELY APOSTOLIC
PAPAW PAPA ASIMEN PAPAIO
ASIMINA CORAZON JASMINE
PAPAYA PAPAW LECHOSA
PAPER LIL WEB BILL BOND BLANK
BROKE ESSAY STUDY THEME
ASTHMA BINDLE CARTEL PAPIER
REPORT RETREE VESSEL CHEVIOT
EXHIBIT JOURNAL WRITING

YOSHINO DOCUMENT
MONOGRAPH NEWSPRINT
ONIONSKIN PARCHMENT
VALENTINE
(— FOLDER) STROKER
(— MAKER) WASHERMAN
(— NAUTILUS) ARGONAUT
(— PULP) WATERLEAF
(— QUANTITY) PAGE REAM QUIRE
SHEET BUNDLE
(— SIZE) SIXMO
(ABSORBENT —) BLOTTER
TOWELLING
(ADVERTISING —) FLIER FLYER
SHOPPER
(ALBUMINIZED —) SAXE
(BUILDING —) FELT
(BUNDLE OF —S) DUFTER DOSSIER
(CHINESE —) INDIA
(COMMERCIAL —) PORTFOLIO
(DAMAGED —) BROKE CASSE SALLE
RETREE
(DEFECTIVE —) BROKES
(DIPLOMATIC —) NOTE
(DRAWING —) TORCHON
(FOLDED —) SADDLE AIRPLANE
(FRILLED —) PAPILLOTE
(GIVING AUTHORITY) POWER
(GLOSS —) GILL
(HARD —) PELURE
(HEAVY —) FELT
(LAVATORY —) BUMF
(LINING —S) SKIPS
(METAL-COATED —) FOIL
(NEGOTIABLE —) STIFF
(OFFICIAL —) TARGE HOOKUM
DOCUMENT
(PARCHMENT —) VELLUM
PERGAMYN
(PHOTOGRAPHIC —) SEPIA
(SIZE OF —) CAP COPY DEMI NOTE
POST POTT TOWN ATLAS CROWN
FOLIO JESUS LARGE LEGAL ROYAL
SIXMO ALBERT BILLET CASING
LETTER MEDIUM THIRDS BASTARD
CABINET EMPEROR THEOREM
ELEPHANT FOOLSCAP IMPERIAL
(SMALL PIECES OF —) CHAD
(STRIP OF —) TAPE
(STRONG —) MANILA MANILLA
(THIN —) FLIMSY PELURE TISSUE
ONIONSKIN
(THROWN —) CONFETTI
(TOILET —) BUMF
(TRANSPARENT —) GLASSINE
(UNCUT —) BOLT
(WALL —) TENTURE
(WATERMARKED —) BATONNE
(WRAPPING —) SKIP KRAFT SEALING
SCREENING
(WRITING —) FLAT LINEN WEDDING
(PREF.) PAPYRO
PAPERBARK CAJEPUT MILKWOOD
PAPERBOARD BENDER VENEER
CARDBOARD CHIPBOARD
PULPBOARD
PAPER FACTOR JUVABIONE
PAPERWORK BUMF BUMPH
PAPIER-MACHE FLONG
PAPILLA CERAS DEIRID NIPPLE
PAPULA MAMMULA THELIUM
(PL.) CERATA
PAPILLOMA ANGLEBERRY

PAPIO MORMON
PAPIST TORY PAPANE CATHOLIC POPELING
PAPPUS DOWN STIPE AIGRETTE PARACHUTE THISTLEDOWN
PAPPY PA DAD PAW PAPA SOFT MUSHY PULPY FATHER SUCCULENT
PAPRIKA PIMENTO PIMIENTO
PAPUA (BAY OF —) DYKE MILNE ACLAND HOLNICOTE
(CAPITAL OF —) PORTMORESBY
(MONEY OF —) KINA
(RIVER OF —) FLY KIKORI PURARI
(TOWN OF —) LAE BUNA DARU WEWAK GOROKA KIKORI MADANG SAMARAI
PAPUAN ARAU BIAK HULA KATE BUANG EKARI KIWAI KWOMA SIVAI SULKA BAITSI BANARO IATMUL KEREWA KOIARI ARAPESH BAINING
PAPULE WHELK PIMPLE
PAPYRUS REED PAPER SEDGE BIBLOS GLUMAL SCROLL BULRUSH
(— STRIP) ORIHON
PAR BY NORM EQUAL NORMAL AVERAGE EQUALITY
(ONE OVER —) BOGIE
(ONE UNDER —) BIRDIE
(TWO UNDER —) EAGLE
PARA FODDA PERAU PARRAH
PARABASIS ODE
PARABLE MYTH TALE FABLE STORY APOLOG BYWORD MASHAL SAMPLE BYSPELL PROVERB ALLEGORY APOLOGUE FORBYSEN LIKENESS SIMILITUDE
PARABOLA ARC CURVE ANTENNA
PARACETAMOL PANADOL
PARACHUTE SILK CHUTE BROLLY DROGUE BALLUTE PATAGIUM STREAMER
(— OF DOWN) PAPPUS
(FOLDED —) PACK
(SEND BY —) DROP
(SMALL —) BALLUTE
PARACHUTIST PATHFINDER
(PL.) STICK
PARACLETE AIDER HELPER PLEADER ADVOCATE CONSOLER COMFORTER
PARADE JET TOP POMP SHOW WALK MARCH STRUT FLAUNT MUSTER REVIEW STROLL CORTEGE DISPLAY EXHIBIT MARSHAL CEREMONY EXERCISE FLOURISH GRANDEUR SPLENDOR PAGEANTRY
(— GROUND) MAIDAN
(— OF BULLFIGHTERS) PASEO
(— OF WORDS) FLOURISH
(UNSUBSTANTIAL —) PAGEANT
PARADED AFFICHE
PARADISE EDEN JODO BLISS JENNA AIDENN GOLOKA HEAVEN PARVIS ELYSIUM NIRVANA
(— OF INDRA) SVARGA SWARGA
(— TREE) ACEITUNA STAVEWOOD
PARADOX KOAN ANTINOMY
PARADOXURE MUSANG PALMCAT PALMCIVET
PARAFFIN ALKANE

PARAGON GEM HERO PINK TYPE IDEAL MODEL PEARL APERSEE PATTERN PEROPUS PHOENIX NONESUCH NONPARIEL
(— OF KNIGHTHOOD) PALADIN
PARAGRAPH ITEM SIGN CAPUT PAUSE CLAUSE NOTICE RUBRIC ARTICLE INITIAL PILCROW SECTION CAUSERIE MATERIAL PEELCROW PERSONAL SUBLEADER
(— MARK) PILCROW
(UNIMPORTANT —S) BALAAM

PARAGUAY

CAPITAL: ASUNCION
COIN: GUARANI
DEPARTMENT: GUAIRA ITAPUA OLIMPO CAAZAPA BOQUERON
LAKE: VERA YPOA YPACARAI
LANGUAGE: GUARANI
MEASURE: PIE LINE LINO VARA LEGUA LINEA CORDEL CUADRA CUARTA FANEGA
PLAIN: CHACO
RIVER: YPANE ACARAY PARANA CONFUSO
TOWN: LUQUE PILAR CAACUPE CAAZAPA TRINIDAD CONCEPCION VILLARRICA
WEIGHT: QUINTAL

PARAGUAY TEA MATE
PARAKEET CONURE PARROT WELLAT ROSELLA ARATINGA KAKARIKI POPINJAY ROSEHILL GREENLEEK
PARALLEL EVEN LIKE ALONG EQUAL MATCH SECOND EXAMPLE FRONTAL PARAGON PENDANT ANALOGUE LIKENESS MULTIPLE QUANTITY
(PREF.) ORTH(O) PAR(A)
PARALLELEPIPED CUBOID
PARALLELISM PARITY ANALOGY
PARALLELOGRAM RHOMB OBLONG SQUARE RHOMBUS RHOMBOID RECTANGLE
PARALYSIS CRAMP PALSY POLIO SHOCK PARESIS DIPLEGIA PARAPLEGIA POLIOMYELITIS
(SUFF.) LYSE LYSIS LYST LYTE LYTIC LYZE
PARALYZE DARE DAZE STUN PALSY SCRAM ASTONY BENUMB CONGEAL IMPALSY PETRIFY TORPEDO TORPEFY
(— WITH EMOTION) TRANSFIX
PARALYZED NUMB PALSIED CRIPPLED
PARAMEDIC EMT
PARAMORPHINE THEBAINE
PARAMOUNT ABOVE CHIEF RULER SOVRAN CAPITAL SUPREME DOMINANT SUPERIOR SUZERAIN SOVEREIGN
PARAMOUR DOLL PRIM PURE LEMAN LOVER WOMAN WOOER AMORET FRIEND MASTER MINION FRANION GALLANT HETAERA RUFFIAN SERVANT SPECIAL SULTANA STALLION BOYFRIEND
PARAPET BUTT WALL BAHUT REDAN BARBET BONNET FLECHE

PARPEN TRENCH BULWARK PLUTEUS RAILING RAMPART BARTIZAN ENVELOPE TRAVERSE
PARAPH RUBRIC
PARAPHERNALIA GEAR EQUIPAGE APPARATUS EQUIPMENT TRAPPINGS
PARAPHRASE FARSE REWORD TARGET TARGUM PREFACE THARGUM VERSION TRANSLATE
PARASITE BUG BUR FLY BURR MOSS SPIV TRYP CHARK DRONE LEECH SHARK TOADY VIRUS FEEDER FUNGUS GNATHO SHADOW SPONGE SUCKER THRIPS BLEEDER BYWONER SPONGER TAGTAIL DICYEMID ENTOZOON EPIPHYTE HANGERON SLAVERER INFESTANT POTHUNTER SACCULINA SPARGANUM SYCOPHANT TOADEATER TURHUNTER
(— ON TROUT) SUG
(PL.) ECTOZOA ENTOZOA DRIFTWOOD
(PREF.) PHYT(I)(O)
(VEGETABLE —) PHYT(I)(O)
PARASITIC CYTOZOIC TRENCHER BIOPHILOUS
(— JAEGER) SHOOI DIRTBIRD
PARASOL SHADE AOGIRI SHADOW ROUNDEL TIRESOL KITTYSOL SUNSHADE UMBRELLA
(— MUSHROOM) LEPIOTA
(PREF.) UMBELL(I)
PARATROOPER SKYMAN
PARAVANE OTTER
PARBOIL CODDLE
PARBOILED LEEPIT
PARCEL DAK LOT DAWK DEAD DEAL DOLE METE PACK PART WISP BULSE BUNCH GROUP PIECE BUNDLE DIVIDE FARDEL PACKET PASSEL CONACRE PACKAGE PORTION COMMODITY
(— OF DIAMONDS) SERIES
(— OF GROUND) LOT PICK CLOSE SOLUM SUERTE CONACRE PENDICLE
(— OF HEMP FIBER) PIG
(— OF JEWELS) BULSE
(— OUT) ALLOT
PARCH DRY FRY BURN COOK SEAR ROAST TOAST PEARCH RIZZER SCORCH BRISTLE BRUSTLE GRADDAN SHRIVEL TORREFY TORRIFY
(PREF.) TORRE XER(O)
PARCHED ARID HUSK SERE ADUST FIERY GIZZEN TORRID THIRSTY SCORCHED
PARCHING URENT
PARCHMENT LARK FOREL CHARTA MEZUZAH PAPYRIN SCYTALE DRUMHEAD SHEEPSKIN PALIMPSEST
(— PAPER) DOCKET PERGAMYN
(FINE —) VEL VELLUM
(PIECE OF —) MEMBRANE
(ROLL OF —) PELL SCROLL
PARD PAL CHUM TIGER FRIEND LEOPARD PANTHER PARTNER COMPANION
PARDON FREE CLEAR COVER

GRACE MERCY REMIT SPARE ACQUIT ASSOIL EXCUSE SHRIVE ABSOLVE AMNESTY CONDONE FORGIVE OVERLOOK REPRIEVE TOLERATE EXCULPATE
PARDONABLE VENIAL VENIABLE EXCUSABLE
PARDONER QUESTOR QUAESTOR
PARE CUP CHIP COPE FLAY PEEL SKIN FRIZZ SHAVE SKELP SKIVE SLIPE SPADE CHISEL REDUCE REMOVE RESECT CURTAIL FLAUGHT WHITTLE
(— LEATHER) SKIVE
(— SOD) BURNBEAT
(— STAVES) BUCK
(— STONE) BOAST
PAREGORIC ANODYNE MITIGATING
PAREL PARELL APPAREL CLOTHING ORNAMENT
PARENCHYMA AMYLOM MESOPHYL
PARENT DAD DAM MAMA PAPA SIRE DADDY ELDER MATER PATER AUTHOR FATHER MOTHER ORIGIN FORBEAR GENITOR ANCESTOR BEGETTER FILICIDE GUARDIAN
PARENTAGE KIND BIRTH BROOD FAMILY ORIGIN PROGENY ENGENDRE
PARENTHESIS HOOK ASIDE PAREN BRACKET TOENAIL INNUENDO INTERVAL INTERLUDE
(PL.) HOOKS CURVES
PAREVE NEUTRAL
PARGET COAT GYPSUM PARIET PLASTER DECORATE WHITEWASH
PARGO MUTTONFISH
PARHELION DOG SUN SUNDOG
PARIAH LEPER PAREA ISHMAEL OUTCAST
PARIAN CHINA MARBLE PORCELAIN
PARIETAL SOMAL SOMALE
PARI-MUTUEL TOTE TOTALIZER
PARING CHIP FOIL SHRED SPECK GUBBIN PARURE PEELING
(FISH —S) GUBBINS
(PL.) BOXING
PARIS ALEXANDER
(— AIRPORT) ORLY
(FATHER OF —) PRIAM
(MOTHER OF —) HECUBA
(PALACE IN —) ELYSEE LOUVRE TUILERIES
(RIVER OF —) SEINE
(STOCK EXCHANGE IN —) BOURSE
(SUBWAY IN —) METRO
(WIFE OF —) OENONE 0ENONE
PARISH CURE HOUSE TITLE CHARGE SOCIETY PECULIAR OUTPARISH
(— HEAD) PASTOR PRIEST MINISTER
(— MEETING) VESTRY
PARISIAN LUTETIAN
PARISINA (BELOVED OF —) HUGO
(HUSBAND OF —) AZO
PARISON BLOW GATHERING
PARITY ANALOGY EQUALITY LIKENESS GRAVIDITY
PARK HAY PEN HOLE STOP WAIT GREEN LEAVE CIRCLE DAPHNE GARDEN PRATER COMMONS DIAMOND PADDOCK TERRACE PARADISE TETRAGON

(AMUSEMENT —) FUNFAIR
(KIND OF —) THEME
PARKA PARCA ANORAK JACKET PULLOVER
PARKING (KIND OF —) VALET
PARKLEAVES TUTSAN
PARLANCE TALK IDIOM SPEECH DICTION DISCOURSE
PARLAY WAGER DOUBLE
PARLEY DODGE PARLE SPEAK TREAT UTTER CONFER INDABA PALTER PAROLI DISCUSS PALAVER PARLING PARLANCE DISCOURSE TEMPORIZE NEGOTIATION
PARLIAMENT DIET RUMP TING COURT SENAT CORTES FANTAN MAJLIS SAEIMA COUNCIL ESTATES KNESSET LAGTING RIKSDAG TYNWALD CONGRESS CONVERSE STORTING VOLKSRAAD SANDHEDRIN
(— HOUSE) DAIL SEANAD
(GREEK —) BOULE
(SCAND. —) THING
PARLIAMENTARIAN APRONEER
PARLOR BEN BOOR HALL SALON FOREROOM LOCUTORY SNUGGERY SOLARIUM
(COUNTRY —) SPENCE
(MILKING —) BAIL
PARLORMAID MATRON
PARLOUS KEEN RISKY CLEVER SHREWD CUNNING CRITICAL PERILOUS DANGEROUS HAZARDOUS
PARMASHTA (FATHER OF —) HAMAN
PARMESAN GRANA
PARNACH (SON OF —) ELIZAPHAN
PAROCHIAL PETTY NARROW PAROCHIAN SECTARIAN
PARODIST SPOOFER
PARODY RIB SKIT PUTON SPOOF SATIRE SENDUP TRAVESTY BURLESQUE IMITATION
PAROLE FAITH PLEDGE LICENSE PROMISE
PARONOMASIA PUN AGNOMINATION
PARONYCHIA FELON PANARIS WHITLOW NAILWORT
PAROTITIS MUMPS
PAROXYSM FIT KINK PANG AGONY COLIC QUIRK SPASM STORM STOUR THROE ACCESS ATTACK FRENZY ORGASM RAPTUS SHOWER RAPTURE EPITASIS AGITATION
PARR PAR SAMLET SCEGGER SKEGGER BRANDLIN BRANDLING
PARROT ARA HIA KEA COPY ECHO JAKO KAKA LORO LORY POLL VAZA ARARA CAGIT MACAW MIMIC POLLY AMAZON CAIQUE CONURE KAKAPO REPEAT TIRIBA CORELLA GRASSIE ITERATE LORILET COCKATOO LORIKEET LOVEBIRD PARAKEET PICARIAN POPINJAY BROADTAIL COCKATEEL BUDGERIGAR
(PREF.) PSITTAC(I)
PARROT FISH LORO SCAR LANIA LAUIA SCAUR VIEJA COTORO

SCARUS LABROID MUDFISH OLDWIFE BLUEFISH
PARRY FEND STOP WARD AVOID BLOCK DODGE EVADE FENCE PRIME QUART SIXTE OCTAVE PARADE QUINTE SECOND THWART TIERCE COUNTER DEFLECT EVASION
PARSE PACE PEARCE ANALYZE DIAGRAM DISSECT CONSTRUE ANATOMIZE
PARSEGHIAN ARA
PARSHANDATHA (FATHER OF —) HAMAN
PARSI ZOROASTRIAN
(— HOLY BOOK) AVESTA
(— PRIEST) MOBED DASTUR
PARSIFAL (CHARACTER IN —) KUNDRY TITUREL AMFORTAS KLINGSOR PARSIFAL GURNEMANZ
(COMPOSER OF —) WAGNER
PARSIMONIOUS GARE MEAN NEAR NIGH CLOSE MINGY NIPPY SCANT SPARE TIGHT FRUGAL NARROW SCARCE SCOTCH SKIMPY SORDID STINGY STRAIT MISERLY SCRIMPY SPARING COVETOUS GRASPING GRUDGING SCREWING WRETCHED MERCENARY NIGGARDLY PENURIOUS RETENTIVE ABERDONIAN
PARSLEY ACHE CUMIN UMBEL CICELY CONIUM ELTROT KARPAS CHERVIL HOGWEED FLUELLIN
PARSLEY CAMPHOR APIOL APIOLE
PARSNIP TANK WYPE UMBEL CONIUM MADNEP CADWEED HOGWEED SKIRRET BUNDWEED QUEENWEED
(WATER —) SIUM
PARSON RECTOR CROAKER PATRICO PERSONA MINISTER PREACHER GUIDEPOST
(COUNTRY —) RUM
(PL.) PARSONRY
PARSONAGE GLEBE MANSE RECTORY PASTORATE PASTORIUM
PARSON BIRD POE TUI KOKO TUWI POEBIRD POYBIRD
PART DEL END LOT PAN DEAL DOLE FECK GRIN HAET HALF HAND NECK PANE ROLE ROVE SECT SHED SIDE SOME TEAR TWIN AUGHT PARTY PIECE QUOTA SEVER SHARE SHODE SNACK SPLIT TWAIN BEHALF CANTON CLEAVE DEPART DETAIL DIVIDE FEEDER FINGER MEMBER MINUTE MOIETY PARCEL PORTIO QUORUM SECTOR SINGLE SUNDER UNYOKE DISJOIN ELEMENT FEATURE FRUSTUM PORTION SECTION SEGMENT SEVERAL ALIENATE DISSEVER DIVISION ELIQUATE FRACTION LIRIPIPE
(— HAIR) SHADE
(— OF ANIMAL'S TAIL) DOCK
(— OF BEEF) CHUCK SKINK
(— OF BLAST FURNACE) BOSH BELLY
(— OF BOW) PEAK
(— OF CAM WHEEL) LOBE
(— OF CANNON) CHASE

(— OF CHAIR) SPLAT
(— OF COMPASS) FLY
(— OF CONCERTO) CEMBALO
(— OF CONFIRMATION SERVICE) ALAPA
(— OF CROSSBOW) LATH
(— OF DIAMOND) BEZEL
(OF FLEECE) LEECH
(— OF FOWL'S COMB) BLADE
(— OF FURNACE) HEARTH
(— OF GUN SHIELD) APRON
(— OF HARBOR) FAIRWAY
(— OF HAWK'S BEAK) CLAP
(— OF HIDE) RANGE
(— OF HOOKAH) CHILLUM
(— OF HORSE) FOREHAND
(— OF JOINT) TABLE
(— OF MASS) INTROIT
(— OF POETIC FOOT) ARSIS
(— OF PORK LOIN) GRISKIN
(— OF RIVER) FRESH
(— OF SADDLE TREE) FORK
(— OF STAIR TREAD) NOSING
(— OF STAMEN) ANTHER
(— OF SWORD) FORTE
(— OF SWORD BLADE) FOIBLE
(— OF TEMPLE) CELLA
(— OF THROAT) GULA FAUCES
(— OF TONGUE) DORSUM
(— OF TURTLE) CALIPEE
(— OF VIOLIN BOW) BAGUET
(— OF WHEEL) SPEECH
(— THAT REVOLVES) ROTOR
(— THE LEGS) STRADDLE
(— WITH) CEDE GIVE LOSE SELL LEAVE DONATE ABANDON
(— WITHIN) INSIDE
(ACCOMPANYING —) BURDEN OBBLIGATO
(ARTIFICIAL —) PROSTHESIS
(ASSIGNED —) QUOTA
(ASSUMED —) FIGURE
(BAGLIKE —) SAC
(BEST —) FAT YOLK CREAM FLOWER MARROW
(BRISTLELIKE —) SETA
(BROADEST — OF PLANK) TOUCH
(CENTRAL —) HUB BODY CORE HEART KERNEL
(CHOICE —) ELITE
(CLEAR — OF LIQUID) SWIM
(CLOSING —) HEEL
(COARSE — OF FLAX) HURDS
(CONCLUDING —) WRAPUP
(CONICAL —) BULLET
(CONNECTING —) NECK PONS UNION
(CURVED —) START
(DEPRESSED —) HOLLOW
(DISTANT —S) FARNESS
(DUPLICATE —) SPARE
(EDIBLE — OF CLAM) CHEEK
(EIGHTH — OF CIRCLE) OCTANT
(ESSENTIAL —) PITH
(ESSENTIAL —S) STAMINA
(FIFTH —) QUINTUS
(FINAL —) LAST SHANK EPILOG
(FIRST —) FRONT PRIME VAUNT INITIAL BEGINNING
(FOURTH —) FARDEL FORPIT FERLING
(FRONT —) VAUNT BREAST FORESIDE

(FURTHEST —) TIP
(GREATER —) HEFT SUBSTANCE
(HARDEST —) BRUNT
(HIGHEST —) CROP CROWN HEIGHT
(HUNDREDTH —) CENTESM
(IMPAIRING —) ALLOY
(IN —) HALVES
(INDETERMINATE —) PERCENTAGE
(INNERMOST —) FUND
(INNERMOST —S) PENETRALIA
(INSTRUMENTAL —) HAND CONTINUO
(INTERLACED —) TWINE
(INTRODUCTORY —) PROTASIS
(LARGE —) FORCE
(LATERAL — OF HEAD) CHEEK
(LATTER —) HEEL SHANK
(LEAST —) STITCH
(LESS DESIRABLE —) RIDDLINGS
(LEVEL —) FLAT
(LOWER —) SECONDO
(LOWER — OF ROBE) BASES
(LOWEST —) FOOT BOTTOM GROUND DESCENT
(MAIN —) BODY BULK SUBSTANCE
(MATERIAL —) GIST
(MIDDLE —) DEEP CENTER
(MIDDLE — OF NIGHT) HOWE
(MINOR —) BIT COG
(MINUTE —) PRICK TITTLE
(MISSING —) LACUNA
(MOST IMPORTANT —) EYE FOREHAND
(MOST SERIOUS —) DICKENS
(NARROW —) STRAIT THROAT
(OF HORSE'S THIGH) GASKIN
(OVERDUE —) ARREAR
(PRINCIPAL —) BODY MAIN GROSS
(PRIVATE —) THING MEMBER
(PROJECTING —) ARM JAG JET JOG APSE LOBE SPURN
(PROTUBERANT —) BOSS BULGE
(REJECTED —S) CHANKINGS
(REMAINING —) BUTT DREG HEEL
(REMOTEST —) EXTREMITY
(RINGLIKE —) ANNULUS
(ROOTLIKE —) RADICLE
(ROTATING —) ROTOR
(ROUNDED —) BULB
(SAWLIKE —) SERRA
(SECRET —) RECESS
(SLENDER —) NECK
(SMALL —) BIT ATOM FLOW TITHE DETAIL MINUTE SNIPPET
(SMALLEST —) ATOM WHIT MINIM
(SOFT — OF BREAD) CRUMB
(SOFT — OF VEIN) LEATH
(SOLO —) CALL
(STAMEN —) ANTHER
(STATIONARY —) STATOR
(STILL — OF WATER) KELD
(SWINGING —) FLAIL
(TELLING —) POINT
(TENTH —) TITHE
(THIN —) LEAF
(THIN — OF WALL) ALLEGE
(THIRD —) THIRDENDEAL
(TOP —) HEADPIECE
(TWELFTH —) INCIA POINT UNCIAL
(UPPER —) CHIEF RIDGE OVERPARTY
(UPPERMOST —) TOP PEAK CHIEF UPSIDE TOPSIDE

(VAUDEVILLE —) OLIO
(VITAL —) HEART
(WINGLIKE —) ALA
(WORST —) DEPTH
(WORTHLESS —) DREGS
(24TH —) CARAT
(360TH —) DEGREE
(PREF.) MER(I)(O) PARTI
(SUFF.) MER(E)(IC)(IS)(OUS)(Y)
TOMA TOME TOMIC TOMOUS
TOMY
PARTAKE BITE PART SHARE DIVIDE
PARTEN PARTICIPATE
(— OF) EAT USE HAVE SHARE TASTE
TOUCH IMPART
PARTAN CRAB
PARTED PARTITE
PARTHAON (FATHER OF —) AGENOR
(MOTHER OF —) EPICASTE
(SON OF —) OENEUS
(WIFE OF —) EURYTE
PARTHENIA (HUSBAND OF —)
ARGALUS
PARTHENIUS (BROTHER OF —)
PANDION
(FATHER OF —) PHINEUS
(MOTHER OF —) CLEOPATRA
PARTHENOGENETIC AGAMIC
AGAMOUS
PARTIAL HALF PART SEMI DIAPED
UNFAIR COLORED HALFWAY
UNEQUAL HARMONIC INCLINED
PARTISAN PROPENSE SKELETON
FAVORABLE SEGMENTAL
PARTICULAR RESPECTIVE
(PREF.) DEMI MER(I)(O) MES(O)
SEMI
PARTIALITY BIAS FAVOR RESPECT
AFFECTION SPECIALTY
PARTIALLY HALF HALFWAY
HALFWISE
PARTICIPANT BOOK ACTOR PARTY
MEMBER PARTNER DUETTIST
PARTABLE PARTISAN
(SUBORDINATE —) STOOGE
(PL.) FIELD
PARTICIPATE JOIN SIDE ENTER
SHARE ENGAGE ENLIST IMPART
COMPETE PARTAKE
(— IN) GO HAVE JOIN STAY STAND
TASTE COMMON STICKLE
PARTICIPATION HAND PLOT
SOCIETY INTEREST
(COMMON —) COMMUNITY
PARTICIPATOR
(SUFF.) STER STRESS
PARTICIPLE VERBID
PARTICLE ACE BIT DOT FIG GRU JOT
PSI RAY ATOM BETA CORN CROT
CURN DUST GRUE HAET IOTA KNIT
MITE MOTE SNIP SPOT STIM WHIT
ALPHA BOSON FLAKE FLECK
GHOST GRAIN MESON OMEGA
POINT PRION QUARK SHRED
SIGMA SPECK STARN STIME
THRUM TWINT FILING GEIGER
LEPTON MOMENT PANGEN
PARTON RIZZOM SMIDGE SMITCH
TITTLE VIRION AMICRON FERMION
GEMMULE GRANULE NUCLEUS
PHOTINO PSYCHON SINGLET
SMIDGIN TACHYON ACCEPTER
GRAVITON NEUTRINO SMIDGEON

SYLLABLE MICROSOME POSITRINO
SCINTILLA
(— IN BLOOD) EMBOLUS
(— IN INTERNAL EAR) OTOCONIUM
(— OF FIRE) SPARK
(— OF GOLD) COLOR
(— OF QUARKS) HADRON
(— OF SOOT) ISEL IZLE SMUT AIZLE
(—S IN BEER) FLOATERS
(—S OF GRAIN) CHOP
(— TO BIND QUARKS) GLUON
(ATOMIC —) ION MUON BARYON
HADRON LEPTON ELECTRON
(BINDING —) GLUON
(COLLECTION OF CHARGED —S)
PLASMA
(COMBINING —) ACCEPTOR
(ELECTRIFIED —) ION ANION
PROTON POSITRON THERMION
(ELEMENTARY —) MUON NEUTRON
NEUTRINO
(FINE ICY —S) SLEET
(GROUP OF —S) MESON
(HYPOTHETICAL —) QUARK
(JAGGED —) SPLINTER
(KIND OF —) ETA TAU
(LEAST POSSIBLE —) MINIM
(LINGUISTIC —) SERVILE
(MASSLESS —) GLUON
(MESON —) UPSILON
(MINUTE —) JOT ORT RAY ATOM
GRAIN SPECK RAMENT GRANULE
MOLECULE RAMENTUM
CORPUSCLE
(NEGATIVE —) NOR NOT
(NUCLEAR —S) FALLOUT
(PHYSICS —) QUARK POSITRON
(POSITIVELY-CHARGED —) CATION
KATION
(PROTEIN —) PRION
(QUARK —S) HADRON
(SMALL —) NIP BLEB CORN MOTE
CRUMB GRAIN SPECK PROTON
AMICRON GRANULE SPRINKLE
SUBMICRON
(SUBATOMIC —) PION LAMBDA
(TINY —) ATOMY
(ULTIMATE —) PSYCHON
(UNCHARGED —) LAMBDA
(PL.) DUST FINES SWARF SIZINGS
CUTTINGS FURFURES
(SUFF.) PLAST
(— OF A KIND) ID
PARTI-COLORED PIED FANCY
MOTLEY PARTED PIEBALD
BUTTERFLY HARLEQUIN
PARTICULAR AND ATOM FIXY ITEM
NICE SELF SOME FUSSY PARTY
POINT THING CHOOSY DAINTY
DETAIL MINUTE MOROSE REGARD
SINGLE STICKY ARTICLE CAREFUL
CERTAIN CORRECT FINICKY
PRECISE PRIVATE RESPECT
SEVERAL SPECIAL UNUSUAL
CLERKISH CONCRETE ESPECIAL
PECULIAR PICKSOME PRECIOUS
SINGULAR SUBALTERN
RESPECTIVE
(NOT —) INCURIOUS
PARTICULARLY ONLY EXTRA
SINGLY SPECIAL EXPRESSLY
SPECIALLY

PARTING DEATH GOODBYE
FAREWELL
(— AS OF HAIR) SHED
PARTISAN PIKE SIDER STAFF
BIASED FACTOR FAUTOR MARIAN
ZEALOT CALOTIN DEVOTEE
GUISARD PARTNER ADHERENT
CRISTINO ESPOUSER FAVORITE
FENNOMAN FOLLOWER
HENCHMAN JACOBITE MOSSBACK
SIDESMAN STALWART URBANIST
HIGHFLIER MAZZINIST OCHLOCRAT
OLIVERIAN SECTARIAN TERRORIST
(NOT —) CATHOLIC
(PL.) FOLLOWING
(SUFF.) CRAT
PARTITION BAR CUT DAM FIN FLAG
SEPT WALL SHOJI SPEER STAGE
WITHE BAFFLE DIVIDE PARPAL
PARPEN SCONCE SCREEN SEPTUM
BARRIER CLOISON ENCLOSE
GRATING PINFOLD PORTION
SCANTLE BRATTICE BULKHEAD
CLEAVAGE DIVISION STOPPING
TRAVERSE DASHBOARD
DAYABHAGA ICONOSTAS
MESENTERY STOOTHING
(— BETWEEN STALLS) TRAVIS
TREVIS TRAVISS
(— IN CHIMNEY) WITH WITHE
(— IN CORAL) TABULA
(— IN COTTAGE) SPEER HALLAN
(— IN FRUIT) REPLUM
(— IN LOUDSPEAKER) BAFFLE
(— IN WATERWHEEL) WREST
(— OF ESTATE) BOEDELSCHEIDING
(— OF LATH AND PLASTER)
STOOTHING
(HORIZONTAL —) STAGE
(MINING —) SOLLAR BRATTICE
STOPPING
(PL.) CANCELLI
PARTLET HEN WOMAN PERTELOT
PARTLY WHAT PARCEL PARTIM
HALFLINGS
(PREF.) SEMI
PARTNER BOY PAL ALLY HALF
MATE PARD WIFE BUDDY BUTTY
PARTY FELLOW MARROW SHARER
COMRADE CONSORT HUSBAND
CAMARADA COPEMATE SIDEKICK
YOKEMATE
(— OF DUMMY) VIVANT
(DANCING —) GIGOLO CAVALIER
(ROMANTIC —) SQUEEZE
(PREF.) CO
PARTNERS INOUT ONOFF TOFRO
COMEGO HEMHAW HITRUN
HUECRY PROCON BILLCOO
DOTDASH DOWNOUT EBBFLOW
FARWIDE FIVETEN HAMEGGS
HIGHDRY HIGHLOW INSOUTS
KITHKIN PATMIKE PUTTAKE
TOUCHGO YINYANG AMOSANDY
BECKCALL GIVETAKE HANDFOOT
HIDESEEK HILLDALE MUCKMIRE
MUTTJEFF ODDSENDS RICKRACK
ROCKROLL SHOWTELL SPICSPAN
TIMETIDE ALASALACK BACKFORTH
BALLCHAIN FACTFANCY
HITHERYON KNIFEFORK
LOSTFOUND READWRITE
ROOMBOARD THICKTHIN

TRIEDTRUE BAGBAGGAGE
BITSPIECES BLACKWHITE
FUSSBOTHER HALEHEARTY
HOOTHOLLER NOOKCRANNY
SPITPOLISH SWITCHBAIT
TARFEATHERS ALIVEKICKING
ROMULUSREMUS STARSSTRIPES
ASSAULTBATTERY
PARTNERSHIP HUI AXIS FIRM
HOUSE FUSION CAHOOTS
COMPANY CONSORT SOCIETY
SOCIETEIT
(MUTUALLY BENEFICIAL —)
SYMBIOSIS
PARTRIDGE HUN BIRD KYAH YUTU
LERWA RUDGE TITAR CHUKAR
REDLEG SEESEE CHEEPER PATRICK
SHRIMPI TINAMOU BOBWHITE
FRANCOLIN FRENCHMAN
TETRAONID
(— NOISE) JUCK
(SAND —) TEHOO
(YOUNG —) CHEEPER SQUEALER
PARTRIDGEBERRY BOXBERRY
COWBERRY EYEBERRY ONEBERRY
SNOWBERRY TWINBERRY
PARTS
(PREF.)
(SIDE —) ALI
PART SONG MADRIGAL
PART-TIME PARCEL
PARTURITION EUTOCIA TRAVAIL
CHILDBED DELIVERY DYSTOCIA
(SUFF.) TOKY
PARTY DO BAL BEE CRY TEA CAMP
CLAN DRUM GALA SECT SIDE
BINGE BLAST BRAWL BUNCH
CABAL COVEY CRUSH FESTA
GROUP LEVEE MIXER COMITE
FIESTA FROLIC FRONDE GERMAN
INFARE JUNKET PERSON SETOUT
SHINDY SHOWER BLOWOUT
CANTICO COMPANY FACTION
GREGORY PATARIA SHINDIG
CLAMBAKE DRINKING FENNOMAN
POTLATCH POUNDING SOCIABLE
SQUANTUM TERTULIA CONCISION
INCLINING MERRIMENT
(— GIVEN AT HOME) HUDDLE
(AFTERNOON —) TEA RECEPTION
(BEACH —) CLAMBAKE
(BOISTEROUS —) BASH HOOLEY
BLOWOUT JAMBOREE
(BRIDAL —) SEND SHOWER
(DANCING —) HOP GERMAN
CANTICO HOEDOWN RIDOTTO
FANDANGO
(DRINKING —) SPREE KNEIPE
MOLLIE POTATION SYMPOSIUM
(DRUNKEN —) BLIND
(EVENING —) BALL SOIREE
GREGORY ROCKING TERTULIA
(FISHING —) HUKILAU
(HUNTING —) FAID
(INFORMAL —) SOCIABLE TERTULIA
(IRISH —) HOOLEY
(LARGE —) ROUT
(MASQUERADE —) GUISE RIDOTTO
(MEMBER OF YOUTH —) YIPPIE
(MEN'S —) STAG SMOKER
(MILITARY —) COMMANDO
(NOISY —) BEANO SHIVOO
(POLITICAL —) SAM SIDE WAFD

HOOKS LABOR CAUCUS FRONDE SWARAJ ZENTRUM MINSEITO KENSEIKAI SQUADRONE OPPOSITION
(POPULAR —) HOOKS
(ROWDY —) BASH BLAST BLOWOUT WINGDING
(SCOUTING —) ESPIAL
(SEARCH —) QUEST
(SPINNING —) ROCKING
(SUPPLY —) BRIGADE
(TEA —) DRUM TEMPEST
(THIRD —) STRANGER
(TYPE OF —) MIXER
(WILD —) WINGDING WHINGDING
(WORKING —) SQUAD
PARUAH (SON OF —) JEHOSHAPHAT
PARULIS GUMBOIL
PARVENU SNOB ARRIVE UPSTART ARRIVIST MUSHROOM ARRIVISTE
PARVIS PARADISE
PARZIFAL (FATHER OF —) GAMURET
(MOTHER OF —) HERZELOIDE
PASACH (FATHER OF —) JAPHLET
PASCH PACE PAQUE EASTER PASSOVER
PASCHAL LAMB CANDLE SUPPER PASSOVER
PAS DE DEUX DUET
PASE FAROL NATURAL VERONICA
PASEAH (FATHER OF —) ESHTON
PASEAR WALK AIRING EXCURSION PROMENADE
PASHA DEY EMIR BASHAW PASAHAW
PASHTO AFGHAN
PASIPHAE (BROTHER OF —) AEETES
(CHILD OF —) ARIADNE PHAEDRA
(DAUGHTER OF —) ARIADNE PHAEDRA
(FATHER OF —) HELIUS
(HUSBAND OF —) MINOS
(MOTHER OF —) PERSA
(SISTER OF —) CIRCE
PASQUEFLOWER BADGER GOSLING APRILFOOL
PASQUINADE PIPE SQUIB SATIRE LAMPOON PASQUIL
PASS BY GO COL DIE END FIG GAP SAG USE ABRA BEAL CEDE CHIT COMP COVE DREE DROP FALL FARE FLIT FOIN GATE GHAT GULF HALS HAND HAVE JARK LANE LEAD PACE RIDE ROLL SEEK SILE SLAP SLIP STEP WADE WALK WEAR WEND WIND ALLOW CANTO DREIE ENACT FLEET GHAUT GORGE HALSE HURRY KOTAL LAPSE LITHE LUNGE NOTCH OCCUR ORDER PAPER PUNTA REACH RELAY SHAKE SHOOT SMITE SPEND STRIP TRADE UTTER WASTE WHELM YODEL BILLET CHALAN CONVEY COUPON DEFILE DEMISE ELAPSE EXCEED HAPPEN PASSUS PERMIT RAVINE SPIRAL TICKET TRAVEL TWOFER ABSOLVE ALLONGE APPROVE BREATHE DESCEND DEVOLVE DIFFUSE ENTREAT LATERAL OVERGET PASSAGE UNDERGO JUNCTURE REBOLERA PURWANNAH SAFEGUARD

(— A BALL) FEED HEEL
(— ABRUPTLY) LEAP
(— ALONG) BANDY DERIVE
(— AWAY) DIE SET FLEE VADE WING DEPART EXPIRE PERISH FORFARE FORTHGO OVERDRIVE
(— BACK AND FORTH) FIG CRISSCROSS
(— BAD COIN) SMASH
(— BETWEEN HILLS) BEAL SLAP SLACK
(— BEYOND) TURN OVERSHOOT
(— BY) COTE OMIT SKIP VADE WEND APASS CLEAR FORGO FOREGO IGNORE OVERGO INTERMIT OVERHEAVE
(— DISCONTINUOUSLY) SKIP
(— FURTIVELY) SNEAK
(— GRADUALLY) FADE
(— IDLY) TRIFLE
(— IMPERCEPTIBLY) SHADE
(— IN BULLFIGHT) SUERTE
(— IN POKER) BREATHE
(— IN SCRUTINY) PERUSE
(— INTO USE) ENURE INURE
(— JUDGMENT ON) DEEM DECERN SENTENCE
(— LIGHTLY) BRUSH SKATE SKITTER
(— OFF) SHAM FOIST
(— ON) LEAK PACE DELATE TRANSMIT PROPAGATE
(— ONE'S LIFE) TRADE
(— OUT) CONK DEBOUCH EXHAUST SKIP SLIP COVER CROSS ELIDE FLEET SCOUR SWEEP TRANCE OVERHIP TRANSIT INTERMIT OVERLOOK OVERPOST PROGRESS TRAVERSE
(— OVER LIGHTLY) SKIM SWEEP OVERSKIP
(— OVER QUICKLY) SCUD FLEET
(— QUICKLY) FLIT SPIN SPEED STRIKE
(— THE NIGHT) LIE LODGE
(— THROUGH) CROSS REEVE TRACE DIVIDE OVERGO PIERCE SUFFER EXCURSE PERVADE OVERPASS OVERRIDE PERMEATE PROGRESS PENETRATE
(— THROUGH A BLOCK) REEVE
(— THROUGH HOLE) REEVE
(— THROUGH NARROW WAY) THRID THREAD
(— TIME) DRIVE SPEND TRADE
(— UNHAPPILY) DREE
(— UP) REJECT DECLINE DISREGARD
(— WITH DIFFICULTY) WADE
(— WITH VIOLENCE) RAKE
(CUSTOMS —) CARNET
(FENCING —) FOIN BOTTE LUNGE PUNTA
(FOOTBALL —) FLY FLARE FORWARD LATERAL PITCHOUT
(FORWARD —) AERIAL
(FREE —) PAPER
(FREE —S) PAPER
(HIGH —) CHIP
(HILL —) SLAP
(HOCKEY —) CENTER
(KIND OF —) SPOT OUTLET
(LONG — IN FOOTBALL) BOMB

(MOUNTAIN —) COL GAP NEK SAG GATE GHAT SLIP CLOVE GHAUT KLOOF KLOOT KOTAL POORT SWIRE SWIRL BEALACH
(NARROW —) ABRA GULF CLOSE SLYPE DEFILE
(SHORT — IN FOOTBALL) FLARE
(SUDDEN —) LUNGE
PASSABLE FIT FAIR SOSO TOLLOL GENUINE ADEQUATE MEDIOCRE MODERATE POSSIBLE TRAVELED PERMEABLE TOLERABLE
(PREF.) BATO
PASSABLENESS INDIFFERENCE
PASSABLY SEEMLY
PASSAGE CUT GAT GUT ROW VIA WAY WRO ADIT BELT BORD DOOR EXIT FARE FLUE FORD GANG GATE HALL ITER LANE PACE PASS PAWN RACE RAMP SLIP SLUM VENT WELL AISLE ALLEY ALURE BAYOU BEARD BOGUE CANAL CHOPS CHUTE CLOSE CREEK CRUSH DRAFT DRIFT DRIVE ENTRY FLYBY FORTE GLADE GOING GORGE INLET JETTY MEUSE PATCH PORCH SHUNT SLYPE SOUND ACCESS ADITUS APORIA ARCADE ATRIUM AVENUE BRIDGE BURROW BYPASS CAREER COURSE DEFILE DROMOS EGRESS ELAPSE FAUCES HIATUS MEATUS PARODE RELIEF SCREEN SLUICE STRAIT TRAJET TRANCE TRAVEL TUNNEL VOYAGE ARCHWAY BALTEUS CHANNEL CHAPTER CHIMNEY CONDUIT COULOIR COUPURE DIAZOMA DOGTROT DRAUGHT ESTUARY EXCERPT FISTULA FRAUGHT GALLERY GANGWAY GATEWAY ISTHMUS JOURNEY MANHOLE OFFTAKE OUTTAKE PARADOS PROCESS TRANSIT APPROACH AQUEDUCT CITATION CLOISTER COMMERCE DEBOUCHE DELETION PARADIGM PERICOPE SENTENCE SHIPPING SINUSOID SPILLWAY
(— ACROSS) TRAVERSE
(— ACROSS WATER) WAFT
(— BACK) REGRESS
(— BETWEEN WALLS) SLYPE
(— FOR MOLTEN METAL) SPRVE RUNNER
(— IN BOOK) WHERE EXCERPT
(— IN CRUIVE) SLAP
(— IN JEWISH SCRIPTURE) PARASHAH
(— OF POETRY OR MUSIC) MORCEAU
(— OF THREAD) FLOAT
(—S OF LITERATURE) BEAUTIES
(— TO STOMACH) SWALLOW
(— TO TOMB) DROMOS SYRINX
(AIR —) FLUE THIRL WINDWAY THIRLING VENTIDUCT
(ANATOMICAL —) ITER
(CENSORED —) CAVIAR
(CONTINUOUS —) LAPSE
(COVERED —) OPE PAWN PEND
(DIFFICULT —) APORIA
(LITERARY —) TEXT QUOTE EXCERPT SNIPPET QUOTATION
(MINE —) RUN ADIT HEAD ROOF

SLUM DRIVE LEVEL SHAFT THIRL AIRWAY STENTON UNDERCAST
(MINUTE —) PORE
(MUSICAL —) CUE CODA LINK BREAK FORTE INTRO STAVE ARIOSO FUGATO LEGATO PRESTO REPEAT CADENZA CODETTA FANFARE STRETTO FLOURISH RITENUTO SPICCATO STACCATO SYMPHONY VOCALISE PIZZICATO RITARDANDO RITORNELLO
(NARROW —) GUT HASS ALLEY CREEP GORGE JETTY NOTCH SLYPE SMOOT DEFILE GULLET NARROW STRAIT
(OPENING —) INTRO INTRODUCTION
(SECRET —) BOLTHOLE
(SECURE — OF) CARRY
(SUBTERRANEAN —) POSTERN
(SWIFT —) FLIGHT
(THROUGH —) TRANCE
(UNDERGROUND —) SUBWAY
(VAULTED —) PEND
(VOCAL —) SPRECHSTIMME
(WATER —) TICKLE TICKLER
(PREF.) MEATO
(SUFF.) PLANIA PORA PORE
PASSAGE HAWK TARTARET PASSENGER
PASSAGE TO INDIA (AUTHOR OF —) FORSTER
(CHARACTER IN —) AZIZ ADELA CECIL MOORE RONALD STELLA GODBOLE HEASLOP QUESTED FIELDING
PASSAGEWAY (ALSO SEE PASSAGE) BORD FLUE GANG HALL LANE PACE PASS PEND PORT RACE SHED SLIP WENT YAWN AISLE ALLEY ALURE CHUTE DRIFT DRONG ENTRY GOING LUMEN RAISE SHOOT SMOOT STULM ACCESS AIRWAY AVENUE COURSE DINGLE FUNNEL GUTTER INTAKE MANWAY RUELLE RUNWAY TRANCE ZAGUAN DOORWAY GALLERY SLIPWAY TWITTEN WALKWAY WAYGATE CALLEJON CORRIDOR HATCHWAY
(CLEARED — IN CROWD) HALL
(COVERED —) ARCADE CLOISTER
(LOCKED —) CANAL
(MINE —) BORD BOARD DRIFT SLANT STULM WINZE
(NARROW —) SLIP AISLE SMOOT BOTTLENECK
(SLOPING —) RAMP
(UNDERGROUND —) CATACOMB
PASSANT PAST CURRENT CURSORY PASSING EPHEMERAL
PASSE AGED PAST WORN DATED FADED BELATED OBSOLETE OUTMODED
PASSED GONE
PASSENGER FARE INSIDE FERRYMAN TRAVELER WAYFARER
(— WHO AVOIDS PAYING FARE) NIP STOWAWAY
(— WITHOUT TICKET) HARE
(AIRPLANE) BIRDMAN
(UNBOOKED —) CAD
(PL.) WAYBILL
PASSEPARTOUT SPANDREL

PASSERBY PASSER PASSANT BYPASSER SAUNTERER

PASSERINE OSCINE PERCHER TANAGER

PASSIFLORA TACSO

PASSING DEATH DYING ELAPSE CURSORY DIADROM PASSADO RUNNING SLIDING ELAPSING FLEETING ENACTMENT EPHEMERAL WAYFARING
(— BETWEEN) INTERCURRENT
(— BY) COTE
(— INTO EACH OTHER) FONDU
(— OF HOURS) TIME
(— OF TIME) EFFLUX
(SLOWLY —) LAG

PASSION IRE WAX RATE FIRE FURY HEAT LOVE LUST PASH RAGA RAGE TEAR TIDE WILL ZEAL ANGER ARDOR BLOOD BRAME CHAFE DEVIL ERROR FLAME LETCH MANIA RAJAS SPUNK WRATH AFFECT CHOLER DESIRE FERVOR MOTHER PELTER SATTVA SPLEEN TALENT WARMTH EARNEST EMOTION EROTISM FEELING OUTRAGE VULTURE APPETITE DISTRESS VIOLENCE PADDYWACK
(— FOR DOING GREAT THINGS) MEGALOMANIA
(— FOR MUSIC) MELOMANIA
(ANGRY —) FUNK
(ANIMAL —) KAMA
(EXALTED —) ALTITUDES
(PREF.) PASSI PATH(O)
(SUFF.) **(— FOR)** MANE MANIA(C)

PASSIONATE HOT FOND WARM WILD FIERY GUTSY QUICK WHITE ARDENT FERVID FIERCE FUMOUS IREFUL STORMY SULTRY TORRID AMOROUS FLAMING PEPPERY THERMAL VIOLENT CHOLERIC FRENETIC VASCULAR VEHEMENT WRATHFUL DIONYSIAN IRASCIBLE

PASSIONATELY HASTILY FERVIDLY

PASSIONFLOWER MAYPOP BULLHOOF

PASSIONLESS COLD FREDDO APATHETIC

PASSIVE INERT STOIC PATHIC STOLID SUPINE PATIENT FEMININE INACTIVE SIGNLESS YIELDING APATHETIC

PASSIVENESS QUIETISM

PASSIVITY INERTIA

PASSOVER PESAH PHASE PASQUE PESACH
(— FESTIVAL) SEDER
(JEWISH —) EASTER

PASSPORT CHOP PASS CONGE CONGEE DUSTUK DUSTUCK FURLOUGH TESCARIA TEZKIRAH SAFEGUARD

PASSUS PACE PART PASS STEP CANTO DIVISION

PASSWORD SIGN WORD TOKEN DUSTUK TESSERA WATCHWORD

PAST BY AGO WAS GONE YOND YORE AFTER AGONE APAST ASIDE ENDED SINCE BEHIND BYGONE FOREBY PRETER ANOTHER FOREGONE PRETERIT COMPLETED
(LONG —) HIGH
(RECENTLY —) OTHER
(TIME IN THE —) LANGSYNE
(TIME NOT LONG —) YESTERDAY
(PREF.) PRETER RETRO

PASTA ORZO ZITI PENNE NOODLE TUFOLI FUSILLI LASAGNA RAVIOLI LINGUINE LINGUINI MACARONI RIGATONI MANICOTTI SPAGHETTI FETTUCELLE TORTELLINI MOSTACCIOLI PERCIATELLI TAGLIATELLE
(— BITS) PASTINA
(TUBULAR —) ZITI
(WAY TO COOK —) ALDENTE

PASTE HIT PAP BEAT BLOW DIKA DUFF GLUE MISO PACK PATE CREAM DOUGH FALSE GESSO HENNA PUNCH STICK ATTACH BATTER CERATE FASTEN GROUND PANADA RASTIK STRASS BUCKETY CLOBBER COLOGNE DRAWOUT FILLING GORACCO GUARANA STICKUM BADIGEON BARBOTINE
(— FOR CAULKING) BLARE
(— FOR LINING HEARTHS) BRASQUE
(— FOR SHOES, BOOTS) CLOBBER BLACKING
(— FROM SESAME SEEDS) TAHINI
(— OF CLAY) RATTER
(— OF SESAME SEEDS) TAHINI
(— TO FILL HOLES IN WOOD AND STONE) BADIGEON
(ALIMENTARY —) PUREE FEDELINI SCUNGILLI SPAGHETTI
(AROMATIC —) PASTILE
(CHICK-PEA —) HOMMOS HUMMUS
(COLORING —) HENNA
(DRIED —) GUARANA
(EARTHY —) ENGOBE
(FISH —) BAGOONG
(MEDICATED —) ELECTUARY
(PORCELAIN —) PATE
(POTTER'S —) BARBOTINE
(TOBACCO —) GORACCO
(WEAVER'S —) SOWENS BUCKETY

PASTEBOARD CARD SHAM CARTON FLIMSY TICKET MATBOARD

PASTEDOWN LINING

PASTEL WOAD LIGHT CRAYON PICTURE DELICATE

PASTEL BLUE OADE WOAD

PASTEN HOBBLE TETHER PASTOUR SHACKLE

PASTILLE CACHOU CANDLE LOZENGE

PASTIME GAY TOY GAME PLOY HOBBY SPORT GOSSIP OLEARY SAILING PASTANCE AMUSEMENT DIVERSION ABRIDGMENT

PASTOR HERD ANGEL RABBI CURATE KEEPER PRIEST RECTOR DOMINIE VICAIRE GUARDIAN MINISTER SHEPHERD

PASTORAL POEM DRAMA RURAL RUSTIC BUCOLIC CROSIER IDYLLIC NOMADIC ROMANCE ARCADIAN THEOCRITEAN

PASTORALIST SQUATTER

PASTRY PIE FLAN HUFF PUFF SOCK TART TUCK CORNET DANISH ECLAIR ABAISSE BRIOCHE CANNOLI CARCAKE STRUDEL BAKEMEAT EMPANADA NAPOLEON TALMOUSE TURNOVER APPLEJACK
(— COOK) PASTLER
(— DOUGH) PHYLLO
(— SHELL) BOUCHEE DARIOLE TIMBALE TALMOUSE
(— STRIPS) LATTICE
(— WHEEL) JAGGER
(KIND OF —) PUFF
(SWEET —) DOUCET
(PL.) PIROZKI PIROSHKI

PASTURAGE FEED GANG GATE STRAY COLLOP EATAGE FORAGE HERBAGE SHEEPGATE

PASTURE ALP FOG HAG HAM ING LEA PEN TYE BENT FEED GAET GANG GATE GIST GIST HAFT HALF HEAF HOGA INGE KEEP PARK RAIK AGIST DRIFT EJIDO GRASS GRAZE LAYER LEASE RANGE VELDT INTAKE MEADOW OUTRUN SAETER COWGATE FOGGAGE GRAZING HERBAGE LEALAND POTRERO VACCARY VICTUAL HERDWICK OUTFIELD SHEEPWALK
(— GRASS) TORE GRAMA
(— IN STUBBLE) GUACK
(— LAND) RAKE TACK LEASOW
(HILL —) HOGA
(MOUNTAIN —) SETER SAETER SHIELING
(SHEEP —) HEAF EWELEASE
(SHETLAND I. —) SETER
(SUMMER —) AGOSTADERO
(WET —) SLINK

PASTURELAND BENT SOUM

PASTURING RELIEF PANNAGE

PASTY PIE PATE SLAB PATTY DOUGHY FRACID SAMBOUSE

PAT APT DAB DIB TAP TIG BLOW CLAP GLIB JUMP PALP TICK CHUCK FITLY FIXED IMPEL THROW CARESS DABBLE PRETTY SMOOGE SOOTHE STRIKE STROKE TIMELY APROPOS CHERISH FITTING PATAPAT READILY SUITABLE PERTINENT SEASONABLE

PATAGIUM TEGULA TIPPET SCAPULA PARACHUTE PTERYGODE

PATAGONIA (DEITY OF —) SETEBOS
(RODENT OF —) CAVY MARA
(TREE OF —) MANIU ALERCE ALERSE

PATAGONIAN HARE MARA

PATAMAR COURIER PATTAMAR MESSENGER

PATAYAN YUMAN

PATCH BIT EKE FLY BOUT LAND MEND SKIP SPOT SWAB SWOB VAMP BLAZE BODGE CLOUT CLUMP COVER FRIAR FUDGE PIECE SAVER SCRAP SPECK SPLAT BLOTCH COBBLE COOPER DOLLOP GORGET MOUCHE PARCEL REVAMP SOLDER SPETCH SWATCH TINKLE CLAMPER CLOBBER INWEAVE PELIOMA REMNANT
(— AS ORNAMENT) MOUCHE
(— CLUMSILY) BOTCH CLOUT CLAMPER
(— IN NEWSPAPER) FUDGE

(— OF COLOR) CLOUP DAPPLE SPLASH SPECULUM
(— OF DARK HAIR) SMUT
(— OF DIRT) MIRE
(— OF FEATHERS) BIB CAP PTERYLA
(— OF ICE) RONE
(— OF LAND) RODHAM
(— OF LEATHER) SPECK
(— OF LIGHT) GLADE
(— OF PRINT) FUDGE
(— OF RUFFLED WATER) ACKER
(— OF SALIVA) SIXPENCE
(— OF TIRE) BOOT
(— ON BIRD'S BEAK) CERE
(— ON BIRD'S WING) SPECULUM
(— ON BOAT) TINGLE
(— ON HORSE) SNIP
(— ON PRINTED PAGE) FRIAR
(— ON THROAT) GORGET
(— TOGETHER) CONSARCINATE
(— UP) HEAL JUMP MEND FUDGE SHUFFLE
(BALD —) AREA
(BLURRED —) FOG
(BOGGY —) LATCH LETCH
(CABBAGE —) KALEYARD
(ISOLATED —) POCKET
(KIND OF —) LOU
(LIVID —) PELIOMA
(OOZY —) SPEW SPUE
(OPEN — IN FOREST) CAMPO
(RANK —) DALLOP DOLLOP
(SHOULDER —) FLASH

PATCHOULI PACCIOLI PATCHLEAF

PATCHWORD WASTEWORD

PATCHWORK OLIO BOTCH CENTO CENTON JUMBLE SCRAPS PATCHERY FRAGMENTS PASTICCIO

PATE PIE TOP HEAD BROWN PASTE PASTY PATTY BADGER NODDLE NOGGIN COSTARD COXCOMB

PATELLA CAP PAN DISH VASE ROTULA KNEECAP KNEEPAN WHIRLBONE

PATEN ARCA DISC DISH DISK PLATE PATINA PLATEN VESSEL

PATENT ARCA BALD OPEN BERAT BROAD OVERT PLAIN SUNNUD CHARTER EVIDENT LICENSE OBVIOUS APPARENT ARCHIVES MANIFEST PALPABLE PRIVILEGE

PATENTED BREVETE

PATER FATHER PRIEST

PATERFAMILIAS MASTER

PATERNAL FATHERLY

PATERNITY FATHER ORIGIN

PATESI ISHSHAKKU

PATH ARC PAD RIG RUN RUT TAN WAY BERM FARE GATE LANE LEAD LINE LODE RACE RACK ROAD TRIG TROD WALK ALLEY BYWAY GOING JETTY ORBIT PISTE ROUTE SPACE TRACK TRACT TRADE TRAIL BOSTAL BYPASS CAMINO CASAUN CIRCLE COMINO COURSE GROOVE SLEUTH SPHERE SWATHE TRENCH CHANNEL ERGODIC FAIRWAY FOOTWAY HIGHWAY LANDWAY MEANDER PASSAGE RODDING SIDEWAY TARIQAT TOWPATH TRAFFIC TRUNDLE WAYGATE BORSTALL CENTRODE CROSSCUT

DRIFTWAY TRAILWAY TWITCHEL CROSSWALK
(— BETWEEN HEDGES) TWITCHEL
(— CUT IN MOWING) SWATH SWATHE
(— FOLLOWED BY ENERGY) ERGODIC
(— MADE BY ANIMAL) PIST PISTE
(— OF CELESTIAL BODY) ORBIT
(— OF CLOUDS) RACK
(— OF ELECTRIC CURRENT) CIRCUIT
(— OF MOVING POINT) CURVE LOCUS
(— OF RACE) STRIP
(— OF SUN) ECLIPTIC
(— UP STEEP HILL) BOSTAL BORSTAL BORSTALL
(BRIDLE —) SPURWAY
(BURIAL —) LICHWAY
(CLOSED —) CIRCUIT
(FORTIFICATION —) RELAIS
(GARDEN —) ALLEE
(NARROW —) BERM RACK TRIG RODDIN TROCHA RODDING
(PHILIPPINE FOOT —) SENDA
(STEEP —) SLIDDER
(STONE-PAVED —) STEEN
(SUFI —) TARIQAT
(WINDING —) ESS
(WINDING —S) AMBAGES
(PREF.) HODO ODO
(SUFF.) ODE OID
PATHAN TURI AFRIDI SIVATI BAJOURI BANGASH PAYTHAN DANGARIK
PATHETIC SAD SILLY TEARY TENDER FORLORN PITIFUL DOLOROSO PATETICO PITIABLE POIGNANT STIRRING TOUCHING AFFECTING
PATHFINDER (AUTHOR OF —) COOPER
(CHARACTER IN —) CAP DAVY MUIR MABEL NATTY BUMPPO DUNHAM JASPER MACNAB CHARLES WESTERN SANGLIER ARROWHEAD CHINGACHGOOK
PATHIC MORBID VICTIM PASSIVE CATAMITE DISEASED SUFFERER SUFFERING
PATHOGEN VIRUS
PATHOLOGICAL
(SUFF.)
(— CONDITION) IA
PATHOLOGIST AMERICAN OPIE ROUS SLYE EWING MOORE SMITH WELCH MOHLER FLEXNER HEKTOEN PRUDDEN WARTHIN WHIPPLE RICKETTS GOODPASTURE
AUSTRALIAN POPPER
CANADIAN WESBROOK
DANISH FIBIGER
ENGLISH ADAMI BOYCE PAGET ANNETT FLOREY WRIGHT SPILSBURY
GERMAN HENLE KLEBS TRAUBE ZENKER VIRCHOW COHNHEIM RECKLINGHAUSEN
IRISH STOKES
ITALIAN GUARNIERI
PATHOS BATHOS SNIVEL POIGNANCY
PATHWAY (ALSO SEE PATH) RUN

LANE PATH RACK SLADE COURSE RAMBLA RAMBLE RODDIN BORSTAL RODDING
(RAISED —) CAUSEY CAUSEWAY
PATIENCE CALM THILD BEARANCE STOICISM COMPOSURE ENDURANCE FORTITUDE
PATIENT CASE CURE MEEK SOBER BOVINE PASSIVE ENDURING THOLEMOD SUFFERANT
(— OF ASYLUM) BEDLAM
(BE —) BEAR
(HYDROPATHIC —) WATERER
(MEDICAL —) CURE
PATIO COURT ATRIUM COURTYARD
PATOIS CANT GOMBO GUMBO CREOLE JARGON PATTER DIALECT GUERNSEY
(FRENCH —) JOUAL
PATOLA SARI GOURD
PATRIARCH JOB ABBA ENOS LEVI NASI NOAH PAPA POPE ALDER ELDER JACOB PITRI DESPOT JOSEPH NESTOR ABRAHAM ANCIENT VETERAN VENERABLE
(ETHIOPIAN —) ABUNA
PATRICIAN NOBLE EMPEROR PATRICK NOBLEMAN GENTLEMAN
PATRIMONY PORTION ANCESTRY HERITAGE LONGACRE
PATRIOT LOVER AMATEUR
PATRIOTIC PUBLIC ENVELOPE NATIONAL
PATRIPASSIAN NOETIAN
PATROCLUS (FATHER OF —) MENOETIUS
(MOTHER OF —) PERIAPIS POLYMELE STHENELE
(SLAYER OF —) HECTOR
PATROL GUARD SCOUT WATCH STOOGE PATROLE PROTECT
PATROLMAN COP GUARD FLATFOOT INSPECTOR
PATRON GOER BUYER GUEST STOOP AVOWRY CLIENT FATHER FAUTOR JAJMAN ACCOUNT PADRONE PATROON PROCTOR SPONSOR ADVOCATE CHAMPION CUSTOMER DEFENDER GUARDIAN MAECENAS
(PL.) FOLLOWING
PATRONAGE AEGIS FAVOR AVOWRY CUSTOM FAVOUR ACCOUNT AUSPICE FOMENTO HEARING AUSPICES BUSINESS PADROADO
(— AND CARE) AUSPICE
(— TO RELATIVES) NEPOTISM
(POLITICAL —) PAP
PATRONAL TITULAR
PATRONIZE USE DEIGN FAVOR DEFEND FATHER PROMOTE PROTECT EMPATRON FREQUENT
PATRON SAINT (OF CRIPPLES) GILES
(OF ENGLAND) GEORGE
(OF FISHERMEN) PETER
(OF FRANCE) DENIS
(OF GOLDSMITHS) ELOY
(OF IRELAND) PATRICK
(OF LAWYERS) IVES
(OF NORWAY) OLAF
(OF PAINTERS) LUKE

(OF SAILORS) ELMO
(OF SCOTLAND) ANDREW
(OF SPAIN) SANTIAGO
(OF THIEVES) DISMAS
(OF WALES) DAVID
PATROON TRACT CAPTAIN SUPPORTER
PATTEE FORMY FORMEE
PATTEN BASE CLOG FOOT SHOE SKATE STAND STILT CHOPIN GALOSH RACKET SANDAL CREEPER RACQUET SUPPORT CIOPPINO SNOWSHOE
PATTER RAP CANT TALK TIRL ARGOT LINGO HAPPER JARGON BLATHER BLATTER CHATTER DIALECT
PATTERING PITAPAT
PATTERN CUT FUR SET BASE CAST COMB COPY FORM GIMP IDEA LAUE MOLD NORM PLAN SEME STAR WAVE BISON BYSEN CHECK DECOR DISME DRAFT EPURE GUIDE IDEAL INLAY MODEL MOIRE MOULD NOTAN PLAID SEMEE SHAPE WATER BASKET BURELE CANVAS CHECKS DESIGN DIAPER ENTAIL ETOILE FABRIC FIGURE FLORAL FORMAT FORMER LACERY MAGPIE MATRIX MIRROR MODULE MUSTER ONDULE PATRON POUNCE RANDOM RECIPE SAMPLE SQUARE STRIPE SYSTEM ALLOVER CHEVRON EXAMPLE FACONNE FILLING FOLKWAY GESTALT GRIZZLE HOBNAIL MEANDER MEANING MULLION PARAGON PROJECT SAMPLER SLEIGHT STENCIL TEMPLET CALENDAR DENTELLE DYNAMICS FILIGREE HATCHING ILLUSION OVERSHOT PARADIGM PLATFORM STRICKLE PROTOTYPE
(— AFTER) COPY
(— IN BRAIN) GYRATION
(— OF BEHAVIOR) HABIT DISPLAY
(— OF CADENCE) CURSUS
(— OF HINDU MUSIC) TALA
(— OF LARGE SQUARES) DAMIER
(— OF SCARS) KELOID
(— OF SEPARATE OBJECTS) SEME
(— OF STRESS) SUPERFIX
(— OF TARTAN) SET SEET SETT SETTE
(— OF THOUGHT) GROUPTHINK
(— ON PAPER) BURELAGE
(— ON STAMP) GRILL GRILLE
(—S ON SILK) ARMURE
(— USED BY SILVERSMITHS) WORK BOROON
(CHARACTERISTIC BEHAVIOR —) BIT
(CROSS-BARRED —) PLAID
(FABRIC —) PAISLEY
(FACIAL —) BLAZE
(FOOTBALL —) FLY
(FRET —) KEY
(GARMENT —) SLOPER
(HAT —) BLOCK
(KNITTING —) ARGYLE
(MASONRY —) SPICATUM
(MELODIC —) RAGA
(METRIC — OF HINDU MUSIC) TALA
(PORCELAIN —) FITZHUGH

(RUG —) AINALEH
(SCANNING —) RASTER
(SHOE —) FORME
(SKATING —) EDGE
(SOCIAL —) FAMILISM
(SPEECH —) IDIOLECT
(SPOTTED —) SEME
(SQUARED FABRIC —) TATTERSALL
(STRIPED —) BARRE
(SYMBOLIC —) MANDALA
(TAILOR'S —) PROTRACTOR
(TATTOO —) MOKO
(TREE —) HOM HOMA
(WEAVING —) DRAW
PATTERNED GOFFERED
PATTY TABLET BOUCHEE PRALINE PATTYPAN VOLAUVENT
(— SHELL) DARIOLE TALMOUSE CROUSTADE
PATTYPAN SQUASH CYMLING
PATULOUS OPEN SPREAD DISTENDED
PAUCITY LACK DEARTH FEWNESS EXIGUITY SCARCITY
PAUL PAOLO
(ASSOCIATE OF —) DEMAS SILAS TITUS ARTEMAS BARNABAS
PAULDRON POLLET EPAULET PALERON POLDRON POLLETTE
PAULINA (HUSBAND OF —) CAMILLO ANTIGONUS
PAULLU (BROTHER OF —) MANCO HUASCAR
PAULOPOST DEUTERIC
PAULOWNIA KIRI
PAUNCH TUN KITE KYTE BELLY PENCH RUMEN ABDOMEN STOMACH GUNDYGUT POTBELLY
PAUNCHY BLOATED
PAUPER BEGGAR INDIGENT ROUNDSMAN
PAUPERISM BEGGARY
PAUSANIAS (FATHER OF —) CLEOMBROTUS
PAUSE HO HEM HALT HANG HOLD LULL REST RUFE STAY STOP WAIT ABIDE BREAK CEASE CHECK COMMA DELAY DEMUR DEVAL DWELL HOVER LETUP LIMMA POISE SELAH TARRY TENOR BREACH BREATH CORONA CUTOFF FALTER HANKER HIATUS PERIOD STANCE CAESURA FERMATA RESPITE VIRGULE BREATHER INTERVAL
(— BEFORE HURDLE) DWELL
(SUDDEN —) CHECK
(PL.) LIMMATA CAESURAE
PAUT PAW POKE POWT STAMP FINGER
PAVANE DANCE PADUAN PASSAMEZZO
PAVE LAY TAR PATH STUD TILE COVER FLOOR CAUSEY COBBLE QUARRY SMOOTH OVERLAY PREPARE RUDERATE MACADAMIZE
(— WITH STONES) STEEN CAUSEY
PAVED COBBLED
PAVEMENT SARN SLAB HEARTH PAEPAE TARMAC ASPHALT MACADAM MADADAM TELFORD ASAROTUM FLAGGING FLOORING

PATHMENT PEDIMENT PITCHING SIDEWALK TROTTOIR WASHBOARD

PAVER CUBER PAVIOR

PAVID TIMID AFRAID FEARFUL

PAVILION BASE FLAG TELD TENT FOLLY KIOSK PINNA ROYAL STAND CANOPY ENSIGN HOWDAH LITTER PANDAL PALLION COVERING GLORIETTE

(— ON ELEPHANT) HOUDAH HOWDAH

PAVILLON CHINOIS CRESCENT

PAVING FLAG SETT BLOCK BRICK DALLE PAVER STEAN STEEN STONE COBBLE TARMAC ASPHALT TELFORD PITCHING FLAGSTONE **(SQUARE —)** MITCHEL

PAVIS COVER PAVADE PAVOIS SHIELD PROTECT

PAW PAT PUD TOE CLAW FOOT GAUM GRAB HAND MAUL PATY PAUT PONT FLAIL PATTE TRICK CLUTCH FUMBLE HANDLE PATTEE CRUBEEN FLIPPER FORELEG FOREFOOT

PAWKY SLY ARCH BOLD CANNY SAUCY CRAFTY LIVELY SHREWD CUNNING FORWARD SQUEAMISH

PAWL COG DOG BOLT HAND GEAR STOP TENT TRIP CATCH CLICK DETENT FINGER PALLET TONGUE CLAWKER RATCHET

PAWN DIP POP WED FINE GAGE HOCK SOAK VAMP WAGE SPOUT SWEAT ENGAGE LUMBER OBLIGE PIGNUS PLEDGE WADSET COUNTER HOSTAGE PEACOCK CHESSMAN MOSKENEER TRIBULATION (PL.) PHALANX

PAWNBROKER MOUNT UNCLE BROKER LUMBERER MONEYLENDER

PAWNEE PANEE SKIDI WATER ALMOND BISCUIT PLEDGEE

PAWNIE PAWN PEACOCK

PAWNSHOP PAWN SPOUT LUMBER LOMBARD POPSHOP **(UNLICENSED —)** TIDDLYWINK

PAX BOARD PEACE TRUCE FRIEND TABLET

PAXWAX WHITLEATHER

PAY DO BUY FEE POP TIP ANTE FOOT FORK GIVE MEET RENT SOLD WAGE BATTA CLEAR COUGH DOUSE PLANK PUTUP REMIT SCREW SHEPE SOUND WAGES YIELD ANSWER BETALL DEFRAY IMPEND PONYUP REWARD SALARY SETTLE COMMUTE DEADRAY HALVANS IMBURSE REQUITE SATISFY SOULDIE STIPEND TRIBUTE RECOMPENSE

(— ATTENTION) DIG SEE COME GAUM HARK HEED TENT ADVERT REGARD AUDIENT

(— COURT TO) NUT SUE GALLANT

(— DOWN) DOUSE

(— FLIRTATIOUS ADVANCES) QUEEN

(— FOR) ABY BUY BYE COUP ABIDE COVER ESCOT STAND ABEGGE

(— FOR LIQUOR) BIRL

(— HEAVY PENALTY) SMART EXPIATE

(— HOMAGE) CHEFE CHEVE CHIVE SALAAM ADULATE

(— IN ADVANCE) IMPRESS

(— MONEY) PINGLE

(— OFF) LIFT SINK ACQUIT

(— OF SOLDIER) SAWDEE

(— OUT) VEER BLEED SPEND STUMP EXPEND DISBURSE

(— PART OF) DEFRAY

(— PENALTY) ABY ABYE

(— TAXES) GILD

(— UP) ANTE QUIT SETTLE LIQUIDATE

(— WITH IOU) VOWEL

(ADVANCE —) IMPREST

(DAILY —) DIET

(EXTRA —) BATTA BONUS KICKBACK

(SMALL —) SCREW

PAYABLE DUE CARTAL

PAYEE HOLDER ENDORSER

PAYMASTER BAKSHI BUKSHI PURSER BUKSHEE PAGADOR

PAYMENT CRO DUE FEE TAX BILL CENS DOES DOLE DUTY ERIC FEAL FINE GALE GILD HIRE LEVY MAIL MISE TACK TOLL BONUS CANON CLAIM GAVEL MAILL MENSE MODUS PREST PRICE YIELD ANGILD BOUNTY CHARGE LINAGE LOBOLA OUTLAY PAYOLA PLEDGE REBATE RETURN REWARD TARIFF ADVANCE ALIMONY ANNUITY BENEFIT CUSTOMS DEPOSIT FOOTAGE GARNISH PANNAGE PENSION PRIMAGE SOLUTIO STIPEND SUBSIDY SUBSIST TREWAGE TUITION CASUALTY FOREGIFT GRATUITY KICKBACK MALIKANA MARITAGE MONEYAGE TREASURY WOODGELD HEADPENNY MALGUZARI

(— BY CLERGYMAN) SYNODAL

(— FOR INJURY) UTU

(— FOR LABOR) MEED

(— FOR OFFENSE) ENACH

(— FOR RELEASE) LOOSING

(— FOR RERUN) RESIDUAL

(— FOR USE) RENT

(— IN ADVANCE) PREST

(— IN GOODS) TRUCK

(— IN KIND) SPECIE

(— OF DEBT) SOLUTION

(— OF FEE) FEAL

(— OF MINERS) FOOTAGE YARDAGE

(— ON DELIVERY) COD

(— TO SECURE FAVOR) PAYOLA

(ADVANCE —) ANTE

(DEMAND —) DUN BILL

(EVADE —) BILK DEFAULT

(FIXED —) FARM MODUS

(HOMICIDE'S —) KELCHIN

(INSURANCE —) PREMIUM

(PARTIAL —) INSTALMENT INSTALLMENT

(PERIODICAL —) GALE GAVEL

(RENT —) GALE

(SECRET —) PAYOLA

PAYNIM PAGAN PANIME HEATHEN INFIDEL PAGANDOM

PAYOFF FIX SOP BRIBE CLIMAX

PROFIT REWARD DECISIVE RECKONING

PDQ ASAP IMMEDIATELY

PEA DAL TUR DHAL GRAM LANG SEED ARHAR CHICK CICER GANDUL LEGUME PIGEON PODDER CARMELE CATJANG KHESARI PODWARE TANGIER GARVANRO MARROWFAT

(— DOVE) ZENAIDA

(— HARVESTER) VINER

(— PETAL) KEEL

(—S AND BEANS) PULSE

(EARLY —S) HASTINGS

(PARCHED —S) CARLS CARLINS (PL.) POIS GRAIN (PREF.) PISI

PEABIRD ORIOLE WRYNECK

PEACE PAX CALM EASE FINE LIOS LISS REST AMITY FRITH GRITH LISSE QUIET TRUCE REPOSE SAUGHT SHALOM CONCORD HARMONY REQUIEM SERENITY

(— MAKER) TREATY

(— OF MIND) ATARAXIA

(GODDESS OF —) IRENE

(SYMBOL OF —) DOVE TOGA OLIVE (PREF.) PACI

PEACEABLE FAIR SOME CIVIL DOUCE QUIET STILL GENTLE SILVER ORDERLY PACIFIC SOLOMON AMICABLE SACKLESS

PEACEFUL CALM SOME SOBER STILL IRENIC PLACID SILVER HALCYON ORDERLY PACIFIC

PEACE PIPE CALUMET

PEACH BLAB PAVY CLING PAVIE SNEAK SPLIT TRUMP ACCUSE BETRAY CARMAN CROSBY FOSTER INDICT INFORM OREJON PEENTO SALWEY BRUNION ELBERTA PERSIAN PIENTAO WHITTLE CRAWFORD ISABELLA RARERIPE ROSEWORT NECTARINE VICTORINE

(— STATE) GEORGIA

(— STONE) PUTAMEN

PEACHBLOW FAKIR

PEACHY FINE DANDY

PEACOCK MAO PAON PAVO PAWN POSE PEKOK STRUT PAJOCK PAVONE POWNIE PEAFOWL PHASIANID

(— TAIL) TRAIN

(CONGO —) AFROPAVO

(EYELIKE SPOT ON —) OCELLUS

PEACOCK BITTERN SUN

PEACOCK BUTTERFLY IO

PEACOCK FISH WRASSE

PEACOCK FLOWER FLAMBEAU POINCIANA

PEA CRAB PINNOTERE

PEAG TAX TOLL BEADS PAAGE PEACK PEAGE PEDAGE WAMPUM

PEAI PIAY PIACHE

PEA JACKET PEACOAT

PEAK ALP BEN NAB NOB PAP PIC TOP TOR ACME APEX BEAK CIMA CUSP DENT DOLT DOME KNOB KNOT PICO PIKE TOLT BLOOM CREST CROWN PIQUE PITCH PITON POINT SI INK SNEAK SPIRE STEAL STUMP CLIMAX CUPULA SHASTA

SHRINK SUMMIT ZENITH EPITOME MAXIMUM PICACHO CENTROID

(— OF ANCHOR) PEE

(— OF CAP) SCOOP

(— OF ENERGY) NUCLEUS

(ICE —) SERAC

(ISOLATED —) TOLT

(SHARP —) HORN AIGUILLE

(SNOW-CAPPED —) DOME CALOTTE (PREF.) ACR(O)

PEAKED WAN PALE THIN DRAWN PIKED SHARP COPPED SICKLY SLIMSY POINTED SLIMPSY

PEAKEDNESS KURTOSIS

PEAL CLAP RING TOLL CHIME CRACK GRILSE SHOVEL MINNING RESOUND SUMMONS THUNDER CARILLON

(— OF THUNDER) CLAP REEL

PEANUT BUR FLAX MANI MEAN PETTY PINDA GOOBER LEGUME PINDAL ARACHIS BEENNUT ARACHIDE EARTHPEA GRASSNUT KATCHUNG VALENCIA MONKEYNUT

(— DISEASE) TIKKA

PEA POD COB PYSE QUASH PESCOD

(POORLY FILLED —) POP

(UNRIPE —) SQUASH

PEAR BOSC BURY DIEGO MELON NELIS SABRA BEURRE BURREL COLMAR PANINI SECKEL WARDEN WINTER KIEFFER PEPERIN PRICKLY AMBRETTE BERGAMOT BLANQUET MUSCATEL TASAJILLO

(PRICKLY —) TUNA NOPAL OPUNTIA (PREF.) PIRI PIRO PYRI

PEAR HAW THORN

PEARL GEM MABE TERN GRAIN NACRE ONION PICOT UNION BOUTON OLIVET ORIENT BAROQUE BLISTER PARAGON BDELLIUM CATARACT MOONBEAM MARGARITE

(— WEIGHT) TANK

(IMITATION —) OLIVET

(IRREGULAR —) SLUG

(KIND OF —) MOBE

(MOCK —) OLIVET

(PIERCED —) WIDOW

(SEED —) ALIOFAR

(SMOKED —) MITRAILLE (PREF.) PERLI

PEARL BLUE METAL

PEARL BLUSH ROSETAN

PEARL FISHERS, THE (CHARACTER IN —) LEILA NADIR ZURGA NOURABAD

(COMPOSER OF —) BIZET

PEARL MILLET KOUS BAJRA CUMBU DUCHN DUKHN KOUSE JONDLA DAGASSA

PEARLSIDES ARGENTIN

PEARLWEED SAGINA POVERTY SEALWORT

PEARLY NACRY NACROUS MARGARIC PRECIOUS

PEARLY EVERLASTING LIVELONG MOONSHINE

PEAR-SHAPED FULL MELLOW ROUNDED PYRIFORM

PEASANT TAO BOND BOOR HERA HIND KERN KONO KOPI PEON RAYA RYOT SERF BAIRU BOWER CHURL

KNAVE KULAK RAYAH SWAIN
CARLOT COTMAN COTTAR
FARMER FELLAH RASCAL RUSTIC
BONDMAN LABORER PAISANO
VILLAIN CHOPSTICK CONTADINO
(— CLASS) JACQUERIE
(— OF INDIA) RYOT KISAN RAIYAT
(ARABIC —) FELLAH
(IRISH —) KERN KERNE
(ITALIAN —) CONTADINO
(RUSSIAN —) KULAK MUZHIK
MUZJIK
PEASANTS (AUTHOR OF —)
REYMONT
(CHARACTER IN —) KUBA ROCH
ANTEK HANKA SIMON YAGNA
YANEK BORYNA NASTKA TERESA
MATTHEW MATTHIAS DOMINIKOVA
PEASCOD (UNRIPE —) SQUASH
PEASE CROW TERN
PEASHOOTER TRUNK BLOWER
PISTOL BLOWGUN
PEAT GOR PET SOD VAG COOM
FUEL MIST MOOR MUCK MULL
TURF COOMB YARFA LAWYER
MINION YARPHA DARLING
FAVORITE
(— BOG) CESS YARPHA
(— CUTTER) PINER
(— SPADE) SLADE TUSKAR TWISCAR
(DRIED — FOR FUEL) VAG
(LAYER OF —) FLAW
PEA TREE KATURAI
PEATY KETTY
PEBA PEVA ARMADILLO
PEBBLE DIB FLAX JACK PLUM
CHUCK SCREE STONE BANTAM
COGGLE GIBBER GRAVEL QUARTZ
SHILLA SYCITE CHUCKIE CRYSTAL
SHINGLE STANNER JACKSTONE
(PL.) BEACH DREIKANTER
(PREF.) CALCULI CHALICO
PSEPH(O) THRIO
PEBBLY BEACHY
PECAN NOGAL PACANE
PECCADILLO FAULT OFFENSE
MISCHIEF
PECCANT FAULTY MORBID
CORRUPT SINNING DISEASED
PECCARY HOG SWINE JAVALI
WARREE TAGASSU TAYASSU
JAVELINA TAYASSUID
PECK DAB DOT JOB NIP BEAK BILL
CARP FOOD GRUB HOLE JERK KISS
PYKE PITCH PRICK STOCK THROW
HATFUL NIBBLE PEGGLE PICKLE
PIERCE STROKE CHIMBLE
(1-4TH OF —) LIPPY FORPET FORPIT
LIPPIE
PECKER BILL NOSE COURAGE
SPIRITS
PECTEN COMB MARSUPIUM
PECTORAL SANDPIPER JACK PERT
PEERT BROWNY BROWNIE
CHOROOK CREAKER FATBIRD
HAYBIRD KRIEKER SQUATTER
TRIDDLER JACKSNIPE
PECULATE STEAL MISUSE
EMBEZZLE
PECULIAR ODD VERY QUEER WEIRD
PROPER QUAINT UNIQUE CURIOUS
PRIVATE SEVERAL SPECIAL

STRANGE UNUSUAL SEPARATE
SINGULAR SPECIFIC
(— TO ONESELF) PRIVATE
(PREF.) IDIO
PECULIARITY KINK IDIOM QUIRK
TRAIT TRICK TWIST IDIASM ODDITY
AEOLISM ANOMALY FEATURE
IRISHRY CROTCHET HEADMARK
MANNERISM PROPRIETY
SINGULARITY
(— IN BOWL) BIAS
(— OF SPEECH) IDIOLOGISM
(CROTCHETY —) FIKE
PECUNIARY POCKET MONETARY
FINANCIAL
PED BASKET HAMPER PANIER
PEDAGOGUE TUTOR PEDANT
DOMINIE SQUEERS TEACHER
THWACKUM
PEDAGOGY SCHOOL DIDACTICS
EDUCATION
PEDAHEL (FATHER OF —) AMMIHUD
PEDAHZUR (SON OF —) GAMALIEL
PEDAIAH (BROTHER OF —)
SALATHIEL
(DAUGHTER OF —) ZEBUDAH
(FATHER OF —) PAROSH
(SON OF —) JOEL
PEDAL LEVER SWELL TREADLE
FOOTFEED PEDALIAN THROTTLE
(— COUPLER) TIRASSE
(BICYCLE —) RATTRAP
(KIND OF —) WAWA WAHWAH
(PIANO —) CELESTE
(PIANO SOFTENING —) CELESTE
PEDAL POINT DRONE
PEDANT PRIG DUNCE TUTOR
DORBEL PURIST TASSEL ACADEME
PEDAGOG GAMALIEL DRYASDUST
OLOFERNES
PEDANTIC BLUE STODGY BOOKISH
DONNISH ERUDITE INKHORN
TEACHING SCHOLASTIC
PEDDLE HAWK SELL CADGE SHOVE
TRANT TRUCK HIGGLE MEDDLE
PIDDLE RETAIL COLPORT
(— OVERPRICED TICKETS) SCALP
PEDDLER ARAB SMOUS BADGER
BODGER CRAMER JAGGER
JOWTER MUGGER STROLL
WALKER YAGGER CHAPMAN
NIGGLER PACKMAN ROADMAN
SANDBOY SWADDER TROGGER
TRUCKER HUCKSTER BOXWALLAH
DUSTYFOOT
(— OF DOPE) FIXER
(— OF DRESS PIECES) DUDDER
(— OF FISH) RIPIER RIPPIER
(— OF SHAM JEWELRY) DUFFER
(BOOK —) COLPORTEUR
(ITINERANT —) SMOUS SMOUSE
SMOUSER STROLLER
(MOHAM. —) BORA
(STREET —) CAMELOT
(WARES OF —) TROGGIN
PEDESTAL ANTA BASE BASIS
BLOCK SOCLE STAND PILLAR
PODIUM ROCKER AKROTER
SUPPORT PADMASANA
ACROTERIUM
(— PART) DADO
PEDESTRIAN PED DULL FOOT
SLOW HIKER FOOTER HOOFER

WALKER FOOTMAN PROSAIC
PLODDING WINGLESS PONDEROUS
VOETGANGER PERIPATETIC
PEDICAB TRISHAW
PEDICEL RAY STEM SCAPE STALK
PEDUNCLE FOOTSTALK
PEDIGREE STEMMA DESCENT
LINEAGE ANCESTRY PETEGREU
PUREBRED
PEDIMENT FRONTAL FRONTON
FASTIGIUM
PEDIPALP
(PL.) LABIUM
PEDOMETER ODOGRAPH
WAYWISER
PEDRERO PERRIER PETRARY
PEDUNCLE STEM SCAPE STALK
STIPES PEDICEL EYESTALK
HYPOCARP
(PL.) CRURA
PEEK PEEP PIKE GLANCE GLIMPSE
PEEKABOO PEEP BOPEEP PEEPEYE
PEEL BARK HARL HULL HUSK PARE
RIND SKIN FLAKE FLIPE SCALE
SLIPE STAKE STRIP CORTEX
SHOVEL SPITTLE UNDRESS
BARKPEEL ORANGEADO
(— OFF) HARL CRAZE FLAKE SHUCK
(BAKER'S —) PALE SPITTLE
(ORANGE OR LEMON —) ZEST
ORANGEAT
PEELER CRAB BOBBY CORER
HUSTLER SHEDDER SPUDDER
PILLAGER
PEELING RIND SKIN PARING PARURE
PEEN PIN PYNE RIVET
PEEP PIP PRY SPY COOK JEEP KEEK
KOOK PEEK PEER PINK PULE SKEG
STEP TOOT TOTE TOUT CHEEP
CHIRP DEKKO GLINT PIPIT SNOOP
TWEET DEGREE GLANCE SQUEAK
SQUINNY PEEKABOO
(— SHOW) RAREE
PEEPER EYE TOM FROG KEEK
VOYEUR
PEEPHOLE PEEP JUDAS EYELET
CREVICE
PEEPING NOSY PRYING
PEEPING TOM VOYEUR
PEER PRY DUKE EARL FEAR GAZE
LOOK LORD MATE PEEP PINK TOOT
TOUT BARON EQUAL GLINT GLOZE
MATCH NOBLE RIVAL STARE STIME
THANE TWIRE APPEAR FELLOW
OLIVER PINKER COMPERE
PEERAGE RANK DEBRETT DIGNITY
BARONAGE NOBILITY TENEMENT
PEER GYNT (AUTHOR OF —) IBSEN
(CHARACTER IN —) ASE BOYG GYNT
PEER ANITRA HEGSTAD SOLVEIG
PEERING SQUINNY
PEERLESS SUPREME MATCHLESS
NONPAREIL UNRIVALED
PEESWEEP FINCH PEWIT LAPWING
PEEWEEP
PEEVE IRK ANNOY GRUDGE NETTLE
IRRITATE
PEEVISH SOUR CROSS DORTY
PENSY SNACK TECHY TEENY TESTY
TETTY THRAW TIFFY WEMOD
CRUSTY FRANZY GIRNIE HIPPED
PATCHY SNARLY SNUFFY SULLEN
TATTER TOUCHY TWARLY TWAZZY

TWITTY UPPISH UPPITY VAPORY
CRABBED FRATCHY FRECKET
FRETFUL FROWARD GROUCHY
PETTISH SPLEENY TEDIOUS TIFFISH
WASPISH CAPTIOUS PERVERSE
PETULANT PHRAMPEL PINDLING
SANSHACH TWANKING
FRAMPOLD,PETULANT
PEEVISHLY CRUSTILY
PEEVISHNESS PET BILE
PETULANCE
PEEWEE BOOT RUNT TINY PEWEE
MARBLE LAPWING
PEG FIX HOB HUB NOB NOG PIN TEE
HOBB KING KNAG PLUG SCOB
SHAG SKEG STEP CLEAT DOWEL
DRINK NOTCH PERCH PITON
PRONG SPELL SPILE SPILL STAKE
THOLE THROW TOOTH WADDY
DEGREE DOWELL FAUCET MARKER
NORMAN PICKET REASON SPIGOT
TAPOUN TIPCAT PINNING PRETEXT
SCOLLOP SPERKET SUPPORT
TRENAIL
(— FOR PLAYING GAME) CAT
SPILIKIN
(— FOR SADDLES) SPERKET
(— OF FAUCET) SPIGOT
(— OF STRINGED INSTRUMENT)
CHEVILLE
(— OUT) DIE FAIL
(BELAYING —) KEVEL
(IRON —) PITON
(THATCH —) SCOB
PEGA REMORA
PEGALL BASKET PACKALL
PEGASUS QUAVIVER HYPOSTOME
PEG TOP PIRY PEERY PEERIE
PEG WOFFINGTON (AUTHOR OF —)
READE
(CHARACTER IN —) PEG RICH VANE
HARRY MABEL CIBBER COLLEY
CHARLES TRIPLET POMANDER
WOFFINGTON BRACEGIRDLE
PEIGNOIR GOWN DRESS KIMONO
NEGLIGEE
PEISE BLOW FORCE PASSE POISE
POIZE IMPACT WEIGHT BALANCE
POISURE
PEKAH (FATHER OF —) REMALIAH
(SLAYER OF —) HOSHEA
PEKAHIAH (FATHER OF —)
MENAHEM
(SLAYER OF —) PEKAH
PEKAN WEJACK
PEKING MAN SINANTHROPUS
PELAGE FUR COAT HAIR PILAGE
PELAGIC MARINE AQUATIC
OCEANIC PELAGIAN
PELAIAH (FATHER OF —) ELIOENAI
PELALIAH (FATHER OF —) AMZI
PELATIAH (FATHER OF —) BENAIAH
HANANIAH
PELEG (BROTHER OF —) JOKTAN
(FATHER OF —) EBER
PELET (FATHER OF —) JAHDAI
AZMAVETH
PELETH (FATHER OF —) JONATHAN
(SON OF —) ON
PELEUS (BROTHER OF —) TELAMON
(FATHER OF —) AEACUS
(HALF-BROTHER OF —) PHOCUS
(MOTHER OF —) ENDEIS

(SON OF —) PELIDES ACHILLES
(WIFE OF —) THETIS ANTIGONE
PELF GAIN BOOTY LUCRE MONEY
SPOIL TRASH PILFER PILFRE
REFUSE RICHES WEALTH
COMPOST
PELIAS (BROTHER OF —) NELEUS
(DAUGHTER OF —) ALCESTIS
(FATHER OF —) POSEIDON
(MOTHER OF —) TYRO
(SON OF —) ACASTUS
(WIFE OF —) ANAXIBIA
PHYLOMACHE
PELICAN DOVE ALCATRAS
ONOCROTAL
(— STATE) LOUISIANA
PELIOOC POSTIN POSTEEN
PELL BEAT PELE PELT HURRY PEELE
HASTEN
PELLAGRA MAIDISM PELAGRA
PELLEAS (BELOVED OF —)
MELISANDE
(BROTHER OF —) GOLAUD
PELLEAS ET MELISANDE
(CHARACTER IN —) ARKEL GOLAUD
YNIOLD PELLEAS ALLEMONDE
GENEVIEVE MELISANDE
(COMPOSER OF —) DEBUSSY
PELLES (DAUGHTER OF —) ELAINE
PELLET BB WAD BALL CAST PILL
SHOT BOLUS PRILL STONE BEEBEE
BULLET FECULA OGRESS PILULE
CASTING GRANULE PALLION
TRATTLE BUCKSHOT GUNSTONE
HAILSTONE
(RAIN —S) HAIL
(SNOW —S) GRAUPEL
(PL.) SHOT
PELLICLE FILM SCUM SKIN CRUST
CUTICLE EPISTASIS
PELLINORE (SLAYER OF —) GAWAIN
(SON OF —) TORRE DORNAR
LAMEROK PERCIVAL AGGLOVALE
PELLITORY BERTRAM BERTRUM
WALLWORT
PELL-MELL RUSH MELPELL
DISORDER HEADLONG
PELLOCK PALACH PORPOISE
PELLUCID CLEAR BRIGHT LIMPID
ORIENT CRYSTAL
PELMA TRACK
PELMET CORNICE VALANCE
PALMETTE
PELOPONNESUS (CITY OF —)
SPARTA
(PEOPLE OF —) MOREOTE
(RIVER GOD OF —) ALPHEUS
PELOPS (FATHER OF —) TANTALUS
(SON OF —) ATREUS TROEZEN
PITTHEUS THYESTES
(WIFE OF —) HIPPODAMIA
PELORIA EPANODY
PELOTA (— BASKET) CESTA
PELT FUR KIT BEAR BEAT BLOW
CAPE CAST CLOD COON DASH
FELL HIDE HURL KITT PELL PUSH
RACK SKIN BESET CHUNK FITCH
HURRY SABLE SLASH SPEED
STONE WHACK BADGER BEAVER
FISHER PELTER PEPPER SERVAL
SPRING BETHUMP COONSKIN
(— OF SEAL, WITH BLUBBER)
SCULP

(— WITH MISSILES) BUM SQUAIL
(— WITH STONES) LAPIDATE
(BEAVER —) BLANKET
PELTAST SOLDIER TARGETEER
PELTATE SCUTATE
PELTER SKEET
PELTING SLASHING
PELTRY FURS SKINS
PELUDO POYOU ARMADILLO
PELVIS
(PREF.) PELVI(O) PELYCO PYEL(O)
(SUFF.) PELLIC
PEN BIC CAN COT CUB GET HOK
MEW PAR PIN STY BOLT CAGE
COOP CROO CROW FAUD FOLD
JAIL STUB WALK YARD BUGHT
CRAWL CREEP CUBBY HUTCH
KRAAL POINT QUILL STYLE WRITE
BOUGHT CORRAL CRUIVE FASTEN
FLIGHT HURDLE INDITE RECORD
STYLUS ZAREBA CONFINE
WARKLOOM
(— BRAND) CLIC
(— CATTLE) STANCE
(— FOR CATTLE) CUB LOT CREW
CRUE LAIR REEVE
(— FOR ELEPHANTS) KRAAL
(— FOR HOGS OR SLAVES) CRAWL
(— OF CUTTLEFISH) GLADIUS
(— POINT) NEB NIB STUB
(— UP) FRANK STIVE
(AUTHOR'S —) STYLE STYLUS
(BALLPOINT —) BIRO
(FOUNTAIN —) STICK
(KIND OF —) POISON
(MUSIC —) RASTRUM
(REED —) CALAMUS
PENALIZE CHECK
PENALTY BETE CAIN COST DOOM
FINE LOSS PAIN BEAST JUISE
MULCT AMENDE AMERCE SOLACE
FORFEIT NEMESIS SURSIZE
BLOODWIT HARDSHIP SCAFFOLD
(DRINKING —) KELTIE
PENANCE TAP SORE SHRIFT
SORROW REMORSE SUFFERING
(DO —) ATONE
PEN CASE PENNER POPPET
PENCEL FLAG PENNON STREAMER
PENNONCEL
PENCHANT BENT TASTE FOIBLE
GENIUS LIKING LEANING
FONDNESS
PENCIL PEN RED WAD BLUE LEAD
WADD LINER SHEAF SKETCH
STYLUS POINTEL CHARCOAL
KEELIVINE
(PART OF —) CASE LEAD POINT
ERASER FERRULE SHOULDER
(SLATE —) CAM CALM SKAILLIE
(PL.) STATIONERY
(PREF.) PENCILLI PENICILLI
PENCILWOOD MORDORE
PEND HANG
PENDANT BOB JAG DROP FLAG
JAGG PEND TAIL AGLET BULLA
GUTTA POINT AIGLET LUSTER
PALAOA PLAYER TABARD TARGET
TASSEL EARDROP LANGUET
SUPPORT LAVALIER
PENDENNIS (AUTHOR OF —)
THACKERAY

(CHARACTER IN —) BELL AMORY
EMILY FANNY FOKER HELEN HENRY
LAURA ARTHUR BOLTON GEORGE
JEMIMA BLANCHE FRANCIS
ALTAMONT COSTIGAN CLAVERING
PENDENNIS WARRINGTON
THISTLEWOOD
PENDENT LOP BAGGED ICICLE
HANGING PROMISS
PENDICLE POFFLE
PENDING NISI
PENDULOUS LOP SLOUCH
HANGING NODDING PENSILE
CERNUOUS DROOPING
PENDULUM SWING PENDLE
SWINGEL SWINGLE VIBRATILE
(INVERTED —) NODDY
PENELOPE (FATHER-IN-LAW OF —)
LAERTES
(FATHER OF —) ICARIUS
(HUSBAND OF —) ULYSSES
ODYSSEUS
(MOTHER OF —) PERIBOEA
(SON OF —) TELEMACHUS
(SUITOR OF —) AGELAUS
PENEPLAIN STRATH ENDRUMPF
PENETRABLE PERVIOUS
PENETRATE CUT DIG DIP SEE BITE
BORE DIVE GORE PASS PINK SINK
STAB WADE BREAK DRILL DRIVE
ENTER IMBUE PROBE SEIZE THIRL
CLEAVE FATHOM FICCHE GIMLET
INVADE PIERCE RIDDLE SEARCH
STRIKE THRILL WIMBLE DISCERN
PERVADE PERCOLATE PERFORATE
(— MENTALLY) ENTER
(— ONE'S MIND) SOAK
PENETRATED (EASILY —) MELLOW
PENETRATING ACID KEEN ACUTE
LEVEL NASAL SHARP ASTUTE
DEADLY SHREWD SHRILL SUBTLE
GIMLETY INGOING INTRANT
KNOWING PUNGENT PERCEANT
PIERCING REACHING TRENCHANT
PENETRATION DEPTH ACUMEN
FATHOM INROAD INGOING INSIGHT
SEEPAGE INCISION INVASION
SAGACITY
(IMAGINATIVE —) INSIGHT
PENEUS (DAUGHTER OF —) DAPHNE
(FATHER OF —) OCEANUS
(MOTHER OF —) TETHYS
(SON OF —) HYPSEUS
PENGUIN AUK DIVER GENTU ADELIE
ARCTIC DIPPER GENTOO JOHNNY
PINWING BREVIPED MACARONI
ROCKHOPPER
(PL.) IMPENNES
(PREF.) SPHENISCI SPHENISCO
PENGUIN ISLAND (AUTHOR OF —)
FRANCE
(CHARACTER IN —) MAEL CLENA
CRRES DRACO OLIVE PYROT TALPA
AGARIC KRAKEN TRINCO VISIRE
EVELINE BOSCENOS CLARENCE
GREATANK JOHANNES OBEROSIA
CHATILLON MARBODIUS
PENINNAH (HUSBAND OF —)
ELKANAH
(SON OF —) SAMUEL
PENINSULA CAPE MULL NECK
INDIA BILAND BYLAND ISLAND
PENILE CHERSONESE

PENIS
(PREF.) BALAN(I)(O) PHALL(O)
POSTH(E)(IO)(O)
PENITENCE RUE REGRET
SORROW PENANCE PENANCY
REMORSE
PENITENT RUER SORRY HUMBLE
WEEPER MOURNER STANDER
CONTRITE
(— OF 3RD STAGE) KNEELER
PENITENTIARY JUG PEN JAIL STIR
TENCH PRISON PENITENT
PENMAN CLERK AUTHOR SCRIBE
WRITER
PENMANSHIP HAND SCRIPT
PENSHIP WRITING
PENNANT FANE FLAG WHIP COLOR
ROGER BANNER BURGEE CORNET
ENSIGN PENCIL PENNON PENSIL
PINION PINNET MEATBALL
REPEATER STREAMER
PENNILESS POOR BROKE NEEDY
SKINT BANKRUPT INDIGENT
STRAPPED PLACKLESS
PENNON FLAG VANE WING ANVIL
BANNER PENCIL PENOUN PINION
FEATHER GONFANON
PENNON SPAR PEGGYMAST

PENNSYLVANIA
CAPITAL: HARRISBURG
COLLEGE: JUNIATA URSINUS
LYCOMING
COUNTY: ELK ERIE PIKE YORK
BERKS BUCKS PERRY TIOGA
LEHIGH CAMBRIA JUNIATA
LUZERNE VENANGO WYOMING
LYCOMING
MOUNTAIN RANGE: POCONO
ALLEGHENY
NATIVE: AMISH DUTCH
PRESIDENT: BUCHANAN
RIVER: LEHIGH CLARION JUNIATA
LICKING TOWANDA CALDWELL
DELAWARE SCHRADER
ALLEGHENY SCHUYLKILL
MONONGAHELA SUSQUEHANNA
STATE BIRD: GROUSE
STATE FLOWER: LAUREL
STATE NICKNAME: KEYSTONE
STATE TREE: HEMLOCK
TOWN: ERIE ETNA PLUM YORK
AVOCA MEDIA EASTON EMMAUS
SHARON ALTOONA EPHRATA
HERSHEY READING TOWANDA
BRYNMAWR SCRANTON
SHAMOKIN BETHLEHEM
CHARLEROI GETTYSBURG
PITTSBURGH
UNIVERSITY: PITT DREXEL LEHIGH
TEMPLE BUCKNELL DUQUESNE
VILLANOVA

PENNY DY AES MEG RED SOU WIN
GILL WING WINN BROON BROWN
OULAP PENCE COPPER FOLLIS
SALTEE STIVER BROWNIE
REDCENT STERLING
(— DREADFUL) HORRIBLE
(DUTCH —) STIVER
(HALF —) HALFLIN
(OLD SCOTCH —) TURNER
(PL.) PENCE FOLLES

PENNYCRESS FANWEED STINKWEED
PENNY-PINCHING STINGY
PENNYROYAL PULIOL HEDEOMA HILLWORT TICKWEED SQUAWWEED
PENNYWEIGHT DWT PENNY WEIGHT STERLING
PENNYWORT ROTGRASS
PENROD (AUTHOR OF —) TARKINGTON
  (CHARACTER IN —) CRIM JONES SARAH PENROD MARJORIE SCHOFIELD
PENSION WAGE PAYMENT STIPEND SUBSIDY TRIBUTE GRATUITY MALIKANA
PENSIONER COD RETIREE
PENSIVE MESTO MOODY PENSY SOBER DREAMY MUSING PENCEY WISTFUL THOUGHTY MELANCHOLY
PENT CAGED PENNED CONFINED ENCLOSED RESERVOIR
PENTACLE STAR HEXAGRAM PENTAGRAM
PENTAD QUINTAD
PENTASTICH POEM UNIT STANZA STROPHE
PENTATEUCH TORAH THORAH
PENTECOST SHABUOTH WHITSUNDAY
PENTHESILEA (SLAYER OF —) ACHILLES
PENTHEUS (FATHER OF —) ECHION
  (GRANDFATHER OF —) CADMUS
  (MOTHER OF —) AGAVE
PENTHIA STARLIGHT
PENTHOUSE CAT PENT ROOF SHED AERIE ANNEX HANGAR LOOKUM SHADOW PLUTEUS BULKHEAD SKEELING SKILLION APPENTICE
PENTOSAN ARABAN
PENTOSE APIOSE RIBOSE
PENTYL AMYL
PENUMBRA AURA
PENURIOUS MEAN POOR BARREN SCANTY STINGY MISERLY WANTING INDIGENT HIDEBOUND NIGGARDLY
PENURY WANT BEGGARY BORASCO POVERTY SCARCITY INDIGENCE PRIVATION
PEON HAND PAWN SERF SLAVE PELADO THRALL FOOTMAN LABORER PEASANT SOLDIER CONSTABLE
PEONY PINY MOUTAN
PEOPLE (ALSO SEE NATIVE AND TRIBE) ARO FUL LOG MEN PUL TAT VAI YAO AKRA ASHA BENI BUGI CHIN CHUD EMIM FOLK FULA GARO GENS HERD HIMA HUMA IRON LAND LEDE LOLO LUBA LURI NOSU PHUD PHUL PHUT RACE RAIS REMI SAFI SARA SEBA SERE TEMA THEY TODA TOMA TULU USUN VITI VOLK WARE AFIFI AVARS BENIN BONGO CATTI CHAGA COURS DEMOS DUALA EDONI ELYMI FOLKS FULAH GENTE GOMER HAUSA JACKS KAREN LAITY LANAO LENDU LUREM MARSI MASAI NOGAI ORANG PUNAN QUADI RAMBO ROTSE SACAE SALAR SAURA SHAKA STOCK TAURI VOLTA WARUA WORLD ABABUA ACHUAS AFSHAR AISSOR ANGAMI ANGLES ARUNTA AVIKOM BAHIMA BAKELE BAKUBA BALUBA BELTIR BOSHAS BULLOM CIMBRI COMMON DAOINE GENTRY GILAKI GILEKI HAUSSA HERERO HERULI KANWAR KPUESI KRUMAN MANTZU MINYAE MOSCHI NATION OVAMPO PAMIRI PUBLIC RAMUSI RUTULI SAFINI SAMBAL SATRAE SEMANG SHARRA TADJIK TAGAUR TELUGU TUNGUZ TURSHA VENETI VOLCAE WACAGO WAHIMA YNDOYS YUECHI ZAMBAL ACHANGO ASTOMOI BAGANDA BAGARRA BAKALAI BANGALA BANGASH BAROTSE BUNYORO DARDANI DENIZEN DURZADA FALISCI GAETULI GENERAL GEPIDAE GOAJIRO GUHAYNA INHABIT IRISHRY ISSEDOI ITALICI KINDRED KURANKO MAKONDE MESHECH MITANNI NABALOI PICENES PICTAVI PUKHTUN ROHILLA SAMBURU SENONES SILURES SUKKIIM TIRURAI VESTINI WABUNGA WACHAGA WAKAMBA WANGONI POPULATE
(— HAVING DISTINCT LANGUAGE) TONGUE
(— OF FASHION) FLOSS
(— OF GOOD BREEDING) GENTRY GENTILITY
(— WITH SIMILAR INTERESTS) MAFIA
(ABORIGINAL —) JAKUN KHMER KODAGU SEKHWAN
(ANCIENT —) CARA CHAM JUNG ELYMI GETAE HURRI ICENI SACAE SERES SICULI DARDANI FALISCI FIRBOLG KIPCHAK SEQUANI SILURES
(BEAUTIFUL —) GLITTERATI
(BIBLICAL —) ALUR IBAD IBAN MAGOG IBANAG SOMALI GADDANG
(CAVE-DWELLING —) HORITE
(COMMON —) DEMOS PLEBE VULGAR VULGUS TILIKUM SNOBBERY
(EXTINCT —) KOT CHONO COFAN COREE CHANGO CHATOT GUINAU HIBITO SAPONI SHIRINO
(FOREST —) SAKAI SAORA SAURA
(GROUP OF —) CAUCUS
(HONORABLE —) HONESTY
(LOWEST CLASS OF —) CANAILLE
(MARITIME —) LAMUT
(MOUNTAIN —) HUZUL HUTZUL
(NOMADIC —) SHUA HORDE IGDYR IHLAT SHUWA HABIRU SHAGIA SARACEN SHAMMAR SHORTZY SHUKRIA
(OLD —) ANCIENTRY
(ORDINARY —) LAYFOLK
(PAGAN —) IRAYA HANUNOO SUBANUN
(POWERFUL GROUP OF —) MAFIA
(PRIMITIVE —) DAFLA IRULA KADIR KURUKH CHENCHU
(WHITE —) ALBICULI
(PL.) MAKHZAN
(PREF.) DEM(O) ETHN(O) PLEBI POPULI
PEOPLED ABAD SETTLED POPULATE
PEORIA MASCOUTEN
PEP GO VIM ZIP DASH MOXIE VERVE VIGOR BOUNCE ENERGY GINGER ANIMATE QUICKEN ACTIVITY
  (— UP) ENLIVEN
PEPLUM GOWN SKIRT TUNIC PEPLOS OVERSKIRT
PEPO GOURD MELON SQUASH PUMPKIN PEPONIDA PEPONIUM
PEPPER CAVA IKMO ITMO KAVA SIRI BETEL CHILI MANGO PIPER SIRIH MATICO TOPEPO CAYENNE PAPRIKA PIMENTA RELIENO JALAPENO KAVAKAVA
  (JAVA —) CUBEB
  (MEXICAN HOT —) SERRANO
  (RED —) LADYFINGER
  (PREF.) PIPERI PIPERO
PEPPER-AND-SALT JASPER
PEPPERGRASS CRESS CANARY ANOUNOU COCKWEED
PEPPERMINT MENTHE LABIATE
PEPPER TREE MOLLE HOROPITO PIMIENTO
PEPPERWORT DITTANDER
PEPPERY HOT FIERY SAUCY SPICY TOUCHY PIQUANT PUNGENT SPIRITED STINGING
PEPPY RAHRAH GINGERY
PEPTIDE KININ AMANITIN
PEPTIDOGLYCAN MUREIN
PEPTONE ASCARON
PER BY THE EACH THROUGH
PERADVENTURE HAP DOUBT MAYBE CHANCE MAPPEN MAYHAP HAPPILY PERHAPS POSSIBLY
PERAMBULATE ROAM WALK RAMBLE STROLL PERAMBLE TRAVERSE
PERAMBULATION WEND
PERAMBULATOR BUGGY WAGON BASSINET VIAMETER WAYWISER PEDOMETER
PERATE OPHITE
PERCEIVE SEE ESPY FEEL FIND GAUM HEAR KNOW LOOK MIND NOTE SCAN TWIG SCENT SENSE SMELL TASTE TOUCH BEHOLD COTTON DESCRY DIVINE FIGURE NOTICE REMARK SURVEY COGNIZE DISCERN OBSERVE REALIZE SENSATE COMPRISE DESCRIBE UNDERNIM RECOGNIZE
  (—CRITICALLY) SAVOR
PERCENTAGE CUT AGIO PART SHARE PROFIT PORTION RAKEOFF SCALAGE CONTANGO DEFLATOR PROPORTION
  (INSURANCE —) FRANCHISE
  (MINING —) LEY
PERCEPT IDEA
PERCEPTIBLE PUBLIC NOTABLE TACTILE VISIBLE APPARENT PALPABLE SENSIBLE TANGIBLE TRACTABLE PERCEIVABLE
  (— BY TASTE) SAPID
  (FAINTLY —) SHADOWY
  (HARDLY —) FAINT
  (PREF.) ESTHETO
PERCEPTION RAY BUMP GAUM TACT SAVOR SCENT SENSE SIGHT ACUMEN VISION CLOSURE FEELING GLIMMER NOSTRIL BEARINGS DELICACY OUTSIGHT COGNITION SENSATION SENTIMENT
  (DIM —) GLIMMER
  (MENTAL —) TACT TOUCH SENSATION
  (NICE —) TASTE
  (SPIRITUAL —) WISDOM
  (UNREAL —) HALLUCINATION
PERCEPTIVE ACUTE QUICK SHARP SUBTLE KNOWING PIERCING SENTIENT SENSITIVE
PERCH BAR BAS LUG PEG ROD SIT BASS JOUK MADO OKOW PERK PIKE POLE POPE RUFF SEAT BARSE BEGTI BEKTI BLOCK LIGHT REACH ROOST RUFFE STAFF STANG ALIGHT ANABAS BUGARA CALLOP COMBER PERCID SANDER SAUGER SETTLE ZANDER ZINGEL ALFIONE HOGFISH STATION ROCKFISH MARTENIKO TRUMPETER MADEMOISELLE
  (KIND OF —) NILE
  (LOFTY —) AERIE
  (2-YEAR OLD —) EGLING
  (PREF.) PERCI
PERCHANCE HAPLY MAYBE AUNTERS FORTUNE PERHAPS POSSIBLY
PERCHER STAKER
PERCHTA BERTHA
PERCOLATE MELT OOZE PERK SEEP SIFT SILT SIPE SOAK WEEP DRILL EXUDE LEACH EXHALE FILTER STRAIN
PERCOLATION SIPING SEEPAGE LEACHING
PERCOLATOR SIPER BIGGIN CAFETIERE DISPLACER
PERCUSSION (ALSO SEE DRUMS) BLOW IMPACT STROKE TOMTOM PNEUMATIC
  (— IN MASSAGE) TAPOTEMENT
PERDITA (FATHER OF —) LEONTES
  (MOTHER OF —) HERMIONE
PERDITION HELL LOSS RUIN BOWWOWS BALLYWACK DAMNATION
PEREGRINATE TOUR WALK TRAVEL WANDER JOURNEY SOJOURN TRAVERSE
PEREGRINE ALIEN NOMAD EXOTIC ROVING PILGRIM STRANGE IMPORTED
PEREGRINE FALCON SAKER GENTLE TASSEL TERCEL
PEREGRINE PICKLE (AUTHOR OF —) SMOLLETT
  (CHARACTER IN —) TOM VANE PIPES SALLY EMILIA HAWSER PICKLE APPLEBY GRIZZLE GAMALIEL GAUNTLET HATCHWAY HORNBECK TRUNNION PEREGRINE CADWALLADER
PEREMPT QUASH DEFEAT DESTROY
PEREMPTORY FLAT FINAL UTTER

EXPRESS HAUGHTY ABSOLUTE
DECISIVE DOGMATIC POSITIVE
ESSENTIAL MASTERFUL
PERENNIAL HERB CAREX LIANA
PEONY SEDUM BANANA CENTRO
BLUEWEED CONSTANT ENDURING
KNAPWEED TOADFLAX CONTINUAL
EVERGREEN PENNYWORT
PERPETUAL RECURRENT
PERESH (FATHER OF —) MACHIR
(MOTHER OF —) MAACHAH
PERFECT ALL AOK BACK BORN
CURE FILL FINE FULL HOLY HONE
PURE SURE TOAT EXACT FINAL
FULLY IDEAL PLAIN RIGHT RIPEN
SHEER SOUND TOTAL UTTER
WHOLE ENTIRE EXPERT FINISH
MATURE POLISH REFINE SPHERE
TIPTOP CERTAIN CONCOCT
CONTENT CORRECT CROWNED
DEVELOP GEMLIKE IMPROVE
PLENARY PRECISE SINLESS
SPHERAL TYPICAL COMPLETE
COPYBOOK FLAWLESS INFINITE
INTEGRAL REPLENISH
(— IN RIGHTEOUSNESS) HOLY
(— SCORE) MAX
(NOT —) IMMATURE
(PREF.) TEL(E)(EO)
PERFECTA EXACTA
PERFECTED EXACT SUMMED
FINISHED PERQUEIR
PERFECTION ACME BEST PINK
BLOOM IDEAL BEAUTY FINISH
PLENTY PARAGON FINALITY
FINENESS FULLNESS MATURITY
RIPENESS ERUDITION
(STATE OF —) SIDDHI
(TO —) NINE
(TYPE OF —) PARAGON
PERFECTIVE TELIC
PERFECTLY SPAN QUITE IDEALLY
PERQUEIR
PERFIDIOUS FALSE SNAKY DISLEAL
SNAKISH DISLOYAL SPITEFUL
FAITHLESS
PERFIDY DECEIT TREASON
FALSEHOOD FALSENESS
TREACHERY
PERFORATE EAT DOCK HOLE DRILL
PRICK PUNCH SIEVE THIRL PIERCE
POUNCE RIDDLE THRILL PINHOLE
PUNCTURE PENETRATE
TEREBRATE
(— A STAMP) CENTER
PERFORATED OPEN CRIBROSE
FENESTRAL PUNCTURED
PERFORATION BORE HOLE THIRL
TORET BROACH EYELET STIGMA
TRESIS FORAMEN PINHOLE
SEPTULA STENCIL FENESTRA
DIABROSIS PERTUSION
(SUFF.) TRESIA
PERFORATOR (SURGICAL —)
TROCAR
PERFORM DO ACT CUT KIP CHAR
FILL FULL HAVE KEEP LAST MAKE
PLAY SHOW STEP CHARE DIGHT
ENACT EXERT FETCH PUTON
THROW ACQUIT COMMIT EFFECT
FULFIL RENDER ACHIEVE EXECUTE
EXHIBIT EXPLOIT FUNGIFY FURNISH

IWURCHE OPERATE PRESENT
PRESTATE PROSECUTE
(— AWKWARDLY) BOGGLE
(— BADLY) BOLLIX
(— BRILLIANTLY) STAR SPARKLE
(— CLUMSILY) THUMB BUNGLE
(— FANCY STUNTS) HOTDOG
(— FULLY) END
(— HASTILY) SKIMP SCAMP,
(— HURRIEDLY) SLUR
(— IN DANCING) FIGURE
(— PERFECTLY) DOTOAT
(— POORLY) CLUTCH
(— SLUTTISHLY) SOZZLE
(— SUCCESSFULLY) CUTIT
(FAIL TO —) CHOKE
(FAIL TO — EFFECTIVELY) CHOKE
PERFORMANCE ACT JOB DEED
FEAT GALA HAND SHOW TEST
WORK CAPER SLANG SPORT
STUNT ACTING ACTION BALLET
EFFECT HORARY MASQUE
ACCOUNT ACROAMA BENEFIT
BOOKING CONCERT EXPLOIT
MATINEE MUMMERY RELEASE
SHOWING FAREWELL FUNCTION
PRACTICE STERACLE OPERATION
(— FOR ONE) SOLO
(— OF DUTY) FEASANCE
(— OF OBLIGATION) SOLUTIO
(— VARIATIONS) COUNTER
(— WITH SENTIMENTALITY) DROOL
(ARAB —) FANTASIA
(BOISTEROUS —) KNOCKABOUT
(BRILLIANT —) BRAVURA
(CHRISTMAS EVE —) GOMBAY
(CLUMSY —) BUNGLE
(DISORDERLY —) SCRAMBLE
(DRAMATIC —) TOPENG
PANTOMIME
(FIRST —) OPENING PREMIERE
(HILARIOUS —) HOOT
(INEPT —) BOMB
(MUSICAL —) LESSON RECITAL
DIVISION
(NO —) RELACHE
(PAST —) FORM
(RENEWED —) REVIVAL
(SHORT —) SPOT
(STAGE —) SCENE
(SURGICAL —) OPERATION
(TRAVELLING —) SLANG
(TRIAL —) AUDITION
(VOCAL —) SPRECHSTIMME
(VULGAR —) BLOWOFF
(WRONG —) MISPRISION
(SUFF.) LOG(ER)(IA)(IAN)(IC)(ICAL)
(IST)(UE)(Y
PERFORMER ACT DOER GEEK
MOKE STAR ACTOR SHINE ARTIST
DANCER KINKER LEADER PLAYER
WORKER ACROAMA ACROBAT
ARTISTE GAMBIST HORNIST
HOTSHOT SOLOIST EXECUTOR
SPARKLER HAMFATTER
HEADLINER
(— ON SEVERAL INSTRUMENTS)
MOKE
(— WITH NEGRO DIALECT)
HAMBONE
(BURLESQUE —) GRINDER
(CIRCUS —) LEAPER

(INFERIOR —) HAM SHINE
(SUFF.) ANT ENT
PERFUME ATAR BALM FUME MUSK
NOSE OTTO AROMA ATTAR CENSE
CIVET MYRRH SCENT SMELL SPICE
CARVOL CHYPRE EMBALM FLAVOR
IONONE BOUQUET CARVONE
DIAPASM ESSENCE INCENSE
JASMINE NOSEGAY ODORIZE
SWEETEN BERGAMOT MARECHAL
ORANGERY PATCHOULI
(— BASE) MUSK CIVET NEROL
NEROLI
(— CENTER) GRASSE
(POWDERY —) PULVIL
PERFUNCTORY CURSORY
CARELESS SLIPSHOD SLOVENLY
APATHETIC
PERGOLA ARBOR BOWER RAMADA
BALCONY TRELLIS
PERHAPS HAPS MAYBE ABLINS
BELIKE HAPPEN MAPPEN MAYHAP
ABLINGS AIBLINS LIGHTLY
PERCASE YIBBLES POSSIBLY
PERCHANCE
PERI ELF FAIRY SPRITE
PERIAPT CHARM AMULET
PERICARP BUR BOLL BURR
BLADDER
PERICHOLE, LA (CHARACTER IN —)
ABDRES PIQUILLO PERICHOLE
(COMPOSER OF —) OFFENBACH
PERICLES (AUTHOR OF —)
SHAKESPEARE
(CHARACTER IN —) BOULT CLEON
DIANA GOWER MARINA THAISA
CERIMON DIONYZA ESCANES
LEONINE PERICLES PHILEMON
THALIARD ANTIOCHUS HELICANUS
LYCHORIDA SIMONIDES
LYSIMACHUS
(FATHER OF —) XANTHIPPUS
(MISTRESS OF —) ASPASIA
(MOTHER OF —) AGARISTE
(SON OF —) PARALUS XANTHIPPUS
(TEACHER OF —) ZENO DAMON
PERICLYMENUS (BROTHER OF —)
NESTOR
(FATHER OF —) NELEUS POSEIDON
(MOTHER OF —) CHLORIS
MELIBOEA
PERICOPE LESSON
PERICRANIUM HEAD BRAIN
PERIDOT OLIVINE
PERIDOTITE PICRITE EULYSITE
JOSEFITE SAXONITE WEHRLITE
PERIERES (FATHER OF —) AEOLUS
(MOTHER OF —) ENARETE
(SON OF —) APHAREUS LEUCIPPUS
(WIFE OF —) GORGOPHONE
PERIGEE EPIGEUM
PERIGYNIUM UTRICLE
PERIL RISK WERE WATHE CRISIS
DANGER HAZARD MENACE SCYLLA
THREAT THRONG TRANCE
DISTRESS JEOPARDY CHARYBDIS
PERILOUS KITTLE DOUBTFUL
DREADFUL INFAMOUS
DANGEROUS HAZARDOUS
PERIMETER RIM CIRCUIT OUTLINE
BOUNDARY PERIPHERY
PERIOD GO AGE DOT END EON ERA
AEON DATE LIFE RACE SPAN STOP

TERM TIDE TIME YEAR AVAIL
CLOSE CYCLE EPACT EPOCH
LABOR LAPSE PATCH POINT SPACE
SPELL STAGE CUTOFF GHURRY
HEMERA MOMENT PARODY
PICTUN SEASON STOUND
ACCOUNT DICOLON FLORUIT
PASTIME SESSION STADIUM
STRETCH DURATION INDUCIAE
INSTANCE LIFETIME SENTENCE
(— ENDING FROST) FRESH
(— FOR WHICH ENJOYED) TENURE
(— IN DEVELOPMENT) STAGE
(— OF ACTION) GO BOUT
(— OF DECLINE) SUNSET EVENING
(— OF DRYNESS) DROUTH
DROUGHT
(— OF DUTY) WATCH
(— OF FAIR WEATHER) SLATCH
(— OF FESTIVITY) WAKES
(— OF FIVE YEARS) LUSTRE PENTAD
LUSTRUM QUINQUENNIUM
(— OF GLOOM) DEAD
(— OF GRACE) DAY
(— OF HAPPINESS) MILLENNIUM
(— OF HEAT) CALLING
(— OF HUMID WEATHER) SIZZARD
(— OF IMMATURITY) SWADDLE
(— OF INSTRUCTION) LESSON
(— OF ISOLATION) QUARANTINE
(— OF LEAVE) SABBATICAL
(— OF LIFE) AGE ELD SPAN
(— OF MILITARY SERVICE) HITCH
(— OF MOTILITY) SWARMING
(— OF MOURNING) SHIVA SHIBAH
(— OF NEW MOON) SYZYGY
(— OF PERFORMING) STANZA
(— OF PLAY) HALF CHUKKER
QUARTER
(— OF RAINFALL) FLUVIAL
(— OF RECREATION) HOLIDAY
VACATION
(— OF REMISSION) JUBILEE
(— OF REST) SMOKO BREATHER
(— OF REVOLUTION OF HEAVENLY
BODY) ORB
(— OF SERVICE) TOUR
(— OF TIME) DAY HOUR WEEK YEAR
MONTH DECADE MINUTE SECOND
(— OF WORK) SHIFT SPELL STINT
(— OF 10 YEARS) DECADE
(— OF 100 YEARS) AGE CENTURY
(— OF 1000 YEARS) CHILIAD
MILLIAD
(— OF 14 MINUTES, 24 SECONDS)
CENTIDAY
(— OF 2 MONTHS) DIMESTER
(— OF 2 YEARS) BIENNIUM
(— OF 20 TUNS) KATUN
(— OF 20 YEARS) KATUN
(— OF 260 DAYS) TONALMATL
(— OF 4 YEARS) QUADRENNIUM
(— OF 5 DAYS) PENTAD
(— OF 5 YEARS) LUSTRE LUSTRUM
(— OF 50 YEARS) JUBILE JUBILEE
(— OF 7 DAYS) HEBDOMAD
(— OF 7 YEARS) SEPTENARY
(— PRECEDING IMPORTANT EVENT)
EVE
(CLASS —) HOUR
(CONTINUOUS —) RUN
(CULTURAL —) HORIZON
(DEFINITE —) MOMENT

(DISTINCTIVE —) EPOCH
(DULL —) SLACK
(EVOLUTIONAL —) HEMERA
(GEOLOGICAL —) JURA KAROO
EOCENE ALGOMAN HORIZON
NEOCENE CAMBRIAN DEVONIAN
JURASSIC SILURIAN TERTIARY
TRANSVAAL
(HAPPY —) MILLENIUM
(HYPOTHETICAL —) ACME
(JAPANESE —) MEIJI
(JAPANESE CULTURAL —) JOMON
(LONG —) EON AEON CYCLE
(MEETING —) SESSION
(MENSTRUAL —) TERMS
(OCCASIONAL —) SNATCH
(OF JAPANESE —) JOMON
(OF JAPANESE CULTURAL —)
YAYOI
(PENITENTIAL —) LENT
(RECOVERY —) REHAB
(RECURRING —) EMBER
(SHORT —) BIT FIT BLINK SHAKE
SPELL SPURT SNATCH
(TELEVISION RATINGS —) SWEEP
(WAITING —) MORATORIUM
(WET —) PLUVIAL
(SUFF.) **(OF A —)** CHRONOUS
PERIODIC ERAL ANNUAL CYCLIC
ETESIAN REGULAR FREQUENT
SEASONAL
(NOT —) LOOSE ACYCLIC
PERIODICAL DAILY ORGAN PAPER
SHEET ANNUAL DIGEST REVIEW
ETESIAN FANZINE JOURNAL
REGULAR TABLOID DREADFUL
EXCHANGE MAGAZINE EPHEMERIS
PICTORIAL
PERIODICALLY TERMLY
PERION (SON OF —) AMADIS
PERIPATETIC ROVING RAMBLING
ITINERANT
PERIPHERAL DEEP OUTER DISTAL
DISTANT EXTERNAL MARGINAL
PERIPHERY LIP RIM BRIM DOME
EDGE AMBIT LIMIT SKIRT AREOLA
BORDER BOUNDS FRINGE
AMBITUS CONTOUR SUBURBS
SURFACE CONFINES PERIMETER
PERIPHRASTIC AMBAGIOUS
PERISCOPE ALTISCOPE HYPOSCOPE
OMNISCOPE
PERISH DIE FADE FALL RUIN TINE
TYNE QUAIL SPILL SWELT WASTE
DEPART EXPIRE STARVE DESTROY
FORFARE MISCARRY
(— GRADUALLY) FADE
PERISHABLE SOFT DYING CADUKE
BRITTLE FUGITIVE
PERISHED MUSHY
PERISTOME FRINGE
PERITE SKILLED
PERITHECIUM ALVEOLA
PERITONEUM RIM SIPHAC
PERIWIG FLASH GALERA PERUKE
TOUPEE GALERUM PERWICK
CHEVELURE
PERIWINKLE PERY PIRE WINK
PERRY SNAIL MYRTLE WINKLE
DOGBANE PINPATCH SENGREEN
BLUEBUTTON
PERJINK NEAT TRIM PRECISE
PERJURE FORSWEAR

PERJURED MANSWORN
PERK BRISK FRILL PERCH PREEN
PRINK FRESHEN SMARTEN
PERKY AIRY PERT COCKY JAUNTY
CHIPPER
PERMANENCE STAY STABILITY
PERMANENT FIXED STABLE
ABIDING DURABLE LASTING
STATIVE CONSTANT ENDURING
REMANENT STANDING INDELIBLE
PERMANENTLY KEEPS
PERMEABLE POROUS PERVIOUS
PERMEATE FILL SEEP SOAK BATHE
IMBUE DRENCH INFORM INVADE
ANIMATE PERVADE DOMINATE
SATURATE PENETRATE
PERMEATED SHOT
PERMEATION SATURATION
PERMIAN DYAS DYASSIC
PERMISSIBLE FREE VENIAL
POSSIBLE CONGEABLE
(NOT —) NEFAS
PERMISSION MAY FIAT LIEF PASS
CONGE DARST FAVOR GRACE
GRANT LEAVE ACCESS ACCORD
PERMIT CONSENT LIBERTY
LICENSE SANCTION
(— TO ACT) POWER
(— TO BE ABSENT) ABSIT
(— TO PRINT) IMPRIMATUR
(— TO PROCEED) GOAHEAD
(— TO USE) LOAN
(LETTER OF —) EXEAT
(WRITTEN —) PASS
PERMISSIVE TOLERANT
CONCESSORY
PERMIT LET CHIT CHOP GIVE LEVE
PASS ADMIT ALLOW CONGE EXEAT
FAVOR GRACE GRANT LEAVE
SERVE ACCORD BETEEM CEDULA
DUSTUK ENDURE ENTREE SUFFER
CONCEDE CONSENT DUSTUCK
FACULTY LICENSE PLACARD
POMPANO WARRANT DISPENSE
(— NEGATIVELY) TOLERATE
(— TO ENTER) INTROMIT
(— TO TAKE) SOAK
(CUSTOMS —) CARNET
PERMITTED FREE LOOT LICIT
ALLOWED INNOCENT SUPPOSED
(— BY LAW) LEGAL
PERMUTATION BARTER CHANGE
EXCHANGE
PERNICIOUS BAD ILL EVIL FATAL
QUICK SWIFT DEADLY MALIGN
WICKED BALEFUL BANEFUL
HARMFUL HURTFUL NOISOME
NOXIOUS RUINOUS
PERNIO CHILBLAIN
PERO (BROTHER OF —) NESTOR
(FATHER OF —) NELEUS
(HUSBAND OF —) BIAS
(MOTHER OF —) CHLORIS
(SON OF —) ASOPUS
PEROPUS PARAGON
PERORATION EPILOG PERIOD
CLOSING PURLICUE
PEROXISOME MICROBODY
PERPEND JUMPER PARPEN PONDER
REFLECT THROUGH
PERPENDICULAR SINE ERECT
PLUMB SHEER ABRUPT NORMAL

APOTHEM UPRIGHT BINORMAL
CATHETUS EVENDOWN VERTICAL
(MUTUALLY —) ORTHOGONAL
PERPENDICULARITY APLOMB
PERPENDICULARLY BOLT SHEER
SHEERLY
PERPETRATE DO PULL COMMIT
EFFECT PERFORM
PERPETUAL ETERN ENDLESS
ETERNAL CONSTANT INFINITO
UNENDING CONTINUAL PERENNIAL
PERPETUALLY EVER ALWAYS
FOREVER
PERPETUATE CONTINUE ETERNIZE
MAINTAIN
PERPLEX CAP MAR SET VEX BEAT
CLOG DOIT DOZE FIKE MAZE STUN
AMAZE BESET BLAIK STUMP TWIST
BAFFLE BOGGLE BOTHER BUNKER
CUMBER DARKEN FEAGUE FICKLE
GRAVEL HAMPER HARASS HOBBLE
KITTLE MAMMER MITHER MOIDER
MUDDLE PLAGUE POTHER POTTER
PUTTER PUZZLE RAFFLE RIDDLE
TWITCH WILDER WRIXLE BEDEVIL
BUMBAZE CONFUSE DIFFUSE
EMBROIL FLUMMOX MYSTIFY
NONPLUS PLUNDER STAGGER
STUMBLE TORMENT BEWILDER
CONFOUND SURPRISE WINDLASS
BAMBOOZLE
PERPLEXED ASEA MAZY ATSEA
ANXIOUS NONPLUS PUZZLED
CONFUSED TROUBLED INTRICATE
TOSTICATED
PERPLEXING HARD MAZY SPINY
CRABBY KNOBBY KNOTTY
CARKING COMPLEX CRABBED
QUISCOS BAFFLING
PERPLEXITY FOG KNOT WERE
BRAKE FOITER HOBBLE PUCKER
PUZZLE TAKING TANGLE ANXIETY
NONPLUS STICKLE TROUBLE
POSEMENT SURPRISE CONFUSION
LABYRINTH PUZZLEMENT
(MENTAL —) STUDY
(RELIEVE OF —) CLEAR
PERQUISITE FEE TIP LOCK PERK
VAIL GOUPIN GOWPEN INCOME
ADJUNCT APANAGE VANTAGE
CONQUEST GRATUITY
(PL.) PICKING
PERRIER PEDRERO
PERRINIST LIBERTINE
PERSE BLUE
(DAUGHTER OF —) CIRCE PASIPHAE
(FATHER OF —) OCEANUS
(HUSBAND OF —) HELIOS
(SON OF —) AEETES PERSES
PERSECUTE VEX BAIT ANNOY
CHASE HARRY HOUND WRACK
WRONG HARASS PESTER PURSUE
AFFLICT CRUCIFY DRAGOON
OPPRESS TORMENT TORTURE
PERSECUTED JOB REFUGEE
PERSECUTOR TORQUEMADA
PERSEPHONE KORE DESPOINA
PRAXIDIKE
(DAUGHTER OF —) CORA KORE
(FATHER OF —) ZEUS JUPITER
(HUSBAND OF —) HADES PLUTO
(MOTHER OF —) CERES DEMETER

PERSES (BROTHER OF —) AEETES
(DAUGHTER OF —) HECATE
(FATHER OF —) CRIUS HELIOS
(MOTHER OF —) PERSE EYRYBIA
(SISTER OF —) CIRCE PASIPHAE
PERSEUS RESCUER CHAMPION
(FATHER OF —) ZEUS JUPITER
(GRANDFATHER OF —) ACRISIUS
(MOTHER OF —) DANAE
(STAR OF —) ATIK ALGOL
(VICTIM OF —) MEDUSA
(WIFE OF —) ANDROMEDA
PERSEVERANCE GRIT MOXIE
STAMINA INDUSTRY PATIENCE
TENACITY CONSTANCY
PERSISTENCE
PERSEVERE PEG CANK KEEP PLUG
TORE ABIDE STICK HANGIN INSIST
REMAIN PERSIST CONTINUE
PERSEVERING BUSY HARD STILL
PATIENT RESOLUTE SEDULOUS
ASSIDUOUS INSISTENT
PERSIA (SEE IRAN)
PERSIAN MEDE FARSI PERSE GILAKI
HAJEMI IRANIC DURZADA HADJEMI
IRANIAN MEMNONIAN
(— RED DEER) MARAL
PERSICARY REDLEG REDLEGS
REDSHANK HEARTEASE
HEARTWEED PEACHWORT
PERSIFLAGE BANTER RAILLERY
PERSIMMON KAKI SIMON SIMMON
ZAPOTE CHAPOTE HYAKUME
TRIUMPH
(— TREE) GAB GAUB LOTUS
PERSIST HOLD KEEP LAST URGE
ADHERE ENDURE INSIST REMAIN
PREVAIL SUBSIST CONTINUE
PERSEVERE
PERSISTENCE GUTS
(SUFF.) STASIA STASIS
PERSISTENCY TENACITY
PERSISTENT SET DREE FIRM HARD
GREAT STOUT TOUGH DOGGED
DREECH GRITTY HECTIC SLEUTH
DURABLE RESTANT RESTIVE
CONSTANT ENDURING HOLDFAST
OBDURATE RESOLUTE SEDULOUS
STUBBORN ASSIDUOUS
OBSTINATE PERENNIAL PRIMITIVE
RELENTLESS
PERSISTING
(PREF.) MENO
PERSON BOD CAT EGG EGO GUY
MAN ONE BABY BODY CHAL CHAP
COVE DUCK FISH FOOD FORM
GINK HOOK LEDE LIFE NABS PRIG
SELF SOUL BEING BLOKE BOSOM
CHILD COOKY GHOST HEART
HUMAN PARTI PARTY PIECE STICK
THING WATCH WIGHT ANIMAL
BUGGER ENTITY FELLOW GALOOT
GAZABO JOHNNY KIPPER NUMBER
SINNER SISTER SPIRIT SPRITE
ARTICLE BLISTER WAGTAIL
SPECIMEN TILLICUM
(— ACTING FOR ANOTHER) PROXY
(— ASSOCIATED WITH WORK)
WALLAH
(— BEARING HEAVY BURDEN)
CAMEL
(— BEHIND THE TIMES) FOGY
FOGEY

(— BRINGING GOOD LUCK)
MASCOT
(— FROM WHOM FAMILY IS
DESCENDED) STIRPS
(— INTERESTED IN FOOD FADS)
FOODIE
(— MEANLY CLAD) SCARECROW
(— NAMED) NOMINEE
(— NOT IN THE KNOW) LAME
(— NOT OF NOBLE BIRTH)
ROTURIER
(— OF AGE) COOT FALDWORTH
(— OF CONSEQUENCE) BIGGIE
BIGWIG TALLBOY
(— OF COURAGE) SPARTAN
(— OF ENERGY) LIVEWIRE
(— OF HONOR) MENSCH
(— OF INFLUENCE) CAPTAIN
HEAVYWEIGHT
(— OF INTEGRITY) MENSCH
(— OF MEAN BIRTH) GUTTERBLOOD
(— OF NO REFINEMENT) SLOB
(— OF RANK) STATE MAGNATE
EMINENCE MAGNIFICO PERSONAGE
(— OF WEAK MIND) FOOL
(— OF WISDOM) SOLOMON
(— OPPOSED TO CHANGE) LUDDITE
(— PREJUDICED AGAINST
ELDERLY) AGIST AGEIST
(— PRETENDING INTELLIGENCE)
PSEUD
(— RESEMBLING ANOTHER) SOSIA
(—S IN AMBASSADOR'S SUITE)
COMES
(— TO BE IMITATED) EXEMPLAR
(— TOO STRONG FOR ASSAILANT)
TARTAR
(— TO SERVE WRIT) ELISOR
(— TRYING TO ATTRACT
ATTENTION) SHOWBOAT
(— WANTING TO BE SOMEONE
ELSE) WANNABE
(— WHO DOESN'T FIT IN) GEEK
(— WHO HOARDS) SQUIRREL
(— WHO IS UP-TO-DATE) SWINGER
(— WHO LOCATES ANTIQUES)
PICKER
(— WHO PERFORMS MENIAL
TASKS) DOGSBODY
(— WHO TAKES AMPHETAMINES)
PILLHEAD
(— WHO TAKES CAPSULES)
PILLHEAD
(— WHO TALKS EXCESSIVELY)
MOTORMOUTH
(— WITH MENTAL TWIST) CRANK
(— WITH MILITANT ATTITUDE)
HAWK
(— WITH NERVOUS DISORDERS)
NEUROTIC
(— WITHOUT EQUAL) NONPAREIL
(— WITHOUT STAMINA) JELLYFISH
(— WITH QUEER IDEAS) ROZUM
(— WITH SHORT HAIR) SKINHEAD
(ABJECT —) SLAVE CRAWLER
(ABSENT-MINDED —) MUSARD
(ACTIVE —) GOER
(ADMIRABLE —) GEM PIPPIN RIPPER
(AFFECTED —) POSEUR MINNICK
GIMCRACK
(AFFECTEDLY INTELLECTUAL —)
PSEUD

(AGGRESSIVE —) SHOVER
HOTSHOT
(AMUSING —) COMIC
(ANNOYING —) FIEND NUDNICK
(ANTIQUATED —) MUMPSIMUS
(ARABIZED —) MOZARAB
(ARROGANT —) HUFF TENGU
(ATTRACTIVE —) DISH CUTEY CUTIE
KILLER KNOCKOUT
(AVARICIOUS —) YISSER
(AWKWARD —) PUT GAWP HICK
MUFF RUBE SLAM STAG STEG
KLUTZ STIFF GALOOT GUFFIN
TUMFIE HOOSIER LOBSTER
SCHLEPP KITHOGUE SHLEPPER
SLOMMACK SPELDRIN
(BAD —) UNSEL
(BALD —) BALLARD BALDHEAD
SKINHEAD BALDICOOT
(BANISHED —) WRETCH
(BAPTIZED —) MEMBER
ILLUMINATO
(BASE —) CUT RASCAL CAITIFF
HILDING PUTTOCK
(BELOVED —) FLAME HEARTROOT
(BIG-BELLIED —) GORBELLY
(BLACK —) BLECK
(BOASTFUL —) BLOWER GASCON
(BOISTEROUS —) TEARER
(BOORISH —) GOOP
(BORING —) SCHMO
(BRUTAL —) RUFFIAN
(BUSTLING —) STIRABOUT
(CALLOW —) GORLIN SMARTY
GOSLING
(CANONIZED —) SAINT
(CARELESS —) HASH TASSEL
(CASTRATED —) SPADO
(CERTAIN —) QUIDAM
(CHARMING —) SMASHER
(CHATTERING —) MAGPIE
(CHICKENHEARTED —) HEN
(CHILDISH —) BAUBLE WHIMLING
(CHUNKY —) JUNT
(CHURLISH —) TIKE TYKE
(CIRCLE OF —S) COTERIE
(CLEVER —) BIRD WHIZ WHIZZ
MERCURY
(CLOWNISH —) BUFFOON HOBNAIL
VILLAIN
(CLUMSY —) DUB LOB BOOB GAWK
SLOB TIKE TYKE JUMBO KLUTZ
STAUP STIFF DUFFER KEFFEL
LUMMOX HODMADOD
(COARSE —) COW STIRK BABOON
MUCKER
(COAXING —) WHILLY WHEEDLE
(COLD —) ICICLE
(COMBATIVE —) DRAGON
GAMECOCK
(COMMONPLACE —) MUT MUTT
BROMIDE
(CONCEITED —) IT HUFF COXCOMB
PRAGMATIC
(CONFUSED —) FOOSTERER
(CONSERVATIVE —) HUNKER
SQUARE MOSSBACK
(CONSPICUOUS —) LIGHT
(CONTEMPTIBLE —) YAP CRUD
HEEL PUKE SCAB SKIN SWAB CATSO
SHRUB SKITE SKUNK SNIPE TWERP
INSECT SHICER STINKER BLIGHTER
WHIFFLER PETTITOES

(COWARDLY —) WIMP FUGIE SISSY
SLINK SQUIB
(CRAFTY —) TOD FILE SHARK JESUIT
(CRAZED —) NUT NUTTER
PSYCHOPATH MESHUGGENAH
(CRINGING —) SNAKE SNOOL
FLUNKY SPANIEL
(CRUEL —) LAMB FIEND MALISON
(CUNNING —) PIE
(CURIOUS —) RUBBERNECK
(DAINTY —) MIMMOCK
(DARK —) MOOR OUSEL OUZEL
MELANO NIGNOG
(DEAD —) DEFUNCT DECEASED
DECEDENT
(DEBAUCHED —) RAKEHELL
(DECREPIT —) CROCK WITHERLING
(DEDICATED —) OBLATE
(DEFORMED —) CRILE CALIBAN
HODMADOD
(DENSE —) DUFFER
(DEPENDENT —) JUNKIE
(DEPRAVED —) SKATE
(DERANGED —) PSYCHE
(DESPICABLE —) SCAB HOUND
SLAVE CAITIFF
(DESTITUTE —) PAUPER
(DEVILISH —) SHAITAN
(DIMINUTIVE —) BANTY MIDGE
BANTAM MIDGET NIFFNAFF
(DIRTY —) SWEEP DRIVEL HOWLET
(DISABLED —) DUCK CRIPPLE
INVALID
(DISAGREEABLE —) GOOP PILL
QUAT SKITE RATBAG
(DISGRUNTLED —) SOREHEAD
(DISHONEST —) ROGUE ROTTER
BEZONIAN
(DISLIKED —) WARLING
(DISREPUTABLE —) RIP QUANDONG
(DISSOLUTE —) RIBALD ROUNDER
STRIKER
(DOLEFUL —) MISERY
(DOLTISH —) BLOCK SWINE
(DRUG-ABUSING —) BURNOUT
(DRUNKEN —) LUSH TUMBREL
TUMBRIL
(DULL —) LOB BORE DODO DRIP
GOON GOOP GRUB LUMP MOME
MOPE SLOB CLUNK DROUD PRUNE
SCHMO STICK STOCK LURDAM
LACKWIT LOBCOCK NUDNICK
OPACITY DEADHEAD
(DULL-WITTED —) DOPE GUMP
DUNCE
(DUMB —) MUTE
(DUMPY —) HODDYDODDY
(DUPED —) GULL
(DWARFISH —) AGATE CROWL
SHURF
(DYING —) MORIBUND
(ECCENTRIC —) COON GINK KOOK
TIKE TYKE GAZABO GAZEBO
FANTAST ODDBALL
(EDUCATED —) SCHOLAR LITERATE
(EFFEMINATE —) SOFTY SQUAW
CODDLE SOFTIE WANTON BADLING
SOFTLING SMOCKFACE
(ELDERLY —) SENIOR SOAKER
GRAYHEAD GERIATRIC
(EMACIATED —) FRAME WASTREL
SKELETON
(EMPTY-HEADED —) NITWIT

(ENERGETIC —) DYNAMO
(ENROLLED —) MEMBER
(ENTERTAINING —) COMEDIAN
(ENTHUSIASTIC —) FANATIC
(ESSENTIAL —) LINCHPIN
(EVIL —) QUED SCUM QUEDE
SHREW
(EXALTED —) PERSONAGE
(EXPERIENCED —) EXPERT SOAKER
STAGER
(EXPERT —) ACE DAB
(EXTORTIONATE —) SCREW
(EXTRAORDINARY —) ONER
BUSTER
(FADED —) SHARGAR SHARGER
(FAINT-HEARTED —) HEN
(FAMOUS —) DON NOTORIETY
(FANTASTIC —) KICKSHAW
(FARSIGHTED —) PRESBYOPE
(FASHIONABLE —) GIMCRACK
(FASTIDIOUS —) MIMMOCK
DELICATE
(FAT —) GURK BLIMP FATSO QUILT
SQUAB STOUT
(FATUOUS —) GOOP
(FAWNING —) COGGER SPANIEL
(FEEBLEMINDED —) FEEB IDIOT
MORON IMBECILE
(FEROCIOUS —) LAMB
(FICKLE —) ROVER MOONCALF
(FILTHY —) HOGG
(FINE —) WHIPPA
(FLABBY —) HUDDERON
(FLAKY —) SPACECADET
(FLASHY —) KID FLASHER
(FLIGHTY —) FLIBBERTIGIBBET
(FOOLISH —) FOP GIT BOZO COOT
GUMP HOIT JERK PUTZ BOOBY
SOFTY BAUBLE DOODLE DOOFUS
DOTARD DRIVEL HOWLET TURKEY
GOSLING GUBBINS HAVEREL
BUBBLEHEAD
(FORCELESS —) DRIP
(FORGETFUL —) SPACECADET
(FOUL —) DREVILL
(FRANK —) TELLTRUTH
(FRIVOLOUS —) HOBBYHORSE
FEATHERBRAIN
(FUSSY —) FAD FADDLE GRANNY
SPOFFY GRANNIE
(GAY —) GRIG HUZZA
(GIDDY —) SCATTERBRAIN
(GLOOMY —) SATURNIST
(GOOD-FOR-NOTHING —) KET PELF
TASSEL WASTER WANHOPE
WASTREL
(GOSSIPING —) SHULER SHUILER
(GOSSIPY —) BIGMOUTH
QUIDNUNC NEWSMONGER
(GOSSIPY, TALKATIVE —) YENTA
(GRASPING —) SHYLOCK
(GRAVE —) SOBERSIDES
(GREEDY —) GORB GANNET
GRASPER PUTTOCK
(GROTESQUE —) GUY GOLLIWOGG
PUNCHINELLO
(GRUMPY —) SOURBELLY
(GULLIBLE —) JAY BOOB GULPIN
LOBSTER FLATHEAD SHLEMIEL
WOODCOCK
(GYPSY —) CHI CHAI
(HANDLESS —) SAMMY
(HARD —) MALISON

(HARD-HEADED —) NUT
(HATEFUL —) TOAD
(HEAVY—) STODGER
(HEAVY-SET —) LUMP
(HETEROSEXUAL —) STRAIGHT
(HOLY —) SAINT
(HOT-TEMPERED —) SPARK
(HUMPBACKED —) LORD
(HUNGRY —) HUNGARIAN
(HYPOCRITICAL —) PHARISEE
(IDENTICAL —) SELF
(IDLE —) BUMMLE RAGABASH SLUGGARD
(IGNORANT —) BABE BOOB PORK IDIOT IGNARO
(ILL-BRED —) BOOR CHURL CLOWN
(ILL-MANNERED —) GRUB SKUNK
(ILL-NATURED) PATCH CROSSPATCH
(ILL-NATURED —) CRAB HUNKS PATCH
(ILL-TEMPERED —) CRAB ETTERCAP TAISTREL
(ILLUSTRIOUS —) HERO
(IMMATURE —) BUD SQUAB GORLIN
(IMMORAL —) REP PERDU IMPURITAN
(IMPASSIVE —) BLOCK
(IMPERTINENT —) PAUK PAWK SNIP
(IMPETUOUS —) HOTHEAD
(IMPISH —) SPRITE
(IMPORTANT —) NIB POT LION HONOR MOGUL NABOB KINGPIN MUGWUMP SOMEBODY
(IMPOTENT —) SPADO
(IMPRACTICAL —) IDEALIST
(IMPUDENT —) SAUCE SQUIRT SAUCEBOX
(INACTIVE —) SLUGGARD
(INANE —) SHAUP
(INCOMPETENT —) BOZO SCHLEP
(INCONSTANT —) ROVER
(INDECISIVE —) INVERTEBRATE
(INEPT —) DWEEB KLUTZ
(INEXPERIENCED —) BABE INGENUE BEGINNER
(INFAMOUS —) NITHING
(INFERIOR —) BATA SHRUB SHABBLE
(INFLEXIBLE —) RAMROD
(INFLUENTIAL —) MOGUL
(INSCRUTABLE —) SPHINX
(INSENSITIVE —) LOG PACHYDERM
(INSIGNIFICANT —) DAB MUT MUTT NERD NURD QUAT BILSH CREEP DWEEB JOKER SHURF SPRAT SQUIB ABLACH PEANUT NEBBISH PINKEEN WHIFFET GNATLING GRILDRIG PIGWIGEON
(INSINUATING —) WHILLY
(INSURED —) LIFE
(INTRACTABLE —) BUCKIE TARTAR HAGGARD HARDCASE
(IRASCIBLE —) TOUCHWOOD
(IRRESPONSIBLE —) PLAYBOY FLYBYNIGHT
(IRRITATING —) BOT
(ISOLATED —) ISOLATO
(LAME —) VULCAN
(LANK —) TANGLE GANGEREL WINDLESTRAW

(LARGE —) CHUNK WHIPPA SKELPER STODGER STRAPPER
(LASCIVIOUS —) SUCCUBUS
(LAST — IN CONTEST) MELL
(LAZY —) BUM DAW HOIT POKE IDLER TRAIL LORDAN LURDAN BLELLUM LAZYLEGS SLUGABED SLUGGARD
(LEAN —) RIBE TANGLE SHARGER THINGUT
(LEARNED —) CLERK ERUDIT ACHARYA SCHOLAR LITERATO WISEACRE LITERATUS
(LECHEROUS —) SATYR
(LEFT-HANDED —) SINISTRAL
(LETHARGIC —) ZOMBI ZOMBIE
(LEWD —) WANTON GAMESTER
(LIGHTHEADED —) BEEHEAD
(LISTLESS —) MOPE
(LITERATE —) SCHOLAR
(LITTLE —) SMOLT SMOUT
(LIVELY —) GRIG BIRKIE HEMPIE WHISKER
(LONG-HAIRED —) HIPPY HIPPIE
(LOUD-VOICED —) STENTOR
(LOW —) PACK SCUM RASCAL BEASTMAN
(LOW-BORN —) GUTTERBLOOD
(LOW SOCIETY —) MUDSILL
(LUBBERLY —) OAF
(LUMBERING —) PUMPKIN TUMBREL TUMBRIL
(LUMPISH —) DROUD
(LUSTY —) BILCH BILSH
(MAD —) MADLING
(MALICIOUS —) SERPENT
(MARRIAGEABLE —) PARTI
(MARRIED —) WIFE SPOUSE HUSBAND MATRIMONY
(MEAN —) RIP SCAB CHURL HOUND MISER SKATE SNEAK SHICER BASTARD DOGBOLT BEZONIAN HUCKSTER STINKARD EARTHWORM
(MEDDLESOME —) BREVIT HESSIAN
(MENTALLY DEFICIENT —) AMENT
(MENTALLY UNBALANCED —) MATTOID
(MISCHIEVOUS —) IMP LIMB PEST TOOL HEMPIE HELLION WHIPSTER
(MISERABLE —) SNAKE SWELP WRETCH
(MISERLY —) SKATE SCROOGE PINCHGUT PINCHBACK
(MONSTROUS —) WAMPUS
(MORAL —) PURITAN
(MORALLY ILL —) SICKO SICKIE
(MOST DISTINGUISHED —) FLOWER
(NAIVE —) JERK CLUCK GUNSEL INGENUE INNOCENT
(NASTY —) BLEEDER
(NEGLECTED —) TACKY TACKEY
(NIMBLE —) MERCURY
(NOISY —) YAP HOWLET
(OBJECTIONABLE —) CUR COYOTE FOUTER
(OBNOXIOUS —) CREEP
(OBSTINATE —) DONKEY STIFFNECK
(ODD —) GIG CURE GEEZER QUIZZY RATBAG CAUTION
(ODD-LOOKING —) QUIZ
(OFFENSIVE —) TICK SKITE SHOCKER STINKER HEDGEHOG
(OLD —) OLDY OLDIE

(OLD-FASHIONED —) FRUMP
(OPINIONATIVE —) PRAGMATIC
(ORACULAR —) PONTIFF
(ORDINARY —) PUNTER
(OVER-LEARNED —) PEDANT
(OVERGROWN —) FUSTILUGS
(OVERSLENDER —) SPINDLING
(PALTRY —) PFI TFR
(PAMPERED —) WANTON
(PASSIONATE —) FUME
(PATIENT —) JOB
(PECULIAR —) BIRD CASE
(PEEVISH —) GRIZZLER SPLENETIC
(PERNICKETY —) FIKE
(PERT —) PIE FLIRT
(PLODDING —) STODGE
(POLISHED —) SMOOTHY SMOOTHIE
(POMPOUS —) PUFFIN POMPIST
(POT-BELLIED —) GORREL
(PRE-EMINENT —) STAR
(PRIGGISH —) PRUDE
(PRIVATE —) JUDEX
(PROMISING —) HOPEFUL
(PROSAIC —) PHILISTINE
(PRYING —) POKER PEEPER SMELLER
(PUDGY —) FATSO FATTY PODGE PUDGE ROLYPOLY
(PUGNOSED —) CAMUS CAMUSE
(PUNY —) SCART SHILP SHRIMP TITMAN
(PURITANICAL —) WOWSER
(QUEER —) RUM SKITE SKYTE GEEZER
(QUEER-LOOKING —) JIGGER
(QUERULOUS —) GRUMP JACKDAW
(QUICK-TEMPERED —) SPUNKIE WILDCAT SPITFIRE
(RAGGED —) ROTO SHAGRAG TATTERWAG
(RAPACIOUS —) SHARK CATERER
(RAWBONED —) SCRAG
(RECKLESS —) MADCAP RAMSTAM RANTIPOLE HELLBENDER
(RED-HAIRED —) BRIQUE
(REFRACTORY —) BUCKIE
(RELENTLESS —) HARDFACE
(REMARKABLE —) PHENOMENON
(RESOLUTE —) STALWART
(RESTLESS —) RAMPLER RAMPLOR RANTIPOLE
(RETICENT —) CLAM
(RICH —) MONEYBAGS
(RIDICULOUS —) GOOF HARE MONIMENT MONUMENT
(RIOTOUS —) ROARER
(ROBUST —) STRAPPER
(ROUGH —) TOWSER
(ROUGH-LOOKING —) RULLION
(RUDE —) HICK PORK RULE CHURL CLOWN GROBIAN
(RUSTIC —) COON KERN KERNE HAYSEED HOMESPUN
(SAINTLY —) SADDIK
(SANGUINE —) OPTIMIST
(SAUCY —) PIET
(SCRAWNY —) SCART SCRAG
(SECRETIVE —) OYSTER
(SELF-ASSERTIVE —) PUSHER
(SELF-CENTERED —) HEEL DEVIL FLANEUR
(SELF-RIGHTEOUS —) PHARISEE

(SELFISH —) HOGG
(SENSUAL —) SWING CARNALIST
(SENTIMENTAL —) MARSHMALLOW
(SEXY —) DISH
(SHAMEFUL —) BISMER
(SHIFTY—) SLICKER
(SHORT —) CRILE FADGE KNURL STUMP
(SHOWY —) FLASH FLASHER HOTSHOT
(SHREWD —) FILE YEPE HARDHEAD SNOLLYGOSTER
(SICK —) SICK MALADE PATIENT AEGROTANT
(SICKLY —) INVALID
(SILENT —) MUM MUMCHANCE
(SILLY —) FOP CAKE DITZ GUMP SOFT DOBBY GOOSE SOFTY SPOON CUCKOO NIMSHI SOFTIE GOOSECAP LIRIPIPE LIRIPOOP SOFTHEAD
(SILLY OR CRAZY —) DINGBAT
(SIMPLE —) DRIP LAMB IDIOT TURKEY PIGWIGEON
(SINGULAR —) ODDITY
(SKINNY —) SCRAE SCARECROW
(SLATTERNLY —) SLATE
(SLIM —) SWABBLE
(SLOTHFUL —) SLOWBELLY
(SLOVENLY —) HASH SLOB SLORP TRAIL STREEL SLOMMACK STREELER
(SLUGGISH —) LUMP DOLDRUM DRUMBLE LOBCOCK
(SLY —) COON SLYBOOTS SNECKDRAW SNICKDRAW
(SMALL —) GRIG TICH TICK AGATE DWARF SPRAT INSECT MORSEL POPPET SACKET GNATLING MUNCHKIN
(SOLEMN —) OWL
(SOPHISTICATED —) WELTKIND
(SPIRITED —) SPUNK SPUNKIE
(SPIRITLESS —) MOPE STICK
(SPITEFUL —) HELLCAT ETTERCAP
(SPRUCE —) SPRUSADO
(STIFF —) POKER STICK
(STINGY —) CHURL HAYNE STINGY
(STOCKY —) STUMP
(STOLID —) CLAM THICKSKIN
(STRANGE —) WAMPUS
(STRANGE OR ECCENTRIC —) WEIRDO
(STRAY —) WAIF
(STUBBORN —) BUCKY STOUT BUCKIE
(STUMPY —) SPUD SQUAB
(STUNTED —) URF SCRUNT SHARGAR
(STUPID —) ASS DIP DUB JAY MUT BETE BOOB DODO DOLT DOPE DRIP GAUM GAWP GOOF GUMP HASH HOIT JERK MOKE MUTT NERD PUTZ BLOCK BUCCA CLUCK CLUNK CUDDY DUMMY DUNCE HOBBY JUKES LOACH MORON SHEEP STIFF STIRK STOCK STUPE SUMPH SWINE THICK WAMUS ZOMBI BOODLE DAWKIN DIMWIT DODUNK DONKEY DOOFUS DUFFER DUMDUM GANDER GILLIE GRANNY GUNSEL LUMMOX LURDAN NITWIT NOODLE SACKET SHMUCK STUPEX TUMFIE TUMPHY TURKEY ZOMBIE AIRHEAD

BLUNTIE DULLARD FATHEAD FUSSOCK HOWFING JACKASS JUGHEAD MUDHEAD PINHEAD SAPHEAD SCHMUCK SCHNOOK BONEHEAD BULLHEAD DOTTEREL DUMBBELL FLATHEAD GAMPHREL IRONHEAD MEATHEAD MOLDWARP MUMPHEAD STUNPOLL THICKWIT HODMANDOD MUMCHANCE THICKHEAD BUBBLEHEAD
(STUPID, FOOLISH —) YOYO
(STURDY —) LUMP CHUNK STALWART
(SUAVE —) SMOOTHIE
(SUBMISSIVE —) SLAVE
(SULKY —) GLUMP GRUMP SUMPH GROUCH
(SUPERLATIVE —) SMASHEROO
(SURLY —) CRUST HUNKS
(TACITURN —) OYSTER
(TALKATIVE —) GASSER BLELLUM BIGMOUTH
(TALL, AWKWARD —) GAMMERSTANG
(TENDER —) LAMBKIN
(THICKSET —) NUGGET
(THIN —) RAKE WRAITH BEANPOLE
(THIRD —) GOOSEBERRY
(THOUGHTLESS —) AIRLING SKIPPER BIRDBRAIN
(TIMID —) MOUSE RABBIT NEBBISH MILQUETOAST
(TIMID OR MEEK —) NEBBISH
(TINY —) KEEROGUE
(TIRESOME) PILL
(TIRESOME —) BORE PILL BROMIDE
(TOUGH —) STUD
(TRADITIONAL —) SQUARE
(TREACHEROUS —) JUDAS SNAKE VIPER GUNSEL SERPENT
(TRICKY —) SLYBOOTS
(TROUBLESOME —) COW PEST HELLION HESSIAN
(TRUSTWORTHY —) TRAIST STANDBY
(TRUSTY —) TROJAN
(TYRANNICAL —) SATRAP
(UNAPPRECIATIVE —) INGRATE
(UNATTRACTIVE —) DRIP GOON GRUB NERD NURD SCUG CREEP DWEEB
(UNBENDING —) STIFF
(UNCHASTE —) SHORTHEELS
(UNCIVILIZED —) VISIGOTH
(UNCOUTH —) APE PUT STIFF YAHOO BABOON SLOMMACK ROUGHNECK
(UNDERSIZED —) DURGAN SPARROW
(UNEMOTIONAL —) ICEBERG
(UNFAITHFUL —) INFIDEL
(UNGAINLY —) CLATCH
(UNGRACIOUS —) NEANY MEANIE
(UNHANDY —) FOUTER
(UNHAPPY —) UNSEL
(UNIMPORTANT —) MINNOW NOTHING SCHNOOK NONENTITY
(UNIQUE —) ONER
(UNKNOWN —) INCONNU STRANGER
(UNLUCKY —) SHLIMAZEL SCHLIMAZEL

(UNMARRIED —) MAIDEN SINGLE AGAMIST BACHELOR CELIBATE SPINSTER
(UNPLEASANT —) NERD NURD SCUMBAG
(UNPRACTICAL —) MUFF
(UNREASONABLE —) DUFFER
(UNRULY —) TURK
(UNSCRUPULOUS —) CATSO KNAVE
(UNSOPHISTICATED —) JAY HICK NYAS HAYSEED CORNBALL INNOCENT
(UNTHANKFUL —) INGRATE
(UNTIDY —) SLOVEN STREEL SLAISTER
(UNUSUALLY INTELLIGENT —) WHIZKID WHIZZKID
(UNWANTED THIRD —) GOOSEBERRY
(UNWIELDY —) FUSTILUGS
(USELESS —) POOP SWAB UNSEL BAUCHLE
(VALOROUS —) HERO
(VENOMOUS —) SPITPOISON
(VIGOROUS —) SNEEZER
(VIOLENT —) DRAGON BANGSTER SPITFIRE
(VIRILE —) STUD
(VORACIOUS —) HUNGARIAN
(VULGAR —) MUCKER
(WANTON —) BIG FLIRT WHIPSTER
(WASTEFUL —) SCATTERGOOD SPENDTHRIFT
(WEAK —) WIMP SCART SHILP SOFTY PUSSYCAT WHIMLING
(WEAK-MINDED —) SAPHEAD TOTTYHEAD
(WEAK-WILLED —) PUTTY
(WEAK OR INEFFECTUAL —) WIMP
(WEALTHY —) MONEYBAGS
(WELL-BORN —) FREE
(WHITE —) FAY OFAY GRIFFIN EUROPEAN PALEFACE
(WICKED —) DEVIL SATAN SHREW UNLEAD UNLEDE SATANIST
(WILD —) HELLICAT RANTIPOLE
(WILY —) PIE
(WITHERED —) RUNT
(WITLESS —) WITHAM WITTOME SLABBERER
(WITTY —) WITSHIP SPARKLER
(WORNOUT —) HUSHEL
(WORTHLESS —) GIT YAP FILE GEAR HOIT JADE LOON SCUM TOOT CRUMB LOREL LOSEL SCOUT SHAND BAUBLE BUGGER FELLOW FOUTRA SHICER BUDMASH GULLION BLIGHTER VAGABOND PHARMAKOS
(WRETCHED —) MISER MISERY
(YOUNG —) CUB KID COLT LAMB CHILD HEMPY SMOLT SMOUT SPRIG YONKE GUNSEL HEMPIE JUNIOR CHICKEN CHOOKIE GRISTLE LAMBKIN JUVENILE STRIPLING
(PL.) FRY PERSONNEL
(PREF.) PROSOP(O)
(SUFF.) (FEMALE —) INE
PERSONABLE COMELY SHAPELY HANDSOME
PERSONAGE DON DUSE NIBS BLOKE FIGURE SHOGUN TYCOON
(EXALTED —) STATE

(GREAT —) MOGUL SOPHI SOPHY SUFFEE
(GROTESQUE —) PUNCHINELLO
PERSONAL SELF PRIVY DIRECT PRIVATE CHATTELS CORPORAL INTIMATE
(— EFFECTS) DUNNAGE
(PREF.) IDIO
PERSONALITY EGO AURA DRAW SELF SOUL BEING ETHOS HEART EGOITY FIGURE CONTROL FACULTY DEMIURGE PRESENCE SELFHOOD SELFNESS
(OF IMPATIENT —) TYPEA
PERSONATE ACT FEIGN MIMIC MASKED PERSON TYPIFY PRESENT
PERSONATION (SHAM —) IDOL
PERSONIFICATION SOUL GENIUS
(— OF DIVINE VIRTUE) EON
(— OF JUSTICE) THEMIS
(— OF PRINCIPLES) AVATAR
PERSONIFY EMBODY INCARNATE PERSONIZE
PERSONNEL BLOOD STAFF KITCHEN PHYSIQUE
PERSPECTIVE ANGLE OPTICS DISTANCE TELESCOPE
PERSPICACIOUS KEEN ACUTE ASTUTE SHREWD
(MAKE —) CLEAR
PERSPICACITY WIT ACUMEN
PERSPICUOUS CLEAR LUCID PLAIN PRECISE VISIBLE MANIFEST LIGHTSOME
PERSPIRATION DEW SUDOR SUINT SWEAT HIDROSIS OLIGIDRIA SUDORESIS
PERSPIRE PUG MELT BREAN SWEAT SWELTER TRANSPIRE
PERSUADE CON GET WIN COAX GAIN MOVE RULE SNOW TICE URGE WISE ARGUE BRING EDUCE SUADE SWADE WEISE ADVISE ARGUFY ASSURE CAJOLE ENGAGE ENTICE INDUCE REMOVE SUBORN CONVERT DISPUTE ENTREAT IMPRESS PREVAIL SATISFY CANOODLE INFLUENCE
(— SUCCESSFULLY) SELL
PERSUADED PLIABLE GULLIBLE RESOLVED SENSIBLE
PERSUASION KIND SORT BELIEF OPINION SUASION JUDGMENT
(AUTHOR OF —) AUSTEN
(CHARACTER IN —) ANNE CLAY MARY CROFT ELLIOT LOUISA WALTER BENWICK CHARLES RUSSELL WILLIAM HARVILLE MUSGROVE ELIZABETH FREDERICK HENRIETTA WENTWORTH
PERSUASIVE COGENT WINNING INDUCTIVE PLAUSIBLE PROTEPTIC
(PREF.) PITHANO
PERT BOLD CHIC FESS FLIP KECK SPRY TRIM ALERT ALIVE BARDY BRISK COCKY DONSY KISKY PEART PERKY PIERT QUICK SASSY SAUCY SMART TAUNT CHEEKY CLEVER COCKET COMELY DAPPER FRISKY SWASHY THWART BOBBISH PAUGHTY INSOLENT PETULANT
(— TALK) CHELP
PERTAIN BE LIE BEAR COME LONG

BELIE TOUCH AFFEIR BEFALL BELIMP BELONG RELATE RETAIN CONCERN
(— TO) RINE
PERTAINING (— TO ABDOMEN) ALVINE
(— TO AFFAIRS OF STATE) PRAGMATIC
(— TO AGRICULTURE) GEORGIC
(— TO AIR) AURAL PNEUMATIC
(— TO ALL NATURE) PAMPHYSIC
(— TO ANIMALS) ZOIC
(— TO ANKLE) TARSAL
(— TO APOLLO) PYTHIAN PAEONIAN
(— TO APOSTLE) PETRINE
(— TO APPETITES) ORECTIC
(— TO ARMPIT) AXILLAR
(— TO ARMY) MARTIAL STRATONIC
(— TO ARROW) SAGITTAL
(— TO ART) TECHNICAL
(— TO ATHENA) PALLADIAN
(— TO BACK) DORSAL TERGAL
(— TO BATH) BALNEAL
(— TO BEAM) TRAGAL
(— TO BEARD) BARBAL
(— TO BED) THORAL
(— TO BEES) APIAN APIARIAN
(— TO BELLY) ALVIN ALVINE VENTRAL VENTRIC
(— TO BIBLICAL LAW) LEVITIC
(— TO BIRDS) AVIAN AVINE ORNITHIC VOLUCRINE
(— TO BIRTH) NATAL
(— TO BISHOP) LAWN
(— TO BITTER TASTE) PICRIC
(— TO BLACK SEA) PONTIC
(— TO BODIES AT REST) STATIC
(— TO BODY) SOMAL SOMATIC
(— TO BONE) OSSAL OSTEAL
(— TO BOSOM) GREMIAL
(— TO BRACELET) ARMILLARY
(— TO BRANCHES) RAMOUS
(— TO BREAD) PANARY
(— TO BREADMAKING) PANARY
(— TO BREAKFAST) ENTACULAR
(— TO BREAST) PECTORAL
(— TO BREASTBONE) STERNAL
(— TO BRISTLES) SETAL
(— TO BROTHEL) STEWISH
(— TO BUNCH) COMAL
(— TO CALF) VITULINE
(— TO CALF OF LEG) SURAL
(— TO CART) PLAUSTRAL
(— TO CARTHAGINIANS) PUNIC
(— TO CARVING) GLYPHIC
(— TO CAVE) SPELEAN SPELUNCAR
(— TO CHAIN) CATENARY
(— TO CHAMBER) CAMERAL
(— TO CHARIOTEER) AURIGAL
(— TO CHEEK) MALAR
(— TO CHESS) SCACCHIC
(— TO CHILDREN) PUERILE
(— TO CHINA) SINIAN SINISIAN
(— TO CITY) CIVIC URBAN
(— TO CLAN) SEPTAL
(— TO CLAY) BOLAR
(— TO CLOTHES) VESTIARY VESTURAL
(— TO COAST) ORARIAN
(— TO COINS) NUMMARY NUMISMATIC
(— TO COLOR) CHROMATIC
(— TO COMB) PECTINAL

(— TO CONSTRUCTION) TECTONIC
(— TO CONTESTS) AGONISTIC
(— TO CORK) SUBERIC SUBEROUS
(— TO COUGH) TUSSAL TUSSIVE
(— TO COURT) AULIC JUDICIAL JUDICIARY
(— TO CROCKERY) PIG
(— TO CROWN) CORONAL
(— TO DANCING) SALTATORY TRIPUDIAL
(— TO DAUGHTER OR SON) FILIAL
(— TO DAWN) EOAN
(— TO DEFENSE) PHYLACTIC
(— TO DESERTS) EREMIC
(— TO DIAPHRAGM) PHRENIC
(— TO DIGESTION) PEPTIC
(— TO DINNER) CENATORY PRANDIAL
(— TO DIVINATION) MANTIC
(— TO DOVE) COLUMBINE
(— TO DREAMS) ONEIRIC ONIROTIC
(— TO DRINKING) BIBITORY
(— TO DUNG) STERCORAL
(— TO EARTH) GEAL TELLURIC TERRANEAN
(— TO EARTHQUAKE) SEISMAL SEISMIC
(— TO EAST) EOAN
(— TO EGGS) OVAL
(— TO ESSENCE) BASIC
(— TO EUNUCH) SPADONIC
(— TO EVENING) VESPER
(— TO EYELIDS) BLEPHARAL
(— TO FACE) PROSOPIC
(— TO FAIR) NUNDINAL
(— TO FAITH) PISTIC
(— TO FEET) PEDAL PEDARY
(— TO FERMENTATION) ZYMIC ZYMOTIC
(— TO FIELDS) AGRARIAN
(— TO FINGERS) DIGITAL
(— TO FISH) PISCINE
(— TO FISHING) HALIEUTIC
(— TO FLEAS) PULICENE PULICOSE
(— TO FLESH) SARCOUS
(— TO FLOCK) GREGAL
(— TO FLOOD) DILUVIAL DILUVIAN
(— TO FLOWERS) FLORAL ANTHINE
(— TO FOREARM) CUBITAL
(— TO FOREHEAD) METOPIC
(— TO FORM) MORPHIC
(— TO FOX) VULPINE
(— TO FRANCE) GALLICAN
(— TO FRESH WATER) LIMNETIC
(— TO FROGS) ANURAN RANINE
(— TO FRUIT) POMONAL POMONIC
(— TO FUNERALS) EXEQUIAL
(— TO FUNGUS) MYCETOID
(— TO FURNACE) FORNACIC
(— TO GALLOWS) PATIBULARY
(— TO GARDEN) HORTULAN
(— TO GARRISON) PRESIDIAL
(— TO GENTILES) ETHNIC
(— TO GLASS) VITREOUS
(— TO GOATS) CAPRIC
(— TO GOVERNMENT) ARCHICAL POLITICAL
(— TO GRANDPARENTS) AVAL
(— TO GRINDING) MOLINARY
(— TO GROIN) INGUINAL
(— TO GROUND) SOLARY
(— TO GROVE) NEMORAL
(— TO GULLS) LARINE

(— TO GUMS) ULETIC GINGIVAL
(— TO HAIR) PILAR CRINAL PILARY
(— TO HAND) CHIRAL MANUAL
(— TO HARE) LEPORINE
(— TO HAWKS) ACCIPITRINE
(— TO HEAD) CEPHALIC
(— TO HEALTH) HYGEIAN
(— TO HEAP) ACERVAL
(— TO HEART) CARDIAC
(— TO HEAT) CALORIC THERMAL THERMIC
(— TO HEAVEN) EMPYREAL EMPYREAN
(— TO HIPS) SCIATIC
(— TO HOLIDAY) FERIAL
(— TO HORIZON) MUNDANE
(— TO HORSE) EQUINE HIPPIC CABALLINE
(— TO HOSPITALITY) XENIAL XENIAN
(— TO HOUSE) DOMAL
(— TO HUNGER) FAMELIC
(— TO HUNTING) VENATIC VENERIAL CYNEGETIC
(— TO INCH) UNCIAL
(— TO INTELLECT) NOETIC
(— TO INTESTINES) ALVIN ALVINE
(— TO JAW) MALAR GNATHAL GNATHIC
(— TO JOURNEY) VIATIC
(— TO KIDNEY) RENAL NEPHRIC
(— TO KNOWLEDGE) GNOSTIC
(— TO LAKES) LACUSTRINE
(— TO LAP) GREMIAL
(— TO LAUGHING) GELASTIC
(— TO LAUGHTER) RISORIAL
(— TO LEARNING) PALLADIAN
(— TO LEG) CRURAL
(— TO LICE) PEDICULAR
(— TO LIFE) VITAL ZOETIC
(— TO LINE) FILAR
(— TO LIPS) LABIAL
(— TO LIVER) HEPATIC JECORAL
(— TO LIVERPOOL) LIVERPUDLIAN
(— TO LOINS) LUMBAR
(— TO LOVE) EROTIC AMATORY
(— TO LUCK) ALEATORY
(— TO LUNGS) PULMONIC PNEUMONIC PULMONARY
(— TO MANCHESTER) MANCUNIAN
(— TO MANKIND) COMMON ANTHROPIC
(— TO MARBLE) MARMORIC
(— TO MARKET) NUNDINAL
(— TO MARRIAGE) MARITAL HYMENEAL
(— TO MARS) AREAN MAMERTINE MAVORTIAL
(— TO MARSHES) PALUDAL PALUDIC
(— TO MASS) MOLAR
(— TO MASTER) HERILE
(— TO MEADOWS) PRATAL
(— TO MEAL) PRANDIAL
(— TO MECCA) MECCAWEE
(— TO MEDICINE) IATRIC IATRICAL
(— TO MEMORY) MNESTIC MNEMONIC
(— TO MIDDAY) MERIDIAN
(— TO MILK) LACTARY LACTEAL
(— TO MILL) MOLINARY
(— TO MIND) MENTAL PHRENIC PSYCHIC PSYCHICAL

(— TO MIRROR) SPECULAR
(— TO MOISTURE) HYGRIC
(— TO MONEY) PECUNIARY
(— TO MOON) LUNAR SELENIC SELENIAN
(— TO MORNING) MATIN MATINAL MATUTINAL
(— TO MOTION) GESTIC KINETIC
(— TO MOUNTAINS) MONTANE
(— TO MOUTH) ORAL OSCULAR STOMATIC
(— TO MUSCLE) SARCOUS
(— TO MUSES) PIERIAN
(— TO MUSIC) HARMONIC
(— TO MYSTERIES) TELESTIC
(— TO NAME) ONOMASTIC
(— TO NAMES) ONOMASTIC
(— TO NAVEL) OMPHALIC
(— TO NECK) JUGULAR
(— TO NEPHEW) NEPOTAL
(— TO NET) RETIARY
(— TO NEW ZEALAND) ZELANIAN
(— TO NIGHT) NOCTURNAL
(— TO NOSE) NASAL RHINAL
(— TO NUT) NUCAL
(— TO NUTRITION) TROPHIC
(— TO OAK) QUERCINE ROBOREOUS
(— TO OCEAN) PELAGIC OCEANOUS THALASSIC
(— TO OCEAN DEPTHS) HADAL
(— TO OLD AGE) SENILE GERATIC GERONTIC
(— TO OPEN SKY) SUBDIAL
(— TO PALACE) PALATINE
(— TO PALM) VOLAR
(— TO PARISH) PAROCHIAL
(— TO PARLOR) BEN BOOR
(— TO PARROTS) PSITTACINE
(— TO PASTURES) PASCUAL
(— TO PAWNBROKER) AVUNCULAR
(— TO PEACOCK) PAVONINE
(— TO PEARL) MARGARIC
(— TO PERSPIRATION) SUDORIC
(— TO PICTURE) ICONIC
(— TO PIGS) PORCINE
(— TO PINE) WARRYN
(— TO PLAGUE) LOIMIC
(— TO PLEASURE) HEDONIC
(— TO POETRY) MUSAL IAMBIC
(— TO POISON) TOXIC
(— TO POTTERY) CERAMIC
(— TO PRIESTS) SACERDOTAL
(— TO PRISON) CARCERAL
(— TO PULSE) SPHYGMIC
(— TO PUNISHMENT) PENAL PUNITIVE
(— TO PURIFICATION) LUSTRAL
(— TO QUEEN) REGINAL
(— TO RAIN) HYETAL PLUVIAL
(— TO RAINBOW) IRIDAL
(— TO REGISTER) MATRICULAR
(— TO REMOTE PLACE) FORANE
(— TO RESONANCE) SYNTONIC
(— TO RING) ARMILLARY
(— TO RISING) ORTIVE
(— TO RIVER) AMNIC POTAMIC RIVERINE FLUMINOSE
(— TO RIVER BANK) RIPARIAN
(— TO ROAD) VIATIC
(— TO ROCK) PETREAN SAXATILE
(— TO ROD) BACULINE
(— TO RUBBISH) RUDERARY

(— TO SABLES) ZIBELINE
(— TO SAIL) VELIC
(— TO SALVATION) SOTERIAL
(— TO SANDARAC) THYINE
(— TO SATURDAY) SABBATINE
(— TO SEAL) PHOCINE SIGILLARY SPHRAGISTIC
(— TO SEAM) SUTURAL
(— TO SEASHORE) LITTORAL
(— TO SEAWEED) ALGOUS
(— TO SENSE OF TASTE) GUSTATIVE
(— TO SEVEN) SEPTIMAL
(— TO SEWING) SUTORIAL SUTORIAN
(— TO SHEEP) VERVECINE
(— TO SHEPHERDS) PASTORAL
(— TO SHERIFF) VICONTIEL
(— TO SHIN) CNEMIAL
(— TO SHIP) NAVICULAR
(— TO SHOPMAN) APOTHECAL
(— TO SHOULDER) ALAR SCAPULAR
(— TO SIGHT) VISUAL
(— TO SIGNS) SEMIC SEMANTIC
(— TO SILVER) LUNAR ARGENTAL
(— TO SISTER) SORORAL
(— TO SKIN) DERIC DERMAL CUTICULAR
(— TO SLAVES) SERVILE
(— TO SLEEP) SOMNIAL MORPHETIC
(— TO SMELLING) OLFACTORY
(— TO SNAKE) ANGUINE
(— TO SNORING) RHONCAL RHONCIAL
(— TO SNOW) NIVAL
(— TO SOFT PALATE) VELAR
(— TO SOIL) DAPHIC
(— TO SOLE) VOLAR
(— TO SONG) MELIC
(— TO SPECTACLE) THEORIC
(— TO SPEECH) PHEMIC
(— TO SPINAL CORD) MYELIC
(— TO SPRING) VERNAL
(— TO STARS) ASTRAL STELLAR SIDEREAL
(— TO STATE AFFAIRS) PRAGMATIC
(— TO STEPMOTHER) NOVERCAL
(— TO STOMACH) GASTRIC
(— TO STONE) LITHIC
(— TO STORKS) PELARGIC
(— TO SULPHUR) THIONIC
(— TO SUMMER) ESTIVAL AESTIVAL
(— TO SUN) SOLAR HELIAC
(— TO SUNDAY) DOMINICAL
(— TO SUNDIAL) SCIATHERIC
(— TO SUPPER) CENATORY
(— TO SURFACE OF ANYTHING) FACIAL
(— TO SWALLOWS) HIRUNDINE
(— TO SWEAT) SUDORIC
(— TO SWIMMING) NATATORY
(— TO SWINEHERD) SYBOTIC
(— TO TAIL) CAUDAL
(— TO TAILOR) SARTORIAL
(— TO TANNING) SC
(— TO TEACHER) MAGISTERIAL
(— TO TEARS) LACRIMAL LACHRYMAL
(— TO TEMPO) AGOGIC
(— TO THE BEAUTIFUL) ESTHETIC AESTHETIC
(— TO THIEVING) KLEPTISTIC

(**— TO THIGH**) CRURAL
(**— TO THREAD**) FILAR
(**— TO THROAT**) GULAR JUGULAR
(**— TO THUNDER**) FULMINEOUS
(**— TO TILE**) TEGULAR
(**— TO TIN**) STANNIC
(**— TO TITHES**) DECIMAL
(**— TO TITMICE**) PARINE
(**— TO TOMB**) TOMBAL
(**— TO TONGUE**) GLOSSAL LINGUAL
(**— TO TORTOISES**) CHELONIAN
(**— TO TOUCH**) TACTILE
(**— TO TOWER**) TURRICAL
(**— TO TREES**) DENDRAL ARBOREAL
(**— TO TWENTY**) VICENARY
(**— TO UNCLE**) AVUNCULAR
(**— TO UNDERGROUND WATER**)
VADOSE PHREATIC
(**— TO VESSEL**) VASAL
(**— TO VIRGIN**) PARTHENIAN
(**— TO VISION**) OCULAR
(**— TO VOW**) VOTAL
(**— TO WAGON**) PLAUSTRAL
(**— TO WALLS**) MURAL PARIETAL
(**— TO WAR**) POLEMICAL
(**— TO WASPS**) VESPAL VESPINE
(**— TO WAX**) CERAL
(**— TO WEAVING**) TEXTORIAL
(**— TO WEIGHT**) BARIC PONDERAL
PONDERARY
(**— TO WELL**) PHREATIC
(**— TO WHALES**) CETIC
(**— TO WHEAT**) VULGARE
(**— TO WHEELS**) ROTAL
(**— TO WHETSTONES**) COTICULAR
(**— TO WIFE**) UXORIAL
(**— TO WILL**) VOLITIVE
(**— TO WIND**) EOLIAN PNEUMATIC
(**— TO WINE**) VINIC VINOUS
(**— TO WINE-MAKING**) OENOPOETIC
(**— TO WINGS**) ALAR PTERIC
EXRUPEAL PTEROTIC
(**— TO WINTER**) HIEMAL
(**— TO WISDOM**) PALLADIAN
(**— TO WOMANKIND**) MULIEBRAL
(**— TO WOODPECKERS**) PICINE
(**— TO WOODS**) SYLVAN NEMORAL
(**— TO WORMS**) VERMICULAR
(**— TO WOUNDS**) VULNERAL
(**— TO WRIST**) CARPAL
(**— TO YESTERDAY**) PRIDIAN
(**— TO YEW**) TAXINE
(**SUFF.**) (**—TO**) AL AR ORIOUS ORY
PERTINACIOUS FIRM STIFF
DOGGED ADHERING STUBBORN
OBSTINATE
PERTINENCE RELEVANCE
PERTINENCY FORCE
PERTINENT APT FIT PAT HAPPY
COGENT PROPER TIMELY ADAPTED
APROPOS GERMANE POINTED
TELLING INCIDENT MATERIAL
RELATIVE RELEVANT
PERTLY CROUSE
PERTURB BITE GRATE UPSET
WORRY DISMAY AGITATE
CONFUSE CONTURB DERANGE
DISTURB TROUBLE
PERTURBATION DISMAY FLIGHT
POTHER UNEASE POOTHER
STICKLE TROUBLE TURMOIL
EVECTION AGITATION

PERTURBED UNEASY
PERTUSSIS COUGH CHINCOF
CHINCOUGH

PERU

CAPITAL: LIMA
COIN: SOL LIBRA DINERO CENTAVO
DEPARTMENT: ICA LIMA PUNO
CUSCO CUZCO JUNIN PIURA
TACNA ANCASH LORETO
TUMBES
DESERT: SECHURA
ISLAND: CHINCHA
LAKE: TITICACA
LANGUAGE: AYMARA QUECHUA
MEASURE: TOPO VARA GALON
CELEMIN FANEGADA
MONEY: INTI
MOUNTAIN: HUAMINA COROPUNA
HUASCARAN
PERIOD: RECUAY
RIVER: NAPU RIMAC SANTA TIGRE
MORONA YAGUAS YAVARI
CURARAY MARANON PASTAZA
UCAYALI AMAZONAS APURIMAC
HUALLAGA URUBAMBA
TOWN: ICA LIMA PUNO CUZCO
PAITA PISCO PIURA TACNA
CALLAO TUMBES IQUITOS
AREQUIPA CHICLAYO TRUJILLO
VOLCANO: MISTI YUCAMANI
WEIGHT: LIBRA QUINTAL

PERUKE WIG FLASH GALERA
TOUPEE GALERUM PERIWIG
WIGGERY
PERUSAL SIGHT LECTURE
SCRUTINY
PERUSE CON READ SCAN STUDY
HANDLE SEARCH SURVEY
EXAMINE INSPECT
(**— QUICKLY**) SKIM
PERUVIAN BARK CALISAYA
CINCHONA
PERVADE FILL BATHE IMBUE
DRENCH INSTIL OCCUPY THREAD
INSTILL PERMEATE TRAVERSE
PERVADED STIFF
PERVASIVE POIGNANT
PERVERSE AUK AWK CAM CAR
AWRY WOGH WRAW CROSS
DONSY GAMMY THRAW WROTH
CUSSED DIVERS LOUCHE THRAWN
THWART WICKED WILFUL WRAIST
AWKWARD CRABBED CROOKED
DIVERSE FORWARD FROWARD
OBLIQUE PEEVISH WAYWARD
CAMSHACH CRANKISH STUBBORN
PERVERSELY AUK AWK AWRY
ATHWART OVERWART
PERVERSION WREST ABUSION
(**— OF TASTE**) MALACIA
PERVERT WRY DRAW RACK RUIN
SKEW TURN WARP ABUSE CROOK
GLOSS TWIST UPSET WREST
DEBASE DETORT DIVERT GARBLE
INVERT MISUSE POISON VOYEUR
WRENCH WRITHE CONTORT
CORRUPT DEGRADE DEPRAVE
DEVIATE DISTORT MISTURN
SUBVERT TRADUCE VITIATE
MISWREST
PERVERTED BAD WICKED ABUSIVE

AWKWARD CORRUPT TWISTED
VICIOUS
PERVERTER WRESTER
PERVIOUS LEACHY PERVIAL
PERVADING
PES NEUME TENOR PODATUS
PESKY VERY PLAGUY ANNOYING
DEVILING EXTREMELY
PESO DURO CONANT DOLLAR
CAROLUS PATACAO
PESSIMISM WELTSCHMERZ
MISERABILISM
PESSIMIST ALARMIST JEREMIAH
WORRYWART
PESSIMISTIC GLOOMY ALARMED
BEARISH CYNICAL DOWNBEAT
PEST BOT BANE GNAT TICK WEED
APHIS MOUSE MYZUS TRAIK
INSECT MENACE PLAGUE SCHELM
SORROW VERMIN HASSLER
NUDNICK SCOURGE MEALYBUG
SANDMITE BUTTINSKY
(**GARDEN —**) APHID
PESTER DUN HOX NAG RAG RIB TIG
HAKE ANNOY DEVIL TEASE WORRY
BADGER BOTHER HARASS INFEST
MOLEST BEDEVIL TORMENT
TROUBLE OBSTRUCT PERSECUTE
PESTHOUSE LAZARET LAZARETTO
PESTICIDE ALAR BIOCIDE
FUMIGANT
PESTILENCE LUES PEST DEATH
QUALM PLAGUE MURRAIN
EPIDEMIC MORTALITY
PESTILENT FATAL DEADLY VEXING
NOXIOUS
PESTLE MIX BRAY GRIND PESTL
PILUM STAMP BEETLE BRAYER
MULLER PISTIL CHAPPER
POUNDER STAMPLER
PET TOY CADE COAX DAUT DEAR
DUCK HUFF LAMB NECK PEAT SNIT
SOCK SULK TIFF DRUNT DUCKY
HUMOR QUIET SPOIL SPOON
TETCH CARESS CODDLE COSHER
COSSET CUDDLE DANDLE DAUTIE
DAWTIE FADDLE FANTAD FANTOD
FONDLE GENTLE PAMPER PETKIN
SMOOCH SQUALL STROKE
WANTON CHERISH DARLING
INDULGE PINKENY TANTRUM
TIDLING UMBRAGE WHITHER
CANOODLE FAVORITE TIDDLING
PADDYWACK
(**— NICKNAME**) DEARIE
PETAL ALA HELM HOOD LEAF WING
BANNER
(**— IN PEA FLOWER**) VEXILLUM
(**— OF IRIS**) STANDARD
(**FLOWER —S**) ALAE
(**UPPER —**) HOOD BANNER
(**PL.**) COROLLA
PETALIA NYCTERIS
PETARD PITTARD FIREWORK
PETATE BANIG
PETECHIA STIGMA
PETER P FADE FAIL PEAK SAFE
WANE CEASE PEDRO PIERS PIERRE
SIGNAL DWINDLE
(**— OUT**) FIZZLE
(**BROTHER OF —**) ANDREW
(**FATHER OF —**) JONAS
PETER GRIMES (**CHARACTER IN —**)

ELLEN PETER GRIMES ORFORD
BALSTRODE
(**COMPOSER OF —**) BRITTEN
PETER IBBETSON (**AUTHOR OF —**)
DUMAURIER
(**CHARACTER IN —**) DEANE MADGE
MIMSY PETER LINTOT GREGORY
PLUNKET IBBETSON PASQUIER
PETERMAN YEGG
PETER PAN (**AUTHOR OF —**) BARRIE
(**CHARACTER IN —**) PAN HOOK
JOHN NIBS SMEE PETER WENDY
TINKER DARLING MICHAEL TOOTLES
MARGARET SLIGHTLY
PETHAHIAH (**FATHER OF —**)
MESHEZABEEL
PETHEUL (**SON OF —**) JOEL
PETIOLE STEM SPINE STALK STIPE
PODEON PEDUNCLE PHYLLODE
LEAFSTALK
PETITE SMALL LITTLE MIGNON
MIGNONNE
PETITION ASK BEG SUE BILL BOON
PLEA PRAY SUIT VOTE WISH APPLY
ORATE PLEAD APPEAL DESIRE
INVOKE MOTION PLACIT PRAYER
STEVEN ADDRESS BESEECH
ENTREAT IMPLORE ORATION
SOLICIT ROGATION SUFFRAGE
(**MAKE —**) SUE
(**PL.**) PRECES
PETITIONER BEGGAR ORATOR
SUITOR BEADSMAN APPLICANT
ENTREATER PLAINTIFF
PETO WAHOO
PETREL BILL TITI CAHOW MITTY
NELLY PRION WITCH FULMAR
SPENCY TEETEE ASSILAG GLUTTON
KAEDING PINTADO SEABIRD
SEAFOWL STINKER ALLAMOTH
FORKTAIL STINKPOT ALLAMOTTI
MALLEMUCK NIGHTHAWK
PETRIFY DAZE APPAL SCARE
APPALL DEADEN STONIFY STUPEFY
FRIGHTEN LAPIDIFY FOSSILIZE
GORGONIZE
PETRIFYING STONY GORGON
PETROL GAS GASOLINE
PETROLATUM VASELINE
PETROLEUM OIL CRUDE PETROL
NAPHTHA
(**— INDUSTRY**) OILDOM
(**CRUDE —**) MAZOUT
PETRUCHIO (**WIFE OF —**) KATHERINE
PE-TSAI PECHAY
PETTED CADE DANDILY
PETTICOAT BAJO GORE KILT SLIP
SOUS DICKY GREEN JUPON PAGNE
SOUSE KIRTLE LUHINGA PLACKET
WHITTLE BALMORAL BASQUINE
WILYCOAT UNDERSKIRT
(**— OF TARGET**) GREEN
PETTIFOG FOG CAVIL BICKER
PETTIFOGGER FOGGER SHYSTER
LEGULEIAN
PETTINESS NAGGLE PARVINIMITY
PETTING COLLING
PETTISH DORTY HUFFY FRETFUL
PEEVISH PLAINTIVE
PETTY TIN BASE JERK MEAN ORRA
PUNY VAIN BANAL GRIMY MINOR
PETIT PUNEE SMALL MEASLY
MINUTE PALTRY PEANUT POKING

PUISNE PUSILL SNIFTY TWOBIT KITLING PIMPING TRIVIAL TWATTLE CHILDISH FIDDLING INFERIOR NIGGLING NUGATORY PEDDLING PICAYUNE PIFFLING SNIPPETY TRIFLING PAROCHIAL
(PREF.) MICR(O)
(SUFF.) (— ONE) EEN

PETULANCE PROCACITY

PETULANT PERT CROSS SAUCY SHORT TESTY TIFFY FEISTY SULLEN WANTON WILFUL CRABBED FRETFUL FROWARD HUFFISH PEEVISH WASPISH PERVERSE SNAPPISH

PEULTHAI (FATHER OF —) OBEDEDOM

PEUMUS BOLDU

PEW BOX PUE BOUT DESK PFUI PUGH SEAT SLIP BENCH BUGHT STALL BOUGHT
(— ATTACHMENT) KNEELER

PEWEE PEWIT PEEWEE PEEWIT

PEWIT PEESWEEP

PEWTER CUP BIDRI BIDRY ETAIN MONEY PUDER BIDERY TRIFLE PEAUDER SADWARE TUTENAG
(— MARK) TOUCHMARK

PEYOTE HIKULI MESCAL

PFENNIG PENNING

PHAEDRA (AUTHOR OF —) RACINE
(CHARACTER IN —) ARICIA OENONE PHAEDRA THESEUS HIPPOLYTUS THERAMENES
(FATHER OF —) MINOS
(HUSBAND OF —) THESEUS
(MOTHER OF —) PASIPHAE
(SISTER OF —) ADRIADNE
(SON OF —) ACAMAS DEMOPHON

PHAETON DUKE FAETON SPIDER STANHOPE

PHAETON BUTTERFLY BALTIMORE

PHALANGER TAIT ARIEL TAPOA CUSCUS TAGUAN OPOSSUM PENTAIL SQUIRREL

PHALAROPE LOBIPED COOTFOOT LOBEFOOT WHALEBIRD

PHALERA BEAD BOSS DISK STUD CAMEO

PHALTI (FATHER OF —) LAISH

PHANTASM DREAM FANCY GHOST VAPOR FIGURE SHADOW SPIRIT FANTASY PHANTOM SPECIES SPECTER SPECTRE

PHANTASMAL EERIE UNREAL SPECTRAL

PHANTASUS (BROTHER OF —) ICELUS MORPHEUS PHOBETOR THANATOS
(FATHER OF —) HYPNOS SOMNUS
(MOTHER OF —) NYX

PHANTASY FANCY FANTASY PHANTASIA

PHANTOM IDOL BOGEY BOGLE DUMMY GHOST IMAGE PHASM SHADE SHAPE UMBRA BOGGLE DOUBLE FANTOM IDOLON IDOLUM SHADOW SPIRIT BUGBEAR EIDOLON ELUSIVE FANTASY FEATURE SPECIES SPECTER ILLUSORY ADAMASTOR SIMULACRUM

PHANUEL (DAUGHTER OF —) ANNA

PHARAOH ALE FARO PHARO TYRANT BUSIRIS

PHARAOH'S HEN VULTURE

PHAREZ (BROTHER OF —) ZARAH
(FATHER OF —) JUDAH
(MOTHER OF —) TAMAR

PHARISEE MUGWUMP NICODEMUS

PHARMACEUTICAL MERCURIAL
(SUFF.) (— PRODUCT) EIN EINE IN INE

PHARMACIST CHEMIST DRUGGIST DISPENSER APOTHECARY

PHARMACY FERMACY DRUGSTORE

PHAROS CLOAK LIGHT TORCH BEACON LANTERN

PHARYNGEAL FAUCAL

PHARYNX MASTAX PROBOSCIS
(PREF.) LAEMO LEM(O)

PHASE EFT END LEG FAZE SIDE ANGLE FACET GRADE STAGE ASPECT AVATAR BACKLASH PASSOVER DICHOTOMY
(INITIAL —) BUD
(LOWEST —) BATHOS
(TRANSITORY —) STREAK

PHASM FANTOM METEOR PHASMA PHANTOM

PHEASANT CHIR GUAN ARGUS CHEER KALIJ MINAL MONAL COUCAL GROUSE LEIPOA MAGPIE MONAUL MOONAL PUKRAS KALLEGE FIREBACK ITHAGINE RINGNECK TRAGOPAN MACARTNEY
(BREEDING PLACE FOR —S) STEW
(BROOD OF —S) NID NYE NIDE
(YOUNG —) POULT

PHEASANT CUCKOO COUCAL

PHEASANT DUCK PINTAIL MERGANSER

PHEASANT FINCH WAXBILL

PHEASANT'S-EYE ROSARUBY

PHEBE (HUSBAND OF —) SILVIUS

PHELLEM CORK SUBER

PHENOBARBITOL LUMINAL

PHENOCRYST INSET

PHENOL BHT LACCOL THYMOL ALOESOL CREOSOL DURENOL EUGENOL ORCINOL CHAVICOL RESORCIN CARVACROL

PHENOMENA
(SUFF.) ICS

PHENOMENON FIRE ANOMY COLOR EVENT IMAGE ARTHUS EFFECT METEOR MIRAGE SHADOW ISOTOPY MIRACLE PARADOX PROCESS SYMPTOM ASTERISM PRAKRITI SIDERISM SUNQUAKE LANDSPOUT
(ATMOSPHERIC —) METEOR
(LUMINOUS —) FIREDRAKE
(METEOROGICAL —) STORM

PHENYLSALICYLATE SALOL

PHERES (BROTHER OF —) AESON AMYTHAON
(DAUGHTER OF —) IDOMENE PERIAPIS
(FATHER OF —) CRETHEUS
(MOTHER OF —) TYRO
(NEPHEW OF —) JASON
(SON OF —) ADMETUS LYCURGUS

PHIAL CUP FIAL VIAL CRUET BOTTLE VESSEL

PHILABEG KILT FILIBEG

PHILANDER FOOL WOLF DALLY FLIRT SMOCK

PHILANTHROPIC HUMANE

PHILANTHROPIST DONOR SHARER ALTRUIST HUMANITARIAN
AMERICAN DIX CASE DUKE FELS HOGG HOLT LICK LOEB MOTT RICE SAGE URIS VAUX YALE AVERY BACHE BRUCE DEPEW EVANS FRICK GERRY GETTY GRATZ HEINZ LENOX LEWYT MILLS ODGEN PEROT PRATT SMITH TRASK TULLY COOPER CRERAR DEDMAN EUSTIS FOLSON GEORGE GIRARD GURLEY HAYDEN HEARST LAMONT LASKER LEHMAN LOWELL MELLON MILLER MORGAN MURPHY PEPPER PHIPPS PUTNAM ROBERT SCHIFF STRAUS TAPPAN TULANE COCHRAN CORNELL DOREMUS FARNHAM GILBERT GRELLET HOPKINS LATHROP LAZARUS MILBANK PARRISH PEABODY RUTGERS RYERSON SHEPARD STEWART WARBURG CARNEGIE CORCORAN HARKNESS HARRIMAN LEWISOHN PHILLIPS ROBINSON STERLING JUILLIARD MEYERHOFF ROSENWALD SHEFFIELD CRITTENTON GUGGENHEIM SULZBERGER VANDERBILT ABERCROMBIE ROCKEFELLER
AUSTRIAN FRANKL
CANADIAN MCGILL
ENGLISH FRY GUY COBBE CORAM CORRY KYRLE MAYER SHARP WAUGH GURNEY KENYON SLOANE COWDRAY HIBBERT MONTAGU PEARSON RYLANDS CHRISTIE KINNAIRD MACAULAY SOMERSET FAITHFULL MONTEFIORE OGLETHORPE SHAFTESBURY WHITTINGTON WILBERFORCE
FRENCH MANCE GIRARD MARBEAU MONTYON MICHELIN MIRAMION
GERMAN FALK HIRSCH MULLER FLIEDNER
INDIAN JEEJEEBHOY
IRISH RICE GONNE MADDEN
ITALIAN KRIM
RUSSIAN NOVIKOV
SCOTTISH DALE HERIOT FINDLAY GUTHRIE
SWEDISH NOBEL
SWISS DUNANT

PHILANTHROPY CHARITY ALMSGIVING

PHILEMATOLOGY KISSING

PHILEMON (WIFE OF —) BAUCIS

PHILIP PIP PHILP SPARROW

PHILIPPIC SATIRE SCREED TIRADE ABUSIVE DIATRIBE

PHILIPPINES
ARCHIPELAGO: SULU
CAPITAL: BAGUIO MANILA
COIN: PESO PISO PESETA CENTAVO SENTIMO
FIBER: ERUC ABACA BUNTAL
ISLAND: CEBU BATAN BOHOL LEYTE LUZON PANAY SAMAR NEGROS MASBATE MINDORO PALAWAN ROMBLON MINDANAO
LAKE: TAAL LANAO
LANGUAGE: MORO BICOL IBANAG ILOCANO TAGALOG VISAYAN
MEASURE: LOAN BRAZA CABAN CAUAN CHUPA GANTA APATAN BALITA QUINON
MOUNTAIN: APO IBA MAYON PULOG BANAHAO
NATIVE: ATA ATI ITA TAO AETA ATTA ETAS MORO SULU BICOL TAGAL VICOL IGOROT TIMAUA BISAYAN TAGALOG FILIPINO
PROVINCE: ABRA CEBU SULU ALBAY CAPIZ DAVAO LANAO RIZAL BATAAN CAVITE IFUGAO ILOILO TARLAC SURIGAO
RIVER: ABRA AGNO MAGAT PASIG AGUSAN LAOANG CAGAYAN MINDANAO PAMPANGA
TOWN: IBA AGOA BOAC CEBU JOLO MATI ALBAY DAVAO DIGOS LAOAG PASAY VIGAN APARRI BAGUIO CAVITE ILAGAN ILOILO MANILA BACOLOD BASILAN DAGUPAN CALOOCAN
TREE: DAO IBA TUA TUI ACLE ANAM ATES BOGO DITA IPIL GUIJO LAUAN LIGAS ALUPAG ANAHAU ARANGA ANONANG APITONG TINDALO ALMACIGA AMPALAYA
VOLCANO: APO TAAL MAYON BULOSAN CANLAON
WEIGHT: CATTY FARDO PICUL PUNTO LACHSA QUILATE CHINANTA

PHILISTINE BOOB GIGMAN MUCKER BABBITT GITTITE BOEOTIAN BARBARIAN BOURGEOIS HYPOCRITE
(— CITY) GATH
(PL.) PULESATI PURASATI CAPHTORIM

PHILOLOGIST LAVENGRO LINGUIST
AMERICAN BUCK COOK HART TODD WOOD ADLER BROWN CHILD CURME GIBBS HEMPL MARCH MARSH BENDER BRIGHT MARDEN PRINCE REEVES CHOMSKY EMERSON GEROULD GUDEMAN HOPKINS KENNEDY LEARNED SHELDON WHITMAN HARRISON TRUMBULL GREENOUGH KORZYBSKI BLOOMFIELD STURTEVANT
AUSTRIAN MINOR MULLER KARAJAN REINISCH SCHONBACH
COLOMBIAN CUERVO MARROQUIN
CZECH HANKA GEBAUER JUNGMANN DOBROVSKY
DANISH RAFN RASK VERNER HEIBERG MOLBECH THOMSEN JESPERSEN WESTERGAARD
DUTCH KATE KERN BRINK VRIES VREESE WINKEL HEINSIUS HEREMANS UHLENBECK HUYDECOPER VALCKENAER HEMSTERHUIS
ENGLISH WYLD ASTON EARLE ELLIS NARES SAYCE SKEAT TOOKE CONWAY CRAGIE GOWERS MORRIS

MURRAY ONIONS THORPE WERNER
WRIGHT ALLEGRO GARNETT
GOMPERZ SKINNER WEEKLEY
BOSWORTH CHADWICK STEPHENS
WEYMOUTH COLERIDGE
DONALDSON FURNIVALL
FINNISH SETALA CASTREN
FRENCH ADAM BREAL DOLET
EGGER HENRY LEBAS MEYER
RENAN BRUNOT LAMBIN WAILLY
BRACHET BURNOUF MEILLET
LEFEBVRE VAUGELAS CHABANEAU
QUICHERAT HOVELACQUE
DARMESTETER
GERMAN AST ABEL BIRT BOPP DIEZ
FICK HIRT JULG KERN MOGK PAUL
POTT WOLF BERGK BLANC BLASS
BOCKH EBERT GREIN GRIMM HAASE
HAGEN HAUPT HEYNE HEYSE JUSTI
KLOTZ KRAPF KRAUS KROLL LEHRS
MEYER NIESE PAULY ZEUSS BECKER
BEKKER BENFEY CHRIST FREUND
FRISCH HENZEN JACOBI JACOBS
KELLER KOCHLY MARTIN MULLER
PASSOW REISKE VAHLEN VIETOR
ADELUNG BARTSCH BERNAYS
BRANDIS BURSIAN CORSSEN
CREUZER CURTIUS DINDORF
DUNTZER GERLAND KIEPERT
KORTING LEPSIUS ESKIEN
MATZNER OSTHOFF RIBBECK
RITSCHL RUHNKEN SANDERS
SCHERER SIEVERS WEIGAND
WELCKER WISSOWA ZARNCKE
ZUPITZA AUFRECHT BEHAGHEL
BISCHOFF BOTTIGER BRUGMANN
FOERSTER GRAEVIUS HOFFMANN
HUMBOLDT MASSMANN SCHRADER
THIERSCH WEINHOLD WESTPHAL
XYLANDER ACIDALIUS BAUMSTARK
BERNHARDY BUSCHMANN
ETTMULLER FRISCHLIN GABELENTZ
HOLTZMANN KIRCHHOFF
KOSCHWITZ STEINTHAL
TRAUTMANN HOLTHAUSEN
MULLENHOFF STREITBERG
THURNEYSEN VOLLMOLLER
BARTHOLOMAE
HUNGARIAN REVAI HUNFALVY
DOBRENTEJ ENDLICHER
ICELANDIC JONSSON EGILSSON
MAGNUSSON VIGFUSSON
ITALIAN ASCOLI MONACI NOVATI
OVIDIO COMPARETTI CASTELVETRO
CASTIGLIONE
NORWEGIAN AASEN BUGGE
KONOW MUNCH
POLISH ZAMENHOF ROZWADOWSKI
PORTUGUESE COELHO
RUMANIAN HASDEU
RUSSIAN GROT VOSTOKOV
SCHIEFNER
SCOTTISH GRANT BAIKIE MURRAY
SPANISH MENENDEZ
SWEDISH IHRE LUNDELL AHLQUIST
SODERWALL ZACHRISSON
SWISS MAHLY ISELIN
PHILOLOGY SEMITICS
PHILOMACHUS MACHETES
PHILOMELA STOP FILOMEL
  (FATHER OF —) PANDION
  (RAVISHER OF —) TEREUS
  (SISTER OF —) PROCNE

  (SLAIN BY —) ITYS
  (VICTIM OF —) ITYS
PHILOSOPHER WIT SAGE CYNIC
STOIC ARTIST IONIAN LEGIST
DOTTORE ELEATIC ERISTIC
SCHOLAR SOPHIST SUMMIST
THINKER ZETETIC ACADEMIC
EPOCHIST MAGICIAN VIRTUOSO
ACADEMIST ALCHEMIST DIALECTIC
PHYSICIAN SCHOOLMAN
AMERICAN AYER HOOK HUME
LADD MEAD MORE ADLER ALBEE
BOWEN BOWNE DEWEY EDMAN
FANON FISKE JAMES LEWIS MOORE
PAINE PERRY QUINE ROYCE UPHAM
WATTS DRAPER HARRIS HICKOK
HOFFER HYSLOP JAEGER KALLEN
LANGER NOZICK PEIRCE SNIDER
BARRETT CALKINS EMERSON
HOCKING HOWISON LOVEJOY
MARCUSE NEWBOLD CALLAHAN
WILLIAMS ALEXANDER SANTAVANA
SANTAYANA
ARAB AVICENNA
ARABIAN GHAZZALI
AUSTRIAN BUBER EXNER DEUBLER
MEINONG STEINER ZIMMERMANN
RATZENHOFER
BELGIAN MERCIER DELBOEUF
BRAZILIAN MAGALHAES
CANADIAN MURRAY STEWART
SCHURMAN
CHINESE MOTI LAOTZU MENCIUS
CONFUCIUS
CZECH MASARYK SMETANA
DANISH SIBBERN HOFFDING
KIERKEGAARD
DUTCH BOLLAND ERASMUS
HEYMANS SPINOZA OPZOOMER
EGYPTIAN ORIGEN PLOTINUS
ENGLISH AYER CASE JOAD MILL
MORE RYLE WARD BACON BROAD
COTES DUNNE GREEN GROTE
HOOKE HULME JONES LAIRD
LEWES LOCKE MOORE PALEY
STOUT SULLY BAYNES BIDDLE
BUTLER FOWLER GODWIN GURNEY
HOBBES LATHAM MCCABE
NEWTON NORRIS OCKHAM TAYLOR
AINSLIE BALFOUR BENTHAM
BRADLEY COLLIER HALDANE
HARTLEY HERBERT HODGSON
INGELBY JACKSON RUSSELL
SPENCER STEPHEN STEWART
WHEWELL CONGREVE CORNFORD
COURTNEY CUDWORTH GLANVILL
HOBHOUSE MUIRHEAD SCHILLER
SIDGWICK BOSANQUET MACKENZIE
WHITEHEAD CUMBERLAND
HUTCHINSON SHAFTESBURY
FINNISH WESTERMARCK
FRENCH DROZ WEIL ALAIN BAYLE
CAMUS COMTE GUYAU HELLO
JANET LEROY LIARD MABLY RAMUS
REVEL SIMON TAINE BERARD
BONALD COUSIN GILSON GOBLOT
LEROUX MARCEL PASCAL QUESNE
RAYNAL SARTRE VALERY ABAUZIT
ABELARD BARTHEZ BERGSON
BURIDAN CABANIS CHARRON
DAMIRON DIDEROT FOURIER
GERANDO HOLBACH MAISTRE
MILHAUD REYNAUD ROMAINS

ALEMBERT BOURDEAU BOUTROUX
CHARTIER FOUCAULT FOUILLEE
GASSENDI GILLOUIN GOBINEAU
JOUFFROY LAFFITTE MARITAIN
MEYERSON ROUSSEAU TEILHARD
VACHEROT VOLTAIRE BALLANCHE
CONDILLAC CONDORCET
DESCARTES HELVITIUS LACHELIER
SCHWEITZER MONTESQUIEU
LAROMIGUIERE
GERMAN BIEL HAYM KANT KRUG
MARX OKEN PREL BAUER CARUS
COHEN DREWS ENGEL FRIES
GROOS HEGEL LIPPS LOTZE MARBE
MEYER RIEHL STEIN UTITZ WAITZ
WOLFF BENEKE CARNAP CAROVE
EUCKEN FICHTE GABLER GEIGER
GEYSER GRUPPE HEINZE HERDER
JACOBI KRAUSE KRONER LASSON
MAIMON MESSER MULLER PRANTL
RITTER SIMMEL STUMPF ULRICI
ZELLER ZIEHEN BRUCKER BRUNNER
CRUSIUS DEUSSEN DILTHEY
DRIESCH DUHRING ECKHART
ERDMANN FECHNER HAECKEL
HENNING HERBART JUNGIUS
KNUTZEN LASAULX LAZARUS
LEIBNIZ PAULSEN STIRNER STRAUSS
VOLKELT CARRIERE CASSIRER
DROBISCH EBERHARD FORTLAGE
HARTMANN HERTLING LASSWITZ
LEIBNITZ MICHELET MICHELIS
PANNWITZ REINHOLD SPENGLER
AVENARIUS BILFINGER CORNELIUS
DIETERICI EHRENFELS FEUERBACH
GOCLENIUS HEIDEGGER LEISEGANG
NIETZSCHE SCHELLING THOMASIUS
TIEDEMANN VAIHINGER
VORLANDER BAUMGARTEN
HILLEBRAND KEYSERLING
ROSENKRANZ FRAUENSTADT
MENDELSSOHN SCHOPENHAUER
TRENDELENBURG
SCHLEIERMACHER
GREEK BION ZENO CEBES DAMON
LYCON PLATO CRATES EUCLID
PHAEDO PYRRHO STRATO THALES
CRANTOR DEMONAX EUDEMUS
PROCLUS TIMAEUS ALCMAEON
APULEIUS CRATYLUS DIODORUS
DIOGENES EPICURUS MELISSUS
MENIPPUS NUMENIUS PHAEDRUS
PORPHYRY SOCRATES ARCHELAUS
ARISTOTLE CARNEADES
CHARMIDES CLEANTHES
CRITOLAUS DAMASCIUS EPICTETUS
EUBULIDES FAVORINUS HIEROCLES
LEUCIPPUS MENEDEMUS
PANAETIUS PANTAENUS PHILOLAUS
ANAXAGORAS ANAXARCHUS
ANAXIMENES ARCESILAUS
ARISTIPPUS CHRYSIPPUS
DEMOCRITUS EMPEDOCLES
HERACLITUS IAMBLICHUS
METRODORUS PARMENIDES
PHERECYDES POSIDONIUS
PROTAGORAS PYTHAGORAS
SIMPLICIUS SPEUSIPPUS
XENOCRATES XENOPHANES
ANAXIMANDER ANTISTHENES
ARISTOXENUS CLITOMACHUS
DICAEARCHUS CALLISTHENES
PHILOSTRATUS THEOPHRASTUS

HUNGARIAN ERDELYI LAKATOS
INDIAN GHOSE IQBAL
KRISHNAMURTI
IRISH BERNARD ERIGENA BERKELEY
MOLYNEUX
ISRAELI BUBER
ITALIAN NIFO VERA VICO ABANO
BRUNO CONTI CROCE FERRI
ARDIGO FICINO PAPINI VANINI
AQUINAS CANTONI CARDANO
FERRARI FRANCHI GENTILE
MAMIANI TELESIO UBERWEG
GIOBERTI GUARDINI ALGAROTTI
CESALPINO CAMPANELLA
FIORENTINO POMPONAZZI
BONAVENTURA MACHIAVELLI
PICCOLOMINI
JAPANESE SUZUKI
NORWEGIAN MONRAD
POLISH LIBELT WRONSKI
LUTOSLAWSKI
PORTUGUESE ACOSTA
ROMAN CICERO SENECA BOETHIUS
CORNUTUS PLOTINUS AUGUSTINE
LUCRETIUS
RUSSIAN BERDYAEV CHICHERIN
RUSSIAN) PLEKHANOV
SCOTTISH BAIN HOME HUME MILL
REID SETH CAIRD FLINT FRASER
VEITCH FERRIER STEWART
WALLACE BREWSTER FERGUSON
HAMILTON STIRLING HUTCHESON
CALDERWOOD MACKINTOSH
SPANISH VIVES BALMES ORTEGA
SUAREZ UNAMUNO AVERROES
MAIMONIDES
SWEDISH BOSTROM ATTERBOM
SWEDENBORG
SWISS WYSS AMIEL HILTY PREVOST
HABERLIN
PHILOSOPHER'S STONE ADROP
MICROCOSM
PHILOSOPHIC SAGE
PHILOSOPHICAL DEEP
PHILOSOPHY YOGA ETHICS GOSPEL
MAGISM SYSTEM TAOISM
APRISMO COSMISM DUALISM
INQUIRY MIMAMSA SANKHYA
SCEPSIS ACTIVISM HINDUISM
HUMANISM IDENTISM IDEOLOGY
LEGALISM OCCAMISM STOICISM
ABSURDISM NOUMENISM
SOCRATISM VEDANTISM
  (— OF LIFE) LIGHTS
  (NATURAL —) PHYSIC
PHILTER DRUG CHARM WANGA
FILTER POTION AMATORY
PHINEHAS (FATHER OF —) ELI
ELEAZAR
  (GRANDFATHER OF —) AARON
PHINEUS (BROTHER OF —) CADMUS
CEPHEUS
  (FATHER OF —) BELUS AGENOR
  (MOTHER OF —) ANCHINOE
TELEPHASSA
  (SISTER OF —) EUROPA
  (WIFE OF —) IDAEA CLEOPATRA
PHLEBOTOMIZE BLEED VENESECT
PHLEBOTOMUS TATUKIRA
PHLEGM FLEM GLEET MUCUS
WATER FLEUME PITUITE
MOUSEWEB
PHLEGMATIC CALM COOL DULL

SLOW INERT MUCOID SLEEPY
WATERY VISCOUS COMPOSED
SLUGGISH APATHETIC IMPASSIVE
PHLEGYAS (DAUGHTER OF —)
CORONIS
(FATHER OF —) ARES MARS
(MOTHER OF —) CHRYSE
(SLAYER OF —) APOLLO
(SON OF —) IXION
PHLOEM BAST LIBER LEPTOME
PHLOGISTIC FIERY HEATED
BURNING FLAMING
PHLOMIS SAGELEAF
PHLOX CYME FLOX ALBION BEACON
COBAEA
PHOCUS (FATHER OF —) AEACUS
ORNYTION
(HALF-BROTHER OF —) PELEUS
TELAMON
(MOTHER OF —) PSAMATHE
(SON OF —) CRISIUS PANOPEUS
(WIFE OF —) ANTIOPE
PHOEBE FEBE FIVE MOON DIANA
PEWEE ARTEMIS
(BROTHER OF —) CASTOR POLLUX
POLYDEUCES
(DAUGHTER OF —) LETO
(FATHER OF —) URANUS LEUCIPPUS
TYNDAREUS
(MOTHER OF —) GAEA LEDA
(SISTER OF —) HELEN
CLYTEMNESTRA
PHOEBUS SOL SUN APOLLO
PHOIBUS
PHOENICIA (COLONY OF —)
CARTHAGE
(GODDESS OF —) TANIT BALTIS
TANITH ASTARTE
(KING OF —) AGENOR
(TOWN OF —) ACRE TYRE SIDON
SAREPTA
PHOENIX FUM FUNG
(BROTHER OF —) CILIX CADMUS
THASUS PHINEUS
(FATHER OF —) AGENOR AMYNTOR
(MOTHER OF —) CLEOBULE
TELEPHASSA
(PUPIL OF —) ACHILLES
(SISTER OF —) EUROPA
PHOLAS PIDDOCK
PHONE CALL DIAL RING CALLUP
RINGUP
PHONEME MORPH TONEME
LARYNGAL
PHONEMIC BROAD
PHONOGRAM LOGOGRAM
SINOGRAM
PHONOGRAPH VIC PHONO
VICTROLA
(— RECORD) DISK PLATTER
PHONY FAKE JIVE SHAM BOGUS
FAKER FALSE BRUMMY BUNYIP
PHONEY PLASTIC IMPOSTOR
SPURIOUS
PHORONEUS (DAUGHTER OF —)
NIOBE
(FATHER OF —) INACHUS
(MOTHER OF —) MELIA
(SISTER OF —) IO
(SON OF —) APIS IASUS AGENOR
PELASGUS
(WIFE OF —) CERDO LAODICE

PHOSPHATE EHLITE FLOATS
APATITE CABOCLE CACOXENE
GRIPHITE MONAZITE
PHOSPHORESCENCE BRIMING
MARFIRE
PHOSPHORESCENT PHOSPHOR
NOCTILUCOUS
PHOTISM SYNOPSY
PHOTO PIC
(— FINISH) MAT MATT MATTE
(ART —) SEPIA
PHOTOENGRAVER ZINCOGRAPHER
PHOTOENGRAVING HALFTONE
HELIOGRAPH
PHOTOGENE AFTERIMAGE
PHOTOGRAPH MUG PIC FILM LENS
SNAP CARTE IMAGE PANEL PHOTO
PINUP PRINT SHOOT STILL CANDID
GLOSSY MOSAIC RETAKE SCENIC
STEREO AIRVIEW MONTAGE
PICTURE TINTYPE LIKENESS
PORTRAIT POSITIVE SNAPSHOT
TABLETOP CYCLOGRAM
MAMMOGRAM
(— OF RENAL EXCRETION)
RENOGRAM
(— SIZE) PANEL
(X-RAY —) SKIAGRAM
(PL.) PIX
PHOTOGRAPHER PHOTOG
LENSMAN CAMERIST CAMERAMAN
PAPARAZZO SHUTTERBUG
PHOTOGRAPHY STEREO CALOTYPE
PHOTOGENY
(— SESSION) SHOOT
(KIND OF —) KIRLIAN
PHOTOMETER LUCIMETER
PHOTOMONTAGE COLLAGE
PHOTON BOSON TROLAND
PHRASE CRY HIT MOT SET CRIB
FUSS HAVE IDEA TERM WORD
COMMA COUCH IDIOM LABEL
LEMMA POINT STATE STYLE TOPIC
TROPE BYWORD CLAUSE CLICHE
DITTON DORISM GRUPPO HOBNOB
NOTION PNEUMA PRAISE SAVING
SLOGAN ATTACCO DICTION
EPITHET PASSAGE CONCEIVE
DIVISION DORICISM FLATTERY
IDEOGRAM IRISHISM LATINISM
LEITMOTIV
(— DIFFERENTLY) TURN
(— UNCTUOUSLY) DROOL
(CANT —) SHIBBOLETH
(JAZZ —) RIFF
(MUSICAL —) RIFF POINT ATTACCO
SUBJECT
(PET —) SHIBBOLETH
(PITHY —) LACONISM LACONICISM
(REDUNDANT —) CHEVILLE
(STOCK —) CANT
(TRITE —) CLICHE
(WELL-TURNED —) STROKE
PHRASEOLOGY CANT STYLE
DIALECT DICTION WORDING
LOCUTION PARLANCE
PHRATRY CLAN
PHRENETIC PYTHIAN FRENETIC
PHRENIC MENTAL
(PL.) PSYCHOLOGY
PHRIXOS (FATHER OF —) ATHAMUS
(MOTHER OF —) NEPHELE
(SISTER OF —) HELLE

PHRONTIS (BROTHER OF —) ARGUS
MELAS CYTISSORUS
(FATHER OF —) PHRIXUS
(HUSBAND OF —) PANTHOUS
(MOTHER OF —) CHALCIOPE
(SON OF —) EUPHORBUS
HYPERENOR POLYDAMAS
PHRYGIA (GOD OF —) ATYS ATTIS
SABAZIOS
(KING OF —) MIDAS
PHRYNIN BUFIDIN
PHTHISIS DECAY
PHUVAH (FATHER OF —) ISSACHAR
PHYLACTERY FILACTERY
(PL.) TEFILLIN TEPHILLIN
PHYLE TRIBE
PHYLLO FILO
PHYLOMACHE (DAUGHTER OF —)
ALCESTIS
(FATHER OF —) AMPHION
(HUSBAND OF —) PELIAS
(SON OF —) ACASTUS
PHYLUM HOKA CLASS HOKAN
NADENE BRYOZOA ANNELATA
ANNELIDA CHORDATA DIVISION
LIGNOSAE PORIFERA
PHYMA TUMOR
PHYSALIS POP POPPER TOMATILLO
PHYSETER CATODON
PHYSIC CURE HEAL FISIC PURGE
TRADE REMEDY MEDICAL
NATURAL RELIEVE DRUGGERY
PHYSICAL ILL LUSTY SOMAL
BODILY CARNAL DISTAL NATURAL
SOMATIC CORPORAL CURATIVE
EXTERNAL MATERIAL CORPOREAL
(PURELY —) BRUTE
PHYSICIAN ASA DOC PILL CURER
GALEN HAKIM LEECH MEDIC
QUACK ARTIST BAIDYA DOCTOR
FELLOW HEALER INTERN MEDICO
DOTTORE EMPIRIC SURGEON
ALIENIST RESIDENT SAWBONES
SUNDOWNER
(— OF GODS) PAEAN
(— OF THE GODS) PAEAN
(PREF.) IATRO JATEO JATO
(SUFF.) IATRIST
AMERICAN ILG LEE RAY BARD COIT
DICK DREW FITZ HARE HOLT KING
LUST MUDD PARK ROCK ROUS SALK
SIMS APGAR APPEL BIGGS BRILL
BRUSH CABOT COHEN CROHN
DRAKE FLINT GOLER GUION KNOPF
KOLFF LILLY LOEWI LOGAN MARAT
MINOT SMITH SPOCK TONER TULLY
TYSON WHITE BARKER BATTEY
BENNET BROOKS CARTER CLARKE
DEVITA ENDERS FISHER FOSTER
GESELL GORGAS GORRIE HEISER
HOOKER HORNER HOSACK JACOBI
JARVIK JOSLIN KEELEY KNIGHT
KOPITS LAZEAR MILLER MIRKIN
MORGAN MORROW MURPHY
ODWYER PARRAN PINCUS SCHICK
STILES STILLE STORER STRONG
TILTON WALKER WATSON WELLER
ALVAREZ CAMMANN CHAPMAN
DARLING DICKSON FRANCIS
GERHARD GILBERT HAGGARD
HEPBURN HOPKINS JACKSON
JANEWAY ROBBINS TROLAND
TRUDEAU WHIPPLE BARTLETT

BILLINGS BOYLSTON CHANNING
FISHBEIN GUERNSEY GWATHMEY
HAMILTON KIRTLAND KNOWLTON
MITCHELL PETERSON RICHARDS
ROCKWELL SHATTUCK SPALDING
TOWNSEND WOODWARD
BLACKWELL BRAZELTON
STERNBERG CLENDENING
GOLDBERGER STEPHENSON
WATERHOUSE ZAKRZEWSKA
CASTIGLIONI WIGGLESWORTH
ARAB AVICENNA ABDALLATIF
ARGENTINIAN BUNGE
AUSTRIAN BARANY BREUER
MESMER OPPOLZER ENNEMOSER
ROKITANSKY
BELGIAN WIER HEYMANS
BRAZILIAN CHAGAS KUBITSCHEK
CANADIAN CRAIK DAFOE FISET
GRANT OSLER REEVE WIGLE
ASHTON MCCRAE BANTING
RODDICK SHULMAN DRUMMOND
GRENFELL MACPHAIL
CZECH VANCURRA
DANISH GRAM WORM LANGE
FINSEN BARTHOLIN
DUTCH GRAAF EIJKMAN
BOERHAAVE INGENHOUSZ
ENGLISH BUDD DALE GOOD HAKE
HALL HUME MEAD PAVY ROSS
SNOW BARRY BRUCE CAIUS DOVER
DOYLE DRAKE FLUDD JAMES JONES
JURIN LOWER PAGET ACLAND
BRIGHT BROWNE CLARKE DARWIN
DOBELL FLOREY GARROD HARVEY
HAVERS HORDER HUNTER JENNER
MANSON PARKES RINGER SLOANE
TREVES WILLIS ADDISON ALLBUTT
BENNETT CHAPMAN CONOLLY
COPLAND DEARDEN FALKNER
GLISSON HODGKIN LINACRE
NABARRO PRINGLE SIMPSON
SKINNER STANTON STEPTOE
WHARTON ANDERSON ANDREWES
BARNARDO BASHFORD BIRKBECK
BUCHANAN CULPEPER GRENFELL
HEBERDEN PRICHARD SYDENHAM
ARBUTHNOT BLACKMORE
BROADBENT LANKESTER RADCLIFFE
FOTHERGILL SUMMERSKILL
FRENCH SUE CLOT DENIS DUPRE
HAYEM PINEL ROGET WIDAL
ANDRAL ASTRUC AUZOUX BERARD
FERNEL LEPINE LITTRE MARTIN
NIEPCE PLANTE VAQUEZ BAILLON
BECHAMP CHARCOT DAVAINE
DUMERIL GRASSET LAENNEC
LAVERAN LEBOYER LECLUSE
MANTOUX MENIERE NICOLLE
PECQUET QUESNAY VINCENT
BOUCHARD DUCHENNE LANDOUZY
LEVADITI BOUILLAUD BROUSSALS
GUILLOTIN LAMETTRIE BAILLARGER
BRETONNEAU CASSEGRAIN
LANCEREAUX POISEUILLE
SCHWEITZER BROUSSONETT
NOSTRADAMUS
GERMAN ERB BINZ EBEL GALL
KOCH MUCH REIL ZINN BLOCH
CARUS FAUST FRANK LINGG OSANN
REMAK BRUCKE CORDUS DOBLIN
DOMAGK KERNER KORTUM LEYDEN
MEIBOM NORDAU OERTEL OLBERS

PEUCER AGRIPPA BASEDOW BERENDT JASPERS KAMPFER NEISSER BRUNFELS ERXLEBEN FLEMMING HARTMANN HOFFMANN HUFELAND ZIEMSSEN DOLLINGER FORSSMANN HAHNEMANN NICOLAIER NOTHNAGEL SCHONLEIN DETTWEILER FRIEDREICH LANGERHANS WASSERMANN **GREEK** GALEN RUFUS AETIOS CTESIAS SORANUS ALCMAEON DEMOCEDES ORIBASIUS PRAXAGORAS ASCLEPIADES DIOSCORIDES HIPPOCRATES ERASISTRATUS PAPANICOLAOU **IRISH** JOYCE STOKES GOGARTY SIGERSON **ITALIAN** REDI BOTTA GOLGI ASELLI FARINI MAZZEI DAGLIVI BELLINI CARDANO GALVANI BACCELLI LOMBROSO SCALIGER BLANDRATA CESALPINO FRACASTORO MONTESSORI TOSCANELLI VALLISNIERI **NORWEGIAN** HANSEN **PARAGUAYAN** BARBERO **PORTUGUESE** EGAS **RUMANIAN** BABES **RUSSIAN** DAHL VERESAEY VORONOFF **SALVADORAN** MOLINA **SCOTTISH** LIND MOIR BLANE BROWN ARNOTT BRIDIE BUCHAN CHEYNE CULLEN FERGUS FORBES MANSON BRUNTON CANTLIE JAMESON MACLEOD SIMPSON GRAINGER ARBUTHNOT ARMSTRONG PITCAIRNE CHRISTISON MACALISTER RUTHERFORD ABERCROMBIE **SPANISH** CHANCA NEGRIN SERVETUS **SWEDISH** BARANY MUNTHE ZANDER ACHARIUS **SWISS** GOLL HESS AMMAN PEYER KOCHER ROLLIER ZWINGER PARACELSUS **VENEZUELAN** VARGAS **PHYSICIST** HYLOZOIST **AMERICAN** CHU AMES CREW GUNN GUTH HALL HESS HULL IVES KAHN LAMB LAND LANE MORE PAGE RABI ROOD ROSA TING TUVE WOOD YANG ZINN ALTER BACHE BARUS BAUER BETHE BLOCH BOLEY COHEN DUANE EWELL FERMI FITCH HENRY KARLE KUSCH LEMON LYMAN MAYER PUPIN SEGRE STERN SWANN YALOW BEDELL BRIGGS CONDON COOPER CRONIN FRANCK GERMER GLASER KARMAN LOOMIS MAIMAN MORLEY NIPHER PIERCE SLOANE TELLER TOLMAN TOWNES VARIAN WIGNER WRIGHT ALLISON ALVAREZ BABCOCK BARDEEN BURGESS CARHART COMPTON FEYNMAN GLASHOW GODDARD GODLOVE LECONTE NICHOLS PENZIAS PURCELL RANDALL RENWIEK RICHTER ROWLAND SZILARD WHEELER ANDERSON BLODGETT BRATTAIN BRIDGMAN

DAVISSON EINSTEIN HASTINGS HAUPTMAN LAWRENCE MILLIKAN SHOCKLEY STRATTON THOMPSON VANALLEN VANVLECK WINTHROP ZWORYKIN BITTINGER GOODSPEED HUMPHREYS INGERSOLL LAURITSEN MICHELSON RAINWATER SCHWINGER HOFSTADTER MENDENHALL RENTSCHLER RUTHERFURD SCHRIEFFER TROWBRIDGE CHAMBERLAIN OPPENHEIMER **ARGENTINIAN** CERNUSCHI **AUSTRIAN** HESS MACH RABI DOPPLER MEITNER PRECHTL BOLTZMANN SCHRODINGER SCHROEDINGER **BELGIAN** PLATEAU **CANADIAN** TORY HILLIER DEMPSTER HERZBERG **DANISH** BOHR OERSTED MOTTELSON **DUTCH** WAALS ZEEMAN HUYGENS LORENTZ ZERNIKE HARTSOEKER KAMERLINGH VANDERMEER MUSSCHENBROEK **ENGLISH** EVE BORN LAMB LEES MOTT ASTON BOYLE BRAGG DEWAR DIRAC DYSON FUCHS GROVE JEANS JOULE LODGE NICOL SALAM AITKEN BARKLA CANTON DALTON DARWIN FRISCH KELVIN STOKES ANDRADE BARRETT BULLARD CROOKES DANIELL FARADAY FLEMING GILBERT GUTHRIE HARTREE MICHELL MOSELEY SIEMENS THOMSON TYNDALL APPLETON BLACKETT CHADWICK HAUKSBEE POYNTING RAYLEIGH SCHUSTER STURGEON CALLENDAR CAVENDISH COCKCROFT HEAVISIDE JOSEPHSON GLAZEBROOK RICHARDSON RUTHERFORD WHEATSTONE **FRENCH** BIOT HIRN NEEL ARAGO CORNU FABRY JAMIN MALUS PAPIN PETIT PITOT WEISS BRANLY CARNOT CLAUDE COTTON DULONG FIZEAU FORTIN JOLIOT NIEPCE NOLLET PERRIN RAOULT SAVART VIOLLE BABINET BEUDANT BLONDEL BROGLIE CHARLES COULOMB FIZERAU FOURIER FRESNEL JOUBERT KASTLER MASCART PELTIER REAUMUR SAUVEUR AMONTONS ARSONVAL DESPRETZ FOUCAULT LANGEVIN LIPPMANN MARIOTTE POUILLET REGNAULT BECQUEREL BRILLOUIN CAILLETET GUILLAUME LISSAJOUS CHARDONNET **GERMAN** MIE OHM BORN DOVE KORN LAUE LENZ REIS WIEN BETHE BOTHE BRAUN BUDDE DEBYE ERMAN HERTZ HOLTZ JOLLY KUNDT MAYER STARK VOIGT WEBER BALMER ELSTER GEIGER HANKEL JENSEN KOENIG LAMONT LENARD LUMMER MAGNUS NERNST PLANCK RIECKE RITTER ZEUNER AEPINUS BEDNORZ BRODHUN CHLADNI FECHNER GEHRCKE HITTORF LAMBERT NEUMANN PLUCKER

PRANDTL QUINCKE REGENER RUDOLPH SCAEFER SEEBECK TOEPLER WULLNER CLAUSIUS EINSTEIN GUERICKE ROENTGEN SCHUMANN FEDDERSEN GOLDSTEIN HALLWACHS KIRCHHOFF MOSSBAUER SCHEIBLER STEINHEIL WIEDEMANN BARKHAUSEN FAHRENHEIT KOHLRAUSCH PRINGSHEIM SCHWEIGGER SIEDENTOPF SOMMERFELD LICHTENBERG **GREEK** CTESIBIUS **HUNGARIAN** WIGNER **INDIAN** BOSE SAHA RAMAN **IRISH** JOLLY KELVIN STONEY WALTON ANDREWS TOWNSEND FITZGERALD **ITALIAN** RIIS FERMI PORTA RIGHI VOLTA ALDINI NOBILI RUBBIA BORELLI CAVALLO GALILEI GALVANI MELLONI VENTURI AVOGADRO BECCARIA BELTRAMI BLASERNA FERRARIS GRIMALDI PALMIERI BOSCOVICH PACINOTTI TORRICELLI **JAPANESE** ESAKI YUKAWA TOMONAGA **NORWEGIAN** GIAEVER BJERKNES HANGSTEEN **POLISH** INFELD WROBLEWSKI **RUSSIAN** TAMM BASOV FRANK LANDAU KAPITZA LEBEDEV SAKHAROV CHERENKOV PROKHOROV **SCOTTISH** KERR TAIT WATT BLACK DEWAR EWING NOBLE WILSON MAXWELL RANKINE STEWART BREWSTER **SWEDISH** EDLEN ALFVEN EDLUND NILSON ANGSTROM SIEGBAHN ARRHENIUS BENEDICKS **SWISS** WILD BLOCH EULER PAULI ARGAND LARIVE PICTET MUELLER PICCARD PREVOST ALLAMAND **WELSH** GROVE **PHYSIC NUT** TUBA CURCAS PIGNON TARTAGO **PHYSICS (— PARTICLE)** QUARK **PHYSIOCRAT** ECONOMIST **PHYSIOGNOMY** MUG FACE PHIZ VIZNOMY PORTRAIT VISENOMY **PHYSIOLOGIST AMERICAN** IVY KEYS LUSK HOUGH CANNON DALTON GASSER HARVEY HOWELL CARLSON SCHALLY COURNAND ECKSTEIN ERLANGER HARTLINE MEYERHOF GUILLEMIN HENDERSON OSTERHOUT **ARGENTINIAN** HOUSSAY **AUSTRALIAN** ECCLES **AUSTRIAN** STEINACH **BELGIAN** HEYMANS **CANADIAN** BEST **CZECH** PURKINJE **DANISH** KROGH **DUTCH** DONDERS EINTHOVEN **ENGLISH** DALE HILL KATZ BEALE HALES LOWER ADRIAN DARWIN FOSTER HUXLEY RIVERS WALLER BAYLISS EDWARDS HERRING HODGKIN BARCROFT MARSHALL STARLING ELLIOTSON SHERRINGTON

FINNISH GRANIT **FRENCH** BERT MAREY RICHET BEAUNIS BERNARD FLOURENS MAGENDIE DUTROCHET POISEUILLE **GERMAN** FICK VOIT BUDGE GOLTZ KUHNE REMAK WUNDT HENSEN HERING LUDWIG MULLER PREYER WAGNER BEHRING BURDACH PFLUGER SCHWANN VERWORN WARBURG MEISSNER MEYERHOF VALENTIN HELMHOLTZ BLUMENBACH HEIDENHAIN **ITALIAN** BOVET MOSSO MANTEGAZZA **RUSSIAN** CYON PAVLOV **SCOTTISH** HALDANE MACLEOD **SWEDISH** EULER GRANIT HOLMGREN **SWISS** HESS **PHYSIOLOGY** BIONOMY ZOONOMY **PHYSIOTHERAPY** PATTERNING **PHYSIQUE** BODY BUILD COOST HABIT FIGURE STRENGTH **PHYSOCARPUS** NEILLIA OPULASTER **PHYSOSTIGMINE** ESERE ESERINE **PHYTOMER** PHYTON PODIUM **PI** JUMBLE CONFUSE PREACHY CONFUSION **PIA** PI GABI GABGAB MARMOT **PIACLE** SIN CRIME GUILT OFFENSE **PIAN** YAWS FRAMBESIA **PIANETTE** PYNOT PIANINO **PIANFORTE** CEMBALO **PIANIST** CEMBALIST CLAVIERIST **PIANO** SOFT FLOOR GRAND GRANT STORY FLUGEL GENTLY SOFTLY SPINET SQUARE CLAVIAL CLAVIER GIRAFFE PIANOLA QUIETLY UPRIGHT MELOTROPE **(— SOFTENING PEDAL)** CELESTE **(AFRICAN —)** KALIMBA **(KIND OF —)** THUMB **(PART OF —)** ARM KEY LEG LID DESK FALL HEEL LYRE PROP CHEEK PEDAL STRING KEYSLIP KEYBOARD **(STYLE OF JAZZ —)** STRIDE **(THUMB —)** KALIMBA **PIASSAVA** IYO JARA BAHIA PIACABA **PIASTER** KURUS **PIATTI** CYMBALS **PIAZZA** PORCH SQUARE BALCONY GALLERY PORTICO VERANDA PIAZZETTA **PIC** PEAK LANCE PHOTO PIQUE PICADOR **PICA** M EM LINE **PICARD** PYKAR **PICARO** KNAVE ROGUE TRAMP BOHEMIAN VAGABOND **PICAROON** ROGUE PICARO PIRATE CORSAIR WRECKER **PICAYUNE** PIC PETTY MEASLY PALTRY TRIVIAL PISTAREEN **PICCADILL** RABATA REBATE REBATO **PICCOLO** BUSBOY JUKEBOX FLAUTINO OTTAVINO **PICHICIAGO** ARMADILLO CHLAMYPHORE **PICK** NAP NIB OPT BILL CULL GAFF HACK LIFT PIKE PILK SHOT WALE

ADORN BEELE BREAK CAVIL ELECT FLANG LEASE PILCH PLUCK PRIDE PRIME CHOICE CHOOSE GATHER PICKAX PUDDLE TWITCH BARGAIN CASCROM DIAMOND DRESSER MANDREL
(— APART) TOW
(— KNOTS FROM) BURL
(— OUT) CULL SPOT TAKE WELE CRONE GLEAN GARBLE SELECT
(— POCKETS) FIG FILE FOIST TOUCH
(— TOBACCO) STRIP
(— UP) SHARK
(FILLING —) ABB

PICKAX PIX BEDE BILL PIKE GURLET TUBBER TWIBIL TWIBILL

PICKED PICK TRIM PIKED CHOSEN DAINTY PEAKED SELECT ADORNED POINTED
(PREF.) LECTO

PICKER COD HOPPER
(BERRY —) HURTER
(PEA —) VINER

PICKEREL JACK SNAKE DUNLIN SAUGER SLINKER WALLEYE

PICKERELWEED TULE WAMPEE

PICKER-UP FINDER

PICKET PEG PALE POST TERN FENCE STAKE FASTEN PALING TETHER ENCLOSE FORTIFY OUTPOST PICQUET PALISADE OUTPICKET

PICKLE BOX ALEC BIND DILL MESS PECK ACHAR BRINE GRAIN MANGO SAUCE SOUSE ATSARA CAPERS DAWDLE HIGDON KERNEL KIMCHI MUDDLE NIBBLE PIDDLE PILFER PLIGHT TRIFLE CONDITE CONFECT GHERKIN TROUBLE VITRIOL MARINADE
(FISH —) ALEC

PICKLED DRUNK OILED UNSOBER MURIATED POWDERED MARINATED

PICKLOCK LOCK PICKER

PICK-ME-UP TONIC BRACER SCREW PICKUP

PICKPOCKET DIP FIG GUN NIP BUNG FILE WIRE DIVER FILER FOIST BULKER BUZZER CANNON DIPPER FIGBOY HOOKER NIPPER RATERO FOISTER MOBSMAN CLYFAKER CUTPURSE KNUCKLER BUZZGLOAK
(HELPER OF —) STALL BULKER

PICKUP BRUSH TRUCK ARREST BRACER ANACRUSIS

PICKWICK PAPERS (AUTHOR OF —) DICKENS
(CHARACTER IN —) BOB SAM MARY ALLEN EMILY TRACY ALFRED HUNTER JINGLE PERKER SAWYER TUPMAN WARDLE WELLER WINKLE BARDELL RACHAEL SLAMMER ARABELLA AUGUSTUS CLUPPINS ISABELLA PICKWICK NATHANIEL SMORLTORK SNODGRASS

PICNIC FRY BALL GIPSY GYPSY BURGOO FROLIC JUNKET MAROON OUTING SHOULDER SQUANTUM SUMMERING WAYZGOOSE
(PRINTERS' —) WAYGOOSE WAYZGOOSE

PICOT LOOP PEARL PERLE

PICOTAH SWEEP PACOTA

PICTOGRAPH GLYPH PICTOGRAM

PICTORIAL GRAPHIC

PICTURE GAY MAP OIL COPY DAUB ICON IKON LIMN SIGN VIEW DECAL FRAME IMAGE LINER PAINT PHOTO PIECE PINAX PRINT SCENE SHAPE STAMP STORY TABLE CACHET CANVAS CHROMO CUTOUT DEPICT EMBLEM MARINE PASTEL SEMBLE SHADOW STEREO TABLET CUTAWAY DIORAMA DIPTYCH EMBLEMA ETCHING EXHIBIT FASHION FEATURE GOUACHE GRAPHIC HISTORY MIZRACH PAYSAGE PORTRAY PORTURE RETRAIT SCENERY TABLEAU VANDYKE AIRSCAPE AUTOTYPE DESCRIBE DROLLERY ENVISION IDEOGRAM KAKEMONO LANDSKIP LIKENESS MAKIMONO MONOTINT OVERDOOR PAINTING PANORAMA PORTRAIT PROSPECT RITRATTO SEASCAPE SINGERIE SKYSCAPE TRIPTYCH VIGNETTE ENCAUSTIC
(— IN BOOK) GAY
(— IN 3 COMPARTMENTS) TRIPTYCH
(— MAT) SPANDREL
(— OF MONKEYS) SINGERIE
(— ON ROLLER) KAKEMONO MAKIMONO
(— PUZZLE) REBUS JIGSAW
(—S IN BOOKS) BABY
(— WOVEN IN SILK) STEVENGRAPH
(COMIC —) DROLLERY
(RELIGIOUS —) TANKA
(STEREOSCOPIC —) ANAGLYPH
(THREE-DIMENSIONAL —) HOLOGRAM
(PREF.) PINAC(O)

PICTURE OF DORIAN GRAY (AUTHOR OF —) WILDE
(CHARACTER IN —) ALAN GRAY VANE BASIL HENRY JAMES SIBYL DORIAN WOTTON CAMPBELL HALLWARD

PICTURESQUE VIVID EXOTIC QUAINT SCENIC GRAPHIC IDYLLIC ROMANTIC PICTORIAL

PICUL TAN PICO PIKOL

PIDDLE PICK PLAY DAWDLE PICKLE PUTTER TRIFLE

PIDDLING JERK MEASLY PALTRY TRIVIAL USELESS FOOTLING TRIFLING JERKWATER

PIDDOCK DACTYL PHOLAD PHOLAS

PIDGIN LANGUAGE SABIR

PIE PAI FLAM FLAN HEAP MESS PATE PILE TART DOWDY FLAWN PASTY PATTY TORTA TOURT AFFAIR BRIDLE CHEWET MAGPIE PASTRY TOURTE COBBLER SMASHER STRUDEL BAKEMEAT CRUSTADE FLAPJACK PANDOWDY SURPRISE TURNOVER SMASHOVER
(CUSTARD —) QUICHE
(GREEK —) SPANAKOPITA SPANOKAPITA SPANAKOPITTA
(MEAT —) FLOATER
(MINCE —) SHREDPIE
(PL.) BAKEMEAT

PIEBALD PIE PIED PIET MIXED PIETY PINTO CALICO MOTLEY SKEWBALD

PIECE BAT BIT COB CUT DAM FIG JOB LAB LOG MAN TUT GIRL MIND PART PISE PLAY BLYPE DAGON DRAMA DWANG FLOOR PEZZO SCRAP SHARD SHERD SHRED SLICE SNODE STECK STUCK THROW COLLOP FARDEL FUGATO GOBBET PARCEL STITCH CANTLET EXAMPLE FLINDER FLITTER MORCEAU OPINION PICTURE PORTION SEGMENT DUOLOGUE EMBOLIUM FANDANGO PAINTING
(— AT END) HEELPIECE
(— FOR TWO) DUET DUOLOGUE
(— IN CHECKERS) DAM
(— IN ORGAN) THUMPER
(— LEFT) STUB
(— OF ARMOR) JAMB JAMBE
(— OF BAD LUCK) DIRDUM
(— OF BLANKET) DAGON
(— OF BLUBBER) BIBLE
(— OF CLOTH) REMNANT
(— OF DECEPTION) BEGUNK
(— OF DECORATED METAL) NIELLO
(— OF EIGHT) PIASTRE
(— OF FALSE HAIR) JANE
(— OF FIBER) NOIL
(— OF FIRED CLAY) TILE
(— OF FOOD) MORSEL
(— OF GOOD FORTUNE) GODSEND
(— OF GROUND SURROUNDED BY WASTE) HOPE
(— OF HARD WOOD) MOOT
(— OF LAND) ERF HAM LOT BUTT GORE PANE PARK PLOT CROFT LEASE PATCH SPONG SQUAT ESTATE GARDEN HUERTA RINCON SECTION CLEARAGE METAIRIE PROPERTY SOLIDATE PENINSULA
(— OF LIGHT ORDNANCE) ASPIC
(— OF LINEN) AMIT AMICE
(— OF LOG) SLAB
(— OF MAST) TONGUE
(— OF MATZOTH) AFIKOMEN
(— OF MEAT) EYE HEEL RAND COLLOP EPIGRAM
(— OF METAL) JAG COIN JAGG SPRAG
(— OF MISCHIEF) LARK
(— OF MONEY) COG SOU SHINER
(— OF NEEDLEWORK) SAMPLER
(— OF NEWS) NOVEL
(— OF NONSENSE) FUDGE TRIMTRAM
(— OF ORE) CHAT
(— OF PROPERTY) CHOSE SUBJECT
(— OF SAIL) HULLOCK
(— OF SCENERY) FLAT
(— OF SEPARATED LAND) BUTT
(— OF SKIN) BLYPE
(— OF SKIN FOR GLOVE) TRANK
(— OF SLATE) SLAT
(— OF SOAP) BALL
(— OF SOMETHING EDIBLE) STULL
(— OF TIMBER) FISH COULISSE FOREHOOK
(— OF TOAST) SLINGER
(— OF TOBACCO) FIG
(— OF TRACK) LEAD RUNBY
(— OF TRICKERY) CROOK CANTRIP

(— OF TURF) FLAG DIVOT SCRAW SHIRREL
(— OF WOOD) KIP LATH APRON BOARD CHUMP CHUNK PLANK SPOON WADDY BILLET COMMON STOWER TIMBER LIPPING
(— OF WORK) JOB CHAR TURN
(— OF WRITING) SCREED SCREEVE
(— OUT) EKE
(—S OF MACARONI) DITALI DITALINI
(— SPLIT OFF) SPLINT
(— TO PREVENT SLIPPING) CLEAT
(ARTILLERY —) DRAKE SAKER LANTACA
(BACKGAMMON —) BLOT STONE
(BROAD —) SHEET
(BROKEN —) BRACK MAMMOCK FRACTION
(BUTTING —) HURTER
(CHESS —) PIN KING PAWN ROOK QUEEN BISHOP CASTLE KNIGHT OFFICER
(DRAMATIC —) SKIT
(DREAMY —) REVERIE
(END — OF BUCKET) CANT
(FLAT —) FLAP FLAKE
(FUR —) PALATINE
(GOLD —) SLUG TALI
(IN —S) LIMBMEAL
(IRREGULAR —) SNAG
(KIND OF —) PERIOD
(LARDED — OF MEAT) DAUB
(LARGE —) HUNK MOLE STULL DOLLOP
(LEFT-OVER —) SCRAP
(LITERARY —) CAMEO
(LITTLE —) STNEKI SCANTLING
(LONG —) STRIP
(MAH JONGG —) TILE
(MISCELLANEOUS —S) ODDS
(MOVABLE — IN VIOLIN BOW) NUT
(MUSICAL —) ITEM CHORO DANCE ETUDE CHASER LESSON ALLEGRO ANDANTE BLUETTE CANZONA CANZONE CONCERTO DUOLOGUE ENTRACTE OVERTURE PASTORAL RHAPSODY BAGATELLE INVENTION DIVERTIMENTO
(NARROW —) LABEL STAVE STRIP
(ODD — OF CARPENTRY) DUTCHMAN
(PIANO —) NOVELETTE
(PROJECTING —) TANG
(ROTATING —) CAM ROTOR SPINDLE
(SAMPLE —) SWATCH
(SHAPELESS —) DUMP MAMMOCK
(SIDE —) RIB JAMB JAMBE
(SINGLE —) LENGTH
(SLENDER —) SPILL SLIVER
(SMALL —) BIT BOB NOB PEA CHIP SNIP TATE CRUMB PATCH PRILL SCRAP SPECK MORSEL SIPPET DRIBLET FLITTER PALLION SPLINTER
(SMALL — OF FLESH) GIGOT
(SMALL — OF WOOD) KIP
(SMALL —S) MATCHWOOD
(STRENGTHENING —) DWANG HURTER
(TAPERING —) GORE GUSSET
(THICK —) JUNK HUNCH
(THIN —) SHIM FLAKE SHIVE SLICE

(WEDGESHAPED — OF WOOD) GLUT SHIM
(100-REAL GOLD —) ISABELLA
(25-CENT —) CUTER
(4-DOLLAR GOLD —) STELLA
(PL.) MATERIAL NOBLEMEN
PIECEWORK SETWORK TUTWORK TASKWORK
PIECEWORKER JOBBER
PIECRUST BREAD COFFIN ABAISSE
PIED PINTO SHELD MAGPIED PIEBALD
PIED ANTELOPE BONTEBOK
PIEDFORT PATAGON
PIED WAGTAIL COB COBB PEER PILE PILLAR WAGGIE WASHER WATERIE SEEDBIRD WASHDISH WASHTAIL
PIEPLANT RHUBARB RHAPONTIC
PIER COB ANTA BELT COBB DOCK MOLE PILE QUAY TILT GROIN JETTY JOWEL JUTTY LEVEE STILT WHARF BRIDGE BUNDER MULLION STAGION PIEDROIT STELLING
(— CAP) SUMMER
(HALF —) RESPONSE
PIERCE CUT DAB DAG DEG DIG JAB JAG RIT BARB BEAR BITE BORE BROB BROD CLOY DART DIRL GORE HOLE HOOK LACE LACK PASS PINK POKE PROB PROG RIVE ROVE STAB STOB TAME TANG WHIP BREAK DRIFT DRILL ENTER GOUGE GRIDE LANCE PERCH PITCH POACH PREEN PROBE PRONG SHEAR SNICK SPEAR SPIKE STEEK STICK STING THIRL ATTAME BROACH CLEAVE DAGGER EMPALE FICCHE GIMLET IMPALE LAUNCH PRITCH RIDDLE SEARCH SKEWER STITCH STRIKE THRILL THRING THRUST WIMBLE ASSAGAI JAVELIN ENTHRILL LACERATE PUNCTURE PENETRATE
(PREF.) FORAMINI
PIERCED AJOURE CRIBRAL PERTUSE CRIBROSE PERFORATE
PIERCING SHY FELL HIGH KEEN LOUD TART ACUTE CLEAR EAGLE SHARP SNELL ARROWY BITTER BORING SHREWD SHRILL SNITHE SNITHY CUTTING GIMLETY POINTED PUNGENT DRILLING INCISIVE PERCEANT POIGNANT POUNCING STABBING STICKING PENETRATIVE
PIERHEAD MOLEHEAD
PIET PYOT DIPPER MAGPIE
PIETIST LABADIST
PIETISTIC DEVOUT
PIETY HONOR LOYALTY PIETISM DEVOTION SANCTION GODLINESS
PIFFLE BUFF FOLDEROL
PIG (ALSO SEE HOG, SWINE) COW FAR HAM HOG SLIP SLOB BACON BONAV BROCK CHEAT CHUCK GRICE INGOT PIGGY SHOAT APEREA BONHAM COCHON FARROW GUSSIE HOGGIE PORKET PORKIN SUCKER TITMAN WEANER BONNIVE GLUTTON GRUMPHY HOGLING PIGLING ROOKLER GRUNTING

(— OUT) GORGE
(BROOD OF —S) TEAM
(CASTRATED —) BARROW
(CASTRATED MALE —) BARROW
(EIGHT —S) FODDER
(FEMALE —) SOW
(MALE —) BOAR
(PART OF —) EAR EYE HAM BUTT HOCK JOWL LOIN POLL TAIL TEAT FLANK SNOUT PICNIC FATBACK FOREFOOT SHOULDER SPARERIB TENDERLOIN
(SMALLEST — OF LITTER) DOLL TITMAN ANTHONY DILLING TANTANY TANTONY
(SUCKLING —) ROASTER
(UNDERSIZED —) RUNT TITMAN TEATMAN
(YOUNG —) ELT FAR SLIP GRICE GURRY
(YOUNG—) SHOAT SHOTE
(YOUNG —) BONEEN BONHAM SQUEAKER
(YOUNG FEMALE —) GILT
(PREF.) HYO
(SUFF.) CHOERUS
PIG DEER BABIRUSA
PIGEON DOO NUN OWL TOY BARB CLAY DOVE JACK KING KITE LUPE RUFF RUNT SPOT BALDY DOWVE FRILL HOMER KOKLA PIPER SQUAB WONGA CULTER CULVER CUSHAT DODLET DRAGON FEEDER HELMET JEWING MAGPIE MANUMA MAUMET MODENA POUTER PRIEST ROCKER SHAKER TRERON TURBIT TURNER WATTLE ANTWERP CARNEAU CARRIER CROPPER FANTAIL FINIKIN JACINTH JACOBIN MALTESE PINTADO SWALLOW TIPPLER TUMBLER BALDHEAD CAPUCHIN FINIKING HORSEMAN MANUTAGI RINGDOVE SASSOROL SQUABBER SQUEAKER SQUEALER FRILLBACK TOOTHBILL
(CLAY —) BIRD GYROPIGEON
(FLIGHTLESS —) SOLITAIRE
(STOOL —) PIG NARK
(YOUNG —) SQUAB
PIGEON BLOOD GARNET
PIGEON HAWK MERLIN
PIGEONHOLE BOX SLOT LABEL SHELVE ANALYZE CELLULE CLASSIFY CUBBYHOLE
(PL.) STOCK
PIGEON HOUSE COT DOOKET DOVECOT COLUMBARY
PIGEON PEA DAL TUR TARE ARHAR DAHIL GANDUL TURNER TURNOR CATJANG
PIGEON WOODPECKER FLICKER
PIGGERY PIGS PIGSTY HOGGERY POTTERY SWINERY CROCKERY
PIGGIE TOE
PIGGIN HANDY PIPKIN
PIGHEADED WILLFUL PERVERSE STUBBORN OBSTINATE
PIGHTLE PIKLE PICKLE PIDDLE PIGTAIL
PIG IRON GRUNDY
PIGLET PORKLING
PIGLIKE SUIFORM SUILINE SWINISH

PIGMENT (ALSO SEE DYE, COLOR) BLUE HEME BROWN COLOR EARTH GREEN HUMIN MORIN MUMMY PAINT STAIN TONER BRONZE CEROID CERUSE IDAEIN LITHOL MALVIN ORANGE PURPLE SIENNA VIOLET BEZETTA GOUACHE PAINTRY PUCCOON STAINER TURACIN ALTHAEIN COLORANT EXTENDER GOSSYPOL MELANOID PAINTURE TINCTURE UROPHEIN VERDITER
(— FOR WOODWORK) KOKOWAI
(— IN BUTTERFLY WING) PTERIN
(BLACK —) ABAISER MELANIN
(BLUE —) BICE SMALT CYANIN ALTHEIN CERULEUM MARENNIN
(BLUE-GREEN —) LEUCOCYAN
(BROWN —) MUMMY SEPIA UMBER BISTER FUSCIN ASTERIN SINOPIA
(BROWNISH-YELLOW —) SIENNA
(GRAPE —) ENIN OENIN
(GREEN —) VERDITER
(MADDER-ROOT —) RUBIATE
(ORANGE-RED —) REALGAR
(PLANT —) CYANIN
(RED —) HAEM LAKE ARUMIN PATISE SANDYX AMATITO KOKOWAI PUCCOON SCARLET SINOPIA CARCUMIN URORUBIN URRHODIN VERMILION
(RED-VIOLET —) TURACIN
(WHITE —) CERUSE ANATASE LITHOPONE
(YELLOW —) MORIN FLAVIN PURREE ETIOLIN FISETIN GAMBOGE PUCCOON CAROTENE DIATOMIN GALANGIN GENTISIN MASSICOT ORPIMENT UROBILIN
(PREF.) CHROM(AT)(ATO)(I)(IDIO)(O)
PIGMENTATION COLOR LENTIL ARGYRIA LENTIGO JAUNDICE NIGRITIES
(SKIN —) ARGYRIA
(SUFF.) CHROMIA
PIGNUS PAWN PLEDGE
PIGNUT ARNOT ARNUT HOGNUT
PIGS' FEET CRUBEEN PETTITOES
PIGSKIN SADDLE FOOTBALL
PIGSNEY EYE DARLING
PIGSTY FRANK CRUIVE HOGCOTE HOGGERY PIGGERY SWINESTY
PIGTAIL BRAID PLAIT QUEUE COLETA
PIGWASH SWILL
PIGWEED QUINOA BEETROOT CARELESS GOOSEFOOT
PIK DRA PICKI PICKL ENDAZE ENDASEH
PIKA CONY HAIR HARE LEPORID LAGOMORPH
PIKE GED DORE DORY GADE GEDD JACK LUCE TANG TOUG TUCK HAKED LUCET SNAKE SNOOK STING VOUGE SALMON SAUGER JAVELIN WALLEYE BLOWFISH GLASSEYE JACKFISH NORTHERN PARTISAN PICKEREL POULAINE TURNPIKE MUSKELLUNGE
PIKELET CRUMPET
PIKEMAN PIKE WATTLEBOY
PIKE PERCH FOGASH PERCID SANDER SAUGER ZANDER

PIKER TRAMP VAGRANT TELLTALE TIGHTWAD VAGABOND
PILASTER ANTA PIER RIDGE ALETTE ALLETTE RESPOND TELAMON
PILCHARD FUMADO ALEWIFE SARDINE MENHADEN
PILCORN OAT
PILDASH (FATHER OF —) NAHOR
(MOTHER OF —) MILCAH
PILE COP FUR LOT NAP PIE TIP BALE BANK BING BULK BUNG BURR COCK DASS DECK DESS DOWN HACK HAIR HEAP LEET LOAD PEEL PIER POLE POOK PYRE REEK RUCK SESS SHAG SPUD AMASS CANCH CLAMP CROWD FAGOT POINT SPILE SPIRE STACK STILT TOWER CASTLE FAGGOT FENDER FILLER GALGAL PILLAR RICKLE RUCKLE FORTUNE JAVELIN PYRAMID REACTOR SPINDLE CROWBILL INCREASE SANDPILE
(— CROSSWISE) COB
(— CURD) CHEDDAR
(— OF BRICKS) HACK CLAMP
(— OF CLOTH) LAY
(— OF HAY) RICK SHOCK DOODLE HAYCOCK HAYRICK
(— OF ICE) HUMMOCK
(— OF LOGS) DECK
(— OF PLATES) BUNG
(— OF REFUSE) DUSTHEAP
(— OF SALT FISH) BULK
(— OF SEALSKINS) PAN
(— OF SHEAVES) SESS
(— OF SHEETS) LIFT
(— OF STONES) ISLAND STONAGE WARLOCK
(— OF TOBACCO) BULK
(— OF WOOD) STRAND
(— TO BE BURNT) PYRE
(— UP) BIG BULK CORD RICK COMPILE ACCUMULATE
(— WHEAT SHOCKS) STITCH
(IRON —) SPINDLE
(LITTLE —) HOT HOTT
(LOOSE —) RICKLE
(ROCK —) HOODOO
(SMALL —) COCK CANCH
(PL.) FIG DRIFT
PILEA ADICEA
PILEATED WOODPECKER LOGCOCK WOODCOCK
PILE DRIVER TUP FISTUCA HERCULES IMPACTER
(— DOLLY) FOLLOWER
(— WEIGHT) RAM TUP MONKEY
PILEUS CAP MITRA PILEOLUS
PILEWORT CRAIN CRANE FICARY FIGWORT CELANDINE
PILFER NIM NIP ROB CRIB HOOK PALM PELF PICK PILK PRIG SMUG SNIG FILCH MICHE MOOCH PILCH PROWL SHARP SLOCK STEAL SWIPE FINGER MAGPIE MOOTCH NIBBLE PICKLE SMOUCH SNITCH CABBAGE MANAVEL PLUNDER PURLOIN SNAFFLE UNHITCH PETTIFOG SCROUNGE
PILFERER PRIG PIKER TAKER SLOCKER FINGERER SLOCKSTER
PILFERING CRIB MICHING PICKING THIEVISH

PILGRIM HADJ HAJI HADJI HAJJI PALMER PELERIN PEREGRIN WAYFARER
(MUSLIM —) HADJ
PILGRIMAGE TRIP TURUS VOYAGE JOURNEY
(— TO MECCA) HADJ
(BRETON —) PARDON
PILGRIM BROWN FRIAR
PILGRIM'S PROGRESS (AUTHOR OF —) BUNYAN
(CHARACTER IN —) POPE PAGAN PIETY SLOTH PLIANT SIMPLE CHARITY DESPAIR HOPEFUL SINCERE APOLLYON FAITHFUL GOODWILL PRUDENCE WATCHFUL CHRISTIAN FORMALISM HYPOCRISY IGNORANCE KNOWLEDGE OBSTINATE DISCRETION EVANGELIST EXPERIENCE PRESUMPTION
(LAND IN —) BEULAH
PILING SPILING STOCKADE
(PL.) STARLING
PILL PIL ROB BALL BARK GOLI PEEL POOL CREEK CACHOU EXTORT TABLET UNHAIR DESPOIL DIURNAL GLOBULE GRANULE PARVULE PILLULE PREFORM BASEBALL GOOFBALL BLACKBALL CIGARETTE
(AROMATIC —) CACHOU
(LARGE —) BALL BOLUS
(LITTLE —) PILULA PILULE
(SLEEPING —) GOOFBALL
(SMALL —) MICRODOT
PILLAGE LOOT PEEL PILL PREY SACK BOOTY FORAY HARRY REAVE RIFLE SPOIL HARROW MARAUD PICORY RAPINE RAVAGE DESPOIL PICKEER PLUNDER RANSACK ROBBERY BOOTHALE EXPILATE PURCHASE SPOLIATE DEVASTATE
PILLAGER PEELER PILLER ROBBER SACKER SPOILER SNAPHANCE
PILLAGING EXECUTION PREDATORY
PILLAR COG HERM JAMB PACK PIER PILE POST PROP STUD TERM JAMBE NEWEL SHAFT STELA STELE STOCK STONE STOOP STUMP CIPPUS COLUMN HERMES PILLER STAPLE BEDPOST DEADMAN TRESTLE TRUMEAU BOUNDARY MASSEBAH PEDESTAL RESPONSE STANCHION
(— CAPPED WITH SLAB) BILITH
(— IN LARGE DOORWAY) TRUMEAU
(— IN MINE) STOOK STUMP
(— OF COAL) SPURN STOOK STOOP
(—S OF HERCULES) ABILA CALPE
(— SUPPORTING ARCH) RESPONSE
(— SURMOUNTED BY HEAD) HERMES
(BUDDHIST —) LAT
(CHANGED TO —) OLENUS
(EARTH —) HOODOO
(MAN-LIKE —) TELAMON
(ROCK —) STACK GENDARME
(SACRED —) ASHERAH
(SEMITE —) MASSEBAH
(STONE —) CIPPUS
(TEMPORARY —) DEADMAN
(UPRIGHT —) STANDARD
(4-SIDED —) OBELISK

(PL.) CRURA
(PREF.) CION(O) STELO STYL(I)(O)
(SUFF.) STELE STYLAR STYLE STYLI(C) STYLOUS
PILLARIST STYLITE
PILLAS PILCORN PILKINS
PILLBOX SCATULA
PILLBUG ISOPOD KEESLIP MILLEPED PILLWORM CHEESELIP
PILLED BALD SHAVEN TONSURED
PILLION PAD PILLOW SADDLE CUSHION
PILLORY CANG THEW JOUGS TRONE CANGUE CRUCIFY HALSFANG
PILLOW COD BOTT DAWN PEEL PILE REST FLOAT WANGER BOLSTER CUSHION FUSTIAN HEADING OREILLER PULVINAR
(PREF.) PULVILLI PULVINI
PILLOWCASE COD BEAR PILL SHAM PILLIVER
PILLOWY PULVINAR
PILM DUST
PILON BONUS LAGNIAPPE
PILOSE HAIRY HIRSUTE PILEOUS
PILOT ACE SPY JOCK KIWI COACH GUARD GUIDE STEER AIRMAN ESCORT MANAGE THAMUS AVIATOR CAPTAIN CONDUCT HOBBLER LODEMAN SHIPMAN WINGMAN AIREDALE GOVERNOR HELMSMAN NAVIGATE NAVIGATOR PALINURUS WHEELSMAN COWCATCHER
(AUTHOR OF —) COOPER
(AUTOMATIC —) GEORGE
(CHARACTER IN —) TOM GRAY ALICE JONES MERRY COFFIN DILLON EDWARD HOWARD MANUAL MUNSON CECILIA PLOWDEN RICHARD GRIFFITH DUNSCOMBE KATHERINE BARNSTABLE CHRISTOPHER BORROUGHCLIFFE
(DUD —) PRUNE
(UNLICENSED —) HOBBLER
PILOT BIRD PLOVER
PILOT FISH ROMERO JACKFISH AMBERFISH
PILOTHOUSE TEXAS CHARTHOUSE CONNINGTOWER
PILUM PESTLE JAVELIN
PIMENTA MYRTAL
PIMENTO PIMENTA ALLSPICE PIMIENTO
PIMP MACK BULLY CADET FAGOT PONCE SNEAK MACRIO PANDER MACKMAN RUFFIAN INFORMER PROCURER PURVEYOR SCOUNDREL SOUTENEUR
PIMPERNEL BURNET WAYWORT EYEBRIGHT MARGELINE WINCOPIPE
PIMPLE GUM NOB PAP WEN ZIT BURL KNOB PUSH QUAT SPOT BLAIN BOTCH HICKY PLOOK PLOUK PLUKE WHELK BLOTCH BOUTON BUTTON PAPULA PAPULE TETTER BUBUKLE PUSTULE PIMGENET WHEYWORM
(— ON NOSE) RUMBUD
(PREF.) CHALAZI CHALAZO PAPULI PAPULO

PIN FID FIX HOB HUB LAG LEG NOG PEG PEN ACUS APEX AXLE BANK BOLT LILL MOOD PEEN POST PRIN PROP PYNE RUNG STUD DRIFT HUMOR KAYLE POINT PREEN SPILL THOLE BOBBIN BODKIN BROACH BROOCH CALIGO COTTER CURLER FASTEN HATPIN JOGGLE NORMAN PINNET SKEWER SPIGOT TEMPER TENPIN TOGGEL TONGUE TRIFLE BAYONET CONFINE ENCLOSE GUDGEON HAIRPIN IMPOUND LOCKPIN PUSHPIN SPINDLE TAMPION TANGENT TUMBLER WOOLDER FORELOCK PINNACLE
(— FOR FITTING PLANKS) SETBOLT
(— IN AXLETREE) LINCHPIN
(— IN RIFLE) TIGE
(— OF DIAL) STYLE GNOMON
(— OF LANTERN PINION) RUNDLE
(— OF WATCH) DART
(— ON CLAVICHORD KEY) TANGENT
(— TO HOLD BEDCLOTHES) BEDSTAFF
(— USED AS TARGET) HOB
(BELAYING —) CAVIL
(BOWLING —) DUCKPIN HEADPIN KINGPIN SLEEPER
(BOWLING —S) DEADWOOD
(CARPENTRY —) DOWEL
(COUPLING —) DRAWBOLT
(ENGAGING —) BAYONET
(HAIR —) BARRETTE
(HEADED —) RIVET
(JEWELED —) PROP
(NECKTIE —) TIETAC TIETACK
(OAR —) THOLE
(ORNAMENTAL —) AGLET AIGLET
(PIVOT —) PINTLE
(SMALL —) LILL MINIKIN MICROPIN
(SPLIT —) COTTER FORELOCK
(SURVEYOR'S —) ARROW
(TAPERED —) DRIFT
(TIRLING —) RISP
(WOODEN —) DOWEL SPILE TRENAIL
(PL.) LEGS KAILS DEADWOOD
(PREF.) PERONEO PERONO
PINACOID BASE HEMIDOME
PINAFORE BRAT SLIP TIDE TIDY TIER TYER DAIDLY PINNER SAVEALL SLIPPER GABERDINE
PINBALL BAGATELLE
PINBALL MACHINE PACHINKO
PINCASE POPPET
PINCE-NEZ NIPPER LORGNON NOSEPINCH
PINCER CLAW
PINCERS TEU TEW CLAM CHELA TUARN PLIERS TURKIS WYNRIS FORCEPS MULLETS NIPPERS PINCHER PINSONS TWEEZERS
PINCH NAB NIP TAD TOP VEX WRY BITE CLAM HURT POOK PUSH STOP TAIT TATE TUCK CHACK CRIMP GRIPE HINCH PUGIL SNUFF SQUAT STEAL STINT TAPER THEFT TWEAK WRING ARREST CLUTCH COLLAR EXTORT HARASS NARROW SNITCH STRAIT STRESS TWITCH SCRINCH SQUEEZE JUNCTURE PRESSURE SHORTAGE STRAITEN VELLICATE

(— OF SNUFF) SNEESH SNEESHIN
(— WITH COLD) NIRL
(— WITH HUNGER) CLAM CLEM
PINCHBECK SHAM CHEAP SPURIOUS PRETENDED
PINCHED CHITTY WASTED HAGGARD PUNGLED SQUINCH
PINCHING CHACK
PINCHPENNY CARL MISER NIGGARD NIGGARDLY
PINDARIC ODE WILD
PINE IE ARA LIM ACHE CHIL CHIR FADE FLAG HALA HONE IEIE KAIL WANT AGGAG DROOP DWAIN GRIEF KAURI MATAI MATSU MOURN OCOTE PINON THUJA WANZE WEARY WRIST YEARN APACHE AROLLA DUSTER FAMINE GRIEVE HUNGER LAMENT PANDAN SHRINK SORROW STARVE TOATOA TORFEL WITHER CYPRESS DAISING DWINDLE FORPINE FOXTAIL JEFFREY LAUHALA TARWOOD TORMENT TORTURE AKAMATSU AUSTRIAN GALAGALA LANGUISH LOBLOLLY LONGLEAF PINASTER STAGHORN TANEKAHA VANQUISH
(— AWAY) PEAK DROOP DWINE SNURP WANZE WINDER FORPINE MACERATE
(AUSTRALIAN —) BEEFWOOD
(GROUND —) FOXTAIL
(KIND OF —) MUGHO JEFFREY
(PITCH —) THYME
(PREF.) PINI PITYO
PINEAPPLE BOMB NANA PINA PINO PITA ANANA ANANAS ABACAXI GRENADE
PINE FINCH SISKIN
PINE MARTEN SABLE
PINE NEEDLE SHAT SPILL PINING ALFILARIA
(PL.) TWINKLES
PINE TREE STATE MAINE
PINFEATHER PEN STUMP STIPULE
PINFISH CHUB SPOT JIMMY PORGY SARGO
PINFOLD POUND
PING KNOCK
PING-PONG SHIFT BOUNCE
PINGRASS ALFILERIA
PINGUIN MAYA ANANAS AGUAMAS PINUELA HUIPILLA
PINGUITUDE FATNESS OBESITY OILINESS
PINING SICK LANGUOR HOMESICK LOVELORN
PINION NOIL WING PINON QUILL PENNON SARCEL SECURE LANTERN PINACLE SHACKLE TRUNDLE FLIGHTER WALLOWER
PINION WHEEL MOBILE
PINITOL SENNITE MATEZITE
PINK JAG PIP CYME DAWN DECK FADE MICE PING STAB WINK ADORN BLINK CORAL ELITE MOVED SWELL WOUND AURORE BISQUE CHERUB FIESTA HEIGHT MINNOW POUNCE SHRIMP SILENE TATTOO ZEPHYR ANNATTO ARBUTUS BEGONIA BERMUDA BLOSSOM CAMPION EXTREME

PARAGON REVEREE SANDUST TUSSORE CONFETTI COQUETTE DECORATE DIANTHUS GILLIVER LIMEWORT RADIANCE RECAMIER
PINKED JAGGED
PINKIE PIRLIE
PINKROOT REDROOT WORMWEED STARBLOOM
PINNA EAR EARFLAP PINNULE APHLEBIA AURICULA PAVILION
PINNACE BARK CROWN WOMAN BARQUE PINNAGE MISTRESS
PINNACLE IT PIN TOP ACME APEX CREST CROWN IDEAL SERAC SPIRE THUMB FINIAL HEIGHT SUMMIT GENDARME
  (ICE —) SERAC
  (ROCKY —) TOR HOODOO AIGUILLE GENDARME
PINNATE WINGED
PINNER PINDER FLANDAN STICKER
PINNIPED SEAL
PINNULE FIN
PINOCHLE BINOCLE GOULASH AIRPLANE
  (— SCORE) MELD
PINPILLOW PIMPLO
PINPOINT ISOLATE
  (— OF LIGHT) GLEAM
PINT O GULL PINNET SWIGGER OCTARIUS
  (FOURTH —) GILL JACK
  (HALF —) CUP NIP GILL JACK CUPFUL NIPPERKIN
  (9-10THS —) MUTCHKIN
PINTADO CERO PIED SIER SEARER SIERRA SPOTTED KINGFISH
PINTAIL DUCK SMEE SPIKE SPRIG GROUSE SMETHE CRACKER LADYBIRD LONGNECK PIKETAIL
PINTANO PILOT COCKEYE CHIRIVITA
PINTID EMPEINE
PINTO PAINT
PINTO BEAN ROSILLO
PINUP CHEESECAKE
PINWEED
  (PL.) LECHEA
PINWHEEL WINDMILL
PINWORM NEMA OXYURID
PIN WRENCH SPANULE
PINZA EZIO
PION MESON
PIONEER BLAZE GUIDE MINER GROPER HALUTZ SETTLE CHALUTZ EXPLORE EARLIEST EMIGRANT ORIGINAL RAWHIDER VOORTREKKER
PIONEERS (AUTHOR OF —) COOPER
  (CHARACTER IN —) JOHN GRANT HIRAM JONES NATTY BUMPPO LOUISA OLIVER TEMPLE EDWARDS RICHARD DOOLITTLE EFFINGHAM ELIZABETH CHINGACHGOOK
PIOUS PI HOLY WISE FROOM GODLY MORAL SEELY DEVOUT DIVINE INWARD PIETIC CANTING DUTIFUL GODDARD PITEOUS SAINTED SAINTLY FAITHFUL REVERENT RELIGIOUS
PIP DIE CHIP ECHO KILL PAIP PEEP SEED SPOT SPECK ACINUS DEFEAT PIPPIN BLACKBALL
PIPAL BO FIG

PIPE TD BIN GUN HUB TAP TEE BONG BUTT CALL CANE DALE DRIP DUCT FLUE HOSE LINE MAIN MUTE PULE REED TILE TUBE WEEP WORM BLAST BRAIL BRIAR BRIER CANAL CANEL CINCH CRANE CROSS CUTTY HOOKA PROBE PUNGI QUILL RIDER RISER SPOUT STAND STRAW TEWEL TRUMP TRUNK VOICE BRANCH BURROW CALEAN CASING DUCTUS DUDEEN FAUCET FILLER GEWGAW HEWGAW HOGGER HOOKAH KINURA NIPPLE NOTICE NOZZLE OFFLET OFFSET POOGYE RANKET SLEEVE SLOUCH SLUICE SUCKER TROWEL TUBULE TUNNEL UPTAKE WEEPER CHANNEL CHANTER CHIBOUK CONDUIT DUCTURE FISTULA HYDRANT SERVICE SPARGER SPINDLE SUCTION TALLBOY TWEEDLE WHISTLE CALIDUCT DOWNTAKE GALOUBET LAMPHOLE MIRLITON NARGHILE NARGILEH PENSTOCK SEMIDOLE SUSPIRAL TELLTALE THRIBBLE
  (— AS NAVIGATION AID) SPINDLE
  (— BENDER) HICKEY
  (— BOWL) STUMMEL
  (— FOR CONDUCTING WATER) LEADER
  (— JOINT) TURNOUT
  (— OF ORE) BUNNY
  (— OF PAN) SYRINX
  (— OF QUEEN BEE) TEET
  (— ON BAGPIPE) DRONE CHANTER
  (— SUPPORT) CRADLE
  (— TAB) TACK
  (— TO MUFFLE TRUMPET) SORDINE
  (— USED IN WELL) STRING
  (— WITH SOCKET ENDS) HUB
  (BOWL AND STEM OF —) STUMMEL
  (CEREMONIAL —) CALUMET
  (CLAMMING —) BRAIL
  (CLEAN A —) REAM
  (CONNECTING —) HOGGER
  (FLUE —) LABIAL
  (HEATING —) CALIDUCT
  (IRISH —) DUDEEN
  (KIND OF —) UILLEANN
  (MUSICAL —) BODY GEWGAW FISTULA SORDINE HORNPIPE SCHWEGEL
  (OATEN —) OAT
  (ORGAN —) FLUE KINURA LABIAL ERZAHLER SCHWEGEL TREMOLANT
  (ORGAN —S) MONTRE
  (PART OF —) BIT BOWL STEM SHANK SHAPE SADDLE MOUTHPIECE
  (PEACE —) CALUMET
  (PROJECTING —) BRACKET
  (RESIDUE IN OPIUM —) YENSHGEE
  (SEWER —) SLANT
  (SHEPHERD'S —) REED LARIGOT CHALUMEAU
  (SNAKE-CHARMER'S —) PUNGI
  (TOBACCO —) GUN CLAY BRIAR BRIER CUTTY HOOKA STRAW CALEAN DUDEEN HOOKAH BULLDOG CHIBOUK CHILLUM CORNCOB BILLIARD CALABASH MEERSCHAUM

  (TOY —) HEWGAG
  (VERTICAL —) STACK LAMPHOLE
  (WATER — FOR ENGINE) SLOUCH
  (4 LENGTHS OF —) FOURBLE
  (PREF.) AUL(O) SIPHON(O) SOLEN(O) SYRING(O) TUBI TUBO TUBULI TUBULO
PIPECLAY CAM CALM CAUM
PIPED DRUNK JETTED
PIPEFISH EARL LONGJAW NEEDLEFISH
PIPELAYER YARNER
PIPESTEM STOPPEL STOPPLE
PIPETTE PIPET TASTER
PIPEWORT HATPIN WOOLWEED
PIPING HOSE SOFT VERY CRYING ROULEAU WAILING WEEPING TRANQUIL
PIPING CROW CASSICAN FLUTEBIRD
PIPIRI PITIRRI
PIPISTRELLE BAT NOCTULE
PIPIT PEEP TEETAN WEKEEN CHEEPER SKYLARK TIETICK TITLARK TITLING WAGTAIL LINGBIRD TWITLARK
PIPPIN PIP APPLE PEPPIN RIBSTON
PIPSISSEWA EVERGREEN WINTERGREEN
PIQUANCY SALT ZEST JUICE FLAVOR GINGER TARTNESS
PIQUANT BOLD RACY JUICY NUTTY SALTY SHARP SPICY TASTY ZESTY LIVELY SEVERE CUTTING PEPPERY PUNGENT POIGNANT STINGING
  (SHARPLY —) ZINGY
PIQUE FRET GOAD PEAK PICK PIKE PYKE TICK ANNOY PRISE SNUFF SPITE STING HARASS MALICE NETTLE PRITCH STRUNT CHIGGER OFFENSE PROVOKE UMBRAGE IRRITATE MARCELLA
PIRACY CAPTURE PIRATISM
PIRAGUA CANOE DUGOUT PIROGUE PETTIAGUA
PIRANHA PIRAI CARIBE PIRAYA
PIRARUCU PAICHE ARAPAIMA
PIRATE CAPER ROVER ROBBER VIKING CATERAN CORSAIR PICKEER SCUMMER ALGERINE MAROONER PICAROON BUCCANEER SALLEEMAN
  (— FLAG) ROGER BLACKJACK
PIRENE (FATHER OF —) ASOPUS ACHELOUS
  (MOTHER OF —) METOPE
  (SON OF —) CENCHRIAS
PIRIPIRI BIRK BIRCH MAPAN
PIRL SPIN TWINE TWIST REVOLVE
PIRN QUILL BOBBIN PIRNIE SPINDLE
PIROGUE CANOE PERIOQUE
PIROPLASM BABESIA
PIROSHKI PIROGEN
PIROUETTE TURN
PISCINA POOL TANK BASIN SACRARY LAVATORY SACRARIUM
PISE CAJON PISAY
PISHOGUE CHARM SPELL SORCERY WITCHERY
PISMIRE ANT EMMET
PISOLITE PEASTONE
PISTACHIO FISTIC PISTICK

PISTIL CHIVE CARPEL UMBONE POINTEL
  (PL.) GYNECIUM
  (PREF.) GYN(AE)(AEO)(E)(EO)(O) GYNAECO GYNANDRO GYNECO
  (SUFF.) GYN
PISTILLATE FEMALE
PISTOL DAG GAT GUN POP ROD BULL COLT DAGG IRON TACK FLUTE RIFLE STICK BARKER BUFFER BULDER BULLER CANNON DRAGON HEATER POTGUN RIFLE ROSCOE BULLDOG DUNGEON SHOOTER TICKLER DERINGER PETRONEL REPORTER REVOLVER PEPPERBOX
  (TOY —) SPARKLER
PISTON BUCKET FORCER PALLET SUCKER EMBOLUS PLUNGER
  (— HUB) SPIDER
PIT PET POT PUT BURY CIST DELF DELL DISC DISK FOSS HELL HOLE KHUD KIST LAKE MINE PLAY PUTT SEED SILO SINK SUMP SWAG TURN WEEM WELL ABYSM ABYSS CRYPT DELFT DITCH FOSSA FOVEA FROST GRAVE LEACH MATCH PITCH PORUS SLACK SLUIG TREAD AREOLE BORROW BUNKER KERNEL OPPOSE RADDLE WALLOW ABADDON ALVEOLA AMPULLA BOTHROS CHARPIT FOSSULA FOXHOLE HANDLER LATRINE MEGARON PINHOLE VARIOLE WINNING CESSPOOL CYPHELLA DOWNFALL FAVEOLUS FENESTRA POCKMARK PUNCTULE WELLHOLE
  (— FOR BAKING) IMU UMU
  (— FOR OFFERINGS) BOTHROS
  (— OF STOMACH) MARK WIND ANTICARDIUM
  (— OF THEATER) GROUND PARTERRE
  (— ON COCKROACH HEAD) FENESTRA
  (— ON LICHENS) LACUNA CYPHELLA
  (— SACRED TO DEMETER) MEGARON
  (AUTHOR OF —) NORRIS
  (BITTER —) STIPPEN
  (BOTTOMLESS —) ABYSS ABADDON BARATHRUM
  (CHARACTER IN —) PAGE WESS LAURA CURTIS GRETRY JADWIN SHELDON CORTHELL CRESSLER DEARBORN
  (COAL —) HEUCH HEUGH WINNING
  (COOKING —) IMU
  (FODDER —) SILO
  (MAORI —) RUA
  (MIRY —) SLUIG
  (RIFLE —) SANGAR
  (ROOFED —) CIST KIST
  (SALT —) VAT PEZOGRAPH
  (SAND —) BUNKER
  (SMALL —) AREOLE LACUNA STAPLE
  (TANNING —) LIME LAYER LEACH HANDLER LAYAWAY SUSPENDER
  (PREF.) BOTHR(I)(IO)(O) FOVEI
PITA PITO YUCCA ARGHAN

PITCH GO DIP FIT KEY LAB MEL PIC TAR BUCK CANT CHAT CODE COOK DING FALL FORK HURL PECK PICK PLUG RAKE TELL TONE TOSS ABODE BOOST BUNCH CHUCK FLING LABOR LURCH PLANT SLENT SLOPE SPIEL THROW TWIRL BINDER CAREEN DIRECT ENCAMP FILLER LENGTH MALTHA MANJAK PLUNGE SQUARE TOTTER TUMBLE VOLLEY WICKET CURRENT NARRATE ALKITRAN OVERHANG
(**— AT A MARK**) LAG
(**— FROM FIR TREES**) ALKITRAN
(**— INSIDE**) JAM
(**— INTO TROUGH OF SEA**) SEND
(**— OF BIRD OF PREY**) PLACE
(**— OF HELIX**) JAW
(**— TENT**) TELD
(**— TENTS**) CAMP
(**ABOVE —**) SHARP
(**AUCTION —**) SETBACK
(**BASEBALL —**) CURVE STRIKE CRIPPLE SPITTER FADEAWAY KNUCKLER SPITBALL BRUSHBACK
(**BELOW —**) FLAT
(**COBBLER'S —**) CODE
(**FULL —**) VOLLEY
(**GLANCE —**) MANJAK MANJACK
(**HIGH —**) BLOOPER
(**HIGHEST —**) PRIDE
(**IDENTITY IN —**) UNISON
(**MINERAL —**) BITUMEN
(**PREF.**) MISERI
PITCH APPLE COPEI CUPAY
PITCHBLENDE CLEVEITE
PITCHED SET
(PREF.) (**— BELOW BASS**) CONTRA
PITCHER JUG JACK OLLA PILL PRIG BUIRE CROCK CRUET GALON GORGE GOTCH AFTABA CROUKE GALLON HURLER POURIE STRAIN URCEUS CANETTE CHUCKER FLINGER GROWLER STARTER STOPPER TWIRLER URCEOLE AIGUIERE ASCIDIUM OENOCHOE SOUTHPAW MOUNDSMAN
(**— AND CATCHER**) BATTERY
(**— FOR BEER**) GROWLER
(**— OF ORCHID**) BUCKET
(**— SHAPED LIKE MAN**) TOBY
(**— WITH ONE HANDLE**) URCEUS
(**BULGING —**) GOTCH
(**EARTHEN —**) GEORG GORGE
(**KIND OF —**) RELIEF
(**RELIEF —**) FIREMAN
(**RELIEF —S**) BULLPEN
(**REMOVE — FROM BASEBALL GAME**) DERRICK
(**WIDEMOUTHED —**) EWER
PITCHER PLANT BISCUIT FLYTRAP FEVERCUP FOXGLOVE WATERCUP NEPENTHES SKUNKWEED
PITCHFORK EVIL PICK PIKE PICKEL SHEPPECK PITCHPIKE
(**THATCHER'S —**) GROOM
(**PL.**) HARD
PITCHHOLE CAHOT
PITCHMAN VENDER SALESMAN
PITCH PINE THYME
PITCH PIPE TUNER EPITONION
PITCHSTONE RETINITE

PITCHY BLACK
PITEOUS MEAN PALTRY PITIFUL MERCIFUL MOURNFUL PIERCING
PITFALL PIT FALL TRAP SNARE DANGER TRAPFALL
PITH JET PUT SAP CORE GIST MEAT PULP PUTT SOLA HEART VIGOR ENERGY KERNEL MARROW ESSENCE EXTRACT MEDULLA NUCLEUS PAPYRUS STRENGTH
(**PREF.**) MEDULLI METR(O) PULPE PULPI PULPO
PITH HELMET TOPI TOPEE
PITHINESS BREVITY
PITHON (FATHER OF —) MICAH
PITH TREE AMBATCH
PITHY CRISP MEATY SAPPY TERSE STRONG CONCISE LACONIC MARROWY SUCCINCT
PITIABLE SAD POOR SEELY WOFUL RUEFUL WOEFUL FORLORN PITIFUL
PITIFUL MEAN MEEK RUTH SILLY SORRY PALTRY RUEFUL TENDER HANGDOG RUESOME RUTHFUL MERCIFUL PATHETIC
PITILESS GRIM CRUEL STERN STONY BRASSY SAVAGE RUTHLESS UNPITIED MERCILESS
PITMAN GEORDIE
PITTANCE BIT ALMS DOLE GIFT MITE SONG TRIFLE BEQUEST
PITTED FOVEATE OPPOSED PUNCTATE ALVEOLATE
PITTER STONER
PITTHEUS (DAUGHTER OF —) AETHRA
(**FATHER OF —**) PELOPS
(**PUPIL OF —**) THESEUS
PITURI BEDGERY PITCHERY
PIT VIPER- MOCCASIN
PITY RUE ACHE MEAN MOAN PETE PITE RUTH MERCY PIETY REIVE SCATH BEMOAN PATHOS MERCIFY REMORSE WAESUCK CLEMENCY SYMPATHY COMPASSION
PIVOT TOE AXIS CRUX SLEW SLUE TURN HEART HINGE CENTER SLOUGH WORDLE GUDGEON TRAVERSE TRUNNION
PIVOTAL KEY POLAR CENTRAL TROCHOID
(**— POINT**) KNUCKLE
PIVOTING DISHRAG
PIVOTMAN CENTER
PIVOT STAND PEDESTAL
PIXILATED DAFT DAFFY DOTTY DRUNK FLAKY KOOKY PIXIE BEMUSED PUCKISH TOUCHED CONFUSED WHIMSICAL
PIXY ELF FAIRY PYGMY ROGUE IMPISH RASCAL SPRITE PUCKISH ROGUISH
PIZE OATH PISE CURSE
PLACABLE WEAK QUIET PACABLE PEACEFUL YIELDING FORGIVING
PLACARD BILL POST TITLE POSTER TICKET AFFICHE REDLINE STOMACHER
PLACATE CALM GENTLE PACIFY PLEASE SOOTHE APPEASE FORGIVE

PLACE L DO BIT FIX PUT SET AREA HOLE LIEU PLAT PLOT POSE POST RANK ROOM SEAT SITE SITU SPOT STEL STEP STOW TEXT VICE YARK BEING ESTER ESTRE HOUSE JOINT LOCUS PLAZA POINT POSIT SCENE SITUS STALL STATE STEAD STELL STOUR WHERE BESTOW CHARGE GROUND IMPOSE INVEST LAYOUT LOCALE LOCATE OFFICE POSSIE RECKON ROOMTH ALLODGE ARRANGE DEPOSIT KITCHEN STATION ABDITORY ALLOCATE DIGGINGS EMPORIUM LOCATION POSITION
(**— ALONE**) ISOLATE
(**— ALTERNATELY**) STAGGER
(**— APART**) ENISLE
(**— BEFORE**) APPOSE PREFIX
(**— BETWEEN**) INTERPOSE
(**— BY FORCE**) PILT
(**— CROSSWISE**) THWART
(**— DEDICATED TO GOD**) TEMENOS
(**— EXACTLY**) PINPOINT
(**— FISH IN SALTING BIN**) KENCH
(**— FOR CATTLE**) CAMP
(**— FOR DUMPING RUBBISH**) SHOOT
(**— FOR GAMES**) GYMKHANA
(**— FOR HAWKING**) RIVER
(**— FOR MILKING**) LOAN
(**— FOR MILKING COWS**) LOAN
(**— FOR MORTAR AND BRICK**) FROG
(**— FOR PHEASANTS**) STEW
(**— FOR PRAYERS**) IDGAH
(**— FOR RABBITS**) WARREN
(**— FOR RECEPTION**) RECEIPT
(**— FOR RUBBISH DEPOSITS**) LAYSTALL
(**— FOR SEETHING**) STEW
(**— FOR SLEEPING**) BED BUNK DOSS FLOP LAIR LIBKIN
(**— FOR STROLLING**) PROMENADE
(**— FOR TORTURE**) CATASTA
(**— FOR TRAINING HORSES**) LONGE
(**— FROM WHICH JURY IS TAKEN**) VENUE
(**— IN**) INNEST
(**— IN COMPACT MASS**) STOW
(**— IN LINE**) RANK
(**— IN OFFICE**) INVEST
(**— IN ORDER**) ARRAY ENRANK
(**— IN WATERFALL**) LEAP
(**— MUCH FREQUENTED**) RESORT
(**— OF ABODE**) LIBKEN
(**— OF ACTION**) GROUND
(**— OF AMUSEMENT**) GAFF
(**— OF ASSEMBLY**) AGORA CURIA KGOTLA SYNAGOG
(**— OF BEAUTY**) TEMPE
(**— OF BLISS**) PARADISE
(**— OF BLOODSHED**) ACELDAMA
(**— OF BURIAL**) AHU KIL KILL LAIR GRAVE LAYSTOW CATACOMB CEMETERY GOLGOTHA LAYSTALL
(**— OF BUSINESS**) BANK AGENCY KNACKERY
(**— OF CARNAGE**) SHAMBLES
(**— OF CONCEALMENT**) DEN BOMA BLIND STALE HIDING HIDEOUT HIDEAWAY
(**— OF CONFINEMENT**) BRIG CAGE COOP LIMBO PRISON BULLPEN

(**— OF CONFUSION**) BABEL TROYTOWN
(**— OF CREMATION**) GHAT GHAUT
(**— OF CRUCIFIXION**) GOLGOTHA
(**— OF DEPARTED SPIRITS**) SHEOL
(**— OF DEPRAVITY**) SODOM
(**— OF DESTRUCTION**) ABADDON
(**— OF DETENTION**) BAGNIO
(**— OF DWELLING**) WANE
(**— OF EMPLOYMENT**) SHOP
(**— OF ENTERTAINMENT**) INN JOINT DANCERY HANGOUT HOSTELRY
(**— OF EXERTION**) ARENA
(**— OF EXILE**) PATMOS
(**— OF FABRICATION**) MINT
(**— OF HAPPINESS**) CAMELOT
(**— OF HONOR**) HEAD PRECEDENCE
(**— OF IDYLLIC BEAUTY**) XANADU
(**— OF JUNCTION**) SYMPHYSIS
(**— OF MISERY**) HELL
(**— OF NETHER DARKNESS**) EREBUS
(**— OF NOISE**) BABEL
(**— OF PLEASURE**) OASIS
(**— OF PROTECTION**) PORT SCUG
(**— OF QUARANTINE**) LAZARET LAZARETTO
(**— OF REFUGE**) ARK BAST HOLD ASYLUM ADULLAM HIDEOUT
(**— OF RESIDENCE**) SOIL DOMICILE
(**— OF RESORT**) PURLIEU
(**— OF REST**) OASIS REPOSE
(**— OF RESTRAINT**) LIMBO PINFOLD
(**— OF REVERENCE**) MECCA
(**— OF SACRIFICE**) ALTAR
(**— OF SAFETY**) GRITH HAVEN WARRANT
(**— OF SECLUSION**) PRIVACY
(**— OF SECURITY**) GRITH ASYLUM CORRAL HARBOR GARRISON
(**— OF SHELTER**) LEW HOLD JOUK COVER
(**— OF SUBMISSION**) CANOSSA
(**— OF THE DEAD**) HELL
(**— OF TORMENT**) GOLGOTHA
(**— OF TRADE**) MART
(**— OF WORSHIP**) HEIAU BETHEL CHAPEL CHURCH DESERT SHRINE TEMPLE GURDWARA SYNAGOGUE TABERNACLE
(**— SIDE-BY-SIDE**) JUXTAPOSE
(**— SIDE BY SIDE**) APPOSE
(**— SPAWNING**) REDD
(**— STRUCK BY LIGHTNING**) BIDENTAL
(**— UNDER RESTRICTIONS**) PROCLAIM
(**— WHERE FOOD IS KEPT**) LARDER
(**— WHERE MEAT IS SMOKED**) BUCAN BUCCAN
(**— WHERE OUTCASTS GATHER**) HELL
(**— WHERE ROADS CROSS**) LEET
(**— WHERE STREAM IS RAPID**) SHARP
(**— WHERE TROOPS HALT OVERNIGHT**) ETAPE
(**— WHERE 4 OR MORE WAYS MEET**) CARFAX
(**ABIDING —**) GRANGE
(**BARE —**) GALL SCAR SCAUR
(**BOGGY —**) SLACK SLUMP
(**BORING —**) DULLSVILLE

(BREEDING —) NIDUS LOOMERY SEMINARY PELICANRY
(BUSHY —) SCROG
(CHAFED —) GALL
(CHIEF —) HEADSHIP
(CIRCULAR —) ORBELL
(CONCEALED —) HIDE
(CONFINED —) CRIB
(CONSECRATED —) HIERON
(COOKING —) GALLEY
(DARK —) GLOOM
(DEEP —) GULF DEPTH GULPH
(DELIGHTFUL —) ELYSIUM
(DILAPIDATED —) DUMP
(DISTASTEFUL —) FLEABAG
(DOME-SHAPED —) IGLOO
(DRINKING —) BOOZER MUMHOUSE
(DRY —) SEARING
(DWELLING —) BY BYE DEN SEE BAWN HAFT HIVE HOME ABODE BEING HOUSE HOWFF SOJOURN HABITACLE
(EATING —) CAFE GRUBBERY
(EMPTY —) BLANK SPACE
(ENCLOSED —) BIN HAY WORTH SEVERAL CLOISTER
(ESSENTIAL —) EYE
(EXOTIC —) XANADU
(FAMILIAR —) KITH
(FAULTY — IN THREAD) TRAP
(FILTHY —) STY
(FIRST —) BLUE LEAD STRAIGHT
(FLAT —) PLAT
(FORTIFIED —) LIS LISS CASTLE FASTNESS
(GARRISONED —) PRESIDIO
(GATHERING —) SHOP AGORA FOYER JOINT LESCHE
(GRASSY —) LAUND
(HALLOWED —) SHRINE
(HALTING —) MARAH
(HIDING —) MEW CACHE HIDEL HOARD STASH COVERT HIDDELS RETREAT STOWAWAY
(HIGH —) EMINENCE
(HIGHEST —) TOP
(HOLLOW —) GULF HOLE HOLL SCOOP CAVITY ALBERCA SINKHOLE
(IDYLLIC —) XANADU BRIGADOON
(IMAGINARY —) FANTASYLAND
(INHABITED —) ABADI
(LANDING —) GHAT HARD HITHE LEVEE SCALE BUNDER PALACE HELIPORT
(LEVEL —) PLANILLA
(LODGING —) CAMP LOGIS BIDING BILLET LIBKEN
(LONELY —) SOLITUDE
(LOOKOUT —) TOOT
(LURKING —) HOLD HOLE HOARD HULSTER
(LYING —) LAY LAIR
(MARKET —) AGORA TRONE MARKET RIALTO
(MARSHY —) SLEW SLOO SLUE SLUMP SLOUGH
(MEETING —) CLUB PNYX COURT FORUM GUILD TRYST TOLSEL TOLZEY AMBALAM KLAVERN TINWALD
(MIDDLE —) MEDIUM
(MUDDY —) SOIL
(NARROW —) NOOK STRAIT

(NESTING —) JUG NIDARY
(OPEN —) ENAJIM
(OTHERWORLDLY —) EMPYREAN
(PARTICULAR —) ROOM
(PASSING —) TURNOUT
(POLLING —) BOOTH
(PRECIPITOUS —) STEEP
(PRIVATE —) SECRET
(RAVELED —) FRAY
(REMOTE —) JERICHO
(RESTING —) LAY CAMP FORM GIST LAIR PARAO CRADLE
(ROCKY —) ROCHER
(SACRED —) HAREM HIERON CHAITYA SANCTUM
(SALTING —) SALADERO
(SECRET —) LAIR ADYTUM CORNER CRANNY
(SECURE —) REDOUBT
(SHADY —) GLOOM SWALE FRESCADE UMBRACLE
(SHELTERED —) NOOK SCUG SUCCOR
(SLEEPING —) ROOST
(SORE —) RAW
(SPAWNING —) REDD
(STARTING —) JUMPOFF
(STEEP —) PITCH
(STOPPING —) HALT MANZIL
(STORAGE —) DEPOT HOARD LODGE SPICERY STORAGE STOWAGE DOCKYARD
(STRONG —) STRENGTH
(SUNKEN —) SWALE
(SWAMPY —) FLUSH SOUGH
(THIRD —) SHOW
(TIGHT —) JAM JAMB
(UNEVEN —) RUB
(WALLOWING —) SOIL
(WATCH —) TOOTHILL
(WATERING —) ABREUVOIR
(WATERY —) SOIL FLUSH
(WEAK —) BLOT
(WET —) DANK
(WORN —) ABRASION
(WRETCHED —) DEN MISERY
(PL.) LOCI
(PREF.) CHOR(O) LOCO TOP(O)
(DRY —) XER(O)
(TAKES — OF) PRO VICE
(SUFF.) ESE THESIS THESTE THETIC TOPE TOPY
(— FOR) ARIUM ORIUM ORY
(— OF) ARY
(— OF DOING) ERY
(— OF GROWING, BREEDING) ERY
(— OF KEEPING) ERY
(— OF SELLING) ERY
PLACEBO SOP TOADY VESPERS PARASITE
PLACED FIXED BESTEAD
(— ON ITS SIDE) LAZY
PLACEHOLDER VARIABLE
PLACE-NAME TOPONYM
PLACENTA MAZA REPLUM
(PREF.) MAZ(O)
PLACENTAL MAZIC
PLACID CALM COOL EVEN MEEK MILD SOFT DOWNY QUIET SUANT SUENT GENTLE SEDATE SERENE SMOOTH PACIFIC TRANQUIL THROBLESS

PLACKET FENT SLIT SPARE WOMAN CLOSING PETTICOAT
PLAGAL MODE
(PREF.) HYPO
PLAGIARISM CRIB PLAGIUM
PLAGIARIST TAKER COPYIST
PLAGIARIZE CRIB LIFT STEAL
PLAGUE DUN IMP POX VEX FRAB FRET GNAW PEST TWIT BESET CURSE DEATH DEUCE HARRY QUALM TEASE TRAIK WEARY WORRY WOUND BOTHER BURDEN HAMPER HARASS INFEST PESTER PESTIS SORROW WANION DESTROY MURRAIN PERPLEX SCOURGE TORMENT TORTURE TROUBLE DEPESTER HANDICAP OUTBREAK PESTILENCE
(PREF.) LEMO LOIMO PESTI PESTO
PLAGUY VERY PESKY VEXING MURRAIN PESTFUL INFERNAL
PLAICE FLUKE FLATFISH FLOUNDER
PLAID CALM FAKE MAUD PLOD TARTAN BRACKEN BRECHAN
(KIND OF —) GLEN
PLAIN DRY LOW BALD BARE CHOL EASY EVEN FLAT OPEN PLAT RIFE VEGA WALD WOLD BLAIR BLUNT BROAD CAMPO CORAH FIELD FRANK GREEN GROSS LAUND LEVEL LLANO MOURN NAKED PAMPA PROSE ROUND SEBKA SECCO SILLY SMALL SOBER TALAO UNORN BEMOAN BEWAIL CHASTE CUESTA GRAITH HOMELY HONEST HUMBLE LENTEN MACHAR MAIDAN PARAMO PUSZTA RUSTIC SABANA SEVERE SIMPLE SINGLE SMOOTH ARTLESS EVIDENT GENUINE IDAVOLL LEGIBLE OBVIOUS POPULAR SAVANNA TERRACE UNARTED VANILLA APPARENT CAMPAIGN DISTINCT EVERYDAY EXPLICIT FAMILIAR HOMEMADE HOMESPUN ITHAVOLL PALPABLE PIEDMONT SEMPLICE STRAIGHT
(— AMONG TREES) LAUND
(— OF ARGENTINA) PAMPA
(— OF RUSSIA) STEPPE
(ALKALI —S) USAR
(ALLUVIAL —) APRON CARSE HAUGH
(ARCTIC —) TUNDRA
(DESOLATE —) CHOL
(HEATHY —) LANDE
(LOW-LYING —) MACHAR MACHAIR
(LUNAR —) MARE
(MARSHY —) BLAIR
(NOT —) MEALYMOUTHED
(SALINE —) SEBKA SEBKHA
(SALT —) SALADA
(SLOPING —) HOPE CUESTA CONOPLAIN
(SMALL GRASSY —) CAMAS CAMASS QUAMASH
(TREELESS —) BLED TUNDRA SAVANNA SAVANNAH
(UNOCCUPIED —) DESERT
(PL.) VIZCACHA
(PREF.) LITI PEDI(O) PLAN(I)
PLAIN CHANT CF
PLAINCLOTHESMAN SPLIT

PLAINLY FAIR BARELY FAIRLY FLATLY SIMPLY BROADLY FRANKLY DIRECTLY
PLAINNESS PROSE INNOCENCE
PLAINSMAN LLANERO
PLAINSONG GROUND
PLAINT WAIL PLANT LAMENT COMPLAINT
PLAINTEXT CLEAR
PLAINTIFF SUER USEE ACTOR ORATOR PURSUER QUERENT
PLAINTIVE SAD CROSS PINING DOLENTE ELEGIAC FRETFUL MOANFUL PEEVISH PETTISH DOLOROSO MANGENDO PETULANT WAILSOME SORROWFUL
PLAIN-VANILLA BASIC
PLAIT CUE PLY KNIT PAIR PLAT RUFF TURN WALE WAND BRAID BREAD CRIMP FETCH FITCH PEDAL PINCH QUEUE QUILL QUIRK TRACE TRESS WEAVE BORDER DOUBLE GATHER GOFFER PLEACH PLIGHT RUMPLE TUSCAN WIMPLE WRITHE CRIMPLE FROUNCE PIGTAIL SCALLOM COMPLECT
(— FOR HAT) DUNSTABLE
(— OF STRAW) MILAN TRACE
(SERIES OF —S) KILTING
PLAITED PLISSE DEVIOUS PLICATE
PLAITING PLISSE LEGHORN NATTIER
PLAN AIM ART LAY WAY CARD CAST COUP DART FOOT GAME HANG IDEA MIND MOOD PLAT PLOT REDE WENT ALLOW BRIEF CHART DARTY DRAFT DRIFT ETTLE FRAME HOBBY MODEL REACH SHAPE TRACE ADVICE AGENDA BEREDE BUDGET CIPHER DECOCT DESIGN DEVISE ENGINE FIGURE INTEND LAYOUT METHOD MODULE ORDAIN PROJET SCHEMA SCHEME SURVEY THEORY ARRANGE CONCERT CONCOCT COUNSEL DRAWING FORELAY NOSTRUM OUTLINE PATTERN PROGRAM PROJECT PURPOSE THOUGHT COGITATE CONSPIRE CONTRIVE ENGINEER FORECAST FOREGAME LANDSKIP MEDITATE PLATFORM PRACTICE SCHEDULE SKELETON STRATEGY BLUEPRINT CALCULATE
(— AHEAD) FORECAST
(— OF FUTURE PROCEDURE) PROGRAM
(— ON A FLOOR) EPURE
(— TOGETHER) CONCERT
(CUNNING —) WHEEZE
(GROUND —) TRACE GRUNDRISS
(INSURANCE —) TONTINE
(KIND OF —) KEOGH
(KIND OF RETIREMENT —) KEOGH
(5-YEAR —) PIATILETKA
PLANARIAN PLATODE TRICLAD FLATWORM PLATYHELMINTH
PLANE BEAD DADO FACE FLAT HOLL MILL AXIAL CHUTE CROZE FACET GLIDE HOULE HOWEL LEVEL MESON SHOOT STICK TABLE WHISK AEQUOR AIRBUS BEADER HOLLOW REEDER ROUTER

SMOKER SNIBEL COURIER INSHAVE JOINTER NONSKED SURFACE WITCHET BULLNOSE DECLINER LEEBOARD MERIDIAN RECLINER SYCAMORE TRAVERSE
(— CURVE) ROSE
(— HANDLE) TOAT TOTE
(— OF CLEAVAGE) BACK
(— OF EARTH'S ORBIT) ECLIPTIC
(— OF ROCK) BED
(—S OF GUNNERY FIRE) SHEAF
(ENEMY —) BANDIT
(INCLINED —) RAMP SLIP
(MOLDING —) HOLL HOULE HOLLOW
(PERSPECTIVE —) TABLE
(RABBET —) PLOW RABAT PLOUGH REBATE FILLETER
(SLOPING —) CUESTA
PLANER JOINTER SURFACER
PLANER TREE HORNBEAM SYCAMORE
PLANET ORB SUN BODY IRIS JOVE MARS MOON STAR EARTH GLOBE HYLEG PLUTO SHREW VENUS WORLD SATURN SPHERE URANUS VULCAN ALMUTEN ANARETA BENEFIC FORTUNE JUPITER MERCURY NEPTUNE PRIMARY CHASUBLE LUMINARY RECEPTOR TERRELLA WANDERER
(— IN A NATIVITY) ALMUTEN
(BENEVOLENT —) FORTUNE
(CONTROLLING —) LORD
(FICTIONAL —) ORK KRYPTON
(HYPOTHETICAL —) VULCAN
(INNER —) MARS EARTH VENUS MERCURY
(MALEFICENT —) SHREW
(MINOR —) VESTA PALLAS PSYCHE
(RULING —) DOMINATOR
(SMALL —) IRIS ASTEROID TERRELLA
PLANETARIUM ORRERY
PLANETOID UNDINE ASTEROID
PLANE TREE CHINAR PLATAN COTONIER PLANTAIN SYCAMORE
PLANET-STRICKEN SIDERATED
PLANISPHERE ASTROLABE METEORSCOPE
PLANK CLAM HOOD PATA PLAT RAIL SOLE WAIR BOARD CLAMP PATTA SHIDE SWALE THEAL DAGGER FLITCH PLANCH ROOFER STRAKE CLAPPER CROSSER DEPOSIT MADRIER RIBBAND STEALER FOREPOLE GARBOARD STRINGER
(— AS PROTECTION) SHOLE
(— OVER BROOK) CLAM
(—S IN BRIDGE) CHESS
(—S LESS THAN 6 FT.) DEAL
(— 6 FT. X 1 FT.) WARE
(CURVED —) SNYING
(ROUGHHEWN —) SLAB
PLANK DRAG RUBBER
PLANK END STUB
PLANKING GORE RACK HATCH SWALE STRAKE CEILING LAGGING BERTHING BRATTICE GARBOARD WATERWAY
PLANKSHEER WATERWAY
PLANKTON KRILL DIATOM SESTON
(GROWTH OF —) BLOOM

PLANNED PREPENSE
(AS —) ONTRACK
PLANNING (KIND OF —) ESTATE
(TECHNIQUE FOR —) PERT
PLANOMILLER SLABBER
PLANT AJI BED SET SOW ACHE ALGA ARUM BURY CROP FAST HERB HIDE MORE RAPE SALT SEED SEGO SLIP TREE WORT ABACA AGAVE AJWAN ARGEL AVENS CAMAS CAROA CHIVE CLOTE CLOVE CUMIN EARLY FANCY GRAFT HEATH INTER INULA JALAP KEIKI ORACH PITCH PUTIN SEDUM SHRUB YERBA ACACIA AJOWAN AKELEY ALASAS ANNUAL BEDDER CACOON CALALU CARROT CLOVER COKERY COSMEA COTTON CUMMIN DERRIS DIBBLE ESCAPE FICOID FORCER GALAXY GROWTH KARREE LENTIL LIGGER MALLOW MANUKA MEDICK MESCAL ORPINE PEPINO SESAME SETTLE SPRING ULLUCU YARROW ABANDON ALKANET ALYSSUM BREWERY BUGLOSS CARAWAY CARDOON CHERVIL CONCEAL CUTTING DAGGERS ENCELIA GENTIAN GINSENG HAEMONY IMPLANT JIKUNGU LETTUCE PALMIET PICKERY RAMBONG SAWMILL ABUTILON AGERATUM AGRIMONY ANGLEPOD BIENNIAL BLUEBELL CAMOMILE CONSOUND DRAWLING DYEHOUSE EMERGENT ENGINERY FOXGLOVE FUMEROOT GASWORKS GERANIUM GROMWELL HAWKWEED HONEWORT JAPONICA KNAPWEED LARKSPUR CHAMOMILE SPIKENARD PHILODENDRON
(— BY SPADING) SPIT
(— DEEPLY) HEEL
(— DISEASE) NECROSIS
(— FIRMLY) BRACE
(— GROWING IN WATER) BILDERS HYDROPHYTE
(— GROWTH MEDIUM) PERLITE
(— IN ROWS) DRILL
(— LIFE) BIOS BIOTA
(— NOT ATTACKED) NONHOST
(— NUTRIENTS) SIDEDRESS
(— OF MEADOWS) POOPHYTE
(— OF THE DEAD) ASPHODEL
(— OUTGROWTH) OVULE
(— ROOTED IN GROUND) LIANA LIANE
(— SUPPORTING PARASITES) SUSCEPT
(— TEMPORARILY) SHEUCH
(— TREE) MOTCH
(— WITH A SPADE) SPIT
(— WITH NO DISTINCT MEMBERS) THALLUS
(— WITH THREE PISTILS) TRIGYN
(— WITH THREE STAMENS) TRIANDER
(— 2ND CROP) ETCH
(AIR —) FLOPPERS
(ANCIENT —) CYCAD
(AQUATIC —) ALISMA NUPHAR SUGAMO TAWKEE AMBULIA

AWLWORT FROGBIT DUCKWEED PONDWEED PICKERELWEED
(AROMATIC —) MINT NARD BASIL CUMIN TANSY THYME AMOMUM CUMMIN CARAWAY DITTANY ALBAHACA CALAMINT LAVENDER SPIKENARD
(AUSTRALIAN —) LILAC STYLO LIGNUM LANCEPOD
(BULBOUS —) GALTONIA
(CENTURY —) PITA
(CLIMBING —) VETCH LAWYER RUNNER ULLUCE ULLUCU CORALITA
(COMPOSITE —) SUCCORY HAWKWEED SNEEZEWEED
(CONSECRATED —) HAOMA
(CREATED —) BARAMIN
(CREEPING —) IPECAC KAREAO KAREAU PENNYWORT
(CROSSBRED —) HYBRID
(CRUSHING —) BREAKER
(DWARF —) CUMIN STUNT
(DYE —) WAD ANIL WOAD WOLD WOALD MADDER
(E. INDIAN —) JATI
(ETIOLATED —) ALBINO
(FIBER —) ALOE FLAX HEMP PITA CAJUN RAMIE SISAL
(FLOWERING —) HOP ROSE DAISY HOLLY POPPY ORCHID VIOLET HAWTHORN LARKSPUR POLYGALA PRIMROSE SNOWDROP
(FORAGE —) RAPE ALFALFA DAINCHA
(FOSSIL —) CALAMITE
(GERMINATING —) SPIRE
(GRAIN —) TEFF
(HEDGE —) ESPINO
(HEMP —) FIMBLE
(IMMATURE —) KEIKI
(LEAFLESS —) ULEX DODDER RESTIAD TRIURID
(MALE —) MAS MACRANDER
(MARSH —) CALL FERN RUSH CALLA JUNCUS BULRUSH CATTAIL BUCKBEAN MARSHMALLOW
(MEDICINAL —) ALOE HERB ERICA ARNICA CATNEP CATNIP IPECAC SIMPLE ACONITE BONESET GENTIAN LOBELIA CAMOMILE
(MEDICINIAL —) SENNA
(NON-FLOWERING —) FERN
(NURSERY —) SEEDLING
(PEPPER —) ARA
(PHILIPPINE —) ABACA
(PISTILLATE —) FEMALE
(POISONOUS —) COWBANE DEATHIN HENBANE MANDRAKE SAMNITIS NIGHTSHADE
(POTTED —) BONSAI LANTANA
(POWER —) HYDRO
(PRICKLY —) BRIAR BRIER CACTUS CARDON NETTLE TEASEL TEAZEL PRICKFOOT
(PUNGENT —) PEPPER
(RAPIDLY-GROWING —) FILLER
(REEDY —) SPRIT
(RENDERING —) KNACKERY
(ROSACEOUS —) AVENS
(SENSITIVE —) MIMOSA
(SIBERIAN —) BADAN
(SPINOUS —) KANTIARA
(STAMINATE —) HUSBAND

(SUBMERGED —) ENALID
(SUCCULENT —) ALOE HERB GASTERIA HAWORTHIA HOUSELEEK
(SWORD-LEAVED —) LEVERS
(THALLOPHYTIC —) LICHEN
(TRAILING —) ARBUTUS
(TUFTED —) DRYAS
(TWINING —) SMII AX WINDER CLIMBER BINDWEED SCAMMONY
(UNIDENTIFIED —) HORDOCK
(WATER —) LIMU LOTUS AQUATILE STARFRUIT
(WEEDY —) DOCK KNAWEL
(YOUNG —) SET SPRINGER
(PL.) FLORA
(PREF.) BOTAN(O) PHYT(I)(O)
(SUFF.) AD CHORE COCCUS OECIA PHYTA PHYTE(S) PHYTIA PHYTIC PHYTUM
PLANTAGENET ANGEVIN
PLANTAIN COCK PALA ABACA ALISMA FINGER PISANG WABRON BENTING NETLEAF RIBWORT SITFAST BALISIER BUCKHORN FIREWEED FLEAWORT ISPAGHUL PLANTANO RATSBANE RIBGRASS ROADWEED WAYBREAD
PLANTAIN EATER TOURACO SPLITBEAK
PLANTAIN LILY HOSTA FUNKIA
PLANTATION PEN HOLT WALK FINCA GROVE BOSKET BOWERY COLONY ESTATE SHAMBA SPRING YERBAL CAFETAL FAZENDA NOPALRY PINETUM THICKET ARBUSTUM HACIENDA TRAPICHE VINEYARD
(HEMP —) LATE
(WILLOW —) SALICETUM
PLANTED LISTED
PLANTER SNAG COLON SOWER FARMER SETTLER PLANTATOR
PLANTING GROVE SATION
PLANTING STICK DIBBLE
PLANT LOUSE APHID PSYLLID PUCERON HOMOPTER
PLANTS
(SUFF.) ACEAE ALES INEAE
PLAQUE CHIP PINAX PLATE PLATEAU SARCOID NAMEPLATE STOMACHER
PLASH LIP DASH BLASH PLOSH PLOUT PLEACH PUDDLE SPLASH SPATTER SPECKLE
PLASMA LATEX PLASM
PLASTER CAST CEIL DAUB HARL LEEP LOCK TEER CLEAM GATCH PARGE SLICK SMALM STAFF TOPIC TREAT CHARGE CHUNAM CLATCH GAGING MORTAR PARGET SPARGE STOOTH STUCCO BLISTER MALAGMA DIACULUM DIAPALMA SINAPISM VESICANT CATAPLASM
(— BETWEEN LATHS) CAT
(— OF PARIS) GESSO GYPSUM
(— WITH COW DUNG) LEEP
(COARSE —) GROUT
(COVER WITH —) CEIL
(MEDICAL —) SALVE TOPIC TREAT CHARGE SPARADRAP
(MUSTARD —) SINAPISM
(2 COATS OF —) RENDERSET

PLASTERBOARD GYPSUM DRYWALL

PLASTERED DRUNK SOUSED SWACKED

PLASTERER DAUBER DAUBSTER PARGETER SPREADER

PLASTERING KEY SETWORK ROUGHCAST

PLASTIC ABS FOAM LOID RICH SIRUP LABILE PLIANT ACETATE CATALIN CRYSTAL DUCTILE FICTILE ORGANIC PERSPEX CREATIVE FLEXIBLE LAMINATE MELAMINE PHENOLIC TECTONIC UNCTUOUS FORMATIVE
(**—S BASE**) RESIN
(**FLEXIBLE —**) SARAN

PLASTICIZER CAMPHOR

PLASTRON DICKEY CALIPEE

PLAT BED FLAT FOOD PLAN PLOT SLAP BRAID LEVEL PLACE PLAIN PLAIT BUFFET WATTLE ARRANGE FLATTEN PLATEAU QUADRAT

PLATANIST SUSU

PLATANUS PLANE COTINIER SYCAMORE

PLATBAND IMPOST LINTEL EPISTYLE

PLATE DAT CAP CUT DIP DOD EAR FIN GIB WEB ANAL BACK BASE BRIN CASE CAST CURB DIAL DISK DROP FISH GILL GONG GULA HOME HOOF LAME LEAF MOLD NAIL ORAL RETE ROSE SHOE SHUT SLAB SOLE STUD TACE TRAY AMPYX ANODE BASAL BELLY BLADE CHAIR CLAMP CLEAT CLOUT FACIA FENCE FLOOR FLUKE FORCE GLAND GUARD GULAR LAMEL PATEN PYGAL SCALE SCUTE SHEET SHOLE SLICE STAMP STAVE STRAP TABLE TASSE TERNE TRAMP UNCUS WATER ADORAL BAFFLE BRIDGE BUCKLE CASTER CIRCLE CLICHE COLLAR COPPER COSTAL CRUSTA DAMPER DASHER EPIGNE FASCIA FILLER FOLIUM FRIZEL GENIAL GNOMON GORGET GUSSET LABIAL LAMINA LOREAL MASCLE MATRIX MENTAL MENTUM MOTHER PALLET PATTEN PLATEN RADIAL SCREEN SCUTUM SEPTUM SERVER SHEATH SHROUD SPLINT STAPLE TARSUS TEGMEN TURTLE TYMPAN VESSEL BESAGNE BOLSTER BRACKET BRACTEA BUCCULA BUCKLER CHARGER CLYPEUS COASTER CORNULE CORONET CRYSTAL DOUBLER ETCHING FRIZZLE FRONTAL GRAVURE HUMERAL INKBLOT MORDANT MYOTOME NEPTUNE PETALON PRIMARY ROSTRAL ROUNDEL SPANGLE STEALER STEELER TERGITE TESSERA VENTRAL ASSIETTE BEDPLATE BIQUARTZ BRACHIAL CELLOCUT DIASCOPE DRAWBACK ELECTRUM EPIGYNUM EPIPROCT EPISTOME FIREBACK FLOUNDER SKEWBACK STAPLING STRINGER SUBPLATE SURPRINT

(**— COVERING KEYHOLE**) DROP
(**— COVERING MIDDLE EAR**) TEGMEN
(**— IN AIRPLANE WING**) SPOILER
(**— IN BATTERY**) GRID
(**— IN ORGAN PIPE**) LANGUET
(**— IN STEAM BOILER**) SPUT DASHER
(**— OF BALEEN**) BLADE
(**— OF BLAST FURNACE**) TYMP
(**— OF CTENOPHORE**) COMB
(**— OF GELATIN**) BAT
(**— OF GLASS**) SLIDE
(**— OF JAW**) AURICLE
(**— OF PRECIOUS METAL**) BRACTEA
(**— OF SOAP FRAME**) SESS
(**— OF SUNDIAL**) GNOMON
(**— ON FIREPLACE**) BLOWER
(**— ON LANCE SHAFT**) VAMPLATE
(**— ON PLOW**) MOLDBOARD
(**— ON SADDLE**) SIDEBAR
(**— ON SATCHEL STRAP**) OLIVE
(**— ON SHOE SOLE**) SEG
(**— ON THROAT OF FISH**) GULAR
(**— ON WATERWHEEL**) SHROUD
(**—S OF CARDING MACHINE**) ARCH
(**—S OF GUN CARRIAGE**) FLASK
(**— TO SUPPORT BEAM**) TASSEL TORSEL
(**ARMOR —**) SPLINT AILETTE PALLETTE
(**COLLECTION —**) BROD
(**COMMUNION —**) PATEN
(**DEEP —**) MAZARINE
(**DERMAL —**) SCUTE
(**DORSAL —**) ELYTRUM ALINOTUM
(**EARTHEN —**) MUFFIN
(**FASHION —**) SWELL
(**FIREPLACE —**) IRONBACK
(**FLAT —**) APRON
(**GOLD — ON FOREHEAD**) PATA PATTA
(**GROOVED TRAM —**) GULLY GULLEY
(**GUARD —**) SHELL
(**HINGED —**) SHUT
(**HOME —**) DISH
(**HOT —**) GRILL GRILLE
(**INSCRIBED —**) TABLET
(**IRON —**) CLOUT STAVE LATTEN MARVER LAPSTONE SKEWBACK MOLDBOARD TURNPLATE TURNSHEET
(**LARGE —**) DOUBLER
(**LOCK —**) SELVEDGE
(**MELTED —**) SOUP
(**METAL —**) ROVE CHROME
(**NAME —**) FACIA
(**PERFORATED —**) DOD GRID WORTLE PINNULE
(**PITCHER'S —**) SLAB MOUND
(**RIMLESS —**) COUPE
(**SIEVE —**) LATTICE
(**SIFTING —**) TROMMEL
(**SKELETAL —**) SCLERITE
(**THIN —**) LAME LAMP LAMINA LAMELLA
(**THIN TIN —**) TAIN LATTEN TAGGERS
(**WALL —**) PAN RASEN TORSEL
(**WOODEN —**) TRENCHER
(**PREF.**) ELASM(O) LAMELLI LAMIN(I) PLAC(O)

(**SUFF.**) (**COVERING —**) STEGE STEGITE

PLATEAU PLAT PUNA FJELD KAROO KARST TABLE CAUSSE HAMADA MESETA NIVEAU PARAMO SABANA UPLAND ANASAZI PLATFORM
(**PL.**) BARRENS

PLATEHOLDER CASSETTE

PLATE-LIKE PLACOID

PLATEN ROLL

PLATER VATMAN CLAIMER COLLARMAN

PLATFORM TOP BANK BEMA DAIS DECK DRIP DROP DUCK FLAT GHAT HEEL KITE PACE PLAT STEP WING ALTAR APRON BENCH BLIND BLOCK CHAIN DUKAN FLAKE FLOAT HEIAU SOLEA STAGE STAND STOEP STOOL STOOP STULL STUMP TOLDO ARBOUR AZOTEA BRIDGE DESIGN GANTRY HURDLE ISLAND MACHAN PAEPAE PALLET PERRON PILLAR PODIUM PULPIT RUNWAY SETTLE SLEDGE ALMEMAR BALCONY BATTERY CATWALK ESTRADE FORETOP GALLERY LANDING LOGEION PADDOCK PATTERN ROLLWAY ROSTRUM SKIDWAY SOAPBOX TRIBUNE BARBETTE FOOTPACE HUSTINGS SCAFFOLD STALLAGE MORTARBOARD
(**— FOR ACTORS**) LOGEION THEOLOGIUM
(**— FOR ALTAR**) PREDELLA
(**— FOR DRYING FISH**) FLAKE
(**— FOR PUBLIC SPEAKING**) BEMA PODIUM TRIBUNE
(**— FOR STORING FOOD**) WHATA
(**— IN CHURCH**) SOLEA
(**— IN SYNAGOGUE**) ALMEMAR
(**— IN TEMPLE**) DUKAN
(**— IN TREE**) MACHAN
(**— OF GALLOWS**) DROP
(**— ON RUNNERS**) SLEDGE
(**— ON STEAMER**) SPONSON
(**— ON TOP OF HOUSE**) AZOTEA
(**— ON WHEELS**) SKID DOLLY FLOAT
(**— TO SUPPORT MINERS**) STULL
(**BOARDING —**) RAMBADE
(**GUN —**) BARBET SPONSON BARBETTE
(**LEADSMAN'S —**) CHAIN
(**MINE —**) STULL SOLLAR SOLLER
(**MOHAMMEDAN STONE —**) MASTABA
(**MOUNTED —**) SKID
(**NAUTICAL —**) FORETOP MAINTOP ROUNDTOP
(**ORE —**) BUDDLE
(**RAILROAD —**) DOCK DOCKEN TRAINWAY
(**RAISED —**) DAIS PYAL STAND STOEP STOOL STOOP EXEDRA LISSOM PANTALAN
(**ROCK —**) STANCE
(**SLEEPING —**) KANG
(**STAIRCASE —**) HALFPACE HATHPACE
(**WOOD —**) PLANCHER

PLATING ARMOR SKIRT

PLATINUM COSTLY PLATINA

PLATITUDE CLICHE TRUISM BROMIDE DULLNESS STALENESS TRITENESS

PLATONIST IDEIST

PLATOON SQUAD VOLLEY PELOTON PLOTTON

PLATTER DISH DISK LANX ASHET GRAIL PLATE RECORD CHARGER TRENCHER

PLATY MOON MOONFISH

PLATYPUS DUCKBILL DUCKMOLE MALLANGONG

PLAUDIT APPLAUD APPROVAL ENCOMIUM
(**PL.**) PRAISE APPLAUSE

PLAUSIBILITY COLOR

PLAUSIBLE FAIR OILY SNOD SLEEK GLOSSY SMOOTH AFFABLE POPULAR CREDIBLE PROBABLE PROVABLE SPECIOUS SUITABLE OSTENSIBLE

PLAY FUN JEU JIG RUN RUX TOY AUTO BEAR COME DAFF DEAL DICE DRAW FAIR GAME JEST LAKE MOVE MUCK PLEE PUNT ROMP SPIN TUNE WAKE CARRY CHARM DALLY DRAMA ENACT FLIRT FROST HORSE SHOOT SOTIE SOUND SPIEL SPORT STOCK WREAK YEDDE ACTION COMEDY COQUET DANDLE DIVIDE FILLER FROLIC GAMBLE GAMBOL GAMING GHOSTS MUSERY NUMBER PIDDLE ROLLIX TRIFLE CONSORT CUTBACK DISPORT EXECUTE EXPLOIT GUIGNOL HISTORY HOLIDAY MIRACLE PAGEANT PASSION PERFORM PRELUDE STAGERY VENTURE BURLETTA MORALITY SKITTLES MELODRAMA
(**— ABOUT**) SPANIEL
(**— A DOMINO**) SET POSE
(**— AGAINST**) BUCK
(**— AN INSTRUMENT**) BOW BLOW SWAY FINGER TWEEDLE
(**— A PART**) DO ACT ENTER GAMMON GUIZARD
(**— A PIPE**) CHARM
(**— AT COURTSHIP**) FLIRT
(**— BAGPIPE**) SKIRL DOODLE DOUDLE
(**— BY STROKES**) STRIKE
(**— FANFARE**) FLOURISH
(**— FAST AND LOOSE**) PALTER
(**— FIRST CARD**) LEAD
(**— FLORIDLY**) DIVIDE
(**— FOR TIME**) STALL
(**— GOLF BALL**) DRIVE
(**— IMPOSTER**) MUMP
(**— IN MUD**) MUDLARK
(**— IN POOL**) BURST
(**— IN STREAKS**) FORK
(**— IN TRIGGER**) CREEP
(**— JAZZ**) BLOW
(**— LEGATO**) SUSTAIN
(**— LOCATION**) SET
(**— LOOSELY**) WAVE
(**— LOUT**) SWAB SLUBBER
(**— MEAN TRICKS**) SHAB
(**— NERVOUSLY**) FIDGET
(**— OF COLORS**) IRIS
(**— OF FOAM**) HOOD
(**— OF LIGHT**) GLORY

(— ON WORDS) PUN CLENCH
CLINCH PARAGRAM CALEMBOUR
PARONOMASIA
(— THE BUFFOON) DROLL
(— THE BULLY) BLUSTER
(— THE FOOL) HOIT
(— THE HYPOCRITE) FACE
(— THE TOADY) SUPE
(— TRICKS) COD JAPE JINK
(— TRUANT) KIP WAG JOUK MICHE
MOOCH MOUCH PLUNK TRONE
MOOTCH
(— UNSKILLFULLY) STRUM FOOZLE
(— WITH) DANDLE
(AMOROUS —) GAME
(BOISTEROUS —) ROMP
(BRIDGE —) COUP ECHO SIGNAL
SQUEEZE
(END —) SHAKE
(FARCICAL —) SOTIE
(FOOTBALL —) DOWN KEEP DELAY
SWING KEEPER SAFETY AUDIBLE
COUNTER CUTBACK ROLLOUT
SPINNER
(IN —) ALIVE
(JAPANESE —) NOH
(MASKED —) GUISE
(MIRACLE —) AUTO GUARY
MIRACLE
(ONE-PERSON —) MONODRAMA
(RAPID CHESS —) SKITTLES
(SHORT —) ONELINER
(USED IN —) LUSORY
(PL.) THEATER VANGELI
PLAYA BEACH SEBKA SALINA
SEBKHA
PLAYBOY RAKE ROMEO LOTHARIO
LIBERTINE
**PLAYBOY OF THE WESTERN
WORLD (AUTHOR OF —)** SYNGE
(CHARACTER IN —) QUIN KEOGH
MAHON SHAWN PEGEEN CHRISTY
FLAHERTY MARGARET
CHRISTOPHER
PLAY-BY-PLAY DETAILED
PLAYER IT CAP END BACK DUCK
SIDE ACTOR BLACK COLOR GUARD
BANKER BUSKER FEEDER STAGER
STROLL TENTER ALTOIST FIELDER
FORWARD GAMBLER STRIKER
TRIFLER TURQUET BUDGETER
GAMESTER HORNSMAN STROLLER
(— IN CHESS) BLACK WHITE
(— IN CHOUETTE) CAPTAIN
(— OF JAZZ) CAT
(— WHO CUTS CARDS) PONE
(— WHO IS IT) HE
(— WHO SCORES ZERO) DUCK
(— WITH LOWEST SCORE) BOOBY
(BACKGAMMON —) TABLER
(BASEBALL —) SHORT SACKER
CATCHER FIELDER LEADOFF
PITCHER BACKSTOP
(BASKETBALL —) PIVOT CAGEMAN
HOOPMAN HOOPSTER PIVOTMAN
(BOWLING —) LEAD
(CARD —) EAST HAND PONE WEST
BLIND DUMMY NORTH OMBRE
SOUTH JUNIOR SENIOR BRAGGER
DECLARER
(CRICKET —) LEG BOWLER INNING
(CROQUET —) MALLET
(DICE —) SHOOTER

(FLUTE —) AULETE
(FOOTBALL —) END BACK GUARD
SLANT BUCKER CENTER TACKLE
BLOCKER FLANKER GRIDDER
SNAPPER FULLBACK HALFBACK
SCATBACK SLOTBACK
(INEPT CHESS —) PATZER
(KEY —) PIVOT
(LACROSSE —) HOME COVER POINT
ATTACK STICKMAN
(LEAPFROG —) BACK
(POKER —) AGE
(RUGBY —) SCRUM HOOKER
(SOCCER —) CAP INNER BOOTER
(STUPID —) HAM
(TENNIS —) SMASHER
(TWO OR MORE —S) PLATOON
(UNSKILLFUL —) DUB
(VOLLEYBALL —) SPIKER
(WEAK —) RABBIT
(PL.) CAST
PLAYFUL SLY ELFIN LUDIC MERRY
FRISKY GAMBOL JOCOSE LUSORY
TOYISH WANTON COLTISH
GIOCOSO JIGGISH JOCULAR
TOYSOME GAMESOME
HUMOROUS LARKSOME
SPORTFUL SPORTIVE KITTENISH
(EXTRAVAGANTLY —) MAD
(IRRESPONSIBLY —) MISCHIEVOUS
PLAYFULLY SCHERZANDO
PLAYFULNESS FUN BANTER
GAMMICK GAMMOCK
PLAYGROUND OVAL CLOSE
TOTLOT PLAYSTOW PLAYSTEAD
PLAYHOUSE HOUSE MOVIE
CINEMA THEATER
PLAYING FROLIC LAKING
(— CARD) ACE JACK KING TREY
DEUCE QUEEN TAROT
(— CARDS) DECK
(— LIGHTLY) LAMBENT
PLAYING FIELD PADANG
PLAYLET SKIT
PLAYTHING DIE TOY HOOP KNACK
PLAIK SPORT BAUBLE LAKING
SUCKER TRIFLE PLAYOCK
PLAYWRIGHT AUTHOR DRAMATIST
PLAYMAKER
AMERICAN ADE LEA BABE BAUM
DALY DELL EYEN HART HOYT INGE
KERR LOOS RABE RICE ROOT SHAW
UHRY AKINS ALBEE BARRY COHAN
DAVIS DOBIE FITCH FRIEL GREEN
HECHT HWANG LEWIS LOGAN
LORTZ MAMET ODETS RIGGS RIVES
SIMON SMITH STEIN WILDE YOUNG
ABBOTT BARAKA BARKER BARRAS
BEAHAN BOLTON BOOTHE BROOKS
COMDEN CROUSE FLAVIN FRINGS
GOLDEN HEGGEN HOWARD
HUGHES KRASNA LAWSON LERNER
LUDLAM MEGRUE MILLER NUGENT
OBOLER ONEILL THOMAS TOTTEN
WALKER WALTER WEXLEY WILDER
ZINDEL ANDREWS BEHRMAN
BELASCO BISSELL BLOSSOM
BURROWS CARROLL COLLIER
HELLMAN HOPWOOD HURLBUT
KAUFMAN LEBLANC LINDSAY
MOELLER NICHOLS PEABODY
RICHMAN RYSKIND SAROYAN
SHELDON SHEPARD SHIPMAN

SHULMAN SPEWACK TEBELAK
VEILLER ANDERSON BOGOSIAN
CARLETON CHODOROV COLLISON
CONNELLY KINGSLEY KIRKLAND
MITCHELL SCHISGAL SCHWARTZ
SHERWOOD TOTHEROH WILLIAMS
BALDERSON CHAYEFSKY
ISHERWOOD MACARTHUR
MIDDLETON MOREHOUSE
NICHOLSON STALLINGS
BOUCICAULT TARKINGTON
WEITZENKORN
AUSTRALIAN CHAMBERS
AUSTRIAN BLEI COLLIN MULLER
NISSEL WERFEL NEUMANN ZEDLITZ
CASTELLI WILDGANS SCHONTHAN
SCHNITZLER GRILLPARZER
HOFMANNSTHAL
BELGIAN CLAUS GHELDERODE
MAETERLINCK
CANADIAN BOLT COOK ROSE
SLADE COULTER DOHERTY
HERBERT TREMBLAY
CZECH HAVEL KLIMA JERABEK
JIRASEK
DANISH EWALD TANDRUP
BERGSTROM BUCHHOLTZ
OEHLENSCHLAGER
DUTCH FEITH HOOFT COSTER
EMANTS VONDEL BREDERO
ENGLISH BAX FRY GAY KYD LEE
BART BEHN BELL FORD HILL LEVY
LONG NASH ROWE SHAW SIMS
TATE TUKE BARRY BROME BYRON
DUKES FIELD FOOTE HOOLE JONES
KEEFE LEMON LEWIS LILLO LODGE
MILNE MOORE MUNRO ORCZY
ORTON PEELE SMITH STORY UDALL
WOODS ALBERY BOADEN BROPHY
CANNAN CASTLE CIBBER COWARD
COWLEY CROWNE DAVIES DEKKER
DENNIS DIBDIN DRYDEN DURFEY
GRAHAM GREENE GRILLO HOWARD
JONSON KENNEY LYTTON MANLEY
MORTON MUNDAY NABBES PINERO
PINTER PORTER PUDNEY ROWLEY
SETTLE STEELE STOREY TAYLOR
TREECE WESKER WILSON ABLEMAN
ACKLAND AMBROSE BAGNOLD
BARNETT BARRETT BENNETT
BURNAND CHAPMAN CHETTLE
EDWARDS FLECKER GILBERT
HARWOOD HEYWOOD HOUSMAN
JERROLD JOHNSON MARLOWE
MARMION MARSTON MERRICK
MITFORD MOTTEUX NICHOLS
OSBORNE PLANCHE PRESTON
SHIRLEY SIMPSON SITWELL
SOWERBY TRAVERS WEBSTER
BEAUMONT CLIFFORD CONGREVE
DAVENANT ETHEREGE FIELDING
FITZBALL FLETCHER HAMILTON
HOLCROFT HOUGHTON JELLICOE
JOHNSTON KNOBLOCK LONSDALE
MORRISON PHILLIPS RATTIGAN
ROBINSON SHADWELL THEOBALD
THURSTON TOURNEUR VANBRUGH
WILLIAMS ZANGWILL BOTTOMLEY
BRIGHOUSE GOLDSMITH
GREENWOOD ISHERWOOD
KILLIGREW MANKOWITZ
MASSINGER MIDDLETON
MONCRIEFF MONKHOUSE

SIEVEKING SOUTHERNE
VANDRUTEN WYCHERLEY
BROADHURST CARTWRIGHT
DRINKWATER GALSWORTHY
PHILLPOTTS SHAKESPEARE
ESTONIAN TAMMSAARE
FINNISH KIVI CHORELL
TAVASTSTJERNA
FRENCH BLUM HUGO JOUY KOCK
PYAT VADE BELOT BLOCH CAMUS
CAPUS CARRE CEARD COLLE CUREL
DUCIS DUMAS FABRE FEVAL FLERS
GENET GIONO JARRY PIRON VIGNY
WOLFF ACHARD AUGIER BAYARD
BECQUE BELLOY BRIEUX COLLIN
COOLUS COPEAU DONNAY DOUCET
FAVART HALEVY LESAGE MAIRET
MARCEL MONVEL MOREAU
PAGNOL PARODI PICARD RACINE
RAYNAL RENARD ROTROU SARDOU
SARTRE SCRIBE SOUMET ANCELOT
ANOUILH BARBIER BERNARD
BORNIER BOUILLY BOUVIER
CLAUDEL COCTEAU DENNERY
FERRIER FEYDEAU GRESSET
HERVIEU IONESCO LABICHE
LAPLACE LARIVEY LAVEDAN
LEGOUVE MAURIAC MEILHAC
MEURICE MOLIERE MORTIER
NUITTER PONSARD PREVOST
ROSTAND SANDEAU SARMENT
SEDAINE VILDRAC ANDRIEUX
BARRIERE BATAILLE BEAUVOIR
BENJAMIN CROISSET DANCOURT
DUMANOIR FAUCHOIS MARIVAUX
MONTEPIN QUINAULT VOLTAIRE
BENSERADE BERNSTEIN
BOURSAULT CORNEILLE DELAVIGNE
DUVEYRIER LEMERCIER VACQUERIE
CAMPISTRON CLAIRVILLE
DESTOUCHES BEAUMARCHAIS
GERMAN BAB BABO BEER KIND
LENZ BLOEM ERNST HALBE JOHST
LAUBE SORGE UNRUH ZWEIG
ANGELY BRECHT DREYER GOETHE
HEBBEL KAISER KLEIST KORNER
REUTER WEISSE BARLACH
BENEDIX BRONNEN GUTZKOW
KLINGER LESSING RAUPACH
REDWITZ VULPIUS BRENTANO
GRYPHIUS HOCHHUTH KATZEBUE
KOTZEBUE LISSAUER SCHILLER
WEDEKIND WOLZOGEN BEYERLEIN
GANGHOFER IMMERMANN
SUDERMANN UECHTRITZ
WILBRANDT ZUCKMAYER
AUFFENBERG BLUMENTHAL
FEUCHTWANGER
GREEK ALEXIS SOPHRON THESPIS
CRATINUS PHILEMON RHINTHON
AESCHYLUS EURIPEDES
SOPHOCLES ANTIPHANES
PHRYNICHUS PHERECRATES
ARISTOPHANES
HUNGARIAN TOTH DOCZI JOKAI
VAJDA MOLNAR ZILAHY BESSENYEI
KISFALUDY SZIGLIGETI
ICELANDIC KAMBAN LAXNESS
SIGURJONSSON
IRISH BEHAN COLUM KEANE KELLY
SYNGE WILDE WILLS YEATS ERVINE
MARTYN OCASEY TREVOR WELDON
BECKETT DUNSANY GREGORY

GRIFFIN LEONARD MATURIN
OKEEFFE SHEILDS ORIORDAN
SHERIDAN BICKERSTAFFE
ITALIAN FO BETTI CECCHI GIRAUD
ALFIERI ARETINO BENELLI CARRERA
GIACOSA GOLDONI MARENCO
PELLICO TORELLI RUCELLAI
SABATINI CHIARELLI NICCOLINI
METASTASIO PIRANDELLO
JAPANESE CHIKAMATSU
MEXICAN GAMBOA FUENTES
NORWEGIAN BOJER IBSEN
HEIBERG BJORNSON KIELLAND
POLISH ASNYK FREDRO SZUJSKI
ZAPOLSKA ZEROMSKI ZULAWSKI
NALKOWSKA WYSPIANSKI
BELCIKOWSKI BOGUSLAWSKI
KORZENIOWSKI
PORTUGUESE SILVA BIESTER
ROMAN SENECA NAEVIUS PLAUTUS
TERENCE PACUVIUS
RUMANIAN BEIN BLAGA
RUSSIAN ADAMOV KRYLOV
CHEKHOV KAPNIST KIRSHON
TOLSTOI BULGAKOV CHIRIKOV
FONVIZIN POTEKHIN SUMBATOV
ABLESIMOV BOBORYKIN
OSTROVSKY KNARITONOV
YUSHKEVICH KHMELNITSKI
LAZHECHNIKOV
SCOTTISH BEITH BARRIE BRIDIE
DAVIDSON ROBERTSON
SOUTH AFRICAN FUGARD
SPANISH CRUZ LARRA ROJAS
RUEDA CANETE ENCINA ESPRIU
ZAMORA ALARCON ARRABAL
MACHADO MORATIN CALDERON
DIAMANTE MARTINEZ CERVANTES
FERNANDEZ
SWEDISH WEISS BESKOW EDGREN
BLANCHE HEDBERG MESSENIUS
LAGERKVIST STREINDBERG
SWISS ILG FAESI
WELSH ABSE EVANS HUGHES
WILLIAMS LLEWELLYN
PLAZA PLACE PLEIN SQUARE
ZOCALO
(— DE TOROS) BULLRING
(— GIRL) ELOISE
PLEA BAR BID PLY MOOT NOLO SUIT
ALIBI CLAIM PLEAD ABATER
APPEAL EXCUSE REFUGE APOLOGY
CONTEND DEFENCE LAWSUIT
PRETEXT QUARREL DILATORY
ENTREATY PLACITUM PRETENSE
PLEACH PLAIT PLASH INTERLACE
PLEAD BEG SUE MOOT PLEA PRAY
PRIG SHOW URGE COUNT ORATE
ALLEGE APPEAL ASSERT PLAYTE
PURSUE ENTREAT IMPLORE
SOLICIT WRANGLE ADVOCATE
LITIGATE
(— FOR) SOLICIT PETITION
PLEADER ACTOR VAKIL PATRON
SUITOR VAKEEL COUNTOR
ADVOCATE
PLEADING PLEA PAROL ANSWER
PAROLE ADVOCACY COGNOVIT
DEMURRER INTENDIT MEMORIAL
PLEASANT FUN GAY BEEN BIEN
BRAW FAIR FINE GLAD GOOD
HEND JOLI NEAT TRIM WEME
AMENE BIGLY BONNY CANNY

COUTH CUSHY DOUCE DRUNK
DUCKY GREEN HAPPY HENDE
HODDY JOLLY LEPID LISTY LUSTY
MERRY NUTTY QUEME SMIRK
SUAVE SWEET TIPSY WALLY
WETHE COMELY DAINTY DULCET
GENIAL KINDLY PRETTY SAVORY
SMOOTH AFFABLE ELEGANT
FARRAND JANNOCK LEESOME
WINSOME DELICATE GLORIOUS
GRATEFUL HEAVENLY LIEFSOME
LIKESOME LOVESOME THANKFUL
TOWARDLY GEMUTLICH
(PREF.) HEDY
PLEASANTLY FAIR WINLY FAIRLY
AFFABLY SWEETLY GENIALLY
LIKINGLY
PLEASANTNESS GAIETY NAAMAN
AMENITY SUAVITY JOCUNDITY
PLEASANTRY WIT JEST JOKE
SPORT BANTER JESTING JOLLITY
WAGGERY
PLEASE PAY GAME LIKE LIST LUST
SUIT WANT WISH AGREE AMUSE
BITTE CHARM ELATE FANCY
HUMOR QUEME SAVOR TASTE
ARRIDE KITTLE OBLIGE REGALE
SOOTHE TICKLE AGGRATE
APPLESE CONTENT DELIGHT
GLADDEN GRATIFY PLACATE
REJOICE SATISFY
(— FORWARD) FS
(— THE PUBLIC) TAKE
PLEASED FAIN FOND GLAD APAID
HAPPY PROUD BUCKED CONTENT
GLADSOME
(BE —) GAME
PLEASING AMEN COOL GLAD
GOOD LIEF NICE SOFT AMENE
DICTY NIFTY SOOTH SWEET
CLEVER COMELY DREAMY FACILE
FLASHY GAINLY LIKING LUSTLY
MELLOW PRETTY AMIABLE
BLESSED CORKING DARLING
LIKABLE LIKEFUL TUNABLE
WELCOME CHARMING DELICATE
FAVOROUS FETCHING GRACEFUL
GRACIOUS GRATEFUL HEAVENLY
INVITING LIKESOME PLACABLE
PLAUSIVE SPECIOUS PLAUSIBLE
PERSONABLE
(— TO EAR) HARMONIC
(— TO EYE) EESOME
(— TO HEAR) FAIR
(VERY —) SNAZZY
PLEASURABLE GOOD JOLLY
ANIMAL MIRTHFUL
PLEASURE JO EST FUN JOY BANG
BOOT EASE ESTE GREE KAMA LIST
LUST PLAY WILL BLISS KICKS
MIRTH SAVOR SOOTH TASTE
DAINTY DEDUIT GAIETY GAYETY
LIKING LUXURY NICETY VOLUPT
COMFORT DELIGHT GRATIFY
JOLLITY JOYANCE VOLUPTY
DELICACY FRUITION GLADNESS
HILARITY VOLUPTAS
(— BY INFLICTING PAIN) SADISM
(INTERJECTION TO EXPRESS —)
YUMYUM
(SELFISH —) LECHERY
(STOLEN —) STOUTH STOWTH
(PL.) DELICIAE

PLEASURE SEEKER FRANION
PLEAT SET FOLD KILT POKE RUCK
FLUTE FRILL PINCH PLAIT PRANK
GUSSET SUNRAY
PLEATED PLICATE SUNBURST
PLEBE PLEBS FRESHMAN
PLEBEIAN LOW BASE PLEB SNOB
COMMON HOMELY VULGAR
IGNOBLE LOWBORN POPULAR
BASEBORN EVERYDAY HOMESPUN
INFERIOR MECHANIC ORDINARY
ROTURIER RUPTUARY
PLEBISCITE VOTE DECREE
PLECTRUM PICK SPUR QUILL
UVULA MALLEUS POINTEL
PLECTRON
(— OF HARP) FESCUE
PLEDGE LAY VAS VOW WAD WED
AFFY BAND CLAP EARL GAGE
HAND HEST HOCK OATH PASS
PAWN WAGE WOID WORD FAITH
SIKER SPOUT STAKE SWEAR
SWEAT TOKEN TROTH TRUTH
WAGER ARREST BORROW
COMMIT ENGAGE IMPAWN
IMPONE LUMBER PAROLE PIGNUS
PLEVIN PLIGHT SICCAR SICKER
VADIUM WADSET BARGAIN
BETROTH CAUTION CREANCE
EARNEST HOSTAGE PROMISE
BOTTOMRY MORTGAGE SECURITY
SPONSION VADIMONY
(— IN DRINKING) PROPINE
(— ONESELF) UNDERTAKE
PLEDGED HIGHT SWORN ASSURED
ENGAGED PIGNORATE
(— TO MARRY) SURE
PLEDGET DOSSIL PENICIL
PLEIADES MAIA MEROPE ALCYONE
CELAENO ELECTRA STEROPE
TAYGETA
PLEIN-AIRIST LUMINIST
PLEISTHENES (FATHER OF —)
ATREUS
(MOTHER OF —) AEROPE
(SON OF —) MENELAUS
AGAMEMNON
PLENARY FULL ENTIRE PLENAL
PERFECT ABSOLUTE COMPLETE
PLENITUDE PLENITY PLEROMA
FULLNESS PLETHORA ABUNDANCE
PLENTEOUS RICH COPIOUS
FERTILE AFFLUENT FRUITFUL
GENEROUS ABOUNDING
EXUBERANT
PLENTIFUL OLD FULL RANK RICH
RIFE AMPLE HEFTY LARGE ROUTH
SONSY STORE ENOUGH FOISON
GALORE LAVISH SONSIE COPIOUS
FERTILE LIBERAL OPULENT
PROFUSE UBEROUS ABUNDANT
FRUITFUL NUMEROUS EXUBERANT
PLENTIFULLY RIFE FREELY GALORE
APLENTY
PLENTY WON BAIT COPY MANY
RAFF SONS AMPLE CHEAP COPIA
FOUTH PRICE ROUTH SONSE
TEEMS FOISON OODLES SCOUTH
UBERTY LASHINGS
(— OF) GALORE
(GREAT —) ABUNDANCE
PLEON TELSON ABDOMEN

PLEONASM ITERATION
MACROLOGY TAUTOLOGY
PLETHORA RASH EXCESS PLENUM
PLURISY FULLNESS PLEURISY
POLYEMIA PROFUSION REPLETION
PLETHORIC TUMID TURGID
SWOLLEN INFLATED
PLEURISY EMPYEMA
PLEURON SCAPULA
PLEXUS RETE GLOMUS NETWORK
PROPLEX GENIPLEX
PLIABLE WAXY WEAK LITHY WAXEN
DOCILE LIMBER PLIANT SEMMIT
SUPPLE BOWABLE FICTILE
FINGENT FLEXILE PLASTIC
WINDING CUSHIONY FLEXIBLE
COMPLIANT
PLIANCY FLEXURE FACILITY
PLIANT APT FLIP SWAK AGILE
BUXOM LITHE SWACK YOUNG
DOCILE LIMBER SUPPLE WANDLE
DUCTILE FLEXILE PLASTIC PLIABLE
SLIPPER WILLOWY APPLIANT
FLEXIBLE SUITABLE WORKABLE
SEQUACIOUS
PLICA FOLD TRICHOMA
PLICATE FOLD PLEAT FOLDED
FANLIKE PLAITED
PLIERS BENDER FLEXOR GRATER
FLECTOR PINCERS
PLIGHT PLY FOLD ARRAY BRAID
DRESS PLAIT POINT STATE WOVEN
ATTIRE ENGAGE PICKLE PLEDGE
PLISKY STRAIT TAKING BETROTH
MISCHIEF QUANDARY
PLIGHTED ASSURATE
PLIM PLUM STOUT SWELL INFLATE
PLIABLE
PLIMSOLL (WHITE —S)
MUTTONDUMMIES
(PL.) RUBBERS
PLINTH ORLE ORLO BLOCK SOCLE
ABACUS PATAND QUADRA
SUBBASE FOOTSTALL SCAMILLUS
PLISTHENES (FATHER OF —)
ATREUS
(MOTHER OF —) CLEOLA
(SON OF —) MENELAUS
AGAMEMNON
(WIFE OF —) AEROPE ERIPHYLE
PLOD JOG GRUB PLOT SLOG STOG
TOIL TORE TROG VAMP POACH
TRAMP TRASH DRUDGE SLOUCH
TRUDGE PLUNTHER
(— ALONG) PEG TORE
(— THROUGH MUD) SLOUGH
PLODDER GRUB DIGGER SLOGGER
PLOIARIA EMESA
PLONK WINE
PLOP FLUMP PLUMP HEAVILY
(— DOWN) SIT
PLOT BREW CAST MARK PACK PLAN
PLAT CABAL DRIFT FRAUD GLEBE
GRAPH GREEN HATCH MODEL
PLECK SCALD STORY STUDY
WATCH ACTION BRIGUE CLIQUE
DESIGN DEVISE GARDEN MALIGN
MYTHOS SCHEME SHAMBA
TAMPER AGITATE COLLUDE
COMPACT COMPASS CONJECT
CONNIVE CONTOUR DRAUGHT
FEEDLOT LAZYBED MACHINE
PRETEND QUADRAT QUARTER

SWIDDEN ARGUMENT COGITATE CONSPIRE CONTRIVE INTRIGUE PRACTICE PROTRACT SEMINARY MACHINATE
(— OF GRASS) SONK
(— OF LAND) ERF LOT PLAT SHOT FORTY MILPA PATCH PLECK SPLAT COMMON PARCEL SCHERM SHAMBA HAGGARD LAZYBED SEVERAL
(— OF 1-2 ACRE) ERF
(— SECRETLY) WHISPER
(GARDEN —) BED ERF QUINTA QUARTER
(UNPRODUCTIVE —) HIRST
PLOTTER PACKER HATCHER JACOBIN SCHEMER DESIGNER ENGINEER
PLOUK KNOB PIMPLE
PLOVER DROME KOLEA OXEYE PILOT SANDY STILT KILDEE QUAILY TURNIX COLLIER COURSER DOTTREL LAPWING MAYCOCK OWLHEAD PAPABOT WRYBILL BULLHEAD DOTTEREL DULWILLY HILLBIRD KILLDEER RINGNECK SPURWING SQUEALER TOADHEAD WHISTLER WIREBIRD SANDERLING
PLOW EAR ERE BOUT DISK FOIL HINT LIST MOLE PLOD RIVE ROVE SLUG STIR SULK SULL TILL BREAK FLUNK SPLIT SULKY THROW ARAIRE BUSTER DIGGER DIPPER FALLOW FURROW GOPHER JUMPER LISTER PLOUGH RAFTER ROOTER RUTTER SULLOW BACKSET BREAKER HUSBAND SCOOTER SULCATE TWISTER FIREPLOW FURROWER GANGPLOW SNOWPLOW TURNPLOW
(— CROSSWISE) THORTER
(— HANDLE) STILT
(— LIGHTLY) SKIM RIFFLE
(— PART) PINHEAD
(— WITH SPACE BETWEEN FURROWS) RIB RIVE
(MOTORIZED —) TRACTOR
(PL.) OUTSIGHT
PLOWBOY YOKEL
PLOWING ARDER EARTH ARDURE ARATION CARUAGE STIRRING
PLOWLAND CARUE CARVE TILTH CARUCATE TEAMLAND
PLOWMAN PLOWER TILLER ACREMAN
PLOWSHARE LAY SLIP SOCK LAVER REEST SHARE JUMPER
(— BONE) VOMER PYGOSTYLE
(PREF.) VOMERO
PLOY BENT BOWED SPORT RAMBLE TACTIC PURSUIT ACTIVITY ESCAPADE
PLUCK GO PUG ROB TUG BOUT CROP CULL DRAG GAME GRAB GRIT PELT PICK PILL POOK PULL RACE RASE RASH SAND TUCK ARBER ARBOR BREAK DRAFT HANGE MOXIE NERVE PILCH PLOAT PLUME RANCH SMITE SPUNK STEAL STRIP AVULSE DECERP EVULSE FLEECE GATHER PIGEON PLITCH PLOUGH QUARRY

SNATCH SPIRIT TWINGE TWITCH COURAGE DEPLUME PLUNDER BOLDNESS DECISION DEMOLISH GAMENESS GUMPTION VELLICATE PURTENANCE
(— APART) DIVELLICATE
(— AS A STRING) TIRL PINCH
(— FEATHERS) STUB
(— LEAVES) BLADE
(— OF SHEEP OR CALF) RACE GATHER
(— UP COURAGE) CHEER
(— WOOL BY HAND) ROO
PLUCKED PLUMED PIZZICATO
PLUCKY GAMY SANDY BANTAM GRITTY SPUNKY FIGHTING
PLUG BUG FID PEG PIN TAP TOP WAD BLOW BONE BOTT BUNG FILL JADE ROOT SHOT SLOG STOP SWAT SWOT BOOST DOWEL DUMMY PILOT PUNCH SHACK SKATE SPILE STUFF SWEAT BOUCHE BOXING BULLET COMEDO DOSSIL DOTTLE FIDDLE SPIGOT BOUCHON BUSHING CHAMBER CHUGGER FERRULE STOPPER STOPPLE DRIVECAP FUSEPLUG PELELITH STOPCOCK
(— FOR CANNON) TAMPION
(— IN GRENADE) BOUCHON
(— IN ORGAN PIPE) STOPPLE TAMPION
(— OF CLAY) BOTT
(— OF OAKUM) FID
(— OF VOLCANO) CORE
(— TO HOLD NAIL) DOOK
(— UP) CLAM STOP ESTOP RAMFORCE
(FIRE —) HYDRANT
(FISHING —) BUG
(LIP —) LABRET
(NOSE —) TEMBETA TEMBETARA
(WASTE —) WASHER
(WATER —) HYDRANT
PLUG-IN JACK
PLUG-UGLY THUG ROWDY TOUGH RUFFIAN ROUGHNECK
PLUM GAGE JOBO RISE ISLAY JAMAN PRUNE SWELL BEAUTY CHENEY DAMSEL DAMSON KELSEY MUSSEL SAPOTE APRICOT BULLACE BURBANK FORTUNE ORLEANS QUETSCH PRUNELLO ROSACEAN ROSEWORT VICTORIA WINDFALL
(COCO —) ICACO
(JAVA —) DUHAT JAMBUL JAMBOOL JAMBOLAN
(WILD —) SKEG SLOE ISLAY
(PREF.) PRUNI
PLUMAGE ROBE RUFF FLUFF HACKLE SHROUD FEATHER FLOCCUS JUVENAL PENNAGE FEATHERS PARADISE PTILOSIS
PLUMB BUNG SHEER BOTTOM BULLET SINKER EXACTLY PLUMMET UTTERLY ABSOLUTE COMPLETE DIRECTLY ENTIRELY VERTICAL
PLUMBAGO LUSTER LUSTRE GRAPHITE LEADWORT
PLUMB BOB PLUMMET
PLUMBISM SATURNISM

PLUMB LINE MERKHET
PLUM CURCULIO TURK WEEVIL
PLUME PEN TIP TUFT CREST EGRET PRIDE PRUNE DEPRIVE DESPOIL FEATHER PANACHE AIGRETTE
(— ON HELMET) CREST PANACHE
(— ON HORSE) PLUMADE
(— ON TURBAN) CULGEE
(EGRET —) OSPREY
(MILITARY —) PANACHE
PLUME NUTMEG SASSAFRAS
PLUMMET LEAD FLOAT PLUMB WEIGHT
PLUMMING BRONZING
PLUMP FAT BOLD FAIR FLOP FULL PLOP SLAP SOSS TIDY BLUNT BONNY BUXOM CLUMP FLUMP FUBBY FUBSY GROUP JOLLY PLUNK PUDGY SAPPY SLEEK SMACK SONSY SQUAB STOUT THICK BONNIE CHUBBY CRUMBY CRUMMY DIRECT FATTEN FLATLY FLESHY FODGEL GAWSIE PLUNGE PUBBLE ROTUND ZAFTIG ZOFTIG BLUNTLY BUNTING CLUSTER DISTEND FULSOME RIBLESS THRODDY CHOPPING FLESHFUL
(— AND ROSY) BUXOM
(— AND ROUND) CHUBBY
(NOT —) ANGULAR
(PLEASINGLY —) ZAFTIG ZOFTIG
PLUM POCKET FOOL
PLUMULE BLASTUS FEATHER GEMMULA GEMMULE GEOBLAST ACROSPIRE
PLUNDER GUT ROB BOOT FANG JUNK LOOT PILL POLL PREY RAID RAPE REIF RIPE RUMP SACK SWAG BEROB BOOTY CHEAT GAINS HARRY PLUCK PREDE RAVEN REAVE RENNE RIFLE SCOFF SHAVE SPOIL STRIP BEZZLE BOODLE CREACH DACOIT FLEECE FORAGE HARROW MARAUD PANYAR PROFIT RAPINE RAVAGE DESPOIL ESCHEAT FREIGHT PILFERY PILLAGE RANSACK SACKAGE SPREAGH SPULZIE BOOTHALE FREEBOOT SPOLIATE
PLUNDERER THIEF BANDIT BUMMER PEELER POLLER RAPTOR ROBBER VANDAL ROUTIER SPOILER MARAUDER RAPPAREE
PLUNDERING PREY SACK MARAUD RAPINE ESCHEAT HERSHIP PURCHASE RAVENOUS SPECHERY SPOILFUL SPOILING PREDATORY
PLUNGE BET DIG DIP CAVE DIVE DOOK DUCK DUMP JUMP PURL PUSH RAKE RISK SINK SOSS BURST DOUSE FLING PITCH PLUMP SOUSE SWOOP FOOTER GAMBLE HEADER LAUNCH SPLASH THRUST WALLOP BRAINGE DEMERGE IMMERSE PLOUNCE SUBMERGE
(— DEEPLY) WHELM
(— INTO) CLAP ENGULF IMMERGE
(— INTO WATER) ENEW
(BETTING —) RAKER
(GAMBLING —) RAKER
PLUNGER RAM SWAB FORCE DUCKER POMMEL BLUNGER STRIKER

PLUNGING FLING
PLUNK DIVE PLONK PLUCK PLUMP DOLLAR SUPPORT SUDDENLY
PLUNTHER PLOD FLOUNDER
PLURAL
(SUFF.) IM
PLURALIST TOTQUOT
PLURALITY MAJORITY MORENESS TRIALITY
(PREF.) POLY
PLURALIZER ESS
PLUS AND GAIN WITH EXTRA BESIDES SURPLUS ADDITION INCREASE POSITIVE
PLUSH EASY BEAVER VELOUR SUPERIOR
PLUSHY SWANK SWANKY
PLUTEUS WAGON PARAPET
PLUTO DIS HADES ORCUS
(BROTHER OF —) JUPITER NEPTUNE
(FATHER OF —) SATURN
(WIFE OF —) PROSERPINE
PLUTOCRAT NABOB RICHARD
PLUTONIC HYPOGENE INTRUSIVE VULCANIAN
PLUTUS (ASSOCIATE OF —) TYCHE EIRENE
(FATHER OF —) IASION
(MOTHER OF —) CERES DEMETER
PLY RUN BEAT BEND BIAS CORD CORE DRAM FOLD MOLD SAIL URGE ADAPT APPLY EXERT LAYER STEER TWIST WIELD YIELD COMPLY DOUBLE HANDLE TRAVEL EXERCISE
(— NEEDLE) SEW
(— WITH DRINK) BIRL ROSIN
(— WITH DRUGS) HOCUS
(— WITH QUESTIONS) HECKLE
(OF ONE —) SINGLE
PLYWOOD (LIKE —) LAMINAR
PNEUMA NEUM SOUL NEUME BREATH SPIRIT
PNEUMATIC HAMMER GUN
PNEUMATOCYST FLOAT
PNEUMONIA PULMONITIS
POACH PUG ROB COOK DROP POKE PUSH SINK BLACK DRIVE FORCE POTCH STEAL BLEACH PLUNGE INTRUDE
POACHED EGGS MOONSHINE
POACHER BLACK POGGE SPOACH LURCHER STALKER WIDGEON BALDPATE BULLHEAD
(SALMON —) REBECCA REBEKAH
(PL.) BLACKS
POALES GLUMALES
POCAHONTAS (HUSBAND OF —) ROLFE
POCHARD DUCK SMEE DIVER POKER SCAUP DUNAIR DUNKER DUNBIRD REDHEAD WHINGER GOLDHEAD WHINYARD
POCHETTE KIT VIOLIN HANDBAG
POCKET BOX CLY FOB PIT CLAY KICK POKE PRAT BASIN BURSE MEANS POUCH PURSE STEAL ACCEPT BECKET CASING CANTINA PLACKET SWALLOW TROUSER ENVELOPE ISOLATED MONETARY PROFONDE SUPPRESS CONDENSED MINIATURE

(— A WRONG) PURSE
(— IN BOOK BINDER) STATION
(— OF NET) BOWL
(BILLIARD —) POT HOLE HAZARD
(KIND OF —) BESOM HACKING
KANGAROO
(MAGICIAN'S —) PROFONDE
(NOODLE —S) KREPLACH
(ORE —) CHURN BONANZA
(SMALL —) FOB
(TROUSER —) PRAT BECKET
(WATCH —) FOB
(WATER —) TINAJA ALBERCA
(PL.) KREPLACH
(PREF.) PERO
POCKETBOOK BAG KICK SKIN
PURSE INCOME READER WALLET
HANDBAG LEATHER BILLFOLD
NOTECASE
POCKET GOPHER TUZA QUACHIL
POCKETING COUP
POCKETKNIFE BARLOW PENKNIFE
PIGSTICKER
POCKMARK PITHOLE
POD BAG COD GAM KID POP SAC
BALL BEAN BOLL HULL HUSK POKE
SWAD BOLLY BURSE CAROB
FLOCK POUCH QUASH SHAUP
SHELL CHUCK SNAIL WILLAUD
CHILLI LEGUME PESCOD SCHOOL
HARICOT PEASCOD SILIQUA
PEASECOD PODOCARP POTBELLY
SEEDCASE TAMARIND
(— FORMING) KID
(— OF LEGUME) KID
(— OF MESQUITE) HONEYPOD
(BARLAH —S) NERNER
(CASSIA —) PUDDINGPIPE
(COILED —) STROMBUS
(EXPLOSIVE —) SANDBOX
(SUBTERRANEAN —) EARTHNUT
(UNRIPE —) SQUASH
(PL.) PIPI SUNT BABUI GARAD
BABLAH GARRAT COWHAGE
GONAKIE ALGAROBA DIVIDIVI
(PREF.) SILIQUI
PODALIRIUS (BROTHER OF —)
MACHAON
(FATHER OF —) ASCLEPIUS
PODARCES (BROTHER OF —)
PROTESILAUS
(FATHER OF —) IPHICLUS
PODDED BOLLED
PODIUM DAIS FOOT WALL LECTERN
PODOCARP YACCA
PODWARE PODDER
PODZOL SPODOSOL
POEM GEM LAI LAY ODE DUAN EPIC
GEST IDYL JOSE MELE POSY RUNE
SONG CENTO DIRGE DITTY EDYLL
GESTE HAIKU IWEIN METER STAFF
VERSE AMHRAN AUBADE BALLAD
CACCIA CARMEN CYCLIC DIXAIN
EPOPEE EROTIC ESTRIF HEROID
MELODY MONODY NOSTOS
PIYYUT SESTET SONNET TENSON
TERCET BUCOLIC CANTARE
CANTATA CANZONE DESCORT
DIZAINE ECLOGUE ELEGIAC
FLITING GEORGIC SOTADIC
TRIOLET VIRELAI VIRELAY
VOLUSPA ACROSTIC AMOEBEUM
BRINDISI CANTICLE DINGDONG

DOGGEREL INVICTUS LIMERICK
MADRIGAL TELESTIC THEOGONY
TRISTICH TROCHAIC VERSICLE
MONORHYME ROUNDELAY
(— ABOUT DEBATE) ESTRIF
(— ABOUT SHEPHERDS) ECLOGUE
(— GREETING DAWN) AUBADE
(— OF LAMENTATION) ELEGY
(— OF RETRACTION) PALINODE
(— OF 10 LINES) DIZAINE
(— OF 14 LINES) SONNET
(AMATORY —) EROTIC SONNET
(EPIC —) EPOS EPOPEE LUSIAD
THEBAID
(HOMELY —) DIT
(IRISH —) AMHRAN
(JAPANESE —) HAIKU HANKA
TANKA SENRYU
(LITURGICAL —) VIDDUI VIDDUY
SELIHOTH
(LOVE —) AMORETTO
(LYRIC —) LAI LAY ODE ALBA EPODE
GHAZEL RONDEL CANZONA
PARTIMEN
(MUSICAL —) RONDO
(PART OF —) PASSUS
(PASTORAL —) IDYL IDYLL BUCOLIC
(PERSIAN —) GHAZAL
(RELIGIOUS —) HYMN
(RURAL —) GEORGIC
(SACRED —) PSALM YIGDAL
(SATIRICAL —) IAMBIC KASIDA
(SHORT —) DIT DITTY EPILOG
RONDEL SONNET CANZONE
EPIGRAM RONDEAU EPILOGUE
EPYLLION
(TONE —) BALLADE
(WELSH —) CYWYDD
(PL.) AZAHROT MAKINGS
(SUFF.) STICH
POET OG RSI BARD FILE FILI FIRI
LARK MUSE SCOP SWAN ARION
LAKER LINOS LINUS LYRIC MAKAR
MAKER ODIST RISHI SAYER SCALD
SKALD FINDER GNOMIC IBYCUS
LAKIST LYRIST SHAPER SINGER
DICHTER ELEGIAC EPICIST IDYLIST
IMAGIST MUSAEUS ORPHEUS
PROPHET CONCRETE FERAMORZ
GEORGIAN LAUREATE LUTANIST
MINSTREL SONGSTER TROUVERE
MINNESINGER
(INSPIRED —) PROPHET
(IRISH —) FILI
(MEDIOCRE —) RIMER RHYMER
(MINOR —) BARDIE
ALBANIAN FISHTA
AMERICAN BLY LOW POE AGAR
AGEE BURR CARY CONE DALY HEAD
KEMP MARX NASH READ REED SAXE
SILL SNOW TABB TATE TOWN VERY
WARE ADAMS AIKEN AKINS ALLEN
AUDEN BACON BEERS BENET
BOGAN BROWN CLAPP CLARK
COLES CORSO CRANE DAMON
DRAKE ENGLE FAUST FICKE FIELD
FINCH FITTS FROST GUEST HAYNE
HECHT HOVEY JOLAS MOODY
OPPEN PIATT POUND PRIME RIDGE
RILEY SIMIC STORY TOWNE WELBY
WILDE WYLIE ARNOLD BARLOW
BRALEY BRANCH BROOKS BRYANT
BURTON CARMER CAWEIN CHENEY

CIARDI CLARKE COATES COFFIN
CRANCH CULLEN CUTTER DARGAN
DUNBAR FISHER GIBRAN GILDER
GIORNO GUINEY HOLMES HOOPER
KEELER KILMER LANIER LEDOUX
LOWELL MILLAY MILLER MONROE
MORGAN MORTON NORTON
OSGOOD PARKER SAVAGE SEEGER
SEXTON SHANGE THOMAS TIMROD
TOOMER VIORST WILCOX WRIGHT
AINSLIE BABCOCK BRODSKY
CARRUTH CHIVERS CROWELL
EMERSON FEARING FRENEAU
HALLECK HILLYER JEFFERS
KNOWLES LAFARGE LAZARUS
LIFSHIN LINDSAY MARKHAM
MIFFLIN MOULTON PARSONS
PATCHEN PEABODY PROCTOR
ROBERTS RUSSELL SHAPIRO
SHERMAN STEDMAN TAGGARD
THAXTER VIERECK WAKOSKI
WATTLES WHITMAN BERRYMAN
BRAINARD CARLETON CONKLING
CORNFORD CUMMINGS DINSMOOR
FISHBACK FLETCHER GINSBURG
HAGEDORN MACLEISH NEIHARDT
PETERSON PHILLIPS PROKOSCH
ROBINSON RUKEYSER SANDBURG
SCOLLARD SPOFFORD STERLING
STODDARD TEASDALE THOMPSON
TIETJENS TRUMBULL WHEATLEY
WHITTIER AUSLANDER COOLBRITH
DICKINSON GUITERMAN
HENDERSON HOLLANDER
HOPKINSON KREYMBORG
OPPENHEIM TUCKERMAN
WURDEMANN COATSWORTH
LONGFELLOW BRAITHWAITE
RITTENHOUSE
ARAB TARAFA
ARGENTINIAN ASCASUBI
ECHEVERRIA
AUSTRALIAN GORDON TURNER
AUSTRIAN VOGL KAFKA BACHER
FRANKL GRAZIE WERFEL NEUMANN
ZEDLITZ CASTELLI WILDGANS
WURZBACH ZINGERLE HAMERLING
HOFMANNSTHAL
BELGIAN CLAUS GILKIN GIRAUD
EEKHOUD ELSKAMP HASSELT
CAMMAERTS RODENBACH
VERHAEREN MAETERLINCK
BRAZILIAN GAMA COSTA AZEVEDO
BANDEIRA GUIMARAES
MAGALHAES
BULGARIAN VAZOV BOTYOV
CANADIAN FISET PRATT SCOTT
SMITH BIRNIE CARMAN MACKAY
MCCRAE FERLAND JOHNSON
LAMPMAN SERVICE CAMPBELL
CRAWFORD DRUMMOND
FRECHETTE MACDONALD
CHILEAN NERUDA MISTRAL
CHINESE LU TU CHAO LIPO TUFU
POCHUI MEISHENG
COLOMBIAN ARBOLEDA
CUBAN VALDES
CZECH CECH GOLL ERBEN FRIDA
HALEK HANKA JEBAVY KVAPIL
MACHAR NERUDA SEIFERT
DANISH BOYE RODE EWALD HAUCH
KINGO PLOUG ARREBO JENSEN
RAHBEK BLICHER CLAUSEN

HOSTRUP KAALUND WINTHER
BAGGESEN BODTCHER INGEMANN
JACOBSEN AARESTRUP GRUNDTVIG
JORGENSEN GERSTENBERG
DUTCH CATS GOES KATE POOT
BEETS BERGH EEDEN FEITH HAREN
HOOFT DECKER EMANTS LENNEP
LOGHEM VERWEY VONDEL
BELLAMY BREDERO HELMERS
TOLLENS BARLEAUS SECUNDUS
ACHTERBERG BILDERDIJK
HEEMSKERCK HUYDECOPER
BROEKHUIZEN
ECUADORIAN OLMEDO
ENGLISH BAX GAY MAY MEW PYE
BELL BIGG COOK CORY DYER GALE
GRAY HAKE HALL HILL HOOD HUNT
KOPS LEAR NOEL OWEN POPE
ROWE TATE VAUX ADAMS AUDEN
BASSE BLAKE BLUNT BROWN
BRYAN BYROM BYRON CAREW
CAREY CLARE COOKE DIXON
DONNE DOYLE GOOGE GOULD
GOWER GREEN JONES KEATS
KEOWN LEWIS MASON MERRY
MILNE MINOT MONRO MOORE
MYERS NADEN NOYES PAYNE PEELE
PERCY PRAED PRIOR SMART SMITH
SWAIN WATTS WAUGH WELLS
WHITE WOLFE WOODS WYATT
YOUNG ABBOTT ANSTEY ARNOLD
AUSTIN BAILEY BARKER BARLOW
BARNES BARTON BINYON BOWLES
BRETON BRONTE BROOKE BROWNE
BUTLER CANTON CAPERN CARTER
CLOUGH CORBET COTTON COWLEY
COWPER CRABBE DANIEL DAVIES
DENHAM DOBELL DOBSON DOMETT
DOWSON DRYDEN EUSDEN FENTON
GIBSON GLOVER GODDEN GODLEY
GRAVES GREENE HARVEY HAWKER
HAYLEY HEMANS HOWARD JONSON
KENYON LANDON LANDOR LARKIN
LYTTON MACKAY MARTIN MASSEY
MCLEOD MILMAN MILNES MILTON
MORRIS MUNDAY NESBIT ROGERS
SAVAGE SCOGAN SEWARD SISSON
STRODE SYMONS TAYLOR THOMAS
TREECE TRENCH WALLER WARNER
WARREN WARTON WATSON
WITHER WOLCOT WOTTON AINSLIE
BAMFORD BARCLAY BLUNDEN
BRIDGES CAEDMON CAMPION
CHAPMAN CHAUCER COKAYNE
COLLINS COPPARD CRASHAW
DARYUSH DOUGHTY DRAYTON
ELLIOTT FAUSSET FLATMAN
FLECKER FRAUNCE FREEMAN
GIBBONS GIFFORD GRIGSON
HERRICK HEWLETT HOPKINS
HOUSMAN INGELOW KENNEDY
KIPLING LAYAMON LYDGATE
MANNYNG MARLOWE MARVELL
MEYNELL MONTAGU NEWBOLT
NICHOLS PATMORE PEACOCK
PHILIPS POMFRET PROCTER
QUARLES SASSOON SEYMOUR
SHELLEY SITWELL SKELTON
SKIPSEY SOUTHEY SPENDER
SPENSER SYMONDS TICKELL
TREVENA VAUGHAN WEBSTER
WOOLNER AKENSIDE BEAUMONT
BETJEMAN BLAGMIRE BRANFORD

BRERELEY BROWNING BUCHANAN
CAMPBELL CHALONER CYNEWULF
DAVENANT FALCONER GASCOYNE
GREVILLE HAMILTON HOCCLEVE
LANGLAND LOVELACE MACNEICE
MOULTRIE OVERBURY ROSSETTI
SHADWELL STERLING SUCKLING
TENNYSON THOMPSON TRAHERNE
WHISTLER ALDINGTON
ARMSTRONG BARNFIELD
BLANCHARD BOTTOMLEY
CALVERLEY CAMBRIDGE CHALKHILL
CHURCHILL CLEVELAND COLERIDGE
CONSTABLE GASCOIGNE
GOLDSMITH HABINGTON
LANGHORNE MASEFIELD
MONKHOUSE ROSCOMMON
SACKVILLE SHENSTONE
SOUTHWELL SWINBURNE
SYLVESTER UNDERHILL WHITEHEAD
BLOOMFIELD BOURDILLON
BRATHWAITE CHATTERTON
DRINKWATER FITZGERALD
MONTGOMERY SOMERVILLE
WORDSWORTH ABERCROMBIE
SHAKESPEARE TURBERVILLE
CHAMBERLAYNE OSHAUGHNESSY
FINNISH MANNINEN RUNEBERG
ARWIDSSON TAVASTSTJERNA
FRENCH NAU AIDE BAIF CHAR FORT
GHIL GRAS KAHN LABE VIAU ARENE
BOREL CARCO DIERX DORAT DUCIS
GACON GREGH GUYAU HARDY
LEGER LOUYS MAROT MURET
PERET PIRON RICTUS SCEVE SULLY
TASTU VIGNY AICARD ARAGON
ARTAUD AUGIER AUTRAN BARTAS
BELLAY BERTIN BRETON BRUNET
COPPEE DANIEL DEREME DUPONT
ELUARD FRANCE GUERIN HUGUES
JAMMES LEBRUN MORICE MUSSET
PARODI PRADON RACINE REBOUL
RICARD RICTUS SAMAIN THIARD
VALERY VILLON ANCELOT AUBANEL
BARBIER BOCCAGE BOILEAU
BONNARD BORNIER BOUCHOR
BOURGET BRIZEUX CARRERE
CAZALIS CHENIER CLAUDEL
COCTEAU DELTEIL FEYDEAU
GAUTIER GILBERT GRESSET
HENRIOT HEREDIA JODELLE
LAPRADE MATHIEU MAYNARD
MISTRAL MOLINET PONSARD
REGNIER RIMBAUD RONSARD
ROSTAND SCARRON SEGRAIS
VICAIRE VILDRAC AJALBERT
ANDRIEUX BEAUVOIR BERANGER
BERGERAT BERTRAND BOUILHET
CHARTIER CHAULIEU COLLERYE
CORBIERE GRECOURT GRINGORE
LAFORGUE MALHERBE MALLARME
PEROCHON PERRAULT QUILLARD
QUINAULT RABELAIS ROUSSEAU
VERLAINE BELMONTET BOUFFLERS
CHAPELAIN CREBILLON DELAVIGNE
DESCHAMPS LAMARTINE
LEMERCIER MONTREUIL
PRUDHOMME ARLINCOURT
BARTHELEMY BAUDELAIRE
BOISROBERT CHENEDOLLE
DESPORTES MALFILATRE
CHANTAVOINE GRANDMOUGIN
DESHOULIERES

GERMAN UZ BAUM BOIE DACH
HUCH KLAJ LENZ RIST VOSS AYRER
BOHME BRANT BUSCH FRANK
GLEIM HARDT HEBEL HEINE HERTZ
HOLTY LANGE LOGAU OPITZ RAABE
RILKE SACHS SORGE STEIN UNRUH
WEBER BECKER BRECHT BROGER
BURGER DEHMEL FOLLEN GEORGE
GOETHE GOTTER GRABBE HAMMER
HEBBEL HERDER HESSUS JORDAN
KARSCH KERNER KLEIST KNEBEL
KOBELL KORNER LEFORT MORIKE
MULLER TIEDGE TOLLER UHLAND
ULRICH WALDIS WEISSE WERNER
ALLMERS BARLACH BARTHEL
BOTTGER BROCKES BUCHNER
FONTANE FORSTER GELLERT
HARRIES HENRICI KALBECK
KASTNER KOPSICH MALTITZ
NEUMARK NOVALIS REDWITZ
RUCKERT VISCHER WALTHER
WIELAND BAUMBACH BIERBAUM
BRENTANO CLAUDIUS ECKSTEIN
FLEMMING FREIDANK GERHARDT
GRYPHIUS HAGEDORN HOFFMANN
JUNGHANS KAUFMANN LISSAUER
MAHLMANN OVERBECK SCHEFFEL
SCHILLER SCHUBART STOLBERG
WERNICKE ACIDALIUS BECHSTEIN
BULTHAUPT HAUPTMANN
HOLDERLIN IMMERMANN
KIRCHBACH KLOPSTOCK
MOSENTHAL NIETZSCHE
RODENBERG WILBRANDT
BODENSTEDT CREIZENACH
FASTENRATH HARDENBERG
KOSEGARTEN MATTHISSON
WECKHERLIN FREILIGRATH
KOLBENHEYER SCHNECKENBURGER
GREEK ION BION AGIAS ARION
HOMER ELYTIS ERINNA HESIOD
IBYCUS NONNUS PALLES PIGRES
PINDAR SAPPHO AGATHON
ALCAEUS ARCHIAS BIKELAS
CORINNA EUPOLIS HERODAS
ISYLLUS LESCHES MOSCHUS
MUSAEUS PALAMAS RHIANUS
SOLOMOS THESPIS ANACREON
COLUTHUS DIAGORAS HIPPONAX
NICANDER PANYASIS PHILETAS
PISANDER STASINUS THEOGNIS
TYRTAEUS AESCHYLUS EUPHORION
LYCOPHRON SIMONIDES
SOPHOCLES TERPANDER
TIMOTHEUS PARTHENIUS
PHOCYLIDES SEFERIADES
THEOCRITUS ASCLEPIADES
BACCHYLIDES HERMESIANAX
STESICHORUS CHRISTOPOULOS
HINDU BHARTRIHARI
HUNGARIAN ADY TOTH AMADE
ARANY GARAY RFVAI SZASZ JOZSEF
MADACH PETOFI BALASSA
CZUCZOR KOLCSEY MAILATH
BACSANYI GYONGYOSI KISFALUDY
VOROSMARTY
ICELANDIC EGILSSON
GUNNARSSON JOCHUMSSON
THORODDSEN HALLGRIMSSON
SIGURJONSSON
INDIAN GHOSE OQBAL TAGORE
BILHANA

IRISH FILI BANIM COLUM DAVIS
JOYCE KEANE MOORE TIGHE TYNAN
WILDE WILLS WOLFE YEATS
ANSTER BROOKE CLARKE DARLEY
DEVERE FIGGIS GRAVES HEANEY
MAGINN MANGAN PEARSE SKRINE
BARRETT DRENNAN DUNSANY
HIGGINS MACGILL STARKEY
CAMPBELL FERGUSON FLECKNOE
KAVANAGH LEDWIDGE MCCARTHY
STEPHENS ALLINGHAM LARMINNIE
MACDONAGH
ISRAELI BIALIK
ITALIAN REDI ROSA VIDA ZENO
BELLI BERNI BETTI BONDI BOSSI
CASTI DANTE GUIDI MOLZA MONTI
PORTA PRAGA PRATI PULCI TASSO
CIAMPI GIUSTI GROSSI MAMELI
MARINI PARINI POERIO REVERE
ALEARDI ALFIERI ARIOSTO BERCHET
BOIARDO FOLENGO FRUGONI
GUARINI MANZONI MARRADI
MAZZONI MONTALE PASCOLI
ZANELLA ALAMANNI BACCELLI
BIBBIENA CARDUCCI CHIARINI
COSTANZO FILICAIA GUERRINI
LEOPARDI MARTELLI NENCIONI
PETRARCH RUCELLAI TANSILLO
ARNABOLDI BARBERINI BROFFERIO
CALZABIGI CESAROTTI CHIABRERA
MARINETTI QUASIMODO RAPISARDI
ANGIOLIERI CANNIZZARO
FIRENZUOLA METASTASIO
PINDEMONTE BRACCIOLINI
CRESCIMBENI FORTEGUERRI
JAPANESE BASHO AKAHITO
MASAOKA NOGUCHI
LITHUANIAN MAIRONIS
MEXICAN PAZ
NEW ZEALAND DUGGAN
NICARAGUAN DARIO
NORWEGIAN MOE KRAG IBSEN
AANRUD HANSEN GARBORG
BJORNSON WELHAVEN
PAKISTANI FAIZ
PERSIAN HAFIZ SAADI ANVARI
DAKIKI HATIFI NIZAMI FIRDAUSI
PERUVIAN CHOCANO
POLISH POL ASNYK LANGE POTOCKI
SZUJSKI UJEJSKI WITTLIN ZALESKI
KLONOWIC KRASICKI ZEROMSKI
ZULAWSKI GASZYNSKI KARPINSKI
KRASINSKI BRODZINSKI
DANILOWSKI KONOPNICKA
LOBODOWSKI MALCZEWSKI
MICKIEWICZ SARBIEWSKI
WIERZYNSKI WYSPIANSKI
KOCHANOWSKI LENARTOWICZ
SZYMONOWICZ
PORTUGUESE DEUS MELO QUITA
BOCAGE CAMOES CASTRO
GONZAGA QUENTAL RESENDE
RIBEIRO CASTILHO FERREIRA
JUNQUEIRO PALMEIRIM
NASCIMENTO
ROMAN CATO OVID CINNA LUCAN
VARRO ACCIUS BAVIUS ENNIUS
HORACE LIVIUS VERGIL VIRGIL
AVIENUS MARTIAL NAEVIUS
STATIUS TERENCE AFRANIUS
CATULLUS LUCILIUS SEDULIUS
TIBULLUS VALERIUS LUCRETIUS
PROPERTIUS

RUMANIAN BLAGA TZARA
EMINESCU ALEXANDRI ALECSANDRI
THEODORESCU
RUSSIAN FET MEI BELY BLOK
BUNIN BUGAEV ESENIN IVANOV
MAIKOV RYLEEV BALMONT
BRYUSOV GNEDICH GUMILEV
KAPNIST KOLTSOV NIKITIN PUSHKIN
NEKRASOV POLONSKI TYUTCHEV
BESTUZHEV DERZHAVIN
KHERASKOV KHOMYAKOV
LERMONTOV LOMONOSOV
PASTERNAK ZHUKOVSKI
BARATYNSKI BATYUSHKOV
EVTUSHENKO MAYAKOVSKI
PLESHCHEEV BOGDANOVICH
VOZNESENSKY YEVTUSHENKO
SCOTTISH ADAM AIRD GRAY HOGG
LANG MURE THOM AYTON BRUCE
BURNS JACOB LOGAN SCOTT
SHARP SMITH YOUNG AYTOUN
DUNBAR GRAHAM HERVEY LEYDEN
MALLET MICKLE MILLER MURRAY
NICOLL POLLOK RAMSAY SPENCE
WILSON BAILLIE BARBOUR
BARCLAY BEATTIE CLELAND
DOUGLAS GRAHAME KENNEDY
LINDSAY MACBETH PRINGLE
TENNANT THOMSON ANDERSON
CAMPBELL COCKBURN DAVIDSON
DRUMMOND HAMILTON HENRYSON
MACNEILL MAITLAND ALEXANDER
BELLENDEN BLACKLOCK
FERGUSSON GILFILLAN
MACDONALD STEVENSON
BALLANTINE CUNNINGHAM
MACDIARMID MOTHERWELL
MONTGOMERIE
SOUTH AFRICAN BREYTENBACH
LANGENHOVEN
SPANISH CRUZ MENA RUIZ VEGA
DURAN LORCA RIOJA CANETE
CETINA ESPRIU GARCIA VIRUES
ALCAZAR BECQUER GALLEGO
GONGORA HERRERA IRIARTE
JIMENEZ MORATIN SALINAS
AGUILERA BALBUENA CORONADO
FIGUEROA MANRIQUE VILLEGAS
CERVANTES ALEIXANDRE
CASTILLEJO CIENFUEGOS
ESPRONCEDA SANTILLANA
VILLAMEDIANA
SWEDISH DALIN BESKOW CREUTZ
LIDNER TEGNER WALLIN DALGREN
EKELUND LEOPOLD RYDBERG
SJOWALL ATTERBOM BELLMAN
BORJESON BOTTIGER BRINKMAN
KELLGREN LAGERLOF LENNGREN
LEVERTIN NICANDER ADLERBETH
KARLFELDT MARTINSON
MESSENIUS FAHLCRANTZ
LAGERKVIST STAGNELIUS
STRANDBERG WENNERBERG
OXENSTIERNA
SWISS ILG AMIEL FAESI MEYER
BODMER GESSNER LAVATER
FROHLICH LEUTHOLD SPITTELER
SYRIAN GIBRAN
TURKISH NABI FUZULI
URUGUAYAN FIGUEROA
WELSH DAVID HUGHES SYMONS
THOMAS VAUGHAN WILLIAMS
YUGOSLAVIAN POPA

POETASTER BARDET BAVIAN BAVIUS POETITO BARDLING VERSEMAN SONNETEER
POETIC ODIC LYRIC STILTED PEGASEAN POEMATIC
POETICAL (NOT —) PROSE
POETRY EPOS SONG BLANK MELIC POEMS VERSE EPOPEE POESIS SONIOU DOGGREL KALEVALA
(FINNISH —) RUNES
(GOD OF —) BRAGI
(HEROIC —) EPOS
(KIND OF —) CONCRETE
(MUSE OF —) ERATO THALIA EUTERPE CALLIOPE
(PASSAGE OF —) MORCEAU
POGGE BULLHEAD
POGROM RIOT PILLAGE MASSACRE
POGY POGIE MENHADEN
POI (— INGREDIENT) TARO
POIGNANT APT HOME KEEN ACUTE SHARP SMART BITING BITTER MOVING SEVERE URGENT CUTTING INTENSE POINTED PUNGENT SATIRIC INCISIVE PIERCING PRESSING STINGING STRIKING TOUCHING AMAREVOLE
POINCIANA DELONIX FLAMBEAU GULMOHAR FLAMBOYER
POINSETTIA BANNER FIREFLOWER
POINT AIM DOT JOT NAK NEB NIB NUB PEG PIN RES WAY APEX BACK BOKE CHAT CUSP FORK GAFF GAME GOOD HEAD HOLD ITEM KNOT LACE LOOK NAIL PEAK PICK PILE PINT SPOT STOP WHET BEARD CHALK DIGIT FOCUS INDEX LEVEL MUCRO PITCH PRICK PUNCH PUNCT PUNTA PUNTO REFER STAND TEACH THING TOOTH ALLUDE BROACH CRAYON CUSPIS CUTOFF DEGREE DIRECT FLECHE JUGALE MATTER NOSING PERIOD THESIS TITTLE VERTEX ZYGION APICULA ARTICLE BENEFIT CACUMEN CRUNODE ESSENCE GATEWAY PUNCTUM PUSHPIN SHARPEN TANJONG TRAGION ANNOUNCE PUNCTULE STRIPPER PARTICULAR
(— AIMED AT) SCOPE
(— AT ISSUE) BEEF CRUX
(— AT WHICH LEAF SPRINGS) AXIL
(— BEHIND EAR) ASTERION
(— FOR PHONOGRAPH RECORD) STYLE
(— IN CAPSTAN) STRIPPER
(— IN CONSONANT) DAGHESH
(— IN DEBATE) ISSUE
(— IN GAME) SHY
(— IN ORBIT OF PLANET) AUGE APSIS APOGEE SYZYGY APOJOVE PERIGEE APASTRON APHELION
(— IN ORBIT OF SPACECRAFT) PERILUNE
(— IN QUESTION) ISSUE
(— IN SEVEN-UP) GIFT
(— IN SOME GAMES) PUNT
(— NEAREST EARTH) PERIGEE
(— OF A BORDER) VANDYKE
(— OF ANCHOR) BILL
(— OF ANTLER) PRONG
(— OF ANVIL) HORN

(— OF CELESTIAL SPHERE) ANTAPEX
(— OF CHIN) BUTTON
(— OF CONTACT) EPHAPSE
(— OF CRESCENT MOON) CUSP
(— OF CURVE) SPINODE
(— OF CUTTING) STYLE
(— OF DECLINE) EBB
(— OF DEVELOPMENT) STAGE
(— OF DIVERGENCE) AXIL
(— OF ECLIPTIC) LAGNA SOLSTICE
(— OF ENERGY) CHAKRA
(— OF EPIGRAM) STING
(— OF FAITH) ARTICLE
(— OF HONOR) PUNDONOR
(— OF INTEREST) CLOU
(— OF INTERSECTION) FOOT STAURION
(— OF JAVELIN) SAGAIE
(— OF JUNCTION) MEET BREGMA LAMBDA
(— OF LABEL) LAMBEAU
(— OF LACE) TAG
(— OF LAND) ODD CAPE SPIT MORRO HEADLAND
(— OF LEAF) MUCRO
(— OF LIFE) HYLEG
(— OF LIGHT) GLINT SPANGLE
(— OF LIGHTNING ROD) AIGRETTE
(— OF LIPS) CHEILION
(— OF MANGO) NAK
(— OF ONSET) BRINK
(— OF ORIGIN) HIVE SOURCE FOUNTAIN
(— OF PEN) NEB NIB
(— OF PETAL) LACINULA
(— OF REFERENCE) STYLION
(— OF ROCK) NUNATAK
(— OF STAG'S HORN) START
(— OF STORY) KNOT
(— OF STYLUS) CUTTER
(— OF SUPPORT) BEARING
(— OF TEMPERATURE) SOLIDUS
(— OF TIME) DATE INSTANT JUNCTURE
(— OF TOOTH) CUSP
(— OF UMBRELLA) FERRULE
(— OF VIEW) EYE ANGLE FRONT SLANT COLORS CORNER GROUND RESPECT FUTURISM
(— OF VIOLIN BOW) HEAD
(— OF WEAPON) ORD BARB
(— ON AUGER OR BIT) SPUR
(— ON BACKGAMMON BOARD) FLECHE
(— ON BILLIARD TABLE) SPOT
(— ON CURVE) TACNODE
(— ON JAW) GONION
(— ON STAG'S HORN) BROACH
(— ON SUNDIAL) NODE
(— OUT) SHOW DIGIT INFER ASSIGN DIRECT ENSIGN FINGER MUSTER NOTIFY REMARK PRESAGE INDICATE
(APPROPRIATE —) PLACE
(ASTROLOGICAL —) INGRESS DESCENDANT
(AT THAT —) THEN THERE
(BARBED —) FORK
(BLUNT —) MORNETTE
(CARBON —) CRAYON
(CARDINAL —) EAST WEST HINGE NORTH SOUTH
(CARDINAL —S) CARDINES

(CENTRAL —) OMPHALOS
(CHIEF —S) SUM
(CHRONOLOGICAL —) ERA EPOCH
(COMPASS —) E N S W NE NW SE SW ENE ESE NNE NNW SSE SSW WNW WSW AIRT AIRTH RHUMB COURSE
(CRITICAL —) JUMP
(CROWNING —) CAPSHEAF CAPSTONE
(CRUCIAL —) CRUX
(CULMINATING —) HEAD COMBLE
(DOUBLE — OF CURVE) ACNODE CRUNODE
(END —) TERMINUS
(ESSENTIAL —) MAIN
(EXACT —) TEE
(EXCESS —S) LAP
(EXCLAMATION —) BANG SCREAMER
(EXTREME —) END
(FARTHEST —) APOGEE SOLSTICE
(FINAL —) UPCOME
(FIXED —) ABUTMENT
(GET THE —) SEE
(GLAZIER'S —) SPRIG
(HALFWAY — IN CRIBBAGE) CORNER
(HEBREW —) SHEVA
(HIGHEST —) TIP ACME APEX AUGE NOON PEAK CREST FLOOD APOGEE CLIMAX CULMEN HEIGHT PERIOD SUMMIT VERTEX ZENITH EVEREST MAXIMUM MERIDIAN SOLSTICE
(HIGHEST SAFE —) REDLINE
(KNOTTY —) CRUX NODUS
(LAST —) END
(LATERAL —) ALARE
(LOW —) TROUGH
(LOWEST —) NADIR BOTTOM BEDROCK
(LOWEST — OF HULL) BILGE
(MAIN —) JET SUM GIST
(MEDIAN —) HORMION
(NICE —) PUNCTILIO
(NO —S) LOVE
(ONE'S STRONG —) FORTE
(PEDAL —) DRONE
(PIVOTAL —) KNUCKLE
(PRECISE —) NICK
(PROJECTING —) CRAG PEAK BEARD
(SELLING —) HOOK
(SHARP —) JAG PRICK PRICKLE
(SIGNIFICANT —) MILESTONE
(SINGLE —) ACE
(SKULL —) TYLION
(SORE —) NERVE
(STARTING —) BASE ORIGIN SCRATCH
(STATIONARY —) SPINODE
(STRIKING —) SALIENCE
(STRONG —) FORTE
(TAPERING —) ACUMEN
(TENNIS —) LET CHASE BISQUE
(TENTH OF —) MOMENT
(TERMINAL —) GOAL BOURN BREAK AIRPORT
(TOP —) TUFT
(TO THE —) BLUNT COGENT
(TURNING —) CARDO EPOCH CRISIS
(UNIPLANAR —) UNODE
(UTMOST —) EXTREME SUBLIME

(VANTAGE —) TOWER
(VOWEL —) SERE SEGOL SEGHOL
(WEAK —) BLOT
(PREF.) KENTRO MUCRONI PUNCTATO PUNCTI PUNCTO STIGMATI STIGMEO STIGMO
POINT-BLANK BLUNT PLAIN POINT DIRECT WHOLLY EXPRESS DIRECTLY
POINT COUNTER POINT (AUTHOR OF —) HUXLEY
(CHARACTER IN —) JOHN LUCY MARK BURLAP ELINOR GILRAY PHILIP RACHEL SIDNEY WALTER WEBLEY BIDLAKE CARLING EVERARD QUARLES RAMPION BEATRICE MARJORIE SPRANDRELL TANTAMOUNT
POINTED SET ERDE HOME ACUTE EXACT FIXED PEAKY PIKED TANGY TERSE ACUATE FITCHE LIVELY OXEOTE PEAKED PECKED PICKED SPIRED ANGULAR FITCHEE LACONIC PRECISE SPICATE ZESTFUL ACICULAR ACULEATE COPATAIN CULTRATE DIACTINE PUNCTUAL STELLATE ACUMINATE **(PREF.)** OXY
POINTEDNESS BARB
POINTER TIP YAD COCK HAND WAND ARROW DUBHE INDEX POINT FESCUE FINGER GUNDOG INDICE SILKER STYLUS FLUSHER INDICANT SIGNITOR
(— IN GREAT BEAR) DUBHE DUBBHE
(— ON ASTROLABE) ALMURY
(— ON GAUGE) ARM
(BUILDER'S —) RAKER
(TEACHER'S —) FESCUE
(PL.) MEN GUARDS YADAYIM
POINTLESS DRY ILL DULL FLAT INANE SILLY VAPID FRIGID STUPID INSIPID WITLESS MUTICOUS
POINTSMAN TRAPPER LATCHMAN SWITCHMAN
POISE PEE CALM HEAD REST SWAY TACT BRACE PEIZE APLOMB OFFSET PONDER BALANCE BEARING DIGNITY OPPRESS POISURE DELIVERY EASINESS SERENITY
(— RECIPROCAL) RHE
POISED SET FACILE HOVERING NERVELESS
(BE —) LIBRATE
POISER HALTER
POISON FIG GAS DANE BIKH DRAB DRUG GALL TUBA VERY ATTER TAINT TOXIN VENOM VIRUS ANTIAR DERRIS INFECT RANKLE TOXIFY TOXOID ACONITE BABASCO CORRUPT ENVENOM FLYBANE MINERAL PERVERT PHALLIN TANGHIN VITIATE ACQUETTA DELETERY RATSBANE VENENATE SAXITOXIN
(— IN DEATH CUP) PHALLIN
(ARROW —) HAYA INEE URALI URARE URARI ANTIAR ANTJAR CURARE CURARI DERRIS OURARI OUABAIN

(FISH —) AKIA CUBE TIMBO DERRIS HAIARI BABASCO BARBASCO
(RAT —) ANTU
(VIRULENT —) BIKH TANGHIN
(PREF.) PHARMACO VENENI VENENO VIRU
POISONED BUCKEYED TOXICATE VENENATE VENOMOUS
POISONER SEPSIN CANIDIA VENEFIC VENOMER
POISON HEMLOCK BUNK CICUTA
POISONING PYEMIA UREMIA ARGYRIA GASSING JIMMIES BOTULISM MYCETISM PLUMBISM CROTALISM FLUOROSIS ICHTHYISM LATHYRISM SATURNISM SELENOSIS INTOXICATION
(ANTIMONY —) STIBIALISM
(LEAD —) SATURNISM
POISON IVY CLIMATH MARKERY MERCURY MARKWEED
POISON OAK YEARA
POISONOUS ATTRY TOXIC ATTERY VENENE VIROSE VIROUS BANEFUL NOISOME NOXIOUS DELETERY MEPHITIC TOXICANT VENENATE VENOMOUS VIRULENT MALIGNANT
(PREF.) TOX(I)(IC)(ICO)(O)
POISON SUMAC BURTREE DOGWOOD
POISON TOBACCO HENBANE
POISONWOOD BUMWOOD
POITREL ARMOR PECTRON
POKE BAG DAB DIG DUB HIT JAB JOG PUG PUR TIG WAD BROD PAUT PORR PROD PROG RAUK RUCK SACK SOCK STAB STIR NIDGE POACH PROKE PROTE PUNCH ROUSE STEER STOKE COWBOY DAWDLE INCITE PIERCE POCKET POUNCE POUTER PUGGLE PUTTER WALLET PRODDLE
(— ABOUT) ROKE ROUT RUMMAGE
(— AROUND) ROOT SCROUNGE
(— FUN) COD
(— LIGHTLY) POTTER PUTTER
(— WITH FOOT) SCUFF
(— WITH NOSE) SNUZZLE
POKE-IN STRANDER
POKELOKEN BOGAN LOGAN
POKER DART DRAW FLIP POIT PORR POTE STUD BLUFF BOGIE CURATE GOBLIN STOKER ACEPOTS FRUGGAN LOWBALL PASSOUT POCHARD SHOTGUN BASEBALL COALRAKE JACKPOTS MISTIGRI SHOWDOWN
(— ACTION) RAISE
(— CHIP) JETON JETTON
(— HAND) RUNT FLUSH SKEET KILTER PELTER STRAIGHT
(— PLANT) TRITOMA
(FORM OF —) DRAW STUD
(HOT —) SALAMANDER
POKEWEED POKE POCAN SCOKE COAKUM GARGET FOXGLOVE INKBERRY REDBERRY
POKEY STIR
POKY DEAD DULL JAIL SLOW DOWDY POKEY POKING SHABBY STODGY STUFFY STUPID CRAMPED TEDIOUS
POLAK BALSA POLLACK

POLAND

CAPITAL: WARSAW
COIN: DUCAT GROSZ MARKA ZLOTY FENNIG HALERZ KORONA
DANCE: POLKA MAZURKA KRAKOWIAK POLONAISE
GENTRY: SZLACHTA
LAKE: GOPLO MAMRY SNIARDWY
MEASURE: CAL MILA MORG PRET LINJA SAZEN STOPA VLOKA WLOKA CWIERK KORZEC KWARTA LOKIEC GARNIEC
MOUNTAIN: RYSY TATRA SUDETEN
NAME: POLONIA SARMATIA
NATIVE: SLAV MARUR SILESIAN
PARLIAMENT: SEJM SEYM SENAT
PROVINCE: OPOLE KIELCE
RIVER: BUG SAN ALLE BRDA GWDA LYNA NYSA ODER STYR BIALA BZURA DRANA DWINA NOTEC SERET WARTA WISTA NEISSE NIEMEN PILICA PRIPET PROSNA STRYPA WIEPRZ VISTULA WISTOKA DNIESTER
TITLE OF ADDRESS: PAN PANI PANIE
TOWN: LWO KOLO LIDA LODZ LVOV OELS BREST BYTOM CHELM POSEN RADOM SRODA TORUN VILNA GDANSK GDYNIA GRODNO KRACOW KRAKOW LUBLIN POZNAN TARNOW WARSAW ZABRZE BEUTHEN BRESLAU CHORZOW GAROCIN GLIWICE LEMBERG LITOUSK WROCLAW GLEIWITZ KATOWICE SZCZECIN TARNOPOL
WEIGHT: LUT FUNT UNCYA KAMIAN CENTNER SKRUPUL

POLAR ARCTIC EMANANT PIVOTAL DIRECTRIX
POLARIS ALRUCABA
POLARITY (WITHOUT —) ASTATIC
POLE BAR LAT LEG LUG POL POY ROD SKY XAT BEAM BIND BROG COPE FALL HOOK KENT MAST NEAP PALO PERK PIKE PROP SKID SPAR TREE UFER CABER FOCUS MASUR MAZUR PERCH QUANT REACH SHAFT SPEAR SPOKE STAFF STANG STILT STING STODE SWAPE SWIPE BEACON BORITY CROTCH FLOWER IMPOSE JUFFER KILHIG RICKER RISSLE RYPECK SPONGE STOWER TONGUE BARLING HEAVENS TOWMAST ALESTAKE FLAGPOLE FOOTPICK POLANDER STANDARD
(— AS EMBLEM OF SOVEREIGNTY) KAHILI
(— AS HOLDFAST FOR BOATS) RYPECK
(— FOR BEARING COFFIN) SPOKE
(— FOR PROPELLING BOAT) POY
(— FOR TOSSING) CABER KEBAR
(— HOLDING SAIL) BOOM MAST SPRIT
(— MARKING SAND DUNE) BALIZE

(— OF TIMBER WAGON) NIB JANKER
(— OF VEHICLE) NEAP
(— ON TWO WHEELS) JANKER
(— SEPARATING HORSES) BAIL
(—S LIVING OUTSIDE POLAND) POLONIA
(— USED AS SIGN) ALEPOLE ALESTAKE
(— WITH BIRD DECOY) STOOL
(BOAT —) SPRIT
(CARRIAGE —) NIB BEAM
(COUPLING —) REACH
(FIR —) UFER UPHER JUFFER
(FISHING —) WAND
(FORKED —) CROTCH
(LOGGING —) JANKER KILHIG KILLIG
(LONG —) PEW
(MANGROVE —) BORITY
(MINE —S) LAGGING
(NEGATIVE —) CATHODE
(PUNT —) QUANT STOWER
(RANGE —) FLAG
(SACRED —) ASHERAH
(SHEPHERD'S —) KENT
(SPRINGY —) BINDER
(STABLE —) BAIL
(STOUT —) KILHIG RICKER
(WATER-RAISING —) SWEEP
(SUFF.) KONT
POLEAX STAFF POLEARM
POLECAT FITCH SKUNK ZORIL FERRET FICHAT WEASEL FOUMART FOULMART PERWITSKY SARMATIER
(— PELT) FITCH
POLE FLOUNDER SOLE
POLEHEAD TADPOLE
POLESTAR STAR GUIDE POLARIS LODESTAR
POLICE MAN FUZZ HEAT GUARD WATCH GOVERN CONTROL JEMADAR OCHRANA POLIZEI PROTECT TOXOTAE OPRICHNIK
(— CAR) PANDACAR
(— FINDING) MO
(— OFFICER) ROZZER
(— STATION) NICK
(SECRET —) CHEKA
POLICEMAN COP JOE KID NAB PIG BOGY BULL FLIC FUZZ GRAB JACK JOHN PEON SLOP TRAP ZARP BOBBY BOGEY BULKY BURLY GAZER PEACE RURAL SCREW SEPOY ASKARI BADGER BOBBIE COPPER FISCAL FLATTY HARMAN JOHNNY PEELER REDCAP ROZZER RUNNER SHAMUS SMOKEY CRUSHER FOOTMAN GHAFFIR GUMSHOE JEMADAR OFFICER SHOOFLY TROOPER ZAPTIAH ZAPTIEH BARGELLO BLUECOAT DOGBERRY FLATFOOT GENDARME MINISTER PATROLMAN
(CANADIAN —) MOUNTY MOUNTIE
(CLUB OF —) BILLY STAFF SPONTOON TRUNCHEON
(MILITARY —) REDCAP SNOWDROP
(MOUNTED —) SOWAR
(PL.) FINEST
POLICE STATION THANA BARGELLO KOTWALEE

POLICY WIT DEAL FRONT ORDER GOVERN NUMBER TICKET WISDOM AUTARKY COUNSEL CUNNING FLOATER LEFTISM LOTTERY TONTINE VOUCHER ACTIVISM ARTIFICE SAGACITY STATEWAY PLURALISM
(CHOSEN —) COURSE
(SOVIET — OF DISCUSSION) GLASNOST
(PL.) APRISMO
POLISH BOB LAP MOP RUB RUD BUFF DUCO FILE POLE CLEAN COUTH FRUSH GLAZE GLOSS GRACE RABAT ROUND SHINE SLICK STONE AFFILE BARREL LUSTER PUNISH REFINE RUMBLE SHAMMY SLIGHT SMOOTH STREAK BEESWAX BURNISH CHAMOIS FURBISH LACQUER PERFECT PLANISH VARNISH ELEGANCE LEVIGATE SIMONIZE URBANIZE SARMATIAN
(— WITH WAX) SIMONIZE
(FINGERNAIL —) ENAMEL
POLISHED FINE COMPT COUTH ROUND SHINY SLICK TERSE BUFFED FACETE GLOSSY INLAND POLITE SMOOTH ELEGANT GALLANT GENTEEL POLITIC REFINED CULTURED
(NOT —) BLIND
POLISHER EMERY BUFFER GLAZER WAGWAG WIGWAG DOLLIER GLOSSER LAPIDARY SMOOTHER
POLISHING SANDING FROTTAGE LIMATION
(— MATERIAL) RABAT
POLITE NEAT TIDY TRIM BLAND CIVIL SUAVE GENTLE HUMANE SMOOTH URBANE COURTLY GALLANT GENTEEL DELICATE DISCREET LUSTROUS ATTENTIVE COURTEOUS
POLITENESS FINISH TASHRIF CIVILITY COURTESY ELEGANCE URBANITY GENTILITY
POLITES (FATHER OF —) PRIAM
(MOTHER OF —) HECUBA
POLITIC WARY WISE SUAVE ARTFUL CRAFTY CUNNING TACTFUL DISCREET PROVIDENT
POLITICAL (— ASSN.) VEREIN
(— PARTY) GOP TORY WHIG LABOR
POLITICIAN BOSS STATIST WARWICK PIPELAYER STATESMAN
POLITY SERFISM
POLIXENES (SON OF —) FLORIZEL
POLL COW DOD NOT POW ROB CHUB COLL DODD HEAD NAPE NOTT PASH CROWN SKULL STRIP CENSUS FLEECE PARROT CANVASS DESPOIL PILLAGE PLUNDER POLLARD
(KIND OF —) EXIT
POLLACK LOB GADE LAIT GADID LYTHE BILLET LAITHE SAITHE BADDOCK SILLOCK WALLEYE BLUEFISH COALFISH GRAYFISH LORICATE MOULRUSH
POLLARD CHU COW DOD BRAN POLL STAG SHEEP CHEVAN

DODDLE DOTARD BOLLING LOPPARD WOODSERE

POLLARD TREE DOTARD RUNNEL

POLLED NOT NOTT POLEY HORNLESS

POLLEN DUST MEAL FLOUR FARINA POWDER BEEBREAD
(**— BEARER**) ANTHER
(**— BRUSH**) SCOPA
(**— TUBE**) SPERMARY

POLLER VOTER BARBER POLLSTER

POLLEX THUMB

POLLINATE SELF FECUNDATE FECUNDIZE FERTILIZE

POLLINATING SIBBING

POLLIWOG TADPOLE

POLLOCK PODLER

POLLSTER HEADCOUNTER

POLLUTE FOIL FOUL SOIL BLEND DIRTY SMEAR TAINT BEFOUL DEFILE INFECT MUDDLE RAVISH ADULTER DEBAUCH PROFANE SLOTTER VIOLATE CONTAMINATE

POLLUTED FOUL DRUNK TURBID CORRUPT

POLLUTING FILTHY

POLLUTION STAIN SULLAGE FOULNESS IMPURITY

POLLUX POL HERCULES
(**BROTHER OF —**) CASTOR
(**MOTHER OF —**) LEDA

POLO (**PERIOD IN —**) CHUKKER

POLONAISE POLACCA FACKELTANZ

POLONIUS CORAMBIS
(**DAUGHTER OF —**) OPHELIA
(**SON OF —**) LAERTES

POLT BLOW THUMP STROKE

POLTERGEIST GHOST SPIRIT

POLTROON IDLER COWARD CRAVEN WRETCH DASTARD COWARDLY SLUGGARD

POLUTANT PCB

POLYA RNA

POLYANDRIUM CEMETERY

POLYBUS (**FATHER OF —**) ANTENOR
(**MOTHER OF —**) THEANO
(**WIFE OF —**) MEROPE PERIBOEA

POLYDAMAS (**BROTHER OF —**) EUPHORBUS HYPERENOR
(**COMPANION OF —**) HECTOR
(**FATHER OF —**) PANTHOUS
(**MOTHER OF —**) PHRONTIS

POLYDORE (**BROTHER OF —**) CASTALIO

POLYDORUS (**FATHER OF —**) PRIAM CADMUS HIPPOMEDON
(**MOTHER OF —**) HECUBA HARMONIA
(**SLAYER OF —**) POLYMNESTOR
(**SON OF —**) LABDACUS
(**WIFE OF —**) NYCTEIS

POLYESTER (**— BRAND**) DACRON

POLYGALA GAYWINGS

POLYGON DECAGON HEXAGON NONAGON HEPTAGON PENTAGON CHILIAGON MULTANGLE

POLYGRAPH KEELER

POLYHEDRON BEAD PRISM PRISMATOID

POLYMER DIMER HYDROL MANNAN MUREIN HEXAMER OLIGOMER
(**— UNIT**) MER

POLYNESIAN MAORI KANAKA TONGAN FUTUNAN

POLYNICES (**BROTHER OF —**) ETEOCLES
(**FATHER OF —**) OEDIPUS
(**MOTHER OF —**) JOCASTA
(**WIFE OF —**) ARGIA

POLYNOMIAL CUBIC

POLYP CORAL HYDRA TUMOR ZOOID ISOPOD HYDRULA OCTOPOD

POLYPARY ZOARIUM

POLYPHONY ORGANUM FABURDEN COUNTERPOINT

POLYPIDOM CORMUS

POLYSACCHARIDE LEVAN GELOSE GLUCAN GLYCAN INULIN IRISIN MANNAN AMYLOSE DEXTRAN FUCOSAN HEXOSAN POLYOSE GALACTAN GLYCOGEN LICHENIN SECALOSE SINISTRIN

POLYTYPE CAST

POLYXENA (**FATHER OF —**) PRIAM
(**MOTHER OF —**) HECUBA

POLYZOAN POLYP CESTODE RADIATE

POMACE MUST RAPE POMMY STOCK STOSH CHEESE

POMADE CIDER POMATUM LIPSTICK OINTMENT

POMANDER CASE POUNCET

POMATO TOPATO

POME BALL APPLE GLOBE JUNEBERRY

POMEGRANATE GRENAT GRENADE BALAUSTA

POMELO SHADDOCK GRAPEFRUIT

POMERANIA (**CAPITAL OF —**) STETTIN
(**CITY IN —**) THORN TORUN ANKLAM
(**ISLAND IN —**) RUGEN USEDOM
(**PROVINCE IN —**) POMORZE

POMFRET BULLY HENFISH

POMME DE TERRE POTATO

POMMEL BOB FIB NOB BEAT HORN KNOB PAIK PAKE TORE NEVEL BRUISE BUFFET CRUTCH FINIAL PLUMMET

POMP BRAG FARE WEAL BOAST PRIDE STATE ESTATE PAMPER PARADE RIALTY SCHEME SPRUNK BOBANCE DISPLAY PAGEANT PANOPLY SPLURGE CEREMONY EQUIPAGE GRANDEUR SEMBLANT SPLENDOR

POMPANO DART JUREL ALLICE CARANX PERMIT ALEWIFE

COBBLER OLDWIFE CARANGID MACKEREL
(**— CLAM**) COQUINA

POMPOSITY TUMOR TUMOUR BIGHEAD BIGNESS BOMBAST

POMPOUS BIG BUG BUDGE JELLY LARGE SHOWY TUMID WIGGY ASTRUT AUGUST TURGID BLOATED BOMBAST FUSTIAN OROTUND STILTED SWOLLEN TURGENT BEWIGGED INFLATED MAGNIFIC SWELLING TOPLOFTY IMPORTANT PONTIFICAL PORTENTOUS

PONCEAU GRANAT

PONCHO MANGA RUANA

POND (**ALSO SEE POOL**) LAY LUM DELF DIKE MOAT PULK SLEW STEW TANK VLEI VLEY CANAL DECOY DELFT LACHE LETCH STANK WAYER CLAIRE LAGOON LAGUNA LAGUNE LOCHAN PUDDLE SALINA SLOUGH SPLASH STAGNE MULLETRY
(**— DRY IN SUMMER**) TURLOUGH
(**— FOR OYSTERS**) CLAIRE
(**— MAN**) JACKER
(**ARTIFICIAL —**) AQUARIUM
(**DIRTY —**) SOAL
(**FISH —**) VIVER GURGES PISCINA
(**FISH STORING —**) STEW
(**SMALL —**) KHAL
(**STAGNANT —**) DUB
(**PREF.**) LACO LIMN(I)(O)

PONDER CON CAST CHAW MUSE PORE ROLL TURN BROOD STUDY VOLVE WEIGH ADVISE EXPEND REASON RECORD REMORD BALANCE COMPASS EXAMINE IMAGINE PERPEND REFLECT REVERIE REVOLVE APPRAISE COGITATE CONSIDER MEDITATE

PONDERABILITY WEIGHT GRAVITY

PONDEROUS DULL SLOW BULKY GRAVE HEAVY SOGGY AWKWARD WEIGHTY UNWIELDY IMPORTANT

PONDEROUSNESS HEFT

POND HEN COOT

PONDMAN JACKER

PONDOKKIE HUT HOVEL

PONE CAKE LUMP WRIT PAUNE PUDDING SWELLING

PONGEE PAUNCHE SHANTUNG

PONGID APE

PONIARD STAB BODKIN DAGGER STYLET POINADO

PONOCRATES (**PUPIL OF —**) GARGANTUA

PONT FERRY FLOAT BRIDGE FERRYBOAT

PONTIANAC JELUTONG

PONTIC DUMMY

PONTICELLO BREAK MAGAS

PONTIFF POPE BISHOP PRIEST PONTIFEX

PONTIFICAL AARONIC

PONTIL PUNTY

PONTOON FLOAT RHINO BRIDGE

PONY CAB RAW TAT CAVY TROT YABU BIDET DALES GRIFF PAINT PINTO POWNY TACKY TRICK WELCH WELSH BASUTO BHUTIA BRONCO CAYUSE EXMOOR GARRAN SHELTY TANGUN TATTOO

ENGLISH HACKNEY MANIPUR MUSTANG SHELTIE FORESTER GALLOWAY SHETLAND
(**— NEW TO RACING**) GRYFON GRIFFIN GRIFFON GRYPHON
(**STUDENT'S —**) CRIB TROT BICYCLE
(**USE A —**) CRIB
(**PL.**) DALES

POODLE SHOCK BARBET

POOH TUSH POWWAW

POOK HEAP PICK PULL PLUCK STACK

POOKA PUCK GOBLIN SPECTER

POOL (**ALSO SEE POND**) CAR DIB DUB LAY LUM PIT POL POT POW BANK BOOK CARR DIKE DUMP FARM FLOW JHIL LAKE LIDO LINN LLYN LUMB MERE PANT PEEL PLUD POLK POND PULE PULK RING SINK SLEW SOIL SWAG TANK TARN WEEL BAYOU BOWLY DECOY FLASH FLUSH FRESH JHEEL KITTY LETCH LOUGH MFARF PLASH PLUMB SLACK STANK STELL STILL THERM TRUNK CARTEL CHARCO FLODGE LAGOON LASHER PLUNGE PUDDLE SILOAM SPLASH STABLE CARLINE CATHOLE CUSHION JACKPOT PLASHET SNOOKER STAGNUM INTERLOT QUINIELA
(**— AT JERUSALEM**) BETHESDA
(**— BELOW WATERFALL**) LIN LINN LLYN
(**— IN BOG**) HAG HAGG
(**— OF MONEY**) KITTY
(**— WITHOUT OUTLET**) STAGNUM
(**— WITH SALMON NETS**) STELL
(**ARTIFICIAL —**) CUSHION
(**AUCTION —**) CAI CUTTA
(**BATHING —**) JACUZZI
(**BETTING —**) EXACTA PERFECTA TRIFECTA
(**DIRTY —**) SUMP
(**FISH —**) TRUNK STEWPOND
(**MEMBER OF —**) STENO
(**MOUNTAIN —**) TARN
(**MUDDY —**) LETCH
(**SWIMMING —**) BATH LIDO PISCINA NATATORY NATATORIUM
(**PREF.**) LIMN(I)(O) STAGNI

POON DILO PEON PUNA DOMBA KEENA TAMANU SIRPOON MASTWOOD

POONGHIE RAHAN PRIEST PUNGYI PHONGHI TALAPOIN

POOP DOCK FIRE GULP TOOT CHEAT COZEN STERN BEFOOL ISLAND DECEIVE EXHAUST HINDDECK OVERCOME

POOR BAD OFF SAD BASE EVIL FOUL LEAN LEWD PUNK SICK SOUR THIN DINKY EXILE FOOTY GROSS JERRY KETTY SCALY SEELY SILLY SOBER SORRY UNORN FEEBLE HUMBLE HUNGRY LEADEN MEAGER MEAGRE MEASLY PILLED PORAIL PRETTY SCANTY SHABBY STREET SUBPAR CODFISH HAPLESS NAUGHTY SCRAWNY SCRUBBY SQUALID TRIVIAL UNLUCKY INDIGENT ORDINARY PRECIOUS SCRANNEL SNEAKING TERRIBLE UNTHENDE PENNILESS PENURIOUS

(— BOY) HERO
(— MAN) PAUPER
(PREF.) MAL(E) PTOCHO
POORHOUSE MEASONDUE
POORLY ILL BADLY SADLY BARELY FEEBLY SIMPLY SLIGHT SHABBILY (PREF.) DYS
POOR SOLDIER FRIARBIRD
POORTITH POVERTY
POOR WHITE (AUTHOR OF —) ANDERSON
(CHARACTER IN —) JIM JOE TOM HUGH CLARA MCVEY SARAH STEVE HUNTER SHEPARD WAINSWORTH BUTTERWORTH
POP GO DOT GUN HIT TRY BLOW DART HOCK JUMP PAWN SODA BREAK CLOOP CRACK KNOCK SHOOT ATTACK EFFORT FATHER POPPER STROKE THRUSH ASSAULT ATTEMPT CONCERT EXPLODE INSTANT REDWING BACKFIRE SUDDENLY
POPDOCK FOXGLOVE
POPE LEO JOHN PAPA PAPE PAUL PIUS RUFF CAIUS FELIX GAIUS PETER URBAN ADRIAN BISHOP CLETUS EUGENE JULIAN LUCIUS PUFFIN SHRIKE SIXTUS VICTOR CLEMENS GREGORY HADRIAN BENEDICT BONIFACE INNOCENT PONTIFEX FISHERMAN
(SPECIFIC —) LEO PAUL PIUS URBAN GREGORY
(PREF.) PAPI PAPO POPO
POPERY POPEISM PAPISTRY
POPE'S-EYE NUT NOIX
POPGUN SCOOT PENGUN POTGUN PLUFFER
POPINJAY PARROT PAPINGO
POPLAR ABBEY ABELE ALAMO ASPEN BAHAN LIARD BALSAM POPPLE BAUMIER ABELTREE WHITEBARK
POPLIN TABINET
POPOLOCA CHOCHO
POPPPYCOCK BUNK
POPPY HEAD BLAVER CANKER COPROSE EARACHE PONCEAU REDWEED ARGEMONE BALEWORT BOCCONIA HEADACHE DANNEBROG SQUATMORE COQUELICOT
(CORN —S) SOLDIERS
(PREF.) MECON(O)
POPPYCOCK BOSH BULL PISH FOLLY STUFF HAVERS HUMBUG HOGWASH
POPPYFISH POMPANO
POPPY SEED MAW MOHNSEED
POPULACE MOB MASS CROWD DEMOS PLEBS MASSES MOBILE PEOPLE PUBLIC COUNTRY MULTITUDE
(PREF.) DEM(O) OCHLO
POPULAR LAY POP COMMON GOLDEN PUBLIC SIMPLE VULGAR CROWDED DEMOTIC VULGATE APPROVED FAVORITE PEOPLISH PLEBEIAN GANGBUSTERS
(EXTREMELY —) HOT REDHOT
POPULARITY VOGUE CLAPTRAP
(— OF BUSINESS) GOODWILL

POPULATE MAN BREED PLANT WORLD PEOPLE INHABIT
POPULATION DEME COLONY FLOTSAM KINDRED TOPODEME UNIVERSE
(— OF A SPECIES) MORPH
(PREF.) DEM(O)
POPULUS SALIX
PORATHA (FATHER OF —) HAMAN
PORBEAGLE LAMNA SHARK LAMNID LAMNOID
PORCELAIN JU KO TING CHINA MURRA SPODE BISQUE MURRHA NANKIN BISCUIT CELADON DRESDEN NANKEEN NANKING MANDARIN STEATITE WORCESTER
(FINE —) SPODE
(JAPANESE —) KUTANI
(VARIETY OF —) CAEN KUAN ARITA HIZEN IMARI KYOTO AMSTEL PARIAN SEVRES BUDWEIS DRESDEN LIMOGES MEISSEN SWANSEA COALPORT HAVILAND KAKIEMON CHANTILLY
PORCH HOOD STOA LANAI STOEP STOOP INGANG PARVIS PIAZZA PORTAL RAMADA BALCONY GALERIE GALILEE NARTHEX PASSAGE POIKILE PORTICO PRONAOS VERANDA ANTENAVE SOLARIUM TRANSEPT VESTIBULE
(FRONT —) ANTICUM
PORCUPINE QUILL URSON CAWQUAW COENDOU ERECTER ERICIUS PORKPEN HEDGEHOG HEDGEPIG
(PREF.) HYSTRICO
PORCUPINE ANTEATER ECHIDNA
PORCUPINE FISH ERIZO ATINGA BURFISH DIODONT
PORCUPINE GRASS SPINIFEX
PORE GAZE GLOSE GLOZE STARE STOMA STUDY TRYPA BROWSE PONDER ALVEOLA CINCLIS OSTIOLE TUBULUS BAJONADO JOLTHEAD LENTICEL POROSITY
PORGY TAI SCUP PARGO PLUMA POGGY BESUGO BRAISE MAMAMU PAGRUS SPARID MARGATE PINFISH MENHADEN SPADEFISH
PORK HAM HOG PIG LARD BACON BRAWN MONEY SWINE BALDRIB LARDOON MIDDLING
(— AND SALMON) LAULAU
(— CHOP) BALDRIB GRISKEN
(— SHOULDER) HAND
(DEEP-FRIED —) CUCHIFRITO
(FRIED CUBE OF —) CUCHIFRITO
(SALT —) BACON SPECK SOWBELLY
PORKFISH SISI CATALINETA
PORKY FAT GREASY
PORNOGRAPHIC LEWD ADULT CURIOUS OBSCENE
PORNOGRAPHY SMUT CURIOSA ESOTERICA
POROUS OPEN LIGHT LEACHY CELLULAR
PORPHYRY ELVAN EURITE ELVANITE GRORUDITE
PORPOISE WHALE PALACH PUFFER COWFISH DOLPHIN HOGFISH PELLOCK PULLOCK SNUFFER CETACEAN GAIRFISH

PORRECT EXTEND TENDER PRESENT
PORRET LEEK ONION PORETT SCALLION
PORRIDGE KHIR MUSH POBS SAMP ATOLE BROSE GROUT GRUEL BURGOO CROWDY SEPAWN SKILLY SOWENS TARTAN BROCHAN BURGOUT OATMEAL POBBIES POLENTA POTTAGE FLUMMERY SAGAMITE
(PREF.) POLTO
PORRINGER TASTER TRINKET
PORT GATE GOAL LEFT MIEN WICK WINE CARRY CREEK HAVEN HITHE SALLY SCALE STATE APPORT HARBOR INPORT REFUGE AIRPORT BEARING DIGNITY LIBERTY OUTPORT ANTEPORT DEMEANOR LARBOARD MALTOLTE PORTHOLE PRESENCE
PORTABLE LAPTOP MOBILE MOVABLE BEARABLE
PORTAGE PACK CARGO CARRY TARBET FREIGHT TONNAGE HAULOVER
PORTAL DOOR GATE ENTRY PORCH DOORWAY ENTRANCE
PORTAMENTO DRAG GLIDE SCOOP SLIDE PORTATO GLISSADE
PORTCULLIS BAR SHUT HERSE ORGUE SARASIN CATARACT SARRASIN
PORTE GATE
PORTE-MONNAIE PURSE
PORTEND BODE AUGUR DIVINE EXTEND BESPEAK BETOKEN PREDICT PRESAGE DENOUNCE FOREBODE FORECAST FORETELL
PORTENT AYAH LUCK SIGN SOUND TOKEN AUGURY MARVEL OSTENT WONDER AUSPICE PREDICT PRESAGE PRODIGY CEREMONY DISASTER SOOTHSAY PROGNOSTIC
PORTENTOUS AWFUL GRAVID BODEFUL DOOMFUL FATEFUL OMINOUS POMPOUS DOOMLIKE DREADFUL INFLATED SINISTER
PORTER ALE BEER MOZO CADDY HAMAL STOUT TAMEN BADGER BEARER CADDIE COOLIE DARWAN DURWAN ENTIRE KHAMAL REDCAP SUISSE DROGHER DVORNIK HUMMAUL JANITOR PITCHER REMOVER BADGEMAN BUMMAREE CARGADOR CHAPRASI LODGEMAN PORTITOR RECEIVER
(— AND STOUT) COOPER
(JAPANESE —) AKABO
(MEAT —) PITCHER
(MEXICAN —) TAMEN
PORTFOLIO BLAD
PORTIA (HUSBAND OF —) BRUTUS
(LOVER OF —) BASSANIO
(MAID OF —) NERISSA
PORTIA TREE MAHO BENDY MAHOE
PORTICO ANTA STOA WALK XYST ORIEL PORCH XYSTA ZAYAT EXEDRA PARVIS PIAZZA SCHOOL XYSTUS BALCONY DISTYLE GALLERY NARTHEX PARVISE PRONAOS TERRACE VERANDA

PORTICUS POSTICUM VERANDAH PENTASTYLE TETRASTYLE
PORTION BIT CUP CUT DAB JAG LAB LOT PAN BLAD DALE DEAL DOLE DOSE FATE FECK JAGG PART SIZE WHAT DOWER PIECE RATIO SHARE SLICE SNACK TASTE WHACK CANTLE CANTON COLLOP DETAIL GOBBET MATTER PARCEL RASHER REGION EXCERPT PARTAGE SCANTLE SECTION SEGMENT TODDICK TRANCHE FRACTION FRAGMENT PITTANCE QUANTITY SCANTLET FODDERING SOMETHING
(— DRUNK) DRAFT DRAUGHT
(— OF ACTOR'S PART) LENGTH
(— OF ARROW) BREAST
(— OF BIRD SONG) TOUR
(— OF BREAD) TOKE
(— OF BREAD OR BEER) CUE
(— OF CITRUS RIND) ALBEDO
(— OF ESTATE) LEGITIM
(— OF FARMLAND) BEREWICK
(— OF FLOODPLAIN) BANCO
(— OF FODDER) JAG
(— OF FOOD) HELP GOBBET HELPING
(— OF HIDE) HEAD
(— OF LAND) BLOCK PATTI INTAKE DIVISION DONATION
(— OF LIQUOR) STICK DIVIDEND
(— OF LITURGY) ANAPHORA
(— OF MAST) HOUSING HOUNDING
(— OF PASTURE) BREAK
(— OF POEM) STRAIN
(— OF RUG) GRIN
(— OF SERPENT'S BODY) TRAIN
(— OF STEM) BOON
(— OF STORY) SNATCH
(— OF STREAM) LAVADERO
(— OF TEA) DRAWING
(— OF TIME) SPAN DISTANCE
(— OF TOBACCO) CUD
(— OF TONGUE) BLADE
(ADDITIONAL —) RASHER
(ALLOTTED —) MOIRA SCANTLING
(BRIDE'S —) DOWRY
(CLOTTED — OF BLOOD) CRUOR
(COARSER —) BOLTINGS
(EARLY —) SPRING
(INHABITED — OF EARTH) ECUMENE
(LARGE —) SKELP
(LATTER —) AUTUMN EVENING
(MAIN —) CORPSE
(MARRIAGE —) DOT DOTE TOCHER
(MINUTE —) GRAIN
(MOST VALUABLE —) CHIEF
(PERCEPTIBLE —) KENNING
(REPRESENTATIVE —) SAMPLE
(SIGNIFICANT —) CHAPTER
(SIZABLE —) DUNT
(SMALL —) BIT DAB DOT DRAM DROP DOSH TAIT TATE CHACK SPICE SPUNK SHADOW KENNING MODICUM REMNANT SCANTLE SMIDGEN SOUPCON SCANTLET
(SMALL — OF LIQUOR) DOLLOP HEELTAP
(TRIFLING —) SMACK
(SUFF.) **(BY A SPECIFIC —)** MEAL
PORTLY FAT FULL AMPLE GAUCY

GAWCY GAWSY STOUT GAUCIE
GOODLY STATELY SWELLING
OVERBLOWN
PORTMANTEAU BAG HOOK VALISE
POCKMANKY
PORTRAIT BUST ICON IKON IMAGE
IMAGO MODEL PIECE PINUP
KITKAT STATUE VISAGE PORTRAY
RETRAIT RETRATE LIKENESS
RITRATTO VERONICA MINIATURE
(— ON COIN) EFFIGY
PORTRAIT OF A LADY (AUTHOR OF
—) JAMES
(CHARACTER IN —) MERLE PANSY
RALPH ARCHER CASPAR EDWARD
GEMINI ISABEL OSMOND ROSIER
GILBERT BANTLING GOODWOOD
TOUCHETT HENRIETTA STACKPOLE
WARBURTON
PORTRAY ACT GIVE LIMN LINE
BLAZE ENACT IMAGE PAINT
CIPHER CLOTHE DEPICT FIGURE
SHADOW FEATURE IMITATE
PICTURE DECIPHER DESCRIBE
RESEMBLE

PORTUGAL

BAY: SETUBAL
CAPE: ROCA MONDEGO ESPICHEL
CAPITAL: LISBON
COIN: JOE REI PECA REAL CONTO
COROA DOBRA INDIO ESCUDO
MACUTA PATACA TESTAO VINTEM
CENTAVO CRUSADO MOIDORE
EQUIPAGA
COLONY: MACAO TIMOR ANGOLA
GUINEA PRINCIPE
DISTRICT: BEJA FARO BRAGA
EVORA HORTA PORTO VISEU
LEIRIA LISBOA
ISLAND: TIMOR
ISLANDS: MADEIRA
MEASURE: PE ALMA BOTA MEIO
MOIO PIPA VARA ALMUD BRACA
FANGA GEIRA LEGOA LINHA
MILHA PALMO ALMUDE CANADA
COVADO QUARTO ALQUIER
ESTADIO FERRADO SELAMIN
ALQUEIRE TONELADA
MOUNTAIN: ACOR GEREZ MARAO
MOUSA PENEDA ESTRELA
MONCHIQUE
RIVER: SOR TUA LIMA MINO MIRA
SADO SEDA TAGO TEJO DOURO
MINHO SABAR TAGUS VOUGA
ZATAS CAVADO CHANCA TAMEGA
ZEZERE MONDEGO GUADIANA
TOWN: BEJA FARO OVAR BRAGA
EVORA HORTA PORTO VISEU
GUARDA OPORTO COIMBRA
FUNCHAL SETUBAL BRAGANCA
UNIVERSITY: COIMBRA
WEIGHT: GRAO ONCA LIBRA
MARCO ARROBA OITAVA
ARRATEL QUINTAL
WINE: PORT

PORTUGUESE
(PREF.) LUSO
PORTULACA MOSS PURSLANE
PORWIGLE TADPOLE
POSADA INN
POSAUNE TROMBONE

POSE ASK SET SIT HOARD MODEL
OFFER PLANT STICK BAFFLE
STANCE NONPLUS PEACOCK
POSTURE PRESENT PROPOSE
POSITION PRETENSE PROPOUND
QUESTION MANNERISM
POSEIDON NEPTUNE EARTHSHAKER
(BROTHER OF —) ZEUS
(FATHER OF —) KRONOS
(MOTHER OF —) RHEA
(WIFE OF —) AMPHITRITE
POSER FACER POSEUR PUZZLE
STAYER STICKER STUMPER
TWISTER EXAMINER STICKLER
BANDARLOG
POSH RITZY SWANKY SWAGGER
POSING OPPOSAL
(— TECHNIQUE) PLASTIQUE
POSIT FIX PUT SET PLACE AFFIRM
ASSUME
POSITING PONENT
POSITION LAY LIE HANG LINE POSE
RANK SITE CENSE COIGN PLANT
POINT POSTE SIEGE SITUS STAND
STATE STEAD ASSIZE FIGURE
HEIGHT OCTAVE OFFICE STANCE
UBIETY VALGUS POSTURE STATION
ATTITUDE CAPACITY DOCTRINE
LOCATION STANDING VOCATION
PLACEMENT SITUATION
(— IN AUTO RACE) POLE
(— IN DISCOURSE) POINT
(— OF AFFAIRS) STATUS
(— OF BODY) AKIMBO
(— OF FEAR) GAZE
(— OF HEAVENLY BODY) HARBOR
(— OF VESSEL) GAUGE HEIGHT
(— OF WEAPON) PORT READY
PRESENT
(— WITH NO ESCAPE) IMPASSE
(— WITH NO RESPONSIBILITY)
SINECURE
(BALLET —) POINTE
(CHESS —) ZUGZWANG
(COMMANDING —) PRESTIGE
(CRICKET —) GULLY GULLEY
(CRITICAL —) PASS
(DEFENSIVE —) WARD OUTWORK
(DIFFICULT —) SPOT
(DISTINGUISHED —) HONOR
(EMBARRASSING —) FIX HOLE
LURCH CORNER
(ESTABLISHED —) TOEHOLD
(FENCING —) CARTE SIXTE SIXTH
QUARTE TIERCE SACCOON
SECONDE SEPTIME
(FIRST —) PRIMACY
(FOREMOST —) HEAD LEAD STEM
(FORTIFIED —) HEDGEHOG
(FRONT —) FOREHEAD
(HABITUAL —) SET
(HINDMOST —) REAR
(HORIZONTAL —) LEVEL
(INCLINED —) SLOPE
(INITIAL —) ANLAUT
(MEDIAL —) INLAUT
(MIDDLE —) MEAN
(NATURAL —) LEVEL
(NEAR —) NEIGHBORHOOD
(OBLIQUE —) SHEER
(OFFICIAL —) RANK
(OPPOSITE —) OPPOSITION

(RELATIVE —) RANK PLACE TERMS
BEARING FOOTING STANDING
(SEATED —) SESSION
(SKIING —) SNOWPLOW
(SOCIAL —) CASTE STATE VALOUR
(SYMBOLIC —) HASTA
(UNFORTUNATE —) PREDICAMENT
(SUFF.) TOPE TOPY
POSITIONAL SITUAL
POSITIVE POS POZ COOL DOWN
FLAT PLUS SURE BASIC SHEER
UTTER ACTIVE DIRECT THETIC
GENUINE HEALTHY ABSOLUTE
CONCRETE DECISIVE DEFINITE
DOGMATIC EXPLICIT INHERENT
RESOLUTE SIGNLESS THETICAL
(THREE —S) KROMOGRAM
POSITIVELY BUT POS FLAT PLUS
QUITE FAIRLY INDEED STRICTLY
POSITIVISM COMTISM CERTAINTY
DOGMATISM
POSITRON LEPTON
POSSESS GET OWE OWN HAVE
HOLD WALD BOAST BROOK
OUGHT REACH WIELD MASTER
OBTAIN OCCUPY BEDEVIL
ENVELOP FURNISH INHABIT
INHERIT INSTALL INSTATE SMITTLE
ACQUAINT DOMINATE INSTRUCT
POSSESSED MAD CALM COOL
OUGHT CRAZED JERUSHA
ENTHEATE
(— BY EVIL SPIRIT) DEMONIAC
(AUTHOR OF —) DOSTOEVSKI
(CHARACTER IN —) BLUM DASHA
FEDKA MARIE MARYA PYOTR YULIA
SHATOV DROZDOV LIPUTIN NIKOLAI
STEPHAN VARVARA KIRILLOV
LIZAVETA LYAMSHIN PETROVNA
SHIGALOV LEBYADKIN STAVROGIN
VIRGINSKY KARMAZINOV
TIMOFYEVNA VERHOVENSKY
POSSESSION AVER HAND HOLD
YHTE AUGHT GRASP STATE
CLUTCH CORNER HAVIOR SASINE
SEISIN SEIZIN WEALTH CONTROL
COUNTER DEMESNE DEWANEE
FINGERS KEEPING MASTERY
SEIZURE TENANCY CONQUEST
DEFIANCE PROPERTY OCCUPANCY
OCCUPATION
(— BY INSPIRATION) ENTHUSIASM
(— OF COMMON FEATURES)
AFFINITY
(— OF KNOWLEDGE) SCIENCE
(— WITH QUIET ENJOYMENT)
SEISIN SEIZIN
(BURDENSOME —) ELEPHANT
(COMMON —) COMMUNION
COMMUNITY
(DEAREST —) EWELAMB
(EXCLUSIVE —) MONOPOLY
(LOST — OF BALL) TURNOVER
(OUTDOOR —S) OUTSIGHT
(PETTY —S) SPRECHERY
(RELIGIOUS —) POWER
(SATISFACTORY —) ENJOYMENT
(TEMPORAL —S) WORLD
(TEMPORARY —) LEND
(PL.) ALLS STORE STUFF WRACK
DOMAIN ESTATE GRAITH PROPER
CAPITAL FORTUNE HAVINGS
LIVINGS

POSSET CURDLE PAMPER
POWSOWDY BALDUCTUM
MERRYBUSH
POSSIBILITY MAY MAYBE POSSE
CHANCE PROSPECT QUESTION
(— OF REFORM) RECLAIM
POSSIBLE ABLE RIFE MAYBE LIKELY
EARTHLY ELIGIBLE FEASIBLE
PROBABLE PROBABLY POTENTIAL
CONTINGENT PRACTICABLE
(BARELY —) OUTSIDE
POSSIBLY MAPPEN LIGHTLY
PERHAPS PERCHANCE
PERADVENTURE
POSSUM TAIT FEIGN PRETEND
POST DAK SET TIE BITT BOMA CAMP
CRIB DAWK DOLE FAST FORT MAIL
META POLE ROOM SPOT SPUD
STOB STUD TREE BERTH CHEEK
CLOSH CRANE NEWEL PLACE
SETUP SPILE SPRAG STAKE STAND
STILT STING STOCK STODE STOOP
STULP STUMP BILLET CIPPUS
COLUMN CROTCH FENDER GIBBET
INFORM OFFICE PICKET PILLAR
SAMSON SCREEN STAPLE STOOTH
STOWER TRUNCH ASHERAH
BOLLARD COURIER GARETTA
PLACARD POSTAGE POSTBOX
QUARTER STATION STUDDLE
UPRIGHT BANISTER DEADHEAD
LEGPIECE MAKEFAST PRESIDIO
PUNCHEON QUINTAIN STRADDLE
STANCHION
(— AS RACE MARKER) META
(— ON PIER) FAST BOLLARD
DEADHEAD
(BOUNDARY —) TERM STOOP
TERMINUS
(CHIMNEY —) SPEER
(CUSTOMS —) CHOKEY
(DECK —) BITT
(DOOR OR GATE —) DURN
(ECCLESIASTIC —) BENEFICE
(FENCE —) DROPPER
(HANGING —) GIBBET
(INDIAN MILITARY —) TANA TANNA
THANA
(MILITARY —) FORT GARRISON
(MOORING —) BITT DOLPHIN
(OBSERVATORY —) CUPOLA
(SACRED —) ASHERAH
(SIGN —) PARSON
(PREF.) STELO
POSTAGE POST INDICIA STAMPAGE
POSTAGE-FREE FRANCO
POSTAGE STAMP DUE HEAD
STICKER
POSTBOY YAMSHIK YEMSCHIK
POSTILION
POSTCARD (— COLLECTOR)
DELTIOLOGIST
POST CHAISE JACK POCHAY
POSCHAY
POSTER BILL CLAP SIGN SNIPE
CLAPPE AFFICHE PLACARD
SHOWING STICKER STREAMER
POSTERIOR BACK REAR CAUDAL
DORSAL POSTIC RETRAL ADAXIAL
BUTTOCKS
(PL.) WHEERIKINS
(PREF.) OPISTH(O) UR(O)
POSTERIORLY RETRAD

POSTERITY SEQUEL KINDRED FUTURITY

POSTERN SIDE CLOCKET KLICKET PRIVATE POSTICUM

POSTHOUSE YAM MUTATION

POSTICHE WIG SHAM SWITCH TOUPEE PRETENSE SPURIOUS

POSTIL HOMILY COMMENT

POSTILION COURIER POSTBOY YAMSHIK

POSTLUDE SORTIE SORTITA EPILOGUE

POSTMAN MAIL CORREO MAILBAG MAILMAN

POST OFFICE BOMA CORREO POSTHOUSE

POSTPONE OFF STAY WAIT DEFER DELAY FRIST REFER REMIT WAIVE FUTURE LINGER RELONG RETARD ADJOURN DEGRADE OVERSET PROLONG RESPECT SUSPEND CONTINUE PROROGUE REPRIEVE WITHHOLD

POSTPONED DEFERRED

POSTPONEMENT MORA STAY DELAY RESPECT RESPITE DEFERRAL

POSTRIDE COURIER POSTILION

POSTSCRIPT EKE ENVOI ENVOY

POST SUPPORT CROWFOOT

POSTULANT NOVICE

POSTULATE AXIOM CLAIM POSIT ASSERT ASSUME DEMAND THESIS PERHAPS PREMISE PETITION PRINCIPLE

POSTULATION PREMISE

POSTURE SET POSE SEAT SITE ASANA FRONT HEART PLACE SHAPE SQUAT STAND LOUNGE SLOUCH STANCE BEARING CROWHOP STATION STATURE ATTITUDE CARRIAGE POSITION
(— **IN BED**) DECUBITUS
(— **OF DEFENSE**) GUARD
(**DANCE** —) HOLD
(**KNEELING** —) SHIKO

POSY POESY TUTTY FLOWER BOUQUET NOSEGAY ANTHOLOGY
(**SMALL** —) FLORET

POT BAG CAN COOP FOOL JUST LEAD OLLA PINT POOL RUIN VASO CREWE CROCK CRUSE DIXIE KITTY SHANT SHOOT ALUDEL CHATTY CHYTRA JORDAN JORDEN KETTLE MARMIT MASLIN MONKEY OUTWIT PINGLE PIPKIN POCKET POSNET BRAISER CHAMBER CUVETTE DECEIVE POTSHOT SEETHER SKILLET YETLING FAVORITE JACKSHEA PRESERVE MARIJUANA
(— **FOR CATCHING FISH**) COOP
(— **FOR MEDICINE**) GALLIPOT
(— **OF BRASS**) LOTA MASLIN
(— **OF DRINK**) SHANT
(— **STICKER**) DUMPLING
(— **WITH 3 FEET**) POSNET
(**BOILING** —) STEW
(**BULGING** —) OLLA
(**BUSHMAN'S** —) JACKSHAY JACKSHEA
(**CHAMBER** —) JERRY JORDAN JORDEN COMMODE JEROBOAM
(**CHIMNEY** —) CAN TUN

(**EARTHEN** —) OLLA CROCK CHATTY PIPKIN
(**FLOWER** —) PLANTER
(**INDIAN** —) LOTA LOTAH
(**LEATHER** —) GISPIN
(**LOBSTER** —) COY TRUNK
(**LONG-HANDLED** —) PINGLE
(**MELTING** —) CREVET CRUCIBLE
(**ORNAMENTAL** —) PLANTER
(**PART OF** —) EAR LIP RIM ANTE BASE BODY FOOT NECK SPOUT HANDLE
(**PEAR-SHAPED** —) ALUDEL
(**SMALL ROUND** —) LOTA LOTAH
(**TEA** —) TRACK
(**THREE-LEGGED** —) TRIVET
(**12-GALLON** —) DIXY DIXIE

POTABLE DRINK BEVERAGE POTATORY

POTAGE SOUP BROTH

POTAMOGETON PONDWEED PONDGRASS

POTASH KALI SALINE PEARLASH POLVERINE
(— **FACTORY**) ASHERY

POTASSIUM K KALIUM POTASS
(— **DICHROMATE**) CHROME

POTASSIUM BICARBONATE SALERATUS

POTASSIUM NITRATE GROUGH

POTATION POT DRAM DRAFT DRINK LIBATION

POTATO PAP YAM CHAT PAPA SPUD YAMP FLUKE IDAHO RURAL TATER TUBER BATATA CAMOTE KUMARA LUMPER MURPHY PRATEY SKERRY BURBANK EPICURE SOLANUM BLUENOSE
(— **BALL**) NOISETTE
(— **CHIP**) CRISP
(— **MASHER**) RICER CHAPPER
(— **S AND CABBAGE**) COLCANNON
(— **SLICES**) LATTICE
(— **STATE**) IDAHO MAINE
(**BAKING** —) IDAHO
(**FRENCH FRIED** —) CHIP
(**FRENCH FRIED** —**S**) GAUFRETTES
(**JAPANESE** —) IMO
(**KIND OF** —) COUCH
(**MASHED** —**ES**) MASH
(**STEWED** —**S**) STOVIES
(**WITH** —**S**) PARMENTIER
(**PL.**) WARE CHUNO

POT BEARER POTIFER

POTBELLIED KEDGE PODDY STOMACHY ABDOMINOUS

POTBELLY PAUNCH TUNBELLY

POTBOY GANYMEDE

POTE KICK MOPE POIT POKE PUSH NUDGE PLATE POKER SHOVE THRUST

POTEEN POTHEEN WHISKEY POTWHISKY

POTENCE STUD CROSS GIBBET

POTENCY FORCE POWER VIGOR ORENDA VIRTUE EFFICACY STRENGTH VITALITY OPERATION
(**TRANSMUTING** —) ALCHEMY

POTENT ABLE MAIN RICH STAY STIFF CAUSAL COGENT CRUTCH MIGHTY STRONG DYNAMIC SUPPORT WARRANT FORCIBLE

POWERFUL PUISSANT VIGOROUS VIRTUOUS VIRULENT

POTENTATE KING RULER HUZOOR POTENT PRINCE SATRAP DICTATOR DOMINION SOVEREIGN

POTENTIAL EH LATENT VIRTUAL IMPLICIT INCHOATE POSSIBLE PREGNANT
(— **ENERGY**) ERGAL
(**ACTION** —) SPIKE
(**EXCESS** —) OVERVOLTAGE

POTENTIALITY POSSE POWER DUNAMIS DYNAMIS POTENCY CAPACITY PREGNANCY

POTGUN PISTOL POPGUN BRAGGART

POTHER ADO VEX FUSS STEW STIR WORRY BOTHER BUSTLE HARASS POTTER PUTTER PUZZLE PERPLEX TURMOIL

POTHERB WORT CLARY WERTE GREENS CHERVIL OLITORY POTWORT QUELITE SPINACH TAMPALA

POTHOLE POT RUT KETTLE TINAJA

POTHOOK HAIK HAKE CROOK HANGLE RACKAN SLOWRIE TRAMMEL COTTEREL

POTHOUSE TAVERN ALEHOUSE MUGHOUSE

POTION DOSE DRUG DRAFT DRINK DWALE STUFF DRENCH POISON AMATORY MIXTURE PHILTER PHILTRE NEPENTHE
(**PALM** —) NIPA

POTIPHERAH (**DAUGHTER OF** —) ASENATH

POTLATCH GIFT FEAST PARTY POTLACH FESTIVAL

POT MARIGOLD GOLD GOLDE SUNFLOWER

POTPOURRI HASH OLIO STEW MASLIN MEDLEY POTPIE RAGOUT FANTASIA PASTICHE JAMBALAYA SALMAGUNDI BOUILLABAISSE

POTRO COLT

POTSHERD BIT PIG TEST CROCK SHARD SHERD FRAGMENT OSTRACON PANSHARD

POTTAGE SEW SOUP SOWL STEW BERRY BROTH BRUET BREWIS BROWET POTAGE OATMEAL PULMENT

POTTED DRUNK CANNED
(— **MEAT**) RILLETT

POTTER FAD FUSS MUCK POKE ANNOY DAKER TRUCK BOTHER DABBLE DACKER DAIDLE DIDDLE DISHER DODDER FIDDLE FOOTLE FOTTER JOTTER KUMHAR MUDDLE NANTLE NIGGLE PETTLE POUTER TIDDLE TIFFIE TIFFLE TRIFLE CLOAMER CROCKER DISTURB FIGURER FOSSICK HANDLER NAUNTLE PERPLEX PLOWTER PRODDLE THROWER TROUBLE CERAMIST TERRAPIN
(— **OFFICIOUSLY**) TEW
(**MACHINE OF** —) JOLLY

POTTERER TWIRLER

POTTERY POT BANK CHUN DELF GROG WARE BIZEN CROCK DELFT GLOST ROUEN SPODE BASALT

FICTIL KASHAN MIMPEI ASTBURY BELLEEK BOCCARO BRISTOL DIPWARE FIGMENT JETWARE KAMARES POTBANK POTWARE POTWORK REDWARE SATSUMA TICKNEY TZUCHOU BUCCHERO CERAMICS FIGULINE GRAYWARE SANTORIN SLIPWARE BROWNWARE
(— **CIVILIZATION**) MINYAN
(— **CULTURE**) PUCARA
(— **DECOR**) MISHIMA
(— **DECORATED WITH SCRATCHING**) GRAFFITO
(**ANCIENT** —) KAMARES GRAYWARE
(**BLACK** —) BASALT BUCCHERO
(**BLUE-AND-WHITE** —) DELFT
(**CHINESE** —) KUAN YIHSING
(**CRUSHED** —) GROG
(**HINDU** —) UDA
(**JAPANESE** —) IMARI
(**RICHLY COLORED** —) MAJOLICA
(**TURKISH** —) IZNIK
(**UNGLAZED** —) BISCUIT

POTTERY TREE CARAIPE

POTTINGER COOK POTYCARY

POTTO LEMUR APOSORO KINKAJOU

POTTY CRAZY FOOLISH TRIVIAL SNOBBISH

POUCH BAG COD JAG POD SAC BELL BOTA CYST POCK POKE BULGE BURSA POKKE PURSE BUDGET CAECUM CRUMEN GIPSER PACKET POCKET PURSET SACHET ALFARGA ALFORJA CANTINA CRUMENA GIPSIRE MAILBAG MOCHILA OVICYST SCROTUM SPORRAN SWALLOW BURSICLE PROTRUDE SPEUCHAN MARSUPIUM
(— **OF FLY**) AEROSTAT
(— **ON DEER'S NECK**) BELL
(— **ON PETAL**) SPUR
(**PILGRIM'S** —) SCRIP
(**TOBACCO** —) DOSS
(**PREF.**) PERO PHASCO PHASCOL(O) THYLAC(O)

POUCHED SACCATE

POUCH OF DOUGLAS
(**PREF.**) CULDO

POUF PUFF OTTOMAN

POULAINE PIKE CRAKOW

POULPE POULP CUTTLE OCTOPUS

POULTICE QUILT STUPA STUPE MALAGMA EPITHEME SINAPISM CATAPLASM

POULTRY FOWL HENS DUCKS GEESE PULLEN PEAFOWL PIGEONS PULLERY TURKEYS CHICKENS PULLAILE VOLAILLE

POUNAMU JADE PUNAMU NEPHRITE

POUNCE NAB CHOP CLAP JUMP POKE SWAP SWOP FLECK PRICK PUNCH SOUSE SWOOP TALON EMBOSS PIERCE TATTOO BOBCOAT DESCEND SPRINKLE
(— **UPON**) TIRE STOOP

POUND L LB BUM DAD LIB PIN PUN SOV BEAT CHAP DRUB FRAM PELT PIND POON POSS PUND QUID SKIT SPCA THUD TRAP TUND CRUSH FRAME KNOCK LABOR LIVRE

NEVEL STAMP THUMP TRAMP WEIGH BATTER BRUISE HAMMER LUMBER NICKER POUNCE PRISON THRASH CONTUND CONTUSE PINFOLD THUNDER LAMBASTE RESTRAIN
(— FINE) BRAY
(— SYMBOL) OCTOTHORP
(FISH —) KEEP MADRAGUE
(ISRAELI —S) LIROTH
(1-8TH OF —) HANDFUL
(100 —S) CENTAL CENTURY
(12 —S OF BUTTER) GAUN
(25 —S) PONY PONEY
(32, 56, OR 75 —S OF RAISINS) FRAIL
(500 —S) MONKEY
POUNDMASTER PINDER PINNER PONDER
POUR JAW RUN TUN YET BIRL BREW DROP EMIT FILL FLOW GOSH GUSH HELD LASH LAVE RAIN TEEM TOOM VENT FLOOD FLUSH HEELD HIELD POWER SLIDE SOUSE SPILL SPOUT SWARM TRILL AFFUSE DECANT SLUICE STREAM CASCADE CHANNEL DIFFUSE SUFFUSE
(— AWAY) STAVE
(— BACK) REFUND
(— BEER OR WINE) BIRL
(— BETWEEN) INTERFUSE
(— CLUMSILY) SLOSH
(— COPIOUSLY) HALE
(— DOWN) RASH SILE SHOWER DESCEND DISPUNGE
(— FORTH) SHED TIDE VENT WELL DISTILL OVERFLOW
(— FREELY) SWILL
(— FROM ONE VESSEL TO ANOTHER) DECANT JIRBLE TRANSFUSE
(— IN) INFUSE INFOUND INHELDE
(— IN DROP BY DROP) INSTIL INSTILL
(— LIKE RAIN OR TEARS) LASH
(— MELTED WAX) BASTE
(— MOLTEN LEAD) YOTE
(— OFF) SLUICE
(— OIL UPON) ANOINT
(— OUT) FILL SEND SHED SKINK STOUR UTTER EFFUSE LIBATE DIFFUND DIFFUSE
(— OVER) PERFUSE SUFFUSE
(— TOGETHER) CONFUSE
(— UNSTEADILY) JIRBLE
(— UPON) AFFUSE
(PREF.) CHYMI
(SUFF.) CHYME
POURBOIRE TIP GRATUITY TRINKGELD
POURER TEEMER INFUSER
POURING AFFUSION EFFUSION INFUSION LIBATION
(SUFF.) ENCHYSIS
POURPOINT GIPON JUPON QUILT DOUBLET
POUT BIB MOP MAID MOUE PUSS SULK BLAIN BOODY GROIN BRASSY BRASSIE CATFISH EELPOUT BULLHEAD PROTRUDE
POUTERIA LUCUMA
POUTING BOUDERIE

POUTY DOUR GLUM MOROSE SULLEN
POVERTY LACK NEED WANE WANT DEARTH PENURY BEGGARY DEFAULT MISEASE TENUITY DISTRESS POORTITH PUIRTITH SCARCITY WANDRETH NECESSITY
(SUFF.) PENIA
POVERTY PLANT HEATH HEATHER LINGWORT
POVERTY-STRICKEN POOR NAKED NEEDY SQUALID SHIRTLESS
POWDER BRAY DUST KISH MILL MULL SAND CHALK CURRY ERBIA FLOUR GRIND HEMOL KOSIN PICRA STOUR CEMENT CHARGE CHINOL DECAMP DERMOL EMPASM ESCAPE FARINA FILITE GERATE KAMALA KERMES KUMKUM MELLON PEYTON PINOLE POUNCE RACHEL SMEETH YTTRIA ALCOHOL BESTREW BROCADE LUPULIN SCATTER SMEDDUM SPACKLE SPODIUM ALGAROTH CATAPASM DYNAMITE FLUMERIN PALEGOLD
(— A SHIELD) GERATE
(— FOR BRONZING) BROCADE
(— FOR EYELIDS) KOHL
(— OBTAINED BY SUBLIMATION) FLOWERS
(— TO MASK SWEAT ODOR) EMPASM EMPASMA
(— USED IN CHOCOLATE) PINOLE
(ABRASIVE —) EMERY
(ANTHELMINTIC —) KOSIN
(ANTIMONY —) KOHL
(ANTISEPTIC —) EUPAD
(APERIENT —) SEIDLITZ
(ASTRINGENT —) BORAL
(BLEACHING —) CHEMIC CHLORIDE
(BROWNISH —) LIGNIN
(CATHARTIC —) KAMALA
(COLORING —) HENNA
(EFFERVESCENT —) SALINE
(FINE —) DUST POUNCE ALCOHOL
(FLUORESCENT —) FLUMERIN
(GOA —) ARAROBA
(GOLD —) VENTURINE
(GRAPHITIC —) KISH
(GRAY —) ANTU
(HAIR —) MUST
(MALT —) SMEDDUM
(PERFUMED —) ABIR PULVIL SACHET
(PINK —) CALAMINE
(POISONOUS —) ROBIN
(PURPLE —) CUDBEAR
(REDDISH —) ABIR KUMKUM SIMMON
(ROSE-COLORED —) ERBIA
(SACHET —) PULVIL
(SILICEOUS —S) SILEX
(SMOKELESS —) FILITE PEYTON CORDITE AMBERITE INDURITE SOLENITE
(WHITE —) CHINOL YTTRIA HYPORIT SCANDIA HALAZONE LANTHANA PARAFORM
(YELLOW —) KOSIN DERMOL MELLON LUPULIN MALARIN SAMARIA TANNIGEN
(PREF.) PUMICI

POWDERED SEME SPICED PICKLED SEASONED
POWDER PUFF PLUFF
POWDER ROOM BATHROOM MAGAZINE
POWDERY MEALY PRUINOSE PULVEROUS
POWER ARM ART JUS ROD SAY SUN VIS BEEF BULK DINT GIFT GRIP HAND HANK HEAP HORN IRON KAMI MAIN MANA MAYA SOUP SWAY WALD WILL AGENT CROWN DEMON DEVIL FORCE GRACE HUACA HYDRO INPUT LURCH MIGHT SINEW SKILL STEAM VALUE VIGOR WAKON WIELD YARAK AGENCY APPEAL BREATH CLUTCH CREDIT DANGER DEGREE DOUGHT EFFORT ENERGY FOISON IMPACT MOLOCH MUSCLE SHAKTI STROIL STROKE SWINGE TALENT VIRTUE WEIGHT ABILITY BALANCE BOSSDOM COMMAND CONTROL DEMESNE DESTINY DUNAMIS DYNAMIS ENTHEOS FACULTY POTENCY VALENCY VOLTAGE WAKONDA ACTIVITY AUTONOMY CAPACITY CLUTCHES COERCION DELEGACY DEMIURGE DISPOSAL DOMINION INTEREST LEVERAGE LORDSHIP SEIGNORY STRENGTH PUISSANCE PREROGATIVE
(— FROM SUPREME BEING) EON AEON
(— OF ACID) BASICITY
(— OF ATTORNEY) PROXY
(— OF ATTRACTION) ALLURE
(— OF CHOICE) LIBERTY
(— OF DETERMINING) VOLITION
(— OF DIVORCE) TAFWIZ
(— OF ENTRY) INGRESS
(— OF GIVING) PROPINE
(— OF HEARING) AUDITION
(— OF IMAGINATION) ESEMPLASY
(— OF KNOWING) JNANASHAKTI
(— OF LIVING) VITALITY
(— OF MANIFESTATION) MAYA
(— OF MOVING AT SEA) YARAGE
(— OF PERFORMING) ART
(— OF RESISTANCE) STAMINA
(— OF RETURNING) REGRESS
(— OF SELF-DETERMINATION) FREEWILL
(— OF SPEECH) TONGUE
(— OF TRANSMUTATION) ALCHEMY
(— OF VISION) KEN
(— OF WINE) SEVE
(—S OF EVIL) HELL
(— TO ATTRACT) DUENDE
(— TO CHARM) DUENDE
(— TO CONVINCE) FORCE
(— TO ENTER) ENTRANCE
(AUTHOR OF —) FEUCHTWANGER
(CHARACTER IN —) REB KARL ISAAC JOSEF MARIE NAEMI ANSELF GABRIEL SIBYLLE LANDAUER MAGDALEN ALEXANDER SELIGMANN WEISSENSEE OPPENHEIMER
(CIVIL —) CAESAR
(COERCIVE —) SWORD
(CURATIVE —) THERAPY
(DIVINE —) MOIRA

(ELEVATING —) LIFT
(EMOTIONAL —) STOMACH
(EXTRAPHYSICAL —) MANA
(FIFTH —) SURSOLID
(FOCAL —) DIOPTRY
(GRIPPING —) HOLD
(GROWTH —) BATHMISM
(HYPOTHETICAL —) FORTUNE
(IMPERSONAL —) WAKAN WAKON WAKANDA
(INHERENT —) VIRTUE
(INTELLECTUAL —) WIT
(LEGAL —) JUS
(MAGIC —) ORENDA
(MAGNETIC —) MAGNES
(MENTAL —) HABITUS
(MILITARY —) SWORDCRAFT
(MORMON —) KEYS
(MOTIVE —) PRINCIPLE
(MYSTERIOUS —) MANA
(NATURAL —) OD
(OCCULT —) MAGIC
(PERSUASIVE —) RHETORIC
(PERUVIAN —) HUACA
(POLITICAL —) DOMINIUM
(RATIONAL —) EYE
(REFLECTIVE —) ALBEDO
(ROYAL —) RIAL
(ROYAL —S) REGALIA
(SACRED —) KAMI
(SECOND —) SQUARE
(SECRET —) MAGIC
(SOLE —) MONOPOLY
(SOVEREIGN —) SWAY THRONE
(SPIRITUAL —) NGAI
(STAYING —) STEEL BOTTOM STAMINA
(STRIKING —) PUNCH
(SUPERNATURAL —) CHARISMA
(SUPREME —) EMPIRE HEAVEN IMPERIUM
(THIRD —) CUBE
(UNLIMITED —) OMNIPOTENCE
(VITAL —) SPIRITS
(ZEST-GIVING —) RELISH
(PREF.) CRATO DYN(A)(AMI)(AMO)
(SUFF.) OD ODIC
(RULING —) CRACY CRAT(IC)
POWERBOAT SEDAN SKIFF GLIDER CRUISER STINKPOT GASOLINER
POWERFUL BIG FAT ABLE DEEP HIGH MAIN RANK RICH VERY FORTE HEFTY HUSKY LUSTY STARK STOUT VALID VIVID WIGHT WILDE COGENT HEROIC MIGHTY POTENT SEVERE STRONG CAPABLE FECKFUL INTENSE POLLENT RICHARD SKOOKUM STAVING VALIANT FORCIBLE PUISSANT VIGOROUS
(PREF.) MEGA
POWERLESS WEAK FEEBLE UNABLE HELPLESS IMPOTENT
POWWOW CHAT PAWAW CONFAB FROLIC COUNCIL MEETING SESSION CONJURER
POX ROUP CANKER PLAGUE VARIOLA
(FOWL —) SOREHEAD
(SHEEP —) OVINIA
POYOU PELUDO ARMADILLO
PRABHU LORD CHIEF WRITER
PRACTICABLE AGIBLE DOABLE

USABLE VIABLE FEASIBLE OPERABLE POSSIBLE

PRACTICAL HARD UTILE ACTIVE ACTUAL THINGY USEFUL OPERARY VIRTUAL WORKING BANAUSIC HOMESPUN PRACTIVE THINGISH DOWNTOEARTH
(— JOKE) WAGGERY
(NOT —) PROFESSORY

PRACTICALLY ALMOST NEARLY REALLY VIRTUALLY

PRACTICE ACT ISM LAW PLY SUE TRY URE USE KEEP LIVE PLAN PLOT ADOPT APPLY ASSAY DRILL FOUND GUISE HABIT HAUNT TRADE TRAIN TREAD USAGE CUSTOM EMPLOY FOLLOW GROOVE OCCUPY PRAXIS RECORD BRUSHUP ENHAUNT KNOCKUP OPERATE PROCEED PROFESS RANDORI USAUNCE ACTIVISM ALARMISM EXERCISE FREQUENT GALENISM REHEARSE OBSERVANCE
(— CHEATING) FOIST
(— DECEPTION) DEACON
(— DILIGENTLY) PLY
(— EXERCISE) DRYRUN
(— FRAUD) SHARK
(— HANDED DOWN) TRADITION
(— HYPOCRISY) CANT
(— OF AN ART) PRAXIS
(— OF MEDICINE) GALENISM
(— QUIETLY) RECORD
(— ROWING) TUB
(— WITCHCRAFT) HEX
(BASEBALL —) FUNGO
(BINDING —) LAW
(CEREMONIAL —) RITE
(COMMUNAL —) SUNNA SCHEME SUNNAH INTRIGUE
(CORRUPT —) ABUSE WHORE
(DIPLOMATIC —) ALTERNAT
(DISHONEST —S) CROSS
(EVIL —) MISUSAGE
(HORTICULTURAL —) CUTTAGE
(MEDICAL —) ALLERGY
(RELIGIOUS —) CULT CULTUS
(SUPERSTITIOUS —) FREET
(TENNIS —) KNOCKUP
(UNDERHAND —) JUGGLING
(VICIOUS —) MOLOCH
(SUFF.) CY ERY ICS ISM

PRACTICED EXPERT VERSED PRACTIC SKILLED VETERAN HACKNEYED

PRACTICING EXERCENT

PRACTITIONER ADEPT DOCTOR HEALER LAWYER NOVICE LEARNER EXERCENT FELDSHER HUMANIST HERBALIST HOMEOPATH NATUROPATH
(SUFF.) ICIAN PATH(IA)(IC)(Y)

PRAD HORSE

PRAENOMEN AULUS CAIUS GAIUS TITUS GNAEUS LUCIUS MANIUS MARCUS SEXTUS SERVIUS SPURIUS MAMERCUS NUMERIUS TIBERIUS

PRAESEPE CRIB CRATCH MANGER BEEHIVE

PRAGMATIC BUSY BUSYBODY

DOGMATIC MEDDLING OFFICIOUS PRACTICAL

PRAGMATIST REALIST

PRAIRIE BAY BLED CAMAS PAMPA PLAIN CAMASS MEADOW PLATEAU QUAMASH
(— STATE) ILLINOIS
(AUTHOR OF —) COOPER
(CHARACTER IN —) ASA BUSH INEZ PAUL WADE ELLEN HOVER NATTY WHITE ABIRAM BUMPPO ESTHER BATTIUS ISHMAEL HARDHEART MIDDLETON

PRAIRIE BERRY TROMPILLO

PRAIRIE CHICKEN GROUSE

PRAIRIE DOG GOPHER MARMOT

PRAIRIE WOLF COYOTE

PRAISE CRY LOF FUME HERY LAUD LOSE LOVE PRES ADORE ALLOW ALOSE BLESS CAROL CHANT CRACK DEIFY EXTOL GLORY HERSE HONOR KUDOS PLAUD PRIZE ROOSE SALVE VALUE WURTH ANTHEM BELAUD EULOGY FRAISE HILLEL KUDIZE LOANGE LOVING ORCHID SALUTE TONGUE ACCLAIM ADULATE APPLAUD COMMEND FLATTER GLORIFY MAGNIFY NOSEGAY PLAUDIT PUFFING TRIBUTE WORSHIP ACCOLADE APPLAUSE BLESSING DOXOLOGY ENCOMIUM EULOGIZE PROCLAIM PANEGYRIC
(— BE TO GOD) LD
(— HIGHLY) MAGNIFY
(— INORDINATELY) FUME
(— IN THANKSGIVING) JOY
(— OF ANOTHER'S FELICITY) MACARISM
(— TO GOD ALWAYS) LDS
(EFFUSIVE —) FUSS
(EXAGGERATED —) PUFFERY
(EXCESSIVE —) FLATTERY ADULATION PANEGYRIC
(EXCLAMATION OF —) BRAVO
(EXTRAVAGANTLY —) PUFF
(INSINCERE —) CLART DAUBING
(PUBLIC —) PRECONY
(SING FALSE —S) CHANT

PRAISED JUDAH JUDITH LAURELED
(UNDULY —) BEPUFFED

PRAISEWORTHY WORTHY AMIABLE GLORIOUS LAUDABLE SPLENDID EXEMPLARY

PRAJAPATI KA PITRI

PRAKRIT PALI MAGADHI

PRAM BUGGY CARRIAGE HANDCART PUSHCART STROLLER

PRANCE STIR BRANK CAPER DANCE JAUNT PRANK CANARY CAREER CAVORT CURVET GAMBOL JAUNCE TITTUP TRANCE PRANKLE SWAGGER CAKEWALK

PRANCER HORSE DANCER CAPERER

PRANK JIG RAG RIG DECK DIDO FOLD GAME GAUD JEST LARK PLOY PRAT REAK ADORN ANTIC CAPER FREAK SHINE SKITE TRICK VAGUE BROGUE CURVET FEGARY FIGARY FROLIC GAMBOL SHAVIE VAGARY MARLOCK SPANGLE ESCAPADE FREDAINE PRANCOME

RIGWIDDIE SHENANIGAN MONKEYSHINE
(PL.) REX GAMES JINKS

PRANKISH TRICKSY

PRANKSTER JOKER FOOLER
(NUDE —) STREAKER

PRASINE LEEK

PRAT PUSH NUDGE TRICK

PRATE GAB BUCK BUKH BUKK CARO CHAT CLAP CLAT TALK BLATE BOAST CLASH SCOLD BABBLE CACKLE CLAVER JANGLE SQUIRT TONGUE BLATHER BLATTER BLETHER CHATTER CLATTER PALAVER PRATTLE TWATTLE

PRATING GAFF CHATTER

PRATIQUE CUSTOM PRODUCT

PRATTLE GUP CHAT CLACK BABBLE BURBLE CACKLE DRIVEL JANNER JAUNER YATTER BLATTER CHATTER CLATTER GABNASH JAUNDER NASHGAB PRITTLE TRATTLE TWADDLE CHITCHAT BAVARDAGE

PRATTLER RATTLE GABNASH PRATTLEBOX

PRATTLING CHAVISH

PRAWN CARID NIPPER PENEID SHRIMP SQUILLA CARIDEAN CARIDOID CREVETTE MACRURAN LANGOSTINO LANGOUSTINE
(SUFF.) CARIS

PRAWN KILLER SQUILLA

PRAXIS HABIT ACTION CUSTOM PRACTICE

PRAY ASK BEG BID BLESS CRAVE DAVEN SOUGH VOUCH INVITE BESEECH ENTREAT IMPLORE REQUEST WRESTLE INVOCATE
(— FOR) BOON

PRAYA BUND BEACH STRAND

PRAYER ACT AHA AVE CRY VOW BEAD BENE BOON PLEA SUIT VOTE AGNUS ALENU NAMAZ SALAT SHEMA ABODAH APPEAL ECTENE ERRAND LITANY MANTRA MATINS ORISON STEVEN VESPER YIZKOR BIDDING COMPLIN FATIHAH GAYATRI GEULLAH KADDISH MEMENTO ORATION PRECULE PREFACE TAHANUN ANAPHORA APOLYSIS CATHISMA DEVOTION KEDUSHAH MISERERE PETITION SUFFRAGE TEHINNAH REQUIESCAT
(— BEADS) ROSARY
(— BEFORE MEAL) GRACE
(— BOOK) MAHZOR MISSAL SERVICE
(— LEADER) IMAM
(— OF DISMISSAL) APOLYSIS
(— RUG) NAMAZLIK
(— SHAWL) TALLITH
(— STICK) BAHO PAHO
(— TOWER) MINARET
(CANONICAL —S) BREVIARY
(CHIEF MOHAMMEDAN —) NAMAZ
(DAILY —) CURSUS
(DEVOTIONAL —) ANGELUS
(HINDU —) GAYATRI
(INAUDIBLE —) SECRET
(INWARD —) ACT
(ISLAM CALL TO —) AZAN

(JEWISH —) ALENU ABODAH GEULLAH HOSHANA KADDISH
(LAST — OF DAY) COMPLIN
(LONG —) CATHISMA
(LORD'S —) PATERNOSTER
(MUSLIM —) SALAH SALAT KHUTBAH
(MUSLIM CALL TO —) AZAN
(OPENING —) COLLECT
(REPETITIVE —) NOVENA
(SECRET —) BREATHING
(SHORT —) GRACE COLLECT
(SILENT —) SECRET
(TABLE —) GRACE
(PL.) HOURS NORITO TIKKUN CHAPLET
(PREF.) EUCHO

PRAYER-BOOK (JEWISH —) MAHZOR MACHZOR

PRAYING ORISON IMPRECANT
(— FIGURE) ORANT

PREACH EDIFY SOUGH TEACH EXHORT GOSPEL SERMON DELIVER HOMILIZE PREDICATE SERMONIZE

PREACHER KHATIB MAGGID PARSON PASTOR TUBMAN DARSHAN LOLLARD MARTEXT PROPHET ROUNDER TEACHER TUBBIST TUBSTER EXHORTER KOHELETH MINISTER PARDONER PULPITER QOHELETH SERMONER SPINTEXT SWADDLER VARTABED BOANERGES
(PL.) PULPIT

PREACHING SPELL PULPIT SERMON HEARING KERUGMA KERYGMA PROPHECY PULPITRY SPELLING

PREACHY DIDACTIC

PREAMBLE PREFACE WHEREAS

PREARRANGED SET

PREBEND CANONRY

PREBENDARY PROVEND

PRE-CAMBRIAN MOINE EOZOIC ARCHEAN PRIMARY HURONIAN TORRIDONIAN

PRECARIOUS NEAR DICKY RISKY SHAKY CASUAL INFIRM NARROW UNSURE DUBIOUS TRICKLE CATCHING DELICATE INSECURE PERILOUS UNSTABLE DANGEROUS UNCERTAIN

PRECAUTION CARE GUARD CAUTEL SAFEGUARD

PRECEDE LEAD FOREGO HERALD FORERUN PREFACE PREVENT ANTECEDE PREAMBLE

PRECEDENCE PAS LEAD PRIMACY HERALDRY PRIORITY
(RIGHT OF —) PAS
(SOCIAL —) LEVEL

PRECEDENT LEAD SIGN MODEL TOKEN USAGE INSTANCE ORIGINAL SPECIMEN STANDARD AUTHORITY

PRECEDING OLD FORE WEST BEFORE FORMER LEADING ADJACENT PREVIOUS
(— ALL OTHERS) FIRST
(PREF.) ANTE

PRECENTOR CANTOR PSALMIST LETTERGAE

PRECEPT LAW HEST LINE RULE TORA WRIT ADAGE AXIOM BREVE

CANON MAXIM ORDER SUTRA SUTTA TENET TORAH BEHEST DICTATE MANDATE WARRANT DOCTRINE DOCUMENT LANDMARK

PRECEPTIVE DIDACTIC MANDATORY

PRECEPTOR TUTOR MASTER

PRECINCT BEAT AMBIT BOUND CLOSE VERGE DOMAIN HIERON VIHARA COLLEGE LENAEUM SOCIETY TEMENOS BANLIEUE DISTRICT ENVIRONS (PL.) AMBIT

PRECIOUS CUTE DEAR FINE LIEF RARE VERY CHARY CHERE GREAT HONEY CHICHI CHOICE COSTLY DAINTY GOLDEN PEARLY POSING SILVER TENDER PRECISE AFFECTED ORIENTAL OVERNICE VALUABLE WORTHFUL PRICELESS

PRECIOUSNESS PRICE

PRECIPICE LIN KHUD LINN LLYN PALI CLIFF KRANS SCREE SHEER STEEP KRANTZ CLOGWYN DOWNFALL HEADWALL

PRECIPITATE GEL CURD HURL RAIN RASH HASTY HURRY SHOOT SPEED STEEP ABRUPT COAGEL HASTEN SLUDGE SUDDEN TUMBLE UNWARY DISTILL LWOOPIN SUBSIDE TRIGGER CATALYZE HEADLONG PROCLIVE SEDIMENT SETTLING (— DYE) STRIKE

PRECIPITATELY HEADLING HEADLONG SLAPDASH

PRECIPITATION HAIL MIST RAIN SNOW HASTE SLEET VIRGA

PRECIPITOUS FULL RASH BRANT BRENT HASTY STEEP ABRUPT CHICHI STEEPY SUDDEN PRERUPT HEADLONG

PRECIS JUNONIA SUMMARY ABSTRACT

PRECISE DRY SET FLAT HARD JUMP JUST NEAT NICE TIDY TRIG TRIM TRUE VERY CLEAN CLOSE EXACT PRESS RIGID SOUND FORMAL NARROW RIGORE STARCH STRICT BUCKRAM CAREFUL CERTAIN CLERKLY CORRECT EXPRESS PERFECT PERJINK STARCHY ABSOLUTE ACCURATE DEFINITE EXPLICIT HAIRLINE PINPOINT PUNCTUAL RIGOROUS

PRECISELY BUT EVEN JUST CLEAN SHARP FINELY JUSTLY STRAIT EXACTLY

PRECISENESS RIGOR RIGOUR PRIMNESS

PRECISIAN PRIG PURITAN

PRECISION NICETY CLARITY ACCURACY DELICACY ELEGANCE JUSTNESS

PRECISIONIST PEDANT

PRECLUDE BAR DENY STOP CLOSE CROSS DEBAR ESTOP FORBID HINDER IMPEDE OBVIATE PREVENT SILENCE CONCLUDE INTERPEL PROHIBIT ANTICIPATE

PRECOCIOUS PRECOX UNRIPE FORWARD PREMATURE RATHERIPE

PRECONCEIVE IDEATE

PRECONCEPTION PRENOTION

PRECONDITION PRIUS

PRECURSOR USHER HERALD INITIAL ANCESTOR PRODROME WAYMAKER HARBINGER HEMIAUXIN PROGENITOR

PREDACITY RAVEN RAVIN

PREDATOR COACTOR

PREDATORY HUNGRY HARMFUL RAVENOUS

PREDECESSOR ANCESTOR FOREGOER (PL.) OLDERS

PREDELLA FOOTPACE

PREDESTINATION FATE DESTINY ELECTION

PREDESTINE DOOM SLATE FOREDOOM FOREPOINT

PREDETERMINE DESTINE FORECAST

PREDICAMENT BOX FIX JAM NODE SOUP SPOT CLASS LURCH STATE STEAD PICKLE PLIGHT SCRAPE DILEMMA IMPASSE CATEGORY JUNCTURE QUANDARY

PREDICANT FRIAR PREACHER DOMINICAN

PREDICATE BASE FOUND AFFIRM ASSERT PRAISE PREACH COMMEND DECLARE EXTREME PREDICT PROCLAIM

PREDICT LAY BODE CALL DOPE READ REDE SPAE AUGUR WEIRD HALSEN FORESAY PRESAGE FOREBODE FORECAST FORETELL PROPHESY SOOTHSAY AUSPICATE PROGNOSTICATE (— EVIL) CROAK

PREDICTION DOPE WEIRD AUGURY BODING BODWORD PORTENT PRESAGE BODEWORD FORECAST PROPHECY VATICINE

PREDILECTION BIAS HANG FANCY FAVOR LIKING RELISH FONDNESS

PREDISPOSE BEND INCLINE SUBJECT

PREDISPOSED PRONE PARTIAL TENDING INCLINED

PREDISPOSITION ITCH DIATHESIS

PREDOMINANCE MAJORITY REGNANCY ASCENDANCY

PREDOMINANT GREAT RULING CAPITAL REIGNING SUPERIOR CULMINANT HEGEMONIC

PREDOMINATE RULE DOMINE EXCEED GOVERN PREVAIL

PREE KISS PRIE TEST TASTE TRIAL PRYING SAMPLE PROVING TASTING

PREEMINENT BIG TOP ARCH HIGH STAR FIRST GRAND GREAT PALMARY PASSING STELLAR SUPREME FOREMOST PRECLARE SPLENDID SUPERIOR PARAMOUNT PREPOTENT (PREF.) ARCH

PREEMPT COLLAR

PREEN PIN PERK PICK TRIM WHET DRESS GLOAT PLUME PRIMP PRINK PRUNE SWELL TRICK BROOCH GODWIT SMOOTH REPLUME (— WINGS) WHET

PREFABRICATED IDENTIKIT

PREFACE FRONT PROEM USHER HERALD PRESAY EPISTLE PRECEDE PREPOSE EXORDIUM FORETALK FOREWORD PREAMBLE PROLOGUE

PREFATORY PROEMIAL PRELIMINARY

PREFECT WALI EPARC GRAVE EPARCH MONITOR PROVOST GOVERNOR PRESIDENT

PREFECTURE EPARCHY (CHINESE —) FU (JAPANESE —) KEN (TIBETAN —) JONG

PREFER LAY LIKE LOVE BRING ELECT EXALT FAVOR OFFER CHOOSE PROFER SELECT OUTRANK PREFECT PRESENT PROMOTE PROPOSE SURPASS

PREFERABLE LIEF RIGHT RATHER ELIGIBLE

PREFERENCE GOO LIKE FAVOR CHOICE DESIRE LIKING RATHER DRUTHERS FAVORITE FOREHAND PRIORITY PRIVILEGE PROMOTION PRECEDENCE

PREFERMENT DIGNITY

PREFIGURE TYPE IDEATE SHADOW TYPIFY FORERUN FORESEE PREDICT FORESHOW PROPHESY ADUMBRATE

PREFIX DUN DOON PREPOSE

PREGNANCY CYESIS TROUBLE ACCYESIS FETATION OOCYESIS GESTATION

PREGNANT BIG GONE OPEN GREAT HEAVY QUICK READY BAGGED CAUGHT COGENT GRAVID PAROUS ENCEINT FERTILE GESTANT TEEMING WEIGHTY CHILDING FORCIBLE GERMINAL PREGGERS PRESSING (— WITH HUMOR) RICH

PREHALLUX CALCAR

PREHEND SEIZE

PREHISTORIC OGYGIAN IMMEMORIAL

PREINDICATE PRESAGE FORESHOW

PREJUDICE BIAS DOWN HARM HURT KINK TURN AGISM DERRY AGEISM DAMAGE IMPAIR INJURY SEXISM SCUNDER SCUNNER JAUNDICE PREJUDGE (— AGAINST ELDERLY) AGISM AGEISM

PREJUDICED BIGOTED INSULAR PARTIAL

PREJUDICIAL BIASED HURTFUL CONTRARY DAMAGING INIMICAL SINISTER

PRELATE CHIEF LEADER PRIEST HIERARCH ORDINARY SUPERIOR MONSIGNOR

PRELIMINARY PRIOR PRELIM PREFACE PRELUDE LIMINARY PREAMBLE PREVIOUS PREFATORY

PRELUDE PROEM VERSET DESCANT FORERUN INTRADA PREFACE ANTELUDE BORSPIEL OVERTURE RITORNEL VERSETTE VORSPIEL

PREMATURE RATH UNRIPE

IMMATURE PREVIOUS TIMELESS UNTIMELY

PREMEDITATE FORNCAST PURPENSE

PREMEDITATED SET STUDIED PREPENSE

PREMIER CHIEF FIRST OLDEST LEADING EARLIEST

PREMISE LEMMA MAJOR ASSUME GROUND REASON SUMPTION

PREMISES (REAR —) BACKSIDE

PREMIUM USE AGIO BACK AWARD BONUS FANCY PRIZE SHAVE USURY BOUNTY DEPORT REWARD GRASSUM CONTANGO DONATIVE FOREGIFT GIVEAWAY (UNDERCOVER —) ICE (UNDERCOVER — FOR SEATS) ICE

PREMIXED INSTANT

PREMONITION OMEN HUNCH VIBES NOTICE BODWORD PRESAGE WARNING BODEWORD FORESCENT

PREMUNE SALTED

PRENATAL INUTERO

PREOCCUPATION HEART INSIGHT FIXATION

PRE-OCCUPIED ABSENTMINDED

PREOCCUPIED DEEP LOST RAPT CRAZY ABSENT FILLED INTENT CRACKED ABSORBED ENGROSSED

PREPARATION DIA FIG GEL BALM DIBS DOPE PREP CREAM FLASH GELEE GLAZE GLOSS JELLY READY ACETUM BLEACH BLUING DERRIS FACIAL LOTION MEGILP NEBULA PEPSIN SIMPLE ADDRESS APPREST CLEANER DIPPING EMANIUM ESSENCE ETHIOPS EXTRACT FITNESS FONDANT LINCTUS MELLITE PLACEBO TRYPSIN VARNISH ABSTRACT CONSERVE COSMETIC FIXATURE GELOSINE INHALANT LAUDANUM MEDICINE RACAHOUT TRAINING MAKEREADY PROVISION (— CONTAINING HONEY) MELLITE (— FOR COLORING LIQUORS) FLASH (— OF GRAPEJUICE) DIBS (AROMATIC —) ELIXIR (CHEESE —) FONDU FONDUTA (CHEESELIKE —) YOGURT CROWDIE YOGHURT (COSMETIC —) HENNA (ENZYME —) KOJI (EYELID —) KOHL (IMPURE RADIOACTIVE —) EMANIUM (INTOXICATING —) BOZA GANJA (MEDICAL —) STUFF (OPIUM —) LAUDANUM (SALINE —) LICK (SLOPPY —) SLIBBERSAUCE (SWEET —) DULCE (UNCTUOUS —) CERATE

PREPARATORY PRIMAL PIONEER PRELIMINARY

PREPARE DO FIT FIX GET LAY ABLE BOUN BUSK COOK GIRD MAKE PARE PLOT PREP TILL YARK ATTLE BLEND BOWNE BRACE DIGHT DRAFT DRESS EQUIP FRAME

ORDER PREDY READY TRAIN
ADJUST DESIGN GRAITH ORDAIN
ADDRESS AFFAITE APPAREL
APPOINT CONCOCT CONFECT
DISPOSE EDUCATE PRODUCE
PROVIDE QUALIFY INSTRUCT
(— BANQUET) COVER
(— BEFOREHAND) PRECONDITION
(— BY BOILING) BREW DECOCT
(— BY HEAT) FRIT
(— CAPON) SAUCE
(— COCAINE) FREEBASE
(— FISH) CALVER
(— FLAX FOR LINEN) RET
(— FOOD) DO COOK
(— FOR BUILDING) FRAME
(— FOR BURIAL) EMBALM
(— FOR DISPLAY) DRESS
(— FOR MARKETING) PROCESS
(— FOR PUBLICATION) EDIT
(— FOR TAKEOFF) STRAPIN
(— HASTILY) RASH
(— HEMP) TAW
(— LAND) CURE
(— ONESELF) ADDRESS
(— TEASEL HEADS) CARP
(— TO DEPART) INSPAN
PREPARED UP APT BUN FIT SET
BAAN BOON BOUN BOWN GIRT
RIPE YARE ALERT BOUND PREST
READY GRAITH CURRIED EQUIPPED
TOGETHER
(— WITH GRAPES) VERONIQUE
(HASTILY —) EXTEMPORARY
(INCOMPLETELY —) GREEN
(QUICKLY —) RUNNING
PREPAREDNESS PROCINCT
PREPENSE DESIGN FORETHOUGHT
PREPONDERANCE MAJORITY
DOMINANCE
PREPONDERATE EXCEED INCLINE
SURPASS DOMINATE OUTWEIGH
PERSUADE
PREPOSSESS BIAS PREVENT
PREPOSSESSING WINNING
PREPOSSESSION BENT BIAS
FETICH FANTASY PREJUDICE
PREPOSTEROUS RICH INEPT
ABSURD FOOLISH LAPUTAN
GROTESQUE RIDICULOUS
PREPUCE
(PREF.) POSTH(E)(I0)(O)
PREROGATIVE GRACE HONOR
RIGHT ESNECY REGALE FACULTY
PECULIAR PRIVILEGE
PRESA LEAD
PRESAGE BODE HINT OMEN OSSE
SIGN ABODE AUGUR TOKEN
AUGURY BETIDE BETOKEN
FORESEE OMINATE PORTEND
PREDICT FOREBODE FORECAST
FOREDOOM FORETELL INDICATE
PREAMBLE PROPHESY
PRESBYTER ELDER PRIEST
PRESTER ANTISTES MINISTER
PRESBYTERIAN WHIG CLASSIC
WHIGGAMORE
PRESBYTERY CLASSIS SENIORY
EXERCISE PARSONAGE
CONSISTORY
PRESCIENCE PRESAGE FORESIGHT
PREVISION
PRESCIND SEVER DETACH

PRESCRIBE SET TAX ALLOT GUIDE
LIMIT ORDER ASSIGN DEFINE
DIRECT ENJOIN INDITE ORDAIN
APPOINT CONFINE CONTROL
DICTATE RESTRAIN
PRESCRIBED SET BASIC THETIC
POSITIVE THETICAL FORMULARY
PRESCRIPT LAW COMMAND
MANDATE PRECEPT
PRESCRIPTION RX BILL FORM
CIPHER RECIPE DICTATE FORMULA
RECEIPT
PRESENCE EYE FACE SELF BEING
ASPECT BEARING COMPANY
ASSEMBLY INSTANCE
(— OF GOD) GLORY
(BODILY —) PERSON
(DIRECT —) IMMEDIACY
(DIVINE —) SHEKINAH SHECHINAH
PRESENT AIM BOX NOW BILL BOON
GIFT GIVE HAND HERE MEED NEAR
NIGH SAND SHOW BEING CUDDY
DOLLY ENTER FEOFF GRANT
NONCE OFFER PLACE RAISE
READY STAGE THERE ACCUSE
ACTUAL ADDUCE ALLEGE AROUND
BESTOW BOUNTY BROACH
CADEAU CLOTHE CUMSHA
DONATE DURANT HANSEL KHILAT
LATTER MODERN NEARBY PREFER
REGALE REGALO RENDER XENIUM
COMMEND CUMSHAW DISPLAY
DOUCEUR ETRENNE EXHIBIT
EXPOUND FAIRING FURNISH
HANDSEL INSTANT LARGESS
PERFORM PORRECT PRETEND
PROPINE RELEASE RESIANT
TASHRIF BLESSING CONGIARY
DONATION GRATUITY INSTANCE
OFFERING PESHKASH RESIDENT
SOULCAKE SPORTULA LAGNIAPPE
(— AS GIFT) DASH
(— FOR ACCEPTANCE) TENDER
(— FORMALLY) SERVE
(— FROM PUPIL TO TEACHER)
MINERVAL
(— IN DETAIL) DISCUSS
(— IN MIND) DEAR
(— OF MONEY) BAKHSHISH
BAKSHEESH BACKSHEESH
(— ONESELF) APPEAR
(— PROMINENTLY) FEATURE
(— TO SOLDIERS) CONGIARY
(— TO STRANGER) XENIUM
(— TO SUPERIOR) NUZZER
(— TO VIEW) YIELD
(— WITHOUT WARRANT) OBTRUDE
(ALWAYS —) CHRONIC
(BRIDEGROOM'S —) HANDSEL
(CEREMONIAL —) KHILAT
(NOT —) ABSENT
(SMALL —) STOCKINGFILLER
PRESENTATION BILL GALA GIFT
SHOW DROLL IMAGE DHARMA
MUSTER SCHEMA BILLING
DISPLAY EPITOME HOOKUPU
MUSICAL PRESENT SPECIES
ANALYSIS BESTOWAL DELIVERY
DONATION EXPOSURE
CANDLEMAS PERFORMANCE
(— IN ART) STUDY
(— TO VIEW) OBJECT
PRESENTIMENT FEELING PRESAGE

BODEMENT FOREFEEL PRENOTION
PREMONITION
PRESENTLY NOW ANON ENOW
SOON SHORTLY DIRECTLY
PRESERVATION FILING SAVING
KEEPING SERVATION
PRESERVATIVE SALT BORAX SPICE
SUGAR CONSERVE TREATMENT
(FOOD —) TINFOIL
PRESERVE CAN JAR CORN HAIN
HOLD KEEP SALT SAVE BLESS
GUARD SERVE SPARE SWEET
WITIE ATHOLD BOTTLE COMFIT
DEFEND EMBALM FREEZE GOGGLE
POWDER RETAIN SECURE SHIELD
UPHOLD CONDITE FORFEND
KYANIZE PROTECT RAISINE
RESERVE SUCCADE SUSTAIN
CHOWCHOW CONSERVE
ENSHRINE MAINTAIN MOTHBALL
PARADISE WITHSAVE
(— BY BOILING WITH SUGAR)
CANDY
(— BY SALTING) CORN CURE SALT
(— OF GRAPES) RAISINE
(— WOOD) KYANIZE PAYNISE
(GAME —) MOOR SHIKARGAH
(HUNTING —) WALK
(PL.) KONFYT
PRESERVED WET CONFECT
BRANDIED POWDERED
PRESERVES JAM JELLY
PRESIDE RULE GUIDE DIRECT
MODERATE
(— OVER) KEEP
PRESIDENCY MADRAS PRYTANY
PRESIDENT MIR FOUD PREX PREXY
PROXY REEVE DEACON RECTOR
PRAESES PREFECT
(— OF COLLEGE) PREX PREXY
(— OF GUILD) DEAN
(— OF LEGISLATURE) SPEAKER
(— OF SUPREME COURT) LAWMAN
(— OF TRADE) DEACON
PRESIGNIFY PRESAGE FORETOKEN
PRESLEY (MIDDLE NAME OF —)
ARON
PRESS FLY HUG JAM SIT BEAR BEND
CRAM DOME DROP DRUK HORN
HUSH IRON JAMB KISS PLOT SERR
THEW TUCK URGE VICE YERK
ARGUE BESET BRIZZ CHAFE CHIRT
CRIMP CROWD CRUSH DRIVE
EXACT FORCE KNEAD MIDST PRIZE
SCREW SHREW SMASH STAMP
STUFF TWIST WEIGH WRING
ASSAIL CHISEL CLOSET COARCT
CRUNCH GOFFER HARASS JOBBER
KVETCH MANGLE NUDDLE PREACE
SQUASH STRAIN STRESS THRAST
THREAP THREAT THREEP THRIMP
THRING THRONG THRUST AFFLICT
ARMOIRE ATTEMPT BESEECH
BESIEGE CONCISE CRUMPLE
EMBRACE ENVIRON FLATBED
IMPRESS MACHINE OPPRESS
SCROOGE SCRUNGE SQUEEZE
THRUTCH AGGRIEVE CALENDER
COMPRESS PRESSURE SCROUNGE
SQUEEGEE SURROUND
(— AGAINST) CONTACT
(— CLOSE) NUDDLE

(— CLOSELY AND PAINFULLY)
MASH
(— DOWN) QUAT
(— FORWARD) DRIVE BREAST
(— FOR WINE) TORCULAR
(— HARSHLY) GRIND
(— IN CHEESE VAT) CHISEL CHIZZEL
(— INTO) THRIMBLE THRUMBLE
(— INTO SERVICE) REQUISITION
(— ON ANVIL) HORN
(— ONWARD) STRETCH
(— OUT) EXTRUDE
(— PAINFULLY) PINCH
(— PAPER) COUCH
(— TOGETHER) PACK KNEAD SERRY
IMPACT CONSTRICT
(— UPON) ELBOW DOWNBEAR
(— WITH FOOT) TREAD
(— WITH HEAD OR HORNS) BOX
(— WITH NOSE) NOUSLE NUZZLE
(— WITH VIOLENCE) DRIVE
(PREF.) PIEZO PRESSI
(SUFF.) (— TOGETHER) ARCTIA
PRESS AGENT FLACK
PRESS-AGENTRY FLACKERY
PRESSED SERRIED
(— WITH BUSINESS) THRONG
(— WITH LEFTHAND FOREFINGER)
BARRED
PRESSES
(SUFF.) (— CLOSE) NASTIC
PRESSING RASH ACUTE CRYING
URGENT CLAMANT EARNEST
EXIGENT INSTANT SQUEEZE
CRITICAL PREGNANT NECESSITOUS
(— HARD) SEVERE
PRESSMAN PIG MINDER PROVER
PRINTER
PRESSURE JAM HEAD HEAT PEND
PUSH SWAY DRIVE FORCE IMAGE
PINCH STAMP BURDEN DURESS
STRESS THRONG WEIGHT BEARING
MERCURY PUSHING SQUEEZE
TENSION URGENCY EXACTION
EXIGENCY FUGACITY PRESSION
(— GROUP) LOBBY
(— OF CIRCUMSTANCE) NECESSITY
(— OF 1 DYNE) BARAD
(— ON INSTRUMENT STRING) STOP
(— UNIT) TORR MICRON
(LIQUID —) HEAD
(MANUAL —) TAXIS
(OSMOTIC —) TONICITY
(UNIT OF —) TORR OSMOL PASCAL
MICROBAR
(VAPOR —) FUGACITY
(PREF.) PIEZO TONO
PRESSURE COOKER STEAMER
AUTOCLAVE
PRESSWORK BACKUP
PRESTIDIGITATOR PALMER
JUGGLER PYTHONIC
PRESTIGE FACE MANA CASTE IKBAL
IZZAT KUDOS PLACE CACHET
STATUS STATURE ILLUSION
INFLUENCE
(HAVING —) STATUSY
PRESTO QUICKLY SPEEDILY
PRESUME BEAR DARE GROW IMPLY
INFER ASSUME EXPECT DARESAY
SUPPOSE ARROGATE
PRESUMED PUTATIVE
PRESUMING ARROGANT FAMILIAR

PRESUMPTION GALL JOLLITY OUTRAGE PRESUME AUDACITY SUCCUDRY SURQUIDY

PRESUMPTUOUS BOLD PERT FRESH PROUD WICKED WILFUL FORWARD HAUGHTY ARROGANT ASSUMING FAMILIAR INSOLENT FOOLHARDY

PRESUPPOSE IMPLY POSIT ASSUME EXPECT PREMISE FORETAKE

PRESUPPOSITION PREMISE

PRETA PETA

PRETEND ACT LET FAKE MAKE MOCK SHAM CLAIM FEIGN LETON AFFECT ASPIRE ASSERT ASSUME GAMMON INTEND OBTEND POSSUM RECKON SEMBLE ATTEMPT PORTEND PRESUME PROFESS SUPPOSE VENTURE SIMULATE

(**— IGNORANCE**) CONNIVE

(**— TO**) FA

PRETENDED FAKE SHAM BOGUS FALSE IRONIC PSEUDO UNREAL ALLEGED ASSUMED COLORED FEIGNED SEEMING SIMULAR AFFECTED IRONICAL SIMULATE

PRETENDER FOP FAKE IDOL CHEAT COWAN FAKER FRAUD POSER QUACK PSEUDO SEEMER AEOLIST CLAIMANT IMPOSTOR INTENDER TARTUFFE MOUNTEBANK

(**— TO LEARNING**) SCIOLIST

PRETENDING FICTION

PRETENSE ACT AIR FACE GRIM MASK MIEN PLEA RUSE SCUG SHAM SHOW SIGN WILE CLOAK COLOR COVER FEINT GLOSS GLOZE GUISE STUDY EXCUSE HUMBUG VENEER CHARADE DAUBERY FAITERY FASHION FICTION GRIMACE PRETEXT PURPOSE UMBRAGE ARTIFICE DISGUISE POSTICHE POSTIQUE SEMBLANT

(**SUPERFICIAL —**) VENEER

PRETENSION AIRS PARADE VANITY PRETEXT

(**—S TO KNOWLEDGE**) SCIOLISM

(**FALSE —**) DISSIMULATION

PRETENTIOUS BIG ARTY BRAG HIGH SIDY BRANK FLASH GAUDY PUFFY SHOWY BRAGGY CHICHI GEWGAW GLOSSY PUFFED ROCOCO SHODDY TINSEL BOMBAST POMPOUS STILTED TINHORN TOPPING BRAGGART OVERBLOWN RECHERCHE

PRETENTIOUSNESS SIDE SWANK

PRETERMIT OMIT NEGLACT SUSPEND INTERRUPT

PRETERNATURAL GOUSTY GOUSTIE STRANGE ABNORMAL UNCOMMON UNEARTHLY

(**— BEING**) MARE

PRETEXT PEG FLAM MASK PLEA RUSE VEIL CLOAK COLOR COVER GLOSS SALVO STALL EXCUSE REFUGE SCONCE APOLOGY UMBRAGE OCCASION PRETENCE PRETENSE

PRETTIFY EYEWASH

PRETTINESS (**ARTFUL —**) COQUETRY)

PRETTY APT GEY PAT ABLE BRAW CUTE DEFT FAIR FEAT FINE GAIN GENT GOOD JOLI MILD MOOI POOR TRIM BONNY DINKY JOLIE POOTY PURTY QUITE SWEET BONITA DIMBER FINELY INCONY MINION PRATTY RATHER TRETIS CLEMENT CUNNING DOLLISH GENTEEL BUDGEREE PRECIOUS

(**— WELL**) GAILY GAYLY

PRETTY-PRETTY KEEPSAKE

PREVAIL WIN BEAR BEAT REIGN WIELD INDUCE OBTAIN CONQUER PERSIST SUCCEED TRIUMPH DOMINATE

(**— BECAUSE BEYOND CONTROL**) RAGE

(**— OVER**) OVERRIDE OVERRULE SURMOUNT

(**— UPON**) GET FOLD LEAD ARGUFY ENTICE INDUCE OBTAIN ENTREAT OVERSWAY

PREVAILING RIFE GOING USUAL CURRENT DOMINANT

PREVALENCE RUN

PREVALENT UP RIFE BRIEF COMMON POTENT VULGAR CURRENT GENERAL POPULAR RAMPANT REGNANT CATHOLIC EPIDEMIC POWERFUL

PREVARICATE LIE EVADE STRAY SKLENT WANDER QUIBBLE SHUFFLE WHIFFLE

PREVARICATOR LIAR JESUIT

PREVENT BAR LET HELP KEEP NILL SHUN STAY STOP TENT WARN AVERT CHECK DEBAR DETER ESTOP ARREST DEFEND FORBID FORLET HINDER OUTRUN RETAIN REVOKE SECURE FORFEND FORLEIT IMPEACH INHIBIT OBVIATE OCCLUDE PRECEDE RETRACT RULEOUT ANTEVERT INTERPEL PARALYZE PRECLUDE PROHIBIT WITHHOLD

(**— OPPONENT FROM SCORING**) CHICAGO

PREVENTION PREFACE ESTOPPEL OBSTACLE PREJUDICE

PREVIEW SNEAK SCREEN FUTURAMA

PREVIOUS HASTY PRIOR BEFORE FORMER RATHER EARLIER LEADING FOREGONE PRECEDING

PREVIOUSLY ERE YET ERST FORE ONCE SUPRA BEFORE ALREADY HASTILY PRIORLY FORMERLY HITHERTO

PREVISION FORESEE FORECAST FORESIGHT

PREY ROB FEED GAME SOYL TIRE BOOTY PREDE RAVEN RAVIN SPOIL QUARRY RAVAGE RAVINE VICTIM CAPTURE PILLAGE PLUNDER ROBBERY SPREATH VULTURE

(**— OF HUNTER**) GAME

(**— UPON**) DEVOUR PICAROON DEPREDATE

(**HAWK'S —**) PELT

PREYER KITE

PRIAM (**DAUGHTER OF —**) CREUSA POLYXENA CASSANDRA

(**GRANDFATHER OF —**) ILUS

(**SLAYER OF —**) PYRRHUS

(**SON OF —**) PARIS HECTOR TROILUS

(**WIFE OF —**) HECUBA

PRIAPISM TENTIGO

PRICE LAY ANTE COST FARE FEER FIAR FIER FOOT ODDS PRYS RATE BRIBE CHEAP CLOSE VALUE WORTH CHARGE FIGURE HANSEL TARIFF AVERAGE CATALOG CRANAGE EXPENSE FURNACE HANDSEL PRETIUM STORAGE CARRIAGE FERRIAGE INTEREST

(**— FOR KEEPING GOODS**) STORAGE

(**— FOR PASTURING CATTLE**) AGISTMENT

(**— OF RECLAMATION**) RANSOM

(**ESTIMATED —**) QUOTATION

(**HIGH —**) DEARTH

(**KIND OF —**) RETAIL STICKER

(**LOW —**) WANWORTH

(**PROPER —**) VALUE

(**REDUCED —**) SALE BARGAIN

(**RISING —S**) BOOM INFLATION

PRICELESS RARE COSTLY UNIQUE UNSALABLE

PRICEY DEAR STEEP

PRICK DOT JAG BROD BROG DROB FOIN GOAD JAGG PECK PING PROG SPUR STAB TANG URGE DRESS ERECT POINT PREEN PUNCH STEEK BROACH GALLOP INDENT LAUNCH POUNCE PRITCH SKEWER STITCH TARGET THRUST TWINGE ACANTHA POINTED BULLSEYE

(**— OUT**) SPOT

(**— PAINFULLY**) STING

(**— WITH NAIL**) CLY CLOY ACCLOY (PREF.) STIGMATI STIGMEO STIGMO

PRICKED PIQUE

(**— UP**) ARRECT

PRICKER PROD NEEDLE STABBER

PRICKET DAG SNUFFER SPITTER

PRICKING SMART PUNGENT RETRACT POIGNANT POINTURE PUNCTION

(SUFF.) NYXIS

PRICKLE PIKE SETA BRIAR BRIER SPEAR SPINE THORN BASKET ACANTHA ACULEUS PRINKLE SPICULA STICKLE STIMULUS (PREF.) ECHIN(O)

PRICKLY BURRY JAGGY SHARP SPINY URCHIN BEARDED SPINOSE SPINOUS STICKLY THISTLY ACULEATE ECHINATE MURICATE SCABROUS SCRATCHY SPICULAR STICKERY STINGING VEXATIOUS (PREF.) CHIN(O)

PRICKLY ASH RUEWORT

PRICKLY HEAT MILIARIA

PRICKLY PEAR TUN TUNA NOPAL SABRA OPUNTIA PINPILLOW

PRICKLY-POINTED PUNGENT

PRICKLY POPPY ARGEMONE COCKSCOMB

PRIDE HEAT HORN LUST POMP RUFF ADORN CREST GLORY ORGUL PLUME PREEN PRIME WLANK EXCESS HUBRIS METTLE NOSISM VANITY COMPANY CONCEIT DISDAIN EGOTISM GLORIFY HAUTEUR STOMACH SMUGNESS SURQUIDY WLONKHEDE

(**— ONESELF**) PIQUE

(**EXCESSIVE —**) SWELLING ARROGANCE

(**MASCULINE —**) MACHISMO

(**SENSE OF MASCULINE —**) MACHISMO

PRIDE AND PREJUDICE (**AUTHOR OF —**) AUSTEN

(**CHARACTER IN —**) JANE MARY DARCY KITTY LUCAS LYDIA BENNET GEORGE BINGLEY COLLINS WICKHAM CAROLINE DEBOURGH GARDINER CATHERINE CHARLOTTE ELIZABETH FITZWILLIAM

PRIDEFUL FASTUOUS

PRIEST EN ABBE CURA CURE DEAN EZRA IMAM MAGA CLERK COHEN EPULO IMAUM ISIAC MOBED PADRE PATER SABIO SARIP VICAR ZADOK ABACES AMAUTA BHIKKU BISHOP DASTUR DIVINE FALMEN FATHER FLAMEN GALLAH GALLUS GELONG GETSUL GOSAIN JETHRO KAHUNA LEVITE POWWOW SHAMAN ANANIAS ARBACES CALCHAS CASSOCK CHANTER DESTOUR DUSTOOR GALLACH LAOCOON PANDITA PAPALOI PATENER PATRICO PHINEAS POONGEE PRESTER STOLIST TEACHER TOHUNGA BABAYLAN BEROSSOS CHRYSEIS HANANIAH KASHYAPA MINISTER PANDARAM PENANCER PONTIFEX POONGHIE SACERDOS SEMINARY SOGGARTH SYRIARCH TALISMAN VARDAPET ZADOKITE OFFICIANT SHAVELING CHAMBERLAIN

((**MISSIONARY —**) REDEMPTORIST

(**— OF APOLLO**) CALCHAS CHRYSEIS

(**— OF CYBELE**) CORYBANT

(**— OF RAMA**) KASHYAPA

(**— OF RHEA**) CURETE

(**BABYLONIAN —**) BEROSSOS

(**BUDDHIST —**) LAMA BHIKKU GELONG POONGEE POONGHIE TALAPOIN

(**BULGARIAN —**) BOGOMIL BOGOMILE

(**CELTIC —**) DRUID

(**CHIEF —**) SYRIARCH

(**CHIEF — OF SHRINE**) EN

(**EGYPTIAN —**) ARBACES CHOACHYTE

(**ETRUSCAN —**) LUCUMO

(**EUNUCH —**) GALLUS

(**FRENCH —**) PERE SULPICIAN

(**GREEK —**) PAPA

(**GYPSY —**) PATRICO

(**HIGH —**) ELI SARIP DASTUR KAHUNA DESTOUR PHINEAS PONTIFF PRELATE CAIAPHAS HIERARCH JEHOIADA PONTIFEX

(**HINDU —**) PANDARAM

(**IGNORANT —**) LACKLATIN

(**INCA —**) AMAUTA

(**INFERIOR —**) LEVITE

(**LAMAIST —**) GETSUL

(MAORI —) TOHUNGA
(MORO —) SARIP PANDITA
(MOSLEM —) ALFAQUI TALISMAN
(NEW —) NEOPHYTE
(PAGAN —) BABAYLAN
(PARISH —) CURA CURE PAPA POPE
PARSON PERSON SECULAR
(PERSIAN —) MAGUS
(ROMAN —) EPULO FLAMEN
(TIBETAN —) LAMA
(VAISHNAVA —) GOSAIN
(VOODOO —) BOCOR BOKOR
(PL.) LUPERCI
PRIEST-DOCTOR SHAMAN
WABENO
PRIESTESS NUN ENTUM HORSE
MAMBO MAMBU BACBUC PYTHIA
DIOTIMA MAMALOI PHOEBAD
PHITONES PYTHONESS
(— OF APOLLO) PYTHIA PHOEBAD
(— OF THE BOTTLE) BACBUC
(BABYLONIAN —) ENTUM
(VOODOO —) HORSE
PRIESTFISH CHERNA ROCKFISH
PRIESTHOOD SALII SACERDOCY
PRIEST-KING PATESI
PRIESTLY AARONIC LEVITIC
SACERDOTAL
PRIG BEG FOP BRAD BUCK NAIL
SMUG DANDY FILCH PLEAD STEAL
THIEF FELLOW HAGGLE PERSON
PILFER TINKER ENTREAT PURITAN
QUIBBLE
PRIGGER THIEF
PRIGGISH PRUDISH
PRIM MIM NEAT TRIG TRIM MIMZY
DEMURE FORMAL MIMSEY PRISSY
PRIVET PROPER STUFFY MISSISH
PERJINK PRECISE PRIMSIE
STARCHY
PRIMACY CHIEFTY PRIMITY
HEADSHIP
PRIMA DONNA DIVA STAR
PRIMARY CYAN MAIN BASIC CHIEF
FIRST PRIME CAUCUS DIRECT
FONTAL MANUAL MAGENTA
RADICAL ARCHICAL CARDINAL
HYPOGENE ORIGINAL PRIMEVAL
PRINCIPAL
(PREF.) ARCHI PROT(E)(EO)
PRIMATE BISHOP GALAGO LEADER
PREMAN PRINCIPAL PREHOMINID
PRIME MAY FANG FILL LOAD MAIN
CHIEF COACH FIRST PRIDE TONIC
YOUTH CHOICE FLOWER SPRING
CENTRAL LEADING LUSTFUL
PREPARE DOMINEER ORIGINAL
YOUTHFUL PRINCIPAL
(— A PUMP) FANG PHANG
(— OF LIFE) FLOWER
PRIME MINISTER DEWAN DIWAN
ATABEG PREMIER
(DEPUTY —) TANAISTE
(IRISH —) TAOISEACH
PRIMER ABC CAP DONAT WAFER
READER CORDERY HORNBOOK
PRIMEVAL OLD NATIVE ANCIENT
OGYGIAN PRIMARY PRISTINE
PRIMITIVE
PRIMING MORSING TWOPENNY
CLEARCOLE
PRIMING IRON DRIFT
PRIMING WIRE PICKER

PRIMITIVE DARK CRUDE EARLY
FIRST GROSS NAIVE PLAIN PRIME
FANTEE GOTHIC PRIMAL SAVAGE
SIMPLE ANCIENT ARCHAIC
PRIMARY PRISCAN BACKVELD
BARBARIC EARLIEST IGNORANT
ORIGINAL PRISTINE ABORIGINAL
PRIMORDIAL NEANDERTHAL
ANTEDILUVIAN
(PREF.) ARCH(AE)(AEO)(E)(EO)(I)
PALAE(O) PALE(O)
PRIMNESS STARCH PRUDERY
PRIMORDIAL CRUDE FIRST
PRIMARY ARCHICAL EARLIEST
PRIMEVAL
PRIMORDIUM BUD ANLAGE
BLASTEMA
PRIMP PRIM ADORN PREEN PRINK
DOLLUP
PRIMROSE GAY OXLIP SPINK
FLOWER SUNCUP COWSLIP
FLOWERY PRIMULA SCABISH
AURICULA PLUMROCK SCURVISH
AFTERGLOW PIMPERNEL
POLYANTHUS
PRIMULA OXLIP COWSLIP
PRIMWORT
PRINCE MIN RAS DUKE EARL EMIR
IMAM KHAN KING KNEZ LORD NASI
RAJA RANA RIAL SAID WANG
ALDER EBLIS EMEER FURST GEBIR
MIRZA PWYLL RAJAH SAYID
ARJUNA DESPOT DYNAST SHERIF
SOLDAN BHARATA ELECTOR
GLAUCUS HELENUS MONARCH
TANCRED TOPARCH ZERBINO
ARCHDUKE ATHELING CARDINAL
FLORIZEL HOSPODAR MAMILIUS
OROONOKO RASSELAS SARPEDON
PENDRAGON
(— OF ABYSSINIA) RAS RASSELAS
(— OF APOSTATE ANGELS) DEVIL
EBLIS
(— OF ARGO) DIOMED DIOMEDES
(— OF BOHEMIA) FLORIZEL
(— OF DARKNESS) DEVIL SATAN
(— OF DEMONS) BEELZEBUB
(— OF DYFED) PWYLL
(— OF SALERNO) TANCRED
(— OF SCOTLAND) ZERBINO
(— SOLD INTO SLAVERY)
OROONOKO
(— WITH CHARLEMAGNE) ASTOLF
ASTOLFO
(ANGLO-SAXON —) ADELING
ATHELING
(ARAB —) SHERIF
(CHINESE —) WANG
(ETRUSCAN —) LUCUMO
(GERMAN —) FURST ELECTOR
(INDIAN —) RAJA RANA RAJAH
BHARATA AHLUWALIA
(LYCIAN —) GLAUCUS SARPEDON
(MESHECH —) GOG
(MOHAMMEDAN —) SOLDAN
(MOSLEM —) IMAM SAID SAYID
SAYYID SHEIKH SOLDAN
(PETTY —) SATRAP VERGOBRET
(SERVIAN —) CRAL
(SLAVIC —) KNEZ
(TROJAN —) HELENUS
(WIFE OF — VALIANT) ALETA

**PRINCE EDWARD ISLAND (BAY OF
—)** ROLLA EGMONT ORWELL
MALPEQUE
(CAPITAL OF —) CHARLOTTETOWN
(TOWN OF —) ABNEY SOURIS
TIGNISH MONTAGUE GEORGETOWN
SUMMERSIDE
PRINCELY NOBLE ROYAL KINGLY
STATELY SOVEREIGN
PRINCE'S FEATHER LILAC
PILEWORT
PRINCESS AIDA ELSA OZMA RANI
DANAE PALLA RANEE SARAH
CREUSA GLAUKE ILDICO MADAME
PSYCHE ANTIOPE CORONIS
PHYLLIS DRAUPADI MAHARANI
(— CHANGED INTO CROW)
CORONIS
(— MOTHER OF ZEUS) ANTIOPA
ANTIOPE
(— OF ARGOS) DANAE
(— OF CORINTH) CREUSA GLAUKE
(— WHO SLEW ATTILA) ILDICO
(MOHAMMEDAN —) BEGUM
(THRACIAN —) PHYLLIS
(TYRIAN —) DIDO
PRINCEWOOD CYP BARIA CYPRE
CERILLO CANALETE SALMWOOD
PRINCIPAL ARCH BOSS HEAD HIGH
LEAD MAIN STAR CHIEF FIRST
GRAND GREAT PRIME STOCK
AUCTOR CORPUS MASTER STAPLE
CAPITAL CAPTAIN CENTRAL
CHATTEL DECUMAN DOMINUS
PREMIER PRIMARY SALIENT
STELLAR CARDINAL ESPECIAL
FOREMOST OFFICIAL PRESTANT
PRINCELY
(— OF SCHOOL) PRECEPTOR
HEADMASTER
(POLITICAL —) PLANK
(PREF.) ARCH PROT(O)
PRINCIPALITY ZUPA ARZAVA
ARZAWA ORANGE SATRAPY
APPANAGE DESPOTAT PRINCEDOM
PRINCIPE (MONEY OF —) DOBRA
PRINCIPLE JUS LAW RTA TAO BASE
FATE RITA RULE SEED YANG
AGENT AXIOM BASIS CANON
CAUSE DATUM ETHOS PRANA
SPARK STUFF TENET ANIMUS
ARABIN CNICIN COGITO CORTIN
ELIXIR EMBRYO FAGINE GOSPEL
ARCHEUS BROCARD BUFAGIN
CLYSSUS ELEMENT FORMULA
GENERAL PRECEPT QUASSIN
RADICAL THEOREM URGRUND
DOCTRINE GOSSYPOL INTIMISM
LANDMARK NICOTINE SANCTION
SPECIFIC TINCTURE
(— ACCEPTED AS TRUE) CANON
(— FROM TOAD) BUFAGIN
(— IN BEECHNUTS) FAGINE
(— OF BLESSED THISTLE) CNICIN
(— OF COTTONSEED) GOSSYPOL
(— OF EXISTENCE) TATTVA
(— OF INDIVIDUATION) AHANKARA
(— OF KEY IN MUSIC) TONALITY
(— OF MENTAL LIFE) PSYCHE
(— OF PARTY) PLANK
(— OF REST) ADHARMA
(— UNDERLYING —) REASON
RATIONALE

(COSMIC —) HEAVEN URGRUND
PRAJAPATI
(DIVINE —) OVERSOUL
(DOGMATIC —) DICTUM
(ELEMENTARY —) BROCARD
(FEMALE —) YIN SAKTI
(FIRST —) ABC SEED ARCHE
(FUNDAMENTAL —) GROUNDSEL
(GERMINAL —) STAMEN
(GOVERNING —) HINGE
(GUIDING —) SQUARE POLESTAR
(KIND OF —) FICK PETER
(LIFE —) SOUL GHOST PRANA
(MALE —) YANG PURUSHA
(MOHAMMEDAN THEOLOGICAL —)
IJMA
(MORAL —) SCRUPLE
(NARCOTIC —) FAGINE
(ONTOLOGICAL —) DHARMA
(POISONOUS —) PICROTOXIN
(PRIMAL —) APEIRON
(PROMINENT —) KEY
(QUICKENING —) LIFE
(RHYTHMICAL —) ACCENT
(SANITARY — S) HYGIENE
(SPIRITUAL —) SOUL
(STOIC —) LOGOS
(SUMMARY OF —S) CREED
(VITAL —) JIVA SPIRIT STAMEN
ARCHAEUS
PRINK PERK PRIG WINK ADORN
PRICK PRIMP PRUNE BEDECK
SMUDGE
PRINT CUT GAY GUM RUN DRUK
MARK TYPE FUDGE PORTY PRESS
SEPIA STAMP BANNER BORDER
CARBON CARBRO ENFACE LETTER
STRIKE BROMOIL DROPOUT
DUOTYPE ENGRAVE GRAPHIC
GRAVURE IMPRESS PUBLISH
TRACING VANDYKE VESTIGE
WOODCUT AQUATONE CALOTYPE
CHLORIDE DRYPOINT HALFTONE
INSCRIBE LEIMTYPE MONOTYPE
POSITIVE URUSHIYE
PHOTOENGRAVING
(— OF WILD MAMMAL) PUG
(— OTHER SIDE) BACK
(— OVER) SURCHARGE
(— PROMINENTLY) SPLASH
(— SECOND SIDE) PERFECT
(— TO RIGHT) ADSCRIPT
(BLOCK —) LINOCUT
(SILK SCREEN —) SERIGRAPH
(UNEDITED —) RUSH
PRINTED FONTED
PRINTER TYPO TWICER PRESSMAN
IMPRIMENT
(AID TO —) DEVIL
(KIND OF —) LINE LASER INKJET
(PL.) TYPOTHETAE
AMERICAN DAY GOUDY GREEN
RUDGE AITKEN BEADLE DRAPER
DUNLAP HUNTER ROGERS SHOLES
THOMAS UPDIKE WILSON ZENGER
DEVINNE GARNETT ROLLINS
BRADFORD WOODWORTH
AUSTRIAN WELSBACH
DUTCH BOMBERG ELZEVIR
ENSCHEDE
ENGLISH CAVE DAYE JONES
WORDE BLOUNT BOWYER BULMER

BUTTER CAXTON OGILBY RAIKES WALKER AWDELAY COPLAND CROWLEY GRAFTON HANSARD NICHOLS BRADSHAW ROYCROFT WOODFALL BASKERVILLE WHITTINGHAM
FRENCH DIDOT DOLET MOREL COLINES PLANTIN RICHARD ESTIENNE
GERMAN FUST ZELL KONIG LUFFT FROBEN MENTEL ZAINER ZENGER PFISTER RATDOLT AMERBACH GRYPHIUS SCHOFFER BREITKOPF GUTENBERG TAUCHNITZ
ITALIAN BODONI GIUNTA CASTALDI MANUTIUS
JAPANESE HARUNOBU
SCOTTISH SMELLIE BALLANTYNE
SWISS GERING
PRINTER'S DEVIL FLY
PRINTING TIRAGE EDITION VIGOREUX CHARACTER IMPRIMERY
(— CHARACTER) SWUNGDASH
(KIND OF —) DNA
(LAST —) THIRTY
PRION PETREL
PRIONID BEETLE
PRIONODON LINSANG
PRIOR ERE OLD FORE PAST EIGNE ELDER FORMER RATHER ALREADY EARLIER FARTHER ANTERIOR FOREHAND HITHERTO PREVIOUS PRECEDING
(PREF.) ANTE EPH EPI
(— TO) ANTE PRAE PRE SUPRA
PRIORITY PRIVILEGE PRECEDENCE PREFERMENT
(PREF.) PRAE PRE
PRIORY ABBEY NUNNERY CLOISTER PRIORATE
PRISCA (HUSBAND OF —) AQUILA
PRISM BLOCK NICOL CYLINDER SPECTRUM WERNICKE REFRACTOR
PRISMATIC SHOWY BRILLIANT
PRISON GIB JUG PEN BRIG COOP GAOL HELL HOCK HOLD HOLE JAIL KEEP LAKE NICK QUAD QUOD SHOP SLAM STIR WARD BAGNE CHOKY CLINK FLEET GRATE JOINT KITTY LIMBO LODGE POUND RATEL TENCH TRONK VAULT BAGNIO BAILEY BUCKET CARCEL CARCER COOLER JIGGER LUMBER RATTLE BASTILE BOCARDO BULLPEN COLLEGE COMPTER CONFINE COUNTER DUNGEON FREEZER GEHENNA KIDCOTE LUDGATE NEWGATE SLAMMER DARTMOOR HOOSEGOW TOLBOOTH TRIBUNAL CALABOOSE PENITENTIARY
(— CAMP) GULAG OFLAG
(— IN ROME) TULLIANUM
(AUSTRALIAN —) TENCH
(IN —) INSIDE
(MILITARY —) GLASSHOUSE GUARDHOUSE
(POLITICAL —) GULAG
(SUBTERRANEAN —) MASSYMORE
(UNIVERSITY —) CARCER
PRISONER CON POW MUTE LIFER DETENU INMATE REMAND TERMER

CAITIFF CAPTIVE CONVICT GAOLBIRD JAILBIRD LONGTIMER
(RELEASED —) EXCON
PRISONER OF ZENDA (AUTHOR OF —) HOPE
(CHARACTER IN —) ROSE SAPT FRITZ FLAVIA RUDOLF MICHAEL DEMAUBAN BURLESDON ANTOINETTE RASSENDYLL TARLENHEIM
PRISONER'S BASE CHEVY CHIVY
PRISSY PRIM FUSSY DAINTY FINICKY PRUDISH PRIGGISH SISSIFIED
PRISTINE NEW PURE FIRST FRESH UNTROD ANCIENT PRIMARY ORIGINAL PRIMEVAL PRIMITIVE UNSPOILED
PRIVACY RECESS SECRET PRIVITY RETREAT SECRECY DARKNESS INTIMACY INTIMITY SOLITUDE SECLUSION
(IN —) ASIDE
(PL.) VERENDA
PRIVATE SNUG ALONE CLOSE GUIDE INNER KHASS PRIVY SHARE CLOSET COVERT INWARD POCKET SECRET STANCH POSTERN SECRECY SEVERAL SOLDIER SQUADDY CIVILIAN DOMESTIC ESOTERIC HOMEFELT INTERNAL INTIMATE PERSONAL SINGULAR UMBRATILE
(BRITISH —) TOMMY
(PREF.) CRYPT(O) KRYPT(O) PRIVI
PRIVATEER CAPER MARQUE PIRATE ALABAMA CORSAIR CRUISER DUNKIRK PICKEER
PRIVATELY ASIDE INWARDLY SECRETLY
PRIVATION LOSS WANT PINCH PENURY PERISH ABSENCE POVERTY HARDSHIP
PRIVET PRIM HEDGE SKEDGE IBOLIUM PRIMWORT PRIMPRINT
PRIVILEGE UP PUT SOC BOTE DOWN HAND STAR TEAM CLAIM ENTRY FAVOR FRANK GRACE HONOR REGAL RIGHT THEAM EXCUSE INDULT MUNITY OCTROI OPTION PATENT WARREN CHARTER FALDAGE FREEDOM LIBERTY MITZVAH PASSAGE GRANDEZA STANDAGE PERQUISITE PREROGATIVE
(— TO USE THINGS) BOTE
(ACQUIRED —) EASEMENT
(POKER —) EDGE
(POOL —) STAR
PRIVILEGED CURULE EXEMPT LICENSED CHARTERED
(— PLACE) WARREN
PRIVY WC AJAX GONG REAR BIFFY DRAFT DUNNY ISSUE JAKES PETTY QUIET SIEGE CLOACA CLOSET OFFICE SECRET DRAUGHT FOREIGN LATRINE PRIVATE DONICKER FAMILIAR INTIMATE OUTHOUSE PERSONAL STEALTHY WARDROBE
(MONASTERY —) REREDORTER
PRIZE CUP FEE GEM PRY BELL BEND GAME GREE PALM PLUM PREY PRIX RATE RISK AWARD BACON

BOOTY LEVER PLATE PLUME PRICE PURSE STAKE VALUE WAGER ESTEEM GLAIVE PRAISE PREMIO TROPHY BENEFIT CAPTURE GARLAND PREMIUM ESTIMATE LEVERAGE PURCHASE REPRISAL TREASURE
(— FOR LAST) MELL
(FIRST —) BLUE
(LOTTERY —) LOT TERN
(THEATER —) OBIE
PRIZE CUP PEWTER
PRIZED DEAR CHARY VALUED
PRIZEFIGHT GO BOUT MILL MATCH SCRAP BARNEY
PRIZEFIGHTER BOXER BLEEDER FIGHTER SLUGGER PUGILIST
PRIZE MONEY GUNNAGE
PRO TO FOR FAVORING
PROA PARO PRAU PROW PAROO PRAHU CARACOA
PROBABILISTIC STOCHASTIC
PROBABILITY ODDS SHOW CHANCE PERCENTAGE
(STRONG —) PRESUMPTION
PROBABLE MAYDE LIKELY PROBAL TOPICAL APPARENT FEASIBLE POSSIBLE INTHECARDS
PROBABLY BELIKE LIKELY
PROBATION TEST PROOF TRIAL PAROLE EVIDENCE
PROBATIONER STIBBLER
PROBE PICK SEEK SIFT STOG TENT DELVE ENTER GROPE SOUND FATHOM SEARCH SEEKER STYLET THRUST TRACER ACCOUNT EXAMINE INQUIRY SOUNDER GYROMELE
PROBITY HONESTY INTEGRITY RECTITUDE
PROBLEM NUT SUM WHY BOYG CRUX DUAL ISSE KNOT BLAIK HYDRA POSER APORIA ENIGMA HANGUP BUGBEAR DILEMMA FUNERAL GORDIAN GRUELER TICKLER EXERCISE HEADACHE JEOPARDY QUESTION STICKLER SITUATION
(CHESS —) DUAL MOVER SUIMATE MINIATURE
PROBLEMATICAL DUBIOUS DOUBTFUL PUZZLING UNCERTAIN UNDECIDED
PROBOSCIS NOSE SNOUT TRUMP TRUNK ANTLIA LINGUA SIPHON SYPHON TONGUE ROSTRUM
PROBOSCIS MONKEY KAHA KAHAU
PROCACIOUS PREY SASSY SAUCY
PROCAINE NOVOCAINE
PROCAVIA HYRAX
PROCEDURE BIAS FORM HAVE VEIN DRAFT ORDER TENOR TRACK AFFAIR COURSE METHOD POLITY SYSTEM DRAUGHT PROCESS PRODUCT ACTIVITY PROTOCOL OPERATION
(PRESCRIBED —S) CEREMONY
(ROUNDABOUT —) CIRCUITY
(SECRET —) STEALTH
(STANDARDIZED —) BIT
(SURGICAL —) BYPASS
(UNWISE —) FOLLY

PROCEED DO GO BANG BEAR FAND FARE FLOW FOND HAVE MAKE MARK MOVE PASS ROAM ROLL SEEK STEP TAKE TOOL TOUR WEAR WEND WIND YEAD YEDE YEED AMBLE ARISE DRESS FOUND FRAME ISSUE MARCH REACH TRACE BREEZE INTEND PURSUE RESULT SPRING STRAKE STRIKE TRAVEL ADVANCE AGGRESS DEVOLVE EMANATE FORTHGO PRETEND STRETCH CONTINUE PROGRESS
(— AIMLESSLY) CIRCLE
(— ALONE) SINGLE
(— AWKWARDLY) SHLEP SCHLEP SCHLEPP
(— BY STEPS) RATCHET
(— CLUMSILY) FLOUNDER
(— INSIDIOUSLY) SAP
(— LINGERINGLY) LOITER
(— OBLIQUELY) CUT
(— RAGGEDLY) HALT
(— RAPIDLY) RAKE STRETCH
(— SECRETLY) MINE
(—S FROM GAMBLING) MOTZA MOTSER
(— SLOWLY) INCH
(— SUCCESSFULLY) COOK
(— THROUGH) PLAY
(— UNSTEADILY) DRIDDLE
(— WITH) PLAY
(— WITH DIFFICULTY) STRUGGLE
(— WITH LITTLE EFFORT) CRUISE
(PL.) TAKE VAIL AVAILS INCOME PROFITS PROVENT RETURNS PREVENUE
PROCEEDING ACT DEED FARE PLOY STEP AFFAIR AMPARO COURSE DOMENT ISSUANT MEASURE ONGOING PASSANT QUIETUS TEMANET WARRANT CONCURSO INSTANCE PLACITUM PRACTICE
(— BY THREES) TERNARY
(— FROM GOD) DIVINE
(— FROM THE EARTH) TELLURIC
(— STEP-BY-STEP) GRADATORY
(COURT —S) ACTA TRIAL ACTION
(INDIRECT —S) AMBAGES
(PARLIAMENTARY —S) HUSTINGS
(PREVIOUS —) PRECEDENT
(RECORDED —S) ACTA
(SECRET —) COVERTURE
(PL.) ONGOINGS
PROCERITY HEIGHT TALLNESS
PROCESS RUN FANG FOOT TINA WRIT CREST FURCA HAMUS MUCRO SPINA CALCAR CAPIAS CILIUM COURSE CRUNCH FEELER HABEAS INTEND METHOD REPORT ACCOUNT BARBULE FURCULA GOBBING HAMULUS ISOLATE LAMELLA MANDATE SPATULA SUMMONS ACROMION ACTIVITY APPENDIX AUTOTYPE FILAMENT FRENULUM GRAINING INSTANCE MANUBRIUM OPERATION
(— OF BONE) HORN
(— OF CHANGE) ACTION
(— OF CREATING VACUUM) EXHAUST
(— OF DYEING) BATIK HANKING
(— OF METALPLATING) ACIERAGE

(— OF PACKING) GOBBING
(— OF REASONING) ALGEBRA
(— OF SUPPLYING WANTAGE) ULLING
(— ON FISH'S HEAD) LACINIA
(— PAPER) CONVERT
(— TO RECOVER LAND) DADENHUDD
(— TO REGAIN USE) RECYCLE
(ABRUPT —) MUCRO
(ALCHEMICAL —) CIBATION DIPLOSIS
(ARTISTIC —) FROTTAGE
(BRISTLE-LIKE —) STILET STYLET
(CALENDERING —) SWISSING
(CARBON —) AUTOTYPE
(CERAMIC —) FIRING
(COATING —) BLOOMING
(CURVED —) HAMUS
(DEVELOPMENTAL —) ANCESTRY
(EARLIKE —) AURICLE
(FALCONRY —) IMPING
(FINISHING —) BRUSHING CRABBING
(FORKED —) FURCA FURCULA
(HAIRLIKE —) VILLUS
(HELMETLIKE —) CASQUE
(HOOKLIKE —) HAMULUS
(HORNSHAPED —) CORNICLE
(INTELLECTUAL —S) COGITO
(KIND OF —) MARKEY MARKOFF
(KNOBLIKE —) BOSS
(LEGAL —) BAIL SUIT CAUSE ATTAINT INSTANCE
(MATHEMATICAL —) ADDITION DIVISION
(MENTAL —) COMPOUND
(MINING —) STOPING
(MOVIE-MAKING —) SLATING
(NERVE-CELL —) DENDRON
(NERVELIKE —) AXON AXONE
(PHOTOGRAPHIC —) CARBRO
(POINTED —) AWN SPINE STYLUS LANGUET
(PRINTING —) OFFSET GRAVURE STENCIL INTAGLIO
(REORGANIZATION —) HEMIXIS
(SMALL POINTED —) AWN
(SPINNING —) JACKING
(SPINOUS —) ACANTHA
(SPINY —) STYLOID
(TEXTILE —) DECATING
(WEAVING —) HATCHING
(WINGLIKE —) ALA FIN
(PREF.) TYP(I)(O)
(DRY —) XER(O)
(SUFF.) AL ANCE ANT ENCE ESIS IAL ING ISATION ISM IZATION OSIS SIS TH TYPAL TYPE TYPIC TYPY
(— OF BECOMING) ESCENCE
PROCESSED DOWN FINISHED
PROCESSION POMP WALK CORSO DRIVE TRACE TRAIN BRIDAL EXEQUY LITANY PARADE STREAM CORTEGE FUNERAL THIASOS TRIONFO TRIUMPH ENTRANCE MOHARRAM PROGRESS MOTORCADE
(— OF THE HOLY CHRIST) SPIRATION
(BOISTEROUS —) SKIMMITY
(FUNERAL —) EXEQUY EXEQUIES
(IRISH CIVIC —) FRINGES

(MUSLIM —) MOHARRAM MUHARRAM MUHARREM
(SUFF.) CADE
PROCESSOR (KIND OF —) WORD
PROCLAIM BID CRY BAWL DEEM HORN OYES OYEZ SCRY SING TOOT TOUT BLARE BLAZE BOAST CLAIM GREDE KNELL SOUND SPEAK BLAZON BOUNCE DEFAME HERALD INDICT OUTCRY CLARION DECLARE DIVULGE PROTEST PUBLISH TRUMPET ANNOUNCE DENOUNCE RENOUNCE PROMULGATE
(— ALOUD) ROAR
(— PUBLICLY) PRECONIZE
(— WITH BIG TALK) BOUNCE
PROCLAMATION CRY HUE BANS FIAT OYES OYEZ RERD SCRY BANDO BANNS BLAZE EDICT UKASE PLACARD PROGRAM PUBLICATION ANNUNCIATION
PROCLIVITY BENT ANLAGE APETITE APTNESS LEANING TENDENCY
PROCNE (FATHER OF —) PANDION
(HUSBAND OF —) TEREUS
(SISTER OF —) PHILOMELA
(SON OF —) ITYS
PROCONSUL GALLIO PROVOST
PROCRASTINATE LAG TIME DEFER DELAY LINGER ADJOURN POSTPONE PROROGUE TEMPORIZE
PROCRASTINATION DELAY CUNCTATION
PROCREANT FRUITFUL
PROCREATE WIN SIRE BEGET ENGENDER GENERATE OCCASION
PROCREATION INCREASE
PROCREATOR AUTHOR
PROCRIS (FATHER OF —) ERECHTHEUS
(HOUND OF —) LAELAPS
(HUSBAND OF —) CEPHALUS
PROCTOR LIAR PROG ACTOR AGENT PROXY BEGGAR RECTOR MONITOR PROCUTOR
PROCUMBENT HUMIFUSE PROSTRATE
PROCURABLE PARABLE
PROCURATOR PROXY PILATE PROCTOR
PROCURE GET WIN FANG FIND GAIN GIVE HALE BRING INFER TOUCH EFFECT INDUCE OBTAIN ACHIEVE ACQUIRE COMPARE CONQUER CONTRIVE PURCHASE
(— TO COMMIT PERJURY) SUBORN
PROCURER PIMP PROXENET PURVEYOR
PROCURESS AUNT BAWD HACK LENA PANDER COMMODE PINNACE
PROD DAB EGG GIG JAB JOB JOG BROD BROG GOAD HEEL POKE PROG URGE GOOSE HURRY NUDGE PROBE INCITE JOSTLE THRUST IRRITATE
(— THE BUTTOCKS) GOOSE
PRODIGAL PROD FLUSH LARGE COSTLY LAVISH WANTON WASTER PROFUSE SPENDER WASTRIE WASTRIFE PROFLIGATE
PRODIGALITY WASTE WASTRY WASTRIFE PROFUSION

PRODIGIOUS HUGE VAST GIANT AMAZING IMMENSE STRANGE ABNORMAL ENORMOUS GIGANTIC MONSTROUS PORTENTOUS
PRODIGY OMEN SIGN MARVEL OSTENT WIZARD WONDER MIRACLE MONSTER PORTENT CEREMONY
PRODITION TREASON BETRAYAL
PRODUCE DO GO ANTE BEAR FORM GIVE GROW MAKE REAR SHOW TEEM WAGE BEGET BIRTH BREED BRING BROOD BUILD CARRY CAUSE DRIVE FORGE FRAME HATCH ISSUE PUTON RAISE SPAWN THROW TRADE YIELD APPORT CREATE EFFECT GROWTH INCOME INVENT INWORK PARENT SECURE TURNIN ADVANCE ANIMATE COMPOSE DEPROME GIGNATE INSPIRE OUTWORK PRODUCT PROLONG PROVENT CONCEIVE CONFLATE ENGENDER GENERATE INCREASE LENGTHEN OFFSPRING
(— A COPY OF) TYPE
(— AN EFFECT) ACT AFFECT
(— ANEW) REGENERATE
(— AS PROFIT) NET NETT
(— AUDIBLE EFFECT) SOUND
(— BY GREAT EFFORT) GRIND
(— CROPS) CARRY
(— DULL APPEARANCE) CHILL
(— EFFECT) OPERATE
(— FREELY) PULLULATE
(— FRUIT) TEEM
(— HEAT) ENRAGE
(— IN SPECIFIED FORM) FORMAT
(— PAID FOR RENT) CAIN
(— SHARP NOISE) CRINK
(AGRICULTURAL —) PODWARE
(FARM —) HUSBANDRY
(GARDEN —) STUFF TRUCK
(MINING —) LEY
(SUFF.) FER(ENCE)(ENT)(OUS) FIC(AL)(ATE)(ATION)(ATIVE)(ATOR) (ATORY)(E)(ENCE)(ENT)(IAL)(IARY) (IENT) FIQUE GEN(E)(ESIA)(ESIS) (ETIC)(IC)(IN)(OUS)(Y)
PRODUCED (ARTIFICIALLY —) FORCED
(SEXUALLY —) GAMIC
(SUFF.) GENETIC
PRODUCER GASMAN BEARING SHOWMAN DIRECTOR GAZOGENE OUTPUTTER
(— OF COMPUTER SYSTEMS) OEM
(SUFF.) ARIAN EER
PRODUCING IN PROCREANT
(PREF.) EXO
(SUFF.) GENIC GEROUS GON(E) (IDIUM)(IMO)(Y) IGEROUS PARA PARQUS
PRODUCT HEIR ITEM BRAND CHILD FRUIT GROSS OUTGO SPAWN ALCLAD EFFORT FABRIC GROWTH RESULT UPCOME FALLOUT OUTTURN PRODUCE PROGENY TURNOUT OUTBIRTH OFFSPRING
(— MADE IN INDIA) SWADESHI
(— OF ROCK DECAY) LATERITE
(—S OF LAND) ESPLEES
(—S OF ORCHARD) BIKKURIM

(ADDITION —) ADDUCT
(CHEESE AND MILK —S) GERVAIS
(CHOICE —) CAVIAR
(COMPLETED —) TURNOFF
(FISH —) SURIMI
(LEGISLATIVE —) ACT
(MATHEMATICAL —) SQUARE
(MINERAL —) HUTCH
(OXIDATION —) SUBSCALE
(RESIDUAL —) LATERITE
(SECONDARY —) CONGENER
(SURPLUS —S) ARISINGS
(TRANSFORMATION —) BAINITE
(WASTE —) RESIDUENT
(WORTHLESS —) CHAFF
(SUFF.) ADE
(COMMERCIAL —) INE
(MANUFACTURED —) ITE
PRODUCTION WORK FORGE FRUIT GROSS PIECE YIELD GROWTH OUTPUT EDITION GUIGNOL PRODUCE ARTIFICE INDUCTION OPERATION
(— OF MEDIUM) APPORT
(— OF YOUNG) INCREASE
(BEST —S) FAT
(SUCCESSFUL —) HIT
(SUFF.) GENY POEIA POEIS POIESIS POIETIC
PRODUCTIVE FAT RICH LOOSE QUICK ACTIVE BATTLE PAROUS STRONG CAUSING FERTILE GAINFUL HEALTHY TEEMFUL TEEMING CHILDING CREATIVE FRUITFUL GERMINAL PLENTEOUS
(SUFF.) POEIA POESIS POIESIS POIETIC
PROEM PREFACE PRELUDE PROHEIM FOREWORD OVERTURE PREAMBLE
PROETUS (BROTHER OF —) ACRISIUS
(DAUGHTER OF —) IPHINOE LYSIPPE IPHIANASSA
(FATHER OF —) ABAS
(MOTHER OF —) OCALEA
(WIFE OF —) ANTEA
PROFANATION VIOLENCE SACRILEGE
PROFANE LAY NOA BLUE FOUL ABUSE COARSE DEBASE DEFILE DEFOIL DEFOUL UNHOLY VULGAR WICKED GODLESS IMPIOUS POLLUTE SECULAR UNGODLY VIOLATE WORLDLY TEMPORAL UNHALLOW
PROFANITY OATH CURSE CURSING LANGUAGE BLASPHEMY
PROFESS OWN AVOW ADMIT CLAIM AFFECT AFFIRM ALLEGE ASSERT ASSUME FOLLOW PRESUME PRETEND PURPORT PRACTICE
(— TO BE) SUBSCRIBE
PROFESSION ART BAR LAW COAT FEAT GAME WALK CRAFT FAITH FORTE TRADE CAREER CHURCH EMPLOY METIER MISTER CALLING FACULTY QUALITY SERVICE ADVOCACY BUSINESS COACHING FUNCTION PEDAGOGY SOLDIERY VOCATION
(— OF LETTERS) QUILL

(JOURNALISTIC —) PRESS
(SUFF.) SHIP
PROFESSIONAL PRO COLT PAID
HIRED EXPERT SKILLED TRAINED
FINISHED
PROFESSOR DON PROF HANIF
KHOJA LAWYER REGENT ADJOINT
ACADEMIC CIVILIAN EMERITUS
PROFESSORSHIP CHAIR FAUTEUIL
PROFFER BID CAP GIVE TEND TENT
DEFER DODGE ESSAY OFFER
EXTEND OPPOSE PREFER PROFRE
TENDER ATTEMPT PRESENT
HESITATE
PROFICIENCY SIGHT SKILL ABILITY
APTNESS MAITRISE
PROFICIENT ADEPT EXPERT
MASTER SALTED VERSED PERFECT
SKILLED SKILLFUL
PROFILE FORM FLANK PURFLE
SKETCH CONTOUR OUTLINE
SECTION PSYCHOGRAPH
(— OF RIVERBED) THALWEG
(— OF RIVER BOTTOM) THALWEG
PROFIT AID GET NET WIN BOOT
GAIN MEND NOTE SKIN VAIL AVAIL
EDIFY FRAME GRIST LUCRE SCALP
SPEED BEHOOF INCOME MAKING
PAYOFF RETURN ACCOUNT
ADVANCE BENEFIT CLEANUP
FURTHER GETTING IMPROVE
MILEAGE PLUNDER REVENUE
VANTAGE WINNING CLEANING
INCREASE INTEREST PERCENTAGE
PERQUISITE
(— BY) BROOK
(ILLICIT —) GRAFT
(INORDINATE —) BUNCE
(UNDERCOVER —) SOUFF7F
(PL.) TAKE GRAVY ISSUE AVAILS
JALKAR ESPLEES
PROFITABLE FAT GOOD UTILE
GOLDEN PLUMMY GAINFUL
HELPFUL PAYABLE BEHOVELY
ECONOMIC PROVABLE REPAYING
VAILABLE REWARDING
PROFITLESS BOOTLESS
PROFLIGATE ROUE ROVE DEFEAT
CORRUPT IMMORAL RIOTOUS
SPENDER VICIOUS WASTREL
DEPRAVED FLAGRANT OVERCOME
RAKEHELL WASTEFUL
ABANDONED
PROFOUND DEEP HARD WISE
ABYSS DEPTH HEAVY OCEAN
SOUND THICK PITCHY STRONG
ABYSMAL INTENSE ABSTRUSE
COMPLETE PREGNANT REACHING
THOROUGH
PROFUNDITY ABYSS DEPTH
FATHOM DEEPNESS
PROFUSE FREE LUSH SLAB FRANK
GALORE LAVISH COPIOUS LIBERAL
OPULENT ABUNDANT GENEROUS
PRODIGAL SQUANDER WASTEFUL
LUXURIANT REDUNDANT
UNSPARING
PROFUSELY HEARTILY
PROFUSION RIOT WASTE EXCESS
LAVISH FLUENCY OPULENCE
REDUNDANCY
PROG FOOD GOAD POKE PROD

PROWL TRAMP BEGGAR FORAGE
PROCTOR
PROGENITOR BURI MANU ROOT
SIRE PITRI STOCK PARENT
ANCESTOR
PROGENY BED GET IMP KIN BURD
CLAN KIND SEED TEAM BROOD
CHILD FRUIT ISSUE STRAIN STRIND
INCROSS KINDRED LINEAGE
OUTCOME PRODUCT CHILDREN
FRUITAGE INCREASE OUTBIRTH
OUTCROSS OFFSPRING
(— OF WATER-BUFFALO AND YAK)
DZO
(— OF WITCH AND DEMON) HOLD
(INSECT —) SOCIETY
PROGNOSIS FORECAST PROPHASIS
PROGNOSTIC OMEN SIGN TOKEN
AUSPICE OMINOUS PRESAGE
PROPHECY
PROGNOSTICATE BODE AUGUR
SPELL BETOKEN CONJECT PREDICT
PRENOTE FOREBODE FORESHOW
FORETELL PROPHESY
PROGNOSTICATION RACE
PRESAGE FOREBODE FORECAST
PROGRESS PROPHECY
PROGNOSTICATOR SEER DOOMER
PROPHET HARUSPEX
PROGRAM CARD SHOW FORUM
AGENDA DESIGN SCHEME
AGENDUM PREFACE CLAMBAKE
FESTIVAL GIVEAWAY GUIDANCE
JAMBOREE PLAYBILL SCHEDULE
SEQUENCE SYLLABUS
(COMPUTER —) DOS EDITOR
FIRMWARE SPREADSHEET
(COMPUTER —S) SOFTWARE
(CURRENT AFFAIRS —) REALITES
(EMPLOYEE —) ESOP
(HEALTH —) MEDICAID MEDICARE
(PART OF COMPUTER —) BRANCH
(PARTY —) PLATFORM
(STOCK —) ESOP
(TELEVISION —) SITCOM
PROGRAMMA EDICT DECREE
PREFACE PROGRAM
PROGRESS WAY BIRL DENT FARE
GAIN GROW MOVE RACE RISE
STEM STEP TOUR WEAR WEND
WENT BUILD DRIFT FORGE GOING
MARCH SWING WEENT ASCENT
BUFFET COURSE GROWTH STREEK
ADVANCE DEVELOP FOOTING
HEADWAY IMPROVE JOURNEY
ONGOING PASSAGE PROCESS
PROFICIENCY
(— CLUMSILY) SCRAMBLE
(— ERRATICALLY) FLAIL
(— FEEBLY) DODDER
(— INTELLIGENTLY PLANNED)
TELESIA TELESIS
(— NOISILY) CHORTLE
(— SLOWLY) CRAWL
(SINGLE —) THROUGH
PROGRESSED FAR
PROGRESSION WAY SWING
COURSE GALLOP ADVANCE
PASSAGE PROGRESS SEQUENCE
(— OF CHORDS) SWIPE
(MUSICAL —) SKIP
(SMOOTH —) SLIDE

PROGRESSIVE ACTIVE ONWARD
FORWARD GRADUAL LIBERAL
(NOT —) SLOW
PROGRESSIVELY STILL
PROHIBIT BAN BAR STOP VETO
BLOCK DEBAR ESTOP DEFEND
ENJOIN FORBID HINDER OUTLAW
FORFEND FORWARN INHIBIT
PREVENT DISALLOW PRECLUDE
SUPPRESS PROSCRIBE
PROHIBITED HOT TABU TABOO
ILLEGAL ILLICIT UNLAWFUL
VERBOTEN
PROHIBITING VETITIVE
PROHIBITION BAN NAY NON VETO
ORDER BARRIER DEFENCE
DEFENSE EMBARGO FORBODE
ESTOPPEL
PROHIBITIONIST DRY PUSSYFOOT
PROJECT GAB GAG JET JUT LAP TUT
BEAM CAST GAME HURL IDEA
PLAN POKE PUSH SAIL SWIM
BULGE CHART DRAFT DRIVE IMAGE
JETTY JUTTY SETUP SHOOT STICK
THROW BEETLE DESIGN DEVICE
ESTATE EXTEND FILLIP OUTJUT
PROPEL SCHEME SCREEN SHELVE
EXTRUDE GOSPLAN IMAGINE
KNUCKLE OUTCROP PATTERN
BUSINESS CONTRIVE OUTREACH
OUTSHOOT OVERHANG PROPOSAL
PROTRUDE SPANGHEW
(UNETHICAL —) SCHEME
(VISIONARY —) BABEL
PROJECTILE BALL BOLT CASE SHOT
SHAFT TRACER OUTCAST
POUNDER FIREBALL SHRAPNEL
**(— DESIGNED TO SET FIRE TO
HOUSES)** CARCASS
(EXPLOSIVE —) BOMB SHELL
(SMALL 6) MITRAILLE
(SUBMARINE —) TORPEDO
(PL.) LEAD SHOT SALVO STUFF
PROJECTING BEETLE SHELVY
EMINENT JUTTING OUTSHOT
PENDENT SALIENT SNAGGLED
PROMINENT OUTSTANDING
(PREF.) PRO
PROJECTION ARM CAM COG DOG
EAR FIN GIB JET JOG JUT NAB NAG
NUT TAB TOE BEAK BOSS BROW
BUHR COAK COCK CROC CUSP
HEEL HORN KEEL KICK KINK KNAG
KNOB KNOP LOBE RIDE SAIL SNUG
SPUD SPUR TEAT WING BULGE
CLEAT EJECT ELBOW FENCE
FURCA JUTTY PRONG SALLY
SCRAG SHANK SHOOT SNOUT
SPIKE TOOTH BRANCH CALCAR
CORBEL CROSET FUSULA HEARTH
ICICLE MENTUM NOSING PALATE
RELIEF RELISH TAPPET BREAKER
CONSOLE DRAWING EPAULET
EYEBROW FETLOCK KNUCKLE
LANGUET ORILLON OUTSHOT
PRICKER PRICKLE RESSAUT
AJUTMENT CASCABEL DENTICLE
EMINENCE FOOTLOCK ORILLION
OVERHANG OVERSAIL SALIENCE
SHOULDER SPROCKET STERIGMA
TRUNNION APOPHYSIS
OUTTHRUST PROMINENCE

(— CONNECTING TIMBER) COAK
(— EXTENDING BACKWARD) BARB
(— FROM CASTING) SPRUE
(— FROM SHIP'S KEEL) SPONSON
(— IN CLOCK) SQUARE
(— IN ORCHIDS) MENTUM
(— OF FOREHEAD) ANTINION
(— OF JAW) GNATHISM
(— OF PEAT) HAG
(— OF RAFTER) SALLY
(— OF TERRITORY) PANHANDLE
(— ON CANNON) CASCABEL
(— ON CHURCH SEAT) MISERICORD
(— ON FOOTWEAR) STUD
(— ON GUN) CROC LUMP
(— ON HARNESS) HAME
(— ON HORSE'S LEG) FETLOCK
(— ON HORSESHOE) STICKER
(— ON LOCK) FENCE STUMP
(— ON MAST) STOP
(— ON OVARY) STIGMA
(— ON POCKETKNIFE) KICK
(— ON SALMON JAW) GIB
(— ON WHEEL) GUB GROUSER
GROUTER
(— OVER AIR PORT) EYEBROW
(CARPENTRY —) TENON
(FIREPLACE —) HOB
(JAGGED —) SNUG
(NARROW —) STRAP TONGUE
(SHARP —) BARB FANG
(SUBMERGED —) KNOLL
(PL.) GRAIN BARLEY
PROJECTOR KINO LANTERN
PLANNER SCHEMER BIOSCOPE
EPISCOPE VITASCOPE
PROLAMIN ZEIN SEINE GLIADIN
HORDEIN KAFIRIN SECALIN
PROLAPSE PTOSIS BLOWOUT
FALLING
PROLETARIAN POPULAR
PROLETARIAT MASSES
PROLIFIC BIRTHY BREEDY BROODY
FECUND FERTILE PROFUSE
TEEMING ABUNDANT FRUITFUL
SPAWNING
(BE —) INCREASE
PROLIX LARGE WORDY DIFFUSE
LENGTHY PROSAIC TEDIOUS
VERBOSE TIRESOME WEARISOME
PROLIXITY REDUNDANCY
PROLOGUE BANS BANNS INDEX
PREFACE
PROLONG DREE LENG LONG SPIN
DEFER DELAY DRIVE ELONG TWINE
DILATE EXTEND LINGER SPREAD
DISPACE PRODUCE RESPITE
SUSTAIN CONTINUE ETERNIZE
LENGTHEN POSTPONE PROROGUE
PROTRACT
PROLONGATION BEAK AORTA
CONUS STIPE STYLE FERMATA
ACROSOME APPENDIX GYNOBASE
LABELLUM
PROLONGED GREAT PROLIX
DELAYED EXTENDED SOSTENUTO
PROMENADE BUND MAIL MALL
PIER PROM WALK CORSO FRONT
PASEO PRADO MARINA PARADE
PASEAR ALAMEDA GALLERY
FRESCADE GALLERIA SEAFRONT
BOULEVARD

(CARRIAGE —) TOUR
(GREEK —) STOA
PROMETHEUS (BROTHER OF —) ATLAS MENOETIUS EPIMETHEUS
(FATHER OF —) IAPETUS
(MOTHER OF —) CLYMENE
PROMETHEUS UNBOUND
(AUTHOR OF —) SHELLEY
(CHARACTER IN —) ASIA IONE EARTH JUPITER MERCURY PANTHEA HERCULES DEMOGORGON PROMETHEUS
PROMINENCE BUR NOB BOSS BURR CUSP KNOB NOOP UMBO AGGER BULLA CREST GRAIN OLIVA SWELL TUBER TYLUS ACCENT CALCAR NODULE TRAGUS BILLING BUTTOCK CONDYLE FASHION HAMULUS KNUCKLE LINGULA AMYGDALA EMINENCY EMPHASIS GLABELLA PULVINAR SALIENCE TUBERCLE MONTICULE PROMONTORY
(PREF.) TUBERCULI TUBERCULO TUBERI
PROMINENT BIG BOLD BEADY BRENT GREAT HEAVY STEEP BEETLE MARKED SIGNAL BLATANT BOLTING CAPITAL EMINENT JUTTING LEADING NOTABLE OBVIOUS SALIENT AQUILINE BEETLING MANIFEST STRIKING NOTICEABLE CONSPICUOUS OUTSTANDING
(SOCIALLY —) SWELL
(UNDULY —) OBTRUSIVE
PROMISCUOUS LIGHT CASUAL RANDOM CARELESS
PROMISCUOUSLY TAGRAG
PROMISE VOW AVOW BAND HEST HETE HOPE HOTE OATH OSSE PASS PLEA SURE WORD FAITH GRANT HIGHT TRUTH ASSURE BEHEST ENGAGE FIANCE HALSEN INSURE PAROLE PLEDGE PLIGHT PROMIT BEHIGHT BETROTH WARRANT CONTRACT COVENANT GUARANTY BETROTHAL OBLIGATION
(— IN MARRIAGE) BETROTH ESPOUSE AFFIANCE
(— OF SUCCESS) LIKELIHOOD
(— RESULTS) PROSPECT
(— TO PAY) NOTE ACCEPT
(— TO TAKE IN MARRIAGE) AFFY
PROMISED VOTARY
(— IN MARRIAGE) SURE HIGHT ENGAGED
(— LAND) CANAAN
PROMISING APT FAIR ROSY BRIGHT LIKELY PROOFY TOWARD GRADELY TOWARDLY
PROMISSORY NOTE IOU HUNDI HOONDI TICKET
PROMONTORY HOE NAB BEAK BILL HEAD MULL NAZE NESS NOOK NOUP PEAK SCAW SKAW TOOT ELBOW MORRO POINT REACH SNOUT SALIENT FORELAND HEADLAND
PROMOTE AID FLOG HELP HYPE LOFT PLUG PUSH AVAIL BOOST EXALT NURSE RAISE SERVE SETON

SPEED ASSIST EXCITE FOMENT FOSTER LAUNCH PREFER ADVANCE DIGNIFY ELEVATE FORWARD FURTHER IMPROVE PREFECT PRODUCE PROMOVE SUCCEED SUPPORT INCREASE SUBSERVE
PROMOTER AGENT FRIEND ABETTOR BOOSTER BUBBLER BROACHER HUMANIST PROJECTOR
(SUFF.) ANT
PROMOTION LIFT REMOVE ADVANCE FLACKERY PROMOVAL
(— OF CONSUMER INTERESTS) NADERISM
PROMOTIONAL PROMO
(— PRONOUNCEMENT) PROMO
PROMPT APT CUE MOVE URGE YARE ALERT FRACK PREST QUICK READY SERVE SWIFT WILLY YEDER EXCITE INDITE MATURE NIMBLE SPEEDY SUDDEN ANIMATE FORWARD PROVOKE SUGGEST PUNCTUAL REMINDER
(— TO EVIL) SUGGEST
PROMPTER CUER CALLER MEMORIST ORDINARY SOUFFLEUR
PROMPTING CALL BEHEST BEHIND MOTIVE
(SPIRITUAL —) LEADING
PROMPTITUDE ALACRITY
PROMPTLY UP PAT TID TIT SOON TITE PRONTO YARELY BETIMES PRESTLY QUICKLY DIRECTLY SPEEDILY
PROMPTNESS ALACRITY CELERITY DISPATCH
PROMULGATE SPREAD DECLARE PUBLISH PROCLAIM
PRONAOS ANTICUM
PRONE APT BENT EASY FLAT FREE GRUF BUXOM GIVEN GROOF JACENT LIABLE SUPINE BEASTLY BESTIAL DORMANT SUBJECT ADDICTED COUCHANT DISPOSED DOWNWARD PROPENSE
(— TO TAKE UP FADS) ISMY
(NATURALLY —) PROLIVE
PRONENESS
(SUFF.)
(— TO) ITIS
PRONG NEB NIB PEG PEW BILL FANG FORK HOOK PUGH SPUR TANG TENG TINE TING GRAIN SPADE SPEAN SPRONG FOURCHE TICKLER GRAINING
(— FOR EXTRACTING BUNG) TICKLER
(— FOR FISH) PEW PUGH
(— OF ANTLER) KNAG TIND TINE POINT
(— OF FORK) SPEAN
PRONGHORN CABREE CABRIT MAZAME BERENDO BERRENDO
PRONOUN HE IT ME MY WE YE ANY HER HIM HIS ONE OUR SHE THY WHO YOU OURS THAT THEM THEY THOU WHAT WHOM YOUR THINE WHICH WHOSE ITSELF MYSELF HERSELF HIMSELF OURSELF WHOEVER YOURSELF OURSELVES
(GENDERLESS —) THON

PRONOUNCE SAY PASS ACUTE SPEAK UTTER PREACH RECITE TONGUE ADJUDGE BEHIGHT CENSURE MOUILLE ASPIRATE
(— FREE) ABSOLVE
(— GUILTY) CONDEMN
(— HOLY) BLESS
PRONOUNCED HIGH MARKED DECIDED HOWLING INTENSE MOVABLE
(— AS FRICATIVE) GRASSEYE
(— PALATALLY) MOUILLE
(NOT —) SOFT
PRONOUNCEMENT FIAT CURSE DICTUM DICTAMEN
PRONTO QUICK ATONCE QUICKLY PROMPTLY
PRONUNCIATION BROGUE DICTION ETACISM LIAISON DELIVERY ENCLISIS ORTHOEPY
(BAD —) CACOEPY CACOLOGY LABDACISM
(BROAD —) PLATEASM
(CORRECT —) ORTHOEPY
(FAULTY —) CACOLOGY
(PLEASING —) EUPHONY EUPHONIA
(ROUGH —) BUR BURR
PROOF SAY MARK PULL SLIP TEST ESSAY PREWE REPRO TOKEN TOUCH TRIAL CLENCH GALLEY ORDEAL REASON RESULT REVISE ATTEMPT OUTCOME PROBATE SHOWING UTTERLY VOUCHER WARRANT ANALYSIS CACOLOGY DOCUMENT EVICTION EVIDENCE GOODNESS MONUMENT
(— AGAINST ATTACK) IMPREGNABLE
(— OF WRONGDOING) GOODS
(— SPIRIT OF WINE) SVT
(ABSOLUTE —) APODIXIS
(CLEAR SHARP —) DUPE REPRO
(INDIRECT —) APAGOGE
(PL.) STRING WARRANTY
PROOFREADER MARK CAP DELE STET CARET
PROP LEG BROB BUNT POST REST SPUR STAY STUD TRIG APPUI BRACE PERCH PUNCH RANCE SCOTE SHORE SHOVE SOUSE SPRAG SPURN STAFF STELL STOOP STULL COLUMN CROTCH CRUTCH PILLAR SCOTCH SHORER STAYER UPHOLD BOLSTER FULCRUM PINNING STUDDLE SUPPORT SUSTAIN BUTTRESS CROTCHET DUTCHMAN UNDERLAY UNDERSET
(— AS TRAP) TEEL
(— FOR CART) NEAP
(— FOR ROOF OF MINE) GIB
(— UP) CUSHION SCAFFOLD
(PREF.) FULCI
PROPAGANDA BOLOISM AGITPROP BALLYHOO
PROPAGATE BREED HATCH LAYER EXTEND SPREAD STRIKE DIFFUSE GEMMATE PRODUCE PUBLISH ENGENDER GENERATE INCREASE MULTIPLY POPULATE TRANSMIT PROCREATE
(— BY LAYERING) PROVINE
PROPAGATION BREED BREEDING

DIVISION INCREASE LAYERAGE OFFSPRING
(SUFF.) GAM(AE)(IST)(OUS)(Y) GAMETE
PROPEL ROW CALL CAST FIRE FLIP KENT POLE PUSH SEND URGE DRIVE FLICK IMPEL KNOCK PRICK RANGE SPANK THROW HURTLE LAUNCH PROJECT
(— BALL) STROKE
(— BOAT) OAR ROW SET KENT POLE SCULL BUSHWACK
(— BOAT WITH FEET) LEG
(— ONESELF) HAUL
(— PUCK) CARRY
(— SUDDENLY) ZAP
(— WITH FORCE) RIFLE
PROPELLANT LOX
PROPELLER FAN HELIX SCREW AIRSCREW WINDMILL
PROPENSITY YEN BENT ITCH LURCH APTNESS IMPULSE LEANING PRONITY APPETITE FONDNESS INTEREST TENDENCY
PROPER FIT OWN GOOD JUST MEET TRUE WELL PREST RIGHT UTTER COMELY DECENT HONEST LAWFUL MODEST SEEMLY CAPITAL CORRECT FITTING GRADELY SEEMING SKILFUL THRIFTY ABSOLUTE BECOMING CONGREVE DECOROUS FORMULAR IDONEOUS PECULIAR RIGHTFUL SORTABLE SUITABLE VIRTUOUS
(APPARENTLY —) SPECIOUS
(BE — TO) BESEEM
(PREF.) CURIO ORTH(O)
PROPERLY DULY WELL FITLY TRULY ARIGHT FAIRLY FEATLY GLADLY MEETLY RIGHTLY
PROPERTY AVER BONA DHAN TOOL WAIF ASSET AUGHT GOODS GRANT MOYEN STATE STOCK THING WORTH APPEAL DEVISE ESTATE HAVIOR KELTER LIVING MUSHAA REALTY TALENT USINGS WEALTH ACQUEST APANAGE CHATTEL DEMESNE ESCHEAT ESSENCE FACULTY FITNESS HARNESS HAVINGS QUALITY WARISON ALLODIAL CATALLUM HOLDINGS PECULIUM POSSESSION PARAPHERNALIA
(— BELONGING TO WOMAN) STRIDHAN
(— FROM WIFE TO HUSBAND) DOS
(— GIVEN BY WILL) DEVISE
(— OF MATTER AT REST) INERTIA
(— SECURED DISHONESTLY) HARL
(— SEIZED BY FORCE) SPOIL
(ABSOLUTE —) ALODIUM
(BEQUEATHED —) DEVISE
(ENEMY —) HEREM
(LANDED —) DOMAIN ESTATE DEMESNE PRAEDIUM
(MOVABLE —) GEAR CHATTEL EFFECTS CATALLUM
(PERSONAL —) FEE BONA GOODS STUFF INSIGHT PLUNDER
(PRIVATE —) SEVERAL
(RURAL —) FINCA
(STOLEN —) PELF MAINOR STEALTH
(THEATRICAL —S) PROPS

(WITHOUT —) LACKLAND
(SUFF.) ISM
PROPHECY SPAE WEIRD EXHORT
PREACH PREDICT BODEMENT
FORECAST FORESHOW SOOTHSAY
VATICINE SIBYLLISH PROGNOSTIC
PROPHESY OSSE SPAE AREAD
AUGUR DIVINE EXHORT PREACH
OMINATE PORTEND PREDICT
ARIOLATE FORETELL
PROPHET GAD AMOS JOEL SEER
ANGEL AUGUR DRUID ELIAS
HOSEA JONAH MICAH MOSES
NAHUM SILAS SYRUS ARIOLE
BALAAM DANIEL ELIJAH HAGGAI
ISAIAH MERLIN MORONI NATHAN
ORACLE PYTHON SAMUEL EZEKIEL
MALACHI SPAEMAN HABAKKUK
JEREMIAH
(WEATHER —) PROGNOSTICATOR
(PL.) VATES NEBIIM
(PREF.) VATI
PROPHETE, LA (CHARACTER IN —)
JOHN FIDES BERTHA OBERTHAL
(COMPOSER OF —) MEYERBEER
PROPHETESS ANNA ANNE HULDA
SIBYL PYTHIA DEBORAH PHOIBAD
SEERESS VOLUSPA DRUIDESS
SPAEWIFE CASSANDRA
PYTHONESS
PROPHETIC FATAL VATIC MANTIC
FATEFUL FATIDIC MANTIAN
DELPHIAN ORACULAR SIBYLLIC
VATICINAL
(— OF DISASTER) APOCALYPTIC
(SUFF.) MANTIC
PROPINE TIP GIFT EXPOSE PLEDGE
PROFFER
PROPINQUITY KINSHIP AFFINITY
NEARNESS VICINITY PROXIMITY
PROPITIATE MILD ATONE PACIFY
APPEASE RECONCILE
PROPITIATORY HILASMIC
PROPITIOUS FAIR KIND HAPPY
LUCKY BENIGN DEXTER KINDLY
HELPFUL PRESENT FRIENDLY
GRACIOUS MERCIFUL TOWARDLY
FAVORABLE PROMISING
AUSPICIOUS
PROPONENT BACKER ADVOCATE
SUPPORTER
PROPORTION END LOT DOSE SIZE
CHIME FRAME QUOTA RATIO
SCALE SHARE ACCORD DEGREE
EXTENT FORMAT QUOTUM
ANALOGY BALANCE COMPASS
CONTENT MEASURE EURYTHMY
QUANTITY SYMMETRY
PERCENTAGE
(— OF CATTLE TO GIVEN AREA)
SOUM
(— OF MALT IN BREWING) STRAIK
(— OF REFLECTED LIGHT) ALBEDO
(ALLOTTED —) STENT STINT
(EXACT —) SQUARE
(SMALL —) TITHE
PROPORTIONAL TOSCALE
PROPORTIONATENESS CONTOUR
PROPOSAL BID KITE MOVE PLAN
PLEA VOEU GRACE OFFER PARTY
DEMAND FEELER MOTION MOTIVE
PROJECT PROPOSE PURPOSE

OVERTURE SCHEDULE SENTENCE
PROPOSITION
(— OF HEALTH) TOAST
(FORMAL —) RESOLUTION
(TENTATIVE —) SNIFF
PROPOSE FACE MOVE PLAN POSE
SHOW WISH OFFER ALLEGE
DESIGN INJECT INTEND MOTION
ADVANCE EXHIBIT IMAGINE
PROPINE PURPOSE SUPPOSE
CONFRONT CONVERSE PROPOUND
(— FOR DISCUSSION) MOOT
(— FOR ELECTION) NOMINATE
(— MARRIAGE) POP
(— RESOLUTION) FIRST
(— TENTATIVELY) SUGGEST
PROPOSITION R FACT AXIOM
MODAL OFFER THEME AFFAIR
CONNEX MEMBER PORISM
GENERAL INVERSE PREMISS
PROBLEM PURPOSE THEOREM
TYCHISM BUSINESS CONTRARY
EMPIREMA IDENTITY IRENICON
JUDGMENT NEGATION OVERTURE
PROPOSAL PROTASIS SENTENCE
SINGULAR SUPPOSAL
(— FOR PEACE) IRENICON
(— IN LOGIC) TERMAL OBVERSE
CONTRARY CONVERSE
(— LEADING TO CONCLUSION)
PREMISE
(PARTICULAR NEGATIVE —) O
(PRELIMINARY —) LEMMA
(UNIVERSAL NEGATIVE —) E
PROPOUND POSE OFFER POSIT
START STATE INVOKE PROPOSE
PURPOSE
PROPOUNDER HYLICIST
PROPRIETOR LORD LAIRD MALIK
OWNER MASTER PATRON TANIST
YEOMAN ESQUIRE PATROON
ABSENTEE BONIFACE SQUARSON
TALUKDAR YEOWOMAN
PROPRIETY GRACE IDIOM MENSE
ESTATE NATURE REASON
DECENCY DECORUM ESSENCE
FITNESS HOLDING MODESTY
CIVILITY PROPERTY ETIQUETTE
PROPROCTOR RECTOR
PROPULSION DRIFT EJECTION
PROPULSIVE ELASTIC
PRORATE ALLOT ASSESS DIVIDE
APPORTION
PROROGUE DEFER ADJOURN
PROLONG POSTPONE PROTRACT
PROSAIC DRAB DULL FLAT FOOT
PROSE PROSY PROLIX STODGY
STOLID STUPID FACTUAL
HUMDRUM INSIPID LITERAL
TEDIOUS SOULLESS TIRESOME
WORKADAY
PROSCENIUM FRAME STAGE
PROSCRIBE BAN TABU EXILE LIMIT
TABOO FORBID OUTLAW REJECT
PROHIBIT
PROSCRIPTION EXILE OUTLAWRY
PROSE CHAT PROSY GOSSIP
PROSAIC TEDIOUS SEQUENCE
ELOQUENCE
PROSECUTE LAW SUE HOLD URGE
CARRY ENSUE ACCUSE CHARGE
DEDUCE FOLLOW INDICT INTEND
PURSUE IMPLEAD PROCESS

PROSECUTION PURSUANCE
PROSECUTOR DA FISCAL PURSUER
SAKEBER PROMOTER QUAESTOR
(PUBLIC —) ACTOR
PROSELYTE CONVERT NICOLAS
NEOPHYTE PURSUANT
(JEWISH —) GER
PROSER HAVERER GRATIANO
PROSODY METER METRICS
PROSPECT HOPE VIEW SCENE
SPECK VISTA CHANCE CHIEVE
FUTURE REGARD SEARCH SURVEY
COMMAND EXPLORE FOSSICK
HORIZON LOOKOUT OUTLOOK
PROJECT RESPECT LANDSKIP
OFFSCAPE
(— FOR GOLD) SPECK
(— OF FUTURE) PERSPECTIVE
(— WITHOUT SYSTEM) GOPHER
(FORBIDDING —) DESERT
PROSPECTING LOAMING
PROSPECTIVE VIEW WATCH
LOOKOUT EXPECTED
PROSPECTOR SNIPER FOSSICKER
SOURDOUGH
(LONE —) HATTER
PROSPECTUS PROGRAM
PROSPER DO DOW FAY HIE LIKE
RISE THEE CHEVE CHIVE EDIFY
FRAME LIGHT SPEED BATTEN
THRIVE BLOSSOM SUCCEED
WELFARE FLOURISH
PROSPERITY HAP BOOM GLEE
GOOD SEEL SONS WEAL IKBAL
SONSE HEALTH THRIFT FORTUNE
SUCCESS THEEDOM WELFARE
FLOURISH
(GOD OF —) FREY
(INCREASE IN —) FREY UPTICK
PROSPERO (DAUGHTER OF —)
MIRANDA
(SERVANT OF —) ARIEL
(SLAVE OF —) CALIBAN
PROSPEROUS UP FAT BEEN BEIN
BIEN BOON GOOD FELIX FLUSH
HAPPY LUCKY PALMY SONSY
EUROUS GILDED SONSIE WELSOM
HALCYON HEALTHY THRIFTY
THRIVEN WEIRDLY SUNSHINE
THRIVING WEALSOME
PROSTITUTE BAG BAT CAT COW
DOG MOB AUNT BAWD DOXY
DRAB HACK MAUX MISS MUFF
PUNK SLUT STEW TART TRUG
BROAD CRACK MAWKS PAGAN
POULE PROSS STALE WHORE
BULKER CALLET CHIPPY DEBASE
GIRLIE HARLOT HOOKER LIMMER
MUTTON PROSTY RANNEL
TOMATO TRADER VIZARD
BAGGAGE BROTHEL CRUISER
CYPRIAN HACKNEY HETAERA
HUSTLER PAPHIAN PINNACE
POLECAT PROSSIE PROSTIE
PUCELLE SELLARY BERDACHE
COMMONER CUSTOMER
HACKSTER MAGDALEN MERETRIX
OCCUPANT RUMBELOW SLATTERN
STRUMPET VENTURER COURTESAN
(PREF.) PORN(O)
PROSTITUTION BORDEL SACKING
BORDELLO HARLOTRY PUTANISM
PROSTRATE LOW FELL FLAT GRUF

RASE RAZE FLING GROOF PRONE
STOOP THROW ATTERR CUMBER
FALLEN REPENT WEAKEN FLATTEN
DEJECTED HELPLESS OVERCOME
PROSTERN DEPRESSED
(— ONESELF) HURKLE
(BECOME —) FALL
PROSTRATION SHOCK KOWTOW
COLLAPSE
(BURMESE —) SHIKO
PROSY DRY DULL JEJUNE
HUMDRUM INSIPID PROSAIC
PROSISH TEDIOUS TIRESOME
PROTAGONIST HERO ACTOR
LEADER PALADIN ADVOCATE
ANTIHERO CHAMPION
PROTAMINE SALMINE STURINE
CLUPEINE
PROTEAN EDESTAN VARIABLE
PROTECT CAP BANK BIEL BIND DIKE
FEND FORT HILL KEEP REDE SAVE
WARD WEAR BLESS CHAIN CLOUT
COURE COVER FENCE GANGE
GRATE GUARD HEDGE PAVIS
SHADE SHEND UMBER ASSERT
BORROW DEFEND SCREEN
SHADOW SHIELD WARISH
BULWARK CHERISH CUSHION
FASCINE FORFEND SECLUDE
SHELTER SUPPORT WARRANT
BESTRIDE CHAMPION DEFILADE
PRESERVE SAFEGUARD
(— AGAINST RAIN) FLASH
(— BY BINDING) KECKLE
(— BY COVERING) HILL
(— BY WINDING WITH WIRE)
GANGE
(— FROM INTRUSION) TILE TYLE
(— IRON OR STEEL) BARFF
PROTECTED SAFE SHADY IMMUNE
CLOUTED GUARDED SHEATHED
SHIELDED
(PREF.) IMMUNO
PROTECTING TUTELAR TUTELARY
SECUREFUL
PROTECTION LEE CARE EGIS HOLD
WARD WING AEGIS ARMOR BIELD
COVER GRITH GUARD SHADE
TARGE TOWER AMULET ASYLUM
AVOWRY CONVOY ESCORT
FENDER REFUGE SAFETY SCONCE
SCREEN SHADOW SHROUD
AUSPICE CUSTODY DEFENCE
HOUSING MANTLET SHELTER
TUITION UMBRAGE WARRANT
BLINDAGE COVERAGE DEFILADE
PASSPORT SECURITY TUTAMENT
TUTELAGE WARDSHIP SAFEGUARD
(— FOR SAILOR) HORSE
(— FROM LOSS) INDEMNITY
(— FROM RAIN) OMBRIFUGE
(— FROM SUN) HAVELOCK
(— FROM WEATHER) LEWTH
(— RIGHT) MUND
(ITEM FOR —) MACE
(VALUABLE —) EDMUND
(WISE —) RAYMOND
PROTECTIVE (— SURFACE) LAGGING
PROTECTOR BIB GUARD BRACER
FAUTOR KEEPER PATRON REGENT
WARRANT DEFENDER GUARDIAN
PECTORAL PRESIDENT

(— OF PROSTITUTE) BULLY
(— OF VINEYARDS) PRIAPUS
(CHEST —) BIB
PROTEGE WARD PUPIL SMIKE
PROTEIN ZEIN ABRIN ACTIN OPSIN
RICIN SOZIN AVIDIN CASEIN FIBRIN
GLOBIN MYOGEN ALBUMIN
AMANDIN ELASTIN GELATIN
GLIADIN HISTONE HORDEIN
KERATIN LIVETIN MUCEDIN
PROTEID SERICIN TUBULIN
ALEURONE COLLAGEN COLLOGEN
FERRITIN GLOBULIN GLUTELIN
GORGONIN IPOMOEIN PROLAMIN
ELEDOISIN PROPERDIN
PROTAMINE
(— IN CEREAL) GLUTENIN
(— PARTICLE) PRION
(POISONOUS —) ABRIN
(RICH IN —S) NARROW
PROTEINASE PAPAIN PEPSIN
PROTEOSE ALBUMOSE ELASTOSE
GELATOSE
PROTESILAUS (BROTHER OF —)
PODARCES
(FATHER OF —) IPHICLUS
(MOTHER OF —) ASTYOCHE
(SLAYER OF —) HECTOR
EUPHORBUS
(WIFE OF —) LAODAMIA POLYDORA
PROTEST AVER BEEF FUSS HOWL
KICK BROCK CROAK DEMUR
AFFIRM ASSERT BOWWOW
EXCEPT HOLLER OBJECT OBTEST
PLAINT SQUAWK SQUEAL
CONTEST INVEIGH PUBLISH
RECLAIM RHUBARB SCRUPLE
TESTIFY HARRUMPH PROCLAIM
(— A CHARGE) TESTIFY
(— AGAINST) ABHOR
(— AGAINST INJUSTICE) HARO
(FORMAL —) REMONSTRANCE
(ORGANIZED —) LIEIN
(TINY —) PEEP
PROTESTANT ALASCAN GENEVAN
GOSPELER HELVETIC HUGUENOT
MORAVIAN SWADDLER
PROTEUS OLM AMOEBA
PROTHESIS CREDENCE PARABEMA
PROTHORAX COLLAR CORSELET
MANITRUNK
PROTOCOL PROCEDURE
PROTOPINE FUMARINE
PROTOPLASM PLASMA PLASSON
SARCODE OVOPLASM PERIPLAST
SOLEPLATE
PROTOPLAST CELL ENERGID
PROTOTYPE IDEAL MODEL FATHER
EXAMPLE PATTERN ANTITYPE
EXEMPLAR
PROTOZOAN AMEBA FORAM
MONAD MONER AMOEBA
AGAMETE ARCELLA BABESIA
BODONID CILIATE PROTIST
RADIATE STENTOR DIDINIUM
HYPOZOAN PARAMECIUM
(HYPOTHETICAL —) MONER
MONERON
(PL.) MICROZOA
PROTRACT DRAG DRAW DREE PLOT
SPIN DEFER DELAY DRIVE TRACT
TRAIL TRAIN DILATE EXTEND
LINGER SPREAD DETRACT

PROLONG CONTINUE LENGTHEN
PROROGUE
PROTRACTED DREE LONG DREICH
PROLIX LENGTHY DRAGGING
EXTENDED
PROTRUDE BUG JUT LILL LOLL
PEER POKE POUT BLEAR BULGE
BUNCH POUCH SHOOT START
STICK STRUT SWELL EXSERT
EXTEND EXTRUDE KNUCKLE
PROJECT PROTEND HERNIATE
OUTPOINT OUTREACH OUTSHOOT
PROTRUDING STEEP ASTRUT
BUNCHY GOGGLE BLABBER
EMINENT JUTTING OBTRUSIVE
PROTRUDINGLY ASTRUT
PROTRUSION JAG LAP NOB BURR
KNOB POUT HERNIA SALIENCE
SHOULDER TYLOSID PROJECTION
PROTUBERANCE BUD HUB JAG
NOB NUB WEN BEAN BOLL BOSS
BULB BUMP HEEL HUMP JAGG
KNAP KNOB KNOP KNOT LUMP
NODE PUFF SCAB SNAG STUB
UMBO WART BULGE BUNCH
CAPUT GLAND GNARL HUNCH
KNURL SWELL TORUS TUBER
TUMOR BREAST CALLUS HUBBLE
PIMPLE POMMEL CRANKLE
EXTANCY PAPILLA EMINENCE
FLANKARD MAMELEON NODOSITY
SWELLING APOPHYSIS
PROJECTION
(— AT BASE OF BIRD'S BILL) CERE
SNOOD
(— BEARING SPINE) UMBO
(— FROM SWELLING) PUFF
(— IN SIDE OF DEER) FLANKARD
(— ON A CASTING) SCAB
(— ON BONE) CONDYLE EMINENCE
(— ON HAND) MOUNT
(— ON HORSE'S HOOF) BUTTRESS
(— ON MANDIBLE OF GEESE) BEAN
(— ON SADDLEBOW) POMMEL
(— ON SALAMANDER) BALANCER
(— ON TONGUE) PAPILLA
(KNOBLIKE —) CAPUT
(OCCIPITAL —) INION
(RAGGED —) JAG JAGG
(ROUGH —) HUB
(SKIN —) WEN MOLE WART PIMPLE
(PREF.) TORO
PROTUBERANT BULGY BUMPY
NODAL PROUD STRUT TUMID
BUCKED EXTANT GOGGLE
BOTTLED BULGING BUNCHED
EMINENT GIBBOUS SALIENT
SWOLLEN PROMINENT
PROTRUSIVE
(REGULARLY —) CONVEX
PROUD FESS GLAD HIGH IKEY LOFT
PERK RANK SIDE VAIN BRANT
CHUFF GELLY GREAT JELLY LOFTY
NOBLE ORGUL PRIDY SAUCY
STEEP STIFF STOUT VOGIE WINDY
WLONK COPPED ELATED FIERCE
LORDLY ORGUIL PENCEY QUAINT
SKEICH SKEIGH UPPISH UPPITY
VAUNTY CHUFFED HAUGHTY
SUBLIME SWOLLEN TOPPING
ARROGANT EXULTANT GLORIOUS
IMPOSING INSOLENT ORGULOUS

SPLENDID STOMACHY TOPLOFTY
OVERBEARING
(TOO — FOR) ABOVE
PROUDLY HIGH
PROVE TRY FAND FOND PREE
SHOW TEST ARGUE ASSAY EVICT
TAINT TASTE TEMPT ARGUFY
EVINCE SUFFER VERIFY BALANCE
CONFESS CONFIRM CONVICT
DERAIGN IMPROVE JUSTIFY
CONCLUDE CONVINCE EVIDENCE
INDICATE INSTRUCT MANIFEST
(— FALSE) BELIE BETRAY FALSIFY
(— GUILTY) ATTAINT
(— ONESELF) ACQUIT
(— OUT) SERVE
(— TITLE) DEDUCE
(— VALID) DEFEND
PROVED TRIED EXPERT PROBATE
PROVENCAL LANGUEDOC
ROMANESQUE
PROVENDER HAY CORN FEED
FOOD OATS STRAW PABULUM
PROVAND PROVIANT
PROVERB SAW SAY REDE WORD
ADAGE AXIOM CREED GNOME
MAXIM SOOTH BALLAD BYWORD
DITTON DIVERB MASHAL SAYING
SPEECH SYMBOL WHEEZE
BYSPELL IMPRESA NAYWORD
PARABLE APHORISM FORBYSEN
PAROEMIA SCHOLION SCHOLIUM
SENTENCE SOOTHSAY
(PREF.) PARAMIO PAROEMIO
PROVIDE DO FIT SEE FEND FILL
FIND GIRD LEND LOOK BLOCK
CATER ENDOW ENDUE EQUIP
SPEED STOCK STORE AFFORD
FOISON PURVEY SUBORN SUPPLY
COMPARE EXHIBIT FORESEE
FURNISH INSTORE PREPARE
ACCOUTER APPANAGE DISPENSE
PURCHASE
(— AHEAD OF TIME) ADVANCE
(— AMUSEMENT) DISTRACT
(— BY STEALTHY MEANS) SUBORN
(— FOOD) GRUB CATER SCAFF
(— FOR) FEND SERVE CHEVEYS
CHEVISE PROVANT
(— STINGILY) SKINCH
(— SUPPORT) ESCOT
(— WITH) BESEE
(— WITH DOWRY) DOT
(— WITH HIP-ROOF) COOT
(— WITH LOAN) ACCOMMODATE
(— WITH MONEY) FUND
PROVIDED IF BODEN FIXED READY
SOBEIT PROVISO INSTRUCT
PREPARED
PROVIDENCE THRIFT ECONOMY
PRUDENCE
PROVIDENT WARY WISE FRUGAL
SAVING CAREFUL PRUDENT
THRIFTY
PROVINCE LAN AREA NOME WALK
AIMAK BANAT FIELD MOUTH
NATAL NOMOS REALM SHENG
SHIRE SUBAH WORLD BANNAT
EMPIRE EYALET MALAGA MONTON
OBLAST REGION SIRCAR SPHERE
SYSSEL YAMATO DEMESNE
DONGOLA EPARCHY MUDIRIA
PURVIEW RECTORY VILAYET

APPANAGE DISTRICT FUNCTION
MUDIRIEH NOMARCHY TERRITORY
(PAPAL —) LEGATION
(ROMAN —) RAETIA RHAETIA
(RUSSIAN —) OBLAST
(SUBDIVISION OF EGYPTIAN —)
KISM
(PL.) OUTLAND
PROVINCIAL HICK BORNE CRUDE
NARROW RUSTIC STUFFY INSULAR
MOFUSSIL SUBURBAN PAROCHIAL
PRESIDIAL
PROVINCIALISM LOCALISM
PROVISION BOARD CHECK GRIST
FODDER MATTER PURVEY STOVER
UNLESS WRAITH APPREST
CAUTION CODICIL DOWNSET
KEEPING SLEEPER VICTUAL
WARNISH WARNISON
(— FOR MAINTENANCE) APANAGE
APPANAGE
(—S FOR JOURNEY) VIATICUM
(BOUGHT —S) ACATES ACATERY
(SUBORDINATE —) ITEM
(PL.) CHOW FOOD JOCK KEEP
LOAN PROG BOUGE CATES CHUCK
SCRAN STORE TERMS TOMMY
ANNONA VIANDS VIVRES
COMMONS WARNAGE WAYFARE
VICTUALS
PROVISO SALVO CAVEAT CLAUSE
CAUTION CONDITION
PROVOCATION TEEN APPEAL
INCENTIVE
PROVOCATIVE GUTTY SALTY
AGACANT PIQUANT IRRITANT
APPEALING
PROVOKE BOG EGG GIG IRE TAR
VEX BEAR DARE HUFF MOVE PICK
STIR TARR TEEN URGE WORK
ANGER ANGRY ANNOY EAGER
EVOKE FRUMP PIQUE TAUNT
TEMPT APPEAL ELICIT EVINCE
EXCITE GRIEVE HARASS INCITE
KINDLE NETTLE PROMPT SUMMON
TICKLE AFFRONT ILLICIT INCENSE
INFLAME INSPIRE VROTHER
CATALYZE IRRITATE
(— AVERSION) REPEL
PROVOKER GADFLY
PROVOKING AGACANT
PROVOST JUDGE PRIOR REEVE
KEEPER WARDEN STEWARD
PROW BOW BEAK SPUR STEM
PRORE SNOUT SPERON STEVEN
DIVIDER GALLANT VALIANT
(— OF GONDOLA) FERRO
PROWESS FEAT PROW VALOR
NOBLEY BRAVERY COURAGE
PROWL OWL PROG ROAM LURCH
MOOCH MOUSE RAVEN BREVIT
RAMBLE
PROWLER WALKER SLASHER
TENEBRION
PROWLIKE PROREAN
PROWLING GRASSANT
PROXIMAL CLOSE
PROXIMATE NEXT CLOSE DIRECT
CLOSEST NEAREST PROXIME
IMMINENT PROXIMAL
PROXIMITY SHADOW NEARNESS
PRESENCE VICINITY PROPINQUITY
NEIGHBORHOOD

PROXY VICE AGENT VICAR BALLOT MANDAT PROCTOR
(PL.) ELECTION

PRUDE PRIG COMSTOCK

PRUDENCE CARE METIS ADVICE CAUTEL WISDOM CAUTION COUNSEL SLEIGHT FORECAST FORELOOK

PRUDENT FIT SAFE SAGE WARE WARY WISE CANNY DOOSE DOUCE SOLID SYKER VERTY FRUGAL QUAINT SEKERE SICCAR POLITIC THRIVEN CAUTIOUS DISCREET PROVIDENT
(NOT —) ADVISED

PRUDISH NICE PRIM MIMZY MIMSEY PRIGGISH PUDIBUND VICTORIA

PRUDISHNESS NICETY PUDENCY

PRUNE COW LOP TOP CLIP COLL COUL GELD PLUM SNED SPUR TAME TRIM CLEAN DRESS KNIFE PLUMB PREEN PRIME PURGE SHEAR SHRAG SHRED SHRUB TRASH TWIST DEHORN REFORM SHRIDE SNATHE SWITCH AMPUTATE CASTRATE RETRENCH
(— SEVERELY) DEHORN
(IMPERFECTLY RIPENED —) FROG

PRUNING HOOK SARPE CALABOZO HANDBILL

PRUNING KNIFE SERPETTE

PRUNING SHEARS SECATEUR

PRURIENCE ITCH

PRURIENT ITCHY

PRURITIS ITCH

PRUSSIA PRUCE SPRUCE

PRUSSIAN PRUTENIC

PRY GAG KEEK NOSE NOTE PEEK PEEP PEER TEET TOOT JIMMY LEVER PRIZE SNOOP BREVIT FERRET PIGGLE POTTER PUTTER CROWBAR GUMSHOE LEVERAGE
(— ABOUT) OWL MOUSE SNOOK SCROUNGE
(— INTO) BREVIT
(— INTO AND REPEAT) RAVE

PRYING NOSY NOSEY PEERY CURIOUS PEEPING

PSALM ODE HYMN SONG DIRGE GATHA TRACT ANTHEM CANTATE CHORALE INTROIT MISERERE
(LENTEN —) TRACT
(100TH —) JUBILATE
(95TH —) VENITE
(98TH —) CANTATE

PSALMS HALLEL
(BOOK OF —) PSALTER

PSALTERIUM BOOK LYRA OMASUM PSALTER PSALTERY

PSALTERY GUSLA CITOLE SAUTREE SAUTERIE

PSEUDO FAKE MOCK SHAM BOGUS FALSE FEIGNED SPURIOUS
(PREF.) NE

PSEUDOCARP HIP

PSEUDOLOGIST LIAR

PSEUDONYM ALIAS ANONYM JUNIUS

PSHAW SHA DARN DRAT POOH SUGAR PHOOEY SHUCKS

PSITTACOSIS ORNITHOSIS

PSORIASIS ALPHOS

PSYCHE MIND SELF SOUL

PSYCHIATRIST SHRINK ANALYST ALIENIST
AMERICAN LIDE BERNE BRILL KLINE MEYER SZASZ OLIVER REUBEN SALMON WILDER RADECKI SPITZKA ABRAMSON MENNINGER DUNBARMFRANK
AUSTRIAN ADLER FRANKL
GERMAN PERLS ZIEHEN JASPERS
ISRAELI LEVY
SCOTTISH LAING
SOUTH AFRICAN COOPER
SWISS JUNG BLEULER RORSCHACH BINSWANGER

PSYCHIC (— POWERS) PSI

PSYCHOANALYST FREUDIAN

PSYCHOLOGIST **AMERICAN** AMES HALL HOLT LADD MEAD SALK BRITT DODGE JANOV LAIRD LEWIN RHINE SEARS SIMON URBAN WELLS ANGELL BORING BRUNER GESELL GINOTT HAINES HUNTER KANNER KOFFKA MASLOW PRINCE STARCH STRONG TERMAN WATSON ALLPORT BALDWIN BATESON CATTELL DOLLARD GODDARD NEWBOLD TROLAND BROTHERS LANGFELD MARSHALL SEASHORE WECHSLER PILLSBURY SCRIPTURE WOODWORTH CARRINGTON HOLLINGWORTH
ARGENTINIAN INGENIEROS
AUSTRIAN ADLER BETTELHEIM
DANISH LANGE
ENGLISH BURT WARD BUCKE ELLIS MYERS OGDEN STOUT SULLY GURNEY MORGAN AVELING BARTLETT MAUDSLEY
FRENCH COUE BINET JANET SIMON BEAUNIS
GERMAN KROH GEISE MARBE STERN WUNDT BENDER KOHLER MULLER PREYER RUBNER ZIEHEN JAENSCH MEUMANN KRONHAUSEN
SCOTTISH BAIN
SWISS JUNG PIAGET

PSYCHOLOGY HORMISM HEDONICS ANIMASTIC FORMALISM

PSYCHOPATH MATTOID

PSYCHOSIS INSANITY PARANOIA SENILITY MELANCHOLIA SCHIZOPHRENIA

PSYCHOTIC MAD CRAZY INSANE

PSYLLA DIMERAN

PSYLLIUM FLEAWORT

PTAH (— EMBODIED) APIS
(ASSOCIATED WITH —) SEKHET

PTARMIGAN RYPE GROUSE LAGOPODE

PTEROCARPUS LINGOUM

PTEROID ALAR

PTEROSAUR DIAPSID

PTERYGIUM WEBEYE

PTERYGOID EXTERNUM

PTERYLA TRACT

PTISAN TEA TISANE

PTOLEMY SOTER
(WIFE OF —) CLEOPATRA

PTOMAINE NEURIN SEPSIN SAPRINE GADININE PUTRESCINE

PTOUS (FATHER OF —) ATHAMAS
(MOTHER OF —) THEMISTO

PUAH (FATHER OF —) ISSACHAR
(SON OF —) TOLA

PUB BAR INN CAFE CAFF BISTRO BOOZER LOUNGE SHANTY TAVERN

PUBBLE FAT FULL PLUMP

PUB-CRAWL BARHOP

PUBERTY
(PREF.) HEBE

PUBES
(PREF.) EPISIO PUBI(O) PUBO

PUBESCENCE DOWN SCURF YOUTH TOMENT TOMENTUM

PUBESCENT HIRSUTE VILLOUS
(PREF.) HEBE

PUBLIC KUNG OPEN TOWN APERT CIVIC OVERT WORLD COMMON SOCIAL VULGAR GENERAL OMNIBUS POPULAR EXTERNAL MATERIAL NATIONAL MULTITUDE
(GENERAL —) GALLERY

PUBLICAN BUNG FARMER KEEPER TAVERNER ZACCHEUS CATCHPOLL

PUBLICATION BOOK ORDO BIBLE FOLIO ISSUE SHEET ANNUAL BLAZON DIGLOT SERIAL WEEKLY ALMANAC BOOKLET ELZEVIR JOURNAL MONTHLY WRITING BIWEEKLY BULLETIN DOCUMENT EMISSION EXCHANGE PRODROME EPHEMERIS PERIODICAL
(KIND OF —) MIMEO NUDIE

PUBLIC HOUSE BAR INN PUB BOOZER PUBLIC SALOON HOSTELRY POTHOUSE

PUBLICIST AGENT SOLON WRITER

PUBLICITY AIR HYPE BLAZE ECLAT BUILDUP PUFFERY RECLAME BALLYHOO BROUHAHA DAYLIGHT FLACKERY HERALDRY PROMOTION
(PROVIDE —) FLACK

PUBLICIZE CRY FLOG HYPE PLUG BLURB BREAK BRUIT HERALD BALLYHOO HEADLINE PROPAGATE

PUBLIC SQUARE PLAZA PLEIN ZOCALO

PUBLISH AIR ASH BLOW CALL EDIT EMIT VEND VENT CARRY ISSUE PRINT SPEAK UTTER BLAZON BROACH DEFAME DELATE EVULGE EXPOSE SPREAD CENSURE DECLARE DIFFUSE DIVULGE GAZETTE PROTEST RELEASE DENOUNCE DISCLOSE EVULGATE PROCLAIM PROMULGE
(— BANNS OF MARRIAGE) CRY SPUR OUTASK
(— IN CHURCH) ASK
(— WITHOUT AUTHORIZATION) PIRATE

PUBLISHER CRIER EDITOR ISSUER PRINTER STATIONER
AMERICAN COX DOW LEA AMES BONI CERF DODD FUNK GINN HOLT HOYT KERN KNOX LOEB LUCE MACY MUIR NAST OCHS ZIFF BOBBS BOEHM BROWN CAREY ENGEL ENOCH FODOR GODEY HECHT HOBBY JONES KNOPF MCRAE SIMON SMITH STERN ZEVIN BOWKER CAPPER CHILDS COVICI CURTIS DUTTON FARRAR FIELDS FORBES GIROUX HARPER HARRIS HEARST HEFNER KEYLOR LAFFAN LESLIE LITTLE MOSHER MUNSEY NIEMAN PAYSON PUTNAM RIDDER RODALE SCHIFF STOKES THOMAS UPDIKE VICTOR WALKER WILSON ZENGER ATTWOOD BINGHAM CAHNERS COLLIER CONNERS DRYFOOS GANNETT GUPTILL LOTHROP MIFFLIN POULSON PRESSER SADLIER SCRIPPS SHUSTER TICKNOR VERONIS WITMARK BANCROFT BARTLETT HOUGHTON PULITZER RINEHART SCHUSTER SCRIBNER WAGNALLS DOUBLEDAY LIVERIGHT MCCORMICK LIPPINCOTT
AUSTRALIAN SHEED MURDOCH THEODORE
CANADIAN SWEET
DUTCH ELZEVIR
ENGLISH DAY BELL BOHN CAPE LANE PAUL ALMON LUCAS MOXON MUDIE UNWIN WARNE WOOLF AITKEN BOOSEY FROWDE HAWKES KNIGHT LINTOT MILLAR NEWNES TONSON TOTTEL BEMROSE BENTLEY BRACKEN CASSELL CHAPMAN DEBRETT DODSLEY JENKINS METHUEN BRITTAIN NEWBERRY QUARITCH RICHARDS WHITAKER HEINEMANN PICKERING RIVINGTON ROUTLEDGE VIZETELLY WHITCHURCH BEAVERBROOK
FRENCH DIDOT HETZEL LEMERRE LITOLFF PLANTIN HACHETTE GALIGNANI
GERMAN COTTA MEYER FROBEN ZENGER PERTHES TEUBNER BAEDEKER SCHIRMER SPRINGER ULLSTEIN BROCKHAUS TAUCHNITZ
IRISH BRACKEN
ITALIAN RICORDI SONZOGNO
SCOTTISH BLACK SMITH CADELL CREECH NELSON CHAMBERS BLACKWOOD CONSTABLE MACMILLAN
SOUTH AFRICAN QOBOZA
WELSH BERRY

PUCCOON GROMYL ALKANET GROMWELL BLOODROOT

PUCE FLEA

PUCK ELF IMP LOB PUG BLOW BUTT DISK POKE POOK DEMON DEVIL FAIRY PEWKE SPORT RUBBER SPRITE STRIKE PUCKREL HOBGOBLIN

PUCKER DRAW FULL RUCK PURSE REEVE RIVEL TIZZY COCKLE COTTER FURROW LUCKEN RUCKLE WRINKLE CONTRACT AGITATION CONSTRICT

PUCKERED PURSY BULLATE COCKLED ROUCHED WRINKLED BULLIFORM

PUCKEREL IMP

PUCKFIST BRAGGART PUFFBALL

PUCKISH PUXY ELFIN IMPISH WHIMSICAL

PUDDING DICK DUFF LINK SAGO BOMBE DOWDY KUGEL MERIT BURGOO FENDER HACKIN HAGGIS HAUPIA JAUDIE SPONGE TANSEY

TARTAN DESSERT ADEQUACY BLOODING HEDGEHOG LIVERING PANDOWDY PLUMDUFF ROLYPOLY STICKJAW WHITEPOT CHARLOTTE
(— CONTAINING KALE) TARTAN
(— INGREDIENT) TAPIOCA
(— OF FLOUR) DUFF
(BOILED —) HOY
(FRUIT —) HEDGEHOG
(HASTY —) MUSH SEPON SUPAWN
(HAWAIIAN —) HAUPIA
(KIND OF —) COTTAGE
(MEAT —) ISING CHEWET HACKIN HACKING
(SUET —) KUGEL
PUDDINGWIFE PUDIANO DONCELLA GLUEFISH
PUDDLE DUB PANT PLUD POOL PULK ROIL SLAB SLOP SOSS SUMP FLUSH PLANT PLASH PUDGE CHARCO FLODGE KENNEL MUDDLE PUDDER SPLASH TAMPER CONFUSE PLASHET SLODDER SPUDDLE BEFUDDLE
(MUD —) DUB SLOP LOBLOLLY
PUDDLEBALL LOOP
PUDDLER'S RABBLE STRIKE
PUDENCY MODESTY DELICACY
PUDGY MIRY BULKY MUDDY PODGY SQUAT CHUBBY SPUDDY ROLYPOLY ROLLABOUT
PUDU VENADA
PUEBLO ANASAZI
PUELCHE PAMPA TEHUELET
PUERILE WEAK SILLY BOYISH JEJUNE TRIVIAL CHILDISH IMMATURE YOUTHFUL

PUERTO RICO
BAY: SUCIA RINCON BOQUERON AQUADILLA
CAPITAL: SANJUAN
ISLAND: MONA CULEBRA VIEQUES
LAKE: LOIZA CARITE CAONILLAS
MEASURE: CUERDA CABALLERIA
RIVER: CAMUY CANAS YAUCO ANASCO TANAMA FAJARDO
TOWN: CAYEY COAMO PONCE ANASCO DORADO MANATI ARECIBO BAYAMON FAJARDO GUAYAMA HUMACAO MAYAGUEZ

PUFF GUF POP BLOW BRAG DRAG FLAM FLAN GASP GUFF GUST HUFF PANT PECH SHOW WAFF WAFT BLURB BLURT ELATE ERUPT EXTOL FLUFF QUIFF SKIFF STECH SWELL WHIFF CAPFUL EXPAND FLATUS BLUSTER EXPLODE GRATIFY INFLATE WHIFFET BRAGGART OVERRATE WINDGALL BOUILLONE
(— FROM SHELL BLAST) BURST
(— OF WIND) FLAM TIFT SCART SLANT FLATUS HUFFLE
(— ON MARIJUANA CIGARETTE) TOKE
(— OUT) BELL BLUB VENT BLOUSE BLUBBER EFFLATE INFLATE
(— OUT SMOKE) EFFUME
(— UP) BLOW HUFF RISE BLOAT HEAVE BLADDER
(— VIOLENTLY) BLAST
(APPLE —) FLAPJACK

(CREAM —) DUCHESSE
(PASTRY —) PROFITEROLE
(SUDDEN —) FLAN FLAW GUST
PUFFBALL FIST FUZZ PUFF SMOKE FUNGUS PUFFIN BULLFICE BULLFIST PUCKFIST SNUFFBOX
PUFFBIRD BARBET MONASE NUNLET DREAMER NUNBIRD BARBACOU
PUFFED BLUB BOLLEN BLOATED SOUFFLE SWOLLEN ARROGANT INFLATED
(— OUT) BAGGY BOUFFANT
(— UP) RANK POBBY ASTRUT BLOATED SWOLLEN TURGENT VENTOSE
(BE — UP) BELL
PUFFER ATINGA BALLER BLOWER SLIMER TAMBOR BURFISH EGGFISH BLOWFISH TOADFISH
PUFFIN LOOM PAPE POPE MARROT MULLET MARROCK WILLOCK COCKANDY PARAKEET TOMNODDY TOMNORRY
(HAWAIIAN —) AO
PUFFY SOFT BAGGY BLOAT FAFFY GUMMY GUSTY PURSY CHUBBY FLUFFY PURFLY PURSIVE SWOLLEN BLADDERY BOUFFANT DROPSICAL
PUG FOX IMP PET BOXER CHAFF GOUGE SPOOR TRACK TRAIL CAMOIS CAMUSE GOBLIN MONKEY MISTRESS PUGILIST FOOTPRINT
PUGENCY TANG
PUGILIST PUG MILLER BRUISER SLOGGER
PUGNACIOUS BELLICOSE
PUG-NOSED CAMUS CAMUSE
PUISNE PUNY LATER PETTY JUNIOR YOUNGER INFERIOR
PUISSANCE ARMY FORCE POWER CONTROL POTENCY PROWESS DOMINION STRENGTH
PUJUNAN MAIDU
PUKKA GOOD REAL GENUINE LASTING COMPLETE SUPERIOR AUTHENTIC
PUKRAS PHEASANT KOKLAS
PULCHRITUDE GRACE BEAUTY
PULE CRY PEEP CHIRP COWRY WHINE SNIVEL WHIMPER
PULING PULY SPINDLY WHINING
PULITZER PRIZE (— IN LETTERS)
BOK LEE NYE AGAR AGEE BATE BUCK CARO COLT DOVE DUYN EDEL FEIS GALE GRAU HART INGE LASH LEVY MACK MOTT RICE TATE UHRY VANN WOOD WOUK AIKEN AKINS ALBEE AUDEN BAKER BAKER BEMIS BENET BRUCE BRUCE BULEY CHASE CLAPP CURTI DAVIS DRURY DUGAN FRANK FROST GLUCK HECHT ISAAC ISSAC JAMES KAMOW KIZER KRAMM KUMIN LEECH LUKAS LURIE MABEE MAMET MOSEL NEELY OPPEN PLATH PLATH PUPIN PUSEY SAGAN SIMIC SIMON SMITH STARR TEALE TOOLE TYLER UNGER WELTY WILLS ABBOTT BAILYN BAILYN BECKER BELLOW BRANCH BUTLER BUTLER CATHER CATTON CREMIN CREMIN CROUSE DEGLER DONALD

DURANT FERBER FRINGS FULLER GARROW GRAZIA HANDIN HARLAN HENLEY HERSEY HORGAN KAMMEN KENNAN KIDDER KIDDER KINNEL LAPINE LARKIN LOWELL MAILER MAILER MARNET MASSIE MASSIE MCCRAW MILLAY MORRIS NAIFEH NORMAN NORMAN OLIVER ONEILL PULLER RHODES SHAARA SMILEY TAYLOR TAYLOR TERKEL TOLAND ULRICH UPDIKE UPDIKE WALKER WALKER WARNER WILBUR WILDER WILSON WILSON YERGIN ZINDEL ASHBERY BURROWS CHEEVER DILLARD ELLMANN ERIKSON JUSTICE JUSTICE KAUFMAN KENNEDY KENNEDY KINNELL KUSHNER LAFARGE LINDSAY LITWACK LITWACK LOESSER MCFEELY MCFEELY NEMEROV POLLOCK RODGERS SAROYAN SHEEHAN SHEEHAN SHIPLER TUCHMAN VIERECK BOORSTIN FAULKNER HIJUELOS KINGSLEY LELYVELD MACLEISH MARQUAND MCMURTRY MEREDITH MICHENER MORRISON SANDBURG SCHORSKE SCHORSKE SCHUYLER SCHUYLER SHERWOOD SINCLAIR SONDHEIM VANDOREN WOODWARD HEMINGWAY MAHARIDGE MCDOUGALL MCPHERSON SCHENKKAN SILVERMAN STEINBECK HOFSTADTER HOFSTADTER HOLLDOBLER MCCULLOUGH WILLIAMSON WASSERSTEIN
(— IN MUSIC) RAN HUSA IVES TOCH WARD CRUMB KUBIK MOORE PERLE RANDS ROREM ROUSE ALBERT BARBER BOLCOM CARTER HANSON PISTON PORTER POWELL ARGENTO BASSETT COPLAND MARTINO MENOTTI SCHUMAN SOWERBY THOMSON WERNICK ZWILICH ZWILICH COLGRASS DRUCKMAN HARBISON KIRCHNER PETERSON REYNOLDS SESSIONS SESSIONS WUORINEN DELLOJOIO DAVIDOVSKY DELTREDICI SCHWANTNER
PULL IN PU EAR LUG POO POU ROG RUG TIT TOW CHUG CLAW DRAG DRAW DUCT HALE HARL HAUL HOOK RUGG SWIG TIRE TREK TUSH TWIG YANK BOUSE BREAK BUNCH CLOUT DRAFT HEAVE HITCH IMPEL JUICE PLUCK POLLE PROOF TRICE TWEAK ASSUME COMMIT GATHER OBTAIN PLITCH RUGGLE SCHLEP SECURE TWITCH UPROOT WRENCH ATTRACT EXTRACT
(— A BELL) SET
(— ABOUT) TEW SOOL TOSE TOZE MOUSLE
(— APART) RAVE REND TEAR DIVULSE
(— AWAY) AVEL AVELL WREST REVULSE
(— BY EARS) SOLE SOWL
(— DOWN) UNPILE DESTROY DEMOLISH
(— FOR) BACK
(— FORCIBLY) TUG

(— HERE AND THERE) TOOZLE TOUSLE
(— IN PIECES) DIVELLICATE
(— NOSE) SNITE
(— OF DRUM) EAR
(— OFF) CROP DRAW STRIP AVULSE
(— ON CIGARETTE) TOKE
(— ON FISHING ROD) STRIKE
(— ON ROPE) BOWSE
(— OUT) RAX UPROOT EXTRACT OUTBRAID
(— QUICKLY) YANK
(— ROUGHLY) WAP TOWSE WOUSE
(— SUDDENLY) TRICE
(— THE LEG) STRING
(— TOGETHER) KNOT ATTRACT
(— TRIGGER) SQUEEZE
(— UP) LOUK
(— UP BY THE ROOTS) ARACE
(— VIOLENTLY) WHAP WHOP WHANG
(— WITH A TWIST) WRENCH
(— WITH JERK) HOICK SWITCH
(ZIPPER —) SLIDER
PULLDEVIL SCROUGER SCRODGILL
PULLER KNOCKER
PULLER-IN CLICKER
PULLET HEN EAROCK EEROCK EIRACK MABYER POULARD POULAINE
PULLEY RIM CONE DRUM BLOCK FUSEE FUZEE IDLER TRICE WHEEL DRIVEN IDLEBY JOCKEY POLYVE RIGGER SHEAVE SHIVER WHARVE CAPSTAN FERRULE TIGHTER TRUCKLE WHARROW PULLISEE PURCHASE TROCHLEA
(PL.) TRISPAST JACKANAPES
PULLOVER JERSEY SWEATER
PULLULATE BUD TEEM BREED SWARM MULTIPLY
PULMONATE LUNGED
PULMONIC PNEUMONIC
PULP MAG PAP PUG CHUM MUSH BROKE JELLY NERVE SLUSH STOCK STUFF MARROW SQUEEZE SQUELCH
(FOOD —) CHYME
PULPIT PEW TUB AMBO BEMA DESK WOOD CHAIR PREACH ROSTRUM TRIBUNE
(— BOARD) TYPE
(— FOR CHOIR BOOKS) ANALOGION
(MOSLEM —) MIMBAR MINBAR
(OPEN-AIR —) TENT
PULPY SOFT SPEWY FLABBY FLESHY SIDDER SIDDOW BACCATE SQUELCHY
PULSATE BEAT BRIM FLAP PANT PUMP THROB COURSE STRIKE PALPITATE
PULSATION BEAT PANT BEATING HEARTBEAT LIFEBLOOD VIBRATION
(— OF ARTERY) ICTUS
PULSE DAL EMP BEAT DOHL TAKT URAD WAVE POUCE STUFF THROB BATTUTA IMPULSE PULSIDGE SPHYGMUS VITALITY
(PREF.) PALMO SPHYGMO
(SUFF.) CROTIC
PULSING VIBRANT
PULVERIZATION TRIPSIS

PULVERIZE BRAY BUCK DRAG FINE MEAL MULL STUB BRAKE CRUSH FLOUR GRIND POUND BRUISE POWDER ATOMIZE DEMOLISH VANQUISH COMMINUTE MICRONIZE

PULVERIZED FINE POWDERED

PULVERIZER MULLER

PULVERULENT DUSTY CRUMBLY POWDERY

PULVILLUS PAD

PUMA COUGAR PAINTER PANTHER

PUME YARURA

PUMICE LAVA PUMEX PUMIE
(**UNCOOLED —**) LAVA

PUMMEL FIB BEAT DRUB PAIK SLAT POUND SLATE THUMP POUNCE

PUMP GIN GUN FORK JACK COURT FORCE HEART PLUMB SLUSH DOCTOR DORSAY FORCER SINKER VOLUTE BOOSTER DOWNTON EJECTOR EVACTOR PITWORK SLUDGER SYRINGE TOEPLER BEERPULL ELEVATOR INFLATER INJECTOR PULSATOR PULSOMETER
(**— ON SHIPS**) DOWNTON
(**— UP**) AERATE INFLATE
(**GAS —**) BOWSER
(**HAND —**) GUN
(**MINE —S**) SET
(**SET OF —S**) LIFT

PUMP DOCTOR GRATHER

PUMPER RACKER

PUMPERNICKEL BOMBERNICKEL

PUMPKIN PEPO CHUMP GOURD PEPON QUASH CASHAW CITRUL CUCURB CUSHAW SQUASH QUASHEY CUCURBIT PEPONIDA

PUMPKINSEED RUFF SUNNY FLATFISH FLOUNDER REDBELLY

PUN NICK WHIM ALLUDE CLINCH GROANER QUIBBLE EQUIVOKE PARAGRAM CALEMBOUR PARANOMASIA ANNOMINATION

PUNCH DAB DIG FIB HUB JAB SET BASH BELT BLOW BOFF BUST DECK DING PLUG POKE SETT SLUG SOAK SOCK TIFF BUMBO DOUSE DRIFT FORCE GLOGG PASTE PENCH SHORT SLOSH CANCEL INCUSE PATRIX PAUNCH SHAPER STINGO STRIKE TRACER MATTOIR PERLOIR SANGRIA SHELLAC STARTER EMBOSSER GROUNDER HAYMAKER PRITCHEL PUNCTURE SWATCHEL THICKSET
(**CHASING —**) TRACER
(**DOG OF —**) TOBY
(**ETCHER'S —**) MATTOIR
(**HORSESHOE —**) PRITCHEL
(**KIND OF —**) RABBIT
(**OVAL —**) PLAISHER
(**RUM —**) RUMBO
(**SWINGING —**) ROUNDHOUSE
(**WIFE OF —**) JUDY

PUNCHBOARD PUSHCARD

PUNCH BOWL SNEAKER

PUNCHCARD (**GROUP OF —S**) DECK

PUNCH-DRUNK PUNCHY SLAPHAPPY

PUNCHED PERTUSE

PUNCHEON CASK PULE SNAP PUNCH

PUNCHER COWBOY SOCKER

PUNCHINELLO CLOWN BUFFOON PUGENELLO

PUNCH PRESS BEAR DROP

PUNCHY POUNCY FORCEFUL

PUNCTILIO PIQUE PUNTO PUNCTO

PUNCTILIOUS NICE EXACT STIFF FORMAL CAREFUL POINTED PRECISE PUNCTUAL

PUNCTUAL DUE EXACT ONTIME PROMPT CAREFUL PRECISE ACCURATE DEFINITE DETAILED EXPLICIT

PUNCTUALLY SHARP

PUNCTUATE MARK STOP POINT EMPHASIZE
(**— JAZZ SOLO**) COMP

PUNCTUATION MARK DOT DASH STOP BRACE COLON COMMA PRICK SLASH HYPHEN PERIOD STIGME BRACKET VIRGULE ELLIPSIS SEMICOLON

PUNCTURE HOLE PICK PINK PROD STAB DRILL POINT PRICK PUNCH STICK NEEDLE PIERCE PIQURE DEFLATE DESTROY PUNCTUM CENTESIS PINPRICK
(**SKIN —**) NEEDLESTICK
(**SUFF.**) NYXIS STIXIS

PUNCTURED CRIBLE

PUNDIT GURU SAGE SVAMI SWAMI CRITIC PANDIT TEACHER

PUNG SLED

PUNGENCY NIP HEAT SALT SNAP ACRIMONY KEENNESS PIQUANCY SALTNESS

PUNGENT HOT TEZ ACID BOLD FELL KEEN RACY RICH SALT TART ACRID ACUTE BRISK NIPPY QUICK SHARP SMART SNELL SPICY TANGY ZESTY BITING BITTER SHRILL SNAPPY CAUSTIC MORDANT PEPPERY PIQUANT POINTED TELLING CAYENNED PIERCING POIGNANT STABBING STINGING
(**— QUALITY**) ZAP

PUNGI BIN

PUNIC PUNICAL FAITHLESS

PUNISH FIT FIX PAY BUCK CANE COLT COOK CUCK FINE FLOG GATE SORT WIPE ABUSE BIRCH CURSE ORDER SCOUR SHEND SLATE SPILL STOCK STRAP TWINK WREAK AMERCE AVENGE CAMPUS FERULE FOLLOW IMMURE LESSON REFORM SCHOOL STRAFE STRIKE CHASTEN CONSUME CORRECT CORRIGE DEPLETE PENANCE REQUITE SCOURGE CARTWHIP CHASTISE DISTRAIN CASTIGATE
(**— BY BLOW ON PALM**) PANDY
(**— BY COMPENSATION**) FINE AMERCE
(**— BY CONFINEMENT**) GATE
(**— BY FINE**) MULCT
(**— BY LASHING WRISTS**) BUCK
(**— IN PRISON**) ISOLATE

PUNISHING HARD GRUELING

PUNISHMENT GIG FINE LASH PAIN PINE RACK SACK WITE YARD BEANS GRUEL LIBEL PANDY PEINE

SMART WRACK WREAK DESERT DIRDUM FERULE LESSON PICKET EXAMPLE GALLOWS GANTLET JANKERS PAYMENT PENALTY PENANCE PENANCY REVENGE SCOURGE HERISSON JUDGMENT PUNITION STOCKING SUPPLICE EXECUTION
(**CAPITAL —**) SCAFFOLD
(**MILITARY —**) JANKERS
(**SCHOOL —**) PANDY

PUNITIVE PENAL PUNITORY

PUNK BAD BOY MUG FUNK JERK MONK POOR PUNG THUG CONCH SPONK SPUNK AMADOU BUNKUM NOVICE HOODLUM RUFFIAN BEGINNER GANGSTER INFERIOR NONSENSE STRUMPET TERRIBLE TOUCHWOOD

PUNKIE MIDGE MIDGET

PUNNING ALLUSIVE BIVERBAL

PUNSCH ARRACK

PUNSTER WAG SPEED

PUNT BET HIT POY KENT KICK QUANT GAMBLE GARVEY SKERRY

PUNTER BIDDER GAMBLER SCALPER SERVITOR

PUNY WEAK DAWNY DEENY DWARF FRAIL PETTY SCRAM WEARY JUNIOR MAUGER NOVICE PUISNE RECENT SICKLY SPROTY MANIKIN PIMPING QUEECHY SHILPIT YOUNGER DROGHLIN INFERIOR PINDLING RECKLING
(**— PERSON**) TITMAN

PUP PUPPY WHELP

PUPA EGG NYMPH PUPPET TUMBLER WIGGLER FLAXSEED WRIGGLER CHRYSALIS

PUPIL BOY GYTE TYRO WARD BLACK CADET CHILD ELEVE NORRY NURRY RAPIN TUTEE ALUMNA GRADER INFANT JUNIOR SENIOR LEARNER PAULINE SCHOLAR SOJOURN STUDENT ABSENTEE BLUECOAT DISCIPLE RUGBEIAN SCHOOLER
(**— AT HEAD OF CLASS**) DUX
(**— GOING TO UNIVERSITY**) ABITURIENT
(**— IN STUDIO**) RAPIN
(**— OF CHRIST'S HOSPITAL**) BLUECOAT
(**— OF EYE**) BLACK PEARL SIGHT
(**— WITH SOME AUTHORITY**) PREFECT PRAEFECT
(**ANGLO-INDIAN —**) CHELA
(**BOARDED —**) SOJOURN
(**GERMAN —**) ABITURIENT
(**PREF.**) COR(E)(O)
(**SUFF.**) CORIA

PUPILAGE (WARDSHIP PEDANTISM

PUPPET BABY DOLL DUPE IDOL MOTE BABBY DROLL DUMMY MAUMET MOTION POPPIN STOOGE WAJANG WAYANG GUIGNOL DROLLERY MARIONET MARIONETTE
(**— PLAY**) WAJANG
(**— SHOW**) VERTEP
(**— THEATER**) BUNRAKU
(**PREF.**) PUPI

PUPPETEER SARG

PUPPIS STERN

PUPPY FOP PUP DOLL DOUGH WHELP PUPPET
(**FEMALE —**) GYP
(**GREYHOUND —**) SAPLING

PURBLIND BISME BISSON

PURCHASABLE VENAL CORRUPT

PURCHASE BUY WIN EARN FISH GAIN KOOP WHIP HEDGE PRIZE DUPLEX EFFECT EMPTIO TACKLE ACQUIRE BARGAIN EMPTION PILLAGE PROCURE BARRATRY
(**— AND FATTEN CATTLE**) HIGGLE

PURCHASER BUYER EMPTOR VENDEE CHAPMAN POULTER SHOPPER CUSTOMER

PURE NET CAST EVEN FAIR FINE FREE FULL GOOD HOLY MERE NEAT PUTE TRUE CLEAN CLEAR FRESH MORAL NAKED SHEER STARK SYCEE UTTER WHITE WHOLE CANDID CHASTE ENTIRE IMMIXT LIMPID PISTIC SIMPLE VESTAL VIRGIN ANGELIC CATHARI GENUINE PERFECT SINCERE ABSOLUTE ABSTRACT COMPLETE DOVELIKE INNOCENT PRISTINE SERAPHIC SPOTLESS VIRGINAL VIRTUOUS SPIRITUAL
(**— IN COLOR**) ORIENT
(**PREF.**) KATHARO

PUREE DAL SOUP CREAM BRANDADE

PURFLE ADORN

PURGATIVE PURGE SENNA CALOMEL DIASENE DRASTIC TURPETH ALOEDARY APERIENT CLEANSER ELATERIN EVACUANT CATHARTIC ABSTERSIVE

PURGATORY PAIN SWAMP

PURGE LAX RID FIRE FLUX SOIL CLEAR RHEUM SCOUR DRENCH PHYSIC REMOVE SEETHE SHRIVE SPURGE CHISTKA CLEANSE DETERGE ABSTERGE

PURIFICATION BAPTISM ELUTION LUSTRUM VASTATION

PURIFIED WHITE

PURIFY TRY BOLT FINE PURE WASH CLEAN PURGE SNUFF BLEACH DISTIL FILTER REFINE SETTLE SPURGE WINNOW BAPTIZE CHASTEN CLEANSE EPURATE EXPIATE LAUNDER MUNDIFY SUBLIME SWEETEN DEPURATE EXORCISE FILTRATE LUSTRATE SANCTIFY SCAVENGE SPRINKLE
(**— ORE**) DILVE
(**— SUGAR**) CLAY

PURIFYING SMECTIC DEPURANT

PURIRI TEAK BULREEDY IRONWOOD

PURIST PRIG PEDANT STICKLER

PURITAN PRIG SAINT CANTER CROPPY BLUENOSE CATHARAN GOSPELER PRECISIAN ROUNDHEAD

PURITANICAL BLUE STRICT GENTEEL PRECISE

PURITANI, I (CHARACTER IN **—**) ARTHUR ELVIRA TALBOT WALTON HENRIETTA
(**COMPOSER OF —**) BELLINI

PURITY PURE ASSAY HONOR WHITE CANDOR SATTVA VIRTUE FINESSE CHASTITY FINENESS PURENESS
(— OF BREED) PEDIGREE
(— OF LUSTER) ORIENT
PURL RIB EDDY KNIT PEARL UPSET RIPPLE TOTTLE CAPSIZE OVERTURN
PURLIEU AREA HAUNT
(PL.) BOUNDS CONFINES ENVIRONS
PURLIN RIB
PURLOIN CAB CRIB WEED ANNEX BRIBE FILCH STEAL SWIPE FINGER PILFER PIRATE CABBAGE SNAFFLE SURREPT ABSTRACT SCROUNGE
PURPLE GAY VIOL LILAC REGAL SHOWY ARGYLE BLATTA BLOODY CROCUS EVEQUE MIGNON ARDOISE FUCHSIA FUCHSIN HEATHEN LOGWOOD PETUNIA PONTIFF PURPURE AMARANTH BURGUNDY CAMERIER CYCLAMEN EGGPLANT EMINENCE IMPERIAL MAUVETTE MULBERRY WISTARIA
(BROWNISH —) PUCE
(DELICATE —) MAUVE
(PALE —) LILAC
(VISIBLE —) RHODOPSIN
(PREF.) PORPHYR(O) PURPUREO PURPURI PURPURO
PURPLE FISH MUREX
PURPLE GALLINULE SULTAN SULTANA HYACINTH
PURPLE LAND (AUTHOR OF —) HUDSON
(CHARACTER IN —) JOHN LAMB ANITA MARCO COLOMA LUCERO MARCOS MONICA SANTOS ANSELMO BARBUDO CALIXTO GANDARA HILARIO ISIDORA PAQUITA PERALTA RICHARD DEMETRIA MARGARITA CARRICKFERGUS
PURPLE LOOSESTRIFE KILLWEED
PURPLE MEDIC ALFALFA
PURPLE RAGWORT JACOBY
PURPLE SANDPIPER REDLEG REDLEGS ROCKBIRD
PURPORT FECK GIST PORT DRIFT SENSE TENOR DESIGN EFFECT IMPART IMPORT INTEND INTENT BEARING MEANING PROFESS PURPOSE COVERING DISGUISE STRENGTH
PURPOSE GO AIM END GOAL IDEA MAIN MEAN MIND MINT PLAN SAKE TALK TEND VIEW WEEN WILL ARTHA CAUSE ETTLE HEART LEVEL POINT SCOPE STUDY THINK DESIGN DEVICE EFFECT INTEND INTENT OBTENT PREFIX REASON SCHEME COMPASS COUNSEL DESTINE EARNEST IMAGINE MEANING PROPOSE THOUGHT DEVOTION FUNCTION PLEASURE PROPOUND DISCOURSE
(ALLEGED —) PRETEXT
(FIXED —) HEART
(INSIDIOUS —) CAUTEL
(MORAL —) ETHOS
(PARTICULAR —) NONCE
(PRESENT —) NONCE

PURPOSEFUL AIMFUL POINTED
PURPOSELESS WASTE RANDOM AIMLESS FECKLESS
PURPOSIVE TELIC HORMIC
PURPURA MUREX PURPLES PELIOSIS
PURPURE GOLP GOLPE PURPLE MERCURY
PURR MURR THRUM WHURL DUNLIN
PURSE BAG CLY JAN BUNG CLAY CLOY FISC KNIT POKE PUSS SKIN BULSE BURSE DUMMY FUNDS MEANS POUCH SPUNG COMMON FOLLIS GIPSER POCKET PUCKER READER SHAMMY ALMONER GIPSIRE LEATHER SPORRAN BUCKSKIN BURSICLE CRUMENAL AUMONIERE POCKETBOOK
(PREF.) BURSI
PURSE CRAB PAGURID
PURSER CLERK BURSAR BOUCHER PINCHGUT NIPCHEESE
PURSING MIMP
(— OF MOUTH) PRIM
PURSLANE PURPIE PUSSLY PIGWEED PUSSLEY PORTULACA
PURSLANE TREE SPEKBOOM
PURSUANCE SUING SEQUENCE
PURSUE BAY RUN SUE HUNT SEEK CHASE CHEVY CHIVY ENSUE HOUND QUEST SLATE STALK TRADE COURSE FOLLOW GALLOP TRAVEL BEDEVIL HOTFOOT CONTINUE PRACTICE
(— ZIGZAG COURSE) TACK
PURSUER FOLLOWER PLAINTIFF QUESTRIST
PURSUIT FAD HUNT SUIT CAPER CAUSE CHASE CHEVY CRAFT HOBBY COURSE SEARCH ASSAULT ACTIVITY ENTREATY PROSECUTION
(— OF PLEASURE) EPICURISM
(— OF WISDOM) PHILOSOPHY
(FAVORITE —) MEAT
PURSUIVANT BUTE MARCH FALCON ORMOND ATHLONE CARRICK ANTELOPE DINGWALL FOLLOWER
PURSY FAT OBESE PUFFY ASTHMATIC
PURULENT PYIC ATTRY ATTERY
PURVEY CATER PANDER SUPPLY FORESEE PROVIDE
PURVEYOR CATER TAKER ACHUAS PROWER CATERER ACHATOUR MANCIPLE
PUS WARE AMPER FESTER MATTER WORSUM QUITTER
(PREF.) PURI PURO PY(O)
(CONTAINING — AND GAS) PYOPNEUMO
PUSH CA DUB JAM JOG JUR PUT BANG BIRR BOIL BOOM BORE BUNT DING DUSH FLOG KENT PICK PILT PING PORR POSS POTE SHOG STOP BLITZ BOOST BRUSH BUNCH CROWD CRUSH DRIVE DUNCH ELBOW GOOSE HUNCH NUDGE PINCH POACH POUSE SCAUT SHOVE SKELP STICK STOVE EXTEND HURTLE HUSTLE JOGGLE

JOSTLE POTTER PROPEL THRING THRONG THRUST ASSAULT IMPETUS IMPULSE OPERATE PERPLEX SHUFFLE THRUTCH CONTRUDE INCREASE SHOULDER STRAITEN DISMISSAL
(— ALONG) TUSH
(— APART) SPREAD
(— ASIDE) SHOG
(— BY STICK) KENT POLE
(— FORWARD) BUCKET ADVANCE
(— GENTLY) NUDGE
(— IN HASTE) RUSH
(— INTO) INVADE
(— INTO PROMINENCE) BOOM
(— MONEY) SPIFF
(— ON) BEAR YERK
(— OUT) DEBOUT LAUNCH
(— OUT LIPS) POUT
(— RUDELY) BARGE HORSE HUSTLE
(— TO FULL STRIDE) EXTEND
(— TOGETHER) CONTRUDE
(— UNDERNEATH) SUBDUCT
(— UP) BOOST
(— VIOLENTLY) WHANG
(— WITH ELBOW) ELBOW HUNCH
(— WITH FEET) DIG SCAUT
(— WITH HEAD) BUNT BUTT
(— WITHIN) INVAGINATE
(STRONG —) BEVEL
PUSH BUTTON PUSH PRESSEL
PUSHCART BARROW TROLLEY
PUSHER PLUNGER TRAILER TRAMMER WHEELER
PUSHING OBTRUSIVE PROTRUSIVE
PUSHOVER SNAP SOFTY SUCKER
PUSHY FORWARD AGGRESSIVE
PUSILLANIMOUS WEAK TIMID FEEBLE COWARDLY TIMOROUS
PUSS CAT FACE HARE CHEET CHILD MOUTH RABBIT BAUDRONS
PUSSYCAT SOFTY
PUSTULE NOB BEAL BURL KNOB POCK PUSH QUAT WART ACHOR AMPER BLAIN WHEAL WHELK BLOTCH FESTER PIMPLE TETTER ANTHRAX BLISTER ERUPTION WHEYWORM
PUT DO BET LAY PIT SET BANG BUTT FILL GIVE GROW PILT REST URGE ADAPT APPLY DIGHT DRIVE FOCUS PLACE STALL STATE STEAD STEEK STELL WAGER ASSIGN BESTOW DECAMP IMPOSE INVEST PHRASE REPOSE SPROUT THRUST DEPOSIT EMPLACE EXPRESS INFLICT SUBJECT
(— AN END TO) DATE SNIB ABATE NAPOO SNUFF SPIKE STASH STILL STINT SOPITE STANCH ABOLISH ASSUAGE EXPIATE SATISFY ABROGATE DEMOLISH FINALIZE SURCEASE
(— ANOTHER IN PLACE OF) RELIEVE
(— APART) DISPART
(— ASHORE) MAROON
(— ASIDE) BLOW HAIN SAVE SHUNT REJECT SHUFFLE
(— ASUNDER) PART
(— AT REST) HUSH
(— AWAY) STOW COVER ELONG HUTCH SHIFT RECOND SAVEUP DIVORCE

(— BACK) REMIT REMISE
(— BACK INTO USE) RESTORE
(— BEFORE) PROFER ANTEPONE
(— DOWN) LAY DEMIT QUASH QUELL DEPOSE SQUASH DEPRESS OPPRESS REPRESS SILENCE DIMINISH SUPPRESS
(— EDGE ON) TED
(— EVASIVELY) SHUFFLE
(— FLAX UPON A DISTAFF) DIZEN
(— FORTH) GEM BLOW CAST GIVE PUSH EXERT LANCE PROFER STRETCH
(— FORTH BLOSSOMS) GEM
(— FORWARD) RUN PLEAD TABLE PREFER PRESENT PROPONE PROPOSE SUGGEST OVERTURE
(— GRAIN IN BARN) END
(— IN) ENTER INSERT INTROMIT
(— IN AGONY) THROE
(— IN CHARGE) COMMIT
(— IN CLAIM) PRETEND
(— IN COMPETITION) PIT
(— IN CONDITION) TUNE
(— IN CUSTODY) REMIT
(— IN DANGER) SCUPPER
(— IN DREAD) ADRAD
(— INFORMATION INTO) ADDRESS
(— IN MOTION) AROUSE
(— IN OPERATION) LAUNCH
(— IN ORDER) DO SET REDD SIDE SORT TRIM DIGHT MENSE SHIFT TRICK ADJUST DAIKER GRAITH ORDAIN SETTLE ARRANGE CLARIFY DISPOSE REDRESS INSTRUCT
(— IN PLACE) POSE
(— IN POSSESSION) SEISE
(— IN PRISON) WARD
(— INTO ACTION) SERVE
(— INTO BARN) END
(— INTO CASE) SHEATHE
(— INTO CIRCULATION) EMIT SPRING
(— INTO ECSTASY) ENTRANCE
(— INTO EFFECT) EXECUTE SANCTION
(— INTO IRONS) BOLT
(— INTO RHYTHM) METER METRE
(— LIQUOR INTO CASK) TUN
(— OFF) DAFF DOFF HAFT DEFER DELAY DEMUR FOIST PARRY REMIT REPRY SHIFT TARRY THROW LINGER RETARD SHELVE ADJOURN FORSLOW PROLONG RESPITE POSTPONE PROROGUE PROCRASTINATE
(— ON) DON HYPE APPLY CRACK DRAPE ENDUE MOUNT STAGE ASSUME INVEST ADDRESS
(— ON AIRS) PROSS FINICK REVEST
(— ON ALERT) ALARM
(— ON BOARD) LADE
(— ON COVER) HACKLE
(— ON GUARD) ALERT CAUTION
(— ON HAT) COVER
(— ON PRETENSE) AFFECT
(— ON RECORD) FILE REGISTER
(— ON SALE) SHOP
(— ON SHORT ALLOWANCE) SCRIMP
(— ON STAGE) PRODUCE
(— ON STRING) ENFILE

(— OUT) GET OUT DOUT OUST DOWSE EVICT EXERT OUTED SLAKE SLOCK RETIRE DISMISS EXCLUDE EXTINCT FORJUDGE
(— OUT BATSMAN) SKITTLE
(— OUT OF ACTION) HAMPER
(— RIGHT) AMEND
(— ROAD METAL ON) STEEN
(— SUDDENLY) CLAP
(— SURREPTITIOUSLY) STEAL
(— THROUGH A STRAINER) TAMMY
(— TO FLIGHT) AFLEY FEAZE FLEME GALLY
(— TOGETHER) ADD JOIN BUILD COMPILE COMPOSE CONCOCT CONFECT PREPARE ASSEMBLE COMPOUND
(— TO PROOF) TEST
(— TO RIGHTS) SORT DIGHT
(— TO SHAME) DASH ABASH SHEND UPBRAID
(— TO SLEEP) OPIATE SOPITE SOPORATE
(— TO THE TEST) SEARCH
(— TO TRIAL) TEMPT
(— TO USE) STOW APPLY BESTOW
(— TO WORK) HARNESS
(— UP) ANTE ERECT FLUSH DISPENSE
(— UP HAY) BOTTLE
(— UPON) GAMMON
(— UP WITH) GO BEAR BIDE HACK ABIDE BROOK ENDURE SUFFER COMPORT STOMACH SWALLOW TOLERATE
(— WITH ANOTHER) APPOSE
(SUFF.) STOLE
PUTAMEN PYRENE
PUTCHER PUTLOG PUTCHEN PUTLOCK
PUT-DOWN SLUR
PUT-ON HYPE

PUTREFACTION ROT DECAY SEPSIS
(SUFF.) SEPTIC
PUTREFACTIVE SEPTIC
(PREF.) SEPTICO
PUTREFIED ROTTEN
PUTREFY ROT ADDLE DECAY SWEAT FESTER POLLUTE PUTRESCE
PUTRESCENT PUTRID ROTTEN
PUTRID FOUL RANK SOUR VILE LOUSY ADDLED RANCID ROTTEN CORRUPT DECAYED FRIABLE VICIOUS DEPRAVED MALODOROUS
(PREF.) SAPR(O) SEPTI SEPTO
(SUFF.) SEPSIS SEPTIC
PUTT CLOWN BORROW GOBBLE
(SHORT —) GIMME TAPIN
PUTTEE PAT PATA GAITER BANDAGE LEGGING
PUTTER FUSS MESS MUCK POKE TRUCK CADDLE DAWDLE MUCKER MUCKLE PIDDLE TINKER FRIGGLE
PUTTY BEDDING
PUTTYROOT CRAWFOOT
PUTZ CRECHE
PUXY SWAMPY QUAGMIRE
PUZZLE CAP GET SET BEAT CRUX DEAD LICK POSE BEFOG GRIPH POSER QUEER REBUS STICK BAFFLE BOTHER ENIGMA FICKLE FOITER GLAIKS JIGSAW KITTLE RIDDLE CONFUSE MYSTERY MYSTIFY NONPLUS PERPLEX STICKER TAISSLE TANGRAM TRANGAM ACROSTIC BEFUDDLE BEWILDER CONFOUND DISTRACT DUMFOUND ENTANGLE INTRIGUE KEMBLERE CROSSWORD METAGRABOLIZE METAGROBOLIZE
(SOPHISTICAL —) SORITES
(TYPE OF —) JIGSAW
PUZZLED ASEA ATSEA PERPLEXED

PUZZLING KNOTTY CURIOUS KNOTTED RIDDLING DIFFICULT PROBLEMATIC
PYCNANTHEMUM KOELLIA
PYCNOGONID SPIDER
PYGARG ADDAX OSPREY
PYGIDIUM PODEX
PYGMALION (AUTHOR OF —) SHAW
(BELOVED OF —) GALATEA
(CHARACTER IN —) HILL LIZA CLARA HENRY ALFRED FREDDY HIGGINS EYNSFORD DOOLITTLE PICKERING
(FATHER OF —) BELUS MUTGO AGENOR
(MURDERED BY —) SICHAEUS
(SISTER OF —) DIDO
(STATUE FASHIONED BY —) GALATEA
PYGMY ELF AKKA AMBA DOKO ACHUA AFIFI ATOMY BATWA DWARF GNOME PIXIE PIGMEW WOCHUA ACHANGO ASHANGO MANIKIN DWARFISH NEGRILLO VAALPENS DANDIPRAT
PYGMY GOOSE GOSLET
PYGMY RATTLESNAKE MASSASAUGA
PYGOSTYLE VOMER
PYKNIC SQUAT STOCKY STHENIC MUSCULAR
PYLADES (COMPANION OF —) ORESTES
(FATHER OF —) STROPHIUS
(MOTHER OF —) ANAXIBIA
(SON OF —) MEDON STROPHIUS
(WIFE OF —) ELECTRA
PYRAMID BENBEN HOPPER TEOCALLI
(— OF CRAYFISH) BUISSON
(DOUBLE —) TWIN ZIRCONOID
(INVERTED —) HOPPER

PYRAMIDAL HUGE ENORMOUS IMPOSING
PYRAMIDICAL TAPER
PYRAMUS (LOVER OF —) THISBE
PYRAZINE ALDINE PIAZIN DIAZINE
PYRE BALE PILE TOPHET BONFIRE BALEFIRE
PYRIDOXIN ADERMIN
PYRITE BALE MUNDIC
(PL.) BRAZIL STANNITE FIRESTONE MAGISTRAL MARCASITE
PYROCLES (BROTHER OF —) CYMOCLES
(FATHER OF —) ACRATES
PYROLA LIMONIUM SHINLEAF
PYROMANIAC FIREBUG ARSONIST
PYRONE CUMALIN
PYROPHYLLITE PENCIL
PYROTECHNICS FIREWORKS
PYROXENE ACMITE AUGITE SALITE SAHLITE AEGIRITE DIALLAGE DIOPSIDE WOLLASTONITE
PYROXENITE ARIEGITE MARCHITE OSTRAITE NIKLESITE
PYRRHIC DIBRACH
PYRRHULOXIA GROSBEAK BULLFINCH
PYRRHUS (FATHER OF —) AEACIDES
(MOTHER OF —) PHTHIA
(SON OF —) PTOLEMY SOPATER
(WIFE OF —) ANTIGONE
PYRROLE AZOLE
PYTHON ADJIGER PEROPOD ANACONDA
PYTHONESS WITCH PHITONES
PYTHONIC HUGE INSPIRED ORACULAR MONSTROUS PROPHETIC
PYX BOX CAPSA CASKET CHRISM VESSEL BINNACLE CHRISMAL CIBORIUM
PYXIDIUM CAPSULE

Q

Q KU CUE KUE QUEEN QUEUE
QUEBEC
QATAR (CAPITAL OF —) DOHA
  (TOWN OF —) RUWAIS UMMSAID
QUA HERON QUABIRD
QUACK PUFF WHACK CROCUS
SALVER SUBTLE EMPIRIC
IMPOSTOR OPERATOR SANGRADO
CHARLATAN
  (PREF.) PSEUD(O)
QUACKERY HUMBUG
QUADRAGESIMA LENT
QUADRANGLE QUAD CLOSE
COURT TETRAGON
QUADRANT BOW RADIAL SQUARE
QUARTER TETRANT ALTIMETER
QUADRATE SUIT AGREE IDEAL
QUADER SQUARE PERFECT
BALANCED
QUADRIC CONICOID
QUADRILATERAL TRAPEZIA
TETRAGRAM
  (PL.) TESSARA
QUADRILLE CONTREDANSE
  (PL.) LANCERS
QUADRILLION
  (PREF.) ASTRA PETA QUEGA
QUADRILLIONTH
  (PREF.) FEMTO
QUADROON QUATERON TERCERON
QUADRUPED BABIRUSA
QUADRUPLE FOURBLE FOURFOLD
QUADRUPLED
  (PREF.) TETRAKIS
QUADRUPLET FOURLING
QUARTOLE
QUAFF QUAX TOOT DRINK QUASS
WAUCHT CAROUSE TRILLIL
QUAG BOG MARSH SHAKE QUIVER
QUAGMIRE BOG FEN GOG HAG
QUA SOG LAIR PUXY QUAW
MARSH MIZZY SWAMP MORASS
PUDDLE SLOUGH BOGMIRE
PUCKSEY WAGMOIRE
QUAHOG CLAM COHOG VENUS
BULLNOSE
QUAIL COW LOWA WEET COLIN
COWER DAUNT ORTYX QUAKE
SPOIL WASTE BLENCH CURDLE
FLINCH SHRINK TURNIX WITHER
DECLINE HEMIPOD TREMBLE
BOBWHITE
  (YOUNG —) SQUEALER
QUAINT DRY ODD TWEE FUNKY
NAIVE BIZARRE STRANGE
FANCIFUL HANDSOME
PICTURESQUE
  (— IN APPEARANCE) FUNKY
QUAKE JAR QUOG RESE CHILL
QUAIL SEISM SHAKE DITHER
QUIVER SHIVER WAMBLE FLUTTER
SHUDDER TREMBLE
  (PREF.) PALLO

QUAKER ASPEN HERON FRIEND
OBADIAH WHACKER HICKSITE
TREMBLER BEACONITE
BROADBRIM SHADBELLY
  (— STATE) PENNA PENNSYLVANIA
QUAKER GRAY ACIER
QUAKING ASPEN QUAKY TREPID
SHAKING TREMBLING
QUAKING GRASS BRIZA
COWQUAKE WAGWANTS
QUALIFICATION NATURE RESERVE
SHADING CAPACITY
QUALIFIED FIT ABLE MEET FITTED
FITTEN LIKELY PASSED CAPABLE
ELIGIBLE SUITABLE AUTHENTIC
  (DULY —) REGULAR
  (NOT —) INAPT INHABILE
QUALIFIER MODIFIER
QUALIFY FIT DASH ADAPT ALLAY
ALLOY EQUIP HEDGE ENABLE
MODIFY SOFTEN TEMPER
ABSOLVE CERTIFY ENTITLE
LICENSE PREPARE GRADUATE
MODERATE RESTRAIN RESTRICT
QUALITIES
  (SUFF.) ERY ICS
QUALITY Y BRAN BUMP CHOP COST
FEEL GUNA LEAD SORT COLOR
GRACE STATE TRAIT ASSIZE
BARREL FABRIC STRAIN THREAD
TIMBER TIMBRE ADJUNCT CALIBER
KINSHIP STATURE ACCIDENT
MOVEMENT PROPERTY
TONEBRAND
  (— OF MIND) CALIBER CALIBRE
  (— OF PERSONAL EMOTIONS)
PATHOS
  (— OF PHOTOGRAPH) CONTRAST
  (— OF SOUND) TONE
  (— OF TONE) TIMBRE
  (— OF VOWELS) LENGTH
  (— PECULIAR TO ONESELF) SEITY
  (AESTHETIC —) TASTE
  (ARTISTIC —) VIRTU
  (ATTRACTIVE —) TAKE
  (BASIC —) GRAIN
  (BASIC —S) STUFF
  (CHARACTERISTIC —) TURN
  (CHIEF —) SPIRIT
  (COLOR —) TONE
  (ESSENTIAL —) ALLOY SPECIES
SUCHNESS
  (GOOD —) THEW
  (HEREDITARY —) STRAIN
  (IMPECCABLE —) FINISH
  (IMPLICIT —) OVERTONE
  (INCISIVE —) BITE
  (INNATE —) LARGESS
  (INTELLECTUAL —) BROW
  (MELODRAMATIC —) SENSATION
  (MORAL —) THEW
  (NATURAL —) TARAGE
  (OBJECTIONABLE —) ANILITY

  (OF HIGH —) FRANK
  (OF HIGHEST —) PRIMO
  (OF LOW —) SHLOCK SCHLOCK
  (OF POOR —) GROTTY
  (PERVASIVE —) AROMA
  (PHYSICAL —S) BOTTOM
  (POSITIVE —) PLUS
  (PRIMAL —) GUNA
  (PUNGENT —) SNAP
  (RELATIVE —) RATE
  (SECONDARY —) OVERTONE
  (SPATIAL —) MAGNITUDE
  (SPRINGY —) SPINE
  (STRUCTURAL —) TEXTURE
  (SUBDUED —) SHADE
  (SUBTLE —) BOUQUET
  (SUPERIOR —) SUPER FINENESS
  (TRIED —) TOUCH
  (UNESSENTIAL —) ACCIDENT
  (UNUSUAL —) SURD
  (USEFUL —) ASSET
  (WAVY — OF HAIR) FLIX
  (SUFF.) ACITY ANCE ANCY CY ENCE
ENCY HEAD HOOD ICE ICITY ILITY
ITY MENT NESS SHIP TY
  (— THAT FILLS) FUL FULL
  (CHARACTERIZED BY —) SOME
QUALITY STREET (AUTHOR OF —)
BARRIE
  (CHARACTER IN —) BROWN LIVVY
PATTY SUSAN BLADES PHOEBE
THROSSEL VALENTINE
QUALM CALM DROW PALL NAUSEA
SQUEAM SCRUPLE
QUALMISH TEWLY SICKISH
SQUEAMISH
QUAMOCLIT MOONFLOWER
QUANDARY FIX PUXY PUZZLE
TANGLE DILEMMA NONPLUS
SWITHER DOLDRUMS JUNCTURE
QUANDONG PEACH
QUANT RYPECK
QUANTIC NONIC OCTIC SEPTIC
SEXTIC QUADRIC QUINTIC
QUANTIFIER PREFIX
QUANTITATIVE METRIC
QUANTITY BAG JAG SUM SUP
BODY DEAL DISH DOSE FECK JAGG
LIFT MASK SOME SOUD WARE
BATCH BREAK CLASH GRIST KITTY
SIEGE TROOP WHEEN ACTION
ADDEND AMOUNT BAGFUL BOTTLE
BUDGET DICKER EFFECT FOTHER
HANTLE NUMBER PARCEL SCALAR
SPINOR THRAVE VOLUME
CONTENT FOOTAGE PORTION
QUANTUM GLASSFUL KNIFEFUL
LADLEFUL PARAMETER
  (— OF ARROWS) SHEAF
  (— OF BUTTER) CHURNING
  (— OF CLOTHES) BUCKING
  (— OF COTTONSEED) CRUSH
  (— OF CUT TREES) FALL

  (— OF DRINK) HOOP DRAFT
DRAUGHT
  (— OF ELECTRICITY) FARADAY
  (— OF EXPLOSIVE) CHARGE
  (— OF FISH OR GAME) TAKE CATCH
DRAFT DRAUGHT
  (— OF GRAIN) GAVEL
  (— OF HAY) LOCK TRUSS
  (— OF IRRIGATION WATER) DUTY
  (— OF LAND) PLOUGHGATE
  (— OF LIQUID) DROP JAUP SLASH
GOBBET JABBLE
  (— OF LIQUOR) HEELTAP
  (— OF LUMBER) RUN
  (— OF MEAL) MELDER
  (— OF METAL) BLOW
  (— OF MUD) CLASH
  (— OF NARCOTICS) BINDLE
  (— OF PAPER) TOKEN
  (— OF PRODUCE) BURY
  (— OF RAISINS) FRAIL
  (— OF THREAD) LEASE
  (— OF WOOD) HAG FATHOM
  (— PRODUCED) OUTPUT
  (DIRECTED —) VECTOR
  (EQUAL —) PART
  (ESTIMATED —) WEY
  (EXCESSIVE —) GLUT SPATE
  (FIXED —) CONSTANT
  (GREAT —) HOST MORT MUCH RAFT
HIRST SHOAL SIGHT STORE BARREL
FOREST SLATHER CHUMELLA
  (INCREASED —) SPATE SPEAT
  (IRRATIONAL —) SURD
  (LARGE —) ACRE BOLT DEAL FECK
HEAP MASS PECK SCAD SLEW
FLOOD FORCE GRIST JORUM
POWER SCADS SHEAF STACK STORE
BUCKET BUSHEL DICKER DOLLOP
GALLON MATTER MELDER CLUTHER
SKINFUL HECATOMB MOUNTAIN
PLURALITY
  (LEAST —) BEDROCK
  (MINUTE —) DRAM DROP SHADE
SCRUPLE PARTICLE
  (NOTEWORTHY —) CHUNK
  (REGULATED —) QUOTA
  (RELATIVE —) DEGREE
  (SETTLED —) SIZE
  (SIZABLE —) SCUMP
  (SLIGHT —) SUSPICION
  (SMALL —) ACE BIT SUP TOT CURN
DASH DUST HAET HAIR HARL IOTA
PEAK SOSH SPOT CANCH PRILL
SMACK SPICE SQUIB TOUCH TRACE
JOBBLE MORSEL PICKLE SAMPLE
SONGLE STIVER CAPSULE CURTSEY
DRIBBLE DRIBLET EPSILON
HANDFUL MODICUM SMICKET
SPATTER TODDICK FARTHING
MOUTHFUL PENNORTH SCANTLET
SPRINKLE PENNYWORTH
SPRINKLING THIMBLEFUL

(UNDIRECTED —) SCALAR
(UNLIMITED —) OCEAN
(VARYING —) SKID
(ZERO —) NOTHING
(SUFF.) **(— THAT FILLS)** FUL FULL SKID
QUANTUM MAGNON PHONON PHOTON ISOSPIN
(— OF ENERGY) PLASMON
QUAPAW KWAPA ARKANSAS
QUARANTINE DETAIN ISOLATE SANCTION
QUARENTENE ROOD FURLONG
QUARK PARTICLE
(PARTICLE TO BIND —S) GLUON
(PROPERTY OF —S) FLAVOR
QUARREL JAR ROW WAP YED BEEF CHIP DEAL FEUD FRAY FUSS JARL JOWL MIFF NIFF ODDS PICK PLEA SPAT TIFF WHID BRACK BRAWL BRIGE BROIL FLITE FLUSK GRUFF HURRY JOWER NOISE PIQUE RUNIN SCOLD SCRAP SHINE STOUR UPSET WRALL AFFRAY BARNEY BLOWUP BREACH BREEZE BRIGUE DEBATE DIFFER DUSTUP FRACAS FRATCH GARROT JANGLE MATTER QUARRY RIPPET SQUARE SOUFAL STRIFE THREAP THREEP THWART BRABBLE BRATTLE DISGUST DISPUTE FACTION OUTCAST PRABBLE RUCTION SIMULTY STASHIE SWAGGER TUILZIE WRANGLE DISAGREE MOORBURN SCRAFFLE SPLUTTER SQUABBLE TRAVERSE
(— IN WORDS) JANGLE
(NOISY —) ROW FRACAS KICKUP
(PETTY —) MIFF SPAT TIFF
QUARRELING BICKER CONTEK CHIDING CONTECK
QUARRELSOME RIXY UGLY ROWTY FEISTY CURRISH SCRAPPY DRAWLING FRAMPOLD FRATCHED PETULANT PHRAMPEL BELLICOSE BUMPTIOUS FRACTIOUS LITIGIOUS CONTENTIOUS
(NOT —) AMICABLE
QUARRELSOMENESS SQUARING WARIANCE
QUARRIED (NOT —) LIVE
(PREF.) ORYCTO
QUARRIER FACEMAN QUARION
QUARRY PIT DELF GAME LODE MEAT CHASE DELFT DELPH PLUCK LATOMY REWARD LATOMIA LOZENGE
(HAWK'S —) MARK
QUARRYMAN SCABBLER SCAPPLER
QUART SHANT WHART
(METRIC —) LITER
(ONE-HALF —) PINT
(TWO —S) MAGNUM
(1-8TH —) GILL
(2 —S) FLAGON
(4 —S) GALLON
QUARTE FOURTH
QUARTER AIRT PART STUD EAVER GRITH TRACT BARRIO BEHALF BESTOW CANTON COLONY FARDEL HARBOR SECTOR TWOBITS CONTRADA FAUBOURG FIERDING STANDARD POBLACION
(— IN BATTLE) GRITH
(— OF A POUND) TRIPPET
(— OF BEEF OR MUTTON) BOUT
(— OF CITY) BLOCK GHETTO
(— OF COMPASS) PLAGE
(— OF FLAG) CANTON
(— OF HOUR) POINT
(— OF HUNDRED) FIERDING
(— OF YEAR) RAITH
(— ONESELF) SORN
(— UPON) LAY
(JEWISH —) ALJAMA
(NATIVE —) MEDINA
QUARTERBACK BOSS
QUARTERING LASKING CHUMMAGE
QUARTER NOTE CROTCHET
QUARTER REST SOSPIRO
QUARTERS BOTHY BILLET BOTHIE LIVERY MENAGE FARDELS CHUMMERY DIGGINGS LODGMENT
(— FOR IMMIGRANTS) HOSTEL
(— OF CREW) FOCSLE FORECASTLE
(— OF SALVATION ARMY) BARRACKS
(GENERAL'S —) PRINCIPIUM
(HIGH —) AERY EYRY AERIE EYRIE
(JUNIOR OFFICERS' —) GUNROOM
(LIVING —) PAD
(MEN'S —) SELAMLIK
(MONASTERY —) FRATRY
(RELIGIOUS —) NOVICIATE NOVITIATE
(TEMPORARY —) CAMP CANTONMENT
(WINTER —) HIBERNACLE
(WOMEN'S —) HAREM SERAGLIO GYNAECEUM
QUARTET FOURSOME
QUARTILE SQUARE TETRAGON
QUARTO FOURS
QUARTZ IRIS ONYX SARD AGATE CHERT FLINT PRASE TARSO TOPAZ JASPER MORION PEBBLE PLASMA SILICA ALENCON CITRINE CRYSTAL RUBASSE SINOPLE AMETHYST BASANITE SARDONYX SIDERITE YENTNITE BUHRSTONE BURRSTONE
QUARTZITE GANISTER SILCRETE
QUASH CASS CRUSH QUELL SPIKE SQUAT SOPITE CASSARE PEREMPT SUPPRESS
QUASI
(PREF.) SEMI
QUASI-ATOM MUONIUM
QUAT FOUR GLUT SQUASH SATIATE UPSTART
QUATERNION TETRAD QUADRATE
QUATREFOIL TRESSURE
(DOUBLE —) EIGHTFOIL
QUAVER QUAP CROMA SHAKE TRILL WAVER CHROMA FALTER QUIVER WABBLE WOBBLE WRIBLE FREDDON VIBRATE
QUAVERY WARBLY UNSTEADY
QUAY KEY POW QUAI LEVEE BUNDER STRAND
QUEACH BOG FEN MARSH THICKET
QUEASINESS KECK SICKNESS

QUEASY NICE SICK SQUEEZY DELICATE NAUSEATED SQUEAMISH
QUEBEC (LAKE OF —) MINTO BIENVILLE MISTASSINI
(TOWN OF —) AMOS HULL AMQUI LAVAL MAGOG PERCE BASSIN VERDUN JOLIETTE MONTREAL LAPRAIRIE
QUEBRACHO BREAKAX AXMASTER IRONWOOD AXBREAKER
QUEBRADA BROOK GULLY RAVINE FISSURE
QUECHUA INCAN KICHUA
QUEEN ENA REG DAME FERS LADY MEDB RANI AEDON BEGUM FIERS RANEE ATOSSA REGINA ROXANA TAILTE TAMARA ARGANTE ATHALIA CANDACE JOCASTE OMPHALE PHEARSE STATIRA TITANIA BRUNHILD GERTRUDE GLORIANA GUINEVER MAHARANI
(— AND KING OF TRUMPS) BELLA
(— CITY) CINCINNATI
(— IN CHESS) FERS LADY FIERS
(— OF CLUBS) SPADILLA
(— OF DENMARK) GERTRUDE
(— OF EGYPTIAN GODS) SATI
(— OF ETHIOPIA) CANDACE
(— OF FAIRY LAND) MEDB GLORIANA
(— OF GEORGIA) TAMARA
(— OF GOTHS) TAMORA
(— OF HEARTS) ELIZABETH
(— OF HEAVEN) HERA
(— OF JUDAH) ATHALIA
(— OF LYDIA) OMPHALE
(— OF SHEBA) BALKIS BILKIS
(— OF SPADES) BASTA LIZZY
(— OF THE ADRIATIC) VENICE
(— OF THE ANTILLES) CUBA
(— OF THEBES) JOCASTA
(— OF THE EAST) ZENOBIA
(— OF THE MAY) MAYLADY MAYQUEEN
(— OF TRUMPS) HONOR
(FAIRY —) MAB ARGANTE TITANIA
(FORMER SPANISH —) ENA
(INDIAN —) RANI SUNK MAHARANI
(MOHAMMEDAN —) BEGUM
(NEIGHBOR OF —) KING BISHOP
QUEEN ANNE'S LACE UMBEL
QUEEN BEE KING
QUEEN ELIZABETH DIANA ORIANA CYNTHIA
QUEENFISH WAHOO CROAKER DRUMFISH
QUEENLY HAUGHTY REGINAL MAJESTIC
QUEENROOT YAWSHRUB
QUEEN'S-DELIGHT YAWSHRUB
QUEENSLAND HEMP SIDA JELLYLEAF
QUEER HEX ODD RUM HARM DICKY DIPPY DROLL FAINT FUNNY GIDDY NUTTY RUMMY COCKLE FIFISH HIPPED QUEASY QUISBY UNIQUE AMUSING COMICAL CURIOUS DISRUPT ERRATIC STRANGE TOUCHED WHIMSIC FANCIFUL OBSESSED PECULIAR
(— THING) QUOZ
QUEERNESS ODDITY

QUEEST RINGDOVE
QUELL DIE CALM FLOW HUSH KILL QUAY SLAY ABATE ALLAY CRUSH QUASH QUIET YIELD PACIFY PERISH REDUCE SOOTHE SPRING STANCH STIFLE KILLING REPRESS SQUELCH SUPPRESS
QUEME QUIM HANDY WHEAM COMELY PLEASE GRATIFY PLEASANT
QUENCH COOL DAMP SIND ALLAY CHECK CRUSH SLAKE SLOCK STILL STANCH STIFLE ASSUAGE SLOCKEN AUSTEMPER
QUENCHED EXTINCT
QUENCHER STANCH
QUENCHING FRITTING
QUENTIN DURWARD (AUTHOR OF —) SCOTT
(CHARACTER IN —) CARL CROYE LOUIS LESLEY PHILIP PIERRE TOISON BALAFRE CHARLES DURWARD EBERSON HERMITE LAMARCK LUDOVIC QUENTIN TRISTAN WILLIAM CRAWFORD HAMELINE ISABELLE HAYRADDIN JAQUELINE MAUGRABIN CREVECOEUR
QUERCINE OAKEN
QUERECHO VAQUERO
QUERELA AUDITA
QUERENT INQUIRER PLAINTIFF
QUERN KERN MILL METATE MILLSTONE
QUERULOUS WHINY FRETFUL PEEVISH NATTERED PETULANT IRRITABLE
QUERY ASK DOUBT DEMAND INQUIRE INQUIRY QUESTION
QUEST ASK BAY GAPE SEEK DEMAND EXAMINE PURSUIT SEEKING VENTURE
QUESTING OUTREACH
QUESTION ASK HOW SPY POSE QUIZ TALK ARGUE DOUBT DREAD QUERY ACCUSE CHANCE CHARGE DEMAND LEADER MATTER PONDER QUAERE REASON SHRIVE EXAMINE INQUIRE INQUIRY PROBLEM PURPOSE SCRUPLE OVERTURE RELEVANT RESEARCH STICKLER CATECHISE
(— AMBIGUOUSLY WORDED) RIDDLE
(— FRETFULLY) RAME
(BAFFLING —) POSER
(BUDDHIST —) KOAN
(CAPTIOUS —) QUIDDIT QUIDDITY
(DIFFICULT —) POSER
(PERPLEXING —) STUMPER
(RHETORICAL —) EROTEMA EROTESIS
(UNSOLVED —) CRUX
(ZEN —) KOAN
QUESTIONABLE FISHY QUEER SHAKY UNSAFE BATABLE CLOUDED DUBIOUS DOUBTFUL PROBLEMATIC
(NOT —) DECENT
QUESTIONER APPOSER INQUIRER
QUESTIONING DUBIOUS QUIZZICAL
QUESTION MARK QUERY QUAERE EROTEME

QUESTIONNAIRE POLL INVENTORY
QUETCH STIR TWITCH
QUETZAL QUESAL TROGON
QUEUE CUE COLA LINE BRAID
PIGTAIL CROCODILE
QUEY KOY WHY WHEY HEIFER
QUIBBLE COG PUN BALK CARP QUIB
QUIP CAVIL DODGE EVADE QUIRK
SALVO AMBAGE BAFFLE BICKER
HAFFLE PALTER SNATCH BRABBLE
CAPTION CHICANE QUIBLET
QUIDDIT QUILLET SHUFFLE
PETTIFOG QUIDDITY QUILLITY
SCRAFFLE CONUNDRUM
PREVARICATE
QUIBBLING CHICANERY
QUICA OPOSSUM SARIGUE
QUICK APT RAD YAP FAST FLIT GLEG
KECK KEEN LISH LIST PERT RATH
RIFE SNAP SOON WHAT WHIT
WICK YARE AGILE ALIVE APACE
BRISK CHEAP FLEET HASTY MERRY
NIFTY NIPPY PREST RAPID READY
SHARP SHORT SNACK SNELL
SWIFT SWITH TOSTO TRICK VISTO
YARRY ACTIVE CLEVER FACILE
KITTLE NIMBLE PROMPT PRONTO
SNAPPY SPEEDY SUDDEN DARTING
SCHNELL SHUTTLE DEXTROUS
TRIPPING CITIGRADE
(— AND NEAT) DEFT
(— AS A FLASH) WHIP
(— IN PERCEPTION) ACID
(— IN RESPONSE) GNIB
(— OF MIND) INTELLIGENT
(— TO DETECT) SMOKY
(— TO FLARE UP) GASSY
(— TO LEARN) APT
(— TO MOVE) YARE
(LIGHT AND —) VOLANT
(PREF.) OXY TACHEO TACHISTO
TACHO TACHY
QUICKEN PEP MEND STIR WHET
HURRY SPEED ACUATE AROUSE
HASTEN INCITE KINDLE REVIVE
VIVIFY ANIMATE ENLIVEN
PROVOKE REFRESH SHARPEN
EXPEDITE INSPIRIT
ACCELERATE
QUICKENING FLICKER REVIVAL
STIRRING
QUICKLY TID TIT ASAP CITO FAST
RIFE SOON TIVY WHIP YARE APACE
NEWLY RADLY RATHE SHARP
SKELP SNACK SNELL SWITH TIGHT
WIGHT YEPLY ASTITE BELIVE
HOURLY PRESTO PRONTO RASHLY
EFTSOON PRESTLY READILY
SPEEDILY WIKIWIKI
(— AND WITH FORCE) SWAP
(MORE —) TIDDER TITTER STRETTO
QUICKNESS HASTE SPEED ACUMEN
AGILITY SMEDDUM ACTIVITY

CELERITY DISPATCH KEENNESS
SAGACITY
(— OF DECISION) PROMPTITUDE
(MENTAL —) NOUS SLEIGHT
LEGERITY
QUICKSAND FLOW SYRT SYRTIS
SWALLOW
QUICK-SELLING LEEFTAIL
QUICKSILVER OREMIX MERCURY
TIERRAS HEAUTARIT
QUICK-SPEAKING PROMPT
QUICK-TEMPERED DONCY DONSY
PEPPERY IRASCIBLE
QUICK-WITTED APT SHARP SMART
NIMBLE KNOWING
QUID FID CHAW CHEW SOVEREIGN
(— OF TOBACCO) CUD FID
QUIDDANY JELLY SYRUP CODINIAC
QUIDDITY QUIBBLE WHATNESS
QUIDNUNC GOSSIP BUSYBODY
QUIESCENCE KAIF REPOSE STASIS
DORMANCY
QUIESCENT QUIET LATENT STATIC
DORMANT RESTING INACTIVE
QUIET QT ST COY LAY CALM COSH
DEAD DUMB EASE EASY HUSH
LOUN LOWN LULL REST ROCK
SNUG SOFT WEME ACCOY CANNY
CIVIL DOWNY LEVEL PEACE PEASE
QUATE QUELL QUEME RESTY
SALVE SHADY SHUSH SILKY SLEEP
SOBER SQUAT STILL SUANT WHIST
DREAMY GENTLE PACIFY PLACID
RETIRE SAUGHT SEDATE SERENE
SETTLE SILENT SMOOTH SOFTLY
SOOTHE SOPITE STEADY STILLY
HUSHFUL ORDERLY REQUIEM
RESTFUL SILENCE COMPOSED
DECOROUS PEACEFUL TRANQUIL
UNRUFFLE
(— DOWN) DILL
(BE —) SSH
(MAKE —) ALLAY
(STEALTHILY —) SLINKY
QUIETEN SEDATE SOPITE SUBDUE
QUIETISM MOLINISM
QUIETLY LOW FAIR CANNY STILL
WINLY EVENLY GENTLY SOFTLY
TIPTOE
QUIETNESS REST REPOSE
SERENITY
QUIETUDE CALM INERTION
QUIETUS REST DEATH RELEASE
QUILL COP PEN RIB PIRN FLOAT
STALK BOBBIN FESCUE PINION
SLEEVE BRISTLE CALAMUS
PRIMARY TRUNDLE
(— FOR WINDING THREAD) COP
(— OF FEATHER) BARREL
(PORCUPINE —) PEN
QUILLBACK SAILFISH SKIMBACK
QUILLWORT ISOETES FERNWORT
QUILT BEAT GULP WALT WELT WHIP

DUVET REZAI CADDOW CHALON
PALLET THRASH SWALLOW
MATTRESS POULTICE COMFORTER
QUILTING MARCELLA
QUIMPER NICE
QUINCE SKEG COYNE ANGERS
SQUINCH JAPONICA
(BENGAL —) BEL BAEL BALE BHEL
QUINCE SEED CYDONIUM
QUININE KINA SPECIFIC
(PREF.) CHIN(O)
QUINK BRANT
QUINONE EMBELIN
QUINSY ANGINA PRUNELLA
QUINTAIN FAN
QUINTE FIFTH
QUINTESSENCE CREAM ELIXIR
CLYSSUS OSMAZOME
QUINTILLION
(PREF.) EXA NEBU
QUINTILLIONTH
(PREF.) ATTO
QUINTUPLE QUINARY FIVEFOLD
QUINIBLE
QUIP GIBE JAPE JEST JOKE CRACK
QUIRK SALLY SCOFF TAUNT
RETORT CONCEIT QUIBBLE
QUIRA CAOBA ROBLE HORMIGO
VENCOLA MACAWOOD
QUIRE CHOR SEXTERN
(20 —S) REAM
(PL.) INSIDES
QUIRK BEND KINK QUIP TURN
CLOCK CROOK TWIST CONCEIT
QUIBBLE FLOURISH PAROXYSM
MANNERISM PECULIARITY
(— OF BEHAVIOR) TIC
QUIRKY ZANY CRAZY DIPPY DOTTY
KINKY
QUIRQUINCHO PICHI PELUDO
QUIRT WHIP ROMAL
QUIS WOODCOCK
QUISLING APOSTATE
QUIT GO DROP NASH PART QUAT
AVOID BELAY CEASE DOUSE LEAVE
SHIFT SHOOT STASH WHITE
BEHAVE CIVITE DESERT DESIST
FOREGO RESIGN SECEDE VACATE
ABANDON FORSAKE RELEASE
UNTENANT
QUITCH COUCH QUICK SCUTCH
TWITCH
QUITCLAIM DEED ACQUIT RELEASE
DISCHARGE
QUITE SO ALL BUT GEY BRAW EVEN
FAIR FREE FULL JUST PLAT WELL
CLEAR CLOSE FULLY SHEER STARK
CLEVER DAMNED ENOUGH JUSTLY
MERELY TOTALLY PERFECTLY
(NOT —) HARDLY
(PREF.) DE
QUITERIA (HUSBAND OF —)
CAMACHO

QUITRENT CANON
QUITS EVEN EVENS UPSIDES
QUITTER PUS SLAG PIKER COWARD
JUMPER SHIRKER TURNBACK
QUIVER DIRL QUAG QUOG BEVER
NIDGE QUAKE SHAKE TRILL WAVER
WIVER BICKER COCKER DIDDER
DINDLE SHEATH SHIMMY SHIVER
TREMOR WAMBLE DORLACH
FLUTTER FRISSON SHUDDER
TREMBLE TWIDDLE TWINKLE
TWITTER VIBRATE FLICHTER
WERSLETE
(PREF.) PALLO
QUIVERING ASPEN AGUISH DIDDER
DITHER QUAGGLE QUAKING
AGITATED ATREMBLE
QUIVER TREE KOKERBOOM
QUIXOTIC ERRANT IMAGINARY
VISIONARY
QUIZ ASK GUY EXAM HOAX MOCK
CHAFF QUEER EXAMINE QUESTION
RIDICULE
QUIZZICAL ODD QUEER QUIZZY
CURIOUS WHIMSICAL
QUO KA
QUOD JAIL QUAD PRISON
QUOIN COIN ANGLE GOIGN CORNER
LOZENGE KEYSTONE VOUSSOIR
QUOIT CIST DISC DISH DISK LINER
DISCUS HOBBER CROMLECH
QUOMODO HOW WAY MEANS
MANNER
QUONDAM OLD ONCE WHILE
FORMER ONETIME SOMETIME
QUORATEAN KAROK
QUORUM CORAM HOUSE MINYAN
MAJORITY
QUOTA PART BOGEY SHARE
QUOTIENT PROPORTION
QUOTATION TAG PRICE QUOTE
EXTRACT SNIPPET EPIGRAPH
(— DEVELOPED INTO ESSAY) CHRIA
(TRITE —) TAG
QUOTATION MARK GUILLEMET
QUOTE CITE COAT COTE MARK
NAME NOTE ADDUCE ALLEGE
RECITE REPEAT EXCERPT EXTRACT
OBSERVE REHEARSE
(— SARCASTICALLY) FLOUT
QUOTH CO KO CUTH QUAD QUOD
SAID SPOKE UTTERED
QUOTIDIAN DAILY TRIVIAL
ORDINARY
QUOTIENT QUOTE FRACTION
MILLESIMAL
QUO VADIS (AUTHOR OF —)
SIENKIEWICZ
(CHARACTER IN —) ACTE NERO
PAUL CHILO LYGIA PETER URSUS
CROTON EUNICE GLAUCUS VINICIUS
PETRONIUS TIGELLINUS
QUTB POLE

R

R AR ROGER ROMEO
  (UVULAR —) BURR
RA RE RAE SHU TEM ATMU BACIS
  HORUS MENTU KHEPERA SOKARIS
RAAMAH (FATHER OF —) CUSH
  (SON OF —) DEDAN SHEBA
RABBAN MASTER TEACHER
RABBET CHECK GROOVE
  BACKJOINT FILLISTER
RABBI TANA AMORA CACAM HAKAM
  TANNA MASTER SABORA
  KHAKHAM TEACHER GAMALIEL
  SABORAIM
  (PL.) AMORAIM TANNAIM
RABBIT BUN REX TAN BUNT CONY
  JACK POLE RACK BUNNY CAPON
  CREAM CUNNY DUTCH FRIER
  LAPIN ANGORA ASTREX CONEEN
  HAVANA OARLOP PARKER POLISH
  SILVER TAPETI WOOLER BEVEREN
  CONYNGE FLEMISH LEPORID
  SNOWSHOE WARRENER
  (— BURROW) CLAPPER
  (— FUR) CONY SCUT CONEY FLICK
  LAPIN FLITCH
  (— MEAT) LAPAN
  (— SKIN) RACK
  (— TAIL) SCUT
  (— WARREN) CONYGER
  (CASTRATED —) CAPON
  (FEMALE —) DOE
  (MALE —) BUCK
  (RELATIVE —) PIKA
  (YOUNG —) KITTEN
  (PL.) FLICK WARREN
RABBITFISH SPINY
RABBLE MOB TAG GING HERD RAFF
  ROUT SCUM FRAPE SCAFF SCUFF
  TRASH MEINIE RADDLE RAFFLE
  RAGTAG RASCAL TAGRAG
  DOGGERY PUDDLER RABBLER
  RANGALE TRAFFIC BRAGGERY
  CANAILLE RAGABASH RIFFRAFF
  VARLETRY RASCALITY
  CLAMJAMFRY
  (DISORDERLY —) HERD
RABBLE-ROUSER FIREBRAND
  DEMAGOG
RABID MAD RAGING FRANTIC
  FURIOUS RABIOUS RABITIC
  FRENZIED RAVENING VIRULENT
RABIES LYSSA MADNESS PIBLOKTO
  RAVENING
  (PREF.) LYSSO RABI
RACCOON COON COATI GUARA
  TEJON AGUARA MAPACH OLINGO
  WASHER AGOUARA ARCTOID
  RATTOON RINGTAIL CRABEATER
  (ANIMAL LIKE A —) OLINGO
  (HIMALAYAN —) PANDA
RACCOON DOG TANUKI
RACE CAP CUP LOG ROD RUN BENT
  CONE DASH DRAG GEST HUMP

KIND LINE NAME RAIS RAZE RING
RINK TEAM TRAM BLOOD BREED
BROOD BRUSH CASTE CHEVY
CORSO DERBY FLESH HOUSE
ISSUE PLATE PURSE RATCH REACH
ROUTE SPEED STAKE STAMM
STIRP STOCK BROOSE CHEVVY
COURSE FAMILY NATION PEOPLE
PHYLON RUNOFF SPRING STIRPS
STRAIN STRIND BIOTYPE CENTURY
CLAIMER CLASSIC HACKNEY
HUNDRED KINDRED LINEAGE
MATINEE NURSERY PROGENY
PROSAPY RACEWAY REGATTA
STADIUM FUTURITY HANDICAP
MARATHON WALKOVER
MOTOCROSS OFFSPRING
ORIENTEERING
  (— A HORSE) CAMPAIGN
  (— AT WEDDING) BROOSE BROUZE
  (— FOR BALL-BEARINGS) CONE
  (— OF BARLEY) BENT
  (— OF GODS) VANIR
  (— OF PEOPLE) VANS AMALS VANIR
  HAZARA SAKAIS YADAVA BAMBUTE
  FIRBOLG GIANTRY NISHADA
  RASENNA REPHAIM AMALINGS
  (— OF UNDERGROUND ELVES)
  DROW
  (— OF WINDMILL) CURB
  (FINAL —) RUNOFF NIGHTCAP
  (HORSE —) AGON DERBY PLATE
  SPRINT MATINEE FUTURITY
  WALKOVER
  (HUMAN —) MAN MANKIND
  SPECIES MORTALITY
  (IMPROMPTU —) BRUSH
  (JUMPING —) SCURRY
  (LENTEN —S) TORPIDS
  (LONG —) ENDURO
  (MILL —) LADE
  (MOTORCYCLE —) SCRAMBLE
  MOTOCROSS
  (PRELIMINARY —) HEAT
  (ROWING —) SCULLS REGATTA
  (RUNNING —) MILE RELAY SPRINT
  HUNDRED HURDLES
  (SHORT —) BICKER
  (SHORT-DISTANCE —) DASH
  SCURRY SPRINT
  (SKI —) SLALOM DAUERLAUF
  (TIDAL —) ROOST
  (PL.) FOURS
  (PREF.) ETHN(O) GEN(O) PHYL(O)
RACECOURSE LIST OVAL PIST RING
  TURF EPSOM CAREER CIRCUS
  CURSUS DROMOS STADIE
  STRETCH GYMKHANA SPEEDWAY
  (PREF.) DROM(O)
  (SUFF.) DROME
RACEHORSE DOG PONY PACER
  RACER CHASER SLEEPER TROTTER
  BANGTAIL

  (— THAT HAS NEVER WON)
  MAIDEN
  (INFERIOR —) PLATER HAYBURNER
  (2-YEAR OLD —) JUVENILE
  (PL.) RUCK
RACEME STRIG PANICLE
RACEMOSE BOTRYOSE
RACER CRACK SNAKE RUNNER
  BICYCLIST CINDERMAN
RACETRACK OVAL DROMOS
  FURLONG AUTODROME
  (— INFORMANT) SPIV TOUT TIPSTER
RACEWAY CANAL TRACK GROOVE
  CHANNEL FISHWAY
RACHEL POWDER
  (FATHER OF —) LABAN
  (HUSBAND OF —) JACOB
  (SISTER OF —) LEAH
  (SON OF —) JOSEPH BENJAMIN
RACHIS SPINE SPINDLE
  (— OF HOP STROBILE) STRIG
RACHITIS RICKETS
RACIAL GENTILE GENTILIC PHYLETIC
RACING (— BET) WIN SHOW PLACE
  DOUBLE EXACTA PARLAY TRIPLE
  PERFECTA QUINELLA TRIFECTA
  (AUTO — PROBLEM) SPINOUT
  (HORSE —) TURF
  (MOTORCYCLE —) MOTOCROSS
RACIST COLOR
RACK GIN RAK RAT TUB BINK BUCK
  CASE HACK HECK SHOG TACK
  AMBLE BRAKE DRIER DRYER
  FLAKE FRAME POKER THROW
  TOUSE TRAIN WRACK WRECK
  WRING CIRCLE CRATCH CUDGEL
  ENGINE NIPPER PULLEY TREBLE
  WRENCH AFFLICT AGONIZE
  PENRACK POTTARO TORMENT
  TORTURE BARBECUE EQUULEUS
  PINEBANK SAWHORSE
  (— ATTACHED TO WAGON)
  SHELVING OUTRIGGER
  (— FOR BARRELS) JIB
  (— FOR CHINAWARE) FIDDLE
  (— FOR DISHES) BINK
  (— FOR FEEDING) HACK HAYRACK
  (— FOR FODDER) HECK CRATCH
  (— FOR PLATES) CREEL
  (— FOR STORAGE) FLAKE
  (— IN THRESHER) SHAKER
  (DRYING —) CRIB TREBLE
  (PLATE —) BINK
  (WOODEN —) BUCAN
RACKED WRUNG TORTURED
RACKET BAT DIN GAME RORT
  BANDY MUSIC RAZOO CLAMOR
  CROSSE DRIVER HUBBUB HUSTLE
  RAQUET RATTLE BUSINESS
  REVELING STRAMASH
  (PART OF —) CAP BUTT CORD GRIP
  HEAD HEEL TAPE YOKE CROWN
  FLAKE SHAFT HANDLE PALLET

STRING THROAT BINDING
SHOULDER THROATPIECE
  (TENNIS —) SCUFE
RACKETEER HOOD HUSTLER
  GANGSTER
RACKETT CERVALET CERVELAT
RACKING FIERCE
RACKMAN TOPMAN
RACON BEACON
RACONTEUR STORYTELLER
RACQUET CROSSE GAZELLE
RACY GAMY LEAN SEXY JUICY
  SALTY SMART SPICY LIVELY
  RISQUE PIQUANT PUNGENT
  ZESTFUL SPIRITED MERACIOUS
RAD COOL MARV EAGER MARVY
  QUICK READY AFRAID ELATED
  FAROUT WAYOUT RADICAL
RADAR (— BEACON) RACON
  (— NAVIGATION SYSTEM) LANAC
  (— RECEPTION) ECHO
  (— SYSTEM) OBOE
RADARSCOPE PPI HSCOPE
RADDAI (BROTHER OF —) DAVID
  (FATHER OF —) JESSE
RADDLE PIT BEAT SCAR RAVEL
  RUDDLE THRASH SEPARATOR
RADHA (FOSTER SON OF —) KARNA
  (HUSBAND OF —) ADHIRATHA
RADIAL RAY TIRE QUADRANT
  (PREF.) RADIO
RADIANCE RAY GLOW LEAM GLARE
  GLEAM GLINT GLORY LIGHT SHINE
  LUSTER AUREOLA GLITTER
  SPLENDOR
RADIANT BEAMY SHEEN SHINY
  ABLAZE BRIGHT GOLDEN LUCENT
  SHEENY AURORAL BEAMFUL
  BEAMING FULGENT LAMBENT
  GLORIOUS LUSTROUS RELUCENT
  SPLENDID BRILLIANT
  (— INTENSITY) J
  (PREF.) STILPNO
RADIATE RAY BEAM POUR SHED
  SHINE EFFUSE SPREAD EFFULGE
  EMANATE ACTINOID
RADIATED PENCILED STELLATE
RADIATING DIADROM
RADIATION AURA LIGHT INFRARED
  (— DOSAGE) REM REP REPP
  (— UNIT) LANGLEY
  (DEVICE TO GENERATE —) LASER
  (ELECTROMAGNETIC —) PUMP
  (SOURCE OF —) PULSAR
  (UNIT OF —) RAD REM
RADIATOR HEATER EMANATOR
  (— FLUID) COOLANT
  (SET OF —S) STACK
RADICAL KEY SURD BASAL CRAZY
  GROUP RADIX ROUGE ULTRA
  CAPRYL HEROIC CAPITAL CAPROYL
  DRASTIC EXTREME FORWARD
  HERETIC JACOBIN LEFTIST

LEVELER LIBERAL PRIMARY CARDINAL LOCOFOCO **(CHEMICAL —)** ACYL AMYL CARYL CETYL GROUP ACETYL ADENYL CAPRYL PHENYL PHYTYL HALOGEN LINALYL CARBAMYL QINNAMAL **(NOT —)** FORMATIVE DERIVATIVE **(SUFF.) (ACID —)** OYL **(BIVALENT —)** YLENE

RADICALISM EXTREMISM JACOBINISM

RADICCHIO CHICORY CHICKORY

RADICEL ROOTLET

RADICLE (— THAT DEVELOPS IN GRAIN) COME

RADIENT ORIENT

RADIO AIR SET WIRELESS **(— OPERATOR)** HAM DEEJAY SPARKS **(— PIONEER)** TESLA **(— PROGRAM)** TALKSHOW **(— SYSTEM)** TBS **(— WAVE EMITTER)** QUASAR

RADIOGRAM FLIMSY

RADIOGRAPH EXOGRAPH SKIAGRAM

RADIOISOTOPE TRACER

RADIO-WAVE (— EMITTER) PULSAR

RADISH RUNCH DAEKON DAIKON RIFART CADLOCK CRADLOCK CRUCIFER CROSSWEED

RADIUS RAYON SPOKE SWEEP THROW ADRADIUS

RADIX BASE ROOT ETYMON RADICLE

RADON NITON THORON ACTINON EXRADIO

RADULA RIBBON TONGUE

RAFF LOW IDLE SCUM SWEEP TRASH COMMON JUMBLE LUMBER RABBLE RAFFLE RAGTAG SNATCH RUBBISH

RAFFISH RAKISH TAWDRY RACKETY UNKEMPT

RAFFLE MOVE RAFF JUMBLE RABBLE REFUSE RUBBISH

RAFT COW CRIB MOKI BALSA BATCH FLOAT TABLE DINGEY DINGHY JANGAR MOKIHI PIPERY RADEAU JANGADA ZATTARE CATAMARAN **(— OF INVERTED POTS)** GHARNAO **(— OF LOGS)** BOOM CRIB **(— WITH CABIN)** COW **(BAMBOO —)** RAKIT **(FIRE —)** CATAMARAN **(LUMBER —)** BATCH

RAFT DOG RAKER

RAFTER HIP BALK BLAD FIRM SILE SOIL SPAR SPUR VIGA BAULK BLADE CABER RIDGE BOUGAR BULKER COUPLE CARLINE CHEVRON RAFFMAN SLEEPER **(— OF TURKEYS)** FLOCK

RAFTY RAW DAMP FUSTY MUSTY RANCID

RAG JAG LAP TAT HAZE HOAX JAGG SAIL ANNOY CLOUT PRANK SCOLD SCRAP SHRED SWIPER GIBBOL LIBBET RAGGLE TAGRAG TATTER FLITTER REMNANT TORMENT RAGSTONE STRAGGLE NEWSPAPER **(— GATHERER)** TATTER

(— USED AS CANDLE) SLUT **(CURLING —)** CRACKER **(FLAPPING —)** WALLOP **(GLAD —S)** GARB **(TARRED —)** HARDS **(TARRED —S)** HARDS HURDS **(PL.)** DUDS CADDIS FITTERS RAGGERY FLITTERS

RAGAMUFFIN MUFFLIN BEGGARLY SHABROON TITMOUSE

RAGAU (FATHER OF —) PHALEC

RAGBAG CATCHALL

RAGE GO AWE FAD RAG WAX BAIT BATE BEEF FARE FOAM FRET FUFF FUME FUNK FUNX FURY GLOW GRIM HEAT PELT RAMP RASE RESE TAVE TEAR WOOD ANGER BRETH CHAFE CRAZE FUROR PADDY STORM TEAVE TEVEL VOGUE WRATH FRENZY FURORE PELTER TYAUVE BLUSTER FASHION MADNESS PASSION RUFFIAN TEMPEST INSANITY WOODNESS PADDYWACK **(BE IN A —)** RANT

RAGFISH ICOSTEID

RAGGED DUDDY HARSH TATTY FRAYED JAGGED SCOURY UNEVEN SHAGRAG SHREDDY TATTERY SCRAGGLY SCRATCHY TATTERED

RAGGED ROBIN ROBIN CUCKOO

RAGGEE MAND RAGI MARUA MANDUA KORAKAN ELEUSINE

RAGGLE-TAGGLE MOTLEY

RAGING HOT GRIM WILD YOND RABID FIERCE FURIAL FERVENT MADDING PELTING VIOLENT FLAGRANT FURIBUND WRATHFUL

RAGOUT SALMI GOULASH HARICOT TERRINE SALPICON CHIPOLATA PULPATONE **(— OF GAME)** SALMI SALMIS

RAGPICKER BUNTER RAGMAN TATTER

RAGWEED HAYWEED HOGWEED AMBROSIA IRONWEED KINGHEAD KINGWEED RICHWEED FRANSERIA

RAGWORT CUSHAG JACOBY BENWEED CAMMOCK SEGGROM LIFEROOT

RAHAM (FATHER OF —) SHEMA **(SON OF —)** JORKOAM

RAID BUST RADE ROAD TALA FORAY HARRY PINCH REISE REIVE BODRAG CREACH FORAGE HARASS INROAD MOLEST PANYAR RAZZIA SORTIE BODRAGE BORDRAG CHAPPOW DESCENT JAYHAWK OUTFALL OUTRAKE OUTRIDE OUTROAD SPREATH COMMANDO SPOILING **(— ORCHARDS)** SCRUMP SKRIMP SKRUMP **(AIR —)** BLITZ **(BOMBING —)** PRANG **(CATTLE —)** SPREAGH SPREATH **(MAKE A — ON)** BUST **(WARLIKE —)** HERSHIP

RAIDER REDLEG BUSHWACK **(SEA —)** VIKING

RAIL BAN BAR BULL COOT GIRD JEST KOKO LIST MOHO RANT RAVE SKID SORA TRAM WEKA WING

CRAKE EASER FENCE GUARD PLATE RAVEL REILE SCOFF SCOLD SLENT STANG STANK STEEL SWEAR BANTER BEDWAY CALLET FENDER RUNNER SKITTY TIKLIN BIDCOCK BILCOCK COURLAN INVEIGH OARCOCK RACKWAY TOPRAIL BULLHEAD CANCELLI CORNBIRD PORTLAST TOADBACK VIGNOLES BRANDRETH BRANDRITH **(— AROUND A WELL)** BRANDRETH **(— AT)** JEST CURSE SCOFF RATTLE REVILE BETONGUE **(— OF BED)** STOCK **(— OF RAILWAY SWITCH)** TONGUE **(— ON GUN PLATFORM)** TRINGLE **(— ON HAY VEHICLE)** THRIPPLE **(— ON SHIP)** FIFE **(ALTAR —)** SEPTUM **(ARCHED —)** HOOPSTICK **(CHAIR —)** LEDGE **(FENCE —)** RIDER **(GROOVED —)** GULLY GULLEY **(PART OF —)** BED TIE FROG JOINT SPIKE BALLAST SLEEPER CROSSTIE BASEPLATE FISHPLATE **(SHUNTING —)** SWITCH **(PL.)** RAILING CANCELLI RAILROAD **(PREF.)** RALLI

RAIL CHAIR CARRIAGE

RAILING BAR SEPT GRATE RAVEL FENDER FIDDLE GITTER VEDIKA BARRIER GALLERY PARAPET CANCELLI ESPALIER HANDRAIL PARCLOSE TRAVERSE

RAILLERY GAFF HASH JEST JOKE RAGE CHAFF RALLY SPORT BANTER BLAGUE HOORAY HURRAH SATIRE TRIFLE MOCKERY BADINAGE DICACITY RABULOUS RIDICULE PERSIFLAGE

RAILROAD EL ROAD YARD STEEL COALER FEEDER GRANGER TRAMWAY CEINTURE ELEVATED **(— CAR)** IDLER **(— FLARE)** FUSEE

RAILROAD CHAIR SADDLE

RAILSPLITTER MAULER

RAILWAY ROAD TUBE COGWAY SUBWAY COGROAD INCLINE TRANVIA WIREWAY ASCENSOR PLATEWAY TRAMROAD FUNICULAR CREMAILLERE **(CARNIVAL —)** ROLLERCOASTER **(KIND OF —)** COG **(MOUNTAIN —)** SWITCHBACK **(UNDERGROUND —)** TUBE METRO SUBWAY

RAIMENT RAY GARB CLOTH ATTIRE APPAREL CLOTHES VESTURE CLOTHING DRESSING WARDROBE **(SPLENDID —)** SHEEN **(SUFF.)** ESTHES

RAIN WET ISLE MIST SMUR ULAN WEET BLASH STORM DELUGE MIZZLE SERENE SHOWER SOAKER DRIZZLE DOWNPOUR SPRINKLE **(— AND SNOW)** SLEET **(— CHECK)** TARP **(— HEAVILY)** TEEM **(— LIGHTLY)** SMUR SPIT SPRINKLE **(— OF SPARKS)** SHOWER

(— SUDDENLY) PLUMP **(DRIZZLING —)** DAG **(FINE —)** MIST SEREIN SERENE **(FROZEN —)** HAIL GRAUPEL **(GOD OF —)** PARJANYA **(HARD —)** SLEET **(HEAVY —)** PASH SPOUT **(LIGHT —)** SEREIN WEATHER HEATDROPS **(SHORT —)** SHOWER **(SMALL —)** ROKE **(SUDDEN —)** SKEW **(WHIRLING —)** SKIRL **(WIND-DRIVEN —)** SCAT **(PL.)** VARSHA **(PREF.)** HYET(O) OMBRI OMBRO PLUVI(O)

RAINBIRD KOEL TOMFOOL STORMBIRD **(— OF JAMAICA)** HUNTER

RAINBOW ARC BOW ARCH IRIS GAMUT METEOR SUNBOW ILLUSION **(AUTHOR OF —)** LAWRENCE **(BROKEN —)** WINDDOG WINDGALL **(CHARACTER IN —)** TOM ANNA WILL ANTON LYDIA LENSKY URSULA BRANGWEN SKREBENSKY **(PREF.)** IRID(O)

RAINBOW FISH GUPPY MAORI

RAINBOW RUNNER SKIPJACK SHOEMAKER

RAINBRINGER KACHINA

RAIN CLOUD NIMBUS

RAINCOAT MAC MACK MINO OILER PONCHO BURSATI OILSKIN SLICKER GOSSAMER MACINTOSH MACKINTOSH

RAINFALL PLOUT SKIFF SKIFT ONDING STEMPLOW

RAIN GAGE UDOMETER

RAINGEAR MAC

RAINMAKER SEEDER

RAINSPOUT RONE

RAINSTORM WET SPATE SCOWTHER

RAIN TREE SAMAN ZAMAN GUANGO ZAMANG ALGAROBA GENISARO MONKEYPOD

RAINY WET KICK FRESH JUICY RAYNE SAPPY WEETY BLASHY DRIPPY HYETAL PLUNGY SPONGY PLUVIAL PLUVINE SHOWERY WEEPING CLUTTERY PLUVIOUS SLATTERY **(— SEASON)** VARSHA

RAISE END SET WIN BUMP BUOY GROW HAIN HEFT HIGH HIKE HOVE JACK KICK LEVY LIFT MAKE OVER REAR ROOF STIR TELD TOSS AREAR BLOCK BOOST BREED BUILD CAIRN CHOCK CRANE DIGHT ELATE ENSKY ERECT EXALT FORCE GREET HANCE HEAVE HEEZE HEVEN HOISE HOIST HORSE LEAVE MOUND MOUNT PRICK PUTUP RISER ROUSE VOICE ARRECT ASSIST BETTER CREATE DOUBLE EMBOSS EXHALE GATHER LEAVEN MUSTER NANTLE PREFER REMOVE RISING UPHOLD UPLIFT ADDRESS ADVANCE COLLECT ELEVATE ENHANCE LIGHTEN NOURISH

PRESENT PROMOTE RECRUIT UPSHOOT ANGELIZE HEIGHTEN INSPIRIT RELEVATE
(— A BUMP) CLOUR
(— ALOFT) SPHERE
(— A NAP) MOZE TEASE TEASEL TEAZLE
(— ANCHOR) CAT
(— A NESTLING) FLEDGE
(— A SIEGE) RISE RELIEVE
(— BRIDGE BID) JUMP
(— BY ASSESSMENT) LEVY
(— BY HAND) NOB
(— CLAMOR) BRAWL
(— IN PITCH) SHARP
(— OBJECTIONS) CAVIL BOGGLE
(— ONESELF) CHIN
(— TO A POWER) INVOLVE
(— TO HIGH DEGREE) STRAIN
(— TO 3RD POWER) CUBE
(— UP) BUOY AREAR ELATE EXALT EXTOL ELEVATE CIVILIZE
RAISED HIGH UPSET ARRECT HOGGED BULLATE EXALTED ELEVATED MOUNTANT UPLIFTED UPRAUGHT
(— A SEMITONE) SHARP
RAISIN FIG PASA PLUM LEXIA ZIBEB REYSON CURRANT SULTANA MUSCATEL
(PL.) SPICE
RAISING ATOLLENT
(— OF BELL) SALLY
(— OF CATTLE) GRAZING
(— OF SIEGE) REMOVE
(— OF TONE) ECBOLE
RAJ RULE REIGN
RAJA KING CHIEF RULER PRINCE PANGLIMA
RAJAB MONTH
RAJAH FABRIC
RAJMAHAL CREEPER JITI CHITI JETEE JEETEE
RAJPUT SAMMA SUMRA GAHRWAL RAZBOOCH
RAKE GO HOE RIP WAY COMB PATH RACK RAFF RAVE REAP ROAM ROUE ROVE RUCK BLOOD CLAUT PITCH SCOOP SCOUR SULKY TIGER PLUNGE RABBLE ROLLER SEARCH RANSACK SCRATCH LOTHARIO SCRAPPLE
(— GRAIN) GAVEL
(— UP IN ROWS) HACK
(— WITH GUNFIRE) SCOUR STRAFE ENFILADE
(— WITHOUT TEETH) LUTE
(BUCK —) SWEEP
(CRANBERRY —) SCOOP
(HORSE-DRAWN —) GLEANER
(OYSTER —) GLEANER
(PART OF —) BOW TANG TINE TOOTH HANDLE FERRULE
RAKEHELL RASCAL IMMORAL LIBERTINE
RAKER GUMMER ROOKER
RAKISH SLANG JAUNTY SPORTY WANTON DASHING CARELESS DEVILISH RANTEPOLE RANTIPOLE
RALE RATTLE SIFFLE SIBILUS RHONCHUS
RALLENTANDO DRAG RITARD
RALLY KID DRAG JOKE MOCK RELY

STIR BULLY JOLLY QUEER BANTER DERIDE REVIVE COLLECT REBOUND CAMPOREE CLAMBAKE RIDICULE SPEAKING
(KIND OF —) PEP
(POLITICAL —) CLAMBAKE
RAM PUN TIP TUP BUCK CRAM PACK RAME STEM TEAP TOOP ARIES CHOKE CRASH POACH ROGER SLIDE BEETLE CHASER RANCID ROSTRUM BULLDOZER WETHERHOG WETHERTEG
(— OF WAR VESSEL) SPUR
(CASTRATED —) WETHER
(FATHER OF —) HEZRON JERAHMEEL
(SON OF —) AMMINADAB
(PREF.) CRIO
RAMA MELCHORA
(FATHER OF —) DASHARATHA
(MOTHER OF —) KAUSHALYA
(WIFE OF —) SITA
RAMADA ARBOR PORCH
RAMAGE WILD RAMMISH UNTAMED
RAMAGE HAWK BRANCHER
RAMBLE RAKE ROAM ROVE SKIR WALK JAUNT PROWL RANGE TRACE TROLL DODDER RUMBLE STROLL VAGARY WAMBLE WANDER ENRANGE EXCURSE SAUNTER SPROGUE TROUNCE FLAGARIE SCRAMBLE SPATIATE
(— AIMLESSLY) HAZE
(— IN TALK) DODDER
RAMBLING GAD RAISE VAGARY CURSORY DEVIOUS WINDING DESULTORY SCATTERED
RAMBUNCTIOUS RUDE WILD ROUGH UNRULY UNTAMED VIOLENT
RAMBUTAN SOAPWORT
RAMENTUM PALEA PALET SCALE SHAVING
RAMIE BAST HEMP RHEA ORTIGA
RAMIFICATION ARM RAMUS BRANCH OFFSHOOT OUTGROWTH
RAMIFY BRANCH SPRANGLE
RAMMAN ADAD ADDA ADDU
RAMMED EARTH PISE
RAMMEL TRASH RUMMLE RUBBISH
RAMMER TUP HEAD BOSER PUNNER WORMER
RAMONA (HUSBAND OF —) ALESSANDRO
RAMOSE CLADOSE BRANCHED
RAMOTH (FATHER OF —) BANI
RAMP ROB RUN BANK EXIT HOAX RAGE RANK SLIP CREEP STORM WAYON EASING FROLIC GARLIC WAYOFF WAYOUT FOOTPAD SLIPWAY SWINDLE GRADIENT
(AIRPORT —) JETWAY
RAMPAGE RAGE ROMP BINGE SPRAY SPREE STORM RANDAN
RAMPAGEOUS UNRULY GLARING RAMPANT VIOLENT
RAMPANT RANK PROFUSE SALIANT SALIENT SEGREANT
RAMPART BRAY LINE WALL AGGER ARGIN ABATIS VALLUM ABATTIS BULWARK DEFENSE PARAPET

RAMPIER BARBICAN MUNITION BARRICADE
RAMPER LAMPREY
RAMPIKE SNAG RAUNPICK ROUNSPIK
RAMROD FORMAL GUNSTICK
RAMSHACKLE RUDE UNRULY RICKETY SHACKLY UNSTEADY
RAMSON RAMP GARLIC BUCKRAM
(PL.) RAMS
RAMSTAM RASH HEADLONG RECKLESS
RAN ARN
(HUSBAND OF —) AESIR
RANCEL SEARCH RANSACK
RANCH RUN FARM TEAR FINCA CHACRA OUTFIT SPREAD WRENCH STATION ESTANCIA HACIENDA
RANCHE NATURAL
RANCHER COWMAN HERDER GRAZIER SHEEPMAN CATTLEMAN
RANCID RAM RANK SOUR FROWY RAFTY RASTY REEST RESTY FROWZY ODIOUS ROTTEN MALODOROUS
RANCOR BILE GALL HATE SPITE ENMITY GRUDGE HATRED MALICE ACRIMONY
RANCOROUS ACRID VENOMOUS MALIGNANT ACRIMONIOUS
(NOT —) GOOD
RAND EDGE ROON RUND BORDER HIGHLAND
RANDAN SPREE RANTAN UPROAR RAMPAGE
RANDOM BANK FORCE LOOSE STRAY CASUAL CHANCE CHANCY AIMLESS RANDALL RENDOUN SHOTGUN UNAIMED VAGRANT ALEATORIC
(AT —) HOBNOB
(SOMEWHAT —) LONG
RANDY LEWD RUDE RUDAS SPREE BEGGAR VIRAGO LUSTFUL RIOTOUS CAROUSAL
RANGE KEN ROW ALLY AREA BEAT GATE GAUT GHAT LINE RAIK RAKE RANK ROAM ROVE SCUM SHOT TOUR WALK ALIGN BLANK CARRY FIELD GAMUT HILLS ORBIT REACH SCOPE SCOUR SHOOT SPACE STAND START STOVE SWEEP SWING VERGE COURSE DANGER EXTEND EXTENT LENGTH RADIUS RAMBLE SCOUTH SPHERE STROLL WANDER BOWSHOT COMPASS DEMESNE EARSHOT GUNSHOT HABITAT HORIZON PURVIEW CLASSIFY DIAPASON EARREACH EYEREACH LATITUDE PANORAMA
(— ABOUT) SCOUR
(— FOR FOOD) FORAGE
(— FOR GAME) QUARTER
(— OF ARROW) FLIGHT
(— OF BRICK) COURSE
(— OF BUILDINGS) CRESCENT
(— OF COLORS) PALETTE SPECTRUM
(— OF COLUMNS) PORTICO COLONNADE PERISTYLE
(— OF FOOD) FARE
(— OF FREQUENCIES) BAND SPECTRUM

(— OF GOVERNANCE) DOMAIN
(— OF GUN) CARRY RANDOM GUNSHOT
(— OF HEARING) EARSHOT
(— OF HILLS) GAUT GHAT HUMP TIER CHAIN GHAUT RIDGE SIERRA SAWBACK BACKBONE
(— OF MOVEMENT) TRAVEL
(— OF ORGANISM) BIOZONE
(— OF PASTURE) GANG
(— OF PLANKS) STRING
(— OF PRINTING TYPES) SERIES
(— OF SIGHT) KEN SCAN EYESHOT KENNING
(— OF TONES) KEY SCALE GRADATION
(— OF VISION) EYE SIGHT KENNING
(— OF WAVELENGTH) BAND
(— OVER) SWEEP
(— TOP) COOKTOP
(— WILDLY) RAMP
(ARCHERY —) BUTTS GREEN
(COOKING —) KITCHENER
(FREE —) SCOUTH SCOWTH LIBERTY
(MOUNTAIN —) CHAIN SERRA SIERRA
(PART OF —) CAP DOOR FLUE HEAD KNOB OVEN RACK TRIM VENT GRATE GUARD GUIDE HINGE PANEL BURNER GASKET HANDLE WINDOW BROILER CONTROL GRIDDLE DRIPPLATE BACKSPLASH
(SHOOTING —) MES GALLERY
(TEMPERATURE —) CONE
RANGE FINDER STADIA MEKOMETER
RANGE POLE PICKET
RANGER ROVER ROBBER MONTERO FIREWARD
RANGOON SHERRY
RANGY OPEN ROOMY SPACIOUS
RANK RAY ROW SEE DANK FOOT FORM FOXY GOLE GREE LINE RAMP RATE ROOM SEED SOUR STEP TIER CENSE CHOIR CLASS FETID FRANK FUSTY GRADE GROSS HONOR LEVEL MARCH ORDER PLACE QUIRE RANGE ROWTY SIEGE SPACE STALL STAND STATE TCHIN TRAIN AFFAIR AGREGE DEGREE ERMINE ESTATE ESTEEM FIGURE LAVISH PARAGE RATING SPHERE STATUS STRONG CALIBER CALLING DIGNITY DUKEDOM EARLDOM FOOTING GLARING RAMMISH RAMPANT STATION WORSHIP ABSOLUTE EARLSHIP ENSIGNCY EQUIPAGE FLAGRANT GENTRICE LADYSHIP PALPABLE STINKING MALODOROUS
(— AND FILE) RUCK RANGALE
(— OF GENTLEMEN) GENTRY GENTILITY
(— OF SERGEANT-AT-LAW) COIF COIFFE
(ACADEMIC —) AGREGE
(BOTTOMMOST —) CELLAR
(HIGH —) PURPLE DIGNITY EMINENCE
(LOWEST —) SCOURING
(MILITARY —) GRADE AIRMAN CORNET CHAOUSH
(NOBLE —) ADELAIDE

(ONE HIGHEST IN —) SUPREMO
(SAME —) KIND
(SOCIAL —) CLASS ESTATE HERALDRY POSITION
(SUFF.) CY HEAD HOOD
RANKLE FRET CHAFE FESTER INJURE RANCOR DESTROY INFLAME
RANSACK RIG DRAG RAKE RIPE SACK SEEK RIFLE DACKER RANCEL SEARCH PLUNDER RUMMAGE
RANSOM FINE RAME REDEEM RESCUE RESGAT EXPIATE
RANSTEAD TOADFLAX
RANT CAVE HUFF RAIL RAND MOUTH REVEL ROUSE SCOLD SPOUT STEVEN BOMBAST CAROUSE DECLAIM FROTHING RODOMONTADE
(— AND RAVE) FAUNCH
RANTAN NOISE
RANTING RANTISM TEARCAT
RANTIPOLE WILD CARROT RAKISH SEESAW ROMPING
RANULA CYST FROGTONGUE
(PREF.) BATRACH(O)
RANUNCULUS MOSS GOLLAND CROWFOOT HEDGEHOG BUTTERCUP
RAOULIA HAASTIA
RAP BOB CON BLOW CHAP GRAB KNAP TIRL TUNK WRAP BLAME CLICK CLINK FLIRT KNOCK STEAL TOUCH BARTER CHARGE HANDLE YANKER
RAPACIOUS CRUEL GREEDY TAKING RAVENING RAVENOUS
RAPACITY RAVEN RAVIN CUPIDITY EXTORTION VULTURISM
RAPE COLE ABUSE COLZA FORCE NAVET NAVEW TOUCH ATTACK CANOLA FELONY RAPEYE TURNIP ASSAULT DESPOIL NAVETTE OPPRESS OUTRAGE PLUNDER RAPTURE STUPRUM VIOLATE COLESEED COLEWORT DISHONOR STUPRATE SUPPRESS
RAPE OF THE LOCK (AUTHOR OF —) POPE
(CHARACTER IN —) ARIEL BETTY PETRE PLUME SPLEEN BELINDA UMBRIEL CLARISSA THALESTRIS
RAPESEED COLZA RAVISON
RAPHA (FATHER OF —) BINEA
RAPHIA JUPATI
RAPHU (SON OF —) PALTI
RAPHUS DIDUS
RAPID GAY FAST CHUTE HASTY MOSSO QUICK ROUND SAULT SHARP SHOOT SHUTE TOSTO WINGY RIFLE SPEEDY WINGED CURSIVE SCHNELL SKELPIN STICKLE TANTIVY SLAPPING SPEEDFUL OVERNIGHT
(—S IN RIVER) SAULT DALLES RIFFLE STICKLE CATARACT
(MORE —) STRETTO
(PREF.) TACHY
RAPIDITY HASTE SPEED RADEUR CELERITY VELOCITY
RAPIDLY APACE CHEAP FLEETLY HASTILY SPEEDILY QUICKFOOT

RAPIER TUCK TUKE BILBO ESTOC SHARP STOCK VERDUN TOASTER
RAPINE FORCE RAVIN PILLAGE PLUNDER VIOLENCE
RAPINI BROCCOLI
RAPPACCINI (DAUGHTER OF —) BEATRICE
RAPPAREE ROBBER CREAGHT VAGABOND
RAPPEE SNUFF
RAPPEL ABSEIL
RAPPORT ACCORD HARMONY RELATION AGREEMENT
(ESTABLISH —) GROK
RAPSCALLION ROGUE RASCAL VILLAIN HOSEBIRD VAGABOND
RAPT LOST WRAP TENSE INTENT RAVISH TRANCE CARRIED ENGAGED RAPTURE ABDUCTED ABSORBED ECSTATIC
RAPTORES RAPACES
RAPTURE JOY BLISS DELIGHT ECSTASY PAROXYSM RHAPSODY
RAPTUROUS ECSTATIC RHAPSODIC
RARA AVIS PHENIX RARITY WONDER PHOENIX
RARE FINE REAL SELD THIN ALONE EARLY GREAT ANTRIN CHOICE GEASON INCONY SCARCE SEENIL SELDOM SINDLE SPARSE SUBTLE SULLEN UNIQUE ANTERIN CURIOUS TENUOUS UNUSUAL CRITICAL SELDSEEN SINGULAR UNCOMMON RECHERCHE
(PREF.) AREO MANO SPAN(I)(O)
RAREFACTION POROSIS
RAREFIED HIGH THIN SUBTILE ABSTRUSE AETHERED ESOTERIC
RAREFY THIN DILUTE EXTENUATE SUBTILIZE
RARELY SELDEN SELDOM
RARENESS RARITY TENUITY SCARCITY
RARITY SWAN CURIO RELIC RARIETY TENUITY RARENESS
(PL.) CURIOSA
RASCAL BOY CAD DOG IMP LOW RAP BASE DUCK FILE KITE LOON MEAN SHAG SMAK CATSO FILTH GANEF GIPSY KNAVE ROGUE SCAMP SHELM SLAVE SMAIK THIEF VIPER ABLACH BEGGAR BRIBER BUDZAT BUGGER COQUIN HARLOT LIMMER RABBLE RAGGIL RIBALD SCHELM SORROW TINKER BLEEDER CAMOOCH CULLION GLUTTON HALLION HESSIAN NEBULON PANURGE PEASANT RAPTRIL SHELLUM SKEEZIX SKELLUM VILLAIN BEZONIAN BLIGHTER HOSEBIRD LIDDERON PALLIARD PICAROON RAKEHELL RUBIATOR SCALAWAG SPALPEEN TAISTREL VAGABOND WIDDIFOW SCAPEGRACE SCARAMOUCH RAPSCALLION SCARAMOUCHE
RASCALITY FOIST RABBLE KNAVERY ROGUING RASCALRY
RASCALLY BASE MEAN ROOKY ARRANT GALLUS LIMMER GALLOWS KNAVISH RAGGILY SHAGRAG WIDDIFOW

RASE PULL RAIS RAZE ERASE PLUCK INCISE SNATCH
RASH ID CUT BRASH HARDY HASTY HEADY SLASH SLICE DARING SUDDEN UNWARY URGENT BULRUSH HOTSPUR RABBISH RAMSTAM ROSEOLA BLIZZARD CARELESS ERUPTION EXANTHEM HEADLONG HEEDLESS MADBRAIN OVERSEEN PRESSING RECKLESS TEMEROUS IMPETUOUS IMPULSIVE
(SUFF.) ANTHEMA
(SKIN —) ID IDE
RASHER SLICE COLLOP TRIFLE COLOPPE
RASHLY HEADILY HEADLONG
RASHNESS RAGE RESE HASTE ACRISY TEMERITY HEADINESS
RASKOLNIK POPOVETS
RASP RUB FILE RAPE ERUCT GRATE TOOTH RAPEYE RUBBER RUGINE RIFFLER DENTICLE
(SHOEMAKER'S —) FLOAT
RASPBERRY AKPEK BAZOO MOLKA AVARIN RASPIS PLUMBOG ARNBERRY BLACKCAP BOGBERRY CUTHBERT MULBERRY RESPASSE ROSACEAN SALMONBERRY
RASPING HARSH ROUGH STOOR STOUR HOARSE RASION RAZZLY GRATING RAUCOUS GUTTERAL
(PL.) SCOBS
RASPY HARSH GRATING SCREAKY SCRABBLY
RASSE CIVET WEASEL
RASSELAS (AUTHOR OF —) JOHNSON
(CHARACTER IN —) IMLAC PEKUAH NEKAYAH RASSELAS
(MENTOR OF —) IMLAC
(SISTER OF —) NEKAYAH
RAT BUCK DAMN DRAT FINK HEEL NOKI ROTN SCAB VOLE KIORE LOUSE METAD RATON SELVA ZEMMI ZEMNI CRABER MURINE RODENT ROTTAN SLEPEZ VERMIN YUNGAS CUSHION CONFOUND INFORMER MYOMORPH SQUEALER
(— ON) SING
(INDIAN —) KOK
RATAPLAN RATTAN RATTLE
RATCH RASH REND ROCH SPOT NOTCH STREAK RATCHET STRETCH
RATCHET DOG PAWL CLICK DETENT ROCHET
RAT CHINCHILLA ABROCOME
RATE LAY RAG SET CESS CHOP DEEM EARN GAIT GIVE HAND KIND RANK RATA ABUSE CULET CURVE PRIZE RATIO REBUT SCOLD STENT STYLE VALUE ZAKAT ASSIZE GALLOP ACCOUNT BESHREW CARTAGE DESERVE FASHION MILLAGE REPROVE CLASSIFY ESTIMATE QUANTIFY
(— HIGHLY) EXALT PRICE
(— OF ASCENT) GRADE
(— OF CHANGE) GRADIENT
(— OF DRAINAGE) FREENESS
(— OF EXCHANGE) BATTA
(— OF FLOW) FLUX DISCHARGE

(— OF INTEREST) COUPON DISCOUNT
(— OF MOTION) BAT SPEED
(— OF MOVEMENT) PACE TEMPO
(— OF RECKONING) FOOT
(— OF SPEED) BAT AGOGE
(— OF TAX) CENSE
(— OF TRANSFER) FLUX
(— OF TUITION) CULET
(— SCHEDULE) TARIFF
(AT ANY —) HURE
(BIRTH —) NATALITY
RATE BOOK STREET
RATEL BADGER BURIER
RATH CAR HILL REUT RUTH EARLY MOUND QUICK REUTE SWIFT BETIMES CHARIOT YOUTHFUL
RATHER Y BUT GEY ATAD LIKE SOON LOURD QUITE ASTITE ATOUCH BEFORE FAIRLY HELDER KINDLY PRETTY RUTHER SEEMLY SORTOF TIDDER TITTER EARLIER INSTEAD MIDDLING SOMEWHAT
(— THAN) ERE BEFORE
RATIFICATION AMEN RATE SANCTION
RATIFY AMEN PASS SEAL SIGN VISA ENSEAL FASTEN OBSIGN APPROVE CONFIRM SCEPTER CANONIZE ROBORATE SANCTION VALIDATE
RATING RANK CENSE CLASS GRADE WRITER STANDING
RATIO Q PI GAIN RATE SINE SLIP INDEX RESON SETUP SHEAR ASPECT CAMBER DECADE QUOTUM REASON REYSON SECANT AVERAGE PORTION CONTRAST SOLIDITY MULTIPLIER PROPORTION
RATIOCINATION MACH LOGIC THOUGHT REASONING
RATION DOLE ALLOT RATIO ALLOCATE
(— OF BREAD) TOMMY
(ANIMAL —) CHOW
(EXTRA —S) BUCKSHEE
(HOG —) SWILL
(PL.) FOOD BOUCH ETAPE COMMON
RATIONAL SANE LUCID SOBER LOGICAL REASONAL SENSIBLE THINKING
RATIONALISM (GERMAN —) NEOLOGY
RATIONALIZE THOB EXPLAIN
RATITE EMU MOA EMEU KIWI RHEA OSTRICH STRUTHIAN
RAT KANGAROO TUNGO POTOROO SQUEAKER
RATOON SHOOT SPROUT SUCKER
RATTAIL MULE ARREST GRENADIER
RATTAN CANE SEGA ROTAN BEJUCO ROTANG SWITCH RATTOON
RATTLE DIN BIRL BURL REEL RICK TIRL CHINK CLACK CROTAL GRAGER HENPEN HURTLE MARACA RACKLE RICKLE RIFFLE ROTTLE RUCKLE RUTTLE CHACKLE CLACKER CLAPPER CLATTER CLICKET CREAKER GNATTER GROGGER SHATTER SISTRUM

SKELLAT CAIXINHA CHOCALHO COWWHEAT NOISEMAKER
(CRIER'S —) CLAPPER
(IRON —) SKELLAT SKILLET
(PREF.) CROTALI
(SUFF.) CROTIC
RATTLEBRAINED MADCAP
RATTLER LIE ROMBLE RUMBLER
RATTLESNAKE BELLTAIL
CASCABEL CASCAVEL CROTALID MASSASAUGA SIDEWINDER
(— PLANTAIN) NETLEAF RATSBANE
RATTLESNAKE ROOT BUGBANE
JOYLEAF
RATTLETRAP HEAP GEWGAW JUNKER TRIFLE RICKETY
RATTLING REEL BRISK HUSKY SLAPPING SPLENDID CREPITANT
RATTY NASTY SHABBY UNKEMPT WORTHLESS
RATWA MUNTJAC
RAUCOUS LOUD HARSH COARSE HOARSE SQUAWKY STRIDENT
RAUN ROE ROWN SPAWN
RAUPO CATTAIL
RAVAGE EAT PREY RIOT RUIN SACK FORAY HARRY HAVOC SPOIL WASTE FORAGE DESPOIL DESTROY OVERRUN PILLAGE PLUNDER DEFLOWER DESOLATE POPULATE SPOLIATE
RAVANA (SISTER OF —) SHURPANAKHA
RAVE MAD RAGE RAND WOOD AWEDE BLURB CRUSH RATHE ROUSE STORM TAVER DELIRE TAIVER WANDER
RAVEL FAG RUN FRAY FRET UNDO REYLE SNARL EVENER LADDER RADDLE RUNNER SLOUGH TANGLE CONFUSE INVOLVE PERPLEX RAILING UNWEAVE
RAVELIN RABLIN OUTWORK DEMILUNE
RAVELING LINT
RAVEN DARK BLACK CRAKE RALPH CORBEL CORBIE CORBIN FORAGE RAVINE WAYBIRD
(BRIGHT —) BERTRAM
(SUFF.) CORAX
RAVENING CRUEL RABIES
RAVENOUS GREEDY LUPINE TOOTHY WOLFISH RAPACIOUS VORACIOUS
RAVINE DEN GAP GUT LIN DELL DRAW GILL GULL KHOR KHUD LINN LLYN SIKE WADI BREAK BUNNY CHASM CHINE CLOVE COULE DONGA FLUME GHYLL GLACK GORGE GOYAL GOYLE GRIFF GRIKE GULCH GULLY HEUCH KLOOF NULLA SLADE SLAKE STRID ARROYO CLEUCH CLOUGH COULEE DIMBLE DINGLE DUMBLE GULLET GULLEY HOLLOW NULLAH RAMBLA SHEUGH STRAIT BARRANCA QUEBRADA
RAVING RAVERY DELIRANT FRENZIED DELIRIOUS
RAVISH ROB RAPE ABUSE CHARM FORCE HARRY SPOIL ABDUCT ATTACK DEFILE AFFORCE CORRUPT DELIGHT ENFORCE

OPPRESS OUTRAGE OVERJOY PLUNDER POLLUTE VIOLATE VITIATE DEFLOWER ENTRANCE STUPRATE SUPPRESS UNMAIDEN
RAVISHER RAPTER RAVENER
RAVISHMENT ECSTASY RAPTURE TRANSPORT
RAW RA RED ROW BRUT LASH REAR RUDE BLEAK CHILL CRUDE FRESH GREEN HARSH NAKED RAFTY SHARP WERSH BITTER CALLOW COARSE CUTCHA KUTCHA UNRIPE VULGAR WAIRSH NATURAL NOUVEAU UNBOUND VERDANT WEARISH WEERISH IMMATURE RAWBONED UNCOOKED UNEDITED VISCERAL
(— AND COLD) CRIMPY
(PREF.) OMO
RAWBONED RAW BONY LEAN GAUNT LANKY SCRAG SCRAWNY
(— PERSON) SCRAG
RAWHIDE WHIP WHANG COWHIDE COWSKIN GREENHIDE PARFLECHE
RAWNESS CRUDITY
RAY BEAM BETA DORN SOIL WIRE ALPHA BRAND DRESS EQUIP FLAIR FLAKE FLATH GLEAM GLEED MANTA ORDER RAYON ROKER SKATE BATOID CHUCHO OBISPO RADIAL RADIUS RAIOID SEPHEN STREAM TRYGON VISUAL BATFISH COWFISH DEWBEAM DRILVIS FIDDLER HOMELYN PLACOID RAIMENT TORPEDO WAIREPO BRACHIUM MOONBEAM NUMBFISH PLOWFISH PYLSTERT STINGRAY STINGAREE
(— OF LIGHT) GLINT SPEAR GLANCE SUNRAY SUNBEAM
(— OF STARFISH) ARM
(FEMALE —) MAID
(FIN —) SPINE
(KIND OF —) GAMMA
(WITHOUT —S) ABACTINAL
(PREF.) BATO
(ELECTRIC —) NARC(O)
RAYED
(PREF.) ACTIN(IO)(O)
(SUFF.) ACT(INE)
(— WITH IMPAIRMENT) LEXIA
RAYON BEAM RADIUS DUCHESS
RAZE CUT FLAT RUIN ARASE ERASE LEVEL STREW ARRACE EFFACE SCRAPE SLIGHT UNPILE DESTROY SCRATCH SUBVERT UNBUILD DEMOLISH
RAZOR SHIV TUSK MUSSEL RASOIR SHAVER RATTLER SLASHER CUTTHROAT
(PREF.) XYR(O)
RAZORBACK STATE ARKANSAS
RAZORBILL MURRE
RAZOR-BILLED AUK FALK TINK MURRE NODDY SCOOT SCOUT SKOOT TINKER SKIMMER WILLOCK ROCKBIRD
RAZOR CLAM PIROT RASOR SOLEN SPOUT RASOIR
RAZZ BOO KID PAN HARRY TEASE CHIACK HECKLE NEEDLE RIDICULE RASPBERRY
RAZZIA RAID FORAY INCURSION

RAZZING RAZOO
RAZZLE-DAZZLE SHOWBIZ
RE RAY ANENT ACTION MATTER REGARDING
REACH GO GET HIT RAX RUN WIN BEAT COME FIND GAIN HAWK HENT MAKE PUSH REEK REIK RYKE SHOT SORT SPAN SPIT TEND BRACE CROSS FETCH GRASP PERCH RANGE RETCH TOUCH ADVENE ARRIVE ATTAIN DANGER EXTEND FATHOM LENGTH OBTAIN SNATCH STREEK STRIKE ACHIEVE COMPASS CONTACT GUNSHOT OVERGET POSSESS RECOVER STRETCH
(— ACROSS) SPAN OVERSTRIDE
(— AN END) STAY
(— BEYOND) OVERREACH
(— BY EFFORT) ATTAIN
(— BY FIGURING) STRIKE
(— FORTH) EXTEND
(— GOAL) HAIL
(— HIGHER) OUTTOP
(— IN TOTAL) RUNTO
(— OF SIGHT) EYESHOT
(— OF WATER) LODE
(— OUT) UTTER SPREAD STRETCH
(— TO) LINE
(— TOTAL) AMOUNT
(— UNDERSTANDING) AGREE
(— WITH END) ABUT
(EXTREME —) PITCH STRETCH
(TRY TO —) ASPIRE
(ULTIMATE —) PITCH
REACHER INGIVER
REACT ACT BUCK BEHAVE RETROACT
REACTION BELT BUZZ KAHN WOHL START WIDAL FAVISM RECOIL BLOWOFF EMOTION FEELING SETBACK BACKLASH BACKWASH EXCHANGE GUARDING KICKBACK RESPONSE RECEPTION COUNTERBUFF
(— TIME) LATENCY
(ADVERSE —) BACKLASH
(ANGRY —) RISE
(DELAYED —) DOUBLETAKE
(KIND OF —) FEULGEN
(NUCLEAR —) SPALLATION
(VIOLENT —) SONG
REACTIONARY WHITE BOURBON BACKWARD
REACTIVATED AWAKE ACTIVE
REACTIVATOR ACTIFIER
REACTOR PILE CHOKER FURNACE INDUCTOR
(SHUTDOWN OF —) SCRAM
READ GO CON KRI QRI SEE CALL KERE QERI TURN CHOKE JUDGE SOLVE WRITE PERUSE RELATE FORESEE LEARNED LECTION PREDICT ABOMASUM DECIPHER FORETELL INDICATE OVERLOOK
(— ALOUD) LINE DEACON
(— BAR CODES) SCAN
(— HERE AND THERE) BROWSE
(— MECHANICALLY) RETINIZE
(— OF) SEE
(— OFF) DICTATE
(— PROOF) HORSE

(— RAPIDLY) DIP SCAN SKIM GOBBLE
(— SLOWLY) SPELL
(— SYSTEMATICALLY) FREQUENT
(— WITH PROFOUND ATTENTION) PORE STUDY
READER PURSE DIPPER LECTOR LISTER MAFTIR GRANTHI PISTLER DEVOURER
(CHILD'S —) TENPENNY
(CHURCH —) LECTOR ANAGNOST
(PUBLIC —) PRELECTOR
(VORACIOUS —) BIBLIOPHAGIST
(PL.) FOLLOWING
READILY PAT LIEF YERN APTLY PREST YERNE EASILY GAINLY PROBABLY SPEEDILY
READINESS ART EASE GIFT PRESS SKILL BELIEF GRAITH ADDRESS FLUENCY FREEDOM ALACRITY FACILITY GOODWILL
(— TO LEARN) APTITUDE
(IN —) APOISE AGAINST
READING KRI QRE QRI KERE KERI QERI KTHIB KETHIB LESSON LECTION LECTURE PERUSAL SETTING CORALENE
(— ANTIPHONALLY) ALTERNATION
(DOCTOR'S —) EEG ERG
(HEAVY —) TOME
(MARGINAL —) KRI
(PL.) PROCINCT
READING DESK AMBO LECTERN
READING ROOM ATHENEUM
READJUST MEND ADVANCE
(— TYPE) OVERRUN
READY UP APT BUN FIT RAD YAP BAAN BAIN BOON BOUN BOWN FREE GIRT GLIB GNIB RIFE RIPE TALL YARF APERT FAGER FRACK HANDY HAPPY ONTAP PREDY PREST PRIME QUICK SWIFT THERE TIGHT ADROIT APPERT FACILE GRAITH HEARTY PROMPT PREPARE PRESENT RENABLE WILLING CHEERFUL DEXTROUS HANDSOME PREGNANT PREPARED PROVIDED SKILLFUL
(— A COMPUTER) BOOT
(— FOR ACTION) ARM EXPEDITE
(— TO GO) ALLSET
(— WITH WORDS) FLUENT
(MAKE —) PREP
(NOT —) SET BOUND GROOM FORWARD DISPOSED IMPROMPT INCLINED
READY-MADE SALE STORE BOUGHT
REAGENT ETCHANT REACTOR TITRANT ALTERANT REACTIVE NINHYDRIN
REAIA (FATHER OF —) MICAH
REAL BODY FAIR GOOD LEAL LEVY PURE RIAL TRUE VERY VRAI PAKKA PUCKA PUKKA RIGHT ROYAL SOLID SOOTH ACTUAL DINKUM ENTIRE HONEST THINGY CORDIAL GENUINE GRADELY SINCERE THINGAL CONCRETE DEFINITE EXISTENT GRAITHLY POSITIVE THINGISH UNFEIGNED VERITABLE
(EXTERNALLY —) TANGIBLE
(HALF —) PICAYUNE

(NOT —) FACTITIOUS INSUBSTANTIAL
(1-8TH —) TLAC TLACO
REALGAR ARSENIC ROSAKER ZARNICH SANDARAC
REALISM VERITE VERITY REALITY LITERALISM NATURALISM
REALISTIC HARD SOBER VIVID EARTHLY LIFELIKE PROBABLE
REALITY FEAT TRUE BEING SOOTH THING TRUTH ACTUAL DASEIN EFFECT VERITY EARNEST SUBJECT IDENTITY OVERSOUL POSITIVE REALNESS TRUENESS
(LIMITED —) SOMEWHAT
(ULTIMATE —) GOD SOURCE DIVINITY SUBSTANCE
(PL.) REALIA
REALIZATION PASS SENSE CRUSHER FRUITION AWAKENING
REALIZE GET EARN GAIN KNOW FETCH LEARN SENSE EFFECT FULFIL ACQUIRE CONCEIVE RECOGNIZE
(— BEFOREHAND) ANTICIPATE
REALIZED BODILY
(FULLY —) COMPLETE
REALLY ARU WIS ARAH HALF JUST ARRAH TRULY WISHA FINELY INDEED SIMPLY SURELY VERILY ACTUALLY
(NOT —) ILL ALMOST
REALM AREA LAND SOIL BOURN CLIME RANGE REIGN REWME RICHE BOURNE CIRCLE DEMAIN EMPIRE HEAVEN REALTY REGION SPHERE DEMESNE GAELDOM KINGDOM NOTALIA ROYALME TERRENE CLUBLAND DEVILDOM DOMINION ELDORADO GHOSTDOM GIPSYDOM NOTOGAEA
(— OF DARKNESS) PO
(— OF FABULOUS RICHNESS) ELDORADO
(— OF THOR) THRUTHHEIM THRUTHVANG
(MARINE —) NOTALIA TROPICALIA
(VISIONARY —) CLOUDLAND
(ZOOLOGICAL —) NOTOGAEA
(SUFF.) DOM
(— OF ANIMAL LIFE) ALIA
REALTY FEALTY REAUTE ROYALTY
REAM FOAM RIME SEED SKIM CHEAT CREAM FROTH FRAISE RHYMER STRETCH
(PL.) INSIDES OUTSIDES
REAMER BUR BURR SPUD DRIFT RIMER BROACH CHERRY FRAISE RANCER RHYMER RIMMER WIDENER
REANIMATE WAKE RENEW REVIVE RECREATE
REANIMATED AWAKE
REAP BAG CUT REP CROP RIPE GLEAN SHEAR GARNER GATHER SICKLE HARVEST
REAPER LORD COCKER TASKER WINNER CRADLER SHEARER SICKLER
(GRIM —) DEATH
REAPING HOOK SICKLE TWIBIL CROTCHET

REAPPEARANCE RENTREE EMERSION
REAR AFT BACK BUNT HIND HINT JUMP LIFT STEN TOSS BREED BUILD CARVE ERECT JUNCH STEND ACHTER AROUSE CRADLE FOSTER NURSLE SUCKLE APPREAR ARRIERE EDUCATE ELEVATE NOURISH NURTURE UPBRING BUTTOCKS HINDMOST REARWARD
(— CAREFULLY) TIDDLE
(NEARER THE —) AFTER
(TO THE —) BACK BEHIND
(TO THE — OF) ABAFT
REARED (— BY HAND) CADE
(DELICATELY —) SOYLED
REARHORSE MANTIS
REARING CABRE FRESNE PESADE FORCENE RAMPANT
(— UP) STEND
REARRANGE DO ALTER AMEND ADJUST JIGGER REORDER READJUST
REARRANGEMENT WAGNER DIAGENESIS
REARWARD AFT BACKWARD
REASON PEG WAY HOTI NOUS REDE SAKE TALK ARGUE CAUSE COLOR COUNT LOGOS PROOF RATIO SCORE SENSE SKILL THING THINK TOPIC EXCUSE GROUND MANNER MATTER MOTION NOESIS ACCOUNT PREMISE QUARREL SUBJECT TUITION ARGUMENT ENCHESON LOGICIZE VERNUNFT
(— AGAINST) OBJECTION
(— FALSELY) PARALOGIZE
(— FOR PRIDE) BOAST
(LACKING —) INEPT
(SUFFICIENT —) GROUND
(PREF.) RATI
REASONABLE FAIR JUST SANE SOBER NATURAL SKILFUL FEASIBLE MODERATE RATIONAL SENSIBLE
REASONABLENESS EPIKY EPIKIKA FITNESS FAIRNESS SOBRIETY
REASONABLY SOON
REASONER (FALLACIOUS —) SOPHIST
REASONING LOGIC THOUGHT ERGOTISM RATIONAL
(CLUMSY —) ARGAL
(DEDUCTIVE —) SYLLOGISM
(FALLACIOUS —) CIRCLE SOPHISTRY PARALOGISM
REASSEMBLE RELY
REASSEMBLY RALLY
REASSUME REVOKE REPRISE
REAVE ROB REFE SEIZE SPLIT REMOVE DESPOIL PILLAGE PLUNDER UNRAVEL
REB RABBI REBEL MISTER
REBAB GUSLE
REBATE BLUNT CHECK LESSEN REFUND RIBBET DIMINISH DISCOUNT DRAWBACK KICKBACK
REBEC LYRE SAROD RIBIBE RUBIBLE
REBECCA (AUTHOR OF —) DUMAURIER
(CHARACTER IN —) JACK BAKER FRANK GILES MAXIM FAVELL

JULYAN CRAWLEY DANVERS BEATRICE DEWINTER
(FATHER OF —) ISAAC
REBEKAH (BROTHER OF —) LABAN
(FATHER OF —) BETHUEL
(HUSBAND OF —) ISAAC
(SON OF —) ESAU JACOB
REBEL REB DEFY KICK RISE TURN ARISE BRAND FAUVE ANARCH CROPPY MUTINE REVOLT FRONDEUR SOLECIST MALCONTENT
(— IN ART) FAUVE
(RELIGIOUS —) APOSTATE
(PL.) REBELDOM
REBELLION MUTINY PUTSCH REVOLT MISRULE UPRISING
REBELLIOUS RUSTY ANARCHIC MUTINOUS AUDACIOUS INSURGENT
REBIRTH REVIVAL
(SPIRITUAL —) REGENERATION
REBOANT AROAR
REBORN REDIVIVUS
REBOUND DAP HOP HANG KISS STOT CANON CAROM STITE BOUNCE CANNON CARROM RECOIL RESILE RESULT BRICOLE REDOUND RICOCHET SNAPBACK
(— ERRATICALLY) KICK
REBOUND CLIP RETAINER
REBUFF NO SLAP SNIB SNUB CHECK FLING NOSER REPEL DEFEAT DENIAL REBUKE REBUTE REFUTE REPULSE SETDOWN
REBUILD MEND
REBUKE NIP WIG BAWL RATE REDD SNEB SNIB SNUB TRIM BARGE BLAME CHECK CHIDE DRESS SAUCE SCOLD SNAPE SNEAP TOUCH DIRDUM GANSEL LESSON PULLUP RATING RATTLE REHETE REMORD THREAP CENSURE CHIDING CORRECT HOTFOOT LECTURE REPROOF REPROVE SARCASM TICKOFF BLESSING BUSINESS CHASTISE KEELHAUL REPROACH SCORCHER THREAPEN UNDERNIM CASTIGATE
REBUS BADGE ENIGMA PUZZLE RIDDLE
REBUT REPEL RECOIL REFUTE REPULSE RETREAT DISPROVE
RECALCITRANT UNRULY RENITENT OBSTINATE RESISTANT
RECALL CITE BRING UNSAY REMAND REMIND RETURN REVOKE UNLOOK BETHINK RECLAIM RETRACE RETRACT REVIVAL UNSHOUT REMEMBER WITHCALL WITHDRAW REPRODUCE
(— FONDLY) CHERISH
(— FROM BANISHMENT) REPEAL
(— OF PURSUERS) RETREAT
RECANT UNSAY ABJURE REVOKE UNSING DISAVOW RETRACT SWALLOW PALINODE RENOUNCE
RECANTATION PALINODE
RECAPITULATE SUM UNITE RECITE REPEAT RECOUNT RESTATE REHEARSE REITERATE SUMMARIZE
RECAPITULATION EPANODOS

RECAPTURE RETAKE RECOVER REPRISAL
RECASTING (— OF LITERARY WORK) RIFACIMENTO
RECEDE DIE EBB BACK FADE STEP VARY RECUR DEPART DIFFER RETIRE SHRINK DECLINE DIGRESS RETREAT CONTRACT DIMINISH ELONGATE WITHDRAW
RECEIPT CHIT RECU RESET APOCHA BINDER RECIPE WARRANT
(PL.) GATE TAKE SALES INCOME ENTRADA
RECEIPTS GATE TAKE
RECEIVE GET BEAR FALL GAIN HAVE HOLD TAKE ADMIT AFONG CATCH GREET GUEST LATCH RESET ACCEPT ASSUME BORROW DERIVE GATHER HARBOR RECULE BELIEVE CONTAIN EMBRACE INHERIT SUSTAIN UNDERFO PERCEIVE
(— A CRIMINAL) RESET
(— A DEGREE) GRADUATE
(— AS GUEST) FANG HOST VANG GREET
(— AS MEMBER) INCEPT
(— AS REWARD) REAP
(— FROM LOTTERY) DRAW
(— INTO RELIGIOUS ORDER) PROFESS
(— PAYMENT) COLLECT
(— SHEETS) FLY
(— STOLEN GOODS) RESET
(— WITH KINDNESS) WELCOME
(— WITH PLEASURE) GRATIFY
(PREF.) RECIPIO
RECEIVER DONEE FENCE PHONE PERNOR SINDICO CYMAPHEN DONATARY REHEATER
(— IN BANKRUPTCY) SINDICO
(— OF INCOME) PERNOR
(— OF PROPERTY) ALIENEE
(— OF STOLEN GOODS) LOCK FENCE
(RADIO —) SET
(SECRET —) TAP
(TELEGRAPH —) INKER INKWRITER
(TELEPHONE —) PHONE CYMAPHEN
RECEIVING PERNANCY
RECENSION REVIEW SURVEY CENSURE CRITIQUE
RECENT HOT NEW LATE PUNY ENDER FRESH GREEN HOURLY LATELY LATTER MODERN CURRENT HOLOCENE NEOTERIC
(MOST —) LAST
(PREF.) CAEN(O) CEN(O) NE(O)
(SUFF.) CENE
RECENTLY ANEW JUST LATE NEWLY LASTLY LATELY FRESHLY LATTERLY
RECENTNESS YOUTH
RECEPTACLE ARK BIN BOX CAN CUP DIP FAT PAN TIN TUB URN VAT BATH BOAT BOWL CASE CELL CIST DOVE DROP FACK FONT HELL HOLD INRO LOOM RACK RECU SAFE SINK TIDY TOUR ARBOR CARRY CREEL KIOSK KITTY RESET SCOOP STEAN STEEN TABLE TORUS BASKET BUCKET BUTLER CARTON CUPULE DIPPER DRAWER HAMPER HOPPER MORTAR PITCHI

POCKET SHRINE TABLET TROUGH ASHTRAY CAPSULE CARRIER CORBULA DUSTBIN ENVELOP HEADBOX LATRINE OMNIBUS OSSUARY PARISON RECEIPT SANDBOX SETTLER SOAPBOX STOWAGE TRAVOIS BURSICLE CANISTER CESSPOOL DUMPSTER FOREBOOT GYNOBASE HONEYPOT LOCKFAST OSSARIUM OVERFLOW PERFUMER SPITTOON STOCKPOT SEPULCHER

(— FOR ABANDONED INFANTS) TOUR
(— FOR BONES) OSSUARY OSSARIUM
(— FOR BROKEN TYPE) HELL
(— FOR BUTTER) RUSKIN
(— FOR COAL) BUNKER
(— FOR CONVEYING) APRON
(— FOR DRY ARTICLES) FAT
(— FOR FOUL THINGS) SINK
(— FOR GLASS BATCH) ARBOR
(— FOR HOLY WATER) FONT
(— FOR ORE-CRUSHING) MORTAR
(— FOR POKER CHIPS) KITTY
(— FOR SACRED RELICS) TABLE SHRINE TABLET SEPULCHRE
(— FOR SAVINGS) SOCK
(— FOR SEWING MATERIALS) TIDY
(— FOR TREASURE) HANAPER
(— FOR TYPE CASES) RACK
(— FOR VOTES) SITULA
(— IN BOTTLE-MAKING MACHINE) PARISON
(— OF CLAY OR STONE) STEAN STEEN
(— OF FLOWER) THALAMUS
(— ON WEIGHING SCALES) PAN
(— OVER ALTAR) DOVE
(CLAY —) BOOT
(DILATED —) GYNOBASE
(ELECTRICAL —) BASEPLUG
(INCENSE —) ACERRA
(OPEN —) TRAY
(PURSELIKE —) BURSICLE
(TAILOR'S —) HELL
(TRASH —) DUMPSTER
(WOODEN —) SEBILLA
(SUFF.) CLINE CLINIC CLINIUM

RECEPTION TEA ROUT COURT CRUSH DIFFA LEVEE SALON TREAT ACCOIL DURBAR RUELLE SOIREE SQUASH ACCUEIL COUCHEE MATINEE OVATION PASSAGE RECEIPT RECUEIL TEMPEST WELCOME ASSEMBLY FUNCTION GREETING PERNANCY REACTION SOCIABLE ACCEPTANCE RECIPIENCE RECIPIENCY
(— AT BEDTIME) COUCHEE
(— OF NATIVE PRINCES) DURBAR
(— OF SOUND) AUDIO
(ARABIC —) DIFFA
(CORDIAL —) WELCOME
(CROWDED —) SQUASH
(FASHIONABLE —) LEVEE SALON
(MORNING —) LEVEE RUELLE
(WEDDING —) INFARE
RECEPTIVE OPEN SENSORY OPENHANDED
RECEPTOR STOCK RECEIVER DOMINATOR

RECERCELEE SARCELLY
RECESS ALA ARK BAY BOX COD CUP PAN BOLE BUNK COVE DEEP HOLE NOOK TRAP AMBRY BOSOM BOWER CANAL CAVUM CLEFT CREEK HAVEN HITCH INLET NICHE ORIEL PRESS SINUS ALCOVE ANCONA CAVERN CENTER CHAPEL CIRQUE CLOSET COFFER CRANNY EXEDRA GROTTO INDENT LOCULE RABBET REBATE BEDSITE CONCAVE CREVICE LOCULUS MANHOLE RETREAT SINKING INTERVAL LOCKHOLE OVERTURE TABLINUM TOKONOMA TRAVERSE VACATION PIGEONHOLE
(— BETWEEN CAPES) BAY
(— FOR FAMILY RECORDS) TABLINUM
(— FOR HINGE LEAF) PAN
(— FOR PIECE OF SCULPTURE) ANCONA
(— FOR URN) LOCULUS
(— IN CHURCH) APSE
(— IN CHURCH WALL) AMBRY AWMRY AUMBRY AUMERY AWMRIE
(— IN COLON) HAUSTRUM
(— IN JAPANESE HOUSE) TOKONOMA
(— IN MOUNTAIN) CIRQUE
(— IN ROCK) HITCH
(— IN SIDE OF HILL) CORRIE
(— IN SIDE OF ROOM) ALA
(— IN WALL) BOLE NICHE ALCOVE
(— ON STAGE) CANOPY
(INMOST —) BOSOM
(PL.) FLASH
RECESSED SUNK SUNKEN
RECESSION BUST RETREAT
RECESSIVE BACKWARD RECEDING RETIRING WITHDRAWN
RECHAB (SON OF —) MALCHIAH JEHONADAB
RECHERCHE RARE CHOICE EXOTIC CURIOUS PRECIOUS UNCOMMON EXQUISITE
RECIDIVIST REPEATER
RECIPE RX FORM RULE FORMULA RECEIPT
RECIPIENT HEIR DONEE ALMSMAN DONATEE DONATORY LAUREATE
(SUFF.) EE
RECIPROCAL CROSS COMMON MUTUAL SECANT SEESAW
(— OF A POISE) RHE
(— OF RADIUS) CURVATURE
(— OF VISCOSITY) FLUIDITY
(PREF.) COUNTER INTER
RECIPROCATE REPAY RETURN REQUITE RETROACT
RECIPROCITY SHU ISOPOLITY MUTUALITY
RECITAL TALE ASHRE CITAL RECIT STORY EXPOSE LITANY PARADE REPEAT TIKKUN READING RELATION REPETITION
(— OF PRAYER) GEULAH HAMOTZI KEDUSHAH
(UNTRUE —) TALE
(SUFF.) LOG(ER)(IA)(IAN)(IC)(ICAL)(IST)(UE)(Y)
RECITATION DHIKR READING RECITAL RHAPSODY

RECITATIVE SCENA CHANSON PARLANDO
RECITE SAY CARP TELL STATE INTONE RECKON RELATE RENDER REPEAT DECLAIM DECLINE DICTATE NARRATE RECOUNT REELOFF REHEARSE
(— AS ELOCUTION EXERCISE) DECLAIM
(— IN MONOTONE) INTONE
(— METRICALLY) SCAN
(— MONOTONOUSLY) CHANT CHAUNT
(— NUMBERS) COUNT
(— PRAYERS) BENSH DAVEN
(— TIRESOMELY) THRUM
(— WITH GREAT EASE) RUSH
RECITER SCALD SKALD ANTERI DISEUR CONTEUR DISEUSE HOMERIST ILIADIST RHAPSODE
RECITING CHARM
RECK RAK CARE DEEM PASS MATTER REGARD CONCERN CONSIDER ESTIMATE
RECKLESS RASH WILD BLIND FOLLE PERDU MADCAP RACKLE SAVAGE GALLOWS RAMSTAM CARELESS HEADLONG HEEDLESS TEARAWAY BLINDFOLD TEMERARIOUS DEVILMAYCARE
RECKLESSLY FAST BLIND RAMSTAM HEADLONG HEADFIRST
RECKLESSNESS BAYARD
RECKON RET ARET CAST DATE ITEM RATE RECK RELY TALE TELL TOTE ALLOT AUDIT CLAIM CLASS COUNT JUDGE PLACE RETTE SCORE TALLY THINK ASSIGN FIGURE IMPUTE NUMBER REPUTE TOTTLE ACCOUNT ASCRIBE COMPUTE INCLUDE PRETEND RECOUNT SUPPOSE SUPPUTE CONSIDER ESTIMATE
(— IN) INCLUDE
(— TOO HIGH) OVERCOUNT
RECKONING TAB BILL NICK POST SHOT TAIL TALE COUNT SCORE TALLY COMPOT LAWING REASON TAILYE TOTTLE ACCOUNT DAYTALE TAILZEE COMPUTUS
(TAVERN —) LAWING
RECLAIM IN TAME ADEEM ASSART OBJECT RECALL REDEEM REFORM RESCUE SUBDUE PROTEST RECOVER RESTORE
(— FOR AGRICULTURE) ASSART
(— FROM SAVAGE STATE) CIVILIZE
RECLAIMANT GOEL
RECLAME FAME
RECLINE LIE LIG LEAN LOLL REST COUCH ACCUMB RECUMB UPLEAN DISCUMB
(— AWKWARDLY) SPRAWL SPRADDLE
(— LANGUIDLY) GAULSH
RECLINING CUMBENT ACCUMBENT RECUMBENT ACCUBATION
(— ON COUCH) ACCUMBENT
RECLUSE NUN MONK CULDEE HERMIT REMOTE ASCETIC EREMITE INCLUSA INCLUSE ANCHORET INCLUSUS SECLUDED SOLITARY SCIOPHYTE SOLITAIRE

(BROWN —) SPIDER
(PL.) SECLUSE
RECLUSIVE HERMETIC
RECOGNITION FAME SPUR HONOR SENSE CREDIT STATUS FEELING KENNING KNOWING AGNITION SANCTION ANAGNOSIS
(— OF ACHIEVEMENT) LAUREL CITATION
(— OF ERROR) RESIPISCENCE
(HONORIFIC —) DISTINCTION
(SUFF.) GNOSIA GNOSIS GNOSTIC GNOSY
RECOGNIZE KEN SEE WIT ESPY FACE KNOW SPOT TELL ADMIT ALLOW BLINK CROWN HONOR KEETH KITHE KYTHE ACCEPT ACKNOW AGNIZE BEKNOW COUTHE REVISE CORRECT DISCERN REALIZE ACCREDIT
(— IN ANY CAPACITY) AGNIZE
RECOGNIZED GOOD CLEAR KNOWN CLASSIC FAMILIAR
RECOIL SHY BALK KICK TURN REBUT SHRUG SHUCK START STRAM BLENCH BOUNCE FLINCH RECULE RESILE RESULT RETORT SHRINK REBOUND REDOUND REVERSE BACKLASH REJOUNCE
(WITHOUT —) DEADBEAT
RECOLLECT RECALL RECORD RETAIN BETHINK COMPOSE RECOVER RECOLETO REMEMBER
RECOLLECTION MIND MEMORY RECALL RECORD MINDING THOUGHT MEMORIAL SOUVENIR ANAMNESIS
RECOMMENCE RENEW REOPEN RESUME REPRISE
RECOMMEND MOVE OSSE PLUG TOUT WISH ADVISE COMMIT PRAISE PREFER COMMEND CONSIGN COUNSEL ENTRUST ADVOCATE RECOMMIT
RECOMMENDATION NAP CHIT VOEU ADVISE COUNSEL TESTIMONY
(PARTY —) COUPON
(SERVANT'S —) CHIT
RECOMPENSE PAY MEED MEND ATONE MENSE QUITS REPAY YIELD AMENDS BOUNTY HADBOT RECOUP REWARD SALARY GUERDON IMBURSE PAYMENT PREMIUM REQUITE RESTORE SATISFY SERVICE
RECONCILE GREE WEAN ADAPT AGREE ATONE ACCORD ADJUST SETTLE SHRIVE REUNITE HARMONIZE
RECONCILED FAIN VAIN SAUGHT
RECONCILIATION ATONE ACCORD SAUGHT REUNION IRENICON
(— OF BELIEFS) SYNCRETISM
RECONDITE DARK DEEP HIGH HIDDEN MYSTIC OCCULT SECRET CRYPTIC CURIOUS OBSCURE RETIRED ABSTRACT ABSTRUSE ESOTERIC
RECONNAISSANCE RECCE RECCO RECCY RECON SURVEY
RECONNOITER CASE SCOUT

RECALL SURVEY EXAMINE PICKEER DISCOVER REMEMBER
RECONSIDER REVIEW FORTHINK
RECONSTRUCT RECAST REPAIR REEVOKE REMODEL RESTORE
RECORD CAN CUT BOOK CARD DATE DISC ITER MARK NICK PAGE ROLL SING SLIP TAPE WICK ALBUM CHART DIARY ENACT ENTER ENTRY FASTI GRAPH JUMBO PRICK QUIPO QUIPU SCORE SIJIL SLATE STYLE TITLE WRITE ANNALS CHARGE DOCKET LEGEND MEMOIR SCROLL SPREAD WARBLE ACCOUNT CALENDS CAPTURE CITATOR DUBBING KALENDS LEXICON MENTION MYOGRAM SHOWING TICKLER TRACING ANAGRAPH ARCHIVES CYLINDER ENTRANCE ERGOGRAM HERDBOOK INSCROLL JUDGMENT KYMOGRAM LAUEGRAM MARIGRAM MELOGRAM MEMORIAL MEMORIZE MONUMENT NOCTUARY ONDOGRAM PANCHART PRESSING REGISTER REMEMBER SCHEDULE STUDBOOK INSCRIPTION OBSERVATION OSCILLOGRAM
(— BY NOTCHES) SCORE
(— OF CAR MOVEMENTS) JUMBO
(— OF DOCUMENT) PROTOCOL
(— OF EVENTS) FASTI
(— OF FOOTPRINTS) STIBOGRAM
(— OF HUMANITY'S FATE) SIJIL SIJILL
(— OF JOURNEY) JOURNAL ITINERARY
(— OF LOAN) CHARGE
(— OF MUHAMMAD'S SAYINGS) HADIT
(— OF MUSCULAR WORK) ERGOGRAM
(— OF PROCEEDINGS) ACTA ITER JOURNAL MINUTES
(COMPUTER —) PRINTOUT
(COURT —) EYRE
(DAILY —) DIARY
(DEMONSTRATION —) DEMO
(FORMAL —) ACT
(HISTORICAL —) STORY
(MAGNETIC —) DISK FLOPPY
(PERSONAL —) BIO VITA RESUME DOSSIER
(PHONOGRAPH —) DISC DISK MONO SINGLE BISCUIT SHELLAC
(PLASTIC MAGNETIC —) DISK
(SHIP'S —) LOG
(TYPE OF —) CD HIFI MONO STEREO MONAURAL
(PL.) LIBER ANNALS ARCHIVE MEMORABILIA
(PREF.) DISC(I)(O)
(SUFF.) GRAM GRAPH(ER)(IA)(IC)(Y)
RECORDED TAPE TAPED ONTAPE
RECORDER VCR FLUTE BOOKER FLAUTO NOTATOR GREFFIER REGISTER FIPPI FFI LITF
(— AND CAMERA) PORTAFAX PORTAPACK
(VIDEOTAPE —) VCR
RECORDING ALBUM ALIVE LABEL

VIDEO CUTTING VIDEODISC VIDEODISK
(— AWARD) GRAMMY
(NARRATION —) VOICEOVER
(TELEVISION —) VIDEOTAPE
RECOUNT MING TELL COUNT DEVISE RECITE REGARD RELATE REPEAT SPREAD EXPRESS HISTORY ITERATE NARRATE CONSIDER DESCRIBE REHEARSE REITERATE
RECOUP DEDUCT REGAIN RECOVER INDEMNIFY
RECOUPLING HOOKUP
RECOURSE SUIT ACCESS APPEAL REFUGE RESORT STRING REGRESS RESTAUR RISORSE
(HAVE —) RECUR
RECOVER DOW COUR COWR CURE FIRM HEAL KERE COVER RALLY REACH UPSET BOUNCE RECURE REGAIN RESCUE RESUME RETAKE RETIRE REVERT REVOKE WARISH DELIVER OVERGET OVERPUT OVERSET READEPT RECLAIM RECRUIT REPAREL REPRISE RESTORE RETRIEVE SNAPBACK
(— LOST TERRITORY) REVENDICATE
RECOVERER DIGESTER
RECOVERY CURE RECOUR RECURE REMEDY RETURN SALVAGE COMEBACK SNAPBACK RECLAMATION
(— OF METAL) CUPELLATION
(— PERIOD) REHAB
(FORCIBLE —) RESCUE
RECREANT FALSE CRAVEN YELLOW APOSTATE COWARDLY DESERTER RECRAYED
RECREATE AMUSE EVOKE REVIVE
RECREATION PLAY SPORT SOLACE RENEWAL ACTIVITY DIVERSION PALINGENY
(PERIOD OF —) HOLIDAY VACATION
RECREATIONAL AMUSIVE
RECREATIVE PLAYING
RECREMENT SLAG DROSS SCORIA
RECRUIT BLEU BOOT FRESH RAISE SPROG GATHER INTAKE MUSTER RECREW REPAIR REVIVE RECOVER REFRESH RESTORE ASSEMBLE BEZONIAN CONSCRIPT
(RAW —) ROOKY ROOKIE
RECTAL
(PREF.) ARCHO
RECTANGLE BOX SQUARE CHECKER
(COTTON —) HUIPIL
(CURVILINEAR —) TESSERA
(EQUILATORAL —) SQUARE
(WOVEN —) SINKER
RECTANGULAR OBLONG SQUARE BOXLIKE EMERALD
RECTIFICATION REFORM LIMATION
RECTIFIER DIODE VALVE COLUMN DETECTOR EXCITRON
RECTIFY AMEND EMEND RIGHT ADJUST BETTER DETECT REFORM REMEDY CORRECT IMPROVE REDRESS EMENDATE REGULATE
RECTITUDE DOOM EQUITY JUSTICE PROBITY
RECTOR RULER LEADER PARSON PERSONA INCUMBENT

RECTUM SIEGE TEWEL
(PREF.) ARCHO PROCT(O) RECTO
RECUMBENT IDLE PRONE JACENT CUMBENT LEANING RESTING INACTIVE REPOSING
RECUPERATE MEND RALLY REFETE REGAIN RECOVER RECRUIT RETRIEVE
RECUR ACTUP CYCLE REFER REPEAT RESORT RETURN REOCCUR REVOLVE REAPPEAR
(— CONSTANTLY) HAUNT
RECURRENCE RESORT RETURN ATAVISM REPRISE ITERANCE ITERANCY RECOURSE FLASHBACK
(— OF SOUND) CADENCE
(REGULAR —) RHYTHM
(SUFF.) LY
RECURRENT CYCLIC FREQUENT PERENNIAL
RECURRING ROLLING CONTINUAL
(— ANNUALLY) ETESIAN
(— EVERY THIRD DAY) TERTIAN
(— EVERY 72 HOURS) QUARTAN
(— ON NINTH DAY) NONAN NONANE
(— ON SEVENTH DAY) SEPTAN
(CONSTANTLY —) ETERNAL
(CONTINUALLY —) CONSTANT
(SUFF.) ENNIAL
RECURVED REFLEX ERICOID
RECUTTING FRESHING
RED (ALSO SEE COLOR) GOYA GULY PINK PUCE ROJO ROSY RUBY ANGRY CANNA CORAL FIERY JUDAS ROUGE RUDDY RUFUS ARCHIL AZALEA BLOODY CERISE FLORID FULGID GARNET HECTIC NECTAR ORCHIL ORIENT RAISIN RUBRIC TITIAN TRYPAN VERMIL WANTON CARMINE GLOWING NACARAT PIMENTO RADICAL RUBELLE RUBIOUS STAMMEL VERMILY ARMENIAN AUBUSSON BORDEAUX CARDINAL CHOLERIC COLORADO FLAGRANT MANDARIN MOROCAIN RUBICUND SANGUINE ARTILLERY RUBINEOUS COQUELICOT SANGDEBOEUF
(— AND INFLAMED) BLOODSHOT
(— PLANET) MARS
(ANTIQUE —) CANNA
(BRICK —) TESTACEOUS
(BRIGHT —) TULY CHERRY PUNICIAL VERMILION
(BRILLIANTLY —) FLAMING
(DARK —) CLARET
(EUREKA —) PUCE
(FIERY —) MINIUM
(GRAYISH —) AZALEA
(HERALDIC —) GULES
(IRON OXIDE —) AGATE TARRAGONA
(ORANGE —) NACARAT
(PURPLISH —) LAKE MURREY MAGENTA
(SEE —) GETMAD
(WAX —) COPPER
(YELLOWISH —) MAROON
(PREF.) ERYTHR(O) PHENIC(O) PHOENIC(O) PYRRH(O) PYRRO RHOD(O) RUBE RUBI RUBO RUBRI RUBRO RUFI RUFO

REDACT EDIT
RED ADMIRAL VANESSA
RED AND THE BLACK (AUTHOR OF —) STENDHAL
(CHARACTER IN —) SOREL FOUQUE JULIEN PIRARD DERENAL VALENOD MATHILDE
RED-BACKED SHRIKE POPE
RED BADGE OF COURAGE (AUTHOR OF —) CRANE
(CHARACTER IN —) JIM HENRY WILSON CONKLIN FLEMING
RED BANEBERRY REDBERRY TOADROOT
RED BAY PERSEA
RED-BELLIED (— TERRAPIN) SLIDER SKILPOT
(— WOODPECKER) CHAB
REDBREAST ROBIN RUDDOCK
RED-BREASTED BREAM FLATFISH FLOUNDER
RED-BREASTED KNOT GRAYBACK GREYBACK
REDBUD CERCIS JUNEBUD
RED CAMPION ROBIN SOLDIER
RED CEDAR SAVIN SABINA JUNIPER
RED CLOVER SAPLING TREFOIL TRIFOLY
RED CURRANT GOYA RIZZLE TIZZAR
REDD RID COMB OPEN LITTER NEATEN REFUSE RESCUE SETTLE ARRANGE DELIVER SMARTEN UNBLOCK UNRAVEL
RED DEER OLEN SPAY STAG
(FEMALE —) HIND
(MALE —) HART STAG
REDDEN RUD FIRE RUBY BLUSH FLUSH LIGHT ROUGE RUDDY BLOODY RUBIFY RUBRIC RUDDLE EMPURPLE
REDDISH REDDY RUDDY RUFUS FLUSHY GINGER RUFOUS COLORADO PYRRHOUS RUBICUND
RED DOG BLITZ
RED DRUM SPOT REDFISH
REDEAR SHELLCRACKER
REDEEM BUY WIN SAVE ALESE CLEAR LOUSE REPRY BORROW OFFSET RANSOM DELIVER FULFILL JUSTIFY RECLAIM WITHBEG AGAINBUY LIBERATE
REDEEMER GOEL SAVIOR
REDEEMING SAVING
REDEMPTION RANSOM REFORM SAFETY SALVATION
REDEYE BASS RUDD VIREO
RED-EYE CATSUP CICADA WHISKY
REDEYE SUNFISH
RED-EYED VIREO REDEYE GRASSET PREACHER
RED-FACED FLUSHED SCARLET
REDFIN DACE SHINER REDHORSE YELLOWFIN
REDFISH SALMON FATHEAD ROSEFISH
RED GOOSEFOOT PIGWEED SOWBANE
RED GROUPER MERO NEGRE REDBELLY
RED GROUSE GORHEN GORCOCK LAGOPODE MOORBIRD MUIRFOWL

RED GUM JARRAH EUCALYPT
RED GURNARD CUR ELLECK
ROCHET SOLDIER
RED-HAIRED RUFUS CARROTY
REDHEAD DIVER FINCH POCHARD
CARROTTOP KIZILBASH
RED HIND GRAYSBY GROUPER
CABRILLA
REDHORSE REDFIN SUCKER
REDIA SPOROSAC
REDIRECT DISPLACE READDRESS
REDISTILL COHOBATE
REDISTRIBUTE FRESHEN REASSIGN
RED LAVER SLOKE
REDNESS RED RUD GLOW HEAT
RUDD RUBOR ERYTHEMA
RUBEDITY
(— OF NOSE) GROGBLOSSOM
(— OF SKIN) EFFLORESCENCE
(— OF SKY) AURORA
REDO REDACT RESTYLE
(— UNSKILLFULLY) BOTCH
RED OCHER TIVER ABRAUM
RUDDLE
REDOLENCE BALM AROMA SCENT
REDOLENT RICH ODOROUS
SCENTED AROMATIC FRAGRANT
SMELLING
RED OSIER WILLOW REDBRUSH
REDOUBLE RECCHO INTENSIFY
REDOUBT FEAR MASK DREAD
SCHANZ SCONCE BULWARK
REDOUND TURN ACCRUE BILLOW
CONDUCE REFLECT OVERFLOW
RED RASPBERRY CUTHBERT
REDRESS HEAL DRESS REDUB
RIGHT AVENGE OFFSET REFORM
RELIEF REMEDE REMEDY REPAIR
ADDRESS CORRECT RECTIFY
REFOUND RELIEVE
RED ROCKFISH TAMBOR
REDROOT PIGWEED
RED ROVER (AUTHOR OF)
COOPER
(CHARACTER IN —) ARK FID DICK
HENRY AFRICA DELACY SCIPIO
WILDER WYLLYS BIGNALL GRAYSON
GERTRUDE RODERICK
RED SAGE LANTANA
RED SALMON SOCKEYE
RED SANDALWOOD CHANDAM
REDSHANK CLEE TEUK SHAKE
GAMBET REDLEG YELPER PELLILE
TATTLER
REDSKIN RED ROJO TAWNY INDIAN
REDSTART YELPER BRANTAIL
FIRETAIL WHITECAP FIREFLIRT
RED STOPPER EUGENIA
IRONWOOD
RED-TAILED (— HAWK) REDTAIL
(— TROPIC BIRD) KOAE
RED TAPE CHICHI
RED-TAPISM BEADLEDOM
RED-THROATED LOON WABBY
REDTOP COUCH FIORIN FINETOP
FINEBENT FURZETOP BLUEJOINT
REDUCE CUT BATE CLIP DOCK DROP
EASE PARE PULL THIN ABASE
ABATE ALLAY APPAL BREAK DRAFT
ELIDE LOWER QUELL SCANT
SHAVE SLAKE SLASH SMELT
ATTRIT DEDUCE DEFALK DEJECT
DELETE DEPOSE DILUTE HUMBLE

LESSEN REBATE REDUCT SHRINK
SUBACT SUBDUE WEAKEN
ABANDON ABRIDGE ASSUAGE
ATOMIZE CHANCER CONQUER
CURTAIL DEFLATE DEGRADE
DEPLETE DWINDLE ECLIPSE
FRITTER INHIBIT RESOLVE
RETREAT SCISSOR SHORTEN
SUBJECT ABSTRACT ATTEMPER
CONDENSE DECREASE DIMINISH
DOWNSIZE MINIMIZE
(— ACCORDING TO FIXED RATIO)
SCALE
(— ANGLE) CHAMFER
(— BULK) BLEND
(— LUMBER) SIZE
(— PROFITS) SQUEEZE
(— PURITY) ALLOY
(— SAIL) REEF
(— STONE BLOCKS) SPALL SPAWL
(— THE VALUE) DECRY BEGGAR
DEPRAVE
(— TO A MEAN) AVERAGE
(— TO ASHES) CREMATE
(— TO CARBON) CHAR
(— TO FINE PARTICLES) ATOMIZE
MICRONIZE
(— TO FLAT SURFACE) LEVEL
(— TO INSIGNIFICANCE) DROWN
(— TO LOWER GRADE) BREAK
DEMOTE DEGRADE
(— TO NIL) CLOSE
(— TO NOTHING) ANNUL
(— TO PASSIVITY) CHINAFY
PROSTRATE
(— TO POWDER) GRIND PULVERIZE
(PREF.) DE
REDUCED SUNK TAIL BROKEN
SHRUNK CURTATE DWARFED
DEGRADED SHRUNKEN WEAKENED
VESTIGIAL
(— TO HELPLESSNESS) PROSTRATE
REDUCING (EXERCISES)
SLIMNASTICS
REDUCTION BUST LETUP SLASH
CUTBACK CUTDOWN DOCKAGE
SHAVING ANALYSIS DILUTION
DISCOUNT DRAWDOWN
ABATEMENT SHRINKAGE
(— IN FORCE) RIF
(— IN PITCH) DROP
(— IN PRICE) SAVING CONCESSION
(— OF POWER) SHUTDOWN
(— OF THICKNESS) OFFSET
(— TO ABSURDITY) APAGOGUE
(PREF.) LY(O)
(SUFF.) LYSIS LYST LYTE
LYTIC LYZE
REDUNDANCY EXCESS NIMIETY
SURPLUS PLEONASM PLETHORA
VERBIAGE MACROLOGY
TAUTOLOGY
REDUNDANT WORDY LAVISH
PROFUSE SURPLUS VERBOSE
SWELLING EXCESSIVE
REDWING POP THRUSH WINDLE
GADWALL WINNARD
REDWOOD MAD AMBOYNA
BARWOOD FURIOUS SEQUOIA
MAHOGANY
RE-ECHO REWORD REBOUND
RESOUND REDOUBLE
REED NAL RIE RIX SAG SAX BENT

JUNK MILL OBOE PIPE PIRN RODE
SLEY TULE ARROW DONAX SPEAR
TWILL BENNEL RADDLE SAGGON
BASSOON CALAMUS FISTULA
WHISTLE WINDING ABOMASUM
CLARINET
(— FOR WARPING) WRAITHE
(— FOR WINDING THREAD) PIRN
SPOOL
(— IN ORGAN) VIBRATOR
(— OF LOOM) COMB
(— OF MUSICAL INSTRUMENT)
TONGUE
(FOXTAIL —) DOD
(GIANT —) DONAX
(MUSICAL —) OAT
(WEAVER'S —) SLAY SLEY RADDLE
SLEIGH
(PL.) SPEAR
(PREF.) ARUNDI CALAM(I)(O)
REED BENT CARRIZO
REEDBIRD BOBOLINK
REEDBUCK BOHOR NAGOR
REITBOK
REED BUNTING RINGBIRD
REED CANARY GRASS SPIRE
DAGGERS
REED END TONGUE
REEDING GADROON MILLING
STRIGIL GRAINING
REED MACE RAUPO CATTAIL
MATREED
REED ORGAN MELODEON
HARMONIUM
REED PIPE MIRLITON
REED WARBLER PITBIRD
REEDY THIN WEAK FRAIL TWILLED
REEF CAY KAY KEY CAYO LODE RYFT
SCAR VEIN ATOLL LEDGE SHELF
STICK BOILER REEFER SADDLE
SKERRY BAGREEF BALANCE
BIOHERM MAKATEA TOMBOLO
REEFER CAR COAT STICK JACKET
MUGGLES
REEK FOG FUG EMIT FUME HEAP
MIST PILE RICK RISE VENT EQUIP
EXUDE FETOR ISSUE NIDOR SMEEK
SMOKE STEAM VAPOR EXHALE
OUTFIT EMANATE
(— WITH CORRUPTION) FESTER
REEL PIRN RANT ROCK SPIN STOT
SWAB SWIM TURN GIDDY SPOOL
SWIFT TRULL WAVER WHEEL
WHIRL WINCE WINCH BOBBIN
RECOIL SWERVE TOTTER TUMULT
WAGGLE WALTER WELTER
WINDER WINDLE WINNLE WINTLE
BALLOON STAGGER SWARBLE
TITUBATE
(— FOR DRAWING SILK) FILATURE
(— FOR WARP DRYING) BALLOON
(— FOR WINDING YARN) PIRN
SWIFT
(— OFF A STORY) SCRIEVE
(— USED FOR YARN) CRIB
(DYEING —) WINCE
(FISHING —) TROW TROLL TRULL
WINCH
(HIGHLAND —) HOOLICAN
HOOLACHAN
(PL.) REVELS
REELER TWINER

REELING TURN AREEL LURCH
FILATURE STAGGERY WAMBLING
REEM MOAN URUS UNICORN
REEVE REE REFE THREAD BAILIFF
PROVOST STEWARD OVERSEER
REFECTION MEAL RELIEF REPAST
HOGMANAY
(NEW YEAR'S —) HOGMANAY
REFECTORY FRATER FRATRY
REFER DEFER LEAVE POINT ADVERT
ALLUDE APPEAL ASSIGN CHARGE
COMMIT DELATE DIRECT IMPUTE
PREFER RELATE SUBMIT ASCRIBE
PERTAIN REJOURN RELEGATE
(— TO) SEE CITE INTEND CONCERN
CONSULT MENTION INTIMATE
(— TO SOMETHING REPEATEDLY)
HARP
REFEREE ZEBRA BREHON UMPIRE
ARBITER AUDITOR
REFERENCE TAB FOLIO REMIT SIGIL
APPEAL REGARD RENVOI BEARING
MEANING RESPECT ALLUSION
HANDBOOK INNUENDO RELATION
(— WORK) OED ATLAS INDEX
ROGET ALMANAC LEXICON
CATALOGUE GAZETTEER
(BRITISH — WORK) OED
(OBLIQUE —) SQUINT
(SATIRICAL —) GLANCE
REFERENDUM POLL MANDATE
REFINE RUN TRY BOLT EDIT FILE
FINE PURE CUPEL EXALT PLAIN
SLICK SMELT AFFINE DECOCT
EXCOCT FILTER GARBLE SMOOTH
CONCOCT ELEVATE PERFECT
SUBLIME SWEETEN CIVILIZE
HUMANIZE URBANIZE
(— AS GOLD) TEST CARAT
(— PULP) JORDAN
(— SUGAR) CLAY
(— WINE) FORCE
REFINED FINE GENT NEAT NICE TRIE
ATTIC EXACT PURED TERSE
CHASTE EXCOCT INLAND NIMINY
POLITE QUAINT SUBTLE URBANE
CLEANLY COURTLY ELEGANT
GENTEEL PRECISE SCRAPED
AUGUSTAN DELICATE ELEVATED
HIGHBRED POLISHED PRECIEUX
PRECIOUS SERAPHIC RECHERCHE
SOPHISTICATED
(AFFECTEDLY —) FOPPISH
(NOT —) CRUDE
(TOO —) FINESPUN
REFINEMENT COUTH GRACE TASTE
NICETY POLISH CULTURE FINESSE
DELICACY ELEGANCE POLITURE
SUBTLETY URBANITY PRECIOSITY
REFINER TRIER JORDAN SMELTER
PURIFIER
REFINERY SMELTER
REFINING HUMAN FINING CULTURE
AFFINAGE
REFINISH ANTIQUE
REFLECT COW CHEW MUSE PORE
SHOW BLAZE FLASH GLASS GLINT
IMAGE SHINE STUDY THINK ADVISE
DAZZLE DEBATE MIRROR MULL
RECORD REFLEX RELUCE RETORT
RETURN REVISE STEVEN EXPRESS
PERPEND REDOUND REFRACT

SHIMMER COGITATE CONSIDER MEDITATE REDOUBLE RUMINATE
(— IRREGULARLY) SCATTER
(— UPON) SPECULATE
REFLECTED DERIVED MIRRORED SPECULAR
REFLECTING
(SUFF.) ESCENT
REFLECTION ECHO FOLD IDEA SKIT BLAME GHOST GLARE GNOME IMAGE DEBATE MUSING PONDER REFLEX RETURN SHADOW CENSURE COUNSEL SPECIES THOUGHT EYESHINE MOONPATH THINKING
(— OF SELF IN ANOTHER'S EYES) BABY
REFLECTIVE PENSIVE THOUGHTFUL
(— POWER) ALBEDO
REFLECTOR DISH FLAT CRITIC HASTER SHINER TAMPER HORIZON DIFFUSER HASTENER SPECULUM
REFLEX COPY IMAGE TROPISM ALLUSION
(NOT —) IDEOMOTOR
REFLUX EBB EBBING REFLOW
REFOREST REBOISE
REFORM MEND AMEND EMEND PRUNE BETTER REBUKE REPAIR CENSURE CORRECT DISBAND RECLAIM RECTIFY REDRESS
REFORMATORY COLLEGE MAGDALEN
REFORMER MOTT APOSTLE UTOPIAN UTOPIAST JANSENIST
(DANISH-AMERICAN —) RIIS
(GREAT SOCIAL —) RIIS
REFRACT DIVIDE REFLECT REFRINGE
REFRACTION REBATE REBOUND DIACLASIS
REFRACTOR PRISM
REFRACTORY TOUGH SULLEN UNRULY WANTON ALUNDUM FROWARD MULLITE RESTIVE VICIOUS WAYWARD MUTINOUS PERVERSE STUBBORN CAMSTEERY REBELLIOUS
REFRAIN BOB TAG CURB DOWN KEEP SHUN AVOID FORGO SPARE WONDE BURDEN CHORUS DESIST FOREGO LUDDEN RETAIN THRAIN ABSTAIN FORBEAR LULLABY REFREIT REPRISE TORNADA FABURDEN FALDERAL OVERCOME OVERWORD REPETEND RESTRAIN WITHDRAW TURNAGAIN
(— FROM) CAN HELP AVOID SPARE WAIVE FOREGO RESIGN ABSTAIN
(— FROM EXACTING) REMIT
(— FROM INDULGENCE) ABSTAIN
(— FROM TELLING) LAYNE
(— FROM USING) BOYCOTT
(— OF SONG) BOB TAG DOWN FOOT WHEEL BURDEN CHORUS FALDEROL
(EPODIC —) HEMISTICH
(MEANINGLESS —) DERRY DUCDAME
(RECURRING —) REPETEND
REFRESH FAN COOL REST CHEER FRESH SLAKE CAUDLE REFECT REFETE REGALE REHETE REPOSE

REVIVE UNTIRE COMFORT FORTIFY FRESHEN QUICKEN RECRUIT IRRIGATE RECREATE
REFRESHING DEWY BALMY CRISP FRESH TONIC CALLER LIVING BRACING COOLING REFRIGERANT
REFRESHMENT BAIT LUNCH CHARITY NUNCHEON REFRESCO COLLATION
(PL.) FOURS
REFRIGERANT ICE FREON COOLER AMMONIA COOLING CRYOGEN
REFRIGERATE CHILL
REFRIGERATION CRYOGENY
REFRIGERATOR FRIG FRIDGE ICEBOX FREEZER CONDENSER
(— CAR) REEFER
REFUEL TANK FILLUP
REFUGE ARK DIVE HOLT HOME PORT ROCK SOIL BIELD GRITH HAVEN OASIS RESET ASYLUM BILBIE COVERT HARBOR REFUTE RESORT SPITAL SUCCOR ALSATIA CRANNOG RESERVE RETREAT SHELTER UMBRAGE WARRANT BOLTHOLE CRANNOGE FORTRESS HIDEAWAY MAGDALEN RESOURCE SAFEHOLD
(FORTIFIED —) STRONGHOLD
(LAST —) SHEETANCHOR
(PLACE OF —) LAIR
(TAKE —) HOLEUP
REFUGEE REFFO COWBOY FUIDHIR FUGITIVE
REFULGENT BRIGHT SHINING RELUCENT BRILLIANT
REFUND REPAY UPSET REBATE REFOUND RESTORE DRAWBACK KICKBACK
REFURBISH DUST RENEW REVAMP FRESHEN BRIGHTEN RENOVATE
REFUSAL NAY VEE WARN WONT DENIAL MITTEN NAYSAY REPULSE ACCISMUS DECLINAL NEGATION NEGATIVE
(— TO SPEAK) APHRASIA
(SLANG —) NOWAY NODICE
(UNEXPECTED —) REBUFF
REFUSE ASH NAY NIL ORT SUD BALK COOM DENY DUST JUNK KEMP NAIT NILL NITE PELF PELT REDD SCUM SKIM SOIL SUDS WARN BAVIN COOMB CRAWN DEADS DRAST DROSS EXPEL FLOCK NITTE OFFAL RENAY REPEL SCRAN STENT STUFF SWASH SWILL TRADE TRASH WAIVE WASTE COLDER DANDER DEBRIS FORBID LITTER LUMBER MIDDEN NAYSAY PALTRY PELTRY RAFFLE RAMMEL RECUSE REFUGE REJECT SCRUFF SCULCH SHORTS SHRUFF SORDES SORDOR SPILTH BACKING BAGGAGE BROCKLE DECLINE DETRACT DETRECT DISAVOW DISOBEY FORSAKE GARBAGE GUBBINS MULLOCK OFFSCUM OUTCAST PRUNING RUBBISH SOILAGE SULLAGE WITHNAY WITHSAY CRASSIER DENEGATE DISALLOW DISCLAIM GARBLING LEAVINGS RIFFRAFF SWEEPAGE WITHHOLD OFFSCOURING

(— ADMISSION) CLOSE
(— FROM CHARCOAL OR COKE) BREEZE
(— FROM COFFEE BERRIES) TAILINGS
(— FROM CUTTING UP WHALE) GURRY
(— FROM MELTING METALS) SLAG DROSS SCORIA
(— FROM SIFTING COFFEE-BEANS) TRIAGE
(— FROM THRESHING) HUSK COLDER
(— FROM WINE-MAKING) RAPE
(— GREASE) COOM COOMB
(— OF CROP) STOVER
(— OF FLAX) PAB POB HARDS HURDS
(— OF FRUITS) MUST
(— OF GRAIN) PUG BRAN
(— OF GRAPES) MARC
(— OF INSECT) FRASS
(— OF MALT) DRAFF
(— OF MINE) BING DEAD
(— OF OIL MILLS) SHODE
(— OF PLANTS) ROSS
(— OF SILK) STRASS
(— OF SPICES) GARBLE
(— OF WHALE) FENKS GURRY TWITTER
(— OF WOOL) BACKINGS
(— TO APPROVE) VETO
(— TO COMPLY) STONEWALL
(— TO GO) JIB BALK
(— TO MOVE) REEST REIST
(— TO RECOGNIZE) CUT
(— TO SUPPORT) BOLT
(— TO TALK) DUMMY
(BREWERY —) DRAFF
(FISH —) CHUM GUBBINS
(FOOD —) SWILL
(LEATHER —) SPETCHES
(PLANT —) SCROFF
(STREET —) FULLAGE SCAVAGE
REFUTATION DISPROOF ELENCHUS HYPOBOLE REBUTTER
REFUTE DENY AVOID BELIE REBUT REFEL ASSOIL CONFUTE CONVELL CONVICT REPROVE REVINCE CONFOUND DISPROVE INFRINGE REDARGUE
REGAIN READEPT RECOVER RETRIEVE RECAPTURE
(— SOMETHING LOST) RECOUP
REGAL REAL ROYAL KINGLY PURPLE RIGGAL RIGOLE STATELY IMPERIAL MAJESTIC PRINCELY REGALIAN SPLENDID
REGALE FETE FEAST TREAT PLEASE DELIGHT REFRESH
REGALIA KIT ROYALTY
REGALO GIFT BONUS TREAT
REGAN (FATHER OF —) LEAR
(HUSBAND OF —) CORNWALL
(SISTER OF —) GONERIL CORDELIA
REGARD CON CARE DEEM FIND GAUM GAZE GIVE HEED HOLD LIKE LOOK MARK MIND RATE RECK SAKE TELL YEME ADORE COUNT FAVOR HONOR TREAT WEIGH ADDEEM ADMIRE ASPECT BEHOLD ESTEEM FIGURE GLANCE HOMAGE IMPUTE INTEND LIKING MOTIVE

NOTICE RECKON REMARK REWARD SURVEY ACCOUNT ADJUDGE CONCERN OBSERVE RESPECT RESPITE CONSIDER ENVISAGE ESTIMATE
(— AS) SEE
(— AS HOPELESS) DEPLORE
(— AS OBJECT OF GREAT INTEREST) LIONIZE
(— AS PROPER) ACCEPT
(— HIGHLY) ADMIRE CONSIDER
(— WITH PROFOUND RESPECT) REVERE VENERATE
(— WITH REPUGNANCE) ABHOR
(ATTENTIVE —) EYE
(MENTAL —) EYE
(PL.) COMPLIMENTS
(SUFF.) SCOPE SCOPIC SCOPUS SCOPY
REGARDED (— WITH AFFECTION) DEAR AFFECTED
REGARDING ABOUT ANENT APROPOS
REGARDLESS DEAF CARELESS HEEDLESS RECKLESS
(— OF THAT) BUT
REGATTA HENLEY LIBERTY
REGEM (FATHER OF —) JAHDAI
REGENCY RULE DOMINION
REGENERATE RENEW REFORM REVIVE RECLAIM GRACIOUS RENOVATE
(NOT —) CIVIL
REGENERATION REBIRTH NEOGENESIS
(GOD OF —) SIVA
REGENT RULER RULING WARDEN SHIKKEN GOVERNOR PANGERANG PROTECTOR
(— DIAMOND) PITT
(— OF NORTH) KUBERA KUVERA
REGIME FASCISM CAFETERIA
REGIMEN CURE DIET KEEP RULE REGIMENT
REGIMENT BUFF RULE COLOR TERCIO GUIDANCE INFANTRY SLASHERS
(BRITISH —) GRAYS GREYS
(COSSACK —) PULK
(FRAMEWORK OF —) CADRE
(INDIA —) PULTON PULTUN
(SPANISH —) TERCIO
(TURKISH —) ALAI
(28TH —) SLASHERS
REGION DO END ERD EYE GAU WON AREA BELT KITH KNOT NECK PART SOIL WONE WOON ZONE CLIME COAST EARTH EXURB INDIA MARCH PAGUS PLACE PLAGE REALM SHIRE TRACT TROAD ALKALI BORDER CENTER DESERT DOMAIN EXTENT GILEAD GROUND GUIANA TATARY CLIMATE CONFINE COUNTRY DEMESNE ENCLAVE IMAMATE KINGDOM MALABAR STATION TARTARY CHIEFDOM CLUBLAND DEMERARA DISTRICT ENVIRONS EPISTOME FLATLAND FORTRESS FRONTIER KRATOGEN LAKELAND LATITUDE NAPHTALI PROVINCE REGIMENT SERICANA STANNARY TERRITORY

(— ABOVE MOUTH) EPISTOMA EPISTOME
(— ADJACENT TO BOUNDARY) MARCH
(— BEYOND ATMOSPHERE) SPACE
(— BEYOND DEATH) CANAAN
(— BORDERING ON HELL) LIMBO
(— FAR AWAY) STRAND
(— IN FIBER) MICELLE
(— NEAR EQUATOR) DOLDRUMS
(— NOTED FOR MANY CONFLICTS) COCKPIT
(— OF AMPLITUDE) ANTINODE
(— OF CHROMOSOME) PUFF
(— OF CLOUDS) WELKIN
(— OF COLD AND DARKNESS) NIFLHEL NIFLHEIM
(— OF DEAD) AMENTI UTGARTHAR
(— OF JAPAN) DO
(— OF MARS) LIBYA
(— OF OCEAN) COUNTRY
(— OF ORIGIN) CRADLE
(— OF PHOTOSPHERE) FACULA
(— OF SHIFTING SAND) ERG
(— OF SIMPLE PLEASURE) ARCADY ARCADIA
(— OF SOURCE OF GOLD) OPHIR
(— OF TISSUE) FIELD
(— OUTSIDE CITY) EXURB
(— WITHOUT LAW) ALSATIA
(— WITHOUT WOODS) WOLD WEALD
(CELESTIAL —S) LANGI
(COASTAL —) LITTORAL
(CULTIVATED —) GARDEN
(DARKISH —S ON MARS) MARE
(DESERT —) ERG HAMADA
(DESERTED —) WASTE
(DESOLATE —) PUNA
(DISTANT —) THULE
(E. INDIAN —) DESH
(ELEVATED —) ALTITUDE
(FOREST —) TAIGA
(FORESTED —) MONTANA
(GEOGRAPHICAL —) BOWL SIDE
(HEAVENLY —) SPHERE
(IDEAL —) JINNESTAN
(INFERNAL —S) ABYSS TARTAR TARTARUS
(LARGE —) COMPAGE
(LIMESTONE —) KARST
(MOUNTAINOUS —) SIERRA
(OPEN —) SAVANNAH
(ORIENTAL —) INDOGAEA
(STAGNANT —) EDDY
(SUPERIOR —) HIGH
(TREELESS —) HIGHMOOR
(UPPER —) HIGH LOFT
(UPPER —S) ETHER
(WOODED —) FOREST
(PL.) DIGGINGS
(PREF.) NESO
(SUFF.) DOM NESE NESIA(N) NESUS
REGIONAL LOCAL SECTIONAL
REGISTER PIE BEAR BOOK FREE LIST MARK PILE POLL READ ROLL STOP ALBUM DIARY ENROL ENTER FASTI GRILL SIJIL SLATE ANNALS BEHAVE ENROLL LEDGER MUSTER RECORD REGEST ALMANAC ASCRIBE CALENDS CATALOG COUCHER DIPTYCH INDORSE

KALENDS NOTITIA ROTULET ANAGRAPH ARCHIVES CADASTER CALENDAR GREFFIER INDICATE INSCRIBE MENOLOGY PEDIGREE POLLBOOK TOLLBOOK STROHBASS
(— OF JUDGMENTS) DOCKET
(LOWEST —) CHALUMEAU
(MIDDLE —) CLARINO
(OFFICIAL —) TABLEAU CADASTER
REGISTRAR GUARD BURSAR ACTUARY PATWARI PUTWARI GREFFIER RESIDENT
REGISTRY FLAG STUDBOOK
REGLET FILET BATTEN FILLET RIGLET
REGRATER HUCKSTER
REGRESS EGRESS RETURN ANALYSIS RECOURSE
REGRET REW RUE RUTH GRIEF DESIRE RELENT REPENT SORROW DEPLORE REGRATE REMORSE FORTHINK REPINING
REGRETFUL BAD SORRY REPINING
REGRETTABLE DIRTY DOLOROUS
REGULAR DUE SET EVEN FULL JUST WEAK SOBER SUANT SUENT USUAL FORMAL GIUSTO NORMAL SQUARE STATED STEADY CANONIC CERTAIN CORRECT NATURAL ORDERED ORDERLY ORDINAL PERFECT TYPICAL UNIFORM COMPLETE CONSTANT DECOROUS FORMULAR HABITUAL ORDINARY ORDINATE TESSERAL
(PREF.) SYM
REGULARITY METHOD SQUARE SYSTEM EVENNESS SYNAPHEA
(— OF NATURE) LAW
REGULARLY DULY EVEN ORDERLY PROPERLY STATEDLY
REGULATE SET PACE RATE RULE WIND BOOST FRAME GUIDE ORDER RIGHT SHAPE ADJUST ASSIZE BEHAVE DIRECT GOVERN MASTER RADDLE SETTLE SQUARE TEMPER ARRANGE CONTROL DISPOSE MEASURE MONITOR QUALIFY RECTIFY ATTEMPER MODERATE MODULIZE
(— FOOD) DIET
(— PITCH) KEY STOP
REGULATED ORDENE ORDERED ORDERLY
(NOT —) INCORRECT
(WELL —) ORDERLY
REGULATING BEHIND
REGULATION LAW RULE BYLAW ORDER REGLE USUAL CURFEW ZABETA CONTROL PRECEPT STATUTE VOICING DISPOSAL STEERAGE
(— OF PRICE) ASSIZE
(DORMITORY —S) PARIETALS
REGULATOR GUIDE DISPOSER GOVERNOR
(GROWTH —) GIBBERELLIN
REGULUS MATTE SLURRY KINGLET
REHABIAH (FATHER OF —) ELIEZER
(GRANDFATHER OF —) MOSES
REHABILITATE REABLE REPONE RESTORE REINSTATE
REHASH RECHAUFFE

REHEARSAL CALL DRYRUN HEARSAL HERSALL PREVIEW CLAMBAKE NARRATION
REHEARSE TELL TRAIN DETAIL RECITE RELATE DECLINE NARRATE RECOUNT DESCRIBE PRACTICE
(— QUICKLY) RUNOVER
REHEAT FLASH
REHOB (SON OF —) HADADEZER
REHOBOAM ROBOAM
(FATHER OF —) SOLOMON
(MOTHER OF —) NAAMAH
REICHSTAG DIET
REIF PLUNDER ROBBERY
REIGN RING RULE REALM RICHE EMPIRE GOVERN KINGDOM PREVAIL REGIMENT REGNANCY
(— IN INDIA) RAJ
REIMBURSE PAY REPAY DEFRAY RECOUP REFUND REBURSE INDEMNIFY
REIN CURB STOP CHECK SWING THONG GOVERN BABICHE LEATHER PLOWLINE RESTRAIN
(PL.) LINES RIBBONS
REINCARNATION AVATAR REBIRTH
REINDEER REIN CERVID TARAND CARIBOU CERVINE CERVOID RANGIFER
REINDEER MOSS SWARD
REINFORCE BAR GUY BACK FACE STAY BRACE FORCE INLAY STUFF SUPER CRADLE DOUBLE GUSSET HARDEN MUSCLE SUPPLY AFFORCE BOLSTER BULWARK ENFORCE GROMMET NERVATE STIFFEN SUPPORT
(— ROAD) SKID
REINFORCED KEYED SPLICED
REINFORCEMENT CREW FUEL STAY BRACE HURTER CUNETTE SPLICING STRAINER
(PL.) SUCCOR SUPPLY
REINVIGORATE QUICK REVIVE RECRUIT RENERVE
REISSUE REPRISE
REITERATE BACK DING REITER REPEAT RESUME ITERATE REHEARSE
REIVER CATERAN
REJECT BEG ORT CAST DEFY DENY DICE FAIL JILT KICK NILL SPIN ABHOR BANDY BELIE BRUSH CHECK EJECT REFEL REPEL SCOUT SPURN WAIVE ABJECT ABJURE DELETE DESERT IGNORE RECUSE REFUSE REFUTE RESPUE RETORT ABANDON CASHIER CONTEMN DECLINE DISCARD DISMISS FORSAKE PROJECT REPROVE REPULSE ABNEGATE ATHETIZE DESELECT DISALLOW DISCLAIM FORSWEAR NEGATIVE RENOUNCE THROWOUT
(— A STUDENT) PLUCK PLOUGH
(— COPY) SPIKE
REJECTED OFFCAST OUTCAST CASTAWAY
(— BY GOD) REPROBATE
REJECTION SACK BRUSH SPURN DENIAL MITTEN REBUFF REFUSAL REPULSE DEFIANCE TURNDOWN
(— AS SPURIOUS) ATHETESIS

(— OF DOCTRINE) HERESY
(INTERJECTION TO EXPRESS —) YUK YECH YUCK YECCH
REJOICE JOY FAIN GAME CHEER ENJOY EXULT GLORY BLITHE PLEASE DELIGHT GLADDEN MAFFICK JUBILATE
REJOICING GLEE MIRTH OVATION FESTIVITY
REJOIN REPLY TAUNT ANSWER REUNITE
REJOINDER REPLY ANSWER COUNTER RESPONSE
REJUVENATE UNOLD
REKEM (FATHER OF —) HEBRON
REKINDLE RELUME REVIVE
RELAPSE SINK WEED LAPSE RECIDE RETURN BACKSET SUBSIDE BACKCAST WITHDRAW RECIDIVISM
RELAPSING (— INTO CRIME) RECIDIVISM
RELATE SAY ALLY BEAR JOIN READ TELL PITCH REFER SPELL STATE TOUCH ALLUDE ASSERT DELATE DETAIL DEVISE RECITE REPORT REPUTE COGNATE CONCERN DECLARE INVOLVE NARRATE PERTAIN RECOUNT CALABASH DESCRIBE REHEARSE APPERTAIN
(— TO) TOUCH
RELATED KIN SIB AKIN ALLIED AFFINED RELEVANT CONNECTED CONSANGUINE
(— BY FATHER'S SIDE) AGNATE
(— INVERSELY) RECIPROCAL
(— ON MOTHER'S SIDE) ENATE ENATIC COGNATE
(RECIPROCALLY —) CONJUGATE
(PREF.) **(— BY REMARRIAGE)** STEP
RELATING (ALSO SEE PERTAINING)
(— TO) AGAINST
(— TO A RECENT PAST) ERST
(SUFF.) **(— TO)** AL ATIVE IAL IC(AL) ILE INE ISH ISTIC ITIC ITIOUS
RELATION KIN SIB TALE BLOOD FETII AFFINE DATIVE REGARD ACCOUNT BEARING HISTORY KINSHIP KINSMAN RAPPORT RESPECT SCHESIS TELLING AFFINITY HABITUDE RELATIVE TENDENCY REFERENCE REHEARSAL RISHTADAR PROPORTION
(— BETWEEN SPECIES) AFFINITY
(— OF LIKENESS) ANALOGY
(BLOOD —) KIN SIB
(FIXED —) RATIO
(FRIENDLY —S) AMITY
(SYNTACTIC —) FUNCTION
(WORKING —) GEAR
RELATIONSHIP KIN BLOOD ACTION AGENCY AMENITY AMITATE ANALOGY ANGULUS BEARING CONTACT KINDRED KINSHIP LIAISON RESPECT SIBNESS SIBREDE SOCIETY AFFINITY AGNATION CONTRAST GOSSIPRY RELATIVE SYMPATHY COGNATION FILIATION
(BUSINESS —) ACCOUNT
(CLOSE —) BOSOM AFFIANCE INTIMACY BELONGING
(FRIENDLY —) ENTENTE

(HARMFUL —) DISOPERATION
(HARMONIOUS —) SYNC
(INHARMONIOUS —) OUTS
(MARITAL —) BED
(MATHEMATICAL —) PARITY
(MUTUAL —) TERMS SYMMETRY
(SEXUAL —) AFFAIR
(SOCIAL —) FOOTING
RELATIVE KIN ALLY BLOOD AFFINE
AGNATE ALLIED COUSIN GERMAN
KINDRED KINSMAN APPOSITE
COGNATUS RELATION RELEVANT
PERTINENT
(PL.) KIN SIB FOLK KINDRED
KINFOLK KINNERY KINSFOLK
RELAX LAX VEG GIVE REST ABATE
BREAK LOOSE REMIT SLACK
DIVERT INKINK LAXATE SOFTEN
UNBEND UNGIVE UNKNIT UNWIND
DEBLOCK RELEASE RESOLVE
SLACKEN UNPURSE MITIGATE
UNBUCKLE UNCLENCH
WINDDOWN
RELAXANT (MUSCLE —) CURARE
CURARI
RELAXATION EASE LAZE REST
ATONY CREEP LETUP RELAX
SOLACE DETENTE LETDOWN
RELACHE BREATHER DIVERSION
(— OF MONASTIC RULES)
MISERICORD MISERICORDE
RELAXED LAX LASH LOOSE SLACK
SONSY REMISS SONSIE INFORMAL
RESOLVED TONELESS UNBENDED
UNBRACED GRASPLESS
RELAXING ANIMAL ANODYNE
DETENTE
(— POINT) SEAR
RELAY SPELL RELIEF REMUDA
AVANTLAY REPEATER
(— OF DOGS) VAUNTLAY
(— OF PALANQUIN BEARERS) DAK
RELEASE LES LET BAIL DROP EMIT
FREE LESE LIOS LISS SHED SLIP
TRIP UNDO ERUPT EXEEM LEISS
LOOSE MUKTI REMIT SLAKE
ACQUIT ASSOIL DEMISE EXCUSE
EXEMPT LAUNCH MOKSHA REMISE
SPRING UNBEND UNTACK
UNWORK ABSOLVE APATHIA
DELIVER DETENTE DISBAND
FREEDOM QUIETUS SOLUTIO
UNSTICK DELIVERY DISPENSE
DISSOLVE LIBERATE DISCHARGE
RELINQUISH
(— AS DOGS) UNLEASH
(— DANCING PARTNER) BREAK
(— EMOTION) ABREAST
(— FROM CENSORSHIP) UNGAG
(— FROM CONFINEMENT) UNMEW
UNPEN SPRING STREET
(— FROM DEBT) FREITH
(— FROM MILITARY) INVALID
(— FROM SLAVERY) MANUMIT
(— ON ONE'S WORD) PAROLE
(PRESS —) HANDOUT
RELEASED OFF FREE EXEMPT
RELEGATE DOOM EXILE BANISH
COMMIT DEMOTE REJECT
DEGRADE
(— TO OBSCURITY) DOWN
RELEGATION (— OF LEGAL
DISPUTE) RENVOI RENVOY

RELENT COME MELT ABATE YIELD
REGRET REPENT LIQUEFY MOLLIFY
SLACKEN
RELENTLESS GRIM HARD HARSH
STERN STONY BITTER SAVAGE
STRICT AUSTERE PITILESS
RIGOROUS
RELEVANCE PRECISION
PERTINENCE
RELEVANT APT VALID GERMAN
APROPOS GERMANE APPOSITE
MATERIAL PERTINENT
RELEVANTLY ADREM
RELIABILITY STEEL CREDENCE
RELIABLE GOOD HARD SAFE SURE
TRUE PUKKA SOLID SOUND THERE
TRIED TRUST WHITE DINKUM
STEADY TRUSTY CERTAIN
FAITHFUL SOOTHFUL STRAIGHT
RELIANCE HOPE TRUST CREDIT
AFFIANCE MAINSTAY
(— ON FAITH) FIDEISM
RELIC HUACO REMAIN ANTIQUE
HALIDOM LEAVING MEMENTO
RELIQUE VESTIGE SOUVENIR
SURVIVAL
(LIFELESS —) SHELL
(PL.) CORPSE HALIDOM REMAINS
(PREF.) LIPSANO
RELICT WIDOW REMANIE RESIDUAL
SURVIVOR EPIBIOTIC
RELIEF AID LAX SOB BOOT BOTE
DOLE EASE HELP RELAY SCRUB
SPELL SWING ESCAPE REMEDY
SUCCOR COMFORT FEEDING
REDRESS RILIEVO EASEMENT
REPOUSSE
(— FROM SIEGE) RESCUE
(TEMPORARY —) HITCH
(SUFF.) LYSE LYSIS LYST LYTE
LYTIC LYZE
RELIEVE ROB BEET EASE FREE HELP
LIOS LISS ALLAY LIGHT LISSE LITHE
RIGHT SLAKE SPARE SPELL ASSIST
LESSEN PHYSIC REMEDY REMOVE
RESCUE SOOTHE SUCCOR
UNMAZE ASSUAGE COMFORT
DELIVER DEPRIVE FRESHEN
LIGHTEN REDRESS REFRESH
SUCCEED SUPPORT SUSTAIN
SWEETEN ALIGHTEN DIMINISH
MITIGATE RELEVATE
(— A SAIL) SPILL
(— OF OFFICE) AX AXE
(— OF SIN) CONFESS
RELIEVED THANKFUL
RELIGIEUSE NUN CLERGESS
RELIGION BON DIN LAW SECT
BONBO CREED DAENA FAITH
OBEAH PIETY SOPHY DHARMA
SHINTO SYSTEM TAOISM ELOHISM
JAINISM JUDAISM MACUMBA
ORPHISM PERSISM RELIGIO
SIKHISM SYNAGOG BUDDHISM
CAODAISM HINDUISM MAZDAISM
PEYOTISM SANTERIA SHAMANISM
(— OF ABRAHAM) HANIFIYA
(— OF TIBET) BON
(— OF WITCHCRAFT) WICCA
(— PRACTICED IN CUBA) SANTERIA
(CHRISTIAN —) WAY
(FALSE —) SUPERSTITION

(GENTILE —) ETHNICISM
(UNORTHODOX —) CULT
RELIGIOSE PIETISTIC
RELIGIOUS PI HOLY EXACT GODLY
PIOUS RIGID DEVOUT DIVINE
SACRED FERVENT GHOSTLY
ZEALOUS SPIRITUAL
(— HOUSE) KELLION
(MORBIDLY —) RELIGIOSE
RELINQUISH LAY LET CEDE DROP
QUIT DEMIT FORGO GRANT LEAVE
WAIVE YIELD CANCEL DESERT
RESIGN ABANDON FORSAKE
RELEASE ABDICATE ABNEGATE
LINQUISH RENOUNCE
RELIQUARY ARCA CHEF CASKET
CHASSE COFFER MEMORY SHRINE
STEEPA TABLET CHORTEN
HALIDOM MEMORIA FERETORY
RELISH CHOW DASH EDGE GOUT
GUST LIKE SOUL SOWL TANG ZEST
ACHAR ENJOY GUSTO RELES
SAVOR SOWLE SPICE TASTE TRACE
ATSARA DEGUST FLAVOR LIKING
PALATE SAVOUR BOTARGO
OUTWORK STOMACH APPETITE
FONDNESS PICCALILLI
(— FOR FOOD) CHAW
(INTELLECTUAL —) TASTE
(MENTAL —) PALATE
(ROMAN —) GARUM
(SALT OR ACID —) ACHAR
RELUCENT RADIANT SHINING
GLEAMING
RELUCT TARROW
RELUCTANCE GRUDGE AVERSION
ANTIPATHY RENITENCE
(— UNIT) REL
RELUCTANT SET SHY CAGY LOTH
NICE CHARY LOATH SWEER
THRAW AFRAID AVERSE DAINTY
FORCED SWEERT UNFAIN
ASHAMED HALTING BACKWARD
GRUDGING LOATHFUL RENITENT
RETICENT THRAWART
RELY AFFY BANK BASE LEAN LITE
REST STAY COUNT RALLY TRUST
DEPEND GROUND RECKON
REPOSE CONFIDE
(— ON) LIPPEN VENTURE
REMAIN LIE SIT BIDE REST STAY
STOP ABIDE CLING DWELL LEAVE
STAND TARRY THOLE BELIVE
ENDURE MANENT RESIDE SUBSIST
SURVIVE CONTINUE
(— ALOFT) HOVER
(— AWAKE) VIGILATE
(— FIRM) INHERE
(— IN DEADLOCK) HANG
(— MOTIONLESS) STAGNATE
(—S IN MASH TUN) GRAINS
(—S IN PIPEBOWL) TOPPER
(—S OF CANE) BEGASS BAGASSE
(—S OF FIRE) EMBER EMBERS
(—S ON STAGE) MANET
(— STATIONARY) FASTEN
(— UNDER HEAT TREATMENT)
SOAK
(— UNDISTURBED AFTER HEAT
TREATMENT) AGE
(— UNUSED) LIE
(— UPRIGHT) STAND
(ANIMAL —S) SPOILS

(FOSSIL —) EXUVIAE
(FOUL —S) SCURF
(PL.) CHAR DUST ASHES DECAY
DRAFF GHOST SHARD SHERD
BURIAL DEBRIS FOSSIL RELIEF
CARCASS REMNANT RESIDUE
RELIQUIAE
(PREF.) MENO
REMAINDER NET HEEL LAVE REST
PLUGS ARREAR EXCESS RELIEF
BALANCE REMNANT RESIDUE
SURPLUS LEAVINGS LEFTOVER
RESIDUAL RESIDUUM
(— OF ATOM) CORE
(PL.) GARBLINGS LEFTMENTS
REMAINING OVER BIDING
REMNANT LEFTOVER REMANENT
RESIDUAL
(PREF.) MENO
REMALIAH (SON OF —) PEKAH
REMARK DIG SAY SEE GIRD HEED
NOTE WORD GLOSS STATE TOKEN
EARFUL GAMBIT NOTICE REGARD
COMMENT DESCANT DISCANT
OBSERVE PERCEIVE OBSERVATION
(— BRIEFLY) GLANCE
(ADVERSE —) STRICTURE
(AGGRESSIVE —) SHOT
(AMIABLE —) DOUCEUR
(AMUSING —) GAG
(BANAL —) PLATITUDE
(BITING —) BARB
(CLEVER —) QUIP NIFTY
(CONCLUDING —S) ENVOI
(CRITICAL —) SWIPE BRICKBAT
(CUTTING —) DIG SPINOSITY
(DULL —) BROMIDE
(EMBARRASSING —) BREAK
(EXPLANATORY —) SCHOLION
SCHOLIUM
(FOOLISH —) INANITY
(ILL-TIMED —) CLANGER
(INSULTING —) SLUR
(JEERING —) JEST SKIT
(LAUGH-PROVOKING —) GAG
(PITHY —) ONELINER
(SARCASTIC —) HIT GIRD SLANT
(SATIRICAL —) JEST SKIT SGAFT
(SHARP —) SWIPE GANSEL STINGER
(SILLY —) FADAISE
(STAGE —) ASIDE
(STALE —S) BILGE
(TEASING —) NEEDLE
(UNCOMPLIMENTARY —) BRICKBAT
(UNKIND —) BARB
(WITTY —) MOT JEST CRACK
ZINGER
REMARKABLE SOME FORBY GREAT
SIGNAL STRONG NOTABLE
STRANGE UNUSUAL FABULOUS
MARKABLE SINGULAR SPANKING
STRIKING UNCOMMON
BODACIOUS NOTICEABLE
PHENOMENAL
(— ONE) LULU
(NOT —) INCURIOUS
REMARKABLY UNCO UNKO JOLLY
UNCOW DEUCED UNCOLY
SIGNALLY
REMEDIAL BONEHEAD RELEVANT
SALUTARY
REMEDILESS BOOTLESS
REMEDY AID BOT BOOT BOTE CURE

GAIN HALE HEAL HELP REDE
AZOTH MANDS REDUB SHERE
TOPIC PHYSIC RECOUR RECURE
RELIEF REPAIR RESIDY URETIC
ANTACID CORRECT DRASTIC
ICTERIC OTALGIC PLASTER
RECTIFY REDRESS RELIEVE
ANTIDOTE MEDICINE PHARMACY
RECOVERY REMEDIAL SPECIFIC
(— COUNTERACTING POISON)
TREACLE ANTIDOTE
(— FOR ALL DISEASES) PANACEA
CATHOLICON
(— FOR DIZZINESS) DINIC
(— FOR JAUNDICE) ICTERIC
(— TO REDUCE FEVER) FEBRIFUGE
(CHINESE —) SENSO
(EXTERNAL —) TOPIC
(FAVORITE —) NOSTRUM
(SECRET —) ARCANUM
(SOVEREIGN —) MAGISTERY
(TAPEWORM —) EMBELIA
(TOOTHACHE —) TONGA
(UNIVERSAL —) AZOTH
CATHOLICON
(WITHOUT —) BOOTLESS
REMEMBER MEM MIN MEAN MIND
MINE MING IDEATE MEMBER
RECALL RECORD REMIND RETAIN
REWARD BETHINK MENTION
RECOLLECT
(— REMORSEFULLY) REMORD
REMEMBRANCE MIN MIND
MEMORY RECORD MEANING
MINDING MINNING MEMORIAL
REMINDER SOUVENIR
**REMEMBRANCE OF THINGS
PAST (AUTHOR OF —)** PROUST
(CHARACTER IN —) MOREL SWANN
MARCEL ODETTE RACHEL ROBERT
VEDURIN GILBERTE VINTEUIL
ALBERTINE DECHARLUS
GUERMANTES
REMIND JOG MIN MIND MINE MING
IMMIND PROMPT REMEMBER
REMINDER CUE MEMO PROD TWIT
TOUCH PROMPT MINDING
MONITOR SOUVENIR REFRESHER
REMINISCENCE MEMORY RECALL
ANAMNESIS
REMISE RETURN RELEASE REPLACE
CARRIAGE
REMISS LAX LAZY MILD PALE FAINT
SLACK TARDY BEHIND DILUTED
LANGUID CARELESS DERELICT
DILATORY HEEDLESS NEGLIGENT
REMISSION CURE LIOS LISS
PARDON REMISE LOOSING
REMITTAL
(— OF BUSINESS) RECESS
(— OF DEBT) ACCEPTILATION
(PARTIAL —) RELAXATION
REMISSNESS LACHES LASHNESS
REMIT SEND COVER LOOSE RELAX
CANCEL EXCUSE PARDON
REMAND REMISS RESIGN ABSOLVE
FORGIVE RELEASE SUSPEND
ABROGATE MITIGATE MODERATE
REMNANT END TAG BUTT DREG
FENT REST RUMP RUND RELIC
STUMP TRACE REMAIN LEAVING
REMAINS SURVIVOR
(— OF CLOTH) FENT

(— OF FOOD) CRUST
(— OF ROCK MASS) KLIP KLIPPE
(— OF VEIL) ANNULUS
(—S OF FILLETS) SCISSEL
(—S OF VEIL) CORTINA
(VESTIGIAL —) SHADOW
(PL.) EPIPLASM
REMODEL MEND RECAST CONVERT
REMONSTRANCE PROOF ADVICE
COUNSEL PROTEST REPROOF
EVIDENCE
REMONSTRANT ARMINIAN
REMONSTRATE ARGUE OBJECT
PROTEST REPROVE COMPLAIN
REMORA CLOG DRAG PEGA SUCKER
GUAICAN PEGADOR ECHENEID
LOOTOMAN OTAYOUIR OTOPOLIIR
SUCKFISH
REMORSE HELL PITY RUTH PRICK
REGRET REMORD AYENBITE
PENITENCE
(— OF CONSCIENCE) GRUDGE
REMORSEFUL BAD PITIFUL
CONTRITE GUILTSICK
REMOTE FAR OFF BACK DEEP FERN
HIGH LONG ALOOF HOARY UTTER
ALENGE DISTAL ELENGE EXEMPT
OTIOSE SECRET DEVIOUS DISSITE
DISTANT EXTREME FAILING
FARAWAY FOREIGN OBSCURE
OUTSIDE ABDITIVE ABSTRUSE
ARMCHAIR BACKVELD INTERIOR
OUTLYING OUTWORLD SECLUDED
SOLITARY OUTLANDISH
(— FROM LIFE) SCHOOLISH
(MOST —) ULTIMA EXTREME
HINDMOST ULTIMATE
(PREF.) DIST(O) PALAE(O) PALE(O)
REMOTELY AFAR CLEAN DISTANTLY
REMOTENESS AWAYNESS
DISTANCE
REMOTER FARTHER ULTERIOR
REMOVABLE DATIVE REMOTIVE
REMOVAL AX AXE EXILE AMOTION
CLEANUP ERASION ABLATION
EXCISION EXERESIS OFFGOING
REMOTION
(— OF COAL) GETTING
(— OF ICE FROM GLACIER)
ATTRITION
(— OF LAND) AVULSION
(DISTANT —) ELOIN ELOIGN
(SUFF.) CENOSIS
(SURGICAL —) ECTOMY
REMOVE GET PUT RID BATE COMB
DELE DRAW FILE FLIT FREE LIFT
MOVE PARE PEEL PULL QUIT RAZE
UNDO VOID WEED APART AUFER
AVOID BLAST BRUSH CLEAR EMITY
ERASE EVOID HEAVE HOIST LIGHT
PLANE RAISE REPEL SHIFT SHUCK
SLASH SLIPE STRIP SWEEP WAIVE
BANISH CANCEL CHANGE CONVEY
DEDUCT DEGREE DEPART DEPOSE
EFFACE ELOIGN EXEMPT EXPORT
MINISH RELEVE REMBLE SPIRIT
ABOLISH AMOLISH DEPRIVE
DESCENT DISMISS DISPOST
DIVORCE EXCERPT RESCIND
RETRACT REVERSE STRANGE
SUBDUCT SUBLATE ABSTRACT
ASPIRATE DISPLACE DISPLANT
ESTRANGE EVACUATE RETRENCH

SUPPLANT TRANSFER WITHDRAW
ELIMINATE OBLITERATE
(— A FAULT) MEND
(— A STITCH) DECREASE
(— BARK FROM LOG) ROSS
(— BIT BY BIT) SCAMBLE
(— BY CUTTING) ABLATE
(— BY DEATH) SNATCH
(— BY SCRAPING) SHAVE
(— CLOTHING) DOFF STRIP
(— COLOR) BLEACH
(— CONTENTS) GUT
(— CORTEX) DECORTICATE
(— COVER) UNCAP
(— DEFECTS) SCARF
(— DIRT) BLADE GARBLE
(— EXCESS METAL) CUT
(— FLOATING MATTER) SKIM
(— FROM CHECKER BOARD) HUFF
(— FROM OFFICE) DEPOSE RECALL
DISMISS
(— FROM REMEMBRANCE) COVER
(— FROM SHEATH) EVAGINATE
(— GILLS) BEARD
(— HAIR) DEPILATE
(— HUSKS AND CHAFF) GELD
(— IMPURITIES) PURGE
(— INSIDES OF FISH) GIB GIP
(— JUDGE) ADDRESS
(— LOWER BRANCHES) BRASH
(— MAST) UNSTEP
(— ORE) EXTRACT
(— PARTICLES OF GOLD LEAF)
SKEW
(— PIECEMEAL) SCAMBLE
**(— PITCHER FROM BASEBALL
GAME)** DERRICK
(— POTATOES) GRABBLE
(— QUEEN BEE) DEMAREE
(— QUIETLY) ABSTRACT
(— ROOTS) GRUB
(— SEED FROM FLAX) RIBBLE
(— SEEDS) STONE
(— SKIN) HULL HUSK
(— SOUND FROM TAPE) BLIP
(— SPROUTS FROM) CHIT
(— STALK FROM) STRIG
(— STAMENS) CASTRATE
(— SURGICALLY) EXTIRPATE
(— TABLECLOTH) DRAW
(— THE TOP OF) COP
(— TO A DISTANCE) ELOIN
(— TO AVOID TAX) SKIM
(— TROUSERS) DEBAG
(— WASTE TO FIBER) GARNETT
(— WOOL) BELLY
(— WORKS OF STOLEN WATCH)
CHURCH
(— WRONGFULLY) MISTAKE
(PREF.) DE
REMOVED UP OFF AWAY ALIEN
ALOOF APART REMOTE DISTANT
SEMOTED ABSTRACT
REMOVER MOVER CROPMAN
KNOTTER
REMUDA CAVY CAVAYARD
CAVYYARD
REMUNERATE PAY REPAY REWARD
GRATIFY SATISFY CONSIDER
REIMBURSE
REMUNERATION PAY REWARD
SALARY PAYMENT

REMUNERATIVE GAINFUL
REWARDING
REMUS (BROTHER OF —) ROMULUS
(FATHER OF —) MARS
RENAISSANCE NARA REBIRTH
REVIVAL
RENAL NEPHRIC NEPHRITIC
RENAME ANABAPTIZE
RENCOUNTER CLASH FIGHT
DEBATE CONTEST CONFLICT
REND PULL RENT RIVE TEAR TOIL
BREAK BURST DIVEL RATCH
ROWEL SEVER SPLIT WREST
CLEAVE SCREED WRENCH
ABSCIND DIVULSE RUPTURE
WREATHE DISPIECE DISTRAIN
FRACTURE LACERATE SPLINTER
(— AND DEVOUR) TIRE
RENDER DO PAY PUT TRY BEAR
DRAW ECHO EMIT MAKE RENT
RIND DEFER PRICK REPAY YIELD
RECITE REPEAT RETURN DELIVER
PRECARY REFLECT REQUITE
RESTORE SERVICE TALLAGE
TRANSMIT
(— ACID) PRICK
(— AGREEABLE) DULCIFY
(— AS LAND) TRY
(— ASSISTANCE TO SHIP) FOY
(— CAPABLE) ACTIVATE
(— CLEAR) OPEN
(— DEFECTIVE) VITIATE
(— DEFENSELESS) DISARM
(— DESTITUTE) DISFURNISH
(— FIT) ADAPT
(— GODLIKE) DEIFY
(— HEAVY WITH FOOD) STODGE
(— HOMAGE) ATTORN
(— IMMUNE) FRANK VASTATE
(— IMPASSIBLE) STOP
(— IMPERFECT) LAME
(— INEFFECTIVE) VITIATE
(— INSANE) DEMENT DISTRACT
(— KNOTTY) GNARL
(— OBLIQUE) SPLAY
(— OBSCURE) DARKLE
(— OF BOON WORK) PRECARY
(— PLAUSIBLE) GLOSS
(— PURE) EXPURGATE
(— QUIET) ACCOY
(— SENSELESS) STUN ASTONISH
(— SUDDENLY) THROW
(— TURBID) ROIL
(— UNFIT) DENATURE
(— UNSTABLE) UNHINGE
(— VERDICT) PASS
(— VOID) CASS DEFEAT
(— WATERTIGHT) CALK CAULK
(— WEAK) EVIRATE
(— LIABLE) ENGAGE PREDISPOSE
(SUFF.) EN
RENDERED RENDU TRIED
RENDERING RENDU ENGLISH
VERSION RENDITION
(— OF SCENE) STUDY
RENDEZVOUS DATE HAUNT TRYST
REFUGE HANGOUT MEETING
RETREAT
(— FOR SHIPS) DOWN
(— OF WITCHES) SABBAT
RENDING SPLITTING
(— ASUNDER) DIVULSION

RENDITION ACCOUNT CONDUCT DELIVERY

RENEGADE DORAX PERVERT TRAITOR APOSTATE DESERTER RECREANT RENEGADO RUNAGADO RUNAGATE TURNCOAT

RENEGE BEG NIG DENY RENIG DESERT REVOKE RETRACT FAINAIGUE

RENEW NEW REST FRESH RECALL REFORM RENOVE REPEAT RESUME REVIVE INSTORE REBUILD REFRESH REPLACE RESTORE OVERHAUL REJUVENATE
(**— MORTAR**) REPOINT
(**— WINE**) STUM

RENEWAL RENEW REVIVAL NOVATION
(**SPIRITUAL-**) REBIRTH

RENNET LAB RUEN VELL STEEP RENNIN RUNNET EARNING ABOMASUM YEARNING CHEESELIP

RENOUNCE PUT CEDE DEFY DENY QUIT DEVOW FORGO RENAY WAIVE ABJURE DISOWN FORLET FORSAY RECANT REFUSE REJECT RENEGE RESIGN REVOKE ABANDON DECLARE FORLEIT FORSAKE RETRACT WITHSAY ABDICATE ABNEGATE DISCLAIM FORSPEAK FORSWEAR MANSWEAR PROCLAIM RELINQUISH
(**— ALLEGIANCE**) REVOLT
(**— AUTHORITY**) REBEL
(**— PROMISE**) RECEDE

RENOVATE DUST RENEW REVIVE FURBISH REFRESH RESTORE OVERHAUL RENOVIZE
(**— HAT**) MOLOKER MOLOCKER

RENOWN BAY BRAG FAME ECLAT GLORY KUDOS PRICE RUMOR ESTEEM LUSTER RENONE REPORT EMPRISE SWAGGER WORSHIP PRESTIGE NOTORIETY

RENOWNED FAMED NOBLE NOTED FAMOUS EMINENT RENOMME GLORIOUS MAGNIFIC RENOMMEE

RENT LET SET TAX FARM GALE GAPE HIRE MAIL RACK RIME RIVE SLIT TEAR TOLL TORN WAGE BREAK CANON CENSO CUDDY ENDOW GANCH GAVEL SPLIT BLANCH BREACH BROKEN CENSUS CHASMA CRANNY CUSTOM GAUNCH INCOME SCHISM SCREED STRENT CHARTER CHIEFRY CORNAGE CRACKED CREVICE FISSURE MAILING MOLLAND ONSTAND RENTAGE REVENUE RUPTURE TRIBUTE CHAMPART CHIEFERY HEADRENT STALLAGE VECTIGAL WAYLEAVE LANDGAFOL
(**— BY BOAR'S TUSK**) GANCH GAUNCH
(**— IN LIEU OF SUPPER**) CUDDY
(**— OF LAND PAID IN KIND**) CAIN
(**ANNUAL —**) CANON
(**EARTHQUAKE —**) SCARLET
(**GROUND —**) CENSO CENSUS
(**OATS IN LIEU OF —**) AVENAGE

RENTAL KAIN PORT TONNAGE TRIBUTE TUNNAGE

RENTED LETTEN

RENTER FARMER RANTER CHIPPER BOXHOLDER
(**— OF GRAZING LAND**) AGIST

RENUNCIATION DENIAL APOSTASY DEFIANCE DISAVOWAL REJECTION SACRIFICE

REORGANIZE (**— SCIENTIFICALLY**) RATIONALIZE

REP CANNELE DROGUET POPELINE

REPAIR DO EIK EKE FIX IMP HEAL HELP MEND TINE AMEND BOTCH DIGHT EMEND HAUNT RALLY REDUB RENEW STORE TRADE UPSET ASTORE BUSHEL COBBLE COGGLE COOPER DOCTOR FETTLE RECURE REDEEM REFORM REMEDY REPASS RESORT RETURN UPKEEP CORRECT INFAINT REDRESS REPAREL RESTORE SERVICE FLOCKING OVERHAUL RETRIEVE REVIVIFY RECONDITION
(**— A SOCK**) DARN
(**— BOAT**) CAREEN
(**— CLUMSILY**) BOTCH
(**— FENCE**) MOUND
(**— ROAD**) SKID
(**— SHOE**) FOX TAP

REPAIRED VAMPED

REPAIRER DOCTOR BOTCHER COBBLER WOFFLER CEMENTER
(**SHOE —**) JACKMAN BENCHMAN
(**TEXTILE —**) SMASHER

REPAIRMAN FETTLER

REPARATION BOTE AMENDS REMEDY REWARD DAMAGES REDRESS REPAIRS REQUITAL
(**— OF LESIONS**) ANAPLASTY
(**PL.**) ATONEMENT

REPARTEE WIT KNACK REPLY BANTER RETORT RIPOST RIPOSTE BACKCHAT BADINAGE COMEBACK GIFFGAFF

REPAST BAIT FEED FOOD MEAL BEVER FEAST TREAT DRINKING COLLATION
(**— BETWEEN MEALS**) BEVER BRUNCH BANQUET
(**HASTY —**) SNACK
(**LIGHT —**) BAIT VOID VOIDEE COLLATION

REPAY MEED QUIT APPAY TALLY YIELD ACQUIT ANSWER AVENGE REFUND RETORT RETURN REWARD IMBURSE REQUITE RESTORE REIMBURSE

REPEAL ANNUL CANCEL RECALL REVOKE ABANDON ABOLISH RESCIND REVERSE ABROGATE DEROGATE DISENACT RENOUNCE

REPEAT SAY ECHO GAIT RAME RANE SHOW TELL DITTO QUOTE RECUR RENEW RESAY REVIE THRUM ANSWER RENDER RESUME RETAIL SECOND DECLINE DIVULGE ITERATE PRESENT RECYCLE REPLICA REPRISE DINGDONG REDOUBLE REHEARSE REPLICATE
(**— BY ROTE**) PARROT
(**— FROM MEMORY**) RECORD
(**— GLIBLY**) SCREED
(**— IN DETAIL**) RETAIL
(**— INSISTENTLY**) PERSIST

(**— LORD'S PRAYER**) PATTER
(**— MONOTONOUSLY**) CUCKOO DINGDONG
(**— OF PATTERN**) GAIT
(**— TIRESOMELY**) DIN

REPEATED OFTEN CONSTANT FREQUENT PERENNIAL

REPEATEDLY OFT EVERY THRICE

REPEATER GUN RIFLE WATCH PISTOL FLOATER HOLDOVER

REPEL FEND TURN WARD FENCE REBUT DEFEND PUTOFF REBEAT REBUFF REFUSE REFUTE REJECT REPUGN RESIST REVOLT DISGUST PELLATE REPULSE PROPULSE

REPELLANT REPUGNANT

REPELLENT DEET DOPE GRIM MACE HARSH CAMPHOR HATEFUL SQUALID
(**INSECT —**) DEET

REPELLING HARD SICKLY

REPENT REW RUE MOURN GRIEVE REGRET REPTANT CREEPING FORTHINK

REPENTANCE REW RUE PITY RUTH RUING REGRET SORROW PENANCE REMORSE

REPENTANT ATTRITE PENITENT

REPERCUSSION ECHO TENOR RECOIL REPULSE BACKWASH

REPERTORY REP BOOK LIST INDEX ARSENAL CATALOG
(**PERFORMER'S —**) REPERTOIRE

REPETITION BIS REP COPY ECHO REPP ROTE PLOCE REVIE TROLL DILOGY REPEAT MENTION RECITAL REPLICA REPRISE IDENTITY ITERANCE ITERANCY NEMBUTSU PALILOGY PARROTRY RECOVERY REDOUBLE REHEARSAL
(**— IN REVERSE ORDER**) EPANODOS
(**— OF HOMOLOGOUS PARTS**) MERISM
(**— OF SPEECH FORMS**) ROTE
(**— OF WORD**) ANAPHORA BATTOLOGY
(**NEEDLESS —**) REDUNDANCY
(**SUCCESSIVE —**) SEQUENCE
(**UNINSPIRED —**) STENCIL
(**UNINTENTIONAL —**) DITTOGRAPHY
(**PREF.**) (**PATHOLOGICAL —**) PALI

REPETITIOUS TATA

REPHAEL (**FATHER OF —**) SHEMAIAH

REPHAH (**FATHER OF —**) EPHRAIM

REPHAIAH (**FATHER OF —**) HUR TOLA BINEA

REPHAIM EMIM

REPINE FRET PINE WEAKEN COMPLAIN

REPINING MURMUR REGRET PLAINTIVE

REPLACE SWAP SWOP RENEW REPAY SHIFT STEAD CHANGE FOLLOW REFUND REMISE REPONE SUPPLY FRESHEN PREEMPT RESTORE SUCCEED DISPLACE SUPPLANT REPLENISH

REPLACEMENT CUT ERSATZ
(**— FOR HAND**) HOOK
(**— OF CONSONANT**) LENITION

REPLAY ECHO

REPLENISH CHUNK REFIT RENEW SUPPLY NOURISH PERFECT

PLENISH REPLETE RESTORE SUFFICE

REPLETE FAT FULL RIFE SATED STOUT STUFF FILLED GORGED IMPLETE COMPLETE HONEYPOT

REPLETION FULTH FULNESS SURFEIT FULLNESS PLETHORA SATURITY

REPLICA BIS PUP COPY IDEA CHARM CLONE IMAGE REVIE FACSIMILE

REPLICATION ECHO REPLY ANSWER REJOINDER

REPLY CAP JAWAB KNACK RESAY ANSWER REJOIN RETORT RETURN REPLIAL RESOUND RESPOND REPARTEE REPLIQUE RESPONSE SIMILITER
(**SECOND —**) DUPLY

REPORT CRY POP SAY FAME ITEM NOTE TELL VENT VOTE WORD AUDIT BRUIT COVER CRACK NOISE REFER ROUND RUMOR SCALE SOUND STATE STORY VOICE BREEZE CAHIER CREDIT DELATE DETAIL FINGER GOSSIP RAPORT RECITE RELATE RENOWN REPUTE RETURN RUMBLE SPEECH STEVEN SURVEY THREAP ACCOUNT HANSARD HEARING HEARSAY INKLING KHUBBER NARRATE OPINION PROCESS RECITAL ADVISORY DECISION DESCRIBE HEMOGRAM VERBATIM GRAPEVINE
(**— NEWS**) COVER
(**— OF GUN**) CLAP
(**— OF INFRACTION**) GIG
(**— OF PROCEEDINGS**) CAHIER
(**— OF TIMBER SURVEYOR**) CRUISE
(**ABSURD —**) CANARD
(**BELIEVED —**) CREDIT
(**CASUAL —**) FABLE
(**COMMON —**) CRY FAME SPEECH
(**FALSE —**) SHAVE CANARD FURPHY SLANDER
(**FLYING —**) SOUGH
(**HONORABLE —**) TONGUE
(**LAW —**) CASE
(**MILITARY —**) STATE SITREP
(**NEWS —**) FLASH SCOOP
(**NOISY —**) RUMBLE
(**OFFICIAL —**) HANSARD
(**POPULAR —**) RUMOR RUMOUR
(**PUBLIC —**) FAME
(**UNFAVORABLE —**) SKIN
(**UNVERIFIED —**) VOICE GRAPEVINE
(**VAGUE —**) BREEZE

REPORTER LEGMAN PISTOL CREEPER NEWSMAN NEWSHAWK PRESSMAN STRINGER PAPARAZZO
(**SOCIETY —**) JENKINS
(**YOUNG —**) CUB

REPORTING BEAT COVERAGE

REPOSE RO BED LIE PUT AFFY CALM EASE RELY REST PEACE PLACE POISE QUIET SLEEP REPAST RECLINE EASINESS QUIETUDE SERENITY
(**— LAZILY**) FROWST
(**DREAMY —**) KEF

REPOSITORY ARK SAFE AMBRY CAPSA DEPOT HOARD VAULT

ARMORY CASKET MUSEUM
VESTRY ARCHIVE CABINET
CAPSULE GENIZAH GRANARY
HANAPER SPICERY ARCHIVES
MAGAZINE TREASURY SEPULCHER
STOREHOUSE
(— FOR DEAD) URN
(SECRET —) SECRETAIRE
REPOSOIR REPOSE
REPOSSESS PULL RECOVER
REPREHEND NIP WARN BLAME
CHIDE REBUKE CENSURE REPRISE
REPROVE CRITICIZE
REPREHENSIBLE ILL AMISS
BLAMABLE CRIMINAL CULPABLE
SCABROUS
REPREHENSION BLAME REBUKE
CENSURE OBLOQUY REPROOF
REPRESENT GIVE LIKE LIMN SHOW
TYPE SHADE DEPICT SEMBLE
TYPIFY DISPLAY EXHIBIT FASHION
PICTURE PORTRAY PROTEST
TRADUCE DEFIGURE DESCRIBE
RESEMBLE PERSONATE
(— CONCRETELY) THING
(— IN LANGUAGE) ACT BODY DRAW
ENACT IMAGE SPEAK BLAZON
CLOTHE EMBODY FIGURE SAMPLE
BETOKEN EXPRESS DECIPHER
(— ON GRAPH) PLOT
(— ON STAGE) ACT
REPRESENTATION SUN BUST
FORM ICON IDEA IDOL IKON SHOW
SWAG ANGLE DRAFT FANCY
IMAGE INSET LABEL MEDAL TABUT
AVOWAL BUDDHA EFFIGY FIGURE
FLEECE MODULE OBJECT SCHEMA
SCHEME SKETCH SUNRAY
WAYANG ANATOMY DIORAMA
DRAUGHT DRAWING EPITOME
EXPRESS EXTRACT FOLIAGE
MAJESTY SCENERY TABLEAU
BESTIARY BLAZONRY CREATION
EPIPHANY EXTERIOR IDIOGRAM
LIKENESS TYPORAMA
SIMULACRUM RESEMBLANCE
(— OF SERPENT) BASIL DRAGON
BASILISK
(— OF SHRINE OF HUSAIN) TABUT
(— OF VISION) AISLING
(DIPLOMATIC —) DEMARCHE
(FACSIMILE —) TYPORAMA
(FAINT —) SHADOW
(FUNERAL —) CADAVER
(GRAPHIC —) CHART BISECT
(HERALDIC —) LEOPARD LIONCEL
(MENTAL —) FANCY IMAGE
(MINIATURE —) MODEL
(SYMBOLIC —) ALLEGORY
REPRESENTATIVE REP FAIR TYPE
AGENT ENVOY VAKIL ASSIGN
COMMON DEPUTY EMBLEM
LEDGER SAMPLE VAKEEL BURGESS
GRIEVER TRIBUNE TYPICAL
DECURION DELEGATE EMISSARY
EXPONENT FIELDMAN GASTALDO
INTIMATE OBSERVER SALESMAN
SPECIMEN
(— AT FOREIGN COURT) RESIDENT
(— OF ATMOSPHERE) AERIAL
(— OF CLERGY) PROCTOR
(LEGAL—) SYNDIC

(MANUFACTURER'S —) BLOCKMAN
(POPE'S —) INTERNUNCIO
(PL.) COMMONS
REPRESS CURB HUSH BLUNT BRIDE
CHAIN CHECK CHOKE CRUSH
DAUNT DROWN QUELL SQUAT
BRIDLE COERCE DEADEN REBUKE
STIFLE SUBDUE CONTROL
DEPRESS INHIBIT REPRIME
SILENCE SWALLOW COMPRESS
OVERBEAR RESTRAIN RESTRICT
RETRENCH REVOCATE STRANGLE
SUPPRESS WITHHOLD
REPRESSED SULLEN STIFLED
REPRIEVE DELAY GRACE ESCAPE
REPRISE RESPITE SUSPEND
POSTPONE
REPRIMAND WIG BAWL CALL
CHEW JACK SKIN SLAP SLON SNEB
SNIB TASK CHECK CREED SLATE
SLOAN SPANK TARGE BOUNCE
CARPET EARFUL REBUKE ROCKET
STRAFE CENSURE CHAPTER
LECTURE REPROOF REPROVE
TICKOFF DRESSING WRAGGING
REPRINT COPY DEPRINT OFFPRINT
REIMPOSE TAUCHNITZ
REPRISAL PRIZE MARQUE REPRISE
REQUITAL RECAPTION
REPROACH ILL TAX BLOT GIBE JIBE
LACK NOSE NOTE RAIL SLUR SPOT
TEEN TWIT WITE ABUSE BLAME
BRAID BRAND CHIDE SCOLD
SHEND TAUNT WHITE AYWORD
BISMER INFAMY REBUKE REVILE
UPCAST VILIFY BLEMISH CENSURE
CONDEMN REPROOF REPROVE
SLANDER UMBRAID UPBRAID
WITHNIM BETONGUE DISHONOR
REDARGUE REVILING CONTUMELY
OPPROBRIUM REFLECTION
REPROACHFUL BITTER ABUSIVE
SHAMEFUL
REPROBATE HARD LOST SCAMP
DISOWN RASCAL REJECT SINNER
ABANDON CENSURE CORRUPT
EXCLUDE REPROVE DEPRAVED
DISALLOW HARDENED SCALAWAG
SKALAWAG
REPRODUCE BUD HIT COPY BREED
SPORE RECITE REPEAT PORTRAY
AUTOTYPE MULTIPLY REFIGURE
REMEMBER PROCREATE
(— ONESELF) CLONE
REPRODUCTION CAST COPY REVI
CLONE IMAGE PRINT ECTYPE
RECALL STEREO EDITION ELECTRO
EXOGAMY FISSION REPLICA
REVIVAL APOMIXIS BLOCKOUT
GAMOGAMY HOMOGAMY
LIKENESS
(— BY FISSION) SCISSIPARITY
(— OF DESIGNS) SPATTERWORK
(— OF SOUND) AUDIO
(— WITHOUT SEX) MONOGENY
(SUFF.) GAM(AE)(IST)(OUS)(Y)
GAMETE GON(E)(IDIUM)(IMO)(IUM)
(Y)
REPRODUCTIVE PROLIFIC
REPROOF PROD RATE BLAME
CHECK LESSON REBUKE CHIDING
LECTURE SETDOWN JOBATION

REPROACH REPROVAL SCOLDING
TAXATION JAWBATION
(GENTLE —) ADMONITION
REPROVE RAG TAP BAWL FLAY FRIE
JOBE RATE SNIB TRIM BLAME
CHECK CHIDE CRAWL SCOLD
SHEND SHENT SNEAP BERATE
CHASTE REBUKE REFORM SCHOOL
THREAT CENSURE CONDEMN
CORRECT IMPROVE LECTURE
UPBRAID WITHNIM ADMONISH
CHASTISE KEELHAUL REDARGUE
REPROACH UNDERNIM WITHTAKE
REPTILE LOW WORM WORM GUANA
SNAKE VIPER GAVIAL LIZARD
MOLOCH TURTLE CRAWLER
CREEPER DIAPSID GHARIAL
PROTEUS SAURIAN SERPENT
TUATARA BASILISK CREEPING
CYNODONT DINOSAUR GALESAUR
MESOSAUR MOSASAUR PLIOSAUR
STEGOMUS SYNAPSID TORTOISE
ALLIGATOR CROCODILE
PELYCOSAUR PLESIOSAUR
(FLYING —) PTEROSAUR
PTERANODON PTERODACTYL
PTERODACTYLE
(PART OF —) EYE JAW PIT BODY
FANG SCALE TOOTH BUTTON
RATTLE SHEATH TONGUE SEGMENT
(PREF.) HERPET(I)(O)
REPTILIAN HERPETIC
REPUBLIC STATE SOVIET POBLACHT
(FRENCH —) MARIANNE
(IDEAL —) ICARIA
(IMAGINARY —) OCEANA
REPUBLICAN RED QUID STALWART
SANSCULOT
REPUDIATE DEFY DENY ABJURE
DISOWN RECANT REFUTE REJECT
DECLINE DISAVOW DISCARD
DIVORCE RETRACT DISCLAIM
DISVOUCH RENOUNCE
(— DEBTS) NOCHEL NOTCHEL
REPUDIATING NAKIR
REPUGNANCE ENMITY HATRED
HORROR DISGUST DISLIKE
DISTASTE LOATHING
REPUGNANT ALIEN DIRTY NASTY
ADVERSE HATEFUL OPPOSED
INIMICAL OPPOSITE ABHORRENT
OBNOXIOUS REPULSIVE
REPULSE FOIL ROUT RUSH CHECK
FLING REBUT REFEL REPEL SMEAR
DEFEAT DENIAL REBUFF REBUTE
REFUSE REJECT
REPULSION UG DISLIKE AVERSION
REPULSIVE COLD DAIN EVIL LOTH
UGLY VILE LOATH GREASY LAIDLY
FULSOME HATEFUL LOATHLY
SQUALID SCABROUS UNHONEST
REPURCHASE (— AGREEMENT)
REPO
REPUTABLE GOOD HONEST
WORTHY CREDIBLE ESTIMABLE
REPUTATION REP FAME LOSE
NAME NOTE ODOR PASS GLORY
HONOR IZZAT NOISE RUMOR
SAVOR VOICE CREDIT ESTEEM
RECORD RENOWN SHADOW
LAURELS OPINION RESPECT
WORSHIP STANDING

(EVIL —) INFAMY
(GOOD —) STANDING
REPUTE FAME ODOR RANK WORD
NOISE SAVOR THINK RECKON
REGARD STATUS OPINION
RESPECT WORSHIP ESTIMATE
JUDGMENT POSITION
(ILL —) SLANDER
REPUTED DIT PUTATIVE
REQUEST ASK BEG BOON CALL
PLEA PRAY SEEK SUIT TELL WISH
CLAIM LIBEL QUEST YEARN
APPEAL BEHEST DEMAND DESIRE
DIRECT ENCORE INVITE MOTION
BESPEAK COMMAND ENTREAT
INQUIRY REQUIRE SOLICIT
ENTREATY INSTANCE PETITION
ROGATION
(— FOR HELP) SOS
(— RECONSIDERATION) RECLAMA
(STRONG —) DUN DEMAND
REQUIEM HYMN MASS REST DIRGE
PEACE QUIET REPOSE REQUIN
REQUIN SHARK TOMMY
REQUIRE ASK HAVE LACK NEED
TAKE WANT CLAIM CRAVE EXACT
FORCE GAVEL COMPEL DEMAND
DEPEND DESIRE ENJOIN ENTAIL
EXPECT GOVERN MISTER OBLIGE
BEHOOVE DICTATE INVOLVE
MANDATE SOLICIT STIPULATE
REQUIRED DUE SET SUPPOSED
NECESSARY REQUISITE
OBLIGATORY
REQUIREMENT CALL MUST NEED
LEGAL ORDER BEHEST DEMAND
NECESSITY
(VEXATIOUS —) FIKE
(PL.) EXIGENCE EXIGENCY
REQUIRING
(PREF.) END(O)
REQUISITE DUE NEED NEEDY VITAL
NEEDFUL ESSENTIAL NECESSARY
REQUISITION ORDER DEMAND
INDENT EMBARGO REQUEST
REQUITAL WAR APPAY MERIT
REPAY SERVE TALLY YIELD ACQUIT
DEFRAY REWARD GRATIFY
PAYMENT REVENGE CONSIDER
FORYIELD REPRISAL
REQUITE SERVE RECOMPENSE
RECIPROCATE
RERAILER DIAMOND
REREAD DOUBLE
RERECORD DUB
REREDOS SCREEN BRAZIER
DRAPERY RETABLO FIREBACK
REARDOSS
REREMOUSE BAT
RERUN (PAYMENT FOR —) RESIDUAL
RES POINT THING MATTER SUBJECT
RESCIND LIFT ANNUL CANCEL
REMOVE REPEAL REVOKE ABOLISH
RETRACT RETREAT ABROGATE
RESCRIPT EDICT ORDER DECREE
LETTER EPISTLE
RESCUE RID FREE HELP REDD SAVE
BORROW RANSOM REDEEM
RESKEW SUCCOR WARISH
BAILOUT DELIVER RECLAIM
RECOVER RELEASE SALVAGE
DELIVERY LIBERATE RECOURSE
(— OF PROPERTY) SALVAGE

RESEARCH ARBEIT SEARCH ENQUIRY INQUIRY

RESECT EXCISE

RESEDA LEEK MENNUET MORILLON

RESELL (— AT INCREASED PRICES) SCALP

RESEMBLANCE SWAP PARITY SIMILE ANALOGY AFFINITY LIKENESS PARALLEL VICINITY SIMILARITY
(DIM HAZY —) BLY
(SLIGHT —) BLUSH

RESEMBLE AGREE BRAID FAVOR IMAGE LIKEN APPEAR DEPICT FIGURE RECALL SEMBLE COMPARE IMITATE PORTRAY ASSEMBLE SIMULATE
(SUFF.) ODE OID OPSIS

RESEMBLING LIKE SAME SEMBLE SIMILAR SEMBLANT
(— AN EGG) OVULARIAN
(— COMB) PECTINAL
(— GOOSE) ANSERINE
(— HORSE) EQUOID
(— IVORY) EBURNEAN EBURNEOID EBURNEOUS
(— LADDER) SCALARIFORM
(— SALT) HALOID
(— STAR) STELLATE
(— WALL) MURAL
(SUFF.) ACEOUS AR ARY EOUS FORM FUL IFORM ITIC OIDAL

RESENT HATE MEAN INDIGN MALIGN STOMACH SUGGEST

RESENTFUL HARD HURT BITTER SULLEN ENVIOUS JEALOUS STOMACHY

RESENTMENT HURT DEPIT PIQUE SNUFF SPITE CHOLER ENMITY GRUDGE HATRED MALICE RANCOR DISDAIN DUDGEON OFFENCE OFFENSE STOMACH UMBRAGE JEALOUSY HEARTBURN
(CAUSE —) OUTRAGE

RESERVATION DIBS SALVO SPACE SAVING UNLESS BOOKING CAUTION KEEPING PROVISO RESERVE FORPRISE RESERVAL
(MENTAL —) SALVO SCRUPLE

RESERVE BOOK CAVE FUND HOJU HOLD KEEP SALT SAVE SPARE BACKUP NICETY SEPONE SEPOSE TRIARY BACKLOG CAUTION CONTROL DIGNITY SEPOSIT SHYNESS TENENUE COLDNESS DISTANCE FALLBACK FORPRISE IMMODEST WITHHOLD STOCKPILE
(HOME —S) LANDSTURM
(IN —) ONICE
(MILITARY —) HOJU YOBI TRIARY TRIARII LANDWEHR
(MONETARY —) CUSHION
(PL.) FAT KOKUMIN STRENGTH

RESERVED COY DRY SHY COLD UNCO ALOOF CHARY SAVED BOOKED CLOSED DEMURE MODEST SILENT STANCH COSTIVE DISTANT RETIRED STRANGE RETICENT RETIRING STANDOFF TACITURN WITHHELD
(— FOR ROYAL USE) KHASS
(NOT —) COMMON

RESERVOIR DAM BOSS FONT KEEP LAKE PENT SUMP TANK BASIN FOUNT STANK STORE CENOTE SIPHON SOURCE SYPHON CISTERN CLEARER FAVISSA FOREBAY IMPOUND PISCINA RECEIPT AFTERBAY DEPOSITO FOUNTAIN MAGAZINE STANDAGE
(— OF WEATHERGLASS) STAGNUM

RESET HELP ABODE ALTER RECEPT RESORT SUCCOR RECEIPT REPLANT SHARPEN WELCOME

RESHEPH (FATHER OF —) EPHRAIM

RESIDE BIG WIN BIDE BIGG HOME LIVE STAY TELD WONT ABIDE DWELL LODGE REMAIN CONSIST SOJOURN HABITATE
(— TEMPORARILY) LIE STOP

RESIDENCE DUN WON DOON HALL HOME SEAT SEMI STAY WENE WONE ABODE COURT DAIRI DEMUR HOUSE MAHAL MANSE YAMUN BIDING DUKERY ELYSEE HOSTEL MANOIR TENSER DEANERY DROSTDY EMBASSY SOJOURN CURATAGE DOMICILE DWELLING LEGATION RESIANCE RESIANCY RESIDUUM SEDIMENT SETTLING PREFECTURE
(— FOR STUDENTS) INN
(— OF ARCHBISHOP) PALACE
(— OF CHIEF OF VILLAGE) TATA
(— OF ECCLESIASTIC) MANSE PRIORY DEANERY RECTORY CURATAGE VICARAGE PARSONAGE
(— OF FRENCH PRESIDENTS) ELYSEE
(— OF MANDARIN) YAMEN YAMUN
(— OF MIKADO) DAIRI
(— OF PRIEST) CONVENTO
(— OF SOVEREIGN) PALACE
(— OF SULTAN) SERAGLIO
(FORTIFIED —) DUN
(HILL —) RATH
(OFFICIAL TURKISH —) KONAK
(RURAL —) SEAT FARMSTEAD
(SUMMER —) MAHAL
(TEMPORARY —) STAY

RESIDENT GER FIXED LEGER LIVER INMATE LEDGER STABLE CITIZEN DENIZEN DWELLER PRESENT RESIANT RESIDER RESTING HABITANT INHERENT KAMAAINA MINISTER OCCUPANT
(— AT A UNIVERSITY) GREMIALE
(— OF HAWAII) KAMAAINA
(— OF NEWFOUNDLAND) LIVYER
(— OF WEST. AUSTRALIA) GROPER
(ALIEN —) GER METIC
(CHINESE — OF TIBET) AMBAN
(FOREIGN-BORN —) ALIEN
(OLD —) STANDARD
(TEMPORARY —) TRANSIENT
(SUFF.) ESETTE
(— OF) ER IER YER

RESIDUAL RELICT REMANIE REMANENT

RESIDUE ASH DREG FOOT GUNK HEEL LAFE LAVE LEES REST SILT SLAG UNIT MAZUT SHARD SHERD BEGASS BORING BOTTOM GRUFFS RELICS BAGASSE CINDERS REMAINS HARDHEAD LEAVINGS LEFTOVER REMANENT RESIDUUM SEMICOKE TAILINGS
(— FROM DISTILLATION) VINASSE
(— FROM FAT) CRAP
(— FROM OLIVES) SANZA
(— FROM REFINING TIN) HARDHEAD
(— IN OPIUM PIPE) YENSHEE
(— IN STILL) BOTTOM BOTTOMS
(— OF COAL) COKE SEMICOKE
(— OF COKE) BREEZE
(— OF COMBUSTION) ASH
(— OF HONEYCOMB) SLUMGUM
(— OF PETROLEUM) MAZUT ASTATKI
(— OF SHINGLES) SPALT
(FRIABLE —) CALX
(INSOLUBLE —) MARC
(SMELTING —) SPEISS
(WORTHLESS —) SNUFF
(PL.) TANKAGE

RESIDUUM TAIL BOTTOM DEPOSIT RESIDUE SEDIMENT

RESIGN QUIT DEMIT FORGO REMIT YIELD PERMIT SUBMIT ABANDON COMMEND DELIVER FORGIVE ABDICATE RENOUNCE RELINQUISH

RESIGNATION PATIENCE DEMISSION SURRENDER

RESILIENCE GIVE LIFE TONE BOUNCE RECOIL SPRING REBOUND BUOYANCY

RESILIENCY TONE

RESILIENT TOUGH BOUNCY LIVELY SUPPLE WHIPPY ELASTIC SPRINGY FLEXIBLE

RESIN ALK LAC BALM BATU BREA HASH TOLU ALKYD AMBER ANIME COPAL CUMAR ELEMI EPOXY GUGAL GUGUL KAURI PITCH ROSEL ROSET SIRUP SYRUP ANTIAR BINDER CHARAS CONIMA DAMMAR GOOGUL GUACIN HARTIN MASTIC STORAX TAMANU ACOUCHI ACRYLIC AMBRITE BENZOIN BISABOL DERRIDE FLUAVIL GAMBOGE IONOMER LADANUM PERSPEX SAGAPEN SHELLAC ALKITRAN ALMACIGA BAKELITE BDELLIUM CACHIBOU CANNABIN COLOPHAN EUOSMITE FORMVAIL GALAGALA GALLIPOT GEDANITE GUAIACUM MALAPAHO MELAMINE OPOPANAX PHENOLIC SANDARAC SCAMMONY
(— DRAWN FROM TREES) CHIP
(— FROM HEMP) CHARAS
(— FROM NORWAY SPRUCE) THUS
(— OF FIR TREE) BLOB
(— PLASTIC) SARAN
(FLEXIBLE —) SARAN
(FOSSIL —) AMBER AMBRITE HARTITE GEDANITE GLESSITE RETINITE
(GRADE OF —) SORTS
(GUM —) ELEMI GUGUL LASER MYRRH ANTIAR BISABOL GAMBOGE BDELLIUM SAGAPENUM
(NARCOTIC —) CHARAS CHURUS
(SYNTHETIC —S) TEFLON
(TURPENTINE —) ALK GALIPOT COLOPHONY

(PREF.) RETIN(O)
(SUFF.) RETIN

RESINOID ALNUIN HELONIN LOBELIN ASCLEPIN CERASEIN CHELONIN TRILLIIN

RESINOUS ROSETY ROSETTY

RESIST BUCK DEFY FACE STAY REPEL STAND DEFEND IMPUGN OPPOSE REPUGN WITHER CONTEST DISPUTE GAINSAY KNUCKLE RESERVE WITHSET OUTBRAVE OUTSTAND
(— AUTHORITY) REBEL DEFORCE
(— SEPARATION) ATTRACT

RESISTANCE DRAG LOAD OHMAGE REBUFF WITHER BALLAST ANTITYPY BLOCKAGE FASTNESS FRICTION HARDNESS OBSTACLE SEDITION
(— OF COTTON FIBERS) DRAG
(— OF KEYS) ACTION
(— THAT EXPLOSIVE MUST OVERCOME) BURDEN BURTHEN
(— TO ATTACK) DEFENCE DEFENSE
(— TO CHANGE) INERTIA
(— TO COLOR CHANGE) FASTNESS
(— TO DISEASE) PREMUNITION
(— TO SLIPPING) BOND
(GREEK — GROUP) EDES ELAS
(PASSIVE —) SATYAGRAHA
(UNIT OF —) OHM

RESISTANT HARD STOUT STABILE STUBBORN
(— TO CHANGE) FAST STICKY
(— TO HEAT) THERMODURIC

RESISTING OBSTANT RELUCTANT

RESISTOR BLEEDER DIVERTOR RHEOSTAT

RESOLUTE BOLD FIRM GRIM BRAVE FIXED HARDY MANLY STERN STIFF STOUT GRITTY MANFUL PLUCKY STABLE STANCH STEADY STUFFY STURDY ANIMOSE ANIMOUS DECIDED CONSTANT FAITHFUL INTREPID POSITIVE STALWART STUBBORN UNSHAKEN
(MAKE —) STEEL

RESOLUTELY TALLY FIRMLY STOUTLY

RESOLUTION VOW SAND THEW NERVE PARTY PLUCK POINT STARCH ACUERDO BESLUIT CENSURE COURAGE MANHEAD MANHOOD PURPOSE RESOLVE THOUGHT ANALYSIS DECISION DIERESIS ENACTURE STRENGTH CONSTANCY

RESOLVE ACT BEND MELT REDE SOIL UNDO LAPSE RELAX SALVE SOLVE SOYLE UNTIE VOUCH ADJUST ADVICE ASSOIL DECIDE DECREE FACTOR INCIDE REDUCE SETTLE STEVEN ABSOLVE ANALYZE APPOINT BETHINK CONSULT PURPOSE CONCLUDE DISSOLVE UNRIDDLE UNTANGLE RECONCILE
(— GRAMMATICALLY) PARSE
(— INTO ELEMENTS) ANALYSE ANALYZE

RESOLVED BENT BOUND INTENT CERTAIN INTENSE RESOLUTE
(HALF —) GOOD

RESONANCE BODY EMPATHY

RAPPORT RESOUND SYNTONY TYMPANY SONORITY VIBRANCY MESOMERISM

RESONANT BIG BRASS RINGY OROTUND RINGING SILVERY VIBRANT CANOROUS PLANGENT SONORANT SONOROUS SOUNDFUL SOUNDING

RESORT GO RUN SPA BEAT DOME HOWF LIDO SEEK TEEM TOUR TURN CAUSE FRAME HAUNT HOWFF JOINT RECUR RESET VISIT ESCORT FINISH REPAIR RETURN REVERT THRONG COMPANY PIMLICO RECOURSE RESOURCE TEETOTUM
(— OF LEARNED) MUSEUM
(— TO) SEEK
(— TO DEVIOUS METHODS) FINAGLE
(— TO EXPEDIENTS) SHIFT
(BATHING —) PLAGE
(DISREPUTABLE —) KEN DIVE
(DRINKING —) DOGGERY
(EVIL —) ROOKERY
(LOW —) KEN DIVE STEW SPITAL
(MEANS OF —) REFUGE
(WORKINGMEN'S —) TEETOTUM

RESOUND DIN DUN ECHO PEAL RING SOUND REECHO EXPLODE REBOUND RESPEAK VIBRATE REDOUBLE

RESOUNDING BRASS REVERB REBOANT EMPHATIC FORCEFUL PLANGENT RESONANT RUMOROUS
(— WITH TALK) ABUZZ

RESOURCE WON BOOT FUND WONE MEANS SHIFT REFUGE RESORT STOPGAP PURCHASE
(PL.) EASE FOND GAIN FUNDS MEANS PURSE SINEW BOTTOM FACULTY FOISONS PURCHASE STRENGTH POCKETBOOK

RESOURCEFUL APT FENDY SHARP SMART ADROIT CLEVER FACILE SHIFTY PLANFUL

RESOURCEFULNESS SENSE SHIFT AGILITY

RESPECT ORE WAY DUTY FACE HEED HORE LOOK MARK DEFER DULIA FRONT HONOR IZZAT PARTY VALUE ASPECT BEHALF DETAIL ESTEEM HALLOW HOMAGE NOTICE REGARD CONCERN OBSERVE RESPITE SUSPECT TASHRIF WORSHIP CONSIDER HABITUDE RELATION VENERATE
(PL.) DEVOIR

RESPECTABLE GOOD NICE SMUG DOUCE DECENT PROPER FRUSANT CULOTTIC

RESPECTFUL AWFUL CIVIL CAREFUL DUTEOUS DUTIFUL HEEDFUL REVERENT

RESPECTIVE SEVERAL

RESPIRATION SIGH EUPNEA ANAPNEA DYSPNEA EUPNOEA ROARING GRUNTING
(PREF.) PNEO PNEUM(A)(O)(ON) (ONO) PNEUMATO SPIRO

RESPIRATOR MUZZLE CUIRASS INHALER
(KIND OF —) DRINKER

RESPIRE BLOW LIVE REST EXHALE REVIVE BREATHE SNUFFLE SUSPIRE

RESPITE SOB REST STAY TRUE DELAY FRIST LETUP PAUSE BARLEY BREATH LAYOFF REGARD REMISE LEISURE RESPECT INTERVAL REPRIEVE SURCEASE

RESPLENDENCE GLORY SHEEN FULGENCE FULGENCY SPLENDOR

RESPLENDENT LUCID SHEEN BRIGHT GILDED ORIENT SILVER AUREATE SHINING GLORIOUS GORGEOUS LUSTROUS SPLENDID SUNSHINY

RESPOND FIELD REACT REPLY ANSWER RETURN TRISAGION
(— TO LURE) STOOL
(— TO PROVOCATION) RISE
(— WARMLY) RISE

RESPONDENT ANSWERER APPELLEE

RESPONSE AMEN ECHO CHORD REPLY SNAFF ANSWER EARFUL VOLLEY INTROIT RESPOND ANTIPHON BEHAVIOR INSTINCT REACTION REANSWER RECEPTION
(— OF KEYS) ACTION
(— OF SHIP) STEERING
(— TO GRAVITY) GEOTAXIS
(INVOLUNTARY —) TIC
(LITURGICAL —) RESPONSORY
(NONCOMMITAL —) ISEE

RESPONSIBILITY BABY BALL CARE DUTY ONUS WITE BLAME GUILT TRUST CHARGE RACKET

RESPONSIBLE GOOD SOLID DIRECT LIABLE AMENABLE
(JOINTLY —) SOLIDARY

RESPONSION REPLY ANSWER
(PL.) SMALLS

RESPONSIVE OPEN SOFT WARM GUILTY MUTUAL NIMBLE SUPPLE TENDER MEETING AMENABLE SENSIBLE
(— TO BEAUTY) ESTHETIC
(— TO STIMULI) SENTIENT
(MUTUALLY —) ANTIPHONIC
(NOT —) IMMUNE

RESPONSIVENESS TOUCH FEELING
(ABNORMAL —) SENSITIVITY

RESPONSORY ANTHEM LIBERA GRADUAL RESPOND

REST BED LAY LIE PUT SET SIT SOB BASE BLOW CALM CAMP EASE HANG HEEL LAIR LAVE LEAN LIOS LISS PROP RELY RIDE RUST STAY STOP COUCH FOUND LEATH LIEBY PAUSE PEACE POISE QUIET RENEW ROOST SLEEP SPELL STAND TRUST WREST ANCHOR BOTTOM FAUCRE FEWTER GROUND INSIST REMAIN REPOSE SETTLE SIESTA STEADY UNTIRE ADHARMA BALANCE BREATHE CAESURA CLARION COMFORT GALLOWS NOONING RECLINE REFRESH RELACHE REMNANT REQUIEM RESIDUE RESPITE SILENCE SLUMBER SOJOURN SUFFLUE SUPPORT SURPLUS AKINESIS INTERVAL QUIETUDE STANDOFF VACATION

(— FOR SPEAR OR LANCE) QUEUE FAUCRE FEWTER
(— FOR SUPPORT) ABUT
(— FOR TYMPAN) GALLOWS
(— HORSE) WIND
(— IDLY) SLUG
(— LAZILY) FROWST
(— ON PLANER) SIDEHEAD
(— ON SUPPORT) BOTTOM
(— UPRIGHT) STAND
(HALF —) MINIM SOSPIRO
(LATHE —) STEADY
(LEG — ON SADDLE) CRUTCH
(MUSKET —) GAFFLE
(NOONDAY —) NAP SIESTA
(QUARTER —) SOSPIRO
(SHORT —) CATNAP
(PREF.) PAULO

RESTATE REHASH

RESTATEMENT SUMMARY

RESTAURANT CAFE DINER GRILL HOUSE PLACE BISTRO BUFFET EATERY AUTOMAT BEANERY CABARET CANTEEN CANTINA OSTERIA TEAROOM HIDEAWAY BRASSERIE CHOPHOUSE TRATTORIA
(— KEEPER) BISTRO TRAITEUR
(SMALL —) CAFF

RESTAURANTEUR (FAMOUS —) SARDI

RESTFUL COOL SOFT QUIET PLACID EASEFUL RELAXED SOOTHFUL TRANQUIL

RESTHARROW WHIN CAMMOCK SITFAST LANDWHIN

RESTHOUSE KHAN SERAI AMBALAM CHHATRI KHANKAH

RESTING DORMANT
(PREF.) STATO

RESTING PLACE (ALSO SEE RESTHOUSE) FORM GIST GITE STAGE CHHATRI DHARMSALA

RESTITUTION AMENDS RETURN RECOVERY
(FINAL —) APOCATASTASIS

RESTIVE ANTSY BALKY FUDGY ITCHY RESTY RUSTY FIDGETY UNRESTY UNWAYED CONTRARY INACTIVE RESTLESS SKITTISH SLUGGISH STUBBORN UNWIELDY

RESTLESS ANTSY FIKIE FUDGY ITCHY FITFUL HAUNTY HECTIC ROVING UNEASY AGITATO ERETHIC FIDGETY FLIGHTY FRETFUL INQUIET RAMPLER RAMPLOR RESTIVE TEWSOME TOSSING UNQUIET UNRESTY VARIANT WAKEFUL FEVERISH FEVEROUS STEERING
(— FLYCATCHER) GRINDER

RESTLESSNESS FIKE STIR FIDGET UNREST DISQUIET ACATHISIA AKATHISIA JACTATION

RESTORATION REPAIR RETURN RENEWAL RESTORE REVIVAL EXCHANGE RECOVERY REMITTER RESTORAL RECLAMATION

RESTORATIVE ACOPON BALSAMIC SALUTARY SANATIVE ANALEPTIC

RESTORE FIX CURE HEAL AMEND BLOCK COVER REDUB REFER RENEW REPAY STORE YIELD

ASTORE DOCTOR RECALL REDEEM REFORM REFUND RELATE RENDER REPONE REVERT REVIVE CONVERT ENSTORE INPAINT REBUILD RECLAIM RECOVER RECRUIT RECYCLE REFOUND REFRESH REPLACE REVOLVE DECOHERE REANSWER RECREATE RESTITUE RETRIEVE RESURRECT
(— CONFIDENCE) REASSURE
(— TO CIVIL RIGHTS) INLAW
(— TO FORMER STATE) REHAB
(— TO HEALTH) CURE HEAL MEND
(— TO LIFE) REVIVIFY
(— TO OFFICE) REPONE
(— TO ORDER) STILL
(—.YOUTH) REJUVENATE

RESTRAIN BAR BIT DAM BATE BIND BOLT BUCK COOP CRIB CURB DAMP GRAB GYVE HEAD HEFT KEEP REIN SHUT SINK SNEB SNIB SNUB STAY STEM STOP STOW BRANK CHAIN CHECK COART CRAMP DETER GUARD LEASH MINCE POUND REPEL SHUNT SOBER STILL STINT TRASH ARREST BOTTLE BRIDLE CHASTE COERCE DETAIN ENJOIN FETTER FORBID GOVERN HALTER HAMPER HINDER KENNEL OBLIGE REBUKE RETAIN RETIRE REVOKE STIFLE STRAIN TEMPER TETHER ABRIDGE ABSTAIN CHASTEN COHIBIT CONFINE CONTAIN CONTROL ENCHAIN EXCLUDE INHIBIT INJUNCT QUALIFY RECLAIM REFRAIN REPRESS RETRACT SHACKLE SNAFFLE SWADDLE BULLDOZE COMPESCE COMPRESS HANDCUFF IMPRISON RESTRICT SIDELINE WITHDRAW WITHHOLD
(— BY FEAR) OVERAWE
(— HAWK'S WING) BRAIL
(— MOTION) SNUB
(PREF.) ISCH(O)

RESTRAINED SOBER CHASTE MODEST SEVERE ASHAMED DISCREET RESERVED RITENUTO

RESTRAINER YOKE

RESTRAINT BIT BEND CLOG CURB HEFT STAY STOP CHECK CRAMP FORCE LEASH SPARE STENT STINT TRASH ARREST BRIDLE DURESS FETTER STAYER TETHER AWEBAND BONDAGE CONTROL DURANCE EMBARGO MANACLE RESERVE SNAFFLE TRAMMEL HEADREST SOBRIETY
(— OF GOODS) HOCK
(BEYOND —) APE
(WITHOUT —) INSPADES

RESTRICT PEG TIE CURB HOLD BOUND CHAIN COART FENCE HEDGE STINT THIRL COARCT COERCE CORRAL CORSET ENTAIL HAMPER NARROW ASTRICT COHIBIT COMBINE QUALIFY REPRESS SCANTLE SWADDLE CONTRACT DEROGATE DIMINISH RESTRAIN STRAITEN
(— MEANING) MODIFY

RESTRICTED CLOSE CRAMP LOCAL

CLOSED FINITE NARROW STRAIT STRICT OBLIGATE PAROCHIAL

RESTRICTION STENT STINT BURDEN DENIAL BARRIER CONFINE RESERVE SQUEEZE BLACKOUT CABOTAGE RESTRAINT
(LEGAL —) LIEN
(PROPERTY —) EASEMENT
(PL.) BARS SWADDLE

RESTRICTIVE SEVERE BINDING STYPTIC COACTIVE LIMITARY LIMITING CONFINING

RESTY LAZY RESTIVE INACTIVE INDOLENT SLUGGISH

RESULT GO END OUT ECHO FALL FATE FAVE GROW RISE TAKE BACON BRING CHILD ENSUE EVENT FRUIT FUDGE ISSUE PROOF EFFECT EFFORT ENDING EVOLVE FINISH FOLLOW GROWTH RECOIL REVERT SEQUEL SPRING UPCOME UPSHOT ENTRAIN FALLOUT FINDING OUTCOME PROCEED PURPOSE REBOUND REDOUND SUCCEED SUCCESS FRUITAGE SEQUENCE OFFSPRING
(— FAVORABLY) SUCCEED
(— FROM) SUE
(ALGEBRAIC —) DUAL EXPANSION
(AS A —) AGAIN
(INCONCLUSIVE —) DOGFALL
(INEVITABLE —) NEMESIS
(PATHOLOGICAL —S) ALCOHOLISM
(REWARDING —) HAY
(SECONDARY —) SEQUELA
(PL.) AFTERINGS
(SUFF.) ISATION IZATION

RESULTANT CONCEPT OUTCOME PROGENY

RESUME RENEW REOPEN RECOVER SUMMARY CONTINUE PURLICUE REASSUME RENOVATE REOCCUPY
(PL.) EXCERPTA

RESURRECTION RISE RIST UPRIST REBIRTH REVIVAL

RESURRECTION PLANT FERNWORT

RESUSCITATE REVIVE QUICKEN SUSCITE REVIVIFY

RESUSCITATION KATSU RENEWAL REVIVAL

RET RAIT RATE SOAK DEWROT

RETABLE PREDELLA

RETAIL REGRATE HUCKSTER
(— OUTLET) MINILAB
(— STORE) WAREHOUSE

RETAILER DEALER CLOTHIER HUCKSTER

RETAIN HAVE HEFT HOLD KEEP SAVE CATCH ATHOLD CONTAIN RESERVE CONTINUE MAINTAIN PRESERVE
(— MOMENTUM) DRIFT

RETAINER FEE FOOL HEWE LACKEY MENIAL RIBALD SEQUEL YEOMAN HOBBLER HUSCARL JACKMAN LACQUEY PANDOUR SERVANT TRAVERS EMPLOYEE FOLLOWER HENCHMAN MYRMIDON BURKUNDAZ PENSIONER
(ARMED —) GALLOGLASS GALLOWGLASS

(JAPANESE —) SAMURAI
(PL.) FOLK

RETALIATE REPAY AVENGE RETORT REQUITE RECIPROCATE

RETALIATION QUITS MARQUE TALION REPRISAL REQUITAL
(MAKE —) TURN
(VINDICTIVE —) REVENGE

RETALIATORY COUNTER

RETARD LAG CHOP DAMP DRAG SLOW STEM BRAKE DEFER DELAY ELONG STUNT TARDY TARRY THROW TRASH BACKEN BELATE DEADEN DETAIN HINDER INHIBIT SLACKEN ENCUMBER OBSTRUCT PROTRACT RESTRAIN

RETARDANT (FIRE —) BORAX

RETARDATION LAG DRAG DELAY ARREST

RETARDED DARK BEHIND LAGGED SIMPLE OVERAGE

RETARDING LENTANDO

RETCH GAG BOKE KECK HEAVE REACH VOMIT KECKLE RECCHE STRAIN

RETCHING HEFT

RETEM JUNIPER

RETENTION MEMORY RETAIN HOLDING KEEPING RETINUE
(SUFF.) STASIA STASIS

RETIARIUS RETIARY GLADIATOR

RETICENCE RESERVE SECRECY RESTRAINT

RETICENT ABED DARK SNUG CLOSE SECRET SILENT MIMMOUD SPARING BOUTONNE

RETICENTLY HEIMLICH

RETICULATE MESHED NETTED

RETICULE BAG CABAS SACHET WORKBAG CARRYALL RIDICULE

RETICULUM NET MITOME NETWORK MATTULLA

RETINOIC ACID TRETINOIN

RETINOL CODOL

RETINOPHORE VITRELLA

RETINUE CREW GING PORT ROUT SUIT TAIL COURT MEINY SUITE TIRED TRAIN FAMILY REPAIR RETAIN COMPANY CORTEGE SOWARRY EQUIPAGE TENDANCE BODYGUARD
(— OF CAVALRY) SOWARRY
(VILLAINOUS —) BLACKGUARD

RETIRE GO GET DRAW GIVE AVOID LEAVE MICHE REBUT DEPART LOCATE RECALL RECEDE RECESS RECOIL SHRINK SURVEY PENSION REGRADE RETRACT RETREAT WITHDRAW
(— IGNOMINIOUSLY) SLINK
(— IN CRICKET) BOWL

RETIRED QUIET SECRET DEVIOUS OBSCURE OUTGONE PRIVATE RETRAIT SECLUSE SHADOWY ABSTRUSE EMERITUS SECLUDED SOLITARY
(— FROM PLAY) DOWN

RETIREMENT SHADE RECESS RETOUR SECESS PRIVACY PRIVATE RETREAT FIRESIDE SOLITUDE

RETIRING SHY NESH TIMID DEMURE

MODEST FUGIENT RESERVED UMBRATIC RECESSIVE
(— ROOM) RECAMERA

RETORT MOT QUIP RISE SNAP VENY QUIRK REPAY REPLY SALLY ANSWER REGEST RETURN RIPOST BOMBOLA CORNUTE CRUSHER PELICAN REFLECT RIPOSTE SQUELCH BACKWORD BLIZZARD COMEBACK MAGAZINE RECEIVER REPARTEE
(CURT —) SNAPHANCE
(GROUP OF —S) SETTING
(PUNNING —) CLINCH
(WITTY —) KNACK ZINGER

RETRACE RECALL FLYBACK RETREAT UNTREAD BACKTRACK

RETRACT BACK UNSAY ABJURE DISOWN RECALL RECANT RECEDE REVOKE SHRINK UNLOOK RESCIND RETREAT SWALLOW PALINODE RENOUNCE WITHDRAW

RETRACTED INNER

RETRACTION PALINODE PALINODY

RETREAT DEN DOME DROP FADE GIVE LAIR NEST ROUT ARBOR AVOID BOWER LODGE NICHE QUAIL QUIET SHADE START ASHRAM ASYLUM BACKUP CASTLE HARBOR RECEDE RECESS REFUGE RESILE RETIRE REVOLT CABINET DESCEND PRIVACY RETIRAL RETRACT SHELTER ANABASIS CRAWFISH DISMARCH FALLBACK FASTNESS NESTLING RECOURSE RECULADE SOLITUDE STAMPEDE WITHDRAW CREEPHOLE KATABASIS
(— FOR FISH) HOD
(FORTIFIED —) REDUIT
(LAST —) REDOUBT
(RELIGIOUS —) ASRAM ASHRAM
(SECURE —) STRENGTH
(SHADY —) ALCOVE
(WINTER —) HIBERNACLE

RETRENCH OMIT EXCISE LESSEN REDUCE ABRIDGE CURTAIL SHORTEN

RETRENCHMENT CUT RAMPART EXCISION RETIRADE LESSENING

RETRIBUTION PAY PAYOFF RETURN REWARD WISSEL MANNAIA PENALTY REVENGE REQUITAL

RETRIBUTIVE VENGEFUL VINDICTIVE

RETRIEVE SHACK RECALL RECURE REGAIN REPAIR RESCUE REVIVE CORRECT RECOVER RESTORE SALVAGE

RETRIEVER LAB FINDER GUNDOG LABRADOR WATERRUG

RETROFLEX DEMAL CORONAL CEREBRAL INVERTED REFLEXED

RETROGRADE RECEDE RETRAL DECLINE INVERSE OPPOSED REGREDE RETREAT BACKWARD DECADENT REARWARD WITHDRAW

RETROGRESS SINK REGRESS BACKSLIDE

RETROGRESSION SINK REGRESS RETREAT FALLBACK

RETROSPECT REVIEW

RETUND DULL TURN BLUNT REFUTE

RETURN EBB GET COME ECHO TURN VAIL RECUR REFER REPAY REPLY VISIT YIELD AIRWAY ANSWER HOMING REMISE RENDER REPAIR REPASS REPORT RESORT RETIRE RETORT RETOUR REVERT CLEANUP PAYMENT REBOUND REDOUND REFLECT REPRISE REQUITE RESTORE REVENUE ATTOURNE DIVIDEND ELECTION EPANODOS FEEDBACK PICKINGS REACCESS REANSWER RECOURSE RECOVERY REDITION REFLECTION RECIPROCATE
(— FOR GOOD) REWARD
(— FROM DEATH) ARISE
(— LIKE FOR LIKE) RETALIATE
(— OF MERCHANDISE) COMEBACK
(— TENNIS BALL) RALLY
(— TO BAD HABITS) LAPSE
(— TO FORMER STATE) RELAPSE
(— TO ORIGINAL CONDITION) RECYCLE
(— TO ZERO) FLYBACK
(GET IN —) REAP
(GROUNDED —) BOND
(TENNIS —) GET BOAST
(TRIFLING —) PEPPERCORN

RETURNING REDIENT REMEANT REDITION

RETURN OF THE NATIVE (AUTHOR OF —) HARDY
(CHARACTER IN —) VYE CLYM VENN DAMON CANTLE JOHNNY DIGGORY NUNSUCH WILDEVE EUSTACIA THOMASIN CHRISTIAN YEOBRIGHT

REUBEN (FATHER OF —) JACOB
(MOTHER OF —) LEAH

REUEL (FATHER OF —) ESAU
(MOTHER OF —) BASHEMATH
(SON OF —) ELIASAPH

REUNE (ONE WHO —S) ALUM ALUMNUS

REUNION COLLEGE ADHESION HERENIGING
(— WITH BRAHMA) NIRVANA

REUNITE RALLY REUNE REJOIN RECONCILE

REUSE RECYCLE

REVEAL BID BARE BLAB HINT JAMB KNOW OPEN SHOW TELL WRAY BREAK EXERT SPEAK SPLIT UNRIP UNTOP UTTER YIELD ACCUSE APPEAR BETRAY BEWRAY DESCRY DETECT EVINCE IMPART OSTEND PATEFY SPRING UNHELE UNLOCK UNMASK UNVEIL UNWRAP BESPEAK CLARIFY CONFESS DEVELOP DISPLAY DIVULGE UNCLOAK UNCOVER UNSHALE UNTRUSS DECIPHER DISCLOSE DISCOVER INDICATE MANIFEST UNBURDEN UNSHADOW UNSHROUD
(— BY SIGNS) EXHIBIT
(— SECRETS) BABBLE
(— UNINTENTIONALLY) BETRAY

REVEILLE DIAN DIANA LEVET ROUSE SIGNAL TRAVALLY

REVEIVER (DISTILLING —) BOLTHOLE

REVEL JOY MASK RANT RIOT BIZLE

COMUS FEAST GLOAT GLORY WATCH BEZZLE FROLIC GAVALL SPLORE TRESCA WALLOW WANTON CAROUSE DELIGHT ROISTER TRESCHE CAROUSAL DOMINEER FESTIVAL WITHDRAW
(NOISY —) JAMBOREE
(PL.) REVELRY
REVELATION TORA TORAH EXPOSE ORACLE REVEAL BATHKOL BATHQOL SHOWING GIVEAWAY OVERTURE APOCALYPSE
(— OF GOD'S WILL) LAW
(SUDDEN —) KICK
REVELER GREEK RANTER RIOTER FRANION PIERROT ROISTER BACCHANT CAROUSER MERRYMAKER
REVELRY JOY ORGY RIOT RIOTISE WASSAIL CARNIVAL CAROUSAL FESTIVAL
REVENANT GHOST WRAITH SPECTER
REVENGE HELL WREAK WROIK AVENGE ULTION REQUITE REQUITAL REVANCHE
(MONTEZUMA'S —) TURISTA
REVENGED EVEN
REVENUE RENT JAGIR MANGE YIELD INCOME ENTRADA FINANCE PROFITS HACIENDA INCOMING
(— FROM WATER RIGHTS) JALKAR
(— REVENUE PAID TO POPE) ANNAT
(CHURCH —) PATRIMONY
(GOVERNMENT —) JAGHIR
(GOVERNMENT —S) JAGIR JAGHIR JAGHIRE
(STATE —) HACIENDA
REVERBERATE DIRL ECHO RING REPEL RETORT REVERB REBOUND REDOUND REFLECT RESOUND
REVERBERATING REBOANT RESONANT SOUNDING
REVERBERATION ECHO REDOUND REBOATION
REVERE ADORE HONOR ADMIRE ESTEEM HALLOW RESPECT WORSHIP VENERATE
REVERED
(PREF.) SEMNO
REVERENCE AWE ORE CULT FEAR DREAD HONOR MENSK PIETY WURTH HOMAGE REGARD WORSHIP DEVOTION VENERANT VENERATE WORTHING
(— FOR ANIMALS) ZOISM
(IRRATIONAL —) FETICH FETISH
(SHOW —) KNEEL
REVEREND SRI SHRI SHREE SVAMI SWAMI PASTOR POTENT STRONG
(PREF.) SEBASTO
REVERENT DEVOUT STRONG AWESOME DUTIFUL
REVERENTIAL PIOUS SOLEMN
REVERIE DUMP DWAM MUSE DREAM DWALM STUDY PONDER MEMENTO MOONING DAYDREAM TRAUMEREI
REVERSAL KNOCK CHANGE DOUBLE SWITCH BACKCAST BACKFLIP OVERTURN THROWBACK TURNABOUT
(PREF.) ALL(O)

REVERSE BACK DOWN FACE FLOP JOLT UNDO ANNUL CHECK UPSET VERSO CHANGE DEFEAT INVERT REPEAL RETURN REVERT REVOKE BACKSET COUNTER INVERSE PUTBACK RETREAT REVERSO SETBACK SNIFTER SUBVERT BACKCAST CONTRARY CONVERSE OPPOSITE OVERRULE OVERTURN RAMVERSE TRAVERSE WATERLOO
(— OARS) SHEAVE
(— OF COIN) PILE TAIL WOMAN
(— OF NOTE) BACK
(— PAGE OF BOOK) VERSO REVERSO
(PREF.) DE DIS DYS
(— ORDER) OB
REVERSED BACK INVERSE REVERTED ROVESCIO
(NOT —) DIRECT
REVERSI QUINOLAS
REVERSION SCRAPS ATAVISM ESCHEAT REMNANT FEEDBACK REVERTAL REVERTER THROWBACK
REVERT ANNUL ADVERT RESORT RESULT RETOUR RETURN REVOKE ESCHEAT RESTORE RECOURSE BACKSLIDE
(— TO A SUPERIOR) FALL
REVETMENT GODWORK
REVIEW HASH VIEW REVIE NOTICE REVISE SURVEY BRUSHUP RECENSE REJUDGE CRITIQUE REVIEWAL REVISION
(— A FLOP) PAN
(— UNSPARINGLY) SLATE
(CRITICAL —) PAN
(ENTHUSIASTIC —) RAVE
(KIND OF —) RAVE
REVIEWER CRITIC
REVILE CALL RAIL ABUSE BLEIR BRAWL REBUT SCOLD SHEND SHENT SLANG MISSAY MISUSE VILIFY INVEIGH MISCALL MISNAME BACKBITE DISGRACE EXECRATE REPROACH CLAPPERCLAW
REVILING ABUSE ABUSION ABUSIVE BLASPHEMY
REVISE EDIT ALTER REDACT REFORM REVIEW CORRECT RECENSE REFLECT REVISIT OVERHAUL
REVISER REDACTOR REFORMER REVIEWER
REVISION REVIEW SURVEY REVISAL REVIEWAL EPANAGOGE
REVITALIZER BRACER
REVIVAL IMAGE PICKUP REBIRTH REPRISE WAKENING
REVIVE DAW EBB WAKE FETCH QUICK RALLY RENEW ROUSE EXHUME GINGER RECALL RELIVE REVERT REVOKE EKPHORE ENLIVEN FRESHEN FURBISH QUICKEN REFRESH RESPIRE RESTORE RECREATE REDIVIVE REKINDLE RENOVATE RETRIEVE
(— FIRE) CHUNK
REVOCATION REPEAL REVERSAL ADEMPTION
REVOICE ECHO
REVOKE LIFT ADEEM ANNUL RENIG CANCEL RECALL RECANT RENEGE

REPEAL REVERT ABOLISH COMMUTE FINAGLE RECLAIM RESCIND RETREAT REVERSE ABROGATE REVOCATE
(— A LEGACY) ADEEM
REVOLT ARISE REBEL REPEL START MUTINY OFFEND RELUCT UPRISE UPROAR MUTATION OUTBREAK SEDITION UPRISING JACQUERIE REBELLION
(RELIGIOUS —) APOSTASY
REVOLTING GARISH HORRID BILIOUS FEARFUL HATEFUL HIDEOUS DREADFUL
REVOLT OF THE ANGELS
(AUTHOR OF —) FRANCE
(CHARACTER IN —) MAX ZITA ISTAR ARCADE AUBELS JULIEN SOPHAR MAURICE GILBERTE SARIETTE ESPARVIEU THEOPHILE EVERDINGEN
REVOLUTION GYRE RIOT TOUR TURN CYCLE WHEEL CHANGE ANARCHY CIRCUIT REVOLVE GYRATION MUTATION NOVATION ROTATION SEDITION REBELLION
(RELIGIOUS —) REFORMATION
REVOLUTIONARY RED RADICAL MUSCADIN ROTATING BOLSHEVIK
REVOLUTIONIST JACOBIN REDSHIRT
REVOLVE BIRL GYRE PIRL ROLL SPIN TIRL TURN WELT ORBIT PIVOT THROW TREND TROLL TWINE VERSE WHEEL WHIRL CENTER CIRCLE GYRATE PONDER ROTATE SPHERE SWINGE WAMBLE AGITATE VERSATE CONSIDER OVERTURN REVOLUTE
(CAUSE TO —) TRUNDLE
REVOLVER GAT GUN ROD RIFLE STICK CANNON CUTTER HEATER HOGLEG PISTOL RIFFLE SIXGUN BULLDOG DUNGEON
(PART OF —) ROD BORE BUTT GATE GRIP SPUR BLADE FRAME GUARD LATCH SIGHT SLIDE STRAP BARREL HAMMER HANDLE MUZZLE CHAMBER TRIGGER CYLINDER BACKSTRAP
REVOLVING ORBY VOLUBLE GYRATORY VOLUTION
(PREF.) (—AROUND) CIRCUM
REVUE SHOW REVIEW FOLLIES
REVULSION FEAR REACTION
REWARD FEE PAY UTU GREE MEED RENT SPUR WAGE AMEED BOOTY BRIBE CROWN LOWER MERIT PLUME SHEPE YIELD BOUNTY DESERT GERSUM PAYOFF SALARY TROPHY WEDFEE AUREOLE GUERDON PREMIUM RENTAGE SOSTRUM STIPEND WARISON CONSIDER DIVIDEND EXACTION REMEMBER REQUITAL ACKNOWLEDGE
(— FOR GOOD NEWS) ALBRICIAS
(— FOR INFORMATION ON CATTLE THIEVES) TASCAL
(— OF VICTORY) CROWN
(— TO HAWK FOR KILL) QUARRY
(— TO HOUNDS) HALLOW

(ILLUSORY —) CARROT
(UNDERCOVER —) PAYOFF PAYOLA
(UNEXPECTED —) JACKPOT
(PREF.) LUCRI
REWARDED APAID BOUNTIED
REWARDING FAT PREMIANT
(FINANCIALLY —) JUICY
REWRITTEN PALIMPSEST
REZAI ROSEI COVERLET MATTRESS
REZON (FATHER OF —) ELIADAH
RHABDUS SCOPULA
RHADAMANTHUS (FATHER OF —) JUPITER
(MOTHER OF —) EUROPA
RHAPSODIC CONFUSED EFFUSIVE RAPTUROUS
RHAPSODY JUMBLE MEDLEY BOMBAST ECSTASY RAPTURE REVERIE
(— SECTION) LASSU
RHATANY LEGUME
RHEA EMU EMEU NANDU NANDOW RATITE OSTRICH AGDISTIS AVESTRUZ
(DAUGHTER OF —) JUNO CERES VESTA
(FATHER OF —) URANUS
(HUSBAND OF —) SATURN
(MOTHER OF —) GAEA
(SON OF —) PLUTO NEPTUNE
RHEBOK PEELE REHBOC
RHEINGOLD, DAS (CHARACTER IN —) ERDA LOGE FREIA WOTAN FAFNER FASOLT FRICKA HUNDING ALBERICH SIEGMUND SIEGLINDE
(COMPOSER OF —) WAGNER
RHENIUM BOHEMIUM
RHEOMETER STROMUHR
RHEOSTAT DIMMER
RHESA (FATHER OF —) ZOROBABEL
RHESUS BANDAR BUNDER MONKEY BHUNDER MACAQUE
(FATHER OF —) EIONEUS STRYMON
(MOTHER OF —) CALLIOPE
RHETORIC SPEECH BOMBAST PROSAIC ELOQUENCE
(ROLLING —) PERIODS
RHETORICAL FLORID PURPLE AUREATE FORENSIC SWELLING
(FLORIDLY —) AUREATE
RHETORICIAN ORATOR RHETOR
RHEUM GORE TEARS CHOLER SPLEEN
RHINARIUM MUFFLE
RHINE REAN DITCH RUNNEL
RHINESTONE DEWDROP
(PL.) GLITTER
RHINO CASH MONEY PONTOON
RHINOCEROS FOW ABADA BADAK RHINO BORELE KEITLOA UNICORN UPEYGAN NASICORN
RHINOCEROS BEETLE UANG SCARABAEID
RHINOCEROS HORNBILL TOPAU
RHINOPLASTY NOSEJOB
RHIPIDION FLABELLUM
RHIZOID RHIZINA ROOTLET
RHIZOME KAVA NARD ARUKE CAAPI STOCK ARALIA ARNICA ASARUM GINGER IPECAC STOLON BERBERY CALAMUS CULVERS GENTIAN SCOPOLA ZEDOARY ASPIDIUM BARBERRY BERBERIS HELONIAS

KAVAKAVA TRILLIUM TRITICUM VERATRUM
(PL.) INULA GERANIUM
RHODE (FATHER OF —) POSEIDON
(MOTHER OF —) HALIA
(SON OF —) PHAETHON

RHODE ISLAND

CAPITAL: PROVIDENCE
COLLEGE: BROWN BRYANT
COUNTY: KENT BRISTOL NEWPORT
INDIAN: NIANTIC
MOTTO: HOPE
NATIVE: GUNFLINT
NICKNAME: LITTLEHODY
RIVER: PAWTUXET PAWCATUCK
BLACKSTONE
STATE FLOWER: VIOLET
STATE TREE: MAPLE
TOWN: BRISTOL NEWPORT
WARWICK CRANSTON KINGSTON
PAWTUCKET

RHODE ISLAND BENT FURZETOP
RHODE ISLANDER GUNFLINT
RHODESIA (SEE ZIMBABWE)
RHODODENDRON ROSEBAY
SPOONHUTCH
(THICKET OF —) SLICK
RHOMB LOZEN WHEEL CIRCLE
LOZENGE
RHOMBUS DIAMOND LOZENGE
RHONCHUS RALE SNORE SNORT
WHEEZE
RHUBARB ROW FLAP RHEUM
HASSEL CITRINE DISPUTE
YAWWEED ARGUMENT PIEPLANT
RHYME CHIME CLINK VERSE
CRAMBO POETRY RHYTHM TINKLE
MEASURE
(— ROYAL) TROILUS
(PL.) RIMUR
RHYOLITE LIPARITE
RHYTHM BEAT STOT TIME CHIME
METER PULSE SWING GROOVE
CADENCE RAGTIME BACKBEAT
MOVEMENT SEQUENCE
(BREEDING —) VOLTINISM
(DISTORTED —) RUBATO
RHYTHMICAL LILTED CADENCED
MEASURED NUMEROUS
ACCENTUAL
(NOT —) RAGGED
RHYTINA SEACOW
RIA CREEK INLET
RIAL COIN RYEL ROYAL KINGLY
SPLENDID
RIALTO MART BRIDGE EXCHANGE
RIANT GAY RIDENT LAUGHING
MIRTHFUL
RIATA LASSO LARIAT
RIB FIN KID BULB CORD DIKE JAPE
JOKE PURL RIDE SLAT WALE WIFE
CORSE COSTA GROIN NERVE
OGIVE PEARL RIDGE TEASE VARIX
VITTA WHELP BRANCH LIERNE
NEEDLE PARODY RIPPLE SCROLL
TIMBER TONGUE BRISTLE
FEATHER NERVURE PLEURAL
STRATUM FORMERET SIDEBONE
(— IN GROINED ROOF) SPRINGER
(— OF INSECT WING) VEIN
(— OF LEAF) NERVE

(— OF SHIP) WRONG
(— OF STOCKING) RIDGE
(— OF VIOLIN) BOUT
(—S OF UMBRELLA) FRAME
(SHORT —S) CROP
(STRENGTHENING —) FEATHER
(VAULTING —) NERVE OGIVE
LIERNE TIERCERON
(PL.) SLATS
(PREF.) COST(I)(O) PLEUR(I)(O)
(SUFF.) COSTAL COSTATE PLEURA
PLEUROUS
RIBALD LEWD ROGUE COARSE
RASCAL VULGAR
RIBALDRY HASH HARLOTRY
RIBAND RIBBON SCROLL
RIBBED RIBBY CORDED COSTATE
RIBBING SPOOFERY
RIBBON BAR BOW FOB PAN BEND
COST PADS BRAID CORSE FILET
LABEL PADOU PIECE RUBAN
SHRED TASTE BENDEL CADDIS
CORDON FERRET FILLET LISERE
RADULA RECORD RIBAND
SHOWER STRING TAENIA TAWDRY
TISSUE TONGUE BANDING
SAUTOIR TORSADE BANDEROL
BOOKMARK FRAGMENT
STREAMER TRESSURE PETERSHAM
(— AS BADGE OF HONOR) CORDON
(— AS HEADDRESS) TRESSOUR
TRESSURE
(— FOR BORDER) LISERE
(— HANGING FROM CROWN) JESS
(— USED FOR GARTERS) CADDIS
CADDICE
(— WORN ON HOSE) FLASH
(COLORED —S) DIVISA
(CORDED —) PETERSHAM
(END OF —S) FATTRELS
(FLOATING —) PAN
(GATHERED —) QUILLING
(KNOT OF —S) SORTIE
(LINGUAL —) TONGUE
(RASPING —) RADULA
(SILK —) CORSE PADOU TASTE
(WATERED —) PADS
(PL.) REINS
(PREF.) TAENI(A)(O)
(SUFF.) TENE
RIBBON FERN PTERIS
RIBBONFISH GARFISH GUAPENA
AGUAVINA BANDFISH DEALFISH
RIBBONLIKE TAENIATE TAENIOID
TAENIFORM
RIBBON TREE AKAROA HOIHERE
HOUHERE LACEBARK
RIBGRASS WINDLES BUCKHORN
HARDHEAD PLANTAIN
RIBWORT KLOPS HEADMAN
RATTAIL SOLDIER WINDLES
HARDHEAD HEADSMAN
PLANTAGO
RICCIARDETTO (SISTER OF —)
BRADAMANTE
RICE AUS AMAN BORO PADI PAGA
RISE SELA TWIG ARROZ BATTY
BIGAS CANIN CHITS GRAIN MACAN
PADDY PALAY PATNA BRANCH
CEREAL CONGEE SIDDHA
ANGKHAK MANOMIN RISOTTO
(— BOILED WITH MEAT) PILAF
PILAU PILAW

(— COOKED WITH MEAT) RISOTTO
JAMBALAYA
(— FIELD) SAWAH
(— IN HUSK) PALAY
(— OF 2ND OR 3RD GRADE) CHITS
(— POLISHINGS) DARAC
(BOILED —) CANIN KANIN
(COLD —) SUSHI
(HUSKED —) CHAL
(INFERIOR —) PAGA
(KIND OF —) DIRTY BASMATI
(LONG-STEMMED —) AMAN
(MOUNTAIN —) SMILO
(SHORT-STEMMED —) AUS
(SPRING —) BORO
(UNCOOKED —) BIGAS
(UNMILLED —) PADI PADDY
(WILD —) MANOMIN
(PREF.) ORYZ(I) RIZI
RICEBIRD BUNTING CACIQUE
SPARROW BOBOLINK
RICE FLOWER PIMELEA
RICEGRASS BARIT SACATE ZACATE
RICH FAT ABLE DEEP FAIR HIGH
LUSH OOFY WARM GLEBY OPIME
PLUMP RITZY ROUND TINNY VIVID
BATFUL COSTLY DAEDAL FRUITY
HEARTY PLUMMY PLUSHY
PODDED SUPERB ULRICA
AMUSING BAITTLE COPIOUS
FERTILE MONEYED OPULENT
PINGUID PLASTIC WEALTHY
ABUNDANT AFFLUENT GENEROUS
HUMOROUS LUSCIOUS
(— IN FAME) RODERICK
(— IN GIFTS) PREMIOUS
(— IN INTEREST) JUICY
(— IN MALT) HEAVY
(— IN METAL) HIGHGRADE
(— IN RESOURCES) STRONG
(— IN SILICA) ACID
(— IN TIMBRE) GOLDEN
(— MAN) DIVES
(— OF SOIL) PINGUID
(MAN —) NABOB
(NOT —) PLAIN
(OSTENTATIOUSLY —) RITZY
(VERY —) WALLOWING
RICHARD DICCON
RICHARD CARVEL (AUTHOR OF —)
CHURCHILL
(CHARACTER IN —) FOX JONES
CARVEL DOROTHY MANNERS
RICHARD WALPOLE
RICHARD II (AUTHOR OF —)
SHAKESPEARE
(CHARACTER IN —) JOHN ROSS
YORK BAGOT BUSHY GAUNT GREEN
HENRY PERCY EDMUND PIERCE
SCROOP SURREY THOMAS
AUMERLE HOTSPUR LANGLEY
MOWBRAY NORFOLK RICHARD
STEPHEN BERKELEY HEREFORD
FITZWATER LANCASTER SALISBURY
WILLOUGHBY BOLINGBROKE
NORTHUMBERLAND
RICHARD III (AUTHOR OF —)
SHAKESPEARE
(CHARACTER IN —) ANNE JOHN
YORK DERBY HENRY JAMES LOVEL
BLOUNT DORSET EDWARD GEORGE
MORTON OXFORD RIVERS ROBERT
SURREY THOMAS TYRREL WALTER

BRANDON CATESBY HERBERT
NORFOLK RICHARD STANLEY
TRESSEL URSWICK VAUGHAN
BERKELEY CLARENCE HASTINGS
MARGARET RATCLIFF RICHMOND
BOURCHIER ELIZABETH
ROTHERHAM BRAKENBURY
BUCKINGHAM GLOUCESTER
CHRISTOPHER
RICHES GOLD PELF WEAL LUCRE
WORTH MAMMON TALENT
WEALTH FORTUNE OPULENCE
RICHESSE TREASURE
RICHLY HIGH AMPLY FATLY FULLY
DEARLY
RICHNESS BODY LUXE SUMEN
LUXURY ELEGANCE FECUNDITY
RICHWEED RAGWEED COOLWEED
RICK GOAF GOFE REKE CANCH
RICKLE SPRAIN WRENCH
CORNRICK
RICKETS RACHITIS
RICKETY SHAKY SHACKY SHACKLY
UNSOUND RACHITIC SHATTERY
UNSTABLE TOTTERING
RAMSHACKLE
RICKMATIC CONCERN BUSINESS
RICOCHET SKIP SKITE GLANCE
REBOUND
RICTUS GRIN GRIMACE
RID FREE QUIT SHED SHUT ANOMY
CLEAR EGEST REDDE SCOUR SHIFT
ACQUIT ANOMIE REMOVE DELIVER
(— OF IMPURITIES) SCORIFY
(— OF INSECTS) BUG
(— OF LICE) CHAT
(— OF WEEDS) CLEAN
(— ONESELF OF) DOFF DEPOSIT
DISPATCH
(GET — OF) DITCH ERASE PALMOFF
PAWNOFF
RIDDANCE SHUT RELIEF DISPATCH
RIDDER SIFT SIEVE RIDDLE
RIDDLE SIFT BLAIK GRIPH REBUS
DEBASE ENIGMA FOITER PUZZLE
RUDDLE SCREEN CORRUPT
CRIBBLE EXPLAIN GRIDDLE
GRIPHUS MYSTIFY PERPLEX
PROBLEM CRATEMAN PERMEATE
(— AS GRAIN) REE
(PL.) MURLEMEWES
RIDDLER CRATEMAN
(— OF OLD) SPHINX
RIDE GO NAG RIB BAIT DOSA HACK
HURL LAST LIFT PRIG SAIL TOOL
CROSS DRIVE TEASE BANTER
CANTER DEPEND DODGEM
GALLOP JUMBLE NEEDLE NOTICE
SADDLE HAYRIDE JOYRIDE
OVERLAP SURVIVE TANTIVY
BESTRIDE
(— A WAVE) BODYSURF
(— FAST) PRICK POWDER
(— HARD) POUND BUCKET
(— IN HIRED VEHICLE) JOB
(— ON) MOUNT
(— ON A WAVE) BODYSURF
(— ON HORSE) BOOT LARK BURST
JOCKEY SCHOOL
(— RECKLESSLY) BRUISE
(— TO HOUNDS) GO
(AMUSEMENT PARK —) SWING
(CYCLE —) SPIN

RIDER TACK ANNEX CROSS HAZER LABEL COWBOY JOCKEY SITTER ALLONGE CODICIL NAGSMAN PRICKER CAVALIER DESULTOR HORSEMAN
(DUKEY —) BRAKEMAN
(DUMMY —) CROSS
RIDERS TO THE SEA (AUTHOR OF —) SYNGE
(CHARACTER IN —) NORA MAURYA BARTLEY MICHAEL
RIDGE AAS ARM BAR FIN RIB RIG RYG BALK BAND BANK BARB BROW BULT BURR BUTT COMB DRUM FRET FULL HACK HILL KEEL LINK LIST PAHA PUFF RAIN REAN ROLL SHIN SPUR WALE WAVE WELT BARGH CHINE COSTA CREST EARTH EAVES GONYS GYRUS JUGUM KNURL LEDGE LINCH RINGE RUDGE SCOUT SHANK SPINE TORUS VARIX WHELP BRIDGE CARINA COLLOP CREASE CRISTA CUESTA CULMEN DIVIDE DORSUM FRENUM RAFTER RIDEAU SADDLE SELION SUMMIT ANNULET APODEMA BREAKER BUCCULA COLLINE COSTULA EYEBROW EYELINE HOGBACK HUMMOCK INTHROW PROPONS RIGGING SOWBACK WINDROW WITHERS WRINKLE YARDANG CATOCTIN CINGULUM FOREDUNE HEADLAND RESTBALK SHOULDER
(— BETWEEN FURROWS) STITCH RESTBALK
(— IN BREASTPLATE) TAPUL
(— IN COAL SEAM) HORSEBACK
(— IN HORSE'S MOUTH) EAR
(— MADE BY PLOWING) HACK SELION
(— MADE BY TOOL) BUR BARB BURR
(— OF BIRD'S BILL) CULM CULMEN
(— OF BRAIN CORAL) COLLINE
(— OF BREASTBONE) KEEL
(— OF CLAY) DOWLE
(— OF EARTH) BALK
(— OF FLESH) COLLOP
(— OF HORSE'S NECK) CREST
(— OF LAND) BULT RAIN SELION STITCH HOGBACK
(— OF SAND IN WATER) REEF SANDBAR
(— OF SCAPULA) SPINE
(— OF SCREW) THREAD
(— OF SNOW) SASTRUGA ZASTRUGA
(— OF UNPLOWED LAND) LINCH LINCHET
(— OF WAVE) CREST
(— ON BOOK) HUB
(— ON CLOTH) WALE
(— ON CROWN OF TOOTH) CINGULUM
(— ON FINGERBOARD OF GUITAR) FRET
(— ON FISH SCALE) CIRCULUS
(— ON FRUITS OF CARROT FAMILY) JUGUM
(— ON GLUMES) CARINA
(— ON MOLLUSK SHELL) COSTULA
(— ON OVULE) RAPHE

(— ON SEA FLOOR) SWELL
(— ON SEASHORE) STANNER
(— ON SHEET METAL) BEAD
(— ON SIDE OF SADDLE) PUFF
(— ON SKIN) WALE
(— ON VIOLIN) NUT
(— PROTECTING CAMP) RIDEAU
(—S ON ROCK) LAPIES
(— WITH SHARP SUMMIT) HOGBACK
(ANATOMICAL —) CARINA
(BEACH —) FULL
(CHEWING —) ENDITE
(CONNECTING —) HAUSE
(CONVOLUTED —) GYRUS
(DRAINAGE —) BREAKER
(GLACIAL —) OS KAME PAHA ARETE ESKAR ESKER SERAC ESCHAR NUNATAK
(HAIRLIKE —) LIRA
(ICE —) SERAC
(ISOLATED —) BARGH
(LONG STONY —) RAND
(MOUNTAIN —) COMB CHINE SIERRA BACKBONE
(NARROW —) DRUM RAZORBACK
(PROJECTING —) HOE SCOUT
(RESIDUAL —) CATOCTIN
(ROCK —) CLEAVER
(SAND —) DUNE ESKER WAVEMARK
(SEEDED —) DRILL
(SHARP-CRESTED —) ARETE ARRIS
(SLIGHT —) PROPONS
(SNOW —) ZASTRUGA
(UNPLOWED —) BALK BAULK
(WOODED —) CHENIER
(PL.) OSAR KNURLING
RIDGED RIDGY SHARP MILLED PORCATE CARINATE
RIDGELING RIG REGALD RIDGIL RIGGOT RIGINAL
RIDGEPOLE ROOFTREE
RIDICULE DO FUN GUY MOD PAN RIG TAX GAME GIBE JEER JEST JIBE JOEY MOCK PLAY QUIZ RAZZ SKIT TROT TWIT BORAK CHAFF CLOWN HORSE IRONY MIMIC MOMUS QUEER RALLY ROAST SCOFF SCOUT SMOKE SNEER TAUNT BANTER DERIDE EXPOSE RAILLY SATIRE BUFFOON LAMPOON MOCKERY SARCASM DERISION RAILLERY SATIRIZE SPOOFERY BURLESQUE
RIDICULOUS DOTTY DROLL FUNNY SILLY ABSURD INSANE COMICAL FOOLISH MOCKING DERISIVE DERISORY FARCICAL INDECENT COCKAMAMY MONSTROUS COCKAMAMIE
RIDING AWHEEL LIVELY OVERLAP PRICKANT SHIVAREE TRITHING CHEVACHIE
(— ACADEMY) MANAGE MANEGE
(— CROP) ROD
(— WHIP) CROP QUIRT
RIDOTTO BALL REDOUTE
RIEM RHEIM RIMPI STRAP THONG
RIENZI (CHARACTER IN —) COLA IRENE PAOLO ORSINI RIENZI ADRIANO COLONNA STEFANO RAIMONDI
(COMPOSER OF —) WAGNER

RIFE EASY FULL RANK QUICK READY ACTIVE FILLED NIMBLE STRONG CURRENT REPLETE ABUNDANT INCLINED MANIFEST NUMEROUS
RIFF BIT SKIM ROUTINE
RIFFLE REEF RIFF WAVE RAPID RIPPLE SHUFFLE WATERFALL
RIFFRAFF MOB RAFF SCUM SCAFF TRASH RABBLE REFUSE RUBBISH CANAILLE POPULACE RAGABASH
RIFLE RIG ROB KRAG LOOT RIPE PIECE YAGER CARBIN JEZAIL JUZAIL RIFFLE SNIDER ARISAKA BULLPUP BUNDOCK BUNDOOK CARABIN CARBINE DESPOIL ENFIELD ESCOPET MARTINI PILLAGE PLUNDER RANSACK SPORTER BANDHOOK REPEATER SPLITTER STRICKLE TAKEDOWN CHASSEPOT
(— BALL CASING) THIMBLE
(— PIN) TIGE
(OPTICAL DEVICE ON —) SNIPERSCOPE
RIFLEMAN JAGER JAEGER
(PL.) RIFLERY
RIFT RIVE BELCH CHASM CRACK SPLIT CLEAVE DIVIDE BLEMISH FISSURE CREVASSE
(— IN TIMBER) LAG
RIG RI FIG REG HOAX JEST JOKE REEK SEMI WIND DRESS EQUIP GETUP PRANK RIDGE SPORT STORM TRICK BANTER CLOTHE GUNTER ROTARY SADDLE SCHEME MARCONI SPUDDER SWINDLE BACKSTAY RIDICULE SEMITRAILER
(DRILLING —) JACKUP
(TRUCKING —) SEMI
RIGADOON DANCE RIGODON
RIGEL REGEL ALGEBAR
RIGGED (FULLY —) ATAUNT
RIGGER CLIMBER SLINGER SCAFFOLD
RIGGING NET GEAR ROOF RIDGE TACKLE APPAREL CLOTHING JACKSTAY TACKLING
RIGHT DUE FEE FIT IUS OFF REE SAY SOC BANG DUTY FAIR FLOP GALE GOOD HAND ITER JUST LIEN REAL RECT REET SANE SLAP SOKE TEAM TRUE WELL CLAIM DRESS DROIT ENTRY EXACT FAVOR FERRY LEGAL RICHT SOUND STRAY TECHT TITLE ACTION ACTUAL ANGARY BALLOT DEMAND DEXTER EATAGE EQUITY PROPER PUTURE ANNUITY APANAGE AUBAINE BENEFIT CORRECT DERECHO DESIRED FACULTY FALDAGE FITTING FOLDAGE FREEDOM GENUINE HAYBOTE LIBERTY LICENSE PRENDER RECTIFY RELIEVE SLAPDAB UPRIGHT WARRANT BANALITY BLOODWIT FIREBOOT FORESTRY HEIRSHIP INTEREST LIFERENT SEIGNORY SLAPDASH STALLAGE STRAIGHT SUFFRAGE SUITABLE THIRLAGE PREROGATIVE
(— AND LEFT) HAY HEY
(— AS COMMAND TO HORSES) REE
(— EYE) OD
(— HAND) MD OPENBAND

(— IN A THING) INTEREST
(— IN WIFE'S INHERITED PROPERTY) CURTESY
(— OF CHOICE) OPTION
(— OF CREDITOR) SECURITY
(— OF EXILE) POSTLIMINY
(— OF EXIT) ISH
(— OF FREE QUARTERS) CORODY
(— OF HOLDING COURT) TEAM
(— OF INQUIRY) SOKEN
(— OF OWNERSHIP) TITLE COMMONTY
(— OF PASTURAGE) FEED STINT EATAGE COWGATE COMMONAGE HORSEGATE
(— OF PRECEDENCE) PAS
(— OF PRESENTATION) ADVOWSON
(— OF PROTECTION) MUND
(— OF RETURNING) REGRESS
(— OF USING ANOTHER'S PROPERTY) EASEMENT
(— OF USING GRASSLAND) EATAGE
(— SIDE) OFFSIDE
(— TIME) TID
(— TO COLLECT REVENUE) DIWANI DEWANEE DEWANNY
(— TO COMMAND) IMPERIUM
(— TO CUT WOOD) VERT GREENHEW
(— TO DECIDE) SAY
(— TO DRAW WATER) HAUSTUS
(— TO DRIVE BEAST) ACTUS
(— TO PASS OVER LAND) ITER
(— TO PAYMENT) RECOURSE
(— TO REJECT) VETO
(— TO SEIZE PROPERTY) ANGARY
(— TO SHOOT FIRST) CAST
(— TO SUE) STANDING
(— TO WORK IN MINE) BEN
(ALL —) HUNK JAKE HUNKY
(EXACTLY —) PAT
(FEUDAL —) CUDDY THIRL MARITAGE THIRLAGE
(FISHING —) PISCARY
(HUNTING —) WARDEN
(INDIAN LEGAL —) HAK HAKH
(JUST —) TOAT TOATEE
(LEGAL —) IUS JUS JURE DROIT ACCESS APPEAL COMMON FISHERY HYPOTHEC
(LEGAL —S) JURA
(MILLER'S —) SOKEN
(MINING —) GALE
(NOT —) AWRY ACUTE
(PROPERTY —) DOMINIUM
(TURN —) GEE
(WIDOW'S —) TERCE TIERCE
(PL.) DIBS JURA
(PREF.) DEXIO DEXTR(O) ORTH(O) RECT(I)
(— HAND) DEXIO DEXTR(O)
RIGHT ANGLE RECTANGLE
(HUNDREDTH OF —) GRAD GRADE
RIGHTEOUS GOOD JUST GODLY MORAL ZADOC ZADOK DEVOUT FITTING PERFECT SKILFUL UPRIGHT INNOCENT VIRTUOUS
RIGHTEOUSNESS DOOM DHARMA EQUITY JUSTICE HOLINESS JUDGMENT JUSTNESS MORALITY RECTITUDE
RIGHTFUL DUE JUST TRUE LEGAL KINDLY LAWFUL PROPER FITTING

RIGHTFULNESS JUSTICE
RIGHT-HANDED RIGHTY DEXTRAL SKILLED DEXTROUS CLOCKWISE
RIGHT-HANDWISE DEASIL DESSIL DEISEAL CLOCKWISE
RIGHTLY RITE FITLY ARIGHT FAIRLY JUSTLY HANDILY PERQUEER SUITABLY
RIGHTS (KIND OF —) MIRANDA
RIGHT WHALE BOWHEAD BALAENID MYSTICETE NORDCAPER
RIGID SET ACID CARK FIRM HARD HIGH FIXED SOLID STARK STERN STIFF STONY STOUT TENSE TONIC TOUGH FORMAL FROZEN MARBLY SEVERE STARCH STICKY STRICT AUSTERE IRONCLAD RIGOROUS STRAIGHT INELASTIC STRINGENT
(— IN SELF-DENIAL) ASCETIC
RIGIDITY FROST RIGOR RIGOUR BUCKRAM SETNESS HARDNESS STIFFNESS
RIGMAREE COIN TRIFLE
RIGMAROLE RANE NOMINY RABBLE RAGMAN SLAMPAMP SLAMPANT AMPHIGORY RIDDLEMEREE
RIGOLETTO (CHARACTER IN —) GILDA MANTUA MADDALENA RIGOLETTO SPARAFUCILE
(COMPOSER OF —) VERDI
RIGOR TYRANNY ASPERITY HARDNESS SEVERITY
RIGOROUS FIRM HARD CLOSE CRUEL EXACT HARSH HEFTY RIGID STERN STIFF TOUGH BITTER FLINTY SEVERE STRAIT STRICT STRONG AUSTERE DRASTIC PRECISE SPARTAN DISTRICT DRACONIC EXACTING IRONCLAD STRAIGHT
(MORALLY —) PURITANIC
(NOT —) INEXACT
(UNDULY —) HARSH
RIKSMAL BOKMAL
RILE VEX ROIL ANGER PEEVE TICKOFF IRRITATE
RILL PURL SIKE CLEFT DRILL PRILL GROOVE RUNLET RILLOCK RIVULET BROOKLET RIVELING TRICKLET ARROYUELO WATERSHUT
RILLSTONE VENTIFACT
RIM HEM LIP BEAD BRIM CURB EDGE SHOE BEZEL BRINK CHIME EAVES FELLY FRAME HELIX SKIRT BORDER CALKER CHOANA FILLET FLANGE MARGIN EXCIPLE
(— HOLDING WATCH CRYSTAL) BEZEL BEZIL
(— OF BASKET) HOOP
(— OF COROLLA) ANNULUS
(— OF CRATER) SOMMA
(— OF EAR) HELIX
(— OF GEM) GIRDLE
(— OF HORSESHOE) WEB
(— OF INSECT'S WING) TERMEN
(— OF JELLYFISH) VELUM
(— OF SANIO) CRASSULA
(— OF TIN) LIST
(— OF WHEEL) FELLY FELLOE STRAKE
(— ON CASK) CHIMB CHIME CHINE
(— ON CLOG) CALKER

(— SURROUNDING FLAGELLUM) CHOANA
(EXTERNAL —) FLANGE
(PROTECTIVE —) BANK
(RAISED —) BOSS
(PREF.) AMBO
RIMA CHINK CLEFT RIMULA FISSURE
RIME RIM HOAR RIND RUNG CRACK CRUST FROST ROUND CRANREUCH
RIMPLE FOLD RIPPLE WRINKLE
RINALDO (BELOVED OF —) ANGELICA
(COUSIN OF —) ORLANDO
(FATHER OF —) AYMON
(HORSE OF —) BAYARD
RIND BARK PEEL PILL RYND SKIN CRUST FROST SWARD CITRON SWARTH
(— OF HAM) SKIN
(— OF MEAT) SPINE
(— OF POMEGRANATE) GRANATUM
(— OF ROASTED PORK) CRACKLING
(PREF.) LEMMO LEPO
(SUFF.) LEMMA
RING GO BEE BOW BUR CUP DEE DIE EKE FAM JOW ORB PIT RIM AMBO BAIL BAND BELL BONG BURR BUZZ CRIC CURB DING DIRL ECHO GYRE HOOP JING LOOP MAIL PASS PEAL RACE RINK RUSH SHUT SING TANG TOLL VIRL WISP AMBON ANLET ARENA BAGUE CAROL CHIME CHINK CLANG CYCLE GRAIN GROUP GUARD GUIDE JEWEL KNELL LUNET PISTE RIGOL ROUND ROWEL TORUS VERGE WAFER WITHE BANGLE BECKET BROUGH BUTTON CIRCLE CIRCUS CIRQUE CLIQUE COLLAR COLLET DINDLE EYELET FAMBLE GIMMER GIRDLE HARROW KEEPER LARIGO LEGLET RINGLE RUNDLE RUNNER SIGNET TORQUE TURRET VIROLE WASHER ANNULUS ARMILLA CIRCLET CIRCUIT CLAPPER COMPASS COUPLER CRINGLE DIAMOND FAMELEN FERRULE GALLERY GARLAND GROMMET GUDGEON MANILLA NUCLEUS PACKING RESOUND ROWLOCK SHACKLE STIRRUP THIMBLE VIBRATE BRACELET BULLRING CINCTURE CORONULE DINGDONG DRAUPNIR DUSTBAND ENCIRCLE FAIRLEAD PACIFIER SONORITY SURROUND TRAVELER
(— AROUND ARTICULAR CAVITY) AMBON
(— AROUND MOON) BROCH
(— AROUND NIPPLE) AREOLA
(— AT EACH END OF CINCH) LARIGO
(— A TREE) FRILL
(— ATTACHED TO JIB) HANK
(— BELLS) FIRE
(— FOR CARRYING SHOT) LADLE
(— FORMING HANDLE OF KEY) BOW
(— FOR SECURING BIRD) VERVEL
(— FOR TRAINING HORSES) LONGE
(— OF ANNULATED COLUMN) BAGUE
(— OF BOILER) STRAKE

(— OF CILIA) TROCHUS
(— OF COLOR) STOCKING
(— OF DNA) PLASTID
(— OF DOTS AROUND EDGE OF COIN) GRAINING
(— OF LIGHT) GLORY
(— OF ODIN) DRAUPNIR
(— OF PILES) STARLING
(— OF RIDING SCHOOL) PISTE
(— OF ROPE) HANK BECKET GARLAND GROMMET SNORTER SNOTTER
(— OF SATURN) ANSA
(— OF SPINES) CORONULE
(— OF STANDING STONES) CAROL
(— OF TWO HOOPS) GEMEL GEMMEL
(— OF WAGONS) CORRAL LAAGER
(— ON BATTLEAX) BUR BURR
(— ON BIRD'S TIBIA) ARMILLA
(— ON DARTBOARD) TREBLE
(— ON DECK) CRANCE
(— ON GUN CARRIAGE) LUNET LUNETTE
(— ON HINGE) GUDGEON
(— ON LAMP) CRIC
(— ON LANCE) BURR
(— ON SPAR) TRAVELER
(— ON UMBRELLA ROD) RUNNER
(— SUPPORTING LAMPSHADE) GALLERY
(— SURROUNDING BUGLE) VIROLE
(— SUSPENDING COMPASS) GIMBAL
(— TO ENCLOSE DEER) TINCHEL TINCHILL
(— UNDER BEEHIVE) EKE
(— USED AS MONEY) MANILLA
(— USED AS VALVE) WAFER
(— WITH GROOVED OUTER EDGE) THIMBLE
(— WITH VIBRATION) DIRL
(BLACKSMITH'S —) BOLSTER
(BRIGHT —) HALATION
(CERVICAL —) TORQUE
(CURTAIN —) EYE
(FINGER —) HOOP
(FLESHY —) ANNULUS
(HARNESS —) DEE BUTTON LARIGO TERRET TORRET TURRET
(HAWK'S —) VERVEL
(INTERLINKED METAL —S) MAIL
(JOINED —) GIMMER GIMMOR
(KIND OF —) MOOD
(LITTLE —) ANNULET
(LUMINOUS —) BROUGH
(MOUNTAINEER'S —) KARABINER
(NECKERCHIEF —) WOGGLE
(NOSE —) PIRN
(OIL —) WIPER
(PACKING —) LUTE
(PART OF —) BAND CLAW PRONG SHANK STONE COLLET SETTING HALLMARK
(PLAITED —) RUSH WISP
(SURGICAL —) CURETTE
(SWIVEL —) TERRET TERRIT
(TAPERING SHANK —) BELCHER
(TARGET —) SOUS SOUSE
(TOOTHED IRON —) HARROW
(TOP OF —) BEZEL BEZIL
(PREF.) CRICO CYCL(O) GYRO
(HAVING OPENED —) SECO

RING AND THE BOOK (AUTHOR OF —) BROWNING
(CHARACTER IN —) PAUL GUIDO PIETRO GIUSEPPE POMPILIA VIOLANTE COMPARINI CAPONSACCHI FRANCESCHINI
RINGDOVE QUIST CUSHAT CUSHIE QUEEST TOOZOO ZOOZOO COWSHOT COWSHUT
RINGED GYRATE ZONATE ANNULAR ANNULOSE
RINGED SNAKE COLUBRID
RINGER CHEER YOUTH COWBOY CROWBAR STOCKMAN
RING FINGER ANNULAR
RINGGIT DOLLAR
RINGHALS COBRA
RINGING BELL BRIGHT FERVID JANGLE CLANGOR OROTUND SINGING DECISIVE RESONANT SONORANT SONOROUS TINNIENT TINNUS
(— IN THE EARS) TINNITUS
(CHANGE —) CINQUES SINGLES
RINGLEADER FUGLEMAN
RINGLET CURL LOCK TRESS TENDRIL
(— ON FOREHEAD) FAVORITE
(PREF.) CIRR(I)(O)
RING-NECKED TORQUATE
RING-NECKED DUCK DOGY SCAUP MOONBILL RINGBILL BLACKJACK
RING OUZEL AMSEL THRUSH WHISTLER
RING PLOVER SANDY COLLIER KILLDEE DULWILLY RINGNECK
RING-SHAPED ANNULAR CRICOID ANNULARY ANNULATE CIRCULAR
RINGTAIL CACOMIXL CACOMISTLE
RINGWORM TINEA KERION TETTER SERPIGO
RINGWORM BUSH SENNA
RINK ALLEY GLACIARIUM
RINSE NET SIND WASH RANGE RENCH RENSH RINGE SCIND SCOUR SWILL BLUING DOUCHE CLEANSE
RINSING NET SIND FLUSH RESIDUE
RIOT DIN HURL BRAWL REVEL WORRY ATTACK CLAMOR EXCESS JUMBLE MEDLEY RANTAN SPLORE TUMULT ANARCHY CONFUSE DESPOIL REVELRY BLOODWIT CAROUSAL TOHUBOHU
RIOTOUS ROID ROYD WILD NOISY RANDY RANTY HEMPIE RANDIE STORMY WANTON BACCHIC PROFUSE ROARING ABUNDANT BACCHIAN
RIP RIT COOP REAT TEAR BREAK SHARK SHRED SLITE UNSEW BASKET RIPPLE UNSEAM
(— OFF) ROB CHEAT FILCH STEAL DEFRAUD
RIPE FIT BOLD LATE DRUNK READY MATURE MELLOW SIDDER SIDDOW SMELLY DIGESTED FINISHED SEASHORE STINKING SUITABLE
(EARLY —) HASTY RARERIPE
(PREF.) HADR(O)
RIPEN AGE ADDLE AUGUST DIGEST MELLOW CONCOCT CRIMSON

DEVELOP PERFECT COMPLETE
MATURATE
RIPENESS MATURITY
RIPHATH (FATHER OF —) GOMER
RIP-OFF GYP THEFT IMITATION
RIPOSTE REPLY RETORT THRUST
REPARTEE
RIPPER RIPSAW BOBSLED
HUMDINGER
RIPPET FUSS TUMULT UPROAR
DISPUTE QUARREL
RIPPING FINE GRAND SWELL
CAPITAL TIPPING SPLENDID
RIPPLE CURL FRET PURL RIFF SEED
WAVE ACKER CRISP TWINE
COCKLE DIMPLE JABBLE LIPPER
RIMPLE RUFFLE RUMBLE WIMPLE
CRINKLE WAVELET WRINKLE
(— ALONG) DADE
RIPPLING BREAK BULGE JABBLE
ARIPPLE
(— OF SEA) LIPPER
(— ON SURFACE) HORROR
RIPSAW RIPPER SPLITSAW
RIPSNORTER SNIFTER HUMDINGER
RISE COME DRAW FLOW GROW
HEAD HIGH HIKE HILL HOLT HOVE
LIFT PLUM SOAR ARISE BEGIN
CANCH CHEER CLIMB ERECT
HEAVE HOIST MOUNT OCCUR
PITCH PLUFF PROVE RAISE ROUSE
SCEND SOURD STAND START
SURGE SWELL TOWER YEAST
ASCEND ASCENT ASPIRE AURORA
BILLOW EMERGE GROWTH
HAPPEN HEIGHT ORIGIN RESULT
RETORT SOURCE SPRING THRIVE
UPDIVE UPREAR UPTICK ADVANCE
APPLAUD HUMMOCK REDOUND
UPHEAVE UPSHOOT EMINENCE
FLOURISH HEIGHTEN INCREASE
LEVITATE SCENSION UPSPRING
(— ABOVE) OVERLOOK SURMOUNT
(— ABRUPTLY) SKYROCKET
(— AGAIN) RESURGE
(— AND FALL) LOOM HEAVE
WELTER
(— AS PRICE) MEND
(— GRADUALLY) LOOM
(— IN BLISTERS) YAW
(— IN CLOUDS) STOOR
(— IN MINE FLOOR) HOGBACK
(— IN PRICES) BULGE
(— IN VALUE) IMPROVE
(— OF CURVE) CAMBER
(— OF HAWK AFTER PREY) MOUNTY
(— OF SHIP'S LINES) FLIGHT
(— OF WATER) FLOOD
(— PRECIPITOUSLY) SKY
(— RAPIDLY) KITE
(— SHARPLY) BREAK
(— SUDDENLY) BOOM SPRING
(— SWIFTLY) BOIL
(— TO BAIT) TAKE
(— TO GREAT HEIGHT) TOWER
(— TO PEAK) SWELL
(— UP) FUME REAR ASCEND
INSURRECT
(CURVED —) HANCE
(GIVE — TO) SPAWN
(SHARP —) HOGBACK
**RISE OF SILAS LAPHAM (AUTHOR
OF —)** HOWELLS

(CHARACTER IN —) TOM COREY
IRENE SILAS LAPHAM PERSIS
ROGERS PENELOPE BROMFIELD
RISER HEAD RAISE FEEDHEAD
INSURGENT
RISHI RSI POET SAGE SAINT
DEVARSHI KASHYAPA MAHARSHI
RISIBLE FUNNY GELASTIC
LAUGHABLE
RISING BOIL BULL RIST ARISE ARIST
ORIENT PUTSCH SOURCE STRAKE
UPREST UPWITH MONTANT
PUSTULE SURGENT EMERGENT
INCREASE MOUNTANT NAISSANT
ONCOMING ASSURGENT
EXCEEDING
(— ABOVE) SUPERIOR
(— ABRUPTLY) BOLD
(— AGAIN) REORIENT
(— AND FALLING) TIDAL
(— AS A BIRD) ROUSANT
(— AS OF HAWK) SOURCE
(— BY DEGREES) GRADIENT
(— FROM DEAD) RESURRECTION
(— GRADUALLY) SOFT
(— HIGH) AERIAL
(— SHARPLY) ABRUPT
(— STEEPLY) BLUFF
(— TO BREATHE) HAURIANT
HAURIENT
(— WITH SUN) COSMICAL
(POPULAR —) EMEUTE
RISK GO RUN SET GAGE JUMP LUCK
PAWN PERIL RISCO STAKE STAND
THROW WAGER WATHE CHANCE
DANGER GAMBLE HAZARD
IMPAWN PLIGHT THREAT BALANCE
IMPERIL VENTURE ENDANGER
EXPOSURE
(PL.) COVERAGE
RISKY BOLD DICEY DODGY CHANCY
DARING KITTLE RISQUE PARLISH
PARLOUS TECHOUS TICKLISH
RISP BUSH RASP STEM TWIG STALK
BRANCH SCRATCH
RISQUE BLUE GAMY RACY SEXY
BROAD DARING SCABROUS
RISSOLE CROQUETTE
(PL.) CECILS
RISS-WURM NEUDECKIAN
RISURREZIONE (CHARACTER IN —)
DIMITRI KATUSHA SIMONSON
(COMPOSER OF —) ALFANO
RIT CUT RIP RUT REND SLIT TEAR
SCRATCH
RITE KEX ASAL BORA BRIS FORM
HAKO SOMA BRITH HONOR RIGHT
SRADH ABDEST AUGURY EXEQUY
FETISH OFFICE PANSIL PIACLE
POOJAH RITUAL BAPTISM
FUNERAL KATCINA LITURGY
MYSTERY OBSEQUY SRADDHA
TASHLIK CEREMONY HIERURGY
HUSKANAW MORTUARY
PIACULUM OBSERVANCE
(FUNERAL —S) EXEQUY EXEQUIES
OBSEQUIES
(INITIATION —) BORA
(RELIGIOUS —) SYMBOL
(SECRET —) ORGY
(PL.) CULT SACRA SERVICE
RITUAL FORM RITE SOLEMN
AGENDUM HAGGADA LITURGY

OBSEQUY SERVICE CEREMONY
VISPARAD VISPERED
(PASSOVER —) AGADAH HAGGADA
HAGGADAH
(PRAYER —) PUJA
RITUALISTIC SACRAL
RITZY SWANKY HAUGHTY SNOBBISH
RIVAGE BANK RIVE COAST SHORE
RIVAL VIE EVEN PEER SIDE MATCH
COMPETE CORRIVE EMULATE
PARAGON CORRIVAL EMULATOR
OPPONENT
(PREF.) ANT(I) ANTH(O)
RIVALRY VIE GAME STRIFE
PARAGON JEALOUSY STRIVING
EMULATION
RIVALS (AUTHOR OF —) SHERIDAN
(CHARACTER IN —) BOB JACK LUCY
ACRES JULIA LYDIA LUCIUS
ANTHONY ABSOLUTE BEVERLEY
LANGUISH MALAPROP MELVILLE
OTRIGGER FAULKLAND
RIVE RIP PLOW REND STAB TEAR
CRACK REAVE SEVER SPLIT WEDGE
CLEAVE SUNDER THRUST SHATTER
FRACTURE
RIVELING RULLION
RIVER EA LE LEE REE RIO TJI ALPH
AVON BAHR GEON ILOG KILL WADI
WADY BAYOU CREEK FLOOD
GANGA GIHON GJOLL GLIDE
HABOR INLET KIANG TCHAI
BARCOO GUTTER KHUBUR NYANZA
STRAIT STREAM CHANNEL
COCYTUS ESTUARY FROEMAN
ILISSUS PHARPAR RUBICON
SENEGAL AFFLUENT ERIDANUS
PACTOLUS STAIRCASE
(— CHANNEL) ALVEUS
(— IN SPIRITUAL) JORDAN
(— NEAR GATE OF HEL'S ABODE)
GJOLL
(— OF ATTICA) ILISSUS
(— OF DAMASCUS) PHARPAR
(— OF HADES) STYX LETHE
(— OF LYDIA) PACTOLUS
(— OF PARADISE) GEON GIHON
(— OF QUEENSLAND) BARCOO
(— OF UNDERGROUND)
PHLEGETHON
(— OF UNDERWORLD) STYX LETHE
ACHERON COCYTUS FLEGETON
(AFRICAN —) NYANZA SENEGAL
(CHINESE —) HO KIANG
(EGYPTIAN —) BAHR NILE
(FULL —) BANKER
(JAVANESE —) TJI
(MINOR —) BAYOU
(SACRED —) ALPH GANGA
(SMALL —) BACHE TCHAI
(TIDAL —) ESTUARY
(PREF.) FLUVI(O) POTAM(O)
(SUFF.) POTAMIA POTAMUS
RIVERBANK RIPA RIPE
RIVERBED LAAGTE BATTURE
(DRY —) WADI WADY
RIVER BLINDNESS
ONCHOCERCIASIS
RIVERBOAT COG BARGE FOIST
PULWAR
RIVER DUCK TEAL MALLARD
WIDGEON GREENWING
RIVERINE (— FISH) HUCHO

RIVERWEED WATERWEED
RIVET STUD CLINK ROOVE PANHEAD
FLATHEAD
(— ATTENTION) GRIP
(— HEAD) CUPHEAD
RIVULET RUN BURN GILL LAKE
MOTH RILL SIKE BACHE BATCH
BAYOU BOURN BROOK GHYLL
RITHE RINDLE RUNLET RUNNEL
STREAM STRIPE STRYPE CHANNEL
RIVERET BROOKLET
RIXY TERN
RIZPAH (LOVER OF —) SAUL
(SON OF —) ARMONI
MEPHIBOSHETH
RIZZAR DRY PARCH RASOUR
RAZOUR CURRANT HADDOCK
RIZZOM BIT EAR RISOM STALK
STRAW RISSOM
RNA POLYA
ROACH HOG BUTT ROCK SPOT
BRAISE BLATTID SUNFISH
ROAD LEG PAD TAO VIA WAY BELT
BORD CASH DRAG DRUN FARE
GAFT GANG GATE LINE LODE LOKE
PASS PATH PAVE PIKE RADE RAID
RIDE RODE ROTE ROUT SLAB SPUR
WENT BARGH BLAZE BYWAY
CLOSE DRIFT DRIVE DROVE FORAY
GAITE GOING METAL PRAYA
ROUTE TRACE TRACK BYROAD
CAMINO CAREER CAUSEY CHEMIN
COURSE DUGWAY FEEDER RIDING
ROUGH RUNWAY SLOUGH
STREET TARMAC TRAJET BEELINE
CALZADA CARTWAY ESTRADA
GANGWAY HIGHWAY LANDWAY
OUTGANG PACKWAY PASSAGE
RAILWAY RAMPIRE ROADWAY
ROLLWAY SKIDWAY TELFORD
AUTOBAHN BEALLACH BLACKTOP
BROADWAY CHAUSSEE
CORDUROY FOOTRILL HORSEWAY
OVERPASS RIDGEWAY SPEEDWAY
TRACKWAY TRAMROAD TRAVERSE
TURNPIKE WAGONWAY
ROADSTEAD
(— BORDERING SHORE) PRAYA
(— FOR LOGGING) SKIDWAY
CROSSHAUL
(— FOR SPACECRAFT)
CRAWLERWAY
(— HAZARD) ESS
(— IN COAL MINE) BORD BOARD
FOOTRILL
(— ON CLIFF) CORNICHE
(— SCRAPER) HARL HARLE
(— SURFACE) TELFORD
(ALTERNATE —) DETOUR
(CEMENT OR CONCRETE —) SLAB
(COUNTRY —) BOREEN DRIFTWAY
(DESCENDING —) BAHADA BAJADA
(IMPASSABLE —) SLOUGH IMPASSE
(IMPROVISED —) CASH
(MILITARY OR PUBLIC —) AGGER
(NARROW —) DRANG DRUNG
RODDIN
(PAVED —) CALZADA CHAUSSEE
(PRINCIPAL —) ARTERY
(PRIVATE —) LOKE DRIVE
DRIVEWAY
(RAISED —) AGGER RAMPIRE
CAUSEWAY

(ROMAN —) ITER CAUSEY
(SIDE —) BRANCH SHUNPIKE
(STEEP —) BRAE PATH BARGH
SPRUNT
(TEMPORARY —) SHOOFLY
(UNIMPROVED —) DROVE
(ZIGZAG —) SWITCHBACK
(PREF.) ODO VIA
(SUFF.) ODE OID
ROADBED BALLAST BITUMEN
ROADBOOK MAP ITINERARY
ROAD DONKEY ROADER
ROADMAN PEDDLER SALESMAN
CANVASSER
ROADMASTER OVERSEER
ROAD RUNNER CUCKOO PAISANO
ROADSIDE HEDGE
ROADSTEAD RAID DOWNS
ROADSTER BUGGY TRAMP DRIVER
BICYCLE RUNABOUT RACEABOUT
SPEEDSTER
ROADWAY DECK EXIT STREET
MACADAM SLIPWAY TRUCKWAY
(— MANEUVER) UTURN
ROAM GO ERR RUN WAG RAKE
RAME RAVE ROIL ROLL ROVE
WALK GIPSY GYPSY KNOCK RANGE
SCAMP SPACE STRAY TAVER
VAGUE WAVER BANGLE RAMBLE
STROLL SWERVE TAIVER VAGARY
WANDER GALLANT PROCEED
SQUANDER VAGABOND
(— FURTIVELY) PROWL
ROAMING ERROR NOMADIC
ROAMAGE FUGITIVE
(PREF.) PLAN(O)
ROAN HORSE GRIZZLE
ROANOKE WAMPUM
ROAR CRY BAWL BEAL BELL BERE
BOOM BRAY CAVE HOWL HURL
RAIR RARE RERD ROIN ROME
ROOP ROUT YELL BLARE BROOL
CRACK RERDE ROUST SHOUT
SNORE BELLOW BULDER BULLER
CLAMOR GOLLAR GOLLER
RUMMES SCREAM SHRIEK STEVEN
BLUSTER RUMMISH THUNDER
ULULATE
(— AS BOAR) FREAM
(— LIKE WIND) HURL
(— OF SURF) ROTE
(LOW —) BROOL
ROARING RUT LOUD AROAR BRISK
ROUST BELLOW BOOMING
RIOTOUS THRIVING
ROARING BOY TWIBIL TWIBILL
ROARING GAME CURLING
ROARING MEG CANNON
ROAST RAZZ ROTI SOAK BREDE
BROWN PARCH ASSATE CODDLE
REMOVE TORREFY TORRIFY
BARBECUE RIDICULE
(— IN ASHES) BRY
(KIND OF —) RIB RUMP
(STUFFED —) FARCI
ROASTED ASADO
(NOT —) GREEN
ROASTER BURNER SCORCHER
ROASTING ASSATION
ROASTING JACK TURNSPIT
ROB COP PAD EASE FAKE FLAP MILL
NICK PEEL PELF PICK PILL POLL

PREY PULL RAMP RIPE ROLL TOBY
BENIM BRIBE FLIMP HARRY HEAVE
HEIST LURCH PINCH PLUCK PLUME
PROWL REAVE RIFLE ROIST SHAKE
SPOIL SPUNG STEAL STRUB
TOUCH HARROW HIJACK HUSTLE
PILFER RAVISH RIPOFF STRIKE
THIEVE BEREAVE DEPRIVE DESPOIL
PLUNDER RUMPADE SNAFFLE
UNPURSE DEFLOWER SPOLIATE
(— HOUSE) MILL
(— OF CHASTITY) DEFILE
(— OF FORCE) COOL
(— OF JOY) DESOLATE
(— OF VIGOR) ETIOLATE
(— WITH VIOLENCE) RAMP
ROBALO FISH PIKE SNOOK SNOWK
SERGEANT
ROBBED RUBATO
(NOT —) UNPILLED
ROBBER PAD CROOK FOMOR
LARON THIEF BANDIT BRIBER
DACOIT FORMOR HOLDUP LATRON
RIFLER BRIGAND CATERAN
FOOTPAD HEISTER LADRONE
MOONMAN PANDOUR PRANCER
RAVENER ROUTIER SPOILER
TOBYMAN BARABBAS FOMORIAN
PILLAGER RABIATOR BANDOLERO
(— ON HIGH SEAS) PIRATE
(— WHO USES VIOLENCE)
RABIATOR
(GRAVE —) GOUL GHOUL
(HIGHWAY —) PAD FOOTPAD
TOBYMAN
(INDIAN MURDEROUS —) DACOIT
(IRISH —) WOODKERN
(MOUNTAIN —) CHOAR
(NIGHT —) MOONMAN
(SEA —) FOMOR FORMOR
FOMORIAN
(WANDERING —) ROUTIER
(PREF.) LESTO
(SUFF.) LESTES
ROBBERY JOB JUMP REIF RIFE
HEIST SCREW STALE FELONY
HOLDUP STOWTH BRIBERY
DACOITY LARCENY PILLAGE
PLUNDER REAVERY STICKUP
THUGGEE PURCHASE SPOLIATION
(— ON HIGH SEAS) PIRACY
(HIGHWAY —) TOBY
ROBE GOWN TOGA VEST KANZU
STOLA CHIMER KIMONO KITTEL
MANTLE PEPLOS REVEST ARISAID
BUFFALO GALABIA SURCOAT
VESTURE PARAMENT WOLFSKIN
(— FOR THE DEAD) HABIT
(— OF HONOR) KHALAT KHILAT
KILLUT KELLAUT
(— OF MONARCH) PLUVIAL
(— PRESENTED BY DIGNITARY)
KHALAT KHILAT
(— REACHING TO ANKLES) TALAR
(ACTOR'S —) SYRMA
(ARAB —) ABA
(BAPTISMAL —) CHRISOM
(BISHOP'S —) CHIMER CHIMERE
(CIRCULAR —) CYCLAS
(CORONATION —) COLOBIUM
DALMATIC
(DERVISH'S —) KHIRKA KHIRKAH
(EMPEROR'S —) PURPLE

(FUNERAL —) SABLE
(JEWISH —) KITTEL
(KING'S —) DALMATIC
(LOOSE —) MANT CAMIS CAMUS
CYMAR SIMAR SYMAR MANTUA
CHIMERE MANTEAU
(MASQUERADE —) VENETIAN
(MEXICAN —) MANGA
(MONK'S —) HAPLOMA
(OLD-FASHIONED —) SAMARE
(OUTER —) JAMA
(PRIEST'S —) ALB
(ROMAN —) TOGA STOLA
(TARTAN —) ARISAID
(TURKISH —) DOLMAN
(WHITE —) CHRISOM
(PL.) ACADEMICALS
ROBERT DOB POP RAB DOBBIN
POPKIN
ROBERT OF LINCOLN BOBOLINK
ROBIN THRUSH PINFISH REDDOCK
RUDDOCK TOOTLER WINGFISH
REDBREAST
ROBIN GOODFELLOW ELF PUCK
FAIRY SPRITE HOBGOBLIN
ROBINIA LOCUST
ROBIN SANDPIPER KNOT
DOWITCHER
ROBORANT TONIC
ROBOT GELEM GOLEM AUTOMAT
TELEVOX
(LIKE A —) FACELESS
ROB ROY (AUTHOR OF —) SCOTT
(CHARACTER IN —) ROB OWEN
DIANA FRANK ANDREW MACFIN
MORRIS VERNON TRESHAM
WILLIAM CAMPBELL FREDERICK
INGLEWOOD MACVITTIE RASHLEIGH
HILDEBRAND FAIRSERVICE
OSBALDISTONE
ROBUST ABLE FIRM HAIL HALE
HARD IRON RUDE BONNY HARDY
HUSKY LUSTY RENKY SOUND
STARK STIFF STOUR STOUT TOUGH
VALID WALLY HEARTY RUGGED
SINEWY STRONG STURDY
HEALTHY NERVOUS STHENIC
VALIANT MUSCULAR PITHSOME
STALWART SWACKING VIGOROUS
STRAPPING
(NOT —) SLENDER
ROBUSTNESS VALIDITY
ROC BIRD BOMB RUKH ROQUE
SIMURG SIMURGH
ROCHET CLOAK SMOCK CAMISIA
ROCK CAP JOW LOG PAY RAG DAZE
HOST KLIP REEL RUKH SIAL SIMA
SWAY SWIG TOSS BRACK CLIFF
FLOOR GREET GRUSS HORSE
LEDGE ROACH ROQUE SHAKE
SHOWD SKARN STONE TRILL
CRADLE FACIES GROUND OOLITE
PELITE TOTTER BRECCIA COUNTRY
FOLIATE GREISEN CIMINITE
PHYLLITE SILTSTONE
(— AROUND DRILL HOLE) COLLAR
(— CHUNK) KNUCKLE
(— DEBRIS) SCREE
(— FRAGMENT) CLAST
(— GROUP FAN) GROUPIE
(— IN ANOTHER ROCK) XENOLITH
(— IN MINE) CAPPING
(— IN SEA) STACK

(— SURFACE) KARREN
(— VIOLENTLY) STAGGER
(ARTIFICIAL —) GRANOLITH
(BALD —) SCALP
(BANDED —) BAR
(BARE —) SCARTH
(BASALTIC —) TEPHRITE
(CAP —) COVER
(COLUMN OF MOLTEN —) PLUME
(COMPACT —) BASEMENT
(CONGLOMERATE —) PSEPHITE
(COUNTRY —) RIDER ROCKABILLY
(CRUSHED —) GREET
(CRYSTALLINE —) ELVAN DUNITE
SCHIST DIORITE GREISEN ECLOGITE
(DECAY OF —S) GEEST LATERITE
(DECOMPOSED —) GOSSAN
GOZZAN
(DENSE —) ADINOLE
(DISINTEGRATED —) SAPROLITE
(EXTRUSIVE —) DACITE SPILITE
ANDESITE CIMINITE
(FELDSPATHIC —) PETUNTSE
(FISSILE —) SHALE SHAUL
(FLUID —) LAVA
(FRAGMENTAL —) PSEPHITE
(FRAGMENT OF —) CLAST
(GABBROITIC —) EUCRITE
(GLASSY —) PITCHSTONE
(GRANULAR —) GABBRO OOLITE
DIORITE IJOLITE KOSWITE
MYLONITE PSAMMITE QUARTZITE
(GRANULATED —) GRUSS
(GREEN —) OPHITE
(HARD —) WHIN KIMGLE
WHINSTONE NOVACULITE
(HIGH —) SCOUT
(IGNEOUS —) BOSS SIAL SIMA TRAP
BASALT DUNITE GABBRO URTITE
FELSITE GRANITE MINETTE PICRITE
SYENITE UNAKITE DOLERITE
ESSEXITE RHYOLITE TONALITE
(IMPURE —) CHERT
(INSULAR —) SKERRY
(INSULATED —) SKERRY
(INTRUSIVE —) HORTITE MINETTE
MAENAITE
(IRON-BEARING —) GAL
(ISOLATED —) SCAR SCARR SCAUR
(JUTTING POINT OF —) KIP
(MANTLE —) REGOLITH
(METAMORPHIC —) SKARN GNEISS
SCHIST BUCHITE GONDITE LEPTITE
ECLOGITE HORNFELS LIMURITE
(MICA-BEARING —) DOMITE
(MOLTEN —) MAGMA
(MOON —) KREEP
(MOTTLED —) SERPENTINE
(PLUTONIC —) TAWITE HOLLAITE
TURJAITE
(POROUS —) TUFA TUFF ARSOITE
(PROJECTING —) CLINT
(PULVERIZED —) FLOUR
(RARE —) ALNOITE
(ROUGH —) CRAG KNAR SCARTH
(ROUNDED —) ROGNON
SHEEPBACK
(SAND —) PSAMMITE
(SEDIMENTARY —) CRAG
IRONSTONE SANDSTONE
(SHARP —) NEEDLE AIGUILLE
(SLATY —) PLATE SCHALSTEIN
(SOFT —) MALM

(SOLID —) GIBBER
(STUDY OF —S) LITHOLOGY
(SUBMERGED —) SHELF
(SURROUNDING —) GROUND
(UNDERLYING —) FLOOR
(UPRIGHT —) PILLAR
(VOLCANIC —) TUFA TUFF BASALT
DACITE DOMITE LATITE TAXITE
PEPERIN ANDESITE ASHSTONE
EUTAXITE RHYOLITE TEPHRITE
TRACHYTE
(WASTE —) MULLOCK
(WORTHLESS —) GANG GANGUE
(WORTHLESS — MATTER) GANGUE
(PL.) ROCHER
(PREF.) FELSO PETR(I)(O) RHYO
RUPI SAXI
(SUFF.) CLAST ITE LITE LITH(IC)
LITIC PHYRE PHYRIC
ROCKAWAY CARRIAGE
ROCK BADGER CONY HYRAX
ROCK BASS REDEYE CABRILLA
ROCK-BREAKER
(SUFF.) FRAGE
ROCKBRUSH ROSILLA
ROCK CEDAR SABINO
ROCK CRESS ARABIS SICKLEPOD
ROCK DEBRIS TALUS
ROCK DOVE SOD
ROCK-DWELLING SAXATILE
ROCK ELM WAHOO
ROCKER CRADLE SHOOFLY
ROCKET DRAKE TITAN REBUKE
STREAK YELLOW CONGREVE
SKYLIGHT STARSHIP FIREDRAKE
(DYER'S —) WELD WOLD WOALD
WOULD
(SYSTEM OF SPACECRAFT —S)
RETROPACK
ROCKET SALAD ROQUETTE
ROCKFISH BASS JACK RENA REINA
VIUVA FLIOMA GOPHER RASHER
TAMBOR CORSAIR GARRUPA
GROUPER BOCACCIO CHINAFISH
GREENLING
ROCK HARE KLIPHAAS
ROCK HIND MERO AGAUJI
ROCKHOPPER PENGUIN
ROCK HOPPER MACARONI
ROCKLING BAUD GADE ROKER
SORGHE WHISTLER
ROCK NATIVE SNAPPER
ROCK OIL NAPHTHA PETROLEUM
ROCK PIPIT TIETICK
ROCK RABBIT PIKA HYRAX
HYRACOID
ROCKROSE CISTUS PINWEED
HUDSONIA ROCKCIST SAGEROSE
DAYFLOWER SUNFLOWER
ROCK SALT EMOL AMOLE HALITE
(BLOCK OF —) PIG
ROCK SANDWORT CYME
ROCKSHAFT SHAFT ROCKER
WEIGHBAR
ROCK TROUT BOREGAT GREENLING
ROCKWEED TANG FUCUS FUCOID
SEATANG SEAWEED
(PREF.) FUCI
ROCK WHITING KELPFISH
STRANGER
ROCKWORK ROCAILLE
(ARTIFICIAL —) ROCAILLE

ROCKY DAFT HARD STONY CLINTY
OBSCENE PETREAN PETROUS
UNCOUTH OBDURATE UNSTABLE
DIFFICULT RUPELLARY
(PREF.) TRACHY
ROCKY MOUNTAIN (— GOAT)
MAZAME
ROCOCO ORNATE QUAINT
BAROCCO BAROQUE OUTMODED
ROD BAR BOW CUE GAD GUY LUG
PIN TIE BOLT CALM CAME CANE
CORE FALL FORK GOAD GONG
LINK MACE POLE RAVE SCOB SNAP
STEM STUD WAND WHIP YARD
ARBOR BIRCH CATCH DOWEL
LYTTA OSIER PERCH POWER
PUNCH REACH REBAR ROUND
SETUP SHOOT SPELK SPILL SPOKE
SPRAG STAFF STANG STEEL STICK
STING TEYNE TOMMY TRACE
VERGE WIPER BALEYS BROACH
CANARY CARBON CENTER CRUTCH
ETALON FERULA FINGER GLOWER
HANGER PISTOL PITMAN PODGER
RADDLE RAMMER SKEWER SPRING
STADIA SWITCH TOGGLE WATTLE
WICKER BACULUS CROPPIE
DRAWROD ELLWAND FEATHER
FESTUCA MANDREL PLUNGER
POINTER POTHOOK PRICKER
PROBANG PROLONG SCALLOM
SCEPTER SPINDLE STADIUM
STICKER TYRANNY VIRGULA
WHISKER WINDING AXOSTYLE
BACKSTAY BILBERRY BODSTICK
BOWSTAVE DIPSTICK JACKSTAY
KINGBOLT REVOLVER STRAINER
TRAVELER WEEDHOOK
(— AS SYMBOL OF OFFICE) VERGE
(— BEARING TRAFFIC SIGNAL)
STANCHION
(— FOR ALIGNING HOLES) PODGER
(— FOR CARRYING GLASS) FORK
(— FOR DISCIPLINE) YARD FERULA
FERULE
(— FOR FASTENING THATCH)
SPELK SPRINGLE
(— FOR FIREARM BORE) WIPER
(— FOR GLASS-MAKING) PUNTY
FASCET PONTEE PONTIL CROPPIE
(— FOR HOLDING MEAT) SPIT
(— FOR TRANSMITTING MOTION)
TRACE
(— IN ARC LAMP) CARBON
(— IN CRICKET) STUMP
(— IN INTERFEROMETER) ETALON
(— IN MINE PUMP) SPEAR
(— IN NERNST LAMP) GLOWER
(— IN SPINNING WHEEL) SPINDLE
(— OF CELLS) NOTOCHORD
(— OF FOUNDRY MOLD) LANCE
(— OF LOOM) SHAFT
(— OF WOOD) SCOB
(— ON DOG SLED) GEEPOLE
(— ON LOGGING TRUCK) RAVE
(— POINTED AT BOTH ENDS)
SKEWER
(— SYMBOLIZING AUTHORITY)
BACULUS
(— TO BIND A CONTRACT) FESTUCA
(— TO FASTEN SAILS) JACKSTAY
(— TO IMMERSE SHEEP) CRUTCH
(— TO URGE BEAST) GOAD PROD

(— UPSET AT ONE END) SETUP
(— USED AS KEY) TOMMY
(— WITH ENDS AT RIGHT ANGLES)
STRAINER
(— WITH SPONGE ON END)
PROBANG
(— WITH T-HEAD) TOGGLE
(AXIAL —) VIRGULA AXOSTYLE
(BASKETRY —) OSIER SLATH
(BUNDLE OF —S) DRIVER
(CARTILAGINOUS —) LYTTA
COLUMELLA
(CLAMMING —) BRAIL
(CONNECTING —) PITMAN
(CURTAIN —) TRINGLE
(DANCER'S —) CROTALUM
(DIVINING —) TWIG DOWSER
(FISHING —) GAD CALCUTTA
(FLEXIBLE —) RADDLE WATTLE
(FORKED —) CRUTCH
(GEM-CUTTING —) SETTER
(GRADUATED —) STADIA STADIUM
(IRON —) SNAP BETTY
(KNITTING —) NEEDLE
(LEAD —) CAME
(LOGGING —) CANARY
(MEASURING —) JUDGE SPILE
STADIA ELLWAND METEWAND
METEYARD
(PLIABLE —) WINDING
(SMALL —) LANCE
(STRENGTHENING —) RIB
(SUPPLE —) SWABBLE
(TETHERING —) STAKE
(THIN —) TEYNE SCALLOM
(TIE —) ANCHOR
(UMBRELLA —) STRETCHER
(WITHE —) BILBERRY
(PREF.) BACULI RHABD(O)
RHAPIDO VERGI
RODENT RAT CONY DEGU HARE
MARA MOCO MOLE PACA PIKA
UTIA VOLE CONEY COYPU GUNDI
HUTIA JUTIA LEROT MOUSE TUCAN
ZOKOR AGOUTI BEAVER BITING
CURURO GERBIL GLIRID GNAWER
GOPHER JERBOA MARMOT
MURINE MUROID RABBIT SOKHOR
BLESMOL CHINCHA DIPODID
GEOMYID GNAWING HAMSTER
LEMMING LEVERET MUSKRAT
ABROCOME CAPIBARA
DORMOUSE LEPORIDE OCTODONT
SEWELLEL SPALACID SQUIRREL
TUCOTUCO VISCACHA VIZCACHA
ANOMALURE PORCUPINE
RODEO ROUNDUP
**RODERICK RANDOM (AUTHOR OF
—)** SMOLLETT
(CHARACTER IN —) TOM STRAP
OAKHUM RANDOM BOWLING
MELINDA SNAPPER CRAMPLEY
NARCISSA RODERICK WILLIAMS
QUIVERWIT
RODLIKE VIRGATE RHABDOID
RODMAN CLASHY CLASHEE
CHAINMAN
RODOMONTADE BRAG RANT
BOAST BLUSTER BOMBAST
BRAGGART
RODOMONTE (BELOVED OF —)
DORALICE
(VICTIM OF —) RUGGIERO

ROD-SHAPED RHABDOID
VIRGULATE
ROE RA DOE FRY PEA RAA RAE DEER
HIND KELK RAUN ROUN ROWN
CORAL TRUBU CAVIAR
ROEBUCK GIRL CHEVREUIL
ROGER RAM HODGE ROGUE
ROGUE BOY GUE IMP NYM HEMP
KEMP KITE LOON ROAG CATSO
CRACK CRANK DROLE GIPSY
GREEK GYPSY HEMPY KNAVE
SCAMP SHELM BEGGAR BORGER
BUGGER CANTER CHOUSE COQUIN
CURTAL HARLOT LIMMER PICARA
PICARO RASCAL SORROW TINKER
BLEEDER ERRATIC FOISTER
HALLION LADRONE PANURGE
SHARPER SKELLUM SWINGER
VILLAIN COMHOGUE HEMPSEED
PICAROON SCALAWAG SWINDLER
WHIPJACK
ROGUE HERRIES (AUTHOR OF —)
WALPOLE
(CHARACTER IN —) ALICE DAVID
PRESS SARAH STARR DEBORAH
DENBURN FRANCIS HERRIES
MARGARET MIRABELL
OSBALDISTONE
ROGUERY ROPERY KNAVERY
LOONERY WAGGERY PATCHERY
PRIGGISM TRICKERY TRUANTRY
ROGUISH SLY ARCH HEMPY ROGUY
WICKED KNAVISH TRICKSY
VAGRANT WAGGISH ESPIEGLE
SCAMPISH DISHONEST
ROGUISHNESS KNAVERY
ARCHNESS
**ROI DE LAHORE, LE (CHARACTER
IN —)** ALIM SITA SCINDIA
(COMPOSER OF —) MASSENET
ROIL VEX FOUL RILE ANNOY
AGITATE BLUNDER DISTURB
STUDDLE BEWILDER DISORDER
IRRITATE
ROILED TURBID
ROISTER REVEL ROIST SCOUR
CAROUSE GALRAVAGE
ROISTERER MUN GREEK HUZZA
BUSTER HECTOR RIOTER SCOURER
TWIBILL EPHESIAN
ROISTERING HOYDEN
ROKE FOG DAMP MIST REEK ROWK
STIR FOGGY SMOKE STEAM VAPOR
ROKELAY ROCOLO
ROLAND (BETROTHED OF —) AUDE
(COMPANION OF —) OLIVER
(HORN OF —) OLIVANT
(SWORD OF —) DURANDAL
(UNCLE OF —) CHARLEMAGNE
ROLE BIT JOB LEAD PART ROTE
HEAVY FIGURE CLOTHES BUSINESS
FUNCTION LIRIPIPE
(CHIEF —) LEAD
(SECONDARY —) COMPRIMARIO
(SMALL —) CAMEO
ROLL BAP BUN ROW WEB BOLT
COIL CURL FILE FLOW FURL LIST
MILL PASS REEL ROAM ROTA
SWAG WELT WIND WRAP BAGEL
BIALY BREAD BUILD DANDY DICKY
ENROL FLUTE ROYLE SPLIT
TOMMY TRILL TROLL WHELM
BILLOW BUNDLE CIRCLE ELAPSE

ENFOLD GOGGLE GROVEL KIPFEL LEGEND MUSTER PONDER RECORD ROSTER ROTATE SCROLL UPWIND VOLUME WAMBLE WANDER WHELVE WINTLE WREATH BISCUIT BOLILLO BRIOCHE CROCKET ENVELOP MANCHET NOTITIA REVOLVE ROTULET ROTULUS ROULEAU STRETCH TERRIER TRINDLE TRUNDLE TWISTER BAGUETTE BROTCHEN CANNELON CONSIDER CRESCENT JACKROLL LAMINATE PORTEOUS REGISTER SEDERUNT SPREADER VOLUTATE

(— A BALL) BOWL
(— ABOUT) WALTER SCAMBLE
(— ALONG) COAST TRUCK
(— AS A SHIP) SEEL LURCH
(— AS STONE) REEL
(— BY) WALK
(— CLOSELY) FURL
(— EYES) WALL WAUL WHAWL GOGGLE
(— GLASS) MARVER
(— INTO A BALL) CLEW CLUE
(— OF BILLS) WAD
(— OF BREAD) BAP SEMMEL TAMMIE
(— OF CLOTH) BOLT DOSSIL WREATH
(— OF COINS) ROULEAU
(— OF DOUGH) TWIST
(— OF DRIED BARK) QUILL
(— OF DRUM) HURRY RATTAN
(— OF DUST) KITTEN
(— OF FIBERS) ROVING
(— OF HAIR) PUFF ROACH ROWEL CROCKET
(— OF HAY) WAKE
(— OF LINT OR LINEN) TENT DOSSIL
(— OF LUGGAGE) SWAG
(— OF MINCED MEAT) RISSOLE
(— OF OFFENDERS) PORTEOUS
(— OF PAPER) SPILL STOMP STUMP
(— OF PARCHMENT) BOOK PELL
(— OF ROULETTE WHEEL) COUP
(— OF SPUN YARN) PRICK
(— OF TOBACCO) CAROT CIGAR PRICK SEGAR CAROTTE
(— OF WALLPAPER) BOLT
(— OF WHEAT BREAD) MANCHET
(— OF WOOL) ROVE ROVING CARDING
(— ON CASTERS) TRUCKLE
(— ON LITTLE WHEELS) TRUNDLE
(— ONWARD) DEVOLVE
(— OVER) COMB JOLL WELTER
(— TOGETHER) CONVOLVE
(— TO RUB DOWN DRAWING) STUMP
(— UP) FURL STOW COLLAR
(— UP SLEEVES) REEVE
(BLANKET —) BINDLE SHIRALEE
(BREAKFAST —) BIALY DANISH
(DANDY —) DANCER
(HOLLOW —) CANNELON
(KIND OF —) KAISER
(LONG —) FLUTE
(ON A —) HOT
(PADDED —) BURLET
(PENNY —) TOMMY

(TWISTED — OF WOOL) SLUB
(WHIP —) BACKREST
(PREF.) HELI(C)(CO)
ROLLED (— IN SUGAR) SANDED
ROLLER FLY BOWL BRAY DRUM JACK LEAD MILL PUCK RUBY WAVE BREAK DANDY FINER GODET INKER RIDER SHELL WAVER WINCH BRAYER BREAST DOFFER DUCTOR FASCIA MANGLE ROWLET RUNNER CARRIER CLEARER MOIETER TRUCKLE HEDGEHOG SQUEEGEE STRIPPER TROUPAND
(— FOR MASSAGER) ROULETTE
(— IN HORSE'S BIT) CRICKET
(— IN ORGAN) TRUNDLE
(— IN STEELWORKS) COGGER
(— TO CLEAR FABRIC) MOIETER
(CARDING —) BREAST WORKER SQUIRREL STRIPPER
(CHINESE —) SIRGANG
(DREDGING —) HEDGEHOG
(DROP —) DUCTOR
(GRINDING —) BREAK
(INKING —) BRAYER
(PLAYER ON — DERBY TEAM) JAMMER
(PRINTING —) DANDY SHELL BRAYER DAMPENER
(ROUND IN — DERBY) JAM
(STONE —) MAMMY TOTER
(SURGICAL —) FASCIA
(TOOTHED —) PRICK PRICKER
(TYPEWRITER —) PLATEN
ROLLER COASTER SWITCHBACK
ROLLER DERBY (ROUND IN —) JAM
ROLLERMAN BRAKER JACKMAN LEVERMAN
ROLLER SKATE PEDOMOTOR
ROLLICK PLAY ROMP CAVORT FROLIC ROLLIX
ROLLICKING GAY WILD MERRY JOVIAL LIVELY
ROLLING CURL GOGGLE WHEELY SWAYING TRILLED LURCHING VOLUTION
(— OF SCROLL) GELILAH
(— OF SHIP) LABOR
(— OF STOMACH) WAMBLE
ROLLTOP TAMBOUR
ROLY-POLY TUBBY ROTUND PUDDING TUMBLER SALTWORT
ROM RO GYPSY ROMANY
ROMAINE COS
ROMAN BRAVE LATIN NOBLE PAPAL ANTIQUA UPRIGHT GOWNSMAN
(— COLLAR) RABAT
ROMAN CATHOLIC ROME ROMAN PAPIST ROMIST JEBUSITE BABYLONIC
ROMANCE WOO GEST ANTAR FANCY FEIGN GESTE KATHA NOVEL STORY AFFAIR ANTARA UTOPIA FANTASY FICTION ROMANZA ROMAUNT
(— LANGUAGE) FRENCH ITALIAN SPANISH
ROMAN-FLEUVE SAGA

ROMANIA

CANAL: BEGA
CAPITAL: BUCHAREST
COIN: BAN LEI LEU LEY

COUNTY: OLT ARAD CLUJ DOLJ GORJ IASI ARGES BACAU BIHOR BUZAU ILFOV MURES NEAMT SALAJ SIBIU TIMIS
DISTRICT: ALBA BANAT BIHOR DOBRUJA DOBROGEA MARAMURES
LAKE: SINOE
MOUNTAIN: BIHOR NEGOI CODRUL RODNEI CALIMAN PIETROSU
OLD NAME: DACIA
PASS: ROSUL
PROVINCE: ARDEAL MOLDAVIA WALACHIA
RIVER: ALT OLT JIUL PRUT ALUTA ARGES BUZDU MOROS MURES OLTUL SCHYL SIRET TIMIS TISZA VEDEA CRASNA DANUBE ARGESUL MURESUL SOMESUL BISTRITA IALOMITA
RIVER PORT: BRAILA GALATI GALATZ
TOWN: ARAD CLUJ IASI BACAU CERNA JASSY NEAMT SIBIU TURNU BRAILA BRASOV GALATI GALATZ LUPENI CRAIOVA FOCSANI PLOESTI SEVERIN CERNAVTI KISHENEF TEMESVAR KOLOZSVAR

ROMANIST MISSARY
ROMANIZATION LATINXUA
ROMANSH LADIN
ROMANTIC AIRY WILD IDEAL ARDENT DREAMY GOTHIC POETIC UNREAL FERVENT FABULOUS FANCIFUL
ROMANY RO ROM GIPSY GYPSY ROMAN
ROMANY RYE (AUTHOR OF —) BORROW
(CHARACTER IN —) DALE JACK BELLE ISOPEL JASPER URSULA BERNERS MURTAGH LAVENGRO SYLVESTER PETULENGRO
ROME (CHAPEL IN —) SISTINE
(FOUNDER OF —) ROMULUS
(HILL IN —) CAELIAN VIMINAL AVENTINE PALATINE QUIRINAL
(OLD PORT OF —) OSTIA
(RIVER IN —) TIBER
ROME HAUL (AUTHOR OF —) EDMONDS
(CHARACTER IN —) BEN DAN JOE RAE SOL LUCY BERRY JACOB KLORE MOLLY WAMPY CALASH GURGET HARROW HECTOR JOTHAM JULIUS SAMSON TINKLE WEAVER WILSON FORTUNE LARKINS TURNESA WILLIAM FRIENDLY CASHDOLLAR BUTTERFIELD
ROMEO AND JULIET (AUTHOR OF —) SHAKESPEARE
(CHARACTER IN —) JOHN PARIS PETER ROMEO JULIET TYBALT ABRAHAM CAPULET ESCALUS GREGORY SAMPSON BENVOLIO LAURENCE MERCUTIO MONTAGUE BALTHASAR
ROMOLA (AUTHOR OF —) ELIOT
(CHARACTER IN —) DINO LUCA TITO BARDO CALVO LILLO MONNA PIERO

TESSA MELEMA ROMOLA BRIGIDA NICCOLO BERNARDO BALDASARRE
ROMP REG RIG HEMP LARK PLAY ROIL FRISK SHIRL SPORT TRAIN FROLIC GAMBOL HOORAY HOYDEN HURRAH RIPPET COURANT GAMMOCK RAMMACK RUNAWAY
ROMPERS JUMPER JUMPERS
ROMPING ROYT HEMPY ROYET
ROMULUS (BROTHER OF —) REMUS
(FATHER OF —) MARS
RONCADOR GRUNT CROAKER SCIAENID
RONDO ROTA
RONE BUSH BRAKE GUTTER THICKET
RONG LEPCHA
RONGA THONGA
RONSDORFER ZIONITE ELLERIAN
ROOD RUD REED ROPE CROSS SPAWN STANG CRUCIFIX
ROODLES RANGDOODLES
ROOF TOP ATAP BACK DECK DOME FLAT ATTAP COVER HOUSE RAISE RISER SHELL THACK AZOTEA BONNET CUPOLA SUMMIT TECTUM CHOPPER CRICKET GAMBREL MANSARD RIGGING TECTURE BULKHEAD HOUSETOP SAWTOOTH SEMIDOME PENTHOUSE
(— MEMBER) PURLIN
(— OF CARRIAGE) IMPERIAL
(— OF CAVERN) DOME
(— OF MINING CAGE) BONNET
(— OF MOUTH) PALATE
(— OF NASOPHARYNX) VAULT
(— OF RAILWAY CAR) DECK
(— OF THE WORLD) PAMIR
(— OVER DOOR) APPENTICE
(— OVER STAGE) SHADOW
(— PORTION) MONITOR
(AUTOMOBILE —) FASTBACK
(CLOTH —) CHUTT
(FALSE —) CRICKET
(FLAT —) LEADS AZOTEA TERRACE
(STEEPLY TAPERING —) SPIRE
(THATCHED —) ATAP ATTAP CHOPPER
(TOWER —) SADDLEBACK
(VAULTED —) DOME
(PREF.) STEG(O) TECTI TECTO
(SUFF.) STEGE STEGITE
ROOFING HEALING SHINDLE PANTILING TECTIFORM
ROOFTOP PEAK
ROOK GYP ROC CROW DUPE RUKH CHEAT CRAKE JUDGE TOWER BLACKY CASTLE DEFRAUD CASTILLO SWINDLER
(NEIGHBOR OF —) KNIGHT
ROOKERY ROOST RUMPUS BUILDING
ROOKIE COLT DRONGO NOVICE RECRUIT BEGINNER
ROOM PAD WON AULA CAFE CRIB FARM HALL KILN LIEU PLAY SALA SEAT SLUM WAME WENE WONE ATTIC BERTH CUDDY DIVAN EWERY HOUSE LODGE OECUS PLACE SALLE SCOPE SHACK SOLAR SPACE STALL STOVE STUDY BELFRY BREAST CAMERA CASINO

CHAPEL ESTUFA EXEDRA
HAMMAM LEEWAY MARGIN
PARVIS SCOUTH SINGLE SMOKER
SOLLAR STANCE STANZA STUDIO
CABINET CAMARIN CHALMER
CHAMBER EPINAOS FREEZER
GALLERY HOLDING HYPOGEE
KITCHEN LAUNDRY LIBRARY
SEMINAR SERVERY SMOKERY
SURGERY AEDICULA ASSEMBLY
BASEMENT CAPACITY DRYHOUSE
HOTHOUSE HYPOGEUM LAVATORY
NYMPHEUM PLAYROOM
SCULLERY SWEATBOX TABLINUM
THALAMUS PRESSROOM
(— ADJOINING SYNAGOGUE)
GENIZAH
(— BEHIND FACADE) ATTIC
(— BELOW STAGE) MEZZANINE
(— BETWEEN KITCHEN AND DINING
ROOM) SERVERY
(— CONTAINING FOUNTAIN)
NYMPHEUM
(— DUG IN CLIFF) HYPOGEE
HYPOGEUM
(— FOR ACTION) LEEWAY
(— FOR BATHING) HAMMAM
(— FOR CONVERSATION) EXEDRA
LOCUTORY
(— FOR DANCING) CASINO
(— FOR FAMILY RECORDS)
TABLINUM
(— FOR KEEPING FOOD) LARDER
PANTRY
(— FOR PAINTINGS) GALLERY
(— FOR PIGEONS) LOFT
(— FOR PRIVATE DEVOTIONS)
ORATORY
(— FOR PUBLIC AMUSEMENTS)
CASINO THEATER
(— FOR STOWAGE) LASTAGE
(— FOR TABLE LINEN) EWERY
(— IN COAL MINE) BREAST
(— IN HAREM) ODA ODAH
(— IN KEEP) DUNGEON
(— IN PREHISTORIC BUILDING)
CELL
(— IN REAR OF TEMPLE) EPINAOS
(— IN SIDE OF LARGER ROOM) ALA
(— IN TOWER) BELFRY
(— OF STUDENTS' SOCIETY) HALL
(— ON SHIP) CABIN STOKEHOLD
(— OVER CHURCH PORCH) PARVIS
(— OVER STAGE) SHADOW
(— TO ADVANCE) WAY
(— TOGETHER) CHUM
(— TO LIVE) LEBENSRAUM
(— UNDER BUILDING) CELLAR
(— UNDER ROOF) LOFT
(CHILDREN'S —) NURSERY
(COTTAGE —) END
(DINING —) CENACLE DINETTE
REFECTORY TRICLINIUM
(DRAWING —) SALON SALOON
(DRESSING —) SHIFT BOUDOIR
CAMARIN VESTUARY WARDROBE
TIREHOUSE
(DRYING —) HOTHOUSE
(ESKIMO ASSEMBLY —) KASHGA
(EXHIBITION —) THEATER
(GRINDING —) HULL
(HEATED —) STEW
(HIGH —) AERY EYRY AERIE EYRIE

(HOSPITAL —) WARD
(INNER —) BEN INBY INBYE SPENCE
THALAMUS
(INSULATED —) FREEZER
(KIND OF —) REC
(KITCHEN —) SCULLERY
(LECTURE —) AUDITORY
(LIVING —) HOUSE LANAI SALON
SERDAB SOLARIUM VOORHUIS
(MONASTERY —) CELL LAVABO
(NARROW —) CRIB
(OCTAGONAL —) TRIBUNA
(PORTER'S —) LODGE
(PRIVATE —) SNUG SCHOLA
SANCTUM CONCLAVE GARDEROBE
(PUBLIC —) SALOON
(PUEBLO ASSEMBLY —) ESTUFA
(READING —) ATHENEUM
(RECEPTION —) DIVAN PARLOR
KURSAAL MANDARAH
(REFRIGERATED —) COOLER
(RETIRING —) RECAMERA
(ROMAN —) ATRIUM AEDICULA
FUMARIUM
(ROUND —) ROTUNDA
(SEA —) BERTH
(SECLUDED —) DEN
(SECRET —) HOLE
(SERIES OF — S) SWEEP
(SITTING —) SEAT SITTER BOUDOIR
(SLEEPING —) DORMER BEDROOM
DORMITORY
(SMALL —) ALA CELL SNUG STEW
ZETA CUBBY CUDDY LOBBY CLOSET
CUBICLE SNUGGERY
(SMOKING —) DIVAN DIWAN
TABAGIE
(SORTING —) SALLE
(STEAM —) STOVE
(STORAGE —) CAMARIN MAGAZINE
THALAMUS
(SWEATING —) SUDARIUM
SUDATORY LACONICUM
(THRONE —) AIWAN
(TOP —) GARRET IMPERIAL
(UPPER —) SOLAR
(VAULTED —) CAMERA
(WRITING —) SCRIPTORIUM
(PREF.) STEG(O)
(SUFF.) STEGE STEGITE
ROOMMATE CHUM ROOMY
ROOMIE
ROOMY WIDE LARGE RANGY SPACY
ROOMSOME SPACIOUS
CAPACIOUS COMMODIOUS
ROOSE RUSE EXTOL PRAISE
FLATTER BOASTING BRAGGING
ROOST EVE SIT BAUK JOUK TIDE
PERCH GARRET HARBOR LODGING
ROOKERY SHELTER
ROOSTER COCK GAME GALLO
MANOC GAMECOCK
(CREST OF A —) COMB
ROOT DIG PRY ROI TAP BASE BULB
CHAY CHOY GRUB MOOR MOOT
MORE PLUG PULL RACE SPUR TAIL
CHEER FIBER FRUIT GROOT GROUT
HEART IREOS LAPPA RADIX STOCK
ALRAUN BOTTOM CARROT
CATGUT GROUND MUZZLE ORIGIN
SENEGA SETTLE SUMBAL SUMBUL
ACONITE ALKANET AZAFRAN
BIACURU BONIATA CALUMBA

CHICORY COLUMBO CRAMPON
GINSENG IMPLANT IPOMOEA
NUNNARI PAREIRA RADICAL
RUMMAGE TURPETH DEDENDUM
EARTHNUT PNEUMATOPHORE
(— BRANCH) TAPOUN
(— CONTAINING STARCH) KOONTI
(— DEEPLY) SCREW
(— OF GINGER) RACE
(— OF ORCHID) CULLIONS
(— OF TARO) EDDO
(— OF TOOTH) FANG
(— OF TREE) TANG SPURN
(— OF WORD) THEME
(— OUT) GRUB STUB STOCK EVULSE
DISPLANT SUPPLANT
(—S FOR SEWING CANOES) WATAP
WATAPEH
(—S OF ACONITE) BIKH NABEE
(— TUBERCLE) CLOG
(— WORD) ETYMON
(— YIELDING RED DYE) CHAY CHOY
CHAYA
(AROMATIC —) ORRIS
(CANDIED —) ERYNGO
(CUSCUS —S) VETIVER
(DRIED —) JALAP ALTHEA SENECA
BRYONIA KRAMERIA LICORICE
SCAMMONY
(DRIED —S) INULA IPECAC
KRAMERIA VERATRUM
(EDIBLE —) YAM BEET EDDO
RADISH TURNIP WASABI PARSNIP
RUTABAGA TUBERCLE
(FERN —) ROI
(FINE —) STRING
(FRAGRANT —S) VETIVER
(KIND OF —) LATENT
(MASS OF FIBROUS —S) SPONGE
(MEDICINAL —) JALAP LAPPA
GINSENG
(PROJECTING —) SPUR
(ROASTED BEET —) BONKA
(STUMP AND —) MOCK
(PL.) CULVERS
(PREF.) RADICI RHIZ(O)
(SUFF.) RHIZA RHIZOUS
ROOTCAP CALYPTRA SPONGIOLE
ROOTED FIXED CHRONIC
(DEEPLY —) BESETTING
ROOTER FAN PLUGGER
ROOTLESS ARRHIZAL
ROOTLESSNESS ANOMIE
ROOTLET VIVER CRAMPON RADICEL
RADICLE
(PL.) COME CULMS
ROOTSTOCK PIP ROI RACE TARO
CROWN ORRIS CASAVA DANNUM
GINGER ORIGIN PANNUM STOLON
BISCUIT MISHMEE TURMERIC
ORRISROOT
ROPE GAD GUY TIE TOW TUG CEEL
COLT CORD FALL FAST GUSS
HEMP JEFF JUNK LIFT LINE ROOD
SEAL SOAM SPAN STAY TACK TAIL
TAUM TOME VANG WARP BRACE
BRAIL CABLE CABUL CHECK
CHORD LASSO LONGE SHANK
STRAP STROP SWEEP TRACE
TWIST WANTY WIDDY WITHE
CABLET HALTER INHAUL LARIAT
LISSOM LIZARD MECATE PINION
RAPEYE RUNNER SHROUD SLATCH

STRAND STRING TETHER WARROK
AWEBAND BEDCORD BOBSTAY
CATFALL CRINGLE ENTRAIL
HALYARD HAYBAND LASHING
LEEFANG OUTHAUL PAINTER
PAZAREE PENDANT PIGTAIL
SEAMING SERPENT SERVICE
STIRRUP SWIFTER BACKBONE
BACKSTAY BUNTLINE CABESTRO
CORDELLE DOWNHAUL DRAGLINE
FOREFOOT FORETACK HALLIARD
HAULYARD INHAULER JACKSTAY
LIFELINE NECKLACE PASSAREE
PROLONGE ROUNDING SEQUENCE
THRAMMLE BREECHING
(— A STEER) HEEL
(— COLLAR) PARRAL PARREL
(— CONNECTING NETS) BALK
BAULK
(— COVERING) QUILTING
(— FOR FASTENING GATE) CRINGLE
(— FOR FISH) STRINGER
(— FOR TRAINING HORSE) LONGE
(— FOR TYING CATTLE) CEEL SEAL
AWEBAND
(— HANDLE) FETTLE SHACKLE
(— HOLDING RAFT TOGETHER)
BRAIL
(— JOINT) TUCK
(— OF HAIR) CABESTRO
(— OF ONIONS) REEVE
(— OF STRAW) GAD SIME VINE
SIMON SUGAN FETTLE SIMMON
SOOGAN
(— OF 10 OR MORE INCHES) CABLE
(— ON DERRICK) TELEGRAF
(— ON FISHING NET) PINION
SEAMING
(— ORNAMENTATION) TORSADE
(— PASSING AROUND DEADEYE)
STRAP STROP
(—S IN RIGGING) CORDAGE
(— STOLEN FROM DOCKYARD)
RUMBO
(— WITH HOOK AND TOGGLE)
PROLONGE
(— WITH SWIVEL AND LOOP)
TOGGEL TOGGLE
(— WOUND AROUND CABLE)
KECKLING
(ANCHOR —) RODE VIOL VOYAL
(BELL —) TYALL HANGER
(CIRCUS —) JEFF
(COWBOY'S —) LASSO NOOSE
RIATA LARIAT
(DESCEND BY —) RAPPEL
(DRAFT —) SOAM
(DRAG —) GUSS
(FLAG-RAISING —) HALYARD
(FOOT —) HORSE
(GRASS —) SOGA
(GUIDE —) DRAGLINE
(HANDLE —) FETTLE
(HANGMAN'S —) HEMP TIPPET
(HARNESS —) TRACE HALTER
(HARPOON —) FOREGOER
(MOORING —) HEADFAST
(NAUTICAL —) TIE TYE COLT FANG
LIFT STAY VANG BRACE BRAIL
SHEET SLING STRAP STROP GILGUY
HAWSER INHAUL LACING RATLIN
SHROUD BOBSTAY BOWLINE
CATFALL GESWARP LANYARD

LEEFANG OUTHAUL PAINTER PAZAREE PENDANT PENNANT PIGTAIL RATLINE SNORTER SNOTTER STIRRUP STOPPER SWIFTER TRIATIC BACKBONE BACKSTAY BUNTLINE DOWNHAUL FORETACK JACKSTAY PASSAREE ROUNDING SELVAGÉE WOOLDING TIMENOGUY
(PART OF —) SLATCH
(SHORT —) SHANK
(SHORT CART —) WANTY
(SMALL HANDMADE —) FOX
(SMUGGLER'S —) LINGTOW
(TALLOWED —) GASKET
(TETHERING —) SPANCEL
(TOW —) CORDELLE
(WIRE —) HAULBACK JACKSTAY
(WORN OR POOR —) JUNK
(PL.) CORDAGE
(PREF.) FUN(I) RESTI SPIR(O)
ROPEBAND RABAND
ROPE-DANCER ACROBAT
ROPEDANCER ACROBAT FUNAMBULIST
ROPEMAKER FOLLOWER RATLINER
ROPEWALKER FUNAMBULO
ROPEWAY TRAMWAY WIREWAY CABLEWAY
ROPY SINEWY STRINGY VISCOUS MUSCULAR GLUTINOUS
ROQUE CROQUET
ROQUELAURE CLOAK ROCOLO ROCKLAY
RORIPA RADICULA
RORQUAL SEI FINBACK
ROSACEA ACNE
ROSADER (BELOVED OF —) ROSALYNDE
(BROTHER OF —) TORRISMOND
ROSAMUNDA (FATHER OF —) CUNIMOND
(HUSBAND OF —) ALBOIN
ROSARY BEADS CORONA TASBIH BEADING PSALTER BEADROLL
(— BEAD) AVE GAUD GAUDY
(MOHAMMEDAN —) COMBOLOIO
ROSE ASH GUL KNOT MOSS ROIS BRIAR BRIDE BUCKY FLUSH RHODA CANKER OPULUS POMPON BOURBON BURBANK GLAIEUL HUGONIS LOZENGE MANETTI MONTHLY OPHELIA RAMBLER AGRIMONY COLUMBIA DOGBERRY LOKELANI PEDELION
(COTTON —) CUDWEED
(DWARF —) POLYANTHA
(HYBRID —) NOISETTE
(KIND OF —) MOSS
(PREF.) RHOD(O) ROSEO ROSI ROSO
(SUFF.) RHODIN
ROSE ACACIA ROBINIA
ROSE APPLE JAMBO JAMBOS JAMBOSA
ROSEATE SPOONBILL AJAJA
ROSE-BREASTED (— COCKATOO) GALAH
ROSEBUSH ROSER BALWARRA
ROSE CAMPION LYCHNIS
ROSE-COLORED OPTIMISTIC
(— STARLING) PASTOR TILYER

ROSEFISH BRIM BREAM BERGYLT REDFISH
(YOUNG —) SNAPPER
ROSE HIP CHOOP CHOUP
ROSELLE SORREL SABDARIFFA
ROSEMARY COSTMARY MOORWORT ROSMARINE
ROSE MOSS PURSLANE PORTULACA
ROSENKAVALIER, DER
(CHARACTER IN —) OCHS SOPHIE FANINAL MARIANDL OCTAVIAN MARSCHALLIN
(COMPOSER OF —) STRAUSS
ROSET BRAZIL
ROSETTE CHOU KNOT ROSACE ROSULA COCKADE
ROSEWOOD BUBINGA MOLOMPI JACARANDA PALISANDER
ROSH (FATHER OF —) BENJAMIN
ROSIN FLUX ROSET COLOPHONY
(— SPIRIT) PINOLIN
ROSS SCALP
ROSSER BARKER PEELER SCALPER SLIPPER
ROSTER LIST ROTA SCROLL REGISTER
ROSTRATE BEAKED
ROSTRUM PEW AMBE BEAK BEMA GUARD SNOUT PULPIT ACROTER TRIBUNE
ROSY ROSEN BLUSHY AURORAL HEALTHY HOPEFUL AUROREAN BLOOMING BLUSHFUL RUBICUND
ROT COE RET DOTE DOZE DROP FOUL JOKE LEAK POKE SOUR WROX DECAY SPOIL TEASE BLUING FESTER MOLDER ROTTEN CORRUPT HOOFRUT PUTREFY NONSENSE STAGNATE
(— BY EXPOSURE) RET
(— OF GRAPES) SLIPSKIN
(APPLE —) FROGEYE
(FOOT —) FOUL
(FRUIT —) BLET LEAK
(LIVER —) COE
(PREF.) PYTHO
ROTA LIST ROLL ROSTER ROTULA
ROTARY CIRCLE GYRATORY ROUNDABOUT
(PREF.) ROTO
ROTATE RUN BIRL GYRE ROLL SPIN TURN PIVOT RABAT SCREW WHEEL GYRATE REVOLVE TRUNDLE ROTIFORM TURNOVER ALTERNATE
(— CAMERA) PAN
(— HIPS) GRIND
ROTATING VOLUBLE
(— PIECE) CAM
ROTATION SPIN TURN ROUND TWIRL GYRATION SPINNING WHIRLING
(— ON BALL) STUFF
(DEVICE INDICATING SPEED OF —) TACH
(KIND OF —) FARADAY
(STOP —) DESPIN
ROTCHE BULL RATCH ROTGE DOVEKEY DOVEKIE BULLBIRD
ROTE CRWTH HEART ROTTA REPEAT
ROTIFER POLYP LIPOPOD LORICATE PLOIMATE
ROTIFORM TROCHAL

ROTL RATTEL WEIGHT ROTTOLO (PL.) ARTAL ARTEL
ROTOGRAVURE ROTO COLOROTO
ROTOR IMPELLER
ROTTED PECKY
ROTTEN BAD FOUL PUNK ROXY SOUR ADDLE DAZED MOSEY PUTID ADDLED AMPERY FRACID MOOSEY PUTRID DECAYED SPOILED DEPRAVED UNSTABLE
(HALF —) DOTED DOATED
(PARTIALLY —) DRUXY
(PREF.) PUTRE PUTRI SAPR(O)
ROTTENSTONE TRIPOLI
ROTTER CAD LOUSE
(INDIAN —) BUDMASH
ROTTING SLEEPY CARIOUS
ROTTLERA KAMALA
ROTULA ROUND TROCHE KNEEPAN PATELLA
ROTUND FAT PLUMP ROUND STOUT CHUBBY SUBROUND
ROTUNDA PANTHEON
ROTURIER PEASANT PLEBEIAN RUPTUARY
ROUE RAKE RAKEHELL DEBAUCHEE
ROUGE RED FARD BLUSH PAINT FUCATE REDDEN RUDDLE CLINKER SCRIMMAGE
(ANIMAL —) CARMINE
ROUGH RU ROW RUF BEAT FOUL GURL HARD HASK LAMB ROID ROYD RUDE THUG WILD ACRID ASPER BLUFF BLUNT BRUTE CHURL CRUDE DIRTY GOBBY GROFF GURLY HAIRY HARSH HEFTY JAGGY LUMPY REWCH ROUCH ROWDY RUGGY RUVID STARK STEER STERN STOUR TOUGH TOUSY WIGHT BORREL BROKEN BRUSHY BURRED CHOPPY COARSE COBBLY CRABBY CRAGGY ELBOIC HACKLY HISPID HOARSE HOBBLY HORRID HUBBLY INCULT JAGGED KEELIE KNAGGY KNOTTY NOGGEN RAGGED RAMAGE RASPED ROBUST RUFFLE RUGGED RUMBLY RUSTIS SEVERE SHAGGY SKETCH STICKY TOOSIE TRYING UNEVEN UNFEEL UNFELE UNFINE UNKIND UNMILD UNRIDE ABUSIVE AUSTERE BOORISH BRISTLY CRABBED HIRSUTE INEQUAL INEXACT JARRING RABBISH RAMMAGE RAPLOCH RAUCOUS RUFFLED SCABRID SCRAGGY STICKLE STICKLY UNCOUTH UNKEMPT VICIOUS ABRASIVE ASPERATE CHURLISH DEPOLISH IMPOLITE LARRIKIN OBDURATE SCABROUS SCRAGGED STUBBORN TACTLESS UNGENTLE UNTENDER MANHANDLE SCABERULOUS
(— EDGES) FASH
(— IT) CAMP SIWASH
(— UP) MESS
(— UP ARROW FEATHERS) SPRANGLE
(MAKE —) SHAG
(PREF.) ASPERI DASI DASY TRACHY
ROUGHAGE FIBER FODDER AVERAGE BALLAST BULKAGE CELLULOSE

ROUGH-AND-READY BURLY TOWSY TOWZIE MAKESHIFT
ROUGHCAST HARL PARGET SPARGE ROUGHHEW SLAPDASH
ROUGH-EDGED JAGGED RAGGED
ROUGHEN CHAP FRET GAIG HACK EMERY FEAZE FLOCK FROST SPRAY TOOTH ABRADE CRISLE STIVER CHIZZLE ENGRAIL SCRATCH SPREAZE ASPERATE SPREATHE UNSMOOTH
(— BRICK WALL) STAB
ROUGHER BULLDOGGER
(PONY —) STRANDER
ROUGH-HOB GASH
ROUGHING IT (AUTHOR OF —) TWAIN CLEMENS
(CHARACTER IN —) HANK MARK SLADE TWAIN YOUNG BRIGHAM ERICKSON
ROUGHLY ABOUT
ROUGH-MILL GASH
ROUGHNECK ROWDY TOUGH MUCKER UNCOUTH BANGSTER
ROUGHNESS GAFF GRAIN SCUFF TOOTH RUFFLE CRIZZLE CRUDITY ACRIMONY ASPERITY
(— OF SEA) LIPPER
(— OF SKIN) GOOSESKIN GOOSEFLESH
(— OF WALL) KEY
ROUGHOMETER VIAGRAPH
ROULADE VOLATA ARPEGGIO
ROULETTE FILET FILLET TROCHOID
(HIGH — NUMBERS) PASSE
(TYPE OF —) RUSSIAN
(1-18 IN —) MANQUE
(13-24 IN —) MILIEU
ROUNCEVAL GIANT LARGE MONSTER GIGANTIC
ROUND BALL BEAT BEND BOLD BOUT FAST FULL GIRO HEAD RICH ROON ROTA TOUR TRIM WALK ABOUT AMPLE BEADY BRISK CATCH DANCE GLOBE HAMBO HARSH LARGE MOONY ORBED PLAIN ROMAN RONDO SPOKE TROLL TUBBY CIRCLE COURSE ENTIRE MELLOW NEARLY ROTUND ROUNDY RUBBER RUNDLE SPHERY SPIRAL STOWER STREAK ZODIAC ANNULAR CIRCUIT SHAPELY CIRCULAR COMPLETE CROSSBAR ENCIRCLE GLOBULAR SONOROUS LABIALIZE
(— EDGES OF TIMBER) BEARD
(— END OF LOG) SNIPE
(— FREQUENTLY GONE OVER) BEAT
(— IN BOWLING) FRAME
(— IN CARDS) GRAND
(— IN ROLLER DERBY) JAM
(— OF ACTIVITIES) SWING
(— OF APPLAUSE) HAND JOLLY SALVO PLAUDIT
(— OF CHAIR) BALUSTER
(— OFF) TOP CROWN FILLET
(— OF KNITTING) BOUT
(— OF LADDER) STAVE
(— OF PLAY) LAP
(— OUT) ORB BELLY INTEGRATE
(— UP) CORRAL WRANGLE SCROUNGE

(FINAL FOUR —S) SEMIS
(PENULTIMATE —) SEMI
(PLUMP AND —) CHUBBY
(SWEDISH —) HAMBO
(TRIAL —) HEAT
(PREF.) GLOBI GLOBO PERI
ROTUNDI ROTUNDO TROCH(I)(LEI)
(O) VENTR(I)(O)
ROUNDABOUT PLUMP DETOUR
ROTARY CURVING DEVIOUS
CAROUSEL CIRCULAR INDIRECT
TORTUOUS AMBAGIOUS
(— MOVEMENT) WINDLASS
ROUNDED FULL BOMBE BOWLY
CONVEX MELLOW ROTUND
TERETE WHELKY ARRONDI
BUNTING COMPASS CONCAVE
GIBBOUS SCUTATE SHAPELY
COMPLETE FINISHED HOOPLIKE
SONOROUS
(— OUT) PLUM
(PREF.) TERETI
ROUNDEL HEURT PLATE POMME
PELLET FOUNTAIN
(— AZURE) HURT
(— GULES) TORTEAU TORTEAUX
(— OR) BEZANT BYZANT
(— PURPURE) GOLP GOLPE
(— SABLE) GUNSTONE
(— SANGUINE) GUZE
(— VERT) POMEY
ROUNDER SOAKER WASTREL
INFORMER
ROUNDERS TUT PATBALL TUTBALL
ROUNDHEAD SWEDE CROPPY
WEAKFISH
ROUND HERRING SHADINE
STRADINE
ROUNDHOUSE BARN POOP
LOCKUP
ROUND-MOUTH HAG HAGFISH
ROUNDNESS ROTUND SPHERICITY
(— OF RIBS) SPRING
ROUND POMPANO PERMIT
PALOMETA
ROUND ROBIN ANGLER SERIES
PANCAKE SEQUENCE
ROUNDSMAN VANMAN
SWINGMAN WATCHMAN
ROUNDUP RODEO CAMBER
GATHER MUSTER
ROUNDWORM NEMA ASCARID
EELWORM GORDIAN HELMINTH
NEMATODE STRONGYL
ROUP ROLP ROOP CROAK CLAMOR
AUCTION SHOUTING
ROUSE DAW GIG HOP JOG BAIT
BEET CALL DRAW FIRK GOAD
MOVE RANT RAVE STIR WAKE
WHET AMOVE ERECT MOUNT
RAISE START STEER UPSET WAKEN
ABRADE ABRAID AROUSE BESTIR
EXCITE FOMENT KINDLE NETTLE
RATTLE REVIVE RUFFLE WECCHE
AGITATE ANIMATE DISTURB
EKPHORE ENLIVEN HEARTEN
INFLAME STARTLE INSPIRIT
IRRITATE
(— TO ACTION) HIE ALARM
ALARUM BESTIR ALACRIFY
ROUSING LIVELY AWAKENING
INCITATION
(— OF GAME) BEATING

ROUSTABOUT LADER FLOORMAN
RAZORBACK
ROUT MOB MOW DRUM FUSS HERD
BRANT CHASE COHUE CROWD
EJECT FLOCK LURCH PASTE
SMEAR SMITE SNORE CLAMOR
DEFEAT FLIGHT NUMBER RABBLE
SOIREE THRONG UPROAR
CONFUSE CONQUER DEBACLE
SCATTER SHELLAC SPARPLE
TEMPEST ASSEMBLY CONFOUND
DISTRESS VANQUISH
(BACCHIC —) THIASUS
ROUTE WAY BELT GATE GEST LINE
PASS PATH SEND TRACE TRACK
AIRWAY CAREER COURSE CUTOFF
SKYWAY TRAJET CHANNEL
CIRCUIT LANDWAY PASSAGE
SHUTTLE CORRIDOR DISTANCE
LIFELINE SHORTCUT TRAVERSE
(— MARKED OUT) ITER
(— TO DEFEAT) SKIDS
(CIRCUITOUS —) DETOUR
(MIGRATION —) FLYWAY
(OCEAN —) LANE
(OVERLAND —) LANDBRIDGE
(PREF.) ODO
ROUTH PLENTY ABUNDANT
ROUTINE RUT RIFF ROTA DRILL
GRIND HEIGH HOHUM ROUND
ROUTE SHTIK TROLL GROOVE
SCHTIK SHTICK HARNESS SCHTICK
EVERYDAY ORDINARY
(— LABOR) SCUTWORK
(COMPUTER —) BOOTSTRAP
(DOMESTIC —) HOMELIFE
(ENTERTAINMENT —) SHTICK
(SHOW BIZ —) SCHTICK
(THEATRICAL —) SCHTICK
(WEARISOME —) TREADMILL
ROVE RUN RAKL HAVE ROAM
GUESS KNOCK RANGE ROWAN
SCOUR SPACE STRAY FORAGE
MARAUD RAMBLE STROLL
WANDER SPATIATE STRAGGLE
TRANSCUR
(— ON THE WING) FLIT
ROVER FLIRT HOYLE STAKE STRAY
MASHER RANGER VIKING GANGREL
SCUMMER MARAUDER SLIVERER
TRAVELER WANDERER
COLORADAN
ROVING END SLUB NOMAD VAGUE
ARRANT ERRANT DEVIOUS
NOMADIC RAMPLER VAGRANT
GADABOUT RAMBLING RESTLESS
SLUBBING VAGABOND MIGRATORY
RANTIPOLE
(— IN SEARCH OF KNIGHTLY
ADVENTURE) ERRANTRY
ROW LAY OAR RIG SET DUST FILE
LINE MUSS PULL RANK RULE TIER
ALLEY BRAWL CHESS FIGHT
MOUTH NOISE ORDER RAMMY
RANGE RINGE SCOLD SCRAP
SCULL SWATH TRAIN BARNEY
BERATE COURSE DUSTUP GARRAY
KICKUP LISSOM PADDLE POTHER
RACKET RUCKUS RUMPUS SHINDY
STREET STROKE BOBBERY
BRULYIE QUARREL RUCTION
SHINDIG CATEGORY OUTBURST
REMIGATE SQUABBLE

(— BACKWARD) STERN
(— OF ARCHES) ARCADE
(— OF BENCHES) STACK
(— OF BUSHES) HEDGE
(— OF CASKS) LONGER
(— OF CORN, BARLEY, ETC.) RIG
(— OF DRY HAY) STADDLE
(— OF GRAIN) SWATH SWATHE
(— OF GRASS) HACK SWATH
(— OF GUNS) TIRE
(— OF HOUSES) CRESCENT
(— OF LAMPS) BATTEN
(— OF SEATS) BARRERA
(— OF SEED) DRILL
(— OF STAKES) ORGUE
(— OF STAMPS) STRIP
(— OF STONES) CORDON
(— OF TREES) SCREEN ESPALIER
(— OF VEGETABLES) RINGE
(—S OF BALCONY) MEZZANINE
(DISORDERLY —) RAG
(DOUBLE — OF TREES) AVENUE
(SHORT —) SPRINT
(PL.) EPEIRA
(PREF.) STICHO
(SUFF.) STICH(OUS)
ROWAN ASH RAN RED RODDIN
ROWAN TREE CARE SORB WICKY
WITCH RODDEN RODDIN WICKEN
WIGGEN QUICKEN RANTREE
WHITTEN WITCHEN ROUNTREE
ROWBOAT GIG OAR BARK OARS
PLAT BARIS COBLE DINGY FUNNY
KOBIL SCULL SKIFF BARQUE
CAIQUE DINGHY LURKER WHERRY
SCULLER
(— SEAT) TAFT
(CLINKER-BUILT —) FUNNY
(FLAT-BOTTOMED —) DORY
(PART OF —) RING SEAT STEM
SOCKET THWART GUNWALE
OARLOCK PAINTER ROWLOCK
TRANSOM
(SMALL —) COG
ROWDY TOU BHOY CASH MONEY
RORTY ROUGH TOUGH TOMBOY
UNRULY VULGAR HOODLUM
RAFFISH BARRATER LARRIKIN
STUBBORN ROUGHNECK
ROWDYISM YAHOOISM
ROWEN EDGROW RAWING
AFTERMATH ROUGHINGS
ROWENA (FATHER OF —) HENGIST
(GUARDIAN OF —) CEDRIC
(HUSBAND OF —) IVANHOE
VORTIGERN
ROWER URGER GALIOT STROKE
OARSMAN STERNMAN CAIQUEJEE
(— ON UPPER SEATS) THRANITE
(OUTERMOST —) THALAMITE
(SECOND LEVEL —) ZYGITE
ROWING CREW
(— EQUIPMENT) OARAGE
ROWLOCK LOCK CRUTCH OARLOCK
RULLOCK
ROXANA (FATHER OF —) OXYARTES
(HUSBAND OF —) ALEXANDER
ROYAL EASY REAL RIAL ELITE
REGAL SMALT AUGUST KINGLY
REGIUS SOVRAN SUPERB BASILIC
GLORIOUS IMPERIAL IMPOSING
MAJESTIC PAVILION PRINCELY
(— MACE) SCEPTER SCEPTRE

ROYAL ANTELOPE MADOQUA
KLEENEBOC
ROYAL FERN OSMOND OSMUND
ROYALIST TORY ULTRA REGIAN
TANTIVY CAVALIER MUSCADIN
(PL.) CHOUANS
ROYALLY PURPLEY
ROYAL PALM COYAL
ROYALTY LOT ALII GALE BONUS
CROWN REGAL REALTY MAJESTY
PENALTY LORDSHIP NOBILITY
REGALITY
ROYET WILD HARSH UNRULY
ROMPING
RUB DUB BARK BILL FILE FRAY FRET
FRIG FROT RISP SHAB WIPE CHAFE
DIGHT FEEZE FRUSH GRATE GRAZE
GRIDE LABOR SCOUR SCRUB
SMEAR STONE FRIDGE RUBBER
STREAK BEESWAX FRICACE
FURBISH MASSAGE
(— AS ANIMALS) SHAB
(— AS A ROPE) SNUG
(— AWAY) ERODE ABRADE
(— BOOT) BONE
(— DOWN) WIPE STRAP
(— ELBOWS) JOSTLE JUSTLE
(— GENTLY) STRIKE STROKE
(— HARD) SCOUR SCRUB
(— HARSHLY) GRIND
(— IN) HARPON
(— LIGHTLY) GRAZE
(— OFF) CROCK ABRADE ABRASE
(— OUT) ERASE EFFACE EXPUNGE
(— ROUGHLY) GRATE
(— SNUFF) DIP
(— THE SKIN OFF) SHAW
(— TOGETHER) FIDDLE
(— VELVET FROM ANTLERS)
BURNISH
(— WITH GREASE) DUB
(— WITH NOSE) NOUSLE NUZZLE
(— WITH OIL) ANOINT
(PREF.) TRIBO
(SUFF.) TRIBE TRIPSIS
RUBABOO SOUP
RUBBED TERSE
RUBBER BUNA FOAM PARA BUTYL
CREPE RASER ALASKA CAUCHO
DAPICO ERASER NIGGER RUNNER
BISCUIT BURUCHA EBONITE
ELASTIC GUAYULE RAMBONG
BORRACHA FRICTION NEOPRENE
SERNAMBY SERWAMBY
SOVPRENE
(— CITY) AKRON
(HARD —) EBONITE
(RECLAIMED —) SHODDY
(PL.) SHAB
RUBBERIZE FRICTION
RUBBERNECK GAPE CRANE STARE
TOURIST SIGHTSEE
RUBBER TREE ULE MILKER
RAMBONG
RUBBING CHAFE CARESS
ABRASION FRICTION FROTTAGE
FRICATION
(SUFF.) TRIPSIS
RUBBISH KET BUNK CRAB CRAP
FLAM FLUM GEAR GWAG MULL
MUSH PELF PELT PUNK RAFF ROSS
TOSH TRAG BILGE BRASH BROCK
CRAWM CULCH OFFAL SCOWL

SLUSH STENT STUFF TRADE TRASH
TRIPE TRUCK WASTE COLDER
DEBRIS GARBLE KELTER LITTER
PALTRY PIFFLE RAFFLE RAMMEL
REFUSE RUBBLE SCULCH SHRUFF
SPILTH BAGGAGE BEGGARY
FLANNEL MULLOCK RUMMAGE
SLITHER TAFFIKE TRAFFIC
FIRETRAP NONSENSE RIFFRAFF
TRASHERY TRUMPERY
CLAMJAMFRY CLAMJAMPHRIE
(VEGETABLE —) WRACK
RUBBISHY POUCY PALTRY TRASHY
BAGGAGE RUMMAGY
RUBBLE BRASH STENT TALUS
RAMMEL BACKING MOELLON
SLITHER
RUBE JAY BOOR HICK JAKE YAHOO
JASPER BUMPKIN BUSHMAN
HAYSEED CORNBALL
RUBELLA ROTELN
RUBELLITE SIBERITE
RUBICUND RED ROSY RUDDY
FLORID FLUSHED
RUBIGINOUS RUSTY
RUBIK ERNO
RUBLE RO RUBLIS
(ONE-HALF —) POLTINIK
RUBRIC RED NAME CANON CLASS
TITLE CONCEPT CATEGORY
RUBRICATE MINIATE
RUBY AGATE BALAS RUBIN PYROPE
ANTHRAX SPARKLE VERMEIL
RUBY SPINEL BALAS ALMANDINE
RUCHING COQUILLE
RUCK RUT HEAP PILE RICK SLEW
CROWD SQUAT STACK TRASH
CREASE FURROW HUDDLE
PUCKER RUBBISH WRINKLE
RUCKUS ADO ROW FIGHT FRACAS
ROOKUS
RUCTION HURRY RUCKUS QUARREL
RUPTION FRACTION
RUDABAH (FATHER OF —) MIHRAB
(HUSBAND OF —) ZAL
(SON OF —) RUSTAM
RUDD REDEYE
RUDDER HELM STEER STERN
TIMON HELLIM RUTHER STEERER
STEERAGE GOVERNAIL
(— BACK) TALON
(— EDGE) BEARDING
(— OF WINDMILL) TAIL
(DIVING —) HYDROVANE
(PART OF —) STOCK
RUDDERFISH CHOPA OPALEYE
RUDDINESS RUBEDITY
RUDDLE RED BOLE KEEL SMIT
ROUGE
RUDDY RED RODE RUDE FRESH
VIVID BLOWSY BLOWZY FLORID
LIVELY GLOWING RUDDISH
BLUSHFUL RUBICUND SANGUINE
(NOT —) PALE
RUDDY DUCK ROOK BOOBY
NODDY PADDY SPRIG BOBBER
DUNBIRD GREASER PINTAIL
SLEEPER SPATTER BLUEBILL
BULLNECK HARDHEAD WIRETAIL
RUDE ILL RAW BOLD IRON LEWD
WILD BLUFF BLUNT CRUDE GREEN
GROSS PLUMP ROUGH STOUR
SURLY UNORN ABRUPT BITTER

BORREL BRASSY CALLOW CHUFFY
CLUMSY COARSE DUDGEN GOTHIC
HOMELY HOYDEN INCULT RIBALD
ROBUST RUGGED RUSTIC SAVAGE
SHAGGY SIMPLE STORMY UNFEEL
UPLAND VULGAR ABUSIVE
ARTLESS BOORISH CARLAGE
CARLISH INCIVIL LOUTISH
LOWBRED NATURAL UNCOUTH
UNHENDE CHURLISH CLUBBISH
HOMESPUN IMPOLITE INSOLENT
MECHANIC PETULANT PORTERLY
STUBBORN SYLVATIC TACTLESS
UNGENTLE UNPOLITE YOKELISH
GRACELESS TASTELESS
(— AND BOLD) HOIDEN HOYDEN
(NOT —) MANNERLY
RUDENESS GAFF
RUDIMENT GERM ANLAGE VESTIGE
BEGINNING PRIMORDIUM
(FIRST —) PRIMORDIUM
(PL.) ABC ALPHABET ELEMENTS
GRAMMATES
RUDIMENTARY BASIC GERMING
ABORTIVE INCHOATE ABECEDARY
ELEMENTAL EMBRYONIC
PRIMITIVE ABECEDARIAN
(MOST —) FIRST
(PREF.) LYO PRO
RUE RU REWE MOURN CATGUT
REGRET REPENT SORROW
BORONIA HARMALA TENTWORT
RUEFUL SAD RUELY WOEFUL
DOLEFUL PITIABLE
RUFF SET APEX FURY PAPE POPE
CREST PRIDE REEVE TEASE TEAZE
TRUMP COLLAR FRAISE RABATO
RUFFLE TIPPET ZENITH ELATION
PARTLET PASSION QUELLIO
REBATER ROTONDE PICKADIL
(FEMALE —) REE
RUFFED BUSTARD HOUBARA
RUFFED LEMUR VARI
RUFFIAN MUN LAMB PIMP PUNK
THUG TORY BRAVO BULLY DEVIL
ROUGH ROWDY TIGER TOUGH
APACHE BRUTAL COARSE CUTTER
CUTTLE MOHAWK MOHOCK
NICKER PANDER TOWSER
HOODLUM SWEATER TUMBLER
HACKSTER HOOLIGAN
RUFFLE VEX BAIT FRET HOOP ROOL
RUFF STIR BULLY CRISP FRILL
GRAZE JABOT PLEAT ROUGH
ROUSE SHIRR ABRADE ATTACK
GATHER NETTLE PEPLUM RIPPLE
BLUSTER BRISTLE DERANGE
FLOUNCE FLUTTER PANUELO
STIFFEN SWAGGER TROUBLE
DISHEVEL DISORDER DISTRACT
FURBELOW IRRITATE QUILLING
SKIRMISH
(— THE TEMPER) ROIL
RUFFLED ROUGH UNKEMPT
**RUFFLING — (ON THE SURFACE OF
WATER)** HORROR
RUFUS (FATHER OF —) SIMON
RUG MAT RYA TUG BAKU COZY
HAUL MAUD PULL SNUG TEAR
WRAP BIJAR HERAT HEREZ HERIZ
JURUK KAZAK KHILA KONIA KULAH
KUMEH LADIK MECCA MELAS
MOSUL NAMDA SENNA SISAL

TEKKE TUZLA USHAK YURUK
ZOFRA AFSHAR BALUCH KANARA
KAROSS KASHAN KIRMAN
MOGHAN NAMMAD PERGAM
RUNNER SHIRAZ SMYRNA TABRIZ
TILPAH TOUPEE WILTON BALUCHI
BERGAMA BOKHARA BUFFALO
DERBEND DRUGGET FERRAHAN
GIORDES GOREVAN HAMADAN
ISPAHAN SHEERAZ SHIRVAN
YARKAND AUBUSSON DOMESTIC
FOOTPACE PANDERMA SARABAND
SEDJADEH SERABEND WOLFSKIN
(— FOR SADDLE) PILCH
(— OF SKINS) KAROSS WOLFSKIN
(GREEK —) FLOKATI
(KIND OF —) AREA SHAG NAVAJO
BRAIDED
(PERSIAN —) HEREZ
(PLAID —) MAUD
(PRAYER —) MELAS MELES
GHIORDES NAMAZLIK
(REVERSIBLE —) KILIM
(SCANDINAVIAN —) RYA
(SMALL —) MAT
RUGA FOLD CREASE WRINKLE
RUGBY FOOTER RUGGER FOOTBALL
(— PLAY) SCRUM
RUGGED RUDE WILD HAIRY HARDY
ROUGH STIFF COARSE CRAGGY
HORRID JAGGED KNAGGY KNOTTY
ROBUST SAVAGE STRONG STURDY
UNEVEN CRABBED GNARLED
OBDURATE SCRAGGED VIGOROUS
RUGGIERO (GUARDIAN OF —)
ATLANTE
(SISTER OF —) MARFISA
(SLAYER OF —) TISAPHERNES
(WIFE OF —) BRADAMANTE
RUIN DO MAR POT BANE BANG
COOK CRAB DAMN DASH DISH
DOOM FALL FATE FELL HELL JACK
KILL LOSS RASE RAZE SINK TALA
BLAST BOTCH BREAK CRUSH
DECAY EXILE GUBAT HUACA LEESE
LEISS SHEND SHOOT SMASH
SPEED SPILL SPLIT SPOIL SWAMP
TRASH WRACK WRAKE WRECK
BANJAX BEDASH BLIGHT CANCEL
COOPER DAMAGE DEFACE DEFEAT
DIDDLE DISMAY FOREDO INJURY
JIGGER MANGLE RAVAGE UNMAKE
BOWWOWS CORRUPT DESTROY
FLATTEN FORLESE FORWORK
LEESING PERVERT SCUPPER
SHATTER SUBVERT TORPEDO
UNDOING BANKRUPT COLLAPSE
DEMOLISH DESOLATE DISASTER
DOWNFALL
(— AT GAMBLING) SHRUB
(SPIRITUAL —) FALL
(PL.) ASHES DEBRIS RELICS
RUDERA ZIMBABWE
RUINATION DOGS
RUINED FLAT GONE LORN BROKE
KAPUT BROKEN FALLEN NAUGHT
NOUGHT FORLORN BANKRUPT
DESOLATE
RUINER MARPLOT
RUINOUS DEADLY BANEFUL
DECAYED SHENDFUL WASTEFUL
CUTTHROAT
RULE LAW MAN RAJ WIN DASH KING

NORM SWAY WALD WARD YARD
AXIOM CANON GUIDE JUDGE
MAXIM NORMA ORDER POWER
REGLE REIGN RICHE RIGHT RULER
SPILE STAFF SUTRA SUTTA WIELD
ALIDAD CUTOFF DECIDE DECREE
DITION DOMINE EMPIRE ENTAIL
GNOMON GOVERN MANAGE
MASTER METHOD REGNUM
REGULA SQUARE VASSAL
BROCARD COMMAND CONTROL
COUNSEL DICTATE DIETARY
FORMULA PLUMMET PRECEPT
PRESIDE REGENCY REGIMEN
THEOREM DICTAMEN DOCTRINE
DOMINATE FUNCTION LEGALISM
MODERATE ORDINARY OVERLEAD
PERSUADE REGIMENT REGNANCY
STANDARD TYRANNIS
OBSERVANCE
(— BY UPSTARTS) NEOCRACY
(— OUT) EXCLUDE
(—S OF CONDUCT) ETIQUETTE
(—S OF DUELING) DUELLO
(— TYRANNICALLY) HORSE
(ABSOLUTE —) EMPERY AUTARCHY
(MOB —) OCHLOCRACY
(OPPOSING —) ANTINOMY
(PREF.) ARCH(AE)(AEO)(E)(EO)(I)
RULER (ALSO SEE CHIEF, TITLE,
LEADER) DEY GOG JAM MIN OBA
AMIR CZAR DAME DUKE EMIR INCA
KING LORD OBBA RULE TSAR TZAR
ALDER AMEER DECAN EMEER
HAKIM MPRET MWAMI NAGID
NAWAB SCALE SOPHI STEER
SUBAH ZUPAN APHETA ARCHON
AUTHOR CAESAR DESPOT DUARCH
DYNAST EPARCH FERULE GERENT
HERSIR ISWARA KABAKA KAISER
MASTER NIMROD PATESI PENLOP
RECTOR REGENT SATRAP
SAWBWA SHERIF SOLDAN SUFFEE
SULTAN TYRANT ADMIRAL
ALIDADE BOURBON DEMARCH
FAIPULE ISHVARA KHEDIVE
MONARCH MOMAER PTOLEMY
RECTRIX REGULUS REIGNER
TOPARCH TRIARCH WIELDER
AUGUSTUS BASILEUS DRIGHTEN
EXILARCH GOVERNOR HEPTARCH
INTERREX OLIGARCH OVERLORD
PADISHAH PENTARCH PHYLARCH
REGINALD TARAFDAR WHIPKING
(— IN A NATIVITY) APHETA
(— OF ENCLOSURE) HENRY
(— OF UNIVERSE) PANTOCRATOR
(ALBANIAN —) MPRET
(CHIEF —) PADISHAH
(CURVED —) SWEEP
(DEIFIED —) THEOCRAT
(ELF —) AUBREY
(INCA —) CURACA
(INDIAN —) NIZAM MAHARAJA
MAHARAJAH
(JAPANESE —) SHOGUN
(JEWISH —) EXILARCH
(MONGOLIAN —) HUTUKTU
(MOSLEM —) SOLDAN
(NAME MEANING —) INCA
(STRONG —) REGINALD
(SUPREME —) SUZERAIN
(TATAR OR MOGUL —) CHAM

(WHITE —S) SERKALI
(PREF.) ARCH(AE)(AEO)(E)(EO)(I)
(SUFF.) ARCHIC ARCHY
RULING CALL CHIEF REGENT
SOVRAN CURRENT HOLDING
REGITIVE HEGEMONIC
RUM ODD ROME OCUBY QUEER
RUMBO TAFIA TAFFIA BACARDI
CACHACA JAMAICA PECULIAR
SWITCHEL EXCELLENT
RUMBLE CROWL DICKY GROWL
MELEE RUMOR SNORE BUMBLE
HOTTER HUMBLE LUMBER
WAMBLE GRUMBLE QUARREL
(— AS A GANG) BOP
RUMBLER VOLCANO
RUMBO RUM GROG LIQUOR
RUMEN CUD PAUNCH STOMACH
RUMINANT OX COW YAK BULL
DEER GOAT CAMEL LLAMA
MOOSE SHEEP STEER TAKIN
ALPACA MAZAME VICUNA GIRAFFE
QUIDDER ANTELOPE TUBICORN
(SUFF.) MERYX
RUMINATE CHAW CHEW MULL
MUSE PONDER CONCOCT REFLECT
SAUNTER CONSIDER
RUMINATION MERYCISM
RUMKIN RUMMER
RUMMAGE COMB GRUB POKE
ROOT ROUT SEEK BUSTLE FORAGE
POWTER TOUSLE UPROAR
FOSSICK RANSACK ROMMACK
DISORDER SKIRMISH UPHEAVAL
(— ABOUT FOR A PROFIT) FOSSICK
(— SALE) JUMBLE
RUMMY GIN RUM TUNK QUEER
CANASTA COONCAN DRUNKARD
OKLAHOMA
RUMOR CRY SAW BUZZ FAMA FAME
TALK WORD BRUIT MUDGE NOISE
SOUGH SOUND STORY VOGUE
GOSSIP MURMUR POTGUN
VOICE BREEZE CANARD FURPHY
RENOWN REPORT RUMBLE
CLATTER HEARING HEARSAY
INKLING OPINION WHISPER
NORATION GRAPEVINE
SCUTTLEBUTT
(SCANDALOUS —S) GOSSIP
RUMORED AFLOAT
RUMP ASS FUD ARSE BEAM CULE
DOCK DOUP DUFF CROUP NACHE
NATCH PODEX STERN BOTTOM
CURPIN CROUPON CRUPPER
HURDIES KEISTER PLUNDER
BANKRUPT BUTTOCKS DERRIERE
(— OF BIRD) UROPYGIUM
(— OF HORSE) CROUP CROUPE
(PREF.) PYG(O)
(SUFF.) PYGAL PYGE PYGIA(N)
PYGOUS PYGUS
RUMPF CORE
RUMPLE FOLD MUSS WISP TOUSE
TOWSE MOUSLE ROMBLE
CRUMPLE SCRUNCH WRINKLE
RUMPUS RAG ROW BRAWL SHINE
CLAMOR FRACAS HUBBUB
RUCKUS SHINDY TOWROW
UPROAR BAGARRE BOBBERY
ROOKERY RUCTION ROWDYDOW
RUMSHOP BAR SALOON TAVERN
BARROOM TAPROOM DRUNKERY

RUN GO BYE ERN FLY FOG GAD HOP
JOG LAM LEG PLY RIN RUB URN
BUNK CALL FLEE FLOW FUSE HARE
HEAT HEEL HUNT IRNE KITE LEAD
LEAP MELT PASS PLAY RACE RAKE
RINN ROAM ROVE SCUD TEND
TRIG TRIP TROT TURN WALK WEEP
WORK ASSAY BLEND BREAK
BRUSH CHASE COAST EXTRA
GOING HURRY NOTCH POINT
SCOUP SPEED SPEND STAND
TABLE TRACE BICKER CAREER
COURSE ELAPSE ESCAPE EXTEND
GALLOP HASTEN LADDER MANAGE
RESORT ROTATE SPRENT SPRINT
STREAM TUMBLE VOLATA
ACCURRE CONDUCT CONTAIN
FLUTTER LIQUEFY OPERATE
PASSAGE RETREAT SCUTTER
SKELTER STRETCH FUNCTION
TRANSCUR
(— ABOUT) TIG FISK DISCURRE
(— ACROSS) STRIKE
(— AGAINST) JOSTLE
(— AGROUND) BEACH GRAVEL
HURTLE STRAND STRIKE
(— ALONG EDGE OF) SKIRT
(— AS DYE) BLEED
(— AS STOCKING) LADDER
(— AT HIGH SPEED) SCORCH
(— AT THE NOSE) SNIVEL
(— AT TOP SPEED) SPRINT
(— AWAY) FLY GUY FLEE HIKE JINK
JUMP SMUG ELOPE SCRAM SMOKE
DECAMP SCAMPER SCARPER
FUGITATE SKEDADDLE
(— AWAY FROM DEBTS) LEVANT
(— AWAY IN PANIC) STAMPEDE
(— BEFORE A GALE) SCUD
(— BEFORE A JUMP) FEAZE FEEZE
(— BETWEEN) INTERCUR
(— BLINDLY) SKITTLE
(— CLUMSILY) LOPPET TUMBLE
(— COUNTER) BELY BELIE CROSS
(— DOWN) SLUR TRASH OVERRUN
(— HARD) DIG
(— HIGH) FLOOD
(— IN CRICKET) BYE WIDE EXTRA
NOTCH
(— IN DROPS) WEEP
(— IN PLACE) IDLE
(— INTO) MEET INCUR
(— ITS COURSE) LAPSE
(— NAKED) STREAK
(— OBLIQUELY) SQUINT
(— OF CLAPBOARDING) STRAKE
(— OFF) BOLT FLEE SCADDLE
(— OF MULE CARRIAGE) DRAW
(— OF SHAD) SPURT
(— OF STAIRS) GOING
(— ON SKIS) SCHUSS
(— OUT) EXCUR ISSUE PETER
ELAPSE EXPIRE
(— OVER) HEAT TRAMP OVERFLOW
(— RAPIDLY) KITE RAKE SCUR
SCOUR SKIRR SPLIT CAREER
(— SHORT) STRAITEN
(— SOAP) FRAME
(— SPEEDILY) CHASE CAREER
(— SWIFTLY) HARE LEAP SCUD
CHEVY CHIVY
(— THE SHOW) EMCEE
(— THROUGH) PIERCE DISCURRE

(— TO) ACCURRE
(— TO EXERCISE HORSE) HEAT
(— TOGETHER) HERD MUDDY
CLUTTER
(— TRAINS) BLOCK
(— WILD) GAD ESCAPE STARTLE
(— WILDLY) STARTLE
**(— WITH AFFECTED
PRECIPITATION)** SCUTTLE
(— WITH SKIPS) SCOUP
(— WITH VELOCITY) DART
(BRIEF —) STREAK FLUTTER
(COMMON —) RUCK
(END —) SWEEP
(GLASS FURNACE —) BLAST
(HOME —) DINGER
(MUSICAL —) TIRADE ARPEGGIO
(OBSTACLE —) GYMKHANA
(RAPID MUSICAL —) TIRADE
VOLATA
(SAILING —) STRETCH
(SHEEP —) SLAIT STATION
(SHORT —) FAIL BICKER SCURRY
FLUTTER RAMRACE SCUTTLE
(SKI —) PISTE SCHUSS LANGLAUF
(WILD —) LAMP
(PREF.) TRECHO TREKO
RUNAGATE APOSTATE FUGITIVE
RENEGADE RUNABOUT VAGABOND
WANDERER
RUNAWAY ROMP FUGIE RUNNER
DECISIVE DESERTER FUGITIVE
RUNAGATE
(PREF.) DRAPETO
RUNDI HUTU
RUNDLE DRUM RUNG STEP ORBIT
CIRCLE SPHERE WINDLASS
RUNDLET KEG BARREL
RUN-DOWN BAD
RUNDOWN INFO CHECK RECAP
SCOOP
RUN-DOWN SEEDY
RUNDOWN REPORT
RUN-DOWN SHODDY SQUALID
RUNDOWN SUMMARY ANALYSIS
RUN-DOWN DERELICT
RUNE WEN WYN AESE WYNN
CHARM OGHAM SPELL THORN
SECRET MYSTERY
RUNG RIM GREE RIME STEP ROUND
SCALE SPELL SPOKE STAFF STAIR
STALE STAVE STEAL TREAD
WRUNG DEGREE RUNDLE STOWER
STREAK CROSSBAR TRAVERSE
(— OF CHAIR) SPELL
(— OF LADDER) RIME STEP RANGE
SPOKE STALE RONDLE STREAK
(— OF ROPE WALK) STAKE
(PL.) STILE
RUNIC ALPHABET FUTHARK
FUTHORC
RUNIC LETTER THORN
RUNLET RUSH RINDLE RUNNEL
STREAM RIVELING
RUNNEL RILL BROOK RHINE RINDLE
RUNLET POLLARD RIVULET
STREAMLET
RUNNER RUG SOW GOER POST
SCUD SHOE SKID BLADE COBIA
FLOAT LOPER MILER RACER
SABOT SCARF SKATE SLIDE SPRAY
TEDGE CURSOR HEELER JOGGER
KANARA RENNER STOLON TOUTER

CHANNEL COURIER HARRIER
NOMINEE SARMENT CURSITOR
SKIPJACK TRAILING CANDIDATE
(— FOR GRINDING STONE) MARTIN
(— WHO SETS PACE) RABBIT
(BLUE —) HARDTAIL
(BOOKMAKER'S —) SPIV
(ERRAND —) CAD GOFER GOPHER
(FLUME —) HERDER
(PAIR OF —S) SLOOP
(RACE —) SCUTTLER
(SLED —S) BOB
(SLEDGE —) SLIP
(SLEDGE —S) SLIPES
(SNOW —) SKI
RUNNING RUN CARF EASY RACE
FLUID QUICK COURSE LIVING
COURANT CURRENT CURSIVE
FLOWING HOTFOOT SCUTTER
SLIDING FUGITIVE
(— ABOUT) COURANT CURSORY
(— ACROSS) DIAGONAL
(— AT SLOW PACE) JOGGING
(— BETWEEN) INTERCURRENT
(— DOWNWARD) DEFLUENT
(— FROM SIDE TO SIDE) SALLY
(— IN) INCURRENT
(— OF SHIPS TOGETHER) ALLISION
(— OVER) OVERFLOWING
(— SIDEWAYS) LATERIGRADE
(— TOGETHER) SLUR
(— TOWARD) APPULSE
(— VERTICALLY) DOWN
(FIRST —S) HEAD
(NOT —) DEAD
(SMOOTHLY —) SWEET
(PREF.) DROM(O)
(SUFF.) DROMOUS
RUNNING GEAR MOBILE
RUN-OF-THE-MILL SOSO AVERAGE
ORDINARY
RUNT BOOR SCRAG SCRUB SLINK
STEER STUMP STUNT HEIFER
PEEWEE SCRUMP SHRIMP TITMAN
URLING BULLOCK SHARGAR
SHARGER SLINKER RECKLING
RUNTY MEAN SURLY SCRUBBY
SCRUNTY STUNTED DWARFISH
RUNWAY RUN TIP DUCT STRIP
TRAIL TARMAC SLIPWAY AIRSTRIP
DOLLYWAY
(— OF HARE) FILE
RUPEE DIB CHIP SICCA ROUPIE
(ONE-SIXTEENTH —) ANNA
(TENS OF —S) RX
(10 MILLION —S) CRORE
(100,000 —S) LAC LAKH
RUPERT'S DROP TEAR
RUPIA RUPEE ERUPTION
(HALF —) PARDO PARDAO
RUPTURE BLOW REND RENT BREAK
BURST CRACK SPLIT BREACH
DIVIDE HERNIA RHEXIS DISRUPT
RUPTION DIVISION FRACTION
FRACTURE HERNIATE
(SUFF.) RHEXIS RRHEXIS
RUPTURED BROKEN
RURAL RUSTIC BUCOLIC COUNTRY
AGRESTIC ARCADIAN LANDWARD
MOFUSSIL PASTORAL PLEASANT
PRAEDIAL VILLATIC
RUSE HOAX ROSE SHIFT STALL
TRICK WREST ARTIFICE TRICKERY

RUSH FLY FOG HIE RIP RIX RUB SAG BANG BENT BOLT CLAP DASH DUSH FALL FLAW GIRD HURL HUSH JUNK KICK LASH LEAP LUSH PASH RACE RACK RASH RESE RISH ROUT SCUD SHOT SLUR SPUR SWIP TEAR TILT WHIP WIND ADRUE CARRY CHASE CHUTE DRASH DRIVE FEEZE FLASH FLUSH FRAIL FRUSH HURRY ONSET PIPES PREEL SCOUR SEAVE SHOOT SPART SPATE SPEED SPRAT SPRIT SPROT START STAVE STORM WHIRL CHARGE DELUGE FESCUE HURTLE JUNCUS POWDER RAMACK RANDOM RAVINE STREAK THRESH THRILL ASSAULT BRATTLE BULRUSH DAILIES DEBACLE JUNCITE RAMMISH RAMRACE SKELTER SMOTHER SWITHER TANTIVY TORNADO VIRETOT WHITHER CATARACT DEERHAIR SALTWEED SPLATTER VANQUISH
(— ABROAD) FLUSH
(— AGAINST) CHARGE
(— AWAY) BOLT FLEE SCUTTLE
(— DOWN) TRACE
(— FOR WEAVING) FRAIL
(— HEADLONG) BOIL RUIN SPURN STAMPEDE
(— OF AIR) WAFT
(— OF LIQUID) HEAD FLUSH
(— OF WATER) FRESH SHOOT SPOUT SWASH
(— OF WORDS) SPATE
(— ON FOOTBALL PLAYER) BLITZ
(— ON PASSER IN FOOTBALL) BLITZ
(— OUT) SALLY
(CLUMP OF —S) RASHBUSS
(COMMON —) FLOSS
(DOWNWARD —) HURL
(FLAT —) SHALDER
(FORCEFUL —) JET
(NOISY —) SCUTTER
(ONWARD —) BIRR SURGE
(PL.) REXEN
(PREF.) JUNCI THRYONO
RUSHED HECTIC
RUSHING HURL SCUD FURIOUS HUDDLING IMPETUOUS
(— OF WIND) GUST
RUSHLIGHT SEAVE
RUSH NUT CHUFA
RUSK ZWIEBACK
RUSSELL'S VIPER DABOIA DABOYA JESSUR KATUKA

RUSSIA (SEE ALSO SPECIFIC REPUBLICS)
CAPITAL: MOSCOW
COIN: KOPEK RUBLE GRIVNA KOPECK
COLLECTIVE FARM: KOLHOZ KOLKHOZ
DISTRICT: KARELIA
FORMER NAME: USSR SOVIET MUSCOVY
FORMER REPUBLIC: UZBEK KAZAKH KIRGIZ LATVIA ARMENIA ESTONIA GEORGIA TADZHIK TURKMEN UKRAINE MOLDAVIA LITHUANIA BYELORUSSIA AZERBAIDZHAN
FORTRESS: KREMLIN

LAKE: ARAL NEVA SEGO CHANY ELTON ILMEN ONEGA BAYKAL LADOGA SELETY TAYMYR TENGIZ ZAYSAN BALKHASH
MEASURE: FUT LOF DUIM FASS LOOF STOF FOUTE KOREC LIGNE OSMIN PAJAK STOFF VEDRO VERST ARSHIN CHARKA LINIYA PALETZ SAGENE TCHAST BOTCHKA CHKALIK GARNETZ VERCHOC BOUTYLKA CHETVERT KROUSHKA
MOUNTAIN: POBEDA BELUKHA
MOUNTAIN RANGE: ALAI URAL CAUCASUS
NAME: CIS
PENINSULA: KOLA CRIMEA KARELIA KAMCHATKA
PORT: EISK ANAPA ODESSA
REPUBLIC: ARMENIA BELARUS MOLDOVA UKRAINE AZERBAIJAN KAZAKHSTAN KYRGYZSTAN TAJIKISTAN UZBEKISTAN TURKMENISTAN RUSSIANFEDERATION
RIVER: IK OB DON ILI KET NER OKA ROS TAZ TYM UFA USA AMGA AMUR KARA LENA NEVA OREL STYR SURA SVIR URAL DESNA ISTRA LOVAT MEZEN NADYM NEMAN ONEGA TEREK TOBOL VOLGA ABAKAN DONETS ENISEI IRTYSH OLEKMA DNIEPER NEMUNAS PECHORA YENISEI
SEA: ARAL AZOV KARA BLACK BAIKAL OKHOTSK
TOWN: BAKU KIEV OMSK OREL PERM RIGA GOMEL ISTRA KASAN KAZAN KYZYL MINSK PENSA PSKOV TOMSK FRUNZE IGARKA KERTCH KURGAN NIZHNI ODESSA ROSTOV SARTOV URALSK ALMAATA BATAISK DONETSK IRKUTSK IVANOVO KALININ KHARKOV RYBINSK TALLINN KOSTROMA ORENBURG SMOLENSK TAGANROG TASHKENT VLADIMIR VORONEZH YAROSLAV
VOLCANO: ALAID SHIVELUCH

RUSSIAN IVAN RUSS SLAV VELIKA MUSCOVITE
(— BRAID) SOUTACHE
(— HEMP) RINE
(— NOT ALLOWED TO EMIGRATE) REFUSNIK REFUSENIK
(— POOL) CARLINE
(LITTLE —) RUSSENE RUTHENE UKRAINIAN
RUSSIAN BANK CRAPETTE
RUSSIAN CALF FUDGE

RUSSIAN FEDERATION (ALSO SEE RUSSIA)
CAPITAL: MOSCOW
COIN: RUBLE
FORT: KREMLIN
ISLAND: KURIL SAKHALIN NOVAYAZEMLYA
LAKE: CHANY ILMEN ONEGA BAIKAL BELOYE BRATSK LADOGA PEIPUS RYBINSK TOPOZERO VYGOZERO

MOUNTAIN: ELBRUS KORYAK SREDINNY NARODNAYA
MOUNTAIN RANGE: URAL ALTAI SAYAN BAIKAL KOLYMA CHERSKY KHIBINY PUTORAN BAIKALIA BYRRANGA CAUCASUS STANOVOY BADZHALSKY DZHUGDZHUR VERKHOYANSK
PENINSULA: KOLA TAIMYR CHUKOTKA KAMCHATKA
PLAIN: KUMA KUBAN KARELIA SIBERIAN
REGION: SIBERIA
REPUBLIC: KOMI MARI TUVA SAKHA BURYAT INGUSH KALMYK UDMURT BASHKIR CHECHEN CHUVASH DAGESTAN KARELIAN MORDOVIAN TATARSTAN NORTHOSSETIAN KABARDINOBALKAR
RIVER: OB DON AMUR KAMA LENA OKA? DVINA VOLGA ANGARA IRTYSH KOLYMA USSURI DNIEPER PECHORA SUKHONA YENISEY VYCHEGDA INDIGIRKA
SEA: KARA BLACK JAPAN WHITE ARCTIC BALTIC BERING LAPTEV BARENTS CASPIAN CHUKCHI OKHOTSK PACIFIC SIBERIAN
SWAMP: VASYUGANE
TERRITORY: ALTAI PRIMORYE KRASNODAR STAVROPOL KHABAROVSK KRASNOYARSK
TOWN: UFA AZOV ORSK PERM GORKY KAZAN MOSCOW ROSTOV SAMARA SARATOV MURMANSK VERONEZH LENINGRAD VOLGOGRAD STALINGRAD CHELYABINSK NOVOSIBIRSK SVERDLOVSK SAINTPETERSBURG
VOLCANO: KLYUCHEVSKAYA

RUSSIAN OLIVE OLEASTER
RUSSIAN THISTLE SALTWORT TUMBLEWEED
RUSSIAN TURNIP RUTABAGA
RUSSIAN WOLFHOUND BORZOI
RUST CLOWN DROSS ROOST ROUST UREDO AERUGO CANKER CORRODE FERRUGO OXIDIZE
(— OF PLANTS) HEMIFORM LEPTOFORM
(KNOT OF —) TUBERCULE
RUSTAM (FATHER OF —) ZAL
(HORSE OF —) RAKSH
(MOTHER OF —) RUDAPAH
(SON OF —) SOHRAB
(WIFE OF —) TAHMINAH
RUSTIC HOB JAY PUT BOOR CARL CHAW HICK HIND JAKE JOCK RUBE RUDE BACON BUSHY CARLE CHUFF CHURL COLIN DAMON DORIC HODGE ROUGH RURAL RURIC SILLY YOKEL AGREST BORREL BUMKIN COARSE FARMER GAFFER HONEST JOBSON RUSSET SAVAGE SCOLOC SCOLOG STURDY SYLVAN UPLAND ARTLESS BOORISH BORRELL BUCOLIC BUMPKIN BUSHMAN COUNTRY DAPHNIS FIELDEN GEORGIC HAYSEED HOBNAIL HOOSIER

LANDMAN PAISANO PEASANT PLOWMAN THYRSIS WAYBACK AGRESTIC ARCADIAN BACKVELD CLOWNISH DAMOETAS GEOPONIC LANDWARD MOSSBACK CHAWBACON CLODHOPPER
(NOT —) CIVIL
(UNCOUTH —) JAKE
(YOUTHFUL —) SWAIN
(PL.) COUNTRYFOLK
RUSTLE TODO FISLE STEAL FISSLE FISTLE HIRSEL REESLE BRUSSEL BRUSTLE CRINKLE REESTLE SKITTER WHISTLE
(— OF SILK) SCROOP
(— UP) SNAVVLE
RUSTLER THIEF WADDY DUFFER WADDIE HUSTLER
RUSTLING ARUSTLE CRINKLY FROUFROU SOUGHING FRICATION SUSURROUS
RUSTY HOARY MOROSE ROOSTY SULLEN CANKERY OUTMODED
RUT RAT BRIM RACK RAIK RUCK TRACK TREAD CREASE FURROW GROOVE STRAKE SULCUS UPROAR CHANNEL OESTRUS WRINKLE
(— IN PATH) GAY
RUTABAGA BAGA SWEDE TURNIP
RUTH BABE PITY MERCY MISERY REGRET SORROW BAMBINO CRUELTY REMORSE SADNESS SYMPATHY
(HUSBAND OF —) BOAZ MAHLON
(MOTHER-IN-LAW OF —) NAOMI
(SON OF —) OBED JESSE
RUTHENIAN RUSSENE RUSSNIAK UKRAINIAN
RUTHLESS FELL GRIM CRUEL BRUTAL PITILESS CUTTHROAT
RUTILE NIGRINE SAGENITE
RUTTER PLOW DRAGOON GALLANT TROOPER
RUTTISH RANK LUSTFUL
RUY BLAS

RWANDA
CAPITAL: KIGALI
LAKE: KIVU
LANGUAGE: KIRUNDI SWAHILI
MOUNTAIN: KARISIMBI
MOUNTAIN RANGE: MITUMBA
PEOPLE: TWA HUTU TUTSI WATUSI
RIVER: KAGERA AKANYARU LUVIRONZA
TOWN: BUTARE GABIRO NYANZA GISENYI
TRIBE: BATWA BAHUTU WATUSI BATUTSI

RYA RUG
RYE RAY RIE ERAY REYE SPELT WHISKY GENTLEMAN
RYEGRASS RAY EAVER DARNEL
RYMANDRA KNIGHTIA
RYND BAIL RHIND MILRIND
RYOT RAYAT FARMER RAIYAT TENANT TILLER PEASANT
RYUKYU ISLANDS (— ISLAND GROUP) AMAMI OKINAWA SAKISHIMA
(OTHER NAME FOR —) LUCHU LOOCHO NANSEI

S

S ESS SUGAR SIERRA
SAARINEN EERO ELIEL
SABBATH SUNDAY SABAOTH
SHABBAT SHABBOS
SABER KUKRI SABRE BANCAL
BASKET TULWAR ATAGHAN
CIMETER TULWAUR YATAGAN
ACINACES SCIMITAR
SABICU JIQUE JIQUI
SABINE (BROTHER OF —) CURIACE
SABLE DWALE SAPLE OGRESS
SATURN DIAMOND ZIBELINE
(ROUNDEL —) PELLET
SABLEFISH SKIL BESHOW
COALFISH SKILFISH
SABOTAGE MASTIC DESTROY
SABRA (FATHER OF —) PTOLEMY
(HUSBAND OF —) GEORGE
(SON OF —) GUY DAVID
ALEXANDER
SABRINA (FATHER OF —) LOCRINE
(MOTHER OF —) ESTRILDIS
SABTAH (FATHER OF —) CUSH
SABTECHA (FATHER OF —) CUSH
SAC BAG GUT POD CYST SACK
ASCUS BURSA FLOAT POUCH
THECA VOLVA ACINUS AMNION
SACCUS VESICA AMPULLA
BLADDER CAPSULE CISTERN
HYGROMA UTRICLE VESICLE
BROODSAC FOLLICLE SACCULUS
SPERMARY
(SPORE —) ASCUS
(PREF.) THEC(A)(I)(O)
SACAR (FATHER OF —) OBEDEDOM
(SON OF —) AHIAM
SACCHARIN SWEET STICKY
SUGARY GLUCOSE GLUSIDE
SACCHAROSE SUCROSE
SACERDOTAL HIERATIC PRIESTLY
SACHEM SAGAMORE
SACK AX AXE BAG BED CAN COT
MAT SAC FIRE LOOT MUID POCK
POKE BAYON GOOSE HARRY
POUCH SPOIL BUDGET POCKET
RAVAGE SACKET SACQUE DISMISS
PILLAGE PLUNDER RANSACK
SACKAGE SACKBAG DESOLATE
PACKSACK PEIGNOIR
(— OF PALM LEAVES) BAYONG
(— OF WOOL) SARPLAR
(MAIL —) BUM
(PACK —) KYACK
(SAD —) BOLO JERK SCHMO
(PREF.) THYLAC(O)
SACKBUT SAMBUKE TROMBONE
SACKING SACK GUNNY CROCUS
SACKEN HESSIAN POLDAVY
SOUTAGE
SACRAMENT RITE BAPTISM
MYSTERY NAGMAAL PENANCE
SACRARIUM PISCINA
SACRED HOLY TABU HUACA PIOUS

SACRE SAINT SANCT SANTO
TABOO DIVINE SACRAL HALLOWED
HEAVENLY NUMINOUS REVEREND
SACROSANCT
(PREF.) HAGI(O) HIER(O) HIERATICO
SACR(I)(O) SEMNO
SACRED FIG PIPAL
SACRED FISH KANNUME
SACREDNESS CHURINGA SANCTITY
TJURUNGA
SACRIFICE GIVE HOST LOSS OFFER
SPEND YAJNA CORBAN FOREGO
VICTIM EXPENSE CHILIOMB
IMMOLATE KAPPARAH LITATION
OBLATION OFFERING PASSOVER
SPHAGION PROPITIATION
(— OF CARGO) JETTISON
(— OF 100 OXEN) HECATOMB
(— OF 1000 OXEN) CHILIOMB
(PL.) HAGIGAH CHAGIGAH
SACRIFICIAL PIACULAR
SACRILEGE PROFANATION
SACRILEGIOUS IMPIOUS
SACRISTAN SEXTON SACRIST
SACRISTY SEXTRY SACRARY
VERGERY PARATORY SACRARIUM
SACROSANCT SACRED
SACRUM
(SUFF.) HIERIC
SAD LOW WAN DARK DOWY DRAM
BLACK DREAR DUSKY MESTO
MOODY SABLE SOBER SORRY
WEARY YEMER DREARY SOLEMN
SULLEN TRISTE WOEFUL BALEFUL
DOLEFUL DUMPISH FORLORN
FUNEBRE LUCTUAL MOANFUL
SOBERLY UNHAPPY DEJECTED
GROANFUL MOURNFUL
MOURNING PATHETIC PITIABLE
SUBTRIST TRISTIVE UNBLITHE
DEPRESSED MELANCHOLY
(PREF.) TRISTI
SADDEN SAD DUMP CLOUD GLOOM
GRIEVE ATTRIST CONTRIST
DISTRESS
SADDENED BROKEN
SADDENING LUCTUAL
SADDLE PAD RIG SAG TAG LOAD
SUNK CHINE PANEL PILCH SELLE
STICK BURDEN HEADER RECADO
PIGSKIN PILLION
(— AND BRIDLE) TACK
(— COVER) MOCHILA
(— FOR ONE-LEGGED RIDER)
SOMERSET
(— STUFFED WITH STRAW) SODS
(— WITH) STICK
(— WORKER) LORIMER
(LIGHT —) PILCH PILLION
(MOTORCYCLE —) PILLION
(PACK —) BAT
(PART OF —) HORN RING SEAT
SKIRT CANTLE FENDER JOCKEY

POMMEL STRING BINDING LEATHER
STIRRUP
(STRAW —) SUNK SUGGAN
(WITHOUT A —) ASELLATE
(PREF.) SELLI
SADDLEBACK JACK JACKBIRD
SADDLEBAG ALFORJA CANTINA
SUMPTER TEETSOOK
(PL.) JAGS JAGGS
SADDLE BLANKET CORONA
SADDLEBOW BOW ARSON
SADDLECLOTH HOUSE NAMDA
HOUSING PADCLOTH SHABRACK
SADDLEMAKER FUSTER KNACKER
SADDLE MAT FLET
SADDLE PAD PANEL NUMNAH
PILLOW
SADDLER CODDER KNACKER
LORIMER WHITTAW
SADISM BRUTALITY
SADISTIC SICK CRUEL SADIC
BRUTAL
SADLY SAD ALAS UNWINLY
SADNESS DUMP RUTH DREAR
DUMPS GLOOM GRIEF UNWIN
SORROW DESPAIR
SAD SACK BOLO
SAFAWID SUFI
SAFE RUG CRIB PETE SURE WELL
AMBRY SALVA SIKER SOUND
SECURE SICCAR HEALTHY SYKERLY
COCKSURE SILVENDY
(— FOR MEAT) KEEP
(— TO DEAL WITH) CANNY
SAFEBLOWER PETEMAN
SAFEBREAKER YEGG YEGGMAN
PETERMAN
SAFE-CONDUCT JARK COWLE
GRITH CONDUCT NAVICERT
PASSPORT
SAFECRACKER YEGG BOXMAN
PETEMAN PETERMAN TORCHMAN
SAFEGUARD SAVE WARD GUARD
HEDGE SALVE DEFEND SAFETY
SECURE BASTION BULWARK
WARRANT FREEWARD PALLADIUM
PRECAUTION
SAFEKEEPING CUSTODY STORAGE
(IN —) ONICE
SAFELY SAFE SICCAR SICKER
SURELY SECURELY
SAFETY REFUGE SALUTE SURETY
WARRANT SECURITY
(PREF.) SOTERIO
SAFETY ZONE ISLET ISLAND
REFUGE
SAFFLOWER KUSUM ALAZOR
SAFFRON
SAFFRON CROCUS AZAFRAN
CROCEUS
(PREF.) CROCEO CROCO
SAFROLE SHIKIMOL
SAG BAG DIP TIE SWAG CREEP

DROOP PLANK SLUMP SAGGON
CURTAIN DEFLATE
SAGA EDDA EPIC MYTH TALE RIMUR
LEGEND NJALSAGA
SAGACIOUS DEEP ACUTE CANNY
SHARP ARGUTE ASTUTE SHREWD
CORDATE POLITIC PRUDENT
SAPIENT
SAGACITY POLICY WISDOM
SMEDDUM YEPHEDE PRUDENCE
SAPIENCE
SAGAMORE SACHEM
SAGE RSI WARE WISE WITE CLARY
HAKAM IMLAC KATHA RISHI SABIO
SOLON SOPHY ABARIS DHARMA
NESTOR SALVIA SAULGE SAVANT
SHREWD WIZARD EYESEED
MAHATMA SAPIENT SOPHIST
TOHUNGA WISEMAN DEVARSHI
MAHARSHI WISEACRE
SAGEBRUSH SAGE HYSSOP
SAGEWOOD ARTEMISIA
SAGENESS SAPIENCE
SAGGER COFFIN SETTER CASSETTE
SAGGING DRAG SWAG PTOSIS
SAGITTA ARROW
SAGITTARIUS ARCHER
SAGO PALM CYCAD
SAGRADA CASCARA
SAGUARO SUAHARO SUWARRO
PITAHAYA
SAHIB SRI BWANA
SAHIDIC THEBAIC
SAIBLING TORGOCH
SAID DIT QUOTH STATED RELATED
SAIL JIB LUG RAG BEAT GALE HAUL
MAIN SCUN SLAT SWAN SWIM
WING DANDY FLEET FLIER FLOAT
FLYER JUMBO RAFFE SCALE
SHEET ACCOST CANVAS COURSE
CRUISE DRIVER JIGGER LATEEN
MIZZEN MUSLIN SINGLE ARTEMON
LUGSAIL SKYSAIL SPANKER
SPENCER TRYSAIL BACKWIND
FORESAIL GAFFSAIL HEADSAIL
MAINSAIL MOONSAIL NAVIGATE
RINGTAIL STAYSAIL STUNSAIL
(— ALONG COAST) COAST ACCOST
(— AROUND) TURN DOUBLE
(— BEFORE THE WIND) SPOON
(— BRISKLY) SPANK
(— BY THE WIND) STRETCH
(— CLOSE TO WIND) PINCH
(— DOWN) AVALE AWALE
(— FASTER) FOOT
(— IN SPECIFIED DIRECTION) STAND
(— OF WINDMILL) ARM AWE EIE
FAN VAN EIGHE FLIER FLYER SWEEP
SWIFT
(— ON COURSE) HAUL WORK
(— QUIETLY) GHOST
(— RAPIDLY) SCUR SKIRR
(— SWIFTLY) RAMP

(— TO WINDWARD) THRASH
(— WITH WIND ABEAM) LASK
(FRAGMENT OF —) HULLOCK
(LIGHT —) SHADOW
(LOWEST —) COURSE
(PART OF —) CLEW FOOT HEAD
LUFF SEAM SLAB TACK LEECH
PANEL POCKET WINDOW ZIPPER
CRINGLE TABLING TELLTALE
HEADBOARD
(REDUCE —) REEF
(SMALL —) ROYAL
(TRIANGULAR —) RAFFE LATEEN
BENTINCK
(WIND —) BADGIR
(3-CORNERED —) JIB TRINKET
(PL.) VELA CLOTH KITES LINENS
SAILAGE CLOTHING
(PREF.) HISTI(O) ISTIO VELI
SAILBOARD (RIDE A —) WINDSURF
SAILBOAT CAT SAIL SCOW BULLY
DANDY NABBY SAPIT SCOUT
SHARP SKIFF SLOOP SNIPE CANGIA
DINGHY QUODDY SAILER SATTIE
CATBOAT SCOOTER SHALLOP
SHARPIE SUNFISH KEELBOAT
SAILSHIP SKIPJACK TRIMARAN
(PART OF —) JIB BOOM BUNK GATE
HEAD HELM KEEL MAST SINK SKEG
SOLE BERTH CLEAT FRAME HATCH
SALON TRUNK WHEEL WINCH
ANCHOR GALLEY JIBTOP LOCKER
PULPIT RUDDER SHROUD YANKEE
BULWARK COAMING COCKPIT
COUNTER GALLOWS PUSHPIT
TOPSAIL BACKSTAY BOWSPRIT
BULKHEAD FOREDECK FOREFOOT
FORESTAY HEADSTAY LIFELINE
MAINSAIL MASTHEAD OVERHEAD
SPREADER STAYSAIL TAFFRAIL
TRAVELER CUBBYHOLE MAINSHEET
PORTLIGHT STANCHION
STATEROOM COMPANIONWAY
(WITCH'S —) SIEVE
SAILFISH BOHO WOOHOO
GUEBUCU LONGJAW VOILIER
VOLADOR BILLFISH
SAILOR (ALSO SEE NAVAL OFFICER)
GOB TAR HAND JACK SALT SWAB
TOTY GUARD KLOSH LAKER LIMEY
CALASH CLASHY DAYMAN DECKIE
HEARTY MARINE MATLOW
SEADOG SEAMAN TARPOT TIERER
TOPMAN COLLIER MARINAL
MARINER MATELOT SHIPMAN
SWABBER WARRIOR YARDMAN
CANOTIER COXSWAIN DECKHAND
FLATFOOT GALIONJI GUNLAYER
LANDSMAN LITHSMAN MASTHEAD
SHIPMATE WATERDOG
WATERMAN WATERRUG
YARDSMAN
(— ON LEAVE) LIBERTYMAN
(CAPTIOUS —) SEALAWYER
(EAST INDIAN —) LASCAR
(INFERIOR —) GREENHAND
(OLD —) SALT SHELLBACK
(SCANDINAVIAN —) KLOSH
(TURKISH —) GALIONGEE
SAILORLIKE TARRISH
SAILOR'S-CHOICE BREAM PIGFISH
PINFISH WHITING
SAIL YARD RAE

SAINFOIN ESPARCET
SAINT PIR RSI DADU HOLY QUTB
WALI ALVAR ARHAT RISHI SANTO
BHAGAT HALLOW PATRON
SANTON CANONIZE MARABOUT
(CHINESE —) IMMORTAL
(PATRON —) AVOWRY
(PILLAR —) STYLITE
(PL.) SS
(PREF.) HAGI
SAINT ELMO'S FIRE HERMO
CASTOR FUROLE HELENA
SAINT JOAN (AUTHOR OF —) SHAW
(CHARACTER IN —) JOAN DUNOIS
ROBERT WARWICK BAUDRICOURT
ST-JOHN'S-BREAD CAROB
ST-JOHN'S-WORT AMBER TUTSAN
CAMMOCK
SAINT KITTS & NEVIS (CAPITAL:)
BASSETERRE
(ISLAND:) NEVIS SOMBRERO
SAINTCHRISTOPHER
SAINTLINESS HOLINESS SANCTITY
SAINT LUCIA (CAPITAL OF —)
CASTRIES
(MOUNTAIN OF —) GIMIE
(MOUNTAINS OF —) PITONS
CANARIES
(VOLCANO OF —) SOUFRIERE
SAINTLY DEVOUT ANGELIC SAINTED
BEATIFIC SAINTISH
(— PERSON) ZADDIK
ST REGIS RANERE
SAINT VINCENT (CAPITAL OF —)
KINGSTOWN
(PART OF —) UNION BEQUIA
GRENADINES
SAITH COALFISH
SAITHE SILLOC POLLACK SILLOCK
SAJ SAIN
SAKE SAKI SCORE ACCOUNT
(SOURCE OF —) RICE
SAKI BISA MONK COUXIA MONKEY
YARKEE
SALA (FATHER OF —) ARPHAXAD
(SON OF —) EBER
SALABLE VENAL SELLING SELLABLE
VENDIBLE
SALACIOUS LEWD SALT RUTTISH
SCARLET SCABROUS
SALAD SALLET COLESLAW
TABBOULEH SILLSALLAT
(CORN —) MACHE FETTICUS
(KIND OF —) CAESAR
(LEBANESE —) TABOULI
TABBOULEH
(TYPE OF —) TOSSED
SALADA SALINA
SALAL SHALLON
SALAMANDER EFT OLM SOW BEAR
NEWT TWEEG GOPHER LIZARD
TRITON AXOLOTL CRAWLER
CREEPER DOGFISH MECODONT
SALAMICH SHADRACH
SALAMI SAUSAGE
(KIND OF —) GENOA
SALAMMBO (AUTHOR OF —)
FLAUBERT
(CHARACTER IN —) NARR GISCO
HANNO HAVAS MATHO TAMIT
HAMILCAR SALAMMBO SPENDIUS
(COMPOSER OF —) REYER
SAL AMMONIAC SPIRIT SALMIAC

SALARY PAY HIRE SCREW WAGES
INCOME PACKET PENSION
STIPEND
SALE FAIR VENT BREAK HEDGE
TOUCH BOURSE VENDUE AUCTION
MOHATRA SELLING HANDSALE
KNOCKOUT PORTSALE
(— BY AUCTION) CANT ROUP
BLOCK VENDUE OUTROOP
(— BY OUTCRY) ROUP ROWP
HAMMER
(— OF OFFICE) BARRATRY
(— OF PERIODICAL) CIRCULATION
(— OF TOBACCO) BREAK
(— ON TRUST) CREDIT
(— TO CONSUMER) RETAIL
(PUBLIC —) AUCTION
(RUMMAGE —) JUMBLE
SALESMAN REP CLERK BAGMAN
RUNNER SELLER BOOKMAN
DRUMMER OUTRIDER PITCHMAN
(— IN FISH MARKET) BUMMAREE
SALESMANSHIP SELLING
SALESPERSON CLERK
SALESWOMAN WINSTER
SHOPGIRL VENDEUSE
SALIENT SPUR BULGE CHIEF
ARGINE BASTION SALTANT
SALIENTIA ANURA ANOURA
ECAUDATA
SALINA SHOR SALINE
SALINE SALT BRINY SALAR SALTY
MARINAL
SALIVA SPIT DROOL WATER DRIVEL
SLAVER SPUTUM SPITTLE
(— FLOW) PTYALISM
(PREF.) PTYAL(O) SIAL(O)
SALIVARY SIALIC
SALIVATION PTYALISM SLOBBERS
SALLET SALADE
SALLOW WAN SALE SICK ADUST
LURID MUDDY SALIX SAUCH
SAUGH PALLID YELLOW
SALLY GRIP JERK PASS QUIP SAIL
QUICK START ESCAPE GAMBIT
SORTIE GAMBADE OUTFALL
OUTLEAP DEMARCHE
SALM (BROTHER OF —) TUR IRAJ
(FATHER OF —) FARIDUN
(MOTHER OF —) SHAHRINAZ
(SLAYER OF —) MINUCHIHR
SALMAGUNDI OLIO SILLSALLAT
SALMON DOG LAX LOX SAM KETA
MASU PINK AMOUT COHOE COUNT
HADDO HOLIA SMOLT SMOOT
SPROD TECON ALEVIN BAGGIT
KIPPER LAUREL MYKISS SAMLET
SAUQUI SILVER TAIMEN ANADROM
ANNATTO BLUECAP BOTCHER
CHINOOK DOGFISH GILLING
GRAVLAX KAHAWAI KOKANEE
NEWFISH QUINNAT REDFISH
RUNFISH SAWMONT SHEDDER
SOCKEYE BLUEBACK BRANDLIN
GOLDFISH GRAVLAKS HUMPBACK
LASPRING SALMONID SPRINGER
OUANANICHE
(— AFTER SPAWNING) KELT BAGGIT
SHEDDER
(— BEFORE SPAWNING) GILLING
GIRLING
(— ENCLOSURE) YAIR
(— IN 2ND OR 3D YEAR) SMOLT

(— IN 2ND YEAR) SPROD HEPPER
GILLING
(— IN 3D YEAR) PUG MORT
(— ON FIRST RETURN FROM SEA)
GRILSE
(BLUEBACK —) NERKA SAUQUI
SOCKEYE
(CURED —) KIPPER GRAVLAX
GRAVLAKS
(DOG —) CHUM KETA
(FATHER OF —) NAHSHON
(FEMALE —) RAUN BAGGIT
(HUMPBACK —) HADDO HOLIA
(MALE —) GIB BUCK COCK
(MILTER —) EKE
(NEWLY HATCHED —) PINK ALEVIN
(SMALL —) PEAL SKIRLING
(SON OF —) BOAZ
(SPENT —) JUDY SLAT LIGGER
RUNFISH
(YOUNG —) FOG PARR PEAL SMOLT
GRILSE HEPPER JERKIN SAMLET
BOTCHER ESSLING SKEGGER
LASPRING SPARLING
SALMONELLOSIS KEEL
SALMONEUS (BROTHER OF —)
SISYPHUS
(DAUGHTER OF —) TYRO
(FATHER OF —) AEOLUS
(MOTHER OF —) ENARETE
(WIFE OF —) ALCIDICE
SALOME (FATHER OF —) HEROD
(HUSBAND OF —) PHILIP ZEBEDEE
ARISTOBULUS
(MOTHER OF —) HERODIAS
SALON HALL SALOON GALLERY
SALOON CAFE CUDDY DIVAN
SALON SHADE BARROOM CANTINA
RUMSHOP SCATTER DEADFALL
DRINKERY DRUNKERY EXCHANGE
BRASSERIE
(RAILWAY —) PULLMAN
SALPA SALP THALIA
SALSIFY GOATBEARD
SALT SAL TAR CORN KERN SAWT
BRINY ZIRAM AMIDOL AURATE
FOLATE GAMMON HALITE MALATE
OLEATE OSMATE POWDER SAILOR
SALIFY SALINE URANIN XENATE
KAINITE LACTATE MALEATE
NIOBATE PHYTATE TROPATE
ABIETATE BRACKISH HALINOUS
PIMELATE PLUMBITE SELENATE
(— FISH) ROIL
(— OUT) CUT GRAIN
(DOUBLE —) ALUM
(HAIR —) ALUNOGEN
(LUMP OF —) SALTCAT
(METAL —) SILICATE
(MIXTURE OF —S) REH USAR
(OLD —) SEADOG
(POISONOUS —) ARSENATE
(ROCK —) PIG HALITE
(ZINC —) ZIRAM
(PREF.) HAL(I)(O) SALI SALIN(I)(O)
(SUFF.) OATE
SALTATE JUMP
SALTATION LEAP
SALT BOILER WELLER
SALTBUSH BLUEBUSH
SALTCELLAR SALT CELLAR SELLER
SHAKER SALTFAT SALTFOOT
SALTED SALEE

SALTICID ATTID
SALT PAN PLAYA
SALTPETER NITER NITRE PETER ANATRON CALICHE PRUNELLA
SALT PIT VAT WICH WYCH
SALT PORK SOWBELLY
SALTWORKS SALINA SALTERN SALTERY SALTPANS
SALTWORT KALI BARILLA SALSOLA KELPWORT
SALTY SALT BRINY SALINE SAVORY HALINOUS
SALU (SLAYER OF —) PHINEHAS
(SON OF —) ZIMRI
SALUBRIOUS BENIGN HEALTHY SALUTARY
SALUTARY GOOD BENIGN HEALTHY HELPFUL BENEDICT
SALUTATION AVE HAIL ALOHA SALUS MIZPAH SALAAM SALUTE REGREET SLAINTE WELCOME DIEUGARD GREETING HAEREMAI
(DRINKING —) SKOAL PROSIT PROFACE WASSAIL
SALUTE CAP HAIL HEIL KISS MOVE YULE CHEER DRINK GREET HALCH HALSE HONOR SALUE SALVO COLORS SALAAM EMBRACE ACCOLADE CONGREET
(— TO DANCING PARTNER) COUPEE
(VICTORY —) VSIGN
SALVADOR BAHIA
SALVAGE SAVE SALVE RECOVERY SCROUNGE
SALVAGER SALVOR
SALVATION BODAI MOKSHA SAFETY NIRVANA KAIVALYA SAVEMENT SOULHEAL
(— APPROACH) MARGA
SALVE SAW TAR SALVO SAUVE NERVAL SUPPLE PLASTER UNGUENT OINTMENT
SALVER TRAY SERVER WAITER PLATEAU
SALVIA CHIA SAGE CLARY MEJORANA MINTWEED
SALVO SALUTE SPREAD PROVISO TRIBUTE STRADDLE
(PL.) LADDER
SAM (FATHER OF —) NARIMAN
(SON OF —) ZAL
SAMARA KEY CHAT
SAMARIA AHOLAH
SAMARITAN CUTHEAN CUTHITE
SAMBA CARIOCA
SAMBAR ELK DEER MAHA RUSA
SAME ID EAD ILK ONE IDEM LIKE MEME SELF VERY DITTO EQUAL SAMEN IDENTIC SELFSAME
(— AS) IQ
(— PLACE) IB
(MUCH THE —) ALIKE
(THAT —) THILK THICKE
(PREF.) AUT(O) AUTH(I) HOM(O)(OI) HOME(O) HOMOE IPSI ISO TAUT(O)
SAMENESS ONENESS EQUALITY IDENTITY MONOTONY
SAMLET PINK
SAMNITES SABELLI
SAMOA (CAPITAL OF —) APIA PAGOPAGO
(COIN OF —) SENE TALA
(ISLAND OF —) OFU TAU ROSE MANUA UPOLU SAVAII OLOSEGA TUTUILA
(MOUNTAIN OF —) FITO SAVAII MATAFAO
SAMOGITIAN ZHMUD
SAMOYED TUBA YURAK BELTIR KAIBAL KOIBAL NENTSI KAMASSIN
SAMPHIRE SALTWEED
SAMPLE DIP SIP CAST PREE CHECK ESSAY TASTE TRIAL CHANCE COUPON FLOWER MUSTER SWATCH TASTER EXAMPLE EXCERPT MONSTER PATTERN SAMPLER TASTING INSTANCE PULLDOWN SPECIMEN
(— OF METAL) DIET
SAMPLING SOUNDING
SAMSON (FATHER OF —) MANOAH
SAMSON ET DALILA (CHARACTER IN —) PRIEST SAMSON DELILAH
(COMPOSER OF —) SAINTSAENS
SAMUEL (FATHER OF —) ELKANAH
(MOTHER OF —) HANNAH
SAMURAI BUSHI RONIN
SAN SAMPI
SANAD SUNNUD
SANBENITO SAMARRA
SAN BLAS TULE
SAN CARLOS ARIVAIPA
SANCTIFICATION HOLINESS
SANCTIFY BLESS SACRE SACRI DEDICATE
SANCTIMONIOUS PI DEVOUT PECKSNIFFIAN
SANCTION AMEN FIAT ALLOW PIETY ASSENT BISHOP RATIFY APPROVE ENDORSE JUSTIFY PASSAGE SUPPORT ACCREDIT APPROVAL CANONIZE COURTESY SUFFRAGE
SANCTIONED CANONICAL
SANCTITY SANTY HALIDOME HOLINESS
SANCTUARY ADYT BAST BEMA FANE HOLY SOIL ABBEY ALTAR BAMAH FRITH GIRTH GRITH SECOS SEKOS TOWER ADYTON ADYTUM ASYLUM CHAPEL HAIKAL REFUGE SENTRY SHRINE SACRARY SHELTER ARCHEION CABIRION DELUBRUM HALIDOME HOLINESS SACRARIUM
(— FOR LAWBREAKERS) ALSATIA
(AUTHOR OF —) FAULKNER
(CHARACTER IN —) LEE RED VAN REBA RUBY DRAKE GOWAN LAMAR TOMMY BENBOW HORACE POPEYE RIVERS SNOPES TEMPLE GOODWIN STEVENS
SANCTUM ADYT ADYTON ADYTUM
SAND DIRT GRIT ARENA GRAIL SONDE GRAVEL ISERINE ISERITE PARTING ASBESTIC BLINDING
(— FOR STREWING ON FLOORS) BREEZE
(— HILL) DENE DUNE
(— IN KIDNEYS) ARENA
(— MIXED WITH GRAVEL) GARD DOBBIN
(— ON SEA BOTTOM) PAAR
(BRAIN —) SABULUM ACERVULUS
(COLOR —) CHIP BEACH
(COLORED —) SMALT
(DEAUVILLE —) STUCCO

(VOLCANIC —) SANTORIN
(WATERY —) QUICKSAND
(PREF.) AMM(O) ARENI PSAMM(O)
SANDAL TIP BAXA FLAT SOCK ZORI TEGUA THONG CALIGA CHARUK PATTEN TATBEB RULLION SCUFFER FOOTHOLD GUARACHE HUARACHO
(JAPANESE —) GETA
(LOOSE —) SLIPSLOP
(RED SILK —) CALCEAMENTUM
(WINGED —) TALARIA
(WINGED —S) TALARIA
SANDAL TREE SANTOL
SANDALWOOD NAIO ALGUM ALMUG MAIRE CHANDAM SAUNDERS
SANDALWOOD TREE ILIAHI
SANDARAC TREE ARAR LIGNUM
SANDBAG CONK SANDCLUB
SAND BANK AIR CHAR MEAL SAND BATCH HURST HYRST KNOCK SHELF SHOAL
SANDBAR BALK LOOP SAND BARRA SHOAL TOMBOLO TOWHEAD
SANDBLASTER FROSTER BLASTMAN
SAND BORER SMELT
SANDBOX TREE ASSACU
SAND COLIC SABURRA
SAND DARTER SPECK
SAND DUNE TOWAN BARCHAN
SAND EEL GRIG SANDFISH
SANDEMANIAN GLASSITE
SANDERLING OXBIRD
SAND FLEA SCREW SCROW SANDBOY
SAND-FLY BUSH TURMERIC
SAND GROUSE GANGA ROCKER ATTAGEN PINTAIL
SAND HOLE BUNKER
SANDIVER NATRON
SAND LAUNCE LANT SMELT WRIGGLE AMMODYTE SANDLING SCRIGGLE
SAND LILY SOAPROOT
SANDMAN DUSTMAN
SANDPAPER TREE CHAPARRO
SANDPIPER JACK KNOT PEEP RUFF STIB WEET OXEYE SNIPE STINT TEREK TIPUP WADER DUNLIN GAMBET OXBIRD PLOVER REDLEG TEETER TILTER TILTUP TRINGA BROWNIE CHOROOK CREEKER FATBIRD FIDDLER HAYBIRD KRIEKER MONGLER MONGREL REDBACK TATTLER TIPTAIL GRAYBACK LEADBACK PEETWEET REDSHANK ROCKBIRD SANDPEEP SHADBIRD SQUATTER SWEESWEE TELLTALE TRIDDLER
(FEMALE —) REEVE
(FLOCK OF —S) FLING
SAND PIT BUNKER
SAND ROCKET FLIXWEED
SAND SHARK BONEDOG
SANDSTONE FAKE FLAG GRES GRIT SAND GAIZE HAZEL ARCOSE ARKOSE DOGGER KINGLE ARENITE HASSOCK CARSTONE COCONINO GANISTER PSAMMITE RUBSTONE SANDROCK
(BLOCK OF —) SARSEN

SANDSTORM BURAN HABOOB TEBBAD
SANDUST VANITY
SANDWICH BLT SUB GYRO HERO BUTTY HOAGY BURGER HOAGIE REUBEN DAGWOOD FALAFEL FELAFEL GRINDER WESTERN
(ITALIAN —) GRINDER
(SUFF.) BURGER
SANDWORT LONGROOT SANDWEED
SANDY DEEP GINGER GRISTY SANDED ARENOSE PSAMMOUS SABULINE SABULOUS
SANDY BROWN LARK
SANE SAFE WISE LUCID RIGHT FORMAL NORMAL HEALTHY PERFECT RATIONAL SENSIBLE
SANGA-SANGA ESSANG
SANGUINARY GORY CRUEL BLOODY CRIMSON SANGUINE
SANGUINE FOND GUZE MURREY HEMATIC HOPEFUL SARDONYX
SANHEDRIN GEROUSIA
SANICLE ALLHEAL SELFHEAL
SANIOUS ICHOROUS
SANITARY HYGIENIC
SANITY SENSE REASON WISDOM BALANCE MARBLES LUCIDITY SANENESS
SAN MARINO (CHURCH OF —) PIEVE
(DISTRICTS OF —) CASTELLI
(MOUNTAIN OF —) TITANO
(SUBURB IN —) BORGO
SANNUP SQUAW
SANSKRIT HINDU
(— SOUND OR SIGN) VISARGA
(— WORK) VEDANGA
SANS SERIF DORIC GOTHIC
SANTA MARIA TREE BIRMA GALBA CALABA
SAN TOME (MONEY OF —) DOBRA
SANTONICA WORMSEED
SAO TOME AND PRINCIPE
(CAPITAL OF —) SAOTOME
(MONEY OF —) DOBRA
(NAME OF —) SAOTHOME SAINTTHOMAS
SAP MUG GOON MINE OOZE RASA SEVE DRAIN HUMBO KEEST LYMPH SAPPER WEAKEN AIRHEAD ALVELOZ FLUXURE JUGHEAD SAPHEAD
(— COURAGE) DAUNT
(— OF RUBBER TREE) LATEX
(FERMENTED PALM —) SURA
(PALM —) TODY TODDY
(POISONOUS —) UPAS
(SUGAR MAPLE —) HUMBO
SAPAJOU SAJOU WARINE
SAPANWOOD BOKOM BRAZIL SIBUCAO
SAPEK DONG
SAPID SIPID FLAVORY
SAPIENT WISE SHREWD KNOWING
SAPI-UTAN ANOA
SAPLING SCOB PLANT SAPLE SPIRE RUNNEL SPRING TILLER STADDLE ASHPLANT SEEDLING SHILLALA SPRINGER
(— AMONG FELLED TREES) WAVER
SAPODILLA GUM CHICA CHICO

DILLY ACHRAS MAMMEE SAPOTA SAPOTE ZAPOTE NISPERO NISBERRY NASEBERRY

SAPONIFYING KILLING

SAPONIN GITONIN SENEGIN CYCLAMIN STRUTHIN

SAPONITE PIOTINE

SAPOTA MATASANO

SAPPHIRE SAFIR TOPAZ ADAMAS ASTERIA ASTRION HYACINTH

SAPPHIRINE GURNARD TUB

SAPPHO (AUTHOR OF —) DAUDET
  (CHARACTER IN —) JEAN ROSA FANNY IRENE DEJOIE POTTER CAOUDAL CESAIRE FLAMANT GAUSSIN LEGRAND BOUCHEREAU DECHELETTE LAGOURNERIE

SAPPY FRIM FRUM SAPFUL

SAPSAP PEPEREK

SAPUCAIA COCO COCOA KAKARALI

SAPWOOD SAP BLEA SPLENT SPLINT GUAYABI LISTING ALBURNUM

SARA (— WOMAN) UBANGI

SARABAITES REMOBOTH

SARACEN CORSAIR

SARAH ATOSSA
  (FATHER OF —) ASHER
  (HUSBAND OF —) ABRAHAM
  (SON OF —) ISAAC

SARAKOLLE WAKORE

SARASVATI VAC VACH BENTEN

SARCASM RUB GIBE WIPE FLING IRONY TAUNT RUBBER SATIRE BROCARD RIDICULE SCORCHER

SARCASTIC ACID ACRID WITTY BITING IRONIC ACERBIC CUTTING MORDANT PUNGENT INCISIVE SARDONIC SATIRICAL ACRIMONIOUS

SARCASTICALLY DRILY DRYLY ACIDLY

SARCOCARP FLESH

SARCOPHAGUS TOMB COFFIN

SARCOPSYLLA TUNGA

SARDINE BANG LOUR SARD SILD CLUPEID PILCHARD SARDELLE

SARDINIA

CAPITAL: CAGLIARI
CHEESE: ROMANO PECORINO
COIN: CARLINE
GREEK COLONY: OLBIA
GULF: OROSEI ASINARA CAGLIARI ORISTANO
MOUNTAIN: RASU FERRY LINAS GALLURA LIMBARA SERPEDDI VITTORIA
NAME: SARDEGNA
PROVINCE: NUORO SASSARI CAGLIARI
RIVER: MANNU TIRSO LASCIA SAMASSI COGHINAS FLUMENDOSA
STRAIT: BONIFACIO
TOWN: IERZU NUORO SASSARI THATARI CAGLIARI CARBONIA IGLESIAS

SARDONIC SARCASTIC

SARGASSUM GULFWEED

SARGO ZEBRA

SARI PATOLA TAMEIN

SAROD LUTE

SARONG PAU KAIN COMBOY KIKEPA TAMEIN

SARPEDON (BROTHER OF —) MINOS RHADAMANTHUS
  (FATHER OF —) ZEUS JUPITER
  (MOTHER OF —) LAODAMIA

SARSAPARILLA NUNNARI SHOTBUSH

SARUCH (FATHER OF —) REU

SASH BAR BELT BENN FAJA GATE TOBE SCARF TAPIS TOWEL VITTA FASCIA GIRDLE BALDRIC BURDASH CHASSIS TUBBECK CASEMENT CORSELET WAISTBAND CUMBERBUND CUMMERBUND
  (JAPANESE —) OBI
  (WINDOW —) CHESS

SASHAY WALK GLIDE STRUT CHASSE TRAIPSE

SASH BAR MUNTIN ASTRAGAL

SASKATCHEWAN (CAPITAL OF —) REGINA
  (LAKE OF —) ROUGE REINDEER ATHABASKA CHURCHILL WOLLASTON
  (RIVER OF —) WOOD MOOSE SOURIS FRENCHMAN
  (TOWN OF —) BIGGAR CLIMAX ESTEVAN MOOSEJAW ROSETOWN SASKATOON

SASQUATCH OMAH BIGFOOT

SASS LIP GUFF

SASSABY TSESSEBE

SASSAFRAS FILE SALOP SALOOP SAXIFRAX

SASSY FLIP KICKY LIPPY MOUTHY SPUNKY

SATAN ANGEL DEVIL EBLIS FIEND SHREW BELIAL LUCIFER SATANAS SHAITAN DIABOLUS SATANAEL

SATANIC SABLE INFERNAL

SATCHEL SCRIP HANDBAG KEESTER

SATE CLOY GLUT ACCLOY SATIATE SATISFY SATURATE

SATED SAD BLASE

SATEEN VENETIAN

SATELLITE MOON ARIEL LUNET DEIMOS MOONET OBERON PHOBOS ACOLYTE ACOLYTH LUNETTE ORBITER SPUTNIK TELSTAR TRABANT UMBRIEL COURTIER FOLLOWER
  (— LAUNCHER) AGENA
  (— OF JUPITER) IO EUROPA CALLISTO GANYMEDE
  (— OF NEPTUNE) NEREID TRITON
  (— OF SATURN) RHEA DIONE MIMAS TITAN PHOEBE TETHYS IAPETUS JAPETUS HYPERION
  (— OF URANUS) ARIEL OBERON MIRANDA TITANIA UMBRIEL
  (U.S. WEATHER —) ESSA
  (WEATHER —) TIROS

SATIATE CLOY FILL GLUT PALL QUAT SADE SATE FLESH GORGE SERVE STALL ENGLUT STODGE RASSASY SATISFY SURFEIT SATURATE

SATIATED SICK BLASE JADED SATED

SATIATING STODGY FULSOME

SATIETY FULNESS SURFEIT CLOYMENT

SATIN SAY RASH ATLAS PANNE CYPRUS MUSHRU COOTHAY CYPRESS SATINET
  (SILK —) DUCHESS

SATINFLOWER SAFFRON

SATINPOD HONESTY LUNARIA

SATINWOOD ZANTE HAREWOOD

SATIRE WIT GRIND IRONY IAMBIC LAMPOON SARCASM SOTADIC RIDICULE PASQUINADE

SATIRIC BITTER IRONIC ABUSIVE CAUSTIC CUTTING POIGNANT SLASHING

SATIRICAL IAMBIC INVECTIVE

SATIRIST GRIND NIPPER SATIRE JUVENAL PASQUIN SILLOGRAPH
  AMERICAN MENCKEN SANDERS
  ENGLISH HONE NIGEL SWIFT WAUGH WOLCOT MARVELL CHURCHILL
  GERMAN BORNE MURNER RABENER
  GREEK LUCIAN SOTADES
  ROMAN HORACE JUVENAL PERSIUS
  SPANISH LARRA

SATIRIZE SKIN SKIT GRIND EXPOSE IAMBIZE LAMPOON PASQUIN RIDICULE
  (— UNFAIRLY) LIBEL

SATISFACTION CRO FIN PAY UTU EASE GREE BELLY ENACH TREAT AMENDS ASSETH CHANGE REASON COMFORT CONTENT DELIGHT GLADNESS PLEASURE REPLETION
  (EXPRESSION OF —) VOILA

SATISFACTORILY SPROWSY CLEVERLY

SATISFACTORY PAT FAIR GOOD JAKE WELL DUCKY HUNKY CLEVER DECENT NOMINAL ADEQUATE LAUDABLE
  (VERY —) COPACETIC

SATISFIED SAD FAIN FULL GLAD PAID VAIN APAID CHUFF PROUD ASSURED CHUFFED CONTENT PERFECT GRUNTLED SENSIBLE WILCWEME

SATISFY PAY EVEN FEED FILL MEET SAIR SATE SUIT ADEEM AGREE APPAY QUEME SERVE SLAKE SPEED ANSWER DEFRAY PLEASE STODGE SUPPLY ASSUAGE CONTENT EXPLETE FULFILL GRATIFY GRUNTLE RESPOND SATIATE STAUNCH SUFFICE SATURATE
  (— APPETITE) STAY
  (— BY PROOF) CONVINCE
  (— IN ADVANCE) PREVENT
  (— NEEDS) DO ADJUST

SATISFYING DUE COOL AMPLE SQUARE PERFECT REWARDING

SATURATE SOG GLUT SATE SOAK DRAWK IMBUE SOUSE STEEP DRENCH IMBIBE SEETHE SODDEN DRUNKEN INGRAIN PERVADE SATIATE SLOCKEN WATERLOG
  (— WITH SYRUP) CANDY

SATURATED SOBBY SOGGY SOPPY SODDEN SPONGY DRUNKEN

SATURATION CHROMA PURITY SATURITY

SATURN (FATHER OF —) URANUS
  (MOTHER OF —) GAEA
  (RING OF —) ANSA
  (SATELLITE OF —) RHEA DIONE MIMAS TITAN TETHYS JAPETUS HYPERION ENCELADUS
  (SON OF —) JUPITER
  (WIFE OF —) OPS CYBELE

SATURNINE SULLEN SATANIC

SATYAGRAHA GANDHISM

SATYR FAUN LECHER SAUMON SALTIER WOODMAN WOODWOSE

SATYRIASIS TENTIGO

SAUCE MOLE SASS SOWL BERCY CHILE CHILI CREAM CREME CURRY GRAVY PESTO SALSA CATSUP COULIS GANSEL MORNAY PANADA ROBERT KETCHUP MARENGO SOUBISE SUPREME TABASCO VELOUTE BECHAMEL CHAWDRON DRESSING DUXELLES MARINADE MATELOTE POIVRADE RAVIGOTE REMOLADE AVGOLEMONO
  (CURRY —) SAMBAL
  (FISH —) ALEC BAGOONG
  (GARLIC —) AIOLI ROUILLE
  (HOT —) SALSA
  (ITALIAN —) RAGU PREGO
  (KIND OF —) MORNAY NANTUA MARINARA
  (KIND OF —) HOLSIN
  (SALAD —) DRESSING
  (SAVORY —) DIP
  (SOY —) TAMARI
  (SPAGHETTI —) PESTO
  (SPICY —) SALSA
  (THICK —) LEAR

SAUCEDISH SAUCER BIRDBATH

SAUCEPAN CHAFER GOBLET POSNET SKILLET STEWPAN PANNIKIN

SAUCER BIRD PATERA PHIALE CAPSULE PANNIKIN
  (— OCCUPANT) ET
  (FLYING —) UFO DISC

SAUCINESS SAUCE DICACITY

SAUCY BOG ARCH BOLD COXY PERT BRASH DONSY DORTY FRESH LIPPY PAWKY POKEY SASSY SMART BANTAM COCKET COPPED CROUSE THWART FORWARD PAUGHTY FLIPPANT MALAPERT PETULANT SANSHACH

SAUDI ARABIA: (CAPITAL OF —) JIDDAH RIYADH
  (COIN OF —) RIYAL HALALA HALALAH
  (DESERT REGION OF —) NEFUD DAHANA ALNAFUD
  (PLATEAU OF —) NEJD
  (TOWN OF —) HAIL HOFUF JIDDA MECCA MEDINA ALHOFUF
  (WEIGHT OF —) OKE

SAUL (FATHER OF —) KISH
  (SON OF —) JONATHAN
  (UNCLE OF —) NER

SAUNTER IDLE ROAM ROVE TOIT AMBLE MOSEY RANGE SHOOL SIDLE STRAY TRAIK BUMMEL DACKER DANDER FAFFLE LINGER LOITER LOUNGE POTTER PUTTER

RAMBLE SOODLE STREEL STROLL
TODDLE WANDER SNAFFLE
STAIVER STRAVAGE
SAURA MAGA
SAUREL SCAD XUREL GASCON
BLUEFISH MACKEREL SKIPJACK
SAURY LONGJAW SKIPPER BILLFISH
GOWDNOOK SKIPJACK
SAUSAGE POT LINK SNAG COPPA
GIGOT BANGER BOUDIN POLONY
SALAMI BOLOGNA BOLONEY
BOTARGO CHORIZO PUDDING
SAVELOY BLACKPOT CERVELAT
DRISHEEN KIELBASA LIVERING
ROLLICHE ANDOUILLE CHIPOLATA
COTECHINO
(KIND OF —) METT
(VIENNA —) WIENER WIENIE
(PREF.) ALLANT(O) BOTULI
SAUTE PANFRY
SAUTERNE YQUEM
SAVAGE ILL FELL GRIM RUDE WILD
BRUTE CRUEL EAGER FELON
FERAL STERN BRUTAL FIERCE
GOTHIC IMMANE BRUTISH
FERVENT HOWLING INHUMAN
MANKEEN MANKIND ROPABLE
UNCIVIL VIOLENT WULBOUN
CANNIBAL PITILESS THEREOID
WARRAGAL
(PREF.) AGRIO
SAVAGELY FELLY UNMANLY
SAVAGERY FURY FERITY FEROCITY
SAVANNA CAMPO SAHEL SABANA
(— LANDS) LALANG
(— REGION) SAHEL
SAVANT ARTIST SCIENT SCHOLAR
VIRTUOSO
SAVE HAR WIN HAIN HELP KEEP
SAFE SALT STOP STOW AMASS
PUTBY SALVE SKIMP SPARE SPELL
DEFEND EXCEPT REDEEM RESCUE
SAVING SCRIMP UNLESS BARRING
DELIVER HUSBAND SALVAGE
WARRANT CONSERVE PRESERVE
SALTAWAY SETASIDE
(— FROM OBJECTION) SALVE
(— PENURIOUSLY) SCRAPE
SNUDGE
(PREF.) SOZ(O)
SAVIN HEATH SABINE JUNIPER
SAVING FRUGAL THRIFT ECONOMY
SPARING THRIFTY PROVIDENT
SAVINGS FAT ADDLINGS
(— CLUB) MENAGE
SAVIOR LORD SAVER SOTER
REDEEMER
SAVOR EDGE SALT SAPOR SMACK
TASTE DEGUST FLAVOR RELISH
RESENT SAVOUR SEASON TASTEN
SAPIDITY
SAVORLESS FOND INSIPID
WEARISH
SAVORY GUSTY MERRY SAPID
TASTY DAINTY SMERVY GUSTFUL
GUSTABLE TASTEFUL
SAVVY SABE
(— ABOUT) UPON
SAW SAG SEY WEB BUCK REDE
ADAGE FREIT GNOME SCEAR
SPOKE CLICHE JIGSAW PITSAW
RIPSAW SAYING SCRIBE BACKSAW
BUCKSAW CONVERT DRAGSAW

FRETSAW HACKSAW HANDSAW
HEADRIG HEADSAW PROVERB
SLABBER WHIPSAW CROSSCUT
SENTENCE
(— INTO LOGS) BUCK
(— LENGTHWISE OF GRAIN) RIP
(— OF SAWFISH) SERRA
(— WITH TWO BLADES) STADDA
(CIRCULAR —) BUR BURR EDGER
DAPPER TRIMMER
(COMB-MAKER'S —) STADDA
(CROSSCUT —) BRIAR
(CYLINDER —) CROWN TREPAN
TREPHINE
(ENDLESS —) RIBBON
(SURGICAL —) TREPAN
(PREF.) PRI(O) PRION(O) SERRATI
SERRATO SERRI
(SUFF.) PRION
SAWAN SRABAN SHRAVAN
SAWBILL MOTMOT
SAWBUCK TENNER
SAWDUST COOM COOMB SCOBS
SAWINGS
(PREF.) SCOBI
SAW FERN DYGAL BUNGWALL
HARDFERN
SAWFISH RAY RATOID COMBFISH
(PREF.) PRISTI(O)
SAWFLY CEPHID SECURIFER
SAW GATE FRAME
SAWHORSE BUCK JACK SETTER
SAWBUCK TRESTLE
SAWING
(PREF.) PRISO
SAW KERF SKAFF
SAWMILL RASPER
(— DEVICE) KICKER
(— WORKER) PONDMAN LEVERMAN
SAWYER WETA SAWER PITMAN
TOPMAN KNOTTER
SAXHORN ALTO TUBA ALTHORN
SAXTUBA BARITONE BARYTONE
SAXIFRAGE BAUERA BENNET
SESELI ASTILBE ROCKFOIL
SELFHEAL SENGREEN MITERWORT
PHILADELPHUS
SAXONIAN MINDEL
SAXOPHONE AX AXE SAX ALTO
TENOR SOPRANINO
SAY DEED MEAN MOVE TAKE TELL
SPEAK SPELL UTTER AUTHOR
QUETHE RELATE REMARK SAYING
REHEARSE PRONOUNCE
(— A BLESSING) BENSH
(— AGAIN) REPEAT ITERATE
(— FOOLISHLY) BLABBER
(— FURTHER) ADD
(— GLIBLY) SCREED
(— IN ANSWER) REPLY
(— INDISTINCTLY) MUMBLE
(— IN RETURN) REJOIN
(— NO TO) NAIT NICK
(— OVER AGAIN) REPEAT
(— REPEATEDLY) DECANTATE
(— SPITEFUL THINGS) BACKBITE
(— SUDDENLY) OUT
(— TOGETHER) CHORUS
(— TOO MUCH) SPILL OVERSAY
(—TRULY) MEAN
(— UNDER OATH) DEPOSE
SAYING DIT SAW SAY TAG DICT
ITEM REDE TEXT WORD ADAGE

AXIOM CHRIA DITTY FREIT MAXIM
SPEAK BALLAD BYWORD DICTUM
DIVERB LOGION DICTION PROVERB
APOTHEGM SENTENCE SPEAKING
(— LITTLE) DUMB
(—S OF JESUS) AGRAPHA
(—S OF RELIGIOUS TEACHER)
LOGIA
(BRIEF —) APHORISM
(CLEVER —) QUIP
(COMMON —) CANT BYWORD
(CONCISE —) EPIGRAM
(CURRENT —) DICTUM
(HABITUAL —) OVERWORD
(NOTEWORTHY —) NOTABILIA
(OBSCURE —) ENIGMA
(PITHY —) GNOME MAXIM
APOTHEGM APOPHTHEGM
(QUICK —) JERK
(SENTENTIOUS —) REASON
(SILLY —) FADAISE
(TERSE —) EPIGRAM
(TRUE —) SOOTHSAW
(WISE —) SCHOLIUM
(WITTY —) MOT SALLY DICTERY
WITNESS
(WITTY —S) FACETIAE
(PL.) LOGIA
(SUFF.) LOGER LOGIAN LOGICAL
LOGIST LOGUE LOGY
SCAB RAT ROIN SHAB SNOB CRUST
SCALD SCALL CANKER ESCHAR
RATTER GREENER RUBBERS
BLACKLEG BLACKNEB
(— ON HORSE'S HEEL) MELLIT
SCABBARD CHAPE SHEATH
PILCHER
SCABBARD FISH HIKU
SCABBLE SCAR SCALP
SCABBY MANGY SCALD ROINISH
SCABIOUS
SCABIES ITCH SCAB PSORA
SCABIOSA KNAUTIA
SCABIOUS SCABIA BLUECAP
BUNDWEED PREMORSE
SCABROUS ROUGH SULTRY
ASPEROUS
SCAD COIN AKULE XUREL DOLLAR
GOGGLER QUIAQUIA
(PL.) ALOT LOTS TONS
SCAFFOLD CAGE PEGMA STAGE
BRIDGE GANTRY CATASTA
HAYLOFT STAGING HOARDING
(MOVABLE —) GANTRY
SCAFFOLDING DOCK STAGING
SCALARE ANGELFISH
SCALAWAG SCAMP
SCALD BURN LEEP PLOT SCAD
BLAST PLOUT SCAUD BLANCH
SCALDER AMBUSTION
SCALDFISH MEGRIM
SCALE PIP LEAF PELA PILL STEP
TAPE CLIMB FLAKE GAMUT GENUS
GULAR MOUNT PALEA PELOG
PELOK PELTA POISE SCUTE SHALE
SHARD SHELL SHERD SHIVE TRUNK
ASCEND CAUDAL CINDER COCCID
FORNIX GUNTER IMBREX KELVIN
LABIAL LADDER LAMINA LIGULE
LOREAL MENTAL NUCHAL OCULAR
PERULE RAMENT RONDLE RUSTRE
SHIELD SQUAMA STRIGA BALANCE
CLINKER ELYTRON FRONTAL

FULCRUM HUMERAL LATERAL
NUCHALE REAUMUR ROSTRUM
VENTRAL VERNIER ANALEMMA
BRACHIAL INDUSIUM LECANIUM
LODICULE MEALYBUG ODOPHONE
RAMENTUM SCRAMBLE
SQUAMULE TEMPORAL UROSTEGE
(— DOWN) DEGRADE
(— OF CORNSTALK) SHIVE
(— OF 7 TONES) SEPTAVE
(— ON BUTTERFLY) PLUMULE
(— ON MOTH) PATAGIUM
(— USED BY TAILORS) LOG
(GRADUATED —) RETE
(GREAT —) GAMUT
(KIND OF —) BRIX MOHS RICHTER
(SHAD —) CENIZO
(PL.) CHAFF DANDER
(PREF.) LEPID(O) LEPO PHOLID(O)
SQUAM(ATO)(ELLI)(I)(O)(OSO)(ULI)
(MUSICAL —) CHORD(O)
(SUFF.) LEPIS PHOLIS
SCALEBOARD SCABBARD
SCALEPAN BASIN
SCALER CULLER SOOTER
SCALES TRON TRONE BALANCE
SCALETAIL SQUIRREL
SCALLION PORRET
SCALLOP DAG CLAM GIMP MUSH
CRENA QUEEN SQUIN PECTEN
COQUILLE DOUGHBOY ESCALLOP
PECTINID
SCALLOPED INVECTED
(SUFF.) CRENATE
SCALP SCAUP SKELP ATTIRE
SCALPEL BISTOURY
SCALPER PUNTER
SCALY SCABBY SQUAMY LEPROSE
PALEATE LEPIDOTE SCABROUS
SQUAMOSE
SCALY ANTEATER PANGOLIN
SCAM DUPE BUNCO BUNKO CHEAT
STING RAMBOOZLE
SCAMP IMP LAD RIP LIMB SLIM
ROGUE SKEMP SKIMP THIEF
BOOGER BUGGER FRIPON NICKUM
RASCAL SINNER SORREL SORROW
URCHIN HALLION HESSIAN
PEASANT RAMMACK SKELLUM
SLUBBER SNOOZER BLIGHTER
SCALAWAG SLYBOOTS SPALPEEN
VAGABOND WIDDIFOW
SCALLYWAG
SCAMPER DASH LAMP CHEVY
SCOUP SCOUR CHIVVY BRATTLE
SKITHER SKITTER
SCAN PIPE GLASS METER DEVISE
SURVEY EXAMINE
(KIND OF —) CAT
SCANDAL GUP CLASH CRACK
ECLAT SHAME CALUMNY OFFENSE
SCANMAG SLANDER NANNYGATE
WATERGATE
SCANDALIZE SHOCK
SCANDALMONGER CLAT
SCANDALOUS UNHOLY SHAMEFUL
SCANDINAVIAN DANE LAPP
NORSE SWEDE VIKING LOCHLIN
NORSEMAN NORTHMAN
SCANDIAN VARANGIAN
(PL.) OSTMEN
SCANT SHY JIMP LEAN MEET POOR
THIN SCAMP SHORT SKIMP SPLAY

BARISH GEASON LITTLE MEAGER MEAGRE SCANTY SKINNY STINGY STINTY SLENDER SCRATCHY (PREF.) OLIG(O)

SCANTILY BARELY FEEBLY SMALLY SCANTLY SPARSELY

SCANTINESS PENURY PARCITY EXIGUITY SPARSITY

SCANTLING STUD FILET JOIST FILLET BOLSTER RIBBAND STUDDING

SCANTY BARE JIMP LANK LEAN POOR SLIM EXILE GNEDE SCANT SHORT SILLY SKIMP SPARE FRUGAL MEAGER MEASLY SCRIMP SKIMPY SLIGHT SPARSE SCRANNY SCRIMPY SLENDER SPARING EXIGUOUS PENURIOUS

SCAPEGOAT PATSY STOOGE FALLGUY

SCAPEGRACE LIMB RASCAL SCALLYWAG SKAINSMATE

SCAPHOID NAVICULAR

SCAPOLITE DIPYRE

SCAPULA BLADE OMOPLATE SPADEBONE

SCAPULAR CUCULLA

SCAR ARR EYE WEM SEAM SEAR WIPE CHALK FESTER KELOID RADDLE STIGMA TRENCH CHELOID SCARIFY CICATRIX SMALLPOX CICATRICE
(— ON SAWED STONE) STUN
(— ON SEED) HILUM
(— ON TREE) CATFACE

SCARAB ATEUCHUS

SCARCE DEAR RARE THIN SLACK DAINTY GEASON CLASSIC UNCOMMON (PREF.) SPAN(I)(O)

SCARCELY ILL VIX JIMP SCANT BARELY HARDLY MERELY ONETHE SCARCE SCRIMP WENETH SCANTLY UNEATHS UNNETHE

SCARCITY LACK WANT FAULT SCANT DEARTH FAMINE RARITY PAUCITY

SCARE COW BOOF BREE FAZE FEAR FLEG FLIG FRAY GAST HUSH SHOO ALARM APPAL GALLY GLIFF GLOFF PSYCH SPOOK AFFRAY FRIGHT GASTER PSYCHE SCARIFY STARTLE TERRIFY AFFRIGHT FRIGHTEN
(— BIRDS) KEEP
(— OFF) SCAT
(— WORD) BOO

SCARECROW BOGLE BUCCA MOGGY SEWEL BOGGLE DUDMAN MALKIN MAUMET MAWKIN SCARER SHEWEL BOGGART BUGABOO DEADMAN HODMADOD SHAWFOWL

SCARED SCART SCARY AFRAID GOOSEY STREAKED

SCAREMONGER ALARMIST

SCARF BARB HOOD SASH ABNET ASCOT BARBE CLOUD CYMAR FICHU LUNGI NUBIA PAGRI SHADE STOCK STOLE TABLE THROW CRAVAT PEPLOS REBOZO SCREEN SQUARE TAPALO TIPPET UPARNA BURDASH DOPATTA FOULARD MANIPLE MUFFLER NECKTIE

ORARIUM OVERLAY PUGGREE SAUTOIR TALLITH CLAUDENT COINTISE DOOPUTTY LIRIPIPE LIRIPOOP MANTILLA MUFFETEE SLENDANG
(— AROUND HAT) PAGRI PUGGERY PUGGREE PUGGAREE
(— ON BISHOP'S STAFF) ORARION ORARIUM VEXILLUM
(— ON KNIGHT'S HELMET) COINTISE
(ARABIAN —) CABAAN
(FEATHER —) BOA
(PRAYER —) TALLIS TALLITH

SCARFING GRAFTING

SCARIFY LIFT

SCARLET LAC RED PINK TULY GRAIN KERMES

SCARLET HAW HAWTHORN

SCARLET IBIS GUARA

SCARLET LETTER (AUTHOR OF —) HAWTHORNE
(CHARACTER IN —) PEARL ROGER ARTHUR HESTER PRYNNE BELLINGHAM DIMMESDALE CHILLINGWORTH

SCARLET LYCHNIS FIREBALL NONESUCH

SCARLETT (LOVE OF —) RHETT

SCARLET TANAGER REDBIRD FIREBIRD

SCARLIKE ULOID

SCARP CLIFF SCARF ESCARP SCARPLET

SCARY EERIE SPOOKY ALARMING FEARSOME TERRIFYING

SCAT (— SINGER) ELLA

SCATHING MORDANT SCALDING

SCATHINGLY ROUNDLY

SCATOLOGICAL BARNYARD

SCATTER DAD SOW TED FLEE ROUT SALT SCAT SEED SHED SPEW VOID FLING SCALE SCHAL SEVER SHAKE SKAIL SPRAY STREW STROW DISPEL PEPPER SHOWER SKIVER SPARGE SPARSE SPREAD SPRENG WINNOW DIFFUSE DISBAND DISJECT FRITTER RESOLVE SCAMBLE SHATTER SKINKLE SKITTER SLATTER SPARKLE SPARPLE SPATTER SWATTER DISPERSE INTERSOW SEPARATE SPLUTTER SPRINKLE SQUANDER SQUATTER
(— BAIT FOR FISH) TOLE TOLL
(— CARELESSLY) LITTER
(— INK) SPLUTTER
(— OVER) BESTREW
(— WATER) SPLASH

SCATTERED LAX OPEN STRAY DAIMEN SPARSE DIFFUSE SPOTTED BESPRENT FUGITIVE SPARSILE (PREF.) LAXI

SCATTERING SOWING DIASPORA SCATTERY

SCATTERSHOT SHOTGUN

SCAUP DUCK DOGS DIVER DUCKER DUNBIRD POCHARD BLUEBILL GRAYBACK SHUFFLER

SCAVAGE SCEWING

SCAVENGE CLEANSE GARBAGE

SCAVENGER BUNGY RAKER

BHANGI BHUNGI MEHTAR REMOVER SCAFFIE CORYDORA HALALCOR RAMSHORN

SCAZON CHOLIAMB

SCEAT SKEAT STYCA

SCENARIO SCRIPT CONTINUITY

SCENE JOG SET CODA CYKE FLAT SITE TODO VIEW ARENA STAGE BRIDGE LOCALE VISION EPISODE PAGEANT TABLEAU COULISSE EXTERIOR INTERIOR PROSPECT TABLETOP
(— IN OPERA) SCENA
(— OF ACTION) STAGE
(— OF ACTIVITY) BEEHIVE
(— OF CONFUSION) BABEL BEDLAM
(— OF HOSTILITIES) FRONT
(CLOSING —) FINALE
(FILM —) FLASHBACK
(FINAL —) CURTAIN EPILOGUE
(INTRODUCTORY —) INDUCTION
(NIGHT —) NOCTURNE

SCENERY DROP FLAT DECOR CUTOUT NATURE IMAGERY PROFILE
(— CHANGER) TRIP
(PIECE OF —) MASKING

SCENESHIFTER GRIP

SCENT AIR DRAG NOSE ODOR VENT WIND CIVET FAULT FLAIR FUMET RELES SAVOR SMACK SMELL SNIFF SNUFF SPOOR TASTE CHYPRE ESSENCE INCENSE NOSEGAY ODORIZE VERDURE FUMIGATE MARECHAL PASTILLE REDOLENCE
(— OF ANIMAL FOLLOWED BY HOUNDS) FEUTE
(— OF COOKING) NIDOR
(— OF FOX) DRAG
(— OF GAME) FUMET FUMETTE
(— OUT) SMOKE
(FALSE —) RIOT
(LOST —) FAULT

SCENTED OLENT ODORATE PERFUMY ESSENCED

SCEPTER ROD WAND VERGE BAUBLE CEPTER FERULA WARDER

SCHEDULE BOOK CARD HOLD LIST SKED TIME PANEL SCRIP SCROW SETUP SLATE TABLE SCROLL CATALOG TABLEAU CALENDAR REGISTER
(— OF COURT CASES) DOCKET
(— OF DUTIES) TARIFF
(— OF GAMES) SEASON
(TELEVISION —) LINEUP

SCHEDULED DUE

SCHEDULING (TECHNIQUE FOR —) PERT

SCHEELITE TUNGSTEN

SCHEHERAZADE (HUSBAND OF —) SCHAHRIAH
(SISTER OF —) DINARZADE

SCHEMA FORM

SCHEMATIC PLAN

SCHEME AIM GIN LAY WAY WEB CAST DART GAME PLAN PLAT PLOT REDE SWIM ANGLE BABEL CADRE DODGE DRAFT DRIFT KNACK PINAX REACH SCALE SETUP SHIFT TABLE THINK TRAIN BRIGUE BUBBLE CIPHER DESIGN DEVICE DEVISE FIGURE HOOKUP POLICY SCHEMA

SYSTEM TAMPER THEORY UTOPIA BUSTOUT COUNSEL DRAUGHT GIMMICK IMAGINE KNAVERY NOSTRUM PROJECT PURPOSE CONSPIRE CONTRIVE FORECAST GIMCRACK IDEOLOGY INTRIGUE MANEUVER PLATFORM PRACTICE TRIPOTER WINDMILL MACHINATE
(— FOR PEACE) IRENICON EIRENICON
(— OF ANCESTRY) PEDIGREE
(— OF RANK) LADDER
(ABORTIVE —) SOOTERKIN
(BETTING —) SYSTEM
(CONFIDENCE —) BUSTOUT
(DECEITFUL —) SHIFT
(DELUSIVE —) BUBBLE
(DIAGRAMMATIC —) PINAX
(FANCIFUL —) WINDMILL
(FAVORITE —) NOSTRUM
(KIND OF —) PONZI
(VERSIFICATION —) METER METRE
(VISIONARY —) BABEL

SCHEMER ARTIST DESIGNER ENGINEER SCHEMIST SLEEVEEN

SCHEMING SCHEMY PLANFUL SPIDERY FETCHING PRACTICE

SCHISM RENT DISUNITY SCISSION SCISSURE

SCHISMATIC HERETIC

SCHIST RAG AMPELITE MICACITE MYLONITE OLLENITE PHYLLITE

SCHIZONT MONONT AGAMONT

SCHIZOPHRENIA CATATONY

SCHLEP LUG

SCHMO JERK

SCHMOOZE CHAT

SCHNAPPER WOLLOMAI

SCHNOZZLE NOSE

SCHOLAR TUG DEMY GAON IMAM CLERK PUPIL DIVINE DOCTOR FELLOW JURIST LAMDEN MASTER PANDIT SABORA SAVANT SCOLOG SHEIKH BIBLIST BOOKMAN DANTIST LATINER LEARNER MAULANA STUDENT BOURSIER DISCIPLE HEBRAEAN HUMANIST ISLAMIST MASORITE TABERDAR THAUMASTE PHILOSOPHER
(— OF QUEENS COLLEGE) TABERDAR
(FOUNDATION —) BOURSIER
(MOSLEM —) ULAMA ULEMA
(PL.) CLERISY LITERATI
AMERICAN LEWIS LOWES POUND BLYDEN CONANT GENUNG KELSEY MILLER NEWELL RIDDLE SARTON BABBITT GUMMERE SEYMOUR GOLDMANN HAMILTON HARKNESS PERCIVAL ROBINSON STERRETT LOUNSBURY
AUSTRIAN SPANN
CANADIAN MACMECHAN
CHINESE YEN
CZECH JIRACEK SAFARIK
DANISH MADVIG GULDBERG
DUTCH COBET BURMAN ERASMUS GROTIUS COORNHERT BILDERDIJK
ENGLISH KER LEE BEDE BYNG LONG BYRON CROFT ELYOT JAMES LEWIS LOWTH MAYOR PALEY ROGET ROWSE YOUNG ALCUIN ALFORD BAXTER BODLEY BRIGHT BROOME

BUTLER COWELL DASENT FARMER GARROD GODLEY GROCYN HARRIS JEVONS MURRAY NECKAM NEWMAN NICOLL YAHUDA ALDHELM ALDRICH BAINTON BUTCHER COGHILL DIODATI DUGDALE HOLLAND HOUSMAN LIDDELL MACKAIL STANLEY CHRISTIE GRIERSON HARRISON MCKERROW PATTISON STRACHAN TUNSTALL TYRWHITT CONINGTON NETTLESHIP

FINNISH LONNROT PORTHAN KOSKENNIEMI

FLEMISH BLOMMAERT

FRENCH BUDE LAMY LUCE AMYOT MAURY PARIS RASHI BAILLY BERARD GAGUIN MAGNIN MENAGE MICHEL BROSSES CAUMONT CHASLES DELISLE LEFRANC LONGNON SOURIAU DEMOGEOT ESTIENNE JAUCOURT BONAPARTE SCALIGER BARTHELEMY TAILLANDIER

GERMAN DIEZ BLEEK HEYNE KLOTZ KROLL LEYEN STAHR FROBEN KOCHLY RAUMER CONRING GOEDEKE GOLTHER HEUSLER LUDWICH MOMMSEN RIBBECK RUHNKEN WILHELM AUFRECHT BERNEKER BUTTMANN HAINISCH PFEIFFER SPANHEIM WEINHOLD KOSCHWITZ CAMERARIUS

GREEK DION GAZA CORAY PALLES DIDYMUS MUSURUS RHIANUS PORPHYRY ATHENAEUS CAECILIUS EUPHORION ZENODOTUS CALLIMACHUS CHRYSOLORAS ERATOSTHENES

HUNGARIAN BEL

ICELANDIC BLONDAL SAEMUND VIGFUSSON

INDIAN PATANJALI

IRISH BALL BUTLER TRENCH MAHAFFY KEIGHTLEY

ITALIAN DONI PRAZ ZENO GNOLI MAFFEI VARCHI ALEANDRO MANUTIUS MARTELLI ROSSETTI MARSILIUS NICCOLINI TIRABOSCHI

JAPANESE NITOBE MABUCHI

MEXICAN GAMA

PERUVIAN MENDIBURU

POLISH CIOLEK CHODZKO RACZYNSKI OSSOLINSKI ZDZIECHOWSKI

PORTUGUESE BRAGA

ROMAN PLINY VARRO AUSONIUS CENSORINUS

RUSSIAN LAVROV CHUKOVSKY LOMONOSOV DRAGOMANOV MANDELSTAM

SCOTTISH LANG BLACKIE GROSART LINDSAY CRICHTON BELLENDEN MACDONALD

SPANISH CARO OCHOA CASTRO VILLENA

SWEDISH MALMSTROM STIERNHIELM

SWISS BODMER BREITINGER PELLICANUS

SCHOLARLY CLERKLY ERUDITE LEARNED ACADEMIC

SCHOLARSHIP ART BOOK BURSE BURSARY DEMYSHIP LEARNING

SCHOLASTIC PEDANTIC

SCHOOL GAM TOL EDDY PREP AGGIE BOOKS ECOLE HEDER LYCEE NYAYA SAKHA TEACH TRADE TRAIN TUTOR ALJAMA CAMPUS CHEDER CHURCH KUTTAB KYAUNG MADHAB MALIKI RABFAK SCHOLA SCHULE SQUEEL TRIPOS ACADEME ACADEMY CRAMMER MADRASA PENSION STUDIUM YESHIVA AUDITORY DOCUMENT EXERCISE EXTERNAT PEDAGOGY SEMINARY

(— FOR JUDO OR KARATE) DOJO

(— FOR SINGERS) MAITRISE

(— OF BLACKFISH) GRIND

(— OF BUDDHISM) CHAN RITSU DHYANA SANRON

(— OF FISH) HERD SCALE SCULL

(— OF HINDU PHILOSOPHY) NYAYA

(— OF OPINION) SECT

(— OF PAINTING) GENRE

(— OF PHILOSOPHY) SECT ACADEMY AUDITORY

(— OF VEDA) SAKHA SHAKHA

(— OF WHALES) GAM POD

(ART —) BAUHAUS LUMINISM

(AZTEC —) CALMECAC

(COMPARATIVE —) FOLKLORE

(DAY —) EXTERNAT

(ELEMENTARY —) GRADES

(HIGH —) HIGH ACADEMY COLLEGE

(KIND OF —) MAGNET

(MARTIAL ARTS —) DOJO

(MOSLEM —) HANAFI KUTTAB SHAFII HANBALI

(PAINTING —) ASHCAN

(REFORM —) BORSTAL

(RELIGIOUS —) ALJAMA YESHIVA

(RIDING —) MANEGE

(SANSKRIT —) TOL

(SCOTCH —) SQUEEL

(SECONDARY —) LYCEE LYCEUM COLEGIO

(WRESTLING —) PALESTRA

SCHOOLBOOK COCKER

SCHOOLBOY SCUG PETTY CLERGION

SCHOOL FOR SCANDAL (AUTHOR OF —) SHERIDAN

(CHARACTER IN —) MARIA MOSES PETER JOSEPH OLIVER ROWLEY TEAZLE CANDOUR CHARLES PREMIUM SURFACE SNEERWELL

SCHOOLHOUSE PORTABLE

SCHOOLING LEARNING

SCHOOLMASTER BEAK CAJI CAXI AKHUN KHOJA KHODJA MASTER PEDANT AKHOOND DOMINIE PEDAGOG ORBILIUS

SCHOOLROOM HOMEROOM

SCHOOL SHARK TOPE TOPER

SCHOOLWORK BOOKWORK

SCHOONER JACK TERN QUART QUINT WUINT PUNGEY BALLAHOO

SCHORL COCKLE

SCHRADAN OMPA

SCHROTHER SHREDDER

SCHUSSBOOMER SKIER

SCHUYT SHOE SCOUT EELBOAT

SCIATICA BONESHAW

SCIENCE ART OLOGY SOPHY MATHESIS SCIENTIA

(— OF ALGAE) ALGOLOGY

(— OF ANIMALS) ZOOLOGY

(— OF AQUEOUS VAPOR) ATMOLOGY

(— OF ARTILLERY) PYROBALLOGY

(— OF ATOMS) ATOMICS

(— OF BEING OR REALITY) ONTOLOGY

(— OF BIOLOGICAL STATISTICS) BIOMETRY

(— OF BREEDING) GENETICS

(— OF CAUSES) ETIOLOGY

(— OF CHARACTER) ETHOLOGY

(— OF CLASSIFICATION) SYSTEMATICS

(— OF CLASSIFICATION OF DISEASES) NOSOLOGY

(— OF COLORS) CHROMATICS

(— OF DISEASES) NOSOLOGY

(— OF DOSES) DOSOLOGY POSOLOGY

(— OF DUTY) DEONTICS DEONTOLOGY

(— OF EARTH'S FORMATION) GEOGONY

(— OF EARTH MEASUREMENTS) GEODESY

(— OF ELECTIONS) PSEPHOLOGY

(— OF ENVIRONMENT) ECOLOGY

(— OF ETHICS) DEONTICS DEONTOLOGY

(— OF EXCHANGE) CAMBISTRY

(— OF FERMENTATION) ZYMOLOGY

(— OF FERNS) PTERIDOLOGY

(— OF FLOW OF MATTER) RHEOLOGY

(— OF FOOTPRINTS) ICHNOLOGY

(— OF FORMS OF SPEECH) GRAMMAR

(— OF FRUIT GROWING) POMOLOGY

(— OF FUNDS MANAGEMENT) FINANCE

(— OF GEMS) GEMMARY GEMOLOGY

(— OF GOD) DIVINITY

(— OF GOVERNMENT) POLITICS

(— OF HEALTH MAINTENANCE) HYGIENE

(— OF HEAT) PYROLOGY THERMOTICS

(— OF HISTORY OF EARTH) GEOLOGY

(— OF HUMAN BODY) SEMATOLOGY

(— OF HUMAN SETTLEMENTS) EKISTICS

(— OF IDEAS) IDEOLOGY

(— OF IMAGINARY SOLUTIONS) PATAPHYSICS

(— OF INSECTS) ENTOMOLOGY

(— OF INTELLECT) NOOLOGY

(— OF INTERPRETATION) HERMENEUTICS

(— OF LANGUAGE) GRAMMAR PHILOLOGY

(— OF LAW) NOMOLOGY

(— OF LIFE) BIOLOGY

(— OF LIFE INFLUENCES) EUGENICS

(— OF LIFE OF TREES) SILVICS

(— OF LIGHT) OPTICS

(— OF LYING) PSEUDOLOGY

(— OF MEANING) SIGNIFICS

(— OF MEASURING TIME) HOROLOGY

(— OF MEDIEVAL CHEMISTRY) ALCHEMY

(— OF MIDWIFERY) TOKOLOGY

(— OF MIND) PSYCHOLOGY

(— OF MOLLUSCS) MALACOLOGY

(— OF MORAL DUTY) ETHICS

(— OF MOSSES) BRYOLOGY

(— OF MOTION) DYNAMICS

(— OF MOUNTAINS) OROLOGY

(— OF MUSCLES) MYOLOGY

(— OF NAVIGATION) NAUTICS

(— OF NUMBERS COMBINATIONS) ALGEBRA

(— OF PERSUADING A GOD) THEURGY

(— OF PLANTS) BOTANY

(— OF QUANTITY) POSOLOGY

(— OF RACIAL IMPROVEMENT) EUGENICS

(— OF REASONING) LOGIC

(— OF RECORDING GENEALOGIES) HERALDRY

(— OF REFRIGERATION) CRYOLOGY

(— OF REMEDIES) ACOLOGY

(— OF RIVERS) POTAMOLOGY

(— OF ROCKS) LITHOLOGY

(— OF SEA) THALASSOGRAPHY

(— OF SERUMS) SEROLOGY

(— OF SMELLS) OSMICS

(— OF SOILS) PEDOLOGY

(— OF SOUND) PHONICS ACOUSTICS

(— OF SPATIAL MAGNITUDES) GEOMETRY

(— OF STRUCTURE OF ANIMALS) ANATOMY

(— OF SUBSTANCES) CHEMISTRY

(— OF SUN) HELIOLOGY

(— OF SYMPTOMS) SEMEIOLOGY

(— OF TEACHING) PEDAGOGY

(— OF TEACHING ADULTS) ANDRAGOGY

(— OF THE EAR) OTOLOGY

(— OF TIDES) TIDOLOGY

(— OF TOUCH DATA) HAPTICS

(— OF VALUES) AXIOLOGY

(— OF VERSIFICATION) PROSODY

(— OF VIRTUE) ARETAICS

(— OF WEIGHT OR GRAVITY) BAROLOGY

(— OF WINES) ENOLOGY OENOLOGY

(— OF WORD MEANINGS) SEMANTICS

(BRANCH OF —) BIONICS

(ESOTERIC —) HERMETICS

(KIND OF —) LIFE

(LEGAL —) LAW

(MILITARY —) STRATEGY

(NATURAL —) STINKS PHYSICS

(PHYSICAL —) PHILOSOPHY

(RELIGIOUS —) THEOLOGY

(SUFF.) LOGER LOGIA(N) LOGIC(AL) LOGIST LOGUE LOGY OLOGY SOPH(ER)(IC)(IST)(Y)

(RELATING TO —) METRIC

SCIENTIST BOFFIN

(KIND OF RUSSIAN —) REFUSNIK REFUSENIK

SCIMITAR SAX SEAX TURK KHEPESH
TULWAUR
SCINDAPSUS POTHOS
SCINTILLA ATOM
SCINTILLATE SNAP FLASH GLEAM
GLANCE GLITTER SPARKLE
TWINKLE
SCINTILLATION SPARKLE
SPARKLET
SCION IMP ROD CION CYON HEIR
ROOT SLIP GRAFT SPRIG BRANCH
SPROUT SARMENT SETLING
SCISSORS SHEARS CLIPPER
SECATEUR
(PREF.) FORFICI
SCLERITE TORMA LABIUM PLANTA
PLAGULA AXILLARY EPIMERON
SCLERODERMA MORPHEA
SCLEROPROTEIN SPONGIN
SCLEROTIUM ERGOT SCLEROTE
TUCKAHOE
SCOFF DOR GAB GALL GECK GIBE
GIRD JEER JIBE MOCK RAIL CURSE
FLEER FLOUT GLEEK SCARF
SCORN SCOUT SNEER TAUNT
DERIDE REPROVE RIDICULE
SCOFFER MOCKER ABDERITE
SCOLD JAW MAG MOB NAG RAG
ROW WIG YAP BAWL CALL CAMP
CANT DING FLAY FRAB FUSS HAZE
JACK JOBE JOWL JUMP RAIL RANT
RATE REDD RICK SHAW SNAG
SNUB TUCK YAFF ABUSE BARGE
BASTE BOAST CHIDE DRESS FLIRT
FLITE PRATE RANDY SCALD SCORE
SHORE SHREW SLANG STORM
TARGE VIXEN BERATE BOUNCE
CALLET CAMPLE CARPET HAMMER
HOORAY HURRAH MAGPIE RATTLE
REHETE REVILE TATTER THREAP
TONGUE YAFFLE YANKIE CHANNER
CHEWOUT REPROVE TRIMMER
TROUNCE UPBRAID BALLYRAG
BERATTLE BETONGUE CHASTISE
CIDESTER DINGDONG RIXATRIX
CLAPPERCLAW
SCOLDING JAW HURL JESSE SCOLD
DIRDUM JAWING RAKING RATTLE
SISERA FLITING HEARING LECTURE
RAGGING WIGGING BLESSING
CARRITCH JOBATION
SCOLEX HEAD
SCOLYTUS IPS
SCONCE SWAPE APPLIQUE
SCONE FARL FARLE
SCOOP BAIL BALE DRAG INFO ROUT
DIDLE GOUGE KEACH SHAUL
SKEET BUCKET DIPPER DISHER
SHOVEL WIMBLE SCRAPER
SCUPPET SKIMMER SKIPPET
SCOOPFUL
(— FOR CANNON) LADLE
(— FOR DAMPENING CANVAS)
SKEET
(— FOR GRAIN) WECHT
(— UP) LAP LAVE GATHER
(— WITH TONGUE) LAP
(CHEESE —) PALE
(GLASSMAKING —) PADDLE
(JAI ALAI —) CHISTERA
(LONG-HANDLED —) DIDLE
(SURGICAL —) CURET CURETTE

SCOOT ZIP DART SCOUT SKEET
SKYHOOT
SCOPE AIM AREA AMBIT POWER
RANGE REACH ROUND SCALE
SCOOP SWEEP VERGE SCOUTH
SPHERE TETHER BREADTH CIRCUIT
COMPASS OPERAND PURVIEW
CONFINES DIAPASON LATITUDE
(— OF VISION) COMMAND
(FREE —) SWING
SCOPOLINE OSCIN OSCINE
SCORBUTUS SCURVY
SCORCH BURN CHAR PLOT SCAM
SEAR ADURE ADUST BROIL PARCH
PLAUT REESE SCALD SCAUM
SINGE SWEAL SWELT BIRSLE
BISHOP DEGREE SMITCH SOTTER
SPARCH SWINGE SWITHE BLISTER
BRISTLE FRIZZLE SCORKLE
SCOWDER SWITHEN SWITHER
TORRIFY FIREFANG SCOUTHER
SCOWTHER
SCORCHED ADUST LEEPIT
SCORCHER SIZZLER
(PREF.) SIRI(O)
SCORCHING BAKING FIRING
ADURENT SCALDING
SCORE ACE CUT LAW RIT RUN CARD
DEBT DROP GAME GOAL HAIL
HOLE MAKE MARK NICK POST RIDE
SLOG CHART CHASE CORGE
COUNT EXTRA NOTCH OPERA
TALLY COOREE FURROW SAFETY
SCOTCH SCRIVE SPADES STRING
TARGET TICKET TWENTY CONVERT
SCORING SCRATCH SQUEEZE
GAMEBALL PARTITUR PLACEKICK
(— FOR ALE) ALESHOT
(— HEAVILY AGAINST) SHELL
(— IN BRIDGE) BOARD BONUS
SWING
(— IN CRIBBAGE) GO PEG FIFTEEN
(— IN CRICKET) BLOB CENTURY
(— IN PIQUET) CAPOT REPIQUE
(— IN RUGBY) TRY
(— OF NOTHING) DUCK
(— OF 100) TON
(APTITUDE —) STANINE
(BASKETBALL —) HOOP
(BILLIARDS —) STRING
(BOWLING —) PINFALL
(GOLF —) ACE PAR BOGEY DEUCE
EAGLE BIRDIE BUZZARD
(INDEX —) APGAR
(KIND OF —) APGAR
(NO —) LOVE
(ORIGINAL MUSICAL —) URTEXT
(PINOCHLE —) LAST
(TENNIS —) CALL FIVE LOVE DEUCE
FORTY FIFTEEN
(THREE —) SHOCK SIXTY
(TIE —) HALVE DEADLOCK
(ZERO —) GOOSEEGG
(PL.) MUSIC
SCORED SULCATE SULCATED
SCOREKEEPER SCORER TALLIER
TALLYMAN
SCORER NIB MARKER NOTCHER
SCORIA SCUM SLAG CINDER
SULLAGE
SCORIFIER CAPSULE
SCORIFY SMELT
SCORN GECK LOUT HOKER SCARN

SPURN BISMER SLIGHT CONTEMN
DESPISE DESPITE DISDAIN
CONTEMPT DERISION MISPRIZE
SCORNFUL SAUCY SCORNY SNIFFY
SNIFTY HAUGHTY FRUMPISH
INSOLENT SARDONIC
SCORNFULLY ASKEW ASWASH
SCORPION NEPA ALACRAN STINGER
UROPYGI ARACHNID PEDIPALP
WHIPTAIL
SCORPION FISH LAPON SERRAN
HOGFISH SCULPIN LORICATE
RASCACIO
SCORPION FLY PANORPID
SCOT (ALSO SEE SCOTSMAN) CELT
JOCK KELT SANDY SAXON SCOTTY
BLUECAP SCOTSMAN
(PL.) SAWNY SAWNEY LALLANS
SCOTCH TRIG SCOAT SCOTS
SCOTTISH
SCOTCHMAN MAC GAUL SANDY
TARTAN SCOTCHY SCOTTIE
SCOTSMAN
SCOTER COOT FILK DIVER SCOUT
WHILK BASQUE DUCKER SURFER
PISHAUG SCOOTER SKUNKTOP
SCOTIA MOUTH
SCOTIST DUNCE
SCOTLAND ALBYN ALBANY ALBION
SCOTIA ALBAINN ALBANIA
(NORTHERN —) PICTLAND

SCOTLAND
BAY: SCAPA
CAPITAL: EDINBURGH
COIN: DEMY BODLE GROAT PLACK RIDER BAWBEE
COUNTY: AYR BUTE FIFE ROSS ANGUS BANFF MORAY NAIRN PERTH ARGYLL LANARK ORKNEY BERWICK KINROSS PEEBLES RENFREW SELKIRK WIGTOWN ABERDEEN AYRSHIRE CROMARTY DUMFRIES ROXBURGH SHETLAND STERLING
FIRTH: LORN CLYDE FORTH MORAY SOLWAY PENTLAND
ISLAND: RUM BUTE IONA JURA MULL RHUM SKYE ARRAN BARRA ISLAY LEWIS HARRIS ORKNEY SHETLAND
ISLANDS: ORKNEY HEBRIDES SHETLAND
LAKE: TAY NESS MORAR LAGGAN LINNHE LOMOND KATRINE RANNOCH
LANGUAGE: ERSE LALLAN LALLAND
MEASURE: COP BOLL CRAN FALL MILE PECK PINT ROOD ROPE SPAN CRANE LIPPY FIRLOT AUCHLET CHALDER CHOPPIN MUTCHKIN STIMPART
MOUNTAIN: HOPE ATTOW DEARG NEVIS TINTO WYVIS CHEVIOT MACDHUI
NATIVE: GAEL PICT SCOT
ORDER: THISTLE
REGION: FIFE BORDERS GRAMPIAN
RESORT: OBAN
RIVER: AYR DEE DON ESK TAY DOON GLEN NITH NORN SPEY AFTON ANNAN CLYDE FORTH GARRY TWEED YTHAN AFFRIC

TEVIOT TUMMEL DEVERON
FINDHORN
SEAPORT: ALLOA LEITH DUNDEE
ABERDEEN
TOWN: AYR DUNS OBAN WICK
ALLOA BRORA CUPAR ELLON
LEITH NAIRN PERTH SALEN
TROON DUNDEE GIRVAN HAWICK
DUNKELD GLASGOW PAISLEY
ABERDEEN DUMFRIES GREENOCK
KIRKWALL STIRLING
WATERFALL: GLOMACH
WEIGHT: BOLL DROP TRONE
BUSHEL

SCOTSMAN SANDY SAWNY
BLUECAP
SCOTTISH SCOTCH SCOTLAND
SCOTTISH TERRIER DIEHARD
SCOTTIE VERMINER
SCOUNDREL RAP PIMP SCAB VILE
WARY BLECK FILTH KNAVE SCAMP
SHREW SMAIK SWEEP THIEF
WHAUP BRIBER LIMMER SLOVEN
VARLET CATAIAN GLUTTON
HALLION NITHING SCROYLE
SKELLUM VILIACO VILLAIN
WARLOCK BEZONIAN LIDDERON
MASCHANT
SCOUNDRELLY VILLAIN
SCOUR ASH BEAT COMB RAKE
SCUM SEEK SIND SKIR SCOOR
SCRUB SKIRR SWEEP DRENCH
SCURRY SLUICE DEGRADE
FURBISH BACKWASH STONEFILE
(PL.) SKIT
SCOURER BLOOMER DOLLIER
PICKLER
SCOURGE EEL TAW LASH WHIP
CURSE FLAIL KNOUT SLASH SWING
BALEYS PLAGUE SWINGE
SCORPION
SCOURGER WHIPSTER
SCOURING BEAT SCOUR HUSHING
SCRUBBING
SCOUT SPY BEAR LION SKIP ROVER
SPIAL VISOR ESPIAL GAYCAT
DESPISE MARINER PICKEER
PIONEER SCOURER WATCHER
EMISSARY OUTRIDER OUTSCOUT
SCURRIER SKIRMISH
(BOY —) CUB BOBCAT SCOUTER
WEBELOS EXPLORER
(CUB — SUBDIVISION) DEN
(GIRL —) DAISY
SCOW ACCON FLOAT GARVEY
SCOWL LOUR FROWN GLARE
GLOOM GLOUT LOWER SKIME
GLOWER VENNER GLOOMING
SCOWLING FROWNY GLARING
SCRABBLE PAW RAKE GROPE
CLAMBER SCRAMBLE
SCRAGGY WEEDY
SCRAM GIT HOP LAM BUNK SCAT
BUGGER BUGOFF SODOFF
BUZZOFF GETLOST
SCRAMBLE MUSS SPURL SCRAWM
SPRAWL CLAMBER LOUSTER
SCRABBLE SCRAFFLE SCRATTLE
SPRACHLE
SCRAP BIT END JAG ORT PIP CRAP
ITEM JAGG JUNK PICK SNAP
BRAWL GRAIN PATCH SCRAN

SHRED THRUM WASTE FRACAS TUSSLE DISCARD MAMMOCK ODDMENT REMNANT SNIPPET FRACTION SCRAPPET SKERRICK SNATTOCK
(— FOR PATCHING) SPETCH
(— OF PAPER) SCRIP
(— OF SONG) CATCH
(— OF WRITING) SCRAPE
(FOOD —S) BROCK
(LEAST —) STITCH
(LITERARY —S) ANA
(METAL —) SCISSEL SCISSIL
(RAGGED —) SCART
(PL.) ORTS SCRAN RELICS SCROFF GARBAGE GUBBINGS
SCRAPE LEG RUB CLAW COMB RAZE CLAUT CURET ERADE ERODE GRATE GRAZE GRIDE SCALP SCART SCUFF SHAVE ABRADE HOBBLE RUGINE SCREED SCROOP SPLORE CORRADE CURETTE JACKPOT SCRATCH SNAPPER TROUBLE SCRABBLE
(— ALONG) HARL HARLE SHOOL
(— GOLF CLUB ON GROUND) SCLAFF
(— OFF) SPUD
(— OUT) ERASE HOLLOW
(— SKINS) MOON SCUD FLESH HARASS
(— TOGETHER) RAKE GLEAN MUCKER SCAMBLE
(— WITH FEET) SCAUT
(PREF.) RAMENTI SCAPI
SCRAPED BRIGHT
SCRAPER PAN PIG HARL SLIP CURET GLOVE HARLE QUIRL RASER SPOON DOCTOR FRESNO GRADER GRATER RASPER CURETTE FLANGER LEVELER RACLOIR SLUSHER STRIGIL GRATTOIR SCRAPPLE TERRACER UNHAIRER
SCRAPING HARL GRIDE RASURE
(CRACKER —S) CUSH
(METAL —S) DIET
(PL.) RAMENTA
SCRAPMAN CHIPMAN
SCRAPPER BREAKER FIGHTER
SCRAPPLE PANHAS PONHAWS
SCRAPPY BITTY SNATCHY
SCRATCH RAT RIT CLAW CRAB RACE RAIN RAKE RAPE RASE RAUK RAZE RISP RIST SHAB SLUG STUN CHALK CLAUT CLAWK CURRY FRUSH GRAZE RANCH SCART SCLUM SCORE SCRAB SCRAT SCROB SCRUB SHRUB SKELP TEASE TOUCH BRUISE CANCEL CRATCH RASURE RIPPLE SCORCH SCOTCH SCRAPE SCRAWK SCRAWL SCRAWM SCRAZE SCRIVE TORACE DECLARE EMERIZE EXPUNGE SCARIFY SCRABBLE SCRATTLE SCRIBBLE
(— OUT MORTAR) POINT
(PREF.) RAMENTI
SCRATCHER RASER
SCRAWL SCRAWM SPRAWL SCRATCH SCRABBLE SCRIBBLE SQUIGGLE
SCRAWNY BONY LEAN SLINK

WEEDY SCRANK SCRAGGY SCRANKY SCRANNY SCRAGGED
(— PERSON OR ANIMAL) RIBE
SCREAM CRY YAW REME WEAK YARM YAUP YAWL YAWP YOWT SKIRL SHRAME SHRIEK SHRILL SQUALL SQUAWL YAMMER SCREECH YELLOCH SKELLOCH
SCREAMER CHAJA ANHIMA
SCREAMING MEEMIES JITTERS HYSTERIA
SCREECH QUAWK QUOCK SCREAM SCREEK SCRITCH SKREIGH ULULATE SKELLOCH
SCREECH OWL STRICH
SCREED BLAUD TIRADE HARANGUE
SCREEN TRY CAGE GOBO HARP HIDE LAWN MASK PICK REJA SCUG SEPT SIFT TENT VEIL ARRAS BLIND CHEEK CHICK CLOAK CLOSE COVER FIGHT GAUZE GRATE HOARD SHADE SHOJI SIEVE SPEER SPIER TATTY BAFFLE BASKET BORDER CANVAS DEFEND ESCORT HALLAN MEDIUM PURDAH RESEAU SCHERM SCONCE SHAKER SHIELD SHROUD THREAD VOIDER CEILING CONCEAL CRIBBLE CURTAIN FLYWIRE GOGGLES GRIZZLY REREDOS SECLUDE SHELTER SHUTTER TESTUDO TROMMEL BACKSTOP BESCREEN BLINDAGE COVERING DIFFUSER ECLIPSER EXCLUDER HOARDING OCCULTER PARAVENT PARCLOSE PAVISADE SCREENER SPLASHER STRAINER TRAVERSE UMBRELLA
(— ALONGSIDE SHIP) PAVISADE
(— BEHIND ALTAR) REREDOS
(— FOR BATTING PRACTICE) CAGE
(— FOR SHIP'S COMBATANTS) FIGHT
(— FOR SIZING ORE) GRATE TROMMEL
(— FOR THEATER LIGHT) JELLY MEDIUM
(— IN BASKETBALL) PICK
(— OF BAMBOO SLIPS) CHEEK CHICK
(— OF BRUSHWOOD) SCHERM
(— OF FIRE) BARRAGE
(— OF SHIELDS FOR TROOPS) TESTUDO
(— OF TAPESTRY) ARRAS CEILING
(— ON AUTOMOBILE) GRILL GRILLE
(— TO PROTECT LOOKOUTS) DODGER
(— USED BY ARCHERS) PANNIER
(BULLETPROOF —) MANTA MANTEL MANTELET
(CHANCEL —) JUBE
(FIRE —) FENDER
(KIND OF —) TOUCH
(MECHANICALLY ACTUATED —) GRIZZLY
(PAPER —) SHOJI
(PL.) CANCELLI
SCREENED BLIND SECLUDED
SCREENINGS CULM SLACK SLECK
SCREENLAND FILMDOM
SCREENPLAY SCRIPT SCENARIO
SCREW HOB VISE WORM CRICK FEEZE SCROW WREST TEMPER

TOGGLE COCHLEA AIRSCREW FLATHEAD SETSCREW THUMBKIN WINDMILL
(KIND OF —) ALLEN MEANTIME
(PART OF —) HEAD ROOT CREST PITCH POINT SHANK THREAD
(PROPELLER —) FAN
SCREWBALL KOOK ZANY FLAKE ECCENTRIC NONSENSICAL
SCREW BEAN MESQUITE SCREWPOD TORNILLA
SCREWDRIVER (KIND OF —) PHILLIPS
SCREWED SQUINCH
SCREWER WORMER
SCREWMAN JACKMAN
SCREW PINE IE ARA HALA IEIE AGGAG PALMA VACOA VACONA LAUHALA PANDANUS
SCREW TREE TWISTY
SCRIBBLE SQUIB DOODLE SCRAWL SCRATCH REMARQUE SCRABBLE SQUIGGLE
SCRIBBLING GRAFFITO
(PL.) GRAFFITI
SCRIBE EZRA CLERK THOTH BOOKER PENMAN SCRIVE SOPHER WRITER GRAFFER MASORET SCRIVAN NOVERINT PENCLERK SCRIPTOR SCRIVANO
(PL.) SOPHERIM
SCRIMMAGE MAUL BULLY ROUGE SCRAP BICKER SPLORE SKIRMISH
SCRIMP HINCH SCREW SKIMP
SCRIP EXONUMIA
SCRIPT BOOK NEUM RONDE SERTA SERTO NASKHI NESKHI SCRITE SOOLOOS THULUTH BASTARDA GURMUKHI HIRAGANA KANARESE MAGHRIBI MAITHILI MEROITIC NASTALIQ SCENARIO
(HINDI —) DEVANAGARI
(KOREAN ALPHABETIC —) HANGUL
(TYPE OF —) RONDE
SCRIPTURE WRIT AGAMA CHING SUTRA SUTTA TANTRA
(HINDU —) VEDA
(PL.) BIBLE GRANTH GRUNTH TANACH TENACH SHASTRA
SCRIVENER PENMAN WRITER GRAFFER SCRIVER NOVERINT TABELLION
SCROFULA EVIL CRUELS STRUMA
SCROLL BEND ROLL LABEL SCRIT AMULET ESCROL LEGEND SCRAWL STEMMA VOLUME VOLUTE EVOLUTE PAPYRUS RINCEAU BANDEROL CARTOUCH MAKIMONO
(— AT END OF HANDRAIL) MONKEYTAIL
(— AT MOUTH OF FIGURE) PHYLACTERY
SCROLL-LIKE TURBINAL
SCROPHULARIA FIGWORT
SCROTUM BAG COD PURSE
(PREF.) OSCHE(O) SCROT(I)(O)
SCROUNGER SCAMBLER
SCRUB FILE ABORT SCOUR SCROG CANCEL COPPET MAQUIS SCODGY CLEANSE SCRUBBER YANNIGAN
SCRUBBY SHRUBBY
SCRUBLAND GARIGUE GARRIGUE

SCRUFF CUFF NAPE SCUFF SCROFF
SCRUFFY DOGEARED
SCRUPLE PASS DEMUR DOUBT FORCE POINT QUALM STAND STICK BOGGLE SCOTCH STRAIN STICKLE STUMBLE
SCRUPULOUS NICE SPICED TENDER CAREFUL FINICKY PRECISE DELICATE QUALMISH
SCRUTINIZE EYE PRY SEE SPY SCAN VIEW AUDIT PROBE SIGHT SOUND VISIT PERUSE SURVEY EXAMINE INSPECT ENSEARCH TRAVERSE
SCRUTINIZING NARROW SCANNING
SCRUTINY EYE SEARCH CANVASS EXAMINE HAWKEYE PERUSAL DOCIMASY
(ELECTION —) CANVAS CANVASS
SCRYER SEER
SCUD RUN RACK RAMP SKID SKIM SKIP SCOOT SPOON
SCUDAMORE (LOVER OF —) AMORETTA
SCUDO FILIPPO
SCUFF SLARE SLIDE SCLAFF SCUFFER SCUFFLE SHUFFLE
SCUFFLE HOE CUFF BUSTLE BUSTUP CLINCH CUFFLE TUSSLE WISTER BAGARRE BRULYIE SHAMBLE SHUFFLE SCRUFFLE
SCULL OAR FUNNY SHELL SKULL WHERRY
SCULLERY SINKROOM
SCULLION GIPPO SCULL SLUSH GALOPIN SWILLER CUSTROUN QUISTRON
SCULPIN COTTID GRUBBY JOHNNY BIGHEAD DRUMMER BULLHEAD BULLPOUT CABEZONE HARDHEAD LORICATE SCALAWAG
SCULPTOR CARVER GRAVER IMAGER MARBLER PLASTIC
AMERICAN FRY BALL GABO HART IVES KECK LADD MEAD RUSH TAFT VOLK WARD ADAMS AKERS ANDRE BEACH BOEHM BROWN CLARK DOYLE EVANS GALLO GOULD HOXLE JONES KELLY KONTI MEARS MILLS PERRY PRATT SEGAL SERRA STONE STORY YOUNG AITKEN BARTHE BENDER BITTER BUFANO CALDER CLARKE COUPER CURTIS DALLIN EAKINS EBERLE ELWELL FRASER FRAZEE FRENCH GRAFLY GRIMES HARVEY HOSMER HUGHES KASKEY KEMEYS KINNEY KITSON LAWRIE LEWITT MILLES MOZIER NAKIAN NEWMAN PALMER POTTER POWERS PUTNAM RIMMER ROGERS ROSZAK RUMSEY SHRADY WALKER WARNER ZORACH BARNARD BISSELL BORGLUM BRENNER BRIGHAM EDSTROM EZEKIEL GELLERT GODDARD GREGORY HANCOCK HARTLEY HOFFMAN JACKSON JAEGERS KENDALL LAESSLE LAURENT LIPPOLD LONGMAN LUKEMAN MACNEIL MANSHIP MARTINY MILMORE NIEHAUS NOGUCHI OCONNOR PROCTOR ROBERTS SCHULER SCUDDER SIEVERS SIMMONS

WHITNEY AGOSTINI ALBRIGHT ATCHISON BARTLETT BREWSTER CONNELLY CRAWFORD DAVIDSON DECREEFT DERIVERA FLANAGAN LACHAISE LENTELLI MCCARTAN MULLIGAN NADELMAN ODONOVAN PARAMINO RINEHART CLEVENGER GREENOUGH HUMPHREYS MACDONALD REMINGTON RUCKSTULL VALENTINE ARCHIPENKO MACMONNIES PAPASHVILY PICCIRILLI ZIOLKOWSKI

ARGENTINIAN ALONZO

ATHENIAN ANTENOR

AUSTRIAN DONNER NATTER TILGNER STRASSER

BELGIAN GEEFS FRAIKIN KESSELS LALAING MEUNIER SIMONIS STAPPEN LAMBEAUX TONGERLOO

CANADIAN HEBERT MACCARTHY

CZECH STRUSA MYSLBEK

DANISH BISSEN JERICHAU WILLUMSEN THORVALDSEN

DUTCH VRIES SLUTER TASSAERT DESJARDINS

ENGLISH BELL CARO FORD GILL JOHN SWAN WARD WOOD ANGEL BACON BAILY BANKS BATES BOEHM COLIN DURST HESSE JONES MOORE RHIND STONE TWEED WATTS ARCHER DOBSON GIBSON JAGGER KENNET LANDAU CHAROUX EPSTEIN FLAXMAN GIBBONS GILBERT STEVENS WOOLNER ARMITAGE ARMSTEAD CHANTREY FRAMPTON HEPWORTH SHERIDAN MACKENNAL KENNINGTON WESTMACOTT THORNYCROFT

FLEMISH BOLOGNE

FRENCH ARP ADAM ETEX RUDE UZES BARYE BOSIO CHAPU CRAUK DALOU DAVID DURET LEMOT PAJOU PILON PUECH RODIN DANTAN DEJOUX DUBOIS DUMONT GOUJON HOUDON ISELIN LEGROS MERCIE MILLET ROCHET ANGUIER BEGUINE BOUCHER CARRIES CHAUDET CLODION COLOMBE COUSTOU DESPIAU FREMIET LEMAIRE LEMOYNE MAILLET MAILLOL PIGALLE PRADIER PREAULT RICHIER CAFFIERI CARPEAUX CAVELIER CHAPLAIN COYSEVOX FALCONET FOYATIER GIRARDON GODEBSKI JOUFFROY LEPAUTRE LIPCHITZ SARRAZIN BARTHOLDI BEAUNEVEU BOURDELLE CLESINGER FALGUIERE INJALBERT LANDOWSKI ROUBILLAC BARTHOLOME CASSEGRAIN CHARPENTIER DELAPLANCHE

GERMAN HAHN KISS LENZ NAHL BEUYS CAUER HAAKE KOLBE KRAFT OESER RAUCH STOSS STUCK WOLFF BANDEL BLASER GEIGER HABICH HAHNEL HALBIG HERTER HOSAUS WAGNER AFINGER BARLACH BELLING KAUPERT KLIMSCH KLINGER KRELING SCHADON SCHAPER EBERHARD EBERLEIN FERNKORN SCHLUTER ZUMBUSCH DANNECKER ENGELHARD LEHMBRUCK MAGNUSSEN RIETSCHEL

SIEMERING UECHTRITZ LEINBERGER SCHWANTHALER RIEMENSCHNEIDER

GREEK MYRON CHARES ONATAS SCOPAS AGASIAS BOETHUS BRYAXIS CALAMIS CRITIUS PHIDIAS SCYLLIS AGELADAS CANACHUS CRESILAS DAMOPHON LYSIPPUS PAEONIUS SOCIBIUS AGESANDER ALCAMENES ARCHERMUS BATHYCLES EUPHRANOR LEOCHARES PASITELES TAURISCUS TIMOTHEUS POLYCLETUS POLYCLITUS POLYEUCTUS PRAXITELES AGORACRITUS ATHENODORUS CALLIMACHUS LYSISTRATUS CEPHISODOTUS

IRISH FOLEY MACDOWELL FITZGERALD

ITALIAN VELA BANCO DANTI DUPRE LEONI PORTA RIZZO VINCI CANOVA GIOTTO MARINI PISANO ROBBIA SOLARI ALGARDI BERNINI CELLINI FIESOLE GIORGIO LAURANA MAZZONI QUERCIA TRIBOLO AGOSTINO AMMANATI ANTELAMI BARBIERE BOCCIONI CAMPAGNA CERACCHI CIVITALI GHIBERTI LOMBARDO MARCHESI TENERANI BARTOLINI BEGARELLI BORROMINI DONATELLO SANSOVINO GIACOMETTI MODIGLIANI MONTEVERDE VERROCCHIO DELLAROBBIA MICHELANGELO

NORWEGIAN VIGELAND

POLISH KALISH

ROMAN COSMATI

RUMANIAN BRANCUSI

RUSSIAN ZADKINS ORLOVSKI ANTOKOLSKI

SPANISH CANO MENA SILOE PICASSO CHILLIDA HERNANDEZ BERRUGUETE

SWEDISH ZORN MILLES SERGEL BYSTROM BORJESON FOGELBERG

SWISS HOERBST KISSLING TINGUELY

VENEZUELAN MARISOL

SCULPTURAL PLASTIC

SCULPTURE CAMEO DRAFT GRAVE SCULP BRONZE ENTAIL GISANT SCULPT CARVING DRAUGHT ENGRAVE GRADINO IMAGERY INSCULP STABILE MORTORIO NATIVITY PORTRAIT PREDELLA SCULLION

SCULPTURED GRAVEN GLYPHIC

SCUM BRAT FOAM GALL HEAD REAM SCUD SILT SKIM SKIN DROSS FROTH SCURF SLOAK SLOKE SLUSH SPUME FLURRY MANTLE MOTHER REFUSE RIDDAM SCRUFF BLANKET CACHAZA OFFSCUM LAITANCE PELLICLE SANDIVER SCOURING SCUMMING
(— OF THE PEOPLE) RIFFRAFF
(— ON FUSED GLASS) SANDIVER
(— ON LIQUOR) PELLICLE
(— ON MELTED METAL) SLAG

SCUP BREAM PORGY SPARID SCUPPAUG

SCURF SCALD SCALL DANDER FURFUR SCRUFF DANDRUFF

SCURFY SCALD SCURVY LEPROSE SCRUFFY LEPIDOTE SCABROUS SCABERULOUS

SCURRILITY ABUSE REPROACH

SCURRILOUS LOW FOUL VILE DIRTY GROSS RIBALD VULGAR ABUSIVE SCURRIL INDECENT

SCURRY HIE RUN ZIP BELT CRAB SKIN CURRY HURRY SCOUR SKICE SKURRY SCUFFLE SCUTTER SCUTTLE SKELTER SKITTER

SCURRYING SKITTER

SCURVY SCALD SCUMMY SHABBY ROYNOUS SCORBUCH SCORBUTE UNLIKING

SCUT BUN

SCUTAGE ESCUAGE

SCUTATE CLYPEATE

SCUTCH SCOTCH SWINGLE

SCUTE PLATE SCUTUM SCUTELLA

SCUTELLATION SCALING

SCUTIFORM PELTATE

SCUTTLE HOD CRAB SINK SKEP BEETLE MANHOLE SCUDDLE SCUTTER SCRATTLE

SCUTTLEBUTT CASK RUMOR GOSSIP FOUNTAIN

SCUZZY NASTY

SCYLLA (FATHER OF —) NISUS TYPHON

SCYLLITOL INOSITOL

SCYPHUS PYXIS

SCYTHE SY LEA HOOK MEAK REAP CRADLE

SCYTHIAN LAMB BAROMETZ

SEA MER ZEE BAHR BLUE BRIM FOAM FRET GULF HOLM LAVE MAIN MARE RACE TIDE WAVE BRINE BRINY FLOAT FLOOD LOUGH OCEAN AEQUOR PONTUS SEALET STRAND TETHYS CHANNEL HYALINE NEPTUNE BOSPORUS DEEPNESS SEAFLOOD THALASSA
(— DIVINITY) TRITON
(— GOD) PROTEUS
(— LETTER) PASSPORT
(AT —) LOST PUZZLED
(HEAVY —) POPPLE
(HIGH —) MAIN
(MODERATE —) SEAWAY
(PREF.) HAL(I)(IO)(O) MARI MER PELAG(O) THALASS(I)(IO)(O) THALATTO

SEA ANCHOR DRAG DROGUE

SEA ANEMONE POLYP DAHLIA OPELET ACTINIA VESTLET ACTINIAN ZOANTHID

SEA BASS HANAHILL HUMPBACK SERRANID TALLYWAG

SEA BEAR OTARIOID

SEABIRD HAGDON

SEA BISCUIT BREAD GALETTE PANTILE

SEABOARD COAST

SEA BREAD HARDTACK

SEA BREAM TAI CARP CHAD PORGY ROMAN BRAISE SARGUS SPARID TARWHINE

SEA BREEZE DOCTOR

SEA BUTTERFLY PTEROPOD

SEACOAST BANK SEABOARD SEASHORE

SEA COW SIREN DUGONG MANATEE RHYTINA SIRENIAN

SEA CUCUMBER BALATE TREPANG CUCUMBER SYNAPTID TEATFISH

SEADOG SALT FOGBOW FOGDOG SAILOR

SEA DOVE DOVEKIE ICEBIRD

SEA DRAGON PEGASID QUAVIVER

SEA DUCK DIVER EIDER DIPPER DUCKER SCOTER

SEA EAGLE ERN ERNE PYGARG PYGARGUS

SEA-EAR ORMER ABALONE

SEAFARER SEAGOER

SEAFOOD (— AND STEAK) SURFANDTURF

SEAFOOD)- ON SKEWERS) YAKITORI

SEA FOX THRASHER

SEA GIRDLE CUVY CUTWEED

SEA GULL COB GOR MEW COBB ANNET COBBE POPELER
(AUTHOR OF —) CHEKHOV
(CHARACTER IN —) NINA IRINA TRIGORIN CONSTANTIN

SEA-GYPSY SELUNG

SEA HOLLY ERYNGO ERYNGIUM

SEA HORSE WALRUS HIPPODAME HIPPOCAMPUS LOPHOBRANCH

SEA KALE COLE

SEAL CAN FIX FOB GUM BULL CHOP CORK HARP HOOD JARK LUTE BLANK BULLA CLOSE EAGLE PHOCA SIGIL STAMP SWILE THONG UGRUG URSUK WAFER ASSEAL BEATER CACHET COCKET DOTARD ENSEAL ENSIGN FASTEN GASKET MAKLUK MATKAH OBSIGN PHOCID RANGER SEALCH SECURE SIGNET CONFIRM CONSIGN COWROID ENGLUTE HOODCAP IMPRESS QUITTER SADDLER SEALING SEALKIE SIGNARY WEDDELL ADHESIVE BACHELOR BEDLAMER BRELOQUE CYLINDER MANDORLA PINNIPED SECRETUM SEECATCH SIGILLUM SIGNACLE TANGFISH VALIDATE
(— FOR WATCH CHAIN) ONION BRELOQUE
(— OFF) CAP
(— OVER CORK) CAPSULE
(BEARDED —) URSUK MAKLUK
(CUSTOM-HOUSE —) COCKET
(EARED —) OTARY
(FEMALE —) MATKA
(GOLD —) BEZEL
(HARBOR —) DOTARD RANGER TANGFISH
(HERD OF —S) PATCH
(IMMATURE —) BEDLAMER
(KIND OF —) HAIR MONK WEDDELL
(MALE —) WIG SADDLER BACHELOR SEECATCH
(NEWFOUNDLAND —) SWILE RANGER
(PAPAL —) BULL BULLA
(SHETLAND —) SILKIE
(YEARLING —) HOPPER
(YOUNG —) PUP BEATER JACKET BLUEBACK
(3-YEAR OLD —) TURNER
(PREF.) PHOC(O) SIGILLO

SEA LACE WHIPLASH
SEA LAVENDER INKROOT STATICE
SEALED CLOSE
SEALER CAPPER GASKET
SEA LETTUCE LAVER SLAKE SLOKE
  SEAWEED
SEA LILY CRINOID
SEA LION OTARY HAIRSEAL
  PINNIPED PINNIPEDE
SEALSKIN SKIN SCULP MATARA
  SAFARI
SEALSKIN COAT NETCHA
SEALYHAM TERRIER
SEAM DRY BAND DART FASH FELL
  PURL REND DEVIL PEARL SPILL
  FAGGOT INSEAM STREAK SUTURE
  SEAMLET JUNCTURE OVERSEAM
  (— IN INGOT) SPILL
  (— IN SHIP'S HULL) DEVIL
  (— OF COAL) RIDER SPLIT STREAK
  (IRREGULAR —) FASH
SEAMAN SALT JACKY MATLO
  ARTIST CALASH LUBBER SAILOR
  MARINER MASTMAN SHIPMAN
  SHIPPER SMASHER WAISTER
  YOUNKER DESERTER SEASONER
SEAMARK MEITH
SEAMED SEAMY RUGGED
SEA MILE NAUT
SEA MONSTER ORC PHOCA
  KRAKEN LEVIATHAN ROSMARINE
  HIPPOCAMPUS
SEAMOUNT GUYOT
SEAMSTER TAILOR SEMPSTER
SEAMSTRESS SEAMER SEWSTER
  NEEDLEWOMAN
SEANCE SITTING
SEA NETTLE BLUBBER
SEA OF GRASS (AUTHOR OF —)
  RICHTER
  (CHARACTER IN —) HAL JIM BRICE
  BROCK HENRY LUTIE SARAH JIMMIE
  BREWTON CAMERON CHARLEY
  BREWSTER MCCURTIN
  CHAMBERLAIN
SEA ONION SCILLA
SEA OTTER KID KALAN
SEA OXEYE SALTWEED SAMPHIRE
SEA PERCH GAPER COMBER
  TRIPLETAIL
SEA PINK THRIFT SABBATIA
SEAPLANE HYDRO AIRBOAT
  AEROBOAT
SEA PLANTAIN GIBBALS
SEA POACHER BULLHEAD
SEAPORT PARA PORT GROIN NATAL
  HARBOR ENTREPOT MACASSAR
SEA PUSS OFFSET
SEAR BURN FIRE SERE FLAME FRIZZ
  ENSEAR SCORCH SIZZLE FRIZZLE
SEA RAVEN SCULPIN
SEARCH FAN SPY BEAT COMB DRAG
  DRAW FAND FISH FOND GAPE
  HUNT LAIT RAKE RIPE ROUT SEEK
  SIFT WAIT FRISK PROBE QUEST
  SCOUR SNOOP VISIT DACKER
  DREDGE FERRET FUMBLE RANCEL
  SLEUTH ENQUIRE EXPLORE
  FOSSICK INQUEST INQUIRE
  INSPECT RANSACK SCRINGE
  ZETETIC FINECOMB OUTREACH
  SCRABBLE SCROUNGE SCRUTINY
  SHAKEDOWN

(— ABOUT) GRUB PROG GROPE
(— AMONG REFUSE) SCAVENGE
(— BY FEELING) GROPE
(— DEEPLY) TENT DELVE
(— DIIGENTLY) SCOUR
(— EVERYWHERE) BUSK SCOUR
(— FOR) FORK HUNT LAIT SNOOK
  REQUIRE SEEKOUT
(— FOR FOX'S TRAIL) CIPHER
(— FOR GAME) DRAW GHOOM
  QUEST
(— FOR GOLD) FOSSICK
(— FOR KNOWLEDGE) OUTREACH
(— FOR PARTNER) CRUISE
(— FOR PROVISIONS) FORAGE
(— FOR SMUGGLED GOODS)
  DACKER JERQUE
(— FOR STOLEN GOODS) RANCEL
  RANSEL RANZEL
(— FOR WEAPONS) FRISK
(— GROPINGLY) GLAMP
(— INTO) EXQUIRE INDAGATE
(— OUT) FERRET INVENT ROOTLE
  EXQUIRE INDAGATE
(— SHIP) RUMMAGE
(— SYSTEMATICALLY) COMB
(— THROUGH) TURN
(— UNDERWATER) FISH
(CAREFUL —) RESEARCH
(SYSTEMATIC —) SWEEP
SEARCHER FINDER
SEARCHING HARD CLOSE SHREWD
  CURIOUS GROPING
SEARED ADUST
SEARING CAUTERY
SEA ROBIN GURNARD WINGFISH
SEA ROVER VIKING SCUMMER
SEASAN NUDE
SEASCAPE MARINE SEAPIECE
SEA SCORPION COBBLER
SEA SERPENT ELOPS
SEASHELL PROP
SEASHORE SEA RIPE CLEVE COAST
  PLAYA MARINE SEASIDE
  SEABEACH SEABOARD SEACOAST
SEASICKNESS HILO NAUPATHIA
SEA SNAIL LIPARIAN
SEA SNAKE CHITAL KERRIL
SEASON BEEK CORN DASH FALL
  PERT SALT SEEL TIDE TIME GRASS
  INURE SAUCE SAVOR SHEMU
  SPICE AUTUMN EASTER FLOWER
  HARDEN HAYING MASTER SPRING
  STEVEN STOUND SUMMER WINTER
  BUDTIME FLYTIME HARVEST
  KITCHEN OATSEED SEEDTIME
(— FOR HERRING FISHING) DRAVE
(— HIGHLY) DEVIL
(— IN THE SUN) HAZE
(— OF JOY) JUBILEE
(— OF MERRYMAKING) CARNIVAL
(CLOSED —) SHUTOFF
(DULL —) SLACK
(EGYPTIAN —) AHET PERT SHEMU
(HAYING —) HAYING HAYSEL
(LENTEN —) CAREME
(RAINLESS —) DRY
(RAINY —) KHARIF VARSHA
(REGULARLY RECURRING —)
  EMBER
(SPRING —) WARE APRIL GRASS
(THE RIGHT —) TID
SEASONABLE PAT TIDY TIMELY

  TIDEFUL TIMEFUL VETERAN
  TOWARDLY OPPORTUNE
SEASONABLY TIMELY APROPOS
  BETIMES
SEASONED SAGY SALT SALTED
  INDIENNE POWDERED
(MILDLY —) SWEET
SEASONER SURFACER
SEASONING SALT SPICE SEASON
  PAPRIKA SPICING OREGANUM
SEA SPIDER PYCNOGONOID
SEA SQUIRT ASCIDIAN
SEA SWALLOW TERN
SEAT BOX CAN SEE SET USH BANK
  BOSS COSY DAIS FLOP FORM
  FROG ROOM SILL SLIP SUNK TOIT
  ASANA BENCH CELLE CHAIR DICKY
  PERCH SELLA SELLE SETTE SIEGE
  SLIDE STALL STOOL USHER
  BOUGHT DODONA EXEDRA
  HUMPTY INSIDE RUMBLE SADDLE
  SEATER SEGGIO SETTEE SETTLE
  THWART BUTTOCK CUSHION
  GRADINE GRADINO INSTALL
  OTTOMAN SEATING TABORET
  TRANSOM BLEACHER ENTHRONE
  PULVINAR SEGGIOLA SUBSELLA
  WOOLPACK
(— AT PUBLIC SPECTACLE)
  PULVINAR
(— FOR CLERGY) SEDILE
(— FOR GRINDER) HORSING
(— FOR PLANE IRON) FROG
(— FOR TWO) SOCIABLE
(— NEAR ALTAR) SEDILIUM
(— OF BIRTH) SIDE
(— OF CHAIR) BOTTOM
(— OF DIGNITY) STATE
(— OF EMOTIONS) CHEST SPLEEN
(— OF FEELINGS) STOMACH
(— OF HARE) FORM
(— OF INTELLECT) HEAD
(— OF KNOWLEDGE) RUACH
(— OF ORACLE) DODONA
(— OF PITY) BOWEL
(— OF POWER) SEE
(— OF REAL LIFE) SOUL
(— OF RESPONSIBILITY) SHOULDER
(— OF RULE) OGDOAD
(— OF THEATRE) STALL
(— OF TURF) SUNK
(— OF UNDERSTANDING) SKULL
(— ON ELEPHANT'S BACK) TOWER
  CASTLE HOWDAH
(— ONESELF) LEAN PITCH
(— SLUNG ON POLES) HORSE
(— WITH BRAZIER BELOW)
  TENDOUR
(— WITHIN WINDOW OPENING)
  CAROL
(AIRPLANE —) DORMETTE
(BACKLESS —) STOOL HASSOCK
(BISHOP'S —) APSE BISHOPRIC
  FALDSTOOL FALDISTORY
  SYNTHRONUS
(BUS —) KNIFEBOARD
(CANOPIED —) COSY COZY
(CARRIAGE —) DICKY
(CHIEF —) METROPOLIS
(CHIMNEY —) SCONCE
(CHURCH —) PEW DESK STALL
  SEDILE
(COACH —) BOOT POOP

(COUNTRY —) TOWER GRANGE
  QUINTA
(DILIGENCE —) BANQUETTE
(DRAPED —) MUSNUD
(DRIVER'S —) BOX DICKY COCKPIT
  FORETOP
(ELEVATED —) PERCH
(FIXED —) DAIS
(GARDEN —) ALCOVE
(JUDGMENT —) TRIBUNAL
(KEY —) KEYWAY
(LONG —) BANK FORM BENCH
(MOTORCYCLE —) PILLION
(NIPPLE —) LUMP
(OARSMAN'S —) TAFT
(PORCH —) GLIDER
(RECLINING —) DORMEUSE
(ROMAN —) PULVINAR
(ROWER'S —) THWART
(ROYAL —) SIEGE STEAD THRONE
(STAGECOACH —S) BASKET
(STRAW —) BOSS
(TIER OF —S) TENDIDO
(TURF —) SUNK BUNKER
(UNRESERVED —S) BLUES
(PREF.) EDRI(O)
(SUFF.) HEDRAL
SEA TANGLE FURBELOW
SEATED (— IN MIND) INWARD
SEATING (— AREA) LOGE
SEA TROUT SEWEN SMELT KIPPER
  HERLING HIRLING BODIERON
(— AFTER SPAWNING) KELT
(YOUNG —) PEAL
SEA TURTLE RIDLEY CHELONID
SEA URCHIN WANA REPKIE
  ARBACIA CIDARID ECHINID
  ECHINUS RADIATE ECHINOID
(FOSSIL —) ECHINITE
(PREF.) ECHIN(O)
SEAWALL BULWARK
SEAWARD OFF MAKAI
SEAWEED ORE AGAR ALGA KELP
  LIMU MOSS NORI OOZE REEK REIT
  TANG WARE DRIFT DULSE KOMBU
  LAVER SLAKE SLOKE VAREC VRAIC
  WRACK DELISK FUCOID FUNORI
  TANGLE HAITSAI OARWEED
  OREWEED OREWOOD REDWARE
  SEATANG SEAWARE CARAGEEN
  GULFWEED HEMPWEED
  ROCKWEED SARGASSO SEABEARD
  WHIPCORD WHIPLASH CORALLINE
  NULLIPORE
(PL.) LUMUT
(PREF.) PHYC(O)
(SUFF.) PHYCEAE
SEA WOLF (AUTHOR OF —) LONDON
  (CHARACTER IN —) HUMP MAUD
  WOLF DEATH LEACH LOUIS LARSEN
  JOHNSON BREWSTER HUMPHREY
  JOHANSEN MUGRIDGE VANWEYDEN
SEA WORM PALOLO SABELLA
SEB (CONSORT OF —) NUT
  (SON OF —) OSIRIS
SEBA (FATHER OF —) CUSH
SEBASTIAN (BROTHER OF —)
  ALONSO
  (SISTER OF —) VIOLA
SEBESTEN MYXA
SECANT SEC CHORD
SECCO FRESCO
SECEDE SPLINTER

SECESSIONIST SECESH SEPARATE
SECLUDE TACKLE ENCLOSE
ISOLATE RECLUSE CLOISTER
SEQUESTER
SECLUDED COY SHY DEEP CLOSE
QUIET HIDDEN REMOTE SECRET
PRIVATE RETIRED RETRAIT
SECLUSE HIDEAWAY MONASTIC
SEPARATE SOLITARY UMBRATIC
CLAUSTRAL
SECLUSION RECESS SHADOW
PRIVACY PRIVITY RETREAT
SECRECY SEQUEST SOLITUDE
ISOLATION
(— OF WOMEN) PURDAH
SECOND AID SEC ABET BACK BETA
TICK OTHER VOUCH ASSIST
LATTER MOMENT TARTAN TIDDER
TOTHER ANOTHER INSTANT
SUPPORT SUSTAIN STICKLER
(— BASE) KEYSTONE
(— IN COMMAND) DEPUTY
(— IN HORSE RACE) PLACE
(— PERSON USE) TUISM
(MAJOR —) TONE
(1000TH OF A —) SIGMA
(60TH OF A —) THIRD
(PREF.) DEUT(O) DEUTER(O)
SECUNDI
SECONDARY BY BYE SUB SLACK
DONKEY SECOND CUBITAL
DERIVED INFERIOR MIDDLING
(PL.) FLAGS
(PREF.) DEUT(ER)(ERO)(O) MES(O)
SECONDHAND USED
SECOND MRS TANQUERAY
(AUTHOR OF —) PINERO
(CHARACTER IN —) RAY HUGH
PAULA ARDALE AUBREY ELLEAN
CORTELYOU TANQUERAY
SECOND-RATE DIMESTORE
COMMON SHODDY INFERIOR
SECOND-RATER PIKER
SECRECY DERN HUSH HIDING
SECRET HIDLING HIDLINS PRIVACY
PRIVITY SILENCE DARKNESS
HIDLINGS SCUGGERY VELATION
SECLUSION HUGGERMUGGER
(STATE OF —) CLOSET
SECRET SLY DARK DERN INLY BLIND
CABAL CLOSE HUSHY PRIVY QUIET
ARCANE CLOSET COVERT HIDDEN
INWARD POCKET STOLEN
ARCANUM COUNSEL CRYPTIC
EPOPTIC FURTIVE MYSTERY
PRIVACY PRIVATE PRIVITY
RECLUSE RESERVE RETIRED
SECRETA UNKNOWN ESOTERIC
HIDLINGS HUSHHUSH MYSTICAL
SNEAKING STEALTHY TETEATETE
HUGGERMUGGER
(PREF.) CRYPT(O) KRYPT(O) SUB
SECRETARY CLERK COPPY BARUCH
MUNSHI RAPTOR SCRIBE
FAMULUS MUNCHEE MOONSHEE
(SENIOR —) QUEENBEE
SECRETE HIDE CACHE NICHE RESET
SECERN SECRET CONCEAL
SECLUDE SALIVATE SEPARATE
(— MILK) LACTATE
(— ONESELF) HIVE
(— SALIVA) DROOL
(PREF.) ECCRINO

SECRETION INK LAC GOWL LAAP
LERP MILT SPIT WOOL HUMOR
LAARP MUCUS SEBUM SEPIA
SLIME SPADE CEMENT SALIVA
SMEGMA CERUMEN CHALONE
FLOCOON HORMONE SPITTLE
AUTACOID ENDOCRIN
(— OF MILK) LACTATION
(FATTY —) SEBUM
(GLAND —) SUCCUS
(OILY —) SEBUM
(THICKENED —) GUM
(VISCOUS —) SLIME
(WAXY —) LERP LAARP PRUINA
SECRETIVE SLY CAGY DARK SNUG
CAGEY CLOSE COVERT SECRET
SILENT INVOLVED
SECRETIVENESS SECRECY
SLYNESS
SECRETLY CLOSE DARKLY DERNLY
SECRET CLOSELY HIDLINGS
INWARDLY
SECRET, THE (CHARACTER IN —)
ROSE KALINA SKRIVANEK
(COMPOSER OF —) SMETANA
SECT SET ZEN BABI CLAN CULT
JODO KIND SHIN ALOGI BHORA
ISAWA PANTH BOHORA DONMEH
HERESY SCHISM SCHOOL CATHARI
DHUNDIA DOCETAE HASIDIM
ISAWIYA KHALSAH RINGATU
SECTARY SEQUELA SHAIKHI
SHINGON SIVAISM SUBSECT
AGNOETAE AHMADIYA AISSAOUA
MURJIITE NAASSENE SECTUARY
SHAKTISM BUCHANITES
(— MEMBER) DRUSE DRUZE
(LEBANESE —) DRUSE
(MEMBER OF —) KHLYST OPHITE
YEZIDI MOLOKAN NUSAIRI
LINGAYAT
SECTARIAN CULTIST HERETIC
MAZHABI SECTARY SECTIST
SECTARY JESUIT HERETIC SECTIST
SECTUARY SEPARATE
SECTION CUT END AREA PACE PART
SECT UNIT CAPUT FRUST PIECE
SHARE TMEMA BILLET BRANCH
BRIDGE CANTON LENGTH MEMBER
PASSUS SECTOR ARTICLE CUTTING
HEADING SEGMENT TRANCHE
ADDENDUM DIVISION FRACTION
(— AROUND HOP KILN) CURB
(— OF A BODY) LAMINA
(— OF AVICENNA'S WORK) FEN
(— OF BLOOM) STAMP
(— OF BUILDING) ENTRY
(— OF FENCE) FLAKE
(— OF FILM) EXPOSURE
(— OF FILTER) LEAF
(— OF FISHING TACKLE) TRACE
(— OF GARMENT) GORE
(— OF GLASS) SHAWL
(— OF HIGH GROUND) DIVIDE
(— OF KORAN) SURA
(— OF LADDER) FLY
(— OF LOG) BOLT FLITCH
(— OF LOOM) LAY
(— OF MELODY) STRAIN
(— OF NET) DEEPING
(— OF NEWSPAPER) LEAD ROTO
(— OF PARLIAMENT) LAGTHING
(— OF PSALTER) CATHISMA

(— OF RHAPSODY) LASSU
(— OF ROOF) SEVERY
(— OF ROOTSTOCK) BIT
(— OF SHIP) STEERAGE
(— OF SONG) STOLLEN
(— OF THREE SHEETS) TERNION
(— OF TORAH) PARASHAH
(— OF TRENCH) BAY
(— OF VIOLIN) BOUT
(— OF WOOD) HAG
(— OF YARN) SLUB
(—S OF SCENERY) BOOK
(CONCLUDING —) ABGESANG
(CONIC —) PARABOLA
(DULL —) LONGUEUR
(LOWEST —) BOTTOM
(MINE —) BORASQUE BORRASCA
(MUSICAL —) CODA EPILOG FINALE
(NARROW —) STRIPE
(NATIVE —) KASBA CASBAH
(ONE-SIXTEENTH OF —) FORTY
(PERCUSSION —) BATTERY
(4-PAGE —) OUTSERT
(SUFF.) TOMA TOME TOMIC
TOMOUS TOMY
SECTIONALISM LOCALISM
SECTOR AREA GORE HOUSE
(45-DEGREE —) OCTANT
SECULAR LAIC CIVIL COMMON
EARTHLY PROFANE WORLDLY
TEMPORAL
SECULARIZE LAICIZE
SECURE FID GET GIB KEY POT RUG
SEW WIN BAIL BOLT BOND CAUK
COCK COLD EASY FAST FIND FIRM
FRAP GAIN GIRD HOOK LAND
MOOR NAIL SAFE SEAL SHOT
SNUG STAY SURE WARM BELAY
BLOCK CINCH CLEAT SLOUR
SOUND STRAP TIGHT TRUST
ANCHOR ASSURE BECKET BUTTON
CLINCH DEFEND ENSURE FASTEN
OBTAIN PLEDGE SETTLE SICCAR
SICKER STABLE STAPLE TRAIST
ACQUIRE BULWARK CONFINE
DUNNAGE FORFEND FORTIFY
RAMPIRE WARRANT GARRISON
PRESERVE
(— AGAINST INTRUSION) TILE
(— AID OF) ENLIST
(— A SAIL) TRICE
(— BAIT) EBB
(— FROM LEAKING) COFFER
(— IN ADVANCE) SCOOP
(— PROMPTLY) SNAP
(— WITH BARS) GRATE
SECURED BOUND SETTLED
SECURELY FAST SAFE SICCAR
SICKER STRAIT SURELY SOLIDLY
SOUNDLY
SECURITY PUP BAIL BAND EASE
GAGE MUNI SEAL WAGE FRITH
GRITH GUARD QUIET STOCK
BORROW CEDULA EQUITY PLEDGE
REFUGE SAFETY SCREEN SEVERE
SURETY VADIUM BULWARK
CAUTION CUSTODY DEFENSE
DEPOSIT FLOATER HOSTAGE
SHELTER SLEEPER WARRANT
COLONIAL COVENANT FASTNESS
GUARANTY HYPOTHEC STRENGTH
VADIMONY MUNICIPAL
(— DEVICE) SENSOR

(BELOW AVERAGE —) LAGGARD
(PL.) PERCENTS PORTFOLIO
SEDAN SEDIA JAMPAN SALOON
TONJON NORIMON TOMJOHN
BROUGHAM
SEDATE CALM COOL DOUCE GRAVE
QUIET SOBER STAID SERENE
EARNEST SERIOUS SETTLED
COMPOSED DECOROUS
SEDATENESS SOBRIETY
SEDATIVE AMYTAL ACONITE
CALMANT CODEINE LUPULIN
BARBITAL LENITIVE QUIETIVE
SOOTHING
SEDENTARY STILL SESSILE
INACTIVE
SEDGE SAG LING RAIT REIT STAR
CAREX CHUFA TIKUG BHABAR
EHUAWA GLUMAL THATCH
TOETOE TOITOI BULRUSH
MONOCOT PAPYRUS SNIDDLE
TUSSOCK GALANGAL JIMSEDGE
PIKERUSH
(PREF.) CARIC(O)
SEDGE FLY GRANAM GRANNOM
SEDGE WARBLER WREN
MOCKBIRD REEDBIRD
SEDGY SAGGY SEGGY TWILLED
SEDIMENT CARR DREG FAEX FOOT
GOBI LEES MULM SILT WARP
DRAST DREGS FECES FOOTS
MAGMA BOTTOM FECULA
SIMMON SLUDGE DREWITE
GROUNDS GRUMMEL SAPROPEL
SETTLING
(— OF BEER OR ALE) CRAP
(IRON —) CAR CARR
(REDDISH —) SIMMON
SEDITION REVOLT TREASON
SEDITIOUS RIOTOUS FACTIOUS
MUTINOUS
SEDUCE DRAW JAPE LOCK DECOY
TEMPT WRONG ALLURE BETRAY
ENTICE DEBAUCH ENSNARE
MISLEAD SUGGEST TRADUCE
INVEIGLE
(— WITH THE EYE) LEER
SEDUCER UNDOER LOTHARIO
SEDUCTION LURE BRIBE CHARM
SEDUCTIVE TEMPTING
SEDULOUS BUSY INTENT STUDIED
DILIGENT UNTIRING
SEDULOUSNESS INDUSTRY
SEDUM MOSS ORPINE SENGREEN
SEE LO EYE KEN SPY VID DATE ESPY
LOOK MIND NOTE PEAT SEGE SEGE
SPOT VIDE VIEW BESEE CATCH
CHAIR SIEGE SIGHT STOOL TENEZ
WATCH ATTEND BEHOLD DESCRY
NOTICE QUAERE REMARK SURVEY
ARCHSEE DISCERN GLIMPSE
OBSERVE WITNESS CATHEDRA
CONCEIVE PERCEIVE
(— ABOVE) VS
(— BELOW) VI
(— FIT) CHOOSE
(— INTO) INSEE PENETRATE
(— THROUGH) RUMBLE
(— TO) FIX
(— VISIONS) SCRY
SEED BEN MAW NIB PIP BEAN BOIL
CHAT CORN DIKA GERM KOLA
LIMA MOTE SETH TARE BEHEN

BERRY CACAO CARAT CARVY GRAIN LUPIN SEMEN SPAWN SPERM SPORE STONE ABILLA ACHENE ACINUS ADZUKI BONDUC CACOON CARNEL FENNEL KERNEL LEGUME LENTIL NICKER NUTLET PIGNON PIPPIN TILLEY ACHIOTE ACHUETE ALPISTE ANISEED BUCKEYE CALINUT FRIJOLE HARICOT HAYSEED SEEDKIN SEEDLET SEMINAL AMBRETTE COKERNUT CYDONIUM DILLSEED FLAXSEED FLEASEED HEMPSEED PIGNOLIA PRINCIPE SEEDLING SEEDNESS PISTACHIO PROPAGULE

(— COATING) TESTA
(— COVER) TESTA
(— OF MAPLE) SAMARA
(AROMATIC —S) ANISE
(COFFEE —) PEABERRY
(COLE —) COLZA
(EDIBLE —) PEA BEAN
(FENUGREEK —) HELBEH
(GRAPE —) ACINUS
(IMMATURE —) OVULE
(MUSTARD —) SENVY SINEWY
(NUTLIKE —) PEANUT
(OILY —) ARGAN ABILLA
(PALM —) COROZO
(POPPY —) MAW MOHNSEED
(SESAME —) JIN JILI GINGELLY
(PL.) ANISE COFFEE SESAME ZERAIM IGNATIA LARKSPUR
(PREF.) COCC(O) GON(O) OVULI SEMINI SEMINULI SPERM(A)(ATI) (ATIO)(ATO)(I)(IO)(O) SPOR(I)(IDI)(O) (ULI)
(BEAK-LIKE —) RYNCO
(SUFF.) COCCAL COCCIC SPERM(A) (AE)(AL)(IA)(IC)(OUS)(UM)(Y) SPORA SPORANGE SPORANGIATE SPORANGIUM SPORE SPORIC SPORIDIA SPORIUM SPOROUS SPORY

SEEDCAKE WIG WIGG
SEEDCASE TEST TESTA THECA
SEED COAT ARIL TESTA SPIRICLE
SEEDED ARABLE
SEEDER SEEDMAN
SEEDLING FREE LINER
SEEDS
(PREF.) GRANI
SEEDY MANGY SCUFFY
SEEING SIGHT SIGHTED
(— THAT) SITH SINCE
SEEK ASK BEG SIC WOO BUSK FAND FEEL FISH FOND FORK HUNT LAIT LOOK SICK SIFT COURT DELVE ESSAY FETCH SCOUR APPETE BOTTOM FERRET FOLLOW FRAIST PURSUE SEARCH FORSEEK INQUIRE RANSACK REQUIRE RUMMAGE SOLICIT ENDEAVOR
(— AFTER) SUE SUIT ENSUE EXPLORE
(— AIMLESSLY) PROG
(— FAVOR) WISH
(— FOR) APPETE EXPLORE
(— IN MARRIAGE) WOO PRETEND
(— OUT) COMB ENSEARCH
(— TO ATTAIN) ASPIRE
(— URGENTLY) PRESS

SEEKER TRACER PETITOR ZETETIC SEARCHER
(— AFTER FACTS) GRADGRIND
(— OF KNOWLEDGE) PHILONIST
(JOB —) CHANCER
(PLEASURE —) FRANION
SEEKING SOKE SOKEN ZETETIC
(SUFF.) PETAL
SEEM BID EYE SEE FARE LOOK PEER SOUND APPEAR BESEEM REGARD
(— TO BE) LIKE
(IT —S) SEMBLE
SEEMING GUISE QUASI LIKELY SEEMLY APPARENT SEMBLANT
(PREF.) QUASI
SEEMINGLY QUASI SEEMLY SEEMING
SEEMLINESS GRACE DECENCY DECORUM
SEEMLY FIT TALL CIVIL COMELY DECENT LIKELY MODEST BECOMING DECOROUS GRACEFUL
SEEP LEAK OOZE SIPE EXUDE PERCOLATE
SEEPAGE SEEP SIPAGE SPRING
SEEPY WEEPY
SEER SIR SWAMI MOPSUS ORACLE SCRYER PROPHET CHALDEAN MELAMPUS
SEERBAND TURBAN
SEERESS SAGA SIBYL VOLVA ALRUNE ALBRUNA PHOIBAD
SEESAW PUMP TILT DANDLE TEETER TIDDLE TILTER TITTER TOTTER
SEETHE FRY JUG BOIL CREE ITCH STEW WALL WALM BULLER HOTTER SIMMER BLUBBER ELIXATE FERMENT
SEETHING ASEETHE BOILING HUMMING ITCHING SCALDING
SEGMENT CUT LAP FALL HAND LITH MERE PART BLANK CHORD ELITE FEMUR FURCA SHARE SLICE TMEMA CANTLE GLOSSA LENGTH SAMPLE SYZYGY ARTICLE DIGITUS EXERGUE FESTOON ISOMERE MYOMERE MYOTOME SECTION SETIGER ANTIMERE BRACHIUM COLUMNAL DACTYLUS DIVISION GONOTOME HYPOMERE INTERVAL MESOMERE METAMERE MYOCOMMA NARICORN
(— OF CASK) CANT
(— OF CAULIFLOWER) FLOWERET
(— OF CIRCLE) SECTION
(— OF COMMUNITY) FACIES
(— OF EARTH'S CRUST) GRABEN
(— OF FIBER) BAND
(— OF INSECT'S LEG) FEMUR TROCHANTER
(— OF IRIS) FALL
(— OF LEAF) LACINIA
(— OF MAXILLA) STIPES SUBGALEA
(— OF RATTLESNAKE'S RATTLE) BUTTON
(— OF SPEECH) DOMAIN
(ABDOMINAL —) URITE UROMERE PROPODEON
(BODY —) SOMITE
(HERALDIC —) FLANCH FLANCHE
(INSTRUCTIONAL —) LESSON
(MERE —) SNAPSHOT

(PEASANT —) HERA
(SUFF.) MERE TMEMA TMESIS
(— OF) ILE
SEGMENTAL MERISTIC
SEGMENTATION CLEAVAGE
(SUFF.) TOMA TOME TOMIC TOMOUS TOMY
SEGMENTED INSECTED
SEGNO SIGN
SEGREGATE SHED SEVER INTERN ISOLATE CLASSIFY INSULATE SEPARATE
SEGREGATION APARTHEID
SEGUB (FATHER OF —) HIEL HEZRON
SEIGNORAGE ROYALTY
SEIGNORY LORDSHIP
SEINE NET FARE TUCK TRAIN POCKET SAGENE SPILLER MADRAGUE
(— SIGHT) ILE
SEISIN VESTURE
SEIZE BAG CAP CLY GET HAP NAB NAP BEAK BONE CLAW CLUM FANG GALL GLOM GRAB GRIP GRUP HAND HENT HOOK JUMP KEEP LEVY NAIL RAMP SMUG SNAP SPAN TAKE TIRE YOKE CATCH CESSE CLASP CLEEK CLICK CRIMP DRIVE GRASP GRIPE LATCH PINCH RAVEN RAVIN REACH REAVE SNACK ARREST ASSUME ATTACH CLUTCH COLLAR EXTEND FASTEN FREEZE GOBBLE NOBBLE QUARRY SECURE SNATCH ASSEIZE CAPTURE ENCLASP ENCLOSE FORHENT GRABBLE GRAPPLE IMPOUND POSSESS PREEMPT PREHEND SCAMBLE SWALLOW ARROGATE COMPRISE DISTRAIN SPUILZIE SURPRISE UNDERNIM
(— AND HOLD FIRMLY) TRUSS
(— BAIT) STRIKE
(— BY NECK) SCRAG COLLAR SCRUFF
(— PREY) CHOP
(— SUDDENLY) NAB NIP SWOOP SNATCH
(— UPON) ATTACK INFECT
(— WITH CLAWS) STRAIN
(— WITHOUT RIGHT) USURP
(— WITH TEETH) BITE
(— WITH WHOLE HAND) GLAUM
SEIZIN SASINE VESTURE
SEIZING FANG GRIP MARQUE CAPTION SEIZURE
SEIZURE PIT BITE HOLD RAPE GRIPE ICTUS SPELL ARREST EXTENT PRISAL RAPTUS SNATCH TAKING ANGARIA CAPTION CONCEIT TELLACH DISTRESS STOPPAGE
(— IN RETALIATION) REPRISAL
(DRUG ADDICT'S —) WINGDING
(SUFF.) LEPSIA LEPSIS LEPSY LEPT(IC)
SELDOM RARE SELD RARELY UNOFTEN
SELDOM-SEEN ANTRIN ANTERIN
SELECT ORT TAP TRY CULL PICK SIFT SORT TAKE WALE DRAFT ELECT ELITE PITCH TRIED ASSIGN BALLOT CHOICE CHOOSE CLUBBY DECIDE DESUME EXEMPT PREFER SAMPLE SINGLE WINNOW

DRAUGHT EMPANEL EXCERPT EXTRACT OUTLOOK EXIMIOUS HANDPICK SELECTED
(— A CAREER) GOINTO
(— BY LOT) DRAW
(— BY PATTERN) SWATCH
(— JURY) STRIKE
SELECTED DRAFT ELECT FANCY DRAUGHT
SELECTING DRAFT GARBLING
SELECTION BLAD CHAP CULL ITEM PICK CHOICE CHOOSE EXCERPT EXTRACT ELECTION HAFTARAH PERICOPE
(— OF PSALMS) HALLEL
(VERSE —) BLAUD SINGSONG
(SUFF.) ECLEXIS
SELECTIVE CHOOSY ECLECTIC
SELED (FATHER OF —) NADAB
SELENE (SISTER OF —) EOS
SELENIDE ZORGITE
SELF EGO SEL SEN JIVA SELL SOUL DAENA NATURE PERSON PSYCHE
(INNER —) ANIMA
(OWN —) AINSELL NAINSEL
(SUPREME UNIVERSAL —) ATTA ATMAN
(PREF.) AUT(O) AUTH(I) EGO
SELF-ACCUSATION GUILT
SELF-ACTING
(PREF.) AUT(O) AUTOMAT(O)
SELF-AGGRANDIZING IMPERIAL
SELF-ASSERTIVE BRASH PERKY CHESTY BLUSTERY BUMPTIOUS
SELF-ASSURANCE CHEEK APLOMB COOLNESS
SELF-ASSURED COCKY CALM PERKY CONFIDENT
SELF-CENTERED SELFISH
SELF-CENTEREDNESS EGOTISM SELFHOOD
SELF-COMMAND NERVE TEMPER
SELF-CONCEIT NOSISM
SELF-CONCEITED COXY PENSY COCKSY PENCEY
SELF-CONFIDENCE CREST HUBRIS HUTZPA CHUTZPA HUTZPAH JOLLITY OPINION CHUTZPAH
SELF-CONFIDENT COCKSURE FLUSH CHESTY
SELF-CONSCIOUS GAWKY BASHFUL
SELF-CONTAINED ABSOLUTE
SELF-CONTAINMENT CLOSURE
SELF-CONTRADICTORY ABSURD
SELF-CONTROL STAY WILL ENCRATY MODESTY RETENUE PATIENCE
(LOSE —) FLIP
SELF-DECEPTION FLATTERY
SELF-DEFENSE (ART OF—) AIKIDO
(ART OF —) KUNGFU
SELF-DENIAL DENIAL
SELF-DENYING ASCETIC
SELF-DESTRUCTION SUICIDE
SELF-DESTRUCTIVE SUICIDAL
SELF-DETERMINATION FREEDOM AUTONOMY
SELF-DISCIPLINE ASCESIS
SELF-ENRICHMENT GROWTH
SELF-ESTEEM EGO PRIDE CONCEIT SELFNESS
SELF-EVIDENT MANIFEST

SELF-EXALTATION NOSISM ELATION
SELF-EXISTENT BEER INCREATE UNCAUSED
SELF-FERTILIZATION AUTOGAMY
SELF-FULFILLMENT FREEDOM SAMADHI
SELF-GENERATION AUTOGENY
SELF-GLORIFICATION VANITY
SELF-GOVERNMENT SWARAJ
SELF-HEAL ALLHEAL HOOKHEAL HOOKWEED BLUECURLS
SELFHOOD SEITY EGOITY IPSEITY OWNHOOD PROPRIUM SELFNESS
SELF-IDENTITY IPSEITY
SELF-IMPORTANT COXY PURDY CHESTY COCKSY BIGGETY POMPOUS BUMPTIOUS
SELF-INDULGENCE NICETY PLEASURE
SELF-INDULGENT WANTON
SELFISH PIGGISH SELFFUL DISSOCIAL
SELFISHNESS EGO SELF EGOTISM SUICISM PHILAUTY SELFHOOD SELFNESS
  (MORBID —) PLEONEXIA
SELF-LOVE CONCEIT PHILAUTY
SELF-ORIGINATION ASEITY
SELF-POLLUTION ONANISM
SELF-POSSESSED COOL ASSURED COMPOSED TOGETHER
SELF-POSSESSION PHLEGM COOL POISE APLOMB COOLNESS SANGFROID
SELF-PRODUCED
  (PREF.) IDIO
SELF-REALIZATION FREEDOM ENERGISM ·
SELF-RELIANT BOLD FREE
SELF-REPROACH GUILT REGRET
SELF-RESTRAINT HO HOO ASCESIS CONTROL RESERVE RETENUE HAVLAGAH
SELF-RIGHTEOUS STUFFY
SELF-SACRIFICING HEROIC GALLANT
SELFSAME SAME VERY SELFSAID IDENTICAL
SELFSAMENESS IDENTITY
SELF-SATISFIED SMUG STODGY ASSURED
SELF-SERVICE
  (SUFF.) TERIA
SELF-SUFFICIENCY ASEITY ASEITAS AUTARKY AUTARCHY
SELF-SUFFICIENT ABSOLUTE
SELF-TAUGHT PRIMITIVE
SELF-WILLED SET SENSUAL STUBBLE WAYWARD CONTRARY PERVERSE
SELION BUTT
SELL DO FLOG GIVE VEND CHEAP PITCH SHAVE TRADE UTTER WRITE AFFORD BARTER MARKET PEDDLE AUCTION BARGAIN
  (— A HORSE) CHANT
  (— AT LOW PRICE) DUMP
  (— BELOW COST) FOOTBALL
  (— BY AUCTION) CANT ROUP
  (— DRUGS ILLEGALLY) PUSH
  (— FOR) BRING FETCH

  (— FRAUDULENTLY) CHANT CHAUNT
  (— IN SMALL QUANTITIES) RETAIL
  (BUY AND —) CHOP
SELLER BOOMER BUSKER CADGER VENDOR CHANTER FLESHER CHANDLER
  (— OF BEER) PINTPOT
  (BEST —) CHARTBUSTER
  (WINE —) ABKAR
SELLING (SPECULATIVE —) AGIOTAGE
SELSYN SYNCHRO
SELVAGE EDGE LIST ROON GOUGE FORREL LISTING STICKING
SEMACHIAH (FATHER OF —) SHEMAIAH
SEMANTEME RHEME
SEMANTICS SEMOLOGY
SEMAPHORE FISHTAIL
SEMBLANCE FACE IDOL SHOW SIGN COLOR GHOST GLOSS GUISE IMAGE SCHEME VISAGE PRETEXT SEEMING UMBRAGE LIKENESS SEMBLANT SKERRICK SIMULACRUM
  (— OF DIGNITY) FACE
  (— OF REALITY) DREAM
  (FALSE —) COLORING
SEME SEMY GUTTY HURTY FLEURY GOUTTE GUTTEE BEZANTE
SEME-DE-LIS FLORETTY
SEMEI (SON OF —) MATTATHIAS
SEMELE (BROTHER OF —) POLYDORUS
  (FATHER OF —) CADMUS
  (MOTHER OF —) HARMONIA
  (SISTER OF —) INO AGAVE AUTONOE
  (SON OF —) BACCHUS
SEMEN SEED SPERM
  (PREF.) GON(O) SPERM(A)(ATI) (ATIO)(ATO)(I)(IO)(O)
  (SUFF.) SPERM(A)(AE)(AL)(IA)(IC) (OUS)(UM)(Y)
SEMESTER HALF
SEMI RIG
SEMIDARKNESS DUSK
SEMIDIAMETER RADIUS
SEMIDOME CONCHA
SEMIFLUID SOFT HUMOR
SEMIGLOSS EGGSHELL
SEMILIQUID SLAB
SEMINARY YESHIVA JUVENATE
SEMIOPAQUE HORNY
SEMIPORCELAIN GOMBROON
SEMIRAMIDE (CHARACTER IN —) ASSUR ARSACE SEMIRAMIS
  (COMPOSER OF —) ROSSINI
SEMIRAMIS (HUSBAND OF —) NINUS
  (MOTHER OF —) DERCETO
SEMITE JEW ARAB HARARI SYRIAN MOABITE SEMITIC SHEMITE ARAMAEAN ASSYRIAN CHALDEAN
SEMITIC JEWISH
  (— LANGUAGE) GAFAT
SEMITONE FEINT LIMMA DEMITONE HEMITONE
SEMITRAILER ARTIC
SEMOLINA SUJI SEMOLA
SENAPO (DAUGHTER OF —) CLORINDA

SENATE BOULE SENATO COUNCIL SENATUS GEROUSIA SENATORY
  (— AND PEOPLE OF ROME) SPQR
  (— DIVISION) PRYTANY
SENATOR SOLON CONSUL FATHER LAWMAKER
  (PL.) ANZIANI
SENATORSHIP TOGA
SEND MIT FAST PACK SHIP ELATE ENVOY SCEND THROW RENDER THRILL ADDRESS CHANNEL COMMAND CONSIGN DELIGHT DELIVER FORWARD DISPATCH TRANSMIT
  (— ABOUT) TROLL
  (— ALOFT) CROSS
  (— AWAY) MAND SHIP AMAND BANISH DISBAND DISMISS RELEGATE
  (— BACK) ECHO TURN WISE REMIT REMAND REMISE RENVOY RESEND RETURN REFRACT
  (— BY MAIL) DROP
  (— BY PARACHUTE) DROP
  (— BY WIRE) FAX
  (— DOWN) DEMIT DIMIT STRIKE
  (— FOR) SUMMON
  (— FORTH) BEAM BEAR CAST EMIT MAND DIMIT FLING LANCH EFFUSE LAUNCH OUTSEND EXPEDITE FULMINATE
  (— FORTH IN RAYS) RADIATE
  (— HURTLING) SPIN
  (— IN) IMMIT IMMISS INTROMIT
  (— MESSAGE) TELEX BLINKER
  (— OFF) POST WING
  (— OFFICIALLY) ISSUE
  (— OFF UNCEREMONIOUSLY) SHANK
  (— OUT) BEAM EMIT AMAND SHOOT SPEED DEDUCE DEPORT LAUNCH DIFFUSE EXPEDITE
  (— OVERSEAS) TRANSPORT
  (— SWIFTLY) SPEED
  (— TO JAIL) LAG MITTIMUS
  (— TO PERDITION) CONFOUND
  (— WITHIN) INTROMIT
  (SUFF.) MISE MISS MIT
SENDING SAND
  (— OF MONEY) REMITTANCE
  (— OUT) EMISSIVE
  (— WITHIN) INSERTION INTROMISSION
SEND-UP PARODY TAKEOFF

SENEGAL
CAPITAL: DAKAR
MOUNTAIN: GOUNOU
NATIVE: PEUL SOCE DIOLA FOULA LAOBE SERER WOLOF FULANI SERERE BAMBARA MALINKE TUKULER MANDINGO
RIVER: FALEME GAMBIA SALOUM SENEGAL CASAMANCE
TOWN: BAKEL LOUGA MATAM THIES DAGANA KAOLACK RUFISQUE

SENILE DOLD ANILE DOTARD
SENILITY DOTAGE CADUCITY PROGERIA
SENIOR AINE DEAN SIRE DOYEN ELDER ANCIENT SUPERIOR

SENIORITY AGE ANCIENTY SIGNEURY
SENNACHERIB (FATHER OF —) SARGON
  (SON OF —) ESARHADDON
SENNET SPET SIGNET
SENOR DON
SENORITA MISS SRTA SRITA
SENSATION FEEL ITCH SOUR STIR SENSE TABET TASTE TIBBIT VEDANA FEELING ESTHESIS EXPERIENCE
  (— OF COLD) RHIGOSIS
  (— OF FRIGHT) FRISSON
  (— OF HEAT) HOTNESS
  (— OF PAIN) ALGESIS
  (ANTICIPATORY —) FOREFEEL
  (BURNING —) ARDOR
  (DARTING —) SHOOT
  (IRRITATING —) ITCH
  (STRONG —) CREEP
  (SUBJECTIVE —) AURA
  (TASTE —) GUST BITTER
  (TINGLING —) DIRL
  (VIBRATING —) FREMITUS
  (VISUAL —) PHOSE PHOTOMA
  (PREF.) AESTHESIO ESTHESIO
SENSATIONAL GORY BOFFO LURID YELLOW SAFFRON SPLASHY TABLOID THRILLY STUNNING MELODRAMATIC
SENSATIONALISM BLARE SENSISM
SENSE WIT FEEL SALT SMELL LETTER MATTER REASON SCONCE WISDOM FEELING HEARING MARBLES MEANING SMEDDUM CARRIAGE GUMPTION JUDGMENT
  (— OF APPREHENSION) ANXIETY
  (— OF DUTY) PIETY
  (— OF HEARING) EAR
  (— OF HUMOR) MUSIC
  (— OF MOVEMENT) KINESTHESIA KINESTHESIS KINAESTHESIS
  (— OF MYSTERY) MYSTIQUE
  (— OF ONENESS) KINSHIP
  (— OF OUTRAGE) SHOCK
  (— OF PANIC) JITTERS
  (— OF RIGHT) GRACE
  (— OF SHAME) PUDOR
  (— OF SIGHT) VISION
  (— OF SMELL) SCENT
  (— OF STYLE) PANACHE
  (— OF SUPERIORITY) EGOTISM
  (— OF TASTE) GUST PALATE GUSTATION
  (— OF TOUCH) FEEL TASTE
  (— OF WORD) ETYMON
  (— ON ONE'S WORTH) PRIDE
  (— THE MEANING OF) READ
  (COMMON —) NOUS SALT BALANCE GUMPTION
  (DISCRIMINATING —) FLAIR
  (GOOD —) MATTER
  (LACKING —) INEPT
  (MAKE —) ADDUP FOLLOW
  (MORAL —) CONSCIENCE
  (PLAIN —) ENGLISH
  (RIGHT —S) MIND
  (SOUND —) MATTER
SENSE AND SENSIBILITY
  (AUTHOR OF —) AUSTEN

(CHARACTER IN —) JOHN LUCY EDWARD ELINOR STEELE BRANDON FERRARS MARIANNE WILLOUGHBY

SENSE-DATUM SENSUM

SENSELESS MAD COLD DUMB SILLY FRIGID STUPID UNWISE WANTON FOOLISH IDIOTIC PEEVISH SOTTISH UNIDEAED POINTLESS REASONLESS

SENSIBILITY HEART SENSE FEELING DELICACY ESTHESIA JUDGMENT **(PL.)** FEELINGS

SENSIBLE SANE WISE AWARE PRIVY WITTY ACTUAL FEELABLE MATERIAL PASSIBLE RATIONAL SENSICAL SENTIENT WISELIKE PERCEPTIBLE

SENSITIVE FINE KEEN SORE ALIVE MIFFY QUICK KITTLY LIABLE NIMBLE TENDER TETCHY FEELING NERVOUS PRICKLY ALLERGIC DELICATE EROGENIC SENSIBLE SENTIENT SKINLESS TOUCHOUS **(— TO PAIN)** TART **(NERVOUSLY —)** TOUCHY **(TOO —)** OVERSTRUNG

SENSITIVENESS SENSE TOUCH ALGESIA DELICACY

SENSITIVE PEA HONEYCUP

SENSITIVE PLANT MIMOSA

SENSITIVITY FLESH ANTENNA DELICACY FINENESS

SENSITIZER CYANINE

SENSORY SENSUAL AFFERENT

SENSUAL LEWD BRUTE MUDDY CARNAL FLESHY SULTRY WANTON BEASTLY BESTIAL BRUTISH FLESHLY LESBIAN SWINISH PANDEMIC SENSUOUS

SENSUALITY FLESH LIKING LUXURY ANIMALISM

SENSUOUS SOFT LYDIAN SATINY SENSAL FLESHLY SENSUAL LUSCIOUS SENSIBLE

SENTENCE BAN DIT RAP SAW DAMN DOOM TIME AWARD FUTWA JUISE TENER TROPE ARREST ASSIZE COMMIT DECREE DEPORT JUWISE KERNEL REASON ADJUDGE CENSURE CONDEMN FLOATER IMPRESA LAGGING FOREDOOM JUDGMENT VERSICLE PALINDROME **(— CONTAINING ALL LETTERS)** PANGRAM **(— CONTAINING EACH LETTER)** PANGRAM **(— INDICATING CHARACTER)** MOTTO **(— OF TEN YEARS IN PRISON)** DIME **(CONCISE —S)** LACONICS **(IMPRISONMENT —)** LAG RAP LIFE LAGGING STRETCH **(KIND OF —)** CLEFT **(MUSICAL —)** PERIOD **(SERVE A —)** DOTIME **(SHORT —)** CLAUSE **(WITTY —)** ATTICISM

SENTENTIOUS CONCISE LACONIC

SENTIENCE SENSE

SENTIENT AWARE FEELING SENSILE SENSIVE SENSEFUL SENSIBLE

SENTIMENT MIND POSY ETHNOS GENIUS HOBNOB NOTION PLEDGE FEELING OPINION **(— IN DRINKING)** HOBNOB **(EXCESSIVE —)** SCHWARMEREI **(FALSE —)** FALSETTO **(SLOPPY —)** DRIP

SENTIMENTAL SLAB SOFT CORNY GOOEY GUSHY MUSHY SAPPY SOBBY SOPPY SOUPY TEARY FRUITY SLUSHY SPOONY SUGARY SYRUPY INSIPID MAUDLIN MAWKISH ROMANTIC SCHMALZY SNIVELLY MOONSTRUCK NOVELETTISH **(MORBIDLY —)** WERTHERIAN **(OVERLY —)** MUSHY

SENTIMENTALISM BATHOS SCHMALZ SCHMALTZ

SENTIMENTALIST SOFTHEAD

SENTIMENTALITY GOO HAM MUSH BLURB SIRUP SYRUP BATHOS **(INTOLERABLE —)** TREACLE **(MAUDLIN —)** GOO

SENTIMENTAL TOMMY (AUTHOR OF —) BARRIE **(CHARACTER IN —)** JEAN AARON LOTTA NYLES TOMMY GRIZEL ELSPETH

SENTINEL WAIT DEINO GUARD WATCH BANTAY PICKET SENTRY WARDEN PICQUET COCKATOO PEPHEDRO WATCHMAN **(MOUNTED —)** VEDET VEDETTE **(PL.)** GRAEAE GRAIAE

SENTINEL BOX STATION WATCHCASE

SENTRY KITE WATCH SENTINEL

SEPAL ALA LEAF HELMET LEAFLET

SEPARATE CUT TOM COMB CULL CURD DEAL FALL FRAY FREE HAZE PART REDD SERE SIFT SORT TEAR TWIN ASIDE BLEED BREAK CALVE ELONG FENCE FLAKE HEDGE PARTY SCALE SEVER SIEVE SKILL SPLIT TWAIN TWIST ABDUCT ABRUPT ASSORT AVULSE BISECT CLEAVE DECIDE DEPART DETACH DIGEST DIVIDE DIVISI FILTER PROPER REMOTE SCREEN SECERN SECRET SEJOIN SETTLE SINGLE SOLUTE SPREAD SUNDER SUNDRY SWATCH UNLUTE WINNOW ABSCISE ABSCISS BRACKET CONCERN DIALYZE DISALLY DISCERP DISJOIN DISLINK DISPAIR DISPART DIVERSE EXPANSE FISSION ISOLATE SCATTER SCIOLTO SECTION SEJUNCT SEVERAL SWINGLE TAKEOUT ABSTRACT BULKHEAD DECOUPLE DETACHED DIFFRACT DISCRETE DISJOINT DISSEVER DISSOLVE DISTINCT DISTRACT DISUNITE DIVIDANT DIVIDUAL FRACTION LAMINATE LEVIGATE LIBERATE PECULIAR SEVERATE SPORADIC UNMINGLE UNSOLDER UNSTRING RESPECTIVE **(— BY BEATING)** SCUTCH **(— BY CROSSWALL)** ABJOINT **(— BY PICKING)** LEASE LEAZE **(— COINS)** JOURNEY

(— COMBATANTS) STICKLE **(— COPIES)** DECOLLATE **(— FIBERS)** HACKLE **(— FROM HERD)** IMPRIME **(— GRAIN FROM CHAFF)** FAN CAVE WINNOW **(— HAIR)** BLOCK **(— INTO COMPONENTS)** STRIP **(— INTO FLOCKS)** DRAFT DRAUGHT **(— INTO SHREDS)** TEASE **(— ONESELF)** ABDICATE **(— ORE)** JIG SMELT DILLUE **(— SHEEP)** DRAW **(— THREADS)** SLEY SLEAVE **(PREF.)** APH APO CHORI(ST)(STO) ECCRINO IDIO

SEPARATED FREE ALONE BROKEN REMOTE DISTANT DIVIDED ABSTRACT ISOLATED RESOLVED **(— BY INTERVAL)** OPEN **(PREF.)** CHORI(ST)(STO) DIALY

SEPARATELY APART SINGLY SUNDRY ASUNDER DIVISIM SEVERAL SUNDERLY ABSOLUTELY

SEPARATING BETWEEN

SEPARATION GAP GULF PART RENT SHED BREAK CHASM SPLIT SCHISM BARRIER DIVORCE ELUTION PARTING ANALYSIS AUTOTOMY AVULSION CREAMING DECISION DIALYSIS DISTANCE DISUNION DIVISION INCISION SHEDDING SOLUTION TWINNING SEQUESTER **(— OF BODY PARTS)** ABDUCTION **(— OF COMPONENTS)** RESOLUTION **(— OF LEAF)** CHORISIS **(— OF MAN AND WIFE)** ZIHAR DIVORCE **(— OF METALS)** DEPART **(— OF PIGMENT)** FLOATING **(— OF SUSPENDED MATTER)** PRECIPITATION **(— OF WORD PARTS)** TMESIS **(— OF YEAST IN BEER)** BREAK **(ABNORMAL —)** SOLUTION **(MENTAL —)** PRECISION **(ORE —)** FLOTATION **(PREF.)** DE

SEPARATIST ZOARITE BIMMELER

SEPARATOR RAVEL PARTER CREAMER SETTLER SEVERER SUBSIDER

SEPARATRIX SLASH DIAGONAL

SEPHESTIA (FATHER OF —) DAMOCLES **(HUSBAND OF —)** MAXIMUS **(LOVER OF —)** MENAPHON **(SON OF —)** PLEUSIDIPPUS

SEPIA COCONUT SEPIARY

SEPOY PANDY TELINGA

SEPT KIN

SEPTEMBER 29 MICHAELMAS

SEPTET SEPTUOR

SEPTIC PURULENT

SEPTIOLITE MEERSCHAUM

SEPTIVALENT HEPTAD

SEPTUAGINT LXX

SEPTUM VITTA TABULA MYOTOME PHRAGMA MYOCOMMA

SEPULCHER BIER GRAVE TITLE CENOTAPH MONUMENT MORTUARY

SEPULCHRAL HOLLOW CHARNEL TUMULARY

SEPULTURE BURIAL

SEQUEL SUITE EFFECT SEQUENT BACKWASH SEQUENCE **(UNEXPECTED —)** AFTERCLAP

SEQUENCE ROPE SUIT ORDER TRACT TRAIN DOCKET ENTAIL SEQUEL SERIES STRING CADENCE CORONET SEQUENT SUCCESS SPECTRUM STRAIGHT **(— IN ACID)** EXON **(— IN MELODY)** AGOGE **(— IN NUCLEIC ACID)** INTRON **(— OF ARCS)** PATH **(— OF BEHAVIOR)** ACT **(— OF BILLIARD SHOTS)** BREAK **(— OF CARDS)** QUART TENACE STRINGER **(— OF CHESS MOVES)** DEFENCE DEFENSE **(— OF EVENTS)** CYCLE SCENARIO **(— OF MELODRAMA)** CHASE **(— OF MESSAGES)** QUEUE **(— OF ROCK UNITS)** SECTION **(— OF SOUNDS)** AFFIX **(— OF 3 NUCLEOTIDES)** CODON **(ACTING —)** EXTERIOR **(CUSTOMARY —)** COURSE **(DNA —)** HOMEOBOX **(FILM)** INTERCUT **(KIND OF —)** CAUCHY **(LITURGICAL —)** CANON

SEQUENT ENSUANT SEQUITUR

SEQUENTIAL SERIATE

SEQUESTER SINGLE ISOLATE RECLUDE

SEQUESTERED LONELY PRIVATE RECLUSE RETIRED SECLUDED SOLITARY

SEQUIN CHICK SPANG VENTIN ZEQUIN CHEQUIN CHEQUEEN VENETIAN ZECCHINO **(PL.)** GLITTER

SERAGLIO HAREM SERAI ZENANA

SERAH (FATHER OF —) ASHER

SERAI INN

SERAIAH (BROTHER OF —) BARUCH OTHNIEL **(FATHER OF —)** KENAZ NERIAH HILKIAH TANHUMETH

SERAPHIC ANGELIC BEATIFIC

SERBOCROATIAN ILLYRIAN

SERE SEAR SERULE UNGREEN HALOSERE

SERED (FATHER OF —) ZEBULUN

SERENADE AUBADE HORNING ALBORADA NOCTURNE SERENATA **(MOCK —)** SHIVAREE

SERENADER WAIT

SERENE CALM EVEN CLEAR LITHE SEDATE SMOOTH HALCYON DECOROUS

SERENITY CALM PEACE REPOSE

SERF BOND THEW CHURL HELOT SLAVE THEOW THETE PENEST SERVUS THRALL BONDMAN COLONUS PEASANT VILLEIN ADSCRIPT PRAEDIAL YANACONA

SERFDOM BONDAGE HELOTRY SERFAGE SERVAGE HELOTISM SERFHOOD SERFSHIP

SERGE SAY SAGATHY

SERGEANT NCO TOP SARGE CHIAUS NONCOM DESKMAN SERVANT TOPKICK HAVILDAR SERIAUNT

SERGEANT-AT-LAW COUNTOR COUNTOUR

SERGEANT FISH LING CABIO COBIA SNOOK BONITO CUBBYYEW

SERGEANT MAJOR PINTANO

SERIAL SEQUENTIAL

SERIALLY SERIATIM

SERIEMA CARIAMA GRUIFORM SCREAMER

SERIES RUN SET ECCA RANK SUIT TIRE CHAIN DRIFT DWYKA ORDER SUITE TALLY TRACE COURSE EOCENE SEQUEL STRING SYSTEM BATTERY CASCADE CATALOG BEADROLL SEQUENCE PROGRESSION
(**— GATHERED TOGETHER**) SORITES
(**— IN LINE**) ROW
(**— OF ABSTRACTS**) SYLLABUS
(**— OF ARCHES**) ARCADE
(**— OF BALLET TURNS**) CHAINE
(**— OF BALLS**) OVER
(**— OF BOAT RACES**) REGATTA
(**— OF CELLS**) FILAMENT
(**— OF CHARACTERS**) CLINE
(**— OF CHESS MOVES**) COOK
(**— OF CLASHES**) CLATTER
(**— OF COMMUNITIES**) SERE
(**— OF DANCE MOVEMENTS**) ADAGIO
(**— OF DRAIN TILES**) FIELD
(**— OF ELEMENTS**) PERIOD
(**— OF EVENTS**) EPOS ACTION
(**— OF EXTRACTS**) CATENA
(**— OF FORTIFICATIONS**) CEINTURE
(**— OF GAMES**) RUBBER
(**— OF IMAGES**) DREAM
(**— OF LEGENDS**) SAGA
(**— OF LIPS**) GILL
(**— OF MASSES**) TRENTAL
(**— OF MEETINGS**) SESSION
(**— OF METAL DISKS**) PILE
(**— OF MILITARY OPERATIONS**) CAMPAIGN
(**— OF MOVEMENTS**) DANCE
(**— OF NEIGHBORING LOTS**) COTE
(**— OF NOTES**) GAMUT GLISSADE
(**— OF PASSES**) FAENA
(**— OF PILES**) DRIFT
(**— OF POEMS**) DIVAN DIWAN
(**— OF PRAYERS**) COURSE SYNAPTE
(**— OF RACES**) CIRCUIT
(**— OF REASONS**) ARGUMENT
(**— OF RINGS**) COIL GIMMAL
(**— OF ROOMS**) SWEEP
(**— OF SHOTS**) BURST
(**— OF SIMILAR STRUCTURES**) STROBILA
(**— OF SLALOM GATES**) FLUSH
(**— OF SLIPS**) DOCK
(**— OF SOILS**) CECIL
(**— OF STAIRS**) FLIGHT
(**— OF STAMPS**) SET
(**— OF STEPS**) STAIR STAIRS
(**— OF STITCHES**) STAY
(**— OF STRAPS**) LADDER
(**— OF STRATA**) KAROO MEASURES
(**— OF STROKES**) RALLY
(**— OF TANKS**) SOAPER

(**— OF THIRTY MASSES**) TRENTAL
(**— OF THREADS**) BINDER STUFFER
(**— OF TONES**) SCALE
(**— OF TRAVELS**) ODYSSEY
(**— OF VERSES**) ANTIPHON
(**— OF WORDS**) ACROSTIC ALPHABET
(**CARD —**) CORONET
(**CONNECTED —**) CATENA
(**CONSECUTIVE —**) STREAK
(**DANCE —**) DOUBLE
(**GEOLOGICAL —**) ECCA LIAS DWYKA KENAI EOCENE MOLASSE KEEWATIN
(**GRADUATED —**) SCALE
(**IMPRESSIVE —**) ARRAY
(**RADIOACTIVE —**) FAMILY
(PREF.) HIRMO

SERIOUS RUM SAD DEEP HIGH ACUTE GRAVE HEAVY SOBER SOLID STAID DEMURE SEDATE SEVERE SOLEMN SOMBER SOMBRE SULLEN AUSTERE CAPITAL EARNEST SERIOSO WEIGHTY GRIEVOUS
(PREF.) SERIO

SERIOUSLY BAD ILL DOWN SADLY DEEPLY GRAVELY SOLIDLY

SERIOUSNESS EARNEST GRAVITY SADNESS GRAVITAS SOBRIETY

SERMON SPELL SUTRA HOMILY POSTIL ADDRESS FUNERAL KHUTBAH SEREMENT SERMONET PREACHMENT
(**MUSLIM —**) KHOTBAH KHOTBEH KHUTBAH

SERMONIZE LECTURE

SERMONIZING MORALITY

SEROPURULENT SANIOUS

SEROUS ICHOROUS

SEROW THAR JAGLA SERAU

SERPENT (ALSO SEE SNAKE) AHI SEPS WORM ABOMA ADDER APEPI ATHER OPHIS SIREN SNAKE TRAIN CHITAL DIPSAS DRAGON GERARD HYDRUS PYTHON APOPHIS PRESTER SCYTALE JARARACA OPHIDIAN
(**— WORSHIPER**) NAASSENE
(**FEATHERED —**) GUCUMATZ KUKULKAN
(**HERALDIC —**) REMORA
(**NORSE —**) GOIN
(**SACRED —**) AVANYU AWANYU
(**SKY —**) AHI
(PREF.) COLUBRI OPHI(O) SERPU VIPERI
(SUFF.) OPHIS

SERPENTINE SNAKY SPIRY OPHITE SNAKISH BOWENITE METAXITE SCROLLED MARMOLITE

SERPENT STAR OPHIURAN

SERRANO PERCOID GITANEMUK

SERRATE SAWED ARGUTE RAFFLE NOTCHED SERRIED

SERRATION SERRA DENTILE

SERUG (**FATHER OF —**) REU

SERUM WHEY FLUID BIOLOGIC
(PREF.) ORO ORRHO SERO

SERVANT BOY FAG KID MAN PUG TAG AMAH BATA COOK DASI DAVY HELP HIND JACK LUCE MATY MOZO ALILA BAGOT BOOTS BOULT

DAVUS GILLY GROOM HAMAL MAMMY SEWER SLAVE SOSIA SPEED USHER ABDIEL ANDREW BATMAN BEARER BILDAR BUTLER CHAKAR CLASHY DORINE EWERER FEEDER FERASH FLUNKY GILLIE GRUMIO HAIDUK HARLOT KHAMAL MENIAL PAMELA SIRCAR SKIVVY SLAVEY TEABOY TEAGUE TRANIO VARLET VASSAL VOIDER ANCILLA BOOTBOY BOUCHAL COURIER DUFTERY FAMULUS FEODARY FERRASH FLUNKEY FOOTMAN GENERAL GHILLIE MALCHUS PANDOUR PANTLER PAPELON PIQUEUR PISANIO WASHPOT ASSIGNEE CHAPRASI CROMWELL DOMESTIC FOLLOWER GRASSCUT HENCHMAN HOUSEBOY MANCIPLE MINISTER OUTRIDER PANTHINO PHILOTUS PINDARUS SERGEANT SERVITOR STANDARD TRENCHER VADELECT WARDMAID KITCHENER OBSERVANT
(**— IN CHARGE OF BREAD**) PANTLER
(**— IN CHARGE OF DAIRY**) DEY
(**— IN OFFICE**) DUFTERY
(**— OF SCHOLAR OR MAGICIAN**) FAMULUS
(**— WHO CARVES**) TRENCHER
(**— WHO CLEARS TABLE**) VOIDER
(**— WHO RUNS BEFORE CARRIAGE**) PIQUEUR
(**— WHO SERVES TABLE**) SEWER
(**ARMED —**) PANDOUR
(**ARMY —**) BATMAN LASCAR
(**BENGAL —**) MEHTAR SIRCAR
(**BODY —**) VALET SIRDAR
(**BOY —**) BOY KNAVE CHOKRA BOUCHAL
(**CAMP —**) BILDAR
(**CLOWNISH —**) SPEED LAUNCE
(**COLLEGE —**) GYP SKIP SCOUT
(**FEMALE —**) AMA NAN AMAH DASI GIRL LASS MAID MAMMY NURSE WENCH PAMELA SKIVVY ANCILLA HANDMAID MUCHACHA WARDMAID
(**GENERAL —**) FACTOTUM
(**HEAD —**) BUTLER TINDAL
(**HIGH PRIEST'S —**) MALCHUS
(**HINDU —**) DAS DASI
(**HOUSE —**) COOK HEWE SEWER DOMESTIC MATRANEE SCULLION
(**INDIAN —**) AYAH
(**KITCHEN —**) COOK WASHPOT
(**LORD OR KING'S —**) THANE
(**LYING —**) FAG
(**MAID —**) NAN BONNE
(**MAN —**) BOY JACK MOZO SWAIN VALET ANDREW GILLIE KNIGHT GHILLIE KHANSAMA MUCHACHO SERVITOR
(**MISCHIEVOUS —**) TEAGUE
(**NON-RESIDENT —**) DAILY
(**PETULANT —**) DORINE
(**PHILIPPINE —**) BATA ALILA
(**SCOTTISH —**) JURR
(**SOLDIER'S —**) PAGE
(**TRUSTY —**) TROUT
(PL.) FOLK VOLK STAFF FAMILIA NETHINIM

SERVE DO KA ACT AID HOP GIVE HELP LEAP SHEW SLAP STAY TEND

TOSS WAIT COVER FRAME HORSE SARRA STAND ANSWER ASSIST FRIEND INTEND SAIRVE SARROW SETTLE SPREAD SUCCOR WAITON ADVANCE ASSERVE BESTEAD CONVENT FORWARD FURTHER SERVICE FUNCTION
(**— A DISH**) MESS
(**— AS ESCORT**) SQUIRE
(**— AS HOST**) GIVE
(**— AS SUBSTITUTE**) PASS
(**— AS WELL AS**) AVAIL
(**— DRINK**) SKINK
(**— FOOD**) HASH KITCHEN
(**— FOR PASTURE**) GRAZE
(**— OBSEQUIOUSLY**) LACKEY LACQUEY
(**— PERFECTLY**) ACE
(SUFF.) (**— FOR**) ORY

SERVER SALVER TUREEN ACOLYTE MINISTER

SERVICE AID FEE CENS DUTY HELP RITE TIDE YOKE FAVOR MUSAF STEAD DEVOIR EMPLOY ERRAND FACTOR OFFICE YIZKOR BENEFIT BONDAGE CHAKARI CORNAGE FUNERAL LITURGY OBSEQUY RETINUE SERVAGE SERVING BREEDING EQUIPAGE FUNCTION HEADWARD KINDNESS MINISTRY ROUNDING TENDANCE SERVITIUM
(**ASSIGNED —**) MYSTERY
(**BODYGUARD —**) INWARD
(**BREAKFAST —**) DEJEUNER
(**CHORAL —**) MATIN
(**CHURCH —**) LAUDS CHAPEL CHURCH HEARING STATION SYNAXIS ASPERGES EVENSONG
(**COFFEE —**) CABARET
(**COMMUNICATION —**) TELEX
(**COMPULSORY —**) ANGARIA
(**DOMESTIC —**) CHAKARI
(**FEUDAL —**) BOON AVERA ARRIAGE CORNAGE SEAWARD HEADWARD
(**FUNERAL —**) HERSE HEARSE
(**MILITARY —**) ARMS CAMP DUTY ESCUAGE
(**MILITIA —**) COMMANDO
(**RELIGIOUS —**) AHA SEDER COMMON
(**SECRET —**) OGPU
(**TENNIS —**) ACE LET

SERVICEABLE UTILE USEFUL DURABLE THRIFTY FRIENDLY VAILABLE

SERVICEBERRY SHADBLOW SHADBUSH SASKATOON

SERVICE TREE SORB SORBUS CHECKER SASKATOON

SERVILE BASE BOND ABJECT MENIAL SUPINE VASSAL CAITIFF SLAVISH VERNILE COISTREL CRAWLING CRINGING SERVIENT THEWLIKE

SERVILITY CRINGE

SERVING OBED SMACK DISHFUL HELPING SERVIENT WHIPPING
(SUFF.) ATORY
(**— FOR**) ORIOUS ORY

SERVITOR FAG GROOM PUNTER SERVANT PUNTSMAN

SERVITUDE USE VIA YOKE BONDAGE PEONAGE SERVICE

SLAVERY SERVITUS THEOWDOM THIRLAGE

SERVOMECHANISM SERVO BOOSTER

SERVOMOTOR RELAY SERVO

SESAME TIL TEEL BENNE BENNI SEMSEM VANGLO GINGILI OILSEED WANGALA AJONJOLI BENISEED SERGELIM

SESBANIA AGATI

SESQUITERPENE CEDROL CLOVENE COPAENE HUMULENE

SESSION DAY BOUT DIET HOUR SEAT COURT CLINIC SCHOOL SEANCE ACUERDO HEARING SEMINAR SITTING CONGRESS SEDERUNT SEMESTER
(COURT —) HILARY
(HAVE A —) SIT
(JAM —) CLAMBAKE
(PL.) ASSIZES
(SUFF.) FEST

SESTERTIUS BRONZE

SESTINA SEXTAIN

SET DO DIP FIX GEL KIT LAY LOT MOB PUT SIC SIT SOT CASE CREW CUBE GAGE GANG GIVE JELL KNIT KNOT NEST PAIR PICK PILT POSE REST SELL SORT STEP SHOW BATCH CLASS CLOCK COVEY CROWD FIXED GAUGE GLADE GROUP INFIX PAVER PLACE POSIT READY STACK STAID STAND STEAD STEEK STICK SUITE ADJUST CIRCLE CLIQUE DEFINE FASTEN FINALE FORMAL GLAZED GROUND HARDEN IMPOSE PARCEL SERIES SETTLE SPREAD SQUARE STATED BATTERY BOILING COMPANY COMPOSE CONFIRM COTERIE DEPOSIT DISPOSE ENCHASE FACTION IMPLANT INSTATE PLATOON SERVICE STATION STIFFEN STRATUM EQUIPAGE PANTALON SEQUENCE SOLIDIFY STANDARD
(— ABOUT) FALL FANG GANG BEGIN ADDRESS
(— ACROSS) TRANSVERSE
(— AFLOAT) LAUNCH
(— APART) MARK SHED DEMARK DESIGN DEVOTE EXEMPT SACRED SEPONE SEPOSE APPOINT ISOLATE RESERVE ALLOCATE DEDICATE INSULATE SEPARATE SEQUESTER
(— A PERIOD) DATE
(— A PRICE) ASK
(— ARMOR) GARNITURE
(— ARROWS IN ORDER) FRUSH
(— ASIDE) BAR DISH DROP HAIN SIDE SINK SLIP BURKE KAPUT SEPOSE BRACKET EARMARK PURLOIN RESERVE SUSPEND ABROGATE DISPENSE OVERRIDE OVERRULE REVERSED
(— AS ONE'S SHARE) ALLOT
(— AT DEFIANCE) BEARD
(— AT LIBERTY) FREE RELEASE LIBERATE
(— BACK TO BACK) ADDORSED ADDOSSED
(— BEFORE) PRESENT

(— BOUNDS) PRESCRIBE
(— CLOSE TOGETHER) PAVEED
(— DOG ON) SIC SLATE
(— DOWN) JOT LAY GIVE LAND PLANK SCORE EXPONE DEPOSIT
(— DOWN IN WRITING) SUBSCRIBE
(— DOWN UNDER NAME) TITLE
(— EDGEWISE) SURBED
(— ERECT) COCK
(— FIRMLY) FIRM STEM EMBED IMBED PLANT POSIT
(— FORTH) DRAW ETCH SHOW GIVEN STATE DEPART DEPICT EXPOSE SPREAD ARTICLE DISPLAY ENOUNCE EXHIBIT EXPOUND PRESENT PROPONE PROPOSE PURPOSE PROPOUND
(— FORWARD) PREFER ADVANCE
(— FREE) BAIL EASE REMIT SKILL SOLVE ACQUIT ASSOIL ABSOLVE DELIVER ENLARGE UNLOOSE WINFREE ABSTRICT DISPLACE DISSOLVE EXPEDITE UNVASSAL
(— GOING) INITIATE
(— IN ACCORD) SORT
(— IN ACTION) TRIGGER
(— IN EARTH) STRIKE
(— IN FROM MARGINS) INDENT
(— IN FRONT) PREFER
(— IN MOTION) SOW
(— IN OPERATION) DRIVE
(— IN OPPOSITION) PIT
(— IN ORDER) ARRAY FRUSH PITCH ADIGHT DAIKER FETTLE INFORM ADDRESS
(— IN POSITION) PLANT POSIT STAND STICK POSITION
(— IN ROWS) RANGE
(— INTO) INLAY
(— INTO A GROOVE) DADO
(— LIMITS TO) SPAN BOUND
(— OF ACTORS) CAST
(— OF ANIMALS) TEAM
(— OF ARMS) CONVEYER
(— OF BARS) CONCAVE
(— OF BELIEFS) CREDO
(— OF BELLS) RING CHIME CARILLON
(— OF BOOKCASES) STACK
(— OF BOOKS) PLENARY
(— OF CARDS) DECK PACK
(— OF CARS) DRAG
(— OF CHARACTERS) FIELD
(— OF CHIMES) DOORBELL
(— OF CIRCUMSTANCES) CASE EGIS FRAME
(— OF CONDITIONS) REGIMEN
(— OF CORDS) SIMPLE
(— OF DISHES) GARNISH SERVICE CUPBOARD
(— OF EIGHT) OGDOAD
(— OF EXERCISES) KATA
(— OFF) FOIL MENSE SEVER SHOOT ACCENT BUNDLE BALANCE COMMEND EMBLAZE CONTRAST DECORATE EMBLAZON
(— OF FACTS) BOOK
(— OF FALSE CURLS) FRONT
(— OF FISH NETS) DRIFT
(— OF FIVE) PENTAD QUINTUPLET
(— OF FOLDED SHEETS) QUIRE
(— OF FOUR) WARP QUATENARY QUATERNION QUATERNITY

(— OFF TO ADVANTAGE) ADORN COMMEND
(— OF FURNITURE) SUITE DINETTE
(— OF GARMENTS) SUIT
(— OF GEARS) GEARSET
(— OF HIDES) KIP
(— OF HORSES) STABLE
(— OF HOUNDS) VANLAY VAUNTLAY
(— OF IDEAS) SYSTEM
(— OF JEWELLED ORNAMENTS) PARURE
(— OF LEAVES) COROLLA
(— OF LETTERS) ALPHABET
(— OF MUSICAL INSTRUMENTS) CONSORT
(— OF NETS) SHOT
(— OF NOTES) ACCORD
(— OF OPINIONS) CREDO
(— OF ORGAN PIPES) STOP
(— OF ORGANS) ARMATURE
(— OF ORNAMENTS) PARURE
(— OF PINS) KAILS KNOCKOUT
(— OF POINTS) INTERVAL
(— OF PUMPS) LIFT
(— OF QUADRILLES) LANCERS
(— OF RADIATORS) STACK
(— OF RAYS) PENCIL
(— OF ROOMS) STORY
(— OF RULES) CODE EQUITY DECALOG
(— OF SAILS) CANVAS
(— OF SHELVES) STAGE BUFFET DRESSER WHATNOT
(— OF SKI FASTENINGS) BINDING
(— OF SKINS) SHODER
(— OF STAVES) SHOOK
(— OF STEPS) LADDER
(— OF SYMBOLS) KATAKANA
(— OF TABLES) COMPUTUS
(— OF TEETH) DENTURE
(— OF TEN) DECADE
(— OF THREE) BALE TERN LEASH
(— OF TOOLS) STRING
(— OF TRAMS) JOURNEY
(— OF TWELVE) ZODIAC
(— OF TWENTY) SCORE
(— OF TYPEFACES) FAMILY
(— OF VALUES) CURRENCY
(— OF VARIATIONS) PARTITA
(— OF VATS) SOLERA
(— OF VERSES) STAVE
(— OF VOWELS) SERIES
(— OF WARP THREADS) LEA
(— OF 3 ANIMALS) LEASH
(— ON) TAR SLATE
(— ON END) UPEND
(— ONESELF) GO
(— ON FIRE) SPIT TIND LIGHT ACCEND IGNIFY IGNITE KINDLE ENFLAME INFLAME ENKINDLE
(— OUT) BOUN MAKE BOWNE FOUND SALLY START INTEND STARTLE
(— OVER) COUCH
(— RIGHT) REDD ADJUST SCHOOL SQUARE CORRECT REDRESS
(— SNARE) TAIL TILL
(— SOLIDLY) EMBED
(— STRAIGHT) DRESS
(— THICKLY) STUD
(— TO MUSIC) AIR DITTY
(— TO WORK) YOKE
(— TRAP) TELD

(— TYPE) KEYBOARD
(— UP) RIG ROAR AREAR ERECT PITCH RAISE ROUSE IMPOSE SETTLE INSTALL UPDRESS ACTIVATE ESTABLISH INSTITUTE
(— UP IN COLUMNS) TABULAR
(— UPON) BESET ATTACK AGGRESS BROWDEN
(— UPRIGHT) ERECT STAND ARRECT
(— UPSIDE DOWN) TURN
(— VALUE) APPRAISE
(— WITH BRISTLES) STRIGOSE
(— WITH GEMS) CHASE
(ANTIGEN —) SEROTYPE
(BECOME —) STRIKE
(CHESS —) MEINY MEINIE
(CHROMOSOME —) GENOME COMPLEX
(COMPLETE —) STAND
(CONSTRUCTION —) ERECTOR
(INFINITE —) FAMILY
(MATHEMATICAL —) LATTICE MANIFOLD
(MINIATURE —) DIORAMA
(RADIO —) BLOOPER
(SMART —) TON
(STAGE —) SCENE
(TELEVISION —) TUBE
(UNALTERABLY —) STOUT
(PL.) DECOR
(SUFF.) STOLE THESIS THETE THETIC

SETA STALK WHISK CHAETA SETULA SETULE CROTCHET PODETIUM

SETBACK DASH JOLT SNAG KNOCK LURCH BLIGHT BACKSET LICKING PUTBACK RELAPSE REVERSE BUSINESS COMEDOWN HAYMAKER CONTRETEMPS
(TEMPORARY —) HICCUP

SETH (BROTHER OF —) ABEL CAIN
(FATHER OF —) ADAM
(MOTHER OF —) EVE
(SON OF —) ENOS

SETHUR (FATHER OF —) MICHAEL

SETLINE GEAR TRAWL BULTOW OUTLINE TROTLINE

SETTEE SETTLE OTTOMAN WINDSOR

SETTER SOFA GUNDOG DROPPER FLUSHER SETTLER

SETTERWORT PIGROOTS

SETTING SET FALL PAVE VAIL CHASE MIDST SCENE SETUP CHATON MILIEU FERMAIL MONTURE SITTING INTERIOR MARQUISE MOUNTING SHOWCASE BRILLIANT BRIOLETTE
(— APART) BETWEEN
(— FORTH) RECITAL PRESENTATION
(— FREE) SOLUTION
(— OF GEM) FOIL OUCH CHASE GALLERY
(— OF REED) CAAMING
(— OF WHEELS) CAMBER
(CAMERA —) BULB
(FAMILIAR —) HOME
(MUSICAL —) CREDO BALLAD BALLADE
(SHUTTER —) TIME
(STAGE —) SCENE

SETTLE BED FIT FIX ICE PAY SAG SET SIT TAX BANK BIND CALM DAIS

DEAS FAST FIRM HAFT LEND NEST
REST ROOT SEAT SINK SNUG TOIT
AGREE CLEAR COUCH ISSUE LIGHT
LODGE ORDER PITCH PLACE
PLANT QUIET SQUAT STATE STILL
ACCORD ADJUST ALIGHT ASSIGN
CLINCH DECIDE DECREE ENCAMP
LOCATE NESTLE PURIFY RESIDE
SCREEN SECURE SOOTHE SOPITE
SQUARE ACCOUNT APPEASE
APPOINT ARRANGE BALANCE
CLARIFY COMPONE COMPOSE
CONCERT CONFIRM DEPOSIT
DERAIGN INHABIT PIONEER
RESOLVE SUBSIDE COLONIZE
REGULATE SQUATTLE CONJOBBLE
RECONCILE
(— ACCOUNTS) WHACK
(— A FINE) AFFEER
(— AMICABLY) COMPOUND
(— AN ACCOUNT) PONYUP
(— BUSINESS) FEEZE PHEESE
PHEEZE
(— DOWN) CAMP SLUMP STEADY
DESCEND
(— ITSELF) INVEST
(— LANDS ON A PERSON) ENTAIL
(— ON) POINT
(— UP) PONY PONEY
(— UPON) AFFIX AGREE TIGHT
(— VERTICALLY) SQUASH
SETTLED SAD SET FIRM FIXED
QUIET STAID FORMED RANGED
SEATED SEDATE SQUARE STAPLE
STATED CERTAIN DECIDED
EMPIGHT STATARY DECOROUS
RESOLVED STANDING SEDENTARY
(NOT —) FARROW
SETTLEMENT AUL DEAL FINE FORK
MISE PACT POST BARRIO COLONY
DIKTAT MOSHAV WINDUP
ACCOUNT BIVOUAC FINANCE
MAABARA OUTPOST STATION
CLERUCHY DECISION DISPATCH
JOINTURE KEVUTZAH PRESIDIO
SETTLING SHOWDOWN TOWNSHIP
PLANTATION
(— OF JERRY-BUILT DWELLINGS)
BIDONVILLE
(— OF MONKS) SCETE SKETE
(— OF SHACKS) FAVELA FAVELLA
(— ON OUTSKIRTS) BIDONVILLE
(COLLECTIVE —) KVUTZA MOSHAV
KIBBUTZ
(HARSH —) DIKTAT
(INDIAN —) BUSTEE
(MARRIAGE —) MAHR ARRAS
DOWNSET
(NEW ZEALAND —) PA PAH
(RAPID —) BOOM
(UPLAND —) BOOLEY
SETTLER METIC SAHIB LIVYER
NESTER GRUELER PEOPLER
PILGRIM PIONEER TRIMMER
FINISHER GACHUPIN HABITANT
SHAGROON SIBERSKI SIBERYAK
(— IN AUSTRALIA) GROPER
(— IN NEW ZEALAND) SHAGROON
(DANISH —S) OSTMEN
SETTLING SIT
(— OF ESTATE) ENTAIL
(PL.) LEES SEDIMENT

SET-TO ROW MELEE BOUT TURN
PLUCK FETTLE TURNUP BRANGLE
SETUP SET SITTER ENTRAPMENT
SEVEN SEPT ZETA ZAYIN HEPTAD
SEPTET HEBDOMAD SEPTETTE
(— OF DIAMONDS) POPE
(— OF TRUMPS) MANILLA
(GROUP OF —) PLEIAD
(PREF.) HEPT(A) SEPT(I) SEPTEM
SEVENFOLD SEPTUPLE
SEVENTEEN (AUTHOR OF —)
TARKINGTON
(CHARACTER IN —) MAY JANE
PRATT BAXTER GEORGE JOHNNY
WATSON GENESIS PARCHER
WILLIAM CLEMATIS
SEVEN-UP PEDRO PITCH SLEDGE
SEVER AX AXE CUT BITE DEAL HACK
REND SLIT TWIN SHEAR SHRED
CLEAVE CUTOFF DEPART DETACH
DIVIDE LOPOFF SAWOFF SUNDER
DISALLY DISCERP DISCIDE DISJOIN
OUTRIVE DISSEVER PRESCIND
SEPARATE SEVERIZE
(PREF.) TEMNO
SEVERAL ODD TEN SERE WHEEN
DIVERS SUNDRY DIVERSE VARIOUS
DISTINCT MULTIPLE
(PREF.) PLURI POLY
SEVERALLY APIECE SEVERAL
SEVERANCE SUNDER SOLUTION
(— OF RELATIONSHIPS) AIR
SEVERE BAD DRY ACID BLUE DEAR
DOUR DURE FIRM HARD IRON
KEEN ROID RUDE SALT SIDE SORE
TART TAUT ACUTE BREME CRUEL
EAGER GRUFF HARSH RETHE RIGID
ROUGH SHARP SMART SNELL
SOBER SOUND STARK STEER
STERN STIFF STOUR TOUGH BITING
BITTER BRUTAL CHASTE COARSE
FROSTY HETTER SIMPLE SOLEMN
STRICT TORVID UNKIND UNMILD
ACERBIC ASCETIC AUSTERE
CAUSTIC CHRONIC CONDIGN
CRUCIAL CUTTING DRASTIC
SERIOUS SPARTAN TORVOUS
UNCANNY VICIOUS VIOLENT
WEIGHTY ACERBATE ACULEATE
CATONIAN EXACTING GRIEVOUS
GRINDING HORRIBLE IRONCLAD
IRONHARD RIGOROUS SCATHING
STALWART STRAIGHT TERMINAL
TERRIBLE STRINGENT
(MOST —) EXTREME
(VERY —) SPLITTING
SEVERELY BAD HARD BADLY STARK
STIFF HARDLY SORELY STRONG
HEAVILY ROUGHLY SMARTLY
SOUNDLY STITHLY SHREWDLY
SEVERIAN AGNOETE AGNOITE
SEVERING
(PREF.) PRISO
SEVERITY FROST RIGOR CRUELTY
TORVITY TYRANNY ACRIMONY
ASPERITY FERVENCY HARDNESS
RIGIDITY SORENESS VIOLENCE
SEW SUE FELL SEAM SLIP PREEN
STEEK NEEDLE STITCH OVERSEW
THIMBLE OVERCAST OVERHAND
(— A CORPSE) SOCK
(— LOOSELY) BASTE
(— TO REINFORCE) BAR

(— UP FERRET'S MOUTH) COPE
(— WAVED PATTERN) DICE
SEWAGE SOIL WASTE SOILAGE
SULLAGE AFFLUENT DRAINAGE
SEWERAGE WASTEWATER
SEWELLEL BEAVER BOOMER
SEWER SINK SIRE DRAFT DRAIN
FLEET ISSUE MAKER SHORE
CLOACA KILTER TACKER VENNEL
BELTMAN COPYIST CULVERT
DRAUGHT GULLION JAWHOLE
SHIRRER PIQUIERE
SEWING TACK SUTURE SEMPSTRY
(SUFF.) RHAPHY RRHAPHY
SEX KIND SECT GENDER
(FEMALE —) SMOCK
(KIND OF —) SAFE
(MALE —) WEPMANKIN
(PREF.) GEN(O)
SEX APPEAL IT OOMPH
SEXLESS NEUTER EPICENE
SEXT MIDDAY
SEXTANT (PART OF —) ARC ARM
DRUM LIMB MARK FRAME GLASS
INDEX LEVER HANDLE MIRROR
SUNSHADE TELESCOPE
SEXTET SESTET SEXTUOR
SESTETTO
SEXTON SAXON BEADLE SHAMUS
WARDEN SACRIST SHAMASH
SHAMMES VESTURER SACRISTAN
SEXTUPLE SENARY
SEXTUPLET SESTOLE SEXTOLE
SESTOLET SEXTOLET
SEXUAL GAMIC CARNAL INTIMATE
(PREF.) GAM(ETO)(O) GON(O)
SEXY FOXY FREUDIAN
SEYCHELLES (CAPITAL OF —)
VICTORIA
(ISLAND OF —) MAHE LADIGUE
PRASLIN
SGANARELLE (BROTHER OF —)
ARISTE
(DAUGHTER OF —) LUCINDE
(WARD OF —) LEONORE ISABELLE
(WIFE OF —) MARTINE
SHA YASHIRO
SHAAPH (FATHER OF —) CALEB
JAHDAI
(MOTHER OF —) MAACHAH
SHAB RUBBERS
SHABBINESS WAFFNESS
SHABBY BASE MEAN POKY WORN
DINGY DIRTY DOWDY MANGY
OURIE POKEY RATTY SCALD SEEDY
SORRY TACKY CHEESY FROWZY
GROTTY GRUBBY GRUNGY SCABBY
SCOURY SCUFFY SCURVY SHODDY
SHROVY SLEAZY TAGRAG BUNTING
MESQUIN SCALLED SCRUBBY
SCRUFFY SCUFFED SHABBED
SQUALID PALTERLY SLIPSHOD
WAFFLIKE
SHABUOTH PENTECOST
SHACHIA (FATHER OF —)
SHAHARAIM
(MOTHER OF —) HODESH
SHACK COE HUT CRIB SHAG HUMPY
HUTCH SHANTY
SHACKLE COP TIE BAND BIND BOLT
BOND GYVE LOCK STAY BASIL
BILBO CLAMP COPSE CRAMP
CRANK HUMPY TRASH TRAVE

FETTER GARTER HAMPER PINION
SHANGY STAYER SWATHE
COTTAGE COUPLER FETLOCK
MANACLE MOUSING PASTERN
SHEBANG SNACKLE TRAMMEL
RESTRAIN
(PL.) IRONS
SHACKLER SLOTTER
SHAD BUCK CHAD ALLIS ALOSE
TRABU ALLICE TWAITE ALEWIFE
ANADROM CLUPEID FLATFISH
SAWBELLY
SHADBUSH DOGWOOD SERVICE
SERVICEBERRY
SHADDOCK LUCBAN POMELO
POMPION PAMPELMOUSE
POMPELMOOSE
SHADE EYE CAST DULL SCUG SHED
TONE VEIL BLEND COLOR ENNUE
GHOST GLIDE GLOOM GRAIN
SCAUM SCOUG SWALE SWILL
TASTE TINCT TINGE TRACE UMBER
UMBRA DEGREE FRESCO SHADOW
SHIELD SHROUD SPRITE STRAIN
STRIPE TONING CURTAIN ECLIPSE
GRADATE HACHURE KENNING
PROTECT SECTION SHADING
UMBRAGE BONGRACE HALFTONE
UMBRELLA
(— OF COLOR) EYE CAST TONE
(— OF DIFFERENCE) NUANCE
(— OFF) GRADUATE
(— OF LINEN) ECRU
(— ON HAT) UGLY
(EYE —) UGLY
(NEUTRAL —) TAUPE
(OVERHANGING —) CANOPY
(WINDOW —) STORE
(PREF.) UMBRI
SHADED OMBRE SHADY DRUMLY
SOMBER SOMBRE DARKLING
SHADINESS GLOOM
SHADING FLUTING LAYERING
SHADOW DOG FOX BLOT SCUG TAIL
CLOUD SCOUG SHADE TRAIL
UMBER UMBRA CLEEKS DARKEN
FINGER SHROUD TAILER ISOGYRE
PHANTOM SCARROW SUGGEST
UMBRAGE UMBRATE PENUMBRA
PHANTASM SHEPHERD
(PREF.) SCI(A)(O) SKIA SKIO
TENEBRI UMBRI
SHADOWED DARKLING
SHADOWINESS GLOOM
SHADOWLESS ASCIAN WHITEOUT
SHADOWS ON THE ROCK
(AUTHOR OF —) CATHER
(CHARACTER IN —) LAVAL CECILE
HECTOR PIERRE AUCLAIR BLINKER
CHARRON EUCLIDE SAINTCYR
FRONTENAC
SHADOWY MISTY VAGUE GLOOMY
GHOSTLY OBSCURE
SHADRACH ANANIAS HANANIAH
SHADY DARK BOSKY BOWERY
CLOUDY LOUCHE SHADOW
SHADOWY UMBROSE ADUMBRAL
SHAFT BAR NIB ROD AXLE BALK
BARB BOLT DART FUST HOLE PILE
POLE TRAM WELL ARBOR HEUGH
QUILL REACH SCAPE SHANK
SHOOT SNEAD SPRAG STAFF
STALE STANG STAVE STEAL STELE

STILT STING THILL TRUNK BOLTEL
CANNON COLUMN GNOMON
SCAPUS STAPLE TILLER TUNNEL
UPRISE VAGINA BOWTELL
CHIMNEY INCLINE MANDREL
SPINDLE CAMSHAFT DOWNCAST
ESCONSON HOISTWAY LAMPHOLE
MISTREAT SHAFTWAY STANDARD
WEIGHBAR WELLHOLE
(— CONNECTING WHEELS) AXLE
(— IN GLACIER) MOULIN
(— IN WATCH) STEM
(— OF CANDLESTICK) BALUSTER
(— OF CARRIAGE) FILL SILL THILL
(— OF CART) ROD TRAM SHARP
STANG
(— OF CAVERN) DOME
(— OF CHARIOT) BEAM
(— OF CLUSTERED PIER) BOLTEL
(— OF COLUMN) FUST TIGE SCAPE
TRUNK VERGE
(— OF FEATHER) SCAPE SCAPUS
AFTERSHAFT
(— OF MINE) PIT WORK GRUFF
HEUCH HEUGH RAISE SLOPE STULM
WINZE GROOVE STAPLE INCL INF
WINNING
(— OF PADDLE) LOOM ROUND
(— OF SPEAR OR LANCE) TREE
STALE
(— OF WAGON) STAVE THILL
LIMBER
(HARNESS —) HEALD
(HOLLOW —) CANNON
(MAIN —) ARBOR
(ORNAMENTAL —) VERGE
(SCYTHE —) SNEAD
(STAIRWAY —) VICE
(TWISTED —) TORSO
(VENTILATION —) UPCAST UPTAKE
WINDHOLE
(PREF.) DORY SCAPI
SHAG PILE
SHAGE (SON OF —) JONATHAN
SHAGGY SHAG SWAG HARSH
NAPPY ROUGH SHOCK TATTY
TOUSY BRUSHY COMATE RAGGED
TOOSIE HIRSUTE SHAGRAG
SQUALID SWAGGED THRUMMY
VILLOUS TATTERED
(PREF.) DASI DASY LASI
SHAGREEN GALUCHAT
SHAGROON PILGRIM
SHAKE BOB DAD JAR JOG ROG
WAG WAP JOLT JOWL PLUM QUAG
RESE ROCK SHOG STIR SWAY TOZE
WEVE WHAP WHOP HOTCH JAUNT
KNOCK NIDGE QUASH SHOCK
SWING TRILL DIDDER DITHER
DODDER DODDLE EXCUSS
GOGGLE HOTTER HUSTLE JOGGLE
JOUNCE JUMBLE QUATCH
QUAVER QUITCH QUIVER ROGGLE
RUFFLE SHIMMY SHIVER TOTTER
WAMBLE WANGLE WARBLE
WEAKEN WOBBLE AGITATE
BRANDLE CHOUNCE CONCUSS
ROULADE SHUDDER STAGGER
SUCCUSS TREMBLE TWITTER
WHIFFLE WHITHER BRANDISH
CONVULSE ENFEEBLE
(— A PURSUER) LOSE
(— FEATHERS) ROUSE

(— HERRING) SCUD
(— LIGHTLY) LIFT
(— OFF) ARISE EXCUSS
(— TO SEPARATE) HOTCH
(— UP) JABBLE JUMBLE RATTLE
(WIND —) ANEMOSIS
SHAKER DUSTER SIFTER DREDGER
JUMBLER POUNCET SANDBOX
SHAKING ASPEN ASHAKE TREMOR
JARRING AGITATED
(— OF AIRPLANE) BUFFET
SHAKTI TARA PRAKRITI
SHAKTIS MATRIS
SHAKUNTALA (FATHER OF —)
VISHVAMITRA
(FOSTER FATHER OF —) KANVA
(HUSBAND OF —) DUSHYANTA
(MOTHER OF —) MENAKA
(SON OF —) BHARATA
SHAKY CRANK DICKY QUAKY ROCKY
TIPSY TOTTY WONKY WOOZY
AGUISH COGGLY CRANKY GROGGY
INFIRM WAMBLY CASALTY
DWAIBLE DWEEBLE PALSIED
RICKETY SHOGGLY TITTUPY
TOTTERY COGGLEDY INSECURE
SHALE BAT BASS BONE CLOD FLAG
KOLM TILL BLAES FAKES METAL
PLATE XALLE KILLAS SHILLET
MUDSTONE SLIGGEEN TORBANITE
PORCELLANITE KUPFERSCHIEFER
SHALL SE MAY MUN MUST SALL
(— NOT) SANNA SHANT SHANNA
SHALLOON CUBICA
SHALLOT CIBOL ALLIUM ESCHALOT
SCALLION
SHALLOW EBB BANK FLAN FLAT
FLUE GLIB FLEET INANE SHOAL
SILLY SMALL FLIMSY FROTHY
LITTLE RIFFLE SLIGHT UNDEEP
CRIPPLE CURSORY TRIVIAL
MAGAZINY
(PL.) FORD
SHALLOW BECOME A —) SHOAL
SHALLOWNESS INANITY
SHALLUM (FATHER OF —) BANI
KORE SHAUL JABESH JOSIAH
HOLOHESH NAPHTALI
(NEPHEW OF —) JEREMIAH
(SON OF —) HOLOHESH MAASEIAH
JEHIZKIAH
(WIFE OF —) HULDAH
SHALLUN (FATHER OF —)
COLHOZEH
SHAM BAM FOB FOX GIG FAKE
HOAX MOCK PUFF BLUFF BOGUS
CHEAT DUMMY FALSE FEIGN FEINT
FRAUD LETON QUEER SHUCK
SNIDE ASSUME BRUMMY BUNYIP
CHOUSE DECEIT DUFFER HUMBUG
PSEUDO SHODDY STUMER FALSITY
FORGERY GRIMACE MOCKISH
PLASTER PRETEND STUMOUR
POSTICHE PRETENSE SPURIOUS
BRUMMAGEM PASTEBOARD
SIMULACRUM
(PREF.) PSEUD(O)
SHAMAN PEAI CURER MACHI
KAHUNA WABENO ANGEKOK
TOHUNGA CONTRARY WITCHMAN
SHAMARIAH (FATHER OF —)
REHOBOAM
SHAMASH (FATHER OF —) SIN

(SISTER OF —) ISHTAR
(WIFE OF —) AA AYA
SHAMBLE SHALE SHOOL CLOUCH
BAUCHLE SCAMBLE SHACHLE
SHACKLE SKEMMEL ABATTOIR
SHAMMOCK
(PL.) BUTCHERY
SHAMBLING SHACKLY
SHAME SISS ABASH AIDOS SHEND
SPITE ASHAME BISMER REBUKE
MORTIFY PUDENCY SCANDAL
SLANDER CONTEMPT DISGRACE
DISHONOR REPROACH SHENDING
VERGOYNE VITUPERY
(— BY CENSURE) TOUCH
SHAMED (FATHER OF —) ELPAAL
SHAMEFACED SHY
SHAMEFACEDNESS PUDENCY
SHAMEFUL BASE FOUL MEAN
GROSS HONTOUS IGNOBLE
FLAGRANT IMPROPER INFAMOUS
SHAMELESS HARD BRASH ARRANT
BRAZEN BASHLESS BROWLESS
IMMODEST IMPUDENT
SHAMELESSNESS BRASS
SHAMGAR (FATHER OF —) ANATH
SHAMIR (FATHER OF —) MICAH
(GRANDFATHER OF —) UZZIEL
SHAMMA (FATHER OF —) ZOPHAH
SHAMMAH (BROTHER OF —) DAVID
(FATHER OF —) JESSE REUEL
SHAMMAI (FATHER OF —) ONAM
REKEM
SHAMMES BEADLE
SHAMMUA (FATHER OF —) DAVID
ZACCUR
(MOTHER OF —) BATHSHEBA
(SON OF —) ABDA
SHAMPOO TRIPSIS
(— INGREDIENT) ALOE
SHAMPOOING TRIPSIS
SHAMROCK OCA SEAMROG
SHAMROOT
SHAMUS TEC SEXTON DETECTIVE
SHANK BODY CRUS GAMB JAMB
TANG FEMUR GAMBE CANNON
NIBBLE TARSUS KNUCKLE
(THREAD —) STEM
SHANNY BULLY
SHANTY SLED BOIST HUMPY
HUTCH SHACK SHEBANG
CHANTIER DOGHOUSE
SHAPE AX ADZ AXE CUT DIE HUE
ADZE BEAT BEND CAST COLE COPE
DRAW FACE FAIR FORM HACK
MOLD NICK BEVEL BLOCK BOAST
BUILT COLOR DRAPE DRESS FEIGN
FORGE FRAME GUISE HORSE
JOLLY LATHE MODEL MOULD
SWAGE BROACH CHISEL CUTOUT
EFFORM FIGURE FORMER FRAISE
HAMMER JIGGER SQUARE
CHANNEL CONFORM CONTOUR
FASHION FEATURE GESTALT
INCLINE OUTLINE PATTERN
TONNEAU CONTRIVE LIKENESS
(— BY HAMMERING) SMITH
(— DIAMOND) BRUTE
(— GARMENTS) BOARD
(— LIKE AN EGG) OVOID
(— METAL) SWAGE EXTRUDE
(— OF BUST) TAILLE
(— OF ENVELOPE FLAP) KNIFE

(— ONE'S COURSE) ETTLE
(— ON POTTER'S WHEEL) THROW
(— RIGHTLY) FIT
(— ROUGHLY) BOAST SCABBLE
SCAPPLE
(— ROUGHLY WITH CHISEL) BOAST
(— STONE) BROACH SCABBLE
(CLAY —) FLOATER
(CONICAL —) BEEHIVE
(GEM —) BAGUET BAGUETTE
(GLOVE —) TRANK
(LIKE A DOUGHNUT) TORIC
(SPIRALLING —) SWIRL
(SURFACE —) GEOMETRY
(UNBLOCKED —) HOOD
(PREF.) MORPH(O)
SHAPED BUILT FITTED BLOCKED
FEATURED
(— LIKE A DOUGHNUT) TORIC
(— LIKE A HORN) LYRATE
(— LIKE ALMOND) AMYGDALOID
(— LIKE ANVIL) INCUS
(— LIKE ARROW) SAGITTAL
SAGITTATE
(— LIKE BASIN) PELVIFORM
(— LIKE BEAN) FABIFORM
(— LIKE BERRY) BACCIFORM
(— LIKE BOAT) SCAPHOID
NAVICULAR
(— LIKE BUCKLER) SCUTATE
(— LIKE CAKE) PLACENTIFORM
(— LIKE CAP) PILEATE PILEATED
(— LIKE CLUB) CLAVATE CLUBBED
(— LIKE COIN) NUMMULAR
(— LIKE COMB) CTENOID
(— LIKE CONE) CONIFORM
(— LIKE CUP) SCYPHATE
(— LIKE DOME) DOMAL
(— LIKE EAR) AURIFORM
(— LIKE FAN) RHIPIDATE
(— LIKE FEATHER) PINNATE
PINNATED PENNIFORM
(— LIKE FIDDLE) PANDURATE
(— LIKE FUNNEL) INFUNDIBULAR
(— LIKE HALBERD) HASTATE
(— LIKE HAMMER) MALLEIFORM
(— LIKE HEART) CORDATE
CORDIFORM
(— LIKE HOOK) ANKYROID
(— LIKE HORN) CORNIFORM
(— LIKE HORSESHOE)
HIPPOCREPIAN
(— LIKE KEEL) CARINATE
(— LIKE KIDNEY) NEPHROID
RENIFORM
(— LIKE LEAF) FOLIATE
(— LIKE LENS) LENTOID PHACOID
(— LIKE LENTIL) PHACOID
PHACOIDAL
(— LIKE NEEDLE) ACUATE
(— LIKE ORANGE) OBLATE
(— LIKE PEA) PISIFORM
(— LIKE PEAR) PYRIFORM
(— LIKE PITCHER) ARYTENOID
ARYTAENOID
(— LIKE POUCH) BURSIFORM
(— LIKE PULLEY) TROCHLEAR
(— LIKE RING) ANNULAR
(— LIKE ROD) BACILLAR
(— LIKE S) SIGMATE
(— LIKE SAUCER) PATELLATE
(— LIKE SAUSAGE) ALLANTOID
(— LIKE SCIMITAR) ACINACIFORM

(— LIKE SHELL) CONCHATE
CONCHIFORM
(— LIKE SHIELD) ASPIDATE
CLYPEATE
(— LIKE SICKLE) FALCULAR
CALCEOLATE
(— LIKE SLIPPER) CALCEIFORM
CALCEOLATE
(— LIKE SNAKE) ANGUIFORM
(— LIKE SOCKET) GLENOID
GLENOIDAL
(— LIKE SPINDLE) FUSOID
FUSIFORM
(— LIKE SPUR) CALCARINE
(— LIKE STAR) ASTROID
(— LIKE STRAP) LIGULATE
(— LIKE SWORD) GLADIATE
(— LIKE THREAD) FILIFORM
(— LIKE TURNIP) NAPIFORM
(— LIKE WATCH GLASS)
MENISCOID
(— LIKE WEDGE) CUNEAL CUNEATE
(— LIKE WHEEL) ROTATE
(— LIKE X) SALTIRE
(— WITH AX) HEWN
SHAPED)- LIKE BELL)
CAMPANIFORM
SHAPELESS DUMPY CLUMPY
DEFORM DUMPTY INFORM
FORMLESS INDIGEST UNSHAPED
AMORPHOUS
SHAPELINESS DELICACY
SHAPELY GENT TIDY TRIM CLEAN
TIGHT DECENT FORMAL GAINLY
FEATOUS FORMFUL SHAPABLE
SHAPHAT (FATHER OF —) HORI
ADLAI SHEMAIAH
(SON OF —) ELISHA
SHAPING DESCENT
SHARAI (FATHER OF —) BANI
SHARAR (SON OF —) AHIAM
SHARD SCAUR SHERD SHRED
SLIVER
(PL.) PITCHER
SHARE CUT END LOT RUG CANT
DALE DEAL DOLE HAND PART
PLOT RENT SCOT SNIP DIVVY
ENTER PARTY QUOTA RATIO
SHEAR SHIFT SLICE SNACK SNICK
SNUCK SPLIT WHACK COMMON
COPART DEPART DIVIDE FINGER
IMPART RATION SHOVEL PARTAGE
PARTAKE PORTION DIVIDEND
DIVISION INTEREST PURPARTY
PERCENTAGE PROPORTION
(— A BED) BUNK
(— DWELLING) STALL
(— EQUALLY) HALVE
(— IN ACTIVITY) PIECE
(— OF CHURCH REVENUE)
PREBEND
(— OF EXPENSES) LAW CLUB
(— OF LAND) DAIL DALE FREEDOM
RUNDALE
(— OF PROFIT) LAY
(— OF STOCK) STOCK ACTION
(— QUARTERS) CHUM
(— SECRETS) CONFIDE
(ALLOTED —) DOLE
(ANCESTRAL —) PATTI
(EQUAL —) PROPORTION
(FULL —) SKINFUL
(GREATER —) FECK
(LEGAL —) HAK

(MINING —S) KANGAROOS
(ONE'S —) AFFERE
(PROPORTIONAL —) QUOTA
(SMALL —) MOIETY
(PL.) STOCK
(PREF.) MER(I)(O) MERISTO
(SUFF.) MER(E)(IC)(IS)(OUS)(Y)
SHARECROPPER RENTER
BYWONER CROPPER
SHARED JOINT BETWEEN
(PREF.) CO
SHAREHOLDER (THEATRE —)
RENTER
SHAREZER (BROTHER OF —)
ESARHADDON ADRAMMELECH
(FATHER OF —) SENNACHERIB
SHARING INON
(— OF EXPENSE) CLUB
(— VICARIOUSLY) ARMCHAIR
SHARK FOX GATA HAYE KULP MAKO
MANO TOPE GUMMY HOMER
HOUND LAMIA TIGER TOMMY
TOPER BEAGLE DAGGAR GALEID
PALOMA REQUIN WHALER
ACRODUS BONEDOG DOGFISH
FOXFISH HUNFYSH PLACOID
REQUIEM SLEEPER SOUPFIN
SQUALID SUNFISH TIBURON
TIGRONE TUBARON BULLHEAD
HYBODONT ROUSETTE SAILFISH
SEAHOUND SKAAMOOG SPEAREYE
SQUATINA THRASHER THRESHER
PORBEAGLE SEALAWYER
SELACHIAN WOBBEGONG
SHOVELHEAD
(KIND OF —) LOAN MAKO NURSE
(YOUNG —) CUB SHARKLET
(PREF.) SQUALI SQUALO
SHARP DRY SHY ACID ACRE CHIC
CUTE EDGY FELL FINE GAIR GASH
GLEG GNIB HARD HIGH KEEN PERT
SALT TART ACERB ACRID ACUTE
ALERT BRASH BREME BRISK CRISP
DOWNY EAGER EDGED FALSE
HARSH NASAL NEBBY NIPPY PEERY
QUICK SMART SNELL SQUAB
STEEP STIFF VIVID YAULD ACIDIC
ACUATE ARGUTE ASTUTE BITING
BITTER BRIGHT CRISPY DIESIS
GLASSY JAGGED PLUCKY SEVERE
SHREWD SHRILL SNELLY SNITHE
STINGY TOOTHY TWEAKY UNRIDE
ANGULAR AUSTERE BRITTLE
CAUSTIC CUTTING GINGERY
NIPPING PIQUANT POINTED
PRECISE PUNGENT SHARPEN
SLICING SPINOUS VARMINT
VIOLENT HATCHETY INCISIVE
POIGNANT ACIDULOUS IRRITABLE
ASTRINGENT ACRIMONIOUS
(NOT —) MILD
(SHAPED AS —) OCTOTHORP
(PREF.) ACET(O) ACUT(I)(O) OXY
SHARP-EDGED VORPAL CULTRATE
SHARPEN EDGE FILE FINE HONE
KEEN WHET BRISK FROST GRIND
POINT RAISE SHARP SLYPE STONE
STROP ACCENT AFFILE STROKE
ENHANCE QUICKEN SMARTEN
EXACUATE HEIGHTEN
(— HORSESHOE) FROST
SHARPENED ACUATE

SHARPENER SHARPER STROPPER
(SCYTHE —) RIP RIFLE
SHARPENING (— OF PITCH) RISE
SHARPER GUE GYP BITE KITE ROOK
SKIN SNAP BITER CHEAT CROOK
GREEK ROGUE SHARK SHARP
BESTER COGGER NICKUM PICARO
ROOKER SHARPY BARNARD
CATALAN GAMBLER SHARKER
SPIELER BLACKLEG DECEIVER
PIGEONER SWINDLER
SHARPLY DAB SHARP SNACK
ACIDLY ROUNDLY SHEERLY
SMARTLY STEEPLY
SHARPNESS WIT EDGE SALT WHET
PLUCK ACRITY ACUITY ACUMEN
ACIDITY ACERBITY ACRIDITY
ACRIMONY ASPERITY EDGINESS
PUNGENCY
SHARP-POINTED ACUATE
ACULEATE
(PREF.) ACUT(I)(O)
SHARPSHOOTER JAGER DEADEYE
VOLTIGEUR TIRAILLEUR
BERSAGLIERE
SHARP-SIGHTED SIGHTY LYNCEAN
SHARP-TAILED GROUSE PINTAIL
SHARP-WITTED ACUTE CANNY
SNELL SHREWD
SHASHAI (FATHER OF —) BANI
SHASHAK (FATHER OF —) ELPAAL
SHASTRA PURANA SASTRA
(— CLASS) SRUTI
SHATTER BLOW DASH DICE BLAST
BREAK BURST CRASH CRAZE
CREEM FRUSH SMASH SMOKE
SPLIT WRECK SHIVER SPIDER
BEGUILE CHATTER CONVELL
EXPLODE SMATTER TORPEDO
DEMOLISH DYNAMITE SPLINTER
(— CLAY TARGET) KILL
SHATTERED BROKEN BROOZLED
DODDERED
SHAUL (FATHER OF —) SIMEON
SHAVE BARB BITE DRAW PARE
RAZE GLACE GRAZE SKIVE SCHAWE
SCRAPE FLATTEN UPRIGHT
SHAVED POLLED SHAVEN
SHAVEN NOT NOTT PILLED
TONSURED
SHAVER PLANE PLANER
SHAVING SHAVE SHRED SPALE
SPELL RAMENT RAMENTUM
(LATHE —S) TURNINGS
(PL.) COOM COOMB SCOBS
MOSLINGS
SHAWL MAUD WRAP LAMBA
MANTA MANTO NUBIA PATTU
RUMAL SCARF TOZIE AFGHAN
ANGORA KAMBAL PEPLOS PEPLUM
PEPLUS PUTTOO SARAPE SERAPE
TAPALO TOILET TONNAG ZEPHYR
AMLIKAR CHUDDAR PAISLEY
WHITTLE WRAPPER ALGERINE
CASHMERE EPIBLEMA KAFFIYEH
SLENDANG TURNOVER
(COARSE —) KAMBAL
(COTTON —) FARDA
(PLAID —) MAUD
(TASSELED —) TALLITH
SHAWM WAIT SHALM BOMBARD
SCHALMEI
(KIN OF —) OBOE

SHE A HE HEO HER SHU ELLE HAEC
SCHO
(AUTHOR OF —) HAGGARD
(CHARACTER IN —) JOB LEO SHE
HOLLY AYESHA LUDWIG USTANE
VINCEY BILLALI MAHOMED
KALLIKRATES
SHEAF TIE BEAT BUNG GAIT GERB
OMER FLASH GAVEL GERBE GLEAN
BATTEN THRAVE DORLACH
HATTOCK CAPSHEAF CORNBOLE
(— LEVIED AS TAX) CORNBOLE
(— OF ARROWS) FLASH
(— OF FLAX OR HEMP) BEAT BEET
GLEAN
(— OF GRAIN) GAIT GARB HOSE
GARBAGE
(LAST — OF CORN) NECK
(LAST — OF HARVEST) KIRN
(PROTECTING —) HATTOCK
(UNBOUND —) REAP GAVEL
SHEAL (FATHER OF —) BANI
SHEALTIEL (SON OF —)
ZERUBBABEL
SHEAR COW CUT DOD LIP NOT CLIP
CROP NOTT TRIM BREAK FORCE
SHARE SHEER SHIRL SLIDE STRIP
FLEECE STRESS
SHEARER SNAGGER
SHEARIAH (FATHER OF —) AZEL
SHEARLING SHEARHOG
(PL.) ALPACA
SHEARS LEWIS SNIPS FORFEX
SHEARER SNOUTER SECATEUR
(PREF.) FORFICI
SHEARWATER HAG CREW COHOW
HAGDON HAGLET PETREL PUFFIN
SCRABE PIMLICO SCRABER
SEABIRD HACKBOLT
SHEATFISH WELS DORAD WALLER
CATFISH SILURID
SHEATH COT NOT BOOT CASE CYST
HOSE HOTT ARMOR CHAPE FOREL
GAINE OCREA SHADE SHEAF SPILL
THECA VOLVA COCOON CONDOM
FORREL MYELIN OCHREA QUIVER
SLOUGH VAGINA AXILEMMA
EPILEMMA SCABBARD STANDARD
VAGINULA NEURILEMMA
(— FOR BOOK) FOREL FORRIL
(— FOR FINGER) STALL
(— FOR GAMECOCK'S SPUR) HOT
HOTT
(— OF CIGARETTE) SPILL
(— OF PLOW) STANDARD
(— OF TISSUE) PERIBLEM
(MEDULLARY —) CORONA
(PREF.) COLE(O) COLI(O) ELYTR(O)
(SUFF.) LEMMA THECA THECIUM
SHEATHBILL PADDY
SHEATHE CLAD COPPER MUZZLE
IMPLATE
SHEATHED THECATE
SHEATHING SKIN ARMOR COPPER
FACING SHEATH INLAYER SHIPLAP
SLITWORK
SHEA TREE KARITE KARITI
SHEAVE SHEAF SHIVER HATTOCK
TRUCKLE
(24 —S OF GRAIN) THRAVE
THREAVE
SHEBA (FATHER OF —) BICHRI
SHEBANG HUT

SHEBER (FATHER OF —) CALEB
(MOTHER OF —) MAACHAH
SHEBUEL (FATHER OF —) HEMAN
SHECHANIAH (FATHER OF —) ARAH
JEHIEL
(SON OF —) SHEMAIAH
SHED BOX CUB SOW ABRI CAST
COTE DROP HELM HULL KILN
MOLT PEEL POUR SHUD SKEO SLIP
BOOTH HIELD HOVEL MOULT
SCALE SHADE SPILL THROW VINEA
ZAYAT BELFRY BROACH DINGLE
EFFUSE GARAGE HANGAR
HEMMEL INFUSE LINHAY MISTAL
PANDAL SLOUGH CHOLTRY
COTTAGE DIFFUSE DISCARD
MUSCLE RADIATE SKIPPER
EXUVIATE SKEELING SKILLION
WOODSHED PENTHOUSE
(— BLOOD) BROACH
(— DROPS) DRIZZLE
(— FEATHERS OR HORNS) MEW
(— FOR LIVESTOCK) SHIPPEN
(— FOR SHEEP) SHEALING
(— LIGHT) ENLIGHT ENLIGHTEN
IRRADIATE
(— OVER MINE SHAFT) COE
(— TEARS) GIVE
(— TO PROTECT SOLDIERS)
TESTUDO
(CATTLE —) CUB HELM LAIR BELFRY
(MOVABLE —) SOW BAIL MUSCLE
(READILY —) FUGACIOUS
(TEMPORARY —) PANDAL
(WEATHER —) DINGLE
SHEDDING FALL SPILTH ECDYSIS
APOLYSIS
(— TEARS) LACHRYMOSE
SHE-DEMON LAMIA
SHEDEUR (SON OF —) ELIZUR
SHEEN GLAZE SHINE LUSTER
LUSTRE SHIMMER
SHEEP SNA TEG DOWN LAMB LONK
MUGS SHIP SOAY URIN ZENU
ANCON BOVID DUMBA HEDER
HUNIA MUGGS OVINE SAIGA
SHORN TAGGE AOUDAD ARGALI
BARHAL BHARAL BIDENT CHURRO
DECCAN DORPER DORSET
EXMOOR HIRSEL MARKER
MASHAM MERINO MUTTON
NAYAUR OXFORD PANAMA
PAULAR ROMNEY WETHER
WOOLIE WOOLLY BIGHORN
BLEATER BRAXIES CHEVIOT
CRIOLLA DELAINE DISHLEY
FREEZER FRONTER JUMBUCK
KARAKUL LINCOLN POLLARD
SUFFOLK TARGHEE TWINTER
VERMONT BIKANERI COMEBACK
COTSWOLD DARTMOOR
HERDWICK LONGWOOL
LUGHDOAN RUMINANT SHEARHOG
SHEARING TALLOWER THRINTER
MONTADALE ROMELDALE
SHROPSHIRE
(— DIFFICULT TO HANDLE)
COBBLER
(— IN 2ND YEAR) HOB TAG TEG
TAGGE TWINTER
**(— THAT HAS SHED PORTION OF
WOOL)** ROSELLA
(— TO BE SHEARED) BOARD

(DEAD —) MORT BRAXY MORLING
(FEMALE —) EWE GIMMER SHEDER
(HORNLESS —) NOT NOTT
(LOST —) WAIF
(MALE —) RAM TUP BUCK HEDER
DINMONT
(MOUNTAIN —) IBEX
(OLD —) GUMMER
(PART OF —) EAR EYE LEG RIB BACK
DOCK FACE LOIN NECK RACK RUMP
FLANK SHANK BREAST MUZZLE
BRISKET FORELEG PASTERN
WITHERS FOREHEAD SHOULDER
FORESHANK
(THICK-WOOLED —) MUG
(UNSHORN —) HOG TEG
(WILD —) SHA ARGAL AUDAD BASSE
URIAL AOUDAD ARGALI BHARAL
SHAPOO BURRHEL MOUFLON
(YOUNG —) HOG HOGG HOGGEREL
(3-YEAR-OLD —) THRINTER
SHEEPBERRY ALISIER VIBURNUM
SHEEPCOTE SHEPPEY
SHEEPDOG PULI KELPIE SHELTY
BOBTAIL MALINOIS SHETLAND
(PL.) PULIK PULIS
SHEEP FLY FAG
SHEEPFOLD REE COTE FANK KRAAL
REEVE STELL BOUGHT BARKARY
SHEPPEY SHEEPCOT
SHEEPHERDER SNOOZER
STOCKMAN
SHEEPISH SHY
SHEEP LAUREL IVY HEATH WICKY
KALMIA LAUREL CALFKILL
LAMBKILL
SHEEPLIKE OVINE
SHEEPMAN HOBBER
SHEEP PLANT RAOULIA
SHEEP ROT CAW
SHEEP RUN STATION
SHEEPSHEAD JAMES JEMMY
JIMMY PARGO PORGY TAUTOG
FATHEAD PERCOID SPAROID
SHEEPSHEARER GUN
SHEEPSKIN ROAN SLAT MOUTON
SOLDIER CAPESKIN LAMBSKIN
WOOLFELL WOOLSKIN
(— TANNED WITH BARK) BASAN
BASIL
(— THAT SWEATS UNEVENLY)
SOLDIER
(ROUGH-TANNED —) CRUST
SHEEP SORREL SOURWEED
SHEEP TICK FAG KEB KED KADE
SHEEPWALK SLAIT
SHEER BOLD FINE MAIN MERE PURE
BLANK BRANT CRUDE FRANK
NAKED STARK STEEP SIMPLE
CLOTTED GAZETTE EVENDOWN
(MADE OF — FABRIC) PEEKABOO
SHEET FIN CARD FILM FINE FLAT
FOIL LEAF SILL BLANK FLONG
FOLIO NAPPE CANVAS CIRCLE
DOUBLE FASCIA FENDER FLIMSY
SHROUD SINDON BLANKET
CHUDDAH CHUDDER FLOGGER
FRISKET LEAFLET PALLIUM
PAPYRUS WRAPPER AIRSHEET
EIGHTEEN FOLLOWER HANDBILL
INTERLAY SHEETLET

(— ADDED TO DEED) FOLLOWER
(— ATTACHED TO INVOICE) APRON
(— FOR BRIDGE SCORES) FLOGGER
(— OF CELLULOID) CEL CELL
(— OF CLOUDS) PALLIUM
(— OF DOUGH) STRUDEL
(— OF FIBER) BAT LAP BATT
(— OF ICE) GLARE GLAZE
(— OF IRON) CRAMPET CRAMPIT
(— OF LAVA) COULEE
(— OF LEAD) SOAKER
(— OF LEATHER) BUFFING
(— OF MICA) FILM
(— OF MICROFILM) FICHE
(— OF MUSCLE) PLATYSMA
(— OF PAPER) FLAT FOLIO FRISKET
LEAFLET HANDBILL
(— OF PARCHMENT) SKIN
FOLLOWER
(— OF RUBBER) DAM
(— OF STAMPS) PANE
(— OF STRAW) YELM
(— OF SUGAR) SLAB
(— OF TISSUE) FASCIA
(— OF TOBACCO) BINDER
(— OF WATER) NAPPE
(— USED FOR MATRIX) FLONG
(HEATED —) CAUL
(METAL —S) LATTENS
(NEWS —) GAZETTE
(ORGANIZATION —) BILL
(PERFORATED —) SIEVE
(PROTECTIVE —) CURTAIN
(THEATRICAL —) SIDE
(THIN —) LAMINA
(THIN —S OF IRON) DOUBLES
(TRANSPARENT —) GELATINE
(WINDING —) SINDON SUDARY
(PREF.) PALLIO
SHEETING PERCALE DOMESTIC
AMERICANI
SHEHARIAH (FATHER OF —)
JEHORAM
SHEKEL (HALF —) BEKAH
SHEKINAH GLORY
SHELAH (FATHER OF —) JUDAH
SHELDRAKE SHELDER BARGOOSE
BERGANDER
SHELEMIAH (FATHER OF —) BANI
ABDEEL
(SON OF —) IRIJAH JEHUCAL
HANANIAH
SHELEPH (FATHER OF —) JOKTAN
SHELESH (FATHER OF —) HELEM
SHELF BANK BERM BINK DECK DESS
STEP TACK BENCH LEDGE SKELF
STAGE STOOL MANTEL SCONCE
SETTLE SHELVE BACKBAR
BRACKET COUNTER PLATEAU
CREDENCE CUPBOARD
(— BEFORE STOVE) HEARTH
(— BEHIND ALTAR) GRADINE
GRADINO RETABLE
(— IN MINE) BUNNING
(— OF ROCK) CAR LENCH
LENCHEON
(ALTAR —) BUTSUDAN
(CONTINENTAL —) PLATFORM
(FIREWORKS —) BALLOON
(RAISED —) SETTLE
SHELL ARD HUD PEN POD BAND
CASK CHOU CLAM CONE HARD
HOOF HULL HUSK MAIL OBUS

PELL PILL PIPI PUKA PUPA SKIN
SWAD UMBO UNIO BALAT CHANK
CHINK CONCH COPIS CRUMP
CRUST DRILL FRITZ GOURD MITER
MITRA MUREX ORMER OVULA
SCAUP SHALE SHARD SHEAL
SHERD SHOCK SHUCK TESTA TIARA
TROCA TURBO VALVE VENUS
ANOMIA ARCHIE BUCKIE BULLET
BURGAU CAPSID CERION COCKLE
CONKER COWRIE CRUSTA DENTAL
DOLIUM ECLAIR JINGLE LORICA
MAROON NOUGAT NUCULA
PULLET PURPLE SANKHA SINGLE
SLOUGH STROMB TRITON TURBAN
VANNET VENTER VOLUTE WINKLE
BALANUS BALLOON CARACOL
CARCASS COCONUT DARIOLE
DISCINA GLADIUS LIMACEL
MARINER PAPBOAT PHILINE
PROJECT SCALLOP SPICULE
SPINDLE SPONDYL TEREBRA
THIMBLE TOHEROA TORPEDO
TOXIFER TROCHID TRUMPET
UNICORN BACULITE BACULOID
CARAPACE CONCHITE COQUILLE
CYLINDER DUCKFOOT EGGSHELL
ENVELOPE ESCALLOP FIGSHELL
FOCALOID FRUSTULE HELICINA
MERINGUE OLIVELLA PUPARIUM
SEASHELL SOLARIUM STROMBUS
UNIVALVE VELUTINA VERMETID
VERMETUS WARRENER WHIZBANG
WOODCOCK
(— CONTAINING MEDICINE)
CAPSULE
(— OF DIATOM) FRUSTULE
(— OF OYSTER) HUSK SHUCK
(— OF SHIP) HULK SKIN
(— OF SLUG) LIMACEL
(— OF THE EARTH) SIAL
(—S FROM GUN) STUFF
(— SYSTEMATICALLY) COMB
(ANTIAIRCRAFT —) FLAK ARCHIE
(CARTRIDGE —S) BRASS
(CAST —S) EXUVIAE
(CUSTARD-FILLED —) ECLAIR
DARIOLE
(EMPTY —) DOP
(FOSSIL —) DOLITE AMMONITE
BACULITE BALANITE CONCHITE
(HOWITZER —) OBUS
(MATHEMATICAL —) HOMEOID
(OYSTER —S) CULCH CULTCH
(PART OF —) EAR LIP RIB TIP APEX
WING HINGE SPIRE VALVE WHORL
MUSCLE SUTURE ADDUCTOR
APERTURE
(PASTA —) TUFOLI
(PASTA —S) MANICOTTI
(PASTRY —) CORNET QUICHE
DARIOLE TIMBALE TALMOUSE
(PROTEIN —) CAPSID
(SNAIL —) CONKER HODMADOD
(SPIRAL —) CHANK
(TORTOISE —) HOOF
(VEGETABLE —) DOLMA
(PREF.) CHITINO CHITO CONCH(O)
LOPO OECO OSTRAC(O) TESTI
(SUFF.) OECA OECIA OSTRACA
SHELLED VINED
SHELLFISH ORM COCK BUCKY
NACRE PIROT BUCKIE LIMPET

WIGGLE MOLLUSK PERIWIG
ASTACIAN
(PART OF —) EYE FAN LEG CLAW
TAIL SHELL TOOTH FEELER RIPPER
TELSON UROPOD ABDOMEN
ANTENNA CRUSHER CARAPACE
SHELLING RATTLES
SHELL-LESS OON
SHELL MONEY UHLLO WAKIKI
SHELOMI (FATHER OF —) ABIHUD
SHELOMITH (FATHER OF —) DIBRI
ZERUBBABEL
SHELTER CAB HUT LEE LOO ABRI
BURY EAVE GIDE GITE HERD HIDE
HIVE JOKE JOUK LOWN ROOF
SCOG SCUG BARTH BELEE BENAB
BERRY BIELD BOIST BOOTH BOTHY
BOWER CABIN CLEAD CLOAK
COVER EMBAY HAVEN HOARD
HOUSE HOVEL HOVER HOWFF
HUTCH LEWTH LITHE RESET
SCOUG SHADE SHEAL ASYLUM
AWNING BELFRY BILBIE BOOLEY
BOUGHT BURROW COVERT
CRADLE DEFEND DUGOUT GABION
GUNYAH HANGAR HARBOR
HOSTEL PANDAL REFUGE SCONCE
SCREEN SHADOW SHIELD SHROUD
SUKKAH BOROUGH CABINET
CARPORT CHAMBER DEFENSE
EMBOSOM EMBOWER HOUSING
NACELLE QUARTER RETREAT
ROOFING TABERNA UMBRAGE
WANIGAN WICKIUP BESCREEN
DOGHOUSE ENSCONCE
LODGMENT PALLIATE SECURITY
SHIELING SNOWSHED WAYHOUSE
PESTHOUSE
(— FOR CATTLE) HELM BOOLY
STELL HEMMEL
(— FOR CROP WATCHERS) KISI
(— FOR DANCES) ENRAMADA
(— FOR SENTRY) GUERITE
(— FROM WEATHER) LEWTH
(— OVER BEEHIVE) HOOD
(BIRD HUNTER'S —) BLIND
(BULLETPROOF —) MANTLET
MANTELET
(CONCRETE-AND-STEEL —)
PILLBOX
(CRAMPED —) HUTCH
(FISH —) CROY
(LEAFY —) LEVESEL
(MINING —) TALPA
(PICNIC —) RAMADA
(PORTABLE —) MANTA CABANA
(ROCK —) KRAPINA
(ROUGH —) JACAL
(TEEPEELIKE —) CHUM
(TEMPORARY —) HALE HOLD CABIN
BIVOUAC
SHELTERED LEE LEW COSY COZY
LOUN LOWN SNUG BIELD LITHE
LOUND LOWND SHADY COVERT
(— SPACE) KILLOGIE
SHELTERED LIFE (AUTHOR OF —)
GLASGOW
(CHARACTER IN —) EVA BENA CORA
ETTA JOHN DELIA JENNY WELCH
BARRON GEORGE JOSEPH PEYTON
CROCKER ARCHBALD BIRDSONG
ISABELLA
SHELTERING BIELDY SHADING

SHELTERLESS HOMELESS
ROOFLESS
SHELUMIEL (FATHER OF —)
ZURISHADDAI
SHELVE DISH BURKE SHELF SHUNT
TABLE PIGEONHOLE
SHELVES STAGE ETAGERE
SHEM (BROTHER OF —) HAM JAPHET
(FATHER OF —) NOAH
SHEMA (FATHER OF —) ELPAAL
SHEMAIAH (FATHER OF —) JOEL
HARIM DELAIAH HASSHUB
ADONIKAM OBEDEDOM ELIZAPHAN
NETHANEEL SHECHANIAH
(SON OF —) ABDA DELAIAH
OBADIAH
SHEMARIAH (FATHER OF —) BANI
SHEMIDA (FATHER OF —) GILEAD
SHEMUEL (FATHER OF —) TOLA
SHENANIGAN ANTIC ESCAPADE
SHENAZAR (FATHER OF —)
JECONIAH
SHENG SANG CHENG SHING
(ONE-HUNDREDTH —) CHAO
SHEOL HELL HADES
SHEPHATHIAH (SON OF —)
MESHULLAM
SHEPHATIAH (FATHER OF —) DAVID
JEHOSHAPHAT
SHEPHERD HERD SHEP TEND COLIN
CORIN GADDI GYGES SWAIN
FEEDER PASTOR TARBOX
CORYDON DAPHNIS DRAFTER
GADARIA KURUMBA THYRSIS
TITYRUS MELIBEUS MENALCAS
PASTORAL SHEEPMAN STREPHON
(GERMAN —) ALSATIAN
SHEPHERDESS DELIA MOPSA
PHEBE DORCAS BERGERE
GALATEA PASTORA PERDITA
AMARYLLIS
SHEPHERD KING, THE
(CHARACTER IN —) ELISA AMINTA
TAMIRI AGENORE ALESSANDRO
(COMPOSER OF —) MOZART
SHEPHERD'S-PURSE TOYWORT
CASEWEED COCOWORT
SHEPHI (FATHER OF —) SHOBAL
SHERAH (FATHER OF —) EPHRAIM
SHERBET ICE GLACE SHRAB
SORBET GRANITA SOUFFLE
SHERD SCARTH
SHERESH (FATHER OF —) MACHIR
(MOTHER OF —) MAACHAH
SHERIFF FOUD FOWD SCULT XERIF
DEPUTY GRIEVE SCHOUT SHIRRA
BAILIFF SHREEVE SHRIEVE
ALGUACIL HUISSIER SHIREMAN
VISCOUNT
SHERRY FINO CLOVE JEREZ XERES
DOCTOR MANCHU SOLERA
OLOROSO RANGOON SHERRIS
MONTILLA MANZANILLA
SHERRY BROWN CLOVE
SHESHAI (FATHER OF —) ANAK
SHE STOOPS TO CONQUER
(AUTHOR OF —) GOLDSMITH
(CHARACTER IN —) KATE TONY
MARLOW CHARLES LUMPKIN
NEVILLE HASTINGS PEDIGREE
CONSTANCE HARDCASTLE
SHEVA (FATHER OF —) CALEB
(MOTHER OF —) MAACHAH

SHEVRI SESBAN
SHIATSU MASSAGE
SHICER DUFFER
SHIELD ECU EGIS HIDE PELT AEGIS
APRON BIELD BOARD CLOAK
COVER FENCE GUARD GULAR
MULGA PATCH PAVIS PELTA PYGAL
SCUTE SHEND TARGE YELDE
ANCILE ANGARA BLAZON CASQUE
DEFEND FENDER GUNTUB
GYROMA LINDEN MENTAL OCULAR
PAUNCH RONDEL SCREEN
SCUTUM SECURE TARGET
BUCKLER CLIPEUS CLYPEUS
CONCEAL LOZENGE PANNIER
PAVISSE PRIDWIN PROTECT
ROSTRAL ROTELLA ROUNDEL
SHELTER SUPPORT TESTUDO
CARTOUCH CUCULLUS HIELAMEN
INSULATE MARGINAL PRESERVE
RONDACHE STERNITE SUNSHADE
BREASTING
(— BELOW A DAM) APRON
(— FOR ARCHERS) PANNIER
(— FOR CAMERA) GOBO
(— FOR HORSE) BIB
(— FOR LAMP) BONNET CHIMNEY
(— FOR MICROPHONE) GOBO
(— OF ABORIGINES) MULGA
HIELAMEN
(— OF A STIRRUP) HOOD
(— OF CONTINENT) CORE
(— OF HIDE) SKILDFEL
(— OF SOMITE) STERNITE
(— OF TRILOBITE) CEPHALON
(— ON MAST) PAUNCH
(— ON THROAT OF FISH) GULAR
(— OVER BASE OF FAN) CANOPY
(— WITHOUT ARMS) ALBERIA
(BONY —) CARAPACE
(BULLETPROOF —) MANTA
MANTLET MANTELET
(HERALDIC —) BLAZON
(KING ARTHUR'S —) PRIWEN
PRIDWIN
(LEATHER —) CHAFE
(PART OF —) RIB BOSS ORLE UMBO
ANTIA
(SACRED —) ANCILE
(SIBERIAN —) ANGARA
(WICKERWORK —) SCIATH
(PREF.) ASPID(O) CLYPEI CLYPEO
PELTATI PELTATO SCUT(I) SCUTATI
SCUTELLI
(SUFF.) ASPIS
SHIELDBEARER SQUIRE ESQUIRE
PELTAST ESCUDERO SCUTIFER
SHIELD BUG STINKBUG
SHIELD FERN FERNGALE
SHIELDMAKER TYCHIOS
SHIELD-SHAPED PELTATE SCUTATE
THYROID
SHIFT JIB BACK CHOP CORE FEND
FLIT HAUL MOVE RUSE SHIP TACK
TOUR TURN VARY VEER WEND
BREAK BUDGE CREEP CYMAR
DRIFT HOTCH QUIRK SHIRK SHUNT
SIMAR SKIFT SLIDE SMOCK SPELL
TRICK BAFFLE CHANGE DENIAL
DEVICE DOUBLE PALTER SKYFTE
SWERVE SWITCH CHEMISE
CUTBACK EVASION FRESHEN
SHUFFLE SLEIGHT WHIFFLE

ARTIFICE DISLODGE DISPLACE
DOGWATCH DOUBLING MUTATION
PINGPONG RESOURCE REVIRADO
TRANSFER TRAVERSE TURNOVER
WINDLASS
(— ABOUT AS THE WIND) LARGE
(— ABRUPTLY) JUMP
(— IN DANCING) BALANCE
(— IN TACKING) JIB
(— ORDER OF BELLS) HUNT
(— RAILROAD EQUIPMENT) DRILL
(— SUDDENLY) FLY CHOP GYBE
JIBE
(— WEIGHT) WING
(KIND OF —) STICK
(MINING —) CORE
SHIFTINESS LUBRICITY
SHIFTING FLUID QUICK AMBULANT
CHOPPING DRIFTING FLOATING
SLIPPAGE VARIABLE VEERABLE
(— BACK AND FORTH) YOYO
SHIFTLESS DRIFTY SOZZLY
DRIFTING FECKLESS HAVELESS
SHIFTLESSNESS SLOUCH
SHIFTY GREASY DEVIOUS EVASIVE
HANGDOG SLIDING SLIPPERY
SHIITE SHIAH SECTARY SHAIKHI
TWELVER
SHILHA SHLU CHLEUH
SHILHI (DAUGHTER OF —) AZUBAH
SHILL STICK BONNET CAPPER
BOOSTER
SHILLEM (FATHER OF —) NAPHTALI
SHILLING BOB HOG ORA CHIP
HOGG LEVY PREST DEENER
HARPER TESTON TEVISS THIRTEEN
(20 —S) POUND
(21 —S) GUINEA
(5 —S) CROWN DECUS
SHILLY-SHALLY HEDGE BACK
BOGGLE
SHILSHAH (FATHER OF —) ZOPHAH
SHIM GLUT LINER SHIMMER
SHIMEA (FATHER OF —) DAVID
SHIMEATH (SON OF —) ZABAD
JOZACHAR
SHIMEI (BROTHER OF —) CONONIAH
ZERUBBABEL
(FATHER OF —) BANI GERA KISH
JAHATH GERSHON PEDAIAH
JEDUTHUN
SHIMMA (BROTHER OF —) DAVID
(FATHER OF —) JESSE
SHIMMER FLASH GLIMMER
SHIMPER SKIMMER
SHIMRI (FATHER OF —) SHEMAIAH
(SON OF —) JEDIAEL
SHIMRITH (SON OF —) JEHOZABAD
SHIMRON (FATHER OF —) ISSACHAR
SHIN SHANK SKINK SWARM CNEMIS
SHINNY
SHINBONE TIBIA
(SUFF.) CNEMA CNEMIA CNEMIC
CNEMUS
SHINDIG SHINDY SHIVOO
SHINDY ROW BOBBERY
SHINE RAY SUN BEAM BUFF GLOW
LAMP LEAM LINK STAR BLARE
BLICK BLINK BLOOM EXCEL GLAIK
GLARE GLEAM GLEIT GLENT GLINT
GLISS GLORE GLORY GLOSS
GLOZE SHEEN SKYRE STARE
BEACON DAZZLE GLANCE LUSTER

LUSTRE POLISH SCANCE EFFULGE
GLIMMER GLISTEN GLITTER
RADIATE REFLECT SHIMMER
SPARKLE RUTILATE
((— IN DARK) PHOSPHORESCE
(— BRIGHTLY) BEEK FLAME LIGHT
(— FAINTLY) SCARROW
(— UPON) SUN SMITE
SHINER CHUB DACE BREAM MOUSE
REDFIN CYPRINID WINDFISH
SHINER-UP PATCHER
SHINGLE SHIM BEACH SHAKE SHIDE
SLATE ASTYLL CHESIL KNOBBLE
STARTER
SHINGLER NOBBLER
SHINGLES ZONA ZOSTER
(PREF.) ZOSTERI ZOSTERO
SHININESS GLARE GLAZE GLOSS
SHINING GLAD NEAT CLEAR GLARY
LIGHT LUCID NITID SHEER WHITE
ARDENT ARGENT ASHINE BRIGHT
FULGID GLOSSY GOLDEN LUCENT
MARBLE NITENT ORIENT SERENE
SHEENY SPUNKY STARRY ADAZZLE
BURNING FULGENT GLARING
GLIMMER LAMPING FLASHING
GLEAMING LUCULENT LUSTRANT
LUSTROUS NITIDOUS RELUCENT
RUTILANT SPLENDID STARLIKE
SUNBEAMY SUNSHINY
(— THROUGH) TRANSLUCENT
(PREF.) STILPNO
SHINLEAF PYROLA
SHINNY PEG SHINTY
SHINTO (— SECT) RYOBU
SHINTY CAMANACHA
SHIP (ALSO SEE BOAT AND VESSEL)
ARK CAT COG HOY NAO BARK
BOAT BOOM GRAB HAND HULK
KEEL LADE NAVY PAHI PINE PINK
SAIL SEND SNOW TREE WOOD
ZULU CHECK LAKER OILER PINTA
PRORE RAZEE SCOUT SCREW
SKIFF WHELP ANDREW ARGOSY
BARKEY BARQUE BOTTOM CARTEL
CASTLE CHASER COALER CODMAN
DECKER DIESEL GALIOT GALLEY
HOLCAD HOPPER LANCHA LATEEN
LORCHA MASTER MISTIC MOTHER
PACKET PUFFER RUNNER SAILER
SALVOR SEALER SMOKER TONNER
TRAVEL VESSEL ADMIRAL
CARRACK CLIPPER COLLIER
CONSORT DROMOND FACTORY
FELUCCA FOREIGN FRIGATE
FRUITER GABBARD GALLEON
GUNBOAT INVOICE MACHINE
MULETTA ONERARY PATAMAR
PINNACE POLACRE SHALLOP
SHIPLET SPITKIT STEAMER
BALANDRA BALINGER BILANDER
CAPITANA CUNARDER DRUMBLER
FLAGSHIP GALLEASS GAYDIANG
INDIAMAN JAPANNER LANCHARA
MAGAZINE PESSONER PIPPINER
REPEATER SAILSHIP SCHOONER
SMUGGLER SPANIARD LEVIATHAN
BRIGANTINE MERCHANTMAN
(— BUILT FROM NAILS OF DEAD)
NAGLFAR
(— FITTED AS CHURCH) BETHEL
(— IN LIQUOR TRADE) COPER
(— OF ARGONAUTS) ARGO

(— OF NORSEMEN) KEEL
(CLUMSY —) TUB HULK
(DEPOT —) TENDER
(ESCORT —) CORVETTE
(FLEET OF —S) ARMADA
(JAPANESE —) MARU
(MALAY —) COUGNAR
(NOVA SCOTIAN —) BLUENOSE
(OBJECT SHAPED LIKE A —) NEF
(PART OF —) BOW CAP GUY RUN
BEAM BOOM GAFF JACK LIFT MAST
RAIL STAY VANG YARD BRACE
CHAIN ROYAL SHEET TRUCK
JUMPER RUDDER SHROUD STRAKE
BOBSTAY BULWARK BUMPKIN
COUNTER FORETOP JIBSTAY
MAINTOP NETTING PENDANT
RATLINE RIGGING SKYSAIL SPANKER
STIRRUP STRIKER SWIFTER
TOPMAST BACKROPE BACKSTAY
CUTWATER FOOTROPE FOREMAST
LIFELINE MAINMAST MAINSTAY
STUDDING CROSSTREE FORESHEET
MAINSHEET NAMEBOARD
WATERLINE MARTINGALE
MIZZENMAST TOPGALLANT
(PIRATE —) GALLIVAT
(PRIZE —) CAPTURE
(QUARANTINE —) LAZARET
(RECEIVING —) GUARDO
(REMOTE-CONTROLLED —) DRONE
(SLOW —) BUCKET
(STORE —) FLUTER
(SUPPLY —) COPER COOPER
(UNTRIM —) BALLAHOO
(VIKING —) DRAKE
(PL.) NAVY MARINE SEACRAFT
SHIPPING
(PREF.) NAU(TI) NAV(I)
SHIPFITTER FITTER ERECTOR
SHIPHI (SON OF —) ZIZA
SHIPHTAN (SON OF —) KEMUEL
SHIPMASTER PADRONE
SHIPMENT CARLOT RAILING
DISPATCH SHIPPAGE
SHIPPING (— UNIT CARLOAD
SHIPSHAPE NEAT TAUT TIDY TRIM
CIVIL TIGHT ATAUNT ORDERLY
SHIP-SHAPED (— UTENSIL) NEF
SHIP SWEEPER TOPASS TOPIWALA
SHIPWAY BERTH
SHIPWORM ARTER BORER COBRA
TEREDO PILEWORM WOODWORM
SHIPWRECK WRACK NAUFRAGE
SHIPWRIGHT WAYMAN BUILDER
SHIRE DERBY SHEER COUNTY
SHIRK BALK FUNK GOOF MIKE
BAULK BLINK BUDGE DODGE
EVADE FEIGN FUDGE SKULK SLACK
RODNEY FINAGLE SHACKLE
SHAFFLE SOLDIER SHAMMOCK
SHIRKER FUNK PIKER SOGER
FUNKER ROTTER BLUDGER
SLACKER SLINKER SUGARER
COBERGER CUTHBERT EMBUSQUE
SCOWBANK
SHIRLEY (AUTHOR OF —) BRONTE
(CHARACTER IN —) JOE DONNE
EMILY LOUIS MOORE PRYOR SCOTT
MALONE ROBERT KEELDAR SHIRLEY
CAROLINE HELSTONE HORTENSE
SWEETING MATTHEWSON
SHIRR SMOCK

SHIRT TOB TOP JUPE SARK TANK
TOBE BLUEY HAIRE JUPON KAMIS
SHIFT BANIAN BANIYA CAMISA
CAMISE PALAKA PARTLET
UNDERGO VAREUSE KAMLEIKA
(— FRONT) DICKY DICKEY
(COLLARLESS —) KURTA KHURTA
(FUR —) PARKA
(HAIR —) HAIRE CILICE
(ROMAN —) SUBUCULA
(SLEEVELESS —) FECKET
(SPORT —) IZOD GUAYABERA
(WORKMAN'S —) FROCK
(WORNOUT —) DICKY
SHIRTING CHEVIOT HARVARD
HOLLAND SARKING
SHIRTWAIST BLOUSE GARIBALDI
SHISHA (SON OF —) AHIAH
ELIHOREPH
SHISH KEBAB SOUVLAKI
SOUVLAKIA
SHITTIMWOOD BOXWOOD
SHIVA (SON OF —) GANESHA
KARTTIKEYA
(WIFE OF —) KALI DURGA
SHIVAREE BELLING CHIVARI
HORNING SERENADE
SHIVER JAR GIRL GRUE BEVER
BREAK CHILL CREEM CREEP FRILL
GROWS QUAKE SHRUG SLICE
CHIVER DITHER DUDDER GROOSE
HOTTER NIDDER NITHER QUIVER
SHRIMP SPLINT TREMOR CHITTER
FLICKER FRISSON SHATTER
SHITHER SHUDDER TREMBLE
KAMLEIKA SPLINTER
(THE —S) AGUE
(PL.) SMITHERS SMITHEREENS
SHIVERING AGUED CHILL OURIE
TREMOR ASHIVER
SHIZA (SON OF —) ADINA
SHNOOK TWERP
SHOAL BAJO BANK FLAT REEF SPIT
BARRA DRAVE FLOTE SCULL SHELF
SCHOOL SHALLOW TOWHEAD
SHOAT GURRY SHOOT SHOTT
SHOBAB (FATHER OF —) CALEB
DAVID
(MOTHER OF —) AZUBAH
BATHSHEBA
SHOBAL (FATHER OF —) SEIR CALEB
SHOBI (FATHER OF —) NAHASH
SHOCK COP JAR BLOW BUMP DINT
JOLT RACK SHOG STUN TURN
APPAL BRUNT GAVEL GLIFF GLOFF
SHAKE STOOK STOUR DISMAY
FRIGHT IMPACT JOSTLE JUMBLE
REJOLT RICKLE ROLLER STRIKE
TRAUMA ASTOUND CANVASS
DISGUST HATTOCK HORRIFY
STAGGER STARTLE STUPEFY
TERRIFY DISEDIFY GLIFFING
SURPRISE
(— OF CORN) STOOK STOUT STITCH
(MENTAL —) TRAUMA
(TYPE OF —) HAIR MANE
SHOCK ABSORBER SHOCK BUFFER
DAMPER DASHPOT SNUBBER
SHOCKED AGHAST
SHOCKER RICKER STOOKER
SHOCKING GRIM AWFUL LURID
HORRID UNHOLY BURNING
FEARFUL FEARING GHASTLY

HIDEOUS DREADFUL ENORMOUS
HORRIBLE DESPERATE
SCANDALOUS
SHOD CALCED
SHODDY SOFT CHEAP FOOTY
MUNGO RATTY SOFTS TACKY
SLEAZY TICKYTACKY
SHOE BAL CUE PAN BOOT BROG
CLOG DRAG FLAT HALF SKID SOCK
TURN BLAKE DERBY KLOMP
MOYLE ROMEO SABOT SCRAE
SLING SPIKE STOGA STOGY STRAP
ANKLET BEAKER BROGAN BROGUE
BUSKIN CALIGA CALIGO CHOPIN
COBCAB COCKER CRAKOW
CREOLE DORSAY GAITER GALOSH
GILLIE KILTIE LOAFER MULLER
PATTEN PINSON POLISH SADDLE
SANDAL SECQUE BAUCHLE
BLUCHER BOTTINE CALCEUS
CHOPINE COWHIDE FLIPPER
GHILLIE OXONIAN RULLION
SHOEPAC SLIPPER SNEAKER
WINGTIP BALMORAL BRODEKIN
CALCEATE COLONIAL PLATFORM
PLIMSOLL SABOTINE SANDSHOE
SKEWBACK SLIPSLOP SOLLERET
(— FOR GRINDING) MULLER
(— FOR MULE) PLANCHE
(— IN TRUSS OR FRAME)
SKEWBACK
(— NOT FASTENED ON) PUMP
(— OF AN OX) CUE
(— OF A SLEDGE) HOB
(— OF COMIC ACTOR) BAXA
(— OF SUBWAY CAR) PAN
(— REPAIRER) JACKMAN
(—S AND STOCKINGS) FEET
(— STYLE) OPENTOE
(— TO CHECK WHEEL) DRAG SKID
(— USED AS BRAKE) SKATE
(— WITH A LONG TONGUE) KILTY
KILTIE
(— WITH POINTED TOE)
WINKLEPICKER
(— WORN ON EITHER FOOT)
STRAIGHT
(ARMORED —) SABBATON
(BABY'S —) CACK
(DOWN-AT-HEEL —) SHAUCHLE
(HOBNAILED —) TACKET
(LARGE —S) GUNBOATS
(LOW-CUT —) SOCK GILLY ANKLET
BUSKIN SLIPPER COLONIAL
(MILITARY —) CALIGA
(OLD —) BAUCHLE
(PART OF —) TIP TOE ARCH FLAP
HEEL LIFT SOLE VAMP WELT AGLET
SHANK COLLAR EYELET FOXING
INSTEP LINING THROAT TONGUE
COUNTER OUTSOLE QUARTER
MUDGUARD PLATFORM SHOELACE
BREASTING
(PIKED —) BEAKER
(RAWHIDE —) HIMMING VELSKOEN
(SPORT —S) NIKES
(SPORTS —S) GILLIES
(STEEL —) SOLLERET
(TENNIS —S) TENNIES SNEAKERS
(THIN —) PINSON SCLAFF
(WINGED —S) TALARIA
(WOODEN —) KLOMP SABOT
PATTEN RACKET RACQUET

(WORN —) SCRAE
(PL.) SHEEN SHOON SHUNE
SCHONE CASUALS FOOTGEAR
(PREF.) CALCEI
SHOEMAKER SNOB FOXER SOLER
ARCHER CHAMAR CODGER COZIER
FUDGER GOUGER SOOTER
SOUTER VAMPER COBBLER
CRISPIN CROWNER SHOEMAN
SNOBBER UPPERER CORVISER
SNOBSCAT CORDWAINER
SHOEMAKING SNOBBING
SHOESTRING LACE LACET
SHOGI (EXPERT LEVEL IN —) DAN
SHOGUN TYCOON
SHOHAM (FATHER OF —) JAAZIAH
SHOMER (SON OF —) JEHOZABAD
SHOO HOOSH DISPEL
SHOOK PACK BLANK SHAKE
SHOOT DAG GUN IMP PAY POT PUT
ROD TIP BANG BOLT BROD CANE
CHIT CION DRAW LEAF PLUG SLIP
WEFT ARROW BLAST BLAZE
BROWN DRILL DRIVE EXPEL FLUSH
FROND GEMMA GLEAM LANCE
LAYER PLUFF SCION SHEET SOBOL
SPEAR SPIRE SPRAY SPRIG SPRIT
SPURT SQUIB STICK STOOL TUBER
TURIO VIMEN BRANCH FLIGHT
FLOWER GERMEN GROWTH
HEADER HURTLE LAUNCH LEADER
OFFSET RATOON SALLOW SOBOLE
SPRING SPROUT STOLON STOUND
STOVEN STRIKE SUCKER TILLER
TURION BUDLING CHIMNEY
DROPPER SCOURGE SPIRING
TENDRIL TENDRON THALLUS
ANAPHYTE APOBLAST CATAPULT
TRAILING
(— A MARBLE) LAG TAW KNUCKLE
(— ASIDE FROM MARK) DRIB
(— AT LONG RANGE) SNIPE
(— A WHALE) STRIKE
(— DOWN) SPLASH
(— DUCKS) SKAG
(— FORTH) JET GLEAM SPIRE
DARTLE
(— FROM DEER'S ANTLER) SPELLER
(— INDISCRIMINATELY) BROWN
(— MOOSE OR DEER) YARD
(— OF A TREE) STOW WHIP LANCE
BRANCH
(— OUT) JUT CHIT DART ERADIATE
(— SEAL) SWATCH
(—S USED AS FODDER) BROWSE
(— UP) SPIRE SPURT
(FIRST —S) BRAIRD
(FLEXIBLE —) BINE
(LATERAL —) ARM
(ORE —) BONANZA
(PAWNBROKER'S —) SPOUT
(SUGARCANE —) LALO
(TENDER —) FLUSH
(WILLOW —) SALLOW
(PREF.) BLAST(O) SOBOLI STOLONI
THALL(I)(O)
(SUFF.) BLAST(IC)(Y) SPERM(A)(AE)
(AL)(IA)(IC)(OUS)(UM)(Y)
SHOOTER SCOOT BLASTER
GUNSTER PLUFFER SHOTMAN
SKEETER
SHOOTING COCKING GUNNING
GUNPLAY HUNTING POTTING

SHOOTING STAR METEOR
COWSLIP SHOOTER PRIMWORT
SHOP CRIB TOKO BOOTH BURSE
STORE TRADE KOSHER PARLOR
SHOPPE TIENDA WINKEL ALMACEN
APOTHEC BOTTEGA CABARET
MERCERY SHEBANG SPICERY
TABERNA TURNERY BOUTIQUE
COOKSHOP CREMERIE EMPORIUM
ESPRESSO EXCHANGE MAGAZINE
SHOWSHOP SLOPSHOP TENDEJON
WAREROOM PERFUMERY
HABERDASHERY
(BARBER —) BARBERY
(BLACKSMITH —) SMITHY
(BUTCHER —) CHARCUTERIE
(DRINKING —) BOUSINGKEN
(DRUGGIST'S —) PHARMACY
(HERB —) BOTANICA
(KIND OF —) HEAD
(LIQUOR —) SALOON
(OLD CLOTHES —) FLIPPERY
(PASTRY —) PATISSERIE
(PAWNBROKER'S —) LUMBER
SPROUT
(REPAIR —) GARAGE
(SUTLER'S —) CANTEEN
(WINE —) BODEGA CANTINA
SHOPKEEPER CIT ARAB BAKAL
BANIAN CHETTY SOUDAGUR
SHOPLIFT BOOST
SHOPLIFTER BOOSTER
SHORE GIB TOM BANK RIPE RIVE
SAND SIDE TRIG BEACH BENCH
CLIFF COAST MARGE RAKER
RANCE SHOAR WARTH RIVAGE
STRAND SEASIDE BUTTRESS
DOCKSIDE LANDFALL LANDSIDE
SEACOAST
SHOREBIRD AVOCET TATTLER
WRYBILL SURFBIRD PHALAROPE
SANDPIPER
SHORE CRAB OCHIDORE
SHOREFISH OPALEYE
SHORER BRACER CRIBBER
SHORN NOT NOTT POLLED
TONSURED
SHORT AIM LAG LOW SHY BAIN
CURT NEAR NIGH SOON BLUFF
BRIEF BUNTY CLOSE CRISP CUTTY
FUBBY FUBSY PUNCH SQUAB
UNDER ABRUPT CRISPY SCANTY
SCARCE STUGGY STUNTY SUDDEN
ULLAGE BRUTAL BRUSQUE
CURTATE LACONIC SQUIDGY
STUBBED SUMMARY SNAPPISH
SUCCINCT
(— AND FLAT) CAMUS
(— AND THICK) CHUNKY STOCKY
STUBBY STUMPY TRUNCH
TRUNCHED
(— AND THICKSET) NUGGETY
(— AS OF WOOL) FRIBBY
(— IN PAYMENT) SHY
(— OF MONEY) HARDUP PUSHED
IMPECUNIOUS
(— PERSON OR ANIMAL) PUNCH
(BRIEF —S) MONOKINI
(STOUT AND —) BUNTY CHUFFY
PLUGGY THICKSET
(PL.) BERMUDAS
(PREF.) BRACHI(O) BRACHY BREVI
(SUFF.) BRACH(ISTO)(Y)

SHORTAGE WANT CRUNCH FAMINE
DROUGHT WANTAGE UNDERAGE
SHORT-BREATHED PURSY
SHORTCHANGE FLUFF SHORT
SHORTCOMING SIN FLAW DEBIT
FAULT DEFECT FOIBLE DRAWBACK
SHORT-COUPLED CHUFFY
SHORTCUT CUTOFF
SHORT-EARED OWL MOMO
SHORTEN CUT CLIP STAG ELIDE
SLASH REDUCE ABRIDGE CURTAIL
EXCERPT SCANTLE CONTRACT
DIMINISH RETRENCH ABBREVIATE
(— AND THICKEN IRON) JUMP
(— A SAIL) REEF
(— GRIP) CHOKE
SHORTENED CURTED BOBTAIL
CURTATE ABRIDGED
SHORTENING LARD
(— IN PRONOUNCIATION)
CORRECTION
(— OF SYLLABLE) SYSTOLE
(— OF WORD) APOCOPE
SHORTEST LEAST
SHORTFALL NEED
SHORTHORN DURHAM TEESWATER
SHORT-LIVED FRAGILE
SHORTLY SOON INABIT DUMPILY
DIRECTLY PRESENTLY
SHORT-NAPPED RAS
SHORTNESS BREVITY CURTNESS
UNLENGTH
(— OF BREATH) ANHELATION
(— OF SIGHT) MYOPIA
(— OF SOUND) QUANTITY
SHORT-RANGE TACTICAL
SHORT-SIGHTED SANDED
PURBLIND
SHORTSIGHTEDNESS MYOPIA
SHORT-TEMPERED CROTCHETY
CROTCHETED CRUSTY SNIPPY
SNUFFY
SHORT-TERM FLOATING
SHORT-WINDED PURSY PURFLY
PURFLED PURSIVE
SHOSHONEAN UTE
SHOT POP SET BLUE CASE JOLT
OVER PLUG SETT SLUG BLANK
FLIER FLING FLUFF FLYER OUTER
PLUFF SHOOT TOWEL WHITE
CARTON CENTER CENTRE FOLLOW
MUDCAP REBOTE ALIIPOE
BOMBARD CUTAWAY DEADEYE
GUNSHOT LANGREL PELICAN
SIGHTER BLIZZARD BUCKSHOT
HAILSHOT LANGRAGE MARKSHOT
SCORCHER
(— BEYOND TARGET) OVER
(— FOR CULVERIN) PELICAN
(— IN FIFTH CIRCLE) WHITE
(— IN FOURTH CIRCLE) BLACK
(— IN THIRD CIRCLE) BLUE
(— OF NARCOTIC) FIX
(— STRIKING BULL'S-EYE) CARTON
(— THAT HITS) CLOUT
(ARCHERY —) GREEN
(BADMINTON —) CLEAR
(BASKETBALL —) BOMB JUMPER
(BIG —) VIP
(BILLIARD —) DRAG STAB CAROM
MASSE SCREW FOLLOW SAFETY
SPREAD BRICOLE SCRATCH
(BOW —) DRAFT

(CAMERA —) PAN INTERCUT
(CROQUET —) SPLIT FOLLOW
(CURLING —) INWICK OUTWICK
(DROP —) DINK
(DUNK —) STUFF
(EASY —) SITTER
(FAULTY —) MISTAKE
(FINAL —) UPSHOT
(FREE —) CORNER MULLIGAN
(GOOD —) SCREAMER
(HIGH —) CHIP
(KIND OF —) MUG
(KIND OF BILLIARD —) BANK
CAROM
(PISTOL —) BARK
(POOL —) BREAK
(SHORT —) HYPO
(SIZE OF —) F T BB FF TT BBB DUST
BUCKSHOT
(SMALL —) PELLET MITRAILLE
(SNOOKER —) POT
(TENNIS —) ACE LOB DINK SERVE
SMASH
(VOLLEY OF —S) BLIZZARD
SHOTGUN DOUBLE TUPARA
PEPPERER SCATTERSHOT
SHOULD MOW SUD WANT OUGHT
(— NOT) SHUDNA SHOULDNA
SHOULDNT
SHOULDER DOD AXLE CLOD DODD
GAIN HUMP SHIP STEP SULD
BOUGH PITCH SPALL SPULE VERGE
AXILLA EPAULE RELISH SCOTCH
SPAULD KNUCKLE RIMBASE
SHOUTHER
(— AROUND TENON) RELISH
(— OF BOLT) NAB
(— OF FIREARM STOCK) RIMBASE
(— OF FLY) CHEEK
(— OF LAMB) BANJO
(— OF PORK) HAND PICNIC
CUSHION
(— OF RABBIT OR HARE) WING
(— OF ROAD) BERM BERME
HAUNCH QUARTER
(— PAIN) OMODYNIA
(BEVELED —) GAIN
(PL.) FOREBOWS
(PREF.) OM(O)
SHOULDER BLADE SPALD SPEAL
SCAPULA OMOPLATE
(PREF.) SCAPUL(I)(O)
SHOUT BAY BOO CRY HOY HUE
BAWL CALL CROW GAPE HAIL
HOCH HOOP HOOT REME ROOT
ROUP ROUT SCRY TOOT YELL
BRAWL CHEER CLAIM CLEPE
CRACK GREDE HALLO HAVOC
HOLLO HUZZA REERE WHEWT
WHOOP ABRAID BOOHOO
CLAMOR GOLLAR GOLLER
HALLOO HOLLER HURRAH HUZZAH
STEVEN YAMMER ACCLAIM
SHILLOO GARDYLOO LULLILOO
SCRONACH
(— AS CHILDREN) BELDER
(— DERISIVELY) BARRACK
(— FOR OR AGAINST) BARRACK
(— OF APPROVAL) BRAVO
(— OF ENCOURAGEMENT) HARK
(— OF HIGHLAND DANCER) HOOCH
(— OF JOY) IO
(HIGHLAND DANCER'S —) HOOCH

(HUNTING —) CHEVY
(SEAMAN'S —) AHOY
SHOUTING HUE GLAM ROUP ROUT HOLLO CLAMOR HOLLOA JUBILEE
SHOVE JUT PUT BUNT DUSH FEND MUCK PICK POTE PUSH SHOG SHUN BOOST CROWD DUNCH ELBOW HUNCH SHIVE SHUNT HUSTLE JOSTLE JUSTLE MUSCLE THRUST SCAMBLE
(— CARELESSLY) BUNG
(— IN MARBLES) FULK
SHOVEL FAN VAN CAST PEEL SPUD SCOOP SHOOL SPADE SPOON BLUNGER SCOPPET SCUPPIT SLUDGER DUCKBILL DUCKFOOT STROCKLE
(— FOR COIN) MAIN
(— FOR DRESSING ORE) VAN
(BAKER'S —) PEEL
(BANKER'S —) MAIN
(BRICKMAKING —) CUCKHOLD
(CASTING —) SCUTTLE
(CHARCOAL BURNER'S —) RABBLE
(FIRE —) PEEL SLICE
(GRATED —) HARP
(MINER'S —) BANJO
(PERFORATED —) SKIMMER
SHOVELER SCOOPER WHINGER BLUEWING SHOUELERD WHINYARD
SHOW DO SAY SEE WIS BOSH CALL DASH HAVE ITEM LEAD MARK MIEN SCAW SEEM SHEW TENT VIEW WEAR WISE ARGUE ASSAY EXERT FLASH GLOSS GLOZE KITHE PRIDE PROVE SHINE SIGHT SLANG SPORT TEACH ACCUSE ASSIGN BETRAY BLAZON CHICHI COUTHE DENOTE DETECT DEVICE DIRECT ENSIGN ESCORT EVINCE EXPOSE FIGURE FLAUNT GAIETY GAYETY LAYOUT MUSTER OBJECT PARADE REVEAL SCHEME SPREAD SPRUNK VANITY ADVANCE ANALYZE BALLOON BESPEAK BETOKEN BRAVURA BREATHE DECLARE DISPLAY DIVULGE EXHIBIT EXPRESS FASHION MONSTER PRESAGE PRODUCE PROPOSE SELLOUT SHOWING SIGNIFY TAMASHA TRIUMPH COLORING CONCLUDE EVIDENCE FLOURISH FORESHOW INDICATE MANIFEST PRETENCE PROCLAIM SEMBLANT SIDESHOW
(— APPROVAL) CLAP APPLAUD
(— BRIEFLY) FLASH
(— CONTEMPT) SCOFF
(— DISCONTENT) GROUCH
(— DISPLEASURE) POUT
(— DOGS) BENCH
(— ENTHUSIASM) DROOL
(— FORTH) BLAZE CIPHER
(— IN PUBLIC CELEBRATION) PAGEANT
(— ITSELF) APPEAR
(— MERCY) SPARE
(— OFF) FLASH PRANK SPORT SWANK HOTDOG PARADE SWAGGER SHOWBOAT
(— OF INDIA) TAMASHA
(— OF LEARNING) SCIOLISM
(— OF LIGHT) BLINK

(— OF REASON) COLOR
(— OF VANITY) AIR
(— ONESELF) BE
(— POSITION OF) MEITH
(— PROMISE) FRAME SHAPE
(— RESPECT FOR) REGARD
(— REVERSE TREND) REACT
(— SIGNS OF GIVING WAY) WAVER
(— SIGNS OF ILLNESS) GRUDGE
(— SPIRIT) SPUNK
(— THE BOTTOM) KEEL
(— THE SIGHTS) LIONIZE
(— THE TEETH) GIRN GRIN
(— THE WAY) LEAD CONDUCT
(— TO BE FALSE) BELIE DISPROVE
(— UNKINDNESS) WAIT
(— WITHOUT SUBSTANCE) FORM
(ARTFUL —) GRIMACE
(CALL-IN RADIO —) PHONEIN
(CINEMA —) FILM MOVIES PICTURES
(DAZZLING —) RAZZLEDAZZLE
(DUMB —) PANTOMINE
(EXTERNAL —) GLOSS
(FALSE —) COLOR FUCUS BUBBLE TINSEL ILLUSION PRETENCE
(FLEETING —) PAGEANTRY
(FLOOR —) CABARET
(GAUDY —) HOOPLA BRAVERY
(KIND OF —) TRUNK
(MERE —) PHANTOM
(MOMENTARY —) FLASH
(ORNATE —) FLUBDUB
(OSTENTATIOUS —) SPRUNK DISPLAY
(OUTSIDE —) VARNISH
(OUTWARD —) FUCUS VISAGE
(PUBLIC —) EXPO
(PUPPET —) DROLL MOTION WAJANG WAYANG GUIGNOL
(RIDICULOUS —) FARCE
(RUDIMENTARY —) SATURA
(RUN THE —) EMCEE
(SPECIOUS —) GLOZE VARNISH
(STREET —) RAREE
(SUPERFICIAL —) GLOSS VENEER
(TELEVISION —) PILOT
(TRAVELLING —) SLANG
(PREF.) PHAENO PHANER(O) PHANTA PHANTO PHENO
(SUFF.) PHANY
SHOW BOAT (AUTHOR OF —) FERBER
(CHARACTER IN —) KIM ANDY ELLY HAWKS JULIE PARTHY GAYLORD RAVENAL MAGNOLIA SCHULTZY
SHOWCASE ISLAND VITRINE
SHOWER WET HAIL RAIN SCAT SUMP AUGER BATHE BLASH SKITE SOUSE FLURRY PELTER PEPPER SHEWER DRIBBLE SHATTER WEATHER COMMORTH SCOUTHER
(CONCENTRATED —) BARRAGE
(HEAVY —) SUMP
(RAIN —) RASH
(SUDDEN —) SCUD SKIT BRASH PLUMP
SHOWERY BRASHY CLASHY SCATTY
SHOWILY GAILY BRAVELY GAUDILY
SHOWINESS DASH GLARE GLITZ PAZAZZ PIZAZZ GLITTER PIZZAZZ FLOURISH GEWGAWRY SPLENDOR
SHOWING SPRANK SPARKLE

(— OFF) EXHIBITION
(— SAME NATURE) AKIN
(— THROUGH THE SKIN) RAW
(ADVANCE —) PREVIEW
(PUBLIC —) EXPO
(SUPERFICIAL —) FACE
(PREF.) PHAEN(O) PHAINO
SHOWMAN IMPRESARIO
SHOWMANSHIP RECLAME
SHOW-ME STATE MISSOURI
SHOW-OFF HAM HOTDOG CUTUP
SHOWY GAY FINE LOUD NICE RORY VAIN DASHY FLARY FLASH FRESH GAUDY GIDDY GRAND JAZZY NOBBY SPICY SWANK TOPPY VAUDY VIEWY BRANKY BRAZEN BRUMMY CHICHI DRESSY FLASHY FLOSSY GARISH GEWGAW GLOSSY JAUNTY PURPLE SHANTY SKYRIN SPANKY SPORTY TAWDRY DASHING FLAUNTY GALLANT GAUDFUL HOTSHOT POMPOUS SHOWFUL SHOWISH SPLASHY SPLURGY CLAPTRAP FASTUOUS GIMCRACK GORGEOUS ORGULOUS SPARKISH SPECIOUS SPLENDID TRUMPERY CLINQUANT OBTRUSIVE
(NOT —) CIVIL LENTEN DISCREET
SHOYU SOY
SHRED DAG HOG JAG RAG ROND ROON SNIP TEAR WISP BLYPE CLOUT GRATE PATCH SHRAG SHRIP CULPON SCREED SLIVER TARGET FRAZZLE FRITTER MAMMOCK SHATTER FILAMENT
(— FISH) SCROD
(— OF CLOTHES) TACK
(— OF FLESH) TAG AGNAIL
(— OF HAIR) TAIL
(PL.) TAVERS CADDICE TAIVERS
SHREDDED CUT
SHREDDER DEVIL
SHREW ERD JES NAG TANA PRESS RANNY SOREX VIXEN CALLET JUMPER MIGALE TARGER TARTAR TUPAIA VIRAGO BLARINA HELLCAT MUSKRAT PENTAIL SCYTALE TUPAIID SINSRING SORICINE SORICOID UROPSILE XANTHIPPE
(TREE —) BANXRING
(PREF.) HYDRAC(O) SORICI
SHREWD DRY SLY ACID ARCH CUTE FELL GASH SAGE TIDY WARE WISE ACUTE CAGEY CANNY HEADY LOOPY PAWKY POKEY SHARP SMART SWACK ARGUTE ARTFUL ASTUTE CALLID CLEVER CRAFTY SPRACK SUBTLE CUNNING GNOSTIC KNOWING PARLISH PARLOUS POLITIC PRACTIC SAPIENT SAGACIOUS PERSPICACIOUS
(— PERSON) FILE
SHREWDLY SLILY CANNILY ASTUTELY
SHREWDNESS NOUS SAVVY ACUMEN POLICY SLYNESS GUMPTION PRUDENCE SAGACITY CALLIDITY
SHREWISH CURST CURSED SHREWD VIXENISH
SHREWMOUSE MYGALE SCYTALE

SHRIEK CRY YIP YARM YELL CHIRK SKIRL SCREAM SCRIKE SHRIKE SKRIKE SPRAICH
SHRIKE POPE BATARA BOUBOU BRUBRU FISCAL FLASHER FLUSHER LOGHEAD MIGRANT MINIVET TRILLER BELLBIRD FALCONET PUFFBACK WOODCHAT
SHRILL HIGH KEEN THIN ACUTE PIPEY SHARP SHILL SHIRL ARGUTE BRASSY GLASSY PIPING SQUEAK TREBLE HAUTAIN MINIKIN SCREAKY PIERCING STRIDENT
(MAKE — NOISE) POTRACK
(PREF.) OXY
SHRIMP GRIT RUNT APANG CARID MYSID PARVA PRAWN NIPPER PANDLE SCAMPI ARTEMIA BROWNIE CAMARON DECAPOD POLYPOD REDTAIL SPECTER SPECTRE CARIDEAN CRAWFISH CREVETTE MACRURAN
(KIND OF —) TIGER
(SUFF.) CARIS
SHRINE ADYT NAOS GUACA HUACA ISEUM MAZAR SEKOS STUPA ZIARA ADYTON ADYTUM CHASSE DAGABA DAGOBA DURGAH HALLOW HIERON MEMORY SAMADH VIMANA ZIARAT CHAITYA CHAPLET CHORTEN EDICULE FANACLE MARTYRY MEMORIA SACRARY TEMENOS THESEUM AEDICULA DELUBRUM FERETORY FERETRUM GURDWARA LARARIUM MARABOUT PANTHEON VALHALLA RELIQUARY
(— FOR MEDITATION) ZENDO
(— STUDY) NAOLOGY
(PREF.) PASTO
SHRINK COY SHY DARE DUCK FULL FUNK GIVE NIRL PEAK ABHOR ARGHE CLING COWER CRINE QUAIL RELAX RIVEL SHRAM SHRUG SHUCK START WINCE BLANCH BLENCH BOGGLE COTTER CRINGE FLINCH LESSEN RECOIL SCRUMP SETTLE SHRIMP WEAZEN ANALYST CRIMPLE CRUMPLE DWINDLE SCUNNER SHRIVEL COLLAPSE CONTRACT
(— FROM DRYNESS) GIZZEN
SHRINKAGE LOSS SETTLE SHRINK SINKAGE
(— OF TYPE) SQUEEZE
SHRINKING COY SHY TIMID BLETHE CREEPS DASTARD FULLING LOATHFUL TIMOROUS
(— FROM REFERENCE TO SELF) AUTOPHOBY
SHRIVE SHRIFT CONFESS SHRIEVE
SHRIVEL NIRL SEAR WELK BLAST CLING CRINE PARCH RIVEL SHRAM SNERP WIZEN BLIGHT COTTER GIZZEN SCORCH SCRUMP SHRINK WEAZEN WITHER CROZZLE
SHRIVELED WEDE CLUNG CORKY THIRL GIZZEN STARKY PUNGLED SHIRPIT WIZENED WRITHEN SHRAMMED WRIZZLED
SHROPSHIRE SALOP
SHROUD HIDE PALL SARK CLOAK CRAPE DRAPE HABIT SHEET SWIFT

EMBOSK HEARSE KITTEL MUFFLE SCREEN SHADOW SINDON SUDARY BENIGHT CONCEAL CURTAIN INVOLVE SWIFTER CEREMENT
(PL.) PUTTOCK

SHROVETIDE SHROVE GUTTIDE CARNIVAL

SHROVE TUESDAY FASTENS GUTTIDE

SHRUB TI BAY HAW KAT MAY QAT TOD AKIA ALEM BUSH COCA HOYA INGA ITEA KARO KEUR KHAT MUSK ULEX AKALA AKELA ALDER ALISO ARUSA BOCCA BROOM BUAZE CEIBO CUMAY ELDER GOOMA GORSE GOUMI HAZEL HENNA IXORA LEDUM LEMON LILAC MAQUI MARIA MUDAR RETEM SALAL SHROG SUMAC THUJA TOYON ZILLA ABELIA AGRITO AKONGE AMULLA ANAGUA ANILAO ARALIA ARUSHA AUCUBA AUPAKA AZALEA BLOLLY CENIZO CHEKAN CHERRY CISTUS CORREA DAPHNE DHAURI DRIMYS FEIJOA FRUTEX JACATE JOJOBA KARAMU KOWHAI LABRUM LARREA LAUREL MATICO MYRTLE NARRAS PENAEA PITURI RAETAM SAVINE STORAX STYRAX ACEROLA AFERNAN AGARITA AMORPHA ARBORET ARRAYAN ARRIMBY AZAROLE BANKSIA BORONIA BUCKEYE BULLACE CANTUTA CHACATE CHAMISE CHANCHE DEUTZIA EHRETIA ENCELIA EPACRID EPHEDRA FUCHSIA GUMWOOD GUTWORT HOPBUSH HOPSAGE JASMINE JETBEAD JEWBUSH JOEWOOD KUMQUAT LANTANA MAHONIA NUNNARI PAVONIA PEABUSH PEARHAW PIMELEA RHODORA SPIRAEA TARBUSH THEEZAN ABELMOSK ALLTHORN BARBERRY CAMELLIA CARAGANA COMEBACK COPALCHE DRACAENA GOATBUSH GOWIDDIE GRAVILEA HARDHACK HARDTACK HAWTHORN HIBISCUS IRONWOOD KEURBOOM KOROMIKO MOORWORT NINEBARK OCOTILLO OLEASTER OSOBERRY PIPEWOOD PONDBUSH ROSEBUSH ROSEMARY SANDSTAY SANDWOOD SASANQUA SHRUBLET SNOWBALL SNOWBELL SNOWBUSH SOAPBARK STANDARD MISTLETOE POINCIANA PHILADELPHUS
(AROMATIC —) THYME CLUSIA BORONIA HOGBUSH ALLSPICE
(AUSTRALIAN —) GOOMA BUDDAH DRIMYS GEEBUNG WARATAH MILKBUSH SANDSTAY
(CHINESE —) KERRIA
(CLIMBING —) CATCLAWS SOLANDRA
(DESERT —) AFERNAN
(EVERGREEN —) BOX BAGO ILEX TITI BOLDO ERICA FURZE HEATH HOLLY KOSAM PYXIE SALAL SAVIN TOYON BAUERA DAHOON KALMIA LAUREL PEPINO PROTEA RUSCUS

SAKAKI ARDISIA BARETTA JASMINE JUNIPER MADRONA MAHONIA CALFKILL CARAUNDA EVONYMUS OLEANDER SASANQUA MANZANITA
(FRAGRANT —) JASMINE HUISACHE MEJORANA MEZEREON ROSEMARY
(HAWAIIAN —) AKALA AKELA ILIMA KOKIO OLONA
(LOW —) AYAPANA
(MEXICAN —) BLUEBUSH
(NEW ZEALAND —) KARO KAWA TUTU KARAMU KIEKIE KAWAKAWA KOROMIKO
(PASTURE —) COWBERRY
(PHILIPPINE —) IPILIPIL
(POISONOUS —) GIF CUBE LITHI SUMAC GIFBLAAR LABURNUM
(PRICKLY —) CAPER COLIMA BRAMBLE CATCLAWS
(SPINY —) ULEX AROMA GORSE JUNCO ESPINO BUMELIA CARISSA CYTISUS GENISTA GOATBUSH GRANJENO GUAJILLO HUAJILLO
(STRONG-SMELLING —) SALTWORT
(STUNTED —) SCRAB SCROG SCRUB
(THORNY —) CHANAR HAWTHORN
(TREELIKE —) ARBUSCLE
(TROPICAL —) INGA MAJO HENNA CAMARA DERRIS MOMBIN OLACAD PERSEA HAMELIA JEWBUSH LANTANA SOAPBARK
(WEST INDIAN —) ANIL RATWOOD MILKWOOD
(XEROPHYTIC —) SAXAUL
(PREF.) THAMN(O)

SHRUBBERY MOGOTE ARBORET

SHRUG SHUG HURKLE SHRINK

SHRUNK WEARISH

SHRUNKEN LANK CLUNG PUNGLED SLUNKEN WIZENED CONTRACT
(— HEAD) TSANTSA

SHTICK ACT BIT GAG GIMMICK ROUTINE

SHUAH (FATHER OF —) ABRAHAM
(MOTHER OF —) KETURAH

SHUAL (FATHER OF —) ZOPHAH

SHUBAEL (FATHER OF —) HEMAN GERSHON

SHUCK HULL HUSK SHACK SHELL SHOCK

SHUCKS DARN DRAT NUTS RATS PSHAW PHOOEY

SHUDDER GRUE CREEP GRISE HIRCH QUAKE SHRUG AGRISE GROOSE HIRTCH HOTTER HURKLE SHIVER FRISSON TREMBLE

SHUDDERING RIGOR

SHUFFLE JANK MAKE MILK SLUR MOSEY SCUFF SHALE SHIFT SHOOL JUGGLE RIFFLE RUFFLE SCLAFF SHOVEL DRAGGLE QUIBBLE SHACKLE SHAFFLE SHAMBLE SLIPPER SLUTHER
(— CARDS DISHONESTLY) PACK STACK
(— DISHONESTLY) PACK

SHUHAM (FATHER OF —) DAN

SHUN FIN SHY BALK FLEE TABU VOID WARE ABHOR AVOID EVADE EVITE SHUNT TABOO ASTART DEVOID ESCAPE ESCHEW REFUSE

SHRINK DECLINE FORBEAR FORSAKE

SHUNI (FATHER OF —) GAD

SHUNT AYRTON BRIDGE BYPASS SWITCH

SHUSH HUSH WHISH SUPPRESS

SHUSWAP ATNAH

SHUT FAST HASP MAKE SEAL SHOT SLAM SLOT SPAR TAKE TEEN TINE CLOSE LATCH STEEK STICK CLOSED CABINET OCCLUSE UPCLOSE
(— DOWN) SCRAM
(— EYES) WINK
(— IN) BAR LAP CAGE COPSE EMBAR EMBAY FORBAR PENTIT TACKLE BELOUKE ENCLAVE
(— OFF) SCREEN SECLUDE SEPARATE
(— OUT) BAR DEBAR REPEL SKUNK HINDER DEPRIVE EXCLUDE OCCLUDE OUTSHUT PRECLUDE
(— SUDDENLY) SNAP
(— TOGETHER) CLASP
(— UP) BAR CUB MEW PENT STOP CHOKE FRANK STIVE STOVE CLOSET EMBOSS ENJAIL IMMURE IMPARK CONDEMN CONFINE DUNGEON ENCLOSE IMPOUND INCLUDE OCCLUDE OPPRESS PARROCK RECLUSE SECLUDE CONCLUDE PRECLUDE
(HALF —) PINK
(PREF.) OCCLUSO

SHUTDOWN LAYOFF
(— OF REACTOR) SCRAM

SHUT-EYE NAP SLEEP

SHUTOUT SKUNK

SHUTTER LID DROP SHUT BLIND SHADE CUTOFF DAMPER DOUSER SLUICE AUTOMAT BUCKLER SHUTTLE JALOUSIE
(— IN ORGAN) SHADE
(— OF TRIPTYCH) VOLET

SHUTTERBUG SNAPPER

SHUTTING CLAUDENT

SHUTTLE FLY FLUTE SHUNT BROCHE LOOPER SWIVEL SHITTLE

SHUTTLECOCK BIRD PETECA VOLANT

SHVANDA THE BAGPIPER
(CHARACTER IN —) DEVIL BABINSKY ICEHEART SCHVANDA
(COMPOSER OF —) WEINBERGER

SHY COY JIB MIM SCAR SHAN SHUN SKIT UNKO WILD BLATE CAGEY CHARY DEMUR FLING PAVID SCARE SHUNT SQUAB TIMID UNCOW BOGGLE BOOGER DEMURE MODEST SHANNY SKIEGH TARTLE BASHFUL GAWKISH RABBITY STRANGE TREMBLY UPSTAGE BACKWARD COCKSHOT DAPHNEAN FAROUCHE RETIRING SHEEPISH SKITTISH SWAIMOUS VERECUND WILLYARD

SHYLOCK (DAUGHTER OF —) JESSICA

SHYNESS COYNESS MODESTY RESERVE TIMIDITY

SHYSTER PETTIFOGGER

SIALAGOGUE SALIVANT

SIAM (SEE THAILAND)

SIAMANG APE UNGKA GIBBON

SIB SEPT AYLLU SIBLING SIBSHIP CALPULLI

SIBERIA (GULF IN —) OB
(MOUNTAIN RANGE IN —) URAL ALTAI
(NATIVE IN —) YAKU SAGAI TATAR KIRGIZ TARTAR KIRGHIZ YUKAGIR
(RIVER IN —) OB ILI KET PUR TAZ TYM AMGA AMUR LENA MAYA ONON UCUR ALDAN ISHIM NADYM SOBOL TOBOL ANGARA IRTYSH OLEKMA VILYUY
(TOWN IN —) OMSK CHITA KYZYL TOMSK IGARKA KURGAN BARNAUL IRKUTSK LENINSK YAKUTSK

SIBERIAN SQUILL SCILLA

SIBILANT HISS

SIBLING TWIN SISTER BROTHER

SIBYL SYBIL SIBYLLA VOLUSPA AMALTHEA

SIC SOOL

SICILIAN
(PREF.) SICULO

SICILIAN VESPERS, THE
(CHARACTER IN —) ELENA ARRIGO MONTFORT FREDERICK
(COMPOSER OF —) VERDI

SICILY		
CAPE: BOEO FARO PASSARO		
CAPITAL: PALERMO		
CATHEDRAL: MONREALE		
COIN: LITRA UNCIA		
GULF: NOTO CATANIA		
ISLAND: EGADI LIPARI USTICA		
MEASURE: SALMA CAFFISO		
MOUNTAIN: EREI ETNA MORO SORI IBREI NEBRODI		
NATIVE: ELYMI SICEL SICANI SICULI		
OLD NAME: TRINACRIA TRIQUETRA		
PROVINCE: ENNA RAGUSA CATANIA MESSINA PALERMO TRAPANI SIRACUSA		
RIVER: SALSO TORTO BELICE SIMETO PLATANI		
SEAPORT: ACI CATANIA MARSALA MESSINA PALERMO TRAPANI		
TOWN: ENNA NOTO RAGUSA CATANIA MARSALA MESSINA TRAPANI SYRACUSE		
VOLCANO: ETNA AETNA		

SICK BAD ILL BADLY CRONK CROOK MORBID MAWKISH SEASICK UNWHOLE CROPSICK MALADIVE PHYSICAL STREAKED

SICKEN TIRE TURN WEARY SUNDER SUNNER WEAKEN DISGUST SCUNNER SURFEIT NAUSEATE

SICKENING FELL SICKLY FULSOME MAWKISH SICKISH NAUSEOUS VOMITOUS

SICKISH DAUNCY

SICKLE HOOK CROOK
(PREF.) DREPANI FALCI ZANCIO

SICKLY WAN FLUE FOND PALE PUKY SICK DAWNY DONCY FAINT GREEN PEAKY SILLY TEWLY WEARY WERSH WISHT AMPERY ANEMIC CLAMMY CRANKY FEEBLE INFIRM PUKISH PULING WANKLY WEAKLY INVALID LANGUID MAWKISH

PEAKING PEAKISH PIMPING QUEECHY SHILPIT SICKISH WEARISH WEERISH DELICATE DISEASED MALADIVE PINDLING

SICKLY-LOOKING SHILPIT

SICKNESS (ALSO SEE DISEASE) MAL SICK SORE TAKING AILMENT DISEASE ILLNESS MALAISE SURFEIT DISORDER
(**INTESTINAL —**) TURISTA
(**MILK —**) SLOWS TIRES
(**MOTION —**) KINETOSIS
(**MOUNTAIN —**) PUNA SOROCHE
(**SUDDEN —**) DWALM

SIDA ILIMA ESCOBA

SIDE CAMP COST EDGE FACE HALF HAND KANT LEAF PANE PART BOARD CHEEK FLANK CATUS PARTY PHASE SITHE BEHALF PTERON ENGLISH PENDANT FORESIDE SIDELONG
(**— BY SIDE**) ACCOLE ABREAST ACCOSTED PARALLEL
(**— OF ATTIC**) SKEELING SKILLING SKILLION
(**— OF BIRD'S HEAD**) LORE
(**— OF BOOM JAW**) HORN
(**— OF BOW**) BELLY
(**— OF BUILDING**) WALL
(**— OF CAVITY**) WALL
(**— OF DECK**) GANGWAY
(**— OF DITCH**) SCARP
(**— OF DIVIDERS**) LEG
(**— OF FACE**) CHEEK
(**— OF GATE**) FOLD
(**— OF GEM**) BEZEL
(**— OF HEAD**) HAFFET
(**— OF HEARTH**) BREAST
(**— OF HILL**) BRAE SCUG SLOPE
(**— OF HOG**) FLITCH
(**— OF HORSESHOE**) BRANCH
(**— OF LACE**) FOOTING
(**— OF LAMB**) CONCERTINA
(**— OF LOG**) RIDE
(**— OF NAVE**) AISLE
(**— OF OPENING**) JAW JAMB
(**— OF PIG**) BACON
(**— OF QUADRANGLE**) PANE
(**— OF RABBET**) LEDGE
(**— OF RACECOURSE**) STRETCH
(**— OF RECTANGLE**) SQUARE
(**— OF ROOF**) CATSLIDE
(**— OF SHIP**) BEAM WALE BOARD BULWARK LARBOARD SEABOARD
(**— OF STAGE**) WING
(**— OF TENNIS RACKET**) ROUGH SMOOTH
(**— OF THEATER GALLERY**) SLIP
(**— OF TRIANGLE**) LEG
(**— OF TYPE**) BACK
(**— OF VALLEY**) COTEAU
(**— OF VIOLIN**) RIB
(**— OF WAGON**) RAVE
(**— PIECE**) RAVE
(**— SHELTERED FROM WIND**) LEE LEW LEEWARD
(**—S OF FIREPLACE**) COVING
(**—S OF GALLERY**) SLIPS
(**— WITH**) SUFFRAGE
(**BACK —**) REAR BEHIND BACKSIDE
(**BY THE —**) ALONG
(**DRESSED —**) FACE
(**FAR —**) OFFSIDE

(**FLAT —**) PANE
(**FOR EACH —**) ALL
(**LEFT —**) PORT
(**MOUNTAIN —**) PUNA VETA SOROCHE
(**OUTER — OF SKIN**) GRAIN
(**RIGHT —**) FACE
(**RIGHT — OF SWORD**) INSIDE
(**UNDERNEATH —**) BOTTOM
(**WINDWARD —**) AWEATHER
(PREF.) LATER(I)(O) PLEUR(I)(O)
(**— BY —**) PAR(A)
(**— PARTS**) ALI
(**BY THE — OF**) JUXTA
(**ON THIS —**) CIS CITRA
(SUFF.) PLEURA PLEUROUS STICH(OUS)

SIDEBAR HOUND

SIDEBOARD ABACUS BUFFET SERVER COMMODE DRESSER CELLARET CREDENCE CREDENZA

SIDE-BY-SIDE ACCOLLE

SIDED (SUFF.) MER

SIDE DISH OUTWORK

SIDEKICK CRONY

SIDEPIECE BAR BOW JAMB WING CHEEK GUSSET EARPIECE LANDSIDE

SIDES (PREF.)
(**ON ALL —**) CIRCUM

SIDESLIP SKID SLIP DRIFT DRILL

SIDESMAN HOGGLER QUESTMAN

SIDESPLITTER RIOT

SIDESTEP BEG AVOID DODGE

SIDETRACK SHUNT

SIDEWALK WALKWAY PAVEMENT TROTTOIR BANQUETTE

SIDEWAYS ASKANT ASKANCE EDGEWAYS EDGEWISE SIDELONG

SIDEWISE ASIDE ASIDEN

SIDING CURB SPUR GARAGE

SIDLE EDGE SLIVE PASSAGE SAUNTER

SIDRA PARASHAH

SIEGE BOUT SEDGE ASSIEGE JOURNEY LEAGUER
(**— ENGINE**) WARWOLF

SIEGFRIED (CHARACTER IN —) MIME WOTAN FAFNER SIEGFRIED BRUNNHILDE
(**COMPOSER OF —**) WAGNER
(**SLAYER OF —**) BRUNHILD
(**WIFE OF —**) KRIEMHILD

SIERRA CERO SERRA SAWBACK KINGFISH

SIERRA LEONE
CAPITAL: FREETOWN
COIN: LEONE
LANGUAGE: KRIO MENDE TEMNE
MEASURE: LOAD KETTLE
MOUNTAIN: LOMA
NATIVE: VAI KONO LOKO SUSU KISSI LIMBA MENDE TEMNE FULANI GALLINA SHERBRO MANDINGO
RIVER: MOA JONG SEWA MONGO ROKEL ROKKEL SCARCY WAANJE
SEAPORT: HEPEL BONTHE SULIMA
TOWN: BO DARU MANO KISSI LUNGI KENEMA MAKENI

SIESTA NAP MERIDIAN

SIEVA BEAN

SIEVE FRY TRY BOLT BUNT DRUM HARP LAWN PREE SCRY SHOE SIFT SILE SIZE TEMS GRATE RANGE SCALP TAMIS TAMMY TEMSE BOLTER RANGER RIDDER RIDDLE SEARCE SEARCH SEMMET SIFTER WEIGHT BOULTEL CHAFFER CRIBBLE DILLUER PRICKLE TIFFANY TROMMEL COLANDER SEARCHER STRAINER
(**— FOR MILK**) MILSEY
(PREF.) COSCINO CRIBRI ETHMO

SIF (HUSBAND OF —) THOR

SIFT REE TRY BOLT DUST SCRY RANGE SCALP SIEVE TEMSE DREDGE GARBLE RIDDER RIDDLE SCREEN SEARCE WINNOW CANVASS CRIBBLE DRIBBLE SIFTAGE CRIBRATE
(**— FLOUR**) DRESS
(**— IN**) INFILTER
(**— IN MINING**) LUE
(**— MEAL**) BUNT
(**— SHOT**) TABLE
(**— WHEAT**) SCALP

SIFTER SIEVE BOLTER CASTER SIEVER WINNOWER

SIFTING DRIFT GARBLING
(PL.) BOLTING FANNINGS SIEVINGS

SIGH SOB PECH SIFE SOCK WIND MOURN SIGHT SITHE SOUGH TWANK BEMOAN BEWAIL SORROW SUTHER DEPLORE SINGULT SUSPIRE

SIGHT AIM EYE KEN RAY BONE ESPY FACE GAZE PEEP SEET VIEW FERLY RAISE SCENE SCOPE SICHT TRACK VISIE VIZZY BEHOLD DESCRY OBJECT TICKET VISION DISCERN DISPLAY EYESHOT GLIMPSE MONSTER CONSPECT DISCOVER EYESIGHT GUNSIGHT
(**— FOR GUN**) BEAD LEAF PEEP SCOPE VISIE VIZZY HAUSSE GUNSIGHT
(**— OF COMPASS**) VANE
(**— ON SURVEYOR'S STAFF**) TARGET
(**—S OF CITY**) LIONS
(**— TO SEE IF LEVEL**) BONE
(**AMAZING —**) STOUND
(**IMAGINARY —**) VISION
(**IMPRESSIVE —**) PICTURE
(**OFFENSIVE —**) EYESORE
(**OUT OF —**) HID
(**PITIFUL —**) RUTH
(**SECOND —**) TAISH TAISCH DEUTEROSCOPY
(**SORRY —**) BYSEN
(**STRANGE —**) FERLY FERLIE
(SUFF.) OPSIA OPSIS OPSY OPTIC OPTICON ORAMA

SIGHTER ALINER ALIGNER

SIGHTING LANDFALL
(**— DEVICE**) ALIDADE

SIGHTLY VIEWLY EYEABLE

SIGHTSEE RUBBERNECK

SIGLOS DARIC

SIGN INK AYAH DASH FIRM HINT HIRE MARK NOTE OMEN TYPE BADGE COLON FRANK GHOST

GUIDA HAMZA INDEX SEGNO SIGIL SINGE SPOOR STAMP TOKEN TRACE ASSIGN AUGURY CARACT EFFECT EMBLEM ENGAGE ENSIGN FUGLER INDICE MOTION NOTICE PARAPH REMARK SIGLUM SIGNAL SIGNET SIGNUM SYMBOL TITTLE WITTER ALEBUSH AUSPICE CHECKER CHEQUER CONSIGN EARMARK ENDORSE INDICIA INSIGNE KNOWING PORTENT PRESAGE PRODIGY PROFFER SHINGLE SHOWING SIGNARY SURMISE SYMPTOM VESTIGE WARNING CEREMONY INDICANT INSTANCE MONUMENT PROCLAIM SIGNACLE SYLLADIC TELLTALE
(**— DOCUMENT**) FIRM
(**— FOR KEYNOTE**) ISON
(**— OF A COVENANT**) SACRAMENT
(**— OF ALEHOUSE**) LATTICE
(**— OF AN IDEA**) EMBLEM
(**— OF APPROVAL**) CACHET
(**— OF CONTEMPT**) FIG
(**— OF DANGER**) SEAMARK
(**— OF GLOTTAL STOP**) HAMZA HAMZAH
(**— OF MULTIPLICATION**) DOT
(**— OF ZODIAC**) LEO RAM BULL CRAB GOAT LION ARIES HOUSE LIBRA TWINS VIRGO ARCHER CANCER FISHES GEMINI PISCES TAURUS VIRGIN BALANCE SCORPIO AQUARIUS SCORPION
(**— ON MAP**) ICON
(**ASTROLOGICAL —**) CIPHER
(**CHARACTERISITC —**) SYMPTOM
(**DIACRITICAL —**) TILDE UMLAUT
(**GLOTTAL STOP —**) HAMZA HAMZAH
(**MATHEMATICAL —**) NAME FUNCTOR
(**MUSICAL —**) CLEF FLAT REST GUIDA NEUME PRESA SEGNO SHARP SWELL SIMILE FERMATA NATURAL
(**OUTWARD —**) EVIDENCE
(**ROAD —**) MERGE
(**SANSKRIT —**) ANUSVARA
(**SHILLING —**) SOLIDUS
(**SHORTHAND —**) DIPHONE
(**SLIGHT —**) SURMISE
(**SUBSCRIPT —**) SUBFIX
(**SUPERSTITIOUS —**) GUEST
(**TAVERN —**) BUSH ALEBUSH ALEPOLE CHECKER CHEQUER ALESTAKE
(**TRAMP'S —**) MONICA MONIKER
(**VOWEL —**) SEGOL SEGHOL
(PL.) INDICIA INSIGNIA
(PREF.) SEMA SEMANT(O) SEMASI(O) SEMATO SEMEIO SEMIO SEMO SYMBOLO
(SUFF.) SEME

SIGNAL OS CUE GUN PST WAG BALK BECK BELL BUZZ CALL COND FLAG GATE HASH SIGN WAFF WAFT WAVE WINK ALARM ALERT BLINK FLARE FUSEE FUZEE LIGHT SHAPE SHORT SPEAK TOKEN WHIFF ALARUM BANNER BEACON BECKON BUZZER ENSIGN HERALD MARKER OFFICE RECALL SIGNET

TARGET WAVING WIGWAG BLINKER CHAMADE COMMAND EMINENT GRIFFIN NOTABLE RETREAT TURNOUT ASSEMBLY CRANTARA DIAPHONE FLAGFALL LOGOGRAM STANDARD STRIKING
(— FISHERMEN) BALK
(— FOR A PARLEY) CHAMADE
(— FOR PLUNDER) HAVOC
(— FOR WHALERS) WAIF
(— IN WHIST) ECHO PETER
(— OF DISTRESS) SOS
(— ON HORN) SEEK BLAST STRAKE
(— ON RADARSCOPE) BLIP
(— TO ATTACK) CHARGE
(— TO BEGIN ACTION) CUE
(— TO RETREAT) RETIRE
(— TO RETURN) RECALL
(— WITH FLAGS) WIGWAG
(AUDIO —) HUM
(BOAT'S —) WAFF WAFT
(DANGER —) RED SEAMARK
(DEATH —) KNELL
(DISTRESS —) FLARE
(FOG —) FOGHORN TORPEDO DIAPHONE
(HUNTER'S —) SEEK PRIZE GIBBET STRAKE
(MILITARY —) FLARE TURNOUT ASSEMBLY
(NAVAL —) SECURE VERYLIGHT
(RADIO —) BEAM
(RAILROAD —) BANJO BOARD FUSEE FUZEE TARGET HIGHBALL SEMAPHORE
(TRAFFIC —) ROBOT
(WARNING —) RED ALARM KLAXON TOCSIN REDFLAG REDLIGHT
(WEATHER —) CONE STORMCONE STORMDRUM
SIGNALIZE MARK
SIGNALLING TICKTACK
SIGNALMAN FLAGS BELLBOY BELLMAN
SIGNATE SENNET
SIGNATORY SIGNEE SIGNER
SIGNATURE BOLT FIRM HAND VISA FRANK SHEET SIGIL THEME SIGNUM TUGHRA SECTION HANDWRIT SIGNATOR
SIGNBOARD SIGN SHINGLE
SIGNET SEAL SIGIL
SIGNIFICANCE WIT BODY PITH SOUND AMOUNT IMPORT INTENT LETTER STRESS WEIGHT BEARING CONTENT GRAVITY MEANING SENTENCE STRENGTH
(DEVOID OF —) JEJUNE
(HIDDEN —) HYPONOIA
(LACKING —) INANE
(MORAL —) ETHOS
SIGNIFICANT REAL RICH GREAT MEATY AUGURAL EPOCHAL OMINOUS POINTED SERIOUS SENSEFUL SPEAKING PERTINENT
SIGNIFICANTLY SENSIBLY
SIGNIFICATION SENSE VALOR VALUE ETYMON IMPORT MOMENT NOTION MEANING CARRIAGE SIGNIFIE
SIGNIFICS SENSIFICS
SIGNIFY BE SAY BEAR GIVE MAKE

MEAN NOTE SIGN WAVE AUGUR IMPLY SKILL SOUND SPEAK SPELL TOKEN UTTER AMOUNT ARGUFY ASSERT BEMEAN DENOTE EMPLOY IMPORT INTEND MATTER SIGNAL BESPEAK BETOKEN CONNOTE DECLARE EXPRESS PORTEND PRETEND DESCRIBE INDICATE INTIMATE MANIFEST
SIGNIFYING DOZENS GOADING NEEDLING
SIGNOR BRUSCHINO, IL
(CHARACTER IN —) SOFIA BRUSCHINO FLORVILLE GAUDENZIO
(COMPOSER OF —) ROSSINI
SIGNPOST GUIDE MERCURY WAYMARK HANDPOST
SIGURD (HORSE OF —) GRANI
(SLAIN BY —) FAFNIR
(SLAYER OF —) HOGNI
(VICTIM OF —) FAFNIR
(WIFE OF —) GUDRUN
SIGYN (HUSBAND OF —) LOKI
SIKH AKALI SINGH UDASI MAZHABI
SIKKIM (CAPITAL OF —) GANGTOK
(NATIVE OF —) RONG BHOTIA LEPCHA
(RIVER OF —) TISTA
SIKSIKA SIHASAPA
SILAS MARNER (AUTHOR OF —) ELIOT
(CHARACTER IN —) CASS AARON DOLLY EPPIE NANCY SILAS MARNER DUNSTAN GODFREY LAMMETER WINTHROP
SILENCE GAG MUM CALK CLUM HIST HUSH REST CHOKE FLOOR PEACE QUIET SHUSH SQUAT STILL CLAMOR MUFFLE SETTLE STIFLE WHISHT CONFUTE SQUELCH DUMBNESS PRECLUDE SUPPRESS
(— OF CONSONANT) QUIESCENCE
(CODE OF —) OMERTA
SILENCED STILL
SILENCER SOURDINE
SILENT MUM CLUM HUSH HUST MUET MUTE SNUG CLOSE MUTED STILL TACIT WHIST MUETTE SOPITE SULLEN TIPTOE WHISHT APHONIC UNWORDY ASPIRATE RESERVED RETICENT TACITURN
SILENT DON (AUTHOR OF —) SHOLOKHOV
(CHARACTER IN —) DARIA DUNIA MAURA GREGOR PIOTRA STEPAN AKSINIA DENIKIN MELEKHOV ILINICHKA PROKOFFEY PANTALEIMON
SILHOUETTE SHADE ISOTYPE OUTLINE SKYLINE
SILICA FLINT SILEX SINTER COESITE TRIPOLI TRIDYMITE
SILICATE MICA ALVITE CERITE IOLITE PINITE EUCLASE ILVAITE LOTRITE ZEOLITE CALAMINE ERIONITE WELLSITE
SILICEOUS SHELLY
SILICLE POD POUCH SILICULE
SILICON (THIN SLICE OF —) WAFER
SILICOSIS CON
SILIQUE POD
SILK SAY SOY CRIN ERIA LOVE MUGA ATLAS FLOSS GREGE

HONAN JAPAN TABBY BLATTA CRACKS CULGEE DUCAPE FRISON MANTUA PONGEE RADIUM SENDAL SHALEE SHILLA SOUPLE TUSSAH ALAMODE CHIFFON HABUTAI PERSIAN SCHAPPE SQUEEZE TIFFANY TSATLEE TUSSORE YAMAMAI ARMOZEEN ARMOZINE LUSTRINE MILANESE
(— FOR LININGS) SARSNET SARCENET
(— TREE) MIMOSA
(CORDED —) PADUASOY
(HEAVY —) CRIN ARMOZINE
(RAW —) GREIGE MARABOU TAYSAAM TSATLEE MARABOUT
(REFUSE —) BUR BURR
(TWILLED —) SURAH TOBINE FOULARD LOUSINE
(UNDYED —) CORAH
(UNTWISTED —) SLEAVE
(UPHOLSTERY —) TABARET
(WASTE —) KNUB NOIL FRISON
(PREF.) SERI(CEO)(CI)(CO)
SILK COTTON KAPOK
SILK-COTTON TREE BULAK SEMUL SIMAL BOMBAX YAXCHE BENTANG MUNGUBA POCHOTE
SILKEN SILL SERIC SILKY SUAVE SEREAN
SILK GRASS KARATAS
SILK GUM SERICIN
SILK OAK LACEWOOD
SILKSMAN SCALPER
SILK TREE SIRIS
SILKWORM ERI ERIA SINA BOMBYX TUSSAH TUSSORE YAMAMAI BOMBYCID
SILKY GLOSSY SILKEN
SILKY CORNEL REDBRUSH
SILKY TAMARIN MARIKINA
SILL GIRD SOLE PLATE PATAND PATTEN SADDLE MUDSILL DOORSILL
SILLINESS BOSH FOLLY BETISE GOOSERY INANITY PORANGI SIMPLES IDLENESS NONSENSE ABSURDITY SIMPLICITY
SILLY TID BETE DAFT FOND FOOL NICE VAIN APISH BALMY BATTY BUGGY CAKEY DENSE DILLY DITSY DITZY DIZZY GIDDY GOOFY INANE KOOKY LOONY SAPPY SEELY WACKY BLASHY CRANKY CUCKOO DAWISH DOTARD DOTTLE FOOTLE FRUITY GUCKED MOPOKE PAULIE SAWNEY SHANNY SIMPLE SINGLE SKIVIE SLIGHT SPOONY VACANT ASININE FATUOUS FOOLISH FOPPISH FRIBBLE GLAIKET PEEVISH PUERILE SCRANNY SHALLOW UNWITTY ANSERINE FEATLESS FOOTLING FOPPERLY
(BE —) DRIVEL
(PREF.) MORO
SILO (PART OF —) BIN DOME PIPE TANK MELON INTAKE LADDER PUMPKIN UMBRELLA PARACHUTE
SILOXANE SILICON
SILPHIUM LASER
SILT DREGS SLEECH DEPOSIT RESIDUE SULLAGE BULLDUST
SILVER LUNA MOON PINA DIANA

PLATE SYCEE WEDGE WHITE ALBATA ARGENT SILLER BULLION VERMEIL ARGENTUM STERLING ARGENTINE
(— INGOT) SYCEE
(— STATE) NEVADA
(DEBASED —) VELLON
(GERMAN —) ALBATA
(GILDED —) VERMEIL
(NICKEL —) PAKTONG
(PREF.) ARGENT(O) ARGYR(O)
SILVER BELL HALESIA BELLWOOD COWLICKS
SILVERFISH SHINER SLICKER FISHTAIL WOODFISH
SILVERING BACKING
SILVERSIDES IAO BRIT TINK BRITT FRIAR SMELT TAILOR TINKER GRUNION ATHERINE PEIXEREY PEJERREY SKIPJACK
SILVERSMITH SONAR
SILVERTIP BEAR
SILVER TREE IRONWOOD
SILVER TREE FERN PITAU
SILVERVINE CATVINE
SILVERWEED TANSY
SILVERWING CINDER
SILVERY WHITE ARGENT SILVER SILVERN
(PREF.) GLAUCO
SILVIA (FATHER OF —) BALLANCE
(LOVER OF —) VALENTINE
SILYBUM MARIANA
SIMAR CYMAR SYMAR ZIMARRA
SIMEON (FATHER OF —) JACOB
(MOTHER OF —) LEAH
SIMILAR AKIN LIKE SAME SUCH ALIKE METOO EVENLY LIKELY SIMILE COGNATE KINDRED SEEMABLE SELFLIKE SUCHLIKE SUITABLE SEMBLANCE
(PREF.) HOL(O) HOM(E)(EO)(O)(OE) (OI)
(SUFF.) (MAKE — TO) FY IFY
SIMILARITY SIMILE ANALOGY HOMOLOGY HOMOTAXY LIKENESS PARALLEL SAMENESS
SIMILARLY EQUALLY LIKEWISE
SIMILE ICON IKON IMAGE FIGURE SUIVEZ COMPARE
SIMILITUDE IMAGE FIGURE ANALOGY PARABLE PORTRAIT
SIMMER FRY CREE SILE STEW SIMPER SOTTER TOTTLE
SIMON ZELOTES
(BROTHER OF —) JESUS
(FATHER OF —) MATTATHIAS
(SON OF —) JUDAS
SIMON BOCCANEGRA
(CHARACTER IN —) MARIA PAOLO SIMON ADORNO AMELIA ANDREA FIESCO GABRIELLE BOCCANEGRA
(COMPOSER OF —) VERDI
SIMONY BARRATRY
SIMOOM SAMUM SAMIEL KHAMSIN
SIMPER MINCE SMIRK BRIDLE
SIMPLE LOW BALD BARE EASY FOND MERE NICE ONLY PURE RUDE SNAP VERY WEAK AFALD BLEAK DIZZY GREEN NAIVE NAKED PLAIN SEELY SILLY SMALL SOBER AEFALD CHASTE GLOBAL HOMELY HONEST HUMBLE NATIVE OAFISH

RUSTIC SEMPLE SEVERE SINGLE STUPID VIRGIN ARTLESS ASININE AUSTERE BABYISH FATUOUS FOOLISH ONEFOLD POPULAR SIMPLEX SPECIES ARCADIAN EXPLICIT HOMEMADE HOMESPUN INNOCENT INORNATE SACKLESS SEMPLICE SOLITARY **(VEGETABLE —)** GALENIC **(PREF.)** APL(O) HAPL(O) LITI

SIMPLE-MINDED SEELY SILLY INNOCENT

SIMPLETON AUF AWF COX DAW FON NUP OAF SAP SOT BABE BABY BOOB CAKE COOT CULL FLAT FOOL GABY GAUP GAWP GOFF GOUK GOWK GOWP GUFF PEAK ROOK SIMP SOFT TONY TOOT ZANY COKES GALAH GOOSE IDIOT IKONA JACOB LOACH NINNY NODDY PRUNE SAMMY SMELT SNIPE SPOON TOMMY BADAUD DAUKIN FONDLE GANDER GAUPUS GAWNEY GOTHAM GREENY GULPIN JOSSER NINCUM NOODLE NUPSON SAWNEY SIMKIN SIMPLE DAWPATE GOMERAL GUBBINS JUGGINS MAFFLIN MUGGINS WIDGEON ABDERITE FLATHEAD FONDLING INNOCENT JEANJEAN JOCRISSE KNOTHEAD MOONCALF MOONLING OMADHAUN PEAGOOSE SILLYTON SOFTHEAD WISEACRE WOODCOCK NINCOMPOOP

SIMPLICITY NICETY PURITY MODESTY NAIVETE ELEGANCE

SIMPLIFY CLARIFY EXPOUND

SIMPLY JUST ALONE FONDLY MERELY PLATLY CRUDELY QUIETLY NATIVELY

SIMULACRUM ICON SHAM IMAGE IMITATION

SIMULATE ACT FAKE MOCK FEIGN MIMIC AFFECT ASSUME SEMBLE SIMULE SKETCH

SIMULATED FAINT FAKED ERSATZ FICTIOUS

SIMULATION ACTING ANALOGUE PRETENCE PRETENSE

SIMULTANEOUS CONJOINT CONJUGATE

SIMULTANEOUSLY ONCE TOGETHER

SIN ERR CULP DEBT ENZU EVIL HELL PAPA VICE BLAME CRIME ERROR FAULT FOLLY GUILT SLOTH WATHE WRONG AGUILT COMMIT FELONY NANNAR OFFEND PIACLE PLIGHT VENIAL FRAILTY OFFENSE HAMARTIA INIQUITY PECCANCY QUEDSHIP TRESPASS **(DAUGHTER OF —)** ISHTAR **(DEADLY —)** ACEDIA **(ORIGINAL —)** ADAM **(SEVEN DEADLY —S)** ENVY LUST ANGER PRIDE SLOTH GLUTTONY COVETOUSNESS **(SON OF —)** NESKU SHAMASH **(WIFE OF —)** NINGAL **(PREF.)** HAMARTIO

SINCALINE CHOLINE

SINCE AS AGO FOR FRO NOW GONE SETH SITH SYNE BEING WHERE FORWHY BECAUSE SITHENS WHEREAS INASMUCH SITHENCE **(PREF.)** CIS CITRA

SINCERE GOOD REAL TRUE AFALD FRANK CANDOR DEVOUT ENTIRE HEARTY HONEST SIMPLE SINGLE CORDIAL EARNEST GENUINE ONEFOLD UPRIGHT FAITHFUL PRAYERFUL **(NOT —)** LIP PLASTIC SYNTHETIC SYNTHETICAL

SINCERELY TRULY SIMPLY SINGLY DEVOUTLY ENTIRELY HEARTILY

SINCERITY FAITH HEART CANDOR VERITY HONESTY REALITY

SINDON CORPORAL

SINE SAGITTA **(VERSED —)** SAGITTA

SINECURE SNAP

SINEW THEW BRAWN FIBER FIBRE FORCE NERVE POWER LEADER SINNER TENDON

SINEWY WIRY NERVY THEWY ROBUST FIBROSE FIBROUS NERVOUS STRINGY TENDINAL

SINFONIA SYMPHONY

SINFUL BAD EVIL VILE NEFAS WRONG WICKED PECCANT UNGODLY VICIOUS PIACULAR

SING HUM JIG LIP CANT CARP GALE HYMN LILT TUNE CAROL CARRY CHANT CHIRL CROON DIRGE DITTY DRING FEIGN LYRIC RAISE TOUCH TROLL YEDDE CHAUNT CHORUS DIVIDE INTONE MELODY RECORD RELISH STRAIN WARBLE CHORTLE COUNTER DESCANT GRIDDLE SINGING TWEEDLE CHERUBIM FALDERAL MODULATE SINGSONG VOCALIZE **(— ABOUT)** RESING **(— ABOVE TRUE PITCH)** SHARP **(— AS A BEGGAR)** GRIDDLE **(— BRISKLY)** KNACK **(— CHEERFULLY)** LILT **(— FLORIDLY)** DIVIDE **(— HARSHLY)** SCREAM **(— IN A CRACKED VOICE)** CRAKE **(— IN CHORUS)** CHOIR **(— IN LOW VOICE)** CROON **(— IN SWISS MANNER)** YODEL **(— LOUDLY)** BELT TROLL TROLLOL **(— PRAISES)** LAUD **(— ROMANCES)** GEST GESTE **(— SECOND PART)** SURCENT **(— SOFTLY)** SOWF SOWTH **(— TO THE MOON)** BAY **(— WITH FLOURISHES)** ROULADE **(— WITH MEANINGLESS SYLLABLES)** SCAT

SINGAPORE (RIVER IN —) SUNGEI SELETAR **(STRAIT OF —)** JOHORE SEMBILAN

SINGE GAS BURN CHAR SEAR SWEAL GENAPP SCORCH SWINGE SCOWDER SWITHEN FIREFANG

SINGER ALTO BARD DIVA LARK SWAN BASSO BUFFA BUFFO SKALD VOICE BULBUL BUSKER CANARY CANTOR LYRIST SONGER BASSIST CHANTER CROONER PRIMOMO SOLOIST SONGMAN

SOPRANO TROLLER WARBLER BAYADERE CANTADOR CASTRATO CHANTEUR FALSETTO GRIDDLER MELODIST MONODIST THAMYRIS VOCALIST CITYBILLY **(— OF FOLK SONGS)** CANTADOR **(— OF ROCK MUSIC)** ROCKER **(— OF THE GODS)** GANDHARVA **(BEWITCHING —)** SIREN **(COUNTRY MUSIC —)** CITYBILLY **(FEMALE —)** SONGBIRD **(MENDICANT —)** BUSKER **(PRINCIPAL —)** PRIMOMO **(PROVENCAL —)** MUSAR **(STROLLING —)** CANTABANK

SINGING CANT SCAT CHANT LYRIC HYMNODY CANOROUS JONGLERY **(— ANTIPHONALLY)** ALTERNATION **(— CAROLS)** PLYGAIN HODENING **(— COACH)** REPETITEUR **(ALTERNATE —)** ANTIPHON **(CANTORIAL —)** HAZANUTH HAZZANUT **(JAZZ —)** SCAT **(SIMULTANEOUS —)** CHORUS

SINGLE ODD ONE LAST ONLY SOLE UNAL AFALD ALONE AEFALD SIMPLE SOLEIN SULLEN UNIQUE VERSAL ALONELY AZYGOUS ONEFOLD SEVERAL SIMPLEX TWOSOME PECULIAR SEPARATE SINGULAR SOLITARY SPORADIC PARTICULAR **(— OUT)** CUT NAP SPOT ISOLATE SEPARATE **(PREF.)** APL(O) HAPL(O) MANI MON(O) UNI

SINGLE-FOOT RACK

SINGLEHANDEDLY SINGLY

SINGLE-MINDED AFALD ONEFOLD DEDICATED

SINGLENESS UNITY ONENESS

SINGLETON ONER UNIT **(— LEAD)** SNEAK

SINGLY SINGLE SOLELY SLONELY

SINGPHO CHINGPAW

SINGSONG CANT SOUGH CHANTING

SINGULAR ODD RARE FERLY QUEER QUAINT SEENIL SINGLE CURIOUS STRANGE PECULIAR

SINGULARISM HENISM

SINGULARITY DOUBLET ONENESS ONLINESS

SINHALESE SINHALA

SINISTER AWK CAR KAY DARK DIRE FELL GRIM DISMAL LOUCHE MALIGN AWKWARD OBLIQUE OMINOUS

SINISTRAL REVERSED

SINK DIP DOP EBB LUM SAG SET SYE BORE DRAU DRAW DROP FADE FAIL FALL GOWT HELD KILL LUMB SILE SWAG AVALE DRAFT DRAIN DROOP DROWN HIELD LAPSE LOWER MERGE POACH SQUAT STOOP SWAMP VERGE CLOACA DEVALL DOLINA DOLINE DRENCH GUTTER JAWBOX PLUNGE PUDDLE RESIDE SETTLE COMMODE DECLINE DESCEND DRAUGHT FOUNDER GULLION IMMERSE RELAPSE SCUPPER

SCUTTLE SUBSIDE SWALLOW DECREASE SINKHOLE SOAKAWAY **(— AND FALL)** TWINE **(— AS IN MUD)** LAIR **(— A WELL)** DRILL **(— DOWN)** BOG AVALE STOOP DECLINE **(— FANGS INTO)** STRIKE **(— FOR MIXING DRINKS)** WETBAR **(— INTO OOZE)** WASEL **(— NAILHEAD)** SET **(— SUDDENLY)** SLUMP **(— UNDER TRIAL)** QUAIL

SINKBOX BOX SINK BATTERY

SINKER BUR BURR SINK DIPSY DONUT PLUMB BULLET

SINKHOLE SINK PONOR UVALA CENOTE COLLECT

SINKING GONE SINKAGE **(— DOWN)** FONDU

SINKIUSE COLUMBIA

SINLESS INNOCENT

SINLESSNESS HOLINESS

SINNER DEBTOR PECCANT

SINNING PECCANT

SINUATE GYROSE

SINUOSITY WRIGGLE

SINUOUS WAVY SNAKEY SINUATE SNAKISH TORTILE WINDING INDENTED SWANLIKE

SINUS BOSOM ANTRUM RECESS LOCULUS TEARPIT **(PL.)** ANTRA

SINUSITIS ROUP

SIOUAN OTOE ABANIC DAKOTA SANTEE SAPONI CATAWBA DACOTAH

SIOUX (— FORCE) WAKAN WAKON

SIP BIB NIP SUP BLEB SEEP SLUP SUCK TIFF KEACH NURSE SNACK WHIFF TIPPLE TICKLER DELIBATE

SIPHON CRANE THIEF VALINCH FLINCHER

SIPPING LIBANT

SIPUNCULOIDEA ACHAETA INERMIA

SIR PO DAN DEN DON PAN AZAM BAAS HERR MIAN STIR TUAN BWANA SAHIB SENOR SEYID SIEUR MESSER SAYYID SIGNOR SIRREE BARONET DOMINUS EFFENDI MESSIRE SIGNIOR SIGNORE GOSPODIN GOVERNOR **(PL.)** LORDINGS

SIRCAR BANIAN

SIRE KING BEGET THROW FATHER GETTER

SIREN BUMMER HOOTER LIGEIA LIGYDA ENTICER LORELEI MERMAID SIRENIAN

SIRENIAN COWFISH MUTILATE

SIRENOMELUS SYMPUS SYMMELUS

SIRICID UROCERID

SIRIS KOKO LEBBEK

SIRIUS SOTHIS TISHIYA CANICULA

SIRLOIN SEY BACKSEY

SIRMUELLERA BANKSIA

SIRUP WAX LICK GOLDY SYRUP GOWDIE GREENS ORGEAT RUNOFF ANTIQUE CLAIRCE ECLEGMA LIQUEUR MOLASSES QUIDDANY

SIRWASH SIDELINE

SISAL RUG CABUYA SISALANA
SISKIN TARIN ABERDEVINE
SISSIFIED PRISSY
SISSOO TALI SHISHAM
SISSY SIS CISSIE SISTER CHICKEN
PANTYWAIST
SISTER NUN SIB SIS GIRL NURSE
SISSY SOEUN TITTY WOMAN
EXTERN PERSON
(YOUNGER —) CADETTE
(PL.) SISTERN SISTREN
(PREF.) SORORI
SISTERHOOD BEGUINES SORORITY
SISTERLY SORORAL
SISYPHUS (BROTHER OF —)
ATHAMAS SALMONEUS
(FATHER OF —) AEOLUS
(MOTHER OF —) ENARETE
(SON OF —) SINON GLAUCUS
ORNYTION
(WIFE OF —) MEROPE
SIT SET LEAN SEAT BENCH PRESS
ROOST SQUAT WEIGH BESTRIDE
(— ABRUPTLY) CLAP
(— ASTRIDE) CROSS HORSE
STRADDLE
(— ERECT LIKE A DOG) BEG
(— FORCIBLY) DOSS
(— IN JUDGMENT) DEEM
(— ON) BROOD COVER
(— OVER EGGS) RUCK BROOD
CLOCK
(— UPRIGHT) PERK
SITA (FATHER OF —) JANAKA
(HUSBAND OF —) RAMA SOMA
SITATUNGA NAKONG
SITE AREA PLOT SEAT SITU SOLE
SPOT TOFT FIELD PLACE SITUS
STAND STANCE BIVOUAC DAMSITE
HABITAT STEADING
(— OF BIRD SEXUAL DISPLAY) LEK
(— OF HUNT) DRIVE
(— OF SMELTER) BOLE
(ARCHAELOGICAL —) EXCAVATION
(BUILDING —) STANCE
(EXCAVATION —) DIG
(FORTIFIED —) KAIM KAME
(THRESHING —) SETTING
SITTER DOLLY DOLLIE INSESSOR
SITTING DIET SEAT ASSIS CLUTCH
SEANCE SEDENT SEJANT SESSION
CONGRESS SEDERUNT
SITUATE PLACE POSITION
SITUATED SET SEATED STATURED
(— OPPOSITE) COUNTER
(GET —) ORIENT
SITUATION JOB LIE CASE CRIB
PASS PLOT POST SEAT SITE SPOT
BERTH SIEGE SITUS STATE STEAD
ASSIZE CHANCE ESTATE OFFICE
PLIGHT STATUS EPISODE PICTURE
PORTENT POSTURE STATION
INCIDENT INSTANCE POSITURE
STANDING UBIQUITY
(— BESET BY DIFFICULTIES)
SCRAPE
(— IN CRIBBAGE) GO
(— IN FARO) CATHOP
(— IN OMBRE) CODILLE
(— OF PERPLEXITY) HOBBLE STRAIT
(AMUSING —) BAR
(AWKWARD —) SCRAPE JACKPOT
(BAD —) SCENE

(CRITICAL —) CLUTCH
(DIFFICULT —) BOX PUXY BOGGLE
NINEHOLES PREDICAMENT
(DISTRESSING —) STYMIE
(EXECRABLE —) ATROCITY
(FAVORABLE —) BREAK
(FINAL — OF ACT) CURTAIN
(HIGH) AERY AERIE
(HOPELESSLY DOOMED —)
RATTRAP
(NECESSITOUS —) BREACH
(PAINFUL —) DISTRESS
(RELATIVE —) BEARING
(TIGHT —) CRUNCH
(TRYING —) COW
(UNPLEASANT —) BUMMER
(UNSATISFACTORY —) DILEMMA
(VEXATIOUS —) HEADACHE
(VILE —) DUNGHILL
(ZODIACAL —) HAYZ
SITZ BATH SITZBAD SEMICUPE
SITZMARK BATHTUB
SIVA RUDRA SHIVA ISVARA SHAMBU
BHAIRAVA MAHADEVA NATARAJA
(SYMBOL OF —) LINGA LINGAM
(WIFE OF —) KALI
SIX VAU WAW SICE SISE HEXAD
HEXADE SENARY SEXTET STIGMA
DIGAMMA SIXSOME
(PREF.) HEX(A) SEX(A)(I) SEXTI
SIXFOLD SEXTUPLE
SIX-FOOTED HEXAPOD
SIXMO SEXTO
SIXPENCE HOG PIG BEND KICK
ZACK SIMON SPRAT TIZZY BENDER
FIDDLE TANNER TESTON CRIPPLE
FIDDLER TESTRIL
SIXTEENTH ANA ANNA
SIXTH
(PREF.) SEXTI
SIXTIETH (— PART OF DAY) GHURRY
SIXTY SAMECH SAMEKH
SIZABLE SNUG HEFTY LARGE
HANDSOME
SIZE WAX AREA BIND BULK MARK
MASS DRESS GIRTH MOUND
PLANK SCALE EXTENT FORMAT
GROWTH MICKLE MOISON PICNIC
SIZING BIGNESS CONTENT
CORSAGE FITTING THIRTEEN
TWELVEMO
(— OF BOOK) FOLIO OCTAVO
QUARTO
(— OF BULLET) CALIBER
(— OF CARDS) TOWN LADIES
(— OF HOLE) BORE
(— OF HOSIERY) POPE
(— OF PAGE) OCTAVO
(— OF PAPERBOARD) LARGE
(— OF PARTICLE) GRIND
(— OF ROPE) GRIST
(— OF SLATE) PEGGY IMPERIAL
(— OF TYPE) GEM PICA RUBY AGATE
CANON ELITE PEARL MINION
PRIMER BREVIER DIAMOND
EMERALD ENGLISH PARAGON
COLUMBIAN
(— YARN) SLASH
(CLOTHING —) LONG SHORT STOUT
JUNIOR PETITE
(EXTRA LARGE —) SUPER
(GREAT —) MAGNITUDE
(MEASURED —) SCANTLING

(PAPER —) SIXMO
(RELATIVE —) SCALE
(UNUSUAL —) OUTSIZE
SIZEABLE HEFTY
SIZING DRESSING SLASHING
(— LIQUID) GLAIR
SIZZLE FRIZZ
SKADI (FATHER OF —) THJAZI
(HUSBAND OF —) NJORD
SKAG SCAG HEROIN
SKANDA (BROTHER OF —) GANESHA
(FATHER OF —) SHIVA
(WIFE OF —) DEVAYANI
VALLIAMMAN
SKASTING (— JUMP) SALCHOW
SKAT CAT NULL TOURNEE
SKATE BOB RAY TUB RAJA RINK
SKIT TINK TUBE FLAIR SCULL
BATOID DOCTOR FLATHE PATENT
PATTEN ROCKER ROLLER RUNNER
SKETCH TINKER CHOPINE FLAPPER
PLACOID SKETCHER
(— MARK) CUSP
(FEMALE —) MAID
(PREF.) BATO
SKATER PATTENER SKETCHER
SKEDADDLE LAM RUN BUNK FLEE
SCAT SCOOT
SKEET FLEE KELTER KILTER PELTER
SKEIN RAP HANK HASP SCAN
BOTTOM SLEAVE SELVAGE
SKEINER RANDER SLIPPER
SKELETIN SPONGIN
SKELETON CUP CAGE MORT RAME
ATOMY BONES FRAME LOOFAH
SICULA SKELET ANATOMY
CARCASS RAWBONE ARMATURE
CORALLUM MANDIBLE OSSATURE
(— OF DRAMATIC WORK) SCENARIO
SKELETON KEY GILT SCREW
TWIRLER
SKELP SCUD
SKEPTIC DOUBTER INFIDEL ZETETIC
APIKOROS APORETIC
SKEPTICAL ACADEMIC APORETIC
DOUBTFUL
SKEPTICALLY ASKANCE
SKEPTICISM HUMISM UNBELIEF
SKETCH BIT DASH DRAW LIMN
PLAN VIEW VITA DRAFT ENTER
PAINT TRACE APERCU DESIGN
DOODLE SCHEME SPLASH
BOZZETO CROQUIS DRAUGHT
DRAWING EBAUCHE ETCHING
OUTLINE SCHIZZO ESQUISSE
MONOGRAM PROFIELE PROSPECT
REMARQUE VIGNETTE
(— BEFOREHAND) INDICATE
(AUTOBIOGRAPHICAL —) VITA
(BIOGRAPHICAL —) ELOGY
ELOGIUM
(FIRST —) ESQUISSE
(HERALDIC —) TRICK
(OUTDOORS —) LANDSKIP
(PRELIMINARY —) DRAFT ABBOZZO
MAQUETTE
(ROUGH —) NOTE CROQUIS
POCHADE ESQUISSE
(SATIRICAL —) SKIT
(THUMBNAIL —) BIO
SKEW ASKEW GAUCHE
SKEWBACK SPRINGER
SKEWBALD PINTO PIEBALD

SKEWED ALOP
SKEWER PIN PROD PROG SPIT STAB
PRICK SPEAR TRUSS SKIVER
TASTER BROCHETTE
SKEWERER TUBER
SKI SKEE SNOWSHOE
(— DOWN AT HIGH SPEED) SCHUSS
(DOWNHILL) WEDEL
(— DOWN SLOPE) SCHUSS
(— METHOD) PASSGANG
(— MOVEMENT) RUADE
(— POSITION) VORLAGE
(— RACE) SLALOM
(— RACING) LANGLAUF
(— SITE) VAIL
(— STYLE) WEDELN
(— TURN) TELEMARK
(— WITH ROLLERS) TURFSKI
(CROSS-COUNTRY RACING ON —S)
LANGLAUF
(ONE WHO —S) SCHUSSBOOMER
(ONE WHO —S DOWNHILL)
SCHUSSBOOMER
(PART OF —) TIP EDGE TAIL SHOVEL
BINDING
(RELATING TO — EVENTS) NORDIC
(TYPE OF —) SNOWBOARD
(PL.) BOARDS
SKID DOG DRAG SLEW SLUE TRIG
DRIFT DRILL SLOUGH SKIDPAN
SLIPPER TRIGGER FISHTAIL
SIDESLIP
(— LOGS) SNAKE TWICH TRAVOY
TWITCH
(— ON RAIL) SKATE
(AUTOMOBILE —) SPINOUT
(FENDER —) GLANCER
(IRON —) SABOT
(ROTATIONAL —) SPINOUT
SKIDDER SNAKER
SKIDI LOUP
SKIDWAY PIT
SKIER KANONE SNOWBIRD
LANGLAUFER SCHUSSBOOMER
(— POSITION) VORLAGE
SKIFF CANOE SHELL SKIFT CAIQUE
DINGHY SAMPAN CURRANE
SKIPPET JOHNBOAT
SKIING TOURING LANGLAUF
(— TURN) TELEMARK
(CROSS-COUNTRY —) LANGLAUF
(DOWNHILL —) WEDELN
(STYLE OF —) WEDELN
SKIL BESHOW SKILFISH
SKILL ART CAN WIT FEAT FEEL
HAND PATE TACT CRAFT DRAFT
HAUNT KNACK TRICK ENGINE
TECHNE ABILITY ADDRESS
APTNESS CUNNING FINESSE
MASTERY MYSTERY PROWESS
SCIENCE SLEIGHT ARTIFICE
CAPACITY CHIVALRY DEFTNESS
FACILITY INDUSTRY LEARNING
(— IN COMMUNICATION) ORACY
(DIPLOMATIC —) TACT
(INTELLECTUAL —) INTELLIGENCE
(LACK OF —) INERTIA
(NAVIGATION —) SEACRAFT
(PREF.) TECHNI TECHNO
(SUFF.) ICS SHIP TECHNIC TECHNY
SKILLED OLD SEEN WISE ADEPT
ASTUTE MASTER PERITE SCIENT

SKILLY VERSED HOTSHOT PRACTIC EDUCATED SKILLFUL
SKILLET PRIG SPIDER
SKILLFUL APT SLY ABLE DEFT FEAT FILE FINE GOOD HEND PERT TIDY WISE ADEPT CANNY FITTY HANDY HENDE READY SLICK SWEET ADROIT ARTFUL CLEVER CRAFTY DAEDAL EXPERT HABILE SCIENT SKILLY SOLERT SUBTLE CUNNING POLITIC SKILLED DEXTROUS PRACTIVE SLEIGHTY TACTICAL PROFICIENT
SKILLFULLY DEFTLY YARELY CRAFTILY
SKILLFULNESS CRAFT
SKIM TOP RIFF SCUD SCUM SCUN SCUR SILE SKIP FLEET GRAZE SCALE SKIFF SKIRR SKIVE BROWSE RABBLE SAMPLE DESPUME SKITTER
(— ON WATER) SCHOON
SKIMMED FLAT FLET
SKIMMER FALK LARI SKEP SCOOP LINGEL SCUMMER CUTWATER
SKIMMINGS SCRUFF
SKIMP JIMP SLUR SCAMP SKINCH
SKIMPY JIMP CHARY SPARE MEAGER MEAGRE SCANTY STINGY
SKIN KIP KIT BACK BARK CASE CAST DERM FELL FLAY FLEA HIDE HILD KITT MORT PEAU PEEL PELT RIND BALAT BLYPE BRAWN FLOAT GENET SLUFF STRIP SWARD CORIUM PELTRY SWARTH UNCASE CUTICLE DOESKIN ENDERON KIDSKIN LEATHER PELLAGE SKIMMER BUCKSKIN DRUMHEAD LAMBSKIN PARADERM PELLICLE SEALSKIN TEGUMENT VITILIGO WOOLFELL
(— AROUND BIRD'S EYE) ORBIT
(— AROUND NAIL) PERIONYCHIUM
(— BETWEEN TOES) WEB
(— FOR BOOKBINDING) BASAN
(— FOR HOLDING WATER) KIRBEH
(— FOR WATER) KIRBEH
(— OF BACON) SWARD
(— OF BOARDS) CARPET
(— OF FRUIT) PEEL
(— OF GOOSE) APRON
(— OF INSECT) CAST
(— OF PLANT) CORTEX
(— OF POTATO) JACKET
(— OF POULTRY NECK) HELZEL
(— OF RABBIT) RACK CONEY
(— OF SEAL) SCULP
(— OF SHARK) SHAGREEN
(— OF THE HEAD) SCALP
(— OF WALNUT) ZEST
(— OF YOUNG CALF) SLINK DEACON
(— WITH WOOL REMAINING ON IT) WOOLFELL
(BARE —) BUFF
(BEAVER —) PLEW
(BOAR'S —) SHIELD
(CAST —) SPOIL SLOUGH EXUVIAE
(CHAFED OR SORE —) IRE
(CHAMOIS —) FURWA
(DEEP LAYER OF THE —) CUTIS
(DRIED —) PARFLECHE
(FAWN —) NEBRIS

(INNER PART OF THE —) DERMA
(LAMB — PREPARED LIKE FUR) BUDGE
(OUTER —) HUSK
(PENDULOUS FOLD OF —) DEWLAP
(ROUGHTANNED —) CRUST
(SHARK —) SHAGREEN
(SHEEP —) BASIL
(SQUIRREL —) VAIR
(SURFACE —) SCARFSKIN
(THICKENED —) BRAWN
(THIN —) FILM PELLICLE STRIFFEN
(TRUE —) ENDERON
(60 —S) TURN
(PREF.) CUT(I)(O) CUTANEO DERM(AT)(ATO)(O) DERO EPIDERM(O) SCYT(O)
(SUFF.) DERM(A)(ATOUS)(IA)(IS)(Y)
SKIN FLICK NUDIE
SKINFLINT SKIN FLINT MISER PIKER SCREW HUDDLE PELTER SCRAPER SCROOGE SKEEZIX TIGHTWAD CHEESEPARER
SKINK ADDA SCINCID SCORPION
(PREF.) SCINCI SCINCO
SKINNY BONY LEAN THIN SLINK
SKIOLD (FATHER OF —) ODIN
SKIP DAP HIP BALK BOUT FOOT JUMP LEAP SLIP TRIP BOUND CAPER DANCE ELIDE FRISK SALTO SCOON SCOPE SCOUP SKITE SMOKE VAULT GAMBOL GLANCE LAUNCH SPRING GUNBOAT SALTATE SKIPPER SKITTER TRIPPLE PORPOISE RICOCHET
(— SCHOOL) TIB
(MINING —) SLIPE
SKIPJACK FOP SKIP BONITO ALEWIFE SKIPPER
SKIPPER IHI SKIP LAODAH LOWDAH SERANG SHIPPER
SKIRMISH FRAY BRUSH CLASH MELEE SKIRM BICKER HASSLE TUSSLE PICKEER RUNNING FIREFIGHT
SKIRMISHER HUSSAR TIRALLEUR
SKIRMISHING SPARRING
SKIRT CUT HUG LAP BANK BASE COAT ENGI JUPE MIDI MINI SAYA TUBE TUTU COAST JUPON LABIE PAREU PASIN STRIP TREND TWIST BASQUE DIRNDL HOBBLE JUMPER KIRTLE PEPLUM SARONG TAMEIN QUARTER BASQUINE PULLBACK SKIRTING
(— STYLE) ALINE
(ARMOR —) TASSES LAMBOYS
(BALLET —) TUTU
(DIVIDED —) CULOTTE
(HOOP —) CRINOLINE
(HOOPED —) TUBTAIL
(LONG —) MAXI
(TARTAN —) KILT ARISAID
(PL.) DOCK DOCKEN
SKIRTING DADE SKIRT PLINTH
(PL.) BROKES
SKIT BLACKOUT
SKITTAGETAN HAIDA
SKITTISH SHY CORKY GOOSY WINDY FLISKY KITTLE SKEIGH SPOOKY FLIGHTY SCADDLE SKADDLE STARTLY BOGGLISH SKITTERY STARTFUL

SKITTLES BOWLS KAYLES KITTLES SQUAILS
SKIVE PARE
SKUA BONXIE JAEGER TEASER TULIAC SEAHAWK STINKPOT WHIPTAIL
SKULDUGGERY JOUKERY PAWKERY
SKULK DERN JOUK LURK LUSK MICHE MOOCH SCOUT SHOOL
SKULL OAR ROW BEAN POLL CRANY MOOCH SCALP SCAUP VAULT COBBRA MAZARD PALLET SCONCE CRANIUM HARNPAN HEADMOLD PANNICLE
(— BONE) VOMER
(— POINT) TYLION
(BACK OF —) OCCIPUT
(INCOMPLETE —) CALVARIA
(PART OF —) INION
(UPPER HALF OF —) SINCIPUT
(PREF.) CRANI(O)
(SUFF.) CRANIA(L)
SKULLCAP COIF PIXY PIXIE SKULL VAULT BEANIE COIFFE CALOTTE CAPELINE HOODWORT
(ARABIAN —) CHECHIA
(JEWISH —) YAMILKE YARMULKE
(STEEL —) SECRET
SKUNK ANNA ATOC ATOK PUSS HURON SKINK SNIPE ZORIL CHINCHA POLECAT SEECAWK SMELLER CONEPATE CONEPATL MUSTELID PHOBYCAT ZORRILLO
(CARTOON —) LEPEW
(JAVANESE —) TELEDU
SKUNK CABBAGE COLLARD POCKWEED
SKY BLUE HIGH LIFT LOFT POLE TIEN AZURE CARRY DYAUS ETHER LANGI VAULT CAELUS CANOPY HEAVEN REGION WELKIN ELEMENT HEAVENS OLYMPUS TENGERE WEATHER
(ICE —) ICEBLINK
(PREF.) CAELI CAELO COELI COELO URAN(I)(O) URANOSO
SKY-BLUE AZURE
(PREF.) CERULEO
SKYLARK LARK YERK
SLAB BAT CANT CLAM LECH PARE SLAT BLADE BOARD DALLE LINER PANEL PLANK SLATE STELA STELE TABLE WADGE ABACUS FLITCH MARVER MIHRAB PAVIOR RUNNER SHEAVE TABLET FLAPPET PLANCHE SHINGLE PORPHYRY PUNCHEON SLABWOOD
(— BESIDE SINK) BUNKER
(— BY SINK) BUNKER
(— INDICATING MECCA) MIHRAB
(— OF CLAY) BAT
(— OF COAL) SKIP SLIP
(— OF GLASS) PANE
(— OF ICE) SCONCE
(— OF LIMESTONE) BALATTE
(— OF MARBLE) DALLE
(— OF PEAT) SCAD
(— OF SANDSTONE) COMAL
(— OVER BROOK) CLAM
(ARCHITECTURAL —) METOPE
(BROKEN-OFF —) BLAUD
(FLOATING —) ICEPAN SCONCE

(GAME —) BOARD
(GRAVE —) LEDGER LEIDGER
(GRINDING —) MULLER
(HOPSCOTCH —) PEEVER
(MEMORIAL —) LEDGER
(PAINTER'S —) SLANT
(PLASTERER'S —) HAWK
(ROOFING —) SLATE
(SQUARE —) QUARRY
(STONE —) PLANK STELA STELE INKSTONE
SLACK DRY LAX OFF CULM DUFF LASH NESH SLOW SOFT VEER CHECK CRANK FLOWN LOOSE SLAKE TARDY ABATED FLARRY FLAPPY REMISS SUPINE UNGIRT BACKING MAKINGS RELAXED SLACKEN SMEDDUM CARELESS DILATORY INACTIVE SLOBBERY NEGLIGENT
(— IN TRIGGER) CREEP
(— OF ROPE) SLATCH
(— SHEET OF SAIL) FLOW
(— SUDDENLY) SURGE
(COAL —) COOM COOMB
(PL.) BAGS
SLACKEN LAG PAY EASE FLAG SLOW DELAY DOWSE LOOSE QUAIL RELAX REMIT SLACK SLAKE START SURGE ASLAKE EXOLVE RELENT UNBEND
(— SPEED) HANG
SLACKENING LETUP DETENTE LETDOWN SLACKAGE
SLACKER SPIV ROTTER COUCHER SLINKER EMBUSQUE
SLACKNESS LACHES LASHNESS
SLADE SOLE
SLAG SCAR DROSS CINDER DANDER SCORIA SLAKIN THOMAS QUITTER SLACKEN
SLAIN FALLEN
SLAKE ABATE SLACK LESSEN QUENCH REFRESH SATISFY
SLAKING FAT
SLAM CLAP DASH FLUB SLOG SLOT VOLE CLASH GRAND PLANK SLOSH STRAM CHELEM FLOUNCE
SLAMMER JAIL STIR PRISON
SLANDER CANT BELIE LIBEL NOISE SMEAR BEFOUL DEFAME INJURE MALIGN MISSAY VILIFY ASPERSE CALUMNY OBTRECT SCANDAL TRADUCE TRUMPET BACKBITE DEROGATE STRUMPET ASPERSION BESPATTER
SLANDERER JUROR BLAZONER
SLANDEROUS FAMOUS SCURRIL SCURRILE VILIPEND SCURRILOUS
SLANG CANT ARGOT FLASH JARGON DIALECT
(THIEVES' —) FLASH
SLANT TIP BIAS CANT FLUE SKEW TILT BEVEL DRAFT SLOPE SPLAY STOOP FLANCH SKLENT DRAUGHT COLORING DIAGONAL
(PREF.) CLIN(O)
SLANTED CANTED BEVELED COLORED COCKEYED
SLANTING AWRY BIAS CANT SKEW BEVEL SLOPE ASLANT ASLOPE SKLENT SQUINT LOXOTIC OBLIQUE

SLANTING SLOPING AVELONGE COLORING OVERWART SIDELONG
SLANTINGLY AHOO ASWASH SLANTLY
SLANT LINE VIRGULA VIRGULE
SLANTWISE (PREF.) LECHRI(O)
SLAP BOX DAB DAFF DLIP DLOW CLAP CUFF FLAP LICK PLAT SCUD SLAT SNUB SPAT TACK BLIBE CLINK CLOUT CRACK PANDY POTCH SKEEG SKELP SKITE SMACK SPANK TWANG TWANK BLEEZE BUFFET SCLAFF SLIGHT STRIKE TINGLER WHERRET BACKSLAP
(— **HARD**) BLAD
(**RANDOM** —) FLAY
SLAPDASH BUCKEYE
SLASH CAG CUT JAG COUP GASH HASH PANE RACE RASH SLIT TOPS KNIFE MINCE SCORE SKICE SLISH RAMMEL SCORCH STREAK SLITTER DIAGONAL SLASHING
SLASHED JAGGED DECOPED TATTERED
SLASHING ABATIS
SLAT BOW LAG FLAT PALE SLOT WAND BLADE SCLAT SLOAT STAVE RIFFLE SPLINE EUPHROE BEDSTAFF
(— **IN SLUICE**) RIFFLE
SLATE RAG SLAT FRAME KILLAS TABLET TICKET SHALDER SHINDLE SLATING
(— **IN SMALL IRREGULAR PIECES**) SCANTLE
(— **OF COURT CASES**) DOCKET
(**BLUE** —) SHIVER SKAILLIE
(**CLAY** —) KILLAS
(**EXPOSED PART OF ROOFING** —) BARI
(**SIZE OF** —) PEGGY QUEEN DUCHESS COUNTESS IMPERIAL PRINCESS MARCHIONESS
(**SURFACE** —) BONE
SLATER HELER HELLIER SLATTER SKIMMITY
(**TOOL OF** —) STAKE
SLATTERN DAB DAW MAB FROW MAUX SLUT TRUB DOLLY FAGOT MAWKS MOGGY MOPSY BLOUSE CLATCH DOLLOP MALKIN SLOVEN STREEL TRAPES LADRONE TROLLOP HUCKMUCK SLUMMOCK
SLATTERNLY DOWDY BLOWSY DAWISH FROWZY SORDID BLOWZED TRAPISH SLATTERN SLOVENLY
SLAUGHTER WAL FELL KILL SLAM SLAY BUTCH HALAL QUELL BATTUE MURDER STRAGE BUTCHER CARNAGE KILLING SCUPPER SHAMBLE BUTCHERY MASSACRE OCCISION SHECHITA HOLOCAUST
(— **ACCORDING TO MOSLEM LAW**) HALAL
(— **OF LARGE NUMBER**) HECATOMB
(**WHOLESALE** —) QUELL
SLAUGHTERER KILLER SHOHET KNACKER SHOCHET
(**HORSE** —) KNACKER

SLAUGHTERHOUSE ABATTOIR BUTCHERY MATADERO SHAMBLES
(— **WORKER**) LIMEMAN
SLAUGHTERING SHEHITA SHECHITA
SLAV VEND WEND CZECH HUNKS HUNKY SLAVE USKOK CROATIAN MORAVIAN POLABIAN
SLAVE BOY DAS ARDU BOND DASI DUPE ESNE MOIL SERF DAVUS HELOT SWINK THEOW ABJECT ALIPIN ALLTUD CUMHAL FORSAR GUINEA HIEROS MAMLUK SLAVEY THRALL VASSAL BONDMAN CAPTIVE CHATTEL FORSADO HACKNEY PEDAGOG SERVANT SLAVISH BONDMAID LORARIUS MAMELUKE MANCIPLE MORGIANA PRAEDIAL SLAVELET THEOWMAN ODALISQUE
(— **IN TEMPLE**) HIEROS
(— **OWNER**) PATRON
(— **WHO WHIPS OTHERS**) LORARIUS
(**DEFORMED** —) CALIBAN
(**FREED** —) CLIENT
(**FUGITIVE** —) MAROON CIMMARON
(**GALLEY** —) FORSAR FORSADO SFORZATO
(**HAREM** —) ODA ODAH ODALISK ODALESQUE
(**HINDU** —) DAS DASI
(**REFUGEE** —) CONTRABAND
(**SLAVE'S** —) GIBEONITE
(**TEMPLE** —) HIERODULE
(**PL.**) CHIURM COFFLE HELOTRY TOXOTAE
SLAVEDRIVER RUSHER
SLAVER DROOL FROTH DRIVEL DRIBBLE SLABBER SLOBBER SALIVATE
SLAVERY YOKE THRALL BONDAGE HELOTRY MIZRAIM THRALDOM SERVITUDE
SLAVEY DRUDGE
SLAVISH MEAN MENIAL
SLAVONIC (— **BEING**) VILA
SLAY DOIN KILL SMITE SPILL MURDER STRIKE BUTCHER EXECUTE STRANGLE SLAUGHTER
SLAYER BANE HOGNI KILLER MURDERER
(— **OF INFIDELS**) GHAZI
(**SUFF.**) CTONUS
SLEAZY FLIMSY TICKYTACKY
SLED LUGE PUNG TODE JUMBO SCOOT SLIDE SLIPE SLOOP HURDLE JUMPER SLEDGE SLEIGH BOBSLED CLIPPER COASTER DOGBOAT DOGSLED KOMATIK MONOSKI POINTER SLIPPER TRAILER TRAVOIS HANDSLED SKELETON TOBOGGAN
(— **RIDER**) BOBBER
SLEDGE DAN DRAG DRAY LUGE PULK SLED GURRY PULKA SLIDE SLIPE TRAIL TRAIN TROLL TRUNK SLEIGH KIBITKA KOMATIK PADDOCK TROLLEY TRAINEAU
(— **FOR CRIMINALS**) HURDLE
(— **FOR STRAIGHTENING RAILS**) GAG
(**LOG** —) SLOOP TIEBOY
(**MINER'S** —) MALLET

SLEDGEHAMMER SMASHER
SLEEK SNOD SOFT CLOSE JOLLY SILKY SLICK TRICK SILKEN SLEEKY SLIGHT SMARMY SMOOTH SVELTE SLEEKIT SOIGNEE SLIPPERY
SLEEKNESS GLOSS
SLEEP BED KIP LIB LIE NAP CALK CAMP DORM DOSS DOZE HALE REST WINK BALMY CRASH DORSE ROOST SWOON DROWSE SIESTA SNOOZE SOMNUS SWEVEN SHUTEYE SLUMBER WINKING
(— **BROKEN BY SNORING**) GRUFF
(— **ON A PERCH**) JOUK
(— **PROBLEM**) APNEA
(**DEEP** —) SOPOR SWOON STUPOR
(**KIND OF** —) REM
(**LIGHT** —) SLOOM
(**PRETENDED** —) DOGSLEEP
(**PROFOUND** —) SOPOR
(**SHORT** —) NAP SIESTA SNOOZE
(**PREF.**) HYPN(O) SOMNI SOPOR
(**DEEP** —) NARC(O)
SLEEPER TIE MOLE FENDER DORMANT CROSSTIE DORMEUSE ELEOTRID STRINGER
SLEEPINESS SOPITION
SLEEPING BED ASLEEP DORMANT DORMIENT
(— **IN HOLY PLACE**) INCUBATION
(— **TABLET**) DALMANE
SLEEPING CAR PULLMAN
SLEEPLESS LIDLESS WAKEFUL RESTLESS WATCHFUL
SLEEPLESSNESS WATCH INSOMNIA
SLEEPY DOZY HEAVY NODDY PEEPY DROWSY GROGGY MORPHIC SLEEPISH SLUMBERY SOMNIFIC SLUMBEROUS
(— **ONE**) NODDER
SLEET STORM
SLEEVE ARM BAND POKE ARMLET MANCHE MOGGAN BUSHING CATHEAD CUBITAL HOUSING THIMBLE
(— **ON A SHAFT**) CANNON
(— **ON GUN**) BAND
(**CANVAS** —) DROGUE
(**HANGING** —) TAB
(**LEG-OF-MUTTON** —) GIGOT
(**LONG** —) POKE
(**ROOMY** —) RAGLAN
(**TAPERED** —) SKEIN
SLEIGH SLO PUNG SLED BOOBY SLIPE TRAIN BERLIN CUTTER SLEDGE CARIOLE TRAINEAU
(**MOTORIZED** —) SNOWMOBILE
SLEIGHT ARTIFICE
SLEIPNER (**OWNER OF** —) ODIN
SLENDER FINE HAIR JIMP LANK LEAN PRIN SLIM THIN DELIE EXILE FAINT LATHY REEDY SLANK SLEEK SMALL SPIRY SWAMP WISPY FILATE SCANTY SEMMIT SLIGHT SPINNY SPIRED STALKY SVELTE TENDER GRACILE LISSOME SLIVERY SPIRLIE SQUINNY TENUOUS THREADY WASPISH ACICULAR ETHEREAL HAIRLIKE PILIFORM SPINDLED ATTENUATE
SLENDERNESS EXILITY TENUITY
SLEUTH TEC DETECTIVE

SLEW LOT ALOT RAFT SLUE STROKE
SLICE CUT BITE CHIP CHOP FLAG FLAP JERK SHED STOW CANCH CAPER GIGOT LEACH SHARE SHAVE SHIVE SKELB SLIPE SLIVE CANTLE COLLOP CORNET CULPON SHIVER SLIVER TARGET THIBLE TRENCH SECTION SHAVING TRANCHE COSSETTE TURNOVER
(— **CUT IN PLOWING**) FLAG
(— **OF BACON**) BARD BARDE LARDON RASHER
(— **OF BREAD**) BUTTY WHANG CROUTE TRENCHER
(— **OF CHEESE**) KEBBOC
(— **OF COAL**) SKIP
(— **OF FISH**) COBBIN
(— **OF MEAT**) STEAK COLLOP CUTLET SCALLOP TAILZIE
(— **OF MEAT OR FISH**) PAUPIETTE
(— **OF SMOKED SALMON**) CORNET
(— **OF TOAST**) ROUND
(— **OF VEAL**) FRICANDEAU
(— **REMOVED FROM ROADWAY**) CANCH
(—**S OF APPLES**) CHOPS
(—**S OF VEAL**) GRENADINE SCALLOPINI
(— **WITH MOTIONS**) SAW
(**LARGE** —) BLAD DODGE
(**POTATO** —) SCALLOP
(**ROLLED** — **OF MEAT**) ROULADE
(**THICK** —) SLAB WHANG
(**THIN** —) CHIP WAFER SECTION
(**THIN** —**S OF MEAT**) PICCATA
SLICED CUT
SLICK LOY MAG GLIB OILY SNUG SLEEK CLASSY GLOSSY SMOOTHY SLIDDERY
SLICKER FLOAT SLICK SMOOTH SLEEKER SMOOTHER
SLIDE SCLY SKID SLEW SLIP SLUR BALOP CHUTE COAST COULE CREEP GLIDE HURRY MOUNT SCOOT SHIRL SLADE FINDER SLOUGH SLIDDER SLITHER SLUTHER FADEAWAY GLISSADE SLIDEWAY TOBOGGAN SCHLEIFER
(— **A DIE**) SLUR
(— **ALONG**) SHOOT
(— **BACK**) RELAPSE
(— **CARDS**) SKIN
(— **DOWN**) RUSE SLUMP
(— **FOR LOWERING CASKS**) POLEYNE
(— **ON DRUMHEAD**) BRACE
(— **SIDEWISE**) SKID SLUE
(**TENT** —) EUPHROE
SLIDER REGISTER
SLIDEWAY PULLEY
SLIDING COULE
SLIGHT CUT OFF EASY FINE HURT POOR PUNY SLAP SLIM SLUR SNUB THIN WEAK FILMY GAUZY LIGHT MINOR SCANT SMALL SOBER FLIMSY FORGET LACHES LITTLE MINUTE REMOTE TWIGGY CONTEMN FRAGILE GRACILE NEGLECT NOMINAL SHALLOW SKETCHY SLENDER SLIGHTY THREADY VILLAIN DELICATE MISPRIZE OVERLOOK SCRANNEL VILIPEND

SLIGHTER LESS
SLIGHTEST FIRST LEAST
SLIGHTINGLY LIGHTLY
SLIGHTLY FAINTLY SOMEWHAT
  (PREF.) MI(O)
  (SUFF.) ESCENT ULOUS
SLIGHTNESS DELICACY GRACILITY
SLIM THIN GAUNT WANDY SLIGHT
  SLENDER TENUOUS
SLIME GLIT GORE OOZE SLAB SLIP
  SLUM GLEET SLAKE SLOAK SLOKE
  SLEECH SLUDGE SCHLICH
  SLUBBER SLUTHER
  (PREF.) MUC(I)(O) MUCOSO MYX(O)
  (SUFF.) MYXA
SLIMMER DIETER
SLIMY EELY OOZY SLAB MUCID
  GLAIRY GLEETY GLETTY LIMOUS
  MUCOUS SNOTTY SLEECHY
  MUCULENT
SLINE JOINT
SLING DUST LOOP FLING HONDA
  SLUNG BRIDGE BRIDLE HALTER
  SLACKIE
  (— FOR HAULING GAME) TUMPLINE
  (— OF BRAIDED FIBERS) MA
  (PREF.) FUNDI
SLINGER FUNDITOR
SLINGSHOT SLING SLAPPY
  TWEAKER CATAPULT SHANGHAI
SLINK SLY CAST HINT LEER LOOP
  LURK PEAK MICHE SHIRK SLING
  SLUNK SNEAK SLINKY
  (— AWAY) SHAG SLOKE FLINCH
  MIZZLE SHRINK
SLIP DIP IMP NOD SLY BALK CARD
  CHIT DOCK FALL JINK LOOP RUSE
  SKEW SKID SLEW SLUR SPEW
  BEWET BEWIT BONER CHECK
  DOGGE ERROR FLIER FLYER GLIDE
  LABEL LAPSE SCAPE SCION SHIFT
  SHIRL SKATE SKITE SLICK SLIDE
  SLIPE SLIVE SLUMP STALK SURGE
  COUPON ENGOBE LAPSUS MISCUE
  SLOUGH SLURRY TICKET UNSLIP
  DELAPSE FOUNDER ILLAPSE
  MISSTEP MORTISE SLIDDER
  SLUTHER SNAPPER STUMBLE
  BOOKMARK GERTRUDE GLISSADE
  HEADBAND QUICKSET SCHEDULE
  SIDESLIP SLIPPAGE SLIPPING
  (— AWAY) GO BILK SKIN WISE
  EVADE ELAPSE
  (— BY) ELAPSE
  (— FROM A PLANT) STALLON
  (— OFF COURSE) SLEW SLOUGH
  (— OF FISH) RAND
  (— OF PAPER) ALLONGE
  (— OF PARCHMENT) PANEL
  (— OF WOOD) SPILL REGLET
  (— ON CARELESSLY) SLIVE
  (— OUT) TIB
  (— SECRETLY) CREEM
  (— SMOOTHLY) SWIM
  (— UP) BLUNDER
  (CERAMICS —) SLOP ENGOBE
  (INFANT'S —) GERTRUDE
  (KIND OF —) FREUDIAN
  (PILLOW —) BIER
  (PREF.) CLAD(O)
  (SUFF.) CLADOUS
SLIPCASE CASE FOREL FORREL

SLIPKNOT BOW SNITTLE
  DRAWKNOT
SLIPMAN JACKER
SLIPOVER OVERSLIP
SLIPPER FLAT MULE NEAP PUMP
  SOCK TURN GLAVE MOYLE ROMEO
  SCUFF BALLET BOOTEE DORSAY
  JULIET PANTON PINSON SANDAL
  SCLAFF SCLIFF BAUCHLE CHINELA
  CRAKOWE EVERETT SCUFFER
  BABOUCHE FEWTERER PANTOFLE
  SCLAFFER SLIPSHOE
  (PREF.) CALCEI
SLIPPERINESS SLIDDER
SLIPPERY EELY GLEG GLIB SLID
  GLARY GLINT SLAPE SLEEK SLICK
  SOAPY SWACK CRAFTY GLINSE
  GREASY LUBRIC SHIFTY SLIPPY
  ELUSIVE EVASIVE GLIDDER
  SHUTTLE SLIDDRY SLIDING
  SLITHER GLIBBERY SLABBERY
  SLICKERY SLIDDERY SLITHERY
  (PREF.) LUBRI
SLIPPERY DICK DONCELLA
SLIPSHOD JERRY RAGGED SLOPPY
  UNKEMPT SLAPDASH SLOVENLY
SLIPSTREAM RACE
SLIPUP FLUFF MISTAKE
SLIT CUT EYE JAG KIN NAG RIT FENT
  GATE NICK PORT RACE RENT SCAR
  SLOT VENT CRACK SPARE BOUCHE
  CRANNY OSTIUM STRENT FISSURE
  PERTUSE PLACKET SLITTED
  SLOTTEN WINDWAY APERTURE
  BOTHRIUM
  (— HIND LEG) HARL
  (— IN EDGE OF SHIELD) BOUCHE
  (— IN ORGAN PIPE) MOUTH
  (— IN SKIRT) SPARE
  (— IN STONE) GRIKE
  (— IN THE THEAD) SIPE
  (— IN WALL) LOOP
  (— MADE BY CUT) KERF
  (ORNAMENTAL —) SLASH
SLITHER SLIDE HIRSEL SLIDDER
  SLUTHER
SLIVER TOP SHAVE SKELF SLICE
  SPELK SPELL SHIVER DELIVERY
  SPLINTER
  (— OF WOOL) ROLL ROVE
  (SPINNING —) END RIBBON
  DELIVERY
SLOB JOKER SLUDGE SLOBBER
  SLOMMACK LITTERBUG
SLOBBER SLOP SLUP SMALM
  SMARM SLAVER SLABBER
  SLATHER SLIVVER BESLAVER
SLOBBERY SLOBBY SMARMY
  SLAVERY
SLOE SLA SNAG SLONE
SLOG PLOD SLOSH STRIKE
SLOGAN CRY CACHET CUTTER
  PHRASE CATCHCRY GRAFFITO
  SLUGHORN WARDWORD
  CATCHWORD SHIBBOLETH
SLOOP STAR BOYER COMET SMACK
  SCHUIT HOOGAARS
SLOP SLAP SOSS SQUAB SWILL
  SOSSLE SOZZLE HOGWASH
  SLATTER
  (— AROUND) SLAISTER
  (PL.) SLIVERS SLIPSLOP SLOPPAGE
SLOPE UP DIP LIE BAND BANK BENT

BRAE CANT CAST CURB DROP FALL
HANG HILL LEAN PALI RAKE RAMP
RISE SIDE SINK TILT BEVEL CLIFF
COAST GAMMA HIELD PINCH
PITCH SCARP SLANT SLENT SLOOP
SPLAY STEEP TALUS VERGE YUNGA
ASCENT BAJADA BATTER BREAST
BROACH ESCARP GLACIS HADING
SHELVE TUMBLE UPBROW UPRISE
CUTBANK DESCENT DOWNSET
FORESET HANDING INCLINE
LEANING PENDANT UPGRADE
VERSANT WEATHER BANKSIDE
DRIPPING GLISSADE GRADIENT
SHOULDER SIDELING SNOWBANK
ACCLIVITY ESCARPMENT
  (— BACK) BATTER
  (— DOWN) SHED
  (— OF CUESTA) INFACE
  (— OF ROOF) CURB
  (— OF STERNPOST) RAKE
  (— ON GOLF GREEN) BURROW
  (— UPWARD) CLIMB ASCEND
  BATTER
  (DOWNWARD —) HANG DEVALL
  DECLINE DESCENT HANGING
  DOWNHILL
  (GENTLE —) GLACIS
  (MARGINAL —) CESS
  (MOUNTAIN —) ADRET
  (SKIING —) SCHUSS
  (STEEP —) BROW HEADWALL
  (TOBOGGANING —) ICEHILL
  (SUFF.) CLINAL CLINE
SLOPING CANT DEVEX SLANT
  SLOPE SLOPY ASLOPE SHELVY
  DECLIVE SCARPED DOWNHILL
  SIDELING
  (— ABRUPTLY) BOLD
  (— BACKWARD) SUPINE
  (STEEPLY —) RAPID
  (SUFF.) CLINAL
SLOPPINESS BLURB
SLOPPY JUICY MESSY SOPPY
  SLABBY SOZZLY SPLOSHY
  SLABBERY SLAPDASH SLATTERN
  SLATTERY SLIPSHOD WATERISH
SLOSH DOWSE SLASH SLUSH
  SOUSE SQUDGE SPLODGE
SLOT COVE DROP SCROLL SPLINE
  KEYHOLE GUIDEWAY
SLOTH AI UNAU TARDO ACEDIA
  IGNAVY ACCIDIE IGNAVIA
  BRADYPOD EDENTATE PIGRITIA
  SLUGGING
SLOTH BEAR BHALU ASWAIL
SLOTHFUL FAT ARGH IDLE LAZY
  INERT LITHER THOKISH UNLUSTY
  DELICATE INDOLENT SLUGGISH
SLOUCH LOUCH LARRUP LOLLOP
  LOUNGE SLIDDER TROLLOP
  SHAMMOCK SLOUCHER
SLOUCH HAT SMASHER
SLOUGH CORE SHED SLEW SLUE
  BAYOU RAVEL SHUCK SLONK
  SLUFF SPOIL SWAMP ESCHAR
  DISCARD LAMMOCK

SLOVEN BESOM CLART SLUSH
  TROLLY GROBIAN HALLION
  TRACHLE HUDDROUN

SLOVENLY DOWDY GAUMY MESSY
  BLOWZY CLATTY FROWZY GRUBBY
  SHABBY SLOPPY SLOVEN TRAILY
  UNTIDY BUNTING RAUNCHY
  SLIVING SLOUCHY UNSONCY
  CARELESS HUDDROUN SLIPSHOD
  SLOBBERY SLUBBERY SLUTTISH
  TROLLOPY
SLOW BOG LAG LAX LEK WET ARGH
  DREE DULL LASH LATE LAZY LENT
  SKID SLUG SOFT SULK BLUNT
  DUNCH DUNNY HEAVY HOOLY
  INERT POKEY SLACK SLOTH
  SWEER TARDE TARDO TARDY
  UNAPT ARREST BEHIND DRIECH
  DUMMEL HINDER RETARD
  SLOOMY SOODLY TRAILY COSTIVE
  DRONISH HALTING LAGGARD
  LANGUID SLACKEN SOAKING
  STRANGE TARDANT TEDIOUS
  UNREADY DILATORY INACTIVE
  LATESOME SLUGGISH
  (— DOWN) SEIZE
  (— DOWN SPACECRAFT) DEBOOST
  (— IN BURNING) SOFT
  (— IN MOVEMENT) GRAVE INERT
  SULKY
  (— OF LEARNING) DULL
  (— OF MIND) STUPID
  (— TO LEARN) BACKWARD
  (— TO RESPOND) GROSS

(— UP) SLACK SLACKEN
(MODERATELY —) ANDANTE
(MUSICALLY —) LENTO
(PLEASANTLY —) SOFT
(VERY —) LARGO
(PREF.) BRADY TARDI
SLOW-BURNING PUNKY
SLOWED STIFF
SLOWER LATTER CALANDO
SLOWING RELENT LENTANDO
RITARDANDO RALLENTANDO
(SUFF.) STASIA STASIS
SLOW LORIS KOKAN
SLOWLY SLOW DULLY GRAVE
HOOLY LENTO ADAGIO GENTLY
HEAVILY
SLOW-MOVING SLEEPY DORMANT
DRAWLING SLUGGISH
SLOWNESS LAG SLOTH LENTOR
TARDITY LATENESS
SLOWPOKE SNAIL TURTLE
ALSORAN DAWDLER
SLOW-WITTED FAT DENSE STUPID
SLOWWORM HAGWORM
SLUDGE GUNK OOZE SLOB
SLUE SLEW PIVOT SWAMP SLOUGH
SLUG BUST LINE MILL PLOW SHOT
SNAG STEW ARION CLUMP LIMAX
SNAIL RATTLE STRIKE SNIFTER
TREPANG GEEPOUND
(PREF.) LIMACI
SLUGGARD DAW SLOW SLUG
DRONE BUZZARD CAYNARD
LUGGARD SWINGER SLOWBACK
SLUGABED
SLUGGISH LAG DOZY DULL FOUL
LATE LAZY LOGY SLOW SOFT
BROSY DOPEY DRONY FAINT
HEAVY INERT LEADY LOURD RESTY
SULKY BOVINE DRAGGY DROWSY
JACENT LEADEN SLEEPY SLOOMY
SLUGGY SUPINE TORPID COSTIVE
DORMANT DRONISH LAGGARD
LANGUID LENTOUS LUMPISH
RESTIVE DILATORY INACTIVE
INDOLENT LOURDISH SLOTHFUL
SLOTTERY SLUGGARD
(PREF.) BRADY
SLUGGISHNESS LEAD SLOTH
APATHY LENTOR PHLEGM INERTIA
LANGUOR
SLUICE CLOW GOOL GOTE GOUT
SASSE SLUSH TRUNK CLOUGH
FENDER LAUNDER PENSTOCK
WASTWEIR
SLUICEGATE ABOIDEAU
SLUICEWAY FLASH
SLUM BUSTI BUSTEE WARREN
SLUMBER DORM DOVE DOZE JOUK
REST ROUT SLEEP SLOOM
DROWSE
SLUMP FALL FLOP SOSS SLOUCH
LETDOWN TROLLOP
SLUR BIND SLIM COULE GLIDE
SLIME SCRUFF SLIGHT SLUBBER
LIGATURE
(— IN PRINTING) SHAKE
SLURRY SLIP
SLUSH MIRE POSH SIND SLOP
FLUSH SLOSH SPOSH STUFF
SWASH SWOSH LOPPER SLUDGE
SLUTCH SLOBBER SLODDER
SLUSHY SLASHY SLOPPY SLOSHY

SLUDGY STICKY SPLASHY
SLOBBERY
SLUT MAUX BITCH FILTH QUEAN
DOLLOP DRAZEL DRAZIL MALKIN
DROSSEL PUCELLE SLAMKIN
SLATTERN
SLUTTISH DRABBY SLUTTY SORDID
SLY ARCH CUTE FOXY SLEE SLID
SLIM CANNY COONY LEERY LOOPY
PAWKY PEERY POKEY SLOAN
SNAKY ARTFUL ASTUTE CRAFTY
FELINE SUBTLE SUPPLE CUNNING
EVASIVE FOXLIKE FURTIVE
LEERING POLITIC SUBTILE
UNFRANK GUILEFUL SLEIGHTY
SNEAKING STEALTHY THIEVISH
CLANDESTINE
SLYNESS CUNNING PAWKERY
STEALTH ARCHNESS
SMACK BANG BARK BIFF BUSS KISS
SALT SCAT SLAP TANG TROW VEIN
WHAM BAWLY GOUFF SAVOR
SNACK SPANG SPICE TASTE
TWANG BARQUE BAWLEY FLAVOR
SMATCH SMACKEE SPANKER
BRAGOZZO SLAPDASH TINCTURE
(— OF) RELISH
SMACKING SKELPING
SMALL BIT SMA WEE BABY MEAN
PINK SEED SLIM TINY WEAK BIJOU
BITTY DAWNY DEENY DINKY ELFIN
PETIT PETTY PINKY POKEY RUNTY
TEENY WEENY BANTAM FRIBBY
GRUBBY INSECT LITTLE MIDGET
MINUTE NARROW PEANUT PETITE
SCANTY SLIGHT SMALLY CAPSULE
MINIMAL NAGGISH NANITIC
NOMINAL PICCOLO QUEECHY
SCRIMPY SLENDER THRIFTY
PEDDLING PILULOUS SNIPPETY
MINIATURE MINISCULE
(— AND NUMEROUS) MILIARY
(— AND THICK) DUMPY DUMPTY
(— BUT TANGIBLE) CERTAIN
(— PORTION) MODICUM
(CONTEMPTIBLY —) MEASLY
(DAINTILY —) MIGNON
(EXCESSIVELY —) BOXY
(NOT —) GOOD
(VERY —) WEE FINE TINY DWARF
MICRO PUSIL PYGMY TEENY
MINUTE MINIKIN TIDDLEY
DWARFISH
(PREF.) LEPT(O) MICR(O) OLIG(O)
PARV(I) PAURO TAPIN(O)
(SUFF.) (— ONE) EL ET IUM LING
OCK ULA ULE ULUM ULUS
SMALLAGE MARCH
SMALLCLOTHES SHORTS SMALLS
SMALL CRANBERRY FENBERRY
SMALLER LESS MINOR LESSER
(PREF.) MEIO MI(O) MINI
SMALLEST FIRST LEAST MINIM
TITMAN MINIMUS
SMALLHOLDER TOFTMAN
SMALL-MINDED PETTY PICAYUNE
SMALLNESS NANISM EXILITY
FEWNESS PAUCITY EXIGUITY
SCARCITY
SMALLPOX POX VARIOLA
ALASTRIM
(PREF.) VARIOLI VARIOLO
SMALL-SCALE MINI

SMALL-TIME PETTY TWOBIT
RINKYDINK INSIGNIFICANT
SMALT ROYAL ESCHEL SMALTZ
ZAFFER ASMALTE
SMART NIP YEP BRAW FESS FLIP
FOXY GNIB NICE PINK POSH RACY
SNAP SPRY SWAG TRIG ACUTE
BRISK CL FAN DINKY FLASH HEADY
JIMMY KIPPY NIFTY NOBBY NUTTY
PEERT PRANK PRIDY RITZY SASSY
SAUCY SHARP SLEEK SLICK SMIRK
SMOKE SMUSH SPICY SPRIG STING
SWANK SWISH TIGHT TIPPY TOFFY
TRICK AKAMAI BRAWLY BRIGHT
CHEESY CLEVER DAPPER GIGOLO
JAUNTY KITTLE PERTLY SHREWD
SPANKY SPIFFY SPRINK SPRUCE
STOUND SWANKY SWIDGE TIDDLY
KNOWING PUNGENT SWAGGER
TOFFISH VOGUISH BRUSHING
SPIFFING
(— IN APPEARANCE) POSH
(— IN DRESS) CHIC CLASSY DRESSY
GALLANT
(AFFECTEDLY —) SMUG
(IMPOSINGLY —) STYLISH
SMART ALECK FLIP SMARTY
WISEASS WISEGUY WISEACRE
WISENHEIMER
SMART-ALECKY CUTE
SMARTEN FINE PUSS SMUG
GROOM PRINK SLICK TITIVATE
SMARTLY SMACK SMART SNACK
YEPLY TIDELY
SMARTNESS TON SNAP SMART
SPIFF SWISH
SMARTWEED CULERAGE
REDKNEES
SMASH GIT BASH BUMP CAVE DASH
PASH RUSH SCAT TRAP BREAK
CRACK CRASH CRAZE PRANG
SOCKO STAVE TRASH WRECK
BANJAX CRACKER SHATTER
SMASHUP DEBRUISE DEMOLISH
OVERHEAD STRAMASH
(— A GAP) BREACH
SMASHED BUNG KAPUT STOVEN
BROOZLED
SMASHING CRACKING
SMASHUP STRAMASH
SMATTERING TANG SMACK
SMATCH SMATTER
SMEAR DAB RUB BLOT BLUR CLAM
DAUB DOPE GAUM GLOB GORM
MOIL CLEAM DITCH GLAIR SLAKE
SLARE SMALM SMARM SULLY
BEDAUB BESLAB DEFILE PLATCH
SLAVER SLURRY SMIRCH SMOOCH
SMUDGE SPREAD STREAK STRIKE
BEPAINT BESMEAR PLASTER
POLLUTE SPLOTCH SLAISTER
(— OVER) ENGLUTE
(— WITH BLOOD) GILD
(— WITH EGG WHITE) GLAIR
(— WITH MUD) CLART SLIME
(— WITH SOMETHING STICKY)
GAUM GORM LIME
(— WITH TAR) PAY
(— WITH WAX) CERE
SMEAR DAB FLATFISH MARYSOLE
SMEARED FOUL BROSY MUSSY
SCOVY BLOODY SMUDGY
BLURRED BEGUMMED

SMEARING (— WITH OINTMENT)
INUNCTION
SMEARY DAUBY GAUMY
SMEDDUM SMITHUM
SMELL FUNK FUST GUSH NOSE
ODOR VENT AROMA FETOR FLAIR
SAVOR SCENT SENSE SMACK
SNIFF SNOOK SNUFF STIFE TASTE
OLFACT RESENT SMEECH
BREATHE PERFUME REFLAIR
VERDURE
(— AFTER PREY) BREVIT
(— OFFENSIVELY) REEK
(BITING —) TANG
(DAMP FUSTY —) RAFT
(DISAGREEABLE —) GOO PONG
STENCH
(HAVING PLEASANT —) SNIFTY
(MUSTY —) FUST
(OFFENSIVE —) FUNK FETOR STINK
MEPHITIS
(PLEASANT —) INCENSE
(STRONG —) HOGO
(SWEET —) SWEET
(PREF.) BROM(O) ODIO ODORI
ODORO OLFACTO OSM(O) OSMIO
OSPHRESIO OZO(NI)(NO)
(SENSE OF —) OSPHRESIO
(SUFF.) OSMA
(SENSE OF —) OSPHRESIA
SMELLY OLID RIPE FETID FUGGY
WHIFFY SMELLFUL
SMELT DECOCT INANGA EPERLAN
ICEFISH ELIQUATE SALMONID
SPARLING SPERLING
(FRY OF —) PRIM
SMEW NUN PIED SMEE DIVER
SMETHE
SMIDGEN BIT DAB JOT SKOSH
SLOSH
SMIDGEON (— OF TEA) SPOT
SMILAX LILY SARSA LILIUM
SMILE BEAM GRIN FLASH FLEER
SMEER ARRIDE SMUDGE SMIRKLE
(— AMOROUSLY) SMICKER
(AFFECTED —) SMIRK
(SELF-CONSCIOUS —) SIMPER
SMILING GOOD BONNY RIANT
SMILY BONNIE RIDENT SMIRKY
TWINKLY SMILEFUL
SMIRCH SMIT SOIL SMEAR SULLY
SLURRY SOILURE TARNISH
SMIRCHED DINGY
SMIRK DRAD YIRN SIMPER SMICKER
SMIRKLE SMURTLE
SMITE DUNT FRAP GIRD SLAY FLING
SKITE STRIKE
(— WITH LIGHTNING) LEVEN
SMITH MIMIR REGIN BOSSER
FORGER SMITHY FARRIER GLUTTER
SMITHER STEELER WAYLAND
FLOORMAN FORGEMAN PANSMITH
SMITHSONITE CALAMINE
SMITHY FORGE SMIDDY STITHY
STUDDIE FARRIERY
SMITTEN EPRISE INLOVE STRICKEN
SMOCK BRAT SLOP CAMIS KAMIS
SMOKE JIBBAH JUMPER CHEMISE
SMICKET
SMOG FOG HAZE
SMOKE PEW USE BLOW FLAN FOGO
FUFF FUME FUNK HAVE LUNT
NAVE PIPE REEK ROKE TOVE DRINK

REECH SMEEK SMORE SMUSH
STIVE VAPOR WHIFF BREATH
BUCCAN POTHER SMEECH
SMUDGE INCENSE SMOLDER
SMOTHER BACONIZE
(— MARIJUANA) BLAST
(AUTHOR OF —) TURGENEV
(CHARACTER IN —) IRINA TANYA
OSININ GRIGORY POTUGIN TATYANA
BAMBAEFF SHESTOFF BINDASOFF
GUBARYOFF LITVINOFF RATMIROFF
KAPITOLINA REISENBACH
(FROST —) BARBER
(HAZE AND —) SMAZE
(OFFENSIVE —) FUNK
(TOBACCO —) BLAST
(PREF.) ATMID(O) CAPNO
FUMAR(O) FUMI
SMOKE-AND-MIRRORS DISGUISE
SMOKE BROWN ASPHALT
SMOKEHOUSE FUMATORY
SMOKEJACK STACKMAN
SMOKER STAG FUNKER NICOTIAN
(MARIJUANA —) VIPER
SMOKESTACK STACK FUNNEL
TUNNEL CHIMNEY
SMOKE TREE ZANTE FUSTET
FUSTIC SCOTINO
SMOKING ROOM DIVAN TABAGIE
SMOKY HAZY ROKY DINGY FUMID
REEKY FUMISH FUMOSE REECHY
REEKIE SMUDGY SMUISTY
SMOLDER SMUSH SMOTHER
SMOLDERING PUNKY
SMOLT SMELT SMOUT SPROD
SMOOCH PET BUSS KISS NECK
SMUDGE LALLYGAG LOLLYGAG
SMOOTH DUB FAT LAP NOT BOSS
COMB DRAG EASE EASY EVEN
FACE FAIR FILE FLAT GLAD GLEG
GLIB HONE IRON LENE NOTT REET
SLID SNOD SOFT TRIM BLAND
BRENT CLEAR COUTH DARBY
DIGHT DOLCE DRESS EMERY
FLOAT FRAZE GLARE GOOSE
HOWEL LEVEL LITHE NAKED PLAIN
PLANE PRESS QUIET SCARF SILKY
SLAPE SLEEK SLICK SMOLT SNUFF
SOAPY SUANT SUAVE SUNET
TERSE ABRASE BUFFED CREAMY
EQUATE EVENLY FETTLE FLUENT
GLOSSY GREASE GREASY LEGATO
LIMBER MANGLE POLITE SCREED
SILKEN SLIGHT STREAK STRIKE
STROKE SVELTE UNFRET BOULDER
ERUGATE FLATTEN SLEEKIT
EXPLICIT GLABRATE GLABROUS
GLIBBERY GRAZIOSO LEVIGATE
SARSENET SLIDDERY SQUEEGEE
STRICKLE UNRUFFLE
(— BY BREAKING LUMPS) BILDER
(— MARBLE) GRIT
(— ONESELF UP) PREEN
(— OVER) GLOZE PLASTER
(— TYPE) KERN
(HYPOCRITICALLY —) SLEEK
(PHONETICALLY —) LENE LENIS
(PREF.) HOMAL(O) LEIO LEUR(O)
LIO LISS(O) LITI OXY
SMOOTHER GLAZER
SMOOTHLY SLICK EASILY EVENLY
GLIBLY SMOOTH SPROWSY
SWEETLY POLITELY

SMOOTH-MANNERED URBANE
SMOOTHNESS EASE FLUENCY
SMOOTH-RUNNING SWEET
SMOOTH-TONGUED WHILLY
SMOOTH WINTERBERRY
CANHOOP
SMOTHER BURKE CHOKE SMEAR
SMOKE SMORE MOIDER SMUDGE
STIFLE FLASKER OPPRESS
QUEASON QUEAZEN SMOLDER
SMUDDER
SMOTHERED ETOUFFE STIFLED
SMUDGE BLUR GAUM SLUR SMUT
SOIL SOOT CROCK SMEAR SMOKE
SMOOCH SMUTCH SMOLDER
SMOTHER SOILURE
SMUDGED BLOTTY SMUTCHY
SMUG SLEEK SMUSH SUAVE
SMUDGE
SMUGGLE RUN STEAL BOOTLEG
SHUFFLE
SMUGGLER OWLER COYOTE
RUNNER SPOTSMAN
(— OF DRUGS) MULE
(— OF IMMIGRANTS) COYOTE
(DOPE —) MULE
(DRUG —) MULE
SMUGGLING OWLING
SMUGLY FATLY
SMUT BUNT COOM PORN BLACK
BLECK COLLY COOMB CROCK
GRIME SMOOT SMITCH SMUTCH
SMATTER COLBRAND
SMUTCH BLOT SMIRCH SMITCH
SMOUCH SMUDGE
SMUT GRASS TUSSOCK
SMUTTINESS RAUNCH
SMUTTY BAWDY DIRTY SOOTY
SULTRY RAUNCHY BARNYARD
FREUDIAN
SMYRNA USHAK
SNACK BIT CUT BAIT BITE GORP
NOSH SNAP TAPA BEVER BUTTY
CHACK CHECK NACHO SHARE
SNICK TASTE GOUTER MUNGEY
NACKET SNATCH ZAKUSKA
ANTOJITO MUNCHIES NUNCHEON
(— SPOT) TEAROOM
(CHOCOLATE —) OREO
SNAFFLE BIT GAG BRIDOON
SNAG KNAG SNUG STUB POINT
GLITCH IMPASSE PLANTER
SNAGGLE
(PL.) EMBARRAS
SNAIL HUA PILA SNAG CHINK DRILL
HELIX OLIVA OVULA PHYSA SHELL
THAIS TURBO WHELK CERION
CONKER DODMAN NERITA NERITA
NERITE PHYSID PURPLE TRITON
WINKLE RISSOID UNICORN
VERTIGO ZONITID CASSIDID
ESCARGOT HODMADOD JANTHINA
LYMNAEID MELANIAN NATICEID
NERITOID RAMSHORN SOLARIUM
WALLFISH PERIWINKLE
(PREF.) STROMBI STROMBULI
(SUFF.) COCHLEI COCHLI(O)
COCHLO
SNAILFLOWER CARACOL
SNAKE (ALSO SEE SERPENT AND
REPTILE) ASP BOA BOM ESS NAG
APOD BOBA BOID BOMA JUBO
NAGA NAJA SEPS SNIG ABOMA

ASPIC COBRA CONGO CRIBO DRILL
JIBOA KRAIT MAMBA PTYAS
RACER SNECK TIGER VIPER BOIGID
BONGAR CANTIL CHITAL DABOIA
DIPSAS ELAPID GOPHER HISSER
JESSUR KERRIL PYTHON ROLLER
RUNNER TAIPAN URAEUS WENONA
ADJIGER ANILIID BOKADAM
CAMOODI CRAWLER CREEPER
CULEBRA DIAPSID HAGWORM
HOGNOSE LABARIA LANGAHA
PRESTER RATTLER REGULUS
REPTILE SCYTALE SERPENT
SPITTER WALPAPI ANACONDA
BONETAIL BUNGARUM CASCAVEL
CERASTES CROTALID EGGEATER
FLATHEAD HAIRWORM JARARACA
KEELBACK MOCCASIN OPHIDIAN
RINGHALS SNAKELET VIPERINE
(— OIL) BUNKUM POPPYCOCK
(TREE —) BOOMSLANG
(TWO-HEADED —) AMPHISBAENA
(PREF.) OPHI(O) SERPU
(SUFF.) OPHIS
SNAKEBARK IRONBARK
SNAKEBIRD DARTER PLOTUS
ANHINGA DUCKLAR
SNAKEHEAD MURRAL
SNAKELIKE ANGUINE VIPEROUS
SNAKE MACKEREL ESCOLAR
SNAKEMOUTH POGONIA
SNAKEPIECE POINTER
SNAKEROOT STEVIA BABROOT
BUGBANE SANGREL SANICLE
SAWWORT POOLWORT RICHWEED
WHITETOP
SNAKESKIN SPOIL HACKLE
SLOUGH
(CASTOFF —S) EXUVIAE
SNAKEWEED BISTORT
SNAP SET ZIP BARK BITE CHOP
GNAP HUFF JERK KNAP LIRP PIPE
SETT BREAK CLACK FILIP FLICK
GANCH KNACK KNICK PHOTO
SMACK SNACK BLUDGE SNAPPY
SNATCH FASTENER PUSHOVER
SNAPHEAD CREPITATE
(— AT) HANCH
(— LIGHTLY) KNICK
(— OFF) SNIP
(— TOGETHER) CRASH
(— UP) SNUP SNAFFLE
(— WITH FINGER) LIRP FILIP THRIP
FILLIP
SNAPBACK PASSBACK
SNAPDRAGON BULL SNAPS
BULLER BULLDOG DOGMOUTH
SNAPE FLINCH
SNAPPER UKU BRIM JOCU SESI
BREAM PARGO VORAZ CUBERA
HUSSAR JENOAR LAWYER NATIVE
TAMURE ULAULA COCKNEY
CRACKER BIAJAIBA CACHUCHO
FLAMENCO GNATSNAP LUTIANID
WOLLOMAI SCHNAPPER
MUTTONFISH SHUTTERBUG
SNAPPING CHACK DOGGISH
SNAPPING BEETLE ELATER
SKIPPER SNAPPER ELATERID
SKIPJACK
SNAPPING TURTLE LOGHEAD
SHAGTAIL
SNAPPISH CRUP EDGY PUXY CROSS

SNACK TESTY WASPY CUTTED
SNAGGY SNAPPY SNARKY SNIPPY
DOGGISH PEEVISH
SNAPPY CRISP JEMMY NIPPY ZIPPY
SNAPSHOT PRINT
SNARE BAG GIN HAY NET PIT SET
BAIT BUKE FANG GIRN GRIN HOOK
LACE LIME TOIL TRAP WAIT WIRE
BRAKE CATCH FRAUD GNARE
LATCH LEASH SINEW SNARL SNIRL
STALE SWEEK TRAIN COBWEB
GILDER PANTER SNATCH SPRINT
TREPAN TUNNEL ENSNARE
MANTRAP OVERNET PITFALL
SETTING SNICKLE SNIGGLE
SPRINGE BIRDLIME INVEIGLE
LIMEBUSH SPRINGLE TENDICLE
MOUSETRAP
(— DEER) WITHE
(— FOR ELEPHANTS) KEDDAH
(— FOR FISH) WEEL
(FISH —) WEEL
SNARL ARR BITE CARL GIRN GNAR
GURR HARL HURR NARR TWIT
WAFF YARR GNARL GNARR GRILL
KNURL RAVEL SNIRL TWINE
BOWWOW BUMBLE GAUNCH
MUCKER TANGLE VENNER GRIZZLE
GRUMBLE
SNARLED SNAFU
SNARLER CYNIC
SNARLING LATRANT
SNATCH HAP NAB NIP RAP GRAB
HINT RACE RASE SNAP SNIP WHIP
WRAP YERK YUCK BRAID CATCH
CLAWK CLICK EREPT GANCH
GRASP GRIPE PLUCK SNACK STRIP
SWIPE SWOOP TWEAK WHIFT
WREST SNITCH STRIKE TWITCH
WRENCH CLAUGHT GRABBLE
SCAMBLE VULTURE
(— MOMENTARY VIEW) GLANCE
SNAZZY CHIC COOL FANCY
SNEAK BLAB GRUB LEER LOOP
LOUT LURK PEAK PIMP SHUG SNIG
LURCH MEECH MOOCH SCOUT
SHARK SHIRK SKULK SLIDE SLINK
SLIPE SLIVE SLOKE SNEAP SNICK
SNOOK BLIFIL MICHER WEASEL
SLOUNGE SNIGGLE SNEAKSBY
(— AWAY) SLIPE
(— OFF) MAG SHAB MIZZLE
(PRYING —) SNOOP
SNEAKER CREEPER GUMSHOE
TENNIES
SNEAKERS TENNIES
SNEAKING HANGDOG PEAKING
SLIVING
SNEAKY FURTIVE MEECHING
SNEER SHY FLON GIBE GIRD GIRN
GULE JEER JERK JIBE MOCK FLEER
FLING FLOUT GLEEK JAUNT SCOFF
SCOUT SLARE SLEER SNIFF SNIRT
SNORT GIZZEN SNEEST TWITCH
WRINKLE RIDICULE
SNEERING FRUMPERY
SNEEZE NEESE NEEZE ARREST
(— AT) CONDEMN DESPISE
SNEEZEWEED ALANT ROSILLA
HELENIUM
SNEEZEWOOD NIESHOUT
SNEEZEWORT HARDHEAD
PTARMICA

SNEEZING PTARMIC
SNELL SNOOD TIPPET GANGING
SNICK TIP SNECK
SNICKER TEEHEE TITTER SMIRKLE
SNIGGER SNIGGLE
SNIDE ORNERY
SNIFF NOSE TIFT VENT WIND SCENT
SMELL SNAFF SNIFT SNUFF SNIVEL
SNAFFLE SNIFFLE SNOTTER
SNIFTER SLUG BALLOON INHALER
SNIGGER NICKER WHICKER
SNIGGLE BRAGGLE
SNIP CUT CLIP CROP MINX NICK
SHRED SNICK SCISSOR
SNIPE JACK NICK WISP SCAPE SNITE
WADER WILLET BLEATER BLITTER
DOWITCH HUMILITY LONGBILL
SHADBIRD WOODCOCK
SNIPER TEASER BUSHWACK
SNIPPET BIT
SNIPPINESS SASS
SNIVEL WHINE BUBBLE SNIFFLE
SNIFTER SNOTTER SNUFFLE
SNIVELY TEARY TEARFUL
SNOB SNAB SNOOT FLUNKY
SHONEEN SNOBBER
SNOBBERY ELITISM
SNOBBISH RITZY DICKTY OFFISH
SNOBBY SNOOTY UPPISH
HAUGHTY UPSTAGE
SNOOK SNOOT ROBALO
SNOOKER CON HOODWINK
SNOOP PRY PEEK PEEP PRIER
SNEAK BREVIT PIROOT GUMSHOE
SNOOPER CREEP BUSYBODY
SNOOPY CURIOUS
SNOOZE NAP NOD DOVER SLEEP
SNOOZLE
SNORE ROUT SNARK SNORK SNORT
SNOCKER SNOTTER
SNORING STERTOR RHONCHUS
SNORT BLOW ROUT SNUR TOOT
VENT BLURT FNESE SNARK SNEER
SNORE SNORK WHOOF EXCLAIM
SNIFTER SNOCKER SNORKEL
SNORTLE SNOTTER
SNOUT NEB SAW BEAK BILL NOSE
WROT GROIN SERRA SNOOT
MUFFLE MUZZLE NOZZLE
GRUNTLE ROSTRUM
(PREF.) PROBOSCI(DI) RHYNCH(O)
(SUFF.) RHYNCHUS RHYNCUS
SNOUT BEETLE CURCULIO
SNOUT MITE BDELLID
SNOW CORN DRIP GRUE COVER
SPOSH STORM SUGAR WHITE
POWDER COCAINE GRAUPEL
RAMPART WEATHER SCOUTHER
WINDSLAB
(— PELLETS) GRAUPEL
(— SLIGHTLY) SPIT
(— UP) STALL
(DISSOLVING —) FLUSH
(DRIFTED —) WINDLE
(GLACIER —) FIRN NEVE BLIZZ
(HEAVY FALL OF —) PASH
(MELTING —) SLUSH
(MUSHY —) SLOB
(NEW-FALLEN —) MANNA
(PARTLY MELTED —) SLUSH
(WHIRLING —) SKIRL
(PREF.) CHIO CHION(O) NIVI
SNOWBERRY MOXA WAXBERRY

SNOWBIRD JUNCO
SNOW BUNTING OATFOWL
SNOWBIRD SNOWFOWL
SNOW COCK JERMONAL
SNOWDRIFT WREATH YOWDEN
SNOWDROP TREE BELLWOOD
COWLICKS TISSWOOD
SNOWFALL PASH SKIFF SKIFT
FLURRY ONDING
SNOWFLAKE FLAG FLAUCHT
SNOW FLEA PODURAN PODURID
SNOW GOOSE WAVY
(— GENUS) CHEN
SNOWINESS NIVOSITY
SNOW LEOPARD IRBIS OUNCE
SNOWLESS GREEN
SNOW MAIDEN, THE (CHARACTER
IN —) LEL BOBYL KUPAVA MIZGIR
SPRING BERENDEY BOBYLIKHA
SNEGUROCHKA
(COMPOSER OF —)
RIMSKYKORSAKOV
SNOWMAN YETI
SNOW MOUNTAIN JOKUL
SNOWSHOE WEB PATIN PATTEN
RACKET RACQUET
SNOWSTORM PURGA DRIFTER
BLIZZARD
SNOWY NIVAL WHITE NIVEOUS
SNUB AIR RITZ SLAP SNIB FRUMP
SNEAP SWANK REBUFF REBUTE
SIMOUS SLIGHT SNOUCH SNUBBY
SETDOWN
SNUBBING MAIL
SNUBBY PUGGISH
SNUB-NOSED SIMOUS
(PREF.) SIMO
SNUFF TOP VENT MUSTY SNIFF
SNUSH TABAC COHOBA PULVIL
RAPPEE SNEESH STIFLE SNUFFLE
BERGAMOT MACCABOY
ORANGERY SMUTCHIN
(UP TO —) ABLE
SNUFFBOX MILL MULL
SNUFFBOX BEAN CACOON
SNUFFER PRICK DOUTER TOPPER
PRICKER
SNUFFLE SNIVEL SNAFFLE SNIFFLE
SNIFTER
SNUG LEW RUG BEIN BIEN COSH
COSY COZY NEAT SNOD TAUT TEAT
TOSH TOSY CANNY CLOSE COMFY
COUTH POVIE QUEME TIGHT
PENTIT COUTHIE SNUGGERY
SNUGGISH
SNUGGLE SNUG BURROW CUDDLE
NESTLE SNUDGE CROODLE
SNUZZLE
SNUGLY SHORT COSILY
SO SAE SUCH THAT THIS THUS
THISSEN INSOMUCH SUCHWISE
THUSWISE
(— AM I) LIKEWISE
(— BE IT) AMEN
(— FAR AS) QUOAD
(— TO SPEAK) FAIRLY
(NOT —) SECUS
(QUITE —) EXACTLY
SOAK RET SOB SOD SOG SOP WET
BOWK BUCK SIPE BINGE DROUK
DROWN SOUSE STEEP STING
TOAST DRENCH EMBAIN IMBIBE
IMBRUE SEETHE SODDEN SPONGE

INSTEEP MICKERY SWELTER
SATURATE
(— A CASK) GROG
(— FLAX) RET RATE
(— IN) SOP FEATHER
(— UP) SOP
SOAKED SOGGY SOPPY SOBBED
SODDEN WATERY DRUNKEN
SOBBING DRAGGLED
SOAKING BATH SUING SOGGING
INFUSION
SOAP SAPO SUDS CHIPS STOCK
CASTILE TALLATE WINDSOR
SANDSOAP SAVONETTE
(— OPERA) SUDSER
(— SUBSTITUTE) AMOLE
(— UNIT) CAKE
(CAKE OF —) TABLET TABULATE
(LIQUID —) FIT
(PREF.) SAP(O) SAPONI
SOAPBARK QUILLAI SOAPWOOD
SOAPFISH JABON
SOAP PLANT AMOLE PALMILLO
SOAPROOT SOAPWEED
SOAPSTONE TALC ALBERENE
POTSTONE STEATITE
SOAPSTONER TALCER
SOAPWORT BORITH COWHERB
SAPONARY SOAPROOT SOAPWEED
SOAR FLY STY KITE FLOAT MOUNT
PLANE SPIRE TOWER ASCEND
ASPIRE AIRPLANE
SOARING ALOFT FLIGHT ICARIAN
SPIRING ESSORANT
SOB YEX SIKE SNOB SNUB SOUGH
BLUBBER SINGULT
SOBBING GREET
SOBER SAD CALM COOL SAGE CIVIL
FRESH GRAVE QUIET STAID
DOULCE SEDATE SEVERE SOLEMN
SOMBER STEADY EARNEST
PENSIVE REGULAR SERIOUS
UNFOXED DECOROUS MODERATE
ABSTEMIOUS
SOBRIETY DRYNESS GRAVITY
ABSTINENCE
SOBRIQUET BYNAME HAWKEYE
SO-CALLED ALLEGED
SOCCER FOOTER FOOTBALL
(— NAME) PELE
(— PLAYER) SWEEPER
SOCIABLE COSY CHUMMY CLUBBY
FOLKSY SOCIAL AFFABLE AMIABLE
INNERLY CLUBABLE FAMILIAR
FELLOWLY INFORMAL
SOCIAL TEA DISTAL PUBLIC SOIREE
SUPPER SOCIABLE SOCIETAL
CONVIVIAL
(— WORKER) ALMONER
SOCIALISM ETATISM MARXISM
GUESDISM
SOCIALIST FABIAN NIHILIST
SOCIALISTIC PINK
SOCIALIZE CIVILIZE
SOCIETY BUND HALL HERD SANG
GUILD MONDE POLIS SABHA
SAMAJ SANGH SOKOL ADMASS
MENAGE NANIGO PARISH SYSTEM
VEREIN ACADEMY COLLEGE
COLORUM COMPANY COUNCIL
KINGDOM SOCIETE THIASOS
EXCHANGE HETAERIA PRECINCT
SOCIETAS SODALITY SORORITY

(— OF RELIGIOUS FANATICS)
COLORUM
(CHORAL —) CHOIR
(CLOWN —) KOSHARE KOYEMSHI
(CRAFT —) ARTEL
(CRIMINAL —) MAFIA MAFFIA
(DEBATING —) POP
(GENTEEL —) FASHION
(GYMNASTIC —) SOKOL
(HIGH —) SWELLDOM
(LITERARY —) HALL
(MEMBER OF CRUDE —) LUMPEN
(POLITICAL —) TAMMANY
(RELIGIOUS —) CHURCH
(SECRET —) HUI EGBO HOEY PORO
TONG LODGE MAFIA OGBONI
PURRAH CAMORRA
(STUDENT —) CORPS
(UTOPIAN —) ANARCHY
(WHITE —) MAN
(PREF.) SOCIO
SOCIETY ISLANDS (CAPITAL OF —)
PAPEETE
(ISLAND OF —) TAHITI
SOCINIAN RACOVIAN
SOCIOLOGIST AMERICAN HUNT
LYND ODUM ROSS WARD BALCH
CAREY BARNES BOGART DEVINE
DUFFEY HUNTER SUMNER VEBLEN
COLLIER DUGDALE ELLWOOD
ETZIONI FRAZIER NEARING STEIZLE
WILLARD ZUEBLIN BOGARDUS
GIDDINGS YANKELOVICH
GOLDENWEISER
ENGLISH KIDD WEBB GLASS
GEDDES TOYNBEE
FRENCH TARDE DURKHEIM
GERMAN LANGE WEBER FREYER
SIMMEL MICHELS SCHAFFLE
THURNWALD
GREEK BARDIS
HUNGARIAN MANNHEIM
ITALIAN LORIA
SCOTTISH GEDDES MCLENNAN
SWEDISH MYRDAL
SOCIOLOGY DEMOTICS
SOCK BOP ONE BIFF BUST HOSE
VAMP ANKLET ARGYLE VAMPEY
STOCKING
(— OF GOAT'S HAIR) UDO
(INFANT'S —) BOOTEE BOOTIE
(JAPANESE —) TABI
SOCKET BOX CUP PAD POD BUSH
CELL HOSE LEAD NOSE SHOE
CHAIR POINT SHANK BUCKET
BUDGET COLLET EYEPIT NOZZLE
POCKET SAUCER SCONCE
ALVEOLE COCKEYE FERRULE
FUTCHEL GUDGEON THIMBLE
TORULUS ALVEOLUS DRAWHEAD
(— FOR BIT) POD
(— FOR CARBINE) BUDGET
(— FOR GEM) OUCH
(— FOR LANCE) PORT
(— FOR LENS) CELL
(— FOR MAST) TABERNACLE
(— FOR MOUTHPIECE) BIRN
(— IN GOLF CLUB HEAD) HOSE
HOSEL
(— OF BONE) POT
(— OF GEM) OUCH
(— OF HINGE) PAN
(— OF LOCK) KEEPER

(— OF MILLSTONE) INK COCKEYE
(— OF WATER PIPE) BELL
(BIT —) POD
(PREF.) GLENO TORMO
SOCKEYE NERKA KOKANEE
BLUEBACK
SOCLE ZOCCO
SOCRATES (— METHOD) MAIEUTIC
(DISCIPLE OF —) XENOPHON
SOD HUB BEAT DELF FAIL FLAG
SCAD SONK TURF DELPH GAZON
GLEBE SCRAW SWARD CLOWER
TERRON SODDING
SODA POP BARILLA
(— FOUNTAIN) SPA
SODA POP TONIC
SODDEN SAMMY SAPPY SOGGY
POACHY DRAGGLED
SODI (SON OF —) GEDDIEL
SODIUM NA SODA NATRIUM
(PREF.) NATR(O)
SODIUM BICARBONATE SODA
BICARB
SODIUM BORATE BORAX
SODIUM CARBONATE SODA
TRONA NATRON ANATRON
BARILLA SALSODA
SODIUM CHLORIDE SALT HALITE
SODIUM THIOSULFATE HYPO
SODOMITE DOG BUGGER SPINTRY
BOUGERON
SOEVER SOME
SOFA BOIST COUCH DIVAN SQUAB
CANAPE LOUNGE SETTEE
CAUSEUSE SOCIABLE
(— IN RESTAURANT) BANQUETTE
SOFFIT GATHER PLAFOND
INTRADOS PLANCIER
SOFRONIA (LOVER OF —) OLINDO
SOFT COY TID FEIL LASH LIMP LUSH
MILD MURE NASH NESH PLUM
SART SLOW TOSY WAXY WEAK
BALMY BLAND CUSHY DABBY
DOLCE DOWNY FAINT GIVEY
HOOLY LENIS LIGHT MALMY
MEALY MELCH MUSHY MUTED
PADDY PAPPY PIANO PLIFF SILKY
SLACK SMALL SOAPY SOOTH
SWASH SWEET WAXEN WETHE
YAPPY CASHIE CREAMY EFFETE
FLAGGY FLOSSY FLUFFY GENTLE
LITHER LYDIAN MELLOW PIPING
PLACID SAMMEL SIDDER SIDDOW
SILKEN SLOPPY SMOOTH SOFTLY
SPONGY SPOONY TENDER
UNDURE CLEMENT COTTONY
CRUMBLY DUCTILE FLESHLY
LENIENT SQUASHY CUSHIONY
FEMININE FLEXIBLE HOTHOUSE
LADYLIKE SARCENET SLUGGISH
SQUELCHY TRANQUIL
(— AND BRITTLE) FROWY FROWIE
FROUGHY
(— AND FLEXIBLE) FLOPPY
(— AND LIFELESS) DOUGHY
(— IN SOUND) SMALL
(— IN TEXTURE) SUPPLE
(VERY —) SQUASHY
(PREF.) LENI MALAC(O) MOLLI
SOFT-COVER PAPERBACK
SOFTEN CUT CREE MELT SOAK
SOFT TAME ALLAY BATCH BREAK
FRIZZ LITHE MALAX TOUCH WOKIE

DIGEST GENTLE LENIFY PACIFY
RELENT SOOTHE SUBDUE SUBMIT
TEMPER WEAKEN APPEASE
ASSUAGE CUSHION LENIATE
MOLLIFY QUALIFY SWEETEN
UNSTEEL AMOLLISH ATTEMPER
ENFEEBLE HUMANIZE MITIGATE
MODULATE PALLIATE PRETTIFY
(— BY BOILING) CREE
(— BY KNEADING) MALAX
MALAXATE
(— BY STEEPING) MACERATE
(— COLOR) CUT SCUMBLE
(— FIBERS) BREAK
(— GRADUALLY) SQUAT
(— JUTE) BATCH
(— LEATHER) BREY FRIZ FRIZZ
(— METAL) ALLAY
(— TONE) SURD
SOFTENED ROXY ANODYNE
MOUILLE FLEXUOUS
SOFTENER (WATER —) CALGON
SOFTENING LENIENT MALACIA
BLETTING
(— OF ARTICULATION) LENITION
SOFTER MANCANDO
SOFTHEARTED TENDER
SOFTLY LOW BAJO SOFT HOOLY
FAIRLY GENTLY SWEETLY
CREAMILY TENDERLY
SOFTNESS SOFT MOLLITIES
(— IN COAL SEAM) LUM LUMB
(TENDER —) LANGUOR
(SUFF.) MALACIA
SOFT-POINTED HEBETATE
SOFT-SHELLED TURTLE FLAPPER
FLIPPER FLAPJACK
SOFT-SOAP CON FLANNEL
SOFT-SPOKEN MEALY
SOFTWARE (COMPUTER —) DRIVER
MONITOR
(DESKTOP — DISPLAY) WYSIWYG
(OF — DISPLAY) WYSIWYG
SOFTY PUSSYCAT
SOGGY SAD DUNCH SOBBY
SODDEN SPONGY WATERY
SOIGNE TRIM SLEEK MODISH
SOIL DAG DUB MUD RAY SOD BLOT
BLUR CLAY CLOD DAUB DIRT DUST
FOIL FOUL GRIT LAND MIRK MOOL
MOSS MUCK MURK MUSS SAUR
SILE SLUR SMUT SOOT TASH BULLI
CROCK EARTH GLEBE GRIME
GUMBO LAYER MUCKY ROSEL
SLUSH SMEAR SOLUM SOULE
SPARK STAIN SULLY BARING
BEDAUB BEFOUL BEMIRE BEMOIL
GROUND PODZOL SLURRY SMIRCH
SMOOCH SMUDGE SPLASH
SUDDLE BEGRIME BENASTY
BESMEAR BESMOKE BETHUMB
FEWMAND PEDOCAL POLLUTE
REGOSOL SEEDBED SLUBBER
TARNISH TRACHLE AGROTYPE
ALLUVIAL BEDABBLE BESMIRCH
BUCKSHOT FLYSPECK LATERITE
PEDALFER PLANOSOL RENDZINA
WOODCOCK SOLONCHAK
CONTAMINATE
(— ABOVE CLAY) KELLY
(— AGGREGATE) PED
(— DEPOSITED BY WIND) ELUVIUM
(— FORMED BY DECAY) GEEST

**(— INTERMEDIATE BETWEEN SAND
AND CLAY)** ROSEL
(— PREPARED FOR SOWING) TILTH
(— REMOVED FROM ORE) BARING
(— WITH GREASE) LARD
(AGGREGATE —) PED
(ALKALINE —) SOLONETZ
(ASHLIKE —) PODSOL PODZOL
(AZONAL —) REGOSOL
(CLAYEY —) GALT MALM MAUM
ADOBE SOLOD SOLOTH
(COTTON —) REGUR
(DRY —) GROOT
(FRIABLE —) CRUMB
(GRAVELLY —) ROACH GROWAN
(HARD —) RAMMEL
(INFERTILE —) GALL
(LEACHED —S) LATOSOL
(PEATY —) YARFA YARPHA
(PLUMBER'S —) SMUDGE
(POROUS —) SPONGE
(POTTING —) COMPOST
(PRAIRIE —) BRUNIZEM
(RED —) LATERITE
(SILTY —) GUMBO
(SPRINGY —) WOODSERE
(ZONAL —) SEROZEM SIEROZEM
(PREF.) AGRI AGRO GE(O) PED(O)
SOLI
SOILAGE SOIL SMUDGE SOILING
SOILED FOUL BLACK DINGY DIRTY
MUSSY SOOTY TARRY SMUDGY
SMUTTY SNUFFY THUMBED
DRAGGLED SHOPWORN
SOIL-EXPOSING EROSIVE
SOIREE EVENING
SOJOURN LIE BIDE STAY STOP
ABIDE ABODE TARRY VISIT RESIDE
ALLODGE MANSION STATION
(— ABROAD) PEREGRINATION
SOJOURNER PILGRIM
SOKOL FALCON
SOL SOH SOU ALCOSOL EMULSOID
HYDROSOL SOLUTION
SOLA SHOLA PAUKPAN
SOLACE CHEER CHEERER
COMFORT CONSOLE SWEETEN
SOLATION
SOLAR HELIAC SOLLER HELIACAL
SOLARIUM
(— REFLECTOR) HELIOSTAT
(— SYSTEM APPARATUS) ORRERY
SOLAR DISK ATEN ATON
(CENTER OF —) CAZIMI
SOLAR ENERGY
(PREF.) HELI
SOLD SELT BOOKED
(ILLICITLY —) BOOTLEG
SOLDER PALE BRAZE FLOAT
SOWDER SPELTER
SOLDERER BROGUER
SOLDERING IRON COPPER
DOCTOR
SOLDIER GI SON TAP BLEU BOLO
GOUM GUGU KERN LEVY SHOT
SWAD TULK WART BERNE CROAT
FRITZ GUARD GUFFY KHAKI LANCE
LIMEY LINER MINER NIZAM PERDU
PIKER PIVOT POILU PONGO
SAMMY SWEAT TOLKE TOMMY
TOPAS ASKARI BONAGH BUMMER
DARTER DIGGER EXPERT GALOOT
GUNNER GURKHA HAIDUK HEINIE

HOSTER LANCER MARKER PIETON
REITER SENTRY SKIEUR SOLDAT
SWADDY THRASO WEAPON
ZOUAVE BAYONET BILLJIM
BLIGHTY BRIGAND CARABIN
CATERAN CORSLET DARTMAN
DOGFACE DRAGOON FEDERAL
FEEDMAN FIGHTER GENETOR
GOUMIER HOBBLER INVALID
JACKMAN MATROSS ORDERLY
PALIKAR PANDOUR PAVISOR
PELTAST PIKEMAN PRIVATE
REDCOAT REGULAR REISTER
SCARLET SLINGER SOLDADO
STRIKER TROOPER VETERAN
WARRIOR ARQUEBUS BEZONIAN
BLUECOAT BUCKSKIN BUFFCOAT
CAMELEER CAVALIER DESERTER
FENCIBLE FUGLEMAN FUSILIER
GALLOPER GENDARME GRAYBACK
GRAYCOAT IRONSIDE JANIZARY
KHANDAIT LANCEMAN LINESMAN
MILITANT MIQUELET MUSTACHE
PIOUPIOU RAPPAREE SENTINEL
SERVITOR SILLADAR SPEARMAN
SWORDMAN TOLPATCH TRANSFER
TRIARIAN WARFARER WHIFFLER
YARDBIRD CATAPHRACT
(— OF MUSCOVITE GUARD)
STRELITZ
(— ON GUARD) SENTRY
(— WITH SIDE WHISKERS) BADGER
(ALBANIAN —) PALIKAR
(ALGERIAN —) ARBI
(AMERICAN —) SAMMY
(ANT —) MAXIM
(ARMY OR MARINE FOOT —)
GRUNT
(ASIAN —) GOOK
(AUSTRALIAN —) ANZAC DIGGER
BILLJIM
(BOMBAY —S) DUCKS
(BRITISH —) LIMEY TOMMY
BLIGHTY LOBSTER REDCOAT
ROOINEK
(BRUTAL —) PANDOUR
(CAREER —) LIFER
(CAVALRY —) REITER TROOPER
(COWARDLY —) CAPITANO
(DISBANDED —) REFORMADO
(EGYPTIAN —) GIPPO GIPPY GYPPO
GYPPY GYPPIE
(FEMALE —) AMAZON
(FILE OF 6 —S) ROT
(FILIPINO —) GUGU
(FOOT —) KERN PAGE PEON GRUNT
PIETON FOOTMAN TOLPATCH
(GERMAN —) HUN FRITZ HEINE
KRAUT HEINIE
(GREEK —) EVZONE HOPLITE
(HORSE —) RUTTER CUIRASSIER
(INCOMPETENT —) BOLL
(INDIAN —) PEON JAWAN SEPOY
GURKHA
(INEPT —) SADSACK
(INVALID —) FOGY FOGEY
(IRREGULAR —) CROAT CATERAN
JAYHAWK SEBUNDY MIQUELET
RAPPAREE SILLADAR
(MERCENARY —) RUTTER HESSIAN
LANSQUENET LANDSKNECHT
(MOROCCAN —) ASKARI
(MOSLEM —) NIZAM

(MOUNTED —) LANCER DRAGOON GENETOR LOBSTER TROOPER VEDETTE CAVALIER
(NEW —) RECRUIT
(NEW ZEALAND —) ANZAC
(NEW ZEALAND OR AUSTRALIAN—) DIGGER
(OLD —) GROGNARD
(PROFESSIONAL —) SAMURAI
(REVOLUTIONARY —) REDCOAT BUCKSKIN
(ROMAN —) FOEDERATUS
(ROMAN —S OF THIRD LINE) TRIARY TRIARII
(RUSSIAN —) IVAN
(SCOTTISH —) JOCK
(SMALL —) BANTAM
(TERRITORIAL —) TERRIER
(TURKISH —) NIZAM REDIF
(U.S. FOOT —) GRUNT
(UNTRAINED —) YARDBIRD
(PL.) FOOT ELITE TERZO TROOP TERTIA CATERVA ENOMOTY MILITIA VELITES FORAGERS INFANTRY SOLDIERY
AMERICAN DIX LEA LEE ORD POE AMES BELL BUTT CARR CLAY DEAN DRUM FISK FORD HAIG HILL HOOD HULL KNOX LANE LEAR LONG LORD LYON MYER OTIS RENO SHAW WOOD WOOL YORK ALLEN BANKS BATES BEALL BLAIR BLISS BLOCH BRAGG BRETT BROWN BUELL BURNS CANBY CATES CHASE CLARK CORSE CRAIG CROOK CROWE DAVIS DODGE EAKER EARLY EATON ELIOT EWELL GATES GAVIN GETTY GRANT GREEN GREGG HAYNE HAZEN HINES HODGE HOVEY HOWZE IRWIN KUTER LEWIS MCCOY MCRAE MEADE MEIGS MILES MOSBY MOWER OHARA ORTIZ PARKE PATCH POORE PRATT ROYCE SCOTT SHAYS SMITH STARK STONE SWIFT SYKES TERRY UPTON VIELE WYMAN ABRAMS ARNOLD BISBEE BOWLEY BUFORD BUTLER CONWAY CULLUM CUSTER DAYTON DEVERS DOZIER EMBICK EMMONS GAINES GIBBON GIBSON GLOVER GORDON GORGAS GRAVES GREENE GROVES HARDEE HARDIN HARMON HARTLE HOOKER HOWARD HUNTER JADWIN JORDAN KEARNY KENNEY LAWTON MACOMB MAHONE MARION MCCOOK MCLAWS MORGAN MORROW NEWTON OLIVER PATTON PHELPS PILLOW PUTNAM RIPLEY ROGERS SCHAFF SEVIER SHARPE SHELBY SPAATZ STRONG STUART SUMNER SUMTER TANNER TAYLOR THAYER TWIGGS VESSEY WARNER WESSON WILCOX ANDREWS BABCOCK BELKNAP BINGHAM BRADLEY BUCKNER BULLARD CARLSON CASWELL CHAFFEE CLINTON CROWDER CROZIER CUSHMAN DICKMAN EDWARDS FERRERO FLEMING FORREST FREMONT FUNSTON GRANGER HALLECK HANCOCK HARBORD HARDING HASKELL HOUSTON INGALLS JACKSON KRUEGER LEDYARD

LEJEUNE LIGGETT LINCOLN MAXWELL MENOHER MERRITT NEVILLE PARROTT PICKETT RAWLINS SHAFTER SHERMAN SLEMMER TORBERT TREMAIN TRIMBLE VANDORN VENABLE WHEELER WINGATE ANDERSON BRERETON BURNSIDE CAMPBELL DONELSON FRANKLIN GAILLARD GOETHALS GRIERSON JOHNSTON MAGRUDER MARSHALL MCDOWELL MCNARNEY MOULTRIE OLMSTEAD PERSHING PRESCOTT REYNOLDS SEDGWICK SHERIDAN SNELLING STILWELL STODDARD SUBLETTE SULLIVAN TOWNSEND VANFLEET AINSWORTH ALEXANDER ARMISTEAD ARMSTRONG BONESTEEL DOOLITTLE DOUBLEDAY FETTERMAN HARTRANFT HUMPHREYS MACARTHUR MCCLELLAN PEMBERTON PETTIGREW QUANTRILL ROSECRANS SCHOFIELD SUMMERALL WILKINSON BEAUREGARD BUFFINGTON EISENHOWER LONGSTREET MCGLACHLIN PLEASONTON WAINWRIGHT BUTTERFIELD
ARGENTINIAN JUSTO
AUSTRALIAN CASEY BLAMEY MACKAY MONASH BENNETT CHAUVEL STURDEE LAVARACK
AUSTRIAN DAUN HESS DANKL HADIK LIGNE GALLAS GYULAI TRENCK BENEDEK GABLENZ ALVINCZY BEAULIEU CLERFAYT RADETZKY PHILIPPOVIC
BOLIVIAN DAZA PANDO CAMPERO BALLIVIAN
BRAZILIAN DUTRA FONSECA PEIXOTO
BULGARIAN SAVOY
CANADIAN BOVEY BISHOP CRERAR HUGHES DENISON LINDSAY
CARTHAGINIAN HANNIBAL
CHILEAN CRUZ BULNES FREIRE IBANEZ PRIETO OHIGGINS
COLOMBIAN REYES HERRAN CORDOBA MOSQUERA
DANISH RANTZAU
DUTCH CHASSE KEPPEL COEHOORN DAENDELS
ECUADORIAN ALFARO FLORES
ENGLISH COX NYE BOLS BYNG DILL DYER GAGE GALE GORT HAIG HEAD HILL LACY LAKE LOWE PILE RICH ROSS SLIM VERE WADE ANDRE BOWER BROCK CAREW CAREY CAVAN CLERY CLIVE CLYDE CRAIG CUTTS GLUBB GOUGH HORNE ISMAY JONES KIRKE MAHON MAUDE MILNE MONCK MOORE NEILL NIXON PLATT SMITH STACK SYKES WARDE AYLMER BLOUNT BROOKE BROWNE BULFIN BURLEY CHURCH CONWAY CREAGH DAWSON DOBELL DUNDAS FORBES FRENCH FULLER GORDON GRAHAM HAKING HARRIS HOWARD INGLIS JARVIS LUGARD MARTEL MILLER MORGAN MURRAY NAPIER NORMAN NUGENT PICTON POPHAM

RAGLAN SAVAGE SCOBIE SIDNEY SIMCOE TEMPLE TURNER UFFORD VYVYAN WALLER WARREN WAVELL WEMYSS ALLENBY AMHERST ATHLONE BARDOLF BINGHAM BOUQUET BRANDON BRIDGES BURNABY CADOGAN CAVALLO CHANDOS CLAYTON CLINTON COLLINS DEMPSEY DOWDING FASTOLF MACMUNN MAXWELL METHUEN MORLAND OCONNOR PEREIRA POWNALL ROBERTS STEWART SWINTON TORRENS VENNING VINCENT WANTAGE WINGATE ALDERSON ANDERSON AUCHMUTY BECKWITH BENTINCK BLAKENEY BRADDOCK BRANCKER BROWNING BURGOYNE CALLWELL CAMPBELL CARDIGAN CARLETON CATHCART CHETWODE COLBORNE CONGREVE CROMWELL FERGUSON GLEICHEN GREVILLE HAMILTON HARDINGE HASTINGS HAVELOCK HORROCKS LAWRENCE LIGONIER LINDSELL LOCKHART MAITLAND MONTFORT POYNINGS SHRAPNEL STANHOPE TARLETON ALEXANDER BEAUCHAMP BERESFORD BROWNRIGG CONSTABLE HARINGTON HENDERSON KITCHENER MACDONALD OCTERLONY POTTINGER REPINGTON ROBERTSON WILKINSON WOODVILLE AUCHINLECK CODRINGTON CORNWALLIS DESBOROUGH MACDOUGALL MONTGOMERY SHERBROOKE WELLINGTON BRACKENBURY WINTRINGHAM
FINNISH MANNERHEIM
FRENCH FAY FOY NEY BUAT FOCH JUIN NIEL SAXE AMADE ANDRE CONTI COSSE DOUAY DUMAS FOREY HENRY HULIN JUNOT LALLY LEVIS LOBAU MENOU MINIE MITRY MURAT TRACY BAYARD BELLAY BOUDET CHABOT CHANZY CISSEY CLARKE CLOSSE DAUMAS DAVOUT DEJEAN DROUOT DUCROT DUNOIS FABERT FAILLY FAVRAS FLEURY FOLARD FRIANT GERARD GIRAUD GOBERT JARNAC JOFFRE KLEBER LACLOS LANNES LATUDE LAUNAY LAUZUN MAGNAN MAISON MANGIN MARBOT MASSUE MONCEY MOREAU PETAIN ROVIGO SUCHET TROCHU BAZAINE BOICHUT BOSQUET BOUILLE CATINAT CATROUX CHAMILY CHARRAS CHAUVIN CLAUSEL CLISSON CRILLON CUSTINE DEBENEY DREYFUS FABVIER GAMELIN GASSION GOURAUD GROUCHY GUIBERT JOUBERT JOURDAN LABORDE LASALLE LEBOEUF LECLERC LEJEUNE LUCKNER LYAUTEY MARCEAU MARMONT MAURICE MOLITOR MONTLUC MORTIER NIVELLE RENAULT REYNIER TALLARD TURENNE VALENCE VENDOME WEYGAND AUGEREAU BARATIER BOURBAKI CHAMBRUN CHAUCHAT CHOISEUL

CLUSERET CONTADES DEGAULLE DEGOUTTE ESTIENNE GALLIENI GOURGAUD GOURGUES GRAZIANI HARCOURT LAMARQUE LANGLOIS LANREZAC LARMINAT LEFEBVRE LORENCEZ MAUNOURY MONTCALM PICHEGRU TAVANNES VANDAMME AIGUILLON ANDREOSSY BERTHELOT BOISSOUDY BOULANGER CANROBERT DAMPIERRE FAIDHERBE GROSSETTI GUEBRIANT HUNTZIGER LAFAYETTE LALLEMAND LAURISTON MACDONALD MONTHOLON NIVERNAIS PELISSIER SCHOMBERG CHASTELLUX GUILLAUMAT KELLERMANN MONTGOMERY ROCHAMBEAU WESTERMANN CHANGARNIER JACQUEMINOT MONTMORENCY CAULAINCOURT LESDIGUIERES
GERMAN EPP JODL KALB ARNIM BOEHN BULOW KLUCK KUNDT HALDER HAUSEN HUTIER KEITEL MOLTKE PAULUS ROMMEL SEECKT BISSING BLUCHER CAPRIVI FISCHER FRITSCH GROENER JOCHMUS SPEIDEL STEUBEN BERNHARD BLOMBERG GALLWITZ GERHARDT GUDERIAN HAESELER HARTMANN LITZMANN RIEDESEL SCHWERIN ZEITZLER ALDRINGEN HAUSHOFER HEERINGEN HINDERSIN LINSINGEN MACKENSEN MANSFIELD REINHARDT RUNDSTEDT THEILMANN WALDERSEE FRUNDSBERG HINDENBURG KESSELRING LUDENDORFF SCHLEICHER SCHLIEFFEN BRAUCHITSCH FALKENHORST FALKENHAUSEN STAUFFENBERG
GREEK ARATUS KALERGES KONDYLES PANGALOS PELOPIDAS ALCIBIADES HIERONYMUS EPAMINONDAS THEMISTOCLES
GUATEMALAN CHACON ORELLANA
HAITIAN PETION RIGAUD SALOMON GEFFRARD
HUNGARIAN GORGEY HUNYADI DAMJANICH SZECHENYI
IRISH LACY WADE COLLEY ODUFFY CADOGAN COLLINS OREILLY OHIGGINS PAKENHAM ALANBROOKE
IRTISH DILL BARRY CUNNINGHAM
ISRAELI ALLON DAYAN ELAZAR NETANYAHU
ITALIAN BIXIO FANTI CANEVA COSENZ DAVILA DOUHET GORGIA NOBILE ABRUZZI CAPELLO BADOGLIO CAVIGLIA CIALDINI COLLEONI GIARDINO GRAZIANI MARSIGLI RAMORINO BARATIERI CAVALLERO DANNUNZIO GARIBALDI LAMARMORA PICCOLOMINI
JAPANESE ABE OKU TOJO ARAKI KOISO NODZU SAITO TAMAI KODAMA KUROKI DOIHARA FUSHIMI KATSURA HASEGAWA SUGIYAMA TERAUCHI FUKUSHIMA HASHIMOTO HIDEYOSHI TAMASHITA
KOREAN PARK
LEBANESE HADDAD
MEXICAN MEJIA ALDAMA ARISTA

CALLES HUERTA ALMAZAN
ALMONTE ALVAREZ AMPUDIA
CAMACHO MIRAMON MORELOS
OBREGON VALLEJO ZULOAGA
CANALIZO CARDENAS ESCOBEDO
GONZALEZ GUERRERO ITURBIDE
VICTORIA BUSTAMANTE
NEW ZEALAND CHAYTOR
FREYBERG
NIGERIAN GOWON
PARAGUAYAN MORINIGO
ESTIGARRIBIA
PERSIAN ARTAPHERNES
PERUVIAN BALTA PRADO CACERES
GAMARRA PIEROLA CASTILLA
IGLESIAS SALAVERRY
POLISH BEM PASEK HALLER
PULASKI CHLOPICKI DEMBINSKI
KOSCIUSKO PILSUDSKI
DOMBROWSKI MALCZEWSKI
SOSNKOWSKI KRUKOWIECKI
PORTUGUESE ALMEIDA PEREIRA
SALDANHA TEIXEIRA
PRUSSIAN GNEISENAU
CLAUSEWITZ
ROMAN SULLA AETIUS ANTONY
BURRUS CAEPIO CAESAR GALLUS
POLLIO POMPEY SCIPIO AGRIPPA
ALBINUS CAECINA CALENUS
CASSIUS CHAEREA CRASSUS
FANNIUS LEPIDUS PLANCUS
AFRANIUS AGRICOLA CEREATIS
DENTATUS DUILLIUS LUCULLUS
FABRICIUS FLAMINIUS PASKEVICH
SERTORIUS CORIOLANUS
CINCINNATUS
RUMANIAN ILIESCU ANTONESCU
RUSSIAN CUI BERK GURKO KONEV
GLINKA NEVSKI PLATOV ZHUKOV
BLUCHER BUDENNY CHAPAEV
CHUIKOV DENIKIN KALEDIN
KAMENEV KUTUZOV SUVOROV
VATUTIN WRANGEL ZHDANOV
AI EKSEEV AVERESCU BOBRIKOV
BRUSILOV GOLITSYN GORBATOV
KAULBARS KORNILOV LINEVICH
MILYUTIN SAMSONOV SKOBELEV
YUDENICH BAGRATION BENNIGSEN
GORCHAKOV LECHITSKI MENSHIKOV
CHERNYAIEV CHERNYSHEV
DRAGOMIROV KUROPATKIN
ROSTOPCHIN TIMOSHENKO
VOROSHILOV ROKOSSOVSKY
SHAPOSHNIKOV
SALVADORAN REGALADO
SCOTTISH HAIG URRY BAIRD
MUNRO ELIOTT RUTHVEN
DRUMMOND IRONSIDE MIDDLETON
SOUTH AFRICAN BOTHA SMUTS
HERTZOG PRETORIUS
SPANISH CID ALVA ELIO MINA
MOLA RADA CROIX GARAY OSUNA
ULLOA AVALOS GUZMAN TOLEDO
ALMAGRO CORDOBA FARNESE
MONCADA NARVAEZ NAVARRO
ODONOJU PORTOLA ALVARADO
CANTERAC CARVAJAL CASTANOS
CASTILLO ESPINOSA MANRIQUE
MUNTANER ORELLANA VALDIVIA
PEDRARIAS REQUESENS
VELASQUEZ CASTELLANOS
SWEDISH HORN TOLL BANER
BRAHE ARMFELT LEWENHAUPT

TORSTENSON ADLERCREUTZ
ADLERSPARRE
SWISS DUFOUR ERLACH JENATSCH
TURKISH BABUR ENVER EVREN
ATATURL
URUGUAYAN ORIBE FLORES
VENEZUELAN PAEZ GOMEZ
CASTRO FALCON MONAGAS
YUGOSLAV ZIVKOVIC MIHAJLOVIC
SOLDIERLY WARLIKE
SOLDIERY HORSE MILITIA SEBUNDY
MILITARY SIBBENDY
SOLE CORK FACE GADE MERE ONLY
SLIP SOCK SPUR AFALD ALONE
CLUMP LEMON OLEPI PELMA
WHOLE GADOID INSOLE ONLEPY
PLANTA SINGLE SOLEYN SULLEN
THENAR TONGUE UNIQUE
ANACANTH FLATFISH HOGCHOKE
MARYSOLE SINGULAR SOLITARY
(— A SHOE) SPECK
(— FOR WALKING OVER SAND)
BACKSTER
(— OF BIRD'S FOOT) PTERNA
(— OF FOOT) PLAT VOLA PELMA
PLANT
(— OF PLANE) FACE
(— OF PLOW) SLADE
(— WITH WOOD) CLOG
(HALF —) SHOULDER
(KIND OF —) DOVER
(TOWARD THE —) PLANTAD
(PREF.) PEDI(O) PELMATO
(SUFF.) PELMOUS
SOLELY SOLE ALONE SIMPLY
SINGLY WHOLLY SHEERLY
ENTIRELY
SOLEMN DEEP SAGE AWFUL BUDGE
SOBER DEVOUT FORMAL RITUAL
EARNEST SERIOUS WEIGHTY
FUNEREAL PORTENTOUS
(STUPIDLY —) POFACED
SOLEMNITY OBIT RITE SACRE
GRAVITY SEVERITY
SOLEMNIZE KEEP SEAL
SOLEMNLY GRAVE HIGHLY
SOLENODONT AGOUTA ALMIQUE
SOLEPIECE SOLE GIRDER
SOL-FA SOLMIZATE
SOLICIT ASK BEG SUE WOO DRUM
MOVE SEEK THIG TOUT URGE
APPLY COURT CRAVE TREAT
ACCOST HUSTLE INVITE INVOKE
BESEECH CANVASS ENTREAT
IMPLORE INSTANT PROCURE
REQUEST APPROACH PETITION
SOLICITATION SUIT QUEST
CANVASS INSTANT REQUEST
SOLICIT ENTREATY INSTANCE
SOLICITOR AVOUE LAWYER WRITER
ADVOCATE ATTORNEY TRAMPLER
SOLICITOUS URGENT CAREFUL
CURIOUS JEALOUS DESIROUS
CONCERNED
SOLICITUDE CARE CARK FEAR
HEED PAIN YEME HEART WORRY
ANXIETY CONCERN BUSINESS
JEALOUSY
SOLID DRY SAD CONE CUBE FAST
FIRM FULL HARD CHAMP CUBIC
LEVEL MASSY MEATY SOUND STIFF
STOUT THICK TIGHT SECURE
STABLE STODGY STRONG STURDY

COMPACT CUPRENE UNIFORM
CONSTANT GROUNDLY MATERIAL
STERLING
(GEOMETRICAL —) CONE CUBE
PRISM CONOID CUPROID FRUSTUM
POLYHEDRON
(NOT —) BUBBLE
(THEORETICAL —) HYPERCUBE
(PL.) POCHE
(PREF.) STERE(O)
SOLIDARITY CIVILITY
SOLIDIFIED SOLID HARDENED
(READILY —) GLACIAL
SOLIDIFY DRY SET CAKE JELL
SHOOT GELATE HARDEN
COMPACT CONGEAL STIFFEN
CONCRETE
SOLIDITY SADNESS FASTNESS
FIRMNESS HARDNESS
SOLIDLY FIRMLY SQUARE STOUTLY
GROUNDLY
SOLIDUS BEZANT NOMISMA
DIAGONAL HYPERPER
(HALF —) SEMIS
SOLIPSISM EGOISM
SOLITAIRE CLARINO CANFIELD
KLONDIKE NAPOLEON PATIENCE
SOLITARY
SOLITARY ODD WAE LONE ONLY
SOLE ALONE ELYNG LONELY
ONLEPY SAVAGE SINGLE SOLEYN
SULLEN DERNFUL EREMITE
PRIVATE RECLUSE UNCOUTH
WIDOWED DESOLATE EREMITIC
ISOLATED LONESOME PEGBOARD
SECLUDED SEPARATE
(PREF.) EREM(O)
SOLITUDE PRIVACY RETREAT
SOLITARY
SOLLERET SABBATON
SOLO ARIA CALL ALONE ARIOSO
CAVATINA SPADILLA
SOLOIST (BASS —) SUCCENTOR
SOLOMON SAM KOHELETH
(BROTHER OF —) ADONIJAH
(FATHER OF —) DAVID
(MOTHER OF —) BATHSHEBA
SOLOMON ISLANDS (CAPITAL:)
HONIARA
(CAPITAL OF —) HONIARA
(ISLAND:) GIZO SAVO FLORIDA
MALAITA RENDOVA CHOISEUL
SANJORGE NEWGEORGIA
GUADALCANAL SANTAISABEL
(ISLAND OF —) BUKA GIZO SAVO
TULAGI FLORISA MALAITA RENDOVA
RUSSELL CHOISEUL GUADALCANAL
BOUGAINVILLE
SOLOMON'S SEAL LILY SEALWORT
SOLON SAGE GNOMIC GNOMIST
SENATOR LAWMAKER
SOLPUGID TARANTULA
SOLSTICE SUNSTAY SUNSTEAD
SOLUBLE FRIM FRUM FIXED
SOLUTE SOLVABLE
SOLUTION IT LYE AQUA EUSOL
STAIN TINCT ACETUM ANSWER
ASSOIL DOCTOR ERASER SALINE
EXTRACT EYEWASH LACQUER
RESOLVE SOLUTIO WORKING
ANALYSIS LEACHATE TINCTURE
(— ADDED FOR GOOD MEASURE)
INCAST

(— OF CHESS PROBLEM) COOK
(— OF FERMENTED BRAN) DRENCH
(— OF GUM TRAGACANTH) BED
(ACID —) SOUR
(ALCOHOLIC —) ESSENCE
(ANTISEPTIC —) EUSOL
(COLLOIDAL —) GEL
(CORROSIVE —) OLEUM
(PICKLING —) SOUSE
(PRESERVING —) BOLIN
(SALINE —) BRINE
(SOAP —) NIGRE
(SOLID —) AUSTENITE
(STERILE —) JOHNIN
(TEMPORARY —) QUICKFIX
(VISCOUS —) GLUE
(WATERY —) EAU SAP
SOLVE DO FIX READ UNDO WORK
BREAK CRACK LOOSE SALVE
ANSWER ASSOIL CIPHER FIGURE
REDUCE RIDDLE SOLUTE RESOLVE
UNRAVEL DECIPHER DISSOLVE
SOLVENT ETHER SOUND CETANE
ELUANT ELUENT SPIRIT TOLUOL
ACETONE ALCOHOL BENZINE
COUPLER DILUENT REMOVER
SPOTTER TOLUENE CARBITOL
PICOLINE SOLVABLE STRIPPER
TEREBENE TETRALIN MENSTRUUM
(UNIVERSAL —) ALKAHEST
SOLVER (PROBLEM —) HACKER
SOMALI SOMAL SHUHALI
(PL.) ASHA
SOMALIA (CAPITAL OF —)
MOGADISHU
(COIN OF —) BESA
(DIVISION OF —) HAWIYA
(MEASURE OF —) TOP CABA CHELA
DARAT TABLA CUBITO
(MOUNTAIN OF —) SURUDAD
(MOUNTAIN RANGE OF —) GUBAN
(NATIVE OF —) GALLA HAWIYA
ISBAAK SOMALI DANAKIL
(RIVER OF —) JUBA NOGAL SCEBELI
(TOWN OF —) MERCA BERBERA
KISMAYU HARGEISA
(WEIGHT OF —) PARSALAH
SOMATIC SOMAL BODILY
SOMBER SAD DERN DULL GRAVE
MORNE SOBER GLOOMY LENTEN
SOLEMN SOMBRE SULLEN
AUSTERE SERIOUS DARKSOME
SOMBROUS
SOME ANY ODD AFEW THIS
CERTAIN
SOMEBODY QUIDAM SOMEONE
SOMEDAY ONCE
SOMEHOW HOW ONEHOW
SOMEWAY SOMEGATE
SOMEONE SUCH
SOMERSAULT FLIP TOPPLE
FLIFFUS SPOTTER TWISTER
BACKFLIP SOMERSET
SOMETHING WHAT ALIQUID
WHATNOT SOMEWHAT
(— ABNORMAL) FREAK
(— ADDED) IMP EXTRA DOCTOR
(— AMUSING) HOOT
(— ATTRACTIVE) DUCK
(— BELIEVED) CREDIT
(— BIG) BOUNCER
(— BRIGHT RED) CORAL
(— CHERISHED) APPLE

(— **COMMONPLACE**) DROSS
(— **CONSECRATED**) SACRUM
(— **CONTRARY TO LOGIC**) ALOGISM
(— **CORRUPT**) CARRION
(— **COUNTERFEIT**) DUFFER PINCHBECK
(— **DIFFICULT**) STINKER
(— **DISLIKED**) DOGMEAT
(— **DONE**) GERENDUM
(— **EASILY ACHIEVED**) GIMME
(— **EASY**) PIPE CAKEWALK
(— **ELABORATE**) DEVICE
(— **ELUSIVE**) FUGITIVE
(— **EXCELLENT**) DANDY
(— **EXCESSIVE**) LUXUS
(— **EXTRAORDINARY**) SNORTER
(— **FALSE**) HOOEY
(— **FAMILIAR**) KNOWN
(— **FIRST-RATE**) CHEESE
(— **FLAWED**) CRIPPLE
(— **FOOLISH**) IDIOCY FATUITY
(— **FORGOTTEN**) CORPSE
(— **FORKED**) CORNUTE
(— **FRAUDULENT**) CROSS
(— **GIVEN WITHOUT CHARGE**) FREEBEE FREEBIE
(— **HORRIFYING**) SHOCKER
(— **IDENTICAL**) ISOMORPH
(— **ILL-DEFINED**) BLOB
(— **IN ADDITION TO ORDINARY**) BONUS
(— **INCOMPLETE**) END
(— **INFERIOR**) DOG CULL LESS CAGMAG
(— **INJURIOUS**) ENEMY
(— **INSIGNIFICANT**) STRAW FEATHER SNICKET FRAGMENT
(— **INTRICATE**) KNOT
(— **LARGE**) GIANT SMASHER
(— **MADE UP**) FIGMENT
(— **NOTABLE**) DEUCE
(— **NOT ESSENTIAL**) FRILL
(— **NOT EXPLAINED**) MYSTERY
(— **OFFERED FOR LOAN**) PREMIUM
(— **OF GREAT VALUE**) EYETOOTH
(— **OF LITTLE VALUE**) SHUCK FOUTER FOUTRA MAKEWEIGHT
(— **OF NO VALUE**) HAW DAMN BAUBEE DOCKEN
(— **OR OTHER**) ANYTHING
(— **OUTSTANDING**) BROTH DOYEN GASSER STANDOUT
(— **PAINFUL**) GAFF
(— **PATCHED UP**) VAMP
(— **POOR**) FLUMMERY
(— **PRECIOUS**) DUMPLING
(— **PREJUDICIAL**) FOE
(— **PROVOKING**) DEVIL
(— **REPELLENT**) SPINACH
(— **RISKED**) HAZARD
(— **SHAPELESS**) DUMP
(— **SHOWY**) FLOSS
(— **SHRIVELED**) SCRUMP
(— **SMALL**) DOT SNIP
(— **SPECTACULAR**) DILLY
(— **STICKY**) CAB
(— **STOLEN**) CRIB
(— **STRANGE**) FANTASIA
(— **SUPERLATIVE**) DARB
(— **TAUGHT**) DOCUMENT
(— **THAT IS LIGHT**) SKIFF SKIFT
(— **THAT WHIRLS**) GIG
(— **TO BIND BARGAIN**) EARNEST

(— **TRIVIAL**) CHIP FLUFF
(— **UNDECIDED**) ACRISY
(— **UNINTELLIGIBLE**) GREEK
(— **UNPLEASANT**) GUCK SOUR
(— **UNSPECIFIED**) ITEM
(— **UNSUBSTANTIAL**) FROTH
(— **UNTRUE**) HOKUM
(— **USELESS**) CRAP BLANK
(— **VILE**) DUNG
(— **WORTHLESS**) BOTH DUST HOKUM DUFFER AMBSACE
(— **WRITTEN**) SCRIPT
SOMETIME FORMER SOMDEL WHILOM ANCIENT QUONDAM SOMEDEAL SOMEPART SOMEWHEN
SOMETIMES NOW TOO WHILE PERDIE WHILES UMQUHILE OCCASIONALLY
SOMEWHAT BIT ATAD POCO SOME ATOUCH PRETTY RATHER SLIGHT SUMMAT ALIQUID SOMEDEAL (PREF.) SEMI
SOMEWHERE SOMERS SOMEGATE
SOMITE ZONITE SEGMENT TERGITE GONOTOME MEROSOME MESOMERE SOMATOME
SOMMER ELKA
SOMNIFEROUS OPIATE SOMNIFIC
SOMNUS HYPNUS
SON BEN BOY LAD ANAC FILS FITZ ZONE CHILD KIBEI MOPSY FILIUS JUNIOR REUBEN EPAPHUS EPIGONUS MONSIEUR
(— **OF CHIEF**) OGTIERN
(— **OF KING OF FRANCE**) DAUPHIN
(— **OF NISEI**) SANSEI
(— **OF PEER**) MASTER
(— **OF SUDRA**) CHANDALA
(**DAVID'S FAVORITE** —) ABSALOM
(**FIRST-BORN** —) HEIR
(**FOURTH** —) MARTLET
(**FREEMASON'S** —) LEWIS
(**ILLEGITIMATE** —) NEPHEW
(**NISEI** —) SANSEI
(**PRIEST'S** —) NEPHEW
(**YOUNG** —) MOPSY
(**YOUNGER** —) CADET
(**YOUNGEST** —) CADET BENJAMIN (PREF.) AP FILI(O)
SONANT VIBRANT
SONAR ASDIC
(— **BLIP**) ECHO
(**KIND OF** —) SIDESCAN
SONCHUS DINDLE
SONG AIR DIT FIT JIG LAY UTA CANT DUAN FOLK GATO GLEE LEED MELE NOTE RANT RUNE SANG TUNE BLUES CANSO CAROL CHANT CHARM CROON DILDO DITTY MELOS MOLPE OLDIE PAEAN VOCAL BALLAD BRANLE BUBBLE CANTIC CANZON CARMEN CHANTY CHORUS HIMENE JINGLE MELODY ORPHIC SHANTY STRAIN VINATA WAIATA WARBLE BACCHIC BALLATA CANCION CANTION CHANSON COMIQUE DESCANT MELISMA MELODIA REQUIEM REVERDI ROMANCE SCOLION SONGLET THRENOS BIRDSONG BRINDISI CANTICLE CANZONET COONJINE FLAMENCO JUBILATE

PALINODE RHAPSODY SERVENTE SINGSONG ZORTZICO ROUNDELAY
(— **ACCOMPANYING TOAST**) BRINDISI
(— **FOR TWO VOICES**) GYMEL
(— **IN GREEK DRAMA**) STROPHE
(— **OF BASQUES**) ZORTZICO
(— **OF BIRD**) LAY KOLLER
(— **OF JOY**) CAROL PAEAN JUBILATE
(— **OF LAMENTATION**) THRENE THRENODY
(— **OF MINSTREL**) YEDDING
(— **OF OCEANIA**) HIMENE
(— **OF PRAISE**) HYMN CAROL ANTHEM CHORALE
(—**S OF BIRDS**) RAMAGE
(— **UNACCOMPANIED**) GLEE
(— **WITH MONOTONOUS RHYME**) VIRELAI VIRELAY
(**ANDALUSIAN** —) SAETA
(**ART** —) LIED
(**BOAT** —) JORRAM
(**CEREMONIAL** —S) AREITO
(**CRADLE** —) HUSHO
(**CUBAN** —) GUAJIRA COMPARSA
(**DANCE** —) BALLAD BAMBUCO
(**DRINKING** —) BACCHIC SCOLION SKOLION WASSAIL
(**EVENING** —) SERENA EVENSONG SERENATA
(**FOLK** —) SON FADO FOLK BLUES DOINA BYLINA CANTIGA JUBILEE STORNELLO
(**FUNERAL** —) DIRGE MONODY EPICEDE THRENODY
(**FUNEREAL** —) ELEGY
(**GAY** —) LILT
(**GERMAN** —) LIED
(**GYPSY** —) FLAMENCO
(**HAWAIIAN** —) MELE
(**HEBREW** —) ELIELI HATIKVAH
(**IMPROMPTU** —) SCOLION
(**JAPANESE** —) UTA
(**LOVE** —) ALBA CANSO CANZO FANCY TORCH AMORET AUBADE SERENA SERENATA
(**MELISMATIC** —) DIVISION
(**MOCKING** —) JIG
(**MORNING** —) MATIN AUBADE
(**MOURNFUL** —) DUMP PLAINT ENDECHA
(**MYSTIC** —) RUNE
(**NEW ZEALAND** —) WAIATA
(**NIGHT** —) COMPLIN
(**NO** —S) UTAI
(**NUPTIAL** —) HYMEN
(**PART** —) CHACE TROLL CACCIA CANZONET FROTTOLA MADRIGAL
(**PASTORAL** —) OAT
(**PLAIN** —) GROUND
(**PORTUGUESE** —) FADO
(**RELIGIOUS** —) HYMN CAROL PSALM SHOUT ANTHEM POLYMNY SIRVENT
(**REVOLUTIONARY** —) CARMAGNOLE
(**ROUND-**) TROLL
(**SACRED** —) MOTET
(**SAILOR'S** —) CHANTY SHANTY
(**SANSKRIT** —) GITA
(**SINGLE** —) CUT
(**SINGLE** — **ON RECORD**) CUT
(**SPIRITED** —) LILT

(**STUPID** —) STROWD
(**VINTAGE** —) VINATA
(**WORK** —) HOLLER
(PL.) ZEMMI AREITO
(PREF.) MELO
(SUFF.) ODE ODIC ODIST ODY
SONGBIRD CHAT IORA LARK WREN MAVIS ROBIN SABIA SHAMA SIREN VEERY VIREO BULBUL CANARY LINNET MOCKER ORIOLE SINGER THRUSH CATBIRD GRASSET TANAGER WARBLER ACCENTOR BENGALEE BLUEBIRD BOBOLINK CARDINAL SONGSTER MEADOWLARK
SONGLIKE ARIOSE
SONG OF BERNADETTE (**AUTHOR OF** —) WERFEL
(**CHARACTER IN** —) LOUISE THERESE FRANCOIS PEYRAMALE SOUBIROUS BERNADETTE
SONG OF HIAWATHA (**AUTHOR OF** —) LONGFELLOW
(**CHARACTER IN** —) KWASIND NOKOMIS WENONAH HIAWATHA CHIBIABOS MINNEHAHA MUDJEKEEWIS
SONG OF ROLAND (**AUTHOR OF** —) UNKNOWN
(**CHARACTER IN** —) ALDA ALORY MILON OGIER BERTHA FERRAU GERARD MEDORO MORGAN OBERTO OLIVER ROLAND SADONE ARGALIA CHARLOT GANELON GODFREY MALAGIS REINOLD ASTOLPHO KARAHEUT BRADAMANT GLORIANDA CHARLEMAGNE MANDRICARDO
SONGSTER SINGER WARBLER
SONG THRUSH MAVIE MAVIS
SON-IN-LAW GENER MAUGH
SONNAMBULA, LA (**CHARACTER IN** —) LISA AMINA ELVINO TERESA RODOLFO
(**COMPOSER OF** —) BELLINI
SONNET AMORET
(— **PART**) SESTET
(**LOVE** —) AMORET
SONOGRAPHY ULTRASOUND
SONORITY RESONANCE
SONOROUS ROUND SHILL TONOUS OROTUND VIBRANT RESONANT SOUNDFUL SOUNDING RESOUNDING
SONOROUSLY DEEPLY
SONS AND LOVERS (**AUTHOR OF** —) LAWRENCE
(**CHARACTER IN** —) LILY PAUL ANNIE CLARA DAWES MOREL ARTHUR BAXTER MIRIAM WALTER LEIVERS WILLIAM GERTRUDE
SONSHIP FILIETY
SONYA (**FATHER OF** —) MARMELADOV
SOOLOOS THULUTH
SOON ERE ANON CITO TITE EARLY NEWLY RADLY RATHE BELIVE INABIT SUDDEN TIMELY BETIMES ERELONG PRESTLY SHORTLY DIRECTLY SPEEDILY PRESENTLY
(**AS** — **AS POSSIBLE**) ASAP
SOONER ERE ERER ERST OKIE FIRST BEFORE TITTER

(— STATE) OKLAHOMA
(— THAN) OR ERE
SOONEST FRST RATHEST
SOOT COOM IZLE SMUT STUP SUMI
BLECK BROOK COLLY COOMB
CROCK GRIME SOTIK FULIGO
SMOUCH SMUTCH SPODIUM
(— ON GRATE BAR) STRANGER
SOOTHE COY DEW BALM CALM
COAX DILL EASE HUSH LULL
ACCOY ALLAY CHARM DULCE
HUMOR QUELL SALVE SLEEK STILL
BECALM PACIFY SETTLE SMOOTH
SOLACE STROKE SUPPLE ADDULCE
APPEASE ASSUAGE COMFORT
COMPOSE CONSOLE DEMULCE
FLATTER GRUNTLE LULLABY
MOLLIFY PLASTER QUALIFY
ATTEMPER BLANDISH MITIGATE
UNRUFFLE
SOOTHER BALM BALSAM ANODYNE
SOOTHING MILD BALMY BLAND
DOWNY DULCE STILL SWEET
ANETIC ANIMAL DREAMY DULCET
GENTLE SMOOTH ANODYNE
BALSAMIC SEDATIVE
SOOTHSAY SORT
SOOTHSAYER SEER AUGUR WEIRD
ARIOLE DIVINE PYTHON ARUSPEX
DIVINER CHALDEAN HARUSPEX
TIRESIAS
SOOTY COLLY REECHY SMUTTY
BROOKIE COLLIED
SOOTY ALBATROSS NELLIE
QUAKER STINKER BLUEBIRD
STINKPOT
SOOTY SHEARWATER TITI
SOP BERRY SIPPET SOAKUP SPONGE
SUGARSOP SWEETSOP
BREADBERRY
SOPATER (FATHER OF —) PYRRHUS
SOPHER SCRIBE
SOPHISM FETCH ELENCH FALLACY
SOPHEME
SOPHIST SOPH DUNCE
SOPHISTICATE GARBLE MONDAINE
SOPHISTICATED WISE BLASE CIVIL
SALTY SVELTE URBANE WORLDLY
SOPHISTICATION CHIC
SOPHISTRY DECEIT FALLACY
SOPHISM CHICANERY
SOPHOCLES (— TRAGEDY) AJAX
SOPHONISBA (BROTHER OF —)
HANNIBAL
(FATHER OF —) HASDRUBAL
(HUSBAND OF —) SYPHAX
SOPORIFIC DWALE DROWSY
HYPNIC OPIATE SLEEPY HYPNOTIC
NARCOTIC SOMNIFIC
SOPPING SQUASHY
SOPPY JUICY SOAKY
SOPRANO CANARY TREBLE
DESCANT CASTRATO
SORA ORTOLAN
SORB OCCLUDE LUSATIAN
SORBIAN WENDISH
SORBOSE ACROSE
SORCERER MAGE BOYLA BRUJO
WITCH BOOLYA NAGUAL VOODOO
WIZARD KORADJI WARLOCK
WIELARE FETISHER MAGICIAN
WITCHMAN
(PL.) GOETAE

SORCERESS BRUJA CIRCE LAMIA
SIBYL WITCH ARMIDA HECATE
BABAJAGA KORRIGAN WALKYRIE
SORCERY OBI MAGIC OBEAH SPELL
MAKUTU PISHOGUE PRESTIGE
SORTIARY WIGELING WITCHERY
WITCHING NECROMANCY
(VOODOO —) OBEAH WANGA
OUANGA
SORDES SABURRA
SORDID RAW BASE GAMY MEAN
VILE DIRTY DUSTY MUCKY SEAMY
CHETIF GRUBBY SODDEN
MESQUIN SQUALID CHURLISH
SORDOR LEES
SORE BUM FOX PET BUBA CHAP
DEAR GALL KIBE KYLE OUCH SAER
BLAIN BOTCH GAMMY AGNAIL
BITTER BOUBAS CANKER FESTER
MELLIT MORMAL RANKLE TAKING
CATHAIR CHANCRE SORANCE
SCALDING
(— ON HORSE'S FOOT) MELLIT
QUITTER
(ARTIFICIAL —) FOX
(SUMMER — S) CALORIS LEECHES
SO RED THE ROSE (AUTHOR OF —)
YOUNG
(CHARACTER IN —) HUGH LUCY
MARY VEAL ZACH AGNES SARAH
AMELIE DUNCAN EDWARD
BALFOUR BEDFORD CHARLES
FRANCES LUCINDA MALCOLM
MCGEHEE SHELTON VALETTE
WILLIAM HARTWELL MIDDLETON
TALIAFERRO
SORE MOUTH ORF
SORENESS FROG
(— OF EYES) LIPPITUDE
SORGHUM CANE CUSH MILO
BATAD DARSO DURRA SORGO
CHOLAM HEGARI IMPHEE KAFFIR
SHALLU FETERITA KAOLIANG
SOROCHE PUNA
SORREL OCA OKA ROAN SORE
CUCKOO HEARTS OXALIS RUBICAN
SOUROCK ALLELUIA STABWORT
SORREL TREE TITI ELKWOOD
SOURWOOD
SORROW WO RUE WOE BALE CARE
DOLE HARM MOAN RUTH SORE
TEEN DOLOR GRAME GRIEF
MOURN RUING SARRA UNWIN
GRIEVE LAMENT MISERY REGRET
STOUND UNLUST ANGUISH
CONDOLE DEPLORE PENANCE
REGRATE REMORSE THOUGHT
TROUBLE WOEFARE CALAMITY
DISTRESS DOLEANCE DREARING
EGRIMONY MOURNING
(— AUDIBLY) WAIL
(— FOR SIN) ATTRITION
(PREF.) LUCTI
SORROWFUL BAD SAD WAN BLUE
GLUM CHARY DREAR TRIST
WOFUL DISMAL DOLENT DREARY
RUEFUL BALEFUL CAREFUL
DOLEFUL LUCTUAL RUESOME
UNHAPPY WAILFUL CONTRITE
DESOLATE DOLESOME DOLOROSO
GRIEFFUL MOURNFUL PITIABLE
SORROWFULLY SADLY WRATH
DERNLY HEAVILY

SORRY BAD SAD WOE HURT VEXED
UNFAIN PITIFUL CONTRITE
PENITENT WRETCHED
SORT ILK KIN LOT BRAN COMB GERE
HUMP KIND RANK SIFT SUIT WING
WORK BRACK BREED GENUS
GRADE SAVOR SPICE ASSORT
BARREL DILLUE GARBLE GENDER
KIDNEY MANNER MISTER NATURE
STRAIN STRIPE FASHION SPECIES
SPECKLE VARIETY CLASSIFY
SEPARATE
(— CHICKS) SEX
(— COTTON BY STAPLE) STAPLE
(— MAIL) CASE
(— MERCHANDISE) BRACK
(— OF) INAWAY
(— OF PERSON) LIKE
(ATHLETIC —) JOCK
(OUT OF —S) GRUMPY
SORTER SHALEMAN
SORTIE RAID ISSUE SALLY ATTACK
OUTFALL
SORTILEGE LOT
SORTING GARBLING
(— ROOM) SALLE
SORTITA ARIA
SORUS AECIUM TELIUM
SORVA BORRACHA
SOT LUSH SOAK DRUNK LOURD
TOPER LOURDY BLOTTER
DASTARD TOSSPOT DRUNKARD
SOTHO SUTO SESUTO
SOTIK SOOT
SOUFFLE FONDU FONDUE
SOUGH MOAN
SOUGHT QUESITED
SOUL BA AME EGO ALMA ANIMA
ATMAN GHOST HEART SHADE
BUDDHI DIBBUK NATURE PNEUMA
PSYCHE SPIRIT SPRITE NEPHESH
PURUSHA INTERNAL
(—S OF THE DEAD) LEMURES
(ANIMAL — IN MAN) NEPHESH
(DISEMBODIED —) KER
(EGYPTIAN IMMORTAL —) BA
(INDIVIDUAL —) JIVA
(LIBERATED —) KEVALIN
(UNIVERSAL —) HANSA
(WANDERING —) DIBBUK DYBBUK
(PREF.) PSYCH(O) THYM(O)
(SUFF.) PSYCHE
SOULFULLY GEISTLICH
SOULLESS TURNIPY
SOU MARQUE STAMPEE
SOUND GO CRY FIT BLOW DING
DRIP FAST FERE FIRM FLOG FLOW
GLUG GOOD HAIL HALE KYLE NOTE
RING SAFE SANE TEST TONE TRIG
WISE AFFIX BLAST BUGLE CHEEP
DREAM FLICK FRESH GLIFF GLUCK
GRIND GROPE HODDY NOISE
PLANG PLUMB PROBE RIGHT
SLUSH SOLID SPANG SPANK SPEAK
SWASH VALID WHOLE BICKER
BIRDIE DORSAL ENDING ENTIRE
FATHOM FAUCAL HEARTY INTACT
LABIAL LAGOON ROBUST SIGNAL
SINGLE SONANT SPLASH STABLE
STRAIN STURDY HEALTHY
HEARING HURLING PERFECT
PHONEME PLUMMET SCRATCH
SONANCE VOCABLE FLAWLESS

FOOTFALL GRINDING GROUNDLY
LAUGHTER RELIABLE SEARCHER
SYLLABIC WAKELESS
(— A BAGPIPE) DOODLE
(— AS IF BY GUN) ZAP
(— BELL) PEAL RING KNELL KNOLL
(— BY PERCUSSION) STRIKE
(— DRUM OR TRUMPET) TUCK
(— FORTH) BOOM
**(— INDEPENDENTLY OF THE
PLAYER)** CIPHER
(— INDISTINCTLY) SLUR
(— IN GREEK AND LATIN) AGMA
(— IN MIND) FORMAL
(— LESS LOUD) FALL
(— LIKE THUNDER) BRONTIDE
(— LOUDLY) TANG LARUM
(— MELODIOUSLY) CHARM
(— OF BAGPIPE) DRONE
(— OF BEATING) RATAPLAN
(— OF BELL) DING PEAL RING KNELL
STROKE DINGDONG TINGTANG
(— OF BIRD) JUG CHURR
(— OF BULLET) ZIP
(— OF CICADA) CHIRR
(— OF CONTEMPT) HUMPH
(— OF CORK) CLOOP CLUNK
(— OF COW) MOO LOWING
(— OF DISAPPROVAL) BOO HOOT
BAZOO
(— OF DOG) ARF YIP BARK BOOK
WOOF YELP YIPE
(— OF DYING PERSON'S VOICE)
TAISCH
(— OF ENGINE) CHUG
(— OF EXPLOSION) BOUNCE
(— OF F) DIGAMMA
(— OF FLUTE) TOOTLE
(— OF FOOTSTEPS) TRAMP
(— OF GLOTTAL STOP) HAMZA
HAMZAH
(— OF HEN) CLUCK
(— OF HOG) OINK GRUNT SQUEAL
(— OF HOOF) CLOP
(— OF HORN) BEEP TOOT
(— OF HORSE) NEIGH SNORT
BLOWING
(— OF KNOCK) RAP
(— OF PLUCKED STRING) TUM
(— OF POURING LIQUID) GLUG
GLUGGLUG
(— OF RAIN) SPAT
(— OF RENDING) SCAT
(— OF REPROACH) FIE
(— OF SCISSORS) SNIP
(— OF SHEEP) BAA BLEAT
(— OF SLAP) SCLAFF
(— OF STEAM ENGINE) CHUFF
(— OF STRAW OR LEAVES) RUSTLE
(— OF SURF) ROTE
(— OF THUNDER) CLAP
(— OF TRUMPET) CLARION
(— OF WIND IN TREES) WOOSH
(— OUT) FEEL
(—S HAVING RHYTHM) MUSIC
(— TO AWAKEN TROOPS) REVEILLE
(ABNORMAL —) BRUIT
(ADVENTITIOUS —) RALE
(BLOWING —) SOUFFLE
(BRAWLING —) CHIDE
(BREATHING —) RALE
(BRONCHIAL —) RHONCHUS
(BUBBLING —) BLATHER

(BUZZING —) Z WHIR WHIRR
(CHARACTERISTIC —) SONG
(CLASHING —) SWASH
(CLICKING —) SNECK
(CONSONANT —) ALVEOLAR
(COOING —) CHIRR TURTUR
(CRACKLING —) RISK
(CRISP —) BLIP
(CRUNCHING —) CRUMP SCRUNCH
(DELICATE —) TINK TINKLE
(DISCORDANT —) JAR BRAY
JANGLE
(DISTINCTIVE —) SONG
(DRUMMING —) RATAPLAN
(DULL —) BUFF THUD CLONK CLUNK
FLUMP SQUELCH
(ELECTRONIC — APPARATUS)
SYNTH SYNTHESIZER
(EXPLOSIVE —) POP BARK CHUG
PUFF SNORT REPORT
(FAINT —) PEEP GLIFF WHISHT
INKLING
(FINAL —) AUSLAUT
(FINANCIALLY —) SOLID
(FLAT —) PLAP
(GENTLE —) TAP
(GROWLING —) SNARL
(GULPING —) GLUCK
(GUTTURAL —) GROWL
(HARSH —) JAR BRAY BLARE CLASH
CRANK TWANG SCROOP DISCORD
STRIDOR
(HEAVY —) DUMP
(HIGH-PITCHED —) BLIP TING BLEEP
(HISSING —) FIZZ SIZZ SWISH SIZZLE
(HOARSE —) ROOP
(HOLLOW —) CHOCK THUNGE
(HUMMING —) HUM BURR SUUM
DRONE SINGING
(INDISTINCT —) BLUR SURD
(INITIAL — OF WORDS) ANLAUT
(JINGLING —) SMIT
(KNOCKING —) RATTAT
(LAPPING —) SLOOSH
(LIGHT REPEATED —) PITAPAT
(LOUD —) PEAL BLARE CLANG
CRASH CLANGOR
(LOW —) WHISPER
(LOW-PITCHED —) BASS
(MEANINGLESS —S) GABBLE
(MEDIAL —) INLAUT
(MENTALLY —) SANE WISE
(MOANING —) SUUM SOUGH
(MOURNFUL —) GROAN
(MUFFLED —) MUFFLE
(MUSICAL —) CHIME
(NASAL —) ANUSVARA
(NON-SIGNIFICANT —) GLIDE
(NONVIBRATORY —) FRICTION
(PLEASING —) EUPHONY EUPHONIA
(QUADRAPHONIC —) QUAD
(RASPING —) BUZZ SKIRR SCROOP
(REPEATED —) ECHO
(RESONANT —) BONG
(REVERBERATING —) PLANG
(RINGING —) CLANG CLANK CLING
TWANG RINGLE DINGDONG
(ROARING —) BEAL
(RUSHING —) SWOOSH HURLING
(RUSTLING —) FISSLE FISTLE
(SCRAPING —) GRIDE
(SCRATCHY —) SCRAICH SCRAIGH

(SHARP —) POP PING SNAP CHINK
CRAKE KNACK SPANG SQUIRK
(SHORT, HIGH-PITCHED —) BLEEP
(SHRILL —) CHEEP KNACK SKIRL
SCREED SQUEAK STRIDOR
(SHUFFLING —) SCUFFLE
(SIBILANT —) HISS SHISH SHUSH
(SLAPPING —) CLATCH
(SLIGHT —) SWISH
(SNORING —) SNORK
(SOBBING —) YOOP
(SPEECH —) SURD DOMAL TENUE
VOWEL APICAL PHONEME
CEREBRAL
(SPLASHING —) LAP CHUNK FLURR
SPLAT SWASH
(SPOKEN —) BREATH
(SQUEAKY —) CREAK
(SQUELCHING —) SQUASH
(STRANGLED —) GLUB GLUG
(SWISHING —) SCHLOOP
(TAPPING —) TACK
(TELEPHONE —) SIDETONE
(TINKLING —) PINK
(TRAMPING —) STUMP
(TREMULOUS —) TRILL
(TRILLING —) CHIRR CHIZZ HIRRIENT
(TUNEFUL —) HARMONY
(UNPLEASANT —) BLOOP
(VIBRATING —) TIRL
(VOWEL —) SHWA SCHWA
(WARNING —) ALARM SIREN
ALARUM TOCSIN
(WHIRRING —) BIRR FLURR SKIRR
(WHISPERING —) SUSURRUS
(WHISTLING —) STRIDOR
(PREF.) AUDIO AUDIT ECHO
PHON(O) SON(I)(O) SONORI
SONORO TONICO TONO
(SUFF.) PHON(E)(IA)(Y) SONANCE
SONANT SONOUS TONE TONIA
TONIC TONOUS TONY
SOUND-ABSORBENT ACOUSTIC
SOUND AND THE FURY (AUTHOR
OF —) FAULKNER
(CHARACTER IN —) HEAD JASON
DILSEY SYDNEY CANDACE
COMPSON QUENTIN BENJAMIN
SOUNDBOARD BELLY
SOUNDED (NOT —) QUIESCENT
SOUNDER TICKER LEADMAN
SOUNDING RAWIN SONANT
INKLING SONDAGE SONATION
(— HARSH) BRAZEN
(— OF BELL) CURFEW
(— OF MUSICAL INSTRUMENT)
SPEECH
(— OF ORGAN PIPE) CIPHER
(— WITH REVERBERATIONS)
PLANGENT
SOUNDLY FAST TIGHT FIRMLY
SOUNDNESS HEAL SANITY FITNESS
SOBRIETY STRENGTH VALIDITY
SOUP BREE KAIL KALE SOPA BRODO
BROTH GUMBO POSOL BISQUE
BORSCH BURGOO CALALU JOUTES
POTAGE POZOLE BILLIBI BILLYBI
BORSCHT CALALOO GARBURE
MARMITE RUBABOO CALLALOO
CALLALOU CONSOMME
GAZPACHO MINESTRA MORTREUX
AVGOLEMONO MINESTRONE

COCKALEEKIE MULLIGATAWNY
MULLIGATAWNEY
(— UP) SUPE
(BARLEY —) SMIGGINS
(BEEFSKIN —) SKINK
(CABBAGE —) SHCHI STCHI
(CLEAR —) CONSOMME JULIENNE
(COLD —) SCHAV
(HAWAIIAN NOODLE —) SAIMIN
(JAPANESE NOODLE —) RAMEN
(JELLIED —) GAZPACHO
(LARGE QUANTITY OF —) SLASH
(NOODLE —) SAIMIN
(POTATO —) TATTIECLAW
(SHINBONE —) SKINK
(THICK —) BISK GUMBO HOOSH
PUREE BISQUE BURGOO CHOWDER
GARBURE POTTAGE HOTCHPOT
MORTREWES
(THIN —) BROTH SKILLY
(VEGETABLE —) PISTOU
SOUR AWA DRY YAR ACID ASIM
CRAB DOUR FOXY GRIM GRUM
HARD TART TURN ACERB ACRID
AIGRE EAGER GOURY GRUFF
MUSTY TEART ACETIC ACIDIC
BITTER CRUETY CURDLE PONTIC
RANCID RUGGED SULLEN TORVID
ACETOSE ACIDIFY AUSTERE
SUBACID ACERBATE VINEGARY
(SLIGHTLY —) BLINK BLINKY
ACESCENT
SOURCE FONS FONT HAND HEAD
HIVE MINE RISE RIST ROOT SEED
FOUNT RADIX SPAWN SURGE
AUCTOR AUTHOR BOTTOM
CENTER FATHER FONTAL ORIGIN
PARENT RESORT STAPLE WHENCE
EDITION FOUNTAIN WELLHEAD
PROVENANCE
(— OF ADVANTAGE) OYSTER
(— OF AID) RECOURSE
(— OF ANCESTRAL LINE) STOCK
(— OF ANNOYANCE) BOGY BOGIE
HARROW BUGBEAR
(— OF ASSURANCE) FORTRESS
(— OF CONCERN) BUGABOO
(— OF CONFIDENCE) ANCHOR
(— OF DANGER) THREAT
(— OF DISPLEASURE) DISGUST
(— OF ENERGY) STEAM TAPAS
(— OF ENLIGHTENMENT) TORCH
(— OF GRATIFICATION) TREAT
(— OF HAPPINESS) SUNSHINE
(— OF HARM) CURSE
(— OF HELP) RESOURCE
(— OF HONOR) CREDIT
(— OF INCOME) TITLE REVENUE
(— OF INFORMATION) CHECK
(— OF INSPIRATION) CASTALIA
CASTILE
(— OF INSTRUCTION) BOOK
(— OF JOY) NUTS
(— OF LAUGHTER) SPLEEN
(— OF LIFE) SPRING
(— OF LIGHT) LAMP
(— OF MERRIMENT) FUN
(— OF MONEY) FUND
(— OF NOURISHMENT) BREAST
(— OF PERPLEXITY) PROBLEM
(— OF POWER) STRENGTH
(— OF QUOTATIONS) QUOTATIVE
(— OF RADIATION) PULSAR

(— OF REGRET) SCATH SCATHE
(— OF STREAM OR RIVER) FILL
(— OF STRENGTH) HORN
(— OF SUPPLY) SHOP FEEDER
ARSENAL
(— OF TROUBLE) HEADACHE
(— OF WATER) BRON SPRING
(— OF WEALTH) GOLCONDA
KLONDIKE
(— OF WORK OF ART) PROVENANCE
PROVENIENCE
(— OF WORRY) HEADACHE
(ABUNDANT —) CORNUCOPIA
(BE THE — OF) SPAWN
(ENCLOSED —) FLOW
(FROM ANOTHER —) ALIUNDE
(GENERATING —) LOINS
(MALIGNANT —) CANCER
(PHYSICAL —) MOTHER
(PRIMARY —) RADIX
(PRIMITIVE —) PRIMORDIUM
(RADIO —) QUASAR
(RICH —) MINE
SOURDOUGH LEAVEN
SOURED FOXY QUARRED
SOURING ACESCENCE
SOURNESS ACIDITY ACERBITY
ACRIMONY ASPERITY TARTNESS
VERJUICE
SOURPUSS CRAB CRANK GROUCH
SOURSOP CORRESOL GUANABANA
SOURWOOD TITI ELKWOOD
SOUSE DIP DUCK TOSH PLUMP
STOOP PLUNGE SOZZLE TOSSPOT
SOUTANE SIMAR ZIMARRA
SOUTH MIDI AUSTER DECANI
MIDDAY MERIDIAN
(FARTHER —) BELOW
(PREF.) AUSTR(O) NOT(O)

SOUTH AFRICA
BAY: ALGOA FALSE
CAPE: AGULHAS
CAPITAL: CAPETOWN PRETORIA
COIN: CENT RAND POUND FLORIN
KRUGERRAND
LANGUAGE: BANTU HINDI TAMIL
TELUGU BUJARATI
MOUNTAIN: AUX KOP KATHKIN
INJASUTI
NATIVE: YOSA BANTU NAMAS
PONDO DAMARA SWAHILI
BECHUANA HOTTENTOT
PROVINCE: NATAL TRANSVAAL
RIVER: MODDER MOLOPO ORANGE
KURUMAM LIMPOPO OLIFANTS
TOWN: AUS MARA STAD BENONI
DURBAN SEVERN UMTATA
KOKSTAD SPRINGS MAFEKING
GERMISTON JOHANNESBURG
WATERFALL: HOWICK TUGELA
AUGRABIES

SOUTH AMERICA
(ALSO SEE SPECIFIC COUNTRIES)
LAKE: MIRIM POOPO TITICACA
MARACAIBO LLANQUIHUE
MOUNTAIN: BAIA ANDES GOIAZ
PARIMA ACARAHY TUMUCHUMAC
NATION: PERU CHILE BRAZIL
GUYANA BOLIVIA ECUADOR
URUGUAY COLOMBIA PARAGUAY

SURINAME ARGENTINA NICARAGUA VENEZUELA
RIVER: NEGRO AMAZON CHUBUT PARANA SALADO ORINOCO RIONEGRO ESSEQUIBO MAGDALENA

SOUTH CAROLINA

CAPITAL: COLUMBIA
COLLEGE: COKER FURMAN LANDER CITADEL CLAFFIN CLEMSON ERSKINE WOFFORD
COUNTY: AIKEN HORRY DILLON JASPER OCONEE SALUDA
FORT: SUMTER
INDIAN: PEDEE SEWEE CUSABO SANTEE WAXHAW CATAWBA SUGEREE WATEREE CONGAREE
ISLAND: EDISTO PARRIS HILTONHEAD
LAKE: MARION MURRAY CATAWBA WATEREE HARTWELL MOULTRIE
MOUNTAIN: SASSAFRAS
NATIVE: WEASEL PALMETTO
NICKNAME: PALMETTO
PLATEAU: PIEDMONT
PRESIDENT: JACKSON
RESERVOIR: SANTEE PINOPOLIS
RIVER: BROAD EDISTO PEEDEE SALUDA SANTEE ASHEPOO TUGALOS WATEREE CONGAREE SAVANNAH
STATE BIRD: WREN
STATE FLOWER: JASMINE
STATE TREE: PALMETTO
TOWN: AIKEN GREER UNION BELTON CAMDEN CHERAW CONWAY DILLON SALUDA SENECA SUMTER BAMBERG LAURENS MANNING BEAUFORT FLORENCE NEWBERRY WALHALLA GREENVILLE SPARTANBURG

SOUTH CAROLINIAN WEASEL PALMETTO

SOUTH DAKOTA

BUTTE: MUD CROW SULLY FINGER SADDLE THUNDER DEERSEARS
CAPITAL: PIERRE
COLLEGE: HURON YANKTON
COUNTY: DAY HYDE BRULE MINER MOODY SPINK SULLY TRIPP CUSTER JERAULD YANKTON MELLETTE
INDIAN: BRULE SIOUX DAKOTA CHEYENNE
LAKE: OAHE BIGSTONE TRAVERSE
MONUMENT: RUSHMORE
MOUNTAIN: BEAR SHEEP TABLE CROOKS HARNEY MOREAU
NICKNAME: COYOTE SUNSHINE
RIVER: JAMES MOREAU CHEYENNE MISSOURI
STATE BIRD: PHEASANT
STATE FLOWER: PASQUE
STATE TREE: SPRUCE
TOWN: LEAD HAYTI HURON LEOLA ONIDA CUSTER DESMET EUREKA KADOKA LEMMON MILLER WINNER STURGIS WEBSTER

YANKTON ABERDEEN DEADWOOD SISSETON

SOUTHERLY AUSTRINE
SOUTHERN SUDIC AUSTRAL MERIDIAN SOUTHRON MERIDIONAL (PREF.) NOTIO
SOUTHERN CROSS CRUX CROSS CROSIER
SOUTHERNER CAVALIER SOUTHRON
SOUTHERN FRANCE MIDI
SOUTHERN ILLINOIS EGYPT
SOUTHERN INDIA DRAVIDA
SOUTHERNWOOD APPLERINGIE

SOUTH KOREA

BAY: KANGHWA
CAPITAL: SEOUL
COIN: WON CHUN HWAN
MONEY: JUN CHON JEON
MOUNTAIN: CHIRI
PROVINCE: CHEJU CHOLLA KANGWON KYONGGI
RIVER: HAN KUM PUKHAN SOMJIN NAKTONG YONGSAN
TOWN: CHEJU MASAN MOKPO PUSAN SUWON TAEGU WONJU CHINJU CHONJU INCHON KUNSAN TAEJON CHONGJU KWANGJU CHUNCHON

SOUTHLAND AUSTER
SOUTH SEA ISLANDER KANAKA
SOUTHWESTER SQUAM
SOUTH YEMEN (CAPITAL OF —) ADEN
　(ISLAND OF —) PERIM KAMARAN SOCOTRA
　(MONEY OF —) DINAR
　(TOWN OF —) SEIYUN MUKALLA
SOUVENIR CURIO RELIC TOKEN FAIRING NICKNACK
SOVEREIGN BEY SIR SOV BEAN CHAM CHIP FREE KHAN QUID SHAH SKIV CROWN JAMES NEGUS NIZAM QUEED RULER CHAGAN COUTER GUINEA KAISER KINGLY MASTER PRINCE SAMORY SHINER SOLDAN SOVRAN SULTAN CROWNED MONARCH ZAMORIN AUTOCRAT DOMINANT IMPERIAL SUFFRAIN SUZERAIN
　(DIVINELY —) THEARCHIC
　(FELLOW —) COUSIN
　(HEAVENLY —) TENNO HEAVEN
　(MOSLEM —) SOLDAN
SOVEREIGNTY SWAY CROWN REIGN DIADEM EMPERY EMPIRE THRONE DEMESNE DYNASTY KINGDOM MAJESTY SCEPTER SCEPTRE AUTARCHY DOMINION IMPERIUM MONARCHY REGALITY REGNANCY SOVRANTY
　(— OF REASON) AUTONOMY
　(JOINT —) SYNARCHY
SOVERIGN DYNAST
SOVIET (ALSO SEE RUSSIA) VOLOST COUNCIL GUBERNIA
　(— POLICY OF DISCUSSION) GLASNOST
SOW ELT HOG GILT SEED SHED YELT

YILT DRILL PLANT PLUMP STREW CHANNEL GRUMPHY IMPLANT OVERSOW SCATTER ENGENDER INTERSOW SEMINATE
　(PREF.) HYO SCROFUL(O)
　(SUFF.) CHOERUS
SOWAR SILLADAR
SOW BUG ISOPOD SLATER ISOPODAN
SOWENS SONS SWEENS FLUMMERY WASHBREW
SOWER SEEDER SEEDMAN SEEDSTER SEMINARY
SOWING SATION SEMENCE SEEDNESS
　(PREF.) SPOR(I)(IDI)(O)(ULI)
　(SUFF.) SPORA SPORE SPORIC SPORIDIA SPORIUM SPOROUS SPORY
SOWN SEME SATIVE SEEDED SEMEED
SOW THISTLE DINDLE GUTWEED HOGWEED MILKWEED
SOY SHOYA SHOYU
　(— SAUCE) TAMARI
SOYBEAN SOJA SOYA
SPA BATH CURE EVIAN HYDRO
SPACE GAP AREA BLUE CORD COSO DENT FACE LUNG PALE RANK ROOM SIDE VOID ABYSS BLOCK CHINK CLEFT FIELD PLACE RANGE CANTON HIATUS INDENT MATTER ROOMTH ARRANGE COMPASS FOREIGN GUNNIES LEGROOM ROOMAGE SPACING SPATIUM DIASTEMA DISTANCE EXOCOELE INTERVAL
　(— ABOVE EARTH) AIRSPACE
　(— AMONG MUSCLES) SINUS
　(— AROUND HOUSE) AMBIT
　(— AT WHARF) BERTHAGE
　(— BEFORE KILN) LOGIE KILLOGIE
　(— BEHIND ALTAR) FERETORY
　(— BETWEEN ARCHES) SPANDREL SPANDRIL
　(— BETWEEN BED AND WALL) RUELLE
　(— BETWEEN BRIDGE PIERS) LOCK
　(— BETWEEN CASKS) CONTLINE
　(— BETWEEN COLUMNS) BAY
　(— BETWEEN CONCENTRIC CIRCLES) ANNULUS
　(— BETWEEN DECKS) LAZARET
　(— BETWEEN DOCKS) SLIPWAY
　(— BETWEEN EYE AND BILL) LORE
　(— BETWEEN FEATHERS) APTERYLA
　(— BETWEEN FLOOR TIMBERS) SPIRKET
　(— BETWEEN FLUTINGS) FILET FILLET GORGERIN
　(— BETWEEN FURROWS) RIG
　(— BETWEEN PAGES) GUTTER
　(— BETWEEN RAILROAD TIES) CRIB
　(— BETWEEN SAW TEETH) GULLET
　(— BETWEEN SHIP'S BOWS AND ANCHOR) HAWSE
　(— BETWEEN STRANDS) CANTLINE
　(— BETWEEN TEETH) DIASTEMA
　(— BETWEEN THUMB AND LITTLE FINGER) SPAN
　(— BETWEEN TIMBERS) SPIRKET
　(— BETWEEN TWO WIRES) DENT

　(— BETWEEN VEINS OF LEAVES) AREOLA
　(— DEVOID OF MATTER) VACUUM VACUITY
　(— FOR SECRETION) BAG
　(— IN CHURCH) KNEELING
　(— IN COIL OF CABLE) TIER
　(— IN FOREST) GLADE
　(— IN MINE) GOB
　(— IN THEATER) BOX
　(— IN TYPE) CORE
　(— OCCUPIED) VOLUME
　(— OF THREE DAYS) TRIDUUM
　(— OF TIME) DAY PULL STEAD GHURRY STITCH INTERVAL
　(— ON BILLIARD TABLE) BALK BAULK
　(— ON COIN) EXERGUE
　(— OVERHEAD) HIGH
　(— OVER STAGE) FLIES
　(— TRANSMITTER) TIROS
　(— UNDER STAGE) DOCK
　(— USED AS LIVING-ROOM) LANAI
　(— WITHIN LIMITS) CONTENT
　(AD —) LINAGE
　(AIR —) CENTRUM
　(ARCHITECTURAL —) METOPE PEDIMENT SACELLUM
　(BACKGAMMON —) POINT
　(BARE — ON BIRD) APTERIUM
　(BLANK —) GAP ALLEY LACUNA
　(BOUNDLESS —) INFINITE
　(BREATHING —) BARLEY
　(CLEAR —) FAIRWAY HEADWAY DAYLIGHT
　(COUNTER —) BACKBAR
　(CRAMPED —) CUBBY
　(EMPTY —) AIR BLANK VACUUM CAPACITY
　(ENCLOSED —) AREA BOWL HATCH VERGE PARVIS CHAMBER CIRCUIT CLOSURE COMPASS PARVISE PTEROMA CLOISTER CONFINES
　(EUCLIDEAN —) FLAT
　(FLAT —) HOMALOID
　(KIND OF —) HILBERT
　(LEVEL —) PLATEA PARTERRE
　(NARROW —) SLOT STRAIT
　(OPEN —) OUT LAWN ALLEY COURT LAUND TAHUA MAIDAN AREAWAY FAIRWAY LOANING APERTURE DAYLIGHT KNEEHOLE
　(OPEN — OF WATER) WAKE
　(OVERHANGING —) DOME
　(POPLITEAL —) HAM HOCK
　(ROOF —) CELL
　(RUSSIAN — STATION) MIR
　(SEATING —) CAVEA
　(SHELTERED —) KILLOGIE
　(SMALL —) AREOLA
　(STORAGE —) ATTIC
　(TRIANGULAR —) SPANDREL
　(UNFILLED —) GAP GAPE CAVITY HOLLOW BREAKAGE
　(VAULTED —) ALCOVE
　(VERTICAL —) HEADROOM
　(WORKING —) COUNTER
　(PREF.) SPATIO
SPACECRAFT BUS SHIP CAPSULE ORBITER
　(CHANNEL SENDING TO —) UPLINK
　(PROCESS OF SLOWING DOWN —) DEBOOST

(SLOW DOWN A —) DEBOOST
(SYSTEM OF — ROCKETS) RETROPACK
SPACED MEATIC
SPACER QUAD
SPACEWALK EVA
SPACIOUS ROOM SIDE WIDE AMPI F RROAD RANGY ROOMY GOLDEN BARONIAL SCOPIOUS
SPADE DIG LOY FECK LILY PEEL PICK SPIT SPUD DELVE DIDLE GRAFF SLADE SLANE TRAMP DIGGER PADDLE PATTLE SERVER SHOVEL TUSKAR GRAFTER SCAFFLE SCUPPIT SPADDLE SPITTER TWISCAR
(LONG NARROW —) LOY
(PART OF —) FROG STEP BLADE HANDLE SOCKET SHOULDER
(PEAT —) SLADE SLANE TUSKAR
(PLASTERER'S —) SERVER
(TRIANGULAR —) DIDLE
SPADEFISH POGY PORGY MOONFISH
SPADEFUL SPIT SPITFUL
SPAGHETTI PASTA SLEEVING
(— SAUCE) RAGU PREGO
SPAGNUOLO LADINO

SPAIN

CAPE: AJO NAO GATA CREUS MORAS PALOS PENAS PRIOR DARTUCH ORTEGAL SALINAS TORTOSA ESPICHEL MARROQUI SACRATIF
CAPITAL: MADRID
COIN: COB DURO PESO REAL DOBLA CUARTO DINERO DOBLON ESCUDO PESETA ALFONSO CENTIMO PISTOLE REALDOR DOUBLOON
DIALECT: BASQUE CATALAN GALICIAN
ISLAND: IBIZA PALMA GOMERA HIERRO ALBORAN MAJORCA MINORCA MALLORCA TAGOMAGO TENERIFE
ISLANDS: CANARY BALEARIC
MEASURE: PIE CODO COPA DEDO MOYO PASO VARA ALMUD BRAZA CAFIZ CAHIZ CARGA LEGUA LINEA MEDIO MILLA PALMO SESMA ARROBA CORDEL CUARTA ESTADO FANEGA RACION YUGADA AZUMBRE CANTARA CELEMIN ESTADEL PULGADA ARANZADA FANEGADA
MOUNTAIN: GATA ANETO ROUCH TEIDE ESTATS NETHOU TELENO BANUELO CERREDO PERDIDO ALMANZOR MONTSENY MULHACEN PENALARA
MOUNTAIN RANGE: CUENCA GREDOS MORENA TOLEDO ALCARAZ DEMANDA MONCAYO MALADETA MONEGROS PYRENEES
NAME: ESPANA IBERIA HISPANIA
NATIVE: CATALAN IBERIAN
PORT: ADRA NOYA VIGO CADIZ GADES GADIR GIJON PALOS ABDERA CORUNA MALAGA ALMERIA ALICANTE BARCELONA

PROVINCE: JAEN LEON LUGO ALAVA AVILA CADIZ SORIA BURGOS CORUNA CUENCA GERONA HUELVA HUESCA LERIDA MADRID MALAGA MURCIA ORENSE OVIEDO TERUEL TOLEDO ZAMORA ALMERIA BADAJOZ CACERES CORDOBA GRANADA LOGRONO NAVARRA SEGOVIA SEVILLA VIZCAYA ALBACETE ALICANTE BALEARES PALENCIA VALENCIA ZARAGOZA
REGION: LEON ARAGON BASQUE MURCIA CASTILE GALICIA NAVARRE ASTURIAS CASTILLA VALENCIA
RIVER: SIL TER CEGA EBRO ESLA LIMA MINO TAJO ULLA ADAJA CINCA DOURO DUERO GENIL JALON JUCAR NAVIA ODIEL RIAZA SEGRE TAGUS TINTO TURIA ALAGON ARAGON ERESMA HUERVA JARAMA ORBIGO SEGURA TOROTE ALMERIA ALMONTE ARLANZA BARBATE CABRIEL DURATON GALLEGO HENARES MIJARES PERALES GUADIANA
TOWN: ROA ASPE BAZA ELDA HARO IRUN JAEN LEON LUGO OLOT REUS ROTA SAMA VIGO BAENA BEJAR CADIZ CIEZA CUETA ECIJA EIBAR ELCHE GIJON IBIZA JEREZ JODAR LORCA OLIVA PALMA RONDA SIERO UBEDA XERES YECLA ZAFRA AVILES AZUAGA BILBAO BURGOS DUENCA GANDIA GERONA GETAFE GUADIX HELLIN HUELVA HUESCA JATIVA LERIDA LUCENA MADRID MALAGA MATARO MERIDA MURCIA ORENSE OVIEDO TERMEL TOLEDO UTRERA ZAMORA BADAJOZ CORDOBA DAIMIEL GRANADA JUMILLA LINARES LOGRONO MANRESA SEGOVIA SEVILLA TARRASA VITORIA BADALONA FIGUERAS PAMPLONA SABADELL SANTIAGO TORRENTE VALENCIA ZARAGOZA
WEIGHT: ONZA FRAIL GRANO LIBRA MARCO TOMIN ADARME ARROBA DINERO DRACMA OCHAVA ARIENZO QUILATE QUINTAL CARACTER TONELADA
WINE: RIOJA SHERRY

SPALL CHIP SCALE SPAWL GALLET
SPAN ARCH BEAM PAIR CHORD SPANG SWING BRIDGE EXTEND SPREAD OPENING QUARTER BESTRIDE
(— OF TIME) PIECE
(— WITH FINGERS) SPEND
(UNSUPPORTED —) BEARING
SPANDREL GROIN ALLEGE SPANDLE
SPANGLE AGLET BEGEM PRANK SPANG INSTAR SEQUIN CHEQUEEN SPANGLET ZECCHINO PAILLETTE
SPANGLED POWDERED SPANKLED
SPANIARD DON DIEGO MULADI
(CHRISTIAN —) MOZARAB

SPANIEL TRASY COCKER SUSSEX CLUMBER BLENHEIM PAPILLON SPRINGER WATERRUG
SPANISH ALJAMIA HISPANIC
(PREF.) HISPANO
SPANISH-AMERICAN LADINO CHINO LADINO
SPANISH BAYONET IZOTE YUCCA
SPANISH BROOM SPART RETAMA
SPANISH FLY CANTHARIS
SPANISH HOGFISH LADYFISH
SPANISH JACINTH SCILLA
SPANISH JASMINE MALATI
SPANISH MACKEREL SIERRA
SPANISH PLUM SIRUELAS
SPANISH STOPPER IRONWOOD
SPANK PRAT SCUD SKELP PADDLE THRASH SLIPPER
SPANKER DRIVER MIZZEN
SPANKING SMACKING
SPANNER KEY WRENCH
SPANNING ASTRIDE
SPAR BEAM BOOM CAUK CLUB GAFF MAST RAFT SPUR YARD CABER SPAAD SPATH SPELK SPRIT STODE BOUGAR BUMKIN RICKER STEEVE BASTITE BUMPKIN DERRICK DOLPHIN JIBBOOM RIBBAND BOWSPRIT CRYOLITE LAZULITE OUTRIGGER MARTINGALE
(BITTER —) DOLOMITE
(HEAVY —) CAUK BARITE BARYTE
SPARE BONY FAIK GASH HAIN LEAN NICE SAVE SLIM THIN FAVOR LANKY SPELL LENTEN MEAGER MEAGRE SKIMPY RESERVE SLENDER PRESERVE
SPARGE PIPE WEEPER
SPARING CHARY GNEDE SCANT SPARE DAINTY FRUGAL STINGY ENVIOUS ECONOMIC SPAREFUL PENURIOUS ABSTEMIOUS
(— IN COMMUNICATION) RETICENT
(— OF WORDS) CURT
(NOT —) HANDSOME
(PREF.) PARCI
SPARINGNESS PARCITY SCARCITY
SPARK FUNK IZLE AIZLE GRAIN LIGHT PURSE SPERK SPUNK BLUETTE FLANKER FLAUGHT SPARKLE SPUNKIE SPARKLET SCINTILLA
(—S OF MOLTEN IRON) NILL
(VITAL —) GHOST LIGHT
(PREF.) SCINTILLO
SPARKER IGNITER
SPARKLE FUNK SNAP WINK BLINK FLASH GLENT GLINT SHINE SPARK GLANCE KINDLE SIMPER CRACKLE EMICATE FLANKER GLIMMER GLISTEN GLISTER GLITTER RADIATE SHIMMER SKINKLE SPANGLE TWINKLE OPALESCE SPRINKLE CORUSCATE
SPARKLER TWINKLER
SPARKLING DEWY CRISP QUICK SUNNY BRIGHT SPUNKY STARRY CREMANT DIAMOND SHINING TWINKLY MOUSSEUX SMIRKING SPERLING BRILLIANT OPALESCENT SCINTILLANT

(MAKE —) AERATE
(NOT —) STILL
(SLIGHTLY —) PETILLANT
SPARK PLUG (PART OF —) CAP GAP SHELL GASKET BUSHING TERMINAL ELECTRODE INSULATOR
SPARLING SMELT
SPARROW SPUG DICKY DONEY FINCH HEMPY ISAAC PADDA PADDY SPRIG SPRUG CHIPPY PHILIP SPRONG TOWHEE CHANTER CHIPPIE DUNNOCK FIELDIE HAYSUCK PINNOCK SPADGER SPURDIE TITLENE TITLING TITTLIN ACCENTOR FIRETAIL HAIRBIRD WHITECAP
(PREF.) PASSERI
SPARROW HAWK MUSKET SPARHAWK
SPARSE BALD THIN MEAGER MEAGRE SCANTY THRIFTY
SPARTAN GREEK LACONIC
SPASM PANG CRICK QUALM TONUS CLONUS ENTASIA FLUTTER RAPTURE SPASMUS MYOTONIA PAROXYSM
(— OF EYELID) BLEPHARISM
(— OF FOOT) PODISMUS
(— OF IRIS) HIPPUS
(— OF PAIN) GRIP
(— OF THE IRIS) HIPPUS
(—S OF WHALE) FLURRY
(MUSCLE —) TRISMUS
(TONIC —) HOLOTONY
(PREF.) CLONICO
SPASMODIC FITFUL SNATCHY SPASMIC SPASTIC SPURTIVE
SPAT SEED TIFF BROOD JOWER GAITER LEGGING BOOTHOSE BOOTIKIN
SPATE ONRUSH SLUICE RAINSTORM
SPATHE CYMBA SHEATH
SPATHIC SPARRY SPATHOSE
SPATIAL LOCAL STERIC
SPATIATE ROVE RAMBLE STROLL
SPATTER DASH JAUP BERAY SKIRP SLART SPARK SPURT DABBLE SPLASH SQUIRT BESPAWL BESPETE SHATTER SMATTER SPATTLE SPIRTLE SPLATTER SPRINKLE
(— WITH FOAM) EMBOSS
(— WITH MUD) JAP BEMUD SPARK
SPATTERDASH SPAT BONNET GAITER CUTIKIN LEGGING BOOTHOSE BOOTIKIN
SPATTERDOCK DUCK CLOTE TUCKY WOKAS NUPHAR BONNETS CANDOCK
SPATTERING JAP JAUP SPAT SQUATTER
SPATULA SPAT SLICE THIBLE THIVEL CESTRUM SPATTLE SPLATTER
SPAVIN JACK SPAVIE VARISSE
SPAWN RUD BLOT RAUN REDD RUDD SILE SPORE TODDER GENERATE
(— OF SHELLFISH) SPAT
(OYSTER —) CULCH CULTCH
SPAWNEATER SHINER
SPAWNING SICK MILKY SEEDING
SPAY FIX GELD ALTER DESEX SPADE

CHANGE DOCTOR SPEAVE CASTRATE

SPEAK ASK CUT SAY CANT CARP MEAN MOOT MOVE TALE TALK TELL WORD BREAK MOUTH NEVEN ORATE PARLE SOUND SPELL SPIEL UTTER ACCENT INTONE PARLEY PATTER QUETHE SERMON SPEECH SQUEAK TONGUE ADDRESS BESPEAK DECLAIM DELIVER EXCLAIM PARRALL CONVERSE REHEARSE
(— ABUSIVELY) JAW
(— AFFECTEDLY) MIMP KNACK
(— AGAINST) ACCUSE GAINSAY FORSPEAK
(— ANGRILY) ROUSE CAMPLE
(— AT LENGTH) DISSERT ENLARGE
(— BROKENLY) FALTER
(— CAJOLINGLY) COLLOGUE
(— CONFUSEDLY) HATTER CLUTTER SPLATHER
(— CONSTANTLY) YAP
(— CONTEMPTUOUSLY) SCOFF
(— CRITICALLY) LAUNCH
(— CURTLY) BIRK SNAP
(— EVIL) BLACKEN
(— FAIR) PALP
(— FALSELY) ABUSE
(— FAMILIARLY) HOBNOB
(— FIRST TO) ACCOST
(— FOOLISHLY) PRATE GIBBER JABBER
(— HALTINGLY) HACK HAMMER STAMMER
(— HESITANTLY) STAMMER
(— HOARSELY) CROAK CROUP
(— ILL OF) KNOCK DEPRAVE DETRACT
(— IMPERFECTLY) LISP
(— IMPUDENTLY) CHEEK
(— IMPULSIVELY) BLURT
(— INDISTINCTLY) FUMBLE JABBER MUFFLE MAUNDER SPLUTTER
(— IN DRAWL) DRANT DRAUNT
(— INEPTLY) BUMBLE
(— IN JEST) FOOL
(— IN ONE'S EAR) HARK
(— IN POINTLESS MANNER) DROOL
(— INSOLENTLY) SNASH
(— IN STUMBLING WAY) STUTTER
(— IN UNDERTONE) WHISPER
(— IN WHINING VOICE) CANT
(— LOUDLY) TANG
(— LOW) WHISPER
(— MINCINGLY) NAB MIMP
(— MONOTONOUSLY) DROLL
(— OBSCURELY) RIDDLE
(— OF) CALL NEVEN MENTION
(— ONE'S MIND) SHOUT
(— OUT) LEVEL SHOOT
(— PLAYFULLY) BANTER
(— POMPOUSLY) CRACK
(— PROFUSELY) PALAVER
(— QUERULOUSLY) CREAK
(— RAPIDLY) TROLL GIBBER JABBER SQUIRT CHATTER
(— RESENTFULLY) HUFF
(— RHETORICALLY) DECLAIM
(— SARCASTICALLY) GIRD
(— SHORTLY) JERK
(— SLIGHTINGLY OF) BELITTLE
(— SLOWLY) DRAWL

(— SNARLINGLY) SNARL
(— TARTLY) SNAP
(— TEDIOUSLY) PROSE
(— THROUGH THE NOSE) SNAFFLE
(— TO ONESELF) SOLILOQUIZE
(— TRUTH) SOOTHSAY
(— WITH EMPHASIS) DWELL
(— WITH LIPS CLOSED) MUMBLE
(— WITH THE HANDS) SIGN
(— WITH UNCERTAINTY) QUAVER
SPEAKEASY SHEBEEN
SPEAKER TRIS VOICE BRYTHON LOCUTOR MOUTHER STYLIST EPILOGUE SPEECHER
(— IN POEM) PERSONA
(OBSCENE —) RIBALD
(ORATORICAL —) SPOUTER
(PUBLIC —) ORATOR STUMPER
SPEAKING STEVEN LOQUENT PARLANCE SPELLING
(— ARTICULATELY) MEROP MEROPIC
(— MANY LANGUAGES) POLYGLOT
(— POMPOUSLY) MAGNILOQUENT
(— WITHOUT SOUND) MUSSITATION
(EVIL —) PRATING
(INDISTINCT —) JABBER
(PUBLIC —) PLATFORM
(SUFF.) LOGER LOGIA(N) LOGIC(AL) LOGIST LOGUE LOGY LOQUENCE LOQUENT LOQUY
SPEAR GAD DART FRAM GAFF PIKE GRAIN LANCE REJON SHAFT STAFF VALET AMGARN BORDUN BROACH FIZGIG FRAMEA GIDJEE GLAIVE WASTER ASSEGAI BOURDON HARPOON IMPALER JAVELIN TRIDENT VERUTUM EELSPEAR GAVELOCK LANCEGAY STANDARD WALSPERE
(BROKEN —) TRUNCHEON
(EEL —) ELGER PILGER
(FISH —) GIG GAFF TREN POACH FIZGIG GRAINS FISHGIG LEISTER SNIGGER
(SALMON —) WASTER
(PREF.) DORI ENCHO HASTATO LANCI
SPEARFISH AGUJA GOGGLE MARLIN BILLFISH LONGJAWS
SPEAR GRASS SPANIARD
SPEARHEAD BUNT GAFF SPUD PRONG CORONAL
SPEARMINT MENTHE LABIATE
SPEAR-SHAPED HASTATE
SPEAR THROWER ATLATL WOMMALA WOOMERAH
SPEARWORT BANEWORT
SPECIAL VERY EXTRA KHASS CONCRETE ESPECIAL PECULIAR SPECIFIC REDLETTER
(NOT —) GENERAL
SPECIALIST SWELL EXPERT HERALD LEGIST ALTAIST ARABIST FAUNIST FEUDIST GRECIAN OLOGIST SURGEON AQUINIST ARBORIST BANTUIST BOTANIST ETHICIST GEMARIST GEOGNOST GEOMETER HEBRAIST HOMERIST LATINIST URBANIST PHYSICIST PEDIATRIST PATHOLOGIST

(SUFF.) ICIAN LOG(ER)(IA)(IAN)(IC) (ICAL)(IST)(UE)(Y)
SPECIALIZE MAJOR
SPECIALTY BAG THING
SPECIES FOLK FORM KIND SORT BROOD CLASS EIDOS GENRE ESPECE MANNER MISTER APOMICT FEATHER SPECIAL ANALOGUE GENOTYPE INDIGENE
(— VARIANT) MORPH
(ATOMIC —) DAUGHTER
SPECIFIC EXPRESS SPECIAL TRIVIAL CONCRETE ESPECIAL
SPECIFICALLY NAMELY
SPECIFICATION MENTION
(WRITE —S) SPEC
SPECIFICITY HECCEITY
SPECIFIED SET GIVEN
SPECIFY ASSIGN DESIGN DETAIL ARTICLE EXPRESS MENTION INDICATE NOMINATE PRESCRIBE
SPECIMEN CAST TEST ESSAY FACER MODEL SPICE CHANCE SAMPLE SWATCH EXAMPLE ICOTYPE ISOTYPE NEOTYPE PATTERN SAMPLER ALLOTYPE EXEMPLAR HOLOTYPE HYPOTYPE IDEOTYPE INSTANCE REPRESENTATIVE
(— OF WORK) PIECE
(ADDITIONAL —) COTYPE
(ANATOMICAL —) PREPARATION
(EXCELLENT —) RATTLER
(EXTRAORDINARY —) BENDER
(FEMALE —) GYNETYPE
(FINEST —) PEARL
(LARGE —) ELEPHANT
(MISERABLE —) RAT
(POOR —) APOLOGY
(SMALL —) MITE
SPECIOUS GAY FAIR FALSE WHITE FACILE GLOSSY HOLLOW TINSEL PAGEANT PLAUSIVE PROBABLE SPURIOUS PLAUSIBLE MERETRICIOUS
SPECIOUSNESS DISGUISE
SPECK DOT JOT PIN PIP MOTE SPOT TICK WHIT BLACK GLEBE PLECK APHTHA SPECKLE FLYSPECK NUBECULA
(— IN LINEN) SPRIT
(— ON FINGERNAIL) GIFT
(BLACK —) DARTROSE
SPECKLE FLECK GARLE SPECK MIZZLE PECKLE STIPPLE
SPECKLED SHELD FIGGED MAILED MENALD SANDED BLOBBED BRACKET PECKLED SPECKED SPECKLY FRECKLED IRONSHOT IRRORATE JASPERED STIPPLED
SPECTACLE POMP SHOW SPEC BYSEN SIGHT CIRCUS DEVICE OBJECT EYEMARK PAGEANT SPECIES TAMASHA MONUMENT NAUMACHY STERACLE NAUMACHIA
(DEPLORABLE —) OBJECT
(ODD —) TRACK
(POMPOUS —) PAGEANTRY
(SORRY —) BIZEN BYSEN BYZEN
(WATER —) AQUACADE
(PL.) LUDI
(SUFF.) CADE ORAMA
SPECTACLES PAIR SPECS BRILLS

LUNETS PEEPER SIGHTS GLASSES GOGGLES WINKERS ANAGLYPH CHEATERS BARNACLES
SPECTACULAR VIEWY PAGEANT
SPECTATOR FAN VIEWER WITNESS BEHOLDER OBSERVER OVERSEER RAILBIRD VIEWSTER SCAFFOLDER
(PL.) DEDANS
SPECTER BUG BOGY MARE BOGIE BOGLE GHOST LARVA POOKA SPOOK TAIPO BOGGLE EMPUSA PHOOKA REDCAP SHADOW SPIRIT SPOORN WRAITH BOGGARD BOGGART BUGBEAR PHANTOM RAWHEAD REDCOWL SPECTRE GUYTRASH PHANTASM PRESENCE REVENANT SPECTRUM
(BROKEN —) GLORY
SPECTRAL SPOOKY GHOSTLY SHADOWY
SPECULATE JOB BEAR RISK STAG GAMBLE PONDER WONDER CONSIDER RUMINATE THEORIZE
(— IN STOCKS) SCALP
SPECULATION THEORY THEORIC VENTURE GAMBLING IDEOLOGY
(ABSTRACT —) IDEOLOGY
(DISHONEST —) BUBBLE
(VAGUE —) MYSTICISM
SPECULATIVE ACADEMIC
SPECULATOR PIKER GAMBLER PLUNGER SCALPER BOURSIER BUMMAREE OPERATOR
SPECULUM METAL MIRROR DILATER DIOPTER DIOPTRIC
SPEECH GOB LIP SAW SAY TAT TOY COAX LEED REDE RUNE TALE DUALA FRUMP GLOZE LEDEN LINGO PARLE SERMO SPEAK SPELL SPIEL SPOKE SQUIB VOICE BREATH DILOGY EPILOG GAELIC GASCON GILAKI JARGON LEDDEN LEMOSI ORISON REASON SALUTE STEVEN TONGUE ACCENTS ADDRESS BROCARD EASTERN MEITHEI ORATION PALABRA VULGATE EPILOGUE GALICIAN HARANGUE LANGUAGE LOCUTION LOQUENCE MORAVIAN PARLANCE QUESTION SONORITY SPEAKING
(— CHARACTERIZED BY SLURRING) SLURVIAN
(— FORM) LEXEME
(— IN GREEK DRAMA) RHESIS
(— IN PLAY) SIDE
(— REDUCER) VOCODER
(ABUSIVE —) REVILEMENT
(AFFECTED —) CANT
(AUSTRALIAN —) STRINE
(BITTER —) DIATRIBE
(BOASTFUL —) BLUSTER
(BOMBASTIC —) SQUIRT HARANGUE
(CHILDISH —) LALLATION
(COARSE —) HARLOTRY
(COCKNEY —) LONDONESE
(CONFUSED —) SPUTTER SPLUTTER
(CONTEMPTUOUS —) FRUMP
(CONVERSATIONAL —) PURPOSE
(DULL IN —) PROSY
(EXTEMPORE —) IMPROMPTU
(IMPUDENT —) SASS
(INCOHERENT —) WORDSALAD

(INDIGENOUS —) VERNACULAR
(INTRODUCTORY —) PROLOGUE PROLOCUTION
(IRRITABLE —) SNAP
(JAVANESE —) KRAMA
(KIND OF —) CUED
(LONG —) MONOLOG
(LONG-DRAWN —) TIRADE
(MISLEADING —) PALAVER
(MOCKING —) TRIFLE
(MONOTONOUS —) DRONE
(NASAL —) RHINOLALIA
(OBSCURE —) ENIGMA
(OFFENSIVE —) INJURY
(PERSUASIVE —) ELOQUENCE
(PERT —) DICACITY
(PRETENTIOUS —) FUSTIAN
(ROUNDABOUT —) CIRCUIT
(SANCTIMONIOUS —) SNUFFLE
(SINGSONG —) CANT
(SLANDEROUS —) EVIL
(SLURRED —) SLURVIAN
(STAGY —) HISTRIONICS
(UNINTELLIGIBLE —) HEBREW
(VAPID —) WASH
(PREF.) LALO LEXI LOG(O) PHON(O)
(SUFF.) ESE LEXIA PHASIA PHEMIA PHEMISM PHEMISTIC PHRASEO PHRASIA PHRASIS
(— DISORDER) LALIA
SPEECHIFIER SPOUTER
SPEECHLESS DUMB MUTE SILENT
SPEECHMAKING SPOUTING
(— TO GAIN APPLAUSE) BUNKUM BUNCOMBE
SPEED BAT HIE REV RIP RUN ZIP FLEE FOOT GAIT HARE HIGH PACE PELT PIKE PIRR POST TEAR TILT ZING BLAST HASTE HURRY SMOKE WHIRL ASSIST CAREER FOURTH HASTEN STREAK QUICKEN WHIZZLE AIRSPEED CELERITY DISPATCH ESCALATE EXPEDITE FASTNESS MOMENTUM RAPIDITY VELOCITY ACCELERATE
(— OF NAUTICAL MILE) KNOT
(— OF PITCH) STUFF
(— OF 100 MILES PER HOUR) TON
(— RELATIVE TO SOUND) MACH
(— UP) HASTEN CATALYZE EXPEDITE
(AT FULL —) AMAIN
(AUTOMOTIVE —) LOW HIGH DRIVE FIRST THIRD FOURTH SECOND REVERSE
(DRIVING —) SWING
(FULL —) RANDOM RANDON
(GOOD —) BONALLY
(HIGH —) CLIP MACH
(UNIT OF —) BAUD
(PREF.) DROM(O) TACHO
SPEEDBOAT HYDRO
SPEEDILY CITO SOON APACE RATHE BELIVE PRESTO BETIMES HYINGLY QUICKLY TANTIVY
SPEEDING HURTLING
SPEEDWELL CATEYE HENBIT FLUELLEN NECKWEED NICKWELL BROOKLIME
SPEEDY FAST SOON HASTY QUICK RATHE SWIFT RAKING SUDDEN POSTING TANTIVY EXPEDITE METEORIC SPEEDFUL SPINNING POSTHASTE

SPELEOLOGIST CAVEMAN
SPELL GO FIT HEX JAG HACK JINX MOJO PULL RUNE SCAT TACK TAKE TIFF TIME TOUR TURN BRIEF CHARM CRAFT CRASH MAGIC PATCH SPACE WANGA WEIRD WHEEL ACCESS GLAMOR GOOFER GRIGRI GUFFER MAKUTU MANTRA PERIOD SNATCH STREAK CANTRIP SORCERY SPELDER CANTRAIP EXORCISM GREEGREE MALEFICE PISHOGUE
(— OF ACTIVITY) BOUT
(— OF EVIL EYE) JETTATURA
(— OF EXERCISE) BREATHER
(— OF INSTRUCTION) LESSON
(— OF LISTLESSNESS) DOLDRUMS
(— OF PROSPERITY) UP
(— OF SHIVERING) AGUE
(— OF WEATHER) SNAP SLANT SEASON
(— OF WEEPING) GREET
(— OF WORK) SLOG
(BREATHING —) BLOW
(BRIEF —) SNATCH
(COLD —) SNAP
(CONTINUOUS —) RUN
(DRINKING —) FUDDLE
(EVIL —) JINX
(FAINTING —) DROW DWALM
(MYSTIC —) RUNE
(NIPPING —) SNAPE
(SHORT —) WINK SPURT SNATCH
(STORMY —) FLAW
(VOODOOISTIC —) WANGA
(WITCH'S —) CANTRIP
SPELLBIND ENCHANT
SPELLBINDING BASILISK
SPELLBOUND HEXED
SPELLING GRAPH WRITING PHONOGRAPHY
(BAD —) CACOGRAPHY
(UNSATISFACTORY —) PSEUDOGRAPHY
SPELT FAR EMMER FITCH SPELTZ
SPELTZ EMMER
SPENCER TRYSAIL
SPEND USE BIRL COST DREE DROP LEAD PASS STOW WARE WEAR DALLY DREIE SERVE SHOOT TRADE BESTOW BEWARE EXPEND LAVISH MOIDER OUTRUN CONSUME DISPEND EXHAUST UNPURSE CONFOUND CONTRIVE DISBURSE
(— FRUITLESSLY) DAWDLE
(— IN IDLENESS) DRONE
(— LAVISHLY) BLUE SPORT DEBAUCH
(— MONEY) MELT
(— RECKLESSLY) BLOW LASH
(— SUMMER) ESTIVATE
(— TIME) DREE FOOL DREIE ENTREAT
(— TIME TEDIOUSLY) DRANT
(— WASTEFULLY) SPILL SQUANDER
SPENDTHRIFT WASTER PANURGE ROUNDER SPENDER WASTREL PRODIGAL PROFLIGATE SCATTERGOOD
SPENSER IMMERITO
SPENT DONE WEARY EFFETE OVERWORN
SPERM SEED SEMINIUM

SPERMACETI SPERM CETACEUM
SPERMOGONIUM PYCNIUM
SPERMOPHILE MARMOT SUSLIK
SPERM WHALE CACHALOT PHYSETER
SPET SIGNET SINNET
SPEW PUKE SPUE VOMIT
SPHAERIUM CYCLAS
SPHAGION HIERA
SPHAGNUM MUSKEG
SPHALERITE JACK BLENDE BLACKJACK
SPHENODON TUATARA HATTERIA
SPHERE ORB AREA BALL BOWL LOKA SHOT FIELD GLOBE ORBIT RANGE REALM SCOPE CIRCLE CROTAL DOMAIN HEAVEN REGION RUNDLE COUNTRY ELEMENT GLOBOID KINGDOM ORBICLE PURVIEW EARTHKIN EMPYREAL EMPYREAN MOVEABLE PROVINCE TERRITORY
(— OF ACTION) AMBIT ARENA WORLD DOMAIN
(— OF ACTIVITY) FIELD FRONT
(— OF AUTHORITY) DIOCESE
(— OF CELLS) BLASTULA
(— OF INFLUENCE) DOMAIN SATRAPY
(— OF LIFE) EARTH WORLD STATION
(— OF OPERATION) AREA AMBIT SCOPE THEATER THEATRE
(— OF WORK) TITLE
(CELESTIAL —) CYCLE ELEMENT
(ENCOMPASSING —) AMBIENT
(HOLLOW —) SHELL
(MAGNETIZED —) EARTHKIN TERRELLA
(METAL —) HAMMER
(SMALL —) ORBICLE SPHERULE
(SUBMERSIBLE —) BENTHOSCOPE
(TINKLING —) CROTAL
(PREF.) GLOBO SPHAER(O) SPHER(O)
SPHERICAL ORBIC GLOBAL ROTUND GLOBATE GLOBOSE ORBICAL SPHERIC GLOBULAR ORBICULAR
(PREF.) GLOBO
SPHEROID QUANTASOME
SPHERULE GLOBULE VARIOLE
SPHINX MUSTANG COLOSSUS HAWKMOTH
(SITE OF —) GIZA
SPICA AZIMECH
SPICCATO PIQUE
SPICE MACE VEIN ZEST AROMA CLOVE EPICE TASTE GINGER NUTMEG PEPPER SEASON STACTE SPICERY SPICING ALLSPICE CINNAMON SEASONER
(ADD — TO) ENLIVEN
(PL.) GARAMMASALA
SPICEBUSH BENZOIN SNAPWOOD
SPICED SPICY POWDERED
SPICKNEL MEW SCLERE BEARWORT
SPICULE OXEA TOXA ASTER CHELA CYMBA DESMA DIACT SIGMA SPINE STYLE ACTINE ANCHOR MONACT SCLERE STYLUS TRIACT TRIPOD TYLOTE CALTROP DIACTIN EUASTER HEXAXON MONAXON

PINULUS RHABDUS SPICKLE SPIRULA TETRACT TORNOTE TRIAENE TRIAXON TYLOTUS HEXASTER ISOCHELA OXYASTER POLYAXON SCLERITE SPHERULA SPICULUM STRONGYL TETRAXON TRICHITE TYLASTER
(SUFF.) AENE
SPICY RACY SEXY GAMEY NUTTY SWEET SPICED GINGERY PEPPERY FRAGRANT SPICEFUL
SPIDER BUG COB ARAIN ATTID COBBE COPPE LOPPE NANCY TAINT ANANSI ARRAND EPEIRA HUNTER KATIPO TRIVET WEAVER ARANEID CREEPER DRASSID EPEIRID JAYHAWK KNOPPIE POKOMOO RETIARY SERPENT SKILLET SOLDIER SPINNER ARACHNID ATTERCOP CTENIZID DICTYNID ETTERCAP KARAKURT ORBITELE PHALANGE PHALANGY PHOLCOID SALTICID SOLPUGID TELARIAN ULOBORID VENANTES WANDERER TARANTULA
(PART OF —) EYE CLAW COXA FEMUR TIBIA TARSUS ABDOMEN PATELLA PEDICEL SCOPULA SPINNERET METATARSUS PEDIPALPUS TROCHANTER CEPHALOTHORAX
(PREF.) ARACHN(O)
SPIDER CRAB MAIAN MAIID
SPIDERFLOWER QUARESMA
SPIDER MONKEY SAJOU COAITA SAPAJOU
SPIDERWORT TRINITY
SPIEL LINE SPEECH
SPIELER BARKER
SPIFF (— UP) ENLIVEN
SPIGNEL MEU
SPIGOT TAP SPILE DOSSIL DOZZLE STOPCOCK
SPIKE GAD BARB BROB PICK PIKE PILE SPUR TINE PITON POINT ROUGH SPEAR SPICA SPICK MOOTER PRITCH SPADIX SPIKER TENTER ALICOLE GADLING PRICKER PRICKET TRENAIL TURNPIN SPIKELET STROBILE WHEATEAR
(— A CANNON) CLOY
(— AS CANDLESTICK) PRICKET
(— OF CEREAL) EAR
(— OF FLOWER) SPIRE
(— ON GAUNTLET) GADLING
(BRACTED —) AMENT
(DRIED —S) CANNABIS
(WILLOW —) CATKIN
SPIKED SPICATE SPINDLED
SPIKELET CHAT ALICOLE LOCUSTA SPICULE
SPIKENARD PHU NARD ARALIA SUMBUL ARALIAD IVYWORT SPIGNET SPIGNUT
SPILE TAP SPILL FOREPOLE
SPILL LET DRIP DUMP SHED SLOP TELL FLOSH SCALE SKAIL SPILE SQUAB STAVE JIRBLE PURLER SLATTER SLOBBER TURNOVER
(— FOR LIGHTING PIPES) FIDIBUS
SPIN CUT BIRL DRAW GYRE HURL PIRL PURL REEL SCREW SPONE

TWIRL TWIST WEAVE WHIRL
FOLLOW GYRATE VRILLE WAMBLE
TWIZZLE TEETOTUM
(— AND MAKE HUM) BUM
(— AROUND) SWING
(— ON BASEBALL) STUFF
(— ON BILLIARD BALL) SIDE
(— OUT) SHOOT
(— SILK) THROW
(— SMOOTHLY) SLEEP
(— UNEVENLY) TWITTER
SPINACH SAVOY EPINARD OLITORY
POTHERB
SPINAL CORD AXION NUCHA
MYELON
(WHITE MATTER OF —) ALBA NUKE
(PREF.) MYEL(O)
(SUFF.) MYELIA
SPINDLE PIN AXLE HASP PIRN SPIT
STEM STUD ARBOR FLOAT QUILL
SPIKE SPILL VERGE BOBBIN
BROACH CANNON FUSEAU
BOLSTER MANDREL SPINNEL
TRENDLE WHARROW
(AXLE —) ARM
(FOURTH OF —) HASP
(ONE 24TH OF —) HEER
(PREF.) FUSI
SPINDLE TREE GAITER DOGWOOD
PEGWOOD EUONYMUS
SPINDLING SPEARY SPINDLY
SPIRLIE
SPINDLY LEGGY PULING
SPINE HORN PIKE PILE SETA SPUR
CHINE PRICK QUILL SPEAR SPIKE
SPINA THORN ACUMEN CHAETA
RACHIS ACANTHA ACICULA
FULCRUM GLOCHIS PAXILLA
PRICKER PRICKLE ROSTRUM
SPINULE STICKLE ACICULUM
BACKBONE ILLICIUM PAXILLUS
PELELITH SPICULUM SPINELET
(— OF FIN) RAY
(— OF SURGEON FISH) TUCK
(CURVATURE OF —) LORDOSIS
(PREF.) ACANTH(O) RACHI(O)
RHACHI(O)
(SUFF.) ACANTHUS CHAETA
CHAETES CHAETUS RACHIDIA
RHACHIS RRHACHIS
SPINEL BALAS CANDITE ESPINEL
GAHNITE VERMEIL PICOTITE
SPINELLE CEYLONITE RUBICELLE
SPINELESS SLAVISH
SPINET PIANO ESPINET GIRAFFE
OCTAVINA SOURDINE VIRGINAL
SPINNER LURE ROTOR
(THREAD OF LIFE —) CLOTHO
SPINNERET GALEA MAMMULA
SPINNER
SPINNING AREEL STROBIC LANIFICE
(— WEB) TELARIAN
SPINNING JENNY MULE JENNY
SPINNING MULE IRONMAN
SPINNING WHEEL TURN CHARKHA
CHURRUCK
(PART OF —) BAND FLYER WHEEL
BOBBIN DISTAFF SPINDLE TREADLE
STANDARD
SPINSTER TABBY VIRGIN
SPINULE
(PL.) CTENII
SPINY PICKED THORNY

(PREF.) ACANTH(O) CENTR(I)(O)
ECHIN(O)
SPINY OYSTER SPONDYLE
SPINY RAT OCTODONT
SPIRACLE STOMA STIGMA
BLOWHOLE
SPIRAEA MAY ROSACEAN
MEADOWSWEET
SPIRAL COIL CURL GYRE SPIN HELIX
SCREW SNARE SPIRE BUTTON
GURGES LITUUS SCREWY SCROLL
SPIRED TWIRLY VOLUTE HELICAL
ROLLING SPIROID STROPHE
WINDING WREATHY GYROIDAL
HELICINE HELICOID
(— OF WIRE) GRID
(LACEWORK —) PURL
(PREF.) GYR(O) HELI HELIC(O)
SPIRANT VAU WAW HISS OPEN
DURATIVE
SPIRANTHES IBIDIUM
SPIRE CROWN SHAFT SIKAR SPEAR
TAPER TOLLY BROACH FLECHE
PRICKET SHIKARA SIKHARA
SPIRALE SPIRELET
SPIRE-BEARER SPIRIFER
SPIREME SKEAN SKEIN
SPIRIT GO AME FLY NAG PEP VIM
AITU AKUA ALMA ATUA BRIO DASH
DOOK ELAN FIRE GALL GIMP HYLE
JINN LIFE MANE MANE MIND
MOOD SOUL TONE ZEMI ZING
AGIEL ARDOR ARIEL ASURA AZOTH
CHEER DEMON DHOUL DJINN
DOBBY ETHOS FLING GEIST GHOST
GORIC GUACA GUSTO HAUNT
HEART HOLDA HUACA JINNI LARVA
MOXIE NUMEN PLUCK POWER
PRETA RALPH SAINT SHADE SHRAB
SPOOK SPUNK VERVE ASTRAL
ASUANG BOTTOM BREATH
CHULPA COURIL DAEMON ESPRIT
FAINTS FLECHE FYLGJA GENIUS
GINGER INWARD KOBOLD LESHEY
METTLE MORALE ORISHA PAZAZZ
PECKER PIZAZZ PNEUMA PYTHON
SPRAWL SPRITE TAFFIA WRAITH
ALCOHOL BRAVERY CONTROL
CORDIAL COURAGE ENTRAIN
EUDEMON KNOCKER MANITOU
PISACHI PIZZAZZ PURUSHA
RAPPIST SMEDDUM STOMACH
CALVADOS ERDGEIST FAMILIAR
FOLLETTO PHANTASM SPIRACLE
SPIRITUS
(— DWELLING IN JEWEL) AZOTH
(— DWELLING IN MINES) KNOCKER
(— HAUNTING PRINTING HOUSES)
RALPH
(— OF DEAD) CHINDI CHINDEE
(— OF DEATH) CHULPA
(— OF DECEASED) AKH
(— OF ENTERPRISE) ADVENTURE
(— OF FERTILITY) YAKSA YAKSHA
YAKSHI
(— OF HOSTILITY) ANIMUS
(— OF LOYALTY) PIETAS
(— OF MAN) AKH
**(— OF ONE WHO HAS MET
VIOLENT DEATH)** PISACHI
(— OF PHYSICAL HEART) AB
(— OF PRIESTHOOD)
SACERDOTALISM

(— OF THE AGE) ZEITGEIST
(— OF THE AIR) SYLPH
(— OF TRAGEDY) COTHURN
(— OF UNBAPTIZED BABE) TARAN
(—S OF LOWER WORLD) INFERI
(—S OF THE DEAD) MANES
(— WHICH ACTUATES CUSTOMS)
ETHOS
(ANCESTRAL —) ANITO KATCHINA
(ARDENT —) RAK RACK ARRACK
(ASTRAL —) AGIEL ASTRAL JOPHIEL
UUCHATON
(AVENGING —) FURY ALECTO
ALASTOR MEGAERA
(CHARACTERISTIC —) VIBE
(COMBATIVE —) SWORD
(DISEMBODIED —) KUEI KWEI SOUL
GHOST LARVA SHADE ASUANG
SPECTER SPECTRE
(DIVINE —) ISVARA ISHVARA
(EARTH —) ERDGEIST
(EFFULGENT —S) ARDORS
(EMANCIPATED —) MUKTATMA
(EVIL —) DEV DIV HAG IMP OKI BAKA
BENG BOKO BOLL DEVA DUSE
MARA OKEE ASURA BUGAN DAEVA
DEMON DEVIL JUMBY OTKON
DAITYA DIBBUK DYBBUK LILITH
AHRIMAN BUGGANE CASZIEL
INCUBUS KANAIMA RAKSHAS
SHAITAN SHEITAN SKOOKUM
WINDIGO ASMODEUS BAALPEOR
BEELPEOR HOBOMOCO SUCCUBUS
NIGHTMARE
(FAMILIAR —) FLY GENIUS HARPIER
(FEMALE —) DUFFY DUPPY DUSIO
HOLDA UNDINE BANSHEE ATAENSIC
BABAJAGA BELFAGOR BELFAZOR
(FIGHTING —) DEVIL
(FOREST —) MIMING
(FULL OF —) CRANK
(FULL OF —S) BRAG
(GOOD —) DEVA EUDEMON
(GOVERNING —) ANIMUS
(GUARDIAN —) ANGEL TOTEM
FYLGJA NAGUAL
(HIGH —) GINGER COURAGE
(HIGH —S) CREST GAIETY HEYDAY
ELATION
(HOSTILE —S) LEMURES
(HOUSEHOLD —S) LARES PENATES
(HUMAN —) JIVATMA
(IMPISH —) PO
(IMPURE —) FAINTS
(INDIAN —) MANITO
(IN VIGOROUS —S) FIERCE
(LOW —S) DUMP BLUES MEGRIM
DISMALS
(MALEVOLENT —) BHUT GORIC
LARVA
(MALICIOUS —) DOBBY
(MALIGNANT —) IMP KER GYRE
DEMON
(MANLY —) SPLEEN
(MISCHIEVOUS —) KOBOLD
TIKOLOSH
(MOUNTAIN —) RUBEZAHL
(MOVING —) SOUL
(MUSICAL —) BRIO
(NATURE —) NAT
(NIGHT —) TENEBRIO
(PARTY —) FACTION
(REFINED —) ELIXIR

(RENEWED —) REFRESHMENT
(RESOLUTE —) SPRAWL
(ROVING —) RAMPLER
(SEA —) TANGIE
(SENSED —) KARMA
(SOOTHSAYING —) PYTHON
(SUPERNATURAL —) FAMILIAR
(SYLVAN —) LESHY SYLVAN
(TRICKSY —) ARIEL
(TUTELARY —S) DIS LARES
(VITAL —) TUCK
(VOLATILE —) ESSENCE
(WATER —) ARIEL KELPY ONDINE
UNDINE
(WICKED —) IMP THURSE
(PL.) GENII IGIGI DAUBER
(PREF.) PNEUMAT(O) PSYCH(O)
THYM(O)
(SUFF.) THYMIA
SPIRITED BRAG FELL GOGO RACY
TALL BEANY BIRKY CRANK EAGER
FIERY FLUSH KEDGE KINKY LIFEY
PEPPY PROUD SASSY SEEDY
SMART SPICY VIVID AUDACE
FIERCE GINGER LIVELY METTLE
PLUCKY SKEIGH SPRUCE SPUNKY
VIVACE ANIMATO DASHING
FORWARD HUMMING NERVOUS
PEPPERY SPIRITY DESIROUS
FRAMPOLD GENEROUS PHRAMPEL
SLASHING STOMACHY VASCULAR
METTLESOME
SPIRITEDLY GAMELY
SPIRITLESS DEAD DOWF MEAN
MEEK POOR TAME AMORT FAINT
MILKY MUSTY SEEDY SOGGY
VAPID ABJECT ANEMIC CRAVEN
DREEPY FLASHY JEJUNE LEADEN
MOPISH SODDEN SOFTLY
WOODEN HILDING INSIPID
LANGUID FECKLESS FLAGGING
LISTLESS THEWLESS
SPIRITLESSLY DAVIELY
SPIRITLESSNESS LANGUOR
SPIRITLIKE ETHEREAL
SPIRITS LACE RAKI HOOCH MANES
METHS FETTLE PECKER FEATHER
LEMURES SAMSHOO WAIPIRO
SPIRITUAL ABOVE DEVOUT INWARD
MISTLY GHOSTLY CHURCHLY
INTERNAL NUMINOUS SUPERIOR
PNEUMATIC
(— LEADER) ZADDIK
SPIRITUALISM SPOOKISM
SPIRITUALITY HEAVEN
SPIRITUALIZE REFINE
SPIRITUOUS HARD
SPIROCHETE BORRELIA
SPIT YEX FUFF RACK FROTH REACH
SPAWL BROACH SPITTLE
SANDSPIT SPITTING
(— AND POLISH) BULL
(— OF LAND) HOOK
(SUFF.) PTYSIS
SPITE ENVY ONDE DEPIT LIVOR
PIQUE VENOM HATRED MALICE
MAUGRE RANCOR SPLEEN
DESPITE AMBITION
SPITEFUL MEAN CATTY NASTY
NEBBY PETTY SNAKY ELVISH
MALIGN SULLEN WANTON WICKED
CATTISH ENVIOUS PEEVISH

SNAKISH VICIOUS WASPISH CANKERED KNAPPISH VENOMOUS

SPITFIRE CACAFOGO PEPPERBOX
(TYPE OF —) VOLCANO

SPITTING FUFF EMPTYSIS

SPITTING SNAKE RINGHALS

SPITTLE SPIT SPAWL SPUTUM SLOBBER
(PREF.) PTYAL(O)

SPITTLEBUG FROGHOPPER

SPITTOON GABOON PIGDAN SPITBOX CRACHOIR CUSPIDOR

SPIV RORTER

SPLAKE MENDIGO

SPLANCHNIC VISCERAL

SPLASH JAW LAP DASH GLOB GOUT JAUP LOSH LUSH SKIT SOSS SPAT WASH BLASH FLASH FLICK FLOOD FLOSH PLASH PLOUT QUASH SKIRP SLART SLASH SLOSH SLUSH SQUAT SWILK BEDASH DABBLE DOLLOP FLOUSE JABBLE LABBER PLATCH SLUNGE SOZZLE SPLOSH SPRENT SQUIRT PLOUTER SPATTER SPIRTLE SPLODGE SPLURGE SWATTER SPLAIRGE SPLATHER SPLATTER SPLOTHER SPLUTHER SPLUTTER
(— OF COLOR) GOUT
(SLIGHT —) GILP

SPLASHBOARD FENDER SPLASHER

SPLASHING SWASH FLASHY JABBLE DASHING SPATTER SPLUTTER SWASHING

SPLASHY BLASHY GLITZY SLOPPY SPRAWLY

SPLATTER DASH BLASH SPLAIRGE

SPLAY FLAN

SPLAYED FLEW FLUE

SPLAYFOOT FLATFOOT

SPLEEN IRE PIP BILE LIEN MELT MILT RHEUM MALICE STOMACH
(PREF.) LIEN(O) SPLEN(I)(O)
(SUFF.) SPLENIA

SPLEENY PEEVISH

SPLENDID GAY BRAW FINE NEAT RIAL BRAVE GRAND JOLLY NOBLE PROUD REGAL ROYAL SHEEN SHOWY STOUT TOUGH WALLY WLONK CANDID COSTLY SIGHTY SOLEMN SPIFFY SUPERB ELEGANT GALLANT SHINING SUBLIME TEARING BARONIAL CHAMPION CLINKING COLOSSAL GLORIOUS GORGEOUS MAJESTIC ORGULOUS RATTLING SLASHING SPANKING STUNNING TERRIFIC
(CHEAPLY —) TINNY

SPLENDIDLY FINE FINELY SPROWSY

SPLENDOR SUN UMA GITE LUXE POMP BLAZE ECLAT GLARE GLEAM GLORY SHEEN SHINE FULGOR LUSTER LUSTRE PARADE RUFFLE CLARITY DISPLAY JOLLITY PANACHE GRANDEUR RADIANCE SUMPTURE

SPLENETIC SULLEN VAPORY PEEVISH

SPLENIC LIENAL

SPLICE FOOT JOIN SCAB PIECE SCARE SKELB CROTCH PIECEN SPLICING

SPLICER STRAPPER

SPLINE FIN SLAT FEATHER

SPLINT SCOB FANON MATCH SPELK SPELL TASSE SPLENT THOMAS CALIPER SPLINTER
(— FOR FRACTURE) JUNK

SPLINTER BROOM BURST PURSE SHAKE SHIDE SHIVE SKELB SKELF SLICE SPAIL SPALE SPALL SPALI SPEEL SPELK SPELL SPILE SPILL SPLIT SPOON SLIVER SPLEET SPLINT FLINDER SHATTER SLITHER SPLITTER

SPLINTERY SKELVY

SPLINTWOOD ALBURNUM

SPLIT AX AXE CUT RIT BUCK CHAP CONE DUNT GAIG MALL MAUL RASH REND RENT RIFT RIVE SKAG SLAT TEAR BLAST BREAK BURST CHECK CHINE LEAVE SHAKE SHEAR SKIVE SLENT SLIVE SMASH SPALD SPALL SPLAT CLEAVE CLOVEN CREASE DEPART DIVIDE FLAGGY FLERRY GOAWAY SCHISM SPRING SUNDER BIVALVE SHATTER SLITHER CREVASSE SCISSION SCISSURE SPLINTER
(— FISH) SCROD
(— IN BOWLING) BEDPOSTS
(— OFF) SPALL SPAWL SCREEVED
(— TICKET) SCRATCH
(KIND OF —) STOCK
(PREF.) SCHISTO SCHIZ(O)

SPLITTERMAN BOLTER

SPLITTING FLAGGY FISSION SCISSION
(— OF PERSONALITY) DISSOCIATION
(— OF WORD) TMESIS
(READILY —) SCISSILE
(PL.) FILMS
(SUFF.) RHEXIS RRHEXIS

SPLOTCH DAB BLOB DASH HALO SPOT FLICK SMUDGE SPECKLE SPLATCH SPLURGE

SPLURGE BINGE SPEND SPRAY SPREE SPLASH

SPLUTTER FUFF GLUTTER SPATTER SPUTTER SPLOTHER

SPODOPTERA LAPHYGMA

SPODUMENE KUNZITE TRIPHANE

SPOIL MAR MUX ROT BLOT BOOT COOK DAZE FANG FOIL FRAB GAIN KILL MANK PELF PREY ADDLE BITCH BLEND BLUNK BOOTY BOTCH CROSS DECAY LOUSE QUAIL QUEER SHEND SPILL STAIN STRIP TOUCH TRASH WALLY BOODLE BUGGER CODDLE COOPER CORPSE COSSET CURDLE DEFACE DEFORM FORAGE INJURE MANGLE PERISH RAVAGE TIDDLE BAUCHLE BEDEVIL BLEMISH CONNACH CORRUMP CORRUPT ESTREPE INDULGE MULLOCK PILLAGE PLUNDER SPOLIUM TARNISH VIOLATE BANKRUPT CONFOUND DISGRACE MISGUIDE SPOLIATE
(— BY SOAKING) RET RAIT RATE

SPOILED BAD BLOWN DAZED MUSTY CADISH STICKIT BRATTISH

(— BY USE) OVERWORN
(EASILY —) GINGER

SPOILER HARROWER

SPOILERS (AUTHOR OF —) BEACH
(CHARACTER IN —) ROY BILL HELEN CHERRY DEXTRY STRUVE CHESTER MALOTTE MCNAMARA STILLMAN GLENISTER

SPOILFIVE MAW

SPOILS BAG LOOT SKIN SWAG BOOTY FORAY SPOLIA PILLAGE PLUNDER PICKINGS

SPOILSPORT NARK PILL GRINCH LETGAME

SPOILT MARDY

SPOKE RUNG QUOTH SPACK SPAKE LOWDER SPONDIL SPONDYL
(— OF WHEEL) RADIUS

SPOKEN ORAL SAID VERBAL VOICED

SPOKESMAN MOUTH HERALD PROPHET SPEAKER TRUMPET MOUTHPIECE
(— OF DEITY) PROPHET

SPOKEWISE RADIAL

SPOLIATION REIF SPOIL RAPINE PILLAGE PLUNDER SPOILING

SPONGE BOT FORM MUMP POLE SILK SORN SWAB ASCON CADGE GRASS LUFFA SCAFF SHARK SHIRK SHOOL SYCON ASCULA BUMMER COSHER LEUCON LOOFAH MALKIN MOPPET RHAGON ROLLER YELLOW BADIAGA BLEEDER GELFOAM RADIATE SCOURER SCRUNGE SYCONID ZIMOCCA DEADBEAT FREELOAD HARDHEAD HEDGEHOG MANDRUKA OLYNTHUS REDBEARD SCROUNGE SILICEAN SPHERIDA SUBERITE ZOOPHYTE PORIFERAN
(TAKE UP LIKE A —) SORB
(YOUNG —) SEEDLING
(SUFF.) AENE

SPONGER BOT BUM TRAMP BUMMER CADGER SPONGE SCAMBLER SMOOTHER

SPONGINESS FOZINESS

SPONGING TRENCHER

SPONGY FOZY FUZZY POACHY QUAGGY FUNGOUS BIBULOUS

SPONSOR COACH GOSSIP SURETY ENDORSE WITNESS
(— AT BAPTISM) HEAVE

SPONSORSHIP EGIS AEGIS

SPONTANEOUS FREE CARELESS FREEWILL UNBIDDEN UNTAUGHT VOLUNTARY

SPONTANEOUSLY KINDLY SELFLY

SPOOF PUTON

SPOOK GYRE GHOST HAUNT SCARE

SPOOL COB COP PIRN REEL QUILL SPILL SPULE TWEEL TWILL BOBBIN BROACH CHEESE COPPIN CARRIER
(— FOR NETS) GURDY
(HERALDIC —) TRUNDLE

SPOON HORN NECK CUTTY LABIS SHELL COCHLEA JUMBLER MUDDLER SKIMMER SPINNER STIRRER BARSPOON COCHLEAR GOBSTICK
(EUCHARISTIC —) LABIS
(FISHING —) TROLL

(FLATTENED —) SPATULA
(LONG-HANDLED —) LADLE
(SKIMMING —) LINGEL SKIMMER
(SNUFF —) PEN
(PREF.) COCHLEARI LIGUL(I)

SPOONBILL AJAJA SPOONY POPELER CICONIID
(PREF.) PLATALEI

SPOONERISM MARROWSKY

SPOONFUL COCHLEARE

SPOON-SHAPED COCHLEAR SPATULAR

SPOONY SILLY FOOLISH

SPOOR SIGN SPUR PISTE

SPORADIC POPPING ISOLATED

SPORANGIUM THECA OOTHECA

SPORE CYST SEED SPORID TELIUM AGAMETE AKINETE BISPORE ISOLANT ISOLATE OOSPORE SEEDLET SPORULE SWARMER CONIDIUM EXOSPORE GONIDIUM PROPAGULE
(— SAC) ASCI ASCUS

SPORES
(PREF.) CONI(DI)

SPOROCYST ZOOCYST SPOROSAC

SPORT FUN GIG KID MUM RIE RUX SEE TOY ALSO GAME GAUD GLEE JEST JOKE LAKE LARK PLAY PLOY RAGE TAIT BOURD BREAK DALLY DROLL FREAK MIRTH FROLIC LAUGHS POPJOY RACING SHIKAR SKIING BOATING CAMOGIE DISPORT DUCKING FOWLING MARLOCK PASTIME ROLLICK ROUNDER SAILING SPANIEL FALCONRY PLEASURE SKYDIVING MOUNTAINEERING
(— OF HAWKING) RIVER
(BOISTEROUS —) HIJINKS
(JAPANESE —) KENDO AIKIDO
(ONE-ON-ONE) EPEE
(ROUGH —) ROMP
(WATER —S) NAUTICS AQUATICS
(WINTER —) SKIJORING
(PREF.) LUDI

SPORTING VARMINT SPORTIVE

SPORTIVE GAY TAIT LARKY MERRY FRISKY JOCUND LIVELY LUSORY TOYFUL TOYING WANTON COLTISH FESTIVE GAMEFUL JESTING JOCULAR PLAYFUL TOYSOME TRICKSY WAGGISH FROLICKY GAMESOME PLAYSOME PLEASANT SPORTFUL

SPORTIVENESS HELL KNAVERY

SPORTS (— OFFICIAL) REF ZEBRA REFEREE

SPORTSMAN SPORT ATHLETE SHIKARI

SPORTSMANLIKE CLEAN SPORTY

SPORTY FLASH RORTY FLASHY RAKISH

SPORULE GRANULE

SPOT BIT DAB PIP SEE WEM BLOT BLUR CHUB DIRT DRAB FLAW GALL MAIL MOIL MOLE PLOT SCAM SITE SKIP SLUR SMUT SOIL SPAT TICK AMPER BLACK CLOUD FLECK GARLE GOODY GUTTA HATCH JIMMY MACLE PATCH PLACE PLECK POINT ROACH SMEAR SPLAT STAIN SULLY TACHE

TAINT WHERE BLANCH BLOTCH
DAPPLE FOGDOG GERATE LOCALE
MACULE MAZUCA MOTTLE
SMUDGE SMUTCH SPLECK STIGMA
BLEMISH CHARBON CHECKER
FLECKER FRECKLE GUTTULA
MASOOKA OCELLUS OLDWIFE
SMATTER SMITTER SPATTER
SPECKLE SPLOTCH SPOTTLE
STATION STIPPLE TERRAIN
FENESTRA LOCALITY MACULATE
PUNCTULE SPARKLET SPRINKLE
(— A SHIELD) GERATE
(— IN CLOTH) YAW
(— IN MARBLE) TERRACE
(— IN MINERAL) MACLE
(— IN PAPER) SHINER
(— IN SAW BLADE) BLOB
(— IN STEEL) STAR
(— IN WOOD) WEM
(— IN YARN) MOTE
(— OF INK) MONK
(— OF PAINT) DAUB
(— OF QUICKSAND) SUCKHOLE
(— ON CAT) BUTTON
(— ON CAT'S FACE) LAVALIER
(— ON EGG) EYE
(— ON FINGERNAIL) GIFT
(— ON FOREHEAD) TILAK TILAKA
(— ON HAWK) GOUT
(— ON HORSE) RACE SNIP STAR
RACHE
(— ON HORSE'S TOOTH) CHARBON
(— ON INSECT WINGS) BULLA
(— ON MOTH'S WINGS) FENESTRA
(— ON PLAYING CARD) PIP
(— ON SUN) FACULA GRANULE
SUNSPOT
(—S IN BOOKS) FOXING
(— WITH MIST) ATOMIZE
(BARREN —) GALL
(BLIND —) SCOTOMA SCOTOSIS
(BROWN —) SPRAIN SPRAING
(CRUSTY —) SCAB
(ESSENTIAL —) EYE
(EYELIKE — ON PEACOCK) OCELLUS
(FERTILE —) OASIS
(FIRM — IN BOG) HAG
(GREEN — IN VALLEY) HAW
(HALLOWED —) BETHEL
(INFLAMED —) AMPER
(LEAF —) TIKKA BLACKARM
(LIVER —S) CHLOASMA
(LIVID —) TOKEN
(LOW —) DIP SWAMP HOLLOW
(MARSHY —) SPEW SPUE
(PAINFUL —) SORE
(PLAGUE —) TOKEN
(RED —) FLEABITE
(RETIRED —) SHADE
(ROUGH — IN WOVEN GOODS) FAG
(ROUND —) BLOB
(SCABBY —) SCALD
(SECLUDED —) ALCOVE CLOISTER
(SHADY —) SWALE
(SKIN —) MOLE BLISTER FRECKLE
LENTIGO PETECHIA
(SMALL —) DOT PLECK STIGMA
LUNULET SPARKLET
(SOILED —) SLOP
(SORE —) BUBU BOTCH
(SPARKLING —) SPANGLE
(SWAMPY —) FLAM

(TIGHT —) JAM JACKPOT
(WEAK —) GALL HOLE CHINK NERVE
(WORN —) FRAY FRET
(PL.) MOONING
(PREF.) MACUL(I)(O) SPIL(O)
SPOTLESS FAIR PURE WEMLESS
INNOCENT
SPOTLIGHT ARC SPOT DEUCE
SPOTTED PIED MARLY SCOVY
SHELD CALICO FIGGED HAWKED
MACLED MAILED MARLED MIRLED
PARDED SPOTTY TICKED BRACKET
BROOKED FINCHED GUTTATE
MOTTLED PARDINE PIEBALD
PINTADO SPARKED SPECKED
SPECKLY TIGROID FRECKLED
LITURATE MACULOSE SPECKLED
STIPPLED
(SUFF.) MACULATE
SPOTTED EAGLE RAY MILLER
OBISPO
SPOTTED FLYCATCHER COBWEB
RAFTER WALLBIRD
SPOTTED GUM EUCALYPT
SPOTTED JEWFISH GUASA
SPOTTED SANDPIPER TIPUP
TILTUP CREEKER TIPTAIL
PEETWEET
SPOTTED SPURGE DOVEWEED
SPOTTED WINTERGREEN
RATSBANE
SPOTTED WOODPECKER PICUS
WITWALL
SPOTTER DOTTER
SPOTTING (— OF LEAVES) HELIOSIS
SPOTTY MEALY PATCHY PLATTY
SCABBY SPOTTED
SPOUSE EX FERE MAKE WIFE BRIDE
MATCH PARTY FELLOW MARROW
CONSORT ESPOUSE HUSBAND
SPOUT JET LIP BEAK DALE GEAT
GUSH NOSE SHOE ORATE SPILE
SPUME SPURT NOZZLE RIGGOT
SPLOIT SPROUT STRONE STROUP
BUBBLER FOUNTAIN GARGOYLE
(RAIN —) RONE
SPOUTER VAPORER
(MEDITERRANEAN —) ETNA
SPOUTING BLOW SALIENT
SPRAG PROP TRAILER
SPRAGGER SCOTCHER
SPRAIN RICK CHINK STAVE THRAW
THROW WRAMP WREST WRICK
STRAIN WRENCH STREMMA
SPRAT SMY BLAY BRIT BRITT SPRET
SPRIT GARVIE ALFIONE GARVOCK
BRISLING
(—S CAUGHT EARLY IN SEASON)
DROVE
SPRAWL LOLL TAVE SPURL SCRAWL
GRABBLE SCAMBLE SPARTLE
SPELDER SCRAMBLE SPRADDLE
SPRANGLE STRADDLE
SPRAWLING SPRANGLY
SPRAY FOG HOSE SCUD SPRY STEW
SPREE STOUR SWISH TRAIL TWIST
WATER HONEST SHOWER SPARGE
SPLASH SPRANG SPRITZ CURTAIN
SPAIRGE SYRINGE INHALANT
SPRANGLE
(— BEHIND MOTORBOAT)
ROOSTERTAIL
(— FROM SMALL WAVES) LIPPER

(— MASH) SPARGE
(— OF GEMS) AIGRETTE
(REDUCE TO —) NEBULIZE
SPREAD BED FAN LAY RUN COAT
DRAW FLUE SPAN TEER TELD TUCK
VEIN WALK APPLY CLEAM CREEP
FLARE KILIM PASTE SCALE SLICE
SPEND SPLAT SPLAY STALK STREW
WIDEN BUTTER EXTEND FLANGE
LARDER LAYOUT MANTLE SETOUT
THRUST UNFOLD UNFURL
BROADEN CANVASS DIFFUSE
DISPLAY DISTEND EXPANSE
EXPLAIN FEATHER OPENING
SCATTER SLATHER STRETCH
DIASPORA DISPENSE DISPERSE
HUMIFUSE INCREASE MULTIPLY
SPLATHER STRAGGLE
(— ABROAD) TOOT BLAZE DELATE
SPRING DIVULGE EMANATE
(— APART) GAPE
(— AS GOSSIP) BUZZ
(— BY REPORT) BLOW NOISE
NORATE
(— DEFAMATION) LIBEL
(— FOR DRYING) TED
(— INTO) INVADE
(— LIKE GRAIN) FLOOR
(— NEWS) HORN
(— ON THICK) COUCH SLATHER
(— OUT) FAN FLOW OPEN ROLL
SPAN ASPAR BREDE SPLAT SPLAY
SPRAY EXPAND FLANGE FRINGE
MANTLE OUTLAY SPRAWL UNLOCK
DIFFUSE DISPAND DISTENT EXPLAIN
FEATHER DIFFUSED SPRADDLE
SPRANGLE STRAGGLY
(— OUTWARD) FLARE
(— OVER) LAP DASH COVER
SUFFUSE
(— PAINT) KNIFE
(— RAPIDLY) MUSHROOM
(— RUMORS) WHISPER
(— SECRETLY) BUZZ
(— THE NEWS) BRUIT
(— THE WORD) TELL
(— THINLY) BRAY DRIVE TOUCH
SCANTY
(— TO) CATCH
(— TO THE WIND) SET
(— WIDE) SPELD SPELDER
(EVENLY —) SUANT
(TAPESTRY-WOVEN —) KILIM
(PREF.) STRATO
(SUFF.) CHORE
SPREADER PLOW PLOUGH SANDER
(HAY —) TEDDER
SPREADING FLAN BUSHY FLANGE
PATENT ASPREAD DIFFUSE
FLARING SPRAYEY PATULENT
PATULOUS SPRANGLY
(— OF LIGHT) HALATION
(— RAPIDLY) RUNNING
(NOT —) ERECT
(SLOW —) CREEPAGE
SPREE BAT BUM JAG BLOW BUST
GELL LARK RANT SOAK TEAR TIME
TOOT BEANO BINGE BOOZE BURST
DRINK DRUNK SOUSE SPRAY
BENDER BUSTER HOORAY
HURRAH JUNKET RANDAN RANTAN
RAZZLE SPLORE BLOWOFF
JAMBOREE WINGDING

SPRIG POINT
(—S FOR MOURNING) CYPRESS
SPRIGGER STRIPPER
SPRIGHTLINESS GAIETY AIRINESS
ALACRITY BUOYANCY VIVACITY
SPRIGHTLY GAY TID AIRY GNIB
PERT WARM ALIVE BRISK CANTY
CRISP DESTO MERRY PERKY QUICK
ALEGER BLITHE BREEZY JAUNTY
LIVELY SPANKY SPRACK WIMBLE
CHIPPER DELIVER JOCULAR
SPARKLY LIFESOME PLEASANT
SPRING EN AIN BUG EYE FLY HOP
JET OJO URN VER WAX BATH BOLT
BOUT BUCK BUNT DART FLOW
FONT GEON HAIR HEAD JUMP
KELD LEAP PERT RISE SEEP SKIP
SOAK STEM URNA WALM WARE
WELL WIND YOAR ARISE BOUND
DANCE FLIRT FOUNT FRESH GIHON
GLENT GRASS ISSUE LYMPH PRIME
QUELL SALLY SOURD SPEND
SPOUT START STEND SURGE
THROW VAULT BOUNCE CHARCO
DERIVE GAMBOL GEYSER JUMPER
LOCKET ORIGIN PIRENE RESORT
RESULT SILOAM SOURCE SPRINT
VENERO BUDTIME EMANATE
ESTUARY FLOUNCE GAMBADO
PROCEED REBOUND WRAPPER
BACKSTAY BANDUSIA CASTALIA
FOUNTAIN SPANGHEW ORIGINATE
PRINTEMPS
(— AWKWARDLY) KEVEL
(— BACK) RECOIL RESULT RETORT
REBOUND
(— DOWN) ALIGHT
(— FORWARD) LAUNCH
(— FROM) DESCEND
(— IN MARSH) WELLHEAD
(— INTO BEING) AWAKEN
(— OF HORSE) GAMBADO
(— OF THE YEAR) VER VOAR
(— ON SHEARS) BACKSTAY
(— SEASON) APRIL GRASS BUDTIME
(— SUDDENLY) FLY BOUNCE
(— TO FASTEN NECKLACE) LOCKET
(— UP) ARISE SHOOT SPROUT
BURGEON UPSPRING
(BOILING —) TUBIG
(CARRIAGE —) ROBBIN
(ERUPTIVE —) WALM GEYSER
(FROM A —) FONTAL
(GUSHING —) CHARCO
(HOT —) SPRUDEL
(INTERMITTENT —) NAILBOURN
(INTERMITTENT —S) GIPSIES
GYPSIES
(LAND —) LAVANT
(MECHANICAL —) RESORT RESSORT
(MINERAL —) SPA BALNEARY
(SALT —) LICK SALINE
(WARM —S) THERMAE
(WATCH —) SLEEVE
(PREF.) CREN(O) CROUNO PEGO
(SUFF.) CRENE
SPRING BEAUTY LETTUCE
SPRINGBOARD BATULE TREMPLIN
SPRINGBOK GAZELLE SPRINGER
SPRING CHAPLET JAMMER
SPRINGE TRAP NOOSE SNARE
SPRINGILY BOUNCILY SPONGILY
SPRINGINESS GIVE LIFE

SPRINGING LAUNCH SALIENT
(**— BACK**) RESULT ELASTIC
(**— FROM STEPS**) GRADY
SPRINGLIKE VERNAL
SPRING ORANGE STYRAX
SPRINGTAIL PODURA FURCULA
PODURID SKIPTAIL
SPRINGTIME VER WARE GERMINAL
SPRINGY WHIPPY ELASTIC FLEXIBLE
SPRINKLE ASH DAG DEG BLOW
DAMP DUST SHED SPIT FLASH
SHAKE SPURT WATER BEDROP
DABBLE POUNCE SPARGE SPRENT
SPRINK SQUIRT ARROUSE
ASPERGE ASPERSE DRIZZLE
RANTIZE SCATTER SKINKLE
SKITTER SPAIRGE SPARKLE
SPARPLE SPATTER SPATTLE
SPERPLE SPURTLE DISPUNGE
INTERSOW SPITTING SPRINGLE
STRINKLE
(**— IN BAPTISM**) RANTIZE
(**— OF RAIN**) SPIT
(**— OF SNOW**) SCOWDERING
SCOUTHERING
(**— SEED**) SPRAIN
(**— TOBACCO**) BLOW
(**— WITH FLOUR**) DREDGE
(**— WITH POWDER**) DUST
(**— WITH SALT**) CORN
(**— WITH SAND**) SAND
SPRINKLED SEEDED SPRENT
(**— OVER**) BESPRENT
SPRINKLER SPARGER SPRAYER
WATERER DAMPENER STRINKLE
(**HOLY WATER —**) HYSSOP
SPRINKLES JIMMIES
SPRINKLING SEME LACING SPARGE
STRANK RANTISM STIPPLE
STOURING
(**— OF PEOPLE**) SALT
SPRINT DASH RACE BICKER SPRENT
SPRUNT
SPRITE ELF HOB IMP PUG PIXY PUCK
ARIEL BUCCA DOBBY FAIRY HOLDA
PIXIE GOBLIN PILWIZ SPIRIT
SPOORN UMBRIEL COLTPIXY
GLAISTIG WATERMAN
(**WATER —**) NIX NECK NIXIE NICKER
SPRITELY WIMBLE
SPROCKET WHELP
SPROUT BUD LAD PUT BROD CHIT
CHUN CION DRAW TOOT CATCH
CHICK SCUTE SHOOT SPEAR SPIRE
SPRIT SPURT BRAIRD GERMEN
RATOON SIRING STOVEN TELLER
TILLER BURGEON COPPICE
SPURTER TENDRON BOURGEON
PULLULATE
(**— OF BARLEY**) TAIL
(**FIRST —S**) BREER BRAIRD BREIRD
(**STUMP —**) TILLER
(PREF.) BLAST(O) CLAD(O) CYM(I)
(O)
(SUFF.) BLAST(IC)(Y) CLADOUS
SPERM(A)(AE)(AL)(IA)(IC)(OUS)(UM)
(Y)
SPRUCE GIM DEFT JIMP NEAT POSH
SMUG SPRY TRIG TRIM BRISK
COMPT CRISP DINKY FRESH
JEMMY JIMMY NATTY NIFTY SLICK
SMART SMIRK SPIFF SPRIG
DAPPER PICKED SPONGE SPRUNT

SPRUSH FINICAL FOPPISH
SMARTEN SMICKER SPRUNNY
EPINETTE SPIFFING TITIVATE
(**KIND OF —**) SITKA
(**TRIMMED —**) LOBSTICK
SPRUE RUNNER PSILOSIS
SPRUER GATER
SPRY AGILE BRISK QUICK NIMBLE
BOBBISH
SPUD SPADE TATER BARKER
PADDLE POTATO WEEDER
SPUDDER
SPUME EST BEES FOAM FROTH
YEAST
SPUNK GUTS GETUP PLUCK
SPRAWL SMEDDUM GUMPTION
SPUNKY GAME GUTSY
SPUR ARM GAD GIG EDGE GAFF
GOAD KNAG MOVE STUD TANG
ARETE DRIVE PRICK PRONG
ROWEL SPICA SPURN BROACH
CALCAR DIGGER EXCITE FILLIP
FOMENT GAFFLE GRIFFE INCITE
MOTIVE OFFSET RIPPON SICKLE
SPERON WEAPON BICYCLE
GABLOCK INCITER LORMERY
SCRATCH COCKSPUR GAVELOCK
(**— OF BIRDS**) SPICA
(**— OF COCK**) HEEL
(**— OF GAMECOCK**) GAFF
(**— ON HORSESHOE**) CALK
(**—S OF COCK**) WEAPON
(**— TO ACTION**) GOOSE
(**PART OF —**) BAND CHAIN ROWEL
BUTTON
(PREF.) CALCARI
SPURGE BALSAM INTISY RICINUS
SUNWEED CATEPUCE DOVEWEED
FLUXWEED MILKBUSH MILKWEED
TITHYMAL WARTWEED
WARTWORT POINSETTIA
SPURIOUS BAD DOG TIN FAKE
SHAM BOGUS FUNNY PHONY
QUEER SHICE SNIDE NOTHAL
PSEUDO BASTARD NOTHOUS
POSTICHE PINCHBECK SYNDIETIC
(PREF.) NOTH(O) PSEUD(O)
SPURN FOOT TACK REPEL SCORN
REFUSE REJECT CONSPUE
CONTEMN DECLINE DESPISE
DISDAIN
SPURRY YARR FRANK COWQUAKE
SANDWEED
SPURT JET GILP GIRD GOUT JAUP
SPAR SPIN BURST CHIRT FLASH
PULSE SALLY SPOUT GEYSER
RANDOM SPLURT SPRING SPROUT
SQUIRT SPATTER
SPUTTER SPIT FIZZLE SOTTER
SPATTER SPLUTTER
SPUTUM SPIT
SPY FLY PRY ESPY MOLE NARK
NOSE STAG TOOT TOUT WAIT
WORM AGENT CALEB LOWER
NINJA PERDU PLANT SCOUT SNEAP
SPIAL SPION SPOOK WATCH
BEAGLE BEHOLD DESCRY GAYCAT
MOUTON PEEPER PERDUE SEARCH
SHADOW SPIRAL TOUTER WAITER
EXAMINE LURCHER OTACUST
SMELLER SPOTTER WATCHER
DISCOVER EMISSARY HIRCARRA
MOUCHARD

(**— ON RACEHORSES**) TOUT
(**— UPON**) LAY
(**AUTHOR OF —**) COOPER
(**BIBLICAL —**) CALEB
(**CHARACTER IN —**) JACK BIRCH
HENRY SARAH CAESAR HARPER
HARVEY LAWTON PEYTON FRANCES
WHARTON ISABELLA JEANETTE
THOMPSON DUNWOODIE
SINGLETON WELLEMERE
(**PLANTED —**) STOOGE
(**POLICE —**) SETTER
SPYBOAT VEDET VEDETTE
SQUAB PIPER SQUABBY SQUEAKER
SQUEALER SQUILGEE
SQUABBLE MUSS TIFF BRAWL
SCRAP BICKER HASSLE JANGLE
SQUALL BOBBERY BRABBLE
BRANGLE CONTEND PRABBLE
QUARREL SWABBLE
SQUAD CREW DECURY TWENTY
PLATOON
(**— OF DETECTIVES**) HOMICIDE
SQUADRON BLUE SOTNIA
SQUADER
(**— OF AIRCRAFT**) ESCADRILLE
(**CAVALRY —**) RESSALAH
(**THREE —S**) WING
SQUALID DINGY DIRTY MANGY
NASTY SEEDY FILTHY FROWZY
SCUZZY SHODDY SLEAZO SLEAZY
SORDID SCABROUS SLOTTERY
SQUALL DROW FRET GUST MEWL
ROAR SCAT WAUL BARAT FRESH
PERRY SKELP BAYAMO FLURRY
SQUAWK BORASCA SUMATRA
TORNADO BLIZZARD BORASQUE
CHUBASCO
SQUALOR DIRT
SQUAMA ALULA TEGULA
SQUANDER SOT BLOW BLUE BURN
GAME LASH WARE SPEND SPILL
SPORT WASTE BEZZLE LAVISH
MAFFLE MUDDLE PADDLE PALTER
PERISH PLUNGE TIPPLE BRANGLE
CONSUME DEBAUCH DEBOISE
DISPEND PROFUSE SCAMBLE
SCATTER SKITTLE SLATHER
SWATTER EMBEZZLE MISSPEND
SQUATTER
SQUANDERER PRODIGAL
SQUANDERING WASTEFUL
(**UNRESTRAINED —**) RIOT
SQUARE FIX EDGE EVEN FOUR FULL
LAME NERD NURD POST QUAD
SUIT AGREE CHECK CROSS FRAME
HUNKY NERDY PLACE PLAIN PLAZA
SUPER BLOCKY DINKUM ISAGON
MICKEY PIAZZA QUARRY ZENZIC
ZOCALO CARREAU CHECKER
COMMONS EMERALD UPRIGHT
QUADRANT QUADRATE
SQUADRON TETRAGON
(**— A STONE**) PITCH
(**— FOR BOWLING SCORE**) FRAME
(**— OF CANVAS**) SKATE
(**— OF CLOTH**) PANE
(**— OF DOUGH**) KNISH
(**— OFF**) BUTT
(**— OF FRAMING**) PAN
(**— OF GLASS**) QUARREL
(**— OF LINEN**) PALL
(**— OF TARTAN**) SET SETT

(**— OF TURF**) DIVOT QUADREL
(**— ON BILLIARD TABLE**) CROTCH
(**— ON CHESSBOARD**) HOUSE
POINT
(**BUILDINGS FORMING —**) INSULA
(**CARPENTER'S —**) NORMA MITER
(**CENTER — IN GAME**) TAC
(**CHURCH —**) PARVIS
(**FROM — ONE**) ANEW
(**KIND OF —**) PUNNETT
(**LINEN —**) SUDARIUM
(**NOT —**) HEP HIP
(**ONE-MILE —**) SECTION
(**PATTERN OF —S**) DAMIER
(**WOVEN —**) SINKER
(PREF.) QUADR(ATO)(I)(U)
SQUARED HEWN QUARTO SQUARE
SQUARE DANCE TUCKER
SQUARE-DEALING WHITE
SQUARELY BUNG FAIR FULL FLUSH
SPANG FAIRLY DIRECTLY
SMACKDAB
(**— AND SHARPLY**) SMACK
SQUARISH BOXY
SQUASH PEPO QUAT GOURD
SQUAB CASHAW CUCURB
CUSHAW MARROW SIMNEL
SQUISH SQUUSH TURBAN
CYMLING HUBBARD PUMPKIN
CUCURBIT CYMBLING PEPONIUM
ZUCCHINI
SQUASH BUG STINKBUG
SQUASHY SWASHY SQUUSHY
SQUAT QUAT RUCK STUB SWAT
SWOT COWER DUMPY FUBSY
HUNCH PUDGY SQUAB FODGEL
HUNKER HURKLE QUATCH STOCKY
STUBBY SQUATTY TAPPISH
SQUATTLE THICKSET
SQUATINA RHINA
SQUATTER NESTER BYWONER
SQUAW JACK WEBB HOUND
WENCH MAHALA SQUARK
SQUAWBUSH SHOVAL
SQUAWFISH CHUB BOXHEAD
BIGMOUTH CHAPPAUL
SQUAWK SCRAWK SQUALL
SQUARK SQUAWL COMPLAIN
SQUAWROOT CLAPWORT
ELOTILLO
SQUEAK GIKE PEEP WEAK CHEEP
CHIRK QUEAK SCRAWK SCROOP
SQUEAL
SQUEAKING SCRANNEL
SQUEAKY CREAKY
SQUEAL PIP RAT FINK HOWL SING
SWEEL SCREAK TATTLE WHISTLE
SQUEALER FINK CANARY
SQUEAMISH HELO NICE NAISH
PAWKY PENSY DAINTY DAUNCH
PENCEY QUAINT QUEASY SPICED
TICKLE WAIRCH WAMBLY FINICAL
MAWKISH WEARISH NAUSEOUS
QVERNICE
SQUEAMISHNESS NICETY
DISGUST MALAISE DELICACY
SQUEEZE EKE HUG JAM NIP CLAM
MULL MURE VISE ZEST BIRSE
BUNCH CHIRT CREEM CROWD
CRUSH PINCH PRESS SQUAB
SQUAT WRING GRUDGE QUEASE
SCRUMP SCRUZE SQUASH STRAIN
THRIMP THRING THRONG TWEEZE

TWITCH SCRINGE SCROOGE
SCROUGE SCRUNCH SCRUNGE
SQUEEGE SQUINCH COMPRESS
CONTRACT PRESSURE SHOEHORN
THRIMBLE THRUMBLE
(— FROM) SPONGE
(— IN) FUDGE
(— INTO) THRIMBLE
(— MONEY FROM) SWEAT
(— OUT) PINCH STRAIN
(ECONOMIC —) CRUNCH
(PREF.) PRESSI
SQUEEZED STRETTA STRETTO
SQUEEZER REAMER ALLIGATOR
SQUELCH QUELCH SQUASH SQUISH
SQUIDGE SLAPDOWN
SQUELCHER BLIZZARD
SQUETEAGUE DRUM DRUMMER
SQUETEE BLUEFISH CHICKWIT
WEAKFISH
SQUIB MOTE SKIT FILLER EXPLODER
SQUID PLUG CALAMARI CALAMARY
SQUIFFED DRUNK BLOTTO STONED
SQUIGGLE SCRIGGLE
SQUILL SCILLA SLANGKOP
(PREF.) SCILLI
SQUINT AWRY GLEE GLEG SKEN
SKEW BAGGE GLENT GLEDGE
GOGGLE SHEYLE SKELLY SQUINCH
SQUINNY STRABISM STRABISMUS
SQUINT-EYED GLEE GLEED
SQUINTING LOUCHE
SQUIRE SWAIN DONZEL JUNKER
TIMIAS ARMIGER ESQUIRE
SQUIRET YOUNKER HENCHMAN
SCUTIGER SERVITOR SQUARSON
SQUIREEN
SQUIRM CURL WIND TWINE WRING
WRITHE WRESTLE WRIGGLE
SCRIGGLE SQUIGGLE
SQUIRREL BUN CON BUNT LEAD
SCUG BUNNY XERUS BOOMER
CHIPPY GOPHER RODENT TAGUAN
ARDILLA SCHILLU SCIURID
CHIPMUNK EGGEATER GRAYBACK
JELERANG RATATOSK CHICKAREE
(— SKIN) VAIR
(FLYING —) TUAN TAGUAN
ASSAPAN
(PREF.) SCIURO
SQUIRRELFISH ALAIHI MARIAN
MOJARRA SERRANO SOLDIER
SANDFISH WELSHMAN
SQUIRREL MONKEY TITI SAIMIRI
TAMARIN
SQUIRREL SHREW TANA TUPAIA
PENTAIL
SQUIRT CHIRT SCOOT SKITE SLIRT
SPIRT SPOUT SPURT SQUIB SQUIT
SPLOIT SPRENT SPRITZ SCOOTER
SQUITTER
SRI BWANA SAHIB

S-SHAPED
(PREF.) SIGMO SIGMOID(O)
ST.CROIX (NATIVE OF —) CRUZAN
STAB DAB DAG JAB JAG JOB DIRK
GORE PINK POKE PROB SHIV STOB
STOG STUG YERK CHIVE KNIFE
POACH PRICK PRONG STICK STOKE
BROACH DAGGER PIERCE POUNCE
SLIVER STITCH THRUST BAYONET
STAGGER PRICKADO STILETTO
STOCCADO STOCCATA
(— IN MIDBREAST) SLOT
STABBING THORNY JABBING
PUNGENT STICKING
(SUFF.) NYXIS
STABILITY POISE FIXURE BALANCE
SADNESS FIRMNESS SECURITY
CONSTANCY
STABILIZE FIX SET EVEN TRIM
POISE SCHOOL STEADY BALANCE
BALLAST STIFFEN
STABILIZER ACARDITE
STABLE BYRE FAST FIRM SURE
HARAS HEMEL SOLID SOUND
STALL STIFF STOUT TAMBO LINTER
LIVERY SECURE SICKER STATIC
STEADY STRONG STURDY
DURABLE EQUERRY LASTING
OXHOUSE SETTLED SHIPPEN
STABLE BALANCED IMMOBILE
RESIDENT STANDING PERMANENT
(EMOTIONALLY —) TOGETHER
(ROYAL —S) MEWS
(PREF.) MONIMO
STABLEBOY LAD MAFU MAFOO
JACKBOY
STABLEMAN OSTLER HOSTLER
STACCATO TUT SECCO DETACHE
SALTATO RICOCHET SALTANDO
(NOT —) LEGATO TENUTO
STACK COB MOW SOW BIKE DESS
LEET PACK PILE POKE RICK CANCH
CLAMP GOAVE POAKE SCROO
SHOCK STAKE STALK STOCK
COLUMN FUNNEL RICKLE
CALENDER STACKAGE
(— BRICKS) CLAMP SCINTLE
(— IN KILN) BOX
(— LUMBER) STICK
(— OF ARMS) PILE
(— OF BRICK) LIFT
(— OF CERAMICS) BUNG
(— OF CHLOROPHYLL) GRANUM
(— OF CORN) SHOCK
(— OF FISH) BULK
(— OF GRAIN) RICK
(— OF HIDES) BED
(— OF PANS) SWEATER
(— OF SHEETS) BOOK
(HAY OR CORN —) HOVEL
(SMALL —) COB CANCH RICKLE
(TILE —) WELL
STACKER CROWDER PITCHER
STACKMAN
STACKING (— OF AIRCRAFT)
HOLDING
STACKYARD MOWIE MOWHAY
HAGGARD

STADIUM BOWL DOME STADE
STAGE FURLONG STADION
COLISEUM
(PRIVATE SEATS IN —) SKYBOX
(ROOFED —) DOME
STAFF MAN PIN ROD TAU TAW
CANE CLUB KENT LIMB MACE
MALL MAUL PIKE POLE RUNG TREE
VARE YARD BATON CROOK CROSS
KEVEL NIBBY PEDUM PERCH
STAVE STICK SUITE VERGE BASTON
CADUCE CEPTER CLEEKY CROCHE
CRUTCH FAMILY FERULE GROUND
LITUUS MULETA POTENT PRITCH
RADIUS RISSLE TAIAHA THYRSE
WARDER BACULUS BOURDON
CAMBUCA CROSIER CRUMMIE
DISTAFF FESTUCA PALSTER
SCEPTER SCEPTRE STADDI F
THYRSUS CADUCEUS CRUMMOCK
PARTISAN PASTORAL PLOWFOOT
TIPSTAFF
(— AT END OF NET) BRAIL
(— OF AUTHORITY) VARE VERGE
(— OF COOKS) BOUCHE
(— OF OFFICIALS) OMLAH
(— WITH CROSSPIECE) POTENT
(BISHOP'S —) BAGLE BACULUS
CROSIER CROZIER PASTORAL
(FIELD MARSHAL'S —) BATON
(FORKED —) LINSTOCK
(GRADUATED —) LIMB
(HOTTENTOT —) KIRVI
(MAGICIAN'S —) RHABDOS
(NEWSPAPER —) DAYSIDE
(NUBIAN —) KUERR
(PILGRIM'S —) BURDEN
(PLASTERER'S —) BEATER
(SHEPHERD'S —) KENT CROOK
(SPARTAN —) SCYTALE
(TEACHING —) FACULTY
(THIEVES' —) FILCH
(PREF.) LITUI SCEPTRO
STAG HART ROYAL SPADE STAIG
WAPITI BULLOCK KNOBBER
POINTER KNOBBLER
(— OF THE 3D YEAR) SPIRE
(— OF 2ND YEAR) BROCKET
(— OF 8 YEARS OR MORE) ROYAL
(— THAT HAS CAST HIS ANTLERS)
POLLARD
(DEAD —) MORT
(HORNLESS —) HUMMEL
(TURNED TO —) ACTAEON
(12-POINT —) ROYAL
(3-YEAR OLD —) SPADE
(PREF.) ELAPH(O)
STAG BEETLE LUCANID
STAGE LEG BANK GEST POST STEP
TREK APRON DUMMY ETAGE
FLAKE GRADE PEGME PHASE
POINT SCENE STAIR STATE
BOARDS DEGREE HEMMEL PERIOD
PHASIS STRIDE CATASTA MANSION
ROSTRUM STADIUM INSTANCE
PLATFORM SCAFFOLD
PROSCENIUM
(— DIRECTION) EXIT ENTER SOLUS
(— FOR DRYING FISH) FLAKE
(— FOR HAY) HEMMEL
(— IN DELIRIUM) TILMUS
(— IN FEVER) FLUSH

(— IN PORCELAIN FURNACE)
HOWELL
(— IN TRAVELING) GEST
(— MANAGER) REGISSEUR
(— OF CUPOLA) LANTERN
(— OF DEVELOPMENT) ERA
BLOSSOM
(— OF FUNGUS) OIDIUM
(— OF GLACIATION) RISS WURM
ACHEN MINDEL
(— OF INSECT) INSTAR
(— OF LIFE) AGE ASRAMA ASHRAMA
(— OF MITOSIS) ANAPHASE
PROPHASE
(— OF PERSONALITY) LATENCY
(— OF ROCKET) BOOSTER
(— OF THEATER) SCAENA
THEATRON
(— WHERE SLAVES WERE SOLD)
CATASTA
(BOTTOMMOST —) CELLAR
(COMIC —) SOCK
(EARLIEST —) PRIME
(FINAL —) CLOSE FINISH STRETCH
(FIRST —) YOUTH SPRING
(FLOATING —) DUMMY
(FLOOD —) CREST
(GEOLOGICAL —) GUNZ GLACIAL
SENONIAN
(GLACIATION —) WURM
(INITIAL —) INFANCY
(LANDING —) STAIR BRIDGE STAITH
STELLING
(MOVING —) PEGMA PEGME
(PART OF —) FLY ARCH DROP FLAT
WING APRON DRAPE BATTEN
BORDER BRIDGE CENTER RETURN
TEASER CURTAIN ENTRANCE
TORMENTOR PROSCENIUM
(RADIO —) STEP
(THIRD —) AUTUMN
(PREF.) SCENO
STAGECOACH DILLY STAGE
STAGEHAND GRIP DAYMAN
GAFFER
STAGER SOAKER
STAGGER REEL ROLL STOT DAVER
DODGE HODGE LURCH PITCH STITE
STOIT DACKER DAIDLE FALTER
GOGGLE STAVER STIVER SWAVER
TOTTER WALTER WAMBLE
WELTER WIGGLE WINTLE
MEGRIMS STACHER STACKER
STAMMER STOITER STOTTER
STUMBLE SWAGGER VANDYKE
WAUCHLE TITUBATE
(— BACK) RECOIL
STAGGERBUSH LAMBKILL
STAGGERED STURTAN STURTIN
STAGGERING AREEL
STAGGERS DUNT GOGGLES
MEGRIMS STAVERS VERTIGO
STAGHEAD SPIKETOP
STAGING STAGE CRIPPLE DERRICK
HURRIES
STAGNANCY STASIS
STAGNANT DEAD DULL INERT
STILL STATIC COBWEBBY
SLUGGISH STAGNATE STANDING
STAGNATION STASIS TORPOR
LANGUOR
STAID SET CIVIL GRAVE SOBER

DEMURE STEADY EARNEST
SERIOUS DECOROUS
STAIN DYE LIT WEM BLOT BLUR
BUFF DIRT DRAB FILE FOIL HURT
MEAL MOLE RUST SCAM SLUR
SMAD SMIT SMUT SOIL SPOT TASH
BLACK BLEND BRAND CLOUD
DIRTY HATCH PAINT PLECK SMEAR
SPECK SULLY TACHE TAINT TINGE
WEMMY BREATH GIEMSA IMBRUE
INFAMY INFECT MACULA SMIRCH
SMUDGE SMUTCH SPLASH STIGMA
SUDDLE ATTAINT BESTAIN
BLEMISH DEPAINT DISTAIN
SLUBBER SOILURE SPATTER
SPLOTCH STADDLE TARNISH
BESMIRCH CARMALUM DISCOLOR
DISGRACE DISHONOR FLYSPECK
MACULATE PYRONINE TAINTURE
(— BLACK) EBONIZE
(— IN LINEN) MELL
(— ON BRICK) SCUMMING
(— WITH BLOOD) ENGORE
(PREF.) MACUL(I)(O) SPIL(O)
STAINED FOXY RUSTY SMUDGY
BLOTCHY SMUTCHY
(— BY DECAY) DOATY
(— WITH BLOOD) BLOODY
IMBRUED
STAINED GLASS VITRAIL
STAINER TRACER
STAINLESS PURE CHASTE
INNOCENT
STAIR STY GREE RUNG STEP
DEGREE COCHLEA ESCALIER
(LANDING —) GHAT GHAUT
(MINING —) LOB
(WINDING —) VICE VISE CARACOL
CARACOLE TURNPIKE
(PL.) PAIR PITCH FLIGHT DANCERS
ESCALIER
STAIRCASE SCALE ESCALIER
(PART OF —) MOLD POST RAIL
NEWEL RISER TREAD NOSING
LANDING BALUSTER BANISTER
HANDRAIL BALUSTRADE
(SHIP'S —) COMPANIONWAY
(SPIRAL —) SPIRAL CARACOLE
STAIRWAY STOOP GREESE PERRON
DESCENT ESCALIER
(— ON RIVER BANK) GHAT
(CURVED —) SWEEP
(SHIP'S —) LADDER
(WINDING —) VICE TURNPIKE
STAITH TIP
STAKE BET HOB LAY SET TAW VIE
WAD WED ANTE BENT GAGE MAIN
PALE PAWN PEEL POOL PUNT RISK
STAB STOB TREE WAGE PITCH
SPILE SPOKE SPRAG STOCK STOOP
STOUR WAGER BAIKIE CAULIS
CHANCE CORNER CROTCH
ENGAGE GAMBLE HAZARD IMPONE
LOGGAT LOGGET PALING PICKET
STOWER TRUNCH WEDFEE
STOATER STUCKEN VENTURE
INTEREST PALISADE PEASTICK
STUCKING
(— HIGHER) REVIE
(— IN PRIMERO) REST
(— SUPPORTING FOUNDATION)
PILE
(CART —) RUNG

(COMPULSORY — IN POKER) BLIND
(GAMBLING —) BET MISE WAGER
(POINTED —) SOULE SOWEL PICKET
(SURVEYORS' —) HUB
(TETHERING —) PUTTO
(TINSMITH'S —) TEEST
(PL.) POOL JACKPOT
STAKE-SHAPED SUDIFORM
STALACE COLUMELLA
STALE OLD COLD FLAT HOAR PALL
SICK WORN BLOWN DATED DUSTY
FROWY HOARY MOLDY MUSTY
RAFTY SANDY TRITE FROWZY
MOULDY STUFFY EXOLETE
FROUGHY INSIPID OVERWORN
STAGNANT TIMEWORN
(DAMP AND —) WAUGH
STALEMATE PATT STALE
STALK BUN RAY CORN HAFT MOTE
POLE RISP STAM STEG STEM TIGE
QUILL SCAPE SHANK SPEAR SPIRE
STAKE STALE STEAL STIPE STUMP
WRIDE COULIS RATOON STIPES
CASTOCK FUNICLE PEDICEL
PETIOLE SPINDLE CAUDICLE
FILAMENT PEDUNCLE PODETIUM
STALKLET STERIGMA PETIOLULE
(— OF BUCKWHEAT) STRAW
(— OF CRINOID) COLUMN
(— OF GRAIN) RESSUM RIZZOM
(— OF GRASS) BENT SPEAR
(— OF HAY) RISP
(— OF MOSS CAPSULE) SETA
(— OF OVULE) FUNICLE
(— OF PLANT) SPINDLE TENACLE
(— OF SPORE) STERIGMA
(— OF SPOROGONIUM) SETA
(— OF STAMEN) FILAMENT
(— OF SUGAR CANE) RATOON
(— OF UMBEL) RAY
(—S OF GRAIN) KARBI STRAW
(CABBAGE —) CASTOCK
(CROSSBOW —) TILLER
(DRY —) KEX KECK BENNET
(FLOWER —) SCAPE
(HOLLOW —) BUN KEX KECK
(PL.) HAULM STRAW WRIDE
IWAIWA
(PREF.) CAUL(I)(O) CULMI
STALKLESS SESSILE
**STALKY AND COMPANY (AUTHOR
OF —)** KIPLING
(CHARACTER IN —) JOHN MTURK
ARTHUR BEETLE STALKY CORKRAN
GILBERT
STALL BAY BIN BOX CUB PEW BULK
CRIB SPAR STAW BOOSE BOOSY
BOOTH CRAME PITCH STAND
STASH CARCER CARREL STANCE
TRAVIS WICKET BALAGAN CABINET
SHAMBLE SHIPPEN BUTCHERY
STANDING TRAVERSE
(FOR TIME) HAVER STRETCH
(— IN CLOISTER) CAROL
(— IN COAL MINE) BREAST WICKET
(— IN MUD) STOG
(— IN ROMAN CIRCUS) CARCER
(BISHOP'S —) TRIBUNE
(CHURCH —) PEW
(THEATER —) LOGE FAUTEUIL
STALLED STOODED
STALLION SIRE STAG STUD ENTRE

HORSE COOSER CUSSER ENTIRE
CUISSER STALLAND STONEHORSE
STALWART RUDE STARK STIFF
WIGHT STRONG STURDY BUIRDLY
VALIANT
STAMEN TAMIN STAMMEL
(PART OF —) ANTHER
(PL.) ANDROECIUM
(PREF.) ANDR(O)
(SUFF.) STEMONOUS
STAMINA GUTS SAND BOTTOM
STAMMER FAM HACK MANT STOT
STUT GANCH WLAFF FAFFLE
FALTER FAMBLE HACKER HAFFLE
HAMMER HOCKER HOTTER
MAFFLE MAMMER YAMMER
FRIBBLE STUMBLE STUTTER
HESITATE SPLUTTER TITUBATE
STAMMERING HACK PSELLISM
TRAULISM BALBUTIES
STAMP DIE CHOP COIL DRUB FAKE
MARK NIXY PAUT POSS RUFF SEAL
SNAP TYPE APPEL BLOCK DOLLY
ERROR FRANK LABEL LOCAL NIXIE
PRINT PUNCH STOCK STOMP
STUNT TENOR TOUCH WRITE
ACCENT CACHET CLICHE DOCKER
FULLER INCUSE INCUTE INDENT
LOCKUP PASTER POUNCE SCRIBE
SHAPER SIGNET STRAMP STRIKE
CARRIER CHARACT EDITION
IMPRESS IMPRINT MINTAGE
POUNDER REPRINT SEEBECK
SPECIAL SQUELCH STICKER
TAXPAID WRAPPER HALLMARK
ORIGINAL PRESSURE PUNCHEON
(— AFTER ASSAY) TOUCH
(— BOOK COVER) BLIND
(— FOR CUTTING DOUGH) DOCKER
(— HERRING BARREL) DUNT
(— HIDES) STOCK
(— HOLES) STOACH
(— OUT) SCOTCH
(— WITH DIE) DINK
(BOOKBINDING —) BLOCK FILLET
(CANCELLING —) KILLER
(HALF OF —) BISECT
(HAND —) CANCELER
(OFFICIAL —) CHOP
(POSTAGE —) AIR DUE CAPE FAKE
HEAD ERROR LABEL LOCAL BUREAU
INVERT AIRMAIL BICOLOR CHARITY
CLASSIC REPRINT STICKER
ADHESIVE COLONIAL ORIGINAL
SPECIMEN PRECANCEL
(REVENUE —) FISCAL TAXPAID
(RUBBER —) YESMAN
(SMART —) APPEL
(PL.) MIXTURE KILOWARE
(PREF.) TIMBRO
STAMP-COLLECTING PHILATELY
TIMBROLOGY
STAMPEDE RUSH BLITZ CHUTE
DEBACLE STAMPEDO
STAMPER FANCIER STOMPER
STAMPING TITLING
STANCE STATION STANDING
(— OF GOLFER) ADDRESS
(— OF HORSE) GATHER
STANCH FIRM STEM STIFF STOUT
HEARTY TRUSTY STAUNCH
FAITHFUL RESOLUTE
STANCHION BAIL PITON CROTCH

CRUTCH STENCIL STANCHEL
STANCHER
STAND GO JIB SET BANK BEAR BIER
DESK HALT RACK RANK REST STAY
STEL ZARF BIPOD BLOCK ERECT
FRAME FRONT KIOSK STALL STICK
STONE STOOL CASTER COLORS
ENDURE HASTER INSIST PILLAR
PILLAR SMOKER STANCE STANZA
STOUND STRIKE TEAPOY TRIPOD
TRIVET CONSIST DIOPTER
EPERGNE FOURBLE LECTERN
STATION TABORET TRESTLE
TROLLEY ATTITUDE BLEACHER
COATRACK CROWFOOT FRIPPERY
GUERIDON HASTENER INKSTAND
POSITION SCAFFOLD STALLAGE
STANDING STANDISH STILLAGE
STILLING STILLION
(— AS SPONSOR) FANG HEAVE
CHRISTEN
(— AT AN ANGLE) CATER
(— AT ATTENTION) BACK
(— BACK) BACCARE BACKARE
(— BEFORE A FIRE) FOOTMAN
(— BEHIND) COVER
(— BY) SERVE STICKTO
(— CLOSE) CROWD ENVIRON
(— DRINKS) SHOUT TREAT
(— ERECT) ROUSE
(— FAST) SUBSIST
(— FASTENED TO MESS TABLE)
CROWFOOT
(— FIRM) STAY
(— FOR) MEAN DENOTE
(— FOR AUCTIONING) BLOCK
(— FOR BARRELS) JIB THRALL
(— FOR COFFIN) BIER
(— FOR COMPASS) BINNACLE
(— FOR CONFINING HEAT) HASTER
HASTENER
(— FOR DRESSES) FRIPPERY
(— FOR DRILL PIPE) FOURBLE
(— FOR FINJAN) ZARF
(— FOR TILES) CRISS
(— FOR WRITING MATERIALS)
STANDISH
(— GUARD) COVER
(— IDLY) LOAF
(— IN AWE) FEAR
(— OFF) AROINT
(— OF FOREST) GROWTH
(— OF PLANTS) STOOL
(— ON AND OFF SHORE) BUSK
(— ON END) STARE UPEND
(— ON HIGH) TOWER
(— ON TWO FEET) BIPOD DUOPOD
(— OUT) CUT TOOT FLAUNT
(— READY) ABIDE
(— STIFFLY) STRUT
(— STILL) HO HOO HALT STAY
(— TO SHOOT) ADDRESS
(— TREAT) MUG SHOUT
(— UNMOVING) FREEZE
(— UNSTEADILY) STAGGER
(— UP) RARE
(— UP FOR) STICKLE
(— UP STIFF) STIVER
(— UP TO) CONFRONT
(— WITH LEGS APART) STRIDE
(BRANCHING —) TREE
(CAKE —) CURATE
(CHEMICAL —) RINGSTAND

(CONCESSION —) JOINT
(FIRECLAY —) CRANK
(HEARTH —) FOOTMAN
(ONE-NIGHT —) GIG
(PRINTER'S —) BANK FRAME
(PULPIT-LIKE —) AMBO
(RAISED —) PERGOLA
(REVOLVING —) KLINOSTAT
(SCULPTOR'S —) CHASSIS
(SHOOTING —) BUTT
(THREE-LEGGED —) TRIVET
STANDARD PAR ALEM DICK FIAR
FLAG GAGE IDEA MARK NORM
SIGN TEST TOUG ALLOY BOGEY
CANON CHECK DOLLY DRAKE
EAGLE GAUGE IDEAL JEDGE
MODEL NORMA SCALE STAND
STOOL AQUILA ASSIZE BANNER
CORNET DOLLIE FILLER NORMAL
SOCKET SQUARE STAPLE TIPONI
TRIPOD VIOLLE ANCIENT CLASSIC
DECORUM DRAPEAU LABARUM
MODULUS STANDER BRATTACH
GONFALON MOUNTING ORIFLAMB
ORTHODOX VEXILLUM
(— IN GATE) STRIKE
(— OF ACCURACY) COCKER
(— OF CONDUCT) LINE GNOMON
(— OF PERFECTION) IDEAL
(— OF PERFORMANCE) BOGY
BOGEY BOGIE
(— OF PITCH) DIAPASON
(— OF QUALITY) GRADE
(—S OF BEHAVIOR) ETHICS
(CONVENTIONAL —) PIETY
(LIGHT —) CARCEL
(NOT —) BASTARD
(TURKISH —) ALEM TOUG
(PL.) LIGHTS HOLSTERS
STANDARD-BEARER CORNET
ENSIGN ALFEREZ ANCIENT
STALLER SIGNIFER STANDARD
VEXILLARY
STANDARDIZE FORDIZE MACHINE
CALIBRATE
STANDEL STORER
STAND-IN SUB STUNTMAN
STANDING RANK BEING ERECT
STATE CREDIT ESTEEM REGULAR
RESPECT PRESTIGE STAGNANT
PERPENDICULAR
(— ALONE) SEPARATE
(— BY ITSELF) ABSOLUTE
DETACHED
(— ERECT) HORRENT
(— FIRM) STABLE
(— INCOORDINATION) ASTASIA
(— IN PROFILE) RAMPANT
(— ON STEPS) DEGRADED
(— OUT) BOLD PROUD EXTANT
RELIEF SALIENT PROMINENT
(— OUT CLEARLY) EMINENT
(— POSITION) OFFHAND
(— UPRIGHT) STANDARD
(HIGH —) RANK WORSHIP POSITION
(MODE OF —) STANCE
(SOCIAL —) LEVEL ESTATE FASHION
STATION
(PREF.) STAT(O)
(— IN SECOND PLACE BEYOND) DVI
EKA
(SUFF.) STASIA STASIS STAT
STATIC STATICS

STANDPATTISM TORYISM
STANDPOINT STANCE
STANDSTILL JIB SET HALT REST
STAY STAND STANCE
STANZA CALL RANN ENVOI ENVOY
STAFF STAND STAVE VERSE
BASTON DIXAIN DIZAIN OCTAVE
SEPTET SESTET SEXTET SIXAIN
STANCE STANZO HUITAIN SESTINA
SEXTAIN STROPHE TRIOLET
TROILUS CINQUAIN OCTONARY
QUATRAIN QUINTAIN RISPETTO
SETTAINE TRISTICH TROPARION
(SUFF.) STICH
STAPES STIRRUP
STAPLE LOOP FLOSS STITCH
SHACKLE STEEPLE VERVELLE
(PL.) BROKES
STAR COR SUN BEID FIRE LAMP
ASTER COMES DWARF EXCEL
GIANT MOLET RISHI SHINE STARN
ALNATH ASTRAL BINARY COUPLE
DOUBLE ETOILE LUCIDA MULLET
NITHAM SHINER SPHERE STELLA
BENEFIC DINGBAT ESTOILE
GEMINID STARLET STARNIE
ASTERISK ASTEROID HEXAGRAM
MALEFICE PENTACLE SUBDWARF
SUBGIANT VARIABLE
(COMPANION —) COMES
(DOG —) ASTA SEPT SOPT TOTO
SEPTI LASSIE SIRIUS RINTINTIN
(EVENING —) VENUS HESPER
VESPER EVESTAR HESPERUS
(FEATHER —) COMATULA
(FILM —) VEDETTE
(FUTURE —) COMER
(GUIDING —) LOADSTAR LODESTAR
(KIND OF —) BETA
(MORNING —) VENUS DAYSTAR
PHOSPHOR
(NEW —) NOVA
(OFFICER'S —) PIP
(OF THE —S) SIDEREAL
(PULSATING —) CEPHEID
(RED —) ANTARES
(SHOOTING —) BOLIDE LEONID
METEOR COWSLIP SHOOTER
(SPECIFIC —) YED ADIB ALYA ATIK
CAPH ENIF ENIR IZAR KIED MAIA
NAOS PHAD SADR VEGA WEGA
ACRAB ACRUX AGENA ALCOR
ALGOL ALKES ANCHA ARNEB
CHARA DABIH DELTA DENEB DUBHE
GIEDI GUIAM GUYAM HAMAL
HAMUL JUGUM MERAK MIZAR
NIBAL NIHAI PHACD PHAET RIGEL
SAIPH SPICA TEJAT WASAT WEZEN
ZOSMA ADHARA ALHENA ALIOTH
ALKAID ALMACH ALTAIR ALUDRA
APOLLO ARIDED CASTOR CELENO
CHELEB DIPHDA ELNATH ETAMIN
GIENAH HYADES KOCHAB LESUTH
MAASYM MARKAB MARKEB MARSIC
MEGREZ MENKAR MENKIB MEROPE
MIRACH MIRFAK MIRZAM NEKKAR
PHECDA POLLUX PROPUS RANICH
SCHEAT SHEDIR SIRIUS THABIT
THUBAN ACUBENS ALBIREO
ALCHIBA ALCYONE ALGENIB
ALGIEBA ALGORAH ALMAACK
ALNILAM ALNITAK ALPHARD
ALPHIRK ALSHAIN ANTARES

AZIMECH BUNGULA CANOPUS
CAPELLA ELECTRA GIANSAR
GOMELZA GRUMIUM MEBSUTA
MELUCTA MENCHIB MINTAKA
MUFRIDE POLARIS PROCYON
REGULUS ROTANIM RUCHBAR
SCHEDAR SEGINUS SHELLAK
STEROPE TARAZED TAYGETA
TEGMINE THEENIM ACHERNAR
ALPHECCA ARCTURUS ASTERION
DENEBOLA GRAFFIAS HERCULES
MULIPHEN PRAESEPE SCALOOIN
SCHEMALI SHERATAN
(THREE —S) KIDS ELLWAND
TRIANGLE
(7 —S OF GREAT BEAR) CAR
(PREF.) ASTER(O) ASTR(I)(O)
SIDERO STELLI
(SUFF.) ASTER ID
STAR APPLE CAIMITO
STARCH AMYL ARUM SAGO STIFF
TIKOR AMYDON AMYLUM CONJEE
FARINA FECULA CASSAVA
CURCUMA FAECULA MARANTA
TALIPOT AMIDULIN DRESSING
FIXATURE GLUCOSAN
(— IN SOLUTION) AMIDIN
(ANIMAL —) GLYCOGEN
(PREF.) AMYL(I)(O)
STARCHED FORMAL
STARE EYE BORE DARE GAPE GAUM
GAUP GAWK GAWP GAZE GOVE
GYPE KIKE LOOK PORE GLARE
GLORE GLOWER GOGGLE EYEBALL
(— DOWN) OUTFACE
(— IDLY) GOVE GOAVE
(— IMPERTINENTLY) OGLE
(— VACANTLY) GOWK
(COLD —) FISHEYE
STARFISH PAD STAR ASTERID
RADIATE ASTEROID OPHIURAN
(PART OF —) ARM ANUS DISC SPINE
EYESPOT TENTACLE MADREPORITE
STARFLOWER ASTER
STAR FRUIT CARAMBOLA
STARING STEEP ASTARE GOGGLE
GOOGLY HAGGARD
STAR JELLY STARSHOT
STARK BUCK CARK FAIR HARD
CRUDE HARSH NAKED STIFF
STARCH DESOLATE METALLIC
STARLIKE ASTRAL SPHERY
STARLING SALI STARE BEAVER
PASTOR TILYER SPREEUW
STARNEL STAYNIL CHEPSTER
CUTWATER SHEPSTER
STARRED LIZARD HARDIM
STARRING FEATURED
STARRY ASTRAL STARNY STELLED
SIDEREAL
STAR SAPPHIRE ASTERIA ASTRION
ASTROITE
STAR-SHAPED ASTROID
START DIG SET BOLT BOUN DART
DASH HEAD JERK JUMP OPEN
TURN WHIP ARISE BEGIN BIRTH
BRAID BREAK BUDGE ENTER FLIRT
GLENT ONSET RAISE ROUSE STORT
THROW ABRADE BOGGLE BROACH
FLINCH INTEND OFFSET OUTSET
SETOFF SETOUT STRIKE TEEOFF
TWITCH GETAWAY OPENERS
OPENING STARTLE SUNRISE

COMMENCE CONCEIVE INCHOATE
OUTSTART
(— A HORSE) WINCE
(— ASIDE) SHY SKIT DODGE
(— A TRIP) EMBARK
(— BACK) RECOIL RESILE
(— BURNING) SPIT KINDLE
(— FERMENTATION) PITCH
(— OF BIRD'S FLIGHT) SOUSE
(— OF FLIGHT) HOPOFF TAKEOFF
(— OF PLAY) ACTONE SCENE1
(— OUT) FRAME INTEND
(— SUDDENLY) SPRING
(— UP) JUMP ASTART ASTERT
(— WITH FEAR) STURT
(FROM THE —) ABOVO
(SUDDEN —) SHY SQUIRT
STARTER KOJI OPENER
(BUNG —) FLOGGER
STAR THISTLE CALTROP CALTHROP
STARTING INCOMING
STARTLE JAR SOHO ALARM SCARE
SHOCK START STURT AFFRAY
BOGGLE BOOGER FRIGHT
FRIGHTEN SURPRISE
STARTLING LURID AI ARMING
SHOCKING
STARVATION LACK PINE FAMINE
STARVE CLEM FAST FAMINE
FAMISH AFFAMISH
STARVED MEAGER MEAGRE
STARVEN
STARVED-LOOKING SLINK
STARVELING SHARGAR SHARGER
STARVING CLUNG
STARWORT ASTER ASTROFEL
ASTROPHEL
STASH QUIT STOP HOARD STORE
STATE WU LAY PUT SAY CASE ETAT
MODE NAME POMP PORT TERM
TIFF COVIN ESTER ESTRE POLIS
SPEAK STADE TERMS TUATH
WHACK AFFIRM AGENCY ASSERT
ASSURE CAESAR EFFEIR EMPIRE
ESTATE IMPORT NATION PLIGHT
POLICY POLITY RENDER RIALTY
SOVIET STATUS STEVEN CIVITAS
DECLARE DESERET DUKEDOM
ENOUNCE EXPOUND EXPRESS
KINSHIP PROPOSE SPECIFY
STATION TERMINE CEREMONY
DEVACHAN DOMINION FRANKLIN
HEGEMONY INDICATE KINGSHIP
REPUBLIC STATELET
PREDICAMENT
(— EXPLICITLY) DEFINE
(— FIRST) PREMISE
(— FORMALLY) ENOUNCE
(— IN NORTH CAROLINA) FRANKLIN
(— OF AFFAIRS) CASE ARRAY
STATUS
(— OF ALARM) GAST FEEZE SCARE
(— OF AMAZEMENT) STOUND
(— OF ANGER) FUME
(— OF APATHY) STUPOR
(— OF BEING) MODE
(— OF BEING CUT) SCISSION
(— OF BEING DRAWN) TRACTION
(— OF BEING OVERFULL)
PLETHORA
(— OF BEING POISONOUS)
TOXICITY
(— OF BEING WORSE) PEJORITY

(— OF BLISS) NIRVANA
(— OF CONCENTRATION) DHARANA SAMADHI
(— OF CONFUSION) FOG FLAP HACK MUSS CHAOS SWIRL HASSLE HUBBUB FLUMMOX TROYTOWN
(— OF CONSECRATION) IHRAM
(— OF COOPERATION) HOOKUP
(— OF DISASTER) SMASH
(— OF DISORDER) HELL MUSS FANTAD ANARCHY
(— OF DISSENSION) SCISSION
(— OF DISTRESS) KATZENJAMMER
(— OF DISTURBANCE) GARBOIL
(— OF DOUBT) MIST
(— OF EAGERNESS) HURRY
(— OF ECSTASY) SWOON
(— OF ENCHANTMENT) SPELL
(— OF ENLIGHTENMENT) BODHI
(— OF EQUALITY) PAR
(— OF EXALTATION) FURY ECSTASY
(— OF EXCITATION) FOMENT
(— OF EXCITEMENT) FRY FLAP GALE HIGH SNIT STEW FEEZE HOIGH DITHER DOODAH HUBBUB FANTEEG FLUSTER KIPPAGE SWELTER FANTIGUE
(— OF EXHAUSTION) GONENESS
(— OF FEAR) FUNK JELLY SCARE
(— OF HAPPINESS) ELYSIUM PARADISE
(— OF HEALTH) EUCRASIA
(— OF HUMILIATION) DUST
(— OF IDEAL PERFECTION) UTOPIA
(— OF IMPERFECTION) SCARCITY
(— OF INACTION) DEADLOCK
(— OF INCIPIENCE) EMBRYO
(— OF INTENSITY) BUILD
(— OF IRRITABILITY) FUME GALL FANTAD
(— OF JOY) JUBILEE
(— OF MELANCHOLY) GLOOM
(— OF MENTAL INACTIVITY) TORPOR
(— OF MENTAL READINESS) ATTITUDE
(— OF MIND) CUE HIP CASE MOOD HUMOR FETTLE CARAPACE
(— OF MISERY) HELL GEHENNA
(— OF NEGLECT) LIMBO
(— OF OPPOSITION) DEFIANCE
(— OF ORDER) HARMONY
(— OF OSTRACISM) COVENTRY
(— OF PERFECTION) SIDDHI
(— OF PERTURBATION) CRISE
(— OF PREOCCUPATION) CARE
(— OF QUIET) PEACE
(— OF READINESS) GUARD
(— OF REALITY) ACT
(— OF REJECTION) GATE
(— OF REPOSE) KEF CALM
(— OF RETIREMENT) GRASS
(— OF REVERIE) DUMP
(— OF SENSITIVITY) NERVES
(— OF SLUGGISHNESS) COMA
(— OF SUBDIVISION) FINENESS
(— OF SUFFERING) PURGATORY
(— OF SUSPENSE) TRANCE
(— OF SUSPENSION) ABEYANCE
(— OF TENSION) FANTEEG STRETCH FANTIGUE
(— OF THE SOUL) BARDO
(— OF THINGS) FARE PASS

(— OF TRANQUILLITY) KEF KIF PEACE
(— OF UNCERTAINTY) FOG FLUX
(— OF UNREST) FERMENT
(— OF WEATHER) FREEZE
(— OF WORRY) TEW SWEAT FANTAD
(— POSITIVELY) AFFIRM
(— PRECISELY) FORMATE
(— UNDER OATH) ALLEGE DEPONE TESTIFY
(AGITATED —) FUSS SNIT STIR CHURN STORM LATHER SWIVET
(BLISSFUL —) NIRVANA
(BUFFER —) GLACIS
(CHINESE —) WU SHU WEI
(DAMAGED —) RUIN RUINS
(DAZED —) DAMP
(DEPRESSED —) GLOOM WALLOW
(DISTURBED —) STIR STORM UNREST
(DOMINANT —) SUZERAIN
(DROWSY —) DOVER
(EMOTIONAL —) FEVER FEELING
(EVIL —) PLIGHT
(FEUDAL —) WEI
(FICTITIOUS —) FABLE
(FILTHY —) DIRT
(FLUSTERED —) JITTERS
(FREE —) SAORSTAT
(GERMAN —) REICH
(GLOOMY —) DUMP
(HIGHEST —) SUPREME
(HOLY —) IHRAM
(HORIZONTAL —) LEVEL
(IMPAIRED —) SHATTER
(INDONESIAN —) NEGARA
(INTERMEDIATE —) LIMBO
(IRISH —) TUATH
(LIQUID —) FLUOR FLUIDITY
(LOWEST —) BEDROCK
(MARRIED —) SPOUSAL
(MENTAL —) EARNEST DELUSION
(MIDDLE —) MEAN
(MIXED —) PI PIE
(MORBID —) HIP IODISM
(MORMON —) DESERET
(NEUTRAL —) BUFFER
(ORDINARY —) NORM
(OVERHEATED —) STEW
(PECUNIARY —) FACULTY
(PERMANENT —) STAY
(PERTURBED —) DEVIL
(PROFOUND —) DEPTH
(PROSPEROUS —) WEAL
(RIGID —) RIGOR
(ROYAL —) MAJESTY
(RUDIMENTARY —) INCHOATION
(SHELTERLESS —) EXPOSURE
(SOCIAL —) LIFE
(SOUTHWESTERN —S) SUNBELT
(SOVEREIGN —) INDEPENDENCY
(SPOTTED —) FOXINESS
(STUPEFIED —) NOD
(SUBORDINATE —) SATELLITE
(SWEATY —) STEW
(SWISS —) CANTON
(TROUBLESOME —) HOWDYDO
(ULTIMATE —) END
(UNCERTAIN —) LIMBO
(UNCONTROLLED —) RANDOM RANDON
(UNCULTIVATED —) FERITY

(UNDECIDED —) PENDENCY
(UNFAVORABLE —) FOULNESS
(VERIFIED —) FACT
(WORST —) PESSIMISM
(PREF.) CRATO TYP(I)(O)
(SUFF.) ANCE ANCY ANDRA ANDRIA ATE ATION CY DOM ENCE ENCY ERY HEAD HOOD ION ISATION ISM ITY IZATION MENT NESS OSIS SHIP TH
(CHARACTERIZED BY —) SOME
(DISEASED —) SIS
(MORBID —) IASIS
STATED GIVEN CERTAIN
(DIRECTLY —) EXPRESS
(DISTINCTLY —) EXPLICIT
STATE DEPARTMENT (— EMPLOYEE) ATTACHE
STATE FAIR (AUTHOR OF —) STONG
(CHARACTER IN —) PAT ABEL WARE EMILY FRAKE HARRY MARGY WAYNE ELEANOR GILBERT MELISSA
STATEHOUSE CAPITOL
STATELINESS STATE DIGNITY MAJESTY GRANDEUR
STATELY DATE BURLY GRAND LARGO LOFTY NOBLE PROUD REGAL STATE STOUT AUGUST COUPON PORTLY SOLEMN SUPERB TOGATE GALLANT BARONIAL IMPOSING MAESTOSO MAJESTIC PALATIAL STATEFUL
STATEMENT SAY BILL VOTE WORD AXIOM BRIEF COUNT DIXIT LIBEL STATE STORY BELIEF DICTUM DOCKET EXPOSE FACTUM RETURN SAYING SPEECH ACCOUNT ADDRESS ANALOGY DISSENT EPITAPH EPITOME FORMULA INVOICE MENTION SHOWING ABSTRACT ANTINOMY ARGUMENT AVERMENT BULLETIN DELIVERY EQUATION EXPLICIT JUDGMENT PROPOSAL SCHEDULE SENTENCE SPEAKING SYNGRAPH SYNOPSIS
(— AS PRECEDENT) AUTHORITY
(— OF FACTS) REPORT
(— OF GRIEVANCE) PLAINT
(— OF OPINION) CHANT
(— OF RELATIONS) THEOREM
(— ON DRUG LABEL) LEGEND
(AUTHORITATIVE —) DICTUM
(CASUAL —) REMARK
(CONCISE —) SCHEME APHORISM
(CONDENSED —) RESUME SYNOPSIS
(DEFAMATORY —) LIBEL
(EXAGGERATED —) STRETCH
(FABRICATED —) CANARD
(FINAL — OF ACCOUNT) AUDIT
(FINANCIAL —) BUDGET
(FOOLISH —) INANITY
(FORMAL —) CITATION
(IRRATIONAL —) ALOGISM
(OBSCURE —) ENIGMA
(PLAINTIFF'S —) BODY
(POMPOUS —) BRAG
(PUBLIC —) OUTGIVING
(SELF-CONTRADICTORY —) PARADOX
(SOOTHING —) SALVE
(UNTRUE —) LIE

STATER COLT TURTLE PEGASUS CYZICENE
STATEROOM BIBBY CABIN
STATESMAN GENRO SOLON FATHER STATIST WARWICK JACOBEAN WEALSMAN
(UNPRINCIPLED —) MACHIAVELLIAN
AMERICAN DIX HAY JAY LEE AMES BURR CASS CLAY FISH GREW HALE HULL OTIS POLK REED ROOT RUSK ADAMS BAKER BLAIR BLAND BORAH DAWES CHASE GENET GERRY GLASS HENRY LODGE MARCY OLNEY WYTHE BARUCH BIDDLE BLAINE BOWLES BROOKE BUNCHE CARTER EVARTS FOSTER GORHAM HURLEY MCKEAN MORRIS NORRIS RODNEY SEWARD SUMNER TOOMBS WALTON ACHESON ALDRICH BARBOUR BULLITT CLINTON CUMMINS DANIELS EVERETT GADSDEN HANCOCK HOUSTON KELLOGG LANSING LAURENS LINCOLN MORRILL SHERMAN STANTON TIMSON WEBSTER FRANKLIN GALLATIN HAMILTON HARRIMAN MILLEDGE PINCKNEY RANDOLPH RUTLEDGE SCHUYLER TRUMBULL DICKINSON ELLSWORTH FULBRIGHT PICKERING WASHINGTON SCHUSCHNIGG BRECKENRIDGE
ARGENTINIAN MITRE ALBERDI CARCANO DORREGO FRONDIZI RIVADAVIA
ATHENIAN SOLON
AUSTRALIAN SEE COOK BRUCE EVATT LYONS PRICE BARTON DEAKIN FISHER HOLDER HUGHES ISSACS LAWSON PARKES SCULLIN NICHOLSON
AUSTRIAN BACH RAAB BRUCK KHESL RAMEK UNGER BADENI GLASER PLENER RENNER SEIPEL TAAFFE BURESCH FIRMIAN HELFERT KAUNITZ KOERBER SCHOBER STADION BELCREDI DOLLFUSS HAYMERLE HUSSAREK LAMMASCH WALDHEIM EGGENBERG BELLEGARDE METTERNICH SCHMERLING BARTENSTEIN GOLUCHOWSKI PILLERSDORF STARHEMBERG
BELGIAN SPAAK DEVAUX HYMANS JACOBS JASPAR MERODE ROGIER ANETHAN NOTHOMB THEUNIS ZEELAND DECHAMPS BEERNAERT DELACROIX SCHOLLAERT VANDERVELDE
BOLIVIAN FRIAS MONTES BALDIVIESO
BRAZILIAN ABREU FEIJO CAXIAS BERNARDES MAGALHAES
BULGARIAN DANEV SAVOY MALINOV TSANKOV LIAPCHEV KARAVELOV STAMBOLOV RADOSLAVOV STAMBOLISKI
BURMESE THANT
CANADIAN KING GOUIN JETTE LEGER SCOTT TACHE VIGER BORDEN BOWELL FISHER FOSTER HUGHES MANION SIFTON TUPPER BALDWIN BENNETT BRODEUR

CARTIER CHAPAIS DOHERTY
LAURIER MEIGHEN PEARSON
RALSTON TRUDEAU MICHENER
THOMPSON MACDONALD
MACKENZIE PELLETIER
CARTWRIGHT LAFONTAINE
DIEFENBAKER FITZPATRICK
CHILEAN CRUZ RIOS EGANA MONTT
FREIRE CRUCHAGA OHIGGINS
BALMACEDA ALESSANDRI
CHINESE WU HUA KOO YEN KUNG
SOONG
COLOMBIAN ZEA HERRAN
COSTA RICAN CASTRO
CUBAN PALMA
CZECH BENES HACHA HODZA
KRAMAR RIEGER SVEHLA UDRZAL
MASARYK
DANISH HALL ZAHLE BLUHME
ESTRUP MONRAD RANTZAU
GULDBERG STAUNING NEERGAARD
GRIFFENFELD
DUTCH CATS COEN FOCK ASSER
DOUSA FAGEL HAREN COLIJN
DEWITT KUYPER GROTIUS HEINSIUS
KLEFFENS HEEMSKERK KARNEBEEK
VANDIEMEN BARNEVELDT
BEEREENBROUCK
ECUADORIAN FLORES
EGYPTIAN SADAT ZIWAR
ENGLISH FOX LAW PYM EDEN HOPE
HYDE LAMB LONG MORE PEEL PITT
VANE WEBB WOOD AMERY BACON
BEVAN BURKE CECIL CLIVE ELIOT
HEATH HOARE JUXON LEWIS NIGEL
PAGET SYKES BLOUNT BRIGHT
COBDEN CRIPPS CURZON GEDDES
GIBSON GRAHAM HARLEY HATTON
HEATON HOLLES MILNER MORELY
MORTON SAVILE SELDEN SIDNEY
SOMERS TEMPLE WOLSEY ASQUITH
BALDWIN BALFOUR CADOGAN
CANNING FAWCETT FORSTER
GERMAIN GIFFARD GOSCHEN
HALDANE HALIFAX HAMPDEN
HERRIES LAMBTON NORWICH
OSBORNE RAFFLES READING
RUSSELL STANLEY STEWART
SWINTON WALDOCK WALPOLE
WINDHAM WYKEHAM WYNDHAM
ADDERLEY ANNESLEY BEAUFORT
CARTERET COURTNEY CROMWELL
DISRAELI GARDINER GOULBURN
HAMILTON HARCOURT HASTINGS
MACAULAY MONTFORT ROBINSON
STANHOPE VILLIERS ADDINGTON
BLEDISLOE CAVENDISH CHURCHILL
CUSHENDUN FITZNEALE FITZPETER
FORTESCUE GAITSKELL GLADSTONE
GLANVILLE GODOLPHIN
GREENWOOD GRENVILLE
HUSKISSON KIMBERLEY
LANSDOWNE LIVERPOOL
MACDONALD NORTHCOTE
STRAFFORD WAKEFIELD
BIRKENHEAD PALMERSTON
ROCKINGHAM WALSINGHAM
WELLINGTON WHITELOCKE
WILLINGDON BOLINGBROKE
CHAMBERLAIN FITZWILLIAM
SHAFTESBURY SOUTHAMPTON
CHESTERFIELD
ESTONIAN PATS STRANDMAN

FINNISH KALLIO TANNER CAJANDER
MECHELIN RELANDER STAHLBERG
MANNERHEIM
FRENCH BLUM COTY DARU MOLE
DUPUY FAURE FAVRE FERRY FOULD
MARET MONIS PASSY RIBOT SIMON
SUGER SULLY AVENOL BARROT
BERNIS BIGNON BRIAND CARNOT
CASSIN DOUMER DUPRAT FLEURY
FOUCHE GUIZOT LOUBET MELINE
NECKER PERIER PETAIN ROUHER
THIERS TURGOT COLBERT DECAZES
GRAMONT HERRIOT MAISTRE
MARIGNY MAUPEOU MAZARIN
MOLLIEN NOGARET REGNIER
ROUVIER SCHUMAN SEGUIER
VILLELE VIVIANI CHOISEUL
CONSTANS DALADIER DELCASSE
FONTANES FRANCOIS GAMBETTA
HANOTAUX LHOPITAL MIRABEAU
PAINLEVE POINCARE POMPIDOU
PORTALIS BONAPARTE BOURGEOIS
CHAMPAGNY CLEMENTEL
DALHOUSIE DOUMERGUE
FALLIERES LAFAYETTE MILLERAND
RICHELIEU VERGENNES
BARTHELEMY CLEMENCEAU
TALLEYRAND WADDINGTON
BASSOMPIERRE CHATEAUBRIAND
GERMAN BLOS CUNO FALK MARX
SOLF BEUST JAGOW NOSKE PAPEN
BRANDT GERBER KRANTZ LUTHER
MAURER MIQUEL MOLTKE WORNER
BRUNING CAPRIVI CURTIUS FABRICE
GESSLER STEPHAN ADENAUER
BISMARCK HAINISCH HERTLING
HOLSTEIN KUHLMANN SEVERING
SPANHEIM BENNIGSEN ERZBERGER
HALLSTEIN MICHAELIS BERNSTORFF
FEHRENBACH HILFERDING
RICHTHOFEN SCHLEICHER
STRESEMANN WINDTHORST
ZIMMERMANN SECKENDORFF
GREEK ZAIMES KANARES KORIZES
RANGABE RHALLES BULGARIS
GOUNARES KONDYLES PANGALOS
PERICLES TIMOLEON ARISTIDES
DINARCHUS DRAGOUMES
HYPERIDES PERIANDER TIMOTHEUS
TRIKOUPES TSALDARES
TSOUDEROS VENIZELOS
ALCIBIADES SKOULOUDES
THEMISTIUS THERAMENES
DEMOSTHENES THRASYBULUS
THEMISTOCLES KOUMOUNDOUROS
MAVROKORDATOS
MICHALAKOPOULOS
HUNGARIAN DEAK NAGY VASS
CSAKY SZELL TISZA BANFFY
BAROSS EOTVOS GOMBOS HORTHY
LONYAY TELEKI BETHLEN HORVATH
HUNYADI KOSSUTH WEKERLE
ANDRASSY SZECHENYI MARTINUZZI
ICELANDIC HAFSTEIN SIGURDSSON
INDIAN NOON GUPTA NEHRU SINHA
BAJPAI GANDHI SASTRI
IRISH HYDE ANDREWS GRATTAN
MCNEILL COSGRAVE DEVALERA
MACBRIDE CRAIGAVON
ISRAELI ALLON DAYAN RABIN
ITALIAN BALBO BERTI CIANO
CROCE DORIA FACTA LANZA MANIN
NITTI ROCCO ROSSI SELLA VOLPI

BONGHI CAVOUR CRISPI FEDELE
GRANDI PEPOLI RUDINI SFORZA
ADRIANI ALFIERI AZEGLIO CADORNA
CAIROLI DURANDO GASPERI
GRAVINA MAMIANI MANCINI
ORLANDO PELLOUX PONTANO
SONNINO TANUCCI TITTONI VILLARI
ALBERONI CIBRARIO CORRENTI
DEPRETIS GIOLITTI LAFARINA
LUZZATTI MATTIOLI MENABREA
NICOTERA RATTAZZI RICASOLI
SALANDRA SCIALOIA ANTONELLI
FEDERZONI GARIBALDI GUERRAZZI
LAMARMORA MINGHETTI
MONTANELLI ZANARDELLI
MACHIAVELLI LAMBRUSCHINI
JAPANESE ITO GOTO HARA KATO
SATO MUTSU OKUBO OKUMA
INOUYE KANEKO KOMURA MAKINO
TANAKA HAYASHI ITAGAKI IWAKURA
IYEYASU KATSURA SAIONJI
HIRANUMA KIYOMORI MATSUOKA
NOBUNAGA TERAUCHI YAMAGATA
YAMAMOTO HAMAGUCHI
HIDEYOSHI MATSUKATA
WAKATSUKI
KOREAN RHEE
LATVIAN KVIESIS ULMANIS
MEIEROVICS
LEBANESE MALIK
LIBERIAN TUBMAN TOLBERT
LITHUANIAN SMETONA
VOLDEMARAS
MEXICAN DIAZ ALAMAN CALLES
OBREGON ZULOAGA IGLESIAS
NEW ZEALAND FOX HALL WARD
ALLEN VOGEL COATES FORBES
FRASER MASSEY SEDDON
ATKINSON STAFFORD
NORWEGIAN BULL KOHT FALSEN
HAMBRO NANSEN HAGERUP
KNUDSEN SVERDRUP MICHELSEN
MOWINCKEL NYGAARDSVOLD
PERUVIAN PRADO CORNEJO
CADLERON BENAVIDES MENDIBURU
PHILIPPINE ROXAS OSMENA
QUEZON ROMULO
POLISH BECK WITOS DMOWSKI
ZALESKI ZALUSKI SIKORSKI
SKRYNSKI KOSCIUSKO PILSUDSKI
PADEREWSKI WOJCIECHOWSKI
PORTUGUESE PAES COSTA
POMBAL ALMEIDA ARRIAGA
CARMONA MACHADO SALAZAR
CARVALHO SALDANHA SANTAREM
PRUSSIAN BULOW
ROMAN CATO CINNA PLINY CAESAR
CICERO POMPEY SENECA AGRIPPA
LAELIUS RUFINUS CAMILLUS
CATILINE GRACCHUS MAECENAS
STILICHO FABRICIUS FLAMINIUS
SERTORIUS SYMMACHUS
CASSIDORUS HORTENSIUS
ROMANIAN CARP MANIU IONESCU
CATARGIU MIRONESCU TITULESCU
MARGHILOMAN KOGALNICEANU
RUSSIAN BIRON GIERS WITTE
BLUDOV CANCRIN KALININ
MOLOTOV MUNNICH SIEVERS
TOLSTOI AVERESCU CHICHKOV
DMITRIEV GOLITSYN IZVOLSKI
LAMSDORF LITVINOV POTMEKIN
STOLYPIN CALINESCU CHICHERIN

GORCHAKOV GOREMYKIN
GRIBOEDOV MENSHIKOV
SPERANSKI NESSELRODE
PROTOPOPOV
SCOTTISH HUME KNOX BEATON
GORDON MURRAY JAMESON
MAITLAND RANDOLPH HORSBRUGH
WARRISTON ELPHINSTONE
SERBIAN GRUIC
SOUTH AFRICAN BOTHA BRAND
REITZ SMUTS STEYN KRUGER
SPRIGG COGHLAN HERTZOG
MERRIMAN
SPANISH LUNA ALAVA GODOY
OSUNA PEREZ GALVEZ MANUEL
TORENO ABASCAL ALARCON
IOTURIZ MENDOZA NARVAEZ
SAGASTA SILVELA ENSENADA
ESCOSURA MANRIQUE OLIVARES
QUINTANA ZORRILLA CALOMARDE
ESCOIQUIZ ESPARTERO REQUESENS
JOVELLANOS MIRAFLORES
SWEDISH EDEN GEER HORN TOLL
BRAHE ESSEN UNDEN HANSSON
LINDMAN SANDLER BRANTING
FORSSELL EHRENSVARD
GYLLENBORG WENNERBERG
OXENSTIERNA OXENSTJERNA
HAMMARSKJOLD
SWISS ADOR DROZ FAZY KERN
MUSY FURER GOBAT MEYER MOTTA
BLUMER ESCHER MINGER MULLER
DEUCHER BLUNTSCHLI
SCHULTHESS
TURKISH INONU SARACOGLU
URUGUAYAN RIVERA
VENEZUELAN VARGAS BOLIVAR
MONAGAS BETANCOURT
YUGOSLAV PASIC PROTIC ZIVKOVIC
DAVIDOVIC MARINKOVIC PRIBICEVIC
STATICE ARMERIA LIMONIUM
STATION BY BYE FIX ORB RUN SET
BASE GARE POST RANK ROOM
SEAT STOP BEING BERTH CHOKY
DEPOT PLACE POSTE SIEGE STAGE
STALL STAND STATE DEGREE
LOCATE STANCE CONTROL
CUARTEL DIGNITY HABITAT
OUTPOST GARRISON PILTDOWN
POSITION STANDING TERMINAL
TERMINUS TRANSFER
(— IN BASEBALL) BASE
(— IN LIFE) BEING CALLING
(— OF HERON) SEDGE SIEGE
(ANIMAL'S —) LIE
(ASSIGNED —) QUARTER
(CONCEALED —) AMBUSH
(CUSTOMS —) CHOKEY
(EXALTED —) PURPLE
(HEALTH —) SANATORIUM
SANITARIUM
(MILITARY —) CAMP
(POLICE —) NICK TANA TANNA
THANAH KOTWALEE
(POST —) DAK
(RADIO —S) CHAIN NETWORK
(RAILWAY —) GARE CABIN
(RUSSIAN SPACE —) MIR
(SAILING —) MARINA
(SIGNALLING —) BANTAY BEACON
(SURVEYING —) STADIA
(TELEVISION —) CHANNEL
(TOLL —) CHOKY CHOKEY

(TRADING —) FACTORY
(WAY —) TAMBO
STATIONARY SET FAST FIXED STILL ATREST LEDGER STATIC DORMANT SITFAST STABILE STATARY IMMOBILE
STATIONERY PAPER PAPETERIE
STATION WAGON WOODY WOODIE MICROBUS SUBURBAN
STATISTICIAN ANALYST STATIST
STATOBLAST SPORE
STATUARY IMAGERY
STATUE HERM ICON IDOL IKON TERM BUSTO HERMA IMAGE MOSES AGALMA BRONZE HERMES MEMNON STATUA WEEPER XOANON ILISSUS PASQUIN PICTURE STATURE STATUTE ACROLITH CARYATID MARFORIO MONUMENT PANTHEUM PORTRAIT VICTORIA
(— ENDOWED WITH LIFE) GALATEA
(— OF ATHENA) PALLADIUM
(— OF GIGANTIC SIZE) COLOSSUS
(COLOSSAL —) GOG MAGOG
STATUETTE WAX CLIO EMMY OSCAR WINNIE TANAGRA FIGURINE FIGURINE SIGILLUM
(— AWARD) REUBEN
(AWARD —) GRAMMY
STATURE PITCH GROWTH HEIGHT INCHES WASTME CAPACITY
STATUS RANK SEAT PLACE STATE ASPECT FOOTING STATURE POSITION STANDING SITUATION
(— OF YOUNGER SON) CADENCY
(HIGH —) CACHET
(LEGAL —) CAPUT
(SECONDARY —) BACKSEAT
STATUTE ACT LAW LEX DOOM EDICT ASSIZE DECREE SETNESS SITTING STATUTUM TANZIMAT
(— FAIR) MOP
STATUTORY LEGAL
STAUNCH FAST STOUT TRUSTY FAITHFUL STALWART
STAVE LAG SLAT STAP SHAKE STAFF STOVE VERSE BASTON STANZA WATTLE
(— IN) BILGE BULGE
(SET OF —S) SHOOK
(PL.) LAGGEN LAGGIN STICKS STAVING
STAY DAY GET LIE BASE HOLD LEND PROP REST SIST STOP WAIT ABIDE ABODE APPUI DEFER DELAY DEMUR DWELL LEAVE STINT TARRY THOLE ARREST ATTEND BIDING DETAIN EXPECT GUSSET POTENT REMAIN TIMBER UPHOLD EMBASSY JIBSTAY LAYOVER MANSION SOJOURN SUSPEND BACKSTAY CONTINUE FORESTAY HORNSTAY MAINSTAY MARTINGALE
(— AWAY) SKIP
(— BEHIND) LAG
(— CLEAR) AVOID
(— FOR) AWAIT
(— IN BED) LIEIN SACKIN
(— THE NIGHT) BUNK HOSTLE
(— WITH) STICK
(PRIEST'S —) STATION

(SHORT —) VISIT
(TAILORING —) BRIDLE
(PL.) JUMPS JUPES BODICE
STAY-AT-HOME HOMEBODY HOMESTER
STAYER BONER
STAYLACE AGLET AIGLET
STAYSAIL JUMBO
STEAD LIEU ROOM VICE PLACE BEHALF
STEADFAST PAT SAD FAST FIRM SURE TRUE ROCKY STAID STEER STABLE STANCH STEADY CERTAIN EXPRESS SETTLED STAUNCH VALIANT CONSTANT FAITHFUL RESOLUTE STALWART
STEADFASTLY FIRM FIRMLY INTENTLY
STEADILY SAD FAST STEADY
STEADINESS NERVE BALANCE
STEADING ONSET ONSTEAD
STEADY GUY SAD BEAU EVEN FIRM SURE TRIG TRUE CANNY FRANK LEVEL SOBER STUDY SUANT TIGHT SICCAR SMOOTH STABLE STANCH BALLAST EQUABLE STABILE STATARY STAUNCH CONSTANT DECOROUS DILIGENT FAITHFUL RESOLUTE TRANQUIL UNSHAKEN
(— AT ANCHOR) HOLSOM
STEAK BROIL SHELL FLITCH TUCKET FLANKEN GRISKIN PORTERHOUSE
(CLUB —) CONTREFILET
(KIND OF —) SHELL SKIRT TBONE
(LOIN —) FILET FILLET TOURNEDOS
STEAL BAG CAB CLY COP FOX GYP LAG MAG NAP NIM NIP RAP RIG BONE CHOR COON CRIB FAKE GLOM HOOK KNAP LIFT LURK MAGG MAKE MILL NAIL NICK PEAK PICK PRIG SLIP SMUG ANNEX BOOST BRIBE CLOUT CREEP FETCH FILCH FLIMP FRISK GLIDE HARRY HEIST HOIST LURCH MOOCH MOUCH PINCH PLUCK POACH SCOFF SHAKE SHARP SHAVE SLIDE SNAKE SNARE SNEAK STALK SWIPE TOUCH TRUFF COLLAR CONVEY FINGER HIJACK MOOTCH NOBBLE PILFER RIPOFF SNITCH STRIKE THIEVE TWITCH BESTEAL CABBAGE PLUNDER PURLOIN SCHLEPP SKYUGLE SNABBLE SNAFFLE SURREPT ABSTRACT CRIBBAGE EMBEZZLE LIBERATE MANARVEL PECULATE SCROUNGE SHOPLIFT PLAGIARIZE
(— A GLANCE) GLIME
(— ALONG) SLIME SLINK
(— A WATCH) FLIMP
(— AWAY) LOOP SLINK
(— BY ALTERING BRANDS) DUFF
(— CALVES) NUGGET
(— CATTLE) DUFF RUSTLE
(— COPPER FROM VESSEL'S BOTTOM) TOSH
(— OFF) RUN
(— SLYLY) SCROUNGE
STEALER (CATTLE —) DUFFER ABACTOR
STEALING STALE
(PREF.) KLEPT(O)

STEALTHILY SIDLINS THIEFLY SIDELINS
STEALTHY CATTY PRIVY ARTFUL FELINE TIPTOE CATLIKE FURTIVE SNEAKING THIEVISH
STEAM IRE OAM ROKE STEM ANGER BLAST SMOKE SWEAT VAPOR BREATH POTHER CUSHION TICKOFF
(PREF.) ATM(O) ATMID(O)
STEAMBOAT KICKUP STEAMER
STEAMER CLAM LINER TENDER CUNARDER
STEAMER DUCK RACER LOGHEAD
STEAMSHIP SCREW STEAM STEAMER SEATRAIN SHOWBOAT
(— OF VENICE) VAPORETTO
STEAM SHOVEL NAVVY NAVVIE
STEATIN MULL
STEATITE LARDITE POTSTONE SOAPROCK
STEATOPYGOUS RUMPY
STEED NAG ROIL HORSE MOUNT STEAD PEGASUS SLEIPNER SLEIPNIR
STEEL RAIL BLOOM BRACE FUSIL TERNE WEAPON WHITTLE FLEERISH
(— FOR STRIKING FIRE) ESLABON
(— FOR USE WITH FLINT) FUSIL FURISON FLEERISH
(— INLAID WITH GOLD) KOFT KOFTGARI
(DAMASCUS —) DAMASK
(INDIAN —) WOOTZ
(KIND OF —) MILD PEDAL
(MOLTEN —) HEAT
STEELER BONER
STEELING ACIERAGE
STEELWORKER HOOKER STICKMAN STRANDER STRANNER
STEELYARD BISMAR BISMER DESEMER DOTCHIN STATERA
STEENBRAS BISKOP
STEEP RET SOP BATE BOLD BOWK BREW BUCK DEAR DRAW DUNG ELIX LIME MASH MASK SOAK STAY STEW STEY BLUFF BRANT BRENT HATCH HEAVY HILLY QUICK SHARP SHEER SOUSE STIFF ABRUPT BLUFFY CLIFFY CLIFTY DECOCT IMBIBE INFUSE SPRUNT STEEPY ARDUOUS BRASQUE CLIVOSE INSTEEP PRERUPT STICKLE HEADLONG MACERATE SATURATE SIDELING STIFFISH STRAIGHT PRECIPITOUS
(— IN VERY HOT WATER) PLOT
STEEPED SODDEN
STEEPING SOUSE INFUSION
STEEPLE SPEAR SPIRE
STEEPLEBUSH HARDHACK
STEEPLECHASE CHASE GRIND
STEER COX PLY AIRT BEEF BULL HELM LEAD STEM STOT GUIDE SPADE SPADO STERN TOLLY CANNER RUDDER BULLOCK STOCKER COWBRUTE MOSSHORN NAVIGATE
(— VEHICLE) DRIVE
(FAT —) BEAST
(HORNLESS —) NOT NOTT
(VICIOUS —) LADINO

(WILD —) YAW YEW COWBRUTE
(YOUNG —) STOT STOTT
STEERAGE STERN
STEERER SLUER CAPPER
STEERSMAN COX PILOT WHEEL PATRON SLEWER CANOPUS SHIPMAN STEERER COXSWAIN HELMSMAN SEACUNNY STERNMAN WHEELMAN COCKSWAIN
STEGOMYIA AEDES
STEIN MUG SHANT
STEINBOCK BOUQUETIN
STELE SHAFT EUSTELE OBELISK
STELLAR STARRY
STELLATE ASTROSE
STEM BUN BASE BEAK BEAM BINE BIRN CANE CULM CURB NOSE PIPE PROW RISP ROOT RUNT SHAW STUD ARISE FILUM HAULM SCAPE SCREW SHAFT SHANK SHOOT SPIRE STALE STALK STEAL STICK STIPE STAVA THEME TRUNK TUBER BRANCH CAUDEX CAULIS DERIVE SCAPUS SPRING CAULOME CONTAIN FULCRUM HOPBINE HOPVINE PEDICEL PETIOLE PLASHER SARMENT SPINDLE STEMLET TIGELLA CAULICLE ENGENDER EPICOTYL FORESTEM PEDUNCLE PIPESTEM TIGELLUM
(— OF ARROW) SHAFT
(— OF BANANAS) COUNT
(— OF GLASS) BALUSTER
(— OF GRAPES) RAPE
(— OF HOOKAH) SNAKE
(— OF MATCH) SHAFT
(— OF MUSHROOM) STIPE
(— OF MUSICAL NOTE) TAIL FILUM VIRGULA
(— OF PIPE) STAPPLE
(— OF PLANT) AXIS RUNT CAULIS
(— OF SHIP) PROW STEMPOST
(— OF TREE) BOLE CAUDEX
(—S OF CULTIVATED PLANTS) HAULM
(BULBLIKE —) CORM
(DRY WITHERED —) BIRN
(EDIBLE —) EDDO
(GRIEF —) KELLY
(MAIN — OF DEER'S ANTLERS) BEAM
(ORNAMENTAL —) STAVE
(PITHY JOINTED —) CANE
(THORNY —) LAWYER
(TWINING —) BINE
(PREF.) CAUL(I) CORM(O) CULMI SCAPI STIRPI
(SUFF.) DENDRON OME
STEMLESS ACAULINE
STEMMA OCELLUS OCELLANA PEDIGREE
STEMMER STRIPPER
STEMWARE CRYSTAL
STENCH FOGO HOGO FETOR SMELL STINK WHIFF FOETOR MEPHITIS
STENCIL THEOREM
(— PROCESS) POCHOIR
STENCILED GOFFERED
STENO TEMP
STENOGRAPHY SHORTHAND
STENOSIS SMALLING

STEP CUT FIT JOG PEG PIP BEMA DESS FOOT GREE LINK PACE PASO PEEP RUNG STAP BRASS CORTE DODGE FLIER FLYER GRECE NOTCH POINT STAGE STAIR TOOTH TRACE TREAD DEGREE GRADIN RUNDLE STRIDE WINDER CURTAIL DESCENT FOOTING GRADINE GRADING COONJINE DEMARCHE DOORSTEP FOOTPACE FOOTSTEP FORESTEP PREDELLA STRATLIN
(— ASIDE) DIGRESS
(— BACKWARD) DODGE
(— BY STEP) GRADATIM
(— DOWNWARD) DESCENT
(— FOR GEM MOUNTING) KITE
(— FORWARD) ADVANCE
(— IN A BEARING) BRASS
(— IN BELL RINGING) DODGE
(— IN DOCK) ALTAR
(— IN SELF-ESTEEM) PEG
(— IN SEQUENCE) PLACE
(— IN SHAFT) STEMPEL STEMPLE
(— IN SOCIAL SCALE) CUT
(— IN TRENCH) BANQUETTE
(— LIVELY) SKELP
(— OF LADDER) RIME RUNG ROUND RUNDLE
(— OF TUSK) TOOTH
(— OUT) DIE
(— PERFORMED BY COMPUTER) OPERATION
(—S OF BOWLER) APPROACH
(— SUPPORTING MILLSTONE) TRAMPOT
(ALTAR —S) GRADUAL
(BALLET —) PLIE FOUETTE SISSONE SISSONNE
(BALLET —S) ALLEGRO
(BOUNDING —) SKIP
(CLUMSY —) STAUP
(DANCE —) DIP PAS SET BUZZ DRAG DRAW FLAT SHAG SKIP BRAWL CHASS COULE GLIDE IRISH STOMP BRANLE CANTER CHASSE DOUBLE INTURN STRIDE BRANSLE BUFFALO FISHTAIL GLISSADE PIGEONWING
(FALSE —) HOB SLIP SPHALM SNAPPER SPHALMA STUMBLE
(FIRST —) STARTER RUDIMENT
(FLIGHT OF —S) GRECE GRICE PERRON GEMONIES
(GLIDING —) CHASSE
(HALF —) HALFTONE SEMITONE
(LIGHT —) PITAPAT
(MINING —) LOB STEMPEL STEMPLE
(POMPOUS —) STRUT
(PRIM —) MINCE
(PROCEED BY —S) RATCHET
(SET OF —S) STILE
(STATELY —) STALK
(PL.) STY GHAT GHAUT STILE LADDER
STEPFATHER FATHER STEPSIRE
STEPLADDER TRAP STEPS
(PART OF —) RAIL REST RUNG SHOE STEP BRACE SPREADER
STEPMOTHER MOTHER HANGNAIL STEPDAME
(RELATING TO —) NOVERCAL
STEPPE PUSZTA

(— REGION) SAHEL
(ARID REGION OF —) POECHORE
STEPPED STOPEN
STEPPENWOLF (AUTHOR OF —) HESSE
(CHARACTER IN —) HARRY MARIA HALLER HERMINE
STEPPING
(SUFF.) GRADE
STEREOISOMER ANOMER EPIMER
STEREOTYPE CAST LABEL CLICHE STEREO TYPECAST
STEREOTYPED CHAIN STAGE TRITE USUAL STEREO IDENTIKIT
STERILE DRY DEAD DEAF GELD POOR AXENIC BARREN GALLED MEAGER MULISH OTIOSE ASEPTIC ACARPOUS BANKRUPT IMPOTENT
(PREF.) STEIRO
STERILITY ATOCIA APHORIA
STERILIZE INSULATE
STERILIZING BURNING
STERLING SOUND
(100,000 POUNDS —) PLUM
STERN GRIL GRIM HARD POOP ASPER CRUEL GRUFF HARSH RIGID ROUGH ROUND STARK STOUR FLINTY GLOOMY GRIMLY SEVERE SHREWD STRICT SULLEN TORVID UNKIND WICKED AUSTERE TORVOUS STEERAGE STERNFUL STRAIGHT
(— OF SHIP) DOCK APLUSTRE
(TOWARD THE —) ABAFT
STERNFAST PROVISO
STERNNESS RIGOR TORVITY SEVERITY
STERNPOST POST STEM MAINPOST
STERNUTATIVE ERRHINE PTARMIC
STERNUTATOR ERRHINE
STEROL AMYRIN STERIN AMBRAIN
STEROPE (FATHER OF —) ATLAS
(MOTHER OF —) PLEIONE
(SON OF —) OENOMAUS
STERTOR SNORE
STEVEDORE STOWER TRIMMER WHARFIE CARGADOR DOCKHAND
STEVENSON, R.L. TUSITALA
STEW JUG FRET ITCH SLUM SNIT SWOT BREDI CIVET CURRY DAUBE SALMI STIVE STOVE SWEAT BRAISE BURGOO HODDLE MUDDLE PAELLA SCOUSE SEETHE SIMMER BROTHEL CALDERA GOULASH HARICOT NAVARIN PUCHERO STOVIES TERRINE BOURRIDE ETOUFFEE FRIJOADA HOTCHPOT MORTREUX MULLIGAN STEWPOND STUFFATA WATERZOOI CARBONNADE RATATOUILLE SLUMGULLION
(— A HARE) JUG
(— IN A SAUCE) DAUBE
(— MADE IN FORECASTLE) HODDLE
(— OF TRAMPS) MULLIGAN
(CAJUN —) ETOUFFEE
(FISH —) STODGE CHOWDER MATELOTE
(GAME —) SALMI
(IN A —) UPSET
(IRISH —) STOVIES
(MUTTON —) NAVARIN
(POT FOR —) OLLA

STEWARD HIND VOGT DEWAN DIWAN GRAFF GRAVE REEVE COMMIS FACTOR FARMER GRIEVE LOOKER SIRCAR SIRDAR BAILIFF CURATOR DAPIFER FLUNKEY GRANGER HUSBAND MAORMOR MORMAOR PESHKAR PROCTOR PROVOST SPENCER SPENDER APPROVER BHANDARI CELLARER CONSUMAH GASTALDO HERENACH KHANSAMA LARDINER MALVOLIO MANCIPLE PROVISOR STEADMAN VILLICUS MAJORDOMO
(JOCKEY CLUB —) STIPE
STEWED SODDEN
STEWING ITCHING
STEWPAN STEW COCOTTE SKILLET
STHENELUS (FATHER OF —) PERSEUS CAPANEUS ANDROGEOS
(MOTHER OF —) EVADNE ANDROMEDA
(SON OF —) EURYSTHEUS
(WIFE OF —) NICIPPE
STHENOBOEA (FATHER OF —) IOBATES
(HUSBAND OF —) PROETUS
STIBNITE SURMA STIBIUM ANTIMONY
STIBOPHEN FUADIN
STICHIC SERIAL
STICK CAT CLA DIP GAD HEW LUG WAN BROG BUFF CHOP CLAG CLAM CLUB CRAB GLUE HANG HURL PALE PALO PICK POLE POTE RICE RUNG STAY TREE YARD BATON BRAIL CAMAN CLAME CLAVE CLEAM CLING CROME DEMUR HURLY PASTE PRICK SPELK STAFF STAKE STANG STAVE STEND STING STOCK STOKE VALET VERGE WADDY ADHERE ATLATL BALLOW BATLER BATLET BATTLE BILLET BROACH BULGER CEMENT CLEAVE CLEEKY COHERE CUDGEL FESCUE HOCKEY INHERE KIERIE KIPPIN LIBBET MALLET RADDLE RAMMER RISSLE STRIKE STRING THIVEL TWITCH BACKSET BATLING CAMMOCK CUMMOCK GAMBREL HURLBAT KILNRIB KIPPEEN MOLINET NOBBLER SHANGAN SPURTLE WOOLDER ASHPLANT BLUDGEON BRINGSEL BRINSELL CATPIECE CATSTICK CRUMMOCK DIPSTICK DUTCHMAN GIBSTAFF GOBSTICK KILNTREE POTSTICK SPREADER
(— AS ARCHERY MARK) WAND
(— AS VIETNAM WEAPON) PUNJI
(— FAST) JAM JAMB SEIZE FITCHER
(— FASTENED TO DOG'S TAIL) SHANGAN
(— FOR ADMITTING TENANTS) VERGE
(— FOR DRIVING OXEN) OXGOAD
(— FOR FIRING CANNON) LINSTOCK
(— FOR KILLING FISH) NOBBLER
(— FOR MAKING FENCE) RADDLE
(— FOR MIXING CHOCOLATE) MOLINET
(— FOR MIXING MORTAR) RAB
(— FOR SNUFF) DIP

(— FOR THATCHING) SPAR GROOM SPELK SPRINGLE
(— IN MUD) STODGE
(— IN OPERATION) FREEZE
(— IT OUT) LAST
(— OF A FAN) BRIN
(— OF CANDY) GIBBY
(— OF CHALK) CRAYON
(— OF ORCHESTRA LEADER) BATON
(— OUT) BUG POKE BULGE SHOOT EXSERT EXTEND EXTRUDE PROTEND
(— REGULATING SLUICEWAY) CATPIECE
(— SEPARATING LUMBER PILES) STICKER
(— TO BEAT CLOTHES) BATLER BATLET
(— TO DISTEND CARCASS) STEND BACKSET
(— TOGETHER) CLOT BLOCK CLING BALTER CEMENT COHERE COAGMENT
(— TO HOLD BOW) TILLER
(— TO HOLD LOG LOAD) DUTCHMAN
(— TO KEEP ANIMAL QUIET) TWITCH
(— TO MARK CROSSING) BROG
(— TO POKE WITH) POTE
(— TO REMOVE HOOK FROM FISH) GOBSTICK
(— TO STRETCH NET) BRAIL
(— TO STUFF DOLLS) RAMMER
(— TO THROW AT BIRDS) SQUAIL
(— TO TIGHTEN KNOT) WOOLDER
(— UP) COCK
(— USED AS POINTER) FESCUE
(BAMBOO —) LATHI LATHEE
(BASKETRY —) LEAGUE
(BENT —) RIFLE
(COLD —) ICICLE
(FIELD HOCKEY —) BULGER CAMMOCK
(FISHING —) GAD
(FORKED —) GROM GROOM
(HOCKEY —) CAMAN HURLY HOCKEY HURLEY SHINNY CAMMOCK CUMMOCK DODDART
(IRON-POINTED —) VALET
(KIND OF —) PUGIL
(KNOBBED —) BILLET
(LACROSSE —) CROSSE
(LARGE —) MOCK
(MARKING —) LEAD
(NOTCHED —) TALLY
(ODD —) JAY
(POLISHING —) BUFF
(PRAYER —) PAHO
(PRINTER'S —) SHOOTER
(RANGE-FINDING —) STADIA
(ROUND —) DOWEL SPINDLE
(STIRRING —) MUNDLE POOLER SPURTLE POTSTICK SWIZZLER
(STOUT —) BAT COSH LOWDER
(TALLY —) TAIL
(THROWING —) ATLATL HORNERAH
(TOBACCO —) LATH
(WALKING —) CANE KEBBY WADDY JAMBEE JOCKEY KEBBIE WHANGEE ASHPLANT GIBSTAFF
(PREF.) RHABD(O)
STICKER HINGE LABEL STRIP

WAFER HOPPER PASTER BLEEDER CROSSER MOPSTICK STICKLER

STICK-IN STRANDER

STICKINESS GAUM TACK ROPINESS

STICKING ADHERENT ADHESION COHESION COHESIVE

STICKLE DEMUR BOGGLE HAGGLE HIGGLE

STICKLEBACK BAGGIE BANDIE HACKLE GHOSTER PINFISH

STICKLER (— FOR FORMALITY) TAPIST

STICKMAN DEALER

STICKS BOONIES BOONDOCKS

STICKUM GLUE PINETAR

STICKY CAB CLAM CLIT ICKY DABBY FATTY GAUMY GLUEY GOOEY GUMMY JAMMY MALMY PUGGY SHORT TACKY TOUGH CLAGGY CLAMMY CLARTY CLINGY CLOGGY GLOPPY PLUCKY SMEARY VISCID VISCOUS ADHESIVE TENACIOUS (PREF.) GLOEO GLOIO

STIFF BUM SAD CARK HARD NASH TRIG BUDGE CLUNG RIGID SOLID STARK STEER STITH STOUR THARF TOUGH BOARDY CLEDGY CLUMSY CLUNCH FORMAL FROZEN PLUGGY STARKY STEEVE STICKY STILTY STOCKY STURDY UNEASY WOODEN ANGULAR BUCKRAM COSTIVE STARCHY STILTED RAMRODDY RIGOROUS STAFFISH (SOMEWHAT —) CARKLED (PREF.) ANKYL(O) TORPI TORPORI

STIFFELIO (CHARACTER IN —) LINA STANKAR RAFFAELE STIFFELIO (COMPOSER OF —) VERDI

STIFFEN GUM SET SIZE BRACE STARK STIFF STRUT TRUSS HARDEN STARCH STOVER CONGEAL STARKEN (— PRICE) HARDEN

STIFFENED FUSED CARKLED

STIFFENER KNEE COUNTER

STIFFENING PUFF DRESS

STIFFNESS KINK RIGOR STARCH BUCKRAM PRIMNESS RIGIDITY SEVERITY (SYMBOL OF —) RAMROD

STIFLE DAMP FUNK SLAY CHOKE CRUSH STIVE STUFF MUFFLE QUENCH FLASKER QUERKEN SMOTHER SCOMFISH STRANGLE SUPPRESS THROTTLE

STIFLED DEAF ETOUFFE

STIFLING CLOSE STIVY SMUDGY POTHERY SMOTHERY

STIGMA BLOT FOIL NOTE SLUR SPOT BRAND ODIUM STAIN TAINT BLOTCH BLEMISH

STIGMATIZE BLOT BRAND DENOUNCE

STILBITE DESMINE

STILE STY STICK TIMBER

STILETTO BODKIN STYLET PIERCER POINTEL

STILL BUT COY LAY YET BODY CALM COSH HUSH LOWN LULL WORM ACCOY CHECK QUIET WHIST HOWEER HUSHED PACIFY QUENCH SETTLE SILENT SOOTHE STATIC SUBDUE WITHAL ALEMBIC

CORNUTE DORMANT HOWEVER PELICAN SILENCE CUCURBIT RECEIVER RESTRAIN STAGNANT STILLERY SUPPRESS (— PART) KELD (PART OF —) HEAD TUBE RETORT CONDENSER

STILLAGE SLOP STILLING STILLION

STILL-HUNT STALK

STILLNESS CALM HUSH REST PEACE LANGUOR SILENCE STATION

STILT KAKI POGO TILT LAWYER PATTEN SCATCH YEGUITA LONGLEGS STILTIFY TRIANGLE

STILTED LOFTY STIFF FORMAL POETIC STILTY POMPOUS

STIMULANT COCA STIM INULA BRACER CINDER FILLIP GINGER HARMAL PHYTIN CAMPHOR CARDIAC OUABAIN REVIVER ADONIDIN AMMONIAC EXCITANT INCITANT LOBELINE PEMOLINE STIMULUS SASSAFRAS WHETSTONE

STIMULATE FAN HOP KEY PEP FUEL GOAD HYPE HYPO MOVE SEED SPUR STIR URGE WHET FILIP IMPEL PIQUE PRIME ROUSE SPARK STING AROUSE BESTIR EXCITE FILLIP INCITE SPIRIT TICKLE UPSTIR ANIMATE ENLIVEN INNERVE INSPIRE PROVOKE QUICKEN SHARPEN ACTIVATE FARADIZE IRRITATE MOTIVATE TITILLATE (FAIL TO —) UNDERWHELM

STIMULATED (ARTIFICIALLY —) HOPPEDUP

STIMULATING PERT SEXY BRISK BRACING PUNGENT EROGENIC EXCITING GENEROUS INCITANT POIGNANT STIRRING (— ANGER) ADRENAL (PREF.) AUXO EXCITO

STIMULATION GINGER IMPETUS (MENTAL —) SPRITE

STIMULUS CUE AURA BROD EDGE GOAD HYPO SPUR STIM STING FILLIP MOTIVE SOURCE BAHNUNG IMPETUS OESTRUS STRESSOR

STING NIP BARB BITE BURN FOIN GOAD SOAK TANG ATTER DEVIL PIQUE PRICK SMART STANG TOUCH NETTLE ACULEUS BUGBITE PIERCER IRRITATE STIMULUS

STINGILY STRAIT SCARCELY

STINGINESS PARSIMONY

STINGING KEEN SMART PEPPERY PIQUANT POINTED PRICKLY PUNGENT ACRIMONY ACULEATE NETTLING POIGNANT SCALDING URTICANT

STINGING ANT KELEP

STINGRAY ANGLER OBISPO SEPHEN TRYGON BATFISH LOPHIID STINGER WAIREPO

STINGY DRY DREE GAIN GAIR HARD MEAN NEAR NIGH CHEAP CLOSE MINGY SCALY TIGHT CHEAPO DRIECH GRIPPY HUNGRY MEASLY NARROW SCABBY SCARCE SCRIMY SKIMPY SKINNY SNIPPY STRAIT CHINCHY CHINTZY COSTIVE

MISERLY NIGGARD PENURIOUS PARSIMONIOUS

STINK FOGO GOAD NIFF PONG STEW SUCK SMELL SMEECH STENCH MEPHITIS (PREF.) BROM(O)

STINKBIRD HOACIN HOATZIN

STINKER RAT BUMMER

STINKING FOUL HIGH FETID PUTID STINKY MALODOROUS

STINKWOOD DOGWOOD

STINT TASK GRIST PINCH SCANT SNAPE SCRIMP SKINCH STINGY TANTUM SCANTLE (SHORT —) SNATCH (WITHOUT —) FREELY

STIPE STEM STALK

STIPEND ANN HIRE ANNAT WAGES SALARY PENSION PREBEND PROVEND COMMENDA

STIPENDIARY BEAK

STIPPLE SPONGE

STIPPLED DOTTED

STIPULATE ARTICLE PROTEST PROVIDE COVENANT

STIPULATION IF ANNEX CLAUSE ARTICLE PREMISE PROVISO STRINGS COVENANT (PL.) TERMS

STIPULE SPINE SHEATH STIPEL STIPULA TENDRIL

STIR DO ADO FAN GOG JEE PUG WAG BEET BUZZ CARD FUSS MOVE PEAL POKE RAUK ROKE TODO WAKE AMOVE BUDGE CHURN CREEP ERECT FUROR HURRY MUDGE POACH QUICH RAISE ROUST SLICE SPARK STING STOOR STURT TEASE TOUCH AROUSE AWAKEN BUBBLE BUSTLE COOLER CRUTCH EXCITE FLURRY GINGER HUBBUB JUMBLE KIAUGH MUDDLE PADDLE POUTER QUINCH QUITCH REMBLE REMOVE ROUNCE STODGE SUMMON TATTER ACTUATE ANIMATE BLATHER CLUTTER COMMOVE FLUTTER PROVOKE STARKLE SWIZZLE TROUBLE SPLUTTER (— ABOUT) KNOCK (— CALICO COLORS) TEER (— DRINK) MUDDLE SWIZZLE (— LIQUID) ROG (— SOIL) CHISEL (— UP) FAN MIX BUZZ DRUM FUSS MOVE PROG ROIL TOSS AMOVE AREAR AWAKE ERECT QUICK ROUSE SNURL SPOOK STOKE TARRY BESTIR BOTHER CHOUSE EXCITE INCITE JOSTLE KINDLE PUDDLE RUMBLE TICKLE UPSTIR AGITATE ANIMATE COMMOVE DISTURB PRODDLE PROVOKE STUDDLE TORMENT UNQUEME DISTRACT ENKINDLE (— UP WITH YEAST) BARM

STIRRER HOG DOLLY ROUSER RUMMAGER

STIRRING RACY ASTIR DEEDFUL ROUSING THRILLY EXCITING PATHETIC

STIRRUP IRON CHAPELET STEELBOW

(PART OF —) EYE PAD TREAD BRANCH (PREF.) STAPED(I)(IO)

STITCH BAR RUN SEW KNIT LOOP PURL WHIP CABLE CLOSE POINT PREEN PUNTO STEEK ACCRUE FESTON SUTURE TRICOT CROCHET POPCORN FAGOTING (— IN) QUILT (— OF CLOTHES) TACK (KIND OF —) FLAME (NEEDLEPOINT —) BARGELLO (SWEATER —) CABLE FAGGOT (TEMPORARY —) TACK (PL.) JOURS FILLING PINWORK

STITCHBIRD IHI

STITCHDOWN SEWROUND

STITCHED BROCHE

STITCHER WHIPPER

STITCHING SERGING FAGOTING STOATING WHIPPING (SUFF.) RHAPHY RRHAPHY

STITCHWORT PAIGLE ALLBONE SNAPPER HEADACHE SNAPJACK SNAPWORT

STITHY STUDY SMITHY STIDDY STUDDY

STOAT VAIR ERMINE WEASEL CLUBSTER FUTTERET WHITRACK

STOCK COP DOG KIN ROD CANT CROP FILL FOND FUND SEED SELL STEM TRIP BLOND BLOOD BROTH CASTE CREAM FLESH HOARD ISSUE PLANT STALE STIRP STORE STUFF TALON BUDGET CHOKER COMMON FUTURE KAFFIR SHARES STOVEN STRAIN SUPPLY CAPITAL DESCENT PILLORY PROSAPY PROVIDE REPLETE RESERVE BONEYARD BOUTIQUE CROSSBAR DIESTOCK GILLIVER GUNSTOCK MAGAZINE MERCHANT ORDINARY SECURITY PROVISIONS (— OF ANCHOR) CROSS (— OF BREEDING MARES) STRUDE (— OF FOOD) FARE (— OF GRAIN) COP (— OF INDIVIDUALS) CLONE (— OF MORPHEMES) LEXICON (— OF WEAPONS) ARSENAL (— OF WHIP) CROP (— OF WINE) CELLAR (— SOLD SHORT) BEAR (— UNIT) SHARE (FARM —) BOW (LANGUAGE —) SALISH SIOUAN BOROTUKE (MEAT —) BLOND BOUILLON (PLASTIC —) BISCUIT (RAILROAD —) GRANGER (PL.) FOODS CIPPUS HARMAN TIMBER CATASTA KAFFIRS (PREF.) STIPI(T)(TI) STIPULI STIRP (SUFF.) STIPULAR STIPULATE

STOCKADE BOMA PEEL ETAPE ZAREBA BARRIER TAMBOUR STOCKADO

STOCK EXCHANGE BOURSE COULISSE

STOCKFISH STOCK LUTFISK TITLING SPELDING SPELDRON (PREF.) SALPI

STOCKING HOSE SOCK SHANK

STOCK CALIGA MOGGAN SCOGGER
SHINNER BOOTHOSE
(— PATTERN) ARGYLE
(FOOTLESS —) HOGGER HUSHION
(PROTECTIVE —) SPATTEE
(SOLELESS —) TRAHEEN
(PL.) HOSE NYLONS BUSKINS
BOOTHOSE
STOCKJOBBING AGIOTAGE
STOCKWORK CARBONA
STOCKY FAT COBBY DUMPY GROSS
SQUAT STOUT CHUMPY CHUNKY
DUMPTY STUBBY STUGGY STUNTY
BUNTING COMPACT HEAVYSET
STOCKISH THICKSET
STODGY STUFFY STUGGY
BOURGEOIS
STOGIE CIGAR
STOIC STOLID APATHETIC
IMPASSIVE
STOKEHOLD FIREROOM
STOKER FIREMAN BLOCKMAN
STOLE BOA FUR STAW ARMIL
ORARY ARMILLA ORARION
PALATINE
STOLEN HOT BENT INOME STOUN
FURTIVE
(— GOODS) MAINOUR
STOLID BEEFY BOVINE CLUMSE
STUPID WOODEN CLUMPST
DEADPAN PASSIVE
STOLIDITY MORGUE
STOLON WIRE SOBOL SOBOLE
SOLENIUM
STOMA PORE OPENING OSTIOLE
STOMACH MAW CROP GUTS KYTE
MARY POKE READ TANK WAME
WOMB BINGY BROOK GORGE
GROUF HEART TUMMY BINGEE
BINGEY BONNET CROPPY GEBBIE
PECHAN VENTER CONCOCT
CRAPPIN GIZZARD ABOMASUM
(— OF ANIMAL) CRAW
(— OF CALF) VELL
(— OF FOWLS) CRAW
(— OF RUMINANT) READ RUMEN
BONNET OMASUM PAUNCH
ABOMASUM MANIFOLD RODDIKIN
RETICULUM
(PIG'S —) JAUDIE
(PREF.) GASTER(O) GASTR(I)(O)
RUMENO
(SUFF.) GASTER GASTRIA
STOMACHACHE FANTAD GULLION
STOMACHER GIMP TRUSS ECHELLE
PLACARD POITREL FOREPART
STOMACHIC COTO CORNUS
BITTERS CALUMBA GENTIAN
LUPULIN ANTHEMIS
STOMATITIS NOMA
STONE DAM GEM RAG BOND DUCK
FLAG HERD KLIP KNAR MARK PELT
ROCK STEN TRIG BAUTA CAPEL
CHUCK DRAKE GUARD LAPIS
PAVER PITCH SCRAE SCREE SNECK
STANE ASHLAR BEDDER BENBEN
CEPHAS CHATON CLOSER COBBLE
GAMAHE GIBBER HEADER JUMPER
LEDGER MARVER METATE MULLER
NUTLET PEEVER PINNER RUNNER
SUMMER TORSEL ANGRITE
CALLAIS DINGBAT DONNOCK
DORNICK GLIDDER KNEELER

KNICKER PERPEND PITCHER
PUTAMEN RATCHEL STANNER
SURFACE THROUGH BAETULUS
CABOCHON DENDRITE EBENEZER
HAGSTONE LAPIDATE LAPILLUS
LAPSTONE MACEHEAD MONOLITH
NAKHLITE SKEWBACK TOPSTONE
(— ADHERING TO LEAD ORE) KEVEL
(— AS AMULET) HAGSTONE
(— AS IT COMES FROM QUARRY)
RUBBLE
(— AS ROAD MARKER) LEAGUE
(— AT DOOR) RYBAT
(— BLOCK) ASSIZE
(— FOR GLASS-ROLLING) MARVER
(— FORMING CAP OF PIER)
SUMMER CUSHION
(— FOR MOUNTING HORSE)
MONTOIR
(— HARD TO MOVE) SITFAST
(— HEAP) MAN CAIRN
(— IN BLAST FURNACE) DAM
(— IN MEMORY OF DEAD)
MONUMENT
(— IN SMALL FRAGMENTS)
RATCHEL
(— IN WALL) PARPEN
(— MARKING CENTER OF WORLD)
OMPHALOS
(— OF FRUIT) COB PIT PAIP COBBE
NUTLET PYRENE PUTAMEN
(— OF PYRAMID SHAPE) BENBEN
**(— PROVIDING CHANGE OF
DIRECTION)** KNEELER
(— RELIC) NEOLITH
(— SET IN RING) CHATON
(—S FROM CRUSHER) TAILINGS
(— SHAPED BY WIND) VENTIFACT
(— SHOT FROM STONE-BOW)
JALET
(—S IN WATER) STANNERS
(— TO DEATH) LAPIDATE
(— USED AS MONUMENT)
MEGALITH
(— USED IN GAME) DUCK DRAKE
(— WITH INTERNAL CAVITY) GEODE
(ARTIFICIAL —) ALBOLITE
(BINDING —) PERPEND THROUGH
PIERPONT
(BOND —) GIRDER KEYSTONE
(BOTTOM — OF ARCH) SPRINGER
(BOUNDARY —) TERM MONUMENT
TERMINUS MERESTONE
(BROKEN —) RIPRAP
(BROKEN — USED FOR ROADS)
BALLAST MACADAM
(BUILDING —) ASHLAR SUMMER
MITCHEL SPERONE
(CARVED —) CAMEO CUVETTE
(CASTING —) TYMP
(CHINA —) PETUNSE
(CLAY —) LECH
(COPING —) SKEW TABLET TABLING
CAPSTONE
(CURLING —) HOG HERD GUARD
LOOFIE POTLID
(CYLINDRICAL —) TAMBOUR
(DESERT —) GIBBER
(DRUID —) SARSEN
(DRYING —) STILLAGE
(EDGING —) SETTER
(FLAT —) PLAT DRAKE LEDGER
(FOUNDATION —) BEDDER

(GLASSY —) TEKTITE
(GLITTERING —) DAZE
(GRAVE —) BAUTA STELE
(GREEN —) CALLAIS
(GRINDING —) METATE MULLER
(HOLY —) BEAR BAETYL
(HOPSCOTCH —) PEEVER PALLALL
(IMAGINARY —) ADAMANT
(KIDNEY —) NEPHRITE
(LAST — IN COURSE) CLOSER
(LOOSE —) GLIDDER
(MAGICAL —) BAETYL
(MEMORIAL —) BAUTA EBENEZER
(METEORIC —) ANGRITE AEROLITE
AEROLITH NAKHLITE
(MIDDLE —) HONEY
(MIDDLE — OF ARCH) KEY
(MONUMENTAL —) LECH
(PAVING —) SET SETT PAVER
REBATE PITCHER
(PHILOSOPHER'S —) ADROP
MAGISTERY TINCTURE
(POLISHING —) SLEEKSTONE
(PRECIOUS —) GEM OPAL RUBY
EWAGE JEWEL TOPAZ ADAMAS
LIGURE SHAMIR ASTERIA ASTRION
CRAPAUD CUVETTE DIAMOND
DIONISE EMERALD GELATIA
JACINTH OLIVINE SARDINE SARDIUS
AMETHYST ASTROITE HYACINTH
PANTARBE SAPPHIRE YDRIADES
(PRECIOUS —S) PERRIE
(REFUSE —) ROACH
(ROCKING —) LOGAN
(SACRED —) BAETYL BAETULUS
(SEMIPRECIOUS —) ONYX SARD
MURRA GARNET CITRINE TIGEREYE
(SHARPENING —) HONE WHET
(SHOEMAKER'S —) LAPSTONE
(SMALL ROUND —) JACK PEBBLE
PELLET
(SOFTENED —) SAP
(STEPPING —) GOAT SARN
(STRATIFIED —) FLAG SLAB
(TALISMANIC —) GAMAHE
(TRANSPARENT —) PHENGITE
(UNSQUARED —) BACKING
(UPRIGHT —) BAUTA MENHIR
MASSEBAH
(PL.) LAPIDES LAPILLI
(PREF.) LAPIDI LAPILLI LITH(O)
(— OF FRUIT) PYREN(O)
(SUFF.) LITE LITH(IC) LITIC
STONEBASS BAFARO WHAPUKU
STONEBOAT DRAY
STONEBOW RODD
STONECHAT CHAT SMICH
SAXICOLA WHEATEAR
STONECROP ORPIN SEDUM ORPINE
PRICKET WALLWORT
STONE CURLEW BUSTARD
STONECUTTER MASON JADDER
LAPICIDE LAPIDARY SCABBLER
SCAPPLER SQUAREMAN
STONED HIGH DRUNK RIPPED
WRECKED
STONEFLY NAIAD
STONEHAND LOCKUP
STONELIKE LITHOID
STONEMAN IMPOSER
STONE MARTEN FOIN
STONEMASON DORBIE
STONE PARSLEY HONEWORT

STONE PINE PINON AROLLA
CEMBRA
STONE ROLLER MAMMY MOMMY
TOTER
STONE TOTER CUTLIPS
STONEWALLER STICKER
STONEWARE GRES BASALT JASPER
BASALTES CANEWARE CHIENYAO
STONEWORKER MASON
STONINESS LAPIDITY PETREITY
STONY RIGID COBBLY PETROUS
LAPIDOSE PETROSAL
STOOGE (THREE —S) MOE CURLY
LARRY
STOOL FORM MORA SEAT STAB
COPPY CROCK HORSE STOLE
TREST BUFFET CREEPY CURRIE
TRIPOD TUFFET COMMODE
CREEPIE KNEELER SHAMBLE
TABORET TRESTLE TUMBREL
BARSTOOL STILLAGE
(CLOSE —) TOM
(CUCKING —) THEW
(LOW —) COPPY SUNKIE CREEPIE
CRICKET
(3-LEGGED —) BUFFET THRESTLE
STOOLBALL TUTBALL
STOOL PIGEON NARK SNITCH
STOOGE STOOLIE DIVULGER
STOOP BOW BEND CURB LEAN
LOUT POKE SINK COUCH COURB
DEIGN STOPE STULP COORIE
CROUCH HUCKLE BALCONY
DECLINE DESCEND RUCKSEY
SUCCUMB
(— OF HAWK) SOUSE
STOOPING DUCK ASTOOP DESCENT
(PREF.) CYPH(O)
STOP HO BAS COG CUT DAM DIE DIT
DOG END HOO KEP LIN MAR NIX
SET BALK BODE BUNG CALK CALL
COOL DROP EASE HALT HELP
HOLD HOOK KILL QUIT REED REST
SIST SNUB SOFT STAP STAY STEM
STOW TEAT TENT TOHO TRIG VIOL
WEAR WHOA ABIDE ABORT AVAST
BASTA BELAY BLOCK BRAKE
BREAK CAULK CEASE CHECK
CHOKE CHUCK CLAMP CLOSE
DELAY EMBAR HITCH LEAVE
MEDIA PAUSE PEACE POINT QUINT
REEST SCOTE SLAKE SPARE SPRAG
STAND STASH STEEK STICK STINT
VIOLA AEOLIN ANCHOR ARREST
ASTINT BIFARA BOGGLE BORROW
CHEESE CLAMOR COLLAR DESIST
DETAIN DEVALL FREEZE GRAVEL
INSTOP LAYOFF MONTRE NASARD
PERIOD SCOTCH SQUASH STANCE
STANCH STIFLE TENUIS TROMBA
BASSOON CAESURA MELODIA
MUSETTE OPPRESS SOJOURN
SQUELCH STATION TERTIAN
TWELFTH ASPIRATA BACKSTOP
BOMBARDE PRECLUDE RECORDER
STOPOVER STOPPAGE SUPPRESS
SURCEASE TENOROON
WALDHORN WITHSPAR
(— AS IF FRIGHTENED) BOGGLE
(— BLAST) DAMP
(— FLOW) BAFFLE STANCH
(— FOR FOOD) BAIT
(— FOR HORSE) BLOW

(**— FROM FERMENTING**) STUM
(**— GROWTH**) BLAST
(**— GUN BREECH**) OBTURATE
(**— IN EARLY STAGES**) ABORT
(**— IN SPEAKING**) HAW
(**— LEAK**) CALK CAULK FOTHER
(**— LIGHT**) RED
(**— ROWING**) EASY
(**— SHORT**) JIB
(**— SPEAKING**) SHUTUP
(**— SWINGING**) SET
(**— UNDESIREDLY**) STALL
(**— UP**) DAM CALK CLOG CLOY FILL PLUG CHINK ESTOP STUFF STANCH OCCLUDE STAUNCH OPPILATE
(**— USING**) SINK
(**— WITH CLAY**) PUG
(**— WORK**) SECURE
(**BRIEF —**) CALL
(**GLOTTAL —**) STOD CATCH STOSS PLOSIVE STOSSTON
(**HARPSICHORD —**) LUTE
(**ROUGH —**) ASPIRATA
(**SUCTION —**) CLICK
(**TEMPORARY —**) PAUSE SUSPEND
(**VOICELESS —**) TENUIS
(**WILL NOT —**) RUNON
(PL.) REEDWORK
(PREF.) ISCH(O)

STOPCOCK BIB BIBB BIBCOCK BALLCOCK TURNCOCK
STOPGAP RESOURCE
STOPLIGHT IMPEDER
STOPOVER LAYOVER
STOPPAGE JAM BLIN ALLAY CHECK HITCH LEATH STICK STINT ARREST DEVALL STASIS EMBARGO GASLOCK REFUSAL SHUTOFF STOPPLE ASTYLLEN SHUTDOWN STOPWORK CESSATION
(**— OF BLOOD**) REMORA
(**— OF DEVELOPMENT**) ATROPHY
(**WORK —**) BUND HARTAL LOWSIN STRIKE
(PREF.) ISCH(O) STASI
(SUFF.) STASIA STASIS
STOPPED PILEATA
(**— WITH HAND**) BOUCHE
STOPPER WAD BUNG CORK PLUG STOP VICE CHECK FIPPLE STANCH BOUCHON CLOSURE SHUTOFF STOPGAP STOPPLE TAMPION STOPCOCK
STOPPERED BOUCHE
STOPPING STAY HOLDUP PHASEOUT STOPPAGE
(**GRADUAL — OF OPERATIONS**) PHASEOUT
STOPPING-PLACE HALT PULLIN OUTSPAN
STORAGE STORE STOWAGE BESTOWAL
STORAX COPALM STACTE STYRAX LORDWOOD
STORE CAVE CRIB DECK FOND FUND HOLD KEEP MART MASS SAVE SHOP STOW TOKO CACHE DEPOT HOUSE HUTCH STASH STOCK UPLAY BAZAAR CELLAR GARNER GIRNEL RECOND STEEVE SUPPLY TIENDA WINKEL ARSENAL BHANDAR BOOTERY GROCERY HARVEST HUSBAND IMBURSE

REPOSIT RESTORE SHEBANG BOUTIQUE EMPORIUM EXCHANGE GARRISON MAGAZINE TENDEJON WAREROOM WARNISON
(**— BEER**) AGE LAGER
(**— CROP**) BARN
(**— FODDER**) ENSILE
(**— IN A MOW**) GOVE
(**— IN LUMBER CAMP**) VAN
(**— IN MOUND**) HOG
(**— KEPT BY CHINESE**) TOKO
(**— OF COMPUTER DATA**) PUSHDOWN
(**— OF FOOD**) LARDER
(**— OF WEALTH**) FORTUNE
(**— POTATOES**) HOG
(**— UP**) FUND POWDER IMBURSE SQUIRREL
(**ABUNDANT —**) MINE
(**BREAD —**) PANARY
(**HIDDEN —**) BIKE
(**LARGE —**) RAFF ANCHOR
(**LIQUOR —**) GROGGERY
(**MARINE —**) DOLLYSHOP
(**MILITARY —**) DUMP
(**MILITARY —S**) DUMP MUNITIONS AMMUNITION
(**READY-TO-EAT FOOD —**) DELI DELLY
(**RESERVE —**) SLUICE
(**RICH —**) ARGOSY
(**SECRET —**) STASH
(**SMALL —S**) SLOPS
(**SUPPLEMENTARY —**) RELAY
(PL.) SAMAN SUPPLY
STORE CHEESE CHEDDAR
STOREHOUSE BIKE GOLA CACHE DEPOT ETAPE STORE ARGOSY ARMORY BODEGA GODOWN PALACE PANARY STAPLE VINTRY ARSENAL BHANDAR CAMALIG CAMARIN GRANARY STORAGE ENTREPOT MAGAZINE SADDLERY TREASURE
(**— FOR BREAD**) PANARY
(**— OF KNOWLEDGE**) THESAURUS
(**RAISED —**) WHATA FUTTAH PATAKA
(**UNDERGROUND —**) PALACE MATTAMORE
STOREKEEPER MERCHANT STOREMAN
STOREROOM CAVE GOLA WARD GOLAH BODEGA CELLAR DINGLE BOXROOM BUTTERY GENIZAH LAZARET POULTRY THALAMUS
(**PAWNBROKER'S —**) LUMBER
STORESHIP FLUTE
STOREY ETAGE ENTRESOL
STORK WADER ARGALA JABIRU SIMBIL HURGILA MAGUARI MARABOU ADJUTANT CICONIID MARABOUT OPENBEAK OPENBILL
(PREF.) CICONI PELANGO
STORKLIKE PELARGIC
STORKSBILL ERODIUM
STORM RIG WAP BLOW HAIL HUFF RAGE RAMP RAND RAVE WIND BLIZZ BLOUT BRASH DEVIL DRIFT FORCE ORAGE STOUR ATTACK BARBER EASTER EXPUGN WESTER BLUSTER BRAVADO CYCLONE DUSTING EQUINOX GAUSTER

PISACHI SHAITAN SNIFTER TEMPEST TORMENT WEATHER BLOWDOWN CALAMITY ERUPTION UPHEAVAL WILLIWAW
(**— OF BLOWS**) STOUR
(**— OF RAGE**) PELT
(**DUST —**) DEVIL DUSTER HABOOB KHAMSIN PEESASH SHAITAN
(**FURIOUS —**) TEMPEST
(**HAWAIIAN —**) KONA
(**SEVERE —**) PEELER SNIFTER
(**VIOLENT —**) FLAW TUFAN CYCLONE SNORTER
STORM DOOR DINGLE
STORMY FOUL GURL RUDE WILD DIRTY DUSTY GURLY GUSTY STARK WINDY WROTH COARSE RUGGED UNFINE WINTRY FURIOUS NIMBOSE RIOTOUS SQUALLY TROUBLE VIOLENT AGITATED BLUSTERY CLUTTERY ORAGIOUS TEMPESTY BOISTEROUS
STORMY PETREL MITTY WITCH SPENCY
STORY GAG SAW DECK DIDO FLAT LORE REDE TALE TEXT YARN ATTIC CRACK ETAGE FABLE FLOOR KATHA PITCH PROSE RECIT SOLAR SPELL SPIEL STAGE STORE CUFFER FABULA FLIGHT PISTLE SCREED SOLLAR ADVANCE HAGGADA HISTORY MANSARD MARCHEN PROCESS RECITAL ANECDOTE DREADFUL ENTRESOL TREATISE NARRATIVE
(**— FROM THE PAST**) LEGEND
(**— OF BEEHIVE**) SUPER
(**— OF BUILDING**) DECK FLAT ATTIC CHESS ETAGE FLOOR PIANO SOLAR STAGE FLIGHT SOLLAR MANSARD ENTRESOL MEZZANINE
(**— OF HEROES**) SAGA
(**ABSURD —**) CANARD
(**ADVENTURE —**) YARN
(**AMUSING —**) BAR DROLLERY
(**BIRTH —**) JATAKA
(**CORNY —**) GROANER
(**DOLEFUL —**) JEREMIAD
(**EERIE —**) CHILLER
(**EXCITING —**) THRILLER
(**FAKE —**) STRING
(**FALSE —**) SHAVE CANARD WHOPPER
(**FISH —**) YARN
(**KIND OF —**) WAR
(**LIFE —**) BIO BIOG
(**LONG, INVOLVED —**) MEGILLA MEGILLAH
(**LOWER —**) DOWNSTAIRS
(**MADE-UP —**) FUDGE
(**MONSTROUS —**) BANGER
(**MORBIDLY SENSATIONAL —**) DREADFUL
(**MYSTERY —**) WHODUNIT
(**NEWS —**) SIDEBAR
(**NEWSPAPER —**) LEAD FEATURE
(**NOTED WAR —**) ILIAD
(**OLD —**) DIDO
(**POMPOUS —**) BRAG
(**PREPOSTEROUS —**) CUFFER
(**RIBALD —**) HARLOTRY
(**SAD —**) TRAGEDY
(**SATIRICAL —**) SKIT

(**SHORT —**) CONTE NOVELLA
(**STALE —**) CHESTNUT
(**UPPER —**) ATTIC GARRET BARBECUE HYPEROON CLERESTORY
(PL.) LEGENDA
STORY BOOK TALEBOOK
STORY OF A BAD BOY (**AUTHOR OF —**) ALDRICH
(**CHARACTER IN —**) BEN TOM BILL EZRA PHIL SETH ADAMS BINNY KITTY MEEKS NELLY SILAS CONWAY MARDEN NUTTER PEPPER ROGERS ABIGAIL ALDRICH CHARLEY COLLINS WALLACE WINGATE GRIMSHAW WHITCOMB TREFETHEN GLENTWORTH
STORY OF AN AFRICAN FARM (**AUTHOR OF —**) SCHREINER
(**CHARACTER IN —**) EM ROSE TANT WALDO SANNIE GREGORY LYNDALL BLENKINS BONAPARTE
STORYTELLER LIAR FIBBER CONTEUR DISCOUR DISSOUR
STOUP STOOP BENITIER
STOUT ALE FAT SAD FIRM STUT TRIM BONNY BROSY BULKY BUNTY BURLY COBBY FRACK FRECK GREAT HARDY KEDGE OBESE PLUMP PODDY PUNCH STARK STERN BONNIE FLESHY PORTER PORTLY PRETTY PYKNIC ROTUND SQUARE STRONG STUFFY STURDY BOWERLY REPLETE FORCIBLE PLUMPISH POWERFUL ROBOREAN STALWART THICKSET
(**— PERSON**) GURK
STOUTHEARTED GOOD VALIANT
STOUTLY FAST HARDILY
STOUTNESS STRENGTH CORPULENCE
STOVE HOD STOW BOGEY CHULA PEACH PLATE CHULHA COCKLE COOKER HEATER PRIMUS BRASERO CHAUFFER FRANKLIN POTBELLY SALAMANDER
(**— FOR DRYING GUNPOWDER**) GLOOM
(**— ON SHIP**) GALLEY
(**PORTABLE —**) SALAMANDER
(**RUSSIAN —**) PEACH
(**WARMING —**) KANGRI
STOVER OVENSMAN
STOW BIN BOX SET CRAM LADE MASS CROWD DOUSE STORE BESTOW COOPER STEEVE DUNNAGE RUMMAGE
STOWAGE BURTON REMBLAI RUMMAGE
STOWAWAY HIDER
STOWED IN
STOWER TOPPER
STOWING BINNING GOBBING
STP DOM
STRABISMUS CAST CROSS SQUINT TROPIA ANOPSIA COCKEYE WALLEYE
STRADDLE SADDLE SPREAD STRIDE BESTRIDE SPRADDLE STRIDDLE
STRADDLER HOE
STRADDLING ATOP
STRAGGLE GAD ROVE TRAIL RAMBLE RANGLE SPRAWL STREEL

TAGGLE WANDER DRAGGLE MEANDER SCRAMBLE SPRANGLE
STRAGGLER STRAY BUMMER
STRAGGLING RAGGED RAGGLED SPRAYEY SCRATCHY VAGULOUS
STRAIGHT BOLT FAIR FULL GAIN NEAT BRANT CLEAN DOGGY FLUSH RIGHT SHORT SPANG ARIGHT DIRECT HONEST STRAIT STRICT BOBTAIL REGULAR UPRIGHT DIRECTLY SEQUENCE
(— AHEAD) ANON PLUMP OUTRIGHT
(— ON) ENDLONG
(— SKINNY) INFO
(— UP AND DOWN) SHEER CLEVER EVENDOWN
(NOT —) WRY AWRY CRAZY
(PREF.) EUTHY ITHO ITHY ORTH(O) RECT(I)
STRAIGHTEDGE LUTE RULE RULER STRICKLE
STRAIGHTEN GAG CONK ORDER STENT EXTEND SQUARE UNKINK COMPOSE RECTIFY STRETCH
(— BY HEATING) SET
(— HAIR) CONK
(— NEEDLE) RUB
(— RAILS) GAG
STRAIGHT-FIBERED BROAD
STRAIGHTFORWARD EVEN PLAT APERT FRANK LEVEL NAKED PLAIN ROUND CANDID DEXTER DIRECT HONEST SIMPLE SQUARE JANNOCK SINCERE EVENDOWN HOMESPUN OUTRIGHT STRAIGHT OPENHEARTED
(NOT —) CROOKED PLAITED
(PREF.) LITI
STRAIGHTFORWARDLY SINGLY SQUARE STRAIGHT
STRAIGHT-THINKING CLEAR
STRAIGHTWAY ANON AWAY RIGHT ARIGHT BEDEEN BEDENE DIRECTLY
STRAIN FIT LAG RAX SIE TAX TRY TUG ACHE BEND CALL DASH DRAG HEAT HEFT LAWN NOTE PULL RACK RANN RICK SILE SINE SOLO SONG VEIN WORK BRUNT CHAFE DEMUR DRAIN FORCE HEAVE PRESS RETCH SHADE SHEAR SIEVE STOCK SURGE TAMMY TOUCH WREST WRICK CLENCH EFFORT EXTEND EXTORT FILTER INTEND KVETCH SPRAIN SPRING STREAK STRESS STRIND THRONG DESCANT DISCANT EUPLOID FATIGUE STRAINT STRETCH STROPHE TENSION TORMENT COLANDER DIAPASON DIATRIBE DIHYBRID FILTRATE SUBBREED
(— EYES) GOGGLE
(— FROM TWISTING) TORSION
(— MILK) SIE SYE
(— OF AN ARCH) THRUST
(— OF CHICKENS) ANCOBAR
(— OF EXCITEMENT) RACKET
(— OF RAILING LANGUAGE) DIATRIBE
(— ON BUGLE) MOT
(— ON HORN) RECHASE RECHEAT
(— THROUGH COLANDER) COIL
(CONCLUDING —) CADENCE

(MELANCHOLY —) DUMP
(MUSICAL —) FIT SOLO POINT
(MUSICAL —S) TOUCH
(MUTANT —) SALTANT
(PREF.) STREMMATO
STRAINED PENT TENSE INTENSE LABORED INTENDED
STRAINER CAGE ROSE SILE RENGE SIEVE STRUM TAMIS TAMMY THEAD SEARCE SEARCH CRIBBLE COLATORY COLATURE SEARCHER
(— OF TWIGS) HUCKMUCK
(COFFEE —) GRECQUE
(MILK —) SAY MILSEY MILSIE
(WICKER —) THEAD THEDE
(PREF.) COLI ETHMO
STRAINING CUTE COILED ASTRAIN INTENSE COLATURE
STRAIT CUT GUT BAND BELT FRET KYLE NECK PACE BRAKE CANAL PHARE PINCH SHARD SOUND ANGUST FRETUM NARROW PLUNGE CHANNEL EURIPUS BOSPORUS JUNCTURE
(IN —S) SET
(LAST —) EXIGENT
(NEWFOUNDLAND —) TICKLER
(PL.) CHOPS PRESS EXTREMES
STRAITEN PINCH SCANT STRAIT
STRAITENED CRIMP NARROW CRIMPED
STRAITJACKET CAMISOLE
STRAITLACED STIFF STUFFY BLUENOSED
STRAKE SHEER COURSE RISING STREAK COAMING SAXBOARD
(PL.) TIRE
STRAMONIUM DEWTRY
STRAND PLY TOP BANK CORE FLAT TOWT WISP BEACH BRAID CLIFF PRAYA READY SHORE LISSOM MAROON SINGLE SLIVER STRAIN STRIKE SUTURE HAIRLINE
(— OF FIBERS) ROVING
(— OF HAIR) LICK SWITCH
(— OF PROTOPLASM) BRIDGE
(— OF TEXTILE) ROVE
(PREF.) CROCO
STRANDED AGROUND ISOLATED
STRANDER EDGER
STRANGE ODD RUM EERY FELL FREM NICE RARE UNCO ALIEN EERIE FREMT FUNNY KINKY NOVEL QUEER UNKET UNKID WOOZY ALANGE FERLIE QUAINT UNIQUE UNKENT UNKIND CURIOUS ERRATIC HEATHEN ODDBALL UNHEARD UNKNOWN UNUSUAL FANCIFUL INSOLENT INSOLITE PECULIAR SELCOUTH SINGULAR UNCOLIKE UNCOMMON UNKENNED UNKINDLY MONSTROUS
(— TO SAY) ODDLY
(PREF.) XEN(O)
STRANGENESS ODDITY
STRANGER COME UNCO UNKO ALIEN GUEST FRENNE GANGER INCOME INMATE FUIDHIR INCOMER UNCOUTH MALIHINI OUTCOMER PEREGRIN OUTLANDER
(SUFF.) XENE XENOUS XENY

STRANGLE CHOKE GRAIN GRANE SNARL WORRY STIFLE GARROTE QUACKLE GARROTTE JUGULATE THROTTLE
STRANGLEHOLD CHANCERY STRANGUL
STRANIERA, LA (CHARACTER IN —) ALAIDE ARTURO ISOLETTA VALDEBURGO
(COMPOSER OF —) BELLINI
STRAP BAR TUG BAND BELT CLIP CURB GIRD HASP RIDE RIEM BRACE CHEEK GIRTH GUIGE PATTE RIDER RISER SABOT SLING STROP THONG TRACE VITTA ANKLET BACKER BILLET COLLAR ENARME GARTER HALTER HANGER LAINER LATIGO SANDAL TOGGLE WARROK BABICHE BOWYANG CRIBBER DOLPHIN LANYARD LATCHET LEATHER RIEMPIE STIRRUP TICKLER WEBBING BACKSTAY BRETELLE SQUILGEE TURNBACK WRISTLET
(— AROUND HORSE'S THROAT) CRIBBER
(— AROUND MAST) DOLPHIN
(— FOR SHIELD) GUIGE ENARME BRETELLE
(— IN FLAIL) TAPLING
(— OF BRIDLE) REIN
(— OF SENNIT) BACKER
(— ON HAWK'S LEAD) JESS JESSE SENDAL
(— WITH SLIT END) TAWS TAWSE
(ANKLE —) BRACELET
(CARRYING —) METUMP TUMPLINE
(DOOR —) HASP
(HARNESS —) TRACE
(MINER'S —) RYARD
(SHOE —) BAR
(STIRRUP —S) CHAPELET
(TIE —) SHANK
(U-SHAPED —) STIRRUP
(PL.) LADDER
(PREF.) LIGUL(I)
STRAP FERN LONGLEAF
STRAPHANGER STANDEE COMMUTER
STRAPPER SPLICER
STRAPPING SWANK BOUNCING CHOPPING SLAPPING SWANKING
STRAP-SHAPED LORATE LIGULAR LIGULATE
STRATA EOCENE TERRANE UNDERAIR
(— OF COAL) MEASURES
STRATAGEM JIG COUP LOCK RUSE TRAM TURN WILE ANGLE DRAFT FETCH FRAUD GUILE JOKER KNACK TRAIN TRICK WREST BLENCH DECEIT DEVICE HUMBUG POLICY TRAPAN TREPAN WOIDRE WRENCH FINESSE SLEIGHT ARTIFICE CONTOISE FARFETCH INTRIGUE LIRIPIPE LIRIPOOP PRACTICE PRACTISE QUENTISE STRATEGY TRICKERY MOUSETRAP
(INDIRECT —) FEELER
STRATEGY GAME FINESSE
(MANUFACTURING —) KANDAN
STRATIFICATION BEDDING
STRATIFIED BEDDED VARVED

STRATIFORM LAYERED
STRATONICE (FATHER OF —) DEMETRIUS
(HUSBAND OF —) SELEUCUS
(MOTHER OF —) PHILA
STRATUM BED CAP CUT LAY RIB FAST LAIN SEAM TIER COUCH ELITE FLOOR LAYER LEDGE SHELF TABLE COUCHE GIRDLE GRAVEL LAYING LISSOM PINNEL AQUAFER AQUIFER ENTIRIS FISHBED SUBSOIL UPRIGHT AQUIFUGE FAHLBAND SUBGRADE
(— OF COAL) BENCH
(— OF FIRECLAY) THILL
(— OF PALE COLOR) FAHLBAND
(— OF SANDSTONE) PINNEL
(— OF SOIL) SOD
(— OF STONE) GIRDLE
(SOCIAL —) CUT
(THIN —) SEAM LENTIL
STRAW BAKU GLOY MOTE REED RUSH TOYO WASE HAULM PEDAL SHILF STALK STREW YEDDA FESCUE FETTLE PANAMA RIZZOM SIPPER TUSCAN BANGKOK SABUTAN STUBBLE WINDLIN STRAMMEL
(— CUT FINE) CHAFF
(— FOR MAKING HATS) SENNIT BANGKOK LEGHORN SABUTAN
(— FOR THATCHING) YELM
(— MEASURE) KEMPLE
(— TO PROTECT PLANTS) MULCH
(BROKEN —) BHUSA BHOOSA
(COOKERY —S) PAILLES
(PLAITED —) SENNIT
(WAXED —) STRASS
(PREF.) CARPHO
STRAWBERRY BERRY DUNLAP FRAISE RUNNER HAUTBOY FRUTILLA HAUTBOIS KLONDIKE ROSACEAN
(— JAR) PLANTER
STRAWBERRY BUSH WAHOO EUONYMUS EVONYMUS FISHWOOD
STRAWBERRY FINCH AMADAVAT AVADAVAT
STRAWBERRY SHRUB BUBBY COWBERRY
STRAWBERRY TOMATO PHYSALIS BLADDERCHERRY
STRAWBERRY TREE ARBUTUS
STRAY ERR ODD FALL RAVE ROVE WAFF WAIF WALK DRIFT RANGE TRAIK VAGUE WAVER ESTRAY RANGLE SWERVE VAGARY WANDER WILDER DEVIATE FORLORN STRAYER DIVAGATE MAVERICK STRAGGLE
STRAYING ASTRAY ERRANT ABERRANT VAGATION
STREAK PAY RAY BAND SEAM VEIN WALE FLAKE FLECK FLICK FREAK GARLE GLADE SLASH FACULA SMUDGE STRAIN STRAKE STREAM STRIPE FLECKER SPRAING STIPPLE DISCOLOR TRAVERSE
(— CAUSED BY BLOOD) VIBEX
(— IN FABRIC) CRACK SHINER
(— IN GLASS) SKIM
(— IN HAIR) BLAZE

(— IN SKY) ICEBLINK
(— IN WOOD) ROE
(— OF BLUBBER) BLANKET
(— OF LIGHT) STREAM
(— ON BEAST'S FACE) RACE RATCH
(— ON SURFACE OF SUN) FACULA
(—S FROM PLANE) CONTRAIL
(—S IN ROCK) SCHLIEREN
(— WITH FINE STRIPES) LACE
(BACTERIOLOGICAL —) STROKE
(LOSING —) SLUMP
(RAISED —) WEAL
(THEATRICAL —) HAM
(WHITE —) SHIM
STREAKED ROWY LACED HAWKED
SMEARY BRINDLE BROCKED
BROOKED FINCHED SPARKED
STRIPED WHIPPED BRINDLED
IRONSHOT PINROWED
STREAKY ROWY SCOVY STREAKED
STREAM EA PUP RIO RUN BECK
BURN FLOW FLUX FORD GILL
GOTE KHAL KILL LAKE OOZE POUR
PUIT PURL RILL SICK SIKE SILE
SPIN TIDE BACHE BATCH BAYOU
BOGUE BOURN BROOK CREEK
DRILL DRINK FLARE FLASH FLEAM
FLOOD FLOSS FLUOR FRESH
GHYLL NYMPH PRILL RITHE RIVER
SWAMP TCHAI TRAIN ARROYO
BANKER BOURNE BRANCH BURNIE
CANADA COULEE FILLER RANDOM
GUZZLE OUTLET PIRATE RANDOM
RUNDLE RUNNEL SLUICE SPRUIT
STRAND STRONE CHANNEL
CURRENT DRIBBLE FLUENCE
FRESHET RIVULET TRICKLE
AFFLUENT INFLUENT MILLSTREAM
(— ALONG) SLIDE
(— FULL TO TOP) BANKER
(— OF AIR OR SMOKE) PEW
(— OF ELECTRODES) BEAM
(— OF LAVA) COULEE
(— OF SIRUP) THREAD
(— OF SPEECH) STRAIN
(— OUT) BREAK
(FLOWING —) NYMPH
(HIGH-SPEED —) JET
(MYTHOLOGICAL —S) ELIVAGAR
(SLOW —) OOZE
(SLOW-MOVING —) POW
(SLUGGISH —) LANE
(SMALL —) BECK LAKE SIKE DRAFT
RITHE COULEE SICKET SQUIRT
STRIPE DRAUGHT GRINDLE
(THIN —) TRICKLE TRICKLET
(TIDAL —) COVE SEAPOOSE
(TRANSIENT —) RILL
(TRICKLING —) DRILL
(TURBID —) DRUVE
(UNDERGROUND —) AAR SWALLET
(VIOLENT —) TORRENT
(WEAK —) DRIP
(PREF.) AMNI FLUVI
(— OF LAVA) RHYACO
STREAMER FLAG VANE FALLAL
GARTER GUIDON LAPPET PENCEL
PENNON PINNET SCROLL SIMPLE
WIMPLE BANDEROL FILAMENT
(— OF MOSS) WEEPER
(— ON HEADDRESS) LIRIPIPE
(PAPER —S) CONFETTI

STREAMING SLUICY ASTREAM
CRINITE CYCLOSIS DOWNPOUR
STREAMLET RILL RILLET RUNDLE
RUNLET RUNNEL RIVULET
STREAMLINE SIMPLIFY
(— FLOW) LAMINAR
STREAMLINED CLEAN SLEEK
STREET ROW RUE WAY CHAR
DRUM GATE PAVE STEM TOBY
BLOCK BORGO CALLE CANON
CHAWK CORSO DRIVE PASEO
AVENUE BOWERY CANYON
CAUSEY CIRCLE RAMBLA POULTRY
TERRACE THROUGH ARTERIAL
BROADWAY BYSTREET CHAUSSEE
CONTRADA PROSPECT
(— IN BARCELONA) RAMBLA
(— IN FLORENCE) BORGO
(MAIN —) CHAWK CHOWK
TOWNGATE
(NARROW —) CHAR ALLEY CHARE
RUELLE
(PRINCIPAL —) ARTERY
(QUIET —) CULDESAC
(SIDE —) HUTUNG
STREETCAR TRAMCAR TRAMWAY
ELECTRIC
STREET CLEANER ORDERLY
CLEANSER
STREET CLEANING SLOPPING
STREET SCENE (AUTHOR OF —)
RICE
(CHARACTER IN —) SAM ROSE
FRANK STEVE KAPLIN SANKEY
WILLIAM MAURRANT
STREETWALKER BULKER CRUISER
STRENGTH EL ARM VIR BEEF DRAW
GRIP GUTS HEAD HORN IRON MAIN
THEW BRAWN CRAFT ETHAN FIBER
FIBRE FORCE HEART JUICE MIGHT
NERVE POWER SINEW VIGOR
ENERGY FOISON MAUGHT MUSCLE
STARCH VIRTUE ABILITY AFFORCE
COURAGE PROWESS STAMINA
STHENIA CAPACITY FIRMNESS
VALIDITY PUISSANCE
(— OF ACID OR BASE) AVIDITY
(— OF ALE) STRIKE
(— OF CARD HAND) BODY
(— OF CHARACTER) GRISTLE
(— OF CURRENT) AMPERAGE
(— OF GRASP) GRIP
(— OF SOLUTION) TITER TITRE
(— OF SPIRITS) PROOF
(— OF TEA) DRAW
(— OF WILL) BACKBONE
(— OF WINE) SEVE
(SUPERIOR —) PREVALENCE
(PREF.) CRATO DYNAM(I)(O)
ISCHY(O)
(SUFF.) DYNAMIA DYNAMOUS
STRENGTHEN IMP ABLE BACK BIND
FIRM FRAP HELP PROP SOUD STAY
BRACE CLEAT FORCE SINEW STEEL
THRAP TONIC TRUSS ANNEAL
ASSURE DEEPEN ENDURE ENFIRM
ENFORT GABION HARDEN INTEND
MUNIFY MUNITE NEEDLE SETTLE
STRING STRONG AFFORCE
BUCKRAM COMFORT CONFIRM
ENFORCE FASCINE FORTIFY
NERVATE QUICKEN RAMPIRE
SUPPORT THICKEN BUTTRESS

ENERGIZE ENTRENCH HEIGHTEN
ROBORATE
STRENGTHENED BULLED
BRANDIED
STRENGTHENING BRACING
ROBORANT
STRENGTHLESS DOWLESS
STRENUOUS HARD EAGER
ARDUOUS WILLING VIGOROUS
STREPHON (BELOVED OF —) CHLOE
STREPSIPTERON STYLOPS
STRESS HIT BIRR BRUNT ICTUS
PINCH SHEAR ACCENT STRAIN
THRONG TENSION CENTROID
DOWNBEAT EMPHASIS PRESSURE
(— OF SOUND) LENGTH
(METRIC —) BEAT
(SYLLABIC —) ARSIS
STRESSED TONIC STRONG
STRETCH EKE LAG LIE RAX RUN
BEAT DRAW LAST MAIN PASS
RACK REAM ROLL RYKE SPAN
TEND BOARD BURST FETCH RATCH
RETCH SIGHT SPELL STENT SWAGE
VERGE EXTEND LENGTH SMOOTH
STRAIN STRAKE STREEK DISPLAY
DISTEND EXPANSE SPELDER
ELONGATE LENGTHEN STRAIGHT
(— CLOTH) TENTER
(— FORCIBLY) RACK
(— FORTH) REACH PORRECT
PRETEND PROTEND
(— INJURIOUSLY) SPRAIN
(— IRREGULARLY) TRAIL
(— LEATHER) DRAFT STAKE
DRAUGHT
(— METAL) FORM
(— OF ARMS) FATHOM
(— OF BROKEN WATER) RIP
(— OF GROUND) BRECK
(— OF INTERVAL) CARSE
(— OF LAND) SWALE COMMON
GALLOP PARCEL COMMONS
(— OF OPEN COUNTRY) RANGE
(— OF ROAD) SIGHT
(— OF SEA) CHOP
(— OF TIME) TIFF
(— OF WALL) CURTAIN
(— OF WATER) GLIDE LEVEL LOGIN
FAIRWAY
(— OF WORK) YOKE
(— OUT) GROW SPIN REACH STENT
STRUT TWINE INTEND OUTLIE
SPRAWL SPREAD SPRING DISTEND
OUTSPAN PORTEND ELONGATE
(— ROPE) WARP
(— SPRAWLINGLY) STRAGGLE
(— THE NECK) CRANE
(— THE WINGS) MANTLE
(CONTINUOUS —) RUN
(GRASSY —) DRINN
(LEVEL —) LAWN
(PREF.) TANY TASI TEN(O)
TENONT(O) TETANI TETANO TINO
(SUFF.) EURYSIS
STRETCHABLE TENSILE
STRETCHED PROSTRATE
(— OUT) PORRECT PROJECT
PROLATE ELONGATE EXTENDED
(TENSELY —) TAUT TORT STIFF
STRETCHER COT STENT GURNEY
LITTER ANGAREP TROLLEY
ANGAREEB BRANCARD STRAINER

STRETCHING
(SUFF.) ECTASIA ECTASIS
STREW BED SOW CLOT DUST LARD
SPEW BESET STRAW STRAY
STROW CARPET LITTER SPREAD
BESTREW SCATTER SKINKLE
SPARKLE
(— WITH BULLETS) SPRAY
STREWED BESPRENT
STREWING SEME
STREWN DOTTED BESPRENT
STRIA CORD STRIOLA DRAGLINE
STRIOLET
STRIATE VEIN
STRIATION STREAK STRIGA
STRICKEN STREAKED
STRICKER TIPPLER
STRICKLE SWEEP STRIKER
STRICT HARD TAUT TRUE CLOSE
EXACT HARSH RIGID STARK STERN
TIGHT GIUSTO SEVERE STRAIT
STRONG ASCETIC AUSTERE
PRECISE REGULAR DISTRICT
RESTRICT RIGOROUS STRINGENT
(NOT —) LAX SCIOLTO
STRICTLY NARROW STRAIT
CLOSELY PROPERLY
STRICTNESS RIGOR RIGIDITY
RIGORISM SEVERITY
STRIDE LAMP SAIL STEP FLOAT
SKELP SPANG STEND STRUT
LAMPER STROAM STROKE
STROME BESTRIDE POINTING
STRIDDLE
(— ALONG) LAMP
(— EXULTANTLY) GALUMPH
GALLUMPH
(— LOFTILY) STALK
(— PURPOSEFULLY) SLING
STRIDENT HARD HARSH BRASSY
GLASSY SHRILL GRATING
RAUCOUS YELLING GRINDING
STRIDULATE CHIRP PITTER
STRIFE TUG WAR WIN BATE FEUD
HOLD PLEA BRIGE CHEST FLITE
JEHAD JIHAD NOISE STOUR
STROW STRUT STURT BARRAT
BICKER BRIGUE DEBATE ESTRIF
MUTINY STRIVE BARGAIN CONTECK
CONTEST DISCORD DISPUTE
HURLING QUARREL CONFLICT
CONTRAST DISPEACE STRUGGLE
CONTENTION
(AUTHOR OF —) GALSWORTHY
(CHARACTER IN —) ENID JOHN
ANNIE DAVID EDGAR SIMON
ANTHONY FRANCIS HARNESS
ROBERTS UNDERWOOD
(CIVIL —) STASIS
STRIGIL COMB SCRAPER
STRIKE GO BAT BOB BOP BOX BUM
COB CUE DAD DUB GET HAB HIT
JOB JOW LAM LAY PUG RAP WAP
ABRE BAFF BEAK BEAT BELT BIFF
BILL BLAD BLIP BUFF BUMP CHAP
CLUB COIN COPE COSH CUFF DING
DINT DONG DUNT FALL FANG FIRK
FLAP FLOG FRAP GIRD GOWF
GRAB HACK HURT JOWL KILL KNEE
LASH LILT LUSH MARK NAIL PAIK
PASH PLAT PUCK ROUT SLAM SLAP
SLAT SLAY SLOG SLUG SOCK SPAR
SPAT SWAP SWAT SWIP TAKE

WHAP WHOP WIPE ZONK ANGLE
BATON CATCH CHECK CHIME
CHINK CLOUT CLUNK CRACK
CRUNT DEVEL DOUSE DOWSE
DRIVE DUNCH FETCH FILCH FILIP
FLAIL KNOCK PANDY PASTE POKER
POTCH SABER SKELP SKITE SLOSH
SMACK SMITE SNICK SOUND
SPANK SQUAP STAMP STEEK
SWACK SWEEP SWIPE SWISH
THROW WHALE WHANG ACOUPE
AFFECT AFFRAP ALIGHT ATTAIN
BATTER BOUNCE BUFFET COURSE
DUNDER FETTLE FILLIP HAMMER
INCUSE INCUTE KEEPER SLOUGH
STOUSH STRICK STRIPE SWITCH
THRASH WALLOP BEARING
FLYFLAP IMPINGE KNUCKLE
PERCUSS STRIKER TURNOUT
WHAMPLE WILDCAT STOPPAGE
STOPWORK STRAMASH STRICKLE
(— **ABOUT)** FLOP
(— **AGAINST)** RAM BANG STUMP
ASSAULT COLLIDE
(— **AND REBOUND)** CAROM
(— **A WICKET)** BREAK
(— **CRICKET BALL)** EDGE
(— **DOWN)** LAY FALL SLAY WEND
FLASH FLOOR AFFLICT SIDERATE
(— **DUMB)** DUMFOUND
(— **FEET TOGETHER)** HITCH
(— **FORCIBLY)** GET CLOUT DEVEL
SLASH
(— **GENTLY)** PAT
(— **GOLF BALL)** HOOK DRIVE
SCLAFF
(— **GROUND IN GOLF)** BAFF DUFF
(— **HEAVILY)** BASH DUNT DUSH
FLOP SLUG CLUMP SLOUGH
CLOBBER
(— **IN CURLING)** WICK
(— **LIGHTLY)** BOB DAB SPAT FLICK
(— **OF LOCK)** KEEPER STRIKER
(— **ON HEAD)** COP NOBBLE
(— **OUT)** FAN DELE POKE TAKE
CROSS ELIDE CANCEL DELETE
EXPUNGE OUTLASH EXCUDATE
(— **REPEATEDLY)** DRUM LICK
(— **SHARPLY)** CUT SNICK
(— **SMARTLY)** NAP RAP KNAP
(— **TEETH TOGETHER)** GNASH
(— **TOGETHER)** CLASH KNACK
(— **UP)** LILT YERK RAISE
(— **VIOLENTLY)** RIP BASH DING
PASH SOUSE BENSEL
(— **WITH AMAZEMENT)** CONFOUND
(— **WITH BAT)** DRIVE
(— **WITH FEAR)** ALARM ASTONISH
(— **WITH FIST)** PLUG NODDLE
(— **WITH FOOT)** KICK BUNCH SPURN
STAMP
(— **WITH HAMMER)** CHAP JOWL
MELL
(— **WITH HORNS)** BUNT BUTT HOOK
(— **WITH SHAME)** ABASH
(— **WITH SPEAR)** STICK
(— **WITH STICK)** SQUAIL
(— **WITH WHIP)** JERK LASH QUIRK
(— **WITH WONDER)** SURPRISE
(**BOWLING —S)** DOUBLE
(**HUNGER —)** ENDURA
(**LABOR —)** STEEK STICK TURNOUT
WALKOUT

(**LUCKY —)** BONANZA
(**MINING —)** TREND
(**THREE —S)** TURKEY
(PREF.) PLESSI PLEXI TYPTO
STRIKEBREAKER FINK BLACKLEG
STRIKER BATMAN DRUMMER
TURNOUT PULSATOR
STRIKER-OUT SETTER
STRIKING FITTY FRESH SHOWY
VIVID DARING SIGNAL STRONG
SALIENT SKELPIN TELLING
COLORFUL CONFLICT DRAMATIC
FRAPPANT KNOCKOUT SENSIBLE
SIZZLING SPANKING SPEAKING
NOTICEABLE PERCUSSION
PHOTOGENIC
STRING LAG BAND BEND CORD FILE
LACE MEAN PAIR SLIP TAPE TAUM
BRAID BRIDE CHORD POINT SINEW
SNEAD STRAP TWINE CORDON
STRAND TREBLE MINIKIN
LIGATURE RHAPSODY
(— **IN BIRD'S EGG)** CHALAZA
(— **OF BEADS)** ROSARY CHAPLET
NECKLACE
(— **OF CASH)** QUAN TIAO
(— **OF DRUM)** SNARE
(— **OF FIDDLE)** THARM
(— **OF FLAGS)** HOIST
(— **OF INVECTIVE)** TIRADE
(— **OF LOCK)** KEEPER
(— **OF LYRE)** MESE NETE TRITE
HYPATE PARAMESE PARAMETE
(— **OF MUSICAL INSTRUMENT)**
WIRE CHORD DRONE THAIRM
CATLING MINIKIN LICHANOSE
(— **OF ONIONS)** REEVE TRACE
(— **OF PHRASES)** CENTO
(— **OF PROPOSITIONS)** SORITES
(— **OF RAILWAY CARS)** SET
(— **OF SUGAR CRYSTALS)** COB
(— **OF VEGETABLES)** STRAP
(— **OF VERSES)** LAISSE
(— **OF VIOL)** MEAN
(— **OF WAGONS)** RAKE
(— **TOBACCO)** SEW
(— **UP)** KILT
(**BONNET —)** BRIDE
(**E —)** QUINT
(**LEADING —)** BAND
(**OAKUM —)** PLEDGET
(**ORNAMENTAL —)** CORDON
(**PULL —S)** PLUCK
(**SURGICAL —)** LIGATURE
(**VIOLIN —)** THAIRM VIBRATOR
(**WEAVING —)** LEASH
(SUFF.) CHORD(AL)
STRING BEAN SNAP HARICOT
SNAPPER
STRINGCOURSE LEDGE TABLE
CORDON STRING
STRINGENCY RIGOR
STRINGENT HARD RIGID TIGHT
SEVERE STRICT EXTREME
STRINGER BALK BAULK
STRINGHALTED CRAMPY
STRINGY ROPY WOOLY SINEWY
THONGY WOOLLY GARGETY
SINEWED THREADY
STRIP BAR LAG TAG BAND BARE
BEAD BELT BEND BUSK DRIP FUSE
GAGE GAIR HILD HUSK LIST MALL
NAKE NUDE PEEL RAND ROLL

SACK SHIM SKIN TIRL TIRR WELT
CLEAN DRIVE EXUTE FILET FLAKE
FLYPE GAUGE GLEAN GUARD
HARRY LABEL LINER LYNCH PANEL
PLUME REEVE SHEAR SHRED
SKELP SLIPE SPEEL SPOIL STRAP
STROP STRUB SWATH UNGUM
UNRIG BORDER BOXING BRIDGE
COLLAR CULPON DENUDE DEVEST
DIVEST FEELER FILLET FLEECE
LIBBET MATRIX PANUNG REGLET
RUNWAY SCROLL SPLINE STREAK
STRIPE TARGET UNBARE UNBARK
UNCASE BANDAGE BEREAVE
CHANNEL DEPLUME DEPRIVE
DESPOIL DISROBE FEATHER
FLOUNCE LAMBEAU LANGUET
NAILROD PINRAIL PLUNDER
UNCLOAK UNCOVER UNDRESS
BOOKMARK COSSETTE DISARRAY
DISENDOW DISTRUSS FOOTBAND
SEPARATE
(— **ACROSS SAIL)** REEFBAND
(— **A PLANT)** SPRIG
(— **BARK)** PILL
(— **BINDING STALKS TO WALL)**
TACK
(— **BLUBBER FROM WHALE)**
FLENSE
(— **EAR OF CORN)** SILK
(— **FOR DRAWING CURVED LINES)**
SPLINE
(— **FOR GUIDING PLASTER)** BEAD
(— **FOR MAKING TUBE)** SKELP
(— **HANGING AROUND SKIRT)**
FLOUNCE
(— **IN BASKETMAKING)** INSIDES
(— **IN BEEHIVE)** STARTER
(— **IN CANING)** SPLENT SPLINT
(— **IN TYPEWRITER)** DRAWBAND
(— **OF ARABLE LAND)** RIDGE
(— **OF BACON)** LARDON LARDOON
(— **OF CANVAS)** FOOTBAND
(— **OF CLOTH)** LIST PATA RIND
ROON GUARD BANNER DUTCHMAN
(— **OF CORK)** SPREADER
(— **OFF)** TIRL FLIPE FLYPE SLIPE
(— **OF FABRIC)** FLIPPER
(— **OF FAT)** FATBACK LARDOON
(— **OF FEATHERS)** PLUCK PLUME
(— **OF FIELD HOCKEY AREA)** ALLEY
(— **OFF SKIN)** CASE FLAY
(— **OF FUR)** GROTZEN
(— **OF GRASS)** VERGE
(— **OF HIDE)** SPECK DEWLAP
(— **OF LAND)** BUTT LAND RAIK RAIN
RAKE TANG BREAK CREEK SLANG
SLIPE SPONG SCREED SELION
STRAKE STRIPE FURLONG ISTHMUS
CORRIDOR SIDELING
(— **OF LEATHER)** LAY RAND WELT
APRON RANGE THONG BACKSTAY
(— **OF LEAVES)** TWIST
(— **OF LINEN)** SETON
(— **OF MASONRY)** ARCHBAND
(— **OF OFFICE)** BREAK
(— **OF OSIER)** SKEIN
(— **OF PALM LEAF)** CADJAN CAJANG
(— **OF PASTRY)** STRAW
(— **OF PLANKING)** APRON
(— **OF PLASTER)** SCREED
(— **OF PRAIRIE)** COVE
(— **OF PROVISIONS)** FORAGE

(— **OF RANK)** DEGRADE
(— **OF RED CLOTH)** COXCOMB
(— **OF ROADWAY)** LANE
(— **OF RUBBER)** CUSHION
(— **OF SHORE)** LITTORAL
(— **OF TERRITORY)** PANHANDLE
(— **OF TURF)** PARKING
(— **OF UNPLOWED LAND)** GAIR
HADE HEADLAND
(— **OF WATER)** INLET
(— **OF WOOD)** LAG LAT LATH LIST
SHAW SLAT WELT CHINK CLEAT
STAVE BATTEN INWALE RADDLE
REEPER REGLET SPLINE SPLINT
FOOTING FURRING STICKER
TRACKER FOOTLING SPLINTER
(— **ON FOLDING DOORS)** ASTRAGAL
(— **ON PRINTER'S GALLEY)** LEDGE
(— **ON SQUASH COURT)** TELLTALE
(— **ON TIRE)** CHAFER
(— **SEPARATING LINES OF TYPE)**
LEAD REGLET
(— **WORN ON ARM)** MANIPLE
(**ARMOR —)** SPLENT SPLINT
(**BOUNDARY —)** PERIMETER
(**CAMOUFLAGING —)** GARI AND
(**COMIC —)** FUNNY
(**CONSTRUCTION —S)** LAGGING
(**CORSET —)** BUSK
(**DEPENDENT —)** LAMBEAU
(**DIVIDING —)** CLOISON
(**ELECTROPHORETIC —)** ZYMOGRAM
(**FASTENING —)** TACK
(**FRIED —)** POPADUM POPPADUM
(**HORSESHOE-SHAPED —)** BAIL
BALE
(**IRON IN —S)** NAILROD
(**LANDING —)** RUNWAY
(**MARINATED —)** FAJITA
(**MEDIAN —)** MALL
(**NARROW —)** SEAM SLAT SLIP TAPE
REEVE STRAKE
(**PAPER —)** ORIHON
(**PERFORATED —)** LAG
(**PROJECTING —)** FEATHER
(**RAISED —)** RIDGE
(**SPACING —)** REGLET
(**STRENGTHENING —)** BEND
(**THATCHING —)** LEDGER
(**UNPLOWED —)** BALK LINCH
LINCHET LYNCHET
STRIPE BAR RAY BAND BEND LIST
PALE SLAT TRIM WALE WEAL
WELT ZONE FLECK PLAGA STRIA
STRIP SWATH VITTA WHEAL
BORDER CLAVUS COTICE FRENUM
LADDER RIBBON STRAKE STREAK
STREAM COTTISE SPRAING
MUSTACHE TRAVERSE
(— **OF CHEVRON)** ARC
(— **OF COLOR ON CHEEK)** FRENUM
FRAENUM
(— **ON ANIMAL'S FACE)** SNIP BLAZE
(— **ON FABRIC)** CROSSBAR
(— **ON MILITARY SLEEVE)** SLASH
(— **ON ROMAN TUNIC)** LATICLAVE
(— **ON SHIELD)** ENDORSE
(**ENCIRCLING —)** ZONE
(**PURPLE —)** CLAVUS
(**SET OF —S)** BAR
STRIPED BANDY PALED PIRNY
RAWED RAYED ROWED WALED
ZONED BARRED CORDED LISTED

PIRNED BROCKED TIGROID
VITTATE FASCIATE STRIPPED
(**— CROSSWISE**) BAYADERE
STRIPED BASS ROCKFISH
SERRANID
STRIPED MAPLE DOGWOOD
STRIPING HAIRLINE
STRIPLIGHT BORDER
STRIPLING LAD SLIP STIRRA
YONKER SPAUGHT YOUNKER
SKIPJACK SPRINGAL SHAVELING
STRIPPED BARE NUDE NAKED
HUSKED PICKED PLUMED
UNPEELED
STRIPPER STEMMER SPRIGGER
STRIPPING STROKINGS
(PL.) JIBBINGS
STRIPTEASE (RELATING TO —)
EXOTIC
STRIPTEASER STRIPPER ECDYSIAST
STRIVE AIM HIE TEW TRY TUG DEAL
FEND PAIN TOIL WORK BANDY
DRIVE EXERT FIGHT FORCE LABOR
PRESS BRIGUE BUCKLE BUFFET
DEBATE INTEND PINGLE STRAIN
STRIKE AGONIZE BARGAIN
CONTEND CONTEST DISPUTE
ENFORCE SCUFFLE CONTRAST
ENDEAVOR PURCHASE STRUGGLE
(**— AFTER**) SEEK FOLLOW CANVASS
(**— AGAINST**) RESIST
(**— FOR SUPERIORITY**) VIE KEMP
(**— IN OPPOSITION**) RIVAL CONTEND
(**— TO EQUAL**) EMULATE
(**— TO OBTAIN**) FOLLOW
(**— TO OVERTAKE**) ENSUE
STRIVING NISUS HORMIC STRIFT
CONATUS CONATION
STRIX SYRNIUM
STROBILE BUR BELL BURR CHAT
CONE BRUSH
STROKE BAT COY CUT DAB FIT JOW
ODD PAT PET POP RUB BAFF BEAT
BLOW CHAP CHOP CLAP COUP
CUFF DASH DENT DING DINT DIRD
DRAW DUNT EDGE FIRK FLAP FLEG
FLIP FLOP FUNG GOWF HAND
HURT JERK JOWL KERF LASH LICK
NACK PAIK PEAL PECK SHOT SMIT
SWAP TILT TIRE TUCK WELT WHAP
WIPE BRUSH CHASE DOUSE
DOWSE DRAFT FLACK FLICK
FORCE HATCH ICTUS MINIM
PANDY PULSE SHOCK SLASH SLING
SLIVE SLOSH STRIP SWEEP SWING
SWIPE THROW TOUCH TRAIT TRICE
WHACK CARESS CENTER FONDLE
FOOZLE GENTLE GLANCE PLAGUE
PLUNGE SMOOTH STRAIK STRAKE
STRIKE STRIPE DRAUGHT OUTLASH
SOLIDUS VIRGULE APOPLEXY
BACKHAND DRUMBEAT FOREHAND
INSTROKE SCORCHER
(**— IN KEEPING TIME**) TACT
(**— IN PAINTING**) HAND
(**— IN PENMANSHIP**) MINIM
(**— IN TENNIS**) LET LOB BOAST
CHASE SMASH BRICOLE BACKHAND
FOREHAND OVERHAND
(**— OF A LETTER**) DUCT STEM SERIF
POTHOOK CROSSBAR
(**— OF ART**) TOUCH
(**— OF BAD FORTUNE**) CLAP

(**— OF BELL**) JOW BELL JOWL
KNELL TELLER
(**— OF BOW**) SCRAPE
(**— OF FORTUNE**) CAST BREAK
BONZER FELICITY
(**— OF LUCK**) HIT FLUKE STRIKE
TURNUP CAPTION
(**— OF MISFORTUNE**) SISERARY
(**— OF SCYTHE**) SWATH SWATHE
(**— OF SHEARS**) SNIP
(**— OF WIT**) FLIRT
(**— OF WORK**) BAT CHAR
(**— ON THE PALM**) LOOFIE
(**— WITH CLAW**) CLOYE
(**BILLIARDS —**) SPOT STUN FLUKE
FORCE MASSE HAZARD
(**CONNECTING —**) LIGATURE
(**CRICKET —**) CUT GLANCE
(**CROQUET —**) ROQUET
(**CURLING —**) INWICK
(**CUTTING —**) GIRD
(**DOUBLE SPINNING —**) DRAW
(**DRUM —**) DRAG
(**FINISHING —**) NOBBLER
(**GOLF —**) ODD BAFF BISK HOOK
LIKE BLAST SLICE BISQUE FOOZLE
SCLAFF APPROACH
(**HOCKEY —**) JOB SCOOP
(**JERKY —**) STAB
(**LIGHTNING —**) BOLT
(**MEDICAL —**) ICTUS APOPLEXY
(**MUSICAL —**) TACT
(**ORNAMENTAL —**) FLOURISH
(**QUICK —**) FLIP
(**SKATING —**) EDGE MOHAWK
CHOCTAW
(**SMART —**) FIRK
(**SOOTHING —**) COY
(**SWIMMING —**) CRAWL TRUDGEN
BUTTERFLY DOGPADDLE
SIDESTROKE
(**SWINGING —**) HEW
(**SWORD —**) MONTANTO
(PREF.) BOLO PLEGA PLEGO
(SUFF.) BOLA BOLE BOLIC BOLISM
BOLIST PLEGIA PLEGY PLEXIA
STROLL JET IDLE ROAM ROVE
AMBLE ANTER JAUNT RANGE
STRAY TRAIK BUMMEL DACKER
DANDER GANDER LOUNGE
PALMER RAMBLE SOODLE
STROAM STROME TODDLE
WANDER SAUNTER TURNOUT
SPATIATE STRAVAGE STRAVAIG
PERAMBULATE
STROLLER SULKY TRAMP SHULER
FLANEUR SHUILER VAGRANT
BOHEMIAN PUSHCHAIR
STROLLING FLANERIE FUGITIVE
STROMA ECOID OECOID
STRONG FAT FIT HOT FELL FERE
FIRM FORT HALE HANG HARD
HIGH IRON KEEN RANK SURE TRIG
TRIM ACRID BONNY FORCY FRECK
FRESH HARDY HEAVY HUSKY
HUSKY JOLLY LUSTY NAPPY NERVY
ORPED PITHY SHARP SMART SOLID
SOUND STARK STEER STERN STIFF
STOUR STOUT SWITH THEWY
VALID VIVID WIGHT YAULD ARDENT
BRAWNY BUCKRA BUNKUM FEIRIE
FIERCE MIGHTY POTENT PRETTY
ROBUST RUGGED SECURE SEVERE

SINEWY STABLE STANCH STARCH
STURDY WIELDY BOARDLY
BUIRDLY DOUGHTY DURABLE
EXALTED FECKFUL HUFFCAP
HUMMING INTENSE LUSTFUL
NERVOUS POLLENT SKOOKUM
STHENIC ATHLETIC BIDDABLE
MUSCULAR REVERENT ROBOREAN
SPANKING STALWART STIFFISH
VIGOROUS MERACIOUS
(PREF.) TRACHY VALE
STRONGBOX ARCA PETE COFFER
DEEDBOX
STRONGEST EXTREME
STRONGHOLD HOLD KEEP PEEL
PIECE PLACE TOWER CASTLE
WARDER BASTION CITADEL
KREMLIN REDOUBT FASTHOLD
FASTNESS FORTRESS FRONTIER
MUNIMENT STRENGTH
(**— ON STEEP PLACE**) AERY EYRY
AERIE EYRIE
STRONGLY BUT SAD BADLY SWITH
FIRMLY STRONG DURABLY
FRESHLY HEFTILY SOLIDLY
STITHLY STOUTLY HEARTILY
STRONG-SCENTED HIGH RANK
STRONG-SMELLING FOXY
STRONTIUM SULPHATE
ACANTHIN
STROP RIP STRAP
STROPHE ALCAIC LAISSE STANZA
SAPPHIC
STROPHIC MELIC
STROPHIUS (FATHER OF —)
CRISSUS
(**MOTHER OF —**) ANTIPHATIA
(**SON OF —**) PYLADES
(**WIFE OF —**) ANAXIBIA ASTYOCHIA
CYDRAGORA
STRUCK (— SHARPLY) SMITTEN
(**— WITH AMAZEMENT**) AGAZED
AGHAST
(**— WITH FEAR**) AFRAID
STRUCTURAL ORGANIC ANATOMIC
TECTONIC
(**— UNIT**) IDANT
STRUCTURE CAGE FALX FORM
MAKE ANNEX BOOTH CABIN FLOAT
FRAME GETUP HOUSE KIOSK
PEGMA SETUP SHAPE STOCK
BRIDGE CAGEOT FABRIC GANTRY
GIRDER ISOGEN KELSON PREFAB
TIMBER COTTAGE EDIFICE FAIRING
FEATURE GATEWAY GESTALT
KEELSON MANSION NURAGHE
OUTCAST PAGEANT STADIUM
TURNOUT ZEUGITE AEDICULA
AIRCRAFT AIRFRAME BUILDING
BUTTRESS COMPAGES CRIBWORK
DOMATIUM ENDOCONE ESCORIAL
HEADWORK MOUNTURE
NEOMORPH SKELETON STANDARD
(**— ALONG WALK**) PERGOLA
(**— BUILT IN WATER**) PIER
(**— CONTAINING KILN**) HOVEL
(**— EXTENDED INTO SEA**) JETTY
(**— FOR PIGEONS**) COTE
(**— FRAMING SHIP**) KEELSON
(**— IN ROCKS**) FLASER
(**— OF CARTRIDGE**) ANVIL
(**— OF EYE**) LENS
(**— OF PRETENSION**) PERRON

(**— ON ROOF**) CUPOLA FEMERELL
(**— ON SHIP**) BLISTER
(**— ON STEAMER**) TEXAS
(**— OVER MINE SHAFT**)
HEADFRAME
(**— OVER WELL**) WELLHEAD
(**— PRODUCING SMOOTH OUTLINE**)
FAIRING
(**— SHELTERING INSECTS**)
DOMATIUM
(**— SUPPORTING AIRSHIP**
PROPELLER) PYLON
(**— TO DEFLECT CURRENT**) SPUR
(**— WITHIN SHELL**) ENDOCONE
(**ANATOMICAL —**) BUD APRON
CARINA CRESCENT
(**ANTICLINAL —**) SWELL
(**ARCHED —**) FORNIX
(**ARTISTIC —**) MOBILE
(**BELL-SHAPED —**) PETTICOAT
(**BODILY —**) FRAME PHYSIQUE
(**BRICK —**) KANG HOVEL
(**BRISTLELIKE —**) ARISTA
(**BRONZE AGE —**) HENGE
(**CABINLIKE —**) CABANA
(**CLIMBING —**) LADDER
(**COAL-SHIPPING —**) STAITH
STAITHE
(**COMPLEX —**) EMBOLUS
(**CONELIKE —**) PYRAMID
(**CONICAL —**) BULLET
(**CREMATION —**) DARGA
(**CROWNLIKE —**) CORONA
(**CRYSTAL —**) POLYTYPE
(**CYLINDRICAL —**) SILO
(**DEADENING —**) BAFFLE
(**DEFENSIVE —**) CAT
(**FLATTENED —**) TABULA
(**FORTIFIED —**) CAVALIER
(**FRAIL —**) SHELL
(**GENERAL —**) GETUP
(**GEOLOGICAL —**) CAMBER
(**GRAMMATICAL —**) SYNTAX
(**HIGH —**) TOWER
(**HOLLOW —**) SHELL
(**KNEE-LIKE —**) GENU
(**LATTICEWORK —**) TRELLIS
(**LENS-SHAPED —**) LENTOID
(**LOFTY —**) BABEL STEEPLE
(**LOGICAL —**) EIDOS
(**MEGALITHIC —**) HENGE
(**ORGANIZED —**) BULK
(**ORIENTAL STORIED —**) PAGODA
(**ORNAMENTAL —**) KIOSK
(**PLANT —**) DISC DISK
(**POINTED —**) BEAK
(**PROTECTIVE —**) SHEATH
(**PUEBLO —**) KIVA
(**RAISED —**) CIMBORIO
(**RAMSHACKLE —**) COOP
(**RINGLIKE —**) ANNULUS
(**RODLIKE —**) RIB
(**RUDE STONE —S**) SPECCHIE
(**SACRIFICIAL —**) ALTAR
(**SENTENCE —**) SYNTAX
(**SHELTERING —**) COT
(**SHIELDING —**) SHELTER
(**SICKLE-SHAPED —**) FALX
(**SLENDER —**) HAIR
(**SPIRY —**) PINNACLE
(**STEMLIKE —**) STOLON
(**STONE —**) TAULA
(**TEMPORARY —**) HUT

(THEATER —) SKENE
(TIERED —) STAGE
(UNDERLYING —) BOTTOM
(UNSTABLE —) COBHOUSE
(VEHICLE —) MONOCOQUE
(WATERTIGHT —) CAMEL COFFERDAM
(WHITE —) ALBEDO
(PREF.) MORPH(O)
(RADIATED —) ACTIN(O)
(SUFF.) (— OF A KIND) ID
(— UNIT) EME
STRUDEL (PASTRY KIN TO —) STOLLEN
STRUGGLE IT TEW TUG VIE WIN AGON CAMP COPE DEAL FEND FICK FRAB GAME PULL TAVE TOIL AGONY FIGHT FLING HEAVE LABOR STRAY SWORD TEAVE TWEIL WORRY WRELE BATTLE BUCKLE BUFFET BUSTLE COMBAT EFFORT HASSLE JOSTLE JUSTLE PINGLE RELUCT SEESAW SPRAWL SPRUNT STIVER STRIFE STRIVE TERVEE TUSSLE WARSLE WIDDLE AGONIZE CLAMBER CONTEND CONTEST DISPUTE FLOUNCE GRAPPLE SCUFFLE TUILYIE WARFARE WAUCHLE WRESTLE CONFLICT ENDEAVOR FLOUNDER SCRAFFLE SCRAMBLE SLUGFEST SPRANGLE SPRATTLE
(— ALONG) HOBBLE
(— CONVULSIVELY) SPRAWL
(— FOR LARGESS) SCAMBLE
(— FORTH) ELUCTATE
(— ON) POUND
(— TO GAIN FOOTING) SCRABBLE SPROTTLE
(AGONIZED —) THROE
(CLOSE —) HANDGRIPS
(CONFUSED —) MUSS
(DEATH —) AGONY
(HAND-TO-HAND —) GRAPPLE
(HAPHAZARD —) SCUFFLE
(SPIRITUAL —) PENIEL
(UNCEREMONIOUS —) SCRAMBLE
STRUGGLER LAOCOON
STRUM THRUM
STRUMA GOITER GOITRE
STRUMPET BRIM PUNK BIMBO TRULL WENCH WHORE BLOWEN BULKER STIVER TOMBOY TOMRIG COCOTTE SUCCUBA DOLLYMOP PUNKLING SUCCUBUS VENTURER
(WORN-OUT —) HARRIDAN
STRUT JET BRAG COCK POMP SPUR BRANK CORSO MAJOR PRINK RANCE SWANK SASHAY SCOTCH STRIDE STROKE STROOT STRUNT NAUNTLE PEACOCK STEMPLE SWAGGER TRANSOM
(KIND OF —) MACPHERSON
STRUTTER HAM
STRUTTING COCKING
STUB BUTT SNAG SPUD STOB STUD CHECK ERGOT GUARD HINGE STUMP SPRUNT
STUBBLE BUN ETCH MANE SHACK ARRISH EDDISH STOVER STUMPS EEGRASS GRATTEN STIBBLE
STUBBORN SOT BALKY ROWDY RUSTY STIFF STOUT STUNT THRAW

TOUGH MULISH STURDY THWART BULLDOG PEEVISH PIGGISH RESTIVE WAYWARD WILLFUL OBDURATE PERVERSE STUNKARD THRAWART OBSTINATE PIGHEADED TENACIOUS REFRACTORY
STUBBORNNESS STOMACH ADAMANCY
STUBBY STUB CUTTY SQUAT STOCKY STUMPY STUBBED
STUCCO ALBARIUM
STUCK FAST MIRED INARUT MASHED WEDGED STICKIT STOODED
STUCK-UP BUG FROSTED
STUD SET BOLT BOSS KNOB KNOP KNOT NAIL RACE SLUG SPOT RESET BULLA CLOUT HARAS JOIST WRIST ASHLAR ENSTAR INSTAR STOOTH STRING CONTACT POTENCE QUARTER STUDDLE PUNCHEON STANDARD STUDDERY
(— FARM) HARAS
(— IN BOOT SOLE) SLUG
(— IN WATCH) POTENCE
(— SHOES) HOBNAIL
(— WITH NAILS) CLOUT
(INTERMEDIATE —) PUNCHEON
(ORNAMENTED —) AGLET AIGLET
STUDDED BOSSY BILLETY STELLED BILLETTE
STUDDLE POST ROIL
STUDENT BOY DIG WIT COED PLUG PREP SMUG SOPH AGGIE BAHUR BEJAN ELEVE FUCHS GRIND MEDIC PUPIL SIZAR SPOON BOCHER BURSAR BURSCH INTERN JUNIOR JURIST MEDICO OPTIME PREMED PRIMAR PRIMER PUISNE SCOLOG SENIOR ADVISEE CHRONIC CLASSIC DANTEAN EDUCAND ETONIAN FAILURE GOLIARD GRECIAN INTERNE INTRANT LEARNER MIDDLER MOOTMAN OPPIDAN PASSMAN PHARMIC PLUGGER SCHOLAR STUDIER TEMPLAR THEOLOG BOTANIST CABALIST COLLEGER DEMOTIST DISCIPLE EDUCATOR FEMINIST HOMERIST HOSTELER ISLAMIST PREMEDIC REPEATER SECONDAR SUBSIZAR TRANSFER
(— IN TALMUDIC ACADEMY) BAHUR
(— LAST IN CLASS) SPOON
(— OF LOW RANK) TERNAR TERNER
(— WHO LIVES IN TOWN) OPPIDAN
(ABNORMALLY ABSORBED —) SAP
(AFTER-DEGREE —) POSTDOC
(DAY —) EXTERN EXTERNE
(DIVINITY —) STIBBLER
(DRUDGING —) PLUG
(ENGLISH SCHOOL —) BLUE SWOT ETONIAN OXONIAN SWOTTER BATTELER
(GRADUATE —) FELLOW
(LAW —) PUNEE JURIST LEGIST PUISNE TEMPLAR STAGIARY
(MILITARY —) CADET
(MOSLEM —) SOFTA
(NON-COLLEGIATE —) TOSHER
(PLODDING —) DIG SMUG

(WANDERING —) GOLIARD
(1ST-YEAR —) FUCHS
(3RD-YEAR —) JUNIOR TERTIAN
(PL.) GOWN CLASS HOUSE SEMINAR
(SUFF.) LOG(ER)(IA)(IAN)(IC)(ICAL) (IST)(UE)(Y)
STUDIED COOL VOULU STUDIOUS
STUDIO LOT SHOT ATELIER BOTTEGA GALLERY
STUDIOUS BOOKY BOOKISH CLERKLY DILIGENT SEDULOUS
STUDY CON BEAT BONE BOOK CASE MUZZ PORE ROOM SIFT STUD GRIND ESTUDY EXAMEN LESSON MUSEUM SCOLEY SURVEY ABBOZZO ACCOUNT ANALYZE CANVASS CROQUIS POCHADE REVOLVE SANCTUM ANALYSIS BOOKWORK CONSIDER EXERCISE MEDITATE SCRUTINY TYPOLOGY
(— ANEW) REVISE
(— BY LAMPLIGHT) LUCUBRATE
(— HARD) DIG MUG SAP BONE CRAM PORE SMUG STEW SWOT
(— OF ALGAE) PHYCOLOGY
(— OF BLINDNESS) TYPHLOLOGY
(— OF BRAMBLES) BATOLOGY
(— OF CLOUDS) NEPHOLOGY
(— OF CODES) CRYPTOLOGY
(— OF CREEDS) SYMBOLICS
(— OF DREAMS) ONEIROLOGY
(— OF EARTHQUAKES) SEISMOLOGY
(— OF EXCREMENT) SCATOLOGY
(— OF FEVERS) PYRETOLOGY
(— OF FLYING OBJECTS) UFOLOGY
(— OF GRASSES) AGROSTOLOGY
(— OF INSECTS) ENTOMOLOGY
(— OF LAKES) LIMNOLOGY
(— OF MOUNTAINS) OROLOGY OREOLOGY
(— OF MOUTH) STOMATOLOGY
(— OF MUSCLES) MYOLOGY
(— OF ONESELF) AUTOLOGY
(— OF PEACE) IRENOLOGY
(— OF PLACE NAMES) TOPONYMY
(— OF PRIMITIVE CUSTOMS) AGRIOLOGY
(— OF PUNISHMENT) PENOLOGY
(— OF RELIGIOUS FEASTS) HEORTOLOGY
(— OF SACRED EDIFICES) NAOLOGY
(— OF SNOW AND ICE) CRYOLOGY
(— OF SOILS) PEDOLOGY
(—OF SPORES) PALYNOLOGY
(— OF TREES) DENDROLOGY
(— OF VALUES) AXIOLOGY
(— OF VERSIFICATION) PROSODY
(— OF WEAPONS) HOPLOLOGY
(— STEADILY) PLOD
(— UNDER PRESSURE) CRAM
(ART —) ABBOZZO CROQUIS POCHADE
(BROWN —) MEMENTO REVERIE
(CLAY —) BOZZETTO
(LABORIOUS —) GRIND
(MUSICAL —) ETUDE
(PRELIMINARY —) SKETCH
(UNINTERESTING —) GRIND
(SUFF.) ICS SOPH(ER)(IC)(IST)(Y)
STUDY IN SCARLET (AUTHOR OF —) DOYLE

(CHARACTER IN —) HOPE JOHN LUCY HOLMES TOBIAS WATSON FERRIER GREGSON LESTRADE SHERLOCK STAMFORD JEFFERSON STANGERSON
STUFF PAD RAM WAD CRAM CRAP GAUM GEAR JAZZ PANG SATE STOP TACK TRIG TUCK WHAT CROWD DUROY FARCE FORCE KEDGE METAL PASTE SQUAB TRADE FABRIC GRAITH KIBOSH MATTER PAUNCH STEEVE STODGE TACKLE TIMBER BOMBARD BOMBAST DRUGGET ELEMENT ENFARCE DIAPHANE MARINATE MATERIAL SPLUTTER WHIPPING
(— AND NONSENSE) HAVERS PICKLE PIFFLE
(— FILLET OF VEAL) BOMBARD
(— FULL) STODGE
(— OF POOR QUALITY SILK) RASH
(— ONESELF) MAST
(— POULTRY) FARCE MARINATE
(— WITH DRESSING) QUILT
(CLAGGY —) STODGE
(COTTON —) CALICO
(HOUSEHOLD —) GEAR
(INFERIOR —) MOCKADO
(PALTRY —) TRASH
(POOR —) TRIPE
(SILKEN —) TARS TARSE DIAPHANE
(SLOPPY —) SLIPSLOP
(STICKY —) GOOK
(TASTELESS —) GLOP
(THIN —) CRAPE
(THIN SILK —) LOVE
(WATERY —) BLASH
(WISHY-WASHY —) BLASH
(WOOLEN —) SAY DUROY TWILLY DRUGGET SAGATHY SHALLOON
(WORSTED —) BUNTING
(WORTHLESS —) GEAR GLOP HOGWASH
STUFFED PANG TRIG BLOAT FARCI STODGY BLOATED BOMBAST
(— DELICACY) DERMA
STUFFING PAD TAR FARCE KAPOK STECH STUFF BOMBAST FARCING SAWDUST SALPICON STUFFAGE
(— FOR MATTRESS) PULU
STUFFY POKY CLOSE FUBBY FUBSY FUGGY STIVY WOOLY WOOLLY AIRLESS FROUSTY
STULTIFY SOT PUPPIFY
STUMBLE CHIP FALL HAMP PECK STOT TRIP HAMEL LURCH SPURN STOIT STUMP BUMBLE CHANCE FALTER HALPER HAMBLE HAPPEN LUMPER OFFEND STEVEL TUMBLE WAGGER BLUNDER FOUNDER MISSTEP SCAMBLE SNAPPER STAMMER STAMPLE STOITER STOTTER STUMMER FLOUNDER THRUMBLE
STUMBLING HACK HURTING OFFENCE OFFENSE
STUMP CAG GET JOB NOG SET BUTT DOCK GRUB LUMP MORE RUNT SNAG STAB STAM STOB STUB STUD CHUNK ORATE SCRAB SCRAG STICK STOCK STOMP STOOL STOOP STOWL DOTARD NUBBIN SCRUNT SPRONG STOVEN

WICKET DODDARD RAMPICK
RAMPIKE SLEEPER STUMMEL
BALDHEAD HUSTINGS STUBBLES
(— AND ROOT) MOCK
(— OF TAIL) STRUNT
(CIGAR —) TOPPER
(CRICKET —) STICKS
(DEAD —) RUNT
(TREE —) MOCK STOW STOCK
STOOP ZUCHE DOTARD NUBBIN
STOVEN DODDARD
(WALNUT —) BUTT
STUMPY SNUB BUNTY SNUBBED
STUN DIN BOWL DAZE ROCK ZONK
DAUNT DAVER DEAVE DOVER
DOZEN DROWN STONY ASTONY
BEDAZE BENUMB DEADEN DEAFEN
DEVVEL NOBBLE STOUND WITHER
ASTOUND DAMMISH SANDBAG
SILENCE STUPEFY STUPEND
ASTONISH PARALYZE
(— BY A SHOT) CREASE
STUNNED SILLY STUPENT
ASTONIED
STUNNER KNOCKER THUMPER
TRIMMER
STUNNING CRASHING SHOCKING
STUNT GAG KIP FEAT NIRL BLAST
CANOE CROWL DWARF STINT
STOCK BARANI BARONI CRADDY
DOLPHIN BACKBEND CATALINA
CRUCIFIX PORPOISE PRATFALL
SUPPRESS
(PUBLICITY —) HYPE
(SWIMMING —) SHARK SPIRAL
STUNTED URLED GRUBBY RUNTISH
SCROGGY SCRUBBY SCRUFFY
SCRUNTY WANTHRIVEN
STUPA TOPE CHORTEN
STUPEFACTION STOUND STUPOR
STUPEFIED MAD DAMP DAZED
DRUNK MAZED SILLY SOTTED
ZONKED BEMAZED BEMUSED
DONNERT DOZENED DOZZLED
STUPENT BESOTTED DATELESS
MINDLESS
STUPEFIER OPIUM
STUPEFY FOX BAZE DAMP DAZE
DOZE DRUG DULL GOOF MAZE
MULL STUN ZONK BESOT DAUNT
DAVER DEAVE DIZZY DOZEN
SHEND SMOKE STONY ASTONE
ASWEVE BEMUSE BENUMB
DUDDLE FUDDLE MOIDER
MUDDLE STOUND ASTOUND
CONFUSE FORDULL SLUMBER
STUPEND ASTONISH BEFUDDLE
BEMUDDLE BEWILDER CONFOUND
MORPHINE PARALYZE SOMNIATE
SOPORATE
STUPEFYING STONY
STUPENDOUS GREAT IMMENSE
ENORMOUS MONSTROUS
STUPID FAT JAY BETE DOWF DULL
DUMB DUNT FOOL HAZY LEWD
NICE NUMB SLOW BLUNT BOOBY
BRUTE CRASS DENSE DORKY
DOTED DUNNY GLAKY GOOSY
GROSS HEAVY INERT MOSSY
MUZZY SILLY THICK ASSISH
BARREN BOVINE CUCKOO DAWKIN
DOITED DROWSY DUMMEL
HEBETE LOGGER LURDAN OBTUSE

OPAQUE SIMPLE SODDEN STOLID
STULTY STURDY SUMPHY TAVERT
URLUCH WOODEN ASININE
BRUTISH CHUCKLE DOLTISH
DONNARD DONNERD DOWFART
DUFFING DUMPISH FATUOUS
FOOLISH FOPPISH GAWKISH
GLAIKIT GULLISH INSULSE
LUMPISH LURDANE PEAKISH
PINHEAD PROSAIC SOTTISH
TAIVERT TOMFOOL VACUOUS
WITLESS ANSERINE BAYARDLY
BESOTTED BLOCKISH BOBBYISH
BOEOTIAN CLODDISH DONNERED
DUNCICAL FOOTLESS GAUMLESS
HEADLESS IMBECILE STOCKISH
PINHEADED SENSELESS
(— PERSON) HOIT NERD JUKES
SUMPH LUMMOX TUMFIE KALLIKAK
(PREF.) MORO
STUPIDITY BETISE TORPOR
BOBBERY DENSITY DUNCERY
FATUITY DULLNESS DUMBNESS
HEBETUDE STOLIDITY
STUPOR FOG SOG COMA DAMP
DOTE SOPOR SWARF STOUND
TORPOR TRANCE NARCOMA
LETHARGY NARCOSIS
(PREF.) NARC(O) TYPH(O)
STURDILY BUFF TOUGH
STURDY GID BUFF DUNT RUDE TALL
THRO BURLY CRANK FELON
HARDY HUSKY LUSTY SOLID
SOUND STARK STERN STIFF STOUT
VAUDY WALLY FEERIE PLUGGY
ROBUST RUGGED RUSTIC SQUARE
STABLE STEADY STEEVE STOCKY
STRONG STUGGY VIRILE FECKFUL
UPRIGHT VALIANT STALWART
STUBBORN VIGOROUS YEOMANLY
STURGEON HUSO ELOPS BELUGA
GANOID MAMMOSE OSSETER
STERLET
STUTTER FAM BUFF HACK MANT
STOT STUT GANCH FAMBLE
HABBER HABBLE STAMMER
STUTTERER RATTLER
STUTTERING TRAULISM
BALBUTIENT
STY PEN QUAT STYE WEST FRANK
CRUIVE PIGPEN STITHE
HORDEOLUM
STYLE AIR CUT DUB PEN SAY TON
WAY CHIC FACE FORM GARB
HAND KIND MODE MOLD NAME
PILE RATE TWIG VEIN GENRE
GETUP GUISE IDIOM SHAPE STATE
SWANK TASTE FESCUE FORMAT
GNOMON GOTHIC PHRASE STEELE
STRAIN STYLUS UMBONE
COSTUME DIALECT DICTION
FASHION INSTYLE QUALITY
EQUIPAGE LANGUAGE MARINISM
NARRANTE PULLBACK
PHRASEOLOGY
(— HAIR) CORNROW
(— OF ARCHITECTURE) ORDER
DRAVIDA GEORGIAN
(— OF COOKING) CUISINE
(— OF DRESS) GUISE
(— OF GEM SETTING) BOX
(— OF HANDWRITING) CHANCERY
SCRIPTION

(— OF HAT) BLOCK
(— OF MOUNTING) SETTING
(— OF MUSIC) BOOGIE
(— OF PAINTING) GENRE
(— OF PENMANSHIP) HAND
(— OF PRINTING) CAMAIEU
(— OF SPEAKING) ADDRESS
(— OF SWIMMING) STROKE
(— OF WRESTLING) SAMBO
(AFFECTED —) EUPHUISM
(ARTISTIC —) GUSTO GOTHIC
ARTIFICE DANDYISM MANNERISM
(BOOKBINDING —) ALDINE MAIOLI
MAJOLI FANFARE GROLIER
ETRUSCAN HARLEIAN ROXBURGH
(CUSTOMARY —) GATE
(DECORATIVE —) ARTDECO
(DISTINCTIVE —) CLOTHES
(FAVORED —) GROOVE
(HAIR —) CROP TETE
(INFLATED —) FUSTIAN
(JAZZ —) TAILGATE
(LACKING —) FUNKY
(LATEST —) KICK
(OF PAST —) RETRO
(PRETENTIOUS —) BOMBAST
(PROPER —) WEAR
(THEATRICAL —) LYCEUM
(WRITING —) MINUSCULE
(SUFF.) (IN THE — OF) ESQUE
STYLET SPEAR STILET STYLUS
TROCAR MANDRIN STILETTE
STYLIDIUM CANDOLEA
STYLISH FLY CHIC DOSS POSH
TONY DOGGY NIFTY NOBBY RITZY
SASSY SHARP SMART SWELL TIPPY
TOPPY CHEESY CLASSY DAPPER
DRESSY FLOSSY JAUNTY SWANKY
TONISH DASHING DOGGISH
GENTEEL KNOWING SWAGGER
TOFFISH
STYLOBATE PODIUM
STYLOID BELONOID
STYLUS GAD PEN STYLE CUTTER
GREFFE TRACER HARPAGO
POINTEL PYROPEN
STYMPHALUS (FATHER OF —)
ELATUS
(MOTHER OF —) LAODICE
STYPTIC ALUM AMADOU MATICO
BAROMETZ STANCHER
STYRENE STYROL CINNAMOL
STYX (— FERRYMAN) CHARON
(FATHER OF —) OCEANUS
(HUSBAND OF —) PALLAS
(MOTHER OF —) TETHYS
SUAEDA DONDIA
SUAH (FATHER OF —) ZOPHAH
SUAN PAN SOROBAN
SUAVE COOL OILY SMUG SOFT
BLAND SOAPY SVELT GLOSSY
SILKEN SMOOTH URBANE
FULSOME POLITIC DEBONAIR
UNCTUOUS
SUAVELY CREAMILY
SUAVITY COMITY URBANITY
SUB GRASS UBOAT
SUBALTERN WART
SUBBASE PLINTH
SUBCINCTORIUM BALTEUS
BALTHEUS
SUBCLASS GENDER BRYALES
CESTODA CYCLIAE DIGENEA

SPECIES AMOEBAEA ANAPSIDA
CESTODES COPEPODA GANOIDEI
SELACHII
SUBCOMPACT MINICAR
SUBCULTURE HIPHOP
SUBCUTANEOUS DEEP
SUBDEACON MINISTER
SUBDIVIDE CARVE MINCE
SUBDIVISION DEN OBE SEX BEAT
CAZA DHER HAPU ITEM TASU
BUNDA CORPS CURIA DEKAN
DHERI FERAE FORTY HSIEN IOWAN
NAHIE OKRUG PHYLE SITIO STAGE
TALUK TARAF TURMA UINTA
ALBIAN ARENIG BANNER BRANCH
BUREAU CERCLE CIRCLE CLAUSE
COHORT COLUMN COMMOT
DAKOTA DANIAN DOGGER FACIES
GUELPH HEMERA IMBREX LENGTH
LUDLOW MARKAZ NAHIYE OBLAST
ONEIDA SANJAK SECTOR SERIAL
SHIRAZ STRAIN SUBAGE TAHSIL
TASSOO TEHSIL BUKEYEF
CENTURY CHEMUNG CHIRIPA
COCHITI COMARCA ECOTYPE
ELEMENT EPARCHY EPISODE
GENESEE MANIPLE MONTANA
ORBITAL PHRATRY RONDOUT
SASTEAN SECTION SEEDBED
SUBAREA SUBLINE SUBPLAT
SUBPLOT SUBRACE SUBZONE
SUPPORT TRENTON TRINITY
WASATCH WASHITA WENLOCK
WICHITA BANOVINA DISTRICT
DIVISION DJAGATAY ENDBRAIN
FLOTILLA GUBERNIA LOCATION
MONTEREY NAUCRARY PARTICLE
PRECINCT STOCKTON SUBCASTE
SUBORDER SUBSTAGE SUBTRIBE
TOWNSHIP PARAGRAPH
(— OF SCOUTS) CREW
(EGYPTIAN —) KISM
(SPARTAN —) ENOMOTY
SUBDOMINANT FOURTH
SUBDUE BOW COW ADAW BEAT
BEND QUAY TAME ACCOY ALLAY
AMATE CHARM CRUSH DAUNT
DOMPT QUAIL QUASH QUELL
SOBER STILL ADAUNT BRIDLE
CHASTE DEBELL DISMAY EVINCE
GENTLE MASTER QUENCH REDUCE
SUBACT SUBMIT UNWILD
ABANDON AFFAITE CAPTURE
CHASTEN CONQUER DAUNTON
OVERAWE REPRESS REPRIME
SUCCUMB CONVINCE OVERCOME
SUPPEDIT SUPPRESS SURMOUNT
VANQUISH
SUBDUED MAK SOFT TAME MUTED
SOBER STILL UNDER BROKEN
CHASTE GENTLE ASHAMED
SUBMISS SOURDINE
SUBFAMILY KHOISAN CUSHITIC
ACRAEINAE
SUBGROUP BAND FAMILY
SUBHEAD BOXHEAD SIDEHEAD
SUBIMAGO DUN
SUBINDEX SUFFIX
SUBIRRIGATE SUB SUBWATER
SUBIRRIGATION SUBBING
SUBJECT DUX PUT ABLE ALLY
BODY BONE ITEM OPEN TEXT
HOBBY PLACE STOOP STUDY

TESTO THEMA THEME TOPIC
GROUND IMPOSE LIABLE PATHIC
REDUCE SACOPE SUBDIT SUBMIT
THRALL VASSAL CAITIVE CITIZEN
FEODARY FEUDARY OBVIOUS
PROBAND SERVILE AMENABLE
ELECTIVE INCIDENT INFERIOR
OBEDIENT OCCASION SENTENCE
SUBJUGAL

(— OF DISCOURSE) NOUN
(— OF FUGUE) GUIDA
(— OF PROPOSITION) EXTREME
(— TO ABUSE) REVILE
(— TO ARGUMENT) MOOT
(— TO BAD TEMPER) MOODY
(— TO CHANGE) MUTABLE FUGITIVE
(— TO CRITICISM) SCOURGE
(— TO FATE) FIE
(— TO PERCOLATION) DISPLACE
(— TO SOME ACTION) TREAT
(CONTROVERTED —) ISSUE
(LOYAL —) LIEGE
(PL.) FOLK

SUBJECTION SLAVERY SERVITUS
THIRLING

SUBJECTIVE IMMANENT INSEEING
INTERNAL PECTORAL EPISTEMIC

SUBJOIN AFFIX ANNEX

SUBJUGATE COW ENSLAVE

SUBJUGATION BONDAGE
SERVITUDE

SUBKINGDOM PHYLUM ANNULOSA
CHORDATA

SUBLEADER HEADMAN

SUBLEASE FARMOUT SUBTACK

SUBLET JOB SUBSET CONACRE
SUBLEASE

SUB-LIEUTENANT CORNET

SUBLIMATE FLOWER ALCOHOL
SUBLIME

SUBLIME BIG FUME GRAND LOFTY
NOBLE AUGUST REFINE SOLEMN
WINGED DANTEAN ELEVATO
EXALTED EMPYREAL EMPYREAN
MAGNIFIC MAJESTIC SERAPHIC
SPLENDID MAGNIFICENT
(— IN STYLE) MILTONIC
(FALSELY —) TUMID

SUBLIMITY GRANDEUR

SUBLUNARY EARTHLY

SUBMARINE SUB BOAT HERO
DIVER EBOAT FRITZ GUPPY HOAGY
UBOAT HOAGIE SUBSEA PIGBOAT
POORBOY TIDDLER
(GERMAN —) UBOAT
(PART OF —) DECK SAIL PLANE
TOWER BRIDGE RUDDER
PROPELLER SAILPLANE
TURTLEBACK FAIRWEATHER

SUBMEDIANT SIXTH

SUBMERGE BOG DIP BURY DIVE
DUNK HIDE SINK SOAK TAKE
DROWN SOUSE SWAMP WHELM
DELUGE DRENCH ENGULF
DEMERGE IMPLUNGE INUNDATE
SUBMERSE SURROUND
OVERWHELM

SUBMERGENCE ONLAP

SUBMISSION VAIL STOOP
PATIENCE

SUBMISSIVE MEEK BUXOM
DEMISS DOCILE DUTIFUL PASSIVE
SERVILE SLAVISH SUBJECT

SUBMISS UNERECT AMENABLE
OBEDIENT RESIGNED YIELDING
(— TO WIFE) UXORIOUS

SUBMISSIVENESS SLAVERY

SUBMIT BOW EAT ABOW BEND
CAVE LEAN OBEY TAKE VAIL AVALE
DEFER HIELD STAND STOOP YIELD
ASSENT CRINGE DELATE RESIGN
CONSIGN KNUCKLE SUBJECT
SUBMISE SUCCUMB TRUCKLE
PROPOUND
(— FOR CONSIDERATION) REMIT
(— TAMELY) EAT
(— TO) ABIDE STAND SUFFER

SUBNORMAL OFF SICK ABNORMAL

SUBORDER LARI ALCAE APODA
APODI GALLI GRUES ARDEAE
COHORT CUCULI SAURIA AGLOSSA
ANSERES ARCACEA ASCONES
CORACII COSTATA SARCURA
SYCONES ACRASIDA ADEPHAGA
BATOIDEI COLUMBAE CORACIAE
CURSORIA ENOPLINA EUSUCHIA
FALCONES FREGATAE SELACHII

SUBORDINARY ENDORSE
ROUNDEL

SUBORDINATE SUB SINK PETTY
SCRUB UNDER EXEMPT MINION
PUISNE SECOND YEOMAN PARTIAL
SERVANT SERVILE SUBJECT
HENCHMAN INFERIOR MYRMIDON
PARERGAL POSTPONE SERVIENT
ANCILLARY SUBALTERN
(PREF.) (— TO) VICE

SUBORN HAVE BRIBE

SUBOVAL PETALOID

SUBPHYLUM EUCHORDA

SUBPOENA SUMMONS

SUBRACE STOCK

SUB ROSA COVERTLY SECRETLY
PROVATELY

SUBSCRIBE SIGN ASSENT ASCRIBE
CONSIGN SUBSIGN
(— AGAIN) RENEW

SUBSCRIBER RAILBIRD

SUBSCRIPT INFERIOR

SUBSCRIPTION APPROVAL
SIGNATURE ABONNEMENT

SUBSEQUENT AFTER LATER
FUTURE PUISNE ENSUING
POSTNATE
(PREF.) POST
(— TO) CIS

SUBSEQUENTLY SO LATER SINCE

SUBSERVIENT OILY UNDER VASSAL
DUTEOUS SERVILE SLAVISH
OFFICIAL

SUBSHRUB STOCK GUAYULE
COLUMNEA PERIWINKLE

SUBSIDE DIE EBB LAY LIE ADAW
CALM FALL LULL SILE SINK VAIL
ABATE ALLAY LAPSE RESIDE
SETTLE ASSUAGE RELAPSE
UNSWELL WITHDRAW

SUBSIDENCE FALL SETTLING

SUBSIDIARY CHILD DONKEY
SUBSIDY ACCESSORY

SUBSIDIZE AID HELP BONUS

SUBSIDY AID BONUS BOUNTY
POUNDAGE

SUBSILICIC BASIC

SUBSIST BE LIVE RELY

SUBSISTENCE DOLE BEING LIVING

SUBSISTENT ENTITY

SUBSOIL PAN LECK SOLE SHRAVE
RATCHEL

SUBSTAGE CARY GUNZ IOWAN
MANKATO STADIAL TAZEWELL

SUBSTANCE FAT SUM BODY CORE
FECK GIST GITE MEAT TACK WHAT
ADROP AGENT ALLOY ARCHE
BEING FOMES GREAT KEEST
METAL MOYEN OUSIA PROOF
SENSE STUFF THING BOTTOM
GADUIN GETTER IMPORT MATTER
STAPLE WEALTH AEROSOL
AGAROID ANTIGEN COLICIN
COLLOID CONTENT ELEIDIN
EMANIUM ERGUSIA ESSENCE
HYALINE MEANING PURPORT
REAGENT SUBJECT SUPTION
ACCEPTOR ADDITIVE ADHESIVE
ALLERGEN AMBEROID ANTIFOAM
BASSORIN HARDNESS MATERIAL
PSORALEN
(— CAPABLE OF EXPANSION)
DILATANT
(— FORMED IN VINEGAR) MOTHER
(— FROM CRUSHED APPLES)
POMACE
(— IN BLOOD) ALEXINE ABLASTIN
(— IN LIGHT BULBS) GETTER
(— IN WOODY TISSUE) LIGNIN
(— OF DENTINE) IVORY
(— OF EXTREME HARDNESS)
ADAMANT DIAMOND
**(— PRODUCING POISONOUS
ATMOSPHERE)** GAS
**(— SURROUNDED BY FOREIGN
TISSUE)** ENCLAVE
(— THAT INDUCES MITOSIS)
MITOGEN
(— THAT STOPS LOCOMOTION)
ARRESTANT
(— TO ADD STABILITY) BALLAST
(— TRANSPORTING GERMS)
FOMES
(— USED AS HYPNOTIC) URAL
(— USED IN DETECTING OTHERS)
REAGENT
(— WITH MOLDY ODOR) CHARACIN
(ADHESIVE —) GLUE GLOEA PASTE
CEMENT STICKER
(AMORPHOUS —) GLASS RESIN
LIGNIN PECTIN FERRITE SAPONIN
(AROMATIC —) BALSAM
(ASTRINGENT —) ALUM CATECHU
(BITTER —) ALOIN LININ ILICIN
(BLACK —) SOOT BLECK
(CLEANSING —) LYE
(COLLOIDAL —) ALGIN EXPANDER
(COMBUSTIBLE —) COAL
(CONDENSED —) PITH
(CORROSIVE —) CAUSTIC
(CRYSTALLINE —) LAURIN ALANINE
HELENIN ELATERIN
(DARK —) ATRAMENT
(DISSOLVED —) SOLUTE
(ETERNAL —) DHARMA ADHARMA
(FATLIKE —) DEGRAS LIPOID
ERGUSIA
(FATTY —) SMEAR SUBERIN
(FERMENTATION —) LEAVEN
(FIBROUS —) COTTON
(FILAMENTOUS —) HARL
(FILMY —) GOSSAMER

(FIRST —) YLEM
(GENERATIVE —) SPERM
(GRINDING —) ABRASIVE
(GROWTH-PROMOTING —) AUXIN
(GUMMY —) GUM GURRY AMYLOID
GLACTAN
(HARD ANIMAL —) BONE ENAMEL
(HORNY —) BALEEN CHITIN
CHONDRIN
(HYPOTHETICAL —) FLUID INOGEN
PROTYL
(IDEAL —) CONTINUUM
(INFLAMMABLE —) BITUMEN
(INSOLUBLE —) CARRIER
HYALOGEN
(LIVERLIKE —) HEPAR
(NARCOTIC —) DRUG
(NITROGENOUS —) LACTENIN
(POISONOUS —) ARSENIC PHRYNIN
EXOTOXIN
(POWDER OF ANY —) FLOUR
(POWDERY —) STOUR
(PREDOMINATING —) BASE
(RESINOUS —) LAC COPAL
CARANNA CARAUNA COPALINE
COPALITE
(SELF-DEFENSIVE —) ACRAEIN
(SEMISOLID —) GEL
(SOUR —) ACID
(STICKY —) GOO GOOP SIZE STICK
GLUTEN BIRDLIME
(SUBTLE —) SPIRIT
(SWEET —) SUGAR
(SYNTHETIC —) HORMONE
(TRANSLUCENT —) HYALINE
CHONDRIN
(UNBREAKABLE —) ADAMANT
(UNCREATED —) ADHARMA
(VISCOUS —) GLAIR GREASE
SLUBBER
(VITAL —) KEEST
(WAXY —) SERIN PROPOLIS
SUBERINE
(PREF.) HYL(O)
(SUFF.) (— HAVING FORM) PHANE
(— PRODUCED THRU PROCESS)
STATE

SUBSTANDARD BAD BAUCH

SUBSTANTIAL FAT FIRM MEATY
PUKKA STOUT ACTUAL BODILY
HEARTY SQUARE STABLE STANCH
STUFFY STURDY MASSIVE
MATERIAL SUBSTANT TANGIBLE

SUBSTANTIATE BACK CONFIRM
SUPPORT VALIDATE

SUBSTANTIVE DIRECT

SUBSTITUTE SUB MOCK TEMP VICE
AKORI EXTRA PINCH PROXY VICAR
BACKUP BEWITH CHANGE DEPUTY
DOUBLE ERSATZ STOOGE
COMMUTE REPLACE RESERVE
STANDBY STANDIN STOPGAP
SUBDEAN SUFFECT SUPPOSE
DISPLACE EMERGENT MAKESHIFT
SURROGATE
(— FOR SIGNATURE) MARK
(— FOR TEA) TIA FAHAM
(— FRAUDULENTLY) SUPPOSE
(NOT —) FULL
(POOR —) APOLOGY
(SOAP —) AMOLE
(TOOTH —) CROWN

(USE OF GRAMMATICAL —) CATAPHORA
(PREF.) PSEUD(O)
(SUFF.) ETTE
SUBSTITUTING (PREF.)
(— FOR) PRO
SUBSTITUTION SHIFT CHANGE ERSATZ ENALLAGE EXCHANGE NOVATION REPLACEMENT
(— OF SOUNDS) LALLATION
SUBSTRATUM SUB GROUND SUBBING SUBJECT
SUBSTREAM MATTER
SUBSTRUCTURE PODIUM FOOTING CENTERING
(— OF DOME) THOLOBATE
SUBSUME COVER EXPLAIN INCLUDE
SUBSUMING GENERIC
SUBTENANT VAVASOUR
SUBTERFUGE MASK BLIND CROOK QUIRK SHIFT TRICK WRINK AMBAGE CHICANE ARTIFICE PRETENCE TRAVERSE VOIDANCE
SUBTILE SUBTLE TENUOUS
SUBTILIZE EXALT
SUBTITLE TITLE LEADER CAPTION
SUBTLE SLY FINE NICE WILY WISE ACUTE ARGUTE ASTUTE CRAFTY SHREWD CUNNING FRAGILE SUBTILE CLERGIAL
(FALLACIOUSLY —) SOPHISTIC
(TOO —) FINESPUN
SUBTLETY NICE FRAUD DECEIT NUANCE EXILITY FINESSE QUILLET DELICACY FINENESS QUIDDITY QUODLIBET REFINEMENT
(— IN ARGUMENT) QUILLET
(CRITICAL —) NICETY
SUBTLY FINE SLILY SLYLY
SUBTRACT BATE PULL TAKE SHAVE DEDUCE DEDUCT DETRACT SUBDUCE SUBDUCT SUBTRAY DIMINISH
SUBTRIBE HAPU SENAAH SEMNONES
SUBURB ANNEX BORGO BARRIO PETTAH BANLIEU ENDSHIP FAUBOURG
(POORLY CONSTRUCTED —) SLURB
(PL.) BURBS SKIRTS ENVIRONS OUTPARTS SUBTOPIA SUBURBIA
SUBURBIA VILLADOM
SUBVERSION FALL SABOTAGE
SUBVERSIVE RUINOUS
SUBVERT SAP KILL RAZE RUIN EVERT UPSET GAINSAY OVERSET REVERSE RUINATE OVERTURN
SUBVERTED LOST
SUBWAY BMT IND IRT DIVE TUBE METRO
SUCCEED GO FAY HIT FARE RISE WORK CLICK ENSUE FADGE PROVE SCORE SPEED COTTON FOLLOW MAKEIT OBTAIN PANOUT SECOND THRIVE ACHIEVE INHERIT PREVAIL PROSPER THROUGH TURNOUT FLOURISH SUPPLANT
(— IN REACHING) RECOVER
(— TO THRONE) ACCEDE ASCEND
SUCCEEDING VICE AFTER CHANGE ULTERIOR

SUCCESS DO GO HIT MAX WIN WOW BANG CESS LUCK SMASH SPEED THRIFT EXPLOIT FORTUNE FURTHER PROWESS THEEDOM FELICITY GODSPEED
(— IN A MATCH) GAME
(ACCIDENTAL —) FLUKE
(BRILLIANT —) ECLAT
(ECONOMIC —) BOOM
(FINANCIAL —) SELLER
(NOT LIKELY TO BE A —) NOWIN
(SUDDEN —) KILLING
(UNEXPECTED —) JACKPOT
(WORLDLY —) ARTHA
SUCCESSFUL HOT MADE SOCK BOFFO LUCKY SPEEDFUL THRIVING GANGBUSTERS
(BARELY —) NARROW
(HIGHLY —) RUNAWAY
SUCCESSFULLY GREAT HAPPILY PROUDLY
SUCCESSION RUN SUIT ROUND SUITE TRACK ASSISE COURSE SEQUEL SERIES STREAM STRING HEIRDOM SUCCESS ANCESTRY DIADOCHE MUTATION SEQUENCE
(— OF CHANGES) FLUX
(— OF CHORDS) CADENCE
(— OF CRUSTS) CALICHE
(— OF LUCK) STREAK
(— OF STAGES) CASCADE
(— OF WAVES) CRIMP
(— RULERS) DYNASTY
SUCCESSIVELY AROW
SUCCESSOR HEIR CALIF HERES CALIPH HAERES EPIGONUS
(— OF CHIEFTAIN) TANIST
(— OF MUHAMMAD) CALIF CALIPH
(ECCLESIASTICAL —) COARB COMARB
(PL.) DIADOCHI
SUCCINCT BRIEF PITHY SHORT TERSE CONCISE LACONIC SUMMARY
SUCCINIC DIACETIC
SUCCOR AID HELP RESET SERVE SPEED ASSIST RELIEF RESCUE SUPPLY UPTAKE COMFORT DELIVER PRESIDY RELIEVE SECOURS SUSTAIN BEFRIEND
SUCCORY CHICORY
SUCCULENT FRIM FRUM LUSH JUICY LUSHY PAPPY PULPY SAPPY YOUNG CASHIE FLESHY TENDER WATERISH
SUCCUMB BREAK QUAIL STOOP TRAIK YIELD
SUCH SIC SICK THAT SWICH
SUCHNESS TATHATA
SUCK SOUK SWIG SWOOP SUCKLE
(— DRY) SOAK
(— UP) DRINK ABSORB TIPPLE
(SUFF.) MYZA MYZON
SUCKEN THIRL
SUCKER CHUB FISH GULL CUIUI PATSY SOBOL THIEF CHUPON CUPULE MULLET RATOON REDFIN SOBOLE SPROUT SQUARE STOLON SUPPER TILLER CUTLIPS GONOTYL LOCULUS OSCULUM PEDICEL SCOURGE BOTHRIUM HUMPBACK LOLLIPOP PUSHOVER REDHORSE SURCULUS QUILLBACK

(PREF.) BDELL(O) BOTHR(I)(IO)(O) MYZO STOLONI SURCULI
(SUFF.) BDELLA
SUCKLE FEED MILK SUCK LACTATE NOURISH
SUCKLING SUCKER LACTANT SUCKLER TEATLING
SUCTION INTAKE
(SUFF.) MYZA MYZON
SUCTORIA ACINETAE

> **SUDAN**
> **CAPITAL:** KHARTOUM
> **DESERT:** NUBIAN
> **LANGUAGE:** GA EWE IBO KRU EFIK MOLE TSHI YORUBA MANDINGO
> **MEASURE:** UD
> **MOUNTAIN:** KINYETI
> **NATIVE:** DAZA GOLO NUER SERE DINKA FULAH HAUSA MOSSI NUBIYIN
> **PROVINCE:** DARFUR KASSALA KORDOFAN
> **REGION:** DARFUR KASSALA KORDOFAN
> **RIVER:** NILE PIBOR
> **TOWN:** WAU JUBA KOSTI MEROE ATBARA ALUBAYD KASSALA MALAKAL OMDURMAN
> **WEIGHT:** HABBA

SUDANESE FULA FULAH
SUDAN GRASS GARAVA GARAWI
SUDDEN BRASH FERLY HASTY ICTIC SWIFT ABRUPT FIERCE SNAPPY SPEEDY PRERUPT HEADLONG SPURTIVE SUBITANY SUBITOUS OVERNIGHT PRECIPITATE
SUDDENLY BOB POP BOLT FLOP SLAP AMAIN SHORT SKELP SOUSE ASTART BOUNCE PRESTO SUBITO ASUDDEN UNAWARES HEYPRESTO
SUDDENNESS ATTACK SUDDENTY
SUDORIFIC SWEAT SWEATER HIDROTIC SUDATORY
SUDRA HINDU VELLALA
SUDS BUCK FOAM SAPPLES SOAPSUDS
SUE LAW WOO SUIT IMPLEAD TROUNCE
SUET TALLOW
(PREF.) STEAR(I)(O) STEAT(O)
(SUFF.) STEARIN
SUFFER BYE GET LET BEAR BIDE DREE FIND GAIN HURT PAIN PINE ALLOW DREIE INCUR LABOR PROVE SMART SMOKE STAND THOLE ABEGGE BETEEM ENDURE PERMIT AGONIZE SUPPORT SUSTAIN UNDERGO TOLERATE
(— AGONY) THROE
(— A PENALTY) PAY
(— AT STAKE) SMOKE
(— DEFEAT) BOW
(— FOR) ABY ABYE ABIDE
(— FROM HEAT) SWELTER
(— FROM TIME) AGE
(— GREAT AFFLICTION) GROAN
(— HUNGER) CLEM STARVE AFFAMISH
(— LOSS OF) GIVE
(— PAIN) STOUND ANGUISH
(— PENALTY) SWEAT

(— REMORSE) RUE
(— RUIN) WRECK
(— SHIPWRECK) SPLIT
(— SYNCOPE) FAINT
(— THE CONSEQUENCES) ANSWER
(— THROUGH) PASS
(— TO ENTER) ADMIT
SUFFERABLE PATIBLE
SUFFERANCE PAIN MISERY PATIENCE THOLANCE
SUFFERER MARTYR AMNESIC DOORMAT PATIENT
(SUFF.) PATH(IA)(IC)(Y)
SUFFERING BALE COST DREE HURT PAIN PINE RACK AGONY DOLOR GRIEF SMART WRAKE PATHIC PATHOS THRALL INVALID LANGUOR PASSION PASSIVE TRAVAIL DISTRESS HARDSHIP MARTYRDOM
(— FROM HANGOVER) CHIPPY
(— FROM ILL HEALTH) DOWN
(— OF MIND) CARE
(—S OF CHRIST) AGONY
(SUFF.) PATH(IA)(IC)(Y)
(— OF) ITIS
SUFFICE DO LAST COVER REACH SERVE SATISFY
SUFFICIENCY ENOUGH PLENTY ADEQUACY BELLYFUL ABUNDANCE PLENITUDE
SUFFICIENT DUE FAIR GOOD AMPLE DECENT ENOUGH PRETTY BASTANT ABUNDANT ADEQUATE RELEVANT COMPETENT
(— LEGALLY) RELEVANT
(BARELY —) SCANT SKIMP NARROW SCRIMPY
(BE — FOR) COVER
SUFFICIENTLY DULY WELL ENOUGH
SUFFIX POSTFIX
(SLANG —) AROO
SUFFOCATE CHOKE DROWN SMOOR STIVE STUFF SWELT SLOKEN STIFLE OVERLIE QUACKLE SMOLDER SMOTHER SCUMFISH STRANGLE THROTTLE
SUFFOCATION APNEA APNOEA ASPHYXIA
SUFFRAGE VOTE VOICE TONGUE VERSICLE
SUFFRAGETTE CATT
SUFFUSE DIP FILL BATHE EMBAY TINGE INFUSE MANTLE
SUFFUSION COLOR
SUGAR CANDY DIOSE IDOSE MELIS PIECE SUCRE THIRD ACROSE ALDOSE ALLOSE FUCOSE GULOSE HEXOSE INVERT KETOSE LYXOSE OCTOSE PANELA TALOSE TRIOSE XYLOSE AGAVOSE ALTROSE BASTARD CHITOSE GLUCOSE GLUTOSE GLYCOSE LACTOSE MALTOSE MANNOSE PAPELON PENOCHI PENTOSE PENUCHE SORBOSE SUCROSE SWEETEN TETROSE THREOSE BROWNING CONCRETE CYMAROSE DEXTROSE FRUCTOSE FURANOSE LEVULOSE PYRANOSE RHAMNOSE RHODEOSE SECALOSE TURANOSE

(BROWN —) CARAIBE JAGGARY DEMERARA JAGGHERY
(COARSE —) RAAB PANOCHA
(CRUDE —) GUR HEAD MELADA CONCRETE
(INFERIOR —) BASTARD
(SIMPLE —) OSE
(UNREFINED —) CASSONADE MUSCOVADO
(PREF.) GLUC(O) GLYC(O) LYXO SACCHAR(I)(O) SUCR(O) THREO
(SUFF.) ULOSE
SUGARCANE CANE GRAIN GLUMAL RATOON MATTRESS
(— SAP) LIQUOR
SUGARHOUSE (PART OF —) PURGERY
SUGARLESS DRY
SUGARPLUM KISS
SUGARY FAT SUGAR SWEET OVERRIPE
SUGGEST JOG BEAR GIVE HINT MINT IMPLY OFFER POSIT SPEAK ADVISE ALLUDE HINTAT INDITE INFUSE MOTION PROMPT RESENT SUBMIT CONNOTE DICTATE INSPIRE INDICATE INTIMATE PROPOUND
(— DRINKING) PROPOSE
(— INSIDIOUSLY) INFUSE
(— STRONGLY) ARGUE
SUGGESTIBLE SOFT
SUGGESTION CUE CAST HINT TANG WIND GLIFF TWANG ADVICE BREATH MOTION SMATCH INKLING LEADING POINTER PROFFER REMNANT SOUPCON WRINKLE INNUENDO INSTANCE PROPOSAL
SUGGESTIVE RACY SEXY RISQUE ANICONIC PREGNANT REDOLENT
(— OF MELODY) CANOROUS
SUICIDAL KAMIKAZE
SUIT DO GO APT DOW FIT GEE HIT SET SIT ACTO LIKE LIST PAIR SEEM SORT VINE ADAPT AGREE APPLY BEFIT BESIT CLUBS COLOR DRAPE DRESS FADGE FANCY FRAME HABIT LEVEL MATCH PLEAD QUEME SAVOR SERVE SHAPE STAND SUING TALLY AFFEIR ANSWER BECOME COHERE COMPLY DITTOS EFFEIR HEARTS PRAYER SPADES SPEECH SQUARE BEHOOVE COMPORT COSTUME COULEUR FASHION PURSUIT REQUEST SEERPAW DIAMONDS INSTANCE QUADRATE SKELETON STANDARD TAILLEUR TROPICAL PINSTRIPE
(— AT LAW) ACTO CASE LAWSUIT
(— OF ARMOR) PANOPLY
(— OF MAIL) CATAPHRACT
(DIVER'S —) SCAPHANDER
(KIND OF —) ZOOT
(SWIMMING —) BATHER BIKINI MAILLOT
SUITABILITY (MUTUAL —) DECENCY IDONEITY SYMPATHY
SUITABLE APT FIT PAT ABLE FEAT GAIN GOOD JUMP JUST MEET TALL WELL WEME DIGNE EQUAL FITTY QUEME RIGHT SUITY COMELY FITTEN GAINLY GIUSTO HABILE

HONEST LIABLE LIKELY PROPER SUITLY AVENANT COMMODE CONDIGN CONGRUE FITTING IDONEAL PLIABLE SEEMING BECOMING DECOROUS ELIGIBLE FEASIBLE HANDSOME IDONEOUS SORTABLE ACCORDING OPPORTUNE
(— FOR MALE AND FEMALE) UNISEX
(— FOR STAGE PERFORMANCE) ACTING
(EXACTLY —) VERY
(NOT —) UNFIT IMPROPER
SUITABLENESS APTNESS HONESTY APTITUDE PROPERTY
SUITABLY FITLY MEETLY TIDELY APROPOS GRADELY
SUITCASE BAG CAP GRIP CAPCASE DORLACH KEESTER PULLMAN
SUITE SET SUIT TAIL SWEEP SWEET TRAIN SERIES PARTITA RETINUE ENSEMBLE EQUIPAGE
(— OF MOLDINGS) LEDGMENT
(— OF ROOMS) FLAT CHAMBER
SUITED FIT ADAPT SEEMLY ADAPTED ASSORTED CONGENIAL
(POORLY —) CROOK
(SUFF.) (— FOR) ILE
SUITING COVERT CHEVIOT SHARKSKIN
SUITOR MAN BEAU SUER SWAIN WOOER GALLANT SERVANT
SUKU WASUKUMA
SULCUS RUT FURROW GROOVE
SULFATE DEX
SULFIDE GLANCE CUBANITE SULFURET COVELLITE
SULFUR BRIMSTONE
(PREF.) THI(O)
SULK DOD PET CHAW CRAB DORT GLUM POUT SULL BOODY FRUMP GLUMP GROUT GRUMP GROUCH SNUDGE THURMUS
(PL.) GEE HUMP GLOUT MUMPS FRUMPS SULLENS BOUDERIE
SULKER MUMPER
SULKINESS DORT GRUMP
SULKING PET BOUDERIE
SULKY BIKE CART CHUFF DODDY DORTY GOURY HUFFY HUMPY CHUFFY GLUMPY GROUTY JINKER SNUFFY STUFFY SULLEN SUMPHY DOGGISH HUFFISH MUMPISH
(NOT —) GOOD
SULLEN DOUR FOUL GLUM GRIM SOUR BLACK CHUFF CROSS DUMPY FELON GRUFF HARSH MOODY RUSTY STERN SULKY SURLY WEMOD CRUSTY DOGGED GLOOMY GLUMMY GLUMPY GLUNCH GROUTY MOROSE MULISH SOMBER SOMBRE STUFFY AUSTERE CRABBED CYNICAL FRETFUL LOURING LUMPISH MUMPISH PEEVISH CHUMPISH CHURLISH FAROUCHE LOWERING PETULANT SPITEFUL STUNKARD
SULLENNESS GEE DORT GLUM MUMPS STOMACH
SULLIED DIRTY SPOTTED
SULLY BLOT BLUR DASH FOUL SLUR SMIT SMUT SOIL CLOUD DIRTY

GRIME SMEAR SMOKE STAIN TAINT BEFOUL DARKEN DEFILE SMIRCH SMUTCH ATTAINT BEGRIME BESMEAR BLEMISH CORRUPT DISTAIN ECLIPSE POLLUTE SLUBBER TARNISH BESMIRCH BESPATTER
SULPHATE ALUM BARITE ILESITE LOWEITE SULFATE VITRIOL KRAUSITE
SULPHIDE HEPAR GLANCE ZARNEC SULFIDE ZARNICH CUBANITE
(PL.) MATTE
SULPHUR ORE SPIRIT SULFUR YELLOW QUEBRITH BRIMSTONE
SULPHURIC ACID VITRIOL
SULTAN SOLDAN
(— OF MOROCCO) SHERIF SHEREEF
SULTANATE SULTANY ZANZIBAR
SULTANESS SOWDONES
SULTRY CLOSE FLUSH FAINTY SMUDGY POTHERY PUTHERY SWELTRY FEVERISH
SUM ALL GOB AGIO CASH DRAB DUMP FARM FINE FOOT FUND MASS TALE DEDIT GROSS KITTY SUMMA TOTAL WHOLE AMOUNT DEMAND DYADIC FIGURE NUMBER DECUPLE INGOING MANBOTE SUBSIDY SUMMARY SUMMATE ENTIRETY OCTONION QUANTITY MOUNTANCE OVERDRAFT POLYNOMIAL
(— AND SUBSTANCE) TOUR SHORT UPSHOT
(— AS COMPENSATION FOR KILLING) MANBOTE
(— FOR REENLISTMENT) GRATUITY
(— FOR SCHOLARSHIP) BURSARY
(— IN BASSET) SEPTLEVA
(— OF) SIGMA
(— OF DETERMINANTS) STIRP
(— OF EXPONENTS) DEGREE
(— OF FACTORS) COMPLEX
(— OF GOOD QUALITIES) ARETE
(— OF MONEY) POT BANK PILE COVER PURSE STOCK BUNDLE ACCOUNT DEPOSIT GRASSUM STIPEND
(— OF 25 POUNDS) PONY PONEY
(— OF 3 FARTHINGS) GILL
(— OF 500 POUNDS) MONKEY
(— PAYABLE AT FIXED INTERVALS) FARM
(— RISKED) STAKE
(— UP) ADD TOT FOOT RECAP ASSESS RECKON SUBSUME SUMMATE COMPRISE CONCLUDE PERORATE
(COMPLETE —) SOLIDUM
(ENTIRE —) SOLIDUM
(EXCESS —) BONUS
(FORFEITED —) DEDIT
(GREAT —) PLUNK SIGHT MICKLE
(LARGE —) GOB SCREAMER
(PETTY —) CENT DIME DRAB
(SMALL — OF MONEY) SPILL DRIBBLE DRIBLET SHOESTRING
(TRIFLING —) HAY GROAT
(UNEXPENDED —S) SAVINGS
(VAST —) MINT
(VECTOR —) GRADIENT
(PL.) BATTELS

SUMAC FUSTET KARREE SUMACH ANACARD BURTREE SCOTINO SHOEMAKE
SUMATRA (ISLAND NEAR —) NIAS
(LANGUAGE IN —) NIAS
(MEASURE OF —) PAAL
(MOUNTAIN IN —) LEUSER KERINTJI
(RIVER IN —) HARI MUSI ROKAN DJAMBI
(TOWN IN —) ACHIN KUALA MEDAN NATAL SOLOK DJAMBI LANGSA PADANG RENGAT BENKULEN
SUMBUL SAMBUL MUSKROOT
SUMERIAN ACCADIAN AKKADIAN
SUMITRA (HUSBAND OF —) DASHARATHA
(SON OF —) LAKSHMANA SHATRUGHNA
SUMMARIZE RECAP PRECIS RESUME WRAPUP ABSTRACT
SUMMARY SUM CURT LEAD BRIEF CHART RECAP SCORE SHORT SUMMA TOTAL APERCU DIGEST PRECIS RESUME SUMMAR CHAPTER CONCISE EPITOME EXTRACT MEDULLA OUTLINE RUNDOWN VIDIMUS ABSTRACT ARGUMENT BREVIARY BREVIATE DRUMHEAD HEADNOTE OVERVIEW SUCCINCT SYNOPSIS
(— OF FAITH) SYMBOL
(— OF PRINCIPLES) CREED
(CONCISE —) PRECIS
SUMMATION SUM DIGEST SUMMARY
SUMMER ETE SHEMU SOMER AESTAS SIMMER DORMANT
(OF —) ESTIVAL
(PREF.) ESTIVO
SUMMER CYPRESS KOCHIA
SUMMER FLOUNDER PLAICE
SUMMERHOUSE FOLLY KIOSK MAHAL TUPEK ALCOVE CASINO GAZEBO PAGODA CABINET BELVEDERE
SUMMER HYACINTH GALTONIA
SUMMER TANAGER REDBIRD
SUMMERWOOD LATEWOOD
SUMMIT CAP DOD SUM TIP TOP VAN ACME APEX BALD CRAP DODD HELM KNAP KNOT PEAK ROOF CREST CROWN SPIRE COMBLE CULMEN HEIGHT VERTEX ZENITH CALOTTE SUMMARY SUMMITY PINNACLE MOUNTAINTOP
(— OF TUBE) MOUTH
(— WITHOUT FOREST) BALD
(ROCKY —) KNOT
(ROUND —) DOD DODD
(SNOW-CAPPED —) CALOTTE
(PREF.) APICO CORY(PH)(PHO)
(SUFF.) ACE
SUMMON BAN CRY BUZZ CALL CITE DRUM HAIL SIST BUGLE CHARM CLEPE EVOKE HIGHT KNELL SOUND VOUCH ACCITE ADVOKE BECALL BECKON COMPEL DEMAND SOMPNE VOCATE ACCERSE COMMAND CONJURE CONVENE CONVENT CONVOKE PROVOKE SUMMONS WHISTLE ASSUMMON EXORCISE
(— FOR HIRING) YARD

(— INTO COURT) DEMAND
(— TOGETHER) BAND MUSTER
ASSEMBLE
(— UP) FIND GATHER COLLECT
SUMMONER SUMNER LOCKMAN
SOMPNER OUTRIDER
SUMMONING CALL ARRAY
(— OF KING'S VASSALS) BAN
SUMMONS CRY CALL BREVE CITAL
TICKET BIDDING CALLING STICKER
WARNING WARRANT CITATION
MONITION VOCATION
(— TO GET UP) REVEILLE
(FALCONER'S —) WO
SUMP SINK STANDAGE
SUMPTUOUS RICH GRAND SHOWY
WLONK COSTLY DELUXE SOLEMN
SUPERB COSTLEW ELEGANT
MAGNIFIC SPLENDID MAGNIFICENT
SUMPTUOUSNESS LUXE DAINTY
SUMPTURE
SUN ORB SOL ATEN ATON BASK INTI
LAMP STAR SENGE SURYA TITAN
SUNLET DAYSTAR IOSKEHA
PHOEBUS SAVITAR JOUSKEHA
(— MOON AND STARS) HOST
(MOCK —) PARHELION
(RISING —) HERAKHTI
(PREF.) HELI(O) SOLARO SOLI
(SUFF.) HELION
SUN ALSO RISES (AUTHOR OF —)
HEMINGWAY
(CHARACTER IN —) BILL COHN JAKE
MIKE BRETT CLYNE PEDRO ASHLEY
BARNES GORTON ROBERT ROMERO
FRANCES MICHAEL MONTOYA
CAMPBELL GEORGETTE
SUNAPEE TROUT SAIBLING
SUNBATHE GETATAN APRICATE
SUNBATHER BAKE
SUNBEAM BANANA
SUN BEAR BRUANG
SUNBIRD MAMO CADET FINFOOT
SUN BITTERN CARLE CAURALE
SUNBIRD
SUN BLIND CHICK UMRELLA
SUNBONNET TILT UGLY CRESIE
KAPPIE SHAKER
SUNBURN GREENING HELIOSIS
(— REMEDY) ALOE
SUNBURNED BRONZED
SUNBURNT ADUST BROWN
TANNED
SUNBURST SUNRAY SUNBREAK
SUNSHINE
SUNDAE GEDUNK
SUNDA ISLANDS (GREATER —)
JAVA BORNEO CELEBES SUMATRA
(LESSER —) BALI TIMOR
SUNDAY EXAUDI JUDICA GAUDETE
TRINITY
(FIFTH — AFTER EASTER) ROGATE
(FIRST — AFTER EASTER)
QUASIMODO
(FIRST — IN LENT) QUADRAGESIMA
(FOURTH — IN LENT) LAETARE
(LOW —) QUASIMODO
(SECOND — BEFORE LENT)
SEXAGESIMA
(THIRD — AFTER EASTER) JUBILATE
SUNDER PART RIVE TWIN BREAK
SEVER TWAIN TWINE DEPART
DIVIDE SINDER ASUNDER DISALLY

DISJOIN DIVORCE DISSEVER
SEJUGATE SEPARATE UNSOLDER
SUNDEW DROSERA EYEBRIGHT
SUNDIAL DIAL GHURRY HOROLOGE
SCAPHION SOLARIUM
(PART OF —) DIAL LINE PLATE
GNOMON DIAGRAM
SUN DISK ATEN ATON CAKHA
CHAKRA
SUNDOG WINDGALL PARHELION
SUNDOWNER HOBO DRINK TRAMP
WHALER TUSSOCKER
SUN-DRIED TILED
SUNDROPS SCABISH
SUNDRY DIVERS DIVERSE SEVERAL
SUNFISH SUN HURO MOLA OPAH
RUFF BREAM FLIER FLYER ROACH
SUNNY KIVVER MOLOID REDEAR
REDEYE CRAPPIE CROPPIE
PANFISH PERCOID BLUEGILL
FLATFISH FLOUNDER HEADFISH
MOONFISH PONDFISH WARMOUTH
REDBREAST PUMPKINSEED
SUNFLOWER GOLD HELIO CANADA
GOLDEN SUNFOIL GIRASOLE
TURNSOLE
(— STATE) KANSAS
SUNGLASSES SHADES
SUN-GREBE FINFOOT SUNBIRD
GRUIFORM
SUNK SUNKEN
(— TO LOW STATE) ABJECT
SUNKEN SUNK LAIGH HOLLOW
SUNKEN BELL (CHARACTER IN —)
MAGDA HEINRICH RAUTENDELEIN
(COMPOSER OF —) RESPIGHI
SUNLESS BLAE
SUNLIGHT GLARE
SUNN SAN SANN DAGGA SANAI
JANAPA MADRAS JANAPAN
SANNHEMP
SUNNITE IHLAT SUNNI SUNNIAH
SUNNY GOOD SUNSHINE
SUN PARLOR SOLARIUM
SUNRISE ARIST SUNUP ORIENT
(KIND OF —) TEQUILA
(TEQUILA —) COCKTAIL
SUNSET SUNFALL
(— STATE) OREGON ARIZONA
SUNSHADE PARASOL ROUNDEL
TIRESOL SOMBRERO
SUNSHINE SUN SHINE SUNLIGHT
(— STATE) FLORIDA
SUNSPOT SPOT FACULA MACULA
SUNSPURGE SUNWEED TURNSOLE
WARTWEED WARTWORT
SUNSTROKE HELIOSIS SIRIASIS
SUNTAN MERIDA
SUN TREE HINOKI
SUNWISE DEASIL DESSIL
SUNYATA VOID
SUP EAT DINE SOWP FEAST
CONSUME SWALLOW
SUPAWN MUSH
SUPER COOL FINE GRAND GREAT
NEATO NIFTY
SUPER-
(PREF.) HYPER
SUPERABOUND OVERFLOW
SUPERABUNDANCE FLOOD
EXCESS CATARACT PLEONASM
PLETHORA PLEURISY PLURISIE

SUPERABUNDANT RANK LAVISH
PROFUSE
SUPERALTAR PREDELLA
SUPERANNUATE RETIRE
OVERYEAR
SUPERB GRAND GOLDEN CLIPPING
GORGEOUS SPLENDID
SUPERCARGO MERCHANT
SUPERCILIOUS GRAND POTTY
PROUD OVERLY SNIFFY SNIPPY
SNOOTY SNOTTY SNUFFY
HAUGHTY ARROGANT CAVALIER
SNIFFISH SUPERIOR
SUPERCLASS AGNATHA
SUPERCONSCIOUSNESS
SAMADHI
SUPERCOOL SUBCOOL SURFUSE
SUPERFAMILY APINA APOIDEA
BOVOIDEA
(SUFF.) OIDA OIDEA OIDEI
SUPERFICIAL GLIB ECTAL SUPER
FACIAL FACILE FLIMSY FORMAL
FROTHY GLASSY OVERLY SLIGHT
CURSORY OUTSIDE OUTWARD
PASSING SHALLOW SKETCHY
SLIGHTY SURFACE SURFACY
COSMETIC EXTERNAL MAGAZINY
SMATTERY DEPTHLESS
SUPERFICIALLY FLEET
SUPERFICIES TERM EXTENT
SUPERFLUITY FAT FRILL LUXUS
EXCESS OVERSET SURFEIT
PLETHORA REDUNDANCY
(CONFUSING —) FLUTHER
SUPERFLUOUS SPARE OTIOSE
USELESS NEEDLESS REDUNDANT
SUPERFRONTAL FRONTLET
SUPERHEATED GASEOUS
SUPERHIGHWAY MOTORWAY
(AVOID —) SHUNPIKE
SUPERHUMAN DEMON DAEMON
DIVINE INHUMAN UNHUMAN
SUPERIMPOSE LAY OVERLAY
SURPRINT
SUPERIMPOSING DISSOLVE
SUPERINTEND CON CONN GUIDE
OVERSEE PRESIDE
SUPERINTENDENCE CARE
CONTROL EPISCOPY GUIDANCE
SUPERINTENDENCY EDILITY
AEDILITY
SUPERINTENDENT BOSS SUPE
EPHOR SUPER EDITOR VENEUR
VIEWER WARDEN CAPTAIN
CURATOR EPHORUS MANAGER
DIRECTOR OVERSEER SURVEYOR
SWINGMAN
SUPERIOR JOE AYNE COOL FINE
MORE OVER TRIE ABBOT ABOVE
CHIEF CREAM EIGNE ELDER ELITE
EXTRA FANCY FRANK GREAT LIEGE
PRIOR PUKKA SWANK UPPER
ABBESS BETTER COCKUP CUSTOS
DOMINA FATHER FORBYE MAHANT
SELECT SENIOR STRONG FORTHBY
PALMARY RANKING ABNORMAL
DOMINANT GUARDIAN SINGULAR
SPLENDID SUPERIAL MARVELOUS
PARAMOUNT
(— IN MANNER) SUPERCILIOUS
(— OF CONVENT) HEGUMEN
(— ONE) LAMA

(— TO) ATOP BEFORE
(PREF.) SUPER
SUPERIORITY DROP GREE PRICE
HEIGHT MASTERY PROWESS
EMINENCE PRIORITY
(MENTAL —) GENIUS
SUPERLATIVE RAVING CURIOUS
ROUSING CRASHING OLYMPIAN
PEERLESS SWINGING ULTIMATE
(ABSOLUTE —) ELATIVE
(SUFF.) EST
SUPERLATIVELY CRACKING
SWINGING
SUPERMAN OVERMAN
OBERMENSCH
SUPERNATURAL FEY ARCANE
DIVINE NUMINOUS SUPERIOR
MARVELOUS PARANORMAL
(— FORCE) WAKANDA
SUPERNUMERARY ORRA
(PREF.) POLY
SUPERORDER GLIRES
SUPERPOSE APPLY
SUPER-REMEDY CUREALL
SUPERSCRIBE DIRECT
SUPERSCRIPT SUPERIOR
SUPERSEDE REPLACE OVERRIDE
SUPPLANT
SUPERSTITION FREIT IDOLATRY
ABERGLAUBE
SUPERSTITIOUS FREITY
SUPERTONIC SECOND
SUPERVENE BEFALL FOLLOW
SUPERVISE BOSS GUIDE DIRECT
GOVERN HANDLE SURVEY
FOREMAN OVERSEE PROCTOR
ENGINEER OVERLOOK CHAPERONE
SUPERVISION EYE CARE DUTY
HAND CHECK CHARGE OVERSIGHT
SUPERVISOR BOSS BULL EPHOR
GUIDE SUPER CENSOR GASMAN
RUNMAN SOURER WARDEN
DESKMAN PROCTOR ALYTARCH
CHAIRMAN FLOORMAN
FOREHAND KNIFEMAN LEACHMAN
MASHGIAH OVERSEER
(— OF STUDENT DISCIPLINE)
HEBDOMADAR HEBDOMADER
SUPINE INERT DROWSY LANGUID
SERVILE UPRIGHT CARELESS
INACTIVE INDOLENT LISTLESS
SLUGGISH
SUPPER CENA MEAL CUDDY
HOCKEY PASCHAL
(— AT HOME) FATIN
(HARVEST-HOME —) HOCKEY
(LAST —) MAUNDY
(LORD'S —) NAGMAAL
SUPPING CENATION
SUPPLANT FOLLOW REMOVE
REPLACE DISPLACE DISPLANT
SUPPLE BAIN FLIP OILY SOFT WIRY
LINGY LITHE SLAMP SWACK
AJOINT LIMBER LITHER LUTHER
PLIANT SUMPLE SVELTE SWANKY
WANDLE LISSOME PLIABLE
SPRINGE FLEXIBLE
SUPPLEJACK SOAPWORT
SUPPLEMENT ARM EKE MEND
TACK ANNEX SUPPLY BOLSTER
CODICIL ADDENDUM APPENDIX
BOUNTITH
(PL.) FIXINGS

SUPPLEMENTAL SPECIAL
PIGGYBACK
SUPPLEMENTARY ADDED SECOND
RIPIENO REMANENT PERIPHERAL
SUPPLENESS WHIP
SUPPLIANT ASKER PLEADING
SUPPLICATE BEG PRAY CRAVE
PLEAD INVOKE OBTEST SUPPLY
BESEECH ENTREAT IMPLORE
REQUEST SOLICIT PETITION
SUPPLICATION CRY VOW BEAD
BILL LIBEL VENIE APPEAL LITANY
PRAYER CRAVING SYNAPTE
ENTREATY PETITION PLEADING
ROGATION ROGATIVE SUFFRAGE
SUPPLICATORY EUCTICAL
SUPPLIED (— WITH FOOD) THORN
(AMPLY —) ABUNDANT
(SCANTILY —) BARE
SUPPLIER SOURCE
SUPPLIES STOCK STUFF DUFFEL
STORES VICTUAL ESTOVERS
ORDNANCE
SUPPLY FEED FILL FIND FRET FUND
GIVE HEEL LEND LINE ARRAY
CATER ENDUE EQUIP INDUE OFFER
SERVE STOCK STORE STUFF YIELD
BUDGET DONATE EMPLOY FOISON
LAYOUT POCKET RENDER SUBMIT
ADVANCE FORTIFY FRAUGHT
FURNISH LISSOME PROVIDE
ACCOMMODATE
(— ABUNDANTLY) SWILL
(— ARRANGED BEFOREHAND)
RELAY
(— EXCESSIVELY) FLOOD
(— FOR AN OCCASION) GRIST
(— FULLY) SATISFY
(— LIQUOR BY SHIP) COPER
COOPER
(— OF FOOD) BOARD
(— OF HORSES) RELAY REMUDA
REMOUNT
(— OF MONEY) BANKROLL
(— OF POTENTIAL JURORS) TALES
(— OF REMOUNTS) REMUDA
(— OF SOLDIERS) GARRISON
(— OF TIN) SERVING
(— PROVISIONS) PURVEY
(— THE NEED) FOR
(— WITH CLOTHES) INFIT
(— WITH FOOD) FODDER
(— WITH FUEL) STOKE
(— WITH LIQUOR) LUBRICATE
(— WITH MONEY) GILD
(— WITH OXYGEN) AERATE
(— WITH WATER) FANG
(CACHED —) CAVE
(CONSTANT —) STREAM
(EXTRA —) RESERVE
(FRESH —) RECRUIT
(FULL —) PLENTY
(HIDDEN —) HOARD
(INADEQUATE —) DEARTH
(LARGE —) TON PILE
(NEW —) RECRUIT
(OVERABUNDANT —) SURFEIT
(PLENTIFUL —) CHOICE
(RENEWED —) RECRUITAL
(RESERVE —) CUSHION
(RICH —) ARGOSY
(SCANTY —) SCANT
(SECRET —) CACHE

SUPPORT AID ARM BAY BED BOW
KAI LEG PEG RIB TIE TOM ABET
ABUT AXIS BACK BASE BEAM BEAR
BUOY CRIB DADE FEND FIND FIRM
FORK FUEL HAVE HELP HOLD
JAMB KEEP KILP LIFT POST PROP
RACK REST ROCK SALT SIDE STAY
STEM STUD TRIG ADOPT AEGIS
ANGEL APPUI ATLAS BIPOD BLOCK
BRACE BROOK CARRY CHAIR
CHEER CHOCK CLEAT CRANK
FAVOR FLOAT FRAME OXTER
PLUNK POISE RANCE SALVE SHORE
SPURN STAFF STAKE STEAD STELL
STIPE STOCK STOOP STRUT STULL
TOWER VOUCH WEIGH ANCHOR
ASSERT ASSIST BARROW BEHALF
CHEVAL COLUMN CORSET CRADLE
CRUTCH DEFEND DONKEY
DUOPOD GARTER PATTEN PILLAR
POTENT PULPIT PUTLOG SADDLE
SECOND SHIELD SOCKET SPLINT
STAYER STEADY SUFFER TASSEL
TIMBER TINGLE TORSEL UPHAND
UPHOLD UPKEEP UPTAKE WHIMSY
ALIMENT ARMREST BACKING
BOLSTER COMFORT CONFIRM
CRIPPLE DEADMAN ENDORSE
ESPOUSE FINDING FULCRUM
GROMMET HOUSING JACKLEG
JUSTIFY KEEPING KNUCKLE
NOURISH NURTURE PABULUM
PROTECT RADICAL SPIRALE
SPONSOR SQUINCH STADDLE
STANDER STIRRUP STIRRUP
SUBSIST SUSTAIN THICKEN
TRESTLE ADJUMENT ADVOCATE
BALUSTER BEFRIEND BESTRIDE
BOOKREST BUTTRESS CAPSHORE
FAIRLEAD FOOTREST FORESTAY
FORTRESS HANDREST HOLDFAST
JACKSTAY KEYSTONE MAINSTAY
MAINTAIN MOUNTING NEEDLING
ORTHOTIC OVERCAST PEDESTAL
PEDIMENT STANDARD STILLAGE
STOCKING STRENGTH SYMPATHY
UNDERLIE UNDERPIN UNDERSET
PATRONAGE MAINTENANCE
(— FINANCIALLY) BANKROLL
(— FOR ANVIL) STOCK
(— FOR BELL CLAPPER) BALDRIC
(— FOR CANDLE) STICK
(— FOR CANOPY) BAIL TESTER
(— FOR CATALYST) CARRIER
(— FOR COLUMN) SOCLE
(— FOR CORSET) BUSK
(— FOR HEAVY MACHINERY)
BUNTING
(— FOR KNEES) STOOL
(— FOR LAUNCHING SHIP) POPPET
(— FOR LEVER) BAIT
(— FOR LIFE-CAR) BAIL
(— FOR MAST) STEP
(— FOR MILL) LOWDER
(— FOR MINE PASSAGE) OVERCAST
(— FOR OARLOCK) OUTRIGGER
(— FOR PICTURE HOOKS) CORNICE
(— FOR PIPE) CHAPLET
(— FOR PLATFORM) STEMPEL
STEMPLE
(— FOR SHAFT) STEMPEL STEMPLE
(— IN A LATHE) DOCTOR
(— IN PAPERMAKING TUB) DONKEY

(— OF COLUMN) SOCLE PLINTH
(— OF COPING) KNEELER
(— OF MOLD CORE) ARBOR
ARBOUR
(— OF RAIL) CHAIR BALUSTER
(— THROUGH BIT AND BRIDLE)
APPUI
(CRUTCHLIKE —) DEADMAN
(ELBOW-SHAPED —) CRANK
(EMBEDDED —) SPURN
(FIREPLACE —) ANDIRON
(GIVE —) FEED
(INCLINED —) RIDER
(LACKING —) FOOTLESS
(LOSE —) ERODE
(MINING —) CAP FRAME
(PORTABLE —) STOOL
(PRINCIPAL —) BACKBONE
(SHOE —) TREE
(TEMPORARY —) NEEDLING
(UPRIGHT —) POPPET BANISTER
(WHEELED —) CARRIAGE
(PL.) SHIPWAY
SUPPORTED BASED BLOCKED
ACCOSTED SUCCINCT
(— BY EVIDENCE) PROBABLE
SUPPORTER ALLY JOCK ATLAS
STOOP COHORT DRAGON SATRAP
APOSTLE BOOSTER DEVOTEE
FAVORER FOUNDER LAUDIAN
PATROON PROPPER SUPPORT
ADHERENT ASSERTER ERASTIAN
ESPOUSER FAVORITE HENCHMAN
STALWART UPHOLDER CHURCHITE
(ATHLETIC —) CUP JOCK
(CHIEF —) STOOP PILLAR
(PL.) SECOND
(SUFF.) CRAT ITE
SUPPORTING BEHIND BEARING
SUPPORTIVE ENGAGE
SUPPOSE SAY SEE SET WIS WIT
DEEM POSE READ TAKE TROW
WEEN ALLOW COUNT ETTLE
FANCY GUESS JUDGE OPINE
SEPAD THINK ASSUME DEVISE
DIVINE EXPECT RECKON BELIEVE
CONCEIT DARESAY IMAGINE
PRESUME PROPOSE SUPPONE
SURMISE CONCEIVE CONCLUDE
CONSIDER OPINIATE
SUPPOSED ALLEGED ASSUMED
PUTATIVE
SUPPOSING IF
SUPPOSITION IDEA FICTION
SURMISE WEENING
SUPPOSITORY BOUGIE CANDLE
PESSARY
SUPPRESS LAY DOWN GULP HIDE
HUSH SINK SLAY SNUB STOP
BLACK BURKE CHOKE CRUSH
ELIDE QUASH QUELL SHUSH
SMORE SPIKE STILL CANCEL
QUENCH SQUASH STIFLE CONTAIN
CUSHION INHIBIT OPPRESS
REPRESS SILENCE SMOLDER
SMOTHER SQUELCH RESTRAIN
STRANGLE SUPPRIME VANQUISH
(— A SYLLABLE) ELIDE
(— IN SPEAKING) MINCE
SUPPRESSED BLIND CENSORED
SUPPRESSION ABEYANCE
AMEIOSIS BLACKOUT
(— OF VOWEL) ELISION

(— OF WORD SOUNDS) SYNCOPE
ECLIPSIS
(PREF.) ISCH(O)
(SUFF.) SCHESIS SCHETIC
SUPPURATE RUN BEAL WHEAL
DIGEST MATTER QUITTER
MATURATE
SUPPURATING
(PREF.) EMPYO
SUPPURATION PYOSIS BEALING
COCTION
SUPPURATIVE DIGERENT
SUPRACLAVICLE SCAPULA
SUPREMACY PALM PRIMACY
DOMINION OVERRULE
SUPREME HIGH LAST CHIEF VITAL
SUBLIME SUMMARY TOPLESS
FOREMOST GREATEST PEERLESS
SURA FATIHA FATIHAH
SURCHARGE PACK
SURCINGLE WANTY ROLLER
SURCOAT JUPON CYCLAS KABAYA
SURD SHARP ATONIC FLATED
SURE COLD SAFE BOUND SECURE
SICCAR SICKER STEADY WITTER
ASSURED CERTAIN PERFECT
COCKSURE POSITIVE UNERRING
SURELY WIS FINE IWIS SURE PARDY
REDLY ATWEEL PARDIE
SURENESS SURETY SECURITY
SURETY VAS ANDI BAIL BAND
BORROW CAUTION ENGAGER
SOVERTY SPONSOR BAILSMAN
SECURITY
SURETYSHIP SPONSION
SURF BREACH KALEMA
(— NOISE) RUT ROTE
SURFACE DAY AREA FACE ORLO
PLAT RYME SIDE ARISE BOSOM
FLOOR STONE SWARF CHROME
EMERGE FINISH GROUND SCRUFF
ASPHALT BLANKET COUNTER
ENVELOP OUTFACE OUTSIDE
STRETCH ADHIBEND CONCRETE
EXTERIOR PLATFORM
(— BESIDE FIREPLACE) HOB
(— BETWEEN FLUTES OF SHAFT)
ORLO
**(— BETWEEN TRIGLYPH
CHANNELS)** MEROS
(— IN BEATER) BACKFALL
(— OF A GEM) BEZEL
(— OF ARCH) INTRADOS
(— OF BEAM) BACK
(— OF BODY) FLESH HABIT
(— OF CLOTH) PILE
(— OF COAL) BUTT
(— OF CRICKET FIELD) CARPET
(— OF DIAMOND) SPREAD
(— OF EARTH) DUST GROUND
TERRENE PENEPLAIN PENEPLANE
(— OF ESCUTCHEON) FIELD
(— OF GEM) FACET TABLE
(— OF GROUND OVER MINE) DAY
(— OF HAND) PALM
(— OF LIQUID) MENISCUS
(— OF MINE) GRASS
(— OF PARACHUTE) CANOPY
(— OF RECESS) REVEAL
(— OF RIFLE BARREL) LAND
(— OF ROOT) RHIZOPLANE
(— OF SAWED LUMBER) FUR
(— OF SHIELD) FIELD

(— OF TOOTH) TRITOR
(— OF VAULT) GROIN
(— OF WATER) RYME SCRUFF
(— WITHIN EARTH) GEOID
(AIRPLANE CONTROL —) ELEVEN
(BOUNDING —) PERIPHERY
(COBBLESTONE —) PITCHING
(CONCAVE —) LAP
(CONCRETE —) PAD
(CONTROL —) RUDDER
(CONVEX —) EXTRADOS
(CURVED —) BELLY
(DULL —) MAT MATTING
(EXTERNAL —) PERIPHERY
(FLAT —) BED FLAT AEQUOR
PAGINA
(FLOOR —) BOWL
(FRONTAL —) METOPE
(GEOMETRIC —) TORE CONOID
SPHERE QUARTIC CONICOID
CYLINDER HELICOID PARABOLOID
(GLASSY —) HYALINE
(GLOSSY —) GLAZE
(GRASSY —) SWARD
(GROOVED —) DROVE
(HAIRY —) NAP
(HORIZONTAL —) LEVEL
(INCLINED —) CANT DESCENT
(MINERAL —) DRUSE
(PAVED —) FOOTWALK
(PILE —) FRIEZE
(PLANE —) AREA FACET
(PRINCIPAL —) FACE
(PRINTING —) CUT
(PROTECTIVE —) LAGGING
(REFLECTING —) MIRROR HORIZON
(ROAD —) MACADAM CORDUROY
(ROUGH —) KEY CRIZZLE STUBBLE
(ROUGHENED —) MAT FOOTGRIP
(SLIPPERY —) GLARE
(SLOPING —) SHELVING
(STRIKING —) BLADE
(UNDER — OF SKI) PALM
(UNGLOSSY PAINT —) FLAT
(UPPER —) NOTAEUM
(UPRIGHT —) JAMB
(WOOLLY —) NAP
(PREF.) **(BENT —)** SINU SINUATO
SURFACER SEASONER
SURFBOARD GUN
(LONG —) GUN BIGGUN
SURF DUCK COOT SCOTER
SURFEIT CLOY FILL GLUT SATE
STAW STALL STUFF AGROTE
ENGLUT SICKEN SATIATE SATIETY
SURCLOY SATURATE REPLETION
SATURATION
SURFEITED SAD SICK BLASE JADED
WEARY REPLETE SATIATED
SURFER GREMMY GREMLIN
GREMMIE
(GIRL —) WAHINE
(INEXPERIENCED —) GREMMY
GREMMIE
SURF FISH PERCH ALFIONA
SURFING (— MANEUVER) CUTBACK
SURF SCOTER COOT SCOTER
SURFER PISHAUG SKUNKTOP
SURF SHINER SPARADA
SURGE JAW GUST TIDE WASH
DRIVE GURGE LUNGE SPURT
SWELL BILLOW BREACH COURSE
ONRUSH SEETHE WALLOW

WALTER ESTUATE REDOUND
AESTUATE UNDULATE
(— OF ELECTRIC POWER) GLITCH
(SHOREWARD —) SUFF
(TIDAL —) EAGRE
SURGEON (AMERICAN) WOOD
COOLEY DEVRIES OCHSNER
THEOREK SEAGRAVE SLAUGHTER
**SURGEON (ALSO SEE PHYSICIAN
AND DOCTOR)** LEECH ARTIST
INTERN MEDICO OPERATOR
SAWBONES
(TREE —) TREEMAN
AMERICAN EVE BULL KEEN LONG
MAYO MOTT REED WOOD AGNEW
COLEY CRILE FLINT GROSS LAHEY
CARREL COOLEY FINNEY KELMAN
KOPITS LAWLER MORRIS MORTON
SHRADY ASHFORD BLALOCK
CUSHING DEVRIES HALSTED
HARTLEY HUGGINS KELLOGG
LAPLACE OCHSNER THEOREK
BEAUMONT MCBURNEY
MCDOWELL METTAUER SEAGRAVE
SLAUGHTER
CANADIAN BETHUNE BIRKETT
ENGLISH POTT REID BRAID HADEN
PAGET BARKER BEDDOE BOWMAN
CHEYNE COOPER FAYRER LISTER
CHARNLEY ERICHSEN MOYNIHAN
ABERNETHY BRIFFAULT CHESELDEN
PARKINSON
FRENCH ANEL PARE BOYER BROCA
PETIT BECHAMP CHOPART CIVIALE
DESAULT NELATON CHAULIAC
CHASSAIGNAC
GERMAN GRAEFE ESMARCH
BILLROTH FORSSMANN
GREEK AMMONIUS
IRISH MADDEN OMEARA
ITALIAN FABRICIUS
RUSSIAN VISHNEVSKY
SCOTTISH BELL SYME BANKS
HUNTER LISTON MACEWEN
SOUTH AFRICAN BARNARD
SPANISH CASTROVIEJO
SWISS KOCHER
SURGEONFISH TANG TANGE
DOCTOR MEDICO BARBERO
SURGEON SAWBONES
SURGERY KNIFE
(VETERINARY —) ZOIATRIA
(SUFF.) CHIRURGIA
SURGING WALE ESTURE ESTUOUS
SURICATE ZENICK MEERKAT
SURINAM (CAPITAL OF —)
PARAMARIBO
(RIVER OF —) ITANY MARONI
COPPENAME SARAMACCA
COURANTYNE
(TOWN OF —) ALBINA KWATTA
TOTNESS LELYDORP
SURINAME (LANGUAGE IN —)
SRANAN
SURINAMINE ANDIRINE ANGELINE
SURINAM TOAD PIPA PIPAL
SURLINESS CYNICISM MOROSITY
SURLY BAD ILL GRUM LUNT BLUFF
CHUFF CYNIC GRUFF GURLY
PURDY ROUGH RUNTY RUSTY
CHUFFY CRUSTY GRUFFY GRUMPY
MOROSE RUGGED SNARLY SULLEN
DOGGISH CHURLISH

SURMISE DEEM REDE GUESS INFER
TWANG SURMIT JALOUSE
SUSPECT WEENING MISTRUST
SURMOUNT TOP BEAT TIDE
CROWN ENSIGN HURDLE MASTER
OUTTOP OVERGO SUBDUE
CONQUER SURPASS OVERCOME
SUPERATE
(— DIFFICULTIES) SWIM
SURMOUNTING ATOP BROCHANT
SURNAME BYNAME SURNOUN
COGNOMEN OVERNAME
SURSTYLE
SURPASS CAP COB TOP WAR BANG
BEAT CAMP COTE DING FLOG FOIL
HEAD PASS SHED WHAP WHOP
EXCEL OUTDO OUTGO TRUMP
ATREDE BETTER EXCEED OUTRAY
OUTRUN OUTVIE OUTWIT OVERDO
PRECEL ECLIPSE FORPASS
OUTPEER OVERTOP PARAGON
PRECEDE ANTECEDE DISTANCE
DOMINATE OUTCLASS OUTMATCH
OUTRANGE OUTREACH OUTSHINE
OUTSTRIP OUTWRITE SURMOUNT
SURPASSING BEST FINE ABOVE
PASSANT PASSING DOMINANT
FRABJOUS TOWERING
(PREF.) PRETER SUPER
SURPLICE SARK COTTA EPHOD
STOLA CHRISOM
(PL.) WHITES
SURPLUS ODD OVER PLUS REST
EXCESS LUMBER SPILTH VELVET
OVERAGE OVERRUN OVERSUM
ARISINGS LEFTOVER OVERCOME
OVERFLOW OVERMUCH
OVERPLUS
SURPRISE CAP SHED SWAN YACH
AMAZE SHOCK SNEAK FERLIE
WAYLAY WONDER ASTOUND
GLOPPEN PERPLEX STARTLE
ASTONISH BEWILDER CONFOUND
DUMFOUND
(BY —) ABACK
(CRY OF —) ACK
(EXCLAMATION OF —) QUOTHA
(EXPRESS —) MIRATE
(INTERJECTION EXPRESSING —)
OOPS WOOPS
(SUDDEN —) KICK
SURPRISING FERLIE STRIKING
SURRA MBORI
SURREJOINDER TRIPLY
SURRENDER HEM LET PUT CEDE
CESS DING FALL QUIT TAKE REMIT
YIELD ADDICT REMISE RENDER
RESIGN SUBMIT ABANDON
CONCEDE DELIVER FORSAKE
KAMERAD ABDICATE ABNEGATE
DEDITION DELIVERY RENOUNCE
UNDERLIE CAPITULATE
(— BY DEED) REMISE
(— OF CLAIM) REMISE
SURREPTITIOUS COVERT SECRET
BOOTLEG FURTIVE SNEAKING
SURROGATE PROXY DEPUTY
SUBSTITUTE
SURROUND HEM LAP ORB BELT
DIKE DYKE FOLD GIRD GIRT HOOP
WRAP BESET BRACE CLASP
EMBAY EMBED FENCE HEDGE
IMBED INARM ROUND BECLIP

BEGIRD BEGIRT CIRCLE COLLET
CORRAL ENFOLD ENWRAP FORSET
GIRDLE IMPALE INCASE INVEST
SPHERE SWATHE ARROUND
BESIEGE BESTAND COMPASS
EMBOSOM ENCLAVE ENCLOSE
ENFEOFF ENROUND ENVELOP
ENVIRON INVOLVE WREATHE
CLOISTER ENCIRCLE ENTRENCH
STOCKADE
(— WITH BOOM) CRIB
(— WITH CORD) GIRT
(— WITH MORTAR) GROUT
SURROUNDED AMID AMONG
AMIDST AMONGST BETWEEN
(— BY WATER) INSULAR
SURROUNDING MIDST ROUND
CIRCUM AMBIENT
(PL.) SCENE HARNESS ENVIRONS
(PREF.) CIRCUM PERI
SURROYALS CROWN
SURVEILLANCE WATCH SCRUTINY
STAKEOUT OVERSIGHT
(— SYSTEM) AWACS
SURVEY EYE SEE DIAL POLL SCAN
VIEW AVIEW STOCK STUDY
PERUSE REGARD REVIEW SEARCH
CANVASS CAPSULE OVERSEE
SURVIEW TERRIER THEORIC
EPISCOPY LUSTRATE OVERLOOK
OVERVIEW PROSPECT SURVEYAL
TRAVERSE RECONNAISANCE
(— RAPIDLY) GLANCE
(— TIMBER) SKYLOOK
(BRIEF —) APERCU
SURVEYING GEODESY GROMATICS
(MINE —) LATCHING
SURVEYOR BOLO ARTIST DIALER
DIALLER NOTEMAN CHAINMAN
GROMATIC LEVELMAN
SURVIVAL ECHO RELIC RELICT
(ANACHRONISTIC —) LEFTOVER
(USELESS —) SNUFF
SURVIVE LAST GETBY BILEVE
OUTLAST OUTLIVE
SURVIVOR RELICT
SURYA (FATHER OF —) ADITI DYAUS
(MESSENGER OF —) PUSHAN
(WIFE OF —) USHAS
SUSCEPTIBILITY CAVIL SENSE
EMOTION FEELING FRAILTY
(— TO ILL-HEALTH) DELICACY
SUSCEPTIBLE EASY SOFT LIABLE
FEELING PATIENT SENSIBLE
TOLERANT
(— TO CHANGE) CASALTY
SUSIAN ELAMITE
SUSLIK SISEL ZIZEL MARMOT
SUSPECT FEAR DOUBT FANCY
GUESS SMOKE THINK BELIEVE
ENDOUTE JALOUSE MISDEEM
SUPPOSE DISTRUST JEALOUSE
MISDOUBT MISTRUST
(NOT —) COLD
SUSPECTED SPOTTED SUSPECT
SUSPEND CALL HALT HANG OUST
SHUT SIST STAY BREAK CLOSE
DEBAR DEFER DEMUR EXPEL
POISE REMIT SLING SWING
APPEND DANGLE ADJOURN
EXCLUDE FLUIDIZE INTERMIT
OVERHANG PROROGUE REPRIEVE
SCAFFOLD SUSPENSE PRETERMIT

(— ANCHOR) COCKBILL
(— FROM ACTIVITY) SIDELINE
(— IN FLUID) ENTRAIN
SUSPENDED SWING AFLOAT
LATENT HANGING PENDANT
PENDENT PENSILE HOVERING
SUSPENSE
(NOT —) VESTED
SUSPENDER GALLUS GARTER
BRETELLE
(PL.) BRACES GALLOWS GALLUSES
SUSPENSE DEMUR POISE
SUSPENSION FOG BREI FUME SIST
STAY STOP DELAY DOUBT MAGMA
SMOKE BREACH CUTOFF SLURRY
AEROSOL FAILURE RESPITE
ABEYANCE BACTERIN EMULSION
INFUSION SHUTDOWN SUSPENSE
WISHBONE
(— OF JUDGMENT) EPOCHE
(— OF NOISE) HUSH
(— OF RESPIRATION) SYNCOPE
(— OF SENTENCE) REPRIEVE
PROBATION
SUSPENSIVENESS DRIVE
SUSPENSORY SUPPORT
SUSPICION HINT DOUBT SOUPCON
SURMISE SUSPECT UMBRAGE
DISTRUST JEALOUSY MISDOUBT
MISTRUST TINCTURE
(IRRATIONAL —) PARANOIA
(SNEAKING —) IDEA
SUSPICIOUS SHY CHARY FISHY
LEERY PEERY QUEER SMOKY
SHODDY JEALOUS SOUPCON
SUSPECT DOUBTFUL WAFFLIKE
SUSPICIOUSLY ASKANCE
SUSQUEHANNA CONESTOGA
SUSTAIN ABET BACK BEAR BUOY
DURE HELP HOLD LAST PROP STAY
ABIDE CARRY FAVOR SINEW
SPRAG STAND ASSIST CONVEY
ENDURE FOSTER SECOND SUCCOR
SUFFER UPHOLD UPSTAY ALIMENT
BOLSTER CONTAIN NOURISH
OUTBEAR PROLONG SUPPORT
UNDERFO BEFRIEND BUTTRESS
CONTINUE MAINTAIN PRESERVE
SCAFFOLD
(PREF.) CO
SUSTAINED TENUTO SOUTENU
SUSTENANCE GEAR MEAT SALT
BREAD FOISON LIVING RELIEF
ALIMENT PABULUM TABLING
SUSU GERIP SOOSOO DOLPHIN
SUSURRUS WHISPER
SUTLER PROVANT VIVANDIER
SUTTEE SATI
SUTURE SEW SEAM RAPHE SETON
STITCH HARMONY PTERION
(SUFF.) RHAPHY RRHAPHY
SVANTOVIT TRIGLAV
SVELTE CHIC TRIM LITHE SLEEK
SUAVE SMOOTH URBANE SLENDER
SVENO (SLAYER OF —) SOLIMANO
SWAB GOB MOP WAD BOSH QTIP
SWOB WIPE PATCH DOSSIL
SPONGE EPAULET SWABBER
SQUILGEE
SWABBIE GOB TAR
SWADDLE BIND SWEEL SWATHE
SWAG DRUM GAME LOOT BOOTY

LUCRE MONEY BOODLE FESTOON
MATILDA
SWAGE BOSS MOUTH UPSET
FULLER JUMPER SHAPER SWAGER
SWEDGE FLATTER
(PL.) OLIVER
SWAGGER JET ROY BRAG COCK
FACE ROLL BOAST BRANK BRAVE
NUTTY STRUT SWANK SWASH
BLAGUE BOUNCE GOSTER HECTOR
PARADO PRANCE RENOWN
RUFFLE SPROSE BLUSTER
BRAVADO GAUSTER PANACHE
ROISTER SOLDIER DOMINEER
TIGERISM
SWAGGERER HUFF SWAG BUCKO
FACER TIGER CUTTLE JETTER
PISTOL BRAVADO HUFFCAP
RUFFLER FANFARON WHIFFLER
SWAGGERING HUFFY FACING
GASCON HUFFCAP TEARCAT
BLUSTERY TIGRISH
SWAGMAN WHALER DRIFTER
DRUMMER TRAVELER
SWAIN BEAU COLIN CUDDY RUSTIC
STREPHON
SWAINSONA INDIGO
SWALE SLASH
SWALLOW OFF SUP BOLT DOWN
DROP GAUP GAWP GLUT GULP
SINK SWIG TAKE CLUNK DRINK
GORGE GURGE POUCH QUILT
SLOCK SWOOP ABSORB ENGLUT
ENGULF GLUTCH GOBBET GOBBLE
GODOWN GUZZLE IMBIBE INGEST
MARTIN POCKET PROGNE SWELLY
CONSUME ENGORGE ARUNDELL
WITCHUCK
(— AGAIN) REGORGE
(— GREEDILY) BEND SLUP GORGE
GULCH SWILL WORRY INHALE
(— HASTILY) SWAP SWOP GLOUP
SLUMMOCK
(— IN AGAIN) RESORB
(— OF LIQUOR) SLUG
(— UP) GULF SWAMP ABSORB
DEVOUR
(— WITH GREEDINESS) ENGORGE
(LOSS OF ABILITY TO —) APHAGIA
(NOISY —) SLURP
(WOMAN TURNED INTO —)
PROCNE
(PREF.) CHELID(O)
SWALLOWTAIL TROILUS
SWALLOWWORT CELANDINE
SWAMP BOG FEN FLAT FLOW MIRE
MOSS SLEW SLUE SOAK SUMP
VLEI VLEY WHAM WHIN FLUSH
LERNA LETCH MARSH SWALE
SWANG URMAN DELUGE DISMAL
ENGULF MORASS MUSKEG
SLOUGH CIENAGA POCOSIN
GREENING INUNDATE QUAGMIRE
SWAMP COTTONWOOD LIAR
SWAMPER BUSHER GOPHER
SWAMPHEN COOT
SWAMP LOOSESTRIFE PEATWEED
PEATWOOD
SWAMP MAHOGANY GUNNUNG
SWAMP MILKWEED DAGGA
SWAMPY PUXY BOGGY POOLY
CALLOW POACHY QUASHY

QUEASY SLUMPY MOORISH
PALUDAL ULIGINOUS
SWAMPY CREE MASKEGON
SWAN COB ELK PEN OLOR CYGNET
HOOPER SWANNET WHOOPER
(FEMALE —) PEN
(FLOCK OF —S) GAME MARK
(KIND OF —) MUTE
SWANFLOWER SWANWORT
SWANHILD (FATHER OF —) SIGURD
(MOTHER OF —) GUDRUN
SWANK CHIC POSH TONY RITZY
SWANKY POSH SWASH SPIFFY
SWAP CHOP SWOP TRADE TRUCK
DICKER EXCHANGE
SWARD SOD TURF SPINE SWARF
SWATH SWARTH
SWARM FRY SNY BIKE CAST FARE
HIVE HOST KNIT NEST SORT SWIM
TEEM CLOUD CROWD FLOCK
FLUSH FRACK HORDE SNARL
FLIGHT HOTTER RABBLE SWARVE
THRONG OVERRUN SUBCAST
PULLULATE
(— IN) FILL
(— OF BEES) BIKE HIVE
(— OF INSECTS) BAND FLIGHT
(— OF PEOPLE) BIKE DRIFT
(THIRD — OF BEES) COLT
SWARMING ALIVE AGWARM
SWARMY
SWARTBACK SWARBIE
SWARTHY DUN DARK BLACK
BROWN DUSKY GRIMY MOORY
SWART MORIAN SWARTH BISTRED
BISTERED
SWASH SWIG SWILL SWATCH
SWABBLE SWASHWAY
SWASHBUCKLER SWASH GASCON
SLASHER SWASHER
SWASTIKA FYLFOT GAMMADION
GAMMATION HAKENKREUZ
SWAT SWOT DEHGAN STRIKE
SWATH SWIPE STADDLE
SWATHE LAP BIND WRAP SWARF
ENWRAP INWRAP SWADDLE
WINDROW
SWATTER FLYSWAT
SWAY NOD WAG BEAR BEND BIAS
FLAP HIKE LILT ROCK ROLL RULE
SHOG SWAB SWAG SWIG TILT
TOSS WALD WAVE CARRY CHARM
LURCH POWER REIGN SHAKE
SWALE SWING WAVER WHEEL
AFFECT ALLURE CAREEN DIRECT
EMPIRE TOTTER WAGGLE
COMMAND SHOGGIE STAGGER
SWABBLE SWIGGLE
(— IN WALKING) WADDLE
(SUFF.) CRACY CRAT(IC)
SWAYBACK WARFA LORDOSIS
RENGUERA
SWAYING ASWAY ROLLING
SWAZILAND (CAPITAL OF —)
MBABANE
(COIN OF —) RAND EMALANGEN
(LANGUAGE OF —) SISWATI
(MONEY OF —) LILANGENI
(RIVER IN —) USUTU KOMATI
MHLATUZE UMBULUZI
(TOWN OF —) STEGI GOLLEL
MANZINI PIGGSPEAK
SWEAR VOW VUM DAMN SINK

SNUM SWAN SWOW TAKE CURSE
ADJURE AFFIRM BEDAMN DEPONE
DEPOSE OBJURE CONJURE
DEJERATE EXECRATE FORSWEAR
(— FALSELY) RAP MOUNT
FORSWEAR MANSWEAR
SWEARING JURANT JURATION
(FALSE —) PERJURY
SWEARWORD CUSS
SWEAT DEW WET STEW WASH
BREAN MADOR SUDOR SUDATE
LAUNDER PARBOIL SWELTER
SWIVVET TRANSUDE
PERSPIRATION
(— SKINS) STALE
(DYNAMITE —) LEAK
(PREF.) HIDR(O) HYDR(O) SUDORI
(SUFF.) IDRUSIS
SWEATBOX HOTBOX
SWEATER FROCK GANSEY JUMPER
WOOLLY CARDIGAN SLIPOVER
(CLOSE-FITTING —) POORBOY
(WOMAN'S SHORT —) SHRINK
SWEATHOUSE TEMESCAL
SWEATING TUB ASWEAT SWELTRY
SUDATION SUDATORY
SWEATY PUGGY ASWEAT PERSPIRY
SUDOROUS SWEATFUL

SWEDEN

CAPITAL: STOCKHOLM
COIN: ORE KRONA SKILLING
COUNTY: KALMAR OREBRO
UPPSALA
DIVISION: AMT LAEN SKANE
OREBRO UPPSALA GOTALAND
JAMTLAND SWEALAND
GULF: BOTHNIA
ISLAND: OLAND GOTALAND
LAKE: SILJA VANERN MALAREN
VATTERN DALALVEN STORAVAN
HJALMAREN
MEASURE: AM ALN FOT MIL REF
TUM FAMN STOP FODER KANNA
KAPPE LINJE NYMIL SPANN
STANG TUNNA FATHOM JUMFRU
KOLLAST OXHUVUD TUNLAND
FJARDING KAPPLAND KOLTUNNA
MOUNTAIN: SARV AMMAR OVIKS
HELAGS SARJEK
PROVINCE: KALMAR OREBRO
GOTLAND HALLAND UPPSALA
ALVSBORG BLEKINGE ELFSBORG
JAMTLAND MALMOHUS
WERMLAND
RIVER: DAL UME GOTA KLAR LULE
KALIX PITEA RANEA LAINIO
LJUSNE TORNEA WINDEL
ANGERMAN
TOWN: UMEA BODEN BORAS
EDANE FALUN GAVLE LULEA
MALMO PITEA VISBY YSTAD
ARVIKA OREBRO LUDVIKA
UPPSALA GOTEBORG NYKOPING
VASTERAS
WATERFALL: HANDOL
TANNFORSEN
WEIGHT: ASS LOD ORT MARK PUND
STEN UNTZ NYLAST LISPUND
SKEPPUND

SWEDISH CLOVER ALSIKE
SWEEP OAR BUCK DUST RAFF SOOP

SWAY TILT BESOM BROOM DIGHT DRIFT FETCH SCOPE SKIRL SWIPE SWOOP BREADTH CLEANSE PICOTAH SHADOOF STRICKLE
(— A NET) BEAT
(— MAJESTICALLY) SWAN
(— OFF) SLIPE
(— OF SCYTHE) SWATH SWATHE
(— ON CULTIVATOR) SKIN
(CHIMNEY —) CHUMMY SWEEPY RAMONEUR
(HAY —) BUCK
SWEEPBOARD STRICKLE
SWEEPER BESOM BUNGY SWEEP TOPAZ BHANGI BHUNGI MEHTAR PRYLER ROADER SOOPER TOPASS BROOMER TUBEMAN BHUNGINI MATRANEE SCRUBBER
SWEEPING SURGE RASANT SWEEPY
(— FOR FISH) DRAFT DRAUGHT
(— OF CURVE) NUTATION
(PL.) DUST FULVIE FULZIE RIFFRAFF
SWEET DOUX DUMP FOOL SOOT SUCK CREAM DILIS DOUCE DULCE FRESH HONEY MERRY SOOTH SPICY SPLIT BREEZE DULCET FRUITY GENTLE SILKEN SILVER SIRUPY SUGARY DARLING FAIRING HONEYED INSIPID MUSICAL PANDROP SUGARED SWEETLY WINNING WINSOME AROMATIC ENGAGING FLUMMERY LIEBLICH LUSCIOUS NECTARED PLEASANT
(SICKLY —) ICKY
(SLIGHTLY —) SEC
(PREF.) DULCI GLYCERO GLYCO HEDY SUAVI
SWEET BAY BREWSTER MAGNOLIA
SWEETBREAD BUR BURR PANCREAS
(— OF DEER) INCHPIN
SWEETBRIER BEDEGUAR EGLANTINE
SWEET CALABASH KURUBA
SWEET CASSAVA AIPI AIPIM
SWEET CHERRY MAZZARD
SWEET CICELY MYRRH
SWEET CLOVER LOTUS MELILOT
SWEET COLTSFOOT LAGWORT
SWEETEN CANDY HONEY SUGAR SWEET PURIFY ADDULCE CLEANSE DULCIFY FRESHEN MOLLIFY PERFUME MITIGATE
SWEETENER SACCHARIN
SWEET FENNEL FINOCHIO FLORENCE
SWEET FERN FERNGALE
SWEETFISH AYU
SWEET FLAG SEDGE BEEWORT CALAMUS
SWEET GALE GOLD GAGEL BAYBUSH FLEAWOOD GALEWORT GALLBUSH
SWEET GUM AMBER COPALM STORAX BILSTED
SWEETHEART JO BOY GRA HON JOE LAD PET PUG SIS AGRA AMIE BABY BEAU DEAR DOLL DOXY DUCK FAIR GILL GIRL JILL LADY LASS LIEF LOVE MASH MORT POUT AGRAH BULLY BUSSY CHERI COOKY DOLLY DONAH DONEY

DONNA DRURY FLAME LEMAN LOVER PUGGY SPARK SWEET COOKIE EMILIA FELLOW FRIEND MOPSEY PIGEON STEADY WAHINE AMOROSA BELOVED PHYLLIS PIGSNEY QUERIDA SPRUNNY SWEETIE TOOTSIE DOWSABEL DULCINEA FOLLOWER LADYBIRD LADYLOVE LIEBCHEN LOVELASS MISTRESS SWEETING TRUELOVE
(— OF HARLEQUIN) COLUMBINE
SWEETIE (— PIE) HON DEAR HONEY DEARIE
SWEETLEAF DYELEAVES SYMPLOCOS
SWEET MARJORAM OREGANO
SWEETMEAT DROP DUMP KISS DULCE FUDGE GOODY PASTE PLATE SPICE TOFFY BONBON BUCAYO COMFIT DRAGEE DREDGE JUNKET ALCORZA BANQUET CARAMEL CARAWAY CLAGGUM CONFECT LOUKOUM PENUCHE SUCCADE CONSERVE HARDBAKE MARZIPAN PASTILLE
(PL.) BALUSHAI CONFETTI
SWEETNESS DULCE HONEY SIRUP SYRUP DULCOR DOUCEUR DULCITY SUAVITY FLORIMEL WORDNESS
SWEET ORANGE CHINA CHINO
SWEET PEA CATGUT LATHYRUS
SWEET PEPPERBUSH CLETHRA SOAPBUSH
SWEET POTATO YAM SWEET BATATA CAMOTE KUMARA OCARINA
SWEET RUSH SQUINANT
SWEET-SMELLING AROMATIC
SWEETSOP ANON ATES ATIS ATTA CORAZON SWEETING
SWEET-SOUNDING MERRY
SWEET-TALK ENAMOR
SWEET VIOLET FINELEAF
SWEET WILLIAM DIANTHUS
SWELL BAG DON NIB NOB BEAL BELL BLAB BLOW BLUB BOLL BULB BULK BUMP BUOY DOME FILL FINE GROW HOVE HUFF HUSH PINK PLIM RISE SWAG TOFF TONY WAVE BELLY BERRY BLAST BLOAT BULGE BUNCH DANDY FLASH NIFTY PLUFF PREEN SMART STOCK STRUT SURGE TULIP BILLOW BOWDEN DILATE EXPAND GROWTH LOVELY SPRING STROUT TUMEFY UPRISE AUGMENT BLUBBER BURGEON DISTEND INFLATE REGULAR SWAGGER OVERBLOW TURGESCE
(— OF GUN MUZZLE) TULIP
(— OF WATER) HUSH SURF FLOOD SURGE
(— OUT) BAG POD BUNT DRAW POUT BOSOM BILLOW SPONGE BALLOON BLADDER
(HEAVY —) RUN SEA
(SEA —) WALLOW BACKWATER
(PREF.) OEDE OEDI TUME
SWELLDOODLE EGGFISH
SWELLED BIAS BLOWN
SWELLFISH BLOWER PUFFER TAMBOR

SWELLING BIG BUR NOB PAP PIN BLAB BOLL BUBO BUMP BURR CLAP COWL CURB FROG FULL GALL KNOB KNOT NODE POKE PONE PUFF AMPER BLAIN BOTCH BOUGE BULGE BUNCH BUNNY CLOUR EDEMA JETTY MOUSE PROUD SURGE SWELL TUBER TUMOR ANCOME ASWELL BOSOMY BUNCHY CALLUS FLATUS GIBBER GROWTH KERNEL PIMPLE RANULA STRUMA SWELTH TURGID WARBLE AMPULLA BOSSING CAPELET CHAGOMA CUSHION GOUNDOU HAPTERE PUSTULE SURGENT TURGENT UREDEMA UROCELE APOSTEME BULLNECK CHEMOSIS DACRYOMA FURUNCLE GLANDULE GOURDING HAPTERON HEMATOMA MUCOCELE NODOSITY PULVINUS PUMPKNOT QUELLUNG SCIRRHUS STYLOPOD VESSICNON TUMESCENCE
(— IN HORSE'S CHEST) ANTICOR
(— IN HORSE'S MOUTH) LAMPAS LAMPASSE
(— IN PLASTER) BLUB
(— OF PLANT TISSUE) GALL
(— OF THE CHEEK) HONE
(— ON ANIMAL'S JOINTS) BUNNY CAPELLET
(— ON HEAD) COWL
(— ON SPLEEN) AGUECAKE
(DISCOLORED —) MOUSE
(EYE —) STY STYE
(ROUNDED —) TUBER
(PREF.) GANGLI GANGLO STRUMI
(SUFF.) EMATOMA PHYMA
SWELTER BAKE BOIL STEW SWELT
SWELTERING STEWY SULTRY SWELTRY
SWERVE BOW CUT LUG YAW BIAS FADE JOUK SKEW VARY VEER WARP SHEER STRAY DEPART DEVIATE DIGRESS DIVERGE INSWING
SWIDDEN CAINGIN KAINGIN
SWIFT CRAN FAST FLIT MAIN VITE FLEET HASTY LIGHT QUICK RAPID SNELL SWITH WIGHT WINDY ARROWY MARLET NIMBLE RAKING SOUPLE SPEEDY STRICT SUDDEN SWIFTY TOTTER WINGED COLLIER DEVELIN FLIGHTY POSTING SWALLOW TANTIVY DEVELING HEPIALID PEGASEAN SCREAMER SCUTTLER SQUEALER SWIFTLET SALANGANE
(PREF.) CITI CYPSELO OCY TACHEO TACHISTO TACHO TACHY
SWIFTLY FAST SWAP APACE SNELL SNELLY LIGHTLY STEEPLY TANTIVY
SWIFTNESS FOOT HASTE SPEED CELERITY FASTNESS VELOCITY
SWIG SCOUR SNORT SWILL SWING SWIGGLE
SWILL SOSS BROCK SLOSH SLUICE HOGWASH PIGWASH SWILLING
SWIM DIP COWD SAIL SOOM SPAN TEEM BATHE CRAWL FLEET FLOAT GLIDE SWARM PLUNGE OVERFLOW

(— IN NEW DIRECTION) MILL
(— IN NUDE) SKINNYDIP
(— IN SHOALS) RUN
(— TOGETHER) SCHOOL
(— TRUNKS) JAMS
(PREF.) NECT(O)
(SUFF.) NECTAE NECTES
SWIMMER NAIAD BATHER NATATOR BUTTERFLYER
SWIMMERET PLEOPOD
SWIMMING ASWIM NATANT FLOTANT NATATION
(— APPARATUS) SCUBA
(— DEVICE) SNORKEL
(— STUNT) MARLIN WALKOVER
SWIMMING POOL POOL THERM PLUNGE THERME PISCINA NATATORY
(— ON LINER) LIDO
SWIMSUIT MAILLOT
SWIN (— IN NUDE) SKINNYDIP
SWINDLE CON GIP GYP JOB RIG BILK BURN DUPE FAKE FLAP HAVE MACE PULL RAMP ROOK ROPE SCAM SWIZ BUNCO BUNKO CHEAT COZEN FLING FOIST GOUGE GRIFT LURCH MULCT PLANT PONZI ROGUE SHARK SHARP SHAVE SHUCK SLANG SPOOF STING SWIZZ UNCLE BOODLE BUBBLE BUCKET CHISEL CHOUSE DIDDLE FIDDLE FLEECE GAZUMP HUSTLE INTAKE NOBBLE SUCKER TREPAN DEFRAUD FINAGLE SKELDER THIMBLE VERNEUK FLIMFLAM BAMBOOZLE
SWINDLER DO FOB GYP LEG BILK FYNK HAWK ROOK SKIN CHEAT CROOK ESROC FAKER GANEF GREEK HARPY KNAVE MACER ROGUE CHIAUS GOUGER INTAKE RINGER ROOKER SALTER SHAVER VERSER BUBBLER GRIFTER HUSTLER MACEMAN MAGSMAN NOBBLER SHARPER SKELDER SLICKER SPIELER BARNACLE BLACKLEG CHISELER FINAGLER GILENYER LUMBERER PIGEONER SHELLMAN TRAMPOSO
(DECOY —) BARNARD
SWINDLING MACE BUNCO BUNKO GRAFT ROOKY SHARK GYPPERY JOUKERY CHEATERY JOOKERIE
SWINE HOG OIC PIG SOW BOAR GALT GILT PORK SUID YILT DUROC ESSEX SWIPE WHITE GUSSIE POLAND PORKER PORKET BUSHPIG LACOMBE OINKERS PECCARY SUFFOLK SUIDIAN CHESHIRE HYOTHERE LANDRACE TAMWORTH
(— AND FOOD) PANNAGE
(— AND MAN) OMNIVORA
(PREF.) HYO
SWINEHERD GURTH HOGMAN EUMAEUS HOGHERD HOGWARD
SWINE-LIKE GADARENE
SWING GO COOK HIKE JUMP LILT SCUP SHOG STOT SWAY SWEE TURN SHAKE SHOWD SLING SWALE TREND DANGLE GYRATE HANDLE SWINGE SWITCH SWIVEL

TOTTER JUMPING SHOGGIE
SWINGEL WAMPISH BRANDISH
FLOURISH OSCILLATE
(— AROUND) JIB SLEW SLUE
SLOUGH
(— A SHIP) SPRING
(— BY BATTER) CUT
(— FROM POSITION) CANT
(— FROM SIDE TO SIDE) JOW
(— FROM THE TIDE) TEND
(— OF PENDULUM) BEAT
(— OF SAIL) GYBE JIBE
(— OF SWORD) MOULINET
(— OUT OF LINE) SWAG
(— THE FOREFEET) DISH
(RHYTHMICAL —) LILT
(WILD —) HAYMAKER
(PREF.) OSCILLO
SWINGER HINGE
SWINGING BANK ASWING SWINGY
SWINGLE SWORD SCUTCH SWIPPLE
SWING SEAT TRANSOM
SWINISH SOWISH HOGGISH
PORCINE SUILLINE
SWIPE COP CHOP GLOM SLOG WIPE
SNAKE STEAL VUI TURE
SWIRL BOIL EDDY GULF HURL PURL
WALM GURGE SWALE SWEEL
SWORL SWOOSH WREATHE
TOURBILLION
(— OF SALMON) BULGE
SWIRLING VORTICAL
SWISH HISH WHIP SMART SWILL
WHISH
SWISS SWISSER HELVETIC
(— PINE) MUGHO
SWISS FAMILY ROBINSON
(AUTHOR OF —) WYSS
(CHARACTER IN —) JACK EMILY
FRITZ ERNEST FRANCIS MONTROSE
ROBINSON
SWITCH GAD TAN LASH TWIG
WAND AZOTE BIRCH BREAK SHUNT
SWISH CHANGE CUTOUT DERAIL
DIPPER FERULA FERULE LARRUP
RATTAN SCUTCH SILENT SPRING
HICKORY KIPPEEN SCOURGE
SQUITCH CRYOTRON HAIRWORK
POSTICHE
(— FOCUS) FADE
(AUTO —) DIMMER
(ELECTRIC —) KEY
(RAILROAD —) GATE POINT
SWITCHBOARD (PRIVATE PHONE
—) PBX
SWITCH ENGINE GOAT
SWITCHMAN SHUNTER SWITCHER

SWIVEL LOPER SWAPE SWIPE
CASTER FIDDLE TIRRET TOGGLE
TONGUE TRAVERSE TRUNNION
SWIVET STEW
SWIZZLE STIR
SWOLLEN BLUB FULL PLIM RANK
BLOWN CHUFF GOUTY GREAT
GUMMY POBBY PROUD PUFFY
TUMID BOLLEN DRAWNY BULLED
GOURDY TURGID BESTRUT
BLOATED BLUBBER BULDOUS
GIBBOSE GIBBOUS GOURDED
GOUTISH STICKLE TURGENT
BEPUFFED BLADDERY TUMOROUS
(PREF.) PHYS(O)
SWOON KEEL SWEB SWIM DOVER
DROWN DWALM FAINT SLOOM
SOUND SWARF SWELT STOUND
SWOUND TRANCE ECSTASY
SWITHER SYNCOPE SWOONING
SWOONING ASWOON SYNCOPE
SWOOP CHOP DIVE JOUK SWAP
SWOP SOUSE STOOP SWOPE
POUNCE SOURCE DESCEND
(KIND OF —) FELL
SWOOPING SOUSE
SWORD FOX SAX BILL DIRK FALX
GRAM IRON PATA SAEX SEAX SPIT
TOOL TUCK TURK BILBO BLADE
BRAND DEGEN DIEGO ESTOC
GULLY KNIFE KUKRI PRICK RIPON
SABER SABRE SHARP STEEL
ANDREW BARONG BILBOA CATTAN
DAMASK DUSACK FLORET GLAIVE
HANGER KHANDA KUKERI MIMING
PARANG PINKER PORKER RAPIER
SMITER SPATHA TILTER TIZONA
TOLEDO WAFTER BALMUNG
BRANDON CURTANA CUTLASH
CUTLASS ESPADON ESTOQUE
FERRARA FLEURET IMPALER

JOYEUSE MALCHUS MORGLAY
SHABBLE SLASHER SNICKER
SPURTLE TOASTER WHIFFLE
WHINGER ACINACES BASELARD
CAMPILAN CLAYMORE DAMASCUS
DURENDAL FALCHION FLAMBERG
SCHLAGER SCIMITAR SPADROON
SPITFROG WACADASH WHINYARD
(— OF CHARLEMAGNE) JOYEUSE
(— OF CID) TIZONA
(— OF HERMES) HARPE
(— OF LANCELOT) ARONDIGHT
(— OF ROLAND) DURENDAL
(— OF SIEGFRIED) GRAM BALMUNG
(— OF SIR BEVIS) MORGLAY
(— OF ST. GEORGE) ASCALON
ASKELON
(— USED BY ST. PETER) MALCHUS
(BLUNT —) WAFTER SCHLAGER
(CELTIC —) SAX SAEX
(CURVED —) SCIMITAR
(DOUBLE-EDGED —) KEN PATA
KHANDA SPATHA
(DUELLING —) EPEE SHARP
(DYAK —) PARANG
(FENCING —) EPEE FOIL SABER
SABRE RAPIER
(HALF OF —) FORTE
(JAPANESE —) CATAN CATTAN
KATANA WACADASH
(LONG —) SPATHA WHIFFLE
(MATADOR'S —) ESTOQUE
(MORO —) BARONG CAMPILAN
(NARROW —) TUCK
(NORMAN —) SPATHA
(PERSIAN —) ACINACES
(POINTLESS —) CURTANA CURTEIN
(RUSTY —) SHABBLE
(SHORT —) DIRK ESTOC KUKRI
SKEAN CREESE HANGER CURTAXE
WHINGER FALCHION WHINYARD
(THRUSTING —) ESTOC STOCK
(TWO-HANDED —) ESPADON
SPADONE CLAYMORE
(WOODEN —) WASTER STRICKLE
SWORD-BEARER VERGER SELICTAR
PORTGLAVE
(PL.) ENSIFERI
SWORD DANCER MATACHIN
SWORDFISH AU ESPADA ESPADON
XIPHIAS ALBACORA BILLFISH
BOATBILL FORKTAIL XIPHIOID
SCOMBROID
(PREF.) XIPH(O)
SWORD-LIKE
(PREF.) XIPH(I)(O)
SWORDPLAY SPADROON
(STYLIZED —) KENDO
SWORD-SHAPED ENSATE
ENSIFORM GLADIATE
SWORDSMAN BLADE BLADER
FENCER SLASHER SWORDER
THRUSTER
SWORDSMANSHIP KENDO
SWORDTAIL HELLERI
SWORN AVOWED
SWOT GRI MUG
SYAGUSH SHARGOSS
SYBARITE EPICURE
SYBARITIC SENSUOUS
SYCAMORE MAY DAROO
COTONIER LACEWOOD PLANTAIN

SYCEE SHOE
SYCOPHANCY FAWNERY
SYCOPHANT TOADY COGGER
FAWNER GNATHO HANGBY
TAGTAIL CLAWBACK PARASITE
PICKTHANK SATELLITE
SYCOPHANTIC FAWNING SERVILE
SLAVISH OBEDIENT TRENCHER
SYCORAX (SON OF —) CALIBAN
SYCOSIS MENTAGRA
SYENITE APPINITE TRACHYTE
SYLLABARY KANA IROFA IROHA
KATAKANA
SYLLABIC SONANT CENTROID
SONANTIC
SYLLABLE ARSIS BREVE GROUP
SHORT DISEME SYLLAB THESIS
TRISEME ASSONANT
(— DENOTING ASSENT) OM
(BOBIZATION —) BO CE DI GA GE LO
MA NI
(IMPROVISE NONSENSE —S) SCAT
(LAST —) ULTIMA
(LAST — BUT ONE) PENULT
(LONG —) LONG
(MUSICAL —) DI DO FA FI LA LE LI
ME MI RA RE RI SE SI SO TA TE TI TO
UT SOL
(REFRAIN —) DILDO
(SHORT —) MORA SHORT
(STRONG —) STRESS
(TERMINAL —) ENDING
(UNACCENTED —) OUTRIDE
(UNACCENTED —S) THESIS
(UNSTRESSED —) OUTRIDE
SYLLABUS PROGRAM VIDIMUS
HEADNOTE SYNOPSIS
PROGRAMME
SYLLOGISM BARBARA ABDUCTION
ENTHYMEME
(SERIES OF —S) SORITES
SYLPH ARIEL SYLPHID
SYLVAN WOODY FOREST SILVAN
WOODEN WOODISH SYLVATIC
SYLVITE HARDSALT
SYMBIOSIS LICHENISM
MUTUALISM NUTRICISM
SYMBOL KEY CODE FISH FOUR
ICON IDOL IKON MARK NEUM SEAL
SIGN TYPE BADGE CREST CROSS
EAGLE IMAGE INDEX PRIME TOKEN
CARACT CIPHER EMBLEM ENSIGN
FIGURE LETTER PNEUME SHADOW
SIGNAL FACIEND MANDALA
PALATAL CEREMONY CONSTANT
DIRECTOR EXPONENT GUTTURAL
IDEOGRAM LIGATURE LOGOGRAM
OPERATOR SWASTIKA SYMBOLUM
TRISKELE IDEOGRAPH METOBELUS
OCTOTHORP ORIFLAMME
PICTOGRAPH PHRASEOGRAM
(— AS ROAD SIGN) GLYPH
(— FOR WAVELENGTH) LAMBDA
(— OF AUTHORITY) MACE
(— OF DEATH) CYPRESS
(— OF DISTINCTION) BELT HONOR
(— OF FAITHFUL DEAD) ORANT
(— OF FRANCE) LILY
(— OF LIFE) ANKH
(— OF MONK) COWL
(— OF PHYSICIAN) CADUCEUS
(— OF RAILROAD) HERALD
(— OF RESURRECTION) PHOENIX

(**— OF SOMETHING SPIRITUAL**)
SACRAMENT
(**— OF SOVEREIGNTY**) ASP URAEUS
SYNAGOGUE SHUL SCHUL ALJAMA
PROSEUCHA
(**— OF SYMBOLS**) CODE
(**— OF TENANCY**) CROFTING
(**— OF SPRING**) KARPAS
SYNAPSIS PAIRING
(**— OF TRANSPORTATION**) AIRLINE
AIRMAIL
(**— OF STRENGTH**) HORN
SYNAPTE ECTENE EKTENE
(**— OF TRUSSING**) CABANE
(**— OF SUN**) DISC DISK
SYNARTHROSIS SUTURE
(**— OF VALUES**) ETHOS
(**— OF UNIVERSE**) MANDALA
SYNCHRO SELSYN
(**— OF WEIGHTS**) TROY
(**— ON UNCHANGEABLENESS**)
LEOPARD
SYNCHRONIZE MESH
(**— OF WIRES**) HARNESS
(**— REPRESENTING THE ABSOLUTE**)
TAIKIH
SYNCHRONIZER SPEEDGUN
(**— OF WORSHIP**) CULT CULTUS
(**ALGEBRAIC —**) EXPONENT
SYNCLINE DOWNFOLD ISOCLINE
(**— OF WRITING**) KANJI BRAILLE
ALPHABET
(**CLAN —**) TOTEM
SYNCOPATED ZOPPA ABRIDGED
(**— TO LOCATE AN OBJECT**) LIDAR
(**CRICKET —**) ASHES
SYNCOPE SWOON COTYPE
FAINTING
(**ACOUSTICAL —**) SODAR
(**CRUSADERS' —**) CROSS
SYNDICATE HUI GROUP CARTEL
COMBINE
(**AGRICULTURAL —**) KOLKOZ
KOLKHOS
(**CURVED —**) HOOK
(**UNIT OF CRIME —**) FAMILY
(**ALARM —**) BUG
(**EFFICIENCY —**) ETA
SYNDICATED CANNED
(**BANKING —**) GIRO
(**EGYPTIAN —**) ANKH SCARAB
SYNDROME (**KIND OF —**) FANCONI
(**BETTING —**) ALEMBERT PERFECTA
QUINELLA MARTINGALE
(**INFORMATION —**) GLYPH
SYNECDOCHE MERISM
(**COLLOIDAL —**) SOL
(**INTERSECTION —**) CAP
SYNERGIST BOOSTER SESAMIN
(**COMMUNICATION —**) BLOWER
CIRCUIT
(**KOREAN —**) TAHGOOK
SYNOD SOBOR
(**COMPUTER —**) KLUGE KLUDGE
TRSDOS
(**MAGIC —**) CARACT
SYNODAL SENAGE
(**MATHEMATICAL —**) KNOWN
FACTOR OBELUS FACIEND
OPERAND PLACEHOLDER
SYNONYM ANTONYM HOMONYM
EUPHONYM POLYONYM
(**COMPUTER DISK OPERATING —**)
MSDOS PCDOS
(**PHALLIC —**) LINGA LINGAM
SYNOPSIS BRIEF TABLE EPITOME
OUTLINE SUMMARY ABSTRACT
ANALYSIS SCENARIO SYLLABUS
ABRIDGMENT
(**CULTURAL —**) ISLAM
(**PICTOGRAPHIC —**) ISOTYPE
(**DEFENSE —**) SAGE
(**PRINTING —**) DIAGONAL
(**DISK OPERATING —**) DOS
(**PRONUNCIATION —**) ENG
SYNSACRUM SACRARY
(**DISPERSE —**) GEL
(**RELIGIOUS —**) CROSS LABRYS
SYNTACTICAL FORMAL
(**ELECTRICAL —**) SELSYN
(**UNION —**) CUP
SYNTHESIS SUMMA FUSION
SYSTASIS
(**ELECTRONIC —**) TELETEXT
(**8 POINTS ON CIRCUMFERENCE —**)
OCTOTHORP
SYNTHESIZER MOOG
(**GEOLOGICAL —**) EOCENE
CAMBRIAN DEVONIAN KEEWATIN
TERTIARY
(**PL.**) KATAKANA
SYNTHETASE LIGASE
(**HAULING —**) DILLY
SYMBOLIC GRAPHIC SHADOWY
ANICONIC
SYNTHETIC ERSATZ PLASTIC
SYSTATIC ARTIFICER
(**HAVERSIAN —**) OSTEON
SYMBOLICAL ALLUSIVE MYSTICAL
SYPHAX (**WIFE OF —**) SOPHENISBA
(**IRRIGATION —**) KAREZ
SYMBOLISM ICONOLOGY
SYPHILIS PIP POX LUES SYPH
CRINKUM GRINCOME
(**LANGUAGE —**) LATINXUA
SYMBOLIZE BODY SIGN TOKEN
FIGURE SAMPLE SHADOW
SYMBOL TYPIFY BETOKEN
EXPRESS PORTEND SIGNIFY
RESEMBLE
(**LOCATING —**) LIDAR
(**NAVIGATING —**) TACAN
(**NAVIGATION —**) GEE DECCA
LANAC TACAN NAVAID SHORAN
NAVARHO OMNIRANGE

SYRIA

CAPITAL: DAMASCUS
COIN: POUND TALENT PIASTER
DISTRICT: ALEPPO HAURAN
LAKE: DJEBOID TIBERIAS
MEASURE: MAKUK GARAVA
MOUNTAIN: HERMON LIBANUS
NAME: ARAM
NATIVE: DRUSE ANSARIE SARACEN
ANSARIEH
RIVER: ASI BALIKH BARADA JORDAN
KNABUR ORONTES EUPHRATES
TOWN: ALEP HAMA HOMS NAWA
BUSRA CALNO DERRA HALAB
HAMAH IDLIB JERUD RAQQA
ALEPPO BALBEL LATAKIA
SELEUCIA
WEIGHT: COLA ROTL ARTAL ARTEL
RATEL TALENT

SYMMETRICAL FORMAL DIMERIC
REGULAR SHAPELY SPHERAL
BALANCED
(**NOT —**) SKEW
SYMMETRY MEASURE
SYMPATHETIC AKIN FERE SOFT
WARM HUMAN FELLOW KINDLY
TENDER PIETOSO SIMPATICO
SYMPATHIZER FABIAN BLACKNEB
SHAYSITE
SYMPATHY PITY RUTH FLESH
PHILIA CONSENT EMPATHY
RAPPORT AFFINITY KINDNESS
SYMPHONY SINFONIA
(**BEETHOVEN'S THIRD —**) EROICA
SYMPOSIUM POTATION
SYMPTOM MARK NOTE SIGN
SHOWER STIGMA INSTANCE
PRODROME
(**DISEASE —**) MERCYISM

SYRINGA PHILADELPHUS
SYRINGE GUN HYPO ENEMA SCOOT
DOUCHE FILLER SQUIRT SCOOTER
SERRING

SYRINGIN LILACIN
SYRINX PANPIPE
SYRNIUM STRIX
SYRUP DIBS LICK SIRUP ORGEAT
ANTIQUE ECLEGMA FALERNUM
QUIDDANY
(**FRUIT —**) ROB
(**STARCH —**) GLUCOSE
SYRUPY FRUITY
SYRYENIAN SYRYAN ZYRIAN
(**PL.**) KAMI KOMI
SYSTEM ISM AREA CREDO FRAME
ORDER CIRCLE METHOD SCHEME
STEREO SYNTAX COMPLEX
DUALISM ECONOMY FAGGERY
NAVARHO REGIMEN ENSEMBLE
GALENISM OVERRIDE RELIGION
UNIVERSE
(**— FOR ROMANIZING IDEOGRAMS**)
PINYIN
(**— OF BARS**) LATTICE
(**— OF BELIEFS**) FAITH
(**— OF BELL CHANGES**) CATERS
QUATERS STEDMAN
(**— OF CORDS**) BRIDLE
(**— OF CROSSING THREADS**)
LEASE
(**— OF DIET**) BANTING
(**— OF ETHICS**) SELFISM
(**— OF EXCHANGE**) KULA
(**— OF EXERCISES**) AEROBICS
(**— OF FAITH**) CREED
(**— OF GEARS**) COMPOUND
(**— OF JOINTS**) CLEAT
(**— OF LANGUAGE SIGNS**) SIGNARY
(**— OF LAW**) EQUITY
(**— OF LINES IN EYEPIECE**) RETICLE
RETICULE
(**— OF LOGIC**) RAMISM
(**— OF MANUAL TRAINING**) SLOJD
SLOYD
(**— OF MARKETING**) ADMASS
(**— OF MEANING**) SEMANTIC
(**— OF MEDICINE**) AYURVEDA
(**— OF MONEY TRANSFER**) GIRO
(**— OF NUMERALS**) ALGORISM
(**— OF OCCULT THEOSOPHY**)
CABALA
(**— OF PHILOSOPHY**) HUMISM
COMTISM HOBBISM SAMKHYA
SANKHYA STOICISM
(**— OF PHONETIC NOTATION**)
ROMIC
(**— OF PRINCIPLES**) CODE
(**— OF RAYS**) ASTER
(**— OF ROCKS**) CENOZOIC
DEVONIAN SILURIAN
(**— OF RULE**) REGIME
(**— OF RULES**) ART
(**— OF SOLMIZATION**) FASOLA
(**— OF SPACES**) LACUNOME
(**— OF SUPPRESSING LITERATURE**)
SAMIZDAT

(**PENAL —**) GULAG
(**RELIGIOUS —**) LAW CULT CULTUS
SHIISM SUNNISM DRUIDISM
(**RHYTHMIC —**) STROPHE GLYCONIC
(**ROMANIZING —**) PINYIN
(**SING-SONG VOWEL —**) ABLAUT
(**SOCIAL —**) CASTE
(**STAR —**) GALAXY
(**TECHNOLOGICAL —**) FORDISM
(**TELEVISION —**) SCOPHONY
(**TRIANGULATION —**) SOFAR
(**TRUCK —**) TOMMY
(**WORK —**) FLEXTIME FLEXITIME
SYSTEMATIC ORDERLY REGULAR
METHODIC
SYSTEMATIZE ORDER CODIFY
ORGANIZE METHODIZE
SYSTEMATIZED CODED ORGANIC
SYSTEMIC DEMETON

T

T TEE TARE TANGO
TAAL AFRIKAANS
TAB JAG PAN TAG BILL COST FLAP
CHECK FLASH PRICE TALLY WATCH
EARTAB EARTAG SIGNAL
TOEPLATE
TABANID GADFLY
TABARD CHIMER CHIMERE
TABARRO, IL (CHARACTER IN —)
LUIGI MICHELE GIORGETTA
(COMPOSER OF —) PUCCINI
TABERNACLE PIX PYX HOVEL
SACRARY
TABES WASTING
TABETIC MARCID
TABITHA DORCAS
TABLATURE LYRAWAY PICTURE
PAINTING
TABLE KEY PIE PYE RUN DANK DUCK
DAIS DESK FORM MESS BELLY
BENCH BOARD CANON CHART
PINAX PLANK SCALE STALL STAND
STONE WAGON COMMON SCHEME
SHELVE TABLET TABULA TARIFF
TEAPOY TRIPOD VANNER CABARET
CAMBIST CONSOLE COUNTER
DIAGRAM DIPTYCH DRESSER
PROJECT SHAMBLE TABLEAU
TESSERA TROLLEY WHIRLER
CALENDAR CREDENCE GUERIDON
PEDIGREE PEMBROKE REGIMENT
SETASIDE SPECULUM STILLAGE
TOILETTE VANITORY NIGHTSTAND
(— DECORATION) DOILY
(— FOR BOWING HAT-BODY) HURL
(— FOR GLAZING LEATHER) BANK
(— FOR ORNAMENT) CARTOUCH
(— FOR PHOTOGRAPHIC PLATES)
WHIRLER
(— FURNISHED WITH MEAL)
SPREAD
(— IN STORE) COUNTER
(— OF ANCESTORS) PEDIGREE
(— OF CONTENTS) INDEX METHOD
(— OF DECLINATIONS) REGIMENT
(— TOP) AMOEBA
(— USED IN FELTING A HAT) BASON
(— WITH BRAZIER BENEATH)
TENDOOR TENDOUR
(ARITHMETIC —) TARIFF
(ASTROLOGICAL —) SPECULUM
(BOTANIC —) KEY
(CIRCULAR —) ROUNDEL
(COMMUNION —) ALTAR
CREDENCE
(DINING —) MAHOGANY
(DRESSING —) TOILET VANITY
TOILETTE
(EUCHARISTIC —) PROTHESIS
(FOLDING —) SERVETTE
(INNER —) HOME
(KIND OF —) PARSONS PERIODIC
(MASSAGE —) PLINTH

(MUSICAL —) DIAGRAM
(NIGHT —) SOMNO
(ONE-FOOTED —) MONOPODE
(PRINCIPAL —) DAIS
(PRINTER'S —) STONE
(PROFUSELY ORNAMENTED —)
PEMBROKE
(SECTIONAL STUDY —) CARREL
(SERVING —) WAGON
(SHAKING —) SLIMER
(SMALL —) KURSI STAND TABORET
TABOURET
(STONE —) DOLMEN
(TEA —) TEAPOY
(WRITING —) DESK
TABLEAU LAYOUT PAGEANT
PICTURE
TABLECLOTH CLOTH COVER
CARPET
TABLE D'HOTE DINNER
TABLELAND PLAT PUNA PUNO
KAROO TABLE KARROO PLATEAU
BALAGHAT
TABLET PAD PAX BRED ALBUM
FACIA PIECE PINAX SLATE TABLE
ABACUS CAPLET TABULA TABULE
TROCHE ASPIRIN CODICIL DIPTYCH
PALETTE PREFORM TABLING
CARTOUCH CHURINGA TABULATE
TRIPTYCH MEDALLION
(— BEARING SYMBOL OF CHRIST)
PAX
(— FOR PUBLISHING LAWS)
PARAPEGM
(— OVER SHOP FRONT) FACIA
FASCIA
(AMPHETAMINE —) BENNY
(DRUG —) QUAALUDE
(MEDICATED —) ASPIRIN JELLOID
TABELLA
(MEDICINAL —) DISC DISK
TROCHE
(MEMORIAL —) BRASS TABUT
(PAINTER'S —) PALETTE
(SLEEPING —) DALMANE
(SQUARE —) ABACK
(UPRIGHT —) STELA STELE
(VOTIVE —) PINAX
(WRITING —) CODICIL TRIPTYCH
(PREF.) PINA PINAC(O) PLAC(O)
TABLEWARE CHINA FLATWARE
HAVILAND
(WOODEN —) TREEN
TABOO KAPU TABU TAPU
FORBIDDEN INEFFABLE
TABOR ATABAL TABRET TIMBRE
TABORIN TIMBREL
TABULATION SCALE SCHEME
TABLING
TABUT TAZIA TAZEEA
TACHOMETER CUTMETER
TACHYGLOSSUS ECHIDNA
TACIT SILENT IMPLICIT

TACITURN DUMB STILL SILENT
LACONIC RESERVED RETICENT
TACK LAY BEAT CAST STAY BASTE
BOARD FETCH ENTAIL LAVEER
TACKET TINGLE SADDLERY
(GLAZIERS' —) BRAD
TACKER GUN SPREADER
TACKLE CAT RIG TAW GEAR SWIG
TACK YOKE ANGLE FALLS ATTACK
BURTON COLLAR GARNET JIGGER
LEDGER RUNNER STEEVE TAGLIA
TEAGLE DERRICK HALYARD
HARNESS RIGGING FISHFALL
PURCHASE TACKLING
(— BY NECK) SCRAG
(— FOR RAISING BOAT) FALLS
(— TO HOIST ANCHOR) CAT
(COMBINATION OF —S) JEER JEERS
(FISHING —) TEW LEGER OTTER
LEDGER
TACO FLAUTA TAQUITO
TACT TOUCH ADDRESS CONDUCT
DELICACY
TACTFUL POLITIC DISCREET
GRACEFUL
TACTFULLY HAPPILY
TACTIC GAME PLOY
TACTICAL THEATER
TACTICS FOOTWORK
TACTLESS BRASH GAUCHE
TAD LAD MOPPET SHAVER SPROUT
TADPOLE POWHEAD BULLHEAD
POLEHEAD POLLIWOG POLLYWOG
PORWIGLE
TAEL LIANG
TAENNIN KOSIN KOUSIN
TAFFETA TABBY ARMOZEEN
FLORENCE
TAFFY GUNDY TOFFY TOFFEE
CLAGGUM
TAG HE DAG EAR TAB TIG TAIL TICK
AGLET DAGGE LABEL TALLY
TOUCH AIGLET EARTAB EARTAG
FOLLOW SWATCH TAGGLE
TAGRAG TICKET TIGTAG HANGTAG
(— OF A LACE) AGLET AIGLET
(ANGLING —) TOUCH
(ORNAMENTED —S) FANCY
TAGALOG PULAHAN
TAGETES MARIGOLD
TAGRAG SHAGRAG
TAHATH (FATHER OF —) BERED
TAHITI (CAPITAL OF —) PAPEETE
(FORMER NAME OF —) OTAHEITE
(MOUNTAIN IN —) OROHENA
TAHMURATH (BROTHER OF —)
YIMA
(FATHER OF —) VIVANGHAO
(SLAYER OF —) AHRIMAN
TAHR KRAS JHARAL
TAHSILDAR TALUKDAR
TAI LI AHOM SHAM THAI PORGY
KHAMTI

TAIGA URMAN
TAIL BOB BUN CUE BUNT BUSH
CLUB FLAG POLE SCUT BRUSH
CAUDA SNAKE START STERN TRAIN
TWIST FLIGHT FOLLOW RUMPLE
SHADOW SWITCH TAILET TAILLE
FANTAIL FOXTAIL RATTAIL
(— OF ARTIFICIAL FLY) TOPPING
(— OF BEAST) QUEUE
(— OF BELL CLAPPER) FLIGHT
(— OF BIRD) FAN
(— OF BIRD OR ANIMAL) CUE POLE
START
(— OF BOAR) WREATH
(— OF CART) ARSE
(— OF COAT) DOCK
(— OF COMET) BEARD STREAM
STREAMER CHEVELURE
(— OF DEER) FLAG SINGLE SHINGLE
(— OF DOG) FLAG STERN
(— OF FISH) UROSOME
(— OF FLY) WHISK
(— OF FOX) BUSH BRUSH FOXTAIL
(— OF HARE OR RABBIT) BUN FUD
BUNT SCUT
(— OF HOOD) LIRIPIPE LIRIPOOP
(— OF HORSE) BOB
(— OF MAN'S TIED HAIR) CLUB
(— OF METEOR) TRAIN
(— OF MUSICAL NOTE) QUEUE
(— OF PUG DOG) TWIST
(— OF SQUIRREL) BUN
(— OF STANZA) CODA
(DRAGON'S —) KETU
(STUMP OF —) STRUNT
(TIP OF —) TAG
(PREF.) CAUD(I)(O) CERC(O) ONCHO
UR(O)
(SUFF.) CERCAL CERCY URA URE
UROUS URUS
TAILBAND FOOTBAND
TAILBOARD ENDGATE ENDBOARD
ENDPIECE
TAILED CAUDATE CAUDATED
(PREF.) UR(O)
(SUFF.) URA URE UROUS URUS
TAILING CHAT
(PL.) SAND TAIL GRUFFS
TAILLE TALLY
TAILLESS ACAUDAL ANUROUS
ACAUDATE ECAUDATE
TAILOR SLOP SNIP BUILD DARZI
GORER SHRED CUTTER DARZEE
FULLER SARTOR SNYDER STITCH
BOTCHER CABBAGE SNIPPER
TIREMAN CLOTHIER SEAMSTER
SEMPSTER SHEPSTER
(ITINERANT —) CARDOOER
TAILORBIRD DARZEE
TAILPIECE QUEUE ANQUERA
TAILRACE AFTERBAY
TAILSPIN FLICKER NOSEDIVE
TAILSTOCK DEADHEAD

TAINO HAITIAN
(**— BELIEFS**) ZEMIISM
TAINT HAUL HOGO MOIL SMUT
SPOT VICE CLOUD STAIN TOUCH
DARKEN INFECT REMORD SMIRCH
SMUTCH ATTAINT BLEMISH
CORRUPT DEBAUCH ENVENOM
FLYBLOW FORRUMP POLLUTE
TARNISH VITIATE EMPOISON
TAINTURE CONTAMINATE
TAINTED BAD OFF GAMY HIGH
BLOWN PINDY SAPPY TAINT
WEMMY RANCID ROTTEN SINFUL
SMUTTY CORRUPT FOUGHTY
FLYBLOWN
TAIWAN (**CAPITAL OF —**) TAIPEI
(**ISLAND GROUP OF —**) MATSU
PENGHU QUEMOY
(**MOUNTAIN IN —**) TZUKAO YUSHAN
HSINKAO
(**OTHER NAME OF —**) FORMOSA
(**RIVER IN —**) WUCHI TACHIA
CHOSHUI HUALIEN TANSHUI
(**TOWN IN —**) CHIAL TAINAN TAIPEI
CHILUNG KEELUNG PINGTUNG
TAICHUNG

TAJIKISTAN (ALSO SEE RUSSIA)
CAPITAL: DUSHANBE STALINABAD
COIN: RUBLE
LAKE: SAREZ KARAKUL
ISKANDERKUL
MOUNTAIN: LENIN COMMUNISM
MOUNTAIN RANGE: KURAMA
MOGOLTAU TIENSHAN
PAMIRALAY TURKESTAN
ZERAVSHAN GISSARALAY
NAME: TAJIK TADZHIK TOJIKISTON
TADZHIKISTAN
RIVER: PANJ MURGAB VAKHSH
AMUDARYA SYRDARYA
KAFIRNIGAN
TOWN: NUREK REGAR KHOROG
KULYAB KHUDZAND URATUYBE
KAYRAKKUM KHUDZHAND
LENINABAD TURSUNZADE
VALLEY: PANJ GISSAR HISSAR
VAKHSH FERGANA OBIKIIK
PYANDZH YAVANSU KAFIRNIGAN
KAFIRNIHAN

TAJIN TOTONAC
TAJ MAHAL (**SITE OF —**) AGRA
TAKE COP HIT NIM NIP NOB BEAR
BONE DRAW FANG GLOM HAVE
LEAD TACK TEEM TOLL ADOPT
AFONG BRING CARRY CATCH
CREEL FETCH GRASP GRIPE LATCH
SEIZE SNAKE ACCEPT CLUTCH
COTTON DERIVE EXTEND FERRET
FINGER RECIPE SNATCH TAKING
ATTRACT CABBAGE CAPTURE
RECEIVE UNPURSE UNDERNIM
(**— A BATH**) TOSH
(**— A CERTAIN POSITION**) SIT
(**— ACROSS**) TRAJECT
(**— ACTION**) ACT
(**— A DIRECTION**) STEER
(**— A DRINK**) PULL SMILE
(**— ADVANTAGE**) DO ABUSE
BLUDGE CLUTCH EXPLOIT
(**— AFTER**) BRAID FOLLOW
(**— AIM**) BEAD

(**— A LITTLE**) DELIBATE
(**— A NAP**) DOSS
(**— APART**) UNRIG
(**— ASIDE**) SINGLE
(**— AS ONE'S OWN**) ADOPT
(**— A STAND**) ASSERT
(**— AWAY**) BATE EASE HENT LIFT
TOLL WISP ADEEM BENIM BLEED
HEAVE REAVE STEAL ABDUCT
CONVEY DEDUCE DEDUCT DEMISE
DEPOSE DEVEST DIVEST ELOIGN
EXEMPT REMOVE UNVEST ABJUDGE
BEREAVE DEPRIVE DETRACT
FORTAKE RETRACT SUBDUCE
SUBLATE ABSTRACT DEROGATE
DIMINISH SUBTRACT
(**— BACK**) RECALL RECANT RECOUP
REGAIN REVOKE RETRACT
RECAPTURE
(**— BACK TO ONESELF**) RESUME
(**— BY ASSAULT**) STORM
(**— BY FORCE**) SPOIL
(**— BY FRAUD**) BOB
(**— BY LEVY**) ESTREAT
(**— BY STEALTH**) HOOK SNITCH
(**— BY STORM**) EXPUGN INVADE
SURPRISE
(**— CARE**) FIX SEE GARE KEEP MIND
TEND WARD YEME NURSE BEWARE
GOVERN INTEND CUIDADO
HUSBAND CHAPERON
(**— CENSUS OF**) MUSTER
(**— CHANCE**) DICE RISK
(**— CHARGE**) ATTEND
(**— CHARGE OF**) CURE SOLICIT
(**— COVER**) COOK
(**— DAMAGE**) BANGE
(**— DINNER**) DINE
(**— DOWN**) STOOP STRIKE
(**— DRUGS ORALLY**) POP
(**— EXCEPTION**) DEMUR STRAIN
(**— FIRE**) SPUNK
(**— FOOD**) EAT DINE GRUB
(**— FORCIBLY**) USURP
(**— FOR GRANTED**) BEG ASSUME
PRESUME
(**— FORM**) FORM INFORM
(**— FOR ONESELF**) CAB
(**— FOR RESALE**) FLOG
(**— FRAUDULENTLY**) STEAL STRIKE
(**— FRIGHT**) BOOGER
(**— FROM**) DETRACT
(**— FROM DEPOSIT**) DRAW
(**— GOLFING STANCE**) ADDRESS
(**— GREAT DELIGHT**) REVEL
(**— HEART**) BRACE
(**— HEED**) RECK TENT
(**— HOLD**) GET BITE GRAB PINCH
SEIZE ARREST BEGRIPE
(**— HOLIDAY**) LAKE
(**— IN**) IN EAT SUP BITE HOAX KEEP
DOWSE DRINK ABSORB DEVOUR
ENFOLD GATHER HARBOR INCEPT
INGEST INSORB INSUME INTAKE
MUZZLE BEGRIPE EMBRACE
INCLUDE
(**— IN BY LEAKING**) LADE
(**— IN LIVESTOCK**) AGIST
(**— IN SAIL**) BRAIL
(**— INTO HANDS**) TOUCH EMBRACE
(**— LEGALLY**) ATTACH
(**— LEVEL OF**) BONE
(**— LUNCH**) TIFFIN

(**— MEALS**) BOARD
(**— NOTE OF**) NB COUNT SMOKE
NOTICE WITNESS
(**— OATH**) ABJURE
(**— OFF**) OFF ROB DOFF EXIT LIFT
VAIL DOUSE SHUCK STRIP DEDUCT
(**— OFFENSE**) DORT HUFF
(**— ON**) HIRE ADOPT MOUNT START
(**— ONE'S LEAVE**) CONGEE
(**— ONESELF**) BETAKE
(**— OUT**) DELE KILL EXCERPT
AIRBRUSH
(**— OUT OF EARTH**) EXTER
(**— OVER**) ABSORB SUBSUME
(**— PAINS**) BOTHER
(**— PART**) LEAD FIGHT ENGAGE
(**— PLACE**) BE DO GO COME GIVE
PASS ARISE BEFALL HAPPEN
(**— PLEASURE IN**) ENJOY ADMIRE
(**— PORTION OF**) PARTAKE
(**— POSITION**) STAND
(**— POSSESSION**) GRIP ANNEX
BESET SEIZE SPOIL EXTEND
CONQUER INHERIT DISTRAIN
(**— REFUGE**) HIDE SOIL EVADE
HAVEN WATCH
(**— ROOT**) MARE MORE ENROOT
STRIKE
(**— SHAPE**) JELL
(**— SHELTER**) HOWF NESTLE
SHROUD
(**— SUPPER**) SUP
(**— THE PLACE OF**) ENSUE SECOND
SUPPLY DISPLACE SUPPLANT
(**— THOUGHT**) ADVISE
(**— TO BE TRUE WITHOUT PROOF**)
PRESUME
(**— TO TASK**) JACK CARPET
CHAPTER
(**— TO WING**) FLUSH
(**— UNAWARE**) DECEIVE
(**— UP**) SORB ENTER MOUNT
ADSORB ASSUME GATHER HANDLE
STRIKE ELEVATE
(**— UP AGAIN**) RESUME
(**— UP WITH**) ALL
(**— WELL OR ILL**) RESENT
(**— WIND ON OPPOSITE QUARTER**)
JIBE
TAKEN TON TAIN
(**— ABACK**) BLANK
(**— AWAY**) ADEMPT
(**— OUT**) EXEMPT
TAKEOFF JATO VTOL SPOOF
SENDUP SCRAMBLE
(**PREPARE FOR —**) STRAPIN
TAKEOUT STACK
(**FOR —**) TOGO
TAKER PERNOR
TAKING HOT TAKY CAPTION
ADOPTION PERNANCY
PREEMPTION
(**— A VOTE**) DIVISION
(**— BACK**) RECAPTION
(**— EVERYTHING INTO ACCOUNT**)
OVERALL
(**— LIBERTIES**) PRESUMPTUOUS
(**— OF LIFE**) BLOOD
(**— PLACE**) AGATE
(**— POSSESSION**) ENTRY
(PREF.) (**— IN**) END(O)
(SUFF.) LEPSIA LEPSIS LEPSY
LEPT(IC)

TALAK AHSAN
TALARI PATACA PATACOON
TALAUS (**FATHER OF —**) BIAS
(**MOTHER OF —**) PERO
(**SON OF —**) ADRASTUS
(**WIFE OF —**) LYSIMACHE
TALC SPAAD TALCUM AGALITE
STEATITE SOAPSTONE
TALE SAW DIDO JEST LEED REDE
TELL BOURD CONTE CRACK FABLE
RECIT SPELL SPOKE STORY WINDY
AITION FABULA LEGEND PISTLE
PURANA FABLIAU FICTION
HISTORY MARCHEN ROMANCE
WHOPPER ANECDOTE FOLKTALE
SPELLING TREATISE
(**— OF ACHIEVEMENTS**) GEST
GESTE
(**— OF ADVENTURE**) CONTE
(**— OF CHIVALRY**) ROMAN
ROMANCE
(**— OF FATE**) WEIRD
(**— OF FOUR**) WARP
(**— OF GOLD COAST NEGROS**)
NANCY
(**— OF GRIEF**) JEREMIAD
(**— OF TERROR**) HAIRRAISER
(**COMIC COARSE —**) FABLIAU
(**DEVISED —**) AITION
(**EPIC —**) TAIN
(**FALSE —**) BAM VANITY SLANDER
(**FATEFUL —**) WEIRD
(**FOLK —**) NANCY THRENE
(**FOLK —S**) LORE
(**HUMOROUS —S**) FACETIAE
(**ICELANDIC —**) SAGA
(**MEDIEVAL —**) LAI
(**MERRY —**) BOURD
(**METRICAL —**) FABLIAU
(**PITIFUL —**) SOBSTORY
(**POETIC NARRATIVE —**) SAGA
(**SENSATIONAL —**) BLOOD
SHOCKER
(**SHORT —**) LAI CONTE
(PREF.) STORIO
TALEBEARER BUZZER GOSSIP
TATTLER TALEPYET TELLTALE
TALEBEARING TALEWISE
TALENT GIFT HEAD NOUS VEIN
DOWER DOWRY VERVE CICHAR
GENIUS ABILITY CHARISM
FACULTY CAPACITY CHARISMA
TALENTED ABLE CLEVER GIFTED
TALE OF TWO CITIES (**AUTHOR OF
—**) DICKENS
(**CHARACTER IN —**) JOHN JERRY
LORRY LUCIE PROSS BARSAD
CARTON DARNAY JARVIS SYDNEY
CHARLES DEFARGE GASPARD
MANETTE STRYVER CRUNCHER
EVREMONDE
TALER ORT THALER
TALES OF HOFFMANN
(**CHARACTER IN —**) ANDRES
LUTHER STELLA ANTONIA CRESPEL
LINDORF MIRACLE OLYMPIA
HOFFMANN SCHLEMIL COPPELIUS
GIULIETTA NICALUSSE DAPERTUTTO
SPALANZANI PITICHINACCHIO
(**COMPOSER OF —**) OFFENBACH
TALIPES CLUBFOOT
TALISMAN ANGLE CHARM IMAGE
OBEAH SAFFI AMULET GRIGRI

SAPHIE SCARAB TELESM ICHTHUS ICHTHYS GREEGREE
(AUTHOR OF —) SCOTT
(CHARACTER IN —) DAVID EDITH PHILIP KENNETH RICHARD SALADIN BERENGARIA MONTFERRAT PLANTAGENET

TALK GAB GAS JAW JIB RAP SAW SAY YAP BLAT BUCK BUKH CANT CARP CHAT CHIN GAFF GIVE GUFF KNAP MEAN TALE TOVE WORD CRACK FABLE MOUTH PARLE PITCH SPEAK SPELL SPIEL SPOKE TUTEL COMMON GAMMON INDABA KORERO PATTER SERMON SPEECH STEVEN TONGUE YABBER ADDRESS CHINWAG DISCUSS JAWBONE LIPWORK PALABRA PALAVER PARRALL PURPOSE WINDJAM CAUSERIE COLLOQUY CONVERSE LANGUAGE PARLANCE QUESTION SCUTTLEBUTT
(— ABOUT) HASH
(— AT LENGTH) RUNON
(— BACK) SASS
(— BIG) SWANK BOUNCE
(— BOASTFULLY) GAS BLATTER
(— BOMBASTICALLY) BEMOUTH
(— CASUALLY) DISH
(— CONFIDENTIALLY) CUTTER
(— CONFUSEDLY) HOTTER
(— DELIRIOUSLY) RAVE
(— DISMALLY) CROAK
(— DRUNKENLY) SLUR
(— EMPTILY) BLOW
(— EXTRAVAGANTLY) ROMANCE
(— FAMILIARLY) TOVE CONFAB
(— FATUOUSLY) BABBLE
(— FONDLY) COO
(— FOOLISHLY) YAK BLAT FLAP YACK HAVER BABBLE DRIVEL FOOTER FOOTLE GABBLE GIBBER CAWNEY TOOTLE BLATHER BLETHER
(— GLIBLY) PATTER SCREED
(— IDLY) GAB GAS BLAB CHAT CHIN GASH YACK FABLE GABBLE JANGLE RABBIT TATTLE CHATTER GNATTER PRATTLE
(— IMPUDENTLY) SASS
(— INACCURATELY) BLAGUE
(— INARTICULATELY) CHUNNER CHUNTER
(— INCESSANTLY) YANK BURBLE RABBIT WAFFLE CHATTER
(— INCOHERENTLY) BABBLE BURBLE HOTTER MITHER MOIDER
(— INCONSIDERATELY) BLAT
(— INDECISIVELY) WAFFLE
(— INFORMALLY) HOBNOB
(— INSOLENTLY) SNASH
(— INTENDED TO DECEIVE) GAMMON PALAVER
(— IRRATIONALLY) RAVE
(— JARGON) JIVE
(— MONOTONOUSLY) DRONE
(— NEEDLESSLY) PALAVER
(— NOISILY) CLAP BLATTER BRABBLE
(— NONSENSE) GAS ROT BLEAT DROOL FUDGE HAVER
(— OFFICIOUSLY) BLEEZE
(— PEEVISHLY) WITTER

(— PERTLY) CHELP
(— PRIVATELY) COLLOGUE
(— RAPIDLY) GABBLE JABBER GNATTER
(— SCANDAL) HORN
(— SNAPPISHLY) KNAP
(— SPORTIVELY) DAFF
(— SUPERFICIALLY) SMATTER
(— TEDIOUSLY) DINGDONG
(— THOUGHTLESSLY) BLAB
(— TOGETHER) DEVISE
(— VAGUELY) WOOZLE
(— VOLUBLY) CHIN PATTER
(— WEAKLY) DRIVEL
(— WITH) CONTACT
(— WITHOUT MEANING) GABBLE
(— WITTILY) SCINTILLATE
(ABSURD —) BOSH
(ABUSIVE —) HOKER JAWING
(ARROGANT —) GUM BRAG
(BACK —) LIP SASS
(BAWDY —) SCULDUDDRY SCULDUDDERY SKULDUDDERY
(BOASTFUL —) BULL GAFF
(BOMBASTIC —) FLASH
(COMMON —) FAME FABLE NOISE HEARSAY
(CONCEITED —) BLAGUE
(CONTINUAL —) CLACK
(COUNTRY —) CLASH
(DECEPTIVE —) GAMMON
(DIFFUSE —) POTTER
(DRIVELLING —) MAUNDERING
(EMPTY —) GAS BOSH GASH FRASE GLOZE FRAISE BLAFLUM GASSING PRATTLE BALLYHOO GALBANUM MOONSHINE POPPYCOCK PRITTLEPRATTLE
(ENTHUSIASTIC —) JAZZ
(EVASIVE —) FLANNEL
(FALSE —) BALLYHOO
(FAMILIAR —) CONFAB CHITCHAT
(FANTASTIC —) GUYVER
(FLATTERING —) FLANNEL
(FLIP —) SASS
(FOOLISH —) GUP GAFF JIVE BLEAT CLACK FABLE BLETHERS COBBLERS
(FORMAL —) ADDRESS
(FRESH —) LIP
(FRIVOLOUS —) PERSIFLAGE
(FUSSY —) PHRASE
(GENERAL —) RUMOR REPORT RUMOUR
(GLIB —) JIVE
(IDLE —) GAB YAK BLAB BUFF CHAT GAFF GEST GUFF YACK FABLE GESTE BABBLE CLAVER GOSSIP JANGLE CHATTER CLATTER PALAVER TWATTLE BABBLING BATTOLOGY BALDERDASH BIBBLEBABBLE
(IMPUDENT —) PRATE SLACK
(INCOHERENT —) GABBER JABBER
(INFORMAL —) CAUSERIE
(INSINCERE —) JAZZ CROCK BUNKUM MALARKEY
(JESTING —) CHAFF JAPERY
(LIGHT —) TRIFLING
(MEANINGLESS —) SLIPSLOP
(NONSENSICAL —) BLABBER BLATHER FOLDEROL
(ORDINARY —) PROSE
(PIOUS OR SANCTIMONIOUS —) PI

(PUBLIC —) NOISE
(RAPID —) GABBLE JABBER CHATTER CLATTER
(SALES —) PITCH
(SCOLDING —) HARANGUE
(SENSELESS —) TWADDLE
(SILLY —) BLAH BUFF CLART CACKLE FOOTLE TWADDLE
(SMALL —) CHAT BACKCHAT CHITCHAT
(SMOOTH —) GLOZE BLARNEY
(STUPID —) MOROLOGY
(TRIFLING —) PRATTLE CHITCHAT
(UNRESTRAINED —) JAWING
(USELESS —) WASTE
(VIOLENT —) BLUSTER
(WEAK —) SLIPSLOP
(WHINING —) BLEAT
(WILD —) RANT
(WORTHLESS —) PIFFLE
(SUFF.) LALIA LOG(ER)(IA)(IAN)(IC)(ICAL)(IST)(UE)(Y)

TALKATIVE COSY GASH GLIB NAWY BUZZY GABBY TALKY CHATTY CLASHY CRACKY FLUENT FUTILE SOCIAL VOLUBLE BIGMOUTH FLIPPANT TELLSOME LOQUACIOUS
TALKATIVENESS FUTILITY
TALKER YENTA CAMPER POTGUN CAUSEUR SPIELER
(IDLE —) WHIFFLER
(NOISY —) BLELLUM
(PROFESSIONAL —) JAWSMITH
(SENSELESS —) RATTLE
TALKING (IDLE —) GASSING
(LOUD —) NORATION
TALKING-TO EARFUL LECTURE
TALKY GABBY
TALL HIGH LANKY LOFTY RANGY STEEP WANDY CRANEY PROCERE
(— AND FEEBLE) TANGLE
(VERY —) TAUNT
TALLAGE CUTTING
TALLER DOMINANT
TALLNESS PROCERITY
TALLOW SUET SEVUM ARMING TAULCH CHERVICE
(PREF.) SEBI SEBO STEAR(O) STEAT(O)
(SUFF.) STEARIN
TALLY TAB JUMP NICK SUIT AGREE CHECK COUNT SCORE STICK STOCK CENSUS STRING SWATCH TAILYE COMPORT TAILZIE
TALMAI (FATHER OF —) AMMIHUD
TALMUD GEMARA
TALON FANG SERE UNCE CLUTCH POUNCE UNGUIS WEAPON
(— OF TOOTH) HEEL
TALONID HEEL
TALPA TESTUDO
TALTHIB GLAGA GLAGAH
TALUS SCREE RUBBLE ASTRAGAL
TAMANDUA ANTEATER
TAMAR (AUTHOR OF —) JEFFERS
(CHARACTER IN —) LEE WILL DAVID JINNY TAMAR STELLA ANDREWS MORELAND CAULDWELL
(FATHER OF —) DAVID ABSALOM
(HUSBAND OF —) ER ONAN
(MOTHER OF —) MAACHAH
(SON OF —) ZARAH PHAREZ
TAMARACK LARCH LARIX EPINETTE

TAMARIN PINCHE JACCHUS LEONCITO MARIKINA MARMOSET
TAMARIND SAMPALOC
TAMARISK ATLE JHOW HEATH MYRICA
TAMASHEK TUAREG
TAMBOURINE RIKK TAAR DAIRA TAMBO TABOUR TIMBER TABORIN TIMBREL
(PART OF —) HEAD TACK SHELL JINGLE
TAMBURLAINE THE GREAT
(AUTHOR OF —) MARLOWE
(CHARACTER IN —) ALMEDA AMYRAS COSROE ZABINA MEANDER MYCETES ORCANES BAJAZETH CALYPHAS MENAPHON CALLAPINE CELEBINUS SIGISMUND TECHELLES ZENOCRATE THERIDAMAS USUMCASANE TAMBURLAINE
TAME MAN CADE DEAD MEEK MILD PACK ACCOY ATAME BREAK DAUNT MILKY SPAKE CADISH ENTAME GENTLE INWARD MEEKEN UNWIFE AFFAITE AMENAGE CORRECT INSIPID SUBDUED CICURATE DOMESTIC MANSUETE
(— FALCON) MAN RECLAIM
TAMED BROKE GENTLE
TAMENESS MANSUETUDE
TAMER (HORSE —) HIPPODAMIST
TAMIL VELLALA
TAMING OF THE SHREW (AUTHOR OF —) SHAKESPEARE
(CHARACTER IN —) SLY BIANCA CURTIS GREMIO GRUMIO TRANIO BAPTISTA LUCENTIO BIONDELLO HORTENSIO KATHARINA PETRUCHIO VINCENTIO CHRISTOPHER
TAMMUZ (FATHER OF —) NINGISHZIDA
TAMMY TAMIS STAMIN
TAMONEA MICONIA
TAM-O-SHANTER TAM TAMMY
TAMP PUG STEM
TAMPER FIX COOK FAKE FOOL GAFF TOUCH DABBLE FIDDLE MEDDLE MONKEY POTTER PUDDLE PUTTER TEMPER FALSIFY TRINKLE
(— WITH HORSE'S TEETH) BISHOP
TAMPION TOMKIN TAMPOON
TAM-TAM GONG
TAN FAN ARAB BARK ADUST ASCOT DRESS TANKA TAWNY ORIOLE COCONUT EMBROWN LEATHER SUNBURN
(BEACH —) SEDGE
(TROTTEUR —) BAY
(PREF.) TANN(I)(O)
TANACETYL THUJYL
TANAGER YENI LINDO REDBIRD WARBIRD CARDINAL EUPHONIA FIREBIRD ORGANIST
TANBARK BARK TAWN AVARAM TURWAR ALGERIAN ALGERINE
TANCRED (FATHER OF —) OTHO
(LOVER OF —) ERMINIA CLORINDA
(MOTHER OF —) EMMA
TANDAN EELFISH
TANEKAHA TOATOA
TANG NIP BITE FANG ODOR TING VEIN SHANK STING STRAP TASTE

TWANG RELISH TANGLE TONGUE SEATANG FAREWELL
TANGELO UGLI
TANGENCY CONTACT
TANGENT SLOPE
TANGERINE NAARTJE MANDARIN
TANGIBLE ACTUAL TACTILE CONCRETE MATERIAL PALPABLE
TANGIER (NATIVE OF —) TANGERINE
TANGLE COT ELF ORE TAT FANK FOUL HARL SHAG TAUT HARLE KNURL SKEIN SNARL SNIRL THRUM TWINE WOPSE BALTER BURBLE ENTRAP FANKLE HANGER JUNGLE MOMBLE MUCKER RAFFLE SLEAVE TAFFLE TARDLE TAUGHT TEIHTE BRANGLE TAISSLE THICKET FURBELOW SCROBBLE
(PL.) COBWEB
TANGLED AFOUL TOUSY MESHED SNARLY TAUTED IMPLICIT INTORTED INVOLVED CESPITOSE
(— UP) HAYWIRE
TANGLEHEAD PILI
TANGUE TENREC
TANGY BRISK
TANHA TRISHNA
TANK DAM DIP TAL VAT BOSH SUMP BASIN MIXER STANK STEEP TRUNK BLOWUP BOILER HOPPER PANZER TROUGH BATTERY BLOWPIT BREAKER CISTERN FLUSHER PISCINA PLUNGER POACHER SETTLER STEEPER BLEACHER DIGESTOR LANDSHIP SUBSIDER
(— FOR DYE OR SOAP) BECK
(— FOR FISH) STEW TRUNK PISCINA AQUARIUM STEWPOND
(— IN SHIP) FOREPEAK
(— ON CANOE) SPONSON
(ARMORED —) FLAIL PANZER WHIPPET LANDSHIP
(KIND OF —) DRUNK SCUBA THINK SEPTIC
(PAPER MANUFACTURING —) POACHER
(PHOTOGRAPHIC —) CUVETTE
(POTTER'S —) PLUNGER
(RECTANGULAR —) BOWLY
(SALT MANUFACTURING —) GRAINER
(SPEEDY —) WHIPPET
(STORAGE —) CHEST
(SUGAR REFINING —) TIGER BLOWUP
(TANNING —) FLOATER
(PL.) HEAVIES
(PREF.) LACO
TANKAGE AMMONATE
TANKARD GUN MUG JACK FACER STOOP STOUP PEWTER POTTLE TANKER GODDARD
TANKER ULCC VLCC BOWSER
(CRUDE-OIL —) ULCC
TANNED BROWN RUDDY TAWNY REECHY BRONZED
(NOT —) RAW
TANNER EGGER SAMAR BARKER STAKER PERCHER
TANNHAUSER (CHARACTER IN —) VENUS HERMANN WOLFRAM ELISABETH TANNHAUSER
(COMPOSER OF —) WAGNER

TANNING PASTING
(— SOLUTION) PLUMPER
TANSY COSTMARY
TANSY MUSTARD FLIXWEED FLUXWEED
TANSY RAGWORT RAGWEED
TANTALIZE GRIG JADE MOCK TEASE HARASS
TANTALUS (— CAPTIVE) IXION
(DAUGHTER OF —) NIOBE
(FATHER OF —) AMPHION JUPITER THYESTES
(MOTHER OF —) NIOBE PLUTO
(SON OF —) PELOPS
(WIFE OF —) DIONE CLYTIA EUPRYTO TAYGETE
TANTAMOUNT SAME
TANTARA BLARE
TANTRA AGAMA
TANTRUM SNIT HISSY SCENE TIRADE TIRRIVEE WINGDING

TANZANIA
CAPITAL: DARESSALAAM
COIN: SENTI SHILINGI
ISLAND: MAFIA PEMBA ZANZIBAR
LAKE: RUKWA
NATIVE: BANTU SUKUMA MAKONDE SWAHILI
REGION: MARA MBEYA PEMBA PWANI TANGA MWANZA RUVUMA TABORA SINGIDA
RIVER: RUVU WAMI RUAHA KAGERA RUFIJI RUVUMA PANGANI MBENKURU
TOWN: WETE KILWA MBEYA MOSHI TANGA ARUSHA DODOMA IRINGA KIGOMA MTWARA MWANZA TABORA MTAWARA MOROGORO ZANZIBAR
VOLCANO: KIBO KILIMANJARO
WATERFALL: KALAMBO
WEIGHT: FARSALAH

TAO MAN PEASANT
(— PRACTICE) WUWEI
TAP BOB DAB PAT TAT TIP TIT TOP BEAT COCK DRUB FLIP JOWL PENK TICK TIRL TUCK TUNK APPEL FLIRT QUILL SNOCK START TOUCH ALETAP BROACH CANNEL DABBLE FAUCET NATTLE SPIGOT TAPLET BIBCOCK BLENDER DRAWOFF HEELTAP PERCUSS
(— A CASK) QUILL STRIKE
(— A DRUM) TUCK
(— FOR A LOAN) TIG
(— ON SHOE) CLUMP UNDERLAY
(— ON THE SHOULDER) FOB
(— REPEATEDLY) DRUM
(— THE GROUND) BEAT
(FENCING —) BEAT
(MASTER —) HOB HUB
(SMART — OF THE FOOT) APPEL
TAPA KAPA SIAPO KIKEPA
TAPACOLO TURCO
TAPE LEAR FERRET GARTER SCOTCH TAPERY YNKELL BINDING MEASURE TAPELINE TELETAPE
(— CARTRIDGE) CASSETTE
(DEMONSTRATION —) DEMO
(FISH —) SNAKE
(KIND OF —) DUCT REELTOREEL

(LAMP —) WICK
(LINEN —) INKLE
(METALLIC —) GALLOON
(NARROW —) TASTE
(PUT ON —) RECORD
(RED —) WIGGERY
(TV —) VIDEO
TAPE GRASS EELGRASS
TAPEMAN CHAINMAN
TAPER DRAW RISE RUSH DRAFT GAUDY PINCH SCARF SNAPE SWAGE CIERGE DRAUGHT LIGHTER PRICKET SHAMMES TRINDLE DIMINISH ACUMINATE
(— OF A SPRING) DRAW
(— OFF) CEASE TONGUE
(— OF PATTERN) STRIP
TAPERED BARRELED BOATTAIL GRADUATED
(SLIGHTLY —) TERETE
TAPERING SHARP SPIRY SPIRAL SPIRED TERETE SPIRING FUSIFORM SUBULATE ATTENUATE
TAPER ROD PODGER
TAPESTRY ARRAS TAPET TAPIS COSTER DORSER DOSSER CEILING GOBELIN HANGING SUSANEE VERDURE AUBUSSON MORTLAKE
TAPEWORM TAPE LIGULA TAENIA CESTODE CESTOID COENURE HYDATID PLATODE BANDWORM COENURUS DAVAINEA FLATWORM HELMINTH STROBILA
(— LARVA) MEASLE
(PL.) CYSTICA
(PREF.) TAENI(A)(O)
TAPHATH (FATHER OF —) SOLOMON
TAPHOLE TAP FLOSS MOUTH
TAPIOCA CASSAVA
TAPIR ANTA KUDA DANTA TENNU TAPIROID
TAPPED ABROACH
TAPPET CAM WIPER
TAPROOM TAP SALOON BARROOM BUVETTE TAPHOUSE
TAPSTER NICKPOT SKINKER
TAPUYAN GE GES GHES BUGRE GESAN JUYAS CAYAPO GOYANA CAMACAN CARAHOS COROADO TIMBIRA APINAGES BOTOCUDO CAINGANG CHAVANTE
TAR PAY BREA LIMEY BINDER SAILOR SEADOG ALKITRAN CREOSOTE
(BIRCH —) DAGGETT
(MINERAL —) MALTHA
TARA DOLMA
TARADIDDLE LIE
TARANTULA HUNTER JAYHAWK MYGALID
TARAS BULBA (AUTHOR OF —) GOGOL
(CHARACTER IN —) BULBA OSTAP TARAS ANDRII YANKEL KIRDYAGA
TARBOOSH FEZ
TARDIGRADA ARCTISCA
TARDILY SLOWLY
TARDINESS SLOTH TARDITY
TARDY LAG LAX DREE LATE SLOW SLACK DREIGH LAGGED REMISS LAGGING OVERDUE DILATORY LATESOME

TARE TINE VETCH LEAKAGE
(PL.) FILTH
TAREA (FATHER OF —) MICAH
TARES ZIZANY
TARGE BUCKLER
TARGET AIM MOT BUTT MARK WAND CLOUT LEVEL PRICK ROVER SCOOP SCOPE TARGE WHITE BANNER NIVEAU OBJECT SLEEVE COCKSHY INCOMER OUTGOER SARACEN POPINJAY
(— OF KNEELING FIGURE) SQUAW
(— OF LEVELING STAFF) VANE
(— OF RIDICULE) GAME
(— RING) SOUS
(EASY —) SITTER
(PIECE OF —) SCAB
(RAILROAD SWITCH —) BANNER
(STRIKE A —) KEYHOLE
(THROWN —) COCKSHY COCKSHUT
(TOWED —) DROGUE
(UNIDENTIFIED —) SKUNK
TARHEEL STATE NORTHCAROLINA
TARIFF ZABETA AVERAGE TRIBUTE
TARNISH DIM BLOT SMIT SOIL CLOUD DIRTY STAIN SULLY TACHE TAINT BREATH DARKEN DEFILE INJURE SMIRCH ASPERSE BEGRIME BESMEAR BLEMISH OBSCURE BESMIRCH DISCOLOR
TARO COCO DALO EDDO GABE KALO MASI TALO COCCO KAROU TANIA TANYA COCKER TARROW YAUTIA COCOYAM DASHEEN MALANGA COCOROOT EDDYROOT
(— PRODUCT) POI
TAROT NAIB TAROCCO
TARPON SABALO
TARRAGON TARCHON ESTRAGON
TARRY BIDE LENG STAY STOP ABIDE DALLY DEMUR PAUSE ARREST LINGER PITCHY REMAIN SOJOURN
TARSIER LEMUR MALMAG
TARSOMETATARSUS SHANK
TARSUS HAND ANKLE DIGITAL
(BIRD'S —) SHANK
TART ACID FLAN SOUR ACERB BOWLA CUPID EAGER SHARP SNIPPY SUNKET PIQUANT POLYNEE PUNGENT SUBACID TARTLET TURNOVER
TARTAN PLAID
(— PATTERN) SETT
TARTAR ARGAL ARGOL CALCULUS
TARTARIN OF TARASCON
(AUTHOR OF —) DAUDET
(CHARACTER IN —) BAIA BRAVIDA GREGORY BEZUQUET TARTARIN BARBASSOU
TARTNESS ACRITY ACIDITY VERDURE ACERBITY ASPERITY VERJUICE
TARTUFFE (AUTHOR OF —) MOLIERE
(CHARACTER IN —) ARGAS DAMIS ORGON DORINE ELMIRE VALERE CLEANTE MARIANE PERNELLE TARTUFFE
TASHMET (HUSBAND OF —) NEBO
TASK FAG JOB TAX CHAR DARG TOIL CHARE CHORE GRIND KNACK LABOR NULLO STINT CHARGE DEVOIR NIYOGA PENSUM RAMSCH

TOURNE FATIGUE SWEATER TRAVAIL BUSINESS EXERCISE TRAUCHLE
(— AS PSYCHOLOGICAL TEST) AUFGABE
(ASSIGNED —) STENT STINT DEVOIR
(DIFFICULT —) BUGGER
(EASY —) PIPE SNAP SETUP PICNIC CAKEWALK
(EXAMINATION —) QUESTION
(ONEROUS —) CORVEE
(ONE WHO PERFORMS MENIAL —S) DOGSBODY
(ROUTINE —) DRUDGE
TASKMASTER DRIVER TASKER RAWHIDER
(BRUTAL —) LEGREE
TASMANIA (CAPITAL OF —) HOBART
(LAKE IN —) ECHO SORELL
(MOUNTAIN IN —) DROME NEVIS BARRON CRADLE LOMOND HUMBOLDT
(RIVER IN —) ESK HUDN TAMAR GORDON JORDAN PIEMAN DERWENT
(TOWN IN —) BURNIF HOBART
TASMANIAN DEVIL DASYURID
TASMANIAN WOLF HYENA TIGER THYLACINE
TASSEL TAG TUFT LABEL THRUM TARCEL TARGET TOORIE CORDELLE
(PL.) ZIZITH
(PREF.) THYSAN(O)
TASSEL)PL.) TZITZIS TZITZIT
TASTABLE GUSTABLE
TASTE FAT GAB GOO LAP SIP CAST DASH GOUT GUST HINT PREE RASA SALT TANG TEST TINT WAFT ASSAY DRINK FANCY GUSTO HEART PROVE RELES SAPOR SAVOR SHADE SKILL SMACK SNACK SPICE TOOTH TOUCH DEGUST FLAVOR GENIUS LIKING PALATE RELISH SAMPLE SMATCH ATTASTE PREGUST SOUPCON THOUGHT APPETITE JUDGMENT PENCHANT SAPIDITY
(— AFTER SWALLOWING) FINISH
(— COMBINED WITH APTITUDE) FLAIR
(— IN MATTERS OF ART) FANCY
(— OF THE CASK) FUST
(BAD —) GOTHISM
(DECIDED —) PENCHANT
(DELICATE —) BREED
(DISCRIMINATING —) SKILL
(GOOD —) DECORUM ELEGANCE
(OF MIDDLE-CLASS —) POLYESTER
(SLIGHT —) TINCTURE
(SOUR —) FOXINESS
(STRONG —) GOO
(PL.) MERIDIAN
(PREF.) SAPORI
(SUFF.) GEUSIA
TASTEFUL NEAT ELEGANT GUSTOSO
TASTELESS DEAF FLAT FLASH MALMY VAPID WERSH WALLON FATUOUS INSIPID INSULSE WEARISH UNSAVORY GRACELESS
TASTER TRIER

TASTING ASSAY
(— OF MALT) CORNY
TASTY SAPID YUMMY GUSTABLE TASTEFUL PALATABLE DELECTABLE
TA-TA TOODLEOO
TATA BYE CIAO LATER CHEERIO
TATAR KIN JUNG KHAN KITAN SOYOT CHAZAR KHAZAR KHITAN KHOZAR SHORTZY MELETSKI
(PL.) HU
TATER SPUD POTATO
TATOUAY CABASSOU
TATTER JAG RAG TAG SHRED FITTER LIBBET TAGRAG TARGET FLITTER TROLLOP
(PL.) DUDS TAVERS FITTERS RIBBONS TAIVERS FLITTERS
TATTERED DUDDY BEATEN TAGGED FORWORN TATTERY TOTTERED
TATTERSALL WINDOWPANE
TATTING LACE
TATTLE BLAB GASH CHEEP CLASH CLYPE PEACH SNEAK TUTEL GOSSIP QUATCH SNITCH TATTER TITTLE CLATTER
TATTLER LAB CLASH SNIPE FABLER GAMBET GOSSIP TUTLER YELPER STOOLIE TITTLER TELLTALE
TATTLETALE REVEALER
TATTLING LEAKY PITTIE
TATTOO TAT MOKO PINK POUNCE RATAPLAN
TATTOOED PINKED
(— MAN) YUN
TATTOOING MOKO
TAUGHT MAK TEACHED INSTRUCT
(EASILY —) DOCIBLE
TAUNT BOB DIG MOB CHIP GIBE GIRD JAPE JEER JEST MOCK PROG SKIT TWIT CHECK FRUMP GLAIK JAUNT SCOFF SCORN SLANT SLARE SLART DERIDE SNEEST UPCAST SARCASM TWITTER RIDICULE
TAUNTING RAIL SARCASTIC
TAUPE MOLESKIN
TAUROTRAGUS OREAS ORIAS
TA-URT THOUERIS
TAUT SNUG TORT STIFF TENSE TIGHT CORDED
TAUTEN SNUB STIFFEN SWIFTER TENSION
TAUTOG CHUB MOLL LABROID
TAVERN BAR INN BUSH HOWF VENT FONDA MITER MITRE TAMBO BISTRO CABACK KNEIPE BUVETTE CABARET CANTEEN OSTERIA TABERNA GASTHAUS ORDINARY POTHOUSE TAPHOUSE
TAW TER ALLY ALLEY SCORE MARBLE GLASSIE SHOOTER
TAWDRY CHEAP GAUDY NASTY GILDED TINSEL RAFFISH DIMESTORE
TAWNY FUSC BRUSK DUSKY FULVID TANNED FULVOUS JACINTH MUSTELINE
(PREF.) CIRRO FUSCO PYRR(O) PYRRH(O)
TAWNY BROWN TENNE CHAMOIS
TAW-SUG SULU
TAX FET LAY LOT TRY CAST CESS

DUTY GELD GELT GILD KAIN LEVY POLL RATE SCAT SCOT SESS TAIL TASK TOLL ABUSE AGIST DONUM FINTA HANSA HANSE LEKIN MAILL OBROK QUINT SCATT STENT TOUST VERGI WATCH ZAKAH ZAKAT ABKARI ASSESS AVANIA BURDEN CEDULA DEMAND EXCISE EXTENT HIDAGE IMPOST JEZIAH KHARAJ MURAGE OCTROI OCTROY PAVAGE PURVEY SENSUS STRAIN SURTAX VINAGE BOOMAGE BOSCAGE CHANCER CHEVAGE CHIVAGE CONDUCT FINANCE GABELLE LASTAGE PATENTE PENSION POLLAGE PONTAGE SCUTAGE STIPEND TAILAGE TERRAGE TOLLAGE TRIBUTE ALCABALA AUXILIUM BONAUGHT CARUCAGE CORNBOLE DANEGELD EXACTION EXERCISE KENNETTY MALTOLTE OBLATION PESHKASH ROMESCOT ROMESHOT STACKAGE SUPERTAX TAXATION WHEELAGE CAPITATION
(— AT HARVESTTIME) CORNBOLE
(— FOR STORING LOGS) BOOMAGE
(— OF ONE-FIFTH) QUINT
(— ON EVERY PLOW) CARUCAGE
(— ON HERRING CATCH) LASTAGE
(— ON LIQUOR) ABKARI
(— ON SALT) GABELLE
(— ON UNBELIEVERS) KHARAJ
(— ON WALLS) MURAGE
(— ON WOOD) BOSCAGE
(— ON WOOL) MALETOTE MALTOLTE
(— TO PETTY PRINCES) KERNETTY
(— TO SYNAGOGUE) FINTA
(— TO TENTH AMOUNT) TITHE
(— UNDULY) STRAIN
(CAPITATION —) JIZYA JIZYAH
(CHINESE —) LEKIN LIKEN LIKIN
(EXCISE —) USERFEE
(EXTRAORDINARY —) AUXILIUM
(FEUDAL —) AID
(IRISH —) BONAGHT
(KIND OF —) SIN
(MOHAMMEDAN —) JEZIAH
(PARISH —) PURVEY
(PHILIPPINES —) CEDULA
(POLL —) TOLL CENSUS
(RUSSIAN —) OBROK
(SPANISH —) ALCABALA ALCAVALA
(TURKISH —) VERGI AVANIA
TAXABLE LISTABLE
TAX COLLECTOR TITHER GABELLER
TAXGATHERER POLLER TAXMAN
TAXI CAB JIXIE CRAWLER
(SMALL —) MINICAB
(THREE-WHEELED —) CYCLO
(3-WHEELED —) CYCLO
TAXICAB CAB HACK CRUISER MOTORCAB
TAXIDERMY NASSOLOGY
TAXING SEVERE GRUELING
TAXON MONERA
TAXONOMIC
(SUFF.)
(— DIVISION) IA
TAXONOMIST LUMPER CLADIST SPLITTER

TAXPAYER FILER
TAYASSU PECARI
TAYGETE (FATHER OF —) ATLAS
(MOTHER OF —) PLEIONE
(SON OF —) EUROTAS LACEDAEMON
TAYRA GALERA
TCHAMBULI CHAMBERI
TEA CHA CHAR CHIA TCHA THAM TSIA ASSAM CAPER CHAIS CONGO FAHAM HYSON MIANG PEKOE STEEP CONGOU KEEMUN OOLONG PTISAN SUNGLO LAPSANG REDROOT TWANKAY AUTUMNAL EARLGREY GOWIDDIE SOUCHONG WORMSEED
(AFRICAN —) CAT KAT QAT KHAT QUAT
(BLACK —) BOHEA CONGO OOPAK CONGOU OOPACK SYCHEE
(COARSE —) BANCHA
(CUP OF —) CUPPA
(GREEN —) TWANKAY
(HIGH-GRADE —) GYOKURO
(INFERIOR —) BOHEA
(KIND OF —) OSWEGO
(MEDICINAL —) TISANE
(MEXICAN —) BASOTE APASOTE
(POOR —) BLASH
(WEAK —) MISERABLE
(PREF.) THEI
TEA BOWL CHAWAN
TEACAKE LUNN SCONE
TEACH ARAL LEAR READ SHOW TECH TENT BREED CARRY COACH EDIFY ENDUE LEARN SPELL TRAIN TUTOR WISSE INFORM PREACH SCHOOL BITECHE EDUCATE EXAMPLE EXPOUND GRAMMAR AMAISTER DISCIPLE DOCUMENT INSTRUCT PUPILIZE
(— TO FIGHT) SPAR
TEACHABLE APT DOCILE DOCIBLE
TEACHABLENESS DOCITY DOSSETY
TEACHER RAB ALIM GURU AKHUN BIDDY CADET GUIDE MOLLA RABBI REBBE TUTOR USHER AKHUND AMAUTA DOCENT DOCTOR DOZENT FATHER MADRIH MAULVI MENTOR MULLAH PANDIT PUNDIT RABBAN READER REGENT RHETOR SUPPLY ACHARYA ALFAQUI DOMINIE MAESTRA MAESTRO MOOLVIE MUNCHEE MURSHID PEDAGOG SHASTRI SOPHIST SPONSOR STARETS TRAINER ALFAQUIN AYUDANTE DIRECTOR EDUCATOR EXTENDER GAMALIEL MAGISTER MELAMMED MISTRESS MOONSHEE MUJTAHID MAHARISHI PEDAGOGUE PRECEPTOR ABECEDARIAN PRIVATDOCENT
(— OF ELOQUENCE) RHETOR
(— OF EMINENCE) MAESTRO
(— OF HIGH LEARNING) SOPHIST
(— OF KORAN) ALFAKI ALFAQUIN
(— OF PAUL) GAMALIEL
(INCA —) AMAUTA
(LANGUAGE —) MUNSHI MOONSHEE
(MOHAMMEDAN —) COJA HODJA KHOJA KHOJAH

(MOSAIC —) SCRIBE
(RELIGIOUS —) STARETS STARETZ
(UNIVERSITY —) SCHOLASTIC
(WALDENSIAN —) GARBE

TEACHING LAW DHARMA DOCENT LESSON LORING ACROAMA TUITION BUDDHISM DIDACTIC DOCTRINE DOCUMENT TUTELAGE
(— **ACTIVITY**) REALIA
(— **OBJECTS**) REALIA
(— **OF CHRIST**) GOSPEL
(PL.) ACOUSMA BROWNISM CACODOXY DIDACTICS

TEAK SAJ DJATI EBONY

TEAKETTLE SUKE SUKEY CHAFER KETTLE POURIE CRESSET

TEAL CRICK BLUEWING GARGANEY SARCELLE

TEAM SET FIVE PLOW SIDE SPAN YOKE DRAFT SWING EQUIPE PLOUGH SEXTET DRAUGHT CARTWARE
(— **HARNESSED ONE BEFORE ANOTHER**) TANDEM
(— **OF CARS**) ECURIE
(— **OF GLASSWORKERS**) SHOP CHAIR
(— **OF OXEN**) SPAN
(— **OF 3 HORSES ABREAST**) TROIKA
(— **THAT FINISHES LAST**) DOORMAT
(— **2 ABREAST, 1 LEADING**) SPIKE UNICORN
(**ATHLETIC** —) CLUB
(**BASEBALL** —) NINE
(**BASKETBALL** —) FIVE
(**FOOTBALL** —) ELEVEN
(**2-HORSE** —) PODANGER
(**3-HORSE** —) RANDOM

TEAMSTER CARTER TEAMEO CARTMAN SKINNER TEAMMAN

TEAPOT TRACK TRACKPOT

TEAR HIE RIP RIT RUG TUT CLAW PILL PULL RACE RASE RASH RAVE REND RIVE RUGG SKAG SNAG STUN BREAK CLAUT LARME PEARL RANCH SHARK SLENT SPALT SPLIT SPREE TOUSE CLEAVE HARROW RANCHE RIPPLE SCHISM SCREED WRENCH CHATTER CONVELL DISCIND EYEDROP SCRATCH DISTRAIN FRACTURE LACERATE LACHRYMA TEARDROP
(— **APART**) REND TEASE DISCERP DIVULSE
(— **A STRIP OFF**) SCOLD
(— **ASUNDER**) DIVEL
(— **AWAY**) AVULSE
(— **DOWN**) UNPILE DESTROY DEMOLISH
(— **IN NEGATIVE**) SLUG
(— **INTO**) LAMBAST LAMBASTE
(— **INTO PIECES**) DRAW TOLE DEVIL SHRED TEASE LANIATE MAMMOCK
(— **INTO SHREDS**) HOG DEVIL TATTER
(— **OFF**) STRIP ABRUPT DISCERP
(— **OPEN**) PROSCIND
(— **TO SHREDS**) RIPUP
(— **UP BY THE ROOTS**) ARACHE
(PL.) DEW BRINE RHEUM EYEWATER

(PREF.) DACRY(O) LACHRYMI LACHRYMO SPARASSO

TEARDROP EYEWATER

TEARFUL SOFT TEARY WEEPY LIQUID WATERY WEEPLY FLEBILE MAUDLIN SHOWERY SNIVELY SNIVELLY

TEARING SCREED
(— **AWAY**) AVULSION

TEARLESS DRYEYED

TEARPIT CRUMEN LARMIER

TEASE COD FUN MAD RAG RIB ROT TAR TRY TUM VEX BAIT CHIP DRAG FASH FRET GRIG HARE HOCK JADE JIVE JOSH LARK NARK RAZZ RIDE SOOL TARR TOUT TWIT WORK CHAFF CHEEK CHEVY CHIAK CHYAK DEVIL FEEZE RALLY TARIE TAUNT TOOSE WRACK BANTER BOTHER CADDLE CHIVVY HARASS HOORAY HURRAH MOLEST MURDER NEEDLE PESTER PLAGUE HATCHEL NEEDLER TERRIFY TORMENT WHERRET

TEASEL KING TASSEL TEASLE MANWEED

TEASELER GIGGER TEASER

TEASELING MOZING

TEASER COMEON TIZEUR

TEASING CHAFF MERRY BANTER DEVILING QUIZZING

TEAT DUG PAP TIT DIDDY SPEAN NIPPLE SUCKLE

TEA TREE TI MANUKA

TEBAH (FATHER OF —) NAHOR

TEBALIAH (FATHER OF —) HOSAH

TECHIQUE SKILL

TECHNICIAN TECHIE SWITCHER
(**MEDICAL** —) EMT

TECHNIQUE FEAT GATE WRINKLE COQUILLE INDUSTRY SPICCATO
(**BILLIARD** —) FOLLOW
(**DANCE** —) HEELWORK
(**DECORATION** —) IKAT
(**DRAMATIC** —) METHOD
(**JUMPING** —) SCISSORS
(**PIANO** —) PIANISM
(**PLANNING** —) PERT
(**SOFT** —) JUJITSU
(**WEAVING** —) SPRANG
(**WRESTLING** —) GLIMA
(**WRITING** —) CUBISM
(SUFF.) URGE URGIC URGY

TECHNOLOGY FISHERY TECHNIC CERAMICS

TECMESSA (FATHER OF —) TELEUTAS
(**HUSBAND OF —**) AJAX
(**SON OF —**) EURYSACES

TECOMIN LAPACHOL

TECTRIX COVERT

TEDDER KICKER

TEDIOUS DEAD DREE DULL LATE LONG POKY PROSY WEARY ALENGE BORING DREECH DREIGH ELENGE MORTAL PROLIX STODGY IRKSOME OPEROSE PREACHY PROSAIC VERBOSE BORESOME DRAGGING TIRESOME WEARIFUL

TEDIUM IRK YAWN ENNUI BOREDOM

TEE COCK TIGHT TOZEE WITTER BULLHEAD

TEEM SNY FLOW SWIM SWARM ABOUND BUSTLE SCRAWL PULLULATE

TEEMER SHOOTMAN

TEEMING BIG ALIVE TUMID FERTILE GUSHING TEEMFUL ABUNDANT BRAWLING PREGNANT SWARMING

TEENAGER TEENY TEENYBOPPER

TEENY SMALL

TEESWATER MUGS MUGGS

TEETER ROCK WAVER JIGGLE QUIVER SEESAW WOBBLE TREMBLE

TEETH CTENII CHOPPERS CRACKERS GRINDERS
(**HAVING** —) IVORIED
(**PETRIFIED** —) BUFONITE
(**SET OF** —) DENTURE
(**WHEEL** —) COGS
(PREF.) DENT(ATO)(I)(INO)(O)
(SUFF.) ODON

TEETHRIDGE ALVEOLE ALVEOLUS

TEETOTUM TOTUM WHIRLIGIG

TEGETICULA PRONUBA

TEGMENTUM ROOF

TEGULA SQUAMA EPAULET SCAPULA PATAGIUM SQUAMULA

TEGUMENT COAT TEGMEN

TEHUELCHE PATAGON

TEJU TEIOID JACUARU TEGUEXIN

TELAMON ATLAS
(**BROTHER OF** —) PELEUS
(**FATHER OF** —) AEACUS
(**MOTHER OF** —) ENDEIS
(**SON OF** —) AJAX TEUCER
(**WIFE OF** —) GLAUCE HESIONE

TELAMONES ATLANTES

TELEDU BADGER STINKARD

TELEGONUS (FATHER OF —) ULYSSES
(**MOTHER OF** —) CIRCE
(**SON OF** —) ITALUS
(**WIFE OF** —) PENELOPE

TELEGRAM TAR WIRE FLASH FLIMSY

TELEGRAPH SEND WIRE CABLE BUZZER TELEGRAM TELOTYPE
(**BUSH** —) GRAPEVINE

TELEMACHUS (FATHER OF —) ULYSSES
(**MOTHER OF** —) PENELOPE
(**SON OF** —) LATINUS

TELENCEPHALON ENDBRAIN

TELEOLOGICAL TELIC FINALIST

TELEOLOGY FINALITY

TELEPHASSA (DAUGHTER OF —) EUROPA
(**HUSBAND OF** —) AGENOR
(**SON OF** —) CADMUS PHOENIX

TELEPHONE CALL DIAL RING PHONE BLOWER HANDSET
(**KIND OF** —) CORDLESS
(**PART OF** —) PAD BASE CORD DIAL HOLE STOP PLATE CRADLE HANDLE HANDSET PLUNGER SPEAKER EARPIECE RECEIVER MOUTHPIECE TRANSMITTER

TELEPHOTE DIAPHOTE

TELEPHUS (FATHER OF —) HERCULES
(**MOTHER OF** —) AUGE
(**WIFE OF** —) ARGIOPE LAODICE ASTYOCHE

TELEPRINTER CREED

TELESCOPE TUBE COUDE GLASS SCOPE TRUNK ALINER FINDER SECTOR ALIGNER BINOCLE TRANSIT PROSPECT SPYGLASS REFRACTOR PERSPECTIVE
(**PART OF** —) LEG CELL LENS TUBE CLAMP GUIDE MOUNT SCOPE CRADLE DEWCAP SLEEVE TRIPOD DIAGONAL DRAWTUBE EYEPIECE MOUNTING SUNSHADE VIEWFINDER
(**SURVEYOR'S** —) LEVEL

TELEVISION TV AIR BOX TELLY VIDEO VIDEOLAND SMALLSCREEN
(— **AFTERNOON FARE**) SOAP
(— **BAND**) UHF
(— **COMEDY PROGRAM**) SITCOM
(— **PROGRAM**) TALKSHOW
(— **PROGRAM FOR CHILDREN**) KIDVID
(— **RATINGS PERIOD**) SWEEP
(— **SERVICE**) PAYTV
(— **SET**) BOX TUBE BOOBTUBE
(— **SHOW**) RERUN SITCOM
(— **STATION**) CHANNEL
(**CHILDREN'S** —) KIDVID
(**EDUCATIONAL** —) ETV
(**ELEMENT ON** — **SCREEN**) PIXEL
(**PERSON FOND OF** —) VIDEOPHILE

TELIOSPORE TELEUTO

TELL HIP SAY DEEM MAKE MEAN MOOT READ SHOW TALE AREAD AREED BREAK BREVE COUNT NEVEN PITCH SPELL STORY TEACH UTTER AUTHOR DEVISE IMPART INFORM MUSTER QUETHE RECITE RELATE REPEAT REPORT REVEAL CONFESS DIVULGE NARRATE PARTAKE RECOUNT ACQUAINT REHEARSE
(— **CONFIDENTIALLY**) CONFIDE
(— **CONFUSEDLY**) SPLATHER
(— **EARNESTLY**) ASSURE
(— **IN ADVANCE**) FORESAY
(— **LIES**) BELY LIGE BELIE
(— **OFF**) JAR
(— **ON**) RAT
(— **ROMANCES**) GEST GESTE
(— **SECRETS**) CHEEP CLYPE SPILL BABBLE
(— **STRIKINGLY**) CRACK
(— **TALES**) BLAB CANT PEACH
(**HOME TO WILLIAM** —) URI

TELLER CASHIER SPINNER STORIER TALLIER FABLEIST FABULIST SENACHIE

TELLING REDE PUNGENT POWERFUL STINGING
(— **OF SECRETS**) BLAB

TELLTALE CLASH TATTLER TITTLER REGISTER

TELL-TALE (— SIGN) TIPOFF

TELLURIDE ALTAITE

TELSON PLEON

TELUGU GENTU GENTOO TELINGA

TEM TUM ATMU ATUM

TEMA (FATHER OF —) ISHMAEL

TEMAN (FATHER OF —) ELIPHAZ
(**MOTHER OF** —) ADAH

TEMENI (FATHER OF —) ASHUR
(**MOTHER OF** —) NAARAH

TEMERITY GALL CHEEK NERVE AUDACITY RASHNESS

TEMP STENO

TEMPER CUE MAD BAIT BATE COOL
DASH DRAW MOOD MULL NEAL
PADD SCOT TONE ALLOY BIRSE
BLOOD CREST DELAY FRAME
GRAIN HUMOR IRISH SAUCE
SOBER TRAMP ADJUST ANIMUS
ANNEAL DANDER MASTER
MONKEY SEASON SPIRIT SPLEEN
STRAIN SUBMIT CHASTEN CLIMATE
COURAGE HACKLES QUALIFY
STOMACH EBENEZER GRADUATE
MITIGATE MODERATE MOORBURN
(— CLAY) TAMPER
(— METAL) ALLAY
(— OF MIND) CUE SPIRIT
(CAPRICIOUS —) SPLEEN

TEMPERAMENT BLOOD GEMUT
HEART HUMOR CRASIS KIDNEY
NATURE TEMPER STOMACH
SANGUINE

TEMPERAMENTAL FITIFIED

TEMPERANCE MEDIETY SOBRIETY

TEMPERATE CALM COOL MILD
SOFT GREEN SOBER STEADY
TEMPRE MODERATE ORDINATE
ABSTINENT CONTINENT
LYSOGENIC ABSTEMIOUS

TEMPERATURE SUN HEAT TEMP
HOTNESS DEWPOINT
(— FACTOR) WINDCHILL
(— UNIT) KELVIN

TEMPERED HARD MILD SOBER
SARCENET

TEMPERING MODULATION

TEMPEST GALE THUD WIND ORAGE
STORM TUMULT TORMENT
TURMOIL WEATHER
(AUTHOR OF —) SHAKESPEARE
(CHARACTER IN —) IRIS JUNO ARIEL
CERES ADRIAN ALONSO ANTONIO
CALIBAN GONZALO MIRANDA
TINCULO PROSPERO STEPHANO
FERDINAND FRANCISCO SEBASTIAN

TEMPESTUOUS WILD GUSTY
STERN WINDY RUGGED STORMY
VIOLENT STALWART

TEMPLATE CURB NORMA TEMPLET
PADSTONE STRICKLE

TEMPLE VAT WAT DEUL FANE NAOS
RATH CANDI GUACA HUACA KIACK
KOVIL MARAE RATHA CHANDI
HAFFET HERION MANDIR SACRUM
SHRINE TEOPAN TJANDI VIHARA
HERAEUM HERAION TEMPLET
TEMPLUM VARELLA OLYMPIUM
PANTHEON RAMESEUM TEOCALLI
VALHALLA PARTHENON
(— AREA) MANDAPA
(CAVE —) SPEOS
(FIJI —) BURE
(HAWAIIAN —) HEIAU
(JAPANESE —) SHA
(PART OF —) PRONAOS
(SHINTO —) SHA JINJA JINSHA
YASHIRO
(STUDY OF —S) NAOLOGY
(TOWERLIKE —) ZIGGURAT
(PREF.) NAO

TEMPLES
(PREF.) TEMPORO

TEMPLET FORMER STRICKLE

TEMPO TAKT TIME AGOGE
MOVEMENT

TEMPORAL LAIC CIVIL CARNAL
TIMELY EARTHLY PROFANE
SECULAR

TEMPORARY ACTING FLYING
INTERIM STOPGAP WHILEND
EPISODAL EPISODIC TEMPORAL
PROVISIONAL
(PREF.) PSEUD(O)

TEMPORIZER DRIFTER POLITIC

TEMPT EGG BAIT FAND FOND LURE
TEMP TENT ASSAY COURT ALLURE
ASSAIL ENTICE INVITE SEDUCE
ASSAULT ATTEMPT SOLICIT
SUGGEST

TEMPTATION BAIT TRIAL ATTEMPT
TESTING SEDUCTION

TEMPTER DEVIL

TEMPTING ALLURING INVITING

TEMPTRESS SIREN DELILAH

TEN ICRE IOTA CHANG DIKER
CHEUNG DECADE DENARY DICKER
ARTICLE BRISQUE
(— OF TRUMPS) GAME
(PREF.) DEC(A)(I)(U) DECEM DEK(A)
(SUFF.) TY

TEN'A KOYUKON

TENACE FORK

TENACIOUS FAST ROPEY STIFF
TOUGH CLAGGY CLEDGY DOGGED
GRIPPY PLUGGY STICKY STRONG
VISCID GRIPPLE VISCOUS
ADHESIVE GRASPING HOLDFAST
RETENTIVE PERTINACIOUS

TENACIOUSNESS TENACY
FASTNESS

TENACITY LENTOR COURAGE

TENACULUM CLASP

TENANCY CONACRE JOINTURE

TENANT KMET LEUD SAER BARON
CEILE DRENG LAIRD BORDAR
COTTAR COTTER DRENGH GENEAT
HOLDER INMATE LESSEE MOLMAN
RADMAN RENTER SOCMAN
VASSAL CHAKDAR COTTIER
FEODARY FEUDARY GAVELER
HOMAGER SOCAGER SOKEMAN
VAVASOR COLIBERT CUSTOMER
SERGEANT SUCKENER
(— OF CROWN) THANE
(— OF THE CROWN) THANE
(FARM —) CROFTER
(LIFE —) LIVIER LIVEYER
(NEW —) INCOME INCOMER

TENCH CYPRINID

TEN COMMANDMENTS DECALOG

TEND HOP NOD RUN SET WRY BABY
BEND DRAW GROW KEEP MAKE
MIND MOVE TENT DRESS GROOM
NURSE OFFER SOUND TREND
VERGE WATCH AFFECT GOVERN
INTEND CHERISH CONDUCE
DECLINE INCLINE PROPEND
(— A FIRE) STOKE
(— IN A CERTAIN DIRECTION) LEAD
(— TO) NURSE
(— TO ONE POINT) CONVERGE
(— TOWARD) AFFECT
(— WHILE AT PASTURE) GRAZE

TENDENCY SET BENT BIAS HAND
TONE VEIN DRAFT DRIFT DRIVE

HABIT KNACK TENOR TREND TWIST
ANIMUS COURSE EONISM GENIUS
MOTION APTNESS CONATUS
DRAUGHT IMPULSE LEANING
NITENCY SAMKARA APTITUDE
INSTINCT STEERING VERGENCY
(— IN NATURE) KIND
(— TO APPROACH) ADIENCE
(— TO GOOD OR EVIL) PROPENSITY
(— TO STICK TOGETHER) CLANSHIP
(— TO WITHDRAW) ABIENCE
(— TO WRATH) TIDE
(INHERITED —) STRAIN
(SUFF.) (— TOWARD) PHIL(A)(AE)(E)
(IA)(ISM)(IST)(OUS)(US)(Y)

TENDER RAW TID BEAR COCK FINE
FOND FRIM FRUM KIND NESH SOFT
SORE TAKE TART TENT WARM
CAGER DEFER FRAIL GREEN
MUSHY OFFER PAPPY DELATE
DRIVER GENTLE GIMPER GINGER
HUMANE LOVELY RAISER SILKEN
ADVANCE AMABILE AMOROSO
AMOROUS CONCHER CRAMPER
FLESHLY MASHMAN OBLATIO
PATACHE PINNACE PITEOUS
PITIFUL PORRECT PROFFER
RUTHFUL STENTER CAMELEER
COCKBOAT EFFETMAN FEMININE
HEATSMAN HERDSMAN LADYLIKE
MERCIFUL MORTISER SPREADER
(KIND OF —) LEGAL
(PREF.) ABRO HABRO

TENDERFOOT DUDE INNOCENT
CHEECHAKO

TENDERHEARTED HUMAN PITIFUL

TENDERIZER PAPAIN

TENDERLOIN FILET PSOAS FILLET
UNDERCUT

TENDERLY FONDLY GENTLY
AMOROSO

TENDERNESS CHERTE TENDER
DELICACY FONDNESS KINDNESS
SYMPATHY TENERITY YEARNING
(— OF FEELING) FLESH

TENDING
(SUFF.) CLINIC CLINOUS
(— TO) ABLE ATIVE ATORY BOND
BUND CUND FUL IBLE

TENDINOUS SINEWY

TENDON CORD TAIL CHORD NERVE
SINEW TENON LEADER PAXWAX
STRING
(PREF.) TENO

TENDRIL CURL CLASP CROOK TWIST
CIRRUS WINDER CAPREOL
CIRRHUS CLASPER TENTACLE
(PREF.) PAMPINI PAMPINO

TENEMENT LAND RENT TACK
CHAWL DECKER LIVING WARREN
HOLDING LETTING ROOKERY
BUILDING PRAEDIUM

TENES (FATHER OF —) CYNCUS
(MOTHER OF —) PROCLEA
PHILONOME
(SISTER OF —) HEMITHEA
(SLAYER OF —) ACHILLES

TENET ISM ADOXY CREDO CREED
DOGMA BELIEF GNOMON
HOLDING MISHNAH PARADOX
DOCTRINE
(PL.) FAITH FAMILISM

TENFOLD DENARY DECUPLE

TENNANTITE FAHLERZ FAHLORE

TENNE TAWNY ORANGE HYACINTH

TENNESSEE
CAPITAL: NASHVILLE
COLLEGE: FISK LANE SIENA BETHEL
BELMONT LAMBUTH LEMOYNE
MILLIGAN TUSCULUM
VANDERBILT
COUNTY: DYER KNOX RHEA COCKE
GILES HENRY MEIGS OBION
COFFEE GRUNDY MCMINN SEVIER
UNICOI BLEDSOE FENTRESS
DAM: WILSON WHEELER
INDIAN: SHAWNEE CHEROKEE
CHICKASAW
LAKE: DOUGLAS CHEROKEE
REELFOOT WATTSBAR
MOUNTAIN: GUYOT LOOKOUT
MOUNTAIN RANGE: SMOKY
NATIONAL PARK: SHILOH
NATIVE: WHELP
NICKNAME: VOLUNTEER
PRESIDENT: POLK JACKSON
RIVER: ELK DUCK CANEY HOLSTON
HIWASSEE CUMBERLAND
STATE BIRD: MOCKINGBIRD
STATE FLOWER: IRIS
STATE TREE: POPLAR
TOWN: ERIN ALAMO ALCOA ERWIN
PARIS CAMDEN CELINA JASPER
SELMER SPARTA BOLIVAR
DICKSON JACKSON MEMPHIS
PULASKI GALLATIN KNOXVILLE
CHATTANOOGA

TENNIES SNEAKERS

TENNIS (— LET) DOOVER
(— NAME) ASHE ILIE
(— PERSONALITY) ASHE ILIE
(— PLAY) RALLY
(— PLAYER) DOD ASHE BETZ BORG
GORE GRAF KING BUDGE BUENO
COURT EVERT LAVER LENDL LLOYD
MOODY MOORE PERRY SEARS
SELES VILAS WILLS WHENN AGASSI
AUSTIN BECKER BROUGH BROWNE
COOPER DUPONT EDBERG JACOBS
LARNED MARBLE STERRY TILDEN
CONNORS COURIER DOHERTY
EMERSON LENGLEN MALLORY
MCENROE NASTASE RENSHAW
SAMPRAS VICARIO WHITMAN
WILDING ATKINSON BADDELEY
CAMPBELL CAPRIATI CHAMBERS
CONNOLLY GONZALES HILLYARD
NEWCOMBE ROSEWALL WILANDER
BJURSTEDT WRIGHTMAN
NAVRATILOVA
(— SCORE) ADIN LOVE ADOUT
DEUCE FORTY THIRTY FIFTEEN
(— SHOT) AD ACE LET LOB ADIN
DINK DROP ADOUT SMASH
(— UNIT) SET GAME MATCH
(ANCIENT —) BANDY
(NAME IN —) WADE
(PERFECT SERVE IN —) ACE
(TABLE —) PINGPONG

TENON COG PIN COAK STUB TUSK
LEWIS TOOTH TABLING DOVETAIL
LEWISSON
(KIND OF —) TUSK

TENOR PES FECK TONE VEIN

COURSE EFFECT TAILLE TENURE CURRENT PURPORT STRENGTH TENDENCY TENORINO

TENOROON FAGOTTINO

TENOR VIOL VIOLET

TENOR VIOLIN ALTO

TEN-PERCENTER AGENT

TENPINS BOWLS NEWPORT

TENPOUNDER AWA CHIRO MACABI BONEFISH BONYFISH LADYFISH SKIPJACK SPRINGER

TENREC TANGUE CENTETES CENTETID HEDGEHOG HEDGEPIG

TENSE EDGY RAPT TAUT STIFF WIRED AORIST CORDED FLINCH FUTURE INTENT NARROW STRAIT STRICT BRITTLE INTENSE PRIMARY FRENETIC PRETERIT STRAINED SYNTONIC

TENSION BENT HEAT DRIVE STEAM SATTVA SPRING STRAIN STRESS TROPPO BALANCE STRAINT TENSURE ISOTONIA

(STATE OF NERVOUS —) YIPS

TENT AUL TOP HALE PAWL TAWN TELD TILT TIPI CABIN CRAME LODGE TEPEE TOPEK TUPIK CANNAT CANVAS DOSSIL SEARCH TEEPEE WIGWAM BALAGAN CABINET KIBITKA MARQUEE SPARVER TABERNA TENTLET TENTORY ZDARSKY PAVILION SHAMIANA TENTICLE TENTWORK SHOOLDARRY

(— FOR WOUNDS) PENICIL

(— WHERE GOODS ARE SOLD) CRAME

(CIRCULAR —) YURT YOURT YURTA KIBITKA

(GENERAL'S —) PRAETORIUM

(INDIAN —) TEPEE WIGWAM

(SAMOYED —) CHUM

(SOUTH AMERICAN —) TOLDO

TENTACLE HORN SAIL PACLE FEELER BRACHIUM

TENTATIVE GINGERLY

TENT CATERPILLAR WEBWORM

TENTERER RACKER RATCHER

TENTH DIME DISME TITHE DECIMA

(— OF CENT) MILL

(— OF LINE) GRY

(PREF.) DECI

TEN THOUSAND

(PREF.) MYRIA MYRIO

TENTWORT RUE

TENUITY EXILITY DELICACY

TENUOUS SLIM FILMY FOGGY FRAIL SUBTLE TENDER FRAGILE GASEOUS SLENDER SUBTILE ETHEREAL GOSSAMER

(TOO —) FINESPUN

TENUOUSNESS FRAILTY

TENURE FEU SORN TACK TAKE TERM GAVEL JAGIR BARONY CAPITE JAGHIR RUNRIG SOCAGE SORREN ALMOIGN BONDAGE BORDAGE BURGAGE CENSIVE CORNAGE CURTESY FARMAGE JAGHEER SOCCAGE SOREHON COPYHOLD DRENGAGE FREEHOLD OVERLAND SOCMANRY SUITHOLD VAVASORY VENVILLE

(LAND —) RUNRIG SOCAGE RUNDALE SOCCAGE

TEPEE CHUM TENT TIPI HOGAN LODGE TEEPEE WICKIUP

TEPHROSIA CRACCA

TEPID LEW WARM WLACH WLECH LUKEWARM

TEQUISLATEC CHONTAL

TERAH (SON OF —) HARAN NAHOR ABRAHAM

TERATOMA EMBRYOMA

TERCET TRISTICH

TEREBINTH TEIL TURPENTINE

TEREDO BORER WOODWORM

TERENTIA (HUSBAND OF —) CICERO

TERETE CENTRIC

TEREUS (FATHER OF —) MARS

(SON OF —) ITYS

(WIFE OF —) PROCNE

TERGITE TERGUM PYGIDIUM

TERGIVERSATION DECEIT

TERGUM PYGIDIUM

TERM HALF NAME NOME WORD LEASE RHEMA SPEAK STYLE TRYST ABBACY GNOMON HILARY NOTION PARODY EPITHET EXTREME SESSION SUBJECT SUMMAND TERMINE VOCABLE EQUIVOKE HEADWORD MAHALATH POCHISMO SEMESTER TERMTIME

(— IN JAIL) JOLT

(— IN LOGIC) CONSTANT

(— IN PROGRESSION) MEAN

(— OF ABUSE) CUSSWORD

(— OF ADDRESS) SIRRAH MADONNA

(— OF CONTEMPT) SLIPE PILCHER TITIVIL

(— OF DEFERENCE) AHUNG

(— OF ENDEARMENT) HON LOVE PEAT ASTOR CHUCK COCKY HONEY JARTA LOVEY MOPSY MOUSE SUGAR YARTA ASTHORE MACHREE STOREEN POSSODIE POWSOWDY PRECIOUS

(— OF IMPRISONMENT) LAG LAGGING STRETCH

(— OF PROPOSITION) REFERENT

(— OF PUNISHMENT) JOB

(— OF RATIO) EXTREME

(— OF REPROACH) GIB BESOM MINGO RONYON

(— OF RESPECT) SAHIB

(— OF SYLLOGISM) EXTREME ARGUMENT

(—S OF REFERENCE) REMIT

(ARITHMETICAL —) NOME GNOMON

(COURT —) HILARY

(DESCRIPTIVE —) EPITHET

(FINAL —S) ULTIMATUM

(HYPHENED —) COMPOUND

(LITERAL —S) LETTER

(POSITIVE —) PLUS

(SOCIAL —S) FOOTING

(UNIVERSAL —) CONCEPT

(PL.) LAY MEANS

(PREF.) HORO

TERMAGANT JADE RUDAS SHREW VIXEN VIRAGO

TERMINABLE FINITE

TERMINAL JACK LAST POLE ANODE DEPOT IMPUT INPUT MUCRO CATHODE POTHEAD DESINENT

(ELECTRIC —) POLE

TERMINATE CUT END ABUT CALL HALT KILL ABORT BLEED CEASE CLOSE ISSUE LAPSE EXPIRE FINISH FOREDO RESULT INCLUDE TERMINE COMPLETE CONCLUDE DISSOLVE

(— A SESSION) PROROGUE

TERMINATED EXPIATE

TERMINATING FINAL

(— ABRUPTLY) BLIND

(SUDDENLY —) ABRUPT

TERMINATION END ISH DATE TERM ABORT CLOSE EVENT ISSUE ENDING EXITUS EXPIRY FINALE PERIOD UPSHOT TERMINUS

(— OF CHURCH CHOIR) CHEVET

(— OF FURNITURE LEGS) FOOT

(— OF RIGHT) LAPSE

(PROSPEROUS —) SUCCESS

TERMINATIVE FINITIVE

TERMINOLOGY JARGON

TERMINUS END FLAT

(— IN FINGERPRINT) DELTA

(— OF PERIOD) TIME

TERMITE ANAI ANAY KING NASUTE WORKER POLILLA

TERMITOPHILE SYMPHILE

TERN KIP DARR INCA LARI NOIO PIRL PIRR RIXY LARID NODDY PEARL SCRAY SKEER SKIRR STERN CHIRRE KERMEW PICKET GOELAND MEDRICK PIRRMAW RITTOCK SCURRIT SEAFOWL STRIKER TARRACK TERNLET MANUSINA SPARLING TIRRACKE

TERPENE CARENE PINENE BORNANE SANTENE THUJENE CAMPHENE FENCHENE LIMONENE NOPINENE

TERRA GE GAEA TELLUS

(DAUGHTER OF —) RHEA THEA PHOEBE TETHYS THEMIS MNEMOSYNE

(HUSBAND OF —) URANUS

(SON OF —) OCEANUS

TERRACE POY DAIS PNYX STEP XYST BEACH BENCH HEIAU LINCH PATIO OFFSET PERRON LINCHET VERANDA BARBETTE CHABUTRA VERANDAH

(— AT ENTRANCE) PERRON

(LOUNGING —) LANAI

(NATURAL —) MESA

(SEA-FRONT —) PROMENADE

TERRA JAPONICA GAMBIR GAMBIER

TERRAPENE CISTUDO

TERRAPIN EMYD COUNT COODLE POTTER SLIDER TURPIN TURTLE EMYDIAN FEUILLE SKILPOT REDBELLY TORTOISE

(FEMALE —) HEIFER

(MALE —) BULL

TERRARIUM VIVARIUM

TERRELLA EARTHKIN

TERRENE EARTHLY

TERRESTRIAL EARTHY EARTHLY TERRENE PLANETAL SUBLUNAR SUBSOLAR TELLURIC PLANETARY SUBASTRAL

TERRET CRINGLE

TERRIBLE DIRE UGLY AWFUL GHAST LURID DEADLY PRETTY TARBLE TRAGIC TURBLE CHRONIC DIREFUL FEARFUL FERDFUL GHASTLY HIDEOUS ALMIGHTY BHAIRAVA FLEYSOME HORRIBLE TERRIFIC TIMOROUS TRAGICAL

(PREF.) DEIN(O) DIN(O)

TERRIBLY FELLY FIERCE GRISLY CONSARN

TERRIER SKYE LHASA SILKY BOSTON DANDIE RATTER SCOTTY DIEHARD SCOTTIE ABERDEEN AIREDALE RATTONER SEALYHAM VERMINER WIREHAIR

(YORKSHIRE) YORKIE

TERRIFIC FINE SWEET GORGON AWESOME FEARFUL DYNAMITE GORGEOUS

TERRIFIED AFRAID AGHAST GHASTLY

TERRIFY AWE COW HAG BREE DARE FEAR FLAY FLEY APPAL DREAD GALLY SCARE ADREAD AFFRAY AGRISE AWHAPE DISMAY FLIGHT FREEZE FRIGHTEN

TERRIFYING GHASTLY HIDEOUS FEARSOME FLEYSOME TERRIBLE

TERRITORIALISM ITOISM

TERRITORY FEE GOA HAN SOC AREA MARK PALE SOKE BANAT DUCHY FIELD MARCH STATE TUATH BORDER COLONY DOMAIN EMPERY EMPIRE GROUND APANAGE CONFINE COUNTRY DEMESNE DUKEDOM EARLDOM ENCLAVE EPARCHY REGENCY SATRAPY APPANAGE CASTLERY CONFINES CONQUEST DISTRICT DOMINION IMPERIUM LIGEANCE LUCUMONY PARMESAN PASHALIK REGALITY SEIGNORY

(FOREIGN —) POSSESSION

(MONASTIC —) ABTHANE

TERROR AWE FEAR FRAY ALARM APPAL DREAD PANIC AFFRAY ALARUM APPALL FRIGHT HORROR DRIDDER AFFRIGHT DREDDOUR SURPRISE

TERRORISM NIHILISM

TERRORIST GOONDA ALARMIST SICARIUS

TERRORIZE FRIGHTEN

TERROR-STRICKEN AWFUL

TERSE CURT SINEWY COMPACT CONCISE LACONIC POINTED SUMMARY UNWORDY SUCCINCT

TERSENESS BREVITY LACONISM

TERTIARY NEOZOIC PALAEIC

TESSELLATED MOSAIC

TESSELLATION AREOLE

TESSERA TILETTE ABACULUS TESSELLA

TESS OF DURBERVILLES (AUTHOR OF —) HARDY

(CHARACTER IN —) ALEC JACK TESS ANGEL CLARE DURBERVILLE DURBEYFIELD

TEST CON SAY TRY FAND FEEL FOND QUIZ SEMI TASK TENT ASSAY AVENA CANON CHECK ESSAY GROPE ISSUE PROBE

PROOF PROVE SENSE SOUND TASTE TEMPT TESTA TOUCH TRIAL SAMPLE TIENTA APPROOF APPROVE AUSSAGE CONTROL EXAMINE GANTLET PLUMMET TESTATE BIOASSAY EXERCISE GAUNTLET SEROLOGY STANDARD
(— CHEESE) PALE
(— EGGS) CANDLE
(— FOR MESSAGES) POLL
(— FOR WEIGHT AND FINENESS) PYX
(— GROUND) BOSE
(— OF COURAGE) SCRATCH
(— OF CRINOID) CALYX
(— OF GUILT) CORSNED
(— OF ORE) VAN
(ASSAY —) ELISA
(COLLEGE —) MIDTERM
(COLLEGE ENTRANCE —) PSAT
(KIND OF —) AMES ORAL MEANS SWEAT DRAIZE LITMUS SCHICK INKBLOT MANTOUX RORSCHACH
(SEROLOGICAL —) COGGINS
(SEVERE —) CRUCIBLE
(SYPHILIS —) KOLMER
(PREF.) DOCIMO OECO
(SUFF.) OECA OECIA

TESTA TEST LORICA EPISPERM
TESTACEOUS SHELLY
TESTAMENT TEST QUETHE WITWORD COVENANT
TESTAR TETARD
TESTATOR LEGATOR
TESTED FIRED TRIED WEIGHED
TESTER TRIER CONNER PROVER SPARVER DENIERER TESTIERE
(BUTTER —) SEARCHER
TESTES
(SUFF.) ORCHISM
TESTICLE STONE BALLOCK DIDYMUS GENITOR
(PREF.) ORCHI(O) ORCHID(O) ORCHO
TESTICLES
(SUFF.) ORCHISM
TESTIFY SPEAK SWEAR AFFIRM DEPONE DEPOSE WITTEN WITNESS EVIDENCE
(— FALSELY) MOUNT
(— TO) BESPEAK
TESTIMONIAL CHIT SCROLL CHARACTER
TESTIMONY TEST ATTEST AVOUCH PROBATE TESTATE TESTIFY WITNESS EVIDENCE
TESTING ASSAY CRUCIAL SHAKEDOWN
(KIND OF —) DNA
TESTIS BALL GONAD STONE BALLOCK CULLION KNOCKER SPERMARY
(PL.) COBS CODS COJONES DOWSETS
TEST TUBE PROOF TESTER PROBATE
TESTUDINATA CHELONIA
TESTUDO SNAIL GALAPAGO TORTOISE
TESTY DONCY MUSTY TUTTY CRANKY DONSIE PATCHY SPUNKY PEEVISH TETTISH TOUSTIE WASPISH SNAPPISH

TETANIC LOCKJAW SPASTIC TRISMUS
TETANUS LOCKJAW HOLOTONY
TETE-A-TETE CHAT TWOSOME CAUSEUSE
TETHER BAND LEASH STAKE PICKET TEDDER TOGGLE PASTERN CABESTRO
(— A HAWK) WEATHER
TETHYS APLYSIA
(DAUGHTERS OF —) OCEANIDES
(FATHER OF —) URANUS
(HUSBAND OF —) OCEANUS
(MOTHER OF —) TERRA
TETHYUM CYNTHIA
TETRA-
(PREF.) QUATER
TETRACHORD GENUS HYPATON LICHANOS
TETRACTYS TETRAD
TETRAD FOURFOLD
TETRADRACHMA OWL
TETRAGONAL DIMETRIC
TETRAHEDRITE FAHLERZ FAHLORE PANABASE
TETRAHEXAHEDRON FLUOROID
TETRAHYDRIDE GERMANE STANNANE
TETRASACCHARIDE LUPEOSE
TETTER DARTRE
TETTIX ACRYDIUM
TEUCER (DAUGHTER OF —) ASTERIA
(FATHER OF —) TELAMON SCAMANDER
(HALF-BROTHER OF —) AJAX
(MOTHER OF —) IDAEA HESIONE
(WIFE OF —) EUNE
TEUTON GOTH LOMBARD
TEUTONIC GOTHIC GERMANIC GOTHONIC

TEXAS
CAPITAL: AUSTIN
COLLEGE: SMU TCU RICE WILEY BAYLOR
COUNTY: BEE CASS COKE JACK REAL RUSK VEGA WEBB WISE BEXAR DELTA ECTOR ERATH GARZA RAINS FANNIN GOLIAD YOAKUM ZAPATA ZAVALA HIDALGO REFUGIO ATASCOSA
FORTRESS: ALAMO
INDIAN: LIPAN BILOXI KICHAI SHUMAN HASINAI COMANCHE TONKAWAN
LAKE: FALCON TEXOMA AMISTAD
MOUNTAIN: GUADALUPE
NATIVE: TEJANO
NICKNAME: LONESTAR
PRESIDENT: JOHNSON EISENHOWER
RIVER: RED PECOS BRAZOS NUECES TRINITY
STATE BIRD: MOCKINGBIRD
STATE FLOWER: BLUEBONNET
STATE TREE: PECAN
TOWN: GAIL VEGA WACO BRYAN MARFA OZONA PAMPA TYLER BORGER DALLAS DENTON ELPASO KILEEN LAREDO ODESSA QUANAH SONORA ABILENE HOUSTON LUBBOCK AMARILLO

BEAUMONT FLOYDADA GALVESTON

TEXAS BUCKTHORN LOTEBUSH
TEXAS FEVER TRISTEZA
TEXT BODY MIQRA PLACE SAKHA TESTO WORDS PURANA SCRIPT SHAKHA TEXTUS TEXTLET ANTETHEM PERICOPE VARIORUM
(— OF ADVERTISEMENT) COPY
(— OF OPERA) LIBRETTO
(— OF PLAY) SCRIPT
(— SET TO MUSIC) ORATORIO
(BIBLICAL —) SCRIPTURE
(REVISED —) RECENSION
(SACRED —) MANTRA
(SHASTRA —) SRUTI SHRUTI
TEXTBOOK DUNCE TUTOR GENETICS
TEXTILE (ALSO SEE FABRIC) SABA STUFF GREIGE MOCKADO SAGURAN SINAMAY TEXTURE TIFFANY
(— MACHINE) WILLOW
(PL.) DRAPE
TEXTURE WEB BONE HAND KNIT WALE WOOF FIBER GRAIN COBWEB FABRIC WEFTAGE FRACTURE
(— OF SOAP) FIT
(— OF STONE) GRIT
THADDEUS OF WARSAW
(AUTHOR OF —) PORTER
(CHARACTER IN —) MARY ROSS SARA DIANA BUTZOU ROBSON VINCENT BEAUFORT EUPHEMIA PEMBROKE SOBIESKI SOMERSET THADDEUS CAVENDISH KOSCIUSKO SACKVILLE TINEMOUTH CONSTANTINE
THAHASH (FATHER OF —) NAHOR
(MOTHER OF —) REUMAH
THAI LAO SIAMESE

THAILAND
CAPITAL: BANKOK BANGKOK
COIN: AT ATT BAHT FUANG TICAL PYNUNG SALUNG SATANG
FORMER NAME: SIAM
ISLAND: PHUKET
ISTHMUS: KRA
LANGUAGE: SHAN
MEASURE: WA KEN NIV NMU RAI SAT SEN SOK WAH YOT KEUP NGAN TANG YOTE KWIEN LAANG SESTI TANAN KABIET KAMMEU CHAIMEU ROENENG CHANGAWN
MOUNTAIN: KHIEO MAELAMUN
MOUNTAIN RANGE: DAWNA BILAUKTAUNG
NATIVE: LAO THAI
PLAIN: KHORAT
RIVER: CHI NAN PING MENAM MEKONG MEPING
TOWN: UBON PUKET RANONG AYUDHYA AYUTHIA BANGKOK LOPBURI RAHAENG SINGORA SONGKLA KHONKAEN KIANGMAI THONBURI
WEIGHT: HAP PAI SEN SOK BAHT HAPH KLAM KLOM CATTY CHANG COYAN PILUL FLUANG SALUNG SOMPAY TAMLUNG

THAIS (CHARACTER IN —) THAIS ATHANAEL
(COMPOSER OF —) MASSENET
THAISA (FATHER OF —) SIMONIDES
(HUSBAND OF —) PERICLES
THALABA (WIFE OF —) ONEIZA
THALER DALER
THALLOGEN AMPHIGEN
THALLOID FRONDOSE
THALLUS FROND THALAMUS THAMNIUM
THAMNOPHIS EUTAENIA
THAMYRAS (FATHER OF —) PHILAMMON
(MOTHER OF —) ARGIOPE
THAN AS NA NE OR TO AND BUT NOR THEN TILL
THANE THEGN BANQUO GESITH ABTHAIN MACDUFF
THANK GRACE MERCY AGGRATE REGRACY REMERCY
THANKFUL GRATEFUL
THANKLESS INGRATE SLOWFUL
THANKS TA DANKE GRACE MERCI MERCY GRACIAS GRAMERCY
THANKSGIVING GLORY DOXOLOGY
THANK-YOU-MA'AM CAHOT
THAT AS AT SE BUT HOW THE THO WHO YAT LEST THAM THIK THON WHAT YOND THICK THILK THOUGH BECAUSE
(— IS) IDEST
(— IS TO SAY) NAMELY
(— ONE) ILLE
(— WHICH HAS TO BE PROVED) IQED
(— YONDER) THON
THATCH NIPA DATCH SIRKI SIRKY STING THRUM CADJAN
(— OVER BEEHIVE) HOOD
THATCHED THACK REEDED
THATCHER HELER CROWDER HELLIER THACKER
THAUMAS (DAUGHTER OF —) IRIS AELLO HARPY OCYPETE
(FATHER OF —) PONTUS NEPTUNE
(MOTHER OF —) GAEA TERRA
(WIFE OF —) ELECTRA
THAUMATURGIST
(PL.) GOETAE
THAUMATURGY MAGIC
THAW GIVE MELT FRESH UNTHAW DEFROST
THE LA LE SE TA THI THAM THEY YARE THERE
(PREF.) AL
THEA CAMELLIA
(FATHER OF —) URANUS
(HUSBAND OF —) HYPERION
(MOTHER OF —) TERRA
THEANO (FATHER OF —) CISSEUS
(HUSBAND OF —) ANTENOR METAPONTUS
(MOTHER OF —) TELECLIA
(SISTER OF —) HECUBA
(SON OF —) ACAMAS AGENOR POLYBUS HELICAON IPHIDAMAS ARCHELOCHUS
THEATER CINE GAFF KINO NABE CAVEA HOUSE LEGIT ODEUM SCENE STAGE CINEMA OZONER ADELPHI COCKPIT GUIGNOL

ORPHEUM THEATRE BIOSCOPE
COLISEUM PANTHEON SHOWSHOP
SPELLKEN STRAWHAT THEATRON
PLAYHOUSE NICKELODEON
(— DISTRICT) RIALTO
(CLASSICAL —) ODEUM
(FULL —) SRO
(HARLEM —) APOLLO
(JAPANESE —) NOH BUNRAKU
(LOCAL —) NABE
(NEIGHBORHOOD —) NABE
(PUPPET —) BUNRAKU
THEATRICAL CAMP HAMMY STAGY
DRAMATIC SCENICAL SINGSONG
THEATRICALITY HAM PANACHE
THEBAN LAIUS NIOBE AMPHION
CADMEAN JOCASTA OEDIPUS
PENTHEUS
THEBE (FATHER OF —) ASOPUS
(HUSBAND OF —) ZETHUS
(MOTHER OF —) METOPE
(SISTER OF —) AEGINA
THECA CUP URN CELL VAGINA
CAPSULE PYXIDIUM VAGINULE
THEELIN ESTRONE FEMININ
OESTRIN
THEFT CRIB LIFT HEIST PINCH
SCORE STALE STEAL FURTUM
RIPOFF STOUTH BRIBERY LARCENY
MICHERY PICKING PILFERY
ROBBERY STEALTH BURGLARY
STEALAGE STEALING
(LITERARY —) PIRACY
(PETTY —) CRIB PICKERY
(PREF.) KLEPT(O)
(SUFF.) KLEPT
THEINE CAFFEINE
THEIR ARE HER ORE HORE YARE
THEIRS HERN THEIRN
THEM A EM HI UM HEM MUN
HEMEN
THEME DUX BASE IDEA TEMA TEXT
DITTY HOBBY LEMMA MOTIF
PLACE SCOPE TESTO THEMA
TOPIC URLAR MATTER MYTHOS
SUBJECT ANTETHEM
(— OF FUGUE) DUX
(HACKNEYED —) CLICHE
(MAIN —) BURDEN
(RECURRING —) BURDEN
(STOCK —) TOPOS
THEMIS (DAUGHTER OF —) DICE
IRENE EUNOMIA
(FATHER OF —) URANUS
(HUSBAND OF —) JUPITER
(MOTHER OF —) TERRA
THEMSELVES HEM HEMSELF
THEN SO AND POI THO ANON SYNE
ALORS
THENCE AWAY THEN THEREFRO
THEOCRACY KHALSA
THEODELINDE (FATHER OF —)
GARIBALD
(HUSBAND OF —) AGO AUTHARI
THEODOLITE TAIPO DIOPTER
TRANSIT TRANSEPT
THEOLOGIAN FAQIH ULEMA DIVINE
MUJTAHID
AMERICAN COX BROWN HATCH
NEVIN SMITH TYLER WOODS
BURTON CURRAN ELIADE FOSTER
GLUECK KOHLER MACHEN SCHAFF
STUART TAYLOR EDWARDS

EVERETT HOPKINS MCCLURE
MOFFATT NIEBUHR PEABODY
SEABURY TILLICH VINCENT
MCGIFFERT WORCESTER
AUSTRIAN MOHR RAHNER
BRUNNER DENIFLE JELLINEK
BELGIAN BAIUS
BRAZILIAN BOFF
CZECH COMENIUS
DANISH MONRAD MULLER
MYNSTER PEDERSEN GRUNDTVIG
PONTOPPIDAN
DUTCH HAAR VOET WITS BEKKER
JANSEN KUENEN KUYPER
GOMARUS ARMINIUS BOGERMAN
LIMBORCH SCHOLTEN EPISCOPIUS
ENGLISH BEDE BULL DODD HORT
OWEN WARD BLUNT COLET HATCH
PALEY PUSEY SWETE WATTS
ALCUIN BUTLER FERRAR HARRIS
HOOKER NEWMAN PECOCK STERNE
WESLEY LANGTON MARBECK
MAURICE PEARSON WHATELY
WHISTON CARDWELL DRUMMOND
PELAGIUS WYCLIFFE CHADERTON
GUILLAUME LIGHTFOOT STAPLETON
WARBURTON GROSSETESTE
CHILLINWORTH
FLEMISH JANSEN
FRENCH BEZE GURY AILLY FAVRE
PAJON SIMON CALVIN GERSON
GLAIRE GOGUEL JURIEU PASCAL
PORREE RICHER SORBON ABELARD
AMYRAUT BASNAGE BAUTAIN
BOCHART CHARRON FENELON
QUESNEL BERENGAR CASAUBON
COURAYER SABATIER CASTELLIO
BOURDALOUE LICHTENBERGER
LABERTHONNIERE
GERMAN ECK ESS ADAM ARND
BAUR DUHM EBER GASS HEIM
MERX RUPP ZAHN AMMON BAUER
BUDDE CALOV EMSER FRANK
GOEZE HAUCK HENKE KNAPP KRAUS
LANGE MAJOR ROTHE STORR
WALCH WEBER WEISS ALSTED
ANDREA BAHRDT BENGEL CRAMER
DALMAN DIPPEL DORNER EBRARD
FICKER GEIGER HEILER HERMES
HERZOG HEUSSI HIRSCH MOHLER
NATORP PEUCER PLANCK REUSCH
SEMLER SPENER UHLICH ZELLER
ZIMMER AGRIPPA AMSDORF
BOUSSET CASPARI CRUSIUS
ECKHART EHRHARD ERNESTI
FORSTER GERHARD HAERING
HARNACK HOFMANN KOSTLIN
LECHLER MOSHEIM MUNSTER
NAUMANN NEANDER NIPPOLD
RITSCHL STRAUSS TILLICH
ULLMANN URSINUS WILHELM
BULTMANN CALIXTUS CANISIUS
CHEMNITZ COCCEIUS CRUCIGER
DIBELIUS DILLMANN EBERHARD
EICHHORN FLIEDNER GERHARDT
GESENIUS HAUSRATH KAUTZSCH
KLIEFOTH MICHELIS MYCONIUS
OETINGER OSIANDER REIMARUS
SCHENKEL AURIFABER BEYSCHLAG
BUSEMBAUM DELITZSCH
DOLLINGER FABRICIUS FREIDRICH
JABLONSKI MICHAELIS NIEMOLLER
OLEVIANUS OLSHAUSEN PFEIDERER

BAUMGARTEN BONHOEFFER
FANNENBERG MARHEINEKE
NEUMEISTER WISLICENUS
TISCHENDORF FROHSCHAMMER
BRETSCHNEIDER SCHLEIERMACHER
GREEK ALLACCI CLEMENT
EUSEBIUS
HUNGARIAN BALLAGI
IRISH DODWELL PLUNKET TYRRELL
ITALIAN OCHINO AQUINAS
LOMBARD PERRONE SOCINUS
PASSAGLIA BELLARMINE
JEWISH HIRSCH
NORWEGIAN MOE
PORTUGUESE ABARBANEL
RUSSIAN BERDYAYEV SCHMEMANN
SCOTTISH CAIRD EADIE BURNET
ALESIUS CAMERON ROLLOCK
TULLOCH CAMPBELL CHALMERS
FAIRBAIRN CUNNINGHAM
RUTHERFORD
SPANISH CANO MOLINA SUAREZ
VALDES ENZINAS CARRANZA
EYMERICO SERVETUS MALDONADO
SEPULVEDA
SWEDISH FRYXELL SODERBLOM
FAHLCRANTZ
SWISS KUNG BARTH GODET VINET
ISELIN BRUNNER DIODATI ERASTUS
LAVATER LECLERC BUCHMANN
HEIDEGGER
SYRIAN AETIUS
THEOLOGY KALAM IRENICS
DIVINITY POIMENIC POLEMICS
THEONOE (BROTHER OF —)
CALCHAS
(FATHER OF —) PROTEUS THESTOR
(MOTHER OF —) LEUCIPPE
PSAMATHE
THEORBO LUTE ARCHLUTE
THEOREM DUAL LEMMA CONVERSE
THEORETIC PURE
THEORETICAL BOOK PURE CLOSET
THEORIC ABSTRACT ACADEMIC
ARMCHAIR NOTIONAL PLATONIC
THEORIST MUSER OPINATOR
THEORIZE SUGGEST
THEORIZING IDEOLOGY
THEORY ISM OVISM EROTIC ETHICS
HOLISM LAXISM SYSTEM AGOGICS
ANIMISM ATOMISM BAASKAP
BIGBANG CAMBISM DUALISM
FORMISM HOBBISM PEELISM
PLENISM THEORIC TYCHISM
ACOSMISM AXIOLOGY DITHEISM
DYNAMISM ENERGISM ESTHETIC
ETIOLOGY FEMINISM FINITISM
GHOSTISM GOBINISM HEDONICS
IDEALISM IDEOLOGY MOLINISM
MONADISM ONTOLOGY PROGRESS
SEMANTIC SEMIOTIC SPERMISM
(— OF GAMES) AGONISTICS
(— OF THE UNIVERSE) SYSTEM
(KIND OF —) DOMINO GALOIS
(METRICAL —) STICHOLOGY
(PHYSICS —) BOHRS
(SUFF.) ISM LOGER LOGIA(N)
LOGIC(AL) LOGIST LOGUE LOGY
OLOGY
THEOW SERF THRALL THEOWMAN
THERAPEUTICS ACEOLOGY
THERAPY PHYSIATRICS
(SUFF.) PATH(IA)(IC)(Y)

THERAVADA HINAYANA
THERE ERE YARE ALONG VOILA
WHERE YONDER THEASUM
THITHER
THEREABOUTS NEARBY
THEREAFTER UPON THENCE
THEREFORE SO ERGO THEN ARGAL
HENCE FORTHY IGITUR THENCE
THEREON UPON
THEREUPON SO SINCE WITHAL
THEREON THEREUP
THEREWITH MIT WITH
THERIACA GALENA
THERMOMETER GLASS HYDRA
CELSIUS REAUMUR
(PART OF —) BORE BULB LENS
SCALE COLUMN GRADUATIONS
CONSTRICTION
THERMOPLASTIC SARAN
THERMOSTAT DETECTOR
PYROSTAT
THERSANDER (FATHER OF —)
POLYNICES
(MOTHER OF —) ARGIA
(SLAYER OF —) TELEPHUS
THESAURUS TREASURE
THESE THIR THIS THEASUM
THESEUS (FATHER OF —) AEGEUS
(MOTHER OF —) AETHRA
(SON OF —) HIPPOLYTUS
(WIFE OF —) PHAEDRA
THESIS ACT PAPER THEMA
DOWNBEAT LOGICISM THESICLE
THESTIUS (DAUGHTER OF —)
ALTHAEA
(FATHER OF —) PARTHAON
(MOTHER OF —) EURYTE
(SON OF —) TOXEUS PLEXIPPUS
THESTOR (DAUGHTER OF —)
THEONOE LEUCIPPE
(FATHER OF —) IDMON APOLLO
(MOTHER OF —) LAOTHOE
(SON OF —) CALCHAS
THETIS (FATHER OF —) NEREUS
(HUSBAND OF —) PELEUS
(MOTHER OF —) DORIS
(SON OF —) ACHILLES
THEY A HI THO THEI ELLAS ELLOS
(— READ) LEG
THIAMINE ANEURIN
THICK FAT SAD HAZY SLAB BLIND
BROAD BURLY BUSHY CLOSE
CRASS DENSE FOGGY GREAT
GROSS MURKY SOLID SQUAB STIFF
STOUT CHUMPY COARSE GREASY
LUBBER SLABBY SPISSY STOCKY
STODGY TURBID BLUBBER
GRUMOUS FAMILIAR LUTULENT
MOTHERED
(— OF A FIGHT) PRESS
(— WITH SMOKE) SMUDGY
(SHORT AND —) SQUAT
(11 POINTS —) HEAVY
(PREF.) CRASSI DASI DASY
HADR(O) PACHY ULO
(— WITH HAIR) DASI DASY
THICKEN GEL BODY CLOT FULL
BREAK KEECH LITHE DEEPEN
HARDEN ENGROSS STIFFEN
(— HEDGE) PLASH
THICKENED BODIED BULLED
FURRED CALLOUS CLUBBED
SPISSATED

THICKENER NAPALM
THICKENING FALX LEAR ROUX
SWELL CALLUS CLAVATE LIAISON
PLACODE ATHEROMA CLUBBING
CRASSULA PYCNOSIS EPHIPPIUM
(— OF ARTERIES) ATHEROMA
(— OF COAL SEAM) SWELLY
(— OF LETTER STROKE) STRESS
THICKET COP BOSK RONE SHAG
SHAW BLUFF BRAKE CLUMP
COPSE COVER DROKE HEDGE
QUICK SHOLA SLICK THICK BOSKET
BUSHET COVERT GREAVE JUNGLE
MALLEE QUEACH SPINNY
BOSCAGE BOSQUET BRUSHET
COPPICE CORYLET SPINNEY
WOODRIS CHAMISAL FERNSHAW
QUICKSET SHINNERY THICKSET
SALICETUM
THICK-HEADED OPAQUE
THICKHEADED DULL DENSE
THICKHEADED FLY CONOPID
THICK-KNEE CURLEW DIKKOP
BUSTARD
THICKLY STEFLY
THICKNESS PLY BODY LAYER
DIAMETER
(— OF CHIP) CUT FEED
(— OF CLOTH) LAY
(— OF METAL) GRIP
(— OF PAPER) BULK CALLIPER
UNDERLAY
(ONE — OVER ANOTHER) LAYER
(SECOND —) DOUBLING
THICKSET STUB BEEFY PUNCH
SQUAT STOUT THICK CHUMPY
CHUNKY HUMPTY PLUGGY ROBUST
STOCKY STUBBY STUGGY
NUGGETY SQUATTY
THIEF GUN NIP PAD CHOR GILT LIFT
MILL PRIG BUDGE CREEP CROOK
FAKER GANEF PIKER SNEAK TAKER
TILER ANGLER BILKER CANNON
CLOYER DISMAS GONOPH
HOOKER KALLAN LIFTER MICHER
NIMMER NIPPER PICKER PIRATE
RATERO ROBBER SNATCH TOSHER
WASTER BOOSTER COLLERY
FOOTMAN GORILLA GRIFTER
HARRIER HEISTER LADRONE
LURCHER MEECHER MERCURY
PRIGGER PRIGMAN PROLLER
PROWLER SNAPPER SPOTTER
STEALER THIEVER CLYFAKER
CONVEYER CUTPURSE FINGERER
HARROWER LARCENER PETERMAN
PICAROON PICKLOCK PILFERER
PRIGSTER SNATCHER
(— AT A MINE) CAVER
(CATTLE —) ABACTOR BLOTTER
PLANTER RUSTLER
(CLEVER —) KID CANNON
(CRUCIFIED —) DISMAS
(FLASHY —) KIDDY
(MOUNTAIN —) CHOAR
(NIGHT —) SCOURER
(PETTY —) HOOKER SLOCKER
(RIVER —) ACKMAN LUMPER
(SNEAK —) LURCHER
(VAGABOND —) WASTER
(WHARF —) TOSHER
(PREF.) KLEPT(O)
(SUFF.) KLEPT

THIEVE MAG NIM
THIEVERY PRIGGERY
THIEVING LAW SHARK PUGGING
PROGGERY STEALING
THIEVING MAGPIE, THE
(CHARACTER IN —) NINETTA
PODESTA GIANETTO
(COMPOSER OF —) ROSSINI
THIEVISH STEALY FURTIVE KLEPTIC
SCADDLE PRIGGISH
THIEVISHNESS PRIGGISM
THIGH HAM HOCK FEMUR FLANK
GAMMON
(— PAIN) MERALGIA
(PREF.) CRURO FEMORO MER(O)
(SUFF.) MERUS
THILL FILL SILL BLADE SHAFT
LIMBER
THIMBLE SKEIN BUSHEL GOBLET
SLEEVE CRINGLE
THIMBLEBERRY MULBERRY
THIN HOE LEW BONY FINE FLUE
FUSE LANK LEAN LIMP PRIN RARE
SLIM WEAK WHEY EXILE FRAIL
GAUNT GAUZY LATHY PEAKY
SHEER SLINK SMALL SPARE
SWAMP THIRL WASHY WIZEN
AERIAL BLASHY DILUTE FLUTED
HOLLOW MAUGER MEAGER
MEAGRE PEAKED SCRANK SEROSE
SEROUS SHELLY SKINNY SLEAZY
SLIGHT SPARSE SPINNY SUBTLE
TENDER TWIGGY WATERY WEAKEN
COVERED FOLIOUS FRAGILE
GRACILE HAGGARD SANIOUS
SCRAGGY SCRAILY SCRANKY
SCRAWNY SHALLOW SHILPIT
SLENDER SPIDERY SPINDLY
TENUOUS THREADY ARANEOUS
CACHECTIC EGGSHELL HAIRLINE
ICHOROUS MACILENT SCRAGGED
SCRANNEL SKINKING VAPORISH
WATERISH ATTENUATE SPINDLING
(— AND PINCHED) CHITTY
(— LEATHER) DOLE
(— OUT) HOE CHOP DISBUD
FEATHER
(— SEEDLINGS) SINGLE
(— THE WALLS) IRON
(MAKE —) EMACIATE
(PREF.) AREO LEPT(O) MANO
TENUI
THINE TUUM
THING JOB RES BABY ITEM SORT
WHAT CHEAT CHOSE AFFAIR
ANIMAL DINGUS FELLOW GILGUY
MATTER ARTICLE DINGBAT
MINIKIN SHEBANG WHATNOT
THINGLET
(— DONE) FACT ACTUS
(— FOUND) TROVE
(— OBSERVED) OBJECT
(— OF LITTLE ACCOUNT) GEWGAW
(— OF LITTLE VALUE) NIFLE TRIFLE
TRINKET
(— OF LITTLE WORTH) STIVER
(— SEEN) REGARD
(—S PROHIBITED) VETANDA
(— TO BE REGRETTED) DAMAGE
(— TO EXHIBIT) BRAVERY
(ADMIRABLE —) GEM
(ANOTHER —) ALIUD
(BIG —) SWAPPER SWOPPER

(CONSECRATED —) ANATHEMA
(CORRECT —) CHEESE
(CREEPING —) SERPENT
(DISAGREEABLE —) STINKER
(EASY —) PIE PUSHOVER
(ENORMOUS —) MONSTER
(ENTIRE —) INTEGRAL
(EXTRAORDINARY —) ONER
(FAIR —) POTATO
(FIT —) CHECKER
(FLAT —) PLAT
(FOOLISH —) FOLLY
(GOOD —) WELFARE
(HOLY —) HALIDOM
(HOLY —S) HAGIA KODASHIM
(IMPORTANT —) ACE
(INSIGNIFICANT —) SCRAT
(INSIGNIFICANT —S) SMATTER
(JEWISH —S) JUDAICA
(LITTLE —S) FEWTRILS
(LIVING —S) BIOTA
(MISSHAPEN —) ABORTION
(NEW —) NEWEL
(OUTMODED —) SNUFF
(PETTY —) SHABBLE
(PRECIOUS —) JEWEL
(PRECISE —) POINT
(REMARKABLE —) UNCO
PHENOMENON
(RIDICULOUS —) MONUMENT
(RIGHT —) POTATO
(ROTTEN —) ROTTOCK
(SAD —) RUTH
(SILLY —) TRIMTRAM
(SINGLE —) UNIT
(SINGULAR —) ODDITY
(SMALL —) SNIPPET
(STRAY —) WAIF
(STUNTED —) SCRUNT SNEESHIN
(SURE —) CERT SNIP
(TERRIFYING —) BOGEYMAN
(TROUBLESOME —) PEST TRIAL
PLAGUE
(UNEXPECTED —) GODSEND
(UNIQUE —) ONER UNICUM
(UNREAL —) NOMINAL
(UNSPECIFIED —S) JAZZ
(UNSUBSTANTIAL —) PUFF
(WITHOUT EQUAL —) NONPAREIL
(WORLDLY —S) EARTH
(WORNOUT —) SNUFF HUSHEL
(PL.) GEAR REALIA SQUARES
(PREF.) REI
(SUFF.) ORIUM ORY SOME
(— USED) ANT
(— USED FOR) ORIUM
THINGAMAJIG GIZMO
THINGAMY DOODAD
THING-IN-ITSELF THINGY
NOUMENON
THINGS
(SUFF.) IA
THINGUMBOB DODAD DINGUS
DOODAD JIGGER THINGUM
THINGAMAJIG
THINGUMMY GISMO GIZMO
THINGAMAJIG
THINK LET SEE WIS WIT DEEM FEEL
HOLD MAKE MEAN MINT MULL
MUSE READ TROW WEEN ALLOW
CENSE FANCY GUESS JUDGE
LOUSE OPINE PANSE SEPAD
ESTEEM EXPECT FIGURE IDEATE

REASON RECKON REPUTE BELIEVE
CONCEIT IMAGINE REFLECT
SUPPOSE SURMISE COGITATE
CONSIDER ENVISAGE
(— BEST) SEEM
(— DIFFERENTLY) DISSENT
(— HARD) YERK
(— HIGHLY OF) RATE
(— IDLY) DREAM
(— ILL) MISDEEM
(— LOGICALLY) DEDUCE
(— OF) MIND PURPENSE
(— OF AS) ACCOUNT
(— OUT) STUDY REASON
(— OVER) BETHINK
(— UP) INVENT
(— UPON) BROOD
(— WELL OF) APPROVE
(— WRONGLY) MISTAKE
THINKER SOPHIST PHILOSOPH
PHILOSOPHER
(CHINESE —) LEGALIST
THINKING CONCEIT THOUGHT
(CLEVER —) HEADWORK
THINLY AIRILY SPARSE SPARSELY
THINNESS RARITY EXILITY FINESSE
TENUITY EXIGUITY
THINNING BALK BAULK PINCH
CLEANING
THIOL MERCAPTAN
THIRD FACE GAMMA TERCE THREE
DITONE TERTIA TIERCE
(PREF.) TRIT(O)
THIRDLY TERTIO
THIRD-RATE C3 HEDGE
THIRD-RATER PIKER
THIRST DRY ADRY CLEM DRYTH
APOSIA DROUTH THRIST DROUGHT
DIPSOSIS POLYDIPSIA
(EXCESSIVE —) POLYDIPSIA
(LOSS OF —) ADIPSIA
(PREF.) DIPS(O)
THIRSTING SITIENT
THIRSTY DRY ADRY ATHIRST
DROUGHTY
THIRTEEN (YOUNGER THAN —)
PRETEEN
THIS HE SO ESTA ESTO THIK DIESE
THILK
THIS ABOVE ALL (AUTHOR OF —)
KNIGHT
(CHARACTER IN —) PRUE CLIVE
MONTY BRIGGS CATHAWAY
PRUDENCE
THISTLE PUHA HOYLE CARDON
DASHEL DINDLE FISTLE TEASEL
CALTROP CARDUUS CARLINA
GUTWEED RAURIKI WARATAH
BEDEGUAR CALTHROP COMPOSIT
ECHINOPS MILKWEED
(PREF.) CARDO
THITHER TO YON YOND THERE
YONDER ULTERIOR YONDWARD
THOAS (BROTHER OF —) EUNEUS
(DAUGHTER OF —) HYPSIPYLE
(FATHER OF —) BACCHUS
ANDRAEMON
(MOTHER OF —) GORGE ARIADNE
HYPSIPYLE
(SON OF —) SICINUS
(WIFE OF —) MYRINE
THOMIST AQUINST

THOMSONITE MESOLE MESOTYPE OZARKITE

THONG LORE RIEM BRAIL GIRTH LASSO LEASH ROMAL STRAP THUNK WHANG WHANK LACING LINGEL STRING TWITCH AMENTUM BABICHE LANIARD LANYARD LATCHET RIEMPIF
(— ON JAVELIN) AMENTUM
(HAWK'S —) BRAIL
(PREF.) HIMANTO

THOR THUNAR THUNOR
(FATHER OF —) ODIN
(HAMMER OF —) MJOLLNIR
(MOTHER OF —) JORDH

THORACIC DORSAL

THORAX CHEST TRUNK BREAST PEREION ALITRUNK CORSELET FOREBODY

THORITE ENALITE ORANGITE

THORN BROD BUSH GOAD PIKE STOB STUG BRIAR BRIER DOORN PRICK SPIKE SPINE FUSTIC JAGGER ACANTHA PRICKER STICKER COCKSPUR THORNLET
(PL.) SPEAR HAYBOTE
(PREF.) ACANTH(O) SPINI SPINO(SO) SPINULI SPINULOSO
(SUFF.) ACANTHUS SPINOSE

THORN APPLE HAW METEL STAMONY

THORNBACK RAY DORN ROKER

THORNBILL TOMTIT

THORNY HARD SPINY PRICKLY SCROGGY SPINOUS THISTLY THORNED

THORON RADON

THOROUGH RUN DEEP FIRM FULL SOUND ERRANT HOLLOW STRICT HOTSHOT INGOING REGULAR COMPLETE GROUNDLY INTIMATE PRECIOUS

THOROUGHBRED HOTBLOOD

THOROUGHFARE BUND DRUM ROAD ALLEY AVENUE STREET BIKEWAY HIGHWAY PARKWAY WHITEHALL

THOROUGH-GOING WHOLEHOG

THOROUGHGOING PAKKA ARRANT ERRANT HEARTY PROPER PUREDEE RADICAL ABSOLUTE PROFOUND TRUEBRED

THOROUGHLY BUT FULL GOOD INLY CLEAN FULLY PROOF DEEPLY GAINLY KINDLY PROPER RICHLY RIPELY WHOLLY ROUNDLY SOAKING SOBBING SOGGING SOUNDLY DRIPPING GROUNDLY HEARTILY INWARDLY
(PREF.) E

THOROUGHWORT BONESET

THOSE THEM THEY YOND

THOTH DHOUTI

THOUGH AS AND SET YET ALTHO ALTHOUGH

THOUGHT CARE IDEA MOOD VIEW FANCY TASTE TRACE NOTION PENSEE CONCEIT CONCEPT COUNSEL OPINION SURMISE PEMMICAN RUMINATE
(— EXPRESSED IN WORDS) SENTIMENT
(— OUT) ADVISED

(CAREFUL —) ADVICE ACCOUNT
(CONTROLLING —) KEYNOTE
(DEEP —) MUSE MEDITATION
(FANCIFUL —) CONCEIT
(HIGHEST —) IDEE
(INMOST —) CONSCIENCE
(INNERMOST —S) PRIVITY
(ORIGINAL —) BRAINCHILD
(REASONED —) STUDY
(UNCLEAN —) SEWERAGE
(WELL-EXPRESSED —) STROKE
(PREF.) LOG(O)

THOUGHTFUL EARNEST PENSIVE SERIOUS STUDIED STUDIOUS THOUGHTY

THOUGHTFULNESS GRACE COUNSEL

THOUGHTLESS RASH VAIN DIZZY GLAKY SUPINE VACANT ETOURDI GLAIKET RAMSTAM HEEDLESS RECKLESS

THOUSAND CHI MIL GRAND MILLE CHILIAD
(FIVE —) EPSILON
(SIX —) DIGAMMA
(TEN —) TOMAN
(10 —) MYRIAD
(100 —) LAC LAKH
(PREF.) CHILI(A) KILO MILLE MILLI
(TEN —) MYRIA MYRIO

THOUSANDTH (— OF CUBIC CENTIMETER) LAMBDA
(— OF INCH) MIL
(HUNDRED —) SSU
(PREF.) MILLI

THRACIAN GETE GETAN GETIC THRAX

THRALL SERF GURTH SLAVE CAPTIVE

THRALLDOM BONDAGE SLAVERY THIRLAGE

THRASH DAD LAM PAY TAN BANG BEAT BELT COMB DING DRUB DUST FLAX JERK LACE LICK LOUK MILL PAIL SOCK SOLE SOWL SWAP SWOP TOSE TRIM WALK WHAP WHIP WHOP YERK BASTE BELAM BLESS CREAM CURRY DRASH FLAIL FRAIL LINCH LINGE NOINT PASTE SLATE SLOSH SWACK SWING TABOR TARGE THUMP TOWEL TWINK WHALE WHANG ANOINT BUMFEG CUDGEL FETTLE JACKET LARRUP LATHER MUZZLE RADDLE STOUSH SWINGE TANCEL THREAP THRESH THWACK WALLOP LAMBACK LEATHER SWADDLE TROLLOP TROUNCE BETHWACK BUMBASTE LAMBASTE LAMBSKIN RIBROAST SPIFLICATE

THRASHER THREAPER THRESHER SICKLEBILL

THRASHING LICK TOCO LALDY HIDING WIPING BELTING LAMMING LICKING WARMING WHALING DRUBBING STRAPPING

THRASYMEDES (FATHER OF —) NESTOR
(MOTHER OF —) ANAXIBIA

THREAD BAR END BAVE CHIP CLEW CLUE CORD DOUP FILE FILM GIMP GOLD LACE LINE POIL PURL ROON SILK TRAM WIRE WORM BRIDE

CHIVE FIBER FIBRE FLOAT FLOSS HYPHA INKLE LISLE LUREX REEVE SCREW SETON SHIVE SHOOT SHUTE STEEK THRUM TWEER TWIRE TWIST WATAP BOTTOM COBWEB COTTON ENFILE FIBRIL INFILE SINGLE STAMEN STITCH STRAIN STRAND STRING TASLAN TISSUE BABICHE BASTING DOUPING SLUBBER SPIREME TWITTER WARPING ACONTIUM FILAMENT GOSSAMER LIGATURE PICKOVER RAVELING SPINNING SPIRICLE
(— AROUND BOWSTRING) SERVING
(— IN SEED COATING) SPIRICLE
(— LEGS OF RABBIT) HARL HARLE
(— OF SCREW) WORM
(— OF WAX) SWARF
(—S THAT CROSS WARP) WEFT WOOF
(— USED FOR COCOON) BAVE
(BADLY TWINED —) SLUBBER
(BALL OF —) CLEW CLUE CLOWE GLOME
(BUTTONHOLE —S) BAR
(COARSE —) GIRD
(COARSEST — IN LACE) GIMP
(COILED —) COP
(FILLING —) PICK
(FINE COTTON —) LISLE
(FLOATING —) PICKOVER
(HARD —) LISLE
(LINEN —) LINE INCLE INKLE
(LOOSELY TWISTED —S) BUMP
(METAL —) LAME WIRE
(OAKUM —) PLEDGET
(PULLED —) SNAG
(REFUSE —S) BUR BURR
(SHOEMAKER'S —) END LINGEL LINGLE
(SILK —) TRAM TRAME DOUPIONI
(SOFT SHORT —) THRUM
(STRONG —) GOUNAU
(SURGICAL —) SETON
(WARP —) END STAMEN
(WAXED —) TACKER
(WEFT —) PICK SHOT
(40 —S) BEER BIER
(PL.) FLOSS
(PREF.) FILI(CI) MIT(O) NEM(A)(O) NEMAT(O) STAMIN(I)
(SUFF.) NEMA NEME STEMONOUS

THREADBARE BARE SEAR SERE USED TRITE PILLED SHABBY NAPLESS

THREADFIN SEER SEIR SULEA BARBUDO KINGFISH SEERFISH

THREADFISH COBBLER SUNFISH

THREADING SCREW STRINGING

THREADLIKE FILATE FILOSE FILIFORM

THREADWORK MACRAME
(KNOTTED —) MACRAME MACRAMI

THREASHOLD BRINK VERGE

THREAT ATTACK MENACE THUNDER
(BOASTFUL —) BRAVADO
(PL.) MINES

THREATEM (— TO RAIN) SCOWDER SCOUTHER SCOWTHER

THREATEN BODE BRAG FACE MINT BOAST SHORE ATTACK IMPEND

MENACE ENDANGER MINATORY OVERHANG
(— TO RAIN) SCOUTHER

THREATENED FRAUGHT

THREATENING BIG GLUM UGLY ANGRY BOAST NASTY SABLE SHORE GREASY BANEFUL BODEFUL OMINOUS RAMPANT MINATORY MINITANT MINACIOUS
(— TO RAIN) HEAVY

THREE TREY GIMEL LEASH TRIAS TERNARY TERNION
(— CENT PIECE) TRIME
(— IN ONE) TRIUNE
(— MILES) LEAGUE
(— OF A KIND) GLEEK BRELAN TRIPLET
(GROUP OF —) TRIO TRIAD TRIPLE TROIKA
(SET OF —) TERN PAIRIAL
(PREF.) TER TERNATI TERNATO TRE TRI(S)
(— DIMENSIONS) STERE(O)
(SUFF.) TERNATE

THREE BLACK PENNIES (AUTHOR OF —) HERGESHEIMER
(CHARACTER IN —) HOWAT JAMES PENNY SUSAN EUNICE JANNAN JASPER POLDER BRUNDON MARIANA LUDOWIKA WINSCOMBE

THREE-CORNERED HAT (AUTHOR OF —) ALARCON
(CHARACTER IN —) LUCAS WEASEL EUGENIO MERCEDES FRASQUITA

THREE-DIMENSIONAL CUBIC CUBICAL

THREEFOLD TERN TRINE TERNAL TREBLE TRINAL TRIPLE TERNARY TRIFOLD TRIPLEX THRIBBLE

THREE-FORKED TRISULC

THREE MUSKETEERS (AUTHOR OF —) DUMAS
(CHARACTER IN —) ATHOS ARAMIS WARDES PORTHOS DEWINTER PLANCHET BONACIEUX CONSTANCE DARTAGNAN RICHELIEU

THREEPENCE JOEY TREY THRIP THRUM TICKEY TICKIE

THREE SISTERS (AUTHOR OF —) CHEKHOV
(CHARACTER IN —) OLGA IRINA MASHA ANDREY SOLENI KULIGIN NATASHA PROSOROV VERSHININ

THREE SOLDIERS (AUTHOR OF —) DOSPASSOS
(CHARACTER IN —) DAN RED ANDY JOHN MABE YVONNE ANDREWS FUSELLI ANDERSON GENEVIEVE CHRISTFIELD

THRENODY DIRGE HEARSE THRENE

THRESH COB BEAT CAVE LUMP WHIP BERRY FLAIL FRAIL SPELT STAMP THRASH

THRESHEL DRASHEL

THRESHER TASKER

THRESHER SHARK FOX FOXFISH WHIPTAIL

THRESHOLD HEAD SILL SOLE DEARN LIMEN DRASHEL DOORSILL
(— OF CONSCIOUSNESS) LIMEN

THRIFT SAVING VIRTUE ECONOMY SEAPINK STATICE THEEDOM PARSIMONY

THRIFTILY NEAR
THRIFTLESS WASTEFUL
THRIFTY CANNY FENDY PUIST FRUGAL SAVING CAREFUL SPARING
THRILL JAG WOW BANG DIRL GIRL KICK RUSH SEND FLUSH SHOOT THIRL DINDLE STOUND TICKLE TINGLE TREMOR ENCHANT FRISSON VIBRATE FREMITUS
(**PROVIDING A —**) KICKY
(**SHARP —**) ZING
THRILLING TINGLY VIBRANT PLANGENT TINGLING
THRINTER FRONTER
THRIPID PHYSOPOD
THRIPS BLACKFLY PHYSOPOD
THRIVE DOW GROW LIKE RISE THEE ADDLE FADGE MOISE PROVE THRAM BATTEN BATTLE CATTER CHIEVE PROSPER STORKEN SUCCEED WELFARE FLOURISH THRODDEN
(**— IN**) LOVE
THRIVING BIEN GRUSHIE ROARING THRIFTY BLOOMING TOWARDLY
THRIVINGLY GAILY GAYLY BRAVELY
THROAT MAW CRAG CROP GOWL GULA HALS HASS LANE GORGE HALSE SWIRE FAUCES GANGET GULLET GUTTUR GUZZLE RICTUS CHANNEL JUGULUM STOMACH SWALLOW WEASAND THRAPPLE THROPPLE THROTTLE
(**— AILMENT**) STREP
(**— OF ANCHOR**) CLUTCH
(**— OF COROLLA**) FAUCES
(**— OF FROG**) KNEE
(**CLEAR —**) HARRUMPH
(**KIND OF —**) STREP
(**MOUTH AND —**) WHISTLE
(**SORE —**) HOUSTY PRUNELLA
(**PREF.**) BRONCH(I)(IO)(O) DER(O) GUTTERO
THROATLATCH FIADOR
THROATY THICK GUTTURAL
THROB ACHE BEAT BELK DRUM DUNT LEAP PANG PANT QUOP WARK FLACK PULSE STANG WARCH STOUND STRIKE STROKE TINGLE WALLOP FLACKER PULSATE VIBRATE FLICHTER PALPITATE
(**— IN PAIN**) SHOOT
(**RAPID —S**) FRIMITTS
THROBBING DUNT ATHROB THRILL BEATING PITAPAT VIBRANT PULSATORY
THROE PANG PULL STOUR SHOWER PAROXYSM
(**—S OF DEATH**) AGONY
THROMBIN PLASMASE
THROMBOPLASTIN COAGULIN CYTOZYME
THROMBOSIS SHOCK CORONARY
THRONE GADI SEAT ASANA GADDI GADHI SELLE SIEGE STALL STATE STEAD STOOL MUSNUD SEGGIO SHINZA TRIBUNE CATHEDRA SEGGIOLA SINHASAN
(**— OF GOD**) MERCYSEAT
(**BISHOP'S —**) SEE APSE CATHEDRA
(**INDIAN —**) GADI

THRONE ROOM AIWAN
THRONG CREW HEAP HOST ROUT CHIRT CROWD FLOCK FRACK HORDE POSSE PRESS SHOAL SWARM RESORT THRAVE THREAT THRIMP THRUST COMPANY TEMPEST THRUTCH SURROUND
(**— OF SEAFOWL**) SAVSSAT
(**CONFUSED —**) LURRY
THRONGED ALIVE FREQUENT NUMEROUS
THROTTLE GUN CHOKE SCRAG STIFLE GARROTE STRANGLE THROPPLE
THROUGH BY PER DONE THRU WITH ROUND AROUND
(**— AND THROUGH**) INGRAIN INGRAINED
(**RIGHT —**) TILL
(**PREF.**) DIA PER
THROUGHOUT OVER ABOUT ROUND ABROAD BEDENE BIDENE DURING ENTIRE PASSIM SEMPRE OVERALL THRUOUT
(**PREF.**) HOL(O)
THROW GO DAB DAD HIP HIT PAT PEG PUT SHY ACES BIFF BUCK BUNG CALE CAST CHIP CLOD COOK CLICK DART DASH DROW DUMP HAIL HANK HIPE HULL HURL HYPE JERK LACE MILL PECK PICK PURL SEND SKIM SLAT SOSS TOSS TURF VANG WARP WURP YEND CHUCK CHUNK DOUSE FLICK FLING FLIRT FLURR HEAVE PITCH SLING SPANG DEVEST ELANCE HAUNCH HURTLE INJECT LAUNCH SLIGHT THRILL BLUNDER BUTTOCK COCKSHY MANGANA UPTHROW VIBRATE CATAPULT JACULATE
(**— A BASEBALL PITCH**) HANG
(**— ABOUT**) BOUNCE
(**— ASIDE**) DEVEST
(**— AT HAZARD**) NICK
(**— AWAY**) DICE DASH BANDY SCRAP WAIVE PROJECT JETTISON SQUANDER
(**— BACK**) REPEL
(**— BASEBALL**) BURN
(**— BY KICKING**) WINCE
(**— CARELESSLY**) COB
(**— DICE**) JEFF
(**— DOWN**) DUSH EVEN PILE FLUMP LODGE ABJECT DETURB THRING FLATTEN
(**— FORTH**) EJECT
(**— FORWARD**) LAUNCH
(**— HEAVILY**) LOB
(**— HEEDLESSLY**) SLIGHT
(**— IN CRAPS**) CRAP PASS CRABS BOXCARS NATURAL
(**— IN QUOITS**) RINGER
(**— INTO CONFUSION**) CLUB EMBROIL FLUTTER CONFOUND CONVULSE
(**— INTO DISORDER**) PIE ADDLE BOLLIX DERANGE DISRANK DISRUPT EMBROIL DISARRAY
(**— INTO PERPLEXITY**) FLUMMOX
(**— INTO WASTE**) BACK
(**— JERKILY**) FLIRT
(**— LIGHT UPON**) ILLUME
(**— LIQUID**) JAW

(**— OF A STEER**) DOGFALL
(**— OFF**) CANT CAST EMIT SLIRT SPILL SLOUGH CONFUSE UNBURDEN
(**— OFF COURSE**) EMIT SHED DERAIL
(**— OF SHUTTLE**) SHOT SHOOT SHUTE
(**— OF THREES**) COCKEYES
(**— ONESELF**) CLAP
(**— OPEN**) DISPARK
(**— OUT**) FIRE HOOF LADE BELCH EJECT ERUPT SPOUT DETURB IGNORE EXTRUDE
(**— OVER**) JILT
(**— QUICKLY**) LASH
(**— REPEATEDLY**) PELT
(**— ROUGHLY**) WAP
(**— SIDEWISE**) SHY
(**— SILK**) THROWST
(**— SMARTLY**) SLAT
(**— STEER**) BUST
(**— STICKS**) SQUAIL
(**— STONES**) ROCK
(**— TOGETHER**) HUDDLE
(**— UNDER**) SUBJECT
(**— UP**) BARF CAVE PICK VOMIT
(**— VIOLENTLY**) BUZZ DING PASH SOCK WHAP WHOP SMASH HURTLE WUTHER WHITHER SPANGHEW PRECIPITATE
(**— WITH A JERK**) JET CANT SQUIRR FLOUNCE
(**— WITH GREAT FORCE**) BUZZ SWACK
(**— WITHOUT VIOLENCE**) HURL
(**CHEATING — OF DICE**) KNAP
(**FOOTBALL —**) GROUND
(**FREE —**) FOUL
(**LARIAT —**) HOOLIAN
(**LOWEST — AT DICE**) AMBSACE AMESACE
(**WRESTLING —**) HANK HIPE HYPE BUTTOCK BACKHEEL
(**SUFF.**) JECT
THROWAWAY DODGER
THROWBACK ATAVISM ATAVIST
THROWER TRAMMER THROWSTER
(**SPEAR —**) ATLATL
THROWING DARTING
THROWING-STICK ATLATL WOMMERA WOOMERA HORNERAH TROMBASH TRUMBASH
THROWN (**— AWAY**) CASTAWAY
(**— DOWN**) DEJECTED
(**PREF.**) (**— OUT**) RHIPTO
THROWSTER TWISTER
THRUM FUM STRUM THUMB FRINGE
THRUSH POP OMAO SOOR APTHA BREVE FRUSH GRIVE MAVIS OUZEL PITTA SABIA SHAMA SHIRL SPREW UZZLE VEERY APHTHA DRAINE JAYPIE KICKUP MISSEL OLOMAO PULISH SHRITE JAYPIET REDWING WAGTAIL BELLBIRD CHERCOCK FORKTAIL PRUNELLA SHAGBARK THRASHER THROSTLE THRUSHEL THRUSTLE URTICATE WOODCHAT SOLITAIRE MONILIASIS NIGHTINGALE
THRUSHLIKE TURDOID

THRUST DAB DEG DIG DUB JAB JAG JAM JOB POP PUG BANG BEAR BIRR BOKE BORE BUCK BUTT CANT CHOP CRAM DART DASH DUSH FOIN HURL KICK LICK MURE PASS PICK PILT POKE PORR POSS POTE PROD PUSH SEND SINK SPAR STAB STOP TILT VENY WHAP WHOP BREAK DRIFT DRIVE EXERT HUNCH LUNGE POACH POINT PROKE PUNCH SHOOT SPANK STAVE STICK STOKE STUFF THROW DARTLE PLUNGE POUNCE STITCH STRAIN STRESS STRIKE STRIPE BEARING IMPULSE PRESSURE SHOULDER STOCCADO
(**— A LANCE**) AVENTRE
(**— ALONG**) SLIDE
(**— ASIDE**) DAFF SHUFFLE
(**— AWAY**) DOFF SHOVE DETRUDE ABSTRUDE
(**— DOWN**) THRING DEPULSE DETRUDE
(**— IN**) INSERT STRIKE INTRUDE
(**— OF ARCH**) DRIFT
(**— OF EXPLOSION**) BLOWOUT
(**— ONESELF**) CHISEL
(**— ONWARD**) STAVE
(**— OUT**) POUT REACH STRUT EXSERT DETRUDE EXTRUDE OBTRUDE PROTRUDE OBTRUSIVE
(**— SUDDENLY**) STRIKE
(**— THROUGH**) ENFILED
(**— WITH ELBOW**) HUNCH
(**— WITH GREAT FORCE**) BUZZ
(**— WITH NOSE**) NUDDLE
(**— WITH WEAPON**) FOIN SHOVE
(**DAGGER —**) DAG
(**FENCING —**) PASS VENY BOTTE PUNTO VENUE REMISE REPOST TIMING PASSADO RIPOSTE STOCCADO STOCCATA
(**HOME —**) HAI HAY
(**MATADOR'S —**) ESTOCADA
(**SARCASTIC —**) GIRD
THUD BAFF DUMP PHUT PLOD SWAG DOYST FLUMP POUND BOUNCE SQUELCH
THUG MUG GOON PUNK GOONDA RODMAN GORILLA HOODLUM MOBSTER GANGSTER
(**LIKE A —**) GOONY
(**SOUTH AFRICAN —**) TSOTSI
THUJA BIOTA
THUJONE SALVIOL
THULUTH SOOLOOS
THUMB THOOM POLLEX THENAR
(**— THROUGH**) SKIM
(**BALL OF —**) THENAR
THUMBHOLE BACKLILL
THUMBSTALL POUCER POUSER
THUMP COB DAD DUB BANG BEAT BLOW BUMP DING DIRD DRUB DUNT KNUB LUMP PAIK PAKE POLT SOSS THUD TUND TUNK YARK YERK BLAFF BLIBE BUNCH CLOUR CLUNK CRUMP KNOCK POUND TABOR THACK WHELK BOUNCE HAMMER PUMMEL THUNGE
THUMPING WHAPPING WHOPPING
THUNDER ROAR SULFUR BRATTLE FOULDRE SULPHUR INTONATE

(PREF.) BRONT(E)(O) CERAUN(O) KERAUN(O)

THUNDERBOLT BOLT FIRE VAJRA FULMEN FOULDRE ARTIFACT FIREBOLT

(SHOOTER OF —S) THOR

(PREF.) CERAUN(O) KERAUN(O)

THUNDERING TONANT

THUNDERSQUALL BAYAMO VENDAVAL

THUNDERSTONE ARTIFACT

THUNDERSTORM HOUVARI TEMPEST TORNADO

THURIBLE CENSER

THUS AS SIC DYCE THUSLY THISWISE THUSGATE

THWACK BLOW DUNT LICK CRUMP SOUSE

THWART BALK FOIL WART BENCH CROOK CROSS SPITE THRAW THROW ZYGON BAFFLE SCOTCH STYMIE SNOOKER CONTRAIR CONTRARY TRAVERSE

THWARTING CROSS CROSSING

THYESTES (BROTHER OF —) ATREUS

(FATHER OF —) PELOPS

(MOTHER OF —) HIPPODAMIA

THYIA (FATHER OF —) CASTALIUS CEPHISSEUS

(SON OF —) DELPHUS

THYINE THUGA THUYA

THYLACINE YABBI

THYME MARUM PELETRE HILLWORT SERPOLET

TI KI TOI TITI

TIAMAT (HUSBAND OF —) APSU

(SLAYER OF —) MARDUK

TIARA MITER REGNUM CIDARIS TIARELLA

TIBBU DAZA TEDA

TIBET (CHINESE NAME:) SITSANG

TIBET

CAPITAL: LASSA LHASA

COIN: TANGA

LAKE: ARU BAM BUM NAM MEMA TOSU JAGOK TABIA DAGTSE GARHUR KASHUN SELING TANGRA YAMDOK KYARING TERINAM TSARING ZILLING JIGGITAI

LANGUAGE: BODSKAD

MOUNTAIN: KAMET SAJUM KAILAS BANDALA

MOUNTAIN RANGE: KAILAS KUNLUN HIMALAYA

NATIVE: BHOTIA BHOTIYA

PEOPLE: NOSU

RIVER: NAK NAU SAK SONG INDUS SUTLEJ MATSANG SALWEEN

TOWN: NOH KARAK LHASA GARTOK TOTLING GYANGTSE SHIGATSE

TIBETAN BALTI DRUPA BHOTIA BHUTIA CHAMPA DROKPA KHAMBA KHAMBU PANAKA SHERPA TANGUT BHOTIYA BHUTANI GYARUNG

TIBIA SHIN SHANK CNEMIS SHINBONE

(SUFF.) CNEMA CNEMIA CNEMIC CNEMUS

TIBOURBOU CORTEZ

TIC FIXATION

(ONE SUBJECT TO —) TIQUEUR

TICAL BAHT

TICK FAG JAR KEB KED BEAT KADE NICK PEAK PICK PIKE CHALK CHICK CRIKE PIQUE STRAP ACARID IXODID PALLET TALAJE TAMPAN ACARIAN ARGASID BEDTICK IXODIAN PINOLIA ARACHNID CARAPATO GARAPATA GARAPATO TURICATA

(— OFF) IRK MIFF RILE STEAM

(— OF TIME) MOMENT

(PREF.) ACAR(I)(O) CROTO

TICKED MACKEREL

TICKET LOT TAG COMP BLANK CHECK DUCAT FICHE TOKEN BALLOT BILLET COUPON DOCKET PIGEON POLICY RETURN BENEFIT ETIQUET CONTRACT DEADHEAD STOPOVER TRANSFER PASTEBOARD

(— GIVEN WITHOUT CHARGE) FREEBEE FREEBIE

(COMMISSION —) SPIFF

(FREE —) PASS FREEBEE FREEBIE

(HOT —) RAGE

(LOTTERY —) BLANK HORSE BENEFIT

(SALES —) TRAVELER

(SEASON —) IVORY

(PL.) PAPER

TICKET WINDOW GUICHET

TICKING KISS TICK BEDTICK

TICKLE AMUSE TEASE EXCITE KITTLE PLEASE THRILL TIDDLE CUITTLE

TICKLISH RISKY GOOSEY KITTLE KITTLY QUEASY TENDER TOUCHY TRICKY KITTLISH

TICKSEED COREOPSIS

TICK TREFOIL BEDSTRAW SAINFOIN TICKSEED

TIDBIT NOSH TRACE SAYNETE BEATILLE KICKSHAW

TIDDLEYWINK SQUAIL

TIDE FLOW NEAP WAVE AGGER EAGRE ROUST SPRING OVERTIDE SEAFLOOD

(— MOVEMENT) LAKIE

(CRIMSON —) BAMA

(KIND OF —) YULE

(PREF.) (HIGH —) PLEMYRA

TIDINGS NEWS WORD RUMOR SOUND UNCOW ADVICE MESSAGE

(GLAD —) GOSPEL

TIDY RID COSH MACK NEAT SIDE SMUG SNOD SNUG TAUT TOSH TRIG WEME CHART DONCY DONSY DOUCE NATTY NIFTY QUEME TIGHT DONSIE FETTLE POLITE SPOONY ORDERLY ALLIGATE MACKLIKE MENSEFUL SHIPSHAPE

TIE BOW LAP TYE BAND BEND BIND BOND CAST DRAW KILT KNOT LACE LASH LOCK ROOT WASH WISP YOKE ASCOT BRACE CADGE LEASH NEXUS POINT THRAP THROW TRICE TRUSS ATTACH BUNDLE CONNEX COPULA COUPLE FASTEN LIGATE SECURE DOGFALL FOULARD JAZZBOW NECKTIE SHACKLE SLEEPER SPANCEL TABLEAU CROSSTIE DEADLOCK

INTERTIE LIGATURE STANDOFF STRINGER VINCULUM

(— BENEATH) SUBNECT

(— IN TENNIS) DEUCE

(— IN WRESTLING) DOGFALL

(— KNOT) CAST

(— LEGS) HOBBLE

(— ONIONS) TRACE

(— SCORE) PEELS

(— THE SCORE) EQUALIZE

(— TOGETHER) KNIT LEASH CONNECT HARNESS

(— UP) SNUB TRAMMEL LIGATURE TWITCHEL

(— UP SHORT) SNUB

(LEATHER —) WANTY

(MADE-UP —) TECK

(NEEDLEWORK —) BRIDE

(STRING —) BOLO

(PL.) GILLIES

TIE BEAM BALK BAULK BINDER

TIED EVEN FAST KNIT EVENED SQUARE

TIEPIN PROP SCARFPIN STICKPIN

TIE PLATE TURTLE

TIER ROW BANK DECK RANK CHESS STORY WITHE DEGREE PINAFORE

(— OF CASKS) RIDER

(— OF GUNS) TIRE

(— OF SEATS) CIRCLE

(— OF SHELVES) STAGE

TIERCE LEASH THIRD UNDERSONG

TIFF MIFF SPAT TIFT

TIFFIN CONDOR

TIGER SHER SHIR TIGRE TIGERKIN

(PREF.) TIGRO

TIGER CAT CHATI MARGAY

TIGERFOOT IPOMOEA

TIGER SHARK DEMOISELLE

TIGER SNAKE ELAPID ELAPOID

TIGHT WET FULL HARD NEAR PANG SNUG TAUT TIDY TRIG CLOSE DENSE DRUNK STENT TENSE STINGY STRAIT STRICT AIRTIGHT

TIGHTEN JAM CALK FIRM FRAP BRACE CAULK CINCH CLOSE FEEZE SCREW THRAP WRENCH STRAITEN

(— WITH ROPE) SWIFT

TIGHTFISTED NARROW STINGY

TIGHT-LIPPED SILENT

TIGHTLY FAST HARD SHORT STRAIT CLOSELY

TIGHTS MAILLOT LEOTARDS

TIGHTWAD FIST MISER PIKER STIFF

TIKVAH (SON OF —) SHALLUM JAHAZIAH

TILDE TIL WAVE TITTLE

(HAVING A —) CURLY

TILE LUMP SLAT FAVUS KASHI LATER SLATE IMBREX LAPPET PAMENT QUARRY SLATER TEGULA AZULEJO CARREAU CONDUIT PANTILE QUARREL STARTER MAINTILE

(— IN HOPSCOTCH) PEEVER

(— USED IN MOSAIC) ABACULUS

(HEXAGONAL —) FAVUS

(HOLLOW —) BACKING

(HOPSCOTCH —) PEEVER

(LARGE —) DALLE QUARL QUARLE

(MAH JONG —) HONOR SEASON

(ONE-HALF —) HEAD

(PERSIAN —) KASHI

(ROUNDED —) CREASE

(SMALL —) TILETTE

(SQUARE —) QUADREL QUARREL

(TURKISH —) IZNIK

(PREF.) OSTRAC(O) PLINTHI

TILER HELER HELLIER

TILL TO EAR FIT LOB CASH FARM PLOW TEAL TOIL DRESS LABOR UNTIL WHILE FURROW MANURE PLOUGH TILLER WHILST HUSBAND SHUTTLE DUCKFOOT OXHARROW

TILLABLE EARABLE

TILLAGE GAINOR MANURE ARATION CULTURE TILTURE

TILLED GEOM TOILED

TILLER HELM STERN STOOL HUSBAND KILLIFER

TILLING EARTH FALLOW

TILON (FATHER OF —) SHIMON

TILT DIP TIP TOP BANK CANT CAVE COCK HEEL LIST PEAK SWAG TRAP BRASH HEELD HIELD JOUST STOOP TIPUP CASTER TILTER TOPPLE CURRENT TOURNEY ATTITUDE COCKBILL QUINTAIN

(— BRICK) HACK

(— IN WATER) DABBLE

(— OF BOWSPRIT) STAVE

(— OF NOSE) KIP KIPP

TILTED ACOCK ASTOOP

TILT HAMMER OLIVER

TILTING DIP JOUSTING

TIMANDRA (FATHER OF —) TYNDAREUS

(HUSBAND OF —) ECHEMUS PHYLEUS

(MOTHER OF —) LEDA

(SISTER OF —) HELEN CLYTEMNESTRA

TIMBAL DRUM TYMBALON

TIMBER CAP LOG RIB BEAM BIBB BUNK BUNT CLOG DRAM FELL FISH FROG GIRT PUMP RAFF SKID SPAR SPUR TREE WOOD CAHUY CAVEL CRUCK FLOOR GRIPE JOIST KEVEL LEDGE ORGUE PLATE RIDER SISSU SPALE STICK BEARER BRIDGE BUMPER CAMBER CORBEL DAGGER FENDER FOREST KNIGHT LIZARD ROOFER SISSOO SUMMER TIMMER BOLSTER CARLING DEADMAN DIVIDER FALLAGE FUTCHEL FUTTOCK GROUSER PARTNER PITWOOD RIBBAND TRANSOM CORDWOOD COULISSE DOGSHORE FOREHOOK STRINGER STUMPAGE TRIPSILL WOODFALL

(— BETWEEN TRIMMERS) HEADER

(— CUT TO LENGTH) JUGGLE

(— IN MINE) COG STULL LIFTER DIVIDER JUGGLER

(— KEPT DRY) BRIGHT

(— ON SCAFFOLD) LIGGER PUTLOG

(— ON SLED) BUNK

(— PIECE) PUTLOG

(— SAWED AND SPLIT) LUMBER

(— SUPPORTING CAP) LEGPIECE

(— SUSTAINING YARDS) MAST

(— TO PROP COAL) BROB

(CONVEX —) CAMBER

(CURVED —) CRUCK

(CUT —) FELL

(FELLED —) HAG

(FLOOR —) JOIST SUMMER

(FLOORING —) BATTEN
(FOUNDATION —) PILE
(FRAMING —) PUNCHEON
(HORIZONTAL —) REASON
(NORWEGIAN —) DRAM
(PHILIPPINE —) LAUAN
(PRINCIPAL — OF VESSEL) KEEL
(ROOF —) LEVER RAFTER
(ROOFING —S) SILE
(SHIP'S —) CANT KEEL KNEE RUNG
SPUR APRON LEDGE WRONG
DAGGER HARPIN LACING SCROLL
BRACKET FUTTOCK STEMSON
DOGSHORE STANDARD
(SHIPBUILDING —S) STOCKS
DEADWOOD HARPINGS
(CLADDED) CANT
(SQUARED —) BALK
(SUPPORT —) SILL GIRDER LEDGER
PUNCHEON STRINGER
(SYSTEM OF —S) BOND
(UNCUT —) STUMPAGE
(WEATHERBEATEN —) DRIKI
TIMBERLAND STICKS WOODLAND
TIMBERMAN BRACER
TIMBO CUBE AJARI
TIMBRE TONE CLANG COLOR KLANG
COLORING
TIMBREL TABOR TABOUR
TIME DAY ELD BELL BOUT HINT
HOUR SELF SITH TIDE WHET
ABYSS CHARE EPOCH FLASH FRIST
KALPA SITHE SPACE STOUN STOUR
TEMPO TEMPS VOLTA WHACK
WHILE COURSE KAIROS PERIOD
SEASON STOUND TEMPUS
CADENCE DEWFALL SESSION
MOVEMENT
(— AFTER) POST
(— ALLOWED FOR PAYMENT)
USANCE
(— AND — AGAIN) OFTEN
(— BEFORE WITHDRAWAL) FLOAT
(— BEING) NONCE
(— FOR PAYING) KIST
(— FOR PAYMENT) CREDIT
(— GRANTED) FRIST
(— HENCE) MORROW
(— IN GRAMMAR) TENSE
(— IN SERVICE) AGE
(— INTERVAL) WINDOW
(— INTERVENING) INTERIM
MEANTIME
(— IN THE PAST) LANGSYNE
(— LONG SINCE PAST) YORE
(— OF BEAUTY) BLOOM
(— OF BEGINNING) SPRING
(— OF CRISIS) EXIGENT
(— OF CURRENCY) TENOR
(— OF DYING) LAST
(— OF ELEVENTH ZONE) SAMOA
(— OF EXPIRY) ISH
(— OF EXUBERANCE) CARNIVAL
(— OF FASTING) LENT
(— OF FEASTING) GUTTIDE
(— OF HAPPINESS) CAMELOT
(— OF HIGHEST STRENGTH)
HEYDAY
(— OF INACTIVITY) INTERIM
NONTERM
(— OF LIGHT) DAY
(— OF MATURITY OR DECLINE)
AUTUMN

(— OF MAXIMUM USE) PEAK
(— OF NEWS STORY) BREAK
(— OF OLD AGE) SUNSET
(— OF QUIET) DEAD
(— OF REST) BREATH SABBATH
(— OF TRIAL) PROBATION
(— OF WOE) WOSITH
(— TO COME) FUTURITY
(ANOTHER —) AGAIN
(AT ANOTHER —) ALIAS
(BRIEF —) TINE FLASH THROW
(BY THE —) AGAINST
(CRITICAL —) PINCH
(EACH —) ONCE
(ENDLESS —) PERPETUITY
(EXTENDED —) TRAIN
(FAST) LENT
(FIT —) TID
(FIXED —) HOUR STEVEN
(FUTURE —) MANANA
(GAY —) FRISK WHOOPEE
(GOOD —) BALL BASH BEANO
JOLLY BARNEY FROLIC HOLIDAY
(HARD —) GYP BUSINESS
(IMMEASURABLY LONG PERIOD OF
—) EON AEON
(INFINITE —) ABYSS
(INTERVENING —) MEANTIME
MEANWHILE
(KIND OF) PRIME
(LONG —) AGE YEARS
(MUSICAL —) METER METRE
(OLD —S) ELD
(OPPORTUNE —) SEAL SEEL SEIL
SELE
(PAST —) FORETIME
(POINT OF —) MOMENT
(PRESCRIBED —) LIMIT
(QUIET —) SLACK
(RIGHT —) TID
(SECOND —) YET EFTSOON
EFTSOONS
(SET —) TRYST
(SHORT —) TIFF SPACE START
MINUTE STOUND
(SINGLE —) ONCE
(SPARE —) TOOM LEISURE
(SPECIAL —) OCCASION
(STRICT —) MEASURE
(TRIPLE —) TRIPLA
(UNENGAGED —) LEISURE
(UNIT OF —) AEON
(WORKING —) CORE
(PL.) SYSE
(PREF.) CHRON(O) HORO
(SUFF.) AD CHRONE CHRONOUS
SEMIC
TIMEAUS (SON OF —) BARTIMAEUS
TIME CLOCK BUNDY TELLTALE
TIME-HONORED VINTAGE
TIMELESS AGELESS ETERNAL
DATELESS ATEMPORAL
TIMELESSNESS ETERNITY
TIMELY PAT DULY TIDY COGENT
TIMEFUL TIMEOUS TOWARDLY
SEASONABLE TEMPESTIVE
TIME OF YOUR LIFE (AUTHOR OF
—) SAROYAN
(CHARACTER IN —) JOE TOM NICK
KITTY MCCARTHY
TIMEPIECE DIAL CLOCK TIMER
VERGE WATCH GHURRY PENDULE
HOROLOGE HOROLOGY

TIMETABLE BRADSHAW SCHEDULE
TIME-WORN RUSTY
TIMID SHY ARGH EERY NESH SELY
SHAN BAUCH BLATE EERIE FAINT
PAVID SCARE SCARY AFRAID
COWARD ASHAMED BASHFUL
CHICKEN FEARFUL FRIGHTY
NEBBISH NERVOUS RABBITY
SCADDLE STRANGE TREMBLY
COWARDLY FEARSOME GHASTFUL
RETIRING TIMOROSO TIMOROUS
PIGEONHEARTED
TIMIDITY SHYNESS TIMERITY
FUNKINESS
TIMIDLY SMALL
TIMNA (BROTHER OF —) LOTAN
(LOVER OF —) ELIPHAZ
(SON OF —) AMALEK
TIMOLEON (FATHER OF —)
TIMODEMUS
(MOTHER OF —) DEMARISTE
TIMON OF ATHENS (AUTHOR OF
—) SHAKESPEARE
(CHARACTER IN —) CUPID TIMON
TITUS CAPHIS LUCIUS FLAVIUS
PHRYNIA LUCILIUS LUCULLUS
PHILOTUS TIMANDRA APEMANTUS
FLAMINIUS SERVILIUS VENTIDIUS
ALCIBIADES HORTENSIUS
SEMPRONIUS
TIMOR (CAPITAL OF —) DILI
(COIN OF —) AVO PATACA
(ISLAND OF —) MOA LETI LAKOR
(LANGUAGE OF —) TETUM
(TOWN IN —) KUPANG ATAMBUA
TIMOROUS ASPEN FAINT MILKY
TIMID AFRAID COWISH TREPID
FEARFUL FERDFUL MEACOCK
NERVOUS FEARSOME SHEEPISH
TEMEROUS TIMOROSO
TIMOTHY (COMPANION OF —) PAUL
(WIFE OF —) SIF
TIN SN DIXY JOVE DIXIE KATIN
SWELL TINNY KHATIN JUPITER
PILLION STANNUM PRILLION
TINGLASS
(MESS —) DIXY DIXIE
(RELATED TO —) STANNIC
(ROOFING —) TERNE
(SHEET —) LATTEN LATTIN
(TIE — CAN TO TAIL) TAILPIPE
(PREF.) STANN(I)(O)
TINAMOU YUTU MACUCA YNAMBU
TATAUPA MARTINET
TINCAL ALTINCAR
TINCTURE BUFO DRUG COLOR
IMBUE SMACK STAIN TAINT TENNE
TINCT ARGENT ARNICA ELIXIR
SATURN DIAMOND SERICON
ARAMAIZE INFUSION LAUDANUM
TAINTURE PAREGORIC
TINDER SPUNK AMADOU TENDRE
FIREBOX
TINE BAY KNAG SNAG TANG GRAIN
OFFER POINT PRONG RIGHT
TOOTH GRAINING TINETARE
TINEWEED
(ANTLER'S —) RIGHT CROCKET
SURROYAL
TIN FOIL TAIN
TINGE DYE EYE HUE CAST DASH
HINT TANG TINT WOAD COLOR
FLUSH IMBUE PAINT SAVOR

SHADE STAIN TAINT TINCT TOUCH
SEASON SMUTCH BEPAINT
DISTAIN GLIMPSE DISCOLOR
TINCTION TINCTURE
TINGED FLORID GILDED
TINGGIAN ITNEG ITANEG
TINGLE SOO BURN DIRL GELL GIRL
THIRL DINDLE SWIDGE TINKLE
PRINGLE PRINKLE TRINKLE
VIBRATE
TINGLY AGOG
TING YAO PORCELAIN
TINHORN ARTY
TINKER PRIG TINK CAIRD FIDDLE
FIDGET MUGGER KETTLER
PROJECT TRAVELER
TINKLE TINK DINDLE DINGLE TINGLE
TRINKLE TWINKLE
TINKLING THIN
TINNER TINKER
TINSEL GAUDY TINSY TINNET
CLINQUANT
TINT DYE EYE COLOR ENNUE GRAIN
SHADE TINCT TINGE SPRAING
(— IN HORSE'S COAT) BLOSSOM
(— WITH COSMETICS) SURFLE
(CLANG —) TIMBRE
TINTED TINCT
TINWORKS STANNARY
TINY TINE BITSY BITTY DEENY
SMALL TEENY TIDDY WEENY
ATOMIC BITTIE WEESHY MINIKIN
ATOMICAL
TIP CAP DIP END FEE NEB TOP APEX
CANT CAVE COCK DUMP HEEL
HELD HORN KEEL LEAD LIST PALM
PIKE PILE SWAG TILT TYPE VAIL
GRIFF HEELD MUCRO POINT
POUCH SPIRE SPURE STEER
CAREEN CENTER CENTRE TICKLE
TIPLET TIPPLE TOPPLE WHEEZE
APICULA CUMSHAW DERTRUM
DOUCEUR GRIFFIN POINTER
PROPINE WRINKLE APICULUS
BONAMANO ENTOMION
FOOTHOLD GRATUITY BAKSHEESH
BACKSHEESH PERQUISITE
(— AT A CASINO) TOKE
(— OF ANTENNA) ARISTA
(— OF BILLIARD CUE) LEATHER
(— OF BIRD'S BILL) DERTRUM
(— OF CHIN) POINT
(— OF CRESCENT) HORN
(— OF ELBOW) NOOP
(— OF FOX'S BRUSH) CHAPE
(— OF SKI) SHOVEL
(— OF SPIDER) BULB
(— OF STAMP) SHOE
(— OF TAIL) TAG
(— OF TOE) POINTE
(— OF TONGUE) CORONA
(— OF UMBO) BEAK
(— OF WHEAT KERNEL) BRUSH
(— OF WHIP) SNAPPER
(— ON ORGAN PIPE) TOE
(— OVER) TOP PURL UPEND
OVERSET
(— UP) CANT COUP COWP
(ABRUPT —) MUCRO
(BOW —) HORN
(GAMBLING —) TOKE
(INWARD —) BANK
(LARGE —S) LARGESS LARGESSE

(RACING —) NAP
(RUBBISH —) TOOM
(PREF.) ACR(O) APIC(O)
TIPCART COUPE COCOPAN TUMBREL
TIPCAT CAT PIGGY PUSSY KITCAT PIGGIE
TIPPED BANKED
(EASILY —) CRANK
TIPPER DUMPER THROWER TIPPLER
TIPPET FUR AMICE SCARF STOLE ALMUCE SINDON LIRIPIPE LIRIPOOP PELERINE VICTORINE
TIPPLE BIB NIP POT SOT DRAM GILL BIBBER BIBBLE FUDDLE PUDDLE SIPPLE TIPPLER TOOTHFUL
TIPPLER SOT SOUSE TOAST WINER BIBBER BOLLER BOOZER BUBBER DRAMMER PANURGE POTATOR TUMBLER WHETTER ALESTAKE MALTWORM
TIPPLING POTTING BIBACITY BIBATION
TIPSTER TOUT PROPHET
TIPSY CUT BOSKY DRUNK FRESH MUSED MUZZY NAPPY OILED ROCKY SLUED TIGHT TOTTY TOZIE BUMPSY GROGGY SCREWY SLEWED SPRUNG SQUIFF EBRIOSE EBRIOUS EXALTED SQUIFFY ELEVATED MUCKIBUS OVERSEEN PLEASANT SQUIFFED
TIPTOE CREEP
TIP-TOP SWELL TIPPY REGULAR TOPPING
TIRADE LAISSE SCREED STOUSH JEREMIAD INVECTIVE PHILIPPIC
TIRAS (FATHER OF —) JAPHETH
TIRE DO FAG HAG LAG SAG BORE CORD FLAT FLOG JADE KILL MOIL SHOE LABOR SPARE WEARY CASING HAGGLE HARASS SICKEN TIRING TUCKER BALLOON EXHAUST FATIGUE FRAZZLE TRACHLE WEAROUT CLINCHER FORSPEND
(— OUT) HAG FLOG THEAD BEJADE HARASS OVERWEARY
(BURST —) FLAT BLOWOUT
(KIND OF —) SNOW RADIAL
(SMOOTH —) SLICK
(USED —) REMOULD RETREAD
(WORN —) CARCASS
TIRED SAD TAM BEAT BOEG DEAD TIRY BLOWN WEARY AWEARY BLEARY BUSHED PLAYED POOPED TAVERT FORWORN SHAGGED TAIVERT FATIGATE FORWAKED
TIREDNESS FATIGUE
TIRESIAS (FATHER OF —) EVERES
(MOTHER OF —) CHARICLO
TIRESOME DRY DREE FAGGY ALANGE BORING DREICH PROLIX IRKSOME PROSAIC TEDIOUS BORESOME BROMIDIC ENNUYANT LONGSOME
(BECOME —) CLOY WEAR
TIRHANAH (FATHER OF —) CALEB
(MOTHER OF —) MAACHAH
TIRIA (FATHER OF —) JEHALELEEL
TIRING DRUDGING
TIRL RISP
TIRO TYRO NEOPHYTE

TIRTHANKARA JINA
TIRZAH (FATHER OF —) ZELOPHEHAD
TISAMENUS (FATHER OF —) ORESTES THERSANDER
(MOTHER OF —) HERMIONE
TISANE PTISAN TILLEUL
TISSUE FAT WEB CORK FOIL PITH TELA TEXT FACIA GLEBA GRAFT SUBER TRAMA CALLUS DARTOS DIPLOE FABRIC FASCIA LIGNUM PANNUS PHLOEM SHEATH TEXTUS ADENOID ALBUMEN BINDWEB CAMBIUM CLYPEUS EPITELA EXPLANT HYDROME KLEENEX MESTOME NEURINE PHLOEUM TEXTURE TWITTER ADHESION BLASTEMA DESMOGEN ECTODERM ENDODERM EPIPLOON HISTOGEN HYPODERM ISOGRAFT MERISTEM OSTEOGEN PERIDERM PERIDESM POLYPARY STEREOME
(— IN PLANT) STEREOME
(— IN SEED) PERISPERM
(— OF FUNGUS) CENTRUM
(— OF SILK) SARSNET SARCENET SARSENET
(— OF SKULL) DIPLOE
(— SURROUNDING TEETH) GUM
(ADIPOSE —) FATDEPOT
(BLACK —) CLYPEUS
(BOTANICAL —) TRACE
(CELL —) CORK
(CONNECTING —) WEB STROMA TENDON LIGAMENT MESENCHYME
(CORK —) SUBER
(DEAD —) SLOUGH
(FATTY —) LARD GREASE
(HARD —) BONE
(HYPOTHETICAL —) COAGULIN
(LYMPHOID —) TONSIL
(NERVE —) GANGLION
(SOFT —) FLAB
(VEGETABLE —) ARMOR
(WOOD —) LIGNUM VITRAIN
(PL.) CHIRATA CHIRETTA MESODERM
(PREF.) FASCIO HIST(I)(IO)(O) HIST(O) HYPHO
(FATTY —) ADIP(O)
(FIBROUS —) FIBR(I)(ILLI)(INO)(O) (OSO) IN(O)
TISWIN TESVINO TEXGUINO
TIT TID MESIA TITTY BLUECAP COLETIT MUFFLIN PINNOCK
TITAN DANA LETO MAIA ASURA ATLAS COEUS CREUS CRIOS DIONE THEIA CRONOS CRONUS PALLAS PHOEBE TETHYS THEMIS IAPETUS OCEANUS HYPERION
(AUTHOR OF —) DREISER
(CHARACTER IN —) FRANK PETER AILEEN BUTLER PLATOW FLEMING BERENICE LAUGHLIN STEPHANIE COWPERWOOD
TITANESS TETHYS
TITANIA (HUSBAND OF —) OBERON
TITANIC HUGE GREAT TITAN IMMENSE COLOSSAL GIGANTIC
TITANITE SPHENE GROTHITE LEDERITE LIGURITE
TITANIUM DIOXIDE ANATASE
TITA ROOT MISHMI MISHMEE

TITHE DIME DISME TEIND TENTH DECIMA PREBEND TITHING
TITHING BORGH BORROW DECIME DENARY DECENARY
TITHINGMAN DEAN DECURION TUTTIMAN
TITHONUS (FATHER OF —) LAOMEDON
(MOTHER OF —) STRYMO
TITI ORA TEETEE WISTIT SAIMIRI WISTITI IRONWOOD MARMOSET ORABASSU OUISTITI
TITILLATE AMUSE KITTLE TICKLE
TITILLATING GAMY SEXY GAMEY
TITIVATE PRIMP
TITLARK PIPIT TEETING
TITLE (ALSO SEE LEADER, CHIEF, GOVERNOR, RULER) AGA AYA BAN BEG BEY DAN DOM DUE FRA JAM LAR MIR PAN SAG SIR ABBA ABBE AGHA AMIR ANBA BABU DAME DEVI EMIR FRAY GAON GRAF HAJI HERR KHAN KNEZ LARS NAME PANI SIDI SLUG ABGAR ABUNA AMEER BABOO BEGUM CCOYA CLAIM CROWN EMEER FRATE GHAZI GOODY GRACE HADJI HAJJI HAKAM HANUM HONOR KNIAZ KNYAZ LEMMA MIRZA MPRET NAWAB NEGUS NIZAM PANNA PASHA RABBI RIGHT SINGH SOPHI SOPHY THANE UNWAN BASHAW BEGANI COUSIN DEGREE DEMAND DESPOT DOMINE EPONYM EXARCH HANDLE HUZOOR LEGEND MADAME MASTER MEHTAR MISTER PESHWA PREFIX SHERIF SQUIRE SUFFEE TITULE VIDAME ALFEREZ ALTESSE ALTEZZA BAHADUR BARONET CANDACE CAPTION CONVITO CRAWLER DIGNITY EFFENDI EPITHET ESQUIRE FIDALGO GAEKWAR GRAVITY HEADING HIDALGO INFANTE KHEDIVE MAHARAO MESSIRE RABBONI SHAREEF TITULUS VOIVODE BANNERET BASILEUS COMMENDA CONVIVIO EMINENCE GOSPODIN HIGHNESS HOLINESS HOSPODAR INTEREST LOKINDRA MAGISTER MAHARAJA MAHARANA MAHARSHI MISTRESS MONSIEUR PADISHAH PRINCIPE RAUGRAVE SUBTITLE TAMBURAN TITULADO
(— ACQUISITION) USUCAPT
(— HOLDER) OWNER
(— OF BOOK) QUARE
(— OF MEMBER OF PRIMROSE LEAGUE) KNIGHT
(— OF RESPECT) SIR SRI COJA LIEF MIAN SHRI SIDI BURRA HODJA KHAJA KHOJA MADAM SAHIB SIEUR KHOJAH MADAME MILADY
(BENEDICTINE —) DOM
(MOCK —) IDLESHIP
TITMOUSE MAG NUN TIT MAGG OXEYE PARUS SPICK FUFFIT HEFFEL PUFFER TOMTIT VERDIN BLUECAP BUSHTIT COLETIT COLMOSE GOLDTIT GRIGNET HAGMALL JACKSAW MUFFLIN PINCHEM PINNOCK TINNOCK TITMALL TOMNOUP CHICADEE

HACKMALL OVENBIRD REEDLING SHABROON SHARPSAW
TITTER GIGGLE CHORTLE SNICKER TWITTER WHICKER
TITTLE DOT JOT IOTA TITLE MINUTE
TITUBATE REEL STAGGER
TITULAR LEGAL NOMINAL HONORARY
TITUS ANDRONICUS (AUTHOR OF —) SHAKESPEARE
(CHARACTER IN —) AARON CAIUS TITUS CHIRON LUCIUS MARCUS MUTIUS TAMORA ALARBUS LAVINIA MARTIUS PUBLIUS QUINTUS AEMILIUS BASSIANUS DEMETRIUS VALENTINE SATURNINUS SEMPRONIUS
TITYUS (FATHER OF —) TERRA JUPITER
(MOTHER OF —) ELARA
TIU ER EAR TIW TYR ZIO ZIU TIWAZ SAXNOT
TIV MUNCHI
TIZZY FLAP SNIT STEW PUCKER SWIVET SWIVVET
TLAKLUIT ECHE LOOT WISHRAM
TLEPOLEMUS (FATHER OF —) HERCULES
(MOTHER OF —) ASTYOCHIA
(SLAYER OF —) SARPEDON
TLINGIT SITKA KOLUSH SUMDUM CHILCAT CHILKAT STIKINE
TMESIS DIACOPE
TNT TROTYL
TO A AD FOR INTO TILL UNTO UPON
(— A CONCLUSION) OUT
(— BE) IBE
(— BE SURE) EVEN
(— COME) BEHIND
(— COMPLETION) DOWN
(— IT) TOOT SESSA
(— PRESS) DOWN
(— SUCH DEGREE) EVEN
(— THAT TIME) UNTIL
(— THE END) AF
(— THE OPPOSITE SIDE) ACROSS
(— THE REAR) ABAFT ASTERN
(— THIS) HERETO
(— THIS PLACE) HERE HITHER
(— VICTORY) ABU ABOO
(— WHAT) WHERETO
(— WIT) NAMELY INNUENDO SCILICET
(PREF.) AC AD AF AG AL AP AS AT INTRO OB
TOAD PAD AGUA BUFO FROG HYLA PIPA PODE HYLID PADDO PADDY PIPAL PIPID TOADY ANURAN CRAPON PEEPER BUFONID CHARLIE CRAPAUD CRAWLER CREEPER FROGLET GANGREL HOPTOAD PADDOCK PODDOCK PUDDOCK QUILKIN REPTILE SERPENT GANGEREL
(PREF.) BATRACHI(O) PHRYN(O)
(SUFF.) BATRACH(O)(US)
TOADFISH SAPO SARPO GRUBBY SLIMER CABEZON FROGFISH LORICATE SCORPION
TOADFLAX FLAX FLAXWEED FLAXWORT FLUELLEN GALLWEED GALLWORT RAMSTEAD
TOAD RUSH SALTWEED

TOADSTONE BUFONITE
TOADSTOOL CANKER FUNGUS
TOADY FAWN SUCK TOAD ZANY
  COTTON EARWIG FAWNER FLUNKY
  GREASE HEELER LACKEY MUCKER
  YESMAN FLUNKEY JENKINS
  LACQUEY PLACEBO SHONEEN
  TRUCKLE BOOTLICK CLAWBACK
  LICKSPIT PARASITE SYCOPHANT
TOADYING GNATHONIC
TOADYISM FLUNKYISM
TOAST WET TOSS BREDE PROST
  ROUSE SANTE SKOAL TRINQ
  BIRSLE BUMPER CHEERS HEALTH
  PLEDGE PROSIT BRISTLE CAROUSE
  CHEERIO FRIZZLE LEHAYIM
  PROFACE PROPINE RESPECT
  SLAINTE WASSAIL BRINDISI
  SCOUTHER
  (— AND ALE) SWIG
  (— ONESELF) LEEP
  (— TO HEALTH) PROSIT
  (DISH WITH —) RAREBIT
  (JACOBITE —) LIMP
TOBACCO CANE CAPA HAND LEAF
  LUGS NAVY POAK POKE QUID ROLL
  SHAG WEED DACCO DACCY DACKY
  BROKE CUBAN DARKS FOGUS
  PETUN REGIE SMOKE SNOUT
  TABAC TWIST BACKER BRIGHT
  BURLEY COLORY COWPEN FILLER
  HAVANA RETURN TOMBAC
  TUMBAK CAPORAL CRACCUS
  GAGROOT GORACCO KNASTER
  LATAKIA NAILROD NICOTIA
  ORONOKO PERIQUE PIGTAIL
  SOTWEED UPPOWOC CANASTER
  HONEYDEW MAKHORKA
  MARYLAND NICOTIAN ORONOOKO
  SEEDLEAF VIRGINIA MUNDUNGUS
  NICOTIANA
  (— AND PAPER) MAKINGS
  (— CAKED IN PIPE BOWL) DOTTEL
  DOTTLE TOPPER
  (— HAVING OFFENSIVE SMELL)
  MUNDUNGO
  (— IN ROPES) BOGIE
  (— JUICE) AMBEER PRAISS
  (— MOISTENED WITH MOLASSES)
  HONEYDEW
  (— MOSAIC) WALLOON
  (— PASTE) GORACCO
  (— ROOM) PRIZERY
  (— WORKER) LOOPER LEAFBOY
  LEAFGIRL
  (CAKED —) HEEL
  (COARSE —) SHAG SCRAP CAPORAL
  (CUT —) CANASTER PICADURA
  (DRIED —) TABACUM
  (HARD-PRESSED —) NAILROD
  (HATING —) MISOCAPNIC
  (INDIAN —) GAGROOT PUKEWEED
  EYEBRIGHT
  (INFERIOR —) LUGS
  (LADIES' —) CUDWEED
  (LOWER LEAVES OF —) FLYING
  (MILD —) RETURN
  (PERSIAN —) SHIRAZ TUMBEK
  TUMBEKI
  (PERUVIAN —) SANA
  (POOR QUALITY —) DOGLEG
  (PULVERIZED —) SNUFF
  (QUID OF —) CUD

  (RAW —) LEAF
  (ROLLED —) CARROT
  (SMALL PIECE OF —) FIG
  (VIRGINIA —) COWPEN VIRGINIA
TOBACCO BROWN TABAC
TOBACCO ROAD (AUTHOR OF —)
  CALDWELL
  (CHARACTER IN —) ADA LOV DUDE
  RICE ELLIE PEARL BENSEY BESSIE
  JEETER LESTER
TOBACCO WORM HORNWORM
TOBOGGAN COAST CARIOLE
  CARRIOLE
TOCHARIAN A AGNEAN
TOCHARIAN B KUCHEAN
TOCSIN ALARUM
TODAY DAY NOW HEUTE
  NOWADAYS
TODDLE TOT FADGE DADDLE
  DIDDLE DODDLE PADDLE TOTTLE
  WADDLE
TODDLER TROT TYKE GANGREL
  TROTTIE
TODDY TOD TUBA TERRY SAGWIRE
TO-DO FUROR HOOHA SCENE
  BROUHAHA HULLABALOO ADO
  FUSS STIR WORK STINK DOMENT
  HOOPLA FLUSTER FOOSTER
  FOOFARAW TRAVALLY
TODY ROBIN
TOE TEN DIGIT DACTYL HALLUX
  PIGGIE MINIMUS TOENAIL TRIPPET
  POULAINE
  (— OF BIRD) HEEL
  (LITTLE —) MINIMUS
  (RUDIMENTARY —) DEWCLAW
  (PL.) TUN TAIS TOON
  (PREF.) DACTYL(O) DACTYLIO
  DIGITI DIGITO
TOENAIL
  (SUFF.) ONYCHA ONYCHES
  ONYCHIA ONYCHIUM ONYCHUS
  ONYX
TOEPLATE SHOD
TOFF NOB GENT
TOFFEE TAFFY HARDBAKE
  BUTTERSCOTCH
TOGA GOWN ROBE TOGUE TRABEA
TOGETHER ONCE SAME ATONE
  YFERE BEDENE INSAME JOINTLY
  ENSEMBLE
  (— WITH) AND INTO
  (PREF.) CO COL COM CON COR
  SYM SYN
TOGGERY DUDS
TOGGLE COTTAR COTTER TOGGEL
  NETSUKE
TOGO (CAPITAL OF —) LOME
  (LANGUAGE OF —) EWE TWI MINA
  HAUSA KABRAIS LOTOCOLI
  (MOUNTAIN IN —) AGOU
  (NATIVE OF —) EWE MINA CABRAI
  KABRAI OUATCHI
  (RIVER IN —) OTI ANIE HAHO MONO
  (TOWN IN —) KANDE ANECHO
  PALIME SOKODE TSEVIE ATAKPAME
TOHUBOHU RIOT CHAOS
  DISORDER CONFUSION
TOI (SON OF —) JORAM
TOIL FAG TUG DARG GRUB HACK
  MOIL MUCK PLOD TASK WORK
  LABOR SCRAT SLAVE SWINK TWEIL
  YAKKA BILDER DRUDGE EFFORT

  HAMMER KIAUGH MITHER MOIDER
  STRIVE UNRUFE YACKER FATIGUE
  TRAVAIL TURMOIL DRUDGERY
  INDUSTRY
TOILER PROLE SLAVE MOILER
  WORKER
TOILET BOG CAN LOO HEAD JOHN
  BIFFY DUNNY PRIVY CRAPPER
  BASEMENT BATHROOM DONNIKER
  LAVATORY PLUMBING DONNICKER
TOILING WORKADAY
TOILSOME HARD SWEATY
  ARDUOUS TOILFUL MOILSOME
  SWEATFUL
TOJOLABAL CHANABAL
TOKAY TUCKTOO
TOKEN BUCK CENT HARP SIGN TYPE
  BADGE CHECK INDEX SCRIP
  BEAVER CASTOR COLLAR COPPER
  COUPON DOLLAR EMBLEM
  JETTON MARKER OSTENT REMARK
  SIGNAL TICKET WITTER AUSPICE
  COUNTER EARNEST INDICIA
  MEMENTO PRESAGE SYMPTOM
  TESSERA BUNGTOWN COINTISE
  EVIDENCE FOOTSTEP FORBYSEN
  INSTANCE KEEPSAKE MONUMENT
  SHILLING SIGNACLE
  (— OF A COVENANT) SACRAMENT
  (— OF LUCK) HANSEL HANDSEL
  (— OF POSSESSION) SEISIN
  (— OF RESPECT) SALUTE
  (— OF SUPERIORITY) PALM
  (— OF VICTORY) LAUREL
  (CANADIAN —) HARP
  (CONFIRMING —) SEAL
  (LOVE —) DRURY AMORET
  (PORCELAIN —S) PI
  (WARNING —) MONUMENT
  (PL.) EXONUMIA
TOKHARI KUCHEAN
TOK PISIN CREOLE
TOKYO (— STREET) GINZA
  (FORMER NAME OF —) EDO YEDO
TOLA (FATHER OF —) ISSACHAR
TOLD (— PRIVATELY) AURICULAR
TOLERABLE GAY SOSO PRETTY
  TARBLE LIVABLE PATIBLE
  BEARABLE PASSABLE PORTABLE
TOLERABLY GAIN GEYAN FAIRLY
  MEETLY MEETERLY MIDDLING
TOLERANCE MERCY SHERE
  LEEWAY REMEDY
TOLERANT SOFT BROAD BENIGN
  PATIENT PLACABLE PERMISSIVE
TOLERATE GO BEAR BIDE HACK
  HAVE ABEAR ABIDE ALLOW
  BROOK SPARE STAND STICK
  THOLE ACCEPT ENDURE PARDON
  PERMIT SUFFER COMPORT
  STOMACH SUPPORT SUSTAIN
TOLERATION WITHGANG
TOLKIEN (— CREATURE) ENT AROD
TOLL JOW TAX JOWL PIKE RENT
  KNELL PEAGE CAPHAR EXCISE
  OCTROI PEDAGE PESAGE
  BOOMAGE KEELAGE LASTAGE
  LOCKAGE MULTURE PASSAGE
  PICCAGE PIERAGE PONTAGE
  SCAVAGE SUMMAGE TERRAGE
  TOLLAGE TRONAGE BERTHAGE
  STALLAGE WEIGHAGE WHEELAGE

  (PL.) CUSTOMS RAHDARI
  RATTAREE
TOLLHOUSE TOLLERY
TOLLIKER DUMMY
TOLSEN FOOTSTEP
TOLUENE DILUENT
TOLYL CRESYL
TOMAHAWK HATCHET NEOLITH
TOMATO TOM BERRY BURBANK
TOMB PIR BIER CIST MOLE GRAVE
  GUACA HUACA MAZAR SPEOS
  TABUT THOLE TURBE BURIAL
  CHULPA DARGAH DURGAH
  GALGAL HEARSE HEROON
  SAMADH SHRINE SYRINX THOLOS
  TROUGH TURBEH CHULLPA
  MASTABA OSSUARY TOMBLET
  TRITAPH CENOTAPH CISTVAEN
  CUBICULO HALLCIST HYPOGEUM
  KISTVAEN MARABOUT MASTABAH
  MONUMENT TREASURY
  MAUSOLEUM SEPULCHER
  (— IN CHURCH) SACELLUM
  (— OF MOSLEM SAINT) ZIARA
  ZIARAT
  (CAVE —) SPEOS
  (PREHISTORIC —) KURGAN
TOMBAC ORSEDE ORSEDUE
TOMBOY HEMP RAMP GAMINE
  HOYDEN MADCAP TOMRIG
TOMBSTONE SLAT TITLE THROUGH
TOMCAT GIB TOMMY PODGER
  THOMAS
TOMCOD GADE GADID SMELT
  GADOID WHITING TOMMYCOD
TOMENTUM WOOL
TOMFOOLERY HELL HORSE
TOM JONES (AUTHOR OF —)
  FIELDING
  (CHARACTER IN —) TOM BETTY
  JENNY JONES NANCY BLIFIL
  GEORGE SOPHIA SQUARE WATERS
  BRIDGET WESTERN THWACKUM
  ALLWORTHY BELLASTON
  PARTRIDGE FITZPATRICK
  NIGHTINGALE
TOMMY FOOL PODGER REQUIN
TOMMYROT WAHOO BALONEY
TOMMY TALKER KAZOO
TOMORROW MANANA MORROW
  TOMORN
TOM SAWYER (AUTHOR OF —)
  TWAIN CLEMENS
  (CHARACTER IN —) AMY JOE SID
  TOM FINN HUCK MARY MUFF BECKY
  POLLY HARPER POTTER SAWYER
  DOUGLAS LAWRENCE ROBINSON
  THATCHER
TOMTATE CAESAR
TON TUN TOUN STYLE
TONALAMATL TZOLKIN
TONALITY KEY
TONE A F DO FA LA MI RE SI SO TI
  DOH KEY SOH SOL CALL FLAT
  NOTE COLOR COUAC DRONE FIFTH
  FORTE PRIME SHARP SIXTH SOUND
  STYLE TONUS ACCENT DEGREE
  FOURTH SECOND FORMANT
  MEDIANT PARTIAL DEMITINT
  ELEVENTH FORENOTE HARMONIC
  HEADNOTE PARAMESE PARANETE
  SONORITY
  (— A DRAWING) STUMP

(— DOWN) DRAB TAME SOFTEN SUBDUE
(— OF TETRACHORD) TRITE
(— UP) BRACE
(ACCENTED —) SFORZANDO
(BROKEN —) CRACK
(COMPLEX —) KLANG
(DEEP —) BASS
(DOMINANT —) ANIMUS
(DRAWLING —) DRANT DRAUNT
(HIGH-PITCHED —) PIP
(KEY —) KEYNOTE
(KIND OF —) FUZZ
(LOUD —) FORTE
(LOW —) SEMISOUN
(MONOTONOUS —) DRONE
(SHARP NASAL —) TWANG
(SIGNIFICANT —) ACCENT
(SINGLE UNVARIED —) MONOTONE
(STRIDENT —) COUAC
(WHINING —) GIRN
(PREF.) PHON(O)
TONGA (CAPITAL OF —) NUKUALOFA
(COIN OF —) PAANGA SENITI
(ISLAND GROUP OF —) TOFUA VAVAU HAAPAI NIUAFOO TONGATAPU NIUATOBUTABU
(ISLAND OF —) ONO TOFUA VAVAU HAAPAI
(TOWN OF —) NEIAFU
TONGS SNAPS SERVER FORCEPS GRAMPUS TUEIRON SCISSORS
TONGUE COG GAB CHIB CLAP KALI NEAP PAWL POLE REED CLACK IDIOM LADIN VOICE GADABA GLOSSA KABYLE KALIKA LADINO LANGUE LINGUA SPEECH CLAPPER DIALECT FEATHER ILOKANO LANGUET DOVETAIL LANGUAGE LORRIKER PLECTRUM
(— IN FLOORING) SPLINE
(— OF BELL) CLAPPER
(— OF JEW'S-HARP) TANG
(— OF LAND) DOAB REACH LANGUE LANGUET
(— OF MOLLUSC) RASP RADULA
(— OF OXCART) COPE
(— OF SHOE) FLAP KILTY KILTIE
(— OF VEHICLE) NEAP SHAFT
(BELLOWS —) GUSSET
(CELTIC —) BRETON
(GIVE —) PRATE
(GOSSIPING —) CLACK CLACKER
(PART OF —) BUD UVULA FAUCES LINGUA SEPTUM
(PIVOTED —) PAWL
(ROMANY —) ROMANES
(PL.) GAURA
(PREF.) GLOSS(O) GLOTT(I)(O) LIGUL(I) LINGU(I)(LI)(O)
(SUFF.) GLOSSA GLOSSIA GLOT
TONGUEFISH SOLE
TONGUE-LASH SCOLD
TONGUE-LASHING RAT TOCO BUSINESS
TONGUELESS AGLOSSAL
TONGUE-TIED SILENT
TONIC DO DOH ALOE KEEP PICHI PRIME BRACER SAMBUL SONANT SUMBUL BONESET CALAMUS CALOMBO CHIRATA COLOMBA DAMIANA FUMARIA GENTIAN KEYNOTE NERVINE SALICIN

TONICAL ANTHEMIS BARBERRY BERBERRY HELONIAS ROBORANT TRILLIUM PIPSISSEWA
TONICITY MYOTONIA
TONKA BEAN GAIAC CUMARU GUAIAC COUMAROU
TONNA DOLIUM
TONNAGE PORTAGE
TONO-BUNGAY (AUTHOR OF —) WELLS
(CHARACTER IN —) RINK EFFIE FRAPP GROVE MOGGS SUSAN ARCHIE EDWARD GEORGE MANTEL MARION OSPREY GARVELL RAMBOAT BEATRICE NORMANDY NICODEMUS PONDEREVO
TONSIL ALMOND KERNEL ADENOID AMYGDAL AMYGDALA
(PREF.) AMYGDAL(O)
TONSILITIS QUINSY
TONSURE CROWN SHAVE SHEAR CORONA DIKSHA RASURE
TONSURED PEELED PILLED SHAVED
TOO SO ALSO OVER TROP LUCKY OVERLY LIKEWISE
(PREF.) OVER
TOOL (ALSO SEE IMPLEMENT AND INSTRUMENT) AX ADZ AWL AXE BIT BUR DIE DIG GIN GUN HOB HOE KEY LAP LOY RIP SAW SAX TAP TIT VOL ZAX ADZE BORE BRAY BURR CLAW COMB DADO DISC DISK DUPE EDGE FILE FLAY FROE FROG FROW GAGE HACK HAWK HONE LEAF LOOM MAUL MILL PICK RASP ROLL SATE SEAX SLED SNAP SPID SPUD STOP TAMP TIER VISE AUGER BLADE BORAL BORER BRAKE BRAND BREAK BRUSH BURIN CROZE DARBY DOLLY DRIFT DRILL DUMMY EDGER FLAKE FLOAT FLUTE GAUGE GOUGE GUIDE HARDY HOBBY HOWEL KNIFE KNURL LEVEL MAKER MISER MODEL PLANE POINT PRUNT PUNCH QUIRK SABER SABRE SCREW SHAVE SHELL SLICE SLICK SNIPE SPADE SPEAR SPLIT STAKE STAMP STING STOCK STRIG STYLE SWAGE TEWEL TOYLE UPSET VALET WAGON BEADER BEATER BIDENT BIFACE BLADER BODKIN BROACH BUDGER BUFFER CALKER CHASER CHISEL CLEAVE COGGLE COLTER CRADLE CRANNY CUTTER DEVICE DIBBLE DIGGER DOCTOR DRIVER ENGINE FASCET FERRET FILLET FLANGE FLORET FLUTER FORMER FRAISE FULLER GIMLET GLAZER GOFFER GRAVER GUMMER HACKER HAMMER HEMMER HOGGER HOLDER HULLER JIGGER JUMPER LADKIN LASTER LIFTER NIBBER PALLET PARTER PICKAX PICKER PLENCH PLIERS PROPER PUPPET REAMER RIPPER ROCKER RUNNER SANDER SAPPER SCRIBE SCUTCH SEATER SHAPER SHAVER SHEARS SHOVEL SKIVER SLATER SOCKET SQUARE STYLET STYLUS SWIVEL TAGGER TASTER TONGUE TREPAN TURNER

TURREL TWILLY VEINER WAGGON WIGWAG WIMBLE WORDLE WORMER YANKEE ABRADER BLOCKER BRADAWL CALIPER CAULKER CHAMFER CHIPPER CHOPPER CLEANER CLEAVER COULTER CREASER DIAMOND DOLABRA DRESSER FISTUCA FLANGER FREEZER FROTTON GRAINER GROOVER GRUBBER GUDGEON JOINTER KNOTTER LOGHEAD MITERER OUSTITI POINTEL POINTER PROFILE RIVETER ROUGHER ROUNDER SCAUPER SCORPER SCRIBER SCRIVER SCURFER SLASHER SLEEKER SLICKER SPLAYER SPUDDER STEMMER STRIKER STROKER TICKLER TREBLET TWIBILL UPRIGHT WRAITHE AIGUILLE BIFACIAL BILLHOOK BOOTJACK BURGOYNE CALLIPER CREATURE CRIPPLER CROSSCUT CROWFOOT DUCKFOOT ELEVATOR EXPANDER FLOUNDER GRAVETTE GRIFFAUN POLISHER PRITCHEL PROPERTY PUNCHEON RAVEHOOK RECAPPER SCRAPPLE SCULPTOR SPLITTER STIPPLER STRICKLE STRINGER SURFACER THWACKER TOLLIKER WARKLOOM WORKLOOM SCRATCHER
(— A BOOK) FINISH
(BORING —) TREPAN
(CHEF'S —) WHISK SPATULA
(PL.) TEW FISH GEAR TRADE CUTLERY GIBBLES PIONERY ENGINERY
TOOLED GOFFERED
(— WITHOUT GILDING) BLIND
TOOLHOLDER TURRET MONITOR
TOOLHOUSE COPHOUSE
TOOLING (— ON BOOK) GOFFERING
TOOLSHED DOGHOUSE
TOON LIM CEDAR TOONWOOD
TOOT BLOW TOWT BINGE BLAST SOUND SPREE TRUMPET
TOOTH BIT COG GAM JAG PEG DENS DENT FANG LEAF RASP SNAG TIND TINE TUSH TUSK CRENA IVORY MOLAR PEARL PRONG RAKER TENON BROACH CANINE CUSPID CUTTER DENTAL INDENT JOGGLE TRIGON TRITOR DENTILE DIVIDER GRINDER INCISOR LATERAL SURDENT UNCINUS ABUTMENT BICUSPID BLEPHARA DENTICLE EYETOOTH GAGTOOTH MARGINAL PREMOLAR SAWTOOTH SPROCKET TOOTHLET TRIGONID CARNASSIAL
(— OF A MOSS) BLEPHARA
(— OF HORSE) DIVIDER
(— OF MOLLUSC) MARGINAL
(— OF PINION) LEAF
(— OF RADULA) UNCINUS
(— ON ROTATING PIECE) WIPER
(ARTIFICIAL —) DUMMY PONTIL
(CANINE —) CUSPID HOLDER LANIARY CYNODONT DOGTOOTH EYETOOTH
(GEAR —) COG GUB DENT ADDENDUM SPROCKET

(HARROW —) TINE
(MOLAR —) WANG
(OF SURFACE OF A —) MESIAL
(PART OF —) GUM NECK PULP ROOT CROWN DENTIN ENAMEL CEMENTUM
(UPPER SURFACE OF —) TABLE
(PREF.) DENT(ATO)(I)(INO)(O)(ODO) ODONT(O)
(SUFF.) DENT(ATE) ODON(T)(TA) (TES)(TIA)(TY) ODUS
TOOTHACHE WORM DENTAGRA
TOOTHED SERRATE VIRGATE SERRATED PECTINATE
(SUFF.) ODON ODUS
TOOTHLESS GUMMY
TOOTHPICK QUILL ARKANSAN
TOOTHSOME SAVORY PALATABLE
TOOTHWORT CROWTOE COOLWORT DENTARIA PEPPERROOT
TOO-TOO ULTRA LADIDA
TOP CAP COP GIG NUN TAP TIP ACME APEX BEAT COCK CULM HEAD HELM ROOF SKIM STOP BLOOM CHIEF COVER CREST CROWN FANCY GIGGE OUTDO PITCH RIDGE SHIRT SPIRE STRIP TOTUM TRUMP UPPER CALASH CAPOTE CULMEN SUMMIT UPWARD VERTEX CACUMEN SPINNER ROUNDTOP SURMOUNT TEETOTUM CULMINATION
(— FOR CHIMNEY OR PIPE) COWL HOOD
(— FOR PEDESTAL) DADOCAP
(— OF ALTAR) MENSA
(— OF AUTOMOBILE) HEAD HOOD
(— OF BIRD'S HEAD) PILEUM
(— OF CAPSTAN) DRUMHEAD
(— OF FURNACE) ARCH
(— OF GLASS) PRETTY
(— OF HEAD) MOLD PATE MOULD SCALP VERTEX
(— OF HELMET) SKULL
(— OF HILL) KNAG KNAP KNOLL
(— OF INGOT) CROPHEAD
(— OF MINING SHAFT) PITHEAD
(— OF MOUNTAIN) MAN
(— OF PLANT OR TREE) CROP
(— OF ROOF) DECK
(— OF SPINDLE) COCKHEAD
(— OF THE LINE) AONE
(— OF THUNDERCLOUD) INCUS
(— OF WAVE) COMB
(— OF WOODEN STAND) CRISS
(—S OF CROP) SHAW
(BLOW ONE'S —) SPEW
(BOOT —) RUFF
(BOX —) COUPON
(CARRIAGE —) CALASH
(PEG —) PEERIE
(RESEMBLING A —) STROBIC
(SITUATED AT —) APICAL
(SPINNING —) PEERY PEERIE
(PREF.) ACR(O)
(SPINNING —) RHOMB(O)
TOPAZ PYCNITE PYCNIUM PHSALITE
TOPCOAT OVERCOAT SIPHONIA
TOPE SOT DHER DHERI STUPA DAGOBA SOUPFIN
TOPER BOUSER CUPMAN POTMAN POTTER SIPPER SOAKER SUPPER

TROUGH BOMBARD POTLING SWILLER TOSSPOT BLACKPOT DRUNKARD MALTWORM

TOPI TIANG
(**MATERIAL FOR —**) PITH

TOPIC HARE ITEM TEXT HOBBY THEMA THEME BURDEN GAMBIT GROUND MATTER SUBJECT OCCASION
(**STOCK —**) TOPOS

TOPKNOT TUFT CREST ONKOS TOPPING

TOPMAN COB

TOPMINNOW GUPPY LIMIA GULARIS HELLERI SAILFIN GAMBUSIA MOLLIENSIS

TOP-NOTCH APLUS

TOPOGRAPHIC TERRAIN

TOPPER CAP FEZ HAT LID TAM BERET

TOPPLE TIP TOP TILT LEVEL UPEND TOTTLE

TOPS AONE

TOPSAIL RAFFE RAFFEE

TOPSOIL KELLY

TOPSTONE CAPSTONE

TOPSWARM TOPCAST

TOPSY-TURVY COCKEYED HEELHALL

TOQUE ZATI MUNGA MACACO RILAWA MACAQUE

TOQUILLA JIPIJAPA

TOR CRAG

TORCEL BURN BERNE BORNE

TORCH DUCK JACK LAMP LINK LUNT PINE TEAD WASE WISP BLAZE BRAND FLARE LIGHT MATCH FOCKLE LAMPAD MASHAL MUSSAL BRANDON CRESSET GRIDDLE LUCIGEN ROUGHIE TORCHET FLAMBEAU
(**KIND OF —**) PLASMA
(**PREF.**) DAD(O) LAMPADE

TORCHBEARER KERYX LINKBOY LINKMAN DADUCHUS TORCHMAN

TOREADOR TORERO CAPEADOR

TORII (**PART OF —**) NYKI DAIWA KASAGI KUSABI LINTEL GAKUZUKA CROSSPIECE

TORIL CHIQUERO

TORMENT WO RAG TAW TRY WOE BAIT BALE FRET MOIL PAIN PANG PINE RACK SOOL TEAR TUCK CHEVY CURSE DEVIL GRILL HARRY SCALD TEASE TWIST WRING CHIVVY HARASS HARROW HECTOR INFEST NEEDLE PLAGUE TRAVEL AFFLICT ANGUISH BEDEVIL CRUCIFY HAGRIDE HATCHEL MALISON PERPLEX PINDING TERRIFY TORTURE TRAVAIL CRUCIATE DISTRAIN LACERATE MACERATE
(**EXTREME —**) AGONY

TORMENTED RODE CRUCIATE

TORMENTIL SEPTFOIL

TORMENTING PLAGUY

TORMINA TORSION

TORN RENT BROKEN RAGGED BLASTED LACERATE LACERATED

TORNADO VORTEX CYCLONE TRAVADO TWISTER

TORPEDO FISH SHELL SQUIB BATOID HOAGIE

TORPID FOUL NUMB BROSY INERT SODDEN STUPID TOGGER LANGUID TORPENT COMATOSE COMATOUS SLUGGISH

TORPIFY DAZE ETHERIZE

TORPOR COMA SLEEP SWOON ACEDIA ACCIDIE SLUMBER LETHARGY
(**PREF.**) NARC(O)

TORQUE BEE SARPE TWIST

TORREFY PARCH

TORRENT FLOW RUSH FLOOD SPATE STREAM NIAGARA CATARACT
(**— OF WORDS**) BLATTER

TORREYA SAVIN TUMION

TORRID HOT SULTRY AUSTRAL BOILING

TORSALO BERNE

TORSION STRESS DIDROMY

TORSK CUSK

TORT LIBEL WRONG

TORTE DOBOS

TORT-FEASOR ACTOR

TORTICOLLIS WRYNECK

TORTILLA TACO BREAD BURRITO TOSTADO ENCHILADA QUESADILLA
(**— CHIP**) NACHO
(**FRIED —**) TACO

TORTOISE EMYD BEKKO GAPER COOTER GOPHER TURTLE EMYDIAN HICATEE MUNGOFA TESTUDO GALAPAGO KASHYAPA SHELLPAD SHELLPOT TERRAPIN
(**PREF.**) CHEL(O)(Y)

TORTOISESHELL CAREY

TORTUOUS CRANKY SCREWY SINUATE WRIGGLY SINUATED

TORTURE GYP TAW BOOT CARD FIRE PAIN PANG PINE RACK AGONY SCREW TWIST ENGINE EXTORT IMPALE MARTYR AFFLICT AGONIZE ANGUISH BOOTING CRUCIFY PERPLEX TORMENT MARTYRDOM STRAPPADO
(**METHOD OF —**) FALANGA

TORTURER BOURREAU

TORUS CORK TORE DONUT BASTON BOLTEL BOUTELL BOWTELL DOUGHNUT THALAMUS

TORY BANDIT OUTLAW ROBBER PEELITE TANTIVY ABHORRER LOYALIST

TOSS BUM COB LAB SHY BUNG CANT CAST CAVE DOSS FLAP FLIP HIKE PASS SHAG SLAT TOUT CHAFE CHUCK FLICK FLING FLIRT FLURR HEAVE PITCH TEAVE THROW BETOSS BOUNCE DANDLE TOTTER WALTER WELTER WENTLE BLANKET TURMOIL WAMPISH WHEMMEL
(**— ABOUT**) VEX SWAB TAVE STREW POPPLE THRASH THRESH TORFLE WAMPISH
(**— A COIN**) SKY
(**— A JACK**) LAG
(**— ASIDE**) BANDY
(**— AWAY**) BLOW
(**— CONTEMPTUOUSLY**) SLIGHT

(**— HEAD**) CAVE GECK BRANK
(**— IN BLANKET**) CANVASS
(**— OFF**) SWAP SWOP
(**— OF HORSE'S HEAD**) CHACK
(**— OF THE HEAD**) HEEZE
(**— ON WAVES**) SURGE
(**— THE LIMBS ABOUT**) SPRAWL
(**— TO AND FRO**) WALK
(**— TOGETHER CONFUSEDLY**) SCRAMBLE
(**— WITH THE HORNS**) DOSS HIKE

TOSSING SURGING
(**— OF BULLFIGHTER**) COGIDA

TOSTAO TESTON

TOT ADD DRAM

TOTAL ADD SUM TAB TOT DEAD MERE TALE COUNT GROSS MOUNT SLUMP SUMMA UTTER WHOLE ENTIRE GLOBAL OMNIUM SUMMED TOTTLE EMBRACE FOOTING GENERAL PERFECT ABSOLUTE COMPLETE ENTIRETY SURMOUNT TEETOTAL
(**REACH THE — OF**) RUNTO
(**PREF.**) HOL(O)

TOTALED KAPUT WRECKED DEMOLISHED

TOTALITY ALL BODY HEAP BEING ALLNESS ECOLOGY ETERNITY HUMANITY INTEGRAL INTERVAL OMNITUDE SUMTOTAL

TOTALLY COLD GOOD QUITE WHOLLY

TOTE ADD LUG LOAD PACK CARRY BURDEN CONVEY

TOTEM HUACA

TO THE LIGHTHOUSE (**AUTHOR OF —**) WOOLF
(**CHARACTER IN —**) LILY PRUE JAMES MCNAB ANDREW BANKES RAMSAY BRISCOE CAMILLA CHARLES TANSLEY WILLIAM CARMICHAEL

TOTTER TOT REEL ROCK TOIT WALT SHAKE WAVER COGGLE DADDLE DODDER DOTTER FALTER HOTTER JOGGLE STAVER SWERVE TITTER TOTTLE WAMBLE WANGLE WAPPER BRANDLE FRIBBLE STAGGER TREMBLE WHITHER TITUBATE VACILLATE
(**PREF.**) LABE

TOTTERING LURCH SHAKY GROGGY CRAMBLY PALSIED RICKETY TOTTERY TITUBANT WAMBLING

TOU (**SON OF —**) HAMATH

TOUCAN TOCO TUCANA ARACARI

TOUCH GET RAP TAG TIG TIP ABUT BILL DASH FEEL HAND KISS KNEE MEET PALP PEAL PLAY RAKE RINE SCAM TACT TAKE FRAUD GLISK GRAZE GROPE SPICE TAINT TASTE TATTO TINGE TRAIT TREAT AFFECT ATTAIN CARESS FINGER GLANCE HANDLE REGARD SCRUFF SMUTCH STRAIN TACTUS TWITCH ATTAINT ATTINGE CONTACT FEELING PALPATE SOUPCON TACTION FLOURISH TINCTURE
(**— A KEY**) STRIKE
(**— BRIEFLY**) GLANCE
(**— CARESSINGLY**) FLATTER
(**— CLOSELY**) IMPINGE

(**— DEEPLY**) PIERCE
(**— FOREHEAD —**) KNUCKLE
(**— GENTLY**) DAB TAT TICK BRUSH
(**— LIGHTLY**) GRAZE SCUFF SKIFF
(**— OF BRUSH**) HAND
(**— OF COLOR**) EYE
(**— OF PAINT**) GLOB
(**— OF PEN**) STROKE
(**— OF PLEASURE**) GLISK
(**— ON**) PERSTRINGE
(**— RIGHTLY**) NICK
(**— UP**) TATT
(**DELICATE —**) STROKE
(**FINISHING —**) HOODER COPESTONE
(**PAINTING —**) ACCENT
(**SLIGHT —**) SKIFF SMATCH
(**SPIRITUALISTIC —**) RAPPORT
(**PREF.**) TAC TACTO TANGO THIGMO THIXO
(**SUFF.**) APHIA
(**HAVING A — OF**) ISH ISTIC

TOUCHDOWN ROUGE
(**MAKE A —**) LAND

TOUCHED FEY DOTTY

TOUCHING ABOUT LIBANT TENDER AGAINST CONTACT TANGENT ADJACENT PATHETIC POIGNANT AFFECTING CONTIGUOUS
(**LIGHTLY**) LAMBENT
(**— THE MIND**) PUNGENT

TOUCHSTONE TEST TOUCH LYDITE BASANITE STANDARD

TOUCHWOOD FUNK MONK PUNK SPUNK PUNKWOOD

TOUCHY HUFFY MIFFY SNAKY TESTY FEISTY KITTLE SNAKEY SNUFFY SPUNKY TENDER TETCHY GROUCHY NERVOUS PEEVISH PEPPERY STROPPY TEMPERY PETULANT TICKLISH

TOUGH RUM BHOY HARD TAUT WIRY BULLY BUTCH CLUNG HARDY STIFF STOUT WITHY BALLSY KNOTTY SINEWY STARCH STRONG HICKORY BULLYBOY LEATHERY UNTENDER ROUGHNECK TENACIOUS
(**NOT —**) TENDER

TOUGHEN TAW ANNEAL ENDURE HARDEN TEMPER
(**— METAL**) PLANISH

TOUGHENED CLUNG

TOUGHIE LULU

TOUGHNESS TUCK FIBER FIBRE STRENGTH TENACITY

TOUPEE RUG DOILY SCALP POSTICHE TOPPIECE

TOUR GIRO TURN SWING TOWER TURUS JUNKET SAFARI JOURNEY INVASION PROGRESS TOURETTE
(**— OF DUTY**) HERD STATION
(**CANARY —**) GLUCK GLUCKE

TOURACO LORY LOURIE TURAKOO

TOURBILLON KARRUSEL

TOUR DE FORCE STUNT

TOURIST TOURER TRIPPER VISITANT RUBBERNECK HOLIDAYMAKER

TOURMALINE SHORL SCHORL DRAVITE ACHROITE SIBERITE

TOURNAMENT TILT JERID JEREED JOUSTS TOURNEY BONSPIEL CAROUSEL

TOURNEUR DEALER
TOURNEY PLAY
TOURNIQUET GARROT STANCH
TWISTER STANCHER TORCULAR
TOUSLE MUSS SOOL SOWL
RUMPLE TOOZLE
TOUSLED TAUTED TOWZIE
TUMBLED UNKEMPT
TOUT SPIV BRUIT PLIER BARKER
STEERER TIPSTER
TOW CRIB HAUL PULL HURDS STUPE
TRACK TRACT CODILLA CORDELLE
(KIND OF —) SKI
TOWAGE TRACKAGE
TOWAI BIRCH KAMAHI
TOWARD AD INTO TORT ANENT
ANENST AGAINST FORNENT
ADVERSUS GAINWARD
(— CENTER) CENTRAD
(— CENTER OF EARTH) DOWN
(— INTERIOR) INBY INBYE
(— ONE SIDE) ASLANT
(— THE END) SF
(— THE HEAD) ANTERIOR
(— THE MOUTH) ORAD
(— THE REAR) ABACK DORSAD
BACKWARD
(— THE RIGHT) DEXTRAD
(— THE SIDE) LATERAD
(— THE STERN) AFTER
(PREF.) AC AD AF AG AL AP AS AT
IL IM IN INTRO IR OB PROS
(SUFF.) AD
(GOING —) PETAL
TOWEL CLOUT WIPER DIAPER
LAVABO RUBBER
(WORD ON —) HIS HERS
TOWER TOR PEEL PIKE REAR RISE
SOAR SPUR TOUR BABEL BROCH
HEAVE MINAR MOUNT PYLON
SIKAR SPIRE STUPA TEXAS ASCEND
ASPIRE BELFRY CASTLE CHULPA
DOKHMA DONJON GOPURA
ROLLER RONDEL SPRING TURRET
BASTIDE CHULLPA DERRICK
GIRALDA LANTERN MIRADOR
NURAGHE SHIKARA SIKHARA
STEEPLE TALAYOT TORREON
TOURNEL TRACKER TURRION
BARBICAN BASTILLE CLOGHEAD
DOMINEER RONDELLE SCRUBBER
TOURELLE TOWERLET PEPPERBOX
(— CONTAINING COKE) SCRUBBER
(— FOR SENTINEL) GUERITE
(— OF FORT) SPUR
(— OF MOSQUE) MINARET
(— OF SILENCE) DAKHMA
(— ON SUMMIT) PIKE
(— OVER) DROWN BESTRIDE
(ATTACHED —) DETAIL
(BELL —) CARILLON CAMPANILE
(BIBLICAL — SITE) EDAR
(CONNING —) SAIL
(FRACTIONATING —) STILL
(KIND OF —) MARTELLO
(PYRAMIDAL —) SIKAR VIMANA
SHIKARA SIKHARA
(SIEGE —) BRATTICE
(SIGNAL —) BANTAYAN
(WIND —) BADGIR
(PREF.) PYRGO TURRI
TOWERING EMINENT SUPERNAL
AMBITIOUS

TOWERMAN LEVERMAN
TOWER MUSTARD CRUCIFER
TOWHEE JOREE CHEWINK
CHEEWINK
TOWING TRACKAGE
TOWLINE CORDELLE
TOWN BY BYE HAM WON BURG
CAMP CITY STAD TOON WENE
WICK BAYAN BORGO BOURH
BRUGH BURGH DERBY MACHI
PLACE PLECK SIEGE STAND STEAD
VILLE CIUDAD HAMMON ORANGE
PUEBLO STAPLE BASTIDE
BOROUGH CHESTER OPPIDUM
QUIVIRA TOWNLET BOOMTOWN
BOURGADE ENCEINTE HOMETOWN
TOWNSHIP
(DESOLATED —) GUBAT
(DULL —) PODUNK
(FORTIFIED —) BURG BURGH
ENCEINTE
(KIND OF —) ONEHORSE
(MILITARY —) CANTONMENT
(MUSHROOM —) CAMP
(MYTHICAL —) QUIVIRA
(SMALL —) SHTETL SHTETEL
(UNFORTIFIED —) BOURGADE
(UNIMPORTANT —) PODUNK
(WALLED —) CHESTER
(PL.) PARGANA
(SUFF.) GRAD
TOWN CRIER BELLMAN
TOWN HALL HALL CABILDO
RATHAUS TOLBOOTH STADHOUSE
TOWNSHIP DEME DORP VILL
BAYAN TREEN BOROUGH
TOWNSMAN CAD CIT DUDE SNOB
TOWNY TOWNEE BURGHER
CITIZEN COCKNEY OPPIDAN
(PL.) BURGWARE
TOWROPE TOW CABLET GUNLINE
TOWLINE CORDELLE
TOXALBUMIN ROBIN PHALLIN
TOXEMIA BLACKLEG ECLAMPSIA
TOXIC VENOMOUS POISONOUS
TOXIN BOTULIN EXOTOXIN
TOY ARK DIE GAY TOP COCK DOLL
FOOL MOVE PLAY YOYO BLOCK
CORAL DALLY FLIRT HAPPY KNACK
LAKIN PLAID SPORT TRICK WALLY
BAUBLE DANDLE DIDDLE DOODLE
FADDLE FINGER FIZGIG GEWGAW
LAKING PRETTY PUPPET RATTLE
SUCKER BLOWOUT CRICKET
DREIDEL PLAYOCK TANGRAM
TRINKET TUMBLER WHIZZER
GIMCRACK KICKSHAW PINWHEEL
SKIPJACK SQUAWKER SQUEAKER
TEETOTUM WINDMILL ZOETROPE
(— AMOROUSLY) MIRD
(— RACER) SLOTCAR
(— WITH) PADDLE
(— WITH FINGERS) PADDLE
(FLYING —) PIGEON
(MUSICAL —) OCARINA
(OPTICAL —) STROBOSCOPE
THAUMATROPE
(SOFT —) GONK
(TOUGH —) GIJOE
TOYING DALLIANCE
TOYON TOLLON CHAMISO
TRABEA TOGA
TRACE RUN TUG WAD CAST ECHO

HINT LICK MARK RACK SCAN
SHOW SIGN STEP TANG TINT TROD
BRING GHOST GLEAM GLIFF GRAIN
PRINT RELIC SHADE SPICE SPOOR
STAMP STEAD THEAT TINGE
TOUCH TRACK TRACT TRAIL TRAIN
TRESS DERIVE ENGRAM HARBOR
LACING RESENT SHADOW SKETCH
SMUTCH STRAIN STREAK SWATHE
COCKEYE GLIMPSE KENNING
MENTION REMNANT SOUPCON
SURMISE SYMPTOM THOUGHT
UMBRAGE VESTIGE WHISPER
DESCRIBE ENGRAMME FOOTSTEP
SKERRICK TINCTURE WAINROPE
SIMULACRUM
(— A BEE) COURSE
(— A CURVE) SWEEP
(— A DESIGN) CALK
(— MATHEMATICALLY) GENERATE
(— OF A HARE) FARE
(— ON CHART) PRICK
(— THE COURSE OF) DEDUCE
(HARNESS —) TUG THEAT TREAT
(HAVE A —) SMACK
(MEMORY —) ENGRAM ENGRAMME
(SLIGHT —) GHOST STAIN SMATCH
SPARKLE
(SLIGHTEST —) SCINTIL
(PL.) FEUTE
(SUFF.) (HAVING A —) ISH ISTIC
TRACER SEEKER OUTLINER
SEARCHER
TRACERY FANWORK FROSTING
TRAILERY
TRACHEA ARTERY WINDPIPE
(— OF CRANE) TRUMP
TRACHEID HYDROID
TRACHYANDESITE ARSOITE
VULSINITE
TRACHYTE PIPERNO
TRACING BAROGRAM POLYGRAM
TRAILING
TRACK DOG PUG RAT RUT TAN WAD
WAY CLEW CLUE DRAW FARE FOIL
FOOT HUNT LANE MARK PAGE
PATH PIST RACE RACK RAIK RAIL
ROAD SHOE SLOT SPUR TROD
VENT BLOCK CHUTE DRIFT FEUTE
HOUND LODGE PISTE PLANE SLIDE
SPACE SPOOR STEAD SWATH
TRACE TRACT TRADE TRAIL TRAIN
TREAD BEARER COURSE GROOVE
HARBOR LADDER RETURN
RUNWAY SIDING SLEUTH STRAIN
STREAM SWATHE CHANNEL
FOILING FOOTING PATHWAY
TANGENT TRAFFIC VESTIGE
BACKBONE FOOTSTEP GUIDEWAY
TRANSFER TRECKPOT TREKPATH
WAGONWAY
(— ALONG CREST) RIDGEWAY
(— BY SMELL) SCENT
(— FOR ROPE) CHANNEL
(— GAME) DRAW
(— OF BLOOD) PERSUE
(— OF DEER) SLOT STRAIN
(— OF GAME IN GRASS) FOILING
(— OF HARE) FILE
(— OF SHIP) WAKE
(— OF WOUNDED BEAST) PERSUE
(— ON PRINTING PRESS) BANK
BEARER

(BEATEN —) PISTE
(BRANCH —) SIDELINE
(CYCLING —) VELODROME
(RACING —) SPEEDWAY
(RAILROAD —) LEAD SPUR STUB
SIDING TANGENT APPROACH
BACKBONE
(RUNNING —) FLAT CINDERS
(SHORT BRANCH —) RETURN
(SIDE —) LIE HOLE
(SKATER'S —) FLAT
(SLIPPERY —) SLIDE
(TEMPORARY —) SHOOFLY
(WINDING —) SERPENTINE
(WORM —) NEREITE
(PREF.) ICHN(O)
TRACKER PUGGI PUGGY TRAILER
TRAILMAN
TRACKLESS INVIOUS PATHLESS
TRACKMAN SPIKER
TRACT AREA BEAT DUAR FLAT ZONE
CAMPO CLIME COAST DRIVE
ESSAY FIELD GRABE HORST PATCH
SWEEP TRACK BARONY BUNDLE
EXTENT PARCEL REGION ENCLAVE
EURIPUS QUARTER ROYALTY
TERRAIN TRACTUS BROCHURE
CAMPAGNA CAMPAIGN CINGULUM
DISTRICT FARMHOLD FORESTRY
PAMPHLET PROVINCE TOWNSITE
TREATISE
(— KEPT IN NATURAL STATE) PARK
(— OF BARREN LAND) BARREN
DERELICT
(— OF BRAIN FIBERS) PEDUNCLE
(— OF GRASSLAND) PRAIRIE
(— OF LAND) CRU DOAB DUAB
DUAR GORE MARK BLOCK CHASE
CLAIM EJIDO FRITH GRANT LAINE
SCOPE SWELL TALUK EIGHTY
ESTATE FOREST GARDEN ISLAND
POLDER STRATH AIRPORT QUILLET
RESERVE TERRAIN BOUNDARY
CLEARING DERELICT FARMHOLD
INTERVAL SCABLAND SLASHING
(— OF MUDDY GROUND) SLOB
(— OF OPEN UPLAND) DOWN
DOWNS
(— OF UNCOVERED ICE) GLADE
(— OF WASTE LAND) HEATH
(BOGGY —) RUNN MORASS
(CLAYEY —) TAKYR
(CLEARED —) JUM JHUM JOOM
(DRY —) SEARING
(FORESTLESS —) STEPPE
(GENITAL —) BEARING
(IRREGULAR —) GORE
(OPEN —) VEGA SLASH
(SANDY —) DEN DENE LANDE
(SHRUBBY —) MONTE
(SWAMPY —) FLOW BAYGALL
**(UNOCCUPIED AND
UNCULTIVATED —)** DESERT
(WATERLESS —) THIRST
TRACTABLE EASY SOFT TAME
BUXOM TAWIE DOCILE GENTLE
TOWARD DUCTILE FLEXILE
PLIABLE AMENABLE FLEXIBLE
GUIDABLE OBEDIENT TOWARDLY
YIELDING MALLEABLE
TRACTARIANISM PUSEYISM
TRACTION DRAFT DRAUGHT
TRACTOR CAT MULE DRAGON

BOBTAIL CRAWLER PEDRAIL AGRIMOTOR

(TRAILER —) RIG

TRADE CHAP CHOP COUP DEAL SELL SWAP CHEAP CRAFT GRAFT PRICE TREAD TROKE TRUCK BAKERY BARTER CHANGE EMPLOY HANDLE METIER MISTER NIFFER OCCUPY SCORCE SCORSE BARGAIN CALLING CHAFFER FACULTY MYSTERY SCIENCE BUSINESS CABOTAGE EXCHANGE PLUMBING MERCHANDISE

(OLD-CLOTHES —) FRIPPERY

(PETTY —) DICKER

(SUBSIDIARY —) SIDELINE

(SUFF.) ERY

TRADEMARK CHOP LOGO MARK BRAND COUPON

TRADER SART BANYA PLIER BALIJA BANIAN BANYAN CHETTY DEALER MONGER NEPMAN TROKER CHAPMAN MARWARI SANGLEY TRUCKER ASTORIAN CHANDLER KURVEYOR MERCHANT OPERATOR

(HORSE —) JOCKEY

(INEXPERIENCED —) LAMB

TRADESMAN CIT BAKAL COOPER EGGLER SELLER TENSOR ARTISAN FRUITER GOLADAR OCCUPIER UPHOLDER

TRADESWOMAN WINSTER

TRADING CABOTAGE

(COASTAL —) CABOTAGE

TRADITION CABAL STORY SUNNA CABALA SMRITI SUNNAH THREAP HALACHA HALAKAH HEREDITY HERITAGE TRANSFER

(PL.) LEGEND

TRADITIONAL CLASSIC POMPIER

TRADUCE ILL SLUR ABUSE DEFAME MALIGN REVILE VILIFY ASPERSE DETRACT SCANDAL SLANDER

TRAFFIC COUP DEAL MANG MART MONG BROKE TRADE BARTER PALTER TRAVEL CHAFFER DEALING PASSAGE BUSINESS CHAFFERY COMMERCE EXCHANGE NAVIGATION

(— CONE) PYLON

(— IN SACRED THINGS) SIMONY

(— IN SLAVES) MAGONIZE

(— JAM) GRIDLOCK

(DRIVE RUDELY IN —) CUTIN

(ILLEGAL —) CONTRABAND

TRAFFICKER COUPER DEALER

TRAGACANTH GUM

TRAGEDY BUSKIN TRAGIC TROIADES

TRAGIC DIRE DREADFUL THESPIAN

TRAGICOMEDY DRAME

TRAGOPAN MONAL

TRAGUS EARLET

TRAIL PAD PUG DRAG FOIL HARL HUNT NECK PATH PIST SIGN SLOT BLAZE CRAWL DRAIL PISTE ROUTE SPOOR STOCK SWEEP TRACE TRADE TRAIN COMING DAGGLE FOLLOW RUNWAY SHADOW SLEUTH STRAIN TAIGLE TRAPES DRAGGLE TRACHLE TRAFFIC OUTTRAIL STRIGGLE TRAILERY

(— ALONG) STREEL TRAPES

(— BY SMELL) SCENT

(— DOWN) FALL

(— OF A FISH) LOOM

(— OF AIRCRAFT) CONTRAIL

(— OF STAG) ABATURE

(— OUT) STREAM

(— THROUGH MUD) DAGGLE

(DESCENDING —) BAHADA BAJADA

(JOGGING —) PARCOURSE

(MOUNTAIN —) CLIMB

(SKI —) PISTE

(WAGON —) RUDLOFF

(WATER —) WAKE

TRAILBLAZER HARBINGER

TRAILER SEMI COACH BOXCAR CARAVAN FLATBED FROGGER GONDOLA ARTMOBILE

TRAILING (— ON GROUND) PROSTRATE

TRAIN SET DRAG GAIT SECT TILL TIRE TURN ZULU BEARD BREED COACH DRESS DRILL ENTER FOCUS LOCAL RANGE TRACE TRACT TRADE TRAIL TRYNE CONVOY DIRECT GENTLE GROUND INFORM MANURE NUZZLE RAPIDE REPAIR SCHOOL SEASON STRING SUBWAY AFFAITE BRIGADE CARAVAN EDUCATE FREIGHT GEARING LIMITED PEDDLER RATTLER RETINUE SHUTTLE VARNISH CIVILIZE DISCIPLE ELECTRIC EQUIPAGE EXERCISE HIGHBALL INSTRUCT MANIFEST REHEARSE

(— AN ANIMAL) BREAK

(— FINE) GAUNT

(— FOR CONTEST) POINT

(— FOR FIGHTING) SPAR

(— OF ANIMALS) COFFLE

(— OF ATTENDANTS) CORTEGE

(— OF COMET) TAIL

(— OF CONSEQUENCES) CONSECUTION

(— OF EXPLOSIVE) FUSE

(— OF FANCY) REVERY REVERIE

(— OF FEATHERS) TAIL

(— OF GOWN) SACK

(— OF MINING CARS) JAG RUN TRIP

(CAMEL —) KAFILA

(FUNERAL —) CONVOY

(PACK —) CONDUCTA

(RAILROAD —) DRAG HOOK LOCAL PICKUP EXPRESS FREIGHT LIMITED RATTLER

TRAINED GOOD MADE ADEPT BROKE BROKEN

TRAINEE BOOT CADET INTERN

TRAINER FEEDER JINETE LANISTA

TRAINING DRILL THEAT ASCESIS ASKESIS CULTURE NURTURE PAIDEIA BREEDING

(— IN HUMANITIES) CIVILITY

(— OF HORSE) DRESSAGE

(EARLY —) TIROCINIUM

(MANUAL —) SLOID SLOYD

(RELIGIOUS —) SADHANA

TRAIPSE GAD WALK TRAMP SASHAY WANDER

TRAIT ITEM LEAD MARK VEIN ANGLE CHARM KNACK TRACT TRICK AMENITY ELEMENT HALLMARK JAPANISM

(CHARACTERISTIC —) TRICK

(CULTURE —) SURVIVAL

(FOREIGN —) EXOTISM

(GOOD —) THEW

(UNDESIRABLE —) DEMON DAEMON

(WELL-DEFINED —) STREAK

(PL.) CORNERS

TRAITOR RAT JUDAS RUSTY NITHING WARLOCK APOSTATE ISCARIOT PRODITOR QUISLING SQUEALER TRADITOR TREACHER

TRAITOROUS FALSE FELON APOSTATE RENEGADE

TRAJECTORY SPORABOLA

TRA-LA-LA TRALIRA

TRAM TUB DRAM TRAMCAR TRAMMEL TRANVIA

(COAL —) TIP

(SET OF —S) JOURNEY

TRAMCAR TRAM DUMMY PICKUP

TRAMMEL TRAM HAMPER STIFLE COTTEREL

TRAMMER PUTTER

TRAMONTANE ALIEN FOREIGN OVERBERG

TRAMP BO BUM PAD BOOM HAKE HIKE HOBO HUMP PUNK SLOG SWAG VAMP WALK YEGG BIMBO BURLY CAIRD CLAMP JAVEL PIKER ROGUE SHACK STIFF STRAG TRAIK TRAIL TRASH TROMP TROUT BAGMAN GAYCAT JOCKER PICARO STODGE STRAMP STROLL TINKER TRANCE TRAPES TRUANT TRUDGE DRUMMER FLOATER RUFFLER SWAGGER SWAGMAN TRAIPSE VAGRANT YEGGMAN CLOCHARD FOOTSLOG GANGEREL STROLLER TRAVELER VAGABOND SUNDOWNER

(— ABOUT) WAG

(LONG —) HUMP

(PL.) MONKERY

TRAMPING MONKERY

TRAMPLE HOX JAM PUG FARE FOIL FULL HOOF CHAMP POACH SCAUT SPURN STOMP TRAMP TRASH TREAD DEFOIL DEFOUL PADDLE SAVAGE STOACH STRAMP WADDLE OPPRESS OVERRUN SCAMBLE FORTREAD OVERRIDE

(— IN MUD) POACH

TRANCE RAPTUS AMENTIA ECSTASY SAMADHI CATALEPSY

TRANQUIL CALM COOL EASY LOWN MILD SOFT EQUAL QUIET STILL GENTLE PACATE PIPING SERENE CALMATO EQUABLE PACIFIC RESTFUL PEACEFUL

TRANQUILIZE CALM LULL QUIET STILL BECALM PACIFY SERENE SETTLE SOFTEN SOOTHE APPEASE COMPOSE

TRANQUILIZER VALIUM DIAZEPAM

TRANQUILIZING ATARAXIC SOOTHING

TRANQUILLITY KEF LEE EASE REST PEACE QUIET SATTVA SERENE HARMONY ATARAXIA QUIETAGE QUIETISM QUIETUDE SERENITY COMPOSURE

TRANQUILLIZER LIBRIUM RESERPINE

TRANS ANTI

TRANSACT DO PASS AGITATE CONDUCT PERFORM

TRANSACTION DEAL DEED GAGE GAGER ACTION AFFAIR FIDDLE MARGIN SPREAD BARGAIN MOHABAT PASSAGE CONTRACT KNOCKOUT OPERATION PROCEEDING

(— AT LOWER PRICE) DOWNTICK

(GAMBLING —) FLUTTER

(STOCK —) STRADDLE

(PL.) ACTA BUSINESS

TRANSCEND PASS SOAR EXCEED OVERTOP SURPASS

TRANSCENDENTAL ACOSMIC

TRANSCENDING EXQUISITE

(PREF.) SUPRA

TRANSCRIBE COPY BRAILLE DESCRIBE EXSCRIBE

TRANSCRIBED CANNED

TRANSCRIBER COPIER COPYIST

TRANSCRIPT COPY SCORE TENOR DOUBLE APOGRAPH EXSCRIPT

TRANSCRIPTION

(PL.) PAZAND PAZEND

TRANSEPT PLACE PORCH

TRANSFER CALL CEDE DEED FLIT GIVE JUMP PASS SALE SELL TURN ALIEN CABLE CARRY CROSS DROGH REFER REMIT SHIFT ASSIGN ATTORN CHANGE DECANT DELATE DONATE REMOVE SWITCH CESSION CONNECT CONSIGN DELIVER DEVOLVE DISPONE MIGRATE TRADUCE ALIENATE ANTEDATE CROCKING DELEGATE DELIVERY DONATION EXCHANGE TRANSACT TRANSUME VIREMENT NEGOTIATE

(— A RECORDING) OVERDUB

(— DYE) EXHAUST

(— HEAT) CONVECT

(— HOMAGE) ATTORN

(— MOLTEN GLASS) LADE

(— OF ENERGY) FLOW

(— OF PROPERTY) DEED GIFT GRANT DISPOSAL

(— PIGMENT) FLUSH

(— WITH POWDER) POUNCE

(DECORATIVE —) DECAL

(TEMPORARY —) SECONDMENT

TRANSFERENCE DEMISE EMOTION REMOVAL DELATION DISPOSAL TRANSFER

(— OF TRIBUTARY) CAPTURE

TRANSFIGURE DEIFY CLARIFY

TRANSFIX FIX DART STAB PITCH STAKE STICK SKEWER THRILL BESTICK

TRANSFORM TURN SHIFT TOUCH CHANGE STRIKE CONVERT FASHION PERMUTE RECYCLE CATALYZE DISGUISE HETERIZE

(— ENERGY) ABSORB

(KIND OF —) FOURIER LAPLACE

TRANSFORMATION CHANGE HAIRWORK

(— IN ATOM) REACTION

TRANSFORMER SET DIMMER

JIGGER TEASER TOROID VARIAC BALANCE BOOSTER HEDGEHOG

TRANSFUSE ENDUE INDUE

TRANSGRESS ERR SIN BREAK OFFEND OVERGO DIGRESS DISOBEY VIOLATE INFRINGE OVERPASS OVERSLIP OVERSTEP TRESPASS

TRANSGRESSION SIN SLIP CRIME FAULT SCAPE BREACH DELICT ESCAPE MISDEED OFFENSE DELICTUM OVERLOUP TRESPASS

TRANSGRESSOR SINNER OFFENDER

TRANSIENCE FUGACITY

TRANSIENT FLEET BUBBLE FLIGHTY PASSING FLEETING FUGITIVE MOMENTARY

TRANSIENTLY HOVERLY

TRANSISTOR FET MOSFET

TRANSIT BINOCLE PASSAGE TRANSEPT

TRANSITION CUT JUMP LEAP SEGUE SHIFT FERMENT PASSAGE

TRANSITIVE ACTIVE

TRANSITORINESS CADUCITY

TRANSITORY FLEET CADUCE FLYING BRITTLE PASSANT PASSING SLIDING VOLATIC WHILEND CADUCOUS FLEETING FLITTING TEMPORAL VOLATILE MOMENTARY

TRANSKEI (CAPITAL OF —) UMTATA **(TOWN OF —)** BUTTERWORTH

TRANSLATE PUT DRAW MAKE TURN WEND RENDER CONVERT ENGLISH EXPOUND TRADUCE CONSTRUE INTERPRET

TRANSLATION CAB KEY CRIB PONY STEP TROT GLOSS HORSE TARGUM UNSEEN BICYCLE CABBAGE ENGLISH THARGUM TRADUCT VERSION SUBTITLE VERBATIM **(— OF BIBLE)** PESHITO **(— OF THE CLASSICS)** JACK **(BIBLICAL —)** PESHITO PESHITTA PESHITTO **(LOAN —)** CALQUE

TRANSLATOR TURNER

TRANSLUCENT CLEAR LUCID LIMPID LUCENT HYALINE **(PREF.)** HYAL(O)

TRANSMIGRATION SAMARA SAMSARA SANSARA

TRANSMISSION CHAIN DRIVE ENTAIL DESCENT GEARBOX PASSAGE SENDING TRANSFER CONDUCTION CONVECTION **(— OF DISEASE)** CONTAGION **(— OF ESTATE)** ENTAIL **(— OF SOUND)** AUDIO **(— TO OFFSPRING)** HEREDITY **(SUFF.)** PHORESIS

TRANSMIT AIR BEAM EMIT SEND CARRY CONVEY DEMISE DERIVE ENTAIL EXPORT IMPACT IMPART RENDER CONDUCT CONSIGN FORWARD TRADUCE TRADUCT TRAJECT BEQUEATH DESCRIBE PROPAGATE **(PREF.)** DIAGO

TRANSMITTER TUBA SLAVE SPARK BEACON JAMMER PINGER SENDER VEHICLE RADIATOR

TRANSMITTING ALIVE

TRANSMUTE CHEMIC CHEMICK ENNOBLE PERMUTE EXCHANGE TRANSMUE TRANSUME

TRANSOM PATIBLE TRAVERSE

TRANSPARENCY SLIDE **(— OF DIAMOND)** WATER

TRANSPARENT THIN CLEAR FILMY LUCID BRIGHT LIMPID LUCENT CRYSTAL FRAGILE HYALINE HYALOID TIFFANY DIOPTRIC LUCULENT LUMINOUS LUSTROUS PELLUCID **(IMPERFECTLY —)** TRANSLUCENT **(PREF.)** DIAPHAN(O) HYAL(O)

TRANSPIRE HAPPEN

TRANSPLANT SPOT SHIFT DEPLANT

TRANSPORT DAK JOY ROB BEAR BOAT BUSS DAWK DRAY HAUL PASS PORT RAPE RAPT RIDE SEND SHIP BLISS CANOE CARRY DROGH FERRY FLUTE GILLY BANISH BARREL CONVEY DEPORT GALLOP KURVEY WAFTER ECSTASY EXPRESS FRAUGHT ONERARY RAPTURE TRADUCE TROOPER CABOTAGE CARRIAGE DAYDREAM ENRAVISH PALANDER **(— BY PACKHORSE)** JAG **(— FOR CRIME)** LAG **(— LOGS)** BOB **(— ORE)** SLUSH **(PREF.)** PEREIO

TRANSPORTATION AIR DAK FARE AIRLIFT BOATAGE FREIGHT MINIVAN TRAJECT TRANSPORT **(AIRPORT —)** LIMO

TRANSPORTED RAPT **(— BY GLACIER)** ERRATIC

TRANSPOSE ADJOINT CONVERT REVERSE

TRANSPOSITION SHIFT ANSWER ANAGRAM

TRANSUBSTANTIATION METUSIA **(BELIEVER IN —)** CAPERNAITE

TRANSUDE SEEP

TRANSVAAL DAISY GERBERA

TRANSVAALER TAKHAAR

TRANSVERSE CROSS FACING THWART OBLIQUE

TRANSVERSELY ATHWART

TRANSVESTISM EONISM

TRANSVESTITE BERDACHE

TRAP COY GET GIN PIT SET FALL GIRN GRIN HOOK LACE LIME NAIL PUTT TIPE TOIL WAIT WEEL BRAKE BRIKE CATCH LEASH PLANT POUND SNARE SPELL STALE SWICK SWIKE TRAIN COBWEB CRUIVE EELPOT ENGINE KEDDAH POCKET QUILEZ SNATCH STAYER WILLOW FLYTRAP PITFALL PITFOLD PUTCHEN PUTCHER RATTRAP SETTING SPRINGE TRAMMEL BIRDLIME COALHOLE DEADFALL DOWNFALL TRAPROCK **(— FOR BIRDS)** SCRAPE **(— FOR LARGE GAME)** HOPO **(— FOR LOBSTER)** POT **(— FOR RABBITS, MICE, ETC)** TIPE TYPE

(— FOR RATS) CLAM **(— FOR SALMON)** PUTT **(— FOR SMALL ANIMALS)** HATCH **(— FOR THE FEET)** CALTROPS **(— IN POKER)** SANDBAG **(— IN THEATER)** SCRUTO **(— INTO SERVICE)** CRIMP **(— OF SCAFFOLD)** DROP **(FISH —)** FYKE KILL LEAP WEEL WEIR CREEL WILLY CORRAL CRUIVE WILLOW **(LOBSTER —)** POT **(MOTH —)** GYPLURE **(RABBIT —)** GATENET **(SAND —)** BUNKER

TRAPDOOR DROP SLOT TRAP SCRUTO VAMPIRE TRAPFALL

TRAPPED CORNERED

TRAPPER WIRER VOYAGEUR

TRAPPINGS GEAR JHOOL ARMORY TOGGERY BARDINGS EQUIPAGE HOUSINGS CAPARISON

TRAPSHOOTING SKEET

TRASH ROT BOSH DREK GEAR GOOK JUNK PELF RAFF TOSH TRAG CLART DRECK DROSS DRUSH SPANK STUFF SWASH THROW TRADE TROKE WASTE WRACK BUSHWA CULTCH KELTER KITSCH LITTER PADDLE PALTRY RAMMEL REFUSE RUBBLE SCULCH TROUSE BAGGAGE BEGGARY FULLAGE GARBAGE PEDLARY RUBBISH TOSHERY TRAFFIC BLATHERY CLAPTRAP FLUMMERY MUCKMENT PEDDLERY SKITTLES SMACHRIE TRASHERY TRUMPERY

TRASHY CHEAP FLASH TOSHY TRIPY PALTRY SHODDY SLUSHY BAGGAGE RUBBISH RIFFRAFF RUBBISHY SIXPENNY TRUMPERY

TRAUMA WOUND INJURY STRESS

TRAVAIL PAIN TASK TOIL AGONY LABOR TORMENT

TRAVEL GO BAT BUS FLY GIG WAG FARE GANG HIKE PASS PATH RIVE TOTE TRIP VAMP WEND WAG KNOCK SLOPE THROW TRACK CRUISE TRANCE VOYAGE EXPRESS JOURNEY TRAVAIL TRUNDLE WAYFARE PROGRESS TRAVERSE **(— ACROSS SNOW)** MUSH **(— AIMLESSLY)** SAUNTER **(— ALONG GROUND)** TAXI **(— AROUND)** TURN COAST CIRCLE GIRDLE COMPASS **(— AT GOOD SPEED)** CRACK **(— AT HIGH SPEED)** HELL BARREL SCORCH **(— AT RANDOM)** DRIFT **(— AT SPEED OF)** DO **(— BACK AND FORTH)** SHUNT COMMUTE **(— BY AIRCRAFT)** AIR FLY AIRPLANE **(— BY OX WAGON)** TREK **(— FAST)** STREAK **(— IN A VEHICLE)** TOOL **(— IN STATE)** PROGRESS **(— IN WATER)** SWIM **(— ON FOOT)** HIKE SHANK KNAPSACK PERAMBULATE PEREGRINATE **(— ON WATER)** SAIL

(— OVER) TRANCE TRAVERSE **(— SPEEDILY)** VROOM **(— THROUGH)** GO **(— THROUGH AIR)** GLIDE **(— THROUGH WOODS)** BUSHWACK **(— WITHOUT EQUIPMENT)** SIWASH **(DAY'S —)** JORNADA JOURNAL JOURNEY

TRAVELER GOER CRAWL FARER GUEST HORSE BAGMAN GANGER KILROY POSTER SAILOR VIATOR CRUISER DRUMMER FOOTMAN HOWADJI LEEFANG PILGRIM SWAGGIE TRAILER TREKKER TRIPPER WAYGOER ARGONAUT EXPLORER MAGELLAN OUTRIDER VOYAGEUR WAYFARER PASSENGER **(COMMERCIAL —)** BAGMAN SALESMAN **(COMPANY OF —S)** CARAVAN

TRAVELER'S JOY HAGROPE BINDWITH CLEMATIS

TRAVELING ERRANT PEREGRINE

TRAVELING SALESMAN RIDER DRUMMER

TRAVELOGUE (— TECHNIQUE) VOICEOVER

TRAVERSE DO GO SEE BURN DENY KNEE LIFT MAKE PASS SPAN WALK COAST COVER CROSS SHEAR SWEEP THIRL TRACE TRACK CIRCLE COURSE DENIAL OVERGO PERCUR TRAVEL VOYAGE WANDER CHANNEL JOURNEY MEASURE OVERRUN PARADOS PERVADE DESCRIBE NAVIGATE OVERPASS OVERWEND SCRAMBLE UNTHREAD PERAMBULATE

TRAVERTINE ONYX TOPHUS ONYCHITE

TRAVESTY EXODE FARCE PARODY SATIRE CHARADE EXODIUM TRAVEST BURLESQUE

TRAVIATA, LA (CHARACTER IN —) FLORA VALERY ALFREDO BERVOIX DOUPHOL GERMONT GIORGIO VIOLETTA **(COMPOSER OF —)** VERDI

TRAVOIS DRAY TRAVOY ALLIGATOR

TRAWL SEINE BOULTER DRAGNET STOWNET TRAWLNET TROTLINE

TRAWLER PAREJA BRAGOZZO

TRAY HOD CASE TILL TRUG BATEA BOARD FLOAT SCALE SLICE SUSAN GALLEY MONKEY SALVER SERVER SERVET VOIDER WAITER BALANCE CABARET COASTER CONSOLE SHALLOW DEJEUNER **(— FOR CRUMBS)** VOIDER **(— FOR DRYING FISH)** FLAKE **(— FOR MATCH SPLINTS)** CAUL MONKEY **(— FOR SHELLFISH)** FLOAT **(— FOR TYPE)** GALLEY **(— TO CATCH OVERFLOW)** SAFE **(CIRCULAR —)** ROUNDEL

TREACHEROUS FOUL CATTY DIRTY FALSE PUNIC SNAKY SWACK FELINE FICKLE HOLLOW ROTTEN YELLOW SNAKISH FRAUDFUL IMPOSING PLOTTING SLIDDERY

TREACHERY GUILE SWICK TRAIN

DECEIT FELONY PERFIDY TREASON
UNTRUTH DASTARDY DISTRUST
TRAHISON TRAITORY

TREACLE DIBS CLAGGUM THERIAC

TREAD FIT PAD BEAT FOOT PATH
POST RUNG STEP VOLT CLAMP
TRACK TRADE DEFOIL DEFOUL
PADDLE CRAWLER FEATHER
FOOTING RETREAD TREADER
FOOTSTEP
(— CLUMSILY) CLUMP BALTER
(— DOWN SHOE HEEL) CAM
(— HEAVILY) SPURN TRAMPLE
(— OF FOWL'S EGG) GRANDO
(— ON) FOIL
(— TO MUSIC) FOOT
(— WARILY) PUSSYFOOT
(TIRE —) COVER

TREADLE PEDAL CHALAZA

TREASON SEDITION TREACHERY

TREASURE POSE ROON HOARD
PRIZE STORE TROVE VALUE
BURSAR COFFER FINDAL GERSUM
WEALTH ASTHORE FINANCE
THESAUR WARISON GARRISON
TREASURY VALUABLE
(— STATE) MONTANA
(— TROVE) STASH
(LITTLE —) STOREEN
(PL.) CIMELIA

TREASURE BOX HANAPER

TREASURED DEAR CHARY
PRECIOUS VALUABLE

**TREASURE ISLAND (AUTHOR OF
—)** STEVENSON
(CHARACTER IN —) BEN JIM PEW
GUNN JOHN BONES HANDS ISRAEL
SILVER HAWKINS LIVESEY
SMOLLETT TRELAWNEY

TREASURER FISC BOWSER BURSAR
FISCAL GABBAI BOUCHER
HOARDER SPENDER BHANDARI
COFFERER HAZNADAR PROVISOR
QUAESTOR RECEIVER

TREASURY FISC FISK KIST CHEST
HOARD PURSE COFFER CORBAN
FISCAL FISCUS BOWSERY
BURSARY CHAMBER CHECKER
CHEQUER HORDARY AERARIUM
THESAURY TREASURE
STOREHOUSE
(PAPAL —) CAMERA

TREAT RUN USE DEAL DOSE HOCK
LEAD PLAY BEANO BESEE COVER
DIGHT GUIDE LEECH SERVE SETUP
SHOUT TRACT TRAIT WRITE
DEMEAN DOCTOR GOVERN
HANDLE LIQUOR PADDLE REGALO
CONDUCT ENTREAT GARNISH
ACTIVATE AIRBRUSH
(— A HIDE) DRUM
(— AS EQUAL) EVEN
(— BADLY) ILLGUIDE
(— BY MELTING) RENDER
(— CARELESSLY) BANG RANDY
(— CLOUDS) SEED
(— CONFIDENTIALLY) HUSH
(— CRUELLY) CRUCIFY
(— DAINTILY) PAMPER
(— DIABOLICALLY) BEDEVIL
(— DISCOURTEOUSLY) DISGRACE
(— FIBERS) GILL
(— FLOUR) AGENIZE

(— FONDLY) DANDLE
(— FUR) CARROT
(— GENTLY) FAVOR
(— HAIR) CONK
(— HARSHLY) STICK
(— ILLNESS) POMSTER
(— IMPROPERLY) MISUSE
(— IMPUDENTLY) NOSE
(— INADEQUATELY) SCANT
(— LIGHTLY) SCRUFF
(— LOVINGLY) COAX
(— MALICIOUSLY) SPITE
(— MASH) LAUTER
(— MERCIFULLY) SPARE
(— OF) DISCOURSE
(— OF DRINKS) SETUP
(— ROUGHLY) BANG MUMBLE
GRABBLE MALTREAT
(— SILK TO RUSTLE) SCROOP
(— SLIGHTINGLY) LIGHTLY
(— STEEL) HARVEY
(— UNFAIRLY) DO SHAFT STICK
(— UNSKILLFULLY) FOOZLE
(— VIOLENTLY) STRONGARM
(— WITH ABUSE) OUTRAGE
(— WITH ACID) SOUR
(— WITH CARE) CODDLE
(— WITH CONSIDERATION)
RESPECT
(— WITH CONTEMPT) HUFF SNUB
BLURT FLIRT FLOCK FLOUT FLAUNT
BAUCHLE
(— WITH HEAT) FOMENT
(— WITH HONOR) RESPECT
(— WITH INATTENTION) FORGET
(— WITH INDULGENCE) FONDLE
(— WITH INJUSTICE) OPPRESS
(— WITH NEGLECT) PIGEONHOLE
(— WITH PARTIALITY) ACCEPT
(— WITH PRIDE) TRAMPLE
(— WITH RESPECT) HONOR
(— WITH RIDICULE) SCOUT
(— WITH RUDENESS) FRUMP
(— WITH TAR) BLACK
(— WITH TENDERNESS) CODDLE
(NEW YEAR'S EVE —) HAGMENA
HOGMANAY

TREATISE AGAMA DONET FAUNA
FLORA LIBEL SILVA SUMMA SYLVA
TRACT TREAT BOTANY POETRY
POMONA SERTUM SYSTEM
ALGEBRA ANATOMY BIOLOGY
COMMENT DIETARY GEOLOGY
GRAMMAR HISTORY PANDECT
PHYSICS PINETUM POETICS
ZOOLOGY ALMAGEST BROCHURE
CALCULUS DIDACTIC ECTHESIS
EXERCISE GENETICS GEOMANCY
GEOMETRY GERMANIA
HORNBOOK LAPIDARY
MONUMENT PANTHEON
PASTORAL PRACTICE SITOLOGY
SPECULUM TRACTATE
MONOGRAPH
(SUFF.) ICS LOGER LOGIA(N)
LOGIC(AL) LOGIST LOGUE LOGY
OLOGY

TREATMENT CURE WORK TREAT
USAGE ANIMUS DETAIL FACIAL
QUARTER BEHAVIOR DEMEANOR
ENTREATY
(— BY MASSAGE) SEANCE
(— BY MUD BATHS) PELOTHERAPY

(— FOR FURS) SECRETAGE
(— FOR WOOLLENS) SPONGING
(— OF DISEASE) ALLOPATHY
(BAD —) MISUSAGE
(COLD —) FREEZE
(COMPASSIONATE —) MERCY
(CONTEMPTUOUS —) SPURN
(CRUEL —) SEVERITY
(DIRE —) DOLE
(HARMFUL —) ABUSE
(HARSH —) SHAFT WHATFOR
(INHUMAN —) CRUELTY
(LUXURIOUS —) DELICACY
(SEVERE —) ROUGH
(PREF.) **(MEDICAL —)** IATR(O)
(SUFF.) PRAXIS
(MEDICAL —) IATRIA IATRIC(S)
IATRIST IATRY

TREATY MISE ACCORD CARTEL
CONCORD ENTENTE LOCARNO
ALLIANCE ASSIENTO PROTOCOL
TREATISE CONCORDAT

TREBLE TRIPLE DESCANT MINIKIN
SOPRANO TRIPLUM

TREBUCHET DONDINE DONDAINE

TREE TI ACH ADY AMA APA ARN ASH
BAY BEL BEN BUR DAK DAR EBO
ELM FIG FIR GUM HAW KOA KOU
LIN NIM OAK SAJ SAL TAL TUI UI F
YEW ACLE AGBA AKEE AMLA
ANAM ANAN ANDA ARAR ASAK
ASOK ATIS ATLE ATTA AULU AUSU
BAEL BAKU BITO BOGO BOOM
BREA BURI BURR CADE COLA
CRAB DATE DHAK DILO DITA DOON
EBOE IPIL JACK KINO KOKO LIME
MABI MORA NEEM OHIA OMBU
PALA PINE POLE POON SADR SORB
SUPA TALA TAWA TCHE TEAK TEIL
TITI TOON TREW TUNG TUNO UPAS
VERA WOOD YATE YAYA AALII
ABETO ABURA ACANA ACAPU
ACOMA AFARA AGATI AGOHO
AKEKI ALAMO ALANI ALDER
ALGUM ALISO ALMON ALMUG
AMAGA AMAPA AMRAK ANABO
ANJAN APPLE ARACA ARBOR
ARECA ARJAN ARJUN ARTAR
ASOKA ASPEN ATLEE BABUL
BALAO BALSA BALTA BANAK
BEECH BEHEN BETIS BIRCH
BONGO BOREE BOSSE BUMBO
CACAO CARAP CAROB CEBIL
CEDAR CEIBO DADAP DHAVA
DHAWA DILLY DRYAD DURIO
ELDER GABUN GAIAC GENIP GINEP
GINKO HAZEL ICICA IXORA JAMBO
JIQUE JIQUI KAPOR KAPUR KEENA
KOKAN KOKIO KOKUM KONGU
KUSAM LANSA LARCH LARIX
LEHUA LEMON LICCA LIMBA LINDE
LINER LINGO MAHOE MAHUA
MAMIE MAPLE MAQUI NARRA
NIEPA NURSE OADAL OSAGE
OSIER PACAY PAPAW PECAN PIPER
RAULI ROBLE ROHAN ROWAN
SALAI SAMAN SASSY SCRAG SIMAL
SIRIS SISSU STICK SUMAC TABOG
TARFA TENIO TERAP TIKUR TIMBO
TINGI TOONA TUART ULMUS UMIRI
URUCA URUCU UVITO WAHOO
YACAL YACCA YULAN ZAMAN
ACAJOU AHKROT AKEAKE ALAGAO

ALERCE ALERSE ALFAJE ALMOND
ALUPAG AMAMAU AMBASH
AMUGIS AMUYON ANAGAP
ANAGUA ANAQUA ANGICO ANILAO
ARALIA ARANGA ARBUTE AUSUBO
AZALEA BABOEN BACURY BAHERA
BAKULA BALSAM BANABA
BANAGO BANANA BANCAL BANIAN
BANYAN BARBAS BATAAN BIRIBA
BOMBAX BONDUC BONETE
BOTONG BRAUNA BUCARE BUSTIC
CALABA CAMARA CANELA CANELO
CAPUMO CARAPA CASSIA CATIVO
CAUCHO CEDRON CHALTA
CHERRY CHICHA CHINAR CHOGAK
CITRON COBOLA COCUYO
CUMBER DATURA DHAMAN
DHAURA DHAURI DRIMYS DURIAN
ELCAJA EMBLIC EMBUIA FEIJOA
FILLER FUSTIC GABOON GINKGO
GUAIAC GURJAN GURJUN IDESIA
IDIGBO ILIAHI ILLIPE ILLUPI
JAGUEY JUJUBE KAMALA KEMPAS
KINDAL KITTUL LANSAT LANSEH
LAUREL LIGNUM LINDEN LITCHI
LOCUST LONGAN MAFURA
MALLET MAYTEN MEDLAR MILKER
MIMOSA ORANGE PANAMA
PAWPAW PICHIA POPLAR RAMBEH
ROHUNA RUNNEL SARICU SARINO
SANDAN SANTOL SAPELE SAPOTA
SAPOTE SATINE SAWYER SERAYA
SINTOC SISSOO SOUARI STYRAX
SUMACH SUNDRI TALUTO TAMANU
TARATA TEETEE TIKOOR TIMBER
TINGUY TOATOA TOTARA TUPELO
URUCUM URUSHI UVALHA
WABAYO WABOOM WAHAHE
WALNUT WAMARA WAMPEE
WANDOO WATTLE YACHAN
YAGHAN YAMBAN ZAMANG
ACHIOTE ACHUETE AILANTO
AKEPIRO AMBATCH AMBOINA
AMUGIS AMUYONG ANABONG
ANNATTO ANONANG APITONG
APRICOT ARARIBA ARAROBA
ARBORET ARBUTUS AROEIRA
ASSAGAI AVOCADO AVODIRE
BANILAD BANKSIA BECUIBA
BENZOIN BILLIAN BOLLING
BUBINGA BUCKEYE BUISSON
CADAMBA CAJAPUT CAJUPUT
CANELLA CARAIPE CASTANA
CATALPA CAUTIVO CERILLO
CHAMPAC CHECHEM CHECKER
CHENGAL COCULLO CONIFER
CURUPAY CYPRESS DEADMAN
DESCENT DETERMA DHAMNOO
EPACRID FRUITER GONDANG
GRIBBLE GUMIHAN HICKORY
HOLLONG HOPBUSH HORMIGO
KAMASSI KAMBALA KICKXIA
KITTOOL KOKOONA KOOMBAR
KUMQUAT LOGWOOD MADRONA
MANJACK MARGOSA NAARTJE
PARAIBA PEREIRA PIMENTO
PULASAN PYRAMID RATWOOD
REDWOOD SERINGA SERVICE
SHITTAH SPINDLE STOPPER
SUNDARI SURETTE TANGELO
TANGHIN TARAIRI TARATAH
TARWOOD TINDALO TREELET
TWISTER URUNDAY VETERAN

WALAHEE WALLABA WEENONG
WONGSHY WONGSKY YAMANAI
YOHIMBE YOHIMBI ZELKOVA
ACEITUNA ALGAROBA ALLSPICE
ALMACIGA ALMANDER ALMENDRO
ALOEWOOD AMARILLO
ARAGUANE ARBOLOCO ARBUSCLE
AVELLANO BAKUPARI BASSWOOD
BAYBERRY BELLWOOD BINDOREE
BITANHOL BLACKBOX BOARWOOD
BORRACHA BREADNUT CABREUVA
CAMELLIA CAMUNING CARAGANA
CARAUNDA CHAMPACA CHESTNUT
CHINCONA CHINOTTO CINNAMON
COCOPLUM COPALCHE
COUMAROU CRABWOOD
CUCUMBOL DEADFALL DOMINANT
DOTTEREL DOVEWOOD
DRACAENA DRUMWOOD ETABALLI
FIREFALL FORESTER GAMDEBOO
GEELHOUT GENISARO GUACACOA
GUAYROTO HALAPEPE HARDTACK
HARDWOOD HOLDOVER
HORNBEAM HOROPITO
IRONWOOD ISHPINGO ITCHWOOD
JELOTONG JELUTONG KAJUGARU
KINGWOOD KNOBWOOD
LACEBARK LEADWOOD
LORDWOOD MAHOGANY
MANDARIN MILKWOOD MOKIHANA
OITICICA OLEASTER ONEBERRY
PEDIGREE PICHURIM PINKWOOD
RAMBUTAN RASAMALA
SANDARAC SANDWOOD SAPUCAIA
SASSWOOD SEBESTEN SHAGBARK
SHAVINGS SILKWOOD SLOGWOOD
SOAPBARK STANDARD SUCUPIRA
SWEETSOP SYCAMORE TAMARACK
TAMARIND TANEKAHA TREELING
TURMERIC ZAPATERO PERSIMMON
PISTACHIO SASSAFRAS
SATINWOOD SANDALWOOD
(— CUT BACK) DOTARD POLLARD
(— FURNISHING SUPPORT TO VINE)
HUSBAND
(— IN STREAM) SAWYER
(— LEFT IN CUTTING) HOLDOVER
(— OF HEAVEN) AILANTO
AILANTHUS
(— ON WALL) RIDER
(— OVER 2 FT. DIAMETER) VETERAN
(—S IN FOREST) STAND
(— SYMBOLIZING UNIVERSE)
YGDRASIL
(— WITH BRANCHES TRIMMED)
LOP LOPSTICK
(AROMATIC —) CLUSIA LABIATE
(AUSTRALIAN —) ASH GUM TOON
BELAH BELAR BOREE BUNDY
BUNYA GIDIA HAZEL KARRI NONDA
PENDA SALLY WILGA BAOBAB
DRIMYS GIDGEE GIMLET GYMPIE
JARRAH KOWHAI MARARA PEROBA
SALLEE DOGWOOD GEEBUNG
PEEBEEN BEEFWOOD CARABEEN
COOLABAH FLINDOSA GRAVILEA
IRONBARK LACEBARK QUANDONG
ROSEBUSH SANDSTAY SOAPWOOD
TILESEED
(BIG —) SEQUOIA
(BORNEO —) BILIAN
(BURMESE —) PADOUK
(CEYLON —) HORA

(CITRUS —) SHADDOCK
(CLOTHES —) COSTUMER
(CLUMP OF —S) TOLL TUMP STELL
(CONTORTED —) SAXAUL
(CUBAN —) JIQUE JIQUI GUACACOA
(CURSED —) WARYTREE
(DEAD —) RUNT SNAG RAMPIKE
(DEAD —S) DRIKI
(DECAYED —) DOTTEREL
(DWARF —) SCRUB ARBUSCLE
(EVERGREEN —) FIR YEW PINE SUGI
TAWA ABIES ATHEL CAROB CEDAR
CLOVE HOLLY LARCH LEMON OLIVE
THUJA BALSAM BIBIRU COIGUE
COIHUE KANAGI KAPUKA LOQUAT
ORANGE SPRUCE ARDISIA BEBEERU
BILIMBI CONIFER HEMLOCK
JUNIPER MADRONA MADRONO
EUCALYPT EUONYMUS SAPODILLA
SANDORICUM
(FAMILY —) STEMMA DESCENT
LINEAGE PEDIGREE
(FRUIT —) CORDON
(GENEALOGICAL —) ARBOR JESSE
(GROWTH OF —S) SYLVAGE
(GUM —) KARI KINO BABUL BALTA
BUMBO ICICA KARRI KIKAR GIMLET
MALLET STORAX TEWART WANDOO
GOMMIER COOLIBAH
(HAWAIIAN —) KOA LEHUA ILIAHI
(INFERNAL —) ZAQQUM
(JAPANESE —) KAYA KIAKI KEYAKI
KADSURA KATSURA SATSUMA
ZELKOVA
(MANDARIN —) SATSUMA
(MEXICAN —) ULE AMAPA DRAGO
EBANO SERON CAPULI CATENA
CHILTE CAPULIN COPALCHE
(MYTHICAL —) TUBA
(NEW ZEALAND —) AKE KARO
KAWA MIRO PUKA RATA RIMU
TAWA TORU WHAU HINAU KAORI
KAURI MAIRE MANGI MAPAU MATAI
TOWAI AKEAKE KAMAHI KANUKA
KAPUKA KARAKA KARAMU KAWAKA
KONINI MANUKA PURIRI TARATA
TITOKI TOATOA TOTARA WAHAHE
AKEPIRO MANGEAO PUKATEA
TARAIRI TARWOOD KAWAKAWA
KOHEKOHE MAKOMAKO
(ORNAMENTAL —) KABIKI
LABURNUM POINCIANA
(PHILIPPINES —) DAO IBA TUA TUI
ATLE BOGO DITA IFIL IPIL AGOHO
AGOJO ALMON AMAGA ANABO
BAYOG BAYOK BETIS DANLI GUIJO
LAUAN LIGAS TABOG YACAL
ALAGAO ALUPAG AMUYON ANAGAP
ANUBIN ARANGA BANUYO BATAAN
BATETE BATINO BOTONG DUNGON
KATMON LANETE MABOLO
MARANG MOLAVE SAGING TALUTO
AMUGUIS AMUYONG ANABONG
ANOBING ANONANG APITONG
BINUKAU CAMAGON DANGLIN
MANCONO MAYAPIS TINDALO
ALMACIGA BITANHOL KALIPAYA
KALUMPIT LUMBAYAO MACAASIM
MALAPAHO TANGUILE
(POISONOUS —) GUAO UPAS LIGAS
TANGHIN TANQUEN MANCHINEEL
(POLYNESIAN —) MACUDA
(SACRED —) CHAMPAC CHAMPAK

(SALT —) ATLE
(SANDARAC —) ARAR
(SHADE —) ELM DILLY GUAMA
HEVEA CATALPA HALESIA INKWOOD
JOEWOOD SYCAMORE
(SHOWY —) ASAK ASOK ASOKA
(SMALL —) AKE BOX TCHE ALDER
CUMAY DWARF HENNA NGAIO
SERON AKEAKE BLOLLY CHANAR
JOJOBA KOWHAI ARBORET
INKWOOD JOEWOOD KADAMBA
STADDLE TREELET EMAJAGUA
HARDTACK HUISACHE OLEASTER
SNOWBELL SOURWOOD TREELING
(SPINY —) LIME AROMA AROMO
HONEY BOOGUM BUCARE BUMELIA
CATECHU COLORIN LAVANGA
COCKSPUR
(STANDING —) FILLER
(STUNTED —) SCRAB SCRUB
SCRUNT
(THORNY —) BEL BAEL BREA
LEMON AMBACH SAMOHU
AMBATCH
(TIMBER —) ASH DAR ENG FIR SAL
ACLE ANDA BAKU COCO CUYA EKKI
IPIL PELU PINE TALA TEAK YANG
ACAPU ALMON AMAPA AMATE
AMBAY ANJAN ARACA ARGAN
BANAK BIRCH CAROB CEDAR
COCOA CULLA EBONY ERIZO FOTUI
HALDU ICICA IROKO KAURI KHAYA
KIAKI KOKAN MANIU MAPLE MVULE
NARRA ROBLE TIMBO ALERCE
ALUPAG BABOEN BACURY BANABA
BANCAL CARBON CHUPON CORTEZ
DAGAME DEGAME DUKUMA ESPAVE
FREIJO GAMARI GUMHAR IMBUIA
JACANA LEBBEK MUERMO PADAUK
SANDAN SATINE SISSOO AMUGUIS
AROEIRA BECUIBA BILLIAN CARAIPI
CYPRESS ESPAVEL GATEADO
GOMAVEL GUARABU GUAYABI
HARPULA HOLLONG KOOMBAR
LAPACHO REDWOOD AMARILLO
BOARWOOD CABREUVA CARACOLI
COCOBOLO CRABWOOD DONCELLA
GUATAMBU GUAYACAN MAHOGANY
SLOGWOOD SUCUPIRA
(TRAINED —) ESPALIER
(TROPICAL —) CYP AKEE AULU DALI
DIKA EBOE EKKI GUAO INGA MABA
MAHO MAJO PALM SHEA ACKEE
BALSA BONGO COUMA DALLI FOTUI
GUAMA GUARA ICICA ILAMA JIGUA
MARIA NEPAL NJAVE POOLI TARFA
ANUBIN BAKULA BALATA BANANA
CASHEW CEDRON CHUPON GENIPA
HACKIA ITAUBA LEBBEK LECYTH
MAMMEE OBECHE PERSEA
ANGELIN ANNATTO CAULOTE
COPAIBA DATTOCK EHRETIA
EUGENIA GATEADO GUACIMO
LAPACHO MAJAGUA MOMBINI
SANDBOX SOURSOP SURETTE
BEEFWOOD CALABASH CAMUNING
CORKWOOD FUNTUMIA
MUSKWOOD PATASHTE SWEETSOP
TAMARIND MONKEYPOD
MANGOSTEEN PRINCEWOOD
(UNARMED —) ALBIZZIA
(VARNISH —) DOON THEETSEE
(XEROPHYTIC —) SAXAUL

(YOUNG —) RUNNEL SPRING TILLER
SAPLING SEEDLING SPRINGER
(PL.) BLUFF RINDS SILVA
OVERSTORY
(PREF.) ARBORI DENDR(O)
(SUFF.) DENDRON
TREE CREEPER TOMTIT
TREE CYPRESS GILIA
TREE DUCK FIDDLER YAGUAZA
TREE EAR FUNGUS
TREE FROG FERREIRO
TREE MOSS USNEA
TREENAIL NOG GUTTA MOOTER
TRUNNEL
TREE PEONY MOUTAN
TREE SHREW TANA BANXRING
BANGSRING
TREE SNAKE BOOMSLANG
TREE TOAD HYLA HYLID ANURAN
TREE TOMATO TAMARILLO
TREETOP LAP LOP
TREFOIL CANCH LOTUS CLAVER
CROWTOE BEDSTRAW SAINFOIN
TICKSEED
TREHALOSE MYCOSE
TRELLIS TRAIL PERGOLA TARLIES
ESPALIER
TREMATODE FLUKE MARITA
STRIGEID
TREMBLE DARE DIRL RESE BEVER
QUAKE SHAKE SLOWS WIVER
AGRISE DIDDER DINGLE DITHER
DODDER FALTER HOTTER HOTTLE
NITHER QUAVER QUIVER SHIMMY
THRILL TITTER TOTTER TREMOR
TRYMLE WABBLE WOBBLE
WUTHER FLICKER SHUDDER
STAGGER TWIDDLE WHITHER
THRIMBLE
(PL.) TIRE TIRES
(PREF.) TREMELLI TROMO
TREMBLER BUZZER HAMMER
VIBRATOR
TREMBLING BEVER SHAKY DITHER
TREMOR TREPID AQUIVER
DODDERY PALSIED QUAKING
QUAVERY QUIVERY TREMBLY
TWITTER
TREMBLY WOOZY
TREMENDOUS BIG AWFUL GIANT
GREAT LARGE HOWLING TEARING
ENORMOUS HORRIBLE TERRIBLE
TERRIFIC MONSTROUS
TREMOLO HURRY TRILLO
TREMOR RIGOR SHAKE DINDLE
QUIVER THRILL SHUDDER
TREMBLE
TREMULOUS ASPEN QUAKY SHAKY
PALSIED SHIVERY TREMBLY
SHIMMERY TINGLING
TRENCH GAW SAP FOSS GRIP GURT
LINE MOAT RILL SICK SIKE TAJO
TRIG BOYAU CHASE DITCH DRAIN
DRILL FLOAT FOSSE GRAFF GRAFT
GRAVE GROOP SEUCH TRINK
COFFER FURROW GULLET GUTTER
SHEUGH ACEQUIA CUNETTE
CUVETTE OPENCUT SLIDDER
ENCROACH LOCKSPIT PARALLEL
SPREADER THOROUGH TRESPASS
(— BELOW FOREST FIRE) GUTTER
(— FOR BURYING POTATOES)
CAMP

(— FOR DRAIN TILES) CHASE
(— FORMED BY BANKING VEGETABLES) GRAVE
(— ON HILLSIDE) SLIDDER
(ARTIFICIAL —) LEAT
(IRRIGATION —) FLOAT SUGSLOOT
(PREF.) BOTHR(O) BOTHRI(O)
TRENCHANT ACID KEEN EDGED SHARP TUANT INCISIVE
TRENCHER PLATTER ROUNDEL
TRENCHERMAN EATER
TREND BEND BIAS HAND TONE TURN BULGE CURVE DRIFT SENSE SLANT SWING TENOR SQUINT STRIKE CURRENT DOWNSIDE MOVEMENT TENDENCY
(LOWERING PRICE —) EASE
TRENDY HIP MOD NOW POP CHIC GROOVY
TREPANG BALATE SWALLO SWALLOW TITFISH TEATFISH
TREPIDATION FEAR ALARM DISMAY
TRESPASS DEBT GILUT POACH BREACH FURTUM INVADE INTRUDE OFFENSE ENCROACH ENTRENCH INFRINGE INTRENCH OVERLOUP
TRESS CURL LOCK TAIL BRAID SWITCH RINGLET WIMPLER
TRES-TINE TRAY ROYAL
TRESTLE MARE HORSE INRUN CHEVALET SAWHORSE
TREVALLY TURRUM
TREWS TROUSERS
TRIACETATE ACETIN EUROBIN
TRIAD MAJOR TRIAS TRINE TRIUNE TERNARY TERNION TRILOGY TRINARY TRINITY TRIMURTI TRIRATNA
TRIAL SAY SHY TRY BOUT DOOM FIRE HACK OYER STAB TEST TURN ASSAY CROSS ESSAY GRIEF ISSUE POINT PROOF TASTE TOUCH WHACK ASSIZE EFFORT EQUITY TRINAL APPROOF ATTEMPT CALVARY DISGUST HEARING PROVING SCRATCH CRUCIBLE EXERCISE JUDGMENT QUAESTIO TENTAMEN PROLUSION
(— BY BATTLE) WAGER
(— BY ORDEAL) ORDALIUM
(— FOR HOUNDS) DERBY
(— OF SPEED) DASH
(— OF STRENGTH) CRUNCH
(— ROUND) HEAT
(AUTHOR OF —) KAFKA
(CHARACTER IN —) LENI JOSEPH ADVOCATE BURSTNER TITORELLI
(EXPERIMENTAL —) TENTAMEN
(RACING —) PREP
(SEVERE —) ORDEAL CRUCIBLE
(PREF.) PEIRA
TRIANGLE APEX CYMBAL OXYGON TRIGON PYRAMID SCALENE TRINITY TRIQUET DINGDONG ISOSCELE
(SPHERICAL —) PENDENTIVE
TRIANGULAR HEATER CUNEATE HASTATE
(— AREA) QUIRK
(— CLOTH) GORE
(— INSET) GODET
(PREF.) TRIGON(O)

TRIBAL GENTILE GENTLIC TRIBULAR
TRIBE (ALSO SEE NATIVE AND PEOPLE) AO GI ATI AUS BOH EVE EWE GOG KHA KIN KRA ROD SUK YAO ADAI AKAN AKHA AKIM AKKA BAYA BONI CLAN DAGO GUHA PURU QUNG RACE RAVI REKI SAHO SEID SHIK SHOR SIOL SOGA SUKU SUSU TOBA TURI TUSH UBII VEPS VILI VIRA YANA AEQUI ANGKA APTAL ARAWA BASSI BATAK BESSI BONGO BROOD CHANG CINEL DADJO DEDAN DIERI FIRCA GIBBI HORDE HOUSE ICENI KAJAR KANDH KEDAR KHOND KIWAI KONGO KOTAR KREPI LANGO MAGOG MARSI MBUBA MENDE MENDI MOSSI MUTER NANDI PHYLE PONDO QUADI SERER SOTIK STAMM SUEVI TAIPI TAULI TCAWI TEKKE TELEI TUATH VEPSE VOLOF WAKHI WARRI WASHO WAYAO YOMUD ADIGHE AGAWAM AMHARA ANAMIM ANTEVA APAYAO ARAINS BANYAI BASOGA BUDUMA BUSAOS CHAMPA CHAWIA CHORAI DOROBO FAMILY HERULI KARLUK KEREWA KHAMTI KONYAK KORANA LOBALE MANGAR MOLALA NATION NERVII PAHARI PHYLON POKOMO RAMNES SHAGIA SICULI SIMEON SUKUMA TAINUI TAMOYO TCHIAM TELEUT THUSHI TUSHIN TYPEES VENETI WABENA WABUMA WAGOMA WAGUHA WAHEHE WARORI WASOGA WAVIRA ZARAMO ZEGUHA ZENAGA ABABDEH ABANTES AIAWONG AKWAPIM AMAKOSA ANOMURA ANTAIVA ARVERNI BAGIRMI BAKATAN BAKONGO BAKUNDA BAMBARA BASONGO CABINDA CHAOUIA CHAUWIA CHONTAL CHUKCHI COLLERY DADAYAG DADSCHO ILLANUN JAZYGES KABINDA KABONGA KHOKANI KOLDAJI KONIAGA KOREISH KUBACHI KURUMBA LLANERO NAIADES PALAUNG PARISII PIMENTO RAURACI SAMBALA SAMBARA SEKHWAN SENONES SEQUANI SHAMMAR SHERANI SHERPAS SHUKRIA SILIPAN SUIONES SUKKIIM TAKELMA TARKANI TURKANA VIDDHAL WAGWENO WAICURI WUMBUGU WAREGGA WASANGO ZONGORA AMAFINGO ANDOROBO ASHANGOS ASSHURIM AWABAKAL BARKINJI BATETELA BOANBURA CHERUSCI CHITRALI GEZRITES JICAQUES KUKURUKU LANDUMAN NEBAIOTH ORUNCHUN PALLIYAN PHASIRON PUPULUCA PURUPURU RAHANWIN SAKALAVA SHINWARI SINGSING SINTSINK TCHUKCHI TENGGRIS USTARANA WANGATTA WAPOGORO WAPOKOMO
(— OF ISRAEL) DAN GAD ASHER REUBEN EPHRAIM ISSACHAR MANASSEH
(CHINESE —S) HU

(PRIVILEGED —) MAGHZEN MAKHZAN
(SEA GYPSY —) SELUNG
(PREF.) PHYL(O)
(SUFF.) INI
TRIBROMOETHANOL AVERTIN
TRIBULATION AGONY CROSS MISERY SORROW DISTRESS
TRIBUNAL BAR FEME ROTA VEHM BENCH COURT FEHME FORUM JUNTA VEHME MAJLIS ACUERDO ESGUARD MEJLISS RIGSRET AREOPAGY KANGAROO
TRIBUNE BEMA VELUTUS
TRIBUTARY ARM BOGAN BRANCH FEEDER TYBURN AFFLUENT ANABRANCH
TRIBUTE AID FEE TAX CAIN GELT KUDO LEVY PORT RENT SCAT CANON GAVEL HANSE MAILL SALVO SCATT CHAUTH HERIOT HIDAGE HOMAGE IMPOST CARATCH CHEVAGE CHIEFRY OVATION PENSION SYNODAL TREWAGE AUXILIUM BRENNAGE HEREGELD PESHKASH ROMESCOT ROMESHOT
(FEUDAL —) HERIOT
TRICE GIRD BLINK THROW INSTANT
TRICHECHUS MANATUS
TRICHINA NEMATODE
TRICHINIZED MEASLY
TRICHION CRINION
TRICHOME SCALE
TRICHOMONIASIS CANKER ABORTION
TRICK DO BAM BOB COG CON CUN DAP DOR FOB FOX FUB FUN GIN GUM JIG JOB PAW RIG BILK BITE BORE CHAW CHIP DIDO DIRT DUPE FAKE FIRK FLAM FLUM FOOL GAFF GAME GAUD GECK GULL HAVE HOAX HOSE JAPE JEST JINK JOUK JUNT LOCK LURK PASS PAWK PRAT PULL RORT RUSE SELL SKIT SLUR TURN WILE WIPE WOOL ANTIC BLEAR BLINK CATCH CHEAT CONNU CRAFT CREEK CROOK CULLY CURVE DODGE DORRE ELUDE FEINT FETCH FOURB FRAUD GLEEK GRIFT GUILE KNACK PAVIE PLANT PRANK SHIFT SHINE SKITE SLICK STUNT TRAIN TRUFF TWIST WHEEL WREST WRINK BAFFLE BANTER BEGUNK BEJAPE BLENCH BROGUE CAUTEL CHOUSE CRADDY DECEIT DELUDE DOUBLE EUCHRE FOURBE HOCKET HUMBUG ILLUDE JOCKEY JUGGLE MANNER PLISKY POLICY SCONCE SHAVIE SPRING TREPAN VAGARY WHEEZE WINNER CANTRIP CHICANE CONCEIT FICELLE FINESSE FORWARD GUILERY KNAVERY MARLOCK PAGEANT SHUFFLE SLEIGHT WHIZZER ARTIFICE CHALDESE CLAPTRAP CLOWNADE CONTOISE CROTCHET DELUSION DOUBLING FLAGARIE FLIMFLAM GILENYIE INTRIGUE JEOPARDY PRACTICE PRANCOME PRESTIGE QUENTISE SLAMPAMP TRAVERSE TRICKING BAMBOOZLE STRATAGEM

(— OUT) FARD FANGLE FINIFY
(BEGUILING —) WILE
(CARD —) CLUB HEART SPADE STICH DIAMOND WEAVING
(FRAUDULENT —) RIG TOP
(JUGGLING —) FOIST
(KIND OF —) ODD
(KNAVISH —) DOGTRICK
(LOVE —) AMORETTO
(MEAN —) TOUCH
(MONKEY —) SINGERIE
(OLD —) CONNU
(PETTY —S) CRANS
(SIX —S) BOOK
(SMART —) LIRIPIPE LIRIPOOP
(STUPID —) SHINE
(VEXING) CHAW
(WRESTLING —) CHIP CLICK FAULX FORWARD
(PL.) DAGS
TRICKER TRUMPER
TRICKERY DOLE GAFF SHAM TRAP TRAY WILE COVIN FRAUD HOCUS SHARK TRAIN CAUTEL COVINE DECEIT JAPERY JUGGLE TREGET DODGERY FALLACY GULLERY JOUKERY KNAVERY PAWKERY SLEIGHT ARTIFICE CHEATING COZENAGE JOOKERIE JUGGLERY PRACTICE TRICKING TRUMPERY SHENANIGAN SHENANIGANS
TRICKILY FOXILY
TRICKINESS PAWKERY
TRICKISH KNAVISH FRAUDFUL
TRICKLE DRIB DRIP DRILL STILL TRILL DISTIL DRIVEL GUTTER SICKER SIGGER STRAIN ZIGGER DISTILL DRIBBLE DRIZZLE DROPPLE TRINTLE
TRICKLET RILL
TRICKSTER GULL SHAM RASCAL TRAPAN SLICKER TRICKER SLEEVEEN TRAMPOSO TREGETOUR
TRICKSY ELFISH QUIRKSEY
TRICKY SLY DEEP BRAID DODGY FIKIE GAUDY ROWDY SNIDE ARTFUL CATCHY LUBRIC QUIRKY SHIFTY SMARTY TWISTY DEVIOUS SLANTER TRICKLE WINDING FLIMFLAM JUGGLING LUBRICAL SHIFTFUL SKITTISH SLIDDERY SLIPPERY TORTUOUS TRICKING
TRICLINIC ANORTHIC
TRICOT JERSEY
TRICYCLE VELO CYCLE TRIKE WHEEL TANDEM TRICAR RANTOON ROADSTER SOCIABLE
TRIDENT SPEAR VAJRA TRISUL TRISULA
TRIED TESTED PROBATE WEIGHED RELIABLE
TRIFECTA TRIPLE
TRIFLE ACE BOB DAB FIG HAW PIN SOU TOY BEAN COOT DOIT FICO FOOL HAIR HOOT JAUK MESS MOCK MOTE PLAY RUSE WHIT DALLY FLIRT FLUKE GLAIK ITEMY NIFLE PLACK POINT SCRAT SPORT TRICK TRUFF BAWBEE BREATH DABBLE DANDLE DAWDLE DELUDE DIBBLE DOODAD DOODLE FADDLE FESCUE FIDDLE FOOTER FOOTLE

FRIVOL GEWGAW MONKEY NIDDLE NIGGLE NIGNAY PADDLE PALTER PETTLE PICKLE PIDDLE PIGGLE PINGLE POTTER PUTTER STIVER TIFFLE VANITY WANTON FEATHER FLAMFEW FRIBBLE NOTHING QUIDDLE THOUGHT TRANEEN TRINKET TRIVIAL WHIFFLE COQUETTE FALDERAL FLIMFLAM FOLDEROL GIMCRACK KICKSHAW MOLEHILL NIFFNAFF NIHILITY NUGAMENT RIGMAREE TRANTLUM BAGATELLE

(— WITH) JANK DANDLE DELUDE NIGGLE

(ATTRACTIVE —) CONCEIT

(LITERARY —) TOY

(MERE —) SONG STRAW

(MEREST —) FIG

(SHOWY —) WALLY

(PL.) NUGAE TRIVIA GIBLETS FEWTRILS NONSENSE

TRIFLER DOODLE PLAYER WANTON FLANEUR FOOTLER FRIBBLE NUGATOR PINGLER TWIDDLER WHIFFLER

TRIFLES

(PREF.) NUGI

TRIFLING AIRY FOND IDLE FUNNY INANE LIGHT PETTY POTTY SILLY SMALL FADDLE FLIMSY FUTILE LEVITY LIMUTE LITTLE PALTRY SIMPLE SLIGHT STRAWY TOYISH FOOLISH FRIBBLE ITEMING NOMINAL PUERILE TRIVIAL TWATTLE COQUETRY FIDDLING FLIMFLAM FRIPPERY IMMOMENT NONSENSE NUGATORY PIDDLING SNIPPING FRIBBLING WHIFFLERY NEGLIGIBLE TOMFOOLERY

TRIFOLIUM CLOVER TREFOIL

TRIG NEAT SNOD TRIM CHIPPER

TRIGGER CAUSE VERGE TRICKER

TRIGGERFISH COCUYO TURBOT OLDWIFE BALISTID FILEFISH OLDWENCH

TRIGON TRINE SABBEKA SACKBUT SAMBUCA TRIGONON

TRIGONOMETRY SPHERICS

(— FUNCTION) SINE COSINE

TRILBY (AUTHOR OF —) DUMAURIER

(CHARACTER IN —) ALICE GECKO SANDY TAFFY BILLEE TRILBY OFERRALL SVENGALI

TRILL BURR FLAP ROLL SHAKE QUAVER THRILL TRILLO WARBLE ROULADE TRILLET

(BEGINNINNG OF A —) RIBATTUTA

TRILLED HIRRIENT

TRILLION

(PREF.) TERA TREG(A)

TRILLIONTH

(PREF.) PICO

TRILLIUM SARA TRUE SARAH TRUMP BENJAMIN TRUELOVE

TRILOBITE EODISCID

TRIM AX AXE CUT DUB GIM LIP LOP MOW NET BARB BEAD BUTT CLIP CROP DEFT DINK FEAT FUSS GASH GIMP HACK JIMP LACE NEAT PICK SNAG SNOD SNUG SPUR STOW TACK TOSH TRIG BRAID BRUSH CLEAN COPSE DRESS FITTY GENTY

HEDGE KEMPT KNIFE NATTY PREEN PRIME PRUNE PURGE SAUCY SHAVE SHEAR SHRAG SHRIP SLEEK SMART SMIRK SPRIG STUMP TIGHT TRICK VERGE BARBER DAPPER DONSIE DOUBLE FETTLE PICKED REFORM SHROUD SOIGNE SPRUCE SVELTE SWITCH TRIMLY CHIPPER FEATHER FLOUNCE SCISSOR MANICURE ORNAMENT TRIMMING SHIPSHAPE

(— A BOAT) SIT

(— ENDS OF HAIR) SHIRL

(— HEDGE) DUB

(— HIDES) ROUND

(— MEAT) CONDITION

(— SAIL) FILL

(— SEAMS) FETTLE

(— SHOE) FOX

(— TREES) PRIME SWAMP

(— WITH EMBROIDERY) GIMP PANEL

(FURNITURE —) SKIRT

TRIMLY SMARTLY SPRUCELY

TRIMMED PEEKABOO

TRIMMER FINER BRIDLE TACKER VOLANT ROUNDER SMOCKER SCRATTER

TRIMMING COQ FUR GIMP LACE BRAID CHAPE COQUE FRILL GUARD INKLE JABOT ROBIN RUCHE ERMINE LACING OSPREY PURFLE ROBING BEADING CASCADE FALBALA FURRING GALLOON MARABOU PUFFING ROULEAU BRAIDING EAVESING FALDERAL FOLDEROL FROSTING FROUFROU FURBELOW JEWELING PAILETTE PEARLING PICKADIL PLASTRON SOUTACHE PAILLETTE SPAGHETTI STRAPPING

(— OF KNOTTED THREAD) MACRAME MACRAMI

(FEATHER —) MARABOU MARABOUT

(PLEATED —) RUCHE

(PL.) LOP FLOTS SHORTS FIXINGS LOPPING BRAIDING FRILLIES

TRIMURTI TRINITY

TRINE TRENE TRIGON

TRINIDAD-TOBAGO (CAPITAL OF —) PORTOFSPAIN

(POINT OF —) GALERA

(RIVER OF —) ORTOIRE

(TOWN OF —) TOCO ARIMA COUVA LABREA MORUGA SIPARIA

TRINITARIAN MATHURIN

TRINITROTOLUENE TNT TOLITE TRITON

TRINITY TRIAD TRIAS TRINE TRIUNE GODHEAD TERNARY TRIMURTI TRINUNITY

TRINKET TOY DIDO GAUD MERE BIJOU HEART KNACK TAHLI BAUBLE CHARME DEVICE DOODAD GEWGAW BIBELOT TRANGAM TRANKUM GIMCRACK KICKSHAW TRANTLUM TRINKLET WHIMWHAM TCHOTCHKE

(PL.) TRINKUMS

TRINKETRY KNAVERY

TRIO GLEEK TERCET TERZET TRIUNE TERZETTO

(THREE —S) NONET

(TWO —S) SEXTET

TRIOLEFIN TRIENE

TRIONYX AMYDA

TRIOPAS (DAUGHTER OF —) IPHIMEDIA

(FATHER OF —) NEPTUNE

(MOTHER OF —) CANACE

(SON OF —) ERYSICHTHON

TRIOPS APUS

TRIP HOP JAG JET JOG TIP BOUT CHIP FOOT GAIT GATE KILT LINK RAKE SKIP TOUR TROT TURN BROAD DANCE DRIVE HITCH JAUNT SALLY CRUISE ERRAND FLIGHT HEGIRA OFFEND OUTING RAMBLE SAFARI SASHAY VOYAGE JOURNEY MISSTEP SAILING SETDOWN STUMBLE TRIPPER CAMPAIGN PERIPLUS

(— ALONG) CHIP LINK

(— BY DOG TEAM) MUSH

(— INTO COUNTRY) CAMPAIGN

(— IN WRESTLING) CHIP CLICK

(— UP) SUPPLANT

(HUNTING —) SHOOT

(KIND OF —) EGO

(MAKE A QUICK —) NIP

(PART OF —) LEG

(PLEASURE —) JUNKET

(SHORT —) HOP

TRIPE GOO PAUNCH ROLPENS TRILLIBUB CODSWALLOP

TRIPLE TRINE TREBLE TERNARY TRIFOLD TRIPLEX THRIBBLE TRIFECTA

TRIPLE BOND

(SUFF.)

(CONTAINING —) OLIC

TRIPLET TRIN CODON BRELAN PARIAL TERCET TRIOLE TRIPLE TERZINA TRIOLET HEMIOLIA TRILLING TRIPLING TRISTICH

(— OF BASES) CODON

TRIPLETAIL SAMA CHOBIE FLASHER GROUPER

TRIPLICITY TRIGON

TRIPOD CAT TRIP SPIDER TEAPOY TRIPOS TRIVET TRESTLE

TRIPODY HEMIEPES

TRIPOLI SILEX TRIPEL

TRIPPER DECKMAN

TRIPTOLEMUS (FATHER OF —) CELEUS

(MOTHER OF —) METANIRA

TRISHAW CYCLO PEDICAB

TRISMUS LOCKJAW TETANUS

TRISTAN UND ISOLDE

(CHARACTER IN —) MARK MELOT ISOLDE TRISTAN BRANGANE KURWENAL

(COMPOSER OF —) WAGNER

TRISTE SAD

TRISTRAM SHANDY (AUTHOR OF —) STERNE

(CHARACTER IN —) SLOP TOBY TRIM BOBBY SHANDY WADMAN WALTER YORICK SUSANNAH TRISTRAM

TRITE FADE HACK WORN BANAL CONNU CORNY HOARY MUSTY STALE TIRED VAPID BEATEN COMMON MODERN HACKNEY

PERCOCT TRIVIAL BROMIDIC SHOPWORN

TRITENESS BATHOS

TRITERPENOID CERIN

TRITON EFT NEWT TRUMPET

(FATHER OF —) NEPTUNE

(MOTHER OF —) AMPHITRITE

TRITURATE POUND POWDER

TRITURATION TRIPSIS

TRITURUS MOLGE

TRIUMPH WIN CROW PALM INSULT PREVAIL VICTORY CONQUEST

(— OVER) SCALP

TRIUMPHANT VICTOR EXULTANT JUBILANT

TRIUMPHING OVANT

TRIUNGULIN CRAWLER

TRIVET SPIDER TRIPOD TRESTLE TRIPPER BRANDISE

TRIVIAL BALD JERK NICE VAIN BANAL LEGER LIGHT PETTY SILLY SMALL TIDDY FIDFAD FOOTLE PALTRY SLIGHT TOYISH COMICAL PIPERLY PUERILE SHALLOW TIDDLEY DOGGEREL FEATHERY FOOTLING GIMCRACK PIDDLING PILULOUS TRIFLING TRINKETY

(NOT —) SOLID EARNEST

TRIVIALITY FOLLY FROTH NIGNAY TRIFLE INANITY IDLENESS NONSENSE NUGACITY

TROCHANTER SCAPULA

TROCHE ROTULA TABLET CACHUNDE PASTILLE

TROCHEE CHOREE CHOREUS TROCHEUS

TROCHLEA PULLEY

TROCTOLITE GABBRO

TRODDEN TRADED

(MUCH —) BEATEN

TROGLODYTIC SPELEAN

TROGON QUEZAL QUETZAL TOCORORO

TROILUS (BELOVED OF —) CRESSIDA

(FATHER OF —) PRIAM

(MOTHER OF —) HECUBA

(SLAYER OF —) ACHILLES

TROILUS AND CRESSIDA

(AUTHOR OF —) SHAKESPEARE

(CHARACTER IN —) AJAX HELEN PARIS PRIAM AENEAS HECTOR NESTOR ANTENOR CALCHAS HELENUS TROILUS ULYSSES ACHILLES CRESSIDA DIOMEDES MENELAUS PANDARUS AGAMEMNON ALEXANDER CASSANDRA DEIPHOBUS PATROCLUS THERSITES ANDROMACHE MARGARELON

TROJAN PARIS TROIC DARDAN HECTOR ANTENOR

(PL.) TEUCRI

TROLL DROW HARL SPIN TROW ANGLE HARLE MOOCH TRAWL TROLLOL

(— WITH LIVE BAIT) ROVE

TROLLER MOOCHER

TROLLEY CORF BOGEY BOGIE DOLLY TRUCK CRADLE PANTOGRAPH

(OFF ONE'S —) BATS CRAZY

TROLLOP CUT DOXY BITCH DOXIE TROLL TRULL DOLLOP

TROMBONE BONE TRAM BUSINE POSAUNE SACKBUT SLIPHORN **(PART OF —)** BOW CUP KEY RIM BELL CROOK FLARE SHANK SLIDE BUMPER FLANGE BALANCER MOUTHPIECE

TRONA URAO

TROOP FARE GANG GING ROUT TURM ROUTE SOLAK STAND TURMA WERED CORNET RISALA ROUGHT SCHOOL THREAT TICHEL TROUPE COMPANY COMITIVA **(— OF ARMED MEN)** CREW **(— OF FOXES)** SKULK **(— OF WORSHIPPERS)** THIASUS **(—S ATTACHED TO SOVEREIGN)** GUARDS **(—S IN BATTLE ARRAY)** SHELTRON **(—S ON WING OF ARMY)** ALARES **(ASSAULTING —S)** WAVE **(BOMBAY —S)** DUCKS **(CAVALRY —)** CORNET **(GIRL SCOUT —)** SHIP **(LIGHT-ARMED —S)** PSILOI **(MOUNTAIN —)** ALPINI **(MOUNTAIN —S)** ALPINI **(SCOTTISH —S)** JOCKS (PL.) GIS PARADE

TROOPER BARGIR REITER RUTTER BARGEER **(INDIAN —)** SOWAR

TROPARION HIRMOS HEIRMOS TROPARY KATABASIS

TROPE IMAGE EVOVAE SIMILE

TROPHONEMA VILLUS

TROPHONIUS (BROTHER OF —) AGAMEDES **(FATHER OF —)** APOLLO ERGINUS

TROPHOZOITE CEPHALIN SPORADIN

TROPHY BAG EMMY HUGO PALM PRIZE SCALP REWARD LAURELS **(WRITING —)** HUGO

TROPIC SOLAR TROPHIC

TROPINE HYOSCINE

TROS (FATHER OF —) ERICTHONIUS ERICHTHONIUS **(MOTHER OF —)** CALLIRRHOE **(SON OF —)** ILUS GANYMEDE ASSARACUS

TROT JOG SPUD TRIG FADGE HURRY PIAFFE **(KIND OF —)** TURKEY

TROTH CERTY TROGS TRUTH CERTIE

TROTTER DRIVER CRUBEEN SPANKER

TROUBADOR BARD MINSTREL SORDELLO

TROUBLE ADO AIL DIK HOE ILL IRK MAL MAR VEX WOE BEAT BUSY CAIN CARK EARN FASH FIKE GRAM JEEL MASH MOIL PAIN PINE ROUT SORE STIR TEEN TINE TRAY UNRO WORK ANNOY BESET CROSS DROVE DUTCH GRIEF HAUNT LABOR ROWEL SMITE SPITE STEER STURT SUSSY THRIE TWEAK WHILE WORRY BARRAT BOTHER BURBLE CADDLE CUMBER DITHER EFFORT GRIEVE GRUDGE HARASS HATTER KIAUGH MOLEST POTHER RATTLE RUBBER SORROW SQUALL TAKING THREAT UNEASE UNRUFE WORRIT

AFFLICT AGITATE ANXIETY CHAGRIN CONCERN DISEASE DISTURB DRUBBLE EMBROIL FASHERY INFLICT PERTURB PILIKIA SCRUPLE SPUTTER THOUGHT TRACHLE TRAVAIL TRIBBLE TURMOIL BUSINESS DARKNESS DISORDER DISQUIET DISTRESS NOISANCE VEXATION WANDRETH **(— ONE'S SELF)** PASS **(EXPRESSION OF —)** UHOH (PL.) CHAGRINS

TROUBLED DRUBLY DRUMLY GRUMLY QUEASY CAREFUL FRETFUL HAUNTED AGITATED HARASSED

TROUBLESHOOTER FIXER

TROUBLESOME DIK ILL SAD BUSY HARD FIKIE PESKY ROWDY SPINY TIGHT PLAGUY SHREWD STICKY THORNY UNEASY BRICKLE HARMFUL ONEROUS PESTFUL PLAGUEY TEWSOME ANNOYING FASHIOUS SPITEFUL UNTOWARD PLAGUESOME

TROUBLESOMENESS BOTHER

TROUBLING CHRONIC

TROU-DE-LOUP TRAPHOLE

TROUGH BOX CUP HOD RUN TOM BACK BOSH BUNK COVE DAIL DALE DISH DORR SHOE SINK TRAY TROW VALE BAKIE CHUTE DITCH LAVER SHOOT SHUTE SLIDE SPOUT STRIP ALVEUS BACKET BUDDLE GUTTER HARBOR HOPPER LAVABO MANGER RUNNER SALTER SINKER SLUICE STRAKE TROGUE VALLEY WALLOW CHENEAU CONDUIT LAUNDER RIFFLER TRENDLE TROFFER LAVATORY PENSTOCK **(— FOR ASHES)** BAKIE **(— FOR COOLING INGOTS)** BOSH **(— FOR KNEADING)** HUTCH **(— FOR PAPER PULP)** RIFFLER **(— FOR WASHING ORE)** TOM HUTCH STRIP BUDDLE STRAKE **(— IN MONASTERY)** LAVABO **(— OF A WAVE)** SULK **(— OF CIDER MILL)** CHASE **(— OF ROCK)** SYNCLINE **(— OF THE SEA)** ALVEUS **(ANNULAR —)** CUP **(BAKER'S —)** HUTCH **(EAVES —)** CANAL CHENEAU **(GLACIAL —)** DORR **(ORE —)** TYE **(SHEEP-DIPPING —)** DUP **(WOODEN —)** TRUG BAKIE TROGUE (PREF.) BOTHR(O) BOTHRI(O) PYEL(O) (SUFF.) SCAPH

TROUNCE MOP FLOG MOPUP THUMP TRAMP WHOMP COURSE CUDGEL DEFEAT CANVASS SHELLAC

TROUNCING LACING WARMING

TROUPE BALLET SERVANTS CUADRILLA

TROUPIAL ORIOLE

TROUSER STROSSER

TROUSERING CASINET

TROUSERS BAGS BELLS CORDS DUCKS JEANS KICKS PANTS SLOPS

TONGS TREWS BRAIES CHINOS DENIMS FLARES SHORTS SKILTS SLACKS WHITES BOTTOMS BRACCAE BROGUES CUTOFFS KERSEYS NANKINS SHALWAR SLIVERS STRIDES BLOOMERS BREECHES FLANNELS KICKSEYS MOLESKIN NANKEENS OVERALLS SHINTYAN PANTALOONS INDESCRIBABLES **(— CUT AT KNEE)** CUTOFFS **(— WITH CREASELESS LEGS)** STOVEPIPE

TROUT CHAR KELT PEAL POGY BROOK BROWN CHARR LAKER LUNGE SCURF SEWEN SEWIN SHARD SQUET SQUIT TRUFF FINNOC KIPPER MYKISS QUASKY SALTER TAIMEN TRUCHA TULADI BOREGAT BROOKIE BROWNIE COASTER HERLING OQUASSA POUNDER RAINBOW SQUETEE SUNAPEE AUREOLUS BODIERON GILLAROO HARDHEAD KAMLOOPS SAIBLING SALMONID SISCOWET **(SMALL —)** SCURLING SKIRLING **(YOUNG —)** WHITLING

TROUVERE BLONDEL

TROVATORE, IL (CHARACTER IN —) INEZ RUIZ DILUNA AZUCENA LEONORA MANRICO FERRANDO **(COMPOSER OF —)** VERDI

TROVE (TREASURE —) STASH

TROW DROW TRUE FAITH BELIEF COVENANT

TROWEL HAWK LEAF PIPE DARBY DERBY FLOAT TAPER TREWEL **(HEARTSHAPED —)** HEART DOGTAIL **(MOLDER'S —)** LEAF TAPER **(PLASTERER'S —)** FLOAT

TROY ILIUN TROIA TROJA **(FOUNDER OF —)** ILUS TROS **(INHABITANT OF —)** ILIAN

TROYENS, LES (CHARACTER IN —) ANNA DIDO IOPAS PRIAM AENEAS HECTOR NARBAL ASCANIUS PANTHEUS CASSANDRA CHOROEBUS **(COMPOSER OF —)** BERLIOZ

TRUANT HOOKY TRONE TROUT MICHER MEECHER TRIVANT VAGRANT

TRUCE PAX BARLEY TREAGUE INDUCIAE

TRUCK DAN UTE BUNK CORF DRAB DRAG DUCK DUMP GUNK RACK WYNN BOGIE BUGGY DILLY DOLLY GILLY LORRY TROKE BARTER BUMMER CAMION DIESEL DROGUE DRUGGE DUMPER JITNEY PICKUP SLOVEN TIPPER TURTLE CARAVAN FOURGON GONDOLA SKIDDER SLEEPER TROLLEY TRUCKLE TRUNDLE DELIVERY HAULAWAY TRANSFER **(COAL —)** DAN **(FIRE —)** PUMPER **(KIND OF —)** PANEL **(LOGGING —)** BUNK BUMMER **(MINING —)** CORF SKIP BARNEY **(PART OF —)** DECK HOOD STEP TANK TIRE GUARD LIGHT STAKE WHEEL BUMPER GRILLE MIRROR

AIRHORN CARRIER EXHAUST MUDFLAP BULKHEAD HEADLIGHT TAILLIGHT COMPRESSOR WINDSHIELD **(TIMBER —)** DRUG WYNN

TRUCKING (— RIG) SEMI

TRUCKLE FAWN TOADY SLAVER

TRUCKLING SERVILE

TRUCULENCE BRAG

TRUCULENT MEAN CRUEL HARSH FIERCE SAVAGE SCATHING

TRUDGE JOG PAD HAKE PLOD STOG JAUNT TRACE TRAIK TRAMP TRASH STODGE TAIGLE TRAIPSE

TRUE SO GOOD JUST LEAL PURE REAL VERY VRAI PLUMB RIGHT SOOTH SOUND VERAY ACTUAL FIDELE LAWFUL DEVOTED GENUINE GERMANE PRECISE SINCERE STAUNCH FAITHFUL RELIABLE RIGHTFUL SOOTHFUL UNERRING **(— TO THE FACT)** LITERAL **(NECESSARILY —)** APODICTIC APODEICTIC **(NOT —)** INEXACT **(QUESTIONABLY —)** ALLEGED **(SEEMINGLY —)** PLAUSIBLE (PREF.) ALETHO ETYMO EU ORTH(O) VERI

TRUFFLE TRUB TRUFF EARTHNUT

TRUISM SOOTH

TRULL DELL BLOWZE CALLET

TRULY YEA AWAT EVEN FEGS IWIS JUST QUITE SOOTH SYKER TIGHT ATWEEL DINKUM INDEED SIMPLY VERILY INSOOTH SOOTHLY VERAMENT WITTERLY

TRUMP DIS DIX LOW PAM LILY RUFF BASTA BASTO DEECE TROMBE MANILLA MATADOR TRIUMPH SPADILLE **(NOT —S)** LAY **(2ND HIGHEST —)** MANILLE

TRUMPERY MOCKADO RUBBISH GIMCRACK PEDDLERY

TRUMPET BEME LURE TUBA SHELL TRUMP BOZINE BUCCIN CORNET KERANA LITUUS TROMBA TULNIC ALCHEMY BUCCINA CLARINO CLARION KERRANA SALPINX NARSINGA SLUGHORN SOURDINE WATERCUP **(— OF DAFFODIL)** CORONA **(— OF FLOWER)** CORONA **(AUSTRALIAN —)** DIDGERIDOO DIDJERIDOO **(CONCH —)** SHELL **(RAM'S HORN —)** SHOFAR SHOPHAR (PREF.) SALPING(O) (SUFF.) SALPINX

TRUMPET BELL CODON PAVILON

TRUMPET CALL DIAN DIANA SENNET

TRUMPET CREEPER TECOMA COWHAGE CREEPER FOXGLOVE HELLVINE

TRUMPETER MOKI AGAMI TRUMP TOOTER JACAMIN TUBICEN YAKAMIK

TRUMPETER FISH MOKI MOKIHI

TRUMPETER PERCH MADO

TRUMPETS WATERCUP
TRUMPET-SHAPED BUCCINAL
TRUMPETWOOD IMBAUBA
TRUNCATED ABRUPT STUBBED
TRUNKED
TRUNCHEON BATON BILLY
WARDER SPONTON PARTISAN
SPONTOON
TRUNDLE HURL RUNG TRILL TROLL
RUNDLE TRUCKLE WALLOWER
TRUNK BOX BODY BOLE BOOT
BULK KIST LICH RUNT STAM STEM
STUD CABER PETER SHAFT STICK
STOCK TORSO ARIGUE BARREL
CAUDEX COFFER LOCKER
CARCASS CORSAGE STOWAGE
TRUNCUS SARATOGA
(ARTERIAL —) AORTA
(DEAD TREE —) RUNT
(ELEPHANT'S —) SNOUT
(FOSSIL —) CYCAD
(SMALL —) HATBOX
(SPLIT —) PUNCHEON
(SWIM —S) JAMS
(TREE —) BOLE BUTT STICK RICKER
**(TREE — OVER 8 INCHES IN
DIAMETER)** MAST
(TRIMMED TREE —) LOG
(WORSHIPPED TREE —S) IRMINSUL
(PREF.) CORM(O) PROBOSCI(DI)
TRUNKFISH CHAPIN BOXFISH
COWFISH
TRUSS TIE BIND GIRD SPAN
WARREN DORLACH
(— OF STRAW) WAP
(— UP) KILT
TRUST AFFY HOPE LITE POOL RELY
REST TICK TREW TROW FAITH
FRIST GROUP TRUTH BELIEF
CARTEL CHARGE CORNER CREDIT
DEPEND FIANCE LIPPEN OFFICE
TICKET BELIEVE BETRUST
COMBINE CONFIDE CREANCE
CRIANCE JAWBONE SECRECY
VENTURE AFFIANCE COMMENDA
CREDENCE MONOPOLY RELIANCE
(KIND OF) TOTTEN
(PLACE IN —) ESCROW
TRUSTED FIDUCIAL
TRUSTEE CURATOR FEOFFEE
SINDICO VISITOR ASSIGNEE
MUTWALLI
TRUSTWORTHINESS HONOR
TRUST CREDIT HONESTY
CREDENCE AXIOPISTY
TRUSTWORTHY SAFE SURE TRIG
SOOTH SOUND SYKER TRIED
HONEST SECRET SECURE SICKER
STABLE TRUSTY COCKSURE
CREDIBLE FIDUCIAL RELIABLE
TRUSTFUL
TRUSTY TRIG FECKFUL STAUNCH
FAITHFUL RELIABLE
TRUTH TAO UNA SOOTH TROTH
WHITE SATTVA VERITY LOWDOWN
REALITY VERITAS VERACITY
VERIDITY VERIMENT
(— TABLE) MATRIX
(FUNDAMENTAL —) PRINCIPLE
(IDEAL —) CHRIST DHARMA
(IN —) CERTES
(RELATING TO —) ALETHIC

(SELF-EVIDENT —) TRUISM
(ULTIMATE —) LIGHT SUNYATA
**TRUTH AND JUSTICE (AUTHOR OF
—)** TAMMSAARE
(CHARACTER IN —) MARI PAAS
KARIN TIINA ANDRES INDREK
TRUTHFUL TRUE VERY SOOTH
HONEST VERIDIC
TRUTHFULLY GOSPELLY
TRUTHFULNESS HONESTY
VERACITY SINCERITY
TRY GO SAY SHY TAX BASH BURL
FAND HACK PASS PENK PREE SEEK
SLAP STAB TEST TIRL TURN AFOND
ASSAY CRACK ESSAY ETTLE FLING
GROPE JUDGE OFFER PROVE
SENSE SOUND TASTE TEMPT
TOUCH WHACK WHIRL APPOSE
ASSAIL FRAIST GRIEVE STRIVE
AFFLICT AFFORCE APPROVE
ATTEMPT DISCUSS ESPROVE
IMITATE STAGGER ENDEAVOR
STRUGGLE
(— DESPERATELY) AGONIZE
(— FOR GOAL) SHOT
(— HARD) STRIVE
(— OUT) SAMPLE AUDITION
(— TO ATTAIN) AFFECT
(CASUAL —) FLING
(QUICK —) SLAP
TRYING NASTY ARDUOUS CRUCIAL
GRUELING
TRYSAIL SPENCER
TSAR SALTAN (CHARACTER IN —)
GUIDON SALTAN MILITRISA
POVARIKHA TKACHIKHA
(COMPOSER OF —)
RIMSKYKORSAKOV
**TSAR'S BRIDE, THE (CHARACTER
IN —)** IVAN LYKOV MARFA
LYUBASHA GRYAZNOY
(COMPOSER OF —)
RIMSKYKORSAKOV
TSETSE FLY KIVU GANDI DIPTERAN
GLOSSINA
T-SHAPED TAU
TSILTADEN CHILION
TSUBO BU
TSWANA CHUANA SECHUANA
TUAREG IMOHAGH IMOSHAGH
TUATARA GUANA GUANO IGUANA
HATTERIA
TUB FAT HOD KID KIT SOE SOW TUN
VAT BACK BOWK COOL CORF
COWL GAWN KNOP MEAL SCOW
TYND TYNE BOWIE ESHIN KEEVE
KIVER SKEEL STAND BUCKET
KEELER KILLER KIMNEL TROUGH
TURNEL BATHTUB BREAKER
SALTFAT TANKARD TRUNDLE
KOOLIMAN LAVATORY
(— FOR ALEWIVES) HOD
(— FOR AMALGAMATING ORES)
TINA
(— FOR BREAD) BARGE
(— OF BUTTER) COOL
(— OF HOGWASH) SWILLTUB
(— USED AS DIPPER) HANDY PIGGIN
(— WITH SLOPING SIDES) SHAUL
(BREWER'S —) BACK KEEVE
(KIND OF —) HOT
(LAUNDRY —) WASHTRAY
(MESS —) KID KIT

(MINING —) CORF
(PICKLING —) SALTFAT
(TANNING —) LEACH
(WATER —) DAN JAILER
(WOODEN —) KIT SOE KIMNEL
TRINDLE
TUBA BASS HELICON BOMBARDON
TUBE TAG BEAK BODY BOOT CANE
CASE CAST CORE CURL DRUM
DUCT HORN HOSE PIPE REED
WORM BATON CANAL CORER
CROOK CRYPT DRAIN GLAND
HEART LINER QUILL SIGHT SKELP
SLIDE SPILE SPOUT THECA THIEF
TRUMP TUBAL VALVE AUDION
BARREL CALCAR CANNEL CANNON
COLUMN CORNET DEWCAP FILTER
GULLET HEADER NOZZLE OCTODE
SLEEVE SUCKER SYRINX THROAT
TRIODE TUBING TUBULE TUNNEL
UPTAKE VESSEL BLOWGUN
CHIMNEY CONDUIT CUVETTE
DROPPER FERRULE FISTULA
HOUSING OOBLAST OVIDUCT
QUILLET ROSTRUM SALPINX
SHALLOT SNORTER SNUFFER
SOXHLET STOPPLE THIMBLE
TUBULUS VENTURI ADJUTAGE
BOMBILLA CORNICLE DIATREME
DRAWTUBE FAIRLEAD GRADUATE
ORTHICON OVARIOLE PENSTOCK
PIPESTEM SAUCISSE SIPHONET
SLEEVING URCEOLUS ZOOECIUM
(— AT BASE OF PETAL) CALCAR
**(— CARRYING BASSOON
MOUTHPIECE)** CROOK
(— COVERING TRACE CHAIN)
PIPING
(— FOR DEPOSITING CONCRETE)
TREMIE
(— FOR DRINKING MATE)
BOMBILLA
(— FOR LINING WELL) WELLRING
(— FOR OBOE REED) STAPLE
(— FOR STIFFENING STRING) TAG
(— FOR TRANSFERRING LIQUID)
SIPHON SYPHON
(— FOR WINDING THREAD) COP
(— FROM SHIP'S PUMP) DALE
(— IN ENGINE CYLINDER) LINER
(— OF BALLOON) APPENDIX
(— OF GUN) BORE BARREL
(— OF RETORT) BEAK ROSTRUM
(— OF SPIRIT LEVEL) BUBBLE
(— OF TOBACCO) CIGARET
(— TO LINE A VENT) BOUCHE
(— TWISTED IN COILS) WORM
(— USED IN WHALING) LULL
(AMPLIFIER —) STAGE
(BONE —) SNUFFER
(BOOB —) TV TELLY
(CAMERA —) VIDICON ORTHICON
(DISCHARGE —) TORUS
(DISTILLING —) TOWER
(ELECTRO —) BULB
(ELECTRODE —) AUDION PENTODE
(ELECTRON —) DIODE DRIVER
TRIODE TETRODE KENOTRON
KLYSTRON PLIOTRON TRINISCOPE
(ELECTRONIC INDICATOR —) NIXIE
(FIREWORKS —) LEADER
(GLANDULAR —) CRYPT
(GLASS —) SIGHT MATRASS

(GLASSBLOWER'S —) BLOWPIPE
(HONEY —) NECTARY SIPHONET
(INDICATOR —) NIXIE
(KIND OF —) PITOT
(KNITTED —) STOCKING
(LABORATORY —) PIPETTE
(PAPER —) LEADER PASTILLE
(PASTRY —) CORNET
(POLLEN —) SPERMARY
(PRIMING —) AUGET
(RECTIFIER —) IGNITRON
(SILK — OF SPIDER) SPIGOT
(SPEAKING —) BLOWER GOSPORT
(SUCKING —) STRAW
(SURGICAL —) CANNULA
(THERMOMETER —) STEM
(VACUUM —) DIODE KEYER
HEXODE HEPTODE DYNATRON
MAGNETRON
(PREF.) FISTULI SIPHON(O)
SOLEN(O) SYRING(O)
TUBELET CIRCLET
TUBER ANU OCA SET ANYU BULB
CLOG COCO ROOT SEED SETT
YAMP COCCO SALEP JICAMA
PIGNUT POTATO WAPATA WINDER
YAUTIA EARTHNUT MURRNONG
(DRIED —S) SALEP
TUBERCLE PEARL NODULE
STEMMA CUSPULE VERRUCA
TUBERCULAR PHTHISIC
TUBERCULOSIS CON LUPUS
CLYERS DECLINE PHTHISIS
SCROFULA
TUBING HOSE TUBAGE
TUBMAN DUCKER
TUBULAR PIPY PIPED TUBATE
QUILLED CANNULAR
(NOT —) FARCTATE
(PREF.) SOLEN(O)
TUBULE TRACHEA TUBULET
TUBULUS CISTERNA
TUCANO BETOYAN
TUCK TOKE STUFF TRUSS FLANGE
(— AWAY) KEEP SAVE STOW
(— IN) TRUSS TROUSS
(— UP) FAKE KILT
TUCKER CORDER KILTER PLEATER
(— OUT) TIRE
**TUESDAY (SECOND — AFTER
EASTER)** HOCKDAY HOKEDAY
TUFA TOPHUS
TUFF TRASS PEPERINO PORODITE
SANTORIN
TUFT COP EAR FAG FOB NOB SOP
TOP COMA DOWN KNOB KNOP
MOCK TAIT TATE TUFF TUSK TUZZ
WISP BEARD BUNCH CREST FLOCK
STUPA THRUM WHISK CATKIN
CIRRUS DOLLOP PAPPUS PENCIL
TASSEL TUFFET CIRRHUS FEATHER
FLOCCUS HOBNAIL PANACHE
SCOPULA TOPKNOT TOPPING
TUSSOCK AIGRETTE FLOCCULE
ARBUSCULE
(— OF BRISTLES) BIRSE
(— OF CLOTH) FAG
(— OF DIRTY WOOL) DAG
(— OF DOWN) FRIEZE
(— OF FEATHERS) EAR HORN HULU
EGRET
(— OF FILAMENTS) BYSSUS
(— OF FLOWERS) TRUSS

(**— OF GRASS**) FAG SOP MOCK HASSOCK TUSSOCK

(**— OF HAIR**) TOP COMA TUZZ BRUSH SWITCH COWLICK FEATHER FLOCCUS SCOPULA TOPKNOT IMPERIAL KROBYLOS

(**— OF HAIR ON HORSE'S HOOF**) FETLOCK

(**— OF HAY**) SOP

(**— OF MALE TURKEY**) BEARD

(**— OF WOOL**) FOB TUSK TUZZ FLOCK

(**— ON BIRD'S HEAD**) COP CUCK EGRET

(**— ON BONNET**) TOORIE

(**— ON CHIN**) GOATEE

(**— ON PINEAPPLE**) CROWN

(**— ON SEED PLANT**) PAPPUS

(**— ON SPIDER'S FEET**) SCOPULA

(**—S OF ROPE YARN**) THRUM

(**VASCULAR —**) GLOMUS

(PREF.) LOPH(O) LOPHI(O)

TUFTED COMOSE TAPPET TAPPIT CRISTATE

TUG LUG PUG RUG TIT TOG CHUG DRAG HALE HAUL PULL TOIL TUCK CHUFF HITCH PLUCK SHRUG TRACE JIGGER RUGGLE TOWBOAT TUGBOAT

TUGBOAT TOW TUG TOWBOAT TRACKER

TUI POE TUA KOKO TUWI POEBIRD

TUITION CUSTODY

TULIP LILY LILIUM BIZARRE BREEDER PICOTEE TURNSOLE

TULIP TREE POPLAR BASSWOOD CUCUMBER

TULIPWOOD AUBURN

TULLE ILLUSION

TULWAR SABER

TUMATAKURU IRISHMAN MATAGORY

TUMBLE TOP COUP WALT LATCH SPILL THROW TIFLE TRACE COTTON GROVEL PURLER TIFFLE TOPPLE WALTER WAMBLE WELTER STUMBLE WHEMMEL

(**— OVER**) TIPPLE WALLOP

TUMBLE-DOWN RUINOUS

TUMBLER NUT CLICK GLASS LEVER WIPER ROLLER ACROBAT DRUMMER TIPPLER TOPPLER VOLTIGEUR

TUMID TURGID BLOATED BULGING FUSTIAN TURGENT INFLATED TUMOROUS

TUMOR PAP WEN BEAL PIAN WART AMPER BOTCH GUMMA MYOMA NEVUS PHYMA SWELL TALPA AMBURY ANBURY EPULIS GLIOMA GYROMA INCOME KELOID LIPOMA MYXOMA NUROMA RISING WARBLE ADENOMA ANGIOMA CYSTOMA DERMOID DESMOID FIBROID FIBROMA LUTEOMA MYELOMA NEUROMA OSTEOMA OSTEOME SARCOMA TESTUDO THYMOMA ULONCUS ATHEROMA BLASTOMA CHLOROMA CHORDOMA CHORIOMA EMBRYOMA GANGLION GLANDULE HEMATOMA HEPATOMA HOLDFAST LYMPHOMA

MELANOMA MELICERA NEOPLASM ODONTOMA PHLEGMON PLASMOMA PSAMMOMA SCIRRHUS SEMINOMA TERATOID TERATOMA WINDGALL CHALAZION PAPILLOMA

(**— OF EYELID**) GRANDO

(**— ON HORSES'S LEGS**) JARDE

(**KIND OF —**) GLOMUS

(**PUSTULAR —**) BLAIN

(**SKIN —**) OUCH

(**STUDY OF —S**) ONCOLOGY

(PREF.) CARCIN(O) GANGLI(O) GANGLO MYOM(O) ONCO SCIRRH(O)

(SUFF.) CELE COELE COELUS OMA ONCUS SCIRRHUS

TUMULT DIN COIL FARE FLAW FRAY FUSS HURL MUSS REEL RIOT ROUT VISE BRAWL BROIL HURLY HURRY LURRY NOISE ROUST STOOR STOUR WHIRL AFFRAY BUSTLE CLAMOR DIRDUM EMEUTE FRACAS HUBBUB MUTINY PUDDER RABBLE RIPPET ROMAGE RUFFLE SHINDY STEERY UPROAR UPSTIR BLUSTER BOBBERY BRATTLE FACTION FERMENT GARBOIL TEMPEST TURMOIL DISORDER SEDITION STIRRING STRAMASH COMMOTION PANDEMONIUM

TUMULTUOUS HIGH LOUD RUDE NOISY ROUGH STORMY FURIOUS HURRIED LAWLESS RIOTOUS VIOLENT AGITATED CONFUSED DRAWLING HURTLING

TUMULUS LOW MOTE TUMP MOUND BARROW BURIAN COTERELL

TUN CASK HAAR

(**ONE-THIRD —**) TERTIAN

(**20 —S**) KATUN

TUNA AHI ATUN TUNNY BLUEFIN PELAMYD ALBACORE KAWAKAWA

(**KIND OF —**) SKIPJACK

TUNE AIR ARIA DUMP FADO LEED LILT NOTE PORT RANT SONG CHARM CHORD DITTY DRANT POINT ATTUNE GROUND MAGGOT STRAIN STRING TEMPER GUAJIRA HALLING MEASURE MELISMA SONANCE ANGLAISE FANDANGO GUARACHA HABANERA QUICKSTEP

(**— A HARP**) WREST

(**— AN INSTRUMENT**) STRING

(**DANCE —**) FURIANT ANGLAISE GALLIARD

(**FOLK —**) FADO

(**HILLBILLY —**) HOEDOWN

(**IN —**) ONKEY

(**LIGHT —**) TOY

(**LITTLE —**) CATCH

(**LIVELY —**) LILT SPRING HORNPIPE

(**MELANCHOLY —**) DUMP

(**SACRED —**) CHORAL CHORALE

(**TRADITIONAL —**) TONE

TUNEBO TAME GUACICO

TUNEFUL TUNY CHANTANT TUNESOME

TUNEFULNESS MELODY

TUNGST-

(PREF.) WOLFRAM

TUNGSTEN W WOLFRAM SCHEELIN

TUNGUS EVENK LAMUT

TUNIC COAT JAMA JUPE VEST AODAI COTTE FROCK GIPON GIPPO JAMAH JUPON PALLA ACHKAN BLIAUT CAMISE CHITON CYCLAS FECKET HARDIE KABAYA KIRTLE TABARD ARISARD BLEAUNT CAMISIA DASHIKI PALTOCK SURCOAT TUNICLE COLOBIUM DAISHIKI GANDOURA SUBTUNIC SUBUCULA SUKKENYE

(**— OF MAIL**) HAUBERK

(**AFRICAN —**) DASHIKI DAISHIKI

(**HOODED FUR —**) SOVIK

TUNICATE SALP SALPA SALPID ASCIDIAN TUNICARY UROCHORD

TUNICLE SACCOS

TUNING ANESIS

TUNING FORK EVEL EVIL FORK TUNER DIAPASE DIAPASON MODULANT

TUNING HAMMER KEY

TUNISIA

CAPE: BON BLANC
CAPITAL: TUNIS
COIN: DINAR
GULF: GABES TUNIS HAMMAMET
ISLAND: DJERBA
LAKE: ACHKEL DJERID BIZERTE
MEASURE: SAA SAH SAAH CAFIZ WHIBA METTAR
PORT: SFAX GABES TUNIS SOUSSE BIZERTE
RIVER: MEDJERDA
TOWN: BEJA DOUZ SFAX SUSA GABES GAFSA THALA MATEUR NABEUL SOUSSE BIZERTE JENDOUBA KAIROUAN TEBOURBA ZAGHOUAN
WEIGHT: SAA ROTL ARTAI ARTEL RATEL UCKIA KANTAR

TUNNEL ADIT BORE CAVE CURL PUKA SINK TUBE DRIFT DRIVE KAREZ STALL BURROW PIERCE

(**— IN ROCK**) SYRINX

(**— INTO AN IGLOO**) TOSSUT

(**IRRIGATION —**) QANAT

(**KIND OF —**) CARPAL

(**PROPOSED —**) CHUNNEL

TUNNY TUNA ALBACORE SCOMBRID

(**YOUNG —**) PELAMYD

TUP TIP TRIP MONKEY BLISSOM

TUR (**BROTHER OF —**) IRAJ SALM

(**FATHER OF —**) FARIDUN

(**MOTHER OF —**) SHAHRINAZ

TURACO LORY

TURANDOT (**CHARACTER IN —**) LIU CALAF TURANDOT

(**COMPOSER OF —**) PUCCINI

TURBAN PAT MOAB PATA SASH TUFT LUNGI MITER MITRE PAGRI PATTI TOWEL TUFFE MANDIL WRAPPER KAFFIYEH PUGGAREE SEERBAND TOLIPANE TULIPANT TURBANTO

TURBELLARIA APROCTA

TURBELLARIAN FLATWORM

TURBID FAT RILY DROVY GUMLY MUDDY RILEY ROILY DRUMLY

GRUMLY QUALLY FECULENT LUTULENT

TURBIDITY RILE

TURBOT BRET BRILL WHIFF FLATFISH

TURBULENCE CAT FURY UPROAR FERMENT RIOTING

(**— IN WATER**) BULLER

TURBULENT GURL HIGH LOUD RUDE WILD ROILY ROUGH WROTH RUGGED STORMY UNRULY YEASTY FURIOUS RABBISH RACKETY TROUBLE VIOLENT MUTINOUS SCAMBLING BOISTEROUS

TURCO IN ITALIA, IL (**CHARACTER IN —**) DAMELEC GERONIO FIORILLA PROSDOCIMO

(**COMPOSER OF —**) ROSSINI

TURDUS MERULA

TUREEN DISH TERRINE

TURF SOD VAG CESS DELF FAIL FALE FEAL FLAG FLAT FLAW PONE SUNK DELFT SCRAW SPINE SWARD TRUFF FLAUGHT SHIRREL SODDING GREENSWARD

(**— CUT BY GOLF STROKE**) DIVOT

(**— FOR LINING PARAPET**) GAZON

(**DRIED — FOR FUEL**) VAG

(**PARED —**) BEAT

(**ROUGH —**) GOR

(**SMALL PIECE OF —**) TAR

(**SMOOTH —**) FAIRWAY

(**THIN LAYER OF —**) FLAW

TURF SPADE SLANE

TURGID ERECT TUMID BLOATED INFLATED PLETHORIC

TURGIDNESS TYMPANY

TURK TURCO TURKO SELJUK CORSAIR OSMANLI OTTOMAN TURQUET KONARIOT

TURKANA ELKUMA

TURKEY BUST FLOP STAG STEG BUSTARD ERECTER ERECTOR FAILURE GOBBLER ALDERMAN

(**BRUSH —**) VULTURN TALEGALLA

(**FLOCK OF —S**) RAFTER

(**KIND OF —**) COLD

(**MALE —**) TOM

(**YOUNG —**) POULT

TURKEY

CAPE: INCE BAFRA ANAMUR HINZIR KARATAS KEREMPE
CAPITAL: ANKARA
COIN: LIRA PARA AKCHA ASPER ATTUN REBIA AKCHEH SEQUIN ZEQUIN ALTILIK BESHLIK PATAQUE PIASTER MEDJIDIE ZECCHINO
DISTRICT: PERA BEYOGLU CILICIA
GULF: COS ANTALYA
LAKE: TUZ VAN EGRIDIR BEYSEHIR
MEASURE: DRA OKA OKE PIK DRAA HATT KHAT KILE ZIRA ALMUD BERRI DONUM KILEH ZIRAI ARSHIN CHINIK DJERIB FORTIN HALEBI PARMAK NOCKTAT
MOUNTAIN: AK ALA KARA HASAN HINIS HONAZ MURAT MURIT ARARAT BINGOL BOLGAR SUPHAN ERCIYAS KARACALI
PROVINCE: MUS VAN AGRI BOLU ICEL KARS ORDU RIZE SERT URFA

USAK AYDIN BURSA IZMIR SIIRT
ANGORA EYALET
REGION: ANATOLIA
RIVER: DICLE FIRAT GEDIZ HALYS
IRMAK KIZIL MESTA SARUS
SEIHUN SEYHAN SEYLAN TIGRIS
SAKARYA MAEANDER
SEAPORT: ENOS IZMIR MERSIN
SAMSUN TRABZON ISTANBUL
TOWN: URFA ADANA BURSA IZMIR
IZNIK KONYA MARAS SIIRT SIVAS
AINTAB EDESSA EDIRNE ELAZIG
MARASH SAMSUN ERZURUM
KAYSERI SCUTARI USKUDAR
ISTANBUL STAMBOUL
WEIGHT: OKA OKE DRAM KILE ROTL
ARTAL ARTEL CEQUI CHEKE
KERAT MAUND OBOLU RATEL
BATMAN DIRHEM KANTAR
MISKAL DRACHMA QUINTAL
YUSDRUM

TURKEY BUZZARD AURA
BROMVOEL BROMVOGEL
GALLINAZO
TURKEY-COCK STAG
TURKEY OAK CERRIS
TURKI KAZAK QAZAQ KAZAKH
TURKISH TURK TURCIC OSMANLI
OTTOMAN
TURKISH DELIGHT LOUKOUM

TURKMENISTAN (ALSO SEE
RUSSIA)
CAPITAL: ASHKHABAD
COIN: RUBLE
DESERT: KARAKUM KARAKUMY
MOUNTAIN RANGE: KOPETDAG
KHAROPETDAG KUGITANGTAU
NAME: TURKMEN TURKMENIA
OASIS: MURGAB TEDZHEN
AMUDARYA KOPETDAG
RIVER: OXUS ATREK MURGAB
TEDZHEN AMUDARYA
SEA: CASPIAN
TOWN: MARY MERV NEBITDAG
CHARDZHOU KRASNOVODSK
TRIBE: TEKKE YOMUT ERSARI

TURKOMAN SEID ERSAR
TURK'S CAP LILY MARTAGON
TURMERIC REA ANGO HALDI OLENA
HULDEE AZAFRAN CURCUMA
TURMIT TURNIP
TURMOIL ADO DIN COIL DUST MOIL
TOIL TOSS BURLE HURLY HURRY
STROW TOUSE WHIRL HASSLE
JABBLE POTHER ROMAGE UPROAR
WELTER CLUTTER EMOTION
FERMENT GARBOIL HURLING
MAKADOO RUMMAGE TEMPEST
DISPEACE DISQUIET
TURN GO BOW CUT GEE JAR RUN
TON WIN AIRT BEND BOUT BOWL
CALE CAST CHAR CHOP COCK
EDDY GIRO HACK HEAD HINT HURL
JAMB KINK PULL PURL QUIP ROLL
ROVE SLEW TIRL TOUR VEER VERT
VICE WAFT WELT WIND AIRTH
ANGLE BLANK CHARE CRANK
CRASH CREEK CRICK CROOK
ELBOW FEEZE GLINT PIVOT PLUCK
PRICK QUIRK SHIFT SPELL SWING

SWIRL TARVE TERVE TREND TRILL
TROLL TWINE TWIST VERSE VOLTI
WHEEL WREST ATTURN BOUGHT
CIRCLE COURSE DEPEND DIRECT
DOUBLE GRUPPO GYRATE INDENT
INTEND INTURN POSSET QUEEVE
RESORT RETURN ROTATE SPIRAL
STRAIN SWIVEL TOURNE TURKEN
VOLUME VOLUTE WIMPLE
CONVERT CRANKLE CRINKLE
DEFLECT DISTURB FLEXION
FLEXURE FLOUNCE INCLINE
INFLECT PASSADE REVERSE
REVOLVE SERPENT SINUATE
TWINGLE TWISTER VERSATE
WREATHE CLINAMEN DOUBLING
FLECTION TOURNURE TRAVERSE
VOLUTION
(— ABOUT) SLEW SLUE SLOUGH
WINDLASS
(— AGAINST) CROSS
(— AROUND) GYRE WELT WEND
RATCH BEWEND SPHERE
(— ASIDE) ERR WRY DAFF SKEW
WARD ABHOR AVERT BLENK DETER
EVADE FENCE GLENT SHEER WAIVE
BLENCH DEPART DETURN DIVERT
SWERVE SWITCH CRINKLE DECLINE
DEFLECT DEVIATE DIGRESS
DIVERGE PERVERT SCRITHE
(— AT DRINKING) TIRL
(— ATTENTION) ADVERT ADDRESS
(— AWAY) DOFF AVERT CHARE
HIELD REPEL AVERSE DESERT
DETURN DIVERT REVOLT ABANDON
DECLINE REVERSE OVERTURN
WITHTURN
(— AWRY) CONTORT
(— BACK) KEP ABORT FLIPE FLYPE
RETORT RETURN REVERT REFLECT
UNTWIST RENVERSE
(— BACK ON) RUMP
(— BROWN) AUGUST
(— BY TOSSING) FLAP
(— CARD FACE UP) BURN
(— DOWN) DIP DENY VETO
(— DOWNWARDS) SLOPE
(— FOR BETTER) CRISIS
(— FOR INFORMATION) REFER
(— IN ARCHERY) END
(— IN CROQUET) BISK BISQUE
(— IN ROPE) NIP RIDER
(— INSIDE OUT) EVERT FLYPE
INVERT
(— INTO ICE) CONGEAL
(— INTO STEEL) ACIERATE
(— INTO VINEGAR) ACETIFY
(— INTO WOOD) LIGNIFY
(— LEAVES OF BOOK) LEAF TOSS
(— LEFT) HAW PORT
(— OF AFFAIRS) GO JOB KICK
(— OF CABLE) BITTER
(— OF DUTY) TOUR SHIFT TRICK
(— OF EVENTS) WENT
(— OF EXPRESSION) CONCETTO
(— OFF) SHUNT DIVERT
(— OF FANCY) GUST
(— OF MIND) FREAK
(— OF STRING) WAP
(— OF TIDE) PINCH
(— OF WIT) FLIRT
(— OF YARN) MOUSING
(— ON) HIT AROUSE

(— ONE'S BACK) TERGIVERSATE
(— ON LATHE) THROW
(— OUT) GO USH BEAR FALL FARE
OUST SORT TAKE CHIVE FUDGE
LOOSE OUTPUT SUCCEED
(— OUT TO BE) PROVE EXFLECT
(— OUTWARD) EVERT SPLAY
(— OVER) CANT FLAP FLIP KEEL
VETTE VOLVE CLINCH DESIGN
AGITATE CAPSIZE OVERSET
(— PAGES) LEAF
(— POINT OF) ABATE
(— RAPIDLY) SPIN TIRL GIDDY
(— RIGHT) GEE HAP HUP
(— SAIL YARD) BRACE
(— SIDEWAYS) TRAVERSE
(— SKIS) STEM
(— SOUR) FOX BLINK PRILL BLEEZE
CHANGE SOUREN
(— SUDDENLY) FLOP SLUE
(— THE BALANCE) PREPONDERATE
(— TO BUY DRINKS) SHOUT
(— TO DUST) MOULDER
(— TO NEAR SIDE) HAW
(— TO OFF SIDE) GEE
(— TO ONE SIDE) CORNER GOGGLE
(— TO STONE) LAPIDIFY
(— TO THE LEFT) HAW PORT WIND
WYND
(— TOWARD WIND) LUFF
(— TO WINDWARD) STAY
(— UP) FACE HAPPEN
(— UP NOSE) FLIRT SNURL
(— UPSIDE DOWN) CANT COUP
WHELM INVERT QUELME WHELVE
WHEMMLE
(— VESSEL IN CIRCLE) CHAPEL
(— WHEELS) CRAMP
(— YELLOW) FIRE
(BALLET —) PIROUETTE
(COMPLETE —) LAP
(DOWNWARD —) SLIDE
(ECCENTRIC —) CRANKUM
(FORTUNATE —) BREAK
(GOOD —) BOON SERVICE
(HALF —) CARACOLE
(IN —) AROUND
(INWARD —) INTROVERT
(SERIES OF —S) CHICANE
(SERIES OF TIGHT —S) CHICANE
(SHARP —) ZAG DOUBLE WRENCH
ZIGZAG HAIRPIN
(SKI —) SWING CHRISTIE TELEMARK
(SUDDEN —) CURL
(TAKE —S) ROTATE
(PL.) ALLEGRO
(PREF.) STREPHO STREPSI
STREPT(O) TREPO TROP(IDO)(O)
VERSI VERTEBR(I)(O) VERTI
(SUFF.) TROPAL TROPE TROPIA
TROPIC TROPY
TURNBUCKLE TURNEL TURNBOUT
TURNCOAT RAT APOSTATE
RENEGADE RENEGADO RENEGATE
TURNED SOUR VERSED COCKEYED
INFLEXED
(— ABOUT) CONVERSE
(— AWAY) FROWARD
(— AWRY) TORTIVE
(— BACK) EVOLUTE RETRORSE
(— DOWNWARD) ABASED
DEFLEXED
(— EDGEWISE) BLIND

(— INWARD) VARUS
(— OUTWARD) SPLAY EXTRORSE
(— TOWARD) ANODIC
(— TOWARD ONE SIDE) AWRY
(— UP) ACOCK URVED RETROUSSE
(— WRONG WAY) AWK
(PREF.) STREPSI
TURNER SLICE BODGER SLIDER
TWIRLER
TURNING HEAD WIND TWIST VOLTA
WRINK DETOUR ROTARY FLEXION
FLEXURE VERSION VOLVENT
FLECTION STREPSIS WHEELERY
ACESCENCE
(— ASIDE) APOTROPAIC
(— BACK) RETORTION REFLECTION
(— FREELY) VERSATILE
(— OF EYE) CAST
(— SOUR) ACESCENT
(— SUNWISE) EUTROPIC
EUTROPOUS
(— TO LEFT) SINISTRAL
LAEOTROPIC
(— TO RIGHT) DEXTRO
(— TOWARD STEM) ADVERSE
(— UP) OCCURRENT
(METAL —S) SWARF
(PL.) SCULL
(PREF.) STROPH(O) TROPIDO
TROPO
(SUFF.) TROPAL TROPE TROPIA
TROPIC(AL) TROPISM TROPOUS
TROPY
TURNIP BAGA NAPE NEEP RAPE
NAVEW SWEDE RAPEYE TURMUT
CRUCIFER RUTABAGA
(KIND OF —) SWEDISH
(PL.) KRAUT RAPPINI
(PREF.) NAPI
TURNIP-SHAPED NAPIFORM
RAPACEUS
TURNIX QUAIL HEMIPOD ORTYGAN
HEMIPODE
TURNKEY SCREW JAILER
LOCKSMAN
**TURN OF THE SCREW (AUTHOR OF
—)** JAMES
(CHARACTER IN —) FLORA MILES
PETER QUINT JESSEL
TURNOUT RIG TEAM SETOUT
EQUIPAGE TRANSFER
TURNOVER PIE PASTY BRIDIE
BRAMBLE CALZONE EMPANADA
FLAPJACK
(PL.) PIROJKI PIROSHKI
TURNPIN TAMPION
TURNSOLE HELIO
TURNSPIT HASTLER
TURNSTILE TIRL STILE MOULINE
TURNGATE TURNPIKE TOURNIQUET
TURNSTONE PLOVER REDLEG
CHICARIC CREDDOCK
TURNTABLE DECK RACER ROTARY
NONSYNC PLAYBACK
TURNUS (FATHER OF —) DAUNUS
(MOTHER OF —) VENILIA
(SLAYER OF —) AENEAS
TURPENTINE THUS TURPS SCRAPE
THINNER OLEORESIN
(BORDEAUX —) GALIPOT
TURPENTINE TREE PEEBEEN
TURPITUDE EVIL FEDITY

TURQUOISE TURKEY TURKIS
  CALAITE CALLAIS
TURRET ROUND BELFRY CUPOLA
  GARRET GAZEBO LOUVER TOURET
  BARMKIN GUERITE MIRADOR
  MONITOR BARBETTE BARTIZAN
  GUNHOUSE PINNACLE TURRICLE
  BELVEDERE PEPPERBOX
  (CORNER —) ROUND
TURTLE EMYD ARRAU CARET CAREY
  TORUP COODLE COOTER JURARA
  RIDLEY SLIDER THURGI TURKLE
  CRAWLER CREEPER EMYDIAN
  JUNIATA LOGHEAD SNAPPER
  TORTUGA CHELONID FLAPJACK
  HAWKBILL MATAMATA SHAGTAIL
  STINKPOT TERRAPIN TORTOISE
  THALASSIAN
  (— HAVING COMMERCIAL SHELL)
  CHICKEN
  (OLD —) MOSSBACK
  (PART OF —) EAR BEAK CLAW
  SHELL SHIELD CARAPACE
  PLASTRON
  (SEA —) RIDLEY
TURTLEHEAD BAI MONY CHELONE
  CODHEAD
TUSCAN BROWN MECCA
  MOHAWK
TUSCANY COLCOTHAR
TUSK GAM CUSK HORN TUSH IVORY
  TOOTH ELEPHANT
  (— OF WILD BOAR) RAZOR
  (ELEPHANT'S —) SCRIVELLO
TUSSLE TUG SCRAP BICKER TASSEL
  TOUSLE WARSLE TUILYIE
TUSSOCK HASSOCK
TUT HOOT TOOT HOOTS
TUTELAGE TUTELE YEMSEL
  NURTURE TEACHING
TUTELARY GENIUS
TUTOR DON ABBE TUTE COACH
  TRACH DOCENT FEEDER GROUND
  MASTER MENTOR PEDANT
  SCHOOL GRINDER TEACHER
  CRANSIER CREANCER GOVERNOR
  PANGLOSS PUPILIZE PRECEPTOR
  REPETITEUR SCHOOLMASTER
TUTTI RIPIENO
TUTU TOOT TUPAKIHI
TUVALU (CAPITAL OF —) FUNAFUTI
  (FORMER NAME OF —)
  ELLICEISLANDS LAGOONISLANDS
  (ISLAND OF —) NANUMEA
  NUKUFETAU NUKULAILAI
TUXEDO TUX SOFA TUCK
TVASHTRI (DAUGHTER OF —)
  SARANYU
TWADDLE ROT BOSH TOSH FUDGE
  HAVER BABBLE DRIVEL FOOTLE
  PIFFLE TOOTLE FADAISE TWATTLE
  NONSENSE SLIPSLOP TOMMYROT
TWANA COLCINE
TWANG TANG PLUCK PLUNK
  SNUFFLE TWANGLE TWANKLE
TWANGY NASAL
TWAYBLADE DUFOIL TWIFOIL
  (PL.) LISTERA
TWEAK FEAK TWIG
TWEED PATTU PATTOO
TWEEZERS TIT TWIRK TWINGE
  TWITCH MULLETS PINCERS
  PINCETTE VOLSELLA

TWELFTH TWALT DOZENTH
  (— OF INCH) SECOND
  (— OF LIGHT PERIOD) INCH
  (— PART) UNCIA
TWELFTH DAY EPIPHANY
TWELFTH NIGHT (AUTHOR OF —)
  SHAKESPEARE
  (CHARACTER IN —) TOBY BELCH
  CURIO FESTE MARIA VIOLA
  ANDREW FABIAN OLIVIA ORSINO
  ANTONIO MALVOLIO AGUECHEEK
  SEBASTIAN VALENTINE
TWELVE TWAL DOZEN DICKER
  DODECADE
  (PREF.) DODEC(A) DUODECIM
TWELVEMONTH TOWMONT
TWELVER IMAMI
TWELVE-TONE SERIAL
TWELVE-TONE-ROW SET
TWENTIETH VIGESIMAL VINGTIEME
TWENTY KAPH CORGE KAPPA
  SCORE COOREE
  (PREF.) ICOS(A) VIGINTI
TWENTY-FIVE QUARTERN
TWENTY-FOURTH CARAT
TWENTY-ONE PONTOON VAN JOHN
  BLACKJACK
20,000 LEAGUES UNDER THE
  SEA (AUTHOR OF —) VERNE
  (CHARACTER IN —) NED LAND
  NEMO PIERRE ARONNAX CONSEIL
TWERP DRIP NERD TWIT DRONGO
  SHNOOK
TWICE BIS DOPPIO
  (— A DAY) BID
  (— IN TIME) AGAIN
  (PREF.) BI BIS DI DIS
TWICE-BORN REGENERATE
TWIDDLE TWEEDLE TWITTER
  (— FEET) CUT
  (— THE FEET) CUT
TWIG COW CHAT RICE RISP SLIP
  WAND YARD BIRCH BRIAR BRIER
  SHRAG SHRED SPRAY SPRIG STICK
  TWIST VIRGA WAVER WITHE
  BALEYS BROWSE FESCUE GREAVE
  SALLOW SPRING SWITCH WATTLE
  WICKER SCOLLOP TWIGLET
  ANAPHYTE
  (— FOR SNUFF) DIP
  (— GROWING FROM STUMP)
  WAVER
  (— IN BIRD SNARE) SWEEK
  (—S FOR BURNING) CHATWOOD
  (—S FOR WATTLING) FRITLES
  (—S MADE INTO BROOM) BESOM
  (— WORN AT SACRIFICES)
  INARCULUM
  (BARE —) COW
  (BROKEN —S) BRUSH
  (CUT —) SARMENT
  (DRIED —) CHAD
  (LITTLE —) SURCLE
  (THATCHING —) SCOLLOP
  (WILLOW —) SALLOW ANAPHYTE
  (SUFF.) CLEMA
TWIGGED VIRGATE
TWIGGY SPRAYEY
TWILIGHT EVE DIMPS DUMPS
  GLOAM TWALE DIMMET DIMMIT
  UGHTEN DUCKISH COCKSHUT
  EVENFALL EVENGLOW EVENTIDE
  GLOAMING GRISPING CREPUSCLE

(— OF THE GODS) RAGNAROK
(DARKER PART OF —) DUSK
(MORNING —) DAWN
TWILL WALE CHINO CADDIS RUSSEL
  CADDICE DUNGAREE
TWILLED CORDED
TWIN DUAL GEMEL SOSIE DIDYMUS
  JUMELLE SIAMESE TWINDLE
  DIDYMATE DIDYMOID DIDYMOUS
  PARASITE TWINLING
  (PL.) GEMEL COUPLET
  (PREF.) DIDYM(O) GEMINI
  (SUFF.) DIDYMUS
TWINE MAT COIL DUNE LACE PIRL
  WIND WRAP TWIRL TWIST ENLACE
  INFOLD INTORT ANAMITE ENTWINE
  SKEENYIE
  (HANK OF —) RAN
  (PITCHED —) WHIPPING
  (PREF.) PLEC(O)
TWINEBUSH PINBUSH
TWINFLOWER LINNAEA
TWINGE ACHE GIRD PANG PULL
  SHOOT TOUCH TWANG STOUND
  (— OF CONSCIENCE) SCRUPLE
  (— OF PAIN) GLISK
TWINING VOLUBLE AMPLECTANT
TWINKLE WINK BLINK TWEER
  TWINK TWIRE BICKER SECOND
  SIMPER WINKLE SPARKLE
TWINKLE-TOED AGILE
TWINKLING TRICE MOMENT
  TWINKLY
TWINLEAF HELMETPOD
TWIRL SPIN TIRL DRILL QUERL TRILL
  TWIRK TWIST WHIRL TRUNDLE
  TWIDDLE TWIZZLE
  (— OF BAGPIPE) WARBLER
TWIST BOB CUE MAT PLY WIN WIP
  CAST COIL CURL DRAW HURL KICK
  KINK PIRL RICK SKEW SLEW SLUB
  SLUE TURN WARP WIND WISP
  WORK CHINK CRANK CRICK CRINK
  CROOK CURVE FEEZE GNARL
  KINCH PLAIT QUIRK QUIRL REEVE
  SCREW SKELL SNAKE SNIRL SNURL
  SPIRE SWIRL THRAW THROW
  TWEAK TWIND TWINE TWIRE
  TWIRL WINCE WITHE WREST
  WRICK BOUGHT DETORT EXTORT
  HANKLE INTORT QUEEVE SLOUGH
  SPRAIN SQUIRL SQUIRM STRAND
  TWEEZE WAMBLE WARPLE
  WASHIN WICKER WIMBLE
  WRABBE WRITHE CHIGNON
  CONTORT CRANKLE CRINKLE
  CROOKLE CRUMPLE DISTORT
  ENTWINE ENTWIST FLOUNCE
  GIMMICK SQUINCH TORTURE
  TWISTER TWISTLE TWIZZLE
  WREATHE WRIGGLE CLINAMEN
  CONVOLVE ENTANGLE FOREHARD
  FORETURN SPRINKLE SQUIGGLE
  VOLUTION
  (— A ROPE) DALLY
  (— AWAY) WAIVE
  (— BACK) RETORT
  (— FORCIBLY) WRING
  (— IN A ROPE) GRIND SQUIRM
  (— IN GRAIN OF A BOW) BOUGHT
  (— IN ONE'S NATURE) KINK
  (— OF FACE) STITCH
  (— OF HAY) HAYBRAND

(— OF PAPER) SPILL
(— OF PEN IN WRITING) QUIRK
(— OF SPEECH) CRANK
(— OF THE MOUTH) DRAD
(— OF TOBACCO) ROLL PIGTAIL
(— OF YARNS) FORETURN
(— OUT OF SHAPE) BUCKLE
  CONTORT
(— SHARPLY) FEAK
(— TOGETHER) CABLE RADDLE
(CAUSE TO —) TORQUE
(DOUBLE —) ESS
(PREF.) SPIR(I)(O) STREMMATO
  STREPHO STREPSI STREPT(O)
  TORSO TORTI
TWISTED CAM KAM WRY AWRY
  TORT KINKY SCREW TORSE WELKT
  WRONG ATWIST GAUCHE HURLED
  KNOTTY SCREWY SKEWED SWIRLY
  THRAWN THROWN TURKEN
  TWISTY WARPED WRITHE CRISPED
  CROOKED GNARLED KNOTTED
  SCREWED TORQUED TORTILE
  TORTIVE WHELKED WREATHY
  COCKEYED IMPLICIT INTORTED
  INVOLVED NONPLANE THRAWART
  WREATHEN
  (PREF.) PLEC(O) PLECT(O) STREPSI
  STREPT(O)
TWISTING DALLY KNECK AJOINT
  TWIRLY WIGWAG ENTRAIL
  TWIDDLY SQUIGGLY STREPSIS
  TORTUOUS
  (PREF.) STROPH(O)
TWIT TIT CHECK TAUNT TEASE
  ETWITE NEEDLE TWITTER
  RIDICULE
TWITCH TIC TIT FEAK FIRK JERK
  JUMP PIRN TWIG WINK YANK
  PLUCK START THRIP TWEAK TWICK
  TWIRK QUATCH QUETCH QUITCH
  TWINGE TWITCHEL VELLICATE
TWITCHING TIC JERKS PALMUS
  WORKING SACCADIC
TWITTER TWIT CHIRM CHIRP GARRE
  TWINK JARGON WARBLE CHIPPER
  CHIRRUP CHITTER QUITTER
  TWITTLE WHITTER
TWO TWA BOTH TWAY TWIN TWAIN
  BINARY COUPLE DOUBLE
  (— LINES) LONGWAYS
  (— OF A KIND) BRACE
  (IN —) ATWO
  (US —) UNC
  (PREF.) BI BIS DUO DY(O) TWI
  (— EACH) BINI
  (IN —) DICH(O)
  (MORE THAN —) MULTI
TWO-COLORED BICHROME
  (PREF.) DICHRO(O)
TWO-DIMENSIONAL FLAT PLANAR
TWO-DOOR COUPE ROADSTER
TWO-FACED FALSE
  DOUBLEDEALING JANUS
  JANIFORM
  (PREF.) JANI
TWO-FIFTEEN PM TIME
TWOFOLD DUAL BINAL DUPLE
  BACKED BIFOLD DOUBLE DUPLEX
  DIGONAL DIPLOID TWIFOLD
  DIDYMATE DIDYMOID DIDYMOUS
  DIPLASIC TWEYFOLD BIFARIOUS
  (PREF.) DI DIPHY DIPL(O)

TWO-FOOTED BIPED
TWO-FORKED BIFURCAL
TWO GENTLEMEN OF VERONA
(AUTHOR OF —) SHAKESPEARE
(CHARACTER IN —) JULIA MILAN
SPEED LAUNCE SILVIA THURIO
ANTONIO LUCETTA PROTEUS
EGLAMOUR PANTHINO VALENTINE
TWO-HANDED BIMANAL
BIMANOUS
TWO-HEADED
(PREF.) DICRANO JANI
TWO-HORNED BICORN BICORNED
TWOPENCE TUPPENCE
TWO-POINTER BASKET
TWOS POT DEUCE
TWO-UP SWY
**TWO WIDOWS, THE (CHARACTER
IN —)** ANEZKA MUMLAL KAROLINA
LADISLAV
(COMPOSER OF —) SMETANA
TWO-WINGED
(PREF.) DIPTER(O)
TYCHICUS (COMPANION OF —)
PAUL
TYCOON SHOGUN TAIKUN
TYDEUS (FATHER OF —) EONEUS
OENEUS
(MOTHER OF —) PERIBOEA
(SON OF —) DIOMEDES
TYKE KIDDIE
TYMPANUM DRUM TYMPAN
EARDRUM EPIPHRAGM
TYNDAREUS (BROTHER OF —)
ICARIUS
(DAUGHTER OF —) PHILOPOE
TIMANDRA CLYTEMNESTRA

(FATHER OF —) OEBALUS PERIERES
(MOTHER OF —) BATIA
GORGOPHONE
(WIFE OF —) LEDA
TYPE CUT ILK CAST KIND MAKE
MOLD NORM SORT TAKE BOGUS
BROOD IMAGE MOULD PRINT
STAMP EMBLEM KICKER KIDNEY
LETTER NATURE SHADOW STRIPE
SYMBOL TAKING TIMBER BATARDE
FASHION PARABLE ANTETYPE
EXEMPLAR
(— BLOCK) QUAD
(— OF EXCELLENCE) PARAGON
(— PLACED BOTTOM UP) TURN
(— SET UP) MATTER
(ASSORTMENT OF —) FONT
(DANCE —) LASYA
(DISARRANGED —) PI PIE
(GERMAN —) FRAKTUR
(HEAVY-FACED —) IONIC
(HIGHEST —) PINK
(IDEAL —) CHRIST
(INVERTED —) TURN
(OPPOSITE —) ANTITYPE
(ORIGINAL —) PROTOTYPE
(PART OF —) BACK BALL BODY
FACE FOOT NICK SIZE STEM
BEARD BELLY BEVEL SERIF SHANK
GROOVE COUNTER ASCENDER
CROSSBAR SHOULDER
DESCENDER
(PHYSICAL —) HABIT
(RACIAL —) DEHWAR
(REMARKABLE —) SPECIMEN
(REPRESENTATIVE —) GENIUS
(SET —) STICK

(SIZE OF —) (SEE SIZE) PICA POINT
DIAMOND ENGLISH
(STYLE OF —) AGATE CANON DORIC
ELITE GOUDY GREEK IONIC KABEL
ROMAN BODONI CASLON CICERO
GOTHIC HEBREW ITALIC JENSON
MODERN BOOKMAN BREVIER
CENTURY ELZEVIR EMERALD
FULLFACE GARAMOND
(PREF.) MORPH(O)
TYPEBAR
(PL.) BASKET
TYPEE (AUTHOR OF —) MELVILLE
(CHARACTER IN —) TOM TOBY
MARNOO MEHEVI FAYAWAY
KORYKORY
TYPEFACE FACE FRAKTUR
BOLDFACE SANSERIF
TYPEHOLDER PALLET
TYPESETTER MONO
TYPESETTING FAT PHAT
TYPEWRITER MILL TYPER TYPIST
PORTABLE
(PART OF —) BAR KEY BAIL KNOB
LOOP STOP GUIDE LEVER PLATE
SCALE SHIFT HOLDER MARGIN
PLATEN RETURN ROLLER SPACER
CONTROL RELEASE SUPPORT
CARRIAGE KEYBOARD REGULATOR
BACKSPACER
TYPHON (FATHER OF —) TARTARUS
(MOTHER OF —) TERRA
TYPHOON WIND CYCLONE
TUFFOON
TYPICAL FAIR TYPAL TYPIC USUAL
AVERAGE CLASSIC PATTERN
PERFECT REGULAR

(PREF.) EU
(SUFF.) (— OF) ISH ISTIC
TYPIFY TYPE IMAGE SHADOW
ADUMBRATE EPITOMIZE
PERSONIFY REPRESENT
SYMBOLIZE
(— BEFOREHAND) FORESHADOW
TYPIFYING GENERIC
TYR ER EAR TIU TYRR
(BROTHER OF —) THOR
(FATHER OF —) ODIN
TYRANNICAL LORDLY SLAVISH
ABSOLUTE DESPOTIC OPPRESSIVE
TYRANNIZE OPPRESS DOMINEER
OVERLORD
TYRANNOUS ABSOLUTE
TYRANNY ROD DESPOTISM
TYRANT ANARCH DESPOT NIMROD
FUEHRER PHARAOH PHALARIS
TYRANT FLYCATCHER PEWEE
TYRE (SITE OF —) SUR
TYRO HAM BABE COLT PUPIL
NOVICE RABBIT TYRONE BEGINNER
NEOPHYTE
(FATHER OF —) SALMONEUS
(HUSBAND OF —) CRETHEUS
(MOTHER OF —) ALCIDICE
(SON OF —) AESON NELEUS PELIAS
PHERES AMYTHAON
TYRRHENIAN ETRUSCAN
TYRRHENUS (BROTHER OF —)
LYDUD TARCHON
(FATHER OF —) ATYS HERCULES
TELEPHUS
(MOTHER OF —) HIERA OMPHALE
CALLITHEA
TYTO ALUCO STRIX

U

U UNCLE UNION
(PREF.) **(— SHAPED)** HY(O)
UDDER BAG DUG TID EWER ELDER
SUMEN VESSEL
UFO (STUDY OF —S) UFOLOGY

UGANDA

AIRPORT: ENTEBBE
CAPITAL: KAMPALA
COLLEGE: MAKERERE
FORMER CAPITAL: ENTEBBE
LAKE: KYOGA ALBERT EDWARD
GEORGE VICTORIA
LANGUAGE: ATESO GANDA
LUGANDA SWAHILI
MOUNTAIN: ELGON MARGHERITA
MOUNTAIN RANGE: RUWENZORI
NATIVE: ATESO BANTU LANGO
ACHOLI ANKOLE BAGISU BAKIGA
BASOGA BATORO BAGANDA
BUNYORO LUGBARA NILOTIC
SUDANIC
PLATEAU: ANKOLE
PROVINCE: BUGANDA
RIVER: ASWA KAFU PAGER
KATONGA
SEAPORT: MOMBASA
TOWN: ARUA JINJA MBALE KITGUM
MOROTO TORORO ENTEBBE
MOMBASA
WATERFALL: KABALEGA

UGH OOF YECH YUCK YECCH
UGLY FOUL AWFUL OUGLE SNIVY
UNKED CRANKY DREEPY GORGON
GROTTY HOMELY LAIDLY ORNERY
CRABBED GRIZZLY HIDEOUS
HOUGHLY VICIOUS GRUESOME
UGLISOME UNLOVELY
MONSTROUS
UGLY-TEMPERED SNARLISH
UGNI BLANC TREBBIANO
UIGHUR JAGATAI
UINTAITE ASPHALT GILSONITE
UITOTAN KAIMO WITOTAN
UKASE ORDER
UKE JARANA

UKRAINE

(ALSO SEE RUSSIA)
BAY: KALAMIT KARKINIT
CANAL: CRIMEAN
CAPITAL: KIEV
COIN: KARBOVANET
GULF: TAGANROG TAHANROH
LAKE: KIEV KANIV LENIN DNIEPER
SVITYAZ DNIESTER KAKHOVKA
MARSH: PRIPET PRYPYAT
MOUNTAIN: KAMULA HOVERLYA
ROMANKOSH MOHYLABELMAK
MOHYLAMECHETNA
MOUNTAIN RANGE: CRIMEAN
KARPATY CARPATHIAN

PENINSULA: KERCH CRIMEAN
RIVER: BUG BUH STRY TYSA DESNA
INHUL SLUCH TISZA DNIPRO
DONETS PRIPET SALHYR ZBRUCH
DNIEPER DNISTER PRYPYAT
TETERIV VORSKLA DNIESTER
SEA: AZOV BLACK
TOWN: KIEV LVIV LVOV KYYIV
ODESSA DONETSK KHARKIV
KHARKOV KRYVYRIH CHERNOBYL
KRIVOYROG ZAPOROZHYE
ZAPORIZHZHYA DNIPROPETROVSK

UKRAINIAN RUSSNIAK
UKULELE UKE TAROPATCH
ULAM (FATHER OF —) ESHEK
ULCER FRET KYLE SORE WOLF
BOTCH ISSUE RUPIA ULCUS
APHTHA MORMAL TETTER
BEDSORE CHANCRE EGILOPS
ENCAUMA FISTULA AEGILOPS
FONTANEL FOSSETTE ULCUSCLE
(ARTIFICIAL —) ISSUE
(PREF.) CHANCRI HELC(O)
ULCERATING EXEDENT
ULCERATION NOMA CANKER
CARIES BEDSORE HELCOSIS
ULCEROUS HELCOID
ULEX LING
ULEXITE TIZA
ULLIKUMMI (FATHER OF —)
KUMARBI
ULNA CUBIT CUBITAL CUBITUS
ULTIMATE IT NTH DIRE LAST FINAL
ULTIME SUPREME ABSOLUTE
EVENTUAL FARTHEST ULTIMITY
ULTIMATELY FINALLY
ULTIMO PAST
ULTRA EXTREME FANATIC
FORWARD
(NE PLUS —) IDEAL
ULTRACONSERVATISM TORYISM
ULTRACONSERVATIVE WHITE
ULTRAFASHIONABLE RITZY SWELL
SWAGGER
ULTRAMONTANISM CURIALISM
ULTRASOUND SONOGRAPHY
ULUA PAPIO PAPIOPIO
ULULATE HOWL
ULYSSES (AUTHOR OF —) JOYCE
(CHARACTER IN —) BUCK RUDY
BLOOM BREEN MOLLY BLAZES
BOYLAN COFFEY GERTIE HAINES
MARION DEDALUS LEOPOLD
PUREFOY STEPHEN MULLIGAN
MACDOWELL
(FATHER OF —) LAERTES
(MOTHER OF —) ANTICLEA
(SLAYER OF —) TELEGONUS
(SON OF —) TELEMACHUS
(WIFE OF —) PENELOPE
UMBEL RAY AXIS RADIUS SERTULE
UMBELLA SERTULUM UMBELLET

UMBELLIFERONE CUMARIN
COUMARIN
UMBER OMER OMBER PARTRIDGE
UMBILICUS NAVEL
(PREF.) OMPHAL(O)
UMBO BEAK UMBONULE
UMBONES NATES
UMBRA DOGFISH MUDFISH
NUCLEUS UMBRINE
UMBRAGE PIQUE SNUFF OFFENSE
UMBRELLA BELL GAMP MUSH
DUMPY BROLLY CHATTA PAYONG
PILEUS CHATTAH GINGHAM
ROUNDEL FITTISOL KITTYSOL
MUSHROOM TYRASOLE
BUMBERSHOOT
(PART OF —) CAP RIB ROD TIP GORE
JOINT PANEL SHAFT BULLET
HANDLE RUNNER SPRING CLOSURE
FERRULE STRETCHER
UMBRELLA BIRD COTINGA
COTINGID
UMBRELLA BUSH MILJEE
UMBRELLA PALM KENTIA
UMBRELLA PLANT SEDGE GLUMAL
UMBRELLA TREE WAHOO
ELKWOOD MAGNOLIA
UMBRETTE UMBRE HOMBRE
UMBRET CICONIID
UMBRIAN IGUVINE
UMBURANA ROBLE
UMLAUT MUTATION METAPHONY
UMPIRE REF UMP JUDGE TRIER
ARBITER DAYSMAN ODDSMAN
REFEREE OVERSMAN STICKLER
BIRLIEMAN BYRLAWMAN
UNABASHED BROWLESS
UNABBREVIATED FULL
UNABLE UNHABILE POWERLESS
UNACCENTED GRAVE LIGHT
ATONIC
UNACCEPTABLE DREADFUL
UNACCOMPANIED BARE SOLO
ALONE SECCO SINGLE
UNACCOUNTABLE STRANGE
UNACCUSTOMED UNUSED
STRANGE INSOLITE WONTLESS
UNACQUAINTED STRANGE
UNCOUTH
UNADORNED DRY BALD PLAIN
SECCO STARK RUSTIC SEVERE
SIMPLE AUSTERE LITERAL
INORNATE
UNADULTERATED NET FRANK
HONEST VIRGIN GENUINE SINCERE
ABSOLUTE
UNADVANTAGEOUSLY ILL
UNAFFECTED EASY REAL PLAIN
HOMELY NATIVE RUSTIC SIMPLE
ARTLESS BUCOLIC SINCERE
SEMPLICE
UNAFRAID BOLD BRAVE DEFIANT
UNAGGRESSIVE AMIABLE

UNALERT SUPINE
UNALLOYED DEEP SOLID VIRGIN
GENUINE
UNALTERABLE IMMUTABLE
UNAMBIGUOUS EXPLICIT
UNANIMATED FLAT VAPID INSIPID
UNANIMITY ATTACK CONSENT
UNANIMOUS SOLID WHOLE
UNANIME UNIVOCAL
UNAPPROACHABLE STATELY
UNARMED BARE INERM UNBARBED
(PREF.) ANOPL(O)
UNASPIRATED LENE
UNASSAILABLE SECURE
UNASSUMED NATURAL
UNASSUMING SHY HUMBLE
MODEST SIMPLE NATURAL
RETIRING
UNATTACHED FREE LOOSE SINGLE
UNATTENDED SINGLE
UNATTRACTIVE BLAH UGLY PLAIN
WORSE HOMELY FRUMPISH
UNLIKELY
UNAVAILING VAIN FUTILE
BOOTLESS GAINLESS NUGATORY
UNAVOIDABLE SHUNLESS
NECESSARY
UNAVOWED SECRET
UNAWARE UNWARE WITLESS
HEEDLESS INNOCENT UNBEWARE
WARELESS OBLIVIOUS
UNAWARES ABACK SHORT
UNBALANCED ALOP HITE DOTTY
NUTTY FRUITY UNEVEN FANATIC
DERANGED LOPSIDED PIXILATED
MOONSTRUCK
UNBAR UNSLOT
UNBARRED UNSTOKEN
UNBEARDED CALLOW
UNBECOMING RUDE INEPT PLAIN
INDIGN UNMEET BENEATH
IMPROPER INDECENT UNSEEMLY
UNWORTHY
UNBEFITTING BENEATH
UNBELIEF UNFAITH
UNBELIEVABLE HOT THIN
UNBELIEVER PAGAN GIAOUR
ATHEIST DOUBTER INFIDEL
SCOFFER SKEPTIC
UNBELIEVING MISCREANT
UNBEND REST THAW FRESE RELAX
UNTIE EXTEND DISBEND UNCROOK
UNBENDING RIGID STARK STERN
STIFF THARF CATONIAN
OBDURATE RAMRODDY RESOLUTE
UNBIASED FAIR JUST DETACHED
UNBIND FREE UNDO UNTIE UNGIRD
UNDRESS
UNBLAMABLE INNOCENT
UNBLEACHED BLAE BLAY ECRU
BEIGE BROWN
UNBLEMISHED FAIR PURE SOUND
WHITE ENTIRE SPOTLESS

UNBLOCK REDD
UNBLOODY INCRUENT
UNBOLT OPEN UNBAR UNPIN
UNBOSOM OPEN
UNBOUGHT UNCOFT
UNBOUND FREE LOOSE
UNBOUNDED HUGE
UNBRANDED SLICK NATIVE
UNBROKEN DEAD FLAT FERAL
FLUSH SHEER SOLID SOUND
SINGLE CERRERO REGULAR
UNRACED STRAIGHT UNBACKED
WAKELESS
UNBUILD DESTROY
UNBUILT UNBIGGED
UNBURDEN EMPTY UNLOAD
UNSHIP
UNBURNISHED WHITE MATTED
UNCALLED (— FOR) GRATUITOUS
UNCANNY EERY UNCO EERIE
SCARY UNCOW UNKID WEIRD
WISHT CREEPY SPOOKY UNCOUTH
ELDRITCH POKERISH
UNCASTRATED INTACT
UNCAUGHT UNHENT
UNCEASING ENDLESS ETERNAL
EASELESS MINUTELY
UNCEREMONIOUS CURT BLUFF
BLUNT SHORT ABRUPT CASUAL
FAMILIAR INFORMAL
UNCERTAIN WAW DARK HAZY
WILD FLUKY SHADY SHAKY
WAUGH CASUAL CLOUDY CRANKY
FITFUL FLUKEY GLEAMY QUEASY
CASALTY CHANCEY COMICAL
DUBIOUS TRICKSY VAGRANT
VARIOUS WILSOME CATCHING
DELICATE FLICKERY FUGITIVE
HOVERING INSECURE SLIPPERY
TECHNOUS TICKLISH
UNCERTAINTY MIST WERE DEMUR
DOUBT MAYBE BAFFLE BALANCE
DUBIETY CASUALTY MISTRUST
SUSPENSE UNSURETY SKEPTICISM
UNCHALLENGED ACCEPTED
UNCHANGEABLE FAST STABLE
DURABLE ETERNAL
UNCHANGING STATIC ETERNAL
UNIFORM CONSTANT STATICAL
UNCHASTE LEWD BAWDY FRAIL
LIGHT LOOSE IMPURE WANTON
FORLAIN HAGGARD SCARLET
IMMODEST
UNCHASTITY BAWDRY STUPRUM
ADULTERY
UNCHECKED LIBERAL RAMPANT
REINLESS
UNCIFORM HAMATUM
UNCINARIA NECATOR
UNCIVIL RUDE BLUFF ROUGH
RUSTY SURLY COARSE CRUSTY
RUGGED UNFEEL IMPOLITE
UNCIVILIZED RUDE WILD MYALL
INCULT SAVAGE UNCIVIL
BARBARIC IGNORANT SYLVATIC
UNCLAD LOOSE UNDRESSED
UNCLE EME OOM TIO YEME BUNKS
NUNKY NUNCLE
UNCLEAN FOUL TREF VILE BLACK
TARRY TERFA TREFA COMMON
FILTHY IMMUND IMPURE DEFILED
UNCLEANLINESS
(PREF.) MYS(O)

UNCLEANNESS DIRT FOULNESS
UNCLEAR DIM HAZY SHAGGY
UNCLEARLY DIMLY
UNCLENCH UNDOUBLE
**UNCLE TOM'S CABIN (AUTHOR OF
—)** STOWE
(CHARACTER IN —) EVA TOM BIRD
CASSY CHLOE ELIZA HALEY HARRY
LOKER MARKS SIMON TOPSY
GEORGE HARRIS LEGREE RACHEL
SHELBY SIMEON OPHELIA STCLAIR
EMMELINE HALLIDAY
UNCLOSE OPE OPEN UNHASP
DISCLOSE
UNCLOTHE TIRL SPOIL UNRIG
DEVEST DESPOIL
UNCLOTHED STARKERS
UNCLOUDED CLEAR SERENE
UNCOIL UNLINK
UNCOLORED FAIR
UNCOMBED TOUSLED UNKAMED
UNTEWED
UNCOMBINED FREE FRANK LOOSE
UNCOMELY INDECENT
UNCOMFORTABLE HOT EVIL POOR
HARSH UNKET UNKID QUEASY
STICKY UNFELE
UNCOMMON MUCH NICE RARE
SELD UNCO BYOUS FORBY
UNCOW VAUDY DAINTY FORBYE
SCARCE SPECIAL STRANGE
UNUSUAL SINGULAR UNWONTED
UNCOMMONLY UNCO BYOUS
EXTRA JOLLY UNCOW UNCOLY
UNCOMMONNESS SCARCITY
UNCOMMUNICATIVE DUMB
SILENT PRIVATE RESERVED
UNCOMPLICATED RURAL HONEST
SIMPLE
UNCOMPOUNDED SIMPLEX
UNCOMPROMISING ACID FIRM
GRIM RIGID STERN STOUT ULTRA
SEVERE STRICT STRONG EXTREME
HARDSHELL BRASSBOUND
UNCONCEALED BARE OPEN OVERT
OUVERT APPARENT
UNCONCERN APATHY EASINESS
UNCONCERNED COOL EASY
BLAND BLASE CASUAL CARELESS
UNCONCERNEDLY LIGHTLY
UNCONDITIONAL FREE FRANK
UTTER SIMPLE ABSOLUTE EXPLICIT
TERMLESS
UNCONDITIONED POSITIVE
UNCONFINED LAX FREE LOOSE
UNCONGENIAL HATEFUL INGRATE
KINDLESS
UNCONNECTED GAPPY REMOTE
DETACHED
UNCONQUERED INVICT INVICTED
UNCONSCIOUS OUT COLD BRUTE
ASLEEP BLOTTO CUCKOO TORPID
UNAWARE WITLESS COMATOSE
IGNORANT SENSELESS INSENSIBLE
UNCONSIDERED WILD
UNCONSTRAINED EASY FREE
UNNET SIMPLE FAMILIAR
UNCONTROLLABLE WILD
UNCONTROLLED FREE MADCAP
LIBERAL ABSOLUTE UNBITTED
UNCONVENTIONAL FLAKY GYPSY
LOOSE CASUAL FLAKEY DEVIOUS

ODDBALL OFFBEAT BOHEMIAN
INFORMAL
(— IN STYLE) MOD
UNCONVINCING LAME THIN FALSE
FISHY FEEBLE
UNCOOKED RAW
UNCOOL UNHIP
UNCOOPERATIVE (TO BE —)
STONEWALL
UNCOUNTABLE SUMLESS
UNCOUPLE CUT UNDOCK DISLINK
UNCOUTH RUDE CRUDE DORIC
GURLY ROUGH UNKED UNKID
GOTHIC JUNGLY QUAINT RENISH
AWKWARD BOORISH CUBBISH
HIRSUTE LOUTISH AGRESTIC
UNGAINLY YOKELISH
(— PERSON) TUG
UNCOVER BARE DOFF HUNT ROOT
ROUT TIRL TIRR BREAK STRIP
TIRVE UNLAP UNLID UNWRY
DETECT EXHUME RAKEUP SEARCH
UNBARE UNCASE UNHALE UNVEIL
UNDRAPE UNEARTH DISCLOSE
DISCOVER UNMANTLE UNMUFFLE
UNCOVERED BARE OVERT
(PREF.) GYMN(O)
UNCTION CHRISM OINTMENT
UNCTIOUS SMUG
UNCTUOUS FAT OILY SALVY SLEEK
SOAPY SUAVE GREASY SMARMY
COURTLY PINGUID OLEAGINOUS
UNCULTIVATED RAW BRUT FERAL
DESERT FALLOW INCULT SAVAGE
SLOVEN WILDERN
UNCULTURED RUDE INCULT
ARTLESS
UNCUT RASPED
UNDAMAGED WHOLE
UNDARKENED CLEAR
UNDAUNTED BOLD BRAVE MANLY
SPARTAN FEARLESS INTREPID
UNDE WAVY UNDEE
UNDECAYED GREEN
UNDECEIVE DISABUSE
UNDECIDED MOOT DUBIOUS
PENDING DOUBTFUL WAVERING
UNDECIDEDLY HUMDRUM
UNDECLARED SECRET
UNDEFENDED UNKEPT
UNDEFILED PURE CHASTE INTACT
VIRGIN
UNDEFINED OBSCURE
UNDELIVERABLE DEAD
UNDEMONSTRATIVE COLD
ASEPTIC LACONIC RESERVED
UNDENIABLE BRUTAL
UNDENIABLY INDEED
UNDEPENDABLE CASUAL FLUFFY
UNDER SUB BAJO BELOW INFRA
NEATH SOTTO ANEATH ANUNDER
BENEATH
(— ORDERS) SUPPOSED
(— THE WORD) IV
(— THE YEAR) SA
(— THIS TITLE) HT
(— THIS WORD) SV SHV
(— WAY) AFOOT
(PREF.) HYPO SUB
UNDERBODICE JUMP BASQUINE
CAMISOLE
UNDERBRUSH FILTH COVERT

GARSIL MAQUIS RAMMEL
ABATURE
UNDERBURNED SOFT SAMEL
UNDERBUTLER WASHPOT
UNDERCARRIAGE BOGY BOGEY
BOGIE
UNDERCLAY THILL WARRANT
UNDERCLOTHES LININGS
UNDERCLOTHING LINEN SHORTS
UNDIES LININGS LINGERIE
BALBRIGGAN
UNDERCOAT PILE ALPACA
SURFACER
(WOOL OF — OF MUSK-OX) QIVIUT
UNDERCOVER SECRET
UNDERCRUST ABAISSE
UNDERCURRENT UNDERLAY
UNDERRUN UNDERSET
UNDERCUT JAD HOLE LAME POOL
SUMP KIRVE NOTCH
UNDERDOG DAVID
UNDERDONE RARE REAR
UNDERDRAWERS FLANNELS
UNDERDRESS SLIP
UNDERESTIMATE DISPRIZE
MINIMIZE
UNDERFLEECE PASHM
UNDERFRAME SOLE
UNDERGARMENT BAND SLIP
CYMAR SIMAR SKIRT SMOCK
TUNIC WAIST BANIAN BANYAN
BODICE CAMISE CILICE CORSET
GIRDLE STAMIN CHEMISE
DOUBLET DRAWERS STAMMEL
TALLITH BLOOMERS KNICKERS
(WOMAN'S —) PANTIHOSE
(WOMEN'S —) LINGERIE
(PL.) SMALLS FLANNELS FLIMSIES
SNUGGIES
UNDERGO PASS SERVE ENDURE
SUFFER SUSTAIN
(— GLADLY) WELCOME
UNDERGOER
(SUFF.) EE
UNDERGRADUATE MAN TASSEL
SERVITOR
(CAMBRIDGE —) SUBSIZAR
(TITLED —) TUFT
UNDERGROWTH RUSH COVER
RAMMEL SPRING BUSHWOOD
UNDERHAND SLY DERN SHADY
BYHAND SECRET CROOKED
OBLIQUE INVOLVED SINISTER
SNEAKING
UNDERHANDED DERN DIRTY
FUNNY FILTHY SECRET SINISTER
UNDERHANDEDLY DIRTY
UNDERIVED ORIGINAL
UNDER JAW
(PREF.) GENYO
UNDERLAYER SLASHING
UNDERLIE SUBTEND
UNDERLING MENIAL SEQUEL
UNDERER HENCHMAN INFERIOR
UNDERLYING COVERT IMPLICIT
UNDERMINE SAP CAVE HOLE POOL
ERODE KNIFE WEAKEN FOSSICK
FOUNDER SUBVERT ENFEEBLE
SUPPLANT
UNDERMINED ROTTEN
UNDERNEATH BELOW BENEATH
UNNEATH
(PREF.) INTRA

UNDERNSONG TIERCE
UNDERPANTS BRIEFS BLOOMERS
  KNICKERS
UNDERPART BELLY
UNDERPASS DIVE SUBWAY
UNDERPINNING GAM
UNDERRATE DECRY DISCOUNT
  EXTENUATE
UNDERRUN BOTTOM
UNDERSACRISTAN CUSTOS
UNDERSHIRT VEST SHIFT SHIRT
  CAMISA JERSEY LINDER SEMMIT
  SINGLET WRAPPER
UNDERSHRUB HEATH PINKEYE
  SEEPWEED SUBSHRUB
  SAGEBRUSH SANTOLINA
UNDERSIDE BOTTOM BREAST
  (— OF CLOUD) BASE
  (— OF FINGER) BALL
  (— OF FLOOR) CEILING
  (— OF STAIRCASE) SOFFIT
  (PREF.) **(ON THE —)** INFERO
UNDERSIZED DEENY SCRUB STUNT
UNDERSKIRT QUILT CRINOLINE
  PETTICOAT
UNDERSONG FABURDEN
UNDERSTAND CAN CON DIG GET
  KEN SEE GAUM HAVE MAKE READ
  TAKE TWIG BRAIN ENTER GRASP
  REACH SAVVY SEIZE SENSE SKILL
  SPELL ACCEPT COTTON FIGURE
  FOLLOW INTAKE INTEND SUBAUD
  UPTAKE CONCEIT DISCERN
  COMPRISE CONCEIVE CONSTRUE
  CONTRIVE FORSTAND PERCEIVE
  PERSTAND UNDERNIM
  (— PROFOUNDLY) GROK
UNDERSTANDABLE PLAIN
UNDERSTANDING KEN WIT GAUM
  HEAD BRAIN CLASP HEART INWIT
  SENSE SKILL ACCORD INTENT
  NOTION REASON TREATY UPTAKE
  COMPACT CONCEIT CONCEPT
  ENTENTE INSIGHT MEANING
  WITNESS DAYLIGHT PREHENSION
  (— WORDS) ISEE
  (HARMONIOUS —) SYMPATHY
  (IMPERFECT —) DARKNESS
  (INSTINCTIVE —) FREEMASONRY
  (WORDS OF —) ISEE
  (PREF.) NOEMA
UNDERSTATEMENT LITOTES
  MEIOSIS
UNDERSTOOD LUCID SUPPOSED
  (— ONLY BY SPECIALLY INITIATED)
  ESOTERIC
  (EASILY —) EASY CLEAR EXTANT
  (NOT —) DARKSOME
UNDERSTUDY DOUBLE
UNDERSURFACE SOLE
  (— OF BRILLIANT) PAVILION
UNDERTAKE GO TRY DARE FANG
  FOND GRANT OFFER ASSUME
  INCEPT PLEDGE SETOUT ATTEMPT
  EMBRACE EMPRISE PRETEND
  UNDERFO CONTRACT PRESTATE
  (— RESPONSIBILITY) ACCEPT
  ANSWER
UNDERTAKER UPHOLDER
  MORTICIAN
UNDERTAKING JOB AVAL TASK
  CAUTIO EFFORT SCHEME VOYAGE

ATTEMPT CALLING PROJECT
  VENTURE COVENANT
  (— IN CARDS) CONTRACT
  (HAZARDOUS —) EMPRISE
  (UNPROFITABLE —) FOLLY
UNDERTEACHER USHER
UNDERTONE INKLING SUBTONE
UNDERTOW SEAPOOSE
UNDER TWO FLAGS (AUTHOR OF
  —) OUIDA
  (CHARACTER IN —) RAKE CECIL
  AMAGUE BERTIE CORONA
  BERKELEY CIGARETTE GUENEVERE
  ROYALLIEU CHATEAUROY
  ROCKINGHAM
UNDERVALUE DECRY DISABLE
  DISPRIZE DISVALUE MISPRISE
  MISPRIZE
UNDERVEST BODICE SEMMIT
  SINGLET
UNDERWAIST CAMISOLE
UNDERWATER (— DEVICE) OTTER
  PARAVANE
UNDERWEAR BRIEFS SHORTS
  SKIVVY UNDIES DESSOUS HEAVIES
  LONGIES LINGERIE PRETTIES
  SCANTIES
  (MEN'S —) SKIVVIES
  (PL.) SMALLS
UNDERWING CATOCALA
UNDERWOOD FRITH BOSCAGE
  COPPICE
UNDERWORLD DUAT DEWAT
  HADES ORCUS SHEOL MICTLAN
  XIBALBA GANGLAND
UNDERWRITE SIGN INSURE
  ENDORSE
UNDERWRITER INSURER
UNDESERVED INDIGN
UNDETERMINED UNSET DUBIOUS
  PENDENT AORISTIC DOUBTFUL
  INFINITE
UNDEVELOPED CRUDE MORON
  LATENT SLOVEN GERMING
  IMMATURE JUVENILE
  (SEXUALLY —) NEUTER
UNDEVIATINGLY SMACK
UNDIFFERENCED ENTIRE
UNDIFFERENTIATED GLOBAL
  AMERISTIC
UNDIGESTED CRUDE
UNDIGNIFIED DOGGREL DOGGEREL
UNDILUTED MERE NEAT PURE
  NAKED SHEER SHORT STRONG
  STRAIGHT
UNDIMINISHED ENTIRE
UNDIMMED CLEAR
UNDINE NIX
  (CHARACTER IN —) HUGO VEIT
  TOBIAS UNDINE BERTHALDA
  KUHLEBORN
  (COMPOSER OF —) LORTZING
UNDISCIPLINED WANTON COLTISH
UNDISCLOSED HIDDEN SEALED
UNDISCRIMINATING GROSS
UNDISGUISED BALD NAKED PLAIN
UNDISMAYED UNFLEMED
UNDISPUTED LIQUID
UNDISTINGUISHED GROSS
  COMMON UNNOBLE FAMELESS
  NAMELESS NOTELESS
UNDISTORTED CLEAR

UNDISTURBED CALM SOUND
  SERENE VIRGIN TRANQUIL
UNDIVIDED WHOLE ENTIRE SINGLE
UNDO DUP COOK POOP SLIP FORDO
  SPEED UNPAY DEFEAT DIDDLE
  FOREDO UNBIND UNKNIT UNLOCK
  UNMAKE UNTUCK UNWORK
  DEFEISE DESTROY NULLIFY
  UNRAVEL UNRIVET UNTWIRL
  UNWEAVE UNWREST DECIPHER
  DISSOLVE DISTRUSS UNFASTEN
UNDOER ACHAN
UNDOGMATIC AGNOSTIC
UNDOING DEFEAT DOWNFALL
  (PREF.) DE DIS
UNDOMESTICATED WILD FERAL
  FERINE
UNDOUBTEDLY SURELY FRANKLY
UNDRESS MOB DOFF FLAY PEEL
  TIRR STRIP UNRAY UNRIG DEVEST
  DIVEST UNBUSK UNCASE UNLACE
  UNRIND UNROBE UNTIRE DISCASE
  UNARRAY UNREADY UNSPOIL
  UNTRUSS NEGLIGEE UNATTIRE
  DESHABILLE DISHABILLE
UNDRESSED UNDIGHT
UNDUE EXTREME
UNDULATE SWAY WAVE WAVY
  FLOAT SWING BILLOW GYROSE
  KELTER RIPPLE UNDATE UNDOSE
  FLICKER UNDATED
UNDULATING SURGING FLEXUOUS
  INDENTED
UNDULATION FOLD ROLL WAVE
  CRIMP TEETER WAVING CRIMPING
UNDULATORY WAVY
UNDUTIFULNESS IMPIETY
UNDYED CORAH
UNDYING IMMORTAL
UNEARTH DIG MOOT DIGUP
  EXPOSE UNCOVER DISCOVER
UNEARTHLY EERY EERIE WEIRD
  AWESOME UNCANNY UNGODLY
UNEASINESS ENVY GENE FIDGET
  NETTLE SORROW UNEASE
  AILMENT ANXIETY DISEASE
  MISEASE TROUBLE DISQUIET
  DISTASTE
UNEASY ANTSY ONEDGE SICKLY
  FIDGETY INQUIET NERVOUS
  RESTIVE UNQUIET WORRIED
  RESTLESS
UNEDUCATED RUDE SIMPLE
  IGNORANT
UNEMBELLISHED DRY PROSE
  STARK AUSTERE
UNEMOTIONAL DRY COLD COOL
  STOIC STONY STOICAL
UNEMOTIONALLY EVENLY
UNEMPLOYED IDLE ORRA VOID
  IDLED ORROW OTIANT OTIOSE
  VACANT IDLESET LEISURE
  UNBUSIED
UNEMPLOYMENT IDLENESS
UNENCUMBERED VACANT
  EXPEDITE
UNENDING ABYSMAL AGELONG
  CHRONIC ENDLESS UNDYING
  TERMLESS TIMELESS
UNENJOYABLE JOYLESS
UNENLIGHTENED MISTY HEATHEN
  IGNORANT
UNENTHUSIASTIC COLD

UNEQUAL IMPAR DISPAR UNEGAL
  UNEVEN INEQUAL INFERIOR
  (— TO STRAIN) FEEBLE
  (PREF.) ANIS(O) IMPARI INEQUI
UNEQUALED UNIQUE NONESUCH
UNEQUIVOCAL DIRECT SQUARE
  PERFECT DEFINITE DISTINCT
  EXPLICIT RESOUNDING
UNERRING DEAD TRUE DEADLY
  INERRANT
UNERRINGLY CLEAN
UNEVEN RUDE EROSE GOBBY
  HAGGY JAGGY MEALY ROUGH
  HOBBLY PLATTY RAGGED RUGGED
  SPOTTY TWITTY UNFAIR UNLIKE
  BLOTCHY DIURNAL ERRATIC
  HOTTERY INEQUAL SCALENE
  STREAKY UNEQUAL HUMMOCKY
  SCRAGGED SCRATCHY SNAGGLED
  ACCIDENTED
  (— IN COLOR) CLOUDY
UNEVENLY AWRY
UNEVENNESS BUMP WAVE FRAZE
  ANOMALY WRINKLE ACCIDENT
  ASPERITY
UNEVENTFUL STILL UNDATED
UNEXCITED LEVEL
UNEXCITING DEAD DULL TAME
  BORING PROSAIC
UNEXPECTED EERY EERIE ABRUPT
  SUDDEN UNWARY INOPINE
  UNLOOKED
UNEXPECTEDLY UNWARES
  UNAWARES
UNEXPIRED ALIVE
UNEXPLAINED HIDDEN
UNEXPOSED RAW
UNEXTINGUISHED LIT LEFTON
UNFADABLE FAST
UNFADED FRESH BRIGHT
UNFAILING SURE DEADLY INFALLID
  UNERRING
UNFAIR FOUL CROOK WRONG
  BIASED SHABBY UNEVEN UNJUST
  DEVIOUS PARTIAL SLANTER
  UNEQUAL UNSEEMLY WRONGFUL
UNFAIRLY HARDLY
UNFAIRNESS CROSS INEQUITY
UNFAITHFUL INFIDEL TRAITOR
  DISLOYAL RECREANT
UNFALTERING SURE TRUE STEADY
  UNERRING
UNFAMILIAR NEW FREMD
  HEATHER STRANGE UNKNOWN
UNFASTEN FREE OPEN UNDO
  LOOSE UNPIN UNBIND UNHASP
  UNLIME UNLINK UNLOCK UNMAKE
  UNTINE UNDIGHT UNHITCH
  UNSTECK UNTRUSS
UNFATHOMABLE ABYSMAL
  ABYSSAL PROFOUND
UNFATHOMED COSMIC
UNFAVORABLE BAD ILL FOUL
  HARD POOR CRONK SHREWD
  UNFAIR UNKIND ADVERSE
  AWKWARD FROWARD HOSTILE
  UNHAPPY BACKWARD CONTRARY
  INIMICAL SINISTER UNKINDLY
  (PREF.) DYS
UNFAVORABLY BADLY CROSS
UNFEATHERED SQUAB
UNFEELING COLD DULL HARD
  CRASS CRUEL HARSH ROCKY

STERN STONY BRUTAL LEADEN MARBLE STOLID CALLOUS OBDURATE

UNFEELINGLY HARSHLY

UNFEELINGNESS APATHY

UNFEIGNED OPEN TRUE HEARTY CORDIAL NATURAL SINCERE

UNFERMENTED AZYMOUS

UNFERTILE BARREN

UNFETTERED FREE UNGYVED

UNFILLED BLANK EMPTY VACANT VACUOUS

UNFINISHED RAW GRAY GREY CRUDE KACHA ROUGH KUTCHA RAGGED KACHCHA STICKIT IMMATURE INCHOATE

UNFIRED GREEN

UNFIRM UNFAST

UNFIT BAD SICK UNAPT WISHT WRONG COMMON FAULTY NOUGHT UNTIDY DISABLE UNFITTY IMPROPER UNFITTEN UNLIKELY UNLIKING

UNFITTING UNMEETLY

UNFIXED AFLOAT

UNFLAPPABLE CALM SURE STOIC SECURE ASSURED

UNFLEDGED SQUAB CALLOW

UNFLINCHING LEVEL STAUNCH

UNFOLD OPEN BREAK BURST SOLVE UNLAP UNTIE DEPLOY EVOLVE EXPAND EXPLAT FLOWER SPREAD UNFURL UNPLAT UNROLL UNTUCK BLOSSOM DEVELOP DISPLAY DIVULGE EXPLAIN UNPLAIT UNRAVEL UNWEAVE UNDOUBLE UNPLIGHT

UNFOLDED OPEN EVOLUTE EXPANDED

UNFOLDING DISPLAY
(— OF EVENTS) ACTION
(— TO VIEW) BURST

UNFORCED EASY GLIB WILLING

UNFORESEEN CASUAL SUDDEN IMPREVU UNAWARE

UNFORGIVING STERN

UNFORMED CALLOW INFORM

UNFORTUNATE ILL EVIL POOR DONCY TOUGH WEARY SHREWD HAPLESS UNHAPPY UNLUCKY LUCKLESS UNTOWARD WANHAPPY WRETCHED

UNFREQUENTED LONE EMPTY UNCOUTH SOLITARY

UNFRIENDLY ILL COLD FOUL CHILL BITTER CHILLY FIERCE FROSTY UNSOME HOSTILE INGRATE STRANGE INIMICAL

UNFROCK DEFROCK DEGRADE DISFROCK UNPRIEST

UNFRUITFUL BLUNT ADDLED BARREN EFFETE WASTED STERILE USELESS INFECUND

UNFULFILLMENT BREACH

UNFURL BREAK SPREAD UNFOLD DEVELOP OUTROOL

UNFURNISHED BARE VACANT

UNGAINLY LANKY SPLAY WEEDY CLUMSY UNGAIN AWKWARD BOORISH NUNTING UNHEPPEN UNLICKED UNWIELDY

UNGENEROUS MEAN SHABBY STINGY GRUDGING

UNGENIAL CHILLY

UNGIRDED DISCINCT

UNGLUED UPSET

UNGODLINESS ATHEISM IMPIETY

UNGODLY SINFUL WICKED GODLESS IMPIOUS PROFANE

UNGOVERNABLE WILD UNRULY FROWARD IMPOTENT

UNGRACEFUL HARD CLUMSY ANGULAR AWKWARD HALTING UNTOWARD

UNGRACEFULLY HARSHLY

UNGRACIOUS GRUFF UNFEEL UNFELE CHURLISH SNAPPISH

UNGRATEFUL UNKIND INGRATE

UNGROOMED UNDRESSED

UNGUARDED OPEN STIFF

UNGUENT SALVE CEROMA CHRISM PIMENT POMADE SMEGMA POMATUM UNCTION OINTMENT
(PREF.) MYRO

UNGULATE HOG PIG DEER HORSE TAKIN TAPIR HOOFED AMBLYPOD ELEPHANT RHINOCEROS

UNGUMMED BRIGHT

UNHALLOWED IMPURE UNHOLY PROFANE

UNHAMPERED FREE DIRECT EXPEDITE

UNHAPPINESS MISERY SORROW ILLFARE SADNESS UNBLISS

UNHAPPY SAD POOR TEARY DISMAL UNLUCKY UNLUSTY WANSOME DEJECTED DOWNBEAT DOWNGONE WOBEGONE WRETCHED

UNHARMED SAFE UNSHENT

UNHARNESS UNGEAR OUTSHUT OUTSPAN UNHORSE UNTACKLE

UNHEALED GREEN

UNHEALTHY BAD MORBID QUEASY SICKLY UNHALE NAUGHTY PECCANT EPINOSIC MALADIVE

UNHEATED COLD

UNHEEDED IGNORED UNTENTED

UNHEEDING DEAF CARELESS

UNHESITATING READY UNPOISED

UNHIDDEN OVERT

UNHITCH OUTSPAN

UNHOLY IMPURE WICKED IMPIOUS PROFANE

UNHORSE PURL THROW UNCOLT DISMOUNT UNSADDLE

UNHURRIED EASY SLOW SOFT SOBER

UNHURT SAFE HARMLESS HURTLESS UNHARMED

UNIAT MALKITE MELCHITE

UNICORN LIN REEM KILIN LICORN LICORNE NARWHAL HOWITZER

UNICORN FISH LIJA UNIE

UNICORN PLANT MARTINOE

UNICUM UNION

UNIDENTIFIED FACELESS INCOGNITO

UNIFICATION SYSTEM ENSEMBLE

UNIFIED GLOBAL

UNIFIER UMBRELLA

UNIFORM KIT DEAD EVEN FLAT JUST LIKE SAME SELF SUIT ALIKE BLUES CLOTH KHAKI SOLID SUITY GLOBAL GREENS LIVERY SINGLE STEADY EQUABLE REGULAR

SIMILAR SUNTANS CONSTANT EQUIFORM EQUIPAGE MEASURED STANDARD UNIVOCAL
(— IN COLOR) SELF
(— IN HUE) FLAT
(LEATHER —) BUFF
(NOT —) MOTLEY RAGTAG SQUALLY UNKEMPT
(PRISONER'S —) STRIPES
(PREF.) IS ISO

UNIFORMITY ONENESS EQUALITY EVENNESS MONOTONY SAMENESS
(— OF MOTION) INSISTURE

UNIFORMLY EVENLY EQUALLY

UNIFY MERGE UNITE CEMENT COMPACT UNITIZE COALESCE

UNILATERAL SECUND

UNIMAGINATIVE DULL SODDEN STUPID LIMITED LITERAL PROSAIC UNIDEAL PEDANTIC PEDESTRIAN

UNIMPAIRED FRESH SOUND ENTIRE INTACT
(— BY) DEVOID

UNIMPASSIONED SOBER WHOLE STEADY

UNIMPEDED FREE EXPEDITE

UNIMPORTANT VAIN LIGHT PETTY SMALL CASUAL SIMPLE TRIVIAL IMMOMENT PEDDLING PIDDLING TRINKETY JERKWATER MINISCULE SMALLTIME INSIGNIFICANT

UNINFLECTED APTOTIC

UNINFORMED GREEN UNTOLD IGNORANT

UNINHABITED WILD EMPTY DESERT VACANT DESOLATE WASTEFUL

UNINHIBITED LARGE

UNINJURED WHOLE INTACT SINCERE

UNINSPIRED HACK STODGY POMPIER DRYASDUST

UNINSPIRING TAME

UNINSTRUCTED NAIVE IGNORANT

UNINTELLIGENT DUMB OBTUSE OPAQUE STUPID ASININE FOOLISH VACUOUS WITLESS

UNINTELLIGIBLE BLIND MISTY OPAQUE MYSTICAL

UNINTENTIONAL UNMEANT

UNINTERESTING DRY ARID COLD DRAB DREE DULL FADE FLAT TAME DREAR SANDY STALE BORING DREICH JEJUNE INSIPID BROMIDIC FRUMPISH

UNINTERMITTENT ITHAND

UNINTERRUPTED SMOOTH STEADY ENDLESS ETERNAL STRAIGHT

UNINTERRUPTEDLY AWAY

UNINVITED (ENTER —) CRASH

UNIO MUSSEL

UNION SUM ZYG BLOC DUAD JOIN ALLOY GROUP JOINT NONOP UNITY ENOSIS FUSION GREMIO TAWHID VEREIN COMPACT CONCERT CONTACT MEETING ONENESS SOCIETY ADHESION ALLIANCE COHESION ESPOUSAL JOINTURE JUNCTION JUNCTURE SODALITY SYSTASIS TRIALISM VINCULUM ZOLLVEREIN
(— OF TWO SETS) CUP

(— OF TWO VOWELS) CRASIS
(MARITAL —) BED
(POLITICAL —) ANSCHLUSS
(SEXUAL —) COPULA COUPLING
(TURKISH —) JETTRU
(PREF.) ZYG(O)(OTO)
(SEXUAL —) GAMO
(SUFF.) APSIS GAM(AE)(IST)(OUS)(Y) GAMETE

UNIONIST REFUGEE

UNIONIZE ALLY

UNION OF SOVIET SOCIALIST REPUBLICS (SEE RUSSIA)

UNIQUE ODD RARE SOLE UNIC ALONE UNION SINGLE SULLEN UNICUM ALONELY SOLEYNE SPECIAL STRANGE ISOLATED SINGULAR

UNIQUENESS SOLITUDE

UNISON FIRST CONCORD HOMOPHONY

UNIT (ALSO SEE MEASURE AND WEIGHT) (ALSO SEE MEASURE) ACE ONE ATOM BARN KLAN FLOOR HUMIT MONAD NEPER ADDRESS DIOPTER ELEMENT ENERGID KLAVERN
(— IN COUNTING FISH) MEASE
(— IN EARTHWORK) FLOAT FLOOR
(— OF ABSORPTION) SABIN
(— OF ACCELERATION) GAL MILLIGAL
(— OF ACOUSTICAL ABSORPTION) SABIN
(— OF ACTION) EPISODE
(— OF ANGULAR MEASURE) CENTRAD
(— OF ARCHEOLOGICAL CLASSIFICATION) ASPECT
(— OF AREA) DEKAR DECARE DEKARE
(— OF BINARY DIGITS) BYTE GIGABYTE
(— OF BRIGHTNESS) NIT STILB LAMBERT
(— OF CAPACITANCE) JAR FARAD
(— OF CAPACITY) COR LAST PIPE ARDAB ARDEB TIERCE AMPHORA
(— OF CARDS) TRICK
(— OF COMIC STRIP) BOX
(— OF CONDUCTANCE) SIEMENS
(— OF COUNTING) POINT
(— OF CURRENT) AMPERE
(— OF DATA TRANSMISSION SPEED) BAUD
(— OF DESIGN) LARME
(— OF DISTANCE) DAY VERST MORGAN PARSEC MEGAPARSEC
(— OF ELASTANCE) DARAF
(— OF ELECTRICAL RESISTANCE) ABOHM
(— OF ELECTRIC CAPACITY) FARAD
(— OF ELECTRIC CONDUCTANCE) MHO
(— OF ELECTRIC FORCE) VOLT KILOVOLT STATVOLT
(— OF ELECTRIC INDUCTANCE) HENRY
(— OF ELECTRIC INTENSITY) AMPERE OERSTED
(— OF ELECTRICITY) ES COULOMB
(— OF ELECTRIC RELUCTANCE) REL STATOHM

(— OF ELECTRIC RESISTANCE)
BEGOHM
(— OF ENERGY) ERG RAD QUAD
JOULE ATOMERG QUANTUM
(— OF FINENESS) CARAT KARAT
(— OF FLOORING) SQUARE
(— OF FLOW) CUSEC
(— OF FLUIDITY) RHE
(— OF FLUX DENSITY) GAUSS
(— OF FORCE) G DYNE STAPP
NEWTON STHENE POUNDAL
(— OF FREQUENCY) HERTZ
FRESNEL GIGAHERTZ MEGAHERTZ
(— OF GEOLOGIC TIME) AEON
(— OF GOVERNMENT) DEME LAND
KREIS GEMEINDE
(— OF HEAT) BTU THERM CALORIE
(— OF ILLUMINANCE) LUX NIT PHOT
MICROLUX
(— OF ILLUMINATION) PHOT
(— OF INFORMATION) NIT GIGABIT
(— OF INSTRUCTION) FRAME
(— OF INSULATION) TOG
(— OF INTERSTELLAR SPACE)
PARSEC
(— OF JET PROPULSION) JATO
(— OF LAND AREA) ARE SULUNG
(— OF LANGUAGE) SYLLABLE
(— OF LENGTH) FERMI STADE
MICRON MICROMETER
(— OF LIGHT) LUMEN
(— OF LIGHT INTENSITY) PYR
PHOTON
(— OF LOUDNESS) PHON SONE
DECIBEL
(— OF LUMINOUS INTENSITY)
CANDELA
(— OF MACHINERY) STAND
(— OF MAGNETIC FLUX) GAUSS
WEBER
(— OF MAGNETIC FLUX DENSITY)
TESLA
(— OF MAGNETIC FORCE) KAPP
GILBERT
(— OF MAGNETIC INTENSITY)
GAMMA OERSTED MAGNETON
(— OF MAGNIFICATION) DIAMETER
(— OF MASS) AMU SLUG CRITH
DALTON AVOGRAM
(— OF MEANING) SEMANTEME
(— OF MEASURE) KILOBASE
(— OF MEMORY) BIT MNEMON
(— OF METRICAL QUANTITY)
MATRA
(— OF MOMENT) DEBYE
(— OF MOMENTUM) BOLE
(— OF NARCOTIC) JOLT
(— OF NYLON FINENESS) DENIER
(— OF ONE INCH) BUTTON
(— OF PAIN INTENSITY) DOL
(— OF PERMEABILITY) DARCY
(— OF PIPE) FOURBLE
(— OF POWER) WATT DYNAM
GIGAWATT KILOWATT PONCELET
TERAWATT
(— OF PRESSURE) BAR TORR
BARAD BARIE BARYE GWELY
OSMOL OSMOLE PASCAL KILOBAR
MEGABAR CENTIBAR MICROBAR
MILLIBAR
(— OF PRESSWORK) TOKEN
(— OF RADIATION) RAD REM REP
GRAY LANGLEY

(— OF RADIOACTIVITY) CURIE
(— OF RESISTANCE) OHM
(— OF ROCKET) STAGE
(— OF SATURATION) SATRON
(— OF SOCIETY) CLAN HORDE
CHAPTER
(— OF SOUND) SONE
(— OF SPACE AND CIRCULATION)
MILLINE
(— OF SPEECH) WORD
(— OF SPEED) BAUD KNOT
(— OF STOCK) SHARE
(— OF STRUCTURE) MICELLE
(— OF TEMPERATURE) KELVIN
(— OF THICKNESS) POINT
(— OF TIME) AEON BEAT SVEDBERG
(— OF TRADING) CONTRACT
(— OF TRANSMISSION SPEED)
BAUD
(— OF USEFULNESS) UTIL
(— OF VELOCITY) VELO
(— OF VERSE METER) FOOT
(— OF VISCOSITY) POISE STOKE
SECONDS
(— OF WAVELENGTH) ANGSTROM
(— OF WEIGHT) SSU TON GERA
GRAM CARAT CATTY GERAH GRAIN
LIANG OUNCE POUND RATTI STEIN
ARROBA GRAMME RUTTEE
(— OF WIRE MEASUREMENT) MIL
(— OF WORK) ERG CROP HOUR
ERGON JOULE KILERG DINAMODE
(— OF YARN) LEA
(— OF YARN SIZE) CUT
(— OF 100 MEN) CENTURY
(— OF 20) CORGE
(ADMINISTRATIVE —) BLOCK HSIEN
AGENCY BUREAU CIRCLE DISTRICT
(ARBITRARY —) OLFACTY
(ARCHERY —) END
(ARMY —) LEGION BRIGADE
COMPANY MAHALLA
(ARTILLERY —) BATTERY
(ATOMIC MASS —) DALTON
(AVAILABLE AS —) MARRIED
(BOWLING —) ALLEY
(BOY SCOUT —) SHIP
(BUILDER'S —) SQUARE
(CIGAR-MANUFACTURING —)
BUCKEYE
(COLLECTIVE —) COMMUNE
(COMBAT —) ARMAMENT
(DISCRETE —) FRACTION
(EDUCATIONAL —) COURSE
(ELECTROMAGNETIC —) ABFARAD
ABHENRY MAXWELL ABAMPERE
(FUNDAMENTAL —) BASE
(GRAMMATICAL —) JUNCTION
(HARMONIC —) CELL
(HOUSING —) HUTMENT
(HYPOTHETICAL —) ID IDANT
MICELLE
(INDIVIDUALLY OWNED LIVING —)
CONDO
(LIFE —) BIOPHORE
(LIVING —) BIONT BIOGEN
(LOGARITHMIC —) BEL
(LOGGING —) CHANCE
(METRIC —) DEKAR DECARE
DEKARE
(MILITARY —) ARMY GOUM CORPS
GROUP LANCE SQUAD BRIGADE

PLATOON SECTION COMMANDO
DIVISION REGIMENT SQUADRON
(NAZI —) FEHME
(ORGANIZATIONAL —) CELL
ACTIVITY
(PHOTOMETRIC —) VIOLLE
(POLITICAL —) POLITY SOVIET
MUNICIPALITY
(RADIOACTIVE DISINTEGRATION —)
RUTHERFORD
(RHYTHMIC —) BASIS COLON
(SELF-PERPETUATING —) BIOSOME
(SHIPPING —) CARLOAD
(SOCIAL —) SEPT GROUP KRAAL
SOCIUS
(STORAGE —) BUFFER
(TELEGRAPHIC —) BAUD
(TEMPERATURE —) KELVIN
(TERRITORIAL —) STAKE STATE
COMMOT CANTRED CANTREF
KINGDOM
(THERMAL —) THERM CALORY
CALORIE
(TRIBAL —) TOWNSHIP
(VOTING —) CENTURY
(SUFF.) MONAS ON
UNITARIAN ARIAN SOCINIAN
UNITE ADD MIX ONE OOP PAN SAM
SEW UNE UNY ALLY BAND BIND
CLUB COAK FUSE HASP JOIN KNIT
KNOT LINK SAMM SEAM SOUD
UNIT WELD BANDY CLOSE GRADE
GRAFT INONE JACOB JOINT
MARRY MERGE NITCH UNIFY
WHOLE ATTACH CEMENT CONCUR
COUPLE EMBODY ENTIRE GATHER
LAUREL LEAGUE SOLDER SPLICE
STRIKE SUTURE ACCRETE
AMALGAM CLUSTER COALITE
COMBINE CONJOIN CONNECT
CONSORT JACOBUS SIAMESE
ALLIGATE ANCYLOSE ANKYLOSE
ASSEMBLE COALESCE COMPOUND
CONCRETE CONSPIRE COPULATE
FEDERATE LAMINATE COLLIGATE
(— ACCURATELY) LAP
(— BY INTERWEAVING) PLEACH
SPLICE
(— BY THREADS) SEW STITCH
(— CLOSELY) FAY YOT WELD
CEMENT COTTON
(— FOR INTRIGUE) CABAL
(— HOSE) COLLECT
(— IN MARRIAGE) WED SACRE
SACRI SPLICE SPOUSE
(— METALS) WELD SWEAT
(— TIMBERS) SCARF
(PREF.) GAMETO GAMO
UNITED ONE TIED ADDED ASONE
ATONE FUSED JOINT ALLIED
CONNATE ENDLESS UNIONED
COMBINED CONCRETE CONJOINT
CONJUNCT FEDERATE
COADUNATE
(PREF.) GAM(ETO)(O)
UNITED ARAB EMIRATES
(CAPITAL OF —) ABUDHABI
(FORMER NAME OF —)
TRUCIALOMAN TRUCIALCOAST
TRUCIALSTATES
(MONEY OF —) DIRHAM
(MOUNTAINS OF —) HAJAR

(STATE OF —) AJMAN DUBAI
SHARJAH FUJAIRAH
(TOWN OF —) DUBAI JEBEL
BURAIMI SHARJAH
UNITED KINGDOM (SEE ENGLAND)
UNITED STATES (ALSO SEE
SPECIFIC STATES)

UNITED STATES
LAKE: ERIE MEAD SALT HURON
TAHOE CRATER ONTARIO
MICHIGAN SUPERIOR CHAMPLAIN
OKEECHOBEE
MOUNTAIN: BEAR BONA SILL
GREEN OZARK ROCKY UINTA
WHITE ANTERO ELBERT SHASTA
SIERRA BELFORD FORAKER
HARVARD MASSIVE RAINIER
SANFORD WASATCH WHITNEY
CATSKILL MCKINLEY WRANGELL
BLACKBURN ADIRONDACK
BITTERROOT APPALACHIAN
PRESIDENT: ABE CAL DDE FDR IKE
JFK LBJ BUSH FORD POLK TAFT
ADAMS GRANT HARRY HAYES
JIMMY NIXON TEDDY TYLER
ARTHUR CARTER HOOVER
MONROE PIERCE REAGAN
TAYLOR TRUMAN WILSON
CLINTON HARDING JACKSON
JOHNSON KENNEDY LINCOLN
MADISON BUCHANAN COOLIDGE
FILLMORE GARFIELD HARRISON
MCKINLEY VANBUREN
JEFFERSON ROOSEVELT
EISENHOWER WASHINGTON
VICE PRESIDENT: BURR BUSH FORD
KING ADAMS AGNEW DAWES
GERRY NIXON TYLER ARTHUR
COLFAX CURTIS DALLAS GARNER
HAMLIN HOBART MORTON
TRUMAN WILSON BARKLEY
CALHOUN CLINTON JOHNSON
MONDALE SHERMAN WALLACE
WHEELER COOLIDGE FILLMORE
HUMPHREY MARSHALL
TOMPKINS VANBUREN FAIRBANKS
HENDRICKS JEFFERSON
ROOSEVELT STEVENSON
ROCKEFELLER BRECKINRIDGE
WATERFALL: TWIN AKAKA SEVEN
NARADA RIBBON FEATHER
PALOUSE PASSAIC SLUISKIN
YOSEMITE BRIDALVEIL
YELLOWSTONE

UNITING SUTURE
UNITS (SUFF.)
(HAVING TIME —) SEMIC
UNITY UNION SYSTEM ONENESS
UNITUDE IDENTITY SODALITY
SYMPATHY TOTALITY
(— OF SPIRIT AND NATURE)
ABSOLUTE
UNIVALENT MONATOMIC
UNIVERSAL ALL LOCAL QUALE
TOTAL WHOLE WORLD COMMON
GLOBAL PUBLIC VERSAL GENERAL
GENERIC CATHOLIC ECUMENIC
PANDEMIC
(TRANSCENDENT —) IDEA
UNIVERSALITY ALLNESS
OMNITUDE

UNIVERSE ALL LOKA MASS OLAM WORLD COSMOS SYSTEM CREATURE EXEMPLAR
(SIDEREAL —) SPACE
(PREF.) COSM(O) COSMETO COSMICO
UNIVERSITY STUDY CAMPUS SCHOOL ACADEMY COLLEGE MADRASA STUDIUM VARSITY MADRASAH REDBRICK
(OF BRITISH —S) REDBRICK
(RELATING TO BRITISH —) OXBRIDGE REDBRICK PLATEGLASS
UNJUST HARD UNFAIR WANTON WICKED UNEQUAL UNRICHT UNRIGHT WRONGFUL
UNJUSTIFIED INVALID
UNJUSTLY UNDULY FALSELY
UNKEELED RATITE
UNKEMPT ROUGH SEEDY FROWZY MOTLEY RAGTAG RUGGED SHAGGY INCOMPT RAFFISH RUFFLED SCRUFFY SHAGRAG TOUSLED DRAGGLED SCRAGGLY SLIPSHOD STRUBBLY UNCOMBED SHAMBOLIC
UNKIND BAD ILL MEAN VILE CRUEL HARSH STERN SEVERE UNMEEK
UNKINDNESS DISFAVOR
UNKNOWABLE SEALED
UNKNOWN IGN UNCO UNKET UNKID IGNOTE MUNKAR SEALED SECRET UNWARE UNWIST FARAWAY OBSCURE UNCOUTH UNHEARD IGNORANT UNAWARES UNKENNED UNWITTING
UNLADEN LEAR LEER
UNLATCH UNSNECK
UNLAWFUL ILLEGAL ILLICIT NONLICET UNLEEFUL UNLEISUM
UNLEARNED LEWD GROSS PLAIN BOOKLESS IGNORANT UNLEARED
UNLEAVENED AZYMOUS
UNLESS BUT NIF LESS LEST NISI SAVE BINNA NOBUT LESSEN ONLESS WITHOUT
(— BEFORE) NIPR NIPRI
(— OTHERWISE NOTED) NAN
UNLETTERED LEWD BORREL IGNORANT
UNLIGHTED BLIND LAMPLESS
UNLIKE DIFFORM DISLIKE DIVERSE DIFFERENT DISSIMILAR
(MOST —) OTHEREST
UNLIKELY REMOTE DUBIOUS
(MOST —) LAST
UNLIMITED VAST SOVRAN ABSOLUTE UNTERMED
(— IN POWER) ALMIGHTY
UNLINED SINGLE
UNLOAD TIP DROP DUMP HOVEL DECANT STRIKE UNLADE UNSHIP UNSTOW DELIVER DEPLETE DETRUCK DISLOAD UNTRUSS DISCHARGE
UNLOCK UNMAKE RESERATE UNLOUKEN
UNLOOSE OUTWIND UNRIVET
UNLUCKY BAD FAY ILL EVIL FOUL DONSY DISMAL DONSIE HOODOO WICKED HAPLESS INFAUST UNHAPPY SINISTER UNCHANCY

UNTOWARD MISCHANCY WANCHANCY
(— THING) AMBSACE
UNMAN UNDO CRUSH UNNERVE
UNMANAGEABLE ROID DONSY RANDY WANTON RESTIVE CHURLISH STAFFISH CAMSTAIRY REFRACTORY
UNMANLY SOFT EPICENE MANLESS UNLUSTY
UNMANNERLY RUDE BOORISH UNCIVIL IMPOLITE UNGENTLE MISLEARED
UNMARKED MAVERICK NOTELESS
UNMARRIED ONE LONE SOLE OLEPI YOUNG ONLEPY SINGLE
UNMASK EXPOSE UNFACE DISMASK UNCLOAK
UNMASKING EXPOSURE
UNMEASURED UNMEET MODELESS
UNMELODIOUS SCRANNEL
UNMERCHANTABLE SALABLE SALEABLE
UNMERCIFUL CRUEL PITILESS RUTHLESS
UNMETHODICAL CURSORY
UNMINDFUL SLOWFUL CARELESS HEEDLESS MINDLESS
UNMISTAKABLE FLAT OPEN BROAD CLEAR FRANK PLAIN PATENT DECIDED EXPRESS APPARENT DECISIVE MANIFEST UNIVOCAL
UNMISTAKABLY SIGNALLY
UNMITIGATED PURE GROSS RUDDY ARRANT DAMNED SOVRAN PERFECT PUREDEE REGULAR ABSOLUTE OUTRIGHT
UNMIX EXSOLVE
UNMIXED NET DEEP MERE NEAT PURE SELF SOLE BLANK SHEER UTTER IMMIXT SIMPLE STRAIGHT
UNMODIFIED BRUTE STRAIGHT
UNMOLESTED SACKLESS
UNMOVED CALM COOL FIRM STONY TIGHT IMMOTE SERENE ADAMANT IMMOVED
UNMOVING INERT IMMOBILE IMMOTIVE
UNMUSICAL NOTELESS SCABROUS
UNNATURAL EERY EERIE STIFF CLAMMY CREEPY FORCED UNKIND STRANGE UNCANNY VIOLENT ABNORMAL ABSONANT FARCICAL KINDLESS STRAINED UNKINDLY MONSTROUS
UNNECESSARY USELESS NEEDLESS SUPERFLUOUS
UNNEEDED WASTE
UNNERVE UNMAN RATTLE UNMAKE WEAKEN ENERVATE PARALYZE
UNNERVED SHOOK
UNNILPENTIUM HAHNIUM
UNNILQUADIUM RUTHERFORDIUM
UNNOTICED SILENT
UNOBJECTIONABLE VENIAL
UNOBSERVANT HEEDLESS
UNOBSTRUCTED FAIR FREE OPEN PATENT THROUGH APPARENT
UNOBTRUSIVE SHY QUIET MODEST SEDATE DISCREET RETIRING

UNOCCUPIED IDLE VOID BLANK EMPTY WASTE OTIOSE VACANT LEISURE UNSEATED WASTEFUL
UNORGANIZED ACOSMIC INCHOATE
UNORTHODOX HERETIC
UNOSTENTATIOUS SHY QUIET LENTEN MODEST
UNPACK UNFARDLE
UNPAID DUE UNQUIT UNWAGED HONORARY WAGELESS OUTSTANDING
UNPAIRED IMPAR AZYGOUS
UNPALATABLE SOD HARD BITTER BRACKISH
UNPARALLELED ALONE UNIQUE EPOCHAL PEERLESS SINGULAR UNPEERED
UNPERTURBED BLAND STILL
UNPLEASANT BAD ACID EVIL HARD NICE SOUR UGLY VILE AWFUL CRUDE GRIMY GUMMY HAIRY HARSH MUCKY NASTY ROUGH TOUGH YUCKY YUKKY BRUTAL CRIMPY RANCID STICKY THRAWN UNFELE UNGAIN UNLIEF BEASTLY BILIOUS GHASTLY INGRATE SPINOUS UNLUSTY UNQUEME UNSONCY CHISELLY DREADFUL HORRIBLE INDECENT SCABROUS UNLOVELY TRAUMATIC ABOMINABLE
(ANNOYINGLY —) CREEPY
(PREF.) CAC(O) CACH
UNPLEASANTLY QUEER HARDLY UNWINLY
UNPLEASANTNESS ILLNESS
UNPLOWED LEA
UNPOETICAL MUSELESS
UNPOLISHED ILL RUDE BLIND CRUDE ROUGH COARSE INCULT RUGGED RUSTIC SAVAGE SHAGGY UPLAND INCOMPT UNKEMPT AGRESTIC
UNPOPULARITY ENVY
UNPRACTICED RAW FRESH UNTRADED
UNPREDICTABILITY CHAOS
UNPREDICTABLE DICEY CHANCY CRANKY ERRATIC
UNPREJUDICED FAIR
UNPREMEDITATED CASUAL
UNPREPARED TARDY
UNPREPOSSESSING SEEDY
UNPRETENDING LOWLY HOMELY HUMBLE
UNPRETENTIOUS HOMY HOMEY PLAIN SOBER COMMON HOMELY HUMBLE MODEST SIMPLE DISCREET HOMESPUN
UNPRINCIPLED LEWD LIMMER
UNPRODUCTIVE DRY SHY ARID DEAD DEAF LEAN POOR VAIN YELD YELL ADDLE DUSTY WASTE BARREN GEASON SAPLESS STERILE WOODSERE
UNPRODUCTIVENESS BORASCO BORASQUE BORRASCA
UNPROFESSIONAL LAY BUSH LAICAL JACKLEG
UNPROFITABLE BAD DRY DEAD LEAN SECK VAIN BARREN BOOTLESS GAINLESS UNGAINLY

UNPROGRESSIVE SLOW DORMANT BACKWARD
UNPROMISING BLUE DUBIOUS
UNPRONOUNCED MUTE
UNPROPITIOUS ILL EVIL FOUL THRAW MALIGN SULLEN ADVERSE AVERTED INFAUST OMINOUS THRAWART
UNPROTECTED NAKED EXPOSED HELPLESS
UNPROVOKED WANTON
UNPUBLISHED INED INEDITED
UNQUALIFIED NET BARE FULL MERE PURE VERY BLACK PLUMP SHEER UNFIT DIRECT ENTIRE UNABLE CLOTTED PLENARY IMPLICIT INHABILE POSITIVE
UNQUESTIONABLE ASSURED CERTAIN DECIDED ABSOLUTE DECISIVE DISTINCT
UNQUESTIONED CLEAR
UNQUESTIONING IMPLICIT
UNRAVEL REDD UNDO BREAK ENODE FEAZE RAVEL RETEX SOLVE EVOLVE TIFFLE UNFOLD UNKNIT UNLACE ENODATE RESOLVE
UNRAVELLING DISCOVERY DENOUEMENT
UNREAL VAIN AERIAL GOTHIC CHEMICK FANCIED SHADOWY AERIFORM CHIMERIC FARCICAL ILLUSORY NOTIONAL SCENICAL VISIONAL
(PREF.) PSEUD(O)
UNREALISTIC CHIMERIC
UNREALIZED BEHIND
UNREASONABLE ABSURD FANATIC ABSONANT
UNREASONABLENESS ALOGY INSANITY
UNREASONABLY SINFULLY
UNREASONING BRUTE RABID
UNRECOGNIZED UNSUNG CRYPTIC UNWITTED
UNRECOVERABLE DEAD
UNRECTIFIED IMPURE
UNREDEEMED CHEAP
UNREFINED RAW DARK LOUD BRUTE CRUDE DORIC GROSS COARSE COMMON EARTHY JUNGLY VULGAR BOORISH UNCOUTH UNKEMPT DREADFUL SWAINISH
UNREFLECTING GLIB VACANT
UNREGENERACY ADAM
UNREGENERATE NATURAL
UNREGENERATELY MANLY
UNREHEARSED IMPROMPTU
UNRELATED FREMD STRAY UNAKIN UNTOLD EXTREME FRAMMIT POSITIVE
UNRELAXED UNSLAKED
UNRELAXING TONIC
UNRELENTING GRIM HARD IRON CRUEL STERN BRASSY SEVERE RIGOROUS
UNRELIABLE FISHY SHADY FICKLE GREASY UNSAFE CASALTY STREAKY WILDCAT FECKLESS GLIBBERY SLIPPERY TICKLISH
UNRELIEVED DEAD BRUTE ABJECT EXQUISITE

UNREMITTING BUSY FAST HARD DOGGED

UNREMUNERATIVE HONORARY

UNRESERVED FREE CLEAN FRANK ROUND COMMON UNCLOSE EXPLICIT

UNRESERVEDNESS FREEDOM

UNRESISTING BUXOM

UNRESPONSIVE DEAD DUMB BARREN SILENT STUBBORN

UNREST ANOMY ANOMIE MOTION AILMENT DISREST WANREST DISQUIET CHEMISTRY PSYCHOSIS

UNRESTRAINED LAX MAD FREE WILD BROAD FANTI FRANK LARGE LOOSE FACILE FANTEE LAVISH UNTIED WANTON FLYAWAY RAMPANT RIOTOUS BARBARIC FAMILIAR FREEHAND LAXATIVE PINDARIC ABANDONED LIBERTINE

UNRESTRAINT LICENSE IMMUNITY

UNRESTRICTED FREE GLOBAL SOVRAN UNZONED ABSOLUTE

UNRETURNED UNYOLDEN

UNREVEALED UNTOLD

UNRHYMED BLANK

UNRIG STRIP

UNRIGHTEOUSNESS ADHARMA

UNRIPE RAW CRUDE GREEN CALLOW UNCURED IMMATURE

UNROBE DISROBE UNDRESS DISARRAY

UNROLL EVOLVE UNCURL DEVELOP OUTROLL TRINDLE UNTREND

UNROOF TIRL TIRR TIRVE DISROOF

UNRUFFLE SMOOTH SOOTHE MOLLIFY

UNRUFFLED CALM COOL EASY EVEN QUIET SOBER STILL ASLEEP PLACID SEDATE SERENE SMOOTH DECOROUS

UNRULY HIGH RAMP ROYT TOUGH HAUNTY WANTON LAWLESS RAMMAGE ROPABLE UNRULED VICIOUS WANRULY WAYWARD INDOCILE MUTINOUS CAMSTAIRY TURBULENT REFRACTORY OBSTREPEROUS RAMBUNCTIOUS

UNSADDLE OUTSPAN UNPANEL

UNSADDLED BAREBACKED

UNSAFE HOT OUT FISHY EXPOSED INSECURE PERILOUS

UNSANCTIFIED PROFANE

UNSATISFACTORY BAD ILL EVIL POOR CROOK LOUSY SHREWD WRETCHED

(— PRODUCT) LEMON

UNSATISFYING DUSTY HOLLOW

UNSATURATED (PREF.) EN

UNSAVORY WERSH INSIPID WEARISH

UNSAY WITHDRAW

UNSCHOLARLY BOOKLESS

UNSCRUPULOUS SKIN CROOK BRAZEN DEVIOUS JACKLEG DEXTROUS RASCALLY

UNSEASONABLE LAT UNRIPE UNTIDY UNCHANCY UNTIMELY

UNSEASONED RAW GREEN

UNSEAT ADDRESS DISSEAT

UNSEEING BLIND GAZELESS

UNSEEMLY HOIDEN UNFAIR

IMPROPER INDECENT SEEMLESS UNMEETLY UNWORTHY

UNSEEN SECRET UNEYED CRYPTIC VIEWLESS INVISIBLE

UNSELFISH (ABSURDLY —) QUIXOTIC

UNSERRIED LOOSE

UNSETTLE JAR TURN UNFIX UNSET UPSET COMMOVE DERANGE DISTURB STAGGER UNHINGE UNQUEME DISORDER DISQUIET DISTRACT

UNSETTLED MOOT LIGHT SHAKY UNSAD VAGUE BROKEN FICKLE QUEASY VAGOUS DUBIOUS NOMADIC SHUTTLE UNSTAID RESTLESS UNSTABLE VAGABOND

UNSETTLING NASTY

UNSHAKABLE DOGGED ADAMANT IRONCLAD

UNSHAKEN FIRM STEADY UNMOVED UNSHOOK CONSTANT RESOLUTE

UNSHAPELY DEFORMED UNMACKLY

UNSHARED SOLE

UNSHEATHE DISCASE

UNSHEATHED BARE

UNSHELTERED BLEAK

UNSHOD BAREFOOT SHOELESS DISCALCED

UNSHORN UNPOLLED

UNSIGHTLY UGLY AWFUL MESSY HOMELY INDECENT

UNSKILLED JAY PUNY GREEN PUISNE UNGAIN UNSEEN STRANGE FECKLESS

UNSKILLFUL ILL EVIL RUDE ARTLESS AWKWARD UNFEATY BUNGLING TINKERLY UNHEPPEN

UNSMILING GLUM AUSTERE

UNSOCIABLE SULLEN FAROUCHE INSOCIAL

UNSOILED CLEAN

UNSOPHISTICATE SQUARE

UNSOPHISTICATED JAY DEWY NAIF PURE FRANK GREEN NAIVE SILLY CALLOW SIMPLE BUCOLIC NATURAL VERDANT HOMEBRED HOMESPUN INNOCENT PROVINCIAL

UNSOUND BAD ILL EVIL SICK ADDLE BARMY CRAZY CRONK DICKY DOTTY DOZED SANDY SHAKY WONKY ABSURD FAULTY FLAWED HOLLOW INFIRM INSANE ROTTEN UNHALE INVALID RICKETY UNWHOLE

UNSOUNDNESS CRACK INSANITY

UNSPARING ROUND SEVERE DRASTIC RIGOROUS RUTHLESS SCATHING SLASHING

UNSPIRITUAL CARNAL

UNSPOILED RACY UNSHENT PRISTINE

UNSPOKEN TACIT SILENT

UNSPORTSMANLIKE DIRTY

UNSPOTTED CLEAR SPOTLESS

UNSPUN RAW

UNSTABLE FLUX BATTY LOOSE SANDY SHAKY BROTEL CHOPPY FICKLE FITFUL FLITTY LABILE LUBRIC ROTTEN SHIFTY TICKLE UNFIRM WANKLE WANKLY ASTATIC DWAIBLE DWAIBLY DWEEBLE RICKETY SLIDDER SLIDDRY VOLUBLE FEVERISH FIRMLESS FUGITIVE INSECURE LUBRICAL REMUABLE SKITTISH SLIPPERY TICKLISH TOTTLISH VARIABLE

(MENTALLY —) BRAINISH

UNSTEADILY GROGGILY

UNSTEADINESS FALTER

UNSTEADY WALT CRANK CRONK DOTTY FLUKY LIGHT NERVY SLACK TIPPY TIPSY TOTTY UNSAD WALTY WONKY COGGLY FICKLE FLICKY FLUFFY GROGGY JIGGLY JOGGLY SWIMMY TOTTIE WAFFLY WAGGLY WAMBLY WANKLE WEEWAW WEEWOW DODDERY GLAIKIT JIGGETY QUAVERY QUEACHY TITTUPY TOTTERY WAYWARD SKITTISH STAGGERY TICKLISH TITUBANT UNSTABLE VARIABLE VERSATILE

UNSTINTED LAVISH ENDLESS

UNSTOPPABLE SUREFIRE

UNSTRESS SLACK

UNSTRESSED SHORT

UNSTRING DISSOLVE

UNSTUDIED GLIB CASUAL CARELESS GLANCING

UNSUBDUED VIRGIN UNBOWED

UNSUBSTANTIAL TOY AIRY LIMP THIN WINDY AERIAL BUBBLE CHAFFY FLIMSY SLEAZY SLEEZY SLIGHT UNREAL FOLIOUS FRAGILE INSOLID SHADOWY TENUOUS FILIGREE FINESPUN FOOTLESS GIMCRACK VAPOROUS PASTEBOARD

UNSUCCESSFUL BAD MANQUE UNSPED STICKIT UNHAPPY ABORTIVE

UNSUITABLE INEPT UNAPT UNDUE UNFIT UNKIND UNMETE UNCOMELY UNGAINLY UNLIKELY INELIGIBLE MALAPROPOS INCONVENIENT

UNSUITABLENESS IMPOLICY

UNSUITED BAD

UNSULLIED FAIR PURE CLEAR VIRGIN INNOCENT SPOTLESS VIRGINAL

UNSUPPLIED HELPLESS

UNSUPPORTED BLIND NAKED BACKWARD STAYLESS

UNSURE TIMID INFIRM DOUBTFUL INSECURE UNSICKER

UNSURPASSED CHAMPION

UNSUSPECTING INNOCENT

UNSWEET UNSOOT

UNSWEETENED BRUT

UNSWERVING FIXED FLUSH LOYAL DIRECT STEADY STRICT STURDY STAUNCH

UNSWERVINGLY HEADLONG

UNSYMMETRICAL LOPSIDED

UNSYMPATHETIC DRY HARD STONY FROZEN GLASSY HOSTILE KINDLESS

UNTAINTED FREE GOOD PURE INNOCENT

UNTAMED WILD FERAL RAMAGE SAVAGE HAGGARD RAMMISH WARRAGAL

UNTANGLE FREE SLEAVE UNLACE

UNTARNISHED PURE

UNTAUGHT WASTE UNLERED IGNORANT

UNTHINKABLE PUERILE

UNTHINKING GLIB BRUTE CASUAL FECKLESS HEEDLESS VISCERAL

UNTHINKINGLY STUPID

UNTIDINESS JAKES LITTER

UNTIDY DOWDY GAUMY MESSY ROOKY BUNTING DRAGGLY LITTERY RUMMAGY SCRUFFY UNSIDED DRAGGLED SLOVENLY STRUBBLY UNHEPPEN SHAMBOLIC

UNTIE UNDO UNBIND UNLASH UNLATCH UNTRUSS UNTWINE UNFASTEN

UNTIL AD OR TO GIN HENT INTO UNTO FORTO TWELL WHILE WHILES WHILST PENDING

(— THEN) BEFORE

UNTILLED INCULT UNEARED

UNTIMELY UNTIDY IMMATURE PREVIOUS TIMELESS

(— ARRIVAL) LATECOMER

UNTIRING BUSY SEDULOUS TIRELESS

UNTITLED (— MEN) AUMAGA

UNTO TILL

UNTOLD VAST UNQUOD

UNTOUCHABLE DOM HARIJAN CHANDALA (PL.) PANCHAMA

UNTOUCHED FREE INTACT PRISTINE (PREF.) INTEGRI

UNTOWARD ILL UNRULY FROWARD WAYWARD

UNTRAINED RAW RUDE GREEN HAGGARD

UNTRAMMELED FREE

UNTRIED MAIDEN UNSOUGHT

UNTRIMMED UNTEWED

UNTRODDEN PATHLESS UNFOOTED

UNTROUBLED CHEERY

UNTRUE FLAM FALSE LEASE WRONG UNFAST DISLOYAL MENDACIOUS (PREF.) PSEUD(O)

UNTRUSTWORTHINESS FALSITY

UNTRUSTWORTHY PUNIC SHAKY LIMBER TRICKY UNSURE SLIDDERY SLIPPERY

UNTRUTH LIE FABLE LEASE SKLENT FALSITY UNTROTH MENDACITY

UNTRUTHFUL SLANTER

UNTUNABLE ABSONANT

UNTUTORED NATURAL IGNORANT PRIMITIVE

UNTWILLED PLAIN

UNTWINE FRESE UNTWIST

UNTWIST RAG REAZE UNLAY UNSPIN UNTWIRL

UNTWISTED SLEIDED

UNUSABLE WASTE INUTILE

UNUSED IDLE FRESH RUSTY WASTE INURED MAIDEN VACANT DERELICT INITIATE UNWONTED

UNUSUAL ODD EERY RARE SELD TALL CRAZY EERIE FORBY NOVEL

UTTER WEIRD EXEMPT FORBYE SCREWY SINGLE UNIQUE STRANGE ABNORMAL DISTINCT ESPECIAL INSOLENT KNOCKOUT SELCOUTH SINGULAR SPANKING UNCOMMON UNTRADED UNWONTED PRODIGIOUS
(PREF.) ANOM(O)

UNUSUALLY EXTRA

UNVARIED SAMELY

UNVARNISHED EVERYDAY

UNVARYING FLAT SAME FRANK LEVEL STABLE UNIFORM

UNVEIL REVEAL UNCOVER UNCROWN UNDRAPE UNSCREEN UNWIMPLE

UNVENTILATED CLOSE

UNVERSED STRANGE

UNWANTED STRAY TRAMP FAULTY

UNWARRANTED UNDUE

UNWARY RASH UNAWARE CARELESS HEEDLESS WARELESS

UNWASHED SOAPLESS

UNWASTEFUL FRUGAL

UNWAVERING FIRM CLEAN LEVEL SOLID GLASSY STABLE EXPRESS STAUNCH

UNWAVERINGLY FAST

UNWEAKENED CLEAR

UNWELL BAD ILL EVIL PUNK SICK BADLY CROOK SEEDY AILING CHIPPY WICKED COMICAL

UNWHOLESOME ILL EVIL SICK CAGMAG IMPURE MORBID SICKLY CORRUPT NOISOME NOXIOUS UNCLEAN DISEASED EPINOSIC

UNWIELDY BULKY CLUMSY UNRIDE AWKWARD HULKING CUMBROUS UNGAINLY

UNWILLING CHARY LOATH SWEER WERSE AVERSE ESCHEW BACKWARD GRUDGING
(— TO GO FORWARD) RESTIVE

UNWILLINGLY MAUGER MAUGRE

UNWILLINGNESS GRUDGE NOLITION

UNWIND UNCLEW UNREEL UNREAVE UNTWINE

UNWISE FALSE INANE SILLY SIMPLE FOOLISH WITLESS

UNWITTING UNWIST WEETLESS

UNWOMANLY MANKIND

UNWORLDLY WEIRD ASTRAL SPIRITUAL

UNWORRIED DOWNBEAT

UNWORTHY BASE INDIGN BENEATH UNDIGNE WANWORDY

UNWOUNDED COLD

UNWREATHE UNPLAT

UNWRINKLED BRANT BRENT

UNWROUGHT RAW LIVE RUDE

UNYIELDING PAT SET ACID DEAF DOUR FAST FIRM GRIM HARD RIGID STARK STEEL STIFF STITH STONY TOUGH FLINTY FROZEN GLASSY KNOBBY MARBLE STEELY STURDY ADAMANT AUSTERE COSTIVE FROWARD CHURLISH OBDURATE OBEDIENT STUBBORN ROCKRIBBED PERTINACIOUS

UNYOKE LOWSE UNTEAM OUTSHUT OUTSPAN

UNYOKED
(PREF.) AZYGO

UP ON ONE OOP ABOUT ASTIR DORMY NORTH DORMIE
(— AND ABOUT) AFOOT
(— TO) TIL INTO UNTIL
(— TO THE TIME) UNTIL
(— YONDER) UPBY UPBYE
(FARTHER —) ABOVE
(HIGH —) ALOFT
(PREF.) ANA ANO SUR

UPANISHAD ISHA KATHA

UPAS DITA ANTIAR CHETTIK

UPBEAT ARSIS AUFTAKT ANACRUSIS

UP-BOW POUSSE

UPBRAID CHEW RAIL SNUB TUCK TWIT ABUSE ROUSE SCOLD TAUNT UPBRAY EMBRAID REPROVE DISGRACE OUTBRAID

UPCARD STARTER

UPCOMING NEXT FUTURE

UPFOLD SADDLE ANTICLINE

UPHEAVAL BOIL STORM UPLIFT RUMMAGE UPTHROW

UPHILL UPBANK UPWITH

UPHOLD AID TOM ABET BACK FAVOR AFFIRM ASSERT DEFEND SOOTHE BOLSTER SUPPORT SUSTAIN CHAMPION MAINTAIN PRESERVE

UPHOLDER DEFENDER ERASTIAN FEUDALIST

UPHOLDING BEHIND

UPHOLSTER SQUAB

UPHOLSTERER TAPISER UPHOLDER

UPKEEP MAINTENANCE

UPLAND DOWN DOWNS MAUKA COTEAU FASTLAND
(PL.) BRAES DOWNS

UPLAND PLOVER QUAILY HILLBIRD PAPABOTE

UPLIFT TOSS BOOST ERECT TOWER UPTHRUST

UPLIFTED ERECT EXALTEE

UPON ON PON SUR INTO OVER ABOVE AGAINST
(— THAT) THEREAT
(PREF.) EP EPH EPI OB

UPPER OVER VAMP SKIVE VAMPEY SUPERIOR
(PL.) FINISH
(PREF.) ANO HYPER SUPERO
(SITUATED ON — SIDE) SUPRA

UPPER CRUST GRATIN

UPPERCUT BOLO

UPPER HURONIAN LAWSON

UPPERMOST UMEST UPMOST OVEREST BUNEMOST OVERMOST

UPPER VOLTA FASO BURKINA

UPRAISED SUBLIME

UPRIGHT FAIR GOOD HARR JUST PROP STUD TIDY TRUE ANEND CHEEK ERECT GUIDE JELLY MORAL ONEND RIGHT ROMAN SETUP STALE STALK STILE ARRECT DIRECT ENTIRE HONEST SQUARE FRIZZEN HOUSING JANNOCK PITPROP SINCERE GOALPOST INNOCENT RIGHTFUL STANDARD STANDING STRAIGHT VERTICAL VIRTUOUS
(NOT —) ATILT BEVEL

(PL.) STUDDING
(PREF.) ORTH(O)

UPRIGHTNESS HONOR TRUTH APLOMB EQUITY HONESTY PROBITY JUSTNESS SINCERITY

UPRISING RIOT EMEUTE MUTINY PUTSCH REVOLT TUMULT UPRISE UPRISAL REBELLION

UPROAR DIN RUT CAIN FLAW GILD HELL MOIL RIOT ROUT BABEL BURLE CHANG FUROR HOOHA HURLY RUMOR STOUN STOUR CLAMOR DIRDUM EMEUTE FRACAS HABBLE HUBBLE HUBBUB RACKET RANDAN RATTLE RIPPET RUCKUS RUMBLE RUMPUS SHINDY STEVEN STOUND TUMULT CATOUSE FERMENT GARBOIL GAUSTER ORATION OUTROAR RUCTION STASHIE TURMOIL BALLYHOO BROUHAHA SCOUTHER STIRRING STRAMASH TINTAMAR CHARIVARI SHEMOZZLE HULLABALOO PANDEMONIUM

UPROARIOUS FURIOUS ROUTOUS ROWDYDOWDY

UPROOT GRUB HACK LOUK MORE UNROUT UNPLANT DISPLANT ROOTWALT SUPPLANT

UPROOTED LUMPEN

UPSET ILL TIP TOP TUP CAVE COUP COWP FUSS JUMP PURL ROCK TILT TURN WELT EVERT FREAK KNOCK ROUSE SHAKE SKAIL SKELL SPILL WHELM BOTHER DISMAY QUELME TICKED TIPPLE TOPPLE UPCAST WALTER CAPSIZE DERANGE DISTURB FRAZZLE HAYWIRE INASTEW OVERSET PERVERT REVERSE SLATTER SUBVERT TEMPEST TURMOIL UNGLUED CAPSIZAL DISTRAIT OVERTILT OVERTURN STREAKED SUPPLANT TURNOVER OVERTHROW
(EASILY —) FUSSY FLAPPABLE

UPSHOT ISSUE SHORT UPSET EFFECT SEQUEL UPPING OUTCOME UPSHOOT UPSTROKE

UPSIDE-DOWN CRAZY REVERSE OVERHAND UPSEDOUN

UPSILON
(PREF.) YPSILI

UPSTAIRS ABOVE

UPSTANDING GRADELY

UPSTART KIP QUAT SNIP SNOB SQUIRT UPSKIP DALTEEN PARVENU ARRIVIST MUSHROOM SKIPJACK UPSPRING

UPTICK RISE INCREASE

UPTIGHT TENSE

UP-TO-DATE AGOGO WITHIT MOD MODERN TRENDY ABREAST TODAYISH

UPWARD ALOFT UPLONG UPWAYS UPWITH SKYWARD UPALONG UPWARDS
(PREF.) ANO

UPWARD-MOVING ANABATIC

URAEUS ASP

URAMIL MUREXAN

URANUS OURANOS HERSCHEL
(WIFE OF —) GAEA

URAO TRONA

URARTAEAN KHALDIAN

URARTU VAN

URATE LITHATE

URBAN TOWN URBIC URBANE BURGHAL OPPIDAN

URBANE CIVIL SUAVE POLITE SVELTE AMIABLE GRACIOUS

URBANITY COMITY SUAVITY COURTESY ELEGANCE

URCHIN IMP TYKE WAIF ELFIN GAMIN SCAMP KEELIE NIPPER HURCHEON
(PREF.) (SEA —) ECHIN(O)

URD MUNGO

URDEE MATELEY

URDU REKHTA REKHTI MOORISH

URDUR (SISTER OF —) SKULD VERTHANDI

URGE ART DUN EGG HIE PLY PUT SIC SUE TAR YEN BROD COAX CRAM EDGE FIRK GOAD ITCH MOVE PING POKE PROD PUSH SICK SPUR WHIP CROWD DRIVE EGGON FILIP FORCE HOOSH IMPEL LABOR PRESS PRICK SPANK TREAT COMPEL DEHORT DESIRE ENGAGE EXCITE FILLIP HARDEN HOICKS HUSTLE INCITE INDUCE INVITE MOTION PROMPT PROPEL STRAIN THREAP THREAT ANIMATE COMMOVE ENFORCE INSTANT OPPRESS PERSIST SOLICIT SUGGEST URGENCY ADMONISH INSTANCE PERSUADE
(— IMPORTUNATELY) DUN PRESS
(— ON) EGG ERT HAG SOOL WHIG ALARM CHIRK CROWD DRIVE FILIP HASTE HURRY IMPEL ROWEL YOICK ALARUM FILLIP HARDEN HASTEN INCITE
(— ON A HORSE) HUP CRAM CHUCK
(— OUT) EXTRUDE
(— STRONGLY) EXHORT SOLICIT
(— WITH VEHEMENCE) DING
(VITAL —) LIBIDO

URGENCY NEED PRESS STRESS COGENCE COGENCY URGENCE EXIGENCY INSTANCE INSTANCY PRESSURE

URGENT HOT DIRE LOUD RASH ACUTE HASTY STRONG BURNING CLAMANT EXIGENT INSTANT URGEFUL CRITICAL PRESSING PRESSIVE NECESSITOUS

URGING QUEST

URI (SON OF —) GEBER BEZALEEL

URIAH (WIFE OF —) BATHSHEBA

URIAL SHA OORIAL

URIEL (DAUGHTER OF —) MAACHAH
(FATHER OF —) TAHATH

URIJAH (FATHER OF —) SHEMAIAH

URINAL DUCK PISSOIR SANITARY

URINATE WET LEAK EMPTY STALE PIDDLE EVACUATE MICTURATE

URINATION MICTION NOCTURIA

URINE MIG SIG LAGE LANT WASH STALE WATER NETTING EMICTION
(— USED AS COSMETIC) LOTIUM
(PREF.) UR(O) URIC(O) URIN(I)(O)
(SUFF.) URIA URIC

URN JAR EWER KIST URNA VASE CAPANNA

(— FOR MAKING TEA) KITCHEN SAMOVAR
(— IN KENO) GOOSE
(BURIAL —) OSSUARY
(CINERARY —) DINOS DEINOS
(STONE —) STEEN
URN-SHAPED URCEOLAR
UROCHORDA ASCIDIA TUNICATA
UROPYGIUM RUMP
UROSTYLE COCCYX
URSA MAJOR OKNARI CHARIOT WAGONER WAGGONER
URSA MINOR CYNOSURE
URSINE ARCTOID
URTICARIA HIVES UREDO CNIDOSIS
URTICACTNUM LAPORTEA
URUBU ZOPILOTE

URUGUAY
CAPITAL: MONTEVIDEO
DEPARTMENT: ROCHA SALTO FLORES RIVERA ARTIGAS COLONIA DURAZNO FLORIDA SORIANO
ESTUARY: PLATA
LAKE: MERIN MIRIM DIFUNTOS
MEASURE: VARA LEGUA CUADRA SUERTE
RIVER: MALO MIRIM NEGRO ULIMAR CUAREIM OUEGUAY YAGUARON CEBOLLATI
TOWN: MELO AIGUA MINAS PANDO ROCHA SALTO VERAS RIVERA DURAZNO FLORIDA MERCEDES PAYSANDU
WEIGHT: QUINTAL

URUGUAYAN ORIENTAL
URUS TUR URE AUROCHS
US HIS HIZ HUZ
U.S.A. (AUTHOR OF —) DOSPASSOS
(CHARACTER IN —) ANN BEN JOE MAC MARY WARD DELLA FAINY JANEY MARGO TRENT FRENCH MAISIE SAVAGE STAPLE STRANG CHARLEY COMPTON DOWLING ELEANOR EVELINE RICHARD SPENCER ANDERSON GERTRUDE HUTCHINS MCCREARY STODDARD WILLIAMS ANNABELLE MOOREHOUSE
USABLE FIT UTIBLE SERVABLE
USAGE USE ASAL FORM WONE HABIT HAUNT SUNNA USURE CUSTOM MANNER FASHION HALACHA HALAKAH USATION PRACTICE
(BAD —) ABUSAGE
(EVIL-) MISUSE
(HARD —) GRIEF
(ILL —) ABUSE
(LEGAL —) PRACTIC
(RELIGIOUS —) RITUS
(PL.) CEREMONY
(PREF.) NOM(O)
(SUFF.) NOMY
USE URE BOOT CALL DUTY HAVE NAIT NOTE USUS WISE APPLY AVAIL GUIDE HABIT SPEND STEAD TREAT USAGE WASTE BEHOOF EMPLOY FINISH HANDLE OCCUPY USANCE ACCOUNT ADHIBIT ENTREAT IMPROVE PURPOSE

SERVICE UTILITY ACCUSTOM EXERCISE FUNCTION PRACTICE
(— AS WONTED) ADOPT
(— DILIGENTLY) PLY
(— EXPERIMENTALLY) TRY
(— FIGURE OF SPEECH) TROPE
(— FOR FIRST TIME) FLESH
(— IMPROPERLY) ABUSE
(— INDISCRIMINATELY) HACK
(— OF MORE WORDS THAN NECESSARY) PLEONASM
(— OF NEW WORD) NEOLOGY
(— OF SUBTERFUGE) CHICANE
(— OSTENTATIOUSLY) SPORT
(— SELFISHLY) HOG
(— SPARINGLY) TAPE SPARE MANAGE
(— UP) EAT TIRE WEAR SHOOT SPEND ABSORB DEVOUR EXPEND GUZZLE PERUSE CONSUME EXHAUST OVERWEAR
(— WASTEFULLY) SPILL
(— WITH FULL COMMAND) WIELD
(EFFICIENT —) ECONOMY
(EXCESSIVE — OF FACE AND HANDS) ABHINAYA
(FIRST —) HANSEL HANDSEL
(FOR TEMPORARY —) JURY
(FRUGAL —) SPARE
(GENERAL —) CURRENCY
(GET EXCLUSIVE — OF) SEWUP
(LITURGICAL —) RITE
(MUCH IN —) GREAT
(UNRESTRICTED —) FREEDOM
(WRONG —) ABUSE
(PREF.) USU
USED WONT
(— CONTINUOUSLY) HOT
(— IN FLIGHT) VOLAR
(— UP) ALL BEAT SHOT SPENT FOREWORN
(CONVENTIONALLY —) STOCK
(MUCH —) GREAT HACKNEY
USEFUL GAIN GOOD UTILE UTIBLE HELPFUL THRIFTY BEHOVELY UTENSILE BEHOVEFUL
(— FOR LONG TIME) HARD
(SUFF.) CHRESIS CHRESTIC CHRESTO
USEFULNESS USE AVAIL VALUE WORTH PROFIT MILEAGE UTILITY
USELESS IDLE LEWD VAIN VOID WIDE EMPTY WASTE DOLESS GROTTY NOUGHT OTIOSE SCREWY TRASHY INUTILE STERILE VAINFUL BOOTLESS FOOTLESS FOOTLING WASTEFUL WORTHLESS INEFFECTIVE
USELESSNESS FUTILITY IDLENESS
USER USUS
(SUFF.) STER STRESS
USH SEAT
USHABTI SHAWABTI
USHER BOW USH SEAT SHOW CRIER ESCORT HERALD ISCHAR SEATER VERGER CHOBDAR HUISHER JANITOR MARSHAL STEWARD
USSR (SEE RUSSIA)
USUAL RIFE NOMIC COMMON FAMOUS NORMAL SOLEMN VULGAR WONTED AVERAGE GENERAL NATURAL REGULAR

TYPICAL USITATE EVERYDAY FREQUENT HABITUAL ORDINARY ORTHODOX ACCUSTOMED
(NOT —) EXTRAORDINARY
USURER SHARK GAVELER HARPAGON
USURP ASSUME INVADE PRESUME ACCROACH ARROGATE
USURY GAVEL OCKER USURE USANCE GOMBEEN

UTAH
CAPITAL: SALTLAKECITY
COLLEGE: WEBER
COUNTY: IRON JUAB CACHE PIUTE CARBON SEVIER TOOELE UINTAH SANPETE
EARLY NAME: DESERET
INDIAN: UTE
LAKE: SALT SWAN SEVIER
MOTTO: INDUSTRY
MOUNTAIN: LENA LION WAAS KINGS PEALE TRAIL FRISCO NAVAJO SWASEY GRANITE GRIFFIN HAWKINS PENNELL LINNAEUS
MOUNTAIN RANGE: CEDAR HENRY HOGUP UINTA WAHWAH TERRACE WASATCH CONFUCION
NATIONAL PARK: ZION
NICKNAME: MORMON BEEHIVE
RIVER: UINTA WEBER JORDAN SEVIER
STATE BIRD: SEAGULL
STATE FLOWER: SEGOLILY
STATE TREE: SPRUCE
TOWN: LOA MOAB OREM DELTA HEBER KANAB LOGAN MAGNA MANTI NEPHI OGDEN PRICE PROVO KEARNS TOOELE VERNAL BRIGHAM BOUNTIFUL COALVILLE

UTENSIL (ALSO SEE IMPLEMENT AND TOOL) HOD BOAT IRON MOLD PECK STEW BAKER FRIER FRYER GRILL KNIFE MOULD RICER SCOOP SHEET SHELL SIEVE SLICE ULLER BEATER BEETLE BREWER COOKER DABBER FUNNEL GRATER GRILLE KETTLE LINGEL MASKER POPPER PUSHER SHAKER SIFTER BRAZIER BROILER DUSTPAN FLIPPER GLUEPOT MUDDLER SCUMMER SKIMMER STEAMER STIRRER TOASTER CALABASH GRIDIRON SAUCEPAN SAUCEPOT SHREDDER SPOUCHER STRAINER
(— FOR COVERING FIRE) CURFEW
(COOKING —) WOK
(LITURGICAL —) ASTERISK
(SHIP-SHAPED —) NEF
(PL.) BATTERY COOKWARE IRONWARE
UTERUS WOMB BELLY METRA MATRIX BEARING
(EXAMINATION OF —) FETOSCOPY
(PREF.) METR(O)
UTHAI (FATHER OF —) BIGVAI AMMIHUD
UTHER (WIFE OF —) IGRAINE
UTILITARIAN USEFUL ECONOMIC
UTILITY USE AVAIL USAGE PROFIT BENEFIT SERVICE

UTILIZE USE EMPLOY ENLIST CONSUME EXPLOIT HARNESS HUSBAND
UTILIZING
(SUFF.) IC(AL)
UTMOST END NTH BEST LAST MOST FINAL EXTREME OUTMOST SUPREME DAMNDEST POSSIBLE UTTEREST
UTOPIA ZION
UTOPIAN IDEAL
UTOPIANISM FUTURISM
UTRAQUIST CALIXTIN
UTRICULUS ALVEUS
UTTER ASK OUT SAY BARK BLOW BOOM DEAD DRIB EMIT FAIR GASP GIVE HURL MAIN MOOT MOVE PASS PURE RANK SEND TELL VENT VERY BLACK COUGH CRUDE FETCH FRAME FRANK GROSS ISSUE MOUTH PLAIN RAISE SHEER SLING SOUND SPEAK SPELL STARK THICK TOTAL VOICE ACCENT ARRANT BROACH DAMNED DIRECT ENTIRE INTONE PARLEY PROFER PROPER TONGUE BLUSTER BREATHE DELIVER ENOUNCE EXCLAIM EXPRESS OUTMOST OUTTELL PERFECT PHONATE PROLATE UPBRAID ABSOLUTE BLINKING COMPLETE CRASHING INTONATE PRONOUNCE BLITHERING PEREMPTORY
(— ABRUPTLY) BLURT
(— AFFECTEDLY) KNAP MINCE
(— ARGUMENTS) BLAZE
(— CASUALLY) DROP
(— EXPLOSIVELY) BOLT
(— FALSEHOODS) FABLE
(— FOOLISHLY) BLABBER
(— GLIBLY) SCREED
(— HALTINGLY) BLUBBER
(— HURRIEDLY) CHOP
(— INADVERTENTLY) SLIP
(— INDISTINCTLY) CHEW
(— IN HARSH VOICE) GRIT GRATE
(— LOUD CRY) BRAY BLARE
(— LOUDLY) CRY BLAT CALL HALLO HALLOO HULLOO PRABBLE
(— LOW SOUNDS) MURMUR WHISPER
(— MEANINGLESS SOUNDS) BABBLE
(— RAPIDLY) FIRE CHATTER
(— RAUCOUSLY) BLAT
(— REPETITIVELY) CHIME
(— RHETORICALLY) DECLAIM
(— RUTTING CALL OF THE ELK) BUGLE
(— SOLEMNLY) SWEAR
(— STUPIDLY) BLUNDER
(— SUDDENLY) CRACK
(— UNCTUOUSLY) DROOL
(— VIGOROUSLY) FLING
(— WITH EFFORT) HEAVE
UTTERANCE CRY GAB CALL OSSE BLURT DITTY PAROL VOICE ACCENT ACTION BREATH CHORUS DRIVEL GIBBER ORACLE PAROLE TONGUE EXPRESS INKLING LALLING STATUTE DELIVERY FOOTNOTE HOMESPUN JUDGMENT LOCUTION SYLLABIC

(— **FROM A DIVINITY**) ORACLE
(— **OF JESUS**) AGRAPHON
(— **OF LOVE**) ENDEARMENT
(— **OF PRAISE**) MAGNIFICAT
(— **OF VOCAL SOUNDS**) PHONESIS
(**CONDEMNATORY** —) INFAMY
(**DEFECTIVE** —) STAMMER
(**ECSTATIC** —) RHAPSODY
(**EMPTY** —) NOTHING
(**FACETIOUS** —) PLEASANTRY
(**FAINT** —) INKLING
(**FLUENT** —) OUTPOURING
(**FOOLISH** —) DRIVEL
(**FOOLISH** —S) GUFF
(**GUSHING** —) EFFUSION
(**HABITUAL** —) SONG
(**IMPULSIVE** —) BLURT
(**INDISTINCT** —) BUMBLE BUMMLE
MUTTER
(**INSIPID** —) INANITY
(**INSPIRED** —) PROPHECY
(**MALICIOUS** —) SLANDER
(**MOMENTOUS** —) MOUTHFUL

(**OFFENSIVE** —) AFFRONT
(**PROPHETIC** —) OSSE
(**PUBLIC** —) AIR OUTGIVING
(**SHORT** —) DITTY
(**SOLEMN** —) EFFATE EFFATUM
(**TRADITIONAL** —) AGRAPHON
(**UNVARIED** —) MONOTONE
(**VAPID** —) CUCKOO
(**VIOLENT** —) INVECTIVE
(**WISE** —) ORACLE
(**PL.**) BYRONICS
UTTERED ORAL SPOKEN
(**BOLDLY** —) OUTSPOKEN
(**INDISTINCTLY** —) INARTICULATE
UTTERLY DOG BONE DEAD BLACK
OUTLY PLUMB PROOF HOLLOW
MERELY BLANKLY OUTERLY
SHEERLY PROPERLY
UTU (**FATHER OF** —) NANNA
UVULA CION UVULE PLECTRUM
STAPHYLE
(**PREF.**) CION(O) STAPHYL(O)
UVULARIA OAKESIA

UZ (**FATHER OF** —) ARAM NAHOR
DISHAN
(**GRANDFATHER OF** —) SEIR SHEM
UZAI (**SON OF** —) PALAL
UZAL (**FATHER OF** —) JOKTAN
UZBEK JAGATAI

UZBEKISTAN (ALSO SEE RUSSIA)
AUTONOMOUS REPUBLIC:
KARAKALPAK KARAKALPAKSTAN
CAPITAL: TASHKENT TOSHKENT
COIN: RUBLE
DESERT: KYZYLKUM QIZILQUM
MIRZACHOL
MOUNTAIN: BESHTOR
MOUNTAIN RANGE: ALAY UGAM
PSKEM GISSAR HISSAR KURAMA
CHATKAL NURATAU MALGUZAR
TIENSHAN TURKESTAN
KARZHANTAU
NAME: UZBEK
PLAIN: TURAN
RIVER: OXUS NARYN AMUDARYA

KARADARYA ZERAVSHAN
KASHKADARYA SURKHANDARYA
SHERABADDARYA
SEA: ARAL
TOWN: KHIVA NAVOI NUKUS
QOQAN ANGREN KOKAND
BEKABAD BUKHARA ANDIZHAN
CHIRCHIK GULISTAN NAMANGAN
YANGIYER YANGIYUL
SAMARKAND
VALLEY: FERGANA ZERAVSHAN

UZZAH (**BROTHER OF** —) AHIO
(**FATHER OF** —) ABINADAB
UZZI (**FATHER OF** —) BANI BELA TOLA
BUKKI
(**SON OF** —) ZERAHIAH
UZZIAH (**FATHER OF** —) AMAZIAH
(**SON OF** —) ATHAIAH JEHONATHAN
UZZIEL (**FATHER OF** —) ISHI KOHATH
HARHAIAH
(**SON OF** —) ZITHRI MISHAEL
ELIZAPHAN

V

V VEE FIVE VICTOR
(INVERTED —) CARET
VACANCY HOLE WANT VACUIT
VACUITY VACATION
(— IN ENERGY BAND) HOLE
VACANT IDLE OPEN VOID BLANK
EMPTY FISHY INANE WASTE
DEVOID HOLLOW DORMANT
UNFILLED
(BECOME —) FALL
(PREF.) VACUO
VACATE QUIT TOLL VOID AVOID
EMPTY WAIVE VACANT ABANDON
RESCIND ABROGATE EVACUATE
VACATION OUT HOLS REST LEAVE
OUTING RECESS HOLIDAY
NONTERM VACANCY
(SUMMER —) LONG
VACCINE (KIND OF —) SALK
VACCINE LYMPH BACTERIN
BIOLOGIC
(KIND OF —) ORAL
VACCINIA COWPOX
VACILLATE HALT SWAG WAVE
WAVER DACKER DITHER HALPER
SEESAW TEETER WABBLE WAFFLE
WOBBLE SHAFFLE STICKLE
SWITHER WHIFFLE HESITATE
VACILLATING INFIRM MOBILE
HALTING
VACILLATION SEESAW WAVERING
VACUITY BLOW VACANCY
FONTANEL NOTHINGNESS
(MENTAL —) INANITY
VACUOLE GUTTA
VACUOUS DULL BLANK EMPTY
SILLY VACANT
VACUUM GAPE VOID HOOVER
VACANCY VACUITY VACATION
VACUUM TUBE
(SUFF.) TRON
VAGABOND BUM VAG HOBO KERN
JAVEL ROGUE SHACK STIFF BRIBER
CANTER HARLOT JOCKEY PICARA
PICARO RODNEY RUNNER TAGRAG
TRUANT WAFFIE COASTER
ERRATIC FAITOUR GADLING
GANGREL OUTCAST SCOURER
SKELDER SWAGMAN SWINGER
TINKLER TRUCKER VAGRANT
VAURIEN WASTREL BOHEMIAN
BRODYAGA CURSITOR CUSTROUN
FUGITIVE GLASSMAN PALLIARD
RAPPAREE RUNABOUT RUNAGATE
WHIPJACK
VAGARY WHIM FANCY FREAK
VAGUE CAPRICE CONCEIT
CRANKUM FLAGARIE
VAGRANCY
(PL.) HUMORS
VAGINA
(PREF.) COLP(O) ELYTR(O)
VAGINATE SHEATHED

VAGRANCY MOPERY ROGUING
NOMADISM
VAGRANT BUM HOBO WAFF WAIF
CAIRD PIKER PIKEY ROGUE SKELB
STRAG TRAMP VAGUE ARRANT
CASUAL SHAKER SHULER TINKER
TRUANT VAGROM VAGUER WAFFIE
DEVIOUS DRIFTER ERRATIC
FLOATER GANGREL ROGUISH
SKILDER SWAGMAN TINKLER
TRAMPER TROGGER BRODYAGA
PLANETIC STROLLER VAGABOND
SHACKLING
(PL.) FLOTSAM
VAGUE LAX DARK HAZY FOGGY
FUZZY GROSS LOOSE MISTY
MUDDY WOOZY CLOUDY DREAMY
MYSTIC SHAGGY BLURRED
EVASIVE OBSCURE SHADOWY
UNFIXED CONFUSED INFINITE
NEBULOUS NUBILOUS
VAGUELY DIMLY DARKLY DUMBLY
DREAMILY
VAIN MAD IDLE NULL PUFF VOID
WANE COCKY EMPTY FLORY
PROUD SAUCY VOGIE WASTE
FLIMSY FUTILE HOLLOW OTIOSE
VAUNTY BIGGITY CARRIED TRIVIAL
USELESS VAINFUL ROOTLESS
CONCEITY NUGATORY PEACOCKY
VAPOROUS WASTEFUL
(NOT —) SOLID
VAINGLORY POMP RUFF GLORY
VANITY ELATION
VAINLY IDLY TOOMLY
VAIR POTENT
VAISRAVANA BISHAMON
VAISYA BAIS BICE
VAJEZATHA (FATHER OF —) HAMAN
VAJRA DORJE
**VAKULA THE SMITH (CHARACTER
IN —)** CHUB DEVIL OXANA PANAS
VAKULA SOLOKHA
(COMPOSER OF —) TCHAIKOVSKY
VAL LACE
VALANCE PAND PELMET FRONTLET
PALMETTE
VALE DALE DEAN DELL BACHE
BATCH ENNIS DINGLE
VALEDICTORY FAREWELL
VALENCE ADICITY ATOMISM
VALENTINE (SISTER OF —)
GRETCHEN
(SLAYER OF —) FAUST
VALERIAN HELIO BENNET SUMBUL
ALLHEAL CUTHEAL SETWALL
CETEWALE
VALERIC PENTOIC
VALET MAN ANDREW JEEVES
SIRDAR TARTAR WALLIE CRISPIN
TIREMAN
VALIANT SAD BOLD BRAG PREU
PROW WILD BRAVE LUSTY ORPED

PROUD STOUT WIGHT FIERCE
HEROIC DOUGHTY GAILLARD
GALLIARD INTREPID STALWART
VIRTUOUS
(SON OF PRINCE —) ARN
(WIFE OF PRINCE —) ALETA
VALID FAIR GOOD JUST LEGAL
SOUND COGENT LAWFUL BINDING
ETERNAL WEIGHTY FORCIBLE
VAILABLE VALIDOUS VALUABLE
(PREF.) RATI
VALIDATE FIRM SEAL VALID AFFIRM
CONFIRM
VALIDATION PROOF
VALIDITY FORCE VIGOR STRENGTH
VALISE BAG GRIP MAIL DORLACH
SATCHEL VALLIES SUITCASE
VALKYRIE BRYNHILD SHIELDMAY
VALLECULA VALLEY
VALLEY DIB CUT COMB COOM
COVE DALE DELL DENE GILL HOLE
HOPE HOWE HOYA PARK VALE
WADI WADY ATRIO BACHE BREAK
CHASM COMBE COOMB DHOON
GHYLL GLACK GOYAL GOYLE
HEUGH SLACK SLADE SWALE
TEMPE YUNGA BOLSON BOTTOM
CANADA CLOUGH COULEE DINGLE
HOLLOW LAAGTE LEEGTE RINCON
STRATH AIJALON BLOWOUT
GEHENNA VAALITE
(— BETWEEN CONES OF VOLCANO)
ATRIO
(— IN OCEAN) DEEP
(— IN THESSALY) TEMPE
(— ON MOON'S SURFACE) RILL
CLEFT RILLE
(— ON MT BLANC) NANT
(BROAD —) STRATH
(CIRCULAR —) RINCON
(DEEP —) CANON GRIKE CANYON
(DROWNED —) RIA VIA
(FLAT-FLOORED DESERT —)
BOLSON
(GRASSY MOUNTAIN —) HOLE
(LOWEST PART OF —) SOLE
(MINIATURE —) GULLY GULLEY
(NARROW —) DEAN DENE GLEN
GLACK GOYLE GRIFF KLOOF
CLOUGH
(RIFT —) GRABEN
(RIVER —) WATER
(SECLUDED —) GLEN DINGLE
(TRENCHLIKE —) COULEE
VALOR ARETE MERIT VALUE
BOUNTY VALOUR BRAVERY
COURAGE HEROISM PROWESS
STOMACH CHIVALRY VALIANCY
VALOROUS BOLD BRAVE VIRTUOUS
VALUABLE DEAR COSTLY PRIZED
WORTHY EMINENT WEALTHY
PRECIOUS PRIZABLE SINGULAR
VALUATION PRIZE VALOR VALUE

ESTEEM EXTENT ESTIMATE
TAXATION
VALUE SET COST FECK FOOT HOLD
RATE TELL AVAIL CARAT CHEAP
COUNT FORCE PRICE PRIZE STAMP
STENT STOCK VALOR WORTH
ASSESS ASSIZE EQUITY ESTEEM
EXTENT FIGURE HIDAGE MATTER
MOMENT PRAISE REGARD VALURE
VALUTA VIRTUE ACCOUNT
ADVANCE APPRIZE CAPITAL
CHERISH COMPUTE PRETIUM
RESPECT VALENCY WERGILD
ESTIMATE EVALUATE GOODWILL
SPLENDOR TREASURE VALIDITY
VALLIDOM
(— HIGHLY) PRIZE ENDEAR
(— OF ANGLE) EPOCH
(— OF COW) SET
(— OF STOCK(S)) OMNIUM
(— OF TIMBER) STUMPAGE
(— WRONGLY) MISRATE
(ABSOLUTE —) MODULUS
(AESTHETIC —) AMENITY
(ANNUAL —) RENTAL
(ESTABLISHED —) PAR
(GOOD —) SNIP
(HIGH —) ESTEEM
(LOWEST —) MINIMUM
(MATHEMATICAL —) EXTREMUM
(MIDDLE —) MEDIAN
(NEGATIVE —) DISVALUE
(OF NO —) IMMOMENT
(SOUND —) POWER
(STUDY OF —) AXIOLOGY
(TESTED —) ASSAY
(PREF.) AXIO TIMO
VALUED DEAR
VALUELESS BAFF STRAWY
NAUGHTY
VALVE TAP COCK DISC DISK GATE
ORAL STOP CHOKE CLACK MIXER
VALVA WAFER BINODE BOTTLE
CUTOUT DAMPER KICKER PALLET
POPPET POTLID SCUTUM SLUICE
SUCKER VENTIL WASHER CLICKET
DRAWOFF PETCOCK REDUCER
SCALLOP SCOLLOP SHUTOFF
VALVULA VALVULE DRAWGATE
EPITHECA EPIVALVE STOPCOCK
THROTTLE
(— OF BARNACLE) SCUTUM
(— OF MUSICAL INSTRUMENT)
PISTON VENTIL
(— OF PUMP BOX) FANG
(ANATOMICAL —) TRICUSPID
(ELECTRODE —) TRIODE
(THERMIONIC —) TUBE
(THIN —) WAFER
(TRIPLE —) KICKER
(PREF.) THYRE(O) THYRO
(SUFF.) THYRIS
VAMBRACE BRACELET

VAMOOSE SCAT SCRAM CHEESE DECAMP SKIDDOO
VAMPIRE LAMIA ALUKAH
VAN WAN FORE LEAD SAIL FRONT TRUCK VAUNT WAGON VAWARD CARAVAN FOURGON FOREWARD KHALDIAN
   (LUGGAGE —) FREIGHTCAR
   (TAKE THE —) LEAD
VANADATE UVANITE TURANITE
VANDAL HUN HUNLIKE SARACEN HOOLIGAN
VANDALIZE MAR TRASH DAMAGE DEFACE RAVAGE
VANE FAN TEE WEB COCK TAIL WING FAINE BUCKET TARGET DOGVANE FLIGHTER VEXILLUM
   (— OF ARROW) FEATHER
   (— OF CONVEYOR BELT) FLIGHT
   (— OF FEATHER) WEB FLUE VEXILLUM
   (— OF SURVEYING STAFF) TRANSOM
   (— OF WINDMILL) FAN FANE TAIL FAINE
   (COOLING — IN BREWING) FLIGHTER
VANESSA PYRAMEIS
VANGUARD LEAD FORLORN
VANIAH (FATHER OF —) BANI
VANILLA PLAIN ORDINARY
VANISH DIE FLY DROP FADE FLEE MELT PASS SANT WEDE WEND CLEAR FLEET SAUNT SLIDE EXHALE EVANISH SCATTER CONQUEST DISSOLVE EVANESCE
   (— BY DEGREES) DRILL
VANISHED LAPSED EXTINCT
VANITY ABEL POMP VAIN FOLLY PRIDE EGOISM CONCEIT FEATHER FOPPERY INANITY SANDUST IDLENESS IDLESHIP PRETENSION
VANITY FAIR (AUTHOR OF —) THACKERAY
   (CHARACTER IN —) JOS PITT BECKY SHARP AMELIA DOBBIN GEORGE JOSEPH RAWDON SEDLEY STEYNE CRAWLEY OSBORNE WILLIAM
VANNER SLIMER
VANNIC KHALDIAN
VANQUISH GET WIN BEAT LICK MILL CREAM PASTE UTTER EXPUGN MASTER OUTRAY SUBDUE THRASH CONQUER OVERWIN SHELLAC SMOTHER CONQUEST OVERCOME SURMOUNT VENKISEN
VANQUISHED CRAVEN
VANUATU (CAPITAL OF —) VILA
   (FORMER NAME OF —) NEWHEBRIDES
   (ISLAND OF —) EPI EFATE MALEKULA PENTECOST ESPIRITUSANTO
   (MONEY OF —) VATU
   (VOLCANO OF —) TANNA AMBRYN LOPEVI
VAPID DRY DULL FADE FLAT STALE TRITE JEJUNE INSIPID WATERISH
VAPOR FOG FUME REEK ROKE STEW BOAST BRUME EWDER HUMOR SMOKE STEAM STIFE BREATH VAPOUR EXHAUST HALITUS

   (FROZEN —) SNOW
   (HOT —) LUNT
   (NOXIOUS —) DAMP
   (PETROL —) JUICE
   (PL.) BRUME
   (PREF.) ATM(O) ATMID(O) MANO PNEUMAT(O) TYPH(O)
VAPORIZATION BURNUP BOILOFF
VAPORIZE DRIVE FLASH STEAM AERATE AERIFY VAPORATE
VAPOROUS FUMY FUMID HUMID FUMISH FUMOSE STEAMY VOLATILE
VARANGIAN VARIAG WARING
   (PL.) ROS
VARGUENO DESK
VARIABILITY HETERISM
VARIABLE FLUX FREE CHOPPY FICKLE FITFUL KITTLE WRAIST CEPHEID FACIENT FLUXILE MUTABLE ROLLING STREAKY UNEQUAL VARIANT VARIOUS ARGUMENT FLOATING FLUXIBLE SHIFTING SKITTISH UNSTABLE VEERABLE
   (EXCEEDINGLY —) PROTEAN
   (MATHEMATICAL —) FUNCTION
   (RANDOM —) STATISTIC
VARIANCE ODDS DISCORD DISPUTE DISCREPANCY
   (ANALYSIS OF —) ANOVA
VARIANT STATE VERSION
   (— IN WHEAT) SPELTOID
   (POSITIONAL —) ALLOPHONE
   (SOUND —) ALTERNANT
   (PL.) DIAPHONE
VARIATION REX TURN ERROR ROGUE SHADE CHANGE DOUBLE JITTER SWITCH CYCLING DESCANT EXTREME SHADING VARIETY WINDING DIVISION DYNAMICS HETERISM MUTATION
   (— IN AIR PRESSURE) ROBBING
   (— IN CURRENT) SURGE
   (— IN FREQUENCY) SWINGING
   (— IN SPEED) HUNTING
   (— OF COLOR) ABRASH
   (— OF PUPIL OF EYE) HIPPUS
   (— OF SHOE) SPRING
   (— OF VOWELS) ABLAUT
   (ALLOWABLE —) LEEWAY
   (BALLET —) ATTITUDE
   (TOPOGRAPHICAL —) BREAK
   (PL.) PIBROCH
VARICOCELE RAMEX
VARIED SORTY DAEDAL SEVERAL VARIANT VARIOUS MANIFOLD
VARIED BUNTING PRUSIANO
VARIEGATE DROP FRET FLECK FREAK SHOOT AUMAIL DAPPLE STRIPE VARIFY CHECKER
VARIEGATED FAW PIED SHOT JASPE LYART PANED SHELD DAEDAL MARLED MENALD MOSAIC MOTLEY SKEWED VEINED BROCKED BROCKIT CHECKED CLOUDED DAPPLED FREAKED FRETTED PECKLED SPARKED VARIOUS DISCOLOR FRECKLED OVERSHOT PANACHED SKEWBALD
   (— AS GLASS BEADS) AGGRI AGGRY

   (NOT —) UNBROKEN
   (PREF.) POECIL(O)
VARIEGATION COLOR
VARIETY BREW FORM KIND MODE SORT BRAND BREED CLASS COLOR SPICE CHANGE FLAVOR NATURE STIRPS STRAIN STRIPE SPECIES VARIENS
   (— OF COLOR) SHADE
   (PERMANENT —) STIRPS
VARIOLA HORSEPOX SMALLPOX
VARIOUS MANY SERE DIVERS SUNDER SUNDRY VARIED DIVERSE SEVERAL VARIANT MANIFOLD MULTIPLE
   (PREF.) PARTI POECIL(O) POEKIL(O)
VARISCITE UTAHITE
VARIX
   (PREF.) CIRS(O)
VARLET BOY CAD LAD GIPPO JIPPO PAVISER COISTREL VARLETTO
VARNISH DOPE JAPAN LACKER MEDIUM PUNDUM FIXATIF LACQUER VEHICLE VERMEIL FIXATIVE OVERGILD THEETSEE
   (— INGREDIENT) ALOE COPAL ROSIN MASTIC
VARY HUNT ALTER BREAK DRIFT SHIFT SPORT CHANGE DIFFER RECEDE VARIFY CHECKER DEVIATE DISSENT DIVERGE VARIATE DISAGREE OSCILLATE
   (— PITCH) MODULATE
VARYING CURRENT
VASE PYX URN OLLA VASA VASO ASKOS CYLIX DINOS DIOTA KYLIX PYXIS BASKET BOWPOT COTULA COTYLA CRATER DEINOS DOLIUM FILLER HYDRIA KALPIS KOTYLE KRATER LEKANE SITULA AMPHORA AMPULLA CANOPUS PATELLA POTICHE PSYKTER SCYPHUS SKYPHOS STAMNOS URCEOLE BOUGHPOT LECYTHUS LEKYTHOS MURRHINE PROCHOUS
   (— FOR PERFUME) CONCH
   (— ON PEDESTAL) TAZZA
   (—S UNDER THEATER SEATS) SCHEA
   (PREF.) POTICHO VAS(I)(O) VASCUL(I)(O)
VASHNI (FATHER OF —) SAMUEL
VASHTI (HUSBAND OF —) AHASUERUS
VASODILATOR KELLIN KHELLIN MINOXIDIL
VASSAL MAN WER BOND LEUD SERF CEILE LIEGE SLAVE CLIENT GENEAT SACOPE BONDMAN FEEDMAN FEODARY HOMAGER RUDIGER SAMURAI SERVANT SUBJECT VAVASOR PALATINE
   (PL.) MANRED
VASSALAGE MANRENT
VAST HUGE BROAD ENORM GREAT LARGE STOUR VASTY COSMIC IMMANE MIGHTY UNTOLD ABYSMAL IMMENSE OCEANIC VASTITY ENORMOUS INFINITE MOUNTAIN SPACIOUS
VASTNESS IMMANE GRANDEUR WIDENESS
VAT ARK BAC DIP FAT PIT TAP TUN

BACK BECK COOM FATE GAAL GAIL GYLE KEEL KIER TINE APRON COOMB FETTE FLOAT KEEVE KIEVE ROUND STAND STEEP KIMNEL MOTHER BLUNGER DRAINER GRAINER KEELVAT STEEPER PRESSFAT
   (— USED IN MEASURING SLIPS) ARK
   (BLEACHING —) KEIR KIER
   (BREWER'S —) BACK FLOAT KEEVE UNION CUMMING
   (CHEESE —) CHESSEL CHESSET CHESSART
   (COOLING —) KELDER
   (DYER'S —) JIG LEAD DYEBECK
   (EVAPORATING —) APRON GRAINER
   (FERMENTING —) TUN COMB COOM GYLE KEEL COOMB FLOAT
   (TANNER'S —) TAP HANGER SPENDER
   (TEXTILE —) KIER
   (WINE —) LAKE CUVEE
   (PREF.) PYEL(O)
VATICAN CITY (BASILICA OF —) STPETERS
   (WALL OF —) LEONINE
VAU DIGAMMA
VAUDEVILLE ZARZUELA
VAULT BOUT COPE JUMP LEAP PEND SKIP TOMB VOLT WOWT AZURE CROFT CRYPT EMBOW VOLTO CELLAR CUPOLA FORNIX SHROUD CONCAVE DUNGEON TESTUDO VALTAGE CATACOMB LEAPFROG MONUMENT
   (— IN CEILING) LACUNAR
   (— OF HEAVEN) WELKIN
   (— OF SKY) CONVEX ZENITH CONCAVE
   (PART OF —) PENDENTIVE
VAULTED CONCAVE CRYPTED EMBOWED
VAULTER VOLTIGEUR
VAULTING POMADA POMMADO
VAUNT GAB BRAG BOAST ROOSE VOUST AVAUNT INSULT BLUSTER GLORIFY FLOURISH
   (— ONESELF) WIND
VAUNTMURE MANURE
VCR (— BUTTON) RESET
VEAL VEAU SLINK FRICANDO
   (— SCALLOPS) SALTIMBOCCA
   (LIKE —) VITULINE
   (PIECE OF —) PAILLARD
   (SCALLOPS OF —) SALTIMBOCCA
   (SLICES OF —) SCALLOPINI
VECTOR I K PHASOR GRADIENT
VEDA SHASTER
VEDDOID PANYAN
VEDIC (— PRINCIPLE) RTA RITA
VEER CUT DIP FLY YAW CAST CHOP SLEW SLUE SWAY TACK WYRE FETCH SHIFT SWOOP BROACH CHANGE SLOUGH SWERVE TUMBLE BOXHAUL DEVIATE WHIFFLE
VEERING DRIFT CHOPPY
VEGA (CONSTELLATION OF —) LYRA
VEGETABLE PEA YAM BEAN BEET CORN KALE LEEK OKRA CHARD GRASS ONION SABZI SALAD VEGIE CARROT CELERY LEGUME LENTIL

POTATO RADISH SQUASH TOMATO TOPEPO TURNIP VEGGIE BLOATER CABBAGE CELTUCE LETTUCE PARSNIP PEASCOD RHUBARB SPINACH VEGETAL BROCCOLI EGGPLANT RUTABAGA
(— MATTER) SUDD
(—S FOR MARKET) TRUCK
(EARLY —) PRIMEUR
(EARLY —S) HASTINGS
(GARDEN —S) SASS SAUCE
(HYBRID —) GARLION
(RAW —S) CRUDITES
(PL.) CRUDITES
(PREF.) PHYT(I)(O)
VEGETARIAN VEGAN VEGIE VEGGIE
VEGETATION HERB COVER GREEN SCRUB GROWTH HERBAGE COVERAGE PLANTAGE PLEUSTON SMELLAGE
(DECOMPOSED —) STAPLE
(SCRUB —) BRUSH
(UNWANTED —) FILTH
(PREF.) PHYT(I)(O)
VEGETATIVE ASEXUAL PLANTAL
VEHEMENCE FURY GLOW HEAT RAGE WARMTH STRENGTH VIOLENCE
VEHEMENT HOT HIGH KEEN LOUD ANGRY EAGER FIERY HEFTY YEDEH ARDENT BITTER FERVID FIERCE FLASHY HEARTY HEATED RAGING STRONG ANIMOSE ANIMOUS FURIOSO INTENSE JEALOUS VIOLENT
VEHEMENTLY AMAIN PELLMELL
VEHICLE BUS CAB CAR FLY VAN ARBA AUTO CART DUKE FLAT GOER JEEP LIMO SLED TAXI TEAM WAIN ARABA BRAKE BREAK BUGGY CARRY DILLY FLAIL GUIDE HANSA NODDY ROVER STAGE WAGON BLADER CAMPER CHARET CISIUM DIESEL HEARSE JITNEY MEDIUM RANDEM SLEDGE SLEIGH SURREY TRISHA TROIKA CARRIER CHARIOT CRUISER HOTSHOT ICEBOAT KIBITKA MACHINE MINIBUS OMNIBUS PEDICAB PEDRAIL SHEBANG SHUTTLE SPEEDER SPRAYER STEAMER STEERER TARTANA TAXICAB TRAVOIS TRISHAW TURNOUT UTILITY AUTORAIL AUTOSLED CARRIAGE CHARETTE CYCLECAR DEADHEAD DELIVERY ELECTRIC FILMOGEN SHOWCASE SOCIABLE UNICYCLE AEROTRAIN SPACESHIP LOCOMOBILE MOTORCYCLE SNOWMOBILE SPACECRAFT
(— DRAWN BY BULLOCK) EKKA
(— FOR COLORS) MEGILP
(— FOR HAULING) TRACTOR
(— FOR SAND USE) DUNEBUGGY
(— IN FINE CONDITION) CREAMPUFF
(— ON RUNNERS) SLED CARRO SLEDGE SLEIGH ICEBOAT AUTOSLED
(— ON SINGLE RAIL) AEROTRAIN
(— PULLED BY MAN) BROUETTE RICKSHAW

(— RUNNING ON RAILS) LORRY TRAIN
(— WITH RUNNERS) SKIBOB
(— WITH 3 HORSES ABREAST) TROIKA
(— WITH 3 HORSES BEHIND EACH OTHER) RANDEM
(AIR-CUSHION —) HOVERCRAFT
(AIRPORT —) SKYLOUNGE
(AMMUNITION —) CAISSON
(AMPHIBIOUS —) BUFFALO
(ARCTIC —) SNOCAT
(AWKWARD —) ARK
(CHILD'S —) PRAM WALKER SCOOTER STROLLER
(COVERED —) SEDAN LANDAU CARAVAN KIBITKA
(DRAG-RACING —) RAIL
(EARTH-MOVING —) SCOOP
(KIND OF —) LAUNCH
(LITTLE —) HINAYANA
(LUMBERING —) TUG TODE
(MILITARY —) WEASEL AMTRACK
(MOON —) LEM
(MOTOR —) WHEELS
(OBSOLETE —) CRATE
(ONE-WHEELED —) BARROW
(OPERATE MOTOR) VROOM
(POOR-QUALITY —) DOG SHANDRYPAN
(RIVER —) HOVERCRAFT
(RUDE —) KIBITKA
(RUSSIAN) TARANTAS TARANTASS
(SATELLITE —) SLV
(SLEDGE-LIKE —) GAMBO
(SNOW —) SKIBOB
(SPACE —) LEM LANDER
(THREE-WHEELED —) PEDICAB
(WHEELLESS —) DRAY
(2-WHEELED —) GIG CART SULKY TONGA CISIUM JINGLE LIMBER BICYCLE CALECHE CROYDON RICKSHAW
(PL.) PARK
(SUFF.) MOBILE
VEIL WRY FALL FILM HIDE MASK WRAP COVER GLOSS RUMAL SCARF SCENE SHADE VELUM VIMPA VOLET WREIL BUMBLE CHRISM FAILLE SHADOW SHROUD VEILER WEEPER WIMPLE CORTINA CURTAIN ENDOTYS PARANJA VEILING CALYPTRA ENDOTHYS HEADRAIL KALYPTRA MAHARMAH MANTILLA TELEBLEM
(— IN CHURCH) AER ENDOTYS ENDOTHYS
(— OF MUSLIM WOMEN) YASHMAK
(— ON FUNGI) CORTINA
(— OVER HELMET) LAMBREQUIN
(BIRTH —) CAUL
(DOUBLE —) YASHMAK
(HUMERAL —) SUDARY
(WIDOW'S —) WEEPER
VEILED COVERT LATENT VELATED SHROUDED
VEILING PURDAH GOSSAMER
VEIN BAR LOB RIB CAVA LODE MOOD RAKE REEF VENA AMPER CLOUD COMES COSTA LEDGE MEDIA NERVE RIDER SCRIN VARIX LEADER MEDIAL STRAIN STREAK

VENULA VENULE AXILLAR AZYGOUS CUBITAL DROPPER JUGULAR NERVURE PRECAVA PRESTER SAPHENA VEINLET AXILLARY EMULGENT PREMEDIA PROFUNDA SUBCOSTA
(— IN MARBLE) CLOUD
(— OF LEAF) RIB COSTA MIDRIB
(— OF MINERAL) STREAK STRINGER
(— OF ORE) LODE ROKE BUNCH LEDGE RIDER SCRIN LEADER STRING DROPPER UNDERSET
(— OF WING) CUBIT RADIUS CUBITAL CUBITUS SUBCOSTA SUBCOSTAL
(—S OF LEAF) SKELETON
(GRANITIC —) ELVAN
(QUARTZ —) SADDLE
(VARICOSE —) AMPER
(PREF.) CIRS(O) PHLEB(O) PYL(E)(O) VENI VENO
(SWOLLEN —) CIRS(O)
VEINED MARBLED NERVOSE
VELA SAILS
VELAR PALATAL GUTTURAL
VELD BUSHVELD SOURVELD
VELELLA SALLYMAN
VELLEITY DESIRE WOULDING
VELLINCH FLINCHER
VELLUM ORIHON
VELOCIPEDE HOBBY STEED TRICAR BICYCLE DICYCLE RANTOON SPEEDER DRAISINE TRICYCLE
VELOCITY DRIFT CELERITY RAPIDITY STRENGTH
(— OF FLOW) CURRENT
(— OF 1 FOOT PER SECOND) VELO
VELOUR SOLEIL
VELOUTE POULETTE
VELUM VEIL VELAMEN VELARIUM
VELVET PILE PANNE YUZEN BIRODO VELURE FRAYING VELLUTE
VELVETEEN TRIPE
VELVET GRASS FOG
VELVETLEAF DAGGA PAREIRA
VENAL CORRUPT SALABLE BRIBABLE HIRELING SALEABLE VENDIBLE
VEND HAWK SELL UTTER MARKET PEDDLE
VENDA (CAPITAL OF —) THOHOYANDOU
(TOWN OF —) SIBASA MAKWARELA
VENDIBLE VENAL SALABLE SALEABLE
VENDITION SALE
VENDOR FAKER SELLER VENDER ALIENOR BUTCHER HUSTLER PITCHER PURI MAN VIANDER PITCHMAN SAUCEMAN VENDITOR
VENEER BURL BURR JAPAN SHOOK OVERLAY SKILLET
VENEERER DUSTER
VENERABLE OLD AGED HOAR SAGE AWFUL HOARY AUGUST SACRED VETUST ANCIENT VENERAL VINTAGE
(PREF.) SEBASTO
VENERATE FEAR DREAD HALLOW REVERE VENERE RESPECT WORSHIP
VENERATED HOLY SACRED HALLOWED

VENERATION AWE CULT DULIA CULTISM RESPECT DEVOTION
VENESECTION PHLEBOTOMY
VENETIAN RED SIENA SIERRA
VENETIAN SUMAC SCOTINO

VENGEANCE WRACK WREAK WRECK AVENGE ULTION WANION ALASTOR REVENGE VINDICT REQUITAL VINDICTA
VENICE (ISLAND NEAR —) LIDO
VENILIA (HUSBAND OF —) DAUNUS
(SISTER OF —) AMATA
(SON OF —) TURNUS
VENISON BILTONG
VENOM GALL ATTER VIRUS POISON SWELTER CROTALIN CROTALUS
VENOMOUS TOXIC ATTERN DEADLY SNAKEY VENOMY BANEFUL NOXIOUS SMITTLE SNAKISH POISONED VIPERINE VIPEROUS VIRULENT POISONOUS
VENT EMIT HOLE REEK BELCH DRAIN FROTH ISSUE TEWEL OUTAGE OUTLET CHIMNEY EXPRESS OPENING ORIFICE OUTCAST OUTFALL OUTTAKE RELEASE VENTAGE APERTURE BREATHER DIATREME FONTANEL MOFFETTE SESPERAL SPIRACLE SUSPIRAL VENTHOLE VOMITORY
(— IN EARTH'S CRUST) VOLCANO
(VOLCANIC —) BOCCA DIATREME SOLFATARA
VENTILATE AIR WIND AERATE EXPRESS
VENTILATED (BADLY —) STUFFY
VENTILATION AERAGE AIRING
VENTILATOR BADGIR LOUVER FEMERELL
VENTING GUST
VENTRAL BELLY HEMAL STERNAL ANTERIOR INFERIOR

(PREF.) (— AREA) GASTER(O) GASTR(I)(O)

VENTRICLE HEART TRICORN DIACOELE
(SUFF.) CELE COELE COELUS

VENTURE HAB RUN SET CAST DARE JUMP KITE LUCK MINT REST RISK WAGE ETTLE FLIER FLYER FROST RISCO SALLY STAKE TEMPT WAGER CHANCE DANGER HAZARD SASHAY FLUTTER IMPERIL JEOPARD PRESUME PRETEND ENDANGER GETPENNY
(— AT DICE) THROW
(— TO SAY) DARESAY
(RISKY —) CRAPSHOOT

VENTURESOME BOLD RASH RISKY DARING PARLOUS TEMEROUS

VENTURESOMELY CHANCILY

VENUS LOVE VESPER LUCIFER HESPERUS PHOSPHOR
(FATHER OF —) JUPITER
(HUSBAND OF —) VULCAN
(MOTHER OF —) DIONE
(SON OF —) AMOR CUPID AENEAS

VENUSIAN VENEREAN

VERACIOUS TRUE VERY TRUTHY SINCERE VERIDIC FAITHFUL TRUTHFUL

VERACITY HSIN TROTH TRUTH VERITY FIDELITY

VERANDA PYAL LANAI PORCH STOEP STOOP PIAZZA BALCONY GALERIE GALLERY

VERB RHEMA ACTIVE NOMINAL PASSIVE DEPONENT VOLITIVE INCEPTIVE INCHOATIVE INDICATIVE INFINITIVE
(AUXILIARY —) BE DO CAN MAY HAVE MUST WILL SHALL
(KIND OF —) ACTIVE PASSIVE PRETERIT TRANSITIVE
(LINKING —) COPULA

VERBAL ORAL WORDY

VERBATIM DIRECT VERBAL LITERAL DIRECTLY

VERBENA ALOYSIA VERVAIN

VERBENALIN CORNIN

VERBIAGE TALK JABBER

VERBOSE WINDY WORDY PROLIX VERBAL DIFFUSE WORDISH
(NOT —) LEAN

VERBOSITY MACROLOGY

VERDANT BOSKY GREEN VIRID

VERDICT WORD VARDI ASSIZE FINDING OPINION DECISION JUDGMENT VEREDICT

VERDIGRIS AERUGO CANKER VERDET

VERDIN GOLDTIT

VERDURE GREENTH GREENERY VIRIDITY
(PREF.) CHLO

VERGE RIM TOP EDGE WAND YARD BRINK POINT TOUCH BORDER TRENCH TRIGGER THRESHOLD

VERGER WANDSMAN

VERGILIAN MARONIAN MARONIST

VERIFICATION AUDIT AVERRAL CHECKUP AVERMENT

VERIFY AVER TRUE AUDIT CHECK PROVE ATTEST RATIFY COLLATE CONFIRM CONTROL JUSTIFY SUPPORT CONSTATE

VERILY YEA AMEN FAITH PARDY CERTES INDEED PARDIE FAITHLY

VERITABLE REAL TRUE VERY ACTUAL HONEST PROPER GENUINE VERIMENT

VERITY TROTH TRUTH REALISM VERIDITY

VERJUICE VARGE

VERMICELLI FEDELINI

VERMICULE VAALITE

VERMICULITE KERRITE MACONITE

VERMIFUGE KOSIN HARMAL HARMEL KAMALA KAMELA KOOSIN COWHAGE HELONIAS PINKROOT WORMWOOD

VERMILION RED GOYA MINIUM MINIATE PAPRIKA PIMENTO VERMEIL ZINOBER CARMETTA CINNABAR TOREADOR

VERMIN FILTH CARRION VARMINT

VERMIS WORM

VERMONT

CAPITAL: MONTPELIER
COLLEGE: BENNINGTON MIDDLEBURY
COUNTY: ESSEX ORANGE ADDISON ORLEANS WINDSOR LAMOILLE
LAKE: CASPIAN DUNMORE SEYMOUR CHAMPLAIN
MOUNTAIN: BROMLEY HOGBACK ASCUTNEY PROSPECT MANSFIELD
MOUNTAIN RANGE: GREEN TACONIC
NICKNAME: GREENMOUNTAIN
PRESIDENT: ARTHUR COOLIDGE
RIVER: SAXTONS LAMOILLE NULHEGAN POULTNEY WINOOSKI
STATE BIRD: THRUSH
STATE FLOWER: CLOVER
STATE TREE: MAPLE
TOWN: BARRE STOWE CHELSEA GRAFTON NEWFANE RUTLAND BENNINGTON BURLINGTON
UNIVERSITY: NORWICH

VERMOUTH CINZANO CHAMBERY

VERNACULAR LINGO COMMON JARGON PATOIS ROMAIC TONGUE VULGAR CHALDEE DIALECT TRIVIAL SCOTTISH

VERNALIZE IAROVIZE JAROVIZE YAROVIZE

VERNE (— CAPTAIN) NEMO

VERNIER NONIUS

VERONICA HEBE SUDARIUM VERNICLE BROOKLIME

VERRUCOSE WARTY WARTED

VERSANT SLOPE

VERSATILE HANDY FICKLE MOBILE FLEXILE

VERSE FIT EPIC LINE POSE RANN RICH HIME SONG BLANK IONIC METER METRE RHYME STAVE STICH TANKA ADONIC ALCAIC BURDEN CHIAVE CYWYDD DIPODY HEROIC JINGLE PANTUN SCAZON STANZA VERSET ANAPEST DICOLON DOGGREL ELEGIAC PAEONIC PANTOUM PENNILL SAPPHIC SAVITRI SOTADIC STICHOS TRIPODY TROILUS CHOLIAMB DACTYLIC DINGDONG DOGGEREL GLYCONIC LEONINES PRIAPEAN RESPONSE SENTENCE SINGSONG TERETISM TRIMETER VERSICLE MACARONIC
(— FORM) VIRELAY KYRIELLE
(— OF FOUR MEASURES) TETRAMETER
(— OF 14 LINES) SONNET
(— OF 2 FEET) DIPODY DIMETER
(— OF 6 FEET) CHOLIAMB SENARIAN SENARIUS
(— WITH LIMPING MOVEMENT) SCAZON
(DEVOTIONAL —) ANTIPHON OFFERTORY
(HINDU —) SLOKA
(JAPANESE —) HAIKU TANKA HAIKAI
(KOREAN — FORM) SIJO
(LINKED —) RENGA
(MEDIEVAL —) SIRVENTE
(NONSENSE —) AMPHIGORY
(NONSENSE —S) AMPHIGORY
(UNMELODIOUS —) TERETISM
(PL.) TRIPOS PINDARICS GALLIAMBICS HUDIBRASTICS

VERSED SEEN WITTY BESEEN TRADED STUDIED FREQUENT OVERSEEN SCIENCED
(WELL —) SKILLFUL

VERSICLE VERSE VERSET STICHOS SUFFRAGE

VERSIFIER BARD POET RHYMER VERSER METERER

VERSIFY METER

VERSION DRAM MODEL DRAUGHT EDITION READING TURNING REDACTION
(SHORT —) BRIEF
(SIMPLIFIED —) KEY
(TRANSLATED —) CONSTRUE

VERSO REVERSE

VERT VERD POMME VENUS PRASINE SINOPLE GREENHEW

VERTEBRA AXIS RACK ATLAS DORSAL LUMBAR SACRAL ACANTHA CENTRUM CERVICAL METAMERE PROATLAS RACKBONE SPONDYLE
(PREF.) ASTRAGAL(O) SPONDYL(O)
(SUFF.) SPONDYLI SPONDYLUS

VERTEBRATA CRANIATA CRANIOTA

VERTEBRATE CRANIATE SAUROPSID

VERTEX APEX COPE NODE POLE CROWN PITCH SUMMIT VERTICAL

VERTICAL APEAK ERECT PLUMB SHEER WHIRL ORTHAL UPRIGHT COLUMNAR SHEERING STRAIGHT
(PREF.) ORTH(O)

VERTICALLY PLUMP ENDLONG SHEERLY DIRECTLY PALEWISE

VERTICIL WHORL

VERTIGINOUS DIZZY

VERTIGO DINUS TIEGO MEGRIM MIRLIGO SWIMMING WHIRLING

VERUMONTANUM COLLICLE

VERVAIN GERVAO FROGFOOT IRONWEED

VERVE PEP BRIO DARE DASH ELAN GUSTO BOUNCE ENERGY PANACHE VITALITY VIVACITY

VERY SO ALL BIG DOG GAY GEY MUY TOO BRAW DEAD FELL FULL JUST MAIN MUCH PURE RARE REAL SAME SEHR SELF SUCH TRES UNCO WELL ASSAI AWFUL BLAME BULLY CRAZY DOOMS JOLLY MOLTO PESKY RIGHT SOWAN SUPER SWITH UNCOW VERRA BITTER BLAMED DAMNED DEUCED FREELY GAINLY LIVING MAINLY MASTER MIGHTY NATION POISON PROPER SORELY STRONG TARNAL THRICE VERRAY WONDER AWFULLY BOILING GALLOWS GREATLY PARLOUS PASSING PRECISE SOPPING STRANGE DEUCEDLY DREADFUL ENORMOUS FAMOUSLY POWERFUL PRECIOUS SPANKING SWINGING WHACKING ABSOLUTELY
(PREF.) ERI MALLO

VESICANT LEWISITE MESEREUM

VESICA PISCIS MANDORLA

VESICATORY BLISTER

VESICLE BLEB CYST APTHA BULLA BURSE FLOAT APHTHA AMPULLA BLADDER BLISTER HYDATID OTOCYST POMPHUS UTRICLE VACUOLE AEROCYST CISTERNA MIDBRAIN VESICULA PHAGOSOME
(SUFF.) YDATIS

VESICULAR BULLOSE BULLOUS

VESPERAL TOWEL

VESPERS LYCHNIC PLACEBO EVENSONG

VESSEL (ALSO SEE BOAT AND SHIP) GO CAN CAT COG CUP FAT GUM HOY KEG NEF PIG POT TUB VAS VAT VIA BARK BOAT BODY BOMB BOOT BOSS BOWL BRIG BUSH BUSS CASK CELL COWL DISH DRIP DUCT GAWN GRAB HORN HULK JACK JUNK KOFF LOTA PINK PINT POST PROW SAIL SHIP SNOW TING YAWL AMULA BAKIE BARGE BASIN BIDET BIKIE BOCAL BOYER CADUS CANNE CHURN COGUE CRACK CRAER CRAFT CRARE CRUET CRUSE DANDY DIOTA DUBBA FLASK GLOBE GUIDE JUBBE KETCH LADLE LAKER LAVER LINER PIECE PYKAR SCOOP SMACK STEAM STILL XEBEC YANKY ZABRA BANKER BARQUE BARREL BILALO BOILER BOTTLE BOUTRE BUCKET BURNER CAIQUE CANNER CAPPIE CHARGE CODMAN COFFIN CONCHA COOLER COPPER CRATER CRAYER CRUISE CUTTER DECKER DEINOS DOGGER DUBBAH ELUTOR FESSEL FIRKIN FLAGON HOLCAD HOOKER JAGGER KERNOS KETTLE KRATER LANCHA LATEEN LEKANE LORCHA MASLIN MONKEY MULLER PACKET PANKIN PATERA PICARD PITHOS POURIE ROLLER SALTER SATTIE SEALER SERVER SETTEE SHIBAR SITULA SMOKER TARTAN TENDER TOPMAN VESICA WHALER BAGGALA BALLOON BALLOON BLICKEY BLICKIE CARAVEL CARRIER CISTERN CLIPPER CORSAIR COUGNAR

CRAGGAN CRESSET CRISSET
CRUISER CUVETTE DRIFTER
DRINKER DROGHER FELUCCA
FLYBOAT FRIGATE GABBARD
GABBART GAIASSA GALASSA
GUNBOAT ORANGER PATAMAR
PINNACE POACHER POLACRE
PSYKTER REDUCER SALTFAT
SCALDER SEEDLIP SETTLER
SPARGER SPOUTER STEAMER
STEEPER TRACHEA TRENDLE
UTENSIL BELANDER BENITIER
BILANDER BILLYBOY BIRDBATH
BLEACHER BUGGALOW CORVETTE
CRUICRLE CRUISKEN CUCURBIT
DECANTER DIGESTER DUTCHMAN
EFFERENT EMISSARY FIREBOAT
FLESHPOT GALLIPOT GALLIVAT
GAROOKUH GAYDIANG HELLSHIP
HONEYPOT INKSTAND INRIGGER
IRONCLAD IRONSIDE KEELBOAT
LATEENER LAVATORY MONOHULL
NITRATOR PICAROON SCHOONER
SMUGGLER SPITTOON WATERPOT
BARKENTINE STIRRUPCUP
(— CUT FROM BLOCK OF WOOD)
DAMBOOS
(— FOR COAL) GEORDIE
(— FOR DYE) TOBY
(— FOR FEEDING ANIMALS)
TROUGH
(— FOR HEATING LIQUIDS) ETNA
(— FOR HOLY WATER) FAT FONT
STOCK STOOP STOUP AMPULLA
BENITIER CHRISMATORY
(— FOR HYPODERMIC USE) AMPUL
AMPULE AMPOULE
(— FOR LIQUID WASTE) DRIP
(— FOR MEASURING ORE) HOPPET
(— FOR MOLTEN METAL) LADLE
(— FOR ORE WASHINGS) LOOL
(— FOR PERFUMES) CENSER
(— FOR PORRIDGE) BICKER
(— FOR SOLDIER'S FOOD) MESSTIN
(— FOR SUGAR) SUCRIER
(— FOR WINE SAMPLING) TASTER
(— HOLDING CONDIMENTS) CRUET
CASTER
(— IN MINE) CORB
(— MADE OF HOLLOW LOG) GUM
(— OF BARK) COOLAMAN
COOLAMON COOLIMAN
(— OF HORN) BUGLE
(— ON TRIPOD) HOLMOS
(— ROWED BY OARS) CATUR
GALLEY
**(— STATIONED IN ENGLISH
CHANNEL)** GROPER
(— USED IN MAKING GLAZE)
HILLER
(ABANDONED —) DERELICT
(ARMORED —) CRUISER IRONCLAD
IRONSIDE
(BAILING —) SCOOP
(BAPTISMAL —) FONT
(BARGELIKE —) PANGARA
(BLOOD —) AORTA ARTERY
BLEEDER EFFERENT
(BREWER'S —) ROUND
(CANDLEMAKING —) JACK
(CHEMIST'S —) BATH FLASK STILL
BEAKER RETORT
(CHINESE —) JUNK SAMPAN

(CIRCULAR —) KIT
(CLUMSY —) CRAY CRARE
HAGBOAT
(COASTING —) DHOW DONI GRAB
PONTIN SHEBAR SHIBAR TRADER
COASTER GRIBANE MISTICO
BILLYBOY HOVELLER
(CODFISHING —) BANKER CODMAN
(COOKING —) MARMITE
(DECORATIVE —) AIGUIERE
(DISTILLING —) BODY STILL RETORT
MATRASS CUCURBIT
(DRINKING —) CAP CUP TIN BOOT
PECE FOUNT GLASS GOURD JORUM
KOVAH POKAL SCALE BICKER
CAFFIE CHOPIN GOOBER COOTIE
DIPPER DUBBER FIRLOT GOBLET
KITTIE KOVSHI QUAICH QUAIGH
RABBIT RUMKIN BIBERON CANAKIN
CANIKIN GALLIOT SCYPHUS SKINKER
SKYPHOS TANKARD CANNIKIN
CYLINDER
(DUTCH —) KOFF YANKY HOOKER
SCHUIT SCHUYT
(EARTHEN —) PIG OLLA BAYAN
PANKIN TINAGE CRAGGAN
(ELECTROPLATING —) TROUGH
(EUCHARISTIC —) AMA PYX AMULA
PIXIS FLAGON COLUMBA
CHRISMAL CIBORIUM
MONSTRANCE
(GLASS —) VERRE UNDINE
BALLOON
(HERRING-FISHING —) BUSS
(HOLLOW METALLIC —) BELL
(INVERTED —) BELL
(LADLING —) GAUN
(LARGE-NECKED —) JORDAN
(LATEEN-RIGGED —) DHOW LATEEN
LATEENER
(LEATHER —) BOOT JACK OLPE
GIRBA DUBBER
(LEVANTINE —) JERM SAIC
(LONG-NECKED —) GOGLET
GUGLET
(LYMPHATIC —) LACTEAL
(MALAYAN —) PROA COUGNAR
(MELTING —) GRISSET
(OPEN —) LOOM
(PERFORATED —) LEACH
(PINECONE-SHAPED —) THYRSE
(PORTUGUESE —) MULET
(RARE —) SNOW
(SEED —) POD BUTTON BIVALVE
(SERVING —) ARGYLE ARGYLL
SERVER
(SHALLOW —) KIVER SKEEL BEDPAN
PANCHION
(SMALL —) CAG HOY VIAL PHIAL
VEDET JIGGER LIEPOT PICARD
TINLET YETLIN FLIVVER VEDETTE
YETLING GALLIPOT
(TOP-HEAVY —) CRANK
(TURKISH —) MAHONE
(WHALING —) WHALER SPOUTER
(WICKER —) POT
(WINE —) AMA AMULA TINAGE
(WOODEN —) COG KIT BOSS BAKIE
KIVER BICKER CAPPIE COOTIE
DUDDIE FIRKIN STOUND
(PL.) CRAFT WAFTAGE
(PREF.) ANGI(O) ARTERI VAS(I)(O)
VASCUL(I)(O)

(HOLLOW —) CYT(O)
(SUFF.) ANGE ANGIUM
VEST GARB GOWN ROBE GILET
ACCRUE ATTACH FECKET INVEST
JACKET JELICK JERKIN LINDER
WESKIT ENFEOFF CLOTHING
(— IN) STATE
VESTA WAX
(FATHER OF —) SATURN
(MOTHER OF —) RHEA
(SISTER OF —) JUNO CERES
VESTED BESTEAD DONATIVE
VESTIBULE HALL ENTRY FOYER
PORCH ATRIUM EXEDRA EPINAOS
NARTHEX PASSAGE PRONAOS
TAMNOUR ANTEROOM VESTIARY
VESTIGE TAG DREG MARK HACK
SIGN PRINT RELIC SPARK TRACE
TRACK TRACT UMBRA SHADOW
MENTION LEFTOVER RUDIMENT
TINCTURE
VESTIGIAL REDUCED OBSOLETE
VESTING ADITIO
VESTITURE TIRE RAIMENT TUNICLE
VESTMENT ALB CAP ALBE COPE
PALL VEST AMICE COTTA EPHOD
FANON RABAT RASON STOLE
RHASON ROCHET SACCOS SAKKOS
VAKASS MANIPLE ORARION
PALLIUM PILLION PLUVIAL
TUNICLE VESTURE CHASUBLE
DALMATIC PHRYGIUM RATIONAL
SCAPULAR SURPLICE VESTIARY
(PL.) GARB GEAR DRESS
CLOTHING
VESTRY SACRISTY VESTIARY
VESTURE COAT
VESUVIANITE EGERAN CYPRINE
IDOCRASE VESUVIAN XANTHITE
VETCH DAL ERS AKRA LUCK TARE
TINE ERVIL FITCH AXSEED FECCHE
THETCH ARVEJON TINETARE
TINEWEED
VETERAN VET CHAUVIN EMERITUS
HARDENED SEASONED
WARHORSE
VETERINARIAN VET LEECH
FARRIER
VETERINARY VET FARRIERY
VETIVER BEN KHUS CUSCUS
KUSKUS KHASGHAS KHUSKHUS
VETO NIX KILL DISALLOW NEGATIVE
VEUGLAIRE FOWLER
VEX FRY IRE NOY TEW CARK CHAW
FASH FAZE FRET FYKE GALL HALE
HUMP ITCH RILE ROIL RUCK TEEN
TOUT YOKE ANGER ANNOY CHAFE
FRUMP GRAME GRILL GRIND
GRIPE HARRY SCALD SPITE STURT
TARRY TEASE WORRY WRACK
WRATH YEARN BOTHER BURDEN
CORSIE COTTER CUMBER GRIEVE
GRUDGE HARASS HARROW INFEST
NETTLE OFFEND PLAGUE POTHER
RUFFLE THREAT WORRIT AFFLICT
BEDEVIL CHAGRIN DESPITE
PERPLEX PROVOKE TORMENT
TROUBLE ACERBATE BEPESTER
BULLYRAG EXERCISE IRRITATE
MACERATE
VEXATION VEX CHAW FASH MOIL
TEEN TRAY CHAFE CROSS ERROR
GRIEF HARRY PIQUE SPITE STEAM

THORN WORRY BOTHER REPINE
CHAGRIN DISGUST NOISANCE
SORENESS
VEXATIOUS MEAN SORE TEEN
NASTY PESKY ACHING FIERCE
SHREWD THORNY VEXFUL
IRKSOME PEEVISH PRICKLY
TARSOME ANNOYING CUMBROUS
FRAMPOLD PHRAMPEL
UNTOWARD VEXATORY WEARIFUL
PESTILENT
VEXATIOUSLY PLAGUY
VEXED DIK MAD RILY SORE TEEN
WAXY WILD WRAW ANGRY NARKY
RAGGY ROILY MIFFED MUFFED
SHIRTY SNUFFY FRABOUS GRIEVED
IRKSOME OUTDONE
(EASILY —) CROSS
VEXILLUM WER VEXIL BANNER
STANDARD
VEXING CHRONIC TECHING
WAYWARD ANNOYING NETTLING
TEACHING
V-GOUGE VEINER
VIABLE VITAL HEALTHY
VIAL AMPUL CRUET PHIAL AMPULE
CASTER CASTOR AMPOULE
(— OF AMYL NITRITE) POPPER
VIANDE CATE DIET FOOD CHEER
VIANDRY VICTUALS
VIBRANT RINGY DRAWLING
RESONANT SONOROUS VIGOROUS
VIBRATE JAR WAG BEAT CAST DIRL
PLAY ROCK TIRL WHIR PULSE
QUAKE SWING THIRL THROB TRILL
WAVER DINDLE HOTTER JUDDER
QUAVER QUIVER SHIMMY SHIVER
THRILL TINGLE WARBLE CHATTER
FLUTTER LIBRATE STAGGER
TREMBLE TWIDDLE EVIBRATE
FLICHTER RESONATE UNDULATE
(— ABNORMALLY) SHIMMY
VIBRATING PLANGENT
(— OF AIRPLANE) BUFFET
VIBRATION BUZZ DIRL FLIP TIRL
VIBE KARMA SWING TRILL DINDLE
JUDDER QUAVER QUIVER THRILL
TREMOR DANCING FLUTTER
TEMBLOR DIADROME FREMITUS
VIBRANCY OSCILLATION
(— OF SAW) CUPPING
(RATTLING —) JAR
VIBRATIONS KARMA
VIBRATO TRILL WHINE TREMOLO
VIBRATOR TREMBLER
VIBRISSA HAIR FEELER SMELLER
VIBURNUM MAE MAY SNOWBALL
ARROWWOOD SHEEPBERRY
VICAR PROXY DEPUTY STALLAR
ALTARIST STALLARY
VICAR OF CHRIST POPE
**VICAR OF WAKEFIELD (AUTHOR
OF —)** GOLDSMITH
(CHARACTER IN —) MOSES GEORGE
OLIVIA SOPHIA WILMOT DEBORAH
ARABELLA BURCHELL PRIMROSE
THORNHILL
VICE SIN EVIL CRIME FAULT TAINT
ULCER DEFECT DEPUTY BUGGERY
OFFENSE INIQUITY
VICE-GERENT EPHOR
VICE-PRESIDENT CROUPIER

VICE PRESIDENT VEEP
VICE-PRESIDENT CROUPIER
(**— OF SANHEDRIN**) ABBETDIN
VICEREGENT VICAR SUBPRIOR
VICEROY EARL VALI NABOB NAWAB
NAZIM SUBAH EXARCH KEHAYA
PROREX PROVES SATRAP WARDEN
PROVOST TSUNGTU SUBAHDAR
VICIA FABA
VICINAGE AREA
VICINITY HERE SHADOW ENVIRONS
(**— OF MINE SHAFT**) COLLAR
(**NEAR —**) SUBURBS
VICIOUS BAD ILL EVIL LAZY LEWD
MEAN UGLY VILE ROWDY TOUGH
SINFUL STRONG VITIAL WICKED
CORRUPT IMMORAL NAUGHTY
SKAITHY DEPRAVED DEVILISH
FRATCHED INFAMOUS THEWLESS
MONSTROUS NEFARIOUS
VICIOUSNESS VICE
VICISSITUDE CHANGE MUTATION
(**— OF FORTUNE**) WEATHER
VICTIM BUTT DUPE GOAT GULL
PREY PATHIC QUARRY CASUALTY
(**— FOR SHARPERS**) JAY
(**INTENDED —**) CHUMP
(**PERPETUAL —**) NEBBISH
(**SACRIFICIAL —**) HOST MERIAH
(**SCAM —**) PATSY
(**SUITABLE —**) MARK
(**UNFORTUNATE —**) BASTARD
VICTIMIZATION RIDE
VICTIMIZE HOAX BUNCO BUNKO
COZEN
VICTOR COCK CAPTOR MASTER
WINNER BANGSTER
VICTORFISH AKU
VICTORIA (**FATHER OF —**) PALLAS
(**MOTHER OF —**) STYX
VICTORIA LAKE PUCE
VICTORIAN GENTEEL
VICTORIOUS FIRST VICTOR
WINNING
VICTORY WIN PALM SIEG PRICE
BETTER SUBDUE VICTOR MASTERY
SACKING TRIUMPH WINNING
CONQUEST DECISION WALKOVER
(**AUTHOR OF —**) CONRAD
(**CHARACTER IN —**) AXEL LENA
WANG HEYST JONES PEDRO
MARTIN RICARDO DAVIDSON
MORRISON SCHOMBERG
(**EASY —**) BREEZE
(**ONE-SIDED —**) BLOWOUT
(**OVERWHELMING —**) SWEEP
VICTUAL BIT VITE VITTLE
(**BROKEN —S**) SCRAN
(PL.) KAI BITE CHOW FOOD GRUB
PROG SAND VIVERS PROVENDER
PROVISIONS
VICTUALER PURVEYOR
VIDELICET NAMELY SCILICET
VIDEO RECORDING
(**— GAME**) ATARI
(**COMPUTER — DEVICE**) MONITOR
VIDEODISC RECORDING
VIDEOTAPE (**— RECORDER**) VCR
VIDEOTEX VIEWDATA
(**— SYSTEM**) VIEWDATA
VIE ENVY JOSTLE STRIVE COMPARE
COMPETE CONTEND CONTEST
EMULATE

VIETNAM (SEE NORTH VIETNAM
AND SOUTH VIETNAM)

VIETNAM
CAPITAL: HANOI
COIN: XU XU DONG DONG
COMMUNIST PARTY: VIETCONG
GULF: TONKIN TONKING
MEASURE: GANG PHAN THON
MOUNTAIN: LINH YANGSIN FANSIPAN
PEOPLE: HOA MAN MEO TAY CHAM KINH NUNG THAI MALAY MUONG
PORT: DANANG HONGAI SAIGON BENTHUY HONGGAI QUINHON HAIPHONG NHATRANG HOCHIMINHCITY
REGION: ANNAM COCHIN TONKIN
RIVER: BO CA DA LO MA CHU GAM KOK XAM CHAY BLACK CLEAR NHIHA MEKONG XONGCA DONGHAI PANLONG
TOWN: HUE VINH HOIAN DANANG BACNINH BIENHOA CAOBANG DONGHOI NAMDINH QUINHON SONGCAU TAYNINH THANHOA VIETTRI HAIPHONG PHANRANG QUANGTRI
WEIGHT: CAN YET UYEN

VIETNAMESE ANNAMESE
VIEW EYE KEN FACE GLOM MAKE
VISE ADVEW AVIEW BLUSH CATCH
MOUTH SCAPE SCENE SIGHT VISTA
VIZZY ADVICE ADVISE ASPECT
DEVICE GLANCE REGARD SURVEY
ALOGISM CONCEIT FEELING
GLIMPSE KENNING LOOKOUT
OFFLOOK OPINION RESPECT
SCENERY SURVIEW THOUGHT
AIRSCAPE CONSPECT EYESIGHT
OFFSCAPE PROSPECT SEASCAPE
SENTENCE SENTIMENT
(**— ATTENTIVELY**) GAZE
(**— CLOSELY**) INSPECT
(**— FROM AFAR**) DESCRY
(**— FROM ANGLE**) SLANT
(**— OF MAN**) DUALISM
(**— WITH SURPRISE**) ADMIRE
(**BACKWARD —**) RETROSPECT
RETROSPECTION
(**BRIEF —**) SNAPSHOT
(**CATCH MOMENTARY —**) GLANCE
(**COMPREHENSIVE —**) PANORAMA
(**DEPRESSING —**) PESSIMISM
(**EXPRESS A —**) OPINE
(**GENERAL —**) LANDSKIP
(**OPEN —**) LIGHT
(**PHYSICAL —**) INSIGHT
(**PUBLIC —**) OPEN
(**SATISFYING —**) EYEFUL
(**SECOND —**) DEUTEROSCOPY
(**SECTIONAL — OF BODY**) CATSCAN
(SUFF.) ORAMA SCOPE SCOPIC
SCOPUS SCOPY
VIEWDATA VIDEOTEX
VIEWER (**TELEVISION —**) GOGGLER
VIEWING
(SUFF.) SCOPE SCOPIC SCOPUS
SCOPY
VIEWPOINT SIGHT LAXISM
STANDPOINT

VIGIL WAKE WATCH WAKING
AGRYPNIA
VIGILANCE WATCH JEALOUSY
VIGILANT AGOG WARE WARY
ALERT AWAKE AWARE CHARY
SHARP JEALOUS LIDLESS
WAKEFUL CAUTIOUS WATCHFUL
VIGODA ABE
VIGOR GO PEP SAP VIM VIR VIS BIRR
DASH EDGE ELAN LUST PITH SEVE
SNAP SOUL TUCK ARDOR DRIVE
FLUSH FORCE GREEN JUICE NERVE
OOMPH POWER PUNCH VERVE
ENERGY ESPRIT FOISON GINGER
SPRAWL SPRING STARCH STINGO
VIGOUR VIRTUS FREEDOM
SMEDDUM STAMINA STHENIA
FLOURISH STRENGTH TONICITY
VITALITY
(**— OF THOUGHT**) FLAME
(**FULL OF —**) LIFESOME
(**MENTAL —**) DOCITY SPIRIT
(**RENEWED —**) REST
VIGOROUS YEP ABLE CANT FRIM
HALE LIVE RUDE SPRY YEPE ALIVE
CRANK EAGER FRACK FRANK
HEFTY JUICY LUSTY NIPPY PEPPY
PITHY PROUD SASSY SOLID STARK
STIFF STOUT TOUGH VIVID FLORID
GOLDEN HEARTY LIVELY MANFUL
POTENT PRETTY RAUCLE ROBUST
RUGGED SINEWY SQUARE STRONG
STURDY BUCKISH CHIPPER
CORDIAL DRASTIC FECKFUL
FURIOUS HEALTHY LUSTFUL
NERVOSE NERVOUS VALIANT
VIBRANT ZEALOUS ATHLETIC
BOUNCING CHOPPING FORCEFUL
MUSCULAR SLAMBANG SLASHING
STUBBORN VEHEMENT VIGOROSO
YOUTHFUL TRENCHANT
(**NOT —**) GENTEEL
VIGOROUSLY DOWN FELL HARD
VERN AMAIN CRANK SNELL TIGHT
VERNE HARDLY SNELLY FRESHLY
SMARTLY STOUTLY WIGHTLY
HEARTILY
VIGOROUSNESS ENERGY
FREEDOM
VIKING DANE WIKING NORSEMAN
VIKRAMADITYA BIKRAM
VILE BAD BASE CLAM FOUL RANK
CHEAP MUCKY POCKY RUSTY
SLIMY WILLE ABJECT CRUSTY
DRAFTY DRASTY FILTHY LECHER
NOUGHT ODIOUS PALTRY SORDID
TURPID UNKIND BEASTLY BENEATH
CAITIFF CORRUPT DEBASED
HATEFUL IGNOBLE SCABBED
SLAVISH VICIOUS BASEBORN
DEPRAVED UNKINDLY
(**OPENLY —**) SCANDALOUS
VILENESS FEDITY VILITY TURPITUDE
VILIFICATION SLANDER REPROACH
VILIFY ILL VILE ABUSE LIBEL SMEAR
STAIN SULLY DEFAME DEFILE
MALIGN REVILE SLIGHT ASPERSE
BLACKEN DEBAUCH DETRACT
SLANDER TRADUCE REPROACH
STRUMPET
VILIPEND SLUR BELITTLE
VILL HAM TOWN TOWNSHIP

VILLA ALDEA DACHA LODGE
CHALET DATCHA QUINTA TRIANON
VILLAGE BY AUL BYE GAV HAM
KOM PAH REW BOMA BURG DORP
HOME MURA TOWN VILL WICK
ALDEA BOURG CASAL PLACE
THORP VICUS ALDEIA BARRIO
BUSTEE CASTLE GOTHAM HAMLET
HAMMON MOUZAH PETTAH
PUEBLO AMBALAM BOROUGH
CAMPODY CASERIO CLACHAN
ENDSHIP MAABARA MISSION
OUTPOST BEREWICK BOURGADE
CAMPOODY CRANFORD TOLDERIA
VILLACHE VILLAGET VILLAKIN
(**— IN WHICH BARLEY IS GROWN**)
BEREWICK
(**— OUTSIDE OF FORT**) PETTAH
(**AFRICAN —**) STAD KRAAL
(**ARABIAN —**) DOUAR
(**ARGENTINE —**) TOLDERIA
(**FRENCH —**) BASTIDE
(**IMAGINARY —**) CRANFORD
(**INDIAN —**) CASTLE PUEBLO
CAMPODY CAMPOODY
(**JAPANESE —**) MURA BUSTI
BUSTEE
(**JAVANESE —**) DESSA
(**JEWISH —**) SHTETL SHTETEL
(**MALAY —**) CAMPONG KAMPONG
(**MAORI —**) KAIK KAIKA KAINGA
(**MEXICAN —**) EJIDO
(**NEWFOUNDLAND —**) OUTPORT
(**NEW ZEALAND FORTIFIED —**) PA
PAH
(**RUSSIAN —**) MIR STANITSA
STANITZA
(**TENT —**) DUAR DOUAR DOWAR
VILLAIN IAGO LOUT SERF BADDY
BRAVO CHURL DEMON DEVIL
FAGIN FELON HEAVY KNAVE
ROGUE SCAMP SHREW VIPER
BADDIE VILIACO SCELERAT
SCOUNDREL
VILLAINOUS BAD EVIL GALLUS
GALLOWS KNAVISH RAFFISH
VILEYNS FLAGRANT RASCALLY
MISCREANT
VILLAINY CRIME KNAVERY
VILLEIN SERF CHURL BORDAR
COTTER VILLAR BONDMAN
TOWNMAN VILLAIN COTARIUS
VILLI (**HAVING —**) ZONARY
VILLOUS SHAGGY
VIM ZIP GIMP ZING FORCE OOMPH
VIGOR ENERGY GINGER SPIRIT
STARCH VINEGAR RAZZMATAZZ
VINA BEN BIN BINA
VINCENTIAN LAZARIST
VINDICATE FREE CLEAR RIGHT
SALVE WREAK ACQUIT ASSERT
AVENGE EXCUSE UPHOLD
ABSOLVE DERAIGN JUSTIFY
PROPUGN REVENGE SUSTAIN
DARRAIGN MAINTAIN
VINDICATION BEHALF APOLOGY
DEFENSE THEODICY
COMPURGATION SATISFACTION
JUSTIFICATION
VINDICATOR VINDEX ASSERTER
DEFENDER
VINDICTIVE HOSTILE PUNITIVE
SPITEFUL VENGEFUL

VINE AKA FIG HOP IVY IYO BINE CARO GOGO ODAL SOMA TINE AKEBI BUAZE BWAZI CAAPI CACUR GUACO KAIWI KUDZU LIANA LIANE MAILE PALAY PRIVY TACSO TIMBO TRAIL TWINE WITHE WONGA BEJUCO CISSUS COBAEA COWAGE DERRIS DODDER ECANDA GERKIN IPOMEA JICAMA LABLAB PIKAKE RUNNER TURURI TWINER ULLUCO WINDER APRICOT BIGROOT BONESET BRAMBLE CALAMUS CATVINE CERIMAN CLIMBER COWHAGE COWITCH CUPSEED EPACRID GHERKIN IPOMOEA LAVANGA PAREIRA PUMPKIN TRAILER VINELET YANGTAO ATRAGENE BINDWEED BOXTHORN CLEMATIS COMEBACK CUCUMBER CUCURBIT DECUMARY DOLICHOS EARDROPS EARTHPEA EVONYMUS GULANCHA HEARTPEA HEMPWEED MUSCATEL REDWITHE TINETARE TINEWEED TRAILERY TRAILING TREEBINE VINIFERA WINETREE WISTARIA WISTERIA OLOLIUQUI (PREF.) AMPEL(O) VITI

VINEGAR VIM EISEL ESILL ACETUM ALEGAR ASCILL SOURING BEEREGAR VINAIGRE (— AND HONEY) OXYMEL (PREF.) ACET(O)

VINEGAR EEL EELWORM

VINEGARY ACETOSE ACETOUS

VINEGROWER VINITOR

VINEYARD CRU CLOS COTE VINER VINERY WINFYARD

VINGT-ET-UN MACAO MACCO

VINOUS WINY

VINTAGE OLD VINT WINE CUVEE ARCHAIC CLASSIC VENDAGE OUTMODED

VIOL GUE GIGA LIRA TURR GIGUE GUDOK TARAU VOYAL VOYOL CHELYS FIDDLE VIELLE VIOLET MINIKIN QUINTON SARINDA SULTANA VIHUELA VIOLONE BARBITON BASSETTE SERINGHI VIOLETTE

VIOLA ALTO QUINT TENOR TENORE VIOLET (BROTHER OF —) SEBASTIAN (HUSBAND OF —) ORSINO

VIOLA BASTARDA BARITONE BARYTONE

VIOLA DA BRACCIO QUINT

VIOLA DA GAMBA GAMBA

VIOLA D'AMORE VIOLET

VIOLATE ERR SIN FLAW ABUSE BREAK CRACK FORCE FRACT HARRY LOOSE VIOLE WRONG BREACH BROACH DEFILE INVADE OFFEND RAVISH DEBAUCH DISOBEY FALSIFY INFRACT OUTRAGE POLLUTE PROFANE VITIATE DEFLOWER DISHONOR FORSWEAR FRACTURE INFRINGE MISTREAT STUPRATE SURPRISE TEMERATE TRESPASS VIOLENCE

VIOLATED FRACTED INFRACT

VIOLATION SIN DEBT ABUSE CRIME ERROR FAULT SALLY BREACH INJURY MISCONDUCT

(HOCKEY —) STICKS (TRIVIAL —) MOPERY

VIOLATOR WRONGER

VIOLENCE FURY NEED RAGE RUFF BRUNT FORCE RIGOR STORM BENSIL ESTURE HUBRIS RANDOM RAPINE STOUSH STRESS BENSAIL BENSALL OUTRAGE FEROCITY SEVERITY SORENESS ROUGHHOUSE (DEPICTING —) SNUFF (LETHAL —) DEATH (OF DEPICTION OF —) SNUFF

VIOLENT BIG HOT TEZ DERF HARD HIGH MAIN RANK RUDE WILD WOOD ACUTE FIERY HEADY HEAVY HEFTY RABID SHARP SMART STARK STERN STIFF STOOR STOUR STOUT WROTH BROTHE FIERCE HEARTY MANIAC MIGHTY SAVAGE SEVERE STORMY STRONG STURDY SUDDEN CRIMSON DRASTIC FURIOUS HOTSPUR RAMMISH RAMPANT RAPEFUL RUFFIAN TEARING VIOLOUS WILSOME CHURLISH DIABOLIC FLAGRANT FORCEFUL IMPOTENT MANIACAL PERACUTE RIGOROUS SEETHING SLAMBANG STALWART VEHEMENT

VIOLENTLY HARD AMAIN HOTLY HARDLY SORELY HOPPING SOUNDLY

VIOLET CANON GRAPE MAUVE VIOLA BLAVER CANYON DAHLIA DAMSON EVEQUE JOHNNY HOOKERS LOBELIA OPHELIA PRELATE PRIMULA PUREAYN CLEMATIS DAMEWORT FINELEAF IANTHINE ROOSTERS WISTERIA (KIND OF,—) AFRICAN (PREF.) IO

VIOLIN GUE KIT ALTO GIGA AMATI CROWD CRWTH GEIGE GIGUE REBAB REBEC STRAD TARAU VIOLA CATGUT CHORUS CROUTH FIDDLE FITHEL REBECK TAILLE VIOLON CATLING CHROTTA CREMONA THEYAOU VIOLAND VIOLINO GUARNERI KEMANCHA VIOLOTTA (PART OF —) NUT PEG TOP FROG HEAD HEEL HOLE NECK BELLY TABLE BRIDGE BUTTON PEGBOX SCROLL STRING PURFLING SOUNDBOARD FINGERBOARD

VIPER ASP HABU ADDER ASPIC ATHER URUTU WYVER ASPIDE DABOIA DABOYA JESSUR KATUKA KUPPER HAGWORM HOGNOSE MAMUSHI VIPERID AMMODYTE CERASTES JARARACA VIPERINE BUSHMASTER (KIND OF —) PIT

VIPER'S BUGLOSS BLUEWEED

VIRAGO NAG RANDY SHREW AMAZON BELDAM CALLET BELDAME TRIMMER VIRAGIN RIXATRIX

VIREO REDEYE GRASSET TEACHER GREENLET PREACHER

VIRGATE YOKE VERGE YARDLAND (HALF —) MANTAL

VIRGILIAN MARONIAN

VIRGIN NEW LIVE MAID PURE FRESH CHASTE MAIDEN VESTAL INITIAL PUCELLE DOROTHEA PARAMOUR (— OF PARADISE) HURI HOURI (PREF.) PARTHEN(O)

VIRGINAL CHERRY INTACT SYMPHONY TRIANGLE

VIRGINIA

CAPITAL: RICHMOND

COLLEGE: AVERETT HOLLINS MADISON RADFORD LONGWOOD

COUNTY: LEE BATH PAGE WISE BLAND CRAIG FLOYD SMYTH SURRY WYTHE AMELIA LOUISA ACCOMAC HENRICO PATRICK PULASKI ROANOKE CULPEPER FLUVANNA TAZEWELL

INDIAN: SAPONI TUTELO MONACAN MANAHOAC MEHERRIN NOTTAWAY POWHATAN

LAKE: KERR SMITH

MOUNTAIN: CEDAR ELLIOT ROGERS BALDKNOB

MOUNTAIN RANGE: CLINCH ALLEGHENY BLUERIDGE

NICKNAME: OLDDOMINION MOTHEROFSTATES MOTHEROFPRESIDENTS

PRESIDENT: TYLER MONROE TAYLOR WILSON MADISON HARRISON JEFFERSON WASHINGTON

RIVER: DAN JAMES POTOMAC RAPIDAN

STATE BIRD: CARDINAL

STATE FLOWER: DOGWOOD

STATE TREE: DOGWOOD

TOWN: GALAX LURAY SALEM MARION BEDFORD BRISTOL EMPORIA NORFOLK PULASKI ROANOKE CULPEPER DANVILLE HOPEWELL MANASSAS STAUNTON TAZEWELL

VIRGINIA COWSLIP LUNGWORT

VIRGINIA CREEPER CREEPER WOODBIND WOODBINE

VIRGINIA KNOTWEED JUMPSEED

VIRGINIAN BEAGLE COOHEE CAVALIER TUCKAHOE (AUTHOR OF —) WISTER (CHARACTER IN —) WOOD HENRY MOLLY STEVE SHORTY TRAMPAS

VIRGINIANS (AUTHOR OF —) THACKERAY (CHARACTER IN —) THEO WILL FANNY HARRY HETTY MARIA MILES ESMOND GEORGE RACHEL LAMBERT MOUNTAIN BERNSTEIN CASTLEWOOD WARRINGTON WASHINGTON

VIRGINIA SNAKEROOT SANGREL SNAGREL

VIRGINIA STICKSEED SOLDIERS

VIRGINIA WATERLEAF SHAWNY

VIRGINIA WILLOW ITEA

VIRGINITY HONOR CHERRY CHASTITY PUCELAGE

VIRGIN MARY DESPOINA THEOTOCOS

VIRGIN'S-BOWER LOVE HONESTY CLEMATIS MOONWORT

VIRGIN SOIL (AUTHOR OF —) TURGENEV (CHARACTER IN —) KOLYA PAHKLIN SOLOMIN MARIANNA MASHURIN SIPYAGIN MARKELOFF VALENTINA NEZHDANOFF OSTRODUMOFF

VIRGO (STAR IN —) SPICA

VIRGULE SLANT VIRGULA DIAGONAL

VIRIDIAN EMERAUDE

VIRILE MALE MACHO MANLY (AGGRESSIVELY —) MACHO

VIRILITY LUST GREEN MANHEAD MANHOOD

VIROLOGIST (FAMOUS —) SABIN

VIRTUAL IMPLICIT PRACTICAL

VIRTUALLY BUT NEARLY MORALLY

VIRTUE JEN HSIN THEW ARETE FAITH GRACE POWER VALOR VERTU WORTH BOUNTY DHARMA FOISON CHARISM CHARITY JUSTICE PROBITY QUALITY CHARISMA CHASTITY EFFICACY GOODNESS MORALITY PARAMITA PROPERTY (CONFUCIAN) LI (PL.) CIVISM (PREF.) ARETO

VIRTUOSO ACE EXPERT SAVANT ESTHETE LAPIDARY

VIRTUOUS GOOD PURE BRAVE CIVIL MORAL PIOUS CHASTE HONEST MODEST GODDARD SAINTED SINCERE UPRIGHT VIRTUAL STRAIGHT

VIRULENCE VIRUS RANCOR RANCOUR

VIRULENT RANK ACRID RABID DEADLY MALIGN VIROSE NOXIOUS VIRIFIC WASPISH VENOMOUS (LESS THAN) MITIS

VIRUS PARVO VENOM POISON PATHOGEN SPECIFIC (AIDS —) HIV (PRESENCE OF —) VIREMIA

VIS PEIKTHA

VISAGE FACE PHIZ CHEER IMAGE VISOR ASPECT FASHION

VISCERA GUTS HASLET INSIDE UMBLES GARBAGE GIBLETS HASSLET INMEATS INNARDS INSIDES NUMBLES ENTRAILS HARIGALS (PREF.) SPLANCHNO

VISCERAL GUT

VISCID SLAB WAXY GOOEY GLAIRY STICKY LENTOUS STRINGY VISCOUS MOTHERED

VISCIDITY LENTOR

VISCOSITY BODY ROPINESS (— UNIT) POISE

VISCOUS LIMY ROPY SIZY SLAB GOBBY GUMMY MUCIC ROPEY SLIMY STIFF TARRY SIRUPY SLABBY SMEARY SNOTTY STICKY THONGY VISCID LENTOUS SQUISHY VISCOSE MUCULENT

VISE GEE CHAP JACK SHOP VICE CHEEK CLAMP CRAMP WINCH (PART OF —) JAW BASE BOLT ANVIL SCREW SLIDE HANDLE SWIVEL

VISHNU RAMA VASU KALKI KRISHNA BALARAMA BHAGAVAT **(AVATAR OF —)** KALKI KURMA BUDDHA MATSYA VAMANA VARAHA KRISHNA NARASINHA PARASHURAMA RAMACHANDRA **(BREAST JEWEL OF —)** KAUSTUBHA **(BREASTMARK OF —)** SHRIVATSA **(VEHICLE OF —)** GARUDA **(WIFE OF —)** SHRI LAKSHMI **(WRIST JEWEL OF —)** SYAMANTAKA

VISIBLE OUT FAIR SEEN CLEAR GROSS EXTANT SIGHTY EVIDENT GLARING OBVIOUS OPTICAL SIGHTLY APPARENT DIOPTRIC EXPLICIT EXTERNAL MANIFEST PROSPECT **(BARELY —)** DARK **(SCARCELY —)** DIM (PREF.) DELO PHANER(O) PHANTA PHANTASMO PHANTO

VISION EYE RAY DREAM FANCY SIGHT FANTAD SEEING SWEVEN AISLING SHOWING SPECTER SPECTRE EYESIGHT PHOTOPIA PROSPECT SPECULATION **(— IN BRIGHT LIGHT)** PHOTOPIA **(— IN DIM LIGHT)** SCOTOPIA **(— PROBLEM)** REDOUT **(BLURRED —)** SWIMMING **(DEFECTIVE —)** ANOPIA **(DOUBLE —)** DIPLOPIA **(FALSE —)** PARABLEPSY PARABLEPSIS **(FANCIED —)** PHANTASM **(IMAGINARY —)** SHADOW **(IMPERFECT —)** CALIGO DARKNESS **(MENTAL —)** VISTA **(MULTIPLE —)** POLYOPIA (PREF.) OPTI(CO) OPTO VISUO **(RANGE OF —)** METROPIA (SUFF.) OPSIA OPSIS OPSY OPTIC OPTICON **(— DEVIATION)** TROPIA

VISIONARY FEY AERY AIRY WILD BIGOT IDEAL VIEWY ASTRAL INSANE SHANDY UNREAL DREAMER FANTAST LAPUTAN UTOPIAN ACADEMIC DELUSIVE FANCIFUL FINESPUN IDEALIST NOTIONAL PHANTAST QUIXOTIC ROMANTIC UTOPIAST VISIONER

VISIT DO GAM SEE VIS CALL CHAT STAY APPLY HAUNT TRYST VIZZY COSHER RESORT RETURN CEILIDH CEILIDHE FREQUENT INVASION **(— BETWEEN WHALERS)** GAM **(— PERSISTENTLY)** INFEST **(— PROFESSIONALLY)** ATTEND **(— RELATIVES)** COUSIN **(— UNEXPECTEDLY)** POPIN DROPIN **(— WRETCHED NEIGHBORHOODS)** SLUM **(CEREMONIAL —)** SELAMLIK

VISITATION SENE VISIT SENDING

VISITING ACTIVE SOCIAL

VISITOR GUEST LAKER CALLER VISITANT **(MEALTIME —)** SCAMBLER (PL.) COMPANY

VISOR BILL SIGHT UMBER UMBRE VIZOR BEAVER MESAIL UMBRIL VIZARD EYESHADE UMBRIERE

VISTA VIEW SCENE OUTLOOK PERSPECTIVE

VISUAL OPTIC OCULAR SCOPIC VISORY VISIBLE

VISUALIZE SEE FANCY IDEATE SYMBOL IMAGINE PICTURE CONCEIVE ENVISAGE

VITAL KEY LIVE BASIC CHIEF FRESH SAPPY LIVELY MOVING VIABLE ZOETIC ANIMATE CAPITAL CORDIAL EXIGENT NEEDFUL ESSENTIAL

VITALITY SAP VIM LIFE COLOR GUSTO JUICE OOMPH PULSE PUNCH BIOSIS BREATH ENERGY FOISON HEALTH MARROW PAZAZZ PIZAZZ STARCH PIZZAZZ VIVENCY STRENGTH **(DEFICIENT —)** ASTHENIA **(LACKING —)** STUFFY TURNIPY

VITALIZE ACTIVATE ENERGIZE

VITAMIN BIOTIN CITRIN NIACIN ADERMIN ANEURIN CHOLINE RETINOL THIAMIN TORULIN ADVITANT INOSITOL NUTRAMIN ORYZANIN VITAMINE

VITAMIN A RETINOL

VITELLINE YOLKY

VITIATE BEAT BLEND SPOIL TAINT CANCEL DEBASE POISON CORRUPT DEBAUCH DEPRAVE

VITIATED PICAL CORRUPT (PREF.) CAC(O) CACH (SUFF.) CACE

VITICULTURIST VIGNERON

VITREOUS GLASSY GLAIZIE VITREAN VITROUS

VITRIFY GLAZE

VITRIOL BLUEJACK COPPERAS (PL.) SORY

VITRIOLIC SHARP BITING BITTER CAUSTIC MORDANT SCATHING

VITRIOS GLASSWARE

VITTLES CHOW

VITUPERATE RAIL ABUSE CURSE SCOLD SLANG BERATE REVILE

VITUPERATION ABUSE VITUPER

VITUPERATIVE ABUSIVE REVILING SHAMEFUL

VIVACE VIVO LEBHAFT

VIVACIOUS GAY AIRY PERT BRISK CRISP MERRY SUNNY ACTIVE BRIGHT LIVELY LIVING SPARKY VIVACE ANIMATE JOCULAR ANIMATED SPIRITED SPORTIVE FLAMBOYANT

VIVACITY BRIO FIRE LIFE ZEAL ARDOR VERVE VIGOR ESPRIT GAIETY GAYETY SPIRIT SPRAWL SPARKLE

VIVARIUM STEW VIVARY STEWPOND

VIVAT HOCH

VIVERRINE CIVET GENET FOUSSA MUSANG LINSANG FALANAKA MONGOOSE SURICATE

VIVIANO (BROTHER OF —) MALAGIGI ALDIGIERI **(SISTER OF —)** BRADAMANTE

VIVID DEEP HARD KEEN LIVE RICH VIVE BRISK FRESH GREEN LURID QUICK RUDDY SHARP GARISH LIVELY LIVING STRONG VISUAL EIDETIC FLAMING FREAKED GLARING GLOWING GRAPHIC INTENSE PEPPERY VIOLENT COLORFUL DISTINCT DRAMATIC SLASHING STRIKING VIGOROUS PICTURESQUE **(NOT —)** PALE

VIVIDNESS COLOR EMPHASIS

VIVIFY LIFE FOMENT ANIMATE QUICKEN SPARKLE

VIVIPARUS PALUDINA

VIXEN BARD FURY RANDY SCOLD SHREW VIRAGO TAGSTER TRIMMER

VIZIER WAZIR ATABEG ATABEK VISIER

VLACH WALLACH

V-MAIL AIRGRAPH

VOCABULARY CANT LEXIS SLANG JARGON DICTION LEXICON POCHISMO WORDBOOK **(FAULTY —)** CACOLOGY **(UNDERWORLD —)** ARGOT (PREF.) LEXICO

VOCAL GLIB ORAL VOWEL FLUENT TONGUED VOCULAR ELOQUENT

VOCALIST BOPPER SINGER BOPPIST BOPSTER SONGSTER VOCALLER

VOCALIZE MOUTH ORATE INTONE PHONATE

VOCATION CALL HOBBY METIER CALLING SCIENCE

VOCATIONAL BANAUSIC

VOCIFERATION CLAMOR OUTCRY

VOCIFEROUS LOUD NOISY BAWLING BLATANT BRAWLING STRIDENT

VODKA SAMOGON SAMOGONKA

VOGUE CUT FAD TON CHIC MODE RAGE TURN STYLE CUSTOM FASHION RECLAME PRACTICE

VOGUL MANSI

VOICE SAY VOX EMIT GIVE HARP PIPE TONE TURN WISH FROTH LEDEN RAISE RUMOR SOUND UTTER ACTIVE ASSERT CHOICE STEVEN TAISCH THROAT TONGUE EXPRESS OPINION SONORIZE DIATHESIS **(— PRAISE)** SLAVER **(ARTIFICIAL —)** FALSETTO **(BELLOWING —)** FOGHORN **(FIFTH —)** QUINTUS **(HOARSE —)** FOGHORN **(LOWEST —)** BASS BASSO **(MIDDLE —)** MOTETUS **(OF LYRIC AND DRAMATIC —)** SPINTO **(PRINCIPAL —)** CANTUS **(PUBLIC —)** CRY **(SINGING —)** ALTO BASS TENOR BREAST SPINTO SOPRANO BARITONE FALSETTO **(SUBDUED —)** UNDERBREATH **(TENOR —)** TAILLE **(UPPER —)** DESCANT DISCANT (PREF.) PHON(O) PHTHONGO VOCI **(LOUD —)** STENTORO (SUFF.) PHON(E)(IA)(Y)

VOICED SOFT WEAK TONIC MEDIAL SONANT VIBRANT PHTHONGAL

VOICELESS MUM DUMB HARD MUTE SURD SHARP ATONIC FLATED SILENT ANAUDIA APHONIC SPIRATE APHONOUS BREATHED NOTELESS

VOID NO BAD FREE KORE LEAR LEER MUTE NULL PASS TOOM ABYSS AVOID BLANK EGEST EJECT EMPTY INEPT LAPSE PURGE SLICE SPACE WASTE DEVOID HOLLOW VACANT VACUUM CONCAVE INVALID VACANCY VACUITY EVACUATE INDIGENT NONBEING **(— OF FEELING)** BLATE **(— OF SENSE)** INANE **(— OF SUBSTANCE)** JEJUNE

VOIDED FALSE CLECHE CLECHY CLECHEE

VOILE NINON ETAMINE

VOLATILE LIGHT FIGENT LIVELY VOLAGE BUOYANT DARTING ELASTIC FLIGHTY FLYAWAY GASEOUS FUGITIVE SKITTISH VAPOROSE VAPOROUS FUGACIOUS (PREF.) PTENO

VOLATILITY LEVITY

VOLCANIC ROCK TRASS

VOLCANO APO DOME ETNA ASKJA PELEE SHASTA VULCAN FURNACE RUMBLER VULCANO FUMAROLE KRAKATOA SPITFIRE VESUVIUS **(MUD —)** SALSE SALINELLE

VOLE CRABER CRICETID CAMPAGNOL

VOLITATION FLIGHT VOLATION

VOLITION WILL CHOICE INTENT VOLENCY VELLEITY

VOLLEY TIRE CROWD DRIFT VOLEE FLIGHT BARRAGE PLATOON BLIZZARD

VOLPLANE GLIDE

VOLPONE (AUTHOR OF —) JONSON **(CHARACTER IN —)** CELIA MOSCA BONARIO CORVINO VOLPONE VOLTORE POLITICK CORBACCIO PEREGRINE

VOLSUNG WAELS

VOLT VOLTA REPOLON **(— AMPERE UNIT)** VAR

VOLTAGE KICKBACK

VOLTAIC GUR GALVANIC

VOLTE-FACE BACKFLIP

VOLUBILITY FLUENCY

VOLUBLE GLIB WORDY FLUENT

VOLUME MO PEN BAND BOOK BULK CODE SIZE TOME CODEX SPACE CUBAGE CONTENT DIURNAL MENAION VOLUMEN CAPACITY CUBATURE SOLIDITY STRENGTH **(— OF SOUND)** STRESS **(— OF WORT)** LENGTH **(PATTERN —)** DUMMY

VOLUMINOUS FULL AMPLE BULKY LARGE BOUFFANT

VOLUMNIA (SON OF —) CORIOLANUS

VOLUNTARILY WILLES WILLICHE

VOLUNTARY FREE WILLY SORTIE WILFUL PRELUDE SORTITA WILLFUL WILLING ELECTIVE

FREEWILL HONORARY OPTIONAL POSTLUDE UNFORCED

VOLUNTEER OFFER ENLIST PROFFER FENCIBLE STRANGER
(— SERVING AS OFFICER) REFORMADO
(— STATE) TENNESSEE

VOLUPTUARY SYBARITE

VOLUPTUOUS ADIN BUXOM LUXIVE LYDIAN SULTRY WANTON SENSUAL DELICATE LUSCIOUS SENSUOUS

VOLUPTUOUSNESS DELICE LUXURY

VOLUTE TURN HELIX SCROLL VOLUTA CILLERY VOLUTION

VOLUTION COIL TWIST WHORL VERTICIL

VOLVA CUP WRAPPER

VOMIT CAT PUT BALK BARF BOCK BOKE CACK CAST PICK PUKE SICK SPEW SPUE VOME WOOM BRAKE EVOME HEAVE RALPH REACH RETCH SHOOT POSSET REJECT VOMITO CASCADE CASTING REGORGE DISGORGE PARBREAK SICKNESS VOMITING

VOMITING BOKE EMESIS PYEMESIS
(PREF.) EMET(O)

VOMITUS SPEW SPUE

VOODOO HEX OBI CHARM OBEAH HOODOO SORCERER
(— DESIGN) VERVER
(— PRIEST) BOCOR BOKOR
(— SPELL) MOJO

VOODOOISM VODUN WANGA VODOUN

VOPHSI (SON OF —) NAHBI

VORACIOUS GORB GREEDY BULIMIC ESURINE GLUTTON THROATY EDACIOUS ESURIENT RAVENING RAVENOUS

VORACITY BULIMIA EDACITY

VORTEX APEX EDDY GYRE SWIRL WHIRL

VOTARESS NUN

VOTARY PALMER ZEALOT DEVOTEE SECTARY ADHERENT DEVOTARY FOLLOWER

VOTE AYE CON NAY PRO ELECT FAGOT GRACE VOICE BALLOT DIVIDE FAGGOT TONGUE APPROVE PLUMPER SUFFRAGE
(— AGAINST) NAY KNIFE NEGATIVE
(— APPROVAL) CONFIRM
(— FOR) AY AYE PRO SUPPORT
(— ILLEGALLY) REPEAT
(— OF ASSENT) PLACET
(AFFIRMATIVE —) YEA YES
(INFORMAL —) STRAW
(KIND OF —) WRITEIN

VOTER BOLTER POLLER CHOOSER ELECTOR FLOATER ASSENTOR
(KIND OF —) CROSSOVER

VOTING POLL
(— FIRST) PREROGATIVE

VOTIVE VOWED

VOTYAK UDMURT

VOUCH ABLE ASSURE ATTEST AVOUCH ENDORSE ACCREDIT

VOUCHER CHIT CHALAN COUPON POLICY TICKET WARRANT

VOUCHSAFE GIVE SEND DEIGN GRANT VOUCH BETEEM PLEASE WITSAFE

VOUSSOIR QUOIN WEDGE KEYSTONE SPRINGER

VOW LAY VUM AVOW OATH SNUM VOTE SWEAR VOUCH BEHEST PLEDGE BEHIGHT PROMISE PROTEST
(MARRIAGE —) IDO
(PREF.) EUCHO

VOWEL SHWA WIDE GLIDE SCHWA VOCOID AUGMENT PALATAL GEMINATE ORINASAL
(— POINT) SERE
(— SOUND) LONGA
(BACK —) VELAR
(CHANGE OF —) UMLAUT
(GLIDE —) MURMUR
(GROUP OF 2 —S) BROAD DIGRAM DIGRAPH
(PREFIXED —) AUGMENT
(SHORT —) MATRA

VOYAGE SAIL TRIP VIAGE COURSE CRUISE FLIGHT TRAVEL CARAVAN JOURNEY PASSAGE SAILING STEAMER PERIPLUS SHIPPING

VOYAGING SEA NAVIGANT

VOYEUR PEEPER

VULCAN MULCIBER
(WORKSHOP OF —) AETNA

VULCANITE EBONITE

VULCANIZATION BURNING

VULCANIZE BURN CURE METALIZE

VULCANIZER CEMENTER

VULGAR LOW LEWD LOUD RUDE BANAL CHEAP FLASH GROSS SLANG SLIMY TOUGH COARSE COMMON PORTER RABBLE VULGUS WOOLEN XRATED BLATANT BOORISH GENERAL KNAVISH LOWBRED MOBBISH OBSCENE POPULAR PROFANE RAFFISH SECULAR TABLOID VILLAIN WOOLLEN BANAUSIC CHURLISH MECHANIC PANDEMIC PLEBEIAN PORTERLY POTHOUSE SOUTERLY

VULGARIAN CAD SLOB TIGER KEELIE RAFFISH

VULGARITY RAUNCH SHODDY FOULNESS HARLOTRY

VULGARIZE PLEBIFY PROFANE

VULGARIZED DEGRADED

VULGARLY CHEAPLY

VULNERABILITY GAP EXPOSURE

VULNERABLE NAKED LIABLE EXPOSED PREGNABLE

VULPINE SLY FOXY CRAFTY ALOPECOID

VULTURE AURA GEIR PAPA AREND GRAAP GRAPE GRIPE SWIPE URUBU CONDOR CORBIE FALCON GRIPHE RAPTOR SNATCH TORGOS GRIFFIN GRIFFON GRYPHON NEKHEBT AASVOGEL DIRTBIRD GEREAGLE NEKHEBET ZOPILOTE GALLINAZO

VULVA DOCK PUDENDUM
(PREF.) EPISIO

VUM SNUM

W

W WAW WHISKEY WILLIAM
WA VU KAWA LAWA
WABBLE COCKLE COGGLE HOBBLE WAGGLE WARBLE WAUBLE WOBBLE
WABBLY COGGLE WAGGLY WOBBLY
WABBY LOON WHABBY
WABRON WAYBERRY
WACKY CRAZY FLAKY WACKO WIGGY FLAKEY INSANE MENTAL ERRATIC OFFBEAT
WAD BAT BET BOB PAD COLF LINE POKE SWAB SWOB WISP WAGER PLEDGE SCOURER GRAPHITE
WADDING BOMBAST
WADDLE WAG DAIDLE HODDLE PODDLE TODDLE WALLOP WIDDLE WAUCHLE
WADDY PEG STICK COWBOY RUSTLER WHADDIE
WADE FORD WYDE SLOSH PLODGE PLOUTER PLUTTER
(— IN MUD) LAIR
WADI OUED WASH GULLY RAVINE
WADSET PAWN PLEDGE MORTGAGE
WAFER HOST ABRET OBLEY CACHET GAUFRE LAVASH MATZOH OFLETE POPADAM FLATBROD PARTICLE
WAFF WAG FLAP GUST ODOR PUFF WAVE WHIFF PALTRY FLUTTER GLIMPSE LOWBORN
WAFFENSCHMIED, DER
(CHARACTER IN —) GEORG MARIE CONRAD LIEBENAU STADINGER
(COMPOSER OF —) LORTZING
WAFFIE VAGRANT VAGABOND
WAFFLE GOFER WAFER WAVER GAUFRE BLATHER
WAFT PUFF WING WHEFT WHIFF BECKON WINNOW
WAG LUG NOD WIG WIT WOG CARD CHAP FLAG WAFF WALK DROLL JOKER ROGUE SHAKE TROLL FARCER JESTER NICKUM WADDLE WAGGLE WAGWIT WIGWAG FARCEUR HUMORIST SLYBOOTS
WAGE FEE PAY WAR HIRE LEVY FIGHT WADGE WEDGE EMPLOY ENGAGE PACKET STIPEND OVERTIME
(— BATTLE) STRIKE
WAGER GO BET LAY PUT SET VIE WED GAGE HOLD PAWN TOSS WOID BOUND PRIZE RAISE REVIE SPORT STAKE STOOP WADGE DEPONE GAMBLE IMPONE LEVANT WEDFEE STOATER QUINELLA
WAGES FEE PAY UTU GAGE HIRE MEED STIP GAGES TUNCA REWARD SALARY PENSION

SERVICE STIPEND GRATUITY LABORAGE PAYCHECK REQUITAL
WAGGERY JEST ROGUERY DROLLERY
WAGGISH ARCH DROLL JOKEY JOCOSE JESTING JOCULAR PARLOUS ROGUISH WAGSOME HUMOROUS SPORTIVE
WAGGLE WAG WIGGLE WOBBLE WOGGLE
WAGON CAR FLY VAN CART CHAR DRAG DRAY PLOW RACK TEAM TRAM WAIN WANE BUGGY DILLY JERKY RULLY TRUCK CAMION ROLLEY SPIDER TELEGA CAISSON CHARIOT COASTER FOURGON SHELVER TUMBREL TUMBRIL DEMOCRAT LANDSHIP RUNABOUT WHITETOP
(— WITHOUT SPRINGS) JERKY TELEGA
(BAGGAGE —) FOURGON
(COVERED —) VAN CARAVAN TARTANA LANDSHIP CONESTOGA
(KIND OF —) PADDY
(LUMBER —) GILLY
(MINING —) TRAM HUTCH RULLY ROLLEY
(ROUNDUP —) HOODLUM
(RUSSIAN —) TELEGA KIBITKA
(SCREENED —) ARABA
(STATION —) MICROBUS SUBURBAN
(TEA —) SERVER
WAGONER AURIGA TREKKER WAINMAN
WAGONETTE BREAK
WAGONLOAD FODDER FOTHER
WAGONMAN FOOTMAN
WAGTAIL MOLLY OATEAR WAGGIE WASHER MOTACIL WATERIE SEEDBIRD WASHDISH WASHTAIL
WAHINE WIFE WOMAN FEMALE VAHINE FEMININE MISTRESS
WAHOO ONO PETO BASSWOOD EUONYMUS GUARAPUCU
WAIF WEFT STRAY FEEBLE PALTRY STRAFE CURRENT IGNOBLE WASTREL
WAIL CRY WOW BAWL GURL HOWL KEEN MOAN RAME YARM CROON MOURN ULULU LAMENT PLAINT YAMMER EJULATE PLANGOR ULULATE ULLAGONE
WAILING WO WOE LAMENT ULULANT
WAIN CART WAGON WEYNE CHARIOT
WAINSCOT CEIL CARDIGAN
WAINSCOTING CEILING PANELING
WAIST JOSIE BASQUE BLOUSE BODICE HALTER MIDDLE TAILLE CORSAGE PIERROT

WAISTCOAT VEST BENJY GILET FECKET JERKIN VESKIT WESKIT SINGLET CAMISOLE
WAISTER TROUNCER
WAIT BIDE HOLD KEEP LITE PARK STAY TEND WHET ABIDE ABODE DEFER HOVER LURCH TARRY WATCH ATTEND DEPEND EXPECT HARKEN LAYOUT LINGER
(— A WHILE) TAIHOA
(— FOR) KEEP ABIDE AWAIT ATTEND EXPECT
(— ON) HOP SEE SERVE INTEND LACKEY
(— TABLE) HASH SERVE
WAITER MOZO CARHOP COMMIS DRAWER FLUNKY GARCON HASHER KIDNEY SALVER TENDER THOMAS DAPIFER FLUNKEY KELLNER PANNIER PICCOLO SERVITOR KITMUDGAR
(APPRENTICE —) COMMIS
(WING —) SOMMELIER
WAITING DORMANT
WAITING ROOM LOBBY ANTEROOM
WAITRESS NIPPY HASHER MOUSMEE PHYLLIS
WAIVE ABEY DEFER EVADE FORGO ABANDON DECLINE FORSAKE POSTPONE RENOUNCE RELINQUISH
WAKA CANOE
WAKE WAK CROW NECK PLAY STIR ALERT REVEL ROUSE TANGI TRAIL VIGIL WATCH AROUSE AWAKEN EXCITE FEATHER
WAKEFUL ALERT WACKER RESTLESS VIGILANT WALKRIFE WATCHFUL
WAKEFULNESS VIGIL WATCH INSOMNIA
WAKE-ROBIN ARUM SARA SARAH TRILLIUM
WAKF WAQF VAKUF VACOUF
WALACHIAN RUMAN VLACH ROMANESE
WALAHEE ALAHEE
WALAPAI HUALPAI
WALDENSIAN LEONIST PATARIN VAUDOIS SABOTIER
WALE RIB BEND PICK WEAL WELT RIDGE WHELP CHOICE HARPIN STROKE
(PL.) BEND HARPINS
WALES CYMRU CAMBRIA
(PREF.) CAMBRO

WALES
BAY: SWANSEA CARDIGAN TREMADOC
CAPITAL: CARDIFF
COUNTY: FLINT RADNOR DENBIGH

ANGLESEY CARDIGAN MONMOUTH PEMBROKE
ISLAND: MONA ANGLESEY HOLYHEAD
LAKE: BALA VYRNWY
LANGUAGE: CYMRAEG
MEASURE: COVER CANTRED CANTREF LESTRAD LISTRED CRANNOCK
MOUNTAIN: SNOWDON
MOUNTAIN RANGE: BERWYN CAMBRIAN
PEOPLE: CYMRY KYMRY WELSH
PORT: CARDIFF
RIVER: DEE USK WYE TAFF TEME TOWY TEIFI SEVERN VYRNWY
TOWN: MOLD RHYL ROSS FLINT TOWYN AMLWCH BANGOR BRECON RUTHIN CARDIFF NEWPORT RHONDDA SWANSEA HEREFORD HOLYHEAD PEMBROKE BRECKNOCK
WATERFALL: CAIN RHAIADR

WALK GO JET MOG FOOT GAIT GANG HIKE HOOF LAMP PACE PAUT REEL STEP TROD ALLEE ALLEY ARBOR LEAVE MARCH PORCH SHANK SLOPE SPACE STALK TRACE TRACK TRADE TRAMP TREAD TROOP ATTEND AVENUE BEHAVE BOUNCE BRIDGE BROGUE DANDER PASEAR SASHAY STROKE TODDLE TRAVEL TRUDGE BALTEUS BERCEAU CRAMBLE FOOTING GALLERY SHUFFLE STRETCH TRACHLE TRAIPSE TURNOUT AMBULATE ARBORWAY FLAGGING FRESCADE NAVIGATE TRAVERSE PROMENADE PEREGRINATE
(— ABOUT) SLOSH
(— AFFECTEDLY) PRINK
(— AIMLESSLY) PAUP POAP
(— ARROGANTLY) STRUT STRIDE
(— ARROGANTLY —) WALTZ
(— AWKWARDLY) STAUP SHAMBLE
(— BEFORE) PREAMBLE
(— BEHIND BATTLEMENTS) ALURE
(— BRISKLY) LEG SKELP
(— CARELESSLY) JAYWALK
(— CAUTIOUSLY) STALK
(— CLUMSILY) JOLL STUMP LOPPET
(— FOR CATTLE) GANG
(— FOR EXAMINING ENGINE) GALLERY
(— FOR EXERCISE) HIKE GRIND
(— HEAVILY) PLOD CLOMP CLUMP STUMP TRAMP LAMPER PLODGE
(— IDLY) DANDER POTTER SAUNTER
(— IN AFFECTED MANNER) MINCE
(— IN SUPERIOR MANNER) SWAGGER

(— LAME) LIMP HIRPLE HOBBLE CRIPPLE
(— LEISURELY) AMBLE DANDER STROLL
(— ON) BEAT TREAD
(— OUT) FLOUNCE
(— PRIMLY) MINCE
(— RAPIDLY) LAMP LINK STAVE
(— SHAKILY) DOTTER
(— SLOWLY) JET LAG
(— SMARTLY) LINK
(— STEADILY) SNOVE SNOOVE
(— THROUGH WATER) WADE
(— UNSTEADILY) REEL DADDLE FALTER STAVER STAGGER STUMBLE
(WAVERINGLY) SHEVEL WARPLE
(— WITH DIFFICULTY) CRAMBLE CRAMMEL LOUTHER
(— WITH JERK) HIRCH
(— WITH LOFTY GAIT) JET
(— WITH LOOSE GAIT) GANGLE
(— WITH OSTENTATION) PRANCE
(— WITHOUT LIFTING FEET) SCUFF
(— WITH SHUFFLE) COONJINE
(— WITH STRIDES) STAG
(— WITH TREES) XYST XYSTUS ALAMEDA
(BACKSTAGE —) BRIDGE
(BOOL —) FRESCADE
(COVERED —) PAWN PORCH CLOISTER
(FOLIAGE-COVERED —) BERCEAU
(HARD —) STRAM SWINGE
(LIMPING —) GIMP
(LONG —) STRAM
(POMPOUS —) STRUT
(PUBLIC —) XYST XYSTUS ALAMEDA
(RAISED —) GALLERY
(SHADED —) MALL ARBOR XYSTUS
(SHORT —) TURN
(TEDIOUS —) TRAIL
(TREE-PLANTED —) XYST XYSTUS
(PL.) BALTEI
(PREF.) AMBULO GRADIO GRADO
WALKER GOER FOOTER FULLER GANGER FOOTMAN TODDLER PEDESTRIAN
(PL.) FEET
WALKING HOTFOOT PASSANT AMBULANT GRADIENT TRIPPING
(— IN SLEEP) SOMNABULISM
(PREF.) BASI BASO
(SUFF.) BAT(ES)(IC) GRADE
WALKING STICK BAT CANE GIBBY KEBBY STICK WADDY KEBBIE PHASMID SPECTER ASHPLANT GIBSTAFF WOODHORSE
WALKOUT STRIKE
WALKURE, DIE (CHARACTER IN —) MIME WOTAN FRICKA HUNDING SIEGMUND SIEGLINDE BRUNNHILDE
(COMPOSER OF —) WAGNER
WALKWAY CATWALK SKYWALK SIDEWALK
WALL WA DAM FIN MUR WAW BAIL BELT CELL CORE CRIB CURB DICK DIKE DRUM DYKE FACE HEAD MURE PACK SKIN SPUR WING WOGE ATTIC BOARD CHEEK CRUST DIGUE EMURE FENCE HEDGE MEURE MURAL PIRCA SHOJI WOGHE WOUGH BAFFLE BAILEY BATTER CUTOFF DOKHMA

IMMURE LEADER PARIES PARPEN PRETIL REBOTE RIPRAP SCREEN SEPTUM SHIELD VALLUM CHEMISE CURTAIN ENCLOSE MIZRACH PARAPET PERPEND PLUTEUS REREDOS TAMBOUR FIREBACK SPANDREL TRAVERSE
(— ABOVE FACADE) ATTIC
(— AROUND) IMMURE
(— BEHIND ALTAR) REREDOS
(— BETWEEN TWO OPENINGS) PIER
(— CARRYING CUPOLA) DRUM
(— CARRYING ROOF) BAHUT
(— CROSSING RAMPART) SPUR
(— HANGING) DRAPERY
(IN) MURE ENTOMB IMMURE IMPRISON
(— IN HOCKEY RINK) BOARD
(— IN ROMAN ARENA) SPINA
(— IN TRUCK) HEADER
(— OF BLAST FURNACE) DAM INWALL FIREBACK
(— OF CASTLE) BARMKIN
(— OF CLAY) COTTLE
(— OF HOOF) CRUST
(— OF MINE) FACE
(— OF MOUTH) CHEEK
(— OF TENT) KANAT CANAUT
(BODY —) MANTLE
(CIRCULAR —) CASHEL
(CORE —) HEARTING
(CURVED —) SWEEP
(DIVIDING —) SEPTUM
(END — OF BUILDING) GABLE
(FISH —) LEADER
(HIGHEST PART OF —) CRAPWA
(INNER SLOPE OF —) BATTER
(KIND OF —) TROMBE
(LOG —) CRIB
(LOW —) BAHUT PODIUM PLUTEUS
(LOWER PART OF —) DADO
(OUTER — OF CASTLE) BAIL BAILEY
(PEAT —) COP
(PUDDLE —) HEARTING
(RETAINING —) CRIB PILING BULKHEAD
(SCARPED —) GHAT
(SEA —) GROIN
(SECONDARY —) CHEMISE
(SOMETHING ATTACHED TO —) PINUP
(SUSTAINING —) RIPRAP
(THINNED PART OF —) ALLEGE
(VENTRAL —) STERNUM
(WING —) AILERON
(PL.) PERICARP
(PREF.) MURI PARIETO TICHO
(SUFF.) (COAT OF SPORE —) SPORIUM
WALLABA APA
WALLABY WURRUP BRUSHER TOOLACH WURRUNG BOONGARY KANGAROO PADMELON WHIPTAIL
WALLACHIAN RUMAN
WALLAROO EURO
WALLBOARD GOBO
WALLET JAG JAGG MAIL POKE BOGET BOUGE BULCH BULGE SCRIP BUDGET READER SACKET ALFARGA ALFORJA LEATHER BILLFOLD NOTECASE POCHETTE
(PREF.) PERO

WALLEYE WHALL SAUGER LEUCOMA WATCHEYE EXOTROPIA
WALLEYED PIKE DORE DORY JACK PERCID SALMON WALLEYE PICKEREL
WALLFLOWER CUBA CHEIR GILLY JACKS KEIRI GELOFER WARRIOR GILLIVER
WALL HAWKWEED LUNGWORT
WALLOP TAN BEAT BEER FLOP SLUG SOCK PASTE POUND VALOP GALLOP IMPACT WALLOW FLUTTER TROUNCE FLOUNDER LAMBASTE
WALLOW FADE LAIR ROLL SOIL SLOSH WALWE GROVEL MUDDLE WALTER WELTER WITHEN SLUDDER SWELTER FLOUNDER KOMMETJE VOLUTATE
WALLOWISH FLAT WELSH INSIPID
WALLPAPER GROUND SCENIC HANGING TENTURE TAPESTRY
WALL PEPPER SEDUM STONECROP
WALL PLATE PAN RASEN
WALL RUE TENTWORT
WALL STREET (— ORDER) BUY HOLD SELL
WALL-TO-WALL UBIQUITOUS
WALLY TOY FINE SPOIL PAMPER ROBUST STRONG STURDY SPLENDID VIGOROUS
WALLY, LA (CHARACTER IN —) WALLY GELLNER HAGENBACH
(COMPOSER OF —) CATALANI
WALNUT ACAPU NOGAL TRYMA AKHROT BANNUT HEARTNUT
(BRAZILIAN —) EMBOYA IMBUIA
(PL.) JUGLANS
WALNUT BROWN TAFFY
WALNUT SHELL BOLSTER
WALPI HUALPI
WALRUS MORSE WALTRON PELAGIAN PINNIPED ROSMARINE
WALT CRANK UNSTEADY
WALTZ LUG CARRY MARCH VALSE BOSTON BREEZE FLOUNCE
WAMARA CLUBWOOD IRONWOOD PANOCOCO
WAMBLE ROLL SPIN WAMEL NAUSEA REVOLVE
WAMBLY FAINT SHAKY
WAME WEM WAMB WYME BELLY
WAMPUM PEAG BEADS DOUGH FADME HAWOK MONEY PAAGE SEWAN FATHOM SEAWAN ROANOKE
WAMUS JACKET WAMPUS WARMUS
WAN DIM HAW ASHY FADE PALE PALY SICK ASHEN BLAKE FAINT WHITE FEEBLE PALLID SALLOW GHASTLY LANGUID
WANAPUM SOKULK
WAND ROD VARE YARD BATON STAFF STICK VERGE VIRGA FERULA THYRSE WATTLE RHABDOS THYRSUS CADUCEUS
(JESTER'S —) BAUBLE
(PREF.) RHABD(O)
WANDER BAT BUM ERR GAD WAG HAAK HAIK HAKE MAZE MUCK RAKE RAVE ROAM ROIL ROLL ROVE WALK WILL WORE DAVER

DRIFT GLAIK KNOCK RANGE ROGUE SHACK SLOSH STRAY TAVER TRAIK VAGUE WAIVE WAVER CANDER CRUISE DANDER DAUNER FORAGE LOITER MITHER MOIDER MUCKER PALMER PERUSE RAMBLE RANGLE STRAKE STROLL SWERVE WILDER MEANDER TRAFFIC TRAIPSE VAGRATE VANDYKE ABERRATE CUTICULA SQUANDER STRAGGLE STRAVAGE STRAVAIG
(— ABOUT) DIVAGATE
(— ABSTRACTEDLY) MOON
(— AIMLESSLY) SWAN SLOSH TRACE MEANDER
(— AS A VAGABOND) SHACK
(— AS A VAGRANT) LOITER
(— AT RANDOM) SQUANDER
(— ERRATICALLY) SWASH
(— FROM DIRECT COURSE) STRAGGLE
(— FROM PLACE TO PLACE) WAG
(— IDLY) HAKE LOUT MAUNDER SHACKLE
(— IN DELIRIUM) DWALE DWALL
(— IN MIND) DAVER DANDER DELIRE
(— LEISURELY) BUMMEL
(— RESTLESSLY) FEEK
WANDERER HOBO WAIF ROVEN TRAMP VAGUE RANGER DRIFTER PILGRIM RAMBLER VAGRANT FUGITIVE RUNAGATE TRAVELER VAGABOND
(AUTHOR OF —) FOURNIER
(CHARACTER IN —) FRANTZ GALAIS MILLIE SEUREL YVONNE AUGUSTIN BLONDEAU FRANCOIS MEAULNES VALENTINE CHARPENTIER
WANDERING GAD ROAM WAFF ERROR STRAY VAGUE ARRANT ASTRAY ERRANT MOBILE ROVING VAGANT VAGOUS DEVIOUS NOMADIC ODYSSEY VAGANCY VAGRANT WINDING ABERRANT FLOATING FUGITIVE PELAGIC PLANETAL PLANETIC RAMBLING RESTLESS TRAILING VAGABOND WINDRING ITINERANT MIGRATORY PEREGRINE
(PREF.) PLAN(O) VAGO
(SUFF.) PLANIA
WANDERING JEW (AUTHOR OF —) SUE
(CHARACTER IN —) ROSE HARDY RODIN SIMON DJALMA SAMUEL BAUDOIN GABRIEL JACQUES ADRIENNE AGRICOLA AIGRIGNY DAGOBERT FRANCOIS HERODIAS RENNEPONT CARDOVILLE
WANDFLOWER GALAX SPARAXIS
WANDOROBO WAASI
WAND-SHAPED VIRGATE
WANE GO EBB SET WELK WILK ABATE DECAY UNWAX WANZE REPINE DECLINE DWINDLE DECREASE
(— OF MOON) WADDLE
WANGA CHARM SPELL OUANGA WONGAH SORCERY
WANGLE FAKE SHAKE WIGGLE FINAGLE

WANIGAN ARK CHEST COFFER WANGUN
WANT HURT LACK LIKE MISS NEED OONT PINE VOID WANE WONT CRAVE FAULT FORGO BESOIN CHOOSE DEARTH DEFECT DESIRE MISTER PENURY PLIGHT ABSENCE BEGGARY BLEMISH BORASCA DEFAULT MISEASE NEEDHAM POVERTY REQUIRE VACANCY MISCHIEF WANTROKE
(— EXCEEDINGLY) DIE ACHE
(— OF APPETITE) ANOREXY ANOREXIA
(— OF CONTROL) ACRASY
(— OF ENERGY) ATONY
(— OF FEELING) APATHY
(— OF GOOD SENSE) FOLLY
(— OF LIBERTY) RESTRAINT
(— OF PROPER CARE) NEGLIGENCE
(— OF REST) UNRO
(— OF SPIRIT) FOZINESS POLTROONERY
(— OF SUCCESS) FAILURE
(— OF VARIETY) MONOPOLY
(— OF VIGOR) DELICACY
WANTAGE ULLAGE
WANTING LACK VOID WANE ALACK MINUS ABSENT LACKING MISSING INDIGENT
(— ORIGINALITY) BANAL
WANTON JAY NAG RIG DAFT GOLE IDLE LEWD NICE RAGE SKIT CADGY DALLY LIGHT SAUCY GIGLET GIGLOT HARLOT HAUNTY LACHES LUBRIC RAKISH RIGSBY TICKLE TOYING TOYISH UNRULY COLTISH FULSOME GIGGISH HAGGARD IMMORAL KITTOCK LUSTFUL PAPHIAN RIGGISH RIOTOUS SMICKER WAYWARD FLAGRANT LUSCIOUS MISTRESS PETULANT PLAYSOME RUMBELOW SKITTISH SLIPPERY SPITEFUL SPORTIVE UNCHASTE
WANTONNESS FOLLY PRIDE SPORT RAGERY SUCCUDRY SURQUIDY
WAP BIND BLOW WHOP WRAP BLAST FIGHT KNOCK STORM TRUSS BUNDLE STRIKE
WAPITI ELK ALCE DEER LOSH LUSH STAG MARAL MOOSE CERVID WAMPOOSE
WAR WIN CAMP FEUD MART FIGHT SWORD WORSE WORST BATTLE CONTEND CRUSADE CONFLICT GUERILLA OVERCOME
(OPPONENT OF —) DOVE PEACENIK
(RELIGIOUS —) JEHAD JIHAD
(PREF.) BELLI MACHO POLEMO
WAR AND PEACE (AUTHOR OF —) TOLSTOY
(CHARACTER IN —) LISE ELLEN MARYA ANDREY PIERRE ROSTOV ANATOLE BEZUHOV KURAGIN KUTUZOV NATASHA NIKOLAY VASSILY NAPOLEON BOLKONSKY NIKOLUSHKA
WARBLE SING CAROL CHANT CHIRL CHIRM SHAKE TRILL YODEL JARGON RALISH RELISH WARNEL

WORMIL DESCANT VIBRATE WOURNIL
WARBLE FLY OXFLY BOTFLY GADFLY OESTRID OESTRIAN
WARBLER CUT KIT CHAT SMEU WREN FITTE PEGGY CANARY EYSOGE REELER SMEUTH SYLVIA TITIEN CREEPER CROMBEC FANTAIL HAYBIRD HAYSUCK PITBIRD REDPOLL SYLVIID TROCHIL BEAMBIRD BLACKCAP FAUVETTE MALURINE MOCKBIRD OVENBIRD PINCPINC REDSTART REEDBIRD RIRORIRO TROCHILUS CHIFFCHAFF
WAR CLUB MAR MER MERE MERAI MARREE
WAR CRY ALALA BANZAI SLOGAN
WARD CARE GUARD MAHAL VICUS WAIRD WATCH ALUMNA BARRIO CALPUL DEFEND ROWENA KEEPING NATUARY PROTEGE CALPOLLI CONTRADA
(— OFF) FEND WEAR WERE AVERT AWARD FENCE PARRY REPEL STAVE SHIELD BUCKLER EXPIATE FORFEND
(— OF WORKHOUSE) SPIKE
(HOSPITAL —) ICU
WARDAGE WARTH
WARDEN ALCADE DIZDAR PORTER RANGER REGENT ROLAND WARNER ALCAIDE HOGMACE LEATMAN ROWLAND BEARWARD CLAVIGER
(AUTHOR OF —) TROLLOPE
(CHARACTER IN —) TOM BOLD JOHN SUSAN FINNEY TOWERS ABRAHAM ELEANOR GRANTLY HARDING SEPTIMUS HAPHAZARD QUIVERFUL THEOPHILUS
WARDER PORTER GUARDER HEIMDAL TURNKEY WATCHMAN BEEFEATER
WARDROBE KAS CLOSET VESTRY ALMIRAH ARMOIRE VESTUARY
WARE CLOTH GOODS SPEND FABRICS SEAWEED SQUANDER
(CERAMIC —) SPODE BENNINGTON
(CLOISONNE —) SHIPPO
(ENAMELED —) BILSTON COALPORT
(GILT —) ORMOLU
(INFERIOR —S) SLUM
(JAPANESE —) IMARI YAYOI
(JAPANESE CERAMIC —) SETO BIZEN KARATSU
(KIND OF —) RAKU SETO TING BIZEN CHIEN SANDA YAYOI KUTANI MINTON KARATSU WHIELDON
(KIND OF JAPANESE POTTERY —) SANDA
(MAJOLICA —) DERUTA
(PORCELAIN —) CHINA IMARI BERLIN
(UNGLAZED —) BISQUE
(PL.) TROKE CHAFFER TROGGIN
WAREHOUSE GOLA HONG ETAPE GOLAH STORE BODEGA FONDUK GODOWN STAITH ALMACEN FUNDUCK SPICERY STOWAGE ENTREPOT MAGAZINE SERAGLIO
WARFARE WAR ARMS IRON ARMOR BATTLE PSYWAR MILITIA CONFLICT
(CHEMICAL — AGENT) SARIN

(NONAGGRESSIVE —) SITZKRIEG
(PETTY —) GUERILLA GUERRILLA
(PSYCHOLOGICAL —) PSYWAR
(SUFF.) MACHIA MACHY
WARHEAD MIRV
WAR-HORSE CHARGER COURSER DESTRER TROOPER DESTRIER
WARILY TIPTOE GINGERLY
WARINESS CAUTEL CAUTION DISTRUST WARESHIP WARIMENT
WARKLOOM TOOL WARKLUME
WARLIKE WARLY MARTIAL CAVALIER FIGHTING MILITARY BELLICOSE
(NOT —) IMBELLIC
WARLOCK IMP WITCH SPRITE WARLOW WIZARD CONJUROR SORCERER
WARLORD TUCHUN
WARM HOT LEW LOO RUG BASK BEEK KEEN LEWD MILD CALID CHAFE EAGER FRESH MALMY MUNGY SLACK TEPID TOAST ACHAFE ARDENT BIRSLE DEVOUT DIGEST FOSTER GENIAL HEARTY HEATED RIZZLE TENDER TOASTY CHERISH CLEMENT CORDIAL GLOWING THERMAL ZEALOUS FRIENDLY PRESSING SANGUINE
(— UP) SCORE
(MODERATELY —) LEW SLACK TEPID
(PREF.) CAL(E)(I)(ORI)
WARMHEARTED KIND TENDER FRIENDLY GENEROUS
WARMING FOVENT
WARMOUTH BIGMOUTH FLATFISH SACALAIT
WARMTH GLOW HEAT LIFE ZEAL ARDOR LEWTH ENERGY FERVOR ARDENCY PASSION CALIDITY FERVENCY
(— OF ADDRESS) UNCTION
(— OF MANNER) EMPRESSEMENT
(INNER —) JUICE
WARN REDE WARD WERN ALERT AREAD DETER WEIRD ADVERT ADVISE EXHORT INFORM CAUTION COMMAND COUNSEL GARNISH PREVISE ADMONISH THREATEN
(— OFF) FORBID
WARNING AHEM ITEM ALARM CHECK KNELL BEACON CAVEAT LESSON NOTICE OFFICE SAMPLE SIGNAL TIPOFF AVISION CALLING CAUTION EXAMPLE GRIFFIN JIGGERS MEMENTO MONITOR PRESAGE SUMMONS DOCUMENT GARDYLOO MONITION PREMONITION
(— OF DISASTER) DIRE
(— ON CHART) VIGIA
(— SIGNAL) RED REDFLAG REDLIGHT
(AIR-RAID —) ALERT
(ARCHERY —) FAST
(DANGER —) VIGIA
WARP CUP WEB BIAS CANE CAST LIFT WARF WERP WIND ANGLE CHAIN CHOKE CRAWL CROOK GEYZE KEDGE PORRY THRAW TWINE WEAVE BUCKLE CHEESE

DEFORM WASHIN DEFLECT DISTORT SKELLER
(— IN WEAVING) CRAM
(PREF.) HIST(O)
WARPED WRY BUCKLED GNARLED HOUSING
WARPER BALLER
WARPING BOW PANDATION
WARRAGAL WILD DINGO HORSE OUTLAW
WARRANT ABLE EARN WARN AMRIT BERAT FIANT PRESS SANAD VOUCH AMRITA ASSERT BRANCH BREVET CAPIAS COUPON DOCKET ENSURE INSURE PARDON PERMIT PLEVIN POLICY POTENT SUNNUD TICKET UPHOLD WARDOG BEHIGHT CAPTION DESERVE JUSTIFY PRECEPT PROMISE GUARANTY MITTIMUS
(CUSTOMS —) TRANSIRE
WARRANTED VALID
WARRANT OFFICER BOSN BOSUN BOATSWAIN
WARRAU GUARANO
WARREN SLUM CONYGER WARRANT
WARRIOR TOA WER EARL HERO KEMP RINK WEER BERNE FREIK FREKE HAGEN LLUDD SEPAD SINGH THANE THEGN OSSIAN WARMAN WEAPON FIGHTER SOLDIER STARKAD WARWOLF ZERBINO CHAMPION RODOMONT SHARDANA STARKATH SWORDMAN WARFARER
(— CLASS) MAGANI
(— OF NOBLE RANK) EARL
(AMERICAN INDIAN —) BRAVE SANNUP
(BOASTFUL —) RODOMONT
(BRYTHONIC —) LLUDD
(BURGUNDIAN —) HAGEN
(FEMALE —) AMAZON SHIELDMAY
(GREEK —) AJAX
(IRISH —) FENIAN
(KAFFIR —S) IMPI
(MUSLIM —) GAZI GHAZI
(NOTED —) THANE THEGN
(SCANDINAVIAN —) BERSERK
(SCOTTISH —) ZERBINO
(TROJAN —) AGENOR
(VALIANT —) TOA
(VIRGIN —) CAMILLA
(PL.) IMPI CHIVALRY GAMMADIM
WARSHIP GUIDE RAZEE WAFTER CRUISER MONITOR SULTANA SULTANE CORVETTE
(— OF OLD) RAM
WART RAT WRAT AMBURY ANBURY SYCOMA PUSTULE VERRUCA VERRUGA EPIDERMA PAPILLOMA
(POTATO —) CANKER
(PREF.) VERRUCI
WART HOG EMGALLA
WARTLIKE PYRENOID
WART SNAKE XENODERM
WARTY MURICATE MURICATED PAPILLOSE
WARY SHY CAGY WISE AWARE CAGEY CANNY DOWNY HOOLY LEERY TENDER CAREFUL

GUARDED PRUDENT WAREFUL CAUTIOUS SKITTISH VIGILANT WATCHFUL

WAS VAS WIS WUZ WYS PAST WISSHE
(— ABLE) COULD
(— NOT) NAS
(I —) CHWAS

WASH DO BOG FEN LAG LAP NET TUB BEER BUCK EDDY HOSE HUSH LAVE SILT SUDS WADI BATHE CLEAN CLEAR DOLLY DRAFF ERODE MARSH RINSE SCRUB SLOSH SOUSE SWILL BUDDLE CRADLE DOLLIE LOTION PURIFY SLOOSH SLUICE SOZZLE STREAM ALLUVIO CLEANSE LAUNDER SHAMPOO ALLUVIUM EYEWATER LAVAMENT LAVATORY
(— A GAS) SCRUB
(— AWAY) GULL
(— BY TREADING IN WATER) TRAMP
(— DOWN) SIND SOOGEE
(— EDGE) LIP
(— FOR GOLD) PAN
(— GIVEN TO SWINE) DRAFF
(— GRAVEL) ROCK
(— HAIR) SHAMPOO
(— IN LYE) BUCK
(— LIGHTLY) RINSE
(— OFF) DETERGE
(— ORE) TYE HUTCH BUDDLE CRADLE STRAKE
(— OUT) SIND ELUTE FLUSH LAVAGE
(— ROUGHLY) SLUSH
(— THOROUGHLY) SCOUR
(— THROAT) GARGLE
(— VIGOROUSLY) SLOSH
(— WITH BROOM) TYE
(— WITH COSMETIC) SURFLE SURPHUL
(DRY —) ARROYA ARROYO
WASHBASIN LAVER LAVABO LAVATORY ALJOFAINA
WASHCLOTH FLANNEL
WASHED ABLUTED
(— UP) SHOT THROUGH
WASHED-OUT ANEMIC ANAEMIC
WASHER BUR BURR DRUM ROVE CLOUT BUTTON RONDEL SOURER GROMMET LEATHER RACCOON COTTEREL LAVENDER RONDELLE SCRUBBER
WASHERMAN DHOBI DHOBIE LAVANDERO
WASHERWOMAN LAUNDER
WASHING LAG BATH LAVAGE SLOOSH LAUNDRY ABLUTION LAVAMENT LAVATION (PL.) ELUATE
WASHING MACHINE DASHWHEEL

WASHOUT FLOP STUMOR FAILURE
WASHROOM BASEMENT LAVATORY
WASHSTAND COMMODE
WASHTUB FLASKET
WASHY SOFT WEAK LOOSE MOIST FEEBLE PALLID WATERY DILUTED SHILPIT
WASP MASON SPHEX WHAMP WOPSE BEMBEX DAUBER DIGGER HORNET TIPHIA TREMEX VESPID CYNIPID DRYINID EUMENID MASARID SCOLIID SERPHID SIRICID SPHECID STINGER ACULEATE MUTILLID POMPILID
(KIND OF —) MASON
WASPISH TART TESTY FRETFUL PEEVISH CHOLERIC SNAPPISH
WASSAIL DRINK TOAST PLEDGE CAROUSE REVELRY CAROUSAL
WASTE EAT FUD GOB TED BURN GNAW JUNK LOSS PASS PEAK ROSS SACK TEAR TINE WEAR WILD DROSS EXILE HAVOC SCRAP SLOOM SLOTH SLOUM SPILL TABID THRUM BANGLE BEZZLE COMMON DEBRIS DESERT DEVOUR DIDDLE DRAFFY DRIVEL ELAPSE EXPEND FOREST GARBLE GOUSTY LAVISH MOLDER MUDDLE PADDLE PERISH RAVAGE REFUSE SCATHE SPILTH WESTEN CONNACH CONSUME EXHAUST FRITTER GARBAGE MULLOCK RUBBISH SLATTER CONFOUND DEMOLISH SLATTERN SQUANDER
(— AWAY) BATE MELT DECAY DWINE SWAIN SWEAL TRAIK WANZE TABEFY WINDLE DWINDLE FORPINE MISLIKE DISSOLVE EMACIATE FORSPEND MACERATE
(— GRADUALLY) WEAR ABSUME
(— IN DRUNKENNESS) SOT
(— IN RIOT) BEZZLE
(— OF INK) INKSHED
(— OF SILK COCOONS) KNUB
(— TIME) FOOL FRIG IDLE DALLY DEFER DRILL DAWDLE DIDDLE FOOTER FOOTLE LOITER DRINGLE FOOSTER GAUSTER
(COAL —) SLUDGE
(COTTON —) FLUKE SLASHER SPOOLER
(FOOD —) SLOP

(LIQUID —) DRIPPING EFFLUENT
(MINING —) GOB GOAF
(RADIOACTIVE —) RADWASTE
(WOOL —) FUD MUNGO GARNETT
(YARN —) THRUM EYEBROW
WASTEBASKET HELL HELLBOX
WASTED IDLE FORWORN RAVAGED DECREPIT
WASTEFUL LAVISH PROFUSE DESOLATE PRODIGAL SPENDFUL
WASTEFULNESS WAIT UNTHRIFT
WASTELAND MOOR HEATH CURAGH DESERT CURRACH
WASTER THIEF LEISTER WASTREL PRODIGAL
WASTING FRET DECAY LIGHT AWASTE ATROPHY CACHEXY EXEDENT MISLIKE PREYING TABIFIC CACHEXIA PHTHISIS SYNTEXIS TABESCENCE CONSUMPTION
(— AWAY) TABES MARASMUS SYNTECTIC TABEFACTION
(PREF.) PHTHISIO TABE TABI TABO
(PROGRESSIVE —) TABO
WASTREL WAIF LOSEL REFUSE WASTER ROUNDER VAGABOND STROYGOOD
WATCH EYE FOB NIT SEE SPY TAB DIAL ESPY GLIM GLOM HACK HEED KEEP LOOK MARK MIND PIPE TOUT TWIG VACH WAIK WAKE WARD YARD CLOCK GUARD SCOUT SPIAL SUPER TIMER VERGE VIGIL VIRGE WAKEN WHEEL BEHOLD DEFEND DIACLE FOLLOW HUNTER PERDUE SENTRY SHADOW TICKER TICTIC TURNIP WAKING YEMING OBSERVE OVERSEE ROSKOPF STRIKER THIMBLE TOMPION HOROLOGE MEDITATE SENTINEL SPECTATE TICKTICK STEMWINDER
(— FOR) TENT ABIDE AWAIT
(— OF ARMY) BIVOUAC
(— ON THE SLY) FOX
(— OVER) HOLD KEEP TEND TENT GUARD ATTEND OVERLOOK
(— OVER DEAD) LIKEWAKE LYKEWALK
(— PEOPLE EATING) GROAK
(— QUIETLY) HINT
(— THAT STRIKES) STRIKER REPEATER
(— UNIT) LIGNE
(— WITH HINGED COVER) HUNTER
(ALARM —) TATLER TATTLER
(CLOSE —) SCRUTINY
(NAUTICAL —) HACK DOGWATCH
(NIGHT —) LICHWAKE LYKEWAKE
(PART OF —) BOW FOB CASE DIAL FACE HAND STEM BEZEL COVER CROWN FRAME CHAPTER CRYSTAL DISPLAY NUMERAL SHOULDER
(SUFF.) SCOPE SCOPIC SCOPUS SCOPY
WATCHBAND WRISTER WRISTLET
WATCH CHAIN GUARD SLANG
WATCH CRYSTAL LUNET LUNETTE
WATCHDOG CUR GARM GARMR MATIN BANDOG KRATIM CERBERUS
WATCHER VEIL ARGUS WAKER

VIEWER WAITER MUSAHAR SPOTTER WATCHMAN
WATCHFUL IRA ALERT AWARE CANNY CHARY ERECT TENTY WAKER TENTIE WACKER ANXIOUS GUARDED JEALOUS LIDLESS WAKEFUL VIGILANT WAKERIFE WAUKRIFE OBSERVANT
WATCHFULNESS OUTLOOK JEALOUSY
WATCH GLASS CRYSTAL LUNETTE
WATCHING VIGIL CUSTODY CONSERVATION
WATCHMAN FLAG MINA WAIT GUARD SCOUT VIGIL WATCH ASKARI BANTAY GHAFIR SENTRY SERENO SHOMER TOOTER WAITER WARDEN WARDER BELLMAN CHARLEY GUARDER TALLIAR WAKEMAN CHOKIDAR SENTINEL
(NIGHT —) SERENO CHARLIE
WATCHTOWER WARD BEACON GARRET MIZPAH SENTRY ATALAYA LOOKOUT MIRADOR BARBICAN SENTINEL SPECCHIE
WATCHWORD CRY MAXIM ALERTA ENSIGN PAROLE SIGNAL NAYWORD PASSWORD
WATCH WORKS MOVFABLE
WATER EAU TJI AGUA AQUA BATH BRIM BROO BURN LAGE LAKE POND POOL TIDE WAVE ABYSS BILGE FLUME LOUGH LYMPH RIVER TABBY TEARS TUBIG BALLOW BAREGE CAMLET CONGEE CONJEE PAWNEE PHLEGM SALIVA STREAM VADOSE WATHER AQUATIC CRYSTAL JAVELLE IRRIGATE SNOWMELT
(— AFTER BOILING RICE) CONGEE CONJEE
(— AS REFUGE FOR GAME) SOIL
(— AT THE MOUTH) DROOL
(— BY CALENDERING) TABBY
(— FOR BREWING) BURN
(— IN SOIL) HOLARD
(— IN WEIR) LASHER
(— REDDISH WITH IRON) RIDDAM
(— RUNNING AGAINST MAIN CURRENT) EDDY
(— SPIRIT) KELPIE
(— SURROUNDED BY ICE) WAKE
(— TRAIL) WAKE
(— UNDER PRESSURE) HUSH
(ARCH OF —) CURL
(BAPTISMAL —) LAVER
(BARLEY —) PTISAN
(BOTTOM — OF SEA) ABYSS
(BOUNDARY —) SHARD
(BUBBLING —) SPRUDEL
(DEEP —) BALLOW
(DIRTY —) SAUR PUDDLE
(FAST-MOVING —) SOUP
(FEN —) SUDS
(FROZEN —) ICE FROST
(FROZEN FLAVORED — ON A STICK) POPSICLE
(HARD —) ICE
(HOLY —) HYSSOP
(HOT —) SOUP
(LIVING —) RASA
(MINERAL —) VICHY SELTER SELTZER APOLLINARIS

(OPEN —) POLYNYA
(QUININE —) TONIC
(RED —) RESP RIDDAM
(ROUGH —) SEA
(RUNNING —) SEA
(SALT —) BRACK BRINE SEAWATER
(SOAPY —) SUDS GRAITH
(SPLASH OF —) FLASH
(STILL —) KELD LOGIN
(SULPHUR —) BAREGE
(SURFACE OF —) RYME
(SWEETENED —) AMRIT AMRITA
(WASHING —) LAVATION
(WHITE — AFTER WAVE) SOUP
(PL.) APSU
(PREF.) AQUA AQUEO AQUI AQUO HIDRO HYDAT(O) HYDR(O)
(GO THROUGH —) SILLO
(STAGNANT —) TELMAT(O)
(SUFF.) LIMNION YDATIS
WATER ARUM DRAGON
WATER BAG CHAGUL MATARA MUSSUK
WATER BATH BAINMARIE
WATERBIRD ALCATRAS
WATER BOA ANACONDA
WATER BOTTLE CARAFE
WATERBRAIN GID
WATERBUCK COB CHUZWI DEFASSA WATERDOE
WATER BUFFALO KERBAU CARABAO
(WILD —) ARNA
WATER CARRIER BHISTI AGUADOR BHEESTY
WATER CART DILLY
WATER CASK WINGER
WATER CHESTNUT LING CALTROP SALIGOT SINGHARA
WATER CHINQUAPIN BONNET NELUMBO WANKAPIN YONCOPIN RATTLENUT
WATER CLOCK GHURRY CLEPSYDRA
WATER CLOSET PETTY PRIVY STOOL SANITARY NECESSARY
WATER COCK KORA
WATERCOLOR GRAPHIC
WATERCOURSE (ALSO SEE STREAM AND RIVER) RUN URN AGOS DIKE DYKE GOTE HAHR KHOR LADE LEAT REAN WADI WADY YORA AUWAI BAYOU BROOK CANAL CANEL COWAL DITCH DRAIN RHINE ARROYO CANNEL COURSE FURROW GUTTER KENNEL NULLAH CHANNEL TRINKET
WATERCRAFT SAILER
WATERCRESS EKER KERS CARSE KERSE BILDERS NOSESMART
WATER DIVINER DOWSER
WATER DOG OTTER WATERRUG
WATER DRINKER HYDROPOT
WATERED MOIRE TABBY
WATERFALL LIN LYN FALL FOSS LINN SALT CHUTE FORCE SAULT SHOOT SPOUT LASHER CASCADE CATADUPE CATARACT OVERFALL
(FROZEN —) ICEFALL
WATER FENNEL EDGEWEED
WATER FERN PILLWORT
WATER FLEA CYCLOPS DAPHNID

WATERFOWL WADER SWIMMER
WATERFRONT PRAYA
WATERGALL WINDDOG WINDGALL JELLYFISH
WATER GATE SLUICE
WATER GERMANDER SCORDIUM
WATER HEMLOCK CICUTA COWBANE DEATHIN JELLICA
WATER HEN GALLINULE
WATER HOG BUSHPIG CAPYBARA
WATER HOLE DUB CHARCO TINAJA ALBERCA
WATER ICE SHERBET
WATERINESS AQUEITY AQUOSITY
WATERING EPIPHORA RIGATION
WATER JUG GAMLA GOMLAH GOOLAH
WATERLEAF SHAWNY NEMOPHILA
WATERLESS
(PREF.) ANHYDR(O)
WATER LETTUCE QUIAPO
WATER LILY DUCK LOTOS LOTUS WOCAS WOKAS BOBBIN CANDOCK NELUMBO CAMALOTE NENUPHAR
WATERLOGGED SOGGY SODDEN SWAMPY EDEMATOUS SATURATED
WATERMAN MERMAN QUENCH OARSMAN
WATERMARK CROWN TIDEMARK
WATERMARKED LAID
WATERMELON PEPO GOURD MELON TSAMA CITRUL SANDIA ANGURIA MILLION CUCURBIT PEPONIDA PEPONIUM SKIPJACK
WATER MOCCASIN CONGO
WATER NEWT ASK TRITON
WATER OPOSSUM YAPOK YAPOCK
WATER OUZEL PIET OOZEL OWZEL DIPPER DUCKER
WATER PARSNIP SKIRRET
WATER PEPPER LAKEWEED
WATER PIMPERNEL BROOKWEED
WATER PLANT LIMU AQUATIC
WATER PLANTAIN ALISMA THRUMWORT
WATERPOT FONTAL
WATERPROOF RAINCOAT
(— MATERIAL) KERATOL
WATER RAIL RUNNER BILCOCK MOORHEN OARCOCK
WATER RAT VOLE CRABER MUSKRAT WATERRUG
WATER SCORPION NEPID
WATERSHED BROW DIVIDE DIVORT SNOWSHED
WATER SHIELD FANWORT DEERFOOD FROGLEAF
WATERSKIN MASHAK MATARA MUSSUK MUSSACK MUSSICK
WATER SOLDIER PONDWORT
WATER SPIRIT ARIEL KELPY KELPIE UNDINE
WATERSPOUT RONE CANAL SPATE SPOUT VORTEX PRESTER TWISTER CATARACT GARGOYLE
WATER SPRITE KELPY KELPIE
WATER STRIDER SKATER SKIMMER SKIPPER SKETCHER
WATER THRUSH KICKUP WAGTAIL
WATER TIGER DYTISCID
WATERTIGHT THEAT THEET TIGHT STANCH THIGHT STAUNCH
WATER WALLY BATAMOTE

WATERWAY GUT CASH DOCK HOLE LODE DITCH INLET ARTERY SEAWAY CULVERT FAIRWAY HIGHWAY IGARAPE
(ARTIFICIAL —) LEAD CANAL
(DUTCH —) ZEE
(PL.) SCUPPERS
WATERWHEEL NORIA SAKIA SAGEER SAKIEH DANAIDE SAKIYEH TYMPANUM
WATERY WET LASH PALE SICK THIN WHEY BOGGY MOIST SAMMY WASHY BLASHY FLASHY LIQUID PALLID SEROSE SEROUS SWASHY AQUATIC AQUEOUS CHOROUS HYDROUS PHLEGMY SANIOUS HUMOROUS HYDATOID ICHOROUS SKINKING
WATT (ONE BILLION —S) GIGAWATT
WATTLE GILL JOWL PLAT SALY TWIG WAND BOREE COOBA FRITH MULGA SALLY SALWE STAVE STICK HURDLE JEWING JOLLOP LAPPET SALLOW BLUEBUSH CARUNCLE
WATTLEBIRD IAO MOHO MINER MANUAO MAOMAO GILLBIRD
WATTLE CROW KOKAKO
WAVE FAN FLY JAW SEA WAW BECK FLAG FLAP GUST LUMP PERM SUFF SULK SWAY WAFF WAFT WAWE YTHE BLESS CRIMP FLASH FLOAT FLOTE PULSE SHAKE SURGE SWELL SWING BILLOW COMBER FLAUNT MARCEL RIPPLE ROLLER WAFFLE WINNOW BREAKER BRIMMER CRIMPLE DECUMAN FEATHER FLICKER FLUTTER TSUNAMI WHIFFLE ARTEFACT BRANDISH FLOURISH GRAYBACK UNDULATE UNIPULSE WHISTLER WHITECAP
(— ABOUT) WAMPISH
(— OF EXCITATION) IMPULSE
(— OF FLAG) DOT DASH
(— OF SHIP) BONE
(ARCH OF —) CURL
(BRAIN —) DELTA
(ELECTRIC —) STRAY CARRIER
(ELECTROMAGNETIC —) ALFVEN
(HAIR —) MARCEL PERMANENT
(LARGE —) HEAVY
(LITTLE —) RIPPLE
(RIDE A —) BODYSURF
(SOLITARY —) SOLITON
(SPIN —) MAGNON
(TIDAL —) AEGIR EAGER EAGRE
(PL.) SURF
(PREF.) CUMA CYM(I)(O) CYMATO KYM(I)(O) KYMATO ONDA ONDO UNDI
WAVER HALT REEL SWAG SWAY VARY CHECK DAKER DOUBT FLOAT SWALE SWING WIVER DACKER DAIKER DITHER FALTER MAMMER QUIVER SWERVE TEETER TOTTER WABBLE WAFFLE WOBBLE BALANCE FLICKER FLITTER FLUTTER STAGGER SWITHER VIBRATE HESITATE VACILLATE
WAVERING WAVY WAVY WEAK WAUCH WAUGH FICKLE GROGGY UNSURE WAVERY WIGGLY DUBIOUS LAMBENT SHUTTLE

DOUBTFUL FLEXUOSE FLEXUOUS FLICKERY HOVERING WAVEROUS PENDULOUS
WAVERLEY (AUTHOR OF —) SCOTT
(CHARACTER IN —) EVAN LEAN ROSE VOHR ALICE COSMO DAVIE FLORA DONALD FERGUS STUART CHARLES EVERARD MACIVOR GARDINER PEMBROKE WAVERLEY GELLATLEY MACCOMBICH BRADWARDINE
WAVINESS CRIMP
WAVING UNDE WAFT AWAVE OUNDY UNDEE WAFTURE FLOURISH
(— OF WEAPON) FLOURISH
WAVY ONDE UNDE UNDY CRISP MOIRE SNAKY UNDEE CRIMPY FLECKY REPAND SNAKEY UNDATE WIGGLY BUCKLED CRINKLY CURVING ENDATED ROLLING SINUATE UNDULAR ENRIDGED FLEXUOUS ONDOYANT SQUIGGLY UNDULATE
(PEOPLE WITH — HAIR) VEDDOID
WAWL HOWL WAIL WOWL SQUALL
WAX WOX CERE CODE GROW RAGE WACE WOXE SCALE BECOME CAPPING CERESIN KLISTER CARNAUBA CERESINE CEROXYLE COCCERIN EPILATOR INCREASE
(— FAINT) APPAL
(— FROM INSECT) PELA
(— IN HONEYCOMB) CAPPING
(— STRONG) PREVAIL
(CHINESE —) PELA
(COBBLER'S —) CODE
(EAR —) CERUMEN
(KIND OF —) MONTAN PINSANG
(POLISH WITH —) SIMONIZE
(SKI —) KLISTER
(PREF.) CER(I)(O) KERO
WAXBILL ASTRILD REDBILL
WAXEN WAX PALLID CEREOUS
WAXER GLAZER WAXMAN
WAXFLOWER EPIPHYTE
WAXING CRESCIVE
WAX LIGHT TAPER CANDLE
WAX MYRTLE ARRAYAN
WAX PALM CARNAUBA
WAX PLANT HOYA
WAXWING WAXBIRD RECOLLET SILKTAIL
WAXY ANGRY VEXED CEREOUS PLIABLE YIELDING
WAY LAW PAD RUE TAO VIA WON WYE FARE FORE FORM GAIT GANG GATE KIND LANE LARK PACE PATH PAWK RAKE ROAD SORT TOBY WISE ALLEY CHANT FORTH GOING GUISE HABIT MOYEN ROUTE SHEAR STEPS STYLE TRACT TRADE ACCESS AVENUE CAREER CHEMIN COURSE MANNER METHOD PHASIS STREET TRAJET CHANNEL FASHION HIGHWAY PASSAGE SKIDWAY APPROACH CONTRADA DISTRICT FOOTPATH THOROUGH VICINITY LAUNCHING
(— OF DEPARTURE) EXIT
(— OF ESCAPE) BOLTHOLE
(— OF LIFE) LARK TRACE HEDONISM
(— OF LOOKING) SLANT

(— OF SPEAKING) AMBAGE
(— OF THINKING) DIET
(— OF WALKING) JET
(— ON OR OFF) RAMP
(— OUT) IT RAD EXIT SALVO
RADICAL
(— THROUGH MINEFIELD) BREACH
(BY ANOTHER —) ALIA
(CLEVER —) KNACK
(COVERED —) CORRIDOR
(DEVIOUS —) ROUNDABOUT
(EVERY —) ROUND
(IN ANY —) SOEVER
(INDIRECT —) AMBAGES
(LONG —) FAR
(MAJOR —) STEM
(NARROW —) DRANG
(ODD —S) JIMJAMS
(PLANK —) BRIDGE
(RAISED —) BANQUETTE
(ROUNDABOUT —) DETOUR
CIRCUIT
(ROUNDABOUT —S) AMBAGES
(SETTLED —) BIAS
(SIDE —) BRANCH
(SLOPING —) RAMP
(UNDEVIATING —) GROOVE
(PL.) DAPS
(PREF.) HODO ODO VIA
(SUFF.) ODE OID WISE
WAYBILL CHALAN WILLIE CHALLAN
WAYFARER SHULER VIATOR
PILGRIM SHUILER TRAVELER
PASSENGER
WAYFARING TREE WHITTEN
COTTONER VIBURNUM
WAYLAY BELAY BESET BLOCK
BRACE AMBUSH FORLAY FORSET
FORELAY OBSTRUCT SURPRISE
WAYLAYER WAIT
WAYMARK AHU
**WAY OF ALL FLESH (AUTHOR OF
—)** BUTLER
(CHARACTER IN —) JOHN ELIZA
ELLEN MARIA PRYER ALLABY
ALTHEA ERNEST GEORGE JOSEPH
OVERTON SKINNER MAITLAND
PONTIFEX THEOBALD CHARLOTTE
CHRISTINA
**WAY OF THE WORLD (AUTHOR OF
—)** CONGREVE
(CHARACTER IN —) FOIBLE FAINALL
MARWOOD ROWLAND WILFULL
WITWOOD MIRABELL WAITWELL
WISHFORT MILLAMANT
WAYSIDE HEDGE
WAYWARD PEEVISH PERVERSE
LOUPTHEDYKE
WEAK DIM LEW COOL DOWY FOND
LAME NESH NICE PALE PUNY SELI
SELY SOFT THIN WASH WAUF
WOKE BAUCH BAUGH CRIMP
DICKY FAINT FLASH FRAIL JERKY
LIGHT NAISH REEDY ROCKY SEELY
SHAKY SILLY SLACK STANK WASHY
WAUGH WEARY WERSH YOUNG
CADUKE DEBILE DILUTE DOTISH
EFFETE FEEBLE FLABBY FLAGGY
FLIMSY FOIBLE GROGGY INFIRM
LIMBER LITTLE MARCID SEMMIT
SICKLY SINGLE SWASHY TENDER
UNSURE UNWISE WAIRCH WATERY
BRICKLE DWAIBLY DWEEBLE

FLACCID FOOLISH FRAGILE INSIPID
INVALID LANGUID PIMPING
PUERILE REGULAR RICKETY
SAUGHEN SHALLOW SHILPIT
SLENDER SPINDLY TOTTERY
UNHARDY UNLUSTY WEARISH
ASTHENIC CHILDISH DECREPIT
DEFINITE FECKLESS FEMININE
FLAGGING GRIPLESS HELPLESS
IMBECILE IMPOTENT LADYLIKE
LANGUENT PHTHISIC RESOLUTE
RUSHLIKE SACKLESS SCRANNEL
THEWLESS UNMIGHTY UNWIELDY
SPINELESS
(— FROM FATIGUE) TANGLE
(— FROM HUNGER) LEER
(— IN RESOLUTION) FRAIL
(MENTALLY —) TOTTY
(PREF.) ASTHEN(O) LEPT(O)
WEAKEN GO LAG SAP DAMP FAIL
HURT MELT PALL SINK THIN ABATE
ALLAY BLUNT BREAK CRAZE DELAY
QUAIL SHAKF SPEND WATER
APPALL ATTRIT DEACON DEADEN
DEFANG DEFEAT DEJECT DENUDE
DILUTE FALTER IMPAIR INFIRM
LABEFY LESSEN PERISH REBATE
REDUCE SICKEN SOFTEN
CORRODE CORRUPT CRIPPLE
DECLINE DEPRESS DISABLE
MOLLIFY QUALIFY RESOLVE
THREADY UNBRACE UNNERVE
CASTRATE DIMINISH EMBEZZLE
ENERVATE ENFEEBLE ETIOLATE
INFRINGE LABEFACT UNSTRENG
WEAKENED GROGGY ANODYNE
INVALID SHOTTEN DECREPIT
LABEFACT STRAINED
WEAKENING CHRONIC FAILURE
FLAGGING
WEAKEST RECKLING
WEAKFISH DRUM TROUT ACOUPA
SALMON CORBINA CORVINA
DRUMMER SQUETEE TOTOABA
TOTUAVA BLUEFISH CHICKWIT
WEAKLING TOY WRIG DUGON
PULER SLINK SOFTIE DILLING
RECKLING SOFTLING
WEAKLY FEEBLY FEMALE SIMPLY
WEAK-MINDED DAFT DOTY DOTED
FOOLISH
WEAKNESS ATONY CRACK CRAZE
FAULT FOLLY TOUCH ATONIA
DEFECT FOIBLE ACRATIA FAILING
FISSURE FRAILTY LANGUOR
ASTHENIA DEBILITY DELICACY
FONDNESS
(— OF DIGESTION) APEPSY APEPSIA
(— OF MIND) FOLLY
(— OF VOICE) PHONASTHENIA
(CARNAL —) FLESH
(SUFF.) (— FOR) ITIS
WEAL WHEAL RICHES STRIPE
WEALTH WELFARE
WEALTH WAD WON DHAN GEAR
GOLD GOOD MUCK WONE MEANS
THING WORTH GRAITH MAMMON
POCKET PURPLE RICHES TALENT
CASHBOX FORTUNE RICHDOM
WARISON WELFARE CATALLUM
OPULENCE OPULENCY PROPERTY
TREASURE WARRISON
MONEYBAGS

(— OF NATION) STOCK
(PATRON OF —) YAKSHA
(PREF.) APHNO PLUT(O)
WEALTHY FAT BEIN BIEN FULL
OOFY RICH WELI AMPLE PURSY
TINNY LOADED OOFIER COUTHIE
MONEYED PURSIVE ABUNDANT
AFFLUENT
(— CLASS) PLUTOCRACY
WEAN CHILD SPAIN SPANE WAYNE
INFANT ESTRANGE
WEANING ABLACTATION
WEAPON (ALSO SEE SPECIFIC TYPE
OF WEAPON) ARM BOW GUN BILL
BOLA BOLO CLUB COSH DART
EDGE EPEE FALX FOIL IRON MACE
NULKF PATU PIKE TOOL WIWI
ADAGA ARROW BILLY CAKRA
DEATH FLAIL KNIFE LANCE ONCIN
ORGUE SHARP SPEAR SQUID
STEEL SWORD VOUGE WAPIN
CANNON CHAKRA DAGGER GLAIVE
MACANA TOMBOC ARCHERY
BAZOOKA FIREARM GISARME
HALBERD HARPOON HURLBAT
JAVELIN LIANGLE POUNAMU
SHOTGUN SLASHER STICKER
STUNGUN TICKLER WHIFFLE
ARBALEST BLOWBACK BLUDGEON
CROSSBOW FAUCHARD
HEDGEHOG LEEANGLE NUNCHAKU
PARTISAN TOMAHAWK TROMBASH
(CELTIC —) PALSTAFF
(DEADLY —) DEATH
(LINE OF —S) RIDGE
(NUCLEAR —) NUKE
(PREHISTORIC —) CELT
(PL.) WAR TACKLE ARCHERY
WEAPONRY
(PREF.) ARMI HOPL(O)
WEAPONRY ARMS
WEAR KIT BEAR FRAY FRET GROW
HAVE PASS CHAFE GUARD SPEND
VOGUE WEARY ABRADE BATTER
BECOME HAVEON BETHUMB
CONSUME DEFENSE DEGRADE
FASHION FATIGUE FRAZZLE
PROCEED WEATHER PROGRESS
(— AND TEAR) GAFF SLITE
GRUELING
(— AN OPENING) BREACH
(— AWAY) EAT FADE FRET GALL
GNAW GULL PINE ERODE GULLY
SCOUR SPEND ABRADE CORRADE
CORRODE CONTRIVE
(— CLOTHES) DRESS
(— DOWN) BRAY GRIND ABRADE
ABRASE GRAVEL
(— FURROWS) GUTTER
(— IN PUBLIC) SPORT
(— OFF) FADE FRAY ABRADE
(— OUT) DO BURN COOK FLOG
FRAY JADE MUSH TIRE TUCK BREAK
SLAVE SLITE SPEND TRASH BUGGER
HATTER MAGGLE PERUSE EXHAUST
FORWEAR FORWORK HACKNEY
INVALID SHACHLE OVERFRET
OVERWEAR
(— SHIP) CAST
(— SHOES OUT OF SHAPE)
SHACHLE SHACKLE
(— TIGHT CORSETS) LACE
(WINTER —) EARMUFF

WEARIED AWEARY FORGONE
FATIGUED WEARIFUL
WEARINESS TIRE FATIGUE
BRAINFAG SICKNESS VEXATION
WEARING DECAY SCUFF BURNING
CLOTHES ABRASION GARMENTS
GRINDING
WEARISOME DRY DULL HARD
SLOW WEARY BORING MORTAL
PROLIX SODDEN IRKSOME
TEDIOUS SAWDUSTY TIRESOME
TOILSOME
WEARISOMENESS TEDIUM
WEARY FAG IRK SAD BEAT BOEG
BORE CLOY MOIL PALL POOP
PUNY SADE TIRE TIRY WEAK WORE
WORN BORED BREAK CURSE
SPENT ABRADE BETOIL HARASS
PLAGUE POOPED SICKLY SQUEAL
TUCKER EXHAUST FATIGUE
IRKSOME SWINKED FATIGATE
FORCHASE GRIEVOUS TIRESOME
WRETCHED FORJASKIT
(— OUT) RAMFEEZLE
(BE —) SAG
(BECOME —) JADE
WEARY WILLIE TRAMP
WEASAND WISEN GULLET THROAT
WIZZEN TRACHEA WINDPIPE
WEASEL CANE VAIR VARE WARE
HULDA HURON SNEAK STOAT
TAIRA TAYRA ERMINE FERRET
HULDAH VERMIN ARCTOID
VORMELA FUTTERET MUISHOND
MUSTELIN WHITRACK
(— OUT OF) EVADE
(— RELATIVE) ZORIL
(PREF.) GALEO
WEASEL CAT LINSANG
WEATHER SKY DIRT RAIN TIME
COLLA STORM WINDWARD
(— CONDITION) WHITEOUT
(— LINE) FRONT
(FAIR —) SHINE
(HOT AND HUMID —) SIZZARD
(INCLEMENT —) SEASON
(INTERVAL OF FAIR —) SLATCH
(OPEN —) FRESH
(OUT OF THE —) ALEE
(UNDER THE —) SEEDY
(VIOLENT —) ELEMENTS
(PREF.) EUDIO METEOR(O)
WEATHERBEATEN GNARLED
SEAGOING
WEATHERCOCK COCK FANE VANE
FAINE FANACLE
WEATHERGLASS BAROMETER
WEAVE CANE HABI HUCK JOIN LACE
LENO LOOM REED ROCK SPIN
WALE WARP WIND WOOF DOBBY
DRAPE PLAIT TWINE UNITE
BROCHE DAMASK DEVISE DIAPER
DOBBIE FABRIC CANILLE ENTWINE
FASHION INDRAPE SATINET
SHUTTLE VANDYKE DIAGONAL
DUCHESSE OVERSHOT
(— PATTERNS INTO) BROCADE
(BASKET —) BARLEYCORN
(CARPET —) FLOSSA
(HERRINGBONE —) SUMAK
SOUMAK SHEMAKA
(LATTICE —) TEE

(OPEN —) LENO BAREGE
(RUG —) RYA
WEAVER KORI TANTI WEBBE DRAWBOY WEBSTER WOBSTER PENELOPE TAPESTER
WEAVERBIRD NUN BAYA MAYA TAHA FINCH MUNIA VIDUA WEBBE BISHOP CANARY OXBIRD WHIDAH WHYDAH BENGALI AMADAVAT AVADAVAT CARDINAL MANNIKIN
WEAVING TANIKO TEXTURE WEBBING
(— MAIDEN) ARACHNE
(— OF WORDS) CONTEXT
(— TOGETHER) PLEXURE
WEAZEN WIZEN SHRINK WIZENED
WEB PLY WOB CAUL FELT MAZE TENT TOIL VANE WARP WEFT SKEIN SNARE THROW TWIST FLEECE TISSUE ENSNARE FEATHER LAYETTE TEXTURE SNOWSHOE VEXILLUM
(— IN EYE) HAW
(CRANK —) THROW
(PREF.) HIST(O) HISTI(O) HYPHO
WEBBED RINGED PALMATE
WEBBING MAT WEB PALAMA
WEB-FOOTED PALMATE PALAMATE PALMIPED
WEB SPINNER EMBIID WEBWORM
WED GET BEWED BRIDE HITCH MARRY STAKE WAGER ENGAGE PLEDGE SPOUSE ESPOUSE WEDLOCK
WEDDING BRIDAL SPLICE NUPTIAL WEDLOCK ESPOUSAL MARRIAGE
(— WORDS) IDO
WEDGE KEY COIN FROE FROW GLUT HORN KYLE PLUG SHIM STOB TRIG TRIP WAGE CHOCK CHUCK CLEAT COIGN HACEK HORSE QUINE QUOIN SCOTE SLICE THROW COTTER CUNEUS QUINET SCOTCH EMBOLUS QUINNET SCHOCHE VOUSSOIR
(— BETWEEN TWO FEATHERS) KEY
(— IN) JAM JAMB
(— OF OATMEAL) FARL FARI F
(— TO PREVENT MOTION) CHOCK
(CURVED —) CAM
(WOODEN —) COW GLUT JACK
(PREF.) CUNEI CUNEO EMBOL(O) SPHEN(O)
WEDGER SPRINGER
WEDGE-SHAPED CUNEAL SPHENIC CUNEATED SPHENOID
(PREF.) CUNEO SPHEN(O)
WEDLOCK WIFE SPOUSAL MARRIAGE SPOUSAGE
WEDNESDAY MIDWEEK
WEE TINY EARLY SMALL TEENY YOUNG LITTLE ITSYBITSY
WEED BUR HOE BURR CHOP CULL DOCK FORB LOUK SHIM SIDA TARE WEID CIGAR DRANK DRAWK DRESS DROKE FLESH BLINKS CASUAL COCKLE DARNEL JIMSON KNAWEL RIPGUT SARCLE SPURGE SPURRY STROIL ASHWORT BUGLOSS COHITRE CUCKOLD EGILOPS GARMENT GOSMORE HOGWORT RAGWEED RAGWORT RIBWORT SANDBUR TOBACCO

VERVAIN VERVINE CHADLOCK COCKSPUR COWWHEAT PIRIPIRI PLANTAIN PURSLANE TOADFLAX ALFILERIA MARIJUANA NIPPLEWORT
(— KILLER) PARAQUAT HERBICIDE
(— OUT) ROGUE
(MEXICAN —) BIRDEYE
(ROADSIDE —) PLANTAGO
(STINGING —) NETTLE
(TROUBLESOME —) KEX TITTER
(WATER —) ANACHARIS
(PL.) FILTH WRACK DISMAL SPRING WEEDAGE TRUMPERY
WEEDER SARCLER
WEEDY FOUL LANKY
WEEK OOK WOK OULK WOKE SENNET STANZA HEBDOMAD SENNIGHT
(TWO —S) FORTNIGHT
WEEKDAY FERIA WARDAY
WEEKLY AWEEK HEBDOMADAL HEBDOMADARY
WEEL LEAP POOL TRAP RIGHT WHIRLPOOL
WEEN MEAN VENE WEND FANCY GUESS EXPECT BELIEVE IMAGINE SUPPOSE CONCEIVE
WEENY TINY SMALL WEESHY
WEEP CRY ORP SOB BAWL BEND GIVE LEAK OOZE PIPE TEAR WAIL GREET BEWAIL BEWEEP BOOHOO BUBBLE LAMENT SHOWER BLUBBER LAPWING SQUINNY COMPLAIN
WEEPER GREETER MOURNER CAPUCHIN
(PL.) FLENTES
WEEPING WOP GREET MILCH RAINY BOOHOO LAMENT OOZING PIPING BLUBBER MAUDLIN TEARFUL DRIPPING LACRIMAL MADIDANS PLORATION
WEEPING SINEW GANGLION
WEEVER JUGULAR STINGBULL
WEEVIL MAX BOUD POPE WHULE PICUDO WFFRLE BILLBUG BRUCHUS VAQUITA CURCULIO WOODWORM
(PLUM —) TURK
WEFT WEB PICK WOOF BLAST FABRIC FILLING
WEIGH GO SIT HEFT PEIS TARE TELL COUNT HEAVE HOIST PEIZE POISE RAISE SCALE BURDEN PONDER ANALYZE BALANCE DEPRESS LIBRATE CONSIDER EVALUATE MEDITATE MILITATE
(— DOWN) LADE SWAY SWEE BESET HEAVY PEISE CADDLE CHARGE CUMBER PESTER DEPRESS FREIGHT INGRATE OPPRESS OVERLAY ENCUMBER
(— UPON) SIT GRIEVE
WEIGHER BOXMAN PEISER SCALER
WEIGHING METAGE
(— MACHINE) TRON SCALE TRONE
WEIGHT (ALSO SEE MEASURE AND UNIT) BOB FEN FOB KIN MAN NET OKE RAM SER SIR TOM TUP ABAS ATOM BEEF CLOG DROP GRAM HEFT IRON KITE LEAD LOAD MACE

MEAL NAIL ONUS PEIS POND PORT ROTL SEAM SEER SINK WAIT ABBAS CLOVE CRITH GARCE LIVRE MAUND PEASE PEISE PICUL POISE POIZE PRESS RIDER SCALE STAMP AUNCEL BURDEN CHARGE DIRHEM HAMMER IMPORT MOMENT MONKEY PASSIR PONDER PONDUS SINKER STRESS BALLAST DOLPHIN GRAVITY MILLIER PAYLOAD PLATINE PLUMMET POSIURE CHALDRON DEMIMARK DUMBBELL ENCUMBER FARASULA LISPOUND PRESSURE PRESTIGE QUINCUNX STANDARD STRENGTH
(— AFTER TARE DEDUCTION) SUTTLE
(— CARRIED BY HORSE) IMPOST
(— CLOTH) FLOCK
(— FOR HURLING) HAMMER
(— FOR LEAD) FOTHER FOTMAL
(— FOR PRECIOUS STONE) CARAT
(— FOR WOOL) TOD SARPLER
(— FOR WOOL, CHEESE, ETC.) CLOVE
(— OF BROADSIDE) GUNPOWER
(— OF COAL) KEEL
(— OF COFFEE) MAT
(— OF EMPTY VEHICLE) TARE
(— OF HYDROGEN) CRITH
(— OF METAL) JOURNEY
(— OF ONE 10TH TAEL) MACE
(— OF ONE 100TH TAEL) FEN
(— OF PENDULUM) BOB
(— OF PILE DRIVER) TUP
(— OF RAW SILK) PARI
(— OF SILK OR RAYON) DRAMMAGE
(— OF 100 LBS.) CENTAL CENTENA CENTNER
(— OF 1000 LIVRES) MILLIER
(— OF 20 OR 21 LBS.) SCORE
(— OF 40 BUSHELS) WEY
(— OF 5 UNCIAE) QUINCUNX
(— ON MINE SWEEPER) KITE
(— ON STEELYARD) PEA
(— ON WATCH CHAIN) FOB
(— TO BEND HOT METAL) DUMPER
(— TO DETECT FALSE COINS) PASSIR
(— TO HINDER MOTION) CLOG
(— WHICH VESSEL CAN CARRY) TONNAGE
(ABYSSINIAN —) FARASULA
(BOXER'S —) FLY HEAVY LIGHT BANTAM MIDDLE WELTER FEATHER
(CARAT —) SILIQUA
(CLOCK —) PEISE
(COUNTERFEIT —) SLANG
(FALSE —) SLANG
(GREATLY VARYING —) MAN MAUND
(HEAVY —) MONKEY
(LIGHT —) SUTTLE
(METRIC —) TONNE
(MONEYER'S —) DROIT
(ORIENTAL —) TAEL CATTY
(SASHCORD —) MOUSE
(SHUFFLEBOARD —) SHIP
(SMALL —) MITE GERAH RIDER
(SPLINE —) DOLPHIN
(UNIT OF —) SER VIS WEY GERA LAST ROTL SEER LIANG LIBRA

LINGO MINAL PECUL PERIT PIKOL KANTAR LINGOE MISKAL POCKET LISPUND PRICKLE QUINTAL ZOLOTNIK
(PREF.) BAR(I)(O)(Y) PONDERO
(SUFF.) BAR(IC)
WEIGHTED BIAS LOADED
WEIGHTER FULLER
WEIGHTLESSNESS MICROGRAVITY
WEIGHT-PRODUCING GRAVIFIC
WEIGHTY GRAVE GREAT HEAVY HEFTY MASSY SOLID VALID COGENT SOLEMN EARNEST MASSIVE ONEROUS PEISANT PESANTE SERIOUS TELLING GRIEVOUS MATERIAL POWERFUL PREGNANT PORTENTOUS SIGNIFICANT
WEIR DAM PEN CRIB KEEP LEAP STOP CAULD DOACH GARTH GORCE HATCH HEDGE SASSE STANK LASHER BURROCK MILLPOND
WEIRD ODD EERY UNCO UNKO EERIE SPACY UNCOW UNKID CREEPY SPACEY ELDRICH ELRITCH UNCANNY UNUSUAL WIZARDLY SPACEDOUT
(— SISTERS) FATES
WEIRDO NUT GEEK KOOK CREEP DINGBAT ECCENTRIC
WEITSPEKAN YUROK
WEKA RAIL WOODHEN RAILBIRD
WELCOME SEE FAIN GOOD HAIL ADOPT ALOHA CHEER GREET RESET TREAT ACCOIL INVITE SALUTE ACCLAIM ACCUEIL EMBRACE GRATIFY BIENVENU GREETING HAEREMAI PLEASANT ACCEPTABLE
WELCOMING HOMEY
WELD SHUT WELL SWAGE UNITE WOALD ACACIA
WELDED SHOT
WELDING FUSION SHUTTING
WELFARE SEL GOOD HALE HEAL SELE WEALTH BENISON BLESSING COMMONWEAL
(PUBLIC —) STATE
WELKIN SKY HEAVENS WALKENE
WELL AIN EYE GAY PIT WEL BENE FINE FLOW GOOD PANT PUIT PURE RITE SAFE SINK WINK AWEEL BOOLY BOWLY GREAT MUSHA OILER QUELL WALLY WISHA ATWEEL BUCKET CENOTE ENOUGH FAIRLY GASSER NICELY OFFSET PUMPER TUNNEL FALLWAY GRADELY HEALTHY WILDCAT BOREHOLE FOUNTAIN GRAITHLY POSTHOLE WATERPIT WEALSOME
(— AND STRONG) BUNKUM
(— IN GLACIER) MOULIN
(— THROUGH FLOORS OF WAREHOUSE) FALLWAY
(— UP) WALL WALM DIGHT
(AS —) TOO ALSO
(FAIRLY —) MIDDLING
(NONPRODUCTIVE —) DUSTER
(NOT —) DONNY SOBER INVALID
(OIL —) OILER GASSER GUSHER SPOUTER WILDCAT STRIPPER

(RECTANGULAR —) BOOLY BOWLY
(REMARKABLY—) RARELY
(SACRED — AT MECCA) ZEMZEM
(TOLERABLY —) GAYLIES GEYLIES
(VERY —) BRAWLY CLEVER
 (PREF.) BENE EU
WELL-BALANCED SOBER
WELL-BEHAVED DECOROUS GOOD
 NICE MODEST MANNERED
WELL-BEING HEAL SKIN WEAL
 HEALTH WEALTH COMFORT
 EUCRASY WELFARE EUCRASIA
 PROSPERITY
WELLBORN GENTLE EUGENIC
WELL-BRED GENTIL POLITE
 GENTEEL REFINED CULTURED
 LADYLIKE
WELL-BUILT TIGHT
WELL CASING STEANING
WELL-CHOSEN CHOICE
WELL-CONDITIONED SONSY
WELL-CONSIDERED THRIFTY
WELL CURB PUTEAL
WELL DEFINED STRICT
WELL-DISPOSED SIB FAIN GOOD
 VAIN
WELL DONE SHABASH
WELL-DRESSED BRAW GASH
 SMART BRAWLY
WELL-FED BLOWSY BLOWZY
 CHUBBY GAWCEY GAWSIE
WELL-FINISHED SOIGNE
WELL-FORMED TIGHT DECENT
 PROPER SEEMLY SHAPELY
WELL-FOUNDED VALID FIRM GOOD
 JUST SOUND WORTHY
WELL-GROOMED SMUG CRISP
 SOIGNE SOIGNEE
WELL-GROUNDED JUST VALID
WELL-GROWN THRODDY
WELL-HUSBANDED THRIFTY
WELL-INFORMED KNOWING
 PERFECT
WELL-INTENTIONED AMIABLE
WELL-KEPT SMUG POLITE
WELL-KNIT WIRY
WELL-KNOWN BREEM BREME
 BEATEN FAMOUS KENNED PUBLIC
 FAMILIAR PROMINENT
WELL-LIKED FANCIED POPULAR
WELL-MADE CLEVER FEATOUS
WELL-MANNERED GENTILE POLITE
 COURTEOUS
WELL-NIGH WELLY ALMOST
 NEARLY WELLMOST
WELL-ORDERED
 (PREF.) COSM(ETO)(ICO)(O)
WELL-ORGANIZED SNOD
WELL-PLEASED FAIN VAIN
WELL-PROPORTIONED SUING
 TRETIS HANDSOME
WELL-READ STUDIED LITERARY
WELL-ROUNDED CHUBBY
WELL-SHAPED CLEANCUT CLEVER
 FEATOUS
WELL-TILLED NOT NOTT
WELL-TO-DO ABLE BEIN BIEN EASY
 WARM PODDED
WELL-TRODDEN TRITE
WELL-WISHER FRIEND FAVORER
WELS WALLER SHEATFISH
WELSH (ALSO SEE WALES) CYMRY

FUDGE TAFFY CYMRIC KYMRIC
 CAMBRIAN
WELSHER SHICER QUITTER
WELSHMAN CELT KELT TAFFY
 BRYTHON CAMBRIAN
WELSH ONION CIBOL CIBOULE
 CHESBOLL
WELT WALE RIDGE STRIP WHELP
 WELTING BANDELET TURNOVER
 (SHOE —S) WATTIS
WELTANSCHAUUNG FAITH
 IDEOLOGY
WELTER REEL RIOT TOSS WILT
 GROVEL TUMBLE WALLOW
 WRITHE SMOTHER STAGGER
 SWELTER
 (— OF SOUNDS) DIN
WELWITSCHIA TUMBOA
WEM FLAW SCAR SPOT STAIN
WEN CYST WYNN CLIER CLYER
 TALPA TUMOR GOITER
WENCH DELL DILL DOXY DRAB GILL
 GIRL JADE MAID MOLL PRIM TRUG
 BIMBO GOUGE KITTY MADAM
 QUEAN TRULL WHORE AUDREY
 BLOUSE BLOWEN BLOWZE
 DRAZEL JILLET KITTIE MOTHER
 POPLET WOTLINK POPLOLLY
 (CLUMSY —) MODER MODDEN
 MOTHER MAUTHER
WENCHER DRABBER STRIKER
WEND BOW END SORB VEND
 STEER BETAKE DEPART DIRECT
 TRAVEL PROCEED SORBIAN
 LUSATIAN
 (— ONE'S WAY) MARK
WENT GODE LANE ROAD YEDE
 ALLEY PASSAGE
 (— ABOUT) WOLK
WENTLETRAP SCALA
WENZEL JACK
WERE (— IT NOT) SAVE
WEREWOLF TURNSKIN VERSIPEL
WERTHER (BELOVED OF —) LOTTE
WEST STY BEWEST PONENT
 OCCIDENT
WESTERN PONENT SCAEAN
 HESPERIC SANDWICH
 (PREF.) HESPER(O)
WESTERN SAMOA (CAPITAL OF —)
 APIA
 (ISLAND OF —) UPOLU MANONO
 SAVAII APOLIMA
 (MONEY OF —) TALA
WEST HIGHLAND KYLOE

WEST INDIES

ISLAND: CAT CUBA LONG ABACO
 EXUMA HAITI NEVIS PELEE TURKS
 ANDROS BAHAMA CAICOS
 CAYMAN INAGUA TOBAGO VIRGIN
 ACKLINS ANTIGUA BONAIRE
 CROOKED CURACAO GRENADA
 JAMAICA LEEWARD STKITTS
 STLUCIA TORTOLA ANGUILLA
 BARBADOS DOMINICA STTHOMAS
 TRINIDAD WINDWARD
 ELEUTHERA MARGARITA
 MAYAGUANA STVINCENT
 GUADELOUPE HISPANIOLA
 MARTINIQUE MONTSERRAT
 PUERTORICO
NATION: BARBADOS

WEST VIRGINIA

CAPITAL: CHARLESTON
COLLEGE: SALEM BETHANY
 CONCORD MARSHALL BLUEFIELD
COUNTY: CLAY WIRT BOONE
 HARDY MINGO ROANE TUCKER
 UPSHUR BARBOUR KANAWHA
INDIAN: MONETON
LAKE: LYNN
NICKNAME: MOUNTAIN
RIVER: ELK OHIO KANAWHA
 POTOMAC GUYANDOT
STATE BIRD: CARDINAL
STATE FLOWER: RHODODENDRON
STATE TREE: MAPLE
TOWN: ELKINS KEYSER RIPLEY
 VIENNA WESTON BECKLEY
 GRAFTON SPENCER WEIRTON
 FAIRMONT WHEELING

WESTWARD WESSEL OCCASIVE
 WESTLINS
WESTWARD HO (AUTHOR OF —)
 KINGSLEY
 (CHARACTER IN —) YEO JOHN LUCY
 ROSE AMYAS FRANK LEIGH DESOTO
 GUZMAN EUSTACE OXENHAM
 RICHARD GRENVILLE SALTERNE
 AYACANORA
WET DEW DIP SOP WAT ASOP DAMP
 DANK LASH MOIL SLOW SOAK
 SOFT UVID BATHE DABBY DROOK
 DRUNK HUMID JUICE JUICY LEACH
 MADID MOIST MOOTH RAINY
 SLAKE SNAPY SOBBY SOPPY
 SPEWY STEEP TIGHT WEAKY
 CLASHY DABBLE DAGGLE DAMPEN
 HUMECT IMBRUE JARBLE LABBER
 MADEFY MASHY MOISTY
 QUASHY SHOWER SLABBY
 SOBBED SPONGY SPOUTY
 SWASHY WATERY ARROUSE
 BLUBBER DRABBLE FLOTTER
 MOISTEN SLOPPED SOBBING
 SPEWING SPRINGY IRRIGATE
 SATURATE SLATTERY SLOBBERY
 SLOTTERY WATERISH
 (— AND STORMY) FOUL
 (— LIGHTLY) SPRINKLE
 (— THOROUGHLY) SOUSE DRENCH
 (DRIPPING —) ASOP
 (SLIGHTLY —) DEWY
 (SOFTLY —) SQUASHY
 (VERY —) SOPPY
 (PREF.) HYGR(O) UDO
WETHER PUR RAM HAMEL DINMAN
 DINMONT
WETNESS DANK
WETTING SOUCE SOUSE SOWSE
 MOILING
WHACK DAD LAM TRY BANG BELT
 BIFF DEAL HACK SWAK TIME
 CLONK DRIVE SHARE STATE
 SWACK WHANG CHANCE DEFFAT
 STROKE THWACK BARGAIN
 LAMBACK PORTION
WHACKING VERY WHALING
 WHOPPING EXTREMELY
WHALE SEI CETE HUEL HULL LASH
 ORCA WALL KOGIA POGGY SCRAG
 SPERM STUNT BALEEN BELUGA
 BLOWER FINNER GIBBAR KILLER

THRASH BOWHEAD DOLPHIN
 FINBACK FINFISH GIBBERT
 GRAMPUS MARSOON RIPSACK
 RORQUAL SPOUTER ZIPHIAN
 BALAENID CACHALOT CETACEAN
 DOEGLING GREYBACK HARDHEAD
 HUMPBACK JUBARTES MUTILATE
 PHYSETER THRASHER ZIPHIOID
 (— BUTCHER) LEMMER
 (— REFUSE) GURRY
 (FINBACK —) GRASO
 (HERD OF —S) GAM
 (KIND OF —) SEI MINKE KILLER
 (NEWBORN —) SUCKER
 (SCHOOL OF —S) GAM POD
 (SMALL —) MINKE
 (YOUNG —) CUB
 (PREF.) BALAENI BALAENO CETI(O)
WHALEBONE BALEEN
WHALER HEADER BUSHMAN
 SPOUTER SWAGMAN WHACKER
 WHOPPER CETICIDE
WHALESKIN MUKTUK
WHAMMY HEX
WHANG BEAT BLOW FLOG CHUNK
 THONG WHACK THRASH RAWHIDE
WHARF KEY POW DOCK GARE PIER
 QUAY SLIP BERTH JETTY LEVEE
 STADE STAITH STRAND LANDING
 PANTALAN STELLING
WHARVE WARVE WHIRL WHORL
WHAT FAT HOT HOW WET WHO
 HOOT HOTE WHEN STUFF WHICH
 MATTER PARTLY
WHATA FUTTAH FUTTER
WHAT EVERY WOMAN KNOWS
 (AUTHOR OF —) BARRIE
 (CHARACTER IN —) JOHN ALICK
 DAVID JAMES SHAND SYBIL WYLIE
 BRIERE MAGGIE CHARLES
 VENABLES TENTERDEN
WHATNOT OMNIUM ETAGERE
WHAT PRICE GLORY (AUTHOR OF
 —) ANDERSON
 (CHARACTER IN —) FLAGG QUIRT
 CHARMAINE
WHATSIT GIZMO WHATSIS
 THINGAMAJIG
WHAT'S-ITS-NAME TIMENOGUY
WHATSOEVER MORTAL
WHEAL HIVE HUEL WALE WELT
 URTICA POMPHUS
WHEAT BLE WIT CORN CONES
 EMMER FULTZ GRAIN SPELT SPICA
 TRIGO BULGUR BURGUL CEREAL
 KANRED STAPLE TURKEY EINKORN
 FORMITY FRUMETY KUBANKA
 MARQUIS POLLARD FRUMENTY
 SPELTOID
 (— BOILED IN MILK) FURMITY
 FRUMENTY
 (— MEASURE) TRUG
 (BEARDED —) RIVETS
 (CRACKED —) GROATS
 (GRANULATED —) SUJI SUJEE
 (HARD —) DURUM
 (PARCHED —) BULGUR
 (PREF.) TRITICO
WHEATCAKE PURI
WHEATEAR CHACK ARLING WITTOL
 CHACKER ORTOLAN SNORTER
 WITTALL CHICKELL SAXICOLA
WHEATGRASS BLUESTEM

WHEATLIKE VULGARE

WHEEDLE COG CANT CLAW COAX CARNY FLUFF GLOSE GLOZE INGLE JOLLY BANTER CAJOLE CUITER FLEECH GLAVER RADDLE SMOOGE WHILLY BLARNEY CUITTLE PALAVER SMOODGE TWEEDLE BLANDISH COLLOGUE SCROUNGE

WHEEDLING BUTTERY COMETHER

WHEEL BOB BUR COG FAN NUT ORB BEAD BUFF GEAR HELM HURL PURL ROLL ROTA RULL STAR TIRL WYLE ATHEY FLIER FLUFF FLYER IDLER NORIA REWET RHOMB ROWEL SWING TRUCK BILOBE CASTER CASTOR CIRCLE DRIVEN DRIVER FANNER HORRAL JAGGER KURUMA LEADER PINION ROLLER ROTATE RUNDLE RUNNER TRACER BALANCE BICYCLE CHUKKER GUDGEON LANTERN PEDRAIL PRICKER REVOLVE STEPNEY TRAILER TRILOBE TRINDLE TROCHUS TRUCKLE TRUNDLE UNILOBE WILDCAT CARACOLE FOLLOWER ODOMETER SPROCKET
(— A SKIN) FLUFF
(— CHARGED WITH DIAMOND DUST) SLITTER
(— CONTROLLING RUDDER) HELM
(— FOR EXECUTIONS) RAT
(— IN KNITTING MACHINE) BUR BURR
(— IN TIMEPIECE) BALANCE
(— OF DAY AND NIGHT) RHOMB
(— OF LIFE) ZOETROPE
(BUCKET —) LIFTER
(DIAMOND —) SKIVE
(GEAR —) DRIVEN HELICAL
(GRINDING —) SHELL
(GROOVED —) PULLEY SHEAVE SHIVER
(INTERRUPTER —) TICKER TIKKER
(LOCOMOTIVE —) DRIVER
(METAL —) FILET FILLET
(MILL —) PIRN
(PAIR OF LOGGING —S) CATYDID KATYDID
(POINTED —) TRACER
(POLISHING —) BOB BUFF SKAIF SKEIF BUFFER SCAIFE
(POTTER'S —) LATHE THROW
(PULLEY —) TRUCKLE
(ROAD-MEASURING —) AMBULATOR
(SPARE —) STEPNEY
(SPINNING —) TURN CHARKA CHARKHA
(SPUR —) ROWEL
(TANK —) BOGY BOGEY BOGIE
(TOOTHED —) GEAR PINION ROULETTE
(TURBINE —) ROTOR
(TWO PAIRS OF —S) CUTS CUTTS
(VANED —) FLIER FLYER
(WATER —) NORIA SAKIA SAKIEH SAKIYEH TYMPANUM
(PL.) KATYDID
(PREF.) CYCL(O) ROTA ROTATO ROTI ROTO TROCH(I)(LEI)(O)
(SUFF.) TROCH(A)(AL)(OUS)(US)
WHEELBARROW GURRY BARROW CARRIAGE

(PART OF —) BED LEG GRIP TIRE TRAY BRACE FRAME WHEEL HANDLE BRACKET SUPPORT

WHEELER POLER PUSHER

WHEEL-SHAPED ROTATE TROCHAL ROTIFORM

WHEELWORK MOTION
(— IN A CLOCK) MOVEMENT

WHEELWRIGHT WHEELER WOODMAN WHEELMAN

WHEEZE JOKE HOOSE HOOZE TRICK COGHLE

WHELK FILK GRUB WELT BUCKIE MAGGOT PAPULE PIMPLE WINKLE PUSTULE

WHELP CUB PUP SON CHIT FAWN PUPPY YELPER KITLING SPROCKET

WHEMMEL UPSET FUMMEL FUMMLE WHAMBLE OVERTURN

WHEN AS BUT FAN FRO GIN THO WON THAN THEN THOA TILL SINCE UNTIL ENOUGH ALTHOUGH

WHENEVER ONCE

WHERE AS FAR FUR FAUR FEAR FERRE PLACE QUAIR THERE WHITHER LOCATION
(— ABOVE MENTIONED) US

WHEREFORE WHY CAUSE FORWHY REASON

WHERENESS UBIETY

WHEREVER THERE

WHEREWITHAL MEANS MONEY RESOURCES

WHERRET BOX CUFF SLAP HURRY TEASE WORRY TROUBLE WHIRRICK

WHERRY BARGE ROWBOAT WHIRREY

WHET WET GOAD HONE TIME TURN GRIND POINT RIFLE ROUSE SLITE WHILE AROUSE EXCITE INCITE STROKE QUICKEN SHARPEN APERITIF EXACUATE

WHETHER IF GIF GIN WHAR WHERE EITHER

WHETSTONE BUR RIP RUB BUHR BURR SLIP STONE RUBBER STRAIK SHARPER WASHITA WHITTLE OILSTONE RUBSTONE STRICKLE

WHEY PALE QUAY WHIG SERUM THRUST WATERY
(PREF.) ORO

WHIBA UEBA

WHICH AS THE WHO THAT QUILK WHILK
(— SEE) QV QQV

WHICKER NEIGH WHINNY WIGHER

WHIDAH BIRD VEUVE WEAVER WHYDAH REDBILL

WHIFF FAN GUF BLOW GUFF GUST HINT PUFF TIFT WAFT WIFT FLUFF QUIFF SMOKE EXHALE MAGRIM MEGRIM WHIFFET

WHIFFLE BLOW FIFE SWAY FLICKER FLUTTER

WHIFFLETREE HEELTREE SWINGLEBAR

WHIG JOG QUIG WHEY

WHIGMALEERIE FANCY

WHILE AS BIT GAM THO YET FILE FYLE TIDE TILL WHEN WHET WOLE FILIE PIECE SPACE STEAD STOUN THROW UNTIL STOUND WHENAS

WHILOM BEGUILE TROUBLE EXERTION OCCASION SOLONGAS
(— AWAY) AMUSE FLEET DIVERT BEGUILE DECEIVE
(LITTLE —) AWEE DRASS WHILEY WHILEEN WHILOCK

WHILES UNTIL SOMETIMES

WHILLY GULL CAJOLE WHEEDLE

WHILOM ERST

WHILST TILL UNTIL

WHIM BEE FAD GIG GIN TOY FIKE FLAM KINK CRANK FANCY FLISK FOLLY FREAK HUMOR MEINY QUIRK THRUM FEGARY FITTEN MAGGOT MEGRIM SPLEEN VAGARY WHIMSY BOUTADE CAPRICE CONCEIT WRINKLE CROTCHET

WHIMBREL JACK SPOW SPOWE CURLEW MAYBIRD MAYFOWL TITTEREL

WHIMPER GIRN MEWL PULE WAIL WEAK BLEAT WHINE SIMPER WHINGE YAMMER GRIZZLE SNIFFLE SNUFFLE WHINDLE WHINNEL WHITTER WHINNOCK

WHIMSICAL FAIRY FANCY BAROCK COCKLE FLISKY NOTION QUAINT BAROQUE BIZARRE GIGGISH PUCKISH TOYSOME BIZZARRO FANCIFUL FREAKISH HUMOROUS NOTIONAL SINGULAR VAPOROUS CROTCHETY FANTASTIC PIXILATED FANTASTICAL

WHIMSY WHIM FREAK VAGARY CAPRICE WHIMWHAM

WHIN FUN ULEX FURZE WHINCOW WOODWAX

WHINCHAT TICK UTICK WHEATEAR

WHINE WOW GIRN GOWL MEWL PULE TIRM TOOT YARM YIRN BLEAT CROON MEECH QUINE TWINE WHAUP WHEWT PEENGE SNIVEL TREBLE WHINGE WINNEL YAMMER WHIMPER WHINDLE

WHINING QUERULOUS

WHINNY HINNY NEIGH PLAIN SNICKER WHICKER

WHINSTONE TRAP WHIN SCURDY

WHINYARD SWORD HANGER POCHARD WHINGER SHOVELER

WHIP CAT EEL FAN GAD ROD TAW BEAT CAST COIL DICK DUST FIRK FLOG FOAM GOAD HIDE JEHU JERK LASH LICK LOUK PLET TAWS URGE WHUP ABUSE AZOTE BASTE BIRCH CRACK FLAIL FLICK FLISK IMPEL KNOUT LEASH PLETE QUILT ROMAL SLASH STRAP SWEPE SWING SWISH TAWSE THONG THUMP AROUSE BREECH CHABUK DEFEAT FEAGUE INCITE LAINER LARRUP LICKER MAIDEN NETTLE PIZZLE QUIPPE SCUTCH SNATCH SWINGE SWITCH THRASH TICKLE CHABOUK CHICOTE COWHIDE COWSKIN CURBASH KURBASH LAMBAST LAYOVER NAGAIKA RAWHIDE SCOURGE SHINGLE SJAMBOK SLASHER TICKLER CHAWBUCK COACHMAN CONFOUND FLAGELLA KOURBASH PEPPERER BLACKSNAKE

(— EGGS) CAST
(— HANDLE) CROP
(— IN PIANO ACTION) WIPPEN
(— WITH 3 LASHES) PLET PLETE
(FURIOUS —) JEHU
(HORSE —) WAND CHABOUK
(JOCKEY'S —) BAT
(RIDING —) CROP DICK QUIRT
(RUSSIAN —) KNOUT
(PREF.) FLAGELLI MASTIG(O)
(SUFF.) MASTIX

WHIPLASH THONG COSAQUE CRACKER

WHIPPED BEATEN BROKEN DEFEATED FOUETTEE CHANTILLY

WHIPPER TICKLER THONGMAN THRASHER THREAPER

WHIPPER-IN PRICKER

WHIPPERSNAPPER SQUIRT WHIFFET WHIPSTER JACKANAPES

WHIPPING LICK TOCO TOKO HIDING CLANKER FANNING SERVING BIRCHING BROWSING SKELPING

WHIPPING POST FORK PILLAR

WHIP SCORPION GRAMPUS PHRYNID PEDIPALP WHIPTAIL

WHIPSOCKET SNEAD

WHIPSTITCH HEM SEC SEAM MINUTE INSTANT OVERCAST

WHIR BIRR ZIZZ WHIRRY

WHIRL BIRL EDDY FURL GYRE HURL PURL REEL RUSH SPIN TIRL DRILL GIDDY SKIRL SQUIR SWIRL THIRL THROW TWIRL TWIST WALTZ WHORL BUSTLE CIRCLE GYRATE HURTLE SWINGE VORTEX WHORLE WINDLE WIRBLE MIZMAZE REVOLVE TRUNDLE TURMOIL VERTICIL
(— ABOUT) DOZE GURGE
(— IN THE AIR) WARP
(— OF ACTIVITY) MERRYGOROUND

WHIRLIGIG GIG TOY SPIN TURN WHEEL FIZGIG FISHGIG

WHIRLING GIDDY WHEELY STROBIC GYRATION GYRATORY VORTICAL PIROUETTE
(PREF.) STROBO

WHIRLPOOL EDDY GULF SUCK WEEL WELL WIEL GORCE GOURD GURGE BULLER GORGES SWELTH VORTEX GURGLET SWALLOW SWILKIE SUCKHOLE MAELSTROM
(PREF.) DINO

WHIRLWIND OE DEVIL VORTEX PRESTER TORNADO TOURBILLON TOURBILLION

WHIRLYBIRD CHOPPER

WHISHT HUSH SILENCE

WHISK ZIP FISK TUFT WHID WHIP WISP CAURI FLICK FLISK HURRY SPEED SWISH CHAURI CHOWRY SWITCH COWTAIL WHISKER
(— OFF) TROUNCE

WHISKER HAIRLINE VIBRISSA
(PL.) BEARD ZIFFS WEEPER GALWAYS VIBRISSA MOUSTACHE SIDEBURNS

WHISKY RYE BOND CORN CIDER IRISH USQUE POTEEN REDEYE SCOTCH BOURBON BLOCKADE BUSTHEAD CREATURE POPSKULL USQUABAE MOONSHINE

TANGLEFOOT USQUEBAUGH MOUNTAINDEW
(GLASS OF —) RUBDOWN
(RAW —) DRUDGE

WHISPER BUZZ HARK HINT ROUN RUNE ROUND RUMOR TRACE TUTEL BREATH BREEZE HARKEN MURMUR SUSURR TITTLE WHISHT HEARKEN SUSURRUS

WHIST MORT VINT QUIET BOSTON SILENT WHEESHT

WHISTLE BLOW CALL PIPE WHEW FLUTE QUILL WHAUP WHEEP WHUTE BUMMER BUZZER CUCKOO FUSSLE HOOTER SIFFLE SISTLE SQUEAL WARBLE YELPER CATCALL TWEEDLE BIRDCALL
(— FEEBLY) WHEEDLE WHEEPLE

WHISTLE FLUTE SIFFLOT

WHISTLER PIPER MARMOT ROARER FLUTIST LAPWING SIFFLEUR

WHISTLING PIPY PIPEY ROARING SIFFLET RHONCHUS SUSSURANT

WHIT BIT JOT RAP ATOM DOIT HATE HOOT IOTA QUAT QUIT AUGHT BODLE GROAT POINT QUITE SPECK CIVITE PARTICLE TWOPENNY

WHITE CUT WAN BAWN FITE HOAR LILY PALE QUAT QUIL ASHEN BLOND HAOLE HOARY LADAN LINEN SNOWY ALBINO ARGENT BLANCH BRIGHT BUCKRA CANDID CIVITE ERMINE SILVER WINTRY CANDENT LEUCOUS NIVEOUS WHITTLE FAVORITE INNOCENT LACTEOUS
(— AND SMOOTH) IVORINE
(— OF EGG) GLAIR ALBUMEN
(— PERSON) OFAY
(POOR —) YAHOO CRACKER
(SHADE OF —) IVORY
(PREF.) ALB(I)(O) CALI CALLI LEUC(O) LEUK(O)

WHITE ALDER CLETHRA

WHITE ANT ANAY NASUTE TERMITE

WHITEBAIT SMELT ICEFISH SALANGID SALMONID

WHITEBEAM ARIA SERVICE MULBERRY

WHITEBOY PET LEVELER

WHITE BRYONY COWBIND MANDRAKE

WHITE CEDAR JUNIPER

WHITE CLOVER LADINO SHAMROCK

WHITE COMPANY (AUTHOR OF —) DOYLE
(CHARACTER IN —) JOHN MAUDE NIGEL HORDLE LORING SAMKIN ALLEYNE AYLWARD EDRICSON

WHITEFACE HEREFORD

WHITEFISH BLOAT CISCO PILOT POWAN BELUGA CHIVEY POLLAN TULIPI VENDIS BLOATER BOWBACK GWYNIAD LAVARET VENDACE BLACKFIN GREYBACK HUMPBACK MENOMINI SALMONID SCHNABEL TULLIBEE

WHITEFLY HOMOPTER MEALYWING

WHITE FRIAR CARMELITE

WHITE GUM TUART

WHITEHEAD MILIUM

WHITE-HEADED GOLDEN FAVORED FORTUNATE

WHITE HEATH BRIAR BRIER

WHITE HELLEBORE ITCHREED ITCHWEED

WHITE IPECAC ITOUBOU

WHITE LEAD CERUSE

WHITE MAPAN PIRIPIRI

WHITE MUSTARD KEDLOCK SINAPIS CRUCIFER

WHITEN CAM CAUM SCURF ALBIFY BLANCH BLANCO BLEACH BLENCH DEALBATE EMBLANCH ETIOLATE PIPECLAY

WHITENED DEALBATE

WHITENESS IVORY ALBEDO ARGENT CANDOR PURITY CANITIES PALENESS

WHITE OAK ROBLE

WHITE POPLAR ABELE ABELTREE

WHITE SNAKEROOT STEVIA POOLWORT RICHWEED WHITETOP

WHITE STURGEON BELUGA

WHITETHROAT JACK MUFF MUFTY MUGGY PEGGY EYSOGE MILLER MUFFET WHISKY WINNEL HAYSUCK WHEYBIRD

WHITEWALL TIRE

WHITEWASH LIME GLASS BLANCH PARGET STIFLE CHICAGO LIMEWASH PALLIATE

WHITEWEED DAISY

WHITE WHALE BELUGA

WHITHER GUST HURL RUSH WHIZ HURRY SHAKE WHERE FLURRY BLUSTER WHERETO

WHITING BARB HAKE CORBINA CORVINA MERLING KINGFISH MOONFISH

WHITING-POUT BIB KLEG BLENS

WHITISH BAWN PALE DILUTE SUBALBID

WHITLOW FELON AGNAIL ANCOME FETLOW BREEDER PANARIS BREDSORE RUNROUND PANARITIUM PARONYCHIA

WHITLOW GRASS DRABA NAILWORT SHADBLOW

WHITRACK WEASEL FUTTERET WHITTRET

WHITSUNDAY TERM

WHITSUNTIDE PINXTER PINGSTER PINKSTER

WHITTLE CUT PARE CARVE KNIFE STEEL TWITE EXCITE MANTLE THWITE BLANKET

WHIZ ACE BUZZ DEAL GIRL PIRR QUIZ SING WHIR ZIZZ BRAIN SOUGH WHISH WHIZZ WIZARD BARGAIN SWITHER WHIDDER WHINNER
(— KID) BRAIN GENIUS EINSTEIN
(COMPUTER —) HACKER

WHIZ-BANG EXPERT NOTABLE

WHO AS HOW THE WHA WHAT WHICH

WHOA WO WAY WHO STOP

WHOEVER WHATSO EVERWHO

WHOLE ALL HOW SUM BODY COOL EVEN HALE HALF HOLY HULL BLOCK GREAT GROSS HAILL SOLID SOUND TOTAL TOTUM TUTTA UNCUT CORPSE ENTIRE HEALED

INTACT VERSAL GENERAL INFRACT INTEGER PERFECT SINCERE SOLIDUM UNITARY COMPLETE ENSEMBLE ENTIRETY GLOBULAR INTEGRAL LIVELONG OUTRIGHT UNBROKEN
(— OF ANY ORGANISM) SOMA
(— OF REALITY) ABSOLUTE
(ORGANIC —) SYSTEM
(ORGANIZED —) GESTALT CONFIGURATION
(PREF.) ALL HOL(O) INTEGRI PAN TOTI TOTO

WHOLEHEARTED HEARTY SINCERE ZESTFUL COMPLETE IMPLICIT

WHOLESALE MASSIVE SWEEPING

WHOLESALER JOBBER EXPORTER

WHOLESOME GOOD CLEAN SOUND SWEET BENIGN SAVORY HEALTHY PRUDENT CURATIVE HALESOME HEALSOME HOMELIKE REMEDIAL SALUTARY HEALTHFUL

WHOLE-SOULED SINCERE

WHOLLY ALL FAIR FLAT HALE ONLY BLACK CLEAR FULLY QUITE STARK ALGATE BODILY FLATLY HOLLOW PURELY SOLELY ALGATES ROUNDLY SOLIDLY TOTALLY DIRECTLY ENTIRELY
(PREF.) TOTI

WHUMP CREAM

WHOOP BOOM HOOP HOOT BOOST RAISE SHOUT EXCITE HALLOO HOOPOE

WHOOPING COUGH KINKHOST CHINCOUGH PERTUSSIS

WHOP TAN WAP BEAT THUD THUMP STRIKE THRASH

WHOPPER LIE TALE SIZER BOUNCER CRUMPER SLAPPER SNAPPER SWAPPER SWINGER SCROUGER STRAPPER WALLOPER

WHOPPING VERY LARGE BANGING RAPPING WAPPING WHALING SWINGING THUMPING WHACKING WALLOPING

WHORE DRAB JILT FILTH QUAIL WENCH HARLOT PUTAIN DEBAUCH PINNACE STRUMPET SUCCUBUS PROSTITUTE

WHOREMONGER HOLOUR

WHORL TURN CYCLE SPIRE SWIRL WHIRL THWORL VOLUTE WHARVE WREATH ANNULUS CALYCLE CALYCULE GYRATION VERTICIL VOLUTION
(PREF.) SPONDYL(O) VERTICILL(I)

WHORLED (NOT —) ACYCLIC

WHORTLEBERRY HOT HURT FRAWN HOOTE FRAGHAN BILBERRY COWBERRY

WHY HOW QUI ENIGMA FORWHY HOWCOME

WICK BAD EVIL FARM TOWN ANGLE CREEK DAIRY MATCH QUICK SEAVE SNAST CORNER LIVING WICKED VILLAGE FARMSTEAD
(— CLOGGED WITH TALLOW) ROUGHIE
(LONG WAXED —) TAPER

WICKED BAD SAD DARK EVIL FAST FOUL IRON LAZY LEWD MEAN PIKY VILE BLACK CURST FELON SHREW

SORRY WRONG WROTH CURSED GUILTY LITHER LUTHER NEFAST PERDIT PITCHY SEVERE SHREWD SINFUL UNHOLY UNJUST UNLEAD UNLEDE UNWELL CAITIFF DARKSUM GODLESS HEINOUS HELLISH IMMORAL NAUGHTY NINETED NOXIOUS PRAVOUS PROFANE ROGUISH UNGODLY UNSEELY UNSOUND UNWREST VICIOUS VILLAIN ACCURSED CRIMINAL DARKSOME DEPRAVED DEVILISH DIABOLIC ENORMOUS FELONOUS FIENDISH FLAGRANT MESCHANT OBDURATE PERVERSE TERRIBLE UNKINDLY ABANDONED NEFARIOUS PERNICIOUS
(— ITEM) CANDLE
(PREF.) PONERO

WICKEDNESS ILL SIN EVIL HARM VICE CRIME FOLLY GUILT BELIAL FELONY NOUGHT UNGOOD ATHEISM DEVILRY ILLNESS PRAVITY DARKNESS DEVILTRY INIQUITY MISCHIEF SATANISM WANGRACE

WICKER SALE

WICKERWORK WEB WEEL TWIGGEN BASKETRY

WICKET GATE HOOP HATCH PITCH STUMP GUICHET
(FALLING OF —S) ROT

WICKETKEEPER STUMP STUMPER

WICKFORD POINT (AUTHOR OF —) MARQUAND
(CHARACTER IN —) JIM JOE BERG MARY ALLEN AVERY BELLA BRILL HARRY STOWE ARCHIE CALDER HOWARD WRIGHT GIFFORD SOUTHBY LEIGHTON PATRICIA CLOTHILDE

WICKIUP HUT WAKIUP SHELTER

WIDDRIM FIT FURY

WIDDY NOOSE WIDOW WITHY HALTER

WIDE FAR LAX DEEP ROOM SIDE AMPLE BROAD LARGE ROOMY SHARP SLACK WRONG ASTRAY ROOMWARD SPACEFUL SPACIOUS
(— OF) BESIDE
(— OF THE MARK) AWRY WILD ABROAD
(LONG AND —) SIDE
(PREF.) EURY LATI

WIDE-AWAKE FLY FOXY KEEN LIVE ALERT FLASH LEERY CADDIE SLIPPY KNOWING WAKEFUL WATCHFUL

WIDELY FAR BROAD ABROAD GREATLY LARGELY

WIDEN FLAN REAM DILATE EXPAND EXTEND FLANCH FLANGE FUNNEL BROADEN

WIDENESS WIDTH BREADTH

WIDESPREAD RIFE DIFFUSE GENERAL POPULAR PROLATE REGNANT CATHOLIC EXTENDED PANDEMIC SWEEPING EXTENSIVE

WIDGEON SMEE WHIM GOOSE WHEWER ZUISIN POACHER POTCHER BALDPATE BLUEBILL WHISTLER

WIDGET PART

WIDOW VID BALO DAME SKAT BLIND KITTY VEUVE WEEDA WIDDY MATRON RELICT TERCER DOWAGER EMPRESS BARONESS DOWERESS
(PL.) VIDUAGE
WIDOWED VIDUOUS
WIDOWHOOD VIDUAGE VIDUITY
WIDTH GAPE SIDE RANGE SCOPE BREADTH OPENING FRONTAGE FULLNESS LARGEOUR LATITUDE WIDENESS
(— OF CUT) KERF
(— OF HORSESHOE) COVER
(— OF PALM) HAND
(— OF PAPER) FILL
(— OF PULLEY) FACE
(— OF SHIP) BEAM
(— OF SHIP'S BAND) STRAKE
(— OF TYPE) SET
(— OF WEB) DECKLE
WIELD PLY RUN BEAR WALT WIND APPLY EXERT SWING VELDE EMPLOY GOVERN HANDLE MANAGE STRAIN CONTROL
WIELDER (— OF AUTHORITY) GAULEITER
(— OF POWER) POTENCY
WIENER FRANK HOTDOG FRANKFURTER
WIFE UX FEM HEN MRS RIB WYF BABY BIBI DAME DORA ENID FEME FERE FRAU FROW JAEL LADY MAKE MAMA MATE RANI UXOR DIRCE DONNA DUTCH FEMME LUCKY MAMMA MATCH MUJER SQUAW WOMAN ELMIRE EMILIA ESPOSA GAMMER KEEPER MATRON MISSIS MISSUS MULIER SPOUSE VENDER WAHINE BEDMATE DIONYZA EMPRESS PARTNER WEDLOCK DEIANIRA DEIDAMIA ERIPHYLE HELPMATE HELPMEET MISTRESS PECULIAR
(— OF COTTER) COTQUEAN
(— OF KNIGHT OR BARONET) DAME
(— OF MOHAMMEDAN) KHADIJA
(AFFIANCED —) FUTURE
(INDIAN'S —) WEBB
(OLD —) GAMMER
(SPEND TIME WITHOUT —) BACHIT
(PL.) PUNALUA
(PREF.) UXOR(I)
WIFTY DITSY DIZZY GIDDY INANE SILLY
WIG BOB JIZ RUG TIE FRIZ GIZZ JANE JIZZ LOCK TETE TOUR BUSBY CAXON FLASH JASEY MAJOR SCALP SCOLD ADONIS BRUTUS FROWZE MERKIN PERUKE REBUKE TOUPEE TOUPET COMBING RAMILIE SCRATCH SHEITEL SPENCER BOBJEROM CHEDREUX CHEWELER DALMAHOY NIGHTCAP PERUKERY POSTICHE ROGERIAN VALLANCY
(— WITH ROUGHLY CROPPED HAIR) BRUTUS
(BUSHY —) BUSBY
(GRAY —) GRIZZLE
(WORSTED —) JASEY
(18TH CENTURY —) ADONIS GEORGE

WIGGLE JET HOTCH JIGGLE WABBLE WANGLE
WIGGLER PUPA LARVA WRYER
WIGGY WACKO WACKY
WIGHT MAN SWIFT STRONG VALIANT CREATURE STALWART
WIGLET TOUPEE
WIGMAKER WIGGER PERUKER PERUKIER
WIGWAG SIGNAL
WIGWAM TIPI LODGE TEPEE WEEKWAM WICKIUP
WIKENO NIKENO HEILTSUK
WILD APE MAD REE SHY FAST RUDE SCAR WOWF CRAZY FANTI FELON FERAL GIDDY MYALL RANDY RANTY ROUGH ROYET SKEER WASTE DESERT FANTEE FERINE FIERCE LAVISH MADCAP NATIVE RAMAGE RANDOM RENISH SAVAGE SHANDY STORMY UNRULY BERSERK BREACHY ERRATIC FRANTIC GALLOUS GALLOWS HAGGARD HOWLING MADDING NATURAL OUTWARD RIOTOUS SKADDLE SKEERED WILDING ABERRANT AGRESTAL BARBARIC CHIMERIC DESOLATE FAROUCHE FRENETIC HALUCKET HELLICAT RECKLESS UNTILLED WARRAGAL WILLYARD BOISTEROUS
(— CARD) FREAK
(PREF.) AGRIO
WILD ASS GOUR KIANG KULAN COTULA KOULAN ONAGER QUAGGA CHIGETAI
WILD BALSAM APPLE CREEPER
WILD BEE KARBI
WILD BOAR APER SUID TUSKER SOUNDER SUIDIAN WILRONE SANGLIER
WILD BUFFALO ARNA ARNEE
WILD BUSH BEAN PHASEMY
WILD CABBAGE YELLOWS
WILD CARDAMOM RUEWORT KNOBWOOD
WILD CARROT DILL ELTROT FIDDLE BIRDNEST HILLTROT
WILDCAT CAT BALU EYRA CHATI CHAUS MANUL TIGER MARGAY SERVAL WAGATI COLOCOLA JAGUARONDI JAGUARUNDI
WILD CELERY ACHE ECHE EELGRASS SMALLAGE
WILD CHERRY GEAN MERRY MAZZARD
WILD CHERVIL KECK COWWEED HONEWORT MILKWEED
WILD CYCLAMEN SOWBREAD
WILD DOG ADJAG DHOLE DINGO GUARA AGUARA AGOUARA CIMARRON WARRAGAL
WILD DUCK (AUTHOR OF —) IBSEN
(CHARACTER IN —) GINA EKDAL SORBY WERLE HANSEN HEDVIG GREGERS HJALMAR RELLING
WILDEBEEST GNU
WILDERNESS BUSH WILD WASTE DESERT FOREST WESTERN SOLITUDE
WILD-EYED HAGGARD RADICAL
WILDFOWL VOLATILE
WILD GARLIC MOLY

WILD GERANIUM ALUMROOT DOVEFOOT FLUXWEED
WILD GOAT TUR IBEX TAHR EVECK PASAN MAZAME MARKHOR AEGAGRUS MARKHOOR
WILD HORSE BRUMBY KUMRAH TARPAN BRUMBIE WARRAGAL WARRIGAL
WILD HYACINTH CUCKOO CROWTOE GREGGLE BRODIAEA CROWFOOT
WILD INDIGO SHOOFLY BAPTISIA TUMBLEWEED
WILD LETTUCE FIREWEED
WILD MAN SAVAGE WOODMAN WOODSMAN
WILD MANGOSTEEN SANTOL
WILD MARJORAM ORGAN ORGAMY ORGANY ORIGAN OREGANO ORGAMENT
WILD MULBERRY YAWWEED
WILD MUSTARD RUNCH CHARLOCK
WILDNESS FERITY HEYDAY HEYDEY FEROCITY SAVAGERY SAVAGISM
WILD OAT DRANK DRAWK DROKE HAVER HEVER EGILOPS
WILD ONION UMBEL UMBELLA
WILD OX BUF YAK ANOA BUFF REEM UNICORN
WILD PARSLEY ELTROT HILLTROT
WILD PEAR DOGBERRY
WILD PLUM SLOE ISLAY
WILD POTATO MANROOT WAPATOO
WILD RADISH RUNCH
WILD RICE MANOMIN
WILD SAGE EYESEED
WILD SARSAPARILLA SHOTBUSH
WILDSCHUTZ, DER (CHARACTER IN —) BACULUS NANETTE EBERBACH FREIMANN GRETCHEN KRONTHAL
(COMPOSER OF —) LORTZING
WILD SERVICE TREE SORB SORBUS
WILD SHEEP SHA AUDAD URIAL AOUDAD ARGALI BHARAL NAYAUR BIGHORN MOUFLON
WILD SWAN ELK
WILD THYME HILLWORT SERPOLET
WILD TOBACCO GAGROOT SOURBUSH MARIJUANA SALVADORA
WILD TURNIP NAVEW
WILD VANILLA LIATRIS
WILE ART PAUK PAWK RUSE FRAUD GUILE TRICK ALLURE BLENCH DECEIT ENGINE ENTICE BEGUILE ARTIFICE TRICKERY
WILGA WILLOW
WILL EGO MAY ULL WAY FATE LIST TEST WISH LEAVE OUGHT SHALL WORST ANIMUS CHOICE CHOOSE DESIRE DEVICE DEVISE LEGATE LIKING QUETHE SCRIPT CODICIL PASSION WITWORD AMBITION APPETITE BEQUEATH PLEASING PLEASURE VOLITION
(— NOT) WONT WINNA WONNA WUNNA WONNOT
(— NOT TO DO) NOLITION
(— OF DEITY) DECREE
(— OF GOD) LAW

(— OF LEGISLATURE) ACT
(— TO LIVE) TANGHA
(FREE —) ACCORD
(GOOD —) GREE
(I —) CHILL
(ILL —) ARR ENVY HEST VENOM ANIMUS ENMITY HATRED UNTHANK AMBITION
(KIND OF —) LIVING
(SUFF.) (CONDITION OF —) THYMIA
(STATE OF —) BOULIA BULIA BULIC
WILLET TATLER TATTLER
WILLFUL HEADY WILLY FEISTY UNRULY HAGGARD WAYWARD WILSOME CAMSTRARY
WILLFULLY WOLDES SCIENTER
WILLIAM TELL (AUTHOR OF —) SCHILLER
(CHARACTER IN —) JOHN TELL FURST HENRY ARNOLD BERTHA ULRICH WALTER WERNER GESSLER WILLIAM MATHILDE BAUMGARTEN
(COMPOSER OF —) ROSSINI
WILLIES JUMPS CREEPS
WILLING BAIN FAIN FREE GAME GLAD LIEF RATH PRONE READY MINDED TOWARD CONTENT OBLIGING UNFORCED
(— TO FORGIVE) PACABLE PLACABLE
WILLINGLY LIEF SOON FREELY GLADLY LIEFLY FRANKLY READILY
(MORE —) RATHER
WILLINGNESS HEART FREEDOM FAINNESS
(— TO FIGHT) DEFIANCE
WILLIWAW STORM WOOLLY TEMPEST
WILLOW DULY ITEA SALE WYLW OSIER SALEW SALIX SAUGH WIDDY WITHY WOODY DUSTER SALLOW TEASER TWILLY WITHEN WUDDIE
(— FOR THATCHING) SPRAYS
(— IN TEXTILES) WOLF
(NATIVE —) COOBA COOBAH
(SIMPLE —) WHIPPER
(PREF.) (— TWIG) LYGO
WILLOWER DULER DUSTER TEASER WILLIER
WILLOW HERB WICOPY EPILOBE FIRETOP PIGWEED ROSEBAY BURNWEED FIREWEED
WILLOW WARBLER SMEU SMEUTH MUDDLER TROCHIL OVENBIRD
WILLOW WREN PEGGY
WILLOWY SUPPLE SLIPPER DELICATE
WILLY-NILLY PERFORCE
WILSON'S PLOVER COLLIER
WILSON'S SNIPE JACK SHADBIRD
WILSON'S TERN MEDRICK
WILSON'S THRUSH VEERY
WILT EBB SAG DROP FADE FLAG WELK DROOP SUCCUMB COLLAPSE
WILTED EMARCID
WILY SLY FOXY CANNY SLICK ARTFUL ASTUTE CLEVER CRAFTY QUAINT SHREWD STALKY SUBTLE TRICKY CUNNING POLITIC VERSUTE WINDING SERPENTINE
WIMBLE BORE AUGER BRISK ACTIVE

GIMLET LIVELY NIMBLE WIBBLE WUMMEL

WIMP NERD

WIMPLE BEND WIND CURVE TWIST GORGET RIPPLE MEANDER WIMLUNGE

WIN BAG COP HIT DRAW GAIN HAVE LAND LICK FORCE SCORE ATTACH CLINCH OBTAIN ACHIEVE ACQUIRE CONQUER DESERVE HARVEST POSSESS TRIUMPH DECISION OVERCOME STRAIGHT
(— AGAINST) BREAK SCOOP
(— AT CHESS) MATE CHECKMATE
(— AWAY) STEAL DEBAUCH
(— BACK) RECOVER
(— BY GUILE) GET POT BEAR CARRY RAISE TRAIN GATHER CAPTURE INVEIGLE PROMERIT
(— EASILY) ROMP
(— EVERY MATCH) SWEEP
(— NARROWLY) SQUEEZE
(— OVER) DEFEAT DISARM NOBBLE
(— OVERWHELMINGLY) SWEEP
(— SKILLFULLY) SNARE
(WRESTLING —) PIN

WINCE KICK CHECK QUECH CRINGE FLINCH QUATCH QUINCH QUITCH RECOIL SHRINK

WINCH CRAB JACK REEL WINK GIPSY WINZE ROLLER WHIMSY WINDLE CATHEAD TRAVELER VARIABLE WINDLASS

WIND AIR COP LAP BALL BIRR BISE BIZE COIL CONE CURL EAST FIST FLAW FOHN GALE GUST KINK PUFF PUNO ROLL WEST WRAP BATCH BLAST BLORE CRANK CREEK CROOK FOEHN QUILL SPOOL STORM TRADE TREND TWINE TWIST WEAVE WITHE BOTTOM BOUGHT BREEZE BUSTER CAURUS COLLAR KECKLE SHAMAL SPIRAL SPIRIT SQUALL WAMPLE WESTER ZEPHYR BREATHE CRANKLE CRINKLE CYCLONE ENTWINE EQUINOX ETESIAN GREGALE INVOLVE MEANDER MISTRAL SERPENT SINUATE TEMPEST TWINGLE TWISTER WEATHER WHIRLER WINDILL ARGESTES DOWNWARD EASTERLY FAVONIUS
(— ABEAM) LASK
(— ABOUT) WIRE SNAKE
(— AFTER DYEING) BATCH
(— DOWN) RELAX UNWIND
(— FROM THE ANDES) ZONDA PAMPERO
(— IN AND OUT) INDENT WINGLE
(— MAGNETS) COMPOUND
(— OF ARGENTINA) ZONDA PAMPERO
(— OF CUBA) BAYAMO
(— OF HAWAII) KONA
(— OF OREGON AND WASHINGTON) CHINOOK
(— OF TUNISIA) CHILE CHILI CHILLI
(— ROPE) WORM WOOLD
(—S OF CHILE AND PERU) SURES
(— THREAD OR YARN) QUILL CHEESE
(— TO PREVENT CHAFING) KECKLE
(— WOOL) TREND

(— YARN) BEAM SERVE WINDLE
(ADRIATIC —) BORA
(BREAKING —) FIST
(BROKEN —) HEAVES
(COLD —) BISE BIZE BORA SARSAR BLIZZARD
(COOLING —) IMBAT
(DEAD —) NOSER
(DESERT —) SAMUM GIBLEH SAMIEL SIMOOM SIMOON KHAMSIN SIROCCO SCIROCCO
(DRYING —) TRADE
(EASTERLY —) LEVANT LEVANTER
(FIERCE —) BUSTER
(GUST OF —) FLAN FLAW
(HAWAIIAN WINTER —) KONA
(HEAD —) NOSER MUZZLE
(HIGH —) RIG
(HOT —) CHILI GIBLEH SAMIEL SOLANO CHAMSIN KHAMSIN SIROCCO SCIROCCO
(LIGHT GENTLE —) BREEZE
(MOUNTAIN —) PUNA
(NORTH —) BISE AQUILO BOREAS AQUILON MISTRAL
(NORTHEAST —) BURAN GREGALE
(NORTHWEST —) CAURUS MAESTRO ARGESTES
(OF —) EOLIAN VENTAL AEOLIAN
(PERIODICAL —) ETESIAN MONSOON
(PERSIAN GULF —) SHAMAL SHARKI SHIMAL
(PERUVIAN —) PUNA PUNO
(ROARING —) BLORE
(SEVERE —) SNIFTER
(SOUTH —) NOTUS AUSTER
(SOUTHEAST —) EURUS SOLANO
(SOUTHEASTERLY —) SHARKI SHURGEE
(SOUTHWEST —) CHINOOK LIBECCIO
(STRONG —) BIRR
(VIOLENT —) BUSTER SQUALL SNORTER
(WARM —) FOHN FOEHN CHINOOK SANTANA
(WEST —) ZEPHYR FAVONIUS ZEPHYRUS
(WHISTLING —) SARSAR
(PREF.) ANEM(O) AURO VENTI VENTO
(SOUTH —) AUSTRO

WINDAGE DRIFT

WIND-BORNE EOLIC EOLIAN AEOLIAN

WINDER REEL WINCH DRUMMER PLUGGER SKEINER SPOOLER TENDRIL

WINDFALL VAIL GRAVY MANNA CADUAC FALLING BLOWDOWN BUCKSHEE

WINDGALL PUFF WINDDOG

WINDING LINK MAZY CRANK LACET SPIRE CREEKY DETOUR GYRATE SCREWY SPIRAL TWISTY WANLAS CRANKLE CRINKLE DEVIOUS MEANDER SINUATE SINUOSE SINUOUS SNAKING WRIGGLY WRINKLE SINUATED TORTUOUS MEANDERING
(PL.) AMBAGES RADDLINGS

WINDING-SHEET SHROUD SUDARY CEREMENT

WINDING STAIR COCKLE COCLEA WINDER COCHLEA

WIND INSTRUMENT
(PREF.) AEOLO

WINDLASS CRAB REEL WINK FEARN WINCH STOWCE STOWSE TACKLE TURNEL WINDAS WINDLE TWISTER WILDCAT ARTIFICE DRAWBEAM MANEUVER

WINDMILL JUMBO MOTOR COPTER PINWHEEL
(— ARM) VANE
(— BAR) UPLONG
(— SAIL) AWE EIE EIGHE FLIER FLYER SWEEP SWIFT
(PART OF —) BAR CAP FAN AXLE CORD HEEL LINE SAIL WHIP BLADE ROTOR STOCK SWEEP TOWER FANTAIL HELMATH CANNISTER WINDSHAFT

WINDOW BAY EYE LOOP ROSE SASH SLIT SLOT CHAFF GLAZE GRILL INLET LIGHT OGIVE SIGHT THURL AWNING DORMER GRILLE LANCET PEEPER ROSACE SPLITE THURLE WICKET BALCONE COUPLET DORMANT FENSTER GUICHET LUTHERN MIRADOR ORIFICE TRANSOM VENTANA WINDOCK WINNOCK CASEMENT FANLIGHT FENESTER FENESTRA JALOUSIE VENETIAN
(— IN ROOF) SKYLIGHT
(— OF TWO LIGHTS) COUPLET
(BAY —) ORIEL MIRADOR
(BLANK —) ORB
(BLIND —) ORB
(CHURCH —) LYCHNOSCOPE
(CRESCENT-SHAPED —) LUNETTE
(DORMER —) OXEYE DORMANT LUCARNE LUTHERN
(HIGH NARROW —) LANCET
(OVAL —) OXEYE
(PART OF —) BEAD JAMB LOCK PANE RAIL SASH STOP YOKE APRON FRAME SKIRT STILE STOOL STRIP CASING MUNTIN BRICKMOLD WINDOWPANE COUNTERWEIGHT
(POINTED —) OGIVE
(ROUND —) OXEYE OCULUS ROUNDEL
(SEMICIRCULAR —) FANLIGHT
(SMALL LOW —) MEZZANINE
(TICKET —) GRILLE GUICHET
(TWIN —) AJIMEZ
(PL.) STORMS

WINDOW DRESSING TRIM FRONT FACADE

WINDOW FRAME SASH REVEAL

WINDOW OYSTER COPIS

WINDOWPANE LIGHT LOZEN QUIRK LOZENGE TATTERSALL

WINDOWSILL SOLE

WINDPIPE HALS ARBER ARBOR ERBER HALSE WIZEN ARTERY GUGGLE STROUP WEEZLE KEACORN TRACHEA WEASAND THRAPPLE THROPPLE THROTTLE
(PREF.) BRONCH(I)(IO)(O) TRACHE(O) TRACHO TRACHY

WINDROW BANK HEAP RIDGE SWATH SWATHE

WINDSOR CHAIR FANBACK

WINDSTORM BLOW BURA THUD BURAN BOURRAN
(HAWAIIAN —) KONA

WINDWARD ALOOF WEATHER AWEATHER
(— SIDE) KOOLAU

WINDY BLOWY EMPTY GASSY GUSTY HUFFY PROUD STARK SWALE FLIMSY STORMY WONDIE BREATHY FEARFUL GUSTFUL NERVOUS VENTOSE VIOLENT BOISTEROUS
(— CITY) CHICAGO

WINE CUP VIN BOIS BUAL CUIT CUTE DEAL PALM PORT RAPE ROSE ROSY TENT TYRE VINO CAPRI GRAPE KRAMA LUNEL MEDOC PETER PLONK PORTO RIOJA SCIAN SHRAB SOAVE TINTO TOKAY VINUM WHITE BAROLO BARSAC CORTON COUTET GRAVES KIJAFA LISBON MASDEU PIMENT ROCHET SAUMUR SHIRAZ SOLERA TIVOLI ALICANT AMBONNA BACCHUS BANYULS BARBERA BASTARD CATAWBA CHACOLI CHATEAU DEZALEY FALERNO MARSALA MISSION MOSELLE ORVIETO PALERMO PIGMENT RHENISH ROSOLIO SERCIAL SILLERY VERNAGE VIDONIA VINTAGE APERITIF BORDEAUX BURGUNDY CHARNECO DELAWARE LACHRYMA LIBATION MALVASIA MARSALLA MOUNTAIN RIESLING ROCHELLE RULANDER RUMBOOZE SPARKLER BARDOLINO LAMBRUSCO ZINFANDEL
(— AND PUNCH) GLOGG
(— BOILED WITH HONEY) MULSE
(— CHEST) TANTALUS
(— FROM VINEGAR) ESILL
(— MIXED WITH WATER) KRASIS
(— OF EXCELLENT QUALITY) VINTAGE
(— OF SACRAMENT) BLOOD
(— SELLER) ABKAR BISTRO WINARE
(— SERVING) VOIDEE
(AROMATIZED —) DUBONNET
(BANANA —) MARAMBA
(BULK —) CUVEE
(CONSECRATED —) CUP
(DRY WHITE —) SANCERRE
(FIRST-GROWTH —) LAFITE LAFITTE
(FRANCONIAN —) STEIN LEISTEN
(GREEK —) RUMNEY RETSINA RESINATA
(HEATED —) WHITEPOT
(INFERIOR —) PLONK
(JAPANESE —) SAKI
(KIND OF —) JUG POP BLUSH
(LIGHT —) BUAL CAPRI BAROLO CANARY
(MULLED —) NEGUS WASSAIL GLUHWEIN
(NEW —) MUST
(NEW — BOILED DOWN) CUIT CUTE
(PALM —) SAGWIRE
(RED —) ZIN GAMAY MACON TINTA BAROLO BEAUNE CLARET MERLOT

CHIANTI HOLLOCK POMMARD ALICANTE BURGUNDY CABERNET FLORENCE BARDOLINO ZINFANDEL
(REVIVED —) STUM
(RHINE —) HOCK SYLVANER
(SPANISH —) SACK TENT DULCE RIOJA OPORTO SHERRY ALICANT ALIKANT BASTARD TARRAGONA
(STILL —) PONTAC PONTACQ
(SWEET —) TYRE DULCE MULSE CANARY BASTARD MALMSEY CHARNECO MUSCATEL
(TENT —) TINTO
(TOKAY —) ESSENCE
(TUSCAN —) VERDEA CHIANTI FLORENCE
(WHITE —) HOCK SACK CAPRI CASEL FORST BARSAC MALAGA BROMIAN CATAWBA CHABLIS CONTHEY LANGOON ANGELICA BUCELLAS MUSCADET RIESLING SANCERRE SAUTERNE VERMOUTH MEURSAULT VERDICCHIO
(WHITE — APERITIF) KIR
(PL.) PALUS
(PREF.) ENO OEN(O) OINO VINI VINO
WINEBERRY MAKO MAKOMAKO
WINEGLASS FLUTE
WINEGROWER WINER VIGNERON
WINESBURG OHIO (AUTHOR OF —) ANDERSON
(CHARACTER IN —) JOHN KATE WING DAVID HARDY HELEN JESSE REEFY SWIFT WHITE CURTIS GEORGE LOUISE BENTLEY HARTMAN WILLARD TRUNNION ELIZABETH BIDDLEBAUM
WINESHOP BISTRO BODEGA
WINE-VAULT SHADE
WING ALA ARM ELL FAN FLY OAR RIB VAN AILE FORE JAMB SAIL TAIL ALULA ANNEX BLOCK FLANK JAMBE PINNA POINT SHEAR VOLET BRANCH FLETCH FLIGHT HALTER PENNON PINION POISER DEMIVOL ELYTRON ELYTRUM AEROFOIL BALANCER DISPATCH TORMENTOR
(— OF ARMY) HORN
(— OF BUILDING) ELL JAMB JAMBE ALETTE ALLETTE FLANKER
(— OF SHELL) AURICLE
(— OF THEATER) COULISSE TORMENTOR
(— OF TRIPTYCH) VOLET
(—S DISPLAYED) VOL
(BASTARD —) ALULA
(BIRD'S —) FLAG
(FLY'S —S) HALTERES
(KIND OF —) DELTA SINGLE
(PL.) PENS FEATHERS
(PREF.) ALI PTER(O) PTERIDO PTERYG(O) PTERYLO PTIL(O)
(SUFF.) PTERA PTERIS PTEROUS PTERUS PTERYX
WING CASE SHEATH ELYTRON
(BEETLE'S —) SHARD
WINGDING GALA
WINGED AILE ALATE LOFTY RAPID SWIFT ALATED PENNED PENNATE ELEVATED
(PREF.) PTENO
(SUFF.) PTENE

WINGED DISK FEROHER
WINGED ELM WAHOO
WING-FOOTED FLEET SWIFT ALIPED
WINGLESS APTERAL
WING-LIKE ALARY ALIFORM PTEROID PTERTGOID
WING SHELL STROMB ELYTRON STROMBUS
WINGS OF THE DOVE (AUTHOR OF —) JAMES
(CHARACTER IN —) CROY KATE MARK MILLY MERTON THEALE DENSHER
WINGTIP SHOE
WINK BAT NAP PINK BLINK DEATH FLASH PRINK SLEEP TWINK CONNIVE FLICKER INSTANT NICTATE SPARKLE TWINKLE NICTITATE
WINKER EYE BLINKER EYELASH
WINKING BLINK
WINKLE PERIWIG TWINKLE
WINNER PLACER VICTOR FACEMAN BANGSTER
(EASY —) SHOOIN
(NOT A —) ALSORAN
(SURE —) SNIP
WINNIE-THE-POOH (AUTHOR OF —) MILNE
(CHARACTER IN —) ROO KANGA ROBIN EEYORE PIGLET RABBIT HEFFALUMP CHRISTOPHER
WINNING GAIN SWEET PROFIT GAINING VICTORY WINSOME CHARMING
(— OF ALL TRICKS) CAPOT SCHWARZ
(PL.) WIN VELVET
WINNOW FAN WIM CHAR SIFT WIND DIGHT SIEVE DELETE REMOVE SELECT WINDER SEPARATE
WINNOWER VAN WINDER DIGHTER
WINSOME GAY BUXOM SWEET CHARMING CHEERFUL PLEASANT
WINTER BISE SNOW YEAR HIEMS HIVER DECEMBER HIBERNATE
(— AILMENT) STREP
(— OVER) HOG
WINTERBERRY PRINOS HOOPWOOD
WINTERBLOOM AZALEA
WINTERGREEN JINKS CHINKS PYROLA DRUNKER BOXBERRY DRUNKARD EYEBERRY GAYWINGS IVYBERRY LIMONIUM RATSBANE SHINLEAF TEABERRY PINEDROPS PIPSISSEWA
WINTERLIKE BRUMAL
WINTERSET (AUTHOR OF —) ANDERSON
(CHARACTER IN —) MIO CARR GARTH GAUNT TROCK ESDRAS SHADOW ROMAGNA MIRIAMNE BARTOLOMEO
WINTER'S TALE (AUTHOR OF —) SHAKESPEARE
(CHARACTER IN —) DION MOPSA DORCAS EMILIA CAMILLO LEONTES PAULINA PERDITA FLORIZEL HERMIONE ANTIGONUS AUTOLYCUS

CLEOMENES MAMILLIUS POLIXENES ARCHIDAMUS
WINTRY AGED COLD WHITE BOREAL HIEMAL STORMY BRUMOUS CHILLING HIBERNAL
WINTUN COPEHAN
WINY VINOUS DRUNKEN
WINZE CURSE RAISE OPENING PASSAGEWAY
WIPE BEAT BLOW DRUB DUST GIBE DICHT DIGHT SWIPE CANCEL SPONGE SPUNGE STRIKE ABOLISH CLEANSE ABSTERGE SQUEEGEE
(— BEAK OF HAWK) FEAK
(— NOSE) SNITE
(— OFF) SCUFF
(— OUT) ERASE SCRUB SWEEP EFFACE DESTROY
(— UP) SWAB SWOB
WIPEOUT MASSACRE
WIPER DUSTER TRIPPET
WIPING TERSION
(— OF INK ON PLATE) RETROUSSAGE
(— OUT) EXTINCTION
WIRE GUY TAP BINE CORE DENT DRAG FILE FUSE PURL BRACE CABLE OUTER RISER SNAKE SWEEP TAPER BRIDGE FESCUE FINGER HEATER JUMPER NEEDLE STAPLE STOLON STRAND DROPPER HAYWIRE LAMETTA LASHING PRICKER SHIFTER SNUFFER FILAMENT LIGATURE PALISADE PULLDOWN STRINGER TELEGRAM
(— BETWEEN TWO VESSELS) SWEEP
(— FASTENED TO TEETH) BRACES
(— FOR CUTTING CLAY) SLING
(— FOR SUSTAINING HAIR) PALISADE
(— HOLDING SPOOL) SPIT
(— IN BLASTING CAP) BRIDGE
(— IN CATHETER) STYLET
(— IN WEAVING LOOM) DENT
(— OF GOLD, SILVER OR BRASS) LAMETTA
(—S BOUND TOGETHER) SELVAGE
(— TO ADJUST WICK) SNUFFER
(— TO CLOSE A BREAK) JUMPER
(— TO REMOVE TUMORS) LIGATURE
(— USED AS POINTER) FESCUE
(— USED IN SPLICING CABLES) TAPER
(ENAMELED —) LITZ
(FENCE —) DROPPER
(FRAYED —) JAGGER
(GOLD —) KINSEN
(LOOPED —) OESE
(PALLET —) PULLDOWN
(PRIMING —) PICKER EPINGLETTE
(SURGICAL —) STYLET
(TWISTED —) HEALD HEADLE HEDDLE
(VENT —) PRICKER
(4 —S TWISTED TOGETHER) QUAD
WIRE CUTTER SECATEUR
WIREDRAW WREST OUTWIT DEFRAUD DISTORT ELONGATE
WIREGLASS FLUTE
WIRE GRASS POA

WIRELESS RADIO
WIRE ROPE JACKSTAY
WIRETAP BUG
(REMOVE —) DEBUG
(REMOVE — DEVICE) DEBUG
WIREWORM ELATER ELATERID MILLIPEDE
WIRY THIN HARDY STIFF WITHY FEEBLE KNOTTY SINEWY STRINGY THREADY
WIS KNOW THINK SURELY SUPPOSE

WISDOM WIT LORE SABE SABBY SAVEY SENSE SOPHY ADVICE GNOSIS HOKMAH POLICY SATTVA SOPHIA WISURE CUNNING MINERVA SAGESSE SLEIGHT AFTERWIT JUDGMENT PRUDENCE SAPIENCE
(DIVINE —) WORD THEOMAGY
(ESOTERIC —) GNOSIS
(SUPREME —) PRAJNA
(UNIVERSAL —) PANSOPHY
(PREF.) SOPH(O) SOPHI(O)
(SUFF.) SOPH(ER)(IC)(IST)(Y)
WISE HEP SLY DEEP GASH GOOD KIND SAGE SANE SEND TURN CANNY FRESH GUIDE SMART SOUND WITTY ADVISE CRAFTY DIRECT QUAINT WITFUL WITTER ANCIENT ERUDITE GNOSTIC KNOWING LEARNED POLITIC PRUDENT SAPIENT THRIVEN PERSUADE PROFOUND SENSIBLE SPACIOUS
(— GUY) SAGE SOLON
(— MAN) MAGI SAGE MAGUS AMAUTA ORACLE
(— ONE) OWL
(PREF.) SOPH(O) SOPHI(O)
(SUFF.) SOPH(ER)(IC)(IST)(Y)
WISEACRE SAGE DUNCE GOTHAM SOLONIST WISEHEAD WISELING
WISECRACK JOKE QUIP
WISE CRACK GASSER
WISENT BISON AUROCH UROCHS BONASUS
WISH CARE GIVE GOAL HOPE LIST LUST MIND VOTE WANT WILL

BOSOM COVET CRAVE DREAM HEART TASTE VOICE DESIRE UTINAM FAREWELL GODSPEED PLEASURE
(— **OTHERWISE**) REGRET
(**DEATH** —) DESTRUDO
(**EARNEST** —) VOW
(**SLIGHT** —) VELLEITY
WISHBONE FURCULA FOURCHET FURCULUM MERRYTHOUGHT
WISHFUL EAGER HOPEFUL LONGING ALLURING
WISHING ANXIOUS DESIROUS
WISHY-WASHY PALE THIN WEAK BLAND VAPID FEEBLE DILUTED INSIPID SLIPSLOP
WISKET BASKET WHISKET
WISP TATE WUSP SCRAP SHRED SKIFF SKIFT TWIST RUMPLE CRUMPLE MASSAGE
(— **OF HAY**) RISP
(— **OF STRAW**) WAP WASE DOSSIL
(— **OF THATCH**) TIPPET
WISPY FRAIL NEBULOUS
WISTERIA FUJI KRAUNHIA
WISTFUL INTENT PENSIVE WISHFUL MOURNFUL YEARNING
WISTITI WISTIT MARMOSET
WIT VAT VIT WAG KNOW NOUS SALT BRAIN HUMOR IRONY SENSE THINK WHITE WOTTE ACUMEN ESPRIT POLICY SANITY SATIRE WISDOM CONCEIT CUNNING PICADOR SARCASM SUPPOSE THINKER WITWORM BADINAGE REPARTEE
(**BITING** —) DICACITY
(**TO** —) NAMELY SCILICET
(**PL.**) SCONCE BUTTONS
WITCH ALP ANI HAG HEG HEX MARE SAGA TRAT WYCH BRUJA BUTCH GREBE HEXER LAMIA SIBYL WEIRD WIGHT ASUANG CARLEY CANDLIN CUMMER DOWSER DUESSA HECATE KIMMER PILWIZ WIZARD AGANICE CANIDIA CARLINE HAGGARD HELLCAT SYCORAX BABAJAGA CAROLINE ERICHTHO SORCERER SPAEWIFE VERSIERA WALKYRIE
(**HOME OF** —) ENDOR
(**MEETING OF** —**S**) ESBAT
(**PL.**) COVEN
WITCHCRAFT CHARM GOETY OBEAH WICCA CUNNING HEXEREI MYALISM SORCERY BRUJERIA DEVILTRY PISHOGUE WIZARDRY
WITCH DOCTOR BOCOR BOKOR GOOFER GUFFER
WITCHERY CHARM SPELL SORCERY SORTIARY
WITCHES'-BROOM STAGHEAD
WITCHGRASS COUCH PANIC PANICLE
WITCH HAZEL FOTHERGILLA
WITE WAT BLAME FAULT WAYTE CENSURE REPROACH HAMESOKEN
WITH BY CUM MID MIT WUD AVEC CHEZ DOWN AMONG ANENT WIGHT AGAINST
(— **HAND ON HIP**) AKIMBO
(— **REGARD TO**) ABOUT
(— **SPEED**) TIVY

(**PREF.**) CO COL COM CON COR META SYM SYN
WITHDRAW GO COY DROP TAKE AVOID DEMIT FREAK LOOSE REVEL SHIFT START UNSAY CHANGE DECEDE DESERT DETACH DETRAY DEVOID EFFACE FLINCH MINISH RECALL RECANT RECEDE RETIRE REVOKE ROGATE SECEDE SHRINK SINGLE SYPHON ABSCOND CONCEAL DESCEND DETRACT FORSAKE INVEIGH RETRACT RETREAT SCRATCH SCUTTLE SECLUDE SUBDUCE SUBDUCT TURNOFF UNSCREW SEPARATE SUBTRACT SEGREGATE SEQUESTER
(— **ATTENTION**) PRESCIND
(— **FROM**) VAIK ABANDON
(— **FROM COMPETITION**) SCRATCH
(— **FROM POKER POT**) DROP
(— **FROM REALITY**) FREAK
(— **FROM USE**) MOTHBALL
(— **SUPPORT**) ABANDON
(— **TEMPORARILY**) STOPOUT
(— **WITHIN**) INVAGINATE
WITHDRAWAL DRAIN FLIGHT HIDING OFFLAP RETIRE SHRINK ABSENCE DUNKIRK PULLOUT REGRESS RETIRAL RETREAT SCUTTLE RECESSION REVULSION RETRACTION
(— **FROM WORLDLY THINGS**) ABSTRACTION
(— **OF BUILDING FACE**) SETBACK
(— **OF PROMISE**) BACKWORD
(— **OF SUIT**) RETRAXIT
WITHDRAWN SHY ASOCIAL INGROWN SECLUSE DISTRAIT ISOLATED SECLUDED RECESSIVE ABSTRACTED
WITHE HANK ROPE TIER TWIG WITHY WATTLE WICKER CHINULL
WITHER BURN DAZE FADE MIFF PINE RUST SEAR STUN WARP WELK WELT BLAST CLING DAVER DECAY QUAIL WIZEN COTTER GIZZEN SHRINK WALLOW WELTER WILTER WINDER AREFACT DECLINE FORWELK SENESCE SHRIVEL LANGUISH PARALYZE
WITHERED DRY ARID SEAR SERE CORKY SCRAM MARCID BLASTED UNGREEN WEARISH WIZENED AUTUMNAL
WITHERING SCATHING
WITHHELD DEFERRED SUSPENSE
WITHHOLD CURB DENY HIDE KEEP STOP CHECK SCANT ABSENT DEPORT DETAIN REFUSE RETAIN ABSTAIN BOYCOTT DEFORCE FORBEAR OUTHOLD REPRESS RESERVE SUSPEND RESTRAIN SUBTRACT
(— **CONSENT**) DECLINE
WITHHOLDING DETAINER
(— **OF DUES**) CHECKOFF
(**CONDITIONAL** —) SUSPENSION
WITHIN IN ON BEN BIN INBY INLY INTRA ABOARD HEREIN INSIDE INWITH INDOORS ENCLOSED INCLUDED INWARDLY

(**PREF.**) END(O) ENT(O) ESO IL IM IN INFRA INTER INTRA INTRO
(**ARISING** —) IDIO
WITHOUT EX BUT OUT SEN BOUT FREE OHNE SANS SINE MINUS SENZA FAILING OUTSIDE WANTING INNOCENT OUTDOORS
(— **ACCENT**) ENCLITIC
(— **ACTION**) DEEDLESS
(— **A FLANGE**) BALD
(— **A MATE**) ODD
(— **BEGINNING OR END**) ETERNAL
(— **BLEMISH**) CHOICE
(— **BRIGHTNESS**) LACKLUSTER
(— **CONTENTS**) INANE
(— **DELAY**) AWAY FOOTHOT SUMMARY
(— **DELIBERATION**) HEADLONG
(— **EFFECT**) EMPTY INSIGNIFICANT
(— **EMOTION**) DRYLY DULLY
(— **END**) ENTERNAL
(— **EXCEPTION**) ALWAYS
(— **FEET**) APOD
(— **FUNDS**) CLEAN
(— **HORNS**) ACEROUS
(— **INTEREST**) BARREN
(— **LIFE**) DULL AZOIC INANIMATE
(— **LIGHT**) APHOTIC
(— **LIMITS OF DURATION**) AGELESS
(— **MONEY**) IMPECUNIOUS
(— **ORDER**) ANYHOW
(— **PAYMENT**) FREE
(— **POWER**) ADRIFT
(— **PROFIT**) FRUITLESS
(— **QUALIFICATION**) FLAT
(— **QUESTION**) EASILY SECURELY
(— **REALITY**) AIRY
(— **REASON**) BLINDLY
(— **REMEDY**) BOOTLESS
(— **ROADS**) INVIOUS
(— **RULE OR LAW**) ANARCHIC
(— **SADDLES**) ASELLATE
(— **SALT**) FRESH
(— **SHAME**) BROWLESS
(— **SIN**) IMPECCANT
(— **STRENGTH**) MEAGER MEAGRE MORNE
(— **THORNS**) INERM
(— **WINGS**) APTEROUS
(**PREF.**) A ECT(O) LIPO
(— **GOVERNMENT**) ANARCH(O)
(**SUFF.**) LESS
WITHSTAND BIDE DEFY TAKE ABIDE OPPOSE OPPUGN RESIST CONTAIN CONTEST FORBEAR SUSTAIN CONFRONT WITHSTAY
WITHY WIRY AGILE OSIER WOODY WILLOW WOODIE WINDING
WITLESS MAD GROSS INANE SILLY INSANE STUPID FATUOUS FOOLISH UNWITTY HEEDLESS SLAPHAPPY
WITLOOF ENDIVE CHICORY
WITNESS SEE TAKE TEST PROOF ATTEST BEHOLD MARTYR RECORD TESTIS TESTOR CURATOR TESTATE TESTIFY EVIDENCE RECORDER SUFFRAGE
(**FALSE** —) JUROR
(**PL.**) SECTA
(**PREF.**) TESTI
WITNESS-BOX STAND
WITOTO HUITOTE

WITTICISM WIT JEER JEST JOKE QUIP SALLY SLENT WHEEZE
WITTING NEWS TIDINGS
WITTINGLY SCIENTER
WITTOL FOOL CUCKOLD WITTALL
WITTY GASH WILY WISE DROLL LEPID PAWKY SHARP SMART CLEVER FACETE JOCOSE JOCULAR KNOWING CONCEITY HUMOROUS
(**NOT** —) INFICETE
WIVERN DRAGON WYVERN
WIZARD MAGE SEER SHIZ FIEND WITCH DOCTOR EXPERT PELLAR WARLOW CHARMED MAGICAL SPAEMAN WARLOCK WISEMAN CONJUROR MAGICIAN SORCERER TROLLMAN WITCHMAN ARCHIMAGE
(**PL.**) GOETAE
WIZARDRY SORCERY
WIZEN DRY WITHER SHRIVEL
WIZENED SERE GIZZEN WEAZEN
WOAD DYE NIL ODE ANIL KERS NILL OADE CRESS ANILLA INDIGO INDIGO PASTEL
(**PREF.**) ISAT(O)
WOADWAXEN ALLELUIA ALLELUJA
WOBBLE COCKLE COGGLE HOBBLE QUAVER SHIMMY TEETER TITTER TOTTER WABBLE WIGGLE TREMBLE NUTATION
(**KIND OF** —) CHANDLER
WOBBLY LOOSE SHAKY COGGLY DRUNKEN DOUBTFUL
WODEN ODIN ALLFATHER
WOE WA WEI BALE BANE DULE PAIN PINE WAWE GRIEF MISERY SORROW TROUBLE WILLAWA CALAMITY DISTRESS WELLADAY WELLAWAY
WOEBEGONE WAFF UNHAPPY DEJECTED DESOLATE DOWNCAST
WOEFUL MEAN DISMAL PALTRY HULI UL DIREFUL DOLEFUL RUTHFUL DOLOROUS PITIABLE WRETCHED
WOLF GLUT LOBO CANID FREKI YABBI CHANCO COYOTE FAMINE FENRIR ISGRIN KABERU LOAFER MASHER SIGRIM THOOID POVERTY ISENGRIM
(**FOX** —) ZORRO
(**KIND OF** —) LONE
(**PREF.**) LUPI LYC(O) VULPI
WOLFBERRY BUCKBUSH
WOLFHOUND ALAN BORZOI PSOVIE
WOLFISH LUPINE RAVENOUS
WOLFLIKE THOOID
WOLFRAMITE CAL TUNGSTEN
WOLFSBANE ACONITE DOGBANE FOXBANE
WOLF SPIDER HUNT JAGER HUNTER JAEGER JAYHAWK LYCOSID TARANTULA
WOLVERINE PIG GLUT GORB MIKER GLOTUM HELLUO GLUTTON GUTLING LURCHER MOOCHER RAVENER SWILLER CARCAJOU DRAFFMAN GOURMAND GULLYGUT
(— **STATE**) MICHIGAN
WOMAN BIM BIT DAM EVE HEN HER

JUG MEG SHE TEG TIT BABE BABY BINT BOSS CONY DAME FAIR FEME FLAG FROW JADE JANE LADY MAMA MARY MORT PERI SLUT WIFE BIDDY BIMBO BLADE BROAD CHINA DONAH FEMME FRAIL JATNI LUBRA LUCKY MAMMA MUJER QUEAN SKIRT SMOCK SQUAW TAGGE TOOTS TWIST UMMAN VROUW BURDIE CALICO CARLIN CUMMER FEMALE GIMMER HEIFER KIMMER LUCKIE MANESS MULIER SISTER TOMATO VIRAGO WAHINE CARLING CHANGAR DISTAFF PARTLET PINNACE PLACKET QUAEDAM MISTRESS PETTICOAT

(— DESERTED BY HUSBAND) AGUNAH

(— OF CONSEQUENCE) HERSELF

(— OF LOW CASTE) DASI

(— OF MEXICAN DESCENT) CHICANA

(— OF RANK) DOMINA

(— OF UNSTEADY CHARACTER) FLAP CALLET

(— OF WEALTH) FORTUNE

(— WHO ACTS AS ADVISER) EGERIA

(— WITH ONE CHILD) UNIPARA

(— WITH 3 CHILDREN) TRIPARA

(ABORIGINAL —) GIN LUBRA

(ABUSIVE —) FISHWIFE

(ALLURING —) DISH

(ATHENIAN — OF HIGH RANK) GERARA GERAERA

(ATTRACTIVE —) FOX DOLLY SHEBA DOLLIE LOOKER CHARMER

(AUSTRALIAN —) BINT

(AWKWARD —) ROIL

(BEAUTIFUL —) HURI PERI BELLE HOURI SIREN SPARK CHERUB EYEFUL MUSIDORA

(BIG COURAGEOUS —) VIRAGO

(BLESSED —) BEATA

(BOISTEROUS —) HOYDEN

(BOLD —) RAMP

(CLEANING —) CHAR

(COARSE —) BEAST RUDAS BLOWZE RULLION

(COOLIE —) CHANGAR

(COY —) HAGGARD

(CREMATED —) SATI SUTTEE

(DEAR —) PEAT

(DIRTY —) SLUT SLATTERN

(DISSOLUTE —) SLAG

(DUTCH OR GERMAN —) FRAU FROW FROKIN FRAULEIN

(ENGAGED —) BONDAGER

(ENTICING —) SIREN

(EVIL OLD —) HAG HELLHAG

(EXCITED —) MAENAD

(FASCINATING —) SIREN

(FASHIONABLE —) MILADY GALLANT ELEGANTE

(FAT —) BOSS FUSTILUGS

(FINE —) SCREAMER

(FIRST —) EMBLA PANDORA

(FLIGHTY —) GILLET JILLET FLIPFLOP

(FLIRTING —) CHIPPY FIZGIG

(FOOLISH —) TAWPIE

(FORWARD —) STRAP

(FOUL-MOUTHED —) RUDAS

(FRENCH HOLY —) STE SAINTE

(FRENZIED —) MAENAD

(GAUDY —) JAY

(GENTLE —) DOVE

(GOSSIPY —) HAIK HAKE BIDDY TABBY

(GOSSIP, TALKATIVE —) YENTA

(GROSS —) SOW

(GYPSY —) ROMI ROMNI GITANA

(ILL-TEMPERED —) VIXEN CATAMARAN

(IMMODEST —) TOMBOY

(IMMORAL —) RIG GITCH FLAPPER HARLOTRY

(IMPUDENT —) YANKIE

(INDIAN —) SQUAW WENCH KLOOCH BUCKEEN

(INSPIRED —) PHOEBAD

(ITALIAN —) DONNA

(LASCIVIOUS —) GIGLET

(LEARNED —) PUNDITA CLERGESS

(LEWD —) REP SLUT BITCH HUSSY HUZZY MALKIN BROTHEL CYPRIAN

(LOOSE —) BAG BIM KIT MOB TIB DRAB FLAP BIMBO TROLL GILLOT HARLOT LIMMER BAGGAGE COCOTTE FRANION TROLLOP

(LOUD-SPOKEN —) RANDY

(LOW OR WORTHLESS —) JADE JURR BUNTER SLINGDUST

(MARRIED — OF LOWLY STATION) GOODY

(MASCULINE —) AMAZON RULLION COTQUEAN

(MEEK —) GRIZEL

(MUSLIM —) BEGUM

(MYTHOLOGICAL —) HEROINE

(NON-JEWISH —) SHIKSA

(ODD-LOOKING —) JUDY

(OLD —) GIB HEN BABA TROT CRONE FAGOT FRUMP LUCKY TROUT BELDAM CARLIN GAMMER GEEZER GRANNY LUCKIE CARLINE GRANDAM HARRIDAN CAILLEACH

(OLD SHRIVELED —) FAGOT FAGGOT

(OVERGROWN —) FUSTILUGS

(PAINTED —) PICT

(PEDANTIC —) BLUE

(PERT —) CHIT

(PERVERSE —) JADE

(PORTUGUESE —) SENHORA

(PREGNANT —) GRAVIDA

(PRIGGISH —) PRUDE

(RAPACIOUS —) HARPY

(RAW-BONED —) RANDLETREE

(RICH OLD —) DOWAGER

(RUDE —) SCOLD

(RUSTIC —) JOAN

(SCOLDING —) RANDY SHREW COTQUEAN RIXATRIX

(SHAMELESS —) JEZEBEL

(SHORT OR STUMPY —) CUTTY

(SHOWY —) ANONYMA

(SHREWISH —) JADE HARPY SKELLAT

(SLATTERNLY —) DRAB FLEABAG SLAMKIN

(SLENDER GRACEFUL —) SYLPH

(SLIPSHOD —) MAUX CLATCH TROLLIMOG

(SLOVENLY —) BAG DAW SOW SLUT BESOM TAWPY TROLL TROLLOP SLATTERN

(SPANISH —) DONA GITANA

(SPANISH-INDIAN —) CHOLA

(SPITEFUL —) CAT FURY BITCH

(SQUAT —) TRUB

(SQUEAMISH —) COCKNEY

(STAID —) MATRON

(STATELY —) JUNO

(STORMY VIOLENT —) FURY

(TRACTABLE —) SHEEP

(UGLY —) HAG GORGON

(UNATTRACTIVE —) SCRUBBER

(UNCHASTE —) JILT

(UNMARRIED —) DAME GIRL SPINSTER MADEMOISELLE

(VIOLENT —) FURY

(VIXENISH —) HARRIDAN

(WANTON —) MINX TRUB QUEAN PARNEL

(WICKED —) JEZEBEL

(WISE —) VOLVA ALRUNA ALRUNE

(WITHERED —) CRONE

(YOUNG —) BIT BIRD BURD CHIT DAME DELL DOLL GIRL LASS PUSS BEAST CHICK FILLY FLUFF TOAST DAMSEL HEIFER PIGEON SHEILA SUBDEB BAGGAGE CHICKEN DAMOZEL FLAPPER WINKLOT DAUGHTER GRISETTE

(PREF.) FEMINO GYN(AE)(AECO) (AEO)(ANDRO)(E)(EO)(O)

(SUFF.) GYN(E)(IST)(OUS)

WOMAN HATER MISOGYNIST

WOMANHOOD MULIEBRITY

WOMAN IN WHITE (AUTHOR OF —) COLLINS

(CHARACTER IN —) ANNE FOSCO GLYDE LAURA PESCA MARIAN WALTER FAIRLIE HALCOMBE PERCIVAL CATHERICK HARTRIGHT

WOMANISH FEMALE FEMININE LADYLIKE PETTICOAT

WOMANIZER ROUE

WOMANKIND WOMEN CALICO MUSLIN FEMINIE

WOMAN'S TONGUE LEBBEK

WOMB BELLY CRADLE UTERUS VENTER

(PREF.) COLP(O) HYSTER(O) METRO UTER(O) VULVI VULVO

(SUFF.) COLPOS METRA METRIUM

WOMBAT KOALA BADGER DIDELPH VOMBATID

WOMEN DISTAFF

(— OF EARLY CHURCH) SETTERS AGAPETAE

WON CITY LIVE ROOM ABIDE DWELL REGION

WONDER AWE MUSE SELI SIGN TROW UNCO UNKO VERY FARLY FERLY SELLE SELLY UNCOW ADMIRE MARVEL MIRATE MAGNALE MIRABLE MIRACLE PORTENT PRODIGY STRANGE UNCOUTH AMERVEIL SELCOUTH SURPRISE

(SMALL —) GEM

(PL.) MIRABILIA

(PREF.) TERAT(O) THAUMA(TO) THAUMO

WONDERFUL KEEN NEAT SELI FERLY GRAND GREAT SELLE SWELL WAKON GEASON MIGHTY AMAZING EPATANT GALLANT MIRABLE MIRIFIC STRANGE FRABJOUS GLORIOUS MIRABILE TERRIFIC WONDROUS

WONDERFULLY AMAZING

WONDER-WORKER THEURGIC THEURGIST

WONDER-WORKING MIRIFIC

WONG FIELD GROVE PLAIN MEADOW

WONKY AWRY SHAKY WRONG UNSTEADY

WONT APT USE FAIN USED VAIN HABIT USAGE CUSTOM INCLINED

WONTED TAME USUAL HAUNTED

WOO SUE LOVE SEEK SUIT WALE COURT SPARK SPOON ASSAIL SPLUNT SUITOR ADDRESS

WOOD (ALSO SEE TREE AND TIMBER) HAG KIP BOIS BOSK BOWL EKKI HOLT HYLE KIRI MASS MOCK PALO SHAW SUPA TREE WOLE ALDER CAHUY CHARK CROWD EDDER FLOUR GROVE HURST HYRST KOKRA RESAK SHOLA STICK STUFF WEALD ALMOND ANGILI AUSUBO BRAZIL EKHIMI FOREST ITAUBA JARANA LUMBER PALING SPINNY TIMBER APITONG AVODIRE BOSCAGE BOSKAGE COPPICE DADDOCK DUDGEON HAYBOTE SATINAY VENESIA BAGTIKAN CRANTARA FIREBOOT CALAMANDER

(— BURNT AS PERFUME) AGALLOCH

(— FOR CARPENTRY) STUFF

(— FOR OARS) ASH

(— FOR REPAIRING HEDGE) TINING HAYBOTE

(— OF SMALL EXTENT) GROVE

(— OF THE VERA) VENESIA

(— ON RAFTER) FUR

(— ROTATED ON STRING) ROMBOS RHOMBOS

(— USEFUL FOR TINDER) PUNK SPONK TOUCHWOOD

(— YIELDING PERFUME) LINALOA

(BABUL —) SUNT

(BLACK —) EBONY

(CONE-SHAPED PIECE OF —) ACORN

(DARK RED —) RATA

(DEAD —) RAMMEL

(DENSIFIED —) STAYPAK

(ELASTIC —) SYCAMORE

(FIR —) DEAL

(FLAT ROUND PIECE OF —) TRENCHER

(FLEXIBLE —) EDDER

(FOSSIL —) PINITE PEUCITES

(FRAGRANT —) CEDAR SANDALWOOD

(FUEL —) ESTOVERS

(HARD —) ASH DAO ELM SAL BAKU IPIL KARI LANA POON ANJAN EBONY GIDYA KARRI KOKRA MAPLE MAZER ZANTE BANUYO CAMARA FREIJO GIDGEE KEMPAS SABICU SAPELE WALNUT CURUPAY DATTOCK HICKORY GUAIACUM IRONBARK MAHOGANY

(HEAVY —) DAO EBON EBONY CHENGAL GUAYABI SUCUPIRA

(LIGHT —) POON BALSA HEMLOCK
(LIMBA —) KORINA
(LOGGED —) CHIP
(LOST —) CHIPPAGE
(LUSTROUS —) LEZA BOARWOOD
(MATCHBOX —) SKILLET
(MOTTLED —) AMBOINA CALAMBOUR
(NARROW BAR OF —) SLAT
(NUMBER 1 —) DRIVER
(NUMBER 2 —) BRASSIE
(NUMBER 3 —) SPOON
(NUMBER 4 —) CLEEK
(OILY —) BATETE
(OLIVE —) COLLIE
(PETRIFIED —) LITHOXYL ROCKWOOD
(PINE —) DEAL
(PINKISH —) BOSSE
(POINTED PIECE OF —) TRIPPET
(REDDISH —) KOA KARI KARRI ARANGA BIMABALA CHERRY DUNGON SATINE KAMBALA
(REDDISH-YELLOW —) GUYO
(ROTTEN —) DADDOCK
(SANDARAC —) ALERCE
(SMALL —) SHAW
(SOFT —) KIRI GABUN GABOON FLKWOOD AGALLOCH ALBURNUM GUATAMBU
(SPONGY —) PUNK
(SQUARE LOG OF —) NOG
(STICK OF —) BILLET
(STRIP OF —) LATH STAVE BATTEN REEPER REGLET SPLINE SPLINT SPLINTER
(WATER-RESISTING —) AMUGIS
(YELLOWISH —) HALDU FUSTIC IDIGBO KADAMBA KAMASSI GUATAMBU
(PREF.) HYL(O) LIGN(I)(O) XYL(O)
(SUFF.) XYLON XYLUM
WOOD ALCOHOL METHANOL
WOOD ANEMONE CYME EMONY ROWBELLA SNOWDROP
WOODBARK SABLE BLONDINE
WOODBINE BIND WIDBIN EGLATERE
WOODCARVER BODGER
WOODCHUCK CHUG CHUCK MONAX MARMOT SUSLIK WEJACK MOONACK GROUNDHOG
WOODCOCK QUIS PEWEE PEWIT SNIPE SNITE SHRUPS BECASSE SIMPLETON
WOODCUT BLOCK
WOODCUTTER AXEMAN LOGGER WOODMAN WOODSMAN
WOOD DUCK SQUEALER BRANCHIER
WOODED BOSKY TREEY HYLEAN SYLVAN FORESTED NEMOROUS
WOODEN DRY DULL STIFF TREEN CLUMSY STICKY STOLID TIMBER AWKWARD DEADPAN TIMBERN LIFELESS
WOOD GUM XYLAN
WOOD HEN WEKA
WOODHEWER PICUCULE
WOOD HOOPOE WHOOP WHOOPE IRRISOR DUNGBIRD PICARIAN
WOOD HYACINTH SCILLA CROWTOE GREGGLE HAREBELL

WOOD IBIS STORK GANNET JABIRU IRONHEAD
WOODLAND DESERT MIOMBO SPRING BOSCAGE
(WASTE —) WEALD
WOOD LOUSE SLATER SOWBUG PILLBUG MILLIPED
WOODPECKER AWL CHAB JYNX KATE PEEK ECCLE HECCO HEWEL ICKLE PICUS SPEKT HECKLE NICKER NICKLE PECKER PIANET PICULE SPRITE TAPPER YAFFLE YUCKER YUKKEL CLIMBER CREEPER FLICKER HEWHOLE HICKWAY LOGCOCK REDHEAD SAPSUCK SNAPPER SPEIGHT WHETILE WITWALL WRYNECK DIRTBIRD HICKWALL PICARIAN PICUCULE POPINJAY RAINBIRD RAINFOWL WALLHICK SAPSUCKER
(LIKE A —) PICIFORM
(PREF.) PICI
WOOD-PIGEON CULVER CUSHAT ZOOZOO RINGDOVE
WOOD PIGEON CUSHAT ZOOZOO
WOODPILE STRAN STRAND WOODRICK
WOOD ROBIN MIRO TOMTIT
WOODRUFF HAIROF MUGGET MUGWET WOODROW HARIFHOF
WOODS BOSK BUSH BOSQUE
(PREF.) NEMO SILVI SYLVI
WOODSMAN BUSHY SILVAN SYLVAN BUSHMAN BUSHWACK
WOOD SORREL OCA COCKOO HEARTS LUJULA OXALIS TREFOIL ALLELUIA ALLELUJA SHAMROCK STABWORT
WOOD SPIRIT METHANOL
WOOD SUGAR XYLOSE
WOOD THRUSH MAYBIRD
WOODTURNER BODGER
WOODWIND OBOE FLUTE BASSOON PIBGORN PICCOLO CLARINET
WOODWORK CEILING
WOODWORKER JOINER TURNER MILLMAN
WOODWORM GRIBBLE
(PREF.) TERMITO
WOODY BOSKY WITHY FRITHY STICKY SYLVAN XYLOID LIGNOSE LIGNEOUS
WOOER BEAU LOVER WOWER SUITOR COURTER WOOSTER COURTIER PARAMOUR
WOOF WEFT WOUGH FILLING TEXTURE
WOOING SUIT WOHLAC
WOOL OO COT DAG HOG VOL WOW BEAT BLUE FRIB PILE PULU ROCK FADGE LAINE MUNGO STUFF TIPPY ALPACA ARGALI BOTANY BREECH FLEECE GREASE JACKET JERSEY KERSEY LUSTER SLIVER WETHER COMBING HASLOCK KASHMIR MORLING STUBBLE WIGGING CASHMERE CLOTHING COMEBACK MORTLING PICKLOCK TOMENTUM
(— AS IT COMES FROM SHEEP) GREASE
(— FROM DEAD SHEEP) MORLING MORTLING

(— FROM LEOMINSTER) ORE
(— FROM RAGS) EXTRACT
(— OF UNDERCOAT OF MUSK-OX) QIVIUT
(— ON SHEEP'S LEG) GARE BREECH
(— ON SHEEP'S THROAT) HASLOCK
(— WEIGHT) TOD
(COARSE —) ABB SHAG BRAID COWTAIL
(COTTON —) CADDIS CADDICE
(DUNGY BIT OF —) FRIB
(FINE —) MERINO
(FINE GRADE OF —) PICKLOCK SPINNERS
(GREASY —) TIPPY
(INFERIOR GRADE OF —) HEAD
(KNOT OF —) NOIL
(LAMB'S —) WASSAIL
(LOCK OF —) FLOCK STAPLE
(LONG —) BLUE
(LOW GRADE OF —) LIVERY
(MATTED —) DAG KET SHAG
(PULLED —) SLIPE
(RECLAIMED —) MUNGO SHODDY
(REFUSE —) COT COTT FLOCK PINION
(ROLL OF —) CARDING
(RUSSIAN —) DONSKY
(SMALL PIECE OF —) TATE
(SPUN —) YARN
(WOUND —) TREND
(PREF.) ERIO LAN(I)(O) MALLO
(SUFF.) LAN
WOOLCLOTH HODDEN
WOOLEN (ALSO SEE FABRIC) CADDIS CAMLET SUCLAT CADDICE PASHMINA
(PL.) LAINAGE
WOOL FAT LANOLIN
WOOLLY SHEEP WOOZY LANATE LANOSE COTTONY FLOCCOSE PERONATE
WOOLLY BEAR WOUBIT
WOOLLY CROTON HOGWORT
WOOLY
(PREF.) DASI DASY ULU
WOOZY SICK DRUNK TIGHT VAGUE BLURRY WOOLLY
WORD GIG MOT EZEL GULE HAIT NEWS RAFF TERM VERB WHID WHUD ADNEX CHEEP COUCH DERRY DILLY FITCH GLOSS HAPAX HOKEY HYNDE LEMMA MAXIM ORDER PAROL RHEMA RUMOR SPELL ACCENT ADVERB AVOWAL BREATH COPULA ETYMON KIBBER LATIVE ONEYER PAROLE PLEDGE QUATCH REMARK REPORT SAYING ACCOUNT ADJUNCT BIGGHED COMMAND COMMENT DICTION DUCDAME GENTILE GITTITH HOMONYM INCIPIT MESSAGE PALABRA PARONYM PRAYFUL PRENZIE PROMISE PROVERB SYNONYM VOCABLE ACROSTIC CATCHCRY CHEVILLE COMPOUND ENCLITIC EQUIVOKE FRABJOUS FRINGENT IDEOGRAM ILLATIVE LATINISM SYLLABLE SYNTAGMA NEOLOGISM PALINDROME PARTICIPLE MONOSYLLABLE
(— AS CALL TO DUCK) DILLY

(— EXPRESSING COMMAND) JUSSIVE
(— FORMED FROM VOWELS) EUOUAE
(— FROM INITIAL LETTERS) ACRONYM
(— IN A PUZZLE) LIGHT
(— MISPRONOUNCED) BEARD
(— OF ADDRESS) SIR
(— OF CONCLUSION) AMEN EXPLICIT
(— OF GOD) LOGOS
(— OF HONOR) PAROLE
(— OF MOUTH) FIDELITY
(— OF OPPOSITE MEANING) ANTONYM
(— OF RESPECT) SIR
(— OF SECONDARY RANK) ABNDK
(— OF SEVERAL MEANINGS) POLYSEME
(— OF UNCERTAIN MEANING) FRINGENT
(— OF UNKNOWN MEANING) KIBBER ONEYER PRAYFUL PRENZIE
(— REPRESENTED BY SIGN) GRAMMALOGUE
(— SEGMENT) SYLLABLE
(—S IN LOW TONE) ASIDE
(—S OF GREETING) SALUTATION
(—S OF OPERA) LIBRETTO
(—S SIGNIFYING UNDERSTANDING) ISEE
(BIBLICAL — OF DOUBTFUL MEANING) EZEL FITCH GITTITH
(BIG —) MOUTHFUL
(CALL —) JINGO
(CHARACTERIZING —) EPITHET
(CODE —) DOG FOX JIG ABLE EASY ECHO GOLF ITEM KING BRAVO DELTA HOTEL INDIA SUGAR GEORGE CHARLIE EUPHEMISM
(DISCOURAGING —) TSK
(EMPTY —S) WAFFLE
(FINE — OF DICK)
(GATHERING —) SLOGAN
(HARSH —) MISWORD
(HONEYED —S) MANNA
(HYPHENATED —) SOLID
(IDENTIFYING —) LABEL
(LAST — OF SPEECH) CUE
(MAGIC —) ABRACADABRA
(MEANINGLESS —) DERRY
(MEANINGLESS —S) NOISE
(METAPHORICAL —) KENNING
(MNEMONIC —) VIBGYOR
(MYSTIC —) ABRAXAS
(NEW —) NEOLOGISM
(NONSENSE —) RAFF RAFFE FRABJOUS RUNCIBLE
(ORIGINAL —) STEM
(PARTING —) ENVOI
(PUT INTO —S) LIMN
(QUOTED —) CITATION
(RECURRING —) REPETEND
(REDUNDANT —) CHEVILLE
(ROOT —) ETYMON PRIMITIVE
(SIGNAL —) NAYWORD SECURITY
(SIGNIFICANT —) ACCENT
(SINGLE —) PHRASE
(SMOOTH —S) SOAP
(SOURCE —) ETYMON
(SPREAD THE —) TELL
(TEST —) SHIBBOLETH

(THIEVES' SLANG —) TWAG WHID
(UNEXPLAINED —) DUCDAME
(UTTERED —S) SPEECH
(WAY WITH —S) TACT
(PL.) LIP TALK LYRIC SPEECH
LANGUAGE DISCOURSE
(PREF.) LEXI LEXICO LOG(O)
ONOMATO RHEMATO VERBI
VERBO
(SUFF.) EPY LEXIA ONYM
WORD-BLINDNESS ALEXIA
DYSLEXIA ALEXIA
WORDBOOK LEXICON SPELLER
LIBRETTO
WORDINESS VERBIAGE
WORDING LEGEND DICTION
PHRASING
WORDLESS DUMB TACIT SILENT
TACITURN
WORDMAKING RHEMATIC
WORDPLAY EQUIVOKE
WORD PROCESSING (— DISPLAY)
WYSIWYG
WORDS TEXT
WORDY PROLIX VERBAL DIFFUSE
VERBOSE WORDISH REDUNDANT
WORK DO GO ACT FAG JOB DIKE
DYKE FEND FRET NOTE OPUS TASK
TEND TOIL ERGON GRAFT GRIND
KARMA KNEAD LABOR PRESS
YAKKA ARBEIT BEAVER BONNET
EFFECT HUSTLE OEUVRE REDUIT
RESULT STRIVE THRIFT CALLING
EXECUTE EXPLOIT FERMENT
HEXAPLA LOUSTER MISSION
OPERATE OPIFICE OPUSCLE
OUVRAGE OVERAGE PICHERY
PURSUIT TRAVAIL ADVOCACY
AGENTING BUSINESS CAPONIER
DEMILUNE DRUDGERY ENDEAVOR
FUNCTION INDUSTRY LABORAGE
OPUSCULE PARERGON RETRENCH
EXECUTION
(— ACROSS GRAIN) THURM
(— ACTIVELY) LOUSTER
(— AGAINST) KNIFE ATTACK
COMBAT
(— AIMLESSLY) FIDDLE
(— AS MUSICIAN) GIG
(— AS REPORTER) HEEL
(— BEYOND ONE'S POWERS)
OVERDO
(— BY THE PIECE) TUT
(— CARELESSLY) RABBLE
(— DILIGENTLY) PEG PLUG STRIKE
BELABOR
(— DOGGEDLY) SLOG
(— DONE) WRIHTE
(— FOR) LABOR SERVE BESWINK
(— FREE) START
(— HARD) TEW MOIL SLOG SWOT
BULLOCK LEATHER
(— HIDES) BEAM
(— IMPERFECTLY) MALFUNCTION
(— INEFFECTUALLY) PINGLE
(— INSIDIOUSLY) WORM
(— INTO A MASS) KNEAD
(— INTO SHAPE) REDACT
(— LAND) FLOAT
(— LEISURELY) DAKER DAIKER
(— OCCASIONALLY) SMOOT
SMOUT

(— OF ACKNOWLEDGED
EXCELLENCE) CLASSIC
(— OF ART) GEM CRAFT ANTIQUE
CAPRICE CREATION EPIPHANY
EXERCISE MANDORLA
(— OF FICTION) SHOCKER
(— OF HISTORY) STORY
(— OF MENIAL KIND) DRUDGE
(— ONE'S WAY) WISE
(— OUT) BLOCK FUDGE SOLVE
TRAIN DESIGN EVOLVE
(— OUT A PROBLEM) PSYCH
PSYCHE
(— OUT IN ADVANCE) FOREPLOT
(— OVER) DIGEST
(— PAID FOR IN ADVANCE) HORSE
(— PART-TIME) TEMP
(— PART TIME) TEMP
(— PERSISTENTLY) HAMMER
(— RESEMBLING PATCHWORK)
CENTO
(— SLIPSHOD) MULLOCK
(— STEADILY) PLY
(— SYSTEM) FLEXTIME FLEXITIME
(— TO EXHAUSTION) FAG
(— TOGETHER) COACT
(— TO WINDWARD) CLAW
(— TRIFLINGLY) PIDDLE
(— UNDER ANOTHER NAME)
ALLONYM
(— UNFAIRLY OR CRUELLY) HORSE
(— UP) MENG MING MENGE SPUNK
SUBACT
(— UPON) TILL LABOR
(— UPWARD) HIKE
(— VIGOROUSLY) BEND
(— WITHOUT FINISHING) SCABBLE
SCAPPLE
(ALLEGORICAL —) BESTIARY
(ANONYMOUS —) ADESPOTA
(BUNGLED —) BOTCH
(CANVAS —) POINT
(CARELESS —) SLAPDASH
(CESSATION OF —) SITIN SITDOWN
(CHASED —) CISELURE
(CLEANING —) CHAR
(CLUMSY —) BOTCH
(COMPLETED —) TRAVAIL
(CONTRACT —) GYPPO
(DAMASCENE —) KOFTGARI
(DAY'S —) DARG DARGUE
(DECORATIVE —) FLOCKING
MARQUETRY
(DIVINE —) THEURGY
(DOING LEGAL —) PROBONO
(DULL —) DRUDGERY
(EMBOSSED —) CELATURE
(FRAUDULENT —) JERRY
(HAND —) CAMAY
(HARD —) TEW MOIL MUCK SWOT
TWIG YERK SWEAT EFFORT MOIDER
LEATHER SLAVERY SLOGGING
(INFERIOR —) KITSCH SLOPWORK
(INLAY —) INTARSIA
(JOINER —) FINISH
(LITERARY —) STUDY CHASER
SEQUEL SERIAL CLASSIC DIPTYCH
PREQUEL PRODUCTION
(LITTLE —) OPUSCLE OPUSCULE
(LURID —) BLOOD
(MANUAL —) FATIGUE
(METAL —) NIELLO
(MINOR —) OPUSCLE OPUSCULUM

(MOSAIC —) EMBLEM
(ORGANIZED ABSENCE FROM —)
SICKOUT
(ORNAMENTAL —) BEADWORK
FILIGREE LEAFWORK
(PIECE OF —) JOB
(REFERENCE —) BIBLE SOURCE
(SACRED —) HIERURGY
(SCHOLASTIC —) SUMMA
(SKILLED MECHANICAL —) SLOJD
SLOYD
(SLOVENLY —) SLAISTER
(SOCIAL —) ALMONING
(USELESS —) BOONDOGGLE
(WOMAN'S —) DISTAFF
(PL.) CANON PLANT STODGE
FACTORY BUSINESS
(PREF.) ERG(O) ERGAT(O) OPERA
(EMBOSSED —) TOREUMATO
(SUFF.) ERGATE ERGY
WORKABLE YOUNG PLIANT VIABLE
FEASIBLE
(EASILY —) SWEET
WORKADAY HUMDRUM PROSAIC
ORDINARY
WORKBASKET CABA CABAS
CALATHUS
WORKBENCH SIEGE DONKEY
TEMPLATE
WORKED INWROUGHT
(— OUT) DEAD
(— UP) ANGRY EXCITED
WORKER (ALSO SEE WORKMAN
AND LABORER) AGER CARL DOER
HAND HIND ICER SCAB AXMAN
BOXER BUTTY DEMAS DRIER
EDGER ENDER FILER FIRER FIXER
FLYER FOXER GLUER GORER
HOLER INKER JERRY LINER LURER
MAXIM MINIM NURSE PROLE
TAPER TOWER ASHMAN BACKER
BAILER BALLER BANDER BEADER
BENDER BINDER BINMAN BLADER
BLOWER BOILER BONDER BOOKER
BOSHER BRACER BUFFER BUMPER
BURNER BURRER CAPPER
CARMAN CASTER CASUAL CHASER
COMBER COOKER DAYMAN
DIPPER DOCKER DOGGER DOTTER
DUMPER ETCHER FACTOR FAGGER
FANMAN FASHER FEEDER FELLER
FILLER FITTER FLAKER FLAMER
FLUTER FLUXER FOILER FOLDER
FORCER FORMER FRAMER
GASSER GOFFER GRADER
GUMMER GUTTER HASHER
HEADER HEELER HELPER HEMMER
HOLDER HOOKER HOOPER
HOPPER HUNKIE INKMAN JOGGER
JOINER LEAFER LEASER LEGGER
NOILER PUGGER READER REEDER
SCORER SEAMAN SEAMER
SHAKER SKIVER SLAKER SLICER
SLIDER SLOPER STAVER STAYER
TOILER TOPPER BUILDER CREATOR
EMPLOYE FIELDER LABORER
OUVRIER
(— IN LEATHER) BEAMER CHUMAR
JACKER BLACKER CHUCKLER
(— IN METALS) SMITH FLAPPER
(ADDITIONAL —) EXTRA
(AGRICULTURAL —) ARKIE KISAN
(AIRCRAFT —) BOOTMAN

(ANT —) MAXIM ERGATES REPLETE
(ASBESTOS —) COBBER
(AUTO —) DISKER
(BAKERY —) BRAKER COOLER
DIVIDER BENCHMAN SPREADER
(BLUE-COLLAR —) STIFF
(BREWERY —) HOPPER STEEPER
STILLMAN
(BRICK —) DAUBER CROWDER
(CANNERY —) SLIMER SCALDER
SHEDMAN
(CLOCK —) STAKER
(CLUMSY —) BODGE BODGER
(COAL —) SUMPER GEORDIE
SPRAGGER
(COMPULSIVE —) WORKAHOLIC
(CONSTRUCTION —) HARDHAT
(DOCK —) BUNGS HOLDMAN
SHENANGO
(DOMESTIC —) HELP
(FARM —) HODGE
(FELLOW —) CONFRERE
(FOREIGN —) GASTARBEITER
(FOUNDRY —) FLOGGER SNAGGER
(GARMENT —) FACER SLEEVER
ASSORTER INSEAMER
(GUN —) BLUER
(HARD —) SLOGGER
(HAT —) CURLER BRIMMER
(HIDE —) HEFTER COLORER
(HOSPITAL —) ALMONER
(HOTEL —) SCRUB
(ICEHOUSE —) AIRMAN
(JEWELRY —) ARBORER
(LIMITED-TIME —) TEMP
(LOGGING —) SNIPER SKIDDER
(MATTRESS —) BEATER
(MIGRATORY —) HOBO OKIE
(MILL —) BILLER SPOUTER
(MINE —) BYEMAN FOOTER
GOPHER LANDER DROPPER
FACEMAN SLEDGER SWAMPER
DRIFTMAN
(NONUNION CONSTRUCTION —S)
LUMP
(OIL WELL —) ROUGHNECK
(ORCHARD —) SMUDGER
(PACKINGHOUSE —) COOK
(PAPERMILL —) SIZER SIZEMAN
(PIANO —) BELLYMAN
(PLODDING —) GRUBBER
(POTTERY —) CASER BATTER
BEDDER FETTLER JOLLIER JUSTLER
(PRINTING —) FLY FLYBOY
(PUERTO RICAN —) GIBARO JIBARO
(QUARRY —) BREAKER
(RAILROAD —) JERRY HERDER
BRAKEMAN
(SAWMILL —) BOLTER SETTER
BOATMAN DECKMAN CHAINMAN
(SHOE —) CASER FOXER ARCHER
FUDGER HEELER CHALKER
BOTTOMER
(SKILLED —) ARTISTE
(SLAUGHTERHOUSE —) FATTER
SHOVER SINGER SLIMER CHEEKER
CHOPPER KNOCKER LIMEMAN
SCALPER SCRIBER STICKER
SNATCHER
(SOCIAL —) ALMONER
(TANNERY —) GATER STONER
CROPPER CURRIER DELIMER
BEAMSMAN SEASONER

(TEXTILE —) DOFFER DOUPER DRAWER GIGGER LAPPER LEASER SINGER CREELER DOUBLER JACKMAN KETTLER SKEINER SPINNER SHUTTLER SOFTENER SPLITTER TEASELER
(THEATER —) FLYMAN STAGEMAN
(TOBACCO —) BULKER SIFTER STEMMER SCRAPMAN SPRIGGER STICKMAN STRIPPER
(UNSKILLED —) HELPER DILUTEE GREENER
(USELESS —) TOOL
(WHITE-COLLAR —) EFFENDI
(YARN —) SOURER CHAINER
(PL.) LABOR
(PREF.) ERG(O) ERGAT(O)
(SUFF.) ERGAT(E) URGE URGIC URGY
WORKHORSE AVER AIVER TRESTLE SAWHORSE
WORKHOUSE UNION FACTORY WORKSHOP
WORKING PLAY GOING OPENCUT FUNCTION LABORAGE OPENCAST OPENWORK OPERATIC OPERATIVE
(— ALONE) HATTING
(— HARD) HOPPING
(— IN THE MIND) MOTION
(— OF MINE) GWAG CROSSCUT
(— ON) PRACTICE
(— TOGETHER) SYNERGIC SYNERGETIC
(DISUSED —) WASTE
(MINE —S) SPLIT
(NOT —) DUFF
WORKMAN (ALSO SEE WORKER AND LABORER) BOSS HAND MATE ROTO CAGER CONER EXTRA FINER FLINT FLUER FROCK LAYER MAJOR MIXER POLER TONER TRIER TUBER BEAMER BLOUSE BOOMER BOWLER BUCKER BUMMER COATER DIPPER DRIVER FORKER GAGGER HANGER LASTER LATHER MASTER NIPPER OILMAN PUFFER RUNNER SAMMER SCORER SHAKER SKIVER SLICER SLIDER SOAKER SPIKER STAGER STAVER TAPPER TARRER TEEMER TILTER TIPMAN TIPPER TOPMAN WARMER WASHER WETTER WRIGHT ARTISAN DRUMMER HOTSHOT LUDDITE SHOPMAN
(CHIEF —) BOSS
(CLUMSY —) BUNGLER COBBLER
(FELLOW —) BULLY BUTTY
(ITINERANT —) HOBO
(PROFICIENT —) DEACON
(SKILLED —) PRUDHOMME
(UNSKILLFUL —) HUNKY BUTCHER
(PL.) VOLK
WORKMANLIKE DEFT ADEPT SKILLFUL
WORKMANSHIP HAND FABRIC FACTURE OVERAGE ARTIFICE ARTISANRY
WORKROOM DEN STUDY ATELIER
WORKS HACIENDA
(— OF CLOCK) WATCH
(SALT —) SALINA
WORKSHOP LAB SHED SHOP FORGE LODGE SMIDDY SMITHY

ATELIER BOTTEGA HOSPITAL OFFICINA PLUMBERY SKINNERY
WORKTABLE BENCH
WORLD ORB LOKA VALE WARD EARTH MONDE WADRU WARDE CAREER PUBLIC KINGDOM MONDIAL CREATION CREATURE UNIVERSE
(— OF BOXING) FISTIANA
(— OF DARKNESS) SHEOL
(— OF DOGS) DOGDOM
(— OF FASHION) STYLEDOM SWELLDOM
(— OF GODS) DEVALOKA
(— OF THE DEAD) DEEP
(— OF WOMEN) FEMINIE
(ACADEMIC —) CAMPUS
(EXTERNAL —) NONEGO
(GREAT —) MACROCOSM
(LITTLE —) MICROCOSM
(LOWER —) ORCUS
(PRIVATE —) AUTOCOSM
(THE —) FOLD
(THIRD —) SOUTH
(TWO-DIMENSIONAL —) FLATLAND
(PREF.) COSM(O) MUNDI
(SUFF.) COSM
WORLDLINESS MAMMON
WORLDLING DIVES
WORLDLY LAY WARLY CARNAL EARTHY MUNDAL EARTHEN EARTHLY FLESHLY MUNDANE PROFANE SECULAR SENSUAL TERRENE
(NOT —) INTERIOR
WORLD'S ILLUSION (AUTHOR OF —) WASSERMANN
(CHARACTER IN —) EVA LAY IVAN VOSS CYRIL DENIS KAREN SOREL BECKER AMADEUS BERNARD CRAMMON CHRISTIAN ENGELSCHALL WAHNSCHAFFE
WORLD-WEARY JADED BLASE
WORLDWIDE GLOBAL ECUMENIC GLOBULAR PLANETAL PLANETARY
(PREF.) GLOBO
WORLD-WISE KNOWING PRUDENT
WORM BOB EEL ESS LOA MAD LURG NAIS NEMA ARTER CADEW FLUKE LYTTA PIPER SCREW SNAKE DRAGON NEREID NEREIS PALMER PALOLO SHAMIR SYLLID SYLLIS TEREDO VERMIS WRETCH ANNELID ASCARID CARBORA ENOPLAN SABELLA SAGITTA SERPENT SERPULA SETARID SHUFFLE SPIONID TAGTAIL TRICLAD WRIGGLE BRANDLIN CEPHALOB CERCARIA CHETOPOD GILTTAIL HELMINTH LEODICID MEASURER NEMATODE POLYCLAD STRONGYL TRICHINA VERMICLE NEMERTEAN TOOTHACHE SCHISTOSOME POGONOPHORAN
(— IN HAWKS) FILANDER
(— OF DOG'S TONGUE) LYTTA
(— USED FOR BAIT) TAGTAIL
(AQUATIC —) TUBIFEX
(BLOODSUCKING —) LEECH
(CADDIS —) CADEW PIPER CADBAIT
(FLUKE —) PLAICE
(MARINE —) RAGWORM
(MEASURING —) LOOPER

(MUD —) IPO LOA
(SHIP —) BROMA COBRA
(PL.) APODA ENTOZOA
(PREF.) HELMINTH(O) LUMBRICI SCOLEC(I)(O) VERMI
(SUFF.) SCOLEX
WORM-EATEN PITTED DECAYED VERMOULU WERMETHE
WORMER JAG
WORMHOLE PIQURE
WORMLIKE VERMIAN
WORMSEED EPAZOTE AMBROSIA
WORMWOOD MOXA ABSINTH CUDWEED MUGWORT ABSINTHE COMPOSIT MINGWORT SANTONICA
WORMY EARTHY
WORN SEAR SERE USED PASSE TRITE MAGGED MIZPAH SHABBY ATTRITE CONTRITE
(— NEXT TO SKIN) INTIMATE
(— OUT) SHOT BANAL JADED SEELY SPENT STALE STANK BEATEN BEDRID BLEARY EFFETE EPUISE SCREWY SHABBY CRIPPLE FORWORN DECREPID FOUGHTEN HARASSED OBSOLETE STRICKEN
(— SMOOTH) BEATEN
WORRICOW DEVIL BUGABOO BUGBEAR HOBGOBLIN
WORRIED TOEY UNEASY ANXIOUS FRETTED STREAKED CONCERNED
WORRIT VEX WORRY DISTRESS
WORRY DOG HOE HOW HOX LUG NAG RUX TEW VEX BAIT BITE CARE CARK FAZE FIKE FRAB FRET FUSS HARE MOIL SOOL STEW ANNOY CHEVY CHOKE DEAVE FEEZE GALLY HARRY HURRY LURRY PHASE SCALD SHAKE TEASE TOUSE TOWSE BOTHER CADDLE CHIVVY COTTER CUMBER FERRET FIDGET GALLOW HARASS HATTER HECTOR INFEST KIAUGH MOIDER PESTER PINGLE PLAGUE POTHER ANXIETY CHAGRIN HATCHEL TROUBLE TURMOIL WHERRET FASHERIE STRANGLE
WORRYING ANXIOUS
WORSE VER WAR SEAMY
WORSEN DESCEND
WORSHIP GOD CULT HERY PUJA RANK ADORE DULIA HONOR NAMAZ WURTH YAJNA CREDIT PRAISE REPUTE REVERE BAALISM ELOHISM ICONISM IDOLISM IDOLIZE IMAGERY OBSERVE BLESSING HIERURGY VENERATE IDOLATRIZE
(— OF ALL GODS) PANTHEISM
(— OF HOST OF HEAVEN) SABAISM
(— OF IMAGES) ICONOLATRY
(— OF SELF) AUTOLATRY
(— OF SHAKESPEARE) BARDOLATRY
(ANCESTOR —) SCIOTHEISM
(DEVIL —) DIABOLISM
(FALSE —) SUPERSTITION
(FORMAL —) EYESERVICE
(FORM OF —) RITUAL
(HERO —) ADULATION
(HIGHEST KIND OF —) LATRIA
(INFERIOR KIND OF —) DULIA

(INSINCERE —) LIPSERVICE
(SERPENT —) OPHISM
(STAR —) SABAISM
(PREF.) LITURGIO THRESKI
(SUFF.) LATER LATRIA LATROUS LATRY
WORSHIPER ISIAC BHAKTA PRAISER IDOLATER
(— OF STARS) AKKUM SABIAN
(FIRE —) PARSI GHEBER GUEBER PARSEE
(SERPENT —) SETHIAN SETHITE
WORSHIPFUL GOOD PROUD NOTABLE REVERENT
WORST ACE GET BEST LAST OUTDO SHEND WREST DEFEAT
(SOMETHING THAT IS THE —) PIT PITS
(PREF.) KAKISTO
WORSTED GARN JERRY SERGE CUBICA VESSES WHIPCORD
WORT GAIL GYLE SWAT PLANT LENGTH TUTSAN FILLING KRAUSEN POTHERB
(FERMENTED —) FEED WASH
(UNFERMENTED —) GROUT
WORTH FECK MEED CARAT MERIT PRICE VALOR VALUE BECOME BOUNTY DESERT ESTEEM REGARD RICHES VALENT VIRTUE WEALTH DIGNITY PRETIUM VALIANT WORSHIP SPLENDOR TREASURE VALIDITY VALLIDOM
(NET —) CAPITAL
(OF LITTLE —) SHLOCK SCHLOCK
(PREF.) AXIO TIMO
WORTHINESS DESERT WORSHIP
WORTHLESS BAD BUM LOW WAF BAFF BALD BARE BASE EVIL IDLE LEWD ORRA PUNK RACA SLIM VAIN VILE WAFF BLANK BLOWN DUSTY FLASH FOUTY LOSEL LOUSY PUTID SLINK SORRY STRAW WASHY ABJECT CHAFFY CHEESY CRUMMY DRAFFY DRASTY DROSSY HOLLOW LIMMER LITHER LUTHER MEASLY NAUGHT PALTRY RASCAL ROTTEN SCREWY TRASHY WOODEN BAGGAGE FUSTIAN MAUVAIS NAUGHTY NOTHING PIPERLY RAFFISH RUBBISH SCABBED SHILPIT USELESS FECKLESS HARLOTRY MAUVAISE NUGATORY PRECIOUS RASCALLY RUBBISHY SIXPENNY TRUMPERY VAGABOND WANWORDY WRETCHED NOACCOUNT STRAMINEOUS
(— THING) AMBSACE
WORTHLESSNESS BELIAL UNTHRIFT
WORTHWHILE TANTI
WORTHY BIG DEAR FAIR GOOD HOLY TIDY AUGHT CANNY DIGNE EXALT HONOR JELLY NOBLE PIOUS GENTLE CONDIGN GRADELY PAREGAL THRIFTY ELIGIBLE VALUABLE WAUREGAN
(— OF BELIEF) CREDIBLE
(— OF DEVOTION) HOLY
(— OF PRAISE) LAUDABLE
(VERY —) SUPERIOR
(SUFF.) ABLE IBLE

WOULD WAD WID WANT WISH
COULD SHOULD
(**— NOT**) NOLD WADNA WADDENT
(**I —**) CHUD CHOLD
WOULD-BE MANQUE
WOUND ARR CUT HEW PIP WIN
BITE CALK CLAW DUNT FAKE FOIN
GALL GORE HARM HURT MAIM
PAIN PINK RASE RAZE RIST SCAR
SKAG SORE STAB TEAR VULN
WING BLESS BROKE GANCH GRIEF
KNIFE KNOCK SHOOT STICK STING
SUGAT THIRL TOUCH BREACH
BRUISE CREASE ENTAME GRIEVE
HARROW INJURE LAUNCH LESION
MARTYR OFFEND PIERCE PLAGUE
SCOTCH TRAUMA AFFLICT ATTAINT
BATTERY BLIGHTY DIACOPE
GUNSHOT SCRATCH DISTRESS
FLANKARD FLEABITE INCISION
LACERATE SPURGALL VULNERATE
(**— FROM BOAR'S TUSK**) GANCH
GAUNCH
(**— FROM BULL'S HORN**) CORNADA
(**— FROM RUBBING**) GALL
(**— IN DEER'S SIDE**) FLANKARD
(**— MADE BY THRUST**) FOIN
(**— ON FOOT**) FIKE
(**— ON HORSE'S ANKLE**) CREPANCE
(**— ON HORSE'S FOOT**) CREPANCE
(**— PRIDE**) PIQUE
(**— WITH POINTED WEAPON**) STAB
SWORD
(**DEEP —**) DIACOPE
(**MINUTE —**) PRICK SCART
(**TRIFLING —**) FLEABITE
(**PL.**) NOUNS
(**PREF.**) HELC(O) TRAUMAT(O)
VULNI
WOUNDED HURT WUND VULNED
WINGED VULNOSE STRICKEN
WOUNDWORT BETONY ALLHEAL
HERCULES
WOU-WOU WAWA WAWAH
CAMPER GIBBON
WOVEN BROCHE BROWDEN
DAMASSE
(**— FULL WIDTH**) SEAMLESS
(**— WIDE**) BROAD
(**— WITH RIB**) SOLEIL
WOW AWE HIT MEW BARK GOSH
HOWL RAVE WAIL GOLLY WHINE
SUCCESS
WOZZECK (**CHARACTER IN —**)
MARIE ANDRES WOZZECK
(**COMPOSER OF —**) BERG
WRACK KELP RACK RUIN VAREC
CUTWEED DESTROY DOWNFALL
EELGRASS WRECKAGE
WRAITH WAFT FETCH GHOST
SPOOK DOUBLE SHADOW SWARTH
SPECTRE
WRANGLE RAG YED CAMP MOIL
SPAR TIFT ARGLE ARGUE BRAWL
CHIDE DAFER FLITE JOWER PLEAD
STRUT ARGUFY BICKER CAFFLE
CAMPLE CANGLE DACKER FRAPLE
FRATCH HAGGLE HASSLE JANGLE
RAGGLE THREAP BRABBLE
BRANGLE DISPUTE PICKEER
QUARREL SCRAFFLE SQUABBLE
TIRRWIRR
WRANGLER CAMPER COWBOY

GRATER HAFTER WRAGER
DEBATER HAGGLER DEFENDER
OPPONENT
WRANGLING JANGLE
WRAP HAP LAP LOT WAP BIND FURL
ROLL WHIP AMICE CLASP CLOAK
LAMBA MANTA NUBIA SERVE
SHAWL TWINE WOOLD AFGHAN
BURLAP CLOTHE COCOON
COOLER DOLMAN EMBALE
MOIDER MUFFLE PATTOO SACQUE
SARAPE SERAPE SWATHE WIMPLE
WRIXLE ENVELOP INVOLVE
SWADDLE UMBELAP BARRACAN
(**— CABLE**) KECKLE
(**— CLOSE**) SNUGGLE
(**— DEAD BODY**) CERE
(**— ONESELF**) HUDDLE
(**— UP**) HAP MAIL CINCH ENROL
IMPLY
(**— UP HEAD**) MOB MOP MOBLE
(**— WIRE AROUND FISHING LINE**)
GANGE
(**— WITH BANDAGE**) SWATHE
(**HEAD —**) NUBIA SNOOD
(**PL.**) SECRECY RESTRAINT
WRAPPER APRON COVER MOTTO
PILCH SHAWL SMOCK COUPON
FARDEL JACKET ENVELOP
OVERALL SARPLER COVERING
MAHARMAH WOOLPACK
(**— FOR BOOK**) JACKET
(**— FOR CUTLET**) PAPILLOTE
(**— WORN IN EGYPT**) GALABIA
GALABEAH
(**COOKING —**) PAPILLOTE
WRAPPING WAP PACK GELILAH
LAPPING COVERING MANTLING
(**— FOR DEAD**) CEREMENT
(**— MATERIAL**) SARAN
(**— OF HEBREW SCROLL**) GELILAH
(**— OF ROPE**) SERVICE
WRASSE COOK BALLAN COMBER
CONNER CUNNER LABRID
HOGFISH PIGFISH SEAWIFE
CORKWING DONCELLA JANIZARY
LADYFISH SENORITA
WRATH IRE FURY GRIM ANGER
WROTH CHOLER FELONY PASSION
VIOLENCE
WRATHFUL IRY EVIL HIGH ANGRY
IRATE WROTH IREFUL RAGING
FURIOUS JEALOUS CHOLERIC
WREAK CAUSE AVENGE EXPEND
GRATIFY INDULGE INFLICT
REVENGE
(**— DESTRUCTION**) ESTREPE
WREATH LEI ORLE PLAY CROWN
GREEN LAURE LORRE OLIVE
TORSE WHORL WRASE ANADEM
CRANTS CREASE LAUREL POTONG
TORTIL CHAPLET CORONAL
CORONET CROWNAL DOLPHIN
FESTOON GARLAND WRINKLE
KELYPHYTE
(**SPIRAL —**) VOLUTION
WREATHE BIND WIND CRISP TWINE
TWIST WRING INTORT WRITHE
CONTORT ENTWINE INTWIST
INVOLVE
WREATHED SPIRY TORTILE TORTIVE
WRITHED INTORTED TORTILLE

WRECK CRAB HULK RUIN BLAST
CRACK CREAM PRANG SHOOT
SMASH TRASH WRACK DEFACE
DESPOIL DESTROY FOUNDER
GODSEND SHATTER TORPEDO
DEMOLISH SABOTAGE SHAMBLES
(**— COMPLETELY**) TOTAL
(**HUMAN —**) DERELICT
WRECKAGE WRACK FINDAL
FLOTSAM GODSEND WAVESON
SHAMBLES
WRECKED NOUGHT
WRECKERS, THE (**CHARACTER IN**
—) AVIS MARK PASCOE THRIZA
(**COMPOSER OF —**) SMYTH
WREN GIRL STAG TOPE CUTTY
JENNY KITTY PEGGY SALLY STAID
TYDIE SCUTTY TIDIFE TIDLEY TINTIE
TOMTIT WRANNY BLUECAP
REGULUS MALURINE WRANNOCK
(**BUSH —**) RIFLEBIRD
WRENCH KEY PIN RUG PULL RACK
RICK RUGG TEAR YERK CRICK
CRINK FORCE THRAW THROW
TWIST WRAMP WREST BEDKEY
SPRAIN STRAIN TWEEZE DISTORT
SPANNER SPANULE SQUINCH
TORTURE TWISTLE
WREST REAR REND EXACT FORCE
TWIST ARREST EXTORT WRENCH
WRITHE ABSTORT WIREDRAW
(**— AWAY**) STRIP DESPOIL
WRESTLE PRAY RASSLE SQUIRM
TUSSLE WRAXLE WRITHE
GRAPPLE SCUFFLE THRIMBLE
THRUMBLE
WRESTLER MATMAN WELTER
CLICKER MATSTER GRAPPLER
(**KIND OF —**) SUMO
WRESTLING SUMO SAMBO
PALESTRA WRAXLING
(**— TECHNIQUE**) GLIMA
(**KIND OF —**) WRIST
(**STYLE OF —**) SAMBO
WRETCH DOG MIX FILE WARY
MISER SLAVE THING BUGGER
PERSON SQUALL BRETHEL CAITIFF
CAMOOCH CHINCHE CULLION
GLUTTON HILDING SCROYLE
BEZONIAN CREATURE MESCHANT
POLTROON RECREANT SCULLION
WRETCHED EVIL FOUL LORN MEAN
POOR DAWNY DEENY GAUNT
SORRY WISHT WOFUL YEMER
ABJECT CAITIF DISMAL MEAGER
PALTRY RASCAL SHABBY SICKLY
SORDID UNLEAD UNLEDE WOEFUL
ABYSMAL BENEATH FORLORN
OUTWORN PITIFUL SQUALID
UNSEELY MESCHANT MISERABLE
(**— PERSON OR ANIMAL**) MISERY
WRIGGLE EEL REG RIG FRIG LASH
WIND WRIG SLIDE WRELE WRING
SQUIRM WAMBLE WANGLE
WARPLE WIDDLE WIMPLE WINTLE
WRITHE EYEBROW SNIGGLE
TWIDDLE TWINGLE WRABILL
WRESTLE SCRIGGLE SQUIGGLE
WRIGGLING EELY SCRIGGLE
SQUIGGLY
WRIGGLY SNAKY SNAKISH
SQUIRMING

WRING RACK DRAIN EXACT SCREW
TWIST WREST EXTORT OPPRESS
SQUEEZE TORMENT TORTURE
(**— THE NECK**) SCRAG
WRINGER RUNG WRUNG SQUEEZER
WRINKLE RUT DRAW FOLD FURL
HINT KNIT LIRK RUCK RUGA SEAM
BREAK CRIMP CRISP DELVE FAULT
FRILL REEVE RIVEL SNIRL BUCKLE
COCKLE CRAVAT CREASE FURROW
METHOD PUCKER RIMPLE RUMPLE
RUNKLE SCRIMP WREATH
BLEMISH CRANKLE CRINKLE
CRUMPLE CRUNKLE FROUNCE
FRUMPLE CONTRACT IRRUGATE
RUGOSITY
(**— OF FLESH**) CRAVAT
(**— REMOVER**) IRON IRONER
(**PREF.**) RUTI RUTID(O)
WRINKLED CRUMP PURFLY RUGATE
RUGGED RUGOSE RUGOUS
SEAMED COCKLED CREASED
ROUCHED SAVOYED CRUMPLED
FURROWED PUCKERED WRITHLED
WRIZZLED
WRINKLING KNIT KNOT FROWN
WRIST CARPUS SHACKLE
(**PREF.**) CARP(O)
WRISTER MUFFETEE
WRISTLET STRAP WRISTER
MUFFETEE
WRISTWATCH BAGUET BAGUETTE
WRIT AIEL CAPE MISE PONE TOLT
ALIAS BREVE BRIEF ERROR RECTO
UTRUM BRIEVE CAPIAS ELEGIT
EXTENT PLAINT VENIRE ACCOUNT
DEDIMUS DETINUE EXIGENT
LATITAT PLURIES PRECEPT
PROCESS SUMMONS WARRANT
CESSAVIT COSINAGE DETAINER
DOCUMENT FORMEDON
MANDAMUS MITTIMUS NOVERINT
PRAECIPE QUOMINUS REPLEVIN
SISERARY SUBPOENA TESTATUM
WARRANTY
(**— FOR SUMMONING EXTRA**
JURORS) TALES
(**LEGAL —**) CERT
WRITE INK PEN BACK BOOK DITE
DRAW READ SELL CLERK DRAFT
STYLE AUTHOR ENFACE INDITE
SCRIBE SCRIVE ADDRESS COMPILE
COMPOSE DICTATE EMPAPER
EXARATE SCREEVE BIOGRAPH
INSCRIBE
(**— ADDRESS**) BACK
(**— BENEATH**) SUBSCRIBE
(**— BETWEEN**) INTERSCRIBE
(**— BRIEFLY**) JOT
(**— CARELESSLY**) DASH SCRAWL
SCRIBBLE
(**— DOWN**) SIGN BREVE DENOTE
RECORD AMORTIZE DESCRIBE
(**— FOR ANOTHER**) GHOSTWRITE
(**— FURTHER**) ADD
(**— HASTILY**) SCRATCH SCRIBBLE
SQUIGGLE
(**— IN A LARGE HAND**) ENGROSS
(**— IN LARGE CHARACTERS**) TEXT
(**— IN SHORTHAND**) STENOGRAPH
(**— LETTER**) CORRESPOND
EPISTOLIZE

(— MUSIC) NOTATE COMPOSE
(— ON FRONT OF BILL) ENFACE
(— PASTORAL POEMS) PHILLIS
(— POMPOUSLY) FUSTIANIZE
(— WHAT IS NOT TRUE) FABLE
(SUFF.) GRAPH(ER)(IA)(IC)(Y)
WRITER (ALSO SEE AUTHOR) PEN
BARD HACK PUFF ALVAR GHOST
ODIST SQUIB AUTHOR FATHER
GLOZER HEROIC LAWYER LETTER
MUNSHI NOTARY PENMAN
PRABHU PROSER PURVOE SCRIBE
TRAGIC YEOMAN ADAPTER
ADSMITH ANALYST DIARIST
ELOHIST ESSAYER GLOSSER
GNOMIST HYMNIST IAMBIST
JUVENAL LAUDIST MUNCHEE
PENSTER PROPHET PROSAIC
REVUIST SCRIVER STYLIST
SUMMIST TEXTMAN AUGUSTAN
BLURBIST COMEDIAN COMPOSER
DECADENT DECADIST DIDACTIC
EMBOSSER EPISTLER ESSAYIST
FABLEIST FABULIST GROMATIC
HUMORIST IDYLLIST MONODIST
MOONSHEE NOVELIST PARODIST
PENWOMAN PREFACER
PRESSMAN PROSAIST PROSEMAN
PSALMIST REVIEWER SATIRIST
SCRIPTER VERSEMAN HISTORIAN
LEGENDARY LEGENDIST
PROSATEUR LIBRETTIST
TRACTARIAN PAMPHLETEER
(— OF BURLESQUE) GABBER
(FAST —) STENO
(FREE-LANCE —) CREEPER
(HACK —) PENSTER
(INCOMPETENT —) BOTCHER
(JESUIT —) BOLLANDIST
(OBITUARY —) NECROGRAPHER
(OBSCENE —) RIBALD
(PROVERB —) PAROEMIOGRAPHER
(SACRED —) HAGIOLOGIST
HAGIOGRAPHER
(SATIRICAL —) SILLOGRAPH
(SPEECH —) LOGOGRAPHER
WRITHE WRY WIND THROW TWIRL
TWIST WRING SQUIRM TERVEE
WAMBLE WRABBE WRENCH

AGONIZE WRESTLE WRIGGLE
WRINGLE CONVOLVE
WRITHING EELY WRING WRITHY
WRITING BOOK DITE FAIT PAGE
POEM KANJI LIBEL SCROW
CADJAN GOSSIP LEGEND LETTER
PAGINE SCRIPT SCRITE SCRIVE
UNCIAL ARTICLE AUTONYM
DIPLOMA ESCRIPT SCREEVE
APOCRYPH CONTRACT DOCUMENT
GRAVAMEN HARANGUE
KAKEMONO LETTRURE LIPOGRAM
PAMPHLET SCRIBING SONNETRY
SMALLHAND JOURNALISM
SCRIVENING
(— FOR ANOTHER) ALLOGRAPH
(— OF LITTLE VALUE) STUFF
SCRIBBLE
(— ON PAPER SCROLL) MAKIMONO
(— ON SILK) KAKEMONO
(— ON WAX) CEROGRAPH
(—S OF VIRGIL) POETICA
(— UNDER SEAL) BOND
(BAWDY —) SCULDUDDRY
SCULDUDDERY SKULDUDDERY
(BIBLICAL —) MENE
(BITTER —) DIATRIBE
(CARELESS —) SCRAWL
(CRAMPED —) NIGGLE
(CURSIVE —) JOINHAND
(EASY —) GOSSIP
(FORMAL —) RECORD
(HINDU —) VEDA
(HUMOROUS —S) FACETIAE
(ILLUMINATED —) FRACTUR
(IN THIS —) HERETO
(IRREGULAR —) SCRAWL
(MUSICAL —) GIMEL GYMEL
(NORSE —) EDDA
(OBSCENE —) BALDERDASH
(PRETENTIOUS —) FUSTIAN
(SACRED —) ARANYAKA BRAHMANA
SCRIPTURE
(SATIRICAL —) PASQUINADE
(SECRET —) SCYTALE
(SHORT —) SCRIP
(SHORTHAND —) PHONOGRAPHY
(SPY —) CODE
(STUPID —) PABLUM PABULUM

(STYLE OF —) ACADEMESE
(SWIFT —) SHORTHAND
(SYLLABIC —) KANA
(VAPID —) WASH
(VERBOSE —) TOOTLE
(VOLUMINOUS —) POLYGRAPHY
(WITTY —S) FACETIAE
(WORTHLESS —) TRIPE
(PL.) LEGENDA ARANYAKA
POSTHUMA
(PREF.) GRAMO GRAPHI GRAPHO
(SUFF.) GRAM GRAPH(ER)(IA)(IC)(Y)
WRITING CASE STANDISH
SCRUTOIRE
WRITTEN KETIB KETHIB KTHIBH
GRAPHIC LITERAL
(— ABOVE) SS
(— AFTER) ADSCRIPT
(— HASTILY) STRAY
(SO —) SIC
(PREF.) GRAPTO
WROCLAW BRESLAU
WRONG BAD CAR ILL MIS OUT WET
AWRY HARM HURT SORE SOUR
TORT WITE AGATE AGLEE AGLEY
AMISS CRIME DUTCH FALSE
GLEED GRIEF MALUM UNFIT
WATHE WOUGH AGUILT ASTRAY
BLOOEY FAULTY INJURE INJURY
NOUGHT OFFEND SARAAD SINFUL
UNTRUE WICKED WONDER
ABUSION ABUSIVE DAMNIFY
DEFRAUD IMMORAL INJURIA
MISBEDE NAUGHTY UNRIGHT
VIOLATE AGGRIEVE COCKEYED
MISTAKEN PERVERSE UNLEEFUL
(CIVIL —) TORT
(IMAGINARY —) WINDMILL
(SHOCKINGLY —) MONSTROUS
(PREF.) MIS
WRONGDOER ACTOR SINNER
FAULTER MISDOER OFFENDER
WRONGDOING MISS CRIME FAULT
DEFAULT MISCONDUCT
MALFEASANCE
WRONGFUL UNFAIR UNJUST
TORTIOUS TORTUOUS UNLAWFUL
WRONGHEADED WRY PERVERSE
WRONGLY AMISS BADLY FALSE

NOUGHT UNRICHT UNRIGHT
OVERWART
WROTH ANGRY IRATE IREFUL
WROUGHT BEATEN CARVEN
FORMED SHAPED VROCHT
CREATED HAMMERED
(ELABORATELY —) LABORED
WRY ASKEW AVERT TWIST WRING
WRONG IRONIC WRITHE DEFLECT
DISTORT TWISTED WRITHEN
SATURNINE
WRYNECK IYNX JYNX SLAB WEET
LOXIA PEABIRD WEETBIRD
TORTICOLLIS
**WUTHERING HEIGHTS (AUTHOR
OF —)** BRONTE
(CHARACTER IN —) DEAN EDGAR
ELLEN JOSEPH LINTON ZILLAH
FRANCES HARETON HINDLEY
EARNSHAW ISABELLA
LOCKWOOD CATHERINE
HEATHCLIFF
WYCH ELM WITCH WITCHEN
WYLIECOAT WALYCOAT
NIGHTGOWN PETTICOAT
WYND HAW ALLEY CLOSE

WYOMING
CAPITAL: CHEYENNE
COUNTY: TETON UINTA GOSHEN
BIGHORN LARAMIE NIOBRARA
INDIAN: ARAPAHO
LAKE: JACKSON
MOUNTAIN: ELK CLOUD GANNET
HOBACK FREMONT ATLANTIC
SHERIDAN
MOUNTAIN RANGE: TETON
ABSARO BIGHORN LARAMIE
RATTLESNAKE
NICKNAME: EQUALITY
RIVER: GREEN SNAKE PLATTE
POWDER BIGHORN
STATE BIRD: MEADOWLARK
STATE FLOWER: PAINTBRUSH
STATE TREE: COTTONWOOD
TOWN: CODY LUSK CASPER
BUFFALO LARAMIE RAWLINS
WORLAND GREYBULL KEMMERER
SHERIDAN SUNDANCE

X

X EX XRAY ERROR MISTAKE
XANADU (SACRED RIVER OF —)
  ALPH
XANTHIC YELLOW
XANTHIPPE NAG SHREW
  (HUSBAND OF —) SOCRATES
XANTHIPPUS (SON OF —) PERICLES
XEBEC SHIP CHEBEC CHEBECK
  SHABEQUE

XENIUM GIFT DAINTY DELICACY
XERES JEREZ SHERRY
XERIC DRY
XHOSA KAFIR KAFFIR
  (PL.) AMAKOSA AMAXOSA
XIPHARES (FATHER OF —)
  MITHRIDATE
XIPHISTERNUM XIFOID
XIPHOSURUS LIMULUS

X-RAY UROGRAM
XUREL SCAD SAUREL
XUTHUS (ADOPTED SON OF —)
  ION
  (BROTHER OF —) DORUS AEOLUS
  (FATHER OF —) HELLEN
  (MOTHER OF —) ORSEIS
  (SON OF —) ION DURUS ACHAEUS
  (WIFE OF —) CREUSA

XYLEM WOOD HADROM HADROME
  XYLOGEN
XYLOID WOODY LIGNEOUS
XYLOPHONE REGAL SARON
  BALAFO GAMBANG GAMELAN
  MARIMBA BALAPHON GAMELANG
  GIGELIRA STICCADO
XYSTUS WALK XYST PORTICO
  TERRACE

Y

Y WY YA WYE YOD YOKE YANKEE
(— **CONNECTION**) SIAMESE
(— **COORDINATE**) SINE
(PREF.) (**LETTER** —) YPSILI
YABBER TALK JABBER LANGUAGE
YABBY CRAWLIE
YACARE CAIMAN CAYMAN JACARE
YACHT SAIL SCOW BRUTE YATCH
DINGHY SONDER YEAGHE CRUISER
KEELBOAT
YAFF YAP BARK YELP
YAFFLE ARMFUL YAFFIL
YAHOO BRUTE CLOWN ROWDY
BUMPKIN
YAHWEH GOD JAVE YHWH JAHVAH
YAHWIST JEHOVIST
YAK GAB GAG GAS JOKE YUCK
LAUGH BULBUL SARLAK SARLYK
YAMMER CHATTER
YAKALA JAGA
YAKKA WORK LABOR
YAKUT SAKHA
YAM HOI UBE UBI UVE JAMB LIMA
RAIL TUGUI IGNAME INAMIA
INHAME POTATO BONIATA
(**TARO** —) KOKO
YAMA (FATHER OF —) VIVASVANT
(**SISTER OF** —) YAMI
YAM BEAN KAMAS JICAMA
WAYAKA SINCAMAS
YAMEN COURT YAMUN OFFICE
YAMEO LLAMEO
YAMMER CRY WAIL SCOLD WHINE
YEARN YOMER GRUMBLE
WHIMPER
YAMP YAMPA SQUAWROOT
YANAN NOZI
YANG HONK GURJUN
YANK FLOG JERK SLAP HOICK
SNAKE BUFFET
YAP BARK YAWP YELP MOUTH
SCOLD WAFFLE BUMPKIN
CHATTER KYOODLE
YAPOK YAPOCK OPOSSUM
OYAPOCK
YAQUI YAKI HIAQUI
YARD HAW HOF YED CREW CROW
DUMP FOLD SKID SPAR TILT
COURT GARTH PATIO STICK
CANCHA HOPPET LOANIN CURTAIN
GARSTON KNACKERY OUTGARTH
(— **OF SAWMILL**) DUMP
(— **WHERE COWS ARE MILKED**)
LOANIN LOANING
(**FINAL** —) FELL
(**GRASSY** —) GARSTON
(**PAVED** —) CAUSEY
(**POULTRY** —) BARTON
(**SAIL** —) RAE
(**1-16TH OF A** —) NAIL
(**1-3RD OF CUBIC** —) CARTLOAD
(**20** —**S**) SCORE
(**5 AND A HALF** —**S**) ROD

YARD GRASS ELEUSINE MANGRASS
YARDLAND VERGE VIRGATE
YARDMASTER DINGER
YARDSTICK VERGE YAIRD METRIC
MEASURE METWAND METEWAND
STANDARD CRITERION
YARE YAR AYRE YORE BRISK READY
LIVELY NIMBLE PROMPT
YARETA LLARETA
YARM WAIL NOISE OUTCRY SHRIEK
YARN ABB END FOX CORD GARN
GIMP PIRN SILK SLIP WEFT WHIP
DYNEL FLOSS GRAIN INKLE LUREX
PITCH SPIEL ALASKA ANGORA
BERLIN BROACH CADDIS COTTON
CREWEL CUFFER DACRON ESTRON
FLORET FRIEZE MERINO MOTTLE
PEELER RATINE SAXONY SINGLE
STRAND TASLAN THREAD VINYON
WOOLEN ZEPHYR ACETATE
CADDICE FILLING GENAPPE
INGRAIN MELANGE RACKING
SCHAPPE VIGOGNE WORSTED
ASBESTOS BOURETTE CHENILLE
FORTISAN METALLIC ROUNDING
SPINNING WHEELING ORGANZINE
VIGOUREUX
(— **FOR WARP**) ABB
(— **FROM FLOSS SILK**) FLORET
(— **MEASURE**) LEA
(— **SIZE**) TYPP
(**BALL OF** —) CLEW CLUE
(**BITS OF ROPE** —) THRUMS
(**BUNDLE OF** —) PAD
(**CONICAL MASS OF** —) COP
(**ELASTIC** —) LASTEX
(**EXAGGERATED** —) STRETCHER
(**FINE SOFT** —) ZEPHYR KASHMIR
CASHMERE
(**LINEN** —) SPINEL
(**ROLL OF** —) PRICK CHEESE
(**ROPE** —**S**) SOOGEE
(**SILK** —) TRAM
(**SMALL PIECE OF SPUN** —) RABAND
ROBBIN ROPEBAND
(**UNEVEN** —) BOUCLE
(PL.) FOX MENDINGS
YARRAN GIDYA MYALL GIDGEA
GIDGEE
YARROW ALLHEAL CAMMOCK
MAUDLIN MILFOIL PELLITORY
YASHIRO SHA
YASHMAK VEIL ASMACK YAKMAK
YATAGHAN SABER ATAGHAN
SIMITAR
YATTER CHATTER PRATTLE
YAUD MARE YADE
YAUPON ASSI HOLLY YUPON
CASINA CASSINE
YAUTIA COCO TARO TANIA COCKER
TANIER MALANGA
YAW GAPE YAWN LURCH SHEER
BROACH SWERVE

YAWL HOWL DANDY MIZZEN
SCREAM SCHOKKER
YAWN GAP GALP GANE GANT GAPE
YANE ABYSM CHAUM CAVITY
TEDIUM DULLNESS OSCITATE
YAWNING HIANT CHASMA GAPING
OSCITANT
YAWP BAWL GAPE RANT YELP
STARE SQUAWK YAMMER
COMPLAIN
YAWS PIAN TUBBA TUBBOE
YAWWEED RHUBARB
YAYA COPA
YEA YA YES YOY YIGH TRULY
ASSENT REALLY VERILY
YEAN EAN LAMB
YEANLING KID LAMB EANLING
YEAR EAR SUN AYRE HAAB TIME
ANNEE ANNUS VAGUE WINTER
ZODIAC TOWMOND TZOLKIN
BIRTHDAY
(— **OF EMANCIPATION**) JUBILEE
(**ACADEMIC** —) SESSION
(**IN THIS** —) HA
(**LAST** —) FERNYEAR
(**MANY** —**S**) AGE
(**MAYAN** —) TUN HAAB
(**ONE BILLION** —**S**) AEON
(**SABBATICAL** —) JUBILE JUBILEE
(**1000** —**S**) MILLENARY MILLENNIUM
(**4320 MILLION** —**S**) KALPA
(PL.) SEASONS
(SUFF.) ENNIAL ENNIUM
YEARBOOK ANNUAL SERIAL
ANNUARY
YEARLING COLT HORNOTINE
(**AUTHOR OF** —) RAWLINGS
(**CHARACTER IN** —) LEM ORA JODY
HUTTO PENNY TWINK BAXTER
NELLIE OLIVER WILSON GINRIGHT
FORRESTER WEATHERBY
FODDERWING
YEARLY ANNUAL SOLEMN
YEARN HO YEN ACHE BURN EARN
GAPE HONE IRNE LONG PANT PINE
SIGH CRAVE GREEN GRIEN ASPIRE
CURDLE GRIEVE HANKER YAMMER
YEARNING EROS DESIRE HANKER
RENNET CRAVING EARNFUL
HOMESICK
YEAST BEE EST BARM BEES EAST
KOJI SOTS FROTH SPUME LEAVEN
NEWING RISING SIZING TORULA
FERMENT SIZZING EMPTINGS
(**FILM** —) FLOR
YEASTY LIGHT FROTHY TRIVIAL
RESTLESS
YEGG ROBBER BURGLAR
YELL CRY CALL GOWL HOWL ROAR
YARM YAUP YOWL YOWT GOLLY
SHOUT TIGER BELLOW GOLLAR
HOLLER SCREAM YAMMER
YELLOCH SCRONACH SKELLOCH

YELLOW (ALSO SEE COLOR) OR
GULL AMBER BLAKE BLOND FAVEL
FLAVE JAUNE PALEW SHELL
YELWE ALMOND BANANA FLAVID
MELINE MIMOSA NUGGET OXGALL
BISCUIT JASMINE JONQUIL
LEGHORN LUTEOUS MEXICAN
MUSTARD NANKEEN OATMEAL
POPCORN SAFFRON TILLEUL
WHEATEN YUCATAN AUREOLIN
GENERALL ICTEROID LUMINOUS
MARIGOLD ORPIMENT PRIMROSE
(— **AS BUTTER**) BLAKE
(— **ORANGE**) SAFFRON
(**BROWNISH** —) FULVID FULVOUS
(**DINGY** —) LURID
(**GOLDEN** —) FLAVID
(**GREENISH** —) ACACIA
(**INDIAN** —) PURI PURREE
(**LEMON** —) GENERALL
(**PALE** —) EGGSHELL
(PREF.) CHLOR(O) CHRYS(O) FLAV(I)
(O) OCHRO XANTH(O) XANTIN(O)
YELLOW ALDER SAGEROSE
YELLOW BEDSTRAW CRUDWORT
CURDWORT FLEAWEED
YELLOW BUGLE IVA IVE IVY
YELLOW CLINTONIA DOGBERRY
YELLOW-DOG MEAN
CONTEMPTIBLE
YELLOW FEVER VOMITO
YELLOW FOXTAIL STICKERS
YELLOW GENTIAN FELWORT
YELLOW GREEN PISTACHE
YELLOWHAMMER SKYTE YITE
AMMER GOWDY SKITE GLADDY
GOLDIE VERDIN YORLIN FLICKER
GLADEYE YELDRIN YOLDRING
(— **STATE**) ALABAMA
YELLOW IRIS SEDGE LEVERS
DAGGERS
YELLOWISH SALLOW ICTERINE
SAFFRONY
(— **GREEN**) GLAUCOUS
(— **RED**) FALLOW
(PREF.) LUTEO
YELLOW JACKET VESPA VESPID
YELLOW JASMINE WOODBINE
YELLOWLEGS KILLCU TATLER
WINTER YELPER TATTLER
YELLOW MACKEREL CREVALLE
YELLOWNESS FLAVEDO
YELLOW POND LILY DUCK CLOTE
CLOTS NUPHAR
YELLOW POPLAR TULIPWOOD
YELLOW PRICKLE RUBIA
YELLOW RATTLE RATEL
COCKSCOMB LOUSEWORT
YELLOW TOADFLAX RAMSTEAD
YELLOW WAGTAIL OATEAR
YELLOW WATER LILY KELP WOKAS
YELLOWWOOD FUSTIC FUSTOC
GOPHER MANGWE VIRGILIA

YELP CRY YAP YIP BAFF BARK KIYI WAFF YAFF YAUP YAWP BOAST YAMPH AVOCET SQUEAL YAFFLE YELLOW
YELPING CRY

YEMEN

ANCIENT KINGDOM: SABA SHEBA
CAPITAL: SANA SANAA
COIN: RIAL RIYAL BUOSHA
MUSLIM SECT: SHIA SUNNI
OFFICIAL NAME:
YEMENARABREPUBLIC
PEOPLE: ZAIDI SHAFAI
PORT: MOKA MOCHA
REGION: TIHAMA
RULER: IMAM
TOWN: MOKA DAMAR MOCHA
TAIZZ HODEIDA

YEN EYES ITCH LONG URGE YEARN DESIRE SUCKER CRAVING LONGING
YENTA GOSSIP TALKER BUSYBODY
YEOMAN CHURL CLERK WRITER GOODMAN GUIDMAN GRAYCOAT RETAINER BEEFEATER
YERBA SANTA TARBUSH
YERK BEAT GOAD HURL JERK KICK STAB YARK THUMP EXCITE THRASH LASHING
YES AY DA IS JA OC SI YA AYE ISS YAS YAW YEA YEP YIS YUH YUS YEAH JOKOL TRULY
YESTERDAY HIER YESTER YESTREEN
(OF —) PRIDIAN
YET AND BUT YIT EVEN STILL ALGATE HOWEER THOUGH FINALLY HOWEVER HITHERTO
(AS —) SOFAR UPTONOW
YETI BIGFOOT SNOWMAN SASQUATCH
YETT GATE
YEUK EWK YUK ITCH YUCK ITCHING
YEW YO HEW UGH YOE YOW VIEW TAXUS TOPIARY CHINWOOD
YEX YOLK
YIDDISH JEWISH
YIELD GO BOW CUT ILD PAN PLY BEAR BEND CAST CEDE CESS COME CROP DRAG DUCK EMIT FOLD GIVE HEAR HELD LOUT QUIT SELL VAIL WAGE AGREE ALLOW AMAIN AVALE AWALE BRING BUDGE CARRY CAUSE DEFER GRANT HIELD HIELD LEAVE OFFER SLAKE STOOP ACCEDE AFFORD BOUNTY BUCKLE COMPLY CONFER FOLLOW IMPART OUTPUT RELENT RENDER RETURN SUBMIT SUPPLY SWERVE UNGIVE UPGIVE ABANDON ANALYZE BEARING CONCEDE DELIVER FURNISH HARVEST KNUCKLE OUTTURN PRODUCE PROVIDE REDOUND RUCKSEY SUCCUMB BEGRUDGE FRUITAGE OVERGIVE PICKINGS UNDERLIE RELINQUISH
(— FRUIT) ADDLE GRAIN
(— GRASS) GRAZE

(— OF FIELD) BURDEN
(— OF MINE) BONANZA
(— ON BOND) BASIS
(— TO) INDULGE
(— TO TEMPTATION) FALL
(— UP) LET FORLET FORLEIT
(— WELL) HIT BLEED
(MINERAL —) PROSPECT
(SUFF.) FER(ENCE)(ENT)(OUS)
YIELDED
(SUFF.) GENETIC
YIELDING ABLE MEEK NESH SOFT TALL WAXY NAISH WAXEN BONAIR CAVING FACILE FEEBLE FLABBY LIMBER LITHER OUTPUT PLIANT QUAGGY SUPPLE BEARING CESSION FINGENT FLACCID DEDITION LADYLIKE RECREANT COMPLIANT COMPLIANCE SUBMISSIVE
(— IRREGULARLY) BUNCHY
(— OF HORSE) FLEXION
(— STAGE) SEAR
(— TO IMPULSES) ABANDON
(— TO INFLUENCE) PLIABLE
(— UNDERFOOT) SINKY
YIN SHANG
YIRMILIK METALLIK
YODEL SONG JODEL WARBLE REFRAIN
YODH IOD JOD
YOGA JOG
(— POSITION) ASANA
YOGI JOGI FAKIR FAKEER
YOKE BOW YOK BAIL CROW DRAG FORK HOOP PAIR POKE SOLE TEAM BANGY FURCA SHEBA SPANG BANGHY COUPLE INSPAN DRAGBAR HARNESS OPPRESS ADJUGATE
(— BAR) SKEY
(— TO HOLD DRILL) CROW
(— TO RAISE CANNON) BAIL
(PREF.) ZYG(O)(OTO)
(SUFF.) ZYGOMATIC ZYGOSIS ZYGOTE
YOKED (NOT —) AZYGOUS
YOKEFELLOW MATE FELLOW PARTNER YOKEMATE
YOKEL YOB BOOR CLUB JAKE JOCK LOUT YAHOO YOBBO FARMER JOSKIN BUMPKIN HAYSEED HOODLUM WAYBACK ABDERITE CHAWBACON
YOKING BOUT CONTEST MUGGING
YOKO ONO
YOLANTA (CHARACTER IN —) RENE ROBERT YOLANTA VAUDEMONT
(COMPOSER OF —) TCHAIKOVSKY
YOLDRING YOWLEY
YOLK CENTER YELLOW ESSENCE LATEBRA VITELLUS PARABLAST
(HAVING A —) LECITHAL
(PREF.) LECITH(O) VITELLI VITELLO
(SUFF.) LECITHAL
YON YONDER THITHER BACKWARD
YONDER THAT THERE THOSE THITHER
YORE PAST YARE YEARS
(OF —) OLDEN

YORKER TICE
YORKSHIREMAN TIKE TYKE LEAROYD
YORUBA NAGO
YOU DU HE IT OW TA TU WE YA YO ONE OWE SHE SIE TOI YOW YUH THOU VOUS YOUSE YOURSELF
YOU CAN'T GO HOME AGAIN
(AUTHOR OF —) WOLFE
(CHARACTER IN —) ELSE JACK LLOYD ESTHER GEORGE KOHLER MCHARG WEBBER EDWARDS FOXHALL
YOU NEVER CAN TELL (AUTHOR OF —) SHAW
(CHARACTER IN —) BOON BOHUM DOLLY GLORIA PHILIP CLANDON MCCOMAS WILLIAM GRAMPTON VALENTINE
YOUNG FRY JUV BIRD CALF DROP BIRTH BROOD FETUS FRUIT GREEN SMALL UNOLD JUNIOR KINDLE JUVENAL IMMATURE YEANLING YOUTHFUL
(— OF ANY ANIMAL) FRY BABY CALF FOAL JOEY LAMB TOTO
(— OF BEAST) SLINK
(— OF BIRD) CHICK
(— OF CAMEL) COLT
(— OF DOG) WHELP
(— OF FISH) FRY
(— OF SEA TROUT) HERLING
(VERY —) SUCKING NEPHIONIC SHIRTTAIL
(PREF.) FETI FETO FOETI FOETO
(SUFF.) (— ONE) LING
(MODE OF HATCHING —) PAEDES
YOUNGER KID LESS PUNEE JUNIOR PUISNE OFFSPRING
YOUNGEST (— OF BROOD) WALLYDRAG
YOUNGSTER KID BIRD COLT CHILD MINOR YOUTH BUTTON SHAVER URCHIN YONKER YOUNKER SPALPEEN
YOUNKER DUPE CHILD KNIGHT NOVICE SQUIRE YUNKER
YOUR OR YO THY YAR YER OURE OWRE SEIN VOTRE YOURN
YOURSELF ITSELF HERSELF HIMSELF ONESELF
YOUTH BOY BUD IMP LAD CHAP COLT PAGE TEEN BAHUR CHABO GROOM HYLAS POULT PRIME SPRIG SWAIN WHELP BOCHUR BURSCH EPHEBE HOYDEN INFANT JUVENT KOUROS MASTER NONAGE SPRING SQUIRT YONKER CALLANT EPHEBOS GOSSOON JUVENAL PUBERTY SAPLING YOUDITH YOUNGTH ENDYMION JUVENILE SPRINGAL
(— WHO SERVES LIQUORS) GANYMEDE
(AWKWARD —) HOBBLEDEHOY
(DELINQUENT —) BODGIE
(GODDESS OF —) HEBE
(IMPUDENT —) SQUIRT
(INEXPERIENCED —) GUNSEL GREENHORN

(NON-JEWISH —) SHEGETZ
(PERT —) PRINCOX
(RUDE —) HOYDEN
(RUSSIAN — ORGANIZATION) KOMSOMOL
(SILLY —) CALF SLENDER
(WELLBORN —) CHILD
(WORLD'S —) PRIME
(PREF.) HEBE
YOUTHFUL RATH FRESH GREEN YOUNG BOYISH GOLDEN JUNIOR MAIDEN NEANIC VERNAL VIRGIN YOUTHY LADDISH PUERILE YOUNGLY IMMATURE JUVENILE SPRINGAL VIGOROUS
YOUTHFULNESS JEUNESSE
YOWL GOWL HOWL WAIL YELL YELP
YO-YO FLUCTUATE VACILLATE
YUAN DOLLAR
YUAPIN YARURA
YUCATAN (— PEOPLE) MAYA MAYAS
YUCATEC MAYA
YUCCA LILY PITA YUCA AGAVE DATIL IZOTE PALMA JOSHUA LILIAL LILIUM PALMITO SOAPWEED
YUCKY ICKY DIRTY NASTY SLIMY DISGUSTING
YUGA KALI

YUGOSLAVIA

CAPITAL: BEOGRAD BELGRADE
COIN: PARA DINAR
FORMER REPUBLIC: BOSNIA CROATIA SLOVENIA
GULF: KOTOR
LAKE: OHRID PRESPA SCUTARI
MEASURE: RIF AKOV RALO DONUM KHVAT LANAZ STOPA MOTYKA PALAZE RALICO
MOUNTAIN: DURMITOR
MOUNTAIN RANGE: DINARIC
PORT: KOTOR NOVISAD BELGRADE
REPUBLIC: SERBIA MONTENEGRO
RIVER: DRIM IBAR SAVA DRINA RASKA TISZA DANUBE MORAVA VARDAR
TOWN: NIS BUDVA USKUB BITOLJ PRILEP TETOVO CATTARO NOVISAD PRIZREN SKOPLJE MONASTIR SUBOTICA
WEIGHT: OKA OKE DRAMM TOVAR WAGON SATLIJK

YUKON TERRITORY (CAPITAL OF —) WHITEHORSE
(LAKE OF —) KLUANE
(MOUNTAIN OF —) LOGAN
(MOUNTAIN RANGE OF —) OGILVIE STIKINE MACKENZIE
(RIVER OF —) PEEL LEWES LIARD PELLY WHITE KLONDIKE PORCUPINE
(TOWN OF —) ELSA MAYO BARLOW DAWSON
YULE NOEL CHRISTMAS
YUMA CUCHAN
YUMAN PATAYAN
YUNX WRYNECK
YURT TENT

Z

Z ZAD ZED ZEE ZETA ZULU IZARD ZEBRA IZZARD
(SHAPED LIKE A —) OPENBAND
ZAAVAN (FATHER OF —) EZER
ZABAD (FATHER OF —) NEBO ZATTU NATHAN
(MOTHER OF —) SHIMEATH
ZABAGLIONE SABAYON
ZABBAI (SON OF —) BARUCH
ZABBUD (FATHER OF —) BIGVAI
ZABDI (FATHER OF —) ASAPH ZERAH
ZABDIEL (SON OF —) JASHOBEAM
ZABUD (FATHER OF —) NATHAN
ZACCUR (FATHER OF —) IMRI ASAPH JAAZIAH
(SON OF —) HANAN SHAMMUA
ZACHARIAH (DAUGHTER OF —) ABIJAH
(FATHER OF —) JEROBOAM
ZACHARIAS (FATHER OF —) BARACHIAS
(SON OF —) JOHN
(WIFE OF —) ELISABETH
ZACHER (FATHER OF —) JEHIEL
(MOTHER OF —) MAACHAH
ZADOK (DAUGHTER OF —) JERUSHAH
(FATHER OF —) BAANA IMMER AHITUB MERAIOTH
ZAFFER SMALT SAFFIOR ZAPHARA
ZAGREUS (FATHER OF —) JUPITER
(MOTHER OF —) PROSERPINE
ZAHAM (FATHER OF —) REHOBOAM
(MOTHER OF —) ABIHAIL

ZAIRE
BOMU UELE
ALTERNATE NAME: CONGO
CAPITAL: KINSHASA
COIN: SENGI LIKUTA MAKUTA
COINS: MAKUTA
LAKE: KIVU MWERU
LANGUAGE: KIKONGO LINGALA SWAHILI TSHILUBA
MONEY: ZAIRE
MOUNTAIN RANGE: MITUMBA VIRUNGA RUWENZORI
PROVINCE: KIVU KASAI SHABA EQUATOR KATANGA BANDUNDU EQUATEUR ORIENTAL
RIVER: RUKI UELE CONGO DENGU IBINA KASAI LINDI ZAIRE LIKATI LOMAMI LUKUGA UBANGI ARUWIMI LUALABA LULONGA
TOWN: BAYA BOMA LEBO AKETI BUKAVU KAMINA KIKWIT MATADI BUTEMBO KANANGA KOLWEZI BAKWANGA YANGAMBI KISANGANI

ZALAPH (SON OF —) HANUN

ZAMBIA
CAPITAL: LUSAKA
COIN: NGWEE KWACHA
FALLS: VICTORIA
LAKE: MWERU BANGWEULU TANGANYIKA
LANGUAGE: LOZI BEMBA TONGA LUVALE NYANJA AFRIKAANS
MOUNTAIN RANGE: MUCHINGA
RIVER: KAFUE LUANGWA LUAPULA ZAMBEZI
TOWN: KITWE NDOLA LUAPULA LUANSHYA MUFULIRA
WATERFALL: VICTORIA

ZAMBO CHINO SAMBO CAFUSO CURIBOCA
ZAMIA BANGA CICAD CYCAD COONTIE
ZAMINDAR MALIK
ZAMOUSE GAMOUS
ZAMPOGNA BAGPIPE PANPIPE
ZANDER ZANT PERCID SANDER SANDRA
ZANTHOXYLUM FAGARA
ZANY NUT FOOL CRAZY TOADY SAWNEY BUFFOON IDIOTIC CLOWNISH SCREWBALL
ZANZIBAR (SEE TANZANIA)
ZAP ZIP ZONK MICROWAVE
ZAPARO IQUITO
ZAPATERO LIMA BOXWOOD CERILLO
ZARA (FATHER OF —) JUDAH
ZARAH KAZOO
ZARPANIT (HUSBAND OF —) MERODACH
ZAZA (FATHER OF —) JONATHAN
ZEAL FIRE MOOD ARDOR FLAME HEART FERVOR WARMTH DEVOTION GOODWILL JEALOUSY
(MORBID —) ZELOTYPIA
(WITH —) DINGDONG
(PREF.) ZELO
ZEALOT BIGOT VOTARY VOTEEN ZELANT DEVOTEE FANATIC CANANEAN SERAPHIC SICARIUS VOTARESS VOTARIST
ZEALOUS HOT AVID HIGH ARDENT FERVID STRING CORDIAL DEVOTED EARNEST EMULOUS FERVENT FORWARD JEALOUS PUSHFUL VIGOROUS PERFERVID RELIGIOUS
(— ABOUT BEAUTY) ESTHETIC
ZEALOUSLY FAST INNERLY HEARTILY
ZEBADIAH (FATHER OF —) ASAHEL ISHMAEL JEROHAM MICHAEL MESHELEMIAH
ZEBAH (SLAYER OF —) GIDEON
ZEBEDEE (SON OF —) JOHN JAMES
(WIFE OF —) SALOME

ZEBINA (FATHER OF —) NEBO
ZEBRA DAUW EQUID HORSE QUAGGA SOLIPED
ZEBRA FISH DANIO
ZEBRAWOOD ARAROBA ZINGANA
ZEBU BRAMIN BRAGMAN BRAHMIN
(HYBRID OF — AND CATTLE) CATTABU
(HYBRID OF — AND YAK) ZOBO
ZEBUDAH (HUSBAND OF —) JOSIAH
(SON OF —) JEHOIAKIM
ZEBULUN (FATHER OF —) JACOB
(SON OF —) ELON
ZECCHINO SEQUIN
ZECHARIAH (DAUGHTER OF —) ABI ABIJAH
(FATHER OF —) IDDO BEDAI HOSAH JEHIEL PASHUR ISSHIAH PHAROSH JEHOIADA JONATHAN BERECHIAH JEBERECHIAH JEHOSHAPHAT MESHELEMIAH
(SON OF —) JAHAZIEL
ZEDEKIAH (BROTHER OF —) JEHOAHAZ
(FATHER OF —) JOSIAH HANANIAH MAASEIAH CHENAANAH
(MOTHER OF —) HAMUTAL
ZEDOARY SETWALL
ZELOPHEHAD (FATHER OF —) HEPHER
ZELUS (FATHER OF —) PALLAS
(MOTHER OF —) STYX
(SISTER OF —) NIKE
ZEMIRA (FATHER OF —) BECHER
ZEN (— PARADOX) KOAN
(— QUESTIONS) MONDO
ZENANA HAREM HARIM SERAGLIO
ZEND AVESTAN
ZENICK SURICATE
ZENITH ACME PEAK HIGHT PITCH HEIGHT SUMMIT VERTEX
ZENOBIA (HUSBAND OF —) ODENATHUS
ZEOLITE ANALCIME ANALCITE STILBITE GMELINITE NATROLITE PHACOLITE
ZEPHANIAH (FATHER OF —) MAASEIAH
(SON OF —) JOSIAH
ZEPHO (FATHER OF —) ELIPHAZ
ZEPHON (FATHER OF —) GAD
ZEPHYR FINE SOFT BERLIN BREEZE
ZEPHYRUS FAVONIUS
(FATHER OF —) AEOLUS ASTRAEUS
(MOTHER OF —) EOS
(SON OF —) CARPOS
(WIFE OF —) CHLORIS
ZEPPELIN ZEP ZEPP AIRSHIP
ZERAH (FATHER OF —) IDDO REUEL SIMEON
ZERBINETTE (FATHER OF —) ARGANTE
ZERBINO (BELOVED OF —) ISABELLA

(COMPANION OF —) ORLANDO
(SISTER OF —) GINEVRA
(SLAYER OF —) MANDRICARDO
ZERESH (HUSBAND OF —) HAMAN
ZERETH (FATHER OF —) ASHUR
(MOTHER OF —) HELAH
ZERI (FATHER OF —) JEDUTHUN
ZERO OH NIL NUL BLOB DUCK NULL AUGHT CLOSE EMPTY OUGHT TRAIN ZILCH ABSENT CIPHER NAUGHT LACKING NOTHING NULLITY SCRATCH NINETEEN
(EQUAL TO —) NILPOTENT
(HAVING — AS LIMIT) NULL
(HAVING VARIABLES EQUAL TO —) TRIVIAL
ZERUAH (FATHER OF —) NEBAT
(SON OF —) JEROBOAM
ZERUIAH (SON OF —) JOAB ASAHEL ABISHAI
ZEST EDGE ELAN JASM LIFE GUSTO SPICE FLAVOR RELISH STINGO MUSTARD PIQUANCY
ZESTFUL RACY SPICY BREEZY
(— QUALITY) ZAP
ZESTY ZINGY
ZETES (BROTHER OF —) CALAIS
(FATHER OF —) BOREAS
(MOTHER OF —) ORITHYIA
ZETHAM (FATHER OF —) LAADAN
ZETHUS (BROTHER OF —) AMPHION
(FATHER OF —) JUPITER
(MOTHER OF —) ANTIOPE
ZEUS ZAN SOTER ALASTOR CRONION KRONION POLIEUS CRONIDES
(BROTHER OF —) HADES POSEIDON
(FATHER OF —) CRONUS KRONOS
(MOTHER OF —) RHEA
(SISTER OF —) HERA HESTIA DEMETER
(SON OF —) ARES ARCAS ARGUS AEACUS AGACUS APOLLO HERMES TITYUS PERSEUS DARDANUS DIONYSUS HERCULES TANTALUS
(WIFE OF —) HERA JUNO METIS THEMIS EURYNOME
(PREF.) ZENO
ZEUXIS UNDERLAY
ZHIVAGO YURI
ZIBEON (SON OF —) ANAH
ZIBIA (FATHER OF —) SHAHARAIM
(MOTHER OF —) HODESH
ZIBIAH (SON OF —) JOASH
ZICHRI (FATHER OF —) ASAPH IZHAR
(SON OF —) JOEL AMASIAH ELIEZER ELISHAPHAT
ZIGZAG BOYAU CRANK BROKEN INDENT SLALOM CRANKLE CHEVRONY FLEXUOSE TRAVERSE
(PREF.) ZYZZO
ZILCH NIL ZAP ZIP ZERO ZING NOTHING

ZILIANTE (BROTHER OF —) ORRIGILLE
(FATHER OF —) MONODANTE
(SISTER OF —) BRANDIMARTE
ZILPAH (SON OF —) GAD ASHER
ZIMARRA CYMAR SIMAR CASSOCK
ZIMB FLY ZEBUB

ZIMBABWE
CAPITAL: HARARE SALISBURY
DIVISION: RHODESIA
LANGUAGE: ILA BANTU SHONA NDEBELE
PEOPLE: BANTU MASHOMA MATABELE BALOKWAKWA
RIVER: SABI GWAII LUNDI LIMPOPO SANYATI ZAMBEZI
TOWN: GWELO UMTALI BULAWAYO
WATERFALL: VICTORIA

ZIMMAH (FATHER OF —) SHIMEI
ZIMRAN (MOTHER OF —) KETURAH
ZIMRI (FATHER OF —) SALU ZERAH
ZINA (FATHER OF —) SHIMEI
ZINC FAR SPELT ZINCUM SPELTER TUTENAG EXCLUDER
(— SALT) ZIRAM
(KIND OF —) MOSSY
ZING PEP VIM ZAP ZIP DASH SNAP ENERGY SPIRIT RAZZMATAZZ
ZINGEL PERCID
ZINGER MOT
ZINGY ZESTY
ZINKE CORNET
ZINNIA CRASSINA
ZION SION ISRAEL UTOPIA
ZIONIST IRGUNIST
ZIP NIL VIM ZAP DASH NADA SEAL SNAP ZERO ZING FORCE OOMPH WHISK ZILCH BUTTON ENERGY STINGO NOTHING
ZIPHAH (FATHER OF —) JEHALELEEL
ZIPHION (FATHER OF —) GAD
ZIPPER FASTENER

(PART OF —) TAB FACE PULL STOP TAPE CHAIN SLIDE TOOTH
ZIPPOR (SON OF —) BALAK
ZIPPORAH (FATHER OF —) REUEL JETHRO
(HUSBAND OF —) MOSES
(SON OF —) ELIEZER GERSHOM
ZIPPY ZAPPY
ZIRCON JARGON AZORITE MALACON HYACINTH STARLITE
ZITHER KIN QIN CANON CANUN GUSLI KANOON CITHARA GITERNE GITTERN AUTOHARP GALEMPONG
(JAPANESE —) KOTO
ZITHER HARP KOTO
ZIZA (FATHER OF —) SHIPHI REHOBOAM
(MOTHER OF —) MAACHAH
ZIZITH SISITH FRINGES TASSELS TSITSITH
ZO DZO ZOH ZOBO
ZOARITE BIMMELER
ZOBEBAH (FATHER OF —) COZ
ZOBO ZO DZO ZOH ZOBU
ZODIAC GIRDLE BALDRIC BAWDRICK SIGNIFIER
(SECTION OF —) TRIGON
(SIGN OF —) LEO RAM BULL CRAB FISH GOAT LION ARIES LIBRA SCALE TWINS VIRGO ARCHER CANCER GEMINI PISCES TAURUS SCORPIO AQUARIUS CAPRICORN
ZOHAR (FATHER OF —) SIMEON
(SON OF —) EPHRON
ZOHETH (FATHER OF —) ISHI
ZOISITE THULITE
ZONA ZOSTER
ZONE BED AREA BAND BEAM BELT HALO PLAGE TRACT CIRCLE REGION ZODIAC CLIMATE HORIZON ZONULET CINCTURE CINGULUM FRONTIER HABENULA HISTOGEN STRINGER
(— OF CONFLICT) FRONT
(— OF FLAME) MANTLE

(— OF MINERALS) CORONA
(— OF VENUS) CEST CESTUS
(ABYSSAL —) BASSALIA
(PALEONTOLOGIC —S) ASSISE
(SAFETY —) ISLET ISLAND REFUGE
(STRATOGRAPHIC —) HEMERA
(WELDING —) ROOT
ZONK WASTE
ZONKED GONZO
ZOO (KIND OF —) PETTING
ZOOECIUM AUTOPORE
ZOOID PERSON SIPHON BRYOZOAN HYDRANTH POLYPIDE ZOOTHOME
ZOOLOGIST AMERICAN DEAN GILL ADAMS ALLEN BAIRD BAKER BIRGE CLARK GOULD GUYER MORSE SHULL BINNEY BROOKS BUTLER CASTLE ELLIOT FISHER GARMAN HOLMES KOFOID MORGAN NEWMAN OLIVER PARKER RIDDLE STILES WILDER WILSON AGASSIZ ANDREWS BARTSCH BIGELOW FERNALD KELLOGG MCCLUNG NUTTING VERRILL WHITMAN CRAMPTON GRINNELL HORNADAY KIRTLAND MELANDER SHELFORD COCKERELL DAVENPORT SANDERSON PETRUNKEVITCH
AUSTRIAN FRISCH
BELGIAN BENEDEN
CANADIAN ANDERSON
DANISH STEENSTRUP
ENGLISH BUSK GRAY OWEN ELTON FLOWER GROGAN LISTER MORGAN MORRIS MURRAY NEWTON PARKER BEDDARD DURRELL GUNTHER HASWELL MEDAWAR POULTON YARRELL GOODRICH MACBRIDE MITCHELL
FRENCH CUVIER DELAGE PERRIER DUJARDIN BLAINVILLE VALENCIENNES
GERMAN VOGT BREHM BRONN CARUS CLAUS DOHRN BOVERI FRISCH LEYDIG MOBIUS MULLER

GRZIMEK HAECKEL HERTWIG SIEBOLD SPEMANN BUTSCHLI GUENTHER BECHSTEIN LEUCKHART SCHAUDINN BLUMENBACH GOLDSCHMIDT REICHENBACH LICHTENSTEIN
ITALIAN GRASSI
NORWEGIAN SARS NANSEN
RUSSIAN PANDER KOVALEVSKI METCHNIKOFF
SWEDISH LOVEN
ZOOM ZAP SPEED
ZOOPHYTE CORAL SPONGE HYDROID
ZOOSPORE MONAD SWARMER ZOOCARP
ZOPHAH (FATHER OF —) HELEM HOTHAM
ZOPHAI (FATHER OF —) ELKANAH
ZORIL SKUNK POWCAT CHINCHE POLECAT MUISHOND
ZOROASTRIAN GABAR PARSI GUEBRE PARSEE
ZOROASTRIANISM MAZDAISM
ZOUAVE ZUZU SCALER ZOUZOU
ZOUNDS OONS WAUNS ZOONS
ZUAR (SON OF —) NETHANEEL
ZUCCHETTO CALOTTE SOLIDEO SKULLCAP
ZUCCHINI COURGETTE
ZULU CAR TRAIN LUGGER MATABELE
ZUNI CIBOLAN SHALAKO
ZUR (FATHER OF —) JEHIEL
(SON OF —) COZBI
ZURIEL (FATHER OF —) ABIHAIL
ZWINGLIAN TIGURINE
ZYGOMATIC JUGAL
ZYGOSPORE COPULA
ZYGOTE OOCYST OOSPERM OOSPORE SPORONT OOKINETE
ZYME YEAST ZYMIN ENZYME FERMENT
ZYMOGEN PEPSINOGEN
ZYRIAN KOMI SYRYAN